Directory of
Special Libraries and
Information Centers

The **Directory of Special Libraries and Information Centers** is Published in Three Volumes:

Volume 1—**Directory of Special Libraries and Information Centers**

Volume 2—**Geographic and Personnel Indexes**

Volume 3—**New Special Libraries** (a periodic supplement to Volume 1)

The **Subject Directory of Special Libraries and Information Centers,** a Subject Classified Edition of Material Taken From Volume 1 of the Basic Directory, is Published in Five Volumes:

Volume 1—**Business and Law Libraries**

Volume 2—**Education and Information Science Libraries**

Volume 3—**Health Science Libraries**

Volume 4—**Social Sciences and Humanities Libraries**

Volume 5—**Science and Technology Libraries**

ISSN 0731-633X

Directory of Special Libraries and Information Centers

9th Edition

A Guide to Special Libraries, Research Libraries,
Information Centers, Archives, and Data Centers Maintained by
Government Agencies, Business, Industry, Newspapers, Educational
Institutions, Nonprofit Organizations, and Societies in the
Fields of Science and Technology, Medicine, Law, Art, Religion,
the Social Sciences, and Humanistic Studies.

BRIGITTE T. DARNAY
Editor

JOHN NIMCHUK
Associate Editor

VOLUME 1
PART 2
O-Z
(Entries 10010–17467)

Appendixes and Subject Index

GALE RESEARCH COMPANY • BOOK TOWER • DETROIT, MICHIGAN 48226

Brigitte T. Darnay, *Editor*

John Nimchuk, *Associate Editor*

Virginia K. Bergman, Dianne E. Boardman, Holly M.G. Leighton, Mary J. Motzko,
Carol Southward, Susan M. Winslow, *Assistant Editors*

Henrietta Krohn, *Editorial Assistant*

Carol Blanchard, *Production Director*
Dorothy Kalleberg, *External Production Associate*
Arthur Chartow, *Art Director*

Laura Bryant, *Internal Production Supervisor*
Louise Gagne, *Internal Production Associate*
Sandy Rock, *Senior Internal Production Assistant*

Lois Lenroot-Ernt, *Contributing Editor*

Frederick G. Ruffner, *Publisher*
James M. Ethridge, *Executive Vice President/Editorial*
Dedria Bryfonski, *Editorial Director*
John Schmittroth, Jr., *Director, Directories Division*
Robert C. Thomas, *Senior Editor, Special Editorial Projects*

Computerized photocomposition by
Computer Composition Corporation,
Madison Heights, Michigan

ISBN 0-8103-1888-1
Library of Congress Catalog Card Number 84-640165 (set)
ISSN 0731-633X

Printed in the United States

Contents

Volume 1, Part 1

Volume 1, Part 2

Description of Listings

A simulated listing is shown below. Each numbered item is explained in the descriptive paragraph bearing the same number.

---

(1) **ECONOMIC ANALYSTS' RESEARCH LABORATORY, INC.**   **(2) INFORMATION CENTER**   **(3)**   (Bus-Fin; Soc Sci)

(4)   Box 5995   **(5)**   Phone: (202) 999-1100
Washington, DC 21112   **(6)**   Justine Comstock, Dir.

(7)   **Founded:** 1975.   **(8)**   **Staff:** Prof 3; Other 5.   **(9)**   **Subjects:** Economics; monetary, credit and fiscal policy; political science; international relations.   **(10)**   **Special Collections:** Economic Growth Center Collection (focuses on national economies of developing countries, their development, plans, budgets, and statistics; 12,000 volumes, 3000 microforms); U.S. census data, 1900 to present (3000 items); Department of Commerce publications (20,000). **(11)**   **Holdings:** 25,000 books; 10,000 bound periodical volumes; 20,000 reports on microfiche; 1000 staff reports; 500 computer tapes; 100 VF drawers of government documents.   **(12)**   **Subscriptions:** 300 journals and other serials; 25 newspapers. **(13)**   **Services:** Interlibrary loans (limited); copying; SDI; center open to public by appointment.   **(14)** **Automated Operations:** Computerized cataloging, acquisitions, and serials. **(15) Computerized Information Services:** SDC, NEXIS, full-text or KWIC form; Earlyon (internal database) **(16) Networks/Consortia:** Member of ECONET.   **(17)**   **Publications:** EARLI Warning (review of journals received), biweekly—for internal distribution only.   **(18) Special Catalogs:** Catalog of staff reports and publications (card). **(19)**   **Special Indexes:** Index to government publications received by the center (computer printout).   **(20)**   **Remarks:** The center is located at 6200 Keynes Ave., N.W., Washington, DC 21114. **(21)**   **Formerly:** Economic Researchers, Inc. **(22)**   **Also Known As:** EARL, Inc.   **(23)**   Formed by the Merger of: Its Professional Library and Government Documents Department.   **(24)**   **Staff:** A.A. Smith, Supv. Libn.; R.J. Johnson, Ref. Libn.; Dolly Brown, Online Supv.

---

(1) NAME OF ORGANIZATION. Name of parent organization, society, or agency which sponsors or is served by the library or information center. Independent libraries and centers and those commonly known by a distinctive name are entered directly under the library's name. Cross-references are included in the body of the work for those entries to which there may be multiple approaches.

(2) NAME OF LIBRARY OR INFORMATION CENTER. Descriptive and memorial names are given as reported. Otherwise the appropriate generic term is used, e.g., library, archives, collection, information center. In many cases the generic term has been supplied by the editors and the inclusion of the term library does not indicate the existence of a formal library.

(3) PRINCIPAL SUBJECT KEYWORD. The major subject or type of material represented by the collection as a whole. When there are two areas of equal importance both are indicated. When collections have more than four major subjects or are general in scope no keyword is used. The keywords offer a classification by broad subject category only; each library's more specialized interests are mentioned in the body of each listing. Both the general keywords and specialized interests are used as entry words in the subject index. The following keywords are employed in the ninth edition.

Agri	- agriculture		Info Sci	- information science
Area-Ethnic	- area ethnic		Law	- law
Art	- art		Med	- medicine
Aud-Vis	- audio visual		Mil	- military
Bus-Fin	- business and finance		Plan	- planning
Comp Sci	- computer science		Publ	- publishing
Educ	- education		Rare Book	- rare book
Energy	- energy		Rec	- recreation
Env-Cons	- environment and conservation		Rel-Theol	- religion and theology
			Sci-Tech	- science-technology
Food-Bev	- food sciences and beverage		Soc Sci	- social sciences
Geog-Map	- geography-map		Theater	- theater
Hist	- history		Trans	- transportation
Hum	- humanities			

(4) MAILING ADDRESS. The permanent mailing address of library or center. In some instances this will differ from the headquarters address of the parent organization and the physical location of the library. When there is a separate location address, it is given under "Remarks" (see item 20).

(5) TELEPHONE NUMBER. Area code and telephone number. When more than one telephone number is supplied, alternate ones are listed under "Remarks" (see item 20). Extensions are not provided, since they are subject to frequent change.

(6) HEAD OF LIBRARY OR INFORMATION CENTER. Name and title of the person directly in charge of library or information center. Where no librarian has been identified or where there is no position as such, the name of the administrative officer may be given. When the directorship is shared by two persons the names of both partners are given in the staff names section (see item 24).

(7) FOUNDING DATE. Year when library or information center was established, either formally or informally.

(8) NUMBER OF STAFF. Number of individuals directly engaged in the operation of the library or center on a regular basis. Part-time employees are included but student assistants and other occasional help generally are not. Professional staff includes librarians, bibliographers, subject specialists, information specialists, and other related specialists. Semi-professionals and clerical assistants are grouped in the second category. Distinction between professional and non-professional staff is made by the respondents. Where the differentiation is not made, the total number of staff is listed.

(9) SUBJECTS. Terms specifically designating the most important subjects represented in the collection as a whole. This section of the listing, obtained from submitted questionnaires, is ordinarily used as the basis of the subject index.

(10) SPECIAL COLLECTIONS. Separately grouped collections of unusual or notable interest that are identifiable either by subject, form, name of donor, or distinctive name.

(11) HOLDINGS. Quantitative data concerning collections. Numbers of books, bound periodical volumes, pamphlets, and technical reports are given separately when supplied by respondents. When the term "volumes" is used, it generally indicates bound units or collections of bound and unbound items which have been accessioned and cataloged. Unbound material is indicated either by unit count, number of vertical file drawers, linear shelf feet, or cubic storage space. Estimates rather than exact statistics have frequently been given. Holdings of non-book materials are also indicated whenever of significant size and importance.

(12) SUBSCRIPTIONS. Figures generally represent the number of journal and serial titles, not separate copies, received by paid subscription, gift, and exchange. Newspaper subscriptions are given separately when numerically significant.

(13) SERVICES. Most special libraries provide bibliographic or reference services primarily for their own organizations. For these, an appropriate statement of service limitations is given. When the library or center provides some form of access to outside clientele, it is so indicated. When services

offered are of an unusual nature they are noted and indication is given whether such services are for internal or external use. Entries for libraries which honor interlibrary loan requests include the appropriate information, as do those for libraries with copying or reproducing facilities. Normally, copying services to outside users are on a fee basis. Some libraries now charge for interlibrary loans and this information is included when supplied by respondent.

(14) AUTOMATED OPERATIONS. Computerized library management functions such as cataloging, circulation, acquisitions, and serials.

(15) COMPUTERIZED INFORMATION SERVICES. This item indicates a special library's access to online information systems, such as MEDLINE, SDC or LEXIS, etc. Also included here are fees for online searches the library may perform for the public, and name and telephone of contact person.

(16) NETWORKS/CONSORTIA. Here is listed the special library's membership in formal or informal groups involved in cooperative sharing of library resources on the local, regional, or national level. Acronyms are used for networks and consortia which are familiar to the library profession (e.g., CLASS, UTLAS). Appendix A lists geographically the names, acronyms, and addresses of the networks and consortia reported by the special libraries in this directory. An alphabetical index follows.

(17) PUBLICATIONS. Periodical, serial, and other publications issued or prepared by the library or information center are included. Title, frequency, and basis of distribution are indicated when known.

(18) SPECIAL CATALOGS. Unique and unusual catalogs which are locally prepared and maintained, including card, book, computer printout, and other forms.

(19) SPECIAL INDEXES. Unique and unusual indexes which are locally prepared and maintained.

(20) REMARKS. Additional information not adaptable to the standard form of entry, including historical data, explanatory notes, and descriptions of unusual activities. Corporate affiliations are often noted here. Also included is the address of a special library's location when it differs from the mailing address in item 4.

(21) FORMERLY. Former names and/or locations of a special library or its parent organization when there is a recent change of names under which they were formerly listed. Cross-references are generally supplied from the former names.

(22) ALSO KNOWN AS. Variant names of a special library or its parent organization. Cross-references from these are provided when needed.

(23) MERGED LIBRARIES. When the special library has been created by the merger of two or more units previously listed separately, the names of the components are identified here. Mergers of parent organizations which affect the special library are also noted here.

(24) STAFF NAMES. Names and titles of professional and supervisory personnel in the special library or information center. Only principal members of the professional staff are listed for operations with large staffs.

Abbreviations and Symbols

An asterisk (*) after the library's name denotes a library that did not answer the four requests for updated information, but that it is one the editors are reasonably certain exists.

A dagger (†) after the library's name denotes a library which did not reply but whose existence was verified in current secondary sources.

AB	— Alberta	Co.	— Company
Acq.	— Acquisitions	Coll.	— Collection, College
Act.	— Acting	COM	— Computer Output Microfilm
Adm.	— Administration, Administrative, Administrator	Comm.	— Committee
		Commn.	— Commission
Adv.	— Advisor	Commnr.	— Commissioner
Aff.	— Affairs	Commun.	— Communications, Community
Agri.	— Agricultural, Agriculture	Comp.	— Computer, Computerized, Computing
AK	— Alaska	Cons.	— Consultant, Consulting, Conservation, Conservator
AL	— Alabama		
Amer.	— American	CONSER	— Conversion of Serials Project
Anl.	— Analysis, Analyst	Coop.	— Cooperating, Cooperation, Cooperative
APO	— Army Post Office	Coord.	— Coordinating, Coordination, Coordinator
AR	— Arkansas	Corp.	— Corporate, Corporation
Arch.	— Architect, Architectural, Architecture	Coun.	— Council
Archeo.	— Archeologist, Archeology	Couns.	— Counsel, Counseling, Counselor
Archv.	— Archives, Archivist	CT	— Connecticut
AS	— American Samoa	Ct.	— Court
Assn.	— Association	Ctr.	— Center, Centre
Assoc.	— Associate	Ctrl.	— Central
Asst.	— Assistant	CUNY	— City University of New York
Att.	— Attorney	Cur.	— Curator
Aud.	— Audio	Curric.	— Curricular, Curriculum
AV	— Audiovisual	Cus.	— Custodian
Ave.	— Avenue	DC	— District of Columbia
AZ	— Arizona	DE	— Delaware
BADADUQ	— Banque de Donnes a Acces Direct de l'Universite du Quebec	Dept.	— Department, Departmental
		Des.	— Design, Designer
BC	— British Columbia	Dev.	— Development, Developmental
Bd.	— Board	Dir.	— Director
Bev.	— Beverages	Distr.	— Distribution
Bibliog.	— Bibliographer, Bibliographical, Bibliography	Div.	— Division, Divisional
Biomed.	— Biomedical, Biomedicine	DOBIS	— Dortmunder Bibliothekssystem
Bk., Bks.	— Book, Books	Doc., Docs.	— Document, Documentation, Documents
Bldg.	— Building	DOE	— U.S. Department of Energy
Blvd.	— Boulevard	DOE/RECON	— U.S. Department of Energy Online Information Retrieval System
Br.	— Branch		
Bro.	— Brother	Dp.	— Deputy
BRS	— Bibliographic Retrieval Services, Inc.	Dr.	— Drive
Bur.	— Bureau	DTIC	— Defense Technical Information Center
Bus.	— Business	E.	— East
CA	— California	Econ.	— Economic(s)
CAN/OLE	— Canadian Online Enquiry System	Ed.	— Editor, Editorial
CAN/SDI	— Canadian Service for the Selective Dissemination of Information	Educ.	— Education, Educational
		Engr.	— Engineer, Engineering
CANSIM	— Canadian Socio-Economic Information Management System	Env.	— Environment, Environmental
		ERIC	— Educational Resources Information Center
Cart.	— Cartographer, Cartographic, Cartography	Exch.	— Exchange
Cat.	— Catalog, Cataloger, Cataloging	Exec.	— Executive
CDC	— Control Data Corporation	Expy.	— Expressway
Ch.	— Child, Children, Children's	Ext.	— Extension
Chem.	— Chemical, Chemist, Chemistry	Fed.	— Federal, Federation
Chf.	— Chief	Fin.	— Finance, Financial
Chm.	— Chairman	FL	— Florida
Circ.	— Circulation	Fl.	— Floor
CIS	— Congressional Information Service, Inc.	Fld.	— Field
Ck.	— Clerk	Found.	— Foundation
Clghse.	— Clearinghouse	Fr.	— Father
CO	— Colorado	Ft.	— Fort

xi

Fwy.	— Freeway	Mtls.	— Materials
GA	— Georgia	Mus.	— Music, Musical
Gen.	— General	Musm.	— Museum
Geneal.	— Genealogical, Genealogist, Genealogy	Myth.	— Mythology
Geog.	— Geographer, Geographical, Geography	N.	— North
Geol.	— Geological, Geologist, Geology	NASA	— National Aeronautics and Space Administration
Govt.	— Government, Governmental	Natl.	— National
GU	— Guam	NB	— New Brunswick
Hd.	— Head	NC	— North Carolina
Hea.	— Health	ND	— North Dakota
HI	— Hawaii	NE	— Nebraska
Hist.	— Historian, Historical, History	NF	— Newfoundland
Hon.	— Honorable, Honorary	NH	— New Hampshire
Hosp.	— Hospital	NJ	— New Jersey
HQ	— Headquarters	NLM	— National Library of Medicine
Hum.	— Humanities	NM	— New Mexico
Hwy.	— Highway	No.	— Number
IA	— Iowa	NS	— Nova Scotia
ID	— Idaho	NT	— Northwest Territories
IL	— Illinois	NTIS	— National Technical Information Service
ILL	— Interlibrary Loan	NV	— Nevada
Illus.	— Illustration, Illustrative, Illustrator	NY	— New York
IN	— Indiana	OCLC	— Online Computer Library Center
Indiv.	— Individual	Off.	— Office, Officer
Info.	— Information, Informational	OH	— Ohio
Inst.	— Institute, Institution, Institutional	OK	— Oklahoma
Instr.	— Instruction, Instructional, Instructor	ON	— Ontario
Int.	— Internal	Oper.	— Operations, Operator
Interp.	— Interpretation, Interpreter, Interpretive	OR	— Oregon
Intl.	— International	P.R.	— Public Relations
Jnl.	— Journal	PA	— Pennsylvania
Jr.	— Junior	PE	— Prince Edward Island
JURIS	— Justice, Retrieval and Inquiry System	Per.	— Periodical(s)
Kpr.	— Keeper	Perf.	— Perform, Performing
KS	— Kansas	Pharm.	— Pharmacy
KWIC	— Keyword in Context	PHILSOM	— Periodical Holdings in Libraries of Schools of Medicine
KWOC	— Keyword out of Context	Photo.	— Photograph(s), Photographer
KY	— Kentucky	Photodup.	— Photoduplication
LA	— Louisiana	Pict.	— Picture(s)
Lab., Labs.	— Laboratory, Laboratories	Pk.	— Park
Lang.	— Language(s)	Pkwy.	— Parkway
Lat.	— Latin	Pl.	— Place
LATCH	— Literature Attached to the Chart (Medical)	Plan.	— Planner, Planning
LCDR	— Lieutenant Commander	PQ	— Quebec
Ldr.	— Leader	PR	— Puerto Rico
Leg.	— Legislation, Legislative, Legislator	Pres.	— President
Lib., Libs.	— Library, Libraries	Prin.	— Principal
Libn., Libns.	— Librarian, Librarians	Proc.	— Process, Processing, Processor
Lit.	— Literary, Literature	Prod.	— Production
Ln.	— Lane	Prof.	— Professional, Professor
LRC	— Learning Resource(s) Center	Prog.	— Program, Programmer, Programming
Lrng. Rsrcs.	— Learning Resources	Proj.	— Project
MA	— Massachusetts	Prov.	— Province, Provincial
Mag.	— Magazine	Psych.	— Psychiatric, Psychiatry, Psychological, Psychology
MB	— Manitoba	Pub.	— Public
MD	— Maryland	Publ.	— Published, Publisher, Publishing
ME	— Maine	Pubn., Pubns.	— Publication, Publications
Med.	— Medical, Medicine	R&D	— Research and Development
MEDLARS	— Medical Literature Analysis and Retrieval System	Rd.	— Reader, Road
MEDLINE	— MEDLARS Online	Rec.	— Record(s), Recreation
Mfg.	— Manufacturing	Ref.	— Reference
Mfr.	— Manufacturer	Reg.	— Region, Regional
Mgr.	— Manager	Rel.	— Relations, Religion, Religious
Mgt.	— Management	Rep.	— Representative
MI	— Michigan	Res.	— Research, Researcher
Mil.	— Military	RESORS	— Remote Sensing On-Line Retrieval System
Mktg.	— Marketing	Ret.	— Retrieval
MN	— Minnesota	Rev.	— Reverend
Mng.	— Managing	RI	— Rhode Island
MO	— Missouri	RLIN	— Research Libraries Information Network
MS	— Mississippi	Rm., Rms.	— Room, Rooms
Ms., Mss.	— Manuscript, Manuscripts		
MT	— Montana		

Rpt.	— Report(s)	Tech.	— Technical, Technological, Technology
Rsrc., Rsrcs.	— Resource, Resources	Techn.	— Technician
Rte.	— Route	Theol.	— Theological, Theology
S.	— South	TN	— Tennessee
SC	— South Carolina	Tpke.	— Turnpike
Sch.	— School	Trans.	— Transportation
Sci.	— Science(s), Scientific, Scientist	Transl.	— Translation, Translator
SD	— South Dakota	Treas.	— Treasurer
SDC	— System Development Corporation	Trng.	— Training
SDI	— Selective Dissemination of Information	TTY	— Teletypewriter
Sec.	— Secretary	TX	— Texas
Sect.	— Section	U.N.	— United Nations
Ser.	— Serials	U.S.	—United States
Serv.	— Service(s)	U.S.D.A.	— U.S. Department of Agriculture
SK	— Saskatchewan	Univ.	— University
SLA	— Special Libraries Association	Unpubl.	— Unpublished
Soc.	— Social, Society	UT	— Utah
Spec.	— Special, Specialist, Specialized	UTLAS	— University of Toronto Library Automation Systems
Sq.	— Square	V.P.	— Vice President
Sr.	— Senior, Sister	VA	— Virginia
St.	— Saint, Street	Vet.	— Veteran(s), Veterinary
Sta.	— Station	VF	— Vertical File(s)
Stat.	— Statistical, Statistics	VI	— Virgin Islands
Ste.	— Sainte, Societe	Vis.	— Visual
Sts.	— Saints, Streets	Vol., Vols.	— Volume, Volumes
Stud.	— Student(s), Studies, Study	VT	— Vermont
SUNY	— State University of New York	W.	— West
Sup.	— Support, Supporting	WA	— Washington
Supt.	— Superintendent	WI	— Wisconsin
Supv.	— Supervising, Supervisor, Supervisory	WV	— West Virginia
Sys.	— System(s)	WY	— Wyoming
Tchg.	— Teaching	YT	— Yukon Territory
TDD	— Telecommunications/Telephone Device for the Deaf		

Directory of
Special Libraries and
Information Centers

Volume 1, Part 2

O-Z

O

O.K. SUPERMARKET
See: The Vineyard

★10010★
OAK FOREST HOSPITAL - PROFESSIONAL LIBRARY (Med)†
15900 S. Cicero Ave.   Phone: (312) 928-4200
Oak Forest, IL 60452   Delores I. Quinn, Libn.
Founded: 1973. **Staff:** Prof 1; Other 2. **Subjects:** Medicine, nursing, paramedical subjects. **Holdings:** 2000 books. **Subscriptions:** 250 journals and other serials. **Services:** Library not open to public. **Staff:** Mary Bell, Asst.Libn.

★10011★
OAK GROVE LUTHERAN CHURCH - MEMORIAL LIBRARY (Rel-Theol)†
71st & Lyndale Ave., S.   Phone: (612) 869-4917
Richfield, MN 55423   Mrs. Forrest Carpenter, Libn.
Founded: 1959. **Staff:** 4. **Subjects:** Bible history and reference, religious education, family life, psychology, children's literature, devotional reading. **Holdings:** 2856 books; tape cassettes; records. **Services:** Interlibrary loans; library open to public.

★10012★
OAK HILLS BIBLE INSTITUTE - LIBRARY (Rel-Theol)
Oak Hills   Phone: (218) 751-8670
Bemidji, MN 56601   John Sanders, Libn.
Founded: 1946. **Staff:** Prof 1; Other 1. **Subjects:** Biblical and theological studies, religious education. **Holdings:** 11,700 books; 500 bound periodical volumes; 150 files of mission material; 550 AV items. **Subscriptions:** 35 journals and other serials. **Services:** Interlibrary loans; copying; library open to public.

★10013★
OAK LAWN PUBLIC LIBRARY - LOCAL HISTORY ROOM (Hist)
9427 S. Raymond Ave.   Phone: (312) 422-4990
Oak Lawn, IL 60453   Gerald R. Anderson, Local Hist.Libn.
Staff: Prof 1; Other 2. **Subjects:** Local history. **Special Collections:** Southtown Economist newspapers (microfilm); Oral History Collection. **Holdings:** 200 books; 300 photographs; 75 files of clippings; 20 boxes of local government records. **Services:** Interlibrary loans; library open to public. **Automated Operations:** CL Systems, Inc.; Computerized circulation and indexing. **Networks/Consortia:** Member of Suburban Library System (SLS). **Special Indexes:** Index of the South Suburban Region Newspapers (booklet).

★10014★
OAK PARK PUBLIC LIBRARY - LOCAL AUTHOR AND LOCAL HISTORY COLLECTIONS (Hist)
834 Lake St.   Phone: (312) 383-8200
Oak Park, IL 60301   Barbara Ballinger, Hd.Libn.
Founded: 1903. **Subjects:** Local history, architecture and authors. **Special Collections:** Ernest Hemingway (268 volumes); Frank Lloyd Wright (305 volumes); Edgar Rice Burroughs (54 volumes); Grant Manson photographs of Wright buildings (350 items); Gilman Lane photographs of Wright buildings (700 items). **Holdings:** 1136 books; 5 VF drawers of Oak Park Landmarks Commission files; 8 VF drawers of local history. **Services:** Interlibrary loans; copying; special collections open to public for reference use only. **Automated Operations:** Computerized cataloging and circulation. **Networks/Consortia:** Member of Suburban Library System (SLS). **Publications:** Frank Lloyd Wright, Prairie School of Architecture, 1974 (bibliography); Ernest Hemingway Collection, revised 1978 (bibliography) - out of print. **Special Indexes:** Local newspaper index (card). **Staff:** William Jerousek, Libn.

★10015★
OAK RIDGE ASSOCIATED UNIVERSITIES - COMPARATIVE ANIMAL RESEARCH LABORATORY LIBRARY
1299 Bethel Valley Rd.
Oak Ridge, TN 37830
Defunct

★10016★

OAK RIDGE ASSOCIATED UNIVERSITIES - MANPOWER EDUCATION, RESEARCH, AND TRAINING DIVISION - LIBRARY (Educ; Info Sci)
Bldg. 2714-F, Rm. E-1
246 Laboratory Rd.
Box 117   Phone: (615) 576-3408
Oak Ridge, TN 37831-0117   Harry T. Burn, Libn.
Founded: 1977. **Staff:** Prof 2. **Subjects:** Libraries, education, employment, manpower, energy. **Holdings:** 200 volumes; 1000 reports. **Subscriptions:** 55 journals and other serials. **Services:** Interlibrary loans; library open to public with restrictions. **Computerized Information Services:** DOE/RECON, DIALOG, BRS; MERT Software Systems (internal database). **Also Known As:** Its MERT Division. **Staff:** Bobbie Newman, Sys.Libn.

★10017★

OAK RIDGE ASSOCIATED UNIVERSITIES - MEDICAL HEALTH SCIENCES DIVISION LIBRARY (Med)
Box 117   Phone: (615) 576-3490
Oak Ridge, TN 37830   Randa Yalcintas, Info.Dir.
Founded: 1974. **Staff:** Prof 1; Other 1. **Subjects:** Nuclear medicine, occupational medicine, biochemistry. **Holdings:** 3250 books; 8060 bound periodical volumes; 9500 microform reports. **Subscriptions:** 115 journals and other serials. **Services:** Interlibrary loans; library not open to public. **Automated Operations:** Computerized cataloging. **Computerized Information Services:** MEDLARS. **Networks/Consortia:** Member of Knoxville Area Health Sciences Library Consortium. **Remarks:** An additional phone number is FTS 626-3490.

★10018★

OAK RIDGE NATIONAL LABORATORY - CONTROLLED FUSION ATOMIC DATA CENTER (Energy; Sci-Tech)
Bldg. 6003, Box X   Phone: (615) 574-4704
Oak Ridge, TN 37830   D.H. Crandall, Dir.
Staff: Prof 2; Other 2. **Subjects:** Heavy particles - heavy particle collisions, particle interactions with electrons, particle penetration into matter, particle interactions with surfaces. **Services:** Collects, stores, evaluates and disseminates atomic and molecular processes information. **Computerized Information Services:** Online systems. **Publications:** Atomic Data for Fusion (bimonthly bulletin); bibliography; reviews and compilations. **Remarks:** The Oak Ridge National Laboratory operates under contract to the U.S. Department of Energy.

★10019★

OAK RIDGE NATIONAL LABORATORY - INFORMATION CENTER FOR INTERNAL EXPOSURE (Sci-Tech)
Box X   Phone: (615) 574-6261
Oak Ridge, TN 37830   S.R. Bernard, Dir.
Staff: Prof 1. **Subjects:** Radiation (internal) dose, metabolic models, trace element matabolism, mathematical models. **Holdings:** 7000 abstracts of literature data. **Services:** Copying; center open to public with restrictions. **Remarks:** The Oak Ridge National Laboratory operates under contract to the U.S. Department of Energy.

★10020★

OAK RIDGE NATIONAL LABORATORY - INFORMATION DIVISION - ENVIRONMENTAL MUTAGEN INFORMATION CENTER (Sci-Tech)
Box Y   Phone: (615) 574-7871
Oak Ridge, TN 37830   John S. Wassom, Dir.
Founded: 1969. **Staff:** Prof 7; Other 3. **Subjects:** Chemical mutagenesis. **Holdings:** 35,000 references on chemical mutagenesis. **Services:** Answers information requests; center open to public. **Computerized Information Services:** TOXLINE, DIALOG, SDC, DOE/RECON. **Publications:** Annual Surveys of the Literature on Chemical Mutagenesis; specialized bibliographies. **Remarks:** The Oak Ridge National Laboratory operates under contract to the U.S. Department of Energy. **Staff:** E.S. Von Halle; B.L. Whitfield; K. Larsen; I.C. Miller; Mary Francis; R.S. Stafford.

★10021★

OAK RIDGE NATIONAL LABORATORY - LIBRARIES (Sci-Tech)†
Box X   Phone: (615) 574-6722
Oak Ridge, TN 37830   R.R. Dickison, Chf.Libn.
Founded: 1946. **Staff:** Prof 16; Other 26. **Subjects:** Chemistry, biology, metallurgy, physics, nuclear science, mathematics, engineering, environmental sciences, ecology. **Holdings:** 60,000 books; 80,000 bound periodical volumes; 400,000 research and development reports. **Subscriptions:** 2800 journals and other serials. **Services:** Interlibrary loans; library not open to public. **Computerized Information Services:** DOE/RECON, DIALOG, SDC, BRS, New York Times Information Service, OCLC. **Networks/Consortia:** Member of SOLINET. **Publications:** Reports Received, weekly; Acquisition List, biweekly - both for internal distribution only. **Remarks:** The Oak Ridge National Laboratory operates under contract to the U.S. Department of Energy. The Oak Ridge National Laboratory Libraries include Central Research Library, Y-12 Technical Library, Biology Division Library and Fusion Energy Library. **Staff:** Cathy Nook, Hd., Tech.Serv.; Nancy Norton, Hd., User Serv.

★10022★

OAK RIDGE NATIONAL LABORATORY - NUCLEAR DATA PROJECT (Sci-Tech)
Box X   Phone: (615) 574-4699
Oak Ridge, TN 37830   M.J. Martin, Dir.
Founded: 1948. **Staff:** Prof 4; Other 4. **Subjects:** Nuclear physics, nuclear levels, nuclear transitions, nuclear structure, radioactivity, isotopes, nuclear reactions. **Special Collections:** Nuclear data tables (400 compilations of measured or calculated quantities). **Holdings:** 200 books; 180 shelf-feet of unbound journals; 9 VF drawers of technical reports. **Subscriptions:** 32 journals and other serials. **Services:** Collection, evaluation, and publication of data on nuclear level structure; answer specific requests for nuclear structure references or data; open to public with special approval. **Computerized Information Services:** DOE/RECON, Evaluated Nuclear Structure Data File (ENSDF), Nuclear Structure References (NSR) File. **Publications:** Nuclear Data Sheets, 12/year - available by subscription. **Special Catalogs:** Maintains computerized bibliographic and keyword files for over 50,000 published references and 30,000 unpublished references in experimental nuclear physics. From these files are produced reference lists for various selectors such as isotope, half-life, specific type of nuclear reaction. **Remarks:** The Oak Ridge National Laboratory operates under contract to the U.S. Department of Energy. **Staff:** Y.A. Ellis, Res.; B. Harmatz, Res.; M.R. Schmorak, Res.; S. Ramavataram, Lit. Scanner.

★10023★

OAK RIDGE NATIONAL LABORATORY - NUCLEAR SAFETY INFORMATION CENTER (Sci-Tech)
Bldg. 9711-1, Box Y   Phone: (615) 483-8611
Oak Ridge, TN 37830   J.R. Buchanan, Dir.
Founded: 1963. **Staff:** Prof 10; Other 6. **Subjects:** Safety of facilities and operations in the nuclear fuel cycle including reactors, nuclear power plants, fuel reprocessing plants, fission product release, transport and removal; meteorological considerations; nuclear instrumentation, control and safety systems; radioactive effluent control, monitoring, movement and dosage; reactor transients, kinetics and stability; operational safety and experience; containment of nuclear facilities. **Special Collections:** Nuclear Reactor Safety Analysis and Environmental Reports; Nuclear Facility Licensing Documents. **Services:** Retrospective bibliographies; questions answered; consultation, free to sponsors and their designees, otherwise fee charged. **Computerized Information Services:** DOE/RECON. **Publications:** State-of-the Art Reports; DOE Nuclear Safety Journal; periodic bibliographies. **Special Catalogs:** Computer file of bibliographic entries with extracts of up to 100 words with keywords as file points (includes over 170,000 items). **Remarks:** The Oak Ridge National Laboratory operates under contract to the U.S. Department of Energy. **Staff:** G.T. Mays, Asst.Dir.

★10024★

OAK RIDGE NATIONAL LABORATORY - RADIATION SHIELDING INFORMATION CENTER (Sci-Tech)
Box X   Phone: (615) 574-6176
Oak Ridge, TN 37830   Betty F. Maskewitz, Dir.
Founded: 1962. **Staff:** Prof 5; Other 10. **Subjects:** Radiation protection, transport and shielding. **Special Collections:** Digital computer code packages to perform shielding calculations; computer-readable data libraries (nuclear cross sections and data from intranuclear cascade calculations). **Holdings:** 9 VF drawers of reports; 12,000 micronegative cards (microfiche); 600 computer code packages; 100 nuclear data packages. **Services:** Literature searches via computer-oriented information retrieval system; dissemination of code/data packages; problem-solving; center open to public. **Computerized Information Services:** DOE/RECON. **Publications:** Bibliographies, irregular; newsletter, monthly; topical reports, irregular; abstracts of code/data packages, annual. **Remarks:** The Oak Ridge National Laboratory operates under contract to the U.S. Department of Energy. D.K. Trubey, Physicist; R.W. Roussin, Nuclear Engr.; B.L. McGill, Mathematician; J.E. White, Mathematician; N.A. Hatmaker, Info.Spec.

★10025★

OAK RIDGE NATIONAL LABORATORY - TOXICOLOGY INFORMATION RESPONSE CENTER (Sci-Tech; Med)
Bldg. 2024, Box X   Phone: (615) 576-1743
Oak Ridge, TN 37830   Susan G. Winslow, Dir.
Founded: 1971. **Staff:** Prof 7; Other 3. **Subjects:** Toxicology, pharmacology, veterinary toxicology, heavy metals, pesticides, chemistry, biology, medicine,

industrial hygiene. **Holdings:** 6000 search files; CA microfilm; BA microfilm; 250 microfiche of published bibliographies; subject files and reprints. **Subscriptions:** 80 journals and other serials. **Services:** SDI; specialized bibliographies; literature searches; library open to public with restrictions. **Computerized Information Services:** DIALOG, SDC, MEDLARS, DOE/RECON. **Publications:** State-of-the-art reviews; list of publications for sale - available on request. **Remarks:** Sponsored by the Toxicology Information Program/National Library of Medicine. The Oak Ridge National Laboratory operates under contract to the U.S. Department of Energy. **Staff:** J.P. Hutson, Info.Ctr.Asst.

★10026★
OAK TERRACE NURSING HOME - DPW FILM LIBRARY
County Rd. 67
Minnetonka, MN 55343
Defunct. Holdings absorbed by Oak Terrace Nursing Home - DPW Library.

★10027★
OAK TERRACE NURSING HOME - DPW LIBRARY (Med)
County Rd. 67   Phone: (612) 934-4100
Minnetonka, MN 55343   Susan F. Ager, Lib.Dir.
Staff: Prof 2; Other 3. **Subjects:** Psychiatry, geriatrics. **Holdings:** 3000 volumes; 1000 16mm films, filmstrips, slide programs and videotapes. **Subscriptions:** 175 journals and other serials. **Services:** Interlibrary loans; copying; library open to public by request. **Automated Operations:** Computerized acquisitions, serials and union lists for the consortia. **Computerized Information Services:** DIALOG, BRS. **Networks/Consortia:** Headquarters of Minnesota Department of Public Welfare Library Consortium; member of MINITEX; Greater Midwest Regional Medical Library Network (Region 3). **Publications:** DPW Library Bibliography, monthly - to consortium members and county mental health centers; SOAR, monthly - to members of consortium; Focus on Films (newsletter), bimonthly - to state residents. **Special Catalogs:** Audiovisuals 1983/1984. **Remarks:** Contains the holdings of the former Minnesota State Department of Public Welfare - Library and of Oak Terrace Nursing Home - DPW Film Library. Also maintains patients' library of 1000 volumes and 34 journal subscriptions. **Formerly:** Its Department of Public Welfare Medical Library. **Staff:** Colleen Spadaccini, Libn.

★10028★
OAKDALE REGIONAL CENTER FOR DEVELOPMENTAL DISABILITIES - STAFF LIBRARY (Med)
2995 W. Genesee St.   Phone: (313) 664-2951
Lapeer, MI 48446   Joanne Erskine, Lib.Coord.
Staff: 1. **Subjects:** Mental retardation, medicine, education, management, nursing, psychiatry. **Holdings:** 2500 books; 1 vertical file collection. **Subscriptions:** 73 journals and other serials. **Services:** Interlibrary loans; copying; library open to public with restrictions. **Networks/Consortia:** Member of Mid-Michigan Health Sciences Libraries (M-MHSL); Flint Area Health Science Library Network. **Remarks:** Library is operated by Lapeer County Library System.

★10029★
OAKITE PRODUCTS INC. - CHEMICAL RESEARCH LIBRARY (Sci-Tech)
50 Valley Rd.   Phone: (201) 464-6900
Berkeley Heights, NJ 07922   Mary Ann Derkach, Lib.Ck.
Staff: 1. **Subjects:** Chemistry. **Holdings:** 1000 books; 1250 bound periodical volumes; 90 reports. **Subscriptions:** 80 journals and other serials. **Services:** Interlibrary loans; library open to public with approval of management.

★10030★
OAKLAND CITY PLANNING DEPARTMENT - LIBRARY*
City Hall, 6th Fl.
Oakland, CA 94612
Founded: 1952. **Subjects:** Urban and regional planning. **Holdings:** 1600 books. **Remarks:** Presently inactive.

OAKLAND COUNTY LAW LIBRARY
See: Adams-Pratt Oakland County Law Library

★10031★
OAKLAND COUNTY PIONEER AND HISTORICAL SOCIETY - LIBRARY & ARCHIVES (Hist)
405 Oakland Ave.   Phone: (313) 338-6732
Pontiac, MI 48058   Mary Ann Treais, Adm.Coord.
Staff: 2. **Subjects:** Local, state and family histories; early Oakland County medical history. **Special Collections:** Howlett Collection of local history on specific families (20 document boxes); Avery Collection of marriages, births and deaths of Oakland County families (7000 cards). **Holdings:** 1500 books; 20 volumes of carbons of historical material; oral histories; clippings;

manuscripts; diaries; scrapbooks; 5 VF drawers of photographs; maps; newspapers; slides. **Services:** Copying; library open to public for reference use only by appointment. **Publications:** Oakland Gazette, 4/year - mailed to members, available free at library.

★10032★
OAKLAND COUNTY REFERENCE LIBRARY (Plan)
1200 N. Telegraph Rd.   Phone: (313) 858-0738
Pontiac, MI 48053   Phyllis Jose, Dir.
Founded: 1972. **Staff:** Prof 1; Other 3. **Subjects:** Planning, solid waste management, transportation, behavioral sciences, census, architecture, municipal government. **Special Collections:** National Research Council publications; Urban Land Institute publications; American Planning Association publications; Southeastern Michigan Council of Government publications. **Holdings:** 10,000 books. **Subscriptions:** 250 journals and other serials. **Services:** Interlibrary loans; copying; library open to public. **Automated Operations:** Computerized circulation. **Networks/Consortia:** Member of Wayne/Oakland Library Federation; Michigan Library Consortium (MLC); Council on Resource Development (CORD). **Publications:** Oakland County Union List of Serials, biennial; new book list, quarterly; bibliographies.

OAKLAND MUSEUM - ARCHIVES OF CALIFORNIA ART
See: Archives of California Art

★10033★
OAKLAND PUBLIC LIBRARY - AMERICAN INDIAN LIBRARY PROJECT (Area-Ethnic)
Dimond Branch Library
3536 Fruitvale Ave.   Phone: (415) 273-3511
Oakland, CA 94602   Marian Nichols, Supv.
Staff: Prof 1. **Subjects:** Native Americans - literature, culture, history. **Holdings:** 1500 books; clippings of current events. **Subscriptions:** 12 journals and other serials. **Services:** Interlibrary loans; library open to public. **Formerly:** Its Intertribal Library Project.

★10034★
OAKLAND PUBLIC LIBRARY - ART, MUSIC, RECREATION (Art; Mus)
125 14th St.   Phone: (415) 273-3178
Oakland, CA 94612   Richard Colvig, Sr.Libn.
Founded: 1961. **Staff:** Prof 3; Other 2. **Subjects:** History of art, architecture, painting, sculpture, decorative and graphic arts, furniture, interior decoration, photography, costume, music and music scores, sports and recreation, theater, cinema, dance. **Holdings:** 20,923 books; 2159 bound periodical volumes; 10,000 music scores; 30,000 choral music copies; 9000 phonograph records and cassettes. **Services:** Interlibrary loans; copying; library open to public. **Networks/Consortia:** Member of Bay Area Library and Information System (BALIS). **Special Indexes:** Card indexes of local events and personalities in music, art and architecture. **Staff:** Clinton Arndt, Libn.; Annabelle Pratt, Jr.Libn.

★10035★
OAKLAND PUBLIC LIBRARY - ASIAN LIBRARY (Area-Ethnic)
449 9th St.   Phone: (415) 273-3400
Oakland, CA 94607   Suzanne Lo, Hd.Libn.
Founded: 1975. **Staff:** Prof 2. **Subjects:** Asian-American experience; adult and juvenile materials in Asian language and literature - Chinese, Tagalog, Japanese, Korean, Vietnamese. **Holdings:** 35,000 books; 8 VF drawers of clippings; 150 historical pictures; 2000 Asian language phonograph records and cassettes; 125 16mm films; 60 sets of filmstrips. **Subscriptions:** 100 journals and other serials; 20 newspapers. **Services:** Interlibrary loans; copying; bilingual staff in all five Asian languages; library tours by bilingual staff; I & R services to Asian Community in East Bay area; library open to public. **Networks/Consortia:** Member of Bay Area Library and Information System (BALIS).

★10036★
OAKLAND PUBLIC LIBRARY - CITYLINE INFORMATION SERVICE (Soc Sci)
Oakland City Hall
1 City Hall Plaza   Phone: (415) 444-2489
Oakland, CA 94612   MaryLou T. Martin, Libn.
Founded: 1977. **Staff:** Prof 1; Other 20. **Subjects:** Local services, community organizations. **Subscriptions:** 10 newspapers. **Services:** Telephone inquiries answered. **Networks/Consortia:** Member of Bay Area Library and Information System (BALIS). **Special Catalogs:** Cityline Resource File.

★10037★
OAKLAND PUBLIC LIBRARY - HANDICAPPED SERVICES (Aud-Vis)
125 14th St.　　　　　　　　　Phone: (415) 273-3133
Oakland, CA 94612　　　　　　　Jean Paeth, Supv.Libn.
Founded: 1981. **Subjects:** Deafness, blindness, physical disabilities. **Special Collections:** Braille catalogs. **Holdings:** Figures not available. **Services:** Interlibrary loans; copying; services open to public. **Publications:** Bay Area Soundings; special bibliographies. **Special Indexes:** Information and Referral File of Agencies Serving the Disabled in the Bay Area. **Remarks:** Handicapped Services is part of the library's Reference Services.

★10038★
OAKLAND PUBLIC LIBRARY - HISTORY/LITERATURE DIVISION (Hist)
125 14th St.　　　　　　　　　Phone: (415) 273-3136
Oakland, CA 94612　　　　　　　Marilyn G. Rowan, Sr.Libn.
Staff: Prof 3; Other 4. **Subjects:** History, travel, biography, English and foreign languages and literature, genealogy, maps. **Special Collections:** Jack London collection (autographed first editions; signed letters; photographs, letters from literary friends; artifacts); logbooks of the cutter BEAR; Ina Coolbrith materials; U.S. Geological Survey Topographical Maps; Schomberg Collection of Black Literature on History (in microform); Negroes of New York, 1939 (Writers Program; in microform); library of American Civilization (in microform); Sutro Library Family History and Local History Subject Catalogs (in microform); Index to Biographies to State and Local Histories in the Library of Congress (in microform). **Holdings:** 100,663 books; genealogy microfilms. **Subscriptions:** 114 journals and other serials. **Services:** Interlibrary loans; copying; division open to public. **Networks/Consortia:** Member of Bay Area Library and Information System (BALIS). **Special Indexes:** Card indexes for Drama, Short Story, Poetry, Literary Criticism; Black Bibliography; local newspapers, 1978 to present; Local History. **Remarks:** The Oakland History Room telephone number is 273-3222. **Staff:** Sherrill Reeves, Libn.; William Sturm, Libn.; Donald Hausler, Libn.

★10039★
OAKLAND PUBLIC LIBRARY - LATIN AMERICAN LIBRARY (Area-Ethnic)
1900 Fruitvale Ave., Suite 1-A　　　Phone: (415) 532-7882
Oakland, CA 94601　　　　　　　Patrick Haggarty, Libn.
Founded: 1966. **Staff:** Prof 2; Other 4. **Subjects:** Spanish-speaking culture and history, Hispanic literature, Chicano history and culture. **Special Collections:** La Raza/Chicano Reference Collection; juvenile and adult materials in Spanish and English (books; magazines; records; newspapers). **Holdings:** 22,000 books; 115 study print sets; 200 slide sets; 190 tapes; 4 VF drawers of Chicano serials. **Subscriptions:** 70 journals and other serials; 17 newspapers. **Services:** Interlibrary loans; library open to public. **Networks/Consortia:** Member of Bay Area Library and Information System (BALIS). **Also Known As:** LAL. **Staff:** Arta Benzie-Youseff, Ch.Libn.; Gladis Carballo, Spanish Lang.Serv.Coord.

★10040★
OAKLAND PUBLIC LIBRARY - SCIENCE/SOCIOLOGY DIVISION (Sci-Tech; Bus-Fin; Soc Sci)
125 14th St.　　　　　　　　　Phone: (415) 273-3138
Oakland, CA 94612　　　　　　　Richard Ragsdale, Sr.Libn.
Staff: Prof 4; Other 5. **Subjects:** Business, technology, natural sciences, useful arts, sociology, philosophy, religion, education, criminology, law, government, psychology. **Special Collections:** Municipal documents (6100); Oakland documents (4900). **Holdings:** 62,183 books; 3800 science pamphlets. **Subscriptions:** 625 journals and other serials. **Services:** Interlibrary loans; copying; division open to public. **Computerized Information Services:** DIALOG, BRS. Performs free searches for Oakland residents. **Networks/Consortia:** Member of Bay Area Library And Information System (BALIS). **Special Indexes:** Municipal Index (cards). **Staff:** Patricia Coffey, Libn.; Mary-Ellen Mort, Libn.; Susan Young Yip, Libn.

★10041★
OAKLAND SCHOOLS - EDUCATIONAL RESOURCE CENTER (Educ)
2100 Pontiac Lake Rd.　　　　　　Phone: (313) 858-1961
Pontiac, MI 48054　　　　　　　Dr. Robert N. Johnson, Dir.
Founded: 1955. **Staff:** Prof 8; Other 15. **Subjects:** Education. **Holdings:** 40,000 books; 500 bound periodical volumes; complete ERIC microfiche collection; 3000 curriculum guides; 5000 curriculum materials; 8000 films; 7000 kits; 20 VF drawers. **Subscriptions:** 700 journals and other serials. **Services:** Interlibrary loans; copying; center open to public for reference use only. **Computerized Information Services:** DIALOG, NEXIS. **Remarks:** Center is also a state document depository. **Staff:** Judith Brooks, Asst.Libn.; Jennie B. Cross, Asst.Dir.; Robert Kramp, Libn.; Patrick Mardney, Media Serv.Spec.; Linda O'Donnell, Instr. TV Coord.; Beverly Palmer, Curric.Rsrc.Cons.; George Hemingway, Graphic Artist.

★10042★
THE (Oakland) TRIBUNE - LIBRARY (Publ)
Box 24424　　　　　　　　　　Phone: (415) 645-2745
Oakland, CA 94623　　　　　　　Yae Shinomiya, Libn.
Founded: 1912. **Staff:** Prof 1; Other 4. **Subjects:** Newspaper reference topics. **Holdings:** Figures not available. **Services:** Library not open to public. **Networks/Consortia:** Member of Bay Area Library and Information System (BALIS).

★10043★
OAKLAND UNIVERSITY - LIBRARY - SPECIAL COLLECTIONS AND ARCHIVES (Hist; Area-Ethnic)
Kresge Library Building　　　　　Phone: (313) 377-2492
Rochester, MI 48063　　　　　Elizabeth A. Titus, Hd. of Archv./Spec.Coll.
Founded: 1959. **Holdings:** James Collection (folklore); Hicks Collection (women in literature, 17th and 18th centuries); Springer Collection (Lincolniana); Anglo-Irish Collection; Underground Press Collection; university archives. **Services:** Interlibrary loans; copying; collections open to public with restrictions. **Automated Operations:** Computerized cataloging and circulation. **Computerized Information Services:** DIALOG, BRS, Dow Jones News/Retrieval, Pergamon InfoLine Ltd., OCLC, CAB Abstracts. Performs searches on partial cost recovery basis. **Networks/Consortia:** Member of Michigan Library Consortium (MLC); Wayne/Oakland Library Federation (WOLF); CLASS; Metropolitan Detroit Medical Library Group (MDMLG). **Publications:** Library Guide Series; Instructional Guide Series, both irregular - campus distribution and by request.

★10044★
OAKLAWN PSYCHIATRIC CENTER - PROFESSIONAL LIBRARY (Med)
2600 Oakland Ave.　　　　　　　Phone: (219) 294-3551
Elkhart, IN 46517　　　　　　　Nancy P. Price, Libn.
Staff: Prof 1. **Subjects:** Psychiatry, mental health, psychology, social work, substance abuse. **Holdings:** 1600 books; 1800 bound periodical volumes; 20 VF drawers. **Subscriptions:** 93 journals and other serials. **Services:** Interlibrary loans; copying; library open to public with restrictions. **Networks/Consortia:** Member of Area Library Services Authority (ALSA), Region 2.

OAKWOOD FORENSIC CENTER
See: Lima State Hospital

★10045★
OAKWOOD HOSPITAL - MC LOUTH MEMORIAL HEALTH SCIENCE LIBRARY (Med)†
18101 Oakwood Blvd.　　　　　　Phone: (313) 593-7685
Dearborn, MI 48124　　　　　　　Sharon A. Phillips, Dir.
Staff: Prof 2; Other 3. **Subjects:** Medicine and allied health sciences. **Holdings:** 13,000 books and bound periodical volumes; AV materials. **Subscriptions:** 435 journals and other serials; 8 newspapers. **Services:** Interlibrary loans; library not open to public. **Computerized Information Services:** MEDLINE, DIALOG, OCLC, BRS. **Networks/Consortia:** Member of Metropolitan Detroit Medical Library Group (MDMLG); Greater Midwest Regional Medical Library Network (Region 3). **Staff:** Lorraine Obrzut, Asst.Libn.

★10046★
OAO CORPORATION - INFORMATION CENTER (Sci-Tech)
7500 Greenway Ctr.　　　　　　　Phone: (301) 345-0750
Greenbelt, MD 20770　　　　　　Joseph Langdon, Corp.Libn.
Staff: Prof 1. **Subjects:** Engineering - aerospace, mechnical; data systems. **Holdings:** 250 books; 1000 bound periodical volumes; 4000 technical reports. **Subscriptions:** 56 journals and other serials. **Services:** Interlibrary loans; copying; SDI (in-house); center open to public with permission of librarian. **Computerized Information Services:** DIALOG, NASA/RECON; internal database.

OAS
See: Organization of American States

★10047★
OBER, KALER, GRIMES & SHRIVER - LIBRARY (Law)
1600 Maryland National Bank Bldg.　Phone: (301) 685-1120
Baltimore, MD 21202　　　　　　Madelyn H. Weschler, Libn.
Staff: 1. **Subjects:** Law - admiralty, hospital/health care, corporate, tax; litigation; estates and trusts. **Holdings:** 20,000 books. **Services:** Copying; library not open to public. **Computerized Information Services:** LEXIS, NEXIS, Shepard's/McGraw-Hill, Auto-Cite, New York Times Information Service.

★10048★
OBERLIN COLLEGE - CLARENCE WARD ART LIBRARY (Art)
Allen Art Bldg.   Phone: (216) 775-8635
Oberlin, OH 44074   Jeffrey Weidman, Art Libn.
Founded: 1917. **Staff:** 3. **Subjects:** Art, architecture, archeology. **Special Collections:** Rare books including duplication of Thomas Jefferson's architectural library (900 books). **Holdings:** 40,000 books and bound periodical volumes; 5000 exhibition catalogs; 8500 art sales catalogs. **Subscriptions:** 250 journals and other serials. **Services:** Interlibrary loans; copying; library open to public for reference use only and to cooperating Great Lakes Colleges Association (GLCA) and NEOMAL libraries with restrictions. **Automated Operations:** Computerized circulation. **Networks/Consortia:** Member of NEOMAL; OHIONET.

★10049★
OBERLIN COLLEGE - CONSERVATORY OF MUSIC LIBRARY (Mus)
                                                   Phone: (216) 775-8280
Oberlin, OH 44074   John E. Druesedow, Jr., Dir.
Staff: Prof 3; Other 7. **Subjects:** Music - chamber, keyboard, vocal, education, history, theory. **Special Collections:** Karl W. Gehrkens Music Education Library; Edmonds Collection of Opera Scores; Rita Benton Collection (reference, research, music librarianship); recital tape archives; Mr. and Mrs. C.W. Best Collection of Autographs. **Holdings:** 67,000 books and scores; 10 VF drawers; 25,000 phonograph records; 4100 microcards; 3000 magnetic tapes; 1300 reels of microfilm; 300 microfiche. **Subscriptions:** 315 journals and other serials. **Services:** Interlibrary loans; copying; library open to public for reference use only and to cooperating NEOMAL libraries with restrictions. **Automated Operations:** Computerized cataloging, acquisitions, circulation and ILL. **Computerized Information Services:** OCLC. **Networks/Consortia:** Member of Cleveland Area Metropolitan Library System (CAMLS); OHIONET; Great Lakes Colleges Association (GLCA); NEOMAL. **Publications:** Recent Additions to the Conservatory Library, irregular. **Special Catalogs:** Catalog of recital tape archives (computer-generated); Catalog of the Mr. and Mrs. C.W. Best Collection of Autographs. **Formerly:** Its Mary M. Vial Music Library. **Staff:** Carolyn Rabson, Libn., Rd.Serv.; David Knapp, Libn., Tech.Serv.

★10050★
OBERLIN COLLEGE - SCIENCE LIBRARY (Sci-Tech)
Kettering Hall   Phone: (216) 775-8310
Oberlin, OH 44074   Alison Ricker, Sci.Libn.
Founded: 1961. **Staff:** Prof 1; Other 1. **Subjects:** Biology, chemistry, earth sciences, physics, astronomy. **Holdings:** 46,000 books and bound periodical volumes; 35 loose-leaf binders of American Petroleum Institute Spectral Data; 800 reels of microfilm. **Subscriptions:** 300 journals and other serials. **Services:** Interlibrary loans; copying; library open to public and to Great Lakes Colleges Association (GLCA) and NEOMAL libraries with restrictions. **Computerized Information Services:** DIALOG. **Networks/Consortia:** Member of OHIONET; NEOMAL. **Formerly:** Its Class of 1904 Science Library and Physics Reading Room.

★10051★
OBICI (Louise) MEMORIAL HOSPITAL - LIBRARY (Med)*
Box 1100   Phone: (804) 539-1511
Suffolk, VA 23434   Patricia D. Herzfeldt, Supv., Med.Rec.
Founded: 1951. **Staff:** Prof 1; Other 1. **Subjects:** Medicine, surgery, obstetrics, pediatrics. **Holdings:** 550 books; 100 Audio-Digest tapes. **Subscriptions:** 25 journals and other serials. **Services:** Interlibrary loans; library not open to public. **Computerized Information Services:** Online systems.

OBLATE COLLEGE - LIBRARY
See: Oblates Theology Library

★10052★
OBLATE FATHERS - BIBLIOTHEQUE DESCHATELETS (Rel-Theol)
175 Main   Phone: (613) 237-0580
Ottawa, ON, Canada K1S 1C3   Leo Laberge, Dir.
Founded: 1885. **Staff:** Prof 1; Other 1. **Subjects:** Theology, spirituality, philosophy, church history, Canadiana, history, literature. **Holdings:** 65,000 books; 15,000 bound periodical volumes. **Subscriptions:** 100 journals and other serials. **Services:** Library not open to public. **Staff:** Gerard Juneau, Libn.

OBLATE FATHERS - UNIVERSITE ST-PAUL
See: Universite St-Paul

★10053★
OBLATE SCHOOL OF THEOLOGY - LIBRARY (Rel-Theol)
285 Oblate Dr.   Phone: (512) 341-1366
San Antonio, TX 78216-6693   James Maney, Lib.Dir.
Founded: 1903. **Staff:** Prof 1; Other 2. **Subjects:** Theology. **Special Collections:** Oblate faculty publications. **Holdings:** 22,000 books; 10,000 bound periodical volumes; 225 pamphlets; 220 AV items. **Subscriptions:** 266 journals and other serials; 8 newspapers. **Services:** Interlibrary loans; copying; library open to public for reference use only; materials circulate to members of consortium only. **Networks/Consortia:** Member of Council of Research & Academic Libraries (CORAL). **Publications:** Library Report, monthly - for internal distribution only.

OBLATES OF MARY IMMACULATE ARCHIVES
See: Oblates Theology Library

OBLATES OF MARY IMMACULATE - ST. CHARLES SCHOLASTICATE
See: St. Charles Scholasticate

★10054★
OBLATES THEOLOGY LIBRARY (Rel-Theol)
391 Michigan Ave., N.E.   Phone: (202) 529-5244
Washington, DC 20017   Ward E. Gongoll, Hd.Libn.
Staff: Prof 4. **Subjects:** Theology, sacred scripture, philosophy. **Special Collections:** Oblates of Mary Immaculate Archives; Special Ministries. **Holdings:** 51,355 books and bound periodical volumes. **Subscriptions:** 247 journals and other serials; 9 newspapers. **Services:** Interlibrary loans; copying; library open to public with restrictions. **Networks/Consortia:** Member of Washington Theological Consortium. **Remarks:** Includes the holdings of the former De Sales Hall School of Theology - Library. **Formerly:** Oblate College - Library.

O'BRIEN (Kevin F.) HEALTH SCIENCES LIBRARY
See: Marquette General Hospital - Kevin F. O'Brien Health Sciences Library

O'CALLAHAN SCIENCE LIBRARY
See: College of the Holy Cross - Science Library

★10055★
OCCIDENTAL CHEMICAL CORPORATION - TECHNICAL INFORMATION CENTER (Sci-Tech)
Box 8   Phone: (716) 773-8531
Niagara Falls, NY 14302   Dr. Irving Gordon, Supv.
Founded: 1916. **Staff:** Prof 5. **Subjects:** Organic chemistry, inorganic chemistry, polymers, textiles, physical chemistry. **Holdings:** 15,000 books; 20,000 bound periodical volumes; 90 VF drawers of technical reports; 10 cabinets of microforms. **Subscriptions:** 500 journals and other serials. **Services:** Interlibrary loans; copying; SDI; library open to public on request. **Computerized Information Services:** DIALOG, SDC, BRS, Pergamon InfoLine Ltd., NLM, NEXIS, CAS Online. **Networks/Consortia:** Member of Western New York Library Resources Council (WNYLRC). **Special Indexes:** Magnetic disc index of internal reports and patents. **Formerly:** Hooker Chemical Corporation. **Staff:** Jane Pattison, Sr.Res.Libn.

★10056★
OCCIDENTAL COLLEGE - MARY NORTON CLAPP LIBRARY (Hum)
1600 Campus Rd.   Phone: (213) 259-2852
Los Angeles, CA 90041   Michael C. Sutherland, Spec.Coll.Libn.
Staff: Prof 1. **Subjects:** Western Americana, mystery and detective fiction, romantic literature, railroad history, fine printing, aviation, Lincoln and the Civil War. **Special Collections:** William Jennings Bryan Collection; William Henry Collection; Upton Sinclair Collection; Ward Ritchie Press Collection; Robinson Jeffers Collection; Doheny Foundation. **Holdings:** 60,000 volumes. **Services:** Copying; library open to public for reference use only. **Publications:** Library Bibliogram, irregular. **Special Indexes:** Index to William Henry Letters (unpublished); Inventory to Guymon Mystery and Detective Fiction Collection (unpublished).

OCCIDENTAL COLLEGE - ROUNCE AND COFFIN CLUB
See: Rounce and Coffin Club, Los Angeles

★10057★
OCCIDENTAL EXPLORATION & PRODUCTION COMPANY - LIBRARY (Energy)
5000 Stockdale Hwy.   Phone: (805) 395-8565
Bakersfield, CA 93309   Barbara Rogers, Libn.
Founded: 1968. **Staff:** Prof 1; Other 2. **Subjects:** Geology, petroleum, engineering, energy resources, environment, law. **Holdings:** 3000 books and

bound periodical volumes; 6000 articles and reprints; 10,000 maps; 538 annual reports. **Subscriptions:** 250 journals and other serials. **Services:** Interlibrary loans; copying; library open to public by appointment with librarian. **Computerized Information Services:** DIALOG, SDC. **Publications:** New Book Lists, bimonthly; Periodical List, monthly; Film List, quarterly.

★10058★

OCCIDENTAL RESEARCH CORPORATION - TECHNICAL INFORMATION CENTER (Energy; Sci-Tech)†
2100 S.E. Main
Box 19601
Irvine, CA 92713
Phone: (714) 957-7450
Patricia M. Petring, Mgr., Tech.Info.Serv.
Staff: Prof 2; Other 4. **Subjects:** Chemical engineering, chemistry, petroleum engineering, energy resources. **Holdings:** 6500 books; 2000 bound periodical volumes; 10,000 documents; 4500 microforms. **Subscriptions:** 500 journals and other serials; 10 newspapers. **Services:** Interlibrary loans; copying; center open to public by appointment. **Automated Operations:** Computerized serials, circulation and document indexing and retrieval. **Computerized Information Services:** DIALOG, SDC, Chemical Information Services, DOE/RECON, BRS, Chemical Abstracts Service, New York Times Information Service; Occidental Universal Retrieval System (OURS; internal database). **Networks/Consortia:** Member of CLASS. **Publications:** Acquisition list, weekly; Alerting Bulletin, weekly; Library Handbook. **Remarks:** Occidental Research Corporation is a subsidiary of Occidental Petroleum Corporation. **Staff:** Nam-Hee Kang, Supv., Tech.Info.Serv.

OCCUPATIONAL SAFETY AND HEALTH ADMINISTRATION
See: U.S. Dept. of Labor - OSHA

★10059★

OCEAN CITY HISTORICAL MUSEUM - LIBRARY (Hist)
409 Wesley Ave.
Ocean City, NJ 08226
Phone: (609) 399-1801
Alberta E. Lamphear, Libn.
Subjects: History of Ocean City. **Holdings:** 200 books; photographs; deeds; documents; periodicals. **Services:** Library open to public for reference use only.

★10060★

OCEAN AND COASTAL LAW CENTER - LIBRARY (Law; Sci-Tech)
School of Law
University of Oregon
Eugene, OR 97403
Phone: (503) 686-3845
Andrea G. Coffman, Libn.
Staff: Prof 1; Other 1. **Subjects:** International law of the sea, coastal zone management, ocean management and policy, fisheries, aquaculture, offshore drilling and mining, marine pollution. **Holdings:** 3800 books; 200 bound periodical volumes; 200 reprints; 100 maps; 80 fishery management plans; 5 VF drawers of documents. **Subscriptions:** 112 journals and other serials. **Services:** Interlibrary loans; copying (limited); library open to public. **Publications:** Recent Acquisitions, monthly; Periodical Holdings, annual with semiannual supplements - both available upon request.

★10061★

OCEAN COUNTY LAW LIBRARY (Law)†
118 Washington St.
Toms River, NJ 08753
Phone: (201) 244-2121
James P. Rutigliano, Asst.Ct.Adm.
Founded: 1930. **Staff:** Prof 1; Other 1. **Subjects:** Law. **Holdings:** 6125 books. **Subscriptions:** 150 journals and other serials. **Services:** Library open to public. **Staff:** Elaine Choppe, Prin.Ck.

OCEAN ENGINEERING INFORMATION CENTRE
See: Memorial University of Newfoundland

★10062★

OCEANIC INSTITUTE - WORKING LIBRARY (Sci-Tech; Env-Cons)
Makapuu Point
Waimanalo, HI 96795
Phone: (808) 259-7951
Ellen Antill, Adm.Asst.
Founded: 1964. **Staff:** 1. **Subjects:** Aquaculture, oceanography, general science, marine biology. **Holdings:** Figures not available for periodicals. **Subscriptions:** 15 journals and other serials. **Services:** Library not open to public.

★10063★

OCEANOGRAPHIC SERVICES, INC. - TECHNICAL LIBRARY (Sci-Tech)
25 Castilian Dr.
Goleta, CA 93117
Phone: (805) 685-4521
Founded: 1973. **Staff:** 1. **Subjects:** Oceanography, meteorology, Arctic research, instrumentation, hydrology, marine geology. **Special Collections:** Nautical charts (400); topographical maps (150); atlases and charts (75). **Holdings:** 3500 books; 50 bound periodical volumes; 2550 technical reports;

1350 reprints; 60 synoptic summaries of meteorological observations; 20 sailing directions; tide tables for 25 years; NTIS publications on microfiche. **Subscriptions:** 49 journals and other serials. **Services:** Interlibrary loans; library not open to public.

★10064★

OCEANROUTES, INC. - TECHNICAL LIBRARY (Sci-Tech)
3260 Hillview Ave.
Palo Alto, CA 94304
Phone: (415) 493-3600
Mari Wilson, Tech.Libn.
Staff: Prof 1. **Subjects:** Weather, shipping and cargo. **Special Collections:** Historical weather data. **Holdings:** 3000 books and bound periodical volumes; 500 technical reports. **Subscriptions:** 125 journals and other serials; 5 newspapers. **Services:** Interlibrary loans; copying; SDI; library open to public by appointment. **Automated Operations:** Computerized cataloging. **Computerized Information Services:** DIALOG. **Networks/Consortia:** Member of South Bay Cooperative Library System (SBCLS); CLASS. **Publications:** Oceanroutes Technical Library Bulletin, bimonthly - distributed in-house and to all foreign offices. **Special Catalogs:** Technical paper file.

OCHSNER (Alton) MEDICAL FOUNDATION
See: Alton Ochsner Medical Foundation

★10065★

OCLC, INC. - LIBRARY (Info Sci)
Box 7777
Dublin, OH 43017
Phone: (614) 764-6000
Ann T. Dodson, Mgr.
Founded: 1977. **Staff:** Prof 5; Other 3. **Subjects:** Library and information science, computer science and engineering, telecommunications, management and business. **Special Collections:** Library Network Newsletters. **Holdings:** 6510 books; 175 bound periodical volumes; 2140 microfiche; 240 cassettes; 1415 slides; 11,385 serial microfiche; 65 maps; 172 microcomputer software packages; 13,950 OCLC and system manuals. **Subscriptions:** 760 journals and other serials; 5 newspapers. **Services:** Interlibrary loans; copying; SDI; current awareness; library open to public with restrictions. **Automated Operations:** Computerized cataloging, acquisitions, serials, circulation and ILL. **Computerized Information Services:** DIALOG, BRS, DIALCOM, Inc., Dun & Bradstreet Corporation, Ohio State University LCS; bibliographies, list of periodicals, software documentation control from internal databases. **Networks/Consortia:** Member of CALICO. **Publications:** OCC Libline; accessions lists. **Also Known As:** Online Computer Library Center, Inc. **Staff:** Trisha L. Davis, Mgr., Tech.Serv.Sect.; Nancy F. Lensenmayer, Mgr., Pub.Serv.Sect.; Paul P. Philbin, Ref.Libn.; Barbara Kriigel, Doc.Libn.

O'CONNOR (Catherine B.) LIBRARY
See: Boston College - Weston Observatory - Catherine B. O'Connor Library

★10066★

O'CONNOR, CAVANAGH, ANDERSON, WESTOVER, KILLINGSWORTH, BESHEARS - LAW LIBRARY (Law)
3003 N. Central Ave., Suite 1800
Phoenix, AZ 85012
Phone: (602) 263-3811
Sharron L. Pettengill, Hd. Law Libn.
Staff: 3. **Subjects:** Law - medical, insurance, corporate, tax, labor, real estate, bond, employment practice, workers compensation. **Holdings:** 19,000 books. **Subscriptions:** 30 journals and other serials. **Services:** Interlibrary loans; copying; library open to attorneys and clients only.

★10067★

O'CONNOR (Lindsay A. & Olive B.) HOSPITAL - LIBRARY (Med)
Andes Road, Route 28
Delhi, NY 13753
Phone: (607) 746-2371
Barbara Green, Libn.
Founded: 1968. **Subjects:** Medicine, nursing. **Holdings:** 200 books; 200 cassettes. **Subscriptions:** 12 journals and other serials. **Services:** Copying; library open to public on request.

★10068★

OCTAMERON ASSOCIATES, INC. - RESEARCH LIBRARY (Educ)
820 Fontaine St.
Alexandria, VA 22302
Phone: (703) 836-1019
Karen Stokstad, Libn.
Founded: 1975. **Staff:** Prof 1; Other 1. **Subjects:** College admissions and financial aid, career information, higher education. **Holdings:** 2100 books; 500 bound periodical volumes; 20 VF drawers of scholarship information; 20 linear feet of pamphlets. **Subscriptions:** 92 journals and other serials. **Services:** Library not open to public. **Computerized Information Services:** College financial aid file (internal database). **Publications:** Annual directories of scholarship information - for sale; internal reports. **Special Indexes:** Financial aid data. **Staff:** Alberta Jane, Cat.

ODELL (Hamilton) LIBRARY
See: New York State Supreme Court - 3rd Judicial District - Hamilton Odell Library

★10069★
ODESSA AMERICAN - EDITORIAL LIBRARY (Publ)
Box 2952   Phone: (915) 337-4661
Odessa, TX 79760   Jo Jones, Libn.
Founded: 1940. **Staff:** 1. **Subjects:** Newspaper reference topics. **Holdings:** Figures not available for books; microfilm; newspaper files. **Subscriptions:** 15 journals and other serials; 35 newspapers. **Services:** Copying; library open to public for reference use only with supervision. **Remarks:** Member of Freedom Newspapers Chain.

O'DONNELL (Mayo Hayes) LIBRARY
See: Monterey History and Art Association - Mayo Hayes O'Donnell Library

O'DONOGHUE MEDICAL LIBRARY
See: St. Anthony Hospital

OESPER CHEMISTRY-BIOLOGY LIBRARY
See: University of Cincinnati

OESTERLE LIBRARY
See: North Central College

★10070★
OFFICE OF BILINGUAL EDUCATION - RESOURCE LIBRARY AND INFORMATION UNIT (Educ; Area-Ethnic)
131 Livingston St., Rm. 204   Phone: (718) 858-5505
Brooklyn, NY 11201   Carmen Gloria Burgos, Libn.
Founded: 1973. **Staff:** Prof 1; Other 1. **Subjects:** Education - bilingual, bicultural; English as a second language. **Special Collections:** Puerto Rican Heritage Collection. **Holdings:** 53,000 books; 410 curriculum guides; 1500 ERIC microfiche; 220 proposals; 3 VF drawers of reports; 9 VF drawers of clippings and articles; AV material. **Subscriptions:** 55 journals and other serials. **Services:** Library open to public. **Networks/Consortia:** Member of Bilingual Education Telecommunications Network (BETNET). **Remarks:** The language groups served include Spanish, Italian, French, Haitian-Creole, Chinese, Greek, Portoguese, Indochinese, Korean and Russian.

OFFICE OF THE COMMISSIONER OF OFFICIAL LANGUAGES
See: Canada - Office of the Commissioner of Official Languages

OFFICE OF THE JUDGE ADVOCATE GENERAL
See: Canada - National Defence

★10071★
OFFICE ON SMOKING AND HEALTH - TECHNICAL INFORMATION CENTER (Med)
Park Bldg., Rm. 1-16
5600 Fishers Lane   Phone: (301) 443-1690
Rockville, MD 20857   Donald R. Shopland, Tech.Info.Off.
Founded: 1965. **Staff:** Prof 3; Other 3. **Subjects:** Smoking and health, tobacco, nicotine, behavioral aspects of smoking, cessation techniques. **Holdings:** 1000 books; 20,000 reprints and journal articles; 12,000 documents on microfilm; 100 dissertation theses; 40,000 technical reports. **Subscriptions:** 60 journals and other serials. **Services:** Interlibrary loans; copying; answers written and telephone requests for information; center open to public. **Computerized Information Services:** Internal database. **Publications:** Smoking and Health Abstract Bulletin, bimonthly; Health Consequences of Smoking, annual; State Legislation on Smoking and Health, annual; Bibliography on Smoking and Health, annual; Directory of On-Going Research in Smoking and Health, biennial - all available to libraries and professionals. **Special Catalogs:** Computerized catalog of collection from 1970 to present. **Remarks:** Center houses the world's leading resource materials on smoking and its effects on health. Information Center located at 12420 Parklawn Dr., Rockville, MD 20857. An alternate telephone number is 443-1575.

OFFICE DU TOURISME DU CANADA
See: Canada - Regional Industrial Expansion - Canadian Government Office of Tourism

OFFUTT AIR FORCE BASE (NE)
See: U.S. Air Force Hospital - Ehrling Bergquist Regional Hospital; U.S. Air Force - Strategic Air Command

★10072★
OGILVY & MATHER, INC. - INFORMATION SERVICES DEPARTMENT (Bus-Fin)
200 E. Randolph Dr., 69th Fl.   Phone: (312) 861-1166
Chicago, IL 60601   Grace A. Villamora, Mgr.
Staff: Prof 1; Other 2. **Subjects:** Advertising, marketing, business, communications. **Holdings:** 1500 volumes; 10 bound periodical volumes; 150 corporate/industry files; Ogilvy & Mather publications, studies and reports; annual reports of Fortune 500 corporations. **Subscriptions:** 469 journals and other serials; 5 newspapers. **Services:** Interlibrary loans; department not open to public. **Automated Operations:** Computerized acquisitions. **Computerized Information Services:** DIALOG, NEXIS, Dow Jones News/Retrieval, SDC; internal database. **Networks/Consortia:** Member of Chicago Library System. **Publications:** New Books, quarterly; Top Resources for Secondary Research, quarterly - for internal distribution only. **Formerly:** Its Library and Information Center.

★10073★
OGILVY & MATHER, INC. - RESEARCH LIBRARY (Bus-Fin)†
2 E. 48th St.   Phone: (212) 907-3502
New York, NY 10017   Joanne Winiarski, Hd.Libn.
Founded: 1955. **Staff:** Prof 3; Other 2. **Subjects:** Advertising, marketing, travel, drugs and cosmetics. **Holdings:** 4000 books and bound periodical volumes; 135 VF drawers of subject files. **Subscriptions:** 243 journals and other serials; 7 newspapers. **Services:** Interlibrary loans; library not open to public. **Computerized Information Services:** New York Times Information Service, DIALOG, SDC. **Staff:** Jennifer Farrar, Libn.; Beth Pollack, Libn.

★10074★
OGILVY, RENAULT - LIBRARY (Law)†
1981 McGill College Ave.   Phone: (514) 286-5424
Montreal, PQ, Canada H3A 3C1   Mrs. M. Elvidge, Libn.
Founded: 1879. **Staff:** Prof 2. **Subjects:** Law - Quebec, Canadian and British. **Holdings:** 12,000 books and bound periodical volumes. **Services:** Library open to clients of the firm only.

★10075★
OGLE PETROLEUM INC. - LIBRARY (Sci-Tech)
4213 State St.   Phone: (805) 964-9911
Santa Barbara, CA 93110   Joyce Foresman, Libn.
Staff: Prof 1. **Subjects:** Geology, geophysics. **Holdings:** 300 books; 70 lateral drawers of files on wells; 10 lateral drawers of microfiche. **Subscriptions:** 18 journals and other serials. **Services:** Library not open to public.

★10076★
OGLEBAY INSTITUTE - MANSION MUSEUM LIBRARY (Hist)
Oglebay Park   Phone: (304) 242-7272
Wheeling, WV 26003   T. Patrick Brennan, Cur.
Founded: 1930. **Staff:** Prof 4. **Subjects:** History - local and tri-state area; glass, china, other decorative arts. **Holdings:** 750 books; 250 items of archival material. **Services:** Interlibrary loans; copying; library open to public for reference use and loan on request. **Staff:** John A. Artzberger, Dir. Mansion Musm.

★10077★
OGLESBY HISTORICAL SOCIETY - LIBRARY (Hist)
Oglesby Public Library
128 W. Walnut   Phone: (815) 883-3619
Oglesby, IL 61348   Albert Moyle, Pres.
Founded: 1919. **Subjects:** Local history. **Holdings:** Figures not available. **Services:** Library open to public.

★10078★
OGLETHORPE UNIVERSITY - LIBRARY - ARCHIVES (Hist)
4484 Peachtree Rd., N.E.   Phone: (404) 261-1441
Atlanta, GA 30319
Subjects: Oglethorpe University, 1835 to present. **Special Collections:** Records of the "Crypt of Civilization" at Oglethorpe; papers and drawings of the original Oglethorpe University buildings in Atlanta, 1913-1930; minutes of the board of trustees, 1835-1871. **Holdings:** 1 file cabinet and 14 boxes of manuscripts and photographs; the Oglethorpe University "Founder's Book," 1916. **Services:** Copying; archives open to public for research only. **Networks/Consortia:** Member of University Center in Georgia, Inc.

★10079★

OHEB ZEDECK SYNAGOGUE CENTER - LIBRARY (Rel-Theol)*
2300 Mahantongo St.   Phone: (717) 622-4320
Pottsville, PA 17901
Staff: Prof 1. **Subjects:** Judaica. **Holdings:** 1900 books; 200 educational materials. **Subscriptions:** 18 journals and other serials. **Services:** Copying; library open to public. **Publications:** Modiin, weekly newspaper - for internal distribution only.

★10080★

OHEV SHALOM SYNAGOGUE - RAY DOBLITZ MEMORIAL LIBRARY (Rel-Theol)
2 Chester Rd.   Phone: (215) 874-1465
Wallingford, PA 19086   Evelyn Schott, Libn.
Founded: 1955. **Staff:** Prof 1. **Subjects:** Judaica. **Holdings:** 5500 books; 120 recordings; pamphlets. **Subscriptions:** 12 journals and other serials. **Services:** Library open to public with references.

★10081★

OHIO BELL - CORPORATE LIBRARY (Bus-Fin)
100 Erieview Plaza, Rm. 112   Phone: (216) 822-2740
Cleveland, OH 44114   Adele R. Kurka, Asst.Mgr.-Libn.
Staff: 7. **Subjects:** Business, management, telecommunications, personnel, psychology, computers, marketing, Ohio Bell and Bell System history. **Special Collections:** Corporate historical photograph collection (30,000 photographs). **Holdings:** 6000 books; 300 bound periodical volumes. **Subscriptions:** 133 journals and other serials. **Services:** Copying; library open to public with approval. **Computerized Information Services:** DIALOG, NEXIS; internal database. **Special Indexes:** Reference file index (loose-leaf). **Staff:** Timothy C. Sharnas, Supv.

★10082★

OHIO COLLEGE OF PODIATRIC MEDICINE - LIBRARY/MEDIA CENTER (Med)
10515 Carnegie Ave.   Phone: (216) 231-3300
Cleveland, OH 44106   Judy Mehl Cowell, Dir.
Founded: 1916. **Staff:** Prof 1; Other 2. **Subjects:** Podiatric medicine, orthopedics, dermatology, biomechanics, sports medicine. **Special Collections:** Archives; podiatric medicine. **Holdings:** 10,000 books; 2000 bound periodical volumes; 4000 AV materials; VF drawers of pamphlet material; 800 reprints; School Papers File; state file. **Subscriptions:** 195 journals and other serials. **Services:** Interlibrary loans; copying; library open to public with restrictions. **Automated Operations:** Computerized cataloging. **Computerized Information Services:** MEDLINE. Performs searches on cost recovery basis.

OHIO COOPERATIVE WILDLIFE RESEARCH UNIT
See: Ohio State University

★10083★

OHIO COUNTY LAW LIBRARY (Law)
City-County Bldg.
1500 Chapline St.   Phone: (304) 234-3634
Wheeling, WV 26003   Nancy C. Obecny, Law Libn.
Founded: 1919. **Staff:** Prof 1. **Subjects:** Law. **Holdings:** 33,000 volumes. **Services:** Copying; library open to public for reference use only. **Remarks:** Maintained by State of West Virginia.

★10084★

OHIO COVERED BRIDGE COMMITTEE - LIBRARY (Hist)*
18 Elm Ave.   Phone: (513) 761-1789
Cincinnati, OH 45215   John A. Diehl, Libn.
Founded: 1940. **Staff:** 1. **Subjects:** Timber bridges (general and Ohio orientation). **Holdings:** 140 books; maps; manuscripts; clippings; black/white and color photographs; checklist of Ohio timber covered bridges. **Services:** Library open to public by appointment.

★10085★

OHIO DOMINICAN COLLEGE - SPANGLER LIBRARY (Soc Sci; Rel-Theol)
1216 Sunbury Rd.   Phone: (614) 253-2741
Columbus, OH 43219   Sr. Rosalie Graham, Dir.
Founded: 1911. **Staff:** Prof 6; Other 3. **Subjects:** Political science, social sciences, theology, philosophy. **Holdings:** 118,000 books; 12,153 bound periodical volumes; 4912 reels of microfilm; 2200 AV materials. **Subscriptions:** 595 journals and other serials; 15 newspapers. **Services:** Interlibrary loans; copying; library open to public. **Automated Operations:** Computerized cataloging. **Computerized Information Services:** OCLC. **Networks/Consortia:** Member of OHIONET. **Staff:** Gabriella Petrovics, Libn.; P. Miller, Cat.Libn.; Larry Cepek, Dir., Media Ctr.; Ken Fromm, Asst.Dir./Media Ctr.

★10086★

OHIO EDISON COMPANY - CORPORATE LIBRARY (Energy)
76 S. Main St.   Phone: (216) 384-5367
Akron, OH 44308   Sharon M. Malumphy, Corp.Libn.
Founded: 1981. **Staff:** Prof 1; Other 1. **Subjects:** Engineering, energy, management. **Special Collections:** Electric Power Research Institute reports (1560); Edison Electric Institute reports (450). **Holdings:** 4200 books; 270 bound periodical volumes; 1440 manufacturers' catalogs; 18 shelves of company references and documents; 4 VF drawers of newsletters and college catalogs; 750 standards. **Subscriptions:** 268 journals and other serials. **Services:** Interlibrary loans; SDI; library open to public with permission. **Computerized Information Services:** DIALOG, SDC, DOE/RECON, The Source, Utility Data Institute (UDI). **Publications:** Library Update, irregular - for internal distribution only. **Special Indexes:** Index to standards.

★10087★

OHIO GENEALOGICAL SOCIETY - LIBRARY (Hist)
Box 2625   Phone: (419) 522-9077
Mansfield, OH 44906   Mrs. Carl Main, Libn.
Staff: Prof 1; Other 2. **Subjects:** History and genealogy. **Special Collections:** Ancestor file (125,000 cards). **Holdings:** 7000 books; census for all Ohio counties, 1820-1860, 1880, 1900, on microfilm; unpublished family history manuscripts. **Services:** Copying; library open to public. **Remarks:** The library is located at 419 W. 3rd St., Mansfield, OH 44903.

★10088★

OHIO HISTORICAL SOCIETY - ARCHIVES-LIBRARY (Hist)
I-71 & 17th Ave.   Phone: (614) 466-1500
Columbus, OH 43211   Dr. Dennis East, Hd.
Founded: 1885. **Staff:** Prof 22; Other 14. **Subjects:** Ohio history, American history, genealogy. **Special Collections:** Audiovisual Archives (5 million feet of motion picture film; 750,000 still pictures; 5000 maps; 3500 broadsides and posters; 10,000 sound recordings including over 400 oral history interviews); local government records (records from Central Ohio counties and municipalities; records from other Ohio regions held by other members of Ohio Network of American History Research Centers); data archives (22 computer data sets); manuscripts (800 large and 4200 small collections of private papers of Ohio individuals and organizations); state archives (9000 linear feet from current and defunct state agencies); Anti-Saloon League temperance material from Westerville (over 100 reels of microfilm). **Holdings:** 132,000 volumes; 55,000 reels of microfilm (newspapers; manuscript collections; government records; theses; dissertations). **Subscriptions:** 1045 journals, serials and newspapers. **Services:** Interlibrary loans; copying; microfilm laboratory; conservation laboratory; reference by mail; library open to public. **Automated Operations:** Computerized cataloging. **Computerized Information Services:** OCLC. **Networks/Consortia:** Member of Ohio Network of American History Research Centers. **Publications:** Guides, inventories, manuals and brochures, 5-25/year. **Staff:** James B. Casey, Hd.Libn.; Gary J. Arnold, Hd., Ref.; Jolene Boettcher, Cat.Libn.; Vernon Will, Hd., Consrv.Lab.; William Myers, Hd., Mss. & AV; David Levine, Act. State Archv.; Robert B. Jones, Hd., Microfilm Lab.

★10089★

OHIO HISTORICAL SOCIETY - CAMPUS MARTIUS MUSEUM - LIBRARY (Hist)
601 Second St.   Phone: (614) 373-3750
Marietta, OH 45750   John B. Briley, Mgr.
Founded: 1920. **Staff:** 2. **Subjects:** Area history and genealogy, river history. **Special Collections:** Early manuscripts; census and legal documents; Blennerhassett materials. **Holdings:** 3000 books. **Services:** Copying; library open to public with staff assistance and a fee.

OHIO INSTITUTE OF TECHNOLOGY
See: Bell & Howell Education Group - De Vry Institute of Technology

★10090★

OHIO NORTHERN UNIVERSITY - COLLEGE OF LAW - JAY P. TAGGART MEMORIAL LAW LIBRARY (Law)
       Phone: (419) 772-2250
Ada, OH 45810   Lynn Foster, Dir./Hd.Libn.
Founded: 1885. **Staff:** Prof 4; Other 5. **Subjects:** Law, international law. **Special Collections:** Papers of Congressman McCullough. **Holdings:** 138,900 books; bound periodical volumes; U.S. Government documents (depository library); 13,900 volumes on microfilm. **Subscriptions:** 2466 journals and other serials; 12 newspapers. **Services:** Interlibrary loans; copying; library open to public. **Automated Operations:** Computerized cataloging. **Computerized Information Services:** LEXIS, Westlaw. Contact Person: Betty Roeske, 772-2255. **Staff:** Marcia Siebesma, Assoc. Law Libn.; Peter Pogacar, Circ./Ref.Libn.; Pam Johnson, Acq.; Josephine Ansley, Govt.Doc.;

Merry Podojil, Docs.; Nancy Biddinger, Circ.; Margaret Appleton, Tech.Proc.; Betty Roeske, Ser.Libn.

★10091★

OHIO NORTHERN UNIVERSITY - HETERICK MEMORIAL LIBRARY (Sci-Tech)
Phone: (419) 772-2180
Ada, OH 45810   Jane Weimer, Act.Lib.Dir.
Staff: Prof 5; Other 9. **Subjects:** Pharmacy, engineering, sciences, humanities, business administration. **Special Collections:** East Europe and Russia; Theodore Roosevelt; ONU authors; Heterick medals; Taggart paperweights. **Holdings:** 136,000 books; 44,949 bound periodical volumes; 48 VF drawers; 137,077 microforms; 84,731 government documents. **Subscriptions:** 960 journals and other serials; 26 newspapers. **Services:** Interlibrary loans; copying; library open to public with circulation to students and area residents only. **Automated Operations:** Computerized cataloging, serials, circulation and ILL. **Computerized Information Services:** OCLC, DIALOG. Performs searches on cost recovery basis. Contact Person: Charles E. Steele, Jr., 772-2189. **Networks/Consortia:** Member of OHIONET; Northwest Ohio Consortium; Western Ohio Regional Library Development System. **Publications:** Library Handbook, annual; bibliographies, irregular. **Staff:** Charles E. Steele, Jr., Sci.Libn.; Cora Layaou, Govt.Doc.Libn.; Sharon Blenkush, Cat.; Paul Logsdon, Ref.Libn.

★10092★

OHIO POETRY THERAPY CENTER - WELCH LIBRARY (Hum; Soc Sci)
2384 Hardesty Dr., S.   Phone: (614) 279-4188
Columbus, OH 43204   Jennifer Groce Welch, Dir.
Founded: 1981. **Staff:** Prof 3. **Subjects:** Poetry, creative arts in therapy, psychology, self-help and motivation, creative writing, social work. **Holdings:** Figures not available for books, bound periodical volumes, dissertations, reports and cassette tapes. **Subscriptions:** 32 journals and other serials. **Services:** Copying; library open to public by appointment. **Publications:** NAPT News (National Association for Poetry Therapy newsletter), 3/year; Pudding Magazine, 3/year; OPTC OHIOGRAM, monthly; list of additional publications - available upon request. **Special Catalogs:** Poetry therapy bibliography (card); printed recommended bibliography, revised yearly - for sale; poetry bibliography: recommended reading for the poetry therapist. **Formerly:** Ohio Valley Regional Training Center - Welch Poetry Therapy Library. **Staff:** Linda Graves Gorrell, Res.Asst.; Rick Welch, Asst.Dir./Mng.Ed.; Doug Swisher, Tech.Ed.

★10093★

OHIO POWER COMPANY - LIBRARY (Energy)
Box 400   Phone: (216) 456-8173
Canton, OH 44701   James M. Beck, Libn.
Founded: 1956. **Staff:** 1. **Subjects:** Public utility regulations, engineering, law and government, statistics, management development. **Holdings:** 2500 volumes; 8 VF drawers. **Subscriptions:** 150 journals and other serials. **Services:** Library open to public for reference use only upon request.

★10094★

OHIO (State) AGRICULTURAL RESEARCH AND DEVELOPMENT CENTER - LIBRARY (Agri)
Phone: (216) 263-3773
Wooster, OH 44691   Constance J. Britton, Libn.
Founded: 1892. **Staff:** Prof 1; Other 2. **Subjects:** Sciences related to agricultural research. **Special Collections:** Virus diseases of corn - Maize Virus Information Service (MAVIS). **Holdings:** 36,900 books and bound periodical volumes; microforms. **Subscriptions:** 1200 journals and other serials. **Services:** Interlibrary loans; copying; library open to public. **Automated Operations:** Computerized cataloging and ILL. **Computerized Information Services:** OCLC, DIALOG. Performs free searches. **Networks/Consortia:** Member of OHIONET. **Publications:** Serials in the Library - available to bio-agricultural libraries. **Special Indexes:** Subject indexes to agricultural documents owned by library, monthly; index to publications of this organization. **Remarks:** Operated by Ohio State University.

★10095★

OHIO STATE ATTORNEY GENERAL'S OFFICE - LAW LIBRARY (Law)
30 E. Broad St., 17th Fl.   Phone: (614) 466-2465
Columbus, OH 43215   Deborah T. Byers, Libn.
Founded: 1846. **Staff:** Prof 1; Other 2. **Subjects:** Law - Ohio, federal. **Holdings:** 19,000 books. **Subscriptions:** 15 journals and other serials; 10 newspapers. **Services:** Interlibrary loans; copying; library open to public. **Computerized Information Services:** LEXIS. **Special Indexes:** Tax, securities, newspaper and magazine indexes.

★10096★

OHIO STATE DEPARTMENT OF DEVELOPMENT - DIVISION OF ENERGY - ENERGY LIBRARY (Energy)
30 E. Broad St., 34th Fl.   Phone: (614) 466-7915
Columbus, OH 43215   Riek A. Oldenquist, Libn.
Founded: 1977. **Staff:** Prof 1. **Subjects:** Energy - sources, research, policy planning; solar energy; coal research. **Special Collections:** Ohio Department of Energy (ODOE) Studies and Reports (250 volumes). **Holdings:** 3000 books and documents; 365 titles on microfiche; 18 films. **Subscriptions:** 130 journals and other serials. **Services:** Interlibrary loans; copying; library open to public for reference use only. **Automated Operations:** Computerized cataloging. **Computerized Information Services:** DOE/RECON. **Formerly:** Ohio State Department of Energy - ODOE Library.

★10097★

OHIO STATE DEPARTMENT OF DEVELOPMENT - RESEARCH LIBRARY (Plan)
Box 1001   Phone: (614) 466-2115
Columbus, OH 43204   Jean Fisher, Libn.
Staff: Prof 1; Other 3. **Subjects:** Census, business, statistics, demography, economics. **Special Collections:** Ohio economic data. **Holdings:** 1000 books; 5000 reports; 12 drawers of microfiche. **Subscriptions:** 438 journals and other serials; 12 newspapers. **Services:** Interlibrary loans; copying; library open to public for reference use only. **Automated Operations:** Computerized cataloging. **Publications:** New Acquisitions List, quarterly; List of Periodicals, annual; Publications Available from ODOD, annual - all for internal distribution and to government, public and private agencies. **Formerly:** Ohio State Department of Economic and Community Development - Ohio Data Users Center Library.

OHIO STATE DEPARTMENT OF ECONOMIC AND COMMUNITY DEVELOPMENT
See: Ohio State Department of Development

OHIO STATE DEPARTMENT OF ENERGY
See: Ohio State Department of Development - Division of Energy

★10098★

OHIO STATE DEPARTMENT OF MENTAL HEALTH - EDUCATIONAL MEDIA CENTER (Aud-Vis; Med)
2401 W. Walnut St.   Phone: (614) 466-6013
Columbus, OH 43223   Portia McDade, Libn.
Staff: Prof 1; Other 1. **Subjects:** Mental health, prevention of mental illness. **Holdings:** 1000 films. **Services:** Center open to public. **Special Catalogs:** Media Catalog.

OHIO STATE DEPARTMENT OF MENTAL HEALTH - PORTSMOUTH RECEIVING HOSPITAL
See: Portsmouth Receiving Hospital

★10099★

OHIO STATE DEPARTMENT OF TAXATION - RESEARCH AND STATISTICS LIBRARY (Bus-Fin)
State Office Tower
Box 530
Columbus, OH 43216   S.L. Shriver, Res.
Founded: 1956. **Subjects:** Taxation, public finance, general statistics. **Holdings:** 2200 books; 95 feet of vertical files. **Services:** Library not open to public.

★10100★

OHIO (State) DEPARTMENT OF TRANSPORTATION - LIBRARY (Trans)
25 S. Front St.
Box 899   Phone: (614) 466-7680
Columbus, OH 43216   Ellen Haider, Libn.
Founded: 1976. **Staff:** Prof 1; Other 1. **Subjects:** Road transportation. **Special Collections:** Ohio Department of Transportation publications; Transportation Research Board publications. **Holdings:** 2500 books; 60 bound periodical volumes; unbound reports. **Subscriptions:** 105 journals and other serials. **Services:** Interlibrary loans; copying; SDI; library open to public. **Automated Operations:** Computerized cataloging. **Computerized Information Services:** DIALOG. **Publications:** New Acquisitions, irregular - distributed in-house or by request.

★10101★

OHIO (State) DIVISION OF GEOLOGICAL SURVEY - LIBRARY (Sci-Tech)
Fountain Sq., Bldg. B   Phone: (614) 265-6605
Columbus, OH 43224   Merrianne Hackathorn, Geologist
Staff: 1. **Subjects:** Geology, mineralogy, hydrology, paleontology, petrology,

mineral resources. **Holdings:** 3200 books. **Services:** Copying; library open to public for reference use only.

★10102★

OHIO STATE ENVIRONMENTAL PROTECTION AGENCY - ENVIRONMENTAL TECHNICAL INFORMATION CENTER (Env-Cons)
361 E. Broad St.   Phone: (614) 466-6058
Columbus, OH 43215   Donna Pittman, Libn.
Staff: Prof 1; Other 4. **Subjects:** Pollution control, environmental law, hazardous waste control, solid waste management. **Holdings:** 25,000 books. **Subscriptions:** 92 journals and other serials. **Services:** Interlibrary loans; copying; center open to public for reference use only. **Automated Operations:** Computerized cataloging. **Computerized Information Services:** DIALOG, SDC, The Source, NIH-EPA Chemical Information System. **Networks/Consortia:** Member of OHIONET. **Publications:** Environmental Acquisitions, quarterly - free upon request.

★10103★

OHIO STATE INDUSTRIAL COMMISSION - DIVISION OF SAFETY AND HYGIENE - RESOURCE CENTER (Med)
246 N. High St.
Box 16512
Columbus, OH 43215   Phone: (614) 466-7388
                                           Rosemary Larkins, Libn.
Founded: 1974. **Staff:** Prof 1; Other 4. **Subjects:** Occupational safety, industrial hygiene. **Holdings:** 4000 books; 850 standards; 200 microfiche; 2500 16mm films; 20 VF drawers of pamphlets; 650 subject headings; 2 VF drawers of clippings. **Subscriptions:** 125 journals and other serials. **Services:** Interlibrary loans; copying; center open to public. **Computerized Information Services:** DIALOG, NLM, Questel; Boss-II, Film Library Circulation (internal database). **Networks/Consortia:** Member of CALICO. **Publications:** Acquisitions, quarterly.

★10104★

OHIO STATE LEGISLATIVE SERVICE COMMISSION - RESEARCH LIBRARY (Soc Sci)
State House   Phone: (614) 466-7434
Columbus, OH 43215   Barbara J. Laughon, Lib.Adm.
Founded: 1953. **Staff:** Prof 2; Other 2. **Subjects:** Public administration, public finance, public education, state government, Ohio history and law. **Special Collections:** Laws of Ohio, 1803 to present; Laws of the Northwest Territory, 1787-1796; Codes for Northwest Territory and State of Ohio; Debates of the Ohio Constitutional Conventions; House and Senate bills and records. **Holdings:** 9000 books; 1000 bound periodical volumes; 50 VF drawers of pamphlets, clippings, unbound and uncataloged documents; 288 reels of microfilm; 120 audiotape cassettes. **Subscriptions:** 262 journals and other serials. **Services:** Copying; library open to public for reference use only. **Automated Operations:** Computerized cataloging. **Computerized Information Services:** DIALOG, Public Affairs Information Service (PAIS), Legislation Information Service (LIS). **Networks/Consortia:** Member of CALICO. **Publications:** Reports submitted to the Ohio General Assembly, monthly; LSC library acquisitions, irregular. **Staff:** Sharon Moore, Asst.Res.Libn.

★10105★

OHIO STATE SCHOOL FOR THE BLIND - LIBRARY (Educ)
5220 N. High St.   Phone: (614) 888-8211
Columbus, OH 43214   Beverly Kessler, Libn.
Staff: Prof 1. **Subjects:** Special education with emphasis on blindness. **Holdings:** 5000 books; 10 bound periodical volumes; 7000 tapes; 300 records; 150 models. **Subscriptions:** 80 journals and other serials. **Services:** Library not open to public.

★10106★

OHIO STATE SUPREME COURT LAW LIBRARY (Law)
30 E. Broad St., 4th Fl.   Phone: (614) 466-2044
Columbus, OH 43215   Paul S. Fu, Law Libn.
Founded: 1858. **Staff:** Prof 4; Other 6. **Subjects:** Law. **Special Collections:** Early laws of Ohio; old legal treatises. **Holdings:** 220,000 volumes. **Subscriptions:** 570 journals and other serials; 23 newspapers. **Services:** Copying; library open to public. **Publications:** Monthly List of Acquisitions; Law Library Handbook. **Staff:** Niann Lao, Asst.Libn. & Cat.; Paula Hidy, Ref.Libn.; Mary Soltesz, Acq.Libn.; Ahmed H. Kanu, AV & Doc.Libn.; Janet Epstein, Circ.Libn.

★10107★

OHIO STATE UNIVERSITY - AGRICULTURAL TECHNICAL INSTITUTE - LIBRARY (Agri)
                                           Phone: (216) 264-3911
Wooster, OH 44691   Phoebe F. Phillips, Hd.Libn.
Founded: 1972. **Staff:** Prof 1; Other 10. **Subjects:** Floriculture, landscape,

nursery, turf, crops, food marketing, greenhouse production, agricultural mechanics, agronomic industries, soil and water management, dairy, horse, livestock, laboratory and research science, wood science, beekeeping. **Special Collections:** Beekeeping journals. **Holdings:** 15,000 books; 1700 bound periodical volumes; 23 VF drawers of pamphlets; journals on microfilm/microfiche; 5 VF drawers of Ohio soil surveys; 14,843 microforms. **Subscriptions:** 547 journals and other serials; 12 newspapers. **Services:** Interlibrary loans; library not open to public. **Automated Operations:** Computerized cataloging.

★10108★

OHIO STATE UNIVERSITY - AGRICULTURE LIBRARY (Agri)
2120 Fyffe Rd.   Phone: (614) 422-6125
Columbus, OH 43210   Mary P. Key, Hd.Libn.
Founded: 1956. **Staff:** Prof 1; Other 3. **Subjects:** Animal science, agriculture and allied subjects, food science and nutrition, forestry, dairy science, plant pathology, rural sociology, horticulture, natural resources, poultry science. **Special Collections:** Arnold Library of Agricultural Credit. **Holdings:** 68,000 volumes; 1500 pamphlets. **Subscriptions:** 1136 journals and other serials. **Services:** Interlibrary loans; copying; library open to public. **Automated Operations:** Computerized cataloging, serials and circulation. **Computerized Information Services:** Online systems.

★10109★

OHIO STATE UNIVERSITY - ARCHIVES (Hist)
2121 Tuttle Park Pl.   Phone: (614) 422-2409
Columbus, OH 43210   Dr. Raimund E. Goerler, Univ.Archv.
Founded: 1963. **Staff:** Prof 2; Other 4. **Subjects:** Ohio State University history. **Special Collections:** Photographic history of OSU (450,000 images). **Holdings:** 4500 cubic feet of archival materials. **Services:** Copying; archives open to public. **Special Catalogs:** Inventories of archival collections. **Staff:** Dr. Robert Bober, Asst.Archv.

★10110★

OHIO STATE UNIVERSITY - BIOLOGICAL SCIENCES LIBRARY (Sci-Tech)
1735 Neil Ave.   Phone: (614) 422-1744
Columbus, OH 43210   Victoria Welborn, Hd.Libn.
Founded: 1916. **Staff:** Prof 1; Other 3. **Subjects:** Zoology, botany, biology, entomology, microbiology, genetics, biochemistry, biophysics. **Holdings:** 86,000 books and bound periodical volumes; 10,000 pamphlets; 3750 dissertations. **Subscriptions:** 904 journals and other serials. **Services:** Interlibrary loans; copying; library open to public. **Automated Operations:** Computerized cataloging, serials and circulation. **Computerized Information Services:** Online systems. **Publications:** Monthly lists of acquisitions.

★10111★

OHIO STATE UNIVERSITY - BLACK STUDIES LIBRARY (Area-Ethnic)
1858 Neil Ave.   Phone: (614) 422-8403
Columbus, OH 43210   Eleanor M. Daniel, Hd.Libn.
Founded: 1971. **Staff:** Prof 1; Other 1. **Subjects:** Black history, African studies. **Special Collections:** Schomburg Collection; Atlanta University Black Culture Collection; Black Newspaper Collection (Bell & Howell); Tuskegee Institute News Clipping File; Martin Luther King, Jr.: Assassination File; W.E.B. DuBois papers; Afro-American Rare Book Collection; Papers of the National Association for the Advancement of Colored People (NAACP), part 1; papers of the Congress of Racial Equality, 1941-1967. **Holdings:** 17,000 books; 6000 microforms; 70 titles of major black U.S. newspapers. **Subscriptions:** 173 journals and other serials; 12 newspapers. **Services:** Interlibrary loans; library open to public. **Automated Operations:** Computerized cataloging, serials and circulation. **Computerized Information Services:** Online systems. **Publications:** Selected List of Titles Received by the Black Studies Library, monthly.

★10112★

OHIO STATE UNIVERSITY - CALCULATOR INFORMATION CENTER
1200 Chambers Rd.
Columbus, OH 43212
Defunct

★10113★

OHIO STATE UNIVERSITY - CENTER FOR HUMAN RESOURCE RESEARCH - LIBRARY (Soc Sci)
5701 N. High St.   Phone: (614) 422-7337
Worthington, OH 43085   Julian Larson, Libn.
Founded: 1965. **Staff:** 1. **Subjects:** Manpower, labor market, education, economics, women, youths, blacks. **Special Collections:** Latin American collection, mostly in Spanish (500 books; reports). **Holdings:** 6000 books; 25 VF drawers of pamphlets, reports, and reprints; 5 VF drawers of microforms; 4 VF drawers of seminar and NLS based research papers. **Subscriptions:** 200

journals and other serials. **Services:** Copying; library open to public with restrictions. **Publications:** NLS (National Longitudinal Surveys) Newsletter, quarterly; NLS Handbook, annual - both available on request.

★10114★

OHIO STATE UNIVERSITY - CENTER FOR LAKE ERIE AREA RESEARCH - LAKE ERIE PROGRAM LIBRARY (Sci-Tech)
484 W. 12th Ave.   Phone: (614) 422-8949
Columbus, OH 43210   Charles E. Herdendorf, Dir.
Staff: Prof 1; Other 1. **Subjects:** Great Lakes limnology, Lake Erie science and technology, Great Lakes Wetlands, oceanography, water quality and treatment, coastal engineering, hydrology. **Special Collections:** Great Lakes topographic maps and lake survey charts; early 1900s Lake Erie Survey Charts. **Holdings:** 9000 books; 200 bound periodical volumes; 100 boxes of pamphlets; 150 boxes of reprints; 300 maps; 3000 slides of Lake Erie activities. **Subscriptions:** 32 monthly Great Lakes Newsletters. **Services:** Copying; library open to public for reference use only on request. **Publications:** Center for Lake Erie Area Research Technical Reports (284); Procedures Manuals (15); Data Reports (10). **Special Indexes:** Bibliography of Lake Erie Environmental Science; Index of Great Lakes Wetlands. **Remarks:** Library also contains the holdings of the Ohio State University Water Resources Library.

★10115★

OHIO STATE UNIVERSITY - CHEMISTRY LIBRARY (Sci-Tech)
140 W. 18th Ave.   Phone: (614) 422-1118
Columbus, OH 43210   Virginia E. Yagello, Hd.Libn.
Founded: 1925. **Staff:** Prof 1; Other 2. **Subjects:** Chemistry, chemical technology and engineering. **Holdings:** 49,000 books and bound periodical volumes. **Subscriptions:** 384 journals and other serials. **Services:** Interlibrary loans; copying. **Automated Operations:** Computerized cataloging, serials and circulation. **Computerized Information Services:** Online systems. **Publications:** Classified List of Serial Holdings in Chemistry Library. **Also Known As:** Charles Cutler Sharp Library.

★10116★

OHIO STATE UNIVERSITY - CHILDREN'S HOSPITAL LIBRARY (Med)
700 Children's Drive   Phone: (614) 461-2375
Columbus, OH 43205   Mary Pat Wilhem, Hd.
Staff: Prof 1; Other 1. **Subjects:** Pediatrics and related subjects. **Holdings:** 10,000 volumes. **Subscriptions:** 300 journals and other serials. **Services:** Interlibrary loans and copying (through KOMILL office of Health Sciences Library); library open to public for reference use only. **Automated Operations:** Computerized cataloging, serials and circulation. **Computerized Information Services:** MEDLINE. **Remarks:** Library is a branch of the Health Sciences Library of Ohio State University.

★10117★

OHIO STATE UNIVERSITY - CLASSICS, GERMAN, LINGUISTICS AND ROMANCE LANGUAGES GRADUATE LIBRARY (Hum)
1858 Neil Ave.   Phone: (614) 422-2594
Columbus, OH 43210
Founded: 1951. **Staff:** Prof 1; Other 1. **Subjects:** French, German, Italian, Spanish, Portuguese, Latin and Greek classics; linguistics; Russian and Scandinavian works of philological and literary importance. **Special Collections:** Linn Collection of works by and about Cervantes (moved to Rare Books Room). **Holdings:** 19,000 books. **Subscriptions:** 458 journals and other serials. **Services:** Interlibrary loans; copying; library open to public. **Automated Operations:** Computerized cataloging, serials and circulation. **Computerized Information Services:** Online systems. **Publications:** Periodicals in the Romance Languages and Literatures at O.S.U. Libraries, compiled by Ana R. Llorens, 2nd edition, 1973. **Special Catalogs:** Catalog of the Talfourd P. Linn Collection of Cervantes Materials, 1963.

★10118★

OHIO STATE UNIVERSITY - COLE MEMORIAL LIBRARY OF THE PHYSICS AND ASTRONOMY DEPARTMENT (Sci-Tech)
174 W. 18th Ave.   Phone: (614) 422-7894
Columbus, OH 43210   Virginia E. Yagello, Hd.Libn.
Founded: 1930. **Staff:** Prof 1; Other 2. **Subjects:** Solid state physics, theoretical physics, mathematical physics, astronomy, astrophysics, infrared spectroscopy, low temperature physics, nuclear physics. **Holdings:** 45,500 books. **Subscriptions:** 307 journals and other serials. **Services:** Interlibrary loans. **Automated Operations:** Computerized cataloging, serials and circulation. **Computerized Information Services:** Online systems.

★10119★

OHIO STATE UNIVERSITY - COMMERCE LIBRARY (Bus-Fin)
1810 College Rd.   Phone: (614) 422-2136
Columbus, OH 43210   Charles Popovich, Hd.Libn.
Founded: 1925. **Staff:** Prof 3; Other 5. **Subjects:** Accounting, business administration, economics, marketing, public administration, geography, finance. **Special Collections:** Annual reports of corporations (84,000 microforms). **Holdings:** 149,000 books and bound periodical volumes; 2000 theses and dissertations; 80 loose-leaf services. **Subscriptions:** 1875 journals and other serials; 10 newspapers. **Services:** Interlibrary loans; copying; library open to public. **Automated Operations:** Computerized cataloging, serials and circulation. **Computerized Information Services:** Online systems.

OHIO STATE UNIVERSITY - DISASTER RESEARCH CENTER
See: University of Delaware, Newark - Disaster Research Center

★10120★

OHIO STATE UNIVERSITY - EAST ASIAN COLLECTION (Area-Ethnic)
1858 Neil Ave. Mall   Phone: (614) 422-3502
Columbus, OH 43210   David Y. Hu, Bibliog.
Staff: Prof 3; Other 3. **Subjects:** Chinese and Japanese studies. **Special Collections:** Creed Collection of Western Language Materials on Chinese and other East Asian languages (16th-20th centuries; 4000 volumes). **Holdings:** 93,000 volumes in Chinese and Japanese; 4329 microforms. **Subscriptions:** 300 journals and other serials; 34 newspapers. **Services:** Interlibrary loans; copying; library open to public. **Automated Operations:** Computerized cataloging, acquisitions, serials and circulation. **Computerized Information Services:** OCLC; Library Control System (LCS, internal database). **Networks/Consortia:** Member of OHIONET. **Publications:** OSU Library East Asian Bibliographical Series; occasional papers. **Staff:** Maureen H. Donovan, Japanese Bibliog./Cat.; Meng-Fen Su, East Asian Cat.

★10121★

OHIO STATE UNIVERSITY - EAST EUROPEAN AND SLAVIC READING ROOM (Area-Ethnic)
Main Library, Rm. 300
1858 Neil Ave. Mall   Phone: (614) 422-2073
Columbus, OH 43210   G. Koolemans Beynen, Slavic Bibliog.
Founded: 1977. **Staff:** Prof 1; Other 2. **Subjects:** Slavic languages and literatures, Eastern Europe. **Holdings:** 7000 books, including reference works and area studies. **Subscriptions:** 294 journals and other serials; 37 newspapers. **Services:** Interlibrary loans; room open to public with restrictions. **Automated Operations:** Computerized cataloging, acquisitions, serials and circulation. **Computerized Information Services:** OCLC. **Publications:** List of Newspapers; List of Journals; List of Bibliographies; Bibliographic Guides. **Special Indexes:** Sources with subject index.

★10122★

OHIO STATE UNIVERSITY - EDGAR DALE EDUCATIONAL MEDIA & INSTRUCTIONAL MATERIALS LABORATORY (Educ)
260 Ramseyer Hall
29 W. Woodruff Ave.   Phone: (614) 422-1177
Columbus, OH 43210   Dr. Betty P. Cleaver, Dir.
Founded: 1979. **Staff:** Prof 2; Other 16. **Subjects:** Children's literature; textbooks and curriculum, K-12; classroom management and methods; media management. **Special Collections:** Historical collection of children's literature and textbooks (500 volumes). **Holdings:** 14,497 books; 2100 AV kits; 3800 microforms; 165 folders of pamphlets; 4 VF drawers of curriculum guides; 4 VF drawers of transparency originals; 200 microcomputer programs. **Subscriptions:** 11 journals and other serials. **Services:** Copying; media production; laboratory open to public for reference use only. **Automated Operations:** Computerized cataloging. **Computerized Information Services:** OCLC. **Networks/Consortia:** Member of OHIONET. **Special Indexes:** Subject mediagraphy file, K-12. **Staff:** Shirley V. Morrison, Media Spec.; Melissa Smith, Lib. Media Tech.Asst.

★10123★

OHIO STATE UNIVERSITY - EDUCATION/PSYCHOLOGY LIBRARY (Educ)
1945 N. High St.   Phone: (614) 422-6275
Columbus, OH 43210   Laura Blomquist, Hd.Libn.
Founded: 1926. **Staff:** Prof 4; Other 7. **Subjects:** Education, psychology. **Holdings:** 153,000 volumes; 250,000 ERIC microfiche. **Subscriptions:** 1100 journals and other serials. **Services:** Interlibrary loans; copying; SDI; retrospective search of ERIC; library open to public for reference use only. **Automated Operations:** Computerized cataloging, serials and circulation. **Computerized Information Services:** Online systems. **Special Indexes:** Supplement to Educational Index, 1919-1961 (card). **Staff:** Toyo S. Kawakami, Asst.Hd.; Mary Gouke, Ref.; Linda Kramer, Ref.

★10124★

OHIO STATE UNIVERSITY - ENGINEERING LIBRARY (Sci-Tech; Plan)
112 Caldwell Lab.
2024 Neil Ave.   Phone: (614) 422-2852
Columbus, OH 43210   Mary Jo Arnold, Hd.Libn.
Staff: Prof 2; Other 3. **Subjects:** Computer science; engineering -
mechanical, aeronautical, civil, electrical; architecture; city and regional
planning; landscape architecture; communications; circuit analyses; physics;
mathematics. **Holdings:** 136,000 volumes. **Subscriptions:** 1010 journals and
other serials. **Services:** Interlibrary loans; copying; SDI; library open to public.
Automated Operations: Computerized cataloging, serials and circulation.
Computerized Information Services: Online systems. **Publications:** Book
List, biweekly - primarily for campus personnel. **Staff:** Jane McMaster,
Ref.Libn.

★10125★

OHIO STATE UNIVERSITY - ENGLISH DEPARTMENT LIBRARY (Hum)
Derby Hall
154 N. Oval Mall   Phone: (614) 422-6357
Columbus, OH 43210   Louise H. Smith, Libn.
Founded: 1934. **Staff:** Prof 1; Other 1. **Subjects:** Literature in English,
literary criticism, biographies of literary figures, linguistics, philosophy and
religion. **Special Collections:** Modern poetry collection; recordings of the
spoken word (especially strong in Shakespeare and modern poetry). **Holdings:**
17,557 books; 542 reprints of articles by English Department faculty; 626
phonograph records.

★10126★

**OHIO STATE UNIVERSITY - ENGLISH, THEATRE AND COMMUNICATION
     GRADUATE LIBRARY** (Theater)
Main Library
1858 Neil Ave. Mall   Phone: (614) 422-2786
Columbus, OH 43210   Richard Centing, Hd.
Founded: 1951. **Staff:** Prof 1; Other 2. **Subjects:** English and American
literature, bibliography, theater, speech communication, speech and hearing
therapy. **Special Collections:** Little Magazines; OSU drama collection (1134
acting editions of 19th and 20th century English language plays). **Holdings:**
20,200 books. **Subscriptions:** 412 journals and other serials. **Services:**
Copying; library open to public for reference use only. **Automated
Operations:** Computerized cataloging, serials and circulation. **Computerized
Information Services:** Online systems. **Special Indexes:** Index by title to OSU
drama collection (card); index by title to Early English Text Society
publications, original and extra series (card).

**OHIO STATE UNIVERSITY - ERIC CLEARINGHOUSE ON ADULT, CAREER
     AND VOCATIONAL EDUCATION**
See: ERIC Clearinghouse on Adult, Career and Vocational Education

**OHIO STATE UNIVERSITY - ERIC CLEARINGHOUSE FOR SCIENCE,
MATHEMATICS AND ENVIRONMENTAL EDUCATION**
See: ERIC Clearinghouse for Science, Mathematics and Environmental
     Education

★10127★

OHIO STATE UNIVERSITY - FINE ARTS LIBRARY (Art)
Sullivant Hall
1813 N. High St.   Phone: (614) 422-6184
Columbus, OH 43210   Susan Wyngaard, Hd.Libn.
Staff: Prof 1; Other 1. **Subjects:** Visual arts (excluding photography), history
of art, archeology, 17th and 18th century art, Serbo-Croatian publications on
Byzantine art, PL480 program - all Polish publications on art. **Holdings:**
68,500 books; 1000 exhibition catalogs; 600 photographs of Ohio W.P.A. art
projects; 12,600 photocards in Decimal Index of the Arts of the Low
Countries (D.I.A.L.); 7 double compartment drawers of Indic journals on
microfiche; 43 reels of microfilm of J.M.W. Turner bequest - water colors,
pencil, pen sketches. **Subscriptions:** 278 journals and other serials. **Services:**
Interlibrary loans; copying; location services for holdings of members of the
Art Research Libraries of Ohio, 1969 to 1980; library open to public for
reference use only. **Automated Operations:** Computerized cataloging, serials
and circulation. **Computerized Information Services:** Online systems.

★10128★

**OHIO STATE UNIVERSITY - FRANZ THEODORE STONE LABORATORY -
     LIBRARY** (Sci-Tech)
Box 119   Phone: (419) 285-2341
Put-In-Bay, OH 43456   Victoria Welborn, Hd.
Founded: 1896. **Staff:** Prof 1. **Subjects:** Great Lakes hydrobiology and
limnology, field biology, botany and zoology. **Special Collections:** Theses and
dissertations (completed at the laboratory or in several departments on the

main campus; 80). **Holdings:** 2000 books; 1000 bound periodical volumes;
300 boxes of reprints. **Subscriptions:** 40 journals and other serials. **Services:**
Interlibrary loans; copying; library open to public. **Publications:** Contributions
from the Franz Theodore Stone Laboratory. **Remarks:** This library is a part of
the Biological Sciences Library of The Ohio State University.

★10129★

OHIO STATE UNIVERSITY - HEALTH SCIENCES LIBRARY (Med)
376 W. 10th Ave.   Phone: (614) 422-9810
Columbus, OH 43210   Elizabeth J. Sawyers, Dir.
Founded: 1849. **Staff:** Prof 7; Other 26. **Subjects:** Clinical medicine,
dentistry, nursing, allied health sciences, experimental medicine, optometry.
Holdings: 155,150 volumes; 3650 government documents. **Subscriptions:**
2132 journals and other serials. **Services:** Interlibrary loans; copying; SDI;
library open to public. **Automated Operations:** Computerized cataloging,
serials and circulation. **Computerized Information Services:** MEDLINE.
Networks/Consortia: Member of Greater Midwest Regional Medical Library
Network (Region 3). **Publications:** Health Sciences Library Services Bulletin,
monthly - distributed to health sciences and library community. **Staff:** Hazel B.
Benson, Asst.Dir.; Barbara Schmidt, ILL; Marcia Anderson, Extramural Coord.;
Jeanne Byrnes, Ref.Libn.; Susan Kroll, Ref.Libn.; Robert Williams, Ref.Libn.

★10130★

OHIO STATE UNIVERSITY - HILANDAR ROOM (Area-Ethnic)
308 Main Library
1858 Neil Ave.   Phone: (614) 422-0634
Columbus, OH 43210   Dr. Predrag Matejic, Cur.
Staff: Prof 1; Other 1. **Subjects:** Medieval Slavic literature, Slavic
paleography, history of Slavic languages, Eastern Orthodox Church. **Special
Collections:** Microfilm collection of the manuscripts and rare books of the
Hilandar Monastery, Mount Athos, Greece; microfilm of Slavic manuscripts
obtained through exchanges or field expeditions. **Holdings:** 1500 volumes;
500,000 pages of Slavic Cyrillic Manuscripts in microform; 3 manuscripts.
Services: Copying; room open to public with restrictions. **Automated
Operations:** Computerized acquisitions, serials and circulation. **Computerized
Information Services:** OCLC. **Publications:** Mateja Matejic, Hilandar Slavic
Codices; Predrag Matejic, Watermarks of the Hilandar Slavic Codices, A
Descriptive Catalog; Mateja Matejic and Predrag Matejic, Hilandar Slavic
Codices, Supplement Number 1. **Remarks:** An alternative telephone number is
422-1327.

★10131★

**OHIO STATE UNIVERSITY - HISTORY, POLITICAL SCIENCE, AND
     PHILOSOPHY GRADUATE LIBRARY** (Hist)
Main Library
1858 Neil Ave.   Phone: (614) 422-2393
Columbus, OH 43210   A. Robert Thorson, Hd.Libn.
Founded: 1951. **Staff:** Prof 1; Other 1. **Subjects:** History, political science,
philosophy. **Holdings:** 21,000 books. **Subscriptions:** 330 journals and other
serials. **Services:** Interlibrary loans; copying; library open to public for
reference use only. **Automated Operations:** Computerized cataloging, serials
and circulation. **Computerized Information Services:** Online systems.

★10132★

OHIO STATE UNIVERSITY - HOME ECONOMICS LIBRARY (Soc Sci; Food-
     Bev)
Campbell Hall
1787 Neil Ave.   Phone: (614) 422-4220
Columbus, OH 43210   Neosha Mackey, Hd.Libn.
Founded: 1962. **Staff:** Prof 1; Other 2. **Subjects:** Family and child
development, foods and nutrition, home economics education, home
management and family economics, housing and furnishings, textiles and
clothing, institution management. **Special Collections:** Cookbooks. **Holdings:**
18,000 books; 4300 pamphlets. **Subscriptions:** 170 journals and other
serials. **Services:** Interlibrary loans; copying; library open to public for
reference use only. **Automated Operations:** Computerized cataloging, serials
and circulation. **Computerized Information Services:** Online systems.

★10133★

**OHIO STATE UNIVERSITY - INSTITUTE OF POLAR STUDIES - GOLDTHWAIT
     POLAR LIBRARY** (Sci-Tech)
125 S. Oval Mall   Phone: (614) 422-6531
Columbus, OH 43210   Lynn B. Lay, Libn.
Founded: 1960. **Staff:** Prof 1. **Subjects:** Agronomy, anthropology, bedrock
geology, botany, civil engineering, coal studies, glacial geology, glaciology,
geophysics, history of polar exploration, ice physics, meteorology,
photogrammetry, zoology. **Holdings:** 1350 books; 70 bound periodical
volumes; 200 unbound periodical volumes; 13,000 reprints and unpublished
reports; 75 report series; 1000 maps. **Subscriptions:** 50 journals and other

serials. **Services:** Interlibrary loans; copying; library open to qualified researchers. **Publications:** Accessions list, quarterly.

★10134★

OHIO STATE UNIVERSITY - JOURNALISM LIBRARY (Info Sci)
242 W. 18th Ave.   Phone: (614) 422-8747
Columbus, OH 43210   Eleanor Block, Hd.Libn.
Founded: 1967. **Staff:** Prof 1; Other 1. **Subjects:** Journalism - newspaper/magazine, radio/television, public relations, mass media, photography and cinema. **Holdings:** 19,000 volumes. **Subscriptions:** 155 journals and other serials; 83 newspapers. **Services:** Interlibrary loans; copying; library open to public for reference use only. **Automated Operations:** Computerized cataloging, serials and circulation. **Computerized Information Services:** Online systems.

★10135★

OHIO STATE UNIVERSITY - JUDAICA LIBRARY (Rel-Theol; Area-Ethnic)
1858 Neil Ave. Mall   Phone: (614) 422-3362
Columbus, OH 43210   Amnon Zipin, Jewish Stud.Libn.
Founded: 1977. **Staff:** Prof 1; Other 2. **Subjects:** Jewish history, Yiddish and modern Hebrew language and literature, rabbinics, Biblical studies. **Holdings:** 52,000 books; 2700 bound periodical volumes; 750 microforms. **Subscriptions:** 210 journals and other serials; 10 newspapers. **Services:** Interlibrary loans; copying; library open to public. **Automated Operations:** Computerized cataloging, acquisitions, serials and circulation. **Publications:** Recent articles in Jewish Studies, irregular - for internal distribution only. **Special Catalogs:** Hebrew title catalog (card).

★10136★

OHIO STATE UNIVERSITY - LATIN AMERICAN STUDIES READING ROOM AND LIBRARY (Hum)
Main Library
1858 Neil Ave.   Phone: (614) 422-8959
Columbus, OH 43210   Dr. Laurence Hallewell, Bibliog.
Staff: Prof 1; Other 2. **Subjects:** Latin America - literature, history, language, bibliography, social and behavioral sciences, current events. **Special Collections:** Bibliography; contemporary Latin American literature; Hispanic-American culture, Brazil; agricultural economics. **Holdings:** 75,000 volumes. **Subscriptions:** 258 journals and other serials; 8 newspapers. **Services:** Interlibrary loans; copying; library open to public with restrictions. **Automated Operations:** Computerized cataloging, acquisitions, serials and circulation. **Computerized Information Services:** DIALOG, OCLC, SDC, BRS, DOE/RECON. **Networks/Consortia:** Member of CRL; CALICO; OHIONET. **Publications:** Occasional papers and bibliographies; Latin American Studies Newsletter, quarterly. **Remarks:** The Latin American Studies Collection is located in the Main Library's stacks and in other departmental libraries. **Staff:** Dr. John M. Bennett, Lib. Media Tech.Asst.

★10137★

OHIO STATE UNIVERSITY - LAW LIBRARY (Law)
College of Law
1659 N. High St.   Phone: (614) 422-6691
Columbus, OH 43210   Ruth Kessler, Act.Dir.
Founded: 1885. **Staff:** Prof 5; Other 9. **Subjects:** Anglo-American law. **Special Collections:** Ohio Supreme Court briefs. **Holdings:** 460,778 volumes; 333,593 microforms. **Subscriptions:** 550 journals and other serials. **Services:** Interlibrary loans; copying; library open to public for legal research. **Automated Operations:** Computerized cataloging. **Computerized Information Services:** Westlaw, LEXIS. **Networks/Consortia:** Member of OHIONET. **Staff:** Nancy E. Miller, Asst.Dir.; Andrew R. Brann, Hd., Cat.Dept.; Barbara Custon-Feinberg, Acq.Libn.; Melanie Solon-Kochneiser, Hd., Pub.Serv.

★10138★

OHIO STATE UNIVERSITY - LIBRARY FOR COMMUNICATION AND GRAPHIC ARTS (Art)
242 W. 18th Ave., Rm. 147   Phone: (614) 422-0538
Columbus, OH 43210   Lucy S. Caswell, Cur.
Staff: Prof 1; Other 1. **Subjects:** Comic strips, editorial cartoons, illustrations, movie posters and stills, mass media arts. **Special Collections:** Milton Caniff Collection of original comic strips and related materials (500,000 items); Jon Whitcomb Collection of magazine illustrations, photographs, tear sheets and correspondence (44 paintings; 33 boxes); Philip Sills Collection of movie posters and stills (110,000 items); Ray Osrin Collection of original editorial cartoons (1700 items); Eugene Craig Collection of original comic strips and editorial cartoons (4000 items); Will Rannells Collection of illustrations (80 paintings; 6 boxes); Katy Keene Collection of comic books (3 boxes); Toni Mendez Collection of business files relating to licensing of comic strip and cartoon feature products (15 boxes); Shel Dorf Collection of historic comic strip materials (30,000 items); Woody Gelman Collection (71 original

cartoons and more than 200 newspaper tearsheets by Winsor McCay); Will Eisner Collection (200 boxes); underground comics (14 boxes); Ned White Collection (editorial cartoons by White and 90 other cartoonists including Herblock, Darling and Kirby); original cartoons of John T. McCutcheon, Jim Larrick, Bill Crawford, Dick Moores, Art Poinier, L.D. Warren and Ed Kuekes. **Holdings:** Representative holdings of original art from editorial cartoonists and comic strip artists; comic strip clippings. **Services:** Copying; library open to public, users are registered. **Automated Operations:** Computerized cataloging.

★10139★

OHIO STATE UNIVERSITY - MAP GRADUATE LIBRARY (Geog-Map)
1858 Neil Ave.   Phone: (614) 422-2393
Columbus, OH 43210   A. Robert Thorson, Hd.Libn.
Founded: 1951. **Staff:** Prof 1; Other 1. **Special Collections:** City maps, atlases, Ohio. **Holdings:** 672 atlases; 114,000 maps. **Services:** Interlibrary loans; copying. **Remarks:** Library is part of History and Political Science Graduate Library.

★10140★

OHIO STATE UNIVERSITY - MATERIALS ENGINEERING LIBRARY (Sci-Tech)
2041 N. College Rd.   Phone: (614) 422-9614
Columbus, OH 43210   Mary Jo Arnold, Hd.Libn.
Staff: Prof 1; Other 1. **Subjects:** Engineering - metallurgic, ceramic; materials science. **Holdings:** 15,500 volumes. **Subscriptions:** 196 journals and other serials. **Services:** Interlibrary loans; copying; SDI; library open to public. **Automated Operations:** Computerized cataloging, serials and circulation. **Computerized Information Services:** Online systems.

★10141★

OHIO STATE UNIVERSITY - MATHEMATICS LIBRARY (Sci-Tech)
231 W. 18th St.   Phone: (614) 422-2009
Columbus, OH 43210
Founded: 1962. **Staff:** Prof 1; Other 1. **Subjects:** Advanced mathematics, mathematical statistics, geodetic sciences. **Holdings:** 41,000 volumes; 3500 pamphlets. **Subscriptions:** 450 journals and other serials. **Services:** Interlibrary loans; copying; Mechanized Information Center; library open to public for reference use only. **Automated Operations:** Computerized cataloging, serials and circulation. **Computerized Information Services:** Online systems. **Special Catalogs:** List of Serial Holdings in the Mathematics Library, published by The Ohio State University Libraries, June 1965.

★10142★

OHIO STATE UNIVERSITY - MECHANIZED INFORMATION CENTER (MIC) (Info Sci)
1858 Neil Ave. Mall   Phone: (614) 422-3480
Columbus, OH 43210   Bernard Bayer, Hd.
Founded: 1970. **Staff:** Prof 4; Other 6. **Subjects:** Science, technology, medicine, social sciences, education, arts and humanities, history, psychology, chemistry. **Holdings:** Institute for Scientific Information's Source Index tapes for Science Citation Index; Social Science Citation Index and Arts and Humanities Citation Index; LC MARC tapes; Current Index to Journals in Education and Resources in Education; census tapes. **Services:** SDI; center open to public. **Computerized Information Services:** DIALOG, BRS, SDC, New York Times Information Service, Mead Data Central, CAS Online; internal databases are leased from ISI and ERIC. **Staff:** Noelle Van Pulis, Info.Spec; Ross Poli, Info.Spec.; Jennifer Kuehn, Info.Spec.; Russ Hand, Prog.

★10143★

OHIO STATE UNIVERSITY - MIDDLE EAST/ISLAMICA READING ROOM (Area-Ethnic)
Thompson Library, Rm. 320
1858 Neil Ave. Mall   Phone: (614) 422-3362
Columbus, OH 43210   Dona S. Straley, Middle East Libn.
Founded: 1977. **Staff:** Prof 1; Other 3. **Subjects:** Arabic, Persian and Turkish languages, literatures, history and general reference; Islam. **Special Collections:** Eliash Collection (Arabic language works on Shi'ism). **Holdings:** 38,000 books and bound periodical volumes. **Subscriptions:** 101 journals and other serials; 34 newspapers. **Services:** Interlibrary loans; copying; room open to public. **Automated Operations:** Computerized acquisitions, serials and circulation. **Computerized Information Services:** OCLC.

★10144★

OHIO STATE UNIVERSITY - MUSIC LIBRARY (Mus)
186 Sullivant Hall
1813 N. High St.   Phone: (614) 422-2319
Columbus, OH 43210   Thomas Heck, Hd.Libn.
Founded: 1946. **Staff:** Prof 2; Other 4. **Subjects:** Music history and literature; music theory; music - opera, piano, organ, vocal, orchestra. **Special**

Collections: Fanny Arms Collection of popular music (late 19th century); Kassel Musikgeschichtliches Archiv (micro film collection representing primary source material of German composers published both in Germany and foreign countries and foreign composers living in Germany, 16th and 17th centuries). **Holdings:** 78,500 volumes of music literature and music scores; 1224 pamphlets; 1390 microprint items; 21,000 phonograph records. **Subscriptions:** 440 journals and other serials. **Services:** Interlibrary loans; library open to public for reference use only. **Automated Operations:** Computerized cataloging, serials and circulation. **Computerized Information Services:** Online systems. **Staff:** Lois Rowell, Cat. & Ref.Libn.

★10145★

OHIO STATE UNIVERSITY - OHIO COOPERATIVE WILDLIFE RESEARCH UNIT - LIBRARY (Env-Cons)
1735 Neil Ave.　　　　　　　　　　Phone: (614) 422-6112
Columbus, OH 43210　　　　Dr. Theodore A. Bookhout, Unit Leader
Founded: 1936. **Subjects:** Wildlife research, wildlife management, animal ecology, pesticide-wildlife relationships. **Holdings:** 270 volumes; 130 theses; 300 unit reprints and releases; 30 VF drawers of other reprints; 2000 35mm color transparencies. **Services:** Interlibrary loans; library open to public with restrictions.

OHIO STATE UNIVERSITY - OHIO (State) AGRICULTURAL RESEARCH AND DEVELOPMENT CENTER
See: Ohio (State) Agricultural Research and Development Center

★10146★

OHIO STATE UNIVERSITY - ORTON MEMORIAL LIBRARY OF GEOLOGY (Sci-Tech)
155 S. Oval Dr.　　　　　　　　　Phone: (614) 422-2428
Columbus, OH 43210　　　　　　　　Regina Brown, Hd.Libn.
Founded: 1917. **Staff:** Prof 1; Other 1. **Subjects:** Geology, paleontology. **Special Collections:** Geologic maps; U.S. Geological Survey topographic maps (75,000 maps). **Holdings:** 57,000 volumes. **Subscriptions:** 610 journals and other serials. **Services:** Interlibrary loans; copying; library open to public for reference use only. **Automated Operations:** Computerized cataloging, serials and circulation. **Computerized Information Services:** Online systems.

★10147★

OHIO STATE UNIVERSITY - PERSONNEL AND CAREER EXPLORATION (PACE) RESOURCE CENTER (Educ)
Ohio Union, Fl. 4
1739 N. High St.　　　　　　　　　Phone: (614) 422-5766
Columbus, OH 43210　　　　　　Jean Brethauer, Career Libn.
Staff: Prof 1; Other 5. **Subjects:** Career and educational information. **Holdings:** 4 VF drawers; 3 card files; 2 rollodex files. **Subscriptions:** 11 journals and other serials; 6 newspapers. **Services:** Copying; library open to public for reference use only and without access to computers. **Computerized Information Services:** Internal databases.

★10148★

OHIO STATE UNIVERSITY - PHARMACY LIBRARY (Med)
Pharmacy Bldg.
500 W. 12th Ave.　　　　　　　　　Phone: (614) 422-6078
Columbus, OH 43210
Founded: 1930. **Staff:** Prof 1; Other 1. **Subjects:** Pharmacy, pharmaceutical chemistry, pharmacology, pharmacognosy, pharmacy administration. **Holdings:** 30,000 volumes; 2100 pamphlets; 785 AV items. **Subscriptions:** 400 journals and other serials. **Services:** Interlibrary loans; library open to public for reference use only. **Automated Operations:** Computerized cataloging, serials and circulation. **Computerized Information Services:** Online systems.

★10149★

OHIO STATE UNIVERSITY - SOCIAL WORK LIBRARY (Soc Sci)
1947 College Rd.　　　　　　　　　Phone: (614) 422-6627
Columbus, OH 43210　　　　　Mrs. Toyo S. Kawakami, Hd.Libn.
Founded: 1938. **Staff:** Prof 1; Other 1. **Subjects:** Social work education, criminology, social group work, family, social casework, mental health. **Holdings:** 39,000 volumes; 16 VF drawers of case records; 5000 pamphlets. **Subscriptions:** 270 journals and other serials. **Services:** Interlibrary loans; copying; library open to public. **Automated Operations:** Computerized cataloging, serials and circulation.

★10150★

OHIO STATE UNIVERSITY - THEATRE RESEARCH INSTITUTE (Theater)
1089 Drake Union
1849 Cannon Dr.　　　　　　　　　Phone: (614) 422-6614
Columbus, OH 43210　　　　　　　　Alan Woods, Dir.
Founded: 1950. **Staff:** 4. **Subjects:** Theater and theater research. **Holdings:**

8450 original documents (posters; scrapbooks; clippings); 520,920 frames of microfilm; 3000 photographs; McDowell Microfilm Archives (5000 separate documents on microfilm). **Services:** Institute open to public. **Publications:** Theatre Studies, annual - by subscription.

★10151★

OHIO STATE UNIVERSITY - TOPAZ MEMORIAL LIBRARY (Med)
College of Optometry
338 W. Tenth Ave.　　　　　　　　　Phone: (614) 422-1888
Columbus, OH 43210　　　　Molly A. Phillips, Libn. Media Tech.Asst.
Founded: 1965. **Staff:** 1. **Subjects:** Optometry, ophthalmology, optics, vision, reading psychology, visual psychology. **Holdings:** 3058 books; 2270 bound periodical volumes; 112 theses; 5 VF drawers of pamphlets, translations and bibliographies. **Subscriptions:** 67 journals and other serials. **Services:** Interlibrary loans; copying. **Automated Operations:** Computerized cataloging, serials and circulation. **Computerized Information Services:** Online systems.

★10152★

OHIO STATE UNIVERSITY - VETERINARY MEDICINE LIBRARY (Med)
1900 Coffey Rd.　　　　　　　　　Phone: (614) 422-6107
Columbus, OH 43210　　　　　　　　Bruce Evans, Hd.Libn.
Founded: 1929. **Staff:** Prof 1; Other 1. **Subjects:** Veterinary medicine, medicine, pharmacology, biochemistry, comparative medicine. **Holdings:** 36,000 books and bound periodical volumes; 6440 pamphlets. **Subscriptions:** 415 journals and other serials. **Services:** Interlibrary loans; copying; library open to public for reference use only. **Automated Operations:** Computerized cataloging, serials and circulation. **Computerized Information Services:** Online systems.

OHIO STATE UNIVERSITY - WATER RESOURCES LIBRARY
See: Ohio State University - Center for Lake Erie Area Research - Lake Erie Program Library

★10153★

OHIO STATE UNIVERSITY - WOMEN'S STUDIES LIBRARY (Soc Sci)
1858 Neil Ave. Mall　　　　　　　　Phone: (614) 422-3035
Columbus, OH 43210　　　　　　Adrienne Zahniser, Hd.Libn.
Founded: 1977. **Staff:** Prof 1; Other 1. **Subjects:** Women's studies. **Holdings:** 7500 books and bound periodical volumes. **Subscriptions:** 80 journals and other serials. **Services:** Interlibrary loans; copying; SDI; library open to public for reference use only. **Automated Operations:** Computerized cataloging, serials and circulation. **Computerized Information Services:** Online systems.

★10154★

OHIO UNIVERSITY - DEPARTMENT OF ARCHIVES AND SPECIAL COLLECTIONS (Rare Book; Hist)
Alden Library　　　　　　　　　　Phone: (614) 594-5755
Athens, OH 45701　　　　　　　　　Gary A. Hunt, Hd.
Founded: 1960. **Staff:** Prof 2; Other 3. **Subjects:** History - Ohio University, Southeastern Ohio; rare books and manuscripts; English literature, 1760-1830 and 1880-1930; 18th-century English drama. **Special Collections:** Ohio University Archives (3569 linear feet); Morgan Collection of the History of Chemistry and Science (1600 volumes); Tennyson (600 volumes); George Moore; H.G. Wells; Thomas Campbell; Thomas Hood; Cowper; Charles Bukowski. **Holdings:** 40,000 volumes; 952 linear feet of local government records; 800 linear feet of private papers; 496 reels of microfilm; 78,804 photographs and slides; 949 maps. **Subscriptions:** 105 journals and other serials. **Services:** Copying; archives open to public. **Automated Operations:** Computerized cataloging. **Computerized Information Services:** OCLC. **Networks/Consortia:** Member of Ohio Network of American History Research Centers. **Publications:** Gatherings, 3/year - for Friends of the Library. **Special Catalogs:** Guide to Local Government Records at Ohio University Library; manuscript inventories and card catalog; rare book card catalog.

★10155★

OHIO UNIVERSITY - FINE ARTS COLLECTION (Art)
Alden Library　　　　　　　　　　Phone: (614) 594-5065
Athens, OH 45701　　　　　　　　Anne Braxton, Fine Arts Libn.
Founded: 1962. **Staff:** Prof 1; Other 1. **Subjects:** Art, architecture, photography, film. **Holdings:** 40,000 volumes; 6000 microfiche; 2400 exhibition catalogs; 7000 study plates. **Subscriptions:** 175 journals and other serials. **Services:** Interlibrary loans; copying; collection open to public. **Automated Operations:** Computerized cataloging. **Computerized Information Services:** OCLC. **Networks/Consortia:** Member of Art Research Libraries of Ohio (ARLO); OHIONET.

★10156★
OHIO UNIVERSITY - HEALTH SCIENCES LIBRARY (Med)
Phone: (614) 594-6731
Athens, OH 45701
Anne S. Goss, Hd.Libn.
Founded: 1977. **Staff:** Prof 3; Other 8. **Subjects:** Medicine, nursing, psychology, basic sciences, allied health fields. **Special Collections:** Osteopathic medicine (350 books). **Holdings:** 18,203 books; 21,233 bound periodical volumes; 15,235 government documents; 3500 reels of microfilm. **Subscriptions:** 963 journals and other serials. **Services:** Interlibrary loans; copying; SDI; library open to public. **Automated Operations:** Computerized cataloging, circulation and ILL. **Computerized Information Services:** DIALOG, SDC, MEDLARS, BRS; internal database. Performs searches on cost recovery basis. Contact Person: Evelyn Constance Powell. **Publications:** Shelf Life. **Staff:** Wayne Evans, Ref.Libn.; Evelyn Constance Powell, Ref.Libn.

★10157★
OHIO UNIVERSITY - MAP COLLECTION (Geog-Map)
Alden Library
Phone: (614) 594-5240
Athens, OH 45701
Theodore Foster, Map Libn.
Founded: 1960. **Staff:** 1. **Subjects:** Maps - U.S. Geological Survey, Defense Mapping Agency, Southeast Asia, East Africa. **Holdings:** 130,000 maps. **Services:** Interlibrary loans; collection open to public. **Computerized Information Services:** OCLC. **Networks/Consortia:** Member of OHIONET.

★10158★
OHIO UNIVERSITY - MUSIC/DANCE LIBRARY (Mus)
Music Bldg.
Phone: (614) 594-5733
Athens, OH 45701
Dan O. Clark, Libn.
Staff: Prof 2; Other 21. **Subjects:** Music and dance. **Holdings:** 25,000 books and scores; 500 bound periodical volumes; 6087 recordings; VF of clippings; 473 college catalogs; microforms; Catalog of Copyright Entries (Music) and Revision Studies. **Subscriptions:** 100 journals and other serials. **Services:** Interlibrary loans; copying; SDI; listening facilities; library open to public. **Automated Operations:** Computerized cataloging. **Computerized Information Services:** DIALOG, OCLC. **Staff:** Shirley Dorman, Lib.Asst.

★10159★
OHIO UNIVERSITY - SOUTHEAST ASIA COLLECTION (Area-Ethnic)
Alden Library
Phone: (614) 594-6958
Athens, OH 45701
Lian The-Mulliner, Hd.
Founded: 1967. **Staff:** Prof 3; Other 14. **Subjects:** Southeast Asia, especially Malaysia/Brunei, Singapore, Philippines, Thailand, Indonesia, Association of Southeast Asian Nations (ASEAN), Asia. **Holdings:** 50,000 books; 7271 bound periodical volumes; 8 VF drawers of clippings on Malaysia and Singapore; 6 VF drawers of pamphlets on Southeast Asia; 20,000 titles on microform. **Subscriptions:** 2500 journals and other serials; 20 newspapers. **Services:** Interlibrary loans; copying; library open to public. **Automated Operations:** Computerized cataloging. **Computerized Information Services:** DIALOG, SDC, OCLC; internal database. **Networks/Consortia:** Member of OHIONET; NPAC; Southeast Asian Microform Project (SEAM). **Special Catalogs:** Dictionary card catalog by country. **Staff:** David Miller, Asst.Libn.; Swee-Lan Quah, Cat.

★10160★
OHIO VALLEY GENERAL HOSPITAL - PROFESSIONAL LIBRARY (Med)
Heckel Rd.
Phone: (412) 777-6159
McKee's Rock, PA 15136
Mary Evans, Libn.
Staff: Prof 1. **Subjects:** Nursing, medicine. **Holdings:** 1925 volumes. **Subscriptions:** 101 journals and other serials. **Services:** Interlibrary loans; copying; library open to public by appointment. **Publications:** Library Bulletin, monthly.

★10161★
OHIO VALLEY HEALTH SERVICES FOUNDATION, INC. - LIBRARY (Med)
One Blue Line Ave.
Phone: (614) 592-4457
Athens, OH 45701
Sandra L. Porter, Adm.Asst.
Founded: 1966. **Staff:** Prof 5; Other 2. **Subjects:** Primary Health Care Management Services - clinic development, implementation and operations, medical/dental recruitment. **Holdings:** 85 books; 56 other items. **Subscriptions:** 12 journals and other serials. **Services:** Library open to public with restrictions.

★10162★
OHIO VALLEY HOSPITAL - HEALTH SCIENCES LIBRARY (Med)
380 Summit Ave.
Phone: (614) 283-7400
Steubenville, OH 43952
Kathie Pasquarella, Med.Libn.
Staff: Prof 1; Other 5. **Subjects:** Nursing, medicine. **Special Collections:** Rare books. **Holdings:** 2106 books; 1673 bound periodical volumes; 12 VF drawers of health sciences ephemeral files; 655 AV items. **Subscriptions:** 70

journals and other serials. **Services:** Interlibrary loans; copying; library open to public for reference use only when librarian is present. **Computerized Information Services:** MEDLINE. **Networks/Consortia:** Member of Greater Midwest Regional Medical Library Network (Region 3). **Publications:** Library Line Newsletter, monthly - for internal distribution only. **Special Catalogs:** Resources and facilities, annual.

★10163★
OHIO VALLEY MEDICAL CENTER - HUPP MEDICAL LIBRARY (Med)
2000 Eoff St.
Phone: (304) 234-8771
Wheeling, WV 26003
Eleanor Shonn, Med.Libn.
Staff: Prof 2. **Subjects:** Medicine, surgery, obstetrics, gynecology, pediatrics, radiology. **Holdings:** 3444 books; 2888 bound periodical volumes; 576 audiotapes. **Subscriptions:** 195 journals and other serials. **Services:** Interlibrary loans; library not open to public except for computer searches. **Computerized Information Services:** MEDLINE.

OHIO VALLEY REGIONAL TRAINING CENTER
See: Ohio Poetry Therapy Center

★10164★
OHIOANA LIBRARY ASSOCIATION - OHIOANA LIBRARY AND ARCHIVES (Hum)
1105 Ohio Departments Bldg.
65 S. Front St.
Phone: (614) 466-3831
Columbus, OH 43215
Kathy A. Babeaux, Libn.
Founded: 1929. **Staff:** Prof 1. **Subjects:** Ohio history, literature and music by or about Ohioans. **Special Collections:** Complete works of William Dean Howells, Sherwood Anderson, Louis Bromfield and other prominent Ohio authors; ''grass roots'' poetry; county histories and atlases. **Holdings:** 30,000 books; 200 bound periodical volumes; 5000 musical compositions; 13 VF drawers of clippings about current Ohio subjects; manuscripts; 28 VF drawers of pamphlets; 69 linear feet of scrapbooks containing biographical information about Ohio authors, artists and composers. **Subscriptions:** 30 journals and other serials. **Services:** Copying; reference by mail; library open to public for reference use only. **Networks/Consortia:** Member of CALICO. **Publications:** Ohioana Quarterly. **Special Catalogs:** The autumn issue of the Ohioana Quarterly includes as a supplement an annual bibliography of books and music by or about Ohioans.

★10165★
OHR KODESH CONGREGATION - SISTERHOOD LIBRARY (Area-Ethnic)
8402 Freyman Dr.
Phone: (301) 589-3880
Chevy Chase, MD 20015
Ethel E. Clemens, Libn.
Founded: 1965. **Staff:** Prof 1; Other 4. **Subjects:** Judaica. **Holdings:** 3700 books. **Services:** Library open to public for reference use only.

OHRSTROM (Elizabeth J.) LIBRARY
See: University of Virginia - Medical Center - Department of Neurology - Elizabeth J. Ohrstrom Library

★10166★
OIL INFORMATION LIBRARY OF WICHITA FALLS (Sci-Tech)
813 Hamilton Bldg.
Phone: (817) 322-4241
Wichita Falls, TX 76301
Dorothy Shilts, Libn.
Founded: 1966. **Staff:** 13. **Subjects:** Oil and gas records, geological information, exploration and development material, well data. **Special Collections:** Original Bess Mason Log File (over 500,000 logs); Independent Operators and Major Oil Companies electric log files (115,000 logs). **Holdings:** 450 books; 81 boxes of microfilm of scout information; 280 miscellaneous county maps; 14 boxes of microfilm of logs; 175 miscellaneous geology maps and plats; other cataloged items; 400 VF drawers of miscellaneous oil information. **Services:** Copying; library open to public with restrictions. **Formerly:** Wichita Scouting Co-op, Inc. - Oil Information Library.

O'KELLY LIBRARY
See: Winston-Salem State University

★10167★
OKLAHOMA ART CENTER - LIBRARY (Art)
3113 Pershing Blvd.
Phone: (405) 946-4477
Oklahoma City, OK 73107
Michael Sanden, Dir.
Subjects: Twentieth century American art. **Holdings:** 1300 volumes. **Services:** Library open to public with restrictions during specified hours.

★10168★

OKLAHOMA CITY METROPOLITAN LIBRARY SYSTEM - BUSINESS-SCIENCE SECTION (Bus-Fin; Sci-Tech)*
131 Dean A. McGee Ave.   Phone: (405) 235-0571
Oklahoma City, OK 73102   Elsie Bell, Chf., Main Lib.
Founded: 1950. **Staff:** Prof 6; Other 1. **Subjects:** Business, geology, geoscience, earth sciences, petroleum engineering, world trade. **Holdings:** 40,000 books; 25,000 bound periodical volumes; 50,000 maps (geologic and topographic); 1650 domestic and foreign telephone and city directories; state and federal reports; 90 periodical and newspaper titles in microform. **Subscriptions:** 425 journals and other serials. **Services:** Interlibrary loans; copying; library open to public. **Automated Operations:** Computerized cataloging, acquisitions and circulation.

★10169★

OKLAHOMA CITY UNIVERSITY - LAW LIBRARY (Law)
                                           Phone: (405) 521-5271
Oklahoma City, OK 73106   William J. Beintema, Law Libn.
Founded: 1956. **Staff:** Prof 5; Other 5. **Subjects:** Law. **Holdings:** 103,000 books. **Subscriptions:** 1250 journals and other serials. **Services:** Interlibrary loans; copying; library open to public. **Computerized Information Services:** Westlaw, OCLC. **Networks/Consortia:** Member of AMIGOS Bibliographic Council, Inc. **Staff:** Frances Deathe, Acq.Libn.; Judith Morgan, Asst.Dir.; Nancy Smith, Hd., Tech.Serv.; Joan Schipper, Ref.

★10170★

OKLAHOMA COLLEGE OF BUSINESS AND TECHNOLOGY - LEARNING RESOURCE CENTER (Bus-Fin)
4821 S. 72nd E. Ave.   Phone: (918) 742-3311
Tulsa, OK 74145   Carolyn S. McCauley, Dir. of Lrng.Rsrcs.
Founded: 1916. **Staff:** Prof 2; Other 1. **Subjects:** Business, accounting, business law, secretarial science, computer science, medical assistance, travel and airlines, electronic technology. **Holdings:** 5800 books; 6 VF drawers of pamphlets; 150 cassettes; 3 boxes of microfiche. **Subscriptions:** 110 journals and other serials. **Services:** Interlibrary loans; copying; subject bibliographies; center open to public. **Networks/Consortia:** Member of Tulsa Area Library Cooperative (TALC). **Formerly:** Oklahoma School of Business - Library.

★10171★

OKLAHOMA COLLEGE OF OSTEOPATHIC MEDICINE & SURGERY - LIBRARY (Med)
1111 W. 17th St.   Phone: (918) 582-1972
Tulsa, OK 74107   Linda L. Roberts, Coll.Libn.
Founded: 1974. **Staff:** Prof 3; Other 4. **Subjects:** Medicine. **Special Collections:** Osteopathy collection. **Holdings:** 16,013 books; 909 bound periodical volumes; 5425 AV items; 15,094 microfiche; 632 reels of microfilm. **Subscriptions:** 568 journals; 162 serials; 5 newspapers. **Services:** Interlibrary loans; copying; library open to public for reference use only. **Automated Operations:** Computerized acquisitions, serials and circulation. **Computerized Information Services:** MEDLARS, DIALOG. **Networks/Consortia:** Member of TALON. **Publications:** Library Newsletter, bimonthly - to faculty and affiliated hospitals and clinics. **Staff:** Anita Sutrick, Asst.Libn.; David Money, Asst.Libn.

★10172★

OKLAHOMA CORPORATION COMMISSION - ENERGY CONSERVATION SERVICES DIVISION - TECHNICAL INFORMATION CENTER (Energy)
4400 N. Lincoln Blvd., Suite 251   Phone: (405) 521-3941
Oklahoma City, OK 73105   Steven Boggs, Prog.Mgr.
Staff: Prof 1; Other 1. **Subjects:** Energy, conservation, renewable energy. **Holdings:** Figures not available. **Services:** Center open to public for reference use only.

★10173★

OKLAHOMA COUNTY LAW LIBRARY (Law)
County Courthouse, Rm. 247   Phone: (405) 236-2727
Oklahoma City, OK 73102   Betty A. Skaggs, Libn.
Staff: Prof 1; Other 3. **Subjects:** Law. **Holdings:** 26,700 books; 5650 microfiche. **Subscriptions:** 27 journals and other serials. **Services:** Copying; library open to public.

OKLAHOMA ENVIRONMENTAL INFORMATION/MEDIA CENTER
See: East Central Oklahoma State University

★10174★

OKLAHOMA GAS AND ELECTRIC COMPANY - LIBRARY (Sci-Tech; Energy)
Box 321   Phone: (405) 272-3191
Oklahoma City, OK 73102   Ms. Pat Tucker, Libn.
Founded: 1928. **Staff:** 1. **Subjects:** Engineering, electronics, mathematics, management, communication, environment, accident prevention, chemistry, physics, private and public power. **Special Collections:** Oklahoma history; the free enterprise system; world power resources; electrical engineering (185 volumes); American Society of Testing and Materials standards. **Holdings:** 5000 volumes. **Subscriptions:** 124 journals and other serials. **Services:** Interlibrary loans; library open to public for reference use only. **Automated Operations:** Computerized circulation. **Remarks:** The library is located at 321 N. Harvey, Oklahoma City, OK 73101.

★10175★

OKLAHOMA GEOLOGICAL SURVEY - OKLAHOMA GEOPHYSICAL OBSERVATORY LIBRARY (Sci-Tech)
Box 8   Phone: (918) 366-4152
Leonard, OK 74043-0008   Charles J. Mankin, Dir.
Founded: 1960. **Staff:** Prof 4; Other 1. **Subjects:** Seismology, geoelectricity, geomagnetism, aeronomy, earth tide gravimetry, meteorology, solar radiation. **Special Collections:** 50 geophysical records are currently recorded on a continuous (24 hour, 7 day) basis (185,000 record days in archives). **Holdings:** 300 books; 1500 other cataloged items. **Subscriptions:** 30 data bulletins. **Services:** Interlibrary loans; library open to public if advance arrangements are made with the chief geophysicist. **Computerized Information Services:** Oklahoma and regional earthquakes (internal database). Performs searches on cost recovery basis. Contact Person: J.E. Lawson, Jr. **Publications:** Reduced seismic data bulletins are sent to 2 world data centers and to several other addresses. This data is redistributed in the World Data Center Bulletins, with a total of about 8000 copies to 3000 addresses; P/PKP Arrival Bulletin, biweekly; Phase Amplitude Bulletin, biweekly; annual listing, maps and discussion of Oklahoma earthquakes published in Oklahoma Geology Notes, Earthquake Notes and United States Earthquakes. **Remarks:** This Geophysical Observatory was previously operated as Leonard Earth Sciences Observatory by the Jersey Production Corporation until 1965, when it was donated to the University of Oklahoma. In 1978 it was transferred to the Oklahoma Geological Survey. **Staff:** J.E. Lawson, Chf. Geophysicist; Paul H. Foster, Cons.; Richard L. Watkins, Electronic Techn.; Shirley A. Jackson, Libn.

★10176★

OKLAHOMA HISTORICAL SOCIETY - ARCHIVES AND MANUSCRIPT DIVISION (Hist)
Historical Bldg.   Phone: (405) 521-2491
Oklahoma City, OK 73105   Mary Lee Ervin Boyle, Sr.Archv.
Staff: Prof 5; Other 4. **Subjects:** Oklahoma and Indian territories, Indian tribes of Oklahoma, pioneer life, missionaries, territorial court records, explorers. **Special Collections:** Records from all state Indian agencies, except Osage Agency (3 million document pages; 5000 volumes); Dawes Commission Records (48 cubic feet; 242 bound volumes); Indian-Pioneer History (interviews; 113 volumes); Whipple Collection (8 cubic feet); Joseph Thoburn Collection (20 cubic feet). **Holdings:** 950 reels of microfilm (Indian affairs); 20,000 historical photographs; 1600 oral history tapes. **Services:** Copying; archives open to public. **Publications:** Microfilm of original materials for sale. **Special Catalogs:** Inventories of Five Civilized Tribes documents; card index of Indian-Pioneer History; catalog listing films for sale. **Staff:** Christine Bittle, Archv.; Robert Nespor, Archv.; William D. Welge, Archv.; Joe L. Todd, Archv./Oral Hist.

★10177★

OKLAHOMA HISTORICAL SOCIETY - CHICKASAW COUNCIL HOUSE LIBRARY (Hist; Area-Ethnic)
Court House Sq.
Box 717   Phone: (405) 371-3351
Tishomingo, OK 73460   Beverly J. Wyatt, Site Dir.
Founded: 1970. **Staff:** 2. **Subjects:** Chickasaw Indian history, including biographies and statistics. **Special Collections:** Oklahoma Chronicles - Chickasaw Constitution and law books. **Holdings:** 1200 books; 150 maps; county and Chickasaw Nation records; 70 reels of microfilm; pamphlets. **Services:** Library open to public.

★10178★

OKLAHOMA HISTORICAL SOCIETY - DIVISION OF LIBRARY RESOURCES (Hist)
Historical Bldg.   Phone: (405) 521-2491
Oklahoma City, OK 73105   Andrea Cantrell Clark, Dir., Lib.Rsrcs.
Founded: 1929. **Staff:** Prof 5; Other 10. **Subjects:** Oklahoma history and genealogy. **Holdings:** 45,000 volumes; 10,000 reels of microfilm of U.S.

Census, 1790-1880; 18,000 reels of microfilm of Oklahoma newspapers, 1893 to present. **Subscriptions:** 300 journals and other serials; 280 newspapers. **Services:** Interlibrary loans (limited); copying; library open to public for reference use only. **Staff:** Charlesa Timmons, Pub.Serv.Libn.; Mary Moran, Supv., Newspaper Dept.;Edward C. Shoemaker, Tech.Serv.Libn.; Fred J. Standley, Archv.

★10179★

OKLAHOMA OSTEOPATHIC HOSPITAL - L.C. BAXTER MEDICAL LIBRARY (Med)
Ninth St. at Jackson Ave.   Phone: (918) 599-5297
Tulsa, OK 74127   S. Jane Cooper, Hd.Med.Libn.
Founded: 1960. **Staff:** Prof 1; Other 2. **Subjects:** General medicine, internal medicine, surgery, ophthalmology, allied health sciences. **Holdings:** 1500 books; 1500 bound periodical volumes; 1600 AV cassettes; 1900 slides. **Subscriptions:** 200 journals and other serials. **Services:** Interlibrary loans; copying; library open to public for reference use only. **Networks/Consortia:** Member of TALON.

★10180★

OKLAHOMA REGIONAL LIBRARY FOR THE BLIND AND PHYSICALLY HANDICAPPED (Aud-Vis)
1108 N.E. 36th St.   Phone: (405) 521-3514
Oklahoma City, OK 73111   Bill McIlvain, Adm.Libn.
Founded: 1933. **Staff:** Prof 8; Other 26. **Subjects:** Recreational and informational reading materials in special media collections. **Special Collections:** Locally recorded books on cassette (1400 titles); hand-copied braille books of radio programs (600 titles); braille books (600); LP textbooks (150). **Holdings:** 19,554 books; 500 magnetic tapes; microfiche materials. **Subscriptions:** 56 journals and other serials. **Services:** Interlibrary loans; LED braille reproduction-machine repair; enlargement of print books; SDI; library not open to public. **Networks/Consortia:** Member of National Library Service for the Blind and Physically Handicapped (NLS). **Publications:** Radio Talking Book schedule, monthly - mail distribution; LP catalog, annual. **Special Catalogs:** Catalog for locally produced cassette books (card); braille catalog for braille books other than those produced by the Library of Congress. **Remarks:** This library is maintained by the Oklahoma State Department of Human Services. **Staff:** Carolyn Baker, Asst.Libn.; Jerome Simpson, Libn.; Linda Ables, Libn.Irma Burr, Libn. Volunteer Coord.; Kent Bowers, Radio Rd.Serv.

★10181★

OKLAHOMA SCHOOL FOR THE BLIND - PARKVIEW LIBRARY (Aud-Vis)
3300 Gibson St.
Box 309   Phone: (918) 682-6641
Muskogee, OK 74402-0309   Marjorie Moske, Libn.
Founded: 1913. **Staff:** 1. **Subjects:** Books in braille and talking books. **Special Collections:** Education of the blind. **Holdings:** 7535 titles; 2175 talking books. **Subscriptions:** 81 journals and other serials. **Services:** Interlibrary loans; library open to blind or partially-seeing. **Remarks:** Maintained by Oklahoma State Department of Human Services.

OKLAHOMA SCHOOL OF BUSINESS
See: Oklahoma College of Business and Technology

★10182★

OKLAHOMA STATE DEPARTMENT OF HEALTH - INFORMATION & REFERRAL HEALTHLINE (Med)†
N.E. 10th & Stonewall
Box 53551   Phone: (405) 271-4725
Oklahoma City, OK 73152   Dorothy Hall, Dir.
Founded: 1938. **Staff:** 1. **Subjects:** Medicine, nursing, psychology, personal health, epidemiology, venereal disease. **Holdings:** 2500 books and bound periodical volumes; 90,000 general health pamphlets covering approximately 300 areas. **Subscriptions:** 30 journals and other serials. **Services:** Library open to public with restrictions.

OKLAHOMA STATE DEPARTMENT OF HUMAN SERVICES - OKLAHOMA SCHOOL FOR THE BLIND
See: Oklahoma School for the Blind

OKLAHOMA STATE DEPARTMENT OF HUMAN SERVICES - REGIONAL LIBRARY FOR THE BLIND AND PHYSICALLY HANDICAPPED
See: Oklahoma Regional Library for the Blind and Physically Handicapped

★10183★

OKLAHOMA STATE DEPARTMENT OF LIBRARIES (Hist; Law)
200 N.E. 18th St.   Phone: (405) 521-2502
Oklahoma City, OK 73105   Robert L. Clark, Jr., Dir.
Founded: 1890. **Staff:** Prof 36; Other 42. **Subjects:** Law; legislative reference materials; Oklahoma government, history and authors; librarianship; juvenile evaluation collection. **Special Collections:** Oklahoma Collection (9000 titles). **Holdings:** 264,227 books; 22,605 cubic feet of state archives and manuscript collections; 13,800 cubic feet of state records; 14,474 linear feet of U.S. Government documents (regional depository); 3200 titles of Oklahoma documents; 1680 motion picture films; 6512 reels of microfilm; 700,000 microfiche; 150 file drawers of pamphlets and clippings; state government publications. **Subscriptions:** 1972 journals and other serials; 25 newspapers. **Services:** Interlibrary loans; copying; legislative and law reference; archival and state research assistance; library open to public for reference use only; loans made to state agency personnel only. **Automated Operations:** Computerized acquisitions. **Computerized Information Services:** OCLC, DIALOG, LEXIS, New York Times Information Service; legislature's index to statutes (internal database). **Networks/Consortia:** Member of AMIGOS Bibliographic Council, Inc.; Western Council of State Libraries. **Publications:** Who Is Who in the Oklahoma Legislature; Annual Report and Directory of Oklahoma Libraries; Oklahoma Register (adminstrative rules and regulations); ODL Source (newsletter), monthly; Automation in Oklahoma (newsletter), monthly; Oklahoma Government Publications (checklist), monthly. **Special Indexes:** Index to status of current state legislation (online). **Staff:** Sandra Ellison, Pub.Lib.Cons.; Dean Doerr, Pub.Lib.Cons.; Cathy Cook, Pub.Lib.Cons.; Denny Stephens, Asst.Dir.; Harriet Barbour, Hd., Govt.Serv.; John Hinkle, Act.Hd., Lib.Serv.; Marilyn Vesely, Pub.Info.Off.; Sue Galloway, Children's Cons.; Jan Blakely, Pub.Div.; Beverly Jones, Chf.Plan.Off.; Marian Patmon, Hd., Lib.Rsrcs.; Betty Brown, Oklahoma Rm.; Mary Hardin, ILL; Virginia Collier, U.S.Govt.Doc.; Oliver Delaney, Legislative Ref.; Geraldine Adams, Acq.; Allan Goode, AV; Howard Lowell, Oklahoma Rsrcs.; Freda Chen, Cat.; Blane Dessy, Pub.Lib.Cons.; Brad Koplowitz, State Archv.

★10184★

OKLAHOMA STATE DEPARTMENT OF VOCATIONAL AND TECHNICAL EDUCATION - CURRICULUM DIVISION - LIBRARY (Educ)
1500 W. 7th Ave.   Phone: (405) 377-2000
Stillwater, OK 74074   Susan K. Hedrick, Libn.
Founded: 1970. **Staff:** Prof 1; Other 2. **Subjects:** Vocational-technical materials, philosophy of vocational education, curriculum development, career education materials. **Holdings:** 4250 books; 1200 pamphlets; 2500 ERIC documents; 7000 microfiche of ERIC materials. **Subscriptions:** 75 journals and other serials. **Services:** Copying; SDI and ERIC search service to state staff and Oklahoma vocational teachers; 16mm films circulated free of charge to Oklahoma state vocational teachers on a reservation basis; library open to public for reference use only. **Networks/Consortia:** Member of Mid-West Curriculum Coordination Network. **Special Catalogs:** Bibliographies upon request of state staff. **Remarks:** The library's main purpose is to keep available all current curriculum materials in the subject area in which it is currently developing curriculum guides. As a new manual is begun, the library attempts to gather all materials by states, federal government and commercial publishers covering that area. **Staff:** Bob Patton, Coord., Curric.Div.

★10185★

OKLAHOMA STATE UNIVERSITY - AUDIO VISUAL CENTER (Aud-Vis)
                                                    Phone: (405) 624-7212
Stillwater, OK 74078   Dr. Woodfin G. Harris, Dir.
Staff: Prof 9; Other 35. **Holdings:** 5000 16mm films; 300 audiotape masters; 50 video cassettes. **Services:** Copying; SDI; audio recording and duplication; graphics production; photography; AV equipment rental and repair; consultations and workshops in various areas of AV communications and operations; films and video cassettes available on rental basis; center open to public. **Automated Operations:** Computerized cataloging and circulation. **Networks/Consortia:** Member of Consortium of University Film Centers (CUFC). **Special Catalogs:** Film Rental Catalog (regional), every 3 years; special catalogs prepared by subject and grade level. **Staff:** Ron G. Payne, Mgr., AV Serv; Claude S. Maxwell, Supv., Photo Serv.; Jane Aston, Supv., Graphics; Jerry D. Harris, Supv., Tech.Serv.

★10186★

OKLAHOMA STATE UNIVERSITY - BIOLOGICAL SCIENCES DIVISION (Sci-Tech)
University Library   Phone: (405) 624-6309
Stillwater, OK 74078   Sheila G. Johnson, Hd.
Founded: 1891. **Staff:** Prof 3; Other 5. **Subjects:** Agriculture, botany, entomology, zoology, bacteriology, anthropology, medicine, home economics. **Holdings:** 76,700 books; 73,803 bound periodical volumes. **Subscriptions:**

1900 journals and other serials. **Services:** Interlibrary loans; copying; division open to Stillwater residents with restrictions. **Computerized Information Services:** DIALOG, BRS, OCLC. **Staff:** Ibraham Hanif, Asst. Biological Sci.Libn.

★10187★
OKLAHOMA STATE UNIVERSITY - CURRICULUM MATERIALS LABORATORY (Educ)
University Library   Phone: (405) 624-6310
Stillwater, OK 74078
Founded: 1957. **Staff:** 2. **Subjects:** Kindergarten through grade 12 library. **Special Collections:** Foreign language children's books (278 books); Indians of North America (children's collections). **Holdings:** 30,000 books; 544 bound periodical volumes; 2082 items in the nonprint media; 5000 textbooks; 5000 courses of study. **Subscriptions:** 150 journals and other serials. **Services:** Interlibrary loans; copying; laboratory open to public with restrictions. **Publications:** Dime a Dozen; Facts of CML; And More to Grow!; Books for Enrichment.

★10188★
OKLAHOMA STATE UNIVERSITY - DOCUMENTS DEPARTMENT (Info Sci)
University Library   Phone: (405) 624-6546
Stillwater, OK 74078   Vicki W. Phillips, Hd.
Founded: 1907. **Staff:** Prof 4; Other 6. **Special Collections:** U.S. Government Regional Depository; NASA depository; U.S. patent depository; Oklahoma documents depository. **Holdings:** 1.2 million items; 157,237 accessioned books and bound periodical volumes; 866,946 microforms. **Subscriptions:** 4411 journals and other serials. **Services:** Interlibrary loans; copying; department open to public with restrictions. **Staff:** John Phillips, Asst.Doc.Libn.; Mary Ann Slater, Asst.Doc.Libn.; Connie Kirby, Asst.Doc.Libn.

★10189★
OKLAHOMA STATE UNIVERSITY - HUMANITIES DIVISION (Hum)
University Library   Phone: (405) 624-6544
Stillwater, OK 74078   Kim Fisher, Hd.
Founded: 1953. **Staff:** Prof 4; Other 3. **Subjects:** Literature, religion, computer science, library science, journalism, language, architecture, film, theater, fine arts, painting, sculpture, interior design, music, sports, recreation. **Holdings:** 127,997 books; 26,890 bound periodical volumes; 77,582 microforms. **Subscriptions:** 1554 journals and other serials. **Services:** Interlibrary loans; copying; division open to public with restrictions. **Computerized Information Services:** DIALOG, BRS, OCLC. **Staff:** Morag Sutherland, Asst.Hum.Libn.; Terry Basford, Asst.Hum.Libn.

★10190★
OKLAHOMA STATE UNIVERSITY - OKLAHOMA CITY BRANCH - TECHNICAL INSTITUTE LIBRARY (Educ)
900 N. Portland   Phone: (405) 947-4421
Oklahoma City, OK 73107   Annette Duffy, Hd.Libn.
Founded: 1963. **Staff:** Prof 2; Other 3. **Subjects:** Computer science, nursing, electronics, police science, horticulture, fire protection. **Holdings:** 10,000 books. **Subscriptions:** 200 journals and other serials. **Services:** Interlibrary loans; copying; library open to public with restrictions. **Computerized Information Services:** OCLC, DIALOG, DataTimes. Performs searches on cost recovery basis. **Networks/Consortia:** Member of AMIGOS Bibliographic Council, Inc. **Publications:** New Book List, 5/year - for internal distribution only. **Staff:** Donna Denniston, Asst.Libn.

★10191★
OKLAHOMA STATE UNIVERSITY - PHYSICAL SCIENCES AND ENGINEERING DIVISION (Sci-Tech)
University Library   Phone: (405) 624-6305
Stillwater, OK 74078   Calvin Brewer, Hd.
Founded: 1928. **Staff:** Prof 3; Other 5. **Subjects:** Chemistry; physics; mathematics; geology; engineering - chemical, aeronautical, civil, electrical, mechanical. **Holdings:** 75,463 books; 106,644 bound periodical volumes; 51,413 microforms. **Subscriptions:** 1588 journals and other serials. **Services:** Interlibrary loans; copying; division open to public with restrictions. **Computerized Information Services:** DIALOG, BRS, OCLC. **Staff:** Elizabeth Struble, Asst. Physical Sci.Libn.; Kevin Kennedy, Asst. Physical Sci.Libn.

★10192★
OKLAHOMA STATE UNIVERSITY - SCHOOL OF TECHNICAL TRAINING - OKMULGEE BRANCH LIBRARY (Sci-Tech)
    Phone: (918) 756-6211
Okmulgee, OK 74447   Becky Kirkbride, Libn.
Founded: 1946. **Staff:** Prof 2; Other 3. **Subjects:** Automotive engineering, electrical-electronics technology, diesel trades, machinist trades, drafting, air conditioning and refrigeration, graphic arts, practical nursing, shoe repair, watch and micro-instrument repair, business education, food trades,

commercial art, building trades, computer graphics, numerical control. **Holdings:** 16,000 books; 225 reels of film. **Subscriptions:** 140 journals and other serials; 7 newspapers. **Services:** Interlibrary loans; copying; library open to public with restrictions. **Computerized Information Services:** The Source. **Staff:** M.F. Christerson, Coord. LRC.

★10193★
OKLAHOMA STATE UNIVERSITY - SOCIAL SCIENCE DIVISION (Soc Sci)
University Library   Phone: (405) 624-6540
Stillwater, OK 74078   Edward G. Hollman, Hd.
Founded: 1953. **Staff:** Prof 4; Other 3. **Subjects:** Business, economics, history, political science, sociology, management, anthropology, geography, education, psychology, philosophy. **Holdings:** 215,000 books; 56,000 bound periodical volumes; 250 VF serials; 28 VF drawers of pamphlets; 250,000 microforms. **Subscriptions:** 2200 journals and other serials; 9 newspapers. **Services:** Interlibrary loans; copying; division open to public with restrictions. **Computerized Information Services:** DIALOG, BRS, OCLC. **Remarks:** Contains the holdings of its Education Division. **Staff:** Jill Holmes, Educ.Libn.

★10194★
OKLAHOMA STATE UNIVERSITY - SPECIAL COLLECTIONS AND MAPS (Geog-Map)
University Library   Phone: (405) 624-6311
Stillwater, OK 74078   Heather M. Lloyd, Hd., Gen.Ref.Dept.
Staff: Prof 2; Other 1. **Subjects:** Oklahoma State University, Oklahoma agriculture and political maps. **Holdings:** OSU publications; U.S. Geological Survey maps (depository); Defense Mapping Agency (DMA) maps (depository); aerial photographs (Oklahoma); state agricultural history; 120,492 maps; papers of Henry Bellman, Henry S. Johnston and Paul Miller. **Services:** Copying; library open to public for reference use only. **Staff:** William C. Richardson, Asst.Ref.Libn.

★10195★
OKLAHOMA STATE UNIVERSITY - VETERINARY MEDICINE LIBRARY (Med)
University Library   Phone: (405) 624-6655
Stillwater, OK 74078   LaVerne K. Jones, Libn.
Founded: 1948. **Staff:** Prof 1; Other 3. **Subjects:** Veterinary medicine, health sciences, laboratory animal medicine. **Holdings:** 3979 books; 7317 bound periodical volumes; 10 reels of microfilm. **Subscriptions:** 307 journals and other serials. **Services:** Interlibrary loans; copying; library open to public with restrictions. **Computerized Information Services:** DIALOG, BRS, NLM, OCLC.

★10196★
OKLAHOMA VETERANS CENTER - TALIHINA DIVISION - LIBRARY (Med)
Box 488   Phone: (918) 567-2251
Talihina, OK 74571   Betty L. Davis, Libn.
Staff: 2. **Subjects:** Internal medicine, nursing. **Holdings:** 250 books; 50 bound periodical volumes; 27 titles on cassette tapes; 1 VF drawer of pamphlets; 24 feet of archives. **Subscriptions:** 98 journals and other serials; 5 newspapers. **Services:** Interlibrary loans; copying; literature searches for medical professionals; library open to public. **Publications:** TVC Newsletter, monthly - distributed to staff, patients, mailing list.

★10197★
OKLAHOMA WATER RESOURCES BOARD - LIBRARY (Sci-Tech)
1000 N.E. 10th, 12th Fl.
Box 53585   Phone: (405) 271-2555
Oklahoma City, OK 73152   Susan E. Lutz, Libn.
Staff: Prof 1. **Subjects:** Water, water quality and planning. **Holdings:** 8200 volumes. **Subscriptions:** 95 journals and other serials. **Services:** Interlibrary loans; copying; library open to public.

★10198★
OKLAHOMA WELL LOG LIBRARY, INC. (Sci-Tech; Energy)
837 Mayo Bldg.   Phone: (918) 582-6188
Tulsa, OK 74103   Jan Jennings, Mgr./Libn.
Staff: Prof 1; Other 6. **Subjects:** Geology, oil and gas. **Special Collections:** Electrical logs (200,000); scout tickets (750,000). **Holdings:** 1000 books and bound periodical volumes; 400 reels of microfilm. **Services:** Copying; library open to public with restrictions.

★10199★
OKRA RIDGE FARM - TENNESSEE LESBIAN ARCHIVES (Soc Sci)
Rte. 2, Box 252   Phone: (615) 992-8423
Luttrell, TN 37779   Catherine R. Moirai, Coord.
Staff: Prof 1. **Subjects:** Lesbian studies. **Holdings:** 450 books; 5 VF drawers of clippings. **Subscriptions:** 15 journals and other serials. **Services:** Archives open to lesbians only, by prior arrangement. **Formerly:** Okra Ridge Farm/East

Tennessee Alliance of Lesbian Activists.

★10200★
OLANA STATE HISTORIC SITE - LIBRARY (Hist; Art)
R.D. 2   Phone: (518) 828-0135
Hudson, NY 12534   James Ryan, Site Mgr.
Staff: Prof 1; Other 2. **Subjects:** Local history. **Special Collections:** Correspondence and paintings of Frederic Edwin Church (19th-century American landscape painter); 19th-century photographs. **Holdings:** 3000 books; 34 bound periodical volumes; theses. **Services:** Library open to public with restrictions. **Publications:** The Crayon, 3/year - to members.

OLCOTT LIBRARY & RESEARCH CENTER
See: Theosophical Society in America

OLD ACADEMY MUSEUM LIBRARY
See: Wethersfield Historical Society

★10201★
OLD AMERICAN INSURANCE COMPANY - LIBRARY (Bus-Fin)*
4900 Oak St.
Kansas City, MO 64112   Catherine Kufahl, Libn.
Staff: 1. **Subjects:** Insurance, law. **Holdings:** 3000 volumes; 4 VF drawers of pamphlets. **Subscriptions:** 207 journals and other serials. **Services:** Interlibrary loans; library not open to public.

OLD BRICK TAVERN MUSEUM
See: Schuyler County Historical Society

★10202★
OLD BRUTUS HISTORICAL SOCIETY, INC. - LIBRARY (Hist)
8943 N. Seneca St.   Phone: (315) 834-6779
Weedsport, NY 13166   Howard J. Finley, Dir.
Staff: 1. **Subjects:** Genealogy, local history. **Special Collections:** Stanley Guppy books on history of Cayuga County (50). **Holdings:** 2000 books; 2000 photographs; 40,000 genealogy sheets. **Services:** Library open to public on a limited schedule.

★10203★
OLD CATHEDRAL PARISH CHURCH - BRUTE LIBRARY (Rare Book; Rel-Theol)
205 Church St.   Phone: (812) 882-7016
Vincennes, IN 47591   Esther Cunningham, Guide/Archv.
Staff: Prof 2. **Subjects:** Rare books, religion. **Special Collections:** Two hand-printed and illuminated documents from the Middle Ages; letter of St. Vincent de Paul dated 1660. **Holdings:** 11,000 books. **Services:** Library open to public for reference use only.

★10204★
OLD CHARLES TOWN LIBRARY, INC. (Hist)
200 E. Washington St.   Phone: (304) 725-2208
Charles Town, WV 25414   Anna M. Shewbridge, Libn.
Founded: 1965. **Staff:** Prof 1; Other 3. **Subjects:** Local history, genealogy, West Virginia history. **Special Collections:** Collection of Jefferson County Historical Society. **Holdings:** 50,426 books; 491 bound periodical volumes. **Subscriptions:** 123 journals and other serials.

★10205★
OLD COLONY HISTORICAL SOCIETY - MUSEUM & LIBRARY (Hist)
66 Church Green   Phone: (617) 822-1622
Taunton, MA 02780   Lisa A. Compton, Dir.
Founded: 1853. **Staff:** Prof 1; Other 1. **Subjects:** Local history, biography, genealogy. **Special Collections:** Books and manuscripts of Francis Baylies. **Holdings:** 6000 books; other cataloged items. **Services:** Copying; museum and library open to public for reference use only.

THE OLD CORNER HOUSE (Norman Rockwell Museum)
See: Norman Rockwell Museum of the Old Corner House

★10206★
OLD DARTMOUTH HISTORICAL SOCIETY - WHALING MUSEUM LIBRARY (Hist)
18 Johnny Cake Hill   Phone: (617) 997-0046
New Bedford, MA 02740   Virginia M. Adams, Libn.
Founded: 1903. **Staff:** Prof 3; Other 1. **Subjects:** History of American whaling, history of New Bedford area. **Special Collections:** Ship log books (1050); Charles F. Batchelder Collection (whaling); Charles A. Goodwin Collection (maritime history); International Marine Archives (whaling and maritime records on microfilm). **Holdings:** 15,000 books; 500 bound periodical volumes; 750 linear feet of manuscripts; 600 maps and charts; 1800 reels of microfilm. **Subscriptions:** 30 journals and other serials. **Services:** Interlibrary loans (microfilm only); copying; library open to public.

OLD ECONOMY VILLAGE
See: Pennsylvania State Historical & Museum Commission

★10207★
OLD FORT NIAGARA ASSOCIATION - LIBRARY (Hist; Mil)
Box 169   Phone: (716) 745-7611
Youngstown, NY 14174   Brian Leigh Dunnigan, Exec.Dir.
Staff: Prof 1. **Subjects:** Local and military history. **Special Collections:** Old Fort Niagara Collection (original diaries, orderly books and post records, 1813-1912). **Holdings:** 400 books. **Subscriptions:** 10 journals and other serials. **Services:** Copying; library open to serious researchers by prior arrangement.

OLD GAOL MUSEUM
See: Old York Historical Society

★10208★
OLD MANSE LIBRARY (Hist)
225 Mary St.   Phone: (506) 622-0453
Newcastle, NB, Canada E1V 1Z3   Catherine Bryan, Libn.
Founded: 1953. **Staff:** Prof 1; Other 2. **Subjects:** Local history and genealogy. **Special Collections:** Lord Beaverbrook Collection; Miramichi Historical Society Records. **Holdings:** 38,000 books. **Subscriptions:** 10 journals and other serials. **Services:** Interlibrary loans; copying; library open to public. **Publications:** Newcastle on the Miramichi; The Old Manse Library, Newcastle, N.B. **Remarks:** Maintained by the town of Newcastle.

★10209★
OLD ST. MARY'S CHURCH - PAULIST LIBRARY (Rel-Theol)
614 Grant Ave.   Phone: (415) 362-0959
San Francisco, CA 94108   Walter Anthony, C.S.P., Dir.
Staff: Prof 1; Other 35. **Subjects:** Catholic religion and history, biography, psychology. **Special Collections:** Rare collection of biographical works. **Holdings:** 5000 books; 3500 cassettes. **Subscriptions:** 25 journals and other serials. **Services:** Library open to public but no borrowing without membership. **Special Catalogs:** Cassette catalog.

★10210★
OLD SALEM, INC. - LIBRARY (Hist; Area-Ethnic)
Drawer F, Salem Sta.   Phone: (919) 723-3688
Winston-Salem, NC 27108   Gene T. Capps, Dir., Dept. of Educ.
Staff: Prof 1; Other 1. **Subjects:** Moravians in North Carolina, North Carolina history, traditional American crafts, historic preservation. **Holdings:** 1800 books; 4 VF drawers of Moraviana, preservation, crafts, interpretation clippings; 26 VF drawers of items on life in early Salem, NC, and restoration of Old Salem. **Subscriptions:** 25 journals and other serials. **Services:** Library open to public with restrictions.

★10211★
OLD SALEM, INC. - MUSEUM OF EARLY SOUTHERN DECORATIVE ARTS (MESDA) - LIBRARY (Art)
Box 10310   Phone: (919) 722-6148
Winston-Salem, NC 27108   Bradford L. Rauschenberg
Founded: 1965. **Staff:** Prof 1. **Subjects:** Decorative arts of southern United States. **Holdings:** 2500 books; 200 bound periodical volumes; data file of 25,000 cards based on source material; 15 VF drawers of photographs and southern decorative art material; 900 reels of microfilmed newspapers, pre-1821. **Services:** Copying (by personal application); library open to public.

★10212★
OLD SLAVE MART MUSEUM - LIBRARY (Hist; Art)
Box 446   Phone: (803) 883-3797
Sullivan's Island, SC 29482   Judith Wragg Chase, Lib.Dir.
Staff: Prof 2; Other 1. **Subjects:** Slave crafts, Afro-American and African arts and crafts, Southern history and history of slavery, modern Afro-American history, history and architecture of Charleston, South Carolina. **Holdings:** 1000 volumes; 1800 photographs; 850 slides; 130 photocopies of documents and 80 original documents; 800 realia; 300 paintings, flatwork and prints; 50 maps. **Subscriptions:** 20 journals and other serials. **Services:** Mail order research service and copying; SDI; selective photographic reproduction rights; slide rental; library open to serious scholars and researchers by appointment only. **Publications:** Monographs; Afro-American Art & Craft, 1971; Catalog of the Old Slave Mart Museum and Library (2 volumes), 1978. **Remarks:** Maintained by Miriam B. Wilson Foundation. The library is the research arm of the Old Slave Mart Museum (located at 6

Chalmers St., Charleston, SC). It offers educational outreach programs and the opportunity for individual research. **Staff:** Barbara Carlson, Cat.; Sabrina Ford, Cat.

OLD SONGS LIBRARY
See: Society for the Preservation and Encouragement of Barber Shop Quartet Singing in America

OLD SPANISH MISSIONS HISTORICAL RESEARCH LIBRARY
See: Our Lady of The Lake University

★10213★
OLD STURBRIDGE VILLAGE - RESEARCH LIBRARY (Hist)
Phone: (617) 347-3362
Sturbridge, MA 01566   Theresa Rini Percy, Libn.
Founded: 1946. **Staff:** Prof 2; Other 3. **Subjects:** New England village life, 1790-1840 - state and local history, agriculture, architecture, fine arts, decorative arts (ceramics, furniture, glass, silver), crafts (blacksmithing, cabinet work, pottery), costume and fabrics, politics, economics, education, law, religion; technology and industry. **Special Collections:** Powell Collection of printed works on agriculture (1000 volumes); Merino/Dudley Wool Company Records, Dudley, Massachusetts, 1811-1845 (35 linear feet); Town of Sturbridge, Massachusetts papers, 1738-1915 (13 boxes). **Holdings:** 26,500 books and bound periodical volumes; 196 shelf feet of manuscripts; 4 VF cabinets of black/white pictures; 13 VF cabinets of pamphlets, archives; 1094 microforms. **Subscriptions:** 125 journals and other serials. **Services:** Interlibrary loans; copying; library open to public for reference use only. **Publications:** Recent Additions (new book list), occasional. **Staff:** Joan Allen, Cat.; Kathleen Pratt Frew, Preservation Techn.

OLD THRESHERS OFFICE - LIBRARY
See: Midwest Old Settlers and Threshers Association

OLD WEST MUSEUM
See: Sunset Trading Post-Old West Museum

★10214★
OLD YORK HISTORICAL SOCIETY - LIBRARY (Hist)
George Marshall Store
Lindsay Rd.
Box 312   Phone: (207) 363-4974
York, ME 03909   Dr. Eldridge H. Pendleton, Dir., Coll. & Prog.
Staff: 5. **Subjects:** Local history, decorative arts, genealogy, Maine history, architecture. **Special Collections:** Rare books (200); local manuscripts (3000); local historic photographs (1000); local genealogies (300). **Holdings:** 4000 books; 200 bound periodical volumes; 55 feet of manuscripts and archives; 12 reels of microfilm; 4 VF drawers. **Services:** Interlibrary loans; copying; library open to public for reference use only. **Publications:** York Maine Then and Now; The Old Gaol Museum; Enchanted Ground - currently for sale. **Formerly:** Old Gaol Museum. **Staff:** Kerry A. O'Brien, Cur.

★10215★
OLD YORK ROAD HISTORICAL SOCIETY - ARCHIVES (Hist)
Abington Library Society   Phone: (215) 884-8058
Jenkintown, PA 19046   Warren Hilton, Libn.
Founded: 1936. **Subjects:** Local history. **Holdings:** Books; newspapers; pamphlets; clippings; photographs. **Services:** Archives open to public for reference use on request. **Publications:** Bulletin, annual - to members and libraries.

OLDHAM (Earl K.) LIBRARY
See: Arlington Baptist College - Earl K. Oldham Library

★10216★
OLDS COLLEGE - LEARNING RESOURCES CENTRE - SPECIAL COLLECTIONS (Agri)
Phone: (403) 556-8243
Olds, AB, Canada T0M 1P0   Garry Grisak, Coord., Lib.Serv.
Holdings: Agricultural Collection; government documents; Agdex (agricultural documents and other pamphlets). **Services:** Interlibrary loans; copying; collections open to public. **Computerized Information Services:** DIALOG.

O'LEARY (Daniel H.) LIBRARY
See: University of Lowell, South Campus - Daniel H. O'Leary Library

★10217★
OLIN CORPORATION - BRASS GROUP LIBRARY (Sci-Tech)†
Phone: (618) 258-3198
East Alton, IL 62024   Barbara A. Allen, Libn.
Staff: 1. **Subjects:** Metallurgy - physical and chemical; metals; metallurgical and alloy engineering; laboratory functions - chemical and physical. **Holdings:** Figures not available. **Subscriptions:** 14 journals and other serials. **Services:** Interlibrary loans (limited); copying; library open to public with restrictions.

★10218★
OLIN CORPORATION - BUSINESS INFORMATION CENTER (Bus-Fin)
120 Long Ridge Rd.   Phone: (203) 356-2498
Stamford, CT 06904   L.A. Magistrate, Mgr., Bus.Onfo.
Staff: Prof 2; Other 2. **Subjects:** Business, law. **Holdings:** 1500 books. **Subscriptions:** 550 journals and other serials. **Services:** Center not open to public. **Computerized Information Services:** DIALOG, SDC, Business International Corporation, Mead Data Central, Trade Information Service, INVESTEXT, Data Resources, Inc. (DRI), Human Resource Information Network, First Boston Corporation.

★10219★
OLIN CORPORATION - CHEMICALS - CHARLESTON TECHNICAL INFORMATION CENTER (Sci-Tech)
Phone: (615) 336-2251
Charleston, TN 37310   Barbara C. Suttles, Supv.
Founded: 1976. **Staff:** Prof 1; Other 2. **Subjects:** Chemistry, chemical engineering, electrochemistry, engineering. **Holdings:** 2000 books; 1000 bound periodical volumes; 3 VF drawers of translations. **Subscriptions:** 100 journals and other serials; 6 newspapers. **Services:** Center not open to public. **Computerized Information Services:** DIALOG, SDC, NLM.

★10220★
OLIN CORPORATION - ECUSTA PAPER AND FILM GROUP - TECHNICAL LIBRARY (Sci-Tech)†
Box 200   Phone: (704) 877-2339
Pisgah Forest, NC 28768   Martha M. Sellers, Tech.Libn.
Founded: 1939. **Staff:** 2. **Subjects:** Cellulose chemistry, polymers and plastics, pulp and paper manufacture, water and air pollution control. **Holdings:** 4176 books; 5075 bound periodical volumes; 550 catalogs; 650 brochures; 15,560 literature separates and patents. **Subscriptions:** 124 journals and other serials. **Services:** Library not open to public. **Staff:** Elizabeth J. Flynn, Mgr., Tech.Adm.

★10221★
OLIN CORPORATION - METALS RESEARCH LABORATORIES - METALS INFORMATION CENTER (Sci-Tech)†
91 Shelton Ave.   Phone: (203) 789-6000
New Haven, CT 06511   Marcella C. Tammard, Libn.
Founded: 1961. **Staff:** Prof 1; Other 1. **Subjects:** Metallurgy, corrosion, aluminum, copper and brass. **Holdings:** 1800 books; 700 bound periodical volumes; 5000 company and outside reports; 5000 patents; 3500 translations. **Subscriptions:** 185 journals and other serials. **Services:** Copying; SDI; center open to public on request. **Computerized Information Services:** DIALOG, SDC, Copper Data Center (CDC).

★10222★
OLIN CORPORATION - RESEARCH CENTER/INFORMATION CENTER (Sci-Tech)
Box 30-275   Phone: (203) 789-6038
New Haven, CT 06511   R.P. Peraza, Mgr.
Founded: 1941. **Staff:** Prof 5; Other 6. **Subjects:** Chemistry, metallurgy, physics. **Holdings:** 25,000 books; 15,000 bound periodical volumes; 16,000 technical reports; journals and patents on microfilm. **Subscriptions:** 500 journals and other serials; 10 newspapers. **Services:** Interlibrary loans; center not open to public. **Automated Operations:** Computerized serials. **Computerized Information Services:** Online systems. **Special Indexes:** Computer-produced indexes. **Staff:** L.D. Campo; T.M. ManningJ. Pitts; V. Pitts

★10223★
OLIN CORPORATION - SOLID PROPELLANT ORGANIZATION - RESEARCH LIBRARY (Sci-Tech)†
Drawer G   Phone: (618) 985-8211
Marion, IL 62959
Founded: 1958. **Subjects:** Chemistry, chemical engineering, electronics, mechanical engineering. **Holdings:** 575 books; 500 bound periodical volumes; 100 VF drawers. **Services:** Library not open to public.

OLIN LIBRARY
See: Washington University - Department of Special Collections

OLIN RESEARCH LIBRARY
See: Cornell University

OLIN SCIENCE LIBRARY
See: Macalester College

OLIPHANT (Jacob T.) LIBRARY
See: Indiana State Board of Health - Jacob T. Oliphant Library

OLIVE VIEW MEDICAL CENTER
See: Los Angeles County/Olive View Medical Center

OLIVER (Monsignor Juan Fremiot Torres) LAW LIBRARY
See: Catholic University of Puerto Rico - Monsignor Juan Fremiot Torres Oliver Law Library

OLIVER (Wrenshall A.) PROFESSIONAL LIBRARY
See: Napa State Hospital - Wrenshall A. Oliver Professional Library

★10224★
OLMSTED COUNTY HISTORICAL SOCIETY - LIBRARY AND ARCHIVES (Hist)
Box 6411   Phone: (507) 282-9447
Rochester, MN 55903   Doris Blinks, Lib.Supv.
Founded: 1926. **Staff:** Prof 2. **Subjects:** Olmsted County history, Minnesota history, genealogy, 19th century farming. **Holdings:** 5000 books; 300 bound periodical volumes; 540 reels of 35mm microfilm of Olmsted County newspapers, 1859 to present; 69 VF drawers of documents, pamphlets and photographs relating to Olmsted County history; Minnesota census records through 1910. **Subscriptions:** 21 journals and other serials. **Services:** Copying; library and archives open to public; fees charged for staff research. **Special Indexes:** Index to newspapers (1859-1912).

OLMSTED (Frederick Law) NATL. HISTORIC SITE
See: U.S. Natl. Park Service - Frederick Law Olmsted Natl. Historic Site

OLSON (Charles) ARCHIVES
See: University of Connecticut - Homer Babbidge Library - Special Collections

OLSON (Otto) MEMORIAL LIBRARY
See: University of Saskatchewan - Lutheran Theological Seminary - Otto Olson Memorial Library

★10225★
OLWINE, CONNELLY, CHASE, O'DONNELL & WEYHER - LAW LIBRARY (Law)
299 Park Ave.   Phone: (212) 207-1800
New York, NY 10171   James T. Roscher, Libn.
Staff: Prof 1; Other 1. **Subjects:** Law - corporate, taxation, trust and estates, patents, real estate. **Holdings:** 14,000 books; 550 bound periodical volumes; 150 pamphlets. **Subscriptions:** 75 journals and other serials; 5 newspapers. **Services:** Interlibrary loans; copying; library open to lawyers only. **Computerized Information Services:** LEXIS, New York Times Information Service.

OLYMPIA FIELDS OSTEOPATHIC MEDICAL CENTER LIBRARY
See: Chicago College of Osteopathic Medicine

OLYMPIC NATL. PARK
See: U.S. Natl. Park Service

★10226★
OLYMPIC SAVINGS AND LOAN ASSOCIATION - LIBRARY
6201 W. Cermak Rd.
Berwyn, IL 60402
Defunct

★10227★
OMAHA-COUNCIL BLUFFS METROPOLITAN AREA PLANNING AGENCY (MAPA) - LIBRARY (Plan)
7000 W. Center Rd., Suite 200   Phone: (402) 444-6866
Omaha, NE 68106   Dagnia Prieiditis, Libn./Info.Off.
Staff: Prof 1. **Subjects:** Planning and community development, transportation, housing, environment, census, local and regional data. **Holdings:** 5000 volumes; 125 periodicals and newsletters; 100 microfiche; 1980 Iowa and Nebraska census tapes; local data; area newspaper clippings; maps; aerial

photographs. **Subscriptions:** 107 journals and other serials. **Services:** Copying; research (fee); library open to public by appointment. **Computerized Information Services:** DIALOG.

★10228★
OMAHA PUBLIC LIBRARY - BUSINESS, SCIENCE & TECHNOLOGY DEPARTMENT (Bus-Fin; Sci-Tech)
215 S. 15th St.   Phone: (402) 444-4817
Omaha, NE 68102   Bernice Johns, Hd.
Founded: 1952. **Staff:** Prof 3; Other 3. **Subjects:** Economics, insurance, mathematics, physics, investments, chemistry, engineering, agriculture, medicine, health, biology, botany. **Special Collections:** Telephone, city and trade directories; trade catalogs; Public Document Room Collection of the Nuclear Regulatory Commission reports. **Holdings:** 38,498 books; 6111 bound periodical volumes; government documents; 75 VF drawers of pamphlets, clippings, house organs and corporate annual reports; maps; microfilm. **Subscriptions:** 525 journals and other serials. **Services:** Interlibrary loans; copying; library open to public. **Publications:** Information Bulletin, monthly - distributed to businesses, corporations and libraries on request. **Staff:** Janet Davenport, Libn.; William Kendra, Libn.

★10229★
OMAHA PUBLIC POWER DISTRICT - MANAGEMENT SYSTEMS SERVICES - LIBRARY (Energy; Comp Sci)
1623 Harney St.   Phone: (402) 536-4295
Omaha, NE 68102   Suzanne Forbes, Libn.
Founded: 1982. **Staff:** Prof 1; Other 1. **Subjects:** Data processing, energy, business, nuclear power. **Holdings:** 500 books. **Subscriptions:** 350 journals and other serials; 30 newspapers. **Services:** Interlibrary loans; library not open to public. **Computerized Information Services:** DIALOG.

★10230★
OMAHA WORLD-HERALD - LIBRARY (Publ)
World Herald Square   Phone: (402) 444-1000
Omaha, NE 68102   Beverly Parisot, Lib.Mgr.
Staff: Prof 1; Other 8. **Subjects:** Newspaper reference topics. **Holdings:** 14 million newspaper clippings; 400 drawers of photographs. **Services:** Library not open to public. **Computerized Information Services:** Omaha World-Herald Data Bank (internal database).

★10231★
O'MELVENY AND MYERS - INFORMATION SERVICES (Law)
400 S. Hope St.   Phone: (213) 669-6000
Los Angeles, CA 90071-2899   Stanley Pearce, Dir., Info.Serv.
Founded: 1885. **Staff:** Prof 7; Other 15. **Subjects:** Law, labor, taxation. **Holdings:** 45,000 volumes; 12,000 research reports (legal memoranda). **Services:** Library not open to public. **Automated Operations:** Computerized cataloging. **Computerized Information Services:** LEXIS, DIALOG, RLIN, Westlaw, BRS. **Networks/Consortia:** Member of CLASS. **Special Catalogs:** Book catalog/index of internal research reports. **Staff:** Maryruth Storer, Law Libn.; Claudia Cook, Ref.Libn.; Kathy Way, Ref.Libn.; Barbara Gabor, Pub.Serv.Libn.; Laura Loring, Tech.Serv.Libn.; Ken Cheong, Cat.Libn.

OMI COLLEGE OF APPLIED SCIENCE
See: University of Cincinnati

★10232★
OMI INTERNATIONAL CORP. - LIBRARY (Sci-Tech)
21441 Hoover Rd.   Phone: (313) 497-9100
Warren, MI 48089   Lynn M. Pefley
Founded: 1955. **Staff:** 1. **Subjects:** Metal finishing and related subjects. **Holdings:** 1600 books; 200 bound periodical volumes. **Subscriptions:** 70 journals and other serials. **Services:** Interlibrary loans; library not open to public. **Formerly:** Oxy Metals Industry Corporation.

★10233★
ONAN CORPORATION - LIBRARY (Sci-Tech)
1400 73rd Ave., N.E.   Phone: (612) 574-5000
Minneapolis, MN 55432   Valera L. Rohrer, Lib.Mgr.
Founded: 1978. **Staff:** Prof 1; Other 1. **Subjects:** Electric generators, gasoline and diesel engines, automotive engineering, control systems. **Holdings:** 1500 books; 15,000 technical reports; 8000 standards. **Subscriptions:** 300 journals and other serials. **Services:** Interlibrary loans; copying; library open to public with restrictions. **Computerized Information Services:** DIALOG, SDC. **Networks/Consortia:** Member of Twin Cities Standards Cooperators.

★10234★
ONE, INC. - BLANCHE M. BAKER MEMORIAL LIBRARY (Soc Sci)
3340 Country Club Dr.   Phone: (213) 735-5252
Los Angeles, CA 90019   David G. Moore, Libn.
Subjects: Homosexuality, homophile movement, gay liberation movement, gay literature, human sexuality, sexual minorities. **Holdings:** 7613 volumes; 60 VF drawers of miscellaneous items including bulletins, newsletters, slides, tapes and pamphlets; archival collections of the organization; personal papers. **Subscriptions:** 152 journals and other serials; 46 newspapers. **Services:** Library open to members and ONE Institute faculty and students.

★10235★
ONE TO ONE - RESOURCE CENTER (Soc Sci)*
One Lincoln Plaza
63rd & Broadway   Phone: (212) 874-2410
New York, NY 10023   Mariette Bates, Resource Ctr.Coord.
Staff: Prof 1. **Subjects:** Mental retardation, community acceptance, sexuality, staff training, legal issues, management of group homes. **Holdings:** 2000 books; 200 videotapes; 40 films; 8 lateral files of documents. **Subscriptions:** 10 journals and other serials. **Services:** Center open to public.

ONEIDA COUNTY COMPREHENSIVE PLANNING PROGRAM
See: Herkimer-Oneida Counties Comprehensive Planning Program

★10236★
ONEIDA HISTORICAL SOCIETY - LIBRARY (Hist)
318 Genesee St.   Phone: (315) 797-0000
Utica, NY 13502   Alice C. Dodge, Libn.
Founded: 1876. **Staff:** Prof 3; Other 4. **Subjects:** History - Oneida County, Utica, Mohawk Valley. **Holdings:** 1300 books and bound periodical volumes; 2500 pamphlets; 250,000 manuscript items. **Subscriptions:** 10 journals and other serials. **Services:** Copying; library open to public. **Publications:** Oniota (newsletter), monthly - for society members. **Special Catalogs:** Catalog of manuscripts (book). **Staff:** Douglas M. Preston, Dir., Hist.Soc.; Francis W. Cunningham, Mss.Cat.

O'NEILL (Eugene) MEMORIAL THEATER CENTER, INC.
See: Eugene O'Neill Memorial Theater Center, Inc.

★10237★
ONGWANADA HOSPITAL - PENROSE & HOPKINS DIVISIONS - PENROSE DIVISION LIBRARY (Med)†
117 Park St.   Phone: (613) 544-9611
Kingston, ON, Canada K7L 1J9   Margaret Garrigan
Founded: 1977. **Staff:** 1. **Subjects:** Mental retardation. **Holdings:** 700 books; 1 VF drawer of reprints; 850 slides and cassettes; 95 AV tapes; 1 film; 5 pieces of training equipment. **Subscriptions:** 23 journals and other serials. **Services:** Interlibrary loans; copying; library open to public.

ONLINE COMPUTER LIBRARY CENTER, INC.
See: OCLC, Inc.

ONLINE INFORMATION RETRIEVAL SYSTEM FOR THE SOCIOLOGY OF LEISURE & SPORT (SIRLS)
See: University of Waterloo

★10238★
ONONDAGA COUNTY PUBLIC LIBRARY - ART AND MUSIC DEPARTMENT (Art; Mus)
335 Montgomery St.   Phone: (415) 473-4492
Syracuse, NY 13202   Beatrice N. Marble, Dept.Hd.
Staff: Prof 2; Other 1. **Subjects:** Art, decorative arts, music. **Holdings:** 17,500 books; 1750 bound periodical volumes; 4000 music scores; 12,000 phonograph records; 175,000 pictures; 700 8mm films. **Subscriptions:** 80 journals and other serials. **Services:** Interlibrary loans; copying; department open to public. **Automated Operations:** Computerized cataloging, acquisitions, serials and circulation. **Computerized Information Services:** DIALOG. Performs free searches. **Staff:** Elizabeth DeMarco, Libn.

★10239★
ONONDAGA COUNTY PUBLIC LIBRARY - BUSINESS AND INDUSTRIAL DEPARTMENT (Bus-Fin; Sci-Tech)
335 Montgomery St.   Phone: (315) 473-4493
Syracuse, NY 13202   Evelyn B. Phelps, Dept.Hd.
Founded: 1931. **Staff:** Prof 5. **Subjects:** Finance, vocations, civil service, management, mathematics. **Special Collections:** Telephone directories (800 U.S. and Canada; 50 foreign); city directories (65). **Holdings:** 20,000 books and bound periodical volumes; 800 annual corporation reports; 600 10K reports; job information center; Patent Gazette, 1872 to present.

Subscriptions: 285 journals and other serials; 70 newspapers. **Services:** Interlibrary loans; copying; department open to public. **Automated Operations:** Computerized cataloging, acquisitions, serials and circulation. **Computerized Information Services:** DIALOG. Performs free searches. **Staff:** William T. Elliot, Libn.; Karen Pitoniak, Libn.; Jeanne Biggins, Libn.; Charles McCabe, Libn.

★10240★
ONONDAGA COUNTY PUBLIC LIBRARY - LOCAL HISTORY AND GENEALOGY DEPARTMENT (Hist)
335 Montgomery St.   Phone: (315) 473-6801
Syracuse, NY 13202   Gerald J. Parsons, Dept.Hd.
Founded: 1852. **Staff:** Prof 2; Other 1. **Subjects:** Genealogy; history - Syracuse, Onondaga County and northeastern U.S. **Holdings:** 32,000 volumes; 24 VF drawers of pamphlets and clippings; 4 VF drawers of genealogical notes; 360 maps; 5650 reels of microfilm. **Subscriptions:** 100 journals and other serials. **Services:** Interlibrary loans; copying; department open to public. **Automated Operations:** Computerized cataloging, acquisitions, serials and circulation. **Computerized Information Services:** DIALOG. Performs free searches. **Special Indexes:** Onondaga County Pioneer Index (8 catalog drawers). **Staff:** William Cook, Libn.; Joyce Cook, Libn.

★10241★
ONONDAGA HISTORICAL ASSOCIATION - LIBRARY (Hist)*
311 Montgomery St.   Phone: (315) 422-9948
Syracuse, NY 13202
Founded: 1862. **Subjects:** Local and regional history, New York State canals. **Holdings:** Figures not available.

★10242★
ONTARIO - ARCHIVES OF ONTARIO - LIBRARY (Hist)
Ministry of Citizenship & Culture
77 Grenville St.   Phone: (416) 965-4030
Toronto, ON, Canada M7A 2R9   Ethelyn Harlow, Libn.
Founded: 1903. **Staff:** Prof 1; Other 1. **Subjects:** Ontario social, political and military history; archival methodology; government records management. **Special Collections:** County and municipal directories; published minutes of Ontario municipalities; British Army Lists (60 volumes); historical atlases. **Holdings:** 5900 books and bound periodical volumes; 12,250 pamphlets; 400 reels of microfilm; 2500 microfiche; 5300 Ontario government publications; 6500 municipal documents. **Subscriptions:** 85 journals and other serials. **Services:** Library open to public with restrictions. **Special Catalogs:** Separate author, title and subject card file for pamphlets received prior to 1968. **Staff:** A.W. Murdoch, Asst.Prov.Archv.

★10243★
ONTARIO BIBLE COLLEGE/ONTARIO THEOLOGICAL SEMINARY - J. WILLIAM HORSEY LIBRARY (Rel-Theol)
25 Ballyconnor Ct.   Phone: (416) 226-6380
Willowdale, ON, Canada M2M 4B3   James Johnson, Libn.
Staff: Prof 2; Other 7. **Subjects:** Biblical studies, theology, pastoral studies, Christian education, missions. **Holdings:** 33,000 books. **Subscriptions:** 650 journals and other serials. **Services:** Interlibrary loans; copying; library open to public for reference use only; membership fee is required for borrowing privileges. **Staff:** Miss C. Church, Supv. of Tech.Serv.; Mrs. M. Ford, Supv. of Pub.Serv.

★10244★
ONTARIO CANCER INSTITUTE - LIBRARY (Med)
500 Sherbourne St.   Phone: (416) 926-4482
Toronto, ON, Canada M4X 1K9   Carol A. Morrison, Libn.
Founded: 1957. **Staff:** Prof 1; Other 3. **Subjects:** Cancer, cytology, electron microscopy, hematology, immunology, radiotherapy, biophysics, virology. **Holdings:** 7000 books; 10,000 bound periodical volumes; archives and pamphlets. **Subscriptions:** 350 journals and other serials. **Services:** Interlibrary loans; library not open to public. **Computerized Information Services:** MEDLARS, DIALOG.

★10245★
ONTARIO CHORAL FEDERATION - LIBRARY (Mus)
Maison Chalmers House
20 St. Joseph St.
Toronto, ON, Canada M5Y 1J9   Norah Bolton, Exec.Adm.
Staff: 1. **Subjects:** Choral music. **Holdings:** Figures not available. **Services:** Library open to members. **Publications:** Newsletter, quarterly.

★10246★
ONTARIO - CIVIL SERVICE COMMISSION - LIBRARY
Frost Bldg. South
Parliament Bldgs., Queen's Park
Toronto, ON, Canada M7A 1Z5
Defunct. Holdings absorbed by Ontario - Ministry of Treasury and Economics - Library Services Branch.

★10247★
ONTARIO COLLEGE OF ART - LIBRARY/AUDIOVISUAL CENTRE (Art; Aud-Vis)
100 McCaul St.   Phone: (416) 977-5311
Toronto, ON, Canada M5T 1W1   Ian Carr-Harris, Dir.
Founded: 1930. **Staff:** Prof 8; Other 4. **Subjects:** Visual arts. **Holdings:** 18,500 books; 3000 bound periodical volumes; 51,000 slides; 318 video cassettes; 32,700 items in picture file; 32 VF drawers of information file. **Subscriptions:** 250 journals and other serials. **Services:** Interlibrary loans; copying; AV production; library open to public with restrictions on borrowing. **Staff:** Richard Milburn, Hd., Pub.Serv.; Diana Myers, Hd., Tech.Serv.; Angelo Rao, Hd., AV Serv.

★10248★
ONTARIO COUNTY HISTORICAL SOCIETY, INC. - ARCHIVES (Hist)
55 N. Main St.   Phone: (716) 394-4975
Canandaigua, NY 14424   Robert Donald Muller, Dir.
Founded: 1902. **Staff:** Prof 2; Other 2. **Subjects:** New York early land dealings, Civil War, history of western New York. **Special Collections:** Oliver Phelps; Oliver L. Phelps; Granger family papers (collection on western New York landholding); Hyland Kirk collection; Jasper Parrish; Judge Smith papers. **Holdings:** 2500 books; bound Ontario County newspapers, 1803-1968; 200 maps; 40,000 manuscripts; Manchester Library Collection (250 volumes); 5000 pieces of ephemera. **Services:** Archives open to public for use on premises with staff assistance.

★10249★
ONTARIO CRAFTS COUNCIL - CRAFT RESOURCE CENTRE (Art)
346 Dundas St., W.   Phone: (416) 977-3551
Toronto, ON, Canada M5T 1G5   Ted Rickard, Mgr.
Founded: 1975. **Staff:** Prof 1; Other 1. **Subjects:** All aspects of craft media. **Special Collections:** Archives (provincial and local craft guilds and prominent individuals; vertical file); health hazards in arts and crafts (files; books). **Holdings:** 600 books; 20 bound periodical volumes; 400 portfolios of practicing craftsmen; 175 exhibition catalogs; slide rental/sales programs. **Subscriptions:** 140 journals and other serials. **Services:** Copying; consulting; center open to public. **Publications:** Annual Craft Fairs in Ontario; Directory of Suppliers of Craft Materials; Directory of Craft Organizations in Canada; Ontario Craft; Craft News - to members; list of craft guides and directories for sale. **Special Indexes:** Indexes to publications of the Ontario Crafts Council; card file of Ontario craftspeople. **Staff:** Sandra Dunn, Info.Serv.Off.

★10250★
ONTARIO ECONOMIC COUNCIL - LIBRARY (Soc Sci)
81 Wellesley St. E.   Phone: (416) 965-4315
Toronto, ON, Canada M4Y 1H6   Diane Wenzel, Libn.
Founded: 1973. **Staff:** Prof 1; Other 1. **Subjects:** Economics - health, labour, urban; education; public administration. **Special Collections:** Statistics Canada publications (selected titles); Ontario Economic Council publications (complete collection); Economic Council of Canada publications, 1973 to present. **Holdings:** 6000 volumes; working papers and reprints from 25 departments of economics of Canadian and U.S. universities. **Subscriptions:** 157 journals and other serials. **Services:** Interlibrary loans; copying; library open to public by appointment. **Computerized Information Services:** DIALOG, Info Globe. **Networks/Consortia:** Member of Ontario Government Libraries' Council (OGLC). **Publications:** Monthly Acquisitions List - for internal distribution only. **Special Catalogs:** Library Serials Holdings List (loose-leaf binder); complete University of Toronto catalog (microfiche). **Remarks:** The Ontario Economic Council Library is a branch library of the Ministry of Treasury, Economics and Intergovernmental Affairs.

ONTARIO EDUCATIONAL COMMUNICATIONS AUTHORITY
See: TV Ontario

★10251★
ONTARIO ENERGY BOARD - LIBRARY (Energy)
14 Carlton St., 9th Fl.   Phone: (416) 598-4000
Toronto, ON, Canada M5B 1J2   Rita Piazza, Lib.Mgr.
Staff: Prof 1. **Subjects:** Energy regulation, natural gas, electricity, gas pipelines, energy rates and pricing, energy economics. **Holdings:** 700 books; decisions and reports. **Subscriptions:** 57 journals and other serials. **Services:**

Interlibrary loans; copying; library open to public by appointment for reference use only.

★10252★
ONTARIO FEDERATION OF LABOUR - RESOURCE CENTRE (Soc Sci)
15 Gervais Dr., Suite 202   Phone: (416) 441-2731
Don Mills, ON, Canada M3C 1Y8   Dr. Jo Surich, Res.Coord.
Founded: 1969. **Staff:** Prof 1. **Subjects:** Labor relations, economic development, labor in politics, labor history. **Special Collections:** OFL Archives. **Holdings:** 800 books; 500 bound periodical volumes. **Subscriptions:** 50 journals and other serials. **Services:** Copying; center open to public. **Computerized Information Services:** CANSIM. **Publications:** Talking Points: Recent Economic, Social and Political Data, biweekly - for internal distribution only.

★10253★
ONTARIO FILM INSTITUTE - LIBRARY & INFORMATION CENTRE (Hum; Theater)
770 Don Mills Rd.   Phone: (416) 429-4100
Don Mills, ON, Canada M3C 1T3   Sherie Brethour, Libn.
Founded: 1969. **Staff:** Prof 4. **Subjects:** All aspects of the cinema. **Special Collections:** Silent Film Music Selections for Piano (100). **Holdings:** 10,000 books; 900 bound periodical volumes; 100 unpublished screenplays; 2500 soundtracks of motion pictures; 200 BBC recordings on motion pictures; 250,000 files by subject, film title and biography for all aspects of film making and the industry. **Subscriptions:** 100 journals and other serials; 15 newspapers. **Services:** Copying; library open to public for reference use only. **Publications:** Film News, quarterly - free upon request. **Remarks:** Maintained by Ontario Science Centre.

★10254★
ONTARIO GENEALOGICAL SOCIETY - LIBRARY (Hist)
c/o Canadiana Collection
North York Public Library
35 Fairview Mall Dr.   Phone: (416) 494-6838
Willowdale, ON, Canada M2J 4S4   Grant Brown, Libn.
Founded: 1963. **Staff:** 1. **Subjects:** Genealogy. **Holdings:** 1550 books; 45 bound periodical volumes; 350 family histories. **Subscriptions:** 30 journals and other serials. **Services:** Copying; library open to public for reference use only.

★10255★
ONTARIO HOSPITAL ASSOCIATION - LIBRARY (Med; Bus-Fin)
150 Ferrand Dr.   Phone: (416) 429-2661
Don Mills, ON, Canada M3C 1H6   John Tagg, Supv.
Staff: Prof 1; Other 1. **Subjects:** Hospital administration, health economics, health insurance, management. **Holdings:** 1500 books. **Subscriptions:** 102 journals and other serials. **Services:** Interlibrary loans; copying; library open to public for reference use only. **Computerized Information Services:** MEDLARS. Performs searches on cost recovery basis.

★10256★
ONTARIO HYDRO - LIBRARY (Sci-Tech)
700 University Ave.   Phone: (416) 592-2719
Toronto, ON, Canada M5G 1X6   Doreen Taylor, Chf.Libn.
Founded: 1916. **Staff:** Prof 13; Other 17. **Subjects:** Electrical engineering, nuclear engineering, electric utilities, management. **Special Collections:** Company reports and documents. **Holdings:** 70,000 volumes; reports; microfiche. **Subscriptions:** 1000 journals and other serials. **Services:** Interlibrary loans; library open to public in Public Reference Centre. **Automated Operations:** Computerized cataloging and serials. **Computerized Information Services:** DIALOG, SDC, QL Systems, CAN/OLE, UTLAS. **Publications:** Accession Lists. **Remarks:** Data given above also include the Research Division Branch Library, the Atrium Building Branch Library and the Public Reference Center. **Staff:** Anita Chui, Sr.Libn.; Sylvia Ernesaks, Sr.Libn.; Lorna Bernard, Jr.Libn.;Deborah Henderson, Jr.Libn.; Tran Dam, Libn.; Kim Cornell, Libn.; Joan Slagt, Translator; Chris Robinson, Libn.; Mary Hanson, Libn.; Martha Courtright, Libn.; Sue Anderson, Libn.; Nancy Fish, Jr.Libn.

★10257★
ONTARIO INSTITUTE FOR STUDIES IN EDUCATION (OISE) - MODERN LANGUAGE CENTRE - LANGUAGE TEACHING LIBRARY (Hum)†
252 Bloor St., W.   Phone: (416) 923-6641
Toronto, ON, Canada M5S 1V6   Alice Weinrib, Res.Assoc./Libn.
Staff: Prof 1; Other 1. **Subjects:** French as a second langauge, English as a second language, theory and methodology of second language teaching, Spanish, German. **Special Collections:** Language curricula resources for the classroom. **Holdings:** 9000 books; 200 bound periodical volumes; 2750 tapes; 60 language tests; 3500 documents; 110 charts and visuals; 70

filmstrip and slide programs. **Subscriptions:** 50 journals and other serials. **Services:** Copying; library open to public with restrictions.

★10258★
ONTARIO INSTITUTE FOR STUDIES IN EDUCATION (OISE) - R.W.B. JACKSON LIBRARY (Educ)
252 Bloor St., W.   Phone: (416) 923-6641
Toronto, ON, Canada M5S 1V6   Shirley K. Wigmore, Chf.Libn.
Staff: Prof 16; Other 26. **Subjects:** Education, psychology, sociology, statistical methodology, linguistics, history, philosophy, computer applications, economics, demography. **Special Collections:** Ontario History of Education Collection (20,000 volumes); Paulo Freire Resource Collection (books and reprints); test collection. **Holdings:** 197,882 books; 19,460 bound periodical volumes; 299,251 microforms; 12,846 films, audio- and videotapes, kits, games, and other multimedia resources; 3982 tests; 85 linear feet of curriculum guides, curriculum publisher and AV distributor catalogs. **Subscriptions:** 4206 journals and other serials. **Services:** Interlibrary loans; copying; library open to public. **Automated Operations:** Computerized cataloging and acquisitions. **Computerized Information Services:** BRS, DIALOG, UTLAS. Performs searches on cost recovery basis. Contact Person: Debbie Kay, 923-6641, ext. 202. **Publications:** Bibliographies. **Special Catalogs:** Catalog of Ontario History of Education Collection (microfiche). **Special Indexes:** Index to the Paulo Freire Resource Collection (typed list); Index to the Test Collection (card). **Staff:** Ann Neveu, Adm.Off.; Ilze Bregzis, Libn., Tech.Serv.; Jan Schmidt, Libn., Pub.Serv.

ONTARIO LABOUR RELATIONS BOARD
See: Ontario - Ministry of Labour

★10259★
ONTARIO - LEGISLATIVE ASSEMBLY - LEGISLATIVE LIBRARY RESEARCH AND INFORMATION SERVICES (Law; Hist)
Legislative Bldg., Queen's Park   Phone: (416) 965-4545
Toronto, ON, Canada M7A 1A2   R. Brian Land, Dir.
Founded: 1867. **Staff:** Prof 29; Other 47. **Subjects:** Political science, especially parliamentary systems; law; public administration and policy; economics; Ontario and Canadian history. **Special Collections:** Full depository for Ontario, Quebec and Canadian government publications; government publications from other provinces, British Parliament and U.S. Congress; U.S. Congressional Information Service on microfiche from 1970; Microlog Service on microfiche from Micromedia Limited; Ontario daily and weekly current newspapers; Canadian and British statutes and law reports; Ambler Pricing Service (weekly product prices of five major food chains). **Holdings:** 76,410 books; 8646 bound periodical volumes; 520,700 microfiche; 6910 reels of microfilm; 1880 current data files; 387 videotapes; 35 audio cassettes. **Subscriptions:** 2145 journals and other serials; 297 newspapers. **Services:** Interlibrary loans; copying; library open to public with restrictions. **Automated Operations:** Computerized cataloging and acquisitions. **Computerized Information Services:** DIALOG, SDC, QL Systems, Info Globe, New York Times Information Service, MEDLINE, CAN/OLE, Westlaw, BRS, Eurolex, TELICHART; internal database. Member of Ontario Government Libraries' Council. **Publications:** Annual Report of the Director; Memo to Members, irregular; Periodical Contents, weekly during session; Periodical Selections, irregular; Selected New Titles, bimonthly. **Staff:** E. Patricia Hay, Exec.Coord.; Mary E. Dickerson, Hd., Info. & Ref.Serv; Pamela Stoksik, Hd., Tech.Serv. & Sys.; Linda M. Grayson, Chf., Leg.Res.Serv.Karen Wierucki, Mgr., Clipping Serv.; Linda L. Reid, Mgr., Checklist/Cat.Serv.

★10260★
ONTARIO LOTTERY CORPORATION - LIBRARY (Rec)
2 Bloor St., W., 24th Fl.   Phone: (416) 961-6262
Toronto, ON, Canada M4W 3H8   Suzanne Kemper, Libn.
Founded: 1978. **Staff:** Prof 1; Other 1. **Subjects:** Lotteries, casinos, off-track betting, gaming and gambling, public relations, draws, community relations. **Holdings:** 40 books; draw cassettes; gaming reports; casino studies; marketing assessments; rules and regulations for social gaming. **Subscriptions:** 18 journals and other serials. **Services:** Library not open to public.

★10261★
ONTARIO MEDICAL ASSOCIATION - LIBRARY (Med; Bus-Fin)
240 St. George St.   Phone: (416) 925-3264
Toronto, ON, Canada M5R 2P4   Jan Greenwood, Libn.
Founded: 1972. **Staff:** Prof 1; Other 2. **Subjects:** Canadian medical economics, medico-legal practices and sociomedical affairs, hospital library service. **Special Collections:** Medical office management; reference collection for hospital library consulting service; PSI Foundation Archives (12 boxes); Trans-Canada Medical Plan Archives (Shillington papers). **Holdings:** 2000 books. **Subscriptions:** 250 journals and other serials. **Services:**

Interlibrary loans; copying; library open to public for reference use only. **Publications:** Health Sciences Library Manual, 1982; Medical Office Management Bibliography, annual; OMA suggested list of basic books and journals, biennial. **Special Indexes:** Ontario Medical Review Index. **Remarks:** Operating under a grant from the PSI Foundation for its collection in Canadian medical economics, the library also provides a consulting service for Ontario hospital libraries.

★10262★
ONTARIO - MINISTRY OF AGRICULTURE AND FOOD - HORTICULTURAL RESEARCH INSTITUTE OF ONTARIO - LIBRARY (Agri)
                                                     Phone: (416) 562-4141
Vineland Station, ON, Canada L0R 2E0   Judith Wanner, Libn.
Staff: Prof 1. **Subjects:** Fruit and vegetable crops, ornamental plants, botany, food science, winemaking, viticulture. **Holdings:** 2000 books; 1500 bound periodical volumes; 2000 pamphlets; annual reports; documents; agricultural statistics. **Subscriptions:** 254 journals and other serials; 6 newspapers. **Services:** Interlibrary loans; copying; library open to public for reference use only. **Computerized Information Services:** CAN/OLE, DIALOG. **Publications:** What's New in the Library, quarterly - to staff and others in the Ministry.

★10263★
ONTARIO - MINISTRY OF AGRICULTURE AND FOOD - LIBRARY (Agri)
801 Bay St., 3rd Fl.   Phone: (416) 965-1816
Toronto, ON, Canada M7A 2B2   Ken Sundquist, Ministry Libn.
Founded: 1969. **Staff:** Prof 1; Other 2. **Subjects:** Agricultural economics, land use, rural agricultural statistics, Ontario and Canadian agriculture, food industry and trade, agriculture and energy, animal husbandry. **Holdings:** 12,000 books; 300 microfiche. **Subscriptions:** 420 journals and other serials. **Services:** Interlibrary loans; copying; library open to public for reference use only. **Automated Operations:** Computerized serials. **Computerized Information Services:** DIALOG. **Networks/Consortia:** Member of Ontario Government Libraries' Council. **Publications:** New Publications, quarterly - to staff and other interested libraries.

ONTARIO - MINISTRY OF AGRICULTURE AND FOOD - RIDGETOWN COLLEGE OF AGRICULTURAL TECHNOLOGY
See: Ridgetown College of Agricultural Technology

★10264★
ONTARIO - MINISTRY OF AGRICULTURE AND FOOD - VETERINARY SERVICES LABORATORY LIBRARY (Med)
P.O. Box 2005   Phone: (613) 258-3804
Kemptville, ON, Canada K0G 1J0   Dr. Peter Lusis, Hd.
Founded: 1948. **Subjects:** Veterinary medicine, pathology, animal science. **Holdings:** Figures not available. **Subscriptions:** 31 journals and other serials. **Services:** Interlibrary loans; copying; library open to veterinarians only.

★10265★
ONTARIO - MINISTRY OF AGRICULTURE AND FOOD - VETERINARY SERVICES LABORATORY LIBRARY (Med)
Box 790   Phone: (705) 647-6701
New Liskeard, ON, Canada P0J 1P0
Founded: 1961. **Subjects:** Veterinary medicine and pathology. **Holdings:** 200 books; 340 bound periodical volumes. **Subscriptions:** 25 journals and other serials; 10 newspapers. **Services:** Library open to veterinarians.

★10266★
ONTARIO - MINISTRY OF THE ATTORNEY GENERAL - LIBRARY (Law)
18 King St., E., 12th Fl.   Phone: (416) 965-4714
Toronto, ON, Canada M5C 1C5   Sharon Day-Feldman, Libn.
Staff: Prof 1; Other 1. **Subjects:** Law - criminal, civil, constitutional. **Special Collections:** English reports (178 volumes); Law Reports (including Appeal Cases, Chancery Division, Probate Division, Queen's Bench and King's Bench: 1000 volumes); All England Law Reports (1500 volumes). **Holdings:** 1500 books; 12,000 bound periodical volumes. **Subscriptions:** 100 journals and other serials. **Services:** Interlibrary loans; library not open to public. **Computerized Information Services:** QL Systems, Westlaw.

★10267★
ONTARIO - MINISTRY OF CITIZENSHIP AND CULTURE - LIBRARIES AND COMMUNITY INFORMATION (Info Sci)
7th Fl., 77 Bloor St., W.   Phone: (416) 965-2696
Toronto, ON, Canada M7A 2R9   Wil Vanderelst, Dir.
Staff: 17. **Subjects:** Professional development in librarianship, public library statistics. **Remarks:** Administers Public Libraries Act, promotes public library and community information services, coordinates library services and provides financial aid to public libraries and information centers. Also administers

Ontario Library Service. **Staff:** Grace Buller, Mgr., Pub.Lib.Serv.; Kelvin Browne, Mgr., Ontario Lib.Serv.; Linda Church, Mgr., Community Info.Serv.

★10268★
ONTARIO - MINISTRY OF CITIZENSHIP AND CULTURE - MAP LIBRARY (Geog-Map)
77 Grenville St.   Phone: (416) 965-4030
Toronto, ON, Canada M7A 2R9   John W. Fortier, Archv.
Founded: 1903. **Staff:** Prof 1. **Subjects:** Land survey, fire insurance, transportation, land tenure, topography, hydrography, geology. **Special Collections:** David Thompson maps (5 maps and 4 volumes); Simcoe maps (106); Canada Company maps (200 maps and 10 volumes); Talbot maps (3 volumes); fire insurance maps (10,000 sheets); survey records maps (3000). **Holdings:** 188 atlases; 31,000 maps. **Services:** Copying; library open to public.

★10269★
ONTARIO - MINISTRY OF CITIZENSHIP AND CULTURE - MINISTRY OF TOURISM AND RECREATION - LIBRARY/RESOURCE CENTRE (Rec)
77 Bloor St., W., 9th Fl.   Phone: (416) 965-6763
Toronto, ON, Canada M7A 2R9   Marjorie Howard, Coord.
Founded: 1975. **Staff:** Prof 1; Other 6. **Subjects:** Recreation and leisure, arts and crafts, sports and fitness, multiculturalism, therapeutic recreation, native peoples. **Special Collections:** Drama Collection (1000 plays); English as a Second Language (2500 books); architectural conservation and preservation reports. **Holdings:** 20,000 books; 1000 unbound periodicals; 4000 pamphlets; 1000 AV items; 7500 slides. **Subscriptions:** 800 journals and other serials; 50 newspapers. **Services:** Interlibrary loans; SDI; library open to residents of the Province of Ontario only. **Networks/Consortia:** Member of Ontario Government Libraries' Council. **Publications:** New Resources, bimonthly; Resume, monthly - both for internal distribution only. **Special Catalogs:** Audio-Visual Catalogue, by subject (book). **Staff:** Renata Grodski, Libn.

★10270★
ONTARIO - MINISTRY OF CITIZENSHIP AND CULTURE - PLANNING AND TECHNICAL SERVICES (Rec)
77 Bloor St., W., 4th Fl.   Phone: (416) 965-0322
Toronto, ON, Canada M7A 2R9   Brian Forsyth, Sr.Arch.Adv.
Founded: 1974. **Staff:** Prof 1. **Subjects:** Recreation and cultural facilities design and planning; management. **Holdings:** 100 books; 4500 documents; 500 clippings; 1500 slides; 600 pieces of product literature; 300 professional brochures. **Services:** Interlibrary loans; copying; services open to public by appointment. **Publications:** Technical reports; list of publications - available upon request.

★10271★
ONTARIO - MINISTRY OF COMMUNITY AND SOCIAL SERVICES - MINISTRY LIBRARY (Soc Sci)†
880 Bay St., Rm. 663   Phone: (416) 965-2314
Toronto, ON, Canada M7A 2B2   Sandra Walsh, Mgr., Lib.Serv.
Founded: 1968. **Staff:** Prof 1; Other 3. **Subjects:** Public welfare, mental retardation, child welfare, rehabilitation, social problems, social work. **Holdings:** 23,000 books; 1000 bound periodical volumes; 200 reports on microfiche; Census of Canada on microfiche (1951, 1956, 1961, 1966); 149 journal titles in microform; 1 cabinet of pamphlets and annual reports; 2 cabinets of reprints; 1 cabinet of newsletters. **Subscriptions:** 433 journals and other serials. **Services:** Interlibrary loans; library open to public for reference use only. **Computerized Information Services:** DIALOG, MEDLARS. **Networks/Consortia:** Member of Ontario Government Libraries' Council (OGLC). **Publications:** Conspectus (acquisitions list), bimonthly; supplement of indexed articles - both distributed to ministry personnel, affiliated agencies and government libraries.

ONTARIO - MINISTRY OF COMMUNITY AND SOCIAL SERVICES - PRINCE EDWARD HEIGHTS
See: Prince Edward Heights

★10272★
ONTARIO - MINISTRY OF COMMUNITY AND SOCIAL SERVICES - RESOURCE LIBRARY (Med)
Highway 59N
P.O. Box 310   Phone: (519) 539-1251
Woodstock, ON, Canada N4S 7X9   Frances Thompson, Libn.
Staff: Prof 1. **Subjects:** Mental retardation, epilepsy, tuberculosis. **Holdings:** 1817 books; 403 films, tapes and cassettes. **Subscriptions:** 69 journals and other serials. **Services:** Interlibrary loans; copying; library open to public with restrictions. **Publications:** Bibliotheca Medica Canadiana, quarterly - to members.

ONTARIO - MINISTRY OF COMMUNITY AND SOCIAL SERVICES - THISTLETOWN REGIONAL CENTRE
See: Thistletown Regional Centre

★10273★
ONTARIO - MINISTRY OF CONSUMER AND COMMERCIAL RELATIONS - CONSUMER INFORMATION CENTRE (Bus-Fin)
555 Yonge St., 1st Fl.   Phone: (416) 963-1111
Toronto, ON, Canada M7A 2H6   Sarah Coombs, Mgr.
Founded: 1978. **Staff:** 11. **Subjects:** Law; business; securities regulation; consumer information, education and protection; insurance. **Holdings:** 5000 books. **Subscriptions:** 180 journals and other serials. **Services:** Interlibrary loans; public inquiry in person, by phone and mail; development of educational material; center open to public for reference use only. **Publications:** New Resources, monthly. **Remarks:** For Ontario residents the toll-free number is (800)268-1142; TTY/TTD (416)963-0808.

★10274★
ONTARIO - MINISTRY OF CORRECTIONAL SERVICES - LIBRARY SERVICES (Soc Sci)
2001 Eglinton Ave., E.   Phone: (416) 750-3481
Toronto, ON, Canada M1L 4P1   T.J.B. Anderson, Chf.Libn.
Founded: 1958. **Staff:** Prof 2; Other 1. **Subjects:** Penology, criminology. **Holdings:** 3600 books; 50 feet of pamphlets and reports. **Subscriptions:** 130 journals and other serials. **Services:** Interlibrary loans; copying; SDI; library open to bona fide students by appointment. **Computerized Information Services:** DIALOG, SDC. **Networks/Consortia:** Member of Ontario Government Libraries' Council. **Publications:** Recent additions list, 3/year - for internal distribution only. **Staff:** Miss H.M. Chan, Libn.

★10275★
ONTARIO - MINISTRY OF EDUCATION - EDUCATION CENTER LIBRARY (Educ)
199 Larch St., 7th Fl.   Phone: (705) 675-4427
Sudbury, ON, Canada P3E 5P9   George Whalen, Libn.
Founded: 1967. **Staff:** Prof 1; Other 3. **Subjects:** Education, psychology. **Special Collections:** Children's literature. **Holdings:** 40,000 books; 5000 unbound periodicals; 1000 microfiche; 1000 records, tapes, cassettes; 1000 slides, pictures, prints; 4000 filmstrips. **Subscriptions:** 200 journals and other serials; 5 newspapers. **Services:** Interlibrary loans; copying.

★10276★
ONTARIO - MINISTRY OF EDUCATION - INFORMATION CENTRE (Educ)
Mowat Block, 13th Fl., Queen's Park   Phone: (416) 965-1451
Toronto, ON, Canada M7A 1L2
Founded: 1979. **Staff:** Prof 10; Other 12. **Subjects:** Education theory and practice at all levels, apprenticeship training, business/management, systems. **Special Collections:** Multi-year plans for Ontario colleges of applied arts and technology; college and university calendars; Ontario Council on University Affairs. **Holdings:** 25,000 books; 22 drawers of microfiche; 45 VF drawers; federal and Ontario sessional papers. **Subscriptions:** 850 journals and other serials; 7 newspapers. **Services:** Interlibrary loans; copying; SDI; center open to public for reference use only. **Automated Operations:** Computerized cataloging and serials. **Computerized Information Services:** DIALOG, BRS, QL Systems, Info Globe, Ontario Education Resources Information System (ONTERIS), CAN/OLE, Questel. **Networks/Consortia:** Member of Ontario Government Libraries' Council; Professional Education Libraries Cataloguing Network. **Publications:** Contents; New Books, monthly. **Special Catalogs:** Film catalog (book); ONTERIS Index. **Staff:** Patricia Grenier, Coord., Info.Serv.; Anna Lau, Coord., Info.Rsrcs.; Nuzhat Jafri, Coord., Current Awareness.

★10277★
ONTARIO - MINISTRY OF ENERGY - LIBRARY (Energy)
56 Wellesley St., W., 12th Fl.   Phone: (416) 965-9175
Toronto, ON, Canada M7A 2B7   Nancy Pierobon, Hd.Libn.
Staff: Prof 1; Other 4. **Subjects:** Energy policy and conservation, conventional and renewable energy. **Special Collections:** ERCB Decisons; NEB Decisions. **Holdings:** 10,000 books; 14 VF drawers of pamphlets. **Subscriptions:** 340 journals and other serials; 10 newspapers. **Services:** Interlibrary loans; copying; library open to public by appointment. **Computerized Information Services:** DIALOG, SDC, QL Systems, Info Globe. **Networks/Consortia:** Member of of Ontario Government Libraries' Council. **Publications:** The Energy Informer, monthly - limited distribution.

★10278★
ONTARIO - MINISTRY OF THE ENVIRONMENT - LIBRARY (Env-Cons)†
135 St. Clair Ave., W., 1st Fl.
Toronto, ON, Canada M4V 1P5   Phone: (416) 965-7978
                                    N.J. McIlroy, Libn.
Founded: 1960. **Staff:** Prof 2; Other 3. **Subjects:** Water pollution, water supply, solid waste, air, noise, engineering, biology, chemistry. **Holdings:** 35,000 books; 2000 bound periodical volumes; 40 VF drawers of reprints, government reports, documents; 34,000 microfiche. **Subscriptions:** 227 journals and other serials. **Services:** Interlibrary loans; library open to public for reference use only. **Computerized Information Services:** SDC, QL Systems, CAN/OLE, DIALOG, MEDLINE. **Publications:** Acquisitions list, monthly. **Remarks:** Includes the holdings of the Ministry of the Environment - Laboratory and Research Library.

★10279★
ONTARIO - MINISTRY OF GOVERNMENT SERVICES - TECHNICAL REFERENCE LIBRARY (Bus-Fin)*
1200 Bay St., 4th Fl.   Phone: (416) 965-2965
Toronto, ON, Canada M5R 2A5   Lynda Magistrale, Educ.Serv.Off.
Founded: 1975. **Subjects:** Data processing. **Holdings:** 200 books; 70 government documents. **Subscriptions:** 75 journals and other serials. **Services:** Library open to government personnel.

★10280★
ONTARIO - MINISTRY OF HEALTH - LIBRARY (Med)
15 Overlea Blvd., 7th Fl.   Phone: (416) 965-7881
Toronto, ON, Canada M4H 1A9   Veronica Brunka, Lib.Supv.
Founded: 1933. **Staff:** Prof 1; Other 5. **Subjects:** Public health, preventive medicine, health care services, hospital administration. **Holdings:** 7600 books; 20 VF drawers; 200 microfiche. **Subscriptions:** 900 journals and other serials. **Services:** Interlibrary loans; library open to public with restrictions. **Computerized Information Services:** MEDLARS, DIALOG, Info Globe. **Networks/Consortia:** Member of Ontario Government Libraries' Council. **Publications:** Library Bulletin, bimonthly - to Ministry personnel.

ONTARIO - MINISTRY OF HEALTH - PSYCHIATRIC BRANCH - HAMILTON PSYCHIATRIC HOSPITAL
See: Hamilton Psychiatric Hospital

★10281★
ONTARIO - MINISTRY OF HEALTH - PUBLIC HEALTH LABORATORIES - LIBRARY (Med; Sci-Tech)
Postal Terminal A, Box 9000   Phone: (416) 248-3165
Toronto, ON, Canada M5W 1R5   Doris A. Standing, Libn.
Staff: Prof 1; Other 1. **Subjects:** Medical microbiology, medical laboratory technology, clinical chemistry. **Holdings:** 4500 volumes; 3 VF drawers of pamphlets. **Subscriptions:** 200 journals and other serials. **Services:** Interlibrary loans; copying; library open to public by special permission. **Staff:** Martha Nunes, Lib.Techn.

★10282★
ONTARIO - MINISTRY OF INDUSTRY AND TRADE - INFORMATION CENTRE (Bus-Fin)
Hearst Block, Queen's Park   Phone: (416) 965-3365
Toronto, ON, Canada M7A 2E1   Dee Phillips, Mgr.
Founded: 1946. **Staff:** Prof 2; Other 1. **Subjects:** Trade, industrial development, small business, management. **Holdings:** 15,000 books. **Subscriptions:** 300 journals and other serials; 5 newspapers. **Services:** Interlibrary loans; copying; center open to public for reference use only. **Computerized Information Services:** Info Globe, DIALOG. **Publications:** Bulletin, monthly - limited distribution. **Staff:** Mrs. N. Chagpar, Ref.Off.; Pam Halpern, Ref.Off.

★10283★
ONTARIO - MINISTRY OF LABOUR - LIBRARY (Soc Sci)
400 University Ave.   Phone: (416) 965-1641
Toronto, ON, Canada M7A 1T7   Jean Collins-Williams, Act.Hd.Libn.
Founded: 1949. **Staff:** Prof 6; Other 10. **Subjects:** Labor relations, occupational health and safety, employment, human rights, women, manpower. **Special Collections:** International Labor Organization materials. **Holdings:** 70,000 books; 1000 bound periodical volumes; 14,000 pamphlets; microforms. **Subscriptions:** 1600 journals; 12,500 serials. **Services:** Interlibrary loans; copying; SDI; library open to public. **Automated Operations:** Computerized cataloging. **Computerized Information Services:** Questel, BRS, DIALOG, SDC, QL Systems, MEDLINE, Info Globe, Occupational Health Services, Inc., CAN/OLE; OMLINE (internal databases). **Publications:** Monthly Bulletins; bibliography series - on topics of labor and occupational health and safety.

★10284★
ONTARIO - MINISTRY OF LABOUR - ONTARIO LABOUR RELATIONS BOARD - LIBRARY (Law)
400 University Ave., 4th Fl.   Phone: (416) 965-0206
Toronto, ON, Canada M7A 1V4   Clare Lyons, Libn.
Staff: Prof 1; Other 2. **Subjects:** Labor law. **Holdings:** 2000 books; Ontario Labour Relations Board reports, 1944 to present; National Labour Relations Board publications, volume 1 to present. **Subscriptions:** 120 journals and other serials. **Services:** Interlibrary loans; copying; library open to public. **Automated Operations:** Computerized cataloging. **Computerized Information Services:** QL Systems; internal database. **Special Indexes:** Index to Ontario Labour Relations Board reports; index to Ontario Labour Relations Board decisions (both on microfiche).

★10285★
ONTARIO - MINISTRY OF MUNICIPAL AFFAIRS & HOUSING - LIBRARY (Plan)
2-777 Bay St.   Phone: (416) 965-9720
Toronto, ON, Canada M5G 2E5   Frank Szucs, Libn.
Founded: 1965. **Staff:** Prof 1; Other 3. **Subjects:** Housing, community planning, urban renewal, city planning, municipal government and finance. **Holdings:** 11,000 books; 8000 microfiche. **Subscriptions:** 260 journals and other serials. **Services:** Interlibrary loans; copying; library open to public. **Computerized Information Services:** SDC, QL Systems. **Publications:** Library Bulletin, irregular - to ministry staff. **Special Indexes:** List of periodical literature.

ONTARIO - MINISTRY OF NATURAL RESOURCES - ALGONQUIN PARK MUSEUM
See: Algonquin Park Museum

★10286★
ONTARIO - MINISTRY OF NATURAL RESOURCES - MINES LIBRARY (Sci-Tech)
77 Grenville St.   Phone: (416) 965-1352
Toronto, ON, Canada M5S 1B3   Nancy Thurston, Libn.
Founded: 1945. **Staff:** Prof 1; Other 3. **Subjects:** Geology of Ontario, mining, Precambrian geology, metallurgy, mineralogy, environmental geology. **Special Collections:** Geological and aeromagnetic maps (20,000 items); annual reports of mining companies. **Holdings:** 2000 texts and reference books; 25,000 government reports. **Subscriptions:** 250 journals and other serials. **Services:** Interlibrary loans; copying; library open to public for reference use only. **Publications:** Accessions list, monthly - distributed to other libraries on request.

★10287★
ONTARIO - MINISTRY OF NATURAL RESOURCES - NATURAL RESOURCES LIBRARY (Env-Cons)
Whitney Block, Rm. 4540
Queen's Park   Phone: (416) 965-6319
Toronto, ON, Canada M7A 1W3   Sandra Louet, Mgr.
Founded: 1972. **Staff:** Prof 3; Other 1. **Subjects:** Forestry, ecology, parks and recreation, land use planning, fish and wildlife. **Holdings:** 80,000 books; 500 bound periodical volumes; 60,000 reprints and unpublished papers. **Subscriptions:** 300 journals and other serials. **Services:** Interlibrary loans; library open to public by appointment for reference use only. **Computerized Information Services:** DIALOG, QL Systems, Info Globe, CAN/OLE, Infomart. **Staff:** Edna Nickie, Libn.; Marusia Borodacz, Libn.

★10288★
ONTARIO - MINISTRY OF NATURAL RESOURCES - NATURAL RESOURCES LIBRARY - MAPLE (Sci-Tech)†
Southern Research Sta.   Phone: (416) 832-2761
Maple, ON, Canada L0J 1E0   Sandra Louet, Mgr.
Founded: 1942. **Staff:** Prof 1; Other 3. **Subjects:** Forestry, fisheries, wildlife. **Special Collections:** Materials from the U.S. Forest Service and the U.S. Fish and Wildlife Service. **Holdings:** Figures not available. **Subscriptions:** 500 journals and other serials. **Services:** Interlibrary loans; copying; library open to public with restrictions. **Computerized Information Services:** DIALOG, SDC, QL Systems. **Publications:** New Materials List, monthly - for internal distribution only.

★10289★
ONTARIO - MINISTRY OF NORTHERN AFFAIRS - LIBRARY AND RECORDS (Area-Ethnic)
10 Wellesley St. E., 8th Fl.   Phone: (416) 965-1417
Toronto, ON, Canada M4Y 1G2   Susan Baumann, Coord.
Founded: 1978. **Staff:** Prof 2; Other 5. **Subjects:** Socioeconomic development, natural resources, community and regional planning, history and

culture of Northern Ontario. **Special Collections:** Ministry Reading Room; Northern Ontario newspapers; college and university calendars for Northern Ontario. **Holdings:** 3000 books and reports; 3 VF drawers of material on Northern Ontario; 3 VF drawers of annual reports. **Subscriptions:** 120 journals and other serials; 55 newspapers. **Services:** Interlibrary loans; library open to public with restrictions. **Publications:** What's New in the Library (list of selected articles and cataloged material), monthly.

★10290★
ONTARIO - MINISTRY OF REVENUE - LIBRARY (Bus-Fin)
33 King St. W.
P.O. Box 627   Phone: (416) 433-6135
Oshawa, ON, Canada L1H 8H5   Penni Lee, Act.Libn.
Founded: 1973. **Staff:** Prof 1; Other 2. **Subjects:** Economics, public finance, taxation, property assessment. **Holdings:** 10,500 books; 390 bound periodical volumes. **Subscriptions:** 250 journals and other serials. **Services:** Interlibrary loans; library open to public for reference use only. **Formerly:** Located in Toronto, ON.

★10291★
ONTARIO - MINISTRY OF THE SOLICITOR GENERAL - CENTRE OF FORENSIC SCIENCES - H. WARD SMITH LIBRARY (Law; Sci-Tech)
25 Grosvenor St., 2nd Fl.   Phone: (416) 965-2561
Toronto, ON, Canada M7A 2G8   Eva Gulbinowicz, Libn.
Founded: 1967. **Staff:** Prof 1; Other 2. **Subjects:** Forensic science, toxicology, biology, chemistry, engineering, firearms, photography, questioned documents. **Special Collections:** Home Office Central Research Establishment (England) reports; slides (5000). **Holdings:** 5000 books; 5500 bound periodical volumes; 510 reports; 9200 reprints; 1000 government documents and pamphlets. **Subscriptions:** 308 journals and other serials. **Services:** Interlibrary loans; copying (limited); library open to criminal justice and medical professionals by telephone appointment. **Automated Operations:** Computerized acquisitions and circulation. **Computerized Information Services:** BRS, DIALOG, MEDLINE. **Publications:** The Scenter (newsletter), irregular. **Special Catalogs:** Journal and reprint file catalog; slide catalog.

★10292★
ONTARIO - MINISTRY OF THE SOLICITOR GENERAL - OFFICE OF THE FIRE MARSHAL LIBRARY (Sci-Tech)
7 Overlea Blvd., 3rd Fl.   Phone: (416) 965-4855
Toronto, ON, Canada M4H 1A8   Iris Becker-Zawadowski, Libn.
Staff: Prof 1; Other 1. **Subjects:** Fire prevention and protection. **Special Collections:** National Fire Protection Association Fire Codes. **Holdings:** 4500 books; 200 bound periodical volumes; 2000 catalogs and pamphlets. **Subscriptions:** 145 journals and other serials. **Services:** Interlibrary loans; copying; library open to public with restrictions. **Computerized Information Services:** DIALOG. **Publications:** Recent Accessions, monthly; bibliographies of library material, irregular - both free upon request.

ONTARIO - MINISTRY OF TOURISM AND RECREATION - HURONIA HISTORICAL PARKS
See: Huronia Historical Parks

★10293★
ONTARIO - MINISTRY OF TOURISM AND RECREATION - PHOTO LIBRARY (Aud-Vis)
10th Fl., Hearst Block
900 Bay St.   Phone: (416) 965-5411
Toronto, ON, Canada M7A 2E1   Linda M. Goodwin, Photo Libn.
Staff: Prof 1. **Subjects:** Ontario - tourist attractions, industry. **Holdings:** 54,000 slides in 29 VF drawers. **Services:** Library open to public by appointment for noncommercial use only.

★10294★
ONTARIO - MINISTRY OF TRANSPORTATION AND COMMUNICATIONS - LIBRARY AND INFORMATION CENTRE (Trans)
Central Bldg., Rm. 149
1201 Wilson Ave.   Phone: (416) 248-3591
Downsview, ON, Canada M3M 1J8   Stefanie A. Pavlin, Hd., Lib.Serv.
Founded: 1956. **Staff:** Prof 3; Other 5. **Subjects:** Highway and bridge design, engineering and maintenance; materials testing; transportation economics; telecommunications; photogrammetry; highway safety and accident statistics; personnel management and supervision; traffic engineering; urban and regional studies; energy conservation; laws and regulations. **Special Collections:** Publications and reports of the Transportation Research Board, the Ministry of Transportation and Communications, the American Association of State Highway and Transportation Officials. **Holdings:** 75,000 books; 2500 bound periodical volumes; 5000 microforms. **Subscriptions:** 900 journals and other serials.

Services: Interlibrary loans; copying; library open to qualified users. **Automated Operations:** Computerized cataloging. **Computerized Information Services:** UTLAS, DIALOG, SDC, Infomart, CAN/OLE. **Networks/Consortia:** Member of Ontario Government Libraries' Council. **Publications:** Library News, semimonthly; Journal Contents, weekly. **Staff:** Laila Zvejnieks, Tech.Serv.; Ian Mann, ILL.

ONTARIO - MINISTRY OF TREASURY, ECONOMICS AND INTERGOVERNMENTAL AFFAIRS - ONTARIO ECONOMIC COUNCIL
See: Ontario Economic Council

★10295★
ONTARIO - MINISTRY OF TREASURY AND ECONOMICS - LIBRARY SERVICES BRANCH (Bus-Fin; Soc Sci)
Frost Bldg. North, 1st Fl.
Queen's Park   Phone: (416) 965-2314
Toronto, ON, Canada M7A 1Y7   Barbara Weatherhead, Dir.
Founded: 1945. **Staff:** Prof 3; Other 8. **Subjects:** Economics, finance (including statistics), all levels of government, management. **Special Collections:** Budgets, estimates and public accounts for Canadian federal and all provincial governments. **Holdings:** 100,000 books; 32 VF drawers; 462 linear feet of Statistics Canada reports; 1600 maps of Ontario. **Subscriptions:** 1200 journals and other serials; 12 newspapers. **Services:** Interlibrary loans; copying; library open to public with permission of librarian. **Automated Operations:** Computerized cataloging and serials. **Computerized Information Services:** SDC, New York Times Information Service, DIALOG, BRS, QL Systems, Info Globe, CAN/OLE, UTLAS. **Networks/Consortia:** Member of Ontario Government Libraries' Council (OGLC). **Publications:** Recent Accessions, weekly; Current Awareness, weekly; bibliographies. **Special Indexes:** Ontario regulations and Ontario debates, both indexed weekly; private acts in Ontario. **Remarks:** Includes the holdings of the former Ontario - Civil Service Commission - Library.

★10296★
ONTARIO - MUNICIPAL BOARD - LIBRARY (Bus-Fin; Plan)
180 Dundas St., W.   Phone: (416) 598-2266
Toronto, ON, Canada M5G 1E5   B.C. Alty, Asst.Sec. & Adm.Off.
Subjects: Appraisal and assessment, land use and values, planning and zoning. **Holdings:** Figures not available. **Services:** Library not open to public.

★10297★
ONTARIO NURSES ASSOCIATION - ONA LIBRARY (Med)
415 Yonge St., 14th Fl.   Phone: (416) 977-1975
Toronto, ON, Canada M5B 2E7   Kathy Bennett O'Hara, Lib.Techn.
Founded: 1977. **Staff:** Prof 2. **Subjects:** Industrial relations, nursing, occupational health and safety, medical and health care. **Holdings:** 2300 books; 100 bound periodical volumes; 4 drawers of ONA archives; 7 VF drawers of nursing and industrial relations materials; 1 drawer of news clippings. **Subscriptions:** 203 journals and other serials. **Services:** Interlibrary loans; copying; library open to public by appointment and for material that is not widely available. **Automated Operations:** Computerized cataloging and acquisitions. **Publications:** ONA Library: Acquisitions, monthly - for internal distribution only. **Special Indexes:** Card index of nursing materials. **Staff:** Jean Buchanan, Lib.Asst.

★10298★
ONTARIO PAPER COMPANY, LTD. - LIBRARY (Sci-Tech)
Allanburg Rd.   Phone: (416) 227-1121
Thorold, ON, Canada L2V 3Z5   Isabelle Ridgway, Libn.
Founded: 1949. **Staff:** 1. **Subjects:** Pulp and paper (newsprint); forestry and logging; chemical byproducts of paper manufacture; chemical engineering; business. **Special Collections:** Patents concerning all phases of pulp and paper manufacture (6000 patents). **Holdings:** 2210 books; 2187 bound periodical volumes; 2025 pamphlets; 1750 unbound company reports; 125 filing boxes of other reports. **Subscriptions:** 310 journals and other serials; 6 newspapers. **Services:** Interlibrary loans; copying; library open to public for reference use only on request. **Automated Operations:** Computerized circulation. **Computerized Information Services:** DIALOG. **Publications:** Monthly Accession List - for internal distribution only.

★10299★
ONTARIO POLICE COLLEGE - LIBRARY (Law)
Box 1190   Phone: (519) 773-5361
Aylmer West, ON, Canada N5H 2T2   Mr. Yen-pin Chao, Libn.
Staff: Prof 1; Other 1. **Subjects:** Police science, criminal law, criminology, sociology. **Holdings:** 7600 volumes. **Subscriptions:** 160 journals and other serials; 8 newspapers. **Services:** Interlibrary loans; copying (limited); library open to public with permission. **Publications:** Acquisitions list.

★10300★

ONTARIO PROVINCIAL POLICE HEADQUARTERS - CAREER MANAGEMENT BRANCH - LIBRARY (Law)
90 Harbour St.   Phone: (416) 965-4468
Toronto, ON, Canada M7A 2S1   Lorna E. Brown, Libn.
Founded: 1979. **Staff:** Prof 1; Other 1. **Subjects:** Criminology, management, laws and regulations of Ontario and Canada. **Holdings:** 6000 book; 200 bound periodical volumes; 30 AV materials. **Subscriptions:** 238 journals and other serials. **Services:** Interlibrary loans; copying; library open to public by appointment for reference use only. **Computerized Information Services:** QL Systems. **Publications:** List of new acquisitions, bimonthly - for internal distribution only.

★10301★

ONTARIO PUPPETRY ASSOCIATION CENTRE - RESOURCE LIBRARY (Theater)
171 Avondale Ave.   Phone: (416) 222-9029
Willowdale, ON, Canada M2N 2V4   Michael Sam Cronk, Musm.Dir./Cur.
Founded: 1980. **Staff:** Prof 1. **Subjects:** Puppetry, education and puppetry, museology, museum exhibitions. **Holdings:** Figures not available for books; 5 VF drawers of research folders. **Services:** Copying; library open to public by appointment. **Publications:** OPAL, bimonthly.

★10302★

ONTARIO RESEARCH FOUNDATION - LIBRARY (Sci-Tech)
Sheridan Park   Phone: (416) 822-4111
Mississauga, ON, Canada L5K 1B3   Carl K. Wei, Libn.
Founded: 1928. **Staff:** Prof 1; Other 4. **Subjects:** Chemistry, engineering, metallurgy, textiles, physics, pollution. **Holdings:** 12,000 books; 26,000 bound periodical volumes; 5000 government documents; 50 boxes of annual reports; 5 drawers of microforms. **Subscriptions:** 550 journals and other serials. **Services:** Interlibrary loans; copying; library open to public. **Computerized Information Services:** CAN/OLE, DIALOG, SDC, NLM, BRS, QL Systems, CAS Online, NIH-EPA Chemical Information System, Info Globe, Questel, Pergamon InfoLine Ltd. **Networks/Consortia:** Member of Sheridan Park Association; Ontario Government Libraries' Council (OGLC); Ontario Technology Centres TIS Network. **Publications:** Library Reminder, biweekly - for internal distribution only.

★10303★

ONTARIO SCIENCE CENTRE - AUDIO VISUAL LIBRARY
770 Don Mills Rd.
Don Mills, ON, Canada M3C 1T3
Defunct. Holdings absorbed by Ontario Science Centre - Library.

★10304★

ONTARIO SCIENCE CENTRE - LIBRARY (Sci-Tech)
770 Don Mills Rd.   Phone: (416) 429-4100
Don Mills, ON, Canada M3C 1T3   Jeanne Duperreault, Libn.
Founded: 1965. **Staff:** Prof 1. **Subjects:** Chemistry, physics, biology, astronomy, mathematics, zoology, botany, technology, engineering, graphic arts, history. **Holdings:** 15,000 books; 30,000 slides; 30,000 prints and negatives; 500 films; 100 videotapes. **Subscriptions:** 80 journals and other serials. **Services:** Interlibrary loans; copying; library open to public by appointment. **Remarks:** Contains the holdings of its Audio Visual Library.

ONTARIO SCIENCE CENTRE - ONTARIO FILM INSTITUTE
See: Ontario Film Institute

★10305★

ONTARIO - SUPREME COURT OF ONTARIO - JUDGES' LIBRARY (Law)†
Osgoode Hall
130 Queen St., W.   Phone: (416) 363-4101
Toronto, ON, Canada M5H 2N5   Anne Brown, Mgr.
Staff: Prof 1. **Subjects:** Law. **Holdings:** 20,000 volumes. **Subscriptions:** 20 journals and other serials. **Services:** Interlibrary loans; library not open to public.

ONTARIO THEOLOGICAL SEMINARY
See: Ontario Bible College/Ontario Theological Seminary

★10306★

OPEN BIBLE COLLEGE - CARRIE HARDY MEMORIAL LIBRARY (Rel-Theol)
2633 Fleur Dr.   Phone: (515) 283-0478
Des Moines, IA 50321   Linda Jones, Libn.
Staff: Prof 1; Other 1. **Subjects:** Theology, Bible, history, literature and Greek. **Holdings:** 19,500 books; 343 bound periodical volumes; 87 reels of microfilm; 480 microfiche; 128 sermons on tape. **Subscriptions:** 182 journals and other serials. **Services:** Interlibrary loans; copying; library open to public.

★10307★

OPEN LANDS PROJECT - LIBRARY (Env-Cons; Plan)
53 W. Jackson Blvd., Rm. 850   Phone: (312) 427-4256
Chicago, IL 60604   Judith M. Stockdale, Exec.Dir.
Founded: 1963. **Staff:** 9. **Subjects:** Flood plains, water resources, outdoor recreation, environmental education, open space preservation, population statistics, urban land preservation. **Special Collections:** NIPC 208 Water Plan, Upper Mississippi River Comprehensive Basin Study; history and planning of Grant Park, Des Plaines River Valley, Kennicott Grove, Indiana Dunes National Lakeshore. **Holdings:** 1000 books; 1000 other cataloged items; 2 VF drawers of clippings; 16 VF drawers of open space subject information. **Subscriptions:** 15 journals and other serials. **Services:** Library open to public by appointment. **Publications:** Newsletter, 6/year; list of publications - available on request. **Special Catalogs:** Catalog of historic and contemporary photographs of Midwest land.

OPENHYM COLLECTION
See: Alfred University - Herrick Memorial Library

OPLIC
See: Minnesota State Department of Education - Office of Public Libraries and Interlibrary Cooperation

★10308★

OPPENHEIMER & CO., INC. - LIBRARY (Bus-Fin)
One New York Plaza, 32nd Fl.   Phone: (212) 825-4264
New York, NY 10004   Carter Crawford, Libn.
Staff: Prof 3; Other 7. **Subjects:** Corporations, investment, government statistics, stock price sources. **Holdings:** 4200 books; 1500 subject files on various industries; 1 million microfiche cards of U.S. Securities and Exchange Commission documents; corporation files of annual reports, proxy statements, prospectuses. **Subscriptions:** 1200 journals and other serials. **Services:** Interlibrary loans; library not open to public. **Automated Operations:** Computerized serials and circulation. **Computerized Information Services:** DIALOG, NEXIS, Dow Jones News/Retrieval, TEXTLINE, Dun & Bradstreet Corporation, Disclosure Inc., SPECTRUM Ownership Profiles Online, Financial Data Bank; internal databases. **Staff:** Jeanne Seyffarth, Sr.Ref.Libn.; Joan Morris, Ref.Libn.

★10309★

OPPENHEIMER, WOLFF, FOSTER, SHEPARD & DONNELLY - LIBRARY (Law)
W-1700 First Bank Bldg.   Phone: (612) 227-7271
St. Paul, MN 55101   Gretchen Haase, Libn.
Staff: Prof 2; Other 1. **Subjects:** Business law. **Holdings:** 24,000 books; 600 bound periodical volumes. **Subscriptions:** 320 journals and other serials; 11 newspapers. **Services:** Interlibrary loans; library not open to public. **Computerized Information Services:** DIALOG, LEXIS. **Networks/Consortia:** Member of Metronet. **Staff:** Kathleen Thielges, Asst.Libn.

★10310★

OPTIKON RESEARCH LABORATORIES - LIBRARY (Sci-Tech)†
Box 947   Phone: (203) 672-6614
West Cornwall, CT 06796   William Covington, Libn.
Staff: Prof 1; Other 3. **Subjects:** Polymer sciences, optics. **Special Collections:** Dioptric materials. **Holdings:** 9000 books; 700 bound periodical volumes. **Services:** Interlibrary loans; library open to public by appointment - request in writing only.

ORAL HISTORY PROJECT IN LABOR HISTORY
See: Roosevelt University

★10311★

ORAL ROBERTS UNIVERSITY - GRADUATE THEOLOGY LIBRARY - JOHN MESSICK LEARNING RESOURCE CENTER (Rel-Theol)
7777 S. Lewis   Phone: (918) 495-6723
Tulsa, OK 74171   Dr. William W. Jernigan, Dir.
Founded: 1962. **Staff:** Prof 3; Other 8. **Subjects:** Biblical literature, historical and theological studies, Christianity and culture, practices of ministry. **Holdings:** 77,106 books and bound periodical volumes; 9045 microforms; 7524 AV materials; 45 VF drawers of pamphlets; 141 tracts. **Subscriptions:** 1208 journals and other serials. **Services:** Interlibrary loans; center open to public with special permission. **Automated Operations:** Computerized cataloging, acquisitions, circulation and reference. **Computerized Information Services:** DIALOG, BRS, OCLC; ALIS (internal database). Performs searches on cost recovery basis. **Networks/Consortia:** Member of AMIGOS Bibliographic Council, Inc. **Staff:** Oon-Chor Khoo, Theol.Libn.

★10312★
ORAL ROBERTS UNIVERSITY - HEALTH SCIENCES LIBRARY (Med)
7777 S. Lewis
Box 2187   Phone: (918) 495-6897
Tulsa, OK 74171   Timothy C. Judkins, Asst.Dir.
Founded: 1976. **Staff:** Prof 3; Other 4. **Subjects:** Medicine, dentistry, nursing. **Holdings:** 20,193 books; 36,088 bound periodical volumes; 700 AV items. **Subscriptions:** 1334 journals and other serials. **Services:** Interlibrary loans; copying; library open to public with restrictions. **Automated Operations:** Computerized cataloging, acquisitions and circulation. **Computerized Information Services:** DIALOG, MEDLINE, BRS, OCLC. **Networks/Consortia:** Member of AMIGOS Bibliographic Council, Inc; South Central Academic Medical Libraries Consortium (SCAMEL). **Publications:** New acquisitions list, quarterly. **Staff:** Carol Liardon, Asst.Libn.; Lola Nair, Cat.

★10313★
ORAL ROBERTS UNIVERSITY - LIBRARY - HOLY SPIRIT RESEARCH CENTER (Rel-Theol)
Box 2187   Phone: (918) 495-6898
Tulsa, OK 74171   Karen Robinson, Libn.
Founded: 1962. **Staff:** Prof 2; Other 2. **Subjects:** History of Pentecostalism, history of Pentecostal/Charismatic denominations and organizations, gifts or manifestations of the Holy Spirit, divine healing, baptism of the Holy Spirit, Neo-Pentecostalism (Charismatic Movement), Catholic Pentecostalism, glossolalia, eschatology. **Special Collections:** Bishop Dan T. Muse (8 boxes of manuscripts; 27 photograph albums); J.G. Lake Photograph Collection (1 box); William Braham Photograph Collection (1 box). **Holdings:** 10,000 books; 1800 bound periodical volumes; 1000 tapes and cassettes; 40 VF drawers of pamphlets; 27 reels of microfilm; 35 theses and dissertations; 30 records; AV materials. **Subscriptions:** 500 journals and other serials. **Services:** Center open to public for reference use only. **Automated Operations:** Computerized cataloging and acquisitions. **Publications:** Bibliographies on Pentecostal and charismatic materials, the Holy Spirit and divine healing; Microfilm Holdings in HSRC; Annotated Bibliography of Catholic Charismatic Materials in HSRC; General Works on the Baptism in the Holy Spirit as Taught by Pentecostals - available for purchase; Oral Roberts books. **Staff:** Dr. W.W. Jernigan, Dir.; Ruth Wells, Cat.

★10314★
ORAL ROBERTS UNIVERSITY - O.W. COBURN LAW LIBRARY (Law)†
School of Law
7777 S. Lewis
Box 2187   Phone: (918) 495-7155
Tulsa, OK 74171   Prof. David W. Dunn, Law Libn.
Founded: 1977. **Staff:** Prof 3; Other 4. **Subjects:** Law. **Holdings:** 73,010 books; 31,045 bound periodical volumes; 97,643 microforms. **Subscriptions:** 3268 journals and other serials. **Services:** Interlibrary loans; copying; library open to members of the Oklahoma Bar Association. **Automated Operations:** Computerized cataloging acquisitions and circulation. **Computerized Information Services:** DIALOG, LEXIS, MEDLARS, BRS. **Staff:** Lorin Lindsay, Asst. Law Libn.; Jean Delts, Cat.

★10315★
ORANGE COUNTY DEPARTMENT OF EDUCATION - LIBRARY (Educ)*
1300 S. Grand Ave., Bldg. B
Box 15029   Phone: (714) 953-3980
Santa Ana, CA 92705   Faith M. Herbert, Lib.Techn.
Staff: 1. **Subjects:** Educational administration, teaching and teachers, philosophy and psychology of education, school buildings, early childhood education, special education. **Special Collections:** Curriculum guides (300). **Holdings:** 9100 books; 20 VF drawers of pamphlets. **Subscriptions:** 125 journals and other serials. **Services:** Interlibrary loans; copying (limited); library open to public for reference use only.

★10316★
ORANGE COUNTY ENVIRONMENTAL MANAGEMENT AGENCY - ADMINISTRATION/PLANNING LIBRARY
Box 4048
Santa Ana, CA 92701
Defunct. Merged with Orange County Environmental Management Agency - Public Works Library to form its EMA Library.

★10317★
ORANGE COUNTY ENVIRONMENTAL MANAGEMENT AGENCY - EMA LIBRARY (Env-Cons; Plan)
400 Civic Center Dr., W.
Box 4048   Phone: (714) 834-6395
Santa Ana, CA 92702   Janet Hilford, Libn.
Founded: 1963. **Staff:** Prof 1. **Subjects:** Environmental management, water resources, hydrology, flood control, transportation engineering, recreational design, urban planning, land use and zoning, public administration, housing/community development. **Holdings:** 7500 books; 20,000 technical reports. **Subscriptions:** 30 journals and other serials. **Services:** Library not open to public. **Formed by the Merger of:** Orange County Environmental Management Agency - Public Works Library and its Administration/Planning Library.

★10318★
ORANGE COUNTY HISTORICAL COMMISSION - MUSEUM LIBRARY (Hist)
812 E. Rollins St.
Loch Haven Park
Orlando, FL 32803   Frank Mendola, Libn.
Staff: Prof 1. **Subjects:** Local and state history, Seminole Indians. **Holdings:** 1025 books and bound periodical volumes; 460 directories and yearbooks; 130 scrapbooks; 50 photograph albums; 2700 pictures; 250 maps; 15 linear feet of vertical file materials; 6000 postcards; newspapers - 12 reels of microfilm, 131 sheets of microfiche. **Subscriptions:** 11 journals and other serials. **Services:** Copying; library open to public when librarian is on duty. **Publications:** Orange County Historical Quarterly - for members and visitors. **Remarks:** Library is a repository for Orange County historical materials.

★10319★
ORANGE COUNTY LAW LIBRARY (Law)
515 N. Flower St.   Phone: (714) 834-3397
Santa Ana, CA 92703   Bethany J. Ochal, Dir.
Founded: 1891. **Staff:** Prof 5; Other 13. **Subjects:** Law. **Special Collections:** Up-to-date codes for the law of all the states, federal government and territories as well as case reports and some administrative regulations and rulings; CIS microfiche service. **Holdings:** 122,500 bound volumes; 4600 tapes; 419,000 microfiche; 2750 ultrafiche; depository for California and U.S. Government documents. **Subscriptions:** 1100 journals and other serials; 9 newspapers. **Services:** Interlibrary loans; copying; library open to public. **Computerized Information Services:** Westlaw. **Networks/Consortia:** Member of CLASS; RLG. **Staff:** Richard Ayotte, Pub.Serv.Libn.; Josephine Miklas, Tech.Serv.Libn.

★10320★
ORANGE COUNTY LAW LIBRARY (Law)†
County Court House, Rm. 558   Phone: (305) 420-3240
Orlando, FL 32801   Sarilou A. Barrow, Libn.
Subjects: Law. **Holdings:** 22,574 volumes. **Services:** Copying; library open to public for reference use only.

★10321★
ORANGE COUNTY LIBRARY DISTRICT - GENEALOGY DEPARTMENT (Hist)
10 N. Rosalind Ave.   Phone: (305) 425-4694
Orlando, FL 32801   Eileen B. Willis, Dept.Hd.
Staff: Prof 3; Other 2. **Subjects:** Genealogy, family history, heraldry, surnames. **Special Collections:** Barber Collection of Connecticut Vital Records (97 reels of microfilm); vital records of 190 Massachusetts towns, to 1850; Florida State Society, Daughters of the American Revolution collection, 1929 to present (5000 volumes); lectures on genealogy (50 tapes). **Holdings:** 10,000 books; 1300 bound periodical volumes; 2900 reels of microfilm; 8 VF drawers of the papers of Beatrice Brown Commander; 12 VF drawers of miscellaneous family papers. **Subscriptions:** 152 journals and other serials. **Services:** Copying; department open to public. **Automated Operations:** Computerized cataloging, acquisitions and circulation. **Computerized Information Services:** OCLC.

★10322★
ORANGE COUNTY SHERIFF/CORONER - FORENSIC SCIENCE SERVICES LIBRARY (Sci-Tech)
550 N. Flower St.
Box 449   Phone: (714) 834-3073
Santa Ana, CA 92702   Mr. J.L. Ragle, Lab.Dir.
Founded: 1948. **Staff:** Prof 1. **Subjects:** Chemistry, criminalistics, toxicology, forensic medicine, investigation. **Holdings:** 2500 books; 4 VF drawers of catalogs and brochures; 2 VF drawers of lab equipment manuals; 2400 reprints; 3 boxes of microfiche and microfilm. **Subscriptions:** 55 journals and other serials. **Services:** Interlibrary loans; library not open to public.

★10323★
ORANGE COUNTY TRANSIT DISTRICT - RESOURCE CENTER (Trans)
11222 Acacia Pkwy.
Box 3005   Phone: (714) 971-6375
Garden Grove, CA 92642   Robin J. Masters, Rsrc.Spec.
Founded: 1973. **Staff:** Prof 1. **Subjects:** Urban mass transit, paratransit, multi-modal transportation. **Special Collections:** History of transit in Orange

County (7 years of documents and pictures). **Holdings:** 4044 books; 2018 technical reports; 500 reports on microfiche; 6515 slides and cassettes. **Subscriptions:** 67 journals and other serials. **Services:** Interlibrary loans; center open to public by appointment. **Automated Operations:** Computerized serials and circulation. **Publications:** Technical Reports.

★10324★

ORANGE AND ROCKLAND UTILITIES, INC. - LIBRARY (Energy)
1 Blue Hill Plaza   Phone: (914) 627-2680
Pearl River, NY 10965   Esther B. Clifford, Libn.
Staff: Prof 1; Other 1. **Subjects:** Electric power, gas industry, energy, environment. **Holdings:** 5000 books; 1200 technical reports and pamphlets; 5 VF drawers of annual reports; special events clippings, 1970 to present. **Subscriptions:** 200 journals and other serials. **Services:** Interlibrary loans; library not open to public.

★10325★

ORANGEBURG-CALHOUN TECHNICAL COLLEGE - GRESSETTE LEARNING RESOURCE CENTER (Sci-Tech)
3250 Matthews Rd.   Phone: (803) 536-0311
Orangeburg, SC 29115   Margaret F. Huff, Dean, LRC
Staff: Prof 4; Other 4. **Subjects:** Science and technology, business, allied health subjects. **Special Collections:** Nontraditional power sources. **Holdings:** 28,184 books; 128 bound periodical volumes; 17,895 documents and pamphlets; 2421 filmstrips; 1227 audiotapes; 1254 AV titles; 2090 other cataloged items and reels of microfilm. **Subscriptions:** 434 journals and other serials; 11 newspapers. **Services:** Interlibrary loans; copying; center open to public. **Publications:** LRC Handbook, irregular - to students; Faculty LRC Handbook, irregular - to faculty; Multi-Media Handbook, irregular - to faculty; Monthly Acquisitions List; Special Bibliographies. **Staff:** Frances D. Ballentine, Multi-Media Coord.; Donna M.L. Tolar, Tech.Serv.Libn.; Hanna Palmer, Rd.Serv.Libn.

★10326★

ORATOIRE ST-JOSEPH - CENTRE DE DOCUMENTATION (Rel-Theol)
3800 Queen Mary Rd.   Phone: (514) 733-8211
Montreal, PQ, Canada H3V 1H6   Aime Trottier, Libn.
Founded: 1950. **Staff:** Prof 3; Other 3. **Subjects:** Saint Joseph and his cult, patrology, Canadiana, iconography, theology, spirituality, religious history. **Holdings:** 70,000 books; 72 VF drawers of archives; 1200 reels of microfilm; 400 titles on microcards. **Subscriptions:** 192 journals and other serials. **Services:** Interlibrary loans; copying; center open to public for reference use only. **Publications:** Cahiers de Josephologie, semiannual - by subscription. **Also Known As:** St. Joseph's Shrine. **Staff:** Roland Gauthier, Dir.

★10327★

ORDER OF DAEDALIANS - NATIONAL HEADQUARTERS - LIBRARY AND INFORMATION CENTER
Bldg. 1635
Kelly Air Force Base
San Antonio, TX 78241
Defunct

ORDER OF FRIARS MINOR (Franciscans) - DUNS SCOTUS LIBRARY
See: Duns Scotus Library

ORDER OF ST. BENEDICT - ABBEY OF REGINA LAUDIS
See: Abbey of Regina Laudis, Order of St. Benedict

★10328★

ORDER OF SERVANTS OF MARY - EASTERN PROVINCE LIBRARY - MORINI MEMORIAL COLLECTION (Rel-Theol; Hist)
3401 S. Home Ave.   Phone: (312) 484-0063
Berwyn, IL 60402   Rev. Conrad M. Borntrager, O.S.M., Archv.
Staff: 1. **Subjects:** Provincial archives. **Holdings:** 2000 books; 230 bound periodical volumes; 320 linear feet of archives; 800 clippings; 40 albums and 2 filing drawers of photographs; 100 blueprints. **Services:** Library open to public with restrictions. **Also Known As:** Servites.

★10329★

ORDRE DES INFIRMIERES ET DES INFIRMIERS DU QUEBEC - CENTRE DE DOCUMENTATION (Med)†
4200 Dorchester, W.   Phone: (514) 935-2501
Montreal, PQ, Canada H3Z 1V4   Denise Mailhot, Libn.
Staff: 3. **Subjects:** Nursing. **Holdings:** 6500 books; 150 bound periodical volumes; 12 films; 8 slide programs; 25 videotapes. **Subscriptions:** 325 journals and other serials. **Services:** Center open to members only. **Publications:** Nursing Quebec, 6/year.

★10330★

OREGON ELECTRIC RAILWAY HISTORICAL SOCIETY, INC. - TROLLEY PARK - LIBRARY (Hist; Trans)
HCR 71
Box 1318 Glenwood   Phone: (503) 357-3574
Forest Grove, OR 97116   William Hayes, Hist.
Staff: 1. **Subjects:** Electric railways, tram and trolley history. **Special Collections:** Tram and trolley business records and employment files from street railway companies. **Holdings:** 200 books; 150 unbound periodicals; 2500 photographs, slides and negatives. **Services:** Copying; library open to public by appointment for reference use only. **Publications:** Trolley Park News, quarterly - to members and by exchange.

★10331★

OREGON GRADUATE CENTER FOR STUDY AND RESEARCH - LIBRARY (Sci-Tech)
19600 N.W. Walker Rd.   Phone: (503) 645-1121
Beaverton, OR 97006   Maureen G. Seaman, Libn.
Staff: Prof 1; Other 2. **Subjects:** Chemistry, biochemistry, laser physics, solid state and surface physics, computer science and engineering, materials science, welding, environmental science. **Holdings:** 10,500 books; 1500 bound periodical volumes; 600 reels of microfilm; 6000 government reports on microfiche. **Subscriptions:** 340 journals and other serials. **Services:** Interlibrary loans; copying; library open to public with telephone request. **Computerized Information Services:** OCLC, CAS Online, DIALOG. **Networks/Consortia:** Member of Washington County Cooperative Library Services. **Publications:** OGC Catalog, annual - available on request.

★10332★

OREGON HEALTH SCIENCES UNIVERSITY - DENTAL BRANCH LIBRARY (Med)
611 S.W. Campus Dr.   Phone: (503) 225-8822
Portland, OR 97201   Dolores Judkins, Dental Libn.
Staff: Prof 1; Other 4. **Subjects:** Dental and oral science. **Special Collections:** History of dentistry (250 books). **Holdings:** 17,650 volumes and bound periodical volumes; 500 AV items. **Subscriptions:** 350 journals and other serials. **Services:** Interlibrary loans (fee); copying; SDI; library open to public for reference use only. **Automated Operations:** Computerized cataloging and serials. **Computerized Information Services:** MEDLINE, OCLC, PHILSOM. **Networks/Consortia:** Member of Pacific Northwest Regional Health Sciences Library Service (PNRHSLS). **Remarks:** Library houses an Independent Learning Center.

★10333★

OREGON HEALTH SCIENCES UNIVERSITY - LIBRARY (Med)
3181 S.W. Sam Jackson Park Rd.
Box 573   Phone: (503) 225-8026
Portland, OR 97207   James E. Morgan, Dir.
Staff: Prof 10; Other 25. **Subjects:** Medicine, dentistry, nursing, allied sciences. **Special Collections:** Pacific Northwest Collection (medical history); History of Medicine Collection. **Holdings:** 178,373 volumes; 1975 AV units. **Subscriptions:** 2619 journals and other serials. **Services:** Interlibrary loans; copying; SDI; library open to public for reference use only. **Computerized Information Services:** NLM, BRS, DIALOG, OCLC, PHILSOM. **Networks/Consortia:** Member of Oregon Health Information Network (OHIN); Pacific Northwest Regional Health Sciences Library Service (PNRHSLS). **Publications:** Accessions list. **Remarks:** Figures include the holdings of its Dental Library. **Staff:** Joan Ash, Assoc.Dir.; Carol Willman, Cat.Libn.; Nancy Hewison, Hd.Ref.Libn.; Betty Jo Keppel, Ser./Acq.Libn.; Heather Rosenwinkel, Coll.Dev.Libn.; Patty Davies, Ref.Libn.; Leslie Cable, Ref.Libn.; Frances Spradlin, ILL Libn.;Steve Teich, OHIN Coord.

★10334★

OREGON HISTORICAL SOCIETY - LIBRARY (Hist)
1230 S.W. Park Ave.   Phone: (503) 222-1741
Portland, OR 97205   Louis Flannery, Chf.Libn.
Founded: 1898. **Staff:** Prof 16; Other 7. **Subjects:** History of the Pacific Northwest and the Oregon Country; social, political and economic growth of the Pacific Northwest; Northwest explorations and voyages; cartography of Northwest. **Special Collections:** Oregon Provisional Government Papers (film); Henry Failing Papers; Oregon Imprints by Belknap; British Collection; Russian-American Studies; Wesley Andrews Collection; M.M. Hazeltine Collection. **Holdings:** 70,000 volumes; 15 million items in 4500 manuscript collections; 16,000 reels of microfilm; 1.5 million photographs; 10,000 maps; 9000 reels of TV film. **Subscriptions:** 600 journals and other serials; 80 newspapers. **Services:** Interlibrary loans; copying; library open to public. **Automated Operations:** Computerized cataloging. **Computerized Information Services:** OCLC. **Special Catalogs:** Guide to Manuscript Collections of the Oregon Historical Society (book with supplements); Catalog

of Microfilm Collections (book); Union Catalog of Photographs Collection in Pacific Northwest.

OREGON INSTITUTE OF MARINE BIOLOGY
See: University of Oregon

★10335★
OREGON INSTITUTE OF TECHNOLOGY - LEARNING RESOURCES CENTER (Sci-Tech)
Oretech Branch P.O. Phone: (503) 882-6321
Klamath Falls, OR 97601 Charles H. Kemp, Dir.
Founded: 1950. Staff: Prof 9; Other 7. Subjects: Engineering, electronics, health sciences, computer science, industrial processes, paramedicine, business. Holdings: 63,000 books; 16,000 bound periodical volumes; microfilm. Subscriptions: 1100 journals and other serials; 37 newspapers. Services: Interlibrary loans; copying; media services; center open to public. Automated Operations: Computerized cataloging. Computerized Information Services: OCLC, DIALOG. Networks/Consortia: Member of Southern Oregon Library Federation (SOLF); CLASS. Staff: Jenny Street, Mgt.Asst.; Robert Weber, Pub.Serv.Libn.; David White, Coord.; Gary Gray, Coord.; Karen Chase, Tech.Serv.Libn.; Johnyne Wascavage, Cir.Libn.; Carol Moore, Doc.Libn.

★10336★
OREGON REGIONAL PRIMATE RESEARCH CENTER - LIBRARY (Sci-Tech; Med)
505 N.W. 185th Ave. Phone: (503) 645-1141
Beaverton, OR 97006 Isabel McDonald, Libn.
Founded: 1961. Staff: Prof 1; Other 1. Subjects: Biomedicine, zoology. Special Collections: Primatology. Holdings: 15,000 books and bound periodical volumes; 35 films; 196 reels of microfilm. Subscriptions: 200 journals and other serials. Services: Interlibrary loans; copying; SDI; library open to visiting scientists and others on request. Automated Operations: Computerized ILL. Computerized Information Services: MEDLINE, BRS. Performs searches on cost recovery basis. Networks/Consortia: Member of Washington County Cooperative Library Services; WLIN; Oregon Health Information Network (OHIN). Special Catalogs: Files on center's publications; files on primate articles, films and theses (both on cards).

★10337★
OREGON RESEARCH INSTITUTE - LIBRARY (Comp Sci)
195 W. 12th Ave.
Eugene, OR 97401 Linda Rangus, Lib.Mgr.
Founded: 1960. Staff: 1. Subjects: Psychology, computers. Holdings: 1000 volumes; 2000 reprints of journal articles. Services: Library not open to public. Computerized Information Services: DIALOG.

★10338★
OREGON SCHOOL OF ARTS AND CRAFTS - LIBRARY (Art)
8245 S.W. Barnes Rd. Phone: (503) 297-5544
Portland, OR 97225 Kristin L. Koester, Libn.
Staff: Prof 1. Subjects: Textiles, ceramics, woodworking, drawing and design, metals, calligraphy. Holdings: 2000 books; 8000 slides; 4 VF drawers of archives. Subscriptions: 90 journals and other serials. Services: Interlibrary loans; copying; library open to public for reference use only.

★10339★
OREGON STATE DEPARTMENT OF AGRICULTURE - INFORMATION SERVICE - LIBRARY (Agri)
Agriculture Bldg.
635 Capitol St., N.E. Phone: (503) 378-3773
Salem, OR 97310
Subjects: Agriculture. Holdings: Figures not available. Services: Library open to public for reference use only.

★10340★
OREGON STATE DEPARTMENT OF EDUCATION - RESOURCE/ DISSEMINATION CENTER (Educ)
700 Pringle Parkway, S.E. Phone: (503) 378-8471
Salem, OR 97310 Juanita Maloney, Lib.Asst.
Founded: 1970. Staff: Prof 1; Other 1. Subjects: General education. Special Collections: Career and vocational education; school standards documents; summarized information packets on selected priority topics; collection of files on cost saving ideas. Holdings: 2200 books; 16 VF drawers; 4000 unbound periodicals and newsletters; 260,000 documents on microfiche; ERIC microfiche collection (complete set). Subscriptions: 200 journals and other serials; 6 newspapers. Services: Interlibrary loans; copying; SDI; center open to public with restrictions. Computerized Information Services: DIALOG, BRS, The Source. Performs free searches.

★10341★
OREGON STATE DEPARTMENT OF FISH AND WILDLIFE - LIBRARY (Sci-Tech)
17330 S.E. Evelyn St.
Clackamas, OR 97015 Shirley M. McKinney, Libn.
Founded: 1957. Subjects: Fisheries biology, fisheries statistics. Holdings: Figures not available. Services: Interlibrary loans; copying; library open to public for reference use only.

OREGON STATE DEPARTMENT OF FISH AND WILDLIFE - NEWPORT LABORATORY LIBRARY
See: Oregon State University - Hatfield Marine Science Center - Library

★10342★
OREGON STATE DEPARTMENT OF GEOLOGY AND MINERAL INDUSTRIES - LIBRARY (Sci-Tech; Energy)
1400 S.W. 5th Ave. Phone: (503) 229-5580
Portland, OR 97201 Klaus Neuendorf, Ed./Libn.
Staff: 1. Subjects: Oregon geology, energy. Special Collections: Publications of the U.S. Geological Survey, the U.S. Bureau of Mines, other state geological surveys and some foreign governments. Holdings: 10,000 volumes; 20 linear yards of maps; 400 unpublished theses and dissertations on Oregon geology; unpublished open-file reports issued by U.S. Geological Survey. Subscriptions: 20 journals and other serials. Services: Interlibrary loans; copying (limited); library open to public with restrictions. Publications: Oregon Geology, monthly; bulletins; special papers; oil and gas investigations; geologic map series; open-file reports. Special Indexes: Bibliography of the geology and mineral resources of Oregon; Bibliography of theses and dissertations on the geology of Oregon. Remarks: Principally a staff library. Public access to this collection is more readily obtained through the Portland State University Science Library or the Oregon State Library in Salem, OR.

★10343★
OREGON STATE DEPARTMENT OF HUMAN RESOURCES - SENIOR SERVICES DIVISION - LIBRARY (Soc Sci)
313 Public Service Bldg. Phone: (503) 378-4728
Salem, OR 97310
Subjects: Aging and the elderly - abuse and crime, long term care and housing, health; management. Holdings: Figures not available.

★10344★
OREGON STATE DEPARTMENT OF LAND CONSERVATION AND DEVELOPMENT - LIBRARY (Env-Cons; Plan)
1175 Court St., N.E. Phone: (503) 378-2980
Salem, OR 97310 Bonnie Putman, Libn./Sec.
Staff: Prof 1. Subjects: Land use and planning. Holdings: 3800 volumes; land use plans. Subscriptions: 122 journals and other serials. Services: Interlibrary loans; copying; library open to public. Publications: Oregon Lands, quarterly.

★10345★
OREGON STATE DEPARTMENT OF REVENUE - RESEARCH LIBRARY (Bus-Fin)
955 Center St., N.E., Rm. 452 Phone: (503) 378-3727
Salem, OR 97310 Marty Orr, Libn.
Founded: 1958. Staff: 1. Subjects: Oregon - laws, administrative rules; taxes; revenue. Special Collections: Tax services for all 50 states and the District of Columbia; two federal income tax services. Holdings: 1029 books; 25 bound periodical volumes; 1606 pamphlets and documents; 2 tax services; legislative bills (1 year). Subscriptions: 178 journals and other serials. Services: Library open to public for research only. Publications: Oregon Property Tax Statistics; Analysis of Oregon Personal Income Tax, both annual.

★10346★
OREGON STATE DEPARTMENT OF TRANSPORTATION - LIBRARY (Trans)
127 Transportation Bldg. Phone: (503) 378-6268
Salem, OR 97310 Marie Elefante, Libn.
Founded: 1938. Staff: Prof 1. Subjects: Transportation, highway engineering, planning, economics, environment, aeronautics, motor vehicles. Holdings: 9000 books. Subscriptions: 80 journals and other serials. Services: Interlibrary loans; copying; library open to public with restrictions. Publications: ODOT Library News, Acquisitions List.

★10347★
OREGON STATE HOSPITAL - MEDICAL LIBRARY (Med)
2600 Center St., N.E. Phone: (503) 378-2266
Salem, OR 97310 Sharon R. Paulsen, Libn.
Founded: 1950. Staff: 1. Subjects: Psychiatry, medicine, psychology, sociology, psychiatric nursing. Special Collections: Complete Psychological

Works of Sigmund Freud (24 volumes). **Holdings:** 2600 books; 138 bound periodical volumes; 3 drawers of cassette tapes; 2 drawers of microfilm. **Subscriptions:** 45 journals and other serials. **Services:** Interlibrary loans; copying; library open to public for reference use only.

★10348★
OREGON STATE LIBRARY (Info Sci)
State Library Bldg.
Summer and Court Sts.
Salem, OR 97310
Phone: (503) 378-4274
Wesley A. Doak, State Libn.
Founded: 1905. **Staff:** Prof 17; Other 37. **Subjects:** Oregon history and government; business; librarianship; social sciences; humanities; science and technology. **Special Collections:** Oregoniana; materials for the blind and physically handicapped; history of Oregon library development; Oregon library statistics. **Holdings:** 349,521 books; 812,277 government documents and other materials; 143,135 microforms; clippings; pamphlets. **Subscriptions:** 1747 journals and other serials; 51 newspapers. **Services:** Interlibrary loans; copying; SDI; library open to public. **Computerized Information Services:** DIALOG, BRS, NLM, EROS Data Center, Oregon Legislative Information System (OLIS). **Publications:** Letter to Libraries; Checklist of Official Publications of State of Oregon, quarterly; What's New, monthly; Directory and Statistics of Oregon Libraries, annual - to all Oregon libraries; Reference Satellite, monthly - to all Oregon public libraries. **Special Catalogs:** Oregoniana (card and microfilm). **Special Indexes:** Subject and biography index to Salem daily newspaper and other publications. **Staff:** Kathleen Grasing, Dp. State Libn.; John Webb, Asst. State Libn.; Merrialyce Kasner, Adm., Tech.Serv.; Marge Wright, Adm., Pub.Serv.

★10349★
OREGON STATE LIBRARY - SERVICES FOR THE BLIND AND PHYSICALLY HANDICAPPED (Aud-Vis)
555 13th St., N.E.
Salem, OR 97301
Phone: (503) 378-3849
Margaret Rader, Act.Dir.
Founded: 1969. **Staff:** Prof 1; Other 10. **Subjects:** General. **Special Collections:** Talking books about Oregon (30 titles; 650 containers); collection of textbooks on cassette (300 titles). **Holdings:** 135,000 volumes, including 10,500 talking book titles; 1981 braille titles; 8832 book titles on cassette tapes; 6000 large print titles. **Subscriptions:** 77 journals and other serials. **Services:** Interlibrary loans; library open to legally blind and physically handicapped in Oregon. **Networks/Consortia:** Member of National Library Service for the Blind & Physically Handicapped (NLS). **Publications:** Newsletter, quarterly - mailed to registered patrons and other regional libraries. **Remarks:** The telephone number for Portland residents is 224-0610. Other in-state residents may call (800)452-0292.

OREGON STATE PARKS DEPARTMENT - COLLIER STATE PARK LOGGING MUSEUM
See: Collier State Park Logging Museum

★10350★
OREGON STATE SCHOOL FOR THE BLIND - MEDIA CENTER (Aud-Vis)
700 Church St., S.E.
Salem, OR 97310
Phone: (503) 378-8025
Delphie Schuberg, Media Coord.
Staff: Prof 1. **Subjects:** Visual and hearing impairment. **Holdings:** 3000 books; 500 bound periodical volumes. **Subscriptions:** 12 journals and other serials and newspapers. **Services:** Center not open to public.

★10351★
OREGON STATE SCHOOL FOR THE DEAF - LIBRARY (Educ)
999 Locust St., N.E.
Salem, OR 97310
Phone: (503) 378-6252
Adoracion A. Alvarez, Curric.Dir.
Staff: Prof 2; Other 1. **Subjects:** Education of deaf child, lipreading, audiology, audio-visual education, vocational education, arts and crafts, science. **Special Collections:** American Annals of the Deaf, 1848 to present; Volta, 1900 to present; Proceedings of Convention of American Instructors of the Deaf, 1870 to present. **Holdings:** 9000 books; 340 bound periodical volumes; 2100 filmstrips; 18 VF drawers of pamphlets. **Subscriptions:** 35 journals and other serials. **Services:** Interlibrary loans; library open to public with restrictions. **Remarks:** This library serves the school students, teachers and staff members, parents of deaf students and students in the Education of the Deaf training programs. **Staff:** Robert Bontrager, Media Spec.; Joyce Virtue, Lib. Teaching Asst.

★10352★
OREGON STATE SECRETARY OF STATE - ARCHIVES AND RECORDS CENTER (Hist)
1005 Broadway, N.E.
Salem, OR 97310
Phone: (503) 378-4240
Subjects: Oregon state and county agency records. **Special Collections:**

Records of the provisional and territorial governments, the governor's office, the Legislative Assembly, the Supreme Court, the Secretary of State's office, the Justice Department, the Treasurer, the Lands Division, the Labor Bureau, the Military Department, and the Highway Division; files from defunct state agencies, such as the Board of Control, the Capitol Reconstruction Commission, the Defense Council, the Finance and Administration Department, the Planning Board, and the World War I Veterans State Aid Commission. **Holdings:** 72,810 cubic feet of records. **Services:** Copying; limited research; center open to public.

★10353★
OREGON STATE SUPREME COURT LIBRARY (Law)
Salem, OR 97310
Phone: (503) 378-6030
Roger Andrus, Law Libn.
Staff: Prof 2; Other 1. **Subjects:** Law. **Holdings:** 145,700 books and bound periodical volumes. **Subscriptions:** 553 journals and other serials. **Services:** Library open to public.

★10354★
OREGON STATE UNIVERSITY - ARCHIVES (Hist)
Ad.Bldg., BO94
Corvallis, OR 97331
Phone: (503) 754-2165
Lauren K. Filson, Archv.
Founded: 1961. **Staff:** Prof 1; Other 4. **Subjects:** University archives. **Holdings:** 200 record groups; 2300 cubic feet of archival material; 3000 reels of microfilm; 120,000 photographs. **Services:** Copying; archives open to public with restrictions.

★10355★
OREGON STATE UNIVERSITY - DEPARTMENT OF CROP SCIENCE - HOP RESEARCH CENTER - WORKING COLLECTION (Sci-Tech)
Corvallis, OR 97331
Phone: (503) 754-2964
Dr. Alfred Hacinold, Res.Sci.
Staff: Prof 1; Other 2. **Subjects:** Hops (humulus lupulus). **Holdings:** 50 books; 50 bound periodical volumes; 200 other cataloged items. **Services:** Collection open to public. **Remarks:** Said to be the only such collection on hops in the U.S.

★10356★
OREGON STATE UNIVERSITY - HATFIELD MARINE SCIENCE CENTER - LIBRARY (Sci-Tech)
Newport, OR 97365
Phone: (503) 867-3011
Marilyn Guin, Libn.
Founded: 1966. **Staff:** Prof 1. **Subjects:** Marine biology and fisheries, mariculture, marine pollution. **Holdings:** 5000 books; 7500 bound periodical volumes; 5000 reprints; microforms. **Subscriptions:** 300 journals and other serials. **Services:** Interlibrary loans; copying; library open to public with restrictions. **Automated Operations:** Computerized cataloging and ILL. **Computerized Information Services:** DIALOG, OCLC. **Remarks:** Contains the holdings of the Oregon State Department of Fish and Wildlife - Newport Laboratory Library.

★10357★
OREGON STATE UNIVERSITY - SCHOOL OF FORESTRY - FRL LIBRARY (Sci-Tech)
Corvallis, OR 97331
Phone: (503) 753-9166
Mary B. Scroggins, Libn.
Founded: 1947. **Staff:** Prof 1. **Subjects:** Forest products, forest management, forest science and engineering, resource recreation. **Holdings:** 4500 books; 550 bound periodical volumes; 600 dissertations; 2 VF drawers of patents; 75 VF drawers of pamphlets. **Subscriptions:** 150 journals and other serials. **Services:** Copying; library open to public for reference use only. **Publications:** Research Notes, Research Bulletins and Research Papers - all available on request; special publications.

★10358★
OREGON STATE UNIVERSITY - WATER RESOURCES RESEARCH INSTITUTE - LIBRARY
Covell Hall 115
Corvallis, OR 97331
Defunct. Holdings absorbed by Oregon State University - William Jasper Kerr Library.

★10359★
OREGON STATE UNIVERSITY - WILLIAM JASPER KERR LIBRARY (Agri; Sci-Tech)
Corvallis, OR 97331
Phone: (503) 754-3411
Melvin R. George, Dir. Of Libs.
Founded: 1887. **Staff:** Prof 29; Other 46. **Subjects:** Agriculture, forestry, engineering, oceanography, pharmacy, veterinary medicine. **Holdings:**

956,813 books and bound periodical volumes; 171,765 maps; 57,955 photographs, pictures and prints; 337,569 government documents (U.S. and U.N.); 23,573 reels of microfilm; 982,010 microforms. **Subscriptions:** 17,004 journals and other serials; 300 newspapers. **Services:** Interlibrary loans; copying; library open to public with restrictions. **Automated Operations:** Computerized cataloging and acquisitions. **Computerized Information Services:** DIALOG, BRS, SDC, OCLC. **Publications:** Bibliography of forestry theses, annual - distributed by OSU Press. **Special Catalogs:** Oregon Union List of Serials. **Remarks:** Includes the holdings of the former Oregon State University - Water Resources Research Institute - Library. **Staff:** Marjorie A. Reeves, Assoc.Dir., Tech.Serv.; Robert Lawrence, Sci.-Tech.Ref.Libn.; Patricia Brandt, Soc.Sci./Hum. & Bus.; Michael Kinch, Agriculture-Forestry; Doris Tilles, ILL.

★10360★
OREGON STATE WATER RESOURCES DEPARTMENT - LIBRARY & INFORMATION CENTER (Env-Cons)
555 13th St., N.E.   Phone: (503) 378-3739
Salem, OR 97310   Darnell Learn, Adm., Policy & Plan.
Founded: 1956. **Subjects:** Water, statistics, dams and reservoirs, water rights, ground water. **Holdings:** 6000 books. **Services:** Interlibrary loans; library open to public. **Publications:** Water Availability reports; water feature maps.

★10361★
OREGONIAN LIBRARY (Publ)
1320 S.W. Broadway   Phone: (503) 221-8131
Portland, OR 97201   Doris N. Smith, Hd.Libn.
Staff: Prof 5; Other 7. **Subjects:** Newspaper reference topics. **Holdings:** News clips from the Oregonian and Oregon Journal; news photographs; microfilm and microfiche of the Oregonian. **Services:** Library not open to public. **Staff:** Sandra Macomber, Asst.Libn.

ORGAN PIPE CACTUS NATL. MONUMENT
See: U.S. Natl. Park Service

★10362★
ORGANIZATION OF AMERICAN STATES - COLUMBUS MEMORIAL LIBRARY (Area-Ethnic)
17th St. & Constitution Ave., N.W.   Phone: (202) 789-6040
Washington, DC 20006   Thomas L. Welch, Dir.
Founded: 1890. **Staff:** Prof 12; Other 13. **Subjects:** Inter-American system, member states, laws, regional development. **Special Collections:** OAS offical documents and technical and information publications; publications of the specialized agencies; documents and publications of other international organizations; official gazettes of member states. **Holdings:** 325,000 books; 133,000 bound periodical volumes; 220,000 documents and publications of OAS, its predecessors and specialized agencies; 200,000 microforms. **Subscriptions:** 3000 journals and other serials; 61 newspapers. **Subscriptions:** Interlibrary loans; copying; library open to public for reference use only. **Automated Operations:** Computerized cataloging and ILL. **Computerized Information Services:** DIALOG; internal database. **Networks/Consortia:** Member of CAPCON. **Publications:** List of Recent Acquisitions; CML Documentation and Information Services. **Special Indexes:** Index to OAS documents; index to Latin American periodical literature. **Also Known As:** OAS. **Staff:** Nora Fernandez, Hd., Cat.; Myriam Figueras, Hd., Reader Serv.; Maria Antonia Roldan, Archv.

★10363★
ORGANIZATION FOR ECONOMIC COOPERATION AND DEVELOPMENT - PUBLICATIONS AND INFORMATION CENTER (Soc Sci)
1750 Pennsylvania Ave., N.W, Suite 1207   Phone: (202) 724-1857
Washington, DC 20006-4582   Hendrikus D. DeVroom, Hd.
Staff: Prof 3; Other 7. **Subjects:** International economic development, comparative statistics, agriculture, energy, educational research, environment, finance, transportation. **Holdings:** 1000 books; 500 bound periodical volumes. **Subscriptions:** 20 journals and other serials. **Services:** Center open to public. **Publications:** Recent OECD Publications, January, March, July and October.

★10364★
ORGANIZATION RESOURCES COUNSELORS, INC. - INFORMATION CENTER (Soc Sci)
1211 Ave. of the Americas   Phone: (212) 719-3400
New York, NY 10036   Mary J. DuVal, Libn.
Founded: 1953. **Staff:** Prof 1; Other 1. **Subjects:** Employee relations, collective bargaining, labor law, labor statistics, human relations in industry, labor economics, wages and salaries, management. **Holdings:** 2000 books; 100 VF drawers. **Subscriptions:** 200 journals and other serials. **Services:**

Interlibrary loans; center not open to public.

★10365★
ORGANON, INC. - MEDICAL LIBRARY (Med)
375 Mt. Pleasant Ave.   Phone: (201) 325-4614
West Orange, NJ 07052   Jane E. Farrands, Libn.
Staff: Prof 1. **Subjects:** Medicine. **Holdings:** Figures not available.

ORI, INC., INFORMATION SYSTEMS DIVISION - ERIC PROCESSING AND REFERENCE FACILITY
See: ERIC Processing and Reference Facility

ORIENTAL INSTITUTE
See: University of Chicago

★10366★
ORLANDO MUNICIPAL REFERENCE LIBRARY (Soc Sci)
City Hall, 400 S. Orange Ave.   Phone: (305) 849-2249
Orlando, FL 32801   Nancy Ahlin, Libn.
Founded: 1973. **Staff:** Prof 1; Other 1. **Subjects:** City of Orlando, public administration, other local governments. **Special Collections:** City publications (450 volumes). **Holdings:** 1500 documents; 11 VF drawers; Orlando reports and studies. **Subscriptions:** 63 journals and other serials. **Services:** Interlibrary loans; copying; library open to public for reference use only. **Computerized Information Services:** Local Government Information Network (LOGIN). Performs searches on cost recovery basis.

★10367★
ORLANDO REGIONAL MEDICAL CENTER - MEDICAL LIBRARY (Med)
1414 S. Kuhl Ave.   Phone: (305) 855-8771
Orlando, FL 32806   Mary C. Garmany, Dir.
Staff: Prof 2; Other 1. **Subjects:** Medicine. **Holdings:** 2500 books; 15,000 bound periodical volumes. **Subscriptions:** 225 journals and other serials. **Services:** Interlibrary loans; copying; SDI; library open to public with permission from Office of Risk Management. **Computerized Information Services:** MEDLARS. **Staff:** Diane Balodis, Assoc.Libn.

★10368★
ORLANDO SENTINEL NEWSPAPER - LIBRARY (Publ)
633 N. Orange Ave.
Box 2833   Phone: (305) 420-5510
Orlando, FL 32802   Judy L. Grimsley, Info.Rsrcs.Supv.
Staff: Prof 6; Other 1. **Subjects:** News and biographical information. **Holdings:** 600 books and bound periodical volumes; 2012 reels of microfilm of newspapers, 1911 to present; clippings; photographs; pamphlets. **Subscriptions:** 15 journals and other serials. **Services:** Interlibrary loans; copying; library open to journalists by special permission. **Staff:** Tom Banks, Dp.Chf.Libn.; Jeannine Delancett, Res.Libn.; Clark McClain, News Libn.; Susan Vitek, News Libn.

ORLEANS-NIAGARA EDUCATIONAL COMMUNICATIONS CENTER
See: BOCES - Orleans-Niagara Educational Communications Center

★10369★
OROVILLE HOSPITAL AND MEDICAL CENTER - EDWARD P. GODDARD, M.D., MEMORIAL LIBRARY (Med)
2767 Olive Hwy.   Phone: (916) 533-8500
Oroville, CA 95965   Gertrude N. Bartley, Libn.
Staff: Prof 1. **Subjects:** Medicine. **Holdings:** 269 books; 110 bound periodical volumes. **Subscriptions:** 26 journals and other serials. **Services:** Interlibrary loans; library not open to public. **Networks/Consortia:** Member of Pacific Southwest Regional Medical Library Service (PSRMLS). **Formerly:** Medical Center Hospital of Oroville.

★10370★
ORPHAN VOYAGE - KAMMANDALE LIBRARY (Hist)
57 N. Dale   Phone: (612) 224-5160
St. Paul, MN 55102   Jeanette G. Kamman, Dir.
Founded: 1975. **Staff:** Prof 4. **Subjects:** Local history, genealogy, graphology. **Special Collections:** Local school yearbooks (500); books on books; authors; nationalities (countries); cartoon scrapbooks (450). **Holdings:** 25,000 books; 5000 bound periodical volumes; pamphlets; maps; obituaries; newspaper clippings. **Services:** Copying; library open to public by appointment. **Staff:** Clark Bradley Hansen, Libn., Bookdealer; Ruth Kudlaty, Libn.; Genevieve Thompson, Soc. Worker.

★10371★

ORPHAN VOYAGE - MUSEUM OF ORPHANHOOD - LIBRARY (Hist; Soc Sci)
2141 Road 2300
Cedaredge, CO 81413

Phone: (303) 856-3937
Jean Paton

Staff: 1. **Subjects:** Orphans as explorers and discoverers, philosophers and religious, fantasy writers, scholars and scientists, painters and poets; fiction by orphans; biographies of orphans in public affairs. **Special Collections:** Americana on orphans; Heritage Press Collection of orphan writers; legislative hearings about adoption. **Holdings:** 850 books; unbound reports; manuscripts; clippings; magnetic tapes; paperbound books. **Subscriptions:** 30 newsletters. **Services:** Copying (limited); library open to public by appointment for reference use. **Publications:** The Adoption Series.

★10372★

ORRICK, HERRINGTON, ROWLEY & SUTCLIFFE - LIBRARY (Law)
600 Montgomery St.
San Francisco, CA 94111

Phone: (415) 392-1122
Cynthia Papermaster, Law Libn.

Staff: Prof 2; Other 2. **Subjects:** Law. **Holdings:** 35,000 volumes; 6 drawers of cassettes; microfiche. **Subscriptions:** 194 journals and other serials; 8 newspapers. **Services:** Interlibrary loans; library open by arrangement to members of the Special Libraries Association and the American Association of Law Libraries. **Computerized Information Services:** LEXIS, DIALOG.

★10373★

ORTHO PHARMACEUTICAL (Canada), LTD. - LIBRARY (Med)
19 Green Belt Dr.
Don Mills, ON, Canada M3C 1L9

Phone: (416) 449-9444
Marta Bodnar, Libn.

Founded: 1967. **Staff:** 2. **Subjects:** Contraception, family planning, diagnostic agents, immunohematology, business management. **Holdings:** 1565 books; 580 bound periodical volumes; microfiche. **Subscriptions:** 272 journals and other serials. **Services:** Interlibrary loans; library open to public by appointment. **Computerized Information Services:** MEDLINE, TOXLINE, DIALOG. **Publications:** Book List, semiannual; Journal Distribution List, semiannual.

★10374★

ORTHO PHARMACEUTICAL CORPORATION - HARTMAN LIBRARY (Med)
U.S. Hwy. 202
Raritan, NJ 08869

Phone: (201) 524-2240
June Bente, Mgr.

Founded: 1944. **Staff:** Prof 2; Other 2. **Subjects:** Medicine, pharmacy, endocrinology, biological sciences, chemistry. **Holdings:** 5000 books; 15,000 bound periodical volumes. **Subscriptions:** 600 journals and other serials. **Services:** Interlibrary loans; library open to public by appointment. **Computerized Information Services:** BRS, DIALOG, SDC, NTIS, MEDLINE. **Networks/Consortia:** Member of Medical Resources Consortium of Central New Jersey (MEDCORE). **Staff:** Jean Shepley, Supv., Tech.Serv.

★10375★

ORTHODOX CHURCH IN AMERICA - DEPARTMENT OF HISTORY AND ARCHIVES (Rel-Theol)
Rte. 25A, Box 675
Syosset, NY 11791

Phone: (516) 922-0550
Rev. Dennis R. Rhodes, Archv.

Staff: Prof 2. **Subjects:** Orthodox Church history - American, Carpatho-Russian, Greek; immigration history - Russian, Syrian, Albanian. **Holdings:** 270 linear feet of archival materials; 240 linear feet of periodicals and other print media; parish and individual collections. **Services:** Copying; archives open to public with restrictions. **Special Catalogs:** Comprehensive guides and catalogs are under preparation. **Staff:** Peg Poeschl, Asst.

★10376★

ORTHOPAEDIC AND ARTHRITIC HOSPITAL - LIBRARY (Med)
43 Wellesley St., E.
Toronto, ON, Canada M4Y 1H1

Phone: (416) 967-8545
Sheila M. Lethbridge, Libn.

Staff: Prof 2. **Subjects:** Orthopedics, arthritis, physical and occupational therapy. **Holdings:** 1000 books; 550 bound periodical volumes. **Subscriptions:** 80 journals and other serials. **Services:** Interlibrary loans; library not open to public.

★10377★

ORTHOPAEDIC HOSPITAL - RUBEL MEMORIAL LIBRARY (Med)
2400 S. Flower St.
Box 60132, Terminal Annex
Los Angeles, CA 90060

Phone: (213) 742-1530
Veena N. Vyas, Dir., Med.Lib.

Staff: Prof 1; Other 1. **Subjects:** Orthopedics. **Holdings:** 3000 books; 3260 bound periodical volumes; 4 VF drawers of staff papers. **Subscriptions:** 285 journals and other serials. **Services:** Interlibrary loans; copying; library open to public but special permission is needed to borrow books. **Computerized Information Services:** DIALOG, SDC, MEDLINE. **Networks/Consortia:** Member of Pacific Southwest Regional Medical Library Service (PSRMLS).

Publications: New Book List, quarterly; Serials List, annual.

★10378★

ORTHOPEDIC FOUNDATION FOR ANIMALS - OFA HIP DYSPLASIA REGISTRY (Med)
Middlebush Farms, Hwy. 63 S.
Columbia, MO 65101

Phone: (314) 442-0418
Dr. Al Corley, Project Dir.

Staff: 5. **Subjects:** Veterinary medicine. **Holdings:** 120,000 radiographs - Hip Registry X-Ray, evaluated for canine hip dysplasia in purebred dogs. **Remarks:** The Hip Dysplasia Registry is a contract project sponsored by the Orthopedic Foundation for Animals at the University of Missouri - College of Veterinary Medicine.

ORTON MEMORIAL LIBRARY OF GEOLOGY
See: Ohio State University

★10379★

OSAWATOMIE STATE HOSPITAL - RAPAPORT PROFESSIONAL LIBRARY - MENTAL HEALTH LIBRARY (Med)

Osawatomie, KS 66064

Phone: (913) 755-3151
Helen Porter, Libn.

Founded: 1949. **Staff:** Prof 1; Other 1. **Subjects:** Psychiatry, psychology, social sciences, medicine, nursing, special education. **Holdings:** 6069 books; 2652 bound periodical volumes; 426 audiotapes; 88 videotapes; 30 VF drawers of dissertations, reprints, pamphlets, documents. **Subscriptions:** 93 journals and other serials. **Services:** Interlibrary loans; copying; library open to public with permission of librarian. **Networks/Consortia:** Member of Midcontinental Regional Medical Library Program.

★10380★

OSBORN LABORATORIES OF MARINE SCIENCES - NEW YORK AQUARIUM LIBRARY (Sci-Tech)
Boardwalk & W. 8th St.
Brooklyn, NY 11224

Phone: (718) 266-8500
G.D. Ruggieri, Ph.D., Dir.

Founded: 1902. **Subjects:** Ichthyology, aquariology, diseases of fish, invertebrates, amphibians and reptiles, marine biochemistry, invertebrate zoology, physiology of fish, marine mammalogy. **Special Collections:** Diseases of aquatic organisms; complete card file of animals of Bay of Naples. **Holdings:** 3000 books; 100 bound periodical volumes; 4000 reprints; 100 theses on aquatic subjects; photographs, films and slides on aquatic organisms. **Services:** Library open to public by special permission. **Also Known As:** New York Zoological Society - New York Aquarium Library.

OSBORN LIBRARY OF VERTEBRATE PALEONTOLOGY
See: American Museum of Natural History

OSBORN (Stanley H.) MEDICAL LIBRARY
See: Connecticut State Department of Health Services - Stanley H. Osborn Medical Library

OSBORNE COLLECTION OF EARLY CHILDREN'S BOOKS
See: Toronto Public Library

OSBORNE LIBRARY
See: Connecticut Agricultural Experiment Station

OSHA
See: U.S. Dept. of Labor - OSHA

O'SHAUGHNESSY LIBRARY
See: College of St. Thomas

★10381★

OSHKOSH PUBLIC MUSEUM - LIBRARY & ARCHIVES (Hist; Sci-Tech)
1331 Algoma Blvd.
Oshkosh, WI 54901

Phone: (414) 424-0452
Kitty A. Hobson, Archv.

Founded: 1924. **Staff:** Prof 1. **Subjects:** Local and state history, anthropology and archeology, arts and crafts, botany and zoology. **Special Collections:** River Steamboat History (3 VF drawers of photographs, clippings and narratives); Lumbering and Logging (3 VF drawers of photographs, clippings and narratives); Inland Lakes Yachting Association minutes, 1899 to present. **Holdings:** 8000 clippings and manuscripts; 200 bound periodical volumes; 68 VF drawers of historical photographs and pamphlets; 400 maps. **Subscriptions:** 25 journals and other serials. **Services:** Interlibrary loans; copying; library open to public for reference use only.

OSLER LIBRARY
See: Mc Gill University

★10382★

OSSINING HISTORICAL SOCIETY MUSEUM - LIBRARY (Hist)
196 Croton Ave.   Phone: (914) 941-0001
Ossining, NY 10562   John B. Drittler, Libn.
Founded: 1931. **Staff:** Prof 2; Other 3. **Subjects:** Local history and genealogy. **Special Collections:** Goodrich Memorial Law Library. **Holdings:** 1100 books; 122 bound periodical volumes; 390 volumes of newspapers; 10 VF drawers of manuscripts, pamphlets, clippings, documents and reports; 300 maps; 1000 photographs. **Services:** Interlibrary loans; library open to public.

OTIS AIR FORCE BASE (MA)
See: U.S. Coast Guard/Air Station

OTIS ART INSTITUTE
See: Parsons School of Design

★10383★

OTTAWA CITIZEN - LIBRARY (Publ)
1101 Baxter Rd.
Box 5020   Phone: (613) 829-9100
Ottawa, ON, Canada K2C 3M4   Steven Proulx, Chf.Libn.
Founded: 1940. **Staff:** Prof 4; Other 1. **Subjects:** Biography - local, national, international; newspaper reference topics. **Holdings:** 400 volumes; 20,000 subject clipping files; 15,000 biographical clipping files. **Subscriptions:** 10 journals and other serials; 10 newspapers. **Services:** Library open to public with restrictions. **Computerized Information Services:** Info Globe, NEWSTEX. **Publications:** Canadian Press (newsletter). **Staff:** Ronald R. Tysick, Photo Libn.; Charlene Rubery, Indexer.

★10384★

OTTAWA CIVIC HOSPITAL - DR. GEORGE S. WILLIAMSON HEALTH SCIENCES LIBRARY (Med)
1053 Carling Ave.   Phone: (613) 725-4450
Ottawa, ON, Canada K1Y 4E9   Mabel C. Brown, Dir., Lib.Serv.
Founded: 1957. **Staff:** Prof 2; Other 6. **Subjects:** Medicine, nursing and allied health sciences. **Holdings:** 3000 books; 5000 bound periodical volumes. **Subscriptions:** 300 journals and other serials. **Services:** Interlibrary loans; copying; SDI; bibliographies; Current Awareness Service; library open to public with restrictions. **Automated Operations:** Computerized acquisitions. **Computerized Information Services:** Info Globe, CAN/OLE, DIALOG, MEDLINE. **Networks/Consortia:** O.H.A. Region 9 Hospital Libraries Group. **Publications:** Acquisition lists, irregular.

★10385★

OTTAWA GENERAL HOSPITAL - MEDICAL LIBRARY (Med)
501 Smyth Rd.   Phone: (613) 737-8530
Ottawa, ON, Canada K1H 8L6   Diane R. Couture, Supv.
Founded: 1936. **Staff:** Prof 1; Other 1. **Subjects:** Medicine. **Holdings:** 994 books; 3000 bound periodical volumes. **Subscriptions:** 245 journals and other serials. **Services:** Interlibrary loans; library not open to public. **Also Known As:** Hopital General d'Ottawa.

★10386★

OTTAWA INSTITUTE - IRENE HOLM MEMORIAL LIBRARY (Hist)
1465 Osborn Dr.   Phone: (614) 486-5028
Columbus, OH 43221   Ms. Bobbi Wilson, Libn.
Founded: 1976. **Staff:** Prof 1; Other 1. **Subjects:** Historic radio broadcasts, archives of Ottawa Institute. **Special Collections:** Edwardian music (200 cassette tapes); Arthur Lindner Memorial Collection of historic radio broadcasts (3000 cassette tapes). **Holdings:** 500 books; 4000 audio cassettes; 30 VF drawers of Institute archives. **Subscriptions:** 11 journals and other serials. **Services:** Interlibrary loans; copying (limited); library open to public with restrictions. **Publications:** Research reports, irregular - by request. **Staff:** Scott-Eric Lindner, Cat.

★10387★

OTTAWA PUBLIC LIBRARY - OTTAWA ROOM (Hist)
120 Metcalfe St.
Ottawa, ON, Canada K1P 5M2   Jean de Temple, Asst.Dir.
Subjects: Ottawa - history, municipal affairs, authors. **Holdings:** 7000 books, (fiction and nonfiction), documents, maps, vertical files, pamphlet boxes, annual reports, archival records, periodicals, city directories and telephone directories.

★10388★

OTTER TAIL COUNTY HISTORICAL SOCIETY - LIBRARY (Hist)
1110 Lincoln Ave., W.   Phone: (218) 736-6038
Fergus Falls, MN 56537   Pamela A. Brunfelt, Libn./Res.
Staff: Prof 1; Other 2. **Subjects:** Local history. **Special Collections:** County newspapers, 1871 to present; War of the Rebellion - Official Records of the Union and Confederate Armies. **Holdings:** 250 books; 100 bound periodical volumes; manuscripts; business records; oral histories; records and newspapers on microfilm; slides; dissertations; maps; photographs. **Subscriptions:** 18 journals and other serials; 7 newspapers. **Services:** Copying; library open to public with restrictions. **Networks/Consortia:** Member of Northern Lights Library Network.

★10389★

OTTER TAIL POWER COMPANY - LIBRARY (Energy)
215 S. Cascade   Phone: (218) 736-5411
Fergus Falls, MN 56537   Janet Johnson, Lib.Asst.
Staff: 1. **Subjects:** Business management, engineering. **Holdings:** 2504 books; 250 Electric Power Research reports; 45 films. **Subscriptions:** 145 journals and other serials; 20 newspapers. **Services:** Copying; library open to public with restrictions. **Publications:** Library Notes, quarterly. **Special Catalogs:** Film catalog, annual.

OTZER HASFORIM OF TELSHE YESHIVA
See: Telshe Yeshiva

★10390★

OUACHITA BAPTIST UNIVERSITY - RILEY LIBRARY (Mus; Hist)
                                           Phone: (501) 246-4531
Arkadelphia, AR 71923   Ray Granade, Libn.
Founded: 1886. **Staff:** Prof 2; Other 5. **Subjects:** Liberal arts, music. **Special Collections:** Francis McBeth Collection (original manuscripts of music compositions, primarily for band and orchestra); John L. McClellan Papers, 1942-1978; Baptis history collection; Arkansas history; university archives. **Holdings:** 115,181 books; 16,333 bound periodical volumes; 226,323 microforms including ERIC; 7557 audiovisual materials including 2990 music scores, 3161 recordings, 904 tapes; 60,571 documents. **Subscriptions:** 684 journals and other serials; 8 newspapers. **Services:** Interlibrary loans; copying; library open to public by request. **Automated Operations:** Computerized cataloging and ILL. **Computerized Information Services:** OCLC. **Networks/Consortia:** Member of AMIGOS Bibliographic Council, Inc. **Staff:** Jean Raybon, Hd., Tech.Proc.; Katherine Sumerlin, Per.Libn.; Marcella Rauch, Circ.Libn.; Kim Patterson, AV Supv.; Janice Savage, Spec.Coll.

★10391★

OUR LADY OF THE LAKE REGIONAL MEDICAL CENTER - SCHOOL OF NURSING LIBRARY (Med)
5000 Hennessy Blvd.   Phone: (504) 769-3100
Baton Rouge, LA 70809   Dorothy D. Romero, Libn.
Founded: 1923. **Staff:** Prof 1. **Subjects:** Nursing and related subjects. **Holdings:** 2366 volumes. **Subscriptions:** 47 journals and other serials. **Services:** Interlibrary loans; library not open to public. **Networks/Consortia:** Member of Community Medical Library Consortium.

★10392★

OUR LADY OF THE LAKE UNIVERSITY - OLD SPANISH MISSIONS HISTORICAL RESEARCH LIBRARY (Hist)
411 S.W. 24th St.   Phone: (512) 434-6711
San Antonio, TX 78285   Fr. Benedict Leutenegger, Archv.
Founded: 1971. **Staff:** Prof 2. **Subjects:** Franciscan missions in Texas, 1682-1834; Spanish shipwrecks off the coast of Texas; Texas Colonial history; Spanish Colonial period in Texas; missions in northern Mexico. **Special Collections:** Microfilm from archives in Mexico, Spain and other European countries (100 reels). **Holdings:** 105 books; 50 maps; 20 photographs; 2000 slides. **Services:** Copying; library open to public with proper identification. **Publications:** Documentary series, numbers 1-5. **Remarks:** The library is maintained by the Franciscan Order. It is a part of the Institute for Intercultural Studies and Research at Our Lady of the Lake University. **Staff:** Sr. Maria Carolina Flores, C.D.P., Asst.Archv.

★10393★

OUR LADY OF THE LAKE UNIVERSITY - WORDEN SCHOOL OF SOCIAL SERVICE - LIBRARY (Soc Sci)
411 S.W. 24th St.   Phone: (512) 434-6711
San Antonio, TX 78285   Margaret Pittman Munke, Libn.
Founded: 1942. **Staff:** Prof 1. **Subjects:** Social work. **Holdings:** 8125 books; 14,353 bound periodical volumes; 325 case records and 259 theses. **Subscriptions:** 98 journals and other serials. **Services:** Interlibrary loans; copying; library open to public.

★10394★

OUR LADY OF LIGHT LIBRARY (Rel-Theol)*
1500 Chapala   Phone: (805) 962-9708
Santa Barbara, CA 93101   Lucile Chinnici, Pres.
Founded: 1949. **Staff:** Prof 1. **Subjects:** Spiritual reading, biography, fiction.
Holdings: 5500 books. **Subscriptions:** 10 journals and other serials.
Services: Library open to public. **Staff:** Sallie May, Cat.Supv.

★10395★

OUR LADY OF LOURDES MEDICAL CENTER - MEDICAL LIBRARY (Med)
1600 Haddon Ave.   Phone: (609) 757-3548
Camden, NJ 08103   Fred Kafes, Dir.
Staff: Prof 1. **Subjects:** Medicine, nursing, allied health sciences, hospital administration. **Holdings:** 1168 books; 1004 textbooks; 1800 periodical volumes; 164 index volumes; 779 audio cassettes; 33 slide/sound sets. **Subscriptions:** 240 journals and other serials. **Services:** Interlibrary loans; copying; SDI; library open to public for reference use only. **Automated Operations:** Computerized cataloging and serials. **Computerized Information Services:** Access to BRS. **Networks/Consortia:** Member of Southwest New Jersey Consortium for Health Information Services.

★10396★

OUR LADY OF LOURDES MEDICAL CENTER - SCHOOL OF NURSING - LIBRARY (Med)
1565 Vesper Blvd.   Phone: (609) 757-3722
Camden, NJ 08103   Eleanor M. Kelly, Libn.
Founded: 1961. **Staff:** Prof 1. **Subjects:** Medicine, nursing and related subjects. **Holdings:** 2800 books and bound periodical volumes; 43 AV programs; 4 VF drawers of clippings, reports, pamphlets. **Subscriptions:** 53 journals and other serials. **Services:** Interlibrary loans; copying; library use restricted to nursing students. **Automated Operations:** Computerized cataloging. **Networks/Consortia:** Member of Southwest New Jersey Consortium for Health Information Services.

★10397★

OUR LADY OF LOURDES REGIONAL MEDICAL & EDUCATION CENTER - LEARNING RESOURCE CENTER (Med)†
611 St. Landry St.
Box 4027C   Phone: (318) 231-2141
Lafayette, LA 70502   Mary Lagroue, Med.Libn.
Staff: Prof 1; Other 1. **Subjects:** Medicine, nursing, pastoral care. **Holdings:** 2500 books; unbound periodicals. **Subscriptions:** 128 journals and other serials. **Services:** Interlibrary loans; copying; center open to public with restrictions. **Networks/Consortia:** Member of TALON.

★10398★

OUR LADY OF PEACE HOSPITAL - MEDICAL LIBRARY (Med)
2020 Newburg Rd.   Phone: (502) 451-3330
Louisville, KY 40232   Sr. Margaret Siena, S.C.N., Dir.
Founded: 1951. **Staff:** Prof 2. **Subjects:** Psychiatry - child, community, forensic; geriatrics; drug addiction; family therapy. **Holdings:** 1605 books; 1186 bound periodical volumes; 239 cassettes (psychiatric series); 15 VF drawers of pamphlets, clippings, and archives. **Subscriptions:** 128 journals and other serials. **Services:** Interlibrary loans; copying; library open to public with registration. **Networks/Consortia:** Member of Kentucky Health Sciences Library Consortium.

★10399★

OUR LADY QUEEN OF MARTYRS - ST. LUCIAN LIBRARY (Rel-Theol)
32460 S. Pierce   Phone: (313) 644-8620
Birmingham, MI 48009   Ruth E. Brady, Hd.Libn.
Founded: 1957. **Staff:** Prof 3; Other 7. **Subjects:** Religion, philosophy, biography, geography, history, travel. **Holdings:** 2500 books. **Services:** Library open to church congregation.

★10400★

OUR LADY OF SORROWS BASILICA - ARCHIVES (Rel-Theol; Hist)
3121 W. Jackson Blvd.   Phone: (312) 638-5800
Chicago, IL 60612   Rev. Conrad M. Borntrager, O.S.M., Archv.
Staff: 1. **Subjects:** Parish archives. **Holdings:** 66 bound periodical volumes; 60 linear feet of archives; 1 filing drawer of photographs; 56 blueprints. **Services:** Archives open to public with restrictions.

★10401★

OUR LADY OF VICTORY HOSPITAL - HOSPITAL LIBRARY (Med)
55 Melroy at Ridge Rd.   Phone: (716) 825-8000
Lackawanna, NY 14218   Ann Hassett, Lib.Ck.
Founded: 1960. **Staff:** 1. **Subjects:** Medicine, surgery, allied health sciences. **Holdings:** 622 books. **Subscriptions:** 48 journals and other serials. **Services:**

Interlibrary loans; library not open to public.

★10402★

OUR LADY OF THE WAY HOSPITAL - MEDICAL LIBRARY (Med)
Box 910   Phone: (606) 285-5181
Martin, KY 41649   Mary Hogans, Act.Libn.
Subjects: Medicine, nursing. **Holdings:** 100 books. **Subscriptions:** 25 journals and other serials. **Services:** Interlibrary loans; library not open to public. **Automated Operations:** Computerized cataloging. **Networks/Consortia:** Member of Eastern Kentucky Health Science Information Network (EKHSIN).

★10403★

OUR REDEEMERS LUTHERAN CHURCH - LIBRARY (Rel-Theol)
Tenth St., S. & Oakwood Ave.   Phone: (612) 843-3151
Benson, MN 56215   Marlene Skold, Libn.
Founded: 1958. **Staff:** 1. **Subjects:** Theology, devotional material. **Holdings:** 1500 books; pamphlets and filmstrips. **Services:** Library open to public with restrictions.

★10404★

OUR SAVIOR'S LUTHERAN CHURCH - LIBRARY (Rel-Theol)
3022 W. Wisconsin Ave.   Phone: (414) 342-5252
Milwaukee, WI 53208   Kenneth E. Nordby, Lay Asst.
Founded: 1955. **Staff:** 1. **Subjects:** Religion. **Special Collections:** Cassette tapes recorded by staff members and members of congregation including concerts, sermons and lectures. **Holdings:** 6000 books; 2000 pictures; 400 filmstrips; 200 phonograph records. **Subscriptions:** 35 journals and other serials. **Services:** Library open to public with restrictions.

★10405★

OUTAGAMIE COUNTY LAW LIBRARY (Law)
410 S. Walnut St.   Phone: (414) 735-5347
Appleton, WI 54911   Diane M. Ebert, Law Ck.
Staff: 1. **Subjects:** Law. **Holdings:** 10,000 volumes. **Services:** Library open to public.

★10406★

OUTBOARD MARINE CORPORATION - RESEARCH CENTER LIBRARY (Sci-Tech)†
4109 N. 27th
Box 663   Phone: (414) 447-5400
Milwaukee, WI 53201   Cynthia Meinhardt, Libn.
Staff: 1. **Subjects:** Mechanical and electrical engineering, mechanics, internal combustion engines, mathematics, metallurgy. **Holdings:** 1900 books and bound periodical volumes; 6000 technical reports; 2000 vendors' catalogs; 200 reels of microfilm; 3000 corporation reports; 9000 technical society papers. **Subscriptions:** 60 journals and other serials. **Services:** Interlibrary loans; copying; library open to other technical organizations by special arrangement. **Automated Operations:** Computerized cataloging. **Computerized Information Services:** Internal database. **Networks/Consortia:** Member of Library Council of Metropolitan Milwaukee, Inc. (LCOMM). **Publications:** Library Information Bulletin, monthly.

OUTDOOR EDUCATION RESOURCE LIBRARY
See: National Outdoor Leadership School

★10407★

OUTLOOK - OUTLOOK ACCESS CENTER (Energy)*
105 Wolpers Rd.   Phone: (312) 481-6168
Park Forest, IL 60466   Elizabeth Hagens, Dir.
Founded: 1976. **Staff:** Prof 2; Other 3. **Subjects:** Solar and alternative energy, appropriate technology, community and international development, environmental planning. **Holdings:** 3000 books; 1000 bound periodical volumes; 4000 other cataloged items. **Subscriptions:** 300 journals and other serials; 5 newspapers. **Publications:** Newsletter, monthly.

★10408★

OVER (W.H.) MUSEUM - LIBRARY (Hist; Sci-Tech)
University of South Dakota   Phone: (605) 677-5228
Vermillion, SD 57069   Julia R. Vodicka, Musm.Dir.
Staff: Prof 2. **Subjects:** Archeology, anthropology, natural history, history, museology, decorative arts, photography. **Special Collections:** Papers of William H. Over; Morrow Photographic Collection (600 items). **Holdings:** 1200 books; 36 bound periodical volumes; 22 museum notebooks of clippings; 50 manuscripts. **Subscriptions:** 15 journals and other serials. **Services:** Copying; library open to public for reference use only. **Special Indexes:** Morrow Photograph Collection. **Remarks:** Maintained by South Dakota State Department of Education and Cultural Affairs. **Staff:** Rebecca

Pipe, Registrar.

★10409★
OVERBROOK SCHOOL FOR THE BLIND - LIBRARY (Aud-Vis)
64th St. & Malvern Ave.   Phone: (215) 877-0313
Philadelphia, PA 19151   Edith L. Willoughby, Libn.
Founded: 1832. **Staff:** Prof 1. **Subjects:** Standard, large print and braille books for kindergarten through high school; general library of braille, talking book, tape and print titles for primary, elementary and high school; library of print for faculty members. **Special Collections:** Historical material on education of the blind and other aspects of blindness; material on deafness. **Holdings:** 12,500 braille books; 5000 printed books; 600 large print books; 3000 talking books, tapes and cassettes. **Subscriptions:** 75 journals and other serials in print and braille. **Services:** Library open to public for reference use only by request.

★10410★
OVERLOOK HOSPITAL - HEALTH SCIENCES LIBRARY (Med)
193 Morris Ave.   Phone: (201) 522-2119
Summit, NJ 07901   Kathleen A. Moeller, Dir., Lib.Serv.
Founded: 1946. **Staff:** Prof 1; Other 3. **Subjects:** Medicine, surgery, nursing, radiology, emergency medicine, psychiatry, pediatrics, orthopedics. **Special Collections:** Consumer Health Information Collection (850 books; 25 journals; free pamphlets). **Holdings:** 6000 books; 12,000 bound periodical volumes; 2000 subject files for LATCH Program; 245 AV programs. **Subscriptions:** 327 journals and other serials. **Services:** Interlibrary loans; copying. **Computerized Information Services:** MEDLARS, DIALOG, BRS. **Networks/Consortia:** Member of Cosmopolitan Biomedical Library Consortium (CBLC); Health Sciences Libraries of New Jersey.

★10411★
OVERSEAS DEVELOPMENT COUNCIL - LIBRARY (Soc Sci)
1717 Massachusetts Ave., N.W.   Phone: (202) 234-8701
Washington, DC 20036   James E. Boyle, Libn.
Staff: Prof 1. **Subjects:** Development policies, developing countries, international trade and finance, economic relations, world food problems and social indicators. **Holdings:** 1000 books. **Subscriptions:** 50 journals and other serials; 10 newspapers. **Services:** Interlibrary loans; copying. **Publications:** ODC Policy Series, quarterly.

★10412★
OVERSEAS PRIVATE INVESTMENT CORPORATION - LIBRARY (Bus-Fin)
1129 20th St., N.W., Rm. 711   Phone: (202) 632-0146
Washington, DC 20527   Myra Norton, Libn.
Founded: 1974. **Staff:** Prof 2; Other 1. **Subjects:** Multinational business, foreign investments, risk insurance, international law, economics of developing countries, foreign relations. **Special Collections:** Legislative histories on foreign assistance and international development (300 volumes); country file (54 linear feet). **Holdings:** 6000 books; 1300 annual reports; 8 linear feet of VF drawers. **Subscriptions:** 240 journals and other serials; 10 newspapers. **Services:** Interlibrary loans; copying; SDI; library open to public by appointment. **Automated Operations:** Computerized cataloging. **Computerized Information Services:** DIALOG, SDC, NEXIS, Dun & Bradstreet Corporation, TEXTLINE, OCLC. **Networks/Consortia:** Member of Metropolitan Washington Library Council; FEDLINK. **Publications:** Ex Libris, bimonthly - for internal distribution only; User's Guide to Information Services. **Remarks:** The corporation (OPIC) is an independent U.S. Government agency which provides financing and political risk insurance to private U.S. businesses to encourage investment in developing countries.

OVIATT LIBRARY
See: California State University, Northridge

★10413★
OWATONNA PUBLIC LIBRARY - TOY LIBRARY (Educ)
105 N. Elm   Phone: (507) 451-4660
Owatonna, MN 55060   Andrea Hoslett, Hd., Children's Serv.
Staff: Prof 1; Other 2. **Subjects:** Manipulative toys, reading readiness, math and science, parenting. **Holdings:** 300 toys; 50 pamphlets. **Services:** Library open to public with restrictions. **Automated Operations:** Computerized cataloging, acquisitions, and circulation. **Computerized Information Services:** ATLAS (internal database). **Special Catalogs:** Illustrated toy catalog (loose-leaf).

OWEN SCIENCE AND ENGINEERING LIBRARY
See: Washington State University

★10414★
OWENS-CORNING FIBERGLAS CORPORATION - LAW DEPARTMENT LIBRARY (Law)
Fiberglas Tower 26   Phone: (419) 248-7787
Toledo, OH 43659   Sandra Sanderson, Law Libn.
Staff: 1. **Subjects:** Law - general, patent and tax. **Holdings:** 4300 books; 48,000 patents. **Subscriptions:** 241 journals and other serials. **Services:** Interlibrary loans; library not open to public. **Publications:** News & Acquisitions List, monthly - for internal distribution only. **Special Indexes:** Index of corporate legal files (book); index of general interest articles in patent and general counsel areas (book).

★10415★
OWENS-CORNING FIBERGLAS CORPORATION - TECHNICAL DATA CENTER (Sci-Tech)
Granville, OH 43023   Betty Nethers, Mgr.
Subjects: Glass, polymers, reinforced plastics, glass textiles, mathematics, chemistry, management, safety engineering. **Holdings:** 26,000 books; 5500 government reports; 2300 translations; 500 annual reports. **Subscriptions:** 600 journals and other serials; 10 newspapers. **Services:** Interlibrary loans; Current Awareness Service; center open to public by request. **Computerized Information Services:** Online systems.

★10416★
OWENS-ILLINOIS - INFORMATION RESEARCH DEPARTMENT (Bus-Fin; Sci-Tech)
One Seagate   Phone: (419) 247-1788
Toledo, OH 43666   Ilga I. Ozolins, Coord.
Subjects: Glass technology; physics; chemistry; chemical engineering; temperature measurement and control; heat transfer; metallurgy; packaging technology; glass, paper and plastics - history, markets, trends, projections and statistics, domestic and international. **Holdings:** 19,700 books; 20,000 bound periodical volumes; 95 VF drawers; 75 shelf feet of association publications; 200 VF drawers of laboratory and engineering reports; VF drawers of translations; 60 VF drawers of translations of federal and state government documents; 500 cartridges of microfilm of periodicals. **Subscriptions:** 450 journals and other serials. **Services:** Department open to public with advance arrangements. **Computerized Information Services:** OCLC; internal database. **Publications:** Technical Publications Bulletin, monthly. **Remarks:** An alternate telephone number is 247-1626. **Formed by the Merger of:** Its Business Information Services and its Technical Information Services. **Staff:** Mrs. P.A. Ajemian, Mgr.

★10417★
OWENS-ILLINOIS - TECHNICAL INFORMATION SERVICES
One Seagate
Toledo, OH 43666
Defunct. Merged with Owens-Illinois - Business Information Services to form its Information Research Department.

OWENS LIBRARY
See: Northwest Missouri State University

★10418★
OWENSBORO AREA MUSEUM - LIBRARY (Sci-Tech)
2829 S. Griffith Ave.   Phone: (502) 683-0296
Owensboro, KY 42301   Joseph M. Ford, Musm.Dir.
Founded: 1969. **Staff:** Prof 8. **Subjects:** Archeology, geology, botany, antiques, astronomy, ornithology. **Holdings:** 300 books; 400 bound periodical volumes; 50 filmstrips; 100 movies; 500 slides; 50 reels of microfilm. **Services:** Library open to public for reference use only. **Staff:** Bonnie Watson, Cat.

★10419★
OWENSBORO-DAVIESS COUNTY PUBLIC LIBRARY - KENTUCKY ROOM (Hist)
450 Griffith Ave.   Phone: (502) 684-0211
Owensboro, KY 42301   Shelia E. Heflin, Supv.
Staff: 3. **Subjects:** Kentucky history, local history, genealogy. **Special Collections:** Photograph collection; Rotary Club records (4 VF drawers). **Holdings:** 2500 volumes; 4 VF drawers of family files; 25 VF drawers of clippings, pamphlets; local newspapers and state censuses on microfilm. **Subscriptions:** 130 journals and other serials. **Services:** Copying; limited research; library open to public.

★10420★
OWENSBORO MESSENGER-INQUIRER - LIBRARY (Publ)
1401 Frederica St.
Owensboro, KY 42301
Phone: (502) 926-0123
Katherine Fiedler, Libn.
Founded: 1973. **Staff:** Prof 1; Other 2. **Subjects:** Newspaper reference topics. **Special Collections:** Chicago Tribune Graphics. **Holdings:** 2500 books; 50 bound periodical volumes; 112,000 clippings; 18,000 photographs; 1500 pamphlets; microfilm of Messenger-Inquirer from 1899 to present. **Subscriptions:** 20 journals and other serials; 22 newspapers. **Services:** Library open to public with restrictions - fee charged for research. **Computerized Information Services:** Info-Ky information retrieval system (internal database). **Special Indexes:** Online systems index to microfiche clippings, photographs, books, pamphlets, maps and graphics.

★10421★
OWYHEE COUNTY HISTORICAL COMPLEX MUSEUM - LIBRARY (Hist)
Murphy, ID 83650
Phone: (208) 495-2319
Linda Morton, Dir.
Staff: 2. **Subjects:** Owyhee County history, agriculture, Indians, mining, ranching. **Holdings:** 1000 books; 10 boxes of reports and manuscripts; 8 VF drawers of clippings and pictures; 20 boxes of archives; 1 drawer of microfilm. **Services:** Copying; library open to public with restrictions. **Publications:** Owyhee Outpost, annual.

★10422★
OXFORD MUSEUM - LIBRARY (Hist)
339 Main St.
Oxford, MA 01540
Phone: (617) 987-2882
Gloria L. Edinburg, Hd.Libn.
Founded: 1978. **Staff:** Prof 1. **Subjects:** Local history, genealogy, Huguenots. **Special Collections:** Town records; local newspapers; books by and about Clara Barton and Dr. Elliott P. Joslin. **Holdings:** 1000 volumes. **Services:** Copying; library open to public for reference use only.

★10423★
OXFORD UNITED METHODIST CHURCH - OSCAR G. COOK MEMORIAL LIBRARY (Rel-Theol)
465 Main St.
Oxford, MA 01540
Phone: (617) 987-5378
Founded: 1965. **Staff:** 2. **Subjects:** Religion and Bible, family living, theology, history, biography. **Holdings:** 450 books; audiovisual material. **Services:** Library open to public. **Staff:** Laura Adams, Co-Libn.; Beth Samuelson, Co-Libn.

★10424★
OXFORD UNIVERSITY PRESS, INC. - LIBRARY (Publ)
200 Madison Ave.
New York, NY 10016
Phone: (212) 679-7300
Clare Marie Hess, Hd.Libn.
Staff: 2. **Subjects:** Publications of the Press. **Holdings:** 8000 books; 42 periodical volumes. **Services:** Library open to public with restrictions.

OXY METALS INDUSTRY CORPORATION
See: OMI International Corp.

OYER MEMORIAL LIBRARY
See: Washington Bible College/Capital Bible Seminary

★10425★
OYSTERPONDS HISTORICAL SOCIETY - LIBRARY (Hist)
Village Lane
Orient, NY 11957
Phone: (516) 323-2480
Constance J. Terry, Archv.
Staff: 2. **Subjects:** Local history, religion, education. **Holdings:** 1350 volumes; 3000 documents and records; 12 VF drawers. **Services:** Library open to public by appointment.

★10426★
OZARK BIBLE COLLEGE - LIBRARY (Rel-Theol)
1111 N. Main St.
Box 518
Joplin, MO 64801
Phone: (417) 624-2518
Loren L. Dickey, Libn.
Founded: 1944. **Staff:** Prof 1; Other 15. **Subjects:** Religion, church history, archeology, Christian education. **Holdings:** 20,900 books; 596 bound periodical volumes; 724 AV items; 3000 audio cassettes; 12 VF drawers of missions files; 240 periodicals; 9 VF drawers of essay files; 7 VF drawers of information about Bible colleges. **Subscriptions:** 261 journals and other serials. **Services:** Interlibrary loans; copying; library open to public. **Networks/Consortia:** Member of Southwest Missouri Library Network. **Special Catalogs:** Audiovisuals Catalog, annual; Audio Cassette Catalog, annual.

★10427★
OZARK FOLK CENTER - LIBRARY (Area-Ethnic)
Mt. View, AR 72560
Phone: (501) 269-3851
W.K. McNeil, Folklorist
Staff: Prof 1; Other 1. **Subjects:** Ozark folklore, crafts, and music. **Holdings:** 3000 books; 50 bound periodical volumes; 100 unbound periodicals; 250 items of ephemera; sheet music; phonograph records. **Subscriptions:** 32 journals and other serials. **Services:** Interlibrary loans; copying; library open to public.

★10428★
OZARK INSTITUTE - RURAL MEDIA CENTER LIBRARY
99 Spring St.
Box 549
Eureka Springs, AR 72632
Founded: 1972. **Subjects:** Ozarkiana, organic agriculture, mountain music and crafts, alternative energy sources, food, nutrition, cooperative development, cultural resources management. **Holdings:** 1650 books; 12,500 papers and pamphlets; 360 state and regional government reports; microfiche; 120 maps. **Remarks:** Presently inactive.

★10429★
OZARK-MAHONING COMPANY - RESEARCH LIBRARY (Sci-Tech)
1870 S. Boulder Ave.
Tulsa, OK 74119
Phone: (918) 585-2661
Judy Tibson, Libn.
Staff: 1. **Subjects:** Chemistry - general, fluorine, inorganic; chemicals for dental application. **Holdings:** 500 books; 300 bound periodical volumes; 50 volumes of unbound journals. **Subscriptions:** 24 journals and other serials. **Services:** Interlibrary loans; copying; library open to public by appointment. **Remarks:** Library is located at 5101 W. 21st St., Tulsa, OK 74107.

P

★10430★
P.T. BOATS, INC. - LIBRARY, ARCHIVES & TECHNICAL INFORMATION CENTER (Mil)
U.S.S. Massachusetts, Battleship Cove   Phone: (617) 678-1100
Fall River, MA 02721   Frank J. Szczepaniak, P.T. Boat Coord.
Founded: 1975. **Staff:** 1. **Subjects:** Patrol Torpedo (P.T.) boats, naval history. **Special Collections:** Personal photo albums of 43 World War II operating squadrons. **Holdings:** 400 books; 300 bound periodical volumes; 150 manuals; 200 P.T. boat blueprints; 100 designs; 5000 photographs; 15 reels of microfilm; 60 reels of P.T. movies. **Services:** Copying; center open to public by appointment. **Publications:** Newspaper, semiannual; 3 books on P.T. boats of World War II. **Remarks:** This is claimed to be the only P.T. Boat Museum and Library in the world. All mail should be sent to the main office of P.T. Boats, Inc., Box 109, Memphis, TN 38101; the telephone number is (901) 272-9980.

★10431★
P.T. BOATS, INC. - LIBRARY, ARCHIVES & TECHNICAL INFORMATION CENTER - NATIONAL HEADQUARTERS (Mil)
Box 109   Phone: (901) 272-9980
Memphis, TN 38101   J.M. "Boats" Newberry, Founder & Dir.
Founded: 1964. **Staff:** Prof 3; Other 3. **Subjects:** Patrol Torpedo (P.T.) boats - World War II operations, squadrons, tenders, bases, training center, P.T. boat builders. **Special Collections:** Photographs (10,000); 78 foot Higgins P.T. Boat; 80 foot Elco P.T. Boat; artifacts, memorabilia, uniforms and weapons. **Holdings:** 500 books; 75 bound periodical volumes; 500 charts; 5000 operation action reports; 5000 clippings; 2000 feet of microfilm; 20,000 feet of World War II film; 20 VF drawers of letters, citations, orders and records of P.T. boaters. **Services:** Interlibrary loans; copying; library open to public by appointment. **Publications:** P.T. Boat All Hands Newspaper, 2/year; Knights of the Sea - for sale; technical manuals on the history of P.T. Boat squadrons. **Special Catalogs:** Rosters of P.T. Boaters on cards (master, alphabetical, by state, by squadron). **Remarks:** The evening phone number is (901) 683-8952. **Staff:** Donald Rhoads, Ref.Libn.; Robert Ferrell, Techn.

PABST BREWING COMPANY - P-L BIOCHEMICALS, INC.
See: **Pharmacia P-L Biochemicals, Inc.**

PACA (William) GARDEN CONSERVATION CENTER
See: **Historic Annapolis, Inc. - William Paca Garden Conservation Center**

PACE (John C.) LIBRARY
See: **University of West Florida - John C. Pace Library**

★10432★
PACE UNIVERSITY - LIBRARY (Bus-Fin)
Pace Plaza   Phone: (212) 488-1331
New York, NY 10038   Henry Birnbaum, Univ.Libn.
Staff: Prof 12; Other 20. **Subjects:** Liberal arts and sciences, accounting, finance, management, marketing, real estate, taxation. **Holdings:** 310,000 books and bound periodical volumes; corporation annual reports for 2500 companies; 19,000 pamphlets; 21,000 reels of microfilm. **Subscriptions:** 1600 journals and other serials; 6 newspapers. **Services:** Interlibrary loans; library not open to public except with special permission. **Automated Operations:** Computerized cataloging. **Computerized Information Services:** BRS. Performs searches on cost recovery basis. Contact Person: Michelle Fanelli. **Networks/Consortia:** Member of METRO. **Staff:** Bruce J. Bergman, Lib.Dir.; Adele Jann, Hd.Cat.; Michelle Fanelli, Rd.Serv.Libn.; Kathleen Clancy, ILL Libn.

★10433★
PACE UNIVERSITY, PLEASANTVILLE/BRIARCLIFF - EDWARD AND DORIS MORTOLA LIBRARY (Bus-Fin)
861 Bedford Rd.   Phone: (914) 769-3200
Pleasantville, NY 10570   William J. Murdock, Lib.Dir.
Founded: 1963. **Staff:** Prof 9; Other 6. **Subjects:** Business administration, period histories, accounting, nursing, 19th century English literature, computer science. **Holdings:** 210,000 books and bound periodical volumes; 4114 pamphlets; 795 corporation reports; 310 college bulletins; 14,000 reels of microfilm. **Subscriptions:** 1150 journals and other serials. **Services:** Interlibrary loans; copying; library open to public for reference use only. **Automated Operations:** Computerized cataloging and serials. **Computerized Information Services:** BRS, OCLC. Performs searches on cost recovery

basis. Contact Person: R. Kuhta, 769-3200, ext. 3384. **Networks/Consortia:** Member of Westchester Library System. **Staff:** R. Yang, Acq.Libn.; R. Kuhta, Rd.Serv.Libn.; Lauren Jackson, Cat.Libn.; P. Chervenie, Per.Libn.; R. Loomis, Ref.Libn.; E. Reiman, Ref.Libn.; J. Lee, Evening Libn.

★10434★
PACE UNIVERSITY - SCHOOL OF LAW LIBRARY (Law)
78 N. Broadway   Phone: (914) 681-4273
White Plains, NY 10603   Bardie C. Wolfe, Jr., Law Libn./Prof.
Founded: 1976. **Staff:** Prof 6; Other 6. **Subjects:** Law - U.S., international. **Special Collections:** Selective U.S. Government documents depository. **Holdings:** 21,485 books; 71,390 bound periodical volumes; 7956 reels of microfilm; 223,506 microfiche. **Subscriptions:** 1754 journals and other serials. **Services:** Interlibrary loans; copying; library open to public by special request. **Automated Operations:** Computerized cataloging. **Computerized Information Services:** LEXIS, WESTLAW, OCLC. **Networks/Consortia:** Member of SUNY/OCLC Library Network; METRO. **Publications:** Acquisitions list, monthly; Informational highlights, bibliographies and reference aids; Government acquisitions list. **Staff:** Martha W. Keister, Hd., Pub.Serv.; Anne Sauter, Ref./Doc.Libn.; Susan Nosseir, Ref./ILL Libn.; Jane Marshall, Hd., Tech.Serv.; Alice Pidgeon, Acq.Libn.

★10435★
PACIFIC AND ASIAN AFFAIRS COUNCIL - PACIFIC HOUSE LIBRARY (Area-Ethnic)*
2004 University Ave.   Phone: (808) 941-5355
Honolulu, HI 96822
Founded: 1925. **Staff:** Prof 3; Other 1. **Subjects:** International affairs, Asia and the Pacific, foreign policy. **Holdings:** 2000 books. **Subscriptions:** 100 journals and other serials; 5 newspapers. **Services:** Interlibrary loans; library open to public.

★10436★
PACIFIC/ASIAN AMERICAN MENTAL HEALTH RESEARCH CENTER - DOCUMENTATION CENTER (Area-Ethnic)
Publications Division
1001 W. Van Buren   Phone: (312) 226-0117
Chicago, IL 60607   Dr. Indu Vohra-Sahu, Dir., Doc.Ctr.
Staff: Prof 3. **Subjects:** Asian, Oceanic, and Pacific Islander Americans. **Holdings:** 50 books; 20 VF drawers of unbound reports and papers. **Subscriptions:** 20 journals and other serials. **Services:** Copying; center open to public. **Publications:** Research Review, quarterly - free. **Special Catalogs:** Pacific/Asian American Research: An Annotated Bibliography, 1981; The Pacific/Asian Americans: A Selected and Annotated Bibliography of Recent Materials, 1983.

PACIFIC BIOLOGICAL STATION
See: **Canada - Fisheries & Oceans**

★10437★
PACIFIC BIO-MARINE LABORATORIES, INC. - RESEARCH LIBRARY (Sci-Tech)†
4134 Del Rey Ave.
Box 536   Phone: (213) 822-5757
Venice, CA 90291   Michael J. Fishman, Libn.
Founded: 1961. **Staff:** 1. **Subjects:** Marine biology, water quality, marine resources. **Special Collections:** Marine resources of southern California. **Holdings:** 2000 books; 500 reports; 2000 reprints. **Subscriptions:** 20 journals and other serials. **Services:** Copying; library open to public for reference use only.

PACIFIC BIO-MEDICAL RESEARCH CENTER
See: **University of Hawaii**

★10438★
PACIFIC CHRISTIAN COLLEGE - HURST MEMORIAL LIBRARY (Rel-Theol)
2500 E. Nutwood Ave.   Phone: (714) 879-3901
Fullerton, CA 92631   Jeffrey L. Wilson, Dir.
Founded: 1929. **Staff:** Prof 2; Other 1. **Subjects:** Theology, Christian education, church history, Bible, missions, sociology, psychology, philosophy, world history. **Holdings:** 44,500 books; 300 bound periodical volumes; 1000 other cataloged items; 6 VF drawers of mission papers of Christian Church; 1600 tapes; 100 reels of microfilm; 1000 microfiche. **Subscriptions:** 289 journals and other serials. **Services:** Interlibrary loans; copying; library open to public with restrictions. **Automated Operations:** Computerized cataloging and ILL. **Computerized Information Services:** OCLC.

★10439★
PACIFIC COAST BANKING SCHOOL - LIBRARY (Bus-Fin)
2001 Sixth Ave., Suite 1710   Phone: (206) 624-7618
Seattle, WA 98121   Mrs. Marciel Tomich, Registrar
Founded: 1950. **Staff:** 4. **Subjects:** Bank capital, bank deposits, marketing and personnel operations, economic studies, international banking, regulatory studies, bank investments, loans, trust department studies. **Holdings:** 400 unbound theses. **Services:** Interlibrary loans; library not open to public. **Staff:** JoAnn McDonald, Libn.

PACIFIC FOREST RESEARCH CENTRE
See: Canada - Canadian Forestry Service

★10440★
PACIFIC GAS AND ELECTRIC COMPANY - CORPORATE LIBRARY (Bus-Fin; Energy)
77 Beale St., Rm. 1220   Phone: (415) 781-4211
San Francisco, CA 94106   Patricia A. Lawrence, Dir.
Staff: Prof 6; Other 2. **Subjects:** Engineering, energy, business, finance. **Special Collections:** Company history. **Holdings:** 6000 books and bound periodical volumes; 53 VF drawers. **Subscriptions:** 350 journals and other serials. **Services:** Interlibrary loans; copying; SDI; library open to public by appointment. **Automated Operations:** Computerized cataloging and ILL. **Computerized Information Services:** DIALOG, SDC, OCLC. **Publications:** Library Bulletin, monthly.

★10441★
PACIFIC GAS AND ELECTRIC COMPANY - LAW LIBRARY (Law)
Box 7442   Phone: (415) 781-4211
San Francisco, CA 94120   Gary L. Stromme, Law Libn.
Founded: 1906. **Staff:** Prof 2; Other 2. **Subjects:** Law. **Holdings:** 22,000 volumes. **Services:** Library not open to public. **Staff:** Betty A. Merritt, Asst. Law Libn.

★10442★
PACIFIC GROVE MUSEUM OF NATURAL HISTORY - LIBRARY (Env-Cons)
165 Forest Ave.
Pacific Grove, CA 93950   Vernal L. Yadon, Musm.Dir.
Subjects: Natural history of Monterey County. **Holdings:** 2000 books. **Services:** Library open to public for reference use only.

★10443★
PACIFIC GROVE PUBLIC LIBRARY - ALVIN SEALE SOUTH SEAS COLLECTION (Area-Ethnic)
550 Central Ave.   Phone: (408) 373-0603
Pacific Grove, CA 93950   Margaret McBride, Lib.Dir.
Subjects: Pacific Islands, voyages. **Holdings:** 1200 volumes. **Services:** Interlibrary loans (limited); copying; collection open to public with restrictions. **Networks/Consortia:** Member of Monterey Bay Area Cooperative Library System (MOBAC).

★10444★
PACIFIC HOSPITAL OF LONG BEACH - MEDICAL STAFF LIBRARY (Med)†
2776 Pacific Ave.
Box 1268   Phone: (213) 595-1911
Long Beach, CA 90801   Lois E. Harris, Dir., Lib. & AV Serv.
Staff: Prof 1; Other 1. **Subjects:** General medicine, nursing, hospital administration, acupuncture. **Special Collections:** Patient Education Program. **Holdings:** 5000 books and bound periodical volumes. **Subscriptions:** 200 journals and other serials. **Services:** Interlibrary loans; SDI; library open to public for reference use only when user is sponsored by physician.

★10445★
PACIFIC INFORMATION INC. - INFORMATION SERVICES (Info Sci)
11684 Ventura Blvd., Suite 295   Phone: (818) 797-7654
Studio City, CA 91604
Staff: Prof 7. **Subjects:** Information science. **Services:** Information management consulting specializing in systems analysis and design, indexing and retrieval methodologies, software selection for automated retrieval systems, systems implementation, building special libraries, archives and records management, and personnel selection and training for information management. **Formerly:** Cibbarelli & Associates Inc., located in Huntington Beach, CA. **Staff:** Kenneth H. Plate, Sr. Partner; Edward J. Kazlauskas, Sr. Partner.

★10446★
PACIFIC LIGHTING CORPORATION - LAW LIBRARY (Law)
810 S. Flower St.   Phone: (213) 689-3352
Los Angeles, CA 90017   Terence Pragnell, Law Libn.
Staff: Prof 2; Other 1. **Subjects:** Law - corporate, utility, oil and gas, energy and environmental. **Holdings:** 23,000 volumes. **Subscriptions:** 350 journals and other serials; 5 newspapers. **Services:** Interlibrary loans; library not open to public. **Automated Operations:** Computerized cataloging, acquisitions and circulation. **Computerized Information Services:** LEXIS, NEXIS, DIALOG; Corporate Library Automated Information Management System (CLAIM; internal database). **Publications:** Law Information Monthly - for internal distribution only; Annotated Bibliography on the California Public Utilities Commission, annual. **Special Indexes:** Index to California PUC General Orders. **Remarks:** Holding company for Southern California Gas Company. **Staff:** Vicki Bustillos, Lib.Asst.

★10447★
PACIFIC LIGHTING GAS SUPPLY COMPANY - REFERENCE CENTER (Energy)
720 W. 8th St. - ML 10MW   Phone: (213) 689-3930
Los Angeles, CA 90017   Janice Moisant, Res. & Info.Supv.
Staff: Prof 1; Other 2. **Subjects:** Energy, natural gas, gas supply. **Holdings:** 250 books. **Subscriptions:** 200 journals and other serials. **Services:** Interlibrary loans; SDI; center not open to public. **Automated Operations:** Computerized cataloging, acquisitions, serials, and circulation. **Computerized Information Services:** DIALOG, SDC, BRS, DOE/RECON, LEXIS. **Publications:** Acquisitions List, monthly.

PACIFIC LUTHERAN THEOLOGICAL SEMINARY
See: Graduate Theological Union

★10448★
PACIFIC MEDICAL CENTER & UNIVERSITY OF THE PACIFIC SCHOOL OF DENTISTRY - HEALTH SCIENCES LIBRARY (Med)
2395 Sacramento St.
Box 7999   Phone: (415) 563-4321
San Francisco, CA 94120   Harold R. Gibson, Libn.
Staff: Prof 2; Other 2. **Subjects:** Medicine, dentistry. **Holdings:** 8767 books; 57,939 bound periodical volumes. **Subscriptions:** 769 journals and other serials. **Services:** Interlibrary loans; library not open to public. **Computerized Information Services:** Online systems.

PACIFIC NORTHWEST FOREST & RANGE EXPERIMENT STATION
See: U.S. Forest Service

PACIFIC NORTHWEST LONG-TERM CARE CENTER
See: University of Washington

★10449★
PACIFIC POWER AND LIGHT COMPANY - LIBRARY (Energy)
920 S.W. Sixth Ave.   Phone: (503) 243-4095
Portland, OR 97204   Susan Jackson, Libn.
Founded: 1960. **Staff:** Prof 1; Other 3. **Subjects:** Electric engineering, electric utility management, energy resources, environment. **Holdings:** 10,000 books and bound periodical volumes; 15,000 U.S. Government documents; 5000 state documents; 10,000 pamphlets, 7500 annual reports and 1000 standards in 150 VF drawers; 1000 reels of microfilm; 5000 microfiche; 200 aperture cards. **Subscriptions:** 560 journals and other serials. **Services:** Interlibrary loans; copying; library open to public for reference use only. **Automated Operations:** Computerized cataloging, acquisitions and ILL. **Computerized Information Services:** DIALOG, Dow Jones News/Retrieval, OCLC. **Networks/Consortia:** Member of CLASS.

★10450★
PACIFIC PRESS, LTD. - PRESS LIBRARY (Publ)
2250 Granville St.   Phone: (604) 732-2519
Vancouver, BC, Canada V6H 3G2   Shirley E. Mooney, Libn.
Staff: Prof 2; Other 17. **Subjects:** Newspaper reference topics. **Holdings:** 1000 volumes; 260 VF drawers of newspaper clipping files; 325,000 microjackets of clipping files; 200 VF drawers of pictures; 250 VF drawers of biographical files; 360 boxes of pamphlets. **Subscriptions:** 37 journals and other serials. **Services:** Library not open to public. **Staff:** Barbara Valle, Asst.Libn.

PACIFIC REGIONAL ORAL HISTORY PROGRAM
See: University of Hawaii - Department of History

PACIFIC SCHOOL OF RELIGION
See: Graduate Theological Union

★10451★
PACIFIC SCIENCE CENTER FOUNDATION - LIBRARY
200 Second Ave., N.
Seattle, WA 98109
Founded: 1978. **Subjects:** Science; science and museum education.
Holdings: 3000 books. **Remarks:** Presently inactive.

★10452★
PACIFIC SCIENTIFIC INFORMATION CENTER
Bernice P. Bishop Museum
1525 Bernice St.
Box 19000-A
Honolulu, HI 96819
Defunct. Holdings absorbed by Bernice P. Bishop Museum - Library.

★10453★
PACIFIC-SIERRA RESEARCH CORPORATION - LIBRARY (Sci-Tech)
12340 Santa Monica Blvd.   Phone: (213) 820-2200
Los Angeles, CA 90025   Letitia A. McIntosh, Res.Libn.
Staff: Prof 1. **Subjects:** Laser optics, nuclear physics, geophysics, foreign
policy, computer science. **Special Collections:** Technical reports on
atmospheric nuclear testing (150). **Holdings:** 700 books; 100 maps; 3500
technical reports. **Subscriptions:** 100 journals and other serials; 5
newspapers. **Services:** Library not open to public. **Computerized Information
Services:** DIALOG, SDC.

PACIFIC SOUTHWEST FOREST & RANGE EXPERIMENT STATION
See: U.S. Forest Service

★10454★
PACIFIC STUDIES CENTER - LIBRARY (Bus-Fin)
222B View St.   Phone: (415) 969-1545
Mountain View, CA 94041   Leonard M. Siegel, Dir.
Founded: 1969. **Staff:** Prof 3. **Subjects:** Multinational corporations, high
technology industry, Southeast Asia, U.S. military and foreign policy. **Holdings:**
6000 books; 120 working research file drawers arranged by geographical
area, country, industry and corporation. **Subscriptions:** 300 periodicals.
Services: Copying; file searches (fee); library open to public. **Publications:**
Pacific Research, quarterly; Global Electronics Information Newsletter,
monthly - both by subscription.

★10455★
PACIFIC-UNION CLUB - LIBRARY (Hist)
1000 California St.   Phone: (415) 775-1234
San Francisco, CA 94108   Barbara Borden, Libn.
Staff: Prof 1. **Special Collections:** Californiana. **Holdings:** 31,750 books.
Services: Library not open to public.

★10456★
PACIFIC UNION COLLEGE - PITCAIRN ISLANDS STUDY CENTER - LIBRARY
(Area-Ethnic)
                    Phone: (707) 965-6241
Angwin, CA 94508   Gary Shearer, Cur.
Founded: 1977. **Staff:** Prof 1; Other 1. **Subjects:** Pitcairn Islands. **Holdings:**
600 books; 400 indexed articles; 300 other indexed items; VF drawers of
pamphlets, articles and clippings; stamp collection, including first day covers;
films; slides; photographs; cassettes; island artifacts and curios;
correspondence of Pitcairn Islanders; complete file of Pitcairn Miscellany;
partial file of Pitcairn Pilhi; obituary file. **Services:** Copying; library open to
public for reference use only.

★10457★
PACIFIC UNIVERSITY - MUSIC DEPARTMENT - LIBRARY (Mus)
College Way   Phone: (503) 357-6151
Forest Grove, OR 97116   Norma M. Cooper, Music Libn.
Staff: Prof 1; Other 4. **Subjects:** Music. **Holdings:** 8600 books and music
scores; 4534 records and tapes. **Services:** Interlibrary loans; library open to
public with restrictions on access. **Remarks:** Most music reference materials,
books and periodicals are housed in the Harvey Scott Memorial Library, Pacific
University.

★10458★
PACIFICA RADIO NETWORK - PACIFICA RADIO ARCHIVE (Aud-Vis)
5316 Venice Blvd.   Phone: (213) 931-1625
Los Angeles, CA 90019   Janice Woo, Libn.
Founded: 1968. **Staff:** Prof 2; Other 3. **Subjects:** Civil rights, public affairs,
politics, Third World, literature, music. **Holdings:** 20,000 sound recordings.
Services: Copying; library open to public by appointment. **Automated
Operations:** Computerized cataloging. **Special Catalogs:** COM catalog. **Staff:**

Helen Kennedy, Dir.

★10459★
**PACKAGING CORPORATION OF AMERICA - INFORMATION SERVICES
DEPARTMENT** (Sci-Tech)
5401 Old Orchard Rd.   Phone: (312) 470-0080
Skokie, IL 60077   Mary S. Senn, Info.Spec.
Staff: Prof 1. **Subjects:** Paper chemistry, packaging, manufacture of paper
and pulpboard. **Holdings:** 1000 books; 2500 bound periodical volumes; 150
VF drawers of publications of Institute of Paper Chemistry, Technical
Association of Pulp & Paper Industry, and Boxboard Research & Development
Association. **Subscriptions:** 51 journals and other serials. **Services:**
Interlibrary loans; copying; department open to public with restrictions.
Computerized Information Services: DIALOG, SDC. Performs free searches.
Networks/Consortia: Member of North Suburban Library System; ILLINET.
Formerly: Its Research and Development Library, located in Grand Rapids, MI.

★10460★
PACKAGING INSTITUTE, USA - LIBRARY AND RESOURCE CENTER
20 E. 46th St., Suite 603
New York, NY 10017
Subjects: Packaging and related fields. **Holdings:** 500 books; 10 VF drawers;
international packaging periodicals, reports and manuscripts. **Publications:**
Directory of Contract Packagers; Glossary of Packaging Terms; Who's Who in
Packaging. **Remarks:** Presently inactive.

PACKARD LIBRARY
See: Columbus College of Art and Design

PACKARD READING ROOM
See: Pennsylvania Hospital - Department for Sick and Injured - Medical
Library

★10461★
PACKER (Robert) HOSPITAL - MEDICAL LIBRARY (Med)*
Guthrie Sq.   Phone: (717) 888-6666
Sayre, PA 18840   E. Jean Antes, Med.Ref.Libn.
Founded: 1929. **Staff:** Prof 3; Other 4. **Subjects:** Medicine, nursing, allied
health sciences. **Holdings:** 3075 books; 3755 bound periodical volumes.
Subscriptions: 449 journals and other serials. **Services:** Interlibrary loans;
copying; library open to medical and health professionals. **Computerized
Information Services:** MEDLINE. **Remarks:** The library provides weekly trips
by medical librarians to 14 hospitals in northern Pennsylvania and south central
New York.

PADDOCK MUSIC LIBRARY
See: Dartmouth College

PAGE (Inman E.) LIBRARY
See: Lincoln University of Missouri - Inman E. Page Library

★10462★
PAIER COLLEGE OF ART, INC. - LIBRARY (Art)
6 Prospect Court
Hamden, CT 06511   Christine de Vallet, Libn.
Staff: Prof 1; Other 2. **Subjects:** Art, photography, graphic design, interior
design. **Holdings:** 6500 books. **Subscriptions:** 52 journals and other serials.
Services: Library open to public for reference use only.

PAIEWONSKY (Ralph M.) LIBRARY
See: College of the Virgin Islands - Foundation Center Regional Collection

★10463★
PAINE ART CENTER AND ARBORETUM - GEORGE P. NEVITT LIBRARY (Art)
1410 Algoma Blvd.   Phone: (414) 235-4530
Oshkosh, WI 54901   Corinne H. Spoo, Hd.
Staff: Prof 2. **Subjects:** Interior decoration, English history. **Holdings:** 800
volumes. **Services:** Interlibrary loans; library open to public.

PAINE (Thomas) HISTORICAL ASSOCIATION OF NEW ROCHELLE
See: Huguenot-Thomas Paine Historical Association of New Rochelle

★10464★
PAINE WEBBER INC. - PAINE WEBBER BLYTH EASTMAN - LIBRARY (Bus-
Fin)
1221 Ave. of the Americas   Phone: (212) 730-8839
New York, NY 10020   Barbara A. Fody, Asst. V.P.
Staff: Prof 3; Other 13. **Subjects:** Finance, investments, money and banking,
economic and business conditions. **Special Collections:** Corporation records.

Holdings: 1500 books; 75 bound periodical volumes; 100 other cataloged items; 700 industry subject files; 500 shelves of corporation records; 75 reels of microfilm; microfiche. **Subscriptions:** 700 journals and other serials; 15 newspapers. **Services:** Interlibrary loans; library open to members of Special Libraries Association. **Computerized Information Services:** New York Times Information Service, DIALOG, Dow Jones News/Retrieval, TEXTLINE, BRS. **Publications:** Blyth Eastman Paine Webber Library Bulletin, monthly - for internal distribution only. **Staff:** Nancy Cohen, Asst.Libn.; Diane Erbeck, Ref.Libn.

★10465★
PAINE WEBBER INC. - PAINE WEBBER MITCHELL HUTCHINS - LIBRARY (Bus-Fin)
140 Broadway　　　　　　　　　　　　Phone: (212) 437-7465
New York, NY 10005　　　　　　　　　　June Fackler, Libn.
Founded: 1967. **Staff:** Prof 1; Other 1. **Subjects:** Finance, business. **Special Collections:** Corporation records. **Holdings:** 200 books; 155 VF drawers of research reports. **Subscriptions:** 200 journals and other serials; 15 newspapers. **Services:** Interlibrary loans; library open to public for limited reference use only.

★10466★
PAJARO VALLEY HISTORICAL ASSOCIATION - WILLIAM H. VOLCK MUSEUM - ARCHIVES (Hist)
261 E. Beach St.　　　　　　　　　　　Phone: (408) 722-0305
Watsonville, CA 95076　　　　　　　　　Alzora Snyder, Archv.
Subjects: History of the Pajaro Valley, 1865 to present. **Holdings:** 90 linear feet of letters, literary manuscripts, genealogical source materials, account books, business and financial records, noncurrent records of schools, city and county government agencies, community groups and associations, architectural drawings, aerial photographs, oral history tapes and transcripts, photographs. **Services:** Copying; archives open to public.

PALENSKE (Maud Preston) MEMORIAL LIBRARY
See: Genealogical Association of Southwestern Michigan - Maud Preston Palenske Memorial Library

★10467★
PALEONTOLOGICAL RESEARCH INSTITUTION - LIBRARY (Sci-Tech)
1259 Trumansburg Rd.　　　　　　　　Phone: (607) 273-6623
Ithaca, NY 14850　　　　　　　　　　　Peter R. Hoover, Dir.
Staff: Prof 1. **Subjects:** Paleontology, geology, conchology, fossils, mollusca. **Holdings:** 50,000 volumes; 48 VF cabinets; microfilm; maps; photographs; 6000 reprints and papers. **Subscriptions:** 400 journals and other serials. **Services:** Interlibrary loans (fee); library open to specialists by appointment. **Publications:** Library Serials List.

PALINET
See: Pennsylvania Area Library Network and Union Library Catalogue of Pennsylvania

★10468★
PALL CORPORATION - LIBRARY (Sci-Tech)
30 Sea Cliff Ave.　　　　　　　　　　Phone: (516) 671-4000
Glen Cove, NY 11724　　　　　　　Patricia J. Iannucci, Mkt.Res.Mgr.
Staff: Prof 1; Other 1. **Subjects:** Filtration, chemistry, technology, medicine. **Holdings:** 1000 books; 500 bound periodical titles; industrial market directories. **Subscriptions:** 503 journals and other serials. **Services:** Interlibrary loans; copying; SDI; library not open to public. **Computerized Information Services:** DIALOG, SDC. **Networks/Consortia:** Member of Long Island Library Resources Council. **Publications:** Acquisitions Report.

★10469★
PALLOTTINE PROVINCIALATE LIBRARY (Rel-Theol)
5424 W. Blue Mound Rd.　　　　　　　Phone: (414) 258-0653
Milwaukee, WI 53208　　　　　　Rev. Jerome Kuskowski, S.A.C., Libn.
Founded: 1923. **Staff:** Prof 1. **Subjects:** Theology, philosophy, hagiography. **Special Collections:** St. Vincent Pallotti Collection (500 items). **Holdings:** 3223 books and bound periodical volumes; 2 VF drawers; 5 shelves of unbound periodicals; 3 shelves of pamphlets. **Subscriptions:** 20 journals and other serials; 15 newspapers. **Services:** Interlibrary loans; copying; library open to public. **Remarks:** Maintained by the Society of the Catholic Apostolate.

★10470★
PALM BEACH COUNTY - LAW LIBRARY (Law)
339 Courthouse　　　　　　　　　　Phone: (305) 837-2928
West Palm Beach, FL 33401　　　　　Marguerite H. Johnson, Law Libn.
Staff: 3. **Subjects:** Law. **Holdings:** 17,936 volumes. **Services:** Copying;

library open to public with restricted hours.

PALMEDO (Roland) NATIONAL SKI LIBRARY
See: National Ski Hall of Fame and Museum - Roland Palmedo National Ski Library

★10471★
PALMER COLLEGE OF CHIROPRACTIC - DAVID D. PALMER LIBRARY (Med)
1000 Brady St.　　　　　　　　　　　Phone: (319) 326-9641
Davenport, IA 52803　　　　　　　Dennis R. Peterson, Interim Dir.
Founded: 1895. **Staff:** Prof 6; Other 12. **Subjects:** Chiropractic, health sciences. **Special Collections:** Chiropractic history and research; conservative health care. **Holdings:** 20,773 books; 6724 bound periodical volumes; 9706 microfiche; 761 reels of microfilm; 394 audiotapes; 287 videotapes; 13,225 slides; 876 biological specimens and models; 1112 x-ray sets. **Subscriptions:** 939 journals and other serials; 14 newspapers. **Services:** Interlibrary loans; copying; library open to public with restrictions. **Automated Operations:** Computerized cataloging and serials. **Computerized Information Services:** MEDLARS, DIALOG, SDC; CLIBCON Union List of Serials (internal database). Performs searches on cost recovery basis. **Networks/Consortia:** Member of Greater Midwest Regional Medical Library Network (Region 3); River Bend Library System; Chiropractic Library Consortium (CLIBCON). **Publications:** NEXUS, biweekly - campus distribution. **Staff:** Alana K. Ferguson, Pub.Serv.Libn.; Georgia Taller, Pub.Serv.Libn.; Glenda C. Wiese, Tech.Serv.Libn.; Richard D. Carr, Tech.Serv.Libn.

★10472★
PALMER COLLEGE OF CHIROPRACTIC - WEST - LIBRARY (Med)
1095 Dunford Way　　　　　　　　　Phone: (408) 244-8907
Sunnyvale, CA 94087　　　　　　　　Phyllis Hazekamp, Libn.
Staff: Prof 1; Other 2. **Subjects:** Chiropractic, health sciences, medicine, basic sciences, education, law. **Special Collections:** Chiropractic history (250 volumes). **Holdings:** 3800 books; 108 skeletal parts; 1548 x-rays; 29 carousels of slides; 12 films and videotapes; periodicals. **Subscriptions:** 109 journals and other serials. **Services:** Interlibrary loans (fee); library open to public for reference use only. **Networks/Consortia:** Member of Chiropractic Library Consortium (CLIBCON); Pacific Southwest Regional Medical Library Service (PSRMLS). **Publications:** New in the Library, bimonthly - for internal distribution only.

PALMER (George B.) MEMORIAL LIBRARY
See: Hunt Memorial Hospital - George B. Palmer Memorial Library

★10473★
PALMER, O'CONNELL, LEGER, TURNBULL & TURNBULL - LAW LIBRARY (Law)†
One Brunswick Sq., Suite 1600
P.O. Box 1324　　　　　　　　　　　Phone: (506) 642-2700
Saint John, NB, Canada E2L 4H8　　　　Peter R. Forestell, Libn.
Staff: Prof 2; Other 1. **Subjects:** Law. **Holdings:** 1000 books; 3000 bound periodical volumes. **Subscriptions:** 20 journals and other serials; 10 newspapers. **Services:** Library open to public with restrictions.

PALMER SCHOOL OF LIBRARY AND INFORMATION SCIENCE
See: Long Island University - C.W. Post Campus

PALMER (Sophia F.) LIBRARY
See: American Journal of Nursing Company - Sophia F. Palmer Library

★10474★
PALO ALTO MEDICAL FOUNDATION - BARNETT-HALL LIBRARY (Med)
860 Bryant St.　　　　　　　　　　Phone: (415) 321-4121
Palo Alto, CA 94301　　　　　　　　Eileen E. Cassidy, Hd.Libn.
Founded: 1950. **Staff:** Prof 3. **Subjects:** Medicine, medical research, basic sciences, nursing, pharmacology. **Holdings:** 11,653 books and bound periodical volumes; 13 VF drawers of pamphlets. **Subscriptions:** 306 journals and other serials. **Services:** Interlibrary loans; copying; library open to physicians and technological researchers of the county. **Computerized Information Services:** MEDLINE. **Networks/Consortia:** Member of Pacific Southwest Regional Medical Library Service (PSRMLS); Northern California Medical Library Group. **Publications:** Annual Report. **Special Indexes:** Periodical holdings visible file index. **Staff:** Natalie Hazen, Ser.Libn.; Judith Cummings, Ref.Libn.

★10475★
PALO ALTO UNIFIED SCHOOL DISTRICT - INSTRUCTIONAL MATERIALS CENTER (Educ)
Greendell School, Rm. 9
4120 Middlefield Rd.　　　　　　　　Phone: (415) 855-8355
Palo Alto, CA 94306　　　　　　　　Jack Gibbany, Prog.Coord.
Founded: 1950. **Staff:** Prof 13; Other 7. **Subjects:** Curriculum materials,

children's fiction. **Holdings:** 200,000 books. **Subscriptions:** 15 journals and other serials; 8 newspapers. **Services:** Interlibrary loans; copying; center open to public for reference use only. **Automated Operations:** Computerized cataloging. **Computerized Information Services:** Picodyne (internal database).

★10476★

PALO VERDE HOSPITAL - MEDICAL LIBRARY†
801 S. Prudence
Tucson, AZ 85710
Founded: 1961. **Subjects:** Psychiatry, psychology, social service, medicine. **Holdings:** 400 books. **Remarks:** Presently inactive.

★10477★

PALOMAR COMMUNITY COLLEGE - LIBRARY - SPECIAL COLLECTIONS (Hum)
1140 Mission Rd.   Phone: (714) 744-1150
San Marcos, CA 92069   Bonnie L. Rogers, Dean, Instr.Rsrcs.
Staff: Prof 5; Other 14. **Holdings:** Fine arts (15,200 volumes); American Indian (3200 volumes); Iceland (200 volumes); World War I poster collection. **Services:** Interlibrary loans; copying; library open to public with restrictions. **Automated Operations:** Computerized cataloging and serials. **Computerized Information Services:** BRS. **Networks/Consortia:** Member of San Diego and Imperial Counties Community Colleges Learning Resources Cooperative; San Diego Greater Metropolitan Area Library & Information Agency Council (METRO); CLASS. **Staff:** Alexis K. Ciurczak, Lib.Dir.; Daniel Arnsan, Pub.Serv.; Judy Cater, Acq.; JoAnne Roake, Ref.Libn.; Carolyn Wood, Ref.Libn.

★10478★

PALOMINO HORSE BREEDERS OF AMERICA - LIBRARY (Rec)
Box 249   Phone: (817) 325-2513
Mineral Wells, TX 76067   Robert J. Shiflet, Exec. V.P.
Subjects: Horses and equine-related activities, the Palomino horse. **Special Collections:** Palomino Horse Breeders of America Stud Book Listings. **Holdings:** Figures not available.

★10479★

PALOS COMMUNITY HOSPITAL - MEDICAL LIBRARY (Med)
80th Ave. at McCarthy Rd.   Phone: (312) 361-4500
Palos Heights, IL 60463   Gail Waldoch, Libn.
Staff: Prof 1. **Subjects:** Medicine and related fields. **Holdings:** 300 books. **Subscriptions:** 83 journals and other serials. **Services:** Interlibrary loans; library not open to public. **Computerized Information Services:** DIALOG. **Networks/Consortia:** Member of Chicago and South Consortium.

PAN AM WORLD SERVICES, INC.
See: Arnold Engineering Development Center Technical Library

PAN-AMERICAN ASSOCIATION OF FORENSIC SCIENCES - SECRETARIAT
See: International Reference Organization in Forensic Medicine and Sciences

★10480★

PAN AMERICAN HEALTH ORGANIZATION - BIBLIOGRAPHIC INFORMATION OFFICE (Med)†
525 23rd St., N.W.   Phone: (202) 861-3300
Washington, DC 20037   Dr. Carlos A. Gamboa, Chf.
Staff: Prof 3; Other 2. **Subjects:** Health sciences. **Special Collections:** Documents of the World Health Organization, Pan American Health Organization and Latin American Ministries of Health. **Holdings:** 34,000 books; 20,000 bound periodical volumes. **Subscriptions:** 130 journals and other serials. **Services:** Interlibrary loans; extramural educational programs; information office open to public. **Publications:** Acquisitions Bulletin. **Remarks:** This is a regional office of the World Health Organization. **Staff:** Jesse Joseph Torres, Asst.Libn.; A. Rovati, ILL Libn.; Maria Tereza Astroza, Ref.Libn.; Emmanuel Quintana, Lib.Acq.

★10481★

PAN AMERICAN SOCIETY OF NEW ENGLAND - SHATTUCK MEMORIAL LIBRARY (Area-Ethnic)
1051 Beacon St.   Phone: (617) 277-9439
Brookline, MA 02146   Vivian P. Quiroga de Ingrao, Exec.Dir.
Subjects: Latin America, Caribbean. **Holdings:** 5000 books. **Services:** Library not open to public.

★10482★

PAN AMERICAN WORLD AIRWAYS - CORPORATE LIBRARY (Trans)
200 Park Ave., Rm. 904   Phone: (212) 880-1917
New York, NY 10166   Liwa Chiu, Libn.
Founded: 1943. **Staff:** Prof 1. **Subjects:** Air transportation world-wide, business, economics, U.S. and foreign travel. **Holdings:** 2000 books; 300 bound periodical volumes; 70 VF drawers of clippings, pamphlets; 1200 microforms. **Subscriptions:** 130 journals and other serials. **Services:** Interlibrary loans; copying; library open to public by appointment. **Publications:** Monthly Acquisition Bulletin. **Special Indexes:** Index of inauguration of services.

★10483★

PANAMA CANAL COMMISSION - LIBRARY (Area-Ethnic)
APO Miami, FL 34011   Beverly C. Williams, Libn.
Founded: 1914. **Staff:** Prof 5; Other 18. **Subjects:** Panama Canal, shipping, engineering, Isthmus of Panama. **Special Collections:** Panama Collection (33,700 items including 20,000 newspaper clippings; 5410 photographs; manuscripts). **Holdings:** 239,900 books; 903 bound periodical volumes; 8041 microforms. **Subscriptions:** 328 journals and other serials; 10 newspapers. **Services:** Copying; library open to researchers and university students referred by other libraries. **Publications:** Bibliography, monthly; Library Resources Up-date, monthly; conference calendar, irregular - all for internal distribution only. **Remarks:** The telephone number for the library is 011-507-52-7761. **Staff:** Naomi A. Wolf, Chf., Rsrcs./Serv.; Nan S. Chong, Libn., Panama Coll.; Mania Nita, Ref.Libn.; Consuelo B. Baker, Cat.

★10484★

PANARCTIC OILS LTD. - LIBRARY (Sci-Tech; Energy)
815 8th Ave., S.W.
Box 190   Phone: (403) 269-0329
Calgary, AB, Canada T2P 2H6   Susan J. Tyrrell, Libn.
Staff: Prof 1; Other 1. **Subjects:** Petroleum exploration, Canadian arctic islands. **Holdings:** 5000 books. **Subscriptions:** 120 journals and other serials. **Services:** Interlibrary loans; library not open to public. **Automated Operations:** Computerized cataloging. **Computerized Information Services:** SDC, QL Systems, CAN/OLE, Info Globe, DIALOG. **Publications:** Library Bulletin, quarterly - for internal distribution only.

★10485★

PANEL DISPLAYS, INC. - TECHNICAL LIBRARY (Sci-Tech)
211 S. Hindry Ave.   Phone: (213) 641-6661
Inglewood, CA 90301   K.O. Fugate, Pres. & Libn.
Staff: Prof 1. **Subjects:** Electronics, electro-acoustics and electro-optics, radar, solid state physics, computers, mathematics, oceanography, ultrasonics. **Holdings:** 2100 books; 5200 bound periodical volumes; 1000 product catalogs; 3000 special subject technical papers. **Subscriptions:** 102 journals and other serials. **Services:** Interlibrary loans; library open to public by appointment.

★10486★

PANHANDLE EASTERN PIPE LINE COMPANY - TECHNICAL INFORMATION CENTER (Sci-Tech; Energy)*
Box 1348   Phone: (816) 753-5600
Kansas City, MO 64141   GeorJane Simmons, Libn.
Founded: 1967. **Staff:** Prof 1. **Subjects:** Engineering, management, natural gas industry, geology, mathematics, finance. **Special Collections:** Conference Board Reports, Stanford Research Institute Reports, SRI Energy Supply and Demand to 1980, Institute of Gas Technology (IGT) and American Gas Association (AGA) Reports. **Holdings:** 2000 books and bound periodical volumes; standards for American National Standards Institute (ANSI), National Fluid Power Association (NFPA), American Society of Mechanical Engineers (ASME), American Petroleum Institute (API). **Subscriptions:** 70 journals and other serials; 6 newspapers. **Services:** Interlibrary loans; copying; answers brief inquiries and makes referrals; center open to public for reference use only on request. **Publications:** Newsletter - for internal distribution only. **Remarks:** Alternate phone number is 753-2849.

★10487★

PANHANDLE-PLAINS HISTORICAL MUSEUM - RESEARCH CENTER (Hist)
Wt. Sta., Box 967   Phone: (806) 655-7191
Canyon, TX 79016   Claire R. Kuehn, Archv./Libn.
Founded: 1932. **Staff:** Prof 2; Other 2. **Subjects:** History - Texas, Southwest; ranching; Indians of the Great Plains; archeology of Texas Panhandle; ethnology; clothing and textiles; fine arts; antiques; museum science. **Special Collections:** Interviews with early settlers collected over a period of 55 years; Bob Wills Memorial Archive of Popular Music, 1915 to present (5000 phonograph records). **Holdings:** 11,000 books; 11,500 cubic feet of manuscripts; 16 VF drawers of pamphlets; 640 maps; 1540 reels of

microfilm; 45 cubic feet of manufacturers' trade literature; 25,000 historic photographs. **Subscriptions:** 250 journals and other serials; 12 newspapers. **Services:** Copying; center open to public. **Special Indexes:** Index to the Panhandle-Plains Historical Review (card); Index to the Canyon (Texas) News. **Remarks:** The center is the Regional Historical Resource Depository for noncurrent county documents for 24 Texas Panhandle counties (a Texas State Library program).

★10488★
PANHANDLE STATE UNIVERSITY - NO MAN'S LAND HISTORICAL MUSEUM - LIBRARY (Hist)
Sewel St.
Box 278   Phone: (405) 349-2670
Goodwell, OK 73939   Dr. Harold S. Kachel, Cur.
Subjects: Western history, No Man's Land, genealogy. **Holdings:** 3000 books; 2000 bound periodical volumes; 2000 other cataloged items. **Services:** Copying; library open to public with restrictions.

★10489★
PANNELL KERR FORSTER - LIBRARY (Bus-Fin)
420 Lexington Ave.   Phone: (212) 867-8000
New York, NY 10170   Pam Wells Newton, Libn.
Founded: 1945. **Staff:** Prof 1; Other 1. **Subjects:** Management advisory services, general business. **Special Collections:** Hotel, real estate, restaurant and health care management; accounting and auditing. **Holdings:** 1000 volumes; pamphlets; clippings; government documents. **Subscriptions:** 300 journals and other serials. **Services:** Interlibrary loans; library not open to public. **Computerized Information Services:** DIALOG, LEXIS, NEXIS, Dun & Bradstreet Corporation, Dow Jones News/Retrieval.

★10490★
PANNELL KERR FORSTER - LIBRARY (Bus-Fin)
601 Jefferson, Suite 745   Phone: (713) 654-1881
Houston, TX 77002   Megan W. Trauth, Off.Serv.Mgr.
Staff: 2. **Subjects:** Hotel operations, travel, tourism. **Holdings:** 5015 books and bound periodical volumes; 5000 manuscripts and studies. **Subscriptions:** 25 journals and other serials; 10 newspapers. **Services:** Library not open to public. **Computerized Information Services:** DIALOG; INFOSTAR, DATASTAR (internal databases). Performs searches for staff. **Publications:** Texas Annual Trends - free upon request; Monthly Trends in the Hotel Industry (for Texas, Houston, Dallas/Fort Worth, San Antonio, Austin).

★10491★
PANNELL KERR FORSTER - MANAGEMENT ADVISORY SERVICES - LIBRARY (Bus-Fin; Food-Bev)
122 S. Michigan Ave.   Phone: (312) 427-7955
Chicago, IL 60603   Carole A. Ditchie, Res.Asst./Libn.
Staff: Prof 1. **Subjects:** Hotels and motels, food service and restaurants, travel and tourism, economics and demographics, commercial real estate. **Holdings:** 100 books; 15 hotel/motel and foodservice operation manuals; statistics and trends of the hotel industry. **Subscriptions:** 34 journals and other serials; 12 newspapers. **Services:** Library not open to public. **Publications:** In-house newsletter. **Special Indexes:** Index of market demand and economic feasibility studies for hotels, motels, condominiums; food and beverage operation studies; economic valuations and data processing studies.

PANZNER MEMORIAL LIBRARY
See: Providence Hospital

★10492★
PAOLI MEMORIAL HOSPITAL - ROBERT M. WHITE MEMORIAL LIBRARY (Med)
Lancaster Pike   Phone: (215) 648-1218
Paoli, PA 19301   Doris J. Rickards, Med.Libn.
Staff: Prof 1. **Subjects:** Clinical and pre-clinical medicine. **Holdings:** 800 books; 110 publications of medical staff members; 4 VF drawers of pamphlets. **Subscriptions:** 100 journals and other serials. **Services:** Interlibrary loans; copying; library open to public for reference use only. **Computerized Information Services:** MEDLARS. **Networks/Consortia:** Member of Consortium for Health Information & Library Services (CHI).

★10493★
PAPANICOLAOU CANCER RESEARCH INSTITUTE AT MIAMI - RESEARCH LIBRARY (Med)
1155 N.W. 14th St.
Box 016188   Phone: (305) 324-5572
Miami, FL 33101
Founded: 1968. **Staff:** Prof 1. **Subjects:** Biochemistry, enzymology, protein chemistry, molecular biology, immunology, cancer research, biophysics,

pathology, genetics, microbiology, virology. **Special Collections:** Russian technical publications (150 items). **Holdings:** 2300 books; 2000 bound periodical volumes; 1500 unbound journals; 5 boxes of archives of staff publications. **Subscriptions:** 90 journals and other serials. **Services:** Interlibrary loans; copying (fee); library open to public with restrictions. **Networks/Consortia:** Member of Miami Health Sciences Library Consortium (MHSLC). **Publications:** Miami Winter Symposium, annual; Institute Annual Report - free to libraries on request; Canscripts, monthly bulletin.

PAPPAS LAW LIBRARY
See: Boston University

★10494★
PARADE PUBLICATIONS, INC. - LIBRARY (Publ)
750 Third Ave., 7th Fl.   Phone: (212) 573-7188
New York, NY 10017   Paul Cook, Lib.Dir.
Staff: Prof 5. **Subjects:** Editorial research materials. **Special Collections:** Parade Magazine, 1941 to present (bound volumes). **Holdings:** 1200 volumes; internal research material; pamphlets; clippings. **Subscriptions:** 100 journals and other serials; 7 newspapers. **Services:** Library not open to public. **Computerized Information Services:** New York Times Information Service (for internal use only). **Publications:** Parade Magazine; Sunday News Magazine. **Staff:** Jean C. Noble, Ed.Libn.; Anita B. Goss, Res.Libn.; Doris Schortman, Res.Libn.; Roger Niles, Res.Libn.

★10495★
PARADISE VALLEY HOSPITAL - MEDICAL LIBRARY (Med)
2400 E. Fourth St.   Phone: (714) 470-6311
National City, CA 92050   Norma A. Reyes, Libn.
Founded: 1974. **Subjects:** Medicine and nursing. **Holdings:** 800 books; 166 bound periodical volumes; 50 other cataloged items. **Subscriptions:** 60 journals and other serials. **Services:** Library not open to public.

★10496★
PARAPSYCHOLOGY FOUNDATION - EILEEN J. GARRETT LIBRARY (Soc Sci)
228 E. 71st St.   Phone: (212) 628-1550
New York, NY 10021   Wayne Norman, Libn.
Founded: 1951. **Staff:** 1. **Subjects:** Experimental parapsychology and related subjects; spiritualism, altered states of consciousness, hypnosis, psi in anthropology, paranormal healing. **Special Collections:** Rare books dealing with the paranormal and occult. **Holdings:** 9300 books; 950 bound periodical volumes; 11 VF drawers; pamphlets; clippings; reprints. **Subscriptions:** 100 journals and other serials. **Services:** Copying (limited); library open to public for reference use only. **Special Indexes:** Index to periodical literature in parapsychology, 1966 to present (card).

★10497★
PARAPSYCHOLOGY SOURCES OF INFORMATION CENTER (Soc Sci)
2 Plane Tree Ln.   Phone: (516) 271-1243
Dix Hills, NY 11746   Rhea A. White, Dir.
Staff: Prof 1; Other 1. **Subjects:** Experimental parapsychology, psychical research, consciousness studies, mysticism, transpersonal psychology, analytical psychology/Jung. **Special Collections:** Sports and mysticism (4000 items); parapsychology from a nonparapsychological viewpoint (12,000 articles); parapsychology and transpersonal psychology organizations (files on 100 organizations); biographies of parapsychologists (350 files). **Holdings:** 4000 books; 40 bound periodical volumes; 65 manuscripts; 16 dissertations; 54 cassette tapes. **Subscriptions:** 105 journals and other serials. **Services:** Copying; center open to scholars by appointment. **Computerized Information Services:** Ps:Line Database System (internal database). **Publications:** Parapsychology Abstracts International, semiannual; PSI Center bibliographies - for sale; Higher degrees granted for work in parapsychology: An international list - for sale. **Special Indexes:** Index to reviews of parapsychology books; parapsychology index; index to biographical information on parapsychologists; index to sports and mysticism collection (all on cards).

PARISH (William J.) MEMORIAL LIBRARY
See: University of New Mexico - William J. Parish Memorial Library

★10498★
PARK AVENUE SYNAGOGUE - ROTHSCHILD LIBRARY (Rel-Theol)
50 E. 87th St.   Phone: (212) 369-2600
New York, NY 10128   Susan Vogelstein, Hd.Libn.
Founded: 1956. **Staff:** Prof 2; Other 1. **Subjects:** Judaica. **Special Collections:** Holocaust; Jewish biographies; early childhood Judaica; Jewish history; Bible; Jewish art and music. **Holdings:** 6000 books; **Subscriptions:** 20 journals and other serials. **Services:** Library open to public with special permission. **Staff:** Salome Cory, Libn.

★10499★
PARK CITY HOSPITAL - CARLSON FOUNDATION MEMORIAL LIBRARY
(Med)
695 Park Ave.   Phone: (203) 579-5097
Bridgeport, CT 06604   Suzanne Porter-Zadera, Dir.
Staff: 1. **Subjects:** Medicine, nursing, dentistry, allied health sciences.
Holdings: 1500 books; 1261 bound periodical volumes; 127 AV materials; 2
VF drawers. **Subscriptions:** 155 journals and other serials. **Services:**
Interlibrary loans; copying; library open to public for reference use only.
Computerized Information Services: MEDLINE. Performs free searches for
staff; on a cost recovery basis for others. **Networks/Consortia:** Member of
Southwestern Connecticut Library Council (SWLC); Connecticut Association of
Health Science Libraries (CAHSL).

★10500★
PARK COUNTY BAR ASSOCIATION - LAW LIBRARY (Law)
Court House
1002 Sheridan Ave.   Phone: (307) 587-2204
Cody, WY 82414   Ernest F. Fuller, Jr., Chm.
Staff: 2. **Subjects:** Law. **Holdings:** 10,600 volumes. **Services:** Copying;
library open to public with restrictions. **Computerized Information Services:**
Westlaw. Performs searches on cost recovery basis.

★10501★
PARK COUNTY MUSEUM ASSOCIATION - MUSEUM LIBRARY (Hist)
118 W. Chinook   Phone: (406) 222-3506
Livingston, MT 59047   Doris Whithorn, Caretaker
Founded: 1976. **Staff:** 5. **Subjects:** State and local history, railroads.
Holdings: 1400 books; 1000 bound periodical volumes; 30,000 newspapers;
39 cassettes; 1000 family history reports; association scrapbooks and
minutes. **Services:** Library open to public with restrictions.

★10502★
**PARK FOREST PUBLIC LIBRARY - ORAL HISTORY OF PARK FOREST
COLLECTION** (Hist)
400 Lakewood Blvd.   Phone: (312) 748-3731
Park Forest, IL 60466   Neal Ney, Adm.Libn.
Subjects: Park Forest history, especially 1948-1960. **Holdings:** 69
audiotapes; 69 transcripts of audiotapes; 4 boxes of ephemera. **Services:**
Interlibrary loans (limited); copying; collection open to public. **Publications:**
Booklet. **Staff:** Gretchen Falk, Ref.Libn.

★10503★
PARK-NICOLLET MEDICAL FOUNDATION - ARNESON LIBRARY (Med)
5000 W. 39th St.   Phone: (612) 927-3097
Minneapolis, MN 55416   Barbara K. Latta, Dir.
Staff: Prof 2; Other 1. **Subjects:** Medicine, nursing, allied health sciences.
Holdings: 1150 books; 3840 bound periodical volumes; 5 boxes of pamphlets
and reprints. **Subscriptions:** 148 journals and other serials. **Services:**
Interlibrary loans (limited); library not open to public. **Computerized
Information Services:** DIALOG, BRS, MEDLARS. Performs searches free of
charge and on cost recovery basis. **Networks/Consortia:** Member of Twin
Cities Biomedical Consortium (TCBC). **Publications:** Bulletin, quarterly.
Formerly: St. Louis Park Medical Center-Research Foundation. **Staff:** Ruth
Amdahl, Libn.

★10504★
PARK PLACE CHURCH OF GOD - CARL KARDATZKE MEMORIAL LIBRARY
(Rel-Theol)
501 College Dr.
Anderson, IN 46012   Hazel Smith, Chm., Lib.Comm.
Subjects: Bibles, religion, Christian education, doctrinal theology, family
ethics, biography, missions, children's books. **Holdings:** 2000 books.

★10505★
PARK RIDGE HOSPITAL - LIBRARY (Med)
1555 Long Pond Rd.   Phone: (716) 225-7150
Rochester, NY 14626   Eileen P. Shirley, Libn.
Founded: 1975. **Staff:** Prof 1. **Subjects:** Medicine, nursing, surgery, hospital
administration. **Holdings:** 1352 books; 1021 bound periodical volumes; 785
audio cassettes; 37 tapes. **Subscriptions:** 114 journals and other serials.
Services: Interlibrary loans; library open to public by request. **Networks/
Consortia:** Member of Rochester Regional Research Library Council (RRRLC).

★10506★
PARK SYNAGOGUE LIBRARY - KRAVITZ MEMORIAL LIBRARY (Rel-Theol)
3300 Mayfield Rd.   Phone: (216) 371-2244
Cleveland Heights, OH 44118   Sharon R. Merklin, Libn.
Staff: Prof 1. **Subjects:** Judaica, Jewish history. **Holdings:** 15,000 books;

100 bound periodical volumes. **Subscriptions:** 70 journals and other serials;
10 newspapers. **Services:** Interlibrary loans; library open to public for
reference use only.

PARK (William Hallock) MEMORIAL LIBRARY
See: New York City - Public Health Laboratories - William Hallock Park
   Memorial Library

PARKE-DAVIS
See: Warner-Lambert/Parke-Davis

★10507★
PARKER, CHAPIN, FLATTAU AND KLIMPL - LIBRARY (Law)
530 Fifth Ave.   Phone: (212) 840-6200
New York, NY 10036   Helene W. Nelson, Mgr., Files/Lib.
Founded: 1940. **Staff:** Prof 2; Other 2. **Subjects:** Law - litigation, antitrust,
tax, labor, trusts and estates, corporations, banking, securities, real estate.
Holdings: 15,500 books; 150 bound periodical volumes; 600 pamphlets.
Subscriptions: 60 journals and other serials. **Services:** Interlibrary loans;
library not open to public. **Computerized Information Services:** LEXIS,
DIALOG. **Publications:** PCF & K Library Memo, monthly. **Special Catalogs:**
Catalog of memoranda and briefs (card); corporate forms catalog (card).
Staff: Emily C. Rose, Libn.

★10508★
PARKER MEMORIAL BAPTIST CHURCH - LIBRARY (Rel-Theol)†
1205 Quintard Ave.   Phone: (205) 236-5628
Anniston, AL 36201   Mrs. Gale Main, Libn.
Founded: 1932. **Staff:** Prof 1; Other 6. **Subjects:** Religion, fiction,
biography, history and geography. **Holdings:** 3500 books; 1 VF drawer of
pamphlets. **Services:** Library open to public.

★10509★
PARKLAND COLLEGE - LEARNING RESOURCE CENTER (Educ)
2400 W. Bradley Ave.   Phone: (217) 351-2241
Champaign, IL 61820   David L. Johnson, Dir.
Founded: 1967. **Staff:** Prof 7; Other 19. **Subjects:** Education. **Holdings:**
80,000 books; 11,000 other cataloged items. **Subscriptions:** 750 journals
and other serials; 38 newspapers. **Services:** Interlibrary loans; copying;
center open to public with restrictions. **Automated Operations:**
Computerized cataloging and acquisitions. **Computerized Information
Services:** OCLC. **Networks/Consortia:** Member of Lincoln Trail Libraries
System; ILLINET. **Staff:** William C. Gaines, Pub.Serv.Libn.; Ann Neely,
Ref.Libn.; Ken Strickler, Tech.Serv.Libn.; Raymond Bial, Acq.Libn.; John
Conley, Media Spec.

PARKLAWN HEALTH LIBRARY
See: U.S. Public Health Service

PARKMAN (Timothy) MEMORIAL LIBRARY
See: St. Thomas More Center - Timothy Parkman Memorial Library

PARKS CANADA
See: Entries filed directly under park name

PARKS COLLEGE OF AERONAUTICAL TECHNOLOGY
See: St. Louis University

★10510★
PARKVIEW EPISCOPAL MEDICAL CENTER - MEDICAL LIBRARY (Med)
400 W. 16th St.   Phone: (303) 584-4582
Pueblo, CO 81003   Ms. Lyn Smith Hammond, Med.Libn.
Founded: 1959. **Staff:** Prof 1; Other 1. **Subjects:** Medicine, nursing, surgery,
hospital administration, allied health sciences. **Holdings:** 2119 books; 1648
bound periodical volumes; pamphlet file. **Subscriptions:** 112 journals and
other serials. **Services:** Interlibrary loans; copying; library open to public with
special permission. **Computerized Information Services:** MEDLARS.
Networks/Consortia: Member of Colorado Council of Medical Librarians;
Peaks and Valleys (Medical) Library Consortium. **Formerly:** Parkview Episcopal
Hospital.

PARKVIEW LIBRARY
See: Oklahoma School for the Blind

★10511★
**PARKVIEW MEMORIAL HOSPITAL - PARKVIEW-METHODIST SCHOOL OF
NURSING - LIBRARY** (Med)
2200 Randallia Dr.   Phone: (219) 484-6636
Fort Wayne, IN 46805   Phyllis Eckman, Libn.
Staff: Prof 1. **Subjects:** Nursing, medicine, allied health sciences. **Holdings:**

2000 books; 87 bound periodical volumes. **Subscriptions:** 74 journals and other serials. **Services:** Interlibrary loans (fee); copying; library open to public with permission. **Computerized Information Services:** MEDLINE, BRS. **Networks/Consortia:** Member of Northeast Indiana Health Science Libraries; TRI-ALSA; Greater Midwest Regional Medical Library Network (Region 3).

★10512★
PARKVIEW OSTEOPATHIC HOSPITAL - LIBRARY (Med)*
1920 Parkwood Ave.   Phone: (419) 242-8471
Toledo, OH 43624   Donna McLain, Lib.Cons.
Staff: Prof 1. **Subjects:** Osteopathy, orthopedics, radiology, surgery, anesthesiology, pediatrics, clinical and family medicine. **Special Collections:** Osteopathic Collection including rare books by the founder of the osteopathic medical profession. **Holdings:** 1050 books; 1450 bound periodical volumes; Audio-Digest tapes. **Subscriptions:** 74 journals and other serials. **Services:** Interlibrary loans; library not open to public. **Computerized Information Services:** MEDLINE.

PARLIN-INGERSOLL LIBRARY - FULTON COUNTY HISTORICAL AND GENEALOGICAL SOCIETY
See: Fulton County Historical and Genealogical Society

PARLOW (A.F.) LIBRARY OF THE HEALTH SCIENCES
See: Los Angeles County Harbor-UCLA Medical Center - A.F. Parlow Library of the Health Sciences

PARMA TECHNICAL CENTER
See: Union Carbide Corporation

★10513★
PARMAR ELDALIEVA LIBRARY (Rec)
1846 Bundy St.
Scranton, PA 18508   Rumil of Cameloford, Libn.
Founded: 1977. **Staff:** Prof 1; Other 1. **Subjects:** J.R.R. Tolkien - fiction, fanzines; mythology; language; scholarly works on Tolkien. **Special Collections:** First editions (18 volumes). **Holdings:** 390 books; 42 bound periodical volumes; 7 VF drawers of clippings. **Subscriptions:** 11 journals and other serials. **Services:** Library not open to public. **Publications:** Lendarin & Danian, semiannual - by subscription.

★10514★
PARMLY BILLINGS LIBRARY - MONTANA ROOM (Hist)
510 N. Broadway   Phone: (406) 657-8290
Billings, MT 59101   Linda Weirather
Staff: Prof 1. **Subjects:** Montana history, Battle of Little Bighorn, Crow Indians. **Special Collections:** Local histories (100 items); city archives (75 items). **Holdings:** 6000 books; 100 bound periodical volumes; 120 filing drawers. **Subscriptions:** 12 journals and other serials; 6 newspapers.

PARNALL TECHNICAL LIBRARY
See: Consumers Power Company

★10515★
PARRISH ART MUSEUM - LIBRARY (Art)
25 Job's Ln.   Phone: (516) 283-2118
Southampton, NY 11968   Eva D. Balamuth, Chm., Lib.Comm.
Founded: 1954. **Subjects:** Art - American, European; architecture; crafts. **Special Collections:** William Merritt Chase Archives; Aline B. Saarinen Library; Moses and Ida Soyer Library; Samuel Parrish Library. **Holdings:** 4300 books; 3000 catalogs. **Services:** Library open to museum members, regional artists and Southampton College students.

PARRISH (June Austin) MEMORIAL LIBRARY
See: Employees Reinsurance Corporation - June Austin Parrish Memorial Library

PARSONNET (Dr. Victor) MEMORIAL LIBRARY
See: Newark Beth Israel Medical Center - Dr. Victor Parsonnet Memorial Library

★10516★
PARSONS, BRINCKERHOFF, QUADE & DOUGLAS - LIBRARY (Plan)
250 W. 34th St.   Phone: (212) 613-5290
New York, NY 10119   Jeanne I. Brown, Libn.
Founded: 1976. **Staff:** Prof 2. **Subjects:** Transportation, civil and structural engineering, urban and environmental planning. **Holdings:** 5500 books; 250 bound periodical volumes; 4500 technical reports. **Subscriptions:** 200 journals and other serials. **Services:** Interlibrary loans; copying; library open to public by appointment. **Automated Operations:** Computerized periodicals

routing. **Computerized Information Services:** BRS, DIALOG, SDC, DOE/RECON. **Staff:** Rachel Cohen, Asst.Libn.

PARSONS (Elbert H.) PUBLIC LAW LIBRARY
See: Madison County - Elbert H. Parsons Public Law Library

★10517★
PARSONS (Ralph M.) COMPANY - CENTRAL LIBRARY (Sci-Tech)
100 W. Walnut St.   Phone: (818) 440-3999
Pasadena, CA 91124   Jennifer Stein, Libn.
Staff: Prof 1; Other 1. **Subjects:** Engineering, mining, nuclear engineering, power. **Holdings:** 6000 books; 1000 bound periodical volumes; 7000 reports; 3500 vendor equipment catalogs. **Subscriptions:** 200 journals and other serials; 5 newspapers. **Services:** Interlibrary loans.

PARSONS (Ralph M.) LABORATORY
See: Massachusetts Institute of Technology - Civil Engineering Dept. - Ralph M. Parsons Laboratory

★10518★
PARSONS SCHOOL OF DESIGN - ADAM AND SOPHIE GIMBEL DESIGN LIBRARY (Art)
66 Fifth Ave.   Phone: (212) 741-8914
New York, NY 10011   Sharon Chickanzeff, Lib.Dir.
Founded: 1896. **Staff:** Prof 2; Other 5. **Subjects:** Art, architecture, costume, crafts, design, environmental design, fashion, graphic arts, photography, typography. **Special Collections:** Sketchbooks by American fashion designer Claire McCardell (125 volumes). **Holdings:** 32,000 books; 31,000 mounted picture plates. **Subscriptions:** 137 journals and other serials. **Services:** Interlibrary loans; library not open to public. **Automated Operations:** Computerized circulation. **Networks/Consortia:** Member of New York University, New School, Cooper Union Consortium; METRO. **Remarks:** Affiliated with New School for Social Research. **Staff:** Claire Petrie, Ref./Tech.Serv.Libn.

★10519★
PARSONS SCHOOL OF DESIGN - OTIS ART INSTITUTE - LIBRARY (Art)
2307 W. 6th St.   Phone: (213) 387-5288
Los Angeles, CA 90057   Justine V. Clancy, Dir.
Founded: 1947. **Staff:** Prof 3; Other 1. **Subjects:** Fine arts, communication design, architecture, fashion, design, photography. **Special Collections:** Artists' books (750 titles); fine prints and artists' realia (54 titles). **Holdings:** 50,000 books; 3000 bound periodical volumes; 60,000 slides; 54 VF drawers of artists' ephemera files; 16 VF drawers of clipping files; 9 VF drawers of art reproduction files; 267 audio cassettes; 123 films; 87 videotapes and cassettes. **Subscriptions:** 207 journals and other serials. **Services:** Copying; library open to public by appointment only. **Automated Operations:** Computerized cataloging. **Staff:** Brian Mains, Slide/Media Cur.; Doug Allen, Circ.&Ser.; Carol Heron, Cat.Libn.

★10520★
PARSONS STATE HOSPITAL AND TRAINING CENTER - RESEARCH LIBRARY (Med)
Box 738   Phone: (316) 421-6550
Parsons, KS 67357   Banny P. Rucker, Asst.Libn.
Founded: 1953. **Staff:** Prof 1; Other 1. **Subjects:** Psychiatry, psychology, mental retardation, psychiatric nursing, social service, speech pathology, audiology, behavioral science, operant conditioning. **Holdings:** 5200 books; 4 VF drawers of pamphlets; 282 working papers. **Subscriptions:** 75 journals and other serials. **Services:** Interlibrary loans; copying; library open to public. **Remarks:** This library is the cooperative effort of P.S.H. and T.C. and the Kansas Bureau of Child Research. CETA employees help to make up the staff. Hospital and Training Center also has an active library for mentally retarded and emotionally disturbed children and young people, ages 6-21.

PASADENA CITY - GREENE AND GREENE LIBRARY
See: Greene and Greene Library

★10521★
PASADENA COLLEGE OF CHIROPRACTIC - LIBRARY (Med)
1505 N. Marengo   Phone: (818) 798-1141
Pasadena, CA 91103   Mary Beth Hayes, Libn.
Staff: Prof 1; Other 1. **Subjects:** Chiropractic. **Holdings:** 7000 books; 900 bound periodical volumes; 5000 unbound periodicals. **Subscriptions:** 60 journals and other serials. **Services:** Copying; library open to public for reference use only. **Networks/Consortia:** Member of Chiropractic Library Consortium (CLIBCON).

★10522★
PASADENA HISTORICAL SOCIETY - LIBRARY (Hist)
470 W. Walnut St.   Phone: (818) 577-1660
Pasadena, CA 91103   Sue F. Schechter, Exec.Dir.
Founded: 1924. **Staff:** Prof 1; other 12. **Subjects:** History of the Pasadena area. **Special Collections:** Photographs and slides of early Pasadena (9000). **Holdings:** 1000 books; pamphlets; clippings; albums; diaries; maps; documents; magazines. **Services:** Library open to public for research only.

★10523★
PASADENA PRESBYTERIAN CHURCH - LIBRARY (Rel-Theol)
100 Pasadena Ave., N.   Phone: (813) 345-0148
St. Petersburg, FL 33710   Elizabeth Howe, Libn.
Founded: 1960. **Staff:** Prof 2; Other 1. **Subjects:** Religion, religious education. **Holdings:** 3000 books; 75 filmstrips; Presbyterian curriculum materials. **Subscriptions:** 12 journals and other serials. **Services:** Copying; library open to public for reference use only. **Staff:** Maxine Perry, Cat.Libn.

★10524★
PASADENA PUBLIC LIBRARY - ALICE COLEMAN BATCHELDER MUSIC LIBRARY (Mus)
285 E. Walnut St.   Phone: (818) 577-4049
Pasadena, CA 91101   Anne Cain, Prin.Libn./Ref.Serv.
Founded: 1955. **Staff:** Prof 4; Other 3. **Subjects:** Music history, theory and biography; dance; musical instruments; cinema. **Special Collections:** Popular sheet music, 1858-1956 (1500 items). **Holdings:** 4850 books; 296 bound periodical volumes; 5342 music scores; 6 VF drawers of clippings and pamphlets; 19 boxes of opera librettos; 33 boxes of miniature scores; 13,056 phonograph records; 22 volumes of scrapbooks; 600 cassettes. **Subscriptions:** 29 journals and other serials. **Services:** Interlibrary loans; copying; library open to public. **Automated Operations:** Computerized circulation. **Networks/Consortia:** Member of Metropolitan Cooperative Library System (MCLS). **Special Indexes:** Card index to song collections; card index to piano, organ and violin music in collections. **Staff:** Laurie Whitcomb; Ruth Quirk .

★10525★
PASADENA PUBLIC LIBRARY - BUSINESS-TECHNOLOGY DIVISION (Bus-Fin)
285 E. Walnut St.   Phone: (818) 577-4052
Pasadena, CA 91101   Anne Cain, Prin.Libn./Ref.Serv.
Founded: 1970. **Staff:** Prof 5; Other 1. **Subjects:** Investments, finance, business management, real estate, taxation, industrial technology, engineering. **Special Collections:** Pasadena industries; state industrial directories; tax and investment services. **Holdings:** 20,485 books; 705 trade and professional directories; 350 company catalogs; 1670 corporate annual reports; 20 VF drawers of clippings and pamphlets; 1450 microfiche; 144 cassettes. **Subscriptions:** 178 journals and other serials; 16 newspapers. **Services:** Interlibrary loans; division open to public. **Automated Operations:** Computerized cataloging, acquisitions and circulation. **Computerized Information Services:** OCLC. **Networks/Consortia:** Member of Metropolitan Cooperative Library System (MCLS). **Special Indexes:** Subject index to trade directories; subject index to company catalogs. **Staff:** Joan Kennedy; Dan Hanne.

★10526★
PASADENA PUBLIC LIBRARY - FINE ARTS DIVISION (Art)
285 E. Walnut St.   Phone: (818) 577-4049
Pasadena, CA 91101   Anne Cain, Prin.Libn./Ref.Serv.
Founded: 1927. **Staff:** Prof 4; Other 3. **Subjects:** Art history and theory, architecture, antiques, crafts, painting, printmaking, photography, costume, art biographies. **Holdings:** 15,126 books; 1550 bound periodical volumes; 377 titles of 16mm films; 12 VF drawers of clippings and pamphlets; 132,568 pictures; 92 volumes of scrapbooks. **Subscriptions:** 94 journals and other serials. **Services:** Interlibrary loans; copying; division open to public. **Automated Operations:** Computerized circulation. **Networks/Consortia:** Member of Metropolitan Cooperative Library System (MCLS). **Special Indexes:** Index to Architectural Digest from 1920-1950 for Southern California Architecture; Picture File Index. **Staff:** Laurie Whitcomb; Ruth Quirk .

★10527★
PASADENA PUBLIC LIBRARY - REFERENCE DIVISION (Hist)
285 E. Walnut St.   Phone: (818) 577-4054
Pasadena, CA 91101   Anne Cain, Prin.Libn./Ref.Serv.
Staff: Prof 5; Other 2. **Special Collections:** California and Pasadena local history, Pasadena Playhouse, genealogy. **Holdings:** 28,057 books; 425 bound periodical volumes; 1752 Pasadena photographs; 210 Pasadena scrapbooks; 47 pamphlet boxes of local city reports; 90,603 U.S. documents; 14,043 California documents; 44 VF drawers; 5047 maps; 8958 reels of microfilm;

8399 pamphlets; 1395 photographs; 109 negatives; 861 telephone directories; 9239 microfiche; 723 college catalogs; 1272 reels of microfilm of Pasadena newspapers. **Subscriptions:** 395 journals and other serials; 30 newspapers. **Services:** Interlibrary loans; copying; division open to public. **Automated Operations:** Computerized cataloging and acquisitions. **Computerized Information Services:** OCLC. **Networks/Consortia:** Member of Metropolitan Cooperative Library System (MCLS). **Staff:** Joan Kennedy .

★10528★
PASCACK VALLEY HOSPITAL - DAVID GOLDBERG MEMORIAL MEDICAL LIBRARY (Med)†
Old Hook Rd.   Phone: (201) 664-4000
Westwood, NJ 07675   Margaret F. DeMarrais, Libn.
Founded: 1968. **Staff:** 1. **Subjects:** Medicine, surgery, nursing. **Holdings:** 1100 books; 500 bound periodical volumes; 4 VF drawers; indexes; 1700 audiotapes. **Subscriptions:** 120 journals. **Services:** Interlibrary loans; copying; library open to public with restrictions. **Networks/Consortia:** Member of Bergen-Passaic Health Sciences Library Consortium; Health Science Libraries of New Jersey.

PASKOW SCIENCE FICTION LIBRARY
See: Temple University - Central Library System - Science Fiction Collection

★10529★
PASQUA HOSPITAL - HEALTH SCIENCES LIBRARY (Med)†
4101 Dewdney Ave.   Phone: (306) 527-9641
Regina, SK, Canada S4T 1A5   Leona Lang, Dir.
Founded: 1953. **Staff:** 1. **Subjects:** Medicine, nursing, administration. **Holdings:** 1200 books; 2800 bound periodical volumes; Audio-Digest tapes; videotapes. **Subscriptions:** 72 journals and other serials. **Services:** Library not open to public.

PASS (Malca) MEMORIAL LIBRARY
See: Agudath Israel Congregation - Malca Pass Memorial Library

★10530★
PASSAIC COUNTY HISTORICAL SOCIETY - LIBRARY (Hist)
Lambert Castle, Valley Rd.   Phone: (201) 881-2761
Paterson, NJ 07503   Catherine Keene, Dir.
Staff: 1. **Subjects:** Local and New Jersey history, local authors, local industry. **Special Collections:** Society for the Establishment of Useful Manufactures papers; Abraham Hewitt papers (iron industry). **Holdings:** 1000 books. **Services:** Copying; library open to public by appointment.

★10531★
PASSAVANT MEMORIAL AREA HOSPITAL ASSOCIATION - SIBERT LIBRARY (Med)
1600 W. Walnut St.   Phone: (217) 245-9541
Jacksonville, IL 62650   Dorothy H. Knight, Libn.
Founded: 1902. **Staff:** Prof 1; Other 1. **Subjects:** Nursing, medicine. **Holdings:** 2160 books; 140 bound periodical volumes; AV material. **Subscriptions:** 267 journals and other serials. **Services:** Interlibrary loans; copying; library open to public with permission for research given on individual basis. **Networks/Consortia:** Member of Greater Midwest Regional Medical Library Network (Region 3); West Central Consortium; Great River Library System.

★10532★
PASSIONIST MONASTIC SEMINARY - LIBRARY (Rel-Theol)
86-45 178th St.   Phone: (718) 739-6502
Jamaica, NY 11432   Br. James G. Johnson, C.P., Libn.
Founded: 1934. **Staff:** Prof 1; Other 1. **Subjects:** Philosophy, theology, history, preaching, suffering, adult education. **Holdings:** 32,648 books; 120 bound periodical volumes. **Subscriptions:** 149 journals and other serials. **Services:** Library not open to public.

PASSIVE SOLAR FOUNDATION
See: Citizens' Energy Project, Inc.

PASTOR (Sherman) MEMORIAL LIBRARY
See: Congregation Shalom - Sherman Pastor Memorial Library

PASTORE LIBRARY
See: Philadelphia College of Textiles and Science

★10533★
PATENT, TRADEMARK AND COPYRIGHT RESEARCH FOUNDATION - LIBRARY (Law)
Franklin Pierce Law Ctr.   Phone: (603) 228-1541
Concord, NH 03301
Staff: Prof 3. **Subjects:** Patents, trademarks, copyright. **Holdings:** 1000 items. **Publications:** IDEA; Journal of Law and Technology, quarterly.

PATERNO LIBRARY
See: Columbia University

★10534★
PATERSON AND CO. - LIBRARY
Box 1196
Palmdale, CA 93550
Defunct

★10535★
PATERSON NEWS - LIBRARY/NEWSPAPER MORGUE (Publ)
1 News Plaza   Phone: (201) 684-3000
Paterson, NJ 07509   Sheldon Matson, Libn.
Founded: 1890. **Staff:** 1. **Subjects:** Newspaper reference topics. **Special Collections:** New Jersey Legislative Directory, 1879 to present; Passaic County Freeholders Reports, 1975 to present; Paterson Morning Call and News, 1889 to present (microfilm). **Holdings:** Photographs; reference books; local sports material. **Services:** Library open to public by appointment. **Subscriptions:** 16 journals and other serials.

PATERSON (Norman) SCHOOL OF INTERNATIONAL AFFAIRS
See: Carleton University - Norman Paterson School of International Affairs

PATERSON (William) COLLEGE OF NEW JERSEY
See: William Paterson College of New Jersey

★10536★
PATIENT CARE COMMUNICATIONS, INC. - LIBRARY (Med; Publ)
16 Thorndal Circle   Phone: (203) 655-8951
Darien, CT 06820   Sylvia Boyd, Libn.
Staff: Prof 1; Other 1. **Subjects:** Medicine, family practice, medical marketing. **Holdings:** 600 books; 30 VF drawers. **Subscriptions:** 122 journals and other serials. **Services:** Interlibrary loans; copying; SDI; library open to public by appointment. **Networks/Consortia:** Member of Southwestern Connecticut Library Council. **Publications:** Library acquisitions, 3/year - for internal distribution only.

PATMOS MEMORIAL LIBRARY
See: Bixby (Emma L.) Hospital

PATRICK AIR FORCE BASE (FL)
See: U.S. Air Force Hospital - Medical Library (FL-Patrick AFB)

★10537★
PATRIOT NEWS COMPANY - NEWS LIBRARY (Publ)
812 Market St.
Box 2265   Phone: (717) 255-8402
Harrisburg, PA 17105   Deanna S. Beeching, Libn.
Staff: Prof 1; Other 1. **Subjects:** Newspaper reference topics. **Holdings:** 200 books; newspapers clipping files on microfiche; 12 VF drawers of photographs; local paper on microfilm, 1911 to present. **Services:** Library not open to public. **Special Indexes:** Clippings index (card); graphics index.

★10538★
PATRIOTIC EDUCATION, INC. - LIBRARY (Soc Sci)
Box 2121   Phone: (904) 252-3414
Daytona Beach, FL 32015   Sedgley Thornbury, Pres.
Founded: 1952. **Staff:** Prof 1. **Subjects:** American history, U.S. Constitution, Declaration of Independence, U.S. flag and other symbols of Americanism. **Special Collections:** Historical Research Studies. **Holdings:** Figures not available.

PATTEE LIBRARY
See: Pennsylvania State University

PATTERSON (A.B.) PROFESSIONAL LIBRARY
See: Scarborough Board of Education - A.B. Patterson Professional Library

★10539★
PATTERSON, BELKNAP, WEBB & TYLER - LIBRARY (Law)
30 Rockefeller Plaza   Phone: (212) 541-4000
New York, NY 10112   Penny Tarpley, Chf.Libn.
Staff: Prof 2; Other 7. **Subjects:** Law - litigation, corporate, tax, patent/copyright, media/communication. **Holdings:** 25,000 volumes; 6000 current annual reports; 15 VF drawers of material; 150 audio cassettes. **Subscriptions:** 360 journals and other serials; 12 newspapers. **Services:** Interlibrary loans; library not open to public. **Computerized Information Services:** Westlaw, New York Times Information Service, DIALOG, Dow Jones News/Retrieval, NewsNet, Inc., BNA Daily SEC Advance, SDC, Mead Data Central. **Networks/Consortia:** Member of Law Library Association of Greater New York. **Publications:** Res Communes (newsletter), monthly - for internal distribution only. **Special Catalogs:** Cataloging Manual (online and printout). **Special Indexes:** Tax Club Memoranda Index; List of On-Line Databases; Annual Reports List; Periodicals List (all online and printout). **Staff:** Lorraine Siegel, Asst.Libn.; Thomas Fedorek, Asst.Libn.

PATTERSON REFERENCE LIBRARY AND ECONOMICS REFERENCE CENTER
See: Midwest Research Institute

PATTILLO (James R.) LIBRARY OF BANKING AND FINANCE
See: University of California, Los Angeles - Management Library

★10540★
PATTON BOGGS AND BLOW - LAW LIBRARY (Law)
2550 M St., N.W.   Phone: (202) 223-4040
Washington, DC 20037   Kevin McCall, Libn.
Staff: Prof 1. **Subjects:** Law. **Holdings:** 7000 books. **Subscriptions:** 36 journals and other serials. **Services:** Interlibrary loans. **Computerized Information Services:** Westlaw, DIALOG.

PATTON MUSEUM OF CAVALRY & ARMOR
See: U.S. Army

★10541★
PATTON STATE HOSPITAL - STAFF LIBRARY (Med)
3102 E. Highland Ave.   Phone: (714) 862-8121
Patton, CA 92369   Mary Sue Stumberg, Libn.
Founded: 1947. **Staff:** Prof 1. **Subjects:** Psychiatry, psychology, neurology, psychiatric nursing. **Holdings:** 3500 books; 2025 bound periodical volumes; 1200 unbound periodical volumes; 2 VF drawers of unbound reports; 2 VF drawers of documents. **Subscriptions:** 65 journals and other serials. **Services:** Interlibrary loans; library open to mental health professionals. **Networks/Consortia:** Member of Pacific Southwest Regional Medical Library Service (PSRMLS); San Bernardino, Inyo, Riverside United Library Services (SIRCULS).

PATUXENT WILDLIFE RESEARCH CENTER LIBRARY
See: U.S. Fish & Wildlife Service

★10542★
PAUL DE HAEN INTERNATIONAL, INC. - DRUG INFORMATION SYSTEMS AND SERVICES (Med)
2750 S. Shoshone St.   Phone: (303) 781-6683
Englewood, CO 80110   Paul E. Groth, Pres.
Founded: 1965. **Staff:** Prof 5. **Subjects:** Drugs and biomedical information. **Holdings:** 500 books; 200,000 scientific reports from international biomedical literature. **Subscriptions:** 1250 journals and other serials. **Services:** Indexing; abstracting; reports; literature translations. **Publications:** List of publications - available upon request. **Formerly:** Micromedex, Inc. - Paul de Haen Drug Information Systems.

★10543★
PAUL, HASTINGS, JANOFSKY AND WALKER - LAW LIBRARY (Law)†
555 S. Flower, 22nd Floor   Phone: (213) 489-4000
Los Angeles, CA 90071   Bobbie Johnson, Hd.Libn.
Founded: 1972. **Staff:** Prof 2; Other 1. **Subjects:** Law (basic U.S. and California). **Holdings:** 15,000 volumes. **Subscriptions:** 185 journals and other serials. **Services:** Interlibrary loans; library open to public on request. **Automated Operations:** Computerized cataloging. **Computerized Information Services:** DIALOG, LEXIS, Predicasts, Inc. **Networks/Consortia:** Member of CLASS. **Special Indexes:** Computerized index to research memos. **Staff:** Suzanne Plessinger, Libn.

★10544★

PAUL SMITH'S COLLEGE OF ARTS AND SCIENCES - FRANK L. CUBLEY LIBRARY (Bus-Fin; Env-Cons)

Paul Smiths, NY 12970

Phone: (518) 327-6313
Theodore D. Mack, Libn.

Staff: Prof 2; Other 4. **Subjects:** Hotel and restaurant management, forestry, environmental science, forest recreation, surveying. **Holdings:** 40,000 books; 23,000 pamphlets. **Subscriptions:** 360 journals and other serials; 9 newspapers. **Services:** Interlibrary loans; copying; library open to public. **Networks/Consortia:** Member of North Country Reference and Research Resources Council (NCRRRC). **Staff:** Neil Surprenant, Asst.Libn.

★10545★

PAUL, WEISS, RIFKIND, WHARTON AND GARRISON - LIBRARY (Law)

345 Park Ave.
New York, NY 10154

Phone: (212) 644-8235
Deborah S. Panella, Chf.Libn.

Founded: 1927. **Staff:** Prof 8; Other 20. **Subjects:** Law. **Holdings:** 60,000 books; 1000 bound periodical volumes; 7500 reels of microfilm. **Subscriptions:** 250 journals and other serials; 25 newspapers. **Services:** Interlibrary loans. **Computerized Information Services:** LEXIS, Westlaw, DIALOG, SDC, RLIN, BRS, I.P. Sharp Associates, Ltd. **Staff:** Gail Beckenstein, Asst.Libn.

PAULIST LIBRARY
See: Old St. Mary's Church

PAVEMENTS AND SOIL TRAFFICABILITY INFORMATION ANALYSIS CENTER
See: U.S. Army - Engineer Waterways Experiment Station

PAVILLON ALBERT-PREVOST
See: Hopital du Sacre-Coeur

★10546★

PAWTUCKET MEMORIAL HOSPITAL - HEALTH SCIENCES LIBRARY (Med)*

Prospect & Pond Sts.
Pawtucket, RI 02860

Phone: (401) 722-6000
Carol-Ann Rausch, Med.Libn.

Founded: 1959. **Staff:** Prof 1; Other 1. **Subjects:** Medicine, family medicine. **Special Collections:** Videocassette Resource Center (Network for Continuing Medical Education - American Medical Association Category Credit Programs). **Holdings:** 485 books; 6822 bound periodical volumes. **Subscriptions:** 150 journals and other serials. **Services:** Interlibrary loans; copying; library open to public upon special request. **Computerized Information Services:** Online systems. **Networks/Consortia:** Member of Association of Rhode Island Health Sciences Librarians (ARIHSL). **Publications:** Newsletter.

★10547★

PAYETTE ASSOCIATES - LIBRARY (Plan)†

40 Isabella St.
Boston, MA 02116

Phone: (617) 423-0070
Sonja M. Nielsen, Corp.Libn.

Founded: 1979. **Staff:** Prof 1; Other 2. **Subjects:** Architecture, design and construction of health care facilities. **Holdings:** 1000 books; 2000 catalogs; 500 samples; 10 VF drawers of reports and clippings; 15 drawers of prints and plans; 17,000 slides. **Subscriptions:** 80 journals and other serials. **Services:** Interlibrary loans; copying; library open to public upon request to librarian.

PAYNE (Bishop) LIBRARY
See: Virginia Theological Seminary - Bishop Payne Library

★10548★

PAYNE THEOLOGICAL SEMINARY - R.C. RANSOM MEMORIAL LIBRARY (Rel-Theol)†

Wilberforce-Clifton Rd.
Wilberforce, OH 45384

Phone: (513) 376-2946
Barbara L. Tyiska, Hd.Libn.

Founded: 1844. **Staff:** Prof 1; Other 2. **Subjects:** Theology, black studies, African Methodist Episcopal Church history. **Special Collections:** Arno Press Black Studies Program - The American Negro, His History and Literature (150 volumes). **Holdings:** 16,907 books; 500 items of archive material; 13 videotapes; 40 filmstrips; 50 microforms. **Subscriptions:** 51 journals and other serials. **Services:** Interlibrary loans; copying; library open to public. **Publications:** Union Serials List of Seminaries, every 4 years.

★10549★

PAYNE WHITNEY PSYCHIATRIC CLINIC LIBRARY (Med)

New York Hospital-
Cornell University Medical College
525 E. 68th St.
New York, NY 10021

Phone: (212) 472-6442
Phyllis Rubinton, Libn.

Staff: Prof 2. **Subjects:** Psychiatry, psychology, behavioral sciences. **Special**

Collections: History of psychiatry; Archives of Psychiatry. **Holdings:** 20,000 books and bound periodical volumes; 125 video cassettes; 50 audio cassettes. **Subscriptions:** 160 journals and other serials. **Services:** Interlibrary loans; library open to qualified researchers. **Networks/Consortia:** Member of Medical Library Center of New York. **Publications:** Acquisitions List, quarterly. **Special Catalogs:** Media Catalog. **Staff:** Mary Mylenki, Sr.Asst.Libn.

PAYSON (Daniel Carroll) MEDICAL LIBRARY
See: North Shore University Hospital - Daniel Carroll Payson Medical Library

★10550★

PCL-BRAUN-SIMONS LTD. - PBS LIBRARY (Sci-Tech)†

1015 4th St., S.W.
Calgary, AB, Canada T2R 1J4

Phone: (403) 260-1592
Kathleen Robertson, Libn.

Staff: Prof 1. **Subjects:** Engineering, project management, construction, procurement. **Special Collections:** Engineering standards (2000). **Holdings:** 500 books; 200 periodical volumes. **Subscriptions:** 22 journals and other serials. **Services:** Interlibrary loans; library not open to public. **Automated Operations:** Computerized cataloging. **Computerized Information Services:** DIALOG, SDC, Sharp (I.P.) Associates Limited, SPIRES.

PEA RIDGE NATL. MILITARY PARK
See: U.S. Natl. Park Service

PEABODY COLLECTION OF BOOKS ON CHILDREN
See: Vanderbilt University - Jean and Alexander Heard Library - Education Library

★10551★

PEABODY CONSERVATORY OF MUSIC - LIBRARY (Mus)

21 E. Mt. Vernon Pl.
Baltimore, MD 21202

Phone: (301) 837-0600
Edwin A. Quist, Libn.

Founded: 1866. **Staff:** Prof 2; Other 3. **Subjects:** Music, dance. **Special Collections:** Caruso Collection (62 volumes); John Charles Thomas Collection; manuscripts of Asger Hamerik, Gustav Strube, Louis Cheslock, Howard Thatcher, Robert L. Paul, Theodore Hemberger and George Boyle. **Holdings:** 56,500 books and scores; 1500 bound periodical volumes; 15,000 recordings; 333 reels of microfilm; 1500 manuscripts; 8 VF drawers; 6 boxes of clippings. **Subscriptions:** 300 journals and other serials. **Services:** Interlibrary loans; copying (nonmusic materials only); library open to public. **Automated Operations:** Computerized cataloging. **Computerized Information Services:** RLIN. **Networks/Consortia:** Member of Maryland Interlibrary Loan Organization (MILO); RLG. **Publications:** Cotage (newsletter), monthly - for internal distribution only. **Special Indexes:** Index to Chrysander edition of Handel's works (card). **Staff:** Christopher Lobingier, Sound Recordings Libn.; Christine Roberts, Asst.Libn./Rd.Serv.

PEABODY (George) COLLECTION
See: Johns Hopkins University - Milton S. Eisenhower Library - George Peabody Collection

★10552★

PEABODY (George) COLLEGE FOR TEACHERS OF VANDERBILT UNIVERSITY - KENNEDY CENTER - MATERIALS LIBRARY (Soc Sci; Educ)

Box 62
Nashville, TN 37203

Phone: (615) 322-8184
Mrs. Jamesie Rodney, Mgr.

Founded: 1968. **Staff:** Prof 1; Other 1. **Subjects:** Special education, psychology, remedial reading, educational and psychological tests. **Holdings:** 4000 books and bound periodical volumes; 23 VF drawers and 50 shelves of 475 test forms; AV equipment. **Subscriptions:** 20 journals and other serials. **Services:** Copying; library is only open to students and faculty. **Also Known As:** John F. Kennedy Center for Research of Education and Human Development.

★10553★

PEABODY HISTORICAL SOCIETY - LIBRARY AND ARCHIVES (Hist)*

35 Washington St.
Peabody, MA 01960

Phone: (617) 535-0805

Founded: 1896. **Staff:** Prof 1. **Subjects:** Local and national history. **Holdings:** 2000 books; 300 bound periodical volumes. **Services:** Library open to public with restrictions.

★10554★

PEABODY INSTITUTE LIBRARY - DANVERS ARCHIVAL CENTER (Hist)

15 Sylvan St.
Danvers, MA 01923

Phone: (617) 774-0554
Richard B. Trask, Town Archv.

Staff: Prof 1; Other 1. **Subjects:** History and development of Danvers and

Salem Village, Salem Village witchcraft. **Special Collections:** Ellerton J. Brehaut Witchcraft Collection (1000 items); Parker Pillsbury Anti-Slavery Collection (179 volumes). **Holdings:** 4000 books; 200,000 manuscript items; 150 reels of microfilm; 600 maps; 50 reels of magnetic tapes. **Subscriptions:** 10 journals and other serials. **Services:** Copying; center open to public. **Special Catalogs:** Catalogs of witchcraft, manuscripts, history.

★10555★
PEABODY MUSEUM OF SALEM - PHILLIPS LIBRARY (Hist)
East India Square   Phone: (617) 745-1876
Salem, MA 01970   Gregor Trinkaus-Randall, Libn.
Founded: 1799. **Staff:** Prof 1; Other 15. **Subjects:** Maritime history, ethnology of non-European peoples, natural history. **Holdings:** 100,000 books and bound periodical volumes; log books; account books; shipping papers. **Subscriptions:** 200 journals and other serials. **Services:** Interlibrary loans; copying; library open to public. **Automated Operations:** Computerized serials.

★10556★
PEABODY (Robert S.) FOUNDATION FOR ARCHEOLOGY - LIBRARY (Soc Sci)
Phillips Academy   Phone: (617) 475-0248
Andover, MA 01810   Dr. Donald W. McNemar, Act.Dir.
Staff: Prof 1; Other 1. **Subjects:** North American archeology and ethnography, particularly Eastern North America; general anthropology. **Holdings:** 4400 books; 100 bound periodical volumes; 5000 reprints and pamphlets. **Services:** Library open to public. **Publications:** Papers of the Robert S. Peabody Foundation for Archeology, irregular; first annual report of the Coxcatlan Project; Prehistory of the Ayacucho Basin, Peru series; First Annual Report of the Belize Archaic Archaeological Reconnaissance.

PEACE COLLECTION
See: Swarthmore College - Friends Historical Library

★10557★
PEALE MUSEUM - REFERENCE CENTER (Hist)
225 Holliday St.   Phone: (301) 396-3523
Baltimore, MD 21202   Richard Flint, Cur., Prints/Photographs
Founded: 1931. **Staff:** Prof 2. **Subjects:** History of Baltimore, especially architectural, maritime and social. **Special Collections:** Hambleton Collection of Baltimore Views (450 historical prints); A. Aubrey Bodine Photographic Collection (25,000 negatives). **Holdings:** 1400 books; 1400 Baltimore prints and ephemera; 25,000 photographs; 15 VF drawers of mixed media subject files. **Subscriptions:** 35 journals and other serials. **Services:** Copying; center open to public for reference use only. **Also Known As:** Municipal Museum of the City of Baltimore, Inc. **Staff:** Dean Krimmel, Musm.Ref.Ctr.Supv.

★10558★
PEARL HARBOR SURVIVORS ASSOCIATION - ARCHIVES (Hist)
1106 Maplewood Ave.   Phone: (603) 436-5835
Portsmouth, NH 03801   Mr. W.M. Cleveland, Hist.
Subjects: Japanese attack on Pearl Harbor. **Holdings:** 5 cubic feet of combat records, reports, artifacts; 10 photograph albums. **Services:** Copying; archives open to public with restrictions. **Publications:** Bibliography of Pearl Harbor Attack; Pearl Harbor Gram, quarterly.

PEARSE (A.S.) MEMORIAL LIBRARY
See: Duke University - Marine Laboratory - A.S. Pearse Memorial Library

★10559★
PEARSON (Lester B.) COLLEGE OF THE PACIFIC - LIBRARY (Hist)
RR 1   Phone: (604) 478-5591
Victoria, BC, Canada V8X 3W9   Margaret McAvity, Libn.
Founded: 1974. **Staff:** Prof 1; Other 1. **Special Collections:** Part of the personal library of the late Lester B. Pearson (1000 titles of history and international affairs). **Services:** Interlibrary loans; copying; SDI; library open to public by appointment. **Remarks:** Lester B. Pearson College of the Pacific is affiliated with the United World Colleges.

★10560★
PEAT, MARWICK, MITCHELL & CO. - AUDIT/MCD LIBRARY (Bus-Fin)
Peat Marwick Plaza
303 E. Wacker Dr.   Phone: (312) 938-1000
Chicago, IL 60601   Mary LaRue Groft, Supv., Info.Serv.
Staff: 3. **Subjects:** Accounting and auditing, business and management consulting. **Holdings:** 2000 books; 107 bound periodical volumes; 2000 unbound periodicals and newsletters; 30,000 public company annual reports and proxies on microfiche. **Subscriptions:** 40 journals and other serials; 6 newspapers. **Services:** Interlibrary loans; library open to public with restrictions. **Computerized Information Services:** LEXIS, National

Automated Accounting Research System (NAARS), Disclosure Inc., New York Times Information Service, DIALOG, Dow Jones News/Retrieval, NEXIS, I.P. Sharp Associates Limited, CompuServe, Inc.

★10561★
PEAT, MARWICK, MITCHELL & CO. - CENTRAL LIBRARY (Bus-Fin)†
555 S. Flower St.   Phone: (213) 972-4000
Los Angeles, CA 90071   Vickie Taylor, Hd.Libn.
Staff: Prof 2; Other 1. **Subjects:** Accounting, auditing, taxation, business. **Holdings:** 3000 books; 85 bound periodical volumes; 3000 company annual reports; 1000 pamphlets. **Subscriptions:** 220 journals and other serials; 7 newspapers. **Services:** Interlibrary loans; library not open to public. **Automated Operations:** Computerized cataloging. **Computerized Information Services:** OCLC, DIALOG, SDC, New York Times Information Service. **Staff:** Ellyn Sato, Tech.Serv.Libn.

★10562★
PEAT, MARWICK, MITCHELL & CO. - INFORMATION AND RESEARCH CENTER (Bus-Fin)
345 Park Ave.   Phone: (212) 872-6531
New York, NY 10154   Michael J. Ready, Hd.Libn.
Founded: 1952. **Staff:** Prof 3; Other 1. **Subjects:** Accounting, auditing, management consulting. **Holdings:** 13,000 books; 300 periodical titles; 80 VF drawers of pamphlets. **Services:** Center not open to public. **Computerized Information Services:** DIALOG, LEXIS, NEXIS, Dow Jones News/Retrieval. **Publications:** Information Update, quarterly - for internal distribution only. **Formerly:** Its Library. **Staff:** Sheldon Wein, Res.Libn.; Janice Thom, Res.Libn.

★10563★
PEAT, MARWICK, MITCHELL & CO. - INFORMATION RESOURCES/CENTRE DE DOCUMENTAION (Bus-Fin)
1155 Dorchester Blvd., W., 20th Fl.   Phone: (514) 879-3428
Montreal, PQ, Canada H3B 2J9   Judy Macfarlane, Mgr.
Staff: Prof 2; Other 1. **Subjects:** Accounting, auditing, taxation, business, data processing, management consulting, transportation. **Holdings:** 5000 books; 500 bound periodical volumes; 17 drawers of annual reports; 16 VF drawers of research files and clippings. **Subscriptions:** 325 journals and other serials; 8 newspapers. **Services:** Interlibrary loans; copying; center open to public by appointment. **Computerized Information Services:** DIALOG, SDC, Info Globe, Dow Jones News/Retrieval, TEXTLINE, Dunserve, Canada Systems Group (CSG). Performs searches on cost recovery basis. **Publications:** Acquisition List, monthly; Information Update, irregular - both for internal distribution only. **Remarks:** Services are available in both English and French.

★10564★
PEAT, MARWICK, MITCHELL & CO. - INFORMATION SERVICES (Bus-Fin)
1601 Elm St., Suite 1400   Phone: (214) 747-8911
Dallas, TX 75201   Celia S. Ellingson, Info.Serv.Dir.
Staff: Prof 2; Other 1. **Subjects:** Taxation, accounting, auditing, oil and gas taxation, insurance taxation. **Holdings:** 2500 books; 500 bound periodical volumes; 1500 unbound periodicals; 500 volumes of loose-leaf services; 100 boxes of legislative history materials and government documents; 4500 corporate annual and 10K reports. **Subscriptions:** 250 journals and other serials; 5 newspapers. **Services:** Copying; SDI; services open to public with permission. **Automated Operations:** Computerized serials. **Computerized Information Services:** DIALOG, SDC, BRS, Dow Jones News/Retrieval, LEXIS; internal database. **Special Indexes:** Index to in-house research memoranda. **Staff:** Jane Byers, Res.Libn.

★10565★
PEAT, MARWICK, MITCHELL & CO. - LIBRARY (Plan; Trans)
San Francisco Intl. Airport
Box 8007   Phone: (415) 347-9521
San Francisco, CA 94128   Karen A. Mayers, Libn.
Staff: Prof 1; Other 1. **Subjects:** Planning - airport, environmental, transportation. **Holdings:** 900 books; 32 VF drawers of reports. **Subscriptions:** 100 journals and other serials. **Services:** Interlibrary loans; library not open to public.

★10566★
PEAT, MARWICK, MITCHELL & CO. - LIBRARY (Bus-Fin)
1990 K St., N.W.   Phone: (202) 223-9525
Washington, DC 20006   Nancy J. Holland, Hd.Libn.
Staff: Prof 2; Other 2. **Subjects:** Accounting, taxation, transportation, business and finance. **Holdings:** 3000 books; 1000 technical reports. **Subscriptions:** 403 journals and other serials. **Services:** Interlibrary loans; copying; SDI; library open to public by appointment. **Computerized Information Services:** DIALOG, SDC, LEXIS. **Networks/Consortia:** Member

of Metropolitan Washington Library Council. **Publications:** Biblionotes, quarterly - for internal distribution only. **Staff:** Gail Kondo, Asst.Libn.

★10567★
PEAT, MARWICK, MITCHELL & CO. - LIBRARY (Bus-Fin)
1700 IDS Center　　　　　　　　　Phone: (612) 341-2222
Minneapolis, MN 55402　　　　　　Donna J. Harnden, Hd.Libn.
Founded: 1973. **Staff:** Prof 1. **Subjects:** Accounting, tax (state, federal and foreign), industry statistics. **Special Collections:** 250 prospectuses. **Holdings:** 3000 books; 40 bound periodical volumes; 12 drawers of annual reports. **Subscriptions:** 150 journals and other serials; 7 newspapers. **Services:** Interlibrary loans; copying; library open to public by request. **Computerized Information Services:** SDC, DIALOG, Dow Jones News/Retrieval. **Special Catalogs:** Catalog of prospectuses and annual reports.

★10568★
PEAT, MARWICK, MITCHELL & CO. - LIBRARY (Bus-Fin)
3000 Republic Bank Center　　　　　Phone: (713) 224-4262
Houston, TX 77002　　　　　　Charlotte Kohrs, Supv., Info.Serv.
Founded: 1968. **Staff:** Prof 3. **Subjects:** Taxation, accounting, management consulting, employee benefits. **Holdings:** 6000 books; 400 bound periodical volumes; annual reports; prospectuses. **Subscriptions:** 300 journals and other serials. **Services:** Interlibrary loans; copying. **Computerized Information Services:** DIALOG, SDC, LEXIS, Dow Jones News/Retrieval. **Staff:** Judith Rosenthal, Info.Spec.; Jeanne Harris, Info.Spec.

★10569★
PEAT, MARWICK & PARTNERS - LIBRARY (Bus-Fin)
Commerce Court West　　　　　　Phone: (416) 863-3440
Toronto, ON, Canada M5L 1B2　　　Mrs. S.A. Layton, Libn.
Founded: 1959. **Staff:** 3. **Subjects:** Finance, corporate organization, transportation planning, urban planning, marketing, electronic data processing. **Special Collections:** Statistics Canada publications (complete set). **Holdings:** 5000 books. **Subscriptions:** 137 journals and other serials. **Services:** Interlibrary loans; library not open to public. **Computerized Information Services:** SDC, DIALOG, Info Globe.

★10570★
PEAVEY COMPANY - CORPORATE INFORMATION CENTER
11 Peavey Rd.
Chaska, MN 55318
Defunct

★10571★
PEDCO GROUP LIBRARY (Env-Cons)
Chester Towers
11499 Chester Rd.　　　　　　Phone: (513) 782-4700
Cincinnati, OH 45246　　　　Janet L. Zieleniewski, Libn.
Founded: 1973. **Staff:** Prof 1; Other 1. **Subjects:** Environment, engineering. **Holdings:** 1500 books; 4000 vertical files; 9000 EPA reports on microfiche. **Subscriptions:** 75 journals and other serials. **Services:** Interlibrary loans; copying; library open to public by appointment. **Publications:** Recent Acquisitions, bimonthly.

★10572★
PEE DEE AREA HEALTH EDUCATION CENTER LIBRARY (Med)
McLeod Regional Medical Ctr.
555 E. Cheves St.　　　　　　Phone: (803) 667-2275
Florence, SC 29501　　　　Lillian Fisher, Regional Libn.
Founded: 1975. **Staff:** Prof 1; Other 2. **Subjects:** Clinical medicine, nursing and allied health areas. **Holdings:** 1469 books; 2446 bound periodical volumes; 2560 AV items. **Subscriptions:** 165 journals and other serials. **Services:** Interlibrary loans; copying; SDI; library open to health personnel and interested patrons. **Automated Operations:** Computerized cataloging. **Computerized Information Services:** MEDLINE and other NLM databases, DIALOG; AVAIL (internal database). **Publications:** Newsletter, irregular. **Special Catalogs:** AVAIL catalg; AV catalog.

PEEL (Bruce) SPECIAL COLLECTIONS LIBRARY
See: University of Alberta - Bruce Peel Special Collections Library

★10573★
PEEL COUNTY BOARD OF EDUCATION - J.A. TURNER PROFESSIONAL LIBRARY (Educ)
73 King St., W.　　　　　　Phone: (416) 279-6010
Mississauga, ON, Canada L5B 1H5　　Dr. K. Kirkwood, Chf.Res.Off.
Founded: 1973. **Staff:** Prof 2. **Subjects:** Education. **Special Collections:** Ministry of Education guidelines. **Holdings:** 10,000 books; 1000 other

cataloged items; 12 VF drawers of clippings, documents and reports; 107 documents and reports on microfiche. **Subscriptions:** 109 journals and other serials. **Services:** Interlibrary loans; copying; library open to public with restrictions. **Computerized Information Services:** Infomart, Info Globe. **Publications:** Research Bulletin, monthly - distributed to Board. **Staff:** Shelley Andrews, Lib.Techn./Res.Asst.

★10574★
PEIRCE JUNIOR COLLEGE - LIBRARY - SPECIAL COLLECTIONS (Bus-Fin)
1420 Pine St.　　　　　　Phone: (215) 545-6400
Philadelphia, PA 19102　　　James R. McAuliffe, Hd.Libn.
Founded: 1963. **Holdings:** Pre-1900 business textbooks. **Services:** Interlibrary loans; library not open to public.

PEIRCE MEMORIAL LIBRARY
See: First Presbyterian Church of Flint

PELL MARINE SCIENCE LIBRARY
See: University of Rhode Island, Narragansett Bay

PELTASON (Paul) LIBRARY
See: Temple Israel - Paul Peltason Library

★10575★
PEMAQUID HISTORICAL ASSOCIATION - HARRINGTON MEETING HOUSE - LIBRARY (Hist)
Old Harrington Road　　　　　Phone: (207) 677-2587
Pemaquid, ME 04558　　　　Stuart P. Gillespie, Pres.
Founded: 1965. **Subjects:** Local history, religion. **Holdings:** 100 books and bound periodical volumes; pamphlets; local maps; hymnals; ledgers; early school books; newspapers; historical documents. **Services:** Library open to public by appointment.

★10576★
PEN AND BRUSH INC. - LIBRARY (Art; Hum)
16 E. Tenth St.　　　　　　Phone: (212) 475-3669
New York, NY 10003　　　　Evelyn C. Kelley, Pres.
Founded: 1893. **Staff:** 1. **Subjects:** Literature, art. **Holdings:** 1200 books.

★10577★
PENDLE HILL - LIBRARY (Rel-Theol)
　　　　　　　　　　　　Phone: (215) 566-4507
Wallingford, PA 19086　　　　Yuki T. Brinton, Libn.
Founded: 1930. **Staff:** Prof 1. **Subjects:** Religion, Quakers. **Special Collections:** Quaker Collection. **Holdings:** 14,000 volumes. **Subscriptions:** 35 journals and other serials. **Services:** Interlibrary loans; library open to public.

★10578★
PENDLETON DISTRICT HISTORICAL AND RECREATIONAL COMMISSION - REFERENCE LIBRARY (Hist)
125 E. Queen St.
Box 565　　　　　　　　Phone: (803) 646-3782
Pendleton, SC 29670　　　　Hurley Badders, Commn.Dir.
Founded: 1974. **Staff:** Prof 2; Other 1. **Subjects:** History - Pendleton district, South Carolina, U.S.; genealogy; church history; travel, tourism and recreation; antiques and historic preservation; archeology. **Special Collections:** Anderson Cotton Mill Records (71 ledgers, 1890-1950s). **Holdings:** 800 books; 200 boxes of clippings, unbound reports and other items; 90 books and documents on microfilm; 10 drawers of photographs and family history; 75 maps; 90 ledgers. **Subscriptions:** 19 journals and other serials. **Services:** Copying; library open to public for reference use only. **Special Indexes:** Index to names mentioned in library materials (card). **Staff:** Donna Roper, Res.Coord.

PENFIELD LIBRARY
See: SUNY - College at Oswego

★10579★
PENICK CORPORATION - PPT LIBRARY (Sci-Tech)
530 New York Ave.　　　　　Phone: (201) 438-6000
Lyndhurst, NJ 07071
Founded: 1920. **Staff:** 1. **Subjects:** Organic chemistry, chemistry of natural products, botany, medicinal drugs, entomology, fish diseases, agricultural chemicals. **Holdings:** 1500 books; 5000 bound periodical volumes; 4000 patents; 700 reprints; 6 VF drawers of literature searches; Chemical Abstracts on microfilm, 1907 to present. **Subscriptions:** 30 journals and other serials. **Services:** Interlibrary loans; library not open to public. **Computerized Information Services:** DIALOG, SDC, CompuServe, Inc.; CPC

International (internal database). **Publications:** Acquisitions List, 3/year - for internal distribution only. **Special Catalogs:** Subject files for pesticides, analytical chemistry, drugs and medicine, industrial engineering and safety (all on cards).

★10580★
PENINSULA COMMUNITY FOUNDATION - COMMUNITY RESOURCE LIBRARY (Soc Sci)
1204 Burlingame Ave.
Box 627   Phone: (415) 342-2505
Burlingame, CA 94011-0627   Cathy Somerton, Libn.
Staff: Prof 1. **Subjects:** Funding sources and management assistance for nonprofit organizations; fundraising activities; proposal writing. **Holdings:** 600 books; 460 foundation annual reports. **Subscriptions:** 50 journals and other serials; 10 newspapers. **Services:** Library open to public. **Computerized Information Services:** DIALOG. Performs searches on cost recovery basis. **Publications:** Community Resource Library News, quarterly - distributed to organizations upon request.

★10581★
PENINSULA CONSERVATION FOUNDATION - LIBRARY OF THE ENVIRONMENT (Env-Cons)
2253 Park Blvd.   Phone: (415) 328-5313
Palo Alto, CA 94306   Nancy S. Olson, Libn.
Founded: 1971. **Staff:** Prof 1. **Subjects:** Conservation, ecology, energy, wildlife and endangered species, pollution control. **Special Collections:** Environmental Volunteers Collection; Audubon Collection (250); Conservation Collection (1000); Trails Collection (125 books and 4 VF drawers). **Holdings:** 2500 books; 636 bound periodical volumes; 43 VF drawers; 2000 maps. **Subscriptions:** 23 journals and other serials; 5 newspapers. **Services:** Interlibrary loans; copying (fee); library open to public. **Networks/Consortia:** Member of Energy Librarians of the Bay Area. **Publications:** The Center View, quarterly - membership and exchange. **Special Indexes:** The Harbinger File - through the Peninsula Conservation Center.

★10582★
PENINSULA HOSPITAL CENTER - MEDICAL LIBRARY (Med)
51-15 Beach Channel Dr.   Phone: (718) 945-7100
Far Rockaway, NY 11691   Edith Rubinstein, Lib.Dir.
Founded: 1970. **Staff:** Prof 1. **Subjects:** Medicine, surgery, nursing, dentistry, podiatry and orthopedics. **Holdings:** 1182 books; 2150 bound periodical volumes; 75 video cassettes; 228 audio cassettes. **Subscriptions:** 108 journals and other serials. **Services:** Interlibrary loans; copying; literature searches; library open to public for reference use only. **Networks/Consortia:** Member of Brooklyn-Queens-Staten Island Health Sciences Librarians (BQSI); Medical & Scientific Libraries of Long Island (MEDLI).

★10583★
PENINSULA HOSPITAL AND MEDICAL CENTER - MEDICAL STAFF LIBRARY (Med)†
1783 El Camino Real   Phone: (415) 697-4061
Burlingame, CA 94010   Prudence Harvey Hamilton, Chf.Libn.
Founded: 1963. **Staff:** 2. **Subjects:** Medicine. **Holdings:** 1400 books; 3000 bound periodical volumes; 600 rare books. **Subscriptions:** 170 journals and other serials. **Services:** Copying; library open to public with approval of administration.

★10584★
PENINSULA LIBRARY AND HISTORICAL SOCIETY (Hist)†
6105 Riverview Rd.   Phone: (216) 657-2291
Peninsula, OH 44264   Edith M. Minns, Libn.
Founded: 1943. **Staff:** Prof 3; Other 2. **Subjects:** History, biography, literature, arts. **Special Collections:** Local history (2000 volumes; manuscripts; clippings; maps; pictures; cemetery records). **Holdings:** 32,884 books; 162 bound periodical volumes; 1050 AV items; depository for U.S. Army Corps of Engineer reports; 24 VF drawers of pamphlets and clippings; 150 maps. **Subscriptions:** 103 journals and other serials; 5 newspapers. **Services:** Interlibrary loans; copying; library open to public. **Publications:** Newsletter, bimonthly - distributed to local area. **Special Indexes:** Index to Local History (card). **Staff:** Margot Jackson, Archv.

★10585★
PENINSULA TEMPLE BETH EL - LIBRARY (Area-Ethnic; Rel-Theol)*
1700 Alameda de Las Pulgas   Phone: (415) 341-7701
San Mateo, CA 94403   Ann Levin, Libn.
Founded: 1961. **Staff:** Prof 1; Other 2. **Subjects:** Philosophy of Judaism; history of Judaism, Jewish religion; fiction of Jewish content or by Jewish authors; Israel - description and travel; history of the Jews in the U.S. **Special Collections:** Biographies of Jewish leaders. **Holdings:** 2625 books. **Services:**

Library open to public.

★10586★
PENINSULA TIMES TRIBUNE - LIBRARY (Publ)
245 Lytton Ave.
Box 300   Phone: (415) 853-5244
Palo Alto, CA 94302   Elizabeth R. Miller, Hd.Libn.
Staff: Prof 2; Other 2. **Subjects:** Newspaper reference topics. **Holdings:** 250 books; 200,000 file folders of clippings; 1404 reels of microfilm; 148,000 pictures; 200 state and county pamphlets and reports. **Subscriptions:** 5 newspapers. **Services:** Copying; library open to public with restrictions. **Staff:** Pam Allen, Asst.Libn.

★10587★
PENN (Annie) MEMORIAL HOSPITAL - MEDICAL LIBRARY (Med)
618 S. Main St.   Phone: (919) 349-8461
Reidsville, NC 27320   Susan Bray, Libn.
Staff: Prof 1. **Subjects:** Medicine, nursing, and allied health sciences. **Holdings:** 500 books. **Subscriptions:** 38 journals and other serials. **Services:** Interlibrary loans; patient education closed-circuit television system; library not open to public.

★10588★
PENN MUTUAL LIFE INSURANCE COMPANY - LAW LIBRARY (Law)
Independence Sq.   Phone: (215) 629-0600
Philadelphia, PA 19172   Doris Nardin, Asst.Libn.
Founded: 1940. **Staff:** 1. **Subjects:** Insurance, law. **Holdings:** 15,000 books; 30 bound periodical volumes. **Subscriptions:** 38 journals and other serials; 7 newspapers. **Services:** Library not open to public. **Publications:** List of periodical holdings, annual; New Books List, irregular.

★10589★
PENN VIRGINIA CORPORATION - LIBRARY (Energy)
2500 Fidelity Bldg.   Phone: (302) 545-6600
Philadelphia, PA 19109   Ben Payne, Libn.
Staff: Prof 1. **Subjects:** Energy, coal, oil, gas, business, environment, mining equipment, industrial minerals. **Holdings:** 300 books; 500 government documents. **Subscriptions:** 40 journals and other serials. **Services:** Interlibrary loans; copying; library open to other professionals with restrictions. **Publications:** Acquisitions report, monthly.

PENN (William) COLLEGE
See: William Penn College

PENN (William) MEMORIAL MUSEUM & ARCHIVES BUILDING
See: Pennsylvania State Historical & Museum Commission - Division of Archives and Manuscripts

PENNAL (George) LIBRARY
See: St. Joseph's Health Centre - George Pennal Library

★10590★
PENNEY (J.C.) COMPANY, INC. - LAW LIBRARY (Law)
1301 Ave. of the Americas   Phone: (212) 957-8488
New York, NY 10019   Eleanor A. Sabo, Legal Libn.
Staff: Prof 1; Other 3. **Subjects:** Law, business. **Holdings:** 20,000 books; 350 bound periodical volumes. **Subscriptions:** 200 journals and other serials; 16 newspapers. **Services:** Interlibrary loans; library not open to public. **Computerized Information Services:** LEXIS, NEXIS, DIALOG.

★10591★
PENNHURST CENTER - STAFF LIBRARY
324 Buchanan Bldg.
Spring City, PA 19475
Founded: 1960. **Subjects:** Mental retardation, medicine, psychology, special education, related therapies, social service. **Special Collections:** Treatment of mental retardation. **Holdings:** 2600 books; articles and pamphlets. **Remarks:** Presently inactive.

★10592★
PENNIE & EDMONDS - LAW LIBRARY (Law)
330 Madison Ave.   Phone: (212) 986-8686
New York, NY 10017   Alfred Baman, Libn.
Founded: 1884. **Staff:** Prof 2; Other 1. **Subjects:** Law - patent, copyright, trademark, federal practice; chemistry; electronics; metallurgy. **Holdings:** 15,000 books and bound periodical volumes. **Subscriptions:** 80 serials. **Services:** Interlibrary loans (limited). **Computerized Information Services:** DIALOG, SDC, LEXIS. **Staff:** Marie DeNino, Asst.Libn.

★10593★

PENNOCK HOSPITAL - MEDICAL LIBRARY (Med)
1009 W. Green St.   Phone: (616) 945-3451
Hastings, MI 49058   Mary Diane Hawkins, Med.Libn.
Staff: Prof 1; Other 1. **Subjects:** Medicine, nursing, pharmacy, and allied health sciences. **Holdings:** 750 books. **Subscriptions:** 125 journals and other serials. **Services:** Interlibrary loans; copying; library open to public by appointment. **Computerized Information Services:** MEDLARS, DIALOG. Performs searches on cost recovery basis. **Networks/Consortia:** Member of Capitol Area Library Network (CALNET); Michigan Library Consortium.

★10594★

PENNSYLVANIA ACADEMY OF THE FINE ARTS - LIBRARY (Art)
Broad & Cherry Sts.   Phone: (215) 972-7611
Philadelphia, PA 19102   Marietta P. Bushnell, Libn.
Founded: 1805. **Staff:** Prof 1. **Subjects:** Art history, painting, sculpture, graphics, with concentration on American art. **Holdings:** 9000 books; 48 VF drawers of artists clippings; 16 VF drawers of subject-idea clippings. **Subscriptions:** 40 journals and other serials. **Services:** Library open to public for reference use only by appointment.

PENNSYLVANIA APPELLATE COURTS LIBRARY
See: Pennsylvania State Superior Court

★10595★

PENNSYLVANIA AREA LIBRARY NETWORK AND UNION LIBRARY CATALOGUE OF PENNSYLVANIA (Info Sci)
3401 Market St., Suite 262   Phone: (215) 382-7031
Philadelphia, PA 19104   Dr. James G. Schoenung, Exec.Dir.
Founded: 1935. **Staff:** Prof 7; Other 4. **Networks/Consortia:** Headquarters of PALINET & Union Library Catalogue of Pennsylvania. **Remarks:** Card file closed in 1975; microfilm available since 1976. Supports full OCLC and microcomputer support services for 270 member libraries in Pennsylvania, New Jersey, Delaware, Maryland and Washington, D.C.

★10596★

PENNSYLVANIA BLUE SHIELD - RESEARCH LIBRARY (Med)
1800 Center St.   Phone: (717) 763-3151
Camp Hill, PA 17011   Charlene Mezellin, Sec.
Founded: 1973. **Staff:** 1. **Subjects:** Health care, health insurance, socioeconomic data, management. **Holdings:** 900 books; 75 unbound reports; 3 file drawers of clippings; 7 VF drawers. **Subscriptions:** 80 journals and other serials. **Services:** Library not open to public.

★10597★

PENNSYLVANIA CANAL SOCIETY - CANAL MUSEUM - RESEARCH LIBRARY (Hist)*
Hugo Moore Park
200 S. Delaware Dr.
Box 877
Easton, PA 18042   Phone: (215) 258-7155
    Marsha L. Kleedorfer, Cur.
Subjects: Canals. **Special Collections:** Richardson Collection (glass slides; news clippings; photographs; reports). **Holdings:** 414 books; 459 bound periodical volumes; 3800 photographs; 4650 slides; 16 oral history tapes; 354 postcards; VF of clippings, reports, business records. **Services:** Copying; library open to public by appointment. **Publications:** Canal Currents, quarterly - to members.

★10598★

PENNSYLVANIA COLLEGE OF OPTOMETRY - ALBERT FITCH MEMORIAL LIBRARY (Med)
1200 W. Godfrey Ave.   Phone: (215) 276-6270
Philadelphia, PA 19141   Marita J. Krivda, Lib.Dir.
Staff: Prof 1; Other 3. **Subjects:** Optometry, ophthalmology, optics theory, ophthalmic optics, contact lenses, low vision rehabilitation, clinical medicine, public health. **Special Collections:** Visual Science Rare Book Collection, 17th-19th centuries (250 books); eye spectacles, turn of the century ophthalmic instruments and ophthalmoscopes. **Holdings:** 4500 books; 7000 bound periodical volumes; 3 VF drawers of government documents; 2 VF drawers of old instruments pamphlets; 50 video cassettes; 800 audio cassettes; 6640 slides. **Subscriptions:** 290 journals and other serials. **Services:** Interlibrary loans; copying; library open to public with restrictions. **Computerized Information Services:** MEDLARS, OCLC, BRS. Performs searches free of charge for students and faculty; on cost recovery basis for others. **Networks/Consortia:** Member of Greater Northeastern Regional Medical Library Program; PALINET and Union Library Catalogue of Pennsylvania; Association of Visual Science Librarians. **Publications:** Acquisitions list, monthly; annual report. **Special Indexes:** Ophthalmic Literature.

★10599★

PENNSYLVANIA COLLEGE OF PODIATRIC MEDICINE - CENTER FOR THE HISTORY OF FOOT CARE AND FOOT WEAR (Med)
Charles E. Krausz Library
Eighth St. at Race   Phone: (215) 629-0300
Philadelphia, PA 19107   Lisabeth M. Holloway, Dir.
Staff: Prof 1; Other 1. **Subjects:** Podiatric medicine, anatomy and diseases of the foot, podiatry/chiropody as a profession, ethnic footwear. **Holdings:** 1000 books; 200 bound periodical volumes; 130 linear feet of archival materials; 500 other cataloged items. **Services:** Copying; center open to public for reference use only. **Publications:** The ClioPedic Items, irregular newsletter - to members of the American Podiatry Association. **Special Indexes:** Index of graduates of chiropody/podiatry colleges in the U.S.; index of foreign practitioners.

★10600★

PENNSYLVANIA COLLEGE OF PODIATRIC MEDICINE - CHARLES E. KRAUSZ LIBRARY (Med)
Eighth St. at Race   Phone: (215) 629-0300
Philadelphia, PA 19107   John C. Harris, Coll.Libn.
Founded: 1962. **Staff:** Prof 2; Other 2. **Subjects:** Podiatry, material on the foot, general medicine. **Special Collections:** Podiatry; Stewart E. Reed historical collection of books on the foot (2500 volumes). **Holdings:** 8500 books; 7000 bound periodical volumes; reprint file of faculty publications; 8 VF drawers of reprints of articles pertaining to the foot; 2400 pamphlets on medical subjects; 233 reels of microfilm; 500 video cassettes; 101 films; 625 audio cassettes; 13,000 slides. **Subscriptions:** 300 journals and other serials. **Services:** Interlibrary loans; library open to public for reference use only on request. **Publications:** List of new acquisitions, semimonthly. **Remarks:** Includes the holdings of the former Audiovisual Library. **Staff:** Frances E. Peters, Libn.

★10601★

PENNSYLVANIA DUTCH FOLK CULTURE SOCIETY, INC. - BAVER MEMORIAL LIBRARY (Hist)
    Phone: (215) 562-4803
Lenhartsville, PA 19534   Florence Baver, Mgr.
Founded: 1978. **Staff:** Prof 1; Other 1. **Subjects:** Genealogy, folklore, local history. **Holdings:** 500 books; 200 bound periodical volumes; pamphlets; photographs; diaries; tape recordings; clippings; postcards; church records. **Services:** Library open to public. **Publications:** Pennsylvania Dutch News & Views, semiannual. **Staff:** Cynthia Spayd, Libn.

★10602★

PENNSYLVANIA ECONOMY LEAGUE - EASTERN DIVISION - LIBRARY (Soc Sci)
1211 Chestnut St.   Phone: (215) 864-9562
Philadelphia, PA 19107   Ellen Brennan, Libn.
Founded: 1916. **Staff:** Prof 1. **Subjects:** Public administration, charters and constitutions, city government, municipal finance. **Holdings:** 16,000 books and bound periodical volumes. **Services:** Interlibrary loans; copying; library open to public with restrictions.

★10603★

PENNSYLVANIA ECONOMY LEAGUE - WESTERN DIVISION - LIBRARY (Soc Sci)
Two Gateway Ctr.   Phone: (412) 471-1477
Pittsburgh, PA 15222   Judith A. Eves, Libn.
Founded: 1932. **Staff:** Prof 1; Other 1. **Subjects:** State and local government, finance, taxation, public personnel. **Holdings:** 1025 books and bound periodical volumes; 2500 pamphlets; 24 VF drawers of financial reports, and news clippings. **Subscriptions:** 160 journals and other serials; 5 newspapers. **Services:** Interlibrary loans; reference services for sponsors and community agencies.

PENNSYLVANIA ETHNIC HERITAGE STUDIES CENTER
See: University of Pittsburgh

★10604★

PENNSYLVANIA FARM MUSEUM OF LANDIS VALLEY - LIBRARY (Hist)
2451 Kissel Hill Rd.   Phone: (717) 569-0401
Lancaster, PA 17601   Robert N. Sieber, Dir.
Founded: 1925. **Subjects:** History, crafts, folklore, agriculture. **Special Collections:** Old manufacturers' catalogs. **Holdings:** 10,000 volumes. **Services:** Library open to researchers by appointment.

★10605★

PENNSYLVANIA HORTICULTURAL SOCIETY - LIBRARY (Agri)
325 Walnut St.　　　　　　　　　Phone: (215) 625-8268
Philadelphia, PA 19106　　　　　　　Mary Lou Wolfe, Libn.
Founded: 1827. **Staff:** Prof 1; Other 2. **Subjects:** Horticulture, botany, landscape design, ornamental horticulture. **Special Collections:** Rare herbals and gardening books; 19th century horticulture; Pennsylvania horticulture. **Holdings:** 14,000 books; 4000 bound periodical volumes; 16 VF drawers of horticultural information; 1000 slides. **Subscriptions:** 200 journals and other serials. **Services:** Interlibrary loans; copying; slides available for rent; library open to public for reference use only. **Special Indexes:** Early and contemporary seed and nursery catalogs (card).

★10606★

PENNSYLVANIA HOSPITAL - DEPARTMENT FOR SICK AND INJURED - HISTORICAL LIBRARY (Med)
Eighth & Spruce Sts.　　　　　　　Phone: (215) 829-3998
Philadelphia, PA 19107　　　　　　Caroline Morris, Libn.-Archv.
Founded: 1761. **Staff:** 1. **Subjects:** Early (pre-1800) chemistry, physics, botany, zoology, natural history and materia medica; medicine and surgery prior to 1940. **Special Collections:** Hospital archives and case reports; early M.D. dissertations. **Holdings:** 8500 books; 4464 bound periodical volumes. **Services:** Library open to public by appointment requested in writing.

★10607★

PENNSYLVANIA HOSPITAL - DEPARTMENT FOR SICK AND INJURED - MEDICAL LIBRARY (Med)
Eighth & Spruce Sts.　　　　　　　Phone: (215) 829-3998
Philadelphia, PA 19107　　　　　　Caroline Morris, Libn.-Archv.
Founded: 1940. **Staff:** Prof 1; Other 2. **Subjects:** Medicine, nursing and allied health sciences. **Holdings:** 2122 books; 9500 bound periodical volumes; 3700 other cataloged items; 2 VF drawers. **Subscriptions:** 540 journals and other serials. **Services:** Interlibrary loans; copying (limited); library open to public by appointment. **Remarks:** Includes holdings of School of Nursing - Lydia Jane Clark Library. **Also Known As:** Packard Reading Room.

PENNSYLVANIA LUMBER MUSEUM
See: Pennsylvania State Historical & Museum Commission

★10608★

PENNSYLVANIA PUBLIC UTILITY COMMISSION - LIBRARY (Energy)
Box 3265　　　　　　　　　　　Phone: (717) 787-4466
Harrisburg, PA 17120　　　　　　　Thais Gardy, Libn.
Staff: Prof 1; Other 1. **Subjects:** Public utility law, energy conservation, economics, transportation, coal, oil, gas technology. **Holdings:** 5500 books; 160 bound periodical volumes; 2400 unbound reports; 22 maps; 2 VF drawers; 16 sets of loose-leaf reporters. **Subscriptions:** 102 journals and other serials. **Services:** Interlibrary loans; copying; library open to public for reference use only.

★10609★

PENNSYLVANIA RESOURCES AND INFORMATION CENTER FOR SPECIAL EDUCATION (Educ)
200 Anderson Rd.　　　　　　　　Phone: (215) 265-7321
King Of Prussia, PA 19406　　　　　Dr. Marianne Price, Dir.
Staff: Prof 8; Other 2. **Subjects:** Education of exceptional students. **Special Collections:** Publishers and supply catalogs (12 VF drawers). **Holdings:** 7000 books; tests on microfiche; special education dissertations on microfiche; ERIC indexes and microfiche. **Subscriptions:** 425 journals and other serials; 200 newsletters. **Services:** Center open to public for reference use only. **Computerized Information Services:** DIALOG, BRS. **Publications:** PRISE, 6/year. **Remarks:** Holdings are shared with Regional Resources Center of Eastern Pennsylvania for Special Education. **Staff:** Philip Juska, Asst.Dir.

★10610★

PENNSYLVANIA SCHOOL FOR THE DEAF - LIBRARY (Educ)
7500 Germantown Ave.　　　　　　Phone: (215) 247-9700
Philadelphia, PA 19119　　　　　　Catherine Lawlor-Fennell, Libn.
Staff: Prof 1; Other 2. **Subjects:** Deafness. **Holdings:** 13,000 books; 205 bound periodical volumes. **Subscriptions:** 120 journals and other serials; 5 newspapers. **Services:** Interlibrary loans; copying; library open to public for reference use only. **Automated Operations:** Computerized cataloging.

PENNSYLVANIA STATE DEPT. OF ENVIRONMENTAL RESOURCES - BUREAU OF OCCUPATIONAL HEALTH LIBRARY
See: Pennsylvania State Dept. of Environmental Resources - Environmental Protection Technical Reference Library

★10611★

PENNSYLVANIA STATE DEPARTMENT OF ENVIRONMENTAL RESOURCES - BUREAU OF TOPOGRAPHIC & GEOLOGIC SURVEY LIB. (Sci-Tech)
916 Executive House Apts.
Second & Chestnut Sts.　　　　　　Phone: (717) 783-8077
Harrisburg, PA 17120　　　　　　　Sandra Blust, Libn.
Founded: 1854. **Staff:** Prof 1; Other 1. **Subjects:** Geology, geography. **Special Collections:** Maps Collection, aerial photographic coverage for Pennsylvania. **Holdings:** 5500 books; 7800 bound periodical volumes; 5000 government publications; 150 unpublished manuscripts; 200 dissertations on Pennsylvania geology (some on microfilm). **Subscriptions:** 83 journals and other serials. **Services:** Interlibrary loans; copying; library open to public for reference use only. **Computerized Information Services:** Geo Ref Information System. **Publications:** Newsletter, weekly - for internal distribution only. **Special Catalogs:** Bibliography of Theses on Pennsylvania Geology; Bibliography of Guidebooks on Pennsylvania to 1977.

★10612★

PENNSYLVANIA STATE DEPT. OF ENVIRONMENTAL RESOURCES - ENVIRONMENTAL PROTECTION TECHNICAL REFERENCE LIBRARY (Env-Cons)
Fulton Bldg., 17th Fl.
Box 2063　　　　　　　　　　　Phone: (717) 787-9647
Harrisburg, PA 17120　　　　　　　Wanda R. Bell, Libn.
Founded: 1965. **Staff:** 2. **Subjects:** Water quality, sewerage, industrial waste, mining and reclamation, air quality, surface mines, solid waste, radiation protection, community environmental control. **Special Collections:** Water Pollution Control Federation Research Series on Clean Water (480 volumes); Pennsylvania State University Special Research Report on Coal (90 volumes); U.S. and Pennsylvania Geological Surveys (700 items). **Holdings:** 2400 books; 215 bound periodical volumes; 10,000 microfiche items in EPA Technology Series to 1974 (cataloged); 200 linear feet of technical material concerning water pollution; 500 river basin and stream file reports. **Subscriptions:** 135 journals and other serials; 10 newsletters. **Services:** Interlibrary loans; library open to public for reference use only. **Automated Operations:** Computerized serials and circulation. **Publications:** New Acquisitions, monthly; User's Guide to the Technical Reference Library. **Remarks:** Contains the holdings of its Bureau of Occupational Health Library. **Staff:** William Carr, Chf.

★10613★

PENNSYLVANIA STATE DEPARTMENT OF HEALTH - BUREAU OF LABORATORIES - HERBERT FOX MEMORIAL LIBRARY (Sci-Tech)
Pickering Way & Welsh Pool Rd.　　Phone: (215) 363-8500
Lionville, PA 19353　　　　　　　Leonard Sideman, Libn.
Staff: Prof 1; Other 2. **Subjects:** Clinical chemistry; microbiology and virology; toxicology; hematology; laboratory legislation. **Holdings:** 500 books. **Subscriptions:** 50 journals and other serials. **Services:** Interlibrary loans; copying; library open to public with restrictions. **Networks/Consortia:** Member of Consortium for Health Information and Library Services (CHI).

PENNSYLVANIA STATE DEPARTMENT OF PUBLIC WELFARE - DIXMONT STATE HOSPITAL
See: Dixmont State Hospital

PENNSYLVANIA STATE DEPARTMENT OF PUBLIC WELFARE - HAMBURG CENTER FOR THE MENTALLY RETARDED
See: Hamburg Center for the Mentally Retarded

★10614★

PENNSYLVANIA STATE DEPARTMENT OF PUBLIC WELFARE - MAYVIEW STATE HOSPITAL - MENTAL HEALTH AND MEDICAL LIBRARY (Med)
1601 Mayview Rd.　　　　　　　　Phone: (412) 221-7500
Bridgeville, PA 15017-1599　　　　William A. Suvak, Jr., Libn.Supv. I
Founded: 1966. **Staff:** Prof 1. **Subjects:** Psychiatry, psychoanalysis, psychiatric nursing, psychology, hospital administration, psychiatric social work, psychopharmacology. **Holdings:** 4000 books; 1200 bound periodical volumes. **Subscriptions:** 135 journals and other serials. **Services:** Interlibrary loans; copying; library open to community mental health professionals. **Networks/Consortia:** Member of Greater Northeastern Regional Medical Library Program. **Publications:** Newsletter, quarterly.

★10615★

PENNSYLVANIA STATE DEPARTMENT OF PUBLIC WELFARE - NORRISTOWN STATE HOSPITAL - PROFESSIONAL/STAFF SERVICES LIBRARY (Med)
c/o Central Professional Library, Bldg. 11　　Phone: (215) 270-1369
Norristown, PA 19401　　　　　　Raymond Frank Roedell, Jr., Dir.
Staff: Prof 1; Other 1. **Subjects:** Psychiatry and neurology; clinical

psychology; psychiatric nursing; psychiatric and clinical social work; activities therapy - recreational, music, occupational, vocational; aging; geriatrics; gerontology. **Holdings:** 12,000 books; 800 AV items; 2 VF drawers; archival material. **Subscriptions:** 300 journals and other serials. **Services:** Interlibrary loans; copying; library open to public with restrictions. **Automated Operations:** Computerized cataloging. **Computerized Information Services:** OCLC. **Networks/Consortia:** Member of Confederation of State & State Related Institutions. **Remarks:** An alternate telephone number is (215) 270-1370.

★10616★
PENNSYLVANIA STATE DEPARTMENT OF PUBLIC WELFARE - PHILIPSBURG STATE GENERAL HOSPITAL - LIBRARY (Med)
Loch Lomond Rd.   Phone: (814) 342-3320
Philipsburg, PA 16866   Elaine G. Filsinger, Libn.
Staff: Prof 1; Other 1. **Subjects:** Medicine, hospital administration, patient education. **Holdings:** 2430 books; 92 bound periodical volumes; 88 videotapes; 39 film loops; 2 drawers of audio cassettes; 2 shelves of patient education materials. **Subscriptions:** 89 journals and other serials. **Services:** Interlibrary loans; copying; library open to public for reference use only. **Networks/Consortia:** Member of Central Pennsylvania Health Sciences Library Association (CPHSLA).

★10617★
PENNSYLVANIA STATE DEPARTMENT OF PUBLIC WELFARE - SOMERSET STATE HOSPITAL - LIBRARY (Med)
Box 631   Phone: (814) 445-6501
Somerset, PA 15501   Eve Kline, Libn./Dir.
Staff: Prof 2; Other 1. **Subjects:** Psychiatry, psychology, mental retardation. **Holdings:** 6500 books; 500 filmstrips; 500 cassettes. **Subscriptions:** 150 journals and other serials; 7 newspapers. **Services:** Interlibrary loans; copying; SDI; computer searches. **Computerized Information Services:** OCLC. Performs free searches. **Networks/Consortia:** Member of Health Information Resources Consortium (HI RESCU); State System of Higher Education Libraries Council (SSHELCO); Greater Northeastern Regional Medical Library Program. **Publications:** Newsletter, weekly. **Staff:** Kathy Plaso, Libn.

★10618★
PENNSYLVANIA STATE DEPARTMENT OF TRANSPORTATION - TRANSPORTATION INFORMATION CENTER (Trans)
903 Transportation & Safety Bldg.   Phone: (717) 787-6527
Harrisburg, PA 17120   Judy H. Gutshall, Libn.
Founded: 1979. **Staff:** Prof 1; Other 1. **Subjects:** Transportation related subjects, management, engineering. **Special Collections:** TRB Publications; U.S. and Pennsylvania Department of Transportation documents; audiovisual collection. **Holdings:** 20,000 publications. **Subscriptions:** 200 journals and other serials. **Services:** Interlibrary loans; copying; center open to public for research purposes. **Computerized Information Services:** DIALOG, VU/TEXT. **Publications:** Information Center Additions.

★10619★
PENNSYLVANIA STATE FISH COMMISSION LIBRARY - BENNER SPRING FISH RESEARCH STATION (Sci-Tech)
R.D. 1, Box 200 C   Phone: (814) 355-4837
Bellefonte, PA 16823   Thomas R. Bender, Jr., Biologist
Staff: 1. **Subjects:** Freshwater fisheries, fish culture, fish disease. **Holdings:** 450 books; 3500 reprints of manuscripts. **Subscriptions:** 50 journals and other serials. **Services:** Library not open to public.

★10620★
PENNSYLVANIA STATE HISTORICAL & MUSEUM COMMISSION - DIVISION OF ARCHIVES AND MANUSCRIPTS (Hist)
William Penn Memorial Museum
& Archives Bldg.
Box 1026   Phone: (717) 787-3051
Harrisburg, PA 17120   Harry E. Whipkey, State Archv.
Founded: 1903. **Staff:** Prof 10; Other 6. **Subjects:** Archives of Pennsylvania and historical manuscripts. **Special Collections:** Record groups of the holdings of state agencies and political subdivisions (52); manuscript collections (350). **Holdings:** 23,000 cubic feet of archives; 8100 cubic feet of personal papers; 14,000 reels of microfilm; 4000 maps. **Services:** Copying; division open to public with restrictions. **Publications:** List of publications - available on request. **Staff:** Roland M. Baumann, Div.Chf.; Robert Dructor, Assoc.Archv.; Frank Suran, Assoc.Archv.

★10621★
PENNSYLVANIA STATE HISTORICAL & MUSEUM COMMISSION - DRAKE WELL MUSEUM - LIBRARY (Hist; Sci-Tech)
R.D. 3   Phone: (814) 827-2797
Titusville, PA 16354
Founded: 1934. **Staff:** 1. **Subjects:** Petroleum industry, local area history, geological surveys. **Special Collections:** Brewer Papers (50 letters and papers of Dr. Francis B. Brewer); Mather Photographic Collection, 1860-1890 (2500 prints, 2761 identified negatives and 1061 unidentified negatives of the oil region). **Holdings:** 1500 books; 900 bound periodical volumes; 1500 other items; 115 cubic feet of Roberts Torpedo Company papers, 1865-1881; 8 cubic feet of John H. Scheide Papers, 1860-1890; 5 cubic feet of Ida M. Tarbell Papers; early maps, atlas, ledgers, scrapbooks. **Subscriptions:** 1300 oil company periodicals and early newspapers of the region. **Services:** Interlibrary loans; copying; library open to public by appointment.

★10622★
PENNSYLVANIA STATE HISTORICAL & MUSEUM COMMISSION - EPHRATA CLOISTER - LIBRARY (Hist)
632 W. Main St.   Phone: (717) 733-6600
Ephrata, PA 17522   James A. Lewars, Act.Adm.
Subjects: History of Ephrata Cloister, Pennsylvania German culture. **Special Collections:** Eighteenth and nineteenth century imprints printed at Ephrata Cloister. **Holdings:** 250 books. **Services:** Copying; library open to public by appointment.

★10623★
PENNSYLVANIA STATE HISTORICAL & MUSEUM COMMISSION - FORT LE BOEUF MUSEUM - LIBRARY (Hist)
123 S. High St.   Phone: (814) 796-4113
Waterford, PA 16441   Patricia P. Leiphart, Hist. Site Mgr.
Founded: 1970. **Subjects:** George Washington, Erie County and Pennsylvania history, Civil War history, archeology, genealogy, American Indians, frontier forts. **Holdings:** 500 books; 15 Bibles of early settlers; 30 ledgers from early businesses; 2 scrapbooks of Amos Judson's letters; 2 drawers of clippings from area newspapers; 10 bound newspapers; 100 magazines. **Services:** Library open to public by appointment. **Remarks:** Holdings are located in the Fort Le Boeuf Museum. The museum and library are under the management of Edinboro University - Anthropology Department. The department's telephone number is (814) 732-2573.

★10624★
PENNSYLVANIA STATE HISTORICAL & MUSEUM COMMISSION - FORT PITT MUSEUM - LIBRARY (Hist)
Point State Park   Phone: (412) 281-9284
Pittsburgh, PA 15222   Robert J. Trombetta, Dir.
Founded: 1967. **Staff:** 5. **Subjects:** French and Indian War, Western Pennsylvania to 1800, 18th century forts and artillery, regimental histories. **Holdings:** 450 volumes; unbound periodicals; 10 French and Indian War letters and documents.

★10625★
PENNSYLVANIA STATE HISTORICAL & MUSEUM COMMISSION - OLD ECONOMY VILLAGE - LIBRARY (Hist)
14th & Church Sts.   Phone: (412) 266-4500
Ambridge, PA 15003   Raymond V. Shepherd, Jr., Dir.
Founded: 1919. **Staff:** Prof 1; Other 20. **Subjects:** History of Harmony Society, communitarian experiments in U.S., social experiments in U.S., industrial and economic history. **Special Collections:** Manuscript music of Harmony Society (6000 items). **Holdings:** 10,000 books. **Services:** Copying; library open to scholars in the field on request. **Remarks:** Historic correspondence, pamphlets and documents have been transferred to the Pennsylvania State Historical & Museum Commission - Division of Archives and Manuscripts.

★10626★
PENNSYLVANIA STATE HISTORICAL & MUSEUM COMMISSION - PENNSYLVANIA LUMBER MUSEUM - LIBRARY (Hist)
Box K   Phone: (814) 435-2652
Galeton, PA 16922   Dolores M. Buchsen, Cur.
Staff: 1. **Subjects:** History of logging, ecology, antique tools, logging railroads. **Special Collections:** Disston Crucible (113 copies on milling, 1912-1926). **Holdings:** 150 books; 24 bound periodical volumes. **Services:** Interlibrary loans; copying (limited); library open to public for reference use only.

★10627★

PENNSYLVANIA STATE HISTORICAL & MUSEUM COMMISSION - REFERENCE LIBRARY (Hist)
William Penn Memorial Museum & Archives Bldg.
Box 1026　　　　　　　　　　　　Phone: (717) 783-9898
Harrisburg, PA 17108-1026　　　　　　Carol W. Tallman, Lib.Techn.
Founded: 1947. **Staff:** 1. **Subjects:** Pennsylvania history, museum technology. **Holdings:** 17,500 books and bound periodical volumes; 15 VF drawers of pamphlets and clippings. **Subscriptions:** 175 journals and other serials. **Services:** Interlibrary loans (limited); library open to students and specialists.

★10628★

PENNSYLVANIA STATE - JOINT STATE GOVERNMENT COMMISSION - LIBRARY (Law)
108 Finance Bldg.　　　　　　　　　Phone: (717) 787-6803
Harrisburg, PA 17120　　　　　　　　Donna Dort, Libn.
Staff: Prof 1. **Subjects:** Education, state legislation, finance, taxes, medical statistics. **Holdings:** 3000 books; 500 bound periodical volumes; 5000 reports and pamphlets; 12 VF drawers of federal and state releases. **Subscriptions:** 30 journals and other serials; 10 newspapers. **Services:** Research on Pennsylvania laws for other states' agencies; library open to members of legislature and authorized visitors. **Publications:** Studies prepared by the staff - limited copies issued.

★10629★

PENNSYLVANIA STATE - LEGISLATIVE REFERENCE BUREAU LIBRARY (Law)
Box 1127　　　　　　　　　　　　Phone: (717) 787-4816
Harrisburg, PA 17120　　　　　　　　Susan K. Zavacky, Libn.
Founded: 1909. **Staff:** Prof 1. **Subjects:** State legislation, law, bill drafting, state court cases. **Special Collections:** Laws of Pennsylvania; Senate and House journals; Senate and House histories; Senate and House bills, 1947 to present. **Holdings:** 8000 volumes; 75 pamphlet files of state documents; 7 VF cases of pamphlets and newspaper clippings. **Subscriptions:** 24 journals and other serials. **Services:** Copying (limited); library open to public for reference use only. **Computerized Information Services:** Internal databases.

★10630★

PENNSYLVANIA STATE LIBRARY (Hist; Law)
Forum Bldg.
Walnut St. & Commonwealth Ave.　　　　Phone: (717) 783-5968
Harrisburg, PA 17105　　　　　　　　Elliot L. Shelkrot, State Libn.
Founded: 1745. **Staff:** Prof 36; Other 71. **Subjects:** Government, law, education, public welfare and administration, Pennsylvania history and biography, Central Pennsylvania genealogy. **Special Collections:** Americana; Pennsylvania Imprints; Colonial Assembly Collection. **Holdings:** 957,871 books; federal and Pennsylvania government publications; Congressional Information Service and American Statistics Index microfiche series; Newsbank, 1977 to present; ERIC microfiche. **Subscriptions:** 3723 journals and other serials; 177 newspapers. **Services:** Interlibrary loans; copying; library open to public. **Automated Operations:** Computerized cataloging, acquisitions and circulation. **Computerized Information Services:** DIALOG, LEXIS, NLM, VU/TEXT; ODIN (internal database). Performs free searches for state government personnel; performs LEXIS searches for public on cost recovery basis. **Networks/Consortia:** Member of PALINET & Union Library Catalogue of Pennsylvania; Interlibrary Delivery Service of Pennsylvania (IDS). **Publications:** The Forum (newsletter), bimonthly. **Special Catalogs:** Pennsylvania Imprints, 1689-1789; Union List of Current Periodical Holdings of the Capitol Hill Libraries and State Library of Pennsylvania; Catalog of Pennsylvania Newspapers and Selected Out-of-State Newspapers. **Staff:** Judith M. Foust, Dir., Lib.Dev.Div.; David R. Hoffman, Dir., Lib.Serv.Div.; Ruth B. Coble, Coord., Tech.Serv.; Donald R. Brown, Coord., Coll.Mgt.; Alice L. Ingraham, Ref./Info.Serv.; Thomas R. Beddoes, Hd., Ref.Sect.

★10631★

PENNSYLVANIA STATE - OFFICE OF ATTORNEY GENERAL - LAW LIBRARY (Law)
1525 Strawberry Square　　　　　　　Phone: (717) 787-3176
Harrisburg, PA 17120　　　　　　　　Ellen R. Chack, Libn.
Founded: 1873. **Staff:** Prof 1; Other 2. **Subjects:** Law. **Holdings:** 30,000 books; 500 bound periodical volumes. **Subscriptions:** 50 journals and other serials; 10 newspapers. **Services:** Library not open to public. **Computerized Information Services:** LEXIS, NEXIS. **Special Indexes:** Pennsylvania Official Opinions of the Attorney General (card).

★10632★

PENNSYLVANIA STATE SUPERIOR COURT - APPELLATE COURTS LIBRARY (Law)
2061 Old Federal Courthouse　　　　　Phone: (215) 351-5840
Philadelphia, PA 19107　　　　　　　Renee Allard Betts, Supv.Libn.
Staff: Prof 1; Other 1. **Subjects:** Law, court administration. **Holdings:** 9550 books and bound periodical volumes; 2350 microfiche. **Subscriptions:** 120 journals and other serials; 5 newspapers. **Services:** Interlibrary loans; SDI; library open to public upon application to librarian. **Automated Operations:** Computerized cataloging. **Computerized Information Services:** LEXIS, NEXIS, OCLC. Performs free searches. **Networks/Consortia:** Member of PALINET & Union Library Catalogue of Pennsylvania. **Publications:** Library Bulletin, monthly - for internal distribution only; quarterly and annual reports.

★10633★

PENNSYLVANIA STATE UNIVERSITY - APPLIED RESEARCH LABORATORY - LIBRARY (Sci-Tech)
Box 30　　　　　　　　　　　　　Phone: (814) 865-6621
State College, PA 16804　　　　　　Charles G. Murphy, Sr.Asst.Libn.
Founded: 1945. **Staff:** Prof 1; Other 1. **Subjects:** Electronics, engineering, acoustics, physics, applied mathematics, hydrodynamics, oceanography. **Holdings:** 3300 books; 1300 bound periodical volumes; 5000 technical reports. **Subscriptions:** 200 journals and other serials. **Services:** Library not open to public. **Computerized Information Services:** DIALOG, DTIC; Library Information Access System (LIAS, internal database). **Publications:** Listing, monthly - to ARL personnel. **Staff:** Wilma Heiser, Lib.Spec.

★10634★

PENNSYLVANIA STATE UNIVERSITY - ARCHITECTURE READING ROOM (Art; Sci-Tech)
207 Engineering Unit C　　　　　　　Phone: (814) 863-0511
University Park, PA 16802　　　　　　Jean Smith, Libn.
Staff: Prof 1; Other 2. **Subjects:** Architecture, history of architecture, building construction, architectural engineering. **Holdings:** 14,350 books. **Subscriptions:** 110 journals. **Services:** Interlibrary loans; copying; reading room open to public. **Automated Operations:** Computerized cataloging, serials and circulation. **Computerized Information Services:** DIALOG.

★10635★

PENNSYLVANIA STATE UNIVERSITY - ARTS LIBRARY (Art)
University Library, Rm. E405　　　　　Phone: (814) 865-6481
University Park, PA 16802　　　　　　Jean Smith, Arts & Arch.Libn.
Founded: 1964. **Staff:** Prof 2; Other 4. **Subjects:** History of art and architecture, painting, sculpture, drawing, graphic arts, decorative arts, music. **Special Collections:** Warren Mack Memorial Collection (505 original prints); Charles Wakefield Cadman Collection. **Holdings:** 60,600 books; 10,061 scores; 1023 spoken word phonograph records; 13,000 music phonograph records and cassette tapes. **Subscriptions:** 462 journals and other serials. **Services:** Interlibrary loans; copying; library open to public. **Automated Operations:** Computerized cataloging, serials and circulation. **Computerized Information Services:** DIALOG, BRS. **Staff:** Daniel Zager, Music Libn.

★10636★

PENNSYLVANIA STATE UNIVERSITY - AUDIOVISUAL SERVICES (Aud-Vis)
Special Services Bldg.　　　　　　　Phone: (814) 865-6314
University Park, PA 16802　　　　　　Robert L. Allen, Dir.
Founded: 1942. **Subjects:** Anthropology, psychology, life sciences, sociology, arts, humanities. **Special Collections:** Psychological Cinema Register (350 film titles); American Archive of Encyclopaedia Cinematographica (2000 film titles). **Holdings:** 16,000 motion picture films. **Services:** Film and video rental and sales; materials available to public with some restrictions. **Computerized Information Services:** Internal database. **Publications:** 16 catalogs in series organized along lines of recognized interest areas; alphabetical listing by title only of 16mm films and video cassettes; reference publication.

★10637★

PENNSYLVANIA STATE UNIVERSITY - CENTER FOR AIR ENVIRONMENT STUDIES - CAES INFORMATION SERVICES (Env-Cons)
225 Fenske Laboratory　　　　　　　Phone: (814) 865-1415
University Park, PA 16802　　　　　　Elizabeth J. Carroll, Adm.Asst.
Founded: 1963. **Staff:** 2. **Subjects:** Air pollution and its effects on health, atmospheric environment research, fossil fuel emissions and acid rain research. **Holdings:** 600 books and bound periodical volumes; 35,000 microfiche and reprints. **Subscriptions:** 35 journals and other serials. **Services:** Interlibrary loans; library open to public. **Automated Operations:** Computerized serials. **Computerized Information Services:** DIALOG; Library Information Access System (LIAS, internal database). Performs searches on cost recovery basis. Contact Person: Eva Brownawell. **Publications:** Air

Pollution Titles, bimonthly - by subscription; CAES reports and publications, irregular - list available upon request.

★10638★

PENNSYLVANIA STATE UNIVERSITY - COLLEGE OF BUSINESS ADMINISTRATION - CENTER FOR RESEARCH - RES. WORKING COLL. (Bus-Fin)

807 Business Administration Bldg.   Phone: (814) 863-0598
University Park, PA 16802   Lydia W. Wasylenko, Libn.
Staff: Prof 1; Other 3. **Subjects:** Accounting and management information systems, business logistics, finance, international business and business law, insurance and real estate, marketing, management science and operations management, organizational behavior. **Holdings:** Doctoral dissertations, masters theses and MBA professional papers; Pennsylvania State University publications; Association for University Business and Economic Research publications; trade association and accounting firm publications; Financial Accounting Standards Board publications; Bureau of National Affairs Tax Management Portfolios; Pennsylvania state and federal government documents. **Subscriptions:** 600 journals and other serials. **Services:** SDI; collection open to public with special permission. **Automated Operations:** Computerized acquisitions and serials. **Computerized Information Services:** DIALOG. **Special Catalogs:** Journal Holdings List (printout).

★10639★

PENNSYLVANIA STATE UNIVERSITY - COLLEGE OF MEDICINE - GEORGE T. HARRELL LIBRARY (Med)

Milton S. Hershey Medical Center   Phone: (717) 534-8629
Hershey, PA 17033   Lois J. Lehman, Libn.
Founded: 1965. **Staff:** Prof 4; Other 9. **Subjects:** Medicine. **Special Collections:** Rare medical books (372 volumes). **Holdings:** 19,315 books; 70,943 bound periodical volumes; 142 motion pictures, videotapes, video discs and cassettes; 2970 audio recordings (discs, tapes, cassettes); 7715 slides; 9 filmstrips. **Subscriptions:** 1588 journals and other serials. **Services:** Interlibrary loans; copying; SDI; library open to public but only local physicians have borrowing privileges. **Computerized Information Services:** Online systems. **Networks/Consortia:** Member of Greater Northeastern Regional Medical Library Program. **Publications:** Library Bulletin, irregular - distributed to state medical school libraries and Hershey Medical Center. **Special Catalogs:** Library Serials Title Catalog; AV Materials. **Staff:** M. Sandra Wood, Assoc.Libn./Hd., Ref.

★10640★

PENNSYLVANIA STATE UNIVERSITY - EARTH AND MINERAL SCIENCES LIBRARY (Sci-Tech; Energy)

105 Deike Bldg.   Phone: (814) 865-9517
University Park, PA 16802   Emilie T. McWilliams, Hd.
Founded: 1931. **Staff:** Prof 1; Other 4. **Subjects:** Geosciences, materials science, meteorology, mineral economics and mineral engineering. **Special Collections:** Coal - mining and processing as a fuel (1300 items). **Holdings:** 71,000 books and bound periodical volumes; 5520 geologic and topographic maps; 1 cabinet NTIS Energy Reports (1983). **Subscriptions:** 1300 journals and other serials. **Services:** Interlibrary loans; copying; library open to public. **Automated Operations:** Computerized circulation. **Computerized Information Services:** DIALOG, SDC, BRS.

★10641★

PENNSYLVANIA STATE UNIVERSITY - ENGINEERING LIBRARY (Sci-Tech)

325 Hammond Bldg.   Phone: (814) 865-3451
University Park, PA 16802   Thomas W. Conkling, Hd.
Founded: 1950. **Staff:** Prof 2; Other 3. **Subjects:** Engineering. **Special Collections:** Schweitzer, diesel engines and diesel research. **Holdings:** 60,000 books and bound periodical volumes; 150,000 technical reports and papers from NASA, National Technical Information Service, American Institute of Aeronautics and Astronautics, Society of Automotive Engineers, Society of Manufacturing Engineers and American Society of Mechanical Engineers. **Subscriptions:** 850 journals and other serials. **Services:** Interlibrary loans; copying; library open to public. **Automated Operations:** Computerized circulation. **Computerized Information Services:** DIALOG, BRS. **Special Catalogs:** Technical Reports Catalog (card). **Staff:** Audrey Powers, Asst.Libn.

★10642★

PENNSYLVANIA STATE UNIVERSITY - FROST ENTOMOLOGICAL MUSEUM - TAXONOMIC RESEARCH LIBRARY (Sci-Tech)

106 Patterson Bldg.   Phone: (814) 865-1895
University Park, PA 16802   Ke Chung Kim, Cur.
Founded: 1972. **Staff:** Prof 2; Other 2. **Subjects:** Taxonomy, entomology, insect identification and information, Anoplura information. **Holdings:** 1000 books; bound volumes, taxonomic references and reprints. **Services:** Library

open for research use by appointment.

★10643★

PENNSYLVANIA STATE UNIVERSITY - INSTITUTE FOR POLICY RESEARCH AND EVALUATION - LIBRARY (Soc Sci)

N253 Burrowes   Phone: (814) 865-5541
University Park, PA 16802   Mary Jane Johnson, Sec.
Founded: 1964. **Subjects:** Human resources, education, manpower, corrections, environment, science policy, welfare, medical care, technology, population. **Holdings:** Vertical file materials. **Publications:** List of publications - available on request. **Services:** Library open to public on a limited basis. **Staff:** Irwin Feller, Dir.

★10644★

PENNSYLVANIA STATE UNIVERSITY - INSTITUTE OF PUBLIC ADMINISTRATION - LIBRARY (Soc Sci)

205 Burrowes Bldg.   Phone: (814) 865-2536
University Park, PA 16802   Robert D. Lee, Jr.
Staff: Prof 1; Other 2. **Subjects:** Public administration, budgeting systems, personnel systems, information systems. **Holdings:** 4059 books; 2043 bound periodical volumes; 1010 masters' degree papers. **Subscriptions:** 45 journals and other serials. **Services:** Copying; library open to public.

★10645★

PENNSYLVANIA STATE UNIVERSITY - INSTITUTE FOR RESEARCH ON LAND AND WATER RESOURCES - LIBRARY (Sci-Tech; Env-Cons)

Land & Water Research Bldg.   Phone: (814) 863-0140
University Park, PA 16802   Eunice Roe, Info.Anl.
Founded: 1963. **Staff:** Prof 1. **Subjects:** Acid precipitation, hazardous waste, land economics, water quality and conservation, land reclamation, acid mine drainage. **Special Collections:** Water Center Reports listed by state; institute publications. **Holdings:** 700 books; 8000 technical reports; pamphlets; 2500 microfiche; maps. **Subscriptions:** 35 journals and other serials; 75 newsletters. **Computerized Information Services:** DIALOG, DOE/RECON, NIH-EPA Chemical Information System. **Publications:** Acquisition list - monthly.

★10646★

PENNSYLVANIA STATE UNIVERSITY - KING OF PRUSSIA CENTER - LIBRARY (Sci-Tech; Educ)

650 S. Henderson Rd.   Phone: (215) 265-7645
King Of Prussia, PA 19406   Vera Hospodka, Hd.Libn.
Founded: 1963. **Staff:** Prof 1; Other 1. **Subjects:** Engineering, public administration, mathematics, regional planning, elementary and special education. **Holdings:** 15,000 books; 1600 bound periodical volumes. **Subscriptions:** 250 journals and other serials. **Services:** Interlibrary loans; copying; library open to public. **Automated Operations:** Computerized cataloging, acquisitions and circulation. **Computerized Information Services:** Online systems; internal database.

★10647★

PENNSYLVANIA STATE UNIVERSITY - LIFE SCIENCES LIBRARY (Sci-Tech; Agri)

E205 E. Pattee Library   Phone: (814) 865-7056
University Park, PA 16802   Keith Roe, Hd.
Founded: 1888. **Staff:** Prof 3; Other 3. **Subjects:** Agriculture, biology, forestry, biophysics, biochemistry, veterinary medicine, health planning and administration, nursing, food science, nutrition. **Special Collections:** Mycology and mushrooms; early American agricultural journals; Lumbering in Pennsylvania Collection (manuscripts, films and slides). **Holdings:** 180,000 books. **Subscriptions:** 3200 journals and other serials. **Services:** Interlibrary loans; library open to public. **Automated Operations:** Computerized cataloging and circulation. **Computerized Information Services:** DIALOG, BRS. **Publications:** Acquisitions List, monthly. **Special Indexes:** Ready-Reference Index to U.S.D.A. Statistical Series. **Staff:** Jane McFall, Assoc.Libn; Judith Anilosky, Asst.Libn.; Robert Seeds, Health Sci.Libn.

★10648★

PENNSYLVANIA STATE UNIVERSITY - MAPS SECTION (Geog-Map)

Pattee Library   Phone: (814) 863-0094
University Park, PA 16802   Karl H. Proehl, Map Libn.
Staff: Prof 1; Other 4. **Subjects:** Topography, city planning, place names, map reading and interpretation. **Special Collections:** Sanborn Fire Insurance maps and atlases of Pennsylvania towns and cities (24,000 sheets); Pennsylvania County boundary maps, 1790-1876. **Holdings:** 800 books; 78 bound periodical volumes; 275,000 maps; 2925 atlases; 8 globes; 5 VF drawers of map interpretation files; 28 VF drawers of travel files. **Subscriptions:** 22 journals and other serials. **Services:** Interlibrary loans; library open to public. **Publications:** Map Collection: New Acquisitions/Cartographic Notes,

quarterly. **Special Indexes:** Atlas Index File (card).

★10649★

PENNSYLVANIA STATE UNIVERSITY - MATHEMATICS LIBRARY (Sci-Tech; Comp Sci)

109 McAllister Bldg.   Phone: (814) 865-6822
University Park, PA 16802   Miriam Pierce, Hd.
Founded: 1966. **Staff:** Prof 1; Other 1. **Subjects:** Mathematics, statistics, computer sciences. **Special Collections:** PSU mathematics dissertations. **Holdings:** 29,101 volumes. **Subscriptions:** 312 journals and other serials. **Services:** Interlibrary loans; copying; library open to public. **Automated Operations:** Computerized cataloging, acquisitions, serials and circulation. **Computerized Information Services:** BRS, DIALOG, SDC; Library Information Access System (LIAS, internal database).

★10650★

PENNSYLVANIA STATE UNIVERSITY - PHYSICAL SCIENCES LIBRARY (Sci-Tech)

230 Davey Laboratory   Phone: (814) 865-7617
University Park, PA 16802   C.J. McKown, Hd.
Staff: Prof 1; Other 4. **Subjects:** Chemistry, physics, chemical engineering, astronomy, biophysics, biochemistry. **Special Collections:** PSU dissertations in chemistry, physics and chemical engineering. **Holdings:** 78,000 volumes. **Subscriptions:** 870 journals and other serials. **Services:** Interlibrary loans; copying. **Automated Operations:** Computerized cataloging, acquisitions, serials and circulation. **Computerized Information Services:** DIALOG, SDC, BRS; Library Information Access System (LIAS, internal database). Performs searches on cost recovery basis. **Publications:** New Books Received, weekly - to faculty.

PENNSYLVANIA STATE UNIVERSITY - SPORTS RESEARCH INSTITUTE
See: Sports Research Institute

★10651★

PENNSYLVANIA STATE UNIVERSITY - TRANSPORTATION INSTITUTE WORKING COLLECTION (Trans)

Research Bldg. B   Phone: (814) 863-3953
University Park, PA 16802   Del Sweeney, Info.Spec.
Founded: 1968. **Staff:** Prof 1; Other 1. **Subjects:** Transportation engineering and materials, automotive research, urban transportation, transportation planning, accident analysis. **Special Collections:** Tire-Pavement Interaction Collection (2600 items); Bureau of Highway Traffic theses. **Holdings:** 3100 books; 700 bound periodical volumes; 6500 reports. **Subscriptions:** 100 journals and other serials. **Services:** Interlibrary loans; copying; collection open to public. **Computerized Information Services:** DIALOG. Performs searches on cost recovery basis.

★10652★

PENNSYLVANIA STATE UNIVERSITY, BERKS CAMPUS - MEMORIAL LIBRARY (Educ)

R.D. 5, Tulpehocken Rd.
Box 2150   Phone: (215) 375-4211
Reading, PA 19608   Sally S. Small, Hd.Libn.
Founded: 1958. **Staff:** Prof 2; Other 4. **Subjects:** Engineering, business, law enforcement, liberal arts, food service, science. **Holdings:** 32,000 books; 2700 bound periodical volumes; 36 VF drawers of pamphlets; 1766 microforms; 700 phonograph records; 65 maps; 287 film loops; 34 art reproductions; 15 videotapes; 17 media kits. **Subscriptions:** 379 journals and other serials; 6 newspapers. **Services:** Interlibrary loans; copying; library open to public with restrictions. **Computerized Information Services:** Library Information Access System (LIAS, internal database). **Publications:** Handbook, annual. **Staff:** Deena H. Morganti, Hd., Pub.Serv.

★10653★

PENNWALT CORPORATION - INFORMATION SERVICES DEPARTMENT (Sci-Tech)

900 First Ave.   Phone: (215) 337-6776
King Of Prussia, PA 19406   Kathryn M. Donovan, Mgr.
Founded: 1944. **Staff:** Prof 4; Other 3. **Subjects:** Chemistry. **Holdings:** 7000 books; 14,000 bound periodical volumes. **Subscriptions:** 500 journals and other serials. **Formerly:** Its Technical Division Library. **Staff:** Betsy Wilhide; Susan Hunsicker; Leah Yocum.

★10654★

PENNWALT CORPORATION - LUCIDOL DIVISION - RESEARCH LIBRARY (Sci-Tech)†

1740 Military Rd.   Phone: (716) 877-1740
Buffalo, NY 14240   David C. Noller, Tech.Info.Spec.
Founded: 1932. **Staff:** Prof 2; Other 1. **Subjects:** Peroxides, organic chemistry, free radicals, chemical safety, polymerization, toxicology. **Holdings:** 6000 monographs; 2500 bound periodical volumes; 15 VF drawers of peroxide literature. **Subscriptions:** 150 journals and other serials. **Services:** Interlibrary loans (fee); copying; library open to public with restrictions. **Networks/Consortia:** Member of Western New York Library Resources Council (WNYLRC). **Special Catalogs:** Peroxides, polymerization, azo compounds catalog (card). **Staff:** Brenda L. Cassoni, Asst.Libn.

★10655★

PENNWALT CORPORATION - PENNWALT PHARMACEUTICAL DIVISION - RESEARCH LIBRARY (Med; Sci-Tech)

755 Jefferson Rd.
Box 1710   Phone: (716) 475-9000
Rochester, NY 14603   Angela Scarfia, Libn.
Staff: Prof 2; Other 1. **Subjects:** Pharmacology, pharmacy, chemistry, bioscience, medicine. **Holdings:** 5561 books; 4750 bound periodical volumes. **Subscriptions:** 400 journals and other serials. **Services:** Interlibrary loans; copying; library open to public by appointment. **Automated Operations:** Computerized interlibrary loans. **Computerized Information Services:** MEDLARS, DIALOG, SDC, BRS, CAS Online, Pergamon InfoLine Ltd., Questel. **Networks/Consortia:** Member of Rochester Regional Research Library Council (RRRLC); Rochester Area Libraries in Healthcare; Rochester OnLine User's Group.

★10656★

PENNZOIL COMPANY - DUVAL RESEARCH & DEVELOPMENT LIBRARY (Sci-Tech)

4715 E. Ft. Lowell Rd.   Phone: (602) 323-5632
Tucson, AZ 85712   Candy L. Gadke, Libn.
Staff: 1. **Subjects:** Mining engineering, chemistry, business development. **Holdings:** 300 books; 88 unbound periodicals. **Subscriptions:** 103 journals and other serials. **Services:** Library open to public with restrictions. **Computerized Information Services:** DIALOG. Performs searches free of charge. **Publications:** Monthly acquisitions list - for internal distribution only.

★10657★

PENNZOIL EXPLORATION AND PRODUCTION COMPANY - TECHNICAL INFORMATION SERVICES (Sci-Tech)

700 Milam
Box 2967   Phone: (713) 546-8793
Houston, TX 77001   Joan K. Baldwin, Libn.
Founded: 1981. **Staff:** Prof 1; Other 1. **Subjects:** Geology, geophysics. **Holdings:** 5000 books; 2000 bound periodical volumes; 1500 technical reports; 2000 maps. **Subscriptions:** 95 journals and other serials. **Services:** Interlibrary loans; copying; services open to public by appointment. **Automated Operations:** Computerized cataloging. **Computerized Information Services:** DIALOG, SDC, Petroleum Data System (PDS), OCLC. **Networks/Consortia:** Member of AMIGOS Bibliographic Council, Inc. **Publications:** Journals Received, weekly; Books Cataloged, monthly - both for internal distribution only.

★10658★

PENNZOIL PRODUCTS COMPANY - RESEARCH DEPARTMENT LIBRARY

8015 St. Vincent Ave.
Box 6199
Shreveport, LA 71106
Defunct

★10659★

PENOBSCOT BAR LIBRARY ASSOCIATION - LIBRARY (Law)†

Penobscot County Court House
Bangor, ME 04401   Norman Minsky, Sec./Tres.
Subjects: Law. **Holdings:** 14,000 volumes. **Services:** Library open to public.

★10660★

PENOBSCOT MARINE MUSEUM - STEPHEN PHILLIPS MEMORIAL LIBRARY (Hist)

Church St.
Box 403   Phone: (207) 548-6634
Searsport, ME 04974   Charles H. Howard, Libn.
Founded: 1936. **Staff:** Prof 3; Other 7. **Subjects:** Maritime history, biography of mariners. **Special Collections:** Ships registers; log books and journals. **Holdings:** 3000 books and bound periodical volumes; archives; clippings; 1900 navigational charts; manuscripts; microfilmed vital records and census data of Knox, Waldo, Hancock counties. **Subscriptions:** 10 journals and other serials. **Services:** Library open to public by appointment.

★10661★
PENROSE HOSPITAL - WEBB MEMORIAL LIBRARY (Med)
2215 N. Cascade Ave.
Box 7021   Phone: (303) 630-5288
Colorado Springs, CO 80933   Elana Heiberger, Med.Libn.
Founded: 1959. **Staff:** Prof 1; Other 1. **Subjects:** Medicine, hospital administration. **Special Collections:** Penrose Cancer Hospital Collection; partial depository for government documents on cancer; history of medicine/ historical medical texts (100 volumes); rare medical books. **Holdings:** 1000 books; 12,000 bound periodical volumes. **Subscriptions:** 300 journals and other serials. **Services:** Interlibrary loans; copying; SDI; library open to persons employed in medical fields and students of local colleges. **Computerized Information Services:** MEDLINE. Performs searches free of charge for physicians and department heads; on cost recovery basis for others. **Networks/Consortia:** Member of Colorado Council of Medical Librarians; Peaks and Valleys (Medical) Library Consortium.

PENROSE LIBRARY
See: University of Denver

★10662★
PENSACOLA HISTORICAL SOCIETY - LELIA ABERCROMBIE HISTORICAL LIBRARY (Hist)
405 S. Adams St.   Phone: (904) 433-1559
Pensacola, FL 32501   Gordon N. Simons, Cur.
Founded: 1960. **Staff:** Prof 3. **Subjects:** Pensacola, Escambia County and West Florida history. **Special Collections:** Stephen R. Mallory letters, 1861- 1870; Brosnaham Collection (land transfers, 1821; letters, deeds, documents and ledgers, 1782-1935); Hollinger manuscript boxes of manuscripts (80). **Holdings:** 2500 books; 700 maps, charts, architectural drawings; 30 hours of oral history recordings by local citizens; 3600 genealogical family data sheets; VF drawers; 140 reels of microfilm; 25,000 photographs; 20,000 glass negatives. **Services:** Copying; library open to public. **Staff:** Claire N. LeMacher, Asst.Cur.; Sandra Johnson, Asst.Cur.

★10663★
PENSACOLA MUSEUM OF ART - HARRY THORNTON MEMORIAL LIBRARY (Art)
407 S. Jefferson St.   Phone: (904) 432-6247
Pensacola, FL 32501
Founded: 1964. **Subjects:** Fine arts and related fields. **Holdings:** 200 books; catalogs; AV materials.

★10664★
PENSION BENEFIT GUARANTY CORPORATION - OFFICE OF THE GENERAL COUNSEL - LIBRARY (Law)
2020 K St., N.W., Suite 7200   Phone: (202) 254-4889
Washington, DC 20006   Anita J. Newman, Libn.
Founded: 1976. **Staff:** Prof 1. **Subjects:** Pension law, pensions. **Holdings:** 5000 books and bound periodical volumes. **Subscriptions:** 150 journals and other serials. **Services:** Interlibrary loans; copying; SDI. **Computerized Information Services:** LEXIS. **Special Indexes:** Indexes to PBGC regulations and notices in the Federal Register; PBGC Congressional testimony. **Remarks:** Pension Benefit Guaranty Corporation is a government corporation that insures private pension plans.

★10665★
PENTON/IPC - MARKETING INFORMATION CENTER (Bus-Fin)
1111 Chester Ave.   Phone: (216) 696-7000
Cleveland, OH 44114   Kenneth Long, Mgr.
Founded: 1960. **Staff:** Prof 3; Other 2. **Subjects:** Industrial and consumer markets, advertising, marketing. **Special Collections:** Penton/IPC market studies. **Holdings:** 3400 books; 3100 government documents; 190 VF drawers of market data, articles, annual reports, company catalogs and government reports. **Subscriptions:** 220 journals and other serials. **Services:** Interlibrary loans; copying; SDI; center open to advertisers and potential advertisers by staff referral. **Computerized Information Services:** NEXIS. **Publications:** Marketing Information Center News, quarterly - to Penton/IPC editors and marketing executives; Market Profiles, annual computation of product sales to consuming industries; industry analyses for Penton/IPC magazines. **Remarks:** The Marketing Information Center is part of Penton/ IPC's Marketing Research & Economic Analysis Department. IPC is the acronym for Industrial Publishing Company. **Staff:** Michael Keating, Sr. Market Anl.; Barbara Pierce, Market Anl.

★10666★
PEOPLES GAS LIGHT AND COKE COMPANY - LIBRARY (Bus-Fin; Energy)
122 S. Michigan Ave., Rm. 727   Phone: (312) 431-4677
Chicago, IL 60603   Anne C. Roess, Chf.Libn.
Founded: 1911. **Staff:** Prof 1; Other 2. **Subjects:** Gas industry - manufactured and natural gas; public utilities; accounting; engineering; energy; management; federal statistics. **Special Collections:** Federal Power Commission Reports; American Gas Association Proceedings. **Holdings:** 6314 books; 1200 reports. **Subscriptions:** 373 journals; 9 newspapers. **Services:** Interlibrary loans; copying; library not open to public. **Automated Operations:** Computerized cataloging. **Computerized Information Services:** DIALOG, SDC, New York Times Information Service, OCLC, DOE/RECON. **Networks/ Consortia:** Member of ILLINET; Chicago Library System. **Special Indexes:** KWOC Index.

PEOPLES LIBRARY
See: Manitoba Indian Cultural Education Centre

★10667★
PEOPLES NATURAL GAS COMPANY - LAW LIBRARY (Law)
2 Gateway Ctr.   Phone: (412) 471-5100
Pittsburgh, PA 15222   Edison W. Keener, Att.
Staff: 1. **Subjects:** Law, oil and gas, public utilities. **Holdings:** 7500 books; 185 bound periodical volumes. **Subscriptions:** 10 journals and other serials. **Services:** Library not open to public.

PEORIA BAHAI ASSEMBLY
See: Bahai Reference Library of Peoria

★10668★
PEORIA COUNTY LAW LIBRARY (Law)
Peoria County Court House, Rm. 209   Phone: (309) 672-6084
Peoria, IL 61602   Mary Louise Jacquin, Libn.
Subjects: Law. **Holdings:** 12,000 volumes. **Subscriptions:** 17 journals and other serials. **Services:** Copying; library open to public. **Networks/Consortia:** Member of Illinois Valley Library System.

★10669★
PEORIA HISTORICAL SOCIETY - HARRY L. SPOONER MEMORIAL LIBRARY (Hist)
Bradley Univ., Cullom-Davis Library
Glenwood & Bradley Aves.   Phone: (309) 676-7611
Peoria, IL 61603   Charles Frey, Spec.Coll.Libn.
Founded: 1962. **Subjects:** Peoria - pictures, biographies, churches, schools, business and industry, authors. **Special Collections:** Ernest E. East Collection; A. Wilson Oakford Collection of Peoria history and pictures (34 volumes of loose-leaf binders); Journal of Illinois State Historical Society, complete with index, 1909 to present; Peoria and Peoria County Atlas; historical encyclopedias, Works Progress Administration (WPA) file. **Holdings:** 1600 books; 27 VF drawers; 12,000 photographic images. **Services:** Copying; library open to public with restrictions.

★10670★
PEPPER, HAMILTON AND SCHEETZ - LAW LIBRARY (Law)
123 S. Broad St.   Phone: (215) 893-3080
Philadelphia, PA 19109   Robyn L. Beyer, Dir., Lib.Serv.
Staff: Prof 2; Other 4. **Subjects:** Law. **Holdings:** 22,000 books and bound periodical volumes. **Subscriptions:** 135 journals and other serials; 5 newspapers. **Services:** Interlibrary loans; SDI; library open to other law libraries and those connected with the firm. **Computerized Information Services:** LEXIS, DIALOG. **Staff:** JoEllen Berger, Asst.Libn.

★10671★
PEPPERDINE UNIVERSITY - LAW LIBRARY (Law)
24255 Pacific Coast Hwy.   Phone: (213) 456-4647
Malibu, CA 90265   Nancy J. Kitchen, Dir.
Founded: 1969. **Staff:** Prof 5; Other 4. **Subjects:** Law. **Holdings:** 85,860 books and bound periodical volumes; 90,130 other cataloged items. **Subscriptions:** 2450 journals and other serials; 18 newspapers. **Services:** Interlibrary loans; copying; library open to public for reference use only. **Automated Operations:** Computerized serials. **Computerized Information Services:** LEXIS, Westlaw, OCLC. **Staff:** Joleen Heather, Acq.; Paula Knecht, Cat.; Ramona Stahl, Circ.; John Wagner, Ref.

★10672★
PEPPERDINE UNIVERSITY - LIBRARY - SPECIAL COLLECTIONS (Hum; Rel-Theol)
24255 Pacific Coast Hwy.   Phone: (213) 456-4243
Malibu, CA 90265   Dr. Harold Holland, Dir.
Subjects: California history, early children's literature. **Special Collections:**

Archives of Churches of Christ, West Coast. **Holdings:** 25 linear feet. **Services:** Interlibrary loans; copying; library open to public. **Automated Operations:** Computerized cataloging and serials. **Computerized Information Services:** DIALOG, OCLC. **Staff:** Virginia Randolph, Spec.Coll.Libn.

★10673★
PEPSICO TECHNICAL CENTER - INFORMATION CENTER (Food-Bev)
100 Stevens Ave.   Phone: (914) 683-0500
Valhalla, NY 10595   Helen Regan, Libn.
Founded: 1950. **Subjects:** Carbonated and other beverages, sweeteners, chemistry, microbiology, food technology, toxicology. **Holdings:** 2000 books and bound periodicals; 33 VF drawers. **Subscriptions:** 170 journals and other serials. **Services:** Interlibrary loans; copying; center open to public to answer telephone or mail inquiries; open to SLA members. **Computerized Information Services:** DIALOG, Pergamon InfoLine, Ltd. **Publications:** Research and Technical Services Library Bulletin - for internal distribution only.

PERE ROUQUETTE LIBRARY
See: St. Joseph Seminary College

★10674★
PERELMAN ANTIQUE TOY MUSEUM - LIBRARY (Hist)
270 S. 2nd St.   Phone: (215) 922-1070
Philadelphia, PA 19106   Harriet Goldfarb, Cur.
Founded: 1969. **Staff:** Prof 1. **Subjects:** Toys, antiques, banks, dolls, historic guidebooks, catalogs. **Special Collections:** Patent papers on antique toy mechanical banks. **Holdings:** 226 books; 100 bound periodical volumes; 100 newsletters; 1 VF drawer of clippings; 2 VF drawers of early toy catalogs. **Subscriptions:** 7 journals and other serials. **Services:** Interlibrary loans; library open to public with restrictions. **Publications:** Perelman Antique Toy Museum (catalog).

PERES OBLATS
See: Oblate Fathers

★10675★
PERGAMON INSTITUTE - LIBRARY (Sci-Tech; Med)
Maxwell House   Phone: (914) 592-7700
Elmsford, NY 10523   Maureen Lyon, Libn.
Founded: 1957. **Staff:** Prof 1; Other 3. **Subjects:** Science, social sciences, technology, humanities and medicine. **Special Collections:** Vergilliana on microfiche; History of Economics (business and annual reports). **Holdings:** 4000 books; 2000 bound periodical volumes; microforms; VF drawers. **Subscriptions:** 250 journals and other serials. **Services:** Library not open to public. **Publications:** Microforms Annual; Librarian's Guide to International Periodicals. **Special Indexes:** Collection Development Guide.

★10676★
PERHAM FOUNDATION - FOOTHILL ELECTRONICS MUSEUM - DE FOREST MEMORIAL ARCHIVES (Sci-Tech; Hist)
12345 El Monte Rd.   Phone: (415) 948-8590
Los Altos Hills, CA 94022   Len Lansdowne, Cur.
Founded: 1973. **Staff:** Prof 2; Other 3. **Subjects:** Early radio, electronics. **Special Collections:** Collections of Dr. Lee de Forest, Dr. Cledo Brunetti, Harold Elliott, Douglas Perham and Royden Thornberg. **Holdings:** 1342 books; 125 bound periodical volumes; 1400 museum artifacts; 30 boxes of manuscripts; 6 boxes of patents; 9 VF drawers of documents and clippings; 10 boxes of scrapbooks; microfilm; pamphlets. **Subscriptions:** 10 journals and other serials. **Services:** Library open to qualified researchers. **Formerly:** Foothill College - Electronics Museum. **Staff:** Cathy Lusk, Act.Dir.

★10677★
PERKIN-ELMER CORPORATION - CORPORATE LIBRARY (Sci-Tech)
Main Ave.   Phone: (203) 834-4798
Norwalk, CT 06856   Margaret D. Wood, Mgr.
Founded: 1958. **Staff:** Prof 4; Other 9. **Subjects:** Instrumentation, optics, electronics, semiconductors. **Holdings:** 25,000 books; 1500 bound periodical volumes; 20,000 documents; 40 VF drawers of reprints, doctoral dissertations, and reprints on microfilm. **Subscriptions:** 600 journals and other serials. **Services:** Interlibrary loans; copying; library open to SLA members, council members, and to the public by appointment. **Automated Operations:** Computerized acquisitions and circulation. **Computerized Information Services:** BRS, NASA/RECON, DTIC; STAIRS (internal database). **Networks/Consortia:** Member of Southwestern Connecticut Library Council (SWLC). **Publications:** List of papers presented by company personnel, annual - for internal distribution only. **Special Catalogs:** Catalog of internal and external engineering reports (book). **Staff:** Evelyn R. Savitzky, Br.Supv.; Elinor M. Hashim, Ref.Supv.; Judy I. Curtis, Tech.Serv.Supv.

★10678★
PERKIN-ELMER DATA SYSTEMS GROUP - LIBRARY (Comp Sci)
106 Apple St.   Phone: (201) 747-7300
Tinton Falls, NJ 07724   Nancy B. Lynott, Libn.
Founded: 1977. **Staff:** Prof 1; Other 1. **Subjects:** Computer science, electrical engineering, math, management. **Holdings:** 2000 books. **Subscriptions:** 150 journals and other serials. **Services:** Interlibrary loans; copying; SDI; library open to public by appointment. **Computerized Information Services:** DIALOG.

PERKIN (Richard S.) LIBRARY
See: American Museum of Natural History - Hayden Planetarium - Richard S. Perkin Library

★10679★
PERKINS, COIE, STONE, OLSEN & WILLIAMS - LAW LIBRARY (Law)
1900 Washington Bldg.   Phone: (206) 682-8770
Seattle, WA 98101   Jane Stewart, Librarian
Staff: Prof 3; Other 5. **Subjects:** Law. **Holdings:** 30,000 volumes. **Subscriptions:** 800 journals and other serials. **Services:** Interlibrary loans; library not open to public. **Staff:** Susan Schulkin, Assoc.Libn.

PERKINS (Ralph) MEMORIAL LIBRARY
See: Archbold (John D.) Memorial Hospital - Ralph Perkins Memorial Library

★10680★
PERKINS SCHOOL FOR THE BLIND - SAMUEL P. HAYES RESEARCH LIBRARY (Soc Sci)
175 N. Beacon St.   Phone: (617) 924-3434
Watertown, MA 02172   Kenneth A. Stuckey, Res.Libn.
Founded: 1880. **Staff:** Prof 1; Other 1. **Subjects:** Nonmedical aspects of blindness and deaf-blindness including education, rehabilitation, and welfare. **Special Collections:** Historical collection of embossed books printed for the blind; pictures of blind people; books by blind and deaf-blind; postage stamps which honor and aid the blind. **Holdings:** 18,000 books and bound periodical volumes; bound newspaper clippings; Helen Keller material. **Subscriptions:** 125 journals and other serials. **Services:** Interlibrary loans; copying (articles and pamphlets only); library open to public for reference use only. **Publications:** Accessions List, biennial - for sale. **Remarks:** Collection also includes a museum showing the history of blindness.

PERKINS SCHOOL OF THEOLOGY
See: Southern Methodist University

★10681★
PERKINS AND WILL ARCHITECTS, INC. - RESOURCE CENTER (Plan; Art)
2 N. LaSalle   Phone: (312) 977-1100
Chicago, IL 60602   Baron Whateley, Specifier
Staff: 1. **Subjects:** Building technology and products, architecture, art, design, planning, interior decorating, engineering. **Holdings:** 2500 books; 300 bound periodical volumes; 12 drawers and 450 linear feet of product literature; 9 drawers of code files. **Subscriptions:** 75 journals and other serials. **Services:** Interlibrary loans; center not open to public. **Staff:** Mary Fugate, Libn.

PERLEY (J. Marshall) HEALTH SCIENCE LIBRARY
See: New Rochelle Hospital Medical Center - J. Marshall Perley Health Science Library

★10682★
PERRY MEMORIAL HOSPITAL - DR. KENNETH O. NELSON LIBRARY OF THE HEALTH SCIENCES (Med)
530 Park Ave., E.   Phone: (815) 875-2811
Princeton, IL 61356   Mary Ann Butler, Lib.Coord.
Staff: Prof 1. **Subjects:** Medicine. **Holdings:** 318 books. **Subscriptions:** 67 journals and other serials. **Services:** Interlibrary loans; copying; library open to public with restrictions. **Automated Operations:** Computerized cataloging, acquisitions, serials and circulation. **Networks/Consortia:** Member of Greater Midwest Regional Medical Library Network (Region 3); Heart of Illinois Library Consortium (HILC); ILLINET; Starved Rock Library System.

PERRY (Merle G.) ARCHIVES
See: Sloan (Alfred P., Jr.) Museum - Merle G. Perry Archives

PERRY'S VICTORY & INTERNATIONAL PEACE MEMORIAL
See: U.S. Natl. Park Service

PERSHING & CO. INC.
See: Donaldson, Lufkin and Jenrette, Inc. - Pershing Division

★10683★
PERSONAL PRODUCTS COMPANY - RESEARCH & DEVELOPMENT LIBRARY (Sci-Tech)
Van Liew Ave.
Milltown, NJ 08850
Phone: (201) 524-7544
Kathryn Hummer, Res.Libn.
Founded: 1954. **Staff:** Prof 1; Other 1. **Subjects:** Chemistry, paper, textiles, medicine, microbiology, cosmetics. **Holdings:** 3150 books; 2550 bound periodical volumes; 2 VF drawers and 21 reels of microfilm of patents; 35 VF drawers and 700 microfiche of company reports; 5 VF drawers of pamphlets. **Subscriptions:** 154 journals and other serials. **Services:** Interlibrary loans; library not open to public. **Automated Operations:** Computerized circulation; indexing of patents and research reports. **Computerized Information Services:** Online systems. **Remarks:** This is a subsidiary of Johnson and Johnson.

★10684★
PERTH AMBOY GENERAL HOSPITAL - HEALTH SCIENCE LIBRARY (Med)
530 New Brunswick Ave.
Perth Amboy, NJ 08861
Phone: (201) 442-3700
Catherine A. Hilman, Health Sci.Libn.
Staff: Prof 1; Other 1. **Subjects:** Medicine, nursing and allied sciences. **Special Collections:** Administrative collection (200 volumes). **Holdings:** 1800 books; 770 bound periodical volumes. **Subscriptions:** 140 journals and other serials. **Services:** Library not open to public.

PERYAM (W.T.) LIBRARY
See: Grand Encampment Museum, Inc. - Library

★10685★
PET, INC. - CORPORATE INFORMATION CENTER (Food-Bev)
Box 392
St. Louis, MO 63166
Phone: (314) 622-6134
Laurence R. Walton, Corp.Libn.
Founded: 1960. **Staff:** Prof 1; Other 1. **Subjects:** Food science and technology, nutrition, microbiology, dairy science, food business, food economics, marketing. **Holdings:** 20,000 books; 2000 bound periodical volumes; microfiche; file of government research reports on food. **Subscriptions:** 450 journals and other serials; 12 newspapers. **Services:** Interlibrary loans; copying; center open to public for reference use only by request. **Automated Operations:** Computerized cataloging. **Computerized Information Services:** DIALOG, Dow Jones News/Retrieval, SDC, NEXIS. **Networks/Consortia:** Member of St. Louis Regional Library Network. **Publications:** PET News Notes, weekly. **Remarks:** Includes the holdings of the former Underwood (William) Company - Library.

PETAWAWA NATIONAL FORESTRY INSTITUTE
See: Canada - Canadian Forestry Service

PETER MEMORIAL LIBRARY
See: Moravian Music Foundation, Inc.

★10686★
PETERBOROUGH HISTORICAL SOCIETY - LIBRARY (Hist)
Grove St.
Box 58
Peterborough, NH 03458
Phone: (603) 924-3235
Gloria Murray, Lib.Chm.
Founded: 1902. **Staff:** Prof 3; Other 4. **Subjects:** History of Peterborough and New Hampshire, antiques. **Special Collections:** 19th century photographs of local people and scenes; early school books; antiques (books and pamphlets). **Holdings:** 1600 books; 130 bound periodical volumes; clippings; early mill account books; maps and letters; early deeds; scrapbooks. **Services:** Library open to public.

PETERS HEALTH SCIENCES LIBRARY
See: Rhode Island Hospital

★10687★
PETERSBURG GENERAL HOSPITAL - MEDICAL LIBRARY MEDIA SERVICES (Med)
801 S. Adams St.
Petersburg, VA 23803
Phone: (804) 732-7220
Mary Grace H. Brown, Med.Lib./Media Serv.Dir.
Founded: 1956. **Staff:** Prof 1; Other 5. **Subjects:** Medicine, nursing. **Special Collections:** Old medical books. **Holdings:** 1002 books; 5230 bound periodical volumes; 4 VF drawers of reprints; 120 video cassettes; 1260 Audio-Digest tapes. **Subscriptions:** 125 journals and other serials. **Services:** Interlibrary loans; copying; library open to public for reference use only. **Networks/Consortia:** Member of Southeastern/Atlantic Regional Medical Library Services. **Publications:** Monthly News-Acquisitions.

PETERSBURG NATL. BATTLEFIELD
See: U.S. Natl. Park Service

★10688★
PETERSHAM HISTORICAL SOCIETY, INC. - LIBRARY (Hist)
Main St.
Petersham, MA 01366
Phone: (617) 724-3380
Mrs. D. Gale Haines, Libn.
Founded: 1930. **Staff:** Prof 1. **Subjects:** Petersham history and genealogy. **Special Collections:** Shays' Rebellion. **Holdings:** 800 books; 600 pamphlets and reports; 15 VF drawers of documents, diaries and pictures; 8 VF drawers of clippings and manuscripts; 20 maps. **Services:** Library open to public with restrictions.

PETERSON (C. Lloyd) MEMORIAL LIBRARY
See: Rocky Mountain Hospital - C. Lloyd Peterson Memorial Library

PETRIFIED FOREST NATL. PARK
See: U.S. Natl. Park Service

★10689★
PETRO-CANADA - LIBRARY SERVICES (Energy)
P.O. Box 2844
Calgary, AB, Canada T2P 3E3
Phone: (403) 296-8000
Beverly Gref, Hd.Libn.
Staff: Prof 6; Other 5. **Subjects:** Petroleum geology and engineering, environment, energy economics, alternative energy sources. **Holdings:** 10,000 books; 100 bound periodical volumes; 1200 company reports. **Subscriptions:** 1200 journals and other serials; 20 newspapers. **Services:** Interlibrary loans; SDI; library open to public with restrictions. **Automated Operations:** Computerized cataloging and serials. **Computerized Information Services:** Online systems. **Publications:** Recent Acquisitions List, monthly. **Staff:** Janet Feero, Tech.Serv.Libn.; Sally Bremmer, Res.Lab.Libn.

PETROLEUM HISTORY AND RESEARCH CENTER LIBRARY
See: University of Wyoming

PETROLEUM RECOVERY INSTITUTE - I.N. MC KINNON MEMORIAL LIBRARY
See: Mc Kinnon (I.N.) Memorial Library

★10690★
PETROLITE CORPORATION - INFORMATION CENTER (Sci-Tech)
369 Marshall Ave.
St. Louis, MO 63119
Phone: (314) 968-6008
Pauline C. Beinbrech, Mgr.
Founded: 1959. **Staff:** Prof 2; Other 1. **Subjects:** Chemistry - organic, petroleum, corrosion; water treatment; wax. **Holdings:** 6000 books; 7500 bound periodical volumes; 89,500 patents; 30,000 microfiche; 10 VF drawers of trade literature. **Subscriptions:** 240 journals and other serials. **Services:** Interlibrary loans; copying; center open to public by appointment. **Automated Operations:** Computerized circulation and periodical routing. **Computerized Information Services:** DIALOG, SDC, NIH-EPA Chemical Information System, CAS Online, OCLC; internal database. **Networks/Consortia:** Member of St. Louis Regional Library Network; Missouri Library Network Corporation. **Publications:** Procedures Manual, irregular; Recent Acquisitions, quarterly. **Staff:** Edward A. Sullivan, III, Info.Spec.

★10691★
PETTAQUAMSCUTT HISTORICAL SOCIETY - LIBRARY (Hist)
1348 Kingstown Rd.
Kingston, RI 02881
Phone: (401) 783-1328
Founded: 1958. **Subjects:** Local history and genealogy, Rhode Island history. **Holdings:** 1000 books; manuscripts; 10 boxes of local government papers. **Services:** Library open to public. **Publications:** Pettaquamscutt Reporter, 5/year - to members.

PETTIGREW MUSEUM
See: Siouxland Heritage Museums

★10692★
PETTIT & MARTIN - LIBRARY (Law)
101 California, 35th Fl.
San Francisco, CA 94111
Phone: (415) 434-4000
Lynn Brazil, Hd.Libn.
Staff: Prof 2; Other 1. **Subjects:** Law. **Holdings:** 23,000 books; 1100 bound periodical volumes. **Subscriptions:** 400 journals and other serials. **Services:** Interlibrary loans; copying; library open to public by permission only. **Computerized Information Services:** LEXIS, NEXIS, DIALOG, RLIN. **Networks/Consortia:** Member of CLASS. **Staff:** Trish McCardy, Asst.Libn.

PETZINGER (Almeda May Castle) LIBRARY
See: The Haggin Museum - Almeda May Castle Petzinger Library

★10693★
P'EYLIM-AMERICAN YESHIVA STUDENT UNION - LIBRARY
3 W. 16th St.
New York, NY 10011
Subjects: Jewish topics. **Holdings:** 2000 periodicals. **Remarks:** Presently inactive.

PFAUDLER COMPANY
See: Standard Oil Company of Ohio

PFEIFFER (Annie Merner) LIBRARY
See: West Virginia Wesleyan College - Annie Merner Pfeiffer Library

PFEIFFER PHYSICS LIBRARY
See: Washington University

★10694★
PFIZER CANADA INC. - MEDICAL LIBRARY (Med)
P.O. Box 800   Phone: (514) 695-0500
Pointe Claire-Dorval, PQ, Canada H9R 4V2   Miriam Hayward, Sci.Info.Coord.
Staff: Prof 1. **Subjects:** Pharmacology, drug therapy, rheumatology, cardiovasology, psychotherapy, microbiology, allergies, dermatology. **Holdings:** 500 books; 450 bound periodical volumes; 50 audio cassettes; 4000 reprints; 125 meeting and symposia proceedings; 90 product information items; 80 other cataloged items. **Subscriptions:** 120 journals and other serials; 12 newspapers. **Services:** Interlibrary loans; SDI; library open to health professionals, sales representatives, and students. **Computerized Information Services:** MEDLARS, DIALOG, Lithium Library; MEDNET (internal database). **Publications:** Bibliographies; Current Awareness - both for internal distribution only.

★10695★
PFIZER, INC. - CENTRAL RESEARCH TECHNICAL INFORMATION SERVICES (Med)
Eastern Point Rd.   Phone: (203) 445-5611
Groton, CT 06340   Dr. Jay S. Buckley, Jr., Dir., Tech.Info.
Founded: 1960. **Staff:** Prof 5; Other 6. **Subjects:** Organic and pharmaceutical chemistry, pharmacology, clinical medicine, antibiotics, fermentation, food chemistry. **Holdings:** 7000 books; 30,000 bound periodical volumes; 2500 reels of patent specifications. **Subscriptions:** 1000 journals and other serials. **Services:** SDI; library open to students and researchers. **Automated Operations:** Computerized acquisitions and serials. **Computerized Information Services:** DIALOG, SDC, NLM, Chemical Abstracts Service (CAS). **Publications:** Periodical Holdings List, semiannual. **Special Indexes:** Central Patents Index - Sections A, B, D and E; Unlisted Drugs (card). **Staff:** John B. Hare, Supv.; Roberta Lewis, Libn.

★10696★
PFIZER, INC. - N.Y.O. LIBRARY (Med)
235 E. 42nd St.   Phone: (212) 573-2966
New York, NY 10017   Veronica Plucinski, Chf.Libn.
Staff: Prof 3. **Subjects:** Pharmaceuticals, pharmacology, clinical medicine. **Holdings:** 14,000 books and bound periodical volumes; 1240 reels of microfilm. **Subscriptions:** 623 journals and other serials. **Services:** Interlibrary loans; SDI; library open by appointment to students and researchers. **Computerized Information Services:** DIALOG, SDC, MEDLARS. **Networks/Consortia:** Member of Medical Library Center of New York (MLCNY). **Publications:** Periodical Subscription List, annual; Periodical Subject List, annual - free upon request. **Staff:** Karen Erani, Assoc.Libn.; Clara Henson, Lib.Asst.

PFOHL (Anthony C.) HEALTH SCIENCE LIBRARY
See: Mercy Health Center - Anthony C. Pfohl Health Science Library

★10697★
PFORZHEIMER (Carl & Lily) FOUNDATION, INC. - CARL H. PFORZHEIMER LIBRARY (Hum)
41 E. 42nd St., Rm. 815   Phone: (212) 697-7217
New York, NY 10017
Founded: 1957. **Staff:** Prof 5; Other 1. **Special Collections:** English literature from Caxton to 1700; Bruce Rogers and other fine presses; George Gissing; first editions of 18th and 19th centuries including manuscript material of Shelley and his Circle; Women Writers, 1790-1840. **Holdings:** Figures not available. **Services:** Library open to scholars on approval of application. **Special Catalogs:** English Literature 1475 to 1700; Shelley and His Circle 1773-1822 (in progress). **Staff:** Donald H. Reiman, Ed., Shelley Project; Mihai H. Handrea, Libn.; Robert Yampolsky, Bibliog.

★10698★
PHARMACEUTICAL MANUFACTURERS ASSOCIATION - LIBRARY (Med)
1100 15th St., N.W.   Phone: (202) 463-2000
Washington, DC 20005   Lucy G. Gritzmacher, Libn.
Founded: 1959. **Staff:** Prof 2. **Subjects:** Pharmacy, medicine, economics, international law, legislation. **Special Collections:** Association Annual Report, 1914 to present. **Holdings:** 1200 books; 1500 reports. **Subscriptions:** 354 journals and other serials. **Services:** Interlibrary loans; library open to public for reference use only, on request **Automated Operations:** Computerized serials. **Computerized Information Services:** NLM, DIALOG. **Special Catalogs:** Catalog of reports, companies, countries. **Formerly:** Its Science Information Sercies. **Staff:** Brenda Semeleer, Asst.Libn.

★10699★
PHARMACEUTICAL SOCIETY OF THE STATE OF NEW YORK - ACADEMY OF PHARMACY LIBRARY
1975 Linden Blvd., 1st Fl.
Elmont, NY 11003
Defunct

★10700★
PHARMACIA P-L BIOCHEMICALS, INC. - RESEARCH LIBRARY (Food-Bev)
2202 N. Bartlett Ave.   Phone: (414) 225-2601
Milwaukee, WI 53202   Marie Fendry, Res.Libn.
Founded: 1944. **Staff:** 1. **Subjects:** Microbiology, biochemistry, chemistry. **Holdings:** 2666 books; 1482 bound periodical volumes; 3208 pamphlets; 8 VF drawers of patents. **Subscriptions:** 75 journals and other serials. **Services:** Library open to public by appointment. **Formerly:** Pabst Brewing Company - P-L Biochemicals, Inc.

★10701★
PHARMACO-MEDICAL DOCUMENTATION, INC. - RESEARCH LIBRARY (Med)†
205 Main St.
Box 401   Phone: (201) 822-9200
Chatham, NJ 07928   Miss G. Wold, Res.Libn.
Founded: 1961. **Staff:** Prof 6; Other 2. **Subjects:** Pharmaceuticals, drug marketing, medicinal chemistry, pharmacology, pharmacotherapy. **Special Collections:** Worldwide Drug Products Compendia (200 volumes). **Holdings:** 2000 books; 500 bound periodical volumes; computer printouts; magnetic tapes; indexes. **Subscriptions:** 400 journals and other serials. **Services:** Copying; consulting on drug information procurement; translating; indexing; SDI; library open to clients of PMD Inc. and subscribers to Unlisted Drugs. **Publications:** Unlisted Drugs, monthly. **Special Indexes:** Unlisted Drugs on file ready Index Cards; Index of Codes for Research Drugs; Unlisted Drugs Index-Guide/5; World Pharmaceuticals Directory. Varied indexes on punched-card and magnetic tape.

PHASE DIAGRAMS FOR CERAMISTS
See: U.S. Natl. Bureau of Standards

PHELAN (Gerald B.) ARCHIVES
See: University of Toronto - Pontifical Institute of Medieval Studies - Library

PHILADELPHIA ACADEMY OF NATURAL SCIENCES
See: Academy of Natural Sciences

★10702★
PHILADELPHIA ASSOCIATION FOR PSYCHOANALYSIS - LOUIS S. KAPLAN MEMORIAL LIBRARY (Med)
15 St. Asaph's Rd.
Bala Cynwyd, PA 19004   June M. Strickland, Libn.
Founded: 1950. **Staff:** Prof 1. **Subjects:** Psychoanalysis, psychiatry. **Holdings:** 2400 books; 2100 bound periodical volumes. **Services:** Library not open to public.

★10703★
PHILADELPHIA BOARD OF EDUCATION - PEDAGOGICAL LIBRARY (Educ)†
22nd St. & Parkway
Adm. Bldg., Rm. 301   Phone: (215) 299-7783
Philadelphia, PA 19103   Helen E. Howe, Hd.Libn.
Founded: 1883. **Staff:** Prof 2; Other 4. **Subjects:** Elementary and secondary education, psychology and testing, intercultural human relations, special education, reading. **Special Collections:** Complete ERIC collection; examination center for textbooks and instructional aids. **Holdings:** 47,000 books and bound periodical volumes; VF drawers of Philadelphia courses of study, pictures, teaching units, bibliographies, pamphlets; 200,000 documents on microfiche. **Subscriptions:** 450 journals and other serials; 6

newspapers. **Services:** Interlibrary loans; SDI; library open to public for reference use; only employees of Philadelphia School District have borrowing privileges. **Publications:** New book lists and flyers, monthly; current list of periodicals, semiannual. **Staff:** Joan B. Myers, Dir.; Patricia Buck, Asst.Libn.

★10704★
PHILADELPHIA - CITY ARCHIVES (Hist)
Dept. of Records
Rm. 523, City Hall Annex   Phone: (215) 686-2272
Philadelphia, PA 19107   Allen Weinberg, City Archv.
Founded: 1952. **Staff:** Prof 3; Other 16. **Subjects:** Archives of the City and County of Philadelphia, 1682 to present. **Special Collections:** Official records of the 1876 Centennial Exhibition, the Sesquicentennial Exposition and 1976 Bicentennial celebration of the city of Philadelphia. **Holdings:** 20,000 cubic feet of archives; 93,000 cubic feet of Records Center holdings. **Services:** Copying; archives open to public. **Publications:** City Archives Newsletter; list of other publications - available on request. **Special Catalogs:** Descriptive Inventory of the Archives of the City and County of Philadelphia (book). **Special Indexes:** Subject Index to the Photograph Collection of the Philadelphia City Archives. **Staff:** Ward Childs, Asst.Archv.; Lee Stanley, Archv. I; Alfonso Harrell, Supv., Rec.Ctr.

★10705★
PHILADELPHIA CITY PLANNING COMMISSION - LIBRARY (Plan)
City Hall Annex, 14th Fl.
Juniper & Filbert Sts.   Phone: (215) 686-4637
Philadelphia, PA 19103
Founded: 1944. **Subjects:** City and regional planning, housing, transportation, government, architecture, engineering, business and industry, sociology, statistics. **Special Collections:** Archives of the Commission; Philadelphia renewal areas (4000 35mm slides). **Holdings:** 22,000 books and pamphlets; 1000 bound periodical volumes; 2 VF drawers of archives. **Subscriptions:** 150 journals and other serials. **Services:** Interlibrary loans (limited); library open to public. **Publications:** List of accessions, quarterly - distributed to staff heads and to other planning libraries on exchange basis.

★10706★
PHILADELPHIA COLLEGE OF ART - AUDIOVISIUAL DEPARTMENT - FILM LIBRARY (Aud-Vis)
Broad & Spruce Sts.   Phone: (215) 893-3204
Philadelphia, PA 19102   Richard Sassaman, AV Coord.
Founded: 1968. **Staff:** Prof 1; Other 5. **Subjects:** Silent films - early experimental and comedy, feature black and white films. **Holdings:** 300 films. **Services:** Library open to public for reference use only. **Networks/Consortia:** Member of Tri-County Library Consortium.

★10707★
PHILADELPHIA COLLEGE OF ART - SLIDE LIBRARY (Art; Aud-Vis)
Broad & Spruce Sts., Anderson Hall   Phone: (215) 893-3117
Philadelphia, PA 19102   John Caldwell, Libn.
Founded: 1958. **Subjects:** Art, crafts, industrial design. **Holdings:** 150,000 slides; 150 VF drawers of pictures. **Services:** Interlibrary loans; copying; library open to public with restrictions. **Computerized Information Services:** Access to OCLC through Albert M. Greenfield Library. **Networks/Consortia:** Member of PALINET & Union Library Catalogue of Pennsylvania; Tristate College Library Cooperative (TCLC).

★10708★
PHILADELPHIA COLLEGE OF BIBLE - LIBRARY (Rel-Theol)
Langhorne Manor   Phone: (215) 752-5800
Langhorne, PA 19047   Julius C. Bosco, Dir.
Founded: 1913. **Staff:** Prof 3; Other 2. **Subjects:** Theology and Bible study, music and arts, Christian education, social work, missions, pre-nursing. **Special Collections:** Hymnals; C.I. Scofield Library of Biblical studies. **Holdings:** 48,500 books, bound periodical volumes and scores; 3481 slides; 1112 reels of microfilm; 17,009 microfiche; 3035 phonograph records; 215 filmstrips; 3 films; 728 cassettes; 159 curriculum materials. **Subscriptions:** 483 journals and other serials; 11 newspapers. **Services:** Interlibrary loans; copying; library open to public for reference use only. **Publications:** Methods and Materials of Library Research, Music Reference Sources, both by D. Black. **Staff:** Dorothy M. Black, Asst. to Dir.; Ruth Homer, Cat., ILL.

★10709★
PHILADELPHIA COLLEGE OF OSTEOPATHIC MEDICINE - O.J. SNYDER MEMORIAL MEDICAL LIBRARY (Med)
4150 City Ave.   Phone: (215) 581-6526
Philadelphia, PA 19131   Dr. Shanker H. Vyas, Prof./Dir. of Libs.
Founded: 1898. **Staff:** Prof 4; Other 8. **Subjects:** Osteopathy, medicine, surgery. **Special Collections:** First editions of works on osteopathy, many autographed; archival collection. **Holdings:** 49,226 books and bound periodical volumes; 3410 audiotapes; 1108 videotapes; 112 35mm reels of microfilm; 3985 slides; 323 view master reels; 946 filmstrips. **Subscriptions:** 689 journals and other serials. **Services:** Interlibrary loans; copying; microfilming; library open to public for reference use only with permission. **Computerized Information Services:** MEDLINE. **Networks/Consortia:** Member of Greater Northeastern Regional Medical Library Program. **Publications:** List of publications - available upon request. **Special Indexes:** Union List of Osteopathic Literature, edited by Dr. S. Vyas. **Staff:** Prof. Hansa S. Vyas, Search Anl./Ref.Libn.; Kathryn Picardo, Asst.Prof./Cat.Libn.; Carol Ann Powers, Instr./Asst.Libn., Ser.

★10710★
PHILADELPHIA COLLEGE OF THE PERFORMING ARTS - LIBRARY (Mus)
250 S. Broad St.   Phone: (215) 875-2200
Philadelphia, PA 19102   Phoebe Law, Hd.Libn.
Staff: Prof 1. **Subjects:** Music, dance, theater arts. **Special Collections:** Lattimore-Nahumck Dance Collection (3000 volumes). **Holdings:** 19,000 books and scores; 13,000 phonograph records. **Subscriptions:** 62 journals and other serials. **Services:** Interlibrary loans; library open to public for reference use only, on request.

★10711★
PHILADELPHIA COLLEGE OF PHARMACY AND SCIENCE - JOSEPH W. ENGLAND LIBRARY (Med; Sci-Tech)
42nd St. & Woodland Ave.   Phone: (215) 596-8960
Philadelphia, PA 19104   Carol Hansen Fenichel, Dir., Lib.Serv.
Founded: 1822. **Staff:** Prof 7; Other 9. **Subjects:** Pharmacy, pharmacology, biological sciences, chemistry, pharmacognosy, toxicology. **Special Collections:** History of pharmacy. **Holdings:** 73,000 books and bound periodical volumes; 4900 reels of microfilm; 20,000 microfiche; 150 audio cassettes; 24 VF drawers of pamphlets; selective AV software. **Subscriptions:** 1000 journals and other serials. **Services:** Interlibrary loans; copying; library open to public for reference use only by appointment. **Automated Operations:** Computerized cataloging, serials and ILL. **Computerized Information Services:** DIALOG, BRS, NLM, NIH-EPA Chemical Information System, OCLC, CAS Online. **Networks/Consortia:** Member of Greater Northeastern Regional Medical Library Program; PALINET & Union Library Catalogue of Pennsylvania; Interlibrary Delivery Service of Pennsylvania (IDS); Philadelphia Area Reference Librarians Information Exchange (PARLIE). **Publications:** J.W. England Newsletter & Booklist, monthly. **Staff:** Karen Albert, Ref.Libn./Search Anl.; Nancy Rainey, Ref.Libn./Search Anl.; Margaret Giles Fallis, Hd., Pub.Serv.; Sherry Montgomery, Hd., AV Dept.; Leslie Bowman, Hd., Tech.Serv./Cat.; Nancy L. Weinstock, Rare Bk.Libn.

★10712★
PHILADELPHIA COLLEGE OF TEXTILES AND SCIENCE - PASTORE LIBRARY (Sci-Tech)
School House Lane & Henry Ave.   Phone: (215) 951-2840
Philadelphia, PA 19144   J. Thomas Vogel, Dir. of Lib.Serv.
Founded: 1949. **Staff:** Prof 4; Other 4. **Subjects:** Textiles, business. **Special Collections:** Textile history. **Holdings:** 70,000 books; 12,000 bound periodical volumes; 6000 reels of microfilm. **Subscriptions:** 1500 journals and other serials; 12 newspapers. **Services:** Interlibrary loans; copying; library open to public for reference use only. **Automated Operations:** Computerized cataloging, acquisitions and serials. **Computerized Information Services:** DIALOG, SDC. **Networks/Consortia:** Member of Tri-State College Library Cooperative; PALINET & Union Library Catalogue of Pennsylvania. **Staff:** Barbara Lowry, Hd., Ref.; Lynn Burns, Cat.; Wilfred Frisby, Ref.Libn.

★10713★
PHILADELPHIA COMMUNITY LEGAL SERVICES, INC. - LAW LIBRARY (Law)
Sylvania House
1324 Locust at Juniper St.   Phone: (215) 893-5368
Philadelphia, PA 19107   Barbara L. Krauss, Libn.
Founded: 1968. **Staff:** Prof 1; Other 1. **Subjects:** Civil and poverty law. **Holdings:** 20,000 books; 200 unbound periodicals; 100 internal publications. **Subscriptions:** 30 journals and other serials; 5 newspapers. **Services:** Interlibrary loans; library not open to public. **Computerized Information Services:** LEXIS, DIALOG; LSC Brief Bank (internal database). **Publications:** Monthly internal newsletters.

★10714★
PHILADELPHIA CORPORATION FOR AGING - LIBRARY (Soc Sci)
Penn Square Bldg.
1317 Filbert St., Rm. 415   Phone: (215) 241-8207
Philadelphia, PA 19107   Steven J. Bell, Ref.Libn.
Founded: 1978. **Staff:** Prof 1; Other 1. **Subjects:** Gerontology,

gerontological literature, programs for the aging. **Special Collections:** Service Center for Aging Information Microfiche Repository Collection (SCAN; 3000 gerontology-related research documents on microfiche). **Holdings:** 950 books; 45 bound periodical volumes; 125 government publications; 5000 documents; 8 VF drawers of pamphlets and reports. **Subscriptions:** 77 journals and other serials; 10 newspapers. **Services:** Interlibrary loans; copying; library open to public for reference use only. **Networks/Consortia:** Member of Greater Northeastern Regional Medical Library Program. **Remarks:** The corporation is an Area Agency on Aging.

★10715★
PHILADELPHIA COURT OF COMMON PLEAS - LAW LIBRARY (Law)
City Hall, Rm. 600   Phone: (215) 686-3799
Philadelphia, PA 19107   James M. Clark, Libn.
Staff: Prof 1; Other 3. **Subjects:** U.S. and Pennsylvania law. **Special Collections:** Philadelphia judges memorial collection. **Holdings:** 24,000 books; 100 bound periodical volumes; 3 VF drawers of Pennsylvania House and Senate bills; 3 VF drawers of Pennsylvania Appellate Court Slip opinions; 40 audio cassettes. **Subscriptions:** 102 journals and other serials; 6 newspapers. **Services:** Interlibrary loans; library not open to public. **Computerized Information Services:** LEXIS. **Special Indexes:** Subject index to Pennsylvania Appellate Court Slip opinions.

PHILADELPHIA DAILY NEWS
See: Philadelphia Newspapers, Inc.

★10716★
PHILADELPHIA ELECTRIC COMPANY - LIBRARY (Energy)
2301 Market St.   Phone: (215) 841-4358
Philadelphia, PA 19101   Sabina D. Tannenbaum, Libn.
Founded: 1909. **Staff:** Prof 2; Other 2. **Subjects:** Engineering - civil, electrical, mechanical, chemical; generating stations - hydro, nuclear, steam; nuclear energy; public utilities; illumination. **Special Collections:** Electric Power Research Institute reports. **Holdings:** 7000 books and bound periodical volumes; 10,000 pamphlets and reports. **Subscriptions:** 250 journals and other serials. **Services:** Interlibrary loans; library open to public by appointment. **Computerized Information Services:** DIALOG, SDC, VU/TEXT, DOE/RECON. **Publications:** Current Topics (abstracts of current articles and books) - for internal distribution only.

PHILADELPHIA EVENING BULLETIN LIBRARY
See: Temple University - Central Library System - Photo-Journalism Collection

PHILADELPHIA FREE LIBRARY
See: Free Library of Philadelphia

★10717★
PHILADELPHIA GERIATRIC CENTER - LIBRARY (Soc Sci)
5307 N. 13th St.   Phone: (215) 455-6100
Philadelphia, PA 19141   Barbara Halpern, Libn.
Staff: Prof 1; Other 1. **Subjects:** Gerontology, geriatrics, psychology, housing, medicine, government reports. **Holdings:** 10,000 books; 1000 bound periodical volumes; 500 titles of unbound periodicals; 1000 reprints; clippings file; 200 cassettes. **Subscriptions:** 300 journals and other serials. **Services:** Interlibrary loans; copying; library open to public for reference use only. **Networks/Consortia:** Member of Greater Northeastern Regional Medical Library Program; Delaware Valley Information Consortium (DEVIC). **Publications:** Quarterly acquisitions list.

★10718★
PHILADELPHIA HISTORICAL COMMISSION - LIBRARY (Hist; Art)
1313 City Hall Annex   Phone: (215) 686-4543
Philadelphia, PA 19107   Dr. Richard Tyler, Hist.
Founded: 1955. **Staff:** Prof 4. **Subjects:** Architectural history of Philadelphia, architecture and history of Philadelphia. **Holdings:** 1200 books; 19 cabinets of manuscript records including insurance surveys, briefs of titles, photostats of old prints and photographs of buildings in Philadelphia. **Subscriptions:** 10 journals and other serials. **Services:** Library open to public.

PHILADELPHIA INQUIRER
See: Philadelphia Newspapers, Inc.

★10719★
PHILADELPHIA JEWISH ARCHIVES CENTER (Rel-Theol)
625 Walnut St.   Phone: (215) 923-2729
Philadelphia, PA 19106   Lee B. Leopold, Archv.
Staff: 3. **Subjects:** Judaica. **Holdings:** 900 books. **Services:** Copying; archives open to public for reference use only. **Publications:** Newsletter,

semiannual; A Guide to the Phildelphia Jewish Archives Center, 1977.

PHILADELPHIA LIBRARY COMPANY
See: Library Company of Philadelphia

★10720★
PHILADELPHIA MARITIME MUSEUM - LIBRARY (Hist)
321 Chestnut St.   Phone: (215) 925-5439
Philadelphia, PA 19106   Dorothy H. Mueller, Libn.
Founded: 1961. **Staff:** 1. **Subjects:** Philadelphia port and general maritime history. **Special Collections:** Vessel registers (1500 volumes). **Holdings:** 8000 books; 12 VF drawers of photographs; manuscripts; oral history tapes; microfilm; pamphlets; charts; maps. **Subscriptions:** 75 journals and other serials. **Services:** Copying; library open to scholars by appointment.

★10721★
PHILADELPHIA MUSEUM OF ART - LIBRARY (Art)
Box 7646   Phone: (215) 763-8100
Philadelphia, PA 19101   Barbara Sevy, Libn.
Founded: 1876. **Staff:** Prof 3; Other 2. **Subjects:** Fine arts. **Special Collections:** Kienbusch Library of Arms and Armour (2000 volumes); museum archives. **Holdings:** 120,000 books, periodicals and pamphlets. **Subscriptions:** 450 journals and other serials. **Services:** Copying; library open to public for reference use only.

★10722★
PHILADELPHIA MUSEUM OF ART - SLIDE LIBRARY (Aud-Vis; Art)
Parkway at 26th St.
Box 7646   Phone: (215) 763-8100
Philadelphia, PA 19101   Thomas Donio, Slide Libn.
Founded: 1939. **Staff:** 1. **Subjects:** History of art and architecture. **Holdings:** 100,000 slides (noncirculating). **Services:** Department not open to public. **Remarks:** Sales requests should be referred to Rosenthal Art Slides, 5456 S. Ridgewood Ct., Chicago, IL 60615.

★10723★
PHILADELPHIA NEWSPAPERS, INC. - INQUIRER AND DAILY NEWS LIBRARY (Publ)
400 N. Broad St.   Phone: (215) 854-2000
Philadelphia, PA 19101   Mary Jo Crowley, Mgr., Lib./Info.Ctr.
Founded: 1925. **Staff:** 11. **Subjects:** Philadelphia Inquirer and Daily News. **Holdings:** 6000 books and bound periodical volumes; 600 pamphlets; clippings and photographs from Inquirer, Daily News and selected New York papers and periodicals; microfilm of Philadelphia Inquirer, 1926 to present, Daily News, 1960 to present, and New York Times, 1958 to present. **Subscriptions:** 30 journals and other serials; 48 newspapers. **Services:** Library not open to public. **Computerized Information Services:** NEXIS, DIALOG, electronic retrieval system for Daily News and Inquirer. **Special Indexes:** Philadelphia Inquirer index, 1926-1954 (card); selective index, 1955-1979.

★10724★
PHILADELPHIA ORCHESTRA ASSOCIATION - LIBRARY (Mus)
Academy of Music
1420 Locust St.   Phone: (215) 893-1929
Philadelphia, PA 19102   Clinton F. Nieweg, Principal Libn.
Founded: 1900. **Staff:** Prof 3. **Subjects:** Symphony orchestra music. **Holdings:** 3500 orchestrations; 3000 choral parts (50 titles); 800 scores. **Services:** Library open for research on premises only. **Staff:** Robert Grossman, Libn.; Nancy M. Bradburd, Libn.

★10725★
PHILADELPHIA PSYCHIATRIC CENTER - PROFESSIONAL LIBRARY (Med)
Ford Rd. & Monument Ave.   Phone: (215) 877-2000
Philadelphia, PA 19131   Ann Vosbergh, Libn.
Staff: Prof 1. **Subjects:** Psychiatry, psychology, psychoanalysis, family therapy. **Holdings:** 7500 books and bound periodical volumes. **Subscriptions:** 90 journals and other serials. **Services:** Interlibrary loans; copying (limited); library open to public with restrictions. **Networks/Consortia:** Member of Greater Northeastern Regional Medical Library Program; PALINET & Union Library Catalogue of Pennsylvania.

★10726★
PHILADELPHIA QUARTZ COMPANY - BUSINESS/CHEMISTRY INFORMATION CENTER (Sci-Tech)
Valley Forge Executive Mall
Box 840   Phone: (215) 293-7363
Valley Forge, PA 19482   Frieda S. Mecray, Info.Spec.
Staff: Prof 1. **Subjects:** Business, marketing, chemistry, engineering.

Holdings: 1500 books. **Subscriptions:** 120 journals and other serials. **Services:** Interlibrary loans; copying; SDI; center open by personal invitation. **Automated Operations:** Computerized cataloging and periodical circulation. **Computerized Information Services:** DIALOG. **Networks/Consortia:** Member of PALINET & Union Library Catalogue of Pennsylvania.

★10727★
PHILADELPHIA STATE HOSPITAL - STAFF LIBRARY (Med)†
Research & Education Bldg.
14000 Roosevelt Blvd.   Phone: (215) 671-4111
Philadelphia, PA 19114   Greta Clark, Libn.
Staff: Prof 1; Other 4. **Subjects:** Psychiatry, psychology, psychiatric nursing, social services, family therapy. **Special Collections:** Robert S. Smith Behavioral Science Library. **Holdings:** 4000 books and bound periodical volumes; 40 dissertations; 4 VF drawers. **Subscriptions:** 185 journals and other serials. **Services:** Interlibrary loans; copying; library open to public at the discretion of librarian. **Publications:** Library information booklet; periodicals list; bibliographies - all irregular.

PHILADELPHIA URBAN SEMESTER
See: Great Lakes Colleges Association

★10728★
PHILATELIC FOUNDATION - ARCHIVES AND LIBRARY (Rec)
270 Madison Ave.   Phone: (212) 889-6483
New York, NY 10016   John F. Dunn, Dir. of Educ.
Staff: 3. **Subjects:** Philately. **Special Collections:** Luff Reference Collection; Ashbrook Correspondence and Special Service. **Holdings:** 1500 books; 200 bound periodical volumes; 5000 documents and archival materials. **Subscriptions:** 25 journals and other serials; 10 newspapers. **Services:** Copying; library open to members.

★10729★
PHILBROOK ART CENTER - LIBRARY (Art)
Box 52510   Phone: (918) 741-7941
Tulsa, OK 74152   Thomas E. Young, Libn.
Founded: 1939. **Staff:** Prof 1. **Subjects:** Art. **Special Collections:** Roberta Campbell Lawson Indian Library (1105 volumes). **Holdings:** 5400 books; 5000 bound periodical volumes; 30 VF drawers; 150 boxes of archives. **Subscriptions:** 92 journals and other serials. **Services:** Interlibrary loans; copying; library open to public by appointment. **Automated Operations:** Computerized cataloging. **Computerized Information Services:** OCLC. **Networks/Consortia:** Member of AMIGOS Bibliographic Council, Inc.; Tulsa Area Library Cooperative (TALC). **Remarks:** Located at 2727 South Rockford Road, Tulsa, OK 74114. **Formerly:** Southwestern Art Association - Philbrook Art Center.

★10730★
PHILIP MORRIS, U.S.A. - RESEARCH CENTER LIBRARY (Sci-Tech)
Box 26583   Phone: (804) 274-2877
Richmond, VA 23261   Marian Z. DeBardeleben, Res.Libn.
Founded: 1959. **Staff:** Prof 3; Other 1. **Subjects:** Tobacco, chemistry, biochemistry, botany, physics, plant physiology. **Holdings:** 20,000 books; 10,000 bound periodical volumes including film volumes; 150 AV items; 500 microfiche; 21 VF drawers of clippings; 4500 reels of microfilm of periodicals. **Subscriptions:** 750 journals and other serials; 6 newspapers. **Services:** Interlibrary loans; selected reference work for the outside; library open to public by appointment. **Automated Operations:** Computerized cataloging, acquisitions, serials and circulation. **Computerized Information Services:** DIALOG, SDC, NLM, Chemical Data Center (CDC), CAS Online, NIH-EPA Chemical Information System, Dow Jones News/Retrieval, Pergamon InfoLine Ltd., International Patent Documentation Center (INPADOC); Philip Morris Information Network (internal database); **Networks/Consortia:** Member of RLIN. **Publications:** TIF Patent Update, monthly - for internal distribution only; Dictionary of Tobacco Terminology (book). **Special Catalogs:** Published Papers and Journal Holdings, annual (both computer printout). **Staff:** Charity McDonald, Assoc.Libn.; Lucy Cook, Asst.Libn.

PHILIPS AUTOGRAPH LIBRARY
See: West Chester University - Francis Harvey Green Library - Special Collections

PHILIPS LABORATORIES RESEARCH LIBRARY
See: North American Philips Corporation

★10731★
PHILIPS ROXANE, INC. - TECHNICAL LIBRARY (Med; Sci-Tech)
2621 N. Belt Hwy.   Phone: (816) 233-1385
St. Joseph, MO 64502   Norma Barnes, Libn.
Staff: Prof 1; Other 1. **Subjects:** Veterinary medicine, bacteriology, virology, pharmaceuticals, immunology, parasitology. **Holdings:** 50,000 books; 15,000 bound periodical volumes; 750 documents and dissertations. **Subscriptions:** 165 journals and other serials. **Services:** Interlibrary loans; copying; library open to public for reference use only with users researching own material. **Networks/Consortia:** Member of Midcontinental Regional Medical Library System.

PHILIPSBURG STATE GENERAL HOSPITAL
See: Pennsylvania State Department of Public Welfare

PHILLIP (Isidore) ARCHIVE AND MEMORIAL LIBRARY
See: University of Louisville - Dwight Anderson Memorial Music Library

PHILLIPS ACADEMY - ADDISON GALLERY OF AMERICAN ART
See: Addison Gallery of American Art

★10732★
PHILLIPS ACADEMY - OLIVER WENDELL HOLMES LIBRARY - SPECIAL COLLECTIONS (Hum)
            Phone: (617) 475-3400
Andover, MA 01810   Lynne C. Robbins, Dir.
Founded: 1796. **Staff:** Prof 5; Other 6. **Special Collections:** Charles H. Forbes Collection of Vergiliana and Bancroft Collection of Vergil Translations (1000 volumes and 450 pamphlets). **Services:** Interlibrary loans; copying; library open to public for reference use only, on request. **Special Catalogs:** Catalog of the Charles H. Forbes Collection of Vergiliana in the Oliver Wendell Holmes Library.

PHILLIPS ACADEMY - ROBERT S. PEABODY FOUNDATION FOR ARCHEOLOGY
See: Peabody (Robert S.) Foundation for Archeology

★10733★
THE PHILLIPS COLLECTION - LIBRARY (Art)
1600 21st St., N.W.   Phone: (202) 387-2151
Washington, DC 20009   Karen Schneider, Libn.
Staff: 1. **Subjects:** 19th and 20th century European and American painting and sculpture. **Special Collections:** Phillips Collection exhibition catalogs; monographs on artists represented in the Phillips Collection. **Holdings:** 4000 books; 65 reels of microfilm of the Phillips Collection correspondence, 1920-1960; 20 VF drawers of exhibition catalogs, clippings, and articles. **Subscriptions:** 40 journals and other serials. **Services:** Copying; library open to researchers by appointment.

★10734★
PHILLIPS (Frank) FOUNDATION, INC. - WOOLAROC MUSEUM - LIBRARY (Art; Area-Ethnic)
Rte. 3   Phone: (918) 336-0307
Bartlesville, OK 74003   Linda Stone, Cur. of Art
Subjects: Native American culture, art, early Americana, weaponry, natural history. **Holdings:** 800 books. **Subscriptions:** 15 journals and other serials. **Services:** Library open to public with director's permission.

PHILLIPS (James Duncan) LIBRARY
See: Essex Institute - James Duncan Phillips Library

PHILLIPS LIBRARY
See: Peabody Museum of Salem

★10735★
PHILLIPS, LYTLE, HITCHCOCK, BLAINE AND HUBER - LIBRARY (Law)
3400 Maine Midland Ctr.   Phone: (716) 847-8400
Buffalo, NY 14203   Ellen M. Reen, Libn.
Staff: Prof 2; Other 2. **Subjects:** New York law, federal law, taxation. **Holdings:** 17,000 books; 500 bound periodical volumes; 150 cassettes; 100 microcards of FPC reports; 100 microcards of New York reports; 500 microcards of U.S. reports. **Subscriptions:** 400 journals and other serials; 7 newspapers. **Services:** Interlibrary loans; copying; users must be cleared by librarian. **Computerized Information Services:** LEXIS, DIALOG. **Publications:** Library Newsletter - for internal distribution only; Legislative Newsletter; Court of Appeals Newsletter; bibliographies, irregular - for internal distribution only. **Special Catalogs:** Tape catalog (card); internal catalogs. **Staff:** Wendy B. Edson, Asst.Libn.

PHILLIPS MEMORIAL LIBRARY
See: Providence College

★10736★
PHILLIPS PETROLEUM COMPANY - ENGINEERING LIBRARY (Sci-Tech)
8 A3 Phillips Bldg.   Phone: (918) 661-5911
Bartlesville, OK 74004   Norma Benefiel, Off.Serv.Supv.
Founded: 1940. **Subjects:** Civil and mechanical engineering, chemical technology, environmental control, metallurgy. **Holdings:** 3000 volumes. **Subscriptions:** 200 journals and other serials. **Services:** Interlibrary loans; copying; library open to public with approval. **Staff:** Charlotte Griggs, Libn.

★10737★
PHILLIPS PETROLEUM COMPANY - EXPLORATION & PRODUCTION GROUP - LIBRARY (Energy)
439 Frank Phillips Bldg.   Phone: (918) 661-5514
Bartlesville, OK 74004   Annabeth Robin, Mgr.
Staff: Prof 1; Other 3. **Subjects:** Geology and petroleum production. **Holdings:** 5000 books; 1000 bound periodical volumes. **Subscriptions:** 600 journals and other serials. **Services:** Interlibrary loans; library open through OCLC only. **Automated Operations:** Computerized serials. **Computerized Information Services:** DIALOG, SDC, NEXIS, OCLC; Library Journal System (internal database). **Networks/Consortia:** Member of AMIGOS Bibliographic Council, Inc.

★10738★
PHILLIPS PETROLEUM COMPANY - GAS & GAS LIQUIDS GROUP - LIBRARY (Energy)
3 D4 Home Savings & Loan Bldg.   Phone: (918) 661-5803
Bartlesville, OK 74004   Ollie Mae Burdett, Rec.Mgt.Supv.
Founded: 1951. **Staff:** 7. **Subjects:** Natural gas industry, natural gas liquids, energy industries. **Holdings:** 300 books; 1100 paperback books. **Subscriptions:** 17 journals and other serials. **Services:** Library not open to public.

★10739★
PHILLIPS PETROLEUM COMPANY - RESEARCH & DEVELOPMENT DEPARTMENT - TECHNICAL INFORMATION BRANCH (Energy)
Phillips Research Ctr.   Phone: (918) 661-0535
Bartlesville, OK 74004   David R. Weiser, Mgr.
Founded: 1945. **Staff:** Prof 11; Other 10. **Subjects:** Chemistry, petroleum science and technology, polymer science and technology, biotechnology, geosciences, plastics, physics, energy minerals, solar power. **Holdings:** 11,500 books; 12,500 bound periodical volumes; 2 million U.S. and foreign patents; 5500 microfilm cartridges; 50 VF drawers; 15,000 U.S. government reports on microfiche. **Subscriptions:** 900 journals and other serials. **Services:** Interlibrary loans; translation; technical editing; literature searching; facilities open to public by appointment. **Automated Operations:** Computerized cataloging, acquisitions and serials. **Computerized Information Services:** SDC, DIALOG, BRS, New York Times Information Service, LEXIS, NEXIS, OCLC, Dow Jones News/Retrieval. **Networks/Consortia:** Member of AMIGOS Bibliographic Council, Inc.; OCLC. **Publications:** Review of Current Periodic Literature; Selected Patent Listings; Library Bulletin - all for internal distribution only. **Special Indexes:** KWIC indexes of R & D Department reports. **Staff:** Paulene Bohannon, Supv., R&D Rec.; Carol Winfield Gill, Tech.Libn.; Joan O'Brien, Info.Spec.; H.R. Jayaraman, Info.Spec.; Lou D. Payne, Info.Spec.; William R. Blake, Transl.; Otokar J. Riha, Transl.; Jeanne Strauss, Transl.; Fima Haimson, Transl./Interpretation.

PHILLIPS (Seymour J.) HEALTH SCIENCES LIBRARY
See: Beth Israel Medical Center - Hospital for Joint Diseases Orthopaedic Institute - Seymour J. Phillips Health Sciences Library

PHILLIPS (Stephen) MEMORIAL LIBRARY
See: Penobscot Marine Museum - Stephen Phillips Memorial Library

★10740★
PHILLIPS UNIVERSITY - GRADUATE SEMINARY LIBRARY (Rel-Theol)
University Sta., Box 2218   Phone: (405) 237-4433
Enid, OK 73701   John L. Sayre, Dir.
Founded: 1907. **Staff:** Prof 5. **Subjects:** Religion. **Special Collections:** Discipliana. **Holdings:** 82,907 books; 8589 bound periodical volumes; 22 VF drawers of pamphlets. **Subscriptions:** 430 journals and other serials. **Services:** Interlibrary loans; copying; library open to public. **Automated Operations:** Computerized cataloging. **Computerized Information Services:** OCLC. **Networks/Consortia:** Member of AMIGOS Bibliographic Council, Inc. **Staff:** Roberta Hamburger, Seminary Libn.; Stephanie Victor, Acq.Libn.; Marilee Pralle, Pub.Serv.Libn.; Patti Harrison, Circ.Libn.

PHILMONT SCOUT RANCH AND EXPLORER BASE - SETON MEMORIAL LIBRARY & MUSEUM
See: Seton Memorial Library

★10741★
PHILOSOPHICAL HERITAGE INSTITUTE - LIBRARY OF ESOTERIC STUDIES (Rel-Theol)
Box 929   Phone: (907) 452-2424
Fairbanks, AK 99707   LaVedi Lafferty, Libn.
Founded: 1971. **Staff:** Prof 1; Other 2. **Subjects:** Esoterics, metaphysics, comparative religions, Tibetan studies, cosmology, New Age interests. **Holdings:** 2900 books; 3 VF drawers of unbound periodicals; 200 magnetic tapes; 1 drawer of past life regression research. **Subscriptions:** 20 journals and other serials. **Services:** Library open to members.

★10742★
PHILOSOPHICAL RESEARCH SOCIETY - RESEARCH LIBRARY (Hum)
3910 Los Feliz Blvd.   Phone: (213) 663-2167
Los Angeles, CA 90027   Pearl M. Thomas, Libn.
Founded: 1934. **Staff:** 12. **Subjects:** Alchemy, Baconiana, Orientalia, comparative religion, mythology, ancient and modern philosophy. **Holdings:** 50,000 books. **Services:** Interlibrary loans; copying; library open to public. **Publications:** Library Bulletin, irregular; Art Bulletin, quarterly.

★10743★
PHOENIX ART MUSEUM - LIBRARY (Art)
1625 N. Central Ave.   Phone: (602) 257-1222
Phoenix, AZ 85004   Clayton C. Kirking, Libn.
Founded: 1959. **Staff:** Prof 1; Other 1. **Subjects:** Painters and sculptors, history of painting and art, Egyptology, prints, museums and galleries (collections and exhibitions). **Special Collections:** Ambrose Lansing Collection of Egyptology (208 volumes); exhibition catalogs for one-man shows (5100); international auction catalogs; museum bulletins (90 boxes); Zervos-Picasso catalog; Orme Lewis Collection of Rembrandt Etching Catalogs; Art Libraries Societies Archives of Arizona Artists. **Holdings:** 20,000 books; 475 bound periodical volumes; 152 file drawers of gallery catalogs, museum publications, artistic biographies, archives. **Subscriptions:** 91 journals and other serials. **Services:** Interlibrary loans; copying; library open to public for reference use only. **Special Indexes:** Index of artists and subjects in exhibition and museum catalogs (card).

★10744★
PHOENIX DAY SCHOOL FOR THE DEAF - LIBRARY/MEDIA CENTER (Aud-Vis; Educ)
1935 W. Hayward Ave.   Phone: (602) 255-3448
Phoenix, AZ 85021   Donna L. Farman, Libn.
Staff: Prof 2. **Subjects:** Juvenile fiction, signed English. **Holdings:** 5600 books. **Subscriptions:** 18 journals and other serials. **Services:** Library not open to public. **Staff:** Lois O. Carlson, Media Coord.

★10745★
PHOENIX ELEMENTARY SCHOOLS - DISTRICT NO. 1 - CURRICULUM MEDIA CENTER (Educ; Aud-Vis)
125 E. Lincoln St.   Phone: (602) 257-3774
Phoenix, AZ 85004   Mary Cook, Coord., Instr.Sup.Serv.
Founded: 1956. **Staff:** Prof 2; Other 9. **Subjects:** Elementary education, Arizona history. **Special Collections:** Juvenile Trade Book Examination Center; 16mm film library. **Holdings:** 12,750 books; 750 bound periodical volumes. **Subscriptions:** 73 journals and other serials. **Services:** Center open to district patrons and staff.

★10746★
PHOENIX GENERAL HOSPITAL - MEDICAL LIBRARY (Med)*
Box 21331   Phone: (602) 279-4411
Phoenix, AZ 85036   Myrtle Idland, Libn.
Founded: 1958. **Staff:** Prof 1. **Subjects:** Internal medicine, surgery, pediatrics, orthopedics, obstetrics/gynecology. **Holdings:** 1294 books; 1784 bound periodical volumes. **Subscriptions:** 90 journals and other serials. **Services:** Interlibrary loans; copying; library open to public for reference use only. **Staff:** Janice Watts, Dir., Med.Rec.

★10747★
PHOENIX INDIAN MEDICAL CENTER - LIBRARY (Med)
4212 N. 16th St.   Phone: (602) 263-1200
Phoenix, AZ 85016   Rebekah G. Hinton, Adm.Libn.
Founded: 1965. **Staff:** Prof 1; Other 1. **Subjects:** Medicine, nursing, dentistry. **Special Collections:** Indian history; Indian health. **Holdings:** 1800 books; 2000 bound periodical volumes; 524 medical tapes; 3000 unbound journals; 5 VF drawers of pamphlets and reprints. **Subscriptions:** 180 journals

and other serials. **Services:** Interlibrary loans; copying; library open to public for reference use only. **Computerized Information Services:** MEDLINE, BRS. **Publications:** List of acquisitions - for internal distribution only.

★10748★
PHOENIX MUTUAL LIFE INSURANCE COMPANY - LIBRARY (Bus-Fin)
One American Row Phone: (203) 278-1212
Hartford, CT 06115 Margaret Colton, Libn.
Founded: 1915. **Staff:** 3. **Subjects:** Insurance, business, salesmanship, management, data processing. **Holdings:** 17,500 volumes. **Subscriptions:** 200 journals and other serials; 5 newspapers. **Services:** Interlibrary loans; copying; library open to public by referral.

★10749★
PHOENIX NEWSPAPERS, INC. - LIBRARY (Publ)
Box 1950 Phone: (602) 271-8555
Phoenix, AZ 85001 Marcy Bagley, Hd.Libn.
Founded: 1947. **Staff:** Prof 1; Other 14. **Subjects:** Newspaper reference topics. **Holdings:** Clippings. **Services:** Library open to law enforcement personnel and other newspaper writers only. **Remarks:** Publishes the Arizona Republic and Phoenix Gazette.

★10750★
PHOENIX PLANNING DEPARTMENT - LONG RANGE PLANNING DIVISION -
   LIBRARY (Plan)
Municipal Bldg., 6th Fl.
251 W. Washington St. Phone: (602) 262-6881
Phoenix, AZ 85003 Catherine N. Donovan, Sec.
Staff: 1. **Subjects:** General urban development, land use, economics, population, community facilities, public utilities, urban renewal, central business district, transportation. **Holdings:** 3200 books; 70 bound periodical volumes. **Subscriptions:** 65 journals and other serials. **Services:** Library open to public.

PHONOGRAPHIC LIBRARY OF CONTEMPORARY POETS
See: CUNY - City College Library - Special Collections

★10751★
PHOTO RESEARCHERS, INC. - LIBRARY (Aud-Vis)
60 E. 56th St. Phone: (212) 758-3420
New York, NY 10022 Jane S. Kinne, Pres.
Founded: 1956. **Staff:** 20. **Subjects:** Color and black/white photographic prints for reproduction in the fields of natural history, geography, social studies, industry, celebrities, anthropology, biology, botany, chemistry, education. **Special Collections:** Edited files of 3000 photographers; Science Library; Osborne Horse Collection; files of Rapho Guillumette and National Audubon Society. **Holdings:** Two million original color transparencies; 1 million custom black/white prints. **Subscriptions:** 27 journals and other serials. **Services:** Library open to public for service fee. **Staff:** Terry Cordasci, Gen. Color Lib.; Karen Nangle, Black/White Lib.; Mary Lynn Sutton, Sci.Libn.; David Christenberry, Nat.Hist.Libn.

★10752★
PHOTO TRENDS - LIBRARY (Aud-Vis)
Box 650 Phone: (516) 379-1440
Freeport, NY 11520 R. Eugene Keesee, Owner
Founded: 1968. **Staff:** Prof 1; Other 2. **Subjects:** Events of the last 60 years; children, education, nature, recent youth trends; science subjects, notably psychology, sociology and medicine, world figures, performers, artists, intellectuals. **Holdings:** 500,000 photographs. **Services:** Library not open to public; sells photographs for reproduction in qualified publications; owner of the former Harris and Ewing print collection of American political figures; represents the library of Syndication International (London Daily Mirror), and Camera Press (London, England). **Remarks:** A conference center is located at 1328 Broadway, New York, NY 10001.

PHOTON AND CHARGED PARTICLE DATA CENTER
See: U.S. Natl. Bureau of Standards

★10753★
PHOTOPHILE - LIBRARY (Aud-Vis)
2311 Kettner Blvd. Phone: (619) 234-4431
San Diego, CA 92101 Linda L. Rill, Dir.
Founded: 1968. **Staff:** 2. **Subjects:** U.S. and international travel, people, recreational sports, industry, nature. **Holdings:** 150,000 color transparencies. **Services:** Library open to public by appointment. **Remarks:** Photophile is a stock photograph agency. Usage is for publications and advertising only.

★10754★
PHYSICS INTERNATIONAL COMPANY - LIBRARY (Sci-Tech)
2700 Merced St.
Box 1538 Phone: (415) 577-7278
San Leandro, CA 94577 Emil Kovtun, Libn.
Staff: Prof 1; Other 2. **Subjects:** Physics, nuclear physics, electronics, mechanical engineering, computer software. **Holdings:** 3000 books; 8000 technical reports; 150 reels of microfilm of military and commercial standards and specifications. **Subscriptions:** 292 journals and other serials. **Services:** Interlibrary loans; library not open to public. **Automated Operations:** Computerized cataloging, acquisitions, serials, and circulation. **Computerized Information Services:** DIALOG, Information Handling Services (IHS); PILIB (internal database). Performs free searches for staff members. **Networks/ Consortia:** Member of Bay Area Library and Information System (BALIS).

★10755★
PIAGET (Jean) SOCIETY - LIBRARY (Educ)
College of Education
University of Delaware Phone: (609) 921-9000
Newark, DE 19716 George Forman, Pres.
Founded: 1971. **Staff:** Prof 1; Other 1. **Subjects:** Psychology, child development, education, language development, cognition. **Special Collections:** Catalog of the archives of Jean Piaget. **Holdings:** 400 books; 150 cataloged articles; 10 shelves of dissertations; journal articles; original manuscripts; speeches; films; cassette tapes. **Services:** Copying; tapes of symposia for sale; library open to public for reference use only. **Publications:** Newsletter, quarterly; Proceedings, annual.

PICATINNY ARSENAL ARCHIVE
See: U.S. Army - Armament Research & Development Center - Scientific and Technical Information Division

PICK (Albert) MUSIC LIBRARY
See: University of Miami - School of Music - Albert Pick Music Library

PICK (Lawrence Mercer) MEMORIAL LIBRARY
See: La Rabida Children's Hospital and Research Center - Lawrence Mercer Pick Memorial Library

★10756★
PICKAWAY COUNTY LAW LIBRARY (Law)†
Courthouse
Box 87 Phone: (614) 474-6026
Circleville, OH 43113 William Ammer, Treas.
Subjects: Law. **Holdings:** 17,000 volumes.

PICKERING (Colonel Timothy) LIBRARY
See: Wenham Historical Association and Museum - Colonel Timothy Pickering Library

PICKLER MEMORIAL LIBRARY
See: Northeast Missouri State University

★10757★
PICTORIAL PARADE INC. - LIBRARY (Aud-Vis)
130 W. 42nd St. Phone: (212) 840-2026
New York, NY 10036 Baer M. Frimer, Pres.
Staff: Prof 6. **Subjects:** Current and historical events, foreign and domestic personalities, picture stories, Hollywood and TV stars. **Holdings:** Black/white photographs and prints; color transparencies. **Services:** Library open to bona fide researchers. **Remarks:** Caters to the publishing and communications fields only.

★10758★
PIEDMONT BIBLE COLLEGE - GEORGE M. MANUEL MEMORIAL LIBRARY
   (Rel-Theol)
716 Franklin St. Phone: (919) 725-8345
Winston-Salem, NC 27101 William P. Thompson, Libn.
Founded: 1947. **Staff:** Prof 2; Other 4. **Subjects:** Religion, theology, philosophy, history, music, science. **Holdings:** 45,026 books; 989 bound periodical volumes; 3545 other cataloged items. **Subscriptions:** 190 journals and other serials; 6 newspapers. **Services:** Interlibrary loans; library open to public with restrictions. **Staff:** Lucille Bowman, Asst.Libn.

★10759★
PIEDMONT HOSPITAL - SAULS MEMORIAL LIBRARY (Med)
1968 Peachtree Rd., N.W. Phone: (404) 350-2222
Atlanta, GA 30309 Alice DeVierno, Med.Libn.
Staff: Prof 2; Other 1. **Subjects:** Clinical medicine, nursing. **Special**

Collections: Patient education (1000 items). **Holdings:** 2500 books; 3500 bound periodical volumes; 200 video cassettes. **Subscriptions:** 200 journals and other serials. **Services:** Interlibrary loans; library not open to public. **Computerized Information Services:** MEDLARS. **Networks/Consortia:** Member of Atlanta Health Libraries Consortium.

PIEDMONT PUBLISHING COMPANY - WINSTON-SALEM JOURNAL AND SENTINEL
See: Winston-Salem Journal and Sentinel

★10760★
PIEDMONT TECHNICAL COLLEGE - LIBRARY (Educ; Sci-Tech)
Emerald Rd.
P.O. Drawer 1467   Phone: (803) 223-8357
Greenwood, SC 29648   Daniel D. Koenig, Dir., Lrng.Rscs.
Staff: Prof 1; Other 3. **Subjects:** Economics, education, science and technology. **Holdings:** 22,500 books; 1225 AV items. **Subscriptions:** 365 journals and other serials; 20 newspapers. **Services:** Interlibrary loans; copying; library open to public. **Automated Operations:** Computerized cataloging. **Computerized Information Services:** OCLC. **Networks/Consortia:** Member of SOLINET. **Staff:** Ruth Nicholson, Ref.Libn.

★10761★
PIERCE COUNTY LAW LIBRARY (Law)†
123 County-City Bldg.   Phone: (206) 593-4346
Tacoma, WA 98402   Faye L. Reese, Libn.
Founded: 1933. **Staff:** 3. **Subjects:** Law. **Holdings:** 18,050 volumes. **Services:** Library open to public with restrictions.

★10762★
PIERCE COUNTY MEDICAL LIBRARY (Med)
315 South K St.
Box 5277   Phone: (206) 572-5340
Tacoma, WA 98405   Ms. Marion VonBruck, Med.Libn.
Staff: 3. **Subjects:** Medicine. **Holdings:** 1400 books; 909 bound periodical volumes; 10 VF drawers. **Subscriptions:** 155 biomedical and administrative journals. **Services:** Interlibrary loans; copying; translations; library open to members of the Medical Society of Pierce County, hospital employees and by private membership to other professionals. **Computerized Information Services:** Online systems. **Networks/Consortia:** Central Resource facility of Pierce County Medical Library Consortium. **Publications:** Pierce County Medical Library Bulletin, monthly. **Special Catalogs:** Union Catalog of consortium's holdings. **Remarks:** The Pierce County Medical Library is part of a consortium that includes the satellite libraries of eight hospitals; holdings of the consortium total 2932 books and 264 journal subscriptions.

★10763★
PIERCE/GOODWIN/ALEXANDER - LIBRARY/RESOURCE CENTER (Plan)
800 Bering Dr.
Box 13319   Phone: (713) 977-5777
Houston, TX 77219   Peggy Kelly, Libn.
Founded: 1980. **Staff:** Prof 1. **Subjects:** Architecture, interiors. **Holdings:** 500 books; 66 bound periodical volumes; 1600 vendor catalogs; vendor samples; 75 maps. **Subscriptions:** 72 journals and other serials. **Services:** Library not open to public. **Special Indexes:** Index to product literature (card).

PIERCE (Lawrence J.) RHODODENDRON LIBRARY
See: Rhododendron Species Foundation - Lawrence J. Pierce Rhododendron Library

PIEROSE (Dean) MEMORIAL HEALTH SCIENCES LIBRARY
See: Moritz Community Hospital - Dean Pierose Memorial Health Sciences Library

★10764★
PIERPONT MORGAN LIBRARY (Rare Book)
29 E. 36th St.   Phone: (212) 685-0008
New York, NY 10016   Charles A. Ryskamp, Dir.
Founded: 1924. **Staff:** Prof 43; Other 29. **Subjects:** Medieval and Renaissance illuminated manuscripts; ancient written records; early printed books; autograph manuscripts, principally English, American, German, French and Italian; autograph letters and documents of Western European and American historical and literary personages, 11th to 20th century; later printed books; bookbindings, from 9th to 20th century; drawings, 14th to 19th century; Rembrandt etchings; music manuscripts; early children's books. **Holdings:** 90,000 volumes. **Services:** Photography; sales desk; exhibition galleries open to public; reading room for accredited scholars. **Staff:** Francis S. Mason, Jr., Asst.Dir.; Paul Needham, Cur., Printed Bks.; Herbert Cahoon, Cur., Autog.Mss.; Cara Dufour Denison, Cur., Draw./Prints; John Plummer, Co-Cur.,

Medv. & Ren.Mss.; William M. Voelkle, Co-Cur., Medv. & Ren.Mss.; Gerald Gottlieb, Cur., Early Ch. Books; Reginald Allen, Cur., Gilbert & Sullivan; Rigbie Turner, Cur., Music Mss. & Books; Anna Lou Ashby, Hd., Ref. & Lib.Serv.

★10765★
PIERSON, BALL & DOWD - LAW LIBRARY (Law)
1200 18th St., N.W.   Phone: (202) 331-8566
Washington, DC 20036   Sandra Parrish, Libn.
Staff: Prof 2; Other 3. **Subjects:** Law - communications, labor; taxation; government contracts. **Holdings:** 10,000 books; 300 bound periodical volumes. **Subscriptions:** 150 journals and other serials; 10 newspapers. **Services:** Interlibrary loans; copying; library open to public with restrictions. **Computerized Information Services:** LEXIS, NEXIS, DIALOG, The Source, LEGI-SLATE. **Staff:** Laura Dacey, Asst.Libn.

PIERSON (William) MEDICAL LIBRARY
See: Hospital Center at Orange - William Pierson Medical Library

★10766★
PIGEON DISTRICT LIBRARY - SPECIAL COLLECTIONS (Hist)
7236 Nitz St.   Phone: (517) 453-2341
Pigeon, MI 48755   Roberta J. Richmond, Libn.
Staff: Prof 3; Other 3. **Special Collections:** Local history (35 volumes); toys (200). **Holdings:** Microfilm of local newspaper, 1880 to present. **Services:** Interlibrary loans; copying; library open to public. **Automated Operations:** Computerized cataloging. **Staff:** Starla Albrecht, Asst.Libn.; Naomi Jantzi, Asst.Libn.

★10767★
PIKES PEAK LIBRARY DISTRICT - LOCAL HISTORY COLLECTION (Hist; Aud-Vis)
20 N. Cascade
Box 1579   Phone: (303) 473-2080
Colorado Springs, CO 80901
Staff: Prof 2; Other 5. **Subjects:** History - Pikes Peak, Colorado High Plains, local gold mining towns. **Special Collections:** Myron Wood photograph collection (5000 photographs documenting the Southwest); Mathews Collection (100 glass negatives, circa 1890); Payne Collection (52,000 negatives from Colorado Springs Gazette, 1950-1975); Stewart Collection (3000 photographs and negatives of Colorado Springs/Pikes Peak area, 1896-1970). **Holdings:** 15,000 books; 2000 bound periodical volumes; 5000 pamphlets; 1000 maps; 27,000 clippings; 100 cubic feet of manuscript material for League of Women Voters of Pikes Peak Region; 30 cubic feet of manuscript material for Mental Health Association; 30 cubic feet of Chase Stone papers; 50 cubic feet of Cliff House papers; 50 Gordon Sweet blueprints; 30 cubic feet of Ghost Town papers; 2 35mm reels of Pike National Forest History file. **Subscriptions:** 110 journals and other serials; 16 newspapers. **Services:** Interlibrary loans; copying; library open to public. **Automated Operations:** Computerized cataloging, acquisitions and circulation. **Computerized Information Services:** Online systems. **Publications:** TIP Sheet, monthly - distributed in-house and by direct mail. **Special Indexes:** Indexes to Gazette Telegraph (book), Free Press (card), Colorado City Iris (book), and Pike National Forest (book); online photoindex. **Staff:** Laura Penny, Asst.Libn.; Mary M. Davis, Lib.Techn.; Ree Mobley, Local Hist.Libn.

PILCH LIBRARY
See: Morris County Law Library

★10768★
PILGRIM PSYCHIATRIC CENTER - HEALTH SCIENCES LIBRARY (Med)
Bldg. 23
Box A   Phone: (516) 231-8000
West Brentwood, NY 11717   Aime Atlas, Sr.Libn.
Founded: 1932. **Staff:** Prof 2; Other 2. **Subjects:** Psychiatry, social sciences, psychology, medicine, nursing. **Holdings:** 6500 books; 120 bound periodical volumes; 8 VF drawers of pamphlets and clippings; 3 VF drawers of reports and manuscripts; 1 VF drawer of documents; 145 reels of microfilm; 90 cassette tapes. **Subscriptions:** 127 journals and other serials; 15 newspapers. **Services:** Interlibrary loans; copying; library open to public for reference use only. **Staff:** Irving Tredwell, Jr., Asst.Libn.

★10769★
PILGRIM SOCIETY - PILGRIM HALL LIBRARY (Hist)
75 Court St.   Phone: (617) 746-1620
Plymouth, MA 02360   Laurence R. Pizer, Dir.
Founded: 1820. **Staff:** Prof 3; Other 1. **Subjects:** Pilgrim history, Plymouth and Plymouth Colony. **Special Collections:** Brewster imprints and other books that belonged to the Pilgrims. **Holdings:** 10,000 books; 1000 bound

periodical volumes; 1500 photographs; 12,000 manuscripts, maps, prints, charts. **Services:** Copying; library open to serious researchers by appointment. **Publications:** Pilgrim Society News; Pilgrim Society Notes. **Special Catalogs:** Index to manuscripts, Rare Book Inventory; catalog of artifacts. **Staff:** Caroline Davis Chapin, Cur., Mss. & Bk.

★10770★
PILLSBURY COMPANY - BUSINESS REFERENCE LIBRARY (Food-Bev; Bus-Fin)
Pillsbury Center, 27th Fl.
Mail Station 2754   Phone: (612) 330-4047
Minneapolis, MN 55402   Rachel Berry, Mgr.
Founded: 1959. **Staff:** Prof 6; Other 2. **Subjects:** Consumer products marketing, marketing research, food industry, foodservice industry, supermarket industry, advertising research, management training. **Special Collections:** Pillsbury primary market research projects (15,000 documents). **Holdings:** 700 books; 790 reference titles; 3500 subject documents; 5000 microfiche. **Subscriptions:** 260 journals and other serials. **Services:** Interlibrary loans (available to employees); library not open to public. **Automated Operations:** Computer-assisted internal document retrieval; word processing. **Computerized Information Services:** Online systems. **Publications:** Extracts from Current Periodicals, weekly; New Products Bulletin, weekly; Consumerism Issues Status, monthly; Acquisitions Listing, monthly - all available to employees. **Special Indexes:** New Products Index, classed by company; Company Index; internally generated subject index; internal materials indexed via library-developed thesaurus. **Remarks:** Maintains a Consumer Service Library specializing in cookbooks and recipe development materials. **Staff:** Barbara Rostad, Res.Libn; Nancy Brenny, Libn.;Sandra Date, Sr. Libn.; Peter Sidney, Sr.Libn.

★10771★
PILLSBURY COMPANY - TECHNICAL INFORMATION CENTER (Food-Bev)
311 Second St., S.E.   Phone: (612) 330-4750
Minneapolis, MN 55414   James B. Tchobanoff, Mgr.
Founded: 1941. **Staff:** Prof 5; Other 3. **Subjects:** Food science and technology, cereal chemistry, microbiology, mathematics, statistics, agriculture, plant science. **Holdings:** 5500 books; 6500 bound periodical volumes; 30,000 patents; 8000 internal reports. **Subscriptions:** 398 journals and other serials. **Services:** Interlibrary loans; SDI; center open to public on limited basis by request. **Automated Operations:** Computerized cataloging and circulation of journals. **Computerized Information Services:** DIALOG, SDC, MEDLINE, CAS Online, Pergamon InfoLine Ltd.; internal database. **Publications:** Library Bulletin, monthly; Food Patent Digest, monthly - for internal distribution only. **Special Indexes:** KWIC index to research notebooks and internal reports. **Remarks:** Contains holdings of the former Green Giant/ Pillsbury Company - Library. **Staff:** Suzanne E. Draper, Tech.Serv.Libn.; Dennis Pedersen, Tech.Info.Sci.; Sally Olson, Cat.; Helen Fett, Tech.Info.Sci.

★10772★
PILLSBURY, MADISON AND SUTRO - LIBRARY (Law)
Box 7880   Phone: (415) 983-1130
San Francisco, CA 94120   Lynn A. Green, Dir., Lib. & Info.Serv.
Staff: Prof 5; Other 17. **Subjects:** Law. **Holdings:** Figures not available. **Services:** Interlibrary loans; library not open to public. **Remarks:** Library is located at 225 Bush St., San Francisco, CA 94104.

★10773★
PILOTS INTERNATIONAL ASSOCIATION - LIBRARY (Sci-Tech)
Box 907   Phone: (612) 588-5175
Minneapolis, MN 55440   Laura E. Dirks, Libn.
Staff: Prof 1; Other 1. **Subjects:** Aviation. **Holdings:** 75 books; 2 VF drawers of aviation clippings; 3 VF drawers of aviation organizations. **Subscriptions:** 15 journals and other serials. **Services:** Interlibrary loans; copying; library open to public with restrictions.

PILSUDSKI ARCHIVES
See: Yale University - Slavic & East European Collections

★10774★
PILSUDSKI (Jozef) INSTITUTE OF AMERICA FOR RESEARCH IN THE MODERN HISTORY OF POLAND - LIBRARY (Hist; Area-Ethnic)
381 Park Ave., S., Suite 701   Phone: (212) 683-4342
New York, NY 10016   Stanislaw Jordanowski, Pres.
Founded: 1943. **Staff:** Prof 1; Other 6. **Subjects:** Poland - history and politics since 1863. **Special Collections:** Diplomatic and military documents of Polish Chief of State Jozef Pilsudski's Military Chancellery (45,000). **Holdings:** 9600 books and bound periodical volumes; 500 linear feet of documents; 30,000 clippings; 1900 titles of cataloged pamphlets; 15,000 pictures; 500 maps; 50 reels of film and microfilm. **Subscriptions:** 50

journals and other serials. **Services:** Interlibrary loans; library open to qualified researchers.

★10775★
PIMA COUNCIL ON AGING - LIBRARY (Soc Sci)
100 E. Alameda, Suite 406   Phone: (602) 624-4419
Tucson, AZ 85701   Mary C. Guilbert, Libn.
Staff: Prof 1; Other 1. **Subjects:** Aging and the elderly, gerontology, long term care. **Holdings:** 100 books; 24 VF drawers; 4000 other cataloged items. **Subscriptions:** 30 journals and other serials; 200 newsletters; 6 newspapers. **Services:** Interlibrary loans; copying; SDI; library open to public by appointment. **Automated Operations:** Computerized cataloging and acquisitions.

★10776★
PIMA COUNTY JUVENILE COURT CENTER - LIBRARY (Law)
2225 E. Ajo Way   Phone: (602) 882-2082
Tucson, AZ 85713   Gwen Reid, Ct.Libn.
Founded: 1978. **Staff:** Prof 1. **Subjects:** Juvenile crime, penal institutions, adolescent problems, drug addiction, status offenses. **Holdings:** 800 books. **Subscriptions:** 30 journals and other serials. **Services:** Copying; library open to public with restrictions.

★10777★
PIMA COUNTY LAW LIBRARY (Law)
111 W. Congress   Phone: (602) 792-8456
Tucson, AZ 85701   Cecilia Torres Zawada, Law Libn.
Founded: 1915. **Staff:** Prof 1; Other 2. **Subjects:** Law. **Holdings:** 37,500 books; 2500 textbooks. **Subscriptions:** 85 journals and other serials. **Services:** Interlibrary loans; copying; library open to public.

★10778★
PIMA COUNTY PLANNING DEPARTMENT - LIBRARY (Geog-Map; Plan)
131 W. Congress St.   Phone: (602) 792-8361
Tucson, AZ 85701   Paul Matty, Libn.
Founded: 1975. **Staff:** Prof 1. **Subjects:** Land use planning, demography, natural features. **Holdings:** 3500 books; 300 maps. **Subscriptions:** 50 journals and other serials. **Services:** Interlibrary loans; copying; SDI; library open to public by appointment.

★10779★
PIMERIA ALTA HISTORICAL SOCIETY - MUSEUM/ARCHIVES (Hist)
223 Grand Ave.
Box 2281   Phone: (602) 287-5402
Nogales, AZ 85621
Subjects: History of Southern Arizona and Northern Sonora, 1000 to present; border history; mining; ranching. **Special Collections:** Logbooks of the Duranzo Mine, Sonora, Mexico; City of Nogales archives; oral history tapes (local history including business activities, ranching, and descendants of Geronimo). **Holdings:** 1500 books; 35 periodicals. **Services:** Museum and archives open to public. **Automated Operations:** Computerized cataloging and acquisitions.

★10780★
PINAL COUNTY HISTORICAL SOCIETY, INC. - LIBRARY (Hist)
2201 S. Main St.
Box 851   Phone: (602) 868-4382
Florence, AZ 85232   Mary A. Faul, Libn.
Staff: Prof 1. **Subjects:** Arizona and Southwest history, Pinal County. **Holdings:** 400 books; 65 bound periodical volumes; clippings and pictures of local history. **Services:** Library open to researchers with restrictions.

★10781★
PINE COUNTY HISTORICAL SOCIETY - LIBRARY (Hist)*
Askov, MN 55704   Ron Nelson, Pres.
Subjects: Finnish culture; local, state and national history. **Holdings:** 1000 books; 10 reels of microfilm. **Services:** Library open to public with restrictions.

★10782★
PINE REST CHRISTIAN HOSPITAL - VAN NOORD HEALTH SCIENCES LIBRARY (Med)
6850 S. Division Ave.   Phone: (616) 455-5000
Grand Rapids, MI 49508   Thomas Van Dam, Libn.
Founded: 1962. **Staff:** Prof 1; Other 1. **Subjects:** Psychiatry, psychiatric nursing, clinical psychology. **Holdings:** 1850 books; 75 other cataloged items; 4 VF drawers of pamphlets. **Subscriptions:** 100 journals and other serials. **Services:** Interlibrary loans (fee); copying; library open to mental health professionals.

PINEL (Philippe) INSTITUT
See: Institut Philippe Pinel

★10783★
PINELAND CENTER - LIBRARY AND MEDIA CENTER (Med)
Box C   Phone: (207) 688-4811
Pownal, ME 04069   Sally Ward, Dir., Staff Dev.
Founded: 1958. **Staff:** 3. **Subjects:** Developmental disabilities, mental retardation, epilepsy, autism, cerebral palsy, medicine. **Holdings:** 400 books; 20 videotapes; 5 films. **Subscriptions:** 20 journals and other serials. **Services:** Interlibrary loans; copying; library open to public. **Computerized Information Services:** BRS, MEDLINE. **Networks/Consortia:** Member of Health Sciences Library and Information Cooperative of Maine (HSLIC).

★10784★
PINELLAS COUNTY JUVENILE WELFARE BOARD - MAILANDE W. HOLLAND LIBRARY (Soc Sci)
4140 49th St., N.   Phone: (813) 521-1853
St. Petersburg, FL 33709   Molly Gill, Libn.
Founded: 1976. **Staff:** Prof 1; Other 1. **Subjects:** Child welfare, marriage and family, therapy, juvenile delinquency, substance abuse, child abuse and neglect, day care and early childhood education. **Special Collections:** Funding collection (20 volumes). **Holdings:** 800 books; 300 government documents; 40 films; 150 AV materials; 4 VF drawers. **Subscriptions:** 82 journals and other serials. **Services:** Interlibrary loans; library open to Pinellas County child-serving agencies only. **Publications:** Bulletin, quarterly.

★10785★
PINELLAS COUNTY LAW LIBRARY - CLEARWATER BRANCH (Law)
315 Court St.   Phone: (813) 448-2411
Clearwater, FL 33516
Staff: 2. **Subjects:** Law and taxes. **Holdings:** 20,100 books and bound periodical volumes. **Subscriptions:** 43 journals and other serials. **Services:** Copying; library open to public for reference use only. **Staff:** Patricia E. Spaulding, Libn.; Margaret Shewell, Libn.

★10786★
PINELLAS COUNTY LAW LIBRARY - ST. PETERSBURG BRANCH (Law)
Judicial Bldg., Rm. 500
545 1st Ave., N.   Phone: (813) 825-1875
St. Petersburg, FL 33701   Martha F. Otting, Libn.
Founded: 1949. **Staff:** 2. **Subjects:** Law and related subjects. **Holdings:** 30,000 volumes. **Subscriptions:** 100 journals and other serials. **Services:** Copying; library open to public for reference use only.

★10787★
PINELLAS COUNTY SCHOOL BOARD - MIRROR LAKE/TOMLINSON EDUCATION CENTER - LIBRARY/MEDIA CENTER (Educ)
709 Mirror Lake Dr.   Phone: (813) 821-4593
St. Petersburg, FL 33701   Helen G. Campbell, Media Spec.
Founded: 1969. **Staff:** Prof 1; Other 3. **Subjects:** Adult education (ABE, high school and GED), art, English for foreign born, medical assistant certification, commercial art and advertising, office training, cosmetology, industrial electronics, jewelry, medical records transcription, watch repair, arts and crafts, cooking, estate planning, foreign languages, music, gemology, travel, reupholstery, sewing, creative writing. **Holdings:** 10,725 books; 1245 filmstrips; 440 phonograph records; 145 transparencies; 8630 slides; 4 16mm films; 1475 tape recordings; 44 microfiche; charts; models; videotapes. **Subscriptions:** 160 journals and other serials. **Services:** Interlibrary loans; copying; center open to public.

★10788★
PIONEER HI-BRED INTERNATIONAL, INC. - CORPORATE LIBRARY (Agri; Bus-Fin)
400 Locust, Suite 700   Phone: (515) 245-3518
Des Moines, IA 50309   Willona Graham Goers, Corp.Libn.
Founded: 1983. **Staff:** Prof 1; Other 1. **Subjects:** Agriculture, agribusiness, law, taxation, business. **Holdings:** 1500 books. **Subscriptions:** 253 journals and other serials. **Services:** Interlibrary loans; copying; SDI; library open to public with restrictions. **Automated Operations:** Computerized cataloging, serials, and circulation. **Computerized Information Services:** DIALOG, SDC, BRS, LEXIS, NEXIS, OCLC, Pergamon International Information Corporation, On-Line Research, I/S Datacentralen, Dow Jones News/Retrieval, Martin Marietta Corporation, HAZARDLINE; BASIS (internal database). Performs searches on cost recovery basis.

PIONEER MEMORIAL MUSEUM
See: U.S. Natl. Park Service - Olympic Natl. Park

PIONEER MUSEUM
See: Clark County Historical Society

★10789★
PIONEER STUDY CENTER (Hist)
Box 1108   Phone: (616) 946-3151
Traverse City, MI 49684   Steve Harold, Dir.
Founded: 1973. **Staff:** Prof 2; Other 2. **Subjects:** History - homesteading, transportation, Cherry Festival; local family history; local lumbering; historical buildings. **Special Collections:** Rare books (30); Campbell-Hobbs Collection (family books, pictures, albums); Roy Steffans Collection; Hannah Rifles pictures, papers and letters; Spanish American War collection. **Holdings:** 100 books; 15 diaries; 2000 photographs; 300 biographies; 1500 negatives; 1500 clippings; 60 oral history tapes; 20 maps. **Services:** Copying; library open to public.

PIONEER VALLEY RESOURCE CENTER
See: Greenfield Community College

★10790★
PIONEERS' MUSEUM - LIBRARY AND ARCHIVES (Hist)
215 S. Tejon St.   Phone: (303) 578-6786
Colorado Springs, CO 80903   Rosemary Hetzler, Hist.-Libn.
Staff: Prof 1; Other 2. **Subjects:** Colorado history, local genealogy. **Special Collections:** Francis W. Cragin Far West Notebooks; Colorado historical manuscripts; William J. Palmer letters and diaries; historical photographs of the Pike's Peak region (20,000). **Holdings:** 6000 books; 3000 bound periodical volumes. **Services:** Copying; library open to public for on-site research.

★10791★
PIPER & MARBURY - LAW LIBRARY (Law)
36 S. Charles St., Suite 1100   Phone: (301) 576-1617
Baltimore, MD 21201   Loretta O. Yaller, Libn.
Staff: Prof 1; Other 5. **Subjects:** Law. **Holdings:** 35,000 volumes. **Subscriptions:** 70 journals and other serials; 6 newspapers. **Services:** Interlibrary loans; library not open to public. **Computerized Information Services:** LEXIS, DIALOG.

PIPESTONE NATL. MONUMENT
See: U.S. Natl. Park Service

PIPPY (Chesley A., Jr.) MEDICAL LIBRARY
See: Grace General Hospital - Chesley A. Pippy, Jr. Medical Library

PIRATE HOUSE LIBRARY
See: Cumberland County Historical Society

PIRNIE (Malcolm), INC.
See: Malcolm Pirnie, Inc.

PIRTLE (George W.) GEOLOGY LIBRARY
See: University of Kentucky - George W. Pirtle Geology Library

★10792★
PISCATAQUIS COUNTY LAW LIBRARY (Law)
Court House Annex   Phone: (207) 564-2181
Dover-Foxcroft, ME 04426   Elaine H. Roberts, Libn.
Staff: 1. **Subjects:** Law. **Holdings:** 5500 volumes. **Services:** Library not open to public.

PITCAIRN ISLANDS STUDY CENTER
See: Pacific Union College

★10793★
PITNEY BOWES - TECHNICAL INFORMATION CENTER (Sci-Tech)†
Walter Wheeler Dr.   Phone: (203) 853-0727
Stamford, CT 06904   Mary Lynn Ainsworth, Mgr., Tech.Info.Ctr.
Founded: 1953. **Staff:** Prof 2; Other 1. **Subjects:** Telecommunications, optics, chemistry, printing technology, business, management, finance, physics, electrophotography. **Special Collections:** Postal technology, postal information. **Holdings:** 5000 volumes; 150 reels of microfilm. **Subscriptions:** 320 journals and other serials. **Services:** Interlibrary loans; copying; center open to SLA members and others by appointment. **Automated Operations:** Computerized cataloging, serials and circulation. **Computerized Information Services:** DIALOG, SDC, BRS, Tech-Net, TECHNOTEC Data Base, Visual Search Microfilm Files (VSMF); internal database. **Networks/Consortia:** Member of Southwestern Connecticut Library Council (SWLC). **Publications:** Table of Contents Packages, 5/month; Library Bulletin, monthly; orientation

sheet. **Special Catalogs:** Technical report file (card). **Staff:** Nancy Bobrek, Asst.Libn.

★10794★
PITNEY, HARDIN, KIPP & SZUCH - LAW LIBRARY (Law)
163 Madison Ave.
CN 1945   Phone: (201) 267-3333
Morristown, NJ 07960   Julie L. von Schrader, Libn.
Staff: Prof 1; Other 2. **Subjects:** Law. **Special Collections:** New Jersey Statutes from 1680 to present (200 publications). **Holdings:** 18,000 books; 1000 bound periodical volumes; 100 video cassettes. **Subscriptions:** 60 journals and other serials; 7 newspapers. **Services:** Library open to attorneys for reference use only on request. **Computerized Information Services:** LEXIS, DIALOG.

PITTS (Amelia White) MEMORIAL LIBRARY
See: Baptist Medical Center - Amelia White Pitts Memorial Library

PITTS THEOLOGY LIBRARY
See: Emory University

PITTSBURG & MIDWAY COAL MINING CO.
See: Gulf Oil Corporation

★10795★
PITTSBURG STATE UNIVERSITY - LEONARD H. AXE LIBRARY - SPECIAL COLLECTIONS (Soc Sci)
S. Joplin   Phone: (316) 231-7000
Pittsburg, KS 66762   Eugene H. De Gruson, Spec.Coll.Libn.
Founded: 1903. **Holdings:** Haldeman-Julius Collection (10,651 items); Southeast Kansas Collection (110,500 items); Kansas and U.S. documents (161,000); college and community archives (21,300 items). **Services:** Interlibrary loans; copying; library open to Kansas residents and students. **Automated Operations:** Computerized cataloging, serials, circulation and ILL. **Computerized Information Services:** DIALOG, SDC, BRS, MEDLARS. **Networks/Consortia:** Member of Southeast Kansas Library System; Bibliographical Center for Research, Rocky Mountain Region Inc. (BCR).

★10796★
PITTSBURGH BOARD OF EDUCATION - PROFESSIONAL LIBRARY (Educ)
635 Ridge Ave.   Phone: (412) 323-4146
Pittsburgh, PA 15212   Dorothy Hopkins, Libn.
Founded: 1928. **Staff:** Prof 1. **Subjects:** Education - all facets from early childhood through high school. **Special Collections:** Depository for Pittsburgh Public School textbooks; courses of study and Board of Education minutes. **Holdings:** 12,500 books; 20 drawers of pamphlets, clippings, reports, articles; 12 VF drawers of archival material. **Subscriptions:** 230 journals, newsletters and other serials; 5 newspapers. **Services:** Interlibrary loans; copying; library open to public for research only. **Computerized Information Services:** BRS, OCLC. **Networks/Consortia:** Member of Pittsburgh Regional Library Center (PRLC). **Staff:** Judy G. Mizik, Dir., Lib.Serv.

★10797★
PITTSBURGH CORNING CORPORATION - TECHNICAL LIBRARY†
800 Presque Isle Dr.
Pittsburgh, PA 15239
Founded: 1962. **Subjects:** Glass, ceramics, chemistry, physics, materials engineering. **Holdings:** 2000 books; 2600 bound periodical volumes; 3500 patents. **Remarks:** Presently inactive.

★10798★
PITTSBURGH-DES MOINES CORPORATION - ENGINEERING LIBRARY (Sci-Tech)
410 Rouser Rd.   Phone: (412) 262-9114
Coraopolis, PA 15108   Louise Franz, Libn.
Staff: Prof 1. **Subjects:** Engineering. **Holdings:** 650 books; 200 bound periodical volumes; 14 VF drawers of technical reports; 500 binders of clippings. **Subscriptions:** 50 journals and other serials. **Services:** Interlibrary loans; library not open to public.

PITTSBURGH HEALTH EDUCATION CENTER
See: Health Education Center Library

★10799★
PITTSBURGH HISTORY & LANDMARKS FOUNDATION - JAMES D. VAN TRUMP LIBRARY (Art; Hist)†
One Landmarks Sq.   Phone: (412) 322-1204
Pittsburgh, PA 15212   Arthur P. Ziegler, Jr., Pres.
Subjects: Architecture, urban planning, landscaping, natural history,

construction technology, engineering. **Special Collections:** Pittsburgh architectural material. **Holdings:** 5000 books; 150 bound periodical volumes; 30 VF drawers of Pittsburgh clippings, brochures. **Subscriptions:** 20 journals and other serials; 5 newspapers.

PITTSBURGH PLATE GLASS COMPANY
See: PPG Industries, Inc.

★10800★
PITTSBURGH POST-GAZETTE PUBLISHING COMPANY - LIBRARY (Publ)
50 Blvd. of the Allies   Phone: (412) 263-1397
Pittsburgh, PA 15222   Angelika Kane, Libn.
Staff: Prof 4. **Subjects:** Newspaper reference topics. **Special Collections:** Movie stills. **Holdings:** 500 books; 30 bound periodical volumes; 280 VF drawers of clippings; 2 VF drawers of subject files; 150,000 picture files; 15 drawers of microfilm. **Subscriptions:** 14 journals and other serials; 24 newspapers. **Services:** Copying (limited); library open to public. **Automated Operations:** Computerized circulation. **Computerized Information Services:** NEXIS. **Special Catalogs:** Photograph catalog (card). **Special Indexes:** Index to newspaper clippings files (notebooks).

★10801★
PITTSBURGH PRESS - LIBRARY (Publ)
Boulevard of the Allies   Phone: (412) 263-1480
Pittsburgh, PA 15230   Eileen E. Finster, Libn.
Founded: 1884. **Staff:** Prof 1; Other 5. **Subjects:** Newspaper reference topics. **Holdings:** 250 books; 600 drawers of clippings; 447 drawers of photographs; Pittsburgh Press, 1884 to present, on microfilm. **Services:** Library not open to public.

★10802★
PITTSBURGH THEOLOGICAL SEMINARY - CLIFFORD E. BARBOUR LIBRARY (Rel-Theol)
616 N. Highland Ave.   Phone: (412) 362-5610
Pittsburgh, PA 15206   Dikran Y. Hadidian, Libn.
Founded: 1794. **Staff:** Prof 2; Other 4. **Subjects:** Theology, philosophy. **Special Collections:** Newburgh Collection (17th and 18th century theological works); James Warrington Collection of hymnology. **Holdings:** 197,389 books and bound periodical volumes; 2055 microforms; 588 phonograph records; 764 theses; 570 tapes; 6000 items of archival materials. **Subscriptions:** 818 journals and other serials. **Services:** Interlibrary loans; library not open to public. **Automated Operations:** Computerized cataloging and serials. **Computerized Information Services:** Online systems. **Networks/Consortia:** Member of Pittsburgh Regional Library Center (PRLC). **Publications:** Bibliographia Tripotamopolitana, irregular. **Staff:** Mary Ellen Scott, Cat./Archv.

PITZER COLLEGE
See: The Claremont Colleges - Library

PIUS XII MEMORIAL LIBRARY
See: St. Louis University

PLACE NAME SURVEY OF THE UNITED STATES
See: American Name Society

★10803★
PLACER COUNTY LAW LIBRARY (Law)
350 Nevada St.   Phone: (916) 823-4391
Auburn, CA 95603   Tanemi Klahn, Law Libn.
Staff: Prof 1. **Subjects:** Law. **Holdings:** 4388 books and bound periodical volumes; 26 cassettes. **Subscriptions:** 102 journals and other serials. **Services:** Interlibrary loans; library open to public.

★10804★
PLACER DEVELOPMENT, LTD. - LIBRARY (Sci-Tech)
Bentall Postal Sta., P.O. Box 49330   Phone: (604) 682-7082
Vancouver, BC, Canada V7X 1P1   Linda Martin, Libn.
Staff: Prof 1; Other 1. **Subjects:** Geology, mining, metallurgy, business and economics. **Holdings:** 10,000 books. **Subscriptions:** 280 journals and other serials; 20 newspapers. **Services:** Interlibrary loans; library not open to public. **Automated Operations:** Computerized serials and acquisitions. **Computerized Information Services:** DIALOG, QL Systems.

★10805★
PLAIN DEALER PUBLISHING COMPANY - LIBRARY (Publ)
1801 Superior Ave.   Phone: (216) 344-4195
Cleveland, OH 44114   Patti A. Graziano, Lib.Dir.
Founded: 1956. **Staff:** Prof 4; Other 7. **Special Collections:** Great Lakes; Ohio and Cleveland history. **Holdings:** 3900 books; 1.5 million pictures; 4.5

million clippings; 4811 reels of microfilm; 38 VF drawers of pamphlets. **Subscriptions:** 200 journals and other serials; 65 newspapers. **Services:** Interlibrary loans; library not open to public. **Special Catalogs:** Subject Authority File on computer printout.

★10806★
PLAINFIELD PUBLIC LIBRARY - GUILFORD TOWNSHIP HISTORICAL COLLECTION (Hist)
1120 Stafford Rd.   Phone: (317) 839-6602
Plainfield, IN 46168   Susan Miller Carter, Hist.Libn.
Staff: Prof 1; Other 2. **Subjects:** State and local history, Society of Friends Western Yearly Meeting. **Holdings:** 3835 books; 120 bound periodical volumes; 24 oral history tapes and transcripts; 2 file drawers of photographs; 14 file drawers of clippings and pamphlets; 84 boxes of manuscripts; obituary file; 254 reels of microfilm of local newspapers; 23 reels of microfilm of census data; 13 reels of microfilm of local history materials. **Subscriptions:** 22 journals and other serials; 7 newspapers. **Services:** Copying; collection open to public by appointment. **Special Indexes:** Card indexes for Hendricks County authors, biographies, 50th wedding anniversaries, place-names, obituaries, local newspapers, Maple Hill cemetery; name indexes for books of local interest (book).

★10807★
PLAINS ART MUSEUM - LIBRARY (Art)
521 Main Ave.   Phone: (218) 236-7171
Moorhead, MN 56560   Susan Talbot-Stanaway, Cur., Educ.
Staff: 1. **Subjects:** Art history, museology. **Holdings:** 40 books; 200 unbound periodicals; 30 videotapes; 30 cassette tapes. **Services:** Library not open to public.

★10808★
PLAINS HEALTH CENTRE - DR. W.A. RIDDELL HEALTH SCIENCES LIBRARY (Med)
4500 Wascana Pkwy.   Phone: (306) 584-6426
Regina, SK, Canada S4S 5W9   Beth Silzer, Dir.
Staff: Prof 1; Other 3. **Subjects:** Medicine, nursing, pharmacy, physiotherapy. **Holdings:** 4764 books; 4500 bound periodical volumes; 800 AV items. **Subscriptions:** 294 journals and other serials. **Services:** Interlibrary loans; SDI; library open to health sciences personnel. **Staff:** Cecilia Yeung, Cat.

PLANETARY IMAGE CENTER
See: Lunar and Planetary Institute

PLANETREE
See: Program Planetree

★10809★
PLANNED PARENTHOOD ASSOCIATION OF ST. LOUIS - FAMILY PLANNING LIBRARY (Soc Sci)
2202 S. Hanley Rd.   Phone: (314) 781-3800
St. Louis, MO 63144   Kathy Kurtz, Info.Ctr.Coord.
Founded: 1972. **Staff:** Prof 1. **Subjects:** Family planning, population, human reproduction, human sexuality, pregnancy, venereal disease, abortion, sterilization, contraception. **Special Collections:** Birth Control Review, 1922-1927 (complete); Social Welfare Forum, 1948-1965. **Holdings:** 500 books; 20 bound periodical volumes; clippings and articles. **Services:** Copying; library open to public with responsibility card signature.

★10810★
PLANNED PARENTHOOD CENTER OF SAN ANTONIO - LIBRARY (Soc Sci)
104 Babcock Rd.   Phone: (512) 736-2244
San Antonio, TX 78201   Karen Glenney, Pub.Aff.Dir.
Founded: 1939. **Staff:** Prof 2. **Subjects:** Birth control, population, human sexuality, sex education, family planning, ecology, environment, women's health, teenage pregnancy. **Holdings:** 1500 books; 500 periodicals; pamphlets, vertical files; 100 films, filmstrips and slide sets. **Subscriptions:** 35 journals and other serials. **Services:** Interlibrary loans; copying; library open to public with restrictions. **Networks/Consortia:** Member of Planned Parenthood Federation of America, Inc. **Publications:** Pamphlets on V.D. and birth control. **Special Catalogs:** Interregional Library Loan Catalog; PPCSA Media Catalog. **Staff:** Janet Alyn, Educ.Coord.

★10811★
PLANNED PARENTHOOD OF CENTRAL INDIANA - RESOURCE CENTER (Soc Sci)
3209 N. Meridian St.   Phone: (317) 925-6686
Indianapolis, IN 46208   Katy Smith, Libn.
Founded: 1980. **Staff:** 1. **Subjects:** Birth control, human sexuality, teen pregnancy, human reproduction, abortion, sex education, women's health.

Holdings: 500 books; 40 films; vertical files. **Subscriptions:** 40 journals and other serials. **Services:** Copying; center open to public.

★10812★
PLANNED PARENTHOOD OF CLEVELAND, INC. - LIBRARY (Soc Sci)
1501 Euclid Ave., Suite 300   Phone: (216) 781-0410
Cleveland, OH 44115   Lyn Cooper Gill, Exec.Dir.
Founded: 1928. **Staff:** 1. **Subjects:** Birth control and contraceptives, family planning, population, sexuality, family life education. **Special Collections:** Historical information on the birth control movement. **Holdings:** 400 books. **Subscriptions:** 10 journals and other serials. **Services:** Copying; library open to health, social and medical professionals for reference use only.

★10813★
PLANNED PARENTHOOD FEDERATION OF AMERICA, INC. - KATHARINE DEXTER MC CORMICK LIBRARY (Soc Sci)
810 Seventh Ave.   Phone: (212) 541-7800
New York, NY 10019   Gloria A. Roberts, Hd.Libn.
Staff: Prof 2; Other 1. **Subjects:** Family planning in the U.S., contraceptives, abortion and sterilization, history of birth control, population, sex and sex education. **Holdings:** 4000 books; 25 bound periodical volumes; 35 VF drawers of journal articles, reprints and unpublished mimeographs. **Subscriptions:** 175 journals and other serials. **Services:** Interlibrary loans (articles only); copying; library open to public for reference use only. **Computerized Information Services:** DIALOG; LINK (Library and Information Network; internal database). Performs searches on cost recovery basis; on fee basis for non PPFA users. **Networks/Consortia:** Member of Association for Population/Family Planning Libraries and Information Centers - International; METRO; Manhattan-Bronx Health Sciences Library Group. **Publications:** A Family Planning Library Manual; A Small Library in Family Planning; Current Literature in Family Planning (review of books and journal articles in the field, annotated and classified), monthly; Directory of Population Research and Family Planning Training Centers in the U.S.A., 1980-1981; Sexuality Education: Results in Review; Sexuality and the Disabled - An Annotated Bibliography. **Staff:** Alice D. Kaplan, Assoc.Libn.

★10814★
PLANNED PARENTHOOD OF MINNESOTA - POPULATION RESOURCE CENTER (Soc Sci)
1965 Ford Pkwy.   Phone: (612) 698-2401
St. Paul, MN 55116   Phyllis Cooksey, Dir. of Educ. & Trng.
Founded: 1972. **Staff:** Prof 2. **Subjects:** Family planning, population growth, human sexuality, abortion, sex education. **Special Collections:** Works of Margaret Sanger (8 volumes). **Holdings:** 2000 books; 12 VF drawers of pamphlets and ephemera; 100 films, filmstrips, video and audio cassettes. **Subscriptions:** 60 journals and other serials. **Services:** Interlibrary loans; copying; literature searches; center open to public. **Publications:** Acquisitions lists, newsnotes, semiannual - free upon request; list of other publications - available upon request. **Staff:** Barbara Lundgren, Rsrc.Coord.; Lynn Woodbury, Rsrc.Libn.

PLANNED PARENTHOOD NEW YORK CITY
See: Sanger (Margaret) Center-Planned Parenthood New York City

★10815★
PLANNED PARENTHOOD OF SOUTHEASTERN PENNSYLVANIA - RESOURCE CENTER (Soc Sci)
1220 Sansom St.   Phone: (215) 629-2828
Philadelphia, PA 19107   Roslyn R. Wright, Dir.
Founded: 1975. **Staff:** Prof 1; Other 1. **Subjects:** Family planning, reproductive health, venereal diseases, childbearing and pregnancy options, sex education. **Holdings:** 2300 books; 40 bound periodical volumes; 10 VF drawers of related materials; 86 films and filmstrips. **Subscriptions:** 53 journals and other serials. **Services:** Interlibrary loans; copying; SDI; center open to public for reference use only. **Networks/Consortia:** Member of Greater Northeastern Regional Medical Library Program. **Publications:** List of publications - available on request.

★10816★
PLANNED PARENTHOOD OF SOUTHWESTERN INDIANA, INC. - LIBRARY (Soc Sci)
1610 S. Weinbach Ave.   Phone: (812) 473-8800
Evansville, IN 47714   Donna Reed, Health Educ.
Subjects: Contraceptives, sexuality, family life education curriculum, women's health, infertility, population. **Holdings:** 300 books; 4 VF drawers. **Subscriptions:** 11 journals and other serials. **Services:** Interlibrary loans; copying; library open to public by appointment for reference use. **Networks/Consortia:** Member of Evansville Area Health Science Library Consortium.

★10817★

PLANNED PARENTHOOD OF WISCONSIN - MAURICE RITZ RESOURCE CENTER (Soc Sci)
1135 W. State St.   Phone: (414) 271-8116
Milwaukee, WI 53233   Ann H. McIntyre, Libn.
Founded: 1972. **Staff:** Prof 1; Other 1. **Subjects:** Birth control, nursing education, human sexuality, sex education, population. **Holdings:** 2600 books; 12 VF drawers of clippings, reports; 125 pamphlets, booklets and reprints; 72 films, slides, tapes, filmstrip kits. **Subscriptions:** 42 journals and other serials. **Services:** Interlibrary loans; copying; center open to public. **Networks/Consortia:** Member of Library Council of Metropolitan Milwaukee, Inc. (LCOMM). **Publications:** Audiovisual list; pamphlets list; material available for rent or purchase; bibliographies; manuals.

PLANNING RESEARCH CORPORATION - PRC CONSOER, TOWNSEND, INC.
See: PRC Consoer, Townsend, Inc.

★10818★

PLANNING RESEARCH CORPORATION - PRC VOORHEES - LIBRARY
1500 Planning Research Dr.
McLean, VA 22102
Defunct. Absorbed by its Technical Library.

★10819★

PLANNING RESEARCH CORPORATION - TECHNICAL LIBRARY (Comp Sci; Plan)
1500 Planning Research Dr.   Phone: (703) 556-1131
McLean, VA 22102   Marion C. Kersey, Lib.Mgr.
Founded: 1961. **Staff:** Prof 5; Other 1. **Subjects:** Computer science, software engineering, military science, planning, land use, information science. **Holdings:** 8000 books; 100 bound periodical volumes; 5000 company reports; 3000 documents. **Subscriptions:** 260 journals and other serials; 10 newspapers. **Services:** Interlibrary loans; copying; SDI; library open to public by appointment. **Automated Operations:** Computerized cataloging. **Computerized Information Services:** DIALOG, SDC, DTIC. **Networks/Consortia:** Member of Metropolitan Washington Library Council; Interlibrary Users Association. **Publications:** Journal Holdings list. **Remarks:** Absorbed its former PRC Voorhees - Library. **Staff:** Patricia A. White, Ref./Info.Serv.Libn.; Baru Rosenblatt, ILL; Patricia Wolf, Acq./Cat.; Patricia Gorman, Docs.

★10820★

PLANTING FIELDS ARBORETUM - HORTICULTURAL LIBRARY (Sci-Tech)
Planting Fields Rd.   Phone: (516) 922-9024
Oyster Bay, NY 11771   Elizabeth K. Reilley, Dir.
Founded: 1975. **Staff:** Prof 2; Other 1. **Subjects:** Horticulture, botany. **Holdings:** 4500 books. **Subscriptions:** 50 journals and other serials. **Services:** Copying; library open to public for reference use only; members may borrow materials. **Staff:** Helen S. Moskowitz, Asst. to Dir.

★10821★

PLASTICS INSTITUTE OF AMERICA - LIBRARY (Sci-Tech)
Stevens Institute of Technology
Castle Point Sta.   Phone: (201) 792-1839
Hoboken, NJ 07030   Albert Spaak, Exec.Dir.
Staff: 6. **Subjects:** Polymer science and engineering. **Holdings:** Figures not available. **Services:** Copying; library open to public with restrictions. **Publications:** Polymer Science and Engineering Programs, biennial - for sale; Institute Reports, 3/year - free upon request.

PLASTICS TECHNICAL EVALUATION CENTER
See: U.S. Army

★10822★

PLATT SACO LOWELL CORPORATION - ENGINEERING LIBRARY (Sci-Tech)
Drawer 2327   Phone: (803) 859-3211
Greenville, SC 29602   Donald H. Feldman, Mgr.
Founded: 1850. **Staff:** Prof 1; Other 1. **Subjects:** Engineering, textile machinery and manufacture, patent and trademark law. **Special Collections:** U.S. and British patents on textile machinery. **Holdings:** 3000 books; 1500 bound periodical volumes; 300,000 patent copies; 1500 microfiche cards of abstracts and patents; 2000 paper copies of abstracts and patents. **Subscriptions:** 85 journals and other serials. **Services:** Library not open to public except with prior permission.

★10823★

PLATTE RIVER POWER AUTHORITY - LIBRARY (Energy)
Timberline & Horsetooth Rds.   Phone: (303) 226-4000
Fort Collins, CO 80525   Rosalie Feldman, Libn.
Staff: Prof 1; Other 1. **Subjects:** Electric energy. **Holdings:** 1000 books;

593 reports; clippings. **Subscriptions:** 240 journals and other serials; 25 newspapers. **Services:** Interlibrary loans; copying; library open to public with restrictions. **Automated Operations:** Computerized cataloging. **Computerized Information Services:** DIALOG. **Networks/Consortia:** Member of High Plains Regional Library Service System. **Publications:** Additions to the Library, quarterly.

★10824★

PLAYBOY ENTERPRISES, INC. - PHOTO LIBRARY (Aud-Vis)†
919 N. Michigan Ave.   Phone: (312) 751-8000
Chicago, IL 60611   Clydia Jones, Pict.Libn.
Staff: 2. **Holdings:** 5 million pictures. **Services:** Library not open to public.

PLEAK (Mariam J.) MEMORIAL LIBRARY AND ARCHIVE
See: Hobart Historical Society, Inc. - Mariam J. Pleak Memorial Library and Archive

PLEASANT VALLEY SCHOOLHOUSE
See: Wolfeboro Historical Society

PLEASANT VALLEY WILDLIFE SANCTUARY
See: Massachusetts Audubon Society - Berkshire Sanctuaries

PLENUM PUBLISHING CORPORATION - IFI/PLENUM DATA COMPANY
See: IFI/Plenum Data Company

★10825★

PLIMOTH PLANTATION, INC. - LIBRARY (Hist)
Warren Ave.
Box 1620   Phone: (617) 746-1622
Plymouth, MA 02360   James W. Baker, Res.Libn.
Founded: 1949. **Staff:** Prof 2. **Subjects:** New England history, 16th and 17th century social history, early travel and exploration, crafts, antiques, colonial archeology. **Holdings:** 3000 books; 1930 pamphlets; 4 volumes of Plymouth Colony wills (photocopy). **Subscriptions:** 65 journals and other serials. **Services:** Library open to public for reference use only. **Staff:** Carolyn Freeman Travers, Res.Assoc.

PLIMPTON LIBRARY
See: Columbia University - Rare Book and Manuscript Library

PLONDKE (Frederick J.) MEDICAL LIBRARY
See: St. John's Hospital - Frederick J. Plondke Medical Library

★10826★

PLOUGH, INC. - RESEARCH LIBRARY (Sci-Tech)
Box 377   Phone: (901) 320-2702
Memphis, TN 38151   Martha Hurst, Libn.
Staff: Prof 1. **Subjects:** Pharmacology, cosmetics, medicine, chemistry. **Holdings:** 1600 books; 1800 bound periodical volumes; 3000 reprints. **Subscriptions:** 113 journals and other serials. **Services:** Interlibrary loans; library open to public by permission only. **Computerized Information Services:** DIALOG, NLM. **Networks/Consortia:** Member of Association of Memphis Area Health Sciences Libraries (AMAHSL).

PLUM ISLAND ANIMAL DISEASE CENTER LIBRARY
See: U.S.D.A. - Agricultural Research Service

★10827★

PLUMAS COUNTY LAW LIBRARY (Law)
Court House
Box 686   Phone: (916) 283-2365
Quincy, CA 95971   Thomas H. Davis, Libn.
Staff: Prof 1. **Subjects:** Law - state and federal. **Holdings:** 7500 volumes. **Services:** Interlibrary loans; copying; library open to public for reference use only.

★10828★

PLUMMER MEMORIAL PUBLIC HOSPITAL - MEDICAL LIBRARY (Med)
969 Queen St., E.   Phone: (705) 254-5161
Sault Ste. Marie, ON, Canada P6A 2C4 Kathy You, Libn.
Founded: 1979. **Staff:** Prof 1. **Subjects:** Medicine, nursing, health care management, psychiatry, social work. **Holdings:** 500 books. **Subscriptions:** 60 journals and other serials. **Services:** Interlibrary loans; copying; library open to public for reference use only.

★10829★
PLYMOUTH CONGREGATIONAL CHURCH - VIDA B. VAREY LIBRARY (Rel-Theol)
1217 6th Ave.
Seattle, WA 98101   Anna F. Chiong, Libn.
Subjects: Religion. **Holdings:** 3000 books. **Services:** Interlibrary loans; library open to public.

★10830★
PLYMOUTH LAW LIBRARY (Law)†
Court House
72 Belmont St.   Phone: (617) 583-8250
Brockton, MA 02401   Kenneth E. MacMullen, Libn.
Staff: Prof 2. **Subjects:** Law. **Holdings:** 30,000 volumes. **Services:** Copying. **Remarks:** Part of the Massachusetts State Trial Court; Marnie Warner, Law Library Coordinator. **Staff:** Rosemary Sullivan, Asst.Libn.

★10831★
PLYMOUTH STATE COLLEGE - GEOGRAPHERS ON FILM COLLECTION (Geog-Map; Aud-Vis)
Ellen Reed House, Off. 4   Phone: (603) 536-1550
Plymouth, NH 03264   Prof. Maynard Weston Dow, Dir.
Staff: Prof 1; Other 1. **Subjects:** Geographers, geography, oral history. **Holdings:** 157 films, including films of special conferences, paper sessions and longer interviews. **Services:** Library open to public for film rental by request. **Publications:** Geographers on Film (brochure) - distributed by request.

★10832★
PLYMOUTH STATE COLLEGE - HERBERT H. LAMSON LIBRARY - ROBERT FROST COLLECTION (Hum)†
                                                    Phone: (604) 536-1550
Plymouth, NH 03264
Subjects: Robert Frost. **Special Collections:** George H. Browne Collection (150 titles and 1 drawer of Robert Frost material). **Holdings:** 200 books; 25 films and recordings; 30 letters from Frost, 1915-1922; 10 typescripts of poems, 1915-1922; 15 photographs, 1915-1920; 200 clippings, memorabilia, pamphlets, lecture notes. **Services:** Copying; collection open to public. **Special Catalogs:** Finding aid - available on request.

★10833★
PLYMOUTH STATE COLLEGE - HERBERT H. LAMSON LIBRARY - SPECIAL COLLECTIONS (Educ; Hist)
                                                    Phone: (603) 536-1550
Plymouth, NH 03264   Philip Wei, Dir.
Founded: 1871. **Subjects:** Education, African affairs, New Hampshire and Plymouth (town) history. **Special Collections:** Ernest L. Silver Collection of Early Textbooks; Educational Materials Center. **Holdings:** 4200 archives; 274,000 microforms (including ERIC); 500 maps. **Services:** Interlibrary loans; copying; remote access system; collections open to public. **Automated Operations:** Computerized cataloging. **Computerized Information Services:** DIALOG, BRS, OCLC. **Networks/Consortia:** Member of NELINET; New Hampshire College & University Council, Library Policy Committee (NHCUC). **Publications:** Handbook; Newsletter, semimonthly; bibliography of holdings in African affairs. **Staff:** Gary A. McCool, Educ.Ctr.Libn.

★10834★
POCONO HOSPITAL - MARSHALL R. METZGAR MEDICAL LIBRARY (Med)
206 E. Brown St.   Phone: (717) 421-4000
East Stroudsburg, PA 18301   Ellen P. Woodhead, Dir.
Staff: Prof 2. **Subjects:** Medicine, nursing. **Holdings:** 545 books; 1100 bound periodical volumes; 16 VF drawers of patient education materials and AV sources. **Subscriptions:** 124 journals and other serials. **Services:** Interlibrary loans; copying; SDI; library open to public by appointment. **Computerized Information Services:** BRS, Dow Jones News/Retrieval. **Networks/Consortia:** Member of Cooperating Hospital Libraries of the Lehigh Valley Area (CHL); Health Information Library Network of Northeastern Pennsylvania. **Publications:** QUEST (library newsletter) - for internal distribution only. **Staff:** Diane Chronister, Tech.Asst.

POCUMTUCK VALLEY MEMORIAL ASSOCIATION
See: Historic Deerfield, Inc. - Henry N. Flynt Library

★10835★
POETRY SOCIETY OF AMERICA - VAN VOORHIS LIBRARY (Hum)†
15 Gramercy Park   Phone: (212) 254-9628
New York, NY 10003   Deborah Gimelson, Adm.Dir.
Founded: 1970. **Staff:** 1. **Subjects:** American poetry and poetics, biography. **Special Collections:** American poetry - turn of the century and contemporary.

Holdings: 5500 books. **Services:** Library open to members only. **Remarks:** Large holograph collection and memorabilia of the Poetry Society of America are included in the Rare Book Division of the New York Public Library.

★10836★
POINT LOMA NAZARENE COLLEGE - RYAN LIBRARY (Rel-Theol)
3900 Lomaland Dr.   Phone: (619) 222-6474
San Diego, CA 92106   James D. Newburg, Act.Dir.
Staff: Prof 6; Other 8. **Subjects:** Religion. **Special Collections:** Arminianism & Wesleyana Collection; 19th & 20th century Christian Holiness movement; Pasadena and Point Loma College authors; college archives (170 linear feet). **Holdings:** 134,680 books; 24,260 bound periodical volumes; 4507 microforms. **Subscriptions:** 816 journals and other serials; 6 newspapers. **Services:** Interlibrary loans; copying; library open to public. **Automated Operations:** Computerized cataloging. **Computerized Information Services:** DIALOG, OCLC. Performs searches on cost recovery basis. **Networks/Consortia:** Member of San Diego Greater Metropolitan Area Library & Information Agency Council (METRO); CLASS. **Staff:** Kimiko Morita, Cat.Libn.; Marilyn Starr, Ref.Libn.Virgil Vail, Media Spec.; Ann Ruppert, Ref./Ser.Libn.

★10837★
POINT PELEE NATIONAL PARK - LIBRARY (Sci-Tech)
R.R. 1   Phone: (519) 326-1161
Leamington, ON, Canada N8H 3V4   Rob Watt, Chf.Pk. Naturalist
Founded: 1968. **Staff:** 4. **Subjects:** Ornithology, botany, biology, natural history, history, geology. **Special Collections:** Herbarium (1000 specimens); live mounts; study skins; insects (300 specimens). **Holdings:** 2000 books; 20,000 35mm slides; 1500 reprints and manuscripts; 1500 black and white prints; 30 16mm film titles. **Subscriptions:** 10 journals and other serials. **Services:** Library not open to public. **Remarks:** Maintained by Parks Canada.

★10838★
POINT OF PURCHASE ADVERTISING INSTITUTE - INFORMATION CENTER (Bus-Fin)
60 E. 42nd St.   Phone: (212) 682-7041
New York, NY 10165   John Kawula
Subjects: Point of purchase information, slide and film presentation. **Holdings:** 162 books and bound periodical volumes; 15 VF drawers; reports and surveys. **Subscriptions:** 90 journals and other serials; 10 newspapers. **Services:** Interlibrary loans; copying; center open to public involved with point of purchase. **Also Known As:** POPAI Information Center.

POINT REYES NATL. SEASHORE
See: U.S. Natl. Park Service

★10839★
POLAR GAS PROJECT - LIBRARY (Energy)
Commerce Court W.
Box 90   Phone: (416) 869-2675
Toronto, ON, Canada M5L 1H3   Carolyn Giovanetti, Libn.
Staff: Prof 1. **Subjects:** Arctic, northern development, gas pipelines, energy. **Special Collections:** Mackenzie Valley Pipeline Hearing before the National Energy Board (transcripts and exhibits). **Holdings:** 3000 books; 300 Polar Gas reports; 4 drawers of microfiche. **Subscriptions:** 75 journals and other serials. **Services:** Interlibrary loans; copying; library open to public by appointment. **Computerized Information Services:** DIALOG, Info Globe, SDC, CAN/OLE, QL Systems. **Publications:** Acquisitions list, monthly - for internal distribution only.

★10840★
POLAROID CORPORATION - RESEARCH LIBRARY (Sci-Tech)
730 Main St.   Phone: (617) 577-3368
Cambridge, MA 02139   Jean M. Vnenchak, Dept.Mgr.
Staff: Prof 3; Other 3. **Subjects:** Photography, chemistry, physics, engineering, mathematics, social sciences, general business. **Special Collections:** Photography and polarized light; Polaroid issued patents; photographs. **Holdings:** 30,000 books; 8000 bound periodical volumes; 60 drawers of annual reports, standards, government documents, translations, scientific papers and technical reports. **Subscriptions:** 1200 journals and other serials; 10 newspapers. **Services:** Interlibrary loans; copying; library open to public for reference use only with approval of the department manager. **Automated Operations:** Computerized cataloging, acquisitions, serials and circulation. **Computerized Information Services:** DIALOG, SDC, BRS, Image Technology Patent Information System (ITPAIS). **Publications:** Library Bulletin, monthly; Journal and Periodical Listings, semiannual - both for internal distribution only. **Staff:** Dorothy M. Morrissey, Assoc.Tech.Libn.; Marjorie J. Kilfoyle, Ref.Libn.; Richard Gurner, Lib.Adm.

POLIER (Shad) MEMORIAL LIBRARY
See: American Jewish Congress - Commission on Law and Social Action - Shad Polier Memorial Library

★10841★
POLISH AMERICAN CONGRESS - SOUTHERN CALIFORNIA-ARIZONA DIVISION - POLAND'S MILLENIUM LIBRARY (Area-Ethnic)
3424 W. Adams Blvd.　　　　　　　　Phone: (213) 664-0662
Los Angeles, CA 90018　　　　　　　Danuta M. Zawadzki, V.P.
Founded: 1966. Staff: Prof 1; Other 2. Subjects: Polish history, literature, sociology, geography with emphasis on the period 1918-1939. Holdings: 5000 books; 120 magazines. Services: Library not open to public. Staff: Wanda Jazwinski, Pres.; Dr. Frances Tuszynski, Libn.

★10842★
POLISH INSTITUTE OF ARTS AND SCIENCES IN AMERICA, INC. - RESEARCH LIBRARY (Area-Ethnic)
59 E. 66th St.　　　　　　　　　　Phone: (212) 988-4338
New York, NY 10021　　　　　　　Krystyna Baron, Libn.
Founded: 1959. Staff: Prof 1; Other 2. Subjects: Poland - humanities, social sciences. Holdings: 17,300 books. Subscriptions: 300 journals and other serials. Services: Library open to faculty and students.

★10843★
POLISH INSTITUTE OF ARTS AND SCIENCES IN CANADA - POLISH LIBRARY (Area-Ethnic)
McGill University
3479 Peel St.　　　　　　　　　　Phone: (514) 392-5958
Montreal, PQ, Canada H3A 1W7　　Dr. Anna Poray-Wybranowski, Chf.Libn.
Staff: Prof 3; Other 2. Subjects: Polish literature, history, social science, political science, art, folklore; East European problems. Special Collections: Wartime publications in English and Polish. Holdings: 30,000 books; 5000 periodicals; reports; manuscripts; clippings; documents; files; 200 engravings; 30 paintings; 700 slides; 15 atlases; 40 maps; 300 photographs. Subscriptions: 65 journals and other serials; 10 newspapers. Services: Interlibrary loans; copying; library open to public. Special Indexes: Index to "Tygodnik Powszechny"; "Kultura," Paris; "Polish Review," New York; "News," London; Abstracts of articles in library periodical holdings in English, French and Polish (4000 cards). Staff: Wanda Stachiewicz, Hon.Cur.

★10844★
POLISH MUSEUM OF AMERICA - ARCHIVES & LIBRARY (Area-Ethnic)
984 Milwaukee Ave.　　　　　　　Phone: (312) 384-3352
Chicago, IL 60622　　　　　　Rev. Donald Bilinski, O.F.M., Dir./Libn.
Founded: 1912. Staff: Prof 1; Other 6. Subjects: Polonica. Special Collections: 16th and 17th century original Polish works; 16th-18th century royal Polish manuscripts; original manuscripts of Kosciuszko, Pulaski, Tyssowski, Paderewski and others; Polish American newspapers and magazines. Holdings: 30,000 books; 4000 bound periodical volumes and reels of microfilm; 400 art pieces, reports, clippings, booklets and museum and archival materials. Services: Interlibrary loans; copying; library open to public by appointment. Remarks: Maintained by the Polish Roman Catholic Union of America.

★10845★
POLISH NOBILITY ASSOCIATION - VILLA ANNESLIE ARCHIVES (Area-Ethnic)
529 Dunkirk Rd.　　　　　　　　Phone: (301) 752-1087
Anneslie, MD 21212　　　　Leonard Suligowski, Dir. of Heraldry
Staff: Prof 2. Subjects: Polish history, heraldry, and nobility. Special Collections: Heraldry of Eastern Europe; nobility-family archives. Holdings: 500 books; 100 other cataloged items. Subscriptions: 10 journals and other serials. Services: Archives not open to public. Staff: Thomas Hollowak, Res. Herald.

★10846★
POLISH SINGERS ALLIANCE OF AMERICA - LIBRARY (Mus)
180 Second Ave.　　　　　　　　Phone: (212) 254-6642
New York, NY 10003　　　　　　　Walter Witkowicki, Libn.
Subjects: Choral and orchestral music. Holdings: 200,000 sheets of music for male, female, mixed choruses and orchestra. Staff: Barbara R. Blyskal, Gen.Sec.

★10847★
POLK COUNTY HISTORICAL AND GENEALOGICAL LIBRARY (Hist)
495 N. Hendry Ave.
Box 1719　　　　　　　　　　　Phone: (813) 533-5146
Bartow, FL 33830　　　　　　LaCona Raines Padgett, Hd.Libn.
Founded: 1937. Staff: Prof 2. Subjects: History - Polk County, Florida,

Southeastern United States; genealogies of Southeastern United States families. Special Collections: Florida history. Holdings: 9000 books; 610 bound periodical volumes; 700 family histories; 3000 reels of microfilm of census reports; 600 reels of microfilm of early newspapers, court records, church records. Subscriptions: 35 journals and other serials; 8 newspapers. Services: Copying; library open to public. Publications: Polk County Historical Quarterly. Remarks: Maintained by Polk County Historical Commission (Board of County Commissioners). Staff: Kathleen M. Greer, Asst.Libn.

★10848★
POLK COUNTY LAW LIBRARY (Law)
Courthouse, Rm. 307　　　　　　Phone: (813) 533-0411
Bartow, FL 33830　　　　　　　Nancy H. Tabler, Libn.
Founded: 1955. Staff: Prof 1. Subjects: Law. Holdings: 14,000 books and bound periodical volumes. Subscriptions: 10 journals and other serials. Services: Copying; library open to public for reference use only. Remarks: Maintained by Polk County Board of County Commissioners.

★10849★
POLK (James K.) ANCESTRAL HOME - LIBRARY (Hist)
301 S. Seventh St.
Box 741　　　　　　　　　　　Phone: (615) 388-2354
Columbia, TN 38401　　　　　　W.H. Bass, Dir.
Founded: 1929. Staff: 2. Subjects: James K. Polk. Holdings: 100 books; 2000 artifacts. Services: Library open to public by written permission. Remarks: Maintained by James K. Polk Memorial Association. Personal letters and memorabilia are on deposit at the State Archives.

★10850★
POLK PUBLIC MUSEUM - MEMORIAL LIBRARY (Hum)
800 E. Palmetto　　　　　　　Phone: (813) 688-7743
Lakeland, FL 33801　　　　　　Ken Rollins, Dir.
Staff: Prof 1; Other 2. Subjects: Art, antiques, history, music, natural history, literature. Holdings: 400 books; 20 bound periodical volumes; 150 clippings. Services: Library open to public for reference use only. Staff: Marjorie Gilvin, Libn.

POLLACK LIBRARY
See: Maimonides Hospital Geriatric Centre

POLLACK LIBRARY
See: Yeshiva University

POLLINS (Calvin E.) MEMORIAL LIBRARY
See: Westmoreland County Historical Society - Calvin E. Pollins Memorial Library

POLLOCK (Channing) THEATRE COLLECTION
See: Howard University - Channing Pollock Theatre Collection

★10851★
POLYCHROME CORPORATION - RESEARCH & DEVELOPMENT LIBRARY (Art; Bus-Fin)†
137 Alexander St.　　　　　　Phone: (914) 965-8800
Yonkers, NY 10702　　　　　　Peg Otis, Libn.
Staff: Prof 1. Subjects: Graphic arts, chemistry, business management. Holdings: 1500 books; 100 unbound periodicals; 4 drawers of U.S. patents; 1 drawer of foreign patents. Subscriptions: 100 journals and other serials. Services: Copying; library open to public for reference use only on request.

★10852★
POLYCLINIC MEDICAL CENTER - MEDICAL STAFF LIBRARY (Med)
Third & Radnor Sts.
Box 3410　　　　　　　　　　Phone: (717) 782-4292
Harrisburg, PA 17105　　　　　Suzanne M. Shultz, Libn.
Founded: 1925. Staff: 1. Subjects: Medicine and medical specialities. Holdings: 1136 books; 4000 bound periodical volumes. Subscriptions: 176 journals and other serials. Services: Interlibrary loans; copying; library open to students and medical professionals. Computerized Information Services: MEDLARS.

★10853★
POLYMER CORPORATION - LIBRARY (Sci-Tech)†
501 Crescent Ave.　　　　　　Phone: (215) 929-5858
Reading, PA 19603
Founded: 1966. Staff: Prof 1. Subjects: Polymer science, polymer technology, engineering, chemistry, physics, management, mathematics. Holdings: 2500 books and bound periodical volumes; 1275 laboratory notebooks. Subscriptions: 100 journals and other serials. Publications:

Periodical Holdings, annual - distributed internally.

★10854★
POLYMER INDUSTRIES - LIBRARY (Sci-Tech)
Roberts Road
Box 2184   Phone: (803) 244-5351
Greenville, SC 29602   Linda F. Gentry, Libn.
Founded: 1964. **Staff:** 1. **Subjects:** Polymers, adhesives, coatings, textile chemicals, packaging. **Holdings:** 500 books; 2000 patents. **Subscriptions:** 40 journals and other serials. **Services:** Interlibrary loans; copying; library open to public by appointment.

★10855★
POLYSAR, LTD. - INFORMATION CENTRE (Sci-Tech)
Vidal St., S.   Phone: (519) 337-8251
Sarnia, ON, Canada N7T 7M2   Dorothy J. Clarkson, Supv.
Founded: 1944. **Staff:** Prof 5; Other 7. **Subjects:** Rubber, latexes, plastics, chemicals, polymer science, organic chemistry. **Holdings:** 12,000 books; 5000 bound periodical volumes; 1800 reels of microfilm; 10,000 microfiche; 33,000 internal reports. **Subscriptions:** 700 journals and other serials; 30 newspapers. **Services:** Interlibrary loans; copying; SDI; center open to public by advance request. **Automated Operations:** Computerized serials. **Computerized Information Services:** DIALOG, SDC, Info Globe, CANSIM; internal databases. **Publications:** Polysar Information Bulletin. **Special Indexes:** Index to internal reports (book). **Staff:** Margaret Vara, Info.Spec.-Bus.; Rosemary O'Donnell, Info.Spec.-Tech.; Tina DeMars, Info.Spec.-Bus./Tech.

★10856★
POLYTECHNIC INSTITUTE OF NEW YORK - LONG ISLAND CENTER LIBRARY (Sci-Tech)
                                             Phone: (516) 694-5500
Long Island, NY 11735   Lorraine Schein, Br.Libn.
Founded: 1960. **Staff:** Prof 1; Other 3. **Subjects:** Electrical engineering, electrophysics, aeronautics, fluid mechanics, physics, mathematics. **Holdings:** NASA depository library; 20 VF drawers of pamphlets; 1 file drawer of cassettes. **Subscriptions:** 250 journals and other serials. **Services:** Interlibrary loans; copying; library open to public. **Networks/Consortia:** Member of Long Island Library Resources Council (LILRC).

★10857★
POLYTECHNIC INSTITUTE OF NEW YORK - SPICER LIBRARY (Sci-Tech)
333 Jay St.   Phone: (718) 643-8690
Brooklyn, NY 11201   James Jarman, Act.Dir. of Libs.
Staff: Prof 8; Other 15. **Subjects:** Aerospace technology; engineering - civil, industrial, electrical; electrophysics; chemistry; industrial management; mathematics; physics. **Special Collections:** Joseph Mattiello collection of works of interest to the paint, varnish, and lacquer industries; history of science and technology collection. **Holdings:** 268,576 books and bound periodical volumes; 429,728 microtexts. **Subscriptions:** 1200 journals and other serials. **Services:** Interlibrary loans; copying; library open to public with letter from parent organization. **Automated Operations:** Computerized cataloging, acquisitions, serials and interlibrary loans. **Computerized Information Services:** DIALOG, OCLC. **Publications:** Serials 1979-80, irregular. **Remarks:** Includes the holdings of the Aerospace Laboratory Library. **Staff:** Zena Jacobs, Hd., Ref.Dept; Lily Middleton, Hd., Circ.Dept.; Heather Walters, Hd., Cat.Dept.; David Turiel, Dir., Tech.Serv.Div.

POMONA COLLEGE - SEELEY G. MUDD SCIENCE LIBRARY
See: The Claremont Colleges - Seeley G. Mudd Science Library

★10858★
POMONA PUBLIC LIBRARY - SPECIAL COLLECTIONS DEPARTMENT (Hist)
625 S. Garey Ave.
Box 2271   Phone: (714) 620-2033
Pomona, CA 91766   David Streeter, Spec.Coll.Libn.
Founded: 1887. **Holdings:** Californiana (3000 items); philately (1200 items); genealogy (2000 items); Citrus Company Records (28 companies); citrus box labels (4200); water company records (16 companies); Frasher photographs (60,000); Cooper photographs (4000); historical photographs (10,000); Tatum photographs (150); post card collection (35,000); glass plate negatives and prints (2500); California Wine Labels (6500); non-California wine labels (1500); Laura Ingalls Wilder Collection (Little House on the Prairie holograph manuscripts; letters; photographs); Clara Webber Collection of Historic Children's Books; Padua Theater Collection (Mexican Players, 15 linear feet of uncataloged manuscripts and photographs). **Services:** Interlibrary loans; copying; department open to public. **Automated Operations:** Computerized cataloging, acquisitions and circulation. **Computerized Information Services:** OCLC. **Networks/Consortia:** Member

of Metropolitan Cooperative Library System (MCLS); Southern California Answering Network (SCAN). **Special Indexes:** Pomona Progress Bulletin Index (card); CULP; CATALIST.

★10859★
POMONA VALLEY COMMUNITY HOSPITAL - MEDICAL LIBRARY (Med)
1798 N. Garey Ave.   Phone: (714) 623-8715
Pomona, CA 91767   Shirley Chervin, Libn.
Staff: 1. **Subjects:** Clinical medicine, nursing, hospital administration. **Holdings:** 1200 books; 5000 bound periodical volumes; 1200 audiotapes. **Subscriptions:** 160 journals and other serials. **Services:** Interlibrary loans; library not open to public. **Computerized Information Services:** DIALOG, MEDLINE. **Networks/Consortia:** Member of Medical Library Group of Southern California and Arizona.

★10860★
PONCA CITY CULTURAL CENTER & MUSEUMS - LIBRARY (Area-Ethnic)
1000 E. Grand Ave.   Phone: (405) 762-6123
Ponca City, OK 74601   LaWanda French, Supv.
Founded: 1938. **Staff:** 1. **Subjects:** American Indian, anthropology, archeology, American cowboy, museology. **Special Collections:** Personal letters and photographs of Bryant Baker, sculptor of the Pioneer Woman; Ponca Indian music (tape recordings). **Holdings:** 200 books; 15 bound periodical volumes; VF drawers of unbound reports, clippings, pamphlets, dissertations and documents. **Subscriptions:** 15 journals and other serials. **Services:** Copying (limited); library open to public. **Publications:** Museum Brochure; Museum Educational Leaflet Series. **Special Catalogs:** Classification, Source, Tribe, Location and Documents Catalogs (card file).

★10861★
PONCE SCHOOL OF MEDICINE - LIBRARY (Med)*
Box 7004   Phone: (809) 844-4150
Ponce, PR 00732   Margarita Arroyo, Libn.
Staff: Prof 2; Other 5. **Subjects:** Clinical and basic sciences. **Holdings:** 5000 books. **Subscriptions:** 613 journals and other serials. **Services:** Interlibrary loans; copying; library open to public. **Publications:** Library guide. **Special Indexes:** Index to the Journal: Asociacion Medica de Puerto Rico Boletin. **Staff:** Roberto Colon, Cat.

★10862★
PONTIAC GENERAL HOSPITAL - LIBRARY (Med)†
Seminole & W. Huron   Phone: (313) 857-7412
Pontiac, MI 48053   Naim K. Sahyoun, Dir. of Libs.
Staff: Prof 2; Other 2. **Subjects:** Health sciences. **Holdings:** 2000 books; 3000 bound periodical volumes; Audio-Digest tapes. **Subscriptions:** 380 journals and other serials. **Services:** Interlibrary loans; copying; SDI; library open to health professionals. **Computerized Information Services:** Online systems. **Networks/Consortia:** Member of Pontiac-Allen Park-Detroit Consortium (PAD).

★10863★
PONTIAC OSTEOPATHIC HOSPITAL - MEDICAL LIBRARY (Med)
50 N. Perry St.   Phone: (313) 338-5000
Pontiac, MI 48058   Janis M. Fox, Libn.
Founded: 1963. **Staff:** 2. **Subjects:** Medicine. **Holdings:** 2586 books; 3100 bound periodical volumes; 125 audiovisual cassettes; 7 drawers of Audio-Digest tapes; 90 slide-cassettes. **Subscriptions:** 149 journals and other serials. **Services:** Interlibrary loans; library not open to public.

★10864★
PONTIFICAL COLLEGE JOSEPHINUM - A.T. WEHRLE MEMORIAL LIBRARY (Rel-Theol)
7625 N. High St.   Phone: (614) 885-5585
Columbus, OH 43085   Peter G. Veracka, Dir./Coll.Libn.
Founded: 1889. **Staff:** Prof 3; Other 2. **Subjects:** Patristics, scholastic philosophy, Catholic theology. **Special Collections:** Dissertations on the work and thought of Bernard Lonergan (53). **Holdings:** 96,726 books; 12,050 bound periodical volumes; 455 microfiche. **Subscriptions:** 404 journals and other serials; 51 newspapers. **Services:** Interlibrary loans; copying; library open to public on request. **Automated Operations:** Computerized cataloging. **Computerized Information Services:** OCLC. **Networks/Consortia:** Member of OHIONET. **Staff:** Matthew Rzeczkowski, O.P., Theology Libn.; Eleanor Byerly, Ref./Bibliog.Instr.Libn.

PONTIFICAL INSTITUTE OF MEDIAEVAL STUDIES
See: University of Toronto

POPAI INFORMATION CENTER
See: Point of Purchase Advertising Institute - Information Center

★10865★
POPE, BALLARD, SHEPARD AND FOWLE - LIBRARY (Law)†
69 W. Washington St.   Phone: (312) 630-4283
Chicago, IL 60602   Ronald E. Feret
Staff: Prof 1; Other 1. Subjects: Law. Holdings: 25,950 books; 200 bound periodical volumes. Subscriptions: 18 journals and other serials. Services: Library not open to public.

★10866★
POPE COUNTY HISTORICAL SOCIETY & MUSEUM - LIBRARY (Hist)
Hwy. No. 104 S. Glenwood   Phone: (612) 634-3293
Glenwood, MN 56334   Merlin Berglin, Off.Supv.
Founded: 1932. Staff: Prof 2. Subjects: History - local, business, personal. Special Collections: Bound newspapers, 1891 to present. Holdings: 1343 volumes. Services: Copying; library open to public for reference use only.

★10867★
POPE JOHN XXIII NATIONAL SEMINARY - LIBRARY (Rel-Theol)
558 South Ave.   Phone: (617) 899-5500
Weston, MA 02193   Rev. James L. Fahey, Libn.
Founded: 1964. Staff: Prof 2; Other 12. Subjects: Theology, philosophy, scripture, humanities, social sciences. Holdings: 40,140 books; 3870 bound periodical volumes; 2 vertical files. Subscriptions: 302 journals and other serials. Services: Interlibrary loans; copying; library open to public for reference use only. Staff: Ann Kidney, Asst.Libn.

★10868★
POPULATION COUNCIL - LIBRARY (Soc Sci)
1 Dag Hammarskjold Plaza   Phone: (212) 644-1620
New York, NY 10017   H. Neil Zimmerman, Libn.
Staff: Prof 1; Other 1. Subjects: Population; demography; family planning; contraception; statistics; public health; development - economic, social, agricultural. Holdings: 12,000 books; 36,000 pamphlets, mimeographs, reprints and other materials. Subscriptions: 350 journals and other serials. Services: Interlibrary loans; library open to researchers by appointment. Automated Operations: Computerized serials. Networks/Consortia: Member of Consortium of Foundation Libraries; Association of Population/ Family Planning Libraries and Information Centers - International; METRO. Publications: Acquisitions List, irregular.

★10869★
POPULATION CRISIS COMMITTEE/DRAPER FUND - LIBRARY (Soc Sci)
1120 19th St., N.W., Suite 550   Phone: (202) 659-1833
Washington, DC 20036   Linda N. Jenks, Sr.Libn./Info.Mgr.
Staff: Prof 2; Other 1. Subjects: Family planning, population, contraceptive technology, food and environment. Special Collections: Population legislative history. Holdings: 5000 books; 65 VF drawers. Subscriptions: 225 journals and other serials. Services: Interlibrary loans; copying; SDI; library open to public by appointment. Computerized Information Services: DIALOG, MEDLARS, SDC. Networks/Consortia: Member of Association for Population/Family Planning Libraries and Information Centers - International. Publications: Library acquisitions list, monthly - free upon request. Staff: Anne Marie B. Amantia, Libn.

★10870★
POPULATION DYNAMICS, INC. - INFORMATION CENTER (Soc Sci)
3829 Aurora Ave., N.   Phone: (206) 632-5030
Seattle, WA 98103
Founded: 1973. Staff: 1. Subjects: Population growth, family planning, contraception, environmental quality. Holdings: Films; 8 rental films (also for sale). Subscriptions: 10 journals and other serials. Services: Copying; center open to public for reference use only.

★10871★
POPULATION REFERENCE BUREAU, INC. - LIBRARY/INFORMATION SERVICE (Soc Sci)
2213 M St., N.W.   Phone: (202) 785-4664
Washington, DC 20037   Janice Beattie, Tech.Info.Spec.
Founded: 1929. Staff: Prof 1; Other 1. Subjects: Demography, U.S. census, family planning, migration, energy/resources. Holdings: 10,000 books; 2500 reprints and papers; 15 VF drawers of pamphlets and clippings (includes reprints); historical U.S. census collection with complete set 1930-1970 census volumes. Subscriptions: 450 journals and other serials. Services: Interlibrary loans; copying; library open to public. Computerized Information Services: MEDLARS, DIALOG.

POPULATION RESOURCE CENTER
See: Planned Parenthood of Minnesota

★10872★
PORT AUTHORITY OF ALLEGHENY COUNTY - TRANSIT RESEARCH LIBRARY (Trans)
Beaver & Island Ave.   Phone: (412) 237-7334
Pittsburgh, PA 15233
Founded: 1974. Staff: Prof 1. Subjects: Rapid transit, para-transit, urban transportation. Holdings: 3500 books; 200 reels of microfilm. Subscriptions: 81 journals and other serials. Services: Interlibrary loans; library open to public by appointment. Publications: List of new acquisitions, monthly; List of Periodicals, annual.

★10873★
PORT AUTHORITY OF NEW YORK AND NEW JERSEY - LIBRARY (Trans)
55 N., One World Trade Ctr.   Phone: (212) 466-4062
New York, NY 10048   Jane M. Janiak, Chf.Libn.
Founded: 1946. Staff: Prof 7; Other 6. Subjects: Transportation, public administration, international trade, business, management, engineering, aviation. Holdings: 25,000 books; 25,000 documents; 150 titles on microfilm; Urban Mass Transportation Administration Depository. Subscriptions: 1200 journals and 500 other serials. Services: Interlibrary loans; library open to students and librarians by appointment. Automated Operations: Computerized cataloging and serials. Computerized Information Services: NEXIS, DIALOG, SDC, DOE/RECON, EBIS (Economic/Business Information System), TECHNOTEC Data Base, TEXTLINE, RLIN, OCLC, LEGI-SLATE. Networks/Consortia: Member of SUNY/OCLC Library Network. Publications: Library Bulletin; Port Authority Bibliography. Staff: Henry Barnard, Asst.Chf.Libn./Cat.; Diane Sciattara, Ref.Libn.; Patricia Cose, Asst.Chf.Libn./Ref.; Donna Nance, Ref.Libn.; Armilda Laats, Cat.; Rhonda Marker, Cat.

★10874★
PORT HURON TIMES HERALD - LIBRARY (Publ)*
911 Military St.   Phone: (313) 985-7171
Port Huron, MI 48060   Joann M. Maxwell, Lib.Ck.
Staff: 1. Subjects: Newspaper reference topics. Holdings: 10,000 files of clippings and photographs; 670 reels of microfilm. Services: Library open to public with permission.

★10875★
PORT OF PORTLAND - LIBRARY (Bus-Fin)
700 N.E. Multnomah   Phone: (503) 231-5000
Portland, OR 97232   Jo Dwyer, Lib.Acq.
Staff: Prof 1; Other 1. Subjects: Commerce - maritime, waterborne; aviation. Special Collections: Port of Portland studies (Port-run airports, ship repair yard, marine terminals); archives. Holdings: 10,000 books. Subscriptions: 350 journals and other serials; 20 newspapers. Services: Interlibrary loans; library open to public.

★10876★
PORT OF SEATTLE - LIBRARY
Box 1209
Seattle, WA 98111
Defunct

★10877★
PORTAGE COUNTY HISTORICAL SOCIETY, INC. - LIBRARY AND MUSEUM (Hist)
6549-51 N. Chestnut St.   Phone: (216) 296-3523
Ravenna, OH 44266
Founded: 1951. Staff: 5. Subjects: Genealogy, county history - families, industries, organizations. Special Collections: Portage County Court House archives, 1808-1950. Holdings: 500 books; 40 family histories. Services: Genealogy and history research; copying; monthly public programs; library open to public with restrictions. Publications: Portage County History (1885, reprint); Portage Heritage; 1874-1978 Bicentennial Atlas of Portage County; Newsletter, quarterly - to members.

PORTER (Dana) ARTS LIBRARY
See: University of Waterloo - Dana Porter Arts Library

PORTER (Sister Esther) MEDICAL-NURSING LIBRARY
See: Bethesda Lutheran Medical Center - Medical-Nursing Library

PORTER (Katherine Anne) ROOM
See: University of Maryland, College Park - Libraries - Katherine Anne Porter Room

PORTER (Langley) PSYCHIATRIC INSTITUTE
See: Langley Porter Psychiatric Institute

★10878★
PORTER MEDICAL CENTER - MEDICAL LIBRARY AND INFORMATION SERVICE (Med)
South St.   Phone: (802) 388-7901
Middlebury, VT 05753   Simone Rollin Lazarus, Libn.
Founded: 1974. **Staff:** 1. **Subjects:** Medicine. **Holdings:** 280 books.
Subscriptions: 85 journals and other serials. **Services:** Interlibrary loans;
library not open to public. **Networks/Consortia:** Member of Vermont/New
Hampshire Health Science Libraries.

★10879★
PORTER MEMORIAL HOSPITAL - HARLEY E. RICE MEMORIAL LIBRARY (Med)
2525 S. Downing St.   Phone: (303) 778-5656
Denver, CO 80210   Karla Britain, Dir.
Staff: Prof 2. **Subjects:** Medicine. **Holdings:** 2000 books; 3250 bound
periodical volumes; 125 audiotapes; 3 VF drawers. **Subscriptions:** 352
journals and other serials. **Services:** Interlibrary loans; copying; library open to
public for reference use only. **Computerized Information Services:** BRS,
MEDLARS. Performs free searches. **Networks/Consortia:** Member of Denver
Area Health Sciences Library Consortium; Bibliographical Center for Research,
Rocky Mountain Region, Inc. (BCR). **Staff:** Roseanne Vercio, Asst.Libn.

★10880★
PORTERVILLE STATE HOSPITAL - MEDICAL LIBRARY (Med)
Box 2000   Phone: (209) 784-2000
Porterville, CA 93257   Mary Jane Berry, Libn.
Staff: Prof 1. **Subjects:** Mental retardation - psychology, medical aspects,
education, social welfare. **Holdings:** 6000 books; 3600 bound periodical
volumes. **Subscriptions:** 125 journals and other serials. **Services:** Interlibrary
loans; copying; library open to public for reference use only on request.

★10881★
PORTLAND ART ASSOCIATION - NORTHWEST FILM STUDY CENTER - CIRCULATING FILM LIBRARY (Aud-Vis)
1219 S.W. Park Ave.   Phone: (503) 221-1156
Portland, OR 97205   Karen Karbo, Regional Serv.
Staff: 2. **Subjects:** Film - experimental, dramatic, documentary. **Special
Collections:** Civilization film series. **Holdings:** 194 films. **Subscriptions:** 15
journals and other serials. **Services:** Film rental; library open to public.
Publications: Exhibition program schedules; Animator, quarterly; NWFSC class
schedules; Filmmaker in the Schools (FIS) brochures. **Special Catalogs:**
Circulating Film Library catalog. **Staff:** Cheryl Bell-Koski, Film Libn.

★10882★
PORTLAND ART MUSEUM - LIBRARY (Art)
1219 S.W. Park   Phone: (503) 226-2811
Portland, OR 97205   Emily Evans Elsner, Libn.
Founded: 1898. **Staff:** Prof 2. **Subjects:** Art and related subjects. **Special
Collections:** Art of Indian tribes of the Pacific Northwest; Oriental art,
especially Japanese prints; English silver books. **Holdings:** 15,260 books;
1026 bound periodical volumes; 365 pamphlet cases of catalogs relating to
artists, movements and exhibitions; 175 pamphlet cases of museum
publications (reports, bulletins); 57,500 slides. **Subscriptions:** 69 journals and
other serials. **Services:** Interlibrary loans; library open to public for reference
use only. **Remarks:** Maintained by the Portland Art Association. **Staff:** Dan
Lucas, Slide Libn.

★10883★
PORTLAND BUREAU OF PLANNING - LIBRARY (Plan)
1120 S.W. 5th Ave., 10th Fl.   Phone: (503) 796-7717
Portland, OR 97204
Founded: 1975. **Staff:** Prof 1; Other 1. **Subjects:** Urban planning, energy
conservation, historic preservation. **Holdings:** 6000 books and bound
periodical volumes. **Subscriptions:** 60 journals and other serials. **Services:**
Interlibrary loans; copying; library open to public with restrictions.

★10884★
PORTLAND CEMENT ASSOCIATION/CONSTRUCTION TECHNOLOGY LABORATORIES - INFORMATION SERVICES SECTION (Sci-Tech)
5420 Old Orchard Rd.   Phone: (312) 966-6200
Skokie, IL 60077   Marilynn Halasz, Mgr., Info.Serv.Sect.
Founded: 1949. **Staff:** Prof 2; Other 2. **Subjects:** Portland cement;
concrete; engineering - structural, civil; pavement; construction. **Special
Collections:** Portland Cement Association literature, 1900 to present (6200
items). **Holdings:** 8100 books; 13,000 bound periodical volumes; 1530 U.S.

patents; 21,150 government, university and foreign reports; 850
translations; 610 bibliographies. **Subscriptions:** 350 journals and other
serials. **Services:** Interlibrary loans; copying; bibliographic searching; library
open to public with fee for services. **Networks/Consortia:** Member of
ILLINET. **Publications:** Literature Review, weekly. **Special Indexes:** Abstract
file on cement/concrete construction literature and related fields (subject,
author, source; 115,000 entries); Cement and Concrete Thesaurus. **Staff:**
Cynthia Spigelman, Assoc.Libn.

★10885★
PORTLAND GENERAL ELECTRIC - CORPORATE AND TECHNICAL LIBRARIES (Bus-Fin; Energy)
121 S.W. Salmon St.   Phone: (503) 226-8695
Portland, OR 97204   Mary K. Devlin-Willis, Br.Mgr., Lib.Serv.
Founded: 1914. **Staff:** Prof 2; Other 3. **Subjects:** Electrical and nuclear
engineering, management, solar and geothermal energy, environmental
sciences. **Special Collections:** Historical material and photograph collection of
early power in Oregon; docketed information for U.S. nuclear power plants
(80,000 reports). **Holdings:** 8000 books; 8000 bound periodical volumes;
40,000 technical reports (hard copy and microfiche); 1500 standards.
Subscriptions: 850 journals and other serials; 30 newspapers. **Services:**
Interlibrary loans; copying; library open to public with restrictions. **Automated
Operations:** Computerized cataloging, acquisitions, serials and ILL.
Computerized Information Services: DIALOG, DOE/RECON, BRS, Evans
Economics, Inc. (EEI), F.W. Faxon Company, Inc. **Networks/Consortia:**
Member of Oregon On-Line Users Group (OOUG). **Special Indexes:** Keyword
index of technical reports, available on microfiche. **Staff:** Donna B. Shaver,
Tech.Libn.

PORTLAND LIBRARY ASSOCIATION
See: Library Association of Portland

PORTLAND PRESS HERALD-EVENING EXPRESS
See: Gannett (Guy) Publishing Company - Press Herald-Evening Express
   Library-Maine Sunday Telegram

★10886★
PORTLAND PUBLIC SCHOOLS - PROFESSIONAL LIBRARY (Educ)
501 N. Dixon St.
Box 3107   Phone: (503) 249-2000
Portland, OR 97208   Connie Stanton, Libn.
Staff: Prof 1; Other 2. **Subjects:** Education. **Holdings:** 15,000 books; 5025
titles of musical scores; archives. **Subscriptions:** 170 journals and other
serials; 7 newspapers. **Services:** Interlibrary loans; copying; SDI; library open
to public with restrictions. **Computerized Information Services:** DIALOG,
OCLC, Tech-Net, ED-LINE. **Networks/Consortia:** Member of WLN.

★10887★
PORTLAND SCHOOL OF ART - LIBRARY (Art)
619 Congress St.   Phone: (207) 761-1772
Portland, ME 04101   Joanne Waxman, Libn.
Founded: 1973. **Staff:** Prof 2; Other 12. **Subjects:** Art and art history,
biographies of artists, local architecture and arts, liberal arts. **Holdings:**
15,000 books; 30,000 slides. **Subscriptions:** 75 journals and other serials.
Services: Interlibrary loans; copying; library open to public with restrictions.
Staff: Jeffory Clough, Asst.Libn.

★10888★
PORTLAND STATE UNIVERSITY - AUDIO-VISUAL SERVICES (Aud-Vis)
Box 1151   Phone: (503) 229-4514
Portland, OR 97207   Frank F. Kuo, Dir.
Founded: 1953. **Staff:** Prof 3; Other 9. **Subjects:** General AV collection to
support university curriculum. **Holdings:** 600 guides and indexes to media
materials; media catalogs; 233 media kits; 50 videotapes; 1300 16mm films;
400 8mm films; 3262 35mm filmstrips; 36,000 35mm slides; 10,457
phonograph records; 7123 phonotapes; 3655 scores; 1802 cassette tapes.
Services: Copying (limited); library open to public for campus use only.
Networks/Consortia: Member of WLN. **Publications:** Film catalog; Foreign
Languages (26) Audiotape Catalog - both for internal distribution only. **Staff:**
Anthony Midson, Asst.Dir.; Stan Nuffer, Supv.

★10889★
PORTLAND STATE UNIVERSITY - CONTINUING EDUCATION FILM LIBRARY (Aud-Vis)
1633 S.W. Park Ave.   Phone: (503) 229-4890
Portland, OR 97207   Anthony J. Midson, Dir.
Founded: 1932. **Staff:** Prof 1; Other 9. **Subjects:** General subjects.
Holdings: 9200 16mm films. **Services:** Rental collection available to public
with restrictions. **Publications:** Film Library News, monthly - available to film

users in 13 Western states only. **Special Catalogs:** Film catalog - free upon request.

★10890★
PORTLAND STATE UNIVERSITY - MIDDLE EAST STUDIES CENTER
Box 751
Portland, OR 97207
Subjects: Arabic, Hebrew, Persian, Turkish. **Holdings:** 31,126 volumes in vernacular languages; additional volumes in Western languages to supplement area studies. **Remarks:** Presently inactive.

★10891★
PORTLAND STATE UNIVERSITY - SCIENCE LIBRARY (Sci-Tech)
Box 1151   Phone: (503) 229-4735
Portland, OR 97207   Robert L. Lockerby, Engr.Libn.
Founded: 1946. **Staff:** Prof 2; Other 2. **Subjects:** Science - history and philosophy, environmental, earth, military, naval, systems; mathematics; physics; astronomy; chemistry; biology; engineering; technology. **Special Collections:** Ivan Bloch Collection of Pacific Northwest natural resources and hydroelectric power; U.S. Geological Survey depository; U.S. Dept. of Energy depository (microfiche). **Holdings:** 148,749 books; 45,165 bound periodical volumes; 130,000 microfiche; 2200 reels of microfilm; 16,300 microcards; NASA documents (microfiche). **Subscriptions:** 2400 journals and other serials. **Services:** Interlibrary loans; copying; library open to public. **Computerized Information Services:** DIALOG, SDC, BRS, NASA/RECON. Performs searches on cost recovery basis. **Networks/Consortia:** Member of WLN. **Remarks:** The public has access to the collection of the Oregon Department of Geology and Mineral Industries through this library. **Staff:** Dr. J.J. Kohut, Sci.Libn.

★10892★
PORTMAN (John) & ASSOCIATES - LIBRARY (Sci-Tech; Plan)
225 Peachtree St.   Phone: (404) 522-8811
Atlanta, GA 30303   Nancy Williams, Libn.
Staff: Prof 2. **Subjects:** Architecture, civil engineering, construction industry, real estate, art. **Special Collections:** Archives of John Portman. **Holdings:** 2750 books; 259 bound periodical volumes; 6 VF drawers of reports and clippings; 7650 sheets of microfilm; drawings; 5700 photographs and slides. **Subscriptions:** 114 journals and other serials; 7 newspapers. **Services:** Interlibrary loans; library not open to public. **Special Catalogs:** File of manufacturers' catalogs (card); microfilm catalog (book). **Staff:** Dannie Martin, P.R.

★10893★
PORTSMOUTH ATHENAEUM - LIBRARY & MUSEUM (Hist)
9 Market Sq.
Box 848
Portsmouth, NH 03801-0848   Phone: (603) 431-2538
Founded: 1817. **Staff:** Prof 2. **Subjects:** Local history, genealogy. **Special Collections:** Local and New England Maritime/Naval History. **Holdings:** 26,000 books; charts and maps; New Hampshire Fire & Marine Insurance Company records, 1801-1823 (450 manuscripts); manuscripts relating to local history, politics and military affairs, 1756-1850; 45 volumes of newspapers. **Subscriptions:** 16 journals and other serials. **Services:** Library open to public for research use by written request for appointment. **Staff:** Mrs. Horace Mitchell, Libn.

PORTSMOUTH BAR ASSOCIATION
See: Norfolk and Portsmouth Bar Association

★10894★
PORTSMOUTH BAR AND LAW LIBRARY (Law)†
Scioto County Court House, 3rd Fl.   Phone: (614) 353-5111
Portsmouth, OH 45662   Otha Sanderlin, Libn.
Staff: 1. **Subjects:** Law. **Holdings:** 25,000 volumes. **Services:** Library not open to public.

★10895★
PORTSMOUTH GENERAL HOSPITAL - MEDICAL LIBRARY (Med)
850 Crawford Pkwy.   Phone: (804) 398-4000
Portsmouth, VA 23704   Linda Wilkinson, Sec.
Staff: 1. **Subjects:** Medicine and related fields. **Special Collections:** Continuing Medical Education Video Cassette Tapes. **Holdings:** 250 books; 50 bound periodical volumes; 60 other items. **Subscriptions:** 75 journals and other serials. **Services:** Interlibrary loans; library not open to public.

PORTSMOUTH PSYCHIATRIC CENTER
See: Virginia Center for Psychiatry

★10896★
PORTSMOUTH PUBLIC LIBRARY - LOCAL HISTORY ROOM (Hist)
601 Court St.   Phone: (804) 393-8501
Portsmouth, VA 23704   Octavia Parrish, Lib.Asst.
Staff: 1. **Subjects:** Local history, lighthouses and lightships, genealogy. **Special Collections:** Judge White Collection. **Holdings:** 2800 books; 200 bound periodical volumes; 35 maps; 280 documents; 1400 photographs. **Services:** Interlibrary loans; copying; SDI; room open to public. **Automated Operations:** Computerized cataloging.

★10897★
PORTSMOUTH PUBLIC LIBRARY - MUNICIPAL REFERENCE
601 Court St.
Portsmouth, VA 23704
Subjects: Municipal government. **Holdings:** 200 books. **Networks/ Consortia:** Member of Virginia Tidewater Consortium for Continuing Higher Education. **Remarks:** Presently inactive.

★10898★
PORTSMOUTH RECEIVING HOSPITAL - MEDICAL LIBRARY (Med)
25th & Elmwood   Phone: (614) 354-2804
Portsmouth, OH 45662   Jack W. Haffner, Educ.Coord.
Founded: 1966. **Staff:** Prof 1. **Subjects:** Psychiatry, psychology and related subjects. **Holdings:** 1509 books; 26 bound periodical volumes. **Subscriptions:** 24 journals and other serials. **Services:** Interlibrary loans; library open to staff and for research to college students. **Networks/ Consortia:** Member of Ohio Valley Area Libraries (OVAL). **Remarks:** Maintained by Ohio State Department of Mental Health.

★10899★
PORTUGUESE CONTINENTAL UNION OF THE U.S.A. - LIBRARY (Area-Ethnic)
899 Boylston St.   Phone: (617) 536-2916
Boston, MA 02115   Francisco J. Mendonca, Supreme Sec.-Libn.
Founded: 1955. **Staff:** 2. **Subjects:** Portugal and overseas provinces - history, geography, statistics, literature. **Holdings:** 2200 volumes. **Services:** Interlibrary loans; library open to public for reference and research work on request. **Staff:** Maria A. Reis, Asst.Libn.

POST (C.W.) CAMPUS
See: Long Island University - C.W. Post Campus

POST-HARVEST DOCUMENTATION SERVICE
See: Kansas State University - Food and Feed Grain Institute

★10900★
POST-TRIBUNE - LIBRARY (Publ)
1065 Broadway   Phone: (219) 881-3134
Gary, IN 46402   Louise K. Tucker, Chf.Libn.
Staff: Prof 1; Other 2. **Subjects:** Newspaper reference topics. **Special Collections:** Gary history; anniversary and special editions. **Holdings:** 300 books; 55 VF drawers of biographical clippings; 67 VF drawers of subject clipping files; 24 VF drawers of local and national photographs; microfilm, 1906 to present. **Services:** Library open to public with restrictions. **Computerized Information Services:** VU/TEXT.

★10901★
POST (Winfred L. and Elizabeth C.) FOUNDATION - MEMORIAL ART REFERENCE LIBRARY (Art)
300 Main St.   Phone: (417) 782-5419
Joplin, MO 64801   Leslie Simpson, Libn./Dir.
Founded: 1981. **Staff:** Prof 1; Other 1. **Subjects:** Visual arts, antiques, architecture, photography, historic preservation, heraldry. **Special Collections:** Picture file (reproductions of works of art; 4000 pictures); 16th- and 17th-century furniture; sculpture and paintings dating from 13th century. **Holdings:** 2000 books; 228 bound periodical volumes; 16 VF drawers of pictures, articles, pamphlets. **Subscriptions:** 31 journals and other serials. **Services:** Copying; library open to public.

POSTAL HISTORY SOCIETY LIBRARY
See: American Philatelic Research Library

★10902★
POSTGRADUATE CENTER FOR MENTAL HEALTH - EMIL A. GUTHEIL MEMORIAL LIBRARY (Med)
124 E. 28th St.   Phone: (212) 689-7700
New York, NY 10016   Mrs. Lee Mackler, Dir., Lib. & Info.Serv.
Founded: 1947. **Staff:** Prof 2; Other 2. **Subjects:** Psychiatry, psychology, community mental health, psychoanalysis. **Holdings:** 9500 books; 150 bound

periodical volumes; 7000 unbound journals; 2 VF cabinets of pamphlets. **Subscriptions:** 125 journals and other serials. **Services:** Interlibrary loans; copying; SDI; library open to professionals on payment of fee. **Computerized Information Services:** BRS. **Networks/Consortia:** Member of Greater Northeastern Regional Medical Library Program; METRO; Manhattan-Bronx Health Sciences Library Group. **Publications:** Acquisitions list, quarterly - staff and fellows. **Staff:** Ruth Schwartz, Asst.Libn.

★10903★
POTLATCH CORPORATION - WESTERN WOOD PRODUCTS DIV. ENGINEERING & TECHNICAL SERV. DEPT. - INFORMATION CTR. (Sci-Tech)
Box 1016   Phone: (208) 799-0123
Lewiston, ID 83501   J.B. Snodgrass, Mgr.
Subjects: Wood technology and engineering. **Holdings:** 800 books and bound periodical volumes; 5000 pamphlets. **Subscriptions:** 60 journals and other serials. **Services:** Center not open to public.

★10904★
POTOMAC ELECTRIC POWER COMPANY - LIBRARY (Energy; Sci-Tech)
1900 Pennsylvania Ave., N.W.   Phone: (202) 872-2361
Washington, DC 20068   Helen C. Jessup, Libn.
Founded: 1932. **Staff:** 1. **Subjects:** Electrical and mechanical engineering, accounting, automation, energy, data processing, personnel management, Washingtoniana. **Holdings:** 8500 books and bound periodical volumes. **Subscriptions:** 176 journals and other serials; 27 newspapers. **Services:** Interlibrary loans; library not open to public. **Publications:** Accessions list of new books.

POTOROKA (William) MEMORIAL LIBRARY
See: Alcoholism Foundation of Manitoba - William Potoroka Memorial Library

★10905★
POTTSTOWN MEMORIAL MEDICAL CENTER - MEDICAL STAFF LIBRARY (Med)
1600 E. High St.   Phone: (215) 327-7000
Pottstown, PA 19464   Marilyn D. Chapis, Med. Staff Libn.
Staff: 1. **Subjects:** Medical and surgical specialties. **Holdings:** 200 books; 700 bound periodical volumes. **Subscriptions:** 50 journals and other serials. **Services:** Interlibrary loans; library not open to public. **Computerized Information Services:** BRS. **Networks/Consortia:** Member of Delaware Valley Information Consortium (DEVIC).

★10906★
POTTSVILLE HOSPITAL AND WARNE CLINIC - MEDICAL LIBRARY (Med)
Jackson & Mauch Chunk Sts.   Phone: (717) 622-6120
Pottsville, PA 17901   Dorothy Rice, Libn.
Founded: 1955. **Staff:** Prof 1. **Subjects:** Medicine, surgery. **Holdings:** 500 books; 1555 bound periodical volumes; audiotapes of surgery, internal medicine, family practice and pediatrics. **Subscriptions:** 65 journals and other serials. **Services:** Interlibrary loans; copying; will answer brief inquiries and make referrals. **Networks/Consortia:** Member of Central Pennsylvania Health Sciences Library Association; Greater Northeastern Regional Medical Library Program.

★10907★
POUDRE VALLEY HOSPITAL - MEDIA RESOURCES LIBRARY (Med)†
1024 Lemay Ave.   Phone: (303) 482-4111
Fort Collins, CO 80524   Carole Trask, Libn.
Founded: 1969. **Staff:** Prof 1. **Subjects:** Medicine, nursing. **Holdings:** 2000 books; 2000 bound periodical volumes; 400 nonprint media items; 300 pamphlets; 200 microfiche. **Subscriptions:** 160 journals and other serials. **Services:** Interlibrary loans; copying; library open to public for reference use only. **Computerized Information Services:** MEDLINE; internal database. **Networks/Consortia:** Member of Colorado Council of Medical Librarians; Midcontinental Regional Medical Library Program; High Plains Regional Library System.

★10908★
POWELL, GOLDSTEIN, FRAZER & MURPHY - LIBRARY (Law)
1100 C & S National Bank Bldg.   Phone: (404) 572-6600
Atlanta, GA 30335   Margarette M. Dye, Libn.
Staff: Prof 2; Other 1. **Subjects:** Law - corporation, banking, securities, tax, labor, real estate. **Holdings:** 23,000 books; 417 bound periodical volumes. **Subscriptions:** 51 journals and other serials. **Services:** Interlibrary loans; copying; library open to public for reference use only on request. **Computerized Information Services:** LEXIS. **Staff:** Renee Ziegler, Asst.Libn.; Irene Hickson, Cat.

★10909★
POWELL (John Wesley) MEMORIAL MUSEUM - LIBRARY (Hist)
6 N. 7th Ave.
Box 747   Phone: (602) 645-2741
Page, AZ 86040
Subjects: John Wesley Powell (1834-1902) and his explorations of the Colorado Plateau areas of Utah and Arizona; Dominguez-Escalante expedition of 1776; Lake Powell Country and the Colorado River, 1776-1909. **Holdings:** 8 file drawers of manuscripts and photographs. **Services:** Library open to public with restrictions from May to October.

POWELL LIBRARY
See: University of California, Los Angeles - Oral History Program Library

POWELL (Robert L.) MEMORIAL LIBRARY
See: Los Angeles Baptist College - Robert L. Powell Memorial Library

POWER (F.B.) PHARMACEUTICAL LIBRARY
See: University of Wisconsin, Madison - F.B. Power Pharmaceutical Library

POWER (Howard Anderson) MEMORIAL LIBRARY
See: Magee-Womens Hospital - Howard Anderson Power Memorial Library

POWER (Patrick) LIBRARY
See: St. Mary's University - Patrick Power Library

★10910★
PPG INDUSTRIES, INC. - C & R GROUP - RESEARCH CENTER LIBRARY (Sci-Tech)
Rosanna Dr.
Box 1009   Phone: (412) 487-4500
Allison Park, PA 15101   Helen Lamrey, Supv., Info.Serv.
Founded: 1924. **Staff:** Prof 1; Other 3. **Subjects:** Chemistry - paint, polymer, organic; plastics; resins. **Holdings:** 4000 books; 6000 bound periodical volumes; 150 linear shelf feet of patents; 105 linear shelf feet of trade literature; 142 linear shelf feet of pamphlets, government documents. **Subscriptions:** 265 journals and other serials. **Services:** Interlibrary loans; copying; library open to public with restrictions. **Automated Operations:** Computerized serials routing list. **Computerized Information Services:** DIALOG, SDC. **Publications:** Research Review, monthly - for internal distribution only. **Formerly:** Its Coatings and Resins Division. **Also Known As:** Pittsburgh Plate Glass Company.

★10911★
PPG INDUSTRIES, INC. - CHEMICAL DIVISION - NATRIUM RESEARCH AND DEVELOPMENT LIBRARY (Sci-Tech)
Box 191   Phone: (304) 455-2200
New Martinsville, WV 26155   Alice K. Johnson, Libn.
Founded: 1945. **Staff:** 1. **Subjects:** Chemistry, chemical engineering. **Holdings:** 9000 books; 3350 bound periodical volumes; 88 VF drawers of confidential company reports; 275 reels of microfilm of U.S. chemical patents; 375 binders of patents, photocopies of articles, translations, pamphlets and correspondence. **Subscriptions:** 196 journals and other serials. **Services:** Interlibrary loans; library not open to public. **Computerized Information Services:** Barberton Information Retrieval System (internal database). **Also Known As:** Pittsburgh Plate Glass Company.

★10912★
PPG INDUSTRIES, INC. - CHEMICAL DIVISION - RESEARCH LIBRARY (Sci-Tech)
Box 31   Phone: (216) 848-4161
Barberton, OH 44203   Diana M. Danko, Supv., Info.Serv.
Founded: 1935. **Staff:** Prof 3; Other 3. **Subjects:** Industrial chemicals, chlorinated solvents, pigments, agricultural chemicals, optical materials. **Holdings:** 10,000 books; 7000 bound periodical volumes; 500 government documents; 5 VF drawers of translations; 100 dissertations; 25 VF drawers of patents. **Subscriptions:** 400 journals and other serials. **Services:** Interlibrary loans; copying; library open to public with restrictions. **Automated Operations:** Computerized cataloging. **Computerized Information Services:** DIALOG, SDC, NLM, CAS Online, OCLC, NIH/EPA Chemical Information System, Pergamon InfoLine Ltd.; internal database. **Publications:** Contents of Periodicals, weekly; Patent Bulletin, biweekly; monthly newsletter. **Staff:** Yvonne Pringle, Info.Spec.; R.L. Russell, Info.Spec.

★10913★
PPG INDUSTRIES, INC. - CHEMICAL DIVISION - RESEARCH LIBRARY (Sci-Tech)*
Box 4026
Corpus Christi, TX 78408
Phone: (512) 883-4301
Ivan C. Trombley, Res.Libn.
Founded: 1946. **Staff:** Prof 1; Other 1. **Subjects:** Chemistry and chemical engineering. **Holdings:** 5000 books; 5000 bound periodical volumes; U.S. patents in microform. **Subscriptions:** 175 journals and other serials. **Services:** Interlibrary loans; library not open to public.

★10914★
PPG INDUSTRIES, INC. - FIBER GLASS RESEARCH CENTER - LIBRARY (Sci-Tech)*
Box 2844
Pittsburgh, PA 15230
Phone: (412) 782-5130
Jacqueline A. Maxin, Supv., Info.Serv.
Staff: Prof 1; Other 1. **Subjects:** Science and technology - fiber glass, glass, plastics, rubber; polymer science. **Special Collections:** Foreign and domestic patents on fiber glass science and technology; Visual Search Microfilm File American Society of Testing and Materials standards/collection. **Holdings:** 750 books; 100 technical reports; 100 translations; 50 college catalogs; internal documents control. **Subscriptions:** 220 journals and other serials. **Services:** Interlibrary loans; copying; SDI; library open to public with permission. **Automated Operations:** Computerized cataloging. **Computerized Information Services:** DIALOG, SDC. **Networks/Consortia:** Member of Pittsburgh Regional Library Center (PRLC). **Publications:** Patent Bulletin, semimonthly; Current Contents, biweekly. **Special Indexes:** Index of internal documents (card).

★10915★
PPG INDUSTRIES, INC. - GENERAL OFFICE LIBRARY
One Gateway Center
Pittsburgh, PA 15222
Defunct

★10916★
PPG INDUSTRIES, INC. - GLASS RESEARCH CENTER - INFORMATION SERVICES (Sci-Tech)
Box 11472
Pittsburgh, PA 15238
Phone: (412) 665-8566
Jane Bookmyer, Supv.
Founded: 1912. **Staff:** Prof 2; Other 1. **Subjects:** Glass technology, physics, mathematics, chemistry, engineering, industrial management. **Special Collections:** U.S. patents on microfilm. **Holdings:** 25,000 books; 18,000 translations and technical reports; 1000 16mm cartridges of journals; 2000 microfiche of technical reports. **Subscriptions:** 400 journals and other serials. **Services:** Interlibrary loans; library not open to public. **Automated Operations:** Computerized cataloging, serials and circulation. **Computerized Information Services:** DIALOG, BRS, OCLC, SDC. **Networks/Consortia:** Member of Pittsburgh Regional Library Center (PRLC). **Publications:** Technical Information Bulletin, monthly - for internal distribution only. **Special Catalogs:** Catalog of internal research reports (card). **Staff:** Hazel Green, Tech.Serv.Libn.

★10917★
PPG INDUSTRIES, INC. - SPECIALTY PRODUCTS UNIT - LIBRARY (Sci-Tech)
12555 W. Higgins Rd.
Box 66251
Chicago, IL 60666
Phone: (312) 694-2700
Pamela R. Fritz, Info.Spec.
Staff: Prof 1; Other 1. **Subjects:** Chemistry - organic, technical, fire retardant; industrial toxicology. **Holdings:** 4000 books; 2000 bound periodical volumes; 200 government documents; 100 manufacturers' catalogs; U.S. chemical patents in microform, 1966 to present; 250 annual reports; 6 VF drawers of pamphlets. **Subscriptions:** 200 journals and other serials; 5 newspapers. **Services:** Interlibrary loans; library not open to public. **Computerized Information Services:** DIALOG, SDC, MEDLINE. **Networks/Consortia:** Member of Chicago Library System. **Publications:** Serials Holding, biennial - for internal distribution and to other special libraries.

★10918★
PQ CORPORATION - RESEARCH LIBRARY (Sci-Tech)
Box 258
Lafayette Hill, PA 19444
Phone: (215) 825-5000
Geraldine R. James, Libn.
Founded: 1927. **Subjects:** Inorganic chemistry, specializing in soluble silicates and silica. **Holdings:** 1700 books; 155 bound periodical volumes; 42 VF drawers of reports and patents. **Subscriptions:** 150 journals and other serials. **Services:** Interlibrary loans; copying; library open to public with approval. **Automated Operations:** Computerized cataloging. **Computerized Information Services:** DIALOG, SDC, Derwent Patents Documentation Services.

★10919★
PQA ENGINEERING - LIBRARY (Sci-Tech)†
90 Riverdale Rd.
Riverdale, NJ 07457
Phone: (201) 831-1500
Kathryn Sullivan, Libn.
Staff: Prof 1; Other 2. **Subjects:** Engineering - civil, environmental. **Holdings:** 4000 books. **Subscriptions:** 53 journals and other serials. **Services:** Interlibrary loans; copying; library open as a professional courtesy. **Computerized Information Services:** DIALOG.

★10920★
PRACTISING LAW INSTITUTE - LIBRARY (Law)
810 Seventh Ave.
New York, NY 10019
Phone: (212) 765-5700
Henry W. Enberg, II, Legal Ed.
Founded: 1933. **Staff:** Prof 1. **Subjects:** Law. **Holdings:** 3000 books. **Subscriptions:** 50 journals and other serials. **Services:** Library not open to public.

★10921★
PRAIRIE AGRICULTURAL MACHINERY INSTITUTE - LIBRARY (Agri; Sci-Tech)
Box 1900
Humboldt, SK, Canada S0K 2A0
Phone: (306) 682-2555
Bernadette Jansen, Lib.Techn.
Staff: Prof 1. **Subjects:** Agriculture, farm machinery testing, electronics, business management, photography. **Holdings:** 2100 books; 80 bound periodical volumes; 10,300 technical papers. **Subscriptions:** 145 journals and other serials; 5 newspapers. **Services:** Interlibrary loans; copying; SDI; library open to public. **Automated Operations:** Computerized cataloging. **Publications:** Evaluation reports - by subscription. **Special Catalogs:** Master bibliography and updates to technical papers.

★10922★
PRAIRIE BIBLE INSTITUTE - LIBRARY (Rel-Theol)
Three Hills, AB, Canada T0M 2A0
Phone: (403) 443-5511
Ron Jordahl, Libn.
Staff: 3. **Subjects:** Biblical studies, Christian missions, Christian biography, Christian education. **Holdings:** 33,000 books; 605 bound periodical volumes; 40 VF drawers of clippings; 240 reels of microfilm; 8750 microfiche; 2400 cassettes. **Subscriptions:** 295 journals and other serials. **Services:** Interlibrary loans; copying; library open to public for reference use only. **Automated Operations:** Computerized acquisitions. **Staff:** Colleen Hertzsprung, Pub.Serv.Libn.; Jacob Geddert, Tech.Serv.Libn.

PRAIRIE FARM REHABILITATION ADMINISTRATION
See: Canada - Prairie Farm Rehabilitation Administration

PRAIRIE MIGRATORY BIRD RESEARCH CENTRE
See: Canada - Canadian Wildlife Service

★10923★
PRAIRIE VIEW A & M COLLEGE OF TEXAS - W.R. BANKS LIBRARY - SPECIAL COLLECTIONS (Hum)†
Third St.
Box T
Prairie View, TX 77445
Phone: (409) 857-2012
Joyce Stimage, Spec.Coll.
Founded: 1912. **Special Collections:** Negro Collection (by and about Negroes); children's literature. **Holdings:** Figures not available. **Services:** Interlibrary loans; collections open to public with restrictions.

PRALL (Margaret) MUSIC LIBRARY
See: Mills College - Margaret Prall Music Library

PRANG-MARK SOCIETY
See: American Life Foundation

PRATT (Enoch) FREE LIBRARY
See: Enoch Pratt Free Library

★10924★
PRATT INSTITUTE - LIBRARY (Art; Sci-Tech)
200 Willoughby Ave.
Brooklyn, NY 11205
Phone: (718) 636-3545
George Lowy, Dean of Libs.
Founded: 1887. **Staff:** Prof 10; Other 13. **Subjects:** Fine arts, architecture, library science, science and technology. **Special Collections:** History of printing (2000 volumes). **Holdings:** 185,000 books; 28,600 bound periodical volumes; 128,000 government documents; 124,000 prints; 67,570 art slides; 16,000 microforms. **Subscriptions:** 750 journals. **Services:** Interlibrary loans; copying; library open to public with restrictions. **Automated Operations:** Computerized cataloging, acquisitions and serials. **Computerized Information Services:** DIALOG. **Networks/Consortia:** Member of METRO.

Special Catalogs: Periodicals in the Library. **Staff:** Tad G. Kumatz, Asst.Dir.; Josephine McSweeney, Ref.Libn.; Laura Noskowitz, Ref.Libn.; Sydney Keaveney, Art & Arch.Libn.; Amy Jo Goldfarb, Art & Arch.Libn.; Margot Karp, Lib.Sci.Libn.; Clare Higgins, Sci.Libn.

★10925★
PRATT INSTITUTE - PRATT/PHOENIX SCHOOL OF DESIGN LIBRARY (Art)
160 Lexington Ave.   Phone: (212) 685-2973
New York, NY 10016   Sharon Lewis, Libn.
Founded: 1974. **Staff:** 1. **Subjects:** Decoration and ornament; textile design; interiors; costumes; furnishings; fashion illustration; portrait, figure, still life and landscape painting; advertising design and illustration; magazine and book illustration; photography and film; furniture design; weaving; airbrush technique. **Special Collections:** History of ornament (3600 plates). **Holdings:** 2000 books; 30 bound periodical volumes; 8 VF drawers; 7500 pictures. **Subscriptions:** 32 journals and other serials. **Services:** Library not open to public. **Networks/Consortia:** Member of METRO. **Remarks:** This is a branch of the Pratt Institute Library, Brooklyn, NY 11205.

PRATT & WHITNEY AIRCRAFT GROUP
See: United Technologies Corporation

★10926★
PRATT AND WHITNEY CANADA, INC. - LIBRARY (Sci-Tech)
P.O. Box 10   Phone: (514) 677-9411
Longueuil, PQ, Canada J4K 4X9   Joyce C. Charlebois, Chf.Libn.
Founded: 1958. **Staff:** Prof 4; Other 3. **Subjects:** Aeronautics, mechanical and materials engineering, gas turbine engines, industrial management. **Holdings:** 6800 books; 2000 periodical volumes; 36,000 reports, patents and standards; 11,900 reports on microfiche. **Subscriptions:** 850 journals and other serials. **Services:** Interlibrary loans; library not open to public. **Automated Operations:** Computerized cataloging and serials routing. **Computerized Information Services:** SDC, CAN/OLE, DIALOG; Engineering Documents Index (EDI; internal database). **Networks/Consortia:** Member of United Technologies Library System. **Publications:** Periodicals in the Library, annual; Library Bulletin, Technical Reports Bulletin, both bimonthly - for internal distribution only. **Special Indexes:** KWOC Index for technical reports (online). **Staff:** Elizabeth Reader, Ref.Libn.; Suzanne Melville, Ref.Libn.Linda Kuchta, Cat.Libn.

★10927★
PRC CONSOER, TOWNSEND, INC. - LIBRARY AND INFORMATION CENTER (Sci-Tech)
3 Illinois Center
303 E. Wacker Dr., Suite 600   Phone: (312) 938-0300
Chicago, IL 60601   Mary T. Schramm, Libn./Mgr., Info.Ctr.
Founded: 1930. **Staff:** Prof 2. **Subjects:** Engineering and architecture. **Holdings:** 12,000 books; 170 bound periodical volumes; 1800 manufacturing catalogs; 2650 project reports (company owned); 28 VF drawers of pamphlets; 8000 microfiche. **Subscriptions:** 150 journals and other serials. **Services:** Interlibrary loans; library not open to public. **Computerized Information Services:** DIALOG, OCLC. **Networks/Consortia:** Member of ILLINET. **Publications:** Monthly report and publications list - for internal distribution only. **Special Catalogs:** Company reports, Contract Specifications, Design Calculations. **Remarks:** PRC Consoer, Townsend, Inc. is a subsidiary of Planning Research Corporation and a unit of PRC Engineering, Inc. **Special Collections:** Delia Ewig, Asst.Libn.

★10928★
PRC SPEAS - TECHNICAL LIBRARY (Sci-Tech; Trans)*
3003 New Hyde Park Rd.   Phone: (516) 488-6930
Lake Success, NY 11042   Maria D. Ferri, Tech.Libn.
Staff: 1. **Subjects:** Commercial aeronautics, airports, aeroplanes, aeronautics, air traffic control, airlines marketing, electronic data processing. **Special Collections:** R. Dixon Speas Associates Client Project Collection. **Holdings:** 1700 books and bound periodical volumes; 1600 volume project collection; 200 VF drawers of aviation reference files. **Subscriptions:** 400 journals and other serials. **Services:** Interlibrary loans; copying; library open to public by advance request. **Publications:** Recent Acquisitions, irregular - for internal distribution only.

★10929★
PRECISION CASTPARTS CORPORATION - TECHNICAL INFORMATION CENTER (Sci-Tech)
4600 S.E. Harney Dr.   Phone: (503) 777-3881
Portland, OR 97206   Pat Spurlock, Tech.Info.Spec.
Staff: Prof 1; Other 1. **Subjects:** Metal casting, alloys, titanium, manufacturing engineering. **Holdings:** 400 books; 400 unbound reports; 900 patents; 1000 government reports; 800 reprints. **Subscriptions:** 100

journals and other serials. **Services:** Interlibrary loans; center not open to public. **Automated Operations:** Computerized cataloging. **Computerized Information Services:** BRS, DIALOG, OCLC.

★10930★
PREFORMED LINE PRODUCTS - RESEARCH & ENGINEERING LIBRARY (Sci-Tech)
Box 91129   Phone: (216) 461-5200
Cleveland, OH 44101   Edwina T. Barron, Libn.
Founded: 1956. **Staff:** Prof 1. **Subjects:** Vibration, fatigue, strains and stresses, pole line hardware, electric power lines, oceanographic cable termination and fittings. **Special Collections:** CIGRE (International Conference on Large Electric Systems); American Institute of Electrical Engineers. **Holdings:** 6500 books; 600 bound periodical volumes; 55 VF drawers of technical papers (indexed); internal reports (indexed, on microfiche); 125 16mm films. **Subscriptions:** 150 journals and other serials. **Services:** Interlibrary loans; copying; library open by permission. **Publications:** R & E Library Bulletin, bimonthly. **Remarks:** Library is located at 660 Beta Dr., Cleveland, OH 44143.

PRENTICE-HALL - GREENVALE EDITORIAL SERVICES, INC.
See: Greenvale Editorial Services, Inc.

PRENTIS MEMORIAL LIBRARY
See: Temple Beth El

★10931★
PRESBYTERIAN CHURCH OF THE ATONEMENT - LIBRARY (Rel-Theol)
10613 Georgia Ave.   Phone: (301) 649-4131
Silver Spring, MD 20902   Lois Walker, Libn.
Staff: 1. **Subjects:** Christian doctrine, life and character, missions, biography and education, Bible. **Holdings:** 8500 books; VF drawer of pictures; 480 AV items; 475 phonograph records; 80 filmstrips; 1150 cassette tapes; 28 maps. **Subscriptions:** 25 journals and other serials. **Services:** Library open to public. **Formerly:** United Presbyterian Church of the Atonement.

★10932★
PRESBYTERIAN CHURCH (U.S.A). - PRESBYTERIAN HISTORICAL SOCIETY - LIBRARY (Hist; Rel-Theol)
425 Lombard St.   Phone: (215) 627-1852
Philadelphia, PA 19147   William B. Miller, Dir.
Founded: 1852. **Staff:** Prof 5; Other 6. **Subjects:** Presbyterian Church history, history of Protestantism, hymnology, slavery. **Special Collections:** Sheldon Jackson Collection (Alaska, circa 1870-1905); Westminster Assembly of Divines Collection (300 17th century pamphlets dealing with British church history); Westminster Press Depository Collection (2800 volumes). **Holdings:** 117,000 books; 500,000 manuscripts and primary source material; 1875 reels of microfilm; 9000 pictures of churches and ministers; 5000 communion tokens; 2.5 million arranged archives. **Subscriptions:** 407 journals and other serials. **Services:** Copying; reference service; library open to public. **Publications:** Journal of Presbyterian History, quarterly - by subscription and membership. **Formerly:** United Presbyterian Church in the U.S.A. **Staff:** Gerald W. Gillette, Mgr., Res. & Lib.Serv.; Jane Ramsay, Rec.Res.; Barbara Roy, Cat.Libn.; Frederic Heuser, Archv.

★10933★
PRESBYTERIAN COLLEGE - LIBRARY (Rel-Theol)
3495 University St.   Phone: (514) 288-5257
Montreal, PQ, Canada H3A 2A8   Rev. Daniel Shute, Libn.
Founded: 1867. **Staff:** Prof 1; Other 2. **Subjects:** Theology, church history, Reformation history, philosophy. **Special Collections:** Patrologia Graeco-Latina (Migne; 382 volumes). **Holdings:** 22,200 books and bound periodical volumes. **Subscriptions:** 50 journals and other serials. **Services:** Interlibrary loans; library open to public from September through May.

★10934★
PRESBYTERIAN DENVER HOSPITAL - BRADFORD MEMORIAL LIBRARY (Med)
1719 E. 19th Ave.   Phone: (303) 839-6440
Denver, CO 80218   Jody Helmer, Libn.
Founded: 1950. **Staff:** Prof 2. **Subjects:** Medicine, nursing, hospital administration, hospital chaplaincy. **Holdings:** 2147 books; 1108 bound periodical volumes; 768 AV items; 2 VF drawers of overhead transparencies; 4 drawers of LATCH files (bibliographies and articles on specific subjects). **Subscriptions:** 55 journals and other serials. **Services:** Interlibrary loans; library not open to public. **Computerized Information Services:** MEDLINE, DIALOG, Octanet. **Networks/Consortia:** Member of Denver Area Health Sciences Library Consortium; Colorado Council of Medical Librarians. **Remarks:** Library contains the holdings of the former Presbyterian/St. Luke's

School of Nursing Library. **Staff:** Mary Lindberg, Asst.Libn.

★10935★
PRESBYTERIAN HOSPITAL - LEARNING RESOURCE CENTER (Med)
Box 33549   Phone: (704) 371-4258
Charlotte, NC 28233   Ellen Cooper, Libn.
Staff: Prof 2; Other 6. **Subjects:** Nursing, medicine, allied health education. **Holdings:** 6000 books; 3 VF drawers; AV programs. **Subscriptions:** 200 journals and other serials. **Services:** Interlibrary loans; center not open to public. **Computerized Information Services:** MEDLINE. **Networks/Consortia:** Member of North Carolina Area Health Education Centers Program.

★10936★
PRESBYTERIAN HOSPITAL - MEDICAL LIBRARY (Med)
1100 Central Ave., S.E.   Phone: (505) 243-9411
Albuquerque, NM 87102   Helen Saylor, Med.Libn.
Founded: 1962. **Staff:** Prof 2; Other 1. **Subjects:** Medicine. **Holdings:** 1000 books; 1287 bound periodical volumes; unbound materials (9840 items). **Services:** Interlibrary loans; copying; library open to public by permission.

★10937★
PRESBYTERIAN HOSPITAL - MEDICAL LIBRARY (Med)
N.E. 13th and Lincoln Blvd.   Phone: (405) 271-4266
Oklahoma City, OK 73104   Dorothy Williams, Lib.Dir.
Founded: 1919. **Staff:** Prof 1; Other 2. **Subjects:** Medicine, nursing, surgery, cardiology. **Holdings:** 4000 books; 6000 bound periodical volumes; 24 boxes of pamphlets; 175 file boxes of unbound periodicals; 2 VF drawers; 800 cassettes. **Subscriptions:** 257 journals and other serials. **Services:** Interlibrary loans; library open to medical and health personnel for reference use only. **Computerized Information Services:** MEDLINE. **Networks/Consortia:** Member of Greater Oklahoma City Area Health Sciences Library Consortium (GOAL); has ILL arrangements with Dallas-Tarrant County Consortium of Health Science Libraries, Health Oriented Libraries of San Antonio (HOLSA) and New Mexico Consortium of Biomedical Libraries.

★10938★
PRESBYTERIAN/ST. LUKE'S SCHOOL OF NURSING - LIBRARY
2025 High St.   Phone: (303) 839-6081
Denver, CO 80205
Defunct. Absorbed by Presbyterian Denver Hospital - Bradford Memorial Library.

PRESBYTERIAN-UNIVERSITY HOSPITAL
See: University of Pittsburgh

★10939★
PRESBYTERIAN-UNIVERSITY OF PENNSYLVANIA MEDICAL CENTER - MARY ELLEN BROWN MEDICAL CENTER LIBRARY (Med)
51 N. 39th St.   Phone: (215) 662-9181
Philadelphia, PA 19104   Kathleen M. Ahrens, Libn.
Staff: Prof 1; Other 4. **Subjects:** Clinical medicine and nursing. **Holdings:** 2200 books; 3500 bound periodical volumes; 300 archival items; 70 AV materials; 3 VF drawers. **Subscriptions:** 246 journals and other serials. **Services:** Interlibrary loans; copying; library open to public with restrictions. **Computerized Information Services:** MEDLARS. **Networks/Consortia:** Member of Delaware Valley Information Consortium (DEVIC); Greater Northeastern Regional Medical Library Program.

PRESBYTERIAN-UNIVERSITY OF PENNSYLVANIA MEDICAL CENTER - SCHEIE EYE INSTITUTE
See: Scheie Eye Institute

PRESCOTT HISTORICAL SOCIETY
See: Sharlot Hall/Prescott Historical Societies

★10940★
PRESENTATION COLLEGE - LIBRARY (Med; Rel-Theol)
1500 North Main   Phone: (605) 225-0420
Aberdeen, SD 57401   Ellen F. Hall, Lib.Dir.
Founded: 1950. **Staff:** Prof 1; Other 2. **Subjects:** Nursing, theology. **Holdings:** 33,135 books; 2650 bound periodical volumes; 2140 recordings, filmstrips, reels of microfilm and cassettes; 8 VF drawers of pamphlets. **Subscriptions:** 190 journals and other serials; 9 newspapers. **Services:** Interlibrary loans; copying; library open to public with restrictions. **Computerized Information Services:** OCLC. **Networks/Consortia:** Member of MINITEX; Bibliographic Center for Research, Rocky Mountain Region, Inc. (BCR). **Staff:** Sr. Judith O'Brien, Cat.

PRESIDENT BENJAMIN HARRISON FOUNDATION
See: Harrison (Benjamin) Memorial Home

PRESIDENTIAL MUSEUM
See: U.S. Presidential Museum

PRESIDENT'S COMMITTEE ON EMPLOYMENT OF THE HANDICAPPED ARCHIVES
See: Marquette University - Department of Special Collections and University Archives

PRESIDENTS HEALTH SCIENCES LIBRARY
See: St. Anne's Hospital

★10941★
PRESS CLUB OF SAN FRANCISCO - WILL AUBREY MEMORIAL LIBRARY
555 Post St.   Phone: (415) 775-7800
San Francisco, CA 94102   Harry R. Illman, Libn.
Founded: 1888. **Subjects:** Biography, Californiana, fiction, history. **Holdings:** 5000 volumes. **Services:** Library not open to public.

PRESTON LIBRARY
See: Virginia Military Institute

PRESTON MEDICAL LIBRARY
See: University of Tennessee - Memorial Research Center and Hospital

★10942★
PRESTON, THORGRIMSON, ELLIS & HOLMAN - LIBRARY (Law)
2000 IBM Bldg.
Box 2927   Phone: (206) 623-7580
Seattle, WA 98111   Margaret Chillingworth, Libn.
Staff: Prof 2; Other 1. **Subjects:** Law. **Holdings:** 14,000 volumes. **Subscriptions:** 161 journals and other serials; 9 newspapers. **Services:** Interlibrary loans; copying; SDI; library open to public with permission. **Computerized Information Services:** LEXIS, DIALOG. Performs searches on abbreviated cost recovery basis. **Networks/Consortia:** Member of Puget Sound Law Librarians. **Publications:** New Acquisitions List, irregular. **Staff:** Marjorie Doyle, Asst.Libn.

PREUS LIBRARY
See: Luther College

PRICE (Isser and Rae) LIBRARY OF JUDAICA
See: University of Florida - Isser and Rae Price Library of Judaica

PRICE & LEE COMPANY DIRECTORY LIBRARY
See: Association of North American Directory Publishers

★10943★
PRICE-POTTENGER NUTRITION FOUNDATION - LIBRARY (Med)
5871 El Cajon Blvd.   Phone: (619) 582-4168
San Diego, CA 92115   Patricia Connolly, Cur.
Founded: 1975. **Subjects:** Nutrition, health, agrobiology, gardening, pesticide, poisoning, medicine. **Special Collections:** Complete works of Dr. Weston A. Price and Dr. Francis M. Pottenger; pesticide research of Dr. G.F. Knight; papers of Dr. William A. Albrecht; scientific studies. **Holdings:** Scientific reprints; tapes; film. **Services:** Copying; distribution of books, reprints and films; library open to PPNF members. **Publications:** PPNF Journal, quarterly.

★10944★
PRICE WATERHOUSE - AUDIT LIBRARY (Bus-Fin)
1075 W. Georgia St., No. 1500   Phone: (604) 682-4711
Vancouver, BC, Canada V6E 3G1   Janet A. Parkinson, Libn.
Staff: Prof 1. **Subjects:** Accounting, auditing, taxation. **Holdings:** 2000 books and bound periodical volumes; newspaper clipping file and financial pages; Price Waterhouse external publications; corporate annual reports for 500 Canadian companies. **Subscriptions:** 30 journals and other serials; 7 newspapers. **Services:** Interlibrary loans; library not open to public. **Computerized Information Services:** Info Globe.

★10945★
PRICE WATERHOUSE - INFORMATION CENTER (Bus-Fin)
3500 One Biscayne Tower   Phone: (305) 358-3682
Miami, FL 33131   Susan Waters, Info.Spec.
Staff: Prof 1; Other 1. **Subjects:** Accounting and auditing, taxation, business. **Holdings:** 1500 books; 600 annual reports; Price Waterhouse external publications; 55 looseleaf services. **Subscriptions:** 80 journals and other

serials; 6 newspapers. **Services:** Interlibrary loans; center open to public by appointment. **Computerized Information Services:** DIALOG, SDC, NewsNet, Inc.

★10946★
PRICE WATERHOUSE - INFORMATION CENTER (Bus-Fin)
One Federal St.   Phone: (617) 423-7330
Boston, MA 02110   Jean M. Scanlan, Mgr.
Founded: 1976. **Staff:** Prof 2. **Subjects:** Accounting, taxation, management, finance. **Holdings:** 2500 books; 60 reels of microfilm; microfiche. **Subscriptions:** 200 journals and other serials. **Services:** Interlibrary loans; copying; SDI; center open to public by appointment. **Computerized Information Services:** Dun & Bradstreet Corporation, DIALOG, SDC, LEXIS. **Publications:** What's New in the Price Waterhouse Information Center, monthly - for internal distribution only. **Staff:** Suzanne Bremer, Asst. to Mgr.

★10947★
PRICE WATERHOUSE - LIBRARY (Bus-Fin)
400 S. Hope St.   Phone: (213) 625-4583
Los Angeles, CA 90071-2889   Mignon Veasley, Hd.Libn.
Staff: Prof 1; Other 2. **Subjects:** Accounting, business, management, investment, auditing, taxation. **Holdings:** Figures not available for books. **Subscriptions:** 200 journals and other serials. **Services:** Interlibrary loans; library not open to public. **Computerized Information Services:** LEXIS, NEXIS, DIALOG. **Publications:** Periodical list.

★10948★
PRICE WATERHOUSE - LIBRARY (Bus-Fin)†
200 E. Randolph Dr., Rm. 6200   Phone: (312) 565-1500
Chicago, IL 60601   E. Ann Raup, Libn.
Founded: 1970. **Staff:** 2. **Subjects:** Accounting, auditing, management. **Holdings:** 1000 books; 120 bound periodical volumes; 49 VF drawers of corporate annual reports. **Subscriptions:** 133 journals and other serials. **Services:** Interlibrary loans (local only); library open to public by appointment.

★10949★
PRICE WATERHOUSE - LIBRARY (Bus-Fin)
1200 McGill College Ave.   Phone: (514) 879-9050
Montreal, PQ, Canada H3B 2G4   Martha Nugent
Founded: 1945. **Staff:** Prof 1. **Subjects:** Accounting, auditing, management, consulting, taxation. **Holdings:** 1800 books; 100 bound periodical volumes. **Subscriptions:** 80 journals and other serials. **Services:** Interlibrary loans; library not open to public.

★10950★
PRICE WATERHOUSE - NATIONAL INFORMATION CENTER (Bus-Fin)
1251 Ave. of the Americas   Phone: (212) 489-8900
New York, NY 10020   Masha Zipper, Mgr.
Staff: Prof 8; Other 10. **Subjects:** Accounting, auditing, business, United States and international taxation. **Holdings:** 15,000 books and bound periodical volumes; 70 VF drawers; 1000 reels of microfilm; 860,000 microfiche. **Services:** Interlibrary loans; center open to clients and Special Libraries Association members. **Automated Operations:** Computerized routing system. **Computerized Information Services:** DIALOG, Dow Jones News/Retrieval, LEXIS, NEXIS, National Automated Accounting Research System (NAARS), SDC, TEXTLINE, BNA Advanceline. **Publications:** National Information Center Acquisitions. **Staff:** Ann Alexanian, Asst. to Mgr; Dennis Dilno, Hd.Cat.; Rita Van Buren, Intl. Tax Spec.; Terry Bennett, Info.Spec.; Nancy Trott, Info.Spec.; Jane Axelrod, U.S. Tax Spec.; Chung Lee, Asst.Cat.

★10951★
PRICE WATERHOUSE - NATIONAL/TORONTO OFFICE LIBRARY (Bus-Fin)
Toronto Dominion Centre
P.O. Box 51   Phone: (416) 863-1133
Toronto, ON, Canada M5K 1G1   Dorothy L. Sedgwick, Hd.Libn.
Staff: Prof 2; Other 2. **Subjects:** Accounting, auditing, business, finance, management. **Holdings:** 5000 volumes; 1200 annual reports (Canadian, U.S. and other); Conference Board publications; annual reports for Canadian companies on microfiche. **Subscriptions:** 150 journals and other serials; 6 newspapers. **Services:** Interlibrary loans; library not open to public. **Computerized Information Services:** SDC, Info Globe, QL Systems, DIALOG, Dun & Bradstreet Corporation. **Publications:** Professional Reading, bimonthly. **Staff:** Nancy Wells, Asst.Libn.

★10952★
PRICE WATERHOUSE - NEW YORK OFFICE INFORMATION CENTER (Bus-Fin)
153 E. 53rd St.   Phone: (212) 371-2000
New York, NY 10022   Patricia R. Pauth, Adm.
Founded: 1972. **Staff:** Prof 4; Other 4. **Subjects:** Accounting. **Holdings:**

4500 books; 180 bound periodical volumes; corporation reports for 3000 companies; securities prices in microform. **Subscriptions:** 350 journals and other serials. **Services:** Interlibrary loans; center open to public by appointment. **Computerized Information Services:** DIALOG, Dow Jones News/Retrieval, LEXIS, NEXIS, SDC, Dun & Bradstreet Corporation. **Staff:** Elizabeth Croft, Asst.Adm.; Victoria De Persiis Vona, Info.Spec.; Deirdre Marks, Info.Spec.

★10953★
PRICE WATERHOUSE - TAX LIBRARY (Bus-Fin; Law)†
153 E. 53rd St.   Phone: (212) 371-2000
New York, NY 10022   Barbara Ferrante, Tax Libn.
Staff: Prof 1. **Subjects:** Taxation law, international tax law. **Holdings:** 3300 books; 324 bound periodical volumes; 150 vertical files on taxation. **Subscriptions:** 22 journals and other serials. **Services:** Interlibrary loans; library open to clients and SLA members. **Computerized Information Services:** LEXIS.

★10954★
PRICHARD (Cleveland) MEMORIAL LIBRARY (Hist)
4559 Old Citronelle Hwy.   Phone: (205) 457-5242
Prichard, AL 36613   Johnnie Andrews, Jr., Dir.
Founded: 1955. **Staff:** Prof 1; Other 4. **Subjects:** City of Mobile and Alabama; genealogy; history of Louisiana, Florida and Mississippi; French, Spanish and English colonial history; black history. **Special Collections:** Manuscripts; early church records dating from 1594 from numerous colonial towns; art collection (1000 prints, etchings and paintings, 1717 to present). **Holdings:** 15,000 books; 1000 colonial manuscripts; 200 Overby photo manuscripts; 300 railroad manuscripts; 300 early maps; 3000 pamphlets; 50,000 clippings in vertical files; 3000 photographs, 1865 to present; 27,000 pages of records on Southern and Colonial history including 16,200 copies of colonial archives. **Subscriptions:** 105 journals and other serials; 20 newspapers. **Services:** Copying; translation of holdings; library open to public. **Publications:** Quarterly publications on Gulf Coast history. **Special Indexes:** Card indexes to library holdings on local history collections in 170 Southern libraries; Index on 150,000 Gulf Coast area residents from 1565-1876 (card).

PRIDE
See: **National Parents' Resource Institute for Drug Education, Inc.**

PRIMATE INFORMATION CENTER
See: **University of Washington - Regional Primate Research Center**

★10955★
PRIME COMPUTER, INC. - INFORMATION CENTER (Comp Sci; Bus-Fin)†
500 Old Connecticut Path   Phone: (617) 879-2960
Framingham, MA 01701   Linda Loring Shea, Corp.Libn.
Founded: 1978. **Staff:** Prof 2; Other 1. **Subjects:** Computer science, business, management, library science. **Holdings:** 1500 books; 3000 technical reports; 80 titles of journals on microfiche. **Subscriptions:** 105 journals and other serials. **Services:** Interlibrary loans; library not open to public. **Automated Operations:** Computerized cataloging. **Computerized Information Services:** OCLC, DIALOG. **Networks/Consortia:** Member of NELINET. **Publications:** Newsletter, monthly - for internal distribution only. **Special Indexes:** KWIC index to technical reports. **Staff:** Susan Keith, Info.Spec.

★10956★
PRINCE COUNTY HOSPITAL - MEDICAL LIBRARY (Med)
                                         Phone: (902) 436-9131
Summerside, PE, Canada C1N 2A9   Dr. J.P. Schaefer, Dir.
Subjects: Medicine. **Holdings:** 2000 books; 200 bound periodical volumes. **Subscriptions:** 20 journals and other serials. **Services:** Interlibrary loans; library open to public with restrictions.

★10957★
PRINCE EDWARD HEIGHTS - RESIDENT RECORDS LIBRARY (Med; Soc Sci)
Box 440   Phone: (613) 476-2104
Picton, ON, Canada K0K 2T0   Deborah Norton, Health Rec.Adm.
Staff: 1. **Subjects:** Mental retardation, psychology, medicine, pharmacy, social work, management. **Holdings:** 758 volumes; 74 files of reference material; 2 educational kits. **Subscriptions:** 34 journals and other serials. **Services:** Interlibrary loans; copying; library open to public. **Remarks:** Maintained by Ontario - Ministry of Community and Social Services.

★10958★
PRINCE EDWARD ISLAND - DEPARTMENT OF EDUCATION - MEDIA CENTRE (Aud-Vis)
202 Richmond St.   Phone: (902) 892-3504
Charlottetown, PE, Canada C1A 1J2   Bill Ledwell, Chf. of Educ. Media
Founded: 1946. **Staff:** Prof 2; Other 5. **Subjects:** General topics. **Holdings:** 3200 16mm films; 600 videotapes; 200 multimedia kits. **Subscriptions:** 13 journals and other serials. **Services:** Center open to public. **Automated Operations:** Computerized circulation. **Remarks:** Media centre serves as distribution outlet for National Film Board in Prince Edward Island.

PRINCE EDWARD ISLAND - DEPARTMENT OF EDUCATION - PLANNING LIBRARY
See: Prince Edward Island - Planning Library

★10959★
PRINCE EDWARD ISLAND - LEGISLATIVE LIBRARY
Confederation Centre Library
P.O. Box 7000
Charlottetown, PE, Canada C1A 7M8
Defunct

★10960★
PRINCE EDWARD ISLAND MUSEUM AND HERITAGE FOUNDATION - GENEALOGICAL COLLECTION (Hist)
2 Kent St.   Phone: (902) 892-9127
Charlottetown, PE, Canada C1A 1M6   Miss Orlo Jones, Prov.Geneal.
Staff: Prof 1. **Subjects:** Genealogy. **Holdings:** 200 books; 10 drawers of manuscript genealogies; 70 bound genealogies; 2 VF drawers of manuscript transcriptions of local cemeteries. **Subscriptions:** 50 journals and other serials. **Services:** Copying (limited); collection open to public. **Special Indexes:** Index to persons having lived on Prince Edward Island (500,000 cards).

★10961★
PRINCE EDWARD ISLAND - PLANNING LIBRARY (Plan; Med)
Box 2000   Phone: (902) 892-3504
Charlottetown, PE, Canada C1A 7N8   Marilyn Bell, Libn.
Founded: 1968. **Staff:** Prof 1. **Subjects:** Planning and development, economics, education, agriculture, recreation and tourism, health services administration. **Holdings:** 8000 books; 500 linear feet of Canadian federal government publications (depository); 66 linear feet of provincial government publications; 8 VF drawers of pamphlets. **Subscriptions:** 250 journals and other serials. **Services:** Interlibrary loans; copying; library open to public. **Remarks:** Maintained by the Department of Education. Includes the holdings of the former Prince Edward Island - Department of Health and Social Services - Health Branch Central Library.

★10962★
PRINCE EDWARD ISLAND - PUBLIC ARCHIVES (Hist)
P.O. Box 1000   Phone: (902) 892-7949
Charlottetown, PE, Canada C1A 7M4   N.J. de Jong, Prov.Archv.
Founded: 1964. **Staff:** Prof 2; Other 1. **Subjects:** History and government of Prince Edward Island. **Holdings:** 600 books; 40 linear meters of bound periodical volumes; 2000 linear meters of archives. **Subscriptions:** 10 journals and other serials. **Services:** Copying; archives open to public.

★10963★
PRINCE GEORGE CITIZEN - NEWSPAPER LIBRARY (Publ)
150 Brunswick St.   Phone: (604) 562-2441
Prince George, BC, Canada V2L 4T1   Sheryl Timmer, Libn.
Staff: Prof 1. **Subjects:** Newspaper reference topics. **Holdings:** 100 books; 1530 files of clippings; 420 files of photographs; 300 reels of microfilm; 200 documents and pamphlets. **Subscriptions:** 16 journals and other serials. **Services:** Library open to public with restrictions. **Special Indexes:** Editorial index (card).

★10964★
PRINCE GEORGE CITY PLANNING DEPARTMENT - PLANNING LIBRARY (Plan)
1100 Patricia Blvd.   Phone: (604) 564-5151
Prince George, BC, Canada V2L 3V9   Kent Sedgwick, Libn.
Subjects: Planning, policy, environmental studies, economic development, design, housing, zoning bylaws. **Holdings:** 1300 books; 50 bound periodical volumes. **Subscriptions:** 25 journals and other serials. **Services:** Library open to public with prior permission of librarian.

★10965★
PRINCE GEORGE'S COUNTY CIRCUIT COURT - LAW LIBRARY (Law)
Courthouse
Box 580   Phone: (301) 952-3438
Upper Marlboro, MD 20772   Pamela J. Gregory, Law Libn.
Staff: Prof 1; Other 2. **Subjects:** Law, Maryland law and history. **Special Collections:** Maryland State documents depository. **Holdings:** 23,000 books; 500 bound periodical volumes; 3 VF drawers of state agency regulations and materials; 15 years of county local legislation. **Subscriptions:** 300 journals and other serials. **Services:** Interlibrary loans; copying; library open to members of the bar and persons representing themselves in litigation. **Computerized Information Services:** Westlaw, DIALOG. **Networks/Consortia:** Member of LAWNET. **Publications:** Selected List of Acquisitions. **Special Indexes:** Index to County Charter; Index to Prince George's County Legislation.

★10966★
PRINCE GEORGE'S COUNTY HEALTH DEPARTMENT - PUBLIC HEALTH RESOURCE CENTER (Med)
Cheverly, MD 20778   Peggy H. Roeder, Libn.
Staff: Prof 1; Other 1. **Subjects:** Public health, health education, nursing, mental health, administration, geriatrics. **Holdings:** 1500 books; educational pamphlets. **Subscriptions:** 100 journals and other serials. **Services:** Interlibrary loans; copying; center open to public. **Publications:** Resource Center Register, quarterly - for internal distribution only.

★10967★
PRINCE GEORGE'S COUNTY MEMORIAL LIBRARY SYSTEM - PUBLIC DOCUMENTS REFERENCE LIBRARY (Plan)
County Adm.Bldg., Rm. 2198   Phone: (301) 952-3904
Upper Marlboro, MD 20772   Marjorie M. Miller, Doc.Libn.
Founded: 1977. **Staff:** Prof 1; Other 1. **Subjects:** County government, regional planning, zoning. **Special Collections:** Published county documents; documents from bi-county and regional agencies, municipalities (3000). **Holdings:** 500 books; 3000 documents; 250 microfilm cartridges; 63 feet of bill files; 192 feet of zoning files. **Subscriptions:** 50 journals and other serials; 8 newspapers. **Services:** Copying; library open to public for reference use only, circulation reserved for county employees. **Publications:** Newsletter, bimonthly - to county departments and selected libraries. **Special Catalogs:** Catalog of county publications. **Special Indexes:** Subject index to county council bills and resolutions (card).

★10968★
PRINCE GEORGE'S COUNTY MEMORIAL LIBRARY SYSTEM - SOJOURNER TRUTH ROOM (Hist)
6200 Oxon Hill Rd.   Phone: (301) 839-2400
Oxon Hill, MD 20745   Cherie P. Barnett, Cur.
Staff: Prof 1; Other 1. **Subjects:** Blacks - women, family, slavery, civil rights. **Special Collections:** Slave narratives (25). **Holdings:** 3000 books; 127 bound periodical volumes; 7 VF drawers of clippings, pamphlets, and government documents; 68 reels of microfilmed periodicals. **Subscriptions:** 17 journals and other serials. **Services:** Copying; library open to public with restrictions. **Automated Operations:** Computerized circulation. **Computerized Information Services:** CLSI (internal database).

★10969★
PRINCE GEORGE'S COUNTY PUBLIC SCHOOLS - PROFESSIONAL LIBRARY (Educ)
8437 Landover Rd.   Phone: (301) 773-9790
Landover, MD 20785   Dr. Edward W. Barth, Supv., Lib. & Media Serv.
Founded: 1960. **Staff:** Prof 4; Other 2. **Subjects:** Education - all subject areas. **Special Collections:** Maryland Collection; Prince George's County Collection (150 books). **Holdings:** 10,000 books; 200 AV materials; 300 public school curriculum guides; 295 journals in microform. **Subscriptions:** 349 journals and other serials. **Services:** Interlibrary loans; copying; library open to public for reference use only. **Computerized Information Services:** Online systems. **Networks/Consortia:** Member of Maryland Interlibrary Loan Organization (MILO); Metropolitan Washington Library Council. **Staff:** Joyce E. Meucci, Lib.Assoc.; Mary Dunn, Libn.; Lida Lou Larsen, Libn.

★10970★
PRINCE GEORGE'S GENERAL HOSPITAL & MEDICAL CENTER - SAUL SCHWARTZBACH MEMORIAL LIBRARY (Med)
                                                    Phone: (301) 341-2440
Cheverly, MD 20785   Eleanor Kleman, Med.Libn.
Staff: Prof 1; Other 1. **Subjects:** Medicine. **Holdings:** 1000 books; 2500 bound periodical volumes; 2350 AV materials. **Subscriptions:** 180 journals and other serials. **Services:** Interlibrary loans; copying; library open to public for reference use only. **Computerized Information Services:** MEDLARS.

Networks/Consortia: Member of Maryland and D.C. Consortium of Resource Sharing (MADCORS).

★10971★
PRINCE OF PEACE LUTHERAN CHURCH - LIBRARY (Rel-Theol)
4419 S. Howell Ave.   Phone: (414) 483-3020
Milwaukee, WI 53207   Mrs. Robert Heinritz, Hd.Libn.
Founded: 1963. **Staff:** 6. **Subjects:** Religion, missions, children's literature. **Special Collections:** Works of Martin Luther. **Holdings:** 3085 books; archives; VF drawers; cassette tapes; maps. **Services:** Library not open to public.

★10972★
PRINCE WILLIAM COUNTY SCHOOLS - STAFF LIBRARY (Educ)
Box 389   Phone: (703) 791-7334
Manassas, VA 22110   Dr. Bobbie J. Bowyer, Staff Libn.
Founded: 1962. **Staff:** Prof 1; Other 1. **Subjects:** Education, psychology, management, library science. **Holdings:** 4936 books; 959 pamphlets; commercial catalog and educational material files; unbound periodicals; newsletters. **Subscriptions:** 120 journals and other serials. **Services:** Library open to public.

★10973★
PRINCETON ANTIQUES BOOKFINDERS - ART MARKETING REFERENCE LIBRARY (Art)
2915-17-31 Atlantic Ave.   Phone: (609) 344-1943
Atlantic City, NJ 08401   Robert Eugene, Cur.
Founded: 1974. **Staff:** Prof 1. **Subjects:** Science and technology, living arts, fiction, collectibles. **Special Collections:** Postcard Photo Library (250,000). **Holdings:** 175,000 books. **Subscriptions:** 25 journals and other serials. **Services:** Library open to public by appointment. **Staff:** Robert E. Ruffolo, II, Pres.

★10974★
PRINCETON LIBRARY IN NEW YORK (Hist)
15 W. 43rd St.   Phone: (212) 840-6400
New York, NY 10036   Paula Matta, Libn.
Founded: 1962. **Subjects:** Princetoniana. **Holdings:** 8500 books. **Subscriptions:** 50 journals and other serials. **Services:** Library is for use of Princeton Club members, alumni, visiting scholars and accredited members of historical, literary or comparable organizations.

★10975★
PRINCETON POLYMER LABORATORIES, INC. - LIBRARY (Sci-Tech)
501 Plainsboro Rd.   Phone: (609) 799-2060
Plainsboro, NJ 08536   Carol Troy, Libn.
Founded: 1970. **Staff:** Prof 1. **Subjects:** Polymer technology; chemistry - organic, inorganic, physical. **Holdings:** 1000 books; 3 VF drawers of U.S. and foreign patents. **Subscriptions:** 30 journals and other serials. **Services:** Library not open to public.

★10976★
PRINCETON THEOLOGICAL SEMINARY - SPEER LIBRARY (Rel-Theol)
Mercer St. & Library Pl.
Box 111   Phone: (609) 921-8300
Princeton, NJ 08540   Dr. Charles Willard, Libn.
Founded: 1812. **Staff:** Prof 6; Other 7. **Subjects:** Theology, Presbyterianism, Semitic philology, Biblical studies, church history. **Special Collections:** Benson Collection of Hymnology; collection of Puritan and English theological literature; Agnew Collection on the Baptism Controversy; Sprague Collection of Early American Pamphlets. **Holdings:** 286,540 books and bound periodical volumes; 57,113 bound pamphlets; 100,000 manuscripts; 1962 reels of microfilm; 3000 cuneiform tablets. **Subscriptions:** 2000 journals and other serials. **Services:** Interlibrary loans; copying; library open to public. **Automated Operations:** Computerized cataloging. **Computerized Information Services:** DIALOG, OCLC, BRS. **Networks/Consortia:** Member of PHUY. **Staff:** Katy Skrebutenas, Ref. Libn.; Dr. James S. Irvine, Asst.Libn., Pub.Serv.

★10977★
PRINCETON UNIVERSITY - ASTRONOMY LIBRARY (Sci-Tech)
Peyton Hall   Phone: (609) 452-3820
Princeton, NJ 08544   Peter Cziffra, Libn.
Staff: Prof 1; Other 1. **Subjects:** Astronomy, astrophysics, astronomical observations. **Holdings:** 15,000 books and bound periodical volumes; 8000 pamphlets. **Subscriptions:** 220 journals and other serials. **Services:** Interlibrary loans; copying; reference and bibliographic services to members of department; library open to others for reference use only. **Computerized Information Services:** RLIN.

★10978★
PRINCETON UNIVERSITY - BIOLOGY LIBRARY (Sci-Tech)
Guyot Hall   Phone: (609) 452-3235
Princeton, NJ 08544   Helen Y. Zimmerberg, Libn.
Staff: Prof 1; Other 3. **Subjects:** Biology, biochemistry, microbiology, zoology, botany, molecular biology, genetics, ecology, population biology. **Holdings:** 18,500 books; 21,500 bound periodical volumes. **Subscriptions:** 1000 journals and other serials. **Services:** Interlibrary loans; copying; library open to public. **Computerized Information Services:** DIALOG, BRS. **Publications:** Acquisitions List.

★10979★
PRINCETON UNIVERSITY - CHEMISTRY & BIOCHEMISTRY LIBRARY (Sci-Tech)
Frick Chemical Laboratory   Phone: (609) 452-3238
Princeton, NJ 08544   Dr. David Goodman, Libn.
Staff: Prof 1; Other 2. **Subjects:** Chemistry - general, physical, organic, inorganic, biochemistry, molecular biology. **Holdings:** 20,000 books; 24,000 bound periodical volumes; 1200 departmental dissertations. **Subscriptions:** 600 journals and other serials. **Services:** Interlibrary loans (through main library); copying; reference, bibliographic and computer database searching services to members of the university; library open to others for reference use only. **Computerized Information Services:** DIALOG, BRS, SDC. **Networks/Consortia:** Member of RLG. **Publications:** New Books and News.

★10980★
PRINCETON UNIVERSITY - DEPARTMENT OF ART & ARCHAEOLOGY - INDEX OF CHRISTIAN ART (Art)
McCormick Hall   Phone: (609) 452-3773
Princeton, NJ 08544   Nigel Morgan, Act.Dir.
Founded: 1917. **Staff:** Prof 4; Other 2. **Subjects:** Christian art before 1400. **Holdings:** Iconographic index (600,000 cards); 250,000 photographs. **Services:** Reference for visiting scholars, mainly in history of art. **Staff:** E.H. Beatson; A.L. Bennett Hagens; R. Melzak.

★10981★
PRINCETON UNIVERSITY - ENGINEERING LIBRARY (Sci-Tech)
Engineering Quadrangle   Phone: (609) 452-3200
Princeton, NJ 08544   Dolores M. Hoelle, Libn.
Staff: Prof 4; Other 7. **Subjects:** Engineering - chemical, civil, electrical, mechanical, nuclear, aeronautical; solid state physics; polymers; computers; transportation; environmental studies; water resources. **Holdings:** 60,000 books; 60,000 bound periodical volumes; 400,000 technical reports and government documents, including 52 file cabinets of microfiche. **Subscriptions:** 1400 journals and other serials. **Services:** Interlibrary loans; copying; bibliographic and reference service for members of school; library open to others for reference use only. **Automated Operations:** Computerized cataloging, acquisitions and circulation. **Computerized Information Services:** DIALOG, BRS, STN International, NASA/RECON; GEAC Circulation System (internal database). Performs searches on cost recovery basis. **Networks/Consortia:** Member of RLG. **Staff:** Lois M. Nase, Asst.Libn.; Alan F. Cook, Asst.Libn.; Ann C. Doyle, Asst.Libn.

★10982★
PRINCETON UNIVERSITY - GEOLOGY LIBRARY (Sci-Tech)
Guyot Hall   Phone: (609) 452-3267
Princeton, NJ 08544   David C. Stager, Geology Libn.
Staff: Prof 2; Other 3. **Subjects:** Geology - crystallography, geochemistry, geomorphology, geophysics, mineralogy, oceanography, paleontology, petrology, sedimentation, stratigraphy, structural geology. **Holdings:** 60,000 books and bound periodical volumes; 900 theses; 127,000 maps; 450 technical reports. **Subscriptions:** 1200 journals and other serials. **Services:** Interlibrary loans; copying; library open to public. **Computerized Information Services:** DIALOG, RLIN; GEOMAP (internal database). Performs searches on cost recovery basis. Contact Person: Patricia Gaspari Bridges, 452-3247. **Staff:** Patricia Gaspari Bridges, Asst.Libn./Map Libn.

★10983★
PRINCETON UNIVERSITY - GEST ORIENTAL LIBRARY AND EAST ASIAN COLLECTIONS (Area-Ethnic; Hum)
317 Palmer Hall   Phone: (609) 452-3182
Princeton, NJ 08544   Diane Perushek, Cur.
Founded: 1926. **Staff:** Prof 8; Other 12. **Subjects:** China, Japan, Korea. **Special Collections:** Buddhist sutras, Sung and Yuan editions (2864 volumes); Ming editions (24,000 volumes); Hishi copies, Ming works reproduced in Japan (2100 volumes); Chinese medicine and materia medica (1700 volumes); "Go" collection (500 volumes); rare books including Mongolian, Tibetan and Manchurian titles (1300). **Holdings:** 369,300 books; 1100 bound periodical volumes; 3000 manuscripts; 12,000 microforms.

Subscriptions: 1100 journals and other serials; 21 newspapers. Services: Interlibrary loans; copying; reference work and information service for outside inquirers on questions relating to China, Japan and Korea. Automated Operations: Computerized cataloging. Computerized Information Services: RLIN catalog (internal database). Contact Person: Min-chih Chou, 452-5336. Networks/Consortia: Member of RLG. Special Indexes: List of Periodicals in Japanese in the Gest Oriental Library and East Asian Collections, 1980. Staff: Iping K. Wei, Hd., Chinese Sect.; Soowan Y. Kim, Hd., Japanese/Korean Sect; David Chang, Chinese Cat.; Min-Chih Chou, Chinese Bibliog.; Charmian Cheng, Chinese Cat.; Mariko Shimomura, Asst.Hd., Japanese Sect.; Shu-Sheng Wang, Chinese/Japanese Cat.

★10984★
PRINCETON UNIVERSITY - INDUSTRIAL RELATIONS LIBRARY (Soc Sci)
Phone: (609) 452-4936
Princeton, NJ 08544   Katherine Bagin, Libn.
Founded: 1922. Staff: Prof 1; Other 2. Subjects: Industrial relations, labor legislation, labor unions, manpower planning, labor economics, social insurance, benefit plans, personnel administration. Holdings: 8000 books and bound periodical volumes; 105 VF drawers; 100,000 pamphlets including company personnel documents and labor union publications, International Labor Organization (ILO) documents. Subscriptions: 650 journals and other serials. Services: Library open to public with restrictions. Computerized Information Services: DIALOG, SDC, BRS. Networks/Consortia: Member of RLG. Publications: Selected References, 5/year - by subscription.

★10985★
PRINCETON UNIVERSITY - MARQUAND LIBRARY (Art)†
McCormick Hall   Phone: (609) 452-3783
Princeton, NJ 08544   Mary M. Schmidt, Libn.
Founded: 1908. Staff: Prof 2; Other 5. Subjects: History of art, history of architecture, archeology. Special Collections: Barr Ferree Collection (architecture); Friend Collection (early Christian and manuscript illumination); sales catalogs; exhibition catalogs. Holdings: 125,000 volumes. Subscriptions: 900 journals and other serials. Services: Copying (limited); library open to public with restrictions. Networks/Consortia: Member of RLG.

★10986★
PRINCETON UNIVERSITY - MATHEMATICS, PHYSICS AND STATISTICS LIBRARY (Sci-Tech)
Phone: (609) 452-3188
Princeton, NJ 08544   Peter Cziffra, Libn.
Staff: Prof 1; Other 4. Subjects: Mathematics, physics and statistics - history, development and philosophy. Holdings: 44,000 books; 35,000 bound periodical volumes; 5000 pamphlets; 10 VF drawers of Princeton theses; 250 VF drawers of uncataloged pamphlets; 16 VF drawers of undergraduate theses. Subscriptions: 805 journals and other serials. Services: Interlibrary loans; copying; library open to qualified readers for reference use only. Automated Operations: Computerized cataloging and acquisitions. Computerized Information Services: DIALOG, RLIN. Performs searches on cost recovery basis.

★10987★
PRINCETON UNIVERSITY - MUSIC COLLECTION (Mus)†
Firestone Library   Phone: (609) 452-3230
Princeton, NJ 08544   Paula Morgan, Music Libn.
Staff: Prof 1; Other 1. Subjects: Music. Holdings: 18,000 books; 3000 bound periodical volumes; 19,000 volumes of music; 2500 microforms. Subscriptions: 150 journals and other serials. Services: Interlibrary loans; copying; collection open to public for reference use only.

★10988★
PRINCETON UNIVERSITY - NEAR EAST COLLECTIONS (Area-Ethnic)†
Firestone Library   Phone: (609) 452-3279
Princeton, NJ 08544   Eric Ormsby, Cur.
Staff: Prof 5; Other 4. Subjects: Arabic, Persian, Turkish and Hebrew languages and literatures. Special Collections: Garrett Collection of Near Eastern Manuscripts. Holdings: 130,000 books and bound periodical volumes; 11,000 volumes of manuscripts. Services: Interlibrary loans; copying; library open to public with payment of fee. Networks/Consortia: Member of RLG; CRL. Staff: Nancy Pressman, Leader, Cat. Team; Mr. J. Rovner; Sergei Shuiskii; Mr. Toby Paff.

★10989★
PRINCETON UNIVERSITY - OFFICE OF POPULATION RESEARCH - LIBRARY (Soc Sci)
21 Prospect Ave.   Phone: (609) 452-4874
Princeton, NJ 08544   Thomas Holzmann, Libn.
Founded: 1936. Staff: Prof 2; Other 1. Subjects: Population studies,

demography (emphasis on methodology), fertility, mortality, census, vital statistics. Holdings: 22,000 volumes; 5500 reprints; 10,000 manuscripts and pamphlets; 850 reels of microfilm. Subscriptions: 400 journals and other serials. Services: Interlibrary loans; copying; library open to public for reference use only. Publications: Acquisitions list - local distribution. Remarks: Population Index, the quarterly index of the demographic field, is published by the Office of Population Research. Staff: Olga Boemeke, Asst.Libn.

★10990★
PRINCETON UNIVERSITY - PHONOGRAPH RECORD LIBRARY (Mus)
Woolworth Center of Musical Studies   Phone: (609) 452-4251
Princeton, NJ 08544   Marjorie Hassen, Record Libn.
Staff: Prof 1; Other 1. Subjects: Music - western classical, nonwestern and jazz. Holdings: 1000 score titles in multiple copies (mainly standard works); 20,000 phonograph records and recordings; 2000 tapes. Subscriptions: 30 journals and other serials. Services: Library not open to public.

★10991★
PRINCETON UNIVERSITY - PLASMA PHYSICS LIBRARY (Sci-Tech)
Box 451   Phone: (609) 452-3567
Princeton, NJ 08544   Elizabeth Graydon, Libn.
Staff: Prof 2; Other 3. Subjects: Fusion reactor technology, plasma physics. Holdings: 5000 books; 5000 bound periodical volumes; 3000 project reports; 17,000 technical reports and reprints; 20,000 microfiche. Subscriptions: 130 journals and other serials. Services: Interlibrary loans; reference and bibliographic service to laboratory staff; library open to public for reference use only. Computerized Information Services: DIALOG, BRS, DOE/RECON. Publications: Accessions List; Monthly Bulletin - both for internal distribution only. Staff: Jane E. Holmquist, Asst.Libn.

★10992★
PRINCETON UNIVERSITY - PLINY FISK LIBRARY OF ECONOMICS AND FINANCE (Bus-Fin)†
Firestone Library   Phone: (609) 452-3211
Princeton, NJ 08544   Louise Tompkins, Libn.
Founded: 1915. Staff: Prof 1; Other 2. Subjects: Economics, finance, international economics. Special Collections: Pliny Fisk Collection of Railroad and Corporation Finance (annual reports and other financial documents, 1830-1900). Holdings: 6042 books; current annual reports of 900 corporations; 21 VF drawers of pamphlets; selected economics working papers. Subscriptions: 1300 journals and other serials. Services: Interlibrary loans; library open to public for reference use with prior arrangement.

★10993★
PRINCETON UNIVERSITY - PSYCHOLOGY LIBRARY (Soc Sci)†
Green Hall   Phone: (609) 452-3239
Princeton, NJ 08544   Janice D. Welburn, Psych.Libn.
Staff: Prof 1; Other 1. Subjects: Psychology - cognitive, developmental, social, experimental, physiological; perception; personality; psychotherapy; psycholinguistics. Holdings: 11,083 books; 9627 bound periodical volumes; 3637 microfiche. Subscriptions: 460 journals and other serials. Services: Interlibrary loans; copying; reference and bibliographic services to members of department; library open to public for reference use only. Computerized Information Services: DIALOG, BRS, RLIN. Networks/Consortia: Member of RLG. Publications: Acquisition list and bibliographies - local distribution.

★10994★
PRINCETON UNIVERSITY - PUBLIC ADMINISTRATION COLLECTION (Soc Sci)†
Firestone Library   Phone: (609) 452-3209
Princeton, NJ 08544   Rosemary Allen Little, Libn.
Founded: 1930. Staff: Prof 1; Other 4. Subjects: Public administration; government on the national, state, county and municipal levels; law; politics; planning. Special Collections: Recent U.S. censuses in housing and population; depository for New Jersey state government documents; official depository for United Nations publications. Holdings: 5000 books; 2000 bound periodical volumes; 18,000 pamphlets; 28 VF drawers of clippings. Subscriptions: 1600 journals and other serials. Services: Interlibrary loans; library open to public. Networks/Consortia: Member of RLG.

★10995★
PRINCETON UNIVERSITY - RARE BOOKS AND SPECIAL COLLECTIONS (Rare Book)
Firestone Library   Phone: (609) 452-3184
Princeton, NJ 08544   Richard M. Ludwig, Asst.Libn.
Subjects: Papyri; Babylonian clay tablets; Medieval, Renaissance, Ethiopian and Batak manuscripts; early printing; English and American literature and history of the 19th and 20th centuries; theatre history; dramatic literature;

New Jerseyana; Western Americana; American Indians; Mormons; history of and examples of bookmaking, printmaking, fine printing, binding and photography; motion picture history; private press books; **Special Collections:** Sylvia Beach Collection; Carton Hunting Collection; Grover Ceveland Library; Cook Chess Collection; College of One Collection of Sheilah Graham; Meirs Collection of George Cruikshank; de Coppet Collection of American Historical Manuscripts; Derrydale Press Collection and The Sporting Books of Eugene V. Connett; general rare books collection; Jonathan Edwards Library; J. Harlin O'Connell Collection of English Literature of the 1890's; Kenneth McKenzie Fable Collection; Sinclair Hamilton Collection of American Illustrated Books; incunabula; Otto von Kienbusch Angling Collection; Charles Scribner Collection of Charles Lamb; James McCosh Library; Robert F. Metzdorf Collection of Victorian Bookbindings; Harry B. Vandeventer Poetry Collection; Orlando F. Weber Collection of Economic History; Goertz Collection; Gryphius Imprints Collection; Laurence Hutton Collection; Miriam Y. Holden Collection on the History of Women (Rare Books Section); Grenville Kane Collection of Americana; Stanley Lieberman Memorial Collection of Hero Fiction; Cyrus McCormick Collection of Americana; William Nelson Collection of New Jerseyana; New Jersey Imprints; Morris L. Parrish Collection of Victorian Novelists; Princeton Borough Collection; Princeton Borough Agricultural Association; Pitney Collection on International Law and Diplomacy (Rare Books Section); Robert Patterson Collection of Horace; Kenneth H. Rockey Angling Collection (Rare Books Section); Junius Spencer Morgan Collection of Virgil; John Shaw Pierson Civil War Collection; John Witherspoon Library; Woodrow Wilson Collection. Also contains over 100 special collections on individual authors and historical figures, and over 200 special collections on other subjects. **Holdings:** 250,000 books; 1000 manuscript collections; 210,000 maps and charts; 25,000 prints and drawings. **Staff:** Stephen Ferguson, Cur. of Rare Books; Jean F. Preston, Cur. of Mss.; Alfred L. Bush, Cur., W. Americana; Brooks Levy, Cur. of Numismatics; Nancy Bressler, Cur., Pub.Aff./Papers; Lawrence Spellman, Cur. of Maps; Dale Roylance, Cur., Graphic Arts; Alexander D. Wainwright, Cur., Parrish Coll.; Karl Buchberg, Consrv.; Mary Ann Jensen, Cur. of Theatre Coll.; Ann Hanson, Cur. of Papyrology.

★10996★
PRINCETON UNIVERSITY - RICHARD HALLIBURTON MAP COLLECTION (Geog-Map)
Firestone Library   Phone: (609) 452-3214
Princeton, NJ 08544   Lawrence E. Spellman, Cur. of Maps
Founded: 1948. **Staff:** Prof 1; Other 3. **Subjects:** Topography, transportation, urban and regional planning, history, navigation. **Holdings:** 2000 books; 100 bound periodical volumes; 235,000 sheet maps; 1100 aerial and satellite photographs; 75 relief models; 26 globes. **Subscriptions:** 40 journals and other serials. **Services:** Interlibrary loans; copying; collection open to public.

★10997★
PRINCETON UNIVERSITY - SCHOOL OF ARCHITECTURE LIBRARY (Plan)
Princeton, NJ 08544   Phone: (609) 452-3256
Frances Chen, Libn.
Founded: 1967. **Staff:** Prof 1; Other 3. **Subjects:** Current architectural practice, urban affairs, physical planning, transportation, sociology. **Special Collections:** Library of the former Bureau of Urban Research. **Holdings:** 22,000 books; 5000 pamphlets. **Subscriptions:** 450 journals and other serials. **Services:** Interlibrary loans; copying; library open to public for reference use only. **Networks/Consortia:** Member of RLG.

★10998★
PRINCETON UNIVERSITY - WILLIAM SEYMOUR THEATRE COLLECTION (Theater)
Firestone Library   Phone: (609) 452-3223
Princeton, NJ 08544   Mary Ann Jensen, Cur.
Founded: 1936. **Staff:** Prof 1; Other 6. **Subjects:** Performing arts - theater, popular music, dance, circus, film. **Special Collections:** Papers of: William Seymour, Fanny Davenport, Otto Kahn, E.L. Davenport, George Crouse Tyler, Sarah Enright and Woody Allen; collections of: Ashton Sly, Lulu Glaser, Max Gordon, Charles Burnham, Joseph McCaddon, Bretaigne Windust, Clinton Wilder, Sam H. Harris; archives of: Warner Bros. Inc., Tams-Witmark, Triangle Club, McCarter Theatre; A.M. Friend Collection of 18th century theatre drawings. **Holdings:** 12,000 books; 3300 VF drawers of programs, pictures and pamphlets; 50 map drawers containing posters; 500 scrap books; 1250 paper bound playbooks. **Subscriptions:** 115 journals and other serials. **Services:** Copying (limited); collection open to qualified scholars. **Networks/Consortia:** Member of RLG.

★10999★
PRINCETON UNIVERSITY - WOODROW WILSON SCHOOL OF PUBLIC AND INTERNATIONAL AFFAIRS - LIBRARY (Soc Sci)
      Phone: (609) 452-4848
Princeton, NJ 08544   Linda Oppenheim, Libn.
Founded: 1964. **Staff:** Prof 1; Other 4. **Subjects:** Political science, economics, international affairs. **Holdings:** 16,202 books; 1143 bound periodical volumes. **Subscriptions:** 302 journals and other serials; 8 newspapers. **Services:** Interlibrary loans; library open to public for reference use only. **Computerized Information Services:** DIALOG, BRS, RLIN. Performs searches on cost recovery basis.

PRINGLE HERBARIUM
See: University of Vermont

PRIOR (Walter F.) MEDICAL LIBRARY
See: Frederick Memorial Hospital - Walter F. Prior Memorial Library

★11000★
PRISON FELLOWSHIP - RESOURCE CENTER (Soc Sci)
Justice Fellowship Resource Center
Box 17181   Phone: (703) 759-4521
Washington, DC 20041   Elizabeth Leahy, Coord.
Staff: Prof 1; Other 2. **Subjects:** Criminal justice and criminal justice reform, Christianity, penology, social welfare, prisons, theology. **Holdings:** 300 books; 400 technical reports; 1100 cassettes; 7 VF drawers of clippings; 2 VF drawers of archives. **Subscriptions:** 96 journals and other serials. **Services:** Interlibrary loans; copying; center open to public with restrictions.

PRITCHARD (H. Wayne) LIBRARY
See: Soil Conservation Society of America - H. Wayne Pritchard Library

PRIVY COUNCIL OFFICE
See: Canada - Privy Council Office

★11001★
PRO FOOTBALL HALL OF FAME - LIBRARY/RESEARCH CENTER (Rec)
2121 Harrison Ave., N.W.   Phone: (216) 456-8207
Canton, OH 44708   Anne Mangus, Libn.
Founded: 1963. **Staff:** 2. **Subjects:** Professional football. **Special Collections:** Spalding football guides, 1892-1940; Scrapbooks of Commissioner Bert Bell; 98 players' personal scrapbooks; pre-NFL rare documents (player contracts and minutes of meetings). **Holdings:** 2437 books; 590 bound periodical volumes; 5000 game programs; 20,000 photographs of players, teams, officials and coaches; 700 slides of player and game action; 50 audiotapes; 1100 16mm films; 525 team media guides; 1500 microforms; 50 VF drawers of player files; 30 VF drawers of team files (present, defunct leagues, semi-pro). **Subscriptions:** 30 journals and other serials; 16 newspapers. **Services:** Interlibrary loans; copying; library open to researchers and writers by appointment. **Also Known As:** National Football Museum. **Staff:** Saundra K. Lang, Lib.Techn.

PRO-LIFE LIBRARY
See: Diocese of Allentown

★11002★
PROCTER & GAMBLE COMPANY - BUCKEYE CELLULOSE CORPORATION - CELLULOSE & SPECIALTIES DIV. TECH. INFO.SERV. (Sci-Tech)
949 Tillman Ave.   Phone: (901) 454-8310
Memphis, TN 38108   Ruth S. McLallen, Tech.Info.Mgr.
Founded: 1953. **Staff:** Prof 1; Other 1. **Subjects:** Chemistry - cellulose, physical, organic, analytical; polymer sciences; colloid science; textiles. **Holdings:** 5000 books; 5000 bound periodical volumes; 10,000 technical reports; 10,000 pamphlets; 8 VF drawers of government documents; 10,000 U.S. and foreign patents; 500 reels of microfilm. **Subscriptions:** 354 journals and other serials. **Services:** Interlibrary loans. **Computerized Information Services:** SDC, NLM, DIALOG, New York Times Information Service.

★11003★
PROCTER & GAMBLE COMPANY - IVORYDALE TECHNICAL CENTER - LIBRARY (Sci-Tech)*
Cincinnati, OH 45217
Holdings: Figures not available. **Services:** Library not open to public. **Remarks:** Library is one of several units comprising the Procter & Gamble Company Information Management Group.

★11004★
PROCTER & GAMBLE COMPANY - LIBRARY (Bus-Fin)
Box 599
Cincinnati, OH 45201 Marcia Cahall, Libn.
Subjects: Detergents, advertising, business. **Holdings:** Figures not available.
Services: Library not open to public.

★11005★
PROCTER & GAMBLE COMPANY - MIAMI VALLEY LABORATORIES - TECHNICAL LIBRARY (Sci-Tech)
Box 39175
Cincinnati, OH 45247 Emelyn L. Hiland, Lib.Mgr.
Staff: Prof 1; Other 3. **Subjects:** Chemistry, surface and colloid science. **Holdings:** 8000 books; 12,000 bound periodical volumes. **Subscriptions:** 600 journals and other serials. **Services:** Library not open to public. **Computerized Information Services:** DIALOG, SDC, OCLC, BRS, CAS Online, NIH-EPA Chemical Information System; internal database.

★11006★
PROCTER & GAMBLE COMPANY - WINTON HILL TECHNICAL CENTER - TECHNICAL LIBRARY (Sci-Tech)
6090 Center Hill Rd. Phone: (513) 977-7257
Cincinnati, OH 45224 Irene L. Myers, Sect.Hd.
Holdings: Figures not available. **Services:** Library not open to public. **Remarks:** Library is one of five units comprising the Procter & Gamble Company Technical Information Service with combined holdings of 35,000 volumes.

★11007★
PROCTOR COMMUNITY HOSPITAL - MEDICAL LIBRARY (Med)
5409 N. Knoxville Ave. Phone: (309) 691-4702
Peoria, IL 61614 Nancy Camacho, Libn.
Founded: 1972. **Staff:** Prof 1. **Subjects:** Medicine, nursing, allied health sciences. **Holdings:** 500 books; 210 bound periodical volumes; 550 unbound journal volumes. **Subscriptions:** 120 journals and other serials. **Services:** Interlibrary loans; copying; SDI; library open to qualified patrons. **Computerized Information Services:** MEDLINE. **Networks/Consortia:** Member of Heart of Illinois Library Consortium (HILC); Illinois Valley Library System; Greater Midwest Regional Medical Library Network (Region 3); ILLINET. **Publications:** Inhouse pamphlets.

★11008★
PROCTOR & REDFERN, CONSULTING ENGINEERS - LIBRARY (Sci-Tech; Plan)
45 Green Belt Dr. Phone: (416) 486-5225
Don Mills, ON, Canada M3C 3K3 Linda Rogachevsky, Hd.Libn.
Staff: Prof 1; Other 1. **Subjects:** Civil and environmental engineering, urban and regional planning, hydrology, transportation, waste management. **Holdings:** 18,000 books; 600 bound periodical volumes. **Subscriptions:** 125 journals and other serials; 20 newspapers. **Services:** Interlibrary loans; copying; library open to public with restrictions. **Automated Operations:** Computerized cataloging. **Computerized Information Services:** DIALOG, SDC, QL Systems. **Publications:** Information Centre News, monthly - for internal distribution only.

★11009★
PROCUREMENT ASSOCIATES - LIBRARY (Bus-Fin)†
733 N. Dodsworth Ave. Phone: (213) 966-4576
Covina, CA 91724 Marie McDonald, Libn.
Staff: Prof 1; Other 2. **Subjects:** Government contracts, business administration. **Holdings:** 3000 books; 4000 government and industry reports; government courses in the field of government contracts. **Subscriptions:** 133 journals and other serials. **Services:** Interlibrary loans; copying; library open to public.

★11010★
PRODUCE MARKETING ASSOCIATION - PMA INFORMATION CENTER (Bus-Fin; Food-Bev)
700 Barksdale Plaza Phone: (302) 738-7100
Newark, DE 19711 J.S. Raybourn, Staff V.P., Commun.
Founded: 1949. **Staff:** 5. **Subjects:** Fresh fruit and vegetables, floral products, packaging, marketing. **Special Collections:** Research reports pertaining to packaging and marketing fresh fruits and vegetables. **Holdings:** Figures not available. **Subscriptions:** 40 journals and other serials; 15 newspapers. **Services:** Interlibrary loans; center not open to public. **Computerized Information Services:** Internal database.

PROESCHER PATHOLOGY LIBRARY
See: Santa Clara Valley Medical Center - Milton J. Chatton Medical Library

★11011★
PROFESSIONAL CONVENTION MANAGEMENT ASSOCIATION - LIBRARY (Bus-Fin)
Commerce Ctr., Suite 1007
2027 First Ave. N. Phone: (205) 251-1717
Birmingham, AL 35203 Roy B. Evans, Exec. V.P.
Subjects: The improvement of management and the increase of effectiveness of meetings and conventions in the fields of medicine, medical sciences and allied professions through the development of ethical principles and sound methods of meeting management. **Holdings:** Figures not available.

PROFESSIONAL CORPORATION OF PHYSICIANS OF QUEBEC
See: Corporation Professionnelle des Medecins du Quebec

★11012★
PROFESSIONAL GOLFERS' ASSOCIATION OF AMERICA - LIBRARY*
100 Ave. of the Champions
Box 12458
Palm Beach Gardens, FL 33410
Subjects: Golf and the golf profession. **Holdings:** 3000 books; 2000 bound periodical volumes; 100 VF drawers. **Remarks:** Presently inactive.

PROGRAM ON PARTICIPATION AND LABOR-MANAGED SYSTEMS
See: Cornell University

★11013★
PROGRAM PLANETREE - HEALTH RESOURCE CENTER (Med)
2040 Webster St. Phone: (415) 346-4636
San Francisco, CA 94115 Rochelle Perrine Schmalz, Med.Libn.
Staff: Prof 2; Other 5. **Subjects:** Consumer health information, preventive medicine, self-care, holistic health, body systems and diseases, nutrition, fitness, pharmaceutical drugs. **Holdings:** 1200 books; 12 VF drawers of clippings; 2000 entries in Information and Reference System. **Subscriptions:** 30 journals and other serials; 5 newspapers. **Services:** Copying; center open to public. **Computerized Information Services:** DIALOG, NLM. **Networks/Consortia:** Member of San Francisco Biomedical Library Network. **Publications:** Planetalk Newsletter, 2/year.

★11014★
PROGRAM PLANNERS, INC. - LIBRARY/INFORMATION CENTER (Soc Sci)
230 W. 41st St. Phone: (212) 840-2600
New York, NY 10036 Patricia Virga, Info.Off.
Founded: 1970. **Staff:** Prof 1; Other 2. **Subjects:** Collective bargaining, education, public employee pensions/retirement systems, local government, urban affairs, health care, insurance, sanitation. **Special Collections:** Annual budgets and financial reports for major U.S. cities and school districts; fire, police, sanitation and transportation departments annual reports; retirement system annual reports; reports of the New York City Special Deputy Comptroller and the New York Financial Control Board, 1976 to present. **Holdings:** 10,000 books and reports; 26 VF drawers of clippings. **Subscriptions:** 110 journals and other serials. **Services:** Interlibrary loans; library open to public by appointment only. **Computerized Information Services:** Internal databases. **Publications:** Monthly New York City Economic Report.

PROGRESS CAMPUS RESOURCE CENTRE
See: Centennial College of Applied Arts & Technology

★11015★
PROGRESSIVE GROCER - RESEARCH LIBRARY (Food-Bev)
1351 Washington Blvd.
Stamford, CT 06902 Shirley Palmer, Res.Libn.
Staff: Prof 2. **Subjects:** Food marketing - retail and wholesale; merchandising. **Special Collections:** Complete bound set of Progressive Grocer, 1927 to present. **Holdings:** Figures not available. **Subscriptions:** 200 journals and other serials. **Services:** Interlibrary loans; library open to clients and librarians by appointment. **Formerly:** Located in New York, NY.

★11016★
PROJECT FOR PUBLIC SPACES - LIBRARY (Plan)
153 Waverly Place Phone: (212) 581-6553
New York, NY 10014 Steven Davies, Project Dir.
Subjects: Pedestrian circulation, urban studies, transportation planning, playground and recreation area research, social behavior in public spaces, landscape architecture. **Holdings:** 25 books; 175 research reports and

articles. **Subscriptions:** 15 journals and other serials. **Services:** Library open to public. **Publications:** List of publications - available on request.

PROJECT SHARE
See: Aspen Systems Corporation

PROJECT TALENT DATA BANK
See: American Institutes for Research

★11017★
PROSKAUER, ROSE, GOETZ & MENDELSOHN - LIBRARY (Law)
300 Park Ave.　　　　　　　　　　　Phone: (212) 909-7208
New York, NY 10022　　　　　　　　　Marsha Pront, Hd.Libn.
Staff: Prof 3; Other 4. **Subjects:** Law. **Holdings:** 25,000 books; 800 bound periodical volumes. **Subscriptions:** 185 journals and other serials; 10 newspapers. **Services:** Interlibrary loans; copying; library open to public with permission. **Computerized Information Services:** LEXIS, NEXIS, DIALOG, New York Times Information Service. **Networks/Consortia:** Member of Law Library Association of Greater New York. **Staff:** Jean O'Grady, Asst.Libn.; Shireen Kumar, Labor Libn.

★11018★
PROSPEROS - LIBRARY (Rel-Theol)
Box 5505　　　　　　　　　　　　　　Phone: (818) 350-3293
El Monte, CA 91734　　　　　　　　　Barbara Hill, Dir./Trustee
Founded: 1956. **Staff:** 1. **Subjects:** Metaphysics, astrology, philosophy, religion. **Holdings:** 4500 volumes. **Services:** Interlibrary loans; library open to public with restrictions. **Publications:** Newsletter, monthly; "Leap into Sanity"; books. **Remarks:** A Fourth Way school which emphasizes self-growth and self-discovery through both specialized classes and regular academics; located at 11724 Alloway St., El Monte, CA.

★11019★
PROTESTANT EPISCOPAL CHURCH - ARCHIVES (Rel-Theol)
Box 2247　　　　　　　　　　　　　　Phone: (512) 472-6816
Austin, TX 78768　　　　　　　Dr. Virginia Nelle Bellamy, Archv.
Staff: Prof 3; Other 1. **Subjects:** Historical materials pertaining to the Protestant Episcopal Church in America. **Special Collections:** Correspondence of the Domestic and Foreign Missionary Society; archives of the General Convention. **Holdings:** 10,000 volumes; manuscripts; documents. **Services:** Copying; archives open to public.

★11020★
PROTESTANT EPISCOPAL CHURCH - DIOCESE OF INDIANAPOLIS, INDIANA - ARCHIVES (Hist)
Indiana State Library
140 N. Senate Ave.　　　　　　　　　Phone: (317) 926-5454
Indianapolis, IN 46208
Subjects: Church history. **Special Collections:** Diocesan manuscripts, 1833 to present (85 file boxes). **Holdings:** 40 books; Bishop's correspondence; church records; personnel jackets. **Services:** Interlibrary loans; copying; archives open to public with restrictions. **Special Catalogs:** Archive inventory; catalog of Bishop's correspondence (card). **Remarks:** Correspondence about the archive or permission to work in it should go to Bishop Edward W. Jones, Episcopal Diocesan Headquarters, 1100 W. 42nd St., Indianapolis, IN, 46208.

★11021★
PROTESTANT EPISCOPAL CHURCH - DIOCESE OF PENNSYLVANIA - INFORMATION CENTER (Rel-Theol)
IVB Bldg., Suite 2616
1700 Market St.　　　　　　　　　　Phone: (215) 567-6650
Philadelphia, PA 19103
Staff: 1. **Subjects:** Episcopal Church, Diocese of Pennsylvania, Anglicanism. **Holdings:** 300 books; parish records; diocesan journals; confirmation records; archives. **Services:** Center open to public.

★11022★
PROTESTANT EPISCOPAL CHURCH - EPISCOPAL DIOCESE OF CONNECTICUT - DIOCESAN LIBRARY AND ARCHIVES (Rel-Theol)
1335 Asylum Ave.　　　　　　　　　Phone: (203) 233-4481
Hartford, CT 06105　　　Rev. Kenneth W. Cameron, Archv./Histographer
Founded: 1850. **Staff:** Prof 1; Other 2. **Subjects:** History of the Protestant Episcopal Church in Connecticut. **Special Collections:** Papers of the Bishops of Connecticut, 1784-1955 (6000 pieces); letters and historical documents relating to the Episcopal Church in Connecticut, 1786-1885 (6000 pieces); early sermons (Colonial period); cathedral and parochial historical materials; parish registers, records of diocesan organizations, 1790 to present; papers of the Standing Committee, 1796 to present; papers of the Society for the

Increase of the Ministry (12,000 pieces); films of reports of the missionaries under the Society for the Propagation of the Gospel in Foreign Parts, 1700-1776; records of the Episcopal Academy of Connecticut at Cheshire. **Holdings:** 100,000 manuscripts and films; 400 reference books; 3000 bound pamphlets. **Services:** Interlibrary loans; copying; library open to public by appointment. **Publications:** Historiographer of the Episcopal Diocese of Connecticut, quarterly - by subscription.

★11023★
PROTESTANT EPISCOPAL CHURCH - EPISCOPAL DIOCESE OF EASTERN OREGON - ARCHIVES (Rel-Theol)
Box 1091　　　　　　　　　　　　　　Phone: (503) 568-4898
LaGrande, OR 97850　　　　　　　　　Rev. Louis L. Perkins
Staff: Prof 1. **Subjects:** Diocese history. **Holdings:** 100 books; 50 bound periodical volumes; manuscripts; correspondence; archival materials; microfilm; pictures; statistics. **Services:** Interlibrary loans; archives open to public. **Formerly:** Located in Cove, OR.

★11024★
PROTESTANT EPISCOPAL CHURCH - EPISCOPAL DIOCESE OF MASSACHUSETTS - DIOCESAN LIBRARY AND ARCHIVES (Rel-Theol; Hist)
1 Joy St.　　　　　　　　　　　　　Phone: (617) 742-4720
Boston, MA 02108　　　　　　　　　Mark J. Duffy, Archv.
Staff: 2. **Subjects:** Historical material relating to churches of The Diocese and published work of the clergy. **Special Collections:** Americana (Colonial sermons); published records of the Society for the Propagation for the Gospel, 1701-1892. **Holdings:** Offical papers of the diocese, its bishops and affiliated agencies; historical manuscripts and pre-1905 vital records of its parishes; 50 linear feet of 19th and 20th century pamphlets. **Services:** Copying; library open to public for reference use only. **Publications:** Guide for Parish Historians, 1961; brochures on history of the Diocese of Massachusetts; Littera Scripta Manet (newsletter); Guide to the Parochial Archives of the Episcopal Church in Boston, 1981. **Remarks:** A description of the manuscript collection was published by Works Progress Administration, Boston, 1939. **Staff:** Margaret A. Dempsey, Asst.Archv.; Ruth S. Leonard, Lib.Cons.

★11025★
PROTESTANT EPISCOPAL CHURCH - EPISCOPAL DIOCESE OF NEW YORK - ARCHIVES (Rel-Theol)
1047 Amsterdam Ave.　　　　　　　　Phone: (212) 678-6977
New York, NY 10025　　　　　　　James E. Templar, Archv.
Staff: Prof 1. **Subjects:** Episcopal Church, Protestant Episcopal Church, local history. **Special Collections:** New York Training School for Deaconnesses (35 linear feet); Episcopal Mission Society (68 linear feet); Seamen's Church Institute of New York and New Jersey (180 linear feet); sermons from the Cathedral of St. John the Divine (300 sound recordings). **Holdings:** 200 books and bound periodical volumes; 1500 linear feet of archival materials; 2500 photographs; baptismal and confirmation records from the Cathedral of St. John the Divine and from some parishes that are now closed. **Services:** Copying; archives open to diocesan staff and clergy only, by appointment. **Special Indexes:** Inventories and Registers (loose-leaf notebook).

★11026★
PROTESTANT EPISCOPAL CHURCH - EPISCOPAL DIOCESE OF SOUTH DAKOTA - ARCHIVES (Rel-Theol)
Center for Western Studies
Augustana College　　　　　　　　　Phone: (605) 336-4007
Sioux Falls, SD 57197　　　　　　Harry F. Thompson, Archv.
Staff: Prof 1; Other 2. **Subjects:** History - Episcopal church, South Dakota, Great Plains, United States; missionary work; Indian culture. **Special Collections:** Bishop William H. Hare papers (10 cubic feet); Rev. Joseph W. Cook registers (28 volumes); Bishop Hugh L. Burleson papers (4 cubic feet); Bishop W. Blair Roberts papers (25 cubic feet); Bishop Conrad H. Gesner papers (50 cubic feet). **Holdings:** 40 volumes of church registers. **Services:** Copying; archives open to public with restrictions.

★11027★
PROTESTANT EPISCOPAL CHURCH - EPISCOPAL DIOCESE OF SPRINGFIELD, ILLINOIS - DIOCESAN CENTER LIBRARY (Hist)
821 S. 2nd St.　　　　　　　　　　Phone: (217) 525-2827
Springfield, IL 62704　　　Philip L. Shutt, Registrar/Historiographer
Staff: Prof 1. **Subjects:** Diocesan archives. **Special Collections:** Journals of Diocese of Illinois, 1835-1877; journals of Diocese of Springfield, 1878 to present; journals of the General Convention of the Episcopal Church, 1823 to present. **Holdings:** 187 books and bound periodical volumes; manuscripts; reports; diocesan records; defunct parish records; maps; photographs. **Services:** Interlibrary loans; library open to public.

★11028★
PROTESTANT EPISCOPAL CHURCH - EPISCOPAL DIOCESE OF UTAH -
ARCHIVES (Rel-Theol)
231 E. First St. Phone: (801) 322-3400
Salt Lake City, UT 84111
Subjects: History of the Episcopal Diocese of Utah, 1867 to present.
Holdings: 65 cubic feet of diocesan records, journals of annual conventions,
confirmation records, financial records, parish statistical reports, and diaries
and registers of the clergy. **Services:** Archives open to public by appointment.

★11029★
PROTESTANT EPISCOPAL CHURCH - EPISCOPAL DIOCESE OF WEST
TEXAS - CATHEDRAL HOUSE ARCHIVES (Rel-Theol)
111 Torcido Dr.
Box 6885 Phone: (512) 824-5387
San Antonio, TX 78209 Zethyl T. LeStourgeon, Dir.
Subjects: Religion, history, education. **Special Collections:** History of the
Episcopal Diocese of West Texas and its institutions, including St. Philip's
College, St. Mary's Hall, and Texas Military Institute, 1874 to present.
Holdings: 5000 books; 50 linear feet of letters, minutes, diaries, records,
scrapbooks, and manuscripts. **Services:** Copying; archives open to other
churches. **Automated Operations:** Computerized cataloging and acquisitions.

★11030★
PROTESTANT EPISCOPAL CHURCH EXECUTIVE COUNCIL - HENRY KNOX
SHERRILL RESOURCE CENTER (Rel-Theol)
Episcopal Church Center
815 Second Ave. Phone: (212) 867-8400
New York, NY 10017 Avis E. Harvey, Rsrcs./Info.Off.
Staff: 1. **Subjects:** Episcopal church. **Services:** Center open to public for
reference use only.

★11031★
PROTESTANT EPISCOPAL CHURCH - MISSOURI DIOCESE - DIOCESAN
ARCHIVES (Hist; Rel-Theol)
1210 Locust St. Phone: (314) 231-1220
St. Louis, MO 63103 Charles F. Rehkopf, Archv./Registrar
Staff: Prof 1; Other 2. **Subjects:** History - diocesan, parish, Anglican Church,
Missouri, St. Louis. **Special Collections:** Journals of the General Convention,
1784 to present (69 volumes); Journals of the Diocese of Missouri, 1841 to
present (144 volumes); The Spirit of Missions and Forth, 1835 to present
(125 volumes); Historical Magazine of the Episcopal Church, 1932 to present.
Holdings: 572 books; 223 bound periodical volumes; 83.5 linear feet of
diocesan archives; 18 linear feet of parish files. **Subscriptions:** 13 journals
and other serials. **Services:** Interlibrary loans; copying; archives open to public
by appointment. **Special Indexes:** Index of diocesan publications and official
records (card); finding aids for diocesan historical collections.

PROTESTANT EPISCOPAL CHURCH IN SOUTH CAROLINA - DALCHO
HISTORICAL SOCIETY
See: Dalcho Historical Society of the Protestant Episcopal Church in
South Carolina

★11032★
PROTESTANT EPISCOPAL CHURCH OF WESTERN WASHINGTON -
DIOCESE OF OLYMPIA - ARCHIVES (Rel-Theol)
1551 Tenth Ave., E.
Box 12126 Phone: (206) 325-4200
Seattle, WA 98102 Peggy Ann Hansen, Archv.
Staff: Prof 1. **Subjects:** Diocesan archives. **Special Collections:** Bishop
Stephen Fielding Bayne Collection; Bishop Simon Arthur Huston Collection.
Holdings: 50 books; bishop's office and diocesan records; journals and
newspapers; pictures; tapes. **Services:** Copying; archives open to public with
restrictions.

★11033★
PROTESTANT EPISCOPAL CHURCH OF WESTERN WASHINGTON -
DIOCESE OF OLYMPIA - EDUCATION RESOURCE CENTER (Rel-Theol;
Educ)
1551 Tenth Ave., E.
Box 12126 Phone: (206) 325-4200
Seattle, WA 98102 Anita Steury, Libn.
Staff: Prof 1. **Subjects:** Religious education, theology, psychology, Christian
life. **Holdings:** 1500 books and bound periodical volumes; 33 films; 300
filmstrips; 650 cassette tapes. **Subscriptions:** 10 journals and other serials.
Services: Interlibrary loans; copying; center open to public with restrictions.

PROTESTANT EPISCOPAL DIOCESE OF LOS ANGELES ARCHIVES
See: School of Theology at Claremont - Theology Library

★11034★
PROTESTANT SCHOOL BOARD OF GREATER MONTREAL - PROFESSIONAL
LIBRARY (Educ)
6000 Fielding Ave. Phone: (514) 482-6000
Montreal, PQ, Canada H3X 1T4 M.E. Montague, Lib.Techn.
Founded: 1963. **Subjects:** Education, child psychology, school administration,
curriculum, special education. **Holdings:** 8000 books; 452 bound periodical
volumes; unbound materials. **Subscriptions:** 150 journals and other serials.
Services: Interlibrary loans; copying; library open to public for reference use
only. **Publications:** Copycat, semiannual.

PROUTY-CHEW MUSEUM AND LIBRARY
See: Geneva Historical Society and Museum

★11035★
PROVIDENCE ATHENAEUM - LIBRARY (Hum)
251 Benefit St. Phone: (401) 421-6970
Providence, RI 02903 Sally Duplaix, Dir.
Founded: 1753. **Staff:** Prof 5; Other 7. **Subjects:** History, literature,
biography, art, voyages and travel, natural history. **Special Collections:**
Bowen Collection; Burns Collection; collections in 19th century fiction and
juvenile literature; rare books. **Holdings:** 152,000 books; 304 periodical
titles. **Subscriptions:** 130 journals and other serials. **Services:** Interlibrary
loans; copying; research facilities; library open to public; free research and
visiting privileges; member's fee. **Networks/Consortia:** Member of Rhode
Island Interrelated Library Network. **Publications:** Providence Athenaeum
Bulletin; Annual Report. **Staff:** Juliet T. Saunders, Asst.Dir.; Risa Gilpin, Hd. of
Pub.Serv.; Dolly Borts, Hd. of Tech.Serv.; Mary Greene, Ch.Libn.

★11036★
PROVIDENCE COLLEGE - PHILLIPS MEMORIAL LIBRARY (Rel-Theol; Soc Sci)
River Ave. at Eaton St. Phone: (401) 865-2242
Providence, RI 02918 Joseph H. Doherty, Dir.
Founded: 1919. **Staff:** Prof 7; Other 22. **Subjects:** Works of St. Thomas
Aquinas, Thomistic philosophy and theology, Dominican Order. **Special
Collections:** John E. Fogarty Papers (500,000 pieces); Dennis J. Roberts
Papers (3000 pieces); William Henry Chamberlin Papers (120 pieces and 40
diaries on microfilm); Louis Francis Budenz Papers (9500 pamphlets and
periodicals); Rhode Island Constitutional Convention Collection, 1964-1968
(1000 pieces); Cornelius Moore Papers (250 pieces); J. Lyons Moore
Collection (3000 pieces); Robert E. Quinn Papers and Oral History Project;
Rhode Island Urban League Papers (200,000 items); Nazi Bund Collection
(300 pieces); John J. Fawcett Collection (3000 drawings); Limited
Constitutional Convention, 1973 (500 pieces); Quonset Point Collection
(9000 pieces); Blackfriars' Guild Collection (2500 pieces); Joseph A. Doorley,
Jr. Collection (60,000 pieces); Black Regiment Collection (600 pieces);
Bonniwell Liturgical Collection (2100 pieces); Coutu Genealogy; Aime J.
Forand Collection (4500 pieces); Irish Literature Collection (50 pieces); John
O. Pastore Collection (100,000 pieces); Rhode Island Library Association
Collection (5000 pieces); Social Justice Collection, 1936-1942 (325 pieces);
Walsh Civil War Diary (30 pages); Black Newspapers, 1932-1957 (8 reels of
microfilm); Confederation Period in Rhode Island Newspapers Collection (47
pieces); Reunification of Ireland Clippings (7 pieces); National Association for
the Advancement of Colored People Collection (pending); English and Colonial
18th Century Trade Statistics Collection (500,000 I.B.M. cards); Alice Lafond
Altieri Collection (925 pieces); Rhode Island Court Records Collection, 1657-
1905 (1 million pieces); J. Howard McGrath Collection (62,000 pieces);
Thomas Matthew McGlynn, O.P. Collection (5000 pieces and art objects);
Edward J. Higgins Collection; Edward P. Beard Collection. **Holdings:** 219,895
books; 41,236 bound periodical volumes; 56,424 government documents;
17,816 microforms; 1143 AV items. **Subscriptions:** 1892 journals and other
serials; 27 newspapers. **Services:** Interlibrary loans (books only); copying;
library open to public for reference use only. **Automated Operations:**
Computerized cataloging and ILL. **Computerized Information Services:**
OCLC. **Networks/Consortia:** Member of Consortium of Rhode Island
Academic and Research Libraries, Inc. (CRIARL); NELINET. **Staff:** Edgar C.
Bailey, Jr., Ref.Libn.; Elaine Shanley, Hd.Cat.Jean A. Sheridan, Acq.Libn.;
Matthew Smith, Archv.; Raynna Genetti, Ref.Libn.; Daniel Eckart, Ref.Libn.

★11037★
PROVIDENCE HOSPITAL, EVERETT - HEALTH INFORMATION NETWORK
SERVICES (HINS) (Med)
Pacific & Nassau
Box 1067 Phone: (206) 258-7558
Everett, WA 98206 Shirley C. Lewis, Dir., Lib.Serv.
Founded: 1974. **Staff:** Prof 1; Other 2. **Subjects:** Medicine, nursing, hospital

management. **Holdings:** Figures not available. **Subscriptions:** 450 journals and other serials. **Services:** Interlibrary loans; copying; SDI; library open to public with restrictions. **Computerized Information Services:** Online systems. **Remarks:** The Health Information Network Services (HINS) is a joint service of Providence Hospital, Everett and the General Hospital of Everett.

★11038★
PROVIDENCE HOSPITAL - HEALTH SCIENCES LIBRARY (Med)
1150 Varnum St., N.E.   Phone: (202) 269-7141
Washington, DC 20017   Sr. Frances Healy, Dir.
Staff: Prof 1; Other 3. **Subjects:** Medicine, nursing, hospital administration, allied health fields. **Holdings:** 3100 books; 3500 bound periodical volumes. **Subscriptions:** 155 journals and other serials. **Services:** Interlibrary loans; library not open to public.

★11039★
PROVIDENCE HOSPITAL - PANZNER MEMORIAL LIBRARY (Med)
16001 W. Nine Mile Rd.
Box 2043   Phone: (313) 424-3294
Southfield, MI 48037   Sharon Cohen, Dir. of Lib.Serv.
Founded: 1965. **Staff:** Prof 1; Other 2. **Subjects:** Medicine, nursing, health sciences, hospitals. **Holdings:** 4800 books; 3600 bound periodical volumes; 550 Audio-Digest tapes; 125 teaching slides. **Subscriptions:** 231 journals and other serials. **Services:** Interlibrary loans; library not open to public. **Computerized Information Services:** DIALOG. **Networks/Consortia:** Member of Metropolitan Detroit Medical Library Group (MDMLG).

★11040★
PROVIDENCE HOSPITAL - SCHOOL OF NURSING MEDIA CENTER (Med)
1912 Hayes Ave.   Phone: (419) 625-8450
Sandusky, OH 44870
Founded: 1905. **Staff:** Prof 1. **Subjects:** Nursing, medicine and related subjects. **Holdings:** 5000 books and bound periodical volumes; 20 VF drawers of pamphlets, leaflets, pictures, articles. **Subscriptions:** 73 journals and other serials. **Services:** Interlibrary loans; copying; center open to public with restrictions.

★11041★
PROVIDENCE HOSPITAL & SCHOOL OF NURSING - PROVIDENCE HEALTH SCIENCE LIBRARY (Med)
Box 208   Phone: (205) 438-7869
Mobile, AL 36601   Mary Ann Donnell, Libn.
Staff: Prof 1; Other 1. **Subjects:** Nursing, medicine and allied health subjects. **Holdings:** 1800 books; bound periodical volumes. **Subscriptions:** 111 journals and other serials. **Services:** Interlibrary loans; copying; library open to public with restrictions. **Networks/Consortia:** Member of National Library of Medicine; Gulf Coast Biomedical Library Consortium.

★11042★
PROVIDENCE JOURNAL COMPANY - NEWS LIBRARY (Publ)
75 Fountain St.   Phone: (401) 277-7390
Providence, RI 02902   Joseph O. Mehr, Libn.
Founded: 1920. **Staff:** Prof 2; Other 9. **Subjects:** Newspaper reference topics. **Special Collections:** Journal Bulletin Almanacs, 1892 to present. **Holdings:** 2500 books; news clippings; picture collection; microforms; pamphlets. **Subscriptions:** 35 journals and other serials; 13 newspapers. **Services:** Copying; library open to public by appointment. **Automated Operations:** Almanac prepared with computer assistance. **Computerized Information Services:** DIALOG, Dow Jones News/Retrieval, BRS, VU/TEXT. **Publications:** Journal Bulletin Almanac. **Special Indexes:** Index to Rhode Island State General Assembly materials. **Staff:** Susan Fedorzyn-Edgar, Asst.Libn.

★11043★
PROVIDENCE MEDICAL CENTER - HORTON HEALTH SCIENCES LIBRARY (Med)
500 17th Ave., C-34008   Phone: (206) 326-5621
Seattle, WA 98124   Kathleen Murray, Dir., Lib.Serv.
Staff: 3. **Subjects:** Clinical medicine, surgery, cardiology, nursing. **Holdings:** 3500 books and bound periodical volumes; 12 VF drawers of material. **Subscriptions:** 300 journals and other serials. **Services:** Interlibrary loans; copying; SDI; library open to patients with approval of physician. **Computerized Information Services:** MEDLINE, BRS. **Networks/Consortia:** Member of Seattle Area Hospital Library Consortium (SAHLC). **Publications:** Medical Library News, bimonthly - to all hospital staff. **Staff:** Sherry Dodson, Libn.

★11044★
PROVIDENCE MEDICAL CENTER - MEDICAL LIBRARY (Med)
4805 N.E. Glisan   Phone: (503) 230-6075
Portland, OR 97213   Miriam Palmer, Med.Libn.
Staff: Prof 1; Other 1. **Subjects:** Nursing, medicine. **Holdings:** 400 books. **Subscriptions:** 140 journals and other serials. **Services:** Interlibrary loans; copying; library open to public with restrictions. **Computerized Information Services:** MEDLARS. **Networks/Consortia:** Member of Oregon Health Information Network (OHIN).

★11045★
PROVIDENCE PUBLIC LIBRARY - ART AND MUSIC DEPARTMENT (Art; Mus)
150 Empire St.   Phone: (401) 521-7722
Providence, RI 02903   Susan R. Waddington, Dept.Hd.
Staff: Prof 3. **Subjects:** Fine arts, music and dance, costume. **Special Collections:** Nickerson Architecture Collection; Richmond Jewelry Collection. **Holdings:** 35,000 books and bound periodical volumes; 13,434 music scores; 5300 phonograph records; 160,000 loose pictures; 8 VF drawers; 400 circulating pictures and posters. **Subscriptions:** 90 journals and other serials. **Services:** Interlibrary loans; copying; department open to public. **Automated Operations:** Computerized acquisitions and circulation. **Computerized Information Services:** DIALOG. Performs searches on cost recovery basis. Contact Person: Richard DesRoches, 521-8751. **Networks/Consortia:** Member of Consortium of Rhode Island Academic and Research Libraries, Inc. (CRIARL); Rhode Island Interrelated Library Network. **Special Indexes:** Song title index for song books in collection; scrapbook of musical performances in Rhode Island from 1929 to present. **Staff:** Richard DesRoches; Margaret Chenan; Barbara Cock; Jane Duggan .

★11046★
PROVIDENCE PUBLIC LIBRARY - BUSINESS-INDUSTRY-SCIENCE DEPARTMENT (Bus-Fin; Sci-Tech)
150 Empire St.   Phone: (401) 521-7722
Providence, RI 02903   Marcia DiGregorio, Dept.Hd.
Founded: 1923. **Staff:** Prof 5; Other 1. **Subjects:** Science (pure and applied), technology, business. **Special Collections:** Textiles (historical). **Holdings:** 18,678 books; 18,500 bound periodical volumes; 20 VF drawers of federal and military specifications; 3400 annual reports; U.S. patents, 1790 to present, on microfilm; indexes to U.S. patents, 1790 to present; official gazettes, 1872 to present, on microfilm; pamphlets. **Subscriptions:** 306 journals and other serials. **Services:** Interlibrary loans; copying; department open to public. **Automated Operations:** Computerized acquisitions and circulation. **Computerized Information Services:** DIALOG. Performs searches on cost recovery basis. Contact Person: Richard DesRoches, 521-8751. **Networks/Consortia:** Member of Consortium of Rhode Island Academic and Research Libraries, Inc. (CRIARL); Rhode Island Interrelated Library Network. **Special Indexes:** Index to Rhode Island Inventors and Inventions. **Staff:** Cheryl R. Hunt, Ref.Asst./Patent Libn.

★11047★
PROVIDENCE-ST. MARGARET HEALTH CENTER - LIBRARY (Med)
8929 Parallel Pkwy.   Phone: (913) 596-4795
Kansas City, KS 66112   Pamela Drayson, Dir.
Staff: Prof 1; Other 1. **Subjects:** Medicine, surgery, nursing, health sciences. **Holdings:** 2000 books; 437 bound periodical volumes; AV materials; video cassettes; cassette tapes; 6 VF drawers. **Subscriptions:** 150 journals and other serials. **Services:** Interlibrary loans; copying; library open to hospital staff and students. **Computerized Information Services:** MEDLINE. DIALOG. **Networks/Consortia:** Member of Kansas City Library Network, Inc. (KCLN).

★11048★
PROVIDENT HOSPITAL - HEALTH SCIENCES LIBRARY
2600 Liberty Heights Ave.
Baltimore, MD 21215
Founded: 1965. **Staff:** Prof 1; Other 1. **Subjects:** Clinical medicine, nursing, hospital administration. **Holdings:** 4236 books; 1021 bound periodical volumes; 1143 unbound periodical volumes; 5 VF drawers of pamphlets; 3698 AV items. **Computerized Information Services:** NLM. **Networks/Consortia:** Member of Baltimore Consortia for Resource Sharing. **Remarks:** Presently inactive.

★11049★
PROVIDENT MUTUAL LIFE INSURANCE COMPANY OF PHILADELPHIA - LIBRARY (Bus-Fin)†
46th & Market Sts.
Box 7378   Phone: (215) 474-7000
Philadelphia, PA 19101   Tikvah S. Shulman, Libn.
Founded: 1915. **Staff:** 2. **Subjects:** Life insurance, actuarial science, banking, economics, finance, general business. **Holdings:** 7000 books; 20 VF

drawers. **Subscriptions:** 155 journals and other serials. **Services:** Interlibrary loans; copying; library open to public by appointment. **Staff:** Cindy A. Pitchon, Asst.Libn.

PROVINCE OF ST. JOSEPH OF THE CAPUCHIN ORDER - ST. LAWRENCE SEMINARY
See: St. Lawrence Seminary

PROVINCIAL ARCHIVES OF NEW BRUNSWICK
See: New Brunswick - Provincial Archives of New Brunswick

★11050★
PROWERS COUNTY HISTORICAL SOCIETY - BIG TIMBERS MUSEUM - LIBRARY (Hist)
North Santa Fe Trail
Box 362   Phone: (303) 336-2472
Lamar, CO 81052   Edith Birchler, Cur.
Subjects: Local history. **Holdings:** 200 books; Prowers County newspapers. **Services:** Library open to public for reference use only.

★11051★
PRUDENTIAL-BACHE SECURITIES INC. - CORPORATE FINANCE DEPARTMENT LIBRARY (Bus-Fin)
100 Gold St., 7th Fl.   Phone: (212) 791-3988
New York, NY 10292   Anne M. Bladstrom, Corp.Fin.Libn.
Founded: 1981. **Staff:** Prof 1; Other 3. **Subjects:** Banks and banking, corporate finance, economic and business conditions, economic forecasting and forecasts, investments, corporate records. **Holdings:** 300 books. **Subscriptions:** 200 journals and other serials. **Services:** Interlibrary loans; library not open to public. **Computerized Information Services:** DIALOG, NEXIS, NewsNet, Dow Jones News/Retrieval, INVESTEXT, VU/TEXT. Performs searches on cost recovery basis. **Formerly:** Its Research Department Library.

★11052★
PRUDENTIAL INSURANCE COMPANY OF AMERICA - BUSINESS LIBRARY (Bus-Fin)
24 Greenway Plaza, Suite 1900   Phone: (713) 993-3526
Houston, TX 77046   Fred Suza
Founded: 1952. **Staff:** 1. **Subjects:** Life insurance, sales promotion, business and business methods, statistics, economics. **Holdings:** 2500 volumes. **Subscriptions:** 51 journals and other serials. **Services:** Interlibrary loans; library open to public for reference use only, on request. **Automated Operations:** Computerized cataloging. **Computerized Information Services:** DIALOG. **Publications:** Annual Report - free upon request to libraries.

★11053★
PRUDENTIAL INSURANCE COMPANY OF AMERICA - DRYDEN BUSINESS LIBRARY (Bus-Fin)
Prudential Plaza - 2W   Phone: (201) 877-6749
Newark, NJ 07101   Robert P. Fallon, Libn.
Founded: 1941. **Staff:** Prof 1; Other 4. **Subjects:** Insurance, personnel management, office management. **Special Collections:** Actuarial proceedings. **Holdings:** 5000 books; 50 VF drawers. **Subscriptions:** 150 journals and other serials. **Services:** Interlibrary loans; library not open to public. **Computerized Information Services:** DIALOG, BRS, NEXIS, The Source, Public Affairs Information Service (PAIS); internal database. **Publications:** Across the Librarian's Desk, bimonthly - for internal distribution only.

★11054★
PRUDENTIAL INSURANCE COMPANY OF AMERICA - EMPLOYEES' BUSINESS & RECREATIONAL LIBRARY (Bus-Fin; Rec)
Prudential Dr.   Phone: (904) 399-2002
Jacksonville, FL 32207   Barbara K. Williams, Libn.
Founded: 1953. **Staff:** Prof 1. **Subjects:** Business, recreation, research. **Holdings:** 4000 books; 750 other cataloged items. **Subscriptions:** 100 journals and other serials; 5 newspapers. **Services:** Library not open to public.

★11055★
PRUDENTIAL INSURANCE COMPANY OF AMERICA - FINANCIAL RESEARCH CENTER (Bus-Fin)
4 Prudential Plaza   Phone: (201) 877-6529
Newark, NJ 07107   Debra R.A. Bowne, Res.Cons.
Staff: Prof 1; Other 2. **Subjects:** Finance, industry. **Holdings:** 1000 books; 100 VF drawers of clippings and pamphlets. **Subscriptions:** 260 journals and other serials; 19 newspapers. **Services:** Interlibrary loans; center not open to public. **Computerized Information Services:** DIALOG. **Publications:** Acquisitions list, bimonthly.

★11056★
PRUDENTIAL INSURANCE COMPANY OF AMERICA - LAW LIBRARY (Law)
Gibralter Bldg., 5th Fl.   Phone: (201) 877-6804
Newark, NJ 07101   Vickie Riccardo-Markot, Law Libn.
Staff: Prof 1; Other 4. **Subjects:** Law, insurance. **Holdings:** 36,000 volumes. **Subscriptions:** 138 journals and other serials and newspapers. **Services:** Interlibrary loans; copying; library open to public on a limited basis. **Computerized Information Services:** DIALOG, Commerce Clearing House Electronic Legislative Search System (ELSS), LEXIS.

★11057★
PRUDENTIAL INSURANCE COMPANY OF AMERICA - MARKETING RESEARCH CENTER (Bus-Fin)
14 Prudential Plaza   Phone: (201) 877-7583
Newark, NJ 07101   Barbara Gurdon Ciccone, Marketing Res.Cons.
Staff: Prof 1; Other 2. **Subjects:** Insurance, marketing and research, census statistics. **Holdings:** 600 books; 24 VF drawers of clippings; 9 VF drawers of research reports; 12 VF drawers of Life Insurance Management and Research Association reports; unbound journals; Conference Board reports; National Regional Economic Projection material; American Council of Life Insurance publications and insurance factbooks; Stanford Research Institute collection; 1980 Census/Current Population reports. **Subscriptions:** 90 journals and other serials; 6 newspapers. **Services:** Interlibrary loans; center not open to public. **Computerized Information Services:** DIALOG. **Publications:** Acquisitions List, bimonthly. **Special Catalogs:** Audio Visual catalog.

★11058★
PRUDENTIAL INSURANCE COMPANY OF AMERICA - WESTERN HOME OFFICE - BUSINESS LIBRARY
111 Lakeview Canyon Rd.
West Lake Village, CA 91362
Defunct

★11059★
PRUDENTIAL LIFE INSURANCE COMPANY OF AMERICA - BUSINESS LIBRARY (Bus-Fin)†
King & Yonge Sts.   Phone: (416) 366-6971
Toronto, ON, Canada M5H 1B7   J. Ireland, Libn.
Founded: 1950. **Staff:** 1. **Subjects:** Insurance. **Holdings:** 800 books. **Services:** Library not open to public.

★11060★
PRYOR, CARNEY AND JOHNSON - LIBRARY (Law)
6200 S. Syracuse, Suite 400   Phone: (303) 771-6200
Englewood, CO 80111   Lavonne Axford, Libn.
Staff: Prof 1; Other 1. **Subjects:** Law. **Holdings:** 5000 books. **Subscriptions:** 225 journals and other serials. **Services:** library not open to public. **Computerized Information Services:** DIALOG, Westlaw; internal database. **Special Indexes:** Internally-generated document file (computerized and on cards).

PSI FOUNDATION ARCHIVES
See: Ontario Medical Association - Library

PSORIASIS EDUCATION AND RESEARCH CENTRE
See: Women's College Hospital

★11061★
PSYCHIATRIC CENTRE - STAFF LIBRARY (Med)
Box 1056   Phone: (306) 842-5461
Weyburn, SK, Canada S4H 2L4   Merle St. Onge, Ck. Stenographer II
Staff: 1. **Subjects:** Psychiatry, psychology, social work, nursing, child and youth services, occupational therapy. **Holdings:** 1117 volumes. **Subscriptions:** 45 journals and other serials; 10 newspapers. **Services:** Interlibrary loans; library open to students.

★11062★
PSYCHICAL RESEARCH FOUNDATION - DAVID WAYNE HOOKS MEMORIAL LIBRARY (Rel-Theol)
214 Pittsboro St.   Phone: (919) 968-4956
Chapel Hill, NC 27514
Founded: 1961. **Subjects:** Parapsychology, death, meditation and religion, mediumship, hauntings and poltergeists, states of consciousness, physics and biophysics, psychology, anthropology. **Special Collections:** Journals and Proceedings of the British Society for Psychical Research, 1882 to present; American Society for Psychical Research Journal, 1941 to present; Journal of Parapsychology, 1937 to present; Proceedings of Parapsychology Association, complete series; Proceedings of American Society for Psychical Research, 1886 to present. **Holdings:** 1500 books; 300 bound periodical

volumes; 200 journals; 4 VF drawers of manuscripts, reprints, articles. **Subscriptions:** 35 journals and other serials. **Services:** Copying; library open to public for reference use only. **Publications:** THETA, quarterly - internationally. **Special Catalogs:** Annotated bibliography of "out-of-body experiences" sheets in file.

PSYCHO-MOTOR SKILL DESIGN ARCHIVE
See: Justice System Training Association

★11063★
PSYCHOANALYTIC ASSOCIATION OF SEATTLE - EDITH BUXBAUM LIBRARY (Med)
4029 E. Madison St.   Phone: (206) 324-6614
Seattle, WA 98112   Adolph M. Gruhn, Chm., Lib.Comm.
Staff: Prof 1; Other 3. **Subjects:** Psychoanalysis and related topics. **Holdings:** 1550 books and bound periodical volumes; 24 pamphlet boxes of journal reprints; 811 unbound journals; videotapes. **Subscriptions:** 20 journals and other serials. **Services:** Library not open to public.

PSYCHOANALYTIC FOUNDATION OF MINNESOTA LIBRARY
See: Ramsey County Medical Society - Boeckmann Library

★11064★
PSYCHOLOGICAL SERVICE OF PITTSBURGH - LIBRARY (Soc Sci)
429 Forbes Ave.   Phone: (412) 261-1333
Pittsburgh, PA 15219   Dina J. Fulmer, Libn.
Staff: Prof 1. **Subjects:** Industrial psychology; counseling - educational, career, personal; mental health; psychological testing; work attitudes and motivation; personnel selection; research techniques and statistical methods. **Holdings:** 950 books and bound periodical volumes; 16 VF drawers of reports, pamphlets, reprints and clippings. **Subscriptions:** 40 journals and other serials. **Services:** Interlibrary loans; copying; SDI and periodical routing; library open to qualified persons by appointment.

PSYCHOLOGY TODAY LIBRARY
See: American Psychological Association

★11065★
PSYNETICS FOUNDATION - LIBRARY (Hum)
1212 E. Lincoln Ave.   Phone: (714) 533-2311
Anaheim, CA 92805   Marilyn Livingston, Off.Mgr.
Staff: 3. **Subjects:** Metaphysics, occultism, philosophy. **Holdings:** Figures not available. **Services:** Library open for reference use to members only.

PTA
See: National Parent Teacher Association

★11066★
PUBLIC AFFAIRS INFORMATION SERVICE (Soc Sci; Publ)
11 W. 40th St.   Phone: (212) 736-6629
New York, NY 10018   Wilhelm Bartenbach, Exec.Dir.
Publications: PAIS Bulletin, semimonthly; PAIS Foreign Language Index, quarterly - both available as publications and online (DIALOG, BRS and Data-Star). **Remarks:** Public Affairs Information Service is housed in the Economic and Public Affairs Division of the New York Public Library but is not part of the library.

★11067★
PUBLIC AFFAIRS RESEARCH COUNCIL OF LOUISIANA - RESEARCH LIBRARY (Soc Sci)
Box 3118   Phone: (504) 343-9204
Baton Rouge, LA 70821   Jan Brashear, Res.Libn.
Founded: 1951. **Staff:** Prof 1. **Subjects:** State and local government and finance; education; statistics; public administration; elections and voting; Louisiana law. **Holdings:** 4000 books; 20 pamphlet boxes of state agency reports. **Subscriptions:** 44 journals and other serials. **Services:** Copying; bibliographic and reference services for members of the council and interested citizens on request; library open to public for reference use only. **Publications:** PAR List of Publications: Selective Subject Index to PAR Research, annual - distributed to members, press and libraries. **Remarks:** The library is located at 300 Louisiana Ave., Baton Rouge, LA 70802.

PUBLIC ARCHIVES OF CANADA
See: Canada - Public Archives of Canada

★11068★
PUBLIC BROADCASTING SERVICE - PTV ARCHIVES (Info Sci)
475 L'Enfant Plaza, S.W.   Phone: (202) 488-5227
Washington, DC 20036   Salomea A. Swaim, Archv.Libn.
Staff: Prof 1. **Subjects:** Fine arts, public affairs, science, history, natural history. **Special Collections:** National Educational Television (NET) Film and Videotape Collection; Public Broadcasting Service (PBS) Videotape Collection; NET and PBS program files. **Holdings:** 38,000 tapes; 18,000 video cassettes. **Services:** Copying; archives open to public by appointment. **Automated Operations:** Computerized inventory of holdings. **Special Catalogs:** Biographical Catalog, 1953-1973 (computer printout).

★11069★
PUBLIC CITIZEN - CONGRESS WATCH - LIBRARY (Soc Sci)
215 Pennsylvania Ave., S.E.   Phone: (202) 546-4996
Washington, DC 20003   Martha Oesch, Libn.
Founded: 1973. **Staff:** Prof 1. **Subjects:** Congressional issues, members of Congress. **Holdings:** 3000 books; 200 bound periodical volumes; Congressional hearings and reports. **Subscriptions:** 15 journals and other serials. **Services:** Copying; library open to public by appointment.

★11070★
PUBLIC EDUCATION ASSOCIATION - LIBRARY AND ARCHIVES (Educ)
20 W. 40th St.   Phone: (212) 354-6100
New York, NY 10018   Judith Baum, Dir., Info.Serv.
Staff: Prof 2. **Subjects:** Education, New York City. **Special Collections:** Integration; decentralization; P.E.A. Archives; collective bargaining; special education (handicapped); alternative education; school finance reform. **Holdings:** 5060 books, bound periodical volumes and documents; 28 VF drawers; 40 historical archives drawers. **Subscriptions:** 31 journals and other serials. **Services:** Interlibrary loans; copying; library open to public by appointment. **Publications:** P.E.A. Reports, 6-8/year. **Special Catalogs:** In-house subject bibliography. **Staff:** Carol Diaz, Adm.Asst.

★11071★
PUBLIC LAW EDUCATION INSTITUTE - LIBRARY (Law)
1346 Connecticut Ave. N.W., Suite 610   Phone: (202) 296-7590
Washington, DC 20036   William J. Straub, Circ.Mgr.
Staff: 2. **Subjects:** Military, civil and criminal law; related federal law; selective service law and administration; veterans law. **Special Collections:** Principal U.S. archive of selective service court opinions (1968-1984); Defense Department regulations on manpower/military justice. **Holdings:** 1100 books and bound periodical volumes; 30 VF drawers of federal court opinions. **Subscriptions:** 50 journals and other serials. **Services:** Interlibrary loans; copying; facsimile service and selective service document locator; library open to public. **Publications:** Military Law Reporter, bimonthly - by subscription. **Special Catalogs:** Catalog of Selected Litigation - Selective Service, 1980-1983.

★11072★
PUBLIC LIBRARY OF CINCINNATI AND HAMILTON COUNTY - ART AND MUSIC DEPARTMENT (Art; Mus)
800 Vine St.   Phone: (513) 369-6955
Cincinnati, OH 45202   R. Jayne Craven, Hd., Art & Music
Founded: 1872. **Staff:** Prof 7; Other 1. **Subjects:** Art, music, architecture, theater arts, photography, cinema, costume. **Special Collections:** Choral Music (208,752 copies of 1840 titles); Delta Omicron Music Composers Library (1200 items). **Holdings:** 122,434 books and cataloged scores; 16,562 periodical volumes; 29,528 pieces of sheet music; 674,440 clippings; 15,938 theater, dance and music programs; 5474 exhibition catalogs; 2345 librettos; 5057 large prints and posters; 768 documents. **Subscriptions:** 661 journals and other serials. **Services:** Interlibrary loans; copying; department open to public. **Computerized Information Services:** OCLC. **Networks/Consortia:** Member of Art Research Libraries of Ohio (ARLO). **Special Indexes:** 26 Symphony Orchestra program notes; Cincinnati Summer Opera Index by season, opera, artist and character; Index to Langstroth Reference Lithographs Collection; Matinee Musicale Recital Series; Analytic Index of Published Songs and Music Collections; Cincinnati Composers Manuscript Collection. **Staff:** Mary Naish, First Asst.; Shirley E. Coffin, Libn.; Charles E. Ishee, Libn.; Anna J. Myers, Libn.; Sheryl R. Pockrose, Libn.; Andrew M. Balterman, Libn.

★11073★
PUBLIC LIBRARY OF CINCINNATI AND HAMILTON COUNTY - CHILDREN'S DEPARTMENT (Educ)
800 Vine St.   Phone: (513) 369-6900
Cincinnati, OH 45202   Consuelo W. Harris, Dept.Hd.
Staff: Prof 3; Other 3. **Subjects:** Children's literature, adult reference pertaining to children's literature. **Special Collections:** Jean Alva Goldsmith

Memorial Collection (juvenile titles - fiction, easy, nonfiction, foreign language, toy books; 5000); Historical Collection (examples of early 20th-century children's books; 1000). **Holdings:** 45,000 books; 230 bound periodical volumes; 3 filing drawers; 20 notebooks on authors and illustrators; 2000 other cataloged items. **Subscriptions:** 58 journals and other serials. **Services:** Interlibrary loans; copying; department open to public. **Staff:** D. Thompson Chase, Libn.; Rebecca Schmidt, First Asst.

★11074★
PUBLIC LIBRARY OF CINCINNATI AND HAMILTON COUNTY - DEPARTMENT OF RARE BOOKS & SPECIAL COLLECTIONS (Rare Book)
800 Vine St.   Phone: (513) 369-6957
Cincinnati, OH 45202   Yeatman Anderson, III, Cur.
Founded: 1955. **Staff:** Prof 2; Other 1. **Subjects:** Discovery and exploration of America; Ohio Valley; Cincinnatiana; Bibles; author collections: Lafcadio Hearn, Mark Twain, William Faulkner, Ernest Hemingway, John Steinbeck, W. Somerset Maugham, Charles Dickens, Sir Winston Churchill, Sinclair Lewis, Pearl Buck, Eugene O'Neill, Edgar Rice Burroughs, A. Edward Newton, Saul Bellow, Isaac B. Singer; English language dictionaries; books about books and fine printing; George Cruikshank; Milestone Books; Mormons and Shakers. **Special Collections:** Inland Rivers Library (books, manuscripts, photographs on commercial transportation on the Ohio and Mississippi Rivers and their navigable tributaries). **Holdings:** 35,000 books; 1356 bound periodical volumes; 20,000 photographs relating to steamboats; 37 VF drawers of pamphlets; 137 boxes, 5 drawers of manuscripts; 15 map case drawers of maps, blueprints, broadsides and prints relating to steamboats. **Subscriptions:** 15 journals and other serials. **Services:** Copying; department open to public. **Publications:** Occasional checklists and brochures describing holdings. **Special Catalogs:** Printed catalog of Inland Rivers Library; Catalog of Kahn English Language Dictionary Collection (both for sale). **Staff:** Jean Hamer, First Asst. & Cat.

★11075★
PUBLIC LIBRARY OF CINCINNATI AND HAMILTON COUNTY - EDUCATION AND RELIGION DEPARTMENT (Educ; Rel-Theol)
800 Vine St.   Phone: (513) 369-6940
Cincinnati, OH 45202   Susan F. Hettinger, Hd.
Founded: 1952. **Staff:** Prof 7; Other 1. **Subjects:** Education, library science, religion, sports and recreation, philosophy, psychology, sociology. **Special Collections:** Theological and Religious Collection (church history and 19th-20th century Protestant theological writings); Foundation Center Regional Collection. **Holdings:** 140,000 books; 17,500 bound periodical volumes; 65 VF drawers of pamphlets and vocational literature; 25 VF drawers of documents; college catalogs of 2400 institutions on microfiche. **Subscriptions:** 500 journals and other serials. **Services:** Interlibrary loans; copying. **Staff:** Joan Hamilton, First Asst.

★11076★
PUBLIC LIBRARY OF CINCINNATI AND HAMILTON COUNTY - EXCEPTIONAL CHILDREN'S DIVISION (Educ)
800 Vine St.   Phone: (513) 369-6065
Cincinnati, OH 45202   Miss Coy K. Hunsucker, Hd.
Founded: 1966. **Staff:** Prof 2; Other 2. **Subjects:** Programs and materials for deaf, mentally handicapped and learning disabled, physically handicapped, socially maladjusted, emotionally disturbed and gifted and talented children and young adults from pre-school through high school ages. **Special Collections:** Deposit collections in 7 hospitals and institutions (2500 books). **Holdings:** 11,378 volumes. **Subscriptions:** 16 journals and other serials. **Services:** Story hours; book talks for parents and children, teachers, and workers with special needs children; bibliographies compiled for individual need. **Publications:** Feelings and Emotions for Younger Children; High Interest Low Vocabulary Books; Dealing with Difficulties. **Staff:** Mark A. Kelso, First Asst.

★11077★
PUBLIC LIBRARY OF CINCINNATI AND HAMILTON COUNTY - FILMS AND RECORDINGS CENTER (Aud-Vis; Mus)
800 Vine St.   Phone: (513) 369-6924
Cincinnati, OH 45202   Robert Hudzik, Hd.
Founded: 1947. **Staff:** Prof 4; Other 8. **Subjects:** Classical and popular music, spoken word, language instruction. **Special Collections:** Slides on the history of Cincinnati (1750); The Fountain Speaks (26 radio programs of local history on 78 rpm); Reference Collection of Cincinnati Symphony recordings (40). **Holdings:** 3287 reels of sound film (2745 titles); 900 8mm films; 1600 35mm filmstrips; 25,000 slides; 35,000 recordings; 5000 tape cassettes; 2000 video cassettes. **Services:** 16mm films and video cassettes loaned to individuals, organizations, schools in Hamilton County and surrounding counties for a fee; circulation of other holdings; center open to public. **Special Catalogs:** 16mm Film Catalog; 35mm Filmstrip Catalog; Slide Catalog; Tape

Cassette Catalog; video cassette pamphlets. **Staff:** Kent Newlon, First Asst.

★11078★
PUBLIC LIBRARY OF CINCINNATI AND HAMILTON COUNTY - GOVERNMENT AND BUSINESS DEPARTMENT (Bus-Fin; Soc Sci)
800 Vine St.   Phone: (513) 369-6932
Cincinnati, OH 45202   Carl G. Marquette, Jr., Hd.
Founded: 1952. **Staff:** Prof 7; Other 6. **Subjects:** Economics, business, labor, accounting, statistics, finance, government, law, insurance. **Special Collections:** Telephone directories (1000); Murray Seasongood Collection of Government, Law and Public Administration (5000 items); Lenke Insurance Library (1000 items). **Holdings:** 123,000 books; 32,000 bound periodical volumes; complete U.S. Government depository since 1884; 60 VF drawers of pamphlets; 80 VF drawers of documents; 24 drawers of microfilm. **Subscriptions:** 1000 journals and other serials. **Services:** Interlibrary loans; copying. **Computerized Information Services:** BRS, NEXIS, Dow Jones News/Retrieval, U.S. Patent Office. Performs U.S. Patent Office searches free of charge; other searches on cost recovery basis. **Staff:** Martha Heitkamp, First Asst.

★11079★
PUBLIC LIBRARY OF CINCINNATI AND HAMILTON COUNTY - HISTORY DEPARTMENT (Hist; Hum)
800 Vine St.   Phone: (513) 369-6905
Cincinnati, OH 45202   J. Richard Abell, Hd.
Staff: Prof 7; Other 4. **Subjects:** History, genealogy, maps, bibliography, geography, travel. **Special Collections:** Travel files; family genealogies; town, county and state histories. **Holdings:** 231,937 books; 24,839 bound periodical volumes; 9542 bound newspaper volumes; 12,356 reels of 35mm microfilm. **Subscriptions:** 801 journals and other serials; 46 newspapers. **Services:** Interlibrary loans; copying. **Formerly:** Its History and Literature Department.

★11080★
PUBLIC LIBRARY OF CINCINNATI AND HAMILTON COUNTY - HISTORY DEPARTMENT - MAP UNIT (Geog-Map)
800 Vine St.   Phone: (513) 369-6909
Cincinnati, OH 45202   Gardner Neely, Map Libn.
Founded: 1955. **Staff:** Prof 1; Other 1. **Subjects:** Maps, atlases, cartography, gazetteers. **Special Collections:** Ohio County Cadastral Atlases (155); maps of Cincinnati. **Holdings:** 137,951 maps; 1857 atlases; 405 gazetteers; 223 carto-bibliographies; 1015 bound periodical volumes. **Subscriptions:** 34 journals and other serials. **Services:** Copying; library open to public.

★11081★
PUBLIC LIBRARY OF CINCINNATI AND HAMILTON COUNTY - INSTITUTIONS/BOOKS BY MAIL (Info Sci)
800 Vine St., Library Sq.   Phone: (513) 369-6070
Cincinnati, OH 45202   Cynthia Whitt-Covalcine, Hd.
Founded: 1969. **Staff:** Prof 2; Other 3. **Subjects:** Fiction and nonfiction. **Special Collections:** Large-print materials (6866 books). **Holdings:** 23,491 volumes; 853 recordings; 158 cassettes. **Subscriptions:** 46 journals and other serials. **Services:** Interlibrary loans; books-by-mail for the homebound; specialized services for the institutionalized; deposit collections for hospitals and senior centers; library not open to public; Special Services Area in main library. **Special Catalogs:** Large-print catalog of holdings, annual; Books-by-Mail catalog, annual.

★11082★
PUBLIC LIBRARY OF CINCINNATI AND HAMILTON COUNTY - LIBRARY FOR THE BLIND AND PHYSICALLY HANDICAPPED (Aud-Vis)
800 Vine St., Library Sq.   Phone: (513) 369-6075
Cincinnati, OH 45202   Carol Heideman, Regional Libn.
Founded: 1901. **Staff:** Prof 1; Other 12. **Subjects:** Books for the blind and physically handicapped in braille, on discs (talking books) and on cassettes. **Holdings:** 14,610 volumes in braille; 69,823 containers of talking books; 45,918 cassette containers. **Subscriptions:** 40 on talking books; 34 in braille; 15 on cassettes. **Services:** Interlibrary loans; library open to public in 33 Ohio counties who must be certified as eligible for services. **Automated Operations:** Computerized circulation; automatic subject selection by reader interest categories. **Publications:** Newsletter, monthly. **Remarks:** WATS line service within Ohio at (800) 582-0335.

★11083★
PUBLIC LIBRARY OF CINCINNATI AND HAMILTON COUNTY - LITERATURE DEPARTMENT (Hum)
800 Vine St.   Phone: (513) 369-6991
Cincinnati, OH 45202   Donna S. Monnig, Hd.
Founded: 1983. **Staff:** Prof 6; Other 2. **Subjects:** Literature, foreign fiction,

folklore, journalism, linguistics. **Special Collections:** Ohio author bibliographies. **Holdings:** 145,318 books; 12,000 bound periodical volumes; 3777 reels of microfilm; dictionaries. **Subscriptions:** 357 journals and other serials. **Services:** Interlibrary loans; copying; department open to public. **Special Indexes:** Ohioana Hamilton County Authors Bibliography (pamphlet), annual. **Staff:** Georganne F. Bradford, First Asst.

★11084★
PUBLIC LIBRARY OF CINCINNATI AND HAMILTON COUNTY - MUNICIPAL REFERENCE LIBRARY (Plan; Soc Sci)
801 Plum St.   Phone: (513) 369-6076
Cincinnati, OH 45202   Sharon Huge
Staff: Prof 1. **Subjects:** Municipal administration, business and economics, criminology and law enforcement, waste collection and management, public health and safety, transportation. **Holdings:** 8000 books; 42,000 other cataloged items. **Subscriptions:** 65 journals and other serials. **Services:** Library open to public. **Computerized Information Services:** BRS, NEXIS. **Special Indexes:** Cincinnati City Ordinance Subject Index (book). **Formerly:** Administered by Cincinnati Planning Commission.

★11085★
PUBLIC LIBRARY OF CINCINNATI AND HAMILTON COUNTY - SCIENCE AND TECHNOLOGY DEPARTMENT (Sci-Tech)
800 Vine St.   Phone: (513) 369-6936
Cincinnati, OH 45202   Rosemary Gaiser, Hd.
Founded: 1902. **Staff:** Prof 7; Other 4. **Subjects:** Pure and applied science, especially chemistry. **Special Collections:** U.S. Depository Library, including U.S. patents, 1871 to present and Official Gazette, 1872 to present. **Holdings:** 178,000 books; 54,200 bound periodical volumes; 53,000 pamphlets. **Subscriptions:** 1100 journals and other serials. **Services:** Interlibrary loans; copying. **Computerized Information Services:** BRS, NEXIS, U.S. Patent Office. Performs U.S. Patent Office searches free of charge, other searches on fee basis. **Staff:** John E. Johns, First Asst.

PUBLIC LIBRARY OF THE HIGH SEAS
See: American Merchant Marine Library Association

★11086★
PUBLIC LIBRARY OF NASHVILLE AND DAVIDSON COUNTY - BUSINESS INFORMATION SERVICE (Bus-Fin)
222 Eighth Ave., N.   Phone: (615) 244-4700
Nashville, TN 37203   Alyne R. Gundlach, Chf.
Founded: 1954. **Staff:** Prof 2; Other 2. **Subjects:** Business, finance, government, economics, technology. **Holdings:** 8000 books; 3000 bound periodical volumes; 15,000 government documents. **Subscriptions:** 450 journals and other serials. **Services:** Interlibrary loans; copying.

★11087★
PUBLIC LIBRARY OF YOUNGSTOWN AND MAHONING COUNTY - SCIENCE AND INDUSTRY COLLECTION (Bus-Fin; Sci-Tech)
305 Wick Ave.   Phone: (216) 744-8636
Youngstown, OH 44503   Orin D. Cole, Hd.
Staff: Prof 4; Other 5. **Subjects:** Science and technology, business and finance. **Holdings:** 50,000 books; 6300 bound periodical volumes; 55 VF drawers of pamphlets, documents, house organs and clippings; 1500 reels of microfilm. **Subscriptions:** 270 journals and other serials. **Services:** Interlibrary loans; copying, library open to public. **Networks/Consortia:** Member of NOLA Regional Library System.

★11088★
PUBLIC/PRIVATE VENTURES - RESOURCE CENTER (Soc Sci)
1701 Arch St.   Phone: (215) 564-4815
Philadelphia, PA 19103   Carol Thomson, Dir. of Pub.Aff.
Staff: Prof 1; Other 1. **Subjects:** Employment, youth unemployment, labor market information, training programs, economic development, disadvantaged populations. **Holdings:** 1000 books; 12 VF drawers of brochures, clippings and annual reports. **Subscriptions:** 43 journals and other serials. **Services:** Copying; SDI; center open to public by appointment. **Publications:** List of publications - available on request.

★11089★
PUBLIC RELATIONS SOCIETY OF AMERICA - INFORMATION CENTER (Bus-Fin)
845 Third Ave.   Phone: (212) 826-1776
New York, NY 10022   Mary W. Wilson, Dir.
Founded: 1955. **Staff:** Prof 2. **Subjects:** Public relations. **Holdings:** 1000 books; 80 VF drawers. **Services:** Center open to public with usage fee.

★11090★
PUBLIC SERVICE COMPANY OF COLORADO - LIBRARY (Bus-Fin)
550 15th St.
Box 840   Phone: (303) 571-7084
Denver, CO 80201   Mary Ann Hamm, Libn.
Staff: 1. **Subjects:** Business management, public utilities, economics, electrical engineering. **Special Collections:** Electric Power Research Institute reports; Conference Board publications. **Holdings:** 3500 books; 500 government documents. **Subscriptions:** 175 journals and other serials; 6 newspapers. **Services:** Interlibrary loans; copying; library open to public through other librarians and for specific research in utility field. **Computerized Information Services:** DIALOG, BRC Associates, Inc., Evans Economics, Inc. (EEI), LEXIS, American Gas Association (AGA). **Publications:** Library bulletin, monthly - for internal distribution only; bibliographies - on request.

★11091★
PUBLIC SERVICE COMPANY OF OKLAHOMA - REFERENCE CENTER (Sci-Tech)
212 E. 6th St.
Box 201   Phone: (918) 599-2367
Tulsa, OK 74119   Carol Hayhurst, Supv.
Founded: 1967. **Staff:** Prof 2; Other 2. **Subjects:** Electric utilities. **Holdings:** 8100 volumes; 6200 technical and conference papers. **Subscriptions:** 450 journals and other serials. **Services:** Interlibrary loans; center not open to public. **Automated Operations:** Computerized serials. **Computerized Information Services:** DIALOG. **Networks/Consortia:** Member of Tulsa Area Library Cooperative. **Publications:** Reference Point (newsletter), monthly. **Special Indexes:** KWIC/KWOC index of technical papers. **Staff:** Susan K. Norris, Libn.

★11092★
PUBLIC SERVICE ELECTRIC AND GAS COMPANY - LIBRARY (Energy)
80 Park Plaza, P3C
Box 570   Phone: (201) 430-7333
Newark, NJ 07101   Florine E. Hunt, Corp.Libn.
Founded: 1911. **Staff:** Prof 4; Other 5. **Subjects:** Public utilities, electric industry, electrical engineering, gas industry, mechanical engineering, management, atomic power. **Holdings:** 13,000 books; 6000 bound periodical volumes; 800 directories; 165 VF drawers of pamphlets, reports and separates; 60 shelves of government documents; 5 shelves of annual reports and prospectuses of public utility companies; 100,000 microfiche of U.S. Government energy related reports. **Subscriptions:** 700 journals and other serials. **Services:** Interlibrary loans; copying; limited service to public by appointment only. **Automated Operations:** Computerized cataloging and serials. **Computerized Information Services:** DIALOG, OCLC, SDC, DOE/RECON, Dun & Bradstreet Corporation, NLM. **Networks/Consortia:** Member of PALINET & Union Library Catalogue of Pennsylvania. **Publications:** Library guide to periodical articles and new books and pamphlets, monthly. **Special Indexes:** Index to selected periodical articles on public utilities (card). **Staff:** Harriet Mayer, Libn.; Mary E. Greene-Cohen, Asst.Libn., Cat.; Sheila E. Cassels, Asst.Libn., Ref.

★11093★
PUBLIC SERVICE ELECTRIC AND GAS COMPANY - NUCLEAR LIBRARY (Energy)
Box 236, MC 150 A   Phone: (609) 339-4135
Hancocks Bridge, NJ 08308   Virginia L. Swichel, Libn.
Founded: 1983. **Staff:** Prof 1; Other 1. **Subjects:** Nuclear power and engineering. **Holdings:** 1700 books; 1 VF drawer of pamphlets; 1 VF drawer of clippings. **Subscriptions:** 125 journals and other serials; 6 newspapers. **Services:** Interlibrary loans; library not open to public. **Automated Operations:** Computerized cataloging, acquisitions and serials. **Computerized Information Services:** DIALOG, SDC, DOE/RECON.

★11094★
PUBLIC SERVICE ELECTRIC AND GAS COMPANY - NUCLEAR TRAINING CENTER LIBRARY (Energy)
244 Chestnut St.   Phone: (609) 339-3773
Salem, NJ 08079   Richard E. Bater, Lrng.Rsrcs.Spec.
Founded: 1983. **Staff:** Prof 1; Other 2. **Subjects:** Nuclear reactor operations - training, engineering, management. **Holdings:** 2000 books; plant documents. **Subscriptions:** 89 journals and other serials. **Services:** Copying; SDI; library open to public with restrictions. **Computerized Information Services:** Internal database. **Publications:** Acquisition lists.

PUBLIC TECHNOLOGY INC. - INFORMATION CENTER
See: National League of Cities - Municipal Reference Service

★11095★
PUBLIC UTILITIES COMMISSION OF OHIO - LIBRARY (Law)
180 E. Broad St.   Phone: (614) 466-5082
Columbus, OH 43215   Elza O. Fodor, Libn.
Founded: 1975. **Staff:** Prof 3; Other 1. **Subjects:** Law, public utilities, economics, accounting, engineering, management. **Special Collections:** PUCO annual reports, 1867 to present; official copies of session and administrative orders, 1913 to present; National Association of Regulatory Utility Commissioners (NARUC) publications, 1922 to present; Public Utilities Fortnightly, 1945 to present. **Holdings:** 12,506 books; 700 bound periodical volumes; 2700 government statistics; 200 unbound reports; 425 staff reports of investigations; 7 VF drawers of studies. **Subscriptions:** 400 journals and other serials; 17 newspapers. **Services:** Interlibrary loans; copying; library open to public with restrictions. **Publications:** PUCO Code of Rules and Regulations, second edition and revisions; Gas Pipeline Safety Code; A Portion of the Laws of Ohio Applying to Railroads; PUC In the News. **Special Catalogs:** Bibliographies (book); PUCO Recent Acquisitions (pamphlets). **Staff:** Ina G. Walker, Asst.Libn.

★11096★
PUBLIC UTILITY COMMISSION OF TEXAS - LIBRARY (Energy)
7800 Shoal Creek Blvd.   Phone: (512) 458-0251
Austin, TX 78757   Martha M. Bartow, Hd.Libn.
Staff: Prof 3. **Subjects:** Utilities, law, energy, economics. **Holdings:** 8500 books. **Subscriptions:** 145 journals and other serials; 12 newspapers. **Services:** Interlibrary loans; copying; library open to public. **Publications:** Informational pamphlets; directories of electric and telephone utilities in Texas; Library Bulletin, irregular. **Special Indexes:** Index to Public Utility Commission of Texas Bulletin; Citation index to Bulletin. **Staff:** Frances Brownlow, Libn. & Cat.; Carol King, Ref.Libn.

PUBLIC WORKS CANADA
See: Canada - Public Works Canada

PUCKETT (Newbell Niles) MEMORIAL ARCHIVES
See: Cleveland Public Library - John G. White Collection of Folklore, Orientalia, & Chess

★11097★
PUEBLO CHIEFTAIN AND STAR-JOURNAL PUBLISHING CORPORATION - LIBRARY (Publ)
825 W. 6th St.   Phone: (303) 544-3520
Pueblo, CO 81003   Betty M. Carnes, Libn.
Staff: Prof 2. **Subjects:** Newspaper reference topics. **Special Collections:** Bound volumes of the Pueblo Daily Chieftain, 1868 to present; bound volumes of the Pueblo Star-Journal, 1901 to present. **Holdings:** 300 books; 735 bound periodical volumes; 6000 filing envelopes of clippings; 10,000 personal files; 1000 historical files. **Services:** Copying; library open to public. **Staff:** Cecil Osborne, Lib.Cons.

★11098★
PUEBLO GRANDE MUSEUM - RESEARCH LIBRARY (Sci-Tech)*
4619 E. Washington St.   Phone: (602) 275-3452
Phoenix, AZ 85034   Chad T. Phinney, Musm.Asst.
Founded: 1926. **Staff:** Prof 1. **Subjects:** Archeology, anthropology. **Services:** Library open to public for reference use on request.

★11099★
PUEBLO REGIONAL PLANNING COMMISSION - LIBRARY (Plan)
Box 1427   Phone: (303) 543-6006
Pueblo, CO 81002   Donald R. Vest, Res.Libn.
Founded: 1960. **Staff:** 1. **Subjects:** Urban and regional planning, social planning, census, environmental quality, land use, zoning. **Special Collections:** Commission reports. **Holdings:** 2000 books and bound periodical volumes; 8 VF drawers; 1000 maps; planning reports. **Subscriptions:** 36 journals and other serials; 6 newspapers. **Services:** Copying; library open to public with restrictions. **Publications:** Planning Reports, 6-10/year. **Remarks:** Library is located at One City Hall Place, Pueblo, CO 81003.

PUENTE (John G.) LIBRARY
See: Capitol Institute of Technology - John G. Puente Library

PUERTO RICAN CENTER
See: University of Connecticut

★11100★
PUERTO RICAN CONGRESS OF MUSIC & ART - LIBRARY (Area-Ethnic; Mus)
2315 W. North Ave.   Phone: (312) 772-4223
Chicago, IL 60647   Carlos C. Ruiz, Exec.Dir.
Founded: 1948. **Staff:** Prof 4. **Subjects:** Music - composition, Latin American; Puerto Rican arts and crafts. **Special Collections:** Post cards of Puerto Rican towns and municipalities; History of the Puerto Ricans in Chicago and Illinois; articles written by local Puerto Rican writers. **Holdings:** 153 books; 500 Latin magazines; Estrellita's Gossip; Latin and Puerto Rican artist information. **Services:** Interlibrary loans; copying; SDI; library open to public by appointment. **Automated Operations:** Computerized circulation.

★11101★
PUERTO RICAN CULTURE INSTITUTE - LUIS MUNOZ RIVERA LIBRARY AND MUSEUM (Hum; Area-Ethnic)
Luis Munoz Rivera St. No.10
Barranquitas, PR 00618   Leticia del Rosario, Inst.Dir.
Founded: 1916. **Staff:** Prof 1; Other 1. **Subjects:** History, literature, language, art, folklore. **Special Collections:** Puerto Rican authors; information about Luis Munoz Rivera and Barranquitas. **Holdings:** 2500 books; 500 pamphlets and journals; 3 VF drawers of clippings and documents. **Services:** Interlibrary loans; library open to public for reference use only. **Publications:** Boletin Cultural, monthly - distributed to high school students. **Remarks:** This library is affiliated with the General Library of Puerto Rico. **Staff:** Maria L. Valencia, Libn.

★11102★
PUERTO RICO - ATENEO PUERTORRIQUENO - BIBLIOTECA (Hist; Area-Ethnic)
Ave. Ponce de Leon
Parada 2, Apartado 1180   Phone: (809) 722-1258
San Juan, PR 00902   Clara S. Lergier, Chf.Libn.
Founded: 1876. **Staff:** Prof 1; Other 2. **Subjects:** Puerto Rico, Puerto Rican literature, history, biography, sciences. **Special Collections:** Late 19th and Early 20th Century General Collection (2500); Puerto Rican Collection; word archive (taped lectures); portrait collection. **Holdings:** 10,500 books; 52 bound periodical volumes; 500 pamphlets; 500 magnetic tapes of conferences, 14 years; 1600 VF drawer items. **Subscriptions:** 124 journals and other serials. **Services:** Interlibrary loans (limited); copying; mail information service; open to public. **Special Catalogs:** Portraits; word archives and lectures catalogs. **Staff:** Marlene Lergier, Asst.Libn.

★11103★
PUERTO RICO - CENTRAL OFFICE OF PERSONNEL ADMINISTRATION - INSTITUTE OF PERSONNEL DEVELOPMENT - LIBRARY (Bus-Fin)*
Fernandez Juncos Sta.
Box 8476   Phone: (809) 721-4300
Santurce, PR 00910   Jose A. Fonseca Molina, Libn.
Founded: 1979. **Staff:** Prof 1. **Subjects:** Public and personnel administration, Puerto Rico history. **Holdings:** 2008 books and bound periodical volumes; 576 pamphlets; 203 reports; 56 scrapbooks of clippings. **Subscriptions:** 14 journals and other serials. **Services:** Interlibrary loans; library open to public. **Automated Operations:** Computerized cataloging and circulation. **Publications:** Boletin Informativo, quarterly. **Special Indexes:** Public Administration (card). **Also Known As:** Puerto Rico - Oficina Central Administracion Personal - Biblioteca Instituto Desarrollo Personal.

★11104★
PUERTO RICO - DEPARTMENT OF HEALTH - MEDICAL LIBRARY (Med)*
Ant. Hospital de Psiquiatria -
Bo. Monacillos
Call Box 70184   Phone: (809) 767-6060
San Juan, PR 00936   Esther Rosario Hernandez, Libn.
Founded: 1952. **Staff:** Prof 1; Other 2. **Subjects:** Public health, emergency and ambulatory services, mental health services, planning and evaluation of hospital development, health services administration, continuing medical education, allied health professions. **Holdings:** 3500 books; 180 bound periodical volumes; 1110 monographs and pamphlets; 600 bound reports and documents; 260 state reports; 558 unbound periodical volumes; 14 VF drawers of leaflets. **Subscriptions:** 563 journals and other serials. **Services:** Interlibrary loans; copying; library open to public for reference use only. **Publications:** Lista de revistas y series recibidas en la biblioteca, annual; bibliographies of publications edited by department, occasional. **Special Catalogs:** Catalog of Puerto Rican agencies publications.

★11105★
PUERTO RICO - DEPARTMENT OF HEALTH - MENTAL HEALTH LIBRARY
(Med)*
Asst. Secretariat for Mental Health
Box G.P.O. 61   Phone: (809) 781-5660
San Juan, PR 00936   Consuelo Serrano Romero, Libn.
Founded: 1957. **Staff:** Prof 1; Other 1. **Subjects:** Psychiatry, drugs,
neurology, psychotherapy, alcoholism, psychology, psychoanalysis, hypnosis,
T-groups. **Special Collections:** Collection of Dr. Luis Morales in psychiatry and
psychoanalysis (2000 items); Dr. Jose Rafael Mayme Collection (200 items).
Holdings: 5665 books; 300 bound periodical volumes; 100 special theme
materials; 200 annual reports of the Mental Health Program; 50 publications
of the Division of Human Resources. **Services:** Interlibrary loans; copying;
library open to public for reference use only. **Automated Operations:**
Computerized cataloging. **Networks/Consortia:** Member of Sociedad de
Bibliotecarios de Puerto Rico (SBPR). **Special Indexes:** Index to magazine
articles (card).

★11106★
PUERTO RICO - DEPARTMENT OF HEALTH - RAMON EMETERIO BETANCES
MEDICAL LIBRARY (Med)
Bo. Sabalos, Carr. no. 2
Box 1868   Phone: (809) 832-8686
Mayaguez, PR 00708   Myrna Y. Ramirez, Libn.
Founded: 1970. **Staff:** Prof 2; Other 1. **Subjects:** Medicine, surgery,
maternity, gynecology, pediatrics, dentistry, laboratory. **Special Collections:**
Ciba Collection. **Holdings:** 2009 books; 614 bound periodical volumes; 13
reports. **Subscriptions:** 66 journals and other serials. **Services:** Interlibrary
loans; copying; library open to public for reference use only. **Computerized
Information Services:** MEDLINE. **Networks/Consortia:** Member of
Consorcio Educativo del Oeste - Recinto Ciencias Medicas. **Staff:** Awilda
Mercado, Auxiliar de Biblioteca.

★11107★
PUERTO RICO - DEPARTMENT OF JUSTICE - LIBRARY (Law)
Box 192   Phone: (809) 721-2900
San Juan, PR 00902   Antonio Nadal, Hd. Law Libn.
Founded: 1936. **Staff:** Prof 2; Other 3. **Subjects:** Law - common, civil.
Special Collections: Puerto Rican law. **Holdings:** 70,000 books and bound
periodical volumes; 10 VF drawers. **Subscriptions:** 260 journals and other
serials; 28 newspapers. **Services:** Interlibrary loans; library open to public
with restrictions. **Publications:** Opiniones del Secretario Justicia, annual;
Informe anual del Secretario de Justicia, Anuario Estadistico.

★11108★
PUERTO RICO - GENERAL COURT OF JUSTICE - OFFICE OF COURT
ADMINISTRATION - LIBRARY DIVISION (Law)
Call Box 22-A   Phone: (809) 764-2739
Hato Rey, PR 00919   Nidia Miranda Graterole, Dir.
Staff: Prof 14; Other 12. **Subjects:** Law - civil, criminal, labor; management;
judicial administration. **Special Collections:** Spain's civil law. **Holdings:**
200,000 books; 33,000 bound periodical volumes; 1100 pamphlets; 500
judicial statistics. **Subscriptions:** 300 journals and other serials; 5
newspapers. **Services:** Interlibrary loans; copying; library open to public with
restrictions. **Remarks:** Library division organizes and supervises the Superior
Court libraries.

★11109★
PUERTO RICO - INSTITUTE OF PUERTO RICAN CULTURE - ARCHIVO
GENERAL DE PUERTO RICO (Hist)
Ponce de Leon 500, Apartado 4184   Phone: (809) 722-2113
San Juan, PR 00905   Miguel Angel Nieves, Dir.
Staff: Prof 9; Other 16. **Subjects:** Public works, municipal records, legislation,
notarial protocols, treasury, court records, health. **Holdings:** 36,000 cubic
feet of documents; 5000 pieces of music; 75 drawers of graphic arts
material; 600 cubic feet of private collections. **Subscriptions:** 15 journals
and other serials. **Services:** Copying; archives open to public. **Publications:**
Guia Al Archivo General De Puerto Rico; Loa Archivos Historicos De Puerto
Rico. **Staff:** Eduardo Leon, Archv; Carmen Alicia Davila, Archv.; Luis De La
Rosa, Archv.; Jose Flores, Archv.; Milagros Pepin, Archv.

★11110★
PUERTO RICO - INSTITUTE OF PUERTO RICAN CULTURE - LA CASA DEL
LIBRO (Publ)
Calle Del Cristo 225
Box 2265   Phone: (809) 723-0354
San Juan, PR 00903   David Jackson McWilliams, Dir.
Founded: 1955. **Staff:** 2. **Subjects:** Typography, history and art of the book,
early printed books especially Spanish, modern press books - fine editions.

Services: Open to public.

★11111★
PUERTO RICO - OFFICE OF BUDGET & MANAGEMENT - LIBRARY (Bus-Fin)
254 Cruz St.
Box 3228   Phone: (809) 725-9420
San Juan, PR 00904   Gladys Santiago, Hd.Libn.
Founded: 1942. **Staff:** Prof 1; Other 2. **Subjects:** Public administration,
budget management, economics, auditing, computers. **Special Collections:**
Puerto Rico and U.S. Law; budget documents of the states and the federal
government. **Holdings:** 5000 books; 500 bound periodical volumes; 18,000
clippings; 5100 pamphlets; 10,000 public documents. **Subscriptions:** 156
journals and other serials. **Services:** Interlibrary loans; library open to public
for reference use only. **Publications:** New acquisitions, quarterly. **Special
Indexes:** Index of professional magazines (card). **Staff:** Sylvette Betancourt,
Asst.Libn.

PUERTO RICO - OFICINA CENTRAL ADMINISTRACION PERSONAL -
BIBLIOTECA INSTITUTO DESARROLLO PERSONAL
See: Puerto Rico - Central Office of Personnel Administration - Institute
of Personnel Development

★11112★
PUERTO RICO - STATE DEPARTMENT OF CONSUMER AFFAIRS - LIBRARY
(Law)*
Minillas Govt. Center
North Tower, 5th Fl.   Phone: (809) 726-7555
Santurce, PR 00940   Israel Rivera, Libn.
Staff: Prof 1. **Subjects:** Law, economics. **Holdings:** 1717 books; 200 bound
periodical volumes. **Subscriptions:** 11 journals and other serials. **Services:**
Interlibrary loans; library open to public with restrictions.

★11113★
PUERTO RICO - SUPREME COURT - LAW LIBRARY (Law)
Box 2392   Phone: (809) 723-3863
San Juan, PR 00903   Doris Asencio-Toro, Hd.Libn.
Founded: 1953. **Staff:** Prof 4; Other 9. **Subjects:** Law. **Special Collections:**
Puerto Rican legal collections; French legal collection. **Holdings:** 77,687
volumes; 24 VF drawers; 53 drawers of microforms. **Subscriptions:** 313
journals and other serials; 7 newspapers. **Services:** Interlibrary loans; copying;
library open to public with restrictions. **Computerized Information Services:**
LEXIS. **Publications:** Nuevas Adquisiciones, monthly. **Special Indexes:** Index
to articles in Spanish and to South American legal periodicals received in the
library; list of magazines and law reviews received, organized by title, country
and subject. **Staff:** Maria E. Montijo, Tech.Serv.Dir.; Mirta Colon, Cat.Libn.;
Emma Bauza, Ref.Libn.

★11114★
PUGET SOUND COUNCIL OF GOVERNMENTS - INFORMATION CENTER
(Plan)
Grand Central on the Park
216 First Ave., S.   Phone: (206) 464-7090
Seattle, WA 98104   Cam McIntosh, Info.Spec.
Founded: 1967. **Staff:** Prof 1; Other 1. **Subjects:** Regional planning,
transportation, housing, population, land use. **Special Collections:** Small area
regional forecasts including population, households and employment. **Holdings:**
3000 books. **Subscriptions:** 110 journals and other serials; 12 newspapers.
Services: Interlibrary loans; center open to public by appointment.
Networks/Consortia: Member of WLN.

PUGET SOUND MARITIME HISTORICAL SOCIETY COLLECTION
See: Historical Society of Seattle & King County - Sophie Frye Bass
Library of Northwest Americana

★11115★
PUGET SOUND POWER AND LIGHT COMPANY LIBRARY (Bus-Fin; Energy)
                                                  Phone: (206) 454-6363
Bellevue, WA 98009   Susan Campbell Ball, Libn.
Founded: 1968. **Staff:** Prof 1; Other 2. **Subjects:** Electric utility operations,
economics, management, energy conservation. **Holdings:** 3000 books; 3000
documents and technical reports; 300 videotapes. **Subscriptions:** 300
journals and other serials. **Services:** Interlibrary loans; copying; SDI; library
open to public by appointment. **Automated Operations:** Computerized
periodical routing. **Computerized Information Services:** DIALOG, Tymshare,
Inc. **Networks/Consortia:** Member of WLN; CLASS.

PUGH (Delia Biddle) LIBRARY
See: Burlington County Historical Society - Delia Biddle Pugh Library

PULASKI COUNTY LAW LIBRARY
See: University of Arkansas at Little Rock

PULLING LAW LIBRARY
See: Villanova University

★11116★
PULP AND PAPER RESEARCH INSTITUTE OF CANADA - LIBRARY (Sci-Tech)
570 St. John's Blvd.　　　　　　　Phone: (514) 697-4110
Pointe Claire, PQ, Canada H9R 3J9　　　Alison Finnemore, Libn.
Founded: 1929. Staff: Prof 3; Other 2. Subjects: Paper, pulp, forestry, mechanical engineering, chemistry, chemical engineering, environmental biology, physics, metallurgy, economics, mathematics. Holdings: 7000 books; 10,000 bound periodical volumes; pamphlets; reports; translations; technical papers; patents. Subscriptions: 375 journals and other serials. Services: Interlibrary loans; copying; SDI. Automated Operations: Computerized search service of pulp and paper literature. Computerized Information Services: DIALOG, SDC, CISTI, Info Globe, Pergamon InfoLine Ltd., QL Systems. Publications: List of Library Books and Periodicals - distributed to libraries on request. Also Known As: Institut Canadien de Recherches sur les Pates et Papiers.

★11117★
PURDUE FREDERICK COMPANY - RESEARCH LIBRARY (Med)
100 Connecticut Ave.　　　　　　Phone: (203) 853-0123
Norwalk, CT 06856　　　　　　　Kathryn Walsh, Libn.
Founded: 1970. Staff: Prof 1; Other 1. Subjects: Pharmacology, pharmacy, chemistry, medicine. Holdings: 2300 books; 7000 bound periodical volumes; patent file. Subscriptions: 450 journals and other serials. Services: Interlibrary loans; library not open to public. Computerized Information Services: DIALOG, BRS, SDC, NLM, Occupational Health Services, Inc., Dow Jones News/Retrieval, Pergamon InfoLine Ltd.; internal database. Publications: News letter.

★11118★
PURDUE UNIVERSITY - AVIATION TECHNOLOGY LIBRARY (Sci-Tech)
Purdue Univ. Airport　　　　　　Phone: (317) 494-7640
West Lafayette, IN 47907　　　　　Dennis H. Parks, Libn.
Founded: 1960. Staff: 2. Subjects: Aviation technology, flight, aerospace education. Special Collections: General Aviation Manufacturers Association designated Aviation Education Resource Center (over 500 educators materials). Holdings: 3000 books; 1100 bound periodical volumes. Subscriptions: 75 journals and other serials. Services: Interlibrary loans; copying; library open to public. Staff: Barbara Stair, Asst.Libn.

★11119★
PURDUE UNIVERSITY - BIOCHEMISTRY LIBRARY (Sci-Tech)
Biochemistry Bldg.　　　　　　Phone: (317) 494-1621
West Lafayette, IN 47907　　　　Martha J. Bailey, Life Sci.Libn.
Founded: 1952. Staff: Prof 1; Other 1. Subjects: Biochemistry, carbohydrate chemistry. Holdings: 4900 books; 5300 bound periodical volumes; 570 dissertations. Subscriptions: 115 journals and other serials. Services: Interlibrary loans; copying; library open to public. Publications: Acquisitions list, quarterly.

★11120★
PURDUE UNIVERSITY - CHEMISTRY LIBRARY (Sci-Tech)
Chemistry Bldg.　　　　　　　Phone: (317) 494-2862
West Lafayette, IN 47907　　　　John Pinzelik, Chem.Libn.
Founded: 1874. Staff: Prof 1; Other 3. Subjects: Chemistry - inorganic, organic, biological, analytical. Special Collections: Archives of Herbert C. Brown, 1979 Nobel Laureate in chemistry. Holdings: 10,000 books; 40,000 bound periodical volumes; 2300 dissertations; 725 pamphlets; patents; 5500 microforms. Subscriptions: 500 journals and other serials. Services: Interlibrary loans; copying; library open to public. Computerized Information Services: DIALOG, SDC. Publications: Biweekly Acquisitions List. Also Known As: M.G. Mellon Library of Chemistry.

★11121★
PURDUE UNIVERSITY - CINDAS - ELECTRONIC PROPERTIES INFORMATION CENTER (Sci-Tech)
2595 Yeager Rd.　　　　　　　Phone: (317) 494-6300
West Lafayette, IN 47906　　　　　C.Y. Ho, Dir.
Founded: 1960. Subjects: Absorption coefficient; dielectric constant; dielectric strength; effective mass; electrical hysteresis; electrical resistivity; energy bands; energy gaps; energy levels; hall coefficient; magnetic hysteresis; magnetic susceptibility; mobility; refractive index; work function; electron emission; luminescence; magnetoelectric, magnetomechanical,

photoelectronic, piezoelectric and thermoelectric properties. Holdings: 95,000 indexed abstracts; 90,000 complete papers on microfiche or microfilm; 6000 new additions/year. Services: Research and special searches; reproductions; center open to public by appointment. Publications: Electronic Properties Research Literature - Retrieval Guide, Basic Edition, 4 volumes, 1979; McGraw-Hill/CINDAS Data Series on Material Properties, 2-4 handbooks/year; Special Studies - list available on request. Remarks: CINDAS is the acronym for Center for Information and Numerical Data Analysis and Synthesis. Staff: Wade H. Shafer, Asst.Dir.

★11122★
PURDUE UNIVERSITY - CINDAS - THERMOPHYSICAL PROPERTIES RESEARCH CENTER - LIBRARY (Sci-Tech)
2595 Yeager Rd.　　　　　　　Phone: (317) 494-6300
West Lafayette, IN 47906　　　　　C.Y. Ho, Dir.
Founded: 1957. Subjects: Thermophysical properties of matter - theoretical, experimental, numerical data; thermal conductivity; accommodation coefficient; thermal contact conductance; thermal diffusivity; specific heat; viscosity; emittance; reflectance; absorptance; transmittance; solar radiation to emittance ratio; Prandtl number; thermal linear expansion coefficient; thermal volumetric expansion coefficient. Holdings: 98,000 indexed abstracts; 97,000 complete papers on microfiche; 4000 new additions/year. Services: Reproductions, research and special searches; center may be visited by appointment. Publications: Thermophysical Properties Research Literature - Retrieval Guide, Basic Edition, 7 volumes, 1981; Masters Theses in the Pure and Applied Sciences, volumes 1-26, published annual; Thermophysical Properties of Matter in 14 volumes (17,000 page data series); McGraw-Hill/CINDAS Data Series on Material Properties, 2-4 handbooks/year. Remarks: CINDAS is the acronym for Center for Information and Numerical Data Analysis and Synthesis. Staff: Wade H. Shafer, Asst.Dir.

★11123★
PURDUE UNIVERSITY - CINDAS - UNDERGROUND EXCAVATION AND ROCK PROPERTIES INFORMATION CENTER
2595 Yeager Rd.
West Lafayette, IN 47906
Founded: 1972. Subjects: Mechanical, thermophysical, electrical and magnetic properties of selected rocks and minerals; codification of the literature on tunnels and other underground excavations. Holdings: 3500 indexed abstracts and complete papers on microfiche; 400 new additions/year. Remarks: CINDAS is the acronym for Center for Information and Numerical Data Analysis and Synthesis. The center is presently inactive.

★11124★
PURDUE UNIVERSITY - CONSUMER AND FAMILY SCIENCES LIBRARY (Food-Bev; Soc Sci)
Stone Hall　　　　　　　　Phone: (317) 494-2914
West Lafayette, IN 47907　　　　Judith Nixon, Libn.
Founded: 1957. Staff: Prof 1; Other 2. Subjects: Clothing and textiles; household equipment; housing and environmental design; foods and nutrition; child development and family life; restaurant, hotel and institutional management; home management; family economics. Holdings: 7700 books; 4500 bound periodical volumes; 760 theses; 15 file drawers of pamphlets and clippings. Subscriptions: 304 journals and other serials. Services: Interlibrary loans; copying; library open to public.

★11125★
PURDUE UNIVERSITY - ENGINEERING LIBRARY (Sci-Tech)
Potter Bldg.　　　　　　　　Phone: (317) 494-2867
West Lafayette, IN 47907　　　　Edwin D. Posey, Engr.Libn.
Founded: 1977. Staff: Prof 3; Other 11. Subjects: Engineering - aeronautical, chemical, civil, electrical, industrial, materials, mechanical, nuclear. Special Collections: Goss History of Engineering Library, with focus on railways and transportation. Holdings: 62,066 books; 50,486 bound periodical volumes; 82,276 technical reports; 12,370 theses; 523,673 microfiche units; 1300 maps. Subscriptions: 1523 journals and other serials. Services: Interlibrary loans; copying; library open to public. Automated Operations: Computerized cataloging and serials. Computerized Information Services: Online systems. Special Catalogs: New books, computer produced. Staff: Jerry Mansfield, Asst.Engr.Libn.; Elizabeth Keeler, Asst.Engr.Libn.

★11126★
PURDUE UNIVERSITY - FILM LIBRARY (Aud-Vis)
Stewart Center　　　　　　　Phone: (317) 494-6742
West Lafayette, IN 47907　　　　Carl E. Snow, Film Libn.
Founded: 1948. Staff: Prof 3; Other 4. Subjects: Agriculture, electrical engineering, aviation technology, home economics, horticulture, psychology. Special Collections: Medieval Archives (10,000 35mm slides of Medieval

illuminations in 500 sets). **Holdings:** 3300 films; 400 filmstrip sets; 8500 other cataloged items; 5700 tape recordings; 150 media kits; 84 film loops; 1900 slide sets. **Services:** Interlibrary loans; library open to organized groups. **Special Catalogs:** Film Catalog - distribution to users of the library; special subject catalogs (computer print-out). **Staff:** R.J. Kovac, Media Ref.Libn.

★11127★
PURDUE UNIVERSITY - GEOSCIENCES LIBRARY (Sci-Tech)
Geosciences Bldg.   Phone: (317) 494-3264
West Lafayette, IN 47907   Dennis H. Parks, Libn.
Founded: 1970. **Staff:** Prof 1; Other 1. **Subjects:** Geology, oceanography, earth science, engineering, remote sensing, stratigraphy, meteorology, paleontology, tectonophysics, astronomy, climatology, mineralogy, sedimentology, geochemistry, biogeography, petrology, geoastrophysical geomorphology, geophysical geography. **Holdings:** 3500 books; 10,000 bound periodical volumes; 140 theses. **Subscriptions:** 445 journals and other serials. **Services:** Interlibrary loans; copying; library open to public. **Computerized Information Services:** DIALOG.

★11128★
PURDUE UNIVERSITY - HUMANITIES, SOCIAL SCIENCE AND EDUCATION LIBRARY (Educ; Soc Sci; Hum)
     Phone: (317) 494-2828
West Lafayette, IN 47907   Laszlo L. Kovacs, Hum.Libn.
Staff: Prof 9; Other 34. **Subjects:** English and American literature, U.S. history, education, audiology and speech science, political science, sociology. **Holdings:** 500,000 books; 178,000 bound periodical volumes; 300,000 government documents; 850,000 microforms; United Nations documents; ERIC documents. **Subscriptions:** 7000 journals and other serials. **Services:** Interlibrary loans; copying; SDI; library open to state residents. **Automated Operations:** Computerized cataloging. **Computerized Information Services:** OCLC. **Networks/Consortia:** Member of INCOLSA. **Staff:** Barbara Pinzelik, Assoc.Hum.Libn.; Mark Tucker, Sr.Ref.Libn.; Helen Schroyer, Govt.Doc.Libn.; Stuart Saunders, Ref.Coll.Dev.; Kathleen McCullough, Hum.Bibliog.; Michael Waldo, Ref.Libn., U.N. Docs.

★11129★
PURDUE UNIVERSITY - LIFE SCIENCE LIBRARY (Agri; Env-Cons)
Lilly Hall of Life Sciences   Phone: (317) 494-2910
West Lafayette, IN 47907   Martha J. Bailey, Life Sci.Libn.
Founded: 1959. **Staff:** Prof 3; Other 6. **Subjects:** Biological sciences, entomology, forestry, horticulture, agronomy, botany, animal science, plant pathology, soil science. **Holdings:** 30,274 books; 38,532 bound periodical volumes; 1330 dissertations; 4785 microforms. **Subscriptions:** 2470 journals and other serials. **Services:** Interlibrary loans; copying; library open to public. **Computerized Information Services:** DIALOG, SDC, MEDLARS. **Publications:** Acquisitions list, monthly. **Staff:** Syed Khan, Asst. Life Sci.Libn.

★11130★
PURDUE UNIVERSITY - MANAGEMENT AND ECONOMICS LIBRARY (Bus-Fin)
Krannert Grad.Sch. of Mgt.   Phone: (317) 494-2922
West Lafayette, IN 47907   Gordon Law, Libn.
Founded: 1959. **Staff:** Prof 3; Other 8. **Subjects:** Business - organization, management; economics - applied, history, principles, theory, systems; industrial relations; agricultural economics; statistics and mathematics; marketing; taxation; real estate; finance; accounting. **Special Collections:** Estey Collection (business cycles); rare books in economics and business history, 16th-19th century (7500 volumes). **Holdings:** 158,000 books; 30,000 bound periodical volumes; 3600 bound annual reports; 100,000 corporate records; newspaper clippings; 25,000 pieces of miscellaneous information; 1250 reels of microfilm; 117,800 microforms; 1400 theses. **Subscriptions:** 2250 journals and other serials. **Services:** Interlibrary loans; copying; library open to public. **Automated Operations:** Computerized serials. **Computerized Information Services:** DIALOG, SDC, BRS, OCLC. **Networks/Consortia:** Member of INCOLSA. **Publications:** Monthly Acquisitions List; occasional publications - on request. **Special Catalogs:** Catalog of rare books (book); catalog of corporation records (microfiche). **Staff:** Priscilla C. Geahigan, Asst.Libn.

★11131★
PURDUE UNIVERSITY - MATHEMATICAL SCIENCES LIBRARY (Sci-Tech)
Mathematical Sciences   Phone: (317) 494-2855
West Lafayette, IN 47907   Richard L. Funkhouser, Libn.
Founded: 1910. **Staff:** Prof 1; Other 3. **Subjects:** Mathematics, statistics, computer sciences. **Holdings:** 22,000 books; 18,000 bound periodical volumes; 493 reels of microfilm; 3600 technical reports; 470 theses. **Subscriptions:** 557 journals and other serials. **Services:** Interlibrary loans; copying; library open to public.

★11132★
PURDUE UNIVERSITY - PHARMACY, NURSING AND HEALTH SCIENCES LIBRARY (Med)
Pharmacy Bldg.   Phone: (317) 494-1416
West Lafayette, IN 47907   Theodora Andrews, Libn.
Founded: 1982. **Staff:** Prof 1; Other 4. **Subjects:** Pharmaceutical sciences, pharmacy, clinical medicine, nursing, bionucleonics, environmental sciences. **Special Collections:** Drug abuse collection (1275 volumes). **Holdings:** 25,000 books; 19,482 bound periodical volumes; 24 VF drawers of pamphlets; 150 audio cassettes; 15 drawers of microfiche. **Subscriptions:** 620 journals and other serials. **Services:** Interlibrary loans; copying; SDI; library open to public. **Automated Operations:** Computerized cataloging and serials (all through General Library). **Computerized Information Services:** Online systems. **Networks/Consortia:** Member of Greater Midwest Regional Medical Library Network (Region 3). **Publications:** Purdue University Pharmacy, Nursing and Health Sciences Library Notes, quarterly - distributed to faculty, graduate students, pharmacy libraries and mailing list.

★11133★
PURDUE UNIVERSITY - PHYSICS LIBRARY (Sci-Tech)
Physics Bldg.   Phone: (317) 494-2858
West Lafayette, IN 47907   Dennis H. Parks, Libn.
Founded: 1905. **Staff:** Prof 1; Other 3. **Subjects:** Physics - classical, mathematical, modern, solid state, nuclear; pure and applied mathematics; astronomy. **Holdings:** 21,000 books; 16,000 bound periodical volumes; 575 theses. **Subscriptions:** 364 journals and other serials. **Services:** Interlibrary loans; copying; library open to public. **Computerized Information Services:** DIALOG. **Publications:** New Acquisitions List, monthly; Library Handbook; Annual Bibliographies - all available on request.

★11134★
PURDUE UNIVERSITY - PSYCHOLOGICAL SCIENCES LIBRARY (Soc Sci)
Peirce Hall   Phone: (317) 494-2969
West Lafayette, IN 47907   Pam Baxter, Psych.Libn.
Founded: 1966. **Staff:** Prof 1; Other 2. **Subjects:** Psychology. **Holdings:** 14,000 books; 6200 bound periodical volumes; 1550 theses. **Subscriptions:** 300 journals and other serials. **Services:** Interlibrary loans; copying; library open to public.

★11135★
PURDUE UNIVERSITY - VETERINARY MEDICAL LIBRARY (Med)
C.V. Lynn Hall, Rm. 108   Phone: (317) 494-2852
West Lafayette, IN 47907   Gretchen Stephens, Libn.
Founded: 1960. **Staff:** Prof 1; Other 3. **Subjects:** Comparative and veterinary medicine, animal behavior, comparative anatomy, neuroanatomy, pathology, laboratory animal medicine. **Holdings:** 17,500 books; 21,600 bound periodical volumes. **Subscriptions:** 860 journals and other serials. **Services:** Interlibrary loans; copying; library open to public. **Automated Operations:** Computerized cataloging. **Computerized Information Services:** OCLC. **Networks/Consortia:** Member of INCOLSA.

★11136★
PURDUE UNIVERSITY, CALUMET - LIBRARY (Educ)
2233 171st St.   Phone: (219) 844-0520
Hammond, IN 46323   Bernard H. Holicky, Dir.
Founded: 1947. **Staff:** Prof 5; Other 12. **Subjects:** Science and technology, humanities, social science. **Holdings:** 160,330 books and bound periodical volumes; 7004 reels of microfilm; 311,745 microforms. **Subscriptions:** 1231 journals and other serials. **Services:** Interlibrary loans; copying; library open to public with limited circulation. **Automated Operations:** Computerized cataloging, acquisitions and ILL. **Computerized Information Services:** BRS, DIALOG, MEDLARS, SDC, OCLC, TEDS. **Networks/Consortia:** Member of INCOLSA; Northwest Indiana Area Library Services Authority. **Staff:** Peter P. Chojenski, Ref.Libn.; Karen M. Corey, Rd.Serv.Libn.; Sheila A. Rezak, Teacher Educ.Rsrcs.; Margaret S. Schoon, Tech.Serv.Libn.

PURDUE UNIVERSITY AT FORT WAYNE
See: Indiana University/Purdue University at Fort Wayne

PURDUE UNIVERSITY AT INDIANAPOLIS
See: Indiana University/Purdue University at Indianapolis

PURDY (G. Flint) LIBRARY
See: Wayne State University - G. Flint Purdy Library

PURDY MEMORIAL LIBRARY
See: Canton Art Institute

PURDY (Ross Coffin) MUSEUM OF CERAMICS
See: American Ceramic Society

★11137★
PURE CARBON CO., INC. - ENGINEERING LIBRARY (Sci-Tech)
441 Hall Ave.   Phone: (814) 781-1573
St. Marys, PA 15857   Betty J. Clark, Libn.
Founded: 1966. **Staff:** 1. **Subjects:** Carbon. **Holdings:** 1190 books; 2025 technical brochures; 1840 U.S. and foreign patents. **Services:** Library not open to public.

★11138★
PUREX CORPORATION - TECHNICAL LIBRARY (Sci-Tech)
24600 S. Main St.
Box 6200   Phone: (213) 775-2111
Carson, CA 90749   Louise Y. Sakamoto, Libn.
Staff: Prof 1. **Subjects:** Chemical technology, chemistry. **Holdings:** 4000 books. **Subscriptions:** 100 journals and other serials. **Services:** Copying; library open to public for reference use only.

PURVIS LIBRARY
See: Kemptville College of Agricultural Technology

PUSEY LIBRARY
See: Harvard University

★11139★
PUTNAM COMPANIES - INVESTMENT RESEARCH LIBRARY (Bus-Fin)
One Post Office Sq.   Phone: (617) 292-1335
Boston, MA 02109   Susan L. Avitabile, Libn./Asst.V.P.
Founded: 1968. **Staff:** Prof 1; Other 2. **Subjects:** Mutual funds, financial and economic data. **Holdings:** 100 books; 3000 files on major American and foreign companies including annual and quarterly reports, 10Ks, brokerage reports. **Subscriptions:** 350 journals and other serials; 20 newspapers. **Services:** Interlibrary loans; library not open to public. **Computerized Information Services:** DIALOG, NEXIS; internal database. **Remarks:** This is a subsidiary of Marsh and McLennan, Inc. **Staff:** Lila Taylor, Asst.Libn.

★11140★
PUTNAM COUNTY HISTORICAL SOCIETY - ARCHIVES (Hist)
Roy O. West Library
DePauw University   Phone: (317) 658-4501
Greencastle, IN 46135
Subjects: County history and genealogy. **Holdings:** 50 books; 21 VF drawers of photos, clippings, letters, diaries, scrapbooks; microfilm, tape recordings, movies. **Services:** Copying; archives open to public. **Staff:** Virginia C. Brann, Sr.Archv.Asst.; Julia J. Young, Sr.Archv.Asst.

★11141★
PUTNAM COUNTY HISTORICAL SOCIETY - FOUNDRY SCHOOL MUSEUM - REFERENCE LIBRARY (Hist)
63 Chestnut St.   Phone: (914) 265-2781
Cold Spring, NY 10516   Carol F. Morse, Libn.
Founded: 1962. **Staff:** 1. **Subjects:** Genealogy; Putnam, Westchester and Dutchess County history; West Point; American Revolution; Hudson River; West Point Foundry. **Special Collections:** Works of Susan and Anna Warner (24 volumes). **Holdings:** 1200 volumes; manuscripts; 2 VF drawers of clippings and newspapers; 30 boxes of archives and letters; 2 VF drawers of maps. **Services:** Library open to public on a limited schedule and by appointment.

★11142★
PUTNAM (Henry W.) MEMORIAL HOSPITAL - MEDICAL LIBRARY (Med)*
100 Hospital Dr.   Phone: (802) 442-6361
Bennington, VT 05201   Jack Hall, Med.Libn.
Staff: Prof 1. **Subjects:** Medicine, surgery. **Holdings:** 1200 books; Audio-Digest tapes. **Subscriptions:** 123 journals and other serials. **Services:** Interlibrary loans; copying; library open to public with restrictions. **Networks/Consortia:** Member of Greater Northeastern Regional Medical Library Program.

★11143★
PUTNAM MUSEUM - LIBRARY (Hist)
1717 W. 12th St.   Phone: (319) 324-1933
Davenport, IA 52804   Michael J. Smith, Dir.
Founded: 1867. **Staff:** 14. **Subjects:** Local and regional history, natural history, anthropology, geology, steamboat history. **Special Collections:** Upper Mississippi River steamboat history; photographs; Civil War; early settlers; newspapers. **Holdings:** 45,000 volumes; 50 VF drawers of documents, pamphlets, maps, broadsides, handbills; 12 VF drawers of Black Store papers; 16 VF drawers of clippings. **Subscriptions:** 15 journals and other serials. **Services:** Library open to public by appointment. **Staff:** Carol Hunt, Cur., Hist.Coll.

★11144★
PUTNEY, TWOMBLY, HALL & HIRSON - LAW LIBRARY (Law)
250 Park Ave.   Phone: (212) 661-8700
New York, NY 10017   Lois Liss, Libn.
Staff: Prof 1. **Subjects:** Law, including labor, corporate, trust, estate and tax law. **Holdings:** 8000 books. **Subscriptions:** 12 journals and other serials. **Services:** Library not open to public.

PU'UHONUA O HONAUNAU NATL. HISTORICAL PARK
See: U.S. Natl. Park Service

PYLE (Howard) LIBRARY
See: Delaware Art Museum - Library

PYMATUNING LABORATORY OF ECOLOGY
See: University of Pittsburgh

Q

★11145★
Q.I.T. - FER ET TITANE INC. - BIBLIOTHEQUE (Sci-Tech)
B.P. 560   Phone: (514) 742-6671
Sorel, PQ, Canada J3P 5P6   C. Stroemgren, Libn.
Founded: 1950. **Subjects:** Chemistry, engineering, business. **Holdings:** Figures not available. **Services:** Interlibrary loans; copying; library open to public by appointment. **Also Known As:** Fer et Titane du Quebec, Inc.; Quebec Iron and Titanium Corporation.

★11146★
QUADREX CORPORATION - LIBRARY (Sci-Tech)
1700 Dell Ave.   Phone: (408) 866-4510
Campbell, CA 95008   Margaret C. Ma, Libn.
Staff: Prof 1; Other 1. **Subjects:** Nuclear science and technology, mechanical and civil engineering, computer application, instrumentation and control. **Holdings:** 2000 books; 200 bound periodical volumes; 800 reports; 30 drawers of technical reports on microfiche; 20 drawers of standards (hard copy and microfiche). **Subscriptions:** 127 journals and other serials. **Services:** Interlibrary loans; library not open to public. **Computerized Information Services:** DIALOG, DOE/RECON. **Publications:** Library Bulletin, quarterly.

★11147★
QUAIN AND RAMSTAD CLINIC - MEDICAL LIBRARY (Med)
622 Ave. A East   Phone: (701) 222-5390
Bismarck, ND 58501   Harriet Kling, Med.Libn.
Founded: 1920. **Staff:** Prof 1; Other 1. **Subjects:** Clinical medicine. **Special Collections:** Pediatric peptic ulcer. **Holdings:** 1600 books; 15,000 bound periodical volumes; 4 VF drawers of pamphlets and reprints. **Subscriptions:** 221 journals and other serials. **Services:** Interlibrary loans; copying; SDI; library open to public with permission. **Computerized Information Services:** MEDLINE. **Networks/Consortia:** Member of Greater Midwest Regional Medical Library Network (Region 3). **Special Catalogs:** Peptic ulcer bibliography; peptic ulcer registry.

★11148★
QUAKER CHEMICAL CORPORATION - INFORMATION RESOURCES CENTER (Sci-Tech)
                                                           Phone: (215) 828-4250
Conshohocken, PA 19428   Ellen B. Morrow, Mgr.
Founded: 1952. **Staff:** Prof 2; Other 6. **Subjects:** Chemical technology for the metals and paper specialty fields. **Holdings:** 3000 books and bound periodical volumes; 4500 pamphlets; 25 VF drawers of vendor literature; 85 VF drawers of documents and miscellaneous materials; chemical patents on microfilm, 1966 to present; 225 reels of microfilm of journals; 60 reels of microfilm of documents; 3 VF drawers of government reports on microfiche; 30 audio cassettes. **Subscriptions:** 130 journals and other serials. **Services:** Interlibrary loans; copying; center open to public by appointment. **Automated Operations:** Computerized circulation. **Computerized Information Services:** DIALOG, SDC, Derwent Publications Ltd.; internal databases. **Publications:** Current awareness lists; Current Contents Alert; Regulatory Alert. **Staff:** Kathryn F. Strang, Coord., Regulatory Aff.; Jane L. Williams, Info.Rsrcs.Coord.

★11149★
QUAKER OATS COMPANY - JOHN STUART RESEARCH LABORATORIES - RESEARCH LIBRARY (Food-Bev)
617 W. Main St.   Phone: (312) 381-1980
Barrington, IL 60010   Geraldine R. Horton, Mgr., Lib.
Staff: Prof 3; Other 2. **Subjects:** Food, biochemistry, nutrition, chemical engineering, organic chemistry. **Holdings:** 10,000 books; 4000 bound periodical volumes; 50 VF drawers of reprints and pamphlets; internal reports. **Subscriptions:** 500 journals and other serials. **Services:** Interlibrary loans; copying (limited); library open to public with permission. **Automated Operations:** Computerized cataloging. **Computerized Information Services:** DIALOG, SDC. **Staff:** Jeanne M. Head, Acq.Libn.; Adrienne Jasnich, Sr.Info.Sci.

★11150★
QUARLES & BRADY - LIBRARY (Law)
780 N. Water St.   Phone: (414) 277-5000
Milwaukee, WI 53202   Susan H. Jankowski, Libn.
Staff: Prof 2; Other 1. **Subjects:** Law - litigation, labor, tax, patent, securities, pension, banking. **Special Collections:** Wisconsin Statutes, 1898

to present. **Holdings:** 40,000 volumes; microfiche. **Subscriptions:** 100 journals and other serials and newspapers. **Services:** Library not open to public. **Computerized Information Services:** LEXIS, DIALOG. **Networks/Consortia:** Member of Library Council of Metropolitan Milwaukee, Inc. (LCOMM); Milwaukee Downtown Law Librarians; Chicago Association of Law Libraries. **Special Catalogs:** Hospital brief, memo and litigation file. **Staff:** Linda Marifke, Sr.Asst.Libn.; Kay Christiansen, Asst.Libn.

QUAYLE RARE BIBLE COLLECTION
See: Baker University

QUEBEC CEREBRAL PALSY ASSOCIATION
See: Association de Paralysie Cerebrale du Quebec, Inc.

QUEBEC CONSERVATORY OF DRAMATIC ART
See: Conservatoire d'Art Dramatique de Quebec

QUEBEC IRON AND TITANIUM CORPORATION
See: Q.I.T. - Fer et Titane Inc.

QUEBEC PENSION BOARD
See: Quebec Province - Regie des Rentes

★11151★
QUEBEC PROVINCE - ARCHIVES NATIONALES DU QUEBEC - BIBLIOTHEQUE (Hist)
C.P. 10450   Phone: (418) 643-2167
Ste. Foy, PQ, Canada G1V 4N1   Colette Barry, Libn.
Founded: 1920. **Staff:** Prof 1; Other 2. **Subjects:** History of Quebec, Canada and French Canada; biography; numismatics; genealogy; church history; sociology. **Holdings:** 40,000 books; 6000 bound periodical volumes; 7000 other cataloged items; 800,000 photographs; 20,000 maps; 260 reels of microfilm of journals. **Subscriptions:** 200 journals and other serials. **Services:** Interlibrary loans; copying; library open to public with permission. **Publications:** Rapport des Archives Nationales du Quebec. **Remarks:** Maintained by the Ministere des Affaires Culturelles. **Also Known As:** Quebec Province National Archives.

★11152★
QUEBEC PROVINCE - BIBLIOTHEQUE DE L'ASSEMBLEE NATIONALE (Law)
Edifice Pamphile-Lemay   Phone: (418) 643-2896
Quebec, PQ, Canada G1A 1A5   Jacques Premont, Dir.
Founded: 1802. **Staff:** Prof 32; Other 56. **Subjects:** Law - Canadian, French, English, American; political science; economics; legislation; Canadiana. **Special Collections:** British Parliamentary Papers. **Holdings:** 446,187 books; 50,708 bound periodical volumes; 24,029 Canadian pamphlets and other cataloged items; 11,520 reels of microfilm of journals and newspapers; 88,323 microfiche of government publications. **Subscriptions:** 1150 journals and other serials. **Services:** Interlibrary loans; copying. **Automated Operations:** Computerized cataloging. **Computerized Information Services:** DIALOG, SDC, Informatech, UTLAS. **Networks/Consortia:** Member of RIBLIN. **Publications:** Bulletin de la Bibliotheque de la Legislature; Bibliographie et Documentation (series); Argus (press reviews). **Special Indexes:** Index to the laws of the Province of Quebec (card). **Formerly:** Quebec Province - Legislature du Quebec - Bibliotheque.

★11153★
QUEBEC PROVINCE - BIBLIOTHEQUE NATIONALE DU QUEBEC (Hist; Hum; Info Sci)
1700, rue St-Denis   Phone: (514) 873-4553
Montreal, PQ, Canada H2X 3K6   M. Jean-Remi Brault, Conservateur en Chef
Founded: 1968. **Staff:** Prof 43; Other 80. **Subjects:** Quebec. **Special Collections:** Books printed before 1821. **Holdings:** 368,200 books and bound periodical volumes; 21,887 reels of microfilm; 7146 monographic maps; 19,710 serial maps; 742.77 linear meters of manuscripts; 20,675 pieces of sheet music. **Subscriptions:** 8686 journals and other serials. **Services:** Interlibrary loans; copying; library open to public. **Automated Operations:** Computerized cataloging. **Computerized Information Services:** UTLAS, Informatech, DOBIS; FMQ (internal database). Performs searches on subscription basis. Contact Person: Philippe Martin, 873-2783. **Networks/Consortia:** Member of CREPUQ. **Publications:** List of publications - available on request. **Special Indexes:** Index to Bulletin de la Bibliotheque nationale du Quebec, 1968-1982. **Staff:** Marcel Fontaine, Conservateur-Adjoint; Roland Auger, Dir., Coll.Dev. & Cons.; Real Bosa, Dir., Pub.Serv.; Pierre Deslauriers, Dir., Bibliog.Serv.; Philippe Martin .

QUEBEC PROVINCE - BIBLIOTHEQUE NATIONALE DU QUEBEC - CINEMATHEQUE QUEBECOISE
See: Cinematheque Quebecoise

★11154★
QUEBEC PROVINCE - BIBLIOTHEQUE NATIONALE DU QUEBEC - SERVICE DES COLLECTIONS SPECIALES - SECTEUR MUSIQUE (Mus)
1700 rue Saint-Denis   Phone: (514) 873-4512
Montreal, PQ, Canada H2X 3K6   Gabrielle Bourbonnais, Hd.
Staff: Prof 2. **Subjects:** Music from Quebec, Canada, and other countries. **Holdings:** 20,000 pieces of sheet music; 90 boxes of clippings; 6300 78rpm phonograph records. **Services:** Copying; section open to public for reference use only. **Remarks:** Books and periodicals relating to music are included in the general collection of the library. **Staff:** Denis Rivest .

★11155★
QUEBEC PROVINCE - CAISSE DE DEPOT ET PLACEMENT DU QUEBEC - LIBRARY (Bus-Fin)†
C.P. 74, Tour de la Bourse   Phone: (514) 873-2460
Montreal, PQ, Canada H4Z 1B4   Pauline Lefebvre Gour, Libn.
Founded: 1967. **Staff:** 2. **Subjects:** Finance, economics, marketing, general statistics. **Holdings:** 2500 books. **Subscriptions:** 175 journals and other serials; 10 newspapers. **Services:** Library not open to public.

★11156★
QUEBEC PROVINCE - CENTRALE DES BIBLIOTHEQUES - CENTRE DOCUMENTAIRE (Info Sci)
1685 Est, Rue Fleury   Phone: (514) 382-0895
Montreal, PQ, Canada H2C 1T1   Gertrude S. DeCarufel, Hd.Libn.
Founded: 1971. **Staff:** Prof 1; Other 2. **Subjects:** Bibliography, reference. **Holdings:** 4500 books; 650 bound periodical volumes. **Subscriptions:** 165 journals and other serials; 6 newspapers. **Services:** Copying; center open to public by appointment. **Remarks:** Centrale des Bibliotheques is a processing center for the college, school and public libraries of Quebec Province. **Staff:** Francine Andre-Angers, Bibliotechnicienne.

QUEBEC PROVINCE - CENTRE DE RECHERCHE INDUSTRIELLE DU QUEBEC
See: Centre de Recherche Industrielle du Quebec

★11157★
QUEBEC PROVINCE - COMMISSION DE LA SANTE ET DE LA SECURITE DU TRAVAIL - CENTRE DE DOCUMENTATION (Soc Sci)
C.P. 6067, Succ. A   Phone: (514) 873-3160
Montreal, PQ, Canada H3C 4E2   Suzanne Heureux
Staff: Prof 8; Other 16. **Subjects:** Occupational health and safety. **Holdings:** 10,000 books. **Subscriptions:** 400 journals and other serials. **Services:** Interlibrary loans; copying; center open to public. **Automated Operations:** Computerized cataloging. **Computerized Information Services:** DIALOG, SDC, MEDLARS, CAN/OLE, QL Systems, COMSHARE, Inc., INFORMATECH, CCH State Tax Review. **Publications:** Sommaire des Periodiques, 25/year.

QUEBEC PROVINCE - DEPARTMENT OF SOCIAL AFFAIRS
See: Quebec Province - Ministere des Affaires Sociales

★11158★
QUEBEC PROVINCE - DIRECTION GENERALE DES MOYENS D'ENSEIGNEMENT - CENTRE DE DOCUMENTATION (Educ)*
600 rue Fullum, 5th Fl.   Phone: (514) 873-3973
Montreal, PQ, Canada H2K 4L1   Chantal Robinson, Assoc.Dir.
Founded: 1969. **Staff:** Prof 2; Other 5. **Subjects:** Educational technology, methods of instruction, correspondence courses. **Holdings:** 12,650 books, bound periodical volumes and pamphlets; 172,000 ERIC microfiche; 4200 AV documents; 650 maps. **Subscriptions:** 485 journals and other serials. **Services:** Interlibrary loans; copying; center open to public for reference use only. **Publications:** Monthly list of new acquisitions; selective list of periodicals, monthly. **Special Indexes:** Index to Quebec provincial laws. **Remarks:** Maintained by Quebec Province Ministere de l'Education.

QUEBEC PROVINCE - ELECTRICITY AND GAS BOARD
See: Quebec Province - Regie de l'Electricite et du Gaz

★11159★
QUEBEC PROVINCE - L'INSPECTEUR GENERAL DES INSTITUTIONS FINANCIERES - BIBLIOTHEQUE (Bus-Fin)
800 Place D'Youville, 7th Fl.   Phone: (418) 643-5236
Quebec, PQ, Canada G1R 4Y5   Sylvie Nadeau, Bibliotechnicienne
Founded: 1969. **Staff:** Prof 1; Other 1. **Subjects:** Financial institutions, finance, insurance, law. **Holdings:** 9000 books; 175 bound periodical volumes; 417 annual reports. **Subscriptions:** 350 journals and other serials; 20 newspapers. **Services:** Interlibrary loans; copying; library open to public with restrictions. **Publications:** Bibliotheque Documentation, monthly. **Formerly:** Quebec Province - Ministere des Consommateurs, Cooperatives et Institutions Financieres.

QUEBEC PROVINCE - LEGISLATURE DU QUEBEC - BIBLIOTHEQUE
See: Quebec Province - Bibliotheque de l'Assemblee Nationale

QUEBEC PROVINCE - MINISTERE DES AFFAIRES CULTURELLES - ARCHIVES NATIONALES DU QUEBEC
See: Quebec Province - Archives Nationales du Quebec

★11160★
QUEBEC PROVINCE - MINISTERE DES AFFAIRES CULTURELLES - CENTRE DE DOCUMENTATION (Hum)†
225 Grande-Allee Est   Phone: (418) 643-6330
Quebec, PQ, Canada G1R 5G5   Real Dumoulin, Chf.
Staff: Prof 3; Other 3. **Subjects:** Politics, humanities, museology, cultural heritage, archeology, architecture, music, theater. **Holdings:** 20,000 books; microcards; microfilm; slides; maps. **Subscriptions:** 600 journals and other serials. **Services:** Interlibrary loans; copying; center open to public. **Automated Operations:** Computerized cataloging. **Networks/Consortia:** Member of RIBLIN. **Publications:** Bulletin of periodicals and monographs. **Staff:** Marie-Therese Thibault, Ref.; Jeannine Morin, Tech.Serv.

QUEBEC PROVINCE - MINISTERE DES AFFAIRES CULTURELLES - MUSEE D'ART CONTEMPORAIN
See: Musee d'Art Contemporain

QUEBEC PROVINCE - MINISTERE DES AFFAIRES CULTURELLES - MUSEE DU QUEBEC
See: Musee du Quebec

★11161★
QUEBEC PROVINCE - MINISTERE DES AFFAIRES MUNICIPALES - CENTRE DE DOCUMENTATION (Plan)
20, rue Chauveau   Phone: (418) 643-6570
Quebec, PQ, Canada G1R 4J3   Ernest Bertrand Roy, Responsable
Founded: 1976. **Staff:** Prof 1; Other 2. **Subjects:** Municipal administration, urban affairs, planning, urbanization, real estate. **Holdings:** 8500 books; 130 bound periodical volumes; maps. **Subscriptions:** 120 journals and other serials. **Services:** Interlibrary loans; copying (limited); center open to public with restrictions. **Automated Operations:** Computerized cataloging and acquisitions. **Computerized Information Services:** UTLAS. **Publications:** Monthly Bulletin for Acquisitions. **Special Indexes:** Computerized card index for authors, titles, subjects, regions.

★11162★
QUEBEC PROVINCE - MINISTERE DES AFFAIRES SOCIALES - SERVICE DE LA DOCUMENTATION (Med; Soc Sci)
6161 rue Saint-Denis, R.C. 07   Phone: (514) 873-3695
Montreal, PQ, Canada H2S 2R5   Gerard Darlington, Libn.
Founded: 1921. **Staff:** Prof 1; Other 2. **Subjects:** Social medicine, sociology, public hygiene, juvenile delinquency, mental hygiene. **Holdings:** 8000 books; 2000 bound periodical volumes; pamphlets, reports, clippings, articles. **Subscriptions:** 264 journals and other serials. **Services:** Interlibrary loans; copying; library open to public for reference use only.

★11163★
QUEBEC PROVINCE - MINISTERE DES AFFAIRES SOCIALES - SERVICE DE LA DOCUMENTATION (Med; Soc Sci)
1075 Chemin Ste-Foy   Phone: (418) 643-6392
Quebec, PQ, Canada G1S 2M1   Yvon Papillon, Hd.Libn.
Staff: Prof 4; Other 5. **Subjects:** Health and social services, medical economics. **Special Collections:** World Health Organization publications. **Holdings:** 35,000 books. **Subscriptions:** 325 journals and other serials. **Services:** Interlibrary loans; copying; SDI; service open to public for reference use only. **Automated Operations:** Computerized cataloging. **Computerized Information Services:** DIALOG, Questel. **Publications:** Informations Documentaires, monthly. **Staff:** Francois Allard, Ref. & Acq.Libn.; Ginette Ruel, Cat.Libn.; Jacqueline Vallee, Ref.Libn.

★11164★
QUEBEC PROVINCE - MINISTERE DE L'AGRICULTURE, DES PECHERIES ET DE L'ALIMENTATION - CENTRE DE DOCUMENTATION (Agri)
200-A, Chemin Ste-Foy   Phone: (418) 643-2428
Quebec, PQ, Canada G1R 4X6   Michele Audette, Responsable
Founded: 1942. **Staff:** Prof 1; Other 2. **Subjects:** Agriculture, food, fisheries, veterinary medicine. **Special Collections:** Ministry publications. **Holdings:** 12,000 books; 1200 bound periodical volumes; 55 AV items. **Subscriptions:** 350 journals and other serials. **Services:** Interlibrary loans; copying; center open to public. **Computerized Information Services:** DIALOG, Informatech. **Networks/Consortia:** Member of ASTED. **Publications:** Agri-Revue.

★11165★

QUEBEC PROVINCE - MINISTERE DES COMMUNICATIONS - BIBLIOTHEQUE ADMINISTRATIVE (Soc Sci)
1037 de la Chevrotiere, Edifice G					Phone: (418) 643-1515
Quebec, PQ, Canada G1R 4Y7					Monique Charbonneau, Lib.Dir.
Founded: 1972. **Staff:** Prof 8; Other 26. **Subjects:** Public administration and management, education, international affairs, labour and manpower, communications. **Holdings:** 150,000 volumes; 125,000 microforms. **Subscriptions:** 1000 journals and other serials. **Services:** Interlibrary loans; copying; library open to Quebec civil servants. **Automated Operations:** Computerized cataloging. **Computerized Information Services:** DIALOG, SDC, CAN/OLE, QL Systems, New York Times Information Service, UTLAS, BADADUQ, Informatech. **Publications:** Sommaires de la documentation courante: Administration & Gestion, Communications, Relations de Travail, Sciences de l'Education, Administration locale et regionale; acces aux publications gouvernementales quebecoises et canadiennes: index permute; Economie et Politique. **Special Catalogs:** Union catalog of periodicals in Quebec government libraries. **Remarks:** The Bibliotheque Administrative includes two libraries which jointly serve sixteen Quebec government departments. **Staff:** Lise Villeneuve-Allaire, Libn., Cat.Dept.; Nelson St-Pierre, Libn., Coll.Dev.; Jean-Marc Labrie, Libn., Online Serv.; Marc Fournier, Depository Prog. & Cat.; Louise Lindsay, Ref.Libn., Edifice G.; Francine Lemieux, Ref., Edifice H.

QUEBEC PROVINCE - MINISTERE DES CONSOMMATEURS, COOPERATIVES ET INSTITUTIONS FINANCIERES
See: Quebec Province - L'Inspecteur General des Institutions Financieres

QUEBEC PROVINCE - MINISTERE DE L'EDUCATION - DIRECTION GENERALE DES MOYENS D'ENSEIGNEMENT
See: Quebec Province - Direction Generale des Moyens d'Enseignement

QUEBEC PROVINCE - MINISTERE DE L'ENERGIE ET DES RESSOURCES - REGIE DE L'ELECTRICITE ET DU GAZ
See: Quebec Province - Regie de l'Electricite et du Gaz

★11166★

QUEBEC PROV. - MIN. DE L'ENERGIE ET DES RESSOURCES - SERVICE DE DOCUMENTATION ET DE RENSEIGNEMENTS (Sci-Tech; Energy)
200B Chemin Ste-Foy, 7th Fl.					Phone: (418) 643-6004
Quebec, PQ, Canada G1R 4X7					Normand Guerette, Dir.
Founded: 1979. **Staff:** Prof 4; Other 17. **Subjects:** Forests and forestry, surveying, geodesy, mines and mining, energy, pollution, geology, metallurgy, mineral chemistry, forest economics, law, conservation, entomology. **Special Collections:** U.S. Bureau of Mines (microfiche); department records (microfiche). **Holdings:** 109,500 volumes; 300 patents; 1500 reels of microfilm; 12,000 microfiche. **Subscriptions:** 1462 journals and other serials; 75 newspapers. **Services:** Interlibrary loans (fee); copying; SDI; open to public with restrictions. **Automated Operations:** Computerized cataloging. **Computerized Information Services:** DIALOG, QL Systems, SDC, CAN/OLE, CAN/SDI, Informatech, Questel, Info Globe. **Networks/Consortia:** Member of RIBLIN. **Publications:** List of Periodicals; Printed Catalog; Info-Mer-Mines, bimonthly; Info-Mer-Terres et Forets, bimonthly; Info-Mer-Energie, monthly - all free upon request. **Special Indexes:** Index of Northern Miner. **Formed by the Merger of:** Ministere des Richesses Naturelles and Ministere des Terres et Forets. **Staff:** Jacques Fournier, SDI; Edward Collister, SDI; Real Fortier, Hd., Info. to Citizens; Claudette Roy, Hd., Automated Sys.

★11167★

QUEBEC PROVINCE - MINISTERE DE L'INDUSTRIE, DU COMMERCE ET DU TOURISME - BIBLIOTHEQUE MINISTERIELLE (Bus-Fin)
710 Place d'Youville, local 203					Phone: (418) 643-5081
Quebec, PQ, Canada G1R 4Y4					Mario Day, Responsable
Founded: 1957. **Staff:** Prof 2; Other 6. **Subjects:** Economics, industrial development, commerce, statistics, tourism, finance, cooperative societies. **Special Collections:** Statistics Canada (32,000 documents); Financial Post Corporation Service Cards (complete set); Stanford Research Institute publications (500). **Holdings:** 14,000 books; 100 bound periodical volumes; 36,000 unbound periodicals. **Subscriptions:** 600 journals and other serials; 25 newspapers. **Services:** Interlibrary loans (limited); copying; library open to public with restrictions. **Automated Operations:** Computerized cataloging. **Computerized Information Services:** DIALOG, Informatech, Info Globe. **Networks/Consortia:** Member of RIBLIN. **Publications:** Bulletin mensuel de la documentation courante, monthly - for internal distribution only; revue de presse quotidienne du MICT, daily - for internal distribution only. **Staff:** Gilbert Plaisance, Ref.

★11168★

QUEBEC PROVINCE - MINISTERE DE LA JUSTICE - BIBLIOTHEQUE (Law)
1200, Route de l'Eglise
Edifice Delta, 4th Fl.					Phone: (418) 643-8409
Ste. Foy, PQ, Canada G1V 4M1					Michel Ricard, Agent de Recherche
Founded: 1965. **Staff:** Prof 1; Other 2. **Subjects:** Law. **Special Collections:** Statutes. **Holdings:** 9800 books; 200 bound periodical volumes; 200 reports and government documents; 400 unbound periodicals; 3967 microfiche. **Subscriptions:** 150 journals and other serials. **Services:** Copying; library open to public. **Computerized Information Services:** QL Systems. **Publications:** New acquisitions list. **Staff:** Francoise Bilodeau, Bibliotechnicienne.

★11169★

QUEBEC PROVINCE - MINISTERE DU LOISIR, DE LA CHASSE ET DE LA PECHE - BIBLIOTHEQUE (Env-Cons)
150 est, Blvd. St-Cyrille					Phone: (418) 643-5300
Quebec, PQ, Canada G1R 4Y3
Founded: 1967. **Staff:** Prof 1; Other 5. **Subjects:** Wildlife management, conservation, ecology, zoology, ornithology, fish culture, game, hunting, sport fishing, recreation. **Holdings:** 8000 books; 1500 bound periodical volumes; 44 VF drawers of reprints and pamphlets; 6000 research reports and manuscripts. **Subscriptions:** 285 journals and other serials. **Services:** Interlibrary loans; copying (limited); library open to public for reference use only. **Automated Operations:** Computerized cataloging.

★11170★

QUEBEC PROVINCE - MINISTERE DU LOISIR, DE LA CHASSE ET DE LA PECHE - BIBLIOTHEQUE DE LA FAUNE (Sci-Tech; Env-Cons)
6255 13th Ave.					Phone: (514) 374-5840
Montreal, PQ, Canada H1X 3E6					Richard Mathieu, Chf.Libn.
Founded: 1945. **Staff:** Prof 1; Other 2. **Subjects:** Aquatic fauna, limnology, mammology, ecology, North American birds, environmental pollution. **Special Collections:** Natural history (16th, 17th and 18th centuries); works of French, American and English naturalists (17th, 18th and 19th centuries). **Holdings:** 8500 books; 160,000 periodical volumes; 3000 reprints. **Subscriptions:** 185 journals and other serials. **Services:** Interlibrary loans; copying; library open to qualified users only. **Networks/Consortia:** Member of ASTED. **Publications:** Monthly recent books list.

★11171★

QUEBEC PROVINCE - MINISTERE DU REVENU - BIBLIOTHEQUE (Bus-Fin)
3800, Rue Marly					Phone: (418) 644-6835
Ste. Foy, PQ, Canada G1X 4A5					Pierre-Paul Blais, Dir.
Staff: 2. **Subjects:** Tax law and administration, management. **Holdings:** 5000 books; 450 bound periodical volumes. **Subscriptions:** 30 journals and other serials; 20 newspapers. **Services:** Interlibrary loans; library open to government employees.

★11172★

QUEBEC PROVINCE - MINISTERE DU TRAVAIL ET DE LA MAIN-D'OEUVRE - BIBLIOTHEQUE
255 Est, Boul. Cremazie
Montreal, PQ, Canada H2M 1L5
Defunct

QUEBEC PROVINCE - NATIONAL ARCHIVES
See: Quebec Province - Archives Nationales du Quebec

★11173★

QUEBEC PROVINCE - OFFICE DES COMMUNICATIONS SOCIALES - BIBLIOTHEQUE ET CENTRE DE DOCUMENTATION (Info Sci)
4005 De Bellechasse					Phone: (514) 729-6391
Montreal, PQ, Canada H1X 1J6					Lucien Labille, Dir.
Founded: 1957. **Staff:** Prof 1; Other 2. **Subjects:** Cinema, radio, television, cablevision, the press. **Holdings:** 6000 books; 400 bound periodical volumes; microfilm; unbound documents. **Subscriptions:** 60 journals and other serials; 10 newspapers. **Services:** Copying; library open to public with restrictions. **Computerized Information Services:** Computerized information and evaluation on 20,000 feature films. **Publications:** List of publications for sale - available on request. **Special Indexes:** Index to film documentation. **Remarks:** Library provides facilities for the office's Centre de Documentation Cinematographique, which produces a continuing series ("Documentation Filmographique") of film documentation available on microfilm.

★11174★

QUEBEC PROVINCE - OFFICE DE PLANIFICATION ET DE DEVELOPPEMENT DU QUEBEC - BIBLIOTHEQUE (Plan)†
1060 Rue Conroy
Complexe G, Bloc 2, 3rd Fl.					Phone: (418) 643-1607
Quebec, PQ, Canada G1R 5E6					Suzanne Plante-Garneau
Staff: 2. **Subjects:** Regional planning, economic development, urbanism.

Holdings: 7000 books; 1000 other cataloged items; 50 annual reports from provincial and federal government departments. **Subscriptions:** 80 journals and other serials. **Services:** Interlibrary loans; copying; library open to public with restrictions. **Publications:** Bulletin HEBDO: acquisitions list, biweekly. **Staff:** Charlotte Bouchard, Bibliotechnicienne.

★11175★
QUEBEC PROVINCE - REGIE DE L'ELECTRICITE ET DU GAZ - BIBLIOTHEQUE
(Bus-Fin; Energy)
2100, rue Drummond   Phone: (514) 873-2452
Montreal, PQ, Canada H3G 1X1   Marielle Bernard, Lib.Techn.
Founded: 1973. **Staff:** Prof 1. **Subjects:** Public utilities, energy, Canadian oil and gas, accounting, law, economics. **Holdings:** 1800 books; 110 bound periodical volumes; 520 other cataloged items; 450 codes and standards; annual reports; conference proceedings; regulations. **Subscriptions:** 45 journals and other serials. **Services:** Interlibrary loans; copying; library open to public by appointment. **Remarks:** Maintained by Ministere de l'Energie et des Ressources. **Also Known As:** Electricity and Gas Board.

★11176★
QUEBEC PROVINCE - REGIE DES RENTES - CENTRE DE DOCUMENTATION
(Soc Sci)
C.P. 5200   Phone: (418) 643-8250
Quebec, PQ, Canada G1K 7S9   Michel Dupuis, Libn.
Founded: 1965. **Staff:** Prof 1; Other 3. **Subjects:** Social security, private pension plans. **Holdings:** 10,000 books and bound periodical volumes; 5500 microfiche; 430 pamphlets and reprints. **Subscriptions:** 299 journals and other serials. **Services:** Interlibrary loans; copying; SDI; center open to public with permission. **Automated Operations:** Computerized cataloging. **Computerized Information Services:** DIALOG, Informatech, QL Systems, Banque de Terminologie du Quebec. Performs searches on cost recovery basis. **Publications:** Nouvelles acquisitions, bimonthly - for exchange; Periodiques recus, annual with supplements - for internal distribution only; Repertoire des periodiques, 1981 - limited distribution. **Also Known As:** Quebec Pension Board.

QUEBEC PROVINCE - SOCIETE DE RADIO-TELEVISION DU QUEBEC - RADIO QUEBEC
See: Radio Quebec

QUEBEC ZOOLOGICAL GARDEN
See: Jardin Zoologique de Quebec

★11177★
QUEEN ANNE'S COUNTY LAW LIBRARY (Law)
Court House   Phone: (301) 758-0216
Centreville, MD 21617   Mary F. Engle, Libn.
Staff: 1. **Subjects:** U.S. and Maryland law. **Holdings:** 3500 books; 158 bound periodical volumes. **Services:** Library open to public with restrictions.

★11178★
QUEEN ELIZABETH II HOSPITAL - MEDICAL LIBRARY (Med)
10409 98th St.
Postal Bag 2600
Grande Prairie, AB, Canada T8V 2E8   Phone: (403) 538-7100
Founded: 1984. **Staff:** 1. **Subjects:** Medicine. **Holdings:** 2000 books; 220 bound periodical volumes. **Subscriptions:** 232 journals and other serials. **Services:** Interlibrary loans; copying; library open to public for reference use only. **Formerly:** Grande Prairie General Hospital - Library.

QUEEN ELIZABETH II LIBRARY
See: Memorial University of Newfoundland

★11179★
QUEEN STREET MENTAL HEALTH CENTRE - HEALTH SCIENCES LIBRARY
(Med)
1001 Queen St., W.   Phone: (416) 535-8501
Toronto, ON, Canada M6J 1H3   Mary Ann Georges, Staff Libn.
Founded: 1965. **Staff:** Prof 1; Other 2. **Subjects:** Psychiatry, psychology, nursing, psychopharmacology, sociology, administration, rehabilitation. **Special Collections:** Hospital History File (history of Queen Street Mental Health Centre); Griffin-Greenland History of Canadian Psychiatry Collection. **Holdings:** 3000 books; 3000 bound periodical volumes; 50 theses; 150 AV cassettes; 4 VF drawers. **Subscriptions:** 202 journals and other serials. **Services:** Interlibrary loans; copying; library open to public for reference use only. **Publications:** Acquisitions list, 3/year; journals list, annual.

★11180★
QUEEN'S BENCH - COURT OF APPEAL JUDGES' LIBRARY (Law)
Law Courts Bldg.
1A Churchill Sq.
Edmonton, AB, Canada T5J 0R2   Shih-Sheng Hu, Chf.Prov. Law Libn.
Subjects: Law. **Holdings:** 6300 volumes. **Services:** Library not open to public. **Remarks:** Housed with Law Society of Alberta - Edmonton Library.

★11181★
QUEENS BOROUGH PUBLIC LIBRARY - ART AND MUSIC DIVISION (Art; Mus)
89-11 Merrick Blvd.   Phone: (718) 990-0755
Jamaica, NY 11432   Dorothea Wu, Div.Hd.
Founded: 1933. **Staff:** Prof 6; Other 3. **Subjects:** Art, music, theatre, dance, games, sports. **Special Collections:** Picture collection (1.5 million reproductions, photographs, postcards, clippings). **Holdings:** 86,000 books; 6736 bound periodical volumes; 10,000 phonograph records; 2500 cassettes; 1407 reels of microfilm; 46 VF drawers of pamphlets; 460 titles of libretti; 180 framed pictures. **Subscriptions:** 275 periodical titles. **Services:** Interlibrary loans; copying. **Special Indexes:** Subject Index to Picture Collection (card, ditto); Song Index (card); Symphonic Program Note Index (card). **Staff:** Claire Kach, Asst.Div.Hd.

★11182★
QUEENS BOROUGH PUBLIC LIBRARY - HISTORY, TRAVEL & BIOGRAPHY DIVISION (Hist)
89-11 Merrick Blvd.   Phone: (718) 990-0762
Jamaica, NY 11432   Deborah Hammer, Div.Hd.
Founded: 1930. **Staff:** Prof 6; Other 3. **Subjects:** History, Indians of North America, biography, geography, travel, exploration. **Special Collections:** U.S. Geographic Survey topographic maps (4800); physical/thematic maps of countries of the world (126); nautical charts (813); jet/ocean/world navigation charts (520); national forest maps (75); Latin American topographic maps (97); New York State planimetric maps (968); New York state, county and road maps (78); railroad transportation zone maps (82); historic/city maps (442). **Holdings:** 130,000 books; 3100 bound periodical volumes; 4100 microforms; 36 VF drawers of pamphlets; New York Daily News on microfilm, 1955 to present. **Subscriptions:** 84 journals and other serials; 24 newspapers. **Services:** Interlibrary loans; copying. **Special Indexes:** Collective biography analytics (card). **Staff:** John Moran, Asst.Div.Hd.; Esther Kluss, Ref.Libn.

★11183★
QUEENS BOROUGH PUBLIC LIBRARY - LANGSTON HUGHES COMMUNITY LIBRARY AND CULTURAL CENTER (Area-Ethnic)
102-09 Northern Blvd.   Phone: (718) 651-1100
Corona, NY 11368   Andrew P. Jackson, Exec.Dir.
Founded: 1969. **Staff:** Prof 9; Other 34. **Subjects:** Black heritage, arts, education, Third World history. **Special Collections:** Langston Hughes Collection (books by and about the author); Black Heritage Center for Queens County; law. **Holdings:** 90,000 books; 150 documents, manuscripts and reels of microfilm. **Subscriptions:** 105 journals and other serials; 15 newspapers. **Services:** Copying; library open to public. **Publications:** Library Center Brochure. **Staff:** Clementine Lewis, Supv.; Rodney Lee, Cur., Black Heritage Ctr.; Grace Holmes, Dir. Homework Assist.Prog; Gale Jackson, Lib.Adv.-Black Heritage; Carl Rogers, Lib.Adv.

★11184★
QUEENS BOROUGH PUBLIC LIBRARY - LANGUAGE & LITERATURE DIVISION (Hum)
89-11 Merrick Blvd.   Phone: (718) 990-0763
Jamaica, NY 11432   Inge M. Judd, Div.Hd.
Founded: 1928. **Staff:** Prof 7; Other 4. **Subjects:** Literature, linguistics, fiction and nonfiction in 75 languages (not including English). **Special Collections:** Foreign language books. **Holdings:** 255,000 books; 5396 bound periodical volumes; 250 sets of phonograph records; 36 VF drawers of pamphlets; 215 microfiche; 2100 reels of microfilm. **Subscriptions:** 665 journals and other serials. **Services:** Interlibrary loans; copying. **Special Indexes:** Play Index (card). **Staff:** Diane Guzzo, Asst.Div.Hd.; Stephan Wroblewski, Ref.Libn.

★11185★
QUEENS BOROUGH PUBLIC LIBRARY - LONG ISLAND DIVISION (Hist)
89-11 Merrick Blvd.   Phone: (718) 990-0770
Jamaica, NY 11432   Nicholas Falco, Div.Hd.
Founded: 1912. **Staff:** Prof 3; Other 2. **Subjects:** Long Island local history and genealogy. **Special Collections:** Books published at Marion Press (private press in Jamaica, NY); publications of Christopher Morley. **Holdings:** 23,000 books; 1600 bound periodical volumes; 60 VF drawers of clippings; 5300

maps; 36,500 manuscripts; 7400 reels of microfilm; 33,000 pictures including prints, photographs, postcards, glass plate negatives. **Subscriptions:** 187 journals and other serials; 48 newspapers. **Services:** Interlibrary loans; copying. **Staff:** William Asadorian, Ref.

★11186★
QUEENS BOROUGH PUBLIC LIBRARY - SCIENCE & TECHNOLOGY DIVISION
(Sci-Tech; Bus-Fin)
89-11 Merrick Blvd.   Phone: (718) 990-0760
Jamaica, NY 11432   John D. Brady, Jr., Div.Hd.
Founded: 1930. **Staff:** Prof 7; Other 4. **Subjects:** Mathematics, engineering, accounting, chemistry, biological sciences, advertising, nursing, physics, business administration, aeronautics, patents. **Special Collections:** Telephone directories for all major U.S. and foreign cities; automobile and household repair manuals. **Holdings:** 180,190 books; 29,494 bound periodical volumes; 9311 reels of microfilm of back issue periodicals; 50 VF drawers. **Subscriptions:** 1645 journals and other serials. **Services:** Interlibrary loans; copying. **Staff:** Hermina Montag, Asst.Div.Hd.

★11187★
QUEENS BOROUGH PUBLIC LIBRARY - SOCIAL SCIENCES DIVISION (Soc Sci; Bus-Fin)
89-11 Merrick Blvd.   Phone: (718) 990-0761
Jamaica, NY 11432   Nathan Shoengold, Div.Hd.
Founded: 1930. **Staff:** Prof 7; Other 5. **Subjects:** Philosophy, psychology, religion, sociology, economics and investments, political science, government, law, education, costumes, folklore. **Special Collections:** Investment, law and tax services; college catalogs; civil service study guides; ERIC documents; corporate reports; curriculum-related pamphlets; Hiler costume collection. **Holdings:** 275,000 books; 26,837 bound periodical volumes; 116 VF drawers; 224 microfiche drawers; 103 newsletters; 8850 reels of microfilm; 154 microcards; 565,000 ERIC microfiche. **Subscriptions:** 1465 journals and other serials; 14 newspapers. **Services:** Interlibrary loans; copying; division open to public. **Staff:** Renee Kaplan, Asst.Div.Hd.

★11188★
QUEENS CHILDREN'S PSYCHIATRIC CENTER - LAURETTA BENDER STAFF LIBRARY (Med)*
74-03 Commonwealth Blvd.   Phone: (718) 464-2900
Bellerose, NY 11426   Mr. L. Feher, Libn.
Staff: Prof 1. **Subjects:** Child psychiatry and psychology, special education, learning disabilities, social work, adolescence, psychoanalysis. **Special Collections:** Collection of reprints from psychiatric journals (300); Lauretta Bender series (books on Bender-gestalt; reprints and limited works of Dr. Paul Ferdinand Schilder). **Holdings:** 5000 books; 300 bound periodical volumes; 650 reprints and pamphlets (cataloged); 300 reels of tape; Audio-Digest tapes on psychiatry. **Subscriptions:** 80 journals and other serials. **Services:** Interlibrary loans; library not open to public.

★11189★
QUEENS COLLEGE OF THE CITY UNIVERSITY OF NEW YORK - CTR. FOR BYZANTINE & MODERN GREEK STUD. - LIB. (Hum; Area-Ethnic)
     Phone: (718) 520-7035
Flushing, NY 11367   Prof. Harry J. Psomiades, Dir.
Staff: Prof 1; Other 2. **Subjects:** Modern Greek language, literature, and history; Greek American community. **Holdings:** 2000 books; 100 other cataloged items. **Subscriptions:** 10 journals and other serials.

★11190★
QUEENS COLLEGE OF THE CITY UNIVERSITY OF NEW YORK - ETHNIC MATERIALS INFORMATION CENTER (Area-Ethnic)
Graduate School of Lib. & Info. Studies
64-15 Kissena Blvd.   Phone: (718) 520-7194
Flushing, NY 11367   David Cohen, Prog.Dir.
Staff: Prof 1; Other 1. **Subjects:** Ethnic studies resources, minority groups in America. **Holdings:** 2000 volumes; 40 filmstrips; 10 tapes; 250 pamphlets. **Services:** Center open to public.

★11191★
QUEENS COLLEGE OF THE CITY UNIVERSITY OF NEW YORK - PAUL KLAPPER LIBRARY - ART LIBRARY (Art)
     Phone: (718) 520-7243
Flushing, NY 11367   Suzanna Simor, Hd.
Founded: 1937. **Staff:** Prof 2; Other 5. **Subjects:** Art, architecture, archeology, design, photography. **Holdings:** 33,000 books; 3600 bound periodical volumes; 15,000 pamphlets; 7000 exhibition catalogs; 27,000 mounted reproductions; 824 microfiche; 11,000 slides. **Subscriptions:** 175 journals and other serials. **Services:** Interlibrary loans; copying; library open to public for reference use only. **Automated Operations:** Computerized

cataloging, serials and circulation. **Computerized Information Services:** DIALOG, RLIN, OCLC. Performs searches on fee basis. **Networks/Consortia:** Member of SUNY/OCLC Library Network. **Publications:** New Books, quarterly; List of Periodicals Available, 2/year - both distributed within Queens College; Collection Development Policy, 1st edition, 1983 - distributed within CUNY and upon request. **Staff:** Irene Avens, Art Libn.

★11192★
QUEENS COLLEGE OF THE CITY UNIVERSITY OF NEW YORK - PAUL KLAPPER LIBRARY - HISTORICAL DOCUMENTS COLLECTION (Hist)
     Phone: (718) 520-7482
Flushing, NY 11367
Subjects: State and local history, 1660-1860. **Holdings:** 18,000 cubic feet of legal records, wills, inventories, administrative papers, assessment lists and criminal court records. **Services:** Copying; collection open to public.

★11193★
QUEENS COLLEGE OF THE CITY UNIVERSITY OF NEW YORK - SCIENCE LIBRARY (Sci-Tech; Med)
65-30 Kissena Blvd.   Phone: (718) 520-7254
Flushing, NY 11367   Jackson B. Cohen, Hd., Sci.Lib.
Staff: Prof 2; Other 2. **Subjects:** Biology, psychology, chemistry, mathematics, physics, earth and environmental sciences, computer science, home economics, speech pathology, audiology, sports physiology and medicine. **Holdings:** 67,000 books; 32,000 bound periodical volumes; 30 VF drawers of pamphlets; microfilm. **Subscriptions:** 1850 journals and other serials. **Services:** Interlibrary loans; copying; library open to public for reference use only. **Automated Operations:** Computerized cataloging, serials and circulation. **Computerized Information Services:** DIALOG, BRS. **Networks/Consortia:** Member of METRO. **Publications:** Science Library Reference Guide series, irregular - to on-site library users. **Staff:** Gail Ronnermann, Sci.Libn.

QUEENS HOSPITAL CENTER
See: Long Island Jewish-Hillside Medical Center

★11194★
QUEEN'S UNIVERSITY AT KINGSTON - ART LIBRARY (Art)
Ontario Hall   Phone: (613) 547-2633
Kingston, ON, Canada K7L 5C4   Eve Albrich, Music/Art Libn.
Founded: 1957. **Staff:** Prof 1; Other 2. **Subjects:** Art history, art education, art conservation. **Holdings:** 22,000 books and bound periodical volumes; 600 microfiche; 118 reels of microfilm; 8500 exhibition catalogs; 100,000 35mm slides; 50,000 photographs. **Subscriptions:** 100 journals and other serials. **Services:** Interlibrary loans; library open to public with restrictions. **Remarks:** Slides and photographs are owned and administered by the Department of Art. They are inaccessible to the public.

★11195★
QUEEN'S UNIVERSITY AT KINGSTON - BIOLOGY LIBRARY (Sci-Tech)
Earl Hall, Barrie St.   Phone: (613) 547-2896
Kingston, ON, Canada K7L 5C4   Mrs. J. Stevenson, Lib.Asst.
Staff: 2. **Subjects:** Biology. **Holdings:** 23,000 books and bound periodical volumes. **Subscriptions:** 358 journals and other serials. **Services:** Interlibrary loans; copying; SDI; library open to teachers and technical staff of local institutions. **Computerized Information Services:** CAN/OLE, QL Systems, BRS, DIALOG.

★11196★
QUEEN'S UNIVERSITY AT KINGSTON - BRACKEN LIBRARY (Med)
     Phone: (613) 547-5753
Kingston, ON, Canada K7L 3N6   Gwen Wright, Libn.
Staff: Prof 4; Other 9. **Subjects:** Medicine, nursing, rehabilitation. **Holdings:** 85,000 volumes. **Subscriptions:** 1342 journals and other serials. **Services:** Interlibrary loans; copying; library open to health sciences personnel. **Automated Operations:** Computerized cataloging, acquisitions and circulation. **Computerized Information Services:** MEDLINE, BRS, DIALOG. **Publications:** Bracken Library New Book List, monthly, September-May; Subscription List, annual. **Staff:** Monica Webster, Ser.Libn.; Vivien Ludwin, Pub.Serv.Libn.; Mr. V. Mahalingam, Tech.Serv.Libn.

QUEEN'S UNIVERSITY AT KINGSTON - CANADIAN INSTITUTE OF GUIDED GROUND TRANSPORT
See: Canadian Institute of Guided Ground Transport

★11197★
QUEEN'S UNIVERSITY AT KINGSTON - CHEMISTRY LIBRARY (Sci-Tech)
Frost Wing, Gordon Hall Phone: (613) 547-2636
Kingston, ON, Canada K7L 5C4 Janet Innis, Lib.Asst.
Staff: 2. **Subjects:** Chemistry. **Holdings:** 10,500 books and bound periodical volumes. **Subscriptions:** 315 journals and other serials. **Services:** Interlibrary loans; copying; SDI; library open to teachers and technical staff of local industries. **Computerized Information Services:** CAN/OLE, QL Systems, BRS.

★11198★
QUEEN'S UNIVERSITY AT KINGSTON - CIVIL ENGINEERING LIBRARY (Sci-Tech)
Ellis Hall Phone: (613) 547-5546
Kingston, ON, Canada K7L 5C4 Stewart Renfrew, Lib.Techn.
Staff: 1. **Subjects:** Civil engineering. **Holdings:** 13,500 books and bound periodical volumes. **Subscriptions:** 266 journals and other serials. **Services:** Interlibrary loans; SDI; library open to public with restrictions. **Automated Operations:** Computerized circulation. **Computerized Information Services:** DIALOG, CAN/OLE, BRS, QL Systems. Performs searches on cost recovery basis.

★11199★
QUEEN'S UNIVERSITY AT KINGSTON - DOCUMENTS LIBRARY (Bus-Fin; Soc Sci)
Mackintosh-Corry Hall Phone: (613) 547-6138
Kingston, ON, Canada K7L 3N6 Peter Girard, Doc.Libn.
Founded: 1960. **Staff:** Prof 4; Other 14. **Subjects:** Economics and business, sociology, political science, urban affairs, planning, history, geography, public administration, ecology. **Special Collections:** Royal Commissions of Canada (3600 volumes); 17th century British documents; pre-Confederation official publications (1500 volumes); Parliamentary publications for Canada (Federal and Provincial); United Nations, EEC and OECD, IMF, ILO documents. **Holdings:** 500,000 volumes; 313,030 microfiche; 324,160 microcards; 5567 reels of microfilm; 85,000 maps; complete Statistics Canada publications; census documents. **Subscriptions:** 3000 journals and other serials. **Services:** Interlibrary loans; copying; library open to public with restrictions. **Automated Operations:** Computerized coding. **Special Indexes:** KWOC index of document holdings. **Remarks:** An alternate phone number is 547-5767. **Staff:** John Offenbeck, Pub.Serv.Libn.; Judith Fraser, Tech.Serv.Libn.; Robyn Zuck, Ref.Libn.

★11200★
QUEEN'S UNIVERSITY AT KINGSTON - DUPUIS HALL LIBRARY (Sci-Tech)
Division & Clergy Sts.
Kingston, ON, Canada K7L 5C4 Mrs. B. Walls, Lib.Asst.
Staff: 2. **Subjects:** Engineering - chemical, mining, metallurgical. **Holdings:** 22,000 books and bound periodical volumes. **Subscriptions:** 360 journals and other serials. **Services:** Interlibrary loans; SDI; library open to teachers and technical staff of local industries. **Computerized Information Services:** QL Systems, BRS, CAN/OLE.

★11201★
QUEEN'S UNIVERSITY AT KINGSTON - EDUCATION LIBRARY (Educ)
Duncan McArthur Hall Phone: (613) 547-6286
Kingston, ON, Canada K7L 3N6 Sandra Casey, Educ.Libn.
Founded: 1966. **Staff:** Prof 2; Other 7. **Subjects:** Education, psychology. **Holdings:** 80,000 books and bound periodical volumes; 4700 pamphlets and miscellaneous government documents; 400,000 microfiche titles; 4000 filmstrips and film loops; 3500 35mm slides; 2000 phonograph records, cassettes and audiotapes; 2000 transparencies. **Subscriptions:** 878 journals and other serials. **Services:** Interlibrary loans; copying; library open to teachers. **Computerized Information Services:** BRS, Ontario Education Resources Information System (ONTERIS). **Publications:** Periodicals List, annual. **Staff:** Melanie Harris, Asst.Libn; Marian Meagher, Supv.Circ.

★11202★
QUEEN'S UNIVERSITY AT KINGSTON - ELECTRICAL ENGINEERING LIBRARY (Sci-Tech)
Fleming Hall
Kingston, ON, Canada K7L 5C4 Christine Bruce, Lib.Asst.
Founded: 1930. **Staff:** 1. **Subjects:** Electrical engineering. **Holdings:** 8048 books and bound periodical volumes. **Subscriptions:** 204 journals and other serials. **Services:** Interlibrary loans; SDI; library open to technical staff of local industries and institutions. **Computerized Information Services:** CAN/OLE, BRS, QL Systems.

★11203★
QUEEN'S UNIVERSITY AT KINGSTON - GEOLOGICAL SCIENCES LIBRARY (Sci-Tech)
Miller Hall, Bruce Wing Phone: (613) 547-2653
Kingston, ON, Canada K7L 5C4 Mary Mayson, Sr.Lib.Techn.
Founded: 1932. **Staff:** 2. **Subjects:** Geological sciences. **Holdings:** 80,000 books and bound periodical volumes; 1020 theses; 35,000 maps; microfiche; microfilm. **Subscriptions:** 450 journals and other serials. **Services:** Interlibrary loans; SDI; library open to public. **Automated Operations:** Computerized circulation. **Computerized Information Services:** CAN/OLE, BRS, QL Systems. **Special Indexes:** Index to maps.

★11204★
QUEEN'S UNIVERSITY AT KINGSTON - INDUSTRIAL RELATIONS CENTRE - LIBRARY (Soc Sci)
Phone: (613) 547-6917
Kingston, ON, Canada K7L 3N6 Carol Williams, Libn.
Founded: 1937. **Staff:** 3. **Subjects:** Industrial relations, labor economics, personnel administration. **Special Collections:** Canadian Government Documents (20,000); United States Government Documents (5000); International Labor Organization Documents (5000). **Holdings:** 5000 books; 2000 bound periodical volumes; 200 VF drawers of pamphlets, reports and dissertations; 343 reels of microfilm. **Subscriptions:** 500 journals and other serials. **Services:** Interlibrary loans; copying; library open to public for reference use only, by request. **Publications:** Bibliographies on various industrial relations topics. **Special Indexes:** Index of Industrial Relations Literature, annual (book). **Staff:** Wendy Gower, Libn.

★11205★
QUEEN'S UNIVERSITY AT KINGSTON - LAW LIBRARY (Law)
Sir John A. Macdonald Hall Phone: (613) 547-5934
Kingston, ON, Canada K7L 3N6 Irene Bessette, Libn.
Founded: 1957. **Staff:** Prof 4; Other 9. **Subjects:** Law. **Special Collections:** Law - international, Quebec, French, labour, criminal and public. **Holdings:** 140,500 books and bound periodical volumes. **Subscriptions:** 3850 journals and other serials. **Services:** Interlibrary loans; copying; library open to public. **Computerized Information Services:** QL Systems. **Staff:** Mrs. Mai Chen, Coord., Tech.Serv.; Jeffrey Johnson, Supv., Pub.Serv.; Elizabeth Fox, Cat.Libn.

★11206★
QUEEN'S UNIVERSITY AT KINGSTON - MAP AND AIR PHOTO LIBRARY (Geog-Map)
Mackintosh-Corry Hall Phone: (613) 547-6193
Kingston, ON, Canada K7L 5C4 Kathy Harding, Sr.Lib.Asst.
Staff: 2. **Subjects:** Cartography, aerial photography, photogrammetry. **Special Collections:** Historical cartography collection. **Holdings:** 850 books; 820 atlases; 85,000 maps; 35,000 aerial photographs; theses; soil surveys; working papers. **Subscriptions:** 50 journals and other serials. **Services:** Interlibrary loans; library open to public with restrictions.

★11207★
QUEEN'S UNIVERSITY AT KINGSTON - MATHEMATICS LIBRARY (Sci-Tech)
Jeffery Hall Phone: (613) 547-5720
Kingston, ON, Canada K7L 5C4 Mrs. D. Nuttall, Lib.Asst.
Staff: 2. **Subjects:** Mathematics. **Holdings:** 23,000 books and bound periodical volumes. **Subscriptions:** 384 journals and other serials.

★11208★
QUEEN'S UNIVERSITY AT KINGSTON - MECHANICAL ENGINEERING LIBRARY (Sci-Tech)
McLaughlin Hall, Stuart St. Phone: (613) 547-2714
Kingston, ON, Canada K7L 5C4 Hilary Richardson, Lib.Asst.
Staff: 1. **Subjects:** Mechanical engineering. **Holdings:** 8200 books and bound periodical volumes. **Subscriptions:** 150 journals and other serials. **Services:** Interlibrary loans; copying; SDI; library open to technical staff of local firms. **Computerized Information Services:** CAN/OLE, QL Systems, BRS, DIALOG.

★11209★
QUEEN'S UNIVERSITY AT KINGSTON - MUSIC LIBRARY (Mus)
Harrison-LeCaine Hall Phone: (613) 547-2873
Kingston, ON, Canada K7L 5C4 Eve Albrich, Music/Art Libn.
Staff: Prof 1; Other 2. **Subjects:** Musicology, music education, ethnomusicology. **Holdings:** 8000 books and bound periodical volumes; 10,500 scores; 50 cassettes; 540 open reel tapes; 230 reels of microfilm; 5500 sound recordings. **Subscriptions:** 120 journals and other serials. **Services:** Interlibrary loans; library open to public with restrictions.

★11210★
QUEEN'S UNIVERSITY AT KINGSTON - PHYSICS LIBRARY (Sci-Tech)
Stirling Hall, Queen's Crescent   Phone: (613) 547-2739
Kingston, ON, Canada K7L 5C4   Catherine Johnson, Lib.Asst.
Staff: 2. **Subjects:** Physics, astronomy. **Holdings:** 20,000 books and bound periodical volumes. **Subscriptions:** 265 journals and other serials. **Services:** Interlibrary loans; SDI; library open to teachers and technical staff of local industries. **Automated Operations:** Computerized circulation. **Computerized Information Services:** CAN/OLE, BRS, QL Systems.

★11211★
QUEEN'S UNIVERSITY AT KINGSTON - PSYCHOLOGY LIBRARY (Soc Sci)
Humphrey Hall   Phone: (613) 547-3172
Kingston, ON, Canada K7L 5C4   Barbara Astbury, Lib.Techn.
Staff: 2. **Subjects:** Psychology. **Holdings:** 12,575 books and bound periodical volumes. **Subscriptions:** 205 journals and other serials. **Services:** Interlibrary loans. **Computerized Information Services:** CAN/OLE, QL Systems, BRS.

★11212★
QUEEN'S UNIVERSITY AT KINGSTON - SPECIAL COLLECTIONS (Hum)
Douglas Library   Phone: (613) 547-3030
Kingston, ON, Canada K7L 5C4   William F.E. Morley, Cur., Spec.Coll.
Founded: 1965. **Staff:** Prof 1; Other 2. **Subjects:** Canadiana; English, Irish and Scottish literature. **Special Collections:** Lorne Pierce, Canadiana (56,000 volumes); John Buchan and T.D. Macgillivray, Scottish (5200 volumes); 18th century British pamphlets (3000 items); McNicol, telecommunications (1200 volumes); Riche-Covington, astrophysics (1000 volumes); Victor Hugo (150 volumes); dated, rare books, published prior to 1700 (1100 volumes); Bible collection (1200 volumes); children's collection (2000 volumes); Gothic Fantasy collection (1000 volumes); F.R. Scott, little magazines (900 items); Dickens British and American first editions (350 volumes); Galsworthy (230 volumes); Masefield (240 volumes); Disraeli (1350 volumes); sample Canadian journals (1500). **Holdings:** 75,000 books, bound periodical volumes and Canadian pamphlets; 1000 non-Canadian pamphlets; 650 volumes in Canadian School Text collection; 200 atlases; 500 items in Canadian Centennial Collection; 94 drawers of microfiche; 3 drawers of information materials; 7000 Canadian programmes; 1000 pieces of Canadian sheet music; 600 maps and plans; 2000 broadsides and posters; 3000 postcards; 500 greeting cards; 2400 ephemera; 1000 bookplates; 17,500 items in papers collections. **Subscriptions:** 135 journals and other serials. **Services:** Interlibrary loans; copying; collections open to public. **Automated Operations:** Computerized cataloging and circulation. **Publications:** Douglas Library Occasional Papers, irregular - to Canadian libraries and others on request. **Special Indexes:** Card indexes - publisher, printer, date, provenance, Canadian imprints in French, 18th century British pamphlets, maps, private presses, broadsides, sheet music, sample journals. Book indexes - Galsworthy, Masefield, sheet music, F.R. Scott, Gothic Fantasy, McNicol, Bible, Dickens, Riche-Covington, Victor Hugo, Canadian School Text, 18th Century British Pamphlets, Bishop Macdonell, Cartwright Kingston and Children's Collections.

QUEENSBURY HISTORICAL ASSOCIATION, INC.
See: Glens Falls-Queensbury Historical Association, Inc.

★11213★
QUEST RESEARCH CORPORATION - LIBRARY (Sci-Tech; Mil)
6858 Old Dominion Dr.   Phone: (703) 821-3200
McLean, VA 22101   Stacey McKinley, Libn.
Founded: 1975. **Staff:** Prof 1. **Subjects:** Electrical engineering, optics, radar, microwaves, military-related subjects. **Special Collections:** M.I.T. Radiation Laboratory Series (complete set - 28 volumes); Selected Rand Abstracts (1963 to present). **Holdings:** 2000 books; 1000 NTIS/DDC documents; 250 documents on microfiche; 14 volumes of data item descriptions; 35 volumes of military regulations, standards and specifications. **Subscriptions:** 50 journals and other serials. **Services:** Interlibrary loans; library not open to public. **Computerized Information Services:** DIALOG.

QUIGLEY (Harold Scott) CENTER OF INTERNATIONAL STUDIES LIBRARY
See: University of Minnesota - Harold Scott Quigley Center of International Studies Library

QUIGLEY (May G.) COLLECTION
See: Grand Rapids Public Library - May G. Quigley Collection

QUIGLEY PHOTOGRAPHIC ARCHIVE
See: Georgetown University - Special Collections Division - Lauinger Memorial Library

QUILLEN-DISHNER COLLEGE OF MEDICINE
See: East Tennessee State University

★11214★
QUINCY HISTORICAL SOCIETY - LIBRARY (Hist)
Adams Academy Bldg., 8 Adams St.   Phone: (617) 773-1144
Quincy, MA 02169   Lawrence J. Yerdon, Musm.Dir./Cur.
Founded: 1893. **Staff:** Prof 1; Other 4. **Subjects:** Quincy area history and genealogy. **Holdings:** 3000 books; 1000 pamphlets; 1000 photographs; manuscripts. **Services:** Copying; library open to public with restrictions.

QUINCY SHIPBUILDING DIVISION LIBRARY
See: General Dynamics Corporation

R

★11215★
R & D ASSOCIATES - TECHNICAL INFORMATION SERVICES (Sci-Tech; Energy)
4640 Admiralty Way
Box 9695   Phone: (213) 822-1715
Marina Del Rey, CA 90295   Margaret R. Anderson, Mgr.
Staff: Prof 4; Other 9. **Subjects:** Defense systems, nuclear physics, electronics, energy systems, systems engineering, weapon systems, computer science, mathematics. **Holdings:** 16,000 books; 100,000 reports. **Subscriptions:** 400 journals and other serials. **Services:** Interlibrary loans; copying; SDI; open to scientists and engineers on request. **Automated Operations:** Computerized cataloging and circulation for classified reports. **Computerized Information Services:** DIALOG, SDC, BRS, Tymshare, Inc., NASA/RECON, RLIN, Data Resources, Inc. (DRI), ESA-QUEST. **Networks/ Consortia:** Member of CLASS. **Staff:** Christine L. Lincoln, Classified Doc.Supv.; Shirley Lee, Unclassified Lib.Supv.; Janet Rocklin Katz, Indexing Libn.

★11216★
R & E RESEARCH ASSOCIATES - LIBRARY
936 Industrial
Palo Alto, CA 94303
Founded: 1966. **Subjects:** Ethnic, history and sociology studies; western Americana; early childhood. **Holdings:** 1500 books; 100 bound periodical volumes; 500 reels of microfilm, theses and dissertations. **Remarks:** Presently inactive.

RABBI NEUHAUS LIBRARY
See: Telshe Yeshiva - Rabbi A.N. Schwartz Library

RABBI SCHIFF LIBRARY
See: Telshe Yeshiva - Rabbi A.N. Schwartz Library

RABINOVITCH (Sam) MEMORIAL COLLECTION
See: Mc Gill University - Education Library - Sam Rabinovitch Memorial Collection

★11217★
RACAL-MILGO, INC. - INFORMATION RESOURCES (Info Sci)†
8600 N.W. 41st St.   Phone: (305) 591-5186
Miami, FL 33166   Jan Stern
Founded: 1963. **Staff:** Prof 2; Other 3. **Subjects:** Telecommunications, computer science and related electronics. **Holdings:** Figures not available. **Services:** Interlibrary loans; center open to public by appointment. **Computerized Information Services:** Online systems; internal database.

★11218★
RACHEL CARSON COUNCIL, INC. - LIBRARY (Sci-Tech)
8940 Jones Mill Rd.   Phone: (301) 652-1877
Chevy Chase, MD 20815   Shirley A. Briggs, Exec.Dir.
Founded: 1965. **Staff:** 5. **Subjects:** Pesticides, toxic substances, government regulation, pest management programs. **Special Collections:** Bioassays of pesticides and other toxic substances for carcinogenicity by National Cancer Institute; government regulatory documents. **Holdings:** 1500 books; 1000 documents and unbound reports; 40 drawers of specialized files; Environmental Protection Agency Pesticide Product Information. **Subscriptions:** 54 journals and other serials. **Services:** Copying (limited); library open to public by appointment. **Publications:** Publications on pesticides, toxic substances and alternatives to use of pesticides, irregular - by subscription and available for sale. **Special Indexes:** Index to pesticides by common name, chemical formula, trade names, and CAS number (card).

RACHMANINOFF ARCHIVES
See: Library of Congress - Music Division

★11219★
RACINE COUNTY HISTORICAL SOCIETY AND MUSEUM, INC. - LOCAL HISTORY AND GENEALOGICAL REFERENCE LIBRARY (Hist)
701 Main St.   Phone: (414) 637-8585
Racine, WI 53403   Jeffrey R. Schultz, Dir.
Founded: 1969. **Subjects:** Local history, Racine County; military history, particularly the Civil War. **Special Collections:** Local history photographs. **Holdings:** 500 books; 32 VF drawers of clippings, pamphlets; ephemera; lineage society materials. **Services:** Copying; library open to public on a limited schedule. **Special Catalogs:** Catalogs for early marriages, name file from histories, cemetery inscriptions, 1858 landowners and vertical files.

RACINE COUNTY LAW LIBRARY
See: Wisconsin State

★11220★
RACINE JOURNAL TIMES - LIBRARY (Publ)*
212 4th St.   Phone: (414) 634-3322
Racine, WI 53403   Karolyn Cotton, Libn.
Founded: 1958. **Staff:** 1. **Subjects:** Newspaper reference topics. **Holdings:** 300 books; 900 reels of microfilm of the Journal Times; miscellaneous pamphlets; 7000 obituaries; 10,000 biographical files. **Subscriptions:** 18 journals and other serials. **Services:** Library not open to public. **Special Indexes:** Clippings, mostly of local stories; biographical files, editorials; business and industry activities (card).

★11221★
RACQUET AND TENNIS CLUB - LIBRARY (Rec)
370 Park Ave.   Phone: (212) 753-9700
New York, NY 10022   Gerard J. Belliveau, Jr., Libn.
Founded: 1916. **Staff:** Prof 2. **Subjects:** Sports, court and lawn tennis, early American sport. **Holdings:** 17,500 books. **Subscriptions:** 45 journals and other serials. **Services:** Mail queries answered; copying; library open to researchers by appointment. **Publications:** Annual Report - to members. **Special Catalogs:** A Dictionary Catalog of the Library of Sports in the Racquet and Tennis Club, 1970. **Staff:** Anthony Toliver, Asst.Libn.

★11222★
RADCLIFFE COLLEGE - ARTHUR AND ELIZABETH SCHLESINGER LIBRARY ON THE HISTORY OF WOMEN IN AMERICA (Hist; Soc Sci)
10 Garden St.   Phone: (617) 495-8647
Cambridge, MA 02138   Dr. Patricia M. King, Dir.
Founded: 1943. **Staff:** Prof 8; Other 5. **Subjects:** Women - suffrage, medicine, education, law, social service, labor, family, organizations; history of American women in all phases of public and private life. **Special Collections:** Beecher-Stowe; Woman's Rights; Blackwell Family; Charlotte Perkins Gilman; Emma Goldman; Somerville-Howorth; Dr. Martha May Eliot; Jeannette Rankin; National Organization for Women; Black Women Oral History Project; cookbooks; etiquette books; picture collection (40,000 items). **Holdings:** 25,000 books and bound periodical volumes; 450 major collections of papers on individual American women, families and women's organizations; 1800 reels of microfilm; 800 magnetic tapes; 40 VF drawers. **Subscriptions:** 350 journals and other serials. **Services:** Interlibrary loans; copying; library open to public. **Automated Operations:** Computerized cataloging. **Publications:** Occasional Reports, sent on request. **Special Catalogs:** Manuscript Inventories; Catalogs of the Manuscripts, Books and Periodicals, 1984 (10 volumes). **Staff:** Eva Moseley, Cur. of Mss.; Barbara Haber, Cur. of Printed Bks.; Ruth E. Hill, Oral Hist.Coord.

★11223★
RADCLIFFE COLLEGE - HENRY A. MURRAY RESEARCH CENTER (Soc Sci)
10 Garden St.   Phone: (617) 495-8140
Cambridge, MA 02138   Anne Colby, Dir.
Founded: 1976. **Staff:** Prof 4; Other 5. **Subjects:** Women's life patterns, self-esteem, work and family life, sex role attitudes, developmental issues, mental and physical health. **Special Collections:** Archival materials dealing with data sets of raw and computer-accessible social science research studies. **Holdings:** 120 data sets; 50 books; 350 boxes of raw data; 35 dissertations; 150 unpublished reports; 25 computer magnetic tapes. **Services:** Center open to public. **Automated Operations:** Computerized acquisitions. **Publications:** Murray Center News, 3/year - by subscription. **Special Indexes:** Guide to the Data Resources of the Henry A. Murray Research Center. **Staff:** Erin Phelps, Res.Assoc.; Sally Powers, Res.Assoc.

RADCLIFFE COLLEGE - MORSE MUSIC LIBRARY
See: Harvard University

★11224★
RADER COMPANIES, INC. - INFORMATION CENTER†
6005 N.E. 82nd Ave.
Portland, OR 97220
Founded: 1970. **Subjects:** Engineering, materials handling, pulp and paper, forest products. **Holdings:** 1045 books; 2700 technical reports; 2200 vendor files. **Remarks:** Presently inactive.

★11225★

RADFORD UNIVERSITY - LIBRARY - VIRGINIA ROOM AND SPECIAL COLLECTIONS (Hist)

Phone: (703) 731-5471
Radford, VA 24142   Ann Swain, Lib.Asst.
Subjects: Southwestern Virginia - institutions, people, culture; Civil War; Christiansburg Institute (originally a black Freedmen's Bureau school); folklore. **Holdings:** 7000 items including manuscripts, photographs, slides, and tapes; unpublished literary manuscripts. **Services:** Copying; collection open to public.

★11226★

RADIAN CORPORATION - LIBRARY (Energy)
8500 Shoal Creek Blvd.
Box 9948   Phone: (512) 454-4797
Austin, TX 78766   Barbara J. Maxey, Sr.Libn.
Staff: Prof 2; Other 4. **Subjects:** Coal conversion processes, air and water pollution control, petroleum refining emissions, geothermal research and development. **Special Collections:** Gasification and liquefaction (14,000 items); sulphur dioxide control (3000 items). **Holdings:** 1882 volumes; 2500 microforms; 20,000 articles, patents and maps; 19,000 technical reports. **Subscriptions:** 380 journals and other serials. **Services:** Interlibrary loans; copying; library open to public by appointment. **Automated Operations:** Computerized circulation. **Computerized Information Services:** Online systems. **Publications:** Library Briefs, irregular; Biweekly List of Books and Reports - both for internal distribution only. **Staff:** Jane E. McDowell, Tech.Libn.

RADIATION BIOLOGY ARCHIVES
See: University of Tennessee - Special Collections

RADIATION SHIELDING INFORMATION CENTER
See: Oak Ridge National Laboratory

★11227★

RADIO ADVERTISING BUREAU - MARKETING INFORMATION CENTER (Bus-Fin)
485 Lexington Ave.   Phone: (212) 599-6666
New York, NY 10017   Erwyn Khan, Dir.
Founded: 1951. **Staff:** Prof 2; Other 3. **Subjects:** Radio, advertising and marketing, consumer markets, competitive media, leading advertisers, retailing. **Special Collections:** Tape Library - 30,000 commercials (separate department); company archives; Broadcasting Yearbook, 1937 to present. **Holdings:** 600 books and bound periodical volumes; 70 VF drawers of clippings. **Subscriptions:** 150 journals and other serials. **Services:** Interlibrary loans (limited); copying; center open to public by special permission. **Computerized Information Services:** DIALOG, NEXIS.

RADIO FREE EUROPE/RADIO LIBERTY LIBRARY
See: Columbia University - Herbert H. Lehman Library

★11228★

RADIO FREE EUROPE/RADIO LIBERTY INC. - REFERENCE LIBRARY (Area-Ethnic)
1775 Broadway   Phone: (212) 397-5343
New York, NY 10019   Irene V. Dutikow, Ref.Libn.
Founded: 1958. **Staff:** Prof 1; Other 2. **Subjects:** Soviet Union and Eastern Europe - cultural, economic and political life. **Special Collections:** Soviet magazines and newspapers (184); biographical file on Soviet personalities; Samizdat materials depository (underground documents; 8 drawers and bound volumes); RFE research papers, 1973 to present; RL Research Bulletin, 1964 to present. **Holdings:** 18,500 books; 98 VF drawers; 3200 reels of microfilm. **Subscriptions:** 340 journals and other serials; 52 newspapers. **Services:** Interlibrary loans; copying; library open to public by appointment.

★11229★

RADIO HISTORICAL ASSOCIATION OF COLORADO, INC. - RENTAL TAPE LIBRARY (Hist)
7213 W. Roxbury Pl.   Phone: (303) 979-0755
Littleton, CO 30123   John Migrala, Treas.-Libn.
Staff: 2. **Subjects:** Radio shows, radio logs. **Holdings:** 400 reels of recorded tape (1600 hours of shows). **Services:** Library not open to public. **Publications:** Return With Us Now, monthly newsletter - to members. **Special Catalogs:** Catalog of all reels of radio shows. **Remarks:** Radio Historical Association of Colorado is a nonprofit corporation whose purpose is to preserve vintage radio shows.

★11230★

RADIO QUEBEC - CENTRE DES RESSOURCES DOCUMENTAIRES (Info Sci)
1000 Fullum   Phone: (514) 521-2424
Montreal, PQ, Canada H2K 3L7   Nicole Charest, Dir.
Founded: 1969. **Staff:** Prof 8; Other 20. **Subjects:** Canadian and Quebec history, communications, television, graphic arts. **Special Collections:** Collection of Radio-Quebec production and administrative documents, 1968 to present (800 documents in French). **Holdings:** 14,000 books; 17,000 phonograph records; 23,000 slides; 6000 photographs; 4000 television programs on videotape; 3 million feet of film; 100 archives; 2000 clipping files; 1000 biographical files. **Subscriptions:** 360 journals and other serials; 30 newspapers. **Services:** Interlibrary loans; center not open to public. **Automated Operations:** Computerized cataloging. **Publications:** List of serials, semiannual; New Books, bimonthly; New Records, bimonthly; Calendar of Events, bimonthly; list of consultants in various fields related to public affairs and news, semiannual. **Remarks:** Maintained by Societe de Radio-Television du Quebec (Quebec Province). **Staff:** Michel Boisvert, Hd. of Ref.Serv.; Micheline Godbout-Mercure, Hd. of Tech.Serv.; Marie Geiser, Hd. of Film Lib.

★11231★

RADIOLOGICAL SOCIETY OF NORTH AMERICA, INC. - LIBRARY (Sci-Tech; Med)
1415 W. 22nd St.
Oak Brook Regency Towers, Suite 1150   Phone: (312) 920-2670
Oak Brook, IL 60521
Subjects: Clinical radiology and allied sciences. **Holdings:** 800 books and bound periodical volumes; records of manuscripts received annually. **Subscriptions:** 120 journals and other serials. **Services:** Library not open to public. **Publications:** Radiology, monthly; Radio Graphics, bimonthly. **Special Indexes:** Indexes of Radiology.

★11232★

RADNOR HISTORICAL SOCIETY - RESEARCH LIBRARY (Hist)
Finley House
113 W. Beech Tree Ln.   Phone: (215) 688-2668
Wayne, PA 19087   K.H. Cummin, Pres.
Founded: 1948. **Subjects:** Local and Pennsylvania history. **Holdings:** 300 volumes; 4 boxes of genealogical papers; 4 drawers of maps; 4 boxes of photographs (1880 to present). **Services:** Library open to public. **Publications:** Bulletin of the Radnor Historical Society, annual - to members and for sale. **Special Indexes:** Index to articles on local history (card).

RADOV (Morris P.) JEWISH CENTER LIBRARY
See: Congregation Brith Shalom - Morris P. Radov Jewish Center Library

RAE COLLECTION ON ARCHITECTURE
See: Monterey Public Library

RAGINSKY (Bernard B.) RESEARCH LIBRARY
See: Institute for Research in Hypnosis - Bernard B. Raginsky Research Library

★11233★

RAHENKAMP (John) & ASSOCIATES, INC. - RSWA PLANNING LIBRARY
1717 Spring Garden St.
Philadelphia, PA 19130
Founded: 1972. **Subjects:** Planning, landscape architecture, planned unit development, watersheds, zoning, growth management. **Holdings:** 5500 books; 25,000 slides; 15,000 VF materials. **Remarks:** Presently inactive.

★11234★

RAHR-WEST MUSEUM - LIBRARY (Art; Hist)
Park St. at N. 8th
Manitowoc, WI 54220
Subjects: Art; county and state history. **Holdings:** 1000 volumes.

RAILROAD COMMISSION OF TEXAS
See: Texas State

★11235★

RAILROAD ENTHUSIASTS NEW YORK DIVISION, INC. - WILLIAMSON LIBRARY (Trans)
Box 1318
New York, NY 10017   Charles Grossman, Libn.
Founded: 1937. **Staff:** 2. **Subjects:** Railroads, electric railroads, engineering. **Special Collections:** Railway and Locomotive Historical Society Bulletins; Railway Age/Railroad Gazette; The RRE Photo Archive. **Holdings:** 1900 books; 200 bound periodical volumes; 500 slides and photographs; 75 feet of

clippings and pamphlets; 1500 prints and negatives; 10,000 feet of movies. **Subscriptions:** 10 journals and other serials. **Services:** Library open to public for research by appointment only. **Staff:** Warren L. Smith, Pres.

★11236★
RAILROAD AND PIONEER MUSEUM, INC. - LIBRARY (Hist)
Box 5126   Phone: (817) 778-6873
Temple, TX 76501   Mary Pat McLaughlin, Libn. & Dir.
Founded: 1977. **Staff:** Prof 1. **Subjects:** Railroads, local and pioneer history. **Special Collections:** Original manuscripts. **Holdings:** 400 books. **Subscriptions:** 18 journals and other serials. **Services:** Interlibrary loans; copying; library and archives open to public for reference use only.

RAILROAD RETIREMENT BOARD
See: U.S. Railroad Retirement Board

★11237★
RAILWAYS TO YESTERDAY, INC. - LEHIGH VALLEY TRANSPORTATION
   RESEARCH CENTER (Trans)*
12th and Cumberland Sts.
2nd Fl., General Office   Phone: (215) 797-3242
Allentown, PA 18103   Douglas E. Peters, Hist./Libn.
Staff: 1. **Subjects:** Electric and steam railways. **Special Collections:** Company records of the Lehigh Valley Transit Company; Howard Sell Collection of photographs and negatives of Lehigh Valley area railways and trolley lines; trolley artifacts; James MacDonald Collection of railway photographs and negatives. **Holdings:** 150 volumes; 10 VF cabinets and 15 boxes of railway material including railway maps and timetables; newspaper clippings. **Subscriptions:** 10 journals and other serials. **Services:** Center open to public by appointment. **Publications:** Trolley Museum Reporter, 6/year.

★11238★
RAINBOW CHILD CARE COUNCIL - TOY AND RESOURCE LIBRARY (Educ)
703 Jefferson St.   Phone: (707) 253-0366
Napa, CA 94559   Katherine Todd, Resource Libn.
Staff: Prof 1. **Subjects:** Toys, family day care, parenting, child development, curricula, cooking for and with children. **Holdings:** 500 books; 3000 toys. **Services:** Copying; library open to county residents. **Publications:** Rainbow Newsletter, monthly - distributed to members and available by request.

★11239★
RAINBOW FLEET, INC. - LIBRARY (Educ)
3016 Paseo   Phone: (405) 521-1426
Oklahoma City, OK 73103   Susan Moore Myers, Exec.Dir.
Staff: Prof 5. **Subjects:** Child development; infant stimulation; pre-school enhancement, including language development, pre-math skills, sensorial development, and practical life skills. **Special Collections:** Toys for handicapped children. **Holdings:** 1750 books; 5000 toys and games. **Services:** Library open to licensed daycare centers and homes enrolled in the program.

★11240★
RAINIER NATIONAL BANK - INFORMATION CENTER (Bus-Fin)
Box 3966
Seattle, WA 98124   Vivienne C. Burke, Asst.V.P./Mgr.
Founded: 1968. **Staff:** Prof 3; Other 1. **Subjects:** Banking and finance. **Holdings:** 3200 books; 8000 pamphlets. **Subscriptions:** 600 journals and other serials; 32 newspapers. **Services:** Interlibrary loans; copying; SDI; center open to public for reference use only with permission. **Automated Operations:** Computerized cataloging. **Computerized Information Services:** DIALOG, Dow Jones News/Retrieval, OCLC. **Staff:** M. Rosemary Clark, Res.Anl.; Vivian Chun, Res.Anl.

RAINIER SCHOOL STAFF LIBRARY
See: Washington State Library

RALSTON (J.K.) MUSEUM AND ART CENTER
See: MonDak Heritage Center

★11241★
RALSTON PURINA COMPANY - INFORMATION CENTER (Food-Bev)
Checkerboard Square, 2RS   Phone: (314) 982-2150
St. Louis, MO 63164   Linda S. Lincks, Mgr.
Founded: 1929. **Staff:** Prof 3; Other 1. **Subjects:** Animal and human nutrition, veterinary medicine, food processing, food sanitation. **Special Collections:** FAO (Food and Agricultural Organization of the United Nations); 20 VF drawers). **Holdings:** 13,000 books and bound periodical volumes; 20 VF drawers of proceedings; 69 VF drawers of government reports. **Subscriptions:** 392 journals and other serials. **Services:** Interlibrary loans;

copying; SDI; center open to public by appointment. **Automated Operations:** Computerized cataloging, acquisitions and ILL. **Computerized Information Services:** DIALOG, SDC, BRS, NLM, Dow Jones News/Retrieval, Mead Data Central, OCLC, I.P. Sharp Associates, Ltd., CAS Online, Pergamon InfoLine Ltd. Contact Person: Peggy Zabel, 982-2807. **Networks/Consortia:** Member of St. Louis Regional Library Network. **Staff:** Deborah Bolas, Libn.; Peggy Zabel, Supv., Search Serv.

RALSTON (Willo) MEMORIAL LIBRARY FOR HISTORICAL RESEARCH
See: MonDak Heritage Center - Willo Ralston Memorial Library for Historical Research

RAMSAYER (Ralph K., M.D.) LIBRARY
See: Mc Kinley Museum of History, Science and Education - Ralph K. Ramsayer, M.D. Library

★11242★
RAMSEY COUNTY HISTORICAL SOCIETY - JOSEPH E. KARTH RESEARCH
   CENTER - LIBRARY (Hist)
75 W. Fifth St., Rm. 323   Phone: (612) 222-0701
St. Paul, MN 55102
Staff: Prof 5. **Subjects:** Local history. **Special Collections:** Heman Gibbs papers. **Holdings:** 300 books; maps, pamphlets, documents, pictures. **Services:** Library open to public for reference use only.

★11243★
RAMSEY COUNTY LAW LIBRARY (Law)
1815 Court House   Phone: (612) 298-5208
St. Paul, MN 55102   Carol C. Florin, Lib.Dir.
Founded: 1935. **Staff:** Prof 1; Other 1. **Subjects:** Law - Minnesota, tax, real property, criminal, corporate; practice. **Special Collections:** Minnesota Supreme Court Briefs and Paperbooks, 1950 to present (1400 volumes). **Holdings:** 20,000 books; 300 bound periodical volumes. **Subscriptions:** 15 journals and other serials. **Services:** Interlibrary loans; copying; library open to public with restrictions. **Networks/Consortia:** Member of Metronet.

★11244★
RAMSEY COUNTY MEDICAL SOCIETY - BOECKMANN LIBRARY (Med)
345 N. Smith Ave.   Phone: (612) 224-3346
St. Paul, MN 55102   Mary Sandra Tarman, Libn.
Founded: 1897. **Staff:** Prof 2; Other 3. **Subjects:** Medicine, nursing, hospital administration. **Special Collections:** Psychoanalytic Foundation of Minnesota Library (300 books; 7 periodicals). **Holdings:** 15,000 books; 28,500 bound periodical volumes; 6500 unbound periodical volumes; 18 VF drawers of pamphlets and clippings; 725 medical instruments and memorabilia (museum items). **Subscriptions:** 400 journals and other serials; 8 newspapers. **Services:** Interlibrary loans; copying; library open to public with restrictions. **Computerized Information Services:** MEDLINE. **Networks/Consortia:** Member of Twin Cities Biomedical Consortium (TCBC); Greater Midwest Regional Medical Library Network (Region 3).

RANCHO BERNARDO TECHNICAL INFORMATION CENTER
See: Burroughs Corporation

★11245★
RANCHO LOS AMIGOS HOSPITAL - MEDICAL LIBRARY (Med)
7601 E. Imperial Hwy.   Phone: (213) 922-7696
Downey, CA 90242   Janet Judson, Med.Libn.
Staff: Prof 1; Other 3. **Subjects:** Medicine and allied health fields. **Holdings:** 5000 books; 12,000 bound periodical volumes; 250 Rancho resident papers; 650 audio cassettes. **Subscriptions:** 631 journals and other serials. **Services:** Interlibrary loans; copying; library open to public. **Computerized Information Services:** MEDLINE, SDC. **Networks/Consortia:** Member of Pacific Southwest Regional Medical Library Service (PSRMLS).

RANCHO LOS CERRITOS MUSEUM
See: Long Beach Public Library

★11246★
RANCHO SANTA ANA BOTANIC GARDEN - LIBRARY (Sci-Tech)
1500 N. College Ave.   Phone: (714) 626-3922
Claremont, CA 91711   Beatrice M. Beck, Libn.
Founded: 1927. **Staff:** Prof 1. **Subjects:** Botany, horticulture. **Special Collections:** Floras of the world. **Holdings:** 30,000 items; reprint collection; nursery catalogs. **Subscriptions:** 450 journals and other serials. **Services:** Interlibrary loans; copying; library open to qualified users. **Publications:** Aliso, Journal of the Rancho Santa Ana Botanic Garden, annual - distributed by subscription and exchange.

RAND (Anne) RESEARCH LIBRARY
See: International Longshoremen's and Warehousemen's Union - Anne Rand Research Library

★11247★
RAND CORPORATION - LIBRARY (Soc Sci)†
1700 Main St.   Phone: (213) 393-0411
Santa Monica, CA 90406   Vivian J. Arterbery, Lib.Dir.
Founded: 1948. **Staff:** Prof 11; Other 20. **Subjects:** Policy analysis, decision-making, military strategy, international affairs, urban development, education, economics of medical care services, criminal and civil justice. **Special Collections:** Russian language collection in economics, political science and military science (8000 monographs, 300 periodical titles). **Holdings:** 65,000 books; 19,000 bound periodical volumes; 225,000 documents and reports; 15,000 maps. **Subscriptions:** 2000 journals and other serials; 52 newspapers. **Services:** Interlibrary loans; library not open to public. **Automated Operations:** Computerized cataloging and serials. **Computerized Information Services:** DIALOG, SDC, BRS, New York Times Information Service, MEDLINE, DOE/RECON, DTIC, Data Resources, Inc.(DRI), Online Acquisitions Systems (OLAS), CIRC, CDC, Petroleum Data System (PDS), I.P. Sharp Associates, Ltd., OnTyme, RLIN, The Computer Company (TCC). **Networks/Consortia:** Member of CLASS. **Publications:** Accessions List, weekly; Interest List, irregular; periodical listing, semiannual. **Special Catalogs:** Microfiche catalog, monthly. **Staff:** Jill Brophy, Adm.Asst.; Andrea Roberts, Hd.Cat.; Doris Small, Hd., Tech.Serv.; Barbara Quint, Hd. Ref.Serv.; Roberta Sharman, Asst.Ref.Libn.; Marge Behrens, Slavic/ Orntl.Libn.; Mike Kurtz, Classified Info.Serv.; Barbara Neff, Hd., ILL; Pamela Harrison, Hd., Per. & Circ.

★11248★
RAND CORPORATION - LIBRARY (Soc Sci)
2100 M St., N.W.   Phone: (202) 296-5000
Washington, DC 20037   Casey Kane, Libn.
Staff: 2. **Subjects:** Social studies, military studies, housing and urban affairs, education. **Holdings:** 10,000 books; 3500 Congressional hearings; 8000 pamphlets. **Subscriptions:** 250 journals and other serials; 6 newspapers. **Services:** Interlibrary loans; library not open to public. **Automated Operations:** Computerized serials. **Computerized Information Services:** DIALOG, NEXIS. **Networks/Consortia:** Member of Interlibrary Users Association.

★11249★
RAND INFORMATION SYSTEMS, INC. - LIBRARY (Comp Sci)
98 Battery St., 4th Fl.   Phone: (415) 392-2500
San Francisco, CA 94111   Diane Huijgen, Libn.
Founded: 1978. **Staff:** Prof 1. **Subjects:** Data processing, business. **Holdings:** 50 books; 4000 computer manuals; 400 data processing vendor documents. **Subscriptions:** 16 journals and other serials; 7 newspapers. **Services:** Library not open to public. **Automated Operations:** Computerized cataloging and circulation. **Special Catalogs:** Catalog of computer manuals holdings.

★11250★
RAND MC NALLY AND COMPANY - LIBRARY (Publ; Geog-Map)
8255 Central Park Ave.   Phone: (312) 673-9100
Skokie, IL 60076   Philip L. Forstall, Libn.
Founded: 1949. **Staff:** Prof 1. **Subjects:** U.S. history, geography, cartography, graphic arts, place names, railroads, business. **Special Collections:** Toponymy (place names); historical collection of company publications; archives. **Holdings:** 17,000 books; 1000 bound periodical volumes; 800 atlases; 30,000 sheet maps (in cartographic department); 400 pamphlets. **Subscriptions:** 120 journals and other serials. **Services:** Interlibrary loans (to libraries and specialized research institutions); geographical reference service to librarians; library open to graduate researchers for reference use. **Publications:** Accessions lists; subject bibliographies.

RANDALL (William Madison) LIBRARY
See: University of North Carolina, Wilmington - William Madison Randall Library

★11251★
RANDOLPH CIRCUIT COURT - LAW LIBRARY (Law)*
Courthouse, Rm. 307   Phone: (317) 584-7070
Winchester, IN 47394   Joan Benson, Libn.
Subjects: Law. **Holdings:** 15,000 volumes. **Services:** Library open to public with restrictions.

RANDOM HOUSE PAPERS AND LIBRARY
See: Columbia University - Rare Book and Manuscript Library

★11252★
RANGE MENTAL HEALTH CENTER - LIBRARY (Med)
624 South 13th St.   Phone: (218) 749-2881
Virginia, MN 55792   JoAnne Matson, Sec.
Staff: 1. **Subjects:** Psychiatry, psychology, social work, behavior, developmental disability, chemical dependency, suicide, mental retardation. **Holdings:** 1000 books; 20 bound periodical volumes; pamphlets. **Subscriptions:** 28 journals and other serials. **Services:** Interlibrary loans; library open to public.

RANKIN (Lydia) TECHNICAL LIBRARY
See: Boeing Vertol Company - Lydia Rankin Technical Library

RANSOM (Harry) HUMANITIES RESEARCH CENTER
See: University of Texas, Austin - Harry Ransom Humanities Research Center

RANSOM (R.C.) MEMORIAL LIBRARY
See: Payne Theological Seminary - R.C. Ransom Memorial Library

RAPAPORT PROFESSIONAL LIBRARY
See: Osawatomie State Hospital

RAPID CITY REGIONAL HOSPITAL
See: Rushmore National Health System

★11253★
RAPIDES GENERAL HOSPITAL - MEDICAL LIBRARY (Med)†
Box 7146   Phone: (318) 487-8111
Alexandria, LA 71301   Mrs. B.T. Dawkins, Libn.
Founded: 1963. **Staff:** Prof 1. **Subjects:** Medicine. **Holdings:** 1800 books; 1112 bound periodical volumes. **Subscriptions:** 65 journals and other serials. **Services:** Interlibrary loans; library open to public with permission of librarian.

RAPIDLY SOLIDIFIED MATERIALS (RaSoMat) - RESOURCE CENTER
See: Battelle-Columbus Laboratories

RASCHE MEMORIAL LIBRARY
See: Milwaukee Area Technical College

RASMUSON (Elmer E.) LIBRARY
See: University of Alaska - Alaska and Polar Regions Department

RATH (Erich) LIBRARY
See: Hollins College - Music Department - Erich Rath Library

RAUB (Jack G.) COMPANY
See: Jack G. Raub Company

RAUH MEMORIAL LIBRARY
See: Children's Museum of Indianapolis

RAVALLI COUNTY MUSEUM
See: Bitter Root Valley Historical Society

★11254★
RAVENSWOOD HOSPITAL MEDICAL CENTER - MEDICAL-NURSING LIBRARY (Med)*
4550 N. Winchester at Wilson   Phone: (312) 878-4300
Chicago, IL 60640   Mr. Zia Solomon Gilliana, Med.Libn.
Founded: 1908. **Staff:** Prof 1; Other 2. **Subjects:** Medicine, nursing. **Special Collections:** History of medicine; history of nursing. **Holdings:** 3747 books; 4415 bound periodical volumes. **Subscriptions:** 201 journals and other serials. **Services:** Interlibrary loans; copying; SDI; library open to public with restrictions. **Publications:** Guide to the Library.

RAWALT (Marguerite) RESOURCE CENTER
See: Business and Professional Women's Foundation - Marguerite Rawalt Resource Center

★11255★
RAWLE AND HENDERSON - LAW LIBRARY (Law)
211 S. Broad St.   Phone: (215) 875-4000
Philadelphia, PA 19107   Hope S. Ridge, Libn.
Founded: 1783. **Staff:** Prof 2; Other 1. **Subjects:** Law - ships and shipping, medical malpractice, tax, securities, general practice. **Holdings:** 10,000

books; 500 Paper Books - bound volumes of firm's important cases. **Subscriptions:** 86 journals and other serials. **Services:** Interlibrary loans; library not open to public. **Computerized Information Services:** LEXIS, DIALOG. **Publications:** Paper Books. **Remarks:** This is said to be the oldest established law firm and law library in Philadelphia. **Staff:** Rosalie Coyle, Asst.Libn.

RAXLER (Alexander) LIBRARY
See: Doctors Hospital - Alexander Raxler Library

RAY (Isaac) MEDICAL LIBRARY
See: Butler Hospital - Isaac Ray Medical Library

RAYBURN (Otto Ernest) LIBRARY OF FOLKLORE
See: University of Arkansas, Fayetteville - Special Collections Division

★11256★
RAYBURN (Sam) FOUNDATION - SAM RAYBURN LIBRARY (Hist)
Phone: (214) 583-2455
Bonham, TX 75418   H.G. Dulaney, Lib.Dir.
Founded: 1957. **Staff:** Prof 4; Other 2. **Subjects:** History of Congress and its leaders; history of political parties; Texas history, especially in 4th Congressional District. **Special Collections:** Congressional documents from the First Continental Congress to present. **Holdings:** 15,000 books; 100 bound periodical volumes; 30 VF drawers of personal papers and correspondence (microfilm) of Honorable Sam Rayburn, Speaker; Presidential letters to the Speaker; original letters from his mother to the Speaker; tape recordings of his speeches. **Services:** Library open to public (research materials are available, subject to restriction of the Board of Trustees). **Special Indexes:** Guide to contents of Speaker's papers.

RAYBURN (Sam) MEMORIAL VETERANS CENTER MEDICAL LIBRARY
See: U.S. Veterans Administration (TX-Bonham) - Sam Rayburn Memorial Veterans Center Medical Library

★11257★
RAYCHEM CORPORATION - CORPORATE LIBRARY (Sci-Tech)†
300 Constitution Dr.   Phone: (415) 329-3282
Menlo Park, CA 94025   Phyllis Oda, Mgr.
Staff: Prof 3; Other 3. **Subjects:** Chemistry, polymer science, electronics. **Holdings:** 6000 books; 8000 bound periodical volumes. **Subscriptions:** 400 journals and other serials. **Services:** Interlibrary loans; library not open to public. **Computerized Information Services:** SDC, DIALOG.

RAYMOND (John) MEMORIAL LIBRARY
See: Waukegan Historical Society - John Raymond Memorial Library

★11258★
RAYMOND KAISER ENGINEERS, INC. - ENGINEERING LIBRARY (Sci-Tech)
300 Lakeside Dr.
Box 23210   Phone: (415) 271-4375
Oakland, CA 94623   Elaine Zacher, Tech.Libn.
Founded: 1951. **Staff:** Prof 1; Other 2. **Subjects:** Engineering - hydraulic, mechanical, mining and metallurgy, sanitary, structural. **Holdings:** 5500 books; 500 pamphlets. **Subscriptions:** 165 journals and other serials; 5 newspapers. **Services:** Interlibrary loans; library open to public by appointment. **Automated Operations:** Computerized serials. **Computerized Information Services:** DIALOG, SDC, DOE/RECON, Dow Jones News/Retrieval. **Networks/Consortia:** Member of Bay Area Library and Information System (BALIS). **Formerly:** Kaiser Engineers, Inc.

★11259★
RAYMOND, PARISH, PINE & WEINER, INC. - LIBRARY (Plan)
555 White Plains Rd.   Phone: (914) 631-9003
Tarrytown, NY 10591   Bertha R. Dwyer, Libn.
Staff: Prof 1. **Subjects:** Land and park planning, environmental studies, traffic and transportation, urban design, zoning and comprehensive planning, economic and market analyses. **Holdings:** 550 books; 175 bound periodical volumes; 12,990 documents; 10 VF drawers of pamphlets. **Subscriptions:** 100 journals and other serials. **Services:** Interlibrary loans; library open to public with restrictions. **Publications:** Current contents, monthly; acquisitions lists, monthly - both for internal distribution only.

★11260★
RAY-O-VAC CORP. - TECHNOLOGY CENTER LIBRARY (Sci-Tech)
630 Forward Dr.   Phone: (608) 252-7400
Madison, WI 53711   C. Saxe, Sr.Tech.Adv.
Founded: 1967. **Staff:** Prof 1. **Subjects:** Electrochemistry, primary batteries, chemical engineering, plastics, management. **Special Collections:** U.S.

government and internal reports (Uniterm collection). **Holdings:** 2200 books; 1100 bound periodical volumes; 3000 patents; 9600 technical reports. **Subscriptions:** 100 journals and other serials. **Services:** Interlibrary loans; copying; library open to public by appointment. **Networks/Consortia:** Member of Madison Area Library Council (MALC). **Publications:** Acquisition List, monthly; Current Awareness Bulletin - both for internal distribution only. **Special Indexes:** Uniterm Index to documents collection.

★11261★
RAYTHEON COMPANY - BADGER AMERICA, INC. - LIBRARY (Sci-Tech)
One Broadway   Phone: (617) 494-7565
Cambridge, MA 02142   Eleanor M. Rice, Libn.
Staff: Prof 1. **Subjects:** Chemical engineering, energy, petroleum refining, environmental engineering. **Holdings:** 4500 books; 1500 bound periodical volumes; 8 VF drawers of patents; 16 VF drawers of codes and specifications; 20 VF drawers of process data files; 41 VF drawers of pamphlets, reprints and special services. **Subscriptions:** 250 journals and other serials. **Services:** Interlibrary loans; library not open to public. **Computerized Information Services:** DIALOG, SDC.

★11262★
RAYTHEON COMPANY - BUSINESS INFORMATION CENTER (Bus-Fin)
141 Spring St.   Phone: (617) 862-6600
Lexington, MA 02173   Dayle Reilly, Mgr.
Founded: 1960. **Staff:** Prof 1; Other 1. **Subjects:** General business, marketing, economics, census, finance. **Special Collections:** Annual reports; Arthur D. Little reports; SRI Long Range Planning reports; Conference Board reports. **Holdings:** 1200 books; 10,000 archives and back copies of journals; 80 VF drawers; 2 cabinets of microfilm. **Subscriptions:** 350 journals and other serials; 15 newspapers. **Services:** Interlibrary loans; center open to public with restrictions. **Publications:** Periodical holdings, annual.

★11263★
RAYTHEON COMPANY - ELECTROMAGNETIC SYSTEMS DIVISION - ENGINEERING LIBRARY (Sci-Tech)
6380 Hollister Ave.   Phone: (805) 967-5511
Goleta, CA 93117   S. Anderson, Libn.
Founded: 1957. **Staff:** Prof 1. **Subjects:** Electronic engineering, general drafting, mathematics, mechanical engineering, microwave and computer technology, radar. **Holdings:** 3000 books and bound periodical volumes; 300 volumes of unbound periodicals; 2 boxes of microfiche of government documents; 2400 microfilm cartridges of specifications, standards, military documents and vendor information; 88 VF drawers of hardcopy specifications and standards. **Subscriptions:** 126 journals and other serials. **Services:** Library open to public by appointment.

★11264★
RAYTHEON COMPANY - EQUIPMENT DIVISION - TECHNICAL INFORMATION CENTER (Sci-Tech)
528 Boston Post Rd.   Phone: (617) 443-9521
Sudbury, MA 01776   Joan Dexter, Libn.
Founded: 1963. **Staff:** Prof 1. **Subjects:** Electronics, computers, communications. **Holdings:** 5000 books; 30 bound periodical volumes; 300 other cataloged items; 330,000 microfiche of NASA reports; 350 tape cassettes; 2 files of reports on microfiche. **Subscriptions:** 160 journals and other serials. **Services:** Interlibrary loans; center not open to public. **Computerized Information Services:** DIALOG, OCLC. **Publications:** Technical Information Center Bulletin, monthly - for internal distribution only. **Special Catalogs:** Raytheon Libraries Union List of Books; Raytheon Libraries Union List of Serials.

★11265★
RAYTHEON COMPANY - EQUIPMENT DIVISION - TECHNICAL INFORMATION CENTER (Sci-Tech)
Boston Post Rd.   Phone: (617) 358-2721
Wayland, MA 01778   Joanne Portsch, Libn.
Founded: 1955. **Staff:** Prof 1; Other 3. **Subjects:** Electronics, electrical engineering, physics, mathematics. **Holdings:** 6000 books; 555 bound periodical volumes; 270 linear feet of military specifications and standards; 2 files of reports on microfiche; 350 tape cassettes. **Subscriptions:** 250 journals and other serials. **Services:** Interlibrary loans; center not open to public. **Automated Operations:** Computerized cataloging. **Computerized Information Services:** DIALOG, OCLC. **Publications:** TIC Bulletin, monthly - for internal distribution only. **Special Catalogs:** Raytheon Libraries Union List of Serials, monthly (computer printout); Raytheon Libraries Union List of Books, quarterly (computer printout). **Special Indexes:** Technical Information Center Index to internal memos and reports, annual (computer printout).

★11266★
RAYTHEON COMPANY - LAW LIBRARY (Law)†
Office of the General Counsel
141 Spring St.   Phone: (617) 862-6600
Lexington, MA 02173   Joan Cook, Libn.
Founded: 1930. **Subjects:** Law. **Holdings:** 2600 volumes. **Subscriptions:** 10 journals and other serials. **Services:** Library not open to public.

★11267★
RAYTHEON COMPANY - MISSILE SYSTEMS DIVISION - BEDFORD LABORATORIES - TECHNICAL INFORMATION CENTER (Sci-Tech)
Hartwell Rd.   Phone: (617) 274-7100
Bedford, MA 01730   Lorraine Bick-Gregoire, Mgr.
Staff: Prof 2; Other 2. **Subjects:** Guided missiles, electronics, aerodynamics, physics, mathematics, management techniques. **Holdings:** 18,000 books; 50,000 research reports; 40,000 microfiche. **Subscriptions:** 125 journals and other serials. **Services:** Interlibrary loans; center not open to public. **Automated Operations:** Computerized circulation. **Computerized Information Services:** DIALOG, DTIC. **Publications:** Technical Abstract Bulletin, monthly - for internal distribution only; Library Scanner. **Special Catalogs:** Book catalog. **Staff:** Patricia Doherty, Ref.Libn.

★11268★
RAYTHEON COMPANY - RESEARCH DIVISION - LIBRARY (Sci-Tech)
131 Spring St.   Phone: (617) 863-5300
Lexington, MA 02173   Martha C. Adamson, Hd.Libn.
Founded: 1952. **Staff:** Prof 3. **Subjects:** Applied physics, advanced materials, semiconductor physics, physical chemistry. **Holdings:** 10,000 books; 5000 bound periodical volumes; 15,000 technical reports; 9000 archival items. **Subscriptions:** 300 journals and other serials. **Services:** Interlibrary loans; library open to public with approval of security officer. **Automated Operations:** Computerized cataloging. **Computerized Information Services:** DIALOG, BRS, DTIC, Electronic Materials Information Service (EMIS). **Networks/Consortia:** Member of NELINET. **Publications:** Accessions Bulletin, quarterly; special bibliographies; Update, biweekly. **Staff:** Irene Buono, Ser. & ILL Libn.; Johanna Grenda, Tech.Info.Spec.

★11269★
RAYTHEON COMPANY - SUBMARINE SIGNAL DIVISION - TECHNICAL INFORMATION CENTER (Sci-Tech)
1847 W. Main Rd.
Box 360   Phone: (401) 847-8000
Portsmouth, RI 02871   Mark F. Baldwin, Mgr., Tech.Info.Ctr.
Founded: 1960. **Staff:** Prof 1; Other 4. **Subjects:** Electronics, acoustics, oceanography, antisubmarine warfare, environmental science. **Holdings:** 10,000 books; 1200 bound periodical volumes; 20,000 reports and documents. **Subscriptions:** 200 journals and other serials. **Services:** Interlibrary loans; center not open to public. **Automated Operations:** Computerized cataloging and circulation. **Computerized Information Services:** DIALOG, DTIC, DMS/ONLINE. **Publications:** Accession Bulletin.

RAYTHEON COMPANY - UNITED ENGINEERS & CONSTRUCTORS INC.
See: United Engineers & Constructors Inc.

★11270★
RAYTHEON DATA SYSTEMS COMPANY - LIBRARY (Comp Sci)
1415 Boston-Providence Tpke.   Phone: (617) 762-6700
Norwood, MA 02062   Vicary Maxant, Libn.
Founded: 1959. **Staff:** Prof 1; Other 1. **Subjects:** Computers and computing, programming, electrical and electronic engineering, business. **Holdings:** 5000 books; 1000 IBM reports. **Subscriptions:** 400 journals and other serials. **Services:** Interlibrary loans; library not open to public. **Automated Operations:** Computerized cataloging and ILL. **Computerized Information Services:** DIALOG. **Publications:** Monthly Bulletin - for internal distribution only.

★11271★
RAYTHEON SERVICE COMPANY - INFORMATION CENTER (Bus-Fin)
2 Wayside Rd., Spencer Laboratory   Phone: (617) 272-9300
Burlington, MA 01803   Jean Cameron, Info.Spec.
Founded: 1970. **Staff:** Prof 1; Other 1. **Subjects:** Business, marketing. **Holdings:** 2000 books; 3000 reports. **Subscriptions:** 100 journals and other serials. **Services:** Interlibrary loans; copying; center open to public by arrangement. **Computerized Information Services:** DIALOG, Dun and Bradstreet Corporation. **Publications:** Accessions bulletin, bimonthly; Current Contents, monthly - both for internal distribution only.

★11272★
RCA CORPORATION - ASTRO-ELECTRONICS-GOVERNMENT SYSTEMS DIVISION - LIBRARY (Sci-Tech)
Box 800   Phone: (609) 448-3400
Princeton, NJ 08540   Mary L. Pfann, Libn.
Founded: 1958. **Staff:** Prof 1; Other 1. **Subjects:** Electronics, astronautics, telecommunications, computers, mechanics, remote sensing. **Special Collections:** NASA formal report series (30 file drawers). **Holdings:** 4000 books; 200 bound periodical volumes; 30 file drawers of unbound reports and pamphlets. **Subscriptions:** 200 journals and other serials. **Services:** Interlibrary loans; copying (both limited); library open to public with restrictions. **Computerized Information Services:** DIALOG, New England Research Application Center (NERAC), NASA/RECON, BRS; internal database.

RCA CORPORATION - C.I.T. FINANCIAL CORPORATION
See: C.I.T. Financial Corporation

★11273★
RCA CORPORATION - DAVID SARNOFF LIBRARY (Sci-Tech)
201 Washington Rd.
Box 432   Phone: (609) 452-2700
Princeton, NJ 08540   Wendy Chu, Mgr., Lib.Serv.
Special Collections: David Sarnoff Collection (history of communications). **Holdings:** 1000 books. **Services:** Copying; library open to public.

★11274★
RCA CORPORATION - ENGINEERING LIBRARY (Sci-Tech)†
Borton Landing Rd., Bldg. 101-222   Phone: (609) 778-3394
Moorestown, NJ 08057   Natalie J. Mamchur, Mgr., Lib.Res.
Founded: 1953. **Staff:** Prof 2; Other 4. **Subjects:** Radar and associated electronics, electrical engineering, computer science, technology, science and mathematics, business. **Holdings:** 25,000 books; 2500 bound periodical volumes; 17,500 reports. **Subscriptions:** 450 journals and other serials; 15 newspapers. **Services:** Interlibrary loans; copying; library open to public by appointment. **Computerized Information Services:** DIALOG, SDC, DTIC, Information Handling Services (IHS). **Special Catalogs:** Computerized holdings list of periodicals and of conference and symposia proceedings.

★11275★
RCA CORPORATION - G & CS - AUTOMATED SYSTEMS - ENGINEERING LIBRARY (Sci-Tech)
Box 588   Phone: (617) 272-4000
Burlington, MA 01803   Veronica Hsu, Tech.Libn.
Founded: 1955. **Staff:** Prof 1; Other 1. **Subjects:** Electronics, electrical engineering, optics, mathematics, computer technology, management. **Holdings:** 5000 books; 2500 bound periodical volumes; 1000 technical reports. **Subscriptions:** 175 journals and other serials. **Services:** Interlibrary loans; library not open to public. **Computerized Information Services:** DIALOG, BRS.

★11276★
RCA CORPORATION - GSD - GOVERNMENT COMMUNICATIONS SYSTEMS - LIBRARY (Sci-Tech)
Delaware Ave. & Cooper St., Bldg. 10-6-5   Phone: (609) 338-4046
Camden, NJ 08102   Nina R. Arrowood, Mgr., Lib.Rsrcs.
Founded: 1927. **Staff:** Prof 2; Other 2. **Subjects:** Electronics, mathematics, physics, computers, telecommunications. **Holdings:** 14,000 books; 3500 bound periodical volumes; 375 VF drawers of reports, reprints, conference proceedings. **Subscriptions:** 300 journals and other serials. **Services:** Interlibrary loans; copying (limited to company); library open to public for reference use of published materials. **Computerized Information Services:** DIALOG, SDC, BRS. **Publications:** Library News; Tables of Contents of Current Periodicals - for internal distribution only. **Special Catalogs:** Catalog of reports (card). **Staff:** Kathleen Gross, Asst.Libn.

★11277★
RCA CORPORATION - LIBRARY (Sci-Tech)
New Holland Pike   Phone: (717) 397-7661
Lancaster, PA 17604   Mary K. Noll, Libn.
Founded: 1943. **Staff:** Prof 1. **Subjects:** Electronics, television, electrical engineering, physics, chemistry, metallurgy, ceramics, mathematics. **Holdings:** 3000 books; 2000 bound periodical volumes; 3000 company reports; 1500 pamphlets and reports; 500 photostats; 450 patents; 2000 reprints; 15 VF drawers of miscellaneous reports and documents. **Subscriptions:** 100 journals and other serials. **Services:** Interlibrary loans; bibliographic and reference services for corporation employees; library open to public. **Computerized Information Services:** DIALOG. **Publications:** Current Technical Literature, weekly; New Acquisitions, monthly - for internal distribution only.

★11278★
RCA CORPORATION - PICTURE TUBE DIVISION - LIBRARY (Sci-Tech)*
3301 S. Adams St.   Phone: (317) 662-1411
Marion, IN 46952   Beth Dewitt, Libn.
Founded: 1950. **Staff:** 1. **Subjects:** Vacuum tubes, television, electronics, physics, chemistry, glass, metals. **Holdings:** 2058 books; 1687 bound periodical volumes; 1200 pamphlets (cataloged); 16 VF drawers of internal reports. **Subscriptions:** 89 journals and other serials. **Services:** Interlibrary loans; library not open to public.

★11279★
RCA CORPORATION - RCA CONSUMER ELECTRONICS DIVISION - ENGINEERING LIBRARY (Sci-Tech)
600 N. Sherman Dr., Bldg. 6-223   Phone: (317) 267-5925
Indianapolis, IN 46201   Susan M. Tamer, Adm., Lib.Serv.
Founded: 1955. **Staff:** Prof 1. **Subjects:** Engineering, electronics, physics, chemistry, television, computers. **Holdings:** 1800 books; 800 bound periodical volumes; 5000 technical reports (indexed). **Subscriptions:** 115 journals and other serials. **Services:** Interlibrary loans; copying; library open to public by appointment. **Automated Operations:** Computerized cataloging. **Computerized Information Services:** DIALOG, BRS, OCLC. **Networks/Consortia:** Member of Central Indiana Area Library Services Authority (CIALSA); INCOLSA. **Publications:** The Elm, quarterly - for internal distribution only.

★11280★
RCA CORPORATION - RCA LABORATORIES - DAVID SARNOFF RESEARCH CENTER - LIBRARY (Sci-Tech)
                                          Phone: (609) 734-2608
Princeton, NJ 08540   Wendy Chu, Mgr.
Founded: 1941. **Staff:** Prof 2; Other 3. **Subjects:** Radio, electronics, television, physics, chemistry, mathematics, metallurgy, acoustics, computers, semiconducting materials, space technology. **Holdings:** 32,000 books; 12,000 bound periodical volumes; 1000 reels of microfilm; 110 VF drawers of company reports; 100 VF drawers of pamphlets. **Subscriptions:** 450 journals and other serials. **Services:** Interlibrary loans; copying; library open to public. **Computerized Information Services:** DIALOG, SDC, BRS. **Publications:** Weekly Bulletin - distributed to RCA Laboratories personnel. **Staff:** Larry Eubank, Lib.Info.Spec.

★11281★
RCA CORPORATION - SELECTAVISION VIDEODISC OPERATIONS - TECHNICAL LIBRARY (Sci-Tech)
Box 91079   Phone: (317) 273-3397
Indianapolis, IN 46291   Joan K. Griffitts, Libn.
Staff: Prof 1. **Subjects:** Engineering, chemistry, computer science, electronics, television. **Holdings:** 1300 books; 50 bound periodical volumes. **Subscriptions:** 151 journals and other serials. **Services:** Interlibrary loans; copying; SDI; library not open to public. **Automated Operations:** Computerized cataloging and ILL. **Computerized Information Services:** DIALOG, BRS, OCLC, INFOLINE; internal database. Performs free searches. **Networks/Consortia:** Member of INCOLSA; Central Indiana Area Library Services Authority (CIALSA). **Publications:** Library Bulletin, monthly.

★11282★
RCA CORPORATION - SOLID STATE DIVISION - LIBRARY (Sci-Tech)
Rte. 202   Phone: (201) 685-6017
Somerville, NJ 08876   Halina S. Kan, Libn.
Founded: 1956. **Staff:** Prof 1. **Subjects:** Solid state electronics, physics, electrochemistry, electronic engineering, materials science, metallurgy. **Holdings:** 3000 books; 5000 bound periodical volumes; 6000 RCA Technical Reports and Engineering Memos. **Subscriptions:** 200 journals and other serials. **Services:** Interlibrary loans; library not open to public. **Computerized Information Services:** DIALOG, SDC, BRS. **Publications:** Library Bulletin.

RCA MUSEUM
See: Royal Canadian Artillery Museum

READ (Sir Herbert) ARCHIVES
See: University of Victoria - Mc Pherson Library - Special Collections

★11283★
READER'S DIGEST - ADVERTISING AND MARKETING LIBRARY (Publ; Bus-Fin)
200 Park Ave.   Phone: (212) 972-3730
New York, NY 10166   Helen Fledderus, Libn.
Staff: 2. **Subjects:** Advertising, marketing, media research. **Holdings:** 800 volumes; 125 VF drawers of commodity and industry data; 6 VF drawers of media information. **Subscriptions:** 116 journals and other serials. **Services:**

Interlibrary loans. **Computerized Information Services:** NEXIS, DIALOG, The Source.

★11284★
READER'S DIGEST - INDEX (Publ)
                                          Phone: (914) 769-7000
Pleasantville, NY 10570   Adrienne M. Bova, Ed.
Founded: 1922. **Staff:** 7. **Holdings:** Articles and book condensations cataloged on computer; anecdotes in the magazine (1922 to present) cataloged on computer. **Services:** Index area not open to public; staff will answer inquiries. **Computerized Information Services:** STAIRS, RAMIS (internal databases).

★11285★
READER'S DIGEST MAGAZINES LIMITED - EDITORIAL LIBRARY (Publ)
215 Redfern Ave.   Phone: (514) 934-0751
Montreal, PQ, Canada H3Z 2V9   Colette Nishizaki, Libn.
Founded: 1973. **Staff:** Prof 1; Other 2. **Subjects:** Canadiana. **Holdings:** 6000 books; 22 VF drawers of newspaper clippings. **Subscriptions:** 200 journals and other serials; 10 newspapers. **Services:** Interlibrary loans; library not open to public. **Computerized Information Services:** Info Globe. **Special Indexes:** Index to Canadian Reader's Digest (card).

★11286★
READING HOSPITAL & MEDICAL CENTER - MEDICAL LIBRARY (Med)
Sixth & Spruce Sts.   Phone: (215) 378-6418
Reading, PA 19603   Melinda Robinson Paquette, Med.Libn.
Founded: 1940. **Staff:** Prof 1. **Subjects:** Medicine and all specialties; medical ethics. **Holdings:** 4000 books; 18,000 bound periodical volumes; 4 VF drawers. **Subscriptions:** 200 journals and other serials. **Services:** Interlibrary loans; copying; SDI; library open to public by appointment for research and reference. **Computerized Information Services:** BRS. **Networks/Consortia:** Member of Greater Northeastern Regional Medical Library Program; Central Pennsylvania Health Sciences Library Association (CPHSLA); Berks County Library Association.

★11287★
READING HOSPITAL & MEDICAL CENTER - SCHOOL OF NURSING LIBRARY (Med)
                                          Phone: (215) 378-6359
Reading, PA 19603   Carolyn V. Unruh, Libn.
Founded: 1935. **Staff:** Prof 1; Other 1. **Subjects:** Nursing, psychiatry, psychology. **Holdings:** 8590 books and bound periodical volumes. **Subscriptions:** 42 journals and other serials. **Services:** Interlibrary loans; library open to public with permission.

★11288★
READING PUBLIC MUSEUM AND ART GALLERY - REFERENCE LIBRARY (Art)†
500 Museum Rd.   Phone: (215) 371-5850
Reading, PA 19611   Bruce L. Dietrich, Dir.
Staff: Prof 1; Other 1. **Subjects:** Art, natural science, anthropology. **Special Collections:** Unger Geology Collection; American Bureau of Ethnology Collection. **Holdings:** 3000 books; 2000 bound periodical volumes; 4 file drawers of catalogs from museum; 4 VF drawers of artist catalogs; 4 VF drawers of art catalogs; 3000 unbound periodicals. **Subscriptions:** 30 journals and other serials. **Services:** Library open to public with advance written permission. **Publications:** List of publications - available upon request.

★11289★
READING REHABILITATION HOSPITAL - MEDICAL LIBRARY (Med)
Rte. 1, Box 250, Morgantown Rd.   Phone: (215) 777-7615
Reading, PA 19607   Toni Wlasniewski, Libn.
Staff: Prof 1. **Subjects:** Medicine, rehabilitation, nursing. **Holdings:** 750 books; 460 bound periodical volumes. **Subscriptions:** 80 journals and other serials. **Services:** Interlibrary loans; copying; library open to public by appointment for reference use. **Networks/Consortia:** Member of Cooperating Hospital Libraries of the Lehigh Valley Area (CHL); Central Pennsylvania Health Sciences Library Association (CPHSLA).

★11290★
READING SCHOOL DISTRICT PLANETARIUM - LIBRARY (Sci-Tech)
1211 Parkside Dr., S.   Phone: (215) 371-5854
Reading, PA 19611   Bruce L. Dietrich, Dir. of Planetarium
Founded: 1969. **Staff:** 1. **Subjects:** Astronomy. **Holdings:** 900 books; 96 bound periodical volumes; 7000 35mm photographic astronomy slides; 1 VF drawer of manuscripts; 500 magnetic tapes; 2 VF drawers of clippings and pamphlets; 25 film loops; 15 movies. **Services:** Library open to public with written permission.

REAL ESTATE INSTITUTE
See: New York University - School of Continuing Education

★11291★
REAL ESTATE RESEARCH CORPORATION - LIBRARY (Plan)
72 W. Adams St.   Phone: (312) 346-5885
Chicago, IL 60603   Mary Oleksy, Libn.
Staff: Prof 2; Other 2. **Subjects:** Real estate management, urban planning, appraisal, land use, housing. **Holdings:** 1100 books; 100 bound periodical volumes; 20,000 company reports on microfiche; 40 VF drawers. **Subscriptions:** 300 journals and other serials; 6 newspapers. **Services:** Interlibrary loans; library open to public with permission of librarian.

REAL ESTATE, SHOPPING CENTER & URBAN DEVELOPMENT INFORMATION CENTER
See: The Vineyard

REASON & EQUITY IN TORT
See: Retort, Inc.

REAVIS (George) LIBRARY
See: Boulder Valley Public Schools, Region 2 - Professional Library

RECON/OPTICAL, INC. - CAI
See: CAI

★11292★
RECONSTRUCTIONIST RABBINICAL COLLEGE - MORDECAI M. KAPLAN LIBRARY (Rel-Theol)
Church Rd. & Greenwood Ave.   Phone: (215) 576-0800
Wyncote, PA 19095   Jennifer Gabriel, Libn.
Founded: 1968. **Staff:** Prof 1; Other 2. **Subjects:** Judaica, Hebraica, Rabbinics, Bible, Jewish history and sociology, religion, philosophy. **Special Collections:** Mordecai M. Kaplan Collection; President's Library. **Holdings:** 25,000 books; 1500 bound periodical volumes. **Subscriptions:** 150 journals and other serials; 20 newspapers. **Services:** Interlibrary loans; copying; library open to public.

RECORDED SOUND ARCHIVE
See: Northwestern University - Music Library

★11293★
RECORDING FOR THE BLIND, INC. - MASTER TAPE LIBRARY (Aud-Vis)
20 Roszel Rd.   Phone: (609) 452-0606
Princeton, NJ 08540   Anne H. Parkison, Dir. of Lib.Serv.
Founded: 1951. **Staff:** Prof 4; Other 1. **Subjects:** Collection consists of recorded textbooks and other educational materials. **Holdings:** 60,000 titles on master tapes. **Services:** Collection available to qualified print-handicapped students who are registered with RFB. **Automated Operations:** Computerized cataloging and circulation. **Computerized Information Services:** BRS, OCLC; internal database. **Networks/Consortia:** Member of FEDLINK. **Special Catalogs:** Catalog of recorded books. **Formerly:** Located in New York, NY.

★11294★
RECORDING INDUSTRY ASSOCIATION OF AMERICA - REFERENCE LIBRARY (Bus-Fin)
888 7th Ave., 9th Fl.   Phone: (212) 765-4330
New York, NY 10019   James Fishel, Exec.Dir.
Subjects: Audio and video recording industry. **Holdings:** Books, magazines, clippings, other materials.

RECYCLING INFORMATION CENTER
See: Earthworm, Inc.

★11295★
RED CROSS OF CONSTANTINE - UNITED GRAND IMPERIAL COUNCIL - EDWARD A. GLAD MEMORIAL LIBRARY (Rec)
14 E. Jackson Blvd., Suite 1700   Phone: (312) 427-5670
Chicago, IL 60604   Paul C. Rodenhauser, Grand Recorder
Founded: 1974. **Staff:** 2. **Subjects:** Freemasonry, American history. **Holdings:** 1700 books; 50 periodical volumes; 200 tapes. **Subscriptions:** 20 journals and other serials; 5 newspapers. **Services:** Library open to Masonic researchers.

★11296★
RED DEER ADVOCATE - NEWSPAPER LIBRARY (Publ)
2950 Bremner Ave.   Phone: (403) 343-2400
Red Deer, AB, Canada T4N 5G3   Patricia J. Goulet, Libn.
Staff: Prof 1. **Subjects:** Newspaper reference topics. **Special Collections:**

Biography files (240). **Holdings:** 100 books; 300 bound periodical volumes; 52 VF drawers of newspaper clippings; 280 reels of microfilm; 15,000 photographs. **Subscriptions:** 10 journals and other serials; 10 newspapers. **Services:** Copying; library open to public.

★11297★
REDDY COMMUNICATIONS, INC. - INFORMATION/RESEARCH SERVICES (Energy)
537 Steamboat Rd.   Phone: (203) 661-4800
Greenwich, CT 06830   Elizabeth A. Muskus, Mgr., Info./Res.Serv.
Staff: Prof 2; Other 1. **Subjects:** Public utilities, energy, communication techniques, public relations. **Holdings:** 700 books; 45 VF drawers of clippings, publications, reports, and speeches. **Subscriptions:** 400 journals and other serials. **Services:** Interlibrary loans; services not open to public. **Computerized Information Services:** DIALOG. **Networks/Consortia:** Member of Southwestern Connecticut Library Council (SWLC). **Staff:** Maureen Young, Info./Res.Spec.

REDINGTON MUSEUM
See: Waterville Historical Society - Library and Archives

REDISH (Jules) MEMORIAL MEDICAL LIBRARY
See: South Nassau Communities Hospital - Jules Redish Memorial Medical Library

★11298★
REDMOND (J.W.) COMPANY - LIBRARY (Bus-Fin)
1750 Pennsylvania Ave., N.W.
Washington, DC 20006   June Johnson, Libn.
Staff: 1. **Subjects:** Stock market. **Holdings:** Figures not available for books; 3000 corporate files. **Services:** Interlibrary loans; copying; library open to public by appointment.

REDSTONE SCIENTIFIC INFORMATION CENTER
See: U.S. Army - Missile Command & Marshall Space Flight Center

★11299★
REDWOOD COMMUNITY ACTION AGENCY - ENERGY DEMONSTRATION CENTER - APPROPRIATE TECHNOLOGY LIBRARY (Energy)
539 T St.   Phone: (707) 444-3831
Eureka, CA 95501   T. Michael Mills, Energy Educ.Coord.
Subjects: Passive solar energy, energy conservation, weatherization, solar retrofits, wind energy, wood stoves. **Holdings:** 1000 books; 18 bound periodical volumes; 2 shelves of energy policy and planning documents; 2 shelves of California Energy Commission reports; 1 shelf of energy curriculum; 3 VF drawers of general information files; 1 VF drawer of organization and agency files. **Subscriptions:** 50 journals and other serials; 20 newspapers. **Services:** Copying; library open to public for reference use only. **Automated Operations:** Computerized cataloging, acquisitions and serials. **Special Catalogs:** Appropriate technology card catalog. **Formerly:** Net Energy - Demonstration Center.

★11300★
REDWOOD EMPIRE ASSOCIATION - LIBRARY (Aud-Vis)
One Market Plaza
Spear St. Tower, Suite 1001   Phone: (415) 543-8334
San Francisco, CA 94105   Stuart Nixon, Gen.Mgr.
Founded: 1925. **Staff:** Prof 4. **Subjects:** Scenic, recreational and travel photos of nine counties in Northwestern California and Southwestern Oregon. **Holdings:** 100 reference books; news releases and fact sheets; 5000 black/white photographic negatives; 500 color transparencies. **Services:** Interlibrary loans; copying; photographs and news releases available without charge; special stories on this area prepared to order; library open to public. **Publications:** Visitors Guide to the Redwood Empire, Wine Country, irregular.

★11301★
REED COLLEGE - PHYSICS LIBRARY (Sci-Tech)*
Dept. of Physics   Phone: (503) 771-1112
Portland, OR 97202   Nicholas A. Wheeler, Prof.
Founded: 1933. **Staff:** 3. **Subjects:** Physics - theoretical, experimental; related technology and history. **Holdings:** 4000 books; 2500 bound periodical volumes; student theses and class materials. **Subscriptions:** 55 journals and other serials. **Services:** Library not open to public.

★11302★
REED LIBRARY OF FOOT & ANKLE (Med)
6000 Waterbury Circle   Phone: (515) 277-5756
Des Moines, IA 50312   Stewart E. Reed, D.P.M.
Founded: 1935. **Staff:** 1. **Subjects:** The foot, club foot, podagra (gout),

podiatry, podology, pedicure, orthopaedic books on the foot and ankle, history of footwear of all nations. **Holdings:** 1400 books; 300 bound periodical volumes; 250 other cataloged items; history of medicine; bibliography of medicine. **Subscriptions:** 15 journals and other serials. **Services:** Library open to public with restrictions. **Special Catalogs:** Catalog of the first Reed Library. **Remarks:** Dr. Reed's first collection of 5000 items on the foot and ankle was donated in 1974 to the Krausz Library of the Pennsylvania College of Podiatric Medicine. Both the new library and the original collection include old and rare books.

★11303★
REED LIGNIN INC. - LIGNIN RESEARCH LIBRARY (Sci-Tech)
100 Hwy. 51, S.   Phone: (715) 359-6544
Rothschild, WI 54474-1198   Julie M. Stephany, Libn.
Founded: 1949. **Subjects:** Lignins. **Holdings:** 1300 books; 850 bound periodical volumes; 800 other volumes. **Subscriptions:** 70 journals and other serials. **Services:** Library open to public with permission. **Formerly:** American Can Company - Research and Development Library.

★11304★
REED INC. - R&D LIBRARY (Sci-Tech)
Box 1487   Phone: (418) 694-7990
Quebec, PQ, Canada G1K 7H9   Jim Drake, Libn.
Founded: 1965. **Staff:** 2. **Subjects:** Pulp and paper, science and engineering. **Holdings:** 3000 books; 700 bound periodical volumes. **Subscriptions:** 120 journals and other serials. **Services:** Interlibrary loans (limited); library open to public by appointment.

★11305★
REED, SMITH, SHAW AND MC CLAY - LAW LIBRARY (Law)
747 Union Trust Bldg.   Phone: (412) 288-3377
Pittsburgh, PA 15219   Barbara Rose Stewart, Hd.Libn.
Staff: Prof 2; Other 3. **Subjects:** Law. **Holdings:** 32,000 books and bound periodical volumes. **Subscriptions:** 130 journals and other serials. **Services:** Library not open to public. **Staff:** Kathleen A. Miller, Libn.

★11306★
REED STENHOUSE, LTD. - RESEARCH DEPARTMENT LIBRARY (Bus-Fin)
Toronto Dominion Centre
P.O. Box 250   Phone: (416) 868-5520
Toronto, ON, Canada M5K 1J6   G.R.E. Bromwich, V.P., Res. & Info.Dept.
Founded: 1957. **Staff:** 3. **Subjects:** Insurance. **Holdings:** 300 books and bound periodical volumes; clippings. **Subscriptions:** 80 journals and other serials. **Services:** Library not open to public.

★11307★
REED INC. - TECHNICAL INFORMATION CENTRE (Sci-Tech)
207 Queen's Quay W.   Phone: (416) 862-5006
Toronto, ON, Canada M5J 1A7   Jim Drake, Info.Spec.
Staff: Prof 1; Other 2. **Subjects:** Pulp and paper. **Holdings:** 7000 books; 30 bound periodical volumes. **Subscriptions:** 200 journals and other serials; 10 newspapers. **Services:** Interlibrary loans; copying; center open to public by appointment. **Automated Operations:** Computerized cataloging, serials and circulation. **Computerized Information Services:** DIALOG. **Publications:** Acquisitions list.

REED (Walter) ARCHIVES
See: **University of Virginia - Medical Center - Claude Moore Health Sciences Library**

REED (Walter) ARMY INSTITUTE OF RESEARCH
See: **U.S. Army - Walter Reed Army Institute of Research**

REED (Walter) ARMY MEDICAL CENTER
See: **U.S. Army - Armed Forces Pest Management Board - Defense Pest Management Information Analysis Center; U.S. Army Hospitals - Walter Reed Army Medical Center**

REED (Walter) ARMY MEDICAL CENTER - U.S. ARMED FORCES INSTITUTE OF PATHOLOGY
See: **U.S. Armed Forces Institute of Pathology**

REEDY (William Marion) LIBRARY
See: **St. Louis Public Library - Carol Mc Donald Gardner Rare Book Room**

REEL THREE-D ENTERPRISES
See: **Stereo Club of Southern California - Library**

★11308★
REES-STEALY MEDICAL GROUP - LIBRARY (Med)
2001 Fourth Ave.   Phone: (619) 234-6261
San Diego, CA 92101   Margaret M. O'Rourke, Libn.
Founded: 1926. **Staff:** Prof 1. **Subjects:** Medicine, biochemistry. **Holdings:** 400 books; 4000 bound periodical volumes. **Subscriptions:** 110 journals and other serials. **Services:** Interlibrary loans; copying; library open to public with restrictions.

REESE AIR FORCE BASE (TX)
See: **U.S. Air Force Hospital - Medical Library (TX-Reese AFB)**

REESE (Michael) HOSPITAL & MEDICAL CENTER
See: **Michael Reese Hospital & Medical Center**

REEVES (David L.) MEDICAL LIBRARY
See: **Cottage Hospital - David L. Reeves Medical Library**

REEVES LIBRARY
See: **Moravian College**

REEVES MEMORIAL LIBRARY
See: **Bridgeport Hospital**

★11309★
REFLECTONE, INC. - ENGINEERING LIBRARY (Sci-Tech)
5125 Tampa West Blvd.   Phone: (813) 885-7481
Tampa, FL 33614   Sue Kaczor, Tech.Libn.
Staff: Prof 1; Other 1. **Subjects:** Aerodynamics of aircraft and helicopters; electronics; engineering. **Special Collections:** Flight simulation; military standards and specifications (20 file cabinets). **Holdings:** 350 books. **Subscriptions:** 80 journals and other serials. **Services:** Interlibrary loans; copying; SDI; library open to public with prior permission. **Computerized Information Services:** DIALOG.

★11310★
REFORM CONGREGATION KENESETH ISRAEL - MEYERS LIBRARY (Rel-Theol)
York Rd. & Township Line   Phone: (215) 887-8700
Elkins Park, PA 19117
Founded: 1870. **Staff:** Prof 1; Other 2. **Subjects:** Judaica. **Holdings:** 10,200 books; 200 bound periodical volumes. **Subscriptions:** 30 journals and other serials. **Services:** Interlibrary loans; library open to public with permission.

★11311★
REFORMED BIBLE COLLEGE - LIBRARY (Rel-Theol)
1869 Robinson Rd., S.E.   Phone: (616) 458-0404
Grand Rapids, MI 49506   Joanne Boehm, Libn.
Staff: Prof 2; Other 6. **Subjects:** Reformed theology, religious education, missions, Bible study, cults. **Holdings:** 39,000 books; 20 VF drawers; 2009 tapes; 699 volumes in microform; 686 filmstrips. **Subscriptions:** 314 journals and other serials. **Services:** Interlibrary loans; copying; library open to public. **Publications:** Library handbook. **Staff:** Lavonne Nettleton, Asst.Libn.

★11312★
REFORMED EPISCOPAL CHURCH - THEOLOGICAL SEMINARY - KUEHNER MEMORIAL LIBRARY (Rel-Theol)
4225 Chestnut St.   Phone: (215) 222-5158
Philadelphia, PA 19104   Walter G. Truesdell, Libn.
Founded: 1886. **Subjects:** Theology, church history, Oxford Movement, English Reformation. **Holdings:** 25,000 books and bound periodical volumes. **Subscriptions:** 85 journals and other serials. **Services:** Interlibrary loans; library open to public for reference use only. **Networks/Consortia:** Member of Southeastern Pennsylvania Theological Libraries Association (SEPTLA).

★11313★
REFORMED PRESBYTERIAN THEOLOGICAL SEMINARY - LIBRARY (Rel-Theol)
7418 Penn Ave.   Phone: (412) 731-8690
Pittsburgh, PA 15208   Rachel George, Libn.
Staff: Prof 1; Other 2. **Subjects:** Biblical studies, systematic and pastoral theology, church history, devotional works, sermons. **Special Collections:** Covenanter history and testimony; Psalms and psalmody. **Holdings:** 21,955 books; 2090 bound periodical volumes; 131 boxes of pamphlets; 865 tapes; 55 reels of microfilm; 163 microfiche. **Subscriptions:** 160 journals and other serials. **Services:** Interlibrary loans; copying; library open to public by appointment, fee for borrowing privilege. **Automated Operations:** Computerized cataloging. **Networks/Consortia:** Member of Pittsburgh

Regional Library Center (PRLC).

★11314★
REFORMED THEOLOGICAL SEMINARY - LIBRARY (Rel-Theol)
5422 Clinton Blvd.
Jackson, MS 39209
Phone: (601) 922-4988
Robert B. Ashlock, Act.Dir.
Founded: 1966. **Staff:** Prof 2; Other 5. **Subjects:** Theology, religion, Biblical studies, Southern Presbyterianism, Christian education. **Special Collections:** Blackburn Memorial Collection - Southern Presbyterian history (1200 volumes and pamphlets, periodicals and manuscripts). **Holdings:** 59,000 books; 1250 bound periodical volumes; 4300 tapes; 18,622 microfiche; 1530 reels of microfilm; manuscripts. **Subscriptions:** 600 journals and other serials; 6 newspapers. **Services:** Interlibrary loans; copying; library open to public. **Automated Operations:** Computerized cataloging. **Networks/Consortia:** Member of SOLINET. **Staff:** Ken Elliott, Circ.Libn.; Ruth Wilson, Cat.Libn.

★11315★
REFRIGERATION RESEARCH FOUNDATION - LIBRARY (Sci-Tech)
Air Rights Bldg.
7315 Wisconsin Ave.
Bethesda, MD 20814
Phone: (301) 652-5674
J. William Hudson, Exec.Dir.
Founded: 1944. **Subjects:** Handling of perishable commodities. **Holdings:** 500 books and bound periodical volumes. **Subscriptions:** 50 journals and other serials. **Services:** Library open to public.

★11316★
REFRIGERATION SERVICE ENGINEERS SOCIETY - LIBRARY (Sci-Tech)
1666 Rand Rd.
Des Plaines, IL 60016
Phone: (312) 297-6464
Mr. Nari Sethna, Exec.Mgr.
Subjects: Refrigeration and air conditioning. **Holdings:** Figures not available.

REGENSTEIN (Joseph) LIBRARY
See: University of Chicago

★11317★
REGINA CITY - PLANNING DEPARTMENT - LIBRARY (Plan)
P.O. Box 1790
Regina, SK, Canada S4P 3C8
Phone: (306) 569-7533
Beth Wignall, Lib.Techn.
Founded: 1976. **Staff:** Prof 1. **Subjects:** Planning; zoning; land use and controls; heritage conservation; housing - native, low income, disabled; day care. **Holdings:** 5000 books and government documents; 60 bound periodical volumes; 2 VF drawers of zoning by-laws; 5 VF drawers of clippings and pamphlets; 1 VF drawer of consultant's reports. **Subscriptions:** 56 journals and other serials. **Services:** Interlibrary loans; copying; library open to public with restrictions. **Publications:** Planning Department Publication Guide, annual.

REGINA CLERI RESOURCE LIBRARY
See: Diocese of Tucson

★11318★
REGINA GENERAL HOSPITAL - HEALTH SCIENCES LIBRARY (Med)
1440 14th Ave.
Regina, SK, Canada S4P 0W5
Phone: (306) 359-4314
Mrs. A. Belva Park, Med.Libn.
Founded: 1942. **Staff:** 2. **Subjects:** Medicine and allied sciences. **Holdings:** 5392 books; 3 VF drawers of reprints and pamphlets. **Subscriptions:** 318 journals and other serials. **Services:** Interlibrary loans; copying; library open to public with permission.

★11319★
REGIONAL MEMORIAL HOSPITAL - HEALTH SCIENCES LIBRARY (Med)
58 Baribeau Dr.
Brunswick, ME 04011
Phone: (207) 729-0181
Lynda K. Willis, Libn.
Founded: 1972. **Staff:** Prof 1. **Subjects:** Internal medicine, orthopedics, surgery, pediatrics. **Holdings:** 800 books; 2971 bound periodical volumes; 100 audio cassettes; 5 VF drawers of pamphlets. **Subscriptions:** 146 journals and other serials. **Services:** Interlibrary loans; copying; SDI; library open to public with restrictions. **Computerized Information Services:** MEDLINE. **Networks/Consortia:** Member of Health Science Library and Information Cooperative of Maine (HSLIC).

★11320★
REGIONAL PLAN ASSOCIATION, INC. - LIBRARY (Plan)
1040 Ave. of the Americas
New York, NY 10018
Phone: (212) 398-1140
Peter Haskel, Libn.
Founded: 1929. **Staff:** Prof 1; Other 1. **Subjects:** Urban and regional planning, housing, transportation, land use, public administration, environment. **Special Collections:** Municipal and county planning reports. **Holdings:** 2000 books; 8000 research and technical reports; 8 file drawers of newspaper clippings; 8 VF drawers. **Subscriptions:** 302 journals and other serials.

Services: Interlibrary loans; copying; library open to members. **Publications:** Accessions list, biennial - distributed to members.

★11321★
REGIONAL PLANNING COUNCIL - LIBRARY (Plan)
2225 N. Charles St.
Baltimore, MD 21218
Phone: (301) 383-5864
Irva B. Nachlas-Gabin, Libn.
Staff: Prof 1; Other 1. **Subjects:** Planning, urban affairs, environment, transportation, demography. **Special Collections:** Maryland and Baltimore region government publications; Regional Planning Council publications. **Holdings:** 10,000 books; 60 bound periodical volumes; 500 technical reports on microfiche. **Subscriptions:** 320 journals and other serials; 15 newspapers. **Services:** Interlibrary loans; copying; library open to public for reference use only. **Networks/Consortia:** Member of Maryland Interlibrary Loan Organization (MILO). **Publications:** Acquisitions list, quarterly; List of current publications of the Regional Planning Council, annual - both free upon request.

REGIONAL RESOURCES CENTER OF EASTERN PENNSYLVANIA FOR SPECIAL EDUCATION
See: Pennsylvania Resources and Information Center for Special Education

★11322★
REGIONAL TRANSPORTATION DISTRICT (Metropolitan Denver Area) - **RESEARCH & RECORDS SERVICES** (Trans; Plan)
1600 Blake St.
Denver, CO 80202
Phone: (303) 628-9000
Rodene Harwood, Supv.
Founded: 1975. **Staff:** 2. **Subjects:** Public transportation, land use, urban planning, civil engineering. **Holdings:** 6073 books; 4068 reports; 7800 slides; 1200 microfiche; 4 films. **Subscriptions:** 263 journals and other serials; 23 newspapers. **Services:** Interlibrary loans; library open to public by appointment. **Automated Operations:** Computerized cataloging, acquisitions, serials and ILL. **Computerized Information Services:** DIALOG. **Networks/Consortia:** Member of Central Colorado Library System (CCLS); Bibliographical Center for Research, Rocky Mountain Region, Inc. (BCR).

★11323★
REGIS COLLEGE - LIBRARY (Rel-Theol)†
15 St. Mary St.
Toronto, ON, Canada M4Y 2R5
Phone: (416) 922-0536
Rev. Vincent MacKenzie, S.J., Chf.Libn.
Founded: 1931. **Staff:** Prof 1; Other 4. **Subjects:** Theology, religion, and related fields. **Special Collections:** Lonergan Centre (manuscripts; books; tapes; off-prints). **Holdings:** 86,127 books; 20,000 bound periodical volumes. **Subscriptions:** 358 journals and other serials. **Services:** Interlibrary loans (fee); copying; library open to public with approval of chief librarian.

★11324★
REGISTER-GUARD - LIBRARY (Publ)
975 High St.
Box 10188
Eugene, OR 97440
Phone: (503) 485-1234
Marijoy Rubaloff, Libn.
Founded: 1950. **Staff:** Prof 1; Other 1. **Subjects:** Newspaper reference topics. **Holdings:** 1500 books; newspaper clippings. **Subscriptions:** 25 journals and other serials; 10 newspapers. **Services:** Library open to public with restrictions. **Formerly:** Eugene Register-Guard.

★11325★
REGISTERED NURSES' ASSOCIATION OF BRITISH COLUMBIA - LIBRARY (Med)
2855 Arbutus St.
Vancouver, BC, Canada V6J 3Y8
Phone: (604) 736-7331
Ilka Abbott, Libn.
Staff: Prof 1; Other 2. **Subjects:** Nursing. **Holdings:** 2000 books; 350 bound periodical volumes; 25 shelves of pamphlets; 375 audiotapes. **Subscriptions:** 70 journals and other serials. **Services:** Interlibrary loans; copying; library open to RNABC members and holders of temporary library cards.

★11326★
REGISTERED NURSES' ASSOCIATION OF ONTARIO - LIBRARY (Med)
33 Price St.
Toronto, ON, Canada M4W 1Z2
Phone: (416) 923-3523
Mary Boite, Libn.
Staff: Prof 1; Other 1. **Subjects:** Nursing, health. **Special Collections:** RNAO Archives. **Holdings:** 2400 books; 258 bound periodical volumes; 8 VF drawers of reports; 20 VF drawers of clippings. **Subscriptions:** 120 journals and other serials. **Services:** Interlibrary loans; copying; library open to public by appointment. **Publications:** RNAO library acquisitions, bimonthly; bibliographies on different aspects of nursing - free upon request.

REGNER HEALTH SCIENCES LIBRARY
See: St. Michael's Hospital

★11327★
REHABILITATION INSTITUTE OF CHICAGO - LEARNING RESOURCES CENTER (Med)
345 E. Superior, Rm. 1671   Phone: (312) 649-2859
Chicago, IL 60611   Carol Ann Lauer, Coord.
Staff: Prof 1. **Subjects:** Rehabilitation, physical medicine. **Holdings:** 600 books; 10 bound periodical volumes; 350 films and videotapes; 50 slide/sound sets and filmstrips; 2000 research reports; 18 VF drawers. **Subscriptions:** 36 journals and other serials. **Services:** Interlibrary loans; copying; center open to public by appointment. **Networks/Consortia:** Member of Greater Midwest Regional Medical Library Network (Region 3); Chicago Library System. **Publications:** Recent Acquisitions, irregular - to staff. **Remarks:** Center is affiliated with Northwestern University - Health Sciences Library.

★11328★
REHABILITATION INSTITUTE, INC. - LEARNING RESOURCES CENTER (Med)
261 Mack Blvd.   Phone: (313) 494-9860
Detroit, MI 48201   Daria Shackelford, Med.Libn./Dir.
Founded: 1958. **Staff:** Prof 1; Other 1. **Subjects:** Physical medicine, rehabilitation, general medicine, physical therapy, occupational therapy, social service, patient education. **Holdings:** 1800 books; 3200 bound periodical volumes; 6 VF drawers of pamphlets; 5 boxes of reports; 1 VF drawer of reprints; 15 16mm films; 1000 35mm slides; 30 videotapes. **Subscriptions:** 125 journals and other serials. **Services:** Interlibrary loans; copying; center open to public with permission. **Computerized Information Services:** BRS, NLM. **Networks/Consortia:** Member of Greater Midwest Regional Medical Library Network (Region 3). **Formed by the Merger of:** Its McPherson Browning Memorial Library and its Patient Education Library.

REHABILITATION INTERNATIONAL
See: International Society for Rehabilitation of the Disabled/Rehabilitation International

★11329★
REICHHOLD CHEMICALS, INC. - RESEARCH LIBRARY (Sci-Tech)
Box 1433   Phone: (904) 433-7621
Pensacola, FL 32596   Rosemary Milner Kiefer, Info.Rsrcs.Mgr.
Founded: 1950. **Staff:** Prof 1. **Subjects:** Chemistry - coatings, ink, resins, adhesives; paper and rubber chemicals. **Holdings:** 500 books; 3000 bound periodical volumes; 5 VF drawers of chemical catalogs; 4 VF drawers of laboratory reports; 4 VF drawers of patents (U.S. and foreign); 4 VF drawers of pamphlets. **Subscriptions:** 110 journals and other serials; 5 newspapers. **Services:** Interlibrary loans; copying; library open to qualified persons with permission. **Computerized Information Services:** DIALOG.

★11330★
REICHHOLD CHEMICALS, INC. - TECHNICAL LIBRARY (Sci-Tech)
2340 Taylor Way   Phone: (206) 572-5600
Tacoma, WA 98401   Deirdre R. Preston, Info. Resource Spec.
Staff: Prof 1; Other 1. **Subjects:** Chemistry, forest products. **Holdings:** 2000 books; 200 bound periodical volumes. **Subscriptions:** 75 journals and other serials. **Services:** Interlibrary loans; copying; SDI; library not open to public. **Computerized Information Services:** DIALOG. **Publications:** Monthly Accessions List. **Remarks:** Library serves the Specialty Chemicals, Specialty Phenolics, and Reichhold Energy divisions of the company.

★11331★
REID AND PRIEST - LAW LIBRARY (Law)
40 W. 57th St.   Phone: (212) 603-2000
New York, NY 10019   Morton Barad, Libn.
Founded: 1935. **Staff:** Prof 2; Other 2. **Subjects:** Law - international, public utilities, securities. **Holdings:** 20,000 volumes; SEC releases. **Services:** Interlibrary loans; library not open to public. **Computerized Information Services:** LEXIS, New York Times Information Service. **Staff:** Eric Olson, Dir. of Lib.Serv.

REIGNER (Charles G.) MEDICAL LIBRARY
See: Lutheran Hospital of Maryland - Charles G. Reigner Medical Library

★11332★
REILLY TRANSLATIONS - LIBRARY (Sci-Tech)
Box 4346   Phone: (213) 515-6839
Carson, CA 90749-4346   Michael M. Reilly, Dir.
Founded: 1967. **Staff:** Prof 1; Other 1. **Subjects:** Linguistics, science and technology. **Holdings:** 1500 books; 587 foreign patents; 200 magnetic

tapes; 50 videotapes. **Subscriptions:** 25 journals and other serials. **Services:** Translations; library not open to public.

REINER (Fritz) LIBRARY
See: Northwestern University - Music Library

REINERT/ALUMNI MEMORIAL LIBRARY
See: Creighton University

REINHARDT (Max) ARCHIVE & LIBRARY
See: SUNY at Binghamton - Special Collections

★11333★
REINHART, BOERNER, VAN DEUREN, NORRIS & RIESELBACH - LIBRARY (Law)
1800 Marine Plaza   Phone: (414) 271-1190
Milwaukee, WI 53202   Carol Bannen, Libn.
Founded: 1975. **Staff:** Prof 1; Other 2. **Subjects:** Law - taxation, real estate, labor, employee benefits, banking, corporate, securities. **Holdings:** 9000 books; 110 cassette tapes; 20 reels of microfilm; 3 boxes of microfiche. **Subscriptions:** 204 journals and other serials. **Services:** Interlibrary loans; copying; SDI; library open to public with restrictions. **Computerized Information Services:** DIALOG, LEXIS. **Networks/Consortia:** Member of Library Council of Metropolitan Milwaukee, Inc. (LCOMM); Milwaukee Downtown Law Librarians. **Publications:** New Book List, monthly; Current Education Opportunities in Law, monthly - for internal distribution only. **Special Indexes:** Information Retrieval Index on computer.

REISMAN MEMORIAL LIBRARY
See: John Jay College of Criminal Justice of the City University of New York

★11334★
REISS-DAVIS CHILD STUDY CENTER - RESEARCH LIBRARY (Soc Sci)
3200 Motor Ave.   Phone: (213) 204-1666
Los Angeles, CA 90034   Leonore Freehling, Libn.
Founded: 1950. **Staff:** Prof 1. **Subjects:** Child psychology, child psychiatry, child development, psychiatric social work, educational psychology, child analysis. **Special Collections:** Freud Collection. **Holdings:** 9500 books; 3500 bound periodical volumes; 5000 reprints; 4000 pamphlets; 25 films; 500 audiotapes. **Subscriptions:** 150 journals and other serials. **Services:** Interlibrary loans; copying; library open to public on payment of membership fee. **Networks/Consortia:** Member of Pacific Southwest Regional Medical Library Service (PSRMLS). **Publications:** Acquisitions list, quarterly. **Special Indexes:** Index to contributions by authors in collections.

★11335★
REL INCORPORATED - CORPORATE LIBRARY (Sci-Tech)
3800 S. Congress Ave.   Phone: (305) 732-0300
Boynton Beach, FL 33435   Linda L. Wyman, Libn.
Staff: Prof 1; Other 1. **Subjects:** Radar, electronic warfare, tropospheric scatter, radio communications, electronics. **Holdings:** 1500 books; 40 bound periodical volumes; 800 Air Force technical orders; 70 VF drawers and 500 microfilm cartridges of vendor catalogs; 60 VF drawers and 824 microfilm cartridges of military specifications and standards. **Subscriptions:** 131 journals and other serials. **Services:** Interlibrary loans; copying; library open to public with restrictions and by appointment. **Publications:** New Titles in the Library, irregular - for internal distribution only.

★11336★
RELIANCE GROUP HOLDINGS, INC. - CORPORATE LIBRARY (Bus-Fin)
Park Ave. Plaza
New York, NY 10055   Ellen Rubin, Corp.Libn.
Founded: 1980. **Staff:** Prof 1; Other 1. **Subjects:** Investment, business, management. **Holdings:** 500 books; 7000 unbound periodicals; 20 VF drawers of microfiche. **Subscriptions:** 200 journals and other serials; 10 newspapers. **Services:** Interlibrary loans; copying; library open to SLA members by appointment. **Computerized Information Services:** DIALOG, SDC, Dun & Bradstreet Corporation, Info Globe, COMPUSTAT Services, Inc., Dow Jones News/Retrieval, LEXIS, NEXIS, INVESTEXT, VU/TEXT, Spectrum Ownership Profiles Online.

★11337★
RELIGIOUS ARTS GUILD - MUSIC LIBRARY (Mus)
25 Beacon St.   Phone: (617) 742-2100
Boston, MA 02108   Barbara M. Hutchins, Exec.Sec.
Founded: 1923. **Subjects:** Poetry, anthem, art scholarship, design awards; worship services promoting the arts. **Holdings:** 325 anthems available for loan to U.U. societies. **Services:** Library not open to public. **Publications:**

Award folders - available on request. **Remarks:** Religious Arts Guild is an affiliate of the Unitarian Universalist Association.

★11338★
RELIGIOUS NEWS SERVICE - LIBRARY AND MORGUE (Rel-Theol; Publ)
104 W. 56th St.   Phone: (212) 688-7094
New York, NY 10019
Founded: 1933. **Staff:** Prof 1. **Subjects:** News stories of the world's religions. **Holdings:** Figures not available. **Services:** Library open on limited basis for research by authorized personnel. **Computerized Information Services:** NewsNet, Inc. **Remarks:** Library carries stories from the past 3-4 years only. Older files are available through the United Presbyterian Church in the U.S.A. - Presbyterian Historical Society in Philadelphia, PA.

★11339★
RELIGIOUS NEWS SERVICE - PHOTOGRAPH LIBRARY (Aud-Vis)
106 W. 56th St.   Phone: (212) 688-7094
New York, NY 10019   Jim Hansen, Photo Ed.
Founded: 1945. **Staff:** Prof 2. **Subjects:** Photographs (black/white only) covering religion, features, social concerns. **Holdings:** 200,000 photographs. **Services:** Library not open to public.

REMBERT-STOKES LEARNING CENTER
See: Wilberforce University

★11340★
REMINGTON ARMS COMPANY, INC. - RESEARCH LIBRARY (Sci-Tech)
Broadbridge Ave.   Phone: (203) 333-1112
Stratford, CT 06497
Subjects: Chemistry, metallurgy, small arms, small ammunition. **Holdings:** 2000 books. **Services:** Library open to staff only.

RENNE (Roland R.) LIBRARY
See: Montana State University - Roland R. Renne Library

★11341★
RENSSELAER COUNTY HISTORICAL SOCIETY - LIBRARY (Hist)
59 Second St.   Phone: (518) 272-7232
Troy, NY 12180   Mrs. Frederick R. Walsh, Dir.
Staff: 1. **Subjects:** Rensselaer County history. **Special Collections:** City directories; collection of photographs of Troy and Rensselaer County; Tibbitts Collection. **Holdings:** 2500 books; letters, local business daybooks and pamphlets. **Services:** Copying; library open to public.

★11342★
RENSSELAER POLYTECHNIC INSTITUTE - ARCHITECTURE LIBRARY (Art)
                                                  Phone: (518) 270-6465
Troy, NY 12181   Virginia S. Bailey
Founded: 1930. **Staff:** Prof 1; Other 2. **Subjects:** Architecture, art, city and regional planning, landscaping. **Holdings:** 24,180 books; 5025 bound periodical volumes; 70 VF drawers of clippings; 12 VF drawers of manufacturers' literature; VF drawers of architectural firms' brochures; 50,000 slides; 1900 maps. **Subscriptions:** 215 journals and other serials. **Services:** Interlibrary loans; library open to public. **Special Indexes:** Selected Periodical Index file (card).

★11343★
RENSSELAER POLYTECHNIC INSTITUTE - FOLSOM LIBRARY (Sci-Tech)
                                                  Phone: (518) 270-6673
Troy, NY 12181   James C. Andrews, Dir. of Lib.
Founded: 1824. **Staff:** Prof 15; Other 28. **Subjects:** Science, engineering, management, social sciences, humanities. **Special Collections:** History of Science and Technology; technical reports; government documents; Geological Survey Quadrangle Maps. **Holdings:** 208,300 books; 117,226 bound periodical volumes; 348,000 microforms; 2500 recordings; 50,000 slides; 46,000 reports and maps. **Subscriptions:** 4975 journals and other serials; 34 newspapers. **Services:** Interlibrary loans; copying; SDI; library open to public. **Automated Operations:** Computerized cataloging, serials and acquisitions. **Computerized Information Services:** BRS, DIALOG, Dow Jones News/Retrieval. **Networks/Consortia:** Member of Capital District Library Council for Reference and Research Resources (CDLC). **Publications:** Library Guide; library use manuals. **Special Catalogs:** Guide to the Roebling Collections. **Staff:** Pat Molholt, Assoc.Dir.; Irving E. Stephens, Hd., Bldg.Serv.; Kingsley W. Greene, Hd., Rd.Serv.; Alice R. Browne, Ref.Libn.; James A. Laviolette, Ref.Libn.; Colette O'Connell, Ref.Libn.; Polly-Alida Farrington, ILL Libn.; Jean K. Sheviak, Ser.Libn.; Flora D. Regnier, Hd., Tech.Serv.; Peter C. Gerdine, Acq.Libn.; Carol T. Lagasse, Cat.Libn.; Kristina MacCormick, Cat.Libn.; Elizabeth Campbell Stewart, Archv.; Samuel V. Johnson, Hd., Automation Serv.

RENTMEISTER WESTERN AMERICANA LIBRARY
See: Brigham City Museum-Gallery

★11344★
REORGANIZED CHURCH OF JESUS CHRIST OF LATTER DAY SAINTS - LIBRARY & ARCHIVES (Hist; Rel-Theol)
RLDS Auditorium
Box 1059   Phone: (816) 833-1000
Independence, MO 64051   Sara Hallier, Libn.
Staff: Prof 2; Other 1. **Subjects:** Mormon history, Reorganized Latter Day Saint thought and doctrine, religion and theology. **Special Collections:** Herald House publications; state histories related to Latter Day Saint movement; Latter Day Saints pamphlets; archival collection (298 linear feet of unpublished records, journals, manuscripts and photographs). **Holdings:** 14,000 books; 2700 bound periodical volumes; 300 reels of microfilm; 200 cassettes. **Subscriptions:** 100 journals and other serials. **Services:** Interlibrary loans; copying; library open to public. **Networks/Consortia:** Member of Kansas City Metropolitan Library Network (KCMLN). **Staff:** Madelon Brunson, Archv.; Shirley Crandall, Asst.Libn.

★11345★
REORGANIZED CHURCH OF JESUS CHRIST OF LATTER DAY SAINTS - SERVICES TO THE BLIND (Rel-Theol; Aud-Vis)
1001 Walnut
Box 1059   Phone: (816) 833-1000
Independence, MO 64051   Stephanie Kelley, Supv.
Staff: 2. **Subjects:** Religious topics. **Holdings:** Figures not available for books in braille; cassettes; large print pamphlets, brochures and instruction manuals. **Services:** Braille transcription instruction and service; thermoform duplication of braille materials; services open to public. **Staff:** Fay Garnier, Asst.

★11346★
REPERTOIRE INTERNATIONAL D'ICONOGRAPHIE MUSICALE - RESEARCH CENTER FOR MUSICAL ICONOGRAPHY - LIBRARY (Mus)
Grad. Ctr., CUNY, Dept. of Music
33 W. 42nd St.   Phone: (212) 790-4282
New York, NY 10036   Dr. Barry S. Brook, Dir.
Staff: Prof 3. **Subjects:** Musical iconography, portraits of musicians, paintings with musical subjects. **Special Collections:** Martin Bernstein Slide Collection; Viennese Classical Period Collection (Haydn, Mozart, Beethoven, Schubert iconography - slides and transparencies); Vienna Gesellschaft der Musikfreunde Portrait Collection (transparencies). **Holdings:** 800 volumes; 1500 documents, pictures with accompanying catalog card; 2000 slides; 8000 pictures. **Services:** Copying; library open to public. **Publications:** RIDIM/RCMI Newsletter, semiannual; The Musical Ensemble, circa 1730-1830, exhibition catalog, 1978; Autour de la viole de gambe, exhibition catalog, 1979. **Special Indexes:** Index to pictures housed in the center.

★11347★
REPUBLIC GEOTHERMAL, INC. - INFORMATION RESOURCES CENTER (Energy)
11823 E. Slauson Ave.   Phone: (213) 945-3661
Santa Fe Springs, CA 90670   Gloria Barnett, Info.Spec.
Founded: 1980. **Staff:** Prof 1. **Subjects:** Geothermal energy, geology. **Holdings:** 100 books; 1400 reports; 3800 maps; 700 clippings; 1000 reports on microfiche; 100 patents. **Subscriptions:** 266 journals and other serials. **Services:** Interlibrary loans; center open to public with restrictions. **Automated Operations:** Computerized cataloging, acquisitions, serials and circulation. **Computerized Information Services:** DIALOG, DOE/RECON, OLIS (Online Library Information System; internal database. **Special Catalogs:** Technical reports catalog (computer printout).

★11348★
REPUBLIC STEEL CORPORATION - RESEARCH CENTER LIBRARY (Sci-Tech)
6801 Brecksville Rd.   Phone: (216) 524-5100
Cleveland, OH 44131   Kathryn A. Woolard, Libn.
Founded: 1958. **Staff:** Prof 1; Other 1. **Subjects:** Metallurgy. **Special Collections:** Brutcher translations. **Holdings:** 11,500 books; 3530 bound periodical volumes. **Subscriptions:** 320 journals and other serials. **Services:** Interlibrary loans; library open to public by appointment. **Automated Operations:** Computerized reports. **Computerized Information Services:** DIALOG. **Staff:** Kathleen A. Schreck, Asst.Libn.

★11349★
REPUBLICAN ASSOCIATES OF LOS ANGELES COUNTY - RESEARCH LIBRARY (Soc Sci)
1153 N. Brand Blvd.   Phone: (818) 240-9100
Glendale, CA 91202   Mark S. Harmsen, Res.Dir.
Founded: 1951. **Staff:** Prof 2; Other 3. **Subjects:** Current issues; state and

federal administrations; political officeholders; assembly, senate and congressional districts. **Special Collections:** Richard Nixon Collection (120 items); campaign materials (100 items); Governor Jerry Brown clipping file; Governor George Deukmejian clipping file; President Reagan and Reagan Administration clipping file. **Holdings:** 126 VF drawers of newspapers clippings; Governor Ronald Reagan Press releases, 1966-1974 (complete and inclusive); Congressional Quarterly Weekly Reports, 1956 to present. **Subscriptions:** 29 journals and other serials; 11 newspapers. **Services:** Copying; library open to public with restrictions (no Democratic candidates or office holders). **Networks/Consortia:** Member of Southern California Answering Network (SCAN). **Publications:** Newsletter, monthly - to members and Republican office holders; campaign material - on request. **Special Catalogs:** Catalog of Judicial appointments. **Special Indexes:** List of speeches by Governor Reagan, 1966-1974; list of appointments by Governor Reagan, 1966-1974; index of past and present political figures; index of current federal and California issues. **Staff:** Gene Wiberg, Exec.Dir.; June Boehle, Libn.

★11350★
REPUBLICAN NATIONAL COMMITTEE - LIBRARY (Soc Sci)
310 First St., S.E.   Phone: (202) 484-6626
Washington, DC 20003   Joanna Evans, Libn.
Founded: 1936. **Staff:** Prof 1; Other 1. **Subjects:** Government, legislation, politics, election results, demographic material, voting statistics, political history, presidential documents. **Special Collections:** Collection of Republican National Committee Proceedings of Nominating Conventions, 1856 to present. **Holdings:** 5000 books; 100 bound periodical volumes; microfilm. **Subscriptions:** 150 journals and other serials; 10 newspapers. **Services:** Interlibrary loans; copying; library open to public with approval of librarian. **Computerized Information Services:** New York Times Information Service, NEXIS, The Source.

★11351★
REPUBLICBANK CORPORATION - ECONOMIC RESEARCH LIBRARY (Bus-Fin)
Box 222105   Phone: (214) 653-5807
Dallas, TX 75222   John W. Brewster, Economic Libn.
Staff: Prof 1; Other 2. **Subjects:** Economics, banking, finance, political science, energy. **Holdings:** 2500 books; 400 bound periodical volumes. **Subscriptions:** 400 journals and other serials; 8 newspapers. **Services:** Interlibrary loans; copying; library open to public by appointment. **Automated Operations:** Computerized serials. **Computerized Information Services:** DIALOG, NEXIS, Data Resources, Inc., Chase Econometrics, Dow Jones News/Retrieval, I.P. Sharp Associates, Ltd., Townsend-Greenspan & Co., Inc.; internal database. **Publications:** Economic Perspective, monthly.

★11352★
RESEARCH FOR BETTER SCHOOLS, INC. - RESOURCE CENTER (Educ)
444 N. Third St.   Phone: (215) 574-9300
Philadelphia, PA 19123   Marian L. Chapman, Dir.
Founded: 1978. **Staff:** Prof 1; Other 1. **Subjects:** Elementary and secondary education. **Special Collections:** Competency-based education (600 documents); educational technology (100 items); Research for Better Schools (750 documents); school improvement (800 documents); school influences (200 documents); training materials (150 documents). **Holdings:** 1500 books; complete ERIC collection on microfiche. **Subscriptions:** 92 journals and other serials. **Services:** SDI; center open to public for reference use only. **Computerized Information Services:** DIALOG, BRS. **Publications:** Tracings, monthly - to all professional staff. **Special Indexes:** Indexes to special collections (card). **Remarks:** The Resource Center provides information services for all RBS using its own collection and those of local university libraries.

RESEARCH CENTER FOR MUSICAL ICONOGRAPHY
See: Repertoire International d'Iconographie Musicale

★11353★
RESEARCH CENTER FOR RELIGION & HUMAN RIGHTS IN CLOSED SOCIETIES - INFORMATION CENTER (Rel-Theol)*
475 Riverside Dr., Suite 448   Phone: (212) 870-2481
New York, NY 10115   Rev. B.S. Hruby, Exec.Dir.
Staff: 2. **Subjects:** Religion and human rights in Communist countries; religious and atheistic literature published in Communist countries. **Holdings:** Periodicals; clippings; reports; occasional papers; underground publications from Communist countries. **Subscriptions:** 100 journals and other serials. **Services:** Center open to members and scholars by special arrangements only. **Publications:** RCDA - Religion in Communist Dominated Areas, quarterly. **Special Indexes:** Index to RCDA, annual.

★11354★
RESEARCH & EDUCATION ASSOCIATION - LIBRARY (Sci-Tech)
505 Eighth Ave.   Phone: (212) 695-9487
New York, NY 10018   Carl Fuchs, Libn.
Staff: Prof 2. **Subjects:** Science and technology, mathematics, physics, chemistry. **Holdings:** 2000 books. **Services:** Library not open to public. **Staff:** P. Weston .

★11355★
RESEARCH FOUNDATION FOR JEWISH IMMIGRATION, INC. - ARCHIVES (Area-Ethnic)
570 7th Ave., 16th Fl.   Phone: (212) 921-3871
New York, NY 10018   Herbert A. Strauss, Coord. of Res.
Subjects: Biography, bibliography, oral history. **Special Collections:** International Biographical Archive of Central European Emigres, 1933-1945 (data on 25,000 individuals). **Holdings:** 300 cassettes of oral history interviews. **Services:** Archives open to public by appointment. **Staff:** Joan C. Lessing, Cur., Oral Hist.Coll.

★11356★
RESEARCH & INFORMATION SERVICES FOR EDUCATION - MONTGOMERY COUNTY INTERMEDIATE UNIT LIBRARY (Educ)
725 Caley Rd.
King of Prussia, PA 19406   Richard R. Brickley, Dir.
Founded: 1966. **Staff:** Prof 1. **Subjects:** Education, curriculum design, educational research, administration, methodology and evaluation, program dissemination. **Special Collections:** ERIC (200,000 documents on microfiche). **Holdings:** 8000 books and bound periodical volumes; 900 literature searches; 4 vertical files of newsletters; 8 VF drawers of general information. **Subscriptions:** 150 journals and other serials; 200 newspapers. **Services:** Copying; library open to public. **Computerized Information Services:** BRS, DIALOG, The Source; internal database. **Publications:** RISE Newsletter, 4/year. **Special Catalogs:** Search catalog (book).

★11357★
RESEARCH INSTITUTE ON ALCOHOLISM - LIBRARY (Med)
1021 Main St.   Phone: (716) 887-2511
Buffalo, NY 14203   Diane Augustino, Res.Sci. I
Staff: Prof 1; Other 1. **Subjects:** Alcoholism and alcohol abuse, including physiological, psychological, sociological, biochemical, and pharmacological aspects; drug abuse. **Holdings:** 3500 books; 550 bound periodical volumes; 10 VF drawers of other cataloged items. **Subscriptions:** 90 journals and other serials; 5 newspapers. **Services:** Interlibrary loans; copying; SDI; library open to public for reference use only. **Automated Operations:** Computerized cataloging. **Networks/Consortia:** Member of Western New York Library Resources Council (WNYLRC); Library Consortium of Health Institutions in Buffalo (LCHIB). **Publications:** RIA Publications List, annual; List of Serials, annual; Library Acquisitions List, monthly.

★11358★
RESEARCH INSTITUTE OF AMERICA - INFORMATION SERVICES CENTER (Bus-Fin)
589 Fifth Ave.   Phone: (212) 755-8900
New York, NY 10017   Mary Summers, Adm. of Info.Serv.
Founded: 1935. **Staff:** Prof 2; Other 1. **Subjects:** Business, economics, labor and personnel relations, international relations, management methods, marketing management. **Holdings:** 3000 books; 30 VF drawers; 5000 microfiche; 200 reels of microfilm. **Subscriptions:** 500 journals and other serials; 5 newspapers. **Services:** Interlibrary loans; center not open to public. **Computerized Information Services:** DIALOG, SDC, Dow Jones News/Retrieval, NewsNet, Inc. **Publications:** InfoAccess, monthly - for internal distribution only. **Staff:** Jamie B. Russell, Info.Spec.

RESEARCH INSTITUTE FOR INNER ASIAN STUDIES
See: Indiana University

★11359★
RESEARCH INSTITUTE FOR THE STUDY OF MAN - LIBRARY (Area-Ethnic)
162 E. 78th St.   Phone: (212) 535-8448
New York, NY 10021   Judith Selakoff, Libn.
Founded: 1955. **Staff:** Prof 2; Other 1. **Subjects:** Social sciences of the Caribbean and non-Hispanic West Indies. **Special Collections:** Caribbeana - pamphlets, dissertations, manuscripts, government publications. **Holdings:** 15,000 books. **Subscriptions:** 200 journals and other serials. **Services:** Interlibrary loans (limited); copying; library open to public for reference use only. **Special Indexes:** Index to West Indian Periodical Literature at RISM; periodical holdings; Listing of RISM Associated Publications (punched card). **Staff:** Sheila Bourne, Libn.

★11360★

RESEARCH MEDICAL CENTER - LOCKWOOD MEMORIAL LIBRARY (Med)
Meyer Blvd. & Prospect Ave.   Phone: (816) 276-4159
Kansas City, MO 64132   Gerald R. Kruse, Dir.
Founded: 1963. **Staff:** Prof 1; Other 4. **Subjects:** Medicine and nursing.
Holdings: 8500 books; 8500 bound periodical volumes; 350 reels of
microfilm; 900 tapes; 150 filmstrips. **Subscriptions:** 330 journals and other
serials. **Services:** Interlibrary loans; copying; library open to public for
reference use only. **Computerized Information Services:** Online systems.

★11361★

RESEARCH AND REVIEW SERVICE OF AMERICA - LIBRARY (Bus-Fin)
6213 La Pas Trail
Box 1727   Phone: (317) 297-4360
Indianapolis, IN 46206
Founded: 1914. **Staff:** Prof 1. **Subjects:** Life insurance industry. **Special
Collections:** Complete collection of all materials published by Research and
Review Services. **Holdings:** 2000 books; 200 bound periodical volumes; 28
VF drawers of pamphlets and clippings; 100 VF drawers of art and copy.
Subscriptions: 90 journals and other serials; 5 newspapers. **Services:**
Copying; library open to public for reference use only. **Publications:** Catalog
of company materials for public use.

★11362★

**RESEARCH SERVICES CORPORATION - THE O.A. BATTISTA RESEARCH
   INSTITUTE - LIBRARY** (Med; Sci-Tech)
3863 Southwest Loop   Phone: (817) 292-4272
Fort Worth, TX 76133   Naomi L. Matous, Libn.
Founded: 1971. **Staff:** Prof 2. **Subjects:** Polymer science and technology,
chemistry, medicine. **Holdings:** 3000 books. **Subscriptions:** 102 journals and
other serials. **Automated Operations:** Computerized cataloging, acquisitions,
serials and circulation. **Publications:** Knowledge Magazine. **Staff:** Dr. O.A.
Battista, Pres.; Howard Callahan, Jr., Institute Mgr.

★11363★

RESIDUALS MANAGEMENT TECHNOLOGY, INC. - LIBRARY (Env-Cons)
1406 E. Washington Ave., Suite 124   Phone: (608) 255-2134
Madison, WI 53703   Mary Jane Kayes, Libn.
Staff: Prof 1; Other 1. **Subjects:** Solid and hazardous waste management,
environmental engineering, industrial hygiene, regulatory compliance,
hydrogeology, consulting engineering. **Holdings:** Figures not available for
books. **Subscriptions:** 200 journals and other serials. **Services:** Interlibrary
loans; copying; SDI; library open to public for reference use only and by
appointment. **Computerized Information Services:** The Source,
Environmental Technical Information System (ETIS). Performs searches for
clients on cost recovery basis. **Networks/Consortia:** Member of Madison
Area Library Council (MALC).

★11364★

**RESOURCE & RESEARCH CENTER FOR BEAVER COUNTY & LOCAL
   HISTORY** (Hist)
Carnegie Free Library
1301 7th Ave.   Phone: (412) 846-4340
Beaver Falls, PA 15010   Vivian C. McLaughlin, Dir.
Founded: 1903. **Staff:** 1. **Subjects:** Local history, genealogy. **Special
Collections:** Beaver County newspapers on microfilm, 1833 to present.
Holdings: 2500 books; marriage and death notices; cemetery listings; census
microfilm; Pennsylvania archives; Daughters of the American Revolution
lineage. **Services:** Interlibrary loans; copying; center open to public for
reference use only. **Publications:** Gleanings (genealogical journal), quarterly.
Special Indexes: Index to census; index to deeds and articles.

RESOURCES FOR THE FUTURE, INC.
See: Brookings Institution - Library

★11365★

RESPONSE ANALYSIS CORPORATION - LIBRARY (Soc Sci)
Research Park
Rte. 206, Box 158   Phone: (609) 921-3333
Princeton, NJ 08542   Anne R. Frihart, Libn.
Staff: Prof 1. **Subjects:** Survey research methodology, energy consumption
and conservation, marketing and market research, advertising and advertising
research, communications and media, employee relations. **Holdings:** 750
books; 1 VF drawer of clippings; 46 reels of microfilm; 700 internal company
reports; 100 corporate annual reports. **Subscriptions:** 38 journals and other
serials. **Services:** Interlibrary loans; copying; library open to public with
restrictions. **Automated Operations:** Computerized serials and reports.
Computerized Information Services: DIALOG, Dow Jones News/Retrieval;
RAC Projects Database (internal database). Performs searches on cost

recovery basis for clients only. **Publications:** BookRAC, monthly - for internal
distribution only. **Special Catalogs:** Catalog of master records for company
reports (book).

★11366★

RESSLER (Martin E.) - PRIVATE MUSIC LIBRARY (Mus)
R.D. 2, Box 173   Phone: (717) 529-2463
Quarryville, PA 17566   Martin E. Ressler, Owner
Founded: 1958. **Subjects:** Hymns, church music. **Special Collections:**
German Hymnals (525 volumes); Collection of Mennonite and Church of the
Brethren publications; complete bound set of The Hymn, 1949-1980;
complete set of Unparteisches Gesangbuch; complete set of Canadian
hymnals. **Holdings:** 4100 books; 250 oblong singing school books; 200 music
reference books; other hymnals and Sunday School songbooks; music
clippings. **Services:** Library open to public by special arrangement.
Publications: Bibliography of Mennonite Hymnals and Songbooks (1742-
1972).

★11367★

**RESURRECTION HOSPITAL - MEDICAL LIBRARY & ALLIED HEALTH
   SCIENCES** (Med)
7435 W. Talcott Rd.   Phone: (312) 774-8000
Chicago, IL 60631   Klara B. Goodrich, Med.Libn.
Founded: 1953. **Staff:** Prof 1; Other 2. **Subjects:** Medicine and allied
sciences. **Holdings:** 3403 books; 3671 bound periodical volumes; 624
cassettes. **Subscriptions:** 104 journals and other serials. **Services:**
Interlibrary loans; library not open to public. **Networks/Consortia:** Member of
Greater Midwest Regional Medical Library Network (Region 3). **Special
Indexes:** Index to surgical articles (vertical file). **Staff:** Sally Brunke,
Asst.Libn.; Renata J. Maslowski, Asst.Libn.

★11368★

RETINA FOUNDATION - JOINT RESEARCH LIBRARY (Med)*
20 Staniford St.   Phone: (617) 742-3140
Boston, MA 02114   Rose M. Miller, Libn.
Founded: 1962. **Staff:** 1. **Subjects:** General biomedicine; eye research -
connective tissue, cornea, muscle, retina. **Holdings:** 200 books; 30 bound
periodical volumes; microfilm. **Subscriptions:** 30 journals and other serials.
Services: Library not open to public.

★11369★

RETORT, INC. - LIBRARY (Bus-Fin)*
Tam O'Shanter Rd.   Phone: (617) 528-6404
Franklin, MA 02038   E.H. Rosenberg, Pres.
Founded: 1976. **Staff:** 2. **Subjects:** Product liability insurance crisis. **Special
Collections:** Clippings of most product liability-related articles published in
many magazines and newspapers since 1975. **Holdings:** Figures not available.
Subscriptions: 50 journals and other serials. **Publications:** RETORT
Newsletter - by subscription or as a benefit of membership in RETORT.
Remarks: The acronym RETORT signifies Reason & Equity in Tort.

REU MEMORIAL LIBRARY
See: Schools of Theology in Dubuque - Libraries

REUTHER (Walter P.) LIBRARY
See: Wayne State University - Archives of Labor and Urban Affairs/
   University Archives

★11370★

REVEILLE UNITED METHODIST CHURCH - REVEILLE MEMORIAL LIBRARY
   (Rel-Theol)
4200 Cary Street Rd.   Phone: (804) 359-6041
Richmond, VA 23221   Janet P. Sigman, Adult Libn.
Staff: Prof 5; Other 6. **Subjects:** Bible studies, devotions, travel, art,
philosophy, psychology. **Holdings:** 8227 books; 10 bound periodical volumes;
tapes; pictures; slides; films; 4 VF drawers. **Subscriptions:** 18 journals and
other serials. **Services:** Interlibrary loans; library open to public. **Publications:**
In-church book reviews, quarterly; reading lists for United Methodist Women's
Circles, annual. **Staff:** Mrs. William Guthrie, Cat.; Mrs. James Macon,
Children's Libn.; Martha Kurtz, AV Room; Mrs. W.G. Binns, Adult Lib.

REVENUE CANADA
See: Canada - Revenue Canada

★11371★

REVIEW & HERALD PUBLISHING ASSOCIATION - LIBRARY (Rel-Theol; Publ)
55 W. Oak Ridge Dr.   Phone: (301) 791-7000
Hagerstown, MD 21740   Betty F. Ullrich, Libn.
Staff: Prof 1; Other 2. **Subjects:** Seventh-Day Adventism, church history.

Special Collections: Early Seventh-Day Adventist publications; William Miller Collection. **Holdings:** 40,000 books; 2600 bound periodical volumes; 2400 pamphlets; 18 VF drawers; microcards for holdings of Review & Herald, 1850-1971. **Subscriptions:** 143 journals and other serials. **Services:** Copying (limited); library open for research on written request to chairman of library committee. **Special Indexes:** Index and catalogs to church periodicals (Adventist Review; Insight). **Remarks:** Contains the holdings of the former Editorial Library of the Southern Publishing Association of the Seventh-Day Adventists. **Formerly:** Located in Washington, DC. **Staff:** Raymond Woolsey, Chm. of Lib.Comm.

★11372★
REVLON HEALTH CARE GROUP - INFORMATION SERVICES (Med)
1 Scarsdale Rd.   Phone: (914) 779-6300
Tuckahoe, NY 10707   Rena Radovich, Mgr., Info.Serv.
Staff: Prof 3; Other 3. **Subjects:** Pharmaceutical sciences, medicine, chemistry, biological sciences, business, management. **Holdings:** 7500 books; 15,000 bound periodical volumes; 50 VF drawers. **Subscriptions:** 700 journals and other serials. **Services:** Interlibrary loans; copying; services open to public by appointment. **Computerized Information Services:** MEDLINE, SDC, DIALOG.

REVLON, INC. - NORCLIFF THAYER MFG. FACILITY
See: Norcliff Thayer Mfg. Facility, Division of Revlon, Inc.

★11373★
REVLON RESEARCH CENTER, INC. - LIBRARY (Sci-Tech)
2121 Rte. 27   Phone: (201) 287-7649
Edison, NJ 08817   Lee J. Tanen, Mgr., Lib./Info.Serv.
Founded: 1955. **Staff:** Prof 2; Other 2. **Subjects:** Cosmetics, soaps, chemistry, perfumery, dermatology, pharmacology, microbiology, aerosols. **Holdings:** 11,000 books; 4000 bound periodical volumes; 650 boxes of reports, pamphlets, reprints, documents; research notebooks. **Subscriptions:** 300 journals and other serials. **Services:** Interlibrary loans; copying; library open to public by appointment. **Computerized Information Services:** DIALOG, NLM; internal database. **Special Indexes:** Index to research notebooks. **Formerly:** Located in Bronx, NY.

★11374★
REX HOSPITAL - LIBRARY (Med)
4420 Lake Boone Trail   Phone: (919) 755-3100
Raleigh, NC 27607   Dorothy T. McCallum, Libn.
Founded: 1937. **Staff:** Prof 1; Other 1. **Subjects:** Medicine, nursing. **Holdings:** 1650 books; 2000 bound periodical volumes; 4 VF drawers of pamphlets, brochures, clippings. **Subscriptions:** 100 journals and other serials. **Services:** Interlibrary loans; library not open to public.

★11375★
REXHAM CORPORATION - PACKAGING TECHNICAL LIBRARY (Sci-Tech)†
Church St. Extension
Box 111   Phone: (201) 782-4000
Flemington, NJ 08822   Anne T. Hand, Exec.Sec.
Founded: 1967. **Subjects:** Packaging, product package testing. **Holdings:** 3 VF drawers of unbound reports; 1 VF drawer of patents. **Subscriptions:** 45 journals and other serials. **Services:** Library not open to public.

★11376★
REXNORD INC. - TECHNICAL LIBRARY (Sci-Tech)†
5101 W. Beloit Rd.
Box 2022   Phone: (414) 643-2725
Milwaukee, WI 53214   Linda L. LeVeille, Info.Spec.
Founded: 1952. **Staff:** Prof 1; Other 1. **Subjects:** Metallurgy, pollution control, science, technology, engineering. **Holdings:** 3750 books; 175 bound periodical volumes; 190 boxes of pamphlets; 2500 EPA publications. **Subscriptions:** 101 journals and other serials. **Services:** Interlibrary loans; copying; library open to public with approval of librarian. **Computerized Information Services:** DIALOG. **Networks/Consortia:** Member of Library Council of Metropolitan Milwaukee, Inc. (LCOMM).

★11377★
REYNOLDA HOUSE, INC. - LIBRARY (Art)*
Reynolda Rd.
Box 11765   Phone: (919) 725-5325
Winston-Salem, NC 27106   Ruth Mullen, Libn.
Staff: Prof 1; Other 2. **Subjects:** American art and literature, art appreciation for children and adults. **Holdings:** 1227 books; 370 catalogs of museums, galleries and special art collections; clippings and other items about American artists and American life; 3000 slides; musical recordings. **Subscriptions:** 23 journals and other serials. **Services:** Copying; library open to public with

restrictions.

REYNOLDS AUDIO-VISUAL DEPARTMENT
See: Rochester Public Library

★11378★
REYNOLDS ELECTRICAL AND ENGINEERING COMPANY, INC. - COORDINATION AND INFORMATION CENTER (Sci-Tech; Energy)
Box 14400   Phone: (702) 295-1000
Las Vegas, NV 89114   Bernardo Maza, Supv.
Founded: 1979. **Staff:** Prof 11; Other 6. **Subjects:** Radioactive fallout, radiation monitoring, nuclear weapons testing, biological effects of radiation. **Special Collections:** U.S. Public Health Service Archive (effects of nuclear weapons testing on health; 76 reels of microfilm; 12,000 documents); Utah State Archives Collection (health effects of radiation; 90 reels of microfilm, 15,000 documents). **Holdings:** 303 books; 8279 reports; 8963 letters and memos; 2379 data documents; 10 photographs; 231 legal documents; 1335 articles; 248 listings; 762 meeting minutes; 372 clippings; 756 press releases; 120 speeches and public statements; 850 other items. **Services:** Copying; center open to public. **Automated Operations:** Computerized cataloging. **Computerized Information Services:** DOE/RECON. **Special Indexes:** KWIC index (microfiche). **Remarks:** The Reynolds Electrical and Engineering Company, Inc. operates under contract to the U.S. Department of Energy. **Staff:** Richard V. Nutley, Logistics Mgt.Spec.

★11379★
REYNOLDS ELECTRICAL AND ENGINEERING COMPANY, INC. - TECHNICAL LIBRARY (Sci-Tech)
Box 14400, M/S 707   Phone: (702) 295-6210
Las Vegas, NV 89114   Mona C. Lupo, Env.Sci.Tech.Libn.
Staff: 1. **Subjects:** Pure and applied sciences, medicine, management, literature. **Holdings:** 3500 books; 40,000 microfiche. **Subscriptions:** 19 journals and other serials. **Services:** Library not open to public.

REYNOLDS (Fred J.) HISTORICAL GENEALOGY COLLECTION
See: Allen County Public Library - Fred J. Reynolds Historical Genealogy Collection

REYNOLDS (Harriet Dickson) ROOM
See: Houston Public Library - Special Collections Department

★11380★
REYNOLDS METALS COMPANY - ALUMINA DIVISION - TECHNICAL INFORMATION CENTER (Sci-Tech)†
One Union National Plaza, Suite 975 Phone: (501) 376-4037
Little Rock, AR 72201   Sherry Townsend, Tech.Libn.
Founded: 1979. **Staff:** Prof 1. **Subjects:** Aluminum - manufacturing, chemical manufacturing technology, ore mining. **Holdings:** 200 books; 50 bound periodical volumes; 5 VF drawers of technical reports; 1 VF drawer of patents; 7 VF drawers of reprints; 6 VF drawers of operations reports. **Subscriptions:** 32 journals and other serials. **Services:** Interlibrary loans; center not open to public. **Computerized Information Services:** Online systems.

★11381★
REYNOLDS METALS COMPANY - CORPORATE LIBRARY SERVICES (Bus-Fin)
6601 W. Broad St.   Phone: (804) 281-2804
Richmond, VA 23261   Carla L. Gregory, Corp.Libn.
Founded: 1958. **Staff:** Prof 1; Other 1. **Subjects:** Aluminum industry, marketing, engineering, business management, patent law, corporate law, international trade. **Holdings:** 8000 books; 2000 bound periodical volumes; 75 VF drawers of annual reports, government statistical releases, and subject files. **Subscriptions:** 240 journals and other serials; 10 newspapers. **Services:** Interlibrary loans; copying; library open to public by appointment. **Automated Operations:** Computerized cataloging. **Computerized Information Services:** DIALOG, SDC, BRS; INQUIRE (internal database).

★11382★
REYNOLDS METALS COMPANY - PACKAGING DIVISION - TECHNOLOGY LIBRARY (Sci-Tech)†
2101 Reymet Rd.   Phone: (804) 743-6649
Richmond, VA 23234   Lorna K. Joyner, Adm.
Staff: 1. **Subjects:** Adhesives, inks and coatings, chemistry, foods and food packaging. **Holdings:** 1200 books; 190 bound periodical volumes; 12 VF drawers of company, project and subject files. **Subscriptions:** 75 journals and other serials. **Services:** Interlibrary loans; copying; library open to public by appointment.

★11383★
REYNOLDS METALS COMPANY - REDUCTION LABORATORY LIBRARY (Sci-Tech)
E. Second St.
Box 1200   Phone: (205) 386-9536
Sheffield, AL 35660   Beth B. Stanford, Libn.
Founded: 1956. **Staff:** Prof 1. **Subjects:** Engineering, electrochemistry, aluminum production, material science, extraction metallurgy of aluminum physics, physical chemistry. **Holdings:** 1800 books; 700 bound periodical volumes; 11 VF drawers of patents. **Subscriptions:** 125 journals and other serials. **Services:** Interlibrary loans; library not open to public. **Automated Operations:** Computerized cataloging and acquisitions. **Computerized Information Services:** DIALOG; INQUIRE (internal database).

★11384★
REYNOLDS METALS COMPANY - TECHNICAL INFORMATION SERVICES LIBRARY (Sci-Tech)
Fourth & Canal Sts.
Box 27003   Phone: (804) 788-7409
Richmond, VA 23261   Mary R. Cameron, Libn.
Founded: 1965. **Staff:** 1. **Subjects:** Metallurgy, materials science, applied sciences, engineering, chemistry, physics. **Holdings:** 14,500 books; 4600 bound periodical volumes; 6000 microfiche; 300 microfilm cartridges; 2000 internal technical reports. **Subscriptions:** 200 journals and other serials. **Services:** Interlibrary loans; copying; library open to public by appointment. **Computerized Information Services:** DIALOG.

★11385★
REYNOLDS MUSEUM - LIBRARY (Hist)
4118 57th St.   Phone: (403) 352-5201
Wetaskiwin, AB, Canada T9A 2B6   Stanley G. Reynolds, Cur.
Founded: 1956. **Staff:** 1. **Subjects:** Antique automobiles, aircraft, gas tractors and steam engines. **Holdings:** 3000 books and catalogs; 20 VF drawers of photographs, photocopies and illustrations. **Subscriptions:** 10 journals and other serials. **Services:** Library not open to public. **Remarks:** Library in process of organization.

★11386★
REYNOLDS (R.J.) INDUSTRIES, INC. - RJR CORPORATE LIBRARY-PLAZA (Bus-Fin)
Plaza Bldg., 1st Fl.   Phone: (919) 777-2092
Winston-Salem, NC 27102   Molly C. Barnett, Plaza Libn.
Founded: 1982. **Staff:** Prof 1; Other 1. **Subjects:** Industrial management, business administration, personnel management, tobacco industry, finance, accounting. **Special Collections:** History of tobacco (books and pamphlets). **Holdings:** 333 books; 501 annual reports; 288 reports. **Subscriptions:** 56 journals and other serials; 7 newspapers. **Services:** Library not open to public. **Automated Operations:** Computerized cataloging, serials and circulation. **Computerized Information Services:** DIALOG, Dow Jones News/Retrieval, TEXTLINE, Pergamon InfoLine Ltd., TOPICS. **Publications:** Update, quarterly - for internal distribution only. **Special Indexes:** Index to company publications. **Remarks:** This is a branch of the RJR World Headquarters Corporate Library.

★11387★
REYNOLDS (R.J.) INDUSTRIES, INC. - RJR WORLD HEADQUARTERS CORPORATE LIBRARY (Bus-Fin)
B4102 World Headquarters Bldg.   Phone: (919) 773-2652
Winston-Salem, NC 27102   Barry K. Miller, Corp.Libn.
Staff: Prof 1; Other 4. **Subjects:** Industrial management, business administration, personnel management, tobacco industry, finance and accounting. **Special Collections:** Corporate archives; history of tobacco (books and pamphlets). **Holdings:** 4736 books; annual reports (microfiche); clippings (microfiche); 100 cassettes; telephone books. **Subscriptions:** 288 journals and other serials. **Services:** Library not open to public. **Automated Operations:** Computerized cataloging, serials and circulation. **Computerized Information Services:** DIALOG, Dow Jones News/Retrieval, TEXTLINE, Pergamon InfoLine Ltd., NEXIS. **Publications:** Update, quarterly - for internal distribution only. **Special Indexes:** Indexes to company publications.

★11388★
REYNOLDS (R.J.) TOBACCO COMPANY - ENGINEERING - TECHNICAL INFORMATION/RECORDS SECTION (Sci-Tech)
RJR Plaza, 11th Fl.   Phone: (919) 777-5842
Winston-Salem, NC 27102   Pansy D. Broughton, Ref.Libn.
Staff: 2. **Subjects:** Mechanical engineering, environmental data, standards and codes. **Holdings:** 3200 books. **Subscriptions:** 140 journals and other serials. **Services:** Interlibrary loans; copying (limited); section open to public with restrictions.

★11389★
REYNOLDS (R.J.) TOBACCO COMPANY - R&D SCIENTIFIC INFORMATION SERVICES LIBRARY (Sci-Tech)
Chestnut at Belews St.   Phone: (919) 773-4360
Winston-Salem, NC 27102   Randy D. Ralph, Sr.Lit.Sci., R&D
Founded: 1951. **Staff:** Prof 6; Other 6. **Subjects:** Tobacco, chemistry, biochemistry, agriculture, chemical engineering. **Holdings:** 19,770 books; 15,562 bound periodical volumes; 9311 unbound periodicals; 6444 internal reports; 940,089 patents on microfilm; 30,209 pamphlets. **Subscriptions:** 500 journals and other serials; 6 newspapers. **Services:** Interlibrary loans; copying; SDI; library open to public with permission. **Publications:** Current awareness bulletin. **Staff:** George Konstantinow, Sr.Lit.Sci.; LeRoy Meek, Sr.Lit.Sci.Nellie W. Sizemore, R&D Libn.; Helen Chung, R&D Libn.

★11390★
REYNOLDS (Russell) ASSOCIATES, INC. - LIBRARY (Bus-Fin)
200 S. Wacker Dr., Suite 3600   Phone: (312) 782-9862
Chicago, IL 60606-4958   Gerri Hilt, Dir. of Res.
Staff: Prof 3; Other 3. **Subjects:** Business, manufacturing, banking. **Holdings:** 300 books; company annual reports; vertical subject files. **Subscriptions:** 34 journals and other serials. **Services:** Interlibrary loans; copying; library open to public by appointment. **Staff:** Nancy Davidson, Sr.Res.Assoc.; Kim Agriesti, Res.Asst.

★11391★
REYNOLDS, SMITH & HILLS - LIBRARY (Sci-Tech)
4019 Blvd. Center Dr.   Phone: (904) 396-2011
Jacksonville, FL 32201   R.C. Frost, Libn.
Founded: 1973. **Staff:** Prof 1; Other 1. **Subjects:** Architecture, engineering, planning. **Holdings:** 12,500 books; 108 bound periodical volumes; 8 VF drawers of pamphlets; 1000 government documents; microforms; maps. **Subscriptions:** 250 journals and other serials; 8 newspapers. **Services:** Interlibrary loans; copying; library open to public by appointment. **Automated Operations:** Computerized cataloging, acquisitions and circulation. **Computerized Information Services:** DIALOG, BRS; internal database. Performs searches on cost recovery basis.

RHOADS (C.P.) MEMORIAL LIBRARY
See: Sloan-Kettering Institute for Cancer Research - Donald S. Walker Laboratory - C.P. Rhoads Memorial Library

★11392★
RHODE ISLAND HISTORICAL SOCIETY - LIBRARY (Hist)
121 Hope St.   Phone: (401) 331-0448
Providence, RI 02906
Founded: 1822. **Staff:** Prof 5; Other 5. **Subjects:** Rhode Island history, New England genealogy and local history. **Special Collections:** Film Archives (feature films, newsreels and TV footage on Rhode Island); Rhode Island newspapers; Rhode Island imprints; business history. **Holdings:** 150,000 books and bound periodical volumes; 1040 feet of manuscripts; 11,000 reels of microfilm of newspapers. **Subscriptions:** 125 journals and other serials; 100 newspapers. **Services:** Copying; library open to public. **Automated Operations:** Computerized cataloging. **Networks/Consortia:** Member of Consortium of Rhode Island Academic and Research Libraries. **Publications:** Rhode Island History, quarterly - free to members, by subscription to institutions; Providence Newspapers on Microfilm 1762 to present: A Bibliography and Subject Guide, 1973. **Special Indexes:** Indexes to the Rhode Island Census for 1850, 1860 and 1865 (card). **Staff:** Paul R. Campbell, Libn.; Christine Lamar, Ref.Libn.; Harold E. Kemble, Mss.Cur.; Maureen Taylor, Graphics Cur.; Nadia McIntosh, Tech.Serv.Libn.

★11393★
RHODE ISLAND HOSPITAL - PETERS HEALTH SCIENCES LIBRARY (Med)
     Phone: (401) 277-4671
Providence, RI 02902   Irene Lathrop, Dir. of Lib.Serv.
Founded: 1931. **Staff:** Prof 3; Other 6. **Subjects:** Medicine and medical specialities, nursing, hospital administration. **Special Collections:** Pratt Collection in Hospital Administration. **Holdings:** 7000 books; 11,000 bound periodical volumes. **Subscriptions:** 600 journals and other serials. **Services:** Interlibrary loans; copying; AV facilities; library open to public with restrictions. **Automated Operations:** Computerized cataloging. **Computerized Information Services:** MEDLINE, OCLC. **Networks/Consortia:** Member of Association of Rhode Island Health Sciences Librarians (ARIHSL); NELINET. **Publications:** Peters Library Newsletter and Guides.

★11394★
RHODE ISLAND JEWISH HISTORICAL ASSOCIATION - LIBRARY (Area-Ethnic)
130 Sessions St.   Phone: (401) 331-1360
Providence, RI 02906   Eleanor F. Horvitz, Libn./Archv.
Founded: 1951. Staff: Prof 1; Other 2. Subjects: History of Rhode Island Jews; Jews in the United States. Special Collections: Family papers; papers and pictures of organizations and institutions; oral history tapes. Holdings: Figures not available. Subscriptions: 13 journals and other serials. Services: Library open to public in presence of librarian. Publications: Rhode Island Jewish Historical Notes, annual - to membership and subscribers; newsletter, annual. Special Indexes: Above Notes are indexed by volume (4 issues).

★11395★
RHODE ISLAND MEDICAL SOCIETY - LIBRARY (Med)
106 Francis St.   Phone: (401) 331-3208
Providence, RI 02903   Marion Sabella, Libn.
Founded: 1879. Staff: Prof 1. Subjects: Medical history, medicine and allied fields, veterinary medicine. Special Collections: Books by and about doctors (scientific and popular). Holdings: 49,000 books and bound periodical volumes; 177 reels of microfilm; manuscripts; clippings; unbound reports; archives; pamphlets; dissertations; documents; photographs; paintings; instruments. Subscriptions: 232 journals and other serials. Services: Interlibrary loans; copying; preparation of bibliographies; library open to public for reference use only. Networks/Consortia: Member of Association of Rhode Island Health Sciences Librarians (ARIHSL). Publications: Rhode Island Medical Journal, monthly, includes library news.

RHODE ISLAND ORAL HISTORY PROJECT
See: University of Rhode Island

★11396★
RHODE ISLAND PUBLIC EXPENDITURE COUNCIL - LIBRARY (Soc Sci)
126 N. Main St.   Phone: (401) 521-6320
Providence, RI 02903   Gary S. Sasse, Exec.Dir.
Founded: 1932. Staff: Prof 2; Other 2. Subjects: State and local government administration and finance. Holdings: 200 books; 500 research reports and government documents. Subscriptions: 100 journals and other serials. Services: Copying; library open to public for reference use only on request. Publications: We the People of Rhode Island, bimonthly; RIPEC Comments on Your Government, irregular - both for members and government officials. Staff: Raymond G. Hewitt, Dir. of Res.

★11397★
RHODE ISLAND SCHOOL OF DESIGN - LIBRARY (Art)
2 College St.   Phone: (401) 331-3511
Providence, RI 02903   James A. Findlay, Dir.
Founded: 1878. Staff: Prof 4; Other 10. Subjects: Fine arts, architecture, applied arts. Special Collections: Lowthorpe Collection of Landscape Architecture (1200 volumes). Holdings: 70,000 books; 8000 bound periodical volumes; 102,000 slides; 290,000 clippings; 30,000 mounted photographs; 1200 posters and color reproductions; 700 phonograph records. Subscriptions: 320 journals and other serials. Services: Interlibrary loans; copying; library open to public for reference use only. Networks/Consortia: Member of Consortium of Rhode Island Academic and Research Libraries, Inc. (CRIARL). Publications: Recent Acquisitions List, 4/year. Staff: Elinor Nacheman, Hd., Cat.Dept; Mark Braunstein, Hd., Slide/Photo Dept.; Laurie Averill, Rd.Serv.Libn.

★11398★
RHODE ISLAND STATE ARCHIVES (Hist)
State House, Rm. 43, Smith St.   Phone: (401) 277-2353
Providence, RI 02903   Phyllis Peloquin Silva, Dir.
Staff: 1. Subjects: Rhode Island history. Special Collections: Private letters of Ellery and Huntington. Holdings: Acts and resolves of the General Assembly; colony records; Revolutionary War records; petitions and reports to the General Assembly; military and maritime charters. Services: Copying; archives open to public with restrictions.

★11399★
RHODE ISLAND STATE DEPARTMENT OF COMMUNITY AFFAIRS - REFERENCE LIBRARY (Soc Sci)
150 Washington St.   Phone: (401) 277-2857
Providence, RI 02903   Donald J. Boisvert, Libn.
Founded: 1969. Staff: Prof 1. Subjects: Planning, government administration, legislation, health, census, land use. Holdings: 8422 volumes. Subscriptions: 14 journals and other serials; 6 newspapers. Services: Interlibrary loans.

★11400★
RHODE ISLAND STATE DEPARTMENT OF ECONOMIC DEVELOPMENT - RESEARCH DIVISION LIBRARY (Bus-Fin)
7 Jackson Walkway   Phone: (401) 277-2601
Providence, RI 02903   John A. Iemma, Asst.Dir., DED
Subjects: Economic statistics. Holdings: Figures not available.

★11401★
RHODE ISLAND STATE DEPARTMENT OF EDUCATION - EDUCATION INFORMATION SERVICES
22 Hayes St.
Providence, RI 02908
Defunct

★11402★
RHODE ISLAND STATE DEPARTMENT OF ELDERLY AFFAIRS - LIBRARY (Soc Sci)
79 Washington St.   Phone: (401) 277-2858
Providence, RI 02903   Eve M. Goldberg, Libn.
Founded: 1958. Staff: Prof 1. Subjects: Gerontology, geriatrics, retirement. Special Collections: Legislation and programs relating to aging; repository for Service Center for Aging Information (SCAN) on microfiche. Holdings: 500 volumes; 50 state studies on aging; 100 pamphlets; 20 films; 10 video cassettes. Subscriptions: 30 journals and other serials. Services: Interlibrary loans; library open to public.

★11403★
RHODE ISLAND STATE DEPARTMENT OF HEALTH - GERTRUDE E. STURGES MEMORIAL LIBRARY (Med)
75 Davis St., Rm. 407   Phone: (401) 277-2506
Providence, RI 02908   A. William Pett, Libn.
Founded: 1939. Staff: Prof 1; Other 1. Subjects: Public health, preventive medicine, nursing. Holdings: 9400 books and pamphlets; 1200 bound periodical volumes; 4 drawers of newsletters; 2 cabinets of vertical files. Subscriptions: 300 journals and other serials; 8 newspapers. Services: Interlibrary loans; copying; library open to public. Computerized Information Services: MEDLARS. Networks/Consortia: Member of Association of Rhode Island Health Sciences Librarians (ARIHSL). Publications: New Book List, quarterly.

★11404★
RHODE ISLAND STATE DEPARTMENT OF SOCIAL AND REHABILITATIVE SERVICES - STAFF DEVELOPMENT LIBRARY (Soc Sci)
600 New London Ave.   Phone: (401) 464-3111
Cranston, RI 02920   Joyce McGee
Staff: 1. Subjects: Social work, psychology, social welfare policy. Holdings: 1000 books. Subscriptions: 14 journals and other serials. Services: Copying; library open to public with restrictions. Automated Operations: Computerized cataloging.

★11405★
RHODE ISLAND STATE DEPARTMENT OF STATE LIBRARY SERVICES (Info Sci)
95 Davis St.   Phone: (401) 277-2726
Providence, RI 02908   Fay Zipkowitz, Dir.
Staff: Prof 20; Other 12. Special Collections: Professional Library Science Collection (3300 volumes); books on handicaps (350 volumes). Holdings: 150,000 books; 410 bound periodical volumes; pamphlet files. Subscriptions: 180 journals and other serials. Services: Interlibrary loans; copying; bookmobile services; library open to librarians, library school students, trustees, and the blind and handicapped. Automated Operations: Computerized cataloging and circulation; electronic mail. Computerized Information Services: DIALOG, OCLC. Contact Person: Frank Iacono. Networks/Consortia: Member of NELINET; Rhode Island Interrelated Library Network; Rhode Island Automated Library Consortium. Publications: Newsletter, quarterly - to libraries. Special Catalogs: Books about Handicaps (book); Non-print Media: Accession List (book). Remarks: This department administers a statewide library program involving all libraries in a network. It administers grants-in-aid to public libraries, serves as the Regional Library for the Blind and Handicapped, and gives professional leadership and consultant services toward the development of improved library service. Staff: Bruce E. Daniels, Deputy Dir.; Barbara Wilson, Chf., Reg.Lib. for Blind; Dorothy Frechette, Lib.Plan., Dev.Info.Serv.; Frank Iacono .

★11406★
RHODE ISLAND STATE LAW LIBRARY (Law)
Providence County Court House
250 Benefit St.   Phone: (401) 277-3275
Providence, RI 02903   Kendall F. Svengalis, State Law Libn.
Founded: 1827. Staff: Prof 2; Other 4. Subjects: Law. Special Collections:

Rare law books. **Holdings:** 92,000 volumes. **Subscriptions:** 240 journals and other serials; 6 newspapers. **Services:** Interlibrary loans; copying; library open to public. **Automated Operations:** Computerized cataloging. **Staff:** Sondra L. Giles, Asst.Libn.

★11407★
RHODE ISLAND STATE LIBRARY (Soc Sci)
State House   Phone: (401) 277-2473
Providence, RI 02903   Beth I. Perry, State Libn.
Founded: 1851. **Staff:** Prof 4; Other 9. **Subjects:** Legislative law; reference and research. **Special Collections:** Rhode Island history and law. **Holdings:** 150,000 books; 250,000 U.S. government documents. **Subscriptions:** 100 journals and other serials; 50 newspapers. **Services:** Interlibrary loans; copying; library open to public with restrictions. **Automated Operations:** Computerized cataloging. **Publications:** List of documents received, quarterly. **Special Catalogs:** Reports filed for all state agencies with special emphasis on governor's office and legislative materials. **Staff:** Linda Walton, Legislative Ref.; Jean Nocera, Govt.Doc.Libn.; Helena Costa, Cat./Gen.Ref.Libn.; Robert Chase, Hd., Doc.Distr.Ctr.; Karen Morris, Asst.Leg.Ref.Libn.

★11408★
RHODODENDRON SPECIES FOUNDATION - LAWRENCE J. PIERCE RHODODENDRON LIBRARY (Agri)
2525 S. 336th St.
Box 3798   Phone: (206) 927-6960
Federal Way, WA 98063-3798   Mrs. George Harrison, Chm.
Staff: Prof 4; Other 3. **Subjects:** Rhododendrons, azaleas, companion plants, trees and shrubs, general horticulture, plant explorers. **Special Collections:** Collections of field notes, photographs, and personal memorabilia of recent plant collectors. **Holdings:** 1000 books; 60 bound periodical volumes; 1500 files of other cataloged items. **Subscriptions:** 20 journals and other serials; 28 newsletters. **Services:** Copying; library open to public. **Automated Operations:** Computerized cataloging. **Computerized Information Services:** Internal database. Performs searches on cost recovery basis. Contact Person: Karen S. Gunderson. **Networks/Consortia:** Member of Council on Botanical Horticultural Libraries. **Publications:** Selected Rhododendron Bibliography. **Remarks:** Library is said to contain most of the printed information on the genus Rhododendron. **Staff:** Janet Binford; Mrs. Rudolph Mate; Margaret Young.

★11409★
RICE COUNTY HISTORICAL SOCIETY - ARCHIVES (Hist)
1814 Second Ave.
Box 5   Phone: (507) 332-2121
Faribault, MN 55021   George Holey, Pres.
Founded: 1926. **Subjects:** Rice County, Minnesota. **Holdings:** 628 books; 350 bound periodical volumes. **Services:** Copying; archives open to public with restrictions.

RICE (Harley E.) MEMORIAL LIBRARY
See: Porter Memorial Hospital - Harley E. Rice Memorial Library

RICE (James E.) POULTRY LIBRARY
See: Cornell University - Albert R. Mann Library

★11410★
RICE MEMORIAL HOSPITAL - HEALTH SCIENCE LIBRARY (Med)
301 Becker Ave., S.W.   Phone: (612) 235-4543
Willmar, MN 56201   Carol Conradi, Libn.
Staff: Prof 1. **Subjects:** Clinical medicine. **Holdings:** 830 books; 800 bound periodical volumes. **Subscriptions:** 103 journals and other serials. **Services:** Interlibrary loans; copying; library open to public with restrictions. **Computerized Information Services:** DIALOG.

★11411★
RICE UNIVERSITY - ART LIBRARY (Art)
Box 1892   Phone: (713) 527-4832
Houston, TX 77251-1892   Jet Marie Prendeville, Art Libn.
Founded: 1964. **Staff:** Prof 1; Other 1. **Subjects:** Art history, archeology, film, photography. **Holdings:** 41,335 books; 6000 exhibition catalogs. **Subscriptions:** 469 journals and other serials. **Services:** Interlibrary loans; copying; library open to public. **Remarks:** Figures include the art and architecture holdings of the university's Fondren Library.

★11412★
RICE UNIVERSITY - GOVERNMENT DOCUMENTS AND MICROFORMS DEPARTMENT (Info Sci)
Fondren Library
Box 1892   Phone: (713) 527-8101
Houston, TX 77251-1892   Barbara Kile, Hd.
Staff: Prof 1; Other 3. **Holdings:** 230,000 government documents; 500,000 technical reports; 1.5 million microforms; U.S. patents: utility, 1962 to present; design, 1842 to present; reissues, 1838 to present; plant, 1978 to present. **Services:** Interlibrary loans; copying; department open to public. **Computerized Information Services:** U.S. Patent Office. Performs free searches. **Publications:** Guides to the collections, irregular - free upon request.

★11413★
RICE UNIVERSITY - JONES GRADUATE SCHOOL OF ADMINISTRATION - BUSINESS INFORMATION CENTER (Bus-Fin)
Herring Hall
Houston, TX 77251   Mary S. Barnard, Bus.Libn.
Staff: Prof 1; Other 8. **Subjects:** Accounting, finance, public administration, management. **Holdings:** 15,000 books. **Subscriptions:** 175 journals and other serials. **Services:** Interlibrary loans; copying; center open to public. **Automated Operations:** Computerized cataloging. **Computerized Information Services:** DIALOG, BRS, SDC. Performs searches on cost recovery basis.

★11414★
RICE UNIVERSITY - MUSIC LIBRARY (Mus)
Fondren Library
Box 1892   Phone: (713) 527-8101
Houston, TX 77251-1892   Ellen J. Burns, Music Libn.
Staff: Prof 1; Other 3. **Subjects:** Music - performance, composition, theory, conducting, history; musicology. **Special Collections:** American music imprints, 1850-1950 (5100 titles); Halford Research Collection (Renaissance and Baroque keyboard, 200 titles); Richard Lert Library (conductor and student of Strauss, 250 books; 260 scores); Sylvester Collection (607 titles of stone lithographed music; 400 acoustical recordings). **Holdings:** 9300 books; 1310 bound periodical volumes; 10,900 scores; 15,975 recordings. **Subscriptions:** 141 journals and other serials. **Services:** Interlibrary loans; copying; library open to public with restrictions. **Automated Operations:** Computerized cataloging, acquisitions, serials and circulation. **Computerized Information Services:** DIALOG, BRS, SDC; OSCAR (internal database). Performs free searches for OSCAR; other searches performed on cost recovery basis. **Networks/Consortia:** Member of Houston Music Librarians' Consort. **Publications:** Rice Notes (newsletter), irregular. **Special Indexes:** Indexes to scores and recordings.

★11415★
RICE UNIVERSITY - WOODSON RESEARCH CENTER (Hist)
Fondren Library, Box 1892   Phone: (713) 527-8101
Houston, TX 77251-1892   Nancy Boothe Parker, Dir.
Staff: Prof 2; Other 1. **Subjects:** Texas history and entrepreneurship, Civil War, Rice University history, history of U.S. spaceflight, 20th century American literature. **Special Collections:** Masterson Texana (1200 volumes); Julian S. Huxley (70 linear feet of papers and 1000 volumes); Johnson Space Center History Archive (405 cubic feet); Axson 18th Century British Drama (5000 volumes); Bartlett Beethoven (600 volumes); Confederate imprints (2500); Carlota and Maximilian manuscript collection (3 linear feet). **Holdings:** 17,000 books and bound periodical volumes; 1215 linear feet of university archives; 1670 linear feet of literary, historical, scientific and artistic manuscript collections; 220 linear feet of faculty papers. **Services:** Copying (limited); library open to public. **Special Catalogs:** Manuscript collection guides: Julian Sorell Huxley papers; Johnson Space Center History Archive, 1952-1980; William Ward Watkin papers; Walter Benona and Estelle Broughton Sharp Collection, 1868-1978; Thomas Moore letters; Walter Gardner Hall papers; Jacobs Collection; George Cranfield Berkeley Collection; James Lockhart Autry papers; William Vaught letters; William Harris Crawford Collection; John Campbell Collection; Hugh H. Wilson papers; Joseph I. Davies papers; Charles Whishaw Clubbe papers; Harris and Carroll Masterson Texana Collection catalog; bibliography of cataloged archival publications in the Fondren Library (book).

★11416★
RICHARDS, LAYTON & FINGER - LAW LIBRARY (Law)
One Rodney Square, 10th Fl.   Phone: (302) 658-6541
Wilmington, DE 19899   Crystal K. Rambo, Law Libn.
Staff: 1. **Subjects:** Law - corporate, commercial, labor, tax. **Holdings:** 12,000 books; 100 bound periodical volumes; 9 VF drawers of unreported Chancery, Supreme, and District Court opinions; 7 VF drawers of current and past Delaware legislation. **Subscriptions:** 115 journals and other serials. **Services:** Interlibrary loans; copying; library open to public by referral only. **Computerized Information Services:** LEXIS, DIALOG. **Special Indexes:** Indexes to unreported court opinions, reference file, and state legislation.

RICHARDSON ARCHIVES
See: University of South Dakota - I.D. Weeks Library

★11417★
RICHARDSON GREENSHIELDS OF CANADA, LTD. - RESEARCH LIBRARY (Bus-Fin)
One Lombard Place, 29th Fl.   Phone: (204) 988-5940
Winnipeg, MB, Canada R3B 0Y2   Agnes Unger, Libn.
Founded: 1921. **Staff:** Prof 1; Other 3. **Subjects:** Securities industry, economics, business, finance. **Holdings:** 3200 books and bound periodical volumes; 4800 classified files. **Subscriptions:** 140 journals and other serials. **Services:** Library open to university students and associate firms. **Publications:** Research Library News Bulletin, monthly - for internal distribution only. **Formerly:** Richardson Securities of Canada, Ltd.

RICHARDSON MEMORIAL LIBRARY
See: St. Louis Art Museum

★11418★
RICHARDSON-VICKS, INC. - MARKETING INFORMATION CENTER (Bus-Fin)
10 Westport Rd.   Phone: (203) 834-5000
Wilton, CT 06897   Mary Lou Wells, Mgr.
Staff: Prof 2; Other 2. **Subjects:** Market research, marketing, drugs. **Holdings:** 500 books; 70 VF drawers of reports, pamphlets, clippings. **Subscriptions:** 130 journals and other serials. **Services:** Interlibrary loans; center open to public by permission.

★11419★
RICHARDSON-VICKS, INC. - VICKS RESEARCH CENTER - LIBRARY (Sci-Tech; Med)
One Far Mill Crossing   Phone: (203) 929-2500
Shelton, CT 06484   Susanne Silverman, Libn.
Founded: 1942. **Staff:** Prof 1; Other 2. **Subjects:** Drugs and pharmaceuticals; medicine; cosmetics and cosmetic science; chemistry - analytical and physical; microbiology; biochemistry; biology; nutrition. **Holdings:** 6500 books; 7000 bound periodical volumes. **Subscriptions:** 275 journals and other serials. **Services:** Interlibrary loans. **Networks/Consortia:** Member of Southwestern Connecticut Library Council (SWLC); Connecticut Association of Health Science Libraries (CAHSL).

★11420★
RICHLAND COLLEGE - EVERYWOMAN PROGRAM - ADULT RESOURCE CENTER (Soc Sci)
12800 Abrams Rd.   Phone: (214) 238-6034
Dallas, TX 75243   Jean Yale, Coord.
Staff: 4. **Subjects:** Personal growth, career development, women's issues. **Holdings:** 105 volumes. **Services:** Center open to clients and community.

★11421★
RICHLAND COUNTY LAW LIBRARY (Law)†
Court House
50 Park Ave., E.   Phone: (419) 524-9944
Mansfield, OH 44902   Arthur W. Negin, Libn./V.P.
Founded: 1896. **Staff:** Prof 1. **Subjects:** Law and all related subjects. **Holdings:** 30,000 books. **Services:** Library open to students on introduction.

★11422★
RICHLAND MEMORIAL HOSPITAL - JOSEY MEMORIAL MEDICAL LIBRARY (Med)
3301 Harden St.   Phone: (803) 765-6312
Columbia, SC 29203   Kay F. Harwood, Libn.
Founded: 1940. **Staff:** Prof 1; Other 1. **Subjects:** Medicine, medical specialities, nursing. **Holdings:** 2025 books; 4000 bound periodical volumes; 175 videotapes; 950 audiotapes (listed); 2800 slides. **Subscriptions:** 220 journals and other serials. **Services:** Interlibrary loans; copying; SDI; library open to public. **Computerized Information Services:** MEDLARS. **Networks/Consortia:** Member of Columbia Area Medical Librarians Association (CAMLA).

★11423★
RICHLAND MEMORIAL HOSPITAL - STAFF LIBRARY (Med)
800 East Locust   Phone: (618) 395-2131
Olney, IL 62450   Jan Nalin, Dir., Med.Rec.Dept.
Staff: 1. **Subjects:** Internal medicine, surgery. **Holdings:** 436 books. **Subscriptions:** 10 journals and other serials. **Services:** Library not open to public. **Staff:** Chandra Varadachari, M.D., Chm., Lib.Comm.

RICHMOND (Mary) ARCHIVES
See: Columbia University - Whitney M. Young, Jr. Memorial Library of Social Work

★11424★
RICHMOND MEMORIAL HOSPITAL - MEDICAL AND NURSING SCHOOL LIBRARY (Med)
1300 Westwood Ave.   Phone: (804) 254-6008
Richmond, VA 23227   Lynne Turman, Libn.
Founded: 1960. **Staff:** Prof 1; Other 1. **Subjects:** Medicine, nursing, health sciences. **Holdings:** 8000 books and bound periodical volumes; nursing AV items. **Subscriptions:** 125 journals and other serials. **Services:** Interlibrary loans; copying; library open to qualified users.

RICHMOND NATL. BATTLEFIELD PARK
See: U.S. Natl. Park Service

★11425★
RICHMOND NEWSPAPERS, INC. - LIBRARY (Publ)
333 E. Grace St.   Phone: (703) 649-6283
Richmond, VA 23213   Charles D. Saunders, Libn.
Staff: 8. **Subjects:** Newspaper reference topics. **Holdings:** 2000 books; 56 file cases of clippings; 59 file cases of pictures; newspapers on microfilm. **Services:** Copying; library open to public.

★11426★
RICHMOND PUBLIC LIBRARY - ART AND MUSIC DEPARTMENT (Art; Mus)
101 E. Franklin St.   Phone: (804) 780-4740
Richmond, VA 23219   Helen M. Ogden, Hd.
Staff: Prof 5; Other 3. **Subjects:** Fine arts, crafts, decoration, music, dance. **Special Collections:** Scott Fund Orchestral Scores (280). **Holdings:** 23,500 books; 2132 bound periodical volumes; 12,400 scores; 271 large print reproductions; 13 VF drawers of art and music clippings; 15 VF drawers of pamphlets; 31 VF drawers of sheet music; 10,900 recordings; 32 VF drawers of pictures. **Subscriptions:** 74 journals and other serials. **Services:** Interlibrary loans; copying (limited); library open to public. **Staff:** Lois Angeletti, Libn.; Raymond Mabry, Libn.; Margaret Harter, Lib.Asst.

★11427★
RICHMOND PUBLIC LIBRARY - BUSINESS, SCIENCE & TECHNOLOGY DEPARTMENT (Bus-Fin; Sci-Tech)
101 E. Franklin St.   Phone: (804) 780-8223
Richmond, VA 23219   Alice L. DeCamps, Hd.
Founded: 1972. **Staff:** Prof 4; Other 6. **Subjects:** Social sciences, business, pure sciences, applied sciences. **Holdings:** Figures not available; Foundation Center Regional Collection, 1100 annual reports of business corporations; government publications; city documents. **Subscriptions:** 415 journals and other serials; 8 newspapers. **Services:** Interlibrary loans; copying (limited); department open to public. **Publications:** Miscellaneous book lists. **Staff:** ; F. Rebecca Walker, Libn.Elizabeth H. Holmes, Libn.; Carol Nichols, Libn.

★11428★
RICHMOND PUBLIC SCHOOLS - CURRICULUM MATERIALS CENTER (Educ)*
301 N. Ninth St.   Phone: (804) 780-5370
Richmond, VA 23219   Delores Z. Pretlow, Coord., Media Serv.
Founded: 1964. **Staff:** Prof 1; Other 3. **Subjects:** Education. **Holdings:** 9967 books; 515 pamphlets; ERIC microfilm, 1970-1972; multimedia kits for grades K-12. **Subscriptions:** 170 journals and other serials; 5 newspapers. **Services:** Interlibrary loans; center open to city employees.

RICHTER LIBRARY
See: Desert Botanical Garden

RICKER LIBRARY OF ARCHITECTURE AND ART
See: University of Illinois

RIDDELL (Dr. W.A.) HEALTH SCIENCES LIBRARY
See: Plains Health Centre - Dr. W.A. Riddell Health Sciences Library

★11429★
RIDER, BENNETT, EGAN & ARUNDEL - LIBRARY (Law)
2500 First Bank Place W.   Phone: (612) 340-7960
Minneapolis, MN 55402   Janet A. Jacobson, Libn.
Staff: Prof 1. **Subjects:** Law. **Holdings:** 5500 books. **Subscriptions:** 50 journals and other serials. **Services:** Library not open to public.

★11430★
RIDER COLLEGE - FRANKLIN F. MOORE LIBRARY (Bus-Fin)
2083 Lawrenceville Rd.   Phone: (609) 896-0800
Lawrenceville, NJ 08648   Ross Stephen, College Libn.
Founded: 1934. **Staff:** Prof 13; Other 13. **Subjects:** Business. **Special Collections:** Kendric C. Hill Shorthand Collection; Riderana. **Holdings:** 325,000 books; 40,000 bound periodical volumes; Delaware Valley

newspapers. **Subscriptions:** 1800 journals and other serials. **Services:** Interlibrary loans; copying; library open to public. **Automated Operations:** Computerized cataloging and circulation. **Computerized Information Services:** DIALOG, OCLC. **Networks/Consortia:** Member of PALINET and Union Library Catalogue of Pennsylvania.

★11431★
RIDGETOWN COLLEGE OF AGRICULTURAL TECHNOLOGY - LIBRARY (Agri)
Ridgetown, ON, Canada N0P 2C0   Phone: (519) 674-5456
                                       Mrs. I.R. Roadhouse, Libn.
Founded: 1951. **Staff:** Prof 1; Other 2. **Subjects:** Soils, crops, horticulture, biology, agricultural engineering and chemistry, farm economics, energy, English and communication. **Holdings:** 10,000 books and bound periodical volumes; 1000 pamphlets and clippings. **Subscriptions:** 140 journals and other serials; 10 newspapers. **Services:** Interlibrary loans; copying; library open to public for reference use only. **Computerized Information Services:** Online systems (through Ontario Ministry of Agriculture and Food). **Special Catalogs:** Bibliographies. **Remarks:** Affiliated with the Ontario Ministry of Agriculture and Food.

RIECKER MEMORIAL LIBRARY
See: Mc Auley (Catherine) Health Center

RIEMENSCHNEIDER BACH INSTITUTE
See: Baldwin-Wallace College

★11432★
RIFKIND CENTER FOR GERMAN EXPRESSIONIST STUDIES - ART LIBRARY
   AND GRAPHICS COLLECTION (Art)
Los Angeles County Museum of Art
5905 Wilshire Blvd.   Phone: (213) 278-0970
Los Angeles, CA 90036   Susan Trauger, Art Libn.
Founded: 1979. **Staff:** Prof 3. **Subjects:** German Expressionist art. **Special Collections:** German Expressionist art exhibition catalogs, monographs, illustrated books and portfolios; Expressionist periodicals; German Expressionist graphics collection. **Holdings:** 5000 volumes. **Services:** Library open to qualified art professionals by appointment only. **Publications:** List of publications - available upon request. **Formerly:** Robert Gore Rifkind Foundation.

★11433★
RIGGS (Austen) CENTER, INC. - AUSTEN FOX RIGGS LIBRARY (Med)
                             Phone: (413) 298-5511
Stockbridge, MA 01262   Helen Linton, Libn.
Founded: 1919. **Staff:** Prof 1. **Subjects:** Psychoanalysis, psychiatry, psychology. **Holdings:** 8543 books; 2013 bound periodical volumes; 54 cassettes. **Subscriptions:** 121 journals and other serials. **Services:** Interlibrary loans; library open to public upon recommendation of staff member or librarian. **Computerized Information Services:** DIALOG. Performs free searches.

★11434★
RIGHT TO LIFE LEAGUE OF SOUTHERN CALIFORNIA - LIBRARY (Soc Sci)
1616 W. 9th St., Suite 220   Phone: (213) 380-8750
Los Angeles, CA 90015   Karen Bodziak, Dir. of Educ.
Founded: 1969. **Staff:** Prof 4; Other 3. **Subjects:** Abortion, pre-natal development, euthanasia, genetic engineering, infanticide, human experimentation, population control. **Holdings:** Books; periodicals; clippings; pamphlets; cassettes; videotapes; films. **Services:** Copying; library open to public. **Publications:** Living (newsletter), quarterly; Lifelines (magazine), quarterly - both free upon request. **Special Catalogs:** Catalog of pro-life materials; catalog of audiovisual aids.

RIIS (Erling) RESEARCH LABORATORY
See: International Paper Company - Erling Riis Research Laboratory

★11435★
RILEY COUNTY GENEALOGICAL SOCIETY - LIBRARY (Hist)
2005 Claflin Rd.   Phone: (913) 537-2205
Manhattan, KS 66502   Mildred Loeffler, Libn.
Founded: 1963. **Staff:** Prof 1; Other 2. **Subjects:** Genealogy, state and local history. **Holdings:** 2800 books; 600 bound periodical volumes; 3 VF drawers of original biographies; 1 VF drawer and 15 card file drawers of genealogical charts of society members' ancestors. **Subscriptions:** 125 journals and other serials. **Services:** Copying; library open to public. **Publications:** Kansas Kin, quarterly - subscription or exchange. **Special Indexes:** Indexes to censuses of Riley County and 1880 census of surrounding counties. **Staff:** Elaine Olney, Asst.Libn.; Evelyn Brown, Ed.

★11436★
RILEY COUNTY HISTORICAL SOCIETY - SEATON MEMORIAL LIBRARY
   (Hist)
2309 Claflin Rd.   Phone: (913) 537-2210
Manhattan, KS 66502   Cheryl Collins, Libn.
Founded: 1914. **Staff:** Prof 2; Other 2. **Subjects:** History of Manhattan City and Riley County, Kansas, Kansas State University. **Holdings:** 3000 books; 100 bound periodical volumes; 100 scrapbooks; 10 filing cabinets of archival materials; 2 VF cabinets of local photographs; 2 architect's filing cabinets of maps, documents, newspaper tear sheets and special issues. **Services:** Copying; library open to public. **Publications:** Newsletter of the Riley County Historical Society, 10/year. **Staff:** Mildred Loeffler; Henrietta Ameel; S. Helen Roberts, Archv.; Jeanne Mithen, Asst.Libn.

RILEY LIBRARY
See: Ouachita Baptist University

★11437★
RILEY STOKER CORPORATION - LIBRARY (Sci-Tech)
Box 547   Phone: (617) 852-7100
Worcester, MA 01613   Cosette M. Kotseas, Info.Spec.
Staff: Prof 1; Other 1. **Subjects:** Steam generation, fuel burning equipment, power generation, boilers and pressure vessels, petroleum chemicals, coal gasification. **Special Collections:** American Society of Mechanical Engineers (ASME) Boiler and Pressure Vessel Codes; Environmental Protection Agency, U.S. Dept. of Energy, and Electric Power Research Institute reports. **Holdings:** 1025 books; 9 VF drawers of reports and documents; 125 patents. **Subscriptions:** 130 journals and other serials; 5 newspapers. **Services:** Interlibrary loans; copying; SDI; library open to public by appointment. **Automated Operations:** Computerized cataloging. **Computerized Information Services:** DIALOG; VAX (internal database). Performs searches on cost recovery basis. **Networks/Consortia:** Member of Worcester Area Cooperating Libraries (WACL). **Publications:** Monthly Bulletin.

★11438★
RINGLING (John and Mable) MUSEUM OF ART - ART RESEARCH LIBRARY
   (Art)
Box 1838   Phone: (813) 355-5101
Sarasota, FL 33578   Lynell A. Morr, Art Libn.
Founded: 1930. **Staff:** Prof 1; Other 1. **Subjects:** Baroque art, 16th, 17th and 18th century European art, Rubens. **Special Collections:** Rare books (16th, 17th and 18th century art history sources); Emblem books; Iconography; Gluck (Gustav) collection of offprints of materials on early Flemish and Dutch painters. **Holdings:** 8000 books; 1400 bound periodical volumes; 25,000 art catalogs; 90 VF drawers of art auction sale catalogs; 4 VF drawers of clippings; 16 VF drawers of Phototeca files. **Subscriptions:** 70 journals and other serials. **Services:** Interlibrary loans; copying; library open to public. **Special Catalogs:** Exhibition Catalogs: Rare Books of the 16th, 17th and 18th centuries from the Library of the Ringling Museum of Art, Sarasota, FL, November 3-23, 1969.

★11439★
RINGLING SCHOOL OF ART AND DESIGN - LIBRARY (Art)
1191 27th St.   Phone: (813) 355-1232
Sarasota, FL 33580   Yvonne Morse, Dir.
Founded: 1928. **Staff:** Prof 2; Other 3. **Subjects:** Art history, interior design, advertising design, architecture, graphics, painting. **Special Collections:** Print Collection of Japanese Art (Robert M. Jackson Collection; 800 items); European prints of 17th and 18th century (500 items). **Holdings:** 10,000 books; 800 bound periodical volumes; 800 museum catalogs; 4 VF drawers of clippings and art prints; 21,000 art slides; 31 16mm films. **Subscriptions:** 192 journals and other serials. **Services:** Interlibrary loans; copying; library open to artists and researchers. **Networks/Consortia:** Member of Florida Library Information Network (FLIN); West Coast Library Consortium (WELCO). **Staff:** Allen R. Novack, AV Libn.

★11440★
RIO ALGOM, LTD. - LIBRARY (Sci-Tech; Energy)
120 Adelaide St., W.   Phone: (416) 365-6800
Toronto, ON, Canada M5H 1W5   Penny Lipman, Libn.
Founded: 1966. **Staff:** Prof 1. **Subjects:** Geology, mining, uranium, copper, tin, coal. **Holdings:** 2000 books; 2000 bound periodical volumes; annual reports for 1500 companies; 1000 Canadian and U.S. federal and provincial geological reports. **Subscriptions:** 150 journals and other serials; 11 newspapers. **Services:** Interlibrary loans; library not open to public. **Computerized Information Services:** DIALOG, SDC, Info Globe, QL Systems, MINESEARCH.

★11441★
RIPON HISTORICAL SOCIETY - LIBRARY (Hist)*
508 Watson St.
Box 274
Ripon, WI 54971   George H. Miller, Cur.
Phone: (414) 748-5354
Subjects: Local history. **Holdings:** 500 books. **Services:** Copying; library open to public.

RITZ (Maurice) RESOURCE CENTER
See: Planned Parenthood of Wisconsin - Maurice Ritz Resource Center

RIVERA (Luis Munoz) LIBRARY AND MUSEUM
See: Puerto Rican Culture Institute - Luis Munoz Rivera Library and Museum

★11442★
RIVERSIDE COMMUNITY MEMORIAL HOSPITAL - HEALTH SCIENCE LIBRARY (Med)
500 Riverside Dr.   Phone: (715) 258-1049
Waupaca, WI 54981   Mary Hanegraaf, Libn.
Staff: 2. **Subjects:** Medicine, nursing, surgery. **Holdings:** 250 books; 40 films; 50 audiotapes. **Subscriptions:** 73 journals and other serials. **Services:** Interlibrary loans; library not open to public. **Networks/Consortia:** Member of Fox River Valley Area Library Consortium. **Staff:** Andrea Crane, Asst.Libn.

RIVERSIDE COUNTY ART & CULTURE CENTER - EDWARD-DEAN MUSEUM OF DECORATIVE ARTS
See: Edward-Dean Museum Art Reference Library

★11443★
RIVERSIDE COUNTY HISTORICAL COMMISSION - LIBRARY (Hist)
4600 Crestmore Rd.
Box 3507   Phone: (714) 787-2551
Rubidoux, CA 92509   Stephen Becker, Dir.
Founded: 1974. **Staff:** Prof 3. **Subjects:** Local and California history, Indian history. **Special Collections:** History of Riverside County. **Holdings:** 500 volumes; manuscripts and ephemera relating to Riverside County history; 90 oral history tapes. **Services:** Library open to public by permission only. **Publications:** Historical Commission Press, annual. **Staff:** Don Kleinhesselink, Cur. of Hist.

★11444★
RIVERSIDE COUNTY LAW LIBRARY (Law)
3535 Tenth St., Suite 100   Phone: (714) 787-2460
Riverside, CA 92501   Gayle Edelman, Law Libn.
Staff: Prof 1; Other 3. **Subjects:** Law. **Holdings:** 25,300 books; 5800 bound periodical volumes; 3560 microforms; 126 cassettes; county ordinances and codes; state and federal statutes; treatises. **Subscriptions:** 62 journals and other serials. **Services:** Copying; SDI; library open to public.

★11445★
RIVERSIDE COUNTY LAW LIBRARY - INDIO LAW LIBRARY (Law)
46-209 Oasis St.
Indio, CA 92201   Marilyn Stafford, Sr.Lib.Ck.
Staff: 1. **Subjects:** Law. **Holdings:** 15,000 volumes. **Services:** Copying; library open to public.

★11446★
RIVERSIDE GENERAL HOSPITAL - MEDICAL LIBRARY (Med)
9851 Magnolia Ave.   Phone: (714) 351-7066
Riverside, CA 92503   Richard M. Butler, Dir., Medical Rec.
Staff: Prof 1; Other 1. **Subjects:** Medicine and allied health sciences. **Holdings:** 898 books; 4737 bound periodical volumes. **Subscriptions:** 213 journals and other serials. **Services:** Interlibrary loans; copying; SDI; library open to public with permission from administration. **Computerized Information Services:** NLM. **Networks/Consortia:** Member of Inland Empire Medical Library Cooperative; Medical Library Group of Southern California and Arizona.

★11447★
RIVERSIDE HOSPITAL - HEALTH SCIENCES LIBRARY (Med)
J. Clyde Morris Blvd.   Phone: (804) 599-2175
Newport News, VA 23601
Staff: Prof 2; Other 5. **Subjects:** Family practice, medicine, pediatrics, obstetrics-gynecology, nursing and allied sciences. **Holdings:** 4400 books; 2473 bound periodical volumes. **Subscriptions:** 168 journals and other serials. **Services:** Interlibrary loans; copying; library open to public for reference use only. **Staff:** Evelyn Kenney, Libn.; Peggy Rogers, Libn.

★11448★
RIVERSIDE HOSPITAL - MEDICAL LIBRARY (Med)
700 Lea Blvd.   Phone: (302) 764-6120
Wilmington, DE 19802   Ruth Irwin, Cons.
Founded: 1967. **Staff:** Prof 1; Other 1. **Subjects:** Osteopathic medicine, internal medicine, nursing. **Holdings:** 251 books and bound periodical volumes; 400 cassettes; 3 VF drawers of pamphlets. **Subscriptions:** 37 journals and other serials. **Services:** Interlibrary loans; library not open to public. **Networks/Consortia:** Member of Wilmington Area Biomedical Library Consortium (WABLC); Libraries in New Castle County System (LINCS). **Staff:** Hilde Ingersoll, Asst.Libn., ILL.

★11449★
RIVERSIDE HOSPITAL - SARAH AND JULIUS STEINBERG MEMORIAL LIBRARY (Med)
1600 N. Superior St.   Phone: (419) 729-6712
Toledo, OH 43604   Kathryn Maluchnik, Libn.
Staff: Prof 1; Other 1. **Subjects:** Medicine, nursing, podiatry, sports medicine, health promotion, hospital management. **Holdings:** 1500 books; 500 bound periodical volumes. **Subscriptions:** 173 journals and other serials. **Services:** Interlibrary loans; copying; library open to qualified users by request. **Computerized Information Services:** MEDLINE, BRS. **Networks/Consortia:** Member of Greater Midwest Regional Medical Library Network (Region 3).

★11450★
RIVERSIDE HOSPITAL - SCOBIE MEMORIAL LIBRARY (Med)
1967 Riverside Dr.   Phone: (613) 731-6710
Ottawa, ON, Canada K1H 7W9   Jean E. White, Libn.
Founded: 1968. **Staff:** Prof 1; Other 5. **Subjects:** Medicine, nursing, hospital administration. **Holdings:** 1000 books; 500 bound periodical volumes; 200 videotapes and cassettes. **Subscriptions:** 175 journals and other serials. **Services:** Interlibrary loans; copying; library open to public.

★11451★
RIVERSIDE MEDICAL CENTER - MEDICAL LIBRARY (Med)†
350 N. Wall St.   Phone: (815) 933-1671
Kankakee, IL 60901
Founded: 1977. **Staff:** Prof 1. **Subjects:** Medicine, nursing, hospital administration, mental health, alcoholism. **Holdings:** 300 books; 200 bound periodical volumes; 110 cassettes; 120 slide/cassette sets. **Subscriptions:** 230 journals and other serials. **Services:** Interlibrary loans; library not open to public. **Computerized Information Services:** MEDLINE. **Networks/Consortia:** Member of Chicago and South Consortium; Bur Oak Library System; Greater Midwest Regional Medical Library Netowrk (Region 3).

★11452★
RIVERSIDE METHODIST HOSPITAL - D.J. VINCENT MEDICAL LIBRARY (Med)
3535 Olentangy River Rd.   Phone: (614) 261-5230
Columbus, OH 43214   Josephine W. Yeoh, Dir.
Staff: Prof 2; Other 4. **Subjects:** Clinical medicine, nursing, hospital administration, microcomputers, management, patient education, fiction. **Special Collections:** Complete collection of American Journal of Nursing, 1901 to present; historical medical books. **Holdings:** 10,000 books; 10,000 bound periodical volumes; 4 Audio-Digest tapes; 20 Network for Continuing Medical Education video cassettes; pamphlet files for patient education; professional reprints file; 500 archives of papers published by professionals connected with the hospital. **Subscriptions:** 420 journals and other serials. **Services:** Interlibrary loans; copying; demand bibliographies; library open to public for reference use only. **Automated Operations:** Computerized cataloging and circulation. **Computerized Information Services:** MEDLINE, DIALOG, OCLC. **Networks/Consortia:** Member of OHIONET; Central Ohio Hospital Library Consortium; CALICO. **Publications:** Newsletter, bimonthly - for internal distribution only. **Staff:** Sandra Theis, Med.Libn.

★11453★
RIVERSIDE MUNICIPAL MUSEUM - LIBRARY (Sci-Tech)
3720 Orange St.   Phone: (714) 787-7273
Riverside, CA 92501
Subjects: History, anthropology, geology and paleontology, botany, zoology. **Holdings:** 1487 books. **Subscriptions:** 15 journals and other serials. **Services:** Library open to public with restrictions.

★11454★
RIVERSIDE OSTEOPATHIC HOSPITAL - RALPH F. LINDBERG MEMORIAL LIBRARY (Med)
150 Truax St.   Phone: (313) 676-4200
Trenton, MI 48183   Susan E. Skoglund, Dir. of Lib.Serv.
Staff: Prof 1; Other 1. **Subjects:** Medicine, nursing. **Holdings:** 1231 books;

1158 bound periodical volumes; 2 VF drawers of pamphlets; 576 Audio-Digest tapes; University of Michigan Media Library programs (slide-cassette). **Subscriptions:** 125 journals and other serials. **Services:** Interlibrary loans; library open to public with restrictions. **Computerized Information Services:** MEDLINE, DIALOG.

★11455★
RIVERSIDE PRESBYTERIAN CHURCH - JEAN MILLER LIBRARY (Rel-Theol)
849 Park St.　　　　　　　　　　　Phone: (904) 355-4585
Jacksonville, FL 32204　　　　　　　Evelyn Parker, Libn.
Staff: Prof 1; Other 1. **Subjects:** General subjects. **Holdings:** 4351 books. **Services:** Library open to public with restrictions.

★11456★
RIVERSIDE PRESS-ENTERPRISE COMPANY - EDITORIAL LIBRARY (Publ)
3512 14th St.　　　　　　　　　　　Phone: (714) 684-1200
Riverside, CA 92502　　　　　　　　Joan Minesinger, Chf.Libn.
Staff: Prof 1; Other 5. **Subjects:** Newspaper reference topics. **Holdings:** 350 books; clippings; microfilm. **Subscriptions:** 10 journals and other serials. **Services:** Copying; library open to public on a limited schedule. **Special Indexes:** Index of newspapers (notebooks and microfiche).

★11457★
RIVERVIEW HOSPITAL - MEDICAL LIBRARY (Med)
35 Union St.　　　　　　　　　　　Phone: (201) 741-2700
Red Bank, NJ 07701　　　　　　　　Cheryl Newman, Med.Libn.
Staff: Prof 1. **Subjects:** Medicine. **Holdings:** 1500 books; 75 Network for Continuing Medical Education (NCME) video cassettes; 900 audio cassettes. **Subscriptions:** 155 journals and other serials. **Services:** Interlibrary loans; copying; library open to health professionals only. **Networks/Consortia:** Member of Monmouth-Ocean Biomedical Information Consortium.

★11458★
RIVERVIEW HOSPITAL - STAFF REFERENCE LIBRARY (Med)
500 Lougheed Hwy.　　　　　　　　Phone: (604) 521-1911
Port Coquitlam, BC, Canada V3C 1J0　Min-Ja Laubental, Dir., Lib.Serv.
Founded: 1949. **Staff:** Prof 1; Other 3. **Subjects:** Psychiatry, psychology, psychiatric nursing, social sciences, medicine, hospital administration, forensic psychiatry. **Special Collections:** Audiovisual collection (125 tapes; 100 filmstrips). **Holdings:** 4450 books; 1510 bound periodical volumes; 160 staff publications; 50 annual reports; 580 pamphlets; 250 bibliographies. **Subscriptions:** 250 journals and other serials. **Services:** Interlibrary loans; copying; library open to public for reference use only, on request. **Automated Operations:** Computerized cataloging. **Computerized Information Services:** MEDLINE. **Publications:** In the Journals, monthly; acquisitions list, bimonthly - both for internal distribution only. **Remarks:** Maintains a Patients Library of 5000 volumes. Also maintains the British Columbia - Ministry of Health - Mental Health Programs - Staff Reference Library.

RKO FILM LIBRARY
See: University of Wisconsin, Madison - Wisconsin Center for Film and Theater Research

★11459★
RMI, INC. - TECHNICAL LIBRARY (Sci-Tech)
225 W. 30th St.　　　　　　　　　　Phone: (619) 474-1076
National City, CA 92050　　　　　　John M. Truesdell, Mgr., Adm.
Staff: Prof 1; Other 1. **Subjects:** Marine engineering, ship building and repair, welding, aluminum fabrication. **Special Collections:** U.S. Navy 3000 Ton Surface Effect Ship Program. **Holdings:** 5000 books; 300 bound periodical volumes. **Subscriptions:** 23 journals and other serials. **Services:** Interlibrary loans; copying; library open to government contractors. **Computerized Information Services:** Online systems. Performs searches on cost recovery basis. **Staff:** Boyd Tullis, Data Mgr.

★11460★
RMS - VS PROGRAM LIBRARY (Mil)
One Neshaminy
Interplex Suite 306
Trevose, PA 19047　　　　　　　　Karen Anderson, Tech.Libn.
Staff: Prof 1; Other 1. **Subjects:** Military specifications, aircraft, weapons. **Special Collections:** Information on the S-3 aircraft used by the U.S. Navy. **Holdings:** 9000 books; 470 tapes; 200 reels of microfilm; 100 microfiche. **Services:** Library not open to public. **Automated Operations:** Computerized cataloging and circulation. **Computerized Information Services:** Internal database.

★11461★
ROA FILMS - LIBRARY (Aud-Vis)
914 N. 4th St.
Box 661　　　　　　　　　　　　　Phone: (414) 271-0861
Milwaukee, WI 53202　　　　　　　Jean Larson, Exec. V.P.
Staff: Prof 1; Other 9. **Subjects:** Motion pictures - religious, industrial, educational and entertainment. **Holdings:** 5000 titles of motion pictures. **Services:** Rental library of films; mailed anywhere in the United States; library open to public. **Publications:** Three rental catalogs a year - entertainment, industrial, religious. **Remarks:** Toll-free telephone number for out of state customers is 1-800-558-9015. **Staff:** Walter Schuh, Asst.Mgr.

★11462★
ROADS AND TRANSPORTATION ASSOCIATION OF CANADA - TECHNICAL INFORMATION SERVICE (Trans)
1765 St. Laurent Blvd.　　　　　　Phone: (613) 521-4052
Ottawa, ON, Canada K1G 3V4　　　Charles James, Tech.Info.Off.
Founded: 1956. **Staff:** 1. **Subjects:** Road construction, surface transportation, urban transit, transportation planning. **Holdings:** 16,000 books. **Subscriptions:** 200 journals and other serials. **Services:** Interlibrary loans; copying; service open to public. **Automated Operations:** Computerized cataloging. **Computerized Information Services:** DIALOG, ESA-QUEST. Performs searches on cost recovery basis. **Publications:** Transportation Research in Canada, annual - by subscription; RTAC News, bimonthly - to members; Transportation Forum, quarterly - by subscription.

★11463★
ROANOKE LAW LIBRARY (Law)
315 Church Ave., S.W.　　　　　　Phone: (703) 981-2268
Roanoke, VA 24016　　　　　　　　Clayne Calhoun, Libn.
Staff: Prof 1. **Subjects:** State and federal law, federal taxation. **Holdings:** 15,000 volumes; 12,000 microfiche. **Subscriptions:** 120 journals and other serials. **Services:** Interlibrary loans; copying; library open to public.

★11464★
ROANOKE MEMORIAL HOSPITALS - MEDICAL LIBRARY (Med)
Belleview at Jefferson St.
Box 13367　　　　　　　　　　　　Phone: (703) 981-7371
Roanoke, VA 24033　　　　　　　　Lucy D. Glenn, Chf.Med.Libn.
Founded: 1959. **Staff:** Prof 2; Other 2. **Subjects:** Medicine, nursing. **Holdings:** 4274 books; 3499 bound periodical volumes; 66 slide sets. **Subscriptions:** 187 journals and other serials. **Services:** Interlibrary loans; copying; library open to public with restrictions. **Computerized Information Services:** MEDLINE. **Staff:** Lois Watson, Asst.Libn.

ROANOKE TIMES & WORLD-NEWS
See: Times-World Corporation

★11465★
ROANOKE VALLEY HISTORICAL SOCIETY - LIBRARY (Hist)
1 Market Square, Center in The Square　Phone: (703) 342-5770
Roanoke, VA 24011　　　　　　　　Clare White, Hd.Libn.
Founded: 1957. **Staff:** 4. **Subjects:** Roanoke and Southwest Virginia history. **Special Collections:** James Breckinridge and William Preston family letters and papers (1030 items). **Holdings:** 300 books. **Services:** Library open to researchers by appointment.

★11466★
ROARING FORK ENERGY CENTER - LIBRARY (Energy)
Box 9950　　　　　　　　　　　　Phone: (303) 925-8885
Aspen, CO 81612
Subjects: Solar energy, alternative energy, solar greenhouses, energy planning, renewable resources, wind and water power. **Holdings:** 150 books. **Subscriptions:** 12 journals and other serials.

★11467★
ROATH & BREGA, P.C. - LAW LIBRARY (Law)
1873 S. Bellaire, Suite 1700
Box 5560, Terminal Annex　　　　　Phone: (303) 691-5400
Denver, CO 80217　　　　　　　　Dorothy Norbie, Law Libn.
Staff: Prof 1; Other 1. **Subjects:** Law. **Holdings:** 10,000 books; 5000 volumes on microfiche. **Subscriptions:** 60 journals and other serials; 5 newspapers. **Services:** Interlibrary loans to local libraries. **Automated Operations:** Computerized cataloging. **Computerized Information Services:** DIALOG, LEXIS. Performs searches on cost recovery basis. **Networks/Consortia:** Member of Colorado Consortium of Law Libraries.

ROBBINS (Jerome) ARCHIVE
See: New York Public Library - Performing Arts Research Center - Dance Collection

ROBBINS LIBRARY
See: Harvard University

ROBERSON CENTER FOR THE ARTS AND SCIENCES - BROOME COUNTY HISTORICAL SOCIETY
See: Broome County Historical Society

ROBERT GORE RIFKIND FOUNDATION
See: Rifkind Center for German Expressionist Studies

ROBERTS (A. Webb) LIBRARY
See: Southwestern Baptist Theological Seminary - A. Webb Roberts Library

★11468★
ROBERTS (H. Armstrong) INC. - STOCK PHOTOGRAPHY LIBRARY (Aud-Vis)
4203 Locust St.   Phone: (215) 386-6300
Philadelphia, PA 19104   H. Armstrong Roberts, III, Pres.
Founded: 1920. **Subjects:** Photography of H. Armstrong Roberts and select contributing photographers. **Special Collections:** Charles Phelps Cushing Collection of historical engravings and photographs. **Holdings:** 1 million black/white original contemporary photographs and color transparencies. **Remarks:** Also maintains offices or representatives in New York City, Chicago, Boston, Atlanta, Los Angeles and Toronto, Canada.

ROBERTS (Oral) UNIVERSITY
See: Oral Roberts University

ROBERTSON LIBRARY
See: University of Prince Edward Island

ROBESON (Paul) LIBRARY
See: SUNY - Syracuse Educational Opportunity Center - Paul Robeson Library

ROBINS (E. Claiborne) SCHOOL OF BUSINESS LIBRARY
See: University of Richmond - E. Claiborne Robins School of Business Library

ROBINSON (Arthur H.) MAP LIBRARY
See: University of Wisconsin, Madison - Cartographic Laboratory - Arthur H. Robinson Map Library

ROBINSON-LEHANE LIBRARY
See: Dorchester Historical Society

ROBINSON LIBRARY
See: Hartford Hospital - Health Science Libraries

ROBINSON (Mary & Louis) LIBRARY
See: Jewish Board of Family & Children Services - Mary & Louis Robinson Library

★11469★
ROBINSON, SHEPPARD, BORENSTEIN, SHAPIRO - LAW LIBRARY (Law)
800 Place Victoria, Suite 4700   Phone: (514) 878-2631
Montreal, PQ, Canada H4Z 1H6   Angela Belle Tietolman, Law Libn.
Staff: Prof 1. **Subjects:** Law - civil, insurance, labour, corporate, criminal, taxation. **Holdings:** Figures not available. **Services:** Interlibrary loans; library not open to public. **Formerly:** Robinson, Cutler, Sheppard, Borenstein, Shapiro, Langlois & Flam.

★11470★
ROBINSON, SILVERMAN, PEARCE, ARONSOHN & BERMAN - LIBRARY & INFORMATION CENTER (Law)
230 Park Ave.   Phone: (212) 687-0400
New York, NY 10169   Mary Cosgrove, Libn.
Staff: Prof 1. **Subjects:** Law. **Holdings:** 12,000 books. **Subscriptions:** 80 journals and other serials; 8 newspapers. **Services:** Interlibrary loans; library not open to public. **Computerized Information Services:** Westlaw. **Networks/Consortia:** Member of Law Library Association of Greater New York.

ROBISON (Sophie) ARCHIVES
See: Adelphi University - Social Work Library

ROBOTICS INTERNATIONAL OF THE SOCIETY OF MANUFACTURING ENGINEERS COLLECTION
See: Society of Manufacturing Engineers - SME Library

★11471★
ROCHESTER ACADEMY OF MEDICINE - LIBRARY (Med)†
1441 East Ave.   Phone: (716) 271-1313
Rochester, NY 14610
Founded: 1900. **Staff:** 1. **Subjects:** Medicine and related health sciences. **Holdings:** 31,300 volumes. **Subscriptions:** 90 journals. **Services:** Interlibrary loans; copying; library open to public. **Networks/Consortia:** Member of Rochester Area Libraries in Healthcare.

★11472★
ROCHESTER BUSINESS INSTITUTE - BETTY CRONK MEMORIAL LIBRARY (Bus-Fin)
107 Clinton Ave., N.   Phone: (716) 325-7290
Rochester, NY 14604   Shirley Nagg, Lib.Aide
Founded: 1970. **Staff:** Prof 1. **Subjects:** Business and related subjects; historic costume; interior decorating. **Holdings:** 2000 books and bound periodical volumes. **Subscriptions:** 31 journals and other serials. **Services:** Interlibrary loans; copying; library open to public by appointment for research.

ROCHESTER DEMOCRAT & CHRONICLE
See: Rochester Times-Union and Rochester Democrat & Chronicle

★11473★
ROCHESTER GAS AND ELECTRIC CORPORATION - TECHNICAL INFORMATION CENTER (Sci-Tech; Energy)
89 East Ave.   Phone: (716) 546-2700
Rochester, NY 14649   Linda L. Phillips, Supv., Off.Serv./Doc.Ctr.
Staff: Prof 2; Other 1. **Subjects:** Electrical power generation, nuclear power, energy, engineering, environment, management. **Special Collections:** Electric Power Research Institute (EPRI) reports (3000). **Holdings:** 2500 books and reports; 3000 items on nuclear power, including codes, standards and regulations; 1500 power plant documents; 500 in-house reports; 8 drawers of pamphlets and company historical information. **Subscriptions:** 125 journals and other serials. **Services:** Interlibrary loans; copying; center library open to public by appointment and with escort. **Automated Operations:** Computerized indexing. **Computerized Information Services:** DIALOG, SDC, Nuclear Network, DOE/RECON. **Networks/Consortia:** Member of Rochester Regional Research Library Council (RRRLC). **Publications:** RG & E News, bimonthly; book review columns and AQ lists. **Special Indexes:** Industry codes & standards (card); technical manuals for power plant systems & components (card); technical reports (computer printout). **Staff:** Sharon Paprocki, Tech.Info.Spec.

★11474★
ROCHESTER GENERAL HOSPITAL - LILLIE B. WERNER HEALTH SCIENCES LIBRARY (Med)
1425 Portland Ave.   Phone: (716) 338-4743
Rochester, NY 14621   Bernie Todd Smith, Lib.Dir.
Founded: 1957. **Staff:** Prof 4; Other 3. **Subjects:** Medicine, psychiatry, nursing. **Special Collections:** Bohrod History of Medicine Collection (200 books). **Holdings:** 5000 books; 6000 bound periodical volumes; 1500 AV items. **Subscriptions:** 350 journals and other serials. **Services:** Interlibrary loans; library not open to public. **Computerized Information Services:** MEDLINE, BRS. **Networks/Consortia:** Member of Rochester Regional Research Library Council (RRRLC). **Publications:** Library Letter, quarterly; Library Guide; Circuit Librarian Program brochure. **Special Catalogs:** Book catalog of AV materials is computer generated and updated quarterly. **Staff:** Edward Lewek, Asst.Libn.; Frederick Pond, Circuit Libn.; Diane Reiman, Circuit Libn.

★11475★
ROCHESTER HISTORICAL SOCIETY - LIBRARY (Hist)
485 East Ave.   Phone: (716) 271-2705
Rochester, NY 14607   Mary Widger, Libn.
Staff: Prof 1. **Subjects:** Local history. **Holdings:** 3000 books; manuscript and archival material, photographs, maps, genealogical material, complete file of Rochester directories, 1827 to present. **Services:** Library open to public with restrictions.

★11476★
ROCHESTER INSTITUTE OF TECHNOLOGY - CHEMISTRY GRADUATE RESEARCH LIBRARY (Sci-Tech)
One Lomb Memorial Dr.   Phone: (716) 475-2520
Rochester, NY 14623   Christine DeGolyer, Chem.Libn.
Founded: 1968. **Staff:** Prof 1; Other 2. **Subjects:** Advanced chemistry. **Holdings:** 3482 books; 4200 bound periodical volumes; 53 masters' theses; 110 pamphlets; 795 microfiche; 51 reels of microfilm. **Subscriptions:** 153 journals and other serials. **Services:** Interlibrary loans; library copying open to public. **Automated Operations:** Computerized cataloging and circulation. **Computerized Information Services:** DIALOG, BRS, NIH-EPA Chemical Information System. Performs searches on fee basis. **Networks/Consortia:** Member of Rochester Regional Research Library Council (RRRLC).

★11477★
ROCHESTER INSTITUTE OF TECHNOLOGY - MELBERT B. CARY, JR. GRAPHIC ARTS COLLECTION (Art; Publ)†
School of Printing   Phone: (716) 475-2408
Rochester, NY 14623   David Pankow, Libn.
Founded: 1969. **Staff:** Prof 2. **Subjects:** Printing history, typography, book arts, press books, calligraphy, papermaking, graphic arts. **Special Collections:** Rudolf Koch; Fritz Kredel; Officina Bodoni; Grabhorn Press; Spiral Press; W.A. Dwiggins; T.M. Cleland; Press of the Woolly Whale; Laboratory Press; Bruce Rogers; Frederic W. Goudy; Type Specimen books; broadsides and posters; fore edge paintings. **Holdings:** 8000 books; 12 VF drawers of clippings; ephemera and pamphlets; 8 boxes of posters, broadsides and drawings. **Subscriptions:** 12 journals and other serials. **Services:** Copying (limited); collection open to public. **Publications:** Festina Lente: The Journal of the Melbert B. Cary, Jr. Graphic Arts Collection, semiannual - by subscription.

★11478★
ROCHESTER INSTITUTE OF TECHNOLOGY - NATIONAL TECHNICAL INSTITUTE FOR THE DEAF - STAFF RESOURCE CENTER (Med)
Lyndon Baines Johnson Bldg., Rm. 2490
1 Lomb Memorial Dr.   Phone: (716) 475-6823
Rochester, NY 14623   Audrey Ritter, Rsrcs.Spec.
Founded: 1978. **Staff:** Prof 1; Other 1. **Subjects:** Deafness. **Special Collections:** National Center on Employment of the Deaf information collection (4 VF drawers). **Holdings:** 1000 books; 200 bound periodical volumes; 600 videotapes; 300 other software items. **Subscriptions:** 41 journals and other serials. **Services:** Interlibrary loans; copying; center open to public by appointment. **Networks/Consortia:** Member of Rochester Regional Research Library Council (RRRLC). **Special Catalogs:** Bibliography of literature and media related to the employment of the deaf.

★11479★
ROCHESTER INSTITUTE OF TECHNOLOGY - TECHNICAL & EDUCATION CENTER FOR THE GRAPHIC ARTS - GRAPHIC ARTS INFO.SERV. (Art)
One Lomb Memorial Dr.   Phone: (716) 475-2791
Rochester, NY 14623   Susan Clark, Tech.Libn.
Founded: 1952. **Staff:** Prof 1; Other 1. **Subjects:** Graphic arts, printing technology, photography in printing operations. **Holdings:** 1000 books; 300 unbound periodical titles; 22,000 articles on microfilm; 12 VF drawers of pamphlets; 4 VF drawers of research reports; printing and photoscience masters' theses. **Subscriptions:** 250 journals and other serials. **Services:** Copying (fee); individual literature searches; service open to public by appointment. **Computerized Information Services:** Image Technology Patent Information System (I.T.P.A.I.S.; internal database). **Publications:** Graphic Arts Literature Abstracts, monthly - by subscription; Photographicconservation, quarterly - by subscription; T & E Center Newsletter - free upon request. **Special Indexes:** Annual Cumulative Author/Keyword Index to Graphic Arts Literature Abstracts (published in December) - with subscription.

★11480★
ROCHESTER INSTITUTE OF TECHNOLOGY - WALLACE MEMORIAL LIBRARY (Art; Sci-Tech)
One Lomb Memorial Dr.   Phone: (716) 475-2565
Rochester, NY 14623   Patricia A. Pitkin, Dir.
Founded: 1688. **Staff:** Prof 23; Other 16. **Subjects:** Art, business, criminal justice, the deaf, printing, photography, social work, engineering, science. **Special Collections:** NASA technical reports; the deaf and deafness. **Holdings:** 218,000 books and bound periodical volumes; 1688 theses; 120 VF drawers of archives; 70,000 slides; 400 films; 14,560 reels of microfilm; 111,330 microfiche. **Subscriptions:** 5360 journals and other serials; 17 newspapers. **Services:** Interlibrary loans; copying; library open to public for in-house use only. **Automated Operations:** Computerized cataloging, acquisitions and circulation. **Computerized Information Services:** Online systems. **Networks/Consortia:** Member of Rochester Regional Research Library Council (RRRLC); Rochester Area Colleges, Inc. (RAC). **Publications:**

Faculty Writings: 1951-1972, Supplements I and II, 2nd edition, 1973-1976, Supplements I, II and III, volume II, 1981; bibliographies. **Staff:** Lois A. Goodman, Asst.Dir., Info.Serv.; Virginia Church, Asst.Dir., Tech.Serv.; Reno Antonietti, Dir., Media Serv.; Gladys Taylor, Archv.

★11481★
ROCHESTER METHODIST HOSPITAL - METHODIST KAHLER LIBRARY (Med)
                                                 Phone: (507) 286-7425
Rochester, MN 55901   Jean M. Brose, Hd.Libn.
Staff: Prof 2; Other 2. **Subjects:** Nursing, hospital administration, health sciences. **Special Collections:** History of Nursing in the United States. **Holdings:** 11,000 books; 450 bound periodical volumes; 500 AV programs, 12 VF drawers of newspaper clippings and pamphlets. **Subscriptions:** 350 journals and other serials. **Services:** Interlibrary loans; copying; library open to public with limited outside circulation. **Computerized Information Services:** DIALOG. Performs searches on cost recovery basis. **Networks/Consortia:** Member of Greater Midwest Regional Medical Library (Region 3). :aff: Karen Larsen, Asst.Libn.

★11482★
ROCHESTER MUSEUM AND SCIENCE CENTER - LIBRARY (Hist; Sci-Tech)
657 East Ave.
Box 1480   Phone: (716) 271-4320
Rochester, NY 14603   Leatrice M. Kemp, Libn.
Founded: 1914. **Staff:** Prof 2; Other 1. **Subjects:** Natural sciences, anthropology, local history, American Indians, antiques, archaeology, costume, technology, museology. **Holdings:** 26,000 volumes; museum bulletins. **Subscriptions:** 60 journals and other serials. **Services:** Copying; library open to public. **Automated Operations:** Computerized cataloging. **Networks/Consortia:** Member of Rochester Regional Research Library Council (RRRLC). **Staff:** Christopher Brennan, Asst.Libn.

★11483★
ROCHESTER MUSEUM AND SCIENCE CENTER - STRASENBURGH PLANETARIUM - TODD LIBRARY (Sci-Tech)
657 East Ave.   Phone: (716) 244-6060
Rochester, NY 14607
Staff: Prof 1. **Subjects:** Astronomy, space science. **Holdings:** 1500 books; 500 bound periodical volumes. **Subscriptions:** 23 journals and other serials. **Services:** Library open to public for reference use only.

★11484★
ROCHESTER POST-BULLETIN - NEWS LIBRARY (Publ)*
18 First Ave., S.E.   Phone: (507) 285-7730
Rochester, MN 55901   Marcy Sawyer, News Libn.
Staff: Prof 1. **Subjects:** Newspaper reference topics. **Holdings:** 100 books; microfilm of Rochester Post-Bulletin. **Subscriptions:** 25 journals and other serials; 20 newspapers. **Services:** Interlibrary loans; copying; library open to public with restrictions.

★11485★
ROCHESTER PSYCHIATRIC CENTER - PROFESSIONAL LIBRARY (Med)†
1600 South Ave.   Phone: (716) 473-3230
Rochester, NY 14620
Staff: Prof 1. **Subjects:** Psychiatry, nursing. **Holdings:** 5042 books; 21 bound periodical volumes; 144 Audio-Digest tapes; 2 VF drawers of pamphlets. **Subscriptions:** 65 journals and other serials. **Services:** Interlibrary loans; copying; library open to public by appointment. **Networks/Consortia:** Member of Rochester Regional Research Library Council (RRRLC).

★11486★
ROCHESTER PUBLIC LIBRARY - ART DIVISION (Art; Mus)
115 South Ave.   Phone: (716) 428-7332
Rochester, NY 14604   Mary Lee Miller, Hd.
Staff: Prof 4; Other 5. **Subjects:** Fine arts, music, photography, film history, antiques, ornamental gardening, architecture, urban planning, crafts. **Special Collections:** Picture file (84 VF drawers). **Holdings:** 39,000 books; 12,000 slides; 20,000 sound recordings; choir music; framed prints. **Subscriptions:** 157 journals and other serials. **Services:** Interlibrary loans; copying. **Networks/Consortia:** Member of Rochester Regional Research Library Council (RRRLC).

★11487★
ROCHESTER PUBLIC LIBRARY - BUSINESS, ECONOMICS AND LEGISLATION DIVISION (Bus-Fin; Soc Sci)
115 South Ave.   Phone: (716) 428-7328
Rochester, NY 14604   Carolyn Johnson, Hd.
Staff: Prof 6; Other 2. **Subjects:** Business, economics, labor, employment,

political science, government, law, sociology. **Special Collections:** Industrial directories; financial services; corporation annual reports; Foundation Center; federal, state and local documents. **Holdings:** 69,000 books; 15 VF drawers of pamphlets and clippings; microcards; microfilm; recordings. **Subscriptions:** 700 journals and other serials. **Services:** Interlibrary loans; copying. **Networks/Consortia:** Member of Rochester Regional Research Library Council (RRRLC).

★11488★
ROCHESTER PUBLIC LIBRARY - EDUCATION, SOCIOLOGY AND RELIGION DIVISION (Educ; Rel-Theol)
115 South Ave.   Phone: (716) 428-7330
Rochester, NY 14604   Robert D. Murphy, Hd.
Staff: Prof 3; Other 2. **Subjects:** Education, religion, philosophy, psychology, psychiatry, ethics. **Special Collections:** College catalog collection (paperback and microfiche); Education/Job Information Center. **Holdings:** 47,000 books; 300 pamphlets. **Subscriptions:** 170 journals and other serials. **Services:** Interlibrary loans; copying; Regents External Degree Advisory Service. **Publications:** New Books for Teachers - distributed to city and county school districts for duplication and distribution to teachers. **Computerized Information Services:** Guidance Information System (GIS). **Networks/Consortia:** Member of Rochester Regional Research Library Council (RRRLC).

★11489★
ROCHESTER PUBLIC LIBRARY - HISTORY, GOVERNMENT AND TRAVEL DIVISION (Hist)
115 South Ave.   Phone: (716) 428-7323
Rochester, NY 14604   Winn McCray, Hd.
Staff: Prof 3; Other 1. **Subjects:** History, travel, international law, international relations, archeology, the military. **Special Collections:** Map collection including topographic maps for New York State. **Holdings:** 53,000 volumes; 26 VF drawers of pamphlets and travel brochures; slides; recordings. **Subscriptions:** 150 journals and other serials. **Services:** Interlibrary loans; copying. **Networks/Consortia:** Member of Rochester Regional Research Library Council (RRRLC). **Publications:** Booklists, irregular.

★11490★
ROCHESTER PUBLIC LIBRARY - LITERATURE, BIOGRAPHY AND SPORTS DIVISION (Hum; Rec)
115 South Ave.   Phone: (716) 428-7315
Rochester, NY 14604   William J. Cuseo, Hd.
Staff: Prof 5; Other 4. **Subjects:** Literature, fiction, biography, language, speech, journalism, folklore, sports and games, etiquette. **Special Collections:** Talking books; books in French, Spanish, German, Italian, Hungarian. **Holdings:** 140,000 books; 3000 large print books; 12 VF drawers of pamphlets and clippings; 2500 record albums; 300 cassettes. **Subscriptions:** 160 journals and other serials. **Services:** Interlibrary loans; copying. **Networks/Consortia:** Member of Rochester Regional Research Library Council (RRRLC).

★11491★
ROCHESTER PUBLIC LIBRARY - LOCAL HISTORY AND GENEALOGY DIVISION (Hist)
115 South Ave.   Phone: (716) 428-7338
Rochester, NY 14604   Wayne Arnold, Hd.
Staff: Prof 3; Other 2. **Subjects:** History of Rochester and the Genesee country, genealogy (primarily New York and New England). **Special Collections:** Local newspapers. **Holdings:** 25,000 books; 15 cases and 400 volumes of manuscripts; 1800 maps; 500 scrapbooks; 145 VF drawers of newspaper clippings; 80 VF drawers of pamphlets and ephemera; 20 VF drawers of pictures; 12 drawers of postcards; 638 reels of microfilm; 120 films. **Subscriptions:** 200 journals and other serials; 78 newspapers. **Services:** Copying (limited). **Networks/Consortia:** Member of Rochester Regional Research Library Council (RRRLC). **Remarks:** The majority of the holdings of the Rochester Historical Society are on permanent loan to the Local History Division.

★11492★
ROCHESTER PUBLIC LIBRARY - REYNOLDS AUDIO-VISUAL DEPARTMENT (Aud-Vis)
115 South Ave.   Phone: (716) 428-7335
Rochester, NY 14604   Robert Barnes, Hd.
Staff: Prof 2; Other 7. **Holdings:** 1472 books; 5500 16mm films; 4100 8mm films; 4000 filmstrips; 250 videotapes. **Subscriptions:** 50 journals and other serials. **Services:** Interlibrary loans; media preview facilities; equipment loans. **Networks/Consortia:** Member of Rochester Regional Research Library Council (RRRLC). **Publications:** Catalogs of 16mm films and video cassette tapes.

★11493★
ROCHESTER PUBLIC LIBRARY - SCIENCE AND TECHNOLOGY DIVISION (Sci-Tech)
115 South Ave.   Phone: (716) 428-7327
Rochester, NY 14604   Judith Prevratil, Hd.
Staff: Prof 4; Other 2. **Subjects:** Physical and natural sciences, applied science and technology, health sciences, environmental sciences, agriculture, home economics. **Special Collections:** Trade catalogs of national firms; automobile shop manuals; Sam's Photofacts Service; Official Gazette of U.S. Patent Office, 1846 to present. **Holdings:** 54,000 books; 15 VF drawers of pamphlets; 130 slide sets; 100 phonograph records; 70 cassettes. **Subscriptions:** 425 journals and other serials. **Services:** Interlibrary loans; copying. **Networks/Consortia:** Member of Rochester Regional Research Library Council (RRRLC). **Publications:** Booklists, irregular.

★11494★
ROCHESTER TIMES-UNION AND ROCHESTER DEMOCRAT & CHRONICLE - LIBRARY (Publ)
55 Exchange St.   Phone: (716) 232-7100
Rochester, NY 14614   Peter Ford, Lib.Dir.
Founded: 1929. **Staff:** Prof 3; Other 3. **Subjects:** Newspaper reference topics. **Holdings:** 1500 books; clippings, photographs, microfilm. **Services:** Library not open to public.

★11495★
ROCK COUNTY HEALTH CARE CENTER - STAFF LIBRARY (Med)
Box 351   Phone: (608) 755-2543
Janesville, WI 53547   Louise Jilbert, Libn.
Founded: 1971. **Staff:** Prof 1. **Subjects:** Psychiatry, psychiatric social work, geriatrics, nursing. **Holdings:** 1052 books; 29 bound periodical volumes; AV materials. **Subscriptions:** 63 journals and other serials. **Services:** Interlibrary loans; copying; library open to public. **Networks/Consortia:** Member of South Central Wisconsin Health Planning Area Cooperative.

★11496★
ROCK COUNTY HISTORICAL SOCIETY - ARCHIVES OF ROCK COUNTY HISTORY (Hist)
10 S. High
Box 896   Phone: (608) 756-4509
Janesville, WI 53545   Maurice J. Montgomery, Archv.
Founded: 1948. **Staff:** Prof 1. **Subjects:** Rock County local history; land speculation. **Special Collections:** Tallman Family papers (3000 items dealing with land speculation, railroad matters and building construction, 1830-1880). **Holdings:** 1500 books; 40 VF drawers of manuscripts and photocopies of clippings; 500 volumes of school records, business records, and diaries; 4 boxes and 15 cubic feet of maps; 50 drawers of cataloged photographs and other miscellaneous items. **Subscriptions:** 15 journals and other serials; 5 newspapers. **Services:** Copying; archives open to public on a limited schedule. **Publications:** Recorder, bimonthly. **Special Catalogs:** Iconographic catalog; artifact catalog (both card). **Special Indexes:** Biographical index to Rock County (card); Cemetery records (card); index to published and nonpublished materials (book).

ROCK CREEK NATURE LIBRARY
See: U.S. Natl. Park Service - Natl. Capital Region

★11497★
ROCKBRIDGE HISTORICAL SOCIETY - LIBRARY/ARCHIVES (Hist)
Randolph St.   Phone: (703) 911-1403
Lexington, VA 24450   Charles W. Turner, Soc.Libn.
Founded: 1939. **Staff:** Prof 3. **Subjects:** Local history and genealogy. **Special Collections:** Davidson Collection; Barcley, Edwardson, Houston, Davidson and Anderson Papers. **Holdings:** 600 books; 200 bound periodical volumes; 40 boxes of local newspapers and local historical material; photograph albums; scrapbooks. **Services:** Interlibrary loans; copying; library open to public. **Publications:** Proceedings, biennial. **Remarks:** Most holdings are housed in the Washington and Lee University Library. An alternative phone number is (703) 463-9111.

ROCKDALE TEMPLE
See: K.K. Bene Israel/Rockdale Temple

ROCKEFELLER (Abby Aldrich) FOLK ART CENTER
See: Abby Aldrich Rockefeller Folk Art Center

★11498★
ROCKEFELLER FOUNDATION - LIBRARY (Soc Sci)
1133 Ave. of the Americas   Phone: (212) 869-8500
New York, NY 10036   Marie Dooling, Libn.
Staff: Prof 2; Other 2. **Subjects:** Philanthropy, social sciences, biography. **Special Collections:** College catalogs; annual reports of philanthropic institutions; Rockefeller Foundation reports and publications. **Holdings:** 8000 volumes. **Subscriptions:** 600 journals and other serials. **Services:** Interlibrary loans; copying; library serves members of staff only. **Automated Operations:** Computerized serials. **Computerized Information Services:** DIALOG, OCLC. **Networks/Consortia:** Member of Consortium of Foundation Libraries; Association for Population/Family Planning Libraries and Information Centers-International (APLIC-Internatl.); METRO; Medical Library Center of New York (MLCNY). **Staff:** Bernadette Adams-Malone, Asst.Libn.

★11499★
ROCKEFELLER UNIVERSITY - LIBRARY (Sci-Tech)
1230 York Ave.
RU Box 263   Phone: (212) 570-8901
New York, NY 10021-6399   Sonya Wohl Mirsky, Univ.Libn./Spec.Coll.Cur.
Founded: 1906. **Staff:** Prof 4; Other 19. **Subjects:** Biological sciences, medicine, chemistry, physics, mathematics. **Holdings:** 210,000 volumes. **Subscriptions:** 1854 journals and other serials. **Services:** Interlibrary loans; library not open to public. **Automated Operations:** Computerized cataloging, acquisitions, serials and circulation. **Computerized Information Services:** DIALOG, BRS, NLM, NEXIS, NASA/RECON. **Networks/Consortia:** Member of Medical Library Center of New York (MLCNY); Greater Northeastern Regional Medical Library Program.

★11500★
ROCKEFELLER UNIVERSITY - NEUROSCIENCES RESEARCH PROGRAM - LIBRARY (Sci-Tech)*
100 York Ave.
New York, NY 10021   Dr. Einar Gall
Staff: Prof 1; Other 2. **Subjects:** Neurosciences, brain sciences, neurobiology. **Holdings:** 5000 books; 50,000 reprints; audiotapes of 60 3-day symposia. **Subscriptions:** 100 journals and other serials. **Services:** Library open to scholars in the field by special arrangement. **Publications:** Bibliographies, reference lists, accessions lists, bibliographies of issues of Neurosciences Research Program Bulletin.

★11501★
ROCKEFELLER UNIVERSITY - ROCKEFELLER ARCHIVE CENTER (Hist; Soc Sci)
Hillcrest, Pocantico Hills   Phone: (914) 631-4505
North Tarrytown, NY 10591   Dr. Joseph W. Ernst, Dir.
Founded: 1975. **Staff:** Prof 7; Other 6. **Subjects:** American philanthropy, Rockefeller family, education, medicine, physical and social science, public health, arts, humanities. **Special Collections:** Rockefeller Foundation (3300 cubic feet); General Education Board (350 cubic feet); Laura Spelman Rockefeller Memorial (58 cubic feet); Bureau of Social Hygiene (32 cubic feet); John D. Rockefeller (550 cubic feet); International Education Board (22 cubic feet); Spelman Fund of New York (42 cubic feet); Rockefeller University (600 cubic feet); China Medical Board (122 cubic feet); Rockefeller Brothers Fund (255 cubic feet); Agricultural Development Council (88 cubic feet); American International Association for Economic and Social Development (33 cubic feet); Population Council (51 cubic feet); Arts, Education and Americans Panel (21 cubic feet); Davison Fund, Inc. (16 cubic feet); John D. Rockefeller, III Fund (143 cubic feet); Memorial Sloan-Kettering Cancer Center (50 cubic feet); Rockefeller Sanitary Commission for the Eradication of Hookworm Disease (6.5. cubic feet); Union Tank Car Company (6 cubic feet). **Holdings:** 8000 cubic feet of archival and manuscript collections; 4000 microfiche cards. **Services:** Copying; center open to visiting scholars by request. **Publications:** Occasional papers. **Special Catalogs:** Archives and Manuscripts in the Rockefeller Archive Center, 1982 (pamphlet). **Staff:** J. William Hess, Assoc.Dir; Claire Collier, Archv.; Thomas Rosenbaum, Archv.; Emily Nager, Archv.; Thomas Reitz, Archv.; Harold Oakhill, Archv.

★11502★
ROCKFORD MEMORIAL HOSPITAL - HEALTH SCIENCE LIBRARY (Med)
2400 N. Rockton Ave.   Phone: (815) 968-6861
Rockford, IL 61101   Prudence Dalrymple, Coord., Lib.Serv.
Staff: Prof 2; Other 1. **Subjects:** Clinical medicine, nursing, health care administration. **Special Collections:** Hunter Memorial Pediatric Library (300 volumes); School of Nursing (3000 volumes). **Holdings:** 2000 books; 2000 bound periodical volumes; 2 VF drawers; 100 nonprint items. **Subscriptions:** 178 journals and other serials. **Services:** Interlibrary loans; copying; library open to public by arrangement. **Computerized Information Services:** MEDLARS. **Networks/Consortia:** Member of Greater Midwest Regional

Medical Library (Region 3); Northern Illinois Library System (NILS); Upstate Illinois Consortium.

★11503★
ROCKFORD PUBLIC LIBRARY - BUSINESS, SCIENCE AND TECHNOLOGY DIVISION (Bus-Fin; Sci-Tech)†
215 N. Wyman   Phone: (815) 965-6731
Rockford, IL 61101   Marie Phillips, Hd.
Founded: 1872. **Staff:** Prof 2; Other 4. **Subjects:** Business, finance (investments), science, technology. **Special Collections:** Telephone books (all cities over 100,000, all Illinois and Wisconsin towns, and all state capitals). **Holdings:** 26,631 volumes; 10,989 items in pamphlet file; 30,496 items in partial federal document depository; Nuclear Regulatory Commission depository for Byron, Illinois nuclear plant. **Subscriptions:** 140 journals and other serials. **Services:** Interlibrary loans; copying; library open to public; telephone reference. **Automated Operations:** Computerized circulation. **Networks/Consortia:** Member of Northern Illinois Library System (NILS); Upstate Consortium of Medical and Allied Libraries in Northern Illinois. **Publications:** Occasional lists to local business, industries and general public.

★11504★
ROCKINGHAM MEMORIAL HOSPITAL - HEALTH SCIENCES LIBRARY (Med)
235 Cantrell Ave.   Phone: (703) 433-8311
Harrisonburg, VA 22801-3293   Ilene N. Smith, Med.Libn.
Founded: 1912. **Staff:** Prof 1. **Subjects:** Clinical medicine, nursing, allied health subjects. **Holdings:** 6000 books and bound periodical volumes; 1150 audiovisuals. **Subscriptions:** 280 journals and other serials. **Services:** Interlibrary loans; SDI; library open to public with restrictions. **Networks/Consortia:** Member of Southwestern Virginia Health Information Librarians.

★11505★
ROCKLAND COUNTY GUIDANCE CENTER - LIBRARY (Soc Sci)
83 Main St.
Nyack, NY 10960   Henrietta Hendrick, Career Info.Asst.
Staff: 3. **Subjects:** Career information, education, employment, status of women. **Holdings:** 500 books; 220 tapes; college catalogs. **Subscriptions:** 12 journals and other serials.

ROCKLAND RESEARCH INSTITUTE
See: Kline (Nathan S.) Institute for Psychiatric Research

★11506★
ROCKVILLE GENERAL HOSPITAL - MEDICAL LIBRARY/RESOURCE ROOM (Med)†
31 Union St.   Phone: (203) 872-0501
Rockville, CT 06066   Dorothea M. Zabilansky, Med.Libn.
Founded: 1960. **Staff:** Prof 1. **Subjects:** Medicine. **Holdings:** 600 books; 300 bound periodical volumes; Audio-Digest tapes, 1960 to present. **Subscriptions:** 102 journals and other serials. **Services:** Interlibrary loans; copying; library open to public by appointment. **Networks/Consortia:** Member of Northeastern Connecticut Hospital Library Consortium; Connecticut Association of Health Science Libraries (CAHSL); Northeastern Association of Health Science Libraries.

ROCKWELL CHEMISTRY LIBRARY
See: Tufts University

★11507★
ROCKWELL INTERNATIONAL - BUSINESS RESEARCH CENTER (Bus-Fin; Sci-Tech)
600 Grant St.   Phone: (412) 565-5880
Pittsburgh, PA 15219   Ruth T. Gunning, Mgr., Bus.Info.Serv.
Founded: 1967. **Staff:** Prof 2. **Subjects:** Business, economic and financial information for the aerospace, automotive, electronic and general industries. **Holdings:** 1000 books; 5000 pamphlets and reports; 5000 Securities and Exchange Commission reports. **Subscriptions:** 300 journals and other serials; 7 newspapers. **Services:** Interlibrary loans; center not open to public. **Computerized Information Services:** DIALOG, Dow Jones News/Retrieval, Chase Econometrics, Compuserve, Data Resources, Inc., Dun & Bradstreet Corporation, NEXIS, NewsNet, Inc., Ontyme. **Publications:** Annotated Checklist of Acquisitions, monthly - for internal distribution only; annual list of periodicals and services; Companies of Interest, annual; Directory of Products/Sales/Services, annual.

ROCKWELL INTERNATIONAL OF CANADA, LTD. - COLLINS CANADA
See: Collins Canada

★11508★
ROCKWELL INTERNATIONAL - COLLINS DIVISIONS - INFORMATION
CENTER (Sci-Tech)
400 Collins Rd., N.E.   Phone: (319) 395-3070
Cedar Rapids, IA 52498   Judith A. Leavitt, Supv., Info.Ctr.
Founded: 1942. Staff: 5. Subjects: Electronics, management, space,
navigation, mathematics, aeronautics, communication equipment, computers,
physics. Holdings: 6000 books and bound periodical volumes; 13,500 Collins
Radio Co. publications; military, federal, and industrial specifications.
Subscriptions: 350 journals and other serials. Services: Center not open to
public. Computerized Information Services: DIALOG, BRS, DTIC, Dow
Jones News/Retrieval, DMS/ONLINE. Networks/Consortia: Member of Linn
County Library Consortium. Publications: Acquisition list, biweekly - for
internal distribution only.

★11509★
ROCKWELL INTERNATIONAL - ELECTRONICS OPERATIONS - DALLAS
INFORMATION CENTER (Sci-Tech)
Dallas Information Center 407-120   Phone: (214) 996-6022
Dallas, TX 75207   Wanda J. Fox, Supv.
Founded: 1960. Staff: Prof 3; Other 5. Subjects: Electronics,
communications. Special Collections: International Business Collection (500
volumes); military, commercial and international specifications and standards.
Holdings: 7000 books; 2000 bound periodical volumes; 55,000 internal
reports and working papers; 1700 financial and marketing files.
Subscriptions: 437 journals and other serials. Services: Interlibrary loans;
copying; center open to public by appointment. Computerized Information
Services: DIALOG, SDC, Data Resources, Inc. (DRI), NEXIS, Dow Jones
News/Retrieval, Dun & Bradstreet Corporation. Publications: Working Paper
Bulletin; Current Awareness Bulletin; Daily News Briefs. Special Indexes:
Working Paper Index. Staff: Joyce Deegan, Libn.; David L. Clifton, Mgr.,
Info.Serv.

★11510★
ROCKWELL INTERNATIONAL - ENERGY SYSTEMS GROUP - LIBRARY
(Energy)
8900 De Soto Ave., NA00   Phone: (818) 700-4406
Canoga Park, CA 91304   Ms. Y.O. Fackler, Mgr.
Founded: 1948. Staff: 2. Subjects: Energy, technology, chemistry, physics,
metallurgy, mathematics, engineering. Holdings: 21,000 books; 8500 bound
periodical volumes; 1600 unbound volumes; 50,000 hard copy reports;
440,000 microfiche. Subscriptions: 250 journals and other serials.
Services: Interlibrary loans; copying; library open to public with restrictions.
Computerized Information Services: SDC, DOE/RECON, DIALOG, DTIC,
BRS, COMSHARE, Inc. Staff: Eriana Ramirez, Acq.

★11511★
ROCKWELL INTERNATIONAL - ENERGY SYSTEMS GROUP - ROCKY FLATS
PLANT - TECHNICAL LIBRARY (Sci-Tech; Energy)†
Box 938   Phone: (303) 497-2863
Golden, CO 80401   Mary Ann Paliani, Lib.Mgr.
Founded: 1952. Staff: Prof 2; Other 3. Subjects: Atomic energy, chemistry,
metallurgy, physics. Holdings: 15,000 books and bound periodical volumes;
10,000 technical reports; 50,000 reports on microcards and microfiche.
Subscriptions: 797 journals and other serials. Services: Interlibrary loans;
library not open to public. Automated Operations: Computerized cataloging,
acquisitions and internal reports. Computerized Information Services:
DIALOG, SDC, New York Times Information Service, DOE/RECON.
Publications: Library and Technical Information Office Bulletin, monthly - for
internal distribution only; Journals Currently Received by the Rocky Flats
Library. Special Indexes: Indexes to classified and unclassified IRF reports
(book).

★11512★
ROCKWELL INTERNATIONAL - FLOW CONTROL DIVISION - TECHNICAL
INFORMATION CENTER (Sci-Tech)
400 N. Lexington Ave.   Phone: (412) 247-3095
Pittsburgh, PA 15208   Kathleen M. Witkowski, Lib.Coord.
Founded: 1950. Staff: Prof 1. Subjects: Engineering - mechanical, hydraulic,
electrical, metallurgy, instrumentation, technology. Holdings: 5750 books;
200 bound periodical volumes; 2500 government research and development
reports; 7 VF drawers of clippings and pamphlets; 240 cartridges of
microfilm; 2200 microfiche. Subscriptions: 140 journals and other serials;
10 newspapers. Services: Interlibrary loans; center not open to public.
Automated Operations: Computerized serials. Computerized Information
Services: DIALOG, SDC, BRS. Publications: Information Bulletin, bimonthly;
List of Standards and Specifications, annual; List of Annual Reports, annual;
List of periodicals, semiannual - all for internal distribution only. Special
Catalogs: Catalog of NTIS Reports (card). Formerly: Its General Industries

Operations.

★11513★
ROCKWELL INTERNATIONAL - GRAPHIC SYSTEMS - TECHNICAL
INFORMATION CENTER (Sci-Tech)
3100 S. Central Ave.   Phone: (312) 656-8600
Chicago, IL 60650   Joyce Tykol, Libn.
Founded: 1965. Staff: 1. Subjects: Engineering, graphic arts, electronics.
Holdings: 3000 books. Subscriptions: 70 journals and other serials.
Services: Center serves staff only. Publications: New Books List, irregular -
for internal distribution only.

★11514★
ROCKWELL INTERNATIONAL - HEAVY VEHICLES COMPONENTS
OPERATION - REFERENCE CENTER (Bus-Fin; Sci-Tech)
2135 W. Maple Rd.   Phone: (313) 435-1668
Troy, MI 48084   Cheryl Hull, Tech.Ref.Asst.
Staff: Prof 1; Other 1. Subjects: Automotive engineering, marketing,
technical sciences. Special Collections: Society of Automotive Engineers
technical papers. Holdings: 2600 books; 33 bound periodical volumes; 250
annual reports; 300 laboratory reports. Subscriptions: 550 journals and other
serials; 5 newspapers. Services: Interlibrary loans; center not open to public.
Computerized Information Services: DIALOG; internal database.
Publications: Reference Center Notes, monthly - for internal distribution only.

★11515★
ROCKWELL INTERNATIONAL - NEWPORT BEACH INFORMATION CENTER
(Sci-Tech; Info Sci)
4311 Jamboree Blvd., (501-345)   Phone: (714) 833-4389
Newport Beach, CA 92660   K.H. Preston, Mgr.
Staff: Prof 1. Subjects: Electronics; communications; data systems/
materials; automatic navigation; sensing, monitoring and reporting;
computers; manufacturing research and development. Special Collections:
Transactions and proceedings of electronics and communications conferences
and societies. Holdings: 8200 books; 550 bound periodical volumes; 20 VF
drawers of working papers (last 5 years, earlier ones on microfilm); 10 VF
drawers of engineers' notebooks; 5 VF drawers of procedures. Subscriptions:
300 journals and other serials. Services: Interlibrary loans; center not open to
public. Computerized Information Services: DIALOG, DTIC.

★11516★
ROCKWELL INTERNATIONAL - NORTH AMERICAN AIRCRAFT OPERATIONS
- TECHNICAL INFORMATION CENTER (Sci-Tech)
Box 92098   Phone: (213) 647-2961
Los Angeles, CA 90009   Linda R. Roberts, Supv.
Founded: 1940. Staff: Prof 5; Other 10. Subjects: Aeronautics, materials,
mathematics and computer sciences, electronics and electrical engineering.
Holdings: 11,500 books; 5400 bound periodical volumes; 282,000 technical
reports; microfiche. Subscriptions: 230 journals and other serials. Services:
Interlibrary loans; center not open to public. Automated Operations:
Computerized cataloging. Computerized Information Services: DTIC,
NASA/RECON, DIALOG, SDC, BRS, Ontyme, ESA-QUEST; Rockwell
International Technical Information Processing System (TIPS; internal
database). Networks/Consortia: Member of CLASS. Staff: Robert Panek,
Ref.Libn.; Margaret Menninger, Cat.; Hildy Buis, Acq.Libn.

★11517★
ROCKWELL INTERNATIONAL - ROCKETDYNE DIVISION - TECHNICAL
INFORMATION CENTER (Sci-Tech)
6633 Canoga Ave.   Phone: (818) 710-2575
Canoga Park, CA 91304   Laura J. Rainey, Mgr.
Founded: 1955. Staff: Prof 4; Other 2. Subjects: Aerospace engineering,
laser technology, fluid dynamics, chemistry, materials science. Holdings:
16,250 books; 3000 bound periodical volumes; 2000 reels of microfilm of
periodicals; 75,000 technical reports. Subscriptions: 325 journals and other
serials. Services: Interlibrary loans; copying; SDI; center open to public by
appointment. Automated Operations: Computerized cataloging.
Computerized Information Services: DIALOG, BRS, NASA/RECON, DTIC,
NEXIS; Rockwell International Technical Information Processing System
(TIPS; internal database). Networks/Consortia: Member of CLASS.
Publications: Current Technical Information; demand bibliographies. Special
Catalogs: Catalog of laser technology (book). Staff: Julia Keim, Lit. SearchK.
Scott Peters, Acq.Libn.Marie Sigari, Cat.

★11518★
ROCKWELL INTERNATIONAL - ROCKWELL HANFORD OPERATIONS -
BASALT WASTE ISOLATION PROJECT - LIBRARY (Sci-Tech)
PBB/1100 Area   Phone: (509) 376-6898
Richland, WA 99352   Betty Jeanne King, Anl.Libn.Res.
Staff: Prof 1; Other 1. Subjects: Nuclear waste, geology, hydrology,

geochemistry, high level radioactive waste, rock mechanics. **Holdings:** Figures not available. **Services:** Library open to public with restrictions. **Automated Operations:** Computerized acquisitions and circulation. **Computerized Information Services:** Internal database. **Publications:** Accessions Listing, weekly.

★11519★
ROCKWELL INTERNATIONAL - ROCKWELL HANFORD OPERATIONS - LEGAL LIBRARY (Law)
Federal Bldg., Rm. 146   Phone: (509) 376-6807
Richland, WA 99352   Bonnie Jean Brown, Libn.
Staff: Prof 1. **Subjects:** Law - federal, Washington state. **Holdings:** 8000 books; 8 bound periodical volumes. **Subscriptions:** 62 journals and other serials. **Services:** Library not open to public. **Computerized Information Services:** LEXIS.

★11520★
ROCKWELL INTERNATIONAL - SCIENCE CENTER LIBRARY (Sci-Tech)
1049 Camino Dos Rios
Box 1085   Phone: (805) 498-4545
Thousand Oaks, CA 91360   Helen M. Coogan, Supv., Lib.
Founded: 1962. **Staff:** Prof 1; Other 1. **Subjects:** Electronics, physics and chemistry, fracture and metal physics, structural materials, semiconductor devices, fluid mechanics, physical metallurgy, computer science. **Holdings:** 10,800 books; 6500 bound periodical volumes; 5500 technical reports; 6000 microfiche. **Subscriptions:** 300 journals and other serials. **Services:** Interlibrary loans; copying; SDI; library open to public by appointment. **Automated Operations:** Computerized cataloging. **Computerized Information Services:** DIALOG, NASA/RECON, DTIC; Rockwell International Technical Information Processing System (TIPS; internal database). **Networks/Consortia:** Member of Total Interlibrary Exchange (TIE). **Publications:** Library Announcements - for internal distribution only. **Special Catalogs:** Catalog of technical report holdings of Rockwell International libraries (machine produced microfiche). **Staff:** Florina Carvalho, ILL

★11521★
ROCKWELL INTERNATIONAL - SPACE BUSINESSES - TECHNICAL INFORMATION CENTER (Sci-Tech; Comp Sci)
12214 Lakewood Blvd.   Phone: (213) 922-4648
Downey, CA 90241   Nan H. Paik, Supv.
Founded: 1947. **Staff:** Prof 5; Other 7. **Subjects:** Aerospace technology, information systems, electronics, astronautics, mathematics, engineering, computer sciences. **Holdings:** 48,000 books; 7000 bound periodical volumes; 75,000 technical reports; 500,000 microfiche. **Subscriptions:** 600 journals and other serials. **Services:** Interlibrary loans; copying; SDI and retrospective search; custom bibliography; center open to public by appointment for reference. **Computerized Information Services:** DIALOG, BRS, SDC, NASA/RECON, DTIC; Rockwell International Technical Information Processing System (TIPS; internal database). **Staff:** Theodore Cranford, Lib.Res.Anl.; Laurraine Tutihasi, Lib.Res.Anl.; Charlotte Baughman, Lib.Res.Anl.; Joan Buck, Lib.Res.Anl.

★11522★
ROCKWELL INTERNATIONAL - TECHNICAL INFORMATION CENTER (Sci-Tech)
3370 Miraloma Ave.   Phone: (714) 632-2089
Anaheim, CA 92803   Carol Glover, Mgr.
Founded: 1955. **Staff:** Prof 4; Other 10. **Subjects:** Electronics, chemistry, physics, solid state electronics, microelectronics, inertial navigation, computers, radar, lasers. **Special Collections:** Management Development. **Holdings:** 68,000 books; 5500 bound periodical volumes; 130,000 technical reports; 80,000 technical reports on microfiche. **Subscriptions:** 519 journals and other serials. **Services:** Interlibrary loans; center not open to public. **Computerized Information Services:** DIALOG. **Publications:** Weekly Accession Bulletin. **Formerly:** Its Anaheim Information Center.

★11523★
ROCKWELL INTERNATIONAL - TECHNICAL INFORMATION CENTER (Sci-Tech)
4300 E. Fifth Ave.
Box 1259   Phone: (614) 239-3131
Columbus, OH 43216
Staff: Prof 2; Other 3. **Subjects:** Aircraft, missiles, aeronautical engineering, military hardware, military directives, product descriptions. **Special Collections:** North American Aircraft Division - Columbus and Missile Systems Division technical reports (3800 volumes). **Holdings:** 7000 books; 1800 bound periodical volumes; 100,000 reports (cataloged); 500,000 microfiche. **Subscriptions:** 250 journals and other serials; 5 newspapers. **Services:** Interlibrary loans; center not open to public. **Automated Operations:**

Computerized cataloging. **Computerized Information Services:** Online systems.

★11524★
ROCKWELL INTERNATIONAL - TECHNICAL INFORMATION CENTER (Sci-Tech)
2000 N. Memorial Dr.
Box 51308   Phone: (918) 835-3111
Tulsa, OK 74151   Mary B. Sewell, Adm.
Founded: 1962. **Staff:** Prof 3. **Subjects:** Aerospace; aircraft; engineering - manufacturing, industrial; management. **Holdings:** 1500 books; 128 bound periodical volumes; 300 bibliography reports; 6000 military and federal specifications; 3000 NASA and DOD reports; 5600 industry technical reports. **Services:** Interlibrary loans (limited); copying; center open to public with restrictions. **Computerized Information Services:** NASA/RECON; Rockwell International Technical Information Processing System (TIPS; internal database). **Publications:** Technical Documents - Rockwell Briefings & Reports. **Special Indexes:** Indexes of Engineering Specifications.

ROCKY FLATS PLANT
See: Rockwell International - Energy Systems Group

★11525★
ROCKY HILL HISTORICAL SOCIETY - ACADEMY HALL MUSEUM - LIBRARY (Hist)
785 Old Main St.
Box 185   Phone: (203) 563-8710
Rocky Hill, CT 06067   Mrs. Dudley S. Cooke, Libn.
Staff: 1. **Subjects:** Local history, 19th century general reading matter, antiques and buildings. **Holdings:** 1000 books; 3 boxes of letters and documents; 20 magnetic tapes (some oral history); local news scrapbooks; school texts (18th and 19th century). **Services:** Library open to public by appointment.

★11526★
ROCKY MOUNT HISTORICAL ASSOCIATION - LIBRARY (Hist)
Route 2, Box 70   Phone: (615) 538-7396
Piney Flats, TN 37686   Cindy Penix, Libn.
Founded: 1961. **Staff:** Prof 1. **Subjects:** Local history, Southwest Territory history, genealogy, technology, biography. **Holdings:** 1000 books; 1000 bound periodical volumes; 7 VF drawers of clippings; 2 VF drawers and 2 boxes of manuscripts; photographs. **Subscriptions:** 10 journals and other serials. **Services:** Copying; library open to public for reference use only.

ROCKY MOUNTAIN COLLEGE - UNITED METHODIST CHURCH - YELLOWSTONE ANNUAL CONFERENCE
See: United Methodist Church - Yellowstone Annual Conference

★11527★
ROCKY MOUNTAIN ENERGY - LIBRARY (Energy)
10 Longs Peak Dr.
Box 2000   Phone: (303) 469-8844
Broomfield, CO 80020   Sunny Adair, Libn.
Founded: 1974. **Staff:** Prof 1. **Subjects:** Coal, trona and uranium mining, mineral economics, marketing, geology, engineering. **Special Collections:** Coal Age, volume 1 to present. **Holdings:** 6500 volumes; 32,000 government publications; 300 reports on microfiche; 20 VF drawers of maps, annual reports, and pamphlets; 400 law books. **Subscriptions:** 350 journals and other serials; 50 newspapers. **Services:** Interlibrary loans; copying; SDI; library open to public with restrictions. **Computerized Information Services:** DIALOG, SDC. **Publications:** Library Newsletter, quarterly. **Remarks:** This is a subsidiary of Union Pacific Corporation.

ROCKY MOUNTAIN FOREST & RANGE EXPERIMENT STATION
See: U.S. Forest Service

★11528★
ROCKY MOUNTAIN HOSPITAL - C. LLOYD PETERSON MEMORIAL LIBRARY (Med)
4701 E. Ninth Ave.   Phone: (303) 388-5588
Denver, CO 80220   Patricia Perry, Libn.
Staff: 1. **Subjects:** Medicine. **Special Collections:** Osteopathic texts (20). **Holdings:** 600 books; 250 bound periodical volumes; 500 cassette tapes; 200 serials. **Subscriptions:** 101 journals and other serials. **Services:** Interlibrary loans; copying; library open to public with restrictions. **Networks/Consortia:** Member of Colorado Council of Medical Librarians; Midcontinental Regional Medical Library Program.

★11529★
ROCKY MOUNTAIN JEWISH HISTORICAL SOCIETY - IRA M. BECK MEMORIAL LIBRARY (Rel-Theol)
Center for Judaic Studies
University of Denver   Phone: (303) 753-3178
Denver, CO 80208   Jeanne Abrams, Archv.
Staff: Prof 1. **Subjects:** Judaica. **Holdings:** Figures not available. **Services:** Copying; library open to public. **Automated Operations:** Computerized cataloging and acquisitions. **Publications:** Rocky Mountain Notes, quarterly; Rocky Mountain Chai newsletter, quarterly.

ROCKY MOUNTAIN LABORATORY LIBRARY
See: U.S. Natl. Institutes of Health - Natl. Institute of Allergy & Infectious Diseases

ROCKY MOUNTAIN NATIONAL PARK
See: U.S. Natl. Park Service

★11530★
ROCKY MOUNTAIN NEWS - LIBRARY (Publ)
400 W. Colfax Ave.   Phone: (303) 892-5000
Denver, CO 80204   Paula Shonkwiler, Hd.Libn.
Founded: 1859. **Staff:** Prof 2; Other 6. **Subjects:** Newspaper reference topics. **Special Collections:** Index to historic houses of Denver. **Holdings:** 300 books; 59 cabinets of newspaper clippings; 53 cabinets of pictures; 4 cabinets of microfilm files. **Services:** Library not open to public. **Staff:** Sue Schwellenbach, Asst.Libn.

RODENBERG (Billie Davis) MEMORIAL LIBRARY
See: Temple Beth El - Billie Davis Rodenberg Memorial Library

RODGERS & HAMMERSTEIN ARCHIVES OF RECORDED SOUND
See: New York Public Library - Performing Arts Research Center

★11531★
RODMAN HALL ARTS CENTRE - ART LIBRARY (Art)
109 St. Paul Crescent   Phone: (416) 684-2925
St. Catharines, ON, Canada L2S 1M3   Debra Attenborough, Educ.Off.
Staff: Prof 1. **Subjects:** Art history - Canadian, American, European; general art. **Holdings:** 400 books; 855 bound periodical volumes; 2000 gallery bulletins. **Services:** Copying; library open to public with restrictions. **Publications:** Monthly bulletin.

RODNEY (L.S.) LIBRARY OF RECREATION ADMINISTRATION
See: University of Oregon - Institute of Recreation Research and Service

ROEHL (Winona) LIBRARY
See: First Christian Church - Winona Roehl Library

ROEMER (Ferdinand) GEOLOGICAL LIBRARY
See: Baylor University - Department of Geology - Ferdinand Roemer Geological Library

ROESCH LIBRARY
See: University of Dayton

★11532★
ROGER WILLIAMS GENERAL HOSPITAL - HEALTH SCIENCES LIBRARY (Med)
825 Chalkstone Ave.   Phone: (401) 456-2036
Providence, RI 02908   Hadassah Stein, Libn.
Staff: Prof 1. **Subjects:** Medicine, nursing, allied subjects. **Holdings:** 2200 books; 2800 bound periodical volumes; 600 indexes, clinics. **Subscriptions:** 182 journals and other serials. **Services:** Interlibrary loans; library not open to public. **Computerized Information Services:** NLM. **Networks/Consortia:** Member of Association of Rhode Island Health Sciences Librarians (ARIHSL). **Staff:** Shirley Halzel, Asst.Libn.

★11533★
ROGER WILLIAMS PARK - PARK MUSEUM OF NATURAL HISTORY & PLANETARIUM - MUSEUM LIBRARY/RESOURCE CENTER
Providence, RI 02905
Founded: 1900. **Subjects:** Natural history, astronomy, Indians of North-America. **Holdings:** 2500 books; 6000 glass plate negatives. **Remarks:** Presently inactive.

★11534★
ROGERS CORPORATION - LURIE LIBRARY (Sci-Tech)
                                           Phone: (203) 774-9605
Rogers, CT 06263   Myrna D. Riquier, Corp.Libn.
Staff: Prof 2. **Subjects:** Polymer science, plastics, chemical engineering, electronics, statistics, business management, graphic arts. **Holdings:** 3200 books; 5500 items of technical literature; 30,000 U.S. and foreign patents (chemical and related). **Subscriptions:** 450 journals and other serials; 23 newspapers. **Services:** Interlibrary loans; copying; library open to public with permission of librarian. **Computerized Information Services:** DIALOG, SDC. **Publications:** Poron Insider newsletter, quarterly; Update, quarterly newsletter - both to customers only; Library Bulletin, monthly list of new acquisitions - for internal distribution only. **Staff:** Nini Davis, Info.Res.; Jackie Whitford, Libn.

ROGERS (Edith Nourse) MEMORIAL VETERANS HOSPITAL
See: U.S. Veterans Administration (MA-Bedford) - Edith Nourse Rogers Memorial Veterans Hospital

★11535★
ROGERS ENVIRONMENTAL EDUCATION CENTER - GEORGE W. HOTCHKIN MEMORIAL LIBRARY (Env-Cons)
Box Q   Phone: (607) 674-2861
Sherburne, NY 13460
Founded: 1971. **Subjects:** Natural history, environmental education, conservation, botany, zoology, ornithology. **Special Collections:** Oran B. Stanley Collection (botany); complete bound sets of the New York State Conservationist and National Wildlife. **Holdings:** 1000 books; 90 bound periodical volumes; 200 magazines, bulletins and pamphlets. **Subscriptions:** 15 journals and other serials. **Services:** Library open to students for reference use only.

ROGERS (Fred) ARCHIVES
See: University of Pittsburgh - School of Library & Information Science - Library

ROGERS (Lauren) MUSEUM OF ART
See: Lauren Rogers Museum of Art

★11536★
ROGERS (Millicent) MUSEUM - LIBRARY (Hist; Art)
Box A   Phone: (505) 758-2462
Taos, NM 87571   May Harrover, Libn.
Staff: 1. **Subjects:** Indians of North America, local history, fine arts, museology, anthropology. **Special Collections:** Registry of Hispanic artists in New Mexico (109 artists). **Holdings:** 904 books; 81 subject classification files. **Subscriptions:** 36 journals and other serials. **Services:** Library open to public by appointment - for reference use only.

★11537★
ROGERS & WELLS - LAW LIBRARY (Law)
200 Park Ave.   Phone: (212) 878-8210
New York, NY 10166   Raphael Gonzalez, Libn.
Staff: Prof 2; Other 3. **Subjects:** Law. **Holdings:** 20,000 volumes. **Services:** Interlibrary loans; library not open to public. **Staff:** Brian J. Mulcahy, Ref.Libn.

★11538★
ROGERS & WELLS - LIBRARY (Law)
1737 H St., N.W.   Phone: (202) 331-7760
Washington, DC 20006   Bart Woodke, Libn.
Subjects: Law. **Holdings:** 5700 volumes; 4.5 shelves of U.S. International Trade Commission publications; U.S. Bureau of the Census statistics and Custom Service decisions and rulings on microfiche. **Subscriptions:** 31 journals and other serials; 8 newspapers. **Services:** Interlibrary loans. **Computerized Information Services:** LEXIS, NEXIS.

ROGERS (Will) LIBRARY
See: Will Rogers Library

★11539★
ROHM & HAAS COMPANY - HOME OFFICE LIBRARY (Bus-Fin)
Independence Mall, W.   Phone: (215) 592-3631
Philadelphia, PA 19105   Sandra F. Hostetter, Bus.Libn./Info.Spec.
Founded: 1965. **Staff:** Prof 1; Other 1. **Subjects:** Law, management, finance, marketing, employee relations. **Holdings:** 5500 books and bound periodical volumes; 500 pamphlets; microfilm. **Subscriptions:** 400 journals and other serials. **Services:** Interlibrary loans; library open to public by appointment. **Automated Operations:** Computerized serials and circulation. **Computerized Information Services:** DIALOG, SDC, Dow Jones News/

Retrieval, NEXIS. **Publications:** Library Bulletin, quarterly - for internal distribution only.

★11540★
ROHM & HAAS COMPANY - RESEARCH DIVISION - INFORMATION SERVICES DEPARTMENT (Sci-Tech)
727 Norristown Rd.   Phone: (215) 641-7816
Spring House, PA 19477   Dr. Frederick H. Owens, Mgr., Info.Serv.
Founded: 1936. **Staff:** Prof 9; Other 12. **Subjects:** Agricultural chemistry, coatings, plastics, textiles and fibers, petroleum chemicals. **Holdings:** 56,000 books and bound periodical volumes; 5600 reels of microfilm; 300 VF drawers of pamphlets, government reports, patents and trade literature. **Subscriptions:** 1000 journals and other serials. **Services:** Interlibrary loans; copying; library open to public by appointment. **Automated Operations:** Computerized cataloging and circulation. **Computerized Information Services:** DIALOG, NIH-EPA Chemical Information System, The Source, CAS Online, OCLC, LEXIS, NEXIS, DARC Pluridata System, SDC, BRS, NLM. Performs searches on cost recovery basis. **Networks/Consortia:** Member of PALINET and Union Library Catalogue of Pennsylvania. **Publications:** Monthly library bulletin - for internal distribution only. **Staff:** Ellen C. Dotterrer, Acq; Joanne L. Witiak, Info.Sci.; Margot B. Licitis, Transl.; Dr. Karl F. Ockert, Adm.Asst.; Dominic R. Falgiatore, Info.Sci.; Helen M. Curran, Libn.

★11541★
ROHM & HAAS COMPANY - RESEARCH DIVISION - INFORMATION SERVICES DEPARTMENT - LIBRARY (Sci-Tech)
Box 718   Phone: (215) 785-8055
Bristol, PA 19007   Barbara G. Prewitt, Res.Lib.Mgr.
Staff: Prof 2; Other 5. **Subjects:** Resins, plastics, chemicals. **Holdings:** 23,000 volumes; government reports. **Subscriptions:** 1000 journals and other serials. **Services:** Interlibrary loans; copying; library open to public by appointment. **Automated Operations:** Computerized serials, circulation and ILL. **Computerized Information Services:** DIALOG, SDC, NLM, BRS, The Source, CAS Online, OCLC. **Networks/Consortia:** Member of PALINET & Union Library Catalogue of Pennsylvania; Greater Northeastern Regional Medical Library Program. **Staff:** Helen Welsh, Info.Chem.

★11542★
ROHR INDUSTRIES - CORPORATE LIBRARY (Sci-Tech)
Box 1516   Phone: (619) 691-3010
Chula Vista, CA 92012   James C. Fuscoe, Chf.Libn.
Staff: Prof 1; Other 2. **Subjects:** Metallurgy, aeronautics, fabrication technology. **Special Collections:** Advanced composites. **Holdings:** 5000 books; 24,000 reports. **Subscriptions:** 148 journals and other serials. **Services:** Interlibrary loans; library not open to public. **Computerized Information Services:** DIALOG, DOE/RECON, DTIC. **Publications:** Library Bulletin, quarterly.

ROHRBACH LIBRARY
See: Kutztown University

ROLFING MEMORIAL LIBRARY
See: Trinity Evangelical Divinity School

★11543★
ROLLINS COLLEGE - BEAL-MALTBIE SHELL MUSEUM - LIBRARY (Sci-Tech)
Box 2753
Winter Park, FL 32789   Linda L. Mojer, Cur.
Subjects: Shells. **Holdings:** Figures not available.

★11544★
ROLLOFF (C.A.) FOUR COUNTY LAW LIBRARY (Law)
Chippewa County Courthouse   Phone: (612) 269-7733
Montevideo, MN 56265   C.A. Rolloff, Sec.
Staff: 1. **Subjects:** Law. **Holdings:** 5000 volumes; Briefs from the Minnesota Supreme Court, 1943 to present. **Services:** Interlibrary loans; library open to public.

★11545★
ROLLS-ROYCE INC. - LIBRARY (Sci-Tech)
1895 Phoenix Blvd.   Phone: (404) 996-8400
Atlanta, GA 30349   Karen L. Bell, Info.Off.
Staff: Prof 1; Other 1. **Subjects:** Jet engine technology, thermodynamics, metallurgy, aeronautics, contract management. **Holdings:** 700 books; 2000 government documents. **Subscriptions:** 150 journals and other serials. **Services:** Library not open to public. **Computerized Information Services:** DIALOG, SDC, DMS/ONLINE, ESA-QUEST. **Networks/Consortia:** Member of Georgia Library Information Network (GLIN).

ROMAN CATHOLIC CHURCH - ARCHDIOCESE OR DIOCESE LIBRARIES
See: Names of individual archdioceses or dioceses, e.g. Archdiocese of Philadelphia; Fresno Diocesan Library

ROMAN CATHOLIC SCHOOL BOARD FOR LABRADOR - LABRADOR CITY COLLEGIATE
See: Labrador City Collegiate

ROMANEK LIBRARY
See: North Shore Congregation Israel

★11546★
ROMANIAN LIBRARY (Area-Ethnic)
200 E. 38th St.   Phone: (212) 687-0180
New York, NY 10016   Aurelian Paraipan, Dir.
Founded: 1971. **Staff:** 2. **Subjects:** Romania - literature, history, arts, science, economy. **Special Collections:** Constantin Brancusi (30 volumes); minorities in Romania (50 volumes); Romania's present day domestic policy; Romania's foreign policy (50 volumes). **Holdings:** 15,000 books; 500 bound periodical volumes; 500 phonograph records; 1000 slides; 500 photographs; films. **Subscriptions:** 100 journals and other serials; 10 newspapers. **Services:** Interlibrary loans; library open to public; Romanian language courses are organized free of charge annually. **Publications:** Romanian Library monthly program - free upon request. **Special Indexes:** Bibliographies on Romanian topics. **Remarks:** The Romanian Library is maintained by the Ministry of Foreign Affairs, Central State Library at Bucharest. **Staff:** Elena Paraipan, Exec.Sec.

ROME AIR DEVELOPMENT CENTER
See: U.S. Air Force

★11547★
ROME HISTORICAL SOCIETY - ELAINE & WILLIAM E. SCRIPTURE MEMORIAL LIBRARY (Hist)
200 Church St.   Phone: (315) 336-5870
Rome, NY 13440   Joseph C. Di Giovanni, Adm.
Founded: 1936. **Staff:** Prof 1; Other 3. **Subjects:** Local history. **Holdings:** 3500 books; 500 bound periodical volumes. **Services:** Copying; library open to public. **Publications:** Annals and Recollections, quarterly. **Staff:** Barbara S. De Himer, Registrar/Conservator.

ROMNEY (Miles) MEMORIAL LIBRARY
See: Bitter Root Valley Historical Society - Ravalli County Museum

★11548★
ROOKS, PITTS, FULLAGAR & POUST - LIBRARY (Law)
55 W. Monroe, Suite 1500   Phone: (312) 372-5600
Chicago, IL 60603   Nancy J. Henry, Hd.Libn.
Staff: Prof 1; Other 2. **Subjects:** Law. **Holdings:** 16,000 volumes. **Services:** Interlibrary loans; library open to public by approval of librarian. **Computerized Information Services:** LEXIS, DIALOG. **Networks/Consortia:** Member of ILLINET; Chicago Library System.

ROOSEVELT (Franklin D.) LIBRARY
See: U.S. Presidential Libraries - Franklin D. Roosevelt Library

★11549★
ROOSEVELT HOSPITAL - HEALTH SCIENCE LIBRARY (Med)
Box 151   Phone: (201) 321-6833
Metuchen, NJ 08840   Karen Rubin, Libn.
Staff: 1. **Subjects:** Medicine, nursing. **Holdings:** 800 books. **Subscriptions:** 60 journals and other serials. **Services:** Library open to public for reference use only; borrowing privileges reserved for hospital personnel only.

★11550★
ROOSEVELT HOSPITAL - MEDICAL LIBRARY (Med)
428 W. 59th St.   Phone: (212) 554-6872
New York, NY 10019   Winifred Lieber, Libn.
Founded: 1955. **Staff:** Prof 1; Other 1. **Subjects:** Medicine, surgery, gerontology, geriatrics, hospital administration, pediatrics, anesthesia. **Holdings:** 25,000 books and bound periodical volumes. **Subscriptions:** 530 journals and other serials. **Services:** Interlibrary loans; copying; library open to public for reference use only by appointment.

ROOSEVELT (Theodore) NATL. PARK
See: U.S. Natl. Park Service - Theodore Roosevelt Natl. Park

★11551★
ROOSEVELT UNIVERSITY - ARCHIVES (Hist)
430 S. Michigan Ave.   Phone: (312) 341-3643
Chicago, IL 60605   Wendy Moorhead, Ref.Libn.
Staff: Prof 1. **Subjects:** University and Chicago history. **Special Collections:** Auditorium Theater records and broadsides (30 boxes; 30 volumes; 80 broadsides). **Holdings:** 30 books; 100 boxes of university records. **Services:** Interlibrary loans; copying; archives open to public.

★11552★
ROOSEVELT UNIVERSITY - MUSIC LIBRARY (Mus)
430 S. Michigan Ave.   Phone: (312) 341-3651
Chicago, IL 60605   Donald Draganski, Libn.
Founded: 1945. **Staff:** Prof 1; Other 3. **Subjects:** Music, music education. **Holdings:** 30,000 volumes; 10,000 phonograph records; 100 reels of microfilm; 200 dissertations; 400 magnetic tapes. **Subscriptions:** 105 journals and other serials. **Services:** Interlibrary loans; copying; library open to public for reference use only. **Computerized Information Services:** OCLC. **Networks/Consortia:** Member of ILLINET. **Remarks:** The Chicago Musical College is affiliated with Roosevelt University.

★11553★
ROOSEVELT UNIVERSITY - ORAL HISTORY PROJECT IN LABOR HISTORY (Hist)
430 S. Michigan Ave.   Phone: (219) 931-9791
Chicago, IL 60605   Elizabeth Balanoff, Dir.
Subjects: Oral histories in labor history. **Holdings:** 150 hours of taped interviews. **Services:** Copying. **Remarks:** The oral history transcripts are held in the Roosevelt University library where they may be read but not checked out. People who desire to read a transcript for scholarly research but are unable to come to Roosevelt University may order the transcript they need through their own university library. Orders should be sent to Director of Oral History Project.

ROOSEVELT-VANDERBILT NATL. HISTORIC SITES
See: U.S. Natl. Park Service

ROPER CENTER
See: University of Connecticut

ROPER CENTER ARCHIVES
See: Yale University - Social Science Library

★11554★
ROPES & GRAY - CENTRAL LIBRARY (Law)
225 Franklin St.   Phone: (617) 423-6100
Boston, MA 02110   Cornelia Trubey, Libn.
Staff: Prof 2; Other 3. **Subjects:** Law. **Holdings:** 21,000 books; 1000 bound periodical volumes. **Subscriptions:** 500 journals and other serials; 10 newspapers. **Services:** Interlibrary loans; library not open to public. **Computerized Information Services:** LEXIS, NEXIS, DIALOG. **Staff:** Catherine FitzGerald, Asst.Libn.

RORER (William H.), INC.
See: William H. Rorer, Inc.

ROSARY COLLEGE LIBRARY - DOMINICAN EDUCATION CENTER
See: Dominican Education Center

ROSE (Billy) THEATRE COLLECTION
See: New York Public Library - Performing Arts Research Center - Billy Rose Theatre Collection

ROSE (David J.) LIBRARY
See: Massachusetts Institute of Technology - Plasma Fusion Center - David J. Rose Library

★11555★
ROSE-HULMAN INSTITUTE OF TECHNOLOGY - JOHN A. LOGAN LIBRARY (Sci-Tech)
5500 E. Wabash Ave.   Phone: (812) 877-1511
Terre Haute, IN 47803   Herman Cole, Jr., Dir.
Founded: 1874. **Staff:** Prof 1; Other 2. **Subjects:** Engineering and science. **Holdings:** 43,000 books; 16,000 bound periodical volumes. **Subscriptions:** 403 journals and other serials; 10 newspapers. **Services:** Interlibrary loans; copying; library open to public. **Computerized Information Services:** OCLC. **Networks/Consortia:** Member of INCOLSA.

★11556★
ROSE MEDICAL CENTER - LIBRARY (Med)
4567 E. 9th Ave.   Phone: (303) 320-2160
Denver, CO 80220   Nancy Simon, Med.Libn.
Founded: 1949. **Staff:** Prof 1. **Subjects:** Medicine. **Holdings:** 795 books; 2989 bound periodical volumes; 257 Audio-Digest tapes. **Subscriptions:** 167 journals and other serials. **Services:** Interlibrary loans; library not open to public. **Computerized Information Services:** MEDLARS, DIALOG. **Networks/Consortia:** Member of Colorado Council of Medical Librarians; Denver Area Health Sciences Library Consortium. **Publications:** Annual report; procedure manual.

ROSE (Sidney G.) MEMORIAL LIBRARY
See: K.K. Bene Israel/Rockdale Temple - Sidney G. Rose Memorial Library

★11557★
ROSELAND COMMUNITY HOSPITAL - HEALTH SCIENCE LIBRARY (Med)
45 W. 111th St.   Phone: (312) 995-3191
Chicago, IL 60628   Mary T. Hanlon, Libn.
Staff: Prof 1. **Subjects:** Medicine and nursing. **Holdings:** 950 books; 2 VF drawers of pamphlets. **Subscriptions:** 37 journals and other serials. **Services:** Interlibrary loans; copying. **Networks/Consortia:** Member of Greater Midwest Regional Medical Library Network (Region 3); Chicago and South Consortium; ILLINET.

ROSEMEAD GRADUATE SCHOOL OF PROFESSIONAL PSYCHOLOGY - LIBRARY
See: Biola University - Library

★11558★
ROSEMONT COLLEGE - GERTRUDE KISTLER MEMORIAL LIBRARY - SPECIAL COLLECTIONS (Educ; Hist)
                                        Phone: (215) 527-0200
Rosemont, PA 19010   Sr. M. Dennis Lynch, S.H.C.J., Lib.Dir.
Founded: 1922. **Staff:** Prof 3; Other 5. **Special Collections:** Early Pennsylvania history; Education Resource Center. **Services:** Interlibrary loans; copying (limited); library open to persons with academic credentials. **Automated Operations:** Computerized cataloging and ILL. **Computerized Information Services:** DIALOG, SDC, OCLC, BRS. Performs searches on cost recovery basis. Contact Person: Deborah G. Holl. **Networks/Consortia:** Member of Tri-State College Library Cooperative (TCLC); PALINET and Union Library Catalogue of Pennsylvania; Interlibrary Delivery Service of Pennsylvania. **Staff:** April Nelson, Tech.Proc.Serv.Libn.; Deborah G. Holl, Rd.Serv.Libn.Anita S. Bolton, Coord., Circ. & ILL.

★11559★
ROSENBACH MUSEUM & LIBRARY (Hist)
2010 De Lancey Pl.   Phone: (215) 732-1600
Philadelphia, PA 19103   Ellen S. Dunlap, Dir.
Founded: 1954. **Staff:** Prof 8; Other 8. **Subjects:** Americana, English literature, incunabula, Judaica, book illustration. **Special Collections:** Marianne Moore Archive; Maurice Sendak original drawings; Latin-American historical manuscripts. **Holdings:** 30,000 books; 130,000 manuscripts. **Subscriptions:** 35 journals and other serials. **Services:** Interlibrary loans; copying; open for tours and exhibitions; library open to scholars by appointment. **Publications:** Recent Acquisitions, irregular; exhibition catalogs on aspects of collection; fine press and facsimile editions of important rare books and manuscripts.

★11560★
ROSENBERG CAPITAL MANAGEMENT - LIBRARY (Bus-Fin)
Four Embarcadero Center, Suite 2900   Phone: (415) 954-5474
San Francisco, CA 94111   Maggie O'Brien, Res.Libn.
Founded: 1976. **Staff:** Prof 1; Other 2. **Subjects:** Investment. **Holdings:** 50 books; 6000 company reports; 5000 broker reports; 20,000 company reports on microfiche. **Subscriptions:** 250 journals and other serials. **Services:** Interlibrary loans; library not open to public. **Computerized Information Services:** DIALOG, Dow Jones News/Retrieval.

★11561★
ROSENBERG LIBRARY - GALVESTON AND TEXAS HISTORY CENTER (Hist)
2310 Sealy Ave.   Phone: (409) 763-8854
Galveston, TX 77550   Jane A. Kenamore, Archv.
Staff: Prof 2; Other 1. **Subjects:** State and local history, Civil War, historic preservation. **Holdings:** 8000 books; 1000 bound periodical volumes; 1400 linear feet of manuscripts; 15,000 photographs; 750 maps; microfilm; architectural drawings; newspapers; vertical files. **Subscriptions:** 75 journals and other serials. **Services:** Copying; center open to public. **Publications:** Manuscript Sources in the Rosenberg Library: A Selective Guide. **Special Catalogs:** Book and manuscript catalogs. **Special Indexes:** News article index;

biographical index; map index; photograph subject index; lists of newspaper holdings; architectural and engineering drawings and films. **Formerly:** Its Archives Department. **Staff:** Uli Haller, Asst.Archv.

★11562★
ROSENBERG (Paul) ASSOCIATES - LIBRARY (Sci-Tech)
330 Fifth Ave.   Phone: (914) 738-2266
Pelham, NY 10803   M. Hill, Libn.
Founded: 1945. **Staff:** Prof 1; Other 1. **Subjects:** Applied physics, engineering, aerospace, photogrammetry, energy, navigation. **Holdings:** 1000 books; 800 bound periodical volumes; 2000 reports and reprints. **Subscriptions:** 40 journals and other serials. **Services:** Library not open to public.

ROSENBLOOM (Sol) LIBRARY
See: Hebrew Institute of Pittsburgh - Sol Rosenbloom Library

ROSENBLUM (Blanche and Ira) MEMORIAL LIBRARY
See: Beth Shalom Congregation - Blanche and Ira Rosenblum Memorial Library

★11563★
ROSENMAN, COLIN, FREUND, LEWIS & COHEN - LAW LIBRARY (Law)
575 Madison Ave.   Phone: (212) 940-8598
New York, NY 10022   Denise Hasil, Hd.Libn.
Staff: Prof 4; Other 7. **Subjects:** Law. **Holdings:** 25,000 books and bound periodical volumes; New York Law Journal, 1964 to present (microfilm); microforms. **Subscriptions:** 400 journals and other serials; 8 newspapers. **Services:** Interlibrary loans; library open to clients and library community by appointment. **Computerized Information Services:** LEXIS, NEXIS, DIALOG. **Staff:** Sheila Parker, Asst.Libn.; Elise Lilly, Tech.Serv.Libn.

★11564★
ROSENN, JENKINS & GREENWALD, ATTORNEYS AT LAW - LIBRARY (Law)
15 S. Franklin St.   Phone: (717) 826-5663
Wilkes-Barre, PA 18711   Sarah P. Carr, Libn.
Staff: Prof 1. **Subjects:** State and federal law. **Holdings:** 8000 books; 200 bound periodical volumes. **Subscriptions:** 350 journals and other serials. **Services:** Interlibrary loans; library not open to public. **Computerized Information Services:** LEXIS.

ROSENSTIEL (Dorothy & Lewis) SCHOOL OF MARINE & ATMOSPHERIC SCIENCES
See: University of Miami - Dorothy & Lewis Rosenstiel School of Marine & Atmospheric Sciences

ROSENTHAL (Samuel) MEMORIAL LIBRARY
See: St. Joseph's Hospital - Samuel Rosenthal Memorial Library

ROSENZWEIG HEALTH SCIENCES LIBRARY
See: St. Luke's Medical Center

★11565★
ROSEVILLE EARLY CHILDHOOD/FAMILY PROGRAMS - PLAY 'N' LEARN LIBRARY (Educ)
Falcon Heights Ctr.
1393 Garden Ave.   Phone: (612) 633-8150
Falcon Heights, MN 55113   Janet Robb, Lib.Mtls.Coord.
Staff: Prof 1. **Subjects:** Educational toys, children's literature, and activity kits for children up to 5 years of age; parenting. **Holdings:** 2300 books; 900 toys; 75 folders of clippings and documents. **Services:** Library open to public for a fee.

★11566★
ROSEWOOD CENTER - MIRIAM LODGE PROFESSIONAL LIBRARY (Med)
                                                    Phone: (301) 363-0300
Owings Mills, MD 21117   June M. Boardman, Supv., Lib./Files
Founded: 1955. **Staff:** Prof 1. **Subjects:** Mental retardation, special education, social work, learning disorders, pediatrics, psychology. **Holdings:** 2500 books; 847 bound periodical volumes; 6 VF drawers of pamphlets; 1 VF drawer of staff papers; 27 manuscripts. **Subscriptions:** 51 journals and other serials. **Services:** Interlibrary loans; copying; library open to public. **Networks/Consortia:** Member of Maryland Association of Health Science Librarians.

★11567★
ROSICRUCIAN FELLOWSHIP - LIBRARY (Rel-Theol)
2220 Mission Ave.   Phone: (619) 757-6601
Oceanside, CA 92054   N.D. Willoughby, Libn.
Staff: 1. **Subjects:** Metaphysics, philosophy, related disciplines, astrology, psychology, health and healing. **Holdings:** 1500 books. **Services:** Library open to members and friends for reference use only.

★11568★
ROSICRUCIAN FRATERNITY - LIBRARY (Rel-Theol)
Beverly Hall
Box 220   Phone: (215) 536-5168
Quakertown, PA 18951   Gerald E. Poesnecker, Pres.
Subjects: Occultism, religion, philosophy. **Holdings:** Figures not available. **Services:** Library not open to public. **Remarks:** Library serves as the archive for the fraternity and as study reference center for students enrolled in the fraternity.

★11569★
ROSICRUCIAN ORDER, AMORC - ROSICRUCIAN RESEARCH LIBRARY (Rel-Theol)
Rosicrucian Park
Park & Naglee Aves.   Phone: (408) 287-9171
San Jose, CA 95191   Clara Campbell, Libn.
Founded: 1939. **Staff:** Prof 1; Other 1. **Subjects:** Egyptology, Rosicrucianism, parapsychology, mysticism, Baconiana. **Holdings:** 13,000 books; 260 bound periodical volumes; 6 VF drawers of pamphlets and manuscripts. **Subscriptions:** 25 journals and other serials. **Services:** Library not open to public. **Publications:** Rosicrucian Digest, monthly - to members and by subscription. **Special Indexes:** Rosicrucian Digest index; Rosicrucian Forum index (card); Index to Rosicrucian books (book); Rosicrucian Lessons (book).

★11570★
ROSS & HARDIES - LAW LIBRARY (Law)
150 N. Michigan Ave., Suite 2500   Phone: (312) 558-1000
Chicago, IL 60601   Janet Collins, Libn.
Founded: 1902. **Staff:** Prof 1; Other 2. **Subjects:** Law, taxation, public utilities, antitrust law, land use and zoning, probate. **Holdings:** 26,196 volumes. **Subscriptions:** 52 journals and other serials. **Services:** Copying; library open to qualified persons.

ROSS HOUSE LIBRARY
See: Audrain County Historical Society

ROSS (Howard) LIBRARY OF MANAGEMENT
See: Mc Gill University - Howard Ross Library of Management

★11571★
ROSS LABORATORIES - LIBRARY (Med)
625 Cleveland Ave.   Phone: (614) 227-3503
Columbus, OH 43216   Linda Mitro Hopkins, Mgr.
Staff: Prof 2; Other 2. **Subjects:** Nutrition, food technology, business, organic analytical chemistry. **Holdings:** 3500 books; 6000 bound periodical volumes; 30 VF drawers of technical information files; 3 VF drawers of patents. **Subscriptions:** 550 journals and other serials. **Services:** Interlibrary loans; copying; SDI; library open to public with restrictions. **Automated Operations:** Computerized cataloging and serials. **Computerized Information Services:** DIALOG, OCLC, MEDLINE. **Networks/Consortia:** Member of OHIONET. **Publications:** Internal newsletter and journal holdings list. **Special Indexes:** Computer Listing - Technical Information Retrieval System Keyword, Title and Project Dictionary.

★11572★
ROSS ROY, INC. - RESEARCH LIBRARY (Bus-Fin)
2751 E. Jefferson Ave.   Phone: (313) 568-6117
Detroit, MI 48207   Eloise Lewis, Libn.
Founded: 1920. **Staff:** 2. **Subjects:** Marketing, sales promotion, automobile data, statistics. **Holdings:** 1750 volumes; 3303 slide films and records; 739 film cassettes; VF drawers of reference data and client information files. **Subscriptions:** 275 journals and other serials; 6 newspapers. **Services:** Interlibrary loans; copying; library open to public with permission of librarian. **Special Indexes:** 5-card cross index for slide film and cassettes. **Staff:** Ann Delargy, Asst.Libn.

★11573★
ROSSLAND HISTORICAL MUSEUM ASSOCIATION - ARCHIVES (Hist)
Box 26   Phone: (604) 362-7722
Rossland, BC, Canada V0G 1Y0   Joyce Tadevic, Archv.
Founded: 1955. **Staff:** 1. **Subjects:** Rossland history including mining, biography, business, entertainment, sports. **Holdings:** 400 books; 50 bound periodical volumes; 50 items of city records; 48 drawers of indexed documents, clippings, reports, letters; 2700 photographs of Rossland area. **Services:** Copying (limited); archives open to public for reference use only.

ROSTAD LIBRARY
See: Evangelical School of Theology

★11574★
ROSWELL MUSEUM AND ART CENTER - ART LIBRARY (Art)
100 W. 11th St.   Phone: (505) 622-4700
Roswell, NM 88201   Wendell Ott, Dir.
Founded: 1937. **Subjects:** Fine arts, rocketry, archeology, architecture. **Special Collections:** American Indian and Spanish colonial art. **Holdings:** 2000 books; 3000 bound periodical volumes; 3000 color slides. **Subscriptions:** 100 journals and other serials. **Services:** Library open to public for reference use only.

★11575★
ROSWELL PARK MEMORIAL INSTITUTE - LIBRARY AND INFORMATION MANAGEMENT SERVICES (Med)
666 Elm St.   Phone: (716) 845-5966
Buffalo, NY 14263   Ann P. Hutchinson, Lib.Dir.
Founded: 1898. **Staff:** Prof 6; Other 10. **Subjects:** Cancer and allied diseases. **Holdings:** 50,000 books and bound periodical volumes; 400 AV items. **Subscriptions:** 1200 journals and other serials. **Services:** Interlibrary loans; copying; SDI; library open to public. **Automated Operations:** Computerized cataloging. **Computerized Information Services:** DIALOG, BRS, OCLC, MEDLINE. **Networks/Consortia:** Member of Western New York Library Resources Council (WNYLRC); Medical Library Center of New York (MLCNY). **Publications:** Library Bulletin, quarterly. **Remarks:** This institution is operated by the New York State Department of Health. **Staff:** Marguerite S. Feldman, Ser. & Circ.; Gail Franke, ILL & Ref.Libn.; Suzanne Zajac, Ref.Libn.; Gayle Ablove, Cat.; Richard Hayden, Clinical Libn.

ROTCH LIBRARY OF ARCHITECTURE AND PLANNING
See: Massachusetts Institute of Technology

ROTCH LIBRARY VISUAL COLLECTIONS
See: Massachusetts Institute of Technology

ROTHMANS OF PALL MALL CANADA, LTD. - CRAVEN FOUNDATION
See: Craven Foundation

ROTHSCHILD LIBRARY
See: Park Avenue Synagogue

ROTHSCHILD MEDICAL LIBRARY
See: Jewish Hospital at Washington University Medical Center

★11576★
ROUNCE AND COFFIN CLUB, LOS ANGELES - LIBRARY (Hum)
Occidental College Library
1600 Campus Rd.   Phone: (213) 259-2852
Los Angeles, CA 90041   Michael C. Sutherland, Spec.Coll.Libn.
Staff: Prof 1. **Subjects:** Western printing, 1938 to present. **Holdings:** 1400 books. **Special Catalogs:** Western Books Catalog, annual.

★11577★
ROWAN MEMORIAL HOSPITAL - MC KENZIE MEMORIAL LIBRARY (Med)
612 Mocksville Ave.   Phone: (704) 636-3311
Salisbury, NC 28144   Mary J. Peck, AHEC Lib.Dir.
Staff: Prof 2; Other 3. **Subjects:** Medicine, nursing and allied health sciences. **Holdings:** Figures not available. **Subscriptions:** 128 journals and other serials. **Services:** Interlibrary loans; copying; SDI; library open to public for reference use only. **Automated Operations:** Computerized cataloging. **Computerized Information Services:** BRS, MEDLARS. **Networks/Consortia:** Member of Northwest AHEC Library Information Network. **Staff:** Frances Fife, AHEC Lib.Asst.Dir.

★11578★
ROWAN PUBLIC LIBRARY - EDITH M. CLARK HISTORY ROOM (Hist)
201 W. Fisher St.
Box 4039   Phone: (704) 633-5578
Salisbury, NC 28144
Staff: Prof 1; Other 1. **Subjects:** Local history and genealogy, North Carolina history, Virginia history and genealogy. **Special Collections:** McCubbins and Smith Collections (court records, wills, deeds, Bible records, correspondence); Archibald Henderson Collection (historical materials of North Carolina and Kentucky). **Holdings:** 4700 books; 226 bound periodical volumes; 920 reels of microfilm; 100 microfiche; 25 VF drawers of personal papers; 100 maps. **Subscriptions:** 45 journals and other serials. **Services:** Copying; room open to public. **Staff:** Shirley W. Hoffman, Hist./Genealogy; Beth Young, Hist./Genealogy.

ROWE MEMORIAL LIBRARY
See: Southeastern Bible College

ROWND HISTORICAL LIBRARY
See: Cedar Falls Historical Society

ROWNTREE (Gradie R.) MEDICAL LIBRARY
See: Humana Hospital University - Gradie R. Rowntree Medical Library

★11579★
ROXBOROUGH MEMORIAL HOSPITAL - SCHOOL OF NURSING AND MEDICAL STAFF LIBRARY (Med)
5800 Ridge Ave.   Phone: (215) 483-9900
Philadelphia, PA 19128   Linda C. Stanley, Libn.
Staff: Prof 1; Other 1. **Subjects:** Nursing, medicine, psychology, sociology, science. **Holdings:** 3000 books; 1300 bound periodical volumes; 4 VF drawers of pamphlets; 3 VF drawers of National League for Nursing pamphlets; 300 pieces of AV material. **Subscriptions:** 75 journals and other serials. **Services:** Interlibrary loans; copying; library open to public for reference use only. **Networks/Consortia:** Member of Greater Northeastern Regional Medical Library Program; Delaware Valley Information Consortium (DEVIC). **Special Indexes:** Classified list of new acquisitions, bimonthly - for internal distribution only.

★11580★
ROYAL ALEXANDRA HOSPITAL - MEDICAL LIBRARY (Med)
10240 Kingsway Ave.   Phone: (403) 474-3431
Edmonton, AB, Canada T5H 3V9   Deana Dryden, Libn.
Founded: 1963. **Staff:** Prof 1; Other 1. **Subjects:** Medicine. **Holdings:** 1200 books; 11 microfiche programs. **Subscriptions:** 150 journals and other serials. **Services:** Interlibrary loans; copying; library open to hospital personnel. **Computerized Information Services:** MEDLINE.

★11581★
ROYAL ALEXANDRA HOSPITAL - SCHOOL OF NURSING LIBRARY (Med)
10240 Kingsway Ave.   Phone: (403) 474-3431
Edmonton, AB, Canada T5H 3V9   E. Pass, Libn.
Founded: 1960. **Staff:** Prof 1; Other 1. **Subjects:** Nursing, medicine, social and behavioral sciences. **Holdings:** 4000 books; 230 bound periodical volumes; 13 drawers of clippings, reports, pamphlets. **Subscriptions:** 41 journals and other serials. **Services:** Interlibrary loans; copying; library open to nursing students, faculty and hospital personnel.

★11582★
ROYAL ASTRONOMICAL SOCIETY OF CANADA - NATIONAL LIBRARY (Sci-Tech)
136 Dupont St.   Phone: (416) 924-7973
Toronto, ON, Canada M5R 1V2   Phil Mozel, Libn.
Subjects: Astronomy and allied sciences. **Holdings:** 2000 books and bound periodical volumes; 600 35mm slides; 11 16mm films. **Subscriptions:** 50 journals and other serials. **Services:** Library open to public.

★11583★
ROYAL BANK OF CANADA - INFORMATION RESOURCES (Bus-Fin)
Royal Bank Plaza, 4th Fl.   Phone: (416) 865-2780
Toronto, ON, Canada M5H 2J5   Jane Dysart, Chf.Libn.
Founded: 1972. **Staff:** Prof 3; Other 3. **Subjects:** Banking, finance, Canadian industry, business, world economic conditions, economics, management. **Holdings:** 9500 books; 250 subject files; 200 association files; 200 country files; 200 industry files; 4 drawers of microfiche of financial statements of Canadian companies. **Subscriptions:** 1000 journals and other serials; 25 newspapers. **Services:** Interlibrary loans; library not open to public. **Automated Operations:** Computerized serials. **Computerized Information Services:** DIALOG, TEXTLINE, Info Globe, BRS, SDC, Dow Jones News/

Retrieval, I.P. Sharp Associates Limited, Canada Systems Group INSIGHT, Questel, QL Systems, InnerLine, NewsNet, Inc. **Publications:** On The Shelf - current awareness bulletin, monthly - for internal distribution only. **Staff:** Deirdre Grimes, Libn.; Rebecca Jones, Libn.

★11584★
ROYAL BANK OF CANADA - INFORMATION RESOURCES (Bus-Fin)
P.O. Box 6001   Phone: (514) 874-2452
Montreal, PQ, Canada H3C 3A9   Anthea Downing, Chf.Libn.
Founded: 1913. **Staff:** Prof 3; Other 6. **Subjects:** Banks and banking; finance and international finance; economics and business; Canadian and world economic conditions; management. **Holdings:** 55,000 books and bound periodical volumes; pamphlets; speeches; archives. **Subscriptions:** 1200 journals and other serials; 50 newspapers. **Services:** Interlibrary loans; copying; library open to public. **Automated Operations:** Computerized serials and circulation. **Computerized Information Services:** SDC, DIALOG, Info Globe, Dow Jones News/Retrieval, QL Systems. **Publications:** New Books, monthly; Notes of the Week. **Staff:** Adelaide Richter, Sr.Libn.; John O'Shaughnessy, Libn.

★11585★
ROYAL BANK OF CANADA - LIBRARY (Energy; Bus-Fin)
335 8th Ave., S.W.
P.O. Box 2534   Phone: (403) 268-3722
Calgary, AB, Canada T2P 2N5   Ms. Myrla J. Koenderink, Libn.
Staff: Prof 2. **Subjects:** Energy economics, banking. **Holdings:** 2500 books. **Subscriptions:** 600 journals and other serials; 10 newspapers. **Services:** Interlibrary loans; copying; library open to public with restrictions. **Automated Operations:** Computerized cataloging. **Computerized Information Services:** Online systems. **Staff:** E. Jane Howe, Asst.Libn.

★11586★
ROYAL BANK OF CANADA - LIBRARY
1055 W. Georgia St.
P.O. Box 11141
Vancouver, BC, Canada V6E 3S5
Defunct

★11587★
ROYAL BANK OF CANADA - TAXATION LIBRARY/INTERNATIONAL (Bus-Fin)
Royal Bank Plaza
Toronto, ON, Canada M5J 2J5   Franki Elliott, Tax Libn.
Founded: 1976. **Staff:** Prof 1; Other 1. **Subjects:** International taxation. **Holdings:** 700 books; 1500 periodicals and journals; government forms. **Subscriptions:** 50 journals and other serials. **Services:** Interlibrary loans; library not open to public. **Formerly:** Located in Montreal, PQ.

★11588★
ROYAL BOTANICAL GARDENS - LIBRARY (Sci-Tech)
Box 399   Phone: (416) 527-1158
Hamilton, ON, Canada L8N 3H8   Ina Vrugtman, Botanical Libn.
Founded: 1947. **Staff:** Prof 1; Other 1. **Subjects:** Botany, ornamental horticulture, natural history and conservation, ornithology. **Special Collections:** Center for Canadian Historical Horticulture Studies (CCHHS). **Holdings:** 5500 books; 1500 bound periodical volumes; 2500 pamphlets and reprints; 6000 nursery and seed trade catalogs. **Subscriptions:** 250 journals and other serials. **Services:** Copying; library open to public; borrowing limited to RBG staff and members. **Special Indexes:** Gray Herbarium card index.

★11589★
ROYAL CANADIAN ARTILLERY MUSEUM - LIBRARY (Mil)
Canadian Forces Base   Phone: (204) 765-2282
Shilo, MB, Canada R0K 2A0   CWO Lunan, Chf.Libn.
Founded: 1956. **Staff:** 1. **Subjects:** Military history. **Special Collections:** War diaries. **Holdings:** 2000 books; maps; pamphlets. **Services:** Copying; library open to public by appointment. **Remarks:** Library maintained by Royal Canadian Artillery. **Also Known As:** RCA Museum.

★11590★
ROYAL CANADIAN MILITARY INSTITUTE - LIBRARY (Mil)
426 University Ave.   Phone: (416) 597-0286
Toronto, ON, Canada M5G 1S9   Lt.Col. W.G. Heard, Cur.
Founded: 1890. **Staff:** Prof 2. **Subjects:** Military science; military, naval and air force history; army, navy and air force technical topics; Canadiana. **Special Collections:** Denison Collection (500 volumes); Frost Collection (200 volumes). **Holdings:** 25,000 books; 2000 bound periodical volumes; 1000 antique volumes; 2500 photographs (World Wars I and II); 500 glass film plates (World War I); 1000 prints (uniforms, equipment). **Subscriptions:** 40

journals and other serials; 6 newspapers. **Services:** Interlibrary loans; library open to public for research on premises only. **Staff:** Capt. N.F. Mallon, Hon.Libn.; Laura C. Body, Libn.

★11591★
ROYAL CANADIAN MOUNTED POLICE - CENTENNIAL MUSEUM LIBRARY (Mil; Hist)
P.O. Box 6500   Phone: (306) 359-5837
Regina, SK, Canada S4P 3J7   Malcolm J.H. Wake, Musm.Dir.
Founded: 1973. **Staff:** 4. **Subjects:** Royal Canadian Mounted Police, military, Saskatchewan and Canadian history. **Special Collections:** History of the Royal Canadian Mounted Police (500 volumes). **Holdings:** 800 books; 200 bound periodical volumes; historical photographs; 8 VF drawers of R.C.M.P. archival material. **Subscriptions:** 10 journals and other serials. **Services:** Copying; library open to public by appointment.

★11592★
ROYAL CANADIAN MOUNTED POLICE - LAW ENFORCEMENT REFERENCE CENTRE (Law)
1200 Alta Vista Dr.   Phone: (613) 993-3225
Ottawa, ON, Canada K1A 0R2   Mrs. G. Wyatt, Mgr.
Founded: 1936. **Staff:** Prof 2; Other 16. **Subjects:** Police science, management, criminology. **Holdings:** 58,000 books; 1200 essays; 40,000 microforms. **Subscriptions:** 3400 journals and other serials; 5 newspapers. **Services:** Interlibrary loans; copying; SDI (internal); center open to public with permission of RCMP Commissioner. **Computerized Information Services:** QL Systems. **Publications:** Bibliographies, irregular - available upon request to libraries. **Also Known As:** Gendarmerie Royale du Canada. **Staff:** Mrs. F. Berube, Ref.Techn.; Mark Fortune, Cat.Techn.; Mrs. S. Wicks, Cat.Techn.

★11593★
ROYAL CANADIAN ORDNANCE CORPS MUSEUM - LIBRARY (Mil)
6560 Hochelaga St.
P.O. Box 6109   Phone: (514) 255-8811
Montreal, PQ, Canada H3C 3H7   Leo Lavigne, Cur.
Founded: 1962. **Staff:** 2. **Subjects:** Military history and equipment, weapons, ammunition and explosives. **Holdings:** 2000 volumes. **Services:** Library open to public by appointment. **Staff:** M. Brown, Asst.Cur.

★11594★
ROYAL COLUMBIAN HOSPITAL - LIBRARY (Med)
330 E. Columbia St.   Phone: (604) 520-4255
New Westminster, BC, Canada V3L 3W7   Ms. S. Abzinger, Libn.
Founded: 1978. **Staff:** 2. **Subjects:** Medicine, allied health sciences. **Holdings:** 900 books; 2200 bound periodical volumes. **Subscriptions:** 125 journals and other serials. **Services:** Interlibrary loans; library not open to public. **Computerized Information Services:** MEDLARS.

★11595★
ROYAL COMMISSION ON THE NORTHERN ENVIRONMENT - LIBRARY
215 Red River Rd., Suite 201
Thunder Bay, ON, Canada P7B 1A5
Defunct. Holdings donated to Lakehead University.

ROYAL JUBILEE HOSPITAL
See: Victoria Medical Society/Royal Jubilee Hospital

★11596★
ROYAL MILITARY COLLEGE OF CANADA - MASSEY LIBRARY & SCIENCE/ENGINEERING LIBRARY (Mil)
                                       Phone: (613) 545-7330
Kingston, ON, Canada K7L 2W3   Keith Crouch, Chf.Libn.
Staff: Prof 6. **Subjects:** Engineering; military history, art and science. **Special Collections:** Military Studies (23,947 volumes). **Holdings:** 170,699 volumes; 32,328 documents; 14,962 technical reports; 9602 microforms; 2353 artifacts, manuscripts, prints and photographs. **Subscriptions:** 998 journals; 14 newspapers. **Services:** Interlibrary loans; copying; library open to public by permission. **Staff:** Mr. D. Kissoore, Hd., Tech.Serv. & Sys; Maj. A.S.J. Bake, Hd., Arts & Spec.Coll.Div; Mrs. N. Turkington, Hd., Sci./Engr.Div.

ROYAL MILITARY COLLEGE, ST. JEAN
See: College Militaire Royal de St-Jean

★11597★
ROYAL ONTARIO MUSEUM - CANADIANA GALLERY LIBRARY (Art; Hist)†
14 Queen's Park Crescent, W.   Phone: (416) 978-6738
Toronto, ON, Canada M5S 2C6   Janet Holmes, Cur.Asst.
Staff: Prof 1; Other 1. **Subjects:** North American decorative arts, Canadian history, 16th and 17th century geographical works. **Holdings:** 4000 books.

Subscriptions: 20 journals and other serials. Services: Interlibrary loans; copying; library open to public for reference use only. Automated Operations: Computerized cataloging.

★11598★
ROYAL ONTARIO MUSEUM - FAR EASTERN LIBRARY (Area-Ethnic; Art)*
100 Queen's Park   Phone: (416) 978-3653
Toronto, ON, Canada M5S 2C6   John Howard, Assoc.Libn.
Founded: 1933. Staff: Prof 2; Other 1. Subjects: Art and archeology of the Far East including China, Japan, India and Southeast Asia. Special Collections: Stone inscriptions and carvings from monuments in China (5000 rubbings). Holdings: 19,000 books and bound periodical volumes; 8 VF drawers. Subscriptions: 150 journals and other serials. Services: Interlibrary loans; copying; library open to public, loans to faculty, librarians and recommended students and nonacademic staff of Ontario universities, academic staff and librarians of art galleries, museums, community colleges and special academic libraries of Ontario. Automated Operations: Computerized cataloging. Computerized Information Services: UTLAS.

★11599★
ROYAL ONTARIO MUSEUM - LIBRARY (Art; Sci-Tech)†
100 Queen's Park   Phone: (416) 928-3671
Toronto, ON, Canada M5S 2C6   Gene Wilburn, Hd.Libn.
Founded: 1961. Staff: Prof 4; Other 6. Subjects: Anthropology, archeology, astronomy, botany, fine arts, geology, mineralogy, museology, paleontology, zoology, decorative arts, ethnology. Holdings: 80,000 volumes. Subscriptions: 557 journals and other serials. Services: Interlibrary loans; copying; SDI; library open to public for reference use only. Computerized Information Services: UTLAS, SDC. Publications: Accessions list, monthly - internal distribution and by request; newsletter, irregular - for internal distribution only. Staff: Sharon Hick, Assoc.Libn.; Mrs. Pat Trunks, ILL; Isabella Guthrie, Asst.Libn.; Marian Press, Assoc.Libn.

★11600★
ROYAL ROADS MILITARY COLLEGE - LIBRARY (Mil; Hist)†
                                          Phone: (604) 388-1483
Victoria, BC, Canada V0S 1B0   C.C. Whitlock, Chf.Libn.
Founded: 1952. Staff: Prof 2; Other 3. Subjects: Academic topics, military science and history, Pacific Northwest history. Holdings: 60,000 books; 14,500 bound periodical volumes. Subscriptions: 550 journals and other serials; 25 newspapers. Services: Interlibrary loans; copying; library open to public by permission only. Special Catalogs: Periodical list (computer printout). Remarks: Maintained by Canada Department of National Defence. Staff: Susan Day, Asst.Libn.

★11601★
ROYAL SOCIETY OF CANADA - LIBRARY (Sci-Tech; Hum)
344 Wellington St.   Phone: (613) 992-3468
Ottawa, ON, Canada K1A 0N4   E.H.P. Garneau, Exec.Sec.
Founded: 1882. Staff: 4. Subjects: Humanities, social sciences, mathematics, chemistry, physics, earth sciences, animal and plant biology, microbiology and biochemistry, applied science, medical science. Special Collections: Proceedings and Transactions, annually, 1882 to present. Holdings: Figures not available; proceedings of symposiums. Services: Copying (limited); library open to public for reference use only. Publications: List of society's publications - available on request. Remarks: Society's collections are stored in the Canada Institute for Scientific and Technical Information and National Library of Canada. Also Known As: Societe Royale du Canada.

★11602★
ROYAL TRUST CORPORATION OF CANADA - INVESTMENT RESEARCH LIBRARY (Bus-Fin)
P.O. Box 7500, Sta. A
Toronto, ON, Canada M5W 1P9   Phone: (416) 867-2928
                                          Anita Frank, Libn.
Founded: 1978. Staff: Prof 1; Other 1. Subjects: Investment, finance, security analysis, Canadian and U.S. corporations and industries. Holdings: Figures not available for books; corporation annual reports. Services: Interlibrary loans; copying; library open to public by appointment. Computerized Information Services: Info Globe, DIALOG, Dow Jones News/Retrieval, TEXTLINE.

★11603★
ROYAL VICTORIA HOSPITAL - MEDICAL LIBRARY (Med)†
687 Pine Ave., W., Rm. H4.01   Phone: (514) 842-1231
Montreal, PQ, Canada H3A 1A1   Sandra R. Duchow, Chf.Med.Libn.
Founded: 1935. Staff: Prof 2; Other 2. Subjects: Medicine, surgery, anesthesia, nursing. Holdings: 2000 books; 10,000 bound periodical volumes. Subscriptions: 225 journals and other serials. Services: Interlibrary

loans; library not open to public. Computerized Information Services: MEDLINE. Networks/Consortia: Member of McGill Medical and Health Libraries Association (MMHLA). Staff: Ada M. Ducas, Asst.Med.Libn.

★11604★
ROYAL VICTORIA HOSPITAL - WOMEN'S PAVILION LIBRARY (Med)
687 Pine Ave., W.   Phone: (514) 842-1251
Montreal, PQ, Canada H3A 1A1   Elaine Waddington, Libn.
Founded: 1957. Staff: Prof 1. Subjects: Gynecology, obstetrics, newborn physiology, neuroendocrinology. Holdings: 700 books; 600 bound periodical volumes; 4 drawers of reprints. Subscriptions: 30 journals and other serials. Services: Interlibrary loans; audiovisual lectures (cassette tapes, slides and prints) on obstetrics and gynecology available to medical students and other interested personnel for use on the premises only; telephone reference service; library open to members of medical and paramedical professions. Computerized Information Services: MEDLINE. Publications: Placenta and Fetus Abstracts; Uterine Physiology Abstracts; Gynaecological Cancer Abstracts, all irregular - distributed to research personnel.

RUBEL MEMORIAL LIBRARY
See: Orthopaedic Hospital

RUBEN LIBRARY
See: Temple Adath Israel

RUBENSTEIN (Bernard) LIBRARY
See: Congregation Agudas Achim - Bernard Rubenstein Library

RUDNYC'KI ARCHIVES
See: Concordia University - Loyola Campus - Georges P. Vanier Library

RUDOFKER (Ida and Matthew) LIBRARY
See: Har Zion Temple - Ida and Matthew Rudofker Library

RUHLE (George C.) LIBRARY
See: U.S. Natl. Park Service - Glacier Natl. Park - George C. Ruhle Library

RUPPEL (Harry) MEMORIAL LIBRARY
See: Vandercook College of Music - Harry Ruppel Memorial Library

RURAL ADVANCEMENT FUND
See: National Sharecroppers Fund/Rural Advancement Fund

RUSH (Charles Andrew) LEARNING CENTER/LIBRARY
See: Birmingham-Southern College - Charles Andrew Rush Learning Center/Library

★11605★
RUSH-PRESBYTERIAN-ST. LUKE'S MEDICAL CENTER - LIBRARY OF RUSH UNIVERSITY (Med)
600 S. Paulina St.   Phone: (312) 942-5950
Chicago, IL 60612   Doris Bolef, Dir.
Founded: 1898. Staff: Prof 10; Other 16. Subjects: Biomedical sciences, hospital administration, health care delivery, nursing, allied health fields. Special Collections: Rare medical books (3250). Holdings: 48,500 books; 44,200 bound periodical volumes. Subscriptions: 2052 journals and other serials. Services: Interlibrary loans; copying; SDI; library open to all health science personnel for reference use only. Automated Operations: Computerized cataloging and serials. Computerized Information Services: MEDLINE, DIALOG, BRS, OCLC, PHILSOM, CDC. Performs searches on cost recovery basis. Contact Person: Marianne Doherty, 942-5952. Networks/Consortia: Member of Rush Affiliates Information Network (RAIN); Greater Midwest Regional Medical Library Network (Region 3); ILLINET. Publications: PULSE. Special Catalogs: Serials list (loose-leaf). Staff: Trudy L. Gardner, Asst.Dir., Info.Serv.; Lucyna Szymanski, Tech.Serv.Coord./Ser.Libn; June Yew, Cat.Libn.; Paul DiMauro, Coll.Dev.Libn.; Marianne Doherty, Hd.Ref.Libn.; Susan Thompson, Ref.Libn.; Sudi Kotecha, Ref.Libn..; Eleanor Hill, ILL Libn.; Colm Hennessy, Circ.Libn.

RUSH RHEES LIBRARY
See: University of Rochester

★11606★
RUSHMORE NATIONAL HEALTH SYSTEM - HEALTH SCIENCES LIBRARY (Med)
353 Fairmont Blvd.   Phone: (605) 341-7101
Rapid City, SD 57701   Bonnie R. Mack, Dept.Mgr./Lib.Serv.
Founded: 1927. Staff: Prof 2; Other 1. Subjects: Natural and social sciences, nursing, medicine. Holdings: 4044 books; 3747 bound periodical

volumes; 2060 government documents. **Subscriptions:** 310 journals and other serials. **Services:** Interlibrary loans; copying; library open to public with restrictions. **Computerized Information Services:** MEDLARS, BRS. **Networks/Consortia:** Member of Greater Midwest Regional Medical Library Network (Region 3). **Formerly:** Rapid City Regional Hospital. **Staff:** Bonne Starks, Ref.Libn.

RUSSELL (Bertrand) SOCIETY, INC.
See: Bertrand Russell Society, Inc.

RUSSELL CAVE NATL. MONUMENT
See: U.S. Natl. Park Service

★11607★
RUSSELL AND DUMOULIN - LIBRARY (Law)
MacMillan Bloedel Bldg., 17th Fl.
1075 W. Georgia St.   Phone: (604) 688-3411
Vancouver, BC, Canada V6E 3G2   Diana E. Hunt, Libn.
Staff: Prof 1; Other 2. **Subjects:** Law. **Holdings:** 12,000 volumes. **Services:** Library not open to public. **Automated Operations:** Computerized cataloging. **Computerized Information Services:** QL Systems, Westlaw.

RUSSELL (Helen Crocker) LIBRARY
See: Strybing Arboretum Society - Helen Crocker Russell Library

RUSSELL (Ina Dillard) LIBRARY
See: Georgia College - Ina Dillard Russell Library

RUSSELL (Richard B.) AGRICULTURAL RESEARCH CENTER LIBRARY
See: U.S.D.A. - Agricultural Research Service - South Atlantic Area - Richard B. Russell Agricultural Res. Ctr. Lib.

RUSSELL (Richard B.) MEMORIAL LIBRARY
See: University of Georgia - Richard B. Russell Memorial Library

★11608★
RUSSELL SAGE FOUNDATION - LIBRARY (Soc Sci)
112 E. 64th St.   Phone: (212) 750-6008
New York, NY 10021   Pauline M. Rothstein, Dir., Info.Serv.
Staff: Prof 1; Other 1. **Subjects:** Social science. **Special Collections:** Foundation archives (15 VF drawers; 6 boxes of letters; photographs). **Holdings:** 1500 books. **Subscriptions:** 100 journals and other serials; 5 newspapers. **Services:** Interlibrary loans; copying; library open to public by appointment. **Automated Operations:** Computerized cataloging. **Computerized Information Services:** DIALOG, OCLC. **Networks/Consortia:** Member of Consortium of Foundation Libraries; METRO. **Publications:** Reporting from the Russell Sage Foundation, irregular - free upon request.

RUSSELL (Susan V.) TAPE LIBRARY
See: Wittenberg University - Thomas Library

RUSSELL VERMONTIANA COLLECTION
See: Canfield Memorial Library

RUSSIAN ORTHODOX DIOCESE OF ALASKA - ARCHIVES
See: St. Herman's Orthodox Theological Seminary - Library

RUSSIAN RESEARCH CENTER
See: Harvard University

★11609★
RUST INTERNATIONAL CORPORATION - LIBRARY (Sci-Tech)
1130 S. 22nd St.
Box 101   Phone: (205) 254-4400
Birmingham, AL 35201   Calberta O. Atkinson, Libn.
Founded: 1957. **Staff:** Prof 1. **Subjects:** Engineering - environmental, civil, chemical, electrical, mechanical; pulp and paper. **Holdings:** 4900 books; 310 bound periodical volumes; 1200 vendors' catalogs; 1260 internal company reports; 3200 technical reports; 70 microfiche cards. **Subscriptions:** 120 journals and other serials. **Services:** Interlibrary loans; copying; library open to public for reference use only. **Computerized Information Services:** DIALOG, Dow Jones News/Retrieval.

★11610★
RUST-OLEUM CORPORATION - R & D LIBRARY (Sci-Tech)
2301 Oakton St.   Phone: (312) 864-8200
Evanston, IL 60204   Shari Capra, Supv.
Founded: 1972. **Staff:** Prof 1; Other 1. **Subjects:** Coatings, resins, corrosion, environment. **Holdings:** 430 books; 100 bound periodical volumes;

100 patents; 100 suppliers' catalogs. **Subscriptions:** 120 journals and other serials; 2 newspapers. **Services:** Library not open to public. **Publications:** Technical Newsletter, quarterly; Book List, Periodical List - annual.

★11611★
RUTAN AND TUCKER - LIBRARY (Law)
611 Anton, Suite 1400   Phone: (714) 641-3460
Costa Mesa, CA 92626   Hazel Bader, Libn.
Subjects: Law. **Holdings:** 23,000 volumes.

RUTGERS CENTER OF ALCOHOL STUDIES
See: Rutgers University, The State University of New Jersey

RUTGERS MEDICAL SCHOOL
See: University of Medicine and Dentistry of New Jersey

★11612★
RUTGERS UNIVERSITY, THE STATE UNIVERSITY OF NEW JERSEY - ALEXANDER LIBRARY - EAST ASIAN LIBRARY (Area-Ethnic)
College Ave.   Phone: (201) 932-7161
New Brunswick, NJ 08903   Dr. Nelson Chou, Libn.
Founded: 1970. **Staff:** Prof 1. **Subjects:** China - language, literature, history, philosophy, religion, arts and sciences; Japanese history; Korean history. **Special Collections:** Complete microfilm collection of the rare books in the National Central Library, Taiwan, up to Series 7; Pamphlet Collection of Tiao-yu-t'ai Problems. **Holdings:** 80,000 books and bound periodical volumes; 4000 reels of cataloged items; 5000 pamphlets. **Subscriptions:** 352 journals and other serials; 12 newspapers. **Services:** Interlibrary loans; library open to public. **Networks/Consortia:** Member of RLG. **Publications:** Serial Holding List, irregular - distributed on request.

★11613★
RUTGERS UNIVERSITY, THE STATE UNIVERSITY OF NEW JERSEY - ART LIBRARY (Art)
Voorhees Hall   Phone: (201) 932-7739
New Brunswick, NJ 08903   Ferris Olin, Art Libn.
Staff: Prof 2. **Subjects:** Art, architecture. **Special Collections:** Louis E. Stern Collection of Modern Art; Bartlett Cowdrey Collection of American Art. **Holdings:** 33,000 books; 5000 bound periodical volumes; 24 VF drawers of exhibition catalogs, museum guides, reports, and ephemeral materials. **Subscriptions:** 75 journals and other serials. **Services:** Copying; library open to public. **Automated Operations:** Computerized cataloging and acquisitions. **Computerized Information Services:** DIALOG; internal database. Performs searches on cost recovery basis. **Networks/Consortia:** Member of RLG. **Staff:** Halina Rusak, Assoc.Art Libn.

★11614★
RUTGERS UNIVERSITY, THE STATE UNIVERSITY OF NEW JERSEY - BLANCHE AND IRVING LAURIE MUSIC LIBRARY (Mus)
Mabel Smith Douglass Library   Phone: (201) 932-9783
New Brunswick, NJ 08903   Jan R. Cody, Music Libn.
Founded: 1982. **Staff:** Prof 3; Other 6. **Subjects:** Music. **Holdings:** 28,000 books; 2250 bound periodical volumes; 15,000 sound recordings. **Subscriptions:** 300 journals and other serials. **Services:** Interlibrary loans; library open to public for reference use only. **Automated Operations:** Computerized acquisitions and circulation. **Computerized Information Services:** DIALOG, BRS, OCLC, RLIN; internal database. Performs searches on cost recovery basis. Contact Person: Lil Maman, 932-9407. **Networks/Consortia:** Member of RLG. **Staff:** Roger Tarman, Chf.Bibliog.; Janet Aaronson, Music Cat.Libn.; M.K. Lane, Media Supv.; John Bewley, Rec.Cat.

★11615★
RUTGERS UNIVERSITY, THE STATE UNIVERSITY OF NEW JERSEY - CENTER FOR COMPUTER AND INFORMATION SERVICES (Comp Sci)
Busch Campus
Computer Reference Ctr.
Box 879 Hill Center   Phone: (201) 932-2296
Piscataway, NJ 08854   Christopher P. Jarocha-Ernst, Coord.
Founded: 1964. **Staff:** Prof 1; Other 2. **Subjects:** Computers, data archives, censuses, electronics. **Special Collections:** University newsletters (200 serials); IBM manuals (1000 volumes); Digital Equipment Corporation (DEC) manuals (200 volumes); U.S. Census tapes; Inter-University Consortium for Political and Social Research (ICPSR) archives. **Holdings:** 1500 books; 500 bound periodical volumes; 500 vendor manuals. **Subscriptions:** 270 journals and other serials; 6 newspapers. **Services:** Library open to public for reference use only. **Automated Operations:** Computerized cataloging, acquisitions and serials. **Computerized Information Services:** Internal database. **Publications:** CCIS Newsletter, CCIS Education Series, both quarterly - by subscription. **Special Catalogs:** CCIS Technical Documents

catalog, Data Archives catalog, ICPSR and Census Material catalog - all online.

★11616★
RUTGERS UNIVERSITY, THE STATE UNIVERSITY OF NEW JERSEY - CENTER FOR URBAN POLICY RESEARCH LIBRARY (Soc Sci; Plan)
Kilmer Area, Bldg. 4051   Phone: (201) 932-3136
Piscataway, NJ 08854   Edward E. Duensing, Jr., Info.Mgr.
Founded: 1962. **Staff:** Prof 1. **Subjects:** Urban/regional planning, urbanization, intergovernmental relations, municipal finance, housing. **Holdings:** 3688 books; 5000 other cataloged items; 45 VF drawers of mimeo papers, manuscripts and government documents. **Subscriptions:** 155 journals and other serials. **Services:** Interlibrary loans; library open to public. **Automated Operations:** Computerized cataloging and acquisitions. **Networks/Consortia:** Member of RLG.

★11617★
RUTGERS UNIVERSITY, THE STATE UNIVERSITY OF NEW JERSEY - CHEMISTRY LIBRARY (Sci-Tech)
Busch Campus
Wright-Riemann Laboratories   Phone: (201) 932-2625
Piscataway, NJ 08854   Dr. Louis P. Torre, Physical Sci.Libn.
Staff: Prof 1; Other 2. **Subjects:** Chemistry. **Holdings:** 7000 books; 10,000 bound periodical volumes. **Subscriptions:** 320 journals and other serials. **Services:** Interlibrary loans; copying; library open to public. **Automated Operations:** Computerized cataloging and acquisitions. **Computerized Information Services:** DIALOG, SDC, BRS, CAS Online, Questel, DARC, Pluridata System. Performs searches on cost recovery basis. **Networks/Consortia:** Member of RLG. **Publications:** Additions to the Chemistry Library, monthly. **Staff:** Gabriel Zalme, Supv.

★11618★
RUTGERS UNIVERSITY, THE STATE UNIVERSITY OF NEW JERSEY - CRIMINAL JUSTICE/NCCD COLLECTION (Soc Sci)
John Cotton Dana Library
185 University Ave.   Phone: (201) 648-5522
Newark, NJ 07102   Phyllis A. Schultze, Libn.
Founded: 1921. **Staff:** Prof 1. **Subjects:** Crime and juvenile delinquency - prevention, control and treatment; criminology and correction. **Holdings:** 7000 books; 500 bound periodical volumes; 37,000 unpublished and published reports, studies, monographs, letters, clippings and pictures. **Subscriptions:** 200 journals and other serials. **Services:** Interlibrary loans to organizations only; copying; telephone information service; collection open to public. **Formerly:** National Council on Crime and Delinquency - Library, located in Hackensack, NJ.

★11619★
RUTGERS UNIVERSITY, THE STATE UNIVERSITY OF NEW JERSEY - DEPARTMENT OF SPECIAL COLLECTIONS AND ARCHIVES (Hist)
Alexander Library
College Ave. & Huntington St.   Phone: (201) 932-1766
New Brunswick, NJ 08903   Ruth J. Simmons, Sr.Archv./Coord.
Founded: 1946. **Staff:** Prof 8; Other 4. **Special Collections:** New Jerseyana; United States history; Social Welfare Archives; Philip Freneau Collection; William Cobbett Collection; Walt Whitman Collection; Robert Morris Papers; William Paterson Papers; American Labor Party Papers; William Elliot Griffis Papers and other primary materials on Westerners in Meiji, Japan (100 cubic feet); Senator Clifford Case Papers (400 cubic feet); Senator Harrison Williams Papers (1000 cubic feet); J. Alexander Symington Collection of 19th and early 20th century British authors (500 cubic feet); Rutgers University Archives. **Holdings:** 100,000 books; 3800 bound periodical volumes; 40,000 newspapers and rare periodicals; 1.8 million manuscripts; 200,000 pictures; 5500 almanacs; 4400 maps; 12,500 broadsides; 72,000 items of genealogical materials; 100 smaller collections; 485 reels of microfilm; 50,000 microcards. **Subscriptions:** 600 journals and other serials; 10 newspapers. **Services:** Interlibrary loans; copying; department open to public. **Automated Operations:** Computerized cataloging, acquisitions and serials. **Computerized Information Services:** Internal database. **Networks/Consortia:** Member of RLG. **Special Catalogs:** A Checklist of New Jersey Periodicals in the Special Collections Department, Rutgers University, 1982 (book); Guide to the Manuscript Collection, 1961; Union List of New Jersey Annual Publications (with New Jersey Historical Society), 1977; Guide to Manuscript Diaries and Journals, 1980. **Staff:** Clark L. Beck, Jr., Mss.Cur.; Ronald L. Becker; Anne Brugh; Marjorie Li; Maxine Lurie; William Miller; Janet Riemer; Jolan Szendrey .

RUTGERS UNIVERSITY, THE STATE UNIVERSITY OF NEW JERSEY - DEPT. OF SPEC.COLL. & ARCHV. - GENEALOGICAL SOC. OF NEW JERSEY
See: Genealogical Society of New Jersey

RUTGERS UNIVERSITY, THE STATE UNIVERSITY OF NEW JERSEY - EAGLETON INSTITUTE - CENTER FOR THE AMERICAN WOMAN & POLITICS
See: Center for the American Woman & Politics

★11620★
RUTGERS UNIVERSITY, THE STATE UNIVERSITY OF NEW JERSEY - GOTTSCHO PACKAGING INFORMATION CENTER (Sci-Tech)
College of Engineering
Box 909   Phone: (201) 932-3044
Piscataway, NJ 08854   Darrell R. Morrow, Dir.
Staff: Prof 3; Other 2. **Subjects:** Packaging. **Holdings:** Periodicals, monographs, pamphlets and government publications. **Subscriptions:** 200 journals and other serials. **Services:** Copying; center open to public. **Publications:** Current Packaging Abstracts, semimonthly - by subscription. **Staff:** Johanna M. Corso, Ed.; John C. Adams, Mng.Ed.

★11621★
RUTGERS UNIVERSITY, THE STATE UNIVERSITY OF NEW JERSEY - JUSTICE HENRY ACKERSON LIBRARY OF LAW & CRIMINAL JUSTICE (Law)
Samuel I. Newhouse Ctr.
for Law & Justice
15 Washington St.   Phone: (201) 648-5675
Newark, NJ 07102   Charlie Harvey, Law Libn.
Founded: 1946. **Staff:** Prof 9; Other 14. **Subjects:** Law, criminology. **Special Collections:** Justice Bradley Law Library (1000 volumes). **Holdings:** 274,000 books and bound periodical volumes; 4475 linear feet of New Jersey and other state records and briefs; 4500 linear feet of U.S. government documents; 50,000 volumes in microform. **Subscriptions:** 3054 journals and other serials; 6 newspapers. **Services:** Interlibrary loans; copying; library open to bar members, university community and public. **Automated Operations:** Computerized cataloging. **Computerized Information Services:** LEXIS, Westlaw. Performs searches for faculty and students. **Networks/Consortia:** Member of RLG. **Publications:** Selected New Acquisitions, monthly - distributed by exchange. **Special Catalogs:** Shelf lists of Federal and New Jersey documents. **Staff:** Ermina Hahn, Hd., Tech.Serv.; Peter Siegel, Hd., User Serv.; Ernest Nardone, Ref.; Paul Axel-Lute, Coll.Dev.Christina Senezak, State Doc.Libn.; Virginia Lemmon, Ref.; William Schroeder, Ref.; Betsy Reidinger, Cat.; Marjorie Crawford, ILL/Circ.

★11622★
RUTGERS UNIVERSITY, THE STATE UNIVERSITY OF NEW JERSEY - INSTITUTE OF JAZZ STUDIES (Mus)
Bradley Hall
Warren St. and Martin Luther King Blvd.   Phone: (201) 648-5595
Newark, NJ 07102   Dan Morgenstern, Dir.
Staff: Prof 4; Other 1. **Subjects:** Jazz. **Special Collections:** National Endowment for the Arts (NEA) Jazz Oral History Project Repository (100 taped interviews and transcriptions). **Holdings:** 5000 books; 600 bound periodical volumes; 65,000 records and transcriptions; 1500 audiotapes; cylinders; 30 VF drawers of clippings; manuscripts; piano rolls; jazz periodicals; sheet music; instruments; dissertations; works of art; photographs; memorabilia. **Subscriptions:** 152 journals and other serials. **Services:** Library open to public by appointment. **Automated Operations:** Computerized cataloging. **Computerized Information Services:** OCLC; IJS Jazz Register and indexes (register of recorded jazz performances cataloged and indexed; internal database). **Networks/Consortia:** Member of RLG. **Publications:** Annual Review of Jazz Studies - by subscription; Studies in Jazz (monograph series): Benny Carter, 1982; Art Tatum, 1982; Erroll Garner, 1984. **Staff:** Edward Berger, Cur.; Marie Griffin, Libn.; Vincent Pelote, Asst.Cur.

★11623★
RUTGERS UNIVERSITY, THE STATE UNIVERSITY OF NEW JERSEY - INSTITUTE OF MANAGEMENT/LABOR RELATIONS LIBRARY (Soc Sci)
     Phone: (201) 932-9513
New Brunswick, NJ 08903   Bernard F. Downey, Libn.
Founded: 1947. **Staff:** Prof 2; Other 2. **Subjects:** Industrial relations, labor education, personnel administration, collective bargaining, labor-management cooperation. **Holdings:** 2724 books; 717 bound periodical volumes; 62 VF drawers of pamphlets; 16 VF drawers of state and federal documents; 27 VF drawers of union and company reports. **Subscriptions:** 524 journals and other serials. **Services:** Interlibrary loans; copying; library open to public for reference use only. **Networks/Consortia:** Member of RLG. **Publications:** Selected Acquisitions List, monthly - available upon request.

★11624★
RUTGERS UNIVERSITY, THE STATE UNIVERSITY OF NEW JERSEY - LIBRARY OF SCIENCE & MEDICINE (Med)
Box 1029   Phone: (201) 932-3850
Piscataway, NJ 08854   Dr. Frank Polach, Dir.
Founded: 1963. Staff: Prof 12; Other 24. Subjects: Medicine, agriculture, biology and biochemistry, engineering, geology, pharmacy, pharmacology, psychology. Holdings: 138,200 books; 134,600 bound periodical volumes; 400,000 government documents. Subscriptions: 3400 periodicals. Services: Interlibrary loans; copying; library open to public. Automated Operations: Computerized circulation. Computerized Information Services: DIALOG, BRS, SDC. Networks/Consortia: Member of RLG.

★11625★
RUTGERS UNIVERSITY, THE STATE UNIVERSITY OF NEW JERSEY - MATHEMATICAL SCIENCES LIBRARY (Sci-Tech; Comp Sci)
                                                Phone: (201) 932-3735
Piscataway, NJ 08854   Sylvia Walsh, Libn.
Founded: 1971. Staff: Prof 1; Other 2. Subjects: Mathematics - pure and applied; computer science; statistics. Holdings: 18,500 books; 11,700 bound periodical volumes; 283 reels of microfilm; 750 technical reports. Subscriptions: 350 journals and other serials. Services: Library open to public. Networks/Consortia: Member of RLG. Publications: Monthly Acquisitions List.

★11626★
RUTGERS UNIVERSITY, THE STATE UNIVERSITY OF NEW JERSEY - NEW JERSEY VOCATIONAL EDUCATION RESOURCE CENTER (Educ)
200 Old Matawan Rd.   Phone: (201) 390-1191
Old Bridge, NJ 08857   Beverly Genetta, Info.Ctr.Dir.
Staff: Prof 3; Other 2. Subjects: Vocational, technical, career, and consumer/homemaker education; curriculum development. Special Collections: Vocational assessment instruments; educational microcomputer software. Holdings: 8000 books; 16 VF drawers; 4200 pieces of AV software; 220,000 ERIC documents on microfiche (complete from 1966 to present); 2200 vocational education doctoral dissertations (1900 on microfilm; 300 manuscripts). Subscriptions: 63 journals and other serials. Services: Interlibrary loans; copying; SDI; center open to public. Computerized Information Services: DIALOG, BRS. Performs searches on cost recovery basis. Contact Person: Marilyn Burk. Staff: Susan Wright, Media Info.Spec.; Joan Eorio, Circ.Supv.

★11627★
RUTGERS UNIVERSITY, THE STATE UNIVERSITY OF NEW JERSEY - PHYSICS LIBRARY (Sci-Tech)
Busch Campus
Serin Physics Laboratory   Phone: (201) 932-2500
Piscataway, NJ 08854   Dr. Louis P. Torre, Physical Sci.Libn.
Staff: Prof 1; Other 2. Subjects: Physics, astronomy. Holdings: 10,000 books; 6000 bound periodical volumes; 4000 preprints; 200 dissertations. Subscriptions: 230 journals and other serials. Services: Interlibrary loans; copying; library open to public. Automated Operations: Computerized cataloging and acquisitions. Computerized Information Services: DIALOG, SDC, BRS. Performs searches on cost recovery basis. Networks/Consortia: Member of RLG. Staff: Barbara Cavallo, Supv.

★11628★
RUTGERS UNIVERSITY, THE STATE UNIVERSITY OF NEW JERSEY - RUTGERS CENTER OF ALCOHOL STUDIES - LIBRARY (Soc Sci)
Busch Campus
Smithers Hall   Phone: (201) 932-4442
Piscataway, NJ 08854   Penny B. Page, Libn.
Founded: 1940. Staff: Prof 2; Other 3. Subjects: Alcohol, drinking, alcoholism. Special Collections: McCarthy Memorial Collection (35,000 documents). Holdings: 7775 books; 134 boxes of archival materials; 20,000 abstracts on 6x7 edge notched cards (Classified Abstract Archive of the Alcohol Literature); 1400 doctoral dissertations on microfilm; 500 alcohol-related bibliographies; 500 questionnaires, interview schedules and survey forms. Subscriptions: 200 journals and other serials. Services: Interlibrary loans; copying; bibliographic and reference services for researchers and students; library open to public.

★11629★
RUTGERS UNIVERSITY, THE STATE UNIVERSITY OF NEW JERSEY - SCHOOL OF LAW LIBRARY (Law)†
Fifth & Penn Sts.   Phone: (609) 757-6173
Camden, NJ 08102   Arno Liivak, Law Libn.
Founded: 1926. Staff: Prof 7; Other 13. Subjects: Law. Special Collections: George Ginsburg's Collection of Soviet Legal Materials, 1945 to present (13,000 volumes). Holdings: 183,500 volumes; 68,600 government documents; 2940 reels of microfilm; 259,000 microfiche. Subscriptions: 1526 journals and other serials. Services: Interlibrary loans; copying; library open to public with restrictions. Automated Operations: Computerized cataloging, acquisitions and serials. Networks/Consortia: Member of RLG; CRL. Staff: Anne Dalesandro, Ref.Libn.; Jabor Kovats, Intl. Law/Doc.Libn.; Jessie Matthews, Night Ref.Libn.; Gloria Chao, Cat.Libn.

★11630★
RUTGERS UNIVERSITY, THE STATE UNIVERSITY OF NEW JERSEY - WAKSMAN INSTITUTE OF MICROBIOLOGY LIBRARY (Sci-Tech)
Box 759   Phone: (201) 932-2906
Piscataway, NJ 08854   Helen Hoffman, Libn.
Founded: 1954. Staff: Prof 1; Other 1. Subjects: Microbiology. Holdings: 7000 books; 9000 bound periodical volumes. Subscriptions: 100 journals and other serials. Services: Interlibrary loans; copying; library open to public for reference use only. Automated Operations: Computerized cataloging and acquisitions. Computerized Information Services: DIALOG, BRS, NLM. Networks/Consortia: Member of RLG. Staff: Mary Jane Werner, Supv.

RUTHERFORD PHYSICS LIBRARY
See: Mc Gill University

★11631★
RUTLAND REGIONAL MEDICAL CENTER - HEALTH SCIENCE LIBRARY (Med)
Allen St.   Phone: (802) 775-7111
Rutland, VT 05701   Cherie L. Goderwis, R.N., Dir.
Founded: 1970. Staff: Prof 1. Subjects: Medicine, nursing, allied health professions, management. Holdings: 2003 books; 35 bound periodical volumes; unbound reports, clippings; journal reprints. Subscriptions: 88 journals and other serials. Services: Interlibrary loans; copying; literature searches. Networks/Consortia: Member of Vermont/New Hampshire Health Science Libraries. Formerly: Rutland Hospital.

RYAN (Calvin T.) LIBRARY
See: Kearney State College - Calvin T. Ryan Library

RYAN LIBRARY
See: Point Loma Nazarene College

RYAN MEMORIAL LIBRARY
See: St. Charles Borromeo Seminary

★11632★
RYDER SYSTEM, INC. - INFORMATION CENTRAL (Trans)
Box 520816   Phone: (305) 593-3456
Miami, FL 33152   Jamie Townsend, Sec., Corp.Plan.
Founded: 1973. Staff: Prof 1; Other 2. Subjects: Transportation, business, economics. Holdings: 250 books; 500 reports; 10 VF drawers of pamphlets; 355 microforms; 100 maps. Subscriptions: 125 journals and other serials; 6 newspapers. Services: Interlibrary loans; copying; library open to company affiliates and public with clearance. Computerized Information Services: Dun & Bradstreet Corporation.

RYERSON AND BURNHAM LIBRARIES
See: Art Institute of Chicago

RYERSON NATURE LIBRARY
See: Lake County Forest Preserve District

★11633★
RYERSON POLYTECHNICAL INSTITUTE - LEARNING RESOURCES CENTRE (Sci-Tech)
350 Victoria St.   Phone: (416) 595-5322
Toronto, ON, Canada M5B 2K3   John North, Dir.
Founded: 1948. Staff: Prof 11; Other 45. Subjects: Business, nursing, engineering, mathematics, technology, architecture, urban planning, interior design, physics, photography, home economics. Special Collections: Energy centre (7900 items); Nutrition Information Service (6500 items); Third World Collection (4900 items); Urban Planning Collection (3900 volumes). Holdings: 237,987 books; 18,824 bound periodical volumes; 25,987 media items; 3567 reels of microfilm; 36,113 microfiche. Subscriptions: 1778 journals and other serials; 32 newspapers. Services: Interlibrary loans (fee); copying; center open to public. Automated Operations: Computerized cataloging, acquisitions and circulation. Computerized Information Services: Internal database. Networks/Consortia: Member of Bibliocentre. Publications: List of publications - available upon request. Staff: Lori Nurse, Info.Ctr.Libn.; Ann Doyle, Sys. & Circ.Libn.; Sue Giles, Coord., Lib.Serv.; Eva Friesen, Tech.Serv.Libn.; Joan Parsons, Hum.Libn.; Olive King, Bus. & Mgt.Libn.;

Elizabeth Bishop, Arts & Lit.Libn.; Lorraine Wilson, Soc.Serv.Libn.; Nancy Grossman, Sci. & Tech.Libn.; Jean Harding, Supv., Media Lib.; Zita Murphy, Soc. & Political Sci.Libn.

★11634★
RYERSON POLYTECHNICAL INSTITUTE - LIBRARY ARTS DEPARTMENT - LIBRARY
50 Gould St.
Toronto, ON, Canada M5B 1E8
Defunct

S

★11635★
S-CUBED - TECHNICAL LIBRARY (Energy)
Box 1620   Phone: (619) 453-0060
La Jolla, CA 92038-1620   LaDonna L. Rowe, Libn.
Staff: Prof 1; Other I. **Subjects:** Physics, geophysics, seismology, energy technology, nuclear technology, chemistry. **Holdings:** 2500 books; 1000 bound periodical volumes. **Subscriptions:** 150 journals and other serials. **Services:** Library open to public by appointment. **Computerized Information Services:** DIALOG. **Networks/Consortia:** Member of San Diego Greater Metropolitan Area Library & Information Agency Council (METRO). **Remarks:** S-Cubed is a division of Maxwell Laboratories, Inc.

★11636★
S.E.R.U. NUCLEAIRE (Canada) LTEE. - LIBRARY (Sci-Tech)
2000 Mansfield, Suite 400   Phone: (514) 282-9369
Montreal, PQ, Canada H3A 2Z1   Elisabeth Lavigueur, Libn.
Staff: Prof 1. **Subjects:** Geology, uranium deposits, earth sciences. **Holdings:** 1200 books; 115 periodicals; 7000 maps; 1500 reports; 150 microfiche. **Subscriptions:** 103 journals and other serials. **Services:** Interlibrary loans (limited); library not open to public.

SAARINEN (Aline B.) LIBRARY
See: Parrish Art Museum - Library

SACHER (C.B.) LIBRARY
See: St. Paul Hospital - C.B. Sacher Library

★11637★
SACRAMENTO AREA COUNCIL OF GOVERNMENTS - LIBRARY (Plan)*
800 H St.   Phone: (916) 441-5930
Sacramento, CA 95814   Rhonda R. Egan, Libn.
Staff: Prof 1. **Subjects:** Planning, census. **Special Collections:** 1975 special census for SACOG region and Placer and Nevada counties. **Holdings:** 5000 books. **Subscriptions:** 40 journals and other serials. **Services:** Interlibrary loans; copying; library open to public with restrictions. **Automated Operations:** Computerized cataloging.

★11638★
SACRAMENTO BEE - REFERENCE LIBRARY (Publ)
21st & Q Sts.
Sacramento, CA 95814   Anna M. Michael, Libn.
Staff: 8. **Subjects:** Newspaper reference topics. **Special Collections:** Sacramento city history. **Holdings:** 500 books; 45 file cabinets of clippings, photographs and pamphlets. **Services:** Library not open to public.

★11639★
SACRAMENTO COUNCIL FOR DELAYED PRESCHOOLERS - DAISY TOY LENDING LIBRARY (Educ)
890 Morse Ave.   Phone: (916) 485-7494
Sacramento, CA 95825   Tammy Guensler, Dir.
Staff: Prof 3. **Subjects:** Infant stimulation - language, creative play, fine and gross motor skills, auditory and tactile skills. **Holdings:** 4000 toys. **Subscriptions:** 12 journals and other serials. **Services:** Library open to families, professionals, and paraprofessionals working with developmentally delayed children. **Publications:** Homemade Toy Book. **Staff:** Marian Geddes, Asst.Libn.; Roberta Snyder, Asst.Libn.

★11640★
SACRAMENTO COUNTY LAW LIBRARY (Law)
Sacramento County Courthouse
720 9th St.   Phone: (916) 444-5910
Sacramento, CA 95814   Shirley H. David, County Law Libn.
Founded: 1903. **Staff:** Prof 1; Other 2. **Subjects:** Law, taxes, California and federal documents. **Holdings:** 37,000 volumes; documents and pamphlets; 2300 cassettes; 8 drawers of microfiche. **Subscriptions:** 210 journals and other serials; 11 newspapers. **Services:** Interlibrary loans; copying; library open to public for reference use only. **Networks/Consortia:** Member of CLASS. **Staff:** Tana S. Smith, Asst.Libn.

★11641★
SACRAMENTO-EL DORADO MEDICAL SOCIETY - PAUL H. GUTTMAN LIBRARY (Med)
5380 Elvas Ave.   Phone: (916) 452-2671
Sacramento, CA 95819   Kathleen D. Proffit, Libn.
Founded: 1949. **Staff:** Prof 1. **Subjects:** Clinical medicine. **Holdings:** 1500 books; 1200 bound periodical volumes. **Subscriptions:** 140 journals and other serials. **Services:** Interlibrary loans; copying; library open to public for reference use only. **Computerized Information Services:** MEDLARS, DIALOG. Performs searches on cost recovery basis. **Networks/Consortia:** Member of Pacific Southwest Regional Medical Library Service (PSRMLS).

★11642★
SACRAMENTO - MUSEUM AND HISTORY DIVISION - LIBRARY (Hist)
1930 J St.   Phone: (916) 447-2958
Sacramento, CA 95814   James E. Henley, Exec.Dir.
Founded: 1960. **Staff:** Prof 7; Other 1. **Subjects:** Sacramento Valley, transportation, railroad and river navigation. **Holdings:** 1500 books; 1 million photographs and negatives; archives of the city and county of Sacramento; maps, lithographs; local NBC-TV affilliate news film library (1955-1973); 3000 linear feet of local government records; 500 linear feet of private papers. **Subscriptions:** 15 journals and other serials. **Services:** Copying; library open to public for reference use only. **Publications:** City of the Plain, Sacramento in the Nineteenth Century, 1969 (book); Old Sacramento, A Reference Point in Time, 1968 (booklet); Guide to Archives (in progress); A Guideline for Signs: Old Sacramento Historic District, 1983 (book). **Staff:** Kathryn Gaeddert, Cur.; Stephen G. Helmich, Hist.; Sherry A. Hatch, Registrar.

SACRAMENTO PEAK NATIONAL OBSERVATORY
See: National Solar Observatory

★11643★
SACRAMENTO PUBLIC LIBRARY - BUSINESS & MUNICIPAL DEPARTMENT (Bus-Fin)†
828 I St.   Phone: (916) 449-5203
Sacramento, CA 95814   Dorothy Harvey, Dept.Hd.
Founded: 1936. **Staff:** Prof 3; Other 1. **Subjects:** Business administration, finance and investments, accounting, real estate, marketing, economics, city and county government. **Special Collections:** Sacramento local history (1000 volumes and 1500 local government documents); U.S. city and telephone directories; picture file of Sacramento scenes, historical and modern; card file of local organizations. **Holdings:** 11,000 volumes; 25 VF drawers of clippings of local history; 1000 annual reports of major U.S. corporations; selective depository for documents of U.S., California, Sacramento City and County. **Subscriptions:** 281 journals and other serials. **Services:** Interlibrary loans; copying (limited); department open to public. **Automated Operations:** Computerized cataloging. **Networks/Consortia:** Member of Mountain-Valley Information Center. **Special Indexes:** Newspaper index (Sacramento Bee and Sacramento Union), 1905-1937, 1974 to present (local items only). **Staff:** Chloris Noblet, Libn.; Diana Gin, Libn.

★11644★
SACRAMENTO UNION - EDITORIAL LIBRARY (Publ)
301 Capitol Mall   Phone: (916) 442-7811
Sacramento, CA 95812   Robin E. Reidy, Libn.
Staff: Prof 1; Other 1. **Subjects:** Newspaper reference topics. **Special Collections:** Sacramento Union, 1846 to present (bound volumes). **Holdings:** 300 books; 180,000 newspaper clipping files. **Subscriptions:** 5 newspapers. **Services:** Interlibrary loans; copying; library open to public by appointment. **Special Indexes:** Index to Sacramento Union, 1977 to present.

★11645★
SACRED HEART GENERAL HOSPITAL AND MEDICAL CENTER - LIBRARY SERVICES (Med)
1255 Hilyard
Box 10905   Phone: (503) 686-6837
Eugene, OR 97440   Deborah Graham, Dir., Lib.Serv.
Founded: 1971. **Staff:** Prof 6; Other 1. **Subjects:** Medicine, nursing, paramedicine, hospital administration, patient education. **Special Collections:** School of Nursing archives, 1942-1970 (2 boxes). **Holdings:** 2000 books; 7000 bound periodical volumes. **Subscriptions:** 400 journals and other serials. **Services:** Interlibrary loans (fee); library open to public with restrictions. **Computerized Information Services:** MEDLARS, Ontyme.

★11646★
SACRED HEART HOSPITAL - HEALTH SCIENCE LIBRARY (Med)*
900 Seton Dr.   Phone: (301) 759-5229
Cumberland, MD 21502   Sr. Martha, Libn.
Founded: 1967. **Staff:** Prof 1; Other 1. **Subjects:** Medicine, nursing, health sciences. **Holdings:** 1900 books; 50 bound periodical volumes. **Subscriptions:** 63 journals and other serials. **Services:** Interlibrary loans; copying; library open to public with restrictions. **Computerized Information Services:** MEDLINE.

★11647★
SACRED HEART HOSPITAL - MEDICAL LIBRARY (Med)
5151 N. 9th Ave.   Phone: (904) 476-7851
Pensacola, FL 32504   Florence V. Ruby, Hosp.Libn.
Founded: 1959. Staff: 2. Subjects: Medicine, pediatrics, nursing, management. Special Collections: Pediatrics library. Holdings: 811 books; 2793 bound periodical volumes. Subscriptions: 101 journals and other serials. Services: Interlibrary loans; copying; library open to public by appointment.

★11648★
SACRED HEART HOSPITAL - MEDICAL LIBRARY (Med)
W. 4th St.   Phone: (605) 665-9371
Yankton, SD 57078   Roxie Olson, Med.Libn.
Founded: 1975. Staff: Prof 1; Other 1. Subjects: Life and health sciences, nursing, hospital administration. Holdings: 2700 volumes; 300 AV items; 5 VF drawers. Subscriptions: 200 journals and other serials. Services: Interlibrary loans; copying; library open to public with restrictions. Automated Operations: Computerized serials Computerized Information Services: NLM. Networks/Consortia: Member of Midcontinental Regional Medical Library Program.

★11649★
SACRED HEART HOSPITAL - MEDICAL LIBRARY (Med)
900 W. Clairemont Ave.   Phone: (715) 839-4330
Eau Claire, WI 54701   Bruno Warner, Libn.
Founded: 1964. Staff: Prof 1. Subjects: Medicine, nursing, dentistry, hospital administration, patient teaching. Holdings: 5000 books; 1000 bound periodical volumes; 2000 unbound periodicals; 4 VF drawers of pamphlets. Subscriptions: 286 journals and other serials. Services: Interlibrary loans; copying; library open to public with the exception of hospital patients. Networks/Consortia: Member of Greater Midwest Regional Medical Library Network (Region 3); West Central Wisconsin Hospital Library Consortium. Publications: Medical Library notes (newsletter), monthly - for internal distribution only.

★11650★
SACRED HEART HOSPITAL - WILLIAM A. HAUSMAN MEDICAL LIBRARY (Med)
4th & Chew Sts.   Phone: (215) 821-3280
Allentown, PA 18102   Sylvia B. Cesanek, Libn.
Founded: 1928. Staff: Prof 1; Other 1. Subjects: Nursing, medicine. Holdings: 1438 books; 5290 bound periodical volumes; 804 Audio-Digest tapes; clippings of Sacred Heart Hospital and School of Nursing history. Subscriptions: 77 journals and other serials. Services: Interlibrary loans; copying; library open to medical, nursing and allied health personnel and students for reference use. Computerized Information Services: MEDLARS.

SACRED HEART JESUIT CENTER
See: California Province of the Society of Jesus

★11651★
SACRED HEART MEDICAL CENTER - HEALTH SCIENCES LIBRARY (Med)
W. 101 8th Ave.   Phone: (509) 455-3094
Spokane, WA 99204   Elizabeth J. Guilfoil, Dir.
Staff: Prof 3; Other 1. Subjects: Medicine and surgery, nursing, dietetics, psychology, administration and personnel, clinical laboratory. Holdings: 5000 books; 3000 bound periodical volumes; 8 VF drawers of clippings, pamphlets and pictures; slides; cassettes; filmstrips. Subscriptions: 210 journals and other serials. Services: Interlibrary loans; copying; library open to public for reference use only. Staff: Agnes Wright, Lib.Techn.; Sandy Keno, Lib.Techn.

★11652★
SACRED HEART MONASTERY - LEO DEHON LIBRARY (Rel-Theol)†
7331 S. Lovers Lane Rd.   Phone: (414) 425-8300
Hales Corners, WI 53130   Sr. Agnese Jasko, P.H.J.C., Libn.
Founded: 1932. Staff: Prof 3; Other 2. Subjects: Dogmatic theology, ascetical theology, canon law, church history, scripture, liturgy, moral theology, comparative religion, philosophy. Special Collections: Sacred Heart Collection (500 titles). Holdings: 55,836 books; 4039 bound periodical volumes; 1000 pamphlets; 319 reels of microfilm; 29 volumes on microfiche; 347 cassette tapes; 10,066 phonograph records. Subscriptions: 312 journals and other serials. Services: Library open to public for reference use only. Staff: Rev. Charles Yost, S.C.J., Cons.; Kathy Jastrab, Lib.Asst.; Joan Metyer, Lib.Asst.

★11653★
SACRED HEART SEMINARY - WARD MEMORIAL LIBRARY (Rel-Theol)
2701 W. Chicago Blvd.   Phone: (313) 868-2700
Detroit, MI 48206   Arnold M. Rzepecki, Libn.
Founded: 1919. Staff: Prof 1; Other 1. Subjects: Catholic theology, scholastic philosophy, modern philosophy, church history. Special Collections: Cardinal Mooney Collection (church and social problems); Michigan Historical Collection (church history in Michigan). Holdings: 55,000 books; 10,000 bound periodical volumes; 500 reels of microfilm. Subscriptions: 250 journals and other serials; 25 newspapers. Services: Interlibrary loans; copying; library open to public with permission of librarian.

★11654★
SACRED HEART UNIVERSITY - LIBRARY (Rel-Theol)
5229 Park Ave.   Phone: (203) 371-7700
Bridgeport, CT 06606   Roch-Josef di Lisio, Act.Dir.
Founded: 1963. Staff: Prof 9; Other 12. Subjects: Mathematics, religious studies, business administration. Special Collections: International Children's Literature Collection; Heywood Hale Broun Collection; Msgr. Ronald Knox Collection. Holdings: 122,000 books; 2250 AV titles. Subscriptions: 650 journals and other serials. Services: Interlibrary loans; copying; library open to public. Automated Operations: Computerized cataloging. Computerized Information Services: OCLC, DIALOG. Networks/Consortia: Member of Southwestern Connecticut Library Council (SWLC); NELINET. Publications: Acquisitions List, monthly - for internal distribution only; Handbook, annual; study guides, AV bibliographies, ethnic studies bibliographies - all free upon request. Staff: Elizabeth Paul, Ref.Libn.; Cara Guerra, Mstr.Libn.; Deborah DeCorso, Asst.Libn./Pub.Serv.; Robert Knapik, Ref.Libn.; Nancy Bobrek, Ref.Libn.; Lucretia Duwel, Ref.Libn.; Marilyn Love, Ref.Libn.; Edward Farrell, Ref.Libn.

★11655★
SADTLER RESEARCH LABORATORIES - LIBRARY (Sci-Tech)
3316 Spring Garden St.   Phone: (215) 382-7800
Philadelphia, PA 19104   Bernadette Steiner, Libn.
Founded: 1966. Staff: 1. Subjects: Spectroscopy - infrared, ultraviolet, nuclear magnetic resonance; gas chromatography; analytical chemistry. Special Collections: Spectra consisting of infrared, ultraviolet, nuclear magnetic resonance, attenuated total reflectance and differential thermal analysis for 70,000 compounds. Holdings: 3500 books; 2500 bound periodical volumes; 2000 reprints and government publications; pamphlets. Subscriptions: 60 journals and other serials. Services: Interlibrary loans; copying; library open to public for reference use only with appointment. Remarks: Sadtler Research Laboratories is a division of Bio-Rad Laboratories, Inc.

★11656★
SAFECO INSURANCE COMPANY - LIBRARY (Bus-Fin)
Safeco Plaza   Phone: (206) 545-5505
Seattle, WA 98185   Esther J. Delaney, Libn.
Founded: 1958. Staff: 2. Subjects: Insurance, finance, management, business. Holdings: 9500 books; 1 VF drawer of unbound materials; 360 AV tapes; 15 phonograph records; 150 16mm films; 20 shelves of archives; 2 VF drawers of pamphlets, brochures; 150 video cassettes. Subscriptions: 210 journals and other serials; 15 newspapers. Services: Interlibrary loans; copying; library open to public with restrictions. Staff: Dorothy Ashburn, Asst.Libn.

★11657★
SAFEWAY STORES, INC. - LIBRARY (Food-Bev)
201 Fourth St.   Phone: (415) 891-3175
Oakland, CA 94660   Virginia A. Veit, Lib.Mgr.
Founded: 1938. Staff: Prof 2; Other 2. Subjects: Food, retail food chains, business. Holdings: 23,500 books; clippings; corporate reports. Subscriptions: 400 journals and other serials. Services: Interlibrary loans; library not open to public. Automated Operations: Computerized serials. Computerized Information Services: DIALOG. Staff: Lee Stoney, Libn.

★11658★
SAGA CORPORATION - MARKETING LIBRARY (Food-Bev; Bus-Fin)
One Saga Ln.   Phone: (415) 854-5150
Menlo Park, CA 94025   Caroline S. Peters, Libn.
Staff: Prof 1. Subjects: Foodservice marketing, business. Holdings: 250 books. Subscriptions: 142 journals and other serials. Services: Library not open to public.

★11659★

SAGADAHOC COUNTY LAW LIBRARY (Law)*
County Court House
752 High St.   Phone: (207) 443-9734
Bath, ME 04530
Subjects: Law. **Holdings:** 5500 books.

SAGALL (Elliot L. and Annette Y.) LIBRARY
See: American Society of Law & Medicine - Elliot L. and Annette Y. Sagall
  Library

★11660★

**SAGAMORE HILLS CHILDREN'S PSYCHIATRIC HOSPITAL - STAFF
MEDICAL LIBRARY** (Med)
11910 Dunham Rd.   Phone: (614) 467-7955
Northfield, OH 44067   Karen Parsons, Libn.
Subjects: Child psychology, institutional care, nursing, activity and educational
therapy, psychiatry. **Holdings:** 950 books; tapes. **Subscriptions:** 15 journals
and other serials. **Services:** Library not open to public.

SAGE (Gardner A.) LIBRARY
See: New Brunswick Theological Seminary - Gardner A. Sage Library

SAGE (RUSSELL) FOUNDATION
See: Russell Sage Foundation

★11661★

SAGINAW COUNTY LAW LIBRARY (Law)
Courthouse, Rm. 215
111 S. Michigan Ave.   Phone: (517) 790-5490
Saginaw, MI 48602   Jannis Corley, Law Libn.
Founded: 1945. **Staff:** Prof 4. **Subjects:** Law. **Holdings:** 20,000 volumes.
Services: Copying; library open to public with restrictions. **Staff:** Cynthia
Brodnex, Law Libn.

★11662★

SAGINAW HEALTH SCIENCES LIBRARY (Med)
1000 Houghton St., Suite 2000   Phone: (517) 771-6846
Saginaw, MI 48602   Stephanie John, Dir.
Founded: 1978. **Staff:** Prof 1; Other 5. **Subjects:** Medicine, nursing, allied
health sciences, dentistry, health care administration. **Holdings:** 6905 books;
13,765 bound periodical volumes; 1448 AV software items; 3 VF drawers of
pamphlets. **Subscriptions:** 494 journals and other serials. **Services:**
Interlibrary loans; copying; library open to public for reference use only.
Computerized Information Services: NLM, BRS, DIALOG. **Networks/
Consortia:** Member of Michigan Library Consortium (MLC). **Publications:**
Library Link, quarterly - to affiliated users. **Remarks:** The library is maintained
by Saginaw Cooperative Hospitals, Inc.

★11663★

SAGINAW NEWS - EDITORIAL LIBRARY (Publ)
201-203 S. Washington Ave.   Phone: (517) 752-7171
Saginaw, MI 48605   Leland R. Watrous, Hd.Libn.
Staff: Prof 2. **Subjects:** Newspaper reference topics. **Holdings:** 1000 books;
5.5 million clippings; area newspapers, 1840 to present, on microfilm.
Subscriptions: 12 journals and other serials; 12 newspapers. **Services:**
Library open to public with restrictions. **Staff:** Judith A. Ahearn, Asst.Libn.

★11664★

SAGINAW OSTEOPATHIC HOSPITAL - LIBRARY (Med)†
515 N. Michigan Ave.   Phone: (517) 771-5100
Saginaw, MI 48602   Patricia A. Wolfgram, Libn.
Subjects: Medicine, allied health fields, management. **Holdings:** 2500 books;
1150 bound periodical volumes; 600 audiotapes. **Subscriptions:** 260 journals
and other serials. **Services:** Interlibrary loans; copying; library open to public
for reference use only, by referral. **Networks/Consortia:** Member of Valley
Regional Health Sciences Librarians.

SAGUENAY REGION HISTORICAL SOCIETY
See: Societe Historique du Saguenay

SAHEL DOCUMENTATION CENTER
See: Michigan State University - International Library

★11665★

SAI/JRB LIBRARY (Sci-Tech)
8400 Westpark Dr.   Phone: (703) 827-8108
McLean, VA 22102   Madeleine Hahn, Libn.
Subjects: Safety, health. **Holdings:** 80 books; 70 journals; 1000

Occupational Safety and Health Administration and National Institute for
Occupational Safety and Health publications; 3500 documents, articles,
patents, dissertations and archival materials. **Subscriptions:** 50 journals and
other serials. **Services:** Interlibrary loans; copying; library not open to public.
Automated Operations: Computerized acquisitions. **Computerized
Information Services:** Online systems. **Networks/Consortia:** Member of
Interlibrary Users Association. **Formed by the Merger of:** SAI and JRB
Associates, Inc.

★11666★

ST. AGNES HOSPITAL - L.P. GUNDRY HEALTH SCIENCES LIBRARY (Med)
900 Caton Ave.   Phone: (301) 368-7565
Baltimore, MD 21229   Joanne Sutt, Dir.
Founded: 1959. **Staff:** Prof 1; Other 2. **Subjects:** Medicine, surgery,
pediatrics, obstetrics, gynecology, pathology, nursing, psychiatry. **Holdings:**
2000 books; 3500 bound periodical volumes. **Subscriptions:** 195 journals
and other serials. **Services:** Interlibrary loans; copying; library open to health
professionals for reference use only. **Computerized Information Services:**
MEDLARS. **Networks/Consortia:** Member of Baltimore Consortia for
Resource Sharing.

★11667★

ST. AGNES HOSPITAL - LIBRARY (Med)
430 E. Division St.   Phone: (414) 921-2300
Fond du Lac, WI 54935   Sr. Mary David Boyle, C.S.A., Libn.
Staff: Prof 1. **Subjects:** Medical science, nursing education, health care
science. **Holdings:** 1430 books. **Subscriptions:** 43 journals and other serials.
Services: Library open to medical and hospital staff and students.

★11668★

ST. AGNES MEDICAL CENTER - HEALTH SCIENCE LIBRARY (Med)
1900 S. Broad St.   Phone: (215) 339-4448
Philadelphia, PA 19145   Angelina Caponigro, Hd.Libn.
Founded: 1975. **Staff:** Prof 2; Other 2. **Subjects:** Medicine, nursing and
allied health sciences. **Holdings:** 5000 books; 2350 bound periodical
volumes; 12 VF drawers. **Subscriptions:** 217 journals and other serials.
Services: Interlibrary loans; library not open to public. **Staff:** Theresa
Africano, Asst.Libn.

★11669★

ST. ALEXIS HOSPITAL - HEALTH SCIENCES LIBRARY (Med)
5163 Broadway Ave.   Phone: (216) 641-3300
Cleveland, OH 44127   Stephen C. Johnson, Dir., Lib.Serv.
Staff: Prof 1; Other 1. **Subjects:** Medicine, allied health sciences, hospitals,
nursing. **Holdings:** 2000 books; 1500 bound periodical volumes; 400 AV
items; pamphlets; reprints. **Subscriptions:** 175 journals and other serials.
Services: Interlibrary loans; library not open to public. **Automated
Operations:** Computerized cataloging. **Computerized Information Services:**
MEDLINE, BRS.

ST. ALPHONSE SEMINARY
See: Seminaire St-Alphonse

★11670★

**ST. ALPHONSUS REGIONAL MEDICAL CENTER - HEALTH SCIENCES
LIBRARY** (Med)
1055 N. Curtis Rd.   Phone: (208) 378-2271
Boise, ID 83706   Martha R. Stolz, Libn.
Founded: 1970. **Staff:** Prof 1; Other 1. **Subjects:** Medicine, nursing and
allied health sciences. **Holdings:** 1000 books; 2 VF drawers of pamphlets
(uncataloged). **Subscriptions:** 200 journals and other serials. **Services:**
Interlibrary loans; copying (limited); library open to the medical community.

★11671★

ST. AMANT CENTRE INC. - MEDICAL LIBRARY (Med)
440 River Rd.
Winnipeg, MB, Canada R2M 3Z9   Pauline Dufresne, Techn.
Staff: Prof 1. **Subjects:** Mental retardation, genetics. **Holdings:** 600 books.
Subscriptions: 20 journals and other serials. **Services:** Copying; library open
to public with restrictions.

ST. ANDREW'S ABBEY - SLOVAK WRITERS AND ARTISTS ASSOCIATION
See: Slovak Writers and Artists Association

ST. ANDREW'S COLLEGE
See: University of Saskatchewan

★11672★
ST. ANDREWS HOSPITAL - MEDICAL LIBRARY (Med)*
3 St. Andrews Lane
Boothbay Harbor, ME 04538
Phone: (207) 633-2121
Karen Roberts, Libn.
Staff: 1. **Subjects:** Medicine, surgery, nursing. **Holdings:** 300 books. **Subscriptions:** 10 journals and other serials. **Services:** Interlibrary loans; library not open to public.

★11673★
ST. ANDREWS PRESBYTERIAN COLLEGE - MUSIC LIBRARY
Laurinburg, NC 28352
Founded: 1961. **Subjects:** Music. **Holdings:** 18,000 scores; 4 VF drawers of unbound scores; 1500 phonograph records. **Remarks:** Presently inactive.

STE-ANNE-DE-LA-POCATIERE COLLEGE
See: College de Ste-Anne-de-la-Pocatiere

★11674★
ST. ANNE'S HOSPITAL - PRESIDENTS HEALTH SCIENCES LIBRARY (Med)
4950 W. Thomas St.
Chicago, IL 60651
Phone: (312) 378-7100
Christina Rudawski, Lib.Dir.
Staff: Prof 1; Other 1. **Subjects:** Medicine, nursing and allied health sciences. **Holdings:** 1700 volumes. **Subscriptions:** 110 journals and other serials. **Services:** Interlibrary loans; library not open to public. **Networks/Consortia:** Member of Metropolitan Consortium. **Formerly:** Its Medical Staff Library.

★11675★
ST. ANNE'S HOSPITAL - SULLIVAN MEDICAL LIBRARY (Med)
795 Middle St.
Fall River, MA 02722
Phone: (617) 674-5741
Elaine M. Crites, Med.Libn.
Founded: 1956. **Staff:** Prof 1. **Subjects:** Oncology, medicine, surgery, allied health sciences. **Holdings:** 100 books; 4000 bound periodical volumes. **Subscriptions:** 80 journals and other serials. **Services:** Interlibrary loans; copying; library open to public with restrictions. **Networks/Consortia:** Member of Southeastern Massachusetts Consortium of Health Science Libraries (SEMCO). **Publications:** Hospital Newsletter - local distribution.

★11676★
ST. ANN'S PASSIONIST MONASTERY - LIBRARY
1230 St. Ann St.
Scranton, PA 18504
Subjects: Theology and religion. **Holdings:** 10,000 books; 400 bound periodical volumes. **Remarks:** Presently inactive.

★11677★
ST. ANSELM'S COLLEGE - GEISEL LIBRARY (Rel-Theol)
Phone: (603) 669-1030
Manchester, NH 03102
James R. Kennedy, Libn.
Founded: 1929. **Staff:** Prof 6; Other 12. **Subjects:** Church history, theology, medieval history, sociology, nursing. **Special Collections:** New England Collection (3000 volumes). **Holdings:** 153,000 books; 15,693 bound periodical volumes; 14,200 reels of microfilm; 30,000 microfiche; 6000 phonograph records and tapes. **Subscriptions:** 1650 journals and other serials; 50 newspapers. **Services:** Interlibrary loans; copying; library open to public with restrictions. **Automated Operations:** Computerized cataloging, acquisitions and ILL. **Computerized Information Services:** DIALOG, OCLC. **Networks/Consortia:** Member of NELINET; New Hampshire College and University Council, Library Policy Committee (NHCUC). **Publications:** Accession list, monthly. **Staff:** Barbara Lerch, Act.Libn.; Barbara Gannon, Ref.; Eunice Wang, Cat.; Patrice Rafail, Online Search; Jeanne Welch, ILLFlorence Cimon, Per.; Sherman Zelinsky, Media.

★11678★
ST. ANSGAR HOSPITAL - HEALTH SCIENCE LIBRARY (Med)
715 N. 11th St.
Moorhead, MN 56560-2088
Phone: (218) 299-2252
Char Myhre, Libn./Educ.Coord.
Staff: Prof 1; Other 1. **Subjects:** Medicine, nursing, hospital administration. **Special Collections:** Hospital archives (3 VF drawers). **Holdings:** 1200 books; 2 VF drawers of documents and reports; 4 VF drawers of other cataloged items. **Subscriptions:** 126 journals and other serials. **Services:** Interlibrary loans; copying; SDI; library open to public with librarian's permission. **Computerized Information Services:** Access to DIALOG, BRS, MEDLARS. **Networks/Consortia:** Member of Valley Medical Network (VMN); Northern Lights Library Network; Greater Midwest Regional Medical Library Network (Region 3).

ST. ANTHONY FALLS HYDRAULIC LABORATORY
See: University of Minnesota

★11679★
ST. ANTHONY HOSPITAL MEDICAL CENTER - MEDICAL LIBRARY (Med)
5666 E. State St.
Rockford, IL 61108
Phone: (815) 226-2000
Nancy Dale, Libn.
Staff: Prof 1. **Subjects:** Clinical medicine. **Holdings:** 300 books; 1400 bound periodical volumes. **Subscriptions:** 100 journals and other serials. **Services:** Interlibrary loans; copying; SDI; library open to public by prior arrangement. **Computerized Information Services:** NLM. **Networks/Consortia:** Member of Greater Midwest Regional Medical Library Network (Region 3); Northern Illinois Library System (NILS); Upstate Consortium of Medical and Allied Libraries in Northern Illinois.

★11680★
ST. ANTHONY HOSPITAL MEDICAL CENTER - SCHOOL OF NURSING - BISHOP LANE LIBRARY (Med)
5666 E. State St.
Rockford, IL 61108
Phone: (815) 226-2000
Mary Patricia Pryor, Libn.
Staff: Prof 1. **Subjects:** Nursing. **Holdings:** 4500 books; 742 bound periodical volumes. **Subscriptions:** 40 journals and other serials. **Services:** Interlibrary loans; library not open to public. **Networks/Consortia:** Member of Upstate Consortium of Medical and Allied Libraries in Northern Illinois. **Special Indexes:** Cumulative index to nursing and allied health literature.

★11681★
ST. ANTHONY HOSPITAL - MEDICAL LIBRARY (Med)
1313 St. Anthony Pl.
Louisville, KY 40204
Phone: (502) 587-1161
Alma Hall Fielden, Adm.Asst., Med. Staff
Subjects: Medicine. **Holdings:** 500 books; 100 bound periodical volumes. **Subscriptions:** 25 journals and other serials. **Services:** Interlibrary loans; library not open to public.

★11682★
ST. ANTHONY HOSPITAL - O'DONOGHUE MEDICAL LIBRARY (Med)
1000 N. Lee St.
Oklahoma City, OK 73102
Phone: (405) 272-6284
Robert J. Lefkowitz, Dir.
Founded: 1950. **Staff:** Prof 1; Other 3. **Subjects:** Cardiovascular medicine, neurosurgery and neurology, general medicine, nursing, community health, allied health sciences. **Holdings:** 4000 books; 3800 bound periodical volumes; 13 VF drawers of pamphlets, reports, clippings, illustrations and reprints. **Subscriptions:** 185 journals and other serials. **Services:** Interlibrary loans; copying; library open to public. **Computerized Information Services:** MEDLINE, TOXLINE. **Networks/Consortia:** Member of Greater Oklahoma City Area Health Sciences Library Consortium (GOAL).

★11683★
ST. ANTHONY HOSPITAL - PHILIP B. HARDYMON LIBRARY (Med)
1450 Hawthorne Ave.
Columbus, OH 43203
Phone: (614) 251-3248
James S. Rucker, Chf.Med.Libn.
Founded: 1956. **Staff:** Prof 1; Other 1. **Subjects:** Medicine, medical specialties. **Special Collections:** Reprint file of articles published by staff physicians (26). **Holdings:** 2800 books; 3500 bound periodical volumes; 92 pamphlets; 392 audio cassettes; holdings in various hospital departments. **Subscriptions:** 200 journals and other serials. **Services:** Interlibrary loans; copying; SDI; bibliographies made for doctors, nursing personnel and administration; library open to public by appointment. **Automated Operations:** Computerized cataloging and ILL. **Computerized Information Services:** DIALOG, NLM. **Networks/Consortia:** Member of Greater Midwest Regional Medical Library Network (Region 3); Central Ohio Hospital Library Consortium. **Special Indexes:** Index to reprint file of articles published by staff physicians.

★11684★
ST. ANTHONY HOSPITAL - SPRAFKA MEMORIAL HEALTH SCIENCE LIBRARY (Med)*
2875 W. 19th St.
Chicago, IL 60623
Phone: (312) 521-1710
Karen Ambrose, Lib.Cons.
Founded: 1945. **Staff:** 2. **Subjects:** Medicine, nursing, administration. **Holdings:** 600 books; 100 bound periodical volumes; 1000 pamphlets. **Subscriptions:** 88 journals and other serials. **Services:** Interlibrary loans; manual and automated bibliographic searches; library open to public with restrictions. **Networks/Consortia:** Member of Greater Midwest Regional Medical Library Network (Region 3); Chicago and South Consortium; Chicago Library System. **Staff:** Irene Szot, Lib.Asst.

★11685★
ST. ANTHONY HOSPITAL SYSTEMS - MEMORIAL MEDICAL LIBRARY (Med)
4231 W. 16th Ave.
Denver, CO 80204
Phone: (303) 629-3790
Christine Yolanda Crespin, Supv.Libn.
Founded: 1948. **Staff:** Prof 1; Other 1. **Subjects:** Emergency medicine, trauma, critical care, allied health sciences. **Holdings:** 900 books; 3500

bound periodical volumes; 50 pamphlets. **Subscriptions:** 254 journals and other serials. **Services:** Interlibrary loans; library not open to public. **Automated Operations:** Computerized cataloging and serials. **Computerized Information Services:** DIALOG. **Networks/Consortia:** Member of Denver Area Health Sciences Library Consortium. **Publications:** Current Awareness Service, monthly.

★11686★
ST. ANTHONY-ON-HUDSON THEOLOGICAL LIBRARY (Rel-Theol)
St. Anthony-On-Hudson   Phone: (518) 463-2261
Rensselaer, NY 12144   Bro. James J. Doyle, Libn.
Founded: 1912. **Staff:** Prof 1. **Subjects:** Theology. **Special Collections:** Franciscana (4000 volumes); Newmaniana (300 volumes); patristic-monastic-medieval theology (10,000 items). **Holdings:** 110,000 books; 15,000 bound periodical volumes; 60 incunabula and post-incunabula; 3 medieval codices; 60 manuscripts; 400 pamphlets; 260 volumes on microfilm; 75 boxes of archival material; 1000 phonograph records. **Subscriptions:** 300 journals and other serials. **Services:** Copying; library open to scholars by appointment.

★11687★
ST. ANTHONY'S HOSPITAL - LIBRARY (Med)
Saint Anthony's Way   Phone: (618) 465-2571
Alton, IL 62002   Dorothy Kulenkamp, Lib.Asst.
Staff: Prof 1. **Subjects:** Medicine, nursing. **Holdings:** 450 books. **Subscriptions:** 89 journals and other serials. **Services:** Interlibrary loans; library not open to public. **Networks/Consortia:** Member of Areawide Hospital Library Consortium of Southwestern Illinois (AHLC).

★11688★
ST. ANTHONY'S HOSPITAL, INC. - MEDICAL LIBRARY (Med)†
718 12th St., N.
Box 12588   Phone: (813) 825-1100
St. Petersburg, FL 33705   Linda Jo Rowe, Libn.
Founded: 1958. **Subjects:** Medicine. **Holdings:** 1000 books; 2500 bound periodical volumes. **Subscriptions:** 77 journals and other serials. **Services:** Interlibrary loans; library not open to public.

★11689★
ST. ANTHONY'S MEMORIAL HOSPITAL - HEALTH SCIENCE LIBRARY (Med)
503 N. Maple St.   Phone: (217) 342-2121
Effingham, IL 62401   Sr. M. Angelus Gardiner, Libn.
Staff: 2. **Subjects:** Health, illness. **Holdings:** 900 books; 250 tapes; archives; 12 VF drawers of other cataloged items. **Subscriptions:** 123 journals and other serials. **Services:** Interlibrary loans; copying; library open to public with restrictions. **Networks/Consortia:** Member of ILLINET; Rolling Prairie Library System.

★11690★
ST. AUGUSTINE HISTORICAL SOCIETY - LIBRARY (Hist)
271 Charlotte St.   Phone: (904) 829-5514
St. Augustine, FL 32084   Jacqueline K. Fretwell, Lib.Dir.
Founded: 1883. **Staff:** 3. **Subjects:** History of St. Augustine and environs and related subjects. **Special Collections:** Cathedral Parish records, St. Augustine, 1594-1763 and 1784-1882 (marriages, baptisms, burials). **Holdings:** 8000 books; photostats; manuscripts; documents; microfilm; photographs; maps; pictures; card calendar of Spanish documents, 1512-1764; card index of St. Augustine people, 1821 to present. **Subscriptions:** 12 journals and other serials. **Services:** Interlibrary loans; copying; library open to public for reference use only. **Publications:** El Escribano, annual - available to members, libraries and institutions by subscription; East Florida Gazette, quarterly.

★11691★
ST. AUGUSTINE'S SEMINARY - LIBRARY (Rel-Theol)
2661 Kingston Rd.   Phone: (416) 261-7207
Scarborough, ON, Canada M1M 1M3   Sr. Madeline Connolly, Libn.
Founded: 1913. **Staff:** Prof 1; Other 1. **Subjects:** Theology, scripture, canon law, church history. **Holdings:** 35,000 books; 3500 bound periodical volumes. **Subscriptions:** 190 journals and other serials; 9 newspapers. **Services:** Interlibrary loans; copying; library open to Toronto School of Theology students, St. Augustine's alumni and occasionally to religious education students. **Staff:** Shirlie Gregoire, Asst.Libn.

★11692★
ST. BARNABAS MEDICAL CENTER - MEDICAL LIBRARY (Med)
Old Short Hills Rd.   Phone: (201) 533-5050
Livingston, NJ 07039   A. Christine Connor, Lib.Dir.
Staff: Prof 1; Other 3. **Subjects:** Medicine, nursing. **Special Collections:** Plastic surgery (225 books). **Holdings:** 4500 books; 6800 bound periodical

volumes. **Subscriptions:** 325 journals and other serials. **Services:** Interlibrary loans (fee); copying; library open to qualified researchers and members of the community with restrictions. **Computerized Information Services:** MEDLINE. **Networks/Consortia:** Member of Medical Library Center of New York (MLCNY); Cosmopolitan Biomedical Library Consortium (CBLC).

★11693★
ST. BENEDICT'S ABBEY - BENET LIBRARY (Rel-Theol)*
                    Phone: (414) 396-4311
Benet Lake, WI 53102   Bro. Vincent Wedig, O.S.B., Libn.
Founded: 1945. **Staff:** Prof 2. **Subjects:** Theology, scripture, psycho-social sciences, history, literature. **Holdings:** 15,000 books; 1000 bound periodical volumes; 200 unbound periodicals. **Subscriptions:** 35 journals and other serials; 10 newspapers. **Services:** Interlibrary loans; copying; library open to public for reference use only. **Staff:** Sr. Mary Benedict, O.S.B., Asst.Libn.

★11694★
ST. BENEDICT'S HOSPITAL - HEALTH SCIENCES LIBRARY (Med)
5475 S. 500 East   Phone: (801) 479-2055
Ogden, UT 84403   Sandy Eckersley, Med.Libn.
Founded: 1947. **Staff:** Prof 1. **Subjects:** Medicine, nursing and allied health sciences. **Special Collections:** Dr. J.G. Olson Cardiovascular Collection (200 volumes). **Holdings:** 2000 books; 150 bound periodical volumes; 125 videotapes; 30 audio cassettes. **Subscriptions:** 200 journals and other serials; 5 newspapers. **Services:** Interlibrary loans; copying; library open to public. **Automated Operations:** Computerized serials. **Computerized Information Services:** MEDLARS, MEDLINE. **Networks/Consortia:** Member of Midcontinental Regional Medical Library Program. **Special Catalogs:** Union List of Serials (book form and machine-readable).

★11695★
ST. BERNARDINE HOSPITAL - NORMAN F. FELDHEYM LIBRARY (Med)
2101 North Waterman Ave.   Phone: (714) 883-8711
San Bernardino, CA 92404   Marilyn L. Popik, Med.Libn.
Founded: 1981. **Staff:** Prof 1; Other 3. **Subjects:** Medicine, paramedical fields, nursing. **Holdings:** 5000 volumes. **Subscriptions:** 120 journals and other serials. **Services:** Interlibrary loans; copying; library open to area nursing students. **Computerized Information Services:** MEDLARS. **Networks/Consortia:** Member of Medical Library Group of Southern California and Arizona; Inland Empire Medical Library Cooperative.

★11696★
ST. BERNARD'S INSTITUTE - LIBRARY (Rel-Theol)
1100 S. Goodman   Phone: (716) 271-1320
Rochester, NY 14620   Rev. Sebastian A. Falcone, Dean
Founded: 1893. **Subjects:** Theology, church history, ecumenism, Roman Catholic studies, liturgy, patristics. **Special Collections:** Nineteenth century Roman Catholic periodicals; McQuaid Papers; Fulton J. Sheen Archives. **Holdings:** 30,000 books; 10,000 bound periodical volumes; 150 reels of microfilm; 1600 cassettes; 1000 tapes. **Subscriptions:** 200 journals and other serials; 20 newspapers. **Services:** Interlibrary loans; copying; library open to public with Rochester Regional Research Library Council access card. **Networks/Consortia:** Member of Rochester Regional Research Library Council (RRRLC). **Remarks:** The institute is affiliated with Colgate Rochester/Bexley Hall/Crozer Theological Seminary, and is located on its campus.

★11697★
ST. BERNARD'S PARISH - HAZARDVILLE CATHOLIC LIBRARY (Rel-Theol)
426 Hazard Ave.
Enfield, CT 06082   Rose Hartman, Libn.
Founded: 1957. **Staff:** 20. **Subjects:** Encyclicals, theology, retreats, religion, Mariology, children's literature. **Holdings:** 8000 volumes; 2000 other cataloged items. **Services:** Library open to public.

ST. BONAVENTURE UNIVERSITY - FRANCISCAN INSTITUTE LIBRARY
See: Franciscan Institute - Library

★11698★
ST. CATHARINES HISTORICAL MUSEUM - LIBRARY (Hist)
343 Merritt St.   Phone: (416) 227-2962
St. Catharines, ON, Canada L2T 1K7   Mr. Arden Phair, Dir.
Staff: 4. **Subjects:** History - St. Catharines, Niagara region, Welland Canal. **Special Collections:** St. Lawrence Seaway Authority Collection (121 maps); Norris Papers (mid-19th century shipping business; 60.95 centimeters); Ingersoll Papers (19th century business and household accounts; 25.4 centimeters); Niagara Grape and Wine Festival Archives. **Holdings:** 1000 books; 600 maps and plans; 350 pamphlets and leaflets; 210 unbound periodicals; 164 reels of microfilm; 79 street directories; 5 drawers of documents; 3400 historical photographs. **Subscriptions:** 11 journals and

other serials. **Services:** Copying; library open to public. **Publications:** A Guide to the Grand River Canal (1982); Recollections of St. Catharines, 1837-1902 (1982); Glimpses Into Our Past, Volume 1 (1984). **Special Catalogs:** Port of St. Catharines Shipping Register (card); Catalog of the Niagara-Heritage Collection. **Remarks:** Library includes the St. Catharines and Lincoln Historical Society Collection.

★11699★
ST. CATHERINE HOSPITAL - MC GUIRE MEMORIAL LIBRARY (Med)
4321 Fir St.   Phone: (219) 392-7494
East Chicago, IN 46312   Madeline E. Downen, Dir., Lib.Serv.
Founded: 1935. **Subjects:** Medicine and allied health sciences. **Holdings:** 8300 volumes. **Subscriptions:** 280 journals and other serials. **Services:** Interlibrary loans; copying; library open to public at discretion of librarian. **Computerized Information Services:** BRS. **Networks/Consortia:** Member of Northwest Indiana Health Science Library Consortium. **Publications:** AV Software, annual update - free upon request.

SAINT CATHERINE LIBRARY
See: College of St. Catherine

★11700★
ST. CATHERINE'S HOSPITAL - MEDICAL LIBRARY (Med)
3556 Seventh Ave.   Phone: (414) 656-3230
Kenosha, WI 53140   Mary Sipsma, Med.Libn.
Founded: 1962. **Staff:** 1. **Subjects:** Medicine, family practice. **Holdings:** 1500 volumes; 300 cassettes. **Subscriptions:** 175 journals and other serials. **Services:** Interlibrary loans; copying; library open to public with restrictions. **Computerized Information Services:** MEDLINE. **Networks/Consortia:** Member of Southeastern Wisconsin Health Sciences Library Consortium; Greater Midwest Regional Medical Library Network (Region 3).

★11701★
ST. CHARLES BORROMEO SEMINARY - RYAN MEMORIAL LIBRARY (Rel-Theol)
Overbrook   Phone: (215) 839-3760
Philadelphia, PA 19151   Rev. John B. DeMayo, Dir. of Libs.
Founded: 1832. **Staff:** Prof 7; Other 4. **Subjects:** Theology, church history, philosophy. **Special Collections:** Ryan Library Archives; historical collections of American Catholic Historical Society of Philadelphia; Pre-1850 Book Collection (incunabula, 16th and 17th century books in sacred sciences; 23,000 volumes). **Holdings:** 181,967 books; 19,505 bound periodical volumes; 5710 AV items and microforms; 398,000 manuscripts; 600 museum pieces; 2000 prints and photographs; 195 paintings. **Subscriptions:** 490 journals and other serials; 23 newspapers. **Services:** Interlibrary loans; copying; library open to public with registration. **Automated Operations:** Computerized cataloging. **Computerized Information Services:** OCLC. **Networks/Consortia:** Member of PALINET & Union Library Catalogue of Pennsylvania; Tri-State College Library Cooperative (TCLC); Southeastern Pennsylvania Theological Libraries Association (SEPTLA). **Publications:** Acquisitions bibliography, bimonthly. **Special Catalogs:** Catalog of holdings of periodicals, newspapers and art (book). **Staff:** Mary J. Giltinan, Rd.Serv.Libn.; Eileen Kearney, Tech.Proc.Libn.; Francis X. Ounan, Per.Libn.; Sr. M. John Aloyse, R.S.M., Rare Bk.Libn.; Rita A. DeStefano, Cat.Libn.; Joseph J. Casino, Archv.; Sr. Rose Lorena, S.S.J., Circ.Libn.

★11702★
ST. CHARLES COUNTY HISTORICAL SOCIETY - ARCHIVES (Hist)
101 S. Main St.   Phone: (314) 723-2939
St. Charles, MO 63301   Gertrude D. Johnson, Archv.
Staff: Prof 1; Other 5. **Subjects:** St. Charles County and Missouri history; genealogy. **Special Collections:** Mrs. Edna McElhiney Olson's Collection (genealogy and local history; 24 VF drawers); St. Charles Banner-News collection of newspapers, 1870-1978 (140 reels of microfilm). **Holdings:** Figures not available for books; 12 VF drawers of court records; 7 VF drawers of miscellaneous materials; 4 VF drawers of photographs; 161 reels of microfilm; deeds; cemetery records; school records. **Services:** Copying; archives open to public for a fee. **Special Indexes:** Card indexes to Mrs. Olson's Collection, court records and genealogy.

★11703★
ST. CHARLES SCHOLASTICATE - LIBRARY (Rel-Theol)
Box 99   Phone: (306) 937-2355
Battleford, SK, Canada S0M 0E0   Ron Zimmer
Founded: 1932. **Staff:** Prof 1; Other 2. **Subjects:** Theology, scripture, philosophy, social sciences. **Holdings:** 30,560 books; 2120 bound periodical volumes. **Subscriptions:** 92 journals and other serials. **Services:** Library not open to public. **Remarks:** Library is operated by the Oblates of Mary Immaculate.

★11704★
ST. CHARLES SEMINARY - LIBRARY
Carthagena, OH 45822
Subjects: Scholastic philosophy, Catholic theology, hagiography. **Holdings:** 28,000 books; 6000 bound periodical volumes. **Remarks:** Presently inactive.

★11705★
ST. CHRISTOPHER'S CHURCH - LIBRARY (Rel-Theol)*
Box 456   Phone: (808) 262-8176
Kailua, HI 96734
Staff: 3. **Subjects:** Religion. **Holdings:** 700 books; tapes; filmstrips. **Subscriptions:** 20 journals and other serials. **Services:** Library open to public.

★11706★
ST. CHRISTOPHER'S HOSPITAL FOR CHILDREN - MEDICAL LIBRARY (Med)
2600 N. Lawrence St.   Phone: (215) 427-5374
Philadelphia, PA 19133   Frances B. Pinnel, Med.Libn.
Subjects: Pediatrics. **Holdings:** 5726 books; 2500 bound periodical volumes. **Subscriptions:** 105 journals and other serials. **Services:** Interlibrary loans; library not open to public. **Publications:** Literature List, monthly; Periodical List, annual.

★11707★
ST. CLAIRE MEDICAL CENTER - MEDICAL LIBRARY (Med)
222 Medical Circle   Phone: (606) 784-6661
Morehead, KY 40351   Patsy Wright, Libn.
Staff: Prof 1. **Subjects:** Medicine, nursing, pharmacy, allied health sciences. **Holdings:** 1501 books; 760 bound periodical volumes; pamphlets. **Subscriptions:** 100 journals and other serials; 10 newspapers. **Services:** Interlibrary loans; copying; library open to public. **Automated Operations:** Computerized cataloging. **Networks/Consortia:** Member of Eastern Kentucky Health Science Information Network (EKHSIN).

★11708★
ST. CLARE'S HOSPITAL & HEALTH CENTER - MEDICAL LIBRARY (Med)
415 W. 51st St.   Phone: (212) 586-1500
New York, NY 10019   James H. Kirk, Libn.
Founded: 1934. **Staff:** Prof 1; Other 1. **Subjects:** Medicine, surgery. **Special Collections:** Surgical Reprints (8 VF drawers). **Holdings:** 1500 books; 7000 bound periodical volumes; tapes. **Subscriptions:** 188 journals and other serials. **Services:** Interlibrary loans; copying; SDI; library open to public at librarian's discretion. **Networks/Consortia:** Member of Manhattan-Bronx Health Sciences Library Group.

★11709★
ST. CLARE'S HOSPITAL - HEALTH SCIENCES LIBRARY (Med)
Pocono Rd.   Phone: (201) 625-6140
Denville, NJ 07834   Rosemary Murphy, Libn.
Staff: 1. **Subjects:** Medicine, surgery, dentistry, mental health, allied health sciences. **Holdings:** 300 books; 300 bound periodical volumes; unbound periodicals; microfiche. **Subscriptions:** 126 journals and other serials. **Services:** Interlibrary loans; copying; library not open to public. **Computerized Information Services:** Access to MEDLINE, TOXLINE. **Networks/Consortia:** Member of Cosmopolitan Biomedical Library Consortium (CBLC).

★11710★
ST. CLARE'S MERCY HOSPITAL - MEDICAL LIBRARY (Med)
St. Clare Ave.   Phone: (709) 778-3414
St. John's, NF, Canada A1C 5B8   Eileen E. Woll, Lib.Techn.
Founded: 1974. **Staff:** 1. **Subjects:** Medicine and related fields. **Holdings:** 800 books. **Subscriptions:** 110 journals and other serials. **Services:** Interlibrary loans; copying; library open to public if material not elsewhere available.

★11711★
ST. CLOUD HOSPITAL - HEALTH SCIENCES LIBRARY (Med)*
1406 Sixth Ave., N.   Phone: (612) 251-2700
St. Cloud, MN 56301   Judy Heeter, Libn.
Staff: Prof 1. **Subjects:** Medicine, nursing, hospital management. **Holdings:** 1000 books; 800 bound periodical volumes; 120 videotapes; 25 16mm films; 50 audio cassettes; 20 AV programs. **Subscriptions:** 100 journals and other serials. **Services:** Interlibrary loans; library not open to public.

ST. CLOUD STATE UNIVERSITY - CENTRAL MINNESOTA HISTORICAL CENTER
See: Central Minnesota Historical Center

ST. CROIX VALLEY ROOM
See: Stillwater Public Library

★11712★
ST. CYRIL AND METHODIUS BYZANTINE CATHOLIC SEMINARY - LIBRARY
(Rel-Theol)
3605 Perrysville Ave.   Phone: (412) 321-8383
Pittsburgh, PA 15214   Rev. Gary Powell, O.F.M.Cap., Libn.
Founded: 1950. **Staff:** Prof 1; Other 2. **Subjects:** Theology, philosophy, Byzantine studies, Ruthenian studies, Slavic studies, Byzantine art. **Special Collections:** Byzantine and Ruthenian theological studies; Slavonic rare books. **Holdings:** 16,603 books; 3155 bound periodical volumes; 2 VF drawers of pamphlets. **Subscriptions:** 60 journals and other serials. **Services:** Library open to public with permission of Rector of the seminary. **Special Catalogs:** Language file; rare book file.

★11713★
ST. DAVID'S UNITED CHURCH - LIBRARY (Rel-Theol)*
3303 Capitol Hill Crescent, N.W.   Phone: (403) 284-2276
Calgary, AB, Canada T2M 2R2   Molly Webb
Founded: 1968. **Subjects:** Religion, theology, Bible. **Holdings:** 480 books; 210 filmstrips and slides; 30 transparencies; 5 tapes. **Services:** Copying; library open to public with restrictions.

★11714★
ST. DOMINIC-JACKSON MEMORIAL HOSPITAL - LUTHER MANSHIP MEDICAL LIBRARY (Med)†
969 Lakeland Drive   Phone: (601) 982-0121
Jackson, MS 39216   Clara Joorfetz, Libn.
Founded: 1973. **Staff:** Prof 1. **Subjects:** Medicine, nursing, mental health. **Holdings:** 1911 books; 439 bound periodical volumes. **Subscriptions:** 127 journals and other serials. **Services:** Interlibrary loans; library not open to public. **Networks/Consortia:** Member of Central Mississippi Library Council; Central Mississippi Council of Medical Libraries.

★11715★
ST. ELIZABETH COMMUNITY HEALTH CENTER - MEDICAL LIBRARY (Med)
555 South 70th St.   Phone: (402) 483-9296
Lincoln, NE 68510   Leslee Shell, Dir.
Staff: Prof 1; Other 1. **Subjects:** Medicine, nursing. **Holdings:** 2783 books; 1643 bound periodical volumes; 38 audiovisual items; 2524 unbound journals; 16 files. **Subscriptions:** 116 journals and other serials. **Services:** Interlibrary loans; copying; library open to public. **Networks/Consortia:** Member of Lincoln Health Science Library Group; Midcontinental Regional Medical Library Program. **Publications:** Lincoln Health Science Library Group Union List of Serials, Directory.

★11716★
ST. ELIZABETH HOSPITAL - HEALTH SCIENCE LIBRARY (Med)
1506 S. Oneida St.   Phone: (414) 738-2324
Appleton, WI 54915   Mary M. Bayorgeon, Dir., Lib.Serv.
Founded: 1973. **Staff:** Prof 1; Other 2. **Subjects:** Medicine, nursing, hospital administration. **Holdings:** 2445 books; 2644 bound periodical volumes; 1129 audiotape cassettes; 229 videotapes. **Subscriptions:** 280 journals and other serials. **Services:** Interlibrary loans; copying; library open to public with restrictions. **Computerized Information Services:** MEDLINE. **Networks/Consortia:** Member of Greater Midwest Regional Medical Library Network (Region 3); Fox River Valley Area Library Consortium; Fox Valley Library Council.

★11717★
ST. ELIZABETH HOSPITAL - HEALTH SCIENCES LIBRARY (Med)
210 Williamson St.   Phone: (201) 527-5371
Elizabeth, NJ 07207   Sally Holdorf, Libn.
Staff: Prof 1; Other 1. **Subjects:** Medicine, nursing, and allied health fields. **Holdings:** 1780 books; 650 bound periodical volumes. **Subscriptions:** 117 journals and other serials. **Services:** Interlibrary loans; copying. **Computerized Information Services:** NLM. **Networks/Consortia:** Member of Cosmopolitan Biomedical Library Consortium (CBLC).

★11718★
ST. ELIZABETH HOSPITAL - HEALTH SCIENCES LIBRARY (Med)†
2830 Calder Ave.
Box 5405
Beaumont, TX 77702   Phone: (409) 892-7171
                                     Deborah West, Health Sci.Libn.
Founded: 1958. **Staff:** Prof 1; Other 2. **Subjects:** Medicine, dentistry, allied health sciences. **Holdings:** 900 books; 5400 bound periodical volumes; AV material. **Subscriptions:** 120 journals and other serials. **Services:** Interlibrary loans; copying; SDI; library open to public. **Computerized Information**

Services: NLM, DIALOG.

★11719★
ST. ELIZABETH HOSPITAL MEDICAL CENTER - BANNON HEALTH SCIENCE LIBRARY (Med)
1501 Hartford St.
Box 7501   Phone: (317) 423-6143
Lafayette, IN 47903   Ruth Pestalozzi Pape, Med.Libn.
Founded: 1941. **Staff:** 1. **Subjects:** Medicine and allied subjects. **Holdings:** 900 books; 3500 bound periodical volumes; 1102 other books in departmental libraries; 1000 audio cassette tapes; 190 video cassette tapes. **Subscriptions:** 275 journals and other serials. **Services:** Interlibrary loans; copying; library open to medical staff, hospital personnel and health care students. **Computerized Information Services:** MEDLINE. **Networks/Consortia:** Member of Greater Midwest Regional Medical Library Network (Region 3).

★11720★
ST. ELIZABETH HOSPITAL MEDICAL CENTER - MEDICAL LIBRARY (Med)†
1044 Belmont Ave.   Phone: (216) 746-7231
Youngstown, OH 44501   Barbara G. Rosenthal, Med.Libn.
Founded: 1929. **Staff:** 3. **Subjects:** Medicine and related subjects. **Holdings:** 2500 books; 7000 bound periodical volumes; 720 reels of microfilm. **Subscriptions:** 289 journals and other serials. **Services:** Interlibrary loans; copying; compiling bibliographies; library open to public with approval of librarian. **Computerized Information Services:** MEDLINE.

★11721★
ST. ELIZABETH HOSPITAL MEDICAL CENTER SCHOOL OF NURSING - LIBRARY (Med)
1044 Belmont Ave.   Phone: (216) 746-7211
Youngstown, OH 44501   Doris L. Crawford, Libn.
Founded: 1911. **Staff:** Prof 1; Other 2. **Subjects:** Nursing, medicine, allied health fields. **Subscriptions:** Historical Collection (nursing). **Holdings:** 7354 books; 1692 bound periodical volumes; 11 VF drawers of pamphlets; 1 VF drawer of photographs; 600 AV materials. **Subscriptions:** 229 journals and other serials. **Services:** Interlibrary loans; copying; library open to public for reference use only. **Automated Operations:** Computerized cataloging. **Computerized Information Services:** DIALOG, MEDLINE. **Networks/Consortia:** Member of Northeastern Ohio Universities College of Medicine (NEOUCOM). **Publications:** Bibliographies; Annual Reports. **Special Catalogs:** Audiovisual Catalog (card and book). **Special Indexes:** Subject Index to New Acquisitions, bimonthly.

★11722★
ST. ELIZABETH HOSPITAL - MEDICAL LIBRARY (Med)
600 Sager   Phone: (217) 442-6300
Danville, IL 61832   Rosemary M. Flanagan, Med.Libn.
Staff: Prof 1; Other 1. **Subjects:** Medicine, nursing. **Holdings:** 537 books. **Subscriptions:** 73 journals and other serials. **Services:** Interlibrary loans; copying; library not open to public. **Automated Operations:** Computerized cataloging and acquisitions. **Networks/Consortia:** Member of Lincoln Trail Libraries System.

★11723★
ST. ELIZABETH MEDICAL CENTER - HEALTH SCIENCES LIBRARY (Med)†
601 Miami Blvd., W.   Phone: (513) 229-6061
Dayton, OH 45408   Ann L. Lewis, Med.Libn.
Staff: 4. **Subjects:** Medicine, sports medicine, rehabilitation, physical medicine, family practice, gastroenterology. **Special Collections:** Archives of St. Elizabeth Medical Center. **Holdings:** 7239 books; 6752 bound periodical volumes; AV materials. **Subscriptions:** 450 journals and other serials. **Services:** Interlibrary loans; copying; SDI; library open to public for reference use only. **Computerized Information Services:** MEDLINE, OCLC, BRS. **Networks/Consortia:** Member of Dayton Area MEDLINE Consortium.

★11724★
ST. ELIZABETH MEDICAL CENTER - HEALTH SCIENCES LIBRARY (Med)
110 S. 9th Ave.   Phone: (509) 575-5000
Yakima, WA 98902   Sr. Irene Charron, S.P., Med.Libn.
Founded: 1969. **Staff:** Prof 1; Other 2. **Subjects:** Medicine, nursing, health sciences, hospital administration. **Holdings:** 3080 books; 494 bound periodical volumes; 4 VF drawers of health sciences material; 124 Audio-Digest tapes; archives (396 books; 222 bound periodical volumes). **Subscriptions:** 251 journals and other serials. **Services:** Interlibrary loans; copying; library open to public. **Computerized Information Services:** MEDLARS. Performs searches on cost recovery basis. **Networks/Consortia:** Member of Pacific Northwest Regional Health Sciences Library Service (PNRHSLS); Sisters of Providence Library Consortium. **Publications:** Health

Sciences Library Newsletter, quarterly. **Special Indexes:** Vertical File Index (notebook); Index to National Library of Medicine Bibliographies.

★11725★
ST. ELIZABETH MEDICAL CENTER - NORTH - MEDICAL LIBRARY (Med)*
401 E. 20th St.   Phone: (606) 292-4048
Covington, KY 41014   Donald R. Smith, Libn.
Staff: Prof 1; Other 1. **Subjects:** Medicine, nursing, psychology, sociology. **Holdings:** 2000 books; 5000 bound periodical volumes; 107 indexes. **Subscriptions:** 220 journals and other serials. **Services:** Interlibrary loans; copying; library open to health sciences professionals. **Computerized Information Services:** Online systems. **Publications:** Interface, bimonthly.

★11726★
ST. ELIZABETH MEDICAL CENTER - ST. ELIZABETH HOSPITAL SCHOOL OF NURSING - LIBRARY (Med)
1508 Tippecanoe St.   Phone: (317) 423-6125
Lafayette, IN 47904   Janet Stroud, Media & Instr.Serv.Coord.
Staff: Prof 1. **Subjects:** Nursing, medicine, sociology, psychiatry. **Holdings:** 4000 books; 302 filmstrips; 6 16mm films; 50 charts. **Subscriptions:** 132 journals and other serials; 10 newspapers. **Services:** Interlibrary loans; copying; library open to public. library. **Publications:** Annual report; bibliographies of various fields in nursing.

★11727★
ST. ELIZABETH MEDICAL CENTER - SOUTH - LIBRARY (Med)
One Medical Village Dr.   Phone: (606) 344-2248
Edgewood, KY 41017   Donald R. Smith, Libn.
Founded: 1978. **Staff:** Prof 1; Other 1. **Subjects:** Health sciences. **Holdings:** 470 books. **Subscriptions:** 43 journals and other serials. **Services:** Interlibrary loans; copying; library open to health professionals. **Computerized Information Services:** BRS. **Networks/Consortia:** Member of Cincinnati Online Consortium for Life Sciences (COCLS); Cincinnati Area Health Sciences Library Association (CAHSLA).

★11728★
ST. ELIZABETH'S HOSPITAL - HEALTH SCIENCE LIBRARY (Med)
211 S. Third St.   Phone: (618) 234-2120
Belleville, IL 62221   Michael A. Campese, Lib.Dir.
Staff: Prof 1; Other 2. **Subjects:** Medicine, nursing, hospital administration. **Special Collections:** Medical books dating from 1879 to 1890. **Holdings:** 2000 books; 1200 bound periodical volumes. **Subscriptions:** 323 journals and other serials. **Services:** Interlibrary loans; copying; literature searches; library open to public on a limited schedule. **Computerized Information Services:** MEDLARS. **Networks/Consortia:** Member of Greater Midwest Regional Medical Library Network (Region 3); Kaskaskia Library System; Areawide Hospital Library Consortium of Southwestern Illinois (AHLC).

★11729★
ST. ELIZABETHS HOSPITAL - HEALTH SCIENCES LIBRARY (Med)
Administration Bldg.
2700 Martin Luther King Jr. Ave., S.E.   Phone: (202) 574-7274
Washington, DC 20032   Toby G. Port, Adm.Libn.
Staff: Prof 2; Other 4. **Subjects:** Psychiatry, occupational therapy, general medicine, Protestant and Catholic chaplaincy, neurology, dance therapy, dentistry, therapeutic recreation, clinical psychology, social work, speech pathology and audiology, psychiatric nursing, psychoanalysis, psychodrama. **Special Collections:** William Alanson White Library. **Holdings:** 20,000 books; 18,000 bound periodical volumes. **Subscriptions:** 300 journals and other serials. **Services:** Interlibrary loans; copying; library open to public for reference use only with librarian's permission. **Automated Operations:** Computerized cataloging. **Computerized Information Services:** MEDLINE. **Networks/Consortia:** Member of District of Columbia Health Sciences Information Network (DOCHSIN). **Publications:** Accessions lists, monthly - for internal distribution only. **Staff:** Marcella Fludd, ILL; Stephen O. Newton, Cat.

★11730★
ST. ELIZABETH'S HOSPITAL - LUKEN HEALTH SCIENCES LIBRARY (Med)
1431 N. Claremont Ave.   Phone: (312) 278-2000
Chicago, IL 60622   Christina Rudawski, Lib.Dir.
Founded: 1955. **Staff:** Prof 1; Other 1. **Subjects:** Medicine, nursing and allied health sciences. **Holdings:** 1500 books; 722 bound periodical volumes; 309 volumes of unbound medical journals; 160 cassette tapes; 81 filmstrips. **Subscriptions:** 101 journals and other serials. **Services:** Interlibrary loans; library not open to public. **Networks/Consortia:** Member of Metropolitan Consortium.

★11731★
ST. ELIZABETH'S HOSPITAL - MEDICAL LIBRARY (Med)†
736 Cambridge St.   Phone: (617) 782-7000
Brighton, MA 02135   Deborah T. Almquist, Libn.
Staff: Prof 1; Other 1. **Subjects:** Medicine. **Holdings:** 2925 books; 4815 bound periodical volumes. **Subscriptions:** 145 journals and other serials. **Services:** Interlibrary loans; copying; library open to public with restrictions. **Computerized Information Services:** MEDLARS. **Networks/Consortia:** Member of Boston Biomedical Library Consortium; Massachusetts Health Sciences Library Network (MAHSLIN).

★11732★
ST. ELIZABETH'S HOSPITAL - NURSING SCHOOL LIBRARY (Med)
2215 Genesee St.   Phone: (315) 798-5209
Utica, NY 13503   Ann M. Kelly, Libn.
Staff: Prof 1; Other 2. **Subjects:** Nursing, medicine, sociology, psychology. **Holdings:** 6603 books; 613 bound periodical volumes; 9 VF drawers; 220 phonograph records; 157 videotapes; 326 AV kits. **Subscriptions:** 110 journals and other serials. **Services:** Interlibrary loans; copying; library open to public for reference use only with permission from librarian.

★11733★
ST. ELIZABETH'S HOSPITAL - SCHOOL OF NURSING - LIBRARY (Med)
159 Washington St.   Phone: (617) 782-7000
Brighton, MA 02135   Robert L. Loud, Libn.
Staff: 1. **Subjects:** Nursing, medicine. **Holdings:** 3000 books and bound periodical volumes. **Subscriptions:** 68 journals and other serials. **Services:** Interlibrary loans; library not open to public. **Networks/Consortia:** Member of Libraries for Nursing Consortium (LINC).

★11734★
ST. FRANCES CABRINI HOSPITAL - MEDICAL LIBRARY (Med)
3330 Masonic Dr.   Phone: (318) 487-1122
Alexandria, LA 71301   Denise Dupont, Act.Libn.
Founded: 1957. **Staff:** Prof 1; Other 1. **Subjects:** Medicine, nursing, and allied health sciences. **Holdings:** 3471 books and bound periodical volumes; 276 tapes and phonograph records; 157 unbound journals. **Subscriptions:** 59 journals and other serials. **Services:** Interlibrary loans; copying; SDI; library open to public with restrictions.

★11735★
ST. FRANCIS CENTER FOR CHRISTIAN RENEWAL - ECUMENICAL LIBRARY
Box 32180
Oklahoma City, OK 73123
Founded: 1967. **Subjects:** Ecumenism, theology, church history, biblical studies. **Holdings:** 36,500 books and bound periodical volumes. **Remarks:** Presently inactive.

ST. FRANCIS CHAPEL INFORMATION CENTER AND FREE-LENDING LIBRARY
See: St. Francis Monastery and Chapel

★11736★
ST. FRANCIS COLLEGE - JAMES A. KELLY INSTITUTE FOR LOCAL HISTORICAL STUDIES - LIBRARY (Hist)
180 Remsen St.   Phone: (718) 522-2300
Brooklyn, NY 11201   Arthur J. Konop, Dir.-Archv.
Founded: 1956. **Staff:** 2. **Subjects:** Local history of Brooklyn. **Holdings:** 10,000 books; 2 million folios of archival material. **Services:** Library open to public for reference use only. **Networks/Consortia:** Member of Long Island Archives Conference; Brooklyn Educational & Cultural Alliance. **Special Catalogs:** Guide to Materials in the John Rooney Collection (book).

★11737★
ST. FRANCIS HOSPITAL - COMMUNITY HEALTH SCIENCE LIBRARY (Med)
415 Oak St.
Breckenridge, MN 56520   Karen Engstrom, Dir. of Lib.Serv.
Founded: 1975. **Staff:** Prof 1; Other 1. **Subjects:** Medicine, nursing and allied health sciences. **Holdings:** 416 books; 4 VF drawers of pamphlets; 23 AV materials. **Subscriptions:** 168 journals and other serials. **Services:** Interlibrary loans; SDI; library open to health care professionals. **Networks/Consortia:** Member of Valley Medical Network; Greater Midwest Regional Medical Library Network (Region 3). **Remarks:** Library contains holdings of the School of Nursing library.

★11738★
ST. FRANCIS HOSPITAL - DOCTORS' LIBRARY (Med)
East Pikes Peak Ave. & Prospect   Phone: (303) 636-8800
Colorado Springs, CO 80903   Sr. Mary Louis Wenzl, Lib.Ck.
Staff: 1. **Subjects:** Medicine, surgery, pediatrics, obstetrics, psychiatry, orthopedics. **Holdings:** 144 books; 182 bound periodical volumes; 1 volume of tape cassettes. **Subscriptions:** 14 journals and other serials. **Services:** Interlibrary loans; copying; library open to public with restrictions.

★11739★
ST. FRANCIS HOSPITAL - HEALTH SCIENCE LEARNING CENTER (Med)
3237 S. 16th St.   Phone: (414) 647-5156
Milwaukee, WI 53215   Joy Shong, Coord.
Founded: 1974. **Staff:** Prof 2; Other 1. **Subjects:** Medicine, nursing, paramedicine. **Special Collections:** Materials relating to and serving patient education. **Holdings:** 2000 books; 2800 bound periodical volumes; 896 AV materials. **Subscriptions:** 245 journals and other serials. **Services:** Interlibrary loans; copying; SDI; Center open to public. **Computerized Information Services:** MEDLINE, BRS. **Networks/Consortia:** Member of Southeastern Wisconsin Health Sciences Library Consortium (SWHSL). **Staff:** Carolyn Barloga, Asst.Libn.

★11740★
ST. FRANCIS HOSPITAL - HEALTH SCIENCE LIBRARY (Med)
North Rd.   Phone: (914) 471-2000
Poughkeepsie, NY 12601   Carol Page, Med.Libn.
Staff: Prof 1; Other 1. **Subjects:** Internal medicine, surgery, dentistry, pediatrics. **Holdings:** 910 books; 74 unbound journals. **Subscriptions:** 77 journals and other serials. **Services:** Interlibrary loans; copying; library open to college students with permission. **Networks/Consortia:** Member of Southeastern New York Library Resources Council (SENYLRC).

★11741★
ST. FRANCIS HOSPITAL - HEALTH SCIENCES LIBRARY (Med)†
6161 S. Yale Ave.   Phone: (918) 494-1210
Tulsa, OK 74177   Darryl Logan, Med.Libn.
Staff: Prof 1; Other 2. **Subjects:** Medical sciences, nursing, hospital management. **Holdings:** 2002 books; 4904 bound periodical volumes; 278 government documents. **Subscriptions:** 250 journals and other serials. **Services:** Interlibrary loans; library not open to public.

★11742★
ST. FRANCIS HOSPITAL - MEDICAL CENTER - MEDICAL LIBRARY (Med)*
530-616 N.E. Glen Oak Ave.   Phone: (309) 672-2210
Peoria, IL 61637   Mary Anne Parr, Med.Libn.
Founded: 1942. **Staff:** Prof 1; Other 4. **Subjects:** Surgery, internal medicine, orthopedics, family practice, pediatrics. **Holdings:** 3500 books; 6600 bound periodical volumes; 300 slide sets; 550 video cassettes; 1000 audio cassettes. **Subscriptions:** 325 journals and other serials. **Services:** Interlibrary loans; copying; library open to public. **Computerized Information Services:** MEDLINE. **Networks/Consortia:** Member of Heart of Illinois Library Consortium (HILC); Greater Midwest Regional Medical Library Network (Region 3). **Publications:** Newsletter, monthly; acquisitions list, monthly.

★11743★
ST. FRANCIS HOSPITAL AND MEDICAL CENTER - SCHOOL OF NURSING LIBRARY (Med)
338 Asylum St.   Phone: (203) 247-4411
Hartford, CT 06103   Ruth P. Carroll, Dir.
Founded: 1942. **Staff:** Prof 2; Other 2. **Subjects:** Nursing, psychiatry, psychology, pre-clinical medicine. **Holdings:** 6000 books; 400 bound periodical volumes; 15 VF drawers. **Subscriptions:** 150 journals and other serials. **Services:** Interlibrary loans; copying; library open to public. **Computerized Information Services:** MEDLARS. **Networks/Consortia:** Member of Capitol Area Association of Medical Library Directors (CAAMLD). **Staff:** Donna Wolfson, Libn.

★11744★
ST. FRANCIS HOSPITAL AND MEDICAL CENTER - WILSON C. JAINSEN LIBRARY (Med)
114 Woodland St.   Phone: (203) 548-4746
Hartford, CT 06105   Ruth Carroll, Dir. of Libs.
Staff: Prof 5; Other 6. **Subjects:** Medicine, nursing, management, psychiatry, psychology. **Holdings:** 9000 books; 300 periodical titles on microfilm. **Subscriptions:** 700 journals and other serials. **Services:** Interlibrary loans; copying; library open to public. **Computerized Information Services:** BRS, NLM, DIALOG. **Networks/Consortia:** Member of Capitol Area Association of Medical Library Directors (CAAMLD). **Publications:** Library Notes. **Staff:** Carolyn Walcox, Hd., Ref.; Ted Friedmann, Clinical Libn.; Jonathan Lord,

Clinical Libn.; Nancy Bianchi, Clinical Libn.

★11745★
ST. FRANCIS HOSPITAL - MEDICAL LIBRARY (Med)
601 E. Micheltorena   Phone: (805) 962-7661
Santa Barbara, CA 93103   Marilyn Shearer, Dir.
Staff: 2. **Subjects:** Medicine and medical specialties. **Holdings:** 1020 books; 469 bound periodical volumes; tapes; cassettes. **Subscriptions:** 38 journals and other serials. **Services:** Library not open to public.

★11746★
ST. FRANCIS HOSPITAL, INC. - MEDICAL LIBRARY (Med)
7th & Clayton Sts.   Phone: (302) 421-4123
Wilmington, DE 19805   Sr. Joan Ignatius McCleary, O.S.F., Libn.
Founded: 1936. **Staff:** Prof 2; Other 1. **Subjects:** Medicine, nursing, surgery, psychiatry, continuing education for acute care. **Holdings:** 3227 books; 123 bound periodical volumes; 12 VF drawers of reprints, original articles and ephemera; 114 audiotapes. **Subscriptions:** 150 journals and other serials. **Services:** Interlibrary loans; copying; library open to public with restrictions. **Networks/Consortia:** Member of Wilmington Area Biomedical Library Consortium (WABLC). **Publications:** Library News, bimonthly - to staff and consortium members. **Special Indexes:** Vertical file subject index (card). **Staff:** Helen E. Gravell, Asst.Libn.

★11747★
ST. FRANCIS HOSPITAL - MEDICAL LIBRARY (Med)
250 W. 63rd St.   Phone: (305) 868-5000
Miami Beach, FL 33141   Wilma S. Grover, Libn.
Founded: 1927. **Staff:** Prof 1. **Subjects:** Medicine and allied health sciences. **Holdings:** 600 books; 2750 bound periodical volumes; 856 audiotapes; 12 phonograph records; 576 slides. **Subscriptions:** 90 journals and other serials. **Services:** Interlibrary loans; copying; library not open to public. **Networks/Consortia:** Member of Miami Health Sciences Library Consortium (MHSLC); Southeastern/Atlantic Regional Medical Library Services.

★11748★
ST. FRANCIS HOSPITAL - MEDICAL LIBRARY (Med)
2230 Liliha St.   Phone: (808) 547-6481
Honolulu, HI 96817   Julie J. Sirois, Libn.
Founded: 1955. **Staff:** Prof 1; Other 2. **Subjects:** Nursing, medicine, hospital administration, sociology, psychology, pre-clinical sciences. **Holdings:** 8000 books; 1500 bound periodical volumes; 500 slides and tapes; 6 VF drawers of pamphlets, medical book reviews, staff publications. **Subscriptions:** 379 journals and other serials. **Services:** Interlibrary loans; copying; SDI; library open to public. **Computerized Information Services:** MEDLARS. Performs searches on cost recovery basis. **Networks/Consortia:** Member of Pacific Southwest Regional Medical Library Service (PSRMLS). **Publications:** Brochure, annual - distributed to users; Library Acquisition List, monthly - for internal distribution only. **Special Indexes:** Index of medical reviews; index to pamphlet file.

★11749★
ST. FRANCIS HOSPITAL - MEDICAL LIBRARY (Med)
Port Washington Blvd.   Phone: (516) 627-6200
Roslyn, NY 11576   John Dwyer, Med.Libn.
Staff: Prof 1; Other 1. **Subjects:** Cardiology, pulmonary diseases, biomedical sciences, hospitals, management. **Special Collections:** Thoracic and cardiovascular surgery. **Holdings:** 2000 books; 1000 bound periodical volumes; pamphlets. **Subscriptions:** 100 journals and other serials. **Services:** Interlibrary loans; library not open to public.

★11750★
ST. FRANCIS HOSPITAL - SCHOOL OF NURSING LIBRARY (Med)
319 Ridge Ave.   Phone: (312) 492-6268
Evanston, IL 60202   Patricia Gibson, Libn.
Staff: Prof 1; Other 1. **Subjects:** Medicine, nursing and allied sciences. **Holdings:** 3000 books; 420 bound periodical volumes; 6 VF drawers of clippings and pamphlets; 234 filmstrip programs; 160 film loops; 60 audio cassettes; 25 video cassettes; 18 16mm films. **Subscriptions:** 50 journals and other serials. **Services:** Interlibrary loans; copying; library open to medical and nursing personnel. **Networks/Consortia:** Member of Metropolitan Consortium; North Suburban Library System (NSLS).

★11751★
ST. FRANCIS MEDICAL CENTER - CAPE COUNTY MEMORIAL MEDICAL LIBRARY, INC. (Med)
211 St. Francis Dr.   Phone: (314) 335-1251
Cape Girardeau, MO 63701   June Johnston, Med.Rec.Dir.
Founded: 1950. **Staff:** Prof 2; Other 2. **Subjects:** Medicine, nursing, hospital

administration, mental health. **Holdings:** 1300 books; 135 bound periodical volumes; 2 shelves of tapes and cassettes. **Subscriptions:** 139 journals and other serials. **Services:** Interlibrary loans; copying; library open with permission of medical and hospital administrative staff. **Networks/Consortia:** Member of Midcontinental Regional Medical Library Program. **Publications:** Cape County Journal, monthly - to members. **Staff:** Mrs. Kilja Israel, Libn.

★11752★
ST. FRANCIS MEDICAL CENTER - HEALTH SCIENCES LIBRARY (Med)
601 Hamilton Ave. Phone: (609) 599-5068
Trenton, NJ 08629 Anita K. Johnson, Dir.
Founded: 1930. **Staff:** Prof 1; Other 2. **Subjects:** Medicine, nursing, allied health sciences. **Holdings:** 5000 books. **Subscriptions:** 300 journals and other serials. **Services:** Interlibrary loans; library not open to public. **Networks/Consortia:** Member of Central Jersey Health Science Libraries Association; Health Sciences Libraries of New Jersey.

★11753★
ST. FRANCIS MEDICAL CENTER - HEALTH SCIENCES LIBRARY (Med)
615 S. 10th St. Phone: (608) 785-0940
La Crosse, WI 54601 Sr. Louise Therese Lotze, Lib.Supv.
Staff: Prof 1; Other 1. **Subjects:** Medicine, dentistry, nursing, allied subjects. **Special Collections:** History of medicine. **Holdings:** 2570 books; 7400 bound periodical volumes; 12 VF drawers of clippings and articles. **Subscriptions:** 360 journals and other serials. **Services:** Interlibrary loans; library open to public.

★11754★
ST. FRANCIS MEDICAL CENTER - MOTHER MACARIA HEALTH SCIENCE LIBRARY (Med)
3630 E. Imperial Hwy. Phone: (213) 603-6045
Lynwood, CA 90262 Eva Kratz, Dir. of Lib.Serv.
Founded: 1971. **Staff:** Prof 1; Other 2. **Subjects:** Medicine, nursing, hospital administration, paramedical fields. **Holdings:** 3000 books; 4000 bound periodical volumes; 120 other cataloged items; 800 audiotapes; 90 boxes of peripheral material; 175 items of archival material; 48 videotapes. **Subscriptions:** 300 journals and other serials. **Services:** Interlibrary loans; copying; SDI; library open to health professionals. **Computerized Information Services:** Online systems. **Publications:** Annual report; Monthly Acquisitions List.

★11755★
ST. FRANCIS MEMORIAL HOSPITAL - WALTER F. SCHALLER MEMORIAL LIBRARY (Med)
Box 7726 Phone: (415) 775-4321
San Francisco, CA 94120 Maryann Zaremska, Dir., Lib.Serv.
Staff: Prof 1; Other 1. **Subjects:** Medicine, nursing. **Special Collections:** Plastic and reconstructive surgery; burns. **Holdings:** 5500 volumes; 650 audiotapes. **Subscriptions:** 145 journals and other serials and newspapers. **Services:** Interlibrary loans; SDI; library open to affiliated personnel only. **Computerized Information Services:** MEDLARS. **Networks/Consortia:** Member of San Francisco Biomedical Library Network; Pacific Southwest Regional Medical Library Service (PSRMLS).

★11756★
ST. FRANCIS MONASTERY AND CHAPEL - ST. FRANCIS CHAPEL INFORMATION CENTER & FREE-LENDING LIBRARY (Rel-Theol)
20 Page St. Phone: (401) 331-6510
Providence, RI 02903 Fr. John Bosco Valente, O.F.M., Libn.
Staff: Prof 1; Other 25. **Subjects:** Religion. **Special Collections:** Franciscana. **Holdings:** 12,000 books; pamphlets and picture files. **Subscriptions:** 20 journals and other serials. **Services:** Interlibrary loans; copying; library open to public.

★11757★
ST. FRANCIS REGIONAL MEDICAL CENTER - PROFESSIONAL LIBRARY (Med)
929 N. St. Francis Phone: (316) 268-5979
Wichita, KS 67214 Betty B. Wood, Libn.
Founded: 1945. **Staff:** Prof 2; Other 3. **Subjects:** Medicine, nursing, surgery, orthopedics, management. **Holdings:** 6000 books; 10,000 bound periodical volumes. **Subscriptions:** 473 journals and other serials. **Services:** Interlibrary loans; copying. **Computerized Information Services:** MEDLINE. **Publications:** Journal Holdings, annual - to hospital staff and local special libraries.

★11758★
ST. FRANCIS-ST. GEORGE HOSPITAL - HEALTH SCIENCES LIBRARY (Med)*
3131 Queen City Ave. Phone: (513) 389-5118
Cincinnati, OH 45238 Carol Mayor, Libn.
Staff: Prof 1. **Subjects:** Medicine, nursing, hospital administration. **Holdings:** 557 books; 365 periodicals. **Subscriptions:** 85 journals and other serials. **Services:** Interlibrary loans; copying; library open to public with special permission.

★11759★
ST. FRANCIS SEMINARY - SALZMANN LIBRARY (Rel-Theol)
3257 South Lake Dr. Phone: (414) 483-1979
Milwaukee, WI 53207 Rev. Lawrence K. Miech, Lib.Dir.
Staff: Prof 3. **Subjects:** Scripture, theology, church history, social science, behavioral science, canon law. **Special Collections:** Wisconsin Catholic Church History; Catholic Americana. **Holdings:** 65,000 books; 13,000 bound periodical volumes; 1600 dissertations; 10 VF drawers of pamphlets, documents; 250 reels of microfilm; 2500 AV materials. **Subscriptions:** 315 journals and other serials; 12 newspapers. **Services:** Interlibrary loans; copying; library open to public for reference use only. **Staff:** Sr. Colette Zirbes, Asst.Libn.; Rev. Thomas Fait, Archv.

★11760★
ST. FRANCIS OF THE WOODS LTD. - EASTERN ORTHODOX CATHOLIC CHURCH IN AMERICA - LIBRARY (Rel-Theol)
Rt. 1 Phone: (405) 466-3774
Coyle, OK 73027 Kay Adair, Libn.
Founded: 1969. **Staff:** Prof 2. **Subjects:** Eastern Orthodox theology, patristics, Biblical theology, liturgics, Byzantine music, philosophy, psychology, homiletics, Roman Catholic theology, Anglican theology. **Special Collections:** Monumentae Musicae Byzantinae - 11th through 17th century Byzantine music manuscripts on microfilm (100); Carl G. Jung. **Holdings:** 12,000 books; 5000 bound periodical volumes; 300 reels of microfilm; 3000 unbound periodicals; 1000 leaflets, pamphlets; 500 phonograph recordings. **Subscriptions:** 12 journals and other serials. **Services:** Library open to public with restrictions. **Formerly:** Eastern Orthodox Catholic Church in America - Cimarron Heights Library **Staff:** James Gleason, Asst.Libn.

★11761★
ST. FRANCIS XAVIER UNIVERSITY - COADY INTERNATIONAL INSTITUTE - MARIE MICHAEL LIBRARY (Soc Sci)†
Phone: (902) 867-3964
Antigonish, NS, Canada B2G 1C0 Sr. Berthold Mackey, Chf.Libn.
Founded: 1974. **Staff:** Prof 1. **Subjects:** Cooperatives, community development, adult education, health education, labor economics, technology. **Holdings:** 4000 volumes; seminar reports. **Subscriptions:** 80 journals and other serials; 11 newspapers. **Services:** Interlibrary loans; copying; library open to public.

★11762★
ST. GABRIEL'S HOSPITAL - LIBRARY (Med)
St. Joseph's Hall Phone: (612) 632-5441
Little Falls, MN 56345 Peggy Martin, Dir. of Educ.
Founded: 1942. **Staff:** Prof 1. **Subjects:** Nursing, medicine, science. **Holdings:** Figures not available. **Services:** Interlibrary loans; copying; library open to public.

ST. HELENA PUBLIC LIBRARY - NAPA VALLEY WINE LIBRARY ASSOCIATION
See: Napa Valley Wine Library Association

★11763★
ST. HELEN'S ISLAND MUSEUM MONTREAL - DAVID M. STEWART LIBRARY (Mil; Hist)†
Sta. A, P.O. Box 1024 Phone: (514) 861-6738
Montreal, PQ, Canada H3C 2W9 Elizabeth F. Hale, Libn.Cons.
Staff: Prof 1. **Subjects:** Canadian history to 1763, including military and social history; American Revolution; War of 1812; Rebellion of 1837-1838. **Special Collections:** Macdonald Stewart Collection of rare books, documents, engravings and 19th century Montreal history; rare books, pre-1764 (1000). **Holdings:** 6000 books. **Subscriptions:** 50 journals and other serials. **Services:** Copying; consultation by appointment; library open to qualified researchers only. **Publications:** 4 M's Bulletins, irregular (both French and English editions) - to members. **Also Known As:** Montreal Military and Maritime Museum.

★11764★
ST. HERMAN'S ORTHODOX THEOLOGICAL SEMINARY - LIBRARY (Rel-Theol)*
414 Mission Rd.
Box 728   Phone: (907) 486-3524
Kodiak, AK 99615   Rev.Fr. Joseph P. Kreta, Dean
Staff: 3. **Subjects:** Church history, patristics, Biblical studies, spirituality, comparative theology, liturgy. **Special Collections:** Archives of the Russian Orthodox Diocese of Alaska. **Holdings:** 6000 books. **Subscriptions:** 35 journals and other serials; 13 newspapers. **Services:** Interlibrary loans; copying; library open to public.

★11765★
ST. JAMES HOSPITAL - HUGO LONG LIBRARY (Med)
1423 Chicago Rd.   Phone: (312) 756-1000
Chicago Heights, IL 60411   Margaret A. Lindstrand, Libn.
Founded: 1940. **Staff:** 1. **Subjects:** Medicine and related subjects. **Holdings:** 800 books; 1350 bound periodical volumes. **Subscriptions:** 70 journals and other serials. **Services:** Interlibrary loans; library open to public with restrictions. **Networks/Consortia:** Member of Chicago and South Consortium.

★11766★
ST. JAMES HOSPITAL - MEDICAL LIBRARY (Med)
610 E. Water St.   Phone: (815) 842-2828
Pontiac, IL 61764   Jill A. Kresse, Lib.Mgr.
Staff: 1. **Subjects:** Medicine and allied health sciences. **Holdings:** 158 volumes; 13 video cassettes. **Subscriptions:** 30 journals and other serials. **Services:** Interlibrary loans; copying; library open to public for reference use only. **Networks/Consortia:** Member of Greater Midwest Regional Medical Library Network (Region 3); Heart of Illinois Library Consortium.

★11767★
ST. JOE MINERALS CORPORATION - INFORMATION CENTER (Sci-Tech)
Box A   Phone: (412) 774-1020
Monaca, PA 15061   Sallie Smith, Tech.Libn.
Staff: Prof 1; Other 1. **Subjects:** Nonferrous metallurgy, materials engineering, electrochemistry. **Holdings:** 4000 books; 300 bound periodical volumes; in-house reports. **Subscriptions:** 270 journals and other serials. **Services:** Interlibrary loans; copying; SDI; center open to public with restrictions. **Computerized Information Services:** DIALOG, SDC, BRS, CAS Online, Occupational Health Servies, Inc., Pergamon Infoline Ltd. **Publications:** New Books. monthly; Thesaurus of Metallurgical Terms, 3rd edition; Announcing Publication, monthly; Technical Literature Update, monthly.

ST. JOHN DEL REY MINING COMPANY ARCHIVES
See: University of Texas, Austin - Benson Latin American Collection

★11768★
ST. JOHN HOSPITAL - MEDICAL LIBRARY (Med)
22101 Moross Rd.   Phone: (313) 343-3733
Detroit, MI 48236   Marie K. Bolanos, Dir.
Founded: 1952. **Staff:** Prof 3; Other 3. **Subjects:** Medicine, nursing and allied health sciences. **Holdings:** 6000 books; 5900 bound periodical volumes; 200 AV programs; 10 VF drawers of pamphlets, documents; 7 series of medical audiotapes; 200 journal titles on microfiche. **Subscriptions:** 425 journals and other serials. **Services:** Interlibrary loans; copying; SDI; library open to public with permission of the director. **Computerized Information Services:** MEDLINE, DIALOG, BRS. **Staff:** Ellen O'Donnell, Ref.Libn.

★11769★
ST. JOHN MEDICAL CENTER - HEALTH SCIENCES LIBRARY (Med)†
1923 S. Utica   Phone: (918) 744-2970
Tulsa, OK 74104   Geneva N. Norvell, Libn.
Founded: 1946. **Staff:** 1. **Subjects:** Medicine, nursing and related subjects. **Holdings:** 3041 books; 7050 bound periodical volumes; Audio-Digest tapes. **Subscriptions:** 148 journals and other serials. **Services:** Interlibrary loans; copying; library open to medical and nursing students.

★11770★
ST. JOHN UNITED CHURCH OF CHRIST - LIBRARY (Rel-Theol)
307 W. Clay St.   Phone: (618) 344-2526
Collinsville, IL 62234   Norma L. Fischer, Libn.
Founded: 1959. **Staff:** Prof 1; Other 7. **Subjects:** Bible, life and teachings of Jesus, prayer and devotions, faith and theology, religions, worship and music. **Holdings:** 6180 books; 30 phonograph records.

★11771★
ST. JOHN VIANNEY COLLEGE SEMINARY - MARY LOUISE MAYTAG MEMORIAL LIBRARY (Rel-Theol)
2900 S.W. 87th Ave.   Phone: (305) 223-4561
Miami, FL 33165   Sr. Mary Julia O'Donnell, Hd.Libn.
Founded: 1960. **Staff:** Prof 2; Other 1. **Subjects:** Religion, philosophy, psychology, sociology, English, Spanish. **Special Collections:** Paintings by Jehan Georges Vibert. **Holdings:** 36,380 books; 2700 bound periodical volumes. **Subscriptions:** 127 journals and other serials; 15 newspapers. **Services:** Interlibrary loans; copying; library open to public. **Publications:** Library handbook. **Special Catalogs:** Periodical directory (booklet). **Staff:** Sr. Charles Marie Parsons, Asst.Supv., Lib.Serv.

★11772★
ST. JOHN AND WEST SHORE HOSPITAL - MEDIA CENTER (Med)
29000 Center Ridge Rd.   Phone: (216) 835-6020
Westlake, OH 44145   Jung Gallant, Dir.
Founded: 1981. **Staff:** Prof 1. **Subjects:** Medicine, nursing, allied health sciences. **Special Collections:** Osteopathic historical collections (35 items). **Holdings:** 2300 books; 130 bound periodical volumes; 2 drawers of pamphlets. **Subscriptions:** 125 journals and other serials. **Services:** Interlibrary loans; copying; Center open to public with restrictions. **Computerized Information Services:** MEDLARS, DIALOG, BRS.

★11773★
ST. JOHN'S ABBEY AND UNIVERSITY - HILL MONASTIC MANUSCRIPT LIBRARY - BUSH CENTER (Rel-Theol; Hist)
     Phone: (612) 363-3514
Collegeville, MN 56321   Dr. Julian G. Plante, Dir.
Founded: 1964. **Staff:** Prof 4; Other 1. **Subjects:** Medieval theology, science, literature, philosophy, medicine, church history, codicology, papyrology, monasticism, paleography, calligraphy, art, liturgy. **Special Collections:** Pre-1600 manuscripts of 76 individual Austrian libraries; manuscripts from Spain, Ethiopia, Malta, England, Germany, Portugal, Italy and Hungary (61,000 manuscript books in all); 100,000 papyri totalling 21 million pages of documentation (all items are on microfilm). **Services:** Copying; research assistance; library open to public with advance notice. **Publications:** Progress Reports; Catalogs, inventories; Festschrift. **Special Catalogs:** Checklists of manuscripts, occasional; Descriptive Inventories of Manuscripts, occasional. **Staff:** Dr. Getatchew Haile, Mss.Cat.; Jonathan Fischer, O.S.B., Field Dir.; Dr. Richard Gerberding, Mss.Cat.

ST. JOHN'S COLLEGE - LIBRARY
See: University of Manitoba

ST. JOHN'S EPISCOPAL HOSPITAL
See: Interfaith Medical Center

★11774★
ST. JOHN'S HOSPITAL - FREDERICK J. PLONDKE MEDICAL LIBRARY (Med)
403 Maria Ave.   Phone: (612) 228-3255
St. Paul, MN 55106   Jan Walton, Lib.Serv.Dir.
Staff: Prof 1. **Subjects:** Medicine, nursing, allied health sciences. **Holdings:** 1200 books; 40 bound periodical volumes; 150 AV materials. **Subscriptions:** 170 journals and other serials. **Services:** Interlibrary loans; copying; library open to students and health professionals by appointment only. **Computerized Information Services:** BRS. **Networks/Consortia:** Member of Twin Cities Biomedical Consortium (TCBC); MINITEX; Greater Midwest Regional Medical Library (Region 3); Metronet. **Publications:** Library newsletter, 9/year - for internal distribution only.

★11775★
ST. JOHN'S HOSPITAL AND HEALTH CENTER - HOSPITAL LIBRARY (Med)
1328 22nd St.   Phone: (213) 829-8494
Santa Monica, CA 90404   Cathey L. Pinckney, Libn.
Founded: 1952. **Staff:** Prof 1; Other 1. **Subjects:** Medicine, nursing and hospital administration. **Holdings:** 5878 books; 2706 bound periodical volumes; 3142 unbound journal volumes. **Subscriptions:** 321 journals and other serials. **Services:** Interlibrary loans; copying; library open to qualified users.

★11776★
ST. JOHN'S HOSPITAL - HEALTH SCIENCE LIBRARY (Med)
800 E. Carpenter   Phone: (217) 544-6464
Springfield, IL 62769   Kathryn Wrigley, Dir.
Staff: Prof 1; Other 2. **Subjects:** Cardiovascular system, surgery, pediatrics, emergency medicine, nursing, pathology, psychiatry. **Holdings:** 3984 books; 2825 bound periodical volumes; 788 AV software items; pamphlets. **Subscriptions:** 268 journals and other serials. **Services:** Interlibrary loans;

copying; library open to public for reference use only on request. **Computerized Information Services:** OCLC. **Networks/Consortia:** Member of Capital Area Consortium; ILLINET; Greater Midwest Regional Medical Library Network (Region 3). **Publications:** Libri (acquisitions list). **Special Catalogs:** Periodical holdings.

★11777★
ST. JOHN'S HOSPITAL - HEALTH SCIENCE LIBRARY (Med)
Hospital Dr.   Phone: (617) 458-1411
Lowell, MA 01852   Gale Cogan, Dir.
Founded: 1970. **Staff:** Prof 1; Other 1. **Subjects:** Medicine and allied health sciences, hospital administration. **Holdings:** 1000 books. **Subscriptions:** 350 journals and other serials. **Services:** Interlibrary loans; copying; library open to public. **Computerized Information Services:** MEDLARS. **Networks/Consortia:** Member of Boston Biomedical Library Consortium; Northeast Consortium for Health Information (NECHI); Massachusetts Health Sciences Library Network (MAHSLIN).

★11778★
ST. JOHN'S HOSPITAL - MEDICAL LIBRARY (Med)
1235 E. Cherokee   Phone: (417) 881-8811
Springfield, MO 65804   Sr. Lillian Clare, Libn.
Founded: 1904. **Staff:** Prof 1; Other 1. **Subjects:** Medicine and allied health sciences. **Holdings:** 500 books; 9000 bound periodical volumes. **Subscriptions:** 92 journals and other serials. **Services:** Interlibrary loans; Interlibrary loans not open to public. **Computerized Information Services:** BRS.

★11779★
ST. JOHN'S HOSPITAL - SCHOOL OF NURSING LIBRARY (Med)
1930 S. National Ave.   Phone: (417) 885-2104
Springfield, MO 65804   Marty Osredker, Libn.
Founded: 1909. **Staff:** Prof 1; Other 2. **Subjects:** Nursing, medicine and allied health sciences. **Holdings:** 4500 books; 155 reels of microfilm; 7 VF drawers of pamphlets; slides; recordings; charts; models; pictures; cassette tapes. **Subscriptions:** 60 journals and other serials. **Services:** Library open to public for reference use only. **Publications:** Book Acquisitions List, monthly.

★11780★
ST. JOHN'S MEDICAL CENTER - HEALTH SCIENCE LIBRARY (Med)†
333 N. F St.   Phone: (805) 487-7861
Oxnard, CA 93030   Joanne Kennedy, Libn.
Founded: 1973. **Staff:** Prof 1. **Subjects:** Clinical medicine, nursing, health management. **Holdings:** 3200 books and bound periodical volumes. **Subscriptions:** 140 journals and other serials. **Services:** Interlibrary loans; copying; library open to health care personnel. **Computerized Information Services:** MEDLINE.

★11781★
ST. JOHN'S MEDICAL CENTER - HEALTH SCIENCES LIBRARY (Med)
2015 Jackson St.   Phone: (317) 646-8264
Anderson, IN 46012   Scott S. Loman, Health Sci.Libn.
Staff: Prof 1. **Subjects:** Medicine, nursing. **Holdings:** 1500 books; 5000 bound periodical volumes; 400 audio cassettes; 50 video cassettes. **Subscriptions:** 180 journals and other serials; 9 newspapers. **Services:** Interlibrary loans; copying; SDI; library open to public with restrictions. **Computerized Information Services:** MEDLINE; BRS. **Networks/Consortia:** Member of Greater Midwest Regional Medical Library Network (Region 3); East Central Indiana Health Science Library Consortium. **Publications:** Library Update (newsletter), monthly.

★11782★
ST. JOHN'S MERCY MEDICAL CENTER - JOHN YOUNG BROWN MEMORIAL LIBRARY (Med)
621 S. New Ballas Rd.   Phone: (314) 569-6340
St. Louis, MO 63141   Saundra H. Hudson, Dir.
Founded: 1912. **Staff:** Prof 2; Other 2. **Subjects:** Medicine. **Holdings:** 1391 books; 4981 bound periodical volumes. **Subscriptions:** 228 journals and other serials. **Services:** Interlibrary loans; copying; SDI; current awareness; library open to users of libraries in the St. Louis Regional Library Network; open to public with physician's permission. **Automated Operations:** Computerized serials and ILL. **Computerized Information Services:** MEDLARS, PHILSOM, Octanet, BRS, DIALOG. Performs searches free of charge. **Networks/Consortia:** Member of St. Louis Regional Library Network. **Staff:** Ann M. Repetto, Asst.Dir.

★11783★
ST. JOHN'S MUSEUM OF ART, INC. - LIBRARY (Art)
114 Orange St.   Phone: (919) 763-0281
Wilmington, NC 28401   Alan Aiches, Dir.
Subjects: Art. **Holdings:** 600 books and periodicals. **Services:** Library open to public by appointment.

★11784★
ST. JOHN'S PROVINCIAL SEMINARY - LIBRARY (Rel-Theol)
44011 Five Mile Rd.   Phone: (313) 453-6200
Plymouth, MI 48170   Jean McGarty, Libn.
Founded: 1949. **Staff:** Prof 2; Other 2. **Subjects:** Theology and Scripture. **Special Collections:** Gabriel Richard Collection. **Holdings:** 45,591 books; 10,300 bound periodical volumes; 1377 cassettes; 2312 microforms. **Subscriptions:** 346 journals and other serials; 19 newspapers. **Services:** Interlibrary loans; copying; library open to public for reference use only. **Publications:** About Books, quarterly. **Staff:** Estelle De Bear, Tech.Serv.Libn.

★11785★
ST. JOHN'S RIVERSIDE HOSPITAL - MEDICAL LIBRARY (Med)
967 N. Broadway   Phone: (914) 963-3535
Yonkers, NY 10701   Helen A. Vocasek, Dir., Med.Rec.
Subjects: Medicine. **Holdings:** 430 books. **Subscriptions:** 31 journals and other serials. **Services:** Library not open to public.

★11786★
ST. JOHN'S SEMINARY - EDWARD LAURENCE DOHENY MEMORIAL LIBRARY (Rel-Theol)
5012 E. Seminary Rd.   Phone: (805) 482-2755
Camarillo, CA 93010   Rev. N.C. Eberhardt, Dir., Lib.Serv.
Founded: 1940. **Staff:** Prof 3; Other 2. **Subjects:** Theology, philosophy, history. **Special Collections:** The Estelle Doheny Collection (illuminated manuscripts); Bibles; incunabula; first editions of English and American literature; Californiana; autograph letters and manuscripts (8000 volumes). **Holdings:** 50,000 volumes. **Subscriptions:** 205 journals and other serials. **Services:** Restricted use to public; visitors may see Doheny Collection by appointment. **Staff:** Rita S. Faulders, Cur., Spec.Coll.; Sr. Angela Woods, S.S.L., Libn.

★11787★
ST. JOHN'S SEMINARY - LIBRARY (Rel-Theol)
99 Lake St.   Phone: (617) 254-2610
Brighton, MA 02135   Rev. L.W. McGrath, Hd.
Staff: Prof 1; Other 3. **Subjects:** Ecclesiastical sciences. **Holdings:** 120,000 books; 7600 bound periodical volumes. **Subscriptions:** 325 journals and other serials. **Services:** Interlibrary loans; copying; library open to accredited scholars. **Automated Operations:** Computerized cataloging. **Computerized Information Services:** OCLC. **Networks/Consortia:** Member of NELINET; Boston Theological Institute Libraries.

★11788★
ST. JOHN'S UNIVERSITY - ARCHIVES (Rel-Theol; Hist; Area-Ethnic)
Grand Central & Utopia Pkwys.   Phone: (718) 990-6161
Jamaica, NY 11439   Rev. John E. Young, C.M., Archv.
Staff: Prof 1. **Special Collections:** James L. Buckley Senatorial Papers; Paul O'Dwyer and Cormac O'Malley Collections (Irish-American affairs); James J. Needham Papers (Wall Street business affairs); American League for an Undivided Ireland Collection, 1947-1963; American Friends of Irish Neutrality Collection; Meehan Collection (ecclesiastical and civic historical clippings); Vincentian Papers (Archives of the Eastern Province of the Congregation of the Mission); university archives; autograph collection. **Holdings:** 1510 books and bound periodical volumes. **Services:** Copying; archives open to public by appointment.

★11789★
ST. JOHN'S UNIVERSITY - ASIAN COLLECTION - LIBRARY (Area-Ethnic)
Grand Central & Utopia Pkwys.   Phone: (718) 990-6161
Jamaica, NY 11439   Mr. Hou Ran Ferng, Hd.Libn.
Founded: 1966. **Staff:** Prof 1; Other 3. **Subjects:** Chinese and Japanese literature, religions, history, arts, philosophy, social sciences. **Special Collections:** Taoism (6250 volumes); Buddhism (8000 volumes); Serial Collections (21,000 volumes). **Holdings:** 55,000 books; 600 bound periodical volumes; survey of China mainland press since 1958; selections from China mainland magazines since 1960; Mainichi Daily News (Japanese daily newspaper on microfilm, 1960 to present); current background since 1958. **Subscriptions:** 120 journals and other serials; 12 newspapers. **Services:** Interlibrary loans; copying; library open to public with restrictions.

★11790★
ST. JOHN'S UNIVERSITY - COLLEGE OF PHARMACY & ALLIED HEALTH PROFESSIONS - HEALTH EDUCATION RESOURCE CENTER (Med)
Grand Central & Utopia Pkwys.　　　　　　Phone: (718) 990-6162
Jamaica, NY 11439　　　　　　　　　　　Mary A. Grant, Dir.
Staff: Prof 3; Other 1. Subjects: Clinical pharmacy, pharmacology, toxicology, pharmacokinetics, industrial pharmacy. Holdings: 1635 books; 25 newsletters; 630 video cassettes and audio slide programs; clipping and pamphlet files; 276 transparencies. Subscriptions: 70 journals and other serials. Services: Center open to health care professionals with a special need. Computerized Information Services: MEDLARS. Staff: Richard Goldberg, Media Spec.; Anne Hurt, Asst. to Dir.

★11791★
ST. JOHN'S UNIVERSITY - GOVERNMENT DOCUMENTS DEPARTMENT (Soc Sci)
Grand Central & Utopia Pkwys.　　　　　　Phone: (718) 990-6161
Jamaica, NY 11439　　　　　　　　Shu-fang Lin, Libn./Assoc.Prof.
Staff: Prof 1; Other 3. Subjects: Politics and government, education, business and economics. Special Collections: Congressional Record, 1st Congress to present; Congressional Serial Set; Joint Publications Research Service and Foreign Broadcast Information Service publications on microfiche. Holdings: 65,023 books; 2390 bound periodical volumes; 3640 reels of microfilm; 62,300 microfiche. Subscriptions: 179 journals and other serials. Services: Interlibrary loans; copying; SDI; department open to public for reference use only. Automated Operations: Computerized cataloging. Computerized Information Services: DIALOG, BRS.

★11792★
ST. JOHN'S UNIVERSITY - INSTRUCTIONAL MATERIALS CENTER (Educ)
Grand Central & Utopia Pkwys.　　　　　　Phone: (718) 990-6161
Jamaica, NY 11439　　　　　　　　Sharon Krauss, Libn./Asst.Prof.
Staff: Prof 1; Other 2. Subjects: Education. Special Collections: Drug and alcohol education books and films; educational and psychological tests. Holdings: 9025 books; 810 curriculum guides; 1510 filmstrips; 1263 study prints; 1284 cassettes; 1650 slides. Services: Copying; center open to public for reference use only. Networks/Consortia: Member of METRO. Special Catalogs: Film catalog (book).

★11793★
ST. JOHN'S UNIVERSITY - LAW LIBRARY (Law)
Fromkes Hall
Grand Central & Utopia Pkwys.　　　　　　Phone: (718) 990-6161
Jamaica, NY 11439　　　　　　Ralph Monaco, Assoc. Law Libn.
Founded: 1925. Staff: Prof 5; Other 19. Subjects: Law - Anglo-American, international, ecclesiastical, foreign, comparative, Roman; jurisprudence. Special Collections: Collected works of St. Thomas More (original editions and works about); canon law. Holdings: 180,991 books; 8654 bound periodical volumes; 1860 reels of microfilm; 46,355 microcards; 633,494 microfiche. Subscriptions: 5074 journals and other serials; 10 newspapers. Services: Interlibrary loans; copying; library open to public with restrictions. Computerized Information Services: LEXIS, Westlaw, NEXIS. Staff: Robert Nagy, Cat.; Karl Christensen, Ref.Libn.Teresa Wrenn, Ser./Ref.Libn.; Julius Marke, Dir.; Andrew Tschinkel, Ref.Libn.

★11794★
ST. JOHN'S UNIVERSITY - LIBRARY AND INFORMATION SCIENCE LIBRARY (Info Sci)
Grand Central & Utopia Pkwys.　　　　　　Phone: (718) 990-6161
Jamaica, NY 11439　　　　　　　　Szilvia Szmuk, Libn./Assoc.Prof.
Staff: Prof 1; Other 1. Subjects: Library and information science. Holdings: 19,000 books; 1600 bound periodical volumes; 1 cabinet of microfilm; 3 cabinets of vertical files and annual reports. Subscriptions: 210 journals and other serials; 185 newsletters. Services: Interlibrary loans; copying; library open to public with identification. Automated Operations: Computerized cataloging. Computerized Information Services: OCLC.

★11795★
ST. JOHN'S UNIVERSITY - SPECIAL COLLECTIONS (Soc Sci)
Grand Central & Utopia Pkwys.　　　　　　Phone: (718) 990-6161
Jamaica, NY 11439　　　　　　　Szilvia E. Szmuk, Spec.Coll.Libn.
Founded: 1870. Staff: Prof 1. Subjects: Lawn tennis, accounting, American literature. Special Collections: Art exhibition catalogs; William M. Fischer Tennis Collection (2500 volumes); Myer Collection (accounting; 170 volumes); Baxter Collection (American literature; 350 volumes); Heller Collection. Holdings: 6000 books; 40 papal letters. Services: Collections open to public by appointment. Automated Operations: Computerized cataloging. Computerized Information Services: DIALOG, SDC. Networks/Consortia: Member of METRO; SUNY/OCLC Library Network.

★11796★
ST. JOHN'S UNIVERSITY, NOTRE DAME CAMPUS - LIBRARY (Bus-Fin)†
300 Howard Ave.　　　　　　　　　　　Phone: (718) 447-4343
Staten Island, NY 10301　　　　　　　　　William V. Stone, Libn.
Subjects: Business administration. Special Collections: Myer collection on accounting. Holdings: 85,000 volumes; 20 VF drawers. Subscriptions: 912 journals and other serials. Services: Interlibrary loans; library open to public.

★11797★
ST. JOSEPH ABBEY - LIBRARY (Rel-Theol)
　　　　　　　　　　　　　　　　　Phone: (504) 892-1800
St. Benedict, LA 70457　　　　　　　Fr. Jules Tate, O.S.B., Libn.
Founded: 1910. Staff: Prof 1; Other 2. Subjects: Theology, scripture, patristics, monastica, church history. Holdings: 14,500 books; 1850 bound periodical volumes. Subscriptions: 65 journals and other serials. Services: Interlibrary loans; library not open to public. Automated Operations: Computerized cataloging.

ST. JOSEPH BAR ASSOCIATION - BUCHANAN COUNTY LAW LIBRARY
See: Buchanan County Law Library

ST. JOSEPH COLLEGE OF ORANGE
See: Loyola Marymount University - Orange Campus Library

★11798★
ST. JOSEPH COMMUNITY HOSPITAL - LIBRARY (Med)
600 N.E. 92nd Ave.
Box 1687　　　　　　　　　　　　　Phone: (206) 256-2045
Vancouver, WA 98668　　　　　　Sylvia E. MacWilliams, Lib.Coord.
Staff: Prof 1. Subjects: Medicine, nursing. Holdings: 320 books. Subscriptions: 130 journals and other serials. Services: Interlibrary loans; library not open to public. Computerized Information Services: MEDLARS. Remarks: Maintained by Southwest Washington Hospitals.

★11799★
ST. JOSEPH COUNTY LAW LIBRARY (Law)
Court House　　　　　　　　　　　　Phone: (219) 284-9657
South Bend, IN 46601　　　　　　　　Conie J. Frank, Libn.
Staff: 1. Subjects: Law. Holdings: 17,310 volumes. Services: Library open to public.

ST. JOSEPH GAZETTE
See: St. Joseph News-Press & Gazette

★11800★
ST. JOSEPH HEALTH CENTER - HEALTH SCIENCE LIBRARY (Med)
300 First Capitol Dr.　　　　　　　　　Phone: (314) 724-2810
St. Charles, MO 63301　　　　　　　Lucille Dykas, Lib.Mgr.
Staff: Prof 1; Other 1. Subjects: Medicine. Holdings: 500 books; 320 bound periodical volumes. Subscriptions: 80 journals and other serials. Services: Interlibrary loans; library not open to public.

★11801★
ST. JOSEPH HOSPITAL - BURLEW MEDICAL LIBRARY (Med)
1100 Stewart Dr.　　　　　　　　　　Phone: (714) 771-8291
Orange, CA 92668　　　　　　　　Julie Smith, Dir., Lib.Serv.
Founded: 1929. Staff: Prof 1; Other 3. Subjects: Medicine. Holdings: 10,000 books; 4798 bound periodical volumes; 1140 AV items. Subscriptions: 713 journals and other serials. Services: Interlibrary loans (fee); copying; library open to health and allied health professionals. Computerized Information Services: MEDLINE, DIALOG. Networks/Consortia: Member of Pacific Southwest Regional Medical Library Service (PSRMLS); Nursing Information Consortium of Orange County (NICOC).

★11802★
ST. JOSEPH HOSPITAL AND HEALTH CARE CENTER - HOSPITAL LIBRARY (Med)
1718 South I St.
Box 2197　　　　　　　　　　　　　Phone: (206) 627-4101
Tacoma, WA 98401　　　　　　　　Cheryl M. Goodwin, Libn.
Staff: Prof 1. Subjects: Medicine, nursing, health sciences, Autism, anorexia nervosa. Holdings: 2000 books; 118 bound periodical volumes. Subscriptions: 75 journals and other serials. Services: Interlibrary loans; copying; library open to public for reference use only. Computerized Information Services: MEDLINE. Networks/Consortia: Member of Pierce County Medical Library Consortium; Pacific Northwest Regional Health Sciences Library Service (PNRHSLS); WLN. Staff: Dan Russell, Pres.

★11803★
ST. JOSEPH HOSPITAL - HEALTH SCIENCE LIBRARY (Med)*
333 N. Madison St.   Phone: (815) 725-7133
Joliet, IL 60435   Catherine Siron, Coord., Lib.Serv.
Founded: 1976. **Staff:** Prof 2; Other 1. **Subjects:** Clinical medicine and nursing. **Special Collections:** Nursing library (4000 volumes). **Holdings:** 2000 books; 2500 bound periodical volumes. **Subscriptions:** 190 journals and other serials. **Services:** Interlibrary loans; copying; literature searches; library open to public for reference use only. **Computerized Information Services:** NLM. **Networks/Consortia:** Member of Chicago and South Consortium; Greater Midwest Regional Medical Library Network (Region 3). **Staff:** Virginia Gale, Lib.Techn.

★11804★
ST. JOSEPH HOSPITAL - HEALTH SCIENCE LIBRARY (Med)
1000 Carondelet Dr.   Phone: (816) 942-4400
Kansas City, MO 64114   Janice Foster, Libn.
Founded: 1929. **Staff:** Prof 1; Other 2. **Subjects:** Medicine, nursing and allied health fields. **Holdings:** 1000 books; 1200 bound periodical volumes. **Subscriptions:** 156 journals and other serials. **Services:** Interlibrary loans; copying. **Computerized Information Services:** MEDLARS, DIALOG. **Networks/Consortia:** Member of Kansas City Library Network, Inc. (KCLN); Midcontinental Regional Medical Library Program.

★11805★
ST. JOSEPH HOSPITAL - HEALTH SCIENCE LIBRARY (Med)*
200 High Service Ave.   Phone: (401) 456-3060
North Providence, RI 02904   Kathleen C. McAvoy, Libn.
Founded: 1977. **Staff:** Prof 1; Other 1. **Subjects:** Medicine, surgery, nursing, allied health sciences. **Holdings:** 3001 books; 2006 bound periodical volumes; 4 VF drawers; 12 files of pamphlets. **Subscriptions:** 130 journals and other serials. **Services:** Interlibrary loans; copying; library open to public by appointment.

★11806★
ST. JOSEPH HOSPITAL - HEALTH SCIENCE LIBRARY (Med)
220 Overton
Box 178
Memphis, TN 38101   Phone: (901) 529-2874
                                      Denise Fesmire, Libn.
Founded: 1938. **Staff:** Prof 1; Other 1. **Subjects:** Medicine, nursing. **Holdings:** 1000 books; 5396 bound periodical volumes. **Subscriptions:** 154 journals and other serials. **Services:** Interlibrary loans; copying; SDI; library open to public for reference use only on request. **Networks/Consortia:** Member of Association of Memphis Area Health Science Libraries (AMAHSL).

★11807★
ST. JOSEPH HOSPITAL - HEALTH SCIENCES LIBRARY (Med)
1835 Franklin St.   Phone: (303) 837-7188
Denver, CO 80218   Margaret Bandy, Libn.
Staff: Prof 1; Other 1. **Subjects:** Medicine, nursing, hospital management. **Holdings:** 2102 books; pamphlets. **Subscriptions:** 208 journals and other serials. **Services:** Interlibrary loans; copying; library open to public. **Automated Operations:** Computerized acquisitions and ILL. **Computerized Information Services:** MEDLINE, DIALOG, OCLC, BRS. **Networks/Consortia:** Member of Denver Area Health Sciences Library Consortium; Midcontinental Regional Medical Library Program.

★11808★
ST. JOSEPH HOSPITAL - HEALTH SCIENCES LIBRARY (Med)
128 Strawberry Hill Ave.   Phone: (203) 327-3500
Stamford, CT 06904-1222   Lucille Lieberman, Dir.
Staff: Prof 1; Other 1. **Subjects:** Medicine, nursing and allied health sciences. **Holdings:** 1200 books; 92 bound periodical volumes; 103 video cassettes. **Subscriptions:** 136 journals and other serials. **Services:** Interlibrary loans; copying; SDI; library open to public by arrangement. **Computerized Information Services:** Online systems. **Networks/Consortia:** Member of Connecticut Association of Health Science Libraries (CAHSL); Southwestern Connecticut Health Science Library Consortium. **Publications:** A Guide to Use of the Health Sciences Library, updated annually - distributed to new employees.

★11809★
ST. JOSEPH HOSPITAL - HEALTH SCIENCES LIBRARY (Med)
302 Kensington Ave.   Phone: (313) 762-8519
Flint, MI 48502   RoseMary Russo, Med.Libn.
Staff: Prof 1; Other 2. **Subjects:** Medicine, nursing. **Holdings:** 2313 books; 5271 bound periodical volumes; 1227 audio cassettes; 108 video cassettes; patient education pamphlets. **Subscriptions:** 220 journals and other serials. **Services:** Interlibrary loans; copying; library open to public for reference use only. **Computerized Information Services:** MEDLINE, DIALOG. **Networks/Consortia:** Member of Flint Area Health Science Library Network (FAHSLN); Michigan Health Sciences Libraries Association. **Publications:** New book lists.

★11810★
ST. JOSEPH HOSPITAL - HEALTH SCIENCES LIBRARY (Med)
12th & Walnut Sts.   Phone: (215) 378-2390
Reading, PA 19603   Kathleen A. Izzo, Libn.
Founded: 1973. **Staff:** Prof 2; Other 2. **Subjects:** Medicine, nursing, patient education, allied health professions, hospital administration, public health. **Holdings:** 2940 books; 3852 bound periodical volumes; 4 VF drawers of pamphlets. **Subscriptions:** 225 journals and other serials; 7 newspapers. **Services:** Interlibrary loans; copying; library open to public. **Computerized Information Services:** BRS. **Networks/Consortia:** Member of Greater Northeastern Regional Medical Library Program; Cooperating Hospital Libraries of the Lehigh Valley Area (CHL); Berks County Library Association; Central Pennsylvania Health Sciences Library Association (CPHSLA). **Publications:** Library Ledger, monthly - for internal distribution only. **Special Catalogs:** AV Catalog (notebook).

★11811★
ST. JOSEPH HOSPITAL - HOSPITAL HEALTH SCIENCE LIBRARY (Med)
1919 LaBranch   Phone: (713) 757-1000
Houston, TX 77002   Shelley G. Mao, Dir.
Founded: 1940. **Staff:** Prof 2; Other 1. **Subjects:** Medicine, sciences, management. **Holdings:** 2144 books; 4260 bound periodical volumes; 127 volumes in microform; 67 volumes of Audio-Digest tapes. **Subscriptions:** 157 journals and other serials. **Services:** Interlibrary loans; copying; library open to professionals by appointment. **Computerized Information Services:** NLM; internal database. **Staff:** Shirley Lukan, Asst.Libn.

★11812★
ST. JOSEPH HOSPITAL - HOSPITAL LIBRARY (Med)
250 College Ave.
Box 3509   Phone: (717) 291-8119
Lancaster, PA 17604   Eileen B. Doudna, Libn.
Founded: 1940. **Staff:** Prof 1; Other 1. **Subjects:** Medicine, nursing, allied health sciences. **Holdings:** 3000 books; 1000 AV items. **Subscriptions:** 108 journals and other serials. **Services:** Interlibrary loans; copying; library open to public. **Computerized Information Services:** MEDLARS.

★11813★
ST. JOSEPH HOSPITAL - INFORMATION SERVICES (Med)
915 E. 5th St.   Phone: (618) 463-5284
Alton, IL 62002   Judith Messerle, Dir.Educ.Rsrcs.
Staff: Prof 2. **Subjects:** Medicine, hospital administration, nursing. **Holdings:** 2800 books and bound periodical volumes; 12 legal files of pamphlets. **Subscriptions:** 200 journals and other serials. **Services:** Interlibrary loans; copying; bibliographic searches; services open to health personnel. **Computerized Information Services:** MEDLINE. **Networks/Consortia:** Member of Areawide Hospital Library Consortium of Southwestern Illinois (AHLC); ILLINET; Greater Midwest Regional Medical Library Network (Region 3). **Publications:** Current Journal Contents, weekly - to department heads and doctors. Betty Byrd, Libn.

★11814★
ST. JOSEPH HOSPITAL - LIBRARY (Med)
2900 N. Lake Shore   Phone: (312) 975-3038
Chicago, IL 60657   Katherine Wimmer, Dir., Lib.Serv.
Staff: Prof 2; Other 2. **Subjects:** Medicine, nursing. **Special Collections:** Hospital archives. **Holdings:** 5000 books; 8000 bound periodical volumes; 2400 audiotapes; 35 sets of slides and filmstrips; 10 VF drawers; 200 videotapes; 50 8mm films. **Subscriptions:** 369 journals and other serials; 10 newspapers. **Services:** Interlibrary loans; copying; LATCH; current awareness; library open to public with director's permission. **Computerized Information Services:** NTIS. **Networks/Consortia:** Member of ILLINET; Metropolitan Consortium; Greater Midwest Regional Medical Library Network (Region 3). **Publications:** Newsletter, quarterly - available to hospital and medical staff. **Special Indexes:** Archival Index. **Staff:** Beverly Ford, Archv./Libn.; Liliana Castaneda, Health Sci.Lib.Coord.

★11815★
ST. JOSEPH HOSPITAL - LIBRARY (Med)*
312 E. Alta Vista   Phone: (515) 684-4651
Ottumwa, IA 52501   Sr. Mary Christine Conaway, Libn./Dir., Media Ctr.
Founded: 1951. **Staff:** Prof 1; Other 1. **Subjects:** Medicine, nursing, health care administration, patient education. **Special Collections:** Pioneer History of Medicine in Iowa, Mississippi River Valley (5 pieces); history of St. Joseph School of Nursing; archives. **Holdings:** 3537 books; 1000 bound periodical

volumes; 2667 pamphlets; 128 maps; 1681 AV items; 8 VF drawers of reprints, clippings, diagrams. **Subscriptions:** 180 journals and other serials; 7 newspapers. **Services:** Interlibrary loans; copying (fee); library open to public for reference use only, with restrictions. **Computerized Information Services:** MEDLINE (through University of Iowa). **Networks/Consortia:** Member of Greater Midwest Regional Library Network (Region 3). **Publications:** Scan, quarterly newsheet. **Special Catalogs:** AV catalog file; bibliographic file (card); vertical file subject catalog (card).

ST. JOSEPH HOSPITAL - LIBRARY (Bellingham, WA)
See: Whatcom/Island Health Services - Library

★11816★
ST. JOSEPH HOSPITAL - SISTER MARY ALVINA NURSING LIBRARY (Med)
7620 York Rd.   Phone: (301) 337-1641
Towson, MD 21204   Mary Weihs, Libn.
Founded: 1949. **Staff:** Prof 1. **Subjects:** Nursing. **Holdings:** 2465 books; 152 bound periodical volumes; 8 VF drawers of pamphlets and clippings; 700 AV items. **Subscriptions:** 62 journals and other serials. **Services:** Interlibrary loans; copying; library open to public for reference use only. **Networks/Consortia:** Member of Baltimore Consortia for Resource Sharing.

★11817★
ST. JOSEPH HOSPITAL - MEDICAL LIBRARY (Med)
One St. Joseph Dr.   Phone: (606) 278-3436
Lexington, KY 40504   Jerri Trimble, Supv.
Staff: 1. **Subjects:** Medicine, nursing, allied health sciences. **Holdings:** 1002 books; 2162 bound periodical volumes; 10 directories; 818 audiotapes; 25 AV tapes. **Subscriptions:** 165 journals and other serials. **Services:** Interlibrary loans; copying; library open to research, medical and nursing students. **Networks/Consortia:** Member of Kentucky Health Sciences Library Consortium.

★11818★
ST. JOSEPH HOSPITAL - MEDICAL LIBRARY (Med)
5325 Faraon   Phone: (816) 271-6075
St. Joseph, MO 64506   Jane Warren Carver, Med.Libn.
Staff: Prof 1. **Subjects:** Medicine. **Holdings:** 450 books; 300 bound periodical volumes. **Subscriptions:** 66 journals and other serials. **Services:** Interlibrary loans; copying; library open to college students conducting research on medical subjects for reference use only. **Networks/Consortia:** Member of Northwest Missouri Library Network (NLN); Midcontinental Regional Medical Library Program.

★11819★
ST. JOSEPH HOSPITAL - MEDICAL LIBRARY (Med)*
400 Walter, N.E.   Phone: (505) 243-8811
Albuquerque, NM 87102   Melba Clark, Libn.
Founded: 1959. **Staff:** 1. **Subjects:** Medicine, nursing, hospital administration, social work, public health. **Holdings:** 700 books; 800 bound periodical volumes. **Subscriptions:** 90 journals and other serials. **Services:** Interlibrary loans; copying; library open to students and workers in health professions. **Remarks:** Hospital is operated by the Sisters of Charity.

★11820★
ST. JOSEPH HOSPITAL - MEDICAL AND NURSING LIBRARY (Med)
1401 S. Main St.   Phone: (817) 336-9371
Fort Worth, TX 76104   Jesse Pierrard, Libn.
Staff: Prof 1. **Subjects:** Medicine, nursing, religion, philosophy. **Holdings:** 2170 books; 350 bound periodical volumes; 8 VF drawers of miscellaneous materials. **Subscriptions:** 60 journals and other serials. **Services:** Interlibrary loans; copying; library open to public. **Networks/Consortia:** Member of Dallas-Tarrant County Consortium of Health Science Libraries.

★11821★
ST. JOSEPH HOSPITAL - MEDICAL STAFF LIBRARY (Med)
205 W. 20th St.   Phone: (216) 245-6851
Lorain, OH 44052   Sue Van Atta, Dir.
Staff: Prof 1; Other 1. **Subjects:** Medicine, nursing. **Holdings:** 2000 books; 1500 bound periodical volumes; 350 video cassettes. **Subscriptions:** 200 journals and other serials. **Services:** Interlibrary loans; copying; library open to public. **Computerized Information Services:** DIALOG. **Networks/Consortia:** Member of Lake Erie Medical Librarians Association.

★11822★
ST. JOSEPH HOSPITAL OF MT. CLEMENS - MEDICAL LIBRARY (Med)
East Site, 215 North Ave.   Phone: (313) 286-8100
Mt. Clemens, MI 48043   Sandra A. Cryderman, Dir.
Staff: Prof 4; Other 2. **Subjects:** Medicine, nursing, allied health sciences,

consumer health, management. **Holdings:** 3000 books; 1600 bound periodical volumes. **Subscriptions:** 350 journals and other serials. **Services:** Interlibrary loans; copying; current awareness; library open to public for reference use only. **Computerized Information Services:** NLM, BRS. **Networks/Consortia:** Member of Metropolitan Detroit Medical Library Group (MDMLG); Macomb Area Libraries Health Information Consortium (MALHIC). **Publications:** Library Services, monthly - for internal distribution only. **Remarks:** The west site of the library is located at 15855 19 Mile Rd., Mt. Clemens, MI 48044. **Staff:** Patricia A. Tomlinson, Libn. (East Site); Mary Lou Hubbard, Libn. (West Site).

★11823★
ST. JOSEPH HOSPITAL - OTTO C. BRANTIGAN MEDICAL LIBRARY (Med)
7620 York Rd.   Phone: (301) 337-1210
Towson, MD 21204   Sr. Francis Marie, Libn.
Founded: 1940. **Staff:** Prof 1; Other 5. **Subjects:** Medicine, surgery, gynecology, obstetrics, pediatrics. **Holdings:** 1800 volumes AV materials. **Subscriptions:** 150 journals and other serials. **Services:** Interlibrary loans; copying; library open to public with restrictions. **Networks/Consortia:** Member of Baltimore Consortia for Resource Sharing; Maryland Association of Health Science Librarians.

★11824★
ST. JOSEPH HOSPITAL, OUR LADY OF PROVIDENCE UNIT - HEALTH SCIENCE LIBRARY (Med)
21 Peace St.   Phone: (401) 456-4035
Providence, RI 02907   Ruth E. Szabo, Coord., Lib.Serv.
Founded: 1940. **Staff:** Prof 1; Other 1. **Subjects:** Medicine, nursing and related sciences. **Holdings:** 3059 books; 4002 bound periodical volumes; 8 VF drawers of pamphlets, reports. **Subscriptions:** 137 journals and other serials. **Services:** Interlibrary loans; copying; library open to public by appointment and with referral from another library. **Networks/Consortia:** Member of Association of Rhode Island Health Sciences Librarians (ARIHSL).

★11825★
ST. JOSEPH INTERCOMMUNITY HOSPITAL - MEDICAL STAFF LIBRARY (Med)
2605 Harlem Rd.   Phone: (716) 896-6300
Cheektowaga, NY 14225   Sr. M. Tiburtia Gorecki, F.S.S.J., Cons.
Staff: Prof 1; Other 1. **Subjects:** Nuclear medicine, radiology. **Holdings:** 1033 books; 57 bound periodical volumes; 1286 reel-to-reel tapes; 663 cassettes; 374 slides. **Subscriptions:** 13 journals and other serials. **Services:** Interlibrary loans; library not open to public. **Computerized Information Services:** Information Dissemination Service (IDS). **Networks/Consortia:** Member of Western New York Library Resources Council (WNYLRC). **Publications:** Library Handbook; Cataloging Handbook.

★11826★
ST. JOSEPH MEDICAL CENTER - HEALTH SCIENCE LIBRARY (Med)
Buena Vista & Alameda Sts.   Phone: (818) 843-5111
Burbank, CA 91505   Sr. Naomi Hurd, S.P., Libn.
Founded: 1953. **Staff:** Prof 2; Other 1. **Subjects:** History of medicine, nursing, hospital administration. **Special Collections:** History of Medicine; rare book collection. **Holdings:** 3749 books; 5818 bound periodical volumes; 1438 audio cassettes; 238 video cassettes; 25 16mm films; 90 filmstrips; 65 slide programs; 4 transparencies; 20 microfiche; 36 miscellaneous items. **Subscriptions:** 607 journals and other serials. **Services:** Interlibrary loans; copying; library open to public for reference use only. **Automated Operations:** Computerized acquisitions and serials. **Computerized Information Services:** MEDLINE. **Networks/Consortia:** Member of CLASS; Pacific Southwest Regional Medical Library Service (PSRMLS). **Publications:** Journal list, annual. **Staff:** Ann Miller, Lib.Asst.

★11827★
ST. JOSEPH MEDICAL CENTER - HOSPITAL LIBRARY (Med)
3600 E. Harry   Phone: (316) 685-1111
Wichita, KS 67218   Carol Matulka, Med.Libn.
Founded: 1942. **Staff:** Prof 1; Other 2. **Subjects:** Medicine, nursing, allied health administration. **Holdings:** 2618 books; 2490 bound periodical volumes; 2440 books and journals in storage for recall; 2 VF drawers of bibliographies; cassettes; records; AV programs and videocassettes. **Subscriptions:** 200 journals and other serials. **Services:** Interlibrary loans; copying; bibliographic searches; library open to hospital personnel and affiliated college/university students. **Computerized Information Services:** Online systems. **Networks/Consortia:** Member of Wichita Area Health Science Libraries; Midcontinental Regional Medical Library Program.

★11828★

ST. JOSEPH MEMORIAL HOSPITAL - HEALTH SCIENCE LIBRARY (Med)
1907 W. Sycamore St.   Phone: (317) 452-5611
Kokomo, IN 46901   Dana Kemp, Med.Libn.
Staff: Prof 1; Other 1. **Subjects:** Medicine, nursing, hospital administration and management. **Holdings:** 1609 books; 736 bound periodical volumes; 348 AV materials; 4 VF drawers. **Subscriptions:** 129 journals and other serials. **Services:** Interlibrary loans; copying; library open to public with limited circulation. **Networks/Consortia:** Member of Greater Midwest Regional Medical Library Network (Region 3); East Central Indiana Health Science Library Consortium.

★11829★

ST. JOSEPH MERCY HOSPITAL - EDUCATIONAL RESOURCES (Med)
900 Woodward   Phone: (313) 858-3495
Pontiac, MI 48053   Mollie S. Lynch, Lib.Mgr.
Staff: Prof 3; Other 2. **Subjects:** Medicine, nursing, health care administration, allied health sciences. **Holdings:** 5000 books; 8000 bound periodical volumes; 300 media items. **Subscriptions:** 600 journals and other serials. **Services:** Interlibrary loans; copying; SDI; LATCH; open to public for reference use only. **Computerized Information Services:** MEDLARS, OCLC, SDC, DIALOG. **Networks/Consortia:** Member of Metropolitan Detroit Medical Library Group (MDMLG); Health Instructional Resources Associated (HIRA); Michigan Health Sciences Libraries Association; Oakland County Union List of Serials (OCULS). Sisters of Mercy Health Corporation AV - Library Group. **Publications:** Acquisitions List, monthly; Info-Pack, semiannual - both for internal distribution only.

★11830★

ST. JOSEPH MERCY HOSPITAL - MEDICAL LIBRARY (Med)
84 Beaumont Dr.   Phone: (515) 424-7699
Mason City, IA 50401   Judy I. Madson, Dir.
Staff: Prof 1; Other 1. **Subjects:** Medicine, nursing, hospital administration. **Holdings:** 4230 volumes. **Subscriptions:** 200 journals and other serials. **Services:** Interlibrary loans; copying; SDI; library open to public with restrictions. **Computerized Information Services:** MEDLARS. **Networks/Consortia:** Member of Greater Midwest Regional Medical Library Network (Region 3).

ST. JOSEPH MERCY HOSPITAL (Ann Arbor, MI)
See: Mc Auley (Catherine) Health Center

★11831★

ST. JOSEPH MUSEUM - LIBRARY (Hist)
Eleventh at Charles   Phone: (816) 232-8471
St. Joseph, MO 64501   Richard A. Nolf, Dir.
Staff: Prof 6; Other 7. **Subjects:** Natural history, North American Indians, Pony Express, history of Western expansion, local and area history. **Special Collections:** American Indian Collection; local history collection of Civil War period; Pony Express, bird, mammal and fish exhibits. **Holdings:** 5000 volumes. **Subscriptions:** 45 journals and other serials. **Services:** Copying; library open to public for reference use only. **Publications:** Newsletter, bimonthly. **Staff:** Bonnie Harlow, Cur., Coll.; Jackie Lewin, Cur., Hist.; Marilyn Taylor, Cur., Ethnology; June Swift, Exec.Sec.; Don L. Reynolds, Cur., Pony Express.

★11832★

ST. JOSEPH NEWS-PRESS & GAZETTE - LIBRARY (Publ)
9th & Edmond Sts.   Phone: (816) 279-5671
St. Joseph, MO 64502   Don E. Thornton, Dir.
Staff: 1. **Subjects:** Newspaper reference topics. **Holdings:** 55,000 clippings; microfilm. **Subscriptions:** 18 newspapers. **Services:** Library open to public with consent of director.

★11833★

ST. JOSEPH SEMINARY COLLEGE - PERE ROUQUETTE LIBRARY (Hum; Rel-Theol)
                                         Phone: (504) 892-9895
St. Benedict, LA 70457   Rev. Timothy J. Burnett, O.S.B., Dir. of Lib.
Staff: Prof 1; Other 15. **Subjects:** Literature, religion, history, social sciences, sciences, languages, fine arts. **Holdings:** 65,000 books; 5700 bound periodical volumes. **Subscriptions:** 232 journals and other serials. **Services:** Interlibrary loans; SDI; library open to public for reference use only on request.

ST. JOSEPH SEMINARY (Trois-Rivieres, PQ)
See: Seminaire St-Joseph

★11834★

ST. JOSEPH STATE HOSPITAL - PROFESSIONAL LIBRARY (Med)†
3400 Frederick Ave.
Box 263   Phone: (816) 232-8431
St. Joseph, MO 64502   Martha Godding, Libn.Dir.
Founded: 1966. **Staff:** Prof 2. **Subjects:** Psychiatry, psychology, social service, nursing, education, alcoholism, chaplaincy, therapy, dietetics, pharmacy. **Special Collections:** Complete works of Sigmund Freud. **Holdings:** 2300 books; 2000 bound periodical volumes; 600 Audio-Digest tapes; 3 films; AV kits; 8 boxes of slides; 53 cassettes; 48 video cassettes. **Subscriptions:** 170 journals and other serials. **Services:** Interlibrary loans; copying; SDI; library open to public with restrictions. **Networks/Consortia:** Member of Midcontinental Regional Medical Library Program; Northwest Missouri Library Network; Health Sciences Library Group of Greater Kansas City. **Publications:** Alcohol and other drugs, quarterly - by mail.

★11835★

ST. JOSEPH'S ABBEY - LIBRARY (Rel-Theol)
Rte. 31, N. Spencer Rd.   Phone: (617) 885-3901
Spencer, MA 01562   Fr. Basil Byrne, Libn.
Founded: 1951. **Staff:** Prof 1. **Subjects:** Theology; Biblical studies; philosophy; patrology; history - church, ancient, Medieval, modern; psychology; sociology. **Holdings:** 40,000 books. **Subscriptions:** 65 journals and other serials; 5 newspapers. **Services:** Interlibrary loans; library open to public with restrictions.

★11836★

ST. JOSEPH'S GENERAL HOSPITAL - MEDICAL LIBRARY (Med)
P.O. Box 3251   Phone: (807) 344-2431
Thunder Bay, ON, Canada P7B 5G7   Laurie J. Hill, Libn.
Subjects: Medicine, nursing, rehabilitation. **Holdings:** 725 books; 460 bound periodical volumes. **Subscriptions:** 42 journals and other serials. **Services:** Interlibrary loans; copying; library open to college and university students. **Networks/Consortia:** Member of Northwestern Ontario Medical Programme Library Network.

★11837★

ST. JOSEPH'S HEALTH CENTRE - GEORGE PENNAL LIBRARY (Med)
30 The Queensway   Phone: (416) 530-6726
Toronto, ON, Canada M6R 1B5   Julia Chan, Med.Libn.
Founded: 1963. **Staff:** Prof 1; Other 1. **Subjects:** Medicine, nursing, pastoral care. **Holdings:** 2000 books; 1300 bound periodical volumes. **Subscriptions:** 200 journals and other serials. **Services:** Interlibrary loans; copying; library open to public for reference use only.

★11838★

ST. JOSEPH'S HOSPITAL - BRUCE COLE MEMORIAL LIBRARY (Med)
350 N. Wilmot   Phone: (602) 296-3211
Tucson, AZ 85732   Polin Lei, Med.Libn.
Staff: Prof 1; Other 4. **Subjects:** Surgery, infection control, ophthalmology, pediatrics, alcoholism. **Holdings:** 1000 books; 150 bound periodical volumes; 100 other cataloged items. **Subscriptions:** 140 journals and other serials; 10 newspapers. **Services:** Interlibrary loans; copying; SDI; library open to public with doctor's referral. **Computerized Information Services:** MEDLARS. **Networks/Consortia:** Member of Pacific Southwest Regional Medical Library Service (PSRMLS). **Publications:** Hoyes; The Link; Times, semiannual. **Special Indexes:** Pharm Index.

★11839★

ST. JOSEPH'S HOSPITAL - DRUG INFORMATION CENTRE (Med)
50 Charlton Ave., E.   Phone: (416) 522-4941
Hamilton, ON, Canada L8N 1Y4   Mrs. D.A. Thompson, Dir. of Pharmacy Serv.
Staff: 1. **Subjects:** Drugs, pharmacology, disease, clinical pharmacy services, pharmaceutical techniques. **Holdings:** 175 books and bound periodical volumes; 75 cassette tapes; 10 videotapes; archives and teaching files. **Subscriptions:** 17 journals and other serials. **Services:** Interlibrary loans; center open to public with approval.

★11840★

ST. JOSEPH'S HOSPITAL AND HEALTH CENTER - MEDICAL LIBRARY (Med)
7th St. W.   Phone: (701) 225-7200
Dickinson, ND 58601   Sr. Salome, Libn.
Founded: 1951. **Staff:** 1. **Subjects:** Nursing, medicine, related subjects. **Holdings:** Figures not available for books; 120 bound periodical volumes. **Subscriptions:** 174 journals and other serials. **Services:** Interlibrary loans; copying; library open to health professionals. **Networks/Consortia:** Member of Greater Midwest Regional Medical Library Network (Region 3).

★11841★

ST. JOSEPH'S HOSPITAL HEALTH CENTER - MEDICAL AND SCHOOL OF NURSING LIBRARIES (Med)
301 Prospect Ave.   Phone: (315) 424-5053
Syracuse, NY 13203   Mr. V. Juchimek, Hd.Libn.
Founded: 1940. **Staff:** Prof 2; Other 3. **Subjects:** Nursing, medicine, psychology, social sciences, religion. **Holdings:** 10,000 books; 2000 bound periodical volumes; 30 VF drawers of pamphlets; 200 cassette programs; models; slides; filmstrips; recordings. **Subscriptions:** 195 journals and other serials. **Services:** Interlibrary loans (limited); library open to public for reference use only. **Publications:** Accessions List, monthly; Exchange List.

★11842★

ST. JOSEPH'S HOSPITAL - HEALTH SCIENCE LIBRARY (Med)
220 Pawtucket St.   Phone: (617) 453-1761
Lowell, MA 01854   Anne C. Dick, Libn.
Founded: 1971. **Staff:** Prof 1; Other 1. **Subjects:** Medicine and nursing. **Holdings:** 3050 books and bound periodical volumes. **Subscriptions:** 200 journals and other serials. **Services:** Interlibrary loans; copying; library open to physicians and medical students. **Networks/Consortia:** Member of Northeastern Consortium for Health Information (NECHI).

★11843★

ST. JOSEPH'S HOSPITAL - HEALTH SCIENCE LIBRARY (Med)*
2661 County Trunk I   Phone: (715) 723-1811
Chippewa Falls, WI 54729   Carolyn Kowalkowski, Dir.
Founded: 1969. **Staff:** Prof 1; Other 1. **Subjects:** Medicine, medical specialties, nursing. **Holdings:** 420 books; tapes; films. **Subscriptions:** 20 journals and other serials. **Services:** Library not open to public.

★11844★

ST. JOSEPH'S HOSPITAL - HELENE FULD LEARNING RESOURCE CENTER (Med)
555 E. Market St.   Phone: (607) 733-6541
Elmira, NY 14902   Arlene C. Pien, Libn.
Founded: 1975. **Staff:** Prof 1; Other 1. **Subjects:** Medicine, nursing. **Holdings:** 5000 books; 4000 bound periodical volumes; 1500 AV items; 10 pamphlet file drawers. **Subscriptions:** 165 journals and other serials. **Services:** Interlibrary loans; copying.

★11845★

ST. JOSEPH'S HOSPITAL - HOSPITAL LIBRARY (Med)
50 Charlton Ave., E.   Phone: (416) 522-4941
Hamilton, ON, Canada L8N 1Y4   Mrs. S.L. Rogers, Hosp.Libn.
Founded: 1964. **Staff:** 2. **Subjects:** Medicine, hospital administration. **Special Collections:** Sir William Osler Collection. **Holdings:** 1600 books; 7000 bound periodical volumes. **Subscriptions:** 150 journals and other serials. **Services:** Library not open to public.

★11846★

ST. JOSEPH'S HOSPITAL - JEROME MEDICAL LIBRARY (Med)
69 W. Exchange St.   Phone: (612) 291-3193
St. Paul, MN 55102   Jacqueline Gionfriddo, Dir.
Founded: 1949. **Staff:** Prof 1. **Subjects:** Medicine, hospital administration, religion and philosophy, nursing. **Holdings:** 5133 books; 4948 bound periodical volumes; 4 VF drawers of clippings and pamphlets. **Subscriptions:** 133 journals and other serials. **Services:** Interlibrary loans; copying; library open to public for reference use only. **Networks/Consortia:** Member of Twin Cities Biomedical Consortium (TCBC).

★11847★

ST. JOSEPH'S HOSPITAL AND MEDICAL CENTER - HEALTH SCIENCES LIBRARY (Med)
703 Main St.   Phone: (201) 977-2104
Paterson, NJ 07503   Patricia May, Lib.Serv.
Staff: Prof 4. **Subjects:** Medicine, biological sciences, dentistry, psychology, nursing. **Holdings:** 4200 books; 4800 bound periodical volumes. **Subscriptions:** 275 journals and other serials. **Services:** Interlibrary loans; copying; library open to public for reference use only. **Computerized Information Services:** MEDLARS, DIALOG. **Networks/Consortia:** Member of Bergen-Passaic Health Sciences Library Consortium. **Staff:** Natalie Richman, Asst.Libn.

★11848★

ST. JOSEPH'S HOSPITAL - MEDICAL LIBRARY (Med)
350 W. Thomas Rd.
Box 2071
Phoenix, AZ 85001   Phone: (605) 285-3299
                                           Evelyn S. Gorman, Dir., Lib.Serv.
Founded: 1942. **Staff:** Prof 1; Other 2. **Subjects:** Medicine. **Special**

Collections: Library of neurological sciences. **Holdings:** 4275 books; 7700 bound periodical volumes. **Subscriptions:** 320 journals and other serials. **Services:** Interlibrary loans; copying; library open to public by permission.

★11849★

ST. JOSEPH'S HOSPITAL - MEDICAL LIBRARY (Med)*
1800 N. California St.   Phone: (209) 943-2000
Stockton, CA 95204   Dr. Bernard
Staff: Prof 1; Other 4. **Subjects:** Medicine, surgery, pediatrics, orthopedics, obstetrics and gynecology, nursing. **Holdings:** 375 books; 29 bound periodical volumes; 8 video cassettes. **Subscriptions:** 80 journals and other serials. **Services:** Interlibrary loans; library not open to public.

★11850★

ST. JOSEPH'S HOSPITAL - MEDICAL LIBRARY (Med)
3000 W. Buffalo Ave.
Box 4227   Phone: (813) 870-4658
Tampa, FL 33677   Adelia P. Seglin, Dir., Med.Lib.
Staff: Prof 2; Other 1. **Subjects:** Medicine, nursing, cancer, pharmacology, management, cardiology. **Holdings:** 1200 books; 5000 bound periodical volumes. **Subscriptions:** 257 journals and other serials. **Services:** Interlibrary loans; copying; library open to public with restrictions. **Computerized Information Services:** MEDLARS, DIALOG, BRS. Performs searches on cost recovery basis. **Networks/Consortia:** Member of Tampa Bay Medical Library Network. **Staff:** Mrs. Gita Halder, Med.Libn.

★11851★

ST. JOSEPH'S HOSPITAL - MEDICAL LIBRARY (Med)*
11705 Mercy Blvd.   Phone: (912) 925-4100
Savannah, GA 31406   Judy G. Henry, Libn.
Staff: Prof 1. **Subjects:** Medicine, surgery, nursing and allied sciences. **Holdings:** 750 books; 150 bound periodical volumes; 100 pamphlets; 80 filmstrips with records; 4 VF drawers. **Subscriptions:** 104 journals and other serials. **Services:** Interlibrary loans; copying; library open to public with restrictions. **Computerized Information Services:** Online systems.

★11852★

ST. JOSEPH'S HOSPITAL - MEDICAL LIBRARY (Med)†
700 Broadway   Phone: (219) 423-2614
Fort Wayne, IN 46802   Michael Sheets, Dir., Med.Lib.
Founded: 1945. **Staff:** Prof 1; Other 1. **Subjects:** Medicine. **Holdings:** 20,000 volumes. **Subscriptions:** 200 journals and other serials. **Services:** Interlibrary loans; copying; library open to public by appointment. **Computerized Information Services:** BRS, NLM. **Networks/Consortia:** Member of Northeastern Indiana Health Science Library Consortium (NIHSLC).

★11853★

ST. JOSEPH'S HOSPITAL - MEDICAL LIBRARY (Med)
268 Grosvenor St.   Phone: (519) 439-3271
London, ON, Canada N6A 4V2   Louise Lin, Coord., Lib.Serv.
Founded: 1966. **Staff:** Prof 1; Other 2. **Subjects:** Clinical medicine, nursing and allied health sciences. **Special Collections:** World Health Organization International Histological Classification of Tumors (books and slides). **Holdings:** 3000 books; 4750 bound periodical volumes; 2000 physical diagnosis teaching slides; 2000 hematology teaching slides; 600 audiotapes. **Subscriptions:** 334 journals and other serials. **Services:** Interlibrary loans; copying; library open to public for reference use only. **Computerized Information Services:** MEDLINE. Performs searches on cost recovery basis.

★11854★

ST. JOSEPH'S HOSPITAL - RUSSELL BELLMAN MEDICAL LIBRARY (Med)†
5665 Peachtree Dunwoody Rd., N.E.   Phone: (404) 256-7040
Atlanta, GA 30342   Gail Waverchak, Med.Libn.
Founded: 1965. **Staff:** Prof 1; Other 1. **Subjects:** Medicine, nursing, hospital administration, allied health sciences. **Special Collections:** Medical Ethics. **Holdings:** 2300 books; 4113 bound periodical volumes. **Subscriptions:** 110 journals and other serials. **Services:** Interlibrary loans; copying. **Networks/Consortia:** Member of Atlanta Health Science Consortium; Georgia Library Information Network (GLIN): Georgia Health Sciences Library Association (GHSLA). **Special Catalogs:** Bibliography and collection of books on death and dying.

★11855★

ST. JOSEPH'S HOSPITAL - SAMUEL ROSENTHAL MEMORIAL LIBRARY (Med)
5000 W. Chambers St.   Phone: (414) 447-2194
Milwaukee, WI 53210   M. Frances McManimon, Med.Libn.
Founded: 1967. **Staff:** Prof 1. **Subjects:** Medicine. **Holdings:** 3000 books; 8000 bound periodical volumes; 150 Audio-Digest tapes. **Subscriptions:** 100

journals and other serials. **Services:** Interlibrary loans; copying; library open to public with permission. **Networks/Consortia:** Member of Southeastern Wisconsin Health Sciences Library (Consortium) (SWHSL); Greater Midwest Regional Medical Library Network (Region 3).

★11856★
ST. JOSEPH'S HOSPITAL - SCHOOL OF NURSING - LEARNING RESOURCE CENTER (Med)
611 St. Joseph Ave.   Phone: (715) 387-7374
Marshfield, WI 54449   Margaret A. Allen, Libn.
Founded: 1914. **Staff:** Prof 1; Other 1. **Subjects:** Nursing. **Holdings:** 3013 books; 771 bound periodical volumes; 7 VF drawers of pamphlets; school archives; 635 AV programs. **Subscriptions:** 100 journals and other serials. **Services:** Interlibrary loans; copying; center open to public with restrictions. **Networks/Consortia:** Member of Northern Wisconsin Health Science Libraries Cooperative. **Publications:** Current Awareness Service, biweekly. **Special Catalogs:** Audiovisual catalog.

★11857★
ST. JOSEPH'S HOSPITAL - SCHOOL OF NURSING LIBRARY (Med)
735 W. Berry St.   Phone: (219) 425-3950
Fort Wayne, IN 46804   Gloria Uptgraft, Libn.
Founded: 1945. **Staff:** 1. **Subjects:** Nursing, medicine. **Holdings:** 2500 volumes. **Subscriptions:** 30 journals and other serials. **Services:** Interlibrary loans (limited); library not open to public. **Networks/Consortia:** Member of Northeastern Indiana Health Science Library Consortium (NIHSLC).

★11858★
ST. JOSEPH'S MEDICAL CENTER - MEDICAL LIBRARY (Med)
811 E. Madison
Box 1935   Phone: (219) 237-7228
South Bend, IN 46634   Donna J. Bayless, Libn.
Staff: Prof 1; Other 1. **Subjects:** Medicine, nursing, pharmacy, health administration, pastoral care. **Holdings:** 1854 books; 2721 unbound periodicals; 380 documents, pamphlets, brochures, and clippings; 3 drawers of microfiche. **Subscriptions:** 174 journals and other serials. **Services:** Interlibrary loans; copying; library open to public. **Computerized Information Services:** BRS. Performs searches free of charge. **Networks/Consortia:** Member of Area Library Services Authority (ALSA), Region 2; INCOLSA.

★11859★
ST. JOSEPH'S MEDICAL CENTER - MEDICAL LIBRARY (Med)
127 S. Broadway   Phone: (914) 965-6700
Yonkers, NY 10701   Ann Gorghan, Med.Libn.
Staff: Prof 1; Other 1. **Subjects:** Medicine. **Holdings:** 2218 books and bound periodical volumes. **Subscriptions:** 110 journals and other serials. **Services:** Library not open to public.

★11860★
ST. JOSEPH'S SEMINARY - ARCHBISHOP CORRIGAN MEMORIAL LIBRARY (Rel-Theol)*
Dunwoodie   Phone: (914) 968-6200
Yonkers, NY 10704   Paul J. Fullam, Lib.Dir.
Founded: 1953. **Staff:** Prof 1; Other 2. **Subjects:** Sacred scripture, moral theology, dogmatic theology, philosophy, church history, canon law, patristics, sociology, education. **Holdings:** 92,000 books; 9892 bound periodical volumes. **Subscriptions:** 400 journals and other serials; 10 newspapers. **Services:** Interlibrary loans; copying; library open to public with restrictions.

★11861★
ST. JOSEPH'S SEMINARY - LIBRARY (Rel-Theol)*
1200 Varnum St., N.E.   Phone: (202) 526-4231
Washington, DC 20017   Laurence A. Schmitt, Libn.
Founded: 1930. **Staff:** Prof 1; Other 1. **Subjects:** Philosophy and theology; black studies. **Holdings:** 24,000 books and bound periodical volumes. **Subscriptions:** 75 journals and other serials. **Services:** Interlibrary loans (limited); library open to public by appointment.

ST. JOSEPH'S SHRINE
See: Oratoire St-Joseph

★11862★
ST. JOSEPH'S UNIVERSITY - ACADEMY OF FOOD MARKETING - CAMPBELL LIBRARY (Food-Bev)
54th & City Line Ave.   Phone: (215) 879-7489
Philadelphia, PA 19131   Anna Mae Penrose, Libn.
Founded: 1965. **Staff:** Prof 1; Other 2. **Subjects:** Food marketing, retailing, consumerism, agricultural products. **Special Collections:** Bound food trade

journals; U.S. Department of Agriculture Yearbooks, 1865 to present. **Holdings:** 3525 books; 1148 bound periodical volumes; 1710 items in corporation files; 230 items in market information; 120 reels of microfilm; journals and doctoral dissertations; 4372 subject information files. **Subscriptions:** 227 journals and other serials. **Services:** Interlibrary loans; copying; library open to public for reference use only, reciprocal privileges extended to food industry libraries and organizations. **Computerized Information Services:** DIALOG. **Publications:** Serials Holdings, annual; Selected Acquisitions; in-house bibliographies.

★11863★
ST. JOSEPH'S UNIVERSITY - DREXEL LIBRARY - INSTITUTE OF INDUSTRIAL RELATIONS
54th & City Line Ave.
Philadelphia, PA 19131
Defunct

★11864★
ST. JOSEPH'S UNIVERSITY - XAVIER-DAMIANS CHRISTIAN LIFE COMMUNITY LIBRARY
54th St. & City Line Ave.
Philadelphia, PA 19131
Defunct

★11865★
ST. JUDE CHILDREN'S RESEARCH HOSPITAL - RESEARCH LIBRARY (Med)
332 N. Lauderdale
Box 318   Phone: (901) 525-0388
Memphis, TN 38101   Mary Edith Walker, Med.Libn.
Founded: 1962. **Staff:** Prof 1; Other 2. **Subjects:** Medicine, biological sciences, chemistry. **Holdings:** 2035 books; 8700 bound periodical volumes; 12 dissertations; 3 VF drawers of reprints by hospital doctors; 210 audio cassettes; 40 AV programs. **Subscriptions:** 255 journals and other serials. **Services:** Interlibrary loans; copying; SDI; library open to medical professionals only for reference use. **Computerized Information Services:** DIALOG, MEDLINE. **Networks/Consortia:** Member of Association of Memphis Area Health Science Libraries (AMAHSL). **Publications:** Library Notes - for internal distribution only.

★11866★
ST. JUDE HOSPITAL & REHABILITATION CENTER - MEDICAL LIBRARY (Med)
101 E. Valencia Mesa Dr.   Phone: (714) 871-3280
Fullerton, CA 92635   Barbara Garside, Med.Libn.
Founded: 1974. **Staff:** Prof 1. **Subjects:** Medicine, nursing. **Holdings:** 500 books; 20 sound-slide sets; 100 video cassettes. **Subscriptions:** 105 journals and other serials. **Services:** Interlibrary loans; copying; SDI; library open to consortia members and local librarians. **Networks/Consortia:** Member of Nursing Information Consortium of Orange County(NICOC); Medical Library Group of Southern California and Arizona.

★11867★
ST. LAWRENCE COLLEGE SAINT-LAURENT - LEARNING RESOURCE CENTRE (Educ)†
2 Belmont St.   Phone: (613) 933-6080
Cornwall, ON, Canada K6H 4Z1   Norah Fourney, Hd.Libn.
Founded: 1967. **Staff:** Prof 1; Other 5. **Subjects:** Education, psychology, social sciences, literature, art, technology. **Holdings:** 41,800 volumes. **Subscriptions:** 400 journals and other serials; 12 newspapers. **Services:** Interlibrary loans; copying; center open to public.

★11868★
ST. LAWRENCE COLLEGE SAINT-LAURENT - LEARNING RESOURCE CENTRE (Hum; Sci-Tech)
King & Portsmouth
Box 6000   Phone: (613) 544-5400
Kingston, ON, Canada K7L 5A6   Sherwin Raichman, Hd.
Founded: 1967. **Staff:** Prof 2; Other 9. **Subjects:** Humanities, technologies, nursing, arts, business. **Holdings:** 65,000 books; 1974 bound periodical volumes; 4200 government documents; 7000 nonprint items. **Subscriptions:** 385 journals and other serials; 16 newspapers. **Services:** Interlibrary loans; copying; center open to public. **Automated Operations:** Computerized cataloging. **Computerized Information Services:** QL Systems, Info Globe; Computerized cataloging. **Special Catalogs:** Union list of college's other two campus libraries in Brockville and Cornwall, Ontario; union list of medical serials in Kingston and area institutions. **Staff:** Barbara Carr, Ref.Libn.; Barbara Love, Ref.Libn.

★11869★

ST. LAWRENCE COUNTY HISTORICAL ASSOCIATION - ARCHIVES (Hist)
3 E. Main St.
Box 8   Phone: (315) 386-2780
Canton, NY 13617   John A. Baule, Dir.
Founded: 1944. **Staff:** Prof 2; Other 6. **Subjects:** St. Lawrence County history. **Special Collections:** David and George Parish papers (2000 items); Silas Wright Papers (250 items); local genealogy (1000 items). **Holdings:** 1500 books; 150 bound periodical volumes; 4000 maps, clippings, pamphlets, documents. **Services:** Copying; archives open to public.

★11870★

ST. LAWRENCE HOSPITAL - MEDICAL LIBRARY (Med)
1210 West Saginaw   Phone: (515) 377-0354
Lansing, MI 48915   Jane B. Claytor, Med.Libn.
Staff: Prof 1. **Subjects:** Medicine, nursing, mental health, hospital management. **Holdings:** 2200 books; 4200 bound periodical volumes. **Subscriptions:** 275 journals and other serials. **Services:** Interlibrary loans; copying; library open to health care professionals. **Computerized Information Services:** MEDLARS, DIALOG. Performs free searches. **Networks/Consortia:** Member of Capital Area Library Network (CALNET); Michigan Library Consortium (MLC); Michigan Health Sciences Libraries Association; Mid-Michigan Health Sciences Libraries (M-MHSL).

ST. LAWRENCE PSYCHIATRIC CENTER
See: New York State Office of Mental Health

ST. LAWRENCE SEAWAY AUTHORITY
See: Canada - Transport Canada

★11871★

ST. LAWRENCE SEMINARY - LIBRARY (Rel-Theol)
                                                Phone: (414) 753-3911
Mount Calvary, WI 53057   Sr. Elaine Basche, Libn.
Staff: Prof 1; Other 1. **Subjects:** Religion, English literature, classical studies. **Holdings:** 13,885 books; 5 VF drawers of pamphlets; 252 reels of microfilm of periodicals; 400 videotapes; 325 sound filmstrip titles. **Subscriptions:** 100 journals and other serials; 10 newspapers. **Services:** Library not open to public. **Remarks:** Maintained by the Province of St. Joseph of the Capuchin Order.

★11872★

ST. LAWRENCE UNIVERSITY - SPECIAL COLLECTIONS (Hist)
Owen D. Young Library   Phone: (315) 379-6398
Canton, NY 13617   Lynn Ekfelt, Cur.
Subjects: 19th century farm, village, and family life in the northern counties of New York; political, cultural, and industrial history of the area. **Special Collections:** Papers of Irving Bacheller, Frederic Remington, David Parish, Nathaniel Hawthorne, Redington, and Silas Wright. **Holdings:** 1500 linear feet of manuscripts, documents, and other materials. **Services:** Interlibrary loans (limited); copying; collections open to public. **Automated Operations:** Computerized cataloging and acquisitions. **Networks/Consortia:** Member of New York State Interlibrary Loan Network (NYSILL); Associated Colleges of the St. Lawrence Valley, Inc.

ST. LOUIS ACADEMY OF SCIENCE ARCHIVES
See: Western Historical Manuscript Collection/State Historical Society of Missouri/Manuscripts Joint Collection (St. Louis, MO)

★11873★

ST. LOUIS ART MUSEUM - RICHARDSON MEMORIAL LIBRARY (Art)
Forest Pk.   Phone: (314) 721-0067
St. Louis, MO 63110   Ann B. Abid, Libn.
Founded: 1915. **Staff:** Prof 2; Other 2. **Subjects:** Painting, sculpture, decorative arts, archeology, history, graphic arts. **Holdings:** 30,000 books and bound periodical volumes; 35,000 pamphlets; 20,000 mounted photographs; 29,000 slides; 15,000 art auction catalogs; 130 VF drawers of pamphlets. **Subscriptions:** 300 journals and other serials. **Services:** Interlibrary loans; copying (both limited); library open to adult public. **Networks/Consortia:** Member of St. Louis Regional Library Network; Missouri Library Network Corporation. **Special Indexes:** Bulletin of St. Louis Art Museum (card index). **Staff:** Doris Sturzenberger, Archv.; Dana Lynn Beth, Asst.Libn./Tech.Serv.

★11874★

ST. LOUIS CHILDREN'S HOSPITAL - BORDEN S. VEEDER LIBRARY (Med)*
500 S. Kingshighway Blvd.
Box 14871   Phone: (314) 367-6880
St. Louis, MO 63178   Ileen R. Upton, Pediatric Libn.
Founded: 1968. **Staff:** 1. **Subjects:** Pediatrics, medicine. **Holdings:** 583

books; 577 bound periodical volumes; annuals; 130 audio cassettes; 25 volumes of staff publications, 1920 to present. **Subscriptions:** 62 journals and other serials. **Services:** Interlibrary loans; library not open to public. **Publications:** Library Guide, handbook for patrons. **Also Known As:** Washington University - School of Medicine - Department of Pediatrics.

★11875★

ST. LOUIS CITY HOSPITAL - ST. LOUIS MUNICIPAL MEDICAL LIBRARY (Med)
1515 Lafayette Ave.   Phone: (314) 622-5255
St. Louis, MO 63104   Mrs. Bernie Ferrell, Libn.
Staff: Prof 1; Other 3. **Subjects:** Medicine, surgery, neurology, pediatrics, radiology, clinical sciences. **Holdings:** 1500 books; 15,000 bound periodical volumes. **Subscriptions:** 150 journals and other serials. **Services:** Interlibrary loans; library not open to public. **Networks/Consortia:** Member of St. Louis Medical Librarian's Association.

★11876★

ST. LOUIS COLLEGE OF PHARMACY - O.J. CLOUGHLY ALUMNI LIBRARY (Med)
4588 Parkview Pl.   Phone: (314) 367-8700
St. Louis, MO 63110   Helen F. Silverman, Libn.
Staff: Prof 2; Other 2. **Subjects:** Pharmacy, pharmacology, medicine, drug information. **Holdings:** 28,000 books; 5000 bound periodical volumes; 500 audiotapes and microforms. **Subscriptions:** 350 journals and other serials; 8 newspapers. **Services:** Interlibrary loans; copying; library open to public for reference use only. **Automated Operations:** Computerized cataloging. **Computerized Information Services:** BRS, DIALOG, **Networks/Consortia:** Member of Missouri Library Network Corporation; St. Louis Regional Library Network. **Publications:** New Accession List, bimonthly. **Staff:** Beth Carlin, Asst.Libn.

★11877★

ST. LOUIS - COMPTROLLERS OFFICE - MICROFILM DEPARTMENT (Hist)
City Hall, Rm. 1
Tucker & Market Sts.   Phone: (314) 622-4274
St. Louis, MO 63103   Edward J. Machowski, Supv.
Staff: Prof 3; Other 15. **Subjects:** St. Louis - fiscal records, vital statistics, inspection reports. **Holdings:** 30,000 reels of microfilm. **Services:** Copying; library open to public with restrictions. **Special Catalogs:** Catalog of contents on microfilm. **Staff:** Ruth Brown, Asst.

★11878★

ST. LOUIS CONSERVATORY AND SCHOOLS FOR THE ARTS (CASA) - MAE M. WHITAKER LIBRARY (Mus)
560 Trinity Ave.   Phone: (314) 863-3033
St. Louis, MO 63130   Marion Sherman, Libn.
Founded: 1974. **Staff:** Prof 1; Other 1. **Subjects:** Music. **Special Collections:** Performance and listening libraries; Thomas B. Sherman Collection; Robert Orchard Opera Collection. **Holdings:** 10,587 volumes (books and scores); 129 bound periodical volumes; 7510 phonograph records and tapes; 2 VF drawers of music publishers' catalogs; 13 volumes on microfiche. **Subscriptions:** 51 journals and other serials. **Services:** Interlibrary loans; library open to public for reference use only. **Special Catalogs:** Catalog of music for performance.

ST. LOUIS COUNTY HISTORICAL SOCIETY - NORTHEAST MINNESOTA HISTORICAL CENTER
See: Northeast Minnesota Historical Center

★11879★

ST. LOUIS COUNTY LAW LIBRARY (Law)
515 St. Louis County Court House   Phone: (218) 723-3563
Duluth, MN 55802   Michele Milinovich, Law Libn.
Founded: 1889. **Staff:** Prof 1. **Subjects:** Law. **Holdings:** 20,000 books. **Services:** Copying; library circulates to members only. **Formerly:** Duluth Bar Library Association.

★11880★

ST. LOUIS COUNTY LAW LIBRARY (Law)*
St. Louis County Govt. Ctr.
7900 Carondelet Ave., Suite 545
Clayton, MO 63105   Phone: (314) 889-2726
                                                 Mary C. Dahm, Libn.
Staff: Prof 1; Other 2. **Subjects:** Law. **Holdings:** 18,600 volumes. **Subscriptions:** 17 journals and other serials. **Services:** Copying; library open to public.

★11881★
ST. LOUIS HEARING AND SPEECH CENTER - LIBRARY (Med)
9526 Manchester   Phone: (314) 968-4710
St. Louis, MO 63119   Peggy Thompson, Exec.Dir.
Staff: 18. **Subjects:** Audiology, speech pathology, sign language, industrial hearing conservation, noise pollution, stutterers, preschool language. **Holdings:** 600 volumes. **Services:** Interlibrary loans; library open to public. **Publications:** Sound of Happiness, quarterly; Health Information.

★11882★
ST. LOUIS MERCANTILE LIBRARY ASSOCIATION - LIBRARY (Hum)
510 Locust St.
Box 633   Phone: (314) 621-0670
St. Louis, MO 63188   Elizabeth Kirchner, Dir./Libn.
Founded: 1846. **Staff:** Prof 6; Other 4. **Subjects:** History, biography, social sciences, science, fine arts, fiction, literature. **Special Collections:** Alchemy, dating to 1420; early Western Americana; early French and German literature; early state papers; Colonial Dames of America (155 items; pamphlets); Waterways Journal River Collection (200 volumes; pamphlets; documents); John W. Barriger, III Railroad Library (11,000 volumes; 250,000 photographs; papers and files). **Holdings:** 255,000 books; manuscripts; broadsides. **Subscriptions:** 241 journals and other serials. **Services:** Interlibrary loans; copying; library open to public with restrictions. **Automated Operations:** Computerized cataloging. **Computerized Information Services:** OCLC. **Networks/Consortia:** Member of St. Louis Regional Library Network. **Publications:** New Books Bulletin, monthly; annual reports. **Staff:** Kathleen Mulligan, Cat.; Mary Mewes, Ref.Libn.; Elizabeth Haspiel, Per. & Mailing Serv.; Jean Marie Deken, Archv.; Karen Faye Kacer, Res.Libn.

★11883★
ST. LOUIS METROPOLITAN MEDICAL SOCIETY - ST. LOUIS SOCIETY FOR MEDICAL AND SCIENTIFIC EDUCATION - LIBRARY (Med)
3839 Lindell Blvd.   Phone: (314) 371-5225
St. Louis, MO 63108   Audrey L. Berkley, Libn.
Founded: 1899. **Staff:** Prof 2; Other 1. **Subjects:** Clinical application of medicine. **Special Collections:** Paracelsus Collection (400 items); St. Louis history of medicine (300 items). **Holdings:** 20,000 books; 44,000 bound periodical volumes; 6 file cabinets of archives. **Subscriptions:** 400 journals and other serials; 8 newspapers. **Services:** Interlibrary loans (fee); copying; library open to public; loans to members only. **Computerized Information Services:** BRS Octanet, AMA/NET. **Networks/Consortia:** Member of Missouri Library Network Corporation. **Staff:** Elizabeth Mueth, Asst.Libn.

ST. LOUIS PARK MEDICAL CENTER-RESEARCH FOUNDATION
See: Park-Nicollet Medical Foundation

★11884★
ST. LOUIS - POLICE LIBRARY (Law)
315 S. Tucker   Phone: (314) 444-5581
St. Louis, MO 63102   Cathy H. Reilly, Libn.
Founded: 1947. **Staff:** Prof 1; Other 1. **Subjects:** Police science, criminology, corrections, juvenile delinquency, criminal law, narcotics. **Special Collections:** Annual Reports; 1861 to present. **Holdings:** 21,000 books; 1002 bound periodical volumes; 515 titles on microfiche; 20 VF drawers of reports, pamphlets, clippings, manuscripts; 466 pictures. **Subscriptions:** 150 journals and other serials; 8 newspapers. **Services:** Interlibrary loans; copying; library open to public. **Networks/Consortia:** Member of St. Louis Regional Library Network; Criminal Justice information Exchange. **Publications:** Bibliographies; directory of law enforcement agencies in metropolitan St. Louis. **Special Indexes:** Index of articles in eight police journals (card).

★11885★
ST. LOUIS POST-DISPATCH - REFERENCE DEPARTMENT (Publ)
900 N. Tucker Blvd.   Phone: (314) 621-1111
St. Louis, MO 63101   Nancy Williams Stoddard, Chf.Libn.
Staff: Prof 2; Other 12. **Subjects:** Newspaper reference topics. **Holdings:** 300 books; 2500 reports and pamphlets; 10 million clippings; 2.5 million photographs. **Subscriptions:** 15 journals and other serials. **Services:** Copying; department open to public by appointment with a fee for services. **Computerized Information Services:** UNIDAS 1100 (internal database). **Remarks:** Microfilm subscription available for purchase - current and back files to 1874.

★11886★
ST. LOUIS PSYCHOANALYTIC INSTITUTE - BETTY GOLDE SMITH MEMORIAL LIBRARY (Med)
4524 Forest Park Blvd.   Phone: (314) 361-7075
St. Louis, MO 63108   Rheba Symeonoglou, Libn.
Founded: 1956. **Staff:** Prof 1; Other 1. **Subjects:** Psychoanalysis and related

subjects. **Holdings:** 6000 volumes. **Subscriptions:** 33 journals and other serials. **Services:** Interlibrary loans; copying; literature searching; library open to public. **Publications:** Newsletter, 3/year - to mailing list.

★11887★
ST. LOUIS PUBLIC LIBRARY - APPLIED SCIENCE DEPARTMENT (Sci-Tech)
1301 Olive St.   Phone: (314) 241-2288
St. Louis, MO 63103   Therese F. Dawson, Supv.
Founded: 1912. **Staff:** Prof 2; Other 1. **Subjects:** Engineering; materials science; manufacturing processes; home remodeling; radio, TV and automobile repair. **Holdings:** 60,000 books; 45,000 bound periodical volumes; U.S. patents, complete collection; British Patents and Abridgements, complete collection; British standards, complete collection; 28 VF drawers of Sams Photofacts; 2000 VF envelopes; 24 VF drawers of industrial standards; 2000 automobile repair manuals. **Subscriptions:** 560 journals and other serials. **Services:** Interlibrary loans; copying; department open to public. **Computerized Information Services:** U.S. Patent Office, BRS. **Staff:** Linda Wright, Libn.

★11888★
ST. LOUIS PUBLIC LIBRARY - ART DEPARTMENT (Art)
1301 Olive St.   Phone: (314) 241-2288
St. Louis, MO 63103   Martha Hilligoss, Supv.
Founded: 1912. **Staff:** Prof 2. **Subjects:** Art and related fields - painting, sculpture, costume, architecture, photography, graphics. **Special Collections:** Steedman Architectural Collection; Bill Collection of Mississippi Riverboat pictures; Boehl photographs of early St. Louis; pictures of St. Louis architecture, past and present. **Holdings:** 50,000 books; VF drawers; 14,500 slides; 131,150 postcards; framed and unframed prints. **Subscriptions:** 105 journals and other serials. **Services:** Interlibrary loans; copying; department open to public. **Special Catalogs:** Steedman Architectural Library Catalog. **Staff:** Gail Mitchell .

★11889★
ST. LOUIS PUBLIC LIBRARY - CAROL MC DONALD GARDNER RARE BOOK ROOM (Rare Book)
1301 Olive St.   Phone: (314) 241-2288
St. Louis, MO 63103   Julanne M. Good, Supv.
Founded: 1971. **Staff:** Prof 2. **Subjects:** St. Louis authors, St. Louis and Missouri imprints (selected); history of the book and printing, natural history. **Special Collections:** Reedy's Mirror, volumes 4-29, 1894-1920; Blake Collection of Bewick materials; William K. Bixby Collection; N.J. Werner Typographic Collection; Benjamin Franklin Shumard Library (selected works); William Marion Reedy Library (selected works); Grolier Collection (history of the book). **Holdings:** 8000 books; archives of St. Louis Public Library manuscripts; 14 clay tablets (2375-394 B.C.). **Subscriptions:** 25 journals and other serials. **Services:** Copying (limited); room open to public with restrictions. **Special Indexes:** Reedys's Mirror Index, 1894-1914 (card). **Staff:** Martha Riley, Libn.

★11890★
ST. LOUIS PUBLIC LIBRARY - CHILDREN'S LITERATURE ROOM (Hum)
1301 Olive St.   Phone: (314) 241-2288
St. Louis, MO 63103   Julanne M. Good, Supv.
Staff: Prof 1; Other 1. **Subjects:** Children's literature, emphasizing fairy tales, folklore; history and criticism of children's literature. **Special Collections:** Award-winning American children's books; Jacob Abbott (50 titles); William Taylor Adams (38 titles); Horatio Alger (60 titles); Beatrix Potter; Charles Austin Fordick (32 titles); early children's literature (2000 books); history of children's literature (500 books); folklore (2000 titles); Mother Goose (50 editions, 1878 to present); St. Nicholas (complete run); story telling; representative collection of early fantasy illustrators including Arthur Rackham, Kay Nielsen, Maxfield Parrish and others. **Holdings:** 28,500 volumes. **Subscriptions:** 20 journals and other serials. **Services:** Interlibrary loans; copying; room open to public.

★11891★
ST. LOUIS PUBLIC LIBRARY - FILM LIBRARY SERVICE (Aud-Vis)
1624 Locust St.   Phone: (314) 241-2288
St. Louis, MO 63103   Rita Broughton, Supv.
Founded: 1948. **Staff:** Prof 1; Other 5. **Holdings:** 2621 16mm sound educational films. **Services:** Service open to public within the City of St. Louis and St. Louis County Library Districts. **Publications:** Catalog of 16mm sound films, annual; new additions list, annual.

★11892★
ST. LOUIS PUBLIC LIBRARY - HISTORY AND GENEALOGY DEPARTMENT
(Hist)
1301 Olive St.   Phone: (314) 241-2288
St. Louis, MO 63103   Noel C. Holobeck, Supv.
Founded: 1973. **Staff:** Prof 3. **Subjects:** U.S. history; local history; genealogy of Missouri, Illinois and most states east of the Mississippi River; heraldry; maps. **Special Collections:** Complete set of St. Louis city directories; early printed records of Eastern States; British learned societies publications; American Colonial and State Papers: passenger lists of the 19th century (microfilm); St. Louis newspapers; Boston Evening Transcript: Genealogical Queries (microfiche); U.S. state and county histories and genealogical materials; Missouri Union and Confederate service records (microfilm); federal population censuses (microfilm) and indexes; territorial papers of U.S.; family histories (3000). **Holdings:** 106,900 volumes; 1200 genealogy files; 10,000 local history files; 8,000 reels of microfilm; U.S. Geological Survey map depository for topographic maps; U.S. Army maps of foreign countries; U.S. and foreign gazetteers. **Subscriptions:** 279 journals and other serials. **Services:** Interlibrary loans; copying; department open to public. **Publications:** Genealogical Materials and Local Histories in the St. Louis Public Library (bibliography of holdings), 1965, 1st supplement, 1971; Heraldry Index of the St. Louis Public Library, 1980 (4 volumes). **Special Indexes:** Genealogy index (card); local history index (card); heraldry index supplement (card); map index; surname and locations file. **Staff:** Cynthia Millar; Leland Hilligoss .

★11893★
ST. LOUIS PUBLIC LIBRARY - HUMANITIES AND SOCIAL SCIENCES DEPARTMENT (Bus-Fin; Hum)
1301 Olive St.   Phone: (314) 241-2288
St. Louis, MO 63103   Edna J. Reinhold, Supv.
Founded: 1973. **Staff:** Prof 2; Other 5. **Subjects:** Business, Religion and philosophy, social sciences, English and American literature, languages, education. **Special Collections:** Career Information Center; Adult Basic Education; Test Information Center. **Holdings:** Books; pamphlets; journals; clippings; 2000 domestic and foreign telephone directories; COLT microfiche library of state industrial directories; vertical file on St. Louis area urban affairs. **Subscriptions:** 300 journals. **Services:** Interlibrary loans; copying; department open to public. **Special Indexes:** Ready reference file (card); local association index (card). **Staff:** Nicolette Ehernberger .

★11894★
ST. LOUIS PUBLIC LIBRARY - POPULAR LIBRARY - MUSIC SECTION (Mus)
1301 Olive St.   Phone: (314) 241-2288
St. Louis, MO 63103   Helen Taylor, Supv.
Founded: 1956. **Staff:** Prof 2; Other 1. **Subjects:** Music. **Holdings:** 5500 books; 119 bound periodical volumes; 24,000 music scores; 25,000 phonograph records; 16 drawers of clippings; 1800 cassette tapes. **Subscriptions:** 65 journals and other serials. **Services:** Interlibrary loans; copying; section open to public. **Special Indexes:** Catalog and indices for songs in songbooks and on phonograph records. **Staff:** Mary Lou Allen .

★11895★
ST. LOUIS PUBLIC LIBRARY - READERS SERVICES/DOCUMENTS DEPARTMENT (Info Sci)
1301 Olive St.   Phone: (314) 241-2288
St. Louis, MO 63103   Anne Watts, Supv.
Founded: 1865. **Staff:** Prof 3; Other 9. **Special Collections:** Defense Mapping Agency map and chart depository; U.S. Geological Survey map depository; Missouri state depository, 1976 to present; U.S. Government depository, 1866 to present. **Holdings:** Missouri documents; St. Louis city documents. **Services:** Interlibrary loans; copying; department open to public. **Staff:** Margaret Ganyard, Libn.; Mary Hutchinson, Libn.

★11896★
ST. LOUIS PUBLIC SCHOOLS - LIBRARY SERVICES CENTER (Educ)
1517 S. Theresa Ave.   Phone: (314) 865-4550
St. Louis, MO 63104   Robert G. Nador, Act.Dir.
Staff: Prof 2; Other 4. **Subjects:** Education. **Holdings:** Figures not available for books; ERIC microfiche. **Services:** Copying; center open to public by appointment. **Networks/Consortia:** Member of St. Louis Regional Library Network. **Staff:** Carolyn Alexander, Act.Coord.

★11897★
ST. LOUIS SCIENCE CENTER - LIBRARY (Sci-Tech)
5050 Oakland Ave.   Phone: (314) 652-5500
St. Louis, MO 63110   Paton R. White, Libn.
Founded: 1984. **Staff:** 1. **Subjects:** General science, natural history, astrology, astronautics. **Holdings:** 3200 books; 18 bound periodical volumes.

Subscriptions: 25 journals and other serials. **Services:** Library not open to public. **Formed by the Merger of:** McDonnell Planetarium, Library and Museum of Science and Natural History, Library.

ST. LOUIS SOCIETY FOR MEDICAL AND SCIENTIFIC EDUCATION
See: St. Louis Metropolitan Medical Society

★11898★
ST. LOUIS UNIVERSITY - COLLEGE OF PHILOSOPHY AND LETTERS - FUSZ MEMORIAL LIBRARY (Hum)
3700 W. Pine Blvd.   Phone: (314) 652-3700
St. Louis, MO 63108   Rev. J. Eugene Coomes, S.J., Libn.
Founded: 1954. **Staff:** 1. **Subjects:** Philosophy, theology, literature, history. **Special Collections:** Philosophy, 1620-1900 (1000 volumes). **Holdings:** 52,000 books; 2000 bound periodical volumes; 525 theses and dissertations. **Subscriptions:** 72 journals and other serials. **Services:** Interlibrary loans; library open to graduate students of the university's philosphy department.

★11899★
ST. LOUIS UNIVERSITY - DIVINITY LIBRARY (Rel-Theol)
Pius XII Memorial Library
3655 W. Pine Blvd.   Phone: (314) 658-3082
St. Louis, MO 63108   Rev. W. Charles Heiser, S.J., Libn.
Founded: 1848. **Staff:** Prof 1; Other 2. **Subjects:** Catholic church, monasticism and religious orders, mysticism, patrology, Bible, canon law. **Holdings:** 115,237 books; 15,793 bound periodical volumes; 145 reels of microfilm; 32 microcards. **Subscriptions:** 1037 journals and other serials. **Services:** Interlibrary loans; copying; library open to public for reference use only. **Staff:** Kathleen E. Casey, Asst.Libn.

★11900★
ST. LOUIS UNIVERSITY - KNIGHTS OF COLUMBUS VATICAN FILM LIBRARY (Rel-Theol)
Pius XII Memorial Library
3655 West Pine Blvd.
St. Louis, MO 63108   Charles J. Ermatinger, Vatican Film Libn.
Founded: 1953. **Staff:** Prof 2; Other 1. **Subjects:** Greek, Latin, Arabic, Ethiopic and Hebrew manuscripts from Vatican Library; Jesuitica and Hispanic Americana from European and Latin American collections; rare and out-of-print books. **Holdings:** 26,470 reels of microfilm (including 40,000 volumes of manuscript material); 50,608 slides of illuminated manuscripts. **Services:** Interlibrary loans; copying (both limited); library open to public with restrictions. **Publications:** Manuscripta, 3/year - available on subscription and exchange. **Special Catalogs:** Published and unpublished catalogs of manuscripts. **Staff:** Rev. Lowrie J. Daly, Microfilm Projects.

★11901★
ST. LOUIS UNIVERSITY - MEDICAL CENTER LIBRARY (Med)
1402 S. Grand Blvd.   Phone: (314) 664-9800
St. Louis, MO 63104   Logan Ludwig, Dir.
Founded: 1890. **Staff:** Prof 5; Other 16. **Subjects:** Medicine, nursing, orthodontics, allied health professions. **Special Collections:** Patrick Henry Griffin Surgical Library. **Holdings:** 35,000 books; 70,000 bound periodical volumes; 15 VF drawers of pamphlets; 400 pictures; 500 historical volumes; instrument collection; 3000 microfiche; 26,000 slides; 700 video cassettes. **Subscriptions:** 1307 journals and other serials. **Services:** Interlibrary loans; copying; SDI; library open to public with restrictions. **Automated Operations:** Computerized serials. **Computerized Information Services:** MEDLINE, BRS, PHILSOM. Performs searches on cost recovery basis. **Networks/Consortia:** Member of CRL; Midcontinental Regional Medical Library Program; St. Louis Regional Library Network. **Staff:** Carolyn L. Taylor, Asst.Libn.; Suzanne Conway, Chf.Ref.Libn.; Mary Anne Sutter, Asst.Ref.Libn.

★11902★
ST. LOUIS UNIVERSITY - PARKS COLLEGE OF AERONAUTICAL TECHNOLOGY - LIBRARY (Sci-Tech)†
                                        Phone: (618) 337-7500
Cahokia, IL 62206   Nancy Nobbe, Libn.
Founded: 1927. **Staff:** Prof 1; Other 1. **Subjects:** Aerospace engineering, aeronautical administration, meteorology, aircraft maintenance engineering. **Holdings:** 25,926 books; 9150 bound periodical volumes; 1497 reels of microfilm; 1016 microfiche; 17,576 government documents. **Subscriptions:** 253 journals and other serials. **Services:** Interlibrary loans; copying; library open to public for reference use only.

★11903★
ST. LOUIS UNIVERSITY - SCHOOL OF LAW - LIBRARY (Law)
3700 Lindell Blvd.   Phone: (314) 658-2755
St. Louis, MO 63108   Eileen H. Searls, Law Libn.
Staff: Prof 6; Other 7. **Subjects:** American law, urban legal problems, jurisprudence, taxation, health and business law. **Special Collections:** U.S. Government documents, 1975 to present; Missouri government documents, 1979 to present; Congressman Leonor Sullivan papers, 1952-1976; Fr. Leo Brown papers; Irish Law Collection. **Holdings:** 190,000 books; 17,200 bound periodical volumes; 2655 reels of microfilm; 36,259 microcards; 120,617 microfiche; 387 cassettes and videotapes. **Subscriptions:** 3700 journals and other serials; 12 newspapers. **Services:** Interlibrary loans; copying; library open to public for reference use only. **Automated Operations:** Computerized cataloging. **Computerized Information Services:** LEXIS, Westlaw, DIALOG, OCLC, Auto-Cite, Commerce Clearing House Electronic Legislative Search System (ELSS). **Networks/Consortia:** Member of Mid-America Law School Library Consortium; Missouri Library Network Corporation; St. Louis Regional Library Network.

★11904★
ST. LOUIS ZOOLOGICAL PARK - LIBRARY (Sci-Tech)*
Forest Park
St. Louis, MO 63108   Charles Hoessle, Dir.
Subjects: Zoos, zoology, mammals, birds, reptiles, animal behavior. **Holdings:** 400 publications; 200 annual reports. **Services:** Library open to public for reference use only by request.

ST. LUC HOSPITAL
See: Hopital St-Luc

ST. LUCIAN LIBRARY
See: Our Lady Queen of Martyrs

★11905★
ST. LUCIE COUNTY HISTORICAL MUSEUM - LIBRARY (Hist)
414 Seaway Dr.   Phone: (305) 464-6635
Fort Pierce, FL 33450   Edward T. McCarron, Dir.
Subjects: History of Indian River area; national, state and local history; genealogy, archives of early families. **Holdings:** 235 volumes. **Services:** Library open to public for reference use only.

★11906★
ST. LUCIE COUNTY - LAW LIBRARY (Law)
County Courthouse, 3rd Fl.   Phone: (305) 464-8904
Fort Pierce, FL 33450   Annie M. Fain, Libn.
Subjects: Law. **Holdings:** 14,000 volumes. **Services:** Library not open to public.

★11907★
ST. LUKE HOSPITAL - MEDICAL LIBRARY (Med)
2632 E. Washington Blvd.
Box 7021   Phone: (818) 797-1141
Pasadena, CA 91109-7021   Jacquelin Erwin, Libn.
Founded: 1948. **Subjects:** Medicine. **Holdings:** 440 books; 600 bound periodical volumes; 300 cassettes. **Subscriptions:** 33 journals and other serials. **Services:** Interlibrary loans; copying; library open to medical and paramedical personnel.

★11908★
ST. LUKE'S EPISCOPAL & TEXAS CHILDREN'S HOSPITALS - MEDICAL LIBRARY (Med)
6621 Fannin St.   Phone: (715) 791-3054
Houston, TX 77030   Robert C. Park, Dir. of Lib.Serv.
Founded: 1954. **Staff:** Prof 1; Other 1. **Subjects:** Medicine and related fields. **Holdings:** 11,000 books. **Subscriptions:** 154 journals and other serials. **Services:** Interlibrary loans; copying; library open to physicians only.

★11909★
ST. LUKE'S HOSPITAL ASSOCIATION - MEDICAL, NURSING AND ALLIED HELP LIBRARY (Med)*
1900 Boulevard   Phone: (904) 356-1992
Jacksonville, FL 32206   Margarette Wally, Libn.
Staff: Prof 1; Other 1. **Subjects:** Medicine, nursing. **Holdings:** 1155 books; 2128 bound periodical volumes. **Subscriptions:** 77 journals and other serials. **Services:** Interlibrary loans; library not open to public. **Computerized Information Services:** Online systems.

★11910★
ST. LUKE'S HOSPITAL OF BETHLEHEM, PENNSYLVANIA - AUDIOVISUAL LIBRARY (Aud-Vis; Med)
801 Ostrum St.   Phone: (215) 691-4341
Bethlehem, PA 18015   Robert Fields, Techn.
Staff: 1. **Subjects:** Medicine, nursing, allied health sciences, patient education. **Holdings:** 650 AV items. **Services:** Interlibrary loans; library open to public with permission of librarian. **Networks/Consortia:** Member of Cooperating Hospital Libraries of the Lehigh Valley Area (CHL).

★11911★
ST. LUKE'S HOSPITAL OF BETHLEHEM, PENNSYLVANIA - SCHOOL OF NURSING - TREXLER NURSES' LIBRARY (Med)
Bishopthorpe & Ostrum Sts.   Phone: (215) 691-4355
Bethlehem, PA 18015   Diane Frantz, Libn.
Staff: Prof 1; Other 2. **Subjects:** Nursing and allied health sciences. **Special Collections:** Historical Nursing Collection. **Holdings:** 4600 books and bound periodical volumes; 15 VF drawers. **Subscriptions:** 63 journals and other serials. **Services:** Interlibrary loans; copying; library open to public for reference use only. **Computerized Information Services:** MEDLINE. **Networks/Consortia:** Member of Cooperating Hospital Libraries of the Lehigh Valley Area (CHL).

★11912★
ST. LUKE'S HOSPITAL OF BETHLEHEM, PENNSYLVANIA - W.L. ESTES, JR. MEMORIAL LIBRARY (Med)
801 Ostrum St.   Phone: (215) 691-4227
Bethlehem, PA 18015   Maria D. Collette, Libn.
Founded: 1947. **Staff:** Prof 2. **Subjects:** Medicine, medical specialities, allied health sciences. **Special Collections:** Historical collection (251 books). **Holdings:** 1700 books; 4000 bound periodical volumes; 150 folders of ephemeral file articles. **Subscriptions:** 175 journals and other serials. **Services:** Interlibrary loans; copying; library open to public for reference use only. **Computerized Information Services:** MEDLINE. **Networks/Consortia:** Member of Cooperating Hospital Libraries of the Lehigh Valley Area (CHL); Greater Northeastern Regional Medical Library Program. **Staff:** Theresa M. Yawornitsky, Asst.Libn.

★11913★
ST. LUKE'S HOSPITAL CENTER - NURSING LIBRARY (Med)*
Amsterdam Ave. at 114th St.   Phone: (212) 870-6195
New York, NY 10025   Geraldine Allerman, Dir., Staff Educ.
Founded: 1928. **Subjects:** Nursing and related subjects. **Holdings:** 6000 books; 500 bound periodical volumes; 2000 pamphlets and clippings; 8 VF drawers. **Subscriptions:** 25 journals and other serials. **Services:** Interlibrary loans; copying; library open to hospital staff and Columbia nursing students. **Publications:** Monthly Library Bulletin (list of new accessions with annotations).

★11914★
ST. LUKE'S HOSPITAL CENTER - RICHARD WALKER BOLLING MEMORIAL MEDICAL LIBRARY (Med)†
Amsterdam Ave. & 114th St.   Phone: (212) 870-1861
New York, NY 10025   Nancy Mary Panella, Libn.
Founded: 1884. **Staff:** Prof 2; Other 2. **Subjects:** Medicine, surgery, psychiatry, child psychiatry, health care administration and planning. **Special Collections:** History of medicine and medical classics; historical collection of St. Luke's Hospital and Women's Hospital. **Holdings:** 8000 books; 17,000 bound periodical volumes; 4 VF drawers of staff reprints. **Subscriptions:** 375 journals and other serials. **Services:** Interlibrary loans; copying; library open to public by appointment. **Automated Operations:** Computerized cataloging. **Computerized Information Services:** MEDLINE, OCLC. **Networks/Consortia:** Member of Medical Library Center of New York; (MLCNY); METRO; Greater Northeastern Regional Medical Library Program. **Publications:** Acquisitions List, quarterly. **Staff:** Marlene Braten, Asst.Libn.

★11915★
ST. LUKE'S HOSPITAL - HEALTH SCIENCES LIBRARY (Med)
601 E. 19th Ave.   Phone: (303) 869-2395
Denver, CO 80203   Karen Guth, Dir.
Founded: 1954. **Staff:** Prof 1. **Subjects:** Medicine, nursing. **Holdings:** 2304 books; 5815 bound periodical volumes. **Subscriptions:** 233 journals and other serials. **Services:** Interlibrary loans; library not open to public. **Computerized Information Services:** SDC, DIALOG, MEDLARS. **Networks/Consortia:** Member of Denver Area Health Sciences Library Consortium; Colorado Council of Medical Libraries.

★11916★
ST. LUKE'S HOSPITAL OF KANSAS CITY - MEDICAL LIBRARY (Med)
Spencer Center for Education
44th & Wornall Rd.   Phone: (816) 932-2333
Kansas City, MO 64111   Karen Horst, Dir. of Lib.Serv.
Founded: 1948. **Staff:** Prof 3; Other 6. **Subjects:** Cardiology, nursing, sports medicine, medicine. **Holdings:** 5000 books; 10,000 bound periodical volumes; 1000 other cataloged items. **Subscriptions:** 349 journals and other serials. **Services:** Interlibrary loans; copying; library open to public for reference use only. **Automated Operations:** Computerized cataloging. **Computerized Information Services:** NLM, DIALOG. **Networks/Consortia:** Member of Kansas City Library Network, Inc. (KCLN); Kansas City Metropolitan Library Network (KCMLN). **Publications:** News and Notes, monthly - for internal distribution only. **Special Catalogs:** AV and serials holdings for the Kansas City area. **Special Indexes:** Index to Medical Staff Publications, biannual; American College of Cardiology Extended Learning Program index, annual. **Staff:** Kathryn Doyle, Asst.Libn.; Michelle Lahey, Ser.Libn.

★11917★
ST. LUKE'S HOSPITAL - LIBRARY (Med)
5535 Delmar Blvd.   Phone: (314) 361-1212
St. Louis, MO 63112   Kathy Mullen, Libn.
Subjects: Medicine. **Holdings:** 2600 volumes; 7 VF drawers of pamphlets and clippings. **Subscriptions:** 110 journals and other serials. **Services:** Interlibrary loans; library not open to public.

★11918★
ST. LUKE'S HOSPITAL - LIBRARY (Med)
5th St. N. at Mills Ave.   Phone: (701) 280-5571
Fargo, ND 58122   Marcia Stephens, Dir. of Lib.Serv.
Founded: 1925. **Staff:** Prof 1; Other 5. **Subjects:** Medicine, paramedicine, nursing. **Holdings:** 3592 books; 2720 bound periodical volumes; 500 AV items. **Subscriptions:** 180 journals and other serials. **Services:** Interlibrary loans; copying; library open to public for reference use only. **Networks/Consortia:** Member of Valley Medical Network.

ST. LUKE'S HOSPITAL - LIBRARY (Bellingham, WA)
See: Whatcom/Island Health Services - Library

★11919★
ST. LUKE'S HOSPITAL - MEDICAL LIBRARY (Med)
3555 Army St.   Phone: (415) 647-8600
San Francisco, CA 94110   Corazon O'S. Ismarin, Libn.
Founded: 1959. **Staff:** Prof 1. **Subjects:** Medicine and nursing. **Holdings:** 6460 books; 4059 bound periodical volumes. **Subscriptions:** 110 journals and other serials. **Services:** Interlibrary loans; library not open to public.

★11920★
ST. LUKE'S HOSPITAL - MEDICAL LIBRARY (Med)†
915 E. First St.   Phone: (218) 726-5320
Duluth, MN 55805   Kirsten Shelstad, Libn.
Founded: 1944. **Staff:** Prof 1; Other 1. **Subjects:** Medicine, nursing. **Holdings:** 10,000 volumes. **Subscriptions:** 270 journals and other serials. **Services:** Interlibrary loans; copying; library not open to public. **Automated Operations:** BRS. **Computerized Information Services:** MEDLINE. **Networks/Consortia:** Member of Arrowhead Professional Libraries Association (APLA).

★11921★
ST. LUKE'S HOSPITAL - MEDICAL LIBRARY (Med)
11311 Shaker Blvd.   Phone: (216) 368-7691
Cleveland, OH 44104   Pam Billick, Dir.
Founded: 1936. **Staff:** Prof 2; Other 1. **Subjects:** Medicine, nursing, management. **Holdings:** 1147 books; 3800 bound periodical volumes. **Subscriptions:** 140 journals and other serials. **Services:** Interlibrary loans; copying; SDI; library open to public. **Automated Operations:** MEDLINE, BRS, DIALOG. **Networks/Consortia:** Member of Medical Library Association of Northeastern Ohio.

★11922★
ST. LUKE'S HOSPITAL - MEDICAL LIBRARY (Med)
2900 W. Oklahoma Ave.   Phone: (414) 649-7357
Milwaukee, WI 53215   Midge Wos, Hd.Libn.
Founded: 1967. **Staff:** Prof 1; Other 3. **Subjects:** Medicine, nursing and paramedicine. **Holdings:** 16,083 books; 6676 bound periodical volumes; 13,958 filmstrips, records, transparencies, slides and reels; 3061 cassettes; 786 video cassettes; 1041 volumes on microfilm. **Subscriptions:** 773 journals and other serials; 21 newspapers. **Services:** Interlibrary loans; copying; SDI; library open to professional staff and employees only. **Computerized Information Services:** MEDLINE, BRS. **Networks/Consortia:** Member of Southeastern Wisconsin Health Sciences Libraries Consortium. **Publications:** New Book List and Audiovisual List, both monthly - distributed to staff and departments.

★11923★
ST. LUKE'S HOSPITAL OF MIDDLEBOROUGH - MEDICAL STAFF LIBRARY (Med)
52 Oak St.   Phone: (617) 947-6000
Middleboro, MA 02346   Gail Twomey, Med.Libn.
Staff: Prof 1. **Subjects:** Medicine and allied health sciences. **Holdings:** 112 books and bound periodical volumes; 2000 unbound periodicals. **Subscriptions:** 45 journals and other serials. **Services:** Interlibrary loans; copying; library open to public with permission. **Networks/Consortia:** Member of Southeastern Massachusetts Health Sciences Libraries ; Massachusetts Health Sciences Library Network.

★11924★
ST. LUKE'S HOSPITAL - SCHOOL OF NURSING LIBRARY (Med)
5555 Delmar Blvd.   Phone: (314) 361-1212
St. Louis, MO 63112   Sarah Deaver, Sch.Libn.
Staff: Prof 1; Other 5. **Subjects:** Nursing, nursing education, secondary education, psychology, sociology, nursing history. **Holdings:** 1857 books; 201 bound periodical volumes; 105 filmstrips; 165 cassette tapes; 817 color slides. **Subscriptions:** 53 journals and other serials. **Services:** Interlibrary loans; copying; library open to public with restrictions. **Staff:** Shelley Phillips, Coord., Adm.Dept.

★11925★
ST. LUKE'S MEDICAL CENTER - ROSENZWEIG HEALTH SCIENCES LIBRARY (Med)
1800 E. Van Buren   Phone: (602) 251-8100
Phoenix, AZ 85006   Kay E. Wellik, Dir.
Founded: 1983. **Staff:** Prof 1. **Subjects:** Cardiology, nursing, behavioral health. **Holdings:** 705 books; 1225 bound periodical volumes. **Subscriptions:** 125 journals and other serials. **Services:** Interlibrary loans; library not open to public. **Computerized Information Services:** DIALOG, MEDLARS. Performs searches free of charge. **Networks/Consortia:** Member of Maricopa Biomedical Librarians (MABL).

★11926★
ST. LUKE'S MEMORIAL HOSPITAL - A.M. JOHNSON MEMORIAL MEDICAL LIBRARY (Med)
711 S. Cowley St.   Phone: (509) 838-4771
Spokane, WA 99210   Loren A. Gothberg, Chm., Lib.Comm.
Staff: 1. **Subjects:** Orthopedics, nursing, medicine, surgery, pathology, neurology. **Holdings:** 400 books; 21 bound periodical volumes; 39 titles of Medcom slides; Audio-Digest tapes. **Subscriptions:** 35 journals and other serials. **Services:** Interlibrary loans; library not open to public. **Staff:** Delores Brewer, Libn.

★11927★
ST. LUKE'S METHODIST HOSPITAL - HEALTH SCIENCE LIBRARY (Med)
1026 A Ave., N.E.   Phone: (319) 398-7358
Cedar Rapids, IA 52402   Sally Harms, Dir.
Staff: Prof 1; Other 5. **Subjects:** Medicine, health administration, nursing and allied health sciences. **Holdings:** 12,000 books; 8000 bound periodical volumes; 1200 AV items. **Subscriptions:** 500 journals and other serials. **Services:** Interlibrary loans; copying; library open to public with restrictions. **Automated Operations:** Computerized cataloging. **Computerized Information Services:** BRS; internal database. **Networks/Consortia:** Member of Linn County Library Consortium (LCLC); Greater Midwest Regional Medical Library Network (Region 3); Educational Telecommunication Consortium. **Special Catalogs:** Book Catalog; Area Serials List.

★11928★
ST. LUKE'S REGIONAL MEDICAL CENTER - LIBRARY-MEDIA CENTER (Med)
2720 Stone Park Blvd.   Phone: (712) 279-3156
Sioux City, IA 51104   Barbara Knight, Lib.-Media Coord.
Staff: Prof 2. **Subjects:** Medicine, nursing. **Holdings:** 1500 books; 200 filmstrips; 250 videotape cassettes. **Subscriptions:** 90 journals and other serials. **Services:** Interlibrary loans; copying; library open to public. **Computerized Information Services:** MEDLINE. **Networks/Consortia:** Member of Siouxland Health Science Library Consortium.

★11929★
ST. LUKE'S REGIONAL MEDICAL CENTER - MEDICAL LIBRARY (Med)
190 E. Bannock   Phone: (208) 386-2277
Boise, ID 83712   Christine K. Vogelheim, Dir.
Staff: Prof 1; Other 2. **Subjects:** Medicine, nursing, administration. **Holdings:** 1000 volumes. **Subscriptions:** 200 journals and other serials. **Services:** Interlibrary loans; copying; SDI; library open to public with restrictions. **Automated Operations:** Computerized cataloging. **Computerized Information Services:** MEDLARS, BRS. **Remarks:** The library also houses the Idaho Health Information Retrieval Center.

ST. MARGARET HEALTH CENTER
See: Providence-St. Margaret Health Center

★11930★
ST. MARGARET HOSPITAL - SALLIE M. TYRRELL, M.D. MEMORIAL LIBRARY (Med)
5454 Hohman Ave.   Phone: (219) 932-2300
Hammond, IN 46320   Laurie Broadus, Libn.Coord.
Staff: Prof 1; Other 1. **Subjects:** Medicine, nursing. **Holdings:** 2000 books; 1500 bound periodical volumes; 1200 pamphlets. **Subscriptions:** 66 journals and other serials. **Services:** Interlibrary loans; library open for reference by request of staff doctors. **Networks/Consortia:** Member of Greater Midwest Regional Medical Library Network (Region 3); Northwest Indiana Health Science Library Consortium.

★11931★
ST. MARGARET MEMORIAL HOSPITAL - PAUL TITUS MEMORIAL LIBRARY AND SCHOOL OF NURSING LIBRARY (Med)
4631 Davison St.   Phone: (412) 622-7090
Pittsburgh, PA 15201   Dorothy Schiff, Libn.
Staff: Prof 2; Other 2. **Subjects:** Medicine, nursing, allied health sciences. **Holdings:** 3200 books; 1500 bound periodical volumes; 8 VF drawers of pamphlets; 3 shelves of archives; audiotapes; filmstrips; slides; AV cassettes. **Subscriptions:** 273 journals and other serials. **Services:** Interlibrary loans; copying. **Networks/Consortia:** Member of Pittsburgh-East Hospital Library Cooperative. **Remarks:** The Paul Titus Memorial Library is located at 815 Freeport Rd., Pittsburgh, PA 15215. **Staff:** Barbara Hartman, Med.Libn.

★11932★
ST. MARIA GORETTI CHURCH LIBRARY (Rel-Theol)*
5405 Flad Ave.   Phone: (608) 271-8244
Madison, WI 53711
Founded: 1962. **Subjects:** Religion and related topics. **Holdings:** 3000 books. **Subscriptions:** 15 journals and other serials. **Services:** Library open to public on a limited schedule.

★11933★
ST. MARK'S HOSPITAL - LIBRARY (Med)
1200 East 3900 South St.   Phone: (801) 268-7004
Salt Lake City, UT 84117   Kerry F. Skidmore, Libn.
Staff: Prof 1; Other 1. **Subjects:** Medicine and allied health sciences. **Holdings:** 1500 books; 500 bound periodical volumes; unbound periodicals; microfiche; 100 pamphlets; 150 AV programs. **Subscriptions:** 321 journals and other serials. **Services:** Interlibrary loans (fee); copying; SDI; patient education instruction; library open to medical librarians only. **Computerized Information Services:** MEDLINE, Octanet. **Networks/Consortia:** Member of Utah Health Sciences Library Consortium. **Special Indexes:** AV index (pamphlet).

ST. MARK'S LIBRARY
See: General Theological Seminary of the Protestant Episcopal Church in the U.S.A.

★11934★
ST. MARK'S PRESBYTERIAN CHURCH - LIBRARY (Rel-Theol)*
3809 E. 3rd St.   Phone: (602) 325-1519
Tucson, AZ 85716
Founded: 1965. **Staff:** 6. **Subjects:** Theology, Bible and Bible study, devotions, church history, social problems. **Holdings:** 2500 books. **Services:** Library open to church members.

★11935★
ST. MARK'S SEMINARY - LIBRARY (Rel-Theol)
429 E. Grandview Blvd.
Erie, PA 16504
Defunct

★11936★
ST. MARTHA'S HOSPITAL - SCHOOL OF NURSING LIBRARY (Med)
25 Bay St.   Phone: (902) 863-2830
Antigonish, NS, Canada B2G 2G5   Sr. Marilyn Curry, Libn.
Staff: Prof 1. **Subjects:** Nursing. **Holdings:** 2000 books; 144 bound periodical volumes; AV materials. **Services:** Interlibrary loans; library not open to public.

★11937★
SAINT MARY COLLEGE - DE PAUL LIBRARY - SPECIAL COLLECTIONS CENTER (Hum; Hist)
                                                  Phone: (913) 682-5151
Leavenworth, KS 66048   Sister Therese Deplazes, Spec.Coll.Libn.
Founded: 1972. **Staff:** Prof 1; Other 1. **Subjects:** Holy Scripture, Abraham Lincoln, William Shakespeare, Charles Dickens, Kansas and regional history, Americana, early missionaries in Kansas. **Holdings:** John and Mary Craig Collection (2000 Bibles and parts in 900 languages; manuscripts, scrolls, codices; incunabula and printed books from 15th century to present; memorabilia); Abraham Lincoln Collection (1500 books and pamphlets; sheet music; postcards; manuscripts; slave papers; letters; documents; photographs; portraits; memorabilia); William Shakespeare Collection (1000 volumes and microfilm titles; scrapbooks of theater programs and photographs; memorabilia); Americana (500 original documents: letters, bills of sale, ships' papers); Kansas Collection (early textbooks; books on Kansas and by Kansas authors); The Church in Kansas; church histories); Charles Dickens (60 rare volumes). **Subscriptions:** 9 journals and other serials. **Services:** Interlibrary loans; copying; center open to public for reference use only. **Networks/Consortia:** Member of Kansas City Regional Council for Higher Education (KCRCHE). **Special Catalogs:** Catalog to Lincoln volumes and pamphlets, portraits and memorabilia (card); catalog to Holy Scripture chronology (card); descriptive bibliographic lists: Holy Scripture, American History (1620-1980), Bibles printed in America (1735 to present), Charles Dickens.

★11938★
ST. MARY-CORWIN HOSPITAL - FINNEY MEMORIAL LIBRARY (Med)
1008 Minnequa Ave.   Phone: (303) 560-5598
Pueblo, CO 81004   Shirley Harper, Med.Libn.
Founded: 1958. **Staff:** Prof 1. **Subjects:** Internal medicine, surgery, pediatrics, pathology, and allied health sciences. **Holdings:** 2568 books and bound periodical volumes; 54 video cassettes; 769 Audio-Digest tapes. **Subscriptions:** 124 journals and other serials. **Services:** Interlibrary loans; copying; library open to public for reference use only. **Automated Operations:** Computerized cataloging. **Computerized Information Services:** MEDLINE, OCLC.

★11939★
ST. MARY HOSPITAL - HEALTH SCIENCE LIBRARY (Med)
3600 Gates Blvd.
Box 3696   Phone: (409) 985-7431
Port Arthur, TX 77642   Sister Mary Patricius, Dir.
Founded: 1930. **Staff:** Prof 2. **Subjects:** Allergic diseases, dermatology, radiology, pathology, genitourinary medicine, physicians and surgeons, family practice, hemodialysis, thoracic and cardiovascular surgery, internal medicine, obstetrics/gynecology, child specialists, dentistry, infection. **Special Collections:** Industrial medicine (340 items). **Holdings:** 3520 books; 642 bound periodical volumes; 400 unbound reports; 168 Audio-Digest tapes; 30 video cassettes. **Subscriptions:** 135 journals and other serials. **Services:** Interlibrary loans; copying; library open to public with approval of administrator. **Automated Operations:** Computerized cataloging, circulation and ILL. **Computerized Information Services:** NLM. **Staff:** Ethel M. Granger, Libn.

★11940★
ST. MARY HOSPITAL - MEDICAL LIBRARY (Med)
36475 Five Mile Road   Phone: (313) 464-4800
Livonia, MI 48154   Sister Mary Clementine, Libn.
Founded: 1959. **Staff:** Prof 1; Other 3. **Subjects:** Internal medicine, surgery, nuclear medicine, obstetrics/gynecology, orthopedics, pathology, hemodialysis, dermatology, pediatrics. **Holdings:** 1000 books; 55 bound periodical volumes; 674 cassettes; 28 slide sets; video cassettes. **Subscriptions:** 33 journals and other serials. **Services:** Interlibrary loans; library not open to public. **Networks/Consortia:** Member of Metropolitan Detroit Medical Library Group (MDMLG). **Remarks:** Hospital is operated by the Felician Sisters.

★11941★
ST. MARY OF THE LAKE SEMINARY - FEEHAN MEMORIAL LIBRARY (Rel-Theol)
Phone: (312) 566-6401
Mundelein, IL 60060   Gloria Sieben, Libn.
Founded: 1929. **Staff:** Prof 1; Other 2. **Subjects:** Ancient Christian literature, medieval theology, Catholic theology. **Special Collections:** Irish history, language, literature. **Holdings:** 140,000 books; 25,000 bound periodical volumes; 610 reels of microfilm; 401 microcards. **Subscriptions:** 450 journals and other serials; 5 newspapers. **Services:** Interlibrary loans; copying.

★11942★
ST. MARY MEDICAL CENTER - BELLIS MEDICAL LIBRARY (Med)
1050 Linden Ave.
Box 887
Long Beach, CA 90801-0887   Phone: (213) 435-4441
                                                    Emily L. Giustino, Dir.
Founded: 1955. **Staff:** Prof 2; Other 1. **Subjects:** Medicine, nursing. **Holdings:** 20,000 books and bound periodical volumes; pamphlet files; history collection. **Subscriptions:** 450 journals and other serials. **Services:** Interlibrary loans; copying; library open to public with restrictions. **Computerized Information Services:** NLM, SDC, BRS.

★11943★
ST. MARY OF NAZARETH HOSPITAL CENTER - SCHOOL OF NURSING LIBRARY (Med)
1127 N. Oakley Blvd.   Phone: (312) 384-5360
Chicago, IL 60622   Phebe Tinker, Libn.
Staff: Prof 1; Other 2. **Subjects:** Nursing and nursing education. **Holdings:** 2870 books; 160 bound periodical volumes; 3 VF drawers of clippings; 4 shelves of pamphlets; AV materials (housed separately). **Subscriptions:** 29 journals and other serials. **Services:** Copying; library open to public.

★11944★
ST. MARY OF NAZARETH HOSPITAL - SISTER STELLA LOUISE HEALTH SCIENCE LIBRARY (Med)†
2233 W. Division St.   Phone: (312) 770-2219
Chicago, IL 60622   Janet S. Klieman, Med.Libn.
Founded: 1949. **Staff:** Prof 1; Other 1. **Subjects:** Medicine, surgery and allied health sciences. **Holdings:** 1300 books; 1500 bound periodical volumes; 300 pamphlets and reprints; 700 Audio-Digest tapes; 65 slide sets; 200 video cassettes. **Subscriptions:** 150 journals and other serials. **Services:** Interlibrary loans; library not open to public. **Computerized Information Services:** MEDLINE. **Networks/Consortia:** Member of Greater Midwest Regional Medical Library Network (Region 3); Metropolitan Consortium. **Publications:** Monthly Acquisitions and Research Grants. **Special Catalogs:** Audiovisual Catalog.

★11945★
ST. MARY SEMINARY - JOSEPH M. BRUENING LIBRARY (Rel-Theol)
1227 Ansel Rd.   Phone: (216) 721-2100
Cleveland, OH 44108   Steven A. Kiczek, Libn.
Founded: 1848. **Staff:** Prof 1; Other 1. **Subjects:** Liturgy, dogmatic and moral theology, history of the Catholic Church, patristic writings, sacred scripture, ecumenism, canon law, religious education, pastoral care. **Special Collections:** Bishop Horstmann Collection (1600 books). **Holdings:** 38,000 books; 7000 bound periodical volumes; 250 drafts and reports of Vatican Council II; 5 boxes of U.S. Catholic Conference pamphlets; 670 cassettes; 288 filmstrips; 367 microfiche; 253 reels of microfilm; 276 theses. **Subscriptions:** 360 journals and other serials; 5 newspapers. **Services:** Interlibrary loans; copying; library open to public by appointment. **Networks/Consortia:** Member of Ohio Theological Librarians; Cleveland Area Metropolitan Library System (CAMLS).

ST. MARY'S OF THE BARRENS LIBRARY
See: St. Mary's Seminary

★11946★
ST. MARY'S CITY COMMISSION - RESEARCH LIBRARY (Hist)
Box 38   Phone: (301) 994-1614
St. Mary's City, MD 20686
Staff: 1. **Subjects:** Historic sites archeology, material culture, folk architecture, Maryland history. **Special Collections:** Transcripts of colonial real estate advertisements and probate inventories (2 VF drawers); abstracts from colonial documents on material culture (2 card files). **Holdings:** 206 books and bound periodical volumes; 20 VF drawers; 30 shelf feet of excavation notes and artifact catalogs. **Services:** Copying; library open to public for reference use only by appointment.

★11947★
SAINT MARY'S COLLEGE - CUSHWA-LEIGHTON LIBRARY - SPECIAL COLLECTIONS (Hum)
Phone: (219) 284-5280
Notre Dame, IN 46556   Sr. Bernice Hollenhorts, CSC, Lib.Dir.
Holdings: Books by and about Dante Alighieri (600 titles). **Services:** Interlibrary loans; copying; collections open to public with restrictions. **Networks/Consortia:** Member of INCOLSA.

★11948★
ST. MARY'S COLLEGE - MUSIC SEMINAR ROOM (Mus)
Moreau Hall, Rm. 322   Phone: (219) 284-4638
Notre Dame, IN 46556   Sr. Rita Claire Lyons, C.S.C., Dir.
Founded: 1957. **Staff:** Prof 2; Other 11. **Subjects:** Music. **Holdings:** 710 books; 2780 scores; 3035 sound recordings; tapes. **Subscriptions:** 11. **Services:** Interlibrary loans; copying; room open to public with limited circulation. **Staff:** Robert Hohl, Cat.

★11949★
ST. MARY'S GENERAL HOSPITAL - HEALTH SCIENCES LIBRARY (Med)
45 Golder St.   Phone: (207) 786-2901
Lewiston, ME 04240   Evelyn A. Greenlaw, Libn.
Founded: 1908. **Staff:** Prof 1. **Subjects:** Medicine, nursing, hospital administration. **Special Collections:** Crisis intervention. **Holdings:** 700 books; 300 bound periodical volumes. **Subscriptions:** 111 journals and other serials. **Services:** Interlibrary loans; copying; SDI; library open to public. **Computerized Information Services:** MEDLINE. **Networks/Consortia:** Member of Health Science Library and Information Cooperative of Maine.

★11950★
ST. MARY'S HEALTH CENTER - HEALTH SCIENCES LIBRARY (Med)
6420 Clayton Rd.   Phone: (314) 768-8112
St. Louis, MO 63117   Candace W. Thayer, Libn.
Founded: 1933. **Staff:** Prof 1; Other 3. **Subjects:** Clinical medicine, nursing, allied health sciences. **Holdings:** 1000 books; 12,000 bound periodical volumes. **Subscriptions:** 200 journals and other serials. **Services:** Interlibrary loans; library not open to public. **Computerized Information Services:** MEDLARS. **Networks/Consortia:** Member of Sisters of St. Mary - System Wide Library Consortium; St. Louis Regional Library Network.

ST. MARY'S HOSPITAL - CATHOLIC MEDICAL CENTER OF BROOKLYN & QUEENS, INC.
See: Catholic Medical Center of Brooklyn & Queens, Inc. - St. Mary's Hospital

★11951★
ST. MARY'S HOSPITAL - FAMILY PRACTICE & PATIENT EDUCATION LIBRARY (Med)†
2900 Baltimore   Phone: (816) 753-5700
Kansas City, MO 64108   Pamela Drayson, Libn.
Founded: 1982. **Staff:** Prof 1. **Subjects:** Family practice, medical business management, bioethics. **Special Collections:** Patient education. **Holdings:** 2000 books. **Subscriptions:** 50 journals and other serials; 10 newspapers. **Services:** Interlibrary loans; copying; library open to public with restrictions. **Computerized Information Services:** MEDLINE, DIALOG. **Networks/Consortia:** Member of Kansas City Library Network, Inc. (KCLN).

★11952★
ST. MARY'S HOSPITAL - FINKELSTEIN LIBRARY (Med)
56 Franklin St.   Phone: (203) 574-6408
Waterbury, CT 06702   Jean Fuller, Libn.
Founded: 1970. **Staff:** Prof 1; Other 2. **Subjects:** Medicine and nursing. **Holdings:** 1000 books; 2584 bound periodical volumes. **Subscriptions:** 143 journals and other serials. **Services:** Interlibrary loans; copying; SDI; library open to public for reference use only.

★11953★
ST. MARY'S HOSPITAL & HEALTH CENTER - RALPH FULLER MEDICAL LIBRARY (Med)
1601 W. St. Mary's Rd.
Box 5386   Phone: (602) 622-5833
Tucson, AZ 85703   Jeffrey W. St. Clair, Med.Libn.
Founded: 1939. **Staff:** Prof 1; Other 1. **Subjects:** Medicine, nursing and allied health sciences, hospital administration, pastoral care. **Holdings:** 800 books; 2500 bound periodical volumes; 4 VF drawers of pamphlets and reprints. **Subscriptions:** 107 journals and other serials. **Services:** Interlibrary loans; copying; SDI; library open to nonstaff and area doctors. **Computerized Information Services:** MEDLINE, DIALOG. **Networks/Consortia:** Member of Pacific Southwest Regional Medical Library Service (PSRMLS). **Publications:**

Serials Holdings List, annual - free upon request.

★11954★
ST. MARY'S HOSPITAL - HEALTH SCIENCE LIBRARY (Med)
1800 E. Lake Shore Dr.   Phone: (217) 429-2966
Decatur, IL 62525   Laura L. Brosamer, Libn.
Staff: Prof 1; Other 1. **Subjects:** Medicine, nursing, hospital administration. **Holdings:** 1194 books; 1600 bound periodical volumes; 184 slide/tape programs; 9 linear feet of vertical files. **Subscriptions:** 234 journals and other serials. **Services:** Interlibrary loans; copying; SDI; library open to public with librarian's permission. **Computerized Information Services:** MEDLARS, DIALOG. **Networks/Consortia:** Member of Rolling Prairie Library System; Greater Midwest Regional Medical Library Network (Region 3); Capitol Area Consortium of Health Science Libraries. **Publications:** The Appendix (a new book list), quarterly.

★11955★
ST. MARY'S HOSPITAL - HEALTH SCIENCES LIBRARY (Med)
901 45th St.   Phone: (305) 844-6300
West Palm Beach, FL 33407   Jennie Glock, Libn.
Founded: 1946. **Staff:** Prof 1; Other 1. **Subjects:** Medicine, nursing, and allied health sciences. **Special Collections:** Historical Collection in Medicine. **Holdings:** 950 books; 6000 bound periodical volumes; 200 rare books. **Subscriptions:** 145 journals and other serials. **Services:** Interlibrary loans; copying; library open to public with restrictions. **Computerized Information Services:** MEDLARS. **Networks/Consortia:** Member of Palm Beach County Health Sciences Library Consortium; Miami Health Sciences Library Consortium.

★11956★
ST. MARY'S HOSPITAL - HEALTH SCIENCES LIBRARY (Med)
5801 Bremo Rd.   Phone: (804) 285-2011
Richmond, VA 23226
Founded: 1966. **Staff:** Prof 2. **Subjects:** Medicine, hospital administration, nursing. **Holdings:** 600 books; 1000 bound periodical volumes. **Subscriptions:** 115 journals and other serials. **Services:** Interlibrary loans; copying; library open to public with permission. **Computerized Information Services:** BRS. **Staff:** Sandra H. Parham, Libn.; Damon Persiani, Libn.

★11957★
ST. MARY'S HOSPITAL - HEALTH SCIENCES LIBRARY (Med)
2323 N. Lake Dr.
Box 503   Phone: (414) 289-7000
Milwaukee, WI 53201   Carolyn J. Barloga, Libn.
Founded: 1959. **Staff:** Prof 1. **Subjects:** Nursing, medicine, management. **Holdings:** 1500 books; 2000 bound periodical volumes. **Subscriptions:** 200 journals and other serials. **Services:** Interlibrary loans; copying; library open to public for reference use only. **Computerized Information Services:** MEDLINE, BRS. **Networks/Consortia:** Member of Southeastern Wisconsin Health Sciences Library Consortium; Great Lakes Regional Medical Library Network.

★11958★
ST. MARY'S HOSPITAL - LIBRARY (Med)
200 Jefferson, S.E.   Phone: (616) 774-6243
Grand Rapids, MI 49503   Mary A. Hanson, Med.Libn.
Founded: 1927. **Staff:** Prof 2; Other 2. **Subjects:** Medicine, nursing. **Special Collections:** Historical medical collections from Kent County Medical Society, St. Mary's Hospital and Mercy Central School of Nursing. **Holdings:** 3500 books; 7500 bound periodical volumes; 12 drawers of VF material. **Subscriptions:** 200 journals and other serials. **Services:** Interlibrary loans; copying; library open to public with restrictions. **Computerized Information Services:** MEDLINE, DIALOG. Performs searches on cost recovery basis. **Networks/Consortia:** Member of Lakeland Area Library Network; Sisters of Mercy Health Corporation AV-Library Group. **Staff:** Yvonne Mathis, Asst.Libn.

★11959★
ST. MARY'S HOSPITAL - LIBRARY (Med)
1216 2nd St., S.W.   Phone: (507) 285-5647
Rochester, MN 55902   Elizabeth Warfield, Libn.
Founded: 1913. **Staff:** Prof 2; Other 6. **Subjects:** Nursing, allied health sciences, nutrition, hospital administration. **Holdings:** 4500 books. **Subscriptions:** 198 journals and other serials. **Services:** Interlibrary loans; literature searches; current awareness. **Publications:** New Books List, monthly; Library News Column, monthly. **Staff:** Mona Stevermer, Asst.Libn.

★11960★
ST. MARY'S HOSPITAL - LIBRARY (Med)
101 Memorial Dr.   Phone: (816) 753-5700
Kansas City, MO 64108   Cheryl A. Postlewait, Libn.
Founded: 1936. **Staff:** Prof 1. **Subjects:** Medicine, nursing and related health fields. **Holdings:** 2000 books; 1000 bound periodical volumes. **Subscriptions:** 126 journals and other serials. **Services:** Interlibrary loans; copying; library open to public with restrictions. **Computerized Information Services:** MEDLINE, DIALOG. **Networks/Consortia:** Member of Kansas City Library Network, Inc.; Sisters of St. Mary - System Wide Library Consortium.

★11961★
ST. MARY'S HOSPITAL - MAX C. FLEISCHMANN MEDICAL LIBRARY (Med)
235 W. Sixth St.   Phone: (702) 789-3108
Reno, NV 89520   Kathleen L. Pratt, Libn.
Founded: 1958. **Staff:** Prof 1. **Subjects:** Medicine, nursing, management. **Holdings:** 750 books; 599 bound periodical volumes. **Subscriptions:** 116 journals and other serials. **Services:** Interlibrary loans; copying; library open to public for reference use only. **Networks/Consortia:** Member of Pacific Southwest Regional Medical Library Service (PSRMLS); Northern California and Nevada Medical Library Group.

★11962★
ST. MARY'S HOSPITAL - MEDICAL ALLIED HEALTH LIBRARY (Med)†
211 Pennington Ave.   Phone: (201) 473-1000
Passaic, NJ 07055   Sister Gertrude, S.C., Libn.
Staff: Prof 1. **Subjects:** Medicine, surgery, orthopedics, vascular surgery, psychiatry, neurology, allied health sciences. **Holdings:** 900 books; 2000 bound periodical volumes. **Subscriptions:** 103 journals and other serials. **Services:** Interlibrary loans; library not open to public. **Automated Operations:** Computerized cataloging, acquisitions and circulation.

★11963★
ST. MARY'S HOSPITAL AND MEDICAL CENTER - MEDICAL LIBRARY (Med)
450 Stanyan St.   Phone: (415) 750-5784
San Francisco, CA 94117   Eleanor Benelisha, Dir., Lib.Serv.
Staff: Prof 2; Other 2. **Subjects:** Medicine, surgery, psychiatry, nursing. **Holdings:** 3700 books; 7000 bound periodical volumes; medical, surgical and psychiatry tape cassettes. **Subscriptions:** 260 journals and other serials. **Services:** Interlibrary loans; copying; library open to public by appointment. **Computerized Information Services:** MEDLINE. **Networks/Consortia:** Member of Pacific Southwest Regional Medical Library Service (PSRMLS); San Francisco Biomedical Library Network.

ST. MARY'S HOSPITAL & MEDICAL CENTER - MUNRO (Dr. E.H.) MEDICAL LIBRARY
See: Munro (Dr. E.H.) Medical Library

★11964★
ST. MARY'S HOSPITAL MEDICAL EDUCATION FOUNDATION - MEDICAL LITERATURE INFORMATION CENTER (Med)
101 Memorial Dr.   Phone: (816) 753-5700
Kansas City, MO 64108   Dr. George X. Trimble, Dir.
Founded: 1947. **Staff:** Prof 1; Other 2. **Subjects:** Clinical medicine, medical education, medical staff organization, toxicology, history of medicine. **Special Collections:** Medical literature reprint technology. **Holdings:** 400 books and bound periodical volumes; 800 monographs; 465,000 medical literature reprints. **Subscriptions:** 150 journals and other serials. **Services:** Copying; will answer brief inquiries and make referrals; center open for medical or academic use by appointment. **Publications:** Reports and critical reviews, irregular; medical literature critiques, irregular. **Special Indexes:** Index and cross-index to medical literature reprints; index to therapeutic drugs in generic and proprietary terms; index of eponyms.

★11965★
ST. MARY'S HOSPITAL - MEDICAL LIBRARY (Med)
305 S. Fifth St.
Box 232   Phone: (405) 233-6100
Enid, OK 73701   Jean McDaniel, Med.Libn.
Staff: Prof 1; Other 1. **Subjects:** Medicine, nursing and hospital administration. **Holdings:** 2405 books; 2292 bound periodical volumes; 246 audiotapes. **Subscriptions:** 310 journals and other serials. **Services:** Interlibrary loans; copying; library open to medical and paramedical professionals.

★11966★

ST. MARY'S HOSPITAL - MEDICAL LIBRARY (Med)†
911B Queen's Blvd.   Phone: (519) 744-3311
Kitchener, ON, Canada N2M 1B2   Marilyn Mathews, Libn.
Founded: 1963. **Staff:** Prof 1. **Subjects:** Medicine, nursing, hospital administration. **Holdings:** 1000 books; 900 bound periodical volumes. **Subscriptions:** 100 journals and other serials. **Services:** Library not open to public.

★11967★

ST. MARY'S HOSPITAL - MEDICAL LIBRARY (Med)
3830 Lacombe   Phone: (514) 344-3317
Montreal, PQ, Canada H3T 1M5   Lucile Lavigueur, Libn.
Founded: 1952. **Staff:** Prof 1; Other 2. **Subjects:** Medicine, nursing, obstetrics, gynecology, psychiatry, surgery. **Holdings:** 3500 books; 5090 bound periodical volumes; 1000 audiotape cassettes. **Subscriptions:** 250 journals and other serials. **Services:** Interlibrary loans; library not open to public.

★11968★

ST. MARY'S HOSPITAL - MEDICAL LIBRARY (Med)
803 E. Dakota Ave.
Pierre, SD 57501   DeAnn DeKay Hilmoe, Med.Libn.
Staff: Prof 1. **Subjects:** Medicine, nursing, allied health sciences. **Holdings:** 2100 books; 25 bound periodical volumes. **Subscriptions:** 115 journals and other serials. **Services:** Interlibrary loans; copying; SDI; library open to public with restrictions. **Computerized Information Services:** MEDLARS. **Networks/Consortia:** Member of Central South Dakota Health Science Library Consortium. **Publications:** CSDHSLC Newsletter, monthly - to members and interested professionals in the region.

★11969★

ST. MARY'S HOSPITAL - MEDICAL LIBRARY (6E) (Med)
       Phone: (304) 696-6807
Huntington, WV 25701-5501   Kay Gibson, Med.Libn.
Founded: 1929. **Staff:** Prof 1; Other 1. **Subjects:** Medicine, surgery and allied health sciences. **Holdings:** 651 books; 1563 bound periodical volumes; 78 pamphlets; 2214 other cataloged items. **Subscriptions:** 177 journals and other serials. **Services:** Interlibrary loans; copying; bibliographic service for physicians; library open to public with restrictions. **Computerized Information Services:** NLM. **Networks/Consortia:** Member of Huntington Health Science Library Consortium. **Special Catalogs:** Huntington Health Science Library Consortium Serial Holdings; listing of serial publications. **Staff:** Catherine Porter, Supv.

★11970★

ST. MARY'S HOSPITAL - MEDICAL STAFF LIBRARY (Med)
1300 Massachusetts Ave.   Phone: (518) 272-5000
Troy, NY 12180   Audna T. Clum, Libn.
Founded: 1960. **Staff:** Prof 1. **Subjects:** Medicine. **Holdings:** 609 books; 1229 bound periodical volumes; 573 other cataloged items. **Subscriptions:** 78 journals and other serials. **Services:** Interlibrary loans; copying; library open to public. **Networks/Consortia:** Member of Capital District Library Council for Reference & Research Resources (CDLC).

★11971★

ST. MARY'S HOSPITAL - STAFF LIBRARY (Med)
2414 S. 7th St.   Phone: (612) 338-2229
Minneapolis, MN 55454   Jacquelynn Carlson, Chf.Libn.
Staff: Prof 1; Other 1. **Subjects:** Medicine and allied fields. **Holdings:** 2000 books; 4500 periodical volumes; 15 boxes of pamphlets; 3 VF drawers of archives; AV materials. **Subscriptions:** 200 journals and other serials; 8 newspapers. **Services:** Interlibrary loans; copying; library open to public for reference use only. **Computerized Information Services:** Access to MEDLINE, BRS. **Networks/Consortia:** Member of Twin Cities Biomedical Consortium (TCBC).

★11972★

ST. MARY'S OF THE LAKE HOSPITAL - GIBSON MEDICAL RESOURCE CENTRE (Med)
340 Union St., W.
Box 3600
Kingston, ON, Canada K7L 5A2   Phone: (613) 544-5220
       Penny G. Levi, Libn.
Founded: 1978. **Staff:** Prof 1; Other 1. **Subjects:** Geriatrics and chronic care, rehabilitation, orthopedics and prosthetics, allied health sciences. **Holdings:** 1330 books; bound and unbound periodicals. **Subscriptions:** 112 journals and other serials. **Services:** Interlibrary loans; copying; centre open to public with restrictions. **Publications:** New Book List, weekly - local distribution on request.

★11973★

ST. MARY'S MEDICAL CENTER - HERMAN M. BAKER, M.D. MEMORIAL LIBRARY (Med)
3700 Washington Ave.   Phone: (812) 479-4151
Evansville, IN 47750   Jane E. Saltzman, Dir.
Staff: Prof 2; Other 4. **Subjects:** Medicine, nursing, health administration. **Holdings:** 1200 books and bound periodical volumes; 300 AV items. **Subscriptions:** 120 journals and other serials; 10 newspapers. **Services:** Interlibrary loans; copying; library open to public with restrictions. **Computerized Information Services:** MEDLARS. **Networks/Consortia:** Member of Greater Midwest Regional Medical Library Network (Region 3); Evansville Area Health Sciences Libraries Consortium. **Publications:** Newsletter, quarterly - for internal distribution only. **Staff:** Toby D. Smith, Asst., Lib.Serv.

★11974★

ST. MARY'S MEDICAL CENTER, INC. - MEDICAL LIBRARY (Med)
Oak Hill Ave.   Phone: (615) 971-7916
Knoxville, TN 37917   Glenda Clark, Libn.
Staff: Prof 1. **Subjects:** Medicine, nursing, hospital administration. **Holdings:** 1500 books; 425 bound periodical volumes; 300 pamphlets. **Subscriptions:** 122 journals and other serials. **Services:** Interlibrary loans; copying; library open to professionals, students, and paraprofessionals in health care fields. **Networks/Consortia:** Member of Knoxville Area Health Sciences Library Consortium.

★11975★

ST. MARY'S MEDICAL CENTER, INC. - SCHOOL OF NURSING LIBRARY (Med)
Celeste Hall, Emerald Ave.   Phone: (615) 971-7839
Knoxville, TN 37917   Beth Barret, Libn.
Founded: 1944. **Staff:** Prof 1; Other 2. **Subjects:** Medicine, nursing. **Holdings:** 3018 volumes; 16 drawers of clippings and pamphlets. **Subscriptions:** 75 journals and other serials. **Services:** Interlibrary loans; copying; library open to public for reference use only. **Networks/Consortia:** Member of Knoxville Area Health Sciences Library Consortium.

★11976★

ST. MARY'S SCHOOL FOR THE DEAF - INFORMATION CENTER (Educ)
2253 Main St.   Phone: (716) 834-7200
Buffalo, NY 14214   Collette Sangster, Dir.
Staff: Prof 2; Other 1. **Subjects:** Deafness, audiology, speech, special education. **Holdings:** 10,096 books; 612 bound periodical volumes; 436 microfiche. **Subscriptions:** 57 journals and other serials. **Services:** Interlibrary loans; copying; center open to public with restrictions. **Automated Operations:** Computerized cataloging. **Staff:** Jean Odien, Libn.

★11977★

ST. MARY'S SEMINARY - CARDINAL BERAN LIBRARY (Rel-Theol)
9845 Memorial Dr.   Phone: (713) 681-5544
Houston, TX 77024   Constance Walker, Libn.
Staff: Prof 1; Other 2. **Subjects:** Philosophy, theology, canon law, church history. **Holdings:** 38,000 books; 3800 bound periodical volumes; 1500 cassette tapes; 1390 microforms; 430 phonograph records. **Subscriptions:** 305 journals and other serials.

★11978★

ST. MARY'S SEMINARY - ST. MARY'S OF THE BARRENS LIBRARY (Rel-Theol)
       Phone: (314) 547-6533
Perryville, MO 63775   Sr. De Paul Schwinn, S.S.N.D., Hd.
Staff: Prof 2; Other 3. **Subjects:** Philosophy, history, religion, literature. **Special Collections:** Rare books (535 volumes); American first editions (836); other special collections (1304 volumes). **Holdings:** 64,248 books; 6565 bound periodical volumes; 24 drawers of St. Mary's Seminary archives; 40 feet of Mississippi Valley historical data; 212 record books of several institutions; 24 VF drawers. **Subscriptions:** 225 journals and other serials; 10 newspapers. **Services:** Interlibrary loans; copying; library open to public by arrangement. **Staff:** Judith Kirn, Asst.Libn.

★11979★

ST. MARY'S UNIVERSITY - LAW LIBRARY (Law)†
One Camino Santa Maria   Phone: (512) 436-3435
San Antonio, TX 78284   Robert L. Summers, Jr., Dir.
Founded: 1937. **Staff:** Prof 6; Other 30. **Subjects:** Law. **Special Collections:** Early Spanish law; land titles (Spanish and American). **Holdings:** 78,865 books; 11,079 bound periodical volumes. **Subscriptions:** 1488 journals and other serials. **Services:** Interlibrary loans; copying (limited); library open to public for reference use only. **Automated Operations:**

Computerized cataloging. **Computerized Information Services:** Westlaw, LEXIS. **Staff:** Douglas Ferrier, Hd., Tech.Serv.; Duane Henricks, Govt.Doc.Libn.; Lee Unterborn, Acq./Ref.Libn.; Caroline Byrd, Hd., Pub.Serv.; James Bass, Cat.

★11980★
ST. MARY'S UNIVERSITY - PATRICK POWER LIBRARY (Rel-Theol; Bus-Fin)
Phone: (902) 429-9780
Halifax, NS, Canada B3H 3C3   Ronald A. Lewis, Univ.Libn.
Staff: Prof 7; Other 36. **Subjects:** Religious studies, Canadiana, business administration. **Special Collections:** Eric Gill Collection (30 volumes); Santamariana Collection (575 volumes). **Holdings:** 250,000 volumes; ERIC microfiche, 1969 to present; 200 titles of Canadian labor newspapers on microfilm; corporate reports for 1331 companies. **Subscriptions:** 1802 journals and other serials; 33 newspapers. **Services:** Interlibrary loans; copying; library open to public with restrictions. **Automated Operations:** Computerized cataloging, acquisitions and serials. **Computerized Information Services:** CAN/OLE, DIALOG, SDC, QL Systems, New York Times Information Service, Info Globe, International Development Research Centre, UTLAS. Performs searches on cost recovery basis with surcharge for outside users. Contact Person: Douglas Vaisey. **Networks/Consortia:** Member of Nova Scotia On-Line Consortium. **Publications:** The Perfect Term Paper: a do-it-yourself guide; Guide to the Patrick Power Library, irregular; statistics collected by the Federal Government of Canada, irregular; The Census of Canada, irregular; statistics published by provincial governments in Canada, irregular; pamphlets on corporate reports and group study rooms - all free upon request. **Staff:** Christine MacGillivray, Adm.Asst.; Rashid Tayyeb, Hd., Tech.Serv.; Margot Schenk, Hd., Pub.Serv.; Paul Rooney, Hd., AV Serv.; Jane Archibald, Coll.Dev./User Educ.

★11981★
ST. MATTHEW'S EPISCOPAL CATHEDRAL - LIBRARY
5100 Ross Ave.
Dallas, TX 75206
Defunct

★11982★
ST. MATTHEW'S & ST. TIMOTHY'S NEIGHBORHOOD CENTER, INC. - TUTORIAL PROGRAM LIBRARY (Educ)
26 W. 84th St.   Phone: (212) 362-6750
New York, NY 10024   Delfa Castillo, Lib.Dir.
Staff: Prof 1. **Subjects:** Remedial reading. **Special Collections:** Remedial reading materials and professional literature; children's literature (600 volumes). **Holdings:** 11,000 books. **Services:** Library open to community residents.

★11983★
ST. MEINRAD ARCHABBEY - COLLEGE & SCHOOL OF THEOLOGY - LIBRARY (Rel-Theol)
Phone: (812) 357-6401
St. Meinrad, IN 47577   Rev. Simeon Daly, O.S.B., Libn.
Staff: Prof 2; Other 7. **Subjects:** Religion, Catholic theology. **Holdings:** 110,000 books; 15,000 bound periodical volumes. **Subscriptions:** 567 journals and other serials. **Services:** Interlibrary loans; copying; library open to public for reference use only. **Automated Operations:** Computerized cataloging and ILL. **Computerized Information Services:** BRS, NEXIS. Performs searches on cost recovery basis. **Networks/Consortia:** Member of INCOLSA; Four Rivers Area Library Services Authority. **Staff:** Rev. Justin DuVall, O.S.B., Asst.Libn.

★11984★
ST. MICHAEL MEDICAL CENTER - AQUINAS MEDICAL LIBRARY (Med)
268 Dr. Martin Luther King Jr. Blvd.   Phone: (201) 877-5471
Newark, NJ 07102   Betty L. Garrison, Dir., Med.Lib.
Staff: Prof 1; Other 1. **Subjects:** Medicine, pediatrics, obstetrics and gynecology, surgery, infectious diseases. **Special Collections:** Podiatry. **Holdings:** 1500 books; 4500 bound periodical volumes; 1 VF drawer of clippings; 2 VF drawers of pamphlets. **Subscriptions:** 85 journals and other serials. **Services:** Interlibrary loans; library not open to public. **Computerized Information Services:** NLM. **Networks/Consortia:** Member of Cosmopolitan Biomedical Library Consortium; Health Science Libraries of New Jersey.

ST. MICHAEL'S COLLEGE
See: University of Toronto

★11985★
ST. MICHAEL'S HOSPITAL - HEALTH SCIENCE LIBRARY (Med)
30 Bond St.   Phone: (416) 360-4941
Toronto, ON, Canada M5B 1W8   Anita Wong, Dir.
Founded: 1956. **Staff:** Prof 1; Other 3. **Subjects:** Medicine and surgery. **Holdings:** 7000 books; 9000 bound periodical volumes; reprints of staff publications. **Subscriptions:** 400 journals and other serials. **Services:** Interlibrary loans; library not open to public. **Computerized Information Services:** MEDLARS, DIALOG. **Publications:** Monthly acquisitions list; library journal holdings by title and by subject, annual.

★11986★
ST. MICHAEL'S HOSPITAL - HEALTH SCIENCES LIBRARY (Med)
900 Illinois Ave.   Phone: (715) 344-4400
Stevens Point, WI 54481   Barbara DeWeerd, Libn.
Founded: 1967. **Staff:** Prof 1; Other 1. **Subjects:** Medicine, nursing. **Holdings:** 900 books. **Subscriptions:** 95 journals and other serials. **Services:** Interlibrary loans; copying; library open to public for reference use only. **Computerized Information Services:** MEDLINE. **Networks/Consortia:** Member of Greater Midwest Regional Medical Library Network (Region 3); Northern Wisconsin Health Science Libraries Cooperative.

★11987★
ST. MICHAEL'S HOSPITAL - REGNER HEALTH SCIENCES LIBRARY (Med)†
2400 W. Villard Ave.   Phone: (414) 263-8477
Milwaukee, WI 53209   Joan Yanicke, Dir., Lib.Serv.
Staff: Prof 1; Other 1. **Subjects:** Medicine, nursing and allied sciences. **Holdings:** 1258 books; 2323 bound periodical volumes. **Subscriptions:** 167 journals and other serials. **Services:** Interlibrary loans; library not open to public. **Automated Operations:** Computerized cataloging. **Computerized Information Services:** DIALOG, NLM. **Networks/Consortia:** Member of Southeastern Wisconsin Health Sciences Library Consortium (SWHSLC).

★11988★
ST. NICHOLAS HOSPITAL - HEALTH SCIENCES LIBRARY (Med)†
1601 N. Taylor Dr.   Phone: (414) 459-4713
Sheboygan, WI 53081   Kathleen Blaser, Libn.
Staff: Prof 1. **Subjects:** Medicine, nursing. **Holdings:** 550 books. **Subscriptions:** 125 journals and other serials. **Services:** Interlibrary loans; copying; literature searches; library open to persons in health fields. **Networks/Consortia:** Member of Fox River Valley Area Library Consortium; Greater Midwest Regional Medical Library Network (Region 3).

★11989★
ST. NORBERT ABBEY - AUGUSTINE LIBRARY (Rel-Theol)
1016 N. Broadway   Phone: (414) 336-1321
De Pere, WI 54115   Rev. Aaron Walschinski, Libn.
Staff: Prof 1. **Subjects:** Theology, philosophy. **Special Collections:** Abbey Archives (1200 rare books); Premonstratensian Order history (1300 books); manuscripts and letters (90,000 items). **Holdings:** 12,000 books; 350 bound periodical volumes. **Subscriptions:** 40 journals and other serials. **Services:** Interlibrary loans; copying; library open to public by appointment.

ST. OLAF COLLEGE - NORWEGIAN-AMERICAN HISTORICAL ASSOCIATION
See: Norwegian-American Historical Association

★11990★
ST. OLAF LUTHERAN CHURCH - CARLSEN MEMORIAL LIBRARY (Rel-Theol)
29th & Emerson Ave., N.   Phone: (612) 529-7726
Minneapolis, MN 55411   Ruth Sivanich, Libn.
Founded: 1962. **Staff:** 2. **Subjects:** Religion and related topics. **Special Collections:** Books in Norwegian. **Holdings:** 1457 books. **Services:** Library not open to public.

★11991★
ST. PATRICK HOSPITAL - LIBRARY (Med)
500 W. Broadway
Box 4587   Phone: (406) 543-7271
Missoula, MT 59806   Jody Anderson, Libn.
Staff: Prof 2. **Subjects:** Nursing, medicine, hospital administration. **Holdings:** 1500 books; 20 VF drawers of pamphlets. **Subscriptions:** 150 journals and other serials. **Services:** Interlibrary loans; copying; library open to public for reference use only. **Networks/Consortia:** Member of Pacific Northwest Regional Health Sciences Library Service (PNRHSLS).

★11992★
ST. PATRICK'S SEMINARY - MC KEON MEMORIAL LIBRARY (Rel-Theol)
320 Middlefield Rd.   Phone: (415) 322-2224
Menlo Park, CA 94025   John F. Mattingly, Dir.
Founded: 1898. **Staff:** Prof 2. **Subjects:** Theology, philosophy, scripture, patrology. **Special Collections:** Bibliotheca Sancti Francisci Archdioceseos. **Holdings:** 58,000 books; 3500 bound periodical volumes; 100 tapes. **Subscriptions:** 250 journals and other serials; 11 newspapers. **Services:** Interlibrary loans; copying; library open to public for reference use only. **Staff:** Pamela Nurse, Asst.Libn.

★11993★
ST. PAUL CITY COUNCIL - RESEARCH LIBRARY (Plan)
502 City Hall
15 W. Kellogg Blvd.   Phone: (612) 298-4163
St. Paul, MN 55102   Theresa M. Jungwirth, Ck.
Founded: 1973. **Subjects:** St. Paul, urban affairs. **Special Collections:** St. Paul city documents. **Holdings:** 1300 books; 500 bound periodical volumes; 29 VF drawers; 8 drawers of microfilm. **Subscriptions:** 153 journals and other serials. **Services:** Interlibrary loans; copying; library open to public with restrictions. **Special Indexes:** Document index (book).

★11994★
ST. PAUL DISPATCH-PIONEER PRESS - LIBRARY (Publ)
55 E. Fourth St.   Phone: (612) 222-5011
St. Paul, MN 55101   Judith Katzung, Hd.Libn.
Founded: 1906. **Staff:** Prof 1; Other 4. **Subjects:** Newspaper reference topics. **Holdings:** 300 books; 1 million clippings; 500,000 pictures. **Services:** Library open to public with special permission only.

★11995★
ST. PAUL FIRE & MARINE INSURANCE COMPANY - LIBRARY (Bus-Fin)
385 Washington St.   Phone: (612) 221-8226
St. Paul, MN 55102   Eleanor Hamilton, Lib.Supv.
Founded: 1953. **Staff:** Prof 1; Other 3. **Subjects:** Insurance, management, data processing. **Special Collections:** Company archives; history of St. Paul and Minnesota; Alexander Wilkin Collection (first president of the company, 1853). **Holdings:** 12,000 volumes. **Subscriptions:** 250 journals and other serials. **Services:** Interlibrary loans; copying; library open to public.

★11996★
ST. PAUL FIRE & MARINE INSURANCE COMPANY - RISK MANAGEMENT SERVICES DIVISION INFORMATION CENTER (Sci-Tech)
385 Washington St.   Phone: (612) 221-7470
St. Paul, MN 55102   Sharon Carter, Info.Spec.
Founded: 1975. **Staff:** Prof 1; Other 1. **Subjects:** Safety and loss prevention, occupational health hazards, product liability, fire prevention, hospital and medical liability. **Holdings:** 1600 titles; 300 linear feet of pamphlets, clippings and standards. **Subscriptions:** 300 journals and other serials. **Services:** Interlibrary loans; copying; center open to public with restrictions. **Computerized Information Services:** DIALOG, SDC, NLM.

★11997★
ST. PAUL HOSPITAL - C.B. SACHER LIBRARY (Med)
5909 Harry Hines Blvd.   Phone: (214) 689-2390
Dallas, TX 75235   Barbara J. Miller, Dir.
Founded: 1900. **Staff:** Prof 2. **Subjects:** Nursing, medicine and allied health sciences. **Holdings:** 3200 books; 1100 bound periodical volumes; 750 audio cassettes. **Subscriptions:** 150 journals and other serials. **Services:** Interlibrary loans; copying; library open to public with restrictions. **Computerized Information Services:** MEDLINE. **Networks/Consortia:** Member of Dallas-Tarrant County Consortium of Health Science Libraries; Metroplex Council of Health Science Librarians. **Staff:** Michael Zimmerman, Libn.Asst.

★11998★
ST. PAUL LUTHERAN CHURCH AND SCHOOL - PARISH LIBRARY (Rel-Theol)*
5201 Galitz   Phone: (312) 673-5030
Skokie, IL 60077   Paula Raabe, Libn.
Founded: 1960. **Staff:** 8. **Subjects:** Religion. **Holdings:** 9000 books; 40 bound periodical volumes; 9 VF drawers of pamphlets; AV materials; pictures, posters, phonograph records, filmstrips. **Subscriptions:** 25 journals and other serials. **Services:** Interlibrary loans; copying; library open to public on request. **Automated Operations:** Computerized cataloging. **Publications:** Book lists, irregular - to parishioners.

★11999★
ST. PAUL PUBLIC LIBRARY - ART AND MUSIC (Art; Mus; Aud-Vis)
90 W. Fourth St.   Phone: (612) 292-6186
St. Paul, MN 55102   Delores Sundbye, Supv.
Staff: Prof 3; Other 3. **Subjects:** Fine and applied arts, music books and scores. **Holdings:** 32,500 books; 2601 bound periodical volumes; 24,000 mounted pictures; 152,000 unmounted pictures; 750 exhibit catalogs; 492 framed pictures; 117 sculptures; 1941 art slides; 10,115 phonograph records; 250 cassettes (music, language). **Subscriptions:** 150 journals and other serials. **Services:** Interlibrary loans; copying; library open to public. **Networks/Consortia:** Member of Metropolitan Library Service Agency (MELSA); Cooperating Libraries in Consortium (CLIC). **Staff:** Carole King, Prof.Asst.

★12000★
ST. PAUL PUBLIC LIBRARY - BUSINESS & SCIENCE ROOM (Bus-Fin; Sci-Tech)
90 W. Fourth St.   Phone: (612) 292-6176
St. Paul, MN 55102   Virginia B. Stavn, Supv.
Staff: Prof 3; Other 4. **Subjects:** Economics, business, labor, finance, science, technology, medicine (popular). **Holdings:** 65,000 books; 7300 bound periodical volumes; 65 VF drawers. **Subscriptions:** 485 journals and other serials. **Services:** Interlibrary loans; copying; library open to public. **Networks/Consortia:** Member of Metropolitan Library Service Agency (MELSA); Cooperating Libraries in Consortium (CLIC). **Special Indexes:** Indexes for handicraft materials and consumer information (card). **Formerly:** Its Science and Industry Room. **Staff:** Richard Hemming, Prof.Asst.; Patricia Gerlach, Libn.

★12001★
ST. PAUL PUBLIC LIBRARY - FILM & VIDEO CENTER (Aud-Vis)
90 W. Fourth St.   Phone: (612) 292-6336
St. Paul, MN 55102   Annette Salo, Supv.
Staff: Prof 1; Other 3. **Subjects:** AV production, film and video software, cable television. **Holdings:** 50 books; 50 catalogs of video software; 486 videotapes and cassettes; 600 16mm films. **Subscriptions:** 15 journals and other serials. **Services:** Interlibrary loans for print material; center open to public with restrictions. **Networks/Consortia:** Member of Metropolitan Library Service Agency (MELSA); MINITEX. **Publications:** Occasional booklists, bibliographies, tapelists, glossaries, instruction guides.

★12002★
ST. PAUL PUBLIC LIBRARY - GOVERNMENT PUBLICATIONS OFFICE (Info Sci)
90 W. 4th St.   Phone: (612) 292-6178
St. Paul, MN 55102   Rosamond T. Jacob, Libn.
Staff: Prof 1; Other 1. **Subjects:** Federal and state depository publications. **Holdings:** 250,000 documents. **Services:** Interlibrary loans; copying; office open to public. **Networks/Consortia:** Member of Metropolitan Library Service Agency (MELSA); Cooperating Libraries in Consortium (CLIC). **Publications:** Documents/Classified, monthly.

★12003★
ST. PAUL PUBLIC LIBRARY - HIGHLAND PARK BRANCH - PERRIE JONES MEMORIAL ROOM (Rare Book)
1974 Ford Pkwy.   Phone: (612) 292-6622
St. Paul, MN 55116   Elizabeth McMonigal, Br.Libn.
Special Collections: Sumerian Clay Tablets (41); Horn Collection: classics published in the 16th, 17th and 18th centuries (154); Cruikshank Collection: books illustrated and/or written by George Cruikshank and his brother (26); Fitzgerald Collection: books by or about F. Scott Fitzgerald and his times (38); Johnston Collection: rare books from the 16th century to present (1430); Local Collection: miscellaneous books on Twin Cities and Minnesota (43); Perrie Jones Collection: books and other material by or related to the late Perrie Jones (50). **Holdings:** 1800 books; letters; manuscripts; photographs; autographs. **Services:** Copying; library open to public for reference use only. **Staff:** Rosalie Guthrie, Asst.Br.Libn.

★12004★
ST. PAUL PUBLIC LIBRARY - REFERENCE ROOM (Soc Sci)
90 W. Fourth St.   Phone: (612) 224-3383
St. Paul, MN 55102   Judith W. Devine, Supv.
Staff: Prof 5; Other 6. **Subjects:** Literature, philosophy, religion, history, biography, sports, geography, travel, education, politics, government. **Special Collections:** St. Paul Collection; selected Minnesota documents; telephone directories (25,000 U.S. cities). **Holdings:** 20,000 volumes. **Subscriptions:** 231 journals; 257 serials; 9 newspapers. **Services:** Interlibrary loans; room open to public. **Computerized Information Services:** DIALOG, SDC, New York Times Information Service. **Networks/Consortia:** Member of

Metropolitan Library Service Agency (MELSA). **Special Indexes:** St. Paul Pioneer Press and St. Paul Dispatch Index, 1967 to present; local organization file. **Staff:** Patricia Ethier, Asst. to Supv.

★12005★
ST. PAUL PUBLIC LIBRARY - SOCIAL SCIENCES & LITERATURE (Hum)
90 W. Fourth St.   Phone: (612) 292-6206
St. Paul, MN 55102   Ortha D. Robbins, Supv.
Staff: Prof 5; Other 5. **Subjects:** Literature, history and travel, philosophy and religion, biography, political and social sciences, sports and games. **Special Collections:** Large print books (2000); costume (300 books); foreign languages (2500 titles in 12 languages); spoken word cassettes (300). **Holdings:** 220,000 volumes. **Services:** Interlibrary loans; copying; library open to public. **Networks/Consortia:** Member of Metropolitan Library Service Agency (MELSA); Cooperating Libraries in Consortium (CLIC). **Special Indexes:** Card indexes to biography and literary criticism file; short story file; drama file; ballet index; dance index; hymn index. **Formerly:** Its Circulation Room. **Staff:** Marti Lybeck, Prof.Asst.

★12006★
ST. PAUL PUBLIC SCHOOLS INDEPENDENT SCHOOL DISTRICT 625 - DISTRICT PROFESSIONAL LIBRARY (Educ)
360 Colborne St.   Phone: (612) 293-7601
St. Paul, MN 55102   Walter M. Ostrem, Libn.
Staff: Prof 1. **Subjects:** Education, psychology, child development. **Special Collections:** Archives of St. Paul School District (1000 items). **Holdings:** 7000 books; 1700 periodicals; 400 reels of microfilm of periodicals; 500 textbooks; 900 documents; 3000 clippings. **Subscriptions:** 184 journals and other serials. **Services:** Interlibrary loans; copying; library open to public. **Networks/Consortia:** Member of MINITEX; Cooperating Libraries in Consortium (CLIC).

★12007★
ST. PAUL RAMSEY MEDICAL CENTER - MEDICAL LIBRARY (Med)
640 Jackson St.   Phone: (612) 221-3607
St. Paul, MN 55101   Mary Dwyer, Hd.Libn.
Founded: 1961. **Staff:** Prof 2; Other 2. **Subjects:** Medicine and nursing. **Holdings:** 4000 books; 6000 bound periodical volumes. **Subscriptions:** 390 journals and other serials. **Services:** Interlibrary loans; copying (hospital use only); library open to professionals only. **Computerized Information Services:** MEDLARS. **Networks/Consortia:** Member of Twin Cities Biomedical Consortium (TCBC). **Staff:** Audrey Woodke, Asst.Libn.

★12008★
ST. PAUL SCHOOL OF THEOLOGY - DANA DAWSON LIBRARY (Rel-Theol)
5123 Truman Rd.   Phone: (816) 483-9600
Kansas City, MO 64127   Dr. William S. Sparks, Libn.
Founded: 1958. **Staff:** Prof 2; Other 4. **Subjects:** Theology. **Holdings:** 63,000 volumes. **Subscriptions:** 350 journals and other serials. **Services:** Interlibrary loans; copying; library open to public with restrictions.

★12009★
ST. PAUL SEMINARY - JOHN IRELAND MEMORIAL LIBRARY (Rel-Theol)
2260 Summit Ave.   Phone: (612) 690-4355
St. Paul, MN 55105   Rev. Leo J. Tibesar, Dir.
Founded: 1894. **Staff:** Prof 4; Other 3. **Subjects:** Biblical studies, Catholic theology, patrology, scholastic philosophy, U.S. Catholic Church history, canon law. **Special Collections:** Papyrology on microfiche; John Ireland papers; Patrologia Graeca; Patrologia Latina; Sources Chretiennes. **Holdings:** 57,000 books; 10,000 bound periodical volumes. **Subscriptions:** 350 journals and other serials. **Services:** Interlibrary loans; copying; library open to public upon request and registration. **Special Catalogs:** Catalog of consortium serials collection (printed); Union Catalog of Consortium Monographic Collection (COM). **Networks/Consortia:** Member of Minnesota Theological Libraries Association (MTLA). **Staff:** Margaret Mary Bannigan, Coord. of Serv.; Mary Knopp, Cat.

★12010★
ST. PAUL TECHNICAL VOCATIONAL LIBRARY (Sci-Tech)
235 Marshall Ave.   Phone: (612) 221-1410
St. Paul, MN 55102   Fred Berndt, Libn.
Founded: 1967. **Staff:** Prof 1; Other 1. **Subjects:** Trades and technical occupations, business subjects. **Holdings:** 7000 books. **Subscriptions:** 185 journals and other serials. **Services:** Copying; library open to public for reference use only.

ST. PAUL UNIVERSITY
See: Universite St-Paul

★12011★
ST. PAUL'S CHURCH - ARCHIVES (Rel-Theol)
605 Reynolds St.   Phone: (404) 724-2485
Augusta, GA 30902
Subjects: St. Paul's Church history, 1755 to present. **Holdings:** 4000 church records, meetings minutes, correspondence of church officers, church registers, and marriage, baptism, and communicant records. **Services:** Archives open to public.

ST. PAUL'S COLLEGE - LIBRARY
See: University of Manitoba

★12012★
ST. PAUL'S COLLEGE - LIBRARY (Rel-Theol)
3015 Fourth St., N.E.   Phone: (202) 832-6262
Washington, DC 20017   Lawrence E. Boadt, C.S.P., Libn.
Founded: 1889. **Staff:** Prof 1; Other 3. **Subjects:** Philosophy, scripture, church history, liturgy, theology, American history, canon law. **Special Collections:** Paulist Fathers Archival Materials (4 filing cases). **Holdings:** 45,000 books; 5000 bound periodical volumes; 2500 pamphlets; 1000 recordings; 100 reels of microfilm. **Subscriptions:** 137 journals and other serials. **Services:** Copying; library open to public with permission of librarian. **Networks/Consortia:** Member of Washington Theological Consortium.

★12013★
ST. PAUL'S EPISCOPAL CHURCH - LIBRARY (Rel-Theol)
815 E. Grace St.   Phone: (804) 643-3589
Richmond, VA 23219   Leigh S. Hulcher, Lib.Cons.
Staff: 1. **Subjects:** Bible, theology, Christian art, worship, meditation, Christian education, church history. **Holdings:** 3500 books; records and tapes. **Subscriptions:** 12 journals and other serials. **Services:** Copying; library open to public.

★12014★
ST. PETER HOSPITAL - PROFESSIONAL LIBRARY (Med)
413 N. Lilly Rd.   Phone: (206) 456-7222
Olympia, WA 98506   Edean Berglund, Dir., Lib.Serv.
Staff: Prof 1. **Subjects:** Health care. **Holdings:** Figures not available. **Subscriptions:** 300 journals and other serials. **Services:** Interlibrary loans; copying; library open to public with restrictions. **Computerized Information Services:** NLM.

★12015★
ST. PETER REGIONAL TREATMENT CENTER - STAFF LIBRARY (Med)
100 Freeman Dr.   Phone: (507) 931-3000
St. Peter, MN 56082   Richard Whitmore, Staff Libn.
Founded: 1869. **Staff:** Prof 1; Other 4. **Subjects:** Medicine, nursing, drug addiction, mental retardation and allied health sciences. **Holdings:** 1300 books; 600 bound periodical volumes; 3 VF drawers; 350 audiotapes; 200 microfiche; clippings. **Subscriptions:** 36 journals and other serials; 10 newspapers. **Services:** Interlibrary loans; copying; library open to public but must register first. **Computerized Information Services:** Access to DIALOG.

★12016★
ST. PETER'S ABBEY & COLLEGE - LIBRARY (Rel-Theol)
Box 10   Phone: (306) 682-5431
Muenster, SK, Canada S0K 2Y0   Andrew M. Britz, Libn.
Founded: 1892. **Staff:** Prof 1; Other 2. **Subjects:** Arts and science, Roman Catholic theology, monasticism. **Holdings:** 35,000 volumes. **Subscriptions:** 100 journals, other serials and newspapers. **Services:** Interlibrary loans; copying; library open to public.

★12017★
ST. PETER'S HOSPITAL - MEDICAL STAFF LIBRARY (Med)
315 S. Manning Blvd.   Phone: (518) 454-1490
Albany, NY 12208   Lynn Siegelman, Libn.
Founded: 1950. **Staff:** Prof 1; Other 1. **Subjects:** Medicine, surgery, nursing. **Holdings:** 1502 books; 4840 bound periodical volumes; 500 audio cassettes. **Subscriptions:** 180 journals and other serials. **Services:** Interlibrary loans; copying; library open to public for reference use only. **Automated Operations:** Computerized serials. **Computerized Information Services:** BRS, NLM. Performs searches on fee basis. **Networks/Consortia:** Member of Capital District Library Council for Reference & Research Resources (CDLC).

★12018★
ST. PETER'S HOSPITAL - PROFESSIONAL LIBRARY (Med)
88 Maplewood Ave.
Hamilton, ON, Canada L8M 1W9   Joan Osburn, Libn.
Founded: 1971. **Staff:** 1. **Subjects:** Geriatrics, nursing. **Holdings:** 1100

books. **Subscriptions:** 33 journals and other serials. **Services:** Interlibrary loans; library not open to public.

★12019★
ST. PETER'S MEDICAL CENTER - LIBRARY (Med)†
254 Easton Ave.   Phone: (201) 745-8545
New Brunswick, NJ 08903   Elizabeth McMullen, Mgr., Lib.Serv.
Founded: 1907. **Staff:** Prof 3; Other 7. **Subjects:** Medicine, nursing, administration. **Holdings:** 10,000 books; 20,000 bound periodical volumes; 3600 AV items. **Subscriptions:** 550 journals and other serials. **Services:** Interlibrary loans; copying; library open to public for reference use only. **Computerized Information Services:** MEDLINE, DIALOG. **Networks/ Consortia:** Member of Medical Resources Consortium of Central New Jersey (MEDCORE). **Publications:** Up-Date, monthly. **Staff:** JoAnn Karcz, AV Coord.; Kerry O'Hara, Ser. & Ref.Libn.Sue Stewart Suretsky, Asst.Libn.

★12020★
ST. PETER'S SEMINARY - LIBRARY (Rel-Theol)
1040 Waterloo St., N.   Phone: (519) 432-1824
London, ON, Canada N6A 3Y1   Lois Cote, Libn.
Founded: 1926. **Staff:** Prof 1; Other 2. **Subjects:** Theology, philosophy. **Holdings:** 37,000 books and bound periodical volumes. **Subscriptions:** 300 journals and other serials. **Services:** Interlibrary loans; copying; library open to public for reference use only.

★12021★
ST. PETERSBURG HISTORICAL SOCIETY - LIBRARY AND ARCHIVES (Hist)
335 Second Ave., N.E.   Phone: (813) 894-1052
St. Petersburg, FL 33701   John Warren, Pres.
Staff: Prof 2. **Subjects:** History - Florida, Civil War. **Special Collections:** Newman Collection (autographs and holographs of American historical figures). **Holdings:** 600 books; manuscripts; documents; records. **Services:** Library open to public. **Staff:** Dorothy K. White, Dir.

★12022★
ST. PETERSBURG TIMES AND EVENING INDEPENDENT - LIBRARY (Publ)
490 First Ave., S.
Box 1121   Phone: (813) 893-8111
St. Petersburg, FL 33731   James S. Scofield, Chf.Libn.
Founded: 1923. **Staff:** 24. **Subjects:** Newspaper reference topics. **Holdings:** 5000 books; 60 VF drawers of reports and pamphlets; newspaper clippings; news and historical photographs; original maps and artwork; newspapers on microfilm. **Subscriptions:** 90 journals and other serials. **Services:** Library not open to public.

★12023★
ST. REGIS CORPORATION - TECHNICAL CENTER LIBRARY (Sci-Tech)
W. Nyack Rd.   Phone: (914) 578-7102
West Nyack, NY 10994   Mary Ruth Bateman, Mgr., Tech.Info.
Staff: Prof 2; Other 1. **Subjects:** Pulp and paper, wood and wood chemistry, paper industry and business. **Holdings:** 2000 books and bound periodical volumes; 75 VF drawers. **Subscriptions:** 287 journals and other serials; 5 newspapers. **Services:** Interlibrary loans; copying; library open to public by appointment. **Computerized Information Services:** DIALOG, SDC, NLM; internal database. **Publications:** Guide to current technical literature, weekly. **Staff:** Shirley A. Rigney, Tech.Info.Libn.

★12024★
ST. RITA'S MEDICAL CENTER - MEDICAL LIBRARY (Med)
730 W. Market St.   Phone: (419) 227-3361
Lima, OH 45801   Sharon Bilopavlovich, Libn.
Staff: 1. **Holdings:** 1030 volumes; 15 pamphlets. **Subscriptions:** 43 journals and other serials. **Services:** Library open to paramedical personnel, medical staff and physicians. **Networks/Consortia:** Member of Greater Midwest Regional Medical Library Network (Region 3).

★12025★
ST. STEPHEN'S COLLEGE - LIBRARY (Rel-Theol)
University of Alberta
Edmonton, AB, Canada T6G 2J6   Phone: (403) 439-7311
                                     Carol Mundie, Act.Libn.
Founded: 1909. **Staff:** 1. **Subjects:** Religion and theology, rare books. **Special Collections:** Dalgleish Collection (old and original printings of Bibles and related literature). **Holdings:** 14,000 books; United Church and World Council of Churches regular publications. **Subscriptions:** 72 journals and other serials. **Services:** Interlibrary loans; library open to public with librarian's approval. **Remarks:** Maintained by the United Church of Canada, the college serves as a Centre for Continuing Education for the professional ministry.

★12026★
ST. THOMAS AQUINAS NEWMAN CENTER - LIBRARY (Rel-Theol)
1815 Las Lomas Rd., N.E.   Phone: (505) 247-1094
Albuquerque, NM 87106   Betty Innerst, Libn.
Founded: 1954. **Staff:** Prof 2; Other 1. **Subjects:** Religion, theology, philosophy and logic, literature, fine arts, Biblical references, biography. **Holdings:** 6000 volumes; 8 VF drawers of clippings and pamphlets; 30 AV items. **Subscriptions:** 28 journals and other serials. **Services:** Interlibrary loans; library open to students, faculty and parishioners. **Staff:** Mercedes Gugisberg, Libn; Evelyn Verstynen, Cons.Libn.; Fr. Anthony E. Romero, O.P., Dir.

★12027★
ST. THOMAS HOSPITAL - MEDICAL LIBRARY (Med)
444 N. Main St.   Phone: (216) 379-1111
Akron, OH 44310   Linda E. Bunyan, Med.Libn.
Founded: 1929. **Staff:** Prof 1; Other 3. **Subjects:** Medicine, nursing and related health sciences. **Holdings:** 1758 books; 3381 bound periodical volumes; 400 cassette tapes; 600 slides; 3 file cases of clippings and pamphlets; AV materials. **Subscriptions:** 130 journals and other serials. **Services:** Interlibrary loans; library not open to public. **Computerized Information Services:** NLM. **Networks/Consortia:** Member of Northeastern Ohio Universities College of Medicine (NEOUCOM).

★12028★
ST. THOMAS INSTITUTE - LIBRARY (Med)
1842 Madison Rd.   Phone: (513) 861-3460
Cincinnati, OH 45206   Sr. M. Virgil Ghering, O.P., Libn.
Founded: 1935. **Staff:** Prof 1. **Subjects:** Biology, experimental medicine, physics, biophysics, chemistry, biochemistry. **Special Collections:** Ph.D. theses; original laboratory notes; Classical Studies (1100 volumes). **Holdings:** 7620 books 20,000 bound periodical volumes; 45 boxes and 4 VF drawers of reprints; 9 volumes of press clippings; 14 boxes of dissertation summaries. **Subscriptions:** 173 journals and other serials. **Services:** Interlibrary loans; copying; library open to public with restrictions. **Networks/Consortia:** Member of Greater Cincinnati Library Consortium (GCLC); Cincinnati Area Health Sciences Library Association (CAHSLA).

★12029★
ST. THOMAS MORE CENTER - TIMOTHY PARKMAN MEMORIAL LIBRARY (Rel-Theol)
1615 E. Second St.   Phone: (602) 327-6662
Tucson, AZ 85719   Thomas DeMan, O.P., Dir.
Founded: 1952. **Staff:** Prof 2. **Subjects:** Catholic religion, theology, philosophy, psychology. **Holdings:** 7500 books; 250 bound periodical volumes. **Subscriptions:** 38 journals and other serials; 5 newspapers. **Services:** Interlibrary loans; library open to center staff, University of Arizona students, local religious and registered members of the center community. **Publications:** List of new acquisitions. **Also Known As:** Newman Catholic Student Center. **Staff:** Sister Dominic, Cat.Libn.

ST. THOMAS MORE COLLEGE
See: University of Saskatchewan

★12030★
ST. THOMAS MORE HOSPITAL - MEDICAL LIBRARY (Med)*
1019 Sheridan St.   Phone: (303) 275-3381
Canon City, CO 81212   Mrs. James G. Bruner, Libn.
Founded: 1965. **Staff:** 1. **Subjects:** Medicine. **Holdings:** 270 books; 30 bound periodical volumes; 3100 unbound journals. **Subjects:** 49 journals and other serials. **Services:** Library open to interested medical personnel for reference.

★12031★
ST. THOMAS PSYCHIATRIC HOSPITAL - LIBRARY SERVICES (Med)
Box 2004   Phone: (519) 631-8510
St. Thomas, ON, Canada N5P 3V9   Lisa McInnis, Libn.
Founded: 1973. **Staff:** Prof 1; Other 1. **Subjects:** Psychiatry, psychology, medicine, nursing, allied health professions. **Holdings:** 2000 books; 1500 bound periodical volumes; 250 videotapes. **Subscriptions:** 175 journals and other serials; 10 newspapers. **Services:** Interlibrary loans; copying; SDI; library open to public with restrictions. **Publications:** Current Awareness, monthly - for internal distribution only.

★12032★
ST. THOMAS SEMINARY - LIBRARY (Rel-Theol)
1300 S. Steele   Phone: (303) 722-4687
Denver, CO 80210   Marguerite W. Travis, Libn.
Founded: 1906. **Staff:** Prof 3; Other 1. **Subjects:** Theology, Bible, social

problems. **Special Collections:** Catholic theology; social problems; Minorities Collection, with emphasis on the Chicano. **Holdings:** 100,000 volumes. **Subscriptions:** 400 journals and other serials. **Services:** Interlibrary loans; copying; library open to those with an identification card. **Staff:** Mr. D. Chinn, Asst.Libn.

★12033★
ST. THOMAS SEMINARY LIBRARY - ALUMNI COLLECTION (Rel-Theol)
467 Bloomfield Ave.   Phone: (201) 242-5573
Bloomfield, CT 06002   Rev. Charles B. Johnson, Dir.
Founded: 1950. **Staff:** Prof 2; Other 1. **Subjects:** Catholic Americana (1790-1860); Catholic theology (incunabula-1853); Bibles (1522 to present), theology. **Holdings:** 13,700 books; 1500 bound periodical volumes; 520 pamphlets; 136 cassette tapes. **Subscriptions:** 100 journals and other serials; 12 newspapers. **Services:** Interlibrary loans; copying; collection open to public for reference use only. **Publications:** Reading Guide for Religious Studies; What Do You Think of the Priest, a bibliographic commentary on the priesthood. **Staff:** Lucille S. Halfpenny, Libn.

★12034★
ST. TIKHON'S SEMINARY - LIBRARY (Rel-Theol)
                                                          Phone: (717) 937-4411
South Canaan, PA 18459   Father John Udics, Libn.
Staff: Prof 1; Other 2. **Subjects:** Theology. **Holdings:** 20,000 books; 500 bound periodical volumes. **Subscriptions:** 40 journals and other serials; 10 newspapers. **Services:** Interlibrary loans; library open to public with restrictions.

★12035★
ST. VINCENT CHARITY HOSPITAL - LIBRARY (Med)
2351 E. 22nd St.   Phone: (216) 861-6200
Cleveland, OH 44115   Joanne Billiar, Hd.Libn.
Founded: 1937. **Staff:** Prof 2; Other 1. **Subjects:** Medicine, nursing, administration, and allied health sciences. **Special Collections:** Ophthalmology (historical). **Holdings:** 2500 titles; 6 audio cassette series. **Subscriptions:** 180 journals and other serials. **Services:** Interlibrary loans; copying; computer and manual bibliographic searches; library open to public for reference use only. **Computerized Information Services:** NLM. **Staff:** Suzanne R. Arnold, Asst.Libn.

★12036★
ST. VINCENT COLLEGE AND ARCHABBEY - LIBRARIES (Rel-Theol)
                                                          Phone: (412) 539-9761
Latrobe, PA 15650   Rev. Chrysostom V. Schlimm, O.S.B., Dir.
Founded: 1846. **Staff:** Prof 5; Other 4. **Subjects:** Liberal arts, Benedictina, patrology, Catholic Church history, medieval studies, Pennsylvaniana, ecclesiastical history. **Special Collections:** Incunabula, Austria-Hungary, England, France, Germany, Switzerland (87 volumes, 15 leaves). **Holdings:** 187,239 books; 31,626 bound periodical volumes; 85,870 microcards; 355 microfiche; 7946 reels of microfilm; 18 cassettes. **Subscriptions:** 756 journals and other serials; 27 newspapers. **Services:** Interlibrary loans; copying; library open to public. **Automated Operations:** Computerized cataloging. **Computerized Information Services:** OCLC. Contact Person: Shirley Dorazio. **Networks/Consortia:** Member of Pittsburgh Regional Library Center (PRLC). **Special Catalogs:** A Descriptive Catalogue of the Incunabula in the St. Vincent College and Archabbey Library (printed, clothbound). **Staff:** Rev. Fintan R. Shoniker, O.S.B., Spec.Coll.; Dr. John F. Macey, Hd.Cat.; John C. Benyo, Asst.Libn.; Rev. Lawrence H. Hill, O.S.B., Ref. & Per.Libn.

★12037★
ST. VINCENT COLLEGE AND ARCHABBEY - MUSIC LIBRARY
Latrobe, PA 15650
Subjects: Music. **Special Collections:** Wimmer Music Collection (1750 to 1900; 2500 items). **Holdings:** 1100 music scores. **Remarks:** Presently inactive.

★12038★
ST. VINCENT COLLEGE AND ARCHABBEY - PHYSICS DEPARTMENTAL LIBRARY
Latrobe, PA 15650
Subjects: Physics, astronomy, mathematics. **Holdings:** 1000 books; 200 bound periodical volumes; 600 unbound periodicals. **Remarks:** Presently inactive.

★12039★
ST. VINCENT DE PAUL REGIONAL SEMINARY - LIBRARY (Rel-Theol)
10701 Military Trail
Box 460   Phone: (305) 732-4424
Boynton Beach, FL 33425   Bro. Frank J. Mazsick, C.F.X., Lib.Dir.
Founded: 1962. **Staff:** Prof 2; Other 2. **Subjects:** Theology, philosophy, Latin

American studies, philosophical and theological classics in Spanish and English. **Holdings:** 48,367 books; 6814 bound periodical volumes; 592 tapes and cassettes; 3740 microforms. **Subscriptions:** 347 journals and other serials; 18 newspapers. **Services:** Interlibrary loans; library open to public for reference use only.

★12040★
ST. VINCENT HEALTH CENTER - HEALTH SCIENCE LIBRARY (Med)
232 W. 25th St.   Phone: (814) 459-4000
Erie, PA 16512   Joni M. Alex, Med.Libn.
Founded: 1894. **Staff:** Prof 1; Other 3. **Subjects:** Clinical medicine, nursing, dentistry. **Holdings:** 3500 books; 5000 bound periodical volumes; 8 filing drawers of pamphlets; 200 cassettes and slides. **Subscriptions:** 205 journals and other serials. **Services:** Interlibrary loans; copying; library open to public for reference use only. **Computerized Information Services:** MEDLINE. **Networks/Consortia:** Member of Greater Northeastern Regional Medical Library Program.

★12041★
ST. VINCENT HOSPITAL - JOHN J. DUMPHY MEMORIAL LIBRARY (Med)
25 Winthrop St.   Phone: (617) 798-6117
Worcester, MA 01604   Theresa B. Davitt, Libn.
Staff: Prof 1; Other 2. **Subjects:** Medicine and allied health sciences. **Holdings:** 950 books; 5500 bound periodical volumes. **Subscriptions:** 162 journals and other serials. **Services:** Interlibrary loans; copying; library open to public by appointment. **Computerized Information Services:** MEDLARS. Performs searches on cost recovery basis. **Networks/Consortia:** Member of Central Massachusetts Consortium of Health Related Libraries.

★12042★
ST. VINCENT HOSPITAL AND MEDICAL CENTER - HEALTH SCIENCES LIBRARY (Med)
9205 S.W. Barnes Rd.   Phone: (503) 299-2257
Portland, OR 97225   Edith H. Throckmorton, Dir.
Staff: Prof 1; Other 2. **Subjects:** Medicine, nursing, hospital administration. **Special Collections:** Patient education (400 books, pamphlets, AV items). **Holdings:** 3800 books; 6000 bound periodical volumes. **Subscriptions:** 425 journals and other serials. **Services:** Interlibrary loans; library not open to public. **Automated Operations:** Computerized cataloging. **Computerized Information Services:** MEDLINE. **Networks/Consortia:** Member of Oregon Health Information Network (OHIN); Washington County Cooperative Library Services (WCCLS); Sisters of Providence Library Consortium.

★12043★
ST. VINCENT HOSPITAL - MEDICAL LIBRARY (Med)
60 Cambridge St., N.   Phone: (613) 233-4041
Ottawa, ON, Canada K1R 7A5   Sr. Germaine Lafleur, Hd. of Dept.
Staff: Prof 2. **Subjects:** Gerontology, physiotherapy, occupational therapy, speech and hearing therapy, long term psychotherapy. **Holdings:** 3989 books; 69 bound periodical volumes; 11 VF drawers. **Subscriptions:** 151 journals and other serials. **Services:** Interlibrary loans; copying; library open to students and medical residents. **Automated Operations:** Computerized cataloging, acquisitions, serials, circulation and audiovisuals.

★12044★
ST. VINCENT HOSPITAL - MEDICAL LIBRARY (Med)
835 S. VanBuren St.
Box 1221   Phone: (414) 433-8171
Green Bay, WI 54305   Margaret Warpinski, Hd.Libn.
Founded: 1955. **Staff:** Prof 1; Other 3. **Subjects:** Medicine, allied health sciences. **Holdings:** 3100 books; 450 bound periodical volumes. **Subscriptions:** 95 journals and other serials. **Services:** Interlibrary loans; copying; library open to public with librarian's approval. **Computerized Information Services:** DIALOG, MEDLINE. **Networks/Consortia:** Member of North East Wisconsin Intertype Libraries (NEWIL); Fox River Valley Area Library Consortium.

★12045★
ST. VINCENT INFIRMARY - MEDICAL LIBRARY (Med)†
Markham & University   Phone: (501) 661-3991
Little Rock, AR 72201   Sr. Jean B. Roberts, S.C.N., Med.Libn.
Founded: 1900. **Staff:** Prof 1; Other 1. **Subjects:** Medicine, medical specialties. **Special Collections:** Hospital Archives (35 volumes). **Holdings:** 4935 books; 3500 bound periodical volumes. **Subscriptions:** 200 journals and other serials. **Services:** Interlibrary loans; copying; library open to students and interns of University of Arkansas Medical Center and open to public with restrictions. **Networks/Consortia:** Member of TALON.

★12046★
ST. VINCENT MEDICAL CENTER - HEALTH SCIENCE LIBRARY (Med)
2213 Cherry St.   Phone: (419) 259-4324
Toledo, OH 43608   Jack W. Shaffer, Dir.
Founded: 1970. Staff: Prof 3; Other 2. Subjects: Clinical medicine and
surgery, nursing, hospital administration. Holdings: 9524 books; 6390 bound
periodical volumes. Subscriptions: 533 journals and other serials. Services:
Interlibrary loans; copying; SDI; library open to public with special permission.
Computerized Information Services: MEDLARS, OCLC, BRS. Staff: Claudia
Grainger, Ref.Libn.; Susan Schafer, Cat.

★12047★
ST. VINCENT MEDICAL CENTER - HEALTH SCIENCES LIBRARY (Med)*
2131 W. Third St.   Phone: (213) 484-5530
Los Angeles, CA 90057   Doreen B. Keough, Libn.
Founded: 1938. Staff: Prof 1. Subjects: Medicine, nursing, nursing
education. Holdings: 1200 books; 400 bound periodical volumes.
Subscriptions: 200 journals and other serials. Services: Interlibrary loans;
copying; SDI; library open to public for reference use only.

★12048★
ST. VINCENT'S HOSPITAL - CUNNINGHAM WILSON LIBRARY (Med)
Box 915   Phone: (205) 320-7830
Birmingham, AL 35201   Joyce Sims, Libn.
Staff: Prof 1; Other 3. Subjects: Medicine, nursing, hospital administration.
Special Collections: Historical Nursing Collection. Holdings: 2537 books;
1316 bound periodical volumes; 335 vertical files; 20 videotapes; 240
audiotapes. Subscriptions: 170 journals and other serials. Services:
Interlibrary loans; copying; SDI; library open to public with restrictions.
Computerized Information Services: MEDLINE. Performs free searches for
physicians; on cost recovery basis to others. Networks/Consortia: Member
of Jefferson County Hospital Librarians' Association.

★12049★
ST. VINCENT'S HOSPITAL - GARCEAU LIBRARY (Med)
2001 W. 86th St.   Phone: (317) 871-2095
Indianapolis, IN 46260   Virginia Durkin, Mgr.,Lib.Serv.
Founded: 1927. Staff: Prof 2. Subjects: Medicine, paramedicine, nursing,
hospital administration. Special Collections: Hospital archives. Holdings:
6980 books and bound periodical volumes; 400 audiotapes; 4 VF drawers of
pamphlets; 200 AV software; microfiche. Subscriptions: 200 journals and
other serials. Services: Interlibrary loans; copying; SDI; library open with
approval of librarian. Automated Operations: Computerized cataloging.
Computerized Information Services: BRS, MEDLINE, OCLC. Networks/
Consortia: Member of Central Indiana Health Science Library Consortium;
Greater midwest Regional Medical Library Network (Region 3); INCOLSA.
Publications: Acquistions list, biannual; library handbook. Staff: Louise Hass,
Asst.Libn.

★12050★
ST. VINCENT'S HOSPITAL AND MEDICAL CENTER - MEDICAL LIBRARY
  (Med)
153 W. Eleventh St.   Phone: (212) 790-7811
New York, NY 10011   Agnes T. Frank, Dir.
Founded: 1934. Staff: Prof 2; Other 1. Subjects: Health sciences,
psychology. Holdings: 8805 books and bound periodical volumes.
Subscriptions: 281 journals and other serials. Services: Interlibrary loans;
library not open to public. Computerized Information Services: MEDLINE,
BRS. Performs searches on cost recovery basis. Networks/Consortia:
Member of Medical Library Center of New York (MLCNY). Staff: Rhona S.
Kelly, Assoc.Libn.

★12051★
ST. VINCENT'S HOSPITAL AND MEDICAL CENTER OF NEW YORK,
  WESTCHESTER BRANCH - MEDICAL LIBRARY (Med)
240 North St.   Phone: (914) 967-6500
Harrison, NY 10528   Ethel Eisenberg, Med.Libn.
Staff: Prof 1. Subjects: Psychiatry, psychology, alcoholism, drug abuse.
Holdings: 3000 books; 2000 bound periodical volumes; cassettes.
Subscriptions: 60 journals and other serials. Services: Interlibrary loans;
library not open to public. Networks/Consortia: Member of Greater
Northeastern Regional Medical Library Program.

★12052★
ST. VINCENT'S HOSPITAL - SCHOOL OF NURSING LIBRARY (Med)
27 Christopher St.   Phone: (212) 790-8486
New York, NY 10014   Marie C. Medici, Libn.
Founded: 1892. Staff: Prof 1. Subjects: Nursing and allied professional
sciences, social sciences, medicine, religion, humanities. Holdings: 4000

books; 225 bound periodical volumes; 8 VF drawers of pamphlets; 700 AV
items. Subscriptions: 95 journals and other serials. Services: Copying; library
open to faculty, students, hospital personnel.

★12053★
ST. VINCENT'S MEDICAL CENTER - DANIEL T. BANKS HEALTH SCIENCE
  LIBRARY (Med)
2800 Main St.   Phone: (203) 576-5336
Bridgeport, CT 06606   Janet Goerig, Dir., Lib.Serv.
Founded: 1903. Staff: Prof 1; Other 5. Subjects: Medicine, nursing, related
subjects. Holdings: 3808 books; 3776 bound periodical volumes; 24 VF
drawers of reprints and pamphlets; 5498 AV materials. Subscriptions: 311
journals and other serials. Services: Interlibrary loans; library not open to
public.

★12054★
ST. VLADIMIR INSTITUTE - UKRAINIAN LIBRARY (Area-Ethnic)†
620 Spadina Ave.   Phone: (416) 923-8266
Toronto, ON, Canada M5S 2H4   Vera Skop, Libn.
Founded: 1969. Staff: Prof 1; Other 1. Subjects: Ukrainian Canadiana;
Ukrainian folk and fine arts, history, politics, literature, language and music;
Ukrainian Orthodox Church. Special Collections: Photograph archives (2
boxes); Ukrainians in Canada 1979 Collection (clippings). Holdings: 15,000
books; 15 VF drawers of clippings and pamphlets; 50 AV tapes; 500
phonograph records; 1 shelf of posters; 500 cassette tapes; 3 boxes of
printed archival material. Subscriptions: 100 journals and other serials; 17
newspapers. Services: Copying; library open to public.

★12055★
ST. VLADIMIR'S ORTHODOX THEOLOGICAL SEMINARY - FR. GEORGES
  FLOROVSKY LIBRARY (Rel-Theol)
575 Scarsdale Rd.   Phone: (914) 961-8313
Tuckahoe, NY 10707   Paul D. Garrett, Libn.
Founded: 1938. Staff: Prof 1; Other 1. Subjects: Russian Orthodox church
history and theology, Byzantine and Balkan church history and theology,
Russian church music, iconography. Special Collections: 19th century
theological periodicals. Holdings: 43,500 books; 200 volumes of
dissertations; 376 sound recordings; 564 titles on microfilm. Subscriptions:
351 journals and other serials. Services: Interlibrary loans; copying; library
open to public for reference use only. Staff: Stephan J. Beskid, Circ.Libn.

★12056★
ST. VLADIMIR'S UKRAINIAN ORTHODOX CULTURAL CENTRE - LIBRARY
  AND ARCHIVES (Area-Ethnic)
400 Meredith Rd., N.E.   Phone: (403) 264-3437
Calgary, AB, Canada T2E 5A6   Mykola Woron, Hd.Libn.
Founded: 1958. Staff: 3. Subjects: Ukraine. Special Collections: Programs
of Ukrainian events (2 boxes). Holdings: 5482 volumes; 61 bound periodical
volumes; 18 maps; 582 clippings; 13 documents; 16 photographs; 27
pictures; 118 items from XXI Olympic Games in Montreal (English, French,
Ukrainian). Subscriptions: 16 journals and other serials; 7 newspapers.
Services: Interlibrary loans; library open to public with restrictions. Formerly:
St. Vladimir's Ukrainian Greek Orthodox Church. Staff: Bill Swityk, Asst.Libn.;
Al Boykiw, Asst.Libn.

★12057★
ST. WALBURG CONVENT OF BENEDICTINE SISTERS OF COVINGTON,
  KENTUCKY - ARCHIVES (Rel-Theol)
2500 Amsterdam Rd.   Phone: (606) 331-6771
Covington, KY 41016   Sr. Teresa Wolking, O.S.B., Archv.
Staff: Prof 1; Other 3. Subjects: History and records of the Benedictine
Sisters of Covington. Holdings: 150 square feet of archival material, peculiar
to religious women. Subscriptions: 12 newspapers. Services: Copying;
archives open to public with restrictions by appointment.

★12058★
STS. MARY AND ELIZABETH HOSPITAL - MEDICAL LIBRARY (Med)
4400 Churchman Ave.   Phone: (502) 361-6319
Louisville, KY 40215   Ruth Gendron, Libn.
Founded: 1897. Staff: Prof 1; Other 1. Subjects: Medicine and nursing.
Holdings: 1500 books; 1600 bound periodical volumes; 1 VF drawer of
clippings and pamphlets; 5 shelves of tapes. Subscriptions: 170 journals and
other serials. Services: Interlibrary loans through Kornhauser Health Sciences
Library; copying; library open to nursing students from surrounding area only.
Networks/Consortia: Member of Kentucky Health Sciences Library
Consortium. Publications: Library Handbook, semiannual.

★12059★
SALEM COUNTY HISTORICAL SOCIETY - LIBRARY (Hist)
79-83 Market St.   Phone: (609) 935-5004
Salem, NJ 08079   Alice G. Boggs
Founded: 1884. **Staff:** Prof 2. **Subjects:** Genealogy and history of Salem
County. **Holdings:** Scrapbooks, photographs, architectural drawings,
microfilm, oral histories, documents. **Subscriptions:** 10 journals and other
serials. **Services:** Copying; library open to public for reference use only during
restricted hours for a fee.

★12060★
SALEM COUNTY LAW LIBRARY (Law)*
Salem County Court House
92 Market St.   Phone: (609) 935-7510
Salem, NJ 08079   Albert Telsey, Law Ck./Libn.
Staff: Prof 2. **Subjects:** Law. **Holdings:** 3500 books; 200 bound periodical
volumes. **Services:** Library open to public with permission of librarian. **Staff:**
Timothy Farrell, Law Ck./Libn.

★12061★
**SALEM COUNTY MEMORIAL HOSPITAL - DAVID W. GREEN MEDICAL
   LIBRARY** (Med)†
                                               Phone: (609) 935-1000
Salem, NJ 08079   Marion E. Schultz, Med.Libn.
Staff: 1. **Subjects:** Medicine and related fields. **Holdings:** 726 books; 750
bound periodical volumes. **Subscriptions:** 31 journals and other serials.
Services: Interlibrary loans; library not open to public.

★12062★
SALEM FREE PUBLIC LIBRARY - SPECIAL COLLECTIONS (Hist)
112 W. Broadway   Phone: (609) 935-0526
Salem, NJ 08079   Elizabeth C. Fogg, Dir.
Staff: Prof 1; Other 1. **Subjects:** South Jersiana, especially Salem County
history. **Holdings:** Granville S. Thomas South Jersey Collection (400 items);
U.S. Nuclear Regulatory Commission/Public Service Electric & Gas Company
Salem I & II Nuclear Power Station document collection (316 linear feet of
reports and documments). **Services:** Interlibrary loans (limited); copying;
collections open to public for reference use only.

★12063★
**SALEM HOSPITAL - HEALTH SCIENCES LIBRARY AND INFORMATION
   CENTER** (Med)
665 Winter St., S.E.
Box 14001   Phone: (503) 370-5377
Salem, OR 97309   Susan Dyer, Health Sci.Libn.
Staff: Prof 1; Other 4. **Subjects:** Clinical medicine and nursing and related
fields. **Special Collections:** Psychiatry; oncology; nursing; veterinary
medicine. **Holdings:** Figures not available. **Subscriptions:** 210 journals and
other serials; 5 newspapers. **Services:** Interlibrary loans (fee); library not open
to public. **Automated Operations:** Computerized cataloging, acquisitions,
serials and circulation. **Computerized Information Services:** Online systems;
internal database. **Networks/Consortia:** Member of Valley Consortium;
Oregon Health Sciences Libraries Association (OHSLA). **Publications:** Current
Awareness Quarterly; bibliograpy, monthly. **Special Indexes:** Citation Index
(punch cards).

★12064★
SALEM HOSPITAL - MACK MEMORIAL HEALTH SCIENCES LIBRARY (Med)
81 Highland Ave.   Phone: (617) 744-6000
Salem, MA 01970   Nancy Fazzone, Dir., Lib.Serv.
Founded: 1928. **Staff:** Prof 1; Other 2. **Subjects:** Medicine, nursing and
allied health fields. **Holdings:** 2000 books; 4000 bound periodical volumes.
Subscriptions: 200 journals and other serials. **Services:** Interlibrary loans;
library open to public by appointment. **Computerized Information Services:**
NLM, BRS; internal database. **Networks/Consortia:** Member of Northeastern
Consortium for Health Information (NECHI).

SALEM MARITIME NATL. HISTORIC SITE
See: U.S. Natl. Park Service

★12065★
SALEM STATE COLLEGE - LIBRARY - SPECIAL COLLECTIONS (Educ)
352 Lafayette St.   Phone: (617) 745-0556
Salem, MA 01970   Neil B. Olson, Dir. of Libs.
Holdings: Congressman William Bates Archives (140 boxes of papers and
books); 19th-century school materials (800 items); U.S. Geological Survey
maps (70,000). **Services:** Interlibrary loans; copying; ERIC microfiche
reproduction; library open to researchers and consortia members; open to
public for reference use only except with payment of term fee. **Automated**

Operations: Computerized cataloging and acquisitions. **Networks/Consortia:**
Member of Massachusetts Conference of Chief Librarians in Public Higher
Educational Institutions (MCCLPHEI); Essex County Cooperating Libraries.
Special Catalogs: Afro-American Holdings. **Staff:** Glenn Macnutt, Lib.Archv.

★12066★
SALEM STATE COLLEGE - PROFESSIONAL STUDIES RESOURCES CENTER
   (Educ)
Library, 352 Lafayette St.   Phone: (617) 745-0556
Salem, MA 01970   Gertrude L. Fox, Libn.
Founded: 1965. **Staff:** Prof 1; Other 1. **Subjects:** Nursing; business; marine
science; education - materials, textbooks and trade books (K-12), nonprint
materials, standardized tests. **Special Collections:** Resource Center for
Marine Science (elementary and secondary). **Holdings:** 15,000 books; 72
bound periodical volumes; 5 filing cabinets of curriculum guides; 2 file drawers
of pamphlets; 1 file drawer of pictures and maps; 2500 curriculum guides on
microfiche. **Services:** Interlibrary loans; center open to public. **Formerly:** its
Curriculum Center.

★12067★
**SALEM STATE COLLEGE - STUDENT GOVERNMENT ASSOCIATION &
   LIBRARY - LIBRARY OF SOCIAL ALTERNATIVES** (Soc Sci)
                                               Phone: (617) 745-0556
Salem, MA 01970   Margaret Andrews, Coord.
Staff: Prof 1; Other 9. **Subjects:** Alternative lifestyles, Third World, social
change, liberation struggles, legal rights, health care, student survival, hobbies,
radical left. **Special Collections:** Community Resource Referral File. **Holdings:**
7000 books; 9 VF drawers of pamphlets; 6 shelves of archives.
Subscriptions: 200 journals and other serials; 50 newspapers. **Services:**
Interlibrary loans; copying; library open to public. **Automated Operations:**
Computerized acquisitions and serials. **Special Catalogs:** Pamphlet file subject
catalog (card). **Staff:** Cindy Glynn, Pub.Serv.Libn.

★12068★
SALES AND MARKETING MANAGEMENT - LIBRARY (Publ; Bus-Fin)
633 Third Ave.   Phone: (212) 986-4800
New York, NY 10017   J. D. Roberts, Libn.
Founded: 1940. **Staff:** Prof 1. **Subjects:** Marketing, sales management,
salesmanship, advertising, general management. **Special Collections:**
Complete bound sets of Sales and Marketing Management, 1918 to present,
and Survey of Buying Power, 1928 to present. **Holdings:** 500 books; 50 VF
drawers. **Subscriptions:** 90 journals and other serials. **Services:** Interlibrary
loans (limited); library open to public by appointment.

★12069★
SALINAS PUBLIC LIBRARY - JOHN STEINBECK LIBRARY (Hum)
110 W. San Luis St.   Phone: (408) 758-7311
Salinas, CA 93901   John Gross, Dir.
Staff: 1. **Holdings:** John Steinbeck collection of first and foreign language
editions of Steinbeck's works; 100 oral interview recordings; 1000
photographs, letters, movie posters, manuscripts and galley proofs. **Services:**
Interlibrary loans; copying; library open to public. **Networks/Consortia:**
Member of Monterey Bay Area Cooperative Library System (MOBAC).
Publications: John Steinbeck: A Guide to the Collection of the Salinas Public
Library, 1979. **Staff:** Mary Gamble, Steinbeck Libn.

★12070★
SALISBURY HISTORICAL SOCIETY - ARCHIVES (Hist)
Box 91, R.D. 1   Phone: (603) 648-2431
Andover, NH 03216   Sylvia P. Barber, Cur.
Founded: 1968. **Staff:** 2. **Subjects:** Local history, genealogy. **Holdings:** 50
books; manuscripts and original documents pertaining to Salisbury. **Services:**
Interlibrary loans; genealogical research; archives open to public by
appointment. **Publications:** News Letter, monthly - to members and friends.

★12071★
**SALISBURY STATE COLLEGE - BLACKWELL LIBRARY - SPECIAL
   COLLECTIONS** (Educ; Hist)
                                               Phone: (301) 546-3261
Salisbury, MD 21801   James R. Thrash, Dir.
Founded: 1925. **Holdings:** Maryland Room (3200 volumes; 12 VF drawers
of clippings); Education Resources Center; U.S. Government documents
depository (selected); Leisure Studies; juvenile literature; Les Callette
Memorial Civil War Collection; Maryland State documents depository.
Services: Interlibrary loans; copying; library open to public. **Automated
Operations:** Computerized cataloging. **Computerized Information Services:**
DIALOG, OCLC. Performs searches on cost recovery basis. **Networks/
Consortia:** Member of PALINET & Union Library Catalogue of Pennsylvania.

★12072★
SALK INSTITUTE FOR BIOLOGICAL STUDIES - LIBRARY (Sci-Tech)
Box 85800   Phone: (619) 453-4100
San Diego, CA 92138   June A. Gittings, Lib.Coord.
Founded: 1962. Staff: 4. Subjects: Biochemistry, molecular biology, plant
biology, chemistry, genetics, philosophy of science. Holdings: 13,400 books
and serials. Subscriptions: 210 journals; 7 newspapers. Services: Interlibrary
loans; copying; library open to public for reference use only by permission.
Computerized Information Services: MEDLINE.

★12073★
SALMAGUNDI CLUB - LIBRARY (Art)
47 Fifth Ave.   Phone: (212) 255-7740
New York, NY 10003   Joseph Levenson, Libn.
Founded: 1899. Subjects: Art. Holdings: 8000 books. Services: Library
open to qualified persons submitting written applications and references.

★12074★
SALMON BROOK HISTORICAL SOCIETY - REFERENCE AND EDUCATIONAL
   CENTER (Hist)
208 Salmon Brook St.   Phone: (203) 653-3965
Granby, CT 06035   Carol Laun, Asst.Cur.
Founded: 1959. Staff: Prof 1; Other 1. Subjects: Local and area history,
genealogy, religion, agriculture and industry, military history. Special
Collections: James L. Loomis Collection (Loomis Store, 1862-1931, and
Connecticut Home Guard, 1917-1918; 600 items); Richard E. Holcomb
Papers (Panama Canal and Civil War; 250 items). Holdings: 1000 books; 6
VF drawers of original documents; 6 VF drawers of research information and
clippings; 20 boxes of pamphlets, booklets and newspapers; 300 deeds; 150
account books. Services: Center open to public by appointment.

SALOMON BROTHERS CENTER FOR THE STUDY OF FINANCIAL
   INSTITUTIONS
See: New York University

★12075★
SALOMON BROTHERS - CORPORATE FINANCE LIBRARY (Bus-Fin)
One New York Plaza, 46th Fl.   Phone: (212) 747-7933
New York, NY 10004   Lydia P. Davies, Lib.Mgr.
Founded: 1976. Staff: Prof 4; Other 21. Subjects: Investment banking,
corporate and international finance, securities industry. Special Collections:
Eurobond prospectuses (5600); underwriting indentures on microfiche
(6500). Holdings: 4750 books; 1000 subject files of clippings, pamphlets,
documents and reports; 2500 international files (annual reports and
prospectuses); 8500 corporate files; transaction files; 406,685 microforms.
Subscriptions: 700 journals and other serials; 25 newspapers. Services:
Interlibrary loans; library not open to public. Automated Operations:
Computerized cataloging and acquisitions. Computerized Information
Services: DIALOG, Dun and Bradstreet Corporation, Data Resources, Inc.
(DRI), Dow Jones News/Retrieval, Info Globe, NEXIS, BRS, Spectrum Data
Base, Securities Data, Wall Street Transcript, OCLC, X/Market. Publications:
Business Publications, quarterly; Financial News Checklist, weekly; Precedent
Document Submissions, monthly; Subject Headings, quarterly; Periodicals in
the Library, semiannual - all for internal distribution only. Staff: Elizabeth
Jacobsen, Hd., Domestic Res.; Gloria McDonald, Hd.,Intl.Res.; Susan
Capozzoli, Doc.Supv.

SALOMON (Sophie and Ivan) LIBRARY COLLECTION
See: Congregation Shearith Israel - Sophie and Ivan Salomon Library
   Collection

SALON (Nate) RESOURCE CENTER
See: Indiana State Department on Aging & Community Services - Nate
   Salon Resource Center

★12076★
SALT LAKE CITY SCHOOLS - DISTRICT LEARNING CENTER (Educ)
1575 S. State   Phone: (801) 328-7279
Salt Lake City, UT 84115   Marian Karpisek, Hd.
Founded: 1965. Staff: Prof 1; Other 8. Subjects: School curriculum related
subjects. Holdings: 2500 audio cassettes; 3326 films; 2465 videotapes;
1919 filmstrips; 1226 sound filmstrips; 1044 kits. Subscriptions: 11
journals and other serials. Services: Center open to teachers in the city school
district. Automated Operations: Computerized cataloging, acquisitions and
circulation.

★12077★
SALT LAKE COUNTY LAW LIBRARY (Law)
240 E. 400 South, Rm. 219   Phone: (801) 535-7518
Salt Lake City, UT 84111   Jean Ann McMurrin, Law Libn.
Founded: 1900. Staff: Prof 1. Subjects: Law. Holdings: 13,000 volumes.
Services: Copying; library open to public with restrictions. Formerly: Utah
State - 3rd Judicial District - Salt Lake County Law Library.

★12078★
SALT LAKE TRIBUNE - LIBRARY (Publ)
143 S. Main St.   Phone: (801) 237-2001
Salt Lake City, UT 84117   Laurene A. Sowby, Hd.Libn.
Staff: 7. Subjects: Newspaper reference topics. Holdings: 2500 books;
photographs; microfilm; clipping files. Services: Interlibrary loans (fee);
copying; library open to public with restrictions. Publications: Annual Index.

★12079★
SALT RIVER PROJECT - LIBRARY (Sci-Tech; Bus-Fin)
Box 1980   Phone: (602) 273-5304
Phoenix, AZ 85001   Bonnie M. Klassen, Libn.
Staff: 1. Subjects: Engineering, energy, electricity, management, utilities,
occupational safety and health. Holdings: 3000 books. Subscriptions: 500
journals and other serials; 18 newspapers. Services: Interlibrary loans; library
not open to public. Automated Operations: Computerized acquisitions.
Computerized Information Services: DIALOG.

★12080★
SALVATION ARMY - ARCHIVES AND RESEARCH CENTER (Hist; Rel-Theol)
145 W. 15th St.   Phone: (212) 620-4392
New York, NY 10011   Thomas Wilsted, Archv./Adm.
Founded: 1975. Staff: Prof 4; Other 3. Subjects: Salvation Army history and
records, social service, churches, religion. Holdings: 2300 books; 800 bound
periodical volumes; 1000 cubic feet of archives; 31 cubic feet of manuscript
collections; 14,000 photographs; 685 reels of microfilm; 750 microfiche; 35
VF drawers; 300 sound recordings; 280 audiotapes; 250 slides; 445 films.
Subscriptions: 15 journals and other serials. Services: Interlibrary loans;
copying; library open to public. Publications: Historical Newsview, quarterly -
available upon request. Special Indexes: Inventories of processed archives
and manuscript collections; Index to Salvation Army Social Service Periodicals
(card); Index to The War Cry (card). Staff: Judith Johnson, Archv.

★12081★
SALVATION ARMY - EDUCATION DEPARTMENT LIBRARY (Rel-Theol; Hist)
120-130 W. 14th St.   Phone: (212) 620-4994
New York, NY 10011   Mrs. Marjorie Sharp
Staff: Prof 1. Subjects: Salvation Army - biography, history, activities.
Holdings: 2400 books; clippings; manuscripts; pamphlets; documents.
Services: Library open to public by appointment.

SALVATION ARMY - GRACE GENERAL HOSPITAL
See: Grace General Hospital

★12082★
SALVATION ARMY GRACE HOSPITAL - LIBRARY (Med)
339 Crawford Ave.   Phone: (519) 255-2245
Windsor, ON, Canada N9A 5C6   Maureen Richards, Act.Libn.
Staff: Prof 1; Other 1. Subjects: Medicine, nursing. Holdings: 1600 books;
880 bound periodical volumes. Subscriptions: 79 journals and other serials.
Services: Interlibrary loans; library not open to public.

★12083★
SALVATION ARMY GRACE HOSPITAL - MEDICAL STAFF LIBRARY (Med)†
1402 8th Ave., N.W.   Phone: (403) 284-1141
Calgary, AB, Canada T2N 1B9   Dr. A. Rothwell, Chm., Lib.Comm.
Founded: 1967. Subjects: Medicine, paramedicine, history of medicine,
poetry of medicine. Holdings: 2000 books; 50 bound periodical volumes; 40
tapes. Subscriptions: 30 journals and other serials. Services: Library not
open to public.

★12084★
SALVATION ARMY SCHOOL FOR OFFICERS TRAINING - ELFTMAN
   MEMORIAL LIBRARY (Rel-Theol)
30840 Hawthorne Blvd.   Phone: (213) 377-0481
Rancho Palos Verdes, CA 90274   Lavonne D. Robertson, Hd.Libn.
Staff: 3. Subjects: Salvation Army history and services, Bible and theology,
social welfare. Holdings: 25,000 books; AV items. Services: Library open to
public by appointment.

SALZMANN LIBRARY
See: St. Francis Seminary

★12085★
SAM HOUSTON STATE UNIVERSITY - LIBRARY - SPECIAL COLLECTIONS (Hist)
Phone: (409) 294-1613
Huntsville, TX 77341 Charles L. Dwyer, Hd., Thomason/Spec.Coll.
Founded: 1879. Holdings: S. Bangs; Confederate and Texana Collection (CLark, Goree, Porter, Shettles); S. Houston; G. Stein; Thomason; Twain; H.G. Wells; WILD DOG (a little magazine); 1000 associated items including archives. Services: Interlibrary loans; copying; library open to public for reference use only. Automated Operations: Computerized cataloging, acquisitions and circulation. Computerized Information Services: DIALOG, SDC, OCLC. Networks/Consortia: Member of AMIGOS Bibliographic Council, Inc. Special Catalogs: Computer printouts of periodical/newspaper holdings.

★12086★
SAMARITAN HOSPITAL - MEDICAL LIBRARY (Med)
2215 Burdett Ave. Phone: (518) 271-3200
Troy, NY 12180 Annie J. Smith, Med.Libn.
Staff: Prof 1. Subjects: Medicine and allied health sciences. Special Collections: Spafford Collection (health-related books for laymen; 450 books). Holdings: 290 books; 1500 bound periodical volumes. Subscriptions: 64 journals and other serials. Services: Interlibrary loans; copying; library open to public with restrictions. Networks/Consortia: Member of SAVE Consortium; Capital District Library Council for Reference & Research Resources (CDLC). Publications: Bookbag.

★12087★
SAMBORN, STEKETEE, OTIS & EVANS, INC. - RESOURCE & INFORMATION CENTER (Sci-Tech)
1001 Madison Ave. Phone: (419) 255-3830
Toledo, OH 43624 Mary Jo Coates
Founded: 1972. Staff: 1. Subjects: Architecture, engineering, planning, building codes. Special Collections: Solid waste. Holdings: 6712 books; 4 VF drawers of technical papers; 16,000 microfilmed engineering drawings; 10 loose-leaf volumes of newspaper clippings; 437 loose-leaf volumes and 12 VF drawers of product catalogs; 42 file drawers of blueprints. Subscriptions: 98 journals and other serials. Services: Center open to public with restrictions.

★12088★
SAMFORD UNIVERSITY - BAPTIST HISTORICAL COLLECTION (Rel-Theol)
Harwell G. Davis Library
800 Lakeshore Dr. Phone: (205) 870-2749
Birmingham, AL 35209 F. Wilbur Helmbold, Cur.
Founded: 1958. Staff: Prof 1; Other 1. Subjects: Alabama Baptist history and biography. Holdings: 2500 books; 2200 bound periodical volumes; 10,000 Baptist Association Annuals; Baptist Church minutes and records; oral history tapes and transcripts. Subscriptions: 55 journals and other serials. Services: Interlibrary loans; copying; collection open to public. Computerized Information Services: DIALOG. Publications: Alabama Baptist Historian. Special Indexes: Index to Alabama Baptist newspaper (card and computerized book form); Annuals, Alabama Baptist State Convention. Remarks: This library is the official depository of the archives of the Alabama Baptist State Convention. Staff: Shirley Hutchens, Archv.

SAMFORD UNIVERSITY - BAPTIST MEDICAL CENTERS
See: Baptist Medical Centers-Samford University

★12089★
SAMFORD UNIVERSITY - CUMBERLAND SCHOOL OF LAW - CORDELL HULL LAW LIBRARY (Law)
800 Lakeshore Dr. Phone: (205) 870-2714
Birmingham, AL 35209 Laurel R. Clapp, Law Libn.
Founded: 1847. Staff: Prof 5; Other 7. Subjects: American law, common law. Holdings: 168,922 books; 21,000 bound periodical volumes; documents; microfilm. Subscriptions: 2567 journals and other serials. Services: Interlibrary loans; copying; library open to public. Automated Operations: Computerized cataloging. Computerized Information Services: Westlaw. Publications: Selected List of Recent Acquisitions, monthly - to faculty. Staff: Linda Jones, Acq.Libn.; Rebecca Hutto, Cat.Libn.; Jewell Miller, Assoc. Law Libn.

★12090★
SAMFORD UNIVERSITY - HARWELL GOODWIN DAVIS LIBRARY - SPECIAL COLLECTION (Hist; Geog-Map)
800 Lakeshore Dr. Phone: (205) 870-2749
Birmingham, AL 35229 Elizabeth C. Wells, Spec.Coll.Libn.
Founded: 1957. Staff: Prof 1; Other 1. Subjects: Alabama history, literature

and imprints; Early Southeast - Indians, travel, law; genealogical source records; Southern Reconstruction; Ireland history and genealogy. Special Collections: William H. Brantley Collection (18th and 19th century maps); Albert E. Casey Collection (maps of Ireland); Douglas C. McMurtrie Collection; John Ruskin Collection; John Masefield Collection; Alfred Tennyson Collection; Lafcadio Hearn Collection. Holdings: 24,147 books; 2499 bound periodical volumes; 806 microcards; 349 phonograph records; 2725 maps; 218,167 manuscripts; 6761 reels of microfilm; 5558 prints and photographs; 2154 microfiche; 150 oral histories; 37 atlases; 1 globe; 60 relief models. Subscriptions: 330 journals and other serials. Services: Interlibrary loans; copying; library open to public. Computerized Information Services: DIALOG. Special Catalogs: Map Catalog; Catalog of the Casey Collection of Irish History and Genealogy. Special Indexes: Analytical Information Index; index to The Alabama Baptist (newspaper). Staff: Shirley Hutchens, Baptist Archv.

★12091★
SAMUEL ROBERTS NOBLE FOUNDATION, INC. - BIOMEDICAL DIVISION LIBRARY (Med)
2510 Hwy. 70 East
Box 2180 Phone: (405) 223-5810
Ardmore, OK 73402 Loretta Cook, Libn.
Founded: 1955. Staff: Prof 1. Subjects: Cancer research, biochemistry, medicine. Holdings: 1525 books; 5500 bound periodical volumes; 1150 annual publications; 2710 reels of microfilm of journals. Subscriptions: 120 journals and other serials. Services: Interlibrary loans; library open to public for reference use only. Computerized Information Services: MEDLINE, Institute for Scientific Information (ISI).

SAMUELS (Bernard) LIBRARY
See: New York Eye and Ear Infirmary - Bernard Samuels Library

★12092★
SAN ANTONIO COLLEGE - SPECIAL COLLECTIONS (Hist)
1001 Howard St. Phone: (512) 734-7311
San Antonio, TX 78284 James O. Wallace, Dir., Lrng.Rsrcs.
Founded: 1927. Special Collections: Morrison Collection of 18th-century British imprints (6000 volumes); McAllister Collection of Texas and Western America (5200 volumes). Holdings: 29,000 volumes. Services: Interlibrary loans; copying; audiovisual production; collections open to public for reference use only. Automated Operations: Computerized cataloging, acquisitions and circulation; computer-assisted instruction. Computerized Information Services: DIALOG, BRS, OCLC. Performs searches for faculty and students. Contact Person: Ralph Domas, 733-2490. Networks/Consortia: Member of Council of Research and Academic Libraries (CORAL); Health Oriented Libraries of San Antonio (HOLSA); Instructional Media Services Group; AMIGOS Bibliographic Council, Inc. Publications: Acquisitions Bulletin. Special Indexes: Periodical index (card).

★12093★
SAN ANTONIO COMMUNITY HOSPITAL - WEBER MEMORIAL LIBRARY (Med)
999 San Bernardino Rd. Phone: (714) 985-2811
Upland, CA 91786 Francena Johnston, Med.Libn.
Staff: 2. Subjects: Clinical medicine, surgery. Holdings: 2500 books; 2250 bound periodical volumes; 390 Audio-Digest tapes; 190 videotapes. Subscriptions: 197 journals and other serials. Services: Interlibrary loans; library not open to public. Computerized Information Services: MEDLINE. Networks/Consortia: Member of Medical Library Group of Southern California and Arizona. Staff: Elizabeth Guerra, Med.Rec.Dir.

★12094★
SAN ANTONIO CONSERVATION SOCIETY - FOUNDATION LIBRARY (Hist)
107 King William St. Phone: (512) 224-6163
San Antonio, TX 78204 Marianna C. Jones, Dir.
Founded: 1971. Staff: Prof 1. Subjects: History of San Antonio; historic preservation; architectural history. Special Collections: Ernst Raba Photograph Collection (250 glass negatives); Texas Heritage Resource Center (300 publications). Holdings: 1500 books; archives; documents; maps; blueprints; pictures; AV items; clippings. Subscriptions: 20 journals and other serials. Services: Interlibrary loans; copying; library open to public on a limited schedule.

★12095★
SAN ANTONIO EXPRESS AND NEWS - LIBRARY (Publ)†
Ave. E. & Third
Box 2171 Phone: (512) 225-7411
San Antonio, TX 78205 Judy Robinson, Hd.Libn.
Founded: 1865. Staff: Prof 2. Subjects: Newspaper reference topics.

Holdings: 14 cabinets of clippings; 60,000 pictures and art; San Antonio Express, 1865 to present, and San Antonio News, 1918 to present, on microfilm. **Subscriptions:** 20 newspapers. **Services:** Copying; library open to public with restrictions. **Remarks:** Published by Express-News Corporation. **Staff:** Rosie Castaneda .

SAN ANTONIO MUSEUM OF ART
See: San Antonio Museum Association - Libraries

★12096★
SAN ANTONIO MUSEUM ASSOCIATION - LIBRARIES (Art)
3801 Broadway
Box 2601   Phone: (512) 226-5544
San Antonio, TX 78299-2601   George Anne Cormier, Asst.Libn.
Founded: 1926. **Staff:** Prof 1; Other 1. **Subjects:** Texana, American art, Indian art, natural history, decorative arts. **Holdings:** 10,000 books; 4000 bound periodical volumes; 20 drawers of documents, maps, pictures; 12 VF drawers; 14 boxes of postcards, stereo scenes; 25 boxes of archival materials; 22,000 slides; photographs. **Subscriptions:** 35 journals and other serials. **Services:** Interlibrary loans; copying; library open to public for reference use only by appointment. **Remarks:** The association maintains libraries at the Witte Memorial Museum, located at 3801 Broadway; the San Antonio Museum of Art, located at 200 West Jones; and the San Antonio Transportation Museum, located at Hemis Fair Plaza.

SAN ANTONIO MUSEUM OF TRANSPORTATION
See: San Antonio Museum Association - Libraries

★12097★
SAN ANTONIO PUBLIC LIBRARY AND INFORMATION CENTER - ART, MUSIC AND FILMS DEPARTMENT (Art; Mus)
203 S. St. Mary's St.   Phone: (512) 299-7795
San Antonio, TX 78205   Mary A. Wright, Hd.
Founded: 1959. **Staff:** Prof 4; Other 7. **Subjects:** Art history and criticism; painting, sculpture and crafts; architecture - history, criticism, design; interior decoration; antiques; glass; graphics; photography; music - history and current; performing arts; sports; stamp and coin collecting. **Holdings:** 60,000 books; picture file; local artists' biographical file; pamphlet file; 9232 phonograph records; 4250 scores; 310 libretti; 8223 slides; 1600 films; 750 video cassettes; 200 audio cassettes. **Subscriptions:** 148 journals and other serials. **Publications:** Selective reading lists; events calendar. **Special Catalogs:** Card catalog for recordings; book catalog of films; index for picture file.

★12098★
SAN ANTONIO PUBLIC LIBRARY AND INFORMATION CENTER - BUSINESS, SCIENCE AND TECHNOLOGY DEPARTMENT (Bus-Fin; Sci-Tech)
203 S. St. Mary's St.   Phone: (512) 299-7800
San Antonio, TX 78205   James Sosa, Hd.
Founded: 1959. **Staff:** Prof 4; Other 2. **Subjects:** Business, science, technology, economics, statistics, population demographics, useful arts, commerce, business and realty law. **Special Collections:** Trade directories; corporate annual reports; Texas business. **Holdings:** 22,911 bound periodical volumes; 16,435 hardbound U.S. Government documents; 70 VF drawers of pamphlets, clippings and reports; 437,049 government pamphlets; 25,179 AEC reports; 65,700 AEC microcards; 164,741 U.S. Government documents on microfiche; 14,000 Texas State documents.

★12099★
SAN ANTONIO PUBLIC LIBRARY AND INFORMATION CENTER - HARRY HERTZBERG CIRCUS COLLECTION (Hist)
210 W. Market St.   Phone: (512) 299-7810
San Antonio, TX 78205   Betty Claire King, Hd.
Founded: 1942. **Staff:** Prof 1; Other 1. **Subjects:** Circus and circus history. **Special Collections:** Jenny Lind; P.T. Barnum; Charles S. Stratton (Tom Thumb); Townsend Walsh Scrapbook Collection; rare books. **Holdings:** 8817 volumes; 5012 lithographs; 200 circus route books; 43 19th century clown songsters; photographs; circus necrological file; archives; memorabilia; letters; documents. **Services:** Copying; collection open to historians, graduate students, publishers, and authors.

★12100★
SAN ANTONIO PUBLIC LIBRARY AND INFORMATION CENTER - HISTORY, SOCIAL SCIENCE & GENERAL REFERENCE DEPT. (Hist; Soc Sci)
203 S. St. Mary's St.   Phone: (512) 299-7813
San Antonio, TX 78205   Marie Berry, Hd.
Founded: 1959. **Staff:** Prof 5; Other 5. **Subjects:** History, travel, biography, social science, Texana, genealogy, education and general reference. **Special Collections:** Texana Collection; genealogy. **Holdings:** 84,400 books; 3545

bound periodical volumes; 13,488 reels of microfilm; 58,457 microfiche; 2397 ultrafiche; San Antonio and Texas vertical file. **Subscriptions:** 241 journals and other serials. **Services:** Interlibrary loans. **Special Indexes:** Index to San Antonio and Texas vertical file.

★12101★
SAN ANTONIO PUBLIC LIBRARY AND INFORMATION CENTER - LITERATURE, PHILOSOPHY AND RELIGION DEPARTMENT (Hum)
203 S. St. Mary's St.   Phone: (512) 299-7817
San Antonio, TX 78205   Helen K. Halloran, Hd.
Founded: 1959. **Staff:** Prof 4; Other 5. **Subjects:** General works, library science, journalism, rare books, literature, philosophy, religion. **Holdings:** 76,038 books; 5489 bound periodical volumes; 1430 reels of microfilm; 5597 microfiche; 200 ultrafiche; 2150 large print books. **Subscriptions:** 165 journals and other serials; 38 newspapers. **Services:** Interlibrary loans; talking and braille books; department open to public.

★12102★
SAN ANTONIO STATE CHEST HOSPITAL - HEALTH SCIENCE LIBRARY (Med)
Highland Hills Sta.
Box 23340   Phone: (512) 534-8857
San Antonio, TX 78223   Patricia Beaman, Libn.
Staff: Prof 1. **Subjects:** Medicine, chest diseases. **Holdings:** 1600 books; 1500 bound periodical volumes; 280 AV items. **Subscriptions:** 114 journals and other serials. **Services:** Interlibrary loans; copying; library open to public for reference use only. **Networks/Consortia:** Member of Health Oriented Libraries of San Antonio (HOLSA). **Publications:** Newsletter (includes recent acquisitions), bimonthly.

★12103★
SAN ANTONIO STATE HOSPITAL - STAFF LIBRARY (Med)
Box 23310, Highland Hills Sta.   Phone: (512) 532-8811
San Antonio, TX 78223   Patricia Small, Med.Libn.
Staff: Prof 1; Other 1. **Subjects:** Medical sciences, psychology, psychiatric medicine, theology, mental health, mental hospitals. **Holdings:** 4000 books and bound periodical volumes; 12 VF drawers of reports, pamphlets and documents; cassette tapes. **Subscriptions:** 130 journals and other serials. **Services:** Interlibrary loans; copying; library open to public; outside users may check out materials only through ILL. **Networks/Consortia:** Member of Health Oriented Libraries of San Antonio (HOLSA); TALON; Texas Department of Mental Health & Mental Retardation Library Association. **Publications:** Current Awareness, monthly - to professional staff.

★12104★
SAN ANTONIO SYMPHONY ORCHESTRA - SYMPHONY LIBRARY (Mus)
109 Lexington Ave., Suite 207   Phone: (512) 222-8573
San Antonio, TX 78205   Gregory Vaught, Libn.
Staff: Prof 3. **Subjects:** Orchestral music and scores, opera. **Holdings:** 1100 orchestrations with operas, full scores and miniature scores. **Services:** Copying; library open to public for reference use only. **Publications:** Report of all performances and timings by the San Antonio Symphony, annual. **Staff:** William Moore, Asst.Libn.

★12105★
SAN BERNARDINO COMMUNITY HOSPITAL - MEDICAL LIBRARY (Med)
1500 W. 17th St.   Phone: (714) 887-6333
San Bernardino, CA 92411   Marlene Goodwin, Med.Libn.
Staff: Prof 1. **Subjects:** Medicine. **Holdings:** 1000 books; 3500 bound periodical volumes. **Subscriptions:** 121 journals and other serials. **Services:** Interlibrary loans; library not open to public. **Computerized Information Services:** DIALOG, MEDLINE. **Networks/Consortia:** Member of Inland Empire Medical Library Cooperative; Medical Library Group of Southern California and Arizona. **Publications:** Library Notes, bimonthly.

★12106★
SAN BERNARDINO COUNTY - ENVIRONMENTAL PUBLIC WORKS AGENCY - RESOURCE CENTER (Env-Cons)
385 N. Arrowhead   Phone: (714) 383-3438
San Bernardino, CA 92415   Jane Young Bellamy, Libn.
Founded: 1977. **Staff:** Prof 2; Other 1. **Subjects:** Land use, planning, water quality, solid waste, transportation, energy. **Special Collections:** Environmental Impact Reports (150). **Holdings:** 4000 books; 50 bound periodical volumes. **Subscriptions:** 50 journals and other serials; 15 newspapers. **Services:** Interlibrary loans; newsclipping services; center open to public by appointment. **Publications:** Library newsletter, monthly - free upon request; EPWA newsletter; Legislative Update.

★12107★

SAN BERNARDINO COUNTY HISTORICAL ARCHIVES (Hist)
104 W. Fourth St.   Phone: (714) 383-3374
San Bernardino, CA 92415   Jeanette Bernthaler, Act.Archv.
Founded: 1979. **Staff:** Prof 1. **Subjects:** County government records.
Special Collections: Sullivan Collection (emphasis on San Bernardino history, 1923-1974, and southern Californian highway system: 25 volumes); W. Jacob Schaefer Collection (Chino, California agricultural history, 1898-1959: journals and ledgers); microfilm of transcripts of Mormon diaries, journals and life sketches. **Holdings:** 7500 books; Works Progress Administration State Reports. **Services:** Interlibrary loans (limited); archives open to public by appointment. **Remarks:** Archives located at 741 S. Lugo, Suite E, San Bernardino, CA 92408.

★12108★

SAN BERNARDINO COUNTY LAW LIBRARY (Law)
Court House Annex, Ground Fl.
351 N. Arrowhead Ave.   Phone: (714) 383-1957
San Bernardino, CA 92415-0015   Duncan C. Webb, Dir.
Founded: 1891. **Staff:** Prof 4; Other 7. **Subjects:** Law, taxation. **Holdings:** 55,000 books; 1500 bound periodical volumes. **Subscriptions:** 372 journals and other serials; 5 newspapers. **Services:** Copying; library open to public. **Automated Operations:** Computerized cataloging. **Computerized Information Services:** Westlaw. Performs searches on fee basis. Contact Person: Terry Lynch, 383-2701. **Networks/Consortia:** Member of San Bernardino, Inyo, Riverside United Library Services (SIRCULS). **Staff:** Alice R. Dement, Tech.Serv.Libn.; Terry R. Lynch, Ref.Libn.; Terrie Zartman, Ref.Libn.

★12109★

SAN BERNARDINO COUNTY MEDICAL CENTER - MEDICAL LIBRARY (Med)
780 E. Gilbert St.   Phone: (714) 383-3367
San Bernardino, CA 92404   Jacqueline M. Wakefield, Med.Libn.
Staff: Prof 1. **Subjects:** Medicine. **Holdings:** 1700 volumes; 1020 Audio-Digest tapes; 4 VF drawers of pamphlets (uncataloged). **Subscriptions:** 201 journals and other serials. **Services:** Interlibrary loans; copying; library open to public for reference use only. **Automated Operations:** Computerized cataloging. **Computerized Information Services:** MEDLINE, DIALOG. **Networks/Consortia:** Member of Pacific Southwest Regional Medical Library Service (PSRMLS); Medical Library Group of Southern California and Arizona; Inland Empire Medical Library Cooperative.

★12110★

SAN BERNARDINO COUNTY MUSEUM - WILSON C. HANNA LIBRARY/ RESEARCH LIBRARY (Hist)†
2024 Orange Tree Lane   Phone: (714) 792-1334
Redlands, CA 92373   Dr. Gerald A. Smith, Dir.
Founded: 1963. **Subjects:** Local history, anthropology, archeology, natural history. **Special Collections:** Ornithology. **Holdings:** 6000 books; 2000 bound periodical volumes. **Subscriptions:** 20 journals and other serials. **Services:** Library not open to public. **Publications:** San Bernardino County Museum Association Quarterly; Technical Series; occasional papers.

★12111★

SAN BERNARDINO SUN-TELEGRAM - LIBRARY (Publ)
399 North D St.   Phone: (714) 889-9666
San Bernardino, CA 92401   Blanche A. Lewis, Libn.
Founded: 1950. **Staff:** Prof 1; Other 1. **Subjects:** Newspaper reference topics. **Holdings:** Clippings; microfilm; photographs.

★12112★

SAN CLEMENTE PRESBYTERIAN CHURCH - SUTHERLAND MEMORIAL LIBRARY (Rel-Theol)
119 Estrella Ave.   Phone: (714) 492-6158
San Clemente, CA 92672   Ethel Wolleson, Libn.
Staff: Prof 1; Other 3. **Subjects:** Bible and Bible study; aids to Christian living; church growth; Christian education; missions. **Holdings:** 3000 books; 100 cassettes. **Subscriptions:** 15 journals and other serials. **Services:** Interlibrary loans; library open to public.

★12113★

SAN DIEGO AERO-SPACE MUSEUM - N. PAUL WHITTIER HISTORICAL AVIATION LIBRARY (Mil; Hist)
2001 Pan America Plaza, Balboa Park   Phone: (619) 234-8291
San Diego, CA 92101   Brewster C. Reynolds, Archv.
Founded: 1980. **Staff:** Prof 5; Other 5. **Subjects:** History of World Wars I and II including military aircraft, civil aircraft, personnel, early aircraft history, Lighter than Air aircraft, rotary wing, gliding engines. **Special Collections:** L.N. Forden Collection (photographs); L.R. Hackney Collection (Air Cargo Library); T.P. Hall Collection; W.F. Schult Collection; E. Cooper Air Mail Pioneers

Collection; Wally Wiberg Collection; Lou E. Gordon Collection; Willard F. Schmitt Air Mail History Collection (3 VF drawers); Early Birds of Aviation Collection (3 file cabinets); U.S. Navy Helicopter Association Collection; George E.A. Hallett Collection; Warren S. Eaton Collection; Frank T. Courtney Collection; Errold G. Bahl Collection; T.C. MacAulay Collection; Hugh M. Rockwell Collection. **Holdings:** 7500 books; 2500 bound and unbound periodicals; 850,000 microfiche; 1176 airline insignia; 3400 aircraft drawings; 2500 aircraft and engine manuals; 20,000 photographs; 1000 negatives; 3000 slides; 85 scrapbooks; 300 aircraft brochures; 80 cassette tapes. **Subscriptions:** 32 journals and other serials. **Services:** Interlibrary loans; copying; library open to public. **Computerized Information Services:** Online systems. **Staff:** Edward H. Rouen, Lib.Asst.; George B. Welsh, Lib.Asst.; Miles Blaine, Lib.Asst.; Neil Saddington, Lib.Asst.

★12114★

SAN DIEGO COUNTY - DEPARTMENT OF PLANNING AND LAND USE - LIBRARY (Plan)
5201 Ruffin Rd., Suite B-2   Phone: (619) 565-3043
San Diego, CA 92123   Sonya Heiserman, Libn.
Staff: Prof 1; Other 1. **Subjects:** Urban planning, zoning, hydrology. **Holdings:** 1000 books; 1500 other cataloged items. **Subscriptions:** 35 journals and other serials; 10 newspapers. **Services:** Library open to public for reference use only.

★12115★

SAN DIEGO COUNTY LAW LIBRARY (Law)
1105 Front St.   Phone: (619) 236-2231
San Diego, CA 92101   O. James Werner, Dir.
Founded: 1891. **Staff:** Prof 8; Other 14. **Subjects:** Law. **Special Collections:** California Appelate Court Briefs (1950 to present); legal history of San Diego County. **Holdings:** 146,830 books and bound periodical volumes; 798 volumes of microcards; 16,160 volumes of microfiche; 1248 audio cassettes; 898 reels of microfilm; 55 videotapes. **Subscriptions:** 814 journals and other serials; 10 newspapers. **Services:** Interlibrary loans; copying; library open to public, but borrowing is restricted to those with deposit accounts. **Computerized Information Services:** Westlaw, OCLC. **Networks/Consortia:** Member of San Diego Greater Metropolitan Area Library and Information Agency Council; CLASS. **Publications:** Recent Acquisitions, monthly - available to mailing list; Guide to San Diego County Law Library, irregular - distributed to patrons and other interested persons. **Special Indexes:** Index of Current Mexican Legal Materials. **Staff:** Norman Stevens, Circ.Libn.; Thomas E. Anderson, Asst.Libn.; Larry Dershem, Asst.Libn.; Thomas Johnsrud, Ref.Libn.; Betty Stephenson, Ref.Libn.; Virginia Piechocki, Acq.Libn.;Elaine Peabody, Ref.Libn.; Florence Ewing, Asst.Ref.Libn.; Colleen Ervin, Asst.Acq.Libn.; Mewail Mebrahtu, Asst.Ref.Libn.

★12116★

SAN DIEGO COUNTY LAW LIBRARY - EAST COUNTY BRANCH (Law)
250 E. Main   Phone: (619) 579-3525
El Cajon, CA 92020   O. James Werner, Dir.
Founded: 1983. **Staff:** Prof 1. **Subjects:** Law. **Holdings:** 4854 books; 146 bound periodical volumes. **Subscriptions:** 31 journals and other serials. **Services:** Copying; library open to public for reference use only. **Staff:** Edna Theil, Br.Asst.

★12117★

SAN DIEGO COUNTY LAW LIBRARY - SOUTH BAY BRANCH (Law)
500 Third Ave.   Phone: (619) 575-4929
Chula Vista, CA 92010   O. James Werner, Dir.
Staff: 1. **Subjects:** Law. **Holdings:** 11,270 books. **Services:** Copying; library open to public for reference use only. **Staff:** Elizabeth Daniels, Br.Asst.

★12118★

SAN DIEGO COUNTY LAW LIBRARY - VISTA BRANCH (Law)
325 S. Melrose   Phone: (619) 758-6247
Vista, CA 92083   O. James Werner, Dir.
Staff: 2. **Subjects:** Law. **Holdings:** 13,221 books and bound periodical volumes. **Subscriptions:** 31 journals and other serials. **Services:** Copying; library open to public for reference use only. **Staff:** Janet M. Beker, Br.Asst.; Marguerite Vollmer, Br.Asst.

★12119★

SAN DIEGO COUNTY LIBRARY - GOVERNMENTAL REFERENCE LIBRARY (Soc Sci; Law)
602 County Administration Center
1600 Pacific Hwy.   Phone: (619) 236-2760
San Diego, CA 92101   Ann Terrell, Govt.Ref.Libn.
Founded: 1946. **Staff:** Prof 1; Other 1. **Subjects:** Local government, public administration, public finance, health and welfare, public works,

transportation, parks and recreation, crime and delinquency, personnel management. **Special Collections:** City and County documents (15,000); surveys and studies by consultants. **Holdings:** 9800 books; 8527 bound periodical volumes; 28,000 pamphlets, surveys, reports. **Subscriptions:** 250 journals and other serials; 7 newspapers. **Services:** Interlibrary loans; copying; library open to public for reference use only. **Computerized Information Services:** DIALOG. **Networks/Consortia:** Member of Serra Cooperative Library System. **Publications:** Timely Topics, bimonthly.

★12120★
SAN DIEGO COUNTY OFFICE OF EDUCATION - PROFESSIONAL INFORMATION AND RESOURCE CENTER (Educ)
6401 Linda Vista Rd.   Phone: (619) 292-3669
San Diego, CA 92111   P. Marvin Barbula, Dir.
Staff: Prof 1; Other 4. **Subjects:** Education and related subjects. **Special Collections:** Administrator's Corner; grant research materials. **Holdings:** 20,000 books and bound periodical volumes; 238,000 ERIC microfiche; 25,000 pamphlets, courses of study; state adopted textbooks for grades K-8; secondary textbook collection; instructional materials. **Subscriptions:** 230 journals and other serials. **Services:** Interlibrary loans; library open to public school personnel within San Diego County. **Computerized Information Services:** DIALOG. **Publications:** Curriculum Currents; bibliographies on request. **Remarks:** An alternate telephone number is 292-3607. **Formerly:** San Diego County - Department of Education - Professional Resource and Development Center.

★12121★
SAN DIEGO ECOLOGY CENTER - LIBRARY (Env-Cons)
430 Olive St.   Phone: (619) 294-2926
San Diego, CA 92103   Gaye M. Dingeman, Libn.
Staff: Prof 1. **Subjects:** Environmental quality, energy, land use, solid waste management, water quality and supply, air quality, wildlife, population, noise, gardening. **Holdings:** 605 books; 2000 handbooks, pamphlets; 44 VF drawers of reports, guidebooks, teaching materials; 12 AV items. **Subscriptions:** 21 journals and other serials. **Services:** Library open to public. **Publications:** Environmental Reporter, bimonthly newsletter - limited distribution.

★12122★
SAN DIEGO GAS AND ELECTRIC COMPANY - LIBRARY (Energy)
Box 1831   Phone: (619) 232-4252
San Diego, CA 92112   Marie A. Peelman, Hd.Libn.
Founded: 1921. **Staff:** Prof 1. **Subjects:** Electrical and gas engineering, power-steam, environment, business, economics, Californiana, science and technology, nuclear science. **Special Collections:** Public Utilities Reports and Digest - opinions and orders of PUC, California. **Holdings:** 1000 books; 10 boxes of microfilm of Electric Power Research Institute (EPRI) reports. **Subscriptions:** 400 journals and other serials; 150 newspapers. **Services:** Interlibrary loans; library not open to public. **Publications:** Acquisitions, monthly - for internal distribution only.

★12123★
SAN DIEGO HALL OF SCIENCE - BERNICE HARDING LIBRARY (Sci-Tech)
Box 33303   Phone: (619) 238-1233
San Diego, CA 92103   Annajean Naylor, Exec.Sec.
Founded: 1976. **Staff:** 1. **Subjects:** Astronomy, photography, scientific research. **Holdings:** 1000 books; 200 bound periodical volumes. **Subscriptions:** 14 journals and other serials. **Services:** Interlibrary loans; library open to members. **Publications:** Space Reflections, bimonthly - to members.

★12124★
SAN DIEGO HISTORICAL SOCIETY - RESEARCH ARCHIVES (Hist)
1649 El Prado, Balboa Pk.   Phone: (619) 232-6203
San Diego, CA 92101   Sylvia Arden, Hd.Libn./Archv.
Founded: 1929. **Staff:** Prof 5. **Subjects:** History - San Diego County, California, Baja California. **Special Collections:** San Diego Biography (374 notebooks); oral history (550 transcripts); Kerr Collection (California ranchos; 19 notebooks). **Holdings:** 9500 volumes; 4500 bound periodical volumes; 500 photostats of documents in the Archivo General, Cuidad de Mejico Collection (1769-1840); business ledgers and reports; census reports; maps; microfilmed newspapers. **Subscriptions:** 15 journals and other serials. **Services:** Copying; clipping service; archives open to public with restrictions. **Publications:** Journal of San Diego History, quarterly; San Diego Historical Society Newsletter, monthly. **Staff:** Rickey D. Best, Asst.Libn.; Gregg Hennessey, Adm.

★12125★
SAN DIEGO HISTORICAL SOCIETY - RESEARCH ARCHIVES - PHOTOGRAPH COLLECTION (Aud-Vis)
Box 81825   Phone: (619) 297-3258
San Diego, CA 92138   Larry Booth, Cur.
Subjects: San Diego city and county, 1867-1984. **Holdings:** 200,000 large format professional negatives and vintage prints. **Services:** Collection open to public on a limited schedule. **Remarks:** Collection is located at Balboa Pk., Casa de Balboa, 1649 El Prado, San Diego, CA 92101.

SAN DIEGO HISTORY RESEARCH CENTER
See: San Diego State University

★12126★
SAN DIEGO MUSEUM OF ART - REFERENCE LIBRARY (Art)
Balboa Park
Box 2107   Phone: (619) 232-7931
San Diego, CA 92112   Nancy J. Andrews, Libn.
Founded: 1926. **Staff:** Prof 1. **Subjects:** Art, especially Spanish Baroque, Oriental and Italian Renaissance. **Holdings:** 9500 books; 1100 bound periodical volumes; 50,000 art exhibition catalogs; 25 cabinets of artists files; 18,000 slides. **Subscriptions:** 35 journals and other serials. **Services:** Copying; library open to members. **Special Catalogs:** Bibliographical card file to artist in art exhibition catalogs.

★12127★
SAN DIEGO MUSEUM OF MAN - SCIENTIFIC LIBRARY (Sci-Tech)
1350 El Prado, Balboa Pk.   Phone: (619) 239-2001
San Diego, CA 92101   Jane Bentley, Libn.
Founded: 1916. **Staff:** Prof 1. **Subjects:** Anthropology, pre-Columbian art, Indians of the Americas, archeology, ethnology, physical anthropology. **Special Collections:** North American Indians. **Holdings:** 5500 books; 2000 bound periodical volumes; 51 archival manuscripts. **Subscriptions:** 325 journals and other serials. **Services:** Interlibrary loans; copying (both limited); library open to public. **Publications:** Ethnic Technology Notes, irregular; San Diego Museum Papers, irregular - both for sale or exchange.

★12128★
SAN DIEGO PUBLIC LIBRARY - ART, MUSIC & RECREATION SECTION (Art; Mus)
820 E St.   Phone: (619) 236-5810
San Diego, CA 92101   Barbara Tuthill, Supv.Libn.
Staff: Prof 5; Other 1. **Subjects:** Art and music history, architecture, sculpture, antiques, interior decoration, crafts, music theory and techniques, painting, drawing, print-making, photography, music scores, libretti, miniature scores, sports, games, theater, cinema, dance. **Special Collections:** Language instruction recordings; pop songs, 1900-1970; World War I and World War II U.S., British, French and Chinese War Posters, organized by illustrator and subject. **Holdings:** 60,000 books; 500,000 pictures; 25,000 picture postcards; 10,000 choral music pieces; 23,000 phonograph records; 17,500 music scores. **Subscriptions:** 339 journals and other serials. **Services:** Chamber music series; monthly art exhibitions. **Networks/Consortia:** Member of Serra Cooperative Library System. **Special Indexes:** Song Title Index; Choral Music Index; Phono-Record Catalog; Film Review File. **Staff:** Linda Griffin, Libn.; Evelyn Kooperman, Libn.; Barbara Carroll, Libn.; Christina Clifford, Libn.

★12129★
SAN DIEGO PUBLIC LIBRARY - CALIFORNIA ROOM (Hist)
820 E St.   Phone: (619) 236-5834
San Diego, CA 92101   Rhoda E. Kruse, Sr.Libn.
Staff: Prof 1. **Subjects:** California - history, politics, government, description, travel, biography; history of San Diego City and County; Baja California description and history; California and San Diego social concerns. **Special Collections:** Records of the Little Landers Colony, San Ysidro, California; Kelly Papers (records of a pioneer family); Hatfield (rainmaker) papers; San Diego Park Department records, including exposition material; official repository of San Diego 200th Anniversary Committee papers; San Diego Great Registers, 1866-1909; Horton House registers. **Holdings:** 15,000 books; 300 maps; 48 VF drawers of pamphlets and clippings; 10 VF drawers of pictures; 800,000 index cards on microfiche, covering San Diego Herald, 1851-1860, San Diego Union, 1868-1903 and 1930 to present. **Subscriptions:** 48 journals and other serials. **Services:** Copying; room open to public for reference use only.

★12130★
SAN DIEGO PUBLIC LIBRARY - GENEALOGY ROOM (Hist)
820 E St.
San Diego, CA 92101 — Rhoda E. Kruse, Sr.Libn.
Founded: 1940. **Subjects:** General genealogy. **Special Collections:** California census on microfilm, 1850-1900. **Holdings:** 2000 books. **Subscriptions:** 38 journals and other serials. **Services:** Copying; room open to public for reference use only.

★12131★
SAN DIEGO PUBLIC LIBRARY - HISTORY & WORLD AFFAIRS SECTION (Hist)
820 E St. — Phone: (619) 236-5820
San Diego, CA 92101 — Jean Hughes, Sr.Libn.
Staff: Prof 3; Other 2. **Subjects:** History, travel, biography, archeology, cartography. **Special Collections:** Western United States history. **Holdings:** Figures not available for books; 2400 maps; 40 VF drawers of pamphlets and clippings. **Subscriptions:** 300 journals and other serials. **Services:** Interlibrary loans; copying; section open to public. **Networks/Consortia:** Member of Serra Cooperative Library System. **Staff:** Don Silva, Libn.; Lynn Whitehouse, Libn.

★12132★
SAN DIEGO PUBLIC LIBRARY - INFORMATION/DIRECTORY SERVICE SECTION (Info Sci)
820 E St. — Phone: (619) 236-5800
San Diego, CA 92101 — Jean Hughes, Sr.Libn.
Staff: Prof 1; Other 6. **Holdings:** 950 telephone directories; 600 trade directories; 75 city directories. **Services:** Copying; library open to public. **Automated Operations:** Computerized cataloging. **Networks/Consortia:** Member of Serra Cooperative Library System. **Special Indexes:** Index to directories (card).

★12133★
SAN DIEGO PUBLIC LIBRARY - LITERATURE & LANGUAGES SECTION (Hum)
820 E St. — Phone: (619) 236-5816
San Diego, CA 92101 — Alyce Archuleta, Sr.Libn.
Staff: Prof 4; Other 2. **Subjects:** Literature, psychology, languages, philosophy, religion. **Special Collections:** Occult sciences; Bacon-Shakespeare controversy; theosophy. **Holdings:** Figures not available for books; 10 VF drawers of pamphlets; large print books; foreign language books (especially Spanish). **Subscriptions:** 500 journals and other serials. **Services:** Copying; shut-in service; section open to public. **Networks/Consortia:** Member of Serra Cooperative Library System. **Publications:** Booklists, irregular. **Staff:** Brinn Vaniman, Libn.; John Vanderby, Libn.; Susanna Hardy, Libn.; Eileen Boyle, Libn.

★12134★
SAN DIEGO PUBLIC LIBRARY - SCIENCE & INDUSTRY SECTION (Bus-Fin; Sci-Tech)
820 E St. — Phone: (619) 236-5813
San Diego, CA 92101 — Joanne Anderson, Sr.Libn.
Staff: Prof 4; Other 4. **Subjects:** Business, industry, science, cookery, automobile repair. **Special Collections:** Space and aeronautics historical collection; depository for U.S., California and San Diego City and County government publications (over 1 million); American National Standards Institute (ANSI) and American Society for Testing and Materials (ASTM) standards on microfiche. **Holdings:** Figures not available for books and bound periodical volumes; microforms; Sams Photofacts (complete collection); American Engineering Council (AEC) and NASA depository collections. **Subscriptions:** 700 journals and other serials. **Services:** Interlibrary loans; copying. **Networks/Consortia:** Member of Serra Cooperative Library System. **Special Indexes:** Subject index to government documents (card). **Staff:** Robert Taylor, Libn.Thomas Karras, Libn.; Carolyn Demaray, Libn.

★12135★
SAN DIEGO PUBLIC LIBRARY - SOCIAL SCIENCES SECTION (Soc Sci)
820 E St. — Phone: (619) 236-5564
San Diego, CA 92101 — Margaret E. Queen, Supv.Libn.
Staff: Prof 4; Other 2. **Subjects:** Sociology, education, political science, law, economics, finance, conservation, transportation, military service. **Holdings:** 7 VF drawers of corporation annual reports; 6 VF drawers of vocational pamphlets; 31 VF drawers of miscellaneous pamphlets; 4610 college catalogs on microfiche; talking books and cassette tapes for the visually handicapped. **Subscriptions:** 511 journals and other serials. **Services:** Interlibrary loans; copying; section open to public. **Automated Operations:** Computerized cataloging. **Networks/Consortia:** Member of Serra Cooperative Library System. **Publications:** Booklists, irregular. **Special Indexes:** Black American

Firsts File (card); Women Firsts File (card). **Staff:** Marian Avila, Libn.; Kathleen Griffin, Libn.; Sharon Jordan, Libn.

★12136★
SAN DIEGO PUBLIC LIBRARY - WANGENHEIM ROOM (Rare Book)
820 E St. — Phone: (619) 236-5807
San Diego, CA 92101 — Eileen Boyle, Libn.
Founded: 1954. **Staff:** Prof 1. **Subjects:** History of printing and the development of the book with specimens ranging from Babylonian tablets to cassettes; famous presses and modern private presses; incunabula; fine book bindings. **Special Collections:** Dime novels (769 volumes); fore-edge paintings (185 volumes); works of John Ruskin (250 volumes); Curtis' North American Indians (20 volumes and 20 portfolios); Monumenta Scenica (12 volumes). **Holdings:** 7600 books; 324 bookplates; selected antiquarian book dealers' catalogs; periodicals; manuscripts; autographs; artifacts. **Services:** Room open to public on a limited schedule. **Special Catalogs:** Chronological card catalog arranged by date and place of publication.

★12137★
SAN DIEGO SOCIETY OF NATURAL HISTORY - NATURAL HISTORY MUSEUM LIBRARY (Sci-Tech)
Box 1390 — Phone: (619) 232-3821
San Diego, CA 92112 — Judith C. Dyer, Libn.
Founded: 1874. **Staff:** Prof 1; Other 1. **Subjects:** Zoology, botany, geology, paleontology, biology. **Special Collections:** A.W. Vodges Library of Geology and Paleontology (20,000 volumes); L. Klauber Herpetological Library (1462 volumes; 19,000 pamphlets and reprints). **Holdings:** 80,000 volumes; maps; 1200 watercolors. **Subscriptions:** 760 journals and other serials. **Services:** Interlibrary loans; copying; library open to public for reference use only.

★12138★
SAN DIEGO STATE UNIVERSITY - BUREAU OF BUSINESS & ECONOMIC RESEARCH LIBRARY (Bus-Fin)*
College of Business Administration — Phone: (619) 265-6873
San Diego, CA 92182 — Robert P. Hungate, Act.Dir.
Founded: 1958. **Staff:** Prof 1; Other 2. **Subjects:** Accounting, auditing, business, business education, economics, finance, management, marketing, labor. **Special Collections:** Research studies of Bureau members; Arthur Young Tax Research Library; regional data on San Diego and southern California; national data by states. **Holdings:** Figures not available. **Subscriptions:** 27 serials. **Services:** Interlibrary loans; library open to public. **Publications:** Monographs; Business Case Studies; Faculty Working Papers.

★12139★
SAN DIEGO STATE UNIVERSITY - CENTER FOR PUBLIC ECONOMICS LIBRARY (Soc Sci)*
— Phone: (619) 286-6707
San Diego, CA 92182-0511 — Dr. George Babilot, Dir.
Staff: Prof 1; Other 3. **Subjects:** Economics, health and welfare, land use and taxation, natural resources and environment, population and demography, poverty, public finance, urban regional studies. **Special Collections:** Fiscal studies from all 50 states; San Diego County documents. **Holdings:** 4000 books. **Subscriptions:** 80 journals and other serials. **Services:** Interlibrary loans; library open to public. **Publications:** Working papers in public economics.

★12140★
SAN DIEGO STATE UNIVERSITY - EUROPEAN STUDIES CENTER - LIBRARY (Hum)
— Phone: (619) 265-5928
San Diego, CA 92182-0511 — Dr. Leon Rosenstein, Dir.
Staff: Prof 12; Other 1. **Subjects:** European studies. **Holdings:** 1500 books; 200 bound periodical volumes; 18,000 slides; 1000 records and tapes. **Services:** Library not open to public.

★12141★
SAN DIEGO STATE UNIVERSITY - GOVERNMENT PUBLICATIONS DEPARTMENT (Info Sci)†
— Phone: (619) 265-5832
San Diego, CA 92182-0511 — Charles Dintrone, Doc.Libn.
Staff: Prof 4; Other 6. **Holdings:** 375,000 U.S., United Nations and California documents; 125,000 maps; 725,000 microforms. **Services:** Interlibrary loans; copying; department open to public. **Special Catalogs:** Monthly Catalog; Index to United Nations Documents; Index to California Documents. **Staff:** Patricia Moore, Ref.Libn.; Joann Goodwin, Ref.Libn.; Walter Posner, Ref.Libn.; Muriel Strickland, Map Cur.

★12142★

SAN DIEGO STATE UNIVERSITY - MALCOLM A. LOVE LIBRARY - SPECIAL COLLECTIONS (Hum; Soc Sci)†

San Diego, CA 92182-0511

Phone: (619) 265-6014
Don L. Bosseau, Univ.Libn.

Founded: 1897. Special Collections: European unification; history and philosophy of science; geological history of Pacific Ocean fauna; developmental biology; Asian Collection of Chinese and Japanese vernacular material; Desi Arnaz television programs. Services: Interlibrary loans; copying; Collections open to public for reference use only; fee required for borrowing. Automated Operations: Computerized cataloging, serials and circulation. Computerized Information Services: DIALOG, SDC, NLM. Networks/Consortia: Member of San Diego Greater Metropolitan Library & Information Agency Council (METRO); Serra Cooperative Library System. Staff: Fidelia Dickinson, Coll.Dev.Libn.; Stephen Fitt, Ref.Dept.; Gerald Palsson, Asst.Univ.Libn.; Ruth Leerhoff, Asst.Univ.Libn.; William Pease, Cat.Dept.

★12143★

SAN DIEGO STATE UNIVERSITY - MEDIA & CURRICULUM CENTER (Educ; Aud-Vis)†

San Diego, CA 92182-0511

Phone: (619) 265-6757
Carole F. Wilson, Chm.

Founded: 1951. Staff: Prof 5; Other 4. Subjects: Textbooks and curriculum materials for K-12, children's literature, nonprint media for all levels. Special Collections: Complete ERIC documents collection with indexes; graduate research papers from the College of Education; classic film collection. Holdings: 20,000 K-12 textbooks; 30,000 K-12 curriculum guides, teachers' resource books and pamphlets; 294,000 microfiche; 13,000 children's books; 10 VF drawers of publishers' and AV producers' catalogs; 16,000 nonbook media. Services: Education and media reference; library instruction program; facilities for previewing and listening. Computerized Information Services: Online systems. Staff: Mary Ada Burns, Sr.Asst.Libn.; Alma Lamb, Asst.Libn.; Ellen Zyroff, Asst.Libn.; Clarissa Erwin, Sr.Asst.Libn.; Judith Arbogast, Media Supv.; Beverly Elliott, Circ.Supv.

★12144★

SAN DIEGO STATE UNIVERSITY - PUBLIC ADMINISTRATION RESEARCH CENTER LIBRARY (Soc Sci)

San Diego, CA 92182-0511

Phone: (619) 286-6084
Elaine Wonsowicz, Mgr.

Founded: 1950. Staff: Prof 1; Other 3. Subjects: American and comparative public administration; urban affairs; public policy and planning; resource utilization; educational administration; criminal justice. Holdings: 3000 books; 70,000 other cataloged items; depository of public institutional reports. Subscriptions: 300 journals and other serials. Services: Copying; library open to public for reference use only.

★12145★

SAN DIEGO STATE UNIVERSITY - SAN DIEGO HISTORY RESEARCH CENTER (Hist)†

University Library
San Diego, CA 92182-0511

Phone: (619) 265-5751
Stephen A. Colston, Dir.

Founded: 1976. Staff: Prof 2; Other 4. Subjects: San Diego history. Special Collections: Archival collections of American Tunaboat Association, Hotel Del Coronado, San Diego Convention and Visitors Bureau, National Conference of Christians and Jews, La Jolla Museum of Contemporary Art, San Diego County Medical Society, San Diego Symphony, U. S. Congressman Robert Carlton Wilson, San Diego Chamber of Commerce, San Diego Center for Children, United Way of San Diego County, and eighty additional archival collections (total holdings, 1300 linear feet). Holdings: 1200 books; 350 oral history tapes; 30 reels of microfilm; 700 photographs; 7000 cores of newsfilm. Subscriptions: 20 journals and other serials; 5 newspapers. Services: Copying; center open to public. Publications: A Guide to the Collections of the San Diego History Research Center, 1978; San Diego History Research Center News, irregular - both available upon request. Special Catalogs: Inventories of archival collections; catalog of published works and archival collections (card); catalog of manuscript collections on the history of the American West (card).

★12146★

SAN DIEGO STATE UNIVERSITY - SCIENCE DEPARTMENT (Sci-Tech)†

University Library
San Diego, CA 92182-0511

Phone: (619) 265-6715
Lillian Chan, Sci.Libn.

Staff: Prof 4; Other 3. Subjects: Biology, chemistry, mathematics, geology, physics, engineering, industrial arts, astronomy, military science, history of sciences, nursing, public health. Special Collections: Ernst Zinner Collection on History of Astronomy and Science (4000 items); Reginald Davis Orchid Collection (200 items); W.M. Pearce Spider Collection (300 items); Calvert E. Norland Collection on the History of Biology. Holdings: 156,364 books;

107,745 bound periodical volumes; 30,764 hard copy science reports; 122,063 microfiche science reports; 1283 reels of microfilms and filmstrips; 197,704 microfiche; 46,668 microcards. Subscriptions: 2858 journals and other serials. Services: Interlibrary loans; copying; department open to public; fee required for borrowing. Automated Operations: Computerized cataloging and serials. Computerized Information Services: DIALOG, SDC, MEDLINE. Publications: Serials printout, quarterly - limited number free upon request; Astronomical Literature in the Ernst Zinner Collection, a checklist; Literature of Time in the Ernst Zinner Collection, a checklist; Copernicus; Johann Kepler, a bibliography; Tycho Brahe, a bibliography; Geology of San Diego County, a bibliography; Geology of Baja California, a bibliography; Botany of San Diego County, guide to research materials; Guide to the Botanical Literature of Baja California in the Collections of the San Diego State University Library; Sunbeams and Solar Energy; Science and Engineering Resource Series. Staff: Gerald Johns, Asst.Sci.Libn.; Katalin Harkanyi, Asst.Sci.Libn.; Mary E. Harris, Asst.Sci.Libn.; Anne Turhollow, Asst.Sci.Libn.

★12147★

SAN DIEGO STATE UNIVERSITY - SOCIAL SCIENCE RESEARCH LABORATORY - LIBRARY (Soc Sci)*

San Diego, CA 92182-0511

Phone: (619) 265-5845
Paul J. Strand, Dir.

Founded: 1974. Staff: Prof 1; Other 25. Subjects: Economics, sociology, geography, political science, social science methodology. Special Collections: San Diego/Tijuana demography; labor economics; international economics; demography studies and census data; international monetary fund data tapes; social science machine-readable data. Holdings: 50,000 books, pamphlets, and brochures; 400 bound periodical volumes; 600 serial titles. Services: Interlibrary loans; copying; library open to public. Staff: Douglas Coe, Res.Tech.; Jeff Green, Res.Tech.; Larry Sharp, Res.Tech.; Carole Outhouse, Res.Tech.

★12148★

SAN DIEGO UNION-TRIBUNE PUBLISHING COMPANY - LIBRARY (Publ)

350 Camino De La Reina
San Diego, CA 92108

Phone: (619) 299-3131
Sharon Stewart Reeves, Dir., Lib.Serv.

Staff: Prof 1; Other 17. Subjects: Newspaper reference topics. Holdings: 2000 books; 240 drawers of newspaper clippings; 4000 reels of microfilm. Subscriptions: 50 journals and other serials; 8 newspapers. Services: Library not open to public. Computerized Information Services: DIALOG, NEXIS. Staff: Linda Ritter, Asst.Libn.

★12149★

SAN FERNANDO VALLEY COLLEGE OF LAW - LAW LIBRARY (Law)†

8353 Sepulveda Blvd.
Sepulveda, CA 91343

Phone: (818) 894-5711
James G. Sherman, Lib.Dir.

Founded: 1962. Staff: Prof 2. Subjects: Law. Holdings: 41,428 books and bound periodical volumes; 25,734 microforms. Subscriptions: 202 journals and other serials. Services: Copying; library open to public.

★12150★

SAN FRANCISCO ACADEMY OF COMIC ART - LIBRARY (Art; Hum)†

2850 Ulloa
San Francisco, CA 94116

Phone: (415) 681-1737
Bill Blackbeard, Dir.

Founded: 1968. Staff: 5. Subjects: Science fiction, crime fiction, popular literature, comic strip art in all aspects, dime novels, pulp and other popular magazines, motion picture data, critical literature. Special Collections: Sherlockiana; Oz books; foreign popular literature; children's books; nationally representative bound newspaper runs, including many rare Hearst papers. Holdings: 50,000 books; one million comic strips; 22,000 unbound periodicals; manuscripts, original comic strips and other graphic work; movie stills and pressbooks; newspaper and magazine ads and art; science fiction fanzines and fanzines of other areas of interest; century-long complete bound newspaper files; segregated editorial pages, columns, film and auto sections, comic strips. Subscriptions: 100 journals and other serials; 100 newspapers. Services: Interlibrary loans; copying; library open to public by appointment. Staff: Dean Dickensheet, Dir.; Shirley Dickensheet, Dir.; Anne Lecture, Dir.; Gale Paulson, Dir.; Barbara Tyger, Dir.

SAN FRANCISCO ART INSTITUTE
See: College of the San Francisco Art Institute

★12151★

SAN FRANCISCO CHRONICLE - LIBRARY (Publ)

5th & Mission Sts.
San Francisco, CA 94103

Phone: (415) 777-1111
Suzanne Caster, Hd.Libn.

Founded: 1879. Staff: Prof 6; Other 8. Subjects: Newspaper reference topics. Holdings: 1500 books; 100 pamphlets; 7.5 million clippings; 3 million news photographs. Services: Copying; library open to public by telephone during limited hours. **Staff:** June Dellapa, Asst.Hd.Libn.

★12152★
SAN FRANCISCO - CITY ATTORNEY'S OFFICE - LIBRARY (Law)
206 City Hall   Phone: (415) 558-4993
San Francisco, CA 94102   Ruth Stevenson, Law Libn.
Staff: Prof 1; Other 3. **Subjects:** San Francisco municipal law and codes; city attorney opinions. **Holdings:** 25,000 volumes. **Subscriptions:** 75 journals and other serials. **Services:** Library not open to public. **Remarks:** Maintains a branch library at 214 Van Ness Ave., San Francisco, CA 94102.

★12153★
SAN FRANCISCO COLLEGE OF MORTUARY SCIENCE - LIBRARY (Sci-Tech)
1450 Post St.   Phone: (415) 567-0674
San Francisco, CA 94109   Dale W. Sly, Pres.
Subjects: Embalming, restorative art, anatomy, pathology, bacteriology, chemistry, funeral directing and management. **Special Collections:** Burial customs of foreign countries (16mm color films); death and dying (20 filmstrips). **Holdings:** 512 books and bound periodical volumes. **Subscriptions:** 12 journals and other serials. **Services:** Library open to public with permission.

★12154★
SAN FRANCISCO CONSERVATORY OF MUSIC - LIBRARY (Mus)
1201 Ortega St.   Phone: (415) 564-8086
San Francisco, CA 94122   Lucretia Wolfe, Libn.
Founded: 1967. **Staff:** Prof 1; Other 3. **Subjects:** Music. **Special Collections:** Guitar music; performance materials. **Holdings:** 17,000 books; 200 bound periodical volumes; 450 tapes; 450 slides; 4000 phonodiscs; 40 holographic scores and some manuscripts of 20th-century music; 450 clippings. **Subscriptions:** 57 journals and other serials. **Services:** Interlibrary loans; copying; library open to public for reference use only. **Publications:** Acquisitions list, semiannual. **Special Indexes:** Periodical file index.

★12155★
SAN FRANCISCO EXAMINER - LIBRARY (Publ)
110 Fifth St.   Phone: (415) 777-7845
San Francisco, CA 94103   Judy Gerritts Canter, Chf.Libn.
Founded: 1865. **Staff:** Prof 1; Other 9. **Subjects:** Newspaper reference topics, state and local history. **Special Collections:** San Francisco Examiner, 1865 to present (microfilm); historical photographs and clippings of San Francisco and California. **Holdings:** 5000 books and pamphlets; 12 million newspaper clippings on micro-jackets; negatives; photographs. **Subscriptions:** 24 journals and other serials; 10 newspapers. **Services:** Interlibrary loans; library not open to public. **Computerized Information Services:** NEXIS. Performs free searches.

SAN FRANCISCO FOUNDATION CENTER
See: Foundation Center - San Francisco Office

★12156★
SAN FRANCISCO GENERAL HOSPITAL MEDICAL CENTER - BARNETT-BRIGGS LIBRARY (Med)
1001 Potrero Ave.   Phone: (415) 821-8553
San Francisco, CA 94110   Miriam Hirsch, Med.Libn.
Founded: 1950. **Staff:** Prof 1; Other 6. **Subjects:** Medicine. **Holdings:** 12,921 books; 15,094 bound periodical volumes. **Subscriptions:** 397 journals and other serials. **Services:** Interlibrary loans; copying; library open to public. **Computerized Information Services:** NLM, BRS, DIALOG. Performs searches on cost recovery basis. **Networks/Consortia:** Member of Pacific Southwest Regional Medical Library Service; San Francisco Biomedical Library Network; CLASS.

★12157★
SAN FRANCISCO LAW LIBRARY (Law)
436 City Hall
400 Van Ness Ave.   Phone: (415) 558-4627
San Francisco, CA 94102-4672   John H. Hauff, Libn.
Founded: 1870. **Staff:** Prof 5; Other 8. **Subjects:** Law. **Holdings:** 271,689 volumes. **Subscriptions:** 436 journals and other serials. **Services:** Library open to public for reference use only. **Remarks:** Maintains branch library at Mills Tower. **Staff:** Coral Henning, Chf.Asst.Libn.; John M. Moore, Br.Libn.

★12158★
SAN FRANCISCO LIGHTHOUSE CENTER FOR THE BLIND - LIBRARY (Aud-Vis)
745 Buchanan St.   Phone: (415) 431-1481
San Francisco, CA 94102   Daniel Forer, Coord.
Founded: 1949. **Staff:** 1. **Subjects:** Fiction, nonfiction, current events.

Holdings: 468 braille titles (1863 volumes); large print books; cassette tapes. **Services:** Copying; library open to blind and visually impaired persons.

★12159★
SAN FRANCISCO MUNICIPAL RAILWAY - LIBRARY (Trans; Plan)
949 Presidio Ave., Rm. 204   Phone: (415) 673-6864
San Francisco, CA 94115   Dr. Marc Hofstadter, Libn.
Staff: Prof 1. **Subjects:** Bay Area transportation planning, public transit. **Holdings:** 2000 books. **Subscriptions:** 40 journals and other serials. **Services:** Interlibrary loans; library open to public by appointment. **Automated Operations:** Computerized cataloging. **Publications:** List of publications - available upon request.

★12160★
SAN FRANCISCO MUSEUM OF MODERN ART - LOUISE S. ACKERMAN FINE ARTS LIBRARY (Art)
McAllister at Van Ness   Phone: (415) 863-8800
San Francisco, CA 94102   Eugenie Candau, Libn.
Founded: 1935. **Staff:** Prof 1; Other 2. **Subjects:** Modern and contemporary visual arts, history of photography. **Special Collections:** Margery Mann Collection of the Literature of Photography. **Holdings:** 8000 books; 69 bound periodical volumes; 40,000 art exhibition catalogs; 68 VF drawers of biographical clippings; 18 files of archives. **Subscriptions:** 47 journals and other serials. **Services:** Copying; library open to public for reference use only. **Networks/Consortia:** Member of Bay Area Reference Center (BARC).

★12161★
SAN FRANCISCO PSYCHOANALYTIC INSTITUTE - LIBRARY (Med)
2420 Sutter St.   Phone: (415) 563-4477
San Francisco, CA 94115   Anne L. Regner, Libn.
Founded: 1954. **Staff:** Prof 1; Other 1. **Subjects:** Psychoanalysis. **Special Collections:** Siegfried Bernfield Collection (300 books); Bernice S. Engle Memorial Collection (80 books). **Holdings:** 3800 books; 1500 bound periodical volumes; 2 VF drawers of pamphlets; 3000 reprints and manuscripts; 5 boxes of audiotapes; 100 audio cassette tapes; 3 VF drawers of archives. **Subscriptions:** 90 journals and other serials. **Services:** Interlibrary loans; copying; SDI; literature searches; library open to institute members, candidates, and to the public upon payment of membership fee. **Networks/Consortia:** Member of Pacific Southwest Regional Medical Library Service (PSRMLS); San Francisco Biomedical Library Network; Northern California and Nevada Medical Library Group. **Publications:** Bulletin of the San Francisco Psychoanalytic Institute and Society, monthly; DIALOGUE: A Journal of Psychoanalytic Perspectives, semiannual. Both publications contain library news, activities and lists of recent acquisitions. Journal holdings list - available on request.

★12162★
SAN FRANCISCO PUBLIC LIBRARY - BUSINESS LIBRARY (Bus-Fin)
530 Kearny St.   Phone: (415) 558-3946
San Francisco, CA 94108   Gilbert McNamee, Prin.Libn.
Staff: Prof 4; Other 3. **Subjects:** Accounting, advertising, economics, finance, banking, business planning, insurance, management, investments, retail, real estate. **Special Collections:** Trade directories; corporation annual reports (1500); bank publications (125); historical insurance collection. **Holdings:** 13,000 books; 434 bound periodical volumes; 200 local, state, and federal publications; 40 business newspapers; 173 business services; 800 VF drawers; newspaper clipping file. **Services:** Copying.

★12163★
SAN FRANCISCO PUBLIC LIBRARY - SAN FRANCISCO ROOM AND ARCHIVES (Hist)
Civic Ctr.   Phone: (415) 558-3949
San Francisco, CA 94102   Gladys Hansen, City Archv.
Founded: 1963. **Staff:** Prof 1; Other 1. **Subjects:** History of San Francisco and California. **Special Collections:** Rotating exhibits. **Holdings:** 2.5 million morgue clips from the San Francisco Examiner, 1906 to present; News-Call-Bulletin morgue photographs, 1925-1965; 125,000 historical San Francisco and California photographs; 299 VF drawers of pamphlets; 6000 postcards; periodicals; newspapers. **Services:** Copying.

★12164★
SAN FRANCISCO PUBLIC LIBRARY - SPECIAL COLLECTIONS DEPARTMENT (Rare Book)
Civic Ctr.   Phone: (415) 558-3940
San Francisco, CA 94102   Johanna Goldschmid, Spec.Coll.Libn.
Founded: 1963. **Staff:** Prof 1; Other 1. **Special Collections:** Robert Grabhorn Collection on the history of printing and the development of the book; Max John Kuhl Collection of printing; Richard Harrison Collection of calligraphy and lettering; James D. Phelan Collection of California authors;

Schmulowitz Collection of wit and humor; George M. Fox Collection of early children's books; Scowrers Sherlockiana Collection; Robert Frost Collection; Panama Canal Collection. **Holdings:** 25,000 books; 100 VF drawers of pamphlets and other ephemera. **Subscriptions:** 40 journals and other serials. **Services:** Copying; collections open to serious researchers and advanced students.

★12165★
SAN FRANCISCO STATE UNIVERSITY - FRANK V. DE BELLIS COLLECTION
    (Area-Ethnic)
1630 Holloway Ave.   Phone: (415) 469-1649
San Francisco, CA 94132   Serena De Bellis, Cur.
Founded: 1963. **Staff:** Prof 1; Other 4. **Subjects:** Italian and Roman civilization, including history, literature, fine arts, music. **Holdings:** 12,500 books; 10,000 music scores; 700 manuscripts; 25,000 sound recordings; 500 reels of microfilm; 450 prints; 356 artifacts; 400 coins. **Subscriptions:** 53 journals. **Services:** Interlibrary loans; copying; collection open to public. **Publications:** The Frank V. de Bellis Collection (revised edition, 1967). **Special Catalogs:** Published catalog of artifacts: Etruscan, Greek and Roman Artifacts in the Frank V. de Bellis Collection (revised edition, 1975).

★12166★
SAN FRANCISCO STATE UNIVERSITY - J. PAUL LEONARD LIBRARY -
    SPECIAL COLLECTIONS/ARCHIVES (Hist; Aud-Vis)
1630 Holloway Ave.   Phone: (415) 469-1856
San Francisco, CA 94132   Helene Whitson, Coord.
Staff: Prof 1; Other 1. **Subjects:** Bay Area news and events, 1967-1980; student protests; gay rights and activities; interviews with local political, social, and cultural figures. **Holdings:** 9000 reels of film; 1 million feet of film in KQED Film Archives. **Services:** Collections open to public for reference use only with permission.

SAN FRANCISCO THEOLOGICAL SEMINARY
See: Graduate Theological Union

★12167★
SAN FRANCISCO THEOSOPHICAL SOCIETY - LIBRARY (Rel-Theol)
809 Mason St.   Phone: (415) 771-8777
San Francisco, CA 94108   Richard Power, Libn.
Founded: 1892. **Staff:** 2. **Subjects:** Theosophy, religion, metaphysics, psychic research, anthropology, healing. **Special Collections:** Popular American metaphysics, circa 1880-1950. **Holdings:** 5000 books; 200 bound periodical volumes; 6 file drawers of pamphlets and clippings; 3 cases of manuscripts. **Services:** Library open to public. **Publications:** Lodge Newsletter, monthly - mailed on request.

★12168★
SAN FRANCISCO UNIFIED SCHOOL DISTRICT - TEACHERS PROFESSIONAL
    LIBRARY (Educ)
135 Van Ness Ave.   Phone: (415) 565-9272
San Francisco, CA 94102   Helen M. Boutin, Lib.Techn.
Staff: 1. **Subjects:** Educational philosophy and psychology, guidance and personnel, human relations, social work, curriculum development, educational administration, educational practices. **Special Collections:** Californiana and San Franciscana (archives files of the school district). **Holdings:** 38,375 books; 2300 bound periodical volumes; 388 reels of microfilm of periodicals; 2251 microfiche; 9 drawers of pamphlets; 135 feet of documents and curriculum guides. **Subscriptions:** 104 journals and other serials. **Services:** Interlibrary loans; copying; library open to public for reference use only. **Publications:** Bibliographies of special collections and recent acquisitions (mimeographed) - distributed to district personnel only.

★12169★
SAN GORGONIO PASS MEMORIAL HOSPITAL - MEDICAL LIBRARY (Med)
600 N. Highland Springs Ave.   Phone: (714) 845-1121
Banning, CA 92220   Elaine Burns, Libn.
Subjects: Medicine. **Holdings:** 783 books and bound periodical volumes; 18 boxes of clippings and pamphlets. **Services:** Library open to professional staff only.

★12170★
SAN JACINTO MUSEUM OF HISTORY ASSOCIATION - LIBRARY (Hist)
3800 Park Rd.   Phone: (409) 479-2421
La Porte, TX 77571   Winston Atkins, Libn.
Founded: 1939. **Staff:** Prof 1. **Subjects:** Texas and regional history. **Holdings:** 10,000 books; 200 linear feet of other cataloged items; maps; pictures; relics; newspapers. **Services:** Copying; library open to qualified scholars by appointment. **Publications:** The Advance, quarterly; occasional monographs.

★12171★
SAN JOAQUIN COLLEGE OF LAW - LIBRARY (Law)†
3385 E. Shields Ave.   Phone: (209) 225-4953
Fresno, CA 93726   Mary Ann Parker, Law Libn.
Staff: Prof 1; Other 2. **Subjects:** Law. **Holdings:** 11,700 books; 2000 bound periodical volumes; 200 audiotapes. **Subscriptions:** 26 journals and other serials. **Services:** Library not open to public.

★12172★
SAN JOAQUIN COUNTY HISTORICAL MUSEUM (Hist)
Micke Grove Pk.
Box 21   Phone: (209) 368-9154
Lodi, CA 95240   Michael W. Bennett, Musm.Dir.
Founded: 1966. **Staff:** 6. **Subjects:** Local and agricultural history. **Holdings:** 2000 books; 1000 bound periodical volumes; clippings; depository for county archives; county maps, plats, survey reports, records; bound newspapers. **Subscriptions:** 11 journals and other serials. **Services:** Museum open to public for reference use only, under supervision.

★12173★
SAN JOAQUIN COUNTY LAW LIBRARY (Law)
County Court House, Rm. 300   Phone: (209) 944-2207
Stockton, CA 95202   Gertrudes J. Ladion, Law Libn.
Founded: 1894. **Staff:** 1. **Subjects:** Law. **Holdings:** 25,560 volumes. **Subscriptions:** 31 journals and other serials. **Services:** Copying; library open to public.

★12174★
SAN JOAQUIN LOCAL HEALTH DISTRICT - LIBRARY (Med)
1601 E. Hazelton Ave.
Box 2009   Phone: (209) 466-6781
Stockton, CA 95201   Doris Beckwith, Libn.
Staff: Prof 1. **Subjects:** Nursing, environmental health, public health. **Holdings:** 372 books; 48 bound periodical volumes; 200 pamphlets; 190 boxes of reference files; Journals of Public Health, 1942 to present. **Subjects:** 80 journals and other serials. **Services:** Interlibrary loans; copying; library open to public with restrictions. **Networks/Consortia:** Member of 49-99 Cooperative Library System.

★12175★
SAN JOSE BIBLE COLLEGE - MEMORIAL LIBRARY (Rel-Theol)
790 S. 12th St.
Box 1090   Phone: (408) 295-1307
San Jose, CA 95108-1090   Minnie Mick, Libn.
Staff: Prof 1; Other 3. **Subjects:** Bible, church history, psychology, Greek, Hebrew. **Special Collections:** History of Christian Church; church music. **Holdings:** 28,259 books; 129 bound periodical volumes; 4529 other cataloged items; 641 unbound periodicals; 320 microfiche; 51 missionary papers. **Subscriptions:** 134 journals and other serials. **Services:** Interlibrary loans; copying; library open to public.

★12176★
SAN JOSE HEALTH CENTER - HEALTH SCIENCE LIBRARY (Med)*
675 E. Santa Clara St.   Phone: (408) 998-3212
San Jose, CA 95114   Susan L. Russell, Mgr.
Founded: 1934. **Staff:** Prof 1; Other 2. **Subjects:** Medicine, nursing, hospital administration. **Holdings:** 3000 books; 3100 bound periodical volumes; 12 VF drawers of pamphlets and clippings; 150 AV cassettes; 80 filmstrips; 19 films; 200 archival items. **Subscriptions:** 317 journals and other serials. **Services:** Interlibrary loans; library not open to public. **Computerized Information Services:** MEDLINE, DIALOG. **Networks/Consortia:** Member of Medical Library Consortium of Santa Clara Valley.

★12177★
SAN JOSE HISTORICAL MUSEUM - ARCHIVES (Hist)
635 Phelan Ave.   Phone: (408) 287-2290
San Jose, CA 95112   Mignon Gibson, Musm.Dir.
Founded: 1971. **Subjects:** California history; local history. **Special Collections:** New Almaden Mines Collection; pueblos and ranchos (original papers). **Holdings:** 200 cubic feet of books, ledgers, pamphlets; 374 linear feet of manuscripts and public records. **Services:** Copying (limited); archives open to public by appointment.

★12178★
SAN JOSE MEDICAL CLINIC - STAFF LIBRARY
45 S. 17th St.
San Jose, CA 95112
Founded: 1953. **Subjects:** Medicine and allied sciences. **Holdings:** 400 books; 900 bound periodical volumes. **Remarks:** Presently inactive.

★12179★
SAN JOSE MERCURY NEWS - LIBRARY (Publ)
750 Ridder Park Dr.　　　　　　　　Phone: (408) 920-5345
San Jose, CA 95190　　　　　　　　Richard Geiger, Lib.Mgr.
Staff: Prof 8; Other 1. **Subjects:** Newspaper reference topics, local history. **Holdings:** 1500 volumes; 2 million clippings; 250,000 photographs; 4000 reels of microfilm of newspapers. **Subscriptions:** 60 journals and other serials; 30 newspapers. **Services:** Interlibrary loans; library not open to public. **Computerized Information Services:** DIALOG, NEXIS, VU/TEXT.

★12180★
SAN JOSE MUSEUM OF ART - LIBRARY (Art)
110 S. Market St.　　　　　　　　Phone: (408) 294-2787
San Jose, CA 95113　　　　　　　　Martha Manson, Cur.
Founded: 1978. **Staff:** Prof 2. **Subjects:** Art. **Holdings:** 1025 books; 1050 exhibition catalogs; 3 VF drawers of information files; 500 art slides. **Services:** Library not open to public.

SAN JOSE PUBLIC LIBRARY - NATIONAL LIBRARY OF SPORTS
See: National Library of Sports

★12181★
SAN JOSE STATE UNIVERSITY - JOHN STEINBECK RESEARCH CENTER
(Hum)
Wahlquist Library
One Washington Square　　　　　　Phone: (408) 277-3377
San Jose, CA 95192-0028　　　　　Robert DeMott, Res.Ctr.Dir.
Staff: Prof 1; Other 1. **Subjects:** John Steinbeck. **Holdings:** 4000 cataloged items. **Services:** Interlibrary loans; copying; SDI; center open to public with restrictions. **Automated Operations:** Computerized cataloging, acquisitions, and circulation. **Computerized Information Services:** DIALOG, BRS, OCLC. Performs searches on partial cost recovery basis. **Special Catalogs:** Steinbeck Research Center catalog (card). **Staff:** Sandra Belanger .

★12182★
SAN JOSE STATE UNIVERSITY - WAHLQUIST LIBRARY - CHICANO LIBRARY RESOURCE CENTER (Area-Ethnic)
1 Washington Sq.　　　　　　　　Phone: (408) 277-3346
San Jose, CA 95192　　　　　　　　Jeff Paul,, Coord.
Staff: Prof 1; Other 2. **Subjects:** Chicano studies. **Special Collections:** Hispanic Link (newspaper articles and editorials on the role of the Hispanic in the United States); National Hispanic Feminist Conference Papers (1980); United Farm Workers Resources (pictures, songs, poems, accounts of Cesar Chavez, a history of the UFW, and announcements of boycotts, 1973-1975). **Holdings:** 1400 books; 100 unbound periodicals; 400 reels of microfilm; 300 clippings and pamphlets; 50 posters. **Subscriptions:** 15 journals and other serials. **Services:** Interlibrary loans; center open to public.

★12183★
SAN JUAN COUNTY ARCHAEOLOGICAL RESEARCH CENTER & LIBRARY
(Sci-Tech)
975 Hwy. 64　　　　　　　　　　Phone: (505) 632-2013
Farmington, NM 87401　　　　　　Ouida Steward, Libn.
Staff: Prof 1; Other 2. **Subjects:** Archeology, history, anthropology, botany. **Special Collections:** Slide/tape programs; historical records of San Juan Basin (3 VF drawers); Rock Art (1700 slides and photographs); archival records of excavation of Salmon Ruin Site (224 feet). **Holdings:** 640 books; 1870 reports, pamphlets, dissertations; 1 VF drawer of clippings; 1 VF drawer of photographs; 24 oral history tapes and transcriptions; 2 reels of microfilm; 3 VF drawers of botany specimens; 5 drawers of historic maps. **Subscriptions:** 38 journals and other serials. **Services:** Copying; library open to public for reference use only. **Publications:** Contributions to Anthropology Series, irregular. **Remarks:** Library is located at the upper level of the Research Center and is maintained by the San Juan County Museum Association.

★12184★
SAN JUAN COUNTY HISTORICAL SOCIETY - ARCHIVE (Hist)
1111 Reese St.　　　　　　　　Phone: (303) 387-5770
Silverton, CO 81433　　　　　　Allen Nossaman, Dir.
Staff: 1. **Subjects:** San Juan County and Colorado history. **Holdings:** 40 books; 500 photographs; 30 reels of microfilm; 75 oral history tapes; 50 cubic feet of maps, slides, correspondence, records. **Services:** Copying; archive open to public. **Publications:** Hillside Cemetery-Silverton - for sale; San Juan County Newspaper Index, 1879-1883. **Special Catalogs:** Oral history catalog.

★12185★
SAN LUIS OBISPO COUNTY LAW LIBRARY (Law)
Courthouse Annex, Rm. 236　　　　Phone: (805) 549-5855
San Luis Obispo, CA 93408　　　　Barbara S. Butler, Libn.
Founded: 1896. **Staff:** Prof 1; Other 1. **Subjects:** Law. **Holdings:** 18,348 volumes; 1000 pamphlets; 200 tapes; 2965 microforms. **Subscriptions:** 43 journals and other serials. **Services:** Interlibrary loans; copying; library open to public with restrictions. **Networks/Consortia:** Member of Total Interlibrary Exchange (TIE).

★12186★
SAN LUIS OBISPO COUNTY PLANNING DEPARTMENT - TECHNICAL INFORMATION LIBRARY (Plan)
County Government Center　　　　　Phone: (805) 549-5600
San Luis Obispo, CA 93408　　　　Paul C. Crawford, Plan.Dir.
Founded: 1969. **Subjects:** Conservation and natural resources, recreation, circulation, land data, social and economic analysis, public utilities and services, aesthetic and historical data, administration data, housing and building research. **Holdings:** 400 books; 1000 pamphlets and documents; 5000 maps. **Subscriptions:** 30 journals and other serials; 7 newspapers. **Services:** Interlibrary loans; library open to public for reference use only, on request. **Staff:** Vivian Lassanske, Libn.

★12187★
SAN MARTIN SOCIETY OF WASHINGTON, DC - INFORMATION CENTER
(Hist)
Box 33　　　　　　　　　　　　Phone: (703) 883-0950
McLean, VA 22101-0033　　　　　Dr. Christian Garcia-Godoy, Pres.
Subjects: General Jose de San Martin; the emancipation of Argentina, Chile, and Peru. **Holdings:** 1200 volumes; microfilms; dissertations; speeches; pamphlets; documents. **Services:** Copying; center open to the public by written request.

★12188★
SAN MATEO COUNTY DEPARTMENT OF HEALTH SERVICES - LIBRARY
(Soc Sci)
225 37th Ave.　　　　　　　　Phone: (415) 573-2520
San Mateo, CA 94403　　　　　　Mark Quinn Constantz, Med.Libn.
Founded: 1967. **Staff:** Prof 1. **Subjects:** Clinical medicine, emergency medicine, psychiatry, public health, mental health, rehabilitation. **Holdings:** 4000 books; 6000 bound periodical volumes. **Subscriptions:** 120 journals and other serials. **Services:** Interlibrary loans; copying; library open to public for reference use only. **Automated Operations:** Computerized cataloging. **Computerized Information Services:** DIALOG, BRS, Tymshare, Inc., MEDLARS; Health Services Bibliographic Source (internal database). **Networks/Consortia:** Member of Pacific Southwest Regional Medical Library Service (PSRMLS); Northern California Medical Library Group; CLASS; San Mateo County Hospital Library Consortia. **Publications:** San Mateo County Hospital Library Consortia Newsletter.

★12189★
SAN MATEO COUNTY EDUCATIONAL RESOURCES CENTER (Educ)
333 Main St.　　　　　　　　Phone: (415) 363-5470
Redwood City, CA 94063　　Dr. Curtis May, Adm., Media & Lib.Serv.
Founded: 1967. **Staff:** Prof 5; Other 36. **Subjects:** Education, microcomputers. **Holdings:** 22,000 books; 2000 textbooks; 350,000 microfiche. **Subscriptions:** 820 education journals. **Services:** Interlibrary loans; copying; center open to public. **Computerized Information Services:** DIALOG; computer retrieval of ERIC materials. **Networks/Consortia:** Member of South Bay Cooperative Library System (SBCLS). **Publications:** Newsnotes, 6/year. **Also Known As:** SMERC. **Staff:** Katherine Clay, Coord., Comp.Serv.; Jean Holbrook, Dir., Info.Ctr.; Ann Lathrop, Coord., Lib.Serv.; Karol Thomas, Coord., Lib.Serv.

★12190★
SAN MATEO COUNTY HISTORICAL ASSOCIATION - LIBRARY (Hist)
1700 W. Hillsdale Blvd.
College of San Mateo Campus　　　Phone: (415) 574-6441
San Mateo, CA 94402　　　　　　Marion C. Holmes, Archv.
Founded: 1935. **Staff:** Prof 1. **Subjects:** San Mateo County history. **Holdings:** 900 books; 718 pamphlets; 15,000 photographs; 326 manuscripts; 350 student monographs; 467 documents including assessment books, diaries, municipal and county records. **Services:** Copying; library open to public. **Publications:** La Peninsula, annual journal - to membership.

★12191★
SAN MATEO COUNTY LAW LIBRARY (Law)*
Hall of Justice & Records
Redwood City, CA 94063
Phone: (415) 363-4160
Robert D. Harrington, Dir.
Staff: 4. **Subjects:** Law. **Holdings:** 40,000 volumes. **Services:** Library open to public.

★12192★
SAN MATEO PUBLIC LIBRARY - BUSINESS SECTION (Bus-Fin)
55 W. Third Ave.
San Mateo, CA 94402
Phone: (415) 574-6955
Cheryl H. Silverblatt, Bus.Ref.Libn.
Staff: Prof 1; Other 2. **Subjects:** Investments, company information, management, small business, personal finance. **Holdings:** 8000 books. **Subscriptions:** 75 journals and other serials; 10 newspapers. **Services:** Interlibrary loans; library open to public. **Automated Operations:** Computerized cataloging and circulation. **Networks/Consortia:** Member of Peninsula Library System. **Special Catalogs:** Business Collection Bibliography (book).

★12193★
SAN PEDRO PENINSULA HOSPITAL - MEDICAL LIBRARY (Med)
1300 W. 7th St.
San Pedro, CA 90732
Phone: (213) 832-3311
James H. Harlan, Libn.
Founded: 1940. **Staff:** Prof 1. **Subjects:** Clinical medicine, nursing. **Holdings:** 2500 books and bound periodical volumes; 170 Audio-Digest tapes; 200 videotapes. **Subscriptions:** 191 journals and other serials. **Services:** Interlibrary loans; library open to public by special permission. **Computerized Information Services:** MEDLINE, DIALOG.

★12194★
SAN RAFAEL INDEPENDENT JOURNAL - NEWSPAPER LIBRARY (Publ)
7100 Alameda del Prado
Novato, CA 94947
Phone: (415) 883-8600
Virginia McKeever, Libn.
Founded: 1957. **Staff:** 3. **Subjects:** Newspaper reference topics. **Holdings:** Bound volumes of back issues; news clips and cut files of Independent Journal; filmed newspapers back to 1861; photographs and history files of Marin County. **Subscriptions:** 10 journals and other serials; 15 newspapers. **Services:** Copying; library open to public for reference use only.

SANBORN HOUSE ENGLISH LIBRARY
See: Dartmouth College

SANDBURG (Carl) HOME NATL. HISTORIC SITE
See: U.S. Natl. Park Service - Carl Sandburg Home Natl. Historic Site

★12195★
SANDERS ASSOCIATES, INC. - LIBRARY SERVICES (Sci-Tech; Mil)
95 Canal St., NCA 1-1342
Nashua, NH 03061-2004
Phone: (603) 885-4143
Art Berlin, Mgr., Lib.Serv.
Founded: 1955. **Staff:** Prof 5; Other 9. **Subjects:** Defense electronics, computer graphics. **Holdings:** 10,000 books; 2000 bound periodical volumes; 20,000 microfiche. **Subscriptions:** 800 journals and other serials; 10 newspapers. **Services:** Interlibrary loans; library open to industrial community by appointment only. **Computerized Information Services:** DIALOG, SDC, DOE/RECON, DTIC. **Staff:** Sue Wolfman, Supv.; Alice Hansen, Supv.

★12196★
SANDERS & THOMAS, INC. - LIBRARY (Sci-Tech)
11 Robinson St.
Pottstown, PA 19464
Phone: (215) 326-4600
Carol S. Leh, Tech.Libn.
Founded: 1962. **Staff:** Prof 1. **Subjects:** Engineering, architecture, planning. **Special Collections:** Solid Waste/Energy Collection (705 titles). **Holdings:** 802 books; catalogs for 2150 companies; 4 information file boxes; 2 films; 495 specifications; 148 transportation reports. **Subscriptions:** 87 journals and other serials. **Services:** Library not open to public.

SANDHAUS (Leonard M.) MEMORIAL LIBRARY
See: Temple Israel - Leonard M. Sandhaus Memorial Library

★12197★
SANDIA NATIONAL LABORATORIES - TECHNICAL LIBRARY (Sci-Tech)†
Box 969
Livermore, CA 94550
Phone: (415) 422-2525
M.A. Pound, Supv.
Founded: 1957. **Staff:** Prof 3; Other 6. **Subjects:** Electronics, electrical engineering, mechanical engineering, engineering materials, physics, chemistry. **Holdings:** 10,000 books; 6000 bound periodical volumes; 900 reels of microfilm of periodicals; 50,000 technical reports. **Subscriptions:** 250 journals and other serials. **Services:** Interlibrary loans; library not open to public. **Remarks:** The Sandia National Laboratories operate under contract to

the U.S. Department of Energy. **Staff:** Susan Coniglio, Ref.Libn.; Matthew J. Connors, Sys.Anl.; Michael Schalit, Ref.Libn.

★12198★
SANDIA NATIONAL LABORATORIES - TECHNICAL LIBRARY (Sci-Tech; Energy)
Dept. 3140
Albuquerque, NM 87185
Phone: (505) 844-2869
Danielle K. Brown, Mgr.
Founded: 1948. **Staff:** Prof 22; Other 33. **Subjects:** Nuclear weapons, nuclear waste management, nuclear safety and security, electronics, explosives, materials, aerodynamics, solid state physics, ordnance, energy research. **Special Collections:** Videotapes on Sandia's weekly colloquia, 1976 to present. **Holdings:** 41,910 volumes; 17,815 bound periodical volumes; 63,000 technical reports (hard copy); 726,000 technical reports on microfiche; 57,000 internal reports. **Subscriptions:** 1532 journals and other serials; 5 newspapers. **Services:** Interlibrary loans; library not open to public. **Automated Operations:** Computerized cataloging, acquisitions, serials and circulation. **Computerized Information Services:** DIALOG, SDC, DOE/RECON, DTIC, NEXIS, NASA/RECON, RLIN, Pergamon InfoLine Ltd., Dortmund/Leuven Library System; internal database. **Publications:** SCAN (Sandia Laboratories Accession News), monthly; Library News Bulletin, weekly. **Special Indexes:** Annual index to computer codes. **Remarks:** The Sandia National Laboratories operate under contract to the U.S. Department of Energy. **Staff:** Sally Landenberger, Supv., Tech.Proc.; Clara Gearhart, Supv., Tech.Proc.; George R. Dalphin, Ref.Supv.; Dennis Rowley, Sys.Supv.; Nancy Pruett, Subject Spec.; Joyce Van Berkel, Subject Spec.; Gloria Zamora, Subject Spec.; Marge Meyer, Subject Spec.; Sue Sozanski, Subject Spec.; Walter R. Roose, Subject Spec.; Gladys E. Rowe, Subject Spec.; Willie M. Servis, Subject Spec.; Jacqueline Stack, Subject Spec.; Patricia Newman, Transl.; Deborah Reinarts, Info.Sys.Anl.; Paul Kirby, Info.Sys.Anl.; Martin L. Dieter, Info.Sys.Anl.; Joe Maloney, Info.Sys.Anl.; Ken Osburn, Info.Sys.Anl.; Chris Morgan, Info.Sys.Anl.; Linda Erickson, Plan.Libn.

★12199★
SANDOZ COLORS & CHEMICALS - INFORMATION CENTER
Route 10
East Hanover, NJ 07936
Defunct

★12200★
SANDOZ COLORS & CHEMICALS - LIBRARY (Sci-Tech)
4000 Monroe Rd.
Charlotte, NC 28205
Phone: (704) 372-0210
Carol D. Zwingli, Libn.
Founded: 1982. **Staff:** 1. **Subjects:** Chemistry, textiles, materials and polymer sciences, economics, business. **Special Collections:** Dyestuff shade cards. **Holdings:** 1500 books; 110 bound periodical volumes; trade literature; internal reports. **Subscriptions:** 67 journals and other serials. **Services:** Interlibrary loans; library not open to public. **Networks/Consortia:** Member of Metrolina Library Association.

★12201★
SANDOZ, INC. - LIBRARY (Med)
Route 10
East Hanover, NJ 07936
Phone: (201) 386-8306
Harriet W. Smith, Mgr., Lib.
Staff: Prof 1; Other 5. **Subjects:** Medicine, chemistry, pharmacology, toxicology, biochemistry. **Holdings:** 2000 books; 4500 bound periodical volumes; 16 drawers of microfilm; 2 drawers of annual reports; 2 drawers of company publications. **Subscriptions:** 446 journals and other serials; 6 newspapers. **Services:** Interlibrary loans; copying; library open to public by appointment. **Publications:** Acquisition list, monthly; Library Journal, updated semiannual - both for internal distribution only.

★12202★
SANDOZ PHARMACEUTICALS - INFORMATION SERVICES (Med)
Route 10
East Hanover, NJ 07936
Phone: (201) 386-8105
Joyce G. Koelle, Mgr.
Founded: 1939. **Staff:** Prof 8; Other 6. **Subjects:** Drug literature - corporation products, biomedical literature, chemistry, business. **Holdings:** Figures not available. **Computerized Information Services:** DIALOG, SDC, NLM; Sandoz Product Information System (internal database). **Publications:** Current Awareness Tools for Science - for internal distribution only.

★12203★
SANDUSKY COUNTY LAW LIBRARY (Law)
Courthouse, 100 N. Park Ave.
Fremont, OH 43420
Phone: (419) 332-6411
Staff: Prof 1. **Subjects:** Law. **Special Collections:** Historical law books (particularly early Ohio legal history). **Holdings:** 11,000 books; 1100 bound periodical volumes; 600 other items. **Subscriptions:** 200 journals and other

serials. **Services:** Library open to public for reference use only, on request. **Staff:** Ann Rooks, Asst. Law Libn.

★12204★
SANDY BAY HISTORICAL SOCIETY AND MUSEUM - LIBRARY (Hist)
40 King St.
Rockport, MA 01966   Dr. William D. Hoyt, Cur.
Founded: 1925. **Staff:** Prof 1. **Subjects:** History of Rockport (Sandy Bay), Cape Ann, Essex County; Rockport families. **Holdings:** 250 books; 7500 manuscripts. **Services:** Library open to qualified researchers.

★12205★
SANDY CORPORATION - LIBRARY (Bus-Fin)
1500 W. Big Beaver Rd.   Phone: (313) 569-4000
Troy, MI 48084   Judith Wilson, Libn.
Founded: 1971. **Staff:** Prof 1; Other 1. **Subjects:** Consulting, training, communication. **Holdings:** 2000 books; 2000 pamphlets; 32 VF drawers of automotive product information; 36 VF drawers of business and management literature; 3000 square feet of periodicals, videodiscs, cartridges, slides, filmstrips, motion pictures, scripts. **Subscriptions:** 150 journals and other serials. **Services:** Library not open to public. **Publications:** Library Bulletin, biweekly; Acquisitions Bulletin, 5/year - both for internal distribution only. **Formerly:** Its Research & Retrieval Center, located in Southfield, MI. **Staff:** George Newhall, Film Libn.

SANDY HOOK LABORATORY
See: U.S. Natl. Marine Fisheries Service

★12206★
SANFORD MUSEUM & PLANETARIUM - LIBRARY (Sci-Tech)
117 E. Willow St.   Phone: (712) 225-3922
Cherokee, IA 51012   J. Terry Walker, Dir.
Founded: 1951. **Staff:** 2. **Subjects:** Archeology, astronomy, geology, history, paleontology, museology. **Holdings:** 5000 volumes. **Services:** Interlibrary loans; library open to public.

★12207★
SANGAMO WESTON GROUP - EMR PHOTOELECTRIC DIVISION - INFORMATION CENTER (Sci-Tech)
Box 44   Phone: (609) 799-1000
Princeton, NJ 08542   Joyce Jordan, Tech.Libn.
Founded: 1954. **Staff:** Prof 1; Other 1. **Subjects:** Photomultiplier tubes, thin films, optical physics, electro-optics, vacuum technology. **Holdings:** 1000 books; 1500 bound periodical volumes; 15 VF drawers of company technical reports; 2 VF drawers of patents. **Subscriptions:** 45 journals and other serials. **Services:** Interlibrary loans; center not open to public. **Computerized Information Services:** DIALOG; internal database. **Publications:** Monthly Library Acquisitions Bulletin. **Remarks:** Company is a division of Schlumberger, Ltd.

★12208★
SANGAMON STATE UNIVERSITY - EAST CENTRAL NETWORK - LIBRARY (Educ)
E22   Phone: (217) 786-6375
Springfield, IL 62708   Susie Shackleton, Libn.
Staff: Prof 4; Other 6. **Subjects:** Education - vocational, career, adult. **Holdings:** 27,340 books; 600 16mm films; 825 AV items; 8 VF drawers of publishers files. **Subscriptions:** 100 journals and other serials. **Services:** Interlibrary loans; copying; library open to public. **Computerized Information Services:** BRS; Task Listing File (internal database). Performs free searches. Contact Person: Jeff Lake. **Networks/Consortia:** East Central Network for Curriculum Coordination (ECNCC). **Publications:** Center Critiques, semiannual; Monthly Memo; occasional papers; subject bibliographies. **Remarks:** The network is funded by the U.S. Dept. of Education. **Staff:** Rebecca Douglass, Dir.; Ruth Patton, Coord.; Jeff Lake, Microcomputer Cons.

★12209★
SANGAMON STATE UNIVERSITY - ORAL HISTORY OFFICE - LIBRARY (Hist)
Brookens Library, Rm. 377   Phone: (217) 786-6521
Springfield, IL 62708   Cullom Davis, Dir.
Founded: 1972. **Staff:** Prof 2; Other 5. **Subjects:** History - 20th century American, Illinois, ethnic and minority, coal mining, labor, agricultural; state and local politics. **Holdings:** 750 oral history memoirs (2000 hours of taped interviews and 45,000 pages of transcript). **Services:** Interlibrary loans; copying; library open to public for reference use only. **Publications:** History with a Tape Recorder: an Oral History Handbook; Oral History: From Tape to Type. **Special Catalogs:** Subject descriptions and inventories for Coal Mining and Union Activities, The Jewish Experience, Agricultural History, Women's History, and Sangamon County History. **Also Known As:** Illinois Oral History

Clearinghouse.

★12210★
SANGER (Margaret) CENTER-PLANNED PARENTHOOD NEW YORK CITY - ABRAHAM STONE LIBRARY (Soc Sci)
380 Second Ave.   Phone: (212) 677-6474
New York, NY 10010   Jeanne Swinton, Libn.
Subjects: Abortion, adolescent sexuality, infertility, sex, family living, demography, population, sexuality of the handicapped. **Holdings:** 6000 books; 3000 bound periodical volumes. **Subscriptions:** 85 journals and other serials. **Services:** Interlibrary loans; copying; library open by appointment to graduate students and agencies.

★12211★
SANTA BARBARA BOTANIC GARDEN - LIBRARY (Sci-Tech)
1212 Mission Canyon Rd.   Phone: (805) 682-4726
Santa Barbara, CA 93105   Nancy Hawver, Libn.
Founded: 1942. **Staff:** Prof 1; Other 2. **Subjects:** Botany; flora of Western North America and Mediterranean climates; California horticulture; California off-shore islands; cactus and succulents. **Holdings:** 6000 books; 600 bound periodical volumes; 1200 reprints; 1000 nursery and seed catalogs; 42 boxes of pamphlets and reports; maps (indexed); 1 file cabinet of reports and newsletters from other gardens. **Subscriptions:** 75 journals and other serials. **Services:** Copying; library open to public with permission. **Networks/Consortia:** Member of Total Interlibrary Exchange (TIE). **Publications:** Recent acquisitions, quarterly.

★12212★
SANTA BARBARA COUNTY GENEALOGICAL SOCIETY - LIBRARY (Hist)
Box 1174
Goleta, CA 93116   Ruth B. Scollin, Libn.
Founded: 1974. **Staff:** Prof 1; Other 8. **Subjects:** Genealogy. **Holdings:** 650 books; 12 boxes of Earl Hazard Family History Papers; family histories; ancestral charts. **Subscriptions:** 110 journals and other serials. **Services:** Library open to members. **Publications:** Ancestors West, quarterly - to members, by subscription or exchange.

★12213★
SANTA BARBARA COUNTY LAW LIBRARY (Law)
Court House   Phone: (805) 966-1611
Santa Barbara, CA 93101   Kathy Jordan, Law Libn.
Founded: 1891. **Staff:** Prof 1; Other 3. **Subjects:** Law. **Holdings:** 40,211 volumes; 3247 microfiche; 495 cassettes. **Services:** Copying; library open to public. **Networks/Consortia:** Member of Total Interlibrary Exchange (TIE). **Remarks:** Figures include holdings of a branch library located in Santa Maria, CA.

★12214★
SANTA BARBARA HISTORICAL SOCIETY - GLEDHILL LIBRARY (Hist)
136 E. De La Guerra St.
Box 578   Phone: (805) 966-1601
Santa Barbara, CA 93102   Michael Redmon, Hd.Libn.
Founded: 1967. **Staff:** Prof 1; Other 2. **Subjects:** Local history and genealogy. **Holdings:** 5000 books; 15,000 photographs. **Subscriptions:** 20 journals and other serials. **Services:** Copying; library open to public.

★12215★
SANTA BARBARA MISSION ARCHIVE-LIBRARY (Hist; Rel-Theol)
Old Mission, Upper Laguna St.   Phone: (805) 682-4713
Santa Barbara, CA 93105   Rev. Francis F. Guest, O.F.M., Archv.-Hist.
Founded: 1786. **Staff:** Prof 1. **Subjects:** Early missions and missionaries in the Santa Barbara area; California and Mexicana, Spain and Hispanic America. **Special Collections:** De la Guerra Collection (12,000 pages of documents on California); Wilson Collection (rare books; globes; works of art); Alexander Taylor Collection (copies of 2300 documents from the Archdiocesan Archives in San Francisco); photographs of the late mission period in California, Spain and Mexico (4000); original mission music (1000 brochures); original mission documents (3500). **Holdings:** 14,000 books; 100 scrapbooks, newspaper clippings; 1000 pamphlets. **Services:** Library open to public. **Publications:** Newsletter, irregular - to Friends of Archive-Library; list of publications available upon request. **Special Catalogs:** Catalog of documents and old books. **Remarks:** Maintained by the Franciscan Fathers of California. **Staff:** Rev. Virgilio Biasiol, O.F.M., Dir.

★12216★
SANTA BARBARA MUSEUM OF ART - MUSEUM LIBRARY AND ARCHIVES (Art)
1130 State St.   Phone: (805) 963-4364
Santa Barbara, CA 93101   Ron Crozier, Libn.
Founded: 1941. **Staff:** Prof 1; Other 2. **Subjects:** Art, artists. **Special**

Collections: Exhibition catalogs (20,000); Single Artist File. **Holdings:** 3000 books; 20,000 exhibition catalogs; 500 linear feet of archives; pamphlet library consisting of museum calendars and artists' exhibition notices; museum and gallery bulletins; annual reports; newspaper clipping file; sale catalogs; slides. **Subscriptions:** 45 journals and other serials. **Services:** Interlibrary loans; copying; library open to public with restrictions.

★12217★
SANTA BARBARA MUSEUM OF NATURAL HISTORY - LIBRARY (Sci-Tech)
2559 Puesta del Sol Rd.   Phone: (805) 682-4711
Santa Barbara, CA 93105   Clifton F. Smith, Libn.
Founded: 1929. **Staff:** Prof 2. **Subjects:** Natural history - anthropology, botany, geology, zoology, astronomy. **Special Collections:** Chumash Indians; Channel Islands Archive; Pacific Voyages Collection. **Holdings:** 13,000 volumes; 100 feet of reprints. **Subscriptions:** 200 journals and other serials. **Services:** Interlibrary loans (limited); copying; library open to public for reference use only. **Publications:** Occasional papers on natural history - by gift and exchange. **Staff:** Shirley R. Morrison, Assoc.Libn.

★12218★
SANTA BARBARA NEWS PRESS - LIBRARY (Publ)
De la Guerra Plaza
Drawer N-N   Phone: (805) 966-3911
Santa Barbara, CA 93102   Carol J. Hardy, Libn.
Staff: Prof 1; Other 3. **Subjects:** Newspaper reference topics. **Holdings:** 1490 books; microfilm; pictures; negatives; 512 linear feet of clippings; 80 pamphlets; 100 maps. **Services:** Copying; library open to public.

★12219★
SANTA CLARA COUNTY HEALTH DEPARTMENT - LIBRARY (Med)*
2220 Moorpark Ave.   Phone: (408) 279-6021
San Jose, CA 95128
Staff: 2. **Subjects:** Public health, psychology, nutrition, environmental health, medicine, alcoholism and drug abuse. **Holdings:** 7000 books; 1200 bound periodical volumes; pamphlets; reprints; hearing reports; clippings. **Subscriptions:** 300 journals and other serials. **Services:** Interlibrary loans; copying; library open to public for reference use only. **Networks/Consortia:** Member of Medical Library Consortium of Santa Clara Valley.

★12220★
SANTA CLARA COUNTY HEALTH SYSTEMS AGENCY - LIBRARY (Med; Soc Sci)
830 N. First St., 2nd Fl.   Phone: (408) 292-9572
San Jose, CA 95112   Scarlett Sato, Health Planner
Founded: 1976. **Staff:** Prof 1. **Subjects:** Health - planning, resources, facilities and services, manpower, law and regulation; special concerns of the aged and minorities; health care costs and financing; consumer and community concerns. **Holdings:** 2500 books; 2000 bound periodical volumes; 600 technical reports and articles; 50 VF drawers of newsletters and pamphlets. **Services:** Library open to public by appointment. **Networks/Consortia:** Member of South Bay Cooperative Library System (SBCLS); Pacific Southwest Regional Medical Library Service (PSRMLS).

★12221★
SANTA CLARA COUNTY LAW LIBRARY (Law)
191 N. First St.   Phone: (408) 299-3567
San Jose, CA 95113   Susan B. Kuklin, County Law Libn.
Founded: 1874. **Staff:** Prof 5; Other 6. **Subjects:** Law. **Holdings:** 55,000 bound volumes. **Subscriptions:** 315 journals and other serials. **Services:** Interlibrary loans; copying.

★12222★
SANTA CLARA COUNTY OFFICE OF EDUCATION - CENTRAL CALIFORNIA CENTER FOR EDUCATIONAL IMPROVEMENT - LIBRARY (Educ)
100 Skyport Dr., Mail Code 223   Phone: (408) 947-6808
San Jose, CA 95115   Dale Winslow Dana, Proj.Coord.
Staff: Prof 3; Other 1. **Subjects:** Education, teacher-developed curriculum, district-developed staff development programs, government funding. **Holdings:** 2250 documents; 1500 microfiche; 200 videotapes; AV materials. **Services:** Copying; library open to nonprofit educators. **Computerized Information Services:** CEI Inquiry System (internal database). Performs free searches, but fee charged for duplication. Contact Person: Donna Akin. **Publications:** Diagnosing A School's Readiness For Change; CEI Newsletter, bimonthly. **Special Catalogs:** Subject bibliographies for 38 subject areas. **Remarks:** One of three centers in California that collect, organize, catalog, and disseminate information about over 400 educational programs developed with state and federal funding. The library is a depository library. **Staff:** Judie Ehret, Rsrcs. Teacher; Donna Akin, Lib.Tech.Asst.

★12223★
SANTA CLARA COUNTY PLANNING AND DEVELOPMENT DEPARTMENT - LIBRARY (Plan)
County Government Center, East Wing
70 W. Hedding St.   Phone: (408) 299-2521
San Jose, CA 95110   W. Eric Carruthers, Prin. Planner
Founded: 1955. **Subjects:** Urban planning, housing, census, economics, transportation, energy, environmental assessment. **Special Collections:** General local plans; energy ordinances from local communities. **Holdings:** 9000 volumes; 250 environmental impact statements; 1300 maps; 9 file drawers of microfiche; 1 VF cabinet of pamphlets. **Subscriptions:** 90 journals and other serials; 5 newspapers. **Services:** Library open to public. **Networks/Consortia:** Member of Bay Area Reference Center (BARC); South Bay Cooperative Library System (SBCLS). **Publications:** Acquisitions Lists, irregular - for internal distribution only.

★12224★
SANTA CLARA VALLEY MEDICAL CENTER - MILTON J. CHATTON MEDICAL LIBRARY (Med)
751 S. Bascom Ave.   Phone: (408) 279-5650
San Jose, CA 95128   Barbara A. Wilson, Med.Libn.
Staff: Prof 2; Other 3. **Subjects:** Clinical medicine, nursing, pathology, physical medicine. **Special Collections:** Tumor Library; Proescher Pathology Library. **Holdings:** 4000 books; 25,000 bound periodical volumes. **Subscriptions:** 650 journals and other serials. **Services:** Interlibrary loans; copying; SDI; library open to students or professionals in the health care field. **Computerized Information Services:** MEDLINE, DIALOG. Performs searches on cost recovery basis. **Networks/Consortia:** Member of Medical Library Consortium of Santa Clara Valley.

★12225★
SANTA CRUZ COUNTY LAW LIBRARY (Law)
701 Ocean St., Courts Bldg.   Phone: (408) 425-2211
Santa Cruz, CA 95060   Patricia J. Pfremmer, Law Libn.
Founded: 1892. **Staff:** Prof 1; Other 1. **Subjects:** Law. **Holdings:** 19,000 books; 1000 bound periodical volumes. **Services:** Interlibrary loans; library open to public with restrictions. **Networks/Consortia:** Member of South Bay Cooperative Library System (SBCLS). **Remarks:** Maintains branch library of 3600 volumes in Watsonville, CA.

★12226★
SANTA CRUZ HISTORICAL SOCIETY, INC. - ARCHIVES (Hist)
Box 246   Phone: (408) 426-9035
Santa Cruz, CA 95061
Subjects: Santa Cruz history, 1844 to present. **Special Collections:** Letters from the Gold Rush era; history of the town band; photographs, 1870-1900. **Holdings:** 450 manuscripts and tapes. **Services:** Archives open to public with written permission.

★12227★
SANTA FE DRILLING COMPANY - LIBRARY (Sci-Tech; Energy)
505 S. Main St.   Phone: (714) 567-8818
Orange, CA 92668-0401   Helen Kramer, Libn.
Staff: Prof 1. **Subjects:** Offshore oil well drilling, ocean engineering, naval architecture, pipelines, petroleum industry, energy industry, hydraulic engineering. **Holdings:** 1600 books; 7 VF drawers of maps; 5 VF drawers of nautical charts; 6000 other cataloged items. **Subscriptions:** 150 journals and other serials. **Services:** Interlibrary loans; copying; library open to public with restrictions. **Computerized Information Services:** DIALOG, SDC, Dun & Bradstreet Corporation. **Publications:** Periodicals list; new books received, irregular.

SANTA FE INTERNATIONAL - C.F. BRAUN COMPANY
See: Braun (C.F.) Company

SANTA FE TRAIL CENTER LIBRARY
See: Fort Larned Historical Society, Inc.

★12228★
SANTA MONICA HOSPITAL MEDICAL CENTER - LIBRARY (Med)
1225 15th St.   Phone: (213) 451-1511
Santa Monica, CA 90404   Lenore F. Orfirer, Librarian
Staff: Prof 1. **Subjects:** Medicine. **Holdings:** 1400 books; 810 bound periodical volumes; 1600 unbound periodical volumes. **Subscriptions:** 185 journals and other serials. **Services:** Interlibrary loans; library not open to public. **Computerized Information Services:** MEDLARS.

★12229★
SANTA MONICA PUBLIC LIBRARY - CALIFORNIA SPECIAL COLLECTION (Hist)
1343 Sixth St.   Phone: (213) 451-5751
Santa Monica, CA 90401   Nancy O'Neill, Hd., Rd.Serv.
Staff: Prof 10. **Subjects:** Local history. **Special Collections:** Photographs of the Santa Monica Bay area, 1875 to present (1000). **Holdings:** 2600 books; 300 bound periodical volumes; Santa Monica Evening Outlook, 1875 to present (microfilm). **Subscriptions:** 10 journals and other serials. **Services:** Interlibrary loans (limited); copying; collection open to public with restrictions. **Networks/Consortia:** Member of Metropolitan Cooperative Library System (MCLS). **Special Indexes:** Selective indexing of Santa Monica Evening Outlook.

★12230★
SANTA ROSA MEDICAL CENTER - HEALTH SCIENCE LIBRARY (Med)
519 W. Houston St.
Sta. A, Box 7330   Phone: (512) 228-2284
San Antonio, TX 78285   Marjorie McFarland, Libn.
Founded: 1939. **Staff:** Prof 1. **Subjects:** Pediatrics, orthopedics, medicine, nursing, hospital administration. **Special Collections:** Terminal Care (30 books). **Holdings:** 1744 books; 4680 bound periodical volumes; 155 audio cassette tapes; 4 file drawers of pamphlets. **Subscriptions:** 191 journals and other serials. **Services:** Interlibrary loans (limited); copying; library open to public with restrictions. **Computerized Information Services:** NLM. **Networks/Consortia:** Member of Health Oriented Libraries of San Antonio (HOLSA).

★12231★
SANTA ROSA PRESS DEMOCRAT - EDITORIAL LIBRARY (Publ)
427 Mendocino Ave.
Box 569   Phone: (707) 546-2020
Santa Rosa, CA 95402   Elaine Cant, Libn.
Staff: Prof 1; Other 2. **Subjects:** Newspaper reference topics. **Holdings:** Figures not available for books and bound periodical volumes; 300 drawers of clippings; 47 drawers of photographs; 670 reels of microfilm of newspapers. **Services:** Copying; SDI; telephone and mail requests only. **Special Indexes:** Criminal card file index; biographical card file index.

★12232★
SANTA YNEZ VALLEY HISTORICAL SOCIETY - ELLEN GLEASON LIBRARY (Hist)
Box 181   Phone: (805) 688-7889
Santa Ynez, CA 93460   Phil Lockwood, Cur.
Subjects: History of Santa Ynez Valley, Santa Barbara County, and early California. **Special Collections:** Early land deeds. **Holdings:** 1000 books. **Services:** Copying; library open to public for reference use only.

SANTE ET BIEN-ETRE SOCIAL CANADA
See: Canada - Health and Welfare Canada

★12233★
SARATOGA COUNTY HISTORICAL SOCIETY - LIBRARY (Hist)
Brookside   Phone: (518) 885-4000
Ballston Spa, NY 12020
Subjects: Saratoga County, New York. **Holdings:** 755 volumes; manuscripts; photographs. **Services:** Library open to public by appointment. **Publications:** Grist Mill, quarterly; Brookside Columns, monthly. **Special Catalogs:** Catalogue of the Manuscript Collection (1979); Genealogical Guide to Saratoga County, NY (1980).

★12234★
SARATOGA GENERAL HOSPITAL - HEALTH SCIENCE LIBRARY (Med)
15000 Gratiot Ave.   Phone: (313) 245-1200
Detroit, MI 48205   Jean Brennan, Med.Libn.
Staff: Prof 1. **Subjects:** Medicine, nursing, hospital administration. **Holdings:** 500 books; 250 bound periodical volumes. **Subscriptions:** 106 journals and other serials. **Services:** Interlibrary loans; library not open to public. **Computerized Information Services:** BRS, MEDLINE.

SARATOGA NATL. HISTORICAL PARK
See: U.S. Natl. Park Service

SARGEANT MEMORIAL ROOM
See: Norfolk Public Library

★12235★
SARGENT & LUNDY ENGINEERS - COMPUTER SOFTWARE LIBRARY (Comp Sci)
55 E. Monroe   Phone: (312) 269-3658
Chicago, IL 60603   William J. Kakish, Chf.Libn.
Staff: Prof 1; Other 3. **Subjects:** Computer applications. **Holdings:** 220 books; 628 computer program manuals; 60 VF drawers of computer program documentation; microfiche. **Subscriptions:** 45 journals and other serials; 5 newspapers. **Services:** Copying; library open to public by appointment. **Automated Operations:** Computerized circulation. **Computerized Information Services:** DIALOG. **Networks/Consortia:** Member of ILLINET.

★12236★
SARGENT & LUNDY ENGINEERS - TECHNICAL LIBRARY (Sci-Tech)
55 E. Monroe St., Rm. 16P41   Phone: (312) 269-3524
Chicago, IL 60603   Helen P. Heisler, Libn.
Founded: 1969. **Staff:** Prof 1; Other 2. **Subjects:** Engineering - civil, mechanical, electrical; nuclear science; public utilities; air and water pollution. **Holdings:** 1000 books; 85 bound periodical volumes; 20 drawers of standards and specifications; 20 VF drawers. **Subscriptions:** 315 journals and other serials. **Services:** Interlibrary loans; copying; library open to public by appointment.

SARNOFF (David) LIBRARY
See: RCA Corporation - David Sarnoff Library

SARNOFF (David) RESEARCH CENTER
See: RCA Corporation - RCA Laboratories - David Sarnoff Research Center

★12237★
SASAKI ASSOCIATES, INC. - LIBRARY (Art)
64 Pleasant St.   Phone: (617) 926-3300
Watertown, MA 02172   Jeanne M. Clancy, Libn.
Staff: Prof 1. **Subjects:** Landscape architecture, architecture, planning, environment, engineering. **Holdings:** 1200 books; 55 bound periodical volumes; 300 office publications. **Subscriptions:** 55 journals and other serials. **Services:** Library not open to public.

★12238★
SASKATCHEWAN ALCOHOLISM COMMISSION - LIBRARY (Soc Sci)
3475 Albert St.   Phone: (306) 565-4656
Regina, SK, Canada S4S 6X6   Karen P. King, Libn.
Staff: Prof 1. **Subjects:** Alcohol and alcoholism, drugs and other dependencies, health care. **Holdings:** 1300 books; 280 bound periodical volumes; 100 archival items; reports; pamphlets; government publications. **Subscriptions:** 60 journals and other serials. **Services:** Interlibrary loans; copying; library open to public. **Computerized Information Services:** BRS, DIALOG. **Networks/Consortia:** Member of Librarians and Information Specialists in Addictions (LISA).

★12239★
SASKATCHEWAN ARCHIVES BOARD (Hist)
University of Regina   Phone: (306) 565-4068
Regina, SK, Canada S4S 0A2   Ian E. Wilson, Prov.Archv.
Founded: 1945. **Staff:** Prof 10; Other 20. **Subjects:** Saskatchewan history. **Holdings:** 600 books; 2000 bound periodical volumes; 25,000 feet of archives; 240,000 historical photographs; 7000 reels of microfilm; 8000 hours of sound recordings. **Services:** Copying; archives open to public. **Publications:** Saskatchewan History, 3/year; Index to Saskatchewan History (volumes 1-30); Saskatchewan Executive and Legislative Directory, 1905-1970, and supplement 1964-1977; biennial reports. **Remarks:** Maintains a branch at the Murray Memorial Bldg., University of Saskatchewan, Saskatoon, SK, S7N 0W0. **Staff:** D.H. Bocking, Assoc.Prov.Archv.; Mr. E.C. Morgan, Staff Archv.; Mr. T.D. Powell, Dir., Rec. & Tech.Serv.; Mr. L.W. Rodwell, Staff Archv.; Mrs. R. Wilson, Staff Archv.; Mr. D. Hande, Staff Archv.; Mr. K.M. Gebhard, Hd., Sound Archv.; Mr. D. Herperger, Staff Archv.; Mrs. K. Szalasznyj, Staff Archv.; Margaret Hutchison, Staff Archv.; Don Richan, Staff Archv.

★12240★
SASKATCHEWAN ARTS BOARD - LIBRARY (Art)
2550 Broad St.   Phone: (306) 565-4056
Regina, SK, Canada S4P 3V7
Staff: 10. **Subjects:** Literary, visual and performing arts. **Holdings:** 5000 books; 1000 bound periodical volumes. **Subscriptions:** 12 journals and other serials; 10 newspapers. **Publications:** Saskatchewan Arts newsletter, 3/year.

★12241★

SASKATCHEWAN CANCER FOUNDATION - ALLAN BLAIR MEMORIAL CLINIC - LIBRARY (Med)
4101 Dewdney Ave.   Phone: (306) 359-2203
Regina, SK, Canada S4T 7T1   Barbara Karchewski, Libn.
Founded: 1948. Staff: 1. Subjects: Cancer, medical and radiation oncology, physics. Holdings: 500 books; 200 bound periodical volumes; 1500 reprint articles on cancer. Subscriptions: 100 journals and other serials; 12 newspapers. Services: Interlibrary loans; copying; library open to medical professionals and some research personnel.

★12242★

SASKATCHEWAN - DEPARTMENT OF ADVANCED EDUCATION AND MANPOWER - WOMEN'S SERVICES - BRANCH RESOURCE CENTRE (Soc Sci)
1855 Victoria Ave.   Phone: (306) 565-2452
Regina, SK, Canada S4P 3V5   Betty Doucette, Educ.Ext.Coord.
Founded: 1976. Staff: 1. Subjects: Career planning and counselling, women's legal rights, women in the labor force, sexism in society, the changing role of women, life options for young women, women in nontraditional roles, day care, health. Holdings: 5000 books; VF drawers. Subscriptions: 40 journals and other serials. Services: Interlibrary loans; copying; library open to public. Special Catalogs: Vertical File Headings, 1983 - free upon request. Formerly: Saskatchewan - Department of Labour - Women's Division - Resource Centre. Staff: Terry Irvine, Lib.Techn.

★12243★

SASKATCHEWAN - DEPARTMENT OF AGRICULTURE - LIBRARY (Agri)
Walter Scott Bldg.
3085 Albert St.   Phone: (306) 565-5151
Regina, SK, Canada S4S 0B1   Helene Stewart, Libn.
Founded: 1974. Staff: Prof 1; Other 2. Subjects: Agricultural economics, marketing, and statistics; current Canadian agriculture. Holdings: 900 books; 360 bound periodical volumes; 5000 pamphlets and technical reports; 1200 government annuals (Canadian, U.S., international); 8 VF drawers. Subscriptions: 600 journals and other serials; 10 newspapers. Services: Interlibrary loans; copying; library open to public for reference use only. Computerized Information Services: BRS, DIALOG, Infomart, CAN/OLE. Publications: Library bulletin (acquisitions list), monthly.

★12244★

SASKATCHEWAN - DEPARTMENT OF THE ATTORNEY GENERAL - COURT OF APPEAL LIBRARY (Law)
Court House, 2425 Victoria Ave.   Phone: (306) 565-5411
Regina, SK, Canada S4P 0S8   Shirley A. Hurnard, Libn.
Staff: Prof 1. Subjects: Law - Canadian, American, English, Indian. Holdings: 2000 volumes. Subscriptions: 30 journals and other serials. Services: Library not open to public.

★12245★

SASKATCHEWAN - DEPARTMENT OF CONSUMER AND COMMERICAL AFFAIRS - CONSUMER INFORMATION CENTRE (Bus-Fin)
1871 Smith St.   Phone: (306) 565-5549
Regina, SK, Canada S4P 3V7   Edith Berg, Coord.
Founded: 1973. Staff: 7. Subjects: Consumer education and information, insurance, credit, advertising and marketing, money management. Special Collections: Consumer product information files; consumer education resources (AV materials). Holdings: 4000 books; 800 audiovisual items; 20 VF drawers; government documents, including Statistics Canada material. Subscriptions: 150 journals and other serials; 10 newspapers. Services: Interlibrary loans; copying; center open to public with restrictions. Networks/Consortia: Member of Association of Saskatchewan Government Libraries (ASGL). Publications: Acquisition List, irregular; special bibliographies.

★12246★

SASKATCHEWAN - DEPARTMENT OF CO-OPERATION - LIBRARY (Agri)
2055 Albert St.   Phone: (306) 565-5807
Regina, SK, Canada S4P 3V7   Rae French, Resource Ctr.Coord.
Founded: 1945. Staff: 1. Subjects: Cooperation, agriculture, credit unions, economics, education. Holdings: 600 books; 800 pamphlets; 500 statutes and gazettes; 2 VF drawers of clippings, newsletters and reports. Subscriptions: 45 journals and other serials; 8 newspapers. Services: Interlibrary loans; copying; library open to public. Publications: Annual Report.

★12247★

SASKATCHEWAN - DEPARTMENT OF EDUCATION - RESOURCE CENTRE (Educ)
2220 College Ave.   Phone: (306) 565-5977
Regina, SK, Canada S4P 3V7   Jane Naisbitt, Libn.
Founded: 1976. Staff: Prof 2; Other 2. Subjects: Education. Holdings:

20,000 books; ERIC microfiche; vertical files; test collections; large print books; audiotapes; braille books. Subscriptions: 200 journals and other serials. Services: Interlibrary loans; copying; center open to public for reference use only. Publications: Bibliographies - for internal distribution only. Staff: Wilma Olmsted, Lib.Techn.

★12248★

SASKATCHEWAN - DEPARTMENT OF THE ENVIRONMENT - LIBRARY (Env-Cons)
5th Fl., 1855 Victoria Ave.   Phone: (306) 565-6125
Regina, SK, Canada S4P 3V5   Shannon G. Bellamy, Libn.
Founded: 1974. Staff: 2. Subjects: Hydrology, water pollution, air pollution, environmental protection and policy, impact assessments. Holdings: 1000 books; 25 bound periodical volumes; 4000 reports; 12 VF drawers of pamphlets; 8 shelves of unbound periodicals. Subscriptions: 90 journals and other serials. Services: Interlibrary loans; library open to other provincial and federal government departments. Publications: Acquisitions list, irregular.

★12249★

SASKATCHEWAN - DEPARTMENT OF HEALTH - LIBRARY (Med)
3475 Albert St.   Phone: (306) 565-3090
Regina, SK, Canada S4S 6X6   M. Smigarowski, Lib.Supv.
Staff: 4. Subjects: Public health, nutrition, public health nursing, medicine. Holdings: 9000 books; 7000 bound periodical volumes; 7000 pamphlets; 2000 technical reports. Subscriptions: 358 journals and other serials. Services: Interlibrary loans; copying (limited); library open to health professionals. Publications: Library Acquisitions, biweekly. Staff: L. Glencross, Asst. to Lib.Supv.

★12250★

SASKATCHEWAN - DEPARTMENT OF HIGHWAYS AND TRANSPORTATION - PLANNING BRANCH LIBRARY (Trans; Plan)
1855 Victoria Ave.   Phone: (306) 565-4777
Regina, SK, Canada S4P 3V5   Dr. M.U. Hassan, Libn.
Founded: 1957. Staff: Prof 1. Subjects: Highway and traffic engineering, transportation planning, urban and regional studies, management. Holdings: 6000 books; 70 bound periodical volumes. Subscriptions: 150 journals and other serials. Services: Library open to employees from other Saskatchewan government departments.

SASKATCHEWAN - DEPARTMENT OF INDUSTRY AND COMMERCE
See: Saskatchewan - Department of Tourism & Small Business

★12251★

SASKATCHEWAN - DEPARTMENT OF LABOUR - LIBRARY (Soc Sci)
1914 Hamilton St.   Phone: (306) 565-2429
Regina, SK, Canada S4P 4V4   Fraser Russell, Libn.
Founded: 1957. Staff: Prof 1; Other 1. Subjects: Labor law and legislation, economic conditions of Canada, industrial relations, income security, trade unions, manpower. Special Collections: Saskatchewan collective labor agreements (500). Holdings: 1500 books; 300 bound periodical volumes; 260 linear feet of Canada and Saskatchewan government publications; 10 drawers of clippings; 10 drawers of pamphlets. Subscriptions: 100 journals and other serials; 5 newspapers. Services: Interlibrary loans; copying; library open to public. Computerized Information Services: DIALOG, SDC, Info Globe, QL Systems. Networks/Consortia: Member of Association of Saskatchewan Government Libraries. Publications: Labour Library (acquisitions) in Saskatchewan Labour Report, monthly - free upon request; Labour Bibliographies, irregular.

★12252★

SASKATCHEWAN - DEPARTMENT OF LABOUR - OCCUPATIONAL HEALTH AND SAFETY DIVISION - LIBRARY (Soc Sci; Med)
1150 Rose St.   Phone: (306) 565-4494
Regina, SK, Canada S4P 3V7   Susan Johnson, Libn.
Founded: 1974. Staff: 1. Subjects: Occupational health. Holdings: 650 books; 200 bound periodical volumes; 129 films; 15 shelves of unbound reports and documents. Subscriptions: 120 journals and other serials. Services: Interlibrary loans; copying; library open to public. Publications: Reports on problem studies, irregular.

SASKATCHEWAN - DEPARTMENT OF LABOUR - WOMEN'S DIVISION
See: Saskatchewan - Department of Advanced Education and Manpower - Women's Services

★12253★
SASKATCHEWAN - DEPARTMENT OF NORTHERN SASKATCHEWAN - LIBRARY
Box 5000
La Ronge, SK, Canada S0J 1L0
Defunct

★12254★
SASKATCHEWAN - DEPARTMENT OF PARKS AND RENEWABLE RESOURCES - FISH ENHANCEMENT DIVISION LIBRARY (Sci-Tech)†
Government Bldg.
Prince Albert, SK, Canada S6V 1B5　　　Brian Christensen, Fisheries Geologist
Staff: 1. **Subjects:** Fisheries management, fisheries and aquatic biology, aquaculture, aquatic habitat protection, commercial and sport fishing. **Holdings:** Figures not available for books, pamphlets, reports, bulletins, periodical volumes. **Subscriptions:** 11 journals and other serials. **Services:** Library open to public.

★12255★
SASKATCHEWAN - DEPARTMENT OF PARKS AND RENEWABLE RESOURCES - FORESTRY DIVISION LIBRARY (Sci-Tech)
P.O. Box 3003　　　　　　　　Phone: (306) 922-3133
Prince Albert, SK, Canada S6V 6G1　　　Janelle D. Johnston, Clerk
Founded: 1946. **Staff:** Prof 1. **Subjects:** Forestry, forest inventory and products, plant ecology, soil science, silviculture, forest injuries, mensuration, wildlife. **Special Collections:** Soil surveys. **Holdings:** 10,000 books; 2000 other cataloged items. **Subscriptions:** 36 journals and other serials. **Services:** Interlibrary loans; copying; library open to public with restrictions on some publications. **Publications:** Technical bulletins, annual. **Formerly:** Saskatchewan - Department of Tourism and Renewable Resources.

★12256★
SASKATCHEWAN - DEPARTMENT OF SOCIAL SERVICES - LIBRARY (Soc Sci)
1920 Broad St.　　　　　　　　Phone: (306) 565-3605
Regina, SK, Canada S4P 3V6　　　Janice Szuch, Lib.Techn.
Staff: 1. **Subjects:** Social work, child welfare, social policy and welfare, management, criminology and corrections, social sciences. **Holdings:** 4300 books; 150 bound periodical volumes. **Subscriptions:** 71 journals and other serials. **Services:** Interlibrary loans; copying; library open to public with restrictions on borrowing.

★12257★
SASKATCHEWAN - DEPARTMENT OF SUPPLY & SERVICES - PHOTOGRAPHIC SERVICES AGENCY - LIBRARY (Aud-Vis)†
Walter Scott Bldg., Rm. 306
3085 Albert St.　　　　　　　　Phone: (306) 565-6298
Regina, SK, Canada S4S 0B1
Staff: Prof 1. **Subjects:** Saskatchewaniana. **Holdings:** 40,000 black and white negatives; 100,000 color negatives; 10,000 slides. **Services:** Library open to public with restrictions.

★12258★
SASKATCHEWAN - DEPARTMENT OF SUPPLY & SERVICES - SYSTEMS CENTRE LIBRARY (Comp Sci)
3rd Fl., T.C. Douglas Bldg.
3475 Albert St.　　　　　　　　Phone: (306) 565-2090
Regina, SK, Canada S4S 6X6　　　Heather D. Henley, Lib.Techn.
Staff: 1. **Subjects:** Computer programming, data processing, business management. **Holdings:** 460 volumes; 65 technical manuals; 3 VF drawer of clippings and pamphlets. **Subscriptions:** 54 journals and other serials. **Services:** Interlibrary loans; library not open to public. **Formerly:** Saskatchewan - Department of Revenue, Supply & Services.

SASKATCHEWAN - DEPARTMENT OF TOURISM AND RENEWABLE RESOURCES
See: Saskatchewan - Department of Parks and Renewable Resources

★12259★
SASKATCHEWAN - DEPARTMENT OF TOURISM & SMALL BUSINESS - BUSINESS INFORMATION CENTRE (Bus-Fin)
Bank of Montreal Bldg., 4th Fl.
2103 11th Ave.　　　　　　　　Phone: (306) 565-2254
Regina, SK, Canada S4P 3V7　　　Rochelle Smith, Coord.
Founded: 1984. **Staff:** Prof 3; Other 2. **Subjects:** Tourism, small business, economic development, trade, economics, marketing. **Holdings:** 1000 books; 1000 reports and clippings; trade directories; government documents; files. **Subscriptions:** 300 journals and other serials; 50 newspapers. **Services:** Interlibrary loans; copying; center open to public. **Computerized Information**

Services: DIALOG, Infomart, SaskComp, DUNSERVE. Performs free searches. **Publications:** Acquisition List, monthly. **Formed by the Merger of:** Saskatchewan - Department of Tourism & Small Business - Library and the Saskatchewan - Department of Industry and Commerce - Library. **Staff:** Jane Mihalyko, Res.Off.

★12260★
SASKATCHEWAN - DEPARTMENT OF URBAN AFFAIRS - LIBRARY
2151 Scarth St.
Regina, SK, Canada S4P 3V7
Founded: 1974. **Subjects:** Urban affairs, community planning, housing. **Holdings:** 1000 books and bound periodical volumes. **Remarks:** Presently inactive.

★12261★
SASKATCHEWAN GENEALOGICAL SOCIETY - LIBRARY (Hist)
Box 1894
Regina, SK, Canada S4P 3E1　　　Laura M. Hanowski, Libn.
Founded: 1970. **Staff:** 2. **Subjects:** Genealogy and genealogical sources, local and family history. **Special Collections:** I.G.I. and Griffiths Valuations (microfiche); Ontario Computerized Land Records (microfiche). **Holdings:** 1500 books; 10 bound periodical volumes; 300 other cataloged items; 3 microfilms. **Subscriptions:** 62 journals and other serials. **Services:** Interlibrary loans; copying; library open to public for reference use only, circulation limited to members. **Special Indexes:** Periodical Index.

★12262★
SASKATCHEWAN HOSPITAL - DEPARTMENT OF PSYCHIATRIC SERVICES - STAFF LIBRARY (Med)
P.O. Box 39　　　　　　　　　Phone: (306) 445-9411
North Battleford, SK, Canada S9A 2X8　　　Doris Allan, Libn.
Staff: 1. **Subjects:** Psychiatry, medicine, psychology, nursing, hospital administration. **Holdings:** 1500 books; 700 bound periodical volumes. **Subscriptions:** 35 journals and other serials; 5 newspapers. **Services:** Interlibrary loans; copying; library open to public with special permission.

★12263★
SASKATCHEWAN INDIAN CULTURAL COLLEGE - LIBRARY (Area-Ethnic)
Box 3085　　　　　　　　　Phone: (306) 244-1146
Saskatoon, SK, Canada S7K 3S9　　　David L. Sparvier, Coord./Libn.
Founded: 1973. **Staff:** Prof 1; Other 4. **Subjects:** North and South American Indian studies. **Special Collections:** Saskatchewan Indian Collection (360 tapes in the Cree language); Canadian Association in Support of the Native Peoples (CASNP) Collection (microfiche); Newstart Documents (microfiche); Saskatchewan Newstart (22 sets of microfiche). **Holdings:** 8285 volumes; 419 16mm films; 79 reels of microfilm; 269 phonograph records; 213 media kits; 363 audio cassettes; 552 audiotapes; 3 slide sets; 58 filmstrips; 27 video cassettes; 93 videotapes; 66 microfiche. **Subscriptions:** 100 journals and other serials. **Services:** Interlibrary loans; copying; consulting; library open to public. **Publications:** Holdings List, monthly.

★12264★
SASKATCHEWAN INDIAN FEDERATED COLLEGE - LIBRARY (Area-Ethnic)
University of Regina
C-4, Classroom Bldg.　　　　　　Phone: (306) 584-8333
Regina, SK, Canada S4S 0A2　　　Heather West, Libn.
Founded: 1977. **Staff:** Prof 1; Other 1. **Subjects:** Indian studies, Indian art. **Special Collections:** Eeniwuk collection. **Holdings:** 8000 books; 112 bound periodical volumes; 20 VF drawers; 32 VF drawers of clippings, pamphlets and reports. **Subscriptions:** 44 journals and other serials; 12 newspapers. **Services:** Interlibrary loans; copying; library open to public with restrictions. **Publications:** Acquisitions list, monthly.

★12265★
SASKATCHEWAN - LEGISLATIVE LIBRARY (Hist; Law)†
234 Legislative Bldg.　　　　　　Phone: (306) 565-2277
Regina, SK, Canada S4S 0B3　　　Christine MacDonald, Legislative Libn.
Founded: 1905. **Staff:** Prof 3; Other 6. **Subjects:** Political and social sciences with emphasis on Canada; history, especially Canadian and Western Canadian; law. **Special Collections:** Saskatchewan, Canadian, and U.S. Government documents; International Labor Organization publications (depository library for all four). **Holdings:** 75,000 books; 17,000 bound periodical volumes; 15,000 microforms; 120 VF drawers of pamphlets and government publications; 23 VF drawers of Statistics Canada materials. **Subscriptions:** 930 journals and other serials; 113 newspapers. **Services:** Interlibrary loans; copying; library open to public with restrictions on borrowing. **Special Catalogs:** Publications of the governments of the North-West Territories, 1876-1905, and the Province of Saskatchewan, 1905-1952; accession lists. **Staff:** Laura Pogue, Ref.Libn.; Craig James, Docs.Libn.

★12266★
SASKATCHEWAN MUSEUM OF NATURAL HISTORY - LIBRARY (Hist)
Dept. of Culture and Recreation
Wascana Park
Regina, SK, Canada S4P 3V7
Phone: (306) 565-2808
Ruby Apperley, Supv., Museum Serv.
Staff: 2. **Subjects:** Natural history, history, archeology, paleontology, museology. **Holdings:** 1200 books; 225 bound periodical volumes. **Subscriptions:** 50 journals and other serials. **Services:** Library open to researchers and students by appointment only.

★12267★
SASKATCHEWAN PIPING INDUSTRY JOINT TRAINING BOARD - LIBRARY (Sci-Tech)
1366 Cornwall St.
Regina, SK, Canada S4R 2H5
Phone: (306) 522-4237
Darlene Pellerin
Founded: 1971. **Staff:** 1. **Subjects:** Plumbing, pipefitting, welding. **Holdings:** 500 volumes; 28 visual aids; training manuals. **Services:** Library not open to public.

★12268★
SASKATCHEWAN POWER CORPORATION - LIBRARY (Energy)†
2025 Victoria Ave.
Regina, SK, Canada S4P 0S1
Phone: (306) 566-2697
H. Philley, Lib.Ck.
Founded: 1959. **Staff:** 2. **Subjects:** Electric power engineering, gas engineering, economics, statistics, management. **Holdings:** 10,000 books; 300 unbound periodical volumes; 6000 reports. **Subscriptions:** 250 journals and other serials; 152 newspapers. **Services:** Interlibrary loans; copying; library open to public. **Computerized Information Services:** DIALOG, SDC, CAN/OLE, QL Systems.

★12269★
SASKATCHEWAN - PROVINCIAL LIBRARY (Info Sci)
1352 Winnipeg St.
Regina, SK, Canada S4P 3V7
Phone: (306) 565-2972
Stan Skrzeszewski, Act.Prov.Libn.
Founded: 1953. **Staff:** Prof 16; Other 42. **Subjects:** Library science, bibliography, Canadiana, Native Indians, foreign languages (24 languages), specialized nonfiction. **Holdings:** 278,000 volumes; 5900 cassettes and tapes; 5000 phonograph records; large print books. **Subscriptions:** 1430 journals and other serials; 45 newspapers. **Services:** Interlibrary loans; coordinates public library services throughout the province; direct services to individuals remote from public libraries; centralized cataloging service to public libraries; library not open to public. **Automated Operations:** Computerized cataloging and serials. **Computerized Information Services:** DIALOG, SDC, BRS, UTLAS. **Publications:** Focus on Saskatchewan Libraries, bimonthly. **Special Catalogs:** Saskatchewan union catalog of books, serials, films; bibliographies, The Saskatchewan Bibliography, 1905-1979. **Staff:** Ved P. Arora, Hd., Bibliog.Serv.; Marie Sakon, Hd., Rd.Serv.; Jim Oxman, Info.Serv; Marcel De Laforest, Hd., Adm.Br.

★12270★
SASKATCHEWAN RESEARCH COUNCIL - INFORMATION CENTRE (Sci-Tech)
30 Campus Dr.
Saskatoon, SK, Canada S7N 0X1
Phone: (306) 664-5488
Margaret Samms, Info.Ctr.Mgr.
Staff: Prof 1; Other 4. **Subjects:** Geology, industrial engineering, chemistry, physics, engineering, hydrology. **Holdings:** 12,000 books; 2000 bound periodical volumes; 15,000 technical reports and government documents. **Subscriptions:** 620 journals and other serials. **Services:** Interlibrary loans; copying; center open to public with restrictions. **Automated Operations:** Computerized cataloging. **Computerized Information Services:** DIALOG, New York Times Information Service, Info Globe, SDC, QL Systems, CAN/OLE.

★12271★
SASKATCHEWAN TEACHERS' FEDERATION - STEWART RESOURCES CENTRE (Educ)
2317 Arlington Ave.
Box 1108
Saskatoon, SK, Canada S7K 3N3
Phone: (306) 373-1660
Ms. S.M. Dyer, Libn.
Founded: 1958. **Staff:** Prof 2; Other 2. **Subjects:** Education, educational psychology, psychology, economic and social conditions. **Special Collections:** Current elementary and secondary school textbooks; Mary Ellen Burgess Drama Library (8000 play titles). **Holdings:** 17,000 books and bound periodical volumes; 4000 pamphlets. **Subscriptions:** 680 journals and other serials; 15 newspapers. **Services:** Interlibrary loans; copying; center open to public with restrictions. **Publications:** Book catalog; acquisition list - both for limited distribution; booklists in subject areas.

★12272★
SASKATCHEWAN TELECOMMUNICATIONS - CORPORATE LIBRARY (Sci-Tech)
2121 Saskatchewan Dr., 2nd Fl.
Regina, SK, Canada S4P 3Y2
Phone: (306) 347-2229
Basil G. Pogue, Corp.Libn.
Staff: Prof 1; Other 2. **Subjects:** Electronics, management, data processing, planning. **Holdings:** 2500 books; 50 bound periodical volumes; 2000 government documents. **Subscriptions:** 550 journals and other serials; 10 newspapers. **Services:** Interlibrary loans; copying; SDI; library open to public with referral from another library. **Automated Operations:** Computerized cataloging and serials. **Computerized Information Services:** DIALOG, BRS, Info Globe, CAN/OLE, QL Systems. **Publications:** New Publications, 11/year - for internal distribution only.

★12273★
SASKATCHEWAN WESTERN DEVELOPMENT MUSEUM - GEORGE SHEPHERD LIBRARY (Trans; Agri)
2935 Melville St.
Saskatoon, SK, Canada S7K 3S5
Phone: (306) 934-1400
Warren A. Clubb, Res.Coord.
Founded: 1972. **Subjects:** Steam and gas tractors, agricultural implements, automobiles, agricultural self-help, railways, aviation, western Canadian history. **Special Collections:** Agricultural implement catalogs dating back to 1880 (70 feet). **Holdings:** 10,000 books; 1500 catalogs and other items; 8 drawers of photographs; 1000 glass slides. **Subscriptions:** 40 journals and other serials; 5 newspapers. **Services:** Copying; library open to serious researchers by appointment.

★12274★
SASKATCHEWAN WHEAT POOL - REFERENCE LIBRARY (Agri)
2625 Victoria Ave.
Regina, SK, Canada S4T 7T9
Phone: (306) 569-4480
A.D. McLeod, Res.Dir.
Founded: 1925. **Staff:** 1. **Subjects:** Agriculture, economics, cooperation. **Holdings:** 2000 books; documents and special reports (Statistics Canada, Royal Commissions and others). **Subscriptions:** 50 journals and other serials; 12 newspapers. **Services:** Interlibrary loans; library open to public for reference use only on a limited basis.

★12275★
SASKATOON CANCER CLINIC - LIBRARY (Med)
University Hospital
Saskatoon, SK, Canada S7N 0X0
Phone: (306) 343-9565
Mrs. A. Oatway, Libn.
Subjects: Treatment and diagnosis of cancer, radiation therapy, physics, nuclear medicine. **Holdings:** 1000 books; 3000 bound periodical volumes; 6 tapes. **Subscriptions:** 50 journals and other serials. **Services:** Interlibrary loans; library open to staff members.

★12276★
SASKATOON GALLERY AND CONSERVATORY CORPORATION - MENDEL ART GALLERY - LIBRARY (Art)
950 Spadina Crescent E.
P.O. Box 569
Saskatoon, SK, Canada S7K 3L6
Phone: (306) 664-9610
Joan Steel, Libn.
Staff: Prof 1. **Subjects:** Art, museology. **Holdings:** 6800 books; 245 bound periodical volumes; 9400 slides; 31 VF drawers of clippings and exhibition announcements; 1000 photographs. **Subscriptions:** 46 journals and other serials. **Services:** Interlibrary loans; copying; library open to public for reference use only.

★12277★
SASKATOON PUBLIC LIBRARY - FINE AND PERFORMING ARTS DEPARTMENT (Art; Mus)
311 23rd St., E.
Saskatoon, SK, Canada S7K 0J6
Phone: (306) 664-5579
Frances Bergles, Dept.Hd.
Staff: Prof 3; Other 9. **Subjects:** Art, music, performing arts, film. **Holdings:** 22,000 books; 980 films; 23,031 recordings. **Subscriptions:** 219 journals and other serials. **Services:** Interlibrary loans; copying; department open to public. **Automated Operations:** Computerized cataloging.

★12278★
SASKATOON STAR-PHOENIX - LIBRARY (Publ)
204 5th Ave., N.
Saskatoon, SK, Canada S7K 2P1
Phone: (306) 664-8223
Lori Hoveland
Staff: 1. **Subjects:** Newspaper reference topics, local and provincial news. **Holdings:** 520 books; 105 drawers of photographs and cuts; 30 VF drawers of clippings; 1080 reels of microfilm. **Subscriptions:** 80 journals and other serials; 21 newspapers. **Services:** Copying; library open to public for reference use only.

★12279★
SATELLITE VIDEO EXCHANGE SOCIETY - VIDEO INN LIBRARY (Aud-Vis)
261 Powell St. Phone: (604) 688-4336
Vancouver, BC, Canada V6A 1G3 Julie Healy
FO 1973. **Staff:** Prof 15. **Subjects:** Media arts, arts, national and international politics, community service. **Special Collections:** International videotapes (1400). **Holdings:** 6000 volumes; 6 VF drawers; clippings. **Subscriptions:** 3000 journals and other serials; 300 newspapers. **Services:** Interlibrary loans; copying; library open to public for reference use only. **Automated Operations:** Computerized cataloging and circulation. **Computerized Information Services:** Online systems. Performs searches on cost recovery basis. Contact Person: Andy Harvey. **Publications:** Video Guide, 5/year - subscription. **Staff:** Andy Harvey .

★12280★
SATURDAY EVENING POST SOCIETY - ARCHIVES (Publ)
1100 Waterway Blvd. Phone: (317) 634-1100
Indianapolis, IN 46202 Carol Brown McShane, Libn./Archv.
Staff: Prof 1; Other 1. **Subjects:** Advertising, marketing, general fiction. **Special Collections:** Correspondence of Cyrus H.K. Curtis, 1900-1930 (15 VF drawers); complete files of Saturday Evening Post, Jack and Jill, Country Gentleman. **Holdings:** 4500 volumes; 4 VF drawers of manuscripts; clippings and pamphlets. **Subscriptions:** 100 journals and other serials. **Services:** Archives not open to public. **Computerized Information Services:** DIALOG. **Special Indexes:** Author, title and subject card index of the Saturday Evening Post, 1900 to present; Saturday Evening Post cartoonists, 1971 to present, and artists, 1920 to present. **Formerly:** Curtis Publishing Company - Archives.

SAUGUS IRON WORKS NATL. HISTORIC SITE
See: U.S. Natl. Park Service

SAUK CENTRE AREA CHAMBER OF COMMERCE - SINCLAIR LEWIS INFORMATION & INTERPRETIVE CENTRE
See: Lewis (Sinclair) Information & Interpretive Center

★12281★
SAUK COUNTY HISTORICAL SOCIETY, INC. - HISTORICAL MUSEUM LIBRARY (Hist)
531 Fourth Ave. Phone: (608) 356-6549
Baraboo, WI 53913 Nijole Etzwiler, Cur.
Founded: 1905. **Staff:** 1. **Subjects:** State and local history, Indian ethnology, religion. **Special Collections:** William H. Canfield writings. **Holdings:** 2000 books; 2000 newspaper clippings. **Services:** Library open to public for reference use only by appointment. **Publications:** Chits and Chats.

★12282★
SAUL, EWING, REMICK & SAUL - LAW LIBRARY (Law)
3800 Centre Square W. Phone: (215) 972-7873
Philadelphia, PA 19102 Judith A. Wishner, Libn.
Staff: 2. **Subjects:** Law. **Holdings:** 15,500 books; 480 bound periodical volumes. **Subscriptions:** 120 journals and other serials; 7 newspapers. **Services:** Interlibrary loans; copying; library not open to public. **Computerized Information Services:** LEXIS, NEXIS, DIALOG, Dow Jones News/Retrieval, VU/TEXT.

SAULS MEMORIAL LIBRARY
See: Piedmont Hospital

SAVAGE (Dr. John E.) MEDICAL STAFF LIBRARY
See: Greater Baltimore Medical Center - Dr. John E. Savage Medical Staff Library

★12283★
SAVANNAH (City) - MUNICIPAL RESEARCH LIBRARY (Plan)†
City Hall, Rm. 402
Box 1027 Phone: (912) 233-9321
Savannah, GA 31402 Glenda E. Anderson, Res.Libn.
Staff: Prof 1. **Subjects:** Urban administration, municipal management, public services, community development, municipal finance/budgeting, public employee labor relations. **Holdings:** 1562 books; local government documents generated by City of Savannah, Chatham County-Savannah Metropolitan Planning Commission and Coastal Area Planning and Development Division. **Subscriptions:** 119 journals and other serials. **Services:** Interlibrary loans; copying; library open to public by appointment. **Networks/Consortia:** Member of Georgia Library Information Network (GLIN); Central Georgia Associated Libraries.

★12284★
SAVANNAH (City) - POLICE DEPARTMENT - LIBRARY (Law)†
323 Oglethorpe Ave.
Box 1027 Phone: (912) 233-9321
Savannah, GA 31402 Glenda E. Anderson, Res.Libn.
Staff: 1. **Subjects:** Police management and organization, criminal justice. **Holdings:** 906 volumes. **Subscriptions:** 21 journals and other serials. **Services:** Interlibrary loans; library not open to public. **Networks/Consortia:** Member of Georgia Library Information Network (GLIN); Criminal Justice Information Exchange.

★12285★
SAVANNAH RIVER PLANT - TECHNICAL LIBRARY (Energy)
E.I. Du Pont de Nemours & Company Phone: (803) 725-2707
Aiken, SC 29808 C. Tom Sutherland, Supv.
Founded: 1952. **Staff:** Prof 2; Other 6. **Subjects:** Nuclear science, chemistry, physics, metallurgy, engineering, mathematics. **Holdings:** 35,000 books; 45,000 bound periodical volumes; 51,000 technical reports. **Subscriptions:** 1200 journals and other serials. **Services:** Interlibrary loans; library not open to public. **Automated Operations:** Computerized cataloging, serials and circulation. **Computerized Information Services:** DIALOG, SDC, DOE/RECON. **Remarks:** The Savannah River Plant operates under contract to the U.S. Department of Energy. **Staff:** Erminia U. Kauer, Info.Spec.

★12286★
SAVANNAH SCIENCE MUSEUM - ENERGY LIBRARY (Energy)*
4405 Paulsen St. Phone: (912) 355-6705
Savannah, GA 31405
Founded: 1981. **Subjects:** Energy - solar, wind, alternative, conservation; appropriate technology. **Holdings:** 400 books; 200 pamphlets; 50 Department of Energy publications. **Services:** Library open to members for reference use only.

★12287★
SAVE THE CHILDREN FOUNDATION, INC. - LIBRARY (Soc Sci)
54 Wilton Rd. Phone: (203) 226-7271
Westport, CT 06880 Nancy N. Faesy, Libn.
Staff: Prof 1; Other 1. **Subjects:** Community development - planning and evaluation; health and nutrition; technical foreign aid; appropriate technology; North American Indians. **Holdings:** 1200 books; 8 VF drawers of pamphlets; 4 VF drawers of information on organizations; 3 VF drawers of United Nations information. **Subscriptions:** 200 journals and other serials; 6 newspapers. **Services:** Interlibrary loans; copying; library open to public with restrictions. **Networks/Consortia:** Member of Information Network for Materials Effecting Development (INFORMED). **Publications:** New materials list, bimonthly.

★12288★
SAVIN CORPORATION - ENGINEERING AND MANUFACTURING DIVISION - SAVIN TECHNICAL INFORMATION CENTER (Sci-Tech)
33 Lewis Rd. Phone: (607) 729-6531
Binghamton, NY 13902 Catherine S. Rybicki,, Lib.Spec.
Staff: Prof 1; Other 1. **Subjects:** Xerography, electronics, engineering, chemistry. **Special Collections:** U.S. patents, 1979 to present (3 cabinets); industrial standards; collection of vendor catalogs (18 linear feet). **Holdings:** 300 books; 25 reels of microfilmed periodicals; 2 file cabinets of vendor pamphlets; 18 linear feet of standards and manuals. **Subscriptions:** 54 journals and other serials. **Services:** Interlibrary loans; copying; SDI; library open to public with restrictions. **Automated Operations:** Computerized cataloging. **Computerized Information Services:** DIALOG, SDC; internal databases. Performs searches on cost recovery basis. **Networks/Consortia:** Member of South Central Research Library Council (SCRLC). **Publications:** Savin Standards Manual Circulation Controls; Savin Training Manual Distribution. **Staff:** Abel Mendes, Mgr., Gen.Serv.

SAVITT MEDICAL LIBRARY
See: University of Nevada, Reno

SAVITZ LIBRARY
See: Glassboro State College

SAWYER (Mildred F.) LIBRARY
See: Suffolk University - Mildred F. Sawyer Library

SAWYER (Ruth) COLLECTION
See: College of St. Catherine - Library - Ruth Sawyer Collection

★12289★

SCARBOROUGH BOARD OF EDUCATION - A.B. PATTERSON PROFESSIONAL LIBRARY (Educ)
140 Borough Dr., Level 2   Phone: (416) 296-7515
Scarborough, ON, Canada M1P 4N6   MaryLu Brennan, Supv.
Founded: 1956. **Staff:** Prof 2; Other 4. **Subjects:** Education, child study, sociology. **Holdings:** 25,000 books; 600 multimedia kits; 600 reels of microfilm; 86,000 microfiche; 12 VF drawers; ONTERIS and ERIC microfiche (1975-1978). **Subscriptions:** 375 journals and other serials; 5 newspapers. **Services:** Interlibrary loans; copying; library open to public by appointment. **Automated Operations:** Computerized cataloging. **Computerized Information Services:** DIALOG, SDC, BRS, UTLAS. **Networks/Consortia:** Member of Professional Education Libraries Cataloguing Network (PEL); Education Libraries Sharing of Resources Network (ELSOR). **Publications:** Multimedia kit list, semiannual; book catalogue, quarterly; journal listing, annual - all for internal distribution only.

★12290★

SCARBOROUGH GENERAL HOSPITAL - HEALTH SCIENCES LIBRARY (Med)
3050 Lawrence Ave., E.   Phone: (416) 438-2911
Scarborough, ON, Canada M1P 2V5
Founded: 1958. **Staff:** Prof 2. **Subjects:** Health sciences. **Holdings:** 1200 books; 85 bound periodical volumes. **Subscriptions:** 151 journals and other serials. **Services:** Interlibrary loans; library not open to public. **Computerized Information Services:** MEDLARS. Performs free searches. **Staff:** Helvi Thomas, Health Sci.Libn.; Anne Kubjas, Health Sci.Libn.

★12291★

SCARBOROUGH PUBLIC LIBRARY - FILM SERVICES (Aud-Vis)
Campbell District Library
496 Birchmount Rd.   Phone: (416) 698-1191
Scarborough, ON, Canada M1K 1N8   Kathy Therrien, Film Coord.
Staff: Prof 1; Other 7. **Subjects:** Leisure and entertainment, community development, continuing education. **Holdings:** 1100 films. **Services:** Library open to public. **Remarks:** Service outlet with viewing facilities for Scarborough Public Library System. Interacts with other Library Boards in Metropolitan Toronto to provide integrated collections and services. Also lends equipment.

★12292★

SCARBOROUGH RESOURCE CENTRE (Plan)
Scarborough Civic Centre
150 Borough Dr.   Phone: (416) 296-7215
Scarborough, ON, Canada M1P 4N7   Dave Hawkins, Mgr.
Founded: 1973. **Staff:** Prof 1; Other 2. **Subjects:** Urban affairs and planning with emphasis on Scarborough and metropolitan Toronto. **Holdings:** 1700 books; 16 VF drawers of reports and documents; 3 VF drawers of zoning by-laws and official plans. **Subscriptions:** 180 journals and other serials; 12 newspapers. **Services:** Interlibrary loans; copying; center open to public. **Publications:** Recent Additions, monthly - distributed to staff and interested individuals and libraries.

★12293★

SCARRITT COLLEGE FOR CHRISTIAN WORKERS - VIRGINIA DAVIS LASKEY LIBRARY (Rel-Theol)
1104 19th Ave., S.   Phone: (615) 327-2700
Nashville, TN 37203   Dale E. Bilbrey, Libn.
Founded: 1892. **Staff:** Prof 2; Other 1. **Subjects:** Christian education, church music education. **Special Collections:** Bibles (297). **Holdings:** 57,250 books; 6101 bound periodical and curriculum volumes; 75 reels of microfilm; 420 recordings; 250 tapes and AV kits. **Subscriptions:** 115 journals and other serials. **Services:** Interlibrary loans; copying; library open to public with restrictions on borrowing. **Remarks:** Library has mutual borrowing privileges with Vanderbilt University Library System. **Staff:** Sharon Thomas, Asst.Libn.

★12294★

SCENIC GENERAL HOSPITAL - STANISLAUS COUNTY MEDICAL LIBRARY (Med)
830 Scenic Dr.
Box 3271
Modesto, CA 95353   Phone: (209) 571-6132
                                     Margie A. Felt, Med.Lib.Asst.
Founded: 1956. **Staff:** Prof 1; Other 1. **Subjects:** General and family practice, orthopedics, surgery, pediatrics, radiology, nursing, psychiatry. **Holdings:** 3563 books; 4330 bound periodical volumes; 931 other cataloged items; 97 slides; Audio-Digest tapes. **Subscriptions:** 162 journals and other serials. **Services:** Interlibrary loans; copying; library open to medical and nursing students and to public with doctor referral. **Formerly:** Stanislaus County Medical Society - Medical Library.

SCHAFF (Philip) LIBRARY
See: Lancaster Theological Seminary of the United Church of Christ - Philip Schaff Library

SCHAFFER LIBRARY
See: Union College

SCHAFFER LIBRARY OF THE HEALTH SCIENCES
See: Union University - Albany Medical College

SCHAFFNER (Franklin J.) FILM LIBRARY
See: Franklin and Marshall College - Shadek-Fackenthal Library - Special Collections

SCHALLER (Walter F.) MEMORIAL LIBRARY
See: St. Francis Memorial Hospital - Walter F. Schaller Memorial Library

SCHARFFENBERG MEMORIAL LIBRARY
See: Narcotics Education, Inc.

★12295★

SCHEIE EYE INSTITUTE - LIBRARY (Med)
Myrin Circle, 51 N. 39th St.   Phone: (215) 662-8148
Philadelphia, PA 19104   Michael P. Toner, Lib.Dir.
Founded: 1972. **Staff:** Prof 1. **Subjects:** Ophthalmology. **Holdings:** 2630 books; 4000 bound periodical volumes; video cassettes; audiotapes. **Subscriptions:** 60 journals and other serials. **Services:** Interlibrary loans; library not open to public. **Networks/Consortia:** Member of Greater Northeastern Regional Medical Library Program. **Publications:** Newsletter, bimonthly - for internal distribution only. **Remarks:** Located at Presbyterian-University of Pennsylvania Medical Center.

SCHENDEL MEMORIAL LIBRARY
See: First Lutheran Church of the Lutheran Church in America

SCHENECTADY ARCHIVES OF SCIENCE AND TECHNOLOGY
See: Union College - Schaffer Library - Special Collections

★12296★

SCHENECTADY CHEMICALS, INC. - W. HOWARD WRIGHT RESEARCH CENTER - LIBRARY (Sci-Tech)
2750 Balltown Rd.   Phone: (518) 370-4200
Schenectady, NY 12309   Elizabeth H. Groot, Mgr., Tech.Info.Serv.
Staff: Prof 1; Other 1. **Subjects:** Polymer and organic chemistry. **Holdings:** 1000 books; 1000 bound periodical volumes. **Subscriptions:** 70 journals and other serials. **Services:** Interlibrary loans; copying; SDI; library open to public with restrictions. **Computerized Information Services:** DIALOG, SDC. **Networks/Consortia:** Member of Capital District Library Council for Reference and Research Resources (CDLC).

★12297★

SCHENECTADY COUNTY HISTORICAL SOCIETY - LIBRARY AND ARCHIVES (Hist)
32 Washington Ave.   Phone: (518) 374-0263
Schenectady, NY 12305   Mrs. C.A. Church, Archv.
Founded: 1905. **Staff:** 2. **Subjects:** History - Schenectady County, New York State; genealogy. **Special Collections:** Local church and cemetery records; Revolutionary War documents; family record file; complete 1850 census of New York State (microfilm); federal census of Schenectady County, 1790-1900; state census of Schenectady County, 1835, 1855. **Holdings:** 1500 volumes; clippings; manuscripts; pamphlets; documents; slides; pictures; maps. **Services:** Copying; family research (fee); library open to public with fee for nonmembers.

★12298★

SCHENECTADY GAZETTE - LIBRARY (Publ)
332 State St.   Phone: (518) 374-4141
Schenectady, NY 12301   Colleen J. Daze, Libn.
Staff: 2. **Subjects:** Newspaper reference topics. **Holdings:** 250 books; 30 state and local documents; 250,000 newspaper clippings; newspaper on microfilm, 1899 to present. **Subscriptions:** 15 journals and other serials. **Services:** Copying; SDI; library open to public by appointment. **Special Indexes:** Index to Schenectady Gazette, 1979 to present.

★12299★

SCHENECTADY MUSEUM - LIBRARY (Art)
Nott Terrace Heights   Phone: (518) 382-7890
Schenectady, NY 12308
Founded: 1934. **Staff:** 22. **Subjects:** Art, science, technology, natural

history. **Holdings:** Figures not available. **Services:** Interlibrary loans; library open to public for reference use only, but primarily serves the staff.

★12300★
SCHERER (R.P.) CORPORATION - LIBRARY (Med)
2075 W. Big Beaver Rd.
Box 160
Troy, MI 48099
Phone: (313) 649-0900
Sandra Abrams, Libn.
Staff: 1. **Subjects:** Chemistry, pharmacy. **Holdings:** 3000 books; 1000 bound periodical volumes. **Subscriptions:** 50 journals and other serials. **Services:** Library not open to public.

SCHERING FOUNDATION LIBRARY OF HEALTH CARE
See: Harvard University - School of Medicine

★12301★
SCHERING-PLOUGH CORPORATION - BUSINESS INFORMATION CENTER - LIBRARY (Bus-Fin)
Galloping Hill Rd.
Kenilworth, NJ 07033
Phone: (201) 558-5121
Esther M. Jankovics, Supv.
Staff: Prof 3; Other 1. **Subjects:** Management, pharmaceutical marketing, business. **Holdings:** 2500 books and bound periodical volumes; 2 drawers of annual reports; 7 card catalog drawers of In the News; 5 VF drawers. **Subscriptions:** 303 journals and other serials; 5 newspapers. **Services:** Interlibrary loans; copying; SDI; library open to public with restrictions. **Computerized Information Services:** Online systems. **Publications:** In the News, 2/week. **Staff:** Amy Mills, Libn.; Virginia Hughes, Ed., In The News.

★12302★
SCHERING-PLOUGH CORPORATION - PHARMACEUTICAL RESEARCH DIVISION - LIBRARY INFORMATION CENTER (Sci-Tech; Med)
60 Orange St.
Bloomfield, NJ 07003
Phone: (201) 429-3727
Rita L. Goodemote, Assoc.Dir.
Founded: 1940. **Staff:** Prof 11; Other 9. **Subjects:** Pharmacy, biomedicine, microbiology, organic chemistry. **Holdings:** 30,000 volumes. **Subscriptions:** 1000 journals and other serials. **Services:** Interlibrary loans; center not open to public. **Automated Operations:** Computerized serials and circulation. **Computerized Information Services:** DIALOG, BRS, CAS Online; SCHOLAR/ Inquire (internal database). **Staff:** Jean Hudson, Supv., Tech.Serv.; Angela Mazella, Sr.Info.Sci.; Mary Pingo, Cat.Libn.; Jean Nocka, Info.Sci.; Elizabeth Hoag, Info.Sci.; Leona Rem, Info.Sci.; Eleanor Shargorodskaya, Info.Sci.; Brian Stephenson, Info.Sci.; Joyce Koehler, Info.sci.; Beverly Brown, Info.Sci.

SCHERING-PLOUGH LIBRARY
See: Massachusetts Institute of Technology

SCHERMAN (Harry) LIBRARY
See: Mannes College of Music - Harry Scherman Library

★12303★
SCHICK SHADEL HOSPITAL - MEDICAL LIBRARY (Med)
Box 48149
Seattle, WA 98148
Phone: (206) 244-8100
Mary Jane McInturff, Med.Libn.
Staff: Prof 1; Other 1. **Subjects:** Medicine, smoking and alcoholism, behavior modification. **Holdings:** 700 books; 100 unbound periodical volumes; 15 VF drawers of reports, reprints, clippings. **Subscriptions:** 80 journals and other serials. **Services:** Interlibrary loans; copying. **Computerized Information Services:** MEDLARS, BRS. **Networks/Consortia:** Member of Seattle Area Hospital Library Consortium (SAHLC).

★12304★
SCHIELE MUSEUM OF NATURAL HISTORY AND PLANETARIUM - LIBRARY (Sci-Tech)
1500 E. Garrison Blvd.
Box 953
Gastonia, NC 28052
Phone: (704) 864-3962
Jackie Ramseur, Registrar/Libn.
Staff: Prof 1; Other 17. **Subjects:** Ecology, natural history, marine biology, archeology, anthropology, land use, zoology, botany, local history. **Holdings:** 6000 books; 141 films and 15,000 slides; 89 planetarium program tapes; 5000 wildflower transparencies; 400 items in research egg collection; serial publications of the Natural History Museum of Los Angeles County; biweekly bulletins of Wildlife Management Institute, 1972 to present. **Subscriptions:** 37 journals and other serials. **Services:** Interlibrary loans; copying; library open to public with restrictions. **Publications:** Newsletter, quarterly; annual report. **Remarks:** Library serves as an Environmental Reference Center for the State of North Carolina and also as a Regional Reference Center for the Library of Congress.

SCHLESINGER (Arthur and Elizabeth) LIBRARY ON THE HISTORY OF WOMEN IN AMERICA
See: Radcliffe College - Arthur and Elizabeth Schlesinger Library on the History of Women in America

SCHLICHTER (Charles H., M.D.) HEALTH SCIENCE LIBRARY
See: Elizabeth General Medical Center - Charles H. Schlichter, M.D. Health Science Library

★12305★
SCHLUMBERGER-DOLL - RESEARCH LIBRARY (Sci-Tech; Energy)
Old Quarry Rd.
Box 307
Ridgefield, CT 06877
Phone: (203) 431-5600
Henry Edmundson, Mgr., Info.
Staff: Prof 3; Other 3. **Subjects:** Oil well logging, physics, nuclear science, mathematics, computer science, chemistry, geology, geoscience, artificial intelligence, petroleum exploration. **Holdings:** 12,000 books; 2500 bound periodical volumes; microforms; 10,000 articles and reports; 3000 government reports. **Subscriptions:** 350 journals and other serials. **Services:** Interlibrary loans; copying; library open to public by appointment. **Automated Operations:** Computerized cataloging, acquisitions and circulation. **Computerized Information Services:** DIALOG, SDC, BRS, SCI-MATE, OCLC; Sigma Data Datalib. **Networks/Consortia:** Member of NELINET; Southwestern Connecticut Library Council. **Staff:** Maureen Jones, Bk./ILL Libn.; Mary Ellen Banks, Lib.Supv.; Amy Loerch Strumolo, Per.Libn.; Karne Lanigan, Doc./Rpts.Libn.

SCHLUMBERGER, LTD. - FAIRCHILD-WESTON SYSTEMS INC.
See: Fairchild-Weston Systems Inc.

SCHLUMBERGER, LTD. - SANGAMO WESTON GROUP
See: Sangamo Weston Group

★12306★
SCHLUMBERGER WELL SERVICES - ENGINEERING LIBRARY (Sci-Tech)
5000 Gulf Fwy.
Box 4594
Houston, TX 77210
Phone: (713) 928-4411
Margaret Kuo, Engr.Libn.
Founded: 1953. **Staff:** Prof 1; Other 1. **Subjects:** Engineering, electronics, geology. **Holdings:** 3700 books; 100 bound periodical volumes; 500 papers; 30 drawers of company reports. **Subscriptions:** 114 journals and other serials. **Services:** Interlibrary loans; library not open to public. **Automated Operations:** Computerized cataloging and circulation. **Computerized Information Services:** SDC, DIALOG; internal database. **Publications:** Monthly New Acquisitions List.

SCHMIDT HERPETOLOGY LIBRARY
See: Field Museum of Natural History

SCHMIDT MEDICAL LIBRARY
See: California College of Podiatric Medicine

SCHMITZ (Dietrich) MEMORIAL LIBRARY
See: Washington Mutual Savings Bank - Information Center & Dietrich Schmitz Memorial Library

★12307★
SCHNADER, HARRISON, SEGAL & LEWIS - LIBRARY (Law)
1600 Market St., Suite 3600
Philadelphia, PA 19103
Phone: (215) 751-2111
Carol Lee Williamson, Libn.
Staff: Prof 1; Other 3. **Subjects:** Law. **Holdings:** 20,000 volumes. **Subscriptions:** 100 journals and other serials; 10 newspapers. **Services:** Interlibrary loans; copying; library open to public with restrictions. **Computerized Information Services:** DIALOG, LEXIS. **Networks/Consortia:** Member of Greater Philadelphia Law Library Association Union List.

SCHNEPP (Kenneth H.) MEDICAL LIBRARY
See: Memorial Medical Center - Kenneth H. Schnepp Medical Library

SCHNITZLER (Arthur) ARCHIVES
See: SUNY at Binghamton - Special Collections

SCHOENBERG (Arnold) INSTITUTE
See: Arnold Schoenberg Institute

SCHOFIELD (William Henry) MEMORIAL LIBRARY
See: American-Scandinavian Foundation - William Henry Schofield Memorial Library

★12308★

SCHOHARIE COUNTY HISTORICAL SOCIETY - REFERENCE LIBRARY (Hist)
Old Stone Fort Museum, N. Main St.   Phone: (518) 295-7192
Schoharie, NY 12157   Helene S. Farrell, Dir.
Founded: 1888. **Subjects:** Schoharie County history and genealogy, regional and New York State history. **Special Collections:** Early Schoharie County land patents. **Holdings:** 1500 books; 200 bound periodical volumes; 500 pamphlets; scrapbooks; maps; pictures. **Services:** Copying; library open to public for reference use only - fee charged to nonmembers and out-of-county residents. **Publications:** Schoharie County Historical Review, semiannual - mailed to society members.

★12309★

SCHOLASTIC MAGAZINES & BOOK SERVICES - EDITORIAL LIBRARY
730 Broadway
New York, NY 10003
Defunct. Merged with its General Library.

★12310★

SCHOLASTIC MAGAZINES & BOOK SERVICES - GENERAL LIBRARY (Publ; Educ)
730 Broadway   Phone: (212) 505-3000
New York, NY 10003   Lucy Evankow, Chf.Libn.
Founded: 1931. **Staff:** Prof 1; Other 2. **Subjects:** Social sciences, youth problems, education of youth, juvenile and teenage literature. **Holdings:** Figures not available for books; periodical volumes; syllabi; photographs. **Services:** Interlibrary loans; library not open to public. **Remarks:** Includes the holdings of its former Scholastic Materials Center - Curriculum Library and its Editorial Library.

★12311★

SCHOLASTIC MAGAZINES & BOOK SERVICES - SCHOLASTIC MATERIALS CENTER - CURRICULUM LIBRARY
730 Broadway
New York, NY 10003
Defunct. Merged with its General Library.

SCHOLES (Samuel R.) LIBRARY OF CERAMICS
See: New York State College of Ceramics at Alfred University - Samuel R. Scholes Library of Ceramics

★12312★

SCHOLL (Dr. William M.) COLLEGE OF PODIATRIC MEDICINE - LIBRARY (Med)
1001 N. Dearborn St.   Phone: (312) 280-2891
Chicago, IL 60610   Richard S. Klein, Dir., Lib.Serv.
Staff: Prof 2; Other 2. **Subjects:** Podiatry, orthopedics, dermatology, anatomy, neurology, sports, medicine. **Special Collections:** Historical shoes; historical podiatry books. **Holdings:** 13,750 books and bound periodical volumes; AV materials. **Subscriptions:** 300 journals and other serials. **Services:** Interlibrary loans; library open to health sciences personnel. **Computerized Information Services:** OCLC, DIALOG, SDC, MEDLINE. **Networks/Consortia:** Member of Greater Midwest Regional Medical Library Network (Region 3); Metropolitan Consortium; Chicago Library System. **Publications:** Acquisitions List, quarterly; Library User's Manual, annual; LibraryReport, annual; Periodicals Holdings List, annual; MEDLINE Fact Sheet. **Staff:** Donald J. Nagolski, Assoc.Dir.

SCHOMBURG CENTER FOR RESEARCH IN BLACK CULTURE
See: New York Public Library

★12313★

SCHOOL OF AMERICAN RESEARCH - LIBRARY (Sci-Tech; Area-Ethnic)
Box 2188   Phone: (505) 982-3583
Santa Fe, NM 87501   Elizabeth Y. Kingman, Libn.
Staff: Prof 1. **Subjects:** Anthropology, archeology, ethnology, Southwest Indian arts. **Holdings:** 6000 books; 300 bound periodical volumes. **Subscriptions:** 25 journals and other serials. **Services:** Interlibrary loans; library open to School of American Research members with restrictions. **Publications:** Exploration, annual; monographs, irregular; advanced seminar publications, annual; Indian Arts Series books; Archaeology of the Grand Canyon series; Arroyo Hondo Archaeological series.

★12314★

SCHOOL OF FINE ARTS - LIBRARY (Art; Mus; Theater)
38660 Mentor Ave.   Phone: (216) 951-7500
Willoughby, OH 44094   Edith Reed, Act.Libn.
Founded: 1978. **Staff:** 2. **Subjects:** Music, theater, art, dance. **Special Collections:** Opera collection. **Holdings:** 3000 books. **Services:** Library not

open to public.

SCHOOL FOR INTERNATIONAL TRAINING
See: Experiment in International Living

★12315★

SCHOOL OF LIVING - RALPH BORSODI MEMORIAL LIBRARY (Soc Sci)
R.D. 7
Box 388   Phone: (717) 755-2666
York, PA 17402   M.J. Loomis, Libn.
Staff: 1. **Subjects:** Major problems of living, modern homesteading, self-sufficiency, balanced living, spiritual development, appropriate technology, adult education. **Special Collections:** Education and Living, Seventeen Problems of Living - both books written by Dr. Ralph Borsodi, founder of School of Living; early American anarchist publications. **Holdings:** 2500 books. **Subscriptions:** 105 journals and other serials. **Services:** Library open to public for reference use only. **Publications:** Green Revolution, 6/year.

SCHOOL OF MEDICINE IN SHREVEPORT
See: Louisiana State University Medical Center

★12316★

SCHOOL OF THE OZARKS - RALPH FOSTER MUSEUM - LOIS BROWNELL RESEARCH LIBRARY (Hist)
                                          Phone: (417) 334-6411
Point Lookout, MO 65726   Robert S. Esworthy, Dir.
Staff: Prof 1; Other 2. **Subjects:** Firearms, archeology, Ozarks regional history, antiques, mineralogy, geology, westward expansion, fine art, natural history, early man. **Holdings:** 1500 books; 550 bound periodical volumes; 4 VF drawers of archives. **Subscriptions:** 15 journals and other serials; 5 newspapers. **Services:** Library open to public.

SCHOOL OF THEOLOGY AT CLAREMONT - CENTER FOR PROCESS STUDIES
See: Center for Process Studies

★12317★

SCHOOL OF THEOLOGY AT CLAREMONT - THEOLOGY LIBRARY (Rel-Theol)
1325 N. College Ave.   Phone: (714) 626-3521
Claremont, CA 91711   Dr. Caroline Becker Whipple, Dir.
Founded: 1968. **Staff:** Prof 4; Other 2. **Subjects:** Bible, Ancient Near East, church history, theology, ethics, pastoral care, homiletics. **Special Collections:** Methodistica; Kirby Page Manuscripts (8 VF drawers); Bishop James C. Baker Manuscripts; archives for the Pacific and Southwest Conference of the United Methodist Church; Protestant Episcopal Diocese of Los Angeles archives. **Holdings:** 99,578 books; 16,728 bound periodical volumes; 1837 mircoforms; 48 audio cassettes; dissertations; manuscripts. **Subscriptions:** 598 journals and other serials. **Services:** Interlibrary loans; copying; library open to public with proper identification. **Automated Operations:** Computerized circulation. **Computerized Information Services:** OCLC. **Publications:** A Selection of Additions to the School of Theology Library at Claremont - to school staff. **Special Catalogs:** Union Catalog of Southern California Theological Seminaries. **Staff:** Richard Denton, Ser.Libn; Jean Cobb, Ref.Libn.; Elsie Freudenberger, Cat.Libn.

★12318★

SCHOOL OF VISUAL ARTS - LIBRARY (Art)
209 E. 23rd St.   Phone: (212) 679-7350
New York, NY 10010   Zuki Landau, Chf.Libn.
Founded: 1961. **Staff:** Prof 4; Other 2. **Subjects:** Fine arts, graphic arts, advertising, photography, film, humanities. **Holdings:** 40,000 books and bound periodical volumes; 900 pamphlets; 10 VF drawers of pictures; 400 mounted reproductions; 70,000 slides. **Subscriptions:** 200 journals and other serials. **Services:** Copying; library open to staff, faculty, students and alumni. **Networks/Consortia:** Member of METRO. **Publications:** Accessions lists, monthly - to staff and students. **Staff:** Rosemary Pandolfi, Cat.; Joan Arnold, Cat.; Doll Mohead, Slide Cur.

★12319★

SCHOOLCRAFT COLLEGE - WOMEN'S RESOURCE CENTER (Soc Sci)
18600 Haggerty Rd.   Phone: (313) 591-6400
Livonia, MI 48152   Virginia Wilhelm, Coord.
Founded: 1975. **Staff:** Prof 1; Other 1. **Subjects:** Women - career information, education, employment, counseling, health. **Holdings:** 500 books; 1000 newsletters, pamphlets, government publications, research reports, reprints; 6 VF drawers. **Subscriptions:** 18 journals and other serials. **Services:** Copying; center open to public for reference use only. **Publications:** Reprints, irregular, Newsletter, quarterly - free upon request.

★12320★
SCHOOLS OF THEOLOGY IN DUBUQUE - LIBRARIES (Rel-Theol)
333 Wartburg Pl. Phone: (319) 589-3215
Dubuque, IA 52001 Duncan Brockway, Dir. of Libs.
Staff: Prof 6; Other 4. **Subjects:** Theology, missions, ecumenical studies. **Special Collections:** Hymnals; Lutheran irenics and polemics. **Holdings:** 222,256 books and bound periodical volumes. **Subscriptions:** 800 journals and other serials; 10 newspapers. **Services:** Interlibrary loans; copying; library open to public. **Automated Operations:** Computerized cataloging, serials and circulation. **Computerized Information Services:** OCLC, DIALOG, BRS. Performs free searches. **Publications:** STD Library Bulletin, monthly - for internal distribution only. **Remarks:** Contains the holdings of the Couchman Memorial Library located at 2050 University Ave. and the Reu Memorial Library located at 333 Wartburg Place. An additional telephone number is 589-0265. **Staff:** Vera L. Robinson, Cat.; Mary Anne Knefel, Ref.Libn.; Gillian S. Gremmels, Ref.Libn.; Mary Timmer, Ref.Libn.; Jim Gingery, Ref.Libn.

SCHOU EDUCATION CENTRE
See: Burnaby School Board

★12321★
SCHREIBER FOODS, INC. - LIBRARY (Food-Bev)
425 Pine St.
Box 610 Phone: (414) 437-7601
Green Bay, WI 54305 Karen K. Braatz, Info.Spec.
Founded: 1977. **Staff:** Prof 1; Other 1. **Subjects:** Cheese, food industry. **Holdings:** 1200 books; 300 bound periodical volumes; government documents. **Subscriptions:** 315 journals and other serials. **Services:** Library not open to public. **Computerized Information Services:** DIALOG.

★12322★
SCHRODER (J. Henry) BANK & TRUST COMPANY - LIBRARY (Bus-Fin)
One State St. Phone: (212) 269-6500
New York, NY 10015 Juliette Levinton, Libn.
Founded: 1930. **Staff:** 2. **Subjects:** Banking, investments, international finance, economic and business conditions, international trade, corporate records. **Special Collections:** Foreign bank letters. **Holdings:** 600 books; 75 bound periodical volumes. **Subscriptions:** 450 journals and other serials. **Services:** Interlibrary loans; library not open to public.

SCHROEDER (Walter) LIBRARY
See: Milwaukee School of Engineering - Walter Schroeder Library

SCHUBERT HALL LIBRARY
See: California Historical Society

★12323★
SCHUMANN MEMORIAL FOUNDATION, INC. - LIBRARY (Mus)
2904 E. Lake Rd. Phone: (716) 346-2745
Livonia, NY 14487 June M. Dickinson, Pres.
Staff: Prof 2. **Subjects:** Music, marked for performance by outstanding performers of past years; musicology; music therapy. **Special Collections:** Dickinson collection of Schumann memorabilia. **Holdings:** 3000 books; 7000 items of sheet music and opera scores; music manuscripts. **Services:** Library is open to serious students by appointment. **Staff:** Dr. Erwin T. Koch, Treas.

★12324★
SCHUMPERT MEDICAL CENTER - MEDICAL LIBRARY (Med)
915 Margaret Place
Box 21976 Phone: (318) 227-4500
Shreveport, LA 71120 Marilyn Willis, Med.Libn.
Staff: Prof 1. **Subjects:** Medicine, surgery and related fields. **Holdings:** 1000 books; 3400 bound periodical volumes. **Subscriptions:** 205 journals and other serials. **Services:** Interlibrary loans; copying; library open to public with restrictions. **Computerized Information Services:** MEDLINE. **Remarks:** Hospital network includes also Pathology, Radiology and Anesthesiology Libraries.

★12325★
SCHUYLER COUNTY HISTORICAL SOCIETY - LEE SCHOOL MUSEUM (Hist)
Rte. 14 South
Box 651 Phone: (607) 535-9741
Montour Falls, NY 14865 Alice M. Wixson, Dir.
Staff: Prof 1; Other 3. **Special Collections:** Schuyler County history. **Holdings:** 500 original textbooks and readers; maps. **Services:** Museum open to public.

★12326★
SCHUYLER COUNTY HISTORICAL SOCIETY - OLD BRICK TAVERN MUSEUM - RESEARCH LIBRARY (Hist)
108 N. Catharine St.
Box 651 Phone: (607) 535-9741
Montour Falls, NY 14865 Alice M. Wixson, Dir.
Founded: 1960. **Staff:** Prof 1; Other 2. **Subjects:** Art, religion, education, agriculture, folklore, genealogy, antiques, history, Indians. **Holdings:** 5000 books; 220 bound periodical volumes; 3000 cemetery records; 3000 clippings; 100 manuscripts; 20 maps; children's toys; Indian relics. **Services:** Interlibrary loans; copying; library open to public. **Publications:** Journal, quarterly. **Special Catalogs:** Newspaper, scrapbook and photograph catalogs.

★12327★
SCHUYLER TECHNICAL LIBRARY (Sci-Tech)
615 Brandywine Dr. Phone: (804) 877-5860
Newport News, VA 23602 Gilbert S. Bahn, Hd.
Founded: 1952. **Subjects:** Chemical thermodynamics, combustion processes, chemical kinetics, analysis of digital imagery. **Special Collections:** Private technical papers of Gilbert S. Bahn. **Services:** Library not open to public. **Remarks:** Most of the library's holdings are now located at the University of Virginia, on permanent loan.

★12328★
SCHUYLKILL COUNTY LAW LIBRARY (Law)
Court House Phone: (717) 622-5570
Pottsville, PA 17901 Patricia G. Kellet, Law Libn.
Staff: Prof 1. **Subjects:** Law. **Holdings:** 24,000 volumes. **Subscriptions:** 25 journals and other serials. **Services:** Copying; library open to public for reference use only; circulation limited to lawyers. **Special Indexes:** Punched card index.

★12329★
SCHUYLKILL VALLEY NATURE CENTER - LIBRARY (Env-Cons)
8480 Hagy's Mill Rd. Phone: (215) 482-7300
Philadelphia, PA 19128 Karin James, Libn.
Founded: 1965. **Staff:** 1. **Subjects:** Natural history, zoology, ornithology, botany, ecology, geology/mineralogy, environmental concerns, astronomy, weather, gardening. **Special Collections:** Rare books on the natural sciences (100 volumes); environmental science teaching resource center (2000 books). **Holdings:** 5200 books; 8 VF drawers of clippings and leaflets; 3 VF drawers of brochures of nature centers; 3 VF drawers of descriptive material of environmental organizations and newsletters. **Subscriptions:** 42 journals and other serials. **Services:** Library open to public for reference use only. **Publications:** The Spider's Web (calendar of events), annual; The Quill (newsletter), 4/year; brochures of courses and workshops - all sent to members; for others on request with The Spider's Web for sale.

SCHWARTZ (Rabbi A.N.) LIBRARY
See: Telshe Yeshiva - Rabbi A.N. Schwartz Library

SCHWARTZ (Arnold & Marie) COLLEGE OF PHARMACY & HEALTH SCIENCES
See: Long Island University - Arnold & Marie Schwartz College of Pharmacy & Health Sciences

SCHWARTZ (Arnold & Marie) LIBRARY
See: Temple Beth-El of Great Neck - Arnold & Marie Schwartz Library

SCHWARTZ (Charles and Bertie G.) JUDAICA READING ROOM & LIBRARY
See: American Jewish Congress - Charles and Bertie G. Schwartz Judaica Reading Room & Library

SCHWARTZ (Dr. Jerrold S.) MEMORIAL LIBRARY
See: University of Medicine and Dentistry of New Jersey - School of Osteopathic Medicine - Dr. Jerrold S. Schwartz Memorial Library

SCHWARTZ (Joseph & Elizabeth) LIBRARY
See: Beth Sholom Congregation - Joseph & Elizabeth Schwartz Library

SCHWARTZ (Marie Smith) MEDICAL LIBRARY
See: Brookdale Hospital Medical Center - Marie Smith Schwartz Medical Library

SCHWARTZBACH (Saul) MEMORIAL LIBRARY
See: Prince George's General Hospital & Medical Center - Saul Schwartzbach Memorial Library

SCHWARZ (Ernst) LIBRARY
See: Zoological Society of San Diego - Ernst Schwarz Library

SCHWARZ (Ted) ARCHIVE
See: Arizona State University - Special Collections

★12330★
SCHWENKFELDER LIBRARY (Rel-Theol)
Phone: (215) 679-7175
Pennsburg, PA 18073
D.K. Moyer, Dir.
Founded: 1946. **Staff:** Prof 1; Other 2. **Subjects:** Schwenkfelder Church history, history of Perkiomen Valley, history of Protestant Reformation in Silesia. **Special Collections:** Writings of Caspar von Schwenkfeld. **Holdings:** 30,000 volumes. **Subscriptions:** 10 journals and other serials. **Services:** Interlibrary loans; copying; library open to public. **Publications:** Annual Library Report - free on request.

SCHWOB (Simon) MEDICAL LIBRARY
See: Medical Center - Simon Schwob Medical Library

★12331★
SCIENCE APPLICATIONS, INC. - FOREIGN SYSTEMS RESEARCH CENTER - LIBRARY (Mil; Soc Sci)
40 DTC W.
7935 E. Prentice Ave.
Phone: (303) 773-6900
Englewood, CO 80111
Jennifer Doran, Libn.
Staff: Prof 1; Other 1. **Subjects:** Military science, international relations, political science, economics. **Special Collections:** Soviet Union source books and journal issues (12,500). **Holdings:** 5000 books; 9000 U.S. and Soviet Union journal issues. **Subscriptions:** 125 journals and other serials; 6 newspapers. **Services:** Library open to government and scholastic researchers with approval. **Computerized Information Services:** FILMS (internal database).

★12332★
SCIENCE ASSOCIATES/INTERNATIONAL, INC. - LIBRARY (Publ; Info Sci)
1841 Broadway
Phone: (212) 265-4995
New York, NY 10023
Roxy Bauer, Libn.
Staff: Prof 4; Other 1. **Subjects:** Information science, library science, documentation, publishing, computer science. **Holdings:** 2500 books; 1000 library and information science reports; 200 newsletters. **Subscriptions:** 250 journals and other serials. **Services:** Library not open to public.

★12333★
SCIENCE CENTER OF PINELLAS - LIBRARY
7701 22nd Ave., N.
St. Petersburg, FL 33710
Defunct

SCIENCE COUNCIL OF CANADA
See: Canada - Science Council of Canada

SCIENCE FICTION SOCIETY
See: Massachusetts Institute of Technology

★12334★
SCIENCE MUSEUM OF MINNESOTA - LOUIS S. HEADLEY MEMORIAL LIBRARY (Sci-Tech)
30 E. 10th St.
Phone: (612) 221-9488
St. Paul, MN 55101
Mary S. Finlayson, Libn.
Founded: 1907. **Staff:** Prof 1. **Subjects:** Geology, anthropology, biology, archeology, paleontology, botany, technology. **Holdings:** 19,000 books; 439 bound periodical volumes; 2437 U.S. Geological Survey publications; International Catalog, 1903-1919; Zoological Record, 1915 to present; 9 VF drawers of pamphlets; 208 file boxes of museum publications. **Subscriptions:** 150 journals and other serials. **Services:** Interlibrary loans; copying; library open to public by special request.

THE SCIENCE PLACE
See: Southwest Museum of Science & Technology/The Science Place

★12335★
SCIENCE RESEARCH ASSOCIATES, INC. - LIBRARY
155 N. Wacker Dr.
Chicago, IL 60606
Defunct

★12336★
SCIENCE SERVICE, INC. - LIBRARY (Sci-Tech; Med)
1719 N St., N.W.
Phone: (202) 785-2255
Washington, DC 20036
Jane M. Livermore, Libn.
Staff: Prof 1; Other 1. **Subjects:** Science, medicine, technology. **Holdings:** 2500 books; 1500 unbound periodicals. **Subscriptions:** 246 journals and other serials. **Services:** Interlibrary loans; copying; library open to public with restrictions.

★12337★
SCIENCE TRENDS - LIBRARY (Sci-Tech)
National Press Bldg., Suite 233
Phone: (202) 393-0031
Washington, DC 20045
Arthur Kranish, Hd.
Founded: 1958. **Subjects:** Government sponsored research and development, science, energy, environment. **Holdings:** Figures not available. **Services:** Maintains information and documents relating to government sponsorship of research and development; subscription includes inquiry service without additional charge. **Publications:** Science Trends, weekly, monthly in July and August - by subscription. **Also Known As:** Trends Publishing, Inc.

★12338★
SCIENTIFIC-ATLANTA, INC. - LIBRARY (Sci-Tech)
3845 Pleasantdale Rd.
Phone: (404) 449-2000
Atlanta, GA 30340
Peggy A. Price, Libn.
Founded: 1965. **Staff:** Prof 1. **Subjects:** Antennas, electronic engineering, mechanical engineering, telecommunications. **Holdings:** 4000 books; 450 bound periodical volumes; 2700 documents and technical reports; manufacturers' catalogs on microfilm; 450 microfiche of technical reports. **Subscriptions:** 230 journals and other serials. **Services:** Interlibrary loans; library not open to public. **Publications:** Acquisitions Bulletin, every 3 weeks - for internal distribution only.

★12339★
SCITUATE HISTORICAL SOCIETY - LIBRARY (Hist)*
Cudworth House, First Parish Rd.
Scituate, MA 02066
Mrs. Philip H. Wood, Libn.
Staff: Prof 1. **Subjects:** Local history, genealogy. **Holdings:** 600 books. **Services:** Library open to public with restrictions. **Publications:** Bulletin, semiannual - distributed to members.

★12340★
SCM CORPORATION - GLIDDEN COATINGS & RESINS DIVISION/DURKEE FOODS DIVISION - TECHNICAL INFORMATION SERVICES (Sci-Tech)
Dwight P. Joyce Research Ctr.
16651 Sprague Rd.
Phone: (216) 826-5260
Strongsville, OH 44136
Ann J. Yancura, Mgr.
Founded: 1962. **Staff:** Prof 4; Other 6. **Subjects:** Coatings and resins, foods, chemistry, particularly polymer chemistry and related topics. **Holdings:** 5500 books. **Subscriptions:** 400 journals and other serials. **Services:** Interlibrary loans; copying; library open to public by appointment. **Computerized Information Services:** DIALOG, SDC, NLM, NIH-EPA Chemical Information System. **Publications:** Newsletters. **Staff:** T.M. Ptak, Supv., External Info.Sys.; D. Klembara, Supv., Internal Info.Sys.; M.E. Swan, Tech.Libn.

★12341★
SCM CORPORATION - ORGANIC CHEMICALS DIVISION - TECHNICAL LIBRARY (Sci-Tech)
Box 389
Phone: (904) 764-1711
Jacksonville, FL 32201
Marian M. Derfer, Mgr., Info.Serv.
Founded: 1958. **Staff:** Prof 1; Other 1. **Subjects:** Organic and analytical chemistry, chemical engineering, flavor and fragrance chemicals, polymers, marketing. **Special Collections:** Catalysis; terpene chemicals; fatty acids; rosin chemistry. **Holdings:** 5730 books; 5000 bound periodical volumes; 5500 patents; 2050 technical reports; chemical abstracts on microfilm; 201,000 abstracts on cards. **Subscriptions:** 75 journals and other serials. **Services:** Library open to public with restrictions. **Automated Operations:** Computerized circulation. **Computerized Information Services:** DIALOG, SDC, NIH/EPA Chemical Information System. **Publications:** Chemical Literature Abstracts Bulletin, monthly; Literature Surveys. **Special Indexes:** Company Division Patents; abstracts and bibliographies of interest to staff members.

★12342★
SCM CORPORATION - PIGMENTS DIVISION - LIBRARY (Sci-Tech)
3901 Glidden Rd.
Phone: (301) 335-3600
Baltimore, MD 21226
Nancy Freeman, Libn.
Founded: 1944. **Staff:** Prof 1. **Subjects:** Chemistry - inorganic, physical, analytical; ceramics; inorganic pigments; paint; paper; colors; rubbers;

plastics; enamels. **Special Collections:** Complete set of National Paint and Coatings Association's Microcard Service Colour Index, Society of Dyers and Colourists (England). **Holdings:** 4000 books and bound periodical volumes; U.S. and foreign patents; reprints; clippings; pamphlets; reports. **Subscriptions:** 135 journals and other serials; 5 newspapers. **Services:** Interlibrary loans; copying; library open to public with prior approval. **Formerly:** Its Glidden-Pigments Division - Adrian Joyce Works Research Center Library.

SCOBIE MEMORIAL LIBRARY
See: Riverside Hospital

SCOTIA-FUNDY REGIONAL LIBRARY
See: Canada - Fisheries & Oceans

SCOTT AIR FORCE BASE (IL)
See: U.S. Air Force Environmental Technical Applications Center; U.S. Air Force Hospital Medical Center - Medical Library (IL-Scott AFB)

SCOTT COUNTY BAR ASSOCIATION - GRANT LAW LIBRARY
See: Grant Law Library

SCOTT-FANTON MUSEUM AND HISTORICAL SOCIETY
See: Danbury Scott-Fanton Museum and Historical Society

★12343★
SCOTT, FORESMAN & COMPANY, INC. - EDITORIAL LIBRARY (Publ; Educ)
1900 E. Lake Ave.   Phone: (312) 729-3000
Glenview, IL 60025   S. Donald Robertson, Hd.Libn.
Staff: Prof 2; Other 1. **Subjects:** Education, children's literature, study and teaching of reading. **Special Collections:** Company publications. **Holdings:** 35,000 books; 3500 bound periodical volumes; 200 phonograph records; 1700 reels of microfilm of periodicals; 12 VF drawers of publishers' catalogs. **Subscriptions:** 400 journals and other serials; 5 newspapers. **Services:** Interlibrary loans; copying; library open to public for reference use only. **Networks/Consortia:** Member of North Suburban Library System. **Publications:** List of Recent Additions, bimonthly. **Staff:** Jane F. Harris, Asst.Libn.

SCOTT (Harvey) MEMORIAL LIBRARY
See: Pacific University - Music Department - Library

SCOTT (John W.) HEALTH SCIENCES LIBRARY
See: University of Alberta - John W. Scott Health Sciences Library

SCOTT LIBRARY
See: York University

SCOTT MEMORIAL LIBRARY
See: Jefferson (Thomas) University

★12344★ .
SCOTT (O.M.) AND SONS - INFORMATION SERVICES (Sci-Tech)
Dwight G. Scott Research Center   Phone: (513) 644-0011
Marysville, OH 43041   Betty Seitz, Supv., Info.Serv.
Staff: 1. **Subjects:** Horticulture, botany, chemistry, business. **Special Collections:** Lawn Care magazine (15 volumes). **Holdings:** 5100 books; 275 bound periodical volumes; 15 VF drawers of research reports. **Subscriptions:** 275 journals and other serials. **Services:** Library open to public with prior arrangement. **Computerized Information Services:** Online systems.

★12345★
SCOTT PAPER COMPANY - MARKETING LIBRARY (Bus-Fin)
Scott Plaza   Phone: (215) 522-6262
Philadelphia, PA 19113   Eva K. Butler, Libn.
Founded: 1960. **Staff:** Prof 1; Other 1. **Subjects:** Paper industry, statistics, marketing, marketing research, management. **Holdings:** 2041 books; 97 bound periodical volumes; 45 VF drawers of pamphlets; 6 drawers of microfiche; 30 VF drawers of internal research reports. **Subscriptions:** 110 journals and other serials. **Services:** Interlibrary loans; library open to public for reference use only on request. **Publications:** Magazine article highlights, monthly; acquisitions bulletin, monthly - both for internal distribution only.

★12346★
SCOTT PAPER COMPANY - RESEARCH LIBRARY & TECHNICAL INFORMATION SERVICE (Sci-Tech)
Scott Plaza 3   Phone: (215) 522-6416
Philadelphia, PA 19113   George Burna, Mgr.
Founded: 1958. **Staff:** Prof 2; Other 1. **Subjects:** Pulp and paper, chemistry,

engineering, physics, textiles, management. **Holdings:** 9844 books and bound periodical volumes; 150,000 patents; internal research reports; microfilm; dissertations. **Subscriptions:** 300 journals and other serials. **Services:** Interlibrary loans; copying; library open to public on request for reference. **Computerized Information Services:** DIALOG, CAS Online, SDC. **Publications:** Biweekly bulletin listing recent acquisitions - for internal distribution only. **Staff:** Cheryl R. Stickle, Libn.

★12347★
SCOTT PAPER COMPANY - S.D. WARREN COMPANY - RESEARCH LIBRARY (Sci-Tech)
Research Laboratory   Phone: (207) 856-6911
Westbrook, ME 04092   Deborah G. Chandler, Info.Spec.
Staff: Prof 1; Other 1. **Subjects:** Papermaking, printing, chemistry, physics, engineering. **Holdings:** 3500 books; 1000 bound periodical volumes; 20 VF drawers of U.S. and foreign patents. **Subscriptions:** 150 journals and other serials. **Services:** Copying (limited); library open to public with prior permission. **Computerized Information Services:** DIALOG, SDC.

★12348★
SCOTT & WHITE MEMORIAL HOSPITAL - MEDICAL LIBRARY (Med)
2401 S. 31st St.   Phone: (817) 774-2228
Temple, TX 76508   Mary H. Spoede, Dir.
Founded: 1897. **Staff:** Prof 3; Other 6. **Subjects:** Clinical medicine, nursing care and education, allied health sciences. **Special Collections:** Historical and Nursing Alumni Collections (400 volumes). **Holdings:** 8894 books; 20,803 bound periodical volumes; 4 VF drawers of clippings and reports. **Subscriptions:** 736 journals and other serials. **Services:** Interlibrary loans; copying; library open to medical and allied health personnel. **Automated Operations:** Computerized serials. **Computerized Information Services:** MEDLINE, MEDLARS, BRS, AMA/NET. Performs free searches for staff; for others on cost recovery basis. Contact Person: Pennie Billings, 774-2379. **Networks/Consortia:** Member of TALON; TAMU Consortium of Medical Libraries. **Publications:** S. & W. Clinic Newsletter Addendum (a monthly list of acquisitions). **Staff:** Pennie Billings, Ref./CML Libn.; Beth McCullough, Pub.Serv.Libn.; Sheila Reynolds, Ser.

SCOTT (William A.) BUSINESS LIBRARY
See: University of Wisconsin, Madison - William A. Scott Business Library

SCOTTISH RESEARCH LIBRARY
See: American-Scottish Foundation, Inc.

★12349★
SCOTTISH RITE BODIES, SAN DIEGO - SCOTTISH RITE MASONIC LIBRARY (Rec)
1895 Camino Del Rio   Phone: (619) 297-0395
San Diego, CA 92108   Alfred D. Sawyer, Chm., Lib.Comm.
Founded: 1974. **Staff:** 15. **Subjects:** Masonic literature and history. **Special Collections:** New Age Magazine, 1904 to present; Quatuor Coronati Research Lodge, London, England, 1880 to present. **Holdings:** 4000 books; 200 bound periodical volumes; cassette tapes. **Subscriptions:** 20 journals and other serials. **Services:** Interlibrary loans (limited); library open to public with restrictions.

★12350★
SCOTTISH RITE SUPREME COUNCIL - LIBRARY (Hist; Rec)
1733 Sixteenth St. N.W.   Phone: (202) 232-3579
Washington, DC 20009   Inge Baum, Libn.
Founded: 1888. **Staff:** Prof 1. **Subjects:** Freemasonry and all its aspects, American history, biography, philosophy, religion. **Special Collections:** Claudy Collection (Goethe); Louis D. Carman Collection (Lincolniana); William R. Smith Collection (Burnsiana); Albert Pike Collection; Maurice H. Thatcher Collection (Panama Canal). **Holdings:** 150,000 books and bound periodical volumes; 15 cases of Masonic patents, documents and clippings; manuscripts; prints; photographs; microfilm. **Subscriptions:** 175 journals and other serials. **Services:** Interlibrary loans; copying; library open to Masons only. **Publications:** Dynamic Freedoms Series; The New Age Magazine, monthly.

SCOTTS BLUFF NATL. MONUMENT
See: U.S. Natl. Park Service

★12351★
SCOTTSDALE MEMORIAL HOSPITAL - DR. ROBERT C. FOREMAN HEALTH SCIENCES LIBRARY (Med)
7400 E. Osborn Rd.   Phone: (602) 994-9616
Scottsdale, AZ 85251   Marihelen O'Connor, Med.Libn.
Founded: 1968. **Staff:** Prof 1; Other 5. **Subjects:** Medicine, surgery, pediatrics, cardiology, orthopedics, radiology, nursing. **Holdings:** 1800 books;

4500 bound periodical volumes; 40 VF items. **Subscriptions:** 145 journals and other serials. **Services:** Interlibrary loans; library not open to public. **Computerized Information Services:** MEDLINE.

★12352★
SCRANTON TRIBUNE AND SCRANTONIAN - LIBRARY (Publ)*
338 N. Washington Ave.   Phone: (717) 344-7221
Scranton, PA 18503   Hal Lewis, Libn.
Staff: Prof 1. **Subjects:** Newspaper reference topics. **Holdings:** 500 books. **Services:** Copying; library open to public with restrictions.

★12353★
SCRIPPS CLINIC & RESEARCH FOUNDATION - KRESGE MEDICAL LIBRARY
   (Med)
10666 N. Torrey Pines Rd.   Phone: (619) 455-8705
La Jolla, CA 92037   Jesse G. Neely, Med.Libn.
Staff: 3. **Subjects:** Immunology, medicine, molecular and cellular biology, biochemistry, psychiatry. **Holdings:** 4166 books; 28,519 bound periodical volumes. **Subscriptions:** 505 journals and other serials. **Services:** Interlibrary loans; copying; library open to public for reference use only on request. **Computerized Information Services:** MEDLINE.

SCRIPPS COLLEGE - ELLA STRONG DENISON LIBRARY
See: The Claremont Colleges - Ella Strong Denison Library

SCRIPPS INSTITUTION OF OCEANOGRAPHY LIBRARY
See: University of California, San Diego

SCRIPTURE (Elaine & William E.) MEMORIAL LIBRARY
See: Rome Historical Society - Elaine & William E. Scripture Memorial Library

SCRUGGS (J. Hubert, Jr.) COLLECTION OF PHILATELY
See: Linn-Henley Library for Southern Historical Research - J. Hubert Scruggs, Jr. Collection of Philately

★12354★
SCUDDER, STEVENS & CLARK - LIBRARY (Bus-Fin)
175 Federal St.   Phone: (617) 482-3990
Boston, MA 02110   Helen Doikos, Libn.
Staff: Prof 1; Other 2. **Subjects:** Investments. **Holdings:** 1750 volumes; 135 drawers of 10K reports, clippings and pamphlets; microfilm. **Subscriptions:** 187 journals and other serials. **Services:** Interlibrary loans; library not open to public. **Computerized Information Services:** COMPUSTAT Services, Inc., Interactive Data Services, Inc., Data Resources, Inc. (DRI), Wharton Econometric Forecasting Associates.

★12355★
SCUDDER, STEVENS & CLARK - LIBRARY (Bus-Fin)
345 Park Ave.   Phone: (212) 350-8371
New York, NY 10154   Linda Osborn, Libn.
Founded: 1926. **Staff:** Prof 2. **Subjects:** Cosmetics, pharmaceuticals, health supplies and services, nonferrous metals, chemicals, general economics, petroleum, gas utilities, construction, paper, forest products, automobiles, steel, railroads, home and leisure. **Holdings:** 2000 books; 300 VF drawers. **Services:** Interlibrary loans; copying; library open to clients and other financial librarians.

★12356★
SDS BIOTECH CORPORATION - CORPORATE LIBRARY (Bus-Fin; Sci-Tech)
Box 348   Phone: (216) 357-3475
Painesville, OH 44077   L. Violet Forgach, Supv., Bus.Info.
Founded: 1980. **Staff:** Prof 6; Other 6. **Subjects:** Chemistry, energy, business, finance, management, statistics, engineering. **Special Collections:** Internal engineering records on microfilm (500 reels). **Holdings:** 10,000 books; 4500 bound periodical volumes; 8800 reels of microfilm; 300,000 patents; 6700 reports; 3000 pamphlets; 550 dissertations. **Subscriptions:** 1002 journals and other serials. **Services:** Interlibrary loans; copying; library open to public. **Automated Operations:** Computerized circulation. **Computerized Information Services:** DIALOG, SDC, BRS, DOE/RECON, NLM, Dow Jones News/Retrieval. **Formerly:** Diamond Shamrock Corporation. **Staff:** Carol Duane, ILL Chem.Info.; Betty Wainio, Chem.Info.Spec.; Mary Darling, Ref.Libn.; Lois Evans, Adm.Libn.; Renee Guttman .

SEA LAMPREY CONTROL CENTRE
See: Canada - Fisheries & Oceans

★12357★
SEA-LAND SERVICE, INC. - CORPORATE INFORMATION CENTER (Trans)†
General Office Port Authority Marine Terminal
Box 1050   Phone: (201) 558-6000
Elizabeth, NJ 07207
Founded: 1970. **Staff:** Prof 2; Other 1. **Subjects:** Containerized ocean shipping, law, water carrier regulation, maritime industry, transportation. **Holdings:** 3000 books; 250 booklets; 5 VF drawers of clippings; 10 VF drawers of documents; 8 VF drawers of unbound reports; 30 newsletters. **Subscriptions:** 50 journals and other serials; 5 newspapers.

★12358★
SEA VIEW HOSPITAL AND HOME - MEDICAL LIBRARY (Med)
460 Brielle Ave.   Phone: (718) 390-8689
Staten Island, NY 10314   Selma Amtzis, Med.Libn.
Founded: 1932. **Staff:** Prof 1; Other 1. **Subjects:** Medicine, nursing, geriatrics, hospital administration. **Holdings:** 2500 books; 4002 bound periodical volumes. **Subscriptions:** 125 journals and other serials. **Services:** Interlibrary loans; copying; library open to public for reference use only. **Computerized Information Services:** NLM. Performs searches on cost recovery basis. **Networks/Consortia:** Member of Brooklyn-Queens-Staten Island Health Sciences Librarians (BQSI). **Staff:** Dr. Arthur Feldstein, Hd. of Lib.Comm.

★12359★
SEA WORLD, INC. - LIBRARY (Env-Cons)
1720 S. Shores Rd.   Phone: (619) 222-6363
San Diego, CA 92109   Carlo A. Mosca, Corp.Dir., Educ.
Founded: 1973. **Staff:** Prof 10. **Subjects:** Oceanography, marine science and related subjects. **Holdings:** 1000 books; 1000 periodicals and scientific and government reports. **Subscriptions:** 40 journals and other serials. **Services:** Interlibrary loans; library open to public for reference use only. **Publications:** Information sheets on marine mammals and curriculum guides on marine life for teachers. **Remarks:** Located in Education Department. Company now owned by Harcourt Brace Jovanovich, Inc. **Staff:** Debbie Anderson, Res./Writer.

★12360★
SEABOARD COAST LINE RAILROAD COMPANY - LAW LIBRARY (Law)*
500 Water St., Rm. 1523   Phone: (904) 353-2011
Jacksonville, FL 32202
Subjects: Law. **Holdings:** 10,000 volumes.

SEABURY-WESTERN THEOLOGICAL SEMINARY
See: Garrett-Evangelical and Seabury-Western Theological Seminaries

★12361★
SEAGRAM (Joseph E.) & SONS, INC. - CORPORATE LIBRARY (Food-Bev;
   Bus-Fin)
800 Third Ave.   Phone: (212) 572-7873
New York, NY 10022   Alice Gross, Mgr., Lib.Serv.
Founded: 1973. **Staff:** Prof 3; Other 3. **Subjects:** Distilled spirits and wine, corporate finance, statistics. **Holdings:** 500 books; 200 newsletters; microfiche. **Subscriptions:** 300 journals and other serials; 75 newspapers. **Services:** Interlibrary loans; library not open to public. **Automated Operations:** Computerized serials. **Computerized Information Services:** DIALOG, NEXIS. Performs searches on cost recovery basis. **Special Catalogs:** Library union catalog. **Remarks:** Individual collections in various departments maintained by Library Union Catalog.

★12362★
SEAGRAM MUSEUM - ARCHIVES AND LIBRARY (Food-Bev)
57 Erb St. W.
P.O. Box 1605   Phone: (519) 885-1857
Waterloo, ON, Canada N2J 4N6   Sandra Lowman, Archv./Libn.
Founded: 1971. **Staff:** Prof 2; Other 2. **Subjects:** Beverage alcohol industry; wine, beer and spirits; alcoholism; prohibition; cooperage; copper-smithing; cork production; glassmaking; decorative arts. **Special Collections:** Photograph, Slide and Film Library (industry and company activities; 25,000 items); Packaging and Bottle Library (2000 items, dating back to 1900); fine art collection (etchings, lithographs and prints related to the art of drinking). **Holdings:** 3000 books; 100 bound periodical volumes; 1200 company reports and industry booklets. **Subscriptions:** 58 journals and other serials. **Services:** Interlibrary loans; copying; library open to public by appointment. **Remarks:** Includes the holdings of the former Wine Museum of San Francisco - Christian Brothers Rare Wine Books Library. **Formerly:** Seagram Company, Ltd. - Information Centre, Library & Archives. **Staff:** Don Spencer, Asst.Archv.

SEALE (Alvin) SOUTH SEAS COLLECTION
See: Pacific Grove Public Library - Alvin Seale South Seas Collection

SEAMAN (Benjamin White) MEDICAL LIBRARY
See: Nassau Hospital - Benjamin White Seaman Medical Library

★12363★
SEAMEN'S CHURCH INSTITUTE OF NEW YORK - JOSEPH CONRAD LIBRARY (Sci-Tech; Trans)
15 State St. Phone: (212) 269-2710
New York, NY 10004 Bonnie Golightly, Libn.
Founded: 1934. **Staff:** Prof 1; Other 3. **Subjects:** Marine engineering, ship registers, maritime history, navigation, shipping, maritime law, seamanship, voyages, naval architecture. **Special Collections:** Ship pictures and photographs; William Bollman collection (biography, history, travel; 3400 volumes); SCI Archives; Untermeyer Collection of Maritime History and Fiction (300 volumes). **Holdings:** 20,000 books; 125 bound periodical volumes; 21 VF cabinets of photographs, pictures of ships and related material; Merchant Marine study guides. **Subscriptions:** 125 journals and other serials; 8 newspapers. **Services:** Copying; library open to researchers and paid subscribers. **Special Indexes:** Subject index to pictures, articles in the vertical file (card); index to scrapbooks of ships.

★12364★
SEAR-BROWN ASSOCIATES, P.C. - INFORMATION CENTER (Sci-Tech)
85 Metro Park Phone: (716) 475-1440
Rochester, NY 14623 Michele Shipley, Info.Ctr.Mgr.
Staff: Prof 1. **Subjects:** Civil and structural engineering, architecture, surveying, water and waste treatment, hydraulics. **Holdings:** 2800 books; 10 VF drawers of product information; 700 manufacturers' catalogs; 4 VF drawers of planning information on local municipalities; 31 VF drawers, 27 shelves, 3 drawing files, and 197 reels of microfilm of Sear-Brown project files and drawings. **Subscriptions:** 125 journals and other serials; 5 newspapers. **Services:** Interlibrary loans; copying; center open to public by appointment. **Automated Operations:** Computerized records management. **Computerized Information Services:** DIALOG. **Networks/Consortia:** Member of Rochester Regional Research Library Council (RRRLC). **Publications:** New From the Information Center (list of new books), bimonthly - for internal distribution only.

★12365★
SEARCH GROUP, INC. - LIBRARY (Law)
925 Secret River Dr. Phone: (916) 392-2550
Sacramento, CA 95831 Thomas F. Wilson, Dir., Info. & Pubns.
Staff: Prof 1; Other 1. **Subjects:** Law enforcement, corrections, courts, identification, statistics. **Holdings:** 250 books; 300 technical reports; 85 unbound periodicals. **Subscriptions:** 11 journals and other serials. **Services:** Library not open to public.

★12366★
SEARLE (G.D.) & CO. OF CANADA, LIMITED - LIBRARY (Med)
400 Iroquois Shore Rd. Phone: (416) 844-1040
Oakville, ON, Canada L6H 1M5
Staff: 1. **Subjects:** Chemistry, biology, medicine, pharmacy. **Holdings:** 1000 books. **Subscriptions:** 100 journals and other serials.

★12367★
SEARLE (G.D.) & CO. - RESEARCH LIBRARY (Med)
4901 Searle Pkwy. Phone: (312) 982-8285
Skokie, IL 60077 Anthony Petrone, Mgr.
Founded: 1952. **Staff:** Prof 3; Other 3. **Subjects:** Chemistry, biology, gastroenterology, gynecology and contraception, hypertension, pharmacology. **Holdings:** 4000 books; 21 periodical titles on microfilm. **Subscriptions:** 900 journals and other serials; 35 newsletters. **Services:** Interlibrary loans; SDI; library available to nonemployees by appointment on a limited basis. **Automated Operations:** Computerized cataloging, acquisitions, serials and circulation. **Computerized Information Services:** DIALOG, SDC, BRS. **Networks/Consortia:** Member of North Suburban Library System; CRL; Greater Midwest Regional Medical Library Network (Region 3). **Publications:** Acquisitions List, monthly; Science Scan, daily - both for internal distribution only. **Staff:** M. Louise Lasworth, Ser.Supv.; Eva B. Koek, Info.Spec.; Joyce Nevins, Bus.Info.Spec.

SEARLS HISTORICAL LIBRARY
See: Nevada County Historical Society

SEARS (Charles B.) LAW LIBRARY
See: SUNY at Buffalo - Charles B. Sears Law Library

SEARS LIBRARY
See: Case Western Reserve University

★12368★
SEARS, ROEBUCK AND CO. - ARCHIVES, BUSINESS HISTORY AND INFORMATION CENTER (Bus-Fin; Hist)
Sears Tower, Dept. 703 Phone: (312) 875-8321
Chicago, IL 60684 Lenore Swoiskin, Dir. of Archv.
Founded: 1955. **Staff:** Prof 2; Other 1. **Subjects:** Historical material covering company development from 1886 to present; biographical collection - papers of officers, directors, key personalities, Americana; retailing. **Special Collections:** Catalog collection of Sears, Roebuck and Co., 1886 to present (6200 volumes). **Holdings:** 160 VF drawers of pamphlets; 36,000 photographs; 250 reels of microfilm. **Services:** Copying; research services available; center open to researchers only with approval. **Staff:** Manny Banayo, Dir. of Info.Ctr.

★12369★
SEARS, ROEBUCK AND CO. - MERCHANDISE DEVELOPMENT AND TESTING LABORATORY - LIBRARY, DEPARTMENT 817 (Sci-Tech)
Sears Tower, 23rd Fl. Phone: (312) 875-5991
Chicago, IL 60684 Mary M. McCarron, Libn.
Founded: 1928. **Staff:** Prof 2. **Subjects:** Textiles. **Holdings:** 10,000 books; 72 VF drawers; government and state publications; specifications and standards of standards organizations. **Subscriptions:** 575 journals and other serials. **Services:** Interlibrary loans. **Staff:** Mariam Syed, Asst.Libn.

SEASONGOOD (Murray) LIBRARY
See: Citizens Forum on Self-Government/National Municipal League, Inc. - Murray Seasongood Library

SEATON MEMORIAL LIBRARY
See: Riley County Historical Society

★12370★
SEATTLE ART MUSEUM - LIBRARY (Art)
Volunteer Park Phone: (206) 447-4686
Seattle, WA 98112 Elizabeth De Fato, Libn.
Founded: 1933. **Staff:** Prof 1; Other 1. **Subjects:** Art, history of art, archeology. **Holdings:** 12,000 books; 4000 exhibition catalogs; 5 drawers of Northwest artists clipping files. **Subscriptions:** 50 journals and other serials. **Services:** Copying; library open to public.

★12371★
SEATTLE-FIRST NATIONAL BANK - LIBRARY (Bus-Fin)
Box 3586 Phone: (206) 583-4056
Seattle, WA 98124 Jeannette M. Privat, A.V.P. & Mgr.
Founded: 1968. **Staff:** Prof 2; Other 5. **Subjects:** Finance and financial institutions; investments and public corporations; economies of Washington state, United States and other countries; small business operations; People's Republic of China. **Holdings:** 8700 books; 100 bound periodical volumes; 300 VF drawers of pamphlets; 4000 microfiche; 10,000 financial reports. **Subscriptions:** 1800 journals and other serials; 25 newspapers. **Services:** Interlibrary loans; copying; library open to public with permission of librarian. **Automated Operations:** Computerized cataloging, acquisitions and serials. **Computerized Information Services:** DIALOG, SDC, Dow Jones News/ Retrieval, TEXTLINE, NEXIS, OCLC, Faxon (F.W.) Company, Inc. **Staff:** James G. Gong, Ref.Libn.

★12372★
SEATTLE POST-INTELLIGENCER - NEWSPAPER LIBRARY (Publ)
6th & Wall Sts. Phone: (206) 628-8000
Seattle, WA 98111 Lytton Smith, Chf.Libn.
Founded: 1890. **Staff:** Prof 1; Other 3. **Subjects:** Newspaper reference topics. **Holdings:** 700 books; historical pictures; clippings; pamphlets; Post-Intelligencer microfilm, 1876 to present. **Services:** Library not open to public.

★12373★
SEATTLE PUBLIC HEALTH HOSPITAL - MEDICAL SERVICE LIBRARY (Med)*
1131 14th Ave. S. Phone: (206) 324-7650
Seattle, WA 98114 Seungja Song, Chf.Libn.
Founded: 1969. **Staff:** Prof 1; Other 1. **Subjects:** Medicine, nursing, dentistry, hospital administration. **Holdings:** 1200 books; 4730 bound periodical volumes. **Subscriptions:** 225 journals and other serials. **Services:** Interlibrary loans; library not open to public. **Computerized Information Services:** NLM, BRS. **Networks/Consortia:** Member of Seattle Area Hospital Library Consortium (SAHLC). **Publications:** Newsletter.

★12374★

SEATTLE PUBLIC LIBRARY - ART AND MUSIC DEPARTMENT (Art; Mus)†
1000 Fourth Ave.　　　　　　　　Phone: (206) 625-2665
Seattle, WA 98104　　　　　　　　Carolyn J. Holmquist, Hd.
Staff: Prof 8; Other 14. **Subjects:** Art, music literature, architecture, music scores, flower and ornamental gardening, dance. **Special Collections:** Scrapbooks containing information on Northwest artists (30,723 items); photographs of Seattle and the Northwest (29,484). **Holdings:** 107,108 books; 10,000 bound periodical volumes; 26,071 pictures; 33,738 pieces of sheet music; 35,854 phonograph records; 681,722 clippings. **Subscriptions:** 570 journals and other serials. **Services:** Interlibrary loans; copying; department open to public. **Computerized Information Services:** DIALOG, SDC. **Special Indexes:** Song Titles Index; premieres index; program notes index - all on cards.

★12375★

SEATTLE PUBLIC LIBRARY - BUSINESS AND SCIENCE DEPARTMENT (Sci-Tech; Bus-Fin)†
1000 Fourth Ave.　　　　　　　　Phone: (206) 625-2665
Seattle, WA 98104
Staff: Prof 13; Other 9. **Subjects:** Aeronautics and space, local marketing and employment information, skilled trades, domestic science, investments, automobiles. **Special Collections:** Aeronautics collection (6500 books; 76 periodicals); Washington Companies Collection (2000 file folders); Pacific Northwest historical telephone and city directory collection (1450 volumes); Ornithology Collection (500 volumes); Clock and Watch Repair Collection (107 volumes); Automotive Repair Collection (2200 volumes). **Holdings:** 232,850 books; 64,000 bound periodical volumes; 106 VF drawers of trade catalogs, directories, clippings, annual reports; 28 VF drawers of standards and specifications; federal document depository (state, local and foreign document holdings). **Subscriptions:** 2500 journals and other serials. **Services:** Interlibrary loans; copying; department open to public. **Automated Operations:** Computerized cataloging. **Computerized Information Services:** DIALOG, SDC, New York Times Information Service; Databnk (internal database of state and local economic statistics). **Networks/Consortia:** Member of WLN. **Special Indexes:** Boat and Ship file; Washington science and business vertical file; Standards.

★12376★

SEATTLE PUBLIC LIBRARY - DOUGLASS-TRUTH BRANCH LIBRARY (Area-Ethnic)
23rd Ave. & E. Yesler Way　　　　Phone: (206) 625-4874
Seattle, WA 98122　　　　　　　　Marcia Myers, South Reg.Libn.
Founded: 1965. **Staff:** Prof 3; Other 4. **Subjects:** Afro-American history and literature. **Special Collections:** Afro-Americana Collection. **Holdings:** 5700 books; 192 bound periodical volumes; 750 portraits, pictures; 1500 pamphlets; 300 phonograph records. **Subscriptions:** 17 journals and other serials. **Services:** Interlibrary loans (fee); copying; library open to public. **Networks/Consortia:** Member of WLN. **Staff:** Ryo Tsai, Pub.Serv.Libn.; Nancy Foley, Coord, Adult Serv.; Mary Ross, Pub.Serv.Libn.

★12377★

SEATTLE PUBLIC LIBRARY - EDUCATION, PSYCHOLOGY, SOCIOLOGY, SPORTS DEPARTMENT (Soc Sci)†
1000 Fourth Ave.　　　　　　　　Phone: (206) 625-2665
Seattle, WA 98104　　　　　　　　Lonita M. Walton, Mng.Libn.
Staff: Prof 6; Other 7. **Subjects:** Education, psychology, sociology, human relations, recreation, sports and games, vocations, occult, etiquette, childbirth, child care, criminology, sex, marriage and family. **Special Collections:** Adult reading and enrichment collection (adult literacy); Career Information Center Collection; Regional Foundation Center Collection. **Holdings:** 68,700 books; microforms; college catalogs. **Services:** Interlibrary loans; department open to public. **Computerized Information Services:** DIALOG, SDC, New York Times Information Service. **Special Catalogs:** Local club file; Seattle-King County social agencies file.

★12378★

SEATTLE PUBLIC LIBRARY - GOVERNMENTAL RESEARCH ASSISTANCE LIBRARY (Soc Sci)†
Municipal Bldg.
600 Fourth Ave.　　　　　　　　Phone: (206) 625-2665
Seattle, WA 98104　　　　　　　　Barbara Guptill, Mng.Libn.
Founded: 1931. **Staff:** Prof 3; Other 4. **Subjects:** Public administration, local government, police science, fire fighting, city planning, public personnel administration, municipal finance. **Special Collections:** City and county documents. **Holdings:** 18,000 volumes; 68 VF drawers. **Subscriptions:** 175 journals and other serials. **Services:** Interlibrary loans; Municipal Reference Exchange Program; library open to public for reference use only. **Computerized Information Services:** DIALOG, SDC, New York Times

Information Service, Local Government Information Network (LOGIN); Databnk (local database). **Publications:** Recent Additions, weekly - distributed to city and county personnel, civic organizations and other municipal reference libraries. **Staff:** Jeannette Voiland, Libn.; Howard Fox, Libn.

★12379★

SEATTLE PUBLIC LIBRARY - HISTORY, GOVERNMENT AND BIOGRAPHY DEPARTMENT (Hist)†
1000 Fourth Ave.　　　　　　　　Phone: (206) 625-2665
Seattle, WA 98104　　　　　　Jean Coberly, Hd., History Dept.
Staff: Prof 10; Other 7. **Subjects:** Northwest history and politics, biography, genealogy, travel. **Special Collections:** Northwest history; Sayre-Carkeek Theater program collection; Balch autograph collection. **Holdings:** General periodicals; microrecords, newspapers, maps. **Services:** Interlibrary loans; copying; department open to public. **Computerized Information Services:** DIALOG, SDC, New York Times Information Service. **Special Indexes:** Northwest history index; Seattle newspaper index.

★12380★

SEATTLE PUBLIC LIBRARY - LITERATURE, LANGUAGES, PHILOSOPHY & RELIGION DEPARTMENT (Hum)†
1000 Fourth Ave.　　　　　　　　Phone: (206) 625-2665
Seattle, WA 98104　　　　　　　　Nancy Wildin, Hd.
Staff: Prof 9; Other 15. **Subjects:** Literature, languages, philosophy, religion, drama, poetry, fiction, general bibliography. **Special Collections:** Multilingual collection (30 languages; 26,000 volumes); young adult collection (6000 volumes); popular library (18,000 volumes). **Holdings:** 200,000 books and bound periodical volumes; 28 VF drawers of unbound plays and scripts; 10 volumes of Seattle Theatre scrapbooks. **Subscriptions:** 800 journals and other serials. **Services:** Interlibrary loans; department open to public.

★12381★

SEATTLE PUBLIC LIBRARY - MEDIA & PROGRAM SERVICES (Aud-Vis)†
1000 Fourth Ave.　　　　　　　　Phone: (206) 625-2665
Seattle, WA 98104　　　　　　　　Kandy B. Brandt, Hd.
Staff: Prof 4; Other 10. **Subjects:** Adult education, child development, general collection. **Special Collections:** 16mm film collection (1850 prints, all subjects); 8mm film collection (475 prints). **Holdings:** 275 books; 52 bound periodical volumes; 250 slide sets; 36 filmstrip sets; 420 video cassettes; 110 videodiscs. **Subscriptions:** 46 journals and other serials. **Services:** Services open to public for reference use only. **Special Catalogs:** Media Catalog (book); resource file (card). **Staff:** Glennie Ruth Webb, Media Libn.; Stephen Goldenberg, Video Libn.; Ray Serebrin, Prog.Libn.

★12382★

SEATTLE PUBLIC LIBRARY - WASHINGTON LIBRARY FOR THE BLIND AND PHYSICALLY HANDICAPPED (Aud-Vis)
821 Lenora St.　　　　　　　　Phone: (206) 464-6930
Seattle, WA 98121　　　　　　　Jan Ames, Regional Libn.
Founded: 1931. **Staff:** 18. **Subjects:** Blindness and disabilities. **Holdings:** 20,000 braille books; 100,000 talking books; 56,000 tape cassettes; 6000 ink print books. **Subscriptions:** 100 journals and other serials. **Services:** Readers' Services; Radio Reading Service; Braille and Taping Service; Aids for Print Handicapped. **Publications:** Newsletter. **Special Catalogs:** Talking book catalogs, braille catalogs and cassette catalogs - most prepared by the National Library Service for the Blind and Physically Handicapped at the Library of Congress, and large print catalogs for distribution to eligible borrowers and libraries. **Staff:** Karen Wallin, Mgr., Volunteer Serv.; Robyn Foreman, Mgr., Rd.Serv.

★12383★

SEATTLE TIMES - LIBRARY (Publ)†
Fairview N. & John
Box 70　　　　　　　　　　　　Phone: (206) 464-2311
Seattle, WA 98111　　　　　　　　Beverly Russell, Libn.
Founded: 1900. **Staff:** Prof 9; Other 11. **Subjects:** Newspaper reference topics. **Holdings:** 6000 books; 1600 bound periodical volumes; 8000 pamphlets and maps; 2 million photographs; 13 million news clippings. **Subscriptions:** 55 journals and other serials. **Services:** Library not open to public. **Computerized Information Services:** DIALOG, SDC, New York Times Information Service. **Staff:** Ann Carver, Asst.Libn.; Sandra Freeman, Asst.Libn.

★12384★

SEATTLE TRUST & SAVINGS BANK - LIBRARY (Bus-Fin)
804 Second Ave.　　　　　　　　Phone: (206) 223-2052
Seattle, WA 98104　　　　　　　　Dorothy S. Hughes, Libn.
Staff: Prof 1. **Subjects:** Banking, business. **Holdings:** 1000 books. **Subscriptions:** 75 journals and other serials; 10 newspapers. **Services:**

Interlibrary loans; copying; SDI; library open to public by prior arrangement.

★12385★
SEATTLE WEAVERS' GUILD - LIBRARY (Art)
1245 10th Ave. E.
Seattle, WA 98102
Staff: 2. **Subjects:** Weaving, textiles, spinning, fibers. **Holdings:** 490 books; 105 bound periodical volumes; slides; 46 other cataloged items. **Subscriptions:** 22 journals and other serials. **Services:** Library not open to public.

★12386★
SEBASTIAN COUNTY LAW LIBRARY (Law)†
503 Stephens Bldg.   Phone: (501) 783-4730
Fort Smith, AR 72901   Frances F. Newhouse, Libn.
Founded: 1972. **Staff:** Prof 1. **Subjects:** Law. **Holdings:** 14,000 volumes. **Services:** Copying; library open to public.

SEBRING MEMORIAL LIBRARY
See: Chevy Chase Baptist Church

SEC
See: U.S. Securities and Exchange Commission

★12387★
SECOND PRESBYTERIAN CHURCH - CAPEN MEMORIAL LIBRARY (Rel-Theol)
313 N. East St.   Phone: (309) 828-6297
Bloomington, IL 61701
Founded: 1939. **Subjects:** Religion, religious education, missions. **Special Collections:** Local church history. **Holdings:** 3200 books; 150 pamphlets; 3 VF drawers. **Services:** Library open to public.

SECURITIES AND EXCHANGE COMMISSION
See: U.S. Securities and Exchange Commission

★12388★
SECURITY BENEFIT LIFE INSURANCE COMPANY - LIBRARY (Bus-Fin)
700 Harrison St.   Phone: (913) 295-3000
Topeka, KS 66636   Kathy Jones, Personnel Ck.
Subjects: Insurance, law, securities, marketing, Life Office Management Association. **Holdings:** 3000 books; company records and annual reports; case histories. **Services:** Library not open to public.

★12389★
SECURITY PACIFIC NATIONAL BANK - ECONOMICS AND BUSINESS LIBRARY (Bus-Fin)
333 S. Hope St.   Phone: (213) 613-8623
Los Angeles, CA 90071   Ann E. Wiedel, Res.Off.
Founded: 1920. **Staff:** Prof 1; Other 1. **Subjects:** Banking and finance, real estate, general business, agriculture. **Special Collections:** California history collection (2500 volumes). **Holdings:** 3000 books; 450 bound periodical volumes; 370 theses; 15,000 VF materials; 370 masters' theses on banking; 50 serials on microfiche. **Subscriptions:** 475 journals and other serials; 30 newspapers. **Services:** Interlibrary loans; copying; library open to public by appointment. **Automated Operations:** Computerized serials. **Computerized Information Services:** LEXIS. **Publications:** Monthly Acquisitions List. **Special Catalogs:** Union Catalog.

★12390★
SEDGWICK COUNTY LAW LIBRARY (Law)†
255 N. Market, Suite 210   Phone: (316) 263-2251
Wichita, KS 67202   Jonalou M. Pinnell, Libn.
Founded: 1915. **Staff:** Prof 1; Other 2. **Subjects:** Law. **Holdings:** 25,700 books; 4000 bound periodical volumes. **Subscriptions:** 5 newspapers. **Services:** Library open to public with circulation restricted to lawyers.

★12391★
SEDGWICK, DETERT, MORAN & ARNOLD - LIBRARY AND INFORMATION CENTER (Law)
111 Pine St.   Phone: (415) 982-0303
San Francisco, CA 94111   Francis Gates, Libn.
Staff: Prof 1; Other 1. **Subjects:** Law. **Holdings:** 7500 books. **Services:** Interlibrary loans; library not open to public. **Computerized Information Services:** LEXIS, Westlaw.

SEED (Lindon) LIBRARY
See: Grant Hospital of Chicago - Lindon Seed Library

SELF MEMORIAL HOSPITAL - UPPER SAVANNAH AREA HEALTH EDUCATION CONSORTIUM
See: Upper Savannah Area Health Education Consortium

SELFRIDGE AIR NATIONAL GUARD BASE
See: U.S. Army - Tacom Support Activity-Selfridge

★12392★
SELIGMAN (J. & W.) & CO. INCORPORATED - RESEARCH LIBRARY (Bus-Fin)
One Bankers Trust Pl.   Phone: (212) 488-0456
New York, NY 10006   Paula A. Gray, Libn.
Founded: 1931. **Staff:** Prof 1; Other 4. **Subjects:** Corporations, finance, investment companies, general business statistics, economics. **Holdings:** 2000 books; 450 bound periodical volumes; 3500 corporate and industry files; 2 drawers of maps; telephone directories; 150 reels of microfilm; 840 microfiche. **Subscriptions:** 500 journals and other serials; 25 newspapers. **Services:** Interlibrary loans; library not open to public. **Publications:** Serials List, annual - for internal distribution only. **Special Catalogs:** Catalog of Company History.

SELIGMAN LIBRARY
See: Columbia University - Rare Book and Manuscript Library

★12393★
SELKIRK MENTAL HEALTH CENTRE - CENTRAL LIBRARY (Med)
Box 9600   Phone: (204) 482-3810
Selkirk, MB, Canada R1A 2B5   John English, Chm., Lib.Comm.
Founded: 1976. **Staff:** Prof 1. **Subjects:** Psychiatry, psychiatric nursing, psychology, social service, nursing, allied health sciences. **Holdings:** 4000 books; 1000 bound periodical volumes; AV material. **Subscriptions:** 110 journals and other serials. **Services:** Interlibrary loans; copying (limited); library open to public with restrictions. **Staff:** Lorna Weiss, Lib.Techn.

SELLES SOLA MEMORIAL COLLECTION
See: University of Puerto Rico - College of Education

SELZNICK (David O.) FILM ARCHIVES
See: University of Texas, Austin - Harry Ransom Humanities Research Center

★12394★
SEMANTODONTICS, INC. - LIBRARY (Med)
Box 15668   Phone: (602) 955-5662
Phoenix, AZ 85060   Jim Rhode, Pres.
Staff: 1. **Subjects:** Dentistry, patient care, dental staff training, psychology, communications, transactional analysis. **Holdings:** 400 books; 50 bound periodical volumes; 200 magnetic tapes; 100 patient education pamphlets. **Subscriptions:** 20 journals and other serials. **Services:** Copying; library open to public by appointment. **Remarks:** Semantodontics means Semantics in Dentistry.

★12395★
SEMINAIRE DE CHICOUTIMI - BIBLIOTHEQUE (Rel-Theol; Hum)
679 Rue Chabanel   Phone: (418) 549-1786
Chicoutimi, PQ, Canada G7H 1Z7   Clement-Jacques Simard, Dir.
Founded: 1873. **Staff:** Prof 2; Other 1. **Subjects:** Religion, theology, science, philosophy, philology, art, history, literature. **Special Collections:** Canadian literature; Latin and ancient Greek literature. **Holdings:** 80,000 books; 20,000 archives. **Subscriptions:** 100 journals and other serials. **Services:** Interlibrary loans; copying; library open to public with restrictions. **Staff:** Jean-Marc Fortin, Lib.Techn./Asst.

★12396★
SEMINAIRE DE QUEBEC - ARCHIVES (Hist)*
Box 460   Phone: (418) 692-3981
Quebec, PQ, Canada G1R 4R7   Rev. Georges Drouin, Archiviste
Founded: 1941. **Staff:** Prof 1; Other 3. **Subjects:** History - local, Canadian, American, economic and religious. **Special Collections:** Canadian public documents, 1763-1867 (250 volumes). **Holdings:** 2000 books; 250 bound periodical volumes; 1500 boxes of manuscripts; 150 feet of bound documents; 200 reels of microfilm. **Services:** Copying; archives open to public with restrictions. **Networks/Consortia:** Member of Association des Archivistes du Quebec.

★12397★
SEMINAIRE ST-ALPHONSE - BIBLIOTHEQUE (Hum)
10026 Rue Royale   Phone: (418) 827-2751
Ste. Anne de Beaupre, PQ, Canada G0A 3C0   Robert Boucher, Dir.
Staff: 3. **Subjects:** Literature, Canadian history, education, art. **Holdings:**
35,500 volumes; 10,000 slides; 2000 phonograph records. **Subscriptions:**
100 journals and other serials and newspapers. **Services:** Copying; library
open to public with restrictions.

★12398★
SEMINAIRE ST-JOSEPH - BIBLIOTHEQUE (Rel-Theol; Hist)
858 Laviolette
C.P. 548
Trois-Rivieres, PQ, Canada G9A 5J1   Phone: (819) 378-5167
                                                 Claude Aubin, Dir.
Founded: 1860. **Staff:** Prof 1; Other 2. **Subjects:** Religion, French literature,
history, foreign literature, sciences. **Special Collections:** Canadiana.
Holdings: 85,000 books; 15,000 bound periodical volumes; 225 films;
18,000 slides; 125 magnetic tapes; 4500 phonograph records.
Subscriptions: 162 journals and other serials; 12 newspapers. **Services:**
Library not open to public.

★12399★
SEMINAIRE DES TROIS RIVIERES - ARCHIVES (Hist)*
858 Laviolette
C.P. 548
Trois-Rivieres, PQ, Canada G9A 5J1   Jules Bettez, Dir.
Staff: Prof 3; Other 1. **Subjects:** Local history and genealogy, Canadiana.
Holdings: 12,000 books; 2000 bound periodical volumes; 28 filing cabinets;
1 filing cabinet of microfiche; 49 reels of microfilm; 20 films; 230
audiotapes. **Subscriptions:** 15 journals and other serials. **Staff:** Suzanne
Girard, Archv.

SEMINARIO EVANGELICO DE PUERTO RICO
See: Evangelical Seminary of Puerto Rico

★12400★
SEMINARY OF THE IMMACULATE CONCEPTION - LIBRARY (Rel-Theol)
West Neck Rd.   Phone: (516) 423-0483
Huntington, NY 11743   Jiri (George) Lipa, Ph.D., Libn.
Founded: 1930. **Staff:** Prof 1; Other 3. **Subjects:** Theology, scripture,
church history, patrology, canon law, liturgy, catechetics. **Holdings:** 45,000
books; 5400 bound periodical volumes. **Subscriptions:** 245 journals and
other serials. **Services:** Interlibrary loans; copying; library open to public by
appointment. **Networks/Consortia:** Member of Long Island Library Resources
Council (LILRC).

★12401★
SEMINARY OF OUR LADY OF PROVIDENCE - LIBRARY
900 Warwick Neck Ave.
Warwick, RI 02889
Defunct

★12402★
SEMINARY OF ST. PIUS X - LIBRARY
Donaldson Rd.
Erlanger, KY 41018
Defunct

SEMINEX LIBRARY
See: Christ Seminary

★12403★
SEMMES, BOWEN & SEMMES - LAW LIBRARY (Law)
10 Light St.   Phone: (301) 539-5040
Baltimore, MD 21202   Helen Y. Harris, Libn.
Staff: Prof 2; Other 2. **Subjects:** Law. **Holdings:** 15,000 books; 475 bound
periodical volumes; 100 bound briefs; 10 VF drawers of memoranda of law.
Subscriptions: 52 journals and other serials. **Services:** Library open to public
with restrictions; prior arrangements must be made by telephone.
Computerized Information Services: DIALOG, LEXIS. **Publications:**
Semmes Library Information Publication (SLIP) - for internal distribution only.
Special Indexes: Index to firm memoranda and briefs (computerized).

★12404★
SEMMES-MURPHEY CLINIC - LIBRARY (Med)
920 Madison Ave., Suite 201   Phone: (901) 522-7700
Memphis, TN 38103   Charles M. Prest, Libn.
Staff: Prof 1. **Subjects:** Neurosurgery, neurology. **Holdings:** 990 books; 639
bound periodical volumes. **Subscriptions:** 26 journals and other serials.

Services: Copying; library not open to public. **Networks/Consortia:** Member
of Association of Memphis Area Health Science Libraries (AMAHSL).

★12405★
SENATE HOUSE STATE HISTORIC SITE - LIBRARY & ARCHIVES (Hist)
296 Fair St.   Phone: (914) 338-2786
Kingston, NY 12401   Leigh R. Jones, Historic Site Mgr.
Founded: 1946. **Subjects:** Art and local history, genealogy. **Special
Collections:** Hoes Collection; VanGaasbeek Collection; Vanderlyn Collection;
Elting Collection; DeWitt Collection. **Holdings:** 975 books; 1000 bound
periodical volumes; 200 pamphlets; 25,000 manuscripts, maps, clippings,
land grants, deeds. **Services:** Copying; library open to public by appointment.
Special Indexes: Vanderlyn Index; DeWitt Index.

★12406★
**SENECA COLLEGE OF APPLIED ARTS AND TECHNOLOGY - LESLIE CAMPUS
RESOURCE CENTRE** (Med)
1255 Sheppard Ave. E.   Phone: (416) 494-8900
Willowdale, ON, Canada M2K 1E2   Vinh P. Le, Ref.Libn.
Staff: Prof 1; Other 4. **Subjects:** Health sciences, nursing, dentistry. **Special
Collections:** International health (450 volumes). **Holdings:** 16,154 books;
800 bound periodical volumes; 100 filmstrips; 200 AV records; 300
audiotapes; 600 videotapes; 50 films; 250 sets of slides; microfilm; 180
slide/tape programs. **Subscriptions:** 71 journals and other serials. **Services:**
Interlibrary loans; copying; center open to public with registration. **Automated
Operations:** Computerized cataloging, acquisitions and circulation.
Computerized Information Services: DIALOG, DOBIS, INET Gateway;
internal database. Performs free searches. **Networks/Consortia:** Member of
Bibliocentre. **Publications:** Bibliographies.

★12407★
SENECA FALLS HISTORICAL SOCIETY - LIBRARY (Hist)
55 Cayuga St.   Phone: (315) 568-8412
Seneca Falls, NY 13148   Lisa F. Johnson, Exec.Dir.
Subjects: Local and state history, Victoriana. **Special Collections:** Women's
Rights Collection (documents, 1848 to present). **Holdings:** 1300 books; 300
bound periodical volumes; 17 VF drawers; local newspaper, 1839 to present
(microfilm). **Services:** Copying; library open to public. **Staff:** Dawn C.
Emerson, Libn.

★12408★
SENECA ZOOLOGICAL SOCIETY - LIBRARY (Sci-Tech)
2222 St. Paul St.   Phone: (716) 342-2744
Rochester, NY 14621   Daniel R. Michalowski, Zoological Pk.Dir.
Founded: 1962. **Staff:** Prof 1. **Subjects:** Zoos, zoo animals, veterinary
medicine, ecology, zoology, herpetology. **Holdings:** 1770 books; 30 zoo
guidebooks. **Subscriptions:** 29 journals and other serials. **Services:** Copying;
library open to public. **Publications:** Zoo Annual Report, free upon request;
Animal Kingdom, 6/year - by subscription.

★12409★
SENTRY INSURANCE COMPANY - LIBRARY (Bus-Fin)†
1800 N. Point Dr.   Phone: (715) 346-6788
Stevens Point, WI 54481   Irene A. Dobbert, Corp.Libn.
Founded: 1930. **Staff:** Prof 1; Other 6. **Subjects:** Insurance - property/
casualty and life; pensions; law; business management. **Holdings:** 21,000
books; 6000 bound periodical volumes; 125 VF drawers of monographs,
booklets, clippings, pamphlets, reports, pictures and archives. **Subscriptions:**
475 journals and other serials; 17 newspapers. **Services:** Interlibrary loans;
copying; library open to public by permission. **Publications:** Acquisition List -
for internal distribution only. **Staff:** Annette Whelihan, Asst.Libn.

SEQUOIA GENEALOGICAL SOCIETY
See: Tulare Public Library - Inez L. Hyde Memorial Collection

★12410★
**SERGENT, HAUSKINS & BECKWITH, CONSULTING GEOTECHNICAL
ENGINEERS - LIBRARY** (Sci-Tech)
3940 W. Clarendon Ave.   Phone: (602) 272-6848
Phoenix, AZ 85019   John A. Cassidy, Libn.
Staff: Prof 1. **Subjects:** Engineering - earthquake, materials, and
geotechnical; hydrology, geophysics. **Special Collections:** Geotechnical
engineering problems in arid regions (1500 volumes). **Holdings:** 2525 books
and bound periodical volumes; 7500 other cataloged items; 18 VF drawers;
70 boxes of unbound periodicals. **Subscriptions:** 94 journals and other serials.
Services: Library open to public with restrictions. **Computerized Information
Services:** DIALOG, SDC.

★12411★
SERVANTS OF THE IMMACULATE HEART OF MARY - ARCHIVES (Rel-Theol)
Villa Maria House of Studies
Immaculata, PA 19345
Phone: (215) 647-2160
Sr. Genevieve Mary, Archv.
Subjects: Congregation history, 1840 to present. **Holdings:** 160 cubic feet of correspondence, journals, financial records, architectural drawings, and photographs. **Services:** Copying; archives open to public on a limited schedule.

SERVICE CENTER FOR AGING INFORMATION (SCAN)
See: Newark Public Library - Social Science Division

SERVITES
See: Order of Servants of Mary

★12412★
SERVO CORPORATION OF AMERICA - TECHNICAL LIBRARY
111 New South Rd.
Hicksville, NY 11802
Defunct

SETON HALL UNIVERSITY - ARCHAEOLOGICAL SOCIETY OF NEW JERSEY
See: Archaeological Society of New Jersey

★12413★
SETON HALL UNIVERSITY - MC LAUGHLIN LIBRARY (Hist)
405 South Orange Ave.
South Orange, NJ 07079
Phone: (201) 762-9000
Rev. James C. Sharp, Univ.Libn.
Staff: Prof 14; Other 32. **Subjects:** Education, science, history, modern languages (including English), Irish culture. **Special Collections:** Gerald Murphy Civil War Collection (1000 volumes); Oriental Collection (10,000 volumes). **Holdings:** 350,000 books; 2600 bound periodical volumes. **Subscriptions:** 2600 journals and other serials; 34 newspapers. **Services:** Interlibrary loans; copying; library open to public, fee charged. **Automated Operations:** Computerized cataloging and ILL. **Computerized Information Services:** OCLC. **Networks/Consortia:** Member of County of Essex Cooperating Libraries (CECLS). **Publications:** Annual report; periodical listings; research guides. **Staff:** Paul Chao, Assoc.Libn.

★12414★
SETON HALL UNIVERSITY - MAC MANUS COLLECTION (Area-Ethnic)
McLaughlin Library
405 South Orange Ave.
South Orange, NJ 07079
Phone: (201) 762-9000
Rev. William Noe Field, Cur., Spec.Coll.
Founded: 1958. **Subjects:** Every phase of Irish literature, history, politics, and particularly the home rule question. **Special Collections:** Complete works of Liam O'Flaherty (300 autographed 1st editions; periodicals and news clippings). **Holdings:** 4000 volumes; autographs; clippings; letters. **Services:** Copying; library open to public with letter of introduction. **Automated Operations:** Computerized cataloging. **Computerized Information Services:** DIALOG, OCLC. Performs on cost recovery basis. **Networks/Consortia:** Member of County of Essex Cooperating Libraries (CECLS).

★12415★
SETON HALL UNIVERSITY - SCHOOL OF LAW - LAW LIBRARY (Law)
1111 Raymond Blvd.
Newark, NJ 07102
Phone: (201) 642-8766
Richard G. Hutchins, Dir.
Founded: 1950. **Staff:** Prof 7; Other 11. **Subjects:** Law. **Holdings:** 135,000 books; 20,000 bound periodical volumes; 63,000 volumes of microforms; 200 titles of audiovisual material. **Subscriptions:** 3500 journals and other serials. **Services:** Interlibrary loans; copying; library open to visitors. **Automated Operations:** Computerized cataloging. **Computerized Information Services:** OCLC, LEXIS, Westlaw. **Networks/Consortia:** Member of PALINET & Union Library Catalogue of Pennsylvania. **Staff:** Gerald A. Garafola, Law Libn.; Constance Nourse, Ref.Libn.; Deborah D. Herrera, Ref.Libn.; Jann Braudis Brown, Cat.Libn.; Jean M. Scott, Acq./Doc.Libn.; Louis M. Adams, Ref.Libn.

★12416★
SETON HALL UNIVERSITY - UNIVERSITY ARCHIVES (Hist; Rel-Theol)
McLaughlin Library
405 South Orange Ave.
South Orange, NJ 07079
Phone: (201) 762-7052
Peter J. Wosh, Univ.Archv.
Founded: 1978. **Staff:** Prof 2; Other 1. **Subjects:** New Jersey Catholicism and Catholic history. **Special Collections:** Archives of the Archdiocese of Newark (300 linear feet); Seton Hall University Archives (250 linear feet); Bernard Shanley Papers (25 linear feet); archives of the Seton family, Leonard Dreyfuss, Chief Justice Richard Hughes; archival and manuscript collections (40 linear feet). **Services:** Copying; archives open to public. **Publications:**

New Jersey Catholic Records Newsletter, 3/year - for sale. **Special Catalogs:** Catholic Parish and Intitutional Histories in the State of New Jersey; Guide to Northern New Jersey Catholic Parish and Institutional Records.

★12417★
SETON, JOHNSON & ODELL, INC. - TECHNICAL INFORMATION CENTER (Sci-Tech)
133 S.W. 2nd Ave.
Portland, OR 97204
Phone: (503) 226-3921
Denise Hiatt, Sec.
Founded: 1978. **Staff:** Prof 1; Other 1. **Subjects:** Engineering - mechanical, structural, civil, electrical, air/noise. **Special Collections:** Environmental Protection Agency materials on air/noise pollution control. **Holdings:** 810 volumes; 50 reports; 8 VF drawers of vendors' brochures. **Subscriptions:** 79 journals and other serials. **Services:** Interlibrary loans; copying; SDI; center open to public with restrictions. **Computerized Information Services:** Online systems.

★12418★
SETON MEDICAL CENTER - LIBRARY (Med)
1900 Sullivan Ave.
Daly City, CA 94015
Phone: (415) 992-4000
Marie Grace Abbruzzese, Libn.
Staff: Prof 1. **Subjects:** Medicine, nursing and hospital administration. **Holdings:** 2000 books; 2000 bound periodical volumes; 8 shelves of audio cassettes and tapes. **Subscriptions:** 125 journals and other serials. **Services:** Interlibrary loans; copying; library open to professionals and referrals. **Publications:** Acquisitions List, irregular - for internal distribution only. **Formerly:** Mary's Help Hospital.

★12419★
SETON MEMORIAL LIBRARY
Philmont Scout Ranch & Explorer Base
Cimarron, NM 87714
Founded: 1967. **Subjects:** Books written by Ernest T. Seton, Boy Scouts, Southwest, natural history, Indian Art, Bureau of American Ethnology. **Special Collections:** Ernest T. Seton Collection (200 volumes; 7 VF drawers of manuscripts and correspondence). **Holdings:** 4100 books; 250 bound periodical volumes; 2000 photographs; 46 boxes of pamphlets; 90 maps; local archeology reports (2 VF drawers). **Remarks:** Maintained by Boy Scouts of America-Philmont Scout Ranch and Explorer Base. Presently inactive.

★12420★
SETTLEMENT MUSIC SCHOOL - BLANCHE WOLF KOHN LIBRARY (Mus)
416 Queen St.
Philadelphia, PA 19147
Phone: (215) 336-0400
Alicia Randisi Hooker, Hd.Libn.
Staff: Prof 2; Other 2. **Subjects:** Music. **Special Collections:** J. Gershon Cohen Chamber Music; William M. Kincaid Flute Music; Mischa Schneider Cello Music; Herman Busch Violin Music; woodwind music. **Holdings:** 1200 books; 10,000 music scores; 100,000 pieces of classical sheet music. **Subscriptions:** 20 journals and other serials. **Services:** Copying; library open to alumni and noted musicians. **Special Catalogs:** Catalogs of special collections and woodwind music (both card).

SEUFERT MEMORIAL LIBRARY
See: Norwegian-American Hospital, Inc.

SEVAREID (Eric) JOURNALISM LIBRARY
See: University of Minnesota - Eric Sevareid Journalism Library

★12421★
SEVENTH-DAY ADVENTISTS - GENERAL CONFERENCE - OFFICE OF ARCHIVES AND STATISTICS (Rel-Theol)
6840 Eastern Ave. N.W.
Washington, DC 20012
Phone: (202) 723-0800
Dr. F. Donald Yost, Archv.
Staff: Prof 3; Other 4. **Subjects:** Seventh-day Adventism - history, theology, missions, institutions. **Special Collections:** Personal collections of prominent SDA leaders. **Holdings:** 100 books; 2000 bound periodical volumes; pamphlets; administrative records. **Services:** Copying; office open to public. **Publications:** Guide to Holdings of Archives. **Staff:** Bert Haloviak, Asst.Dir.; Jim Ford, Rec.Mgr.

★12422★
SEVENTH DAY BAPTIST HISTORICAL SOCIETY - LIBRARY (Rel-Theol; Hist)
Box 1678
Janesville, WI 53547
Phone: (608) 752-5055
D. Scott Smith, Hist.
Founded: 1916. **Staff:** Prof 2. **Subjects:** Seventh Day Baptist history; Sabbatarian literature, church history, religion; New England history; genealogy. **Special Collections:** Julius F. Sachse Ephrata Collection; Nyasaland-Malawi Collection; 1895-1915. **Holdings:** 6000 books; 500 bound and indexed periodical volumes; 250 society record books; tracts;

reports; church records; letters; manuscripts. **Subscriptions:** 5 journals and other serials. **Services:** Interlibrary loans; copying; library open to public. **Publications:** Annual Report; occasional bulletins. **Remarks:** Library is located at 3120 Kennedy Rd., Janesville, WI. **Staff:** Janet Thorngate, Libn.

SEWARD HOUSE
See: Foundation Historical Association

★12423★
SEWARD & KISSEL - LIBRARY (Law)
Wall Street Plaza   Phone: (212) 248-2800
New York, NY 10005   Robert J. Davis, Libn.
Staff: Prof 1; Other 2. **Subjects:** Law. **Holdings:** 16,000 volumes; 17 VF drawers of pamphlets. **Subscriptions:** 110 journals and other serials. **Services:** Interlibrary loans; library not open to public. **Computerized Information Services:** LEXIS, DIALOG, Dow Jones News/Retrieval, NEXIS.

★12424★
SEX INFORMATION & EDUCATION COUNCIL OF THE U.S. - SIECUS INFORMATION SERVICE AND LIBRARY (Soc Sci)
715 Broadway, Rm. 213   Phone: (212) 673-3850
New York, NY 10003   Leigh Hallingby, Libn.
Founded: 1979. **Staff:** Prof 1. **Subjects:** Sex education, behavior and research; human sexuality; family life education. **Holdings:** 2000 books; 120 curriculum items; 7 VF drawers; 150 pamphlets and booklets. **Subscriptions:** 70 journals and other serials; 5 newspapers. **Services:** Copying; library open to professionals and students. **Networks/Consortia:** Member of Association for Population/Family Planning Libraries and Information Centers-International (APLIC-International).

★12425★
SEYFARTH, SHAW, FAIRWEATHER & GERALDSON - LIBRARY (Law)
2029 Century Park East, Suite 3300   Phone: (213) 277-7200
Los Angeles, CA 90067   Beth Bernstein, Libn.
Staff: Prof 1; Other 1. **Subjects:** Labor and agricultural labor law. **Special Collections:** California Agricultural Labor Relations Board decisions, 1975 to present. **Holdings:** 12,000 books. **Services:** Interlibrary loans; library open to area law firms. **Automated Operations:** Computerized cataloging. **Computerized Information Services:** LEXIS, DIALOG. **Special Indexes:** Index to Agricultural Labor Relations Board decisions.

★12426★
SEYFARTH, SHAW, FAIRWEATHER & GERALDSON - LIBRARY (Law)
55 E. Monroe St.   Phone: (312) 346-8000
Chicago, IL 60603   Kenneth C. Halicki, Libn.
Staff: Prof 3; Other 3. **Subjects:** Labor law, industrial relations, taxation. **Holdings:** 25,000 books and bound periodical volumes; 96 VF drawers of pamphlets, decisions, briefs, agreements. **Subscriptions:** 275 journals and other serials. **Services:** Interlibrary loans; library not open to public. **Automated Operations:** Computerized cataloging. **Computerized Information Services:** DIALOG, LEXIS, LABOR LAW. **Staff:** Joseph Hoonicki, Ref.; Deborah Pearson, Cat.

★12427★
SEYFARTH, SHAW, FAIRWEATHER & GERALDSON - LIBRARY (Law)
520 Madison Ave.   Phone: (212) 715-9635
New York, NY 10022   Catherine Inglis, Libn.
Staff: Prof 1; Other 1. **Subjects:** Law - labor, securities, corporate, tax, real estate. **Holdings:** 9050 books; 100 bound periodical volumes. **Subscriptions:** 48 journals and other serials; 8 newspapers. **Services:** Interlibrary loans; copying; library open to public with permission. **Automated Operations:** Computerized cataloging and serials. **Computerized Information Services:** DIALOG, LEXIS, New York Times Information Service. Performs searches on cost recovery basis. **Networks/Consortia:** Member of Law Library Association of Greater New York.

SEYMOUR (William) THEATRE COLLECTION
See: Princeton University - William Seymour Theatre Collection

SHADEK-FACKENTHAL LIBRARY
See: Franklin and Marshall College

SHADELANDS RANCH HISTORICAL MUSEUM
See: Walnut Creek Historical Society

★12428★
SHADYSIDE HOSPITAL - JAMES FRAZER HILLMAN HEALTH SCIENCES LIBRARY (Med)
5230 Centre Ave.   Phone: (412) 622-2415
Pittsburgh, PA 15232   Malinda Fetkovich, Dir.
Staff: Prof 2; Other 6. **Subjects:** Medicine, nursing. **Holdings:** 3000 books; 7000 bound periodical volumes. **Subscriptions:** 200 journals and other serials. **Services:** Interlibrary loans; library not open to public. **Networks/Consortia:** Member of Pittsburgh-East Hospital Library Cooperative.

★12429★
SHAKER COMMUNITY, INC. - LIBRARY (Hist)
Box 898   Phone: (413) 447-7284
Pittsfield, MA 01202   Jerry V. Grant, Dir.
Founded: 1960. **Staff:** 2. **Subjects:** Shaker history, Utopian history, music, herbs and botany, crafts, agriculture. **Holdings:** 1000 books; 75 Shaker tracts, 200 Shaker manuscripts; 7 oral history tapes; 171 reels of microfilm; 600 microfiche. **Services:** Copying; library open to public by appointment. **Staff:** Robert F.W. Meader, Libn.

★12430★
SHAKER HEIGHTS CITY SCHOOL DISTRICT - GARVIN LIBRARY (Educ)
15600 Parkland Dr.   Phone: (216) 921-1400
Shaker Heights, OH 44120   Ellen M. Stepanian, Dir. of Lib. Media
Staff: Prof 1; Other 1. **Subjects:** Education. **Holdings:** 1292 books; VF items; 761 microforms. **Subscriptions:** 38 journals and other serials. **Services:** Library not open to public. **Automated Operations:** Computerized cataloging. **Networks/Consortia:** Member of Cleveland Area Metropolitan Library System (CAMLS).

SHAKER LIBRARY
See: United Society of Believers - The Shaker Library

SHAKER LIBRARY
See: Warren County Historical Society - Museum and Library

★12431★
SHAKER MUSEUM FOUNDATION - EMMA B. KING LIBRARY (Rel-Theol)
                                             Phone: (518) 794-9100
Old Chatham, NY 12136   Ann Kelly, Libn./Archv.
Founded: 1950. **Staff:** Prof 1; Other 1. **Subjects:** Society of Shaker material covering 2 centuries and 19 communities: books and diaries, account books, drawings, music, theology, membership, vision. **Holdings:** 2000 books; 50 bound periodical volumes; 550 pamphlets; 2500 other cataloged items; 2500 slides; 120 reels of microfilm; AV material; 2409 manuscripts; 3000 photographs; 40 maps. **Subscriptions:** 20 journals and other serials. **Services:** Copying; research facilities granted to qualified people on application to the librarian; library open to public by appointment. **Publications:** List of publications - available on request. **Special Catalogs:** Catalog of the Emma B. King Library, 1970. **Remarks:** Library is a repository of Shaker Society manuscripts and records. **Staff:** Ann Kelly, Libn./Archv.

★12432★
SHAKESPEARE SOCIETY OF AMERICA - NEW PLACE RARE BOOK LIBRARY (Hum; Rare Book)
1107 N. Kings Rd.   Phone: (213) 654-5623
Los Angeles, CA 90069   Thad Taylor, Pres.
Founded: 1967. **Staff:** Prof 3; Other 2. **Subjects:** Shakespeare - all aspects of his works. **Special Collections:** Renaissance literature; early science; antique furniture; Shakespeare Stamp Collection; Shakespeare coins and medals. **Holdings:** 3000 books; 1500 bound periodical volumes; 1000 catalogs; 500 magazines and pamphlets; 450 clippings and articles; 2000 photographs and slides; 100 tapes and phonograph records. **Subscriptions:** 50 journals and other serials; 5 newspapers. **Services:** Interlibrary loans; library open to public with request in writing. **Publications:** Shakespeare's Proclamation - free to members, for sale to others. **Remarks:** The library is adjacent to a one-half scale replica of Shakespeare's Globe Theatre.

★12433★
SHAND, MORAHAN & COMPANY, INC. - LIBRARY (Bus-Fin)
One American Plaza   Phone: (312) 866-2800
Evanston, IL 60201   Deborah A. Schaffer, Libn.
Staff: Prof 1. **Subjects:** Property and casualty insurance, reinsurance, professional liability, management. **Holdings:** 400 books; 150 bound periodical volumes; 15 boxes of pamphlets and clippings. **Subscriptions:** 160 journals and other serials. **Services:** Interlibrary loans; copying; SDI; library open to public by appointment. **Computerized Information Services:** DIALOG, OCLC. **Networks/Consortia:** Member of ILLINET. **Publications:** Library Bulletin, bimonthly - for internal distribution only.

SHAND (William, Jr.) MEMORIAL LIBRARY
See: Franklin and Marshall College - Chemistry Department - William Shand, Jr. Memorial Library

SHANK MEMORIAL LIBRARY
See: Good Samaritan Hospital

★12434★
SHANLEY & FISHER - LAW LIBRARY (Law)
550 Broad St.   Phone: (201) 643-1220
Newark, NJ 07102   Susan C. Cunningham, Libn.
Staff: Prof 2; Other 2. Subjects: Law. Holdings: 20,000 volumes. Computerized Information Services: LEXIS.

SHANNON LIBRARY
See: University of Saskatchewan - St. Thomas More College

★12435★
SHANNON & WILSON, INC. - TECHNICAL LIBRARY (Sci-Tech)†
1105 N. 38th St.
Box C-30313
Seattle, WA 98103   Phone: (206) 632-8020
                                 Phyllis Jean Boucher, Libn.
Staff: Prof 1; Other 1. Subjects: Geotechnical engineering, rock mechanics, applied geophysics, earthquake effects on soils. Holdings: 2100 books and bound periodical volumes; 4820 reports, documents and clippings; 1200 maps. Subscriptions: 220 journals and other serials. Services: Interlibrary loans; copying; library open to public with permission of librarian. Computerized Information Services: SDC. Networks/Consortia: Member of WLN. Publications: Recent acquisitions, monthly.

SHAPIRO LIBRARY
See: New Hampshire College

SHAPIRO (Max) LIBRARY
See: Beth El Synagogue - Max Shapiro Library

★12436★
SHAPIRO (Samuel H.) DEVELOPMENTAL CENTER - PROFESSIONAL LIBRARY (Med)
100 E. Jeffery St.   Phone: (815) 939-8419
Kankakee, IL 60901   Juanita Licht, Resident Staff Libn.
Founded: 1877. Staff: 1. Subjects: Developmental disabilities, mental retardation. Holdings: 2200 volumes; videotapes; educational games. Subscriptions: 62 journals and other serials. Services: Interlibrary loans; library open to public by appointment. Remarks: Maintained by the Bur Oak Library System.

★12437★
SHARLOT HALL/PRESCOTT HISTORICAL SOCIETIES - LIBRARY/ARCHIVES (Hist)
415 W. Gurley St.   Phone: (602) 445-3122
Prescott, AZ 86301   Sue Abbey, Archv.
Founded: 1929. Staff: Prof 6; Other 7. Subjects: Anglo and Indian history of the Southwest, especially Arizona. Special Collections: Hartzell Collection of Indian Artifacts. Holdings: 5200 volumes; manuscripts; diaries; artifacts; letters; newspapers. Subscriptions: 8 journals and other serials. Services: Interlibrary loans (fee); copying; library/archives open to public. Publications: Quarterly newsletter.

★12438★
SHARON GENERAL HOSPITAL - MEDICAL STAFF LIBRARY (Med)
740 E. State St.   Phone: (412) 983-3911
Sharon, PA 16146   Eugenia Christenson, Libn.
Staff: 1. Subjects: Medicine and related fields. Holdings: 283 books; 679 bound periodical volumes; 2422 unbound journals; 2 VF drawers of clip sheets and pamphlets. Subscriptions: 33 journals and other serials. Services: Interlibrary loans; copying; library open to community residents.

★12439★
SHARON GENERAL HOSPITAL - SCHOOL OF NURSING - LIBRARY (Med)
740 E. State St.   Phone: (412) 983-3911
Sharon, PA 16146   Eugenia Christenson, Libn.
Staff: 1. Subjects: Nursing, medicine, nutrition and related sciences. Holdings: 1500 books; 200 bound periodical volumes; 50 volumes of unbound journals; 4 VF drawers of clipsheets and pamphlets; 117 videotapes; 261 filmstrips and records; 14 slide cassette programs; 23 audio cassettes. Subscriptions: 25 journals and other serials. Services: Interlibrary loans; copying; library open to community residents.

★12440★
SHARON HOSPITAL - HEALTH SCIENCES LIBRARY (Med)
W. Main St.   Phone: (203) 364-5511
Sharon, CT 06069
Subjects: Medicine. Holdings: 400 books; 1440 bound periodical volumes. Subscriptions: 107 journals and other serials. Services: Interlibrary loans; copying; library open to public for reference use only. Networks/Consortia: Member of Northwestern Connecticut Health Science Library Consortium. Staff: Lucie Collins, Co-Dir.; Jean Moore, Libn./Co-Dir.

SHARP (Charles Cutler) LIBRARY
See: Ohio State University - Chemistry Library

★12441★
SHARP (Ella) MUSEUM - LIBRARY/ARCHIVES (Hist)
3225 Fourth St.   Phone: (517) 787-2320
Jackson, MI 49203   Lynnea Loftis, Dir., Educ.
Founded: 1965. Subjects: Local history, Victorian culture, art. Special Collections: Merriman-Sharp Collection (family papers, 1835-1912). Holdings: 1200 books; 20 bound periodical volumes; 66 document cases and 34 storage boxes of periodicals; 20 document cases and 17 storage boxes of archival material. Subscriptions: 15 journals and other serials. Services: Interlibrary loans; copying; library open for scholarly research at the museum's convenience.

★12442★
SHARP MEMORIAL HOSPITAL - HEALTH SCIENCE LIBRARY (Med)
7901 Frost St.   Phone: (619) 292-2538
San Diego, CA 92123   Estelle Davis, Dir. of Lib.Serv.
Founded: 1970. Staff: 6. Subjects: Medicine and health science. Holdings: 1000 books; 2000 bound periodical volumes. Subscriptions: 250 journals and other serials. Services: Interlibrary loans; library not open to public. Computerized Information Services: MEDLINE, BRS.

SHARP (Reuben L.) HEALTH SCIENCE LIBRARY
See: Cooper Hospital/University Medical Center - Reuben L. Sharp Health Science Library

SHARPE ARMY DEPOT
See: U.S. Army - Special Services Division

★12443★
SHASTA COUNTY LAW LIBRARY (Law)
Court House
Redding, CA 96001   Joan Odell, Law Libn.
Founded: 1851. Subjects: Law. Holdings: 12,000 books and bound periodical volumes. Services: Library open to public for reference use only.

★12444★
SHATTUCK (Lemuel) HOSPITAL - MEDICAL LIBRARY (Med)
170 Morton St.   Phone: (617) 522-8110
Jamaica Plain, MA 02130   Beth C. Poisson, Libn.
Founded: 1954. Staff: Prof 1; Other 1. Subjects: Medicine and allied health sciences. Special Collections: Alcoholism (55 books). Holdings: 940 books; 4360 bound periodical volumes; 320 audio cassettes. Subscriptions: 205 journals and other serials. Services: Interlibrary loans; copying; library open to public. Computerized Information Services: NLM. Networks/Consortia: Member of Boston Biomedical Library Consortium.

SHATTUCK MEMORIAL LIBRARY
See: Pan American Society of New England

★12445★
SHAVER HOSPITAL FOR CHEST DISEASES - HEALTH SCIENCES LIBRARY (Med)
541 Glenridge Ave.   Phone: (416) 685-1381
St. Catharines, ON, Canada L2R 6S5   Ruth Servos, Dir.
Staff: 1. Subjects: Medicine, nursing and allied health sciences. Special Collections: Canadian Tuberculosis Association, 1927 to present; Tuberculosis in Industry, 1941 to present; Financial & Medical Statistics of Sanitoria of Ontario, 1930 to present. Holdings: 3000 books; 300 bound periodical volumes; manuscripts; reports and clippings. Subscriptions: 31 journals and other serials. Services: Interlibrary loans; copying; library open to medical personnel.

SHAVER (Robert E.) LIBRARY OF ENGINEERING
See: University of Kentucky - Robert E. Shaver Library of Engineering

SHAW (Alfred) AND EDWARD DURELL STONE LIBRARY
See: Boston Architectural Center - Alfred Shaw and Edward Durell Stone Library

SHAW (Charles E.) HERPETOLOGICAL LIBRARY
See: Zoological Society of San Diego - Ernst Schwarz Library

SHAW (Edwin) ARCHIVES
See: Akron Art Museum - Library

SHAW (J. Porter) LIBRARY
See: National Maritime Museum - J. Porter Shaw Library

★12446★
SHAW, PITTMAN, POTTS & TROWBRIDGE - LIBRARY (Law)
1800 M St., N.W.   Phone: (202) 822-1317
Washington, DC 20036   Carolyn P. Ahearn, Libn.
Staff: Prof 2; Other 5. Subjects: Law. Holdings: 20,000 books; 550 bound periodical volumes; 1000 congressional hearings; 8 VF drawers of pamphlets. Subscriptions: 200 journals and other serials. Services: Interlibrary loans; copying; library open to public with restrictions. Computerized Information Services: LEXIS, DIALOG.

★12447★
SHAWINIGAN CONSULTANTS INC. - LIBRARY (Sci-Tech)
620 Dorchester West   Phone: (514) 878-6294
Montreal, PQ, Canada H3B 1N8   Carol Lacourte, Libn.
Founded: 1965. Staff: Prof 1; Other 2. Subjects: Engineering, mining, economics, water resources development, applied mathematics, chemical technology, management. Holdings: 10,000 books; 3000 specifications; 700 reports, transactions, reprints; 10 drawers of technical clippings and pamphlets; maps. Subscriptions: 350 journals and other serials; 15 newspapers. Services: Interlibrary loans; copying; library open to public by appointment. Staff: Mrs. C. Perreault, ILL.

★12448★
SHAWINIGAN GROUP INCORPORATED - ENERGY LIBRARY (Energy; Sci-Tech)
620 University Ave.   Phone: (416) 365-7290
Toronto, ON, Canada M5G 2C1   Pearl H. Weisbaum, Libn.
Staff: Prof 1. Subjects: Fossil power, advanced thermal technology, district heating, geology, environment, energy conservation. Holdings: 2500 books; 875 trade catalogs; 600 reports; 500 microfiche. Subscriptions: 200 journals and other serials; 10 newspapers. Services: Interlibrary loans; library not open to public.

★12449★
SHAWMUT BANK OF BOSTON, N.A. - LIBRARY (Bus-Fin)
1 Federal St., 8th Fl.   Phone: (617) 292-2550
Boston, MA 02211   Amy A. Ribuoli, Libn.
Founded: 1981. Staff: Prof 1. Subjects: Banking, finance, business. Special Collections: D.T. Trigg Collection on Lending and Credit Practices (100 items). Holdings: 2000 books; 120 bound periodical volumes; 220 other cataloged items; 32 VF drawers of subject files. Subscriptions: 90 journals and other serials; 20 newspapers. Services: Interlibrary loans; library not open to public. Publications: Library Morning News Service; Monthly Bulletin; Library Review - all for internal distribution only.

SHAWNEE COUNTY MEDICAL SOCIETY
See: Stormont-Vail Regional Medical Center and Shawnee County Medical Society

★12450★
SHAWNEE MISSION MEDICAL CENTER - MEDICAL LIBRARY (Med)
74th & Grandview
Box 2923   Phone: (913) 676-2101
Shawnee Mission, KS 66201   Clifford L. Nestell, Dir. of Lib.Serv.
Staff: Prof 1; Other 3. Subjects: Medicine. Holdings: 4139 books; 5593 bound periodical volumes; 1454 audiotapes; 215 videotapes. Subscriptions: 576 journals and other serials. Services: Interlibrary loans; copying; SDI; library open to public with restrictions. Automated Operations: Computerized cataloging, acquisitions, serials and ILL. Computerized Information Services: BRS, DIALOG, NLM, OCLC, AMA/NET. Networks/Consortia: Member of Kansas City Library Network, Inc. (KCLN); Kansas City Metropolitan Library Network (KCMLN).

★12451★
SHAWNEE SOLAR PROJECT, INC. - ENERGY CONSERVATION & SOLAR RETROFIT DEMONSTRATION CENTER (Energy)
808 S. Forest   Phone: (618) 457-8172
Carbondale, IL 62901   Yolande Tullar, Dir.
Staff: 2. Subjects: Solar energy, renewable resources, appropriate technology, energy conservation, energy policy, self-help construction. Holdings: 1000 books; 6 VF drawers; 1750 slides and cassettes; blueprints and plans; 1 VF drawer of manufacturers' files and catalogs. Subscriptions: 32 journals and other serials. Services: Interlibrary loans; copying; center open to public. Networks/Consortia: Member of Shawnee Library System.

★12452★
SHEA & GARDNER - LIBRARY (Law)
1800 Massachusetts Ave., N.W.   Phone: (202) 828-2069
Washington, DC 20036   Susan Perrine, Libn.
Founded: 1950. Staff: Prof 1; Other 3. Subjects: Law - labor, transportation, environment. Special Collections: Legislative histories (500 volumes). Holdings: 25,000 books; 600 bound periodical volumes; 1500 other items. Subscriptions: 40 journals and other serials. Services: Interlibrary loans; library not open to public. Computerized Information Services: LEXIS, NEXIS, DIALOG, INFOBANK.

★12453★
SHEARMAN & STERLING - LIBRARY (Law)
53 Wall St., Rm. 718   Phone: (212) 483-1000
New York, NY 10005   Jack S. Ellenberger, Libn.
Staff: Prof 5. Subjects: Law. Holdings: 60,000 volumes. Services: Interlibrary loans; library not open to public. Automated Operations: Computerized cataloging. Computerized Information Services: Dow Jones News/Retrieval, LEXIS, WESTLAW, DIALOG. Remarks: A branch library is located at 153 E. 53rd St., Rm. 3205, New York, NY 10020. Staff: Ralph G. Lombardi, Assoc.Libn.; Joseph Florio, Ref.Libn.; Eileen Dolan, Cat.; Jane Huston, Branch Libn.

★12454★
SHEARSON LEHMAN/AMERICAN EXPRESS INC. - LIBRARY (Bus-Fin)
55 Water St.   Phone: (212) 558-2134
New York, NY 10041   Ronald F. Dow, Mgr., Lib.Serv.
Founded: 1930. Staff: Prof 6; Other 18. Subjects: Finance. Special Collections: Annual reports. Holdings: 1000 volumes; 900 VF drawers of pamphlets. Subscriptions: 700 journals and other serials; 20 newspapers. Services: Interlibrary loans; library not open to public. Automated Operations: Computerized cataloging, acquisitions and serials. Computerized Information Services: DIALOG, NEXIS, Dow Jones News/Retrieval, International Data Corporation, I.P. Sharp Associates, Inc., Spectrum Ownership Profiles Online, Vickers Institutional Stock System, I.P. Sharp Associates, Inc., Spectrum Ownership Profiles Online, Dun and Bradstreet Corporation, Disclosure Inc. Formed by the Merger of: Lehman Brothers Kuhn Loeb Inc. and Shearson/American Express. Staff: Louise Gent-Sandford, Libn; Harriet Wisner, Libn.; Delores Antonetz, Libn.; Sizeekumar Menon, Libn.

★12455★
SHEARSON LEHMAN/AMERICAN EXPRESS INC. - RESEARCH LIBRARY (Bus-Fin)
2 World Trade Ctr., 101st Fl.   Phone: (212) 321-5745
New York, NY 10048   Elizabeth R. Boutinon, Chf.Libn.
Founded: 1962. Staff: Prof 3; Other 6. Subjects: Investments, finance, economics, industries. Holdings: 3000 books; 500 bound periodical volumes; annual reports and interims; prospectuses; industry pamphlets; government documents; Securities and Exchange Commission (SEC) documents on microfiche. Subscriptions: 500 journals and other serials. Services: Interlibrary loans; copying; library open to other librarians. Formed by the Merger of: Lehman Brothers Kuhn Loeb and Shearson/American Express, Inc. Staff: Ruth Martin, Asst.Libn.

★12456★
SHEBOYGAN PRESS LIBRARY (Publ)
632 Center Ave.   Phone: (414) 457-7711
Sheboygan, WI 53081   Janice Hildebrand, Libn.
Staff: Prof 1. Subjects: Newspaper reference topics. Special Collections: Wisconsin Blue Books, city directories, local and state histories. Holdings: 200 books; 600 bound periodical volumes; newspapers on microfilm, 1907 to present. Subscriptions: 10 journals and other serials; 30 newspapers. Services: Copying; library open to public. Special Catalogs: Local obituaries from 1968 to present.

★12457★
SHEDD (John G.) AQUARIUM - LIBRARY (Sci-Tech)
1200 S. Lake Shore Dr.   Phone: (312) 939-2426
Chicago, IL 60605   Janet E. Powers, Libn.
Founded: 1975. Staff: Prof 1. Subjects: Marine and freshwater biology, fishes, water pollution, fisheries, Lake Michigan, aquatic education. Holdings: 5500 books; 300 file folders of clippings, reprints, pamphlets. Subscriptions: 180 journals and other serials. Services: Interlibrary loans (limited); copying; library open to public by appointment. Automated Operations: Computerized cataloging. Networks/Consortia: Member of Chicago Library System. Publications: Aquaticus, 4/year - to Shedd Aquarium Society members.

SHEELY-LEE LAW LIBRARY
See: Dickinson School of Law

★12458★
SHELBURNE MUSEUM, INC. - RESEARCH LIBRARY (Hist)
                                           Phone: (802) 985-3346
Shelburne, VT 05482   Leslie A. Hasker, Lib.Asst.
Founded: 1947. Subjects: Antiques, art, Vermontiana, furniture, architecture, textiles, transportation. Holdings: 7000 books; 600 bound periodical volumes; 1400 pamphlets; 164 magazines on antiques; 260 manuscripts; 600 volumes of records of museum holdings. Subscriptions: 85 journals and other serials. Services: Copying; library is open for reference use to researchers and museum friends or members by appointment only.

★12459★
SHELBY COUNTY LAW LIBRARY (Law)*
Courthouse   Phone: (513) 498-4541
Sidney, OH 45365   Rita Miller, Libn.
Staff: 2. Subjects: Law. Holdings: 18,000 books; microfiche. Subscriptions: 75 journals and other serials. Services: Copying; library open to public; circulation privileges for members only.

★12460★
SHELDON ART MUSEUM - GOVERNOR JOHN W. STEWART & MR. & MRS. CHARLES M. SWIFT RESEARCH CENTER LIBRARY (Hist)
1 Park St.   Phone: (802) 388-2117
Middlebury, VT 05753   Polly C. Darnell, Libn.
Founded: 1882. Staff: 1. Subjects: Addison County and Vermont history. Special Collections: Newspapers published in Middlebury, 1801 to present (bound); letters filed by date (30,000). Holdings: 3000 books; pamphlets; 200 scrapbooks compiled by Henry L. Sheldon; 300 linear feet of manuscripts, account books and diaries; 200 photographs of local scenes and people. Services: Center open to public. Publications: Annual report; newsletter - to members. Special Indexes: Index of letters (author and subject; card).

THE SHELDON MUSEUM & CULTURAL CENTER
See: Chilkat Valley Historical Society

★12461★
SHELL CANADA LIMITED - OAKVILLE RESEARCH CENTRE - SHELL RESEARCH CENTRE LIBRARY (Energy)
P.O. Box 2100   Phone: (416) 827-1141
Oakville, ON, Canada L6J 5C7   Mr. Lan C. Sun, Libn.
Founded: 1970. Staff: Prof 1; Other 4. Subjects: Petroleum technology - products and processes. Holdings: 5000 books and bound periodical volumes; 40,000 proprietary research and technical reports; 6000 pamphlets, journal articles and patents. Subscriptions: 110 journals and other serials; 5 newspapers. Services: Interlibrary loans; copying; library open to public with restrictions on proprietary materials. Automated Operations: Computerized cataloging, circulation and ILL. Computerized Information Services: CAN/OLE, DIALOG, NLM, SDC; SCATILS (internal database). Networks/Consortia: Member of Shell Canada Technical Information System. Publications: Monthly Accession List of Final Reports and Monographs; Monthly Subject List of Routine Report Articles. Special Catalogs: Eight separate indexes produced cumulatively every month on COM microfiche from computer tape and merged annually with previous years (corporate author, title, personal author, series, project, subject, KWIC index and shelf list or master file). Remarks: The Shell Research Centre Library and the Shell Technical Library in Toronto form the Shell Canada Technical Information and Library Service, a coordinated service network for Shell research/technical staff and refineries across Canada.

★12462★
SHELL CANADA LIMITED - TECHNICAL LIBRARY (Energy)
505 University Ave.
Toronto, ON, Canada M5G 1X4   Miss S. Tattershall, Hd., Lib.Sect.
Subjects: Petroleum industry. Holdings: Figures not available. Services:

Library not open to public. Remarks: The technical library is affiliated with the Shell Research Centre Library in Oakville, ON, and is operated as an integral part of the Shell Canada Technical Information and Library Service System.

★12463★
SHELL CANADA RESOURCES LIMITED - TECHNICAL LIBRARY (Energy)
400 4th Ave., S.W.   Phone: (403) 232-3512
Calgary, AB, Canada T2P 2H5   Mila E. Carozzi, Sr.Libn.
Founded: 1950. Staff: Prof 1; Other 4. Subjects: Geology, earth sciences, petroleum and chemical engineering, minerals, economics. Special Collections: Geology of the Western Canadian Foothills. Holdings: 4400 books; 875 bound periodical volumes; 8400 government documents; 10,200 technical reports; 160 microfiche; 200 reels of microfilm; 575 theses; 90 feet of geological maps. Subscriptions: 302 journals and other serials. Services: Interlibrary loans (limited); library not open to public. Automated Operations: Computerized cataloging. Computerized Information Services: SDC, DIALOG, CAN/OLE, Info Globe; SCROLL (internal database). Performs searches on cost recovery basis. Publications: Current Awareness Bulletin, monthly - for internal distribution only.

★12464★
SHELL DEVELOPMENT COMPANY - BELLAIRE RESEARCH CENTER LIBRARY (Energy)
Box 481   Phone: (713) 663-2293
Houston, TX 77001   Aphrodite Mamoulides, Lib.Supv.
Founded: 1946. Staff: Prof 2; Other 1. Subjects: Geology, geophysics, petroleum-reservoir engineering, drilling and production, computer science. Holdings: 14,000 books; 6000 bound periodical volumes; 3000 pamphlets; 18,000 government reports; 2500 dissertations. Subscriptions: 600 journals and other serials. Services: Interlibrary loans; copying; library open by appointment to research personnel. Computerized Information Services: SDC. Publications: Weekly Acquisitions List; Weekly Library Bulletin. Staff: F.B. Melde, Libn.

★12465★
SHELL DEVELOPMENT COMPANY - BIOLOGICAL SCIENCES RESEARCH CENTER - LIBRARY (Sci-Tech)
Box 4248   Phone: (209) 545-8224
Modesto, CA 95352   Patt Snyder, Supv.
Staff: Prof 3; Other 4. Subjects: Chemistry, biochemistry, entomology, plant physiology, molecular biology. Holdings: 9917 books; 9453 bound periodical volumes. Subscriptions: 531 journals and other serials. Services: Interlibrary loans; library open to valid researchers by appointment.

★12466★
SHELL DEVELOPMENT COMPANY - WESTHOLLOW RESEARCH CENTER LIBRARY (Sci-Tech)†
3333 Hwy. 6 S.
Box 1380   Phone: (713) 493-7530
Houston, TX 77001   Esther Ando, Supv. of Lib.
Founded: 1975. Subjects: Corrosion, petrochemicals, petroleum refining, toxicology. Holdings: 14,000 volumes. Subscriptions: 1430 journals and other serials. Computerized Information Services: DIALOG, SDC.

SHELL (John N.) LIBRARY
See: Nassau County Medical Society - Nassau Academy of Medicine - John N. Shell Library

★12467★
SHELL OIL COMPANY - DEER PARK MANUFACTURING COMPLEX - LIBRARY SERVICES (Sci-Tech)†
Box 999   Phone: (713) 476-6565
Deer Park, TX 77536   Julia C. Smith, Libn.
Founded: 1952. Staff: Prof 1; Other 1. Subjects: Chemistry, chemical engineering, and other process engineering. Holdings: 10,000 books; 1700 bound periodical volumes; 20,000 company reports; 18 VF drawers of pamphlets; 10,000 microcards; 130,000 technical abstracts (cards). Subscriptions: 168 journals and other serials. Services: Interlibrary loans; library not open to public. Publications: Literature Searches, weekly; Technical Reports, weekly; Periodical Abstracts, weekly.

★12468★
SHELL OIL COMPANY - INFORMATION & LIBRARY SERVICES (Energy)
Box 587   Phone: (713) 241-1017
Houston, TX 77001   Jane C. Rodgers, Supv.
Founded: 1971. Staff: Prof 8; Other 20. Subjects: Petroleum, business, chemistry. Holdings: 13,000 volumes. Subscriptions: 900 journals and other serials. Services: Interlibrary loans; copying. Automated Operations: Computerized cataloging, serials and circulation. Computerized Information

Services: DIALOG, SDC, Dow Jones News/Retrieval, NEXIS, RLIN. **Staff:** Barbara G. Wells, Info.Ret. & Sys.Sup.; Tom S. Brodie, Acq. & Dist.

★12469★
SHELTER ISLAND HISTORICAL SOCIETY - ARCHIVES (Hist)*
Havens House   Phone: (516) 749-0025
Shelter Island, NY 11964   Margaret Joyce, Chairwoman
Staff: 9. **Subjects:** Local history. **Special Collections:** Worthington journals and notebooks (ornithology). **Holdings:** 168 books; 18 bound periodical volumes; 400 literary documents; 100 financial documents; 100 legal documents; 1600 maps, clippings, genealogies. **Services:** Copying; archives open to public for reference use only.

★12470★
SHENANDOAH COLLEGE & CONSERVATORY OF MUSIC - HOWE LIBRARY (Mus)
                                              Phone: (703) 667-8714
Winchester, VA 22601   Nancy H. Moore, Dir.
Staff: Prof 3; Other 7. **Subjects:** Music, nursing, respiratory therapy, liberal arts, management. **Special Collections:** History of Evangelical United Brethren Church. **Holdings:** 82,000 books; 5200 bound periodical volumes; 8800 phonograph records. **Subscriptions:** 500 journals and other serials; 15 newspapers. **Services:** Interlibrary loans; copying; library open to public, registration required. **Computerized Information Services:** DIALOG. Performs searches on cost recovery basis. **Special Indexes:** Periodical Index (computer printout). **Staff:** Sharon M. Kleptach, Tech.Serv.Libn.; Rosemary Green, Asst.Libn.

★12471★
SHENANGO VALLEY OSTEOPATHIC HOSPITAL - MEDICAL LIBRARY (Med)
2200 Memorial Dr. Extended   Phone: (412) 981-3500
Farrell, PA 16121   Ethelnel Baron, Staff Sec.
Staff: 1. **Subjects:** Medicine. **Holdings:** 500 books; 110 video cassette tapes; 86 cassette tapes. **Subscriptions:** 45 journals and other serials. **Services:** Interlibrary loans; library not open to public. **Networks/Consortia:** Member of Greater Northeastern Regional Medical Library Program.

SHEPARD (Carl F.) MEMORIAL LIBRARY
See: Illinois College of Optometry - Carl F. Shepard Memorial Library

SHEPARD (Edward M.) MEMORIAL ROOM
See: Springfield-Greene County Public Libraries - Edward M. Shepard Memorial Room

SHEPARD (J.E.) LIBRARY
See: North Carolina Central University - School of Library Science - Library

★12472★
SHEPARD'S/MC GRAW-HILL - LIBRARY (Law)
420 N. Cascade Ave.
Box 1235
Colorado Springs, CO 80901   Phone: (303) 475-7230
                                     Gregory P. Harris, Libn.
Founded: 1873. **Staff:** Prof 3. **Subjects:** Law. **Holdings:** 60,000 books; 30,000 reports; 20,000 statutes, digests. **Subscriptions:** 500 journals and other serials. **Services:** Library not open to public. **Computerized Information Services:** Westlaw, LEXIS.

SHEPHERD (George) LIBRARY
See: Saskatchewan Western Development Museum - George Shepherd Library

SHEPPARD AIR FORCE BASE (TX)
See: U.S. Air Force Hospital - Sheppard Regional Hospital; U.S. Air Force School of Health Care Sciences

SHEPPARD LIBRARY
See: Massachusetts College of Pharmacy & Allied Health Sciences

★12473★
SHEPPARD, MULLIN, RICHTER & HAMPTON - LAW LIBRARY (Law)†
333 S. Hope St., 47th Fl.   Phone: (213) 620-1780
Los Angeles, CA 90071   Debra K. Hogan, Libn.
Staff: Prof 1. **Subjects:** Law. **Holdings:** 17,000 books. **Subscriptions:** 75 journals and other serials. **Services:** Library not open to public.

★12474★
SHERBURNE COUNTY SOCIAL SERVICES - THE BORROWING CORNER, INC. (Educ)
County Office Building
1810 1st St. W.   Phone: (612) 441-1880
Becker, MN 55319   Christine Rudnicki, Coord.
Staff: Prof 1; Other 1. **Subjects:** Educational play equipment. **Holdings:** 135 books; toys. **Services:** Service open to members.

★12475★
SHERIDAN COLLEGE OF APPLIED ARTS AND TECHNOLOGY - SCHOOL OF DESIGN - LIBRARY (Art)
1460 S. Sheridan Way   Phone: (416) 274-3685
Mississauga, ON, Canada L5H 1Z7   Madeleine La Pointe, Lib.Techn.
Founded: 1967. **Staff:** 1. **Subjects:** Crafts, ceramics, textiles, design, furniture, art history, architecture, metals, glass. **Holdings:** 5133 books; 270 bound periodical volumes; 10 VF drawers of pamphlets; 100 audio cassettes (music); 49 video cassettes (curriculum-based); 20,000 slides (arts and crafts); 62 rare books. **Subscriptions:** 122 journals and other serials. **Services:** Interlibrary loans (limited); library open to public by special arrangement only.

★12476★
SHERIDAN COUNTY HISTORICAL SOCIETY, INC. - AGNES & CLARENCE BENSCHOTER MEMORIAL LIBRARY (Hist)
Box 274   Phone: (308) 327-2961
Rushville, NE 69360   Robert Buchan, Cur.
Founded: 1958. **Staff:** Prof 1; Other 1. **Subjects:** Western and Nebraska history; military; genealogy. **Special Collections:** Camp Sheridan, Nebraska archives, 1874-1881. **Holdings:** 700 books; 100 bound periodical volumes; clippings; manuscripts; albums. **Services:** Copying; library open to public by appointment; tours. **Publications:** Recollections of Sheridan County.

SHERMAN ART LIBRARY
See: Dartmouth College

★12477★
SHERMAN COLLEGE OF STRAIGHT CHIROPRACTIC - TOM AND MAE BAHAN LIBRARY (Med)
Box 1452   Phone: (803) 578-8770
Spartanburg, SC 29304   Susan Matusak, Hd.Libn.
Staff: Prof 1; Other 5. **Subjects:** Chiropractic, clinical and basic sciences. **Special Collections:** B.J. Palmer Collection. **Holdings:** 6500 books; 815 bound periodical volumes; 150 audiotapes; 50 videotapes; 2471 slides; 3 16mm films; 8 phonograph records; 4 VF drawers. **Subscriptions:** 108 journals and other serials; 5 newspapers. **Services:** Interlibrary loans; library not open to public.

★12478★
SHERMAN GRINBERG FILM LIBRARIES, INC. (Aud-Vis)
630 Ninth Ave.   Phone: (212) 765-5170
New York, NY 10036   Bernard Chertok, Pres.
Staff: Prof 29; Other 2. **Subjects:** News on film and videotape. **Special Collections:** Pathe, Paramount, American Broadcasting Corporation and other private film libraries. **Holdings:** 5 million feet of film; 500,000 video cassettes. **Subscriptions:** 11 journals and other serials. **Services:** Copying; library open to public for purchase of copies. **Staff:** Nancy Casey, Sec.; Doug Gillette, Chf.Libn.; William Memeriz, Libn.

★12479★
SHERMAN RESEARCH LIBRARY (Hist)
614 Dahlia Ave.   Phone: (714) 673-1880
Corona Del Mar, CA 92625   Dr. William O. Hendricks, Dir.
Founded: 1966. **Staff:** Prof 3. **Subjects:** Pacific Southwest history since 1870 - economic development, land and water, transportation, immigration. **Special Collections:** Sherman papers; Brant papers; Colorado River Land Company documents. **Holdings:** 15,000 books; 400 bound periodical volumes; 2500 pamphlets; 375 document boxes of business papers; 1475 reels of microfilm of newspapers; 200 theses and dissertations on microfilm; 2000 maps. **Subscriptions:** 30 journals and other serials. **Services:** Interlibrary loans; library open to public. **Special Catalogs:** Inventory catalogs to the papers. **Staff:** Edwin W. Tomlinson, Libn.; Reva McFarlane, Res.Asst.

SHERRILL (Henry Knox) RESOURCE CENTER
See: Protestant Episcopal Church Executive Council - Henry Knox Sherrill Resource Center

★12480★
SHERRITT GORDON MINES, LTD. - RESEARCH CENTRE LIBRARY (Sci-Tech)
　　　　　　　　　　　　　　　　Phone: (403) 998-6419
Fort Saskatchewan, AB, Canada T8L 2P2　　J. Derek Sim, Libn.
Founded: 1953. **Staff:** Prof 1; Other 1. **Subjects:** Hydrometallurgy, inorganic chemistry, physical chemistry, fertilizers. **Holdings:** 7000 books and bound periodical volumes; 5000 pamphlets; 1500 slides; 800 laboratory reports, pilot plant reports and Sherritt published papers. **Subscriptions:** 250 journals and other serials. **Services:** Interlibrary loans. **Publications:** Acquisitions report, monthly - for internal distribution only.

★12481★
SHERWIN-WILLIAMS COMPANY OF CANADA, LTD. - TECHNICAL LIBRARY
P.O Box 489
Montreal, PQ, Canada H3C 2Z4
Defunct

★12482★
SHERWIN-WILLIAMS COMPANY - INFORMATION CENTER (Bus-Fin; Comp Sci)
13 Midland Bldg.
101 Prospect Ave., N.W.　　　　　Phone: (216) 234-6444
Cleveland, OH 44115　　　　　　Gary Weske, Info.Ctr.Dir.
Founded: 1982. **Staff:** Prof 5. **Subjects:** Data processing, business. **Holdings:** 200 books; 2000 computer listings; 100 technical manuals; 2 VF drawers of hardware/software product brochures. **Subscriptions:** 50 journals and other serials; 5 newspapers. **Services:** Center not open to public. **Automated Operations:** Computerized cataloging, serials, circulation and routing. **Computerized Information Services:** Internal database. **Publications:** Information Center Bulletin, monthly - for internal distribution only. **Staff:** Pamela J. Kuzma, Anl./Libn.; Edward Boehnlein, Anl.; Robert Holland, Anl.; Patrick Mullin, Anl./Educ.Coord.

★12483★
SHERWIN-WILLIAMS COMPANY - TECHNICAL LIBRARY
601 Canal Rd.
Cleveland, OH 44113
Defunct

SHERWOOD (K.K.) LIBRARY
See: **University of Washington - Health Sciences Library - K.K. Sherwood Library**

★12484★
SHEVCHENKO SCIENTIFIC SOCIETY, INC. - LIBRARY AND ARCHIVES (Area-Ethnic)
63 4th Ave.　　　　　　　　　Phone: (212) 254-5130
New York, NY 10003　　　　　Svetlana Andrushkiv, Dir.
Founded: 1873. **Staff:** Prof 2; Other 1. **Subjects:** Ukrainian and Slavic language, literature, history, arts, music, geography, ethnography, sciences. **Special Collections:** World Wars I and II. **Holdings:** 18,000 books; 1500 periodicals; 3000 manuscripts, archives, pamphlets. **Subscriptions:** 21 journals and other serials; 17 newspapers. **Services:** Library open for research only. **Publications:** Publications catalog; pamphlets. **Staff:** Anna Kobrynska, Acq.; Bohdan Kowal, Cat.

SHIFFMAN (Vera Parshall) MEDICAL LIBRARY
See: **Wayne State University - School of Medicine - Vera Parshall Shiffman Medical Library**

★12485★
SHILOH MILITARY TRAIL, INC. - LIBRARY (Hist)
Box 17386　　　　　　　　　Phone: (901) 454-5600
Memphis, TN 38117　　　　Edward F. Williams, III, Res.Hist.
Founded: 1961. **Staff:** 1. **Subjects:** Civil War history and American history. **Special Collections:** Civil War manuscripts and material related to the Battle of Shiloh and Confederate General Nathan Bedford Forrest (4 VF drawers). **Holdings:** 1000 books; 20 bound periodical volumes. **Subscriptions:** 10 journals and other serials. **Services:** Library open to public by appointment. **Remarks:** Located in Memphis Pink Palace Museum Library, 232 Tilton, Memphis, TN 38111.

SHILOH NATL. MILITARY PARK
See: **U.S. Natl. Park Service**

★12486★
SHIPPENSBURG HISTORICAL SOCIETY - ARCHIVES (Hist)*
Shippensburg Public Library
West King St.　　　　　　　　Phone: (717) 532-4508
Shippensburg, PA 17257
Subjects: History and genealogy of Shippensburg area. **Services:** Archives open to public by appointment.

★12487★
SHIPPENSBURG UNIVERSITY - EZRA LEHMAN LIBRARY (Educ)
　　　　　　　　　　　　　　　　Phone: (717) 532-1463
Shippensburg, PA 17257　　Gene Hanson, Dir., Lib. & Media Serv.
Founded: 1871. **Staff:** Prof 10. **Special Collections:** Media/Curricular Center; Pennsylvaniana; rare books; university archives (546 linear feet). **Holdings:** 105,000 books; 420 bound periodical volumes; 24 VF drawers. **Subscriptions:** 32 journals and other serials. **Services:** Interlibrary loans; copying; library open to public for serious research. **Automated Operations:** Computerized cataloging. **Computerized Information Services:** DIALOG. Performs searches on cost recovery basis. Contact Person: Madelyn Valunas, 532-1479. **Networks/Consortia:** Member of Associated College Libraries of Central Pennsylvania. **Staff:** Berkley Laite, Ctr.Libn.; Madelyn Valunas; Marjorie Shoap, Ctr.Lib.Techn.

SHOALS MARINE LABORATORY
See: **Cornell University**

SHOCK AND VIBRATION INFORMATION CENTER
See: **U.S. Navy - Naval Research Laboratory**

★12488★
SHODAIR CHILDREN'S HOSPITAL - MEDICAL REFERENCE LIBRARY (Med)
Box 5539　　　　　　　　　　Phone: (406) 442-1980
Helena, MT 59604　　　　　　Suzy Holt, Info.Spec.
Founded: 1979. **Staff:** Prof 1; Other 1. **Subjects:** Genetics - human medical, disorders, counseling; cytogenetics; prenatal diagnosis; pediatrics. **Holdings:** 2000 books; 1000 bound periodical volumes; 15,000 reprints. **Subscriptions:** 65 journals and other serials. **Services:** Interlibrary loans; copying; library open to public. **Computerized Information Services:** Birth Defects Information System (BDIS), MEDLARS. **Networks/Consortia:** Member of Helena Area Health Sciences Library Consortium (HAHSLC).

SHOENBERG (Moses) MEMORIAL LIBRARY
See: **Jewish Hospital at Washington University Medical Center - School of Nursing - Moses Shoenberg Memorial Library**

★12489★
SHOOK, HARDY & BACON - LIBRARY (Law)
Mercantile Bank Tower, 20th Fl.
1101 Walnut　　　　　　　　Phone: (816) 474-6550
Kansas City, MO 64106　　　Marianne L. Griffin, Libn.
Staff: Prof 2; Other 1. **Subjects:** Law - federal and state, products liability, antitrust, corporate, tax. **Holdings:** 18,000 books; legal memoranda; 700 documents; 2000 ultrafiche. **Subscriptions:** 105 journals and other serials. **Services:** Interlibrary loans; library not open to public. **Computerized Information Services:** LEXIS. **Networks/Consortia:** Member of Kansas City Library Network, Inc. (KCLN). **Publications:** Library Information Bulletin, quarterly. **Special Indexes:** Index to legal memoranda file (card); Expert Witness Index (book). **Staff:** Sara J. Hibbeler, Asst.Libn.

★12490★
SHORTER COLLEGE - MEMORABILIA ROOM (Hist)
　　　　　　　　　　　　　　　　Phone: (404) 291-2121
Rome, GA 30161　　　　Robert Gardner, College Historian
Subjects: History of Shorter College. **Holdings:** 300 books; 20 VF drawers of archives, manuscripts, documents, unbound reports and clippings; 250 artifacts. **Services:** Copying; room open to public by appointment.

SHORTT LIBRARY OF CANADIANA
See: **University of Saskatchewan - Special Collections**

★12491★
SHOSTAL ASSOCIATES, INC. (Aud-Vis)
164 Madison Ave.　　　　　　Phone: (212) 686-8850
New York, NY 10016
Founded: 1940. **Subjects:** Complete, up-to-date file of stock color transparencies of subjects of general interest with world-wide geographical coverage; special emphasis on educational projects and advertising. **Special Collections:** Large format original color transparencies representing hundreds of photographers from around the world. **Holdings:** Figures not available.

SHOULDICE (Kenneth J.) LIBRARY
See: Lake Superior State College - Kenneth J. Shouldice Library

★12492★
THE (Shreveport) TIMES - LIBRARY (Publ)
222 Lake St.   Phone: (318) 459-3283
Shreveport, LA 71130   Johnny L. King, Libn.
Founded: 1951. Staff: Prof 1; Other 5. Subjects: Newspaper reference topics. Special Collections: Shreveport Times bound and on microfilm, 1871 to present; bound issues of the Sunday Magazine with index. Holdings: 2300 books; 20 bound periodical volumes; 50,000 newspaper clippings; 113 reels of microfilm; 15 VF drawers of photographs; caricatures; files of art work; 300 VF drawers. Subscriptions: 20 journals and other serials; 20 newspapers. Services: Library not open to public. Special Indexes: Index to Sunday Magazine; index of daily clippings; index to Shreveport Magazine. Remarks: This paper is operated by Gannett Newspapers.

★12493★
SHREWSBURY DAILY-SUNDAY REGISTER - LIBRARY (Publ)
One Register Plaza   Phone: (201) 542-4000
Shrewsbury, NJ 07701   Olga Boeckel, Hd.Libn.
Staff: Prof 1; Other 1. Subjects: Newspaper reference topics. Holdings: 400 books; 75 bound periodical volumes; newspapers on microfilm, 1878 to present; pamphlets; photographs; clippings. Services: Interlibrary loans; library not open to public.

★12494★
SHRINE TO MUSIC MUSEUM (Mus)
University of South Dakota
Box 194   Phone: (605) 677-5306
Vermillion, SD 57069   Andre P. Larson, Dir.
Founded: 1966. Staff: Prof 3; Other 1. Subjects: Musical instruments, musical history including American music, sheet and wind music. Holdings: Figures not available for books; 3000 musical instruments; music; photographs; sound recordings. Services: Copying; library open to public with permission of director. Publications: Newsletter, quarterly - distributed free on request. Remarks: Maintained by Center for Study of the History of Musical Instruments of the University of South Dakota. Staff: Arne B. Larson, Res.Cons.; Margaret Downie, Assoc.Cur.; Gary Stewart, Consrv.

★12495★
SHRINERS HOSPITAL FOR CRIPPLED CHILDREN - ORTHOPEDIC LIBRARY (Med)*
1402 Outerbelt Dr.   Phone: (713) 797-1616
Houston, TX 77030   Lillian Nicholson, Libn.
Staff: Prof 2. Subjects: Orthopedics. Holdings: 1200 books; 200 bound periodical volumes. Subscriptions: 22 journals and other serials. Services: Library not open to public. Staff: Susanna G. Baxter, Libn.

★12496★
SHRIVER (Eunice Kennedy) CENTER FOR MENTAL RETARDATION, INC. - LIBRARY (Med)
200 Trapelo Rd.   Phone: (617) 893-3500
Waltham, MA 02154   Jacklyn Collette, Libn.
Founded: 1970. Staff: Prof 1. Subjects: Biochemistry, chemistry, genetics. Holdings: 200 books; 100 bound periodical volumes; 50 pamphlets. Subscriptions: 30 journals and other serials. Services: Library not open to public. Computerized Information Services: DIALOG.

SHULMAN (Max) ZIONIST LIBRARY
See: Hebrew Theological College - Saul Silber Memorial Library

★12497★
SHUMAKER, LOOP & KENDRICK - LIBRARY (Law)
1000 Jackson   Phone: (419) 241-4201
Toledo, OH 43624   Martha Esbin, Law Libn.
Staff: Prof 1. Subjects: Law. Holdings: 9000 books; 500 bound periodical volumes; 600 research memoranda; 800 pieces of employee benefit material. Subscriptions: 128 journals and other serials. Services: Interlibrary loans; library not open to public. Computerized Information Services: LEXIS. Publications: S,L&K Library Letter (newsletter) - for internal distribution only. Special Indexes: Index to research and employee benefits files.

SHUMARD (Benjamin Franklin) LIBRARY
See: St. Louis Public Library - Carol Mc Donald Gardner Rare Book Room

SIBERT LIBRARY
See: Passavant Memorial Area Hospital Association

SIBLEY (Clyde L.) MEDICAL LIBRARY
See: Baptist Medical Center - Medical Library

★12498★
SIBLEY MEMORIAL HOSPITAL - MEDICAL LIBRARY (Med)
5255 Loughboro Rd., N.W.   Phone: (202) 537-4110
Washington, DC 20016   Annie B. Footman, Libn.
Founded: 1903. Staff: Prof 1. Subjects: Medicine. Holdings: 3240 books; 1913 bound periodical volumes; 150 pamphlets; 30 pamphlet boxes of pamphlets and maps; 8 VF drawers of clippings, reports and documents. Subscriptions: 152 journals and other serials. Services: Interlibrary loans; library not open to public. Networks/Consortia: Member of Southeastern/ Atlantic Regional Medical Library Services; Maryland and D.C. Consortium of Resource Sharing (MADCORS).

SIBLEY MUSIC LIBRARY
See: University of Rochester - Eastman School of Music

★12499★
SIDBEC-DOSCO INC. - CENTRE DE DOCUMENTATION (Sci-Tech; Bus-Fin)
C.P. 1000   Phone: (514) 587-2091
Contrecoeur, PQ, Canada J0L 1C0   L. Seguin, Coord.
Founded: 1971. Staff: 1. Subjects: Metallurgy (iron and steel), marketing and management, automation. Holdings: 5800 books. Subscriptions: 100 journals and other serials. Services: Interlibrary loans; center not open to public.

★12500★
SIDLEY AND AUSTIN - LIBRARY (Law)
One First National Plaza, Suite 4800   Phone: (312) 853-7475
Chicago, IL 60603   Allyson D. Withers, Hd. Law Libn.
Staff: Prof 1; Other 7. Subjects: Law. Holdings: 40,000 volumes. Services: Interlibrary loans; library open to area law firms. Automated Operations: Computerized cataloging. Computerized Information Services: LEXIS, DIALOG. Performs searches on subscription basis. Networks/Consortia: Member of ILLINET.

★12501★
SIECOR CORPORATION - TECHNICAL INFORMATION CENTER (Sci-Tech)
1928 Main Ave., S.E.
Box 489   Phone: (704) 328-2171
Hickory, NC 28601   Nola V. Callahan, Tech.Libn.
Staff: Prof 1; Other 1. Subjects: Telephone and cable industries, telecommunications, fiber optics. Holdings: 1000 books; 100 bound periodical volumes; 6000 reports and documents. Subscriptions: 97 journals and other serials. Services: Interlibrary loans; copying; SDI. Automated Operations: Computerized cataloging. Computerized Information Services: DIALOG, BRS. Performs free searches for staff.

SIECUS
See: Sex Information & Education Council of the U.S.

★12502★
SIEMENS GAMMASONICS, INC. - NUCLEAR MEDICAL DIVISION - RESEARCH LIBRARY (Sci-Tech)
2000 Nuclear Dr.   Phone: (312) 635-3643
Des Plaines, IL 60018   Arlene M. Lowden, Libn.
Founded: 1957. Staff: Prof 1. Subjects: Nuclear instrumentation, computers, engineering, electronics, gamma camera imaging, nuclear medicine, nuclear cardiology, mathematics, software, computed tomography. Holdings: 4000 books; 1000 bound periodical volumes; 200 reports. Subscriptions: 84 journals and other serials. Services: Interlibrary loans (limited); library open to public by appointment. Networks/Consortia: Member of North Suburban Library System.

★12503★
SIERRA CLUB - ENVIRONMENTAL LIBRARY & INFORMATION CENTER
1709 Paseo De Peralta
Santa Fe, NM 87501
Defunct

★12504★
SIERRA CLUB - WILLIAM E. COLBY MEMORIAL LIBRARY (Env-Cons)
530 Bush St.   Phone: (415) 981-8634
San Francisco, CA 94108   Barbara Lekisch, Rsrcs.Libn.
Founded: 1892. Staff: Prof 2. Subjects: Environmental policy, conservation, energy policy, mountaineering, natural history, Sierra Nevada. Special Collections: Foreign mountaineering journals (800 bound volumes); selected Sierra Club archives and memorabilia (500 items). Holdings: 7000 books;

1300 bound periodical volumes; 10,000 documents and reports (indexed); 10 VF drawers of maps; 5000 slides; 5 file boxes of photographs. **Subscriptions:** 300 journals and other serials; 10 newspapers. **Services:** Interlibrary loans; copying; library open to public for reference use only. **Networks/Consortia:** Member of Bay Area Reference Center (BARC). **Publications:** New Environmental Literature, annual; Sierra Club Periodicals Holdings List, 1982. **Special Indexes:** Subject index to documents holdings. **Staff:** Jean Stefancic, Cat., Asst.Libn.

★12505★
SIERRA COUNTY LAW LIBRARY (Law)
Courthouse
Downieville, CA 95936   Phone: (916) 289-3269
Founded: 1920. **Staff:** 2. **Subjects:** Law. **Holdings:** 4000 volumes. **Services:** Library open to public with restrictions.

★12506★
SIERRA VIEW DISTRICT HOSPITAL - MEDICAL LIBRARY (Med)
465 W. Putnam Ave.   Phone: (209) 784-1110
Porterville, CA 93257   Marilyn R. Pankey, Dir., Med.Rec.
Staff: 1. **Subjects:** Anatomy, physiology, medicine, surgery. **Holdings:** 150 books. **Subscriptions:** 22 journals and other serials. **Services:** Library not open to public. **Networks/Consortia:** Member of Areawide Library Network (AWLNET).

★12507★
SIGNAL UOP RESEARCH CENTER - TECHNICAL INFORMATION CENTER
(Energy)
50 UOP Plaza
Algonquin & Mt. Prospect Rds.   Phone: (312) 391-3361
Des Plaines, IL 60016-6187   Leonore Rogalski, Mgr.
Founded: 1926. **Staff:** Prof 5; Other 7. **Subjects:** Petroleum refining processes and technology, petrochemical processes, chemical engineering, air and water conservation, special purpose chemicals, catalysis, patents, trademarks, copyrights. **Special Collections:** American Petroleum Institute project publications; Technical Oil Mission reports (microfilm); official patent publications of Australia, Brazil, Canada, France, Germany, Great Britain, India, South Africa and United States. **Holdings:** 15,500 books; 12,000 bound periodical volumes; 25 VF drawers of clippings; 50 VF drawers and 2500 microfiche of government documents; 400,000 U.S. patents; 150,000 foreign patents. **Subscriptions:** 400 journals and other serials. **Services:** Interlibrary loans; SDI; center open to public by appointment. **Computerized Information Services:** DIALOG, SDC, BRS, I.P. Sharp Associates, Ltd., NIH-EPA Chemical Information System (CIS), Data Resources, Inc. (DRI), Data Communications; Research Reports (internal database). Performs searches on cost recovery basis. **Publications:** What's New/Current Reading List, monthly; Current Awareness Report, weekly - both for internal distribution only. **Special Indexes:** Research Reports. **Remarks:** UOP stands for Universal Oil Products Company. Center contains holdings of the former UOP Inc. - Patent Library. **Formerly:** UOP Inc. **Staff:** Else Weber, Asst.Mgr.; Adelaide Kass, Sr.Lit. Searcher; Crisencia Liwag, Sr.Lit. Searcher; Kay Kim, Sr.Lit. Searcher.

★12508★
SIGNETICS CORPORATION - LIBRARY (Sci-Tech)
811 E. Arques Ave.   Phone: (408) 739-7700
Sunnyvale, CA 94086   Stephanie Jang, Libn.
Founded: 1970. **Staff:** Prof 1. **Subjects:** Electronics, semiconductors. **Holdings:** 800 books; 1900 bound periodical volumes. **Subscriptions:** 90 journals and other serials. **Services:** Interlibrary loans; library not open to public. **Computerized Information Services:** DIALOG. **Networks/Consortia:** Member of South Bay Cooperative Library System. **Remarks:** Signetics is a subsidiary of U.S. Phillips Corporation.

SIKORSKY AIRCRAFT
See: United Technologies Corporation - Sikorsky Aircraft Division

SILBER (Saul) MEMORIAL LIBRARY
See: Hebrew Theological College - Saul Silber Memorial Library

SILCOX MEMORIAL LIBRARY
See: Huron College

SILVA (Luigi) COLLECTION
See: University of North Carolina, Greensboro - Luigi Silva Collection

★12509★
SILVER BURDETT COMPANY - EDITORIAL LIBRARY (Educ; Bus-Fin)
250 James St.   Phone: (201) 538-0400
Morristown, NJ 07960   Jane Marie Schrader, Hd.Libn.
Staff: Prof 1. **Subjects:** General education, business, marketing research. **Special Collections:** Silver Burdett publications. **Holdings:** 12,450 books; 1000 government documents. **Subscriptions:** 200 journals and other serials. **Services:** Interlibrary loans; copying; library open to public on request. **Networks/Consortia:** Member of New Jersey Library Network Services. **Publications:** Bibliographies on sexism; Guidelines for Developing Bias-Free Instructional Materials. **Special Catalogs:** Guide to Library Holdings; Report.

★12510★
SILVER CROSS HOSPITAL - MEDICAL LIBRARY (Med)
1200 Maple Rd.   Phone: (815) 740-1100
Joliet, IL 60432   Mary Ingmire, Libn.
Founded: 1956. **Staff:** 1. **Subjects:** Medicine, nursing, hospital administration, social science. **Holdings:** 750 books; 1500 bound periodical volumes; 8 VF drawers of articles and pamphlets; 1500 AV items. **Subscriptions:** 98 journals and other serials. **Services:** Interlibrary loans; copying; library open to public with referrals. **Networks/Consortia:** Member of Chicago and South Consortium.

SILVER (Abba Hillel) ARCHIVES
See: Temple Library

★12511★
SILVER INSTITUTE - LIBRARY (Sci-Tech)
1001 Connecticut Ave., N.W., Suite 1138   Phone: (202) 331-1485
Washington, DC 20036   Richard L. Davies, Exec.Dir.
Staff: Prof 4; Other 6. **Subjects:** Silver. **Holdings:** 100 volumes; newsletters. **Subscriptions:** 15 journals and other serials. **Services:** Library open to public. **Special Catalogs:** Catalog of abstracts on silver (11,000 items).

★12512★
SILVERADO MUSEUM (Hum)
1490 Library Lane
Box 409   Phone: (707) 963-3757
St. Helena, CA 94574   Ellen Shaffer, Cur.
Staff: Prof 1. **Subjects:** Robert Louis Stevenson - life and works. **Holdings:** 3000 books; 1200 original letters; 110 manuscripts; 1000 photographs; 120 paintings, prints and drawings; 8 sculptures; memorabilia. **Services:** Copying; museum open to qualified research workers.

★12513★
SILVERMINE SCHOOL OF THE ARTS - LIBRARY
1037 Silvermine Rd.
New Canaan, CT 06840
Founded: 1959. **Subjects:** Art and related subjects. **Holdings:** 3000 books. **Remarks:** Maintained by Silvermine Guild of Artists, Inc. Presently inactive.

SILVERWOOD INDUSTRIES, LTD.
See: Ault Foods, Ltd.

★12514★
SIMAT, HELLIESEN AND EICHNER - LIBRARY (Trans)
708 Third Ave., 17th Fl.   Phone: (212) 682-8455
New York, NY 10017   William J. Ehlers, Libn.
Founded: 1963. **Staff:** 1. **Subjects:** Transportation, airport planning, travel, economics, marketing. **Holdings:** 10,000 books; 100 bound periodical volumes; 500 statistical volumes. **Subscriptions:** 100 journals and other serials. **Services:** Interlibrary loans; library not open to public.

★12515★
SIMCOE COUNTY ARCHIVES (Hist)
R.R. 2   Phone: (705) 726-9300
Minesing, ON, Canada L0L 1Y0   Peter P. Moran, Archv.
Founded: 1966. **Staff:** Prof 2; Other 1. **Subjects:** Simcoe County history, business and genealogy, cartography, lumbering history. **Special Collections:** Jacques and Hay Papers, 1854 to 1872 (the operation of New Lowell, Ontario; 2000 items, mainly letters); A.F. Hunter Papers (personal notes of local historian); Clarke Collection (500 books; 200 maps; 20,000 photographs, slides and negatives; correspondence). **Holdings:** 1500 books; 500 bound periodical volumes; 50 Women's Institute histories; 130 county assessment rolls; 800 feet of municipal records; 150 magnetic tapes; 50 feet of Georgian Bay Lumber Company papers; 400 maps; microfilm (census records). **Subscriptions:** 29 journals and other serials. **Special Collections:** Copying; archives open to public. **Special Indexes:** Index of newspaper Barrie Northern Advance, 1847-1940 (card); index of photographs (card); index of

maps (card). **Staff:** Bruce Beacock, Archv.Techn.

★12516★

SIMCOE COUNTY LAW ASSOCIATION - LIBRARY (Law)†
30 Poyntz St.   Phone: (715) 728-1221
Barrie, ON, Canada L4M 1M1   Eleanor Garner, Act.Libn.
Staff: 1. **Subjects:** Law - criminal, civil, family, income tax, corporate.
Special Collections: Ontario Municipal Board Decisions; Ontario Government
Bills and Statutes (revisions). **Holdings:** 6600 books and bound periodical
volumes. **Services:** Library not open to public.

★12517★

SIMI VALLEY HISTORICAL SOCIETY - ARCHIVES (Hist)
R.P. Strathearn Historical Park
137 Strathearn Place
Box 351
Simi Valley, CA 93065   Phone: (805) 526-6453
Subjects: Simi Valley history, 1874-1960. **Holdings:** 500 letters and archival
items. **Services:** Archives open to public by appointment.

SIMMEL-FENICHEL LIBRARY
See: Los Angeles Psychoanalytic Society and Institute

★12518★

SIMMONS COLLEGE - GRADUATE SCHOOL OF LIBRARY AND
    INFORMATION SCIENCE - LIBRARY (Info Sci)
300 The Fenway   Phone: (617) 738-2226
Boston, MA 02115   Linda H. Watkins, Libn.
Founded: 1902. **Staff:** Prof 1; Other 14. **Subjects:** Library and information
science, publishing, media resources and study, library management,
librarianship. **Special Collections:** NEBIC File; annual reports of New England
libraries; History of Publishing. **Holdings:** 22,827 books; 7040 bound
periodical volumes; 4935 microfiche; 800 reels of microfilm; 34 VF drawers;
13 videotapes; 20 cassettes; School of Library Science doctoral field studies;
information files (100 library-related subjects); doctoral dissertations
(microfilm). **Subscriptions:** 500 journals and other serials; 153 newsletters.
Services: Interlibrary loans; copying; library open to public for reference use
only. **Automated Operations:** Computerized reserve holdings, Union
periodicals list. **Computerized Information Services:** OCLC, DIALOG, BRS.
Networks/Consortia: Member of NELINET; Fenway Library Consortium.
Publications: Bibliographic Instruction Brochure; acquisitions list. **Special
Catalogs:** Reserve list file.

★12519★

SIMMONS COLLEGE - SCHOOL OF SOCIAL WORK LIBRARY (Soc Sci)
51 Commonwealth Ave.   Phone: (617) 266-0806
Boston, MA 02116   Marilyn Smith Bregoli, Libn.
Founded: 1904. **Staff:** Prof 1; Other 2. **Subjects:** Social work, public
welfare, psychiatry. **Holdings:** 19,500 books; 2600 bound periodical
volumes; 1200 theses. **Subscriptions:** 160 journals and other serials.
Services: Interlibrary loans; library open to public for research. **Automated
Operations:** Computerized cataloging.

★12520★

SIMON FRASER UNIVERSITY - LIBRARY - SPECIAL COLLECTIONS (Hum)
                                        Phone: (604) 291-3261
Burnaby, BC, Canada V5A 1S6   Percilla Groves, Spec.Coll.Libn.
Special Collections: Canadiana; Africana; Contemporary Literature Collection
(Canadian and American avant-garde poetry and prose since 1945; books,
manuscripts, tapes, little magazines and ephemera related to Ezra Pound,
Charles Olson, Gary Snyder, Michael McClure, and over thirty others);
Government Documents Collection (Canadian, British Columbian, and African).
Services: Interlibrary loans; copying; SDI; library open to public for reference
use only. **Computerized Information Services:** DIALOG, SDC, MEDLINE,
CAN/OLE, UTLAS.

SIMON (Norton) MUSEUM OF ART AT PASADENA
See: Norton Simon Museum of Art at Pasadena

SIMONS (Harry) LIBRARY
See: Beth David Congregation - Harry Simons Library

SIMONS (Leonard N.) RESEARCH LIBRARY
See: Michigan Cancer Foundation - Leonard N. Simons Research Library

SIMONS (Menno) HISTORICAL LIBRARY AND ARCHIVES
See: Eastern Mennonite College - Menno Simons Historical Library and
    Archives

SIMPSON GEOGRAPHIC RESEARCH CENTER
See: University of Wisconsin, Eau Claire

★12521★

SIMPSON, THACHER & BARTLETT - LIBRARY (Law)†
1 Battery Park Plaza   Phone: (212) 483-9000
New York, NY 10004   John S. Marsh, Libn.
Founded: 1884. **Staff:** Prof 2; Other 6. **Subjects:** Law - antitrust, corporate,
labor, banking, trade regulations, public utilities, taxation, securities. **Holdings:**
30,000 volumes. **Services:** Interlibrary loans; library not open to public.
Computerized Information Services: LEXIS, New York Times Information
Service, DIALOG, Dow Jones News/Retrieval. **Remarks:** Branch library
located at 350 Park Ave., New York, NY 10022. **Staff:** Lynn Abraham,
Assoc.Libn.

SIMS (L.A.) MEMORIAL LIBRARY
See: Southeastern Louisiana University - L.A. Sims Memorial Library

★12522★

SIMSBURY HISTORICAL SOCIETY - SIMSBURY RESEARCH LIBRARY (Hist)
800 Hopmeadow St.   Phone: (203) 658-2500
Simsbury, CT 06070   Robert A. Hawley, Dir.
Founded: 1975. **Subjects:** Simsbury area history and genealogy. **Holdings:**
2000 books and bound periodical volumes; extensive uncataloged materials.
Services: Library open to public by request. **Remarks:** Established as a
bicentennial project, the library is based on materials that had been in storage
since 1911.

★12523★

SINAI HOSPITAL OF BALTIMORE, INC. - EISENBERG MEDICAL STAFF
    LIBRARY (Med)
Belvedere & Greenspring   Phone: (301) 578-5015
Baltimore, MD 21215   Rita Matcher, Dir., Lib.Serv.
Staff: Prof 1; Other 2. **Subjects:** Medicine, nursing. **Holdings:** 4441 books;
9000 bound periodical volumes. **Subscriptions:** 232 journals and other
serials. **Services:** Interlibrary loans; library not open to public. **Computerized
Information Services:** MEDLINE. **Networks/Consortia:** Member of
Baltimore Consortia for Resource Sharing.

★12524★

SINAI HOSPITAL OF DETROIT - SAMUEL FRANK MEDICAL LIBRARY (Med)
6767 W. Outer Dr.   Phone: (313) 493-5140
Detroit, MI 48235   Barbara L. Finn, Dir. of Med.Lib.
Founded: 1953. **Staff:** Prof 3; Other 5. **Subjects:** Medicine, nursing and
allied health sciences. **Special Collections:** History of Medicine (emphasis on
Jewish contributions). **Holdings:** 9600 books; 15,135 bound periodical
volumes; 9 VF drawers of reprints and pamphlets; cassettes and Audio-Digest
tapes. **Subscriptions:** 571 journals and other serials. **Services:** Interlibrary
loans; copying; SDI; library open to those connected with medical and
paramedical fields. **Computerized Information Services:** Online systems.
Publications: Accession list of new books, monthly - for internal distribution
only. **Staff:** Cathy Palmer, Lib.Supv.; Laura Grab, Asst.Dir.

SINCLAIR LIBRARY
See: University of Hawaii - Special Collections - Archives

★12525★

SINGER COMPANY - EDUCATION DIVISION - TECHNICAL LIBRARY*
3750 Monroe Ave.
Rochester, NY 14603
Founded: 1964. **Staff:** 1. **Subjects:** Physics, electronics, fine arts,
management, mathematics, engineering, optics, photography. **Holdings:** 485
volumes. **Remarks:** Presently inactive.

★12526★

SINGER COMPANY - HRB-SINGER, INC. - TECHNICAL INFORMATION
    CENTER (Sci-Tech)
Science Pk.   Phone: (814) 238-4311
State College, PA 16804   Peggy A. Hayden, Tech.Libn.
Founded: 1948. **Staff:** 1. **Subjects:** Electronics, mathematics, physics,
electrical engineering, psychology, photography. **Holdings:** 14,000 books and
bound periodical volumes. **Subscriptions:** 54 journals and other serials.
Services: Interlibrary loans; center not open to public.

★12527★

SINGER COMPANY - KEARFOTT DIVISION - TECHNICAL INFORMATION
    CENTER (Sci-Tech)
150 Totowa Rd.   Phone: (201) 785-6462
Wayne, NJ 07470   B.R. Meade, Supv.
Founded: 1956. **Staff:** Prof 2; Other 1. **Subjects:** Aerospace sciences,

electronic engineering. **Holdings:** 21,500 books; 5000 bound periodical volumes; 1600 bound serials; 40,000 reports, pamphlets, reprints; 3500 microforms. **Subscriptions:** 215 journals and other serials. **Services:** Interlibrary loans; center not open to public. **Computerized Information Services:** DIALOG.

★12528★
SINGER COMPANY - LIBRASCOPE DIVISION - TECHNICAL INFORMATION CENTER (Sci-Tech; Comp Sci)
833 Sonora Ave.   Phone: (818) 244-6541
Glendale, CA 91201   Nathan J. Sands, Mgr.
Founded: 1954. **Staff:** Prof 2; Other 2. **Subjects:** Computers; engineering - systems, electronic, mechanical, electrical; data processing; military electronics; electro-optics; instruments; mathematics; management. **Holdings:** 20,000 books; 1000 bound periodical volumes; 20,000 reports; VSMF microfilm files; 25,000 microfiche; 12 VF drawers of pamphlets. **Subscriptions:** 250 journals and other serials. **Services:** Interlibrary loans; copying; project data bank management; center open to company personnel only, to others by appointment. **Automated Operations:** Computerized cataloging and circulation. **Computerized Information Services:** Internal database. **Publications:** Accessions List, monthly; computer-generated data bank lists. **Staff:** Saundra Murray, Libn.; Clarine Miller, Spec. Control.

★12529★
SINGER COMPANY - LINK DIVISION - TECHNICAL LIBRARY (Sci-Tech)
1077 E. Arques Ave.   Phone: (408) 720-5719
Sunnyvale, CA 94088-3484   Shu-nan T. Chiang, Tech.Libn.
Staff: Prof 1. **Subjects:** Computer science, electrical engineering, computer graphics, simulation, Link trainers, flight simulation, flight trainers, radar, electronics. **Holdings:** 1200 volumes; 500 technical reports. **Subscriptions:** 75 journals and other serials. **Services:** Interlibrary loans; library not open to public. **Networks/Consortia:** Member of CLASS. **Publications:** Information from the Technical Library, monthly - for internal distribution only.

★12530★
SINGER COMPANY - LINK FLIGHT SIMULATION DIVISION - INFORMATION CENTER (Sci-Tech)
Colesville Rd.
Binghamton, NY 13902   Eileen M. Hamlin, Supv.
Founded: 1951. **Staff:** Prof 3; Other 3. **Subjects:** Electrical and electronic engineering; aeronautics; economics; mathematics; computers. **Holdings:** Figures not available for books, internal reports, technical reports, manuals, reprints, handbooks, microforms. **Subscriptions:** 530 journals and other serials. **Services:** Interlibrary loans; copying; center open to public by appointment. **Computerized Information Services:** DIALOG, BRS, DTIC, NASA/RECON, Dun & Bradstreet Corporation; Engineering Information Service (internal database). **Networks/Consortia:** Member of South Central Regional Library Council (SCRLC). **Staff:** Robert Walliant, Info.Spec.-Sys.; Dale Carpenter, Info.Spec.Sandra P. Stiles, Info.Couns.

★12531★
SINGER COMPANY - SPG ENGINEERING - SEWING PRODUCTS GROUP - ENGINEERING LIBRARY
70 New Dutch Ln.
Fairfield, NJ 07006
Defunct

★12532★
SINGER (H. Douglas) MENTAL HEALTH CENTER - LIBRARY (Med)
4402 North Main St.   Phone: (815) 987-7092
Rockford, IL 61105   Pat Ellison, Lib.Assoc.
Founded: 1966. **Staff:** Prof 1. **Subjects:** Mental health, psychology, psychiatry, psychotherapy, sociology, religion, medicine. **Holdings:** 2000 books. **Subscriptions:** 100 journals and other serials. **Services:** Interlibrary loans; copying (staff only); library open to public with restrictions. **Networks/Consortia:** Member of Upstate Illinois Consortium; Northern Illinois Library System (NILS). **Remarks:** Maintained by Illinois State Department of Mental Health and Developmental Disabilities.

SINGEWALD READING ROOM
See: **Johns Hopkins University - Department of Earth and Planetary Sciences**

★12533★
SINGING RIVER HOSPITAL - MEDICAL LIBRARY (Med)
2809 Denny Ave.   Phone: (601) 938-5040
Pascagoula, MS 39567   Mary Evelyn Dowell, Dir., Med.Lib.
Staff: Prof 1; Other 1. **Subjects:** Medicine, nursing, allied health sciences, hospital administration. **Holdings:** 1000 books; 6000 bound periodical

volumes. **Subscriptions:** 160 journals and other serials. **Services:** Interlibrary loans; copying; library open to Jackson County students. **Computerized Information Services:** MEDLARS. **Networks/Consortia:** Member of Gulf Coast Biomedical Library Consortium; Mississippi Biomedical Library Consortium.

★12534★
SINGLE DAD'S LIFESTYLE MAGAZINE - LIBRARY (Publ)
Box 4842   Phone: (602) 998-0980
Scottsdale, AZ 85258   Robert A. Hirschfeld, Ed./Publ.
Founded: 1978. **Staff:** 1. **Subjects:** Father's rights, divorce law, psychology of divorce, paternal custody, visitation and child support, child rearing by single parents. **Special Collections:** Father's Rights/Divorce Reform Organization newsletters (400); case law collection of paternal custody, visitation, child support materials (50 items). **Holdings:** 210 books and bound periodical volumes; 15 videotapes. **Subscriptions:** 13 journals and other serials. **Services:** Library not open to public. **Publications:** Single Dad's Lifestyle Magazine, monthly - by subscription; Father's Rights/Divorce Reform Newsletter, monthly - free to bona fide Father's Rights groups. **Special Indexes:** Annual blue list of Father's Rights/Divorce Reform organizations.

SINOLOGICAL SEMINAR LIBRARY
See: **Yale University - East Asian Collection**

★12535★
SIOUX CITY ART CENTER ASSOCIATION - LIBRARY (Art)
513 Nebraska St.   Phone: (712) 279-6272
Sioux City, IA 51101   Marilyn Laufer, Educ.Cur.
Subjects: Art and art history. **Holdings:** 800 books; exhibition catalogs; reproduction slides. **Subscriptions:** 15 journals and other serials. **Services:** Library open to public for reference use only. **Publications:** Artifact, monthly; exhibition catalogs.

★12536★
SIOUX FALLS ARGUS-LEADER - LIBRARY (Publ)★
200 S. Minnesota   Phone: (605) 331-2300
Sioux Falls, SD 57102
Staff: 1. **Subjects:** Newspaper reference topics. **Holdings:** Figures not available. **Services:** Library for firm's use only; newspaper copies on microfilm are available at Sioux Falls Public Library.

SIOUX FALLS PARK & RECREATION DEPARTMENT - GREAT PLAINS ZOO & MUSEUM
See: **Great Plains Zoo & Museum**

★12537★
SIOUX VALLEY HOSPITAL - MEDICAL LIBRARY (Med)
1100 S. Euclid Ave.
Box 5039   Phone: (605) 333-1000
Sioux Falls, SD 57117   Kay Hasegawa, Libn.
Founded: 1954. **Staff:** 3. **Subjects:** Medicine, nursing, and related health fields. **Holdings:** 4195 books; 3925 bound periodical volumes; 4 VF drawers of pamphlets, reprints, articles, and clippings. **Subscriptions:** 153 journals and other serials. **Services:** Interlibrary loans; copying; library open to public for reference use only. **Computerized Information Services:** MEDLINE.

★12538★
SIOUXLAND HERITAGE MUSEUMS - PETTIGREW MUSEUM - LIBRARY (Hist)
131 N. Duluth Ave.   Phone: (605) 339-7097
Sioux Falls, SD 57104   Ms. Lee N. McLaird, Cur. of Collections
Founded: 1926. **Staff:** Prof 1. **Subjects:** South Dakota history; U.S. history - silver question; 19th century works on ethnology and natural science; Indians. **Special Collections:** R.F. Pettigrew Collection (1000 volumes); Arthur C. Phillips Collection; Northern League Baseball records (4 linear feet); library and private papers of U.S. Senator R.F. Pettigrew (1000 volumes); South Dakota history (1500 items). **Holdings:** 9000 books; 200 bound periodical volumes; 50 maps; 20 linear feet of manuscripts; 2500 photographs. **Subscriptions:** 10 journals and other serials. **Services:** Copying; library open to public. **Publications:** Prairie People, quarterly - by subscription.

★12539★
SIR MORTIMER B. DAVIS JEWISH GENERAL HOSPITAL - INSTITUTE OF COMMUNITY & FAMILY PSYCHIATRY - LIBRARY (Med)
4333 Cote St. Catherine Rd.   Phone: (514) 341-6211
Montreal, PQ, Canada H3T 1E2   Ruth Stilman, Libn.
Founded: 1969. **Staff:** Prof 1; Other 1. **Subjects:** Psychiatry, psychotherapy, family therapy, community mental health, psychopharmacology. **Holdings:** 5380 books; 1150 bound periodical volumes; 300 VF items; 325 audiotapes.

Subscriptions: 90 journals and other serials. **Services:** Interlibrary loans; copying; library open to public for consultation. **Computerized Information Services:** MEDLINE. **Networks/Consortia:** Member of McGill Medical and Health Libraries Association; Montreal Health Libraries Association.

★12540★
SIR MORTIMER B. DAVIS JEWISH GENERAL HOSPITAL - LADY DAVIS INSTITUTE FOR MEDICAL RESEARCH - RESEARCH LIBRARY (Med)
3755 Cote St. Catherine Rd.   Phone: (514) 342-3620
Montreal, PQ, Canada H3T 1E2   Arlene Greenberg, Chf.Med.Libn.
Founded: 1969. **Staff:** Prof 1. **Subjects:** Biochemistry, molecular biology, cancer research, cell genetics, diabetes. **Holdings:** 7000 books and bound periodical volumes. **Subscriptions:** 70 journals and other serials. **Services:** Interlibrary loans; copying; library open to public for reference use only. **Computerized Information Services:** BRS, MEDLINE. **Networks/Consortia:** Member of McGill Medical and Health Libraries Association; Montreal Health Libraries Association. **Remarks:** All services are coordinated through the Sir Mortimer B. Davis Jewish General Hospital - Medical Library.

★12541★
SIR MORTIMER B. DAVIS JEWISH GENERAL HOSPITAL - MEDICAL LIBRARY (Med)
3755 Cote St. Catherine Rd.   Phone: (514) 342-3111
Montreal, PQ, Canada H3T 1E2   Arlene Greenberg, Chf.Med.Libn.
Founded: 1950. **Staff:** Prof 1; Other 3. **Subjects:** Medicine, nursing, social work, administration. **Holdings:** 22,000 books and bound periodical volumes. **Subscriptions:** 370 journals and other serials. **Services:** Interlibrary loans; copying; library open to public for reference use only. **Computerized Information Services:** BRS, MEDLINE. **Networks/Consortia:** Member of McGill Medical and Health Libraries Association; Montreal Health Libraries Association. **Publications:** Library Newsletter, semiannual; Acquisitions List, bimonthly - both for internal distribution only.

★12542★
SIR SANDFORD FLEMING COLLEGE OF APPLIED ARTS & TECHNOLOGY - EDUCATIONAL RESOURCE CENTER (Sci-Tech)
Sutherland Campus
Brealey Bldg.   Phone: (705) 743-5610
Peterborough, ON, Canada K9J 7B1   Janice Coughlin, Dir.
Founded: 1968. **Staff:** Prof 1; Other 20. **Subjects:** Forestry, business, electro-mechanical technology, fine arts, psychology, sociology, nursing, natural resources. **Holdings:** 35,000 books; 500 bound periodical volumes; 2000 nonprint items; 500 vertical files. **Subscriptions:** 550 journals and other serials; 10 newspapers. **Services:** Interlibrary loans; copying; library open to public. **Automated Operations:** Computerized cataloging and acquisitions. **Networks/Consortia:** Member of Bibliocentre. **Remarks:** Above data includes the holdings of the Brealey, Daniel and Lindsay campus libraries.

★12543★
SIROTE, PERMUTT, FRIEND, FRIEDMAN, HELD & APOLINSKY, P.C. - LAW LIBRARY (Law)
2222 Arlington Ave., S.   Phone: (205) 933-7111
Birmingham, AL 35205   Patricia L. Mennicke, Libn.
Staff: Prof 1; Other 1. **Subjects:** Law - taxation, litigation, business, collection. **Holdings:** 15,000 volumes; 100 cassettes; 82 binders of legal briefs and memos; 50 speech outlines. **Subscriptions:** 79 journals and other serials. **Services:** Interlibrary loans; copying; library open to public with permission of member of the firm. **Computerized Information Services:** Westlaw. **Special Indexes:** Legal Brief/Memo index (card); holdings list of tax materials (card).

★12544★
SIRRINE (J.E.) COMPANY - TECHNICAL LIBRARY
Box 42286
Houston, TX 77042
Defunct. Merged with Caudill Rowlett Scott to form CRS Serrine.

★12545★
SISKIYOU COUNTY HISTORICAL SOCIETY - LIBRARY (Hist)
910 S. Main St.   Phone: (916) 842-3836
Yreka, CA 96097   Eleanor Brown, Musm.Cur.
Founded: 1950. **Staff:** Prof 2; Other 1. **Subjects:** History of California and Siskiyou County. **Holdings:** 1000 books; 21 bound periodical volumes; 75 ledgers and account books; 10 manuscripts; 550 documents; 3 VF cabinets of photographs; 248 bound volumes of county newspapers, 1915-1952. **Subscriptions:** 10 journals and other serials. **Services:** Library open to public. **Publications:** Siskiyou Pioneer, annual; occasional papers. **Special Indexes:** Index to Siskiyou Pioneer.

★12546★
SISKIYOU COUNTY LAW LIBRARY (Law)
311 Fourth St., Courthouse   Phone: (916) 842-3531
Yreka, CA 96097   Patricia Howard, Libn.
Staff: 1. **Subjects:** Law. **Holdings:** 12,500 volumes; 12 bound periodical volumes. **Services:** Library open to public.

SISTER KENNY INSTITUTE
See: Abbott-Northwestern Hospital Corporation

SISTER MARY ALVINA NURSING LIBRARY
See: St. Joseph Hospital

SISTER STELLA LOUISE HEALTH SCIENCE LIBRARY
See: St. Mary of Nazareth Hospital

★12547★
SISTERS OF CHARITY HOSPITAL - MEDICAL STAFF LIBRARY (Med)
2157 Main St.   Phone: (716) 862-2846
Buffalo, NY 14214   Anne Cohen, Med.Libn.
Founded: 1948. **Staff:** Prof 1. **Subjects:** Medicine, surgery, obstetrics and gynecology, pediatrics. **Holdings:** 5049 books and bound periodical volumes. **Subscriptions:** 99 journals and other serials. **Services:** Interlibrary loans; copying; library open to medical staff only.

SISTERS OF CHARITY - ST. JOSEPH HOSPITAL
See: St. Joseph Hospital - Medical Library (Albuquerque, NM)

SISTERS OF THE HOLY FAMILY - HOLY FAMILY COLLEGE
See: Holy Family College - Mother Dolores Memorial Library

★12548★
SISTERS OF THE HOLY FAMILY OF NAZARETH - IMMACULATE CONCEPTION B.V.M. - ARCHIVES (Rel-Theol; Hist)
Grant & Frankford Aves.   Phone: (215) 637-6464
Philadelphia, PA 19114   Sr. M. Theodosette, Archv.
Founded: 1973. **Staff:** Prof 1. **Subjects:** History of the Sisters of the Holy Family of Nazareth and the Immaculate Conception Province. **Special Collections:** Autobiography and biographies of the Foundress of the Sisters of the Holy Family of Nazareth; Constitutions of the Congregation, 1887-1980; Proceedings of the General Chapters, 1895-1983; Books of Customs, 1894-1966; Reports of Provincial Superiors, 1951-1974; Educational Conference Proceedings, 1941-1979; correspondence and circular letters of the General and Provincial Superiors; Album of Fine Arts of the Sisters of the Holy Family of Nazareth (CSFN); Provincial Superior Correspondence with Prelates and Clergy; Provincial Superior Statistical Reports; information on various programs held in the Province; Inter-Province News Letters. **Holdings:** 1150 books; 41 bound periodical volumes; 118 doctoral and masters' dissertations; active files of convents and members; chronicles and annals of Homes; necrologies of deceased Sisters. **Services:** Interlibrary loans; copying; archives open to public with restrictions. **Publications:** Guide to Nazareth Literature, 1873-1973 (1st edition).

★12549★
SISTERS OF NOTRE DAME DE NAMUR - OHIO PROVINCE - ARCHIVES (Rel-Theol)
Provincial House
701 E. Columbia Ave.   Phone: (513) 821-7448
Cincinnati, OH 45215
Subjects: Houses, institutions, and works of the Ohio Province of the Sisters of Notre Dame de Namur, 1840 to present; work of St. Julie Billiart. **Special Collections:** Manuscripts (original and copied letters of church officials, and sisters of the convent); biographies and memoirs of sisters, Catholic women, and clergy. **Holdings:** 650 cubic feet of church records, conference proceedings, catechisms, educational writings, academic theses, institutional histories, cemetery records and necrologies, church rules, prayers; photographs; slides. **Services:** Copying; archives open to public with permission.

★12550★
SISTERS OF PROVIDENCE - SACRED HEART PROVINCE - ARCHIVES (Rel-Theol)
4800 37th Ave., S.W.   Phone: (206) 937-4600
Seattle, WA 98126   Sr. Rita Bergamini, S.P., Archv.
Founded: 1972. **Subjects:** Sisters of Providence; history of health care, education, Catholic church, Indians. **Special Collections:** Mother Joseph, a Sister of Providence (1823-1902); medical history of the Sisters of Providence hospitals and health care institutions in the Pacific Northwest states including Alaska and California from 1857 to present; education history

of the Sisters of Providence schools in the Pacific Northwest states including Alaska and California from 1856 to present. **Services:** Copying; archives open to public by appointment.

★12551★

SISTERS OF ST. JOSEPH OF CARONDELET - ST. PAUL PROVINCE - ARCHIVES (Rel-Theol)
1884 Randolph Ave.   Phone: (612) 690-7000
St. Paul, MN 55105   Mary E. Kraft, C.S.J., Archv.
Staff: Prof 1; Other 1. **Subjects:** Religious life, education, health care, social justice, women. **Holdings:** Archival collections. **Services:** Copying; archives open to public with restrictions.

★12552★

SISTERS OF ST. MARY OF NAMUR - MOUNT ST. MARY RESEARCH CENTER (Rel-Theol; Hist)
3756 Delaware Ave.   Phone: (716) 875-4705
Kenmore, NY 14217   Sr. M. Xavier Hefner, Archv./Libn.
Founded: 1975. **Staff:** Prof 1. **Subjects:** History of Sisters of St. Mary. **Special Collections:** Slides of Dante. **Holdings:** 300 volumes; 7 boxes of dissertations. **Subscriptions:** 25 journals and other serials. **Services:** Interlibrary loans; copying; center open to public.

★12553★

SISTERS OF SOCIAL SERVICE - ARCHIVES
1120 Westchester Pl.
Los Angeles, CA 90019
Subjects: History of the Sisters of Social Service, social change in Hungary and U.S., social change in the Catholic Church and in religious life. **Holdings:** Manuscripts; letters; photographs; work reports. **Remarks:** Presently inactive.

SITKA NATL. HISTORICAL PARK
See: U.S. Natl. Park Service

★12554★

SKADDEN, ARPS, SLATE, MEAGHER & FLOM - LIBRARY (Law)†
919 3rd Ave.   Phone: (212) 371-6000
New York, NY 10022   Carrie Hirtz, Libn.
Staff: Prof 5; Other 10. **Subjects:** Law. **Holdings:** 30,000 books; 500 bound periodical volumes; 98 VF drawers of prospectuses and legal memoranda. **Subscriptions:** 150 journals and other serials; 6 newspapers. **Services:** Interlibrary loans; library not open to public. **Automated Operations:** Computerized circulation. **Computerized Information Services:** DIALOG, Westlaw, Dow Jones News/Retrieval, SDC, LEXIS, New York Times Information Service.

★12555★

SKAGIT COUNTY HISTORICAL MUSEUM - HISTORICAL REFERENCE LIBRARY (Hist)
Box 818   Phone: (206) 466-3365
La Conner, WA 98257   David J. van Meer, Cur.
Founded: 1968. **Staff:** Prof 3; Other 2. **Subjects:** Local history (Skagit County), pioneer family genealogies, local Indian histories, late 19th century novels and periodicals, old American popular music (1866-1954), local newspapers (1900 to present). **Special Collections:** Diaries of Grant Sisson, W.J. Cornelius, Arthur Champenois, and others from 1844 to 1964; Darius Kinsey Photographs; personal and legal papers of Key Pittman, U.S. Senator from Nevada, 1913-1940. **Holdings:** 1500 books; 308 bound periodical volumes; 4829 photographs; 599 newspapers; 658 business documents; 109 old letters; 106 old district school accounts/records; 81 maps; 626 clippings and clipping scrapbooks; 183 old programs/announcements; 64 pioneer diaries; 220 oral history tapes with transcripts. **Subscriptions:** 14 journals and other serials. **Services:** Copying; library open to public by appointment. **Staff:** Eunice Darvill, Dir; David J. Van Meer, Cur.

★12556★

SKAGIT COUNTY LAW LIBRARY (Law)
County Court House, 2nd Fl.   Phone: (206) 336-9313
Mount Vernon, WA 98273   Pat Ryan, Libn.
Subjects: Law, decisions of appellate courts. **Holdings:** 6500 books and bound periodical volumes. **Services:** Library open to public for reference use only.

SKIDAWAY INSTITUTE OF OCEANOGRAPHY
See: University of Georgia

SKIDMORE (Louis) ROOM
See: Massachusetts Institute of Technology - Rotch Library Visual Collections - Louis Skidmore Room

★12557★

SKIDMORE, OWINGS & MERRILL - INFORMATION SERVICES DEPARTMENT (Art; Sci-Tech)
220 E. 42nd St.   Phone: (212) 309-9500
New York, NY 10017   Frances C. Gretes, Mgr., Info.Serv.
Staff: Prof 1; Other 3. **Subjects:** Architecture, art, engineering, interior design, New York history. **Special Collections:** Archives. **Holdings:** 2000 books; 145 bound periodical volumes; 100 catalogs; 200 master plans; 10,000 drawings; specifications; 300 reels of microfilm; 5000 project clippings; 5000 photographs; 1000 unbound periodicals. **Subscriptions:** 133 journals and other serials. **Services:** Interlibrary loans (limited); copying; SDI; department open to other librarians and students for reference use only. **Computerized Information Services:** DIALOG, RLIN, NewsNet. **Publications:** Monthly list of new publications. **Special Catalogs:** Bibliography on the work of the firm (published articles).

★12558★

SKIDMORE, OWINGS & MERRILL - LIBRARY (Sci-Tech; Art)
1675 Broadway   Phone: (303) 825-3100
Denver, CO 80202   Jay Schafer, Libn.
Staff: Prof 1. **Subjects:** Architecture, engineering. **Holdings:** 300 books; 500 volumes of manufacturer's literature; product samples. **Subscriptions:** 20 journals and other serials. **Services:** Library not open to public.

★12559★

SKIDMORE, OWINGS & MERRILL - LIBRARY (Plan; Art)
1201 Pennsylvania Ave., N.W.   Phone: (202) 393-1400
Washington, DC 20004   Gail Markowitz, Libn.
Founded: 1976. **Staff:** Prof 1. **Subjects:** Architecture, interior design, urban planning and transportation, landscape architecture. **Holdings:** 3000 books; 100 bound periodical volumes; 1000 SOM reports; 500 SOM proposals; slides; maps; photographs; clippings. **Services:** Interlibrary loans; copying; library open to public by appointment.

★12560★

SKIDMORE, OWINGS & MERRILL - LIBRARY (Plan)
33 W. Monroe St.   Phone: (312) 641-5959
Chicago, IL 60603   Mary K. Woolever, Libn.
Staff: 1. **Subjects:** Manufacturing product information, building laws and regulations, environmental control, city and urban planning, architectural design. **Holdings:** 5138 books; 24 bound periodical volumes; 20 VF drawers of photographs and pamphlets. **Subscriptions:** 50 journals and other serials. **Services:** Interlibrary loans; library open to architectural firms.

SKILLMANN (David Bishop) LIBRARY
See: Lafayette College - American Friends of Lafayette Collection

SLA
See: Special Libraries Association

SLAC HIGH ENERGY PREPRINT LIBRARY
See: University of California, Los Angeles - Physics Library

SLADEN (Frank J.) LIBRARY
See: Henry Ford Hospital - Frank J. Sladen Library

★12561★

SLATER MILL HISTORIC SITE - RESEARCH LIBRARY (Hist)
Roosevelt Ave.
Box 727   Phone: (401) 725-8638
Pawtucket, RI 02862   T.E. Leary, Cur.
Founded: 1955. **Staff:** 1. **Subjects:** Handicraft and factory textile production, machine tools, local industrial and social history. **Holdings:** 500 volumes. **Services:** Library open to public by appointment. **Publications:** The Flyer, bimonthly.

★12562★

SLAVIA LIBRARY (Area-Ethnic)
418 W. Nittany Ave.   Phone: (814) 238-5215
State College, PA 16801   Dr. W.O. Luciw, Dir.
Staff: Prof 2; Other 2. **Subjects:** Ukrainian history, literature, language, social studies, art, and science. **Special Collections:** Ukrainian and Slavic archives. **Holdings:** 45,000 books; 5000 unbound periodical volumes; 17,000 other cataloged items; 40,000 items in microform. **Subscriptions:** 60 journals and other serials. **Services:** Copying; SDI; library open to public by appointment for reference use only. **Publications:** Life and School, 5/year; Free World. **Special Catalogs:** Book publications catalog.

★12563★

SLAVONIC BENEVOLENT ORDER OF THE STATE OF TEXAS - LIBRARY, ARCHIVES, MUSEUM (Area-Ethnic)
520 N. Main St.   Phone: (817) 773-1575
Temple, TX 76501   Otto Hanus, Libn./Cur.
Staff: Prof 1. **Subjects:** Education, medicine, religion, history, music. **Holdings:** 20,000 volumes (mostly in Czech language); over 500 Czech plays. **Services:** Interlibrary loans; copying; library open to public.

★12564★

SLEEPY HOLLOW RESTORATIONS, INC. - SPECIAL LIBRARY & ARCHIVES (Art; Hist)
150 White Plains Rd.   Phone: (914) 631-8200
Tarrytown, NY 10591   Hollee Haswell, Libn.
Founded: 1951. **Staff:** Prof 2. **Subjects:** 17th-, 18th- and 19th-century Hudson River Valley history; decorative arts and architecture; Washington Irving. **Special Collections:** Manuscript holdings of Van Cortlandt and Philipse families; Washington Irving manuscripts. **Holdings:** 12,000 volumes; pamphlets; 49 VF drawers of maps, plans and graphics; 19 microfilm files; unpublished reports; archives; plans and blueprints of Sleepy Hollow Restorations restored buildings. **Subscriptions:** 130 journals and other serials. **Services:** Copying (limited); library open to scholars, authors and researchers by appointment. **Networks/Consortia:** Member of METRO. **Staff:** Sherri Paul

SLICK (Thomas Baker) MEMORIAL LIBRARY
See: Southwest Research Institute - Thomas Baker Slick Memorial Library

★12565★

SLOAN (Alfred P., Jr.) MUSEUM - MERLE G. PERRY ARCHIVES (Hist; Trans)
1221 E. Kearsley St.   Phone: (313) 762-1170
Flint, MI 48503   Phillip C. Kwiatkowski, Dir.
Subjects: Automotive history, carriage industry, local history. **Special Collections:** Automotive catalogs (300). **Holdings:** 750 volumes. **Subscriptions:** 24 journals and other serials. **Services:** Copying; archives open to public for reference use only. **Staff:** Scott M. Peters, Cur. of Coll.; James Johnson, Assoc.Dir.; Neil Yake, Dir., Health Inst.; Carol deKalands, Archv.; David White, Registrar.

SLOAN FINE ARTS LIBRARY
See: Williamsport Area Community College

SLOAN (John) MEMORIAL LIBRARY
See: Delaware Art Museum - Library

★12566★

SLOAN-KETTERING INSTITUTE FOR CANCER RESEARCH - DONALD S. WALKER LABORATORY - C.P. RHOADS MEMORIAL LIBRARY (Med)
145 Boston Post Rd.   Phone: (914) 698-1100
Rye, NY 10580   Virginia Gregory, Libn.
Founded: 1959. **Staff:** Prof 1; Other 1. **Subjects:** Cancer and allied diseases, biochemistry, cytology and cytogenetics, immunology. **Holdings:** 2999 books; 6322 bound periodical volumes; 1 file of staff reprints; 6 catalog drawers of microcards; 8 drawers of microfilm. **Subscriptions:** 177 journals and other serials. **Services:** Interlibrary loans; copying; library open to professionals only. **Computerized Information Services:** NLM. **Networks/Consortia:** Member of Medical Library Center of New York (MLCNY). **Publications:** Quarterly list of new accessions; list of journal subscriptions, annual - both to staff only.

SLOAN MATHEMATICS CENTER
See: Stanford University - Mathematical and Computer Sciences Library

SLOCUM SOCIETY LIBRARY
See: Jefferson County Historical Society - Museum

SLOTKIN (Dr. Barney A.) MEMORIAL LIBRARY
See: Kennedy Memorial Hospitals - Cherry Hill Division - Dr. Barney A. Slotkin Memorial Library

★12567★

SLOVAK CATHOLIC CHARITABLE ORGANIZATION - SLOVAK CULTURAL CENTER - LIBRARY (Area-Ethnic)
5900 W. 147th St.   Phone: (312) 687-2877
Oak Forest, IL 60452   Sr. M. Methodia Machalica, Dir.
Staff: Prof 1. **Subjects:** Slovakia. **Holdings:** 2030 books and bound periodical volumes; Slovak encyclopedias, periodicals, and stamps; manuscripts; clippings; archival materials; documents; magnetic tapes. **Services:** Library open to public with restrictions.

★12568★

SLOVAK WRITERS AND ARTISTS ASSOCIATION - SLOVAK INSTITUTE - LIBRARY (Area-Ethnic)
St. Andrew's Abbey
2900 East Blvd.   Phone: (216) 521-7288
Cleveland, OH 44104   Fr. Nicholas Sprinc, Sec.
Staff: Prof 2. **Subjects:** Slovak history, Slovak art, Slovak literature, cultural achievements of Americans of Slovak ancestry. **Holdings:** 5000 books. **Services:** Library open to public for reference use only by special arrangement.

SMALL BUSINESS ADMINISTRATION
See: U.S. Small Business Administration

SMALL BUSINESS CENTER (SBC)
See: District of Columbia Public Library - Business, Economics & Vocations Division

SMALL BUSINESS DEVELOPMENT CENTER
See: Georgia State University

SMALL BUSINESS DEVELOPMENT & RECREATION CENTER
See: University of Wisconsin, Madison - Small Business Development & Recreation Center

★12569★

SMALL, CRAIG & WERKENTHIN - LIBRARY (Law)
2500 Interfirst Tower   Phone: (512) 472-8355
Austin, TX 78701   Candice Cortes Kennington, Libn.
Staff: Prof 1; Other 1. **Subjects:** Law. **Holdings:** 9950 books; 50 bound periodical volumes. **Subscriptions:** 50 journals and other serials. **Services:** Interlibrary loans; copying; library open to public by appointment. **Automated Operations:** Computerized cataloging. **Computerized Information Services:** DIALOG, LEXIS, NEXIS; Research Retrieval (internal database).

SMALL (Robert Scott) LIBRARY
See: College of Charleston - Robert Scott Small Library

SMALL (Walter M.) GEOLOGY LIBRARY
See: Allegheny College - Walter M. Small Geology Library

SMALLEY LIBRARY OF SOCIAL WORK
See: University of Pennsylvania - School of Social Work

★12570★

SMATHERS & THOMPSON - LAW LIBRARY (Law)
1301 Alfred I. duPont Bldg.   Phone: (305) 379-6523
Miami, FL 33131   Sid Kaskey, Libn.
Staff: Prof 1; Other 1. **Subjects:** Law - general, civil practice, corporation, estate planning, taxation, probate, real estate, banking, international, maritime. **Holdings:** 13,000 volumes. **Subscriptions:** 525 journals and other serials. **Services:** Library open to attorneys only.

SMERC
See: San Mateo County Educational Resources Center

SMILEY (A.K.) PUBLIC LIBRARY - LINCOLN MEMORIAL SHRINE
See: Lincoln Memorial Shrine

SMISER (Mary Miller) HERITAGE LIBRARY
See: Johnson County Historical Society - Mary Miller Smiser Heritage Library

★12571★

SMITH (A.O.) CORPORATION - TECHNICAL LIBRARY (Sci-Tech)
Box 584   Phone: (414) 447-4683
Milwaukee, WI 53201   Larry Medley, Libn.
Founded: 1950. **Staff:** Prof 1; Other 1. **Subjects:** Engineering, business, industrial management, metals. **Holdings:** 15,000 volumes; 2000 technical reports; 7 VF drawers of standards. **Subscriptions:** 400 journals and other serials. **Services:** Interlibrary loans; copying; library open to public for reference use only with permission. **Computerized Information Services:** DIALOG, Pergamon InfoLine Ltd., NewsNet, Inc.

★12572★

SMITH, ANDERSON, BLOUNT, DORSETT, MITCHELL & JERNIGAN - LIBRARY (Law)
1300 St. Mary's St.
Box 12807   Phone: (919) 821-1220
Raleigh, NC 27605   Constance M. Matzen, Libn.
Staff: Prof 1. **Subjects:** Law. **Holdings:** 2000 volumes. **Services:** Library not

open to public. **Computerized Information Services:** LEXIS, DIALOG. Performs searches on cost recovery basis.

SMITH (Andre) COLLECTION
See: Maitland Public Library - Andre Smith Collection

★12573★
SMITH BARNEY, HARRIS UPHAM & COMPANY, INC. - LIBRARY (Bus-Fin)
1345 Ave. of the Americas   Phone: (212) 399-6294
New York, NY 10105   Morton R. Brown, Libn.
Founded: 1922. **Staff:** Prof 3; Other 7. **Subjects:** Investments and securities. **Special Collections:** Corporation records. **Holdings:** 1000 books and bound periodical volumes; 500 VF drawers. **Subscriptions:** 450 journals and other serials. **Services:** Interlibrary loans; library open to clients only.

SMITH (Bertha) LIBRARY
See: Luther Rice Seminary - Bertha Smith Library

SMITH (Betty Golde) MEMORIAL LIBRARY
See: St. Louis Psychoanalytic Institute - Betty Golde Smith Memorial Library

SMITH (Dr. C.W.) TECHNICAL INFORMATION CENTER
See: General Electric Company - Aircraft Engine Business Group - Dr. C.W. Smith Technical Information Center, 24001

★12574★
SMITH COLLEGE - ARCHIVES (Hist)
Phone: (413) 584-2700
Northampton, MA 01063
Founded: 1922. **Staff:** Prof 2; Other 1. **Subjects:** Smith College - alumnae and faculty files, department records, presidential papers, trustee's minutes, faculty meeting agenda, activities, publications, photographs, tapes. **Special Collections:** Among many others William Allan Neilson Papers (College president, 1917-1939); Smith College Relief Unit, 1918-1920; World War I work; Harriet Hawes (Instructor of Greek, 1900-1906; unpublished records and other material). **Holdings:** 1800 linear feet of document boxes. **Services:** Copying (limited); archives open to public. **Staff:** Mary B. Trott, Asst.Archv.

★12575★
SMITH COLLEGE - CLARK SCIENCE LIBRARY (Sci-Tech)
Phone: (413) 584-2700
Northampton, MA 01063   David Vikre, Sci.Libn.
Founded: 1966. **Staff:** Prof 1; Other 3. **Subjects:** Astronomy, biological sciences, chemistry, geology, mathematics, physics, psychology, computer science. **Holdings:** 98,730 volumes; 30,000 government documents and pamphlets; 7423 microforms; 83 audiotapes. **Subscriptions:** 745 journals and other serials. **Services:** Interlibrary loans; copying; library open to public for reference use only. **Automated Operations:** Computerized cataloging. **Computerized Information Services:** BRS, DIALOG.

★12576★
SMITH COLLEGE - HILLYER ART LIBRARY (Art)
Fine Arts Ctr.   Phone: (413) 584-2700
Northampton, MA 01063   Karen J. Harvey, Libn.
Staff: Prof 1; Other 4. **Subjects:** History of art, painting, design, architecture, sculpture, graphic arts, landscape architecture. **Holdings:** 43,500 books and bound periodical volumes; 68,000 study photographs; color reproductions; 6200 microfiche. **Subscriptions:** 198 journals and other serials. **Services:** Interlibrary loans; copying; library open to public for reference use only, by special permission.

★12577★
SMITH COLLEGE - RARE BOOK ROOM (Rare Book)
Phone: (413) 584-2700
Northampton, MA 01063   Ruth Mortimer, Cur.
Staff: Prof 2. **Subjects:** 18th-century English literature, early science, history of printing, economics, 19th-century English lithography. **Special Collections:** English and American children's books, 17th-20th centuries (525 titles); Rudyard Kipling (275 items); William Faulkner (100 items); George Bernard Shaw (264 items); Ernest Hemingway (250 items); Sylvia Plath (700 items, including 400 pages of manuscripts); E. Thornton Botanical Books (89 titles). **Holdings:** 16,000 books. **Services:** Copying; room open to public by appointment. **Special Indexes:** Chronological index (card). **Staff:** Ritsuko T. Ozawa, Asst.Cur.

★12578★
SMITH COLLEGE - SOPHIA SMITH COLLECTION - WOMEN'S HISTORY ARCHIVE (Hist; Soc Sci)
Phone: (413) 584-2700
Northampton, MA 01063
Founded: 1942. **Staff:** Prof 5. **Subjects:** Women's intellectual and social history - retrospective, contemporary and world-wide emphasis; social reform; suffrage; birth control; professions; women's rights. **Special Collections:** 163 major collections including Margaret Sanger (200 document boxes); Blanche Ames Ames (suffragist, artist; 120 document boxes); Hale Family (150 document boxes); Clara Barton (4 document boxes); Garrison Family (extensive); Ellen Gates Starr (19 document boxes). **Holdings:** 600 books; 2100 linear feet of document boxes. **Subscriptions:** 87 journals and other serials. **Services:** Copying (limited); archive open to public. **Publications:** Catalog of the Sophia Smith Collection; Picture Catalog of the Sophia Smith Collection - both available for purchase. **Special Catalogs:** Collection inventories. **Staff:** Virginia Christenson, Asst. to Dir.; Susan L. Boone, Cur.; Eleanor Lewis, Res.Assoc.; Dorothy Green, Res.Assoc.

★12579★
SMITH COLLEGE - WERNER JOSTEN LIBRARY OF THE PERFORMING ARTS (Mus; Theater)
Mendenhall Ctr.   Phone: (413) 584-2700
Northampton, MA 01063   Marlene M. Wong, Libn.
Staff: Prof 2; Other 4. **Subjects:** Music, theater, dance. **Special Collections:** Einstein Collection of music of the 16th and 17th centuries copied in score by Alfred Einstein; music and correspondence of Werner Josten; collection of reproductions of holographs of early twentieth century American composers. **Holdings:** 27,000 books and bound periodical volumes; 34,500 scores; 43,000 phonograph records; 125 reels of microfilm. **Subscriptions:** 425 journals and other serials. **Services:** Interlibrary loans; copying; library open to public for reference use only. **Automated Operations:** Computerized cataloging. **Computerized Information Services:** OCLC. **Networks/ Consortia:** Member of NELINET. **Special Indexes:** Index to articles in periodicals owned by the library prior to 1949; index to Americana collection; index to selected song collections. **Staff:** Kathryn E. Burnett, Assoc.Libn.

★12580★
SMITH, CURRIE & HANCOCK - LAW LIBRARY (Law)
233 Peachtree St., N.E.
2600 Peachtree Ctr., Harris Tower   Phone: (404) 521-3800
Atlanta, GA 30303   Elisa F. Kadish, Libn.
Founded: 1972. **Staff:** Prof 1; Other 1. **Subjects:** Law - building and construction, government contract, labor. **Holdings:** 8500 volumes; 1300 other cataloged items; 1100 in-house materials. **Subscriptions:** 59 journals and other serials. **Services:** Interlibrary loans; library open to members of the Atlanta Law Libraries Association. **Computerized Information Services:** DIALOG, Westlaw. **Publications:** Library Newsletter, monthly - for internal distribution only. **Special Catalogs:** Construction Law Books; Labor Law Books - both annotated bibliographies.

SMITH (David Eugene) MATHEMATICAL LIBRARY
See: Columbia University - Rare Book and Manuscript Library

SMITH (Edgar Fahs) MEMORIAL COLLECTION IN THE HISTORY OF CHEMISTRY
See: University of Pennsylvania - Edgar Fahs Smith Memorial Collection in the History of Chemistry

★12581★
SMITH (Frederick C.) CLINIC - MEDICAL LIBRARY (Med)
1040 Delaware Ave.   Phone: (614) 387-0850
Marion, OH 43302   Doris P. Hurn, Libn.
Staff: Prof 1. **Subjects:** Medicine. **Holdings:** 650 books; 2000 bound periodical volumes. **Subscriptions:** 153 journals and other serials. **Services:** Interlibrary loans; copying; library open to public by appointment. **Networks/ Consortia:** Member of Central Ohio Hospital Library Consortium.

SMITH (Frederick Madison) LIBRARY
See: Graceland College - Frederick Madison Smith Library

SMITH (Furman) LAW LIBRARY
See: Mercer University - Law School - Furman Smith Law Library

SMITH (George F.) LIBRARY
See: University of Medicine and Dentistry of New Jersey at Newark - George F. Smith Library

★12582★
SMITH (George Walter Vincent) ART MUSEUM - LIBRARY (Art)
222 State St.   Phone: (413) 733-4214
Springfield, MA 01103   Richard Muhlberger, Dir.
Staff: 1. Subjects: Chinese and Japanese decorative arts. Holdings: 2500 volumes. Services: Library not open to public.

SMITH (H. Ward) LIBRARY
See: Ontario - Ministry of the Solicitor General - Centre of Forensic Sciences - H. Ward Smith Library

SMITH (Herman) ASSOCIATES
See: Herman Smith Associates

SMITH (Hervey Garrett) RESEARCH LIBRARY
See: Suffolk Marine Museum - Hervey Garrett Smith Research Library

SMITH (J.D.) MEMORIAL LIBRARY
See: Akron General Medical Center - J.D. Smith Memorial Library

SMITH (J. Eugene) LIBRARY
See: Eastern Connecticut State University - Center for Connecticut Studies

SMITH (John Peter) HOSPITAL
See: John Peter Smith Hospital

SMITH (Johnson C.) UNIVERSITY THEOLOGICAL SEMINARY LIBRARY OF CHARLOTTE, NC
See: Atlanta University Center - Robert W. Woodruff Library - Interdenominational Theological Center Archives

SMITH (Joseph F.) LIBRARY AND MEDIA CENTER
See: Brigham Young University, Hawaii Campus - Joseph F. Smith Library and Media Center

SMITH (Kent H.) LIBRARY
See: Foundation Center - Cleveland - Kent H. Smith Library

★12583★
SMITH, KLINE & FRENCH CANADA, LTD. - MEDICAL/MARKETING LIBRARY (Med; Sci-Tech)
1940 Argentia Rd.   Phone: (416) 821-2200
Mississauga, ON, Canada L5N 2V7   Janet B. Hillis, Lib.Techn.
Founded: 1960. Staff: 1. Subjects: Medicine, pharmacy, pharmacology, biochemistry, chemistry, microbiology, marketing. Holdings: 1000 books; 650 bound periodical volumes; 600 volumes of reprints; 170 reels of microfilm. Subscriptions: 160 journals and other serials. Services: Interlibrary loans; library not open to public.

★12584★
SMITH, KLINE & FRENCH LABORATORIES - MARKETING RESEARCH DEPARTMENT - INFORMATION CENTER (Bus-Fin)
1500 Spring Garden St.   Phone: (215) 854-5328
Philadelphia, PA 19101   Anna M. Smyth, Info.Ctr.Coord.
Founded: 1965. Staff: 2. Subjects: Business and marketing aspects of the pharmaceutical industry; general marketing and advertising. Holdings: 1200 books and bound periodical volumes; 10,000 internal reports; 30 VF drawers of clippings and pamphlets. Subscriptions: 180 journals and other serials. Services: Center not open to public. Computerized Information Services: New York Times Information Service; RYSTS (internal database). Publications: Marketing Research Reports, monthly; MarkAlert, 4/year - both for internal distribution only.

★12585★
SMITH, KLINE & FRENCH LABORATORIES - RESEARCH AND DEVELOPMENT LIBRARY (Med)
F-121
1500 Spring Garden St.   Phone: (215) 751-5593
Philadelphia, PA 19101   Penny Young, Libn.
Founded: 1947. Staff: Prof 5; Other 3. Subjects: Medicine, chemistry, pharmacology, pharmacy, biological sciences. Holdings: 20,000 books and bound periodical volumes; 2500 reels of microfilm. Subscriptions: 1100 journals and other serials. Services: Interlibrary loans; library not open to public. Computerized Information Services: DIALOG, SDC, BRS, NLM, AMA/NET, Mead Data Central, Institute for Scientific Information (ISI). Publications: Recent Acquisitions, bimonthly - for internal distribution only. Remarks: A branch library is located at 709 Swedeland Rd., Swedeland, PA 19479. Its telephone number is (215) 278-7325.

SMITH (Lillian H.) COLLECTION OF CHILDREN'S BOOKS
See: Toronto Public Library - Lillian H. Smith Collection of Children's Books

★12586★
SMITH (Margaret Chase) LIBRARY CENTER (Hist)
Norridgewock Avenue
Box 366   Phone: (207) 474-8844
Skowhegan, ME 04976   James C. MacCampbell, Dir.
Founded: 1982. Staff: Prof 1; Other 3. Subjects: Senator Margaret Chase Smith's personal and professional records. Holdings: Figures not available. Services: Copying; library open to qualified scholars. Remarks: Center operates under the auspices of Northwood Institute, Midland, Michigan.

SMITH (Marjorie) LIBRARY
See: University of British Columbia - Marjorie Smith Library

★12587★
SMITH MEMORIAL LIBRARY (Hum)
Pratt & Miller Ave.   Phone: (716) 357-5844
Chautauqua, NY 14722   Mrs. Torrey Isaac, Libn.
Founded: 1906. Staff: 12. Subjects: Chautauqua, education, art, music. Special Collections: Books and history from 1874 of the Chautauqua Institution. Holdings: 23,400 books; 141 bound periodical volumes; 2000 phonograph records. Subscriptions: 100 journals and other serials. Services: Interlibrary loans; copying; library open to public. Networks/Consortia: Member of Chautauqua-Cattaraugus Library System. Remarks: Library is part of the Chautauqua Institution. Staff: Barbara Haug, Hist.

SMITH (Percy Kendall) LIBRARY FOR HISTORICAL RESEARCH
See: Lake County Historical Society - Percy Kendall Smith Library for Historical Research

SMITH (Richard Root) LIBRARY
See: Blodgett Memorial Medical Center - Richard Root Smith Library

SMITH (Robert S.) BEHAVIORAL SCIENCE LIBRARY
See: Philadelphia State Hospital - Staff Library

SMITH (Sophia) COLLECTION
See: Smith College - Sophia Smith Collection

SMITH (Wilbur) AND ASSOCIATES
See: Wilbur Smith and Associates

SMITH (William Henry) MEMORIAL LIBRARY
See: Indiana Historical Society - William Henry Smith Memorial Library

★12588★
SMITHSONIAN INSTITUTION - ARCHIVES (Hist)
Arts and Industries Bldg., Rm. 2135   Phone: (202) 381-4075
Washington, DC 20560
Subjects: Smithsonian Institution, history of American art and science. Special Collections: Papers of Joseph Henry, Spencer F. Baird, Samuel P. Langley, Charles D. Walcott, Charles G. Abbot, and Alexander Wetmore (Smithsonian Secretaries). Holdings: 7929 cubic feet of records, manuscripts, private papers, and collections relating to the Smithsonian, its staff members, and other scientists. Services: Copying; archives open to public. Publications: Guide to the Smithsonian Archives, 1983.

SMITHSONIAN INSTITUTION - ARCHIVES OF AMERICAN ART
See: Archives of American Art/Smithsonian Institution

★12589★
SMITHSONIAN INSTITUTION - FREER GALLERY OF ART - LIBRARY (Art)
Twelfth & Jefferson Dr., S.W.   Phone: (202) 357-2091
Washington, DC 20560   Ellen A. Nollman, Hd.Libn.
Founded: 1923. Staff: Prof 2. Subjects: Art and cultures of the Far East, Near East, and South Asia; history and civilization; art and art history; archeology; pottery; painting. Special Collections: Washington Biblical manuscripts; C.L. Freer Letter Books (30 volumes); letters of Whistler, Tryon, Dewing, Thayer, Freer acquaintances, dealers and business associates (2500-3000). Holdings: 30,000 books and bound periodical volumes (both Western and Oriental languages); 500 rubbings from Chinese monuments; 4 VF drawers of maps; 12 VF drawers of study photographs; 50,000 slides. Subscriptions: 100 journals. Services: Copying; library open to public for reference use only; slides loaned to public. Special Indexes: Index to KOKKA and Index to sales catalogs.

★12590★

SMITHSONIAN INSTITUTION - HIRSHHORN MUSEUM AND SCULPTURE GARDEN - LIBRARY (Art)
Independence Ave. & 8th St., S.W.
Washington, DC 20560
Phone: (202) 357-3223
Anna Brooke, Libn.
Founded: 1966. **Staff:** Prof 1; Other 2. **Subjects:** Fine arts, European and American 20th century painting and sculpture, American 19th century painting. **Special Collections:** Samuel Murray scrapbooks; Thomas Eakins memorabilia. **Holdings:** 12,000 books; exhibition catalogs; 31 VF drawers of artist files. **Subscriptions:** 50 journals and other serials. **Services:** Copying; library open to scholars by appointment.

★12591★

SMITHSONIAN INSTITUTION LIBRARIES (Sci-Tech; Art; Hist)
National Museum of Natural History
10th & Constitution Ave., N.W.
Washington, DC 20560
Phone: (202) 357-2240
Robert Maloy, Dir.
Founded: 1846. **Staff:** Prof 42; Other 62. **Subjects:** Natural history and ethnology; ecology; history of science, technology and flight; American history and culture; decorative and graphic arts; American and contemporary art. **Holdings:** 451,000 books; 454,000 bound periodical volumes; 35,000 items of archival materials; manuscripts; 1.5 million pictures; photographs and clippings. **Subscriptions:** 16,005 journals and other serials. **Services:** Interlibrary loans; copying; open to qualified scholars. **Automated Operations:** Computerized cataloging and acquisitions. **Computerized Information Services:** DIALOG. **Networks/Consortia:** Member of FEDLINK. **Remarks:** Figures given above represent combined holdings and staff for all branches. The Smithsonian Tropical Research Institute's address is P.O. Box 2072, Balboa, Republic de Panama. **Staff:** Vija L. Karklins, Assoc.Dir.; Margaret Child, Asst.Dir.; Nancy E. Gwinn, Asst.Dir.; Mary Augusta Rosenfeld, Adm.Libn.; Mildred Raitt, Chf., Acq.Serv.; Victoria Avera, Chf., Auto.Bibliog.Cont.; Mary Jane Linn, Chf., Original Indexing; Brooke Henley, Chf., Cat.Rec.; Sylvia Churgin, Chf., STRI Lib.

★12592★

SMITHSONIAN INSTITUTION LIBRARIES - ASTROPHYSICAL OBSERVATORY - LIBRARY (Sci-Tech)†
60 Garden St.
Cambridge, MA 02138
Phone: (617) 495-7264
Joyce Rey, Libn.
Founded: 1959. **Staff:** Prof 1. **Subjects:** Astrophysics, astronomy, physics, mathematics, satellite and earth geophysics. **Holdings:** 12,000 books; 3500 bound periodical volumes; 12,000 unbound reports; 20,000 microfiche. **Subscriptions:** 400 journals and other serials. **Services:** Interlibrary loans; copying; library open to public by arrangement.

★12593★

SMITHSONIAN INSTITUTION LIBRARIES - CENTRAL REFERENCE SERVICES (Sci-Tech)†
Central Library
10th & Constitution Ave., N.W.
Washington, DC 20560
Phone: (202) 357-2139
Mary Clare Gray, Chf.
Subjects: Museology, exploration and travel, ecology, oceanography. **Special Collections:** Publications of scientific societies; printed library catalogs. **Holdings:** 60,000 volumes. **Services:** Interlibrary loans; copying; open to qualified scholars.

★12594★

SMITHSONIAN INSTITUTION LIBRARIES - COOPER-HEWITT MUSEUM OF DESIGN - DORIS & HENRY DREYFUSS MEMORIAL STUDY CENTER (Art)
2 E. 91st St.
New York, NY 10128
Phone: (212) 860-6887
Katharine Martinez, Chf.Libn.
Staff: Prof 1; Other 4. **Subjects:** Decorative arts, design, textiles, architecture. **Special Collections:** American and foreign auction catalogs; George W. Kubler Collection of 18th- and 19th-century line engravings; Color Archive; Henry Dreyfuss Archive; Donald Deskey Archive; Ladislav Sutnar Archive; Therese Bonney photographs; trade catalogs. **Holdings:** 35,000 books; 3500 bound periodical volumes; 16 VF drawers; picture collection of over 1.5 million items arranged by subject for designers. **Subscriptions:** 275 journals and other serials. **Services:** Interlibrary loans; copying; center open to public. **Automated Operations:** Computerized cataloging, acquisitions, serials and circulation. **Computerized Information Services:** OCLC.

★12595★

SMITHSONIAN INSTITUTION LIBRARIES - MUSEUM REFERENCE CENTER (Hum)
Arts & Industries Bldg., Rm. 2235
900 Jefferson Dr., S.W.
Washington, DC 20560
Phone: (202) 357-3101
Catherine D. Scott, Libn.
Founded: 1974. **Staff:** Prof 1. **Subjects:** Museology. **Holdings:** 1600 books;

165 linear feet of files on museology; 15 linear feet of annual reports. **Subscriptions:** 1200 journals and other serials. **Services:** Interlibrary loans; copying; center open to public. **Remarks:** The Museum Reference Center contains resources on all aspects of museum operations. It is the only central source of museological information in the United States that makes such materials available to researchers and all members of the museum community.

★12596★

SMITHSONIAN INSTITUTION LIBRARIES - MUSEUM SUPPORT CENTER LIBRARY (Sci-Tech)
Museum of American History, AB-070
Washington, DC 20560
Phone: (202) 357-2444
Karen Preslock, Chf.Libn.
Founded: 1964. **Staff:** Prof 1. **Subjects:** Conservation of materials and museum objects; conservation science, including archaeometry, study of museum environments and analysis of materials by such means as x-ray diffraction and gas chromatography; occupational health hazards; medical entomology; taxonomic aspects of marine and estuarine fauna. **Holdings:** 8500 books; 1800 bound periodical volumes; 13,000 reprints; 12 reels of microfilm; 280 microfiche. **Subscriptions:** 160 journals and other serials. **Services:** Interlibrary loans; copying; SDI; library open to public by appointment only. **Automated Operations:** Computerized cataloging and acquisitions. **Computerized Information Services:** DIALOG, OCLC. **Formerly:** Its Conservation Analytical Laboratory.

★12597★

SMITHSONIAN INSTITUTION LIBRARIES - NATIONAL AIR AND SPACE MUSEUM - LIBRARY (Sci-Tech)
National Air & Space Museum, Rm. 3100
Independence Ave. & Seventh St., S.W.
Washington, DC 20560
Phone: (202) 357-3133
Frank A. Pietropaoli, Libn.
Founded: 1972. **Staff:** Prof 5; Other 4. **Subjects:** Aeronautics, astronautics, astronomy, earth and planetary sciences. **Special Collections:** Sherman Fairchild Photographic Collection; William A.M. Burden Collection of early ballooning works and aeronautica; Bella Landauer aeronautical sheet music collection (1500 pieces); Jerome Hunsaker papers; Samuel P. Langley aerodrome manuscripts; Harold E. Morehouse biographical files on early aircraft pioneers; Juan Trippe correspondence and papers. **Holdings:** 25,000 books; 9500 bound periodical volumes; 2000 motion pictures; 30,000 document files of aeronautical and astronautical archives and photographic files; 10,000 technical reports; 200 scrapbooks; 500,000 NASA and NACA technical reports on microfiche; 18,750 files of German and Japanese aircraft companies captured in World War II (on microfilm); U.S. Air Force and Navy Aircraft History cards; 95 reels of microfilm of periodicals; 17,500 NASM archival documents on microfiche; 700 audiotapes; 900,000 photographs. **Subscriptions:** 450 journals and other serials; 8 newspapers. **Services:** Interlibrary loans; copying; library open to public by appointment. **Automated Operations:** Computerized cataloging, acquisitions and circulation. **Computerized Information Services:** OCLC. **Networks/Consortia:** Member of FEDLINK. **Publications:** NASM Library Brochure. **Special Indexes:** Aerospace periodical index (automated). **Staff:** Monica Knuds, Ref.Libn.; Amy Levin, Ref.Libn.; Philip Edwards, Ref.Spec.

★12598★

SMITHSONIAN INSTITUTION LIBRARIES - NATIONAL MUSEUM OF AFRICAN ART - BRANCH LIBRARY (Art; Area-Ethnic)
318 A St., N.E.
Washington, DC 20002
Phone: (202) 287-3490
Janet L. Stanley, Chf.Libn.
Founded: 1971. **Staff:** Prof 1; Other 1. **Subjects:** Africa - art, anthropology, folklore history; Afro-American arts. **Holdings:** 6000 books; 300 VF drawers. **Subscriptions:** 50 journals and other serials. **Services:** Interlibrary loans; copying; SDI; library open to public by appointment. **Publications:** National Museum of African Art Library Acquisitions List, monthly.

★12599★

SMITHSONIAN INSTITUTION LIBRARIES - NATIONAL MUSEUM OF AFRICAN ART - ELIOT ELISOFON ARCHIVES (Art)
318 A St., N.E.
Washington, DC 20002
Phone: (202) 287-3490
Edward Lifschitz, Archv.
Staff: Prof 3. **Subjects:** Africa, African art. **Holdings:** 33,000 color slides; 35,000 black and white negatives. **Services:** Library open to public by appointment. **Staff:** Jonathan Reel, Archv.Techn.; Bryna Freyer, Res.Asst.

★12600★

SMITHSONIAN INSTITUTION LIBRARIES - NATIONAL MUSEUM OF AMERICAN HISTORY - ARCHIVES CENTER (Hist)
3rd Fl., NMAH
14th St. & Constitution Ave., N.W.
Washington, DC 20560
Phone: (202) 357-3270
John A. Fleckner, Archv.
Staff: Prof 6. **Subjects:** Business advertising, history of science and

technology. **Special Collections:** Warshaw Collection of Business Americana (800 cubic feet); Clark Radioana Collection (early history of radio; 300 cubic feet). **Holdings:** 3000 cubic feet of manuscripts and other items. **Services:** Copying; center open to public.

★12601★

SMITHSONIAN INSTITUTION LIBRARIES - NATIONAL MUSEUM OF AMERICAN HISTORY - LIBRARY (Sci-Tech; Hist)
Museum of American History   Phone: (202) 357-2414
Washington, DC 20560   Rhoda Ratner, Chf.Libn.
Staff: Prof 2; Other 4. **Subjects:** American history, history of science and technology, applied science, decorative arts, domestic and community life. **Special Collections:** Exhibitions and expositions (1500 items); trade catalogs (275,000 items). **Holdings:** 165,000 volumes. **Services:** Interlibrary loans; copying; library open to public with restrictions.

★12602★

SMITHSONIAN INSTITUTION LIBRARIES - NATIONAL MUSEUM OF NATURAL HISTORY - ANTHROPOLOGY BRANCH LIBRARY (Soc Sci)
Natural History Bldg., Rm. 330/331   Phone: (202) 357-1819
Washington, DC 20560   Angeline Smith, Libn.
Staff: 2. **Subjects:** Anthropology, physical anthropology, archeology, ethnology, linguistics. **Special Collections:** Bureau of American Ethnology Library Collection; Hrdlicka Collection (physical anthropology). **Holdings:** 54,000 books and bound periodicals. **Subscriptions:** 1200 journals and other serials. **Services:** Interlibrary loans; copying; library open to public by appointment.

★12603★

SMITHSONIAN INSTITUTION LIBRARIES - NATIONAL MUSEUM OF NATURAL HISTORY - BOTANY BRANCH LIBRARY (Sci-Tech)
Natural History Bldg.
10th & Constitution Ave.   Phone: (202) 357-2715
Washington, DC 20560   Ruth Schallert, Libn.
Subjects: Taxonomic botany, history of botany. **Special Collections:** Hitchcock-Chase Collection on grasses (1500 books and reprints); Dawson Collection on algae (1000 books and reprints). **Holdings:** 32,000 volumes; 14 shelves of collectors' field notebooks; 325 boxes of reprints; 21 herbaria on microfiche. **Subscriptions:** 400 journals and other serials. **Services:** Interlibrary loans; copying; library open to public.

★12604★

SMITHSONIAN INSTITUTION LIBRARIES - NATIONAL MUSEUM OF NATURAL HISTORY - ENTOMOLOGY BRANCH LIBRARY (Sci-Tech)
Natural History Bldg.   Phone: (202) 357-2354
Washington, DC 20560   Ruth Schallert, Libn.
Staff: 1. **Subjects:** Taxonomic and medical entomology. **Special Collections:** Casey Collection (Coleoptera). **Holdings:** 17,500 volumes. **Subscriptions:** 280 journals and other serials. **Services:** Interlibrary loans; copying; library open to public.

★12605★

SMITHSONIAN INSTITUTION LIBRARIES - NATIONAL MUSEUM OF NATURAL HISTORY - LIBRARY (Sci-Tech)
Natural History Bldg.
10th & Constitution Ave.   Phone: (202) 357-1496
Washington, DC 20560   Ruth Schallert, Act.Nat.Hist.Libn.
Subjects: Paleobiology, systematic botany, zoology, oceanography, ecology, entomology, limnology, anthropology, North and South American Indians. **Special Collections:** J.D. Smith Collection (botany); Cushman Collection (Foraminifera); Springer Collection (crinoids); Wilson Collection (copepoda); Remington-Kellogg Collection of Marine Mammalogy. **Holdings:** Figures not available. **Services:** Interlibrary loans.

★12606★

SMITHSONIAN INSTITUTION LIBRARIES - NATIONAL ZOOLOGICAL PARK - LIBRARY (Sci-Tech)
3001 Connecticut Ave., N.W.   Phone: (202) 673-4771
Washington, DC 20008   Kay A. Kenyon, Chf.Libn.
Staff: Prof 1. **Subjects:** Capture and care of animals in captivity, zoology, animal behavior, veterinary medicine, pathology, animal nutrition, conservation of endangered species. **Special Collections:** Zoo publications. **Holdings:** 5000 volumes. **Subscriptions:** 350 journals and other serials. **Services:** Interlibrary loans; copying; library open to public by appointment. **Automated Operations:** Computerized cataloging. **Computerized Information Services:** DIALOG.

★12607★

SMITHSONIAN INSTITUTION LIBRARIES - SMITHSONIAN ENVIRONMENTAL RESEARCH CENTER LIBRARY-EDGEWATER (Env-Cons)
R.R. 4, Box 622   Phone: (202) 261-4190
Edgewater, MD 21037   Angela N. Haggins, Chf.
Founded: 1972. **Staff:** 1. **Subjects:** Environment, ecology, estuarine research, marine ecology, aquatic microbiology. **Holdings:** 825 books; 300 bound periodical volumes; 950 technical reports. **Subscriptions:** 65 journals and other serials. **Services:** Interlibrary loans; copying; library open to public by appointment. **Special Indexes:** Computerized list of technical reports. **Formed by the Merger of:** Its Chesapeake Bay Center for Environmental Studies and its Radiation Biology Branch.

★12608★

SMITHSONIAN INSTITUTION LIBRARIES - SMITHSONIAN ENVIRONMENTAL RESEARCH CENTER LIBRARY-ROCKVILLE (Sci-Tech)
12441 Parklawn Dr.   Phone: (301) 443-2307
Rockville, MD 20852   Angela Haggins, Chf.
Staff: Prof 1; Other 1. **Subjects:** Plant physiology, regulatory biology, biophysics, solar radiation, environmental biology, cell biology, carbon dating, photobiology. **Holdings:** Figures not available. **Subscriptions:** 156 journals and other serials. **Services:** Interlibrary loans; library open to public for reference use only. **Formed by the Merger of:** Its Chesapeake Bay Center for Environmental Studies and its Radiation Biology Branch.

★12609★

SMITHSONIAN INSTITUTION LIBRARIES - SPECIAL COLLECTIONS BRANCH (Sci-Tech)
MAH 5016   Phone: (202) 357-1568
Washington, DC 20560   Ellen B. Wells, Chf.
Staff: Prof 1. **Subjects:** Physical sciences, natural history, technology, applied arts. **Special Collections:** Smithson Collection (200 books and offprints); Wetmore Ornithology Collection (400 books); Dibner Library (Americana and science and technology; 10,000 books); Comegys Library (19th-century Philadelphia family library; 900 volumes). **Holdings:** 20,000 books and bound periodical volumes; 350 bound manuscripts; 1500 engraved portraits; 200 science medals. **Services:** Copying; library open to public by appointment for reference use only. **Publications:** Operations of the Geometric and Military Compass 1606, 1978; Heralds of Science, 1980.

★12610★

SMITHSONIAN INSTITUTION - NATIONAL ANTHROPOLOGICAL ARCHIVES (Soc Sci)
Natl. Museum of
Natural History Bldg., Rm. 60-A, MRC 152
10th & Constitution Ave., N.W.   Phone: (202) 357-1976
Washington, DC 20560   Dr. Herman J. Viola, Dir.
Founded: 1879. **Staff:** Prof 6; Other 3. **Subjects:** Anthropology, linguistics, archeology, history of anthropology, history of American Indians, history of geography. **Special Collections:** Bureau of American Ethnology manuscript collection (5000 items); photographs of American Indians (60,000 items); John P. Harrington Papers; Center for the Study of Man; Department of Anthropology records; Institute for Social Anthropology records; River Basin Surveys. **Holdings:** 4000 cubic feet of archives and private papers; 250,000 photographs; 500 recordings; 100 reels of microfilm. **Services:** Copying; archives open to public. **Computerized Information Services:** Smithsonian Institution - SELGEM System. **Special Catalogs:** Manuscripts catalog (card, book form published); catalog of photographs (card); inventory and registers (booklets). **Staff:** James R. Glenn, Sr. Archv.; Paula J. Fleming, Asst.Dir.; Elaine L. Mills, Ed.

★12611★

SMITHSONIAN INSTITUTION - NATL. MUSEUM OF AMERICAN ART - INVENTORY OF AMERICAN PAINTINGS EXECUTED BEFORE 1914 (Art)
8th and G Sts., N.W.   Phone: (202) 357-2941
Washington, DC 20560   Martha Shipman Andrews, Coord.
Founded: 1971. **Staff:** Prof 1; Other 2. **Subjects:** American painting. **Holdings:** Photographic study collection of over 45,000 images of American paintings. **Services:** Library open to public with restrictions. **Automated Operations:** Computerized cataloging. **Publications:** Directory to the Bicentennial Inventory of American Paintings Executed Before 1914 (published 1976). **Special Indexes:** Listings of approximately 215,000 American paintings indexed by artist, subject matter, owner/location and title. **Staff:** Pamela U. Jenkins, Asst. to Coord.

★12612★
SMITHSONIAN INSTITUTION - NATIONAL MUSEUM OF AMERICAN ART/ NATIONAL PORTRAIT GALLERY - LIBRARY (Art)
8th & F Sts., N.W.   Phone: (202) 357-1886
Washington, DC 20560   Cecilia Chin, Chf.Libn.
Founded: 1930. **Staff:** Prof 3; Other 7. **Subjects:** American painting, sculpture, graphic arts, biography, history, photography; portraiture; contemporary art. **Special Collections:** Ferdinand Perret Collection (scrapbooks on California and West Coast art). **Holdings:** 47,000 books and bound periodical volumes; 350 VF drawers of clippings, pamphlets, correspondence and photographs. **Subscriptions:** 1000 journals and other serials. **Services:** Interlibrary loans; copying; library open to adult researchers and graduate students. **Staff:** Susan Gurney, Ref.Libn.; Charles H. King, Jr., Cat.

★12613★
SMITHSONIAN INSTITUTION - NATIONAL MUSEUM OF AMERICAN ART - OFFICE OF VISUAL RSRCS. - SLIDE/PHOTOGRAPH ARCHIVE (Art)
8th & G Sts., N.W.   Phone: (202) 357-1626
Washington, DC 20560   Eleanor E. Fink, Chf.
Founded: 1973. **Staff:** Prof 4; Other 1. **Subjects:** American art, painting, sculpture, graphics, decorative arts. **Special Collections:** Photographic negatives for the New York photographic firm of Peter Juley and Son (127,000 negatives). The collection documents 80 years of American artists and their works of art. **Services:** Archive open to public with restrictions. **Automated Operations:** Computerized cataloging. **Special Indexes:** Computer-generated indexes by artist, subject, source and location. **Staff:** Rachel M. Allen, Asst.Dir.; Diane Mallos, Slide Libn.

SMITHSONIAN INSTITUTION - WOODROW WILSON INTERNATIONAL CENTER FOR SCHOLARS
See: Wilson (Woodrow) International Center for Scholars

SMITHSONIAN TROPICAL RESEARCH INSTITUTE
See: Smithsonian Institution Libraries

★12614★
SMITHTOWN HISTORICAL SOCIETY - LIBRARY (Hist)†
Route 25A
Box 69   Phone: (516) 265-6768
Smithtown, NY 11787   Louise P. Hall, Dir.
Staff: 2. **Subjects:** Local history and genealogy. **Holdings:** 1000 books; deeds; documents; letters. **Services:** Copying; library open to public by appointment.

★12615★
SMITHTOWN LIBRARY - SPECIAL COLLECTIONS (Hist)
1 North Country Rd.   Phone: (516) 265-2072
Smithtown, NY 11787   Peter McCann Gillard, Dir.
Founded: 1907. **Special Collections:** Long Island Collection (23,075 items). **Services:** Interlibrary loans; copying; library open to public. **Automated Operations:** Computerized acquisitions and circulation. **Networks/Consortia:** Member of Suffolk Cooperative Library System; Long Island Library Resources Council (LILRC). **Publications:** Pamphlets on Long Island History, irregular. **Staff:** Vera Toman, L.I. Coll.Libn.

★12616★
SMYTHE (R.M.) AND COMPANY - OBSOLETE AND INACTIVE SECURITIES LIBRARY (Bus-Fin)
24 Broadway   Phone: (212) 668-1880
New York, NY 10004   Diana E. Herzog, Vice Pres.
Staff: 3. **Subjects:** Obsolete securities, inactive U.S. securities, foreign securities, active securities, collector's certificate reference. **Holdings:** 5000 books and bound periodical volumes; 35 VF drawers of correspondence; 20 boxes of pamphlets; 250,000 cards of company records; 50,000 cards of company reports; lost stockholder tracing reference material; reference material for antique certificate collectors. **Services:** Copying; library open to public with restrictions.

SNAKE RIVER CONSERVATION RESEARCH CENTER
See: U.S.D.A. - Agricultural Research Service

★12617★
SNC GROUP - LIBRARY (Sci-Tech)
1 Complexe Desjardins
C.P. 10   Phone: (514) 282-9551
Montreal, PQ, Canada H5B 1C8   Andree Nicole, Lib.Supv.
Founded: 1911. **Staff:** Prof 1; Other 1. **Subjects:** Construction, electricity, power, mining, hydraulics, engineering. **Holdings:** 9500 books; 2800 specifications and standards. **Subscriptions:** 450 journals and other serials. **Services:** Interlibrary loans; copying; library open to public by appointment only. **Automated Operations:** Computerized serials and circulation. **Computerized Information Services:** DIALOG, SDC, New York Times Information Service, CAN/OLE, QL Systems. **Publications:** Library News, irregular - for internal distribution only.

★12618★
SNELL & WILMER - LAW LIBRARY (Law)
3100 Valley Bank Center   Phone: (602) 257-7316
Phoenix, AZ 85073   Mary Grace Oakes, Libn.
Staff: Prof 1; Other 2. **Subjects:** Law - tax, utilities, real estate, water, corporate, securities. **Special Collections:** Arizona archival law materials. **Holdings:** 20,000 books; 325 bound periodical volumes; 700 other cataloged items. **Services:** Interlibrary loans; copying; library not open to public. **Computerized Information Services:** LEXIS. Performs searches on cost recovery basis.

SNITE MUSEUM OF ART
See: University of Notre Dame

★12619★
SNOHOMISH COUNTY LAW LIBRARY (Law)
County Court House   Phone: (206) 259-5326
Everett WA 98201   Betty Z. Scott, Libn.
Staff: Prof 1; Other 1. **Subjects:** Law - federal, state, local. **Holdings:** 18,000 volumes. **Subscriptions:** 17 journals and other serials. **Services:** Interlibrary loans; copying; library open to public with restrictions on circulation.

SNYDER COLLECTION OF AMERICANA
See: University of Missouri, Kansas City

★12620★
SNYDER COUNTY HISTORICAL SOCIETY, INC. - LIBRARY (Hist)
30 E. Market St.
Box 276   Phone: (717) 837-6191
Middleburg, PA 17842   Kathryn Gift, Libn.
Staff: Prof 1. **Subjects:** Local history, Pennsylvania history, Pennsylvania military history, genealogy. **Special Collections:** Civil War letters; Dr. Charles A. Fisher Collection. **Holdings:** 3000 volumes; 1000 historical bulletins, early land grants, warrants, deeds. **Services:** Copying; library open to public with permission. **Publications:** Snyder County Yearly Bulletin.

★12621★
SNYDER (H.L.) MEMORIAL RESEARCH FOUNDATION - LIBRARY (Med)†
1407 Wheat Rd.   Phone: (316) 221-4080
Winfield, KS 67156   Barbara Smith, Libn.
Founded: 1947. **Staff:** Prof 1. **Subjects:** Biochemistry, medicine, clinical chemistry. **Holdings:** 2000 books; 3000 bound periodical volumes. **Subscriptions:** 65 journals and other serials. **Services:** Interlibrary loans; library open to public. **Networks/Consortia:** Member of Midcontinental Regional Medical Library Program. **Remarks:** Includes holdings of the Snyder Clinic Library.

SNYDER (O.J.) MEMORIAL MEDICAL LIBRARY
See: Philadelphia College of Osteopathic Medicine - O.J. Snyder Memorial Medical Library

★12622★
SOAP AND DETERGENT ASSOCIATION - LIBRARY (Sci-Tech)
475 Park Ave., S.   Phone: (212) 725-1262
New York, NY 10016   Rose D. Api, Off.Mgr.
Staff: 1. **Subjects:** Detergents. **Holdings:** 1000 books; 200 bound periodical volumes. **Subscriptions:** 205 journals and other serials. **Services:** Copying; library open to public by appointment.

★12623★
SOCIAL LAW LIBRARY (Law)
1200 Court House   Phone: (617) 523-0018
Boston, MA 02108   Edgar J. Bellefontaine, Libn.
Founded: 1804. **Staff:** Prof 22; Other 21. **Subjects:** Anglo-American law. **Holdings:** 243,866 books and bound periodical volumes; 130,000 microfiche; 905 audio cassettes. **Subscriptions:** 3436 journals and other serials; 16 newspapers. **Services:** Interlibrary loans (limited); copying; library open to members and other authorized persons. **Computerized Information Services:** Westlaw. **Publications:** Newsletter, quarterly - to members.

SOCIAL SCIENCE EDUCATION CONSORTIUM
See: ERIC Clearinghouse for Social Studies/Social Science Education - Resource & Demonstration Center

SOCIAL SECURITY ADMINISTRATION
See: U.S. Social Security Administration

SOCIAL WELFARE HISTORY ARCHIVES
See: University of Minnesota

★12624★
SOCIETE D'ARCHEOLOGIE ET DE NUMISMATIQUE DE MONTREAL - BIBLIOTHEQUE (Hist)†
280 est, rue Notre-Dame   Phone: (514) 861-7182
Montreal, PQ, Canada H2Y 1C5   Margot Albert, Sec.
Founded: 1895. **Staff:** 1. **Subjects:** Canadian history, numismatics. **Holdings:** 10,000 books; manuscripts, archives, documents. **Services:** Library not open to public, but the society will consider appropriate requests by researchers. **Remarks:** Library is in process of reorganization after being inactive for over twenty years. **Also Known As:** Antiquarian and Numismatic Society of Montreal.

SOCIETE CANADIENNE D'HYPOTHEQUES ET DE LOGEMENT
See: Canada - Mortgage and Housing Corporation

SOCIETE CANADIENNE DE PSYCHANALYSE
See: Canadian Psychoanalytic Society

★12625★
SOCIETE CULINAIRE PHILANTHROPIQUE DE NEW YORK, INC. - LIBRARY (Food-Bev)
250 W. 57th St., Rm. 1532   Phone: (212) 246-6754
New York, NY 10019   Henri Deltieure, Pres.
Subjects: Professional cooking. **Holdings:** Cookbooks. **Services:** Library open to members only.

★12626★
SOCIETE DE DEVELOPPEMENT DE LA BAIE JAMES - DOCUMENTATION CENTRE (Soc Sci; Plan)
800 de Maisonneuve Blvd., E.   Phone: (514) 284-0270
Montreal, PQ, Canada H2L 4M6   Diane Lefebvre, Dir.
Staff: Prof 1. **Subjects:** Regional planning, environment, Amerindian studies, energy, municipal organization, management. **Holdings:** 11,400 books; 3000 topographic maps; 200 ecologic maps; 1500 aerial photographs. **Subscriptions:** 500 journals and other serials. **Services:** Interlibrary loans; copying; center open to public. **Publications:** DOC-SDBJ, quarterly; acquisitions list. **Also Known As:** James Bay Development Corporation.

★12627★
SOCIETE D'ENERGIE DE LA BAIE JAMES - CENTRE DE DOCUMENTATION-ENVIRONNEMENT
800 de Maisonneuve Blvd., E.
Place Dupuis, 8th Floor
Montreal, PQ, Canada H2L 4M8
Defunct

★12628★
SOCIETE D'HISTOIRE DES CANTONS DE L'EST - BIBLIOTHEQUE (Hist)
C.P. 2117   Phone: (819) 562-0616
Sherbrooke, PQ, Canada J1J 3Y1   Andree Desilets, Pres.
Founded: 1927. **Staff:** Prof 2. **Subjects:** Local and regional history of the Eastern Townships. **Holdings:** 3000 volumes; 2000 photographs; 250 maps; archives. **Also Known As:** Eastern Townships Historical Society. **Staff:** Danielle Potvin, Sec./Archv.

SOCIETE HISTORIQUE-DE-LA-COTE-DU-SUD
See: College de Ste-Anne-de-la-Pocatiere

★12629★
SOCIETE HISTORIQUE DU SAGUENAY - BIBLIOTHEQUE (Hist)
C.P. 456
Chicoutimi, PQ, Canada G7H 5C8   Roland Belanger, Archv.
Founded: 1934. **Staff:** Prof 1. **Subjects:** Regional history and geography, genealogy, oral history, folklore. **Special Collections:** Newspaper clippings, 1859 to present, concerning the Saguenay region. **Holdings:** 8000 books; 200 bound periodical volumes; 150,000 photographs; 65,000 negatives; 1500 maps. **Subscriptions:** 50 journals and other serials; 30 newspapers. **Services:** Copying; library open to public for reference use only. **Automated Operations:** Computerized cataloging. **Publications:** Saguenayensia,

quarterly.

★12630★
SOCIETE NATIONALE DE DIFFUSION EDUCATIVE ET CULTURELLE - SERVICE D'INFORMATION SONDEC (Info Sci)
8770 Langelier, Suite 230   Phone: (514) 324-4010
St. Leonard, PQ, Canada H1P 3E8   Micheline Lestage, Dir.
Staff: Prof 2; Other 3. **Subjects:** Encyclopedias, home, crafts, sports. **Special Collections:** Encyclopedi Famille. **Holdings:** 500 books; 3000 subject files. **Subscriptions:** 28 journals and other serials. **Services:** Service not open to public. **Remarks:** This is an information center providing internal documents and outside investigations for private clients. **Staff:** Georgette Murray, Asst.

★12631★
SOCIETE QUEBECOISE D'INITIATIVES PETROLIERES - DOCUMENTATION CENTRE (Sci-Tech; Energy)†
1175 de Lavigerie   Phone: (418) 651-9543
Ste. Foy, PQ, Canada G1V 4P1   Gilles Dion, Chf.
Founded: 1970. **Staff:** Prof 3; Other 1. **Subjects:** Geology, geophysics, petroleum, engineering, well drilling, energy policy. **Holdings:** 10,000 volumes; 2200 aerial photographs; archives; 5000 confidential maps; 3000 other maps; 1500 magnetic tapes (seismic); 2000 seismic lines. **Subscriptions:** 80 journals and other serials. **Services:** Interlibrary loans; copying; center open to public with restrictions. **Automated Operations:** Computerized cataloging, acquisitions and serials. **Publications:** Monthly accessions list. **Staff:** Miss Marjolaine Simard, Archv.; Gilles Dube, Map Div.; Diane Lemire, Aid Libn.

SOCIETE RADIO-CANADA
See: Canadian Broadcasting Corporation

SOCIETE ROYALE DU CANADA
See: Royal Society of Canada

★12632★
SOCIETY FOR ACADEMIC ACHIEVEMENT - LIBRARY (Educ)
220 WCU Bldg.
510 Maine St.   Phone: (217) 224-0570
Quincy, IL 62301   Leo W. Manning, Exec.Dir./Libn.
Staff: 1. **Subjects:** Academic excellence, communication skills. **Holdings:** 1075 volumes. **Subscriptions:** 15 journals and other serials. **Services:** Library not open to public.

SOCIETY OF AMERICAN FORESTERS - ARCHIVES
See: Forest History Society, Inc. - Library and Archives

★12633★
SOCIETY OF AMERICAN FORESTERS - LIBRARY (Sci-Tech)
5400 Grosvenor Ln.   Phone: (301) 897-8720
Bethesda, MD 20814   Philip V. Petersen, Dir, Info./Member Serv.
Subjects: Forestry education, forest economics, silviculture, forest fires, forest land use, history of professional forestry. **Holdings:** Figures not available. **Services:** Collection open to members.

★12634★
SOCIETY OF AUTOMOTIVE ENGINEERS - SAE LIBRARY (Sci-Tech)
400 Commonwealth Dr.   Phone: (412) 776-4841
Warrendale, PA 15096   Janet Jedlicka, Libn./Res.Ck.
Founded: 1905. **Staff:** Prof 1. **Subjects:** Automotive and aerospace engineering. **Holdings:** 1147 books; 222 bound periodical volumes; 20,000 technical papers; 2500 aerospace material specifications; 1700 automotive standards. **Subscriptions:** 41 journals and other serials. **Services:** Copying; library open to public. **Computerized Information Services:** SDC. **Publications:** Quarterly Abstracts. **Special Catalogs:** Publications catalog.

★12635★
SOCIETY OF CALIFORNIA PIONEERS - JOSEPH A. MOORE LIBRARY (Hist)
456 McAllister St.   Phone: (415) 861-5278
San Francisco, CA 94102   Grace E. Baker, Libn.
Founded: 1850. **Staff:** Prof 1. **Subjects:** California - primarily pre-1870 with emphasis on the activities of 1849ers. **Special Collections:** Correspondence of Thomas Starr King, Unitarian Minister, 1861-1864; letters of Jessie Benton Fremont, writer; Jacob Rink Snyder Collection (California Battalion documents; 295 items); handwritten diaries of forty-niners and other pioneers (200); reminiscences of pioneers (8 volumes); photographs of the San Francisco Bay Area and California (25,000); political scrapbooks, 1863-1910 (18 linear feet); scrapbooks on early San Francisco history and prominent figures (9 linear feet); Cooper-Molera Papers, 1828-1910 (ship logs, account

books, business papers, legal documents, taxation and assessment papers for Monterey County, Mexican mining deeds, household papers of Monterey adobe; 10 linear feet); Patterson Ranch Papers, 1849-1965 (ranch history; 81 linear feet); Sherman Music Collection, 1852-1923 (early theatrical posters and biographical sketches of California musicians; rare sheet music; playbills; musical manuscripts); mining company stock certificates and business records dating from 1850. **Holdings:** Diaries and county histories on microfilm. **Services:** Copying; photographs made of paintings and duplicate prints made of photos; library open to public. **Publications:** The Pioneer - to members and by mailing list. **Special Catalogs:** Catalog of pioneers (card).

SOCIETY OF THE CATHOLIC APOSTOLATE - PALLOTTINE PROVINCIALATE LIBRARY
See: Pallottine Provincialate Library

★12636★
SOCIETY OF THE CINCINNATI - ANDERSON HOUSE LIBRARY AND MUSEUM (Hist)
2118 Massachusetts Ave., N.W.   Phone: (202) 785-2040
Washington, DC 20008   John D. Kilbourne, Dir.
Founded: 1783. **Staff:** Prof 2; Other 1. **Subjects:** U.S. history, American Revolution. **Holdings:** 12,000 books; 25,000 items in manuscript archives of the society; 500 items in manuscript collections of the society. **Subscriptions:** 52 journals and other serials. **Services:** Interlibrary loans; copying; library open to public. **Publications:** Annual Report of Museum; Cincinnati 14 (newsletter), semiannual; George Rogers Clark Lecture Series.

SOCIETY OF CIVIL WAR SURGEONS - LIBRARY
See: Lincoln Memorial University - Abraham Lincoln Library and Museum

SOCIETY OF COLLECTORS, INC. - DUNHAM TAVERN MUSEUM
See: Dunham Tavern Museum

★12637★
SOCIETY OF COSMETIC CHEMISTS - LIBRARY (Sci-Tech)
1995 Broadway, 17th Fl.   Phone: (212) 532-7320
New York, NY 10023   George L. Cohen, Ph.D., Chm., Lib.Comm.
Subjects: Chemistry, pharmacy, cosmetic sciences. **Holdings:** 550 volumes. **Subscriptions:** 25 journals and other serials. **Services:** Interlibrary loans; library open to public. **Publications:** Journal of the Society of Cosmetic Chemists.

★12638★
SOCIETY OF COSTA RICA COLLECTORS (SOCORICO) - EARL FOSSOM MEMORIAL LIBRARY (Rec)
Box 14831
Baton Rouge LA 70808   Hector R. Mena, Libn.
Subjects: Costa Rican philatelics, postal history. **Holdings:** 84 volumes; 15 volumes of articles, pamphlets and manuscripts; unbound periodicals. **Services:** Library not open to public. **Publications:** Index to Costa Rican Philatelic Literature, 1863-1973. **Special Catalogs:** Catalogo de Sellos Postales de Costa Rica, 1978. **Formerly:** Located in Sellersville, PA.

★12639★
SOCIETY FOR CRIPPLED CHILDREN AND ADULTS OF MANITOBA - STEPHEN SPARLING LIBRARY (Soc Sci)
825 Sherbrook St.   Phone: (204) 786-5601
Winnipeg, MB, Canada R3A 1M5   Barbara Wolfe, Libn.
Founded: 1957. **Staff:** 1. **Subjects:** Rehabilitation, social work, learning disorders, physical disabilities, therapy, psychology, psychiatry. **Holdings:** 1082 books and bound periodical volumes; 1000 monographs, reprints and pamphlets. **Subscriptions:** 70 journals and other serials. **Services:** Interlibrary loans; copying; library open to public. **Publications:** Monthly Library Additions.

★12640★
SOCIETY OF THE FOUNDERS OF NORWICH, CONNECTICUT - LEFFINGWELL INN LIBRARY (Hist)
348 Washington St.
Norwich, CT 06360   Linda Kate Edgerton, Libn.
Staff: Prof 1; Other 1. **Subjects:** Local history and genealogy. **Holdings:** 400 books; 32 bound periodical volumes; 15 linear feet of documents and letters. **Services:** Interlibrary loans (limited); copying; library open to public by appointment.

★12641★
SOCIETY OF THE FOUR ARTS - LIBRARY (Art)
Four Arts Plaza   Phone: (305) 655-7226
Palm Beach, FL 33480   Winnifred Romoser, Libn.
Founded: 1936. **Subjects:** Fine arts. **Holdings:** 28,000 books and bound

periodical volumes. **Services:** Interlibrary loans; library open to public with membership fee.

★12642★
SOCIETY OF FRIENDS - FRIENDS HOUSE LIBRARY (Rel-Theol)
60 Lowther Ave.   Phone: (416) 921-0368
Toronto, ON, Canada M5R 1C7   Jane Sweet, Lib.Coord.
Founded: 1890. **Subjects:** History of Quakerism, peace and nonviolence, native concerns. **Holdings:** 4600 books; 102 bound periodical volumes; 12 boxes of pamphlets and reports. **Subscriptions:** 25 journals and other serials. **Services:** Interlibrary loans; library open to public.

★12643★
SOCIETY OF FRIENDS - FRIENDS MEETING OF WASHINGTON - LIBRARY (Rel-Theol)*
2111 Florida Ave., N.W.   Phone: (202) 483-3310
Washington, DC 20008   Stephen McNeil, Ck.
Founded: 1932. **Staff:** Prof 1; Other 2. **Subjects:** Quaker history and beliefs. **Holdings:** 4000 books. **Subscriptions:** 12 journals and other serials. **Services:** Interlibrary loans; bibliographic and reference service on request; library open to public by appointment.

★12644★
SOCIETY OF FRIENDS - NEW ENGLAND YEARLY MEETING OF FRIENDS - ARCHIVES (Rel-Theol)
121 Hope St.   Phone: (401) 331-8575
Providence, RI 02906   Rosalind Wiggins, Cur.
Founded: 1661. **Staff:** 1. **Subjects:** Archives and records of Society of Friends in New England; Quaker historical material. **Special Collections:** Moses and Obadiah Brown Libraries (512 volumes); Moses Brown Papers and Pamphlets, 1774-1836 (29 file boxes). **Holdings:** 1570 books; 155 bound periodical volumes; 635 volumes of archives; 112 file boxes of pamphlets and papers; 47 boxes of unbound periodicals; 173 reels of microfilm of archives; 1 box of newspaper clippings; 7 dissertations; 40 magnetic tapes. **Services:** Copying; archives open to public upon written request to curator. **Special Catalogs:** Guide to the Records of Yearly Meetings of New England Friends and Subordinate Meetings; chart of vital statistics of all meetings since 1657.

★12645★
SOCIETY OF FRIENDS - NEW YORK YEARLY MEETING - RECORDS COMMITTEE - HAVILAND RECORDS ROOM (Rel-Theol)
15 Rutherford Pl.   Phone: (212) 673-6866
New York, NY 10003   Elizabeth Haas Moger, Kpr.
Founded: 1900. **Staff:** 1. **Subjects:** Quaker genealogy and history in New York and surrounding states. **Special Collections:** New York Quaker imprints - Samuel Wood, Mahlon Day, Isaac T. Hopper (70 volumes); papers relating to Friends and New York State Indians in the 19th century. **Holdings:** 2500 books; 2000 manuscript records. **Services:** Records room open to public by appointment. **Special Catalogs:** Catalog of manuscript records (card). **Remarks:** Official depository for New York Yearly Meeting and its subordinate meetings in New York State, western Vermont, Connecticut, and northern New Jersey.

★12646★
SOCIETY OF FRIENDS - OHIO YEARLY MEETING - WESTGATE FRIENDS LIBRARY (Rel-Theol)
3750 Sullivant Ave.   Phone: (614) 274-5131
Columbus, OH 43228   William T. Peters, Lit.Coord.
Founded: 1968. **Staff:** Prof 1. **Subjects:** Quaker history and theology. **Holdings:** 1900 books and pamphlets; 10 VF drawers. **Subscriptions:** 58 journals and other serials. **Services:** Interlibrary loans; library open to public with restrictions. **Remarks:** Maintained by Evangelical Friends Church, Eastern Region.

★12647★
SOCIETY OF FRIENDS - PHILADELPHIA YEARLY MEETING - LIBRARY (Rel-Theol; Soc Sci)
1515 Cherry St.   Phone: (215) 241-7220
Philadelphia, PA 19102   Mary Davidson, Libn.
Founded: 1960. **Staff:** Prof 1; Other 1. **Subjects:** Quakerism; education; religious education; social concerns - religion, native Americans, criminal justice, race, service, sex, family relations, hunger, poverty, nuclear energy, peace education, nuclear weapons and disarmament. **Special Collections:** Dora Wilson Collection (religion and psychology); E. Vesta Haines Collection of Christmas Literature; Jean C. Hollingshead Poetry Corner; Peace Education Resource Center; Frances Ferris Collection (books for and about children). **Holdings:** 16,500 books. **Subscriptions:** 104 journals and other serials. **Services:** Interlibrary loans; copying; library open to public for reference use

only. **Publications:** Subject reading lists. **Remarks:** Includes the holdings of the American Friends Service Committee, Inc. - Library.

★12648★
SOCIETY FOR THE INVESTIGATION OF THE UNEXPLAINED - LIBRARY (Sci-Tech)
Box 265
Little Silver, NJ 07739
Phone: (201) 842-5229
N. Warth, Sec.
Founded: 1965. **Staff:** Prof 2; Other 3. **Subjects:** Forteana (works on tangible objects or events not yet accepted by orthodox science, i.e., sea monsters, abominable snowmen, poltergeists, UFOs); geology and geography; natural history; biology (all phases); cultural anthropology; astronomy; physics; chemistry; mathematics. **Special Collections:** Personal papers, original manuscripts and drawings of Society's former Director, the late Ivan T. Sanderson. **Holdings:** 2000 books; 105 bound periodical volumes; 95 shelf feet of unbound periodicals; 22 boxes of pamphlets; 260 ring binders of clippings, original reports, tear sheets; 300 maps; 2 map case drawers and 1 VF drawer of charts, diagrams, original drawings; 6 VF drawers of photographs and clippings, slides; 25 magnetic tapes. **Subscriptions:** 59 journals and other serials. **Services:** Copying (for members only); library open to members only for research. **Publications:** Pursuit Quarterly Journal - to members by subscription.

SOCIETY OF JESUS
See: Compagnie de Jesus

SOCIETY OF JESUS (Maryland Province) - ARCHIVES
See: Georgetown University - Special Collections Division - Lauinger Memorial Library

★12649★
SOCIETY OF JESUS - OREGON PROVINCE ARCHIVES (Rel-Theol; Hist)
Crosby Library, Gonzaga University
E. 502 Boone Ave.
Spokane, WA 92588
Phone: (509) 328-4220
Rev. Clifford Carroll, S.J., Archv.
Founded: 1931. **Staff:** Prof 1; Other 2. **Subjects:** Northwest Church history, Alaska Church history (including mission history), Doukhobor history, local history, Alaskan and Indian languages. **Special Collections:** Joset Papers; Cataldo Papers; Crimont Papers; Neil Byrne Papers; Monaghan Papers; Cowley Papers; Prando Papers; Jesuit Mission Papers. **Holdings:** 3600 books; 400 bound periodical volumes; 122,000 manuscripts; 24,000 photographs. **Subscriptions:** 35 journals and other serials; 18 newspapers. **Services:** Copying; library open to those with scholarly credentials. **Automated Operations:** Computerized cataloging. **Networks/Consortia:** Member of WLN. **Publications:** Guides to Microfilm Editions of the Oregon Province Archives of the Society of Jesus Indian Language Collection: (1) The Alaska Native Languages; (2) The Pacific Northwest Tribes; The Alaska Mission Papers. **Staff:** Bro.Ed Jennings, S.J., Asst.Archv.

★12650★
SOCIETY OF MANAGEMENT ACCOUNTANTS OF CANADA - RESOURCE CENTRE (Bus-Fin)
154 Main St., E.
Box 176
Hamilton, ON, Canada L8N 3C3
Phone: (416) 525-4100
Helen Hill, Libn.
Founded: 1920. **Staff:** Prof 1. **Subjects:** Accounting, management, systems, communication, economics, marketing, mathematics, production, taxation. **Holdings:** 8000 books; 2000 clippings. **Subscriptions:** 80 journals and other serials. **Services:** Interlibrary loans; copying (limited); center open to public for reference use only. **Publications:** Index, biennial.

★12651★
SOCIETY OF MANUFACTURING ENGINEERS - SME LIBRARY (Sci-Tech)
One SME Dr.
Box 930
Dearborn, MI 48121
Phone: (313) 271-1500
Paulette Groen, Libn.
Founded: 1932. **Staff:** 1. **Subjects:** Business, manufacturing engineering and materials, metallurgical processing, robotics, computerized automation in manufacturing. **Special Collections:** SME annual reports, minutes, papers and other publications; Computerized Automation and Robotics Information Center (CARIC; books, documents, related resource materials). **Holdings:** 2200 books; 8 VF drawers of clippings; 11,000 technical reports, 1951 to present. **Subscriptions:** 300 journals and other serials. **Services:** Library not open to public. **Computerized Information Services:** DIALOG; INTIME (internal database). Performs searches on fee basis. **Remarks:** Library contains Robotics International of the Society of Manufacturing Engineers Collection.

★12652★
SOCIETY OF MARY - CINCINNATI PROVINCE - ARCHIVES (Rel-Theol)
University of Dayton
Box 445
Dayton, OH 45469
Phone: (513) 229-2724
Bro. Bernard Laurinaitis, S.M., Archv.
Founded: 1938. **Staff:** Prof 1. **Subjects:** Church history, theology and philosophy. **Special Collections:** Archives of the Society of Mary (Marianists) from its origin in U.S., 1850 to present. **Holdings:** 2800 storage boxes of archival material; 15 oral history tapes of the University of Dayton; collection of slides and photographs about various schools conducted by Marianists. **Services:** Copying; archives open to public by appointment. **Special Indexes:** Indexes of Serial Publications of Marianists (card). **Remarks:** Archives located in Room 313, Roesch Library at the University of Dayton.

★12653★
SOCIETY OF MAYFLOWER DESCENDANTS IN THE STATE OF CALIFORNIA - LIBRARY (Hist)
Terrace Level
405 14th St.
Oakland, CA 94612
Phone: (415) 451-9599
Oliver S. Hayward, Libn.
Founded: 1907. **Staff:** Prof 2. **Subjects:** Genealogy. **Special Collections:** Folger Collection (family group sheets with references; 85 volumes). **Holdings:** 1400 books; 400 bound periodical volumes; 3000 pedigree papers of members in 20 volumes. **Services:** Library open to public on a limited schedule. **Remarks:** "This is a specialized collection of old books which are helpful to those trying to prove descent from the Mayflower passengers." **Staff:** Ralph George, Asst.Libn.

★12654★
SOCIETY FOR NUTRITION EDUCATION - SNE RESOURCE CENTER
1736 Franklin St., 9th Fl.
Oakland, CA 94612
Defunct

★12655★
SOCIETY OF PHILATICIANS - LIBRARY (Rec)
154 Laguna Ct.
St. Augustine, FL 32086
Gustav Detjen, Jr., Libn.
Founded: 1972. **Staff:** Prof 1. **Subjects:** Philately and Rooseveltiana. **Holdings:** 620 books. **Subscriptions:** 15 journals and other serials; 6 newspapers. **Services:** Interlibrary loans; copying. **Publications:** The Philatelic Journalist; Philatelic Directory, Handbook for Philatelic Writers.

★12656★
SOCIETY FOR THE PRESERVATION OF COLONIAL CULTURE - LIBRARY (Hist)
c/o 10th Foot Royal
Lincolnshire Regimental Assn.
52 New Spalding St.
Lowell, MA 01851
Founded: 1966. **Staff:** 3. **Subjects:** British military history, 1768-1783; history of America from discovery-1783; Iroquois Indians. **Holdings:** 9000 books, artifacts and reproductions; 25 boxes of unbound materials; 20,000 feet of films; 3500 slides. **Subscriptions:** 19 journals and other serials. **Services:** Copying; library open to public by appointment.

★12657★
SOCIETY FOR THE PRESERVATION AND ENCOURAGEMENT OF BARBER SHOP QUARTET SINGING IN AMERICA - OLD SONGS LIBRARY (Mus)
6315 Third Ave.
Box 575
Kenosha, WI 53141
Phone: (414) 654-9111
Ruth Marks, Harmony Found.Adm.
Staff: 1. **Subjects:** Piano-vocal sheet music from 1880s to present. **Special Collections:** Walter F. Wade Collection; Ken Grant Collection. **Holdings:** 65,000 pieces. **Services:** Library open to public with restrictions. **Also Known As:** Harmony Foundation.

★12658★
SOCIETY FOR THE PRESERVATION OF NEW ENGLAND ANTIQUITIES - LIBRARY (Hist)
141 Cambridge St.
Boston, MA 02114
Phone: (617) 227-3956
Elinor Reichlin, Libn.
Founded: 1910. **Staff:** 3. **Subjects:** New England architecture, local history, transportation, history of photography. **Special Collections:** Photographic collections: N.L. Stebbins, Henry Peabody, Baldwin Coolidge, Soule Art Photo Company, Halliday Historic Photograph Company, New England News Company, George Noyes, Arthur Haskell, Wilfred French, Mary Northend, Emma Coleman, Fred Quimby, Boston and Albany Railroad, Wallace Nutting, and other regional photographers; Manuscript collections: Codman Family

Papers (100 linear feet); Rundlet-May Papers (5 linear feet); Sayward Family Papers (2 linear feet); Casey Family papers (40 linear feet); Harrison Gray Otis business records (1 linear foot); architectural drawings, originals, and blueprints including works of Asher Benjamin, Luther Briggs, Ogden Codman, Jr., Frank Chouteau Brown, Arthur Little, Herbert Brown, George Clough and Arland Dirlham (7000 items); rare architectural pattern books (18th and 19th centuries; 500). **Holdings:** 400,000 photographic prints, including 8000 stereoptician views, 8000 postcards, 125 albums, 2500 cartes de visite portraits, 100,000 standard size prints, 800 daguerreotypes and ambrotypes; 70,000 negatives including 40,000 glass plates; 2500 prints and drawings of topographical subjects relating to New England architecture and landscape. **Services:** Copying; photography; library open to public by appointment only. **Special Catalogs:** Printed catalog to N.L. Stebbins marine photographs. **Special Indexes:** Typed inventories to photograph albums, prints and drawings, account books, maps, Soule Art Company photographs, and trade catalogs and manuscripts; card index to rare architectural pattern books.

★12659★
SOCIETY OF REAL ESTATE APPRAISERS - LIBRARY (Bus-Fin)
645 N. Michigan Ave.   Phone: (312) 346-7422
Chicago, IL 60611
Founded: 1957. **Subjects:** Appraising, real estate, mortgage lending, real estate market studies. **Holdings:** 1000 books; 37 bound periodical volumes; 408 pamphlets.

★12660★
SOCIETY OF ST. VINCENT DE PAUL - LIBRARY (Rel-Theol; Soc Sci)
4140 Lindell Blvd.   Phone: (314) 371-4980
St. Louis, MO 63108   Dudley L. Baker, Exec.Sec.
Subjects: History and work of the Society of St. Vincent de Paul. **Holdings:** Figures not available.

★12661★
SOCIETY OF SEPARATIONISTS - CHARLES E. STEVENS AMERICAN ATHEIST LIBRARY AND ARCHIVES INC. (Rel-Theol)
2210 Hancock Dr.   Phone: (512) 458-1244
Austin, TX 78756   R. Murray-O'Hair, Dir.
Founded: 1971. **Staff:** 4. **Subjects:** Atheism, agnosticism, freethought, humanism, objectivism, rationalism, iconoclasm, ethical culturism, separation of state and church. **Special Collections:** Atheist and Freethought magazines from pre-Civil War to present. **Holdings:** 20,000 books; 1000 bound periodical volumes; 500,000 pamphlets, booklets, throw-aways, manuscripts, documents, clippings, leaflets; 500 radio tapes. **Services:** Copying; library open to scholars.

SOCIETY FOR SOUTHEASTERN FLORA AND FAUNA
See: Brookgreen Gardens

★12662★
SOCIETY OF WIRELESS PIONEERS, INC. - BRENIMAN NAUTICAL-WIRELESS LIBRARY & MUSEUM OF COMMUNICATIONS (Sci-Tech)
Box 530   Phone: (707) 542-0898
Santa Rosa, CA 95402   Elmer Burgman, Dir.
Staff: Prof 2; Other 5. **Subjects:** Wireless telegraphy, communication, radio and television broadcasting; ships and shipping. **Special Collections:** Dickow Wireless Collection; Brown Lighthouses of the World. **Holdings:** 1400 books; 1500 bound periodical volumes; 4500 maps and other cataloged items. **Subscriptions:** 23 journals and other serials. **Services:** Copying; library open to public with restrictions.

★12663★
SOCIETY OF WOMEN ENGINEERS - INFORMATION CENTER (Soc Sci)
345 E. 47th St., Rm. 305   Phone: (212) 705-7855
New York, NY 10017
Subjects: Women in engineering. **Holdings:** Figures not available. **Services:** Center not open to public. **Publications:** Career guidance brochures; article reprints; Survey of Women Engineers; U.S. Woman Engineer. **Remarks:** This is an information center on women in engineering with emphasis on career guidance for the younger girl.

★12664★
SOD TOWN PIONEER HOMESTEAD MUSEUM - LIBRARY (Hist)*
U.S. Hwy. 24, East
Box 393
Colby, KS 67701   Phone: (913) 462-2021
                Ronald E. Thiel, Dir.
Founded: 1955. **Staff:** 2. **Subjects:** Sod houses, dugouts, adobe buildings, pioneer homestead history. **Special Collections:** Old photographs of sod buildings in North America (500). **Holdings:** 20,000 personal letters and family history reports from persons with sod house heritage. **Services:** Sod

House Survey; library open to public for reference use only. **Publications:** Sod Houses and Dugouts in North America - for sale. **Remarks:** Maintained by Sod House Society of America.

SODARCAN, LTD. - GESTAS INC.
See: Gestas Inc.

★12665★
SOHIO ALASKA PETROLEUM COMPANY - INFORMATION RESOURCE CENTER (Env-Cons; Energy)
3111 C St., Pouch 6-612   Phone: (907) 267-4574
Anchorage, AK 99502   Lorraine M. Culbert, Libn.
Staff: Prof 1. **Subjects:** Geology, environmental aspects of petroleum development, management, engineering, maintenance, petroleum production. **Holdings:** 6000 books; 1500 uncataloged reports and binders; 1500 reels of microfilm of industry standards and vendor catalogs; 480 reels of microfilm of journals. **Subscriptions:** 140 journals and other serials. **Services:** Interlibrary loans; copying; SDI (limited); center open to public by appointment. **Computerized Information Services:** DIALOG, SDC. **Publications:** Acquisitions List, monthly - for internal distribution only; subscription list, annual; special bibliographies and handouts, irregular.

★12666★
SOHIO CHEMCIAL COMPANY - INFORMATION CENTER (Sci-Tech; Agri)
1875 Guildhall Bldg.   Phone: (216) 575-5715
Cleveland, OH 44115   Christine Kikta, Mgr., Info.Serv.
Staff: Prof 2; Other 2. **Subjects:** Business, petrochemicals, agriculture, market research. **Special Collections:** Petrochemicals. **Holdings:** 6000 books; annual reports for 1500 companies. **Subscriptions:** 350 journals and other serials; 8 newspapers. **Services:** Interlibrary loans; library not open to public. **Automated Operations:** Computerized cataloging, acquisitions, serials and circulation. **Computerized Information Services:** DIALOG, SDC, BRS, OCLC, Data Resources, Inc. (DRI), EPCA, Sage; Info Center (internal database). **Networks/Consortia:** Member of OHIONET. **Publications:** Acquisitions List, monthly. **Staff:** Laura Gusby, Asst.Mgr.

★12667★
SOHIO PETROLEUM COMPANY - CENTRAL LIBRARY AND INFORMATION SERVICES (Sci-Tech)
50 Fremont St.   Phone: (415) 445-9511
San Francisco, CA 94105   Aileen M. Donovan, Mgr.
Staff: Prof 3; Other 3. **Subjects:** Petroleum industry and engineering, geology, paleontology, engineering, business, economics. **Holdings:** 15,000 books. **Subscriptions:** 500 journals and other serials. **Services:** Interlibrary loans; library not open to public. **Automated Operations:** Computerized cataloging and serials. **Computerized Information Services:** DIALOG, SDC, New York Times Information Service, RLIN, BRS, I.P Sharp Associates, Ltd., Pergamon InfoLine Ltd. **Remarks:** Standard Oil Company of Ohio is the parent organization. **Staff:** Annemarie Welteke, Asst.Libn.; Linnea Christiani, Asst.Libn.

SOHN MEMORIAL HEALTH SERVICES LIBRARY
See: Fort Hamilton-Hughes Memorial Hospital Center

★12668★
SOHO CENTER FOR VISUAL ARTISTS - LIBRARY (Art)
110 Prince St.   Phone: (212) 226-1993
New York, NY 10012   Rhonda Wall, Libn.
Founded: 1974. **Staff:** Prof 1; Other 1. **Subjects:** Twentieth century painting, sculpture, photography and film; architecture; crafts. **Holdings:** 2000 volumes; exhibition catalogs; unbound reference materials; 10 VF drawers of limited edition print portfolios and reproductions of art work. **Subscriptions:** 50 journals and other serials. **Services:** Library open to visual artists. **Remarks:** Includes the library of the Aldrich Museum of Contemporary Art, Ridgefield, CT. The Soho Center consists of the library and an Exhibition Gallery at 114 Prince St.

★12669★
SOIL CONSERVATION SOCIETY OF AMERICA - H. WAYNE PRITCHARD LIBRARY (Env-Cons)
7515 N.E. Ankeny Rd.   Phone: (515) 289-2331
Ankeny, IA 50021   James L. Sanders, Asst.Ed.
Subjects: Soil and water conservation, land use planning, natural resources management. **Special Collections:** Papers of Hugh Hammond Bennett, Father of Soil Conservation, and of other leaders in soil and water conservation. **Holdings:** 2500 books. **Services:** Copying; library open to public for reference use only.

SOIL MECHANICS INFORMATION ANALYSIS CENTER
See: U.S. Army - Engineer Waterways Experiment Station

SOIL SCIENCE SOCIETY OF AMERICA
See: American Society of Agronomy

SOILAND (Albert) MEMORIAL LIBRARY
See: California Hospital Medical Center - Medical Staff Library

SOJOURNER TRUTH ROOM
See: Prince George's County Memorial Library System

★12670★
SOLANO COUNTY LAW LIBRARY (Law)
Hall of Justice
600 Union Ave.   Phone: (707) 429-6655
Fairfield, CA 94533   Hon. Richard M. Harris, Pres., Lib. Trustees
Staff: 1. Subjects: Law. Holdings: 15,000 books. Subscriptions: 16 journals and other serials. Services: Copying; library open to public. Staff: Marion Grant, Libn.

★12671★
SOLAR ENERGY RESEARCH INSTITUTE - SERI TECHNICAL LIBRARY (Energy)
1617 Cole Blvd.   Phone: (303) 231-1415
Golden, CO 80401   Jerome T. Maddock, Br.Chf.
Founded: 1977. Staff: Prof 5; Other 4. Subjects: Energy - solar, wind, ocean, biomass; photovoltaics. Holdings: 10,500 books; 3500 bound periodical volumes; 20,000 technical reports; 7380 patents; 43,000 reports on microfiche. Subscriptions: 800 journals and other serials; 5 newspapers. Services: Interlibrary loans; library open to public by appointment. Automated Operations: Computerized cataloging and serials. Computerized Information Services: DIALOG, SDC, DOE/RECON, RLIN, OCLC, BRS. Publications: Serials Holdings List; New Acquisitions Lists, both irregular. Remarks: The Solar Energy Research Institute operates under contract to the U.S. Department of Energy. Staff: Nancy Greer, Hd., Tech.Serv.; Joe Chervenak, Acq.; Soon Duck Kim, Cat.; Al Berger, Ref.

★12672★
SOLAR TURBINES INCORPORATED - LIBRARY (Energy)
Box 80966   Phone: (619) 238-5992
San Diego, CA 92138   George Hall, Libn.
Founded: 1959. Staff: Prof 1. Subjects: Gas turbines, ceramics, high temperature metals. Holdings: 2700 books; 700 bound periodical volumes; 5000 technical reports and society papers. Subscriptions: 30 journals and other serials; 10 newspapers. Services: Interlibrary loans; library not open to public. Computerized Information Services: DIALOG. Publications: New Material Bulletin, monthly. Remarks: Solar Turbines Incorporated is a subsidiary of Caterpillar Tractor Company.

SOLAR USE NOW FOR RESOURCES AND EMPLOYMENT - LEARNING RESOURCES CENTER
See: SUNRAE Learning Resources Center

SOLAR AND WIND ENERGY RESEARCH PROGRAM INFORMATION CENTRE
See: Alberta Research Council

★12673★
SOLDIERS AND SAILORS MEMORIAL HOSPITAL - HEALTH SCIENCE LIBRARY (Med)
Central Ave.   Phone: (717) 724-1631
Wellsboro, PA 16901   Charlean Patterson, Libn.
Staff: 1. Subjects: Clinical medicine, nursing, hospital administration, allied health sciences, patient education. Holdings: 750 books; 300 bound periodical volumes; 200 NCME (Network for Continuing Medical Education) videotapes. Subscriptions: 115 journals and other serials. Services: Interlibrary loans; copying; SDI; library open to public. Networks/Consortia: Member of Susquehanna Library Cooperative; Central Pennsylvania Health Sciences Library Association; Greater Northeastern Regional Medical Library Program.

★12674★
SOLEIL LIMITEE - CENTRE DE DOCUMENTATION (Publ)
390 E. St. Vallier   Phone: (418) 647-3369
Quebec, PQ, Canada G1K 7J6   Mr. Berthold Landry, Adm.Asst.
Founded: 1967. Staff: Prof 4; Other 5. Subjects: Newspaper reference topics. Holdings: 1500 books; 50 bound periodical volumes; one million clippings; 20,000 reels of microfilm; 150 VF drawers. Subscriptions: 120 journals and other serials; 30 newspapers. Services: Copying; center open to

public by appointment. Staff: Claudine Gagnon, Coord.

SOLERI (Paolo) ARCHIVES
See: Arizona State University - Howe Architecture Library

SOMERS (Gerald G.) GRADUATE REFERENCE ROOM
See: University of Wisconsin, Madison - Gerald G. Somers Graduate Reference Room

★12675★
SOMERS HISTORICAL SOCIETY - ARCHIVES (Hist)
574 Main St.   Phone: (203) 749-7273
Somers, CT 06071   Jeanne K. DeBell, Cur.
Staff: 3. Subjects: Local and state history; genealogy. Special Collections: Civil War Letters; Sermons 1750-1865; Public School Readers 1830-1890. Holdings: 200 books; 1 VF drawer of local history material; 1 box of early deeds and letters, 1730-1865. Services: Archives open to public with restrictions. Publications: Somers, History of a Connecticut Town, 1973; Somers, Connecticut Through the Camera's Eye, 1978 - both available for sale. Special Indexes: Genealogical File of Somers Families.

★12676★
SOMERS HISTORICAL SOCIETY - LIBRARY AND ARCHIVES (Hist)
Box 336   Phone: (914) 277-4977
Somers, NY 10589   Florence S. Oliver, Archv.
Staff: 1. Subjects: Circus, local history. Special Collections: Dr. Hugh Grant Rowell Collection (1000 items on the American circus). Holdings: 600 books; pamphlets and manuscripts; 4 VF drawers of uncataloged pamphlets and manuscripts; 10 maps. Services: Library open to public for research by appointment.

★12677★
SOMERSET COUNTY LAW LIBRARY (Law)
Court House   Phone: (201) 231-7000
Somerville, NJ 08876   Helen W. Leavitt, Law Libn.
Staff: 1. Subjects: Law. Holdings: 20,000 volumes. Services: Copying; library open to public for reference use only.

★12678★
SOMERSET COUNTY LAW LIBRARY (Law)★
                                            Phone: (814) 445-5545
Somerset, PA 15501   Irene Coffroth, Libn.
Subjects: Law. Holdings: 20,500 volumes. Services: Library not open to public.

SOMERSET HISTORICAL CENTER
See: Historical and Genealogical Society of Somerset County - County Historical Library and Research Center

SOMERSET STATE HOSPITAL
See: Pennsylvania State Department of Public Welfare

★12679★
SOMERVILLE HOSPITAL - CARR HEALTH SCIENCES LIBRARY (Med)
230 Highland Ave.   Phone: (617) 666-4400
Somerville, MA 02143   Celeste F. Kozlowski, Libn.
Staff: Prof 1; Other 7. Subjects: Medicine and nursing. Holdings: 2500 books; 118 bound periodical volumes; 360 pamphlets; 400 transparencies; 16 filmloops. Subscriptions: 113 journals and other serials. Services: Interlibrary loans; copying; library open to public with permission. Networks/Consortia: Member of Libraries for Nursing Consortium (LINC).

★12680★
SONAT INC. - CORPORATE LIBRARY (Bus-Fin; Energy)
Box 2563   Phone: (205) 325-7409
Birmingham, AL 35202   Gina Hinkle, Corp.Libn.
Staff: Prof 1; Other 1. Subjects: Energy, natural gas industry, alternative fuels, oil industry, business, corporate law. Special Collections: Financial data on major natural gas pipeline companies (53 VF drawers). Holdings: 8200 books; 400 bound periodical volumes; 8 VF drawers of clippings; 6 VF drawers of speeches. Subscriptions: 400 journals and other serials; 10 newspapers. Services: Copying; SDI; library open to public for reference use only. Computerized Information Services: NEXIS. Performs searches free of charge and on subscription basis.

★12681★
SONNENSCHEIN CARLIN NATH & ROSENTHAL - LIBRARY (Law)
8000 Sears Tower
233 S. Wacker Dr.   Phone: (312) 876-7906
Chicago, IL 60606   Colleen L. McCarroll, Libn.
Staff: Prof 2; Other 3. **Subjects:** Law. **Special Collections:** Insurance
statutes and regulations for all states. **Holdings:** 25,000 books; 240 bound
periodical volumes; 500 microfiche; 45 documents; 300 in-house research
reports. **Services:** Interlibrary loans; copying; SDI; library open to public upon
approval by head librarian. **Automated Operations:** Computerized cataloging
and serials. **Computerized Information Services:** DIALOG, OCLC, LEXIS,
Westlaw, SDC, Dow Jones News/Retrieval, Commerce Clearing House
Electronic Legislative Search System (ELSS). **Networks/Consortia:** Member
of Chicago Library System. **Special Indexes:** In-house research index (book
and magnetic disk); corporate precedents file (card). **Staff:** Serpil de Costa,
Asst.Libn.

SONNTAG LIBRARY
See: Manhattan College

★12682★
SONOMA COUNTY LAW LIBRARY (Law)
Hall of Justice, Rm. 213-J
600 Administration Dr.   Phone: (707) 527-2668
Santa Rosa, CA 95401   Charlotte S. von Gunten, Law Libn.
Founded: 1891. **Staff:** Prof 1; Other 1. **Subjects:** Law. **Holdings:** 17,155
volumes; 5005 pamphlets; 265 tapes. **Subscriptions:** 80 journals and other
serials. **Services:** Interlibrary loans; copying; SDI; library open to public.
Publications: List of holdings; Union List of Legal Periodicals in Sonoma
County Libraries, both irregular.

★12683★
SONOMA COUNTY PLANNING DEPARTMENT - LIBRARY (Plan)
575 Administration Dr.   Phone: (707) 527-2931
Santa Rosa, CA 95401   Ruth Lund, Supv.Ck.
Founded: 1961. **Staff:** Prof 1. **Subjects:** Planning, transportation, land use,
housing, zoning and environmental impact information related to Sonoma
County and surrounding areas. **Holdings:** Figures not available for books,
reports and special studies. **Services:** Copying; library open to public with
restrictions.

★12684★
**SONOMA STATE HOSPITAL AND DEVELOPMENTAL CENTER - STAFF
LIBRARY** (Med)
Box 1400   Phone: (707) 938-6561
Eldridge, CA 95431   Barbara Fetesoff, Sr.Libn.
Founded: 1951. **Staff:** Prof 1. **Subjects:** Mental retardation, psychology,
nursing, social work, rehabilitation therapy, medicine. **Special Collections:**
History of the hospital. **Holdings:** 7401 books; 8417 bound periodical
volumes; 70 AV programs. **Subscriptions:** 105 journals and other serials.
Services: Interlibrary loans; copying; library open to public. **Computerized
Information Services:** MEDLARS. Performs free searches for staff.

SONORA DESERT MUSEUM
See: Arizona-Sonora Desert Museum

SONS OF THE AMERICAN REVOLUTION
See: National Society of the Sons of the American Revolution

★12685★
SONS OF NORWAY - NORTH STAR LIBRARY (Area-Ethnic)
1455 W. Lake St.   Phone: (612) 827-3611
Minneapolis, MN 55408   Bent Vanberg, Cons.
Staff: Prof 1. **Subjects:** Literature, travel, history, World War II, art, social
studies, children, insurance, general business. **Special Collections:** Norwegian
Pictorial Review (55); Norwegian-American Studies (20); Norwegian-
American Emigration Lists (15); 19th-century Norwegian literary classics.
Holdings: 1150 books (half in Norwegian, half in English); insurance reports;
census and legal reference materials; photographs. **Services:** Copying
(limited); library open to nonmembers with restrictions.

★12686★
**SONS OF THE REVOLUTION IN THE STATE OF CALIFORNIA SOCIETY -
LIBRARY** (Hist)
600 S. Central Ave.   Phone: (818) 240-1775
Glendale, CA 91204   Richard E. Coe, Lib.Dir.
Founded: 1893. **Subjects:** Genealogy, history, biography. **Holdings:** 22,000
volumes; 2000 family genealogies. **Subscriptions:** 10 journals and other
serials. **Services:** Copying; genealogical research; library open to public with

donation.

★12687★
SONS OF THE REVOLUTION IN THE STATE OF NEW YORK - LIBRARY (Hist)
Fraunces Tavern Museum
Broad & 54 Pearl Sts.   Phone: (212) 425-1776
New York, NY 10004   Patricia Kesling, Act.Adm.
Subjects: Colonial and Revolutionary War period. **Holdings:** Figures not
available. **Services:** Library open to members by appointment.

★12688★
**SOURIS VALLEY REGIONAL CARE CENTER - MEDICAL & HEALTH
SCIENCES LIBRARY** (Med)
Box 2001   Phone: (306) 842-7481
Weyburn, SK, Canada S4H 2L7   Melva Cooke, Libn.
Founded: 1971. **Staff:** 1. **Subjects:** Gerontology, psychiatry, nursing,
nutrition, physical and occupational therapy. **Holdings:** 800 books; 90 bound
periodical volumes; 300 articles; 3 VF drawers of clippings. **Subscriptions:**
75 journals and other serials; 7 newspapers. **Services:** Interlibrary loans;
library not open to public.

★12689★
SOUTH BALTIMORE GENERAL HOSPITAL - MEDICAL LIBRARY (Med)
3001 S. Hanover St.   Phone: (301) 354-1000
Baltimore, MD 21230   Kristine M. Scannell, Med.Libn.
Staff: Prof 1; Other 1. **Subjects:** Medicine and related sciences. **Holdings:**
1000 books; 2000 bound periodical volumes; educational materials.
Subscriptions: 110 journals and other serials. **Services:** Interlibrary loans;
library not open to public. **Computerized Information Services:** MEDLARS,
DIALOG. **Networks/Consortia:** Member of Maryland Association of Health
Science Librarians; Baltimore Consortia for Resource Sharing.

★12690★
SOUTH BEND OSTEOPATHIC HOSPITAL - MEDICAL LIBRARY (Med)
2515 E. Jefferson Blvd.   Phone: (219) 288-8311
South Bend, IN 46615   Helga R. Wehrhan, Lib.Mgr.
Staff: Prof 1. **Subjects:** Medicine. **Special Collections:** History of osteopathy
(25 volumes). **Holdings:** 1100 books; 160 bound periodical volumes; 50
video cassettes; Audio-Digest tapes. **Subscriptions:** 42 journals and other
serials. **Services:** Interlibrary loans; copying; library open to students.
Networks/Consortia: Member of Area Library Services Authority (ALSA),
Region 2.

★12691★
SOUTH CAROLINA CONFEDERATE RELIC ROOM & MUSEUM - LIBRARY
(Hist)
World War Memorial Bldg.
920 Sumter St.   Phone: (803) 758-2144
Columbia, SC 29201
Founded: 1896. **Staff:** 5. **Subjects:** South Carolina history, Southern
Confederacy, Revolutionary history. **Special Collections:** Civil War era
histories (225 volumes); War of the Rebellion (150 volumes). **Holdings:** 450
books; 50 bound periodical volumes; scrapbooks, diaries, Muster Rolls; 100
pamphlets; 50 newspapers. **Subscriptions:** 10 journals and other serials.
Services: Research on request; library open to public for reference use only.

★12692★
SOUTH CAROLINA HISTORICAL SOCIETY - LIBRARY (Hist)
Fireproof Bldg.
Meeting & Chalmers Sts.   Phone: (803) 723-3225
Charleston, SC 29401   Gene Waddell, Dir.
Staff: Prof 7; Other 3. **Subjects:** South Carolina history, architecture,
economy, genealogy. **Holdings:** 15,000 books and bound periodical volumes;
9000 pamphlets; 1500 linear feet of manuscripts; microfiche. **Subscriptions:**
70 journals and other serials. **Services:** Copying; library open to public for
reference use only. **Publications:** South Carolina Historical Magazine,
quarterly. **Staff:** David Moltke-Hansen, Assoc.Dir.; Harlan Greene, Archv.

★12693★
**SOUTH CAROLINA STATE ATTORNEY GENERAL'S OFFICE - LEGAL
LIBRARY** (Law)
1000 Assembly St., Suite 701
Box 11549   Phone: (803) 758-3094
Columbia, SC 29211   Susan Husman, Libn.
Staff: Prof 1; Other 1. **Subjects:** Law. **Special Collections:** South Carolina
Attorney Generals' opinions (published and unpublished). **Holdings:** 8200
books; 53 bound periodical volumes. **Subscriptions:** 15 journals and other
serials. **Services:** Interlibrary loans; copying; library open to public.
Automated Operations: Computerized opinion index. **Publications:** Annual

Report of the Attorney General of South Carolina. **Special Indexes:** Index of published and unpublished opinions.

★12694★
SOUTH CAROLINA STATE COMMISSION ON ALCOHOL AND DRUG ABUSE - RESOURCE CENTER (Med)
3700 Forest Dr.   Phone: (803) 758-3866
Columbia, SC 29204   Sarah B. Clarkson, Libn.
Staff: Prof 1; Other 1. **Subjects:** Alcohol and drug abuse - education, prevention, intervention, treatment. **Special Collections:** South Carolina State Commission on Alcohol and Drug Abuse publications (complete set). **Holdings:** 1500 books; 150 bound periodical volumes; 16 VF drawers; 50 pamphlet titles; 200 16mm films. **Subscriptions:** 44 journals and other serials. **Services:** Interlibrary loans; copying; center open to public with restrictions. **Networks/Consortia:** Member of Columbia Area Medical Library Association (CAMLA). **Publications:** SCCADA Data, quarterly - to county alcohol and drug abuse programs, consortium members, agency personnel, and Substance Abuse Librarians & Information Specialists (SALIS). **Special Catalogs:** AV catalog (book).

★12695★
SOUTH CAROLINA STATE DEPARTMENT OF ARCHIVES & HISTORY - ARCHIVES SEARCH ROOM (Hist)
Capitol Sta., Box 11669   Phone: (803) 758-5816
Columbia, SC 29211   Charles E. Lee, Dir.
Founded: 1905. **Staff:** 120. **Subjects:** History of South Carolina - political, constitutional, legal, economic, social, religious. **Special Collections:** Noncurrent public records of South Carolina, including: land records of the colony and state; Revolutionary War accounts; confederate service records; executive, legislative and judicial records of the colony and state; probate records of the colony; county records (13,000 cubic feet of records; 15,000 reels of microfilm). **Holdings:** 2000 books; 250 bound periodical volumes. **Subscriptions:** 200 journals and other serials. **Services:** Copying; archives and records for reference use only. **Publications:** Colonial Records of South Carolina, 15 volumes; State Records of South Carolina, 8 volumes; The Papers of John C. Calhoun, 15 volumes; South Carolina Archives Microcopies, 12 series; New South Carolina State Gazette, quarterly newsletter; other documentary publications. **Special Catalogs:** Catalog of reference library (card). **Special Indexes:** Published Summary Guide to Archives; consolidated computer output microfilm index to documents; bound volume indexes to land plats and grants, marriage settlements and other records; map catalog (card); Revolutionary and Confederate War service records (card). **Remarks:** Library is located at 1430 Senate St., Columbia, SC 29201. **Staff:** William L. McDowell, Jr., Dp.Dir.; Charles H. Lesser, Asst.Dir./Archv. & Pubn.

★12696★
SOUTH CAROLINA STATE DEPARTMENT OF HEALTH & ENVIRONMENTAL CONTROL - EDUCATIONAL RESOURCE CENTER (Med)
2600 Bull St.   Phone: (803) 758-5448
Columbia, SC 29201   Michael Kronenfeld, Dir.
Founded: 1981. **Staff:** Prof 1; Other 8. **Subjects:** Public health, medicine, nursing, epidemiology, environmental sciences, nutrition, health education. **Holdings:** 3000 books; 3000 bound periodical volumes; 1500 films; 60,000 pamphlets and posters. **Subscriptions:** 190 journals and other serials. **Services:** Interlibrary loans; copying; library open to public with restrictions. **Computerized Information Services:** DIALOG, MEDLARS, Occupational Health Services, Inc. **Networks/Consortia:** Member of Columbia Area Medical Librarians Association (CAMLA).

★12697★
SOUTH CAROLINA STATE DEPARTMENT OF MENTAL RETARDATION - MIDLANDS CENTER LIBRARY (Educ)†
8301 Farrow Rd.   Phone: (803) 758-4434
Columbia, SC 29203   Mrs. Clannie H. Washington, Libn.
Staff: Prof 1; Other 1. **Subjects:** Mental retardation, special education. **Holdings:** 7590 books; 10 video cassettes; 6 16mm films; 295 slides. **Subscriptions:** 45 journals and other serials. **Services:** Interlibrary loans; copying; library open to state employees.

★12698★
SOUTH CAROLINA STATE DEPARTMENT OF MENTAL RETARDATION - WHITTEN CENTER LIBRARY & MEDIA RESOURCE SERVICES (Educ)
Box 239   Phone: (803) 833-2736
Clinton, SC 29325   Mr. Hsiu-Yun Keng, Dir.
Founded: 1965. **Staff:** Prof 1; Other 1. **Subjects:** Mental retardation, social services for mentally retarded, special education, special media for mentally retarded, psychology. **Special Collections:** Mental retardation; low reading level/high interest books for mentally retarded; special education. **Holdings:** 21,000 books; 170 bound periodical volumes; 18 volumes of South Carolina

laws; 250 microfiche; 16,500 AV items. **Subscriptions:** 60 journals and other serials. **Services:** Interlibrary loans; copying; library open to residents and employees of state institutions for the mentally retarded. **Publications:** Bibliography of Professional Materials on Mental Retardation, 2nd edition and annual supplements. **Special Catalogs:** Simplified card catalog for mentally retarded people; Audiovisual Materials in Teaching Mentally Retarded; Subject Headings and Classification Index in Mental Retardation, 1979.

★12699★
SOUTH CAROLINA STATE ENERGY EXTENSION SERVICE - ENERGY INFORMATION CENTER (Energy)
111 Executive Center Dr., Rm. 118   Phone: (803) 758-6925
Columbia, SC 29210   Debbie Bowdler, Energy Info.Spec.
Staff: Prof 1. **Subjects:** Energy conservation; energy - solar, wind, ocean, thermal, wood, water; alcohol fuels. **Holdings:** 2000 items. **Services:** Interlibrary loans; copying; center open to public with restrictions. **Computerized Information Services:** DIALOG, DOE/RECON. **Publications:** S.C. Energy Extension Service Energy News, monthly - by request.

★12700★
SOUTH CAROLINA (State) GEOLOGICAL SURVEY - LIBRARY (Sci-Tech)
Harbison Forest Rd.   Phone: (803) 758-6431
Columbia, SC 29210   Alan-Jun Zupan, Prin. Geologist
Subjects: Geology, earth science. **Holdings:** Figures not available. **Services:** Copying; library open to public for reference use only. **Publications:** South Carolina Geology.

★12701★
SOUTH CAROLINA STATE LIBRARY (Info Sci)
1500 Senate St.
Box 11469   Phone: (803) 758-3181
Columbia, SC 29211   Betty E. Callaham, State Libn.
Founded: 1943. **Staff:** Prof 20; Other 28. **Subjects:** Reference, government, business, political science, education, history, fine arts, South Caroliniana. **Special Collections:** Foundation Center Regional Depository. **Holdings:** 165,752 books; 1636 bound periodical volumes; 30,869 South Carolina state documents; 13,859 reels of microfilm of periodicals; 257,450 ERIC microfiche; 59,902 government documents; 32,081 government documents on microfiche; 1018 filmstrips; 1353 slides; 1381 films; 4273 large type books. **Subscriptions:** 1945 journals and other serials; 23 newspapers. **Services:** Interlibrary loans; copying; library open to public with written referral from public or college library. **Automated Operations:** Computerized periodicals list. **Computerized Information Services:** DIALOG, OCLC. **Networks/Consortia:** Member of SOLINET. **Publications:** News for South Carolina Libraries, monthly - to trustees, public and academic libraries; New Resources for State Government and Agencies - to state government agencies; Checklist of State Documents, quarterly; News about library services for the blind and physically handicapped, quarterly - to handicapped readers; News about the AV scene, quarterly - to public libraries; South Carolina Foundation Directory, irregular - available for sale. **Special Catalogs:** Microfilm catalogs of State Library, Clemson University and the University of South Carolina Libraries. **Special Indexes:** Computer index. **Staff:** James Johnson, Jr., Dp. State Libn.; Margie E. Herron, Dir. of Field Serv.; Frances Case, Dir., Div. of Blind; John H. Landrum, Dir. of Rd.Serv.; Marjorie Mazur, Dir. of Tech.Serv.; Theresa Mills, Inst.Cons.; Mary B. Toll, Doc.Libn.; Mary Cross, Cat.Libn.; Libby Law, Field Serv.Libn.; Barbara Kasper, Field Serv.Libn.; Alice I. Nolte, Field Serv.Libn.; Anne K. Middleton, Ref.Libn.; Jane Gardner, Field Serv.Libn./Ch.; Lea Walsh, ILL Libn.; Ron Anderson, Field Serv.Libn./AV; Iris Shirley, Handicapped Serv; Deborah Hotchkiss, Ref.Libn.; Edna White, Asst.Ref.Libn.; William Ellett, Cat.

★12702★
SOUTH CAROLINA STATE SUPREME COURT - LIBRARY (Law)
Box 11330   Phone: (803) 758-3741
Columbia, SC 29211   Elizabeth A. Tomlinson, Libn.
Staff: Prof 1; Other 1. **Subjects:** Law. **Holdings:** 51,440 books; 1005 bound periodical volumes. **Subscriptions:** 75 journals and other serials. **Services:** Copying; library open to public.

★12703★
SOUTH CAROLINA STATE WILDLIFE AND MARINE RESOURCES DEPARTMENT - LIBRARY (Sci-Tech)
P.O. Box 12559   Phone: (803) 795-6350
Charleston, SC 29412   Marilyn L. Lewis, Marine Rsrcs.Libn.
Founded: 1972. **Staff:** Prof 1; Other 2. **Subjects:** Marine biology and ecology; fisheries; aquaculture; marine resources management. **Holdings:** 12,750 books; 6600 bound periodical volumes; 20,000 reprints. **Subscriptions:** 335 journals and other serials. **Services:** Interlibrary loans; copying; library open to public with restrictions. **Automated Operations:**

Computerized cataloging. **Networks/Consortia:** Member of Charleston Higher Education Consortium (CHEC).

★12704★
SOUTH CENTRAL BELL TELEPHONE COMPANY - RESOURCE CENTER (Info Sci)
600 N. 19th St., 12th Fl.
Box 771   Phone: (205) 321-2064
Birmingham, AL 35201   Bonnie B. Browning, Asst. Staff Supv.
Subjects: Telecommunications. **Holdings:** 500 books. **Subscriptions:** 62 journals and other serials. **Services:** Interlibrary loans; copying; center open to public on a limited basis. **Computerized Information Services:** NEXIS.

★12705★
SOUTH CENTRAL MONTANA REGIONAL MENTAL HEALTH CENTER - LIBRARY (Med)
1245 N. 29th St.   Phone: (406) 252-5658
Billings, MT 59101   ElRene A. Dorn, Libn.
Staff: Prof 1. **Subjects:** Psychiatry, psychology, drugs and alcohol, nursing. **Holdings:** 300 books; vertical files. **Services:** Interlibrary loans; copying; library open to patients and students. **Networks/Consortia:** Member of Billings Area Health Sciences Information Cooperative (BAHSIC).

★12706★
SOUTH CHICAGO COMMUNITY HOSPITAL - DEPARTMENT OF LIBRARY SERVICES (Med)
2320 E. 93rd St.   Phone: (312) 978-2000
Chicago, IL 60617   Bruce Ardis, Dir.
Staff: Prof 2; Other 2. **Subjects:** Clinical medicine, nursing. **Holdings:** 3333 books; 2500 bound periodical volumes. **Subscriptions:** 250 journals and other serials. **Services:** Interlibrary loans; library not open to public. **Automated Operations:** Computerized cataloging. **Computerized Information Services:** DIALOG, NLM. **Networks/Consortia:** Member of Chicago and South Consortium; Greater Midwest Regional Medical Library Network (Region 3). **Staff:** Eleanor Adams, Sch.Libn.; Joyce Styler, AV Coord.

★12707★
SOUTH CONGREGATIONAL CHURCH - ETHEL L. AUSTIN LIBRARY (Rel-Theol)
242 Salmon Brook St.
Box 779   Phone: (203) 653-7289
Granby, CT 06035   Joan Griswold, Libn.
Staff: 1. **Subjects:** Christian living, devotions, Bible study, biography. **Holdings:** 1650 books. **Services:** Library open to public.

★12708★
SOUTH DAKOTA HUMAN SERVICES CENTER - MEDICAL LIBRARY (Med)
Box 76   Phone: (605) 665-3671
Yankton, SD 57078   Mary Lou Kostel, Libn.
Staff: 1. **Subjects:** Psychiatry, psychology, nursing, medicine, psychiatric social work. **Holdings:** 1582 books; 131 bound periodical volumes; 353 audiotapes; VF drawers of pamphlets; manuscripts; historical clippings. **Subscriptions:** 54 journals and other serials. **Services:** Interlibrary loans; copying; library open to staff, students and professionals. **Automated Operations:** Computerized serials.

★12709★
SOUTH DAKOTA SCHOOL OF MINES & TECHNOLOGY - DEVEREAUX LIBRARY (Sci-Tech)
500 St. Joseph St.   Phone: (605) 394-2418
Rapid City, SD 57701   Bernice E. McKibben, Dir.
Staff: Prof 4; Other 6. **Subjects:** Mining and minerals, geology, engineering. **Holdings:** 190,000 volumes; 1500 theses and dissertations; 18,000 archival items; 110,000 microforms. **Subscriptions:** 1300 journals and other serials; 25 newspapers. **Services:** Interlibrary loans; copying; library open to public. **Automated Operations:** Computerized cataloging. **Computerized Information Services:** DIALOG, SDC, BRS, QL Systems. **Networks/Consortia:** Member of Bibliographical Center for Research, Rocky Mountain Region, Inc. (BCR); MINITEX. **Publications:** Selected Acquisitions; Location Guide; General Information Tips; Guide Series. **Special Catalogs:** Thesis/Dissertation listing; periodical listing. **Staff:** Philip F. McCauley, Cur./Archv.; Margaret Sandine, Tech.Serv.; Charlotte A. Erdmann, Info.Serv.

SOUTH DAKOTA STATE DEPARTMENT OF EDUCATION & CULTURAL AFFAIRS - ARCHIVES RESOURCE CENTER
See: **South Dakota State Library & Archives - South Dakota State Archives**

SOUTH DAKOTA STATE DEPARTMENT OF EDUCATION & CULTURAL AFFAIRS - W.H. OVER MUSEUM
See: **Over (W.H.) Museum**

★12710★
SOUTH DAKOTA STATE HISTORICAL RESOURCE CENTER (Hist)
Memorial Bldg.   Phone: (605) 773-3615
Pierre, SD 57501   Rosemary Evetts, Libn.
Founded: 1901. **Staff:** Prof 1; Other 1. **Subjects:** South Dakota history, Sioux and Plains Indian culture and history, genealogy, fur trade. **Special Collections:** John E. Pfeiffer German-Russian Collection (36 titles); Smithsonian Institution Annual Reports (122 volumes). **Holdings:** 34,000 items, 8000 cataloged; 2000 maps; 700 manuscript collections; 50,000 photographs. **Services:** Interlibrary loans; copying; center open to public for reference use only. **Computerized Information Services:** OCLC. **Networks/Consortia:** Member of MINITEX. **Publications:** South Dakota Historical Collections, biennial; South Dakota History, quarterly.

★12711★
SOUTH DAKOTA STATE LIBRARY & ARCHIVES (Info Sci)
800 N. Illinois St.   Phone: (605) 773-3131
Pierre, SD 57501   Clarence L. Coffindaffer, State Libn.
Founded: 1913. **Staff:** Prof 11; Other 38. **Subjects:** General collection. **Special Collections:** South Dakota; large print; South Dakota documents. **Holdings:** 117,805 volumes; 94,030 documents; 6147 pictures; 581 maps; 4064 slides; 5178 films, filmstrips, videotapes and other media; 21,930 talking book titles; 284,623 microfiche; 8839 reels of microfilm. **Subscriptions:** 1179 journals and other serials. **Services:** Interlibrary loans; copying; library open to South Dakota residents. **Automated Operations:** Computerized cataloging and ILL. **Computerized Information Services:** DIALOG, SDC, BRS, OnTyme II, ALANET, OCLC. **Networks/Consortia:** Member of Bibliographical Center for Research, Rocky Mountain Region, Inc.; CLASS; MINITEX; Western Council of State Libraries. **Publications:** South Dakota State Library & Archives Newsletter. **Special Catalogs:** South Dakota Union Card Catalog (microfiche). **Staff:** Dorothy Liegl, Dp. State Libn.; Rebecca Bell, Tech.Serv.Libn.; Ann Eichinger, Ref.Libn.; Constance Scofield, Interlib.Coop.Libn.; Rose Oniewski, Doc.Libn.; Ron MacIntyre, Film Serv.Libn.; Daniel Boyd, Dir., Handicapped Serv.; Donna Gilliland, Sch.Lib.Cons.; Gene Meyer, Inst.Lib.Cons.

★12712★
SOUTH DAKOTA STATE LIBRARY & ARCHIVES - SOUTH DAKOTA STATE ARCHIVES (Hist)
800 N. Illinois St.   Phone: (605) 773-3173
Pierre, SD 57501   Lawrence E. Hibpshman, State Archv.
Founded: 1974. **Staff:** Prof 2; Other 1. **Subjects:** South Dakota history, culture and government; Great Plains; government administration. **Holdings:** 500 volumes; 1500 cubic feet of records; 5 cubic feet of photographs; 2000 maps. **Services:** Interlibrary loans (limited); copying; center open to outside users. **Publications:** Guide to holdings; Where Are They Now: Guide to Noncurrent South Dakota School Records. **Formed by the Merger of:** South Dakota State Library and South Dakota State Department of Education & Cultural Affairs - Archives Resource Center.

★12713★
SOUTH DAKOTA STATE SUPREME COURT - LIBRARY (Law)†
State Capitol
Pierre, SD 57501   V. Biddle, Asst.Libn.
Staff: Prof 1; Other 1. **Subjects:** Law. **Holdings:** 27,802 volumes. **Subscriptions:** 53 journals and other serials. **Services:** Library open to public.

★12714★
SOUTH DAKOTA STATE UNIVERSITY - DEPARTMENT OF WILDLIFE & FISHERIES SCIENCES - RESEARCH LIBRARY
Brookings, SD 57007
Founded: 1956. **Subjects:** Wildlife biology, ecology, fishery biology, environmental sciences. **Holdings:** 850 books and bound periodical volumes; 15,000 pamphlets. **Remarks:** Presently inactive.

★12715★
SOUTH DAKOTA STATE UNIVERSITY - HILTON M. BRIGGS LIBRARY (Agri; Sci-Tech)
Box 2115   Phone: (605) 688-5106
Brookings, SD 57007-1098   Dr. Leon Raney, Dean of Lib.
Founded: 1886. **Staff:** Prof 12; Other 15. **Subjects:** Agriculture; pharmacy; engineering - civil, mechanical, electrical; chemistry; entomology; plant pathology; biological sciences; nursing; home economics. **Holdings:** 353,099 books and bound periodical volumes; 345,272 documents; 102,280 microforms. **Subscriptions:** 3187 journals and other serials; 50 newspapers.

Services: Interlibrary loans; library open to public. **Automated Operations:** Computerized cataloging and acquisitions. **Computerized Information Services:** OCLC, DIALOG, BRS. Performs searches on cost recovery basis. Contact Person: Clark Hallman. **Publications:** South Dakota Union List of Serials, 1979. **Special Indexes:** Sioux Falls Argus Leader Index, 1979 to present; Index to SDSU Agricultural Experiment Station and Extension Service Publications, 1975 (punched card; book); South Dakota Farm and Home Research, KWIC Index, 1976 (punched card; book). **Staff:** Iqbal Junaid, Hd., Cat.Dept.; Mary Brady, Hd., Ser.Dept.; Clark Hallman, Hd., Ref.Dept.; Karen Blank, Hd., Circ.Dept.; Bang Kim, Hd., Doc.; Gary Hudson, Hd., Acq.Dept.; Philip Brown, Pub.Serv.Libn.

★12716★
SOUTH FLORIDA REGIONAL PLANNING COUNCIL - LIBRARY (Plan)
3440 Hollywood Blvd., Suite 140   Phone: (305) 961-2999
Hollywood, FL 33021   M. Keegan, Info.Spec.
Founded: 1971. **Staff:** Prof 1. **Subjects:** Planning - regional, transportation, housing, land use, coastal zone, energy. **Holdings:** 8000 books. **Subscriptions:** 150 journals and other serials. **Services:** Interlibrary loans; copying; library open to public. **Automated Operations:** Computerized cataloging. **Formerly:** Located in Miami, FL.

★12717★
SOUTH FLORIDA STATE HOSPITAL - MEDICAL AND PROFESSIONAL LIBRARY (Med)†
1000 S.W. 84th Ave.   Phone: (305) 983-4321
Hollywood, FL 33025   Mabel E. Harvey, Med.Libn.
Staff: 1. **Subjects:** Psychiatry, neurology, psychology, nursing, social work. **Holdings:** 2650 books; 230 bound periodical volumes; cassettes; 3 masters' theses; tape cassettes. **Subscriptions:** 63 journals and other serials. **Services:** Interlibrary loans; copying; library open to public with restrictions.

★12718★
SOUTH GEORGIA MEDICAL CENTER - MEDICAL LIBRARY (Med)
Box 1727   Phone: (912) 333-1160
Valdosta, GA 31603-1727   Susan T. Danner, Med.Libn.
Staff: Prof 1. **Subjects:** Medicine, nursing and allied sciences. **Holdings:** 175 books; 200 bound periodical volumes. **Subscriptions:** 60 journals and other serials. **Services:** Interlibrary loans; copying; current awareness; library open to public with restrictions. **Computerized Information Services:** NLM. **Networks/Consortia:** Member of Southwest Georgia Health Science Library Consortium (SWGHSLC); South Georgia Associated Libraries (SGAL).

★12719★
SOUTH HIGHLANDS HOSPITAL - MEDICAL LIBRARY (Med)*
1127 S. 12th St.   Phone: (205) 250-7703
Birmingham, AL 35205   Dena Metts, Libn.
Founded: 1910. **Staff:** 1. **Subjects:** Medicine, nursing and allied health sciences. **Holdings:** 500 books; 450 bound periodical volumes. **Subscriptions:** 125 journals and other serials. **Services:** Interlibrary loans; library not open to public. **Publications:** Reports of the Hospital, annual.

★12720★
SOUTH HILLS HEALTH SYSTEM - BEHAN HEALTH SCIENCE LIBRARY (Med)
Coal Valley Rd.
Box 18119   Phone: (412) 664-5786
Pittsburgh, PA 15236   William Rose, Dir., Lib./Media Serv.
Founded: 1975. **Staff:** Prof 1. **Subjects:** Medicine, nursing and allied health sciences. **Special Collections:** Dr. Richard J. Behan Memorial Collection (cancer, trauma, legal aspects of medicine, pain, medical monographs). **Holdings:** 2000 books; 150 video cassettes. **Subscriptions:** 80 journals and other serials. **Services:** Interlibrary loans; library not open to public. **Networks/Consortia:** Member of Greater Northeastern Regional Medical Library Program.

★12721★
SOUTH JERSEY REGIONAL FILM LIBRARY (Aud-Vis)
Echelon Urban Ctr., Laurel Rd.   Phone: (609) 772-1642
Voorhees, NJ 08043   Katherine Schalk-Greene, Dir.
Founded: 1970. **Staff:** Prof 1; Other 4. **Subjects:** Films - entertainment, social documentaries, film art, health & safety, classic features, cartoons. **Special Collections:** State Department films; Canadian travelogue documentaries. **Holdings:** 1800 16mm films. **Services:** Interlibrary loans; library open to public with restrictions. **Automated Operations:** Computerized cataloging. **Networks/Consortia:** Member of New Jersey State Library Regional Film Centers. **Publications:** Catalogs, annual.

SOUTH MACOMB HOSPITAL LIBRARY
See: Detroit Macomb Hospital Corporation - South Macomb Hospital Library

★12722★
SOUTH MOUNTAIN LABORATORIES, INC. - LIBRARY (Med)
380 Lackawanna Pl.   Phone: (201) 762-0045
South Orange, NJ 07079   C.N. Mangieri, Dir.
Staff: 15. **Subjects:** Biology, chemistry, medicine, pharmaceutics. **Holdings:** 1000 books; 500 bound periodical volumes. **Subscriptions:** 14 journals and other serials. **Services:** Library not open to public.

★12723★
SOUTH NASSAU COMMUNITIES HOSPITAL - JULES REDISH MEMORIAL MEDICAL LIBRARY (Med)
Oceanside Rd.   Phone: (516) 536-1600
Oceanside, NY 11572   Claire Joseph, Dir.
Subjects: Medicine, surgery, nursing. **Holdings:** 1000 books; 6000 bound periodical volumes. **Subscriptions:** 111 journals and other serials. **Services:** Interlibrary loans; copying; library open to public for reference use only.

★12724★
SOUTH SHORE HOSPITAL - MEDICAL STAFF LIBRARY (Med)*
8015 S. Luella Ave.   Phone: (312) 768-0810
Chicago, IL 60617   Maline Mars, Sec./Libn.
Staff: 1. **Subjects:** Medicine, nursing. **Holdings:** 236 books; 15 sets of bound periodical volumes. **Subscriptions:** 12 journals and other serials. **Services:** Library not open to public. **Automated Operations:** Computerized cataloging.

★12725★
SOUTH STREET SEAPORT MUSEUM - LIBRARY (Hist)
207 Front St.   Phone: (212) 669-9422
New York, NY 10038   Norman J. Brouwer, Ship Hist.
Staff: Prof 1; Other 1. **Subjects:** Maritime history, technology, New York City. **Holdings:** 4000 books; 100 bound periodical volumes. **Services:** Library open to public. **Publications:** Seaport Magazine, quarterly.

★12726★
SOUTH SUBURBAN GENEALOGICAL & HISTORICAL SOCIETY - LIBRARY (Hist)*
Box 96
South Holland, IL 60473   Marilyn Poe Laird, Hd.Libn.
Subjects: Genealogy, local history. **Special Collections:** Eddy Collection; Bishop Collection. **Holdings:** 2131 books; 450 bound periodical volumes; 99 reels of microfilm; federal census, land indexed wills, Bible records, obituaries, family work sheet files. **Subscriptions:** 110 journals and other serials. **Services:** Copying; library open to public. **Publications:** Where the Trails Cross, quarterly. **Special Indexes:** Family sheets of members, wills, Bibles and obituary notices.

★12727★
SOUTH TEXAS COLLEGE OF LAW - LIBRARY (Law)
1220 Polk St.   Phone: (713) 659-8040
Houston, TX 77002   F.H. Thompson, Law Libn.
Founded: 1923. **Staff:** Prof 7; Other 4. **Subjects:** Law. **Holdings:** 203,000 volumes.

★12728★
SOUTHAM COMMUNICATIONS LTD. - LIBRARY (Publ)
1450 Don Mills Rd.   Phone: (416) 445-6641
Don Mills, ON, Canada M3B 2X7   Eileen M. Wise, Libn.
Founded: 1957. **Staff:** Prof 1. **Subjects:** Business, journalism, print advertising, business periodical publishing. **Special Collections:** Southam publications. **Holdings:** 700 books; 500 bound periodical volumes. **Subscriptions:** 38 journals and other serials. **Services:** Copying (limited); library open to outside users with restrictions.

★12729★
SOUTHEAST ALABAMA MEDICAL CENTER - MEDICAL LIBRARY (Med)
Box 6987   Phone: (205) 793-8111
Dothan, AL 36302   Ruth Baxter, Med.Lib.Dir.
Founded: 1963. **Staff:** Prof 1. **Subjects:** General medicine, hospital administration, nursing. **Holdings:** 500 books; 1900 bound periodical volumes; 50 unbound volumes. **Subscriptions:** 75 journals and other serials. **Services:** Copying; library open to public with doctor's permission. **Computerized Information Services:** MEDLARS.

★12730★

SOUTHEAST ASIA RESOURCE CENTER (Area-Ethnic)
Box 4000-D   Phone: (415) 548-2546
Berkeley, CA 94704   Joel Rocamora, Dir.
Staff: Prof 5. **Subjects:** Vietnam, Laos, Kampuchea, Thailand, Philippines, Indonesia. **Holdings:** 500 volumes; 13 drawers of Indochina clipping files, 1971 to present; 15 drawers of other Southeast Asia clipping files, 1976 to present; photograph files; films and video cassettes; anti-war posters; slide programs. **Subscriptions:** 34 journals and other serials; 7 newspapers. **Services:** Copying; center open to public with restrictions. **Publications:** Southeast Asia Chronicle, 6/year - by subscription. **Staff:** Martha Winnacker, Res.Assoc.; Meredith Meek, Off.Mgr.

★12731★

SOUTHEAST HUMAN SERVICES CENTER - LIBRARY (Med)
700 1st Ave., S.   Phone: (701) 235-5354
Fargo, ND 58103   Diane Nordeng, Libn.
Staff: Prof 1. **Subjects:** Mental health, child growth and development, counseling. **Holdings:** 210 books; 4 VF drawers. **Subscriptions:** 12 journals and other serials. **Services:** Interlibrary loans; copying; library open to public with restrictions. **Networks/Consortia:** Member of Valley Medical Network.

★12732★

SOUTHEAST INSTITUTE - LIBRARY (Soc Sci)
Edwards Mountain
Box 2183   Phone: (919) 929-1171
Chapel Hill, NC 27514   Vann Joines, Pres.
Founded: 1969. **Staff:** 5. **Subjects:** Transactional analysis, psychotherapy, family therapy, race relations, Gestalt therapy. **Special Collections:** Audio- and videotapes on racism (not available to public). **Holdings:** 2500 volumes. **Services:** Library open only to institute students.

★12733★

SOUTHEAST LOUISIANA HOSPITAL - PROFESSIONAL LIBRARY (Med)
Box 3850   Phone: (504) 626-8161
Mandeville, LA 70448   Carol C. Adams, Libn.
Staff: Prof 1; Other 1. **Subjects:** Psychiatry, psychology, sociology, psychiatric nursing, human physiology, biochemistry, philosophy. **Holdings:** 3000 books; 2800 bound periodical volumes; 70 other items; 3 VF drawers of doctoral dissertations, pamphlets, state vital statistics reports; 10 newsletters; 216 cassette tapes. **Subscriptions:** 110 journals and other serials; 12 newspapers. **Services:** Interlibrary loans; copying; SDI; library open to public with restrictions. **Publications:** Brochure of Professional Library Services - for internal distribution only.

★12734★

SOUTHEAST METROPOLITAN BOARD OF COOPERATIVE SERVICES - PROFESSIONAL INFORMATION CENTER (Educ)
3301 S. Monaco   Phone: (303) 757-6201
Denver, CO 80222   Lynda Welborn, Mgr./Info.Spec.
Founded: 1968. **Staff:** Prof 2; Other 3. **Subjects:** Education - elementary, secondary, early childhood, special. **Holdings:** 3000 books; textbooks. **Subscriptions:** 300 journals and other serials. **Services:** Interlibrary loans; copying; center open to public for reference use only. **Automated Operations:** Computerized cataloging. **Computerized Information Services:** DIALOG, BRS. **Publications:** SEMBCS Occasional Report, irregular - available by request. **Staff:** Jessica Swaim, Info.Spec.

★12735★

SOUTHEAST MICHIGAN COUNCIL OF GOVERNMENTS - SEMCOG LIBRARY (Plan)
800 Book Bldg.
1249 Washington Blvd.   Phone: (313) 961-4266
Detroit, MI 48226   Pamela L. Lazar, Libn.
Staff: Prof 2. **Subjects:** Economic development, transportation, environmental issues, intergovernmental cooperation, regional planning, public safety. **Holdings:** 9800 books and reports; 23 VF drawers of publications; 9 VF drawers of SEMCOG archives; 7 VF drawers of zoning ordinances; 2900 reports on microfiche. **Subscriptions:** 320 journals and other serials; 13 newspapers. **Services:** Interlibrary loans; copying; SDI; library open to public for reference use only. **Computerized Information Services:** CDC. Performs free searches for members. **Networks/Consortia:** Member of Detroit Associated Libraries Region of Cooperation. **Publications:** Bibliographic accession list, monthly; periodical master list, annual - both for internal distribution only. **Staff:** Katherine Smith, Lib.Techn.

★12736★

SOUTHEAST MICHIGAN REGIONAL FILM LIBRARY (Aud-Vis)
c/o Monroe County Library System
3700 S. Custer Rd.   Phone: (313) 241-5277
Monroe, MI 48161   Bernard A. Margolis, Dir.
Founded: 1975. **Staff:** Prof 1; Other 4. **Special Collections:** 16mm feature films. **Holdings:** 1600 reels of film. **Services:** Library not open to public. **Special Catalogs:** Film catalog, annual. **Staff:** Barbara Bradley, Hd., AV Dept.

★12737★

SOUTHEASTERN BIBLE COLLEGE - ROWE MEMORIAL LIBRARY (Rel-Theol)
2901 Pawnee Ave., S.   Phone: (205) 251-2311
Birmingham, AL 35256   Edith Taff, Libn.
Staff: Prof 1. **Subjects:** Theology, Christian education, missions, church music. **Holdings:** 28,000 books and bound periodical volumes. **Subscriptions:** 159 journals and other serials; 5 newspapers. **Services:** Interlibrary loans; copying; library open to public with restrictions.

★12738★

SOUTHEASTERN COLLEGE OF OSTEOPATHIC MEDICINE - MEDICAL LIBRARY (Med)
1750 N.E. 168th St.   Phone: (305) 947-6130
North Miami Beach, FL 33162   Naomi E. Prussiano, Hd.Med.Libn.
Staff: Prof 2. **Subjects:** Clinical medicine, basic sciences, osteopathy. **Special Collections:** Osteopathic medicine. **Holdings:** 4000 books; 663 bound periodical volumes. **Subscriptions:** 340 journals and other serials. **Services:** Interlibrary loans; copying; library open to public. **Networks/Consortia:** Member of Miami Health Sciences Library Consortium (MHSLC). **Staff:** Jeannette Neushaefer, Asst.Libn.

★12739★

SOUTHEASTERN GENERAL HOSPITAL, INC. - LIBRARY (Med)
300 W. 27th St.
Box 1408   Phone: (919) 738-6441
Lumberton, NC 28358   Ann Stephens, Libn.
Staff: Prof 1. **Subjects:** Medicine, surgery, nursing. **Holdings:** 250 books. **Subscriptions:** 51 journals and other serials. **Services:** Interlibrary loans; copying; SDI; library open to public for reference use only. **Computerized Information Services:** MEDLINE. **Networks/Consortia:** Member of Cape Fear Health Sciences Information Consortium.

★12740★

SOUTHEASTERN LOUISIANA UNIVERSITY - L.A. SIMS MEMORIAL LIBRARY (Educ)
Drawer 896, Univ. Sta.   Phone: (504) 549-2234
Hammond, LA 70402   F. Landon Greaves, Jr., Lib.Dir.
Founded: 1925. **Staff:** Prof 8; Other 16. **Subjects:** Education, mathematics, music, American history. **Special Collections:** Papers of Congressman James H. Morrison. **Holdings:** 235,000 books; 47,000 bound periodical volumes; 91,266 AV items. **Subscriptions:** 1700 journals and other serials; 23 newspapers. **Services:** Interlibrary loans; copying; library open to public for reference use only. **Computerized Information Services:** DIALOG, OCLC. **Networks/Consortia:** Member of SOLINET.

SOUTHEASTERN NEWSPAPERS CORPORATION - AUGUSTA CHRONICLE-HERALD NEWS
See: Augusta Chronicle-Herald News

SOUTHEASTERN OKLAHOMA STATE UNIVERSITY - KERR INDUSTRIAL APPLICATIONS CENTER
See: Kerr Industrial Applications Center

★12741★

SOUTHEASTERN PENNSYLVANIA TRANSPORTATION AUTHORITY - SEPTA LIBRARY (Trans)
841 Chestnut St., 11th Fl.   Phone: (215) 472-1287
Philadelphia, PA 19107   Rena E. Hawes, Libn.
Founded: 1966. **Staff:** Prof 1; Other 1. **Subjects:** Public transportation, commuter railroads, urban planning. **Special Collections:** Urban Traffic and Transportation Board Collection (history and early planning of public transportation in Philadelphia, 300 items). **Holdings:** 5000 books and technical reports; 8 VF drawers of pamphlets; 4 VF drawers of annual reports of other agencies; 8 VF drawers of clippings. **Subscriptions:** 61 journals and other serials; 5 newspapers. **Services:** Interlibrary loans; copying; library open to public by appointment. **Networks/Consortia:** Member of PALINET & Union Library Catalogue of Pennsylvania. **Publications:** Acquisitions List, bimonthly - for internal distribution only; Annual Reports of Agency, 1964 to present - free.

★12742★

SOUTHEASTERN WISCONSIN HEALTH SYSTEMS AGENCY - RESOURCE INFORMATION CENTER (Med)
735 W. Wisconsin Ave., Suite 600   Phone: (414) 271-9788
Milwaukee, WI 53211   Suzy Weisman, Coord.
Founded: 1976. **Staff:** Prof 1. **Subjects:** Health and health facility planning, health care cost containment, health promotion/wellness, hospitals. **Holdings:** 2000 books and unbound reports. **Subscriptions:** 79 journals and other serials. **Services:** Interlibrary loans; copying; center open to public with restrictions on circulation.

★12743★

SOUTHEASTERN WISCONSIN REGIONAL PLANNING COMMISSION - REFERENCE LIBRARY (Plan)
916 N. East Ave.
Box 769
Waukesha, WI 53187-1607   Phone: (414) 547-6721
                                                    Edell M. Peters, Libn.
Founded: 1960. **Staff:** 1. **Subjects:** Regional planning, land use, transportation, population, housing, sewerage, drainage and flood control, environmental quality, parks and open space. **Special Collections:** Publications of Transportation Research Board, Southeastern Wisconsin Regional Planning Commission, Urban Land Institute, American Society of Planning Officials and American Society of Civil Engineers. **Holdings:** 6500 books; census data; weather maps; climatological data. **Subscriptions:** 100 journals and other serials. **Services:** Interlibrary loans; copying; library open to public for reference use only. **Networks/Consortia:** Member of Library Council of Metropolitan Milwaukee, Inc. (LCOMM).

★12744★

SOUTHERN ALBERTA INSTITUTE OF TECHNOLOGY - LEARNING RESOURCES CENTRE (Sci-Tech)
1301 16th Ave., N.W.   Phone: (403) 284-8647
Calgary, AB, Canada T2M 0L4   R.F. Peters, Hd., LRC
Founded: 1920. **Staff:** Prof 7; Other 30. **Subjects:** Electronics, computer technology, business, chemical technology, engineering technology, drafting, art. **Holdings:** 73,628 books; 629 bound periodical volumes; 1260 film titles; 926 videotapes; 615 audiotapes; 14,000 microfiche; 3148 reels of microfilm; 417 film loop and filmstrip titles; 50 VF drawers of pamphlets. **Subscriptions:** 950 journals and newspapers. **Services:** Interlibrary loans; copying; center open to public with permission. **Automated Operations:** Computerized cataloging, acquisitions and circulation. **Computerized Information Services:** DIALOG, SDC, CAN/OLE, Info Globe. **Publications:** Periodicals List, annual; Handbook; Pathfinders. **Staff:** Robert Wilson, Hd., Pub.Serv.Thomas Skinner, Hd., Tech.Serv.

★12745★

SOUTHERN ALBERTA INSTITUTE OF TECHNOLOGY - LEARNING RESOURCES CENTRE - ALBERTA COLLEGE OF ART BRANCH (Art)
1301 16th Ave., N.W.   Phone: (403) 284-8665
Calgary, AB, Canada T2M 0L4   Christine E. Sammon, Libn.
Staff: Prof 2; Other 2. **Subjects:** Art, art history, painting, sculpture, graphic arts, weaving, textiles, pottery, photography, ceramics, advertising art, animation. **Holdings:** 6800 books; 250 bound periodical volumes; 60,000 slides; 3000 mounted prints; 1000 picture clippings; 800 exhibition catalogs. **Subscriptions:** 85 journals and other serials. **Services:** Interlibrary loans; copying; center open to public. **Automated Operations:** Computerized cataloging, acquisitions and circulation. **Publications:** Periodical holdings list. **Special Indexes:** Card indexes for picture, print, pamphlet and art school calendar collections; printouts listing slide collection, generated from a modified Santa Cruz slide classification system; KWIC and KWOC indexes for exhibition catalogs. **Staff:** Monika Croydon, Slide Libn.

SOUTHERN APPALACHIAN ARCHIVES
See: Berea College - Hutchins Library - Special Collections

★12746★

SOUTHERN BAPTIST CONVENTION - FOREIGN MISSION BOARD - ARCHIVES CENTER (Rel-Theol)
3806 Monument Ave.
Box 6767
Richmond, VA 23230   Mary Virginia Currie Jones, Mgr., Rec.Mgt.Sect.
Subjects: Missions. **Holdings:** Board minutes; minutes of missions; administrative correspondence; correspondence with missionaries in the field. **Services:** Center open to qualified users upon request.

★12747★

SOUTHERN BAPTIST CONVENTION - FOREIGN MISSION BOARD - JENKINS RESEARCH CENTER (Rel-Theol)
3806 Monument Ave.
Box 6767
Richmond, VA 23230   Phone: (804) 353-0151
                                                    Mary Virginia Currie Jones, Mgr.
Founded: 1960. **Staff:** Prof 1; Other 2. **Subjects:** Missions, management theory and practice, history, anthropology, travel. **Holdings:** 15,000 books. **Subscriptions:** 500 journals and other serials. **Services:** Interlibrary loans; copying (limited); center open to public by written request and appointment scheduled in advance. **Computerized Information Services:** DIALOG, NEXIS.

★12748★

SOUTHERN BAPTIST CONVENTION - FOREIGN MISSION BOARD - MISSIONARY LEARNING CENTER LIBRARY (Rel-Theol)
Box 6767
Richmond, VA 23230   Cary Ann Geron, Libn.
Founded: 1967. **Staff:** Prof 1. **Subjects:** Religions of the world, theology, culture and customs, history, geography, travel. **Special Collections:** Foreign language Bibles (42). **Holdings:** 4815 books; 24 bound periodical volumes; 28 drawers of country files; slides; filmstrips; tapes; cassette tapes; records. **Subscriptions:** 92 journals and other serials; 20 newspapers. **Services:** Interlibrary loans; library not open to public. **Formerly:** Its Missionary Orientation Library, located in Pine Mountain, GA.

★12749★

SOUTHERN BAPTIST CONVENTION - HISTORICAL COMMISSION - SOUTHERN BAPTIST HISTORICAL LIBRARY & ARCHIVES (Rel-Theol; Hist)
901 Commerce St.   Phone: (615) 251-2660
Nashville, TN 37203   A. Ronald Tonks, Asst.Exec.Dir.
Founded: 1938. **Staff:** Prof 2; Other 1. **Subjects:** Baptist history. **Holdings:** 20,000 books; 1100 linear feet of archival material; 15,000 reels of microfilm. **Subscriptions:** 116 journals and other serials; 100 newspapers. **Automated Operations:** Computerized cataloging. **Computerized Information Services:** Baptist Information Retrieval System (internal database). Contact Person: Charles W. Deweese, 251-2664. **Publications:** Baptist History and Heritage, quarterly - by subscription. **Special Catalogs:** Microfilm catalog. **Special Indexes:** Southern Baptist Periodical Index. **Staff:** Pat Brown, Libn.; Bill Sumners, Archv.; Charles W. Deweese.

SOUTHERN BAPTIST CONVENTION - SUNDAY SCHOOL BOARD - DARGAN-CARVER LIBRARY
See: Dargan-Carver Library

★12750★

SOUTHERN BAPTIST HOSPITAL - LEARNING RESOURCE CENTER (Med)
2700 Napoleon Ave.   Phone: (504) 899-9311
New Orleans, LA 70115   Pauline Fulda, Dir.
Staff: Prof 2; Other 1. **Subjects:** Medicine, nursing, allied health sciences, pastoral care and counseling. **Special Collections:** Harriet L. Mather Archives. **Holdings:** 3333 books; 461 bound periodical volumes; 1509 AV items. **Subscriptions:** 175 journals and other serials; 9 newspapers. **Services:** Interlibrary loans; center not open to public. **Publications:** Library Users' Handbook. **Staff:** Marylynn Rooney, Lib.Asst.

★12751★

SOUTHERN BAPTIST THEOLOGICAL SEMINARY - AUDIOVISUAL CENTER (Aud-Vis)
2825 Lexington Rd.   Phone: (502) 897-4508
Louisville, KY 40280   Andrew B. Rawls, AV Libn.
Staff: Prof 1; Other 4. **Subjects:** Sermons, religious education, theology, church history, Christian missions, pastoral counseling. **Holdings:** 1882 filmstrips; 8421 reel and cassette tapes; 287 16mm motion pictures; 26,792 slides; 2089 phonograph records. **Services:** Center open to public for reference use only.

★12752★

SOUTHERN BAPTIST THEOLOGICAL SEMINARY - BILLY GRAHAM ROOM (Rel-Theol)
2825 Lexington Rd.   Phone: (502) 897-4807
Louisville, KY 40280   Dr. Ronald F. Deering, Libn.
Founded: 1960. **Subjects:** Ministry of Billy Graham - books, sermons, movies and records of revivals throughout the world. **Holdings:** Figures not available. **Services:** Copying; room open to public.

★12753★
SOUTHERN BAPTIST THEOLOGICAL SEMINARY - CHURCH MUSIC LIBRARY
(Mus)
2825 Lexington Rd.   Phone: (502) 897-4712
Louisville, KY 40280   Martha C. Powell, Church Music Libn.
Founded: 1944. Staff: Prof 1; Other 3. Subjects: Hymnody; music - history, education, instruments, choral, folk; musicians; voice; worship. Special Collections: Converse Hymnal Collection; Ingersoll Evangelistic Music Collection (3000 titles); Everett B. Helm Score Collection. Holdings: 15,511 books; 1603 bound periodical volumes; 7464 phonograph records; 3512 phonotapes; 131,728 scores; 269 titles on microfilm. Subscriptions: 96 journals and other serials. Services: Interlibrary loans; copying; library open to public.

★12754★
SOUTHERN BAPTIST THEOLOGICAL SEMINARY - JAMES P. BOYCE
CENTENNIAL LIBRARY (Rel-Theol)
2825 Lexington Rd.   Phone: (502) 897-4807
Louisville, KY 40280   Dr. Ronald F. Deering, Libn.
Founded: 1859. Staff: Prof 7; Other 20. Subjects: Bible, theology, philosophy, psychology, religious education, church history and music, comparative religions, sociology. Special Collections: Baptist Historical Collection. Holdings: 294,700 volumes; 99,032 pamphlets; 26,329 microforms. Subscriptions: 1280 journals and other serials. Services: Interlibrary loans; copying; library open to public. Staff: Nancy Robinson, Cat.; Elsa A. Miller, Acq./Circ.Libn.; Paul M. Debusman, Ref./Ser.Libn.

★12755★
SOUTHERN BELL TELEPHONE AND TELEGRAPH COMPANY - LAW LIBRARY
(Law)
4300 Southern Bell Ctr.   Phone: (404) 529-7937
Atlanta, GA 30375   Cheryl L. McKenzie, Libn.
Staff: Prof 1. Subjects: Law. Holdings: 14,000 volumes. Services: Library not open to public. Networks/Consortia: Member of Atlanta Law Libraries Association.

SOUTHERN BIBLE COLLEGE
See: Messenger College

★12756★
SOUTHERN CALIFORNIA ASSOCIATION OF GOVERNMENTS -
INFORMATION RESOURCE CENTER (Plan)
600 S. Commonwealth Ave.   Phone: (213) 385-1000
Los Angeles, CA 90005   Shelli Snyder, Libn.
Founded: 1974. Staff: Prof 1. Subjects: Transportation, population, land use, housing, water and air quality, public administration, urban planning. Special Collections: Legislative materials. Holdings: 6500 books, reports; 2000 unbound volumes. Subscriptions: 75 journals and other serials. Services: National report distribution; report acquisitions; maps; regional census data center; center open to public by appointment. Special Indexes: Bibliography of association's publications.

SOUTHERN CALIFORNIA CENTER FOR EDUCATIONAL IMPROVEMENT
See: Los Angeles County Superintendent of Schools

★12757★
SOUTHERN CALIFORNIA COLLEGE OF OPTOMETRY - M.B. KETCHUM
MEMORIAL LIBRARY (Med)
2001 Associated Rd.   Phone: (714) 870-7226
Fullerton, CA 92631   Mrs. Pat Carlson, Hd.Libn.
Founded: 1948. Staff: Prof 1; Other 2. Subjects: Optometry, optics, ophthalmology, learning disabilities. Holdings: 7000 books; 4000 bound periodical volumes; 380 theses; 325 AV titles. Subscriptions: 300 serials. Services: Interlibrary loans; copying; SDI; library open to public with restrictions. Computerized Information Services: DIALOG, MEDLINE. Publications: Recent Publications Received, bimonthly - by request.

★12758★
SOUTHERN CALIFORNIA EDISON COMPANY - LIBRARY (Sci-Tech)
2244 Walnut Grove Ave.
Box 800
Rosemead, CA 91770   Phone: (213) 572-2096
     Mary L. Parker, Corp.Libn.
Founded: 1905. Staff: Prof 3; Other 4. Subjects: Electrical engineering and allied fields, nuclear engineering, management. Holdings: 12,332 books; 1253 bound periodical volumes; 33 VF drawers; 67 shelves of government documents; 14 shelves of reports; 1600 reels of microfilm of periodicals. Subscriptions: 570 journals and other serials. Services: Interlibrary loans; copying (limited); library open to public by appointment only. Automated Operations: Computerized cataloging, serials listing and routing.

Computerized Information Services: DIALOG, SDC, BRS, DOE/RECON; internal database. Publications: Library Bulletin, monthly. Staff: Barbara L. Netzley, Asst.Libn.

★12759★
SOUTHERN CALIFORNIA GAS COMPANY - ENGINEERING INFORMATION
CENTER (Energy)
Box 3249, Terminal Annex, ML730D   Phone: (818) 307-2872
Los Angeles, CA 90051   Gordon L. Sandviken, Info.Ctr.Spec.
Founded: 1975. Staff: Prof 1; Other 2. Subjects: Engineering - civil, mechanical, structural; natural gas; energy. Special Collections: Project Collection (20 project holdings). Holdings: 3000 books; 1000 codes. Subscriptions: 252 journals and other serials. Services: Interlibrary loans; copying; center open to public. Automated Operations: Computerized cataloging, acquisitions, serials and circulation. Computerized Information Services: DIALOG, SDC. Performs searches free of charge. Contact Person: Charmaine Hintson, 307-2871. Publications: Acquisitions list, monthly.

SOUTHERN CALIFORNIA GAS COMPANY - PACIFIC LIGHTING
CORPORATION
See: Pacific Lighting Corporation

★12760★
SOUTHERN CALIFORNIA INSTITUTE OF ARCHITECTURE - ARCHITECTURE
AND URBAN PLANNING LIBRARY (Plan)
1800 Berkeley St.   Phone: (213) 829-3482
Santa Monica, CA 90404   Rose Marie Rabin, Libn.
Founded: 1974. Staff: Prof 1; Other 1. Subjects: Urban planning, land use, architecture, environmental protection, future studies. Special Collections: Victor Gruen Collection of speeches and project reprints. Holdings: 3000 books; 7000 pamphlets and VF material; 143 notebooks of newspaper clippings; 10,000 slides; 200 audiotapes; 500 videotapes. Subscriptions: 151 journals and other serials. Services: Interlibrary loans; copying; library open to public for reference use only. Networks/Consortia: Member of The Source Network. Publications: Modern Architecture: Mexico.

★12761★
SOUTHERN CALIFORNIA LIBRARY FOR SOCIAL STUDIES AND RESEARCH
(Soc Sci)
6120 S. Vermont Ave.   Phone: (213) 759-6063
Los Angeles, CA 90044   Sarah Cooper, Dir.
Founded: 1963. Staff: Prof 3; Other 8. Subjects: Labor; Communism; Marxism; liberalism; black, Chicano and women's movements; southern California grassroots organizations. Special Collections: Civil Rights Congress (Los Angeles area) archival records; Harry Bridges papers on deportation trials; Los Angeles Committee for the Protection of the Foreign Born records; personal manuscript collections from Charlotta A. Bass, Richard Gladstein, Robert W. Kenny and Earl Robinson. Holdings: 35,000 books; 30,000 pamphlets; 3500 tapes; 500,000 news clippings; 600 VF drawers of periodicals and files from labor, peace and civil rights organizations, 1930s to the present; 50 documentary films, 1930s-1970s. Services: Copying; library open to public. Publications: Catalog of surplus books, pamphlets, tapes; Heritage (newsletter), bimonthly.

★12762★
SOUTHERN CALIFORNIA PERMANENTE MEDICAL CENTER - HEALTH
SCIENCES LIBRARY/MEDIA CENTER (Med)
9400 E. Rosecrans Ave.   Phone: (213) 920-4247
Bellflower, CA 90706   Geraldine N. Graves, Dir., Lib.Serv.
Founded: 1965. Staff: Prof 2; Other 4. Subjects: Medicine and medical specialties, nursing. Holdings: 3662 books; 3600 bound periodical volumes; 1200 Audio-Digest tapes; 2 VF drawers of pamphlets; AV materials. Subscriptions: 319 journals and other serials. Services: Interlibrary loans; copying; library open to community physicians and paramedical personnel, students majoring in health sciences. Automated Operations: Computerized cataloging, serials and circulation. Computerized Information Services: MEDLINE; KENO (internal database). Networks/Consortia: Member of Pacific Southwest Regional Medical Library Service (PSRMLS). Publications: Library Newsletter - for internal distribution only. Special Catalogs: Computerized union book catalog of all Kaiser libraries in southern region. Staff: Dennis Ritchey, Asst.Dir.

★12763★
SOUTHERN CALIFORNIA PSYCHOANALYTIC INSTITUTE - FRANZ
ALEXANDER LIBRARY (Med)
9024 Olympic Blvd.   Phone: (213) 276-2455
Beverly Hills, CA 90211   Lena Pincus, Libn.
Founded: 1950. Staff: Prof 1. Subjects: Psychoanalysis, psychiatry, psychology. Holdings: 3800 books and bound periodical volumes; 2200

reprints. **Subscriptions:** 34 journals and other serials. **Services:** Interlibrary loans; copying; library open to public with restrictions. **Publications:** Bulletin: Southern California Psychoanalytic Institute and Society, 3/year - to members.

★12764★
SOUTHERN CALIFORNIA RAPID TRANSIT DISTRICT - INFORMATION CENTER LIBRARY (Trans)
425 S. Main St.   Phone: (213) 972-6467
Los Angeles, CA 90013   Nola Wolf, Libn.
Founded: 1971. **Staff:** Prof 3. **Subjects:** Urban mass transit, parent organization history. **Holdings:** 20,000 books and bound periodical volumes; 1100 reports on microfiche; 50 maps. **Subscriptions:** 75 journals and other serials. **Services:** Interlibrary loans; copying; library open to public with restrictions. **Automated Operations:** Computerized cataloging. **Computerized Information Services:** DIALOG, LEXIS, NEXIS, OCLC. **Staff:** Robert Bremer, Asst.Libn.

★12765★
SOUTHERN CALIFORNIA SOCIETY FOR PSYCHICAL RESEARCH, INC. - LIBRARY (Rel-Theol)
Box 3901   Phone: (213) 936-0904
Thousand Oaks, CA 91359   Andrew T. Shields, Lib.Coord.
Founded: 1968. **Subjects:** Parapsychology. **Special Collections:** Journal of Parapsychology (50); Journal of the American Society for Psychic Research (300); rare books by early psychical researchers (100); UFOs (15 books). **Holdings:** 1000 books; 18 bound periodical volumes. **Subscriptions:** 8 journals and other serials. **Services:** Library open to public for reference use only by appointment. **Publications:** Southern California Society for Psychical Research Monthly Bulletin.

SOUTHERN CENTER FOR STUDIES IN PUBLIC POLICY
See: Clark College

★12766★
SOUTHERN COLLEGE - LIBRARY (Sci-Tech; Bus-Fin)*
5600 Lake Underhill Rd.   Phone: (305) 273-1000
Orlando, FL 32807   Mary Love Hammond, Libn.
Staff: Prof 1; Other 2. **Subjects:** Dental assistance and laboratory technology, interior design, data processing and computer programming, fashion merchandising, law. **Holdings:** 4340 books; 1574 unbound periodicals; 1747 slides; 16 film cassettes; 8 filmstrips. **Subscriptions:** 39 journals and other serials. **Services:** Copying; library open to public for reference use only.

★12767★
SOUTHERN COLLEGE OF OPTOMETRY - WILLIAM P. MAC CRACKEN, JR. MEMORIAL LIBRARY (Med)
1245 Madison Ave.   Phone: (901) 725-0180
Memphis, TN 38104   Nancy Gatlin, Dir.
Founded: 1938. **Staff:** Prof 2; Other 2. **Subjects:** Optometry, optics, ophthalmology, psychology, exceptional education. **Holdings:** 13,458 books; 3506 bound periodical volumes; 12,302 slides; 332 microfiche; 156 reels of microfilm; 191 video cassettes. **Subscriptions:** 207 journals and other serials. **Services:** Interlibrary loans; copying; library open to public for reference use only. **Automated Operations:** Computerized cataloging, acquisitions and serials. **Computerized Information Services:** DIALOG; internal database. Performs searches on cost recovery basis. **Networks/Consortia:** Member of Association of Memphis Area Health Science Libraries; Association of Visual Science Librarians. **Special Indexes:** Vision Science Index (online); ocular pathology slide index. **Staff:** Deborah Lawless, Asst.Dir.

SOUTHERN COLLEGE OF PHARMACY
See: Mercer University

★12768★
SOUTHERN COLORADO ECONOMIC DEVELOPMENT DISTRICT - REGIONAL PLANNING & DEVELOPMENT CENTER - DATA FILE (Plan)
3418 N. Elizabeth   Phone: (303) 543-6006
Pueblo, CO 81008   Don Vest, Libn.
Founded: 1967. **Staff:** 1. **Subjects:** Regional development for Southern Colorado - cities, counties, regional data, industrial location. **Holdings:** 1700 books and bound periodical volumes. **Services:** Compilation of statistical data for public agencies on request; library open to public with restrictions. **Publications:** District Digest (newsletter), monthly; annual report.

★12769★
SOUTHERN CONNECTICUT STATE UNIVERSITY - H.C. BULEY LIBRARY - SPECIAL COLLECTIONS (Hist; Hum)
501 Crescent St.   Phone: (203) 397-4505
New Haven, CT 06515   Claire Bennett, Spec.Coll.Libn.
Founded: 1893. **Special Collections:** Connecticut Room (6300 volumes; 24 VF drawers); Carolyn Sherwin Bailey Historical Collection of Children's Books (2300 volumes); government documents (120,000); archives (25 VF drawers); Hartford Times newspaper morgue (300 VF drawers). **Services:** Interlibrary loans; copying; collections open to public with restrictions. **Special Catalogs:** Catalog of Carolyn Sherwin Bailey Children's Collection (printed). **Staff:** Julia Kobus, Docs.

SOUTHERN ENERGY/ENVIRONMENTAL INFORMATION CENTER (SEEIC)
See: Southern States Energy Board (SSEB)

SOUTHERN FOREST EXPERIMENT STATION LIBRARY
See: U.S. Forest Service

★12770★
SOUTHERN FOREST PRODUCTS ASSOCIATION - LIBRARY (Bus-Fin)
Box 52468   Phone: (504) 443-4464
New Orleans, LA 70152   Ivy Riley, Libn.
Staff: Prof 1. **Subjects:** Lumber industry economics. **Special Collections:** History of Southern Pine Association/Southern Forest Products Association. **Holdings:** Figures not available. **Subscriptions:** 18 journals and other serials. **Services:** Interlibrary loans; library not open to public. **Publications:** List of association publications and films available for purchase - free upon request.

★12771★
SOUTHERN HIGHLAND HANDICRAFT GUILD - FOLK ART CENTER LIBRARY (Art)
Box 9545   Phone: (704) 298-7928
Asheville, NC 28815   James Gentry, Dir.
Staff: Prof 1; Other 6. **Subjects:** History and traditional and contemporary crafts of the southern highlands. **Special Collections:** Goodrich Collection; textiles study collection; craft objects (750). **Holdings:** 1600 books; historical materials. **Subscriptions:** 15 journals and other serials. **Services:** Library open to public on a limited schedule and by appointment. **Publications:** Bibliographies. **Remarks:** Library located at Blue Ridge Parkway and Riceville Road, Asheville, NC 28805.

SOUTHERN HIGHLANDS RESEARCH CENTER
See: University of North Carolina, Asheville

★12772★
SOUTHERN ILLINOIS UNIVERSITY - SCHOOL OF MEDICINE - MEDICAL LIBRARY (Med)
801 N. Rutledge
Box 3926   Phone: (217) 782-2658
Springfield, IL 62708   Rick Dilley, Act.Dir.
Founded: 1970. **Staff:** Prof 7; Other 16. **Subjects:** Medical sciences. **Special Collections:** History of medicine (3000 volumes). **Holdings:** 39,000 books; 45,000 bound periodical volumes; 1200 reels of microfilm; 3500 AV items. **Subscriptions:** 1800 journals and other serials. **Services:** Interlibrary loans; copying; library open to public. **Automated Operations:** Computerized cataloging, serials and circulation. **Computerized Information Services:** MEDLINE, DIALOG, OCLC, BRS, Library Computer System (LCS). Performs free searches for primary users; on cost recovery basis to others. Contact Person: Jean Crampon. **Networks/Consortia:** Member of Greater Midwest Regional Medical Library Network (Region 3); ILLINET; Sangamon Valley Academic Library Consortium. **Special Catalogs:** Subject and title listings of current subscriptions; subject guide to AV collection. **Staff:** Jean Crampon, Hd.Ref.Libn.; Gail Hitchcock, Acq.Libn.; Kathryn Harris, User Serv.; Joyce Horney, ILL Libn.; Philip Metzger, Spec.Coll.Libn.

★12773★
SOUTHERN ILLINOIS UNIVERSITY, CARBONDALE - EDUCATION AND PSYCHOLOGY DIVISION LIBRARY (Educ; Info Sci)
Morris Library   Phone: (618) 453-2274
Carbondale, IL 62901   Dr. Ruth Bauner, Educ. & Psych.Libn.
Founded: 1950. **Staff:** Prof 4; Other 1. **Subjects:** Education, guidance, psychology, sports and recreation, library science. **Special Collections:** John Dewey Collection; historical children's book collection. **Holdings:** 128,500 books; 31,670 bound periodical volumes; 33,000 other volumes in instructional materials center (curriculum guides, children's literature, textbooks). **Subscriptions:** 1300 journals and other serials. **Services:** Interlibrary loans; copying; library open to public for reference use only. **Automated Operations:** Computerized cataloging and circulation.

Computerized Information Services: DIALOG, SDC, OCLC, BRS. Networks/ Consortia: Member of ILLINET. Publications: Periodicals List, cumulative supplements, printed; Index to Theses and Dissertations, 1949-1972, printed - both sent to libraries in state, and for sale. Staff: Dr. Kathy Cook, Asst.Libn.Mary Isbell, Asst.Libn.; Lorene Pixley, Asst.Libn.

★12774★
SOUTHERN ILLINOIS UNIVERSITY, CARBONDALE - HUMANITIES DIVISION LIBRARY (Hum)
Morris Library   Phone: (618) 536-3391
Carbondale, IL 62901   Alan M. Cohn, Hum.Libn.
Founded: 1956. Staff: Prof 4; Other 1. Subjects: Literature, linguistics, music, art, philosophy, religion, speech, theater, journalism. Holdings: 505,000 books; 83,000 bound periodical volumes; 85,000 microtexts; 15,500 phonograph records; 25,000 prints. Subscriptions: 3600 journals and other serials. Services: Interlibrary loans; copying; library open to public for reference use only. Automated Operations: Computerized cataloging and circulation. Computerized Information Services: OCLC, DIALOG, SDC. Networks/Consortia: Member of ILLINET. Publications: Periodicals List, cumulative supplements, printed; Index to Theses and Dissertations, 1949-1972, printed - both sent to libraries in state, and for sale. Staff: Angela Rubin, Asst.Libn.; Dr. Theophil Otto, Asst.Libn.; Annie Woodbridge, Asst.Libn.

★12775★
SOUTHERN ILLINOIS UNIVERSITY, CARBONDALE - SCHOOL OF LAW LIBRARY (Law)
                                              Phone: (618) 536-7711
Carbondale, IL 62901   Elizabeth Slusser Kelly, Law Lib.Dir.
Founded: 1973. Staff: Prof 6; Other 12. Subjects: Law. Special Collections: Mining law; water law (208 water quality plans); federal and state government documents depository. Holdings: 225,000 volumes. Subscriptions: 5820 journals and other serials. Services: Interlibrary loans; copying; library open to public. Automated Operations: Computerized cataloging and ILL. Computerized Information Services: Westlaw, LEXIS, OCLC. Networks/Consortia: Member of ILLINET; Mid-America Law School Library Consortium. Publications: Recent Acquisitions and Developments, irregular - to campus and other libraries. Staff: Christopher J. Noe, Ref./Instr.Serv.Libn.; Elizabeth W. Matthews, Cat.Libn.; Kay L. Andrus, Rd.Serv.Libn.; Heija B. Ryoo, Acq./Ser.Libn.; Laurel A. Wendt, Automation/Res.Libn.

★12776★
SOUTHERN ILLINOIS UNIVERSITY, CARBONDALE - SCIENCE DIVISION LIBRARY (Sci-Tech)
Morris Library   Phone: (618) 453-2700
Carbondale, IL 62901   George W. Black, Sci.Libn.
Founded: 1956. Staff: Prof 4; Other 1. Subjects: Agriculture, science, medicine, engineering. Holdings: 180,000 books; 150,000 bound periodical volumes; 2200 theses; 205,000 maps and aerial photographs; 9600 serial reports on microfilm; 1500 books on microfilm. Subscriptions: 5000 journals and other serials. Services: Interlibrary loans; copying; library open for reference to nonregistered users. Automated Operations: Computerized cataloging and circulation. Computerized Information Services: DIALOG, SDC, BRS, OCLC. Networks/Consortia: Member of ILLINET. Publications: Index to Theses and Dissertations, 1949-1972, printed - sent to libraries in state, and for sale. Staff: Kathy Fahey, Asst.Sci.Libn.; Jean Ray, Asst.Sci./Map Libn.; Andrew Tax, Asst.Sci./Med.Libn.

★12777★
SOUTHERN ILLINOIS UNIVERSITY, CARBONDALE - SOCIAL STUDIES DIVISION LIBRARY (Soc Sci)
Morris Library   Phone: (618) 453-2708
Carbondale, IL 62901   James Fox, Soc.Stud.Libn.
Founded: 1956. Staff: Prof 5; Other 1. Subjects: Anthropology, business, economics, geography, history, political science, sociology, Latin American studies. Holdings: 299,000 books; 95,000 bound periodical volumes; 307,000 U.S. government documents in hardcopy; 140,350 government documents on microfiche; 57 cabinets of Human Relations Area Files; one file of Classified Abstract Archive of Alcohol Literature; 10 VF drawers; microprints of U.S. government documents (1953-1976 ND, 1956-1976 D), British Sessional Papers (1731 to present), and American Antiquarian Society's early American newspapers and imprints; 53,950 reels of microfilm of newspapers, journals, National Archives material. Subscriptions: 3476 journals and other serials; 84 newspapers. Services: Interlibrary loans; copying; library open to public. Automated Operations: Computerized cataloging and circulation. Computerized Information Services: DIALOG, SDC, OCLC. Networks/Consortia: Member of ILLINET. Publications: Periodicals list, cumulative supplements, printed; Index to Theses and Dissertations, 1949-1972, printed - both sent to libraries in state, and for

sale. Staff: Charles Holliday, Asst.Soc.Stud.Libn.Carlos Marquez-Sterling, Asst.Soc.Stud.Libn.; Catherine Martinsek, Asst.Soc.Stud.Libn.; Walter Stubbs, Asst.Soc.Stud.Libn.

★12778★
SOUTHERN ILLINOIS UNIVERSITY, CARBONDALE - SPECIAL COLLECTIONS (Rare Book)
Morris Library   Phone: (618) 453-2516
Carbondale, IL 62901   David V. Koch, Cur./Archv.
Founded: 1956. Staff: Prof 5; Other 2. Special Collections: Irish Literary Renaissance; 20th century British and American literature, theater and philosophy; private press books (Black Sun, Trovillion, Nash, Cuala); Southern Illinois history; Ulysses S. Grant; John Dewey; Paul Weiss; James K. Feibleman; Open Court Press; Christian Century Magazine; Henry Nelson Wieman; Robert Graves; James Joyce; D.H. Lawrence; Richard Aldington; Lawrence Durrell; Erwin Piscator; Henry Miller; Kay Boyle; university archives. Holdings: 40,000 books; 600,000 manuscripts and letters. Services: Copying; collection open to qualified scholars. Automated Operations: Computerized cataloging and circulation. Computerized Information Services: OCLC. Networks/Consortia: Member of ILLINET. Publications: Catalogs of special exhibits; Bibliographic Contributions; ICarbS, semiannual journal. Staff: Jane Lockrem, Libn.; Shelley Cox, Libn.; Louisa Bowen, Mss.;Anne Sims, Archv.

★12779★
SOUTHERN ILLINOIS UNIVERSITY, CARBONDALE - UNDERGRADUATE LIBRARY
Morris Library   Phone: (618) 453-2818
Carbondale, IL 62901   Dr. Judith Ann Harwood, Libn.
Founded: 1971. Staff: Prof 4; Other 3. Subjects: Automotive technology, thanatology, cinema and photography, women's studies, radio and television, general studies. Holdings: 92,686 books; 7529 bound periodical volumes; 2086 reels of microfilm. Subscriptions: 503 journals and other serials. Services: Interlibrary loans; library open to public. Automated Operations: Computerized cataloging and circulation. Computerized Information Services: DIALOG, BRS, OCLC. Networks/Consortia: Member of ILLINET. Publications: Periodicals list, cumulative supplements, printed; Index to Theses and Dissertations, 1949-1972, printed - both sent to libraries in state, and for sale. Staff: Wilma Lampman, Asst.Libn.; Roland Person, Asst.Libn.; Willie Scott, Asst.Libn.

★12780★
SOUTHERN ILLINOIS UNIVERSITY, EDWARDSVILLE - DOCUMENTS COLLECTION (Info Sci)
Lovejoy Library   Phone: (618) 692-2606
Edwardsville, IL 62026-1001   Robert J. Fortado, Doc.Libn.
Staff: Prof 1; Other 1. Holdings: 422,401 U.S. government documents (U.S. Depository). Services: Interlibrary loans; copying; collection open to public. Automated Operations: Computerized cataloging and circulation. Computerized Information Services: OCLC, Library Computer System (LCS), DIALOG; internal database.

★12781★
SOUTHERN ILLINOIS UNIVERSITY, EDWARDSVILLE - EDUCATION LIBRARY (Educ)†
Lovejoy Library   Phone: (618) 692-2906
Edwardsville, IL 62026-1001   Don Smith, Educ.Libn.
Founded: 1964. Staff: Prof 2; Other 1. Subjects: Education, guidance, physical education, psychology, library science. Special Collections: Instructional materials (13,014); rare textbooks (29 shelves). Holdings: 59,698 books; 18 shelves of pamphlets; periodicals on microfilm; 3000 college catalogs; ERIC microfiche (182,536 titles). Services: Interlibrary loans; copying; library open to public for reference use only. Computerized Information Services: DIALOG. Special Indexes: School texts; curriculum guides; college catalogs; teaching aids; children's collection.

★12782★
SOUTHERN ILLINOIS UNIVERSITY, EDWARDSVILLE - HUMAN SERVICES LIBRARY (Soc Sci)
SIU Box 24   Phone: (618) 692-2881
Edwardsville, IL 62026   Nancy Bramhall, Sec.
Founded: 1971. Staff: 1. Subjects: Law enforcement, organization and administration, research methodology, community based programs, juvenile delinquency, corrections, minority groups, urban affairs, sociology, psychology, education. Holdings: 1200 books; 50 bound periodical volumes. Subscriptions: 21 journals and other serials. Services: Library open to S.I.U. students and staff. Automated Operations: Computerized serials. Publications: Human Services Library Inventory and Supplement, semiannual.

★12783★
SOUTHERN ILLINOIS UNIVERSITY, EDWARDSVILLE - HUMANITIES & FINE
    ARTS LIBRARY (Art; Hum)
Lovejoy Library   Phone: (618) 692-2670
Edwardsville, IL 62026-1001
Founded: 1963. Staff: Prof 2; Other 2. Subjects: Literature, art, music,
philosophy, religion, speech, theater, mass communication. Holdings:
177,939 books; 26,000 bound periodical volumes; 25,000 phonograph
records; 250,000 items in music collections; 19th and early 20th century
sheet music; silent movie orchestra scores; stock band charts from a radio
orchestra library; violin and flute music. Subscriptions: 1591 journals and
other serials. Services: Interlibrary loans; copying; library open to public.
Automated Operations: Computerized cataloging and circulation.
Computerized Information Services: BRS, DIALOG, OCLC, Library Computer
System (LCS). Performs searches on cost recovery basis. Contact Person:
Charlotte Johnson, 692-3828. Staff: John Neal Hoover, Fine Arts Libn.;
Richard Reilly, Hum.Libn.

★12784★
SOUTHERN ILLINOIS UNIVERSITY, EDWARDSVILLE - RESEARCH &
    PROJECTS OFFICE LIBRARY (Info Sci)
Graduate School   Phone: (618) 692-3162
Edwardsville, IL 62026-1001   Kate Chappell, Rsrcs.Anl.
Founded: 1970. Staff: Prof 1. Subjects: Federal, state and private grant
support; federal legislation. Holdings: 15 VF drawers of federal and state
program guidelines and applications; education directories; foundation annual
reports; directories of federal and private grant support. Subscriptions: 20
newsletters. Services: Library open to public for reference use only.
Computerized Information Services: IRIS (Illinois Researcher Information
System; internal database). Publications: Research Highlights, monthly -
distributed to faculty and staff.

★12785★
SOUTHERN ILLINOIS UNIVERSITY, EDWARDSVILLE - SCIENCE LIBRARY
    (Sci-Tech)
Lovejoy Library   Phone: (618) 692-3828
Edwardsville, IL 62026-1001   Charlotte Johnson, Sci.Libn.
Founded: 1962. Staff: Prof 1; Other 1. Subjects: Biology, chemistry,
mathematics, nursing, physics, engineering. Holdings: 102,140 books;
33,500 bound periodical volumes. Subscriptions: 1636 journals and other
serials. Services: Interlibrary loans; copying; library open to public.
Computerized Information Services: DIALOG.

★12786★
SOUTHERN ILLINOIS UNIVERSITY, EDWARDSVILLE - SOCIAL SCIENCE/
    BUSINESS/MAP LIBRARY (Soc Sci; Bus-Fin)†
Lovejoy Library   Phone: (618) 692-2422
Edwardsville, IL 62026-1001   Marvin Soloman, Soc.Sci./Map Libn.
Founded: 1962. Staff: Prof 2; Other 3. Subjects: History, business,
economics, earth science, anthropology, government, sociology, social work,
law, geography, military and naval science, urban affairs. Special Collections:
Commissioner Gordon Bush papers (26 linear feet); Etienne Cabet collection
(1600 manuscript pages; 33 volumes); Flagg Collection (11 manuscript
boxes); Congressman Frank Fries papers (20 linear feet); Harold J. Gibbons
papers (160 linear feet); Illinois Coal Reports (70 volumes); Mayor William E.
Mason papers (100 linear feet); Metro-East Journal (East St. Louis, IL)
Collection (135 VF drawers of clippings; 1300 pamphlets; 600 reels of
microfilm); proceedings of the East St. Louis City Council, 1959-1974 (3
reels of microfilm); Waldo E. Stephens Collection (7 linear feet; 200 titles);
Slavic American Collection; Mayor James E. Williams Papers (60 linear feet);
London; arctic regions; Mayor Alvin G. Fields Collection (5 VF drawers);
George T. Wilkens papers (33 linear feet). Holdings: 230,700 books; 32,240
bound periodical volumes; 77,930 other cataloged items; 111,830 maps; 94
shelves of U.N. documents; 6145 aerial photographs; 450 reels of
microfilmed dissertations. Subscriptions: 4043 journals and other serials.
Services: Interlibrary loans; copying; library open to public. Computerized
Information Services: DIALOG, RLIN, OCLC. Networks/Consortia: Member
of ILLINET. Staff: Donald Thompson, Bus.Libn.

★12787★
SOUTHERN MAINE VOCATIONAL TECHNICAL INSTITUTE - LIBRARY (Sci-
    Tech)
Fort Rd.   Phone: (207) 799-7303
South Portland, ME 04106   Donald A. Bertsch, Jr., Libn.
Staff: Prof 1; Other 1. Subjects: Electronics, marine science, building
technology, culinary arts, plant and soil sciences, nursing and allied health
sciences. Holdings: 15,000 books. Subscriptions: 250 journals and other
serials; 10 newspapers. Services: Interlibrary loans; copying; SDI; library
open to public. Networks/Consortia: Member of Health Science Library and

Information Cooperative of Maine.

★12788★
SOUTHERN METHODIST UNIVERSITY - BRIDWELL LIBRARY - CENTER FOR
    METHODIST STUDIES (Rel-Theol)
                                        Phone: (214) 692-2363
Dallas, TX 75275   Rev. Roger L. Loyd, Assoc.Libn.
Founded: 1956. Staff: Prof 1. Subjects: Methodist Church (U.S.), Methodist
Church in England, Church of England, Wesleyana, 18th century theological
literature, Methodist hymnology. Special Collections: Bishop Edwin D.
Mouzon Collection; Bishop John M. Moore Collection; Bishop Frederick D.
Leete Collection; Papers of Bishops Charles C. Selecman, A. Frank Smith,
Hiram Abiff Boaz, Paul E. Martin, William C. Martin, Lance Webb, O. Eugene
Slater, William X. Ninde, Kenneth Pope. Holdings: 205 VF drawers of
manuscripts. Services: Center open to qualified scholars. Formerly: Its
Methodist Historical Collections. Staff: Richard Heitzenrater, Dir.; Wanda
Smith, Res.Assoc.

★12789★
SOUTHERN METHODIST UNIVERSITY - DEGOLYER LIBRARY - FIKES HALL
    OF SPECIAL COLLECTIONS (Hist; Trans)
Central University Libraries, SMU Sta. Phone: (214) 692-2253
Dallas, TX 75275   Clifton H. Jones, Dir.
Founded: 1956. Staff: Prof 5; Other 4. Subjects: Western United States
history, history of the Spanish borderlands, history of the American railroad,
history and technology of transportation. Special Collections: E.L. DeGolyer,
Sr. papers; Baldwin Locomotive Works papers; S.M. Vauclain papers; John
Insley Blair papers; Texas and Pacific Railway papers; Muskogee Corporation
papers; archival collections reported regularly to National Union Catalog of
Manuscript Collection. Holdings: 80,000 monographs; 5000 periodical
volumes; 300,000 railroad photographs; 1500 cubic feet of manuscript and
archival collections; 3000 reels of microfilm. Subscriptions: 400 journals and
other serials. Services: Copying; library open to public. Automated
Operations: Computerized indexing and processing of manuscripts and
photographs. Computerized Information Services: OCLC; internal database.
Networks/Consortia: Member of AMIGOS Bibliographic Council, Inc.
Publications: DeGolyer Library Publication Series, irregular; occasional
publications, irregular. Special Catalogs: Finding aids to processed
manuscript, serial, photograph and archival collections available; chronological
file to all printed holdings. Staff: James W. Phillips, Sr.Bibliog.; Dawn Letson,
Mss.Cur.; Sally Gross, Assoc.Cur./Printed Coll.; Deborah Carpenter,
Asst.Libn./Printed Coll.

★12790★
SOUTHERN METHODIST UNIVERSITY - FORT BURGWIN RESEARCH
    CENTER - LIBRARY & HERBARIUM (Sci-Tech)*
Box 314   Phone: (505) 758-8322
Ranchos de Taos, NM 87557
Founded: 1957. Staff: Prof 1; Other 3. Subjects: Anthropology, biology,
ecology, geology, linguistics. Special Collections: Herbarium of flora of
Carson National Forest; Pollen Reference Collection for modern and
paleoenvironments; Taos and Llano Estacado. Holdings: 2500 books; 800
bound periodical volumes. Subscriptions: 80 journals and other serials.
Services: Library open to visiting scholars by arrangement. Publications: List
of publications - available upon request.

★12791★
SOUTHERN METHODIST UNIVERSITY - MC CORD THEATER COLLECTION
    (Theater)
Fondren Library   Phone: (214) 692-2400
Dallas, TX 75275   Edyth Renshaw, Cur.
Staff: 1. Subjects: Theater, opera, vaudeville, cinema, dance, radio,
television. Special Collections: Texas Theater; Dallas Little Theater; Arden
Club Collection; Corsicana Opera House Collections (records and artifacts);
Harriet Bacon McDonald Collection of photographs. Holdings: Archival
material, photographs and clippings; theater and cinema realia. Services:
Copying; library open to public by appointment. Publications: McCord Theater
Collection (pamphlet).

★12792★
SOUTHERN METHODIST UNIVERSITY - PERKINS SCHOOL OF THEOLOGY -
    LIBRARY (Rel-Theol)
Bridwell Library   Phone: (214) 692-3483
Dallas, TX 75275   Jerry D. Campbell, Libn.
Founded: 1915. Staff: Prof 6; Other 6. Subjects: Theology, history of the
Methodist Church, Texas history, Judaica, archeology as related to biblical
study, linguistics (Greek and Hebrew), art, Egyptology, early printing. Special
Collections: New Thought Archive; Levi Olan Collection of Fine Books; Robert
and Lessie Curl Collection of New Testament Literature; Joseph Walker Elston

III Collection of David Hume; Violet Hayden Joyce Collection; George Leinwall James Joyce Collection; Corey Collection; Thomas J. Harrison Bible Collection; Ferguson Collection of Texana and Americana; Gutenberg Leaf Collection; Laura and Carl Brannin Collection of Religion in Social Action; Selecman Savonarola Collection; Margaret Bridwell Bowdle Collection of Fifteenth Century Printing; Bridwell-DeBellis Collection of Fifteenth Century Printing; Steindorff Collection of Egyptology; William Perry Bentley Collection on psychical research, parapsychology and cognate subjects; Archives of the Perkins School of Theology (56 boxes); Methodist manuscripts collection (108 boxes). **Holdings:** 175,700 books; 26,300 bound periodical volumes; 2183 reels of microfilm; 52,046 microfiche. **Subscriptions:** 554 journals and other serials. **Services:** Interlibrary loans; copying; library restricted to registered patrons. **Automated Operations:** Computerized cataloging and ILL. **Computerized Information Services:** OCLC. **Networks/Consortia:** Member of AMIGOS Bibliographic Council, Inc. **Staff:** Roger L. Loyd, Assoc.Libn.; Page Thomas, Tech.Serv. & ILL; Laura Randall, Cat.; Linda Umoh, Cat.; Alice Mongold, Per.

★12793★
SOUTHERN METHODIST UNIVERSITY - SCIENCE/ENGINEERING LIBRARY (Sci-Tech)
Phone: (214) 692-2276
Dallas, TX 75275 Devertt D. Bickston, Libn.
Founded: 1961. **Staff:** Prof 5; Other 7. **Subjects:** Biology, botany, chemistry, engineering, geology, mathematics, physics, statistics. **Special Collections:** E. DeGolyer Collection (petroleum, history of geology, guide books); Edwin Foscue Map Library; SMU Herbarium with Lloyd Shinners Collection of Taxonomic Botany. **Holdings:** 173,000 books; 69,000 bound periodical volumes; 360,000 government documents; 182,000 maps. **Subscriptions:** 1500 journals and other serials. **Services:** Interlibrary loans; copying; library open to public. **Computerized Information Services:** DIALOG, SDC, BRS. Performs searches on cost recovery basis. **Networks/Consortia:** Member of Association for Higher Education of North Texas - Library Committee (AHE). **Publications:** Proofs S/E Library Bulletin - for internal distribution only. **Remarks:** Business and industrial special libraries should contact Industrial Information Services at (214) 692-2271 for service. **Staff:** Jim Stephens, Spec. Projects Libn.; Sandra Setnick, Ref.Libn.; Mary Ellen Batchelor, Ref.Libn.; Leslie Green, Ref.Libn.

★12794★
SOUTHERN METHODIST UNIVERSITY - UNDERWOOD LAW LIBRARY (Law)
Phone: (214) 692-3258
Dallas, TX 75275 Earl C. Borgeson, Libn.
Staff: Prof 10; Other 13. **Subjects:** International law and business, commercial transactions, corporations, securities, taxation, jurisprudence, oil and gas. **Holdings:** 304,248 volumes. **Subscriptions:** 4828 journals and other serials. **Services:** Interlibrary loans; copying. **Automated Operations:** Computerized cataloging. **Computerized Information Services:** LEXIS, Westlaw. Performs searches for law school only. **Publications:** Doing Business Abroad, 1982; Doing Business with the People's Republic of China, 1983 - both for sale; pamphlets.

★12795★
SOUTHERN MINNESOTA HISTORICAL CENTER - LIBRARY (Hist)
Mankato State University Phone: (507) 389-1029
Mankato, MN 56001 Dr. William E. Lass, Dir.
Founded: 1969. **Staff:** 2. **Subjects:** Mankato civic affairs, Minnesota politics and government, business, oral history. **Special Collections:** Mankato State University archives; H.H. King Flour Mills Company records; Mankato YWCA records. **Holdings:** 1100 linear feet of local history materials and university archives; oral history cassettes; microfilm. **Services:** Copying; library open to public. **Remarks:** The center is maintained by Mankato State University.

★12796★
SOUTHERN MISSIONARY COLLEGE - MC KEE LIBRARY - SPECIAL COLLECTIONS (Rel-Theol; Hist)
Box 629 Phone: (615) 396-4290
Collegedale, TN 37315 Charles E. Davis, Dir. of Libs./Archv.
Staff: Prof 6; Other 10. **Special Collections:** Dr. Vernon Thomas Memorial Civil War Collection (1400 books; 2000 letters; manuscripts; newspapers; pamphlets; pictures; maps); Dr. Vernon Thomas Memorial Abraham Lincoln Collection (2000 books, letters, manuscripts, newspapers, pamphlets, pictures, paintings, maps, artifacts); Seventh-day Adventist Church publications (10,000 books, current periodicals, bound periodicals, microforms, archives). **Services:** Interlibrary loans; copying; library open to public with restrictions. **Automated Operations:** Computerized cataloging. **Computerized Information Services:** OCLC. **Networks/Consortia:** Member of SOLINET. **Staff:** Mrs. Pat Morrison, Pub.Serv. & ILL; Lorann Grace, Per. & Exch.; Peggy Bennett, Cat.

★12797★
SOUTHERN NEVADA MEMORIAL HOSPITAL - MEDICAL LIBRARY (Med)
2040 W. Charleston Blvd. Phone: (702) 383-2368
Las Vegas, NV 89102 Aldona Lautenschlager, Dir., Lib.Serv.
Founded: 1964. **Staff:** Prof 1; Other 2. **Subjects:** Medicine and nursing. **Holdings:** 3224 books; 5835 bound periodical volumes; 246 bound indexes; 100 vertical files; 5 boxes of staff publications; 550 symposiums; 324 cassettes. **Subscriptions:** 205 journals and other serials. **Services:** Interlibrary loans; copying (for staff and hospital personnel only); library open to public for reference use only. **Publications:** Medical Library Bulletin - distributed to medical and allied health professionals, hospital personnel and consortium members.

★12798★
SOUTHERN OHIO GENEALOGICAL SOCIETY - REFERENCE LIBRARY (Hist)
879 W. Main St.
Box 414 Phone: (513) 393-2452
Hillsboro, OH 45133 Marie A. Knott, Libn.
Founded: 1978. **Staff:** 6. **Subjects:** Genealogy, local history. **Special Collections:** Jewish genealogical records; international genealogical index on microfiche (65 million names and accompanying information). **Holdings:** 700 books; family files; 25 reels of microfilm; 85 family history files; 3700 burial records of veterans buried in Highland County, OH; 53 volumes of published family histories; 90 family history manuscripts. **Services:** Library open to public. **Publications:** Roots & Shoots Quarterly - by subscription. **Special Indexes:** Surname/Locality Index, annual; Visitors Surname Index (card); Family File Index (card). **Remarks:** The society acts as a clearinghouse for local and out-of-state patrons in finding and establishing their genealogical lines.

★12799★
SOUTHERN OREGON HISTORICAL SOCIETY - RESEARCH LIBRARY (Hist)
206 N. 5th St.
Box 480 Phone: (503) 899-1847
Jacksonville, OR 97530 Alan C. Miller, Libn./Archv.
Staff: Prof 1; Other 2. **Subjects:** County and state history, historic preservation, museum techniques. **Special Collections:** Peter Britt photographic collection and work of other photographers (30,000 photographs dealing with southern Oregon subjects). **Holdings:** 3100 books; 100 bound periodical volumes; 460 manuscript collections; 240 oral histories. **Subscriptions:** 55 journals and other serials; 8 newspapers. **Services:** Interlibrary loans (limited); copying; library open to public. **Special Catalogs:** Preliminary Guide to Local History Materials, 1978 (booklet).

★12800★
SOUTHERN OREGON STATE COLLEGE - LIBRARY (Educ)
1250 Siskiyou Blvd. Phone: (503) 482-6445
Ashland, OR 97520 Ruth Monical, Act.Lib.Dir.
Founded: 1926. **Staff:** Prof 10; Other 15. **Subjects:** Education, liberal arts. **Special Collections:** Margery Bailey Renaissance Collection (6000 volumes); Southern Oregon History (1120 volumes). **Holdings:** 205,000 books and bound periodical volumes; 26,857 maps; 2817 photographs and pamphlets; 172,000 state and federal government documents; 452,895 microforms. **Subscriptions:** 4900 journals and other serials; 29 newspapers. **Services:** Interlibrary loans; copying; library open to public. **Computerized Information Services:** OCLC. **Networks/Consortia:** Member of Southern Oregon Library Federation. **Publications:** Bibliography series, irregular; list of serials, annual. **Special Indexes:** Index to Ashland Daily Tidings, 1958 to present. **Staff:** Harry Gates; Deborah Hollens; Patricia Larsen; Harold Otness ; Constance Battaile; David Russell; Ray Anne Kibbey; Richard Moore; Timothy Shove .

★12801★
SOUTHERN POVERTY LAW CENTER - KLANWATCH - LIBRARY (Soc Sci)
1001 S. Hull St. Phone: (205) 264-0286
Montgomery, AL 36104 Randall Williams, Dir.
Founded: 1980. **Staff:** 3. **Subjects:** Ku Klux Klan, neo-Nazi organizations, other right-wing extremists, anti-KKK information. **Holdings:** 50 books; 100 legal documents; 10,000 news clippings; 50 videotapes and audiotapes; 1000 letters. **Subscriptions:** 30 journals and other serials. **Services:** Copying; library open to public with restrictions. **Publications:** Klanwatch Intelligence Report, bimonthly - for internal distribution only.

SOUTHERN RAILWAY PREDECESSORS ARCHIVE
See: Virginia Polytechnic Institute and State University - Carol M. Newman Library

★12802★

SOUTHERN REGIONAL COUNCIL, INC. - REFERENCE LIBRARY (Soc Sci)
75 Marietta St., N.W.   Phone: (404) 522-8764
Atlanta, GA 30303   Stephen T. Suitts, Exec.Dir.
Subjects: Civil rights, civil liberties, politics, suffrage. **Holdings:** 950 books; special studies. **Services:** Library open to public with restrictions. **Publications:** Southern Changes; Special Reports and Studies - by subscription.

★12803★

SOUTHERN REGIONAL EDUCATION BOARD - LIBRARY (Educ)
1340 Spring St., N.W.   Phone: (404) 875-9211
Atlanta, GA 30345   Ann Hadley Carter, Res.Asst./Libn.
Founded: 1949. **Staff:** Prof 1. **Subjects:** Higher education in the South, southern education, mental health, computer science, nursing, medical education. **Holdings:** 3000 books; 4 VF drawers of pamphlets; 15 linear shelf feet of college catalogs; 22 drawers of documents on microfiche. **Subscriptions:** 100 journals and other serials. **Services:** Interlibrary loans; written requests for information will be answered. **Publications:** Acquisition list, quarterly - for internal distribution only.

★12804★

SOUTHERN RESEARCH INSTITUTE - THOMAS W. MARTIN MEMORIAL LIBRARY (Sci-Tech; Energy)
2000 Ninth Ave., S.
Box 55305   Phone: (205) 323-6592
Birmingham, AL 35255-5305   Mary L. Pullen, Lib.Mgr.
Founded: 1945. **Staff:** Prof 2; Other 2. **Subjects:** Chemistry, biology, biomaterials, engineering, energy, pollution, metallurgy, physics. **Holdings:** 12,000 books; 27,000 bound periodical volumes. **Subscriptions:** 800 journals and other serials. **Services:** Interlibrary loans; copying; library open to qualified users. **Staff:** Richard Remy, Info.Sci.; Mary W. White, Doc.Libn.

★12805★

SOUTHERN STATES ENERGY BOARD (SSEB) - SOUTHERN ENERGY/ ENVIRONMENTAL INFORMATION CENTER (SEEIC) (Energy)
One Exchange Place, Suite 1230
2300 Peachford Rd.   Phone: (404) 455-8841
Atlanta, GA 30338   Jane F. Clark, Dir.
Staff: Prof 2; Other 1. **Subjects:** Energy - policy, legislation, development; nuclear energy; energy facility site selection. **Holdings:** 100 books; 2000 technical reports; 200 state publications relating to energy; VF drawers of energy information. **Subscriptions:** 154 journals and other serials. **Services:** Interlibrary loans; copying (limited); center open to public. **Computerized Information Services:** DIALOG, DOE/RECON, NEXIS. **Publications:** List of publications - available upon request. **Staff:** Nancy E. Kaiser, Res.Libn.

★12806★

SOUTHERN TECHNICAL INSTITUTE - LIBRARY (Sci-Tech)
Clay St.   Phone: (404) 424-7275
Marietta, GA 30060   John W. Pattillo, Dir.
Founded: 1948. **Staff:** Prof 4; Other 2. **Subjects:** Engineering and technology - apparel, architectural, civil, computer, electrical, industrial, mechanical, textile. **Holdings:** 59,000 books; 13,600 bound periodical volumes; 9000 serials; 26,033 AV items; 5500 company reports. **Subscriptions:** 1500 journals and other serials. **Services:** Interlibrary loans; copying; library open to public with restrictions. **Automated Operations:** Computerized cataloging. **Computerized Information Services:** OCLC. **Networks/Consortia:** Member of SOLINET. **Staff:** Nancy S. Shofner, Asst.Dir.; Dorothy Stamps, Ser.Libn.

★12807★

SOUTHERN UNION COMPANY - LEGAL LIBRARY (Law)
InterFirst Two, Suite 1800   Phone: (214) 748-8511
Dallas, TX 75270
Staff: Prof 5; Other 3. **Subjects:** Law. **Holdings:** 5920 books. **Subscriptions:** 10 journals and other serials. **Services:** Library not open to public.

★12808★

SOUTHERN UNION COMPANY - PLANNING RESEARCH LIBRARY (Bus-Fin; Energy)
InterFirst Two, Suite 1800   Phone: (214) 748-8511
Dallas, TX 75270   Charles B. Woodard, Res.Libn.
Staff: Prof 1. **Subjects:** Management, petroleum and gas, accounting, finance, government, economics. **Holdings:** 950 books; 59 binders of Duff and Phelps reports; 200 Gas Research Association documents; 150 American Gas Association publications. **Subscriptions:** 47 journals and other serials. **Services:** Copying; library open to public with restrictions. **Publications:** Statistical Report on General Business and Oil & Gas Industry, monthly - for internal distribution only.

★12809★

SOUTHERN UNIVERSITY - LAW SCHOOL LIBRARY (Law)
Southern Branch Post Office   Phone: (504) 771-4900
Baton Rouge, LA 70813   Ann Jones, Law Libn.
Staff: Prof 4, Other 7. **Subjects:** Law. **Special Collections:** U.S. government and state of Louisiana documents depository. **Holdings:** 137,728 volumes; 12 VF drawers. **Subscriptions:** 4476 journals and other serials; 11 newspapers. **Services:** Interlibrary loans; copying; library open to public with restrictions. **Automated Operations:** Computerized cataloging. **Computerized Information Services:** OCLC, Westlaw. **Networks/Consortia:** Member of SOLINET. **Publications:** Periodical list; acquisitions list. **Staff:** Melbarose Manuel, Act.Libn.Roberta S. Cummings, Asst. Law Libn./Acq.; Harold Isadore, Asst. Law Libn./Ref./Res.; Clarence T. Nalls, Asst. Law Libn./Circ.; Elaine Simmon, Cat.Dept.

★12810★

SOUTHERN UTAH STATE COLLEGE - LIBRARY - SPECIAL COLLECTIONS DEPARTMENT (Hist; Hum)
300 W. Center St.   Phone: (801) 586-7945
Cedar City, UT 84720
Founded: 1962. **Staff:** Prof 1; Other 3. **Subjects:** Local history, college history, Shakespeare, art, music, opera, theater. **Special Collections:** William Rees and Kate Vilate Isom Palmer Western History Collection; Gladys McConnell Collection; Rhoda M. Wood Collection; E.D. Woolley Collection; Amasa Redd Collection; Alva and Zella Matheson Collection; Belle Armstrong Collection; John Laurence Seymour Collection (music, theater, humanities). **Holdings:** 6890 volumes; 400 oral history tapes; 457 phonograph records; 1445 linear feet of manuscript collections; 11,200 pictures and negatives; 3068 pamphlets; 804 linear feet of archives; 3250 microforms. **Services:** Copying; department open to public for reference use only. **Networks/Consortia:** Member of Utah College Library Council; Conference of Intermountain Archivists. **Special Indexes:** Index of Library's holdings on women; index of Library's holdings of Latter Day Saints periodicals; index to Palmer Western History Collection.

★12811★

SOUTHERN WISCONSIN CENTER FOR THE DEVELOPMENTALLY DISABLED - LIBRARY (Soc Sci)*
2145 Spring St.
Box 100   Phone: (414) 878-2411
Union Grove, WI 53182   Joyce Dabbs
Founded: 1919. **Staff:** 1. **Subjects:** Mental retardation, learning disabilities, social work, institutional care, food service, children's collection. **Holdings:** 2500 books; 500 filmstrips; 250 phonograph records. **Subscriptions:** 88 journals and other serials. **Services:** Library not open to public.

SOUTHERN WOMEN'S ARCHIVES
See: Birmingham Public and Jefferson County Free Library

★12812★

SOUTHLAND CORPORATION - CORPORATE BUSINESS RESEARCH CENTER (Bus-Fin)
2828 N. Haskell   Phone: (214) 828-7840
Dallas, TX 75204   Debra H. Marshall, Mgr.
Staff: Prof 2; Other 1. **Subjects:** Business, convenience stores, energy, investment, public companies, Southland Corporation history. **Special Collections:** Company files (1000 files containing annual and 10K reports, news releases, and clippings). **Holdings:** 800 books; 200 cassettes; 500 videotapes; 100 audiotapes; 2000 slides. **Subscriptions:** 400 journals and other serials; 15 newspapers. **Services:** Copying; center not open to public. **Automated Operations:** Computerized cataloging, acquisitions, serials, and circulation. **Computerized Information Services:** DIALOG, BRS, Dow Jones News/Retrieval. **Staff:** Elizabeth A. Laurent, Corp.Libn.

★12813★

SOUTHOLD HISTORICAL SOCIETY MUSEUM - LIBRARY (Hist)
Main Rd. & Maple Ln.   Phone: (516) 765-5500
Southold, NY 11971   George D. Wagoner, Dir.
Founded: 1960. **Subjects:** Local and state history, local fishing and farming, early textbooks, decorative arts, local cabinet makers. **Special Collections:** Early and local music; doll collection, unique doll house from 1903. **Holdings:** 3000 books; diaries. **Services:** Library open to public by appointment. **Publications:** Newsletter, annual; Guide to Historic Markers, 1960.

★12814★

SOUTHSIDE HOSPITAL - MEDICAL LIBRARY (Med)
Montauk Hwy.
Bay Shore, NY 11706
Phone: (516) 859-3111
May Chariton, Libn.
Founded: 1955. **Staff:** Prof 1. **Subjects:** Medicine and related topics. **Holdings:** 600 books; 2123 bound periodical volumes; 5 VF drawers of pamphlets; 150 audio cassette programs. **Subscriptions:** 90 journals and other serials; 12 newspapers. **Services:** Interlibrary loans; library not open to public. **Automated Operations:** Computerized cataloging. **Networks/Consortia:** Member of Greater Northeastern Regional Medical Library Program; Medical and Scientific Libraries of Long Island (MEDLI); Brooklyn-Queens-Staten Island Health Sciences Librarians (BQSI).

★12815★

SOUTHWEST ARKANSAS REGIONAL ARCHIVES (SARA) (Hist)
Box 134
Washington, AR 71862
Phone: (501) 983-2633
Mary Medearis, Dir.
Founded: 1978. **Staff:** Prof 1. **Subjects:** History of Southwest Arkansas, Caddo Indians. **Special Collections:** Rare books collection on Southwest Arkansas and Texas; Dawson Collection (research on Nicholas Trammel and Trammel's Trace); Claud Garner Collection (first editions and manuscripts); census and court records for twelve southwest Arkansas counties; newspapers of southwest Arkansas; index and service records for Civil War soldiers who served in Arkansas units. **Holdings:** 1000 books; 3000 reels of microfilm; 280 original court records of Hempstead County; 500 pictures; 10 scrapbooks; family collections and genealogical records. **Services:** Copying; archives open to public for reference use only.

★12816★

SOUTHWEST FOUNDATION FOR AUDIOVISUAL RESOURCES - AV COLLECTION
Box 522
Santa Fe, NM 87501
Founded: 1972. **Subjects:** Southwest arts and crafts. **Holdings:** Figures not available. **Special Indexes:** Index of New Mexico AV resources. **Remarks:** Presently inactive.

★12817★

SOUTHWEST FOUNDATION FOR BIOMEDICAL RESEARCH - PRESTON G. NORTHROP MEMORIAL LIBRARY (Med)
Box 28147
San Antonio, TX 78284
Phone: (512) 674-1410
Maureen D. Funnell, Libn.
Founded: 1959. **Staff:** Prof 3; Other 1. **Subjects:** Biomedicine. **Special Collections:** Primatology. **Holdings:** 7800 books; 30,000 bound periodical volumes. **Subscriptions:** 776 journals and other serials. **Services:** Interlibrary loans; copying; library open to public. **Automated Operations:** Computerized cataloging, acquisitions, serials and circulation. **Computerized Information Services:** DIALOG, SDC, MEDLARS, CAS Online. **Networks/Consortia:** Member of TALON; Council of Research and Academic Libraries (CORAL); Health Oriented Libraries of San Antonio (HOLSA); AMIGOS Bibliographic Council, Inc. **Formerly:** Southwest Foundation for Research and Education. **Staff:** Ruth H. Brooks, Asst.Libn.; Mary Ann Smith, ILL.

★12818★

SOUTHWEST MINNESOTA HISTORICAL CENTER - LIBRARY (Hist)
Southwest State University
Marshall, MN 56258
Phone: (507) 537-7373
Thaddeus Radzialowski, Dir.
Founded: 1972. **Staff:** Prof 1; Other 4. **Subjects:** Local history, church histories, Iceland, agricultural history, genealogy. **Special Collections:** Minnesota Farm Holiday Association (tapes); Globe Land and Loan Company records; Verzlunarfelag Islendinga records; regional newspapers. **Holdings:** 150 books; 300 bound periodical volumes; 700 feet of manuscripts; 50 reels of microfilm of church records; 200 oral history interviews. **Services:** Interlibrary loans; copying; library open to public on a varying schedule. **Remarks:** The center is maintained by Southwest State University.

★12819★

SOUTHWEST MISSOURI STATE UNIVERSITY - MAP COLLECTION (Geog-Map)
Box 175, Duane G. Meyer Library
Springfield, MO 65804-0095
Phone: (417) 836-5105
James A. Coombs, Map Libn.
Founded: 1980. **Staff:** Prof 1; Other 2. **Subjects:** Cartography, spatial analysis, land use, outdoor recreation. **Special Collections:** Tourist information (2500 items); pre-1920 U.S. Geological Survey topographic quadrangles; U.S. Geological Survey Geologic Atlas of the United States (219 volumes). **Holdings:** 129 books; 86,357 maps; 33,022 aerial photographs; 776 atlases; 4 globes; 6 raised relief maps; 154 micorforms; 3 gazetteers. **Subscriptions:** 18 journals and other serials. **Services:** Interlibrary loans; copying; collection open to public. **Automated Operations:** Computerized cataloging. **Special Indexes:** Indexes to U.S. Geological Survey geologic atlases and small- and medium-scale maps in U.S.

★12820★

SOUTHWEST MUSEUM - RESEARCH LIBRARY (Hist)†
Highland Park Sta., Box 42128
Los Angeles, CA 90042
Phone: (213) 221-2163
Ruth M. Christensen, Libn.
Founded: 1907. **Staff:** Prof 1. **Subjects:** Indians of the Western Hemisphere, with emphasis on the New Southwest; Western Americana; Arizoniana; Californiana; Western and American Indian art; ethnobotany; archeology. **Special Collections:** Munk Library of Arizoniana; Hector Alliott Memorial Library of Archaeology; Charles F. Lummis Collection; George Wharton James Collection; papers of Frank Hamilton Cushing, John Charles Fremont, George Bird Grinnell, Frederick Webb Hodge, Charles F. Lummis, Maurice H. and Marco R. Newmark. **Holdings:** 100,000 pamphlets and manuscripts; government publications; VF drawers. **Services:** Library open to public for reference use only, on a limited schedule. **Publications:** An Introduction to the Southwest Museum Research Library (brochure); price list of publications - available on request. **Remarks:** Library located at 234 Museum Dr., Los Angeles, CA 90065.

★12821★

SOUTHWEST MUSEUM OF SCIENCE & TECHNOLOGY/THE SCIENCE PLACE - LIBRARY
Fair Park, Box 11158
Dallas, TX 75223
Founded: 1961. **Subjects:** Health, astronomy, medicine, earth sciences, astronautics, sex education, natural science. **Holdings:** 1600 books and bound periodical volumes. **Remarks:** Presently inactive.

★12822★

SOUTHWEST REGIONAL LABORATORY FOR EDUCATIONAL RESEARCH AND DEVELOPMENT - LIBRARY (Educ)*
4665 Lampson Ave.
Los Alamitos, CA 90720
Phone: (213) 598-7661
Louise D. Riedel, Libn.
Founded: 1967. **Staff:** Prof 1. **Subjects:** Education, psychology, linguistics, computer sciences, music, art. **Holdings:** 5500 books; 819 bound periodical volumes; 1675 other cataloged items; 2 million archives; 70,000 ERIC microfiche; 1800 items in Curriculum Library; 250 items in Juvenile Library; 93 VF drawers of pamphlets and miscellaneous information. **Subscriptions:** 625 journals and other serials. **Services:** Interlibrary loans; library not open to public. **Also Known As:** SWRL.

★12823★

SOUTHWEST RESEARCH & INFORMATION CENTER (Soc Sci)
Box 4524
Albuquerque, NM 87106
Phone: (505) 262-1862
Paul Robinson, Exec.Dir.
Founded: 1971. **Staff:** Prof 2; Other 1. **Subjects:** Environmental, consumer and social issues. **Special Collections:** Uranium publications and clippings (3000 items); nuclear waste management publications and clippings. **Holdings:** 3000 books; 7 cabinets of clippings in 1000 categories; 100 sourcebooks. **Subscriptions:** 350 journals and other serials; 15 newspapers. **Services:** Copying; center open to public for reference use only. **Publications:** The Workbook, quarterly; Nuclear Waste News (newsletter), bimonthly. **Staff:** Don Hancock, Info.Coord.

★12824★

SOUTHWEST RESEARCH INSTITUTE - NONDESTRUCTIVE TESTING INFORMATION ANALYSIS CENTER (Sci-Tech)
Drawer 28510
San Antonio, TX 78284
Phone: (512) 684-5111
George A. Matzkanin, Dir.
Founded: 1974. **Staff:** Prof 2; Other 1. **Subjects:** Nondestructive evaluation (NDE), quality control, inspection using liquid penetrants, radiography, electricity and magnetism, ultrasonics, heat, optical-visual devices, audible-sonic devices. **Special Collections:** Series of abstracts devoted to nondestructive evaluation. **Holdings:** 26,000 reports and patents. **Services:** Rapid response literature searching; consultation; center open to qualified researchers. **Computerized Information Services:** DIALOG, SDC, NTIAC (internal database). Performs searches on cost recovery basis. Contact Person: Frances P. Hicks. **Publications:** Quarterly newsletter; list of additional publications - available upon request. **Remarks:** Center is an official DOD Information Analysis Center. Operated by SWRI for the U.S. Department of Defense under technical cognizance of U.S. Army - Materials & Mechanics Research Center. Sponsors a biennial symposium on NDE. **Staff:** Frances P. Hicks, Info.Anl.

★12825★
SOUTHWEST RESEARCH INSTITUTE - THOMAS BAKER SLICK MEMORIAL
   LIBRARY (Sci-Tech)
Drawer 28510   Phone: (512) 684-5111
San Antonio, TX 78284   Robert D. Armor, Libn.
Founded: 1948. Staff: Prof 3; Other 4. Subjects: Engineering - chemical,
electrical, mechanical, aeronautical; chemistry; geology; physics;
mathematics. Holdings: 30,000 books; 13,500 bound periodical volumes;
20,500 unbound periodicals; 77,000 reports on microfiche. Subscriptions:
1600 journals and other serials. Services: Interlibrary loans; copying; library
open to public for reference use only. Computerized Information Services:
DIALOG, SDC. Networks/Consortia: Member of Council of Research and
Academic Libraries (CORAL); Health Oriented Libraries of San Antonio
(HOLSA). Staff: Oralia R. Ruiz, Assoc.Libn.; Anita Lang, Asst.Libn.

SOUTHWEST   STATE   UNIVERSITY - SOUTHWEST   MINNESOTA
   HISTORICAL CENTER
See: Southwest Minnesota Historical Center

★12826★
SOUTHWEST TEXAS METHODIST HOSPITAL - LIBRARY (Med)
7700 Floyd Curl Dr.   Phone: (512) 696-4583
San Antonio, TX 78229   Eileen T. Lively, Libn.
Staff: Prof 1. Subjects: Medicine, nursing. Holdings: 1250 books; 192
bound periodical volumes. Subscriptions: 50 journals and other serials.
Services: Interlibrary loans; copying; library open to nurses and doctors
without restrictions; to students with restrictions.

SOUTHWEST WASHINGTON HOSPITALS - ST. JOSEPH COMMUNITY
   HOSPITAL
See: St. Joseph Community Hospital

★12827★
SOUTHWEST   WISCONSIN   VOCATIONAL-TECHNICAL   INSTITUTE   -
   LEARNING RESOURCES CENTER (Bus-Fin; Sci-Tech)
Bronson Blvd.
Rte. 1, Box 500   Phone: (608) 822-3262
Fennimore, WI 53809   Patricia Payson, Libn.
Founded: 1971. Staff: Prof 1; Other 3. Subjects: Business education,
agriculture, automotive mechanics, home economics, health occupations,
technical and industrial occupations. Holdings: 28,000 books; 2500 AV kits;
18 drawers of pamphlets; 1147 pages of microforms. Subscriptions: 250
journals and other serials. Services: Interlibrary loans; copying; center open to
public.

SOUTHWESTERN ART ASSOCIATION - PHILBROOK ART CENTER
See: Philbrook Art Center

★12828★
SOUTHWESTERN   ASSEMBLIES   OF   GOD   COLLEGE   - P.C. NELSON
   MEMORIAL LIBRARY (Rel-Theol)
1200 Sycamore   Phone: (214) 937-4010
Waxahachie, TX 75165   Mr. Murl M. Winters, Dir.
Founded: 1927. Staff: Prof 2; Other 2. Subjects: Bible, liberal arts,
education. Special Collections: Pentecostal Materials Collection (1463
volumes); William Burton McCafferty Pentecostal Periodical Collection (4
cabinets). Holdings: 64,165 books; 5087 bound periodical volumes; 8526
pamphlets; 550 flannelgraphs; 632 tapes; 1355 slides; 105 maps; 1299
phonograph records; 712 filmstrips; 867 reels of microfilm; 5421 microfiche;
1234 directories and catalogs; 402 documents; 1649 ultrafiche; 54 puppets.
Subscriptions: 500 journals and other serials. Services: Interlibrary loans;
copying; library open to public, fee for circulation card to nonstudents. Special
Indexes: Index to Pentecostal Evangel (1920, 1926, 1930-1961; card);
index to Pentecost Magazine (card); index to Church of God Evangel (card; in
preparation); index to Missionary Challenge (card; in preparation). Staff:
Pearl Ellis, Asst.Dir.

★12829★
SOUTHWESTERN BAPTIST THEOLOGICAL SEMINARY - A. WEBB ROBERTS
   LIBRARY (Rel-Theol)
Box 22000-2E   Phone: (817) 923-1921
Fort Worth, TX 76122   Keith C. Wills, Dir. of Libs.
Founded: 1909. Staff: Prof 11; Other 26. Subjects: Religion and theology,
Bible, music and hymnology, Baptist history, religious education. Special
Collections: Personal items and correspondence of B.H. Carroll, L.R.
Scarborough, George W. Truett, M.E. Dodd, James M. Carroll (Baptist
leaders); Texas Baptist Historical Collection (63,737 items). Holdings:
238,750 books; 68,445 bound periodical volumes; 83,031 convention and
association annuals; 124,145 items of printed music; 32,919 tapes and

discs; 2528 films and filmstrips; 832 videotapes; 234 VF drawers of
manuscripts; church minutes and histories. Subscriptions: 1472 journals and
other serials. Services: Interlibrary loans; copying; SDI; library open to public.
Automated   Operations: Computerized   cataloging,   acquisitions   and
circulation. Computerized Information Services: OCLC, BRS. Performs
searches on cost recovery basis. Contact Person: Robert Phillips, 294-7142.
Networks/Consortia: Member of AMIGOS Bibliographic Council, Inc.
Publications: Book Reviews of the Month (index); New Titles Added, monthly.
Special Indexes: Baptist biography index (card). Staff: Phil Sims, Music Libn.;
Robert Phillips, Asst.Libn./Pub.Serv.; Carol Bastien, Acq.Libn.; Lori Robertson,
Circ.Libn.; Myrta Garrett, Ser.Libn.; Bob Trimble, AV Libn.; Steve Story, Media
Coord.; Barbara Russell, Cat.Libn.; Ben Rogers, Archv.

★12830★
SOUTHWESTERN BELL TELEPHONE COMPANY - BUSINESS INFORMATION
   RESOURCE SERVICE (Bus-Fin)*
112 N. Fourth St., Rm. 1323   Phone: (314) 247-8696
St. Louis, MO 63102
Founded: 1978. Staff: Prof 1. Subjects: Marketing, management,
telecommunications, research. Holdings: 600 books; 300 technical reports;
200 video cassettes; 9 lateral file drawers of slides, films and cassettes; 2
lateral file drawers of pamphlets and annual reports. Subscriptions: 88
journals and other serials. Services: Interlibrary loans; library not open to
public.

SOUTHWESTERN COLLEGE LIBRARY - UNITED METHODIST CHURCH -
   KANSAS WEST CONFERENCE
See: United Methodist Church - Kansas West Conference

★12831★
SOUTHWESTERN ILLINOIS METROPOLITAN AND REGIONAL PLANNING
   COMMISSION - TECHNICAL LIBRARY (Plan)
203 W. Main St.   Phone: (618) 344-4250
Collinsville, IL 62234   Bonnie C. Moore, Info.Mgr.
Founded: 1965. Staff: Prof 1. Subjects: Urban and regional planning, census
data, legislation, codes and ordinances, transportation, recreation, water and
sewage. Holdings: 4000 books and bound periodical volumes. Subscriptions:
65 journals and other serials. Services: Interlibrary loans; copying; library
open to public.

★12832★
SOUTHWESTERN INDIAN POLYTECHNIC INSTITUTE - INSTRUCTIONAL
   MATERIALS CENTER (Educ)
9169 Coors Rd., N.W.   Phone: (505) 766-3266
Albuquerque, NM 87184   Dollie D. Watson, Dir., Spec.Serv.
Founded: 1972. Staff: Prof 4; Other 2. Subjects: Vocational-technical
curriculum, American Indians, recreational reading. Holdings: 20,000 books.
Subscriptions: 150 journals and other serials; 17 newspapers. Services:
Interlibrary loans; center open to public for reference use only by
appointment. Staff: Nellie Buffalomeat, Libn.

★12833★
SOUTHWESTERN INDIANA MENTAL HEALTH CENTER, INC. - LIBRARY
   (Med)
415 Mulberry St.   Phone: (812) 423-7791
Evansville, IN 47713   Donna Yuschak, Libn.
Staff: Prof 1. Subjects: Psychology, psychiatry, social work, child
development, sexuality, therapeutic recreation, drug abuse. Holdings: 1000
books; 700 pamphlets; 125 AV materials. Subscriptions: 80 journals and
other serials. Services: Interlibrary loans; copying; library open to public for
reference use only. Networks/Consortia: Member of Evansville Area Health
Sciences Libraries Consortium; Four Rivers Area Library Services Authority.

★12834★
SOUTHWESTERN OKLAHOMA STATE UNIVERSITY - AL HARRIS LIBRARY
   (Educ)
                                       Phone: (405) 772-6611
Weatherford, OK 73096   Sheila Wilder Hoke, Lib.Dir.
Founded: 1902. Staff: Prof 6; Other 9. Subjects: Pharmacy, education,
psychology, business administration. Holdings: 217,033 books and bound
periodical volumes; 14,953 reels of microfilm; 559,957 microfiche;
104,557 microcards; 25,318 government documents. Subscriptions: 1676
journals and other serials. Services: Interlibrary loans; library not open to
public. Staff: Charles Ingram, Acq./Pharmacy Libn.; Marinelle Harris,
Ser.Libn.; George Alsbach, Cat.;Caroline Armold Torrence, Ref./ILL/
Govt.Docs.

★12835★
SOUTHWESTERN PUBLIC SERVICE COMPANY - LIBRARY (Energy; Bus-Fin)
Box 1261   Phone: (806) 378-2741
Amarillo, TX 79170   Gloria Branham, Libn.
Founded: 1971. **Staff:** Prof 1. **Subjects:** Engineering, power transmission and distribution, business administration, finance, economics, agriculture, data processing, law. **Special Collections:** Electric Power Research Institute Reports; Texas Water Development Board Reports. **Holdings:** 3000 books; 250 bound periodical volumes; 80 audio cassettes; 3 drawers of microfilm; 3 drawers of microfiche; 63 films; 2 VF drawers of standards; 3 VF drawers of annual reports. **Subscriptions:** 400 journals and other serials; 9 newspapers. **Services:** Interlibrary loans; library not open to public. **Automated Operations:** Computerized cataloging and serials. **Computerized Information Services:** DIALOG. **Publications:** Film catalog - on request.

★12836★
SOUTHWESTERN STATE HOSPITAL - PROFESSIONAL LIBRARY (Med)
E. Main St.
Box 670   Phone: (703) 783-3171
Marion, VA 24354   Kathleen G. Overbay, Dir., Lib.Serv.
Founded: 1941. **Staff:** Prof 1; Other 1. **Subjects:** Psychiatry. **Special Collections:** Historical collection (166 items). **Holdings:** 804 volumes; 479 AV items. **Subscriptions:** 32 journals and other serials. **Services:** Interlibrary loans; copying; library open to public.

★12837★
SOUTHWESTERN UNIVERSITY - A.J. GERUNTINO LIBRARY (Educ; Sci-Tech)
2525 North Country Club Rd.   Phone: (602) 327-3156
Tucson, AZ 85716   Dr. Geruntino
Founded: 1982. **Staff:** 1. **Subjects:** Nutrition, psychology, business-finance, experiential education. **Special Collections:** Donald G. Minnich Collection of Railroad Books of Western and Southwestern U.S. (120 books); Southwest College of Medical and Health Sciences Collection of Naturopathic medicine (500 volumes). **Holdings:** 7500 books; 10 bound periodical volumes; 125 unbound theses; 1 vertical file drawer of reports on university faculty, students and history. **Subscriptions:** 20 journals and other serials; 5 newspapers. **Services:** Copying; library open to public for reference use only with permission from director. **Publications:** New acquisitions list, monthly.

★12838★
SOUTHWESTERN UNIVERSITY - SCHOOL OF LAW LIBRARY (Law)
675 S. Westmoreland Ave.   Phone: (213) 738-6725
Los Angeles, CA 90005   Linda Whisman, Dir.
Founded: 1913. **Staff:** Prof 8; Other 12. **Subjects:** Law. **Holdings:** 132,100 books; 20,312 bound periodical volumes; 824 audiotapes; 278,224 microforms. **Subscriptions:** 3477 journals and other serials; 25 newspapers. **Services:** Interlibrary loans; copying; library open to public. **Automated Operations:** Computerized cataloging. **Computerized Information Services:** LEXIS, RLIN, Westlaw. **Networks/Consortia:** Member of CLASS. **Staff:** C. Ebbinghouse, Ref./Media; D. Johnson-Champ, Ref.; B. Nazarro, Cat.; C. Weiner, Circ.; C. McClamma, Doc.Libn.; P. Lambert, Cat.

★12839★
SOUTHWIRE COMPANY - R & D TECHNICAL LIBRARY (Sci-Tech)
Fertilla St.   Phone: (404) 832-5080
Carrollton, GA 30119   Linda League, Libn.
Founded: 1964. **Staff:** 1. **Subjects:** Aluminum, copper, rod, wire and cable, metallurgy, environment, management. **Holdings:** 1000 books; 500 bound periodical volumes; 4000 information files. **Subscriptions:** 62 journals and other serials. **Services:** Library open to company employees only. **Computerized Information Services:** DIALOG.

★12840★
SOUTHWOOD COMMUNITY HOSPITAL - MEDICAL LIBRARY (Med)
111 Dedham St.   Phone: (617) 668-0385
Norfolk, MA 02056   Isabella M. Callahan, Med.Libn.
Founded: 1927. **Staff:** Prof 1; Other 1. **Subjects:** Cancer and allied diseases. **Holdings:** 1896 books and bound periodical volumes. **Subscriptions:** 94 journals and other serials. **Services:** Interlibrary loans; copying; library serves professional and paraprofessional staff of hospital, open to researchers and others upon request. **Computerized Information Services:** MEDLINE, BRS. **Networks/Consortia:** Member of Boston Biomedical Library Consortium; Southeastern Massachusetts Health Sciences Libraries; Consortium for Information Resources.

★12841★
SOVEREIGN HOSPITALLER ORDER OF ST. JOHN - VILLA ANNESLIE - ARCHIVES (Rel-Theol)
529 Dunkirk Rd.   Phone: (301) 752-1087
Anneslie, MD 21212   Rev. Robert Woodside, H.O.S.J., Dir.
Staff: Prof 1. **Subjects:** History of the Order of St. John. **Holdings:** 1000 books and documents. **Subscriptions:** 34 journals and other serials. **Services:** Archives open to public by appointment.

★12842★
SOVRAN BANK, N.A. - LIBRARY (Bus-Fin)
Two Commercial Pl.
Box 600   Phone: (804) 441-4419
Norfolk, VA 23501   Victoria Strickland-Cordial, Libn.
Founded: 1968. **Staff:** Prof 1; Other 1. **Subjects:** Banks and banking, personnel administration, international business, law, accounting. **Holdings:** 3000 books; 130 bound periodical volumes; 10 VF drawers; 150 cassettes; 5 directories; 62 theses. **Subscriptions:** 104 journals and other serials. **Services:** Interlibrary loans; copying; library open to public for reference use only. **Publications:** Recent Acquisitions, bimonthly - for internal distribution only. **Formed by the Merger of:** First & Merchants Bank and Virginia National Bank.

SOYER (Moses and Ida) LIBRARY
See: Parrish Art Museum - Library

★12843★
SOYFOODS CENTER LIBRARY (Food-Bev)
Box 234   Phone: (415) 283-2991
Lafayette, CA 94549   William R. Shurtleff, Dir.
Staff: Prof 2; Other 1. **Subjects:** Soyfoods and soybeans - history, food technology, nutrition, industrial statistics, marketing information. **Special Collections:** Traditional, low technology soyfoods; East Asian soyfoods; European soyfoods; historical collection. **Holdings:** 300 books; 8000 articles and letters. **Subscriptions:** 15 journals and other serials. **Services:** Library open to public by appointment. **Publications:** International Bibliography of Soyfoods, biennial; Soyfoods Industry and Market: Directory and Databook, annual; eight other books about soyfoods - for sale.

SPACE IMAGERY CENTER
See: University of Arizona

★12844★
SPACE AND UNEXPLAINED CELESTIAL EVENTS RESEARCH SOCIETY - LIBRARY (Sci-Tech)
Box 2228   Phone: (304) 269-2719
Clarksburg, WV 26301   Gray Barker, Dir.
Staff: 1. **Subjects:** Unidentified flying objects (UFO). **Holdings:** 200 books; 3000 other cataloged items. **Services:** Copying; research services are available.

SPACED-OUT LIBRARY
See: Toronto Public Library

SPANGLER LIBRARY
See: Ohio Dominican College

SPANISH AMERICAN WAR MUSEUM
See: Veterans Home of California - Lincoln Memorial Library

SPANISH ARCHIVES
See: Florida State Dept. of Natural Resources - Division of State Lands - Bureau of State Land Mgmt. - Title Section

★12845★
SPAR AEROSPACE LTD. - LIBRARY (Sci-Tech)
21025 Trans Canada Hwy.   Phone: (514) 457-2150
Ste. Anne de Bellevue, PQ, Canada H9X 3R2   Margaret B. Gross, Libn.
Staff: Prof 1. **Subjects:** Electronics, satellite communications, telecommunications, radar, aeronautics, space research. **Holdings:** 3000 books; 500 bound periodical volumes; 4000 NASA reports; 4000 technical reports; 500 internal reports. **Subscriptions:** 153 journals and other serials. **Services:** Interlibrary loans; library not open to public. **Computerized Information Services:** DIALOG, CAN/OLE.

★12846★
SPARKS REGIONAL MEDICAL CENTER - REGIONAL HEALTH SCIENCES LIBRARY (Med)*
1311 S. Eye St.   Phone: (501) 441-4221
Fort Smith, AR 72901   Grace Anderson, Libn.
Founded: 1951. **Staff:** Prof 1; Other 1. **Subjects:** Medicine and biological sciences. **Holdings:** 2000 books; 3000 bound periodical volumes. **Subscriptions:** 237 journals and other serials. **Services:** Interlibrary loans (fee); copying; library open to public for reference use only. **Computerized Information Services:** MEDLINE. **Remarks:** Designated as an Area Health Education Center Library.

SPARLING (Stephen) LIBRARY
See: Society for Crippled Children and Adults of Manitoba - Stephen Sparling Library

★12847★
SPARROW (Edward W.) HOSPITAL - MEDICAL LIBRARY (Med)
1215 E. Michigan Ave.
Box 30480   Phone: (517) 483-2274
Lansing, MI 48909   Doris H. Asher, Med.Libn.
Founded: 1950. **Staff:** 1. **Subjects:** Medicine and nursing. **Holdings:** 3300 books. **Subscriptions:** 310 journals and other serials. **Services:** Interlibrary loans; copying; library open to health care professionals.

★12848★
SPARTANBURG GENERAL HOSPITAL - HEALTH SCIENCES LIBRARY (Med)
101 E. Wood St.   Phone: (803) 573-6220
Spartanburg, SC 29303   Fay J. Towell, Dir., Lib.Serv.
Staff: Prof 1; Other 1. **Subjects:** Medicine, nursing, allied health sciences, hospital administration. **Holdings:** 3000 books; 3000 bound periodical volumes; 200 AV items. **Subscriptions:** 200 journals and other serials. **Services:** Interlibrary loans; copying; library open to public for reference use only. **Computerized Information Services:** NLM, DIALOG. **Networks/Consortia:** Member of Health Communications Network; Area Health Education Center of South Carolina.

SPAULDING (Harriet M.) LIBRARY
See: New England Conservatory of Music - Harriet M. Spaulding Library

SPEARE (Martin) MEMORIAL LIBRARY
See: New Mexico Institute of Mining and Technology - Martin Speare Memorial Library

★12849★
SPEARS, LUBERSKY, CAMPBELL, BLEDSOE, ANDERSON & YOUNG - LIBRARY (Law)
800 Pacific Bldg.
520 S.W. Yamhill St.   Phone: (503) 226-6151
Portland, OR 97204   Bob Newby, Libn.
Staff: Prof 1; Other 1. **Subjects:** Law. **Holdings:** 16,000 volumes; 2000 internal legal memoranda. **Subscriptions:** 320 journals and other serials. **Services:** Interlibrary loans; library not open to public. **Computerized Information Services:** LEXIS. **Special Indexes:** Index to legal memoranda (punch cards).

★12850★
SPECIAL LIBRARIES ASSOCIATION - INFORMATION RESOURCES CENTER (Info Sci)
235 Park Ave., S.   Phone: (212) 477-9250
New York, NY 10003   Mr. Chris R. Ikehara, Mgr., Info.Rsrcs.
Staff: Prof 1. **Subjects:** Special libraries, librarianship, information science. **Special Collections:** Association's Archives. **Holdings:** 3000 volumes. **Subscriptions:** 140 journals and other serials. **Services:** Center open to public by appointment. **Also Known As:** SLA.

★12851★
SPECIAL METALS CORPORATION - TECHNICAL LIBRARY/INFORMATION CENTER (Sci-Tech)
Middle Settlement Rd.   Phone: (315) 798-2936
New Hartford, NY 13413   Elizabeth A. Lazore, Libn.
Founded: 1957. **Staff:** Prof 1; Other 1. **Subjects:** Metallurgy, business management, ceramics, vacuum melting, industrial maintenance. **Holdings:** 2500 books and bound periodical volumes; 5000 technical documents; 900 technical reports; company records. **Subscriptions:** 126 journals and other serials. **Services:** Interlibrary loans; library open to public upon request.

SPECK (John) MEMORIAL LIBRARY
See: Chicago Mountaineering Club - John Speck Memorial Library

★12852★
SPECTROL ELECTRONICS CORPORATION - LIBRARY (Sci-Tech)*
17070 E. Gale Ave.
Box 1220   Phone: (213) 964-6565
Industry, CA 91749   James Roehrich, Engr. Standards Supv.
Subjects: Engineering. **Holdings:** 200 books. **Services:** Library not open to public.

★12853★
SPEED (J.B.) ART MUSEUM - LIBRARY (Art)
2035 S. Third St.   Phone: (502) 636-2893
Louisville, KY 40208   Mary Jane Benedict, Libn.
Staff: Prof 1. **Subjects:** Art, decorative arts, architecture, archeology, film, photography. **Special Collections:** J.B. Speed's Lincoln collection; Weygold Indian collection. **Holdings:** 12,000 books and bound periodical volumes; 48 VF drawers. **Subscriptions:** 50 journals and other serials. **Services:** Copying; library open to public for reference use only. **Special Indexes:** Speed Bulletin Index; Speed Scrapbook Index; Kennedy Quarterly Index; Index of Contemporary Artists file; Index of Reproduction file; Index to Gallery Catalogs (all on cards).

SPEER LIBRARY
See: Princeton Theological Seminary

SPELLMAN (Cardinal) PHILATELIC MUSEUM , INC.
See: Cardinal Spellman Philatelic Museum, Inc.

★12854★
SPENCE-CHAPIN SERVICES TO FAMILIES AND CHILDREN - CHARLOTTE TOWLE MEMORIAL LIBRARY (Soc Sci)
6 E. 94th St.   Phone: (212) 369-0300
New York, NY 10028   Leilani Straw, Asst.Dir.
Founded: 1967. **Staff:** 1. **Subjects:** Child welfare, social work. **Holdings:** 932 volumes; pamphlets. **Services:** Library open to agency staff only.

SPENCE (David) LIBRARY
See: University of Southern California - Science & Engineering Library

SPENCER ART REFERENCE LIBRARY
See: Nelson-Atkins Museum of Art

SPENCER CENTER FOR EDUCATION
See: St. Luke's Hospital of Kansas City - Medical Library

SPENCER COLLECTION
See: New York Public Library

SPENCER ENTOMOLOGICAL MUSEUM
See: University of British Columbia

SPENCER (Helen Foresman) MUSEUM OF ART
See: University of Kansas - Murphy Library of Art History

SPENCER KELLOGG
See: Textron, Inc. - Spencer Kellogg Division

SPENCER RESEARCH LIBRARY
See: University of Kansas

★12855★
SPERRY - BUSINESS PLANNING LIBRARY (Bus-Fin; Comp Sci)
1290 Avenue of the Americas   Phone: (212) 956-3476
New York, NY 10104   William C. Patterson, Dir.
Staff: Prof 1. **Subjects:** Computer industry, farm equipment, flight systems, communications, security, publications. **Holdings:** 300 books and bound periodical volumes; 100 other cataloged items; 75 research reports; 75 government publications. **Subscriptions:** 80 journals and other serials; 9 newspapers. **Services:** Interlibrary loans; library not open to public. **Staff:** Clare T. Thompson, Libn.

★12856★
SPERRY COMPUTER SYSTEMS - DEFENSE SYSTEMS DIVISION - INFORMATION SERVICE CENTER (Sci-Tech; Comp Sci)
M.S. UOR25, Box 43525   Phone: (612) 456-2580
St. Paul, MN 55164-0525   Faye V. Peterson, Supv.
Staff: Prof 2; Other 2. **Subjects:** Computers, electronics, data processing,

management, physics, chemistry, mathematics. **Holdings:** 25,000 books. **Subscriptions:** 500 journals and other serials. **Services:** Interlibrary loans; copying; center open to public with restrictions. **Computerized Information Services:** DIALOG, SDC, NEXIS. **Publications:** Bulletin, monthly - selected magazine articles and new book list. **Staff:** Virginia Van Horn, Libn.

★12857★
SPERRY COMPUTER SYSTEMS - INFORMATION CENTER (Sci-Tech)†
Township Line & Union Meeting Rds.
Box 500   Phone: (215) 542-2458
Blue Bell, PA 19424   Alma B. Campbell, Mgr.
Founded: 1952. **Staff:** Prof 3; Other 2. **Subjects:** Computers, programming, management, marketing, electrical engineering, mathematics, physics, chemistry. **Holdings:** 20,000 books and bound periodical volumes; 2500 reels of microfilm. **Subscriptions:** 700 journals and other serials; 10 newspapers. **Services:** Interlibrary loans; SDI; center open to public with permission. **Computerized Information Services:** OCLC, DIALOG, SDC, New York Times Information Service, Dow Jones News/Retrieval, BRS, Mead Data Central, The Source, IN/FORM Data Services. **Networks/Consortia:** Member of PALINET & Union Library Catalogue of Pennsylvania. **Publications:** Information Center Bulletin, biweekly; newsletters; Current Awareness Services. **Staff:** Elaine S. Harris, Info.Res.Anl.; Mary Ann Zaborowski, Info.Res.Anl.

★12858★
SPERRY COMPUTER SYSTEMS - LIBRARY (Sci-Tech)*
55 City Centre Dr.   Phone: (416) 270-3030
Mississauga, ON, Canada L5B 1M4 Laurie Bennett, Libn.
Founded: 1977. **Staff:** Prof 1. **Subjects:** Finance, marketing, computers, management. **Holdings:** 400 books; 10 bound periodical volumes; 3000 clippings; 200 in-house publications. **Subscriptions:** 70 journals and other serials; 7 newspapers. **Services:** Interlibrary loans; copying; library open to public with restrictions. **Publications:** Newsletter, monthly - for internal distribution only.

★12859★
SPERRY COMPUTER SYSTEMS - LIBRARY/TECHNICAL INFORMATION CENTER (Sci-Tech; Comp Sci)
322 North 2200 West   Phone: (801) 539-5222
Salt Lake City, UT 84116   Phyllis J. Nye, Libn.
Founded: 1956. **Staff:** Prof 1; Other 1. **Subjects:** Computer science, engineering, management and business, manufacturing. **Holdings:** 3000 books; 500 symposia proceedings; 5000 technical reports and manuals. **Subscriptions:** 250 journals and other serials. **Services:** Interlibrary loans; library not open to public. **Computerized Information Services:** NEXIS, DIALOG. **Publications:** Acquisition list, monthly.

★12860★
SPERRY COMPUTER SYSTEMS - ROSEVILLE INFORMATION CENTER (Sci-Tech; Comp Sci)
2276 Highcrest Rd.   Phone: (612) 633-6170
Roseville, MN 55113   Mary C. Steele, Mgr.
Staff: Prof 3; Other 2. **Subjects:** Computers, electrical engineering, electronics, management, production methods. **Holdings:** 15,000 volumes; 22,000 technical reports; 1000 audio cassette tapes; 6 VF drawers of microfiche. **Subscriptions:** 650 journals and other serials; 14 newspapers. **Services:** Interlibrary loans (limited); center not open to public. **Automated Operations:** Computerized serials. **Computerized Information Services:** Online systems. **Special Indexes:** Online and KWIC indexes to internal documents; journal articles and proceedings. **Formerly:** Its Commercial Division - Information Service Center.

★12861★
SPERRY ELECTRONIC SYSTEMS - ENGINEERING LIBRARY (Sci-Tech; Comp Sci)
Rte. 29 North   Phone: (804) 973-0100
Charlottesville, VA 22906   Ora Bray, Libn.
Staff: 1. **Subjects:** Engineering - electrical, mechanical; computer technology. **Holdings:** 2000 books; 300 bound periodical volumes; 20,000 technical reports; 175 volumes of standards; 1500 patents; 1000 reels of microfilm. **Subscriptions:** 15 journals and other serials. **Services:** Library not open to public. **Publications:** Acquisitions Bulletin, bimonthly - for internal distribution only. **Formerly:** Sperry Marine Systems.

★12862★
SPERRY FLIGHT SYSTEMS - ENGINEERING LIBRARY (Sci-Tech)
Box 21111   Phone: (602) 869-2278
Phoenix, AZ 85036   Pat DeVillier, Libn.
Founded: 1960. **Staff:** Prof 1; Other 1. **Subjects:** Electronic engineering,

computer sciences, flight instrumentation. **Holdings:** 3000 books; 2000 technical reports; 1000 other cataloged items. **Subscriptions:** 150 journals and other serials. **Services:** Interlibrary loans; copying; library open to public by appointment. **Computerized Information Services:** DIALOG. Performs searches on cost recovery basis. **Publications:** Quarterly Library Acquisitions.

★12863★
SPERRY AND HUTCHINSON COMPANY - MARKET RESEARCH LIBRARY
330 Madison Ave., 9th Fl.
New York, NY 10017
Founded: 1960. **Subjects:** Trading stamps, promotions, incentives, retailing, marketing, demography. **Holdings:** Figures not available. **Special Catalogs:** Card catalog of Sperry and Hutchinson Market Research Reports; book catalog of Sperry and Hutchinson Accounts-Redemption Centers. **Remarks:** Presently inactive.

★12864★
SPERRY - LAW LIBRARY (Law)
1290 Avenue of the Americas   Phone: (212) 484-4444
New York, NY 10104   Rosemarie Scirica, Lib.Adm.
Founded: 1955. **Staff:** 2. **Subjects:** Law. **Holdings:** 2000 volumes. **Subscriptions:** 1004 journals and other serials. **Services:** Interlibrary loans; library not open to public. **Staff:** G. Huertas .

SPERRY MARINE SYSTEMS
See: Sperry Electronic Systems

★12865★
SPERRY - NEW HOLLAND ENGINEERING LIBRARY (Sci-Tech; Agri)
500 Diller Ave.   Phone: (717) 354-1358
New Holland, PA 17557   Tammy A. Houck, Libn.
Staff: Prof 1. **Subjects:** Engineering - agricultural, mechanical; agriculture. **Holdings:** 625 books and bound periodical volumes. **Subscriptions:** 64 journals and other serials. **Services:** Interlibrary loans; copying; library open to public with permission.

★12866★
SPERRY - RESEARCH CENTER LIBRARY (Sci-Tech)†
North Rd.   Phone: (617) 369-4000
Sudbury, MA 01776   H. Alan Steeves, Libn.
Founded: 1961. **Staff:** Prof 1; Other 1. **Subjects:** Physics, chemistry, mathematics. **Holdings:** 7000 books; 7000 bound periodical volumes; 200 pamphlets. **Subscriptions:** 250 journals and other serials. **Services:** Interlibrary loans; library not open to public. **Computerized Information Services:** DIALOG, DOE/RECON, DTIC.

★12867★
SPERRY - SPERRY ELECTRONIC SYSTEMS - TECHNICAL INFORMATION CENTER (Sci-Tech)
Box 4648   Phone: (813) 577-1900
Clearwater, FL 33518   Margaret M. Cort, Hd.Libn.
Founded: 1959. **Staff:** 3. **Subjects:** Electronic engineering, physics, mathematics, mechanical engineering. **Holdings:** 2100 books; 4000 reports. **Subscriptions:** 53 journals and other serials. **Services:** Interlibrary loans; center not open to public. **Computerized Information Services:** DIALOG; internal database. **Remarks:** The center is located at 13133 34th St., Clearwater, FL 33520. **Formerly:** Sperry - Sperry Gyroscope Division - Engineering Library.

★12868★
SPERRY - SPERRY ELECTRONIC SYSTEMS - TECHNICAL INFORMATION CENTER (Sci-Tech)
Lakeville Rd. & Marcus Ave.   Phone: (516) 574-1001
Great Neck, NY 11020   Catherine L. Marcoux, Libn.
Staff: Prof 2. **Subjects:** Navigation, radar, electronics, telecommunications, optics, systems engineering. **Holdings:** 5600 books and bound periodical volumes. **Subscriptions:** 170 journals and other serials. **Services:** Interlibrary loans; center not open to public. **Computerized Information Services:** DIALOG, DTIC, New England Research Application Center (NERAC). **Networks/Consortia:** Member of Long Island Library Resources Council. **Publications:** Acquisitions Bulletin, monthly - for internal distribution only. **Formerly:** Sperry - Sperry Library. **Staff:** James Montalbano, Asst.Libn.

★12869★
SPERRY - TECHNICAL LIBRARY (Comp Sci)
1290 Avenue of the Americas   Phone: (212) 484-4444
New York, NY 10104   Graham Gurney, Dist.Mgr.
Founded: 1960. **Staff:** Prof 1. **Subjects:** Computer industry - hardware, software, sales, applications, research, self-study. **Holdings:** 10,000

volumes. **Services:** Interlibrary loans; copying; library open to public with restrictions. **Publications:** Technical manuals; sales and applications literature; self-study booklets; computer industry research manuals; list of other publications - available upon request.

★12870★
SPERTUS COLLEGE OF JUDAICA - NORMAN AND HELEN ASHER LIBRARY
(Rel-Theol; Area-Ethnic)
618 S. Michigan Ave. Phone: (312) 922-9012
Chicago, IL 60605 Richard W. Marcus, Dir.
Founded: 1925. **Staff:** Prof 4; Other 2. **Subjects:** Judaica, Hebraica, Rabbinica, Yiddish language and literature, Zionism, Israel, Jewish current events. **Special Collections:** Badona Spertus Art Collection; Chicago Jewish Archives; Levin Microform Collection. **Holdings:** 72,000 books; 8300 bound periodical volumes; 300 reels of microfilm. **Subscriptions:** 625 journals and other serials; 9 newspapers. **Services:** Interlibrary loans; copying; library open to public. **Networks/Consortia:** Member of Chicago Library System; Judaica Library Network of Chicago. **Staff:** Dan Sharon, Libn.; Robbin Saltzman, Libn.; Chava Feferman, Per.Asst.

SPICER LIBRARY
See: Polytechnic Institute of New York

★12871★
**SPIE - THE INTERNATIONAL SOCIETY FOR OPTICAL ENGINEERING -
LIBRARY** (Sci-Tech)
Box 10 Phone: (206) 676-3290
Bellingham, WA 98227-0010 Joseph Yaver, Exec.Dir.
Subjects: Optical and electo-optical technology - electro-optics, laser, infrared and photographic. **Holdings:** 500 books. **Services:** Library open to public. **Publications:** S.P.I.E. Proceedings of approximately 70 conferences per year; Optical Engineering journal, bimonthly. **Remarks:** Library is located at 1022 19th St., Bellingham, WA 98225.

★12872★
SPILL CONTROL ASSOCIATION OF AMERICA - LIBRARY (Env-Cons)
17117 W. Nine Mile Rd., Suite 1040 Phone: (313) 552-0500
Southfield, MI 48075 Marc K. Shaye, General Counsel
Founded: 1972. **Staff:** 2. **Subjects:** Federal and state water laws, current proposed legislation, equipment and contractor listings, government agencies, oil and hazardous substances spill statistics, industry history. **Special Collections:** Current abstracts of technical documents relating to oil and hazardous substances spill control and containment research and techniques employed in the United States, Canada and around the world. **Holdings:** Figures not available for books; SCAA Newsletters. **Services:** Interlibrary loans; copying; library open to public upon request. **Remarks:** Library includes the most current information regarding laws and regulations relating to oil and hazardous materials spill control, cleanup, transport, and disposal.

★12873★
**SPIRIT OF THE FUTURE CREATIVE INSTITUTE - CENTRAL LIBRARY
ARCHIVES** (Sci-Tech; Soc Sci)
3027 22nd St., Suite 3
Box 40296 Phone: (415) 821-7800
San Francisco, CA 94110 Gary Marchi, Creative Dir.
Staff: Prof 1. **Subjects:** Future science, space technology and innovations, new business development, vital growth industries, pure economics, mental development. **Holdings:** 350 books; 100 cassette tapes; 2000 clippings; other cataloged items. **Subscriptions:** 30 journals and other serials; 10 newspapers. **Services:** Copying; library not open to public.

★12874★
SPIRITUAL COMMUNITY PUBLICATIONS - INFORMATION CENTER
Box 1080
San Rafael, CA 94902
Founded: 1971. **Subjects:** Eastern religions, natural foods, growth centers, meditation, yoga, occult, psychology, ecology, health. **Holdings:** 600 volumes; original manuscripts and photographs. **Remarks:** Presently inactive.

★12875★
SPIRITUAL FRONTIERS FELLOWSHIP - LIBRARY (Rel-Theol)
10819 Winner Rd. Phone: (816) 254-8585
Independence, MO 64052
Founded: 1956. **Staff:** 1. **Subjects:** Psychic research, psychic experiences, spiritual healing, prayer, mysticism, meditation, spiritual development. **Special Collections:** Gertrude Tubby Collection - papers and books from the former secretary of the American Society for Psychical Research. **Holdings:** 8000 books. **Subscriptions:** 25 journals and other serials. **Services:** Library open to members only. **Special Catalogs:** Progressive Reading List, Lending Library

Catalog.

SPITZ (Rene A.) PSYCHIATRIC LIBRARY
See: **University of Colorado Health Sciences Center - Rene A. Spitz
Psychiatric Library**

★12876★
SPOHN HOSPITAL - MEDICAL LIBRARY (Med)
600 Elizabeth St. Phone: (512) 881-3261
Corpus Christi, TX 78404 Linda Neargardner-Shake, Med.Libn.
Staff: Prof 1; Other 2. **Subjects:** Medicine, nursing, medical technology, management, x-ray. **Holdings:** 3500 books; 1200 bound periodical volumes; 8 VF drawers of pamphlets; AV material. **Subscriptions:** 50 journals and other serials. **Services:** Interlibrary loans; library open to public for reference use only. **Networks/Consortia:** Member of Coastal Bend Health Sciences Library Consortium. **Staff:** Gloria Henson, Dept.Hd.

SPOKANE CHRONICLE
See: **Spokane Spokesman-Review and Spokane Chronicle**

★12877★
SPOKANE COUNTY LAW LIBRARY (Law)
1020 Paulsen Bldg. Phone: (509) 456-3680
Spokane, WA 99201 Emily E. Wadden, Law Libn.
Founded: 1909. **Staff:** Prof 1; Other 1. **Subjects:** Law. **Holdings:** 22,000 volumes. **Services:** Interlibrary loans; copying; library open to public.

★12878★
SPOKANE MEDICAL LIBRARY (Med)
W. 35 8th Ave. Phone: (509) 747-5777
Spokane, WA 99204 Lisa Veium, Dir.
Founded: 1929. **Staff:** Prof 2; Other 1. **Subjects:** Clinical medicine. **Holdings:** 2000 books; 23,000 bound periodical volumes. **Subscriptions:** 250 journals and other serials. **Services:** Interlibrary loans; copying; library open to public with restrictions. **Automated Operations:** Computerized cataloging. **Computerized Information Services:** DIALOG, MEDLINE. Performs searches on cost recovery basis. **Networks/Consortia:** Member of EWNIC. **Remarks:** Maintained by the Spokane County Medical Society. **Staff:** Neva Henning, Libn.

★12879★
**SPOKANE SPOKESMAN-REVIEW AND SPOKANE CHRONICLE -
NEWSPAPER REFERENCE LIBRARY** (Publ)†
508 Chronicle Bldg. Phone: (509) 455-6891
Spokane, WA 99210 Robert A. Neswick, Mgr.
Staff: 5. **Subjects:** Newspaper reference topics. **Holdings:** 3000 books; newspapers on microfilm from 1881; newspaper clipping files; pictures. **Services:** Library not open to public. **Remarks:** Both newspapers are published by the Cowles Publishing Company.

★12880★
SPOKANE VALLEY PIONEER MUSEUM, INC. - LIBRARY
Box 141245
Spokane, WA 99206
Defunct

SPOKESWOMAN MAGAZINE ARCHIVES
See: **Northwestern University - Special Collections Department -
Women's Collection**

SPOONER (Harry L.) MEMORIAL LIBRARY
See: **Peoria Historical Society - Harry L. Spooner Memorial Library**

★12881★
SPORT INFORMATION RESOURCE CENTRE (Rec)
333 River Rd. Phone: (613) 746-5357
Ottawa, ON, Canada K1L 8H9 Gilles Chiasson, Mgr.
Founded: 1973. **Staff:** Prof 6; Other 6. **Subjects:** Sport, physical education, recreation, physical fitness, sport medicine. **Holdings:** 15,000 books; 3000 bound periodical volumes; 5000 microfiche; 300 boxes of pamphlets. **Subscriptions:** 1400 journals and other serials. **Services:** Interlibrary loans; copying; SDI; center open to public. **Automated Operations:** Computerized cataloging and acquisitions. **Computerized Information Services:** DIALOG, SDC, Info Globe, CAN/OLE. Performs searches on fee basis. Contact Person: Linda Wheeler. **Publications:** Sport Bibliography, 1981-1982, 8 volumes with annual update. **Special Indexes:** Sport and Fitness Index, a monthly indexing journal - available by subscription. **Remarks:** Maintained by Coaching Association of Canada. The Resource Centre creates SPORT, an online database containing 145,000 documents. **Staff:** Richard Stark, Chf. Indexer;

Linda Wheeler, Hd., Ref.Serv.; Christine Lalande, Asst.Mgr.

★12882★
SPORTS RESEARCH INSTITUTE - LIBRARY (Rec)
109 Sports Research Bldg.
Pennsylvania State University   Phone: (814) 865-9543
University Park, PA 16802   Patricia McMullen, Sec.
Founded: 1969. **Staff:** 1. **Subjects:** Sports - research, safety, injuries; biomechanics of sport. **Holdings:** 150 books; 250 bound periodical volumes; 2 VF drawers of reprints; 15 theses. **Subscriptions:** 6 journals and other serials. **Services:** Copying; library open to public for reference use only.

★12883★
SPOTSYLVANIA HISTORICAL ASSOCIATION, INC. - RESEARCH MUSEUM AND LIBRARY (Hist)
Court House, Box 64   Phone: (703) 582-5672
Spotsylvania, VA 22553   Frances L.N. Waller, Dir.
Founded: 1962. **Staff:** Prof 4; Other 2. **Subjects:** Spotsylvania County history, Civil War battlefields, colonial settlers and forts since 1671, genealogy statistics, Lafayette's campaign through Spotsylvania County 1781. **Special Collections:** Early medicine; Civil War arms; Indian artifacts; colonial farm implements; many family histories and collection of old home and church histories in the county. **Holdings:** 2500 books; 100 bound periodical volumes; 800 booklets; 1 bookcase Ohio and Virginia historical reports; 4 VF drawers of local manuscripts; maps, tapes, photostats, slides, reels. **Subscriptions:** 10 journals and other serials. **Services:** Interlibrary loans; copying; library open to public for reference use only. **Publications:** Association reports; Revolutionary Times in Spotsylvania County, 1976; Spotsylvania County Historical Map, 1978; Spotsylvania County Patriots, 1774-1786. **Staff:** Merle Strickler; John E. Pruitt, Jr.A.N. Waller; Monica Blount; Sonya Harvison.

SPRAFKA MEMORIAL HEALTH SCIENCE LIBRARY
See: St. Anthony Hospital

★12884★
SPRAGUE ELECTRIC COMPANY - RESEARCH LIBRARY (Sci-Tech)*
87 Marshall St.   Phone: (413) 664-4411
North Adams, MA 01247   Virginia Kemp, Libn.
Founded: 1944. **Staff:** Prof 1. **Subjects:** Electronics, chemistry, physics, materials sciences, mathematics, engineering. **Holdings:** 5800 books; 1100 bound periodical volumes; 24 VF drawers of internal company reports; government documents on microfiche. **Subscriptions:** 240 journals and other serials. **Services:** Interlibrary loans; copying; use of library for reference may be requested.

SPRAGUE (Harry A.) LIBRARY
See: Montclair State College - Harry A. Sprague Library

SPRAGUE (Norman F.) MEMORIAL LIBRARY
See: The Claremont Colleges - Norman F. Sprague Memorial Library

SPRIGG (William Mercer) MEMORIAL LIBRARY
See: Capitol Hill Hospital - William Mercer Sprigg Memorial Library

★12885★
SPRING GARDEN COLLEGE - LIBRARY (Sci-Tech)
102 E. Mermaid Ln.   Phone: (215) 242-3700
Chestnut Hill, PA 19118   Mildred Glushakow, Dir.
Staff: Prof 2. **Subjects:** Electrical, electronic, civil, mechanical and computer engineering; building construction; architecture; medical technology; business management. **Holdings:** 21,900 volumes; 8 VF drawers of catalogs and pamphlets. **Subscriptions:** 454 journals and other serials. **Services:** Interlibrary loans; copying; library open to public. **Automated Operations:** Computerized cataloging. **Networks/Consortia:** Member of Tri-State College Library Cooperative (TCLC). **Publications:** Library Handbook; Library Research Quiz; Alphabetical and Subject Lists of Periodicals - students and faculty. **Staff:** Ella Strattis, Asst.Libn.

★12886★
SPRING GROVE HOSPITAL CENTER - SULZBACHER MEMORIAL LIBRARY (Med)†
Wade Ave., Isidore Tuerk Bldg.   Phone: (301) 455-7824
Baltimore, MD 21228   Charles H. Johnson, Supv. of Lib.
Founded: 1938. **Staff:** 1. **Subjects:** Psychiatry, psychology, psychotherapy, pharmacology, sociology, social work, neurology, pastoral care, nursing education, therapy. **Special Collections:** History of Spring Grove Hospital Center; Rare Book Collection. **Holdings:** 7000 books; 1000 bound periodical volumes; 600 cassettes; 10 films; 15 phonograph records; 500 pamphlets;

13 AV units. **Subscriptions:** 316 journals and other serials. **Services:** Interlibrary loans; copying; bibliographies; library open to staff and students. **Computerized Information Services:** MEDLINE.

★12887★
SPRINGFIELD ACADEMY OF MEDICINE - HEALTH SCIENCE LIBRARY (Med)
1400 State St.   Phone: (413) 734-5445
Springfield, MA 01109   Margaret Stoler, Lib.Dir.
Founded: 1907. **Staff:** Prof 1; Other 2. **Subjects:** Medicine and allied medical fields, dentistry, nursing. **Special Collections:** Medical history. **Holdings:** 10,000 books; 18,000 bound periodical volumes; 4 drawers of reports; 2 drawers of manuscripts; 6 drawers of clippings. **Subscriptions:** 187 journals and other serials. **Services:** Interlibrary loans; copying; library open to public for reference use only. **Networks/Consortia:** Member of Western Massachusetts Health Information Consortium. **Remarks:** Affiliated with the Hampden District Medical Society.

★12888★
SPRINGFIELD ART ASSOCIATION - MICHAEL VICTOR II ART LIBRARY (Art)
700 N. Fourth St.   Phone: (217) 523-2631
Springfield, IL 62702   Florence Irene Boyer, Libn.
Staff: Prof 1; Other 4. **Subjects:** Visual and related arts. **Holdings:** 2500 books; prints; booklets; exhibition catalogs. **Subscriptions:** 12 journals and other serials. **Services:** Library open to public for reference use only.

★12889★
SPRINGFIELD ART CENTER - LIBRARY (Art)
107 Cliff Park Rd.   Phone: (513) 325-4673
Springfield, OH 45501   Mary McG. Miller, Chm. of Lib.Comm.
Subjects: Art, art history, photography. **Special Collections:** Axel Bahnson Collection (historical photographic books and periodicals). **Holdings:** 2500 books. **Subscriptions:** 15 journals and other serials. **Services:** Library open to public with restrictions. **Publications:** Newsletter - issued to members.

★12890★
SPRINGFIELD ART MUSEUM - ART REFERENCE LIBRARY (Art)
1111 E. Brookside Dr.   Phone: (417) 866-2716
Springfield, MO 65807   Alice Brooker, Libn.
Staff: Prof 1. **Subjects:** Painting, sculpture, graphics, ceramics, art history, appreciation of aesthetics, social history. **Holdings:** 4000 books; 1000 slides; 5000 clippings and pictures; 3000 unbound magazines; 2000 brochures and pamphlets of art exhibitions. **Subscriptions:** 47 journals and other serials; 15 newspapers. **Services:** Interlibrary loans; copying (limited); library open to public with limited circulation to nonresidents. **Automated Operations:** Computerized cataloging, acquisitions, serials and circulation.

★12891★
SPRINGFIELD BAR AND LAW LIBRARY ASSOCIATION - LIBRARY (Law)†
Clark County Court House, 3rd Fl.   Phone: (513) 428-2478
Springfield, OH 45502   Rita M. Harnish, Libn.
Staff: Prof 1. **Subjects:** Law. **Holdings:** 30,000 volumes. **Subscriptions:** 80 journals and other serials. **Services:** Library open to public with restrictions.

★12892★
SPRINGFIELD CITY LIBRARY - FINE ARTS DEPARTMENT (Art; Mus)
220 State St.   Phone: (413) 739-3871
Springfield, MA 01103   Karen A. Dorval, Supv./Art Libn.
Founded: 1857. **Staff:** Prof 4; Other 3. **Subjects:** Art, crafts, needlework, music, photography, coins. **Special Collections:** Aston collection of wood-engravings (2250 prints). **Holdings:** 33,250 books; 3200 bound periodical volumes; 18,000 recordings; 125,000 pictures; 8000 pamphlets. **Subscriptions:** 112 journals and other serials. **Services:** Interlibrary loans; copying; library open to public, card required to borrow books. **Staff:** Sylvia St. Amand, Mus.Libn.

★12893★
SPRINGFIELD CITY LIBRARY - WARTIME PROPAGANDA COLLECTION (Hist)†
220 State St., Rice Hall   Phone: (413) 739-3871
Springfield, MA 01103   Joseph Carvalho, III, Coll.Libn.
Subjects: World Wars I and II. **Holdings:** 1200 World War I pamphlets; 200 World War I periodical issues; 25 World War I posters; 1500 World War II pamphlets and periodicals; 100 World War II air-drop leaflets. **Services:** Copying; library open to public. **Publications:** Propaganda: A Collection of Wartime Materials Owned by the Springfield City Library (1979) - available to collection users.

★12894★
SPRINGFIELD COLLEGE - BABSON LIBRARY - SPECIAL COLLECTIONS (Educ)
263 Alden St.
Springfield, MA 01109
Phone: (413) 788-3307
Gerald F. Davis, Lib.Dir.
Founded: 1885. **Special Collections:** Physical education; recreation. **Holdings:** Figures not available. **Services:** Interlibrary loans; copying; library open to public with permission. **Computerized Information Services:** DIALOG. Performs searches on cost recovery basis for college community. Contact Person: Henry Dutcher, 788-3315. **Networks/Consortia:** Member of Cooperating Libraries of Greater Springfield. **Staff:** Henry Dutcher, Ref.Libn.; Raymond Lin, Cat.

★12895★
SPRINGFIELD-GREENE COUNTY PUBLIC LIBRARIES - EDWARD M. SHEPARD MEMORIAL ROOM (Hist)
397 E. Central
Springfield, MO 65801
Phone: (417) 869-4621
Michael D. Glenn, Ref.Libn.
Founded: 1961. **Staff:** Prof 1; Other 3. **Subjects:** Missouri, Greene County, Springfield and the Ozarks - history, biography, genealogy, literature, Missouri authors, archeology, geology, religion, language. **Special Collections:** Edward M. Shepard Collection of Rare Missouri and Ozark books; Justus R. Moll Collection of Missouriana; Collection of Ozarks poetry; Collection of Historical Photographs; Max Hunter Collection of Ozark Folksong (1000 songs on cassette tapes). **Holdings:** 6000 books; Federal Census, Missouri (1830-1880; 1900; 1910) on microfilm; 1100 reels of microfilm of Springfield newspapers, 1870 to present; 54 reels of miscellaneous genealogical material; 16 VF drawers of pictures and clippings. **Subscriptions:** 75 journals and other serials. **Services:** Copying; collections open to public. **Automated Operations:** Computerized circulation. **Computerized Information Services:** CLSI (internal database). **Networks/Consortia:** Member of Southwest Missouri Library Network. **Special Indexes:** Card index to Springfield newspapers (articles pertaining primarily to Springfield and Greene County, also includes Missouri and the Ozarks).

★12896★
SPRINGFIELD HISTORICAL SOCIETY - LIBRARY (Hist)
126 Morris Ave.
Box 124
Springfield, NJ 07081
Phone: (201) 376-7737
Kenneth D. Hendrix, Pres.
Founded: 1956. **Subjects:** Local history, genealogy, New Jersey history. **Holdings:** 1000 books. **Services:** Library open to public by appointment for reference use only; Cannon Ball House, circa 1741, open to public on a limited schedule. **Staff:** Howard Wiseman, V.P.

★12897★
SPRINGFIELD HOSPITAL CENTER - MEDICAL LIBRARY (Med)
Phone: (301) 795-2100
Sykesville, MD 21784
Elizabeth D. Mercer, Libn.
Founded: 1954. **Staff:** 1. **Subjects:** Psychiatry, neurology, clinical psychology, psychotherapy, psychiatric nursing, psychiatric social work, medicine, practical nursing. **Holdings:** 2000 books; 1000 bound periodical volumes. **Subscriptions:** 84 journals and other serials. **Services:** Interlibrary loans; library open to public for reference use only on request. **Publications:** Acquisition lists, quarterly.

★12898★
SPRINGFIELD HOSPITAL - INFORMATION CENTER LIBRARY (Med)
25 Ridgewood Rd.
Springfield, VT 05156
Phone: (802) 885-2151
Holly H. Eddy, Med.Libn.
Staff: 2. **Subjects:** Medicine. **Holdings:** 280 books. **Subscriptions:** 39 journals and other serials. **Services:** Center open to others in medical or allied health fields. **Networks/Consortia:** Member of Vermont/New Hampshire Health Science Libraries.

★12899★
SPRINGFIELD, ILLINOIS STATE JOURNAL & REGISTER - EDITORIAL LIBRARY (Publ)
1 Copley Plaza
Springfield, IL 62705
Phone: (217) 788-1300
Sandra Vance, Libn.
Staff: 2. **Subjects:** Newspaper reference topics. **Holdings:** 460 books; 90 bound periodical volumes; 2.9 million newspaper clippings on microfiche; newspapers on microfilm; photo negative file, photos of subjects and people. **Services:** Library open to public.

★12900★
SPRINGFIELD LIBRARY AND MUSEUMS ASSOCIATION - CATHERINE E. HOWARD MEMORIAL LIBRARY (Sci-Tech)
236 State St.
Springfield, MA 01103
Founded: 1899. **Subjects:** Astronomy, physical geology, historical geology, anthropology, ethnology, botany, zoology, ornithology. **Holdings:** 4000 books; 200 bound periodical volumes; 200 pamphlets. **Remarks:** Presently inactive.

★12901★
SPRINGFIELD NEWSPAPERS - LIBRARY (Publ)*
1860 Main St.
Springfield, MA 01101
Phone: (413) 787-2411
Diane A. Blais, Supv.
Staff: Prof 1; Other 5. **Subjects:** Newspaper reference topics. **Special Collections:** Springfield city directories, 1852 to present; Springfield Union Index, 1912-1941. **Holdings:** 80,000 subject headings of clippings and microfiche. **Services:** Library not open to public.

★12902★
SPRINGHOUSE CORPORATION - CORPORATE LIBRARY (Med; Publ)
1111 Bethlehem Pike
Spring House, PA 19477
Phone: (215) 646-8700
Vonda Heller, Libn./Rec.Coord.
Staff: Prof 2. **Subjects:** Nursing, health care, publishing. **Holdings:** 3000 books. **Subscriptions:** 131 journals and other serials. **Services:** Interlibrary loans; copying; library not open to public. **Networks/Consortia:** Member of Delaware Valley Information Consortium (DEVIC); Greater Northeastern Regional Medical Library Program. **Publications:** Editorial Resources Bulletin, monthly. **Formerly:** Intermed Communications, Inc. **Staff:** Elaine Shelly, Art Libn.

SPROUL OBSERVATORY LIBRARY
See: Swarthmore College

★12903★
SPROULE ASSOCIATES, LTD. - LIBRARY
505 2nd St., S.W., 3rd Fl.
Calgary, AB, Canada T2P 1N8
Defunct

SPRUANCE LIBRARY
See: Bucks County Historical Society

★12904★
SPS TECHNOLOGIES, INC. - RESEARCH AND DEVELOPMENT LABORATORIES - CORPORATE TECHNICAL LIBRARY (Sci-Tech)
Highland Ave.
Jenkintown, PA 19046
Phone: (215) 572-3564
Michele R. Thomas, Corp.Libn./Editor
Staff: Prof 1. **Subjects:** Fastener engineering and technology, mechanical engineering, metallurgy, management. **Holdings:** 1500 books; 10,000 internal technical reports; 250 technical reports; specifications; industry standards; annual reports. **Subscriptions:** 53 journals and other serials. **Services:** Interlibrary loans; copying; SDI; library open to public by appointment. **Computerized Information Services:** DIALOG, BRS; internal database. Performs searches on cost recovery basis. **Publications:** Acquisitions List, monthly; Technical Reports Issued by the Corporation, monthly - both for internal distribution only. **Special Indexes:** Chronological, author, and subject indexes to SPS technical reports and lab notes (book), annual.

★12905★
SQUARE D COMPANY - LIBRARY (Sci-Tech)
4041 N. Richards St.
Milwaukee, WI 53212
Phone: (414) 332-2000
Julie Schwartz, Libn.
Founded: 1960. **Staff:** 1. **Subjects:** Electrical engineering. **Holdings:** 3000 books. **Subscriptions:** 150 journals and other serials. **Services:** Interlibrary loans; library not open to public.

★12906★
SQUIBB CANADA INC. - MEDICAL LIBRARY (Med)
2365 Cote de Liesse Rd.
Montreal, PQ, Canada H4N 2M7
Phone: (514) 337-7423
Carole Schneider, Sec./Libn.
Staff: 1. **Subjects:** Medicine, pharmacology. **Holdings:** 500 unbound periodical volumes. **Subscriptions:** 40 journals and other serials; 5 newspapers. **Services:** Interlibrary loans; copying; library open to public with restrictions.

★12907★
SQUIBB (E.R.) AND SONS, INC. - SQUIBB INSTITUTE FOR MEDICAL RESEARCH - SCIENCE INFORMATION DEPARTMENT (Med)
Box 4000   Phone: (609) 921-4844
Princeton, NJ 08540   Dr. Frank L. Weisenborn, Dir.
Founded: 1925. **Staff:** Prof 9; Other 10. **Subjects:** Pharmacology, chemistry, medicine, pharmacy. **Holdings:** 17,300 books; 40,000 bound periodical volumes; 7000 volumes on microfilm; 100 VF drawers. **Subscriptions:** 1000 journals and other serials. **Services:** Interlibrary loans; copying; department open to public by appointment. **Automated Operations:** Computerized cataloging AND serials. **Computerized Information Services:** DIALOG, SDC, OCLC, MEDLINE, Derwent Publications Ltd. **Networks/Consortia:** Member of Medical Resources Consortium of Central New Jersey (MEDCORE). **Publications:** Index Squibbicus, bimonthly - for internal distribution only; Monthly Acquisitions Bulletin. **Staff:** Dr. Nick Semenuk, Sec.Hd., Lit. Search; Helen Kosowski, Supv., Lib.Oper.

★12908★
SQUIBB (E.R.) & SONS, INC. - SQUIBB INST. FOR MEDICAL RES. - SCIENCE INFO. DEPT. - NEW BRUNSWICK LIBRARY (Med)
Georges Rd.   Phone: (201) 545-1300
New Brunswick, NJ 08903   Muriel S. George, Supv., Lib.Oper.
Staff: Prof 1; Other 2. **Subjects:** Chemistry, pharmaceutics, science and technology, microbiology, quality control. **Holdings:** 3000 books; 4900 bound periodical volumes. **Subscriptions:** 200 journals and other serials. **Services:** Interlibrary loans; copying; library open to other librarians and researchers with authorization. **Computerized Information Services:** DIALOG, SDC, BRS, CAS Online. **Networks/Consortia:** Member of Medical Resources Consortium of Central New Jersey (MEDCORE).

SQUIRE (Eleanor) LIBRARY
See: Garden Center of Greater Cleveland - Eleanor Squire Library

★12909★
SQUIRE, SANDERS & DEMPSEY - LAW LIBRARY (Law)
1800 Union Commerce Bldg.   Phone: (216) 696-9200
Cleveland, OH 44115   Vivian S. Balester, Hd.Libn.
Founded: 1890. **Staff:** Prof 9; Other 6. **Subjects:** Law. **Special Collections:** International law and trade; Cleveland and Ohio history (300 titles). **Holdings:** 47,000 volumes. **Subscriptions:** 700 journals and other serials; 35 newspapers. **Services:** Interlibrary loans; library not open to public. **Computerized Information Services:** LEXIS, Westlaw, Auto-Cite, DIALOG, BRS, SDC. **Special Indexes:** Indexes to internal legal memoranda (card). **Remarks:** Maintains other libraries in Washington, DC; Brussels, Belgium; Miami, FL; Columbus, OH; Phoenix, AZ; New York, NY. **Staff:** Leslie Bitman, Assoc.Libn.; Nanna Frye, Assoc.Libn.; Donna Shumaker, Br.Libn., Washington; Zelma Palestrant, Br.Libn., Columbus.

★12910★
SRI INTERNATIONAL - BUSINESS INTELLIGENCE PROGRAM - INFORMATION CENTER (Bus-Fin)†
333 Ravenswood Ave.   Phone: (415) 859-2400
Menlo Park, CA 94025   Edward F. Christie, Mgr., Inquiry Serv.
Founded: 1958. **Staff:** 13. **Subjects:** Trends - business and industrial, technological, government, sociological; business planning. **Holdings:** 400 books; 75,000 clippings, pamphlets and reports indexed by subject. **Subscriptions:** 450 journals and other serials. **Services:** Center use restricted to SRI staff and subscribers to Business Intelligence Program Service. **Computerized Information Services:** DIALOG, NEXIS. **Special Indexes:** Index to BIP publications, annual.

★12911★
SRI INTERNATIONAL - LIBRARY AND RESEARCH INFORMATION SERVICES DEPARTMENT (Sci-Tech)
333 Ravenswood Ave.   Phone: (415) 326-6200
Menlo Park, CA 94025   Elizabeth D. Gill, Dir.
Founded: 1946. **Staff:** Prof 9; Other 17. **Subjects:** Engineering, physical sciences, life sciences, management sciences, research and development, economics. **Holdings:** 56,990 books; 8000 bound periodical volumes; 59,473 technical reports; 15,400 corporate annual reports; 6332 pamphlets; 128,674 government documents. **Subscriptions:** 1648 journals and other serials. **Services:** Interlibrary loans; copying; SDI; information systems design; indexing and abstracting; department open to public for reference use only by prior arrangement. **Automated Operations:** Computerized cataloging, acquisitions and serials. **Computerized Information Services:** Alternate Fuels Data Bank, BRS, CAS Online, NIH-EPA Chemical Information System. DIALOG, DOE/RECON, Dow Jones News/Retrieval, DTIC, Dun and Bradstreet Corporation, INVESTEXT, MEDLARS, NASA/RECON, NewsNet, Inc., NEXIS, Occupational Health Services, Inc., SDC, Pergamon InfoLine Ltd.,

Questel, RLIN; LIBRI (internal database). Performs searches on cost recovery basis plus fee. Contact Person: Donna Kleiner, 859-5983. **Networks/Consortia:** Member of South Bay Area Reference Network (SBARN); CLASS. **Staff:** Donna Kleiner, Sr.Info.Spec.; Helen Rolen, Supv., Tech.Serv.; Stephen Dennett, Sys.Anl.; Lucille Steelman, Rsrcs.Coord.

★12912★
SRI INTERNATIONAL - STRATEGIC CENTER LIBRARY (Mil)
1611 N. Kent St.   Phone: (703) 524-2053
Arlington, VA 22209   Helga Brennan, Res.Anl.
Subjects: Defense, political science, economics (all in Russian). **Holdings:** 4500 books; 500 SRI research reports; 1000 items in telecommunications project file. **Subscriptions:** 84 journals and other serials. **Services:** Interlibrary loans; copying (limited); library open to public by appointment. **Publications:** SRI Reports, 12/year - distributed to clients and scholars.

STAATS (Joan) LIBRARY
See: Jackson Laboratory - Joan Staats Library

STABINS (Samuel J., M.D.) HEALTH SCIENCES LIBRARY
See: Genesee Hospital - Samuel J. Stabins, M.D., Health Sciences Library

STACK GAS EMISSION CONTROL COORDINATION CENTER
See: Battelle-Columbus Laboratories

★12913★
STACK'S RARE COIN COMPANY OF NEW YORK - TECHNICAL INFORMATION CENTER (Rec)
123 W. 57th St.   Phone: (212) 582-2580
New York, NY 10019   James C. Risk, Mgr., Tech.Oper.
Staff: Prof 2. **Subjects:** Rare coins - U.S., ancient, foreign; medals and decorations. **Special Collections:** Historical busts of famous world personalities. **Holdings:** 15,000 books; 5000 bound periodical volumes. **Services:** Center open to public with permission and by appointment.

★12914★
STAGECOACH LIBRARY FOR GENEALOGICAL RESEARCH (Hist)
1840 S. Wolcott Ct.   Phone: (303) 922-8856
Denver, CO 80219   Donna J. Porter, Owner
Staff: Prof 1; Other 1. **Subjects:** Genealogy, local history. **Holdings:** 2800 books. **Services:** Copying; library open to public by mail only. **Publications:** Stagecoach Library Bulletin, bimonthly - to members. **Formerly:** Located in Magnolia, TX.

STAIGER (Ralph C.) LIBRARY
See: International Reading Association - Ralph C. Staiger Library

★12915★
STALEY (A.E.) MANUFACTURING COMPANY - TECHNICAL INFORMATION CENTER (Food-Bev)
2200 E. Eldorado St.   Phone: (217) 423-4411
Decatur, IL 62525   Ann M. Seidman, Mgr.
Founded: 1920. **Staff:** Prof 2; Other 3. **Subjects:** Carbohydrates, sweeteners, fats-oils, soybean products, corn products. **Holdings:** 10,000 books; 23,000 bound periodical volumes; 3000 reprints, translations, pamphlets. **Subscriptions:** 500 journals and other serials. **Services:** Interlibrary loans; copying; center open to public with restrictions. **Computerized Information Services:** DIALOG, SDC. **Networks/Consortia:** Member of Rolling Prairie Library System. **Publications:** Abstracts, weekly; New Additions to the Library, bimonthly. **Staff:** Julie Ostrow, Tech.Libn.

STALEY LIBRARY
See: Millikin University

STALLMAN (J. Kenneth) MEMORIAL LIBRARY
See: Atlantic Salmon Federation - J. Kenneth Stallman Memorial Library

STAMATS (Herbert S.) ART LIBRARY
See: Cedar Rapids Museum of Art - Herbert S. Stamats Art Library

★12916★
STAMFORD CATHOLIC LIBRARY, INC. (Rel-Theol)†
195 Glenbrook Rd.   Phone: (203) 348-4422
Stamford, CT 06902   Mary C. Cash, Libn.
Founded: 1948. **Staff:** Prof 1. **Subjects:** Religion, theology, American literature, history, biography, psychology. **Holdings:** 5000 books; 25 documentary series; 200 pre-Vatican II pamphlets; 20 encyclicals; 12 scripture studies; 100 papal and episcopal documents; 24 tapes. **Services:** Interlibrary loans; library open to public (fee charged). **Publications:** Annual

Report.

★12917★
STAMFORD HISTORICAL SOCIETY - LIBRARY (Hist)
713 Bedford St.   Phone: (203) 323-1975
Stamford, CT 06901   Ann M. Hermann, Dir.
Founded: 1901. **Staff:** 2. **Subjects:** History - Stamford, Fairfield County, State of Connecticut. **Special Collections:** Lewis Ruscoe Collection on Stamford government, 1700-1892; Charles Kurz Photographic Collection on Stamford, 1868-1941; Eaton, Yale and Towne Collection on Yale and Towne Manufacturing Company of Stamford, 1868-1949; F. Stewart Andrews Collection on Stamford Foundry Company, 1850-1950; Katharine Murphy Collection (Holly and Welles family papers, 1749-1950). **Holdings:** 700 books; 50 Stamford tax lists manuscripts, 1712-1876; 136 Stamford Revolutionary War damage claims manuscripts, 1776-1783; 300 Stamford newspapers, 1829-1925; 2000 Stamford pictures, 1870-1940; 1000 Stamford slides, 1870-1920; 25 Stamford maps, 1800-1961; 65 Stamford account books manuscripts, 1787-1941; 12 Stamford diaries, 1850-1929; 450 Stamford pamphlets, 1800-1953; 8 VF drawers of documents and clippings. **Services:** Copying; library open to public. **Publications:** Stamford Revolutionary War Damage Claims; Stamford - Pictures from the Past; Stamford - Journey through Time; Fort Stamford; Stamford in the Gilded Age - The Political Life of a Connecticut Town 1868-1893; Stamford from Puritan to Patriot 1641-1774; list of other publications - available on request. **Staff:** Greg Mecca, Asst.Dir.; Lois Dater, Cur.; Ronald Marcus, Libn.

★12918★
STAMFORD HOSPITAL - HEALTH SCIENCES LIBRARY (Med)
Shelburne Rd.
Box 9317   Phone: (203) 325-7522
Stamford, CT 06904-9317   Joanna Faraday, Dir.
Staff: Prof 2; Other 1. **Subjects:** Clinical medicine, nursing. **Holdings:** 1900 books; 2893 bound periodical volumes; 6454 microfiche; 1189 tapes; 3607 slides. **Subscriptions:** 350 journals and other serials. **Services:** Interlibrary loans; copying; library open to public by appointment only. **Computerized Information Services:** BRS, NLM. **Networks/Consortia:** Member of Connecticut Association of Health Science Libraries (CAHSL); Health Information Libraries of Westchester; Southwestern Connecticut Library Council. **Publications:** Newsletter, quarterly - to hospital staff and Connecticut medical libraries. **Staff:** Christina Russo, Asst.Libn.

★12919★
STANDARD EDUCATIONAL CORPORATION - EDITORIAL LIBRARY (Publ)
200 W. Monroe St.   Phone: (312) 346-7440
Chicago, IL 60606   David E. King, Libn.
Staff: 2. **Subjects:** General reference. **Holdings:** 8000 books; 400 microforms; 88 VF drawers. **Subscriptions:** 161 journals and other serials. **Services:** Interlibrary loans; copying; library open to public by appointment. **Networks/Consortia:** Member of ILLINET. **Publications:** New Books List, monthly; Serials List, annual.

★12920★
STANDARD OIL OF CALIFORNIA - CHEVRON U.S.A., INC. - EASTERN REGION LIBRARY (Sci-Tech; Energy)
935 Gravier St.   Phone: (504) 521-6292
New Orleans, LA 70112   Bob Hatten, Libn.
Staff: 2. **Subjects:** Geology, engineering, paleontology. **Holdings:** 5000 volumes. **Subscriptions:** 200 journals and other serials; 10 newspapers. **Services:** Interlibrary loans; library not open to public. **Computerized Information Services:** SDC.

★12921★
STANDARD OIL COMPANY OF CALIFORNIA - CORPORATE LIBRARY (Bus-Fin; Energy)
225 Bush St.   Phone: (415) 894-2945
San Francisco, CA 94104   Margaret J. Linden, Mgr.
Founded: 1917. **Staff:** Prof 10; Other 13. **Subjects:** Oil economics and technology. **Holdings:** Figures not available. **Subscriptions:** 2200 journals and other serials. **Services:** Library open to public for reference use only by special request. **Automated Operations:** Computerized cataloging and acquisitions. **Computerized Information Services:** RLIN, NEXIS, SDC, BRS, Info Globe, DIALOG, Dow Jones News/Retrieval; internal database. **Staff:** Sandra Menegaux, Supv., Ref.Serv.; Elena Herdman, Supv., Tech.Serv.

STANDARD OIL COMPANY OF INDIANA - AMOCO PRODUCTION COMPANY INTERNATIONAL
See: Amoco Production Company International

★12922★
STANDARD OIL COMPANY OF INDIANA - CENTRAL RESEARCH LIBRARY (Energy)
Amoco Research Center, Box 400   Phone: (312) 420-5545
Naperville, IL 60566   B. Camille Stryck, Res.Supv.
Founded: 1920. **Staff:** Prof 4; Other 6. **Subjects:** Petroleum chemistry, physics, engineering, chemistry, chemical engineering, economics, polymers. **Holdings:** 25,000 books; 35,000 bound periodical volumes; 15,000 reports; 7000 cartridges of journals on microfilm; U.S. chemical patents on microfilm, 1970 to present. **Subscriptions:** 900 journals and other serials. **Services:** Interlibrary loans; copying; SDI; library open to public with restrictions. **Automated Operations:** Computerized cataloging, serials and journal routing. **Computerized Information Services:** DIALOG, SDC, DOE/RECON, OCLC. **Networks/Consortia:** Member of ILLINET. **Publications:** Library Bulletin, monthly; Reports Alert, monthly. **Staff:** May S. Avery, Info.Spec.; Cheryl Kirk, Info.Spec.; Janet Zupko, Info.Spec.

★12923★
STANDARD OIL COMPANY OF INDIANA - LIBRARY/INFORMATION CENTER (Bus-Fin; Energy)
200 E. Randolph St.   Phone: (312) 856-5961
Chicago, IL 60601   Vicky A. Perlman, Mgr.
Founded: 1973. **Staff:** Prof 8; Other 11. **Subjects:** Petroleum technology, business, law, geology, chemistry, engineering. **Holdings:** 65,000 books and bound periodical volumes; technical reports; patents; business and technical information files; microforms. **Subscriptions:** 1200 journals and other serials; 20 newspapers. **Services:** Interlibrary loans; library open to researchers by appointment. **Automated Operations:** Computerized cataloging, serials and documents. **Computerized Information Services:** Online systems. **Publications:** Current Acquisitions List, weekly - for internal distribution only. **Staff:** E. Bears, Supv.; M. Dorigan, Supv.; S. Crosby, Supv.; L. Matera, Info.Spec.; M. Stowawy, Info.Spec.; N. Kelly, Info.Spec.; S. Robertson, Info.Spec.

★12924★
STANDARD OIL COMPANY OF OHIO - CORPORATE ENGINEERING LIBRARY (Sci-Tech)
Midland Bldg., 826HB   Phone: (216) 575-8006
Cleveland, OH 44115   Dorothy A. Jankowski, Supv., Tech.Info.Serv.
Staff: Prof 4; Other 2. **Subjects:** Engineering. **Holdings:** 2800 books; 7600 government reports; 1100 internal reports; 140 VF drawers of engineering project files; 275 reels of microfilm; 22 drawers of microfiche. **Subscriptions:** 100 journals and other serials. **Services:** Interlibrary loans; copying; library open to public with prior permission. **Computerized Information Services:** DIALOG, SDC; CHEERS, PROPS, DEVELOP, PRONODA (internal databases). **Publications:** Infomania, monthly - for internal distribution only. **Formerly:** Its EHEA Library. **Staff:** Pamela McConnell, Tech.Info.Spec.; Pamela Melick, Tech. Indexer; Beth Maher, Tech. Indexer; Lauren Morgan, Info.Spec.

★12925★
STANDARD OIL COMPANY OF OHIO - THE PFAUDLER COMPANY - TECHNICAL LIBRARY (Sci-Tech)
1000 West Ave.
Box 1600   Phone: (716) 235-1000
Rochester, NY 14692   Candice M. Johnson, Libn.
Founded: 1960. **Staff:** 1. **Subjects:** Metallurgy - steel and refractory metal fabrication; protective coatings - ceramic, metallic, plastic; chemical engineering. **Holdings:** 1900 books; 1065 bound periodical volumes; 6 VF drawers of government reports; 4 VF drawers of patents; 3 VF drawers of microforms; 8 VF drawers of internal reports. **Subscriptions:** 250 journals and other serials. **Services:** Interlibrary loans; copying; translations; library open to public by appointment. **Automated Operations:** Computerized serials. **Computerized Information Services:** DIALOG. **Networks/Consortia:** Member of Rochester Regional Research Library Council (RRRLC). **Special Catalogs:** Book catalog; journal catalog. **Special Indexes:** Patent and internal reports indexes.

STANDARD OIL COMPANY OF OHIO - SOHIO PETROLEUM COMPANY
See: Sohio Petroleum Company

★12926★
STANDARD & POOR'S COMPUSTAT SERVICES, INC. - DATA RESOURCE CENTER (Bus-Fin)
7400 S. Alton Court   Phone: (303) 771-6510
Engelwood, CO 80112   Nancy Bundren, Oper. Control Supv.
Founded: 1968. **Staff:** Prof 2; Other 3. **Subjects:** Financial reports. **Special Collections:** Daily Stock Price Record Books; Moody publications. **Holdings:** 50 books; 7 filing cabinets of Federal Reserve publications; 100,000

microfiche of financial reports; financial reports from over 8000 companies; Standard & Poor's publications; Canadian Stock Exchange listings. **Subscriptions:** 30 journals and other serials; 5 newspapers. **Services:** Center open to public by appointment. **Automated Operations:** Computerized cataloging. **Publications:** Compustat; Financial Dynamics, both weekly.

★12927★
STANDARD & POOR'S CORPORATION - RESEARCH LIBRARY (Bus-Fin)
25 Broadway Phone: (212) 208-8514
New York, NY 10004 Dennis F. Jensen, Lib.Mgr.
Founded: 1917. **Staff:** Prof 5; Other 15. **Subjects:** Corporations and industries, securities and investments, finance and banking, public utilities. **Special Collections:** Annual and quarterly reports, prospectuses, documents describing corporations and their activities (800 VF drawers); Standard & Poor's publications, 1860 to present; disclosure reports to Securities and Exchange Commission (SEC) on microfiche, 1968 to present (800,000 pieces). **Holdings:** 22,000 volumes; 600 reels of microfilm; 100 VF drawers of pamphlets and newsletters. **Subscriptions:** 2000 journals and other serials; 40 newspapers. **Services:** Copying (limited); library open to public with restrictions. **Automated Operations:** Computerized serials. **Computerized Information Services:** DIALOG, Dow Jones News/Retrieval, Data Resources Inc. **Publications:** Acquisitions list/newsletter, monthly - for internal distribution, and available to others on request. **Staff:** Mary C. Burns, Corp. Files Mgr.; Walter Nixon, Ref.Libn.; Richard ZainEldeen, Tech.Serv.; Linda Payne, Cent. Inquiry Libn.

★12928★
STANDARD REGISTER COMPANY - CORPORATE LIBRARY (Sci-Tech)
Box 1167 Phone: (513) 223-6181
Dayton, OH 45401 Dorothea P. Adkinson, Libn.
Staff: Prof 1. **Subjects:** Chemistry, printing, paper, physics, chemical engineering, business, mechanical engineering, electronic engineering. **Holdings:** 5500 books; 104 bound periodical volumes; 3000 company catalogs. **Subscriptions:** 250 journals and other serials. **Services:** Interlibrary loans; library not open to public. **Networks/Consortia:** Member of Ohio-Kentucky Cooperating Libraries: Union List of Serials.

STANDARDBRED CANADA LIBRARY
See: Canadian Trotting Association

★12929★
STANDARDS COUNCIL OF CANADA - STANDARDS INFORMATION DIVISION (Sci-Tech)
350 Sparks St., Suite 1210 Phone: (613) 238-3222
Ottawa, ON, Canada K1R 7S8 M. Crainey, Mgr.
Founded: 1977. **Staff:** Prof 6; Other 2. **Subjects:** Standards, specifications, codes and related documents, technical regulations. **Holdings:** 300,000 documents. **Subscriptions:** 90 journals and other serials. **Services:** Copying; division open to public. **Computerized Information Services:** DIALOG; CANSTAN/CAN-NORM (internal database). **Special Indexes:** KWIC Directory and Index of Standards and Specifications; Directory of Standards Referenced in Federal Legislation. **Remarks:** The toll free telephone number in Canada is 1 (800) 267-8220. **Also Known As:** Conseil Canadien des normes. **Staff:** D. Thompson, Asst.Mgr.

STANFORD ARCHIVE OF RECORDED SOUND
See: Stanford University - Music Library

★12930★
STANFORD ENVIRONMENTAL LAW SOCIETY - LIBRARY (Law)
Stanford University Law School Phone: (415) 497-4421
Stanford, CA 94305 Jack Haugrud, Pres.
Subjects: Water law, resource management, toxic waste disposal, land use, beverage container laws, smoking regulations. **Holdings:** Figures not available. **Services:** Library open to public. **Publications:** List of publications - available on request.

★12931★
STANFORD LINEAR ACCELERATOR CENTER - LIBRARY (Sci-Tech)
Box 4349 Phone: (415) 854-3300
Stanford, CA 94305 Robert C. Gex, Chf.Libn.
Staff: Prof 5; Other 4. **Subjects:** High energy physics, particle accelerators. **Holdings:** 12,000 books; 6000 bound periodical volumes; 98,000 technical reports and preprints; 20,000 microfiche reports. **Subscriptions:** 1214 journals and other serials. **Services:** Interlibrary loans; copying; library open to public. **Automated Operations:** Computerized cataloging, acquisitions and serials. **Computerized Information Services:** DIALOG, NIH-EPA Chemical Information System. Contact Person: Louise Addis. **Publications:** Preprints in Particles and Fields, weekly - by subscription; Anti-Preprint Cumulation, annual

- for sale. **Remarks:** The Stanford Linear Acceleralor Center operates under contract to the U.S. Department of Energy. Located at 2575 Sand Hill Rd., Menlo Park, CA 94305. **Staff:** Louise Addis, Assoc.Hd.Libn.; Arsella Raman, Ser.Libn.; Rita Taylor, Libn.; Shirley Livengood, Tech. Data Libn.

STANFORD MEMORIAL LIBRARY OF MUSIC
See: Stanford University - Music Library

★12932★
STANFORD UNIVERSITY - ART AND ARCHITECTURE LIBRARY (Art)
Nathan Cummings Art Bldg. Phone: (415) 497-3408
Stanford, CA 94305 Alexander D. Ross, Hd.Libn.
Staff: Prof 2; Other 4. **Subjects:** Art - 19th and 20th century, Medieval, Renaissance, Baroque, Far Eastern, ancient; classical archeology; architectural history. **Special Collections:** Thomas Rowlandson Collection; Paris Salon Catalogues, 1673-1952; J.D. Chen Collection of material on Chinese art and archeology. **Holdings:** 111,000 books and bound periodical volumes. **Subscriptions:** 452 journals and other serials. **Services:** Copying; library use limited to library card holders. **Computerized Information Services:** DIALOG, BRS; Socrates (internal database). **Networks/Consortia:** Member of CLASS; South Bay Cooperative Library System; University of California Berkeley/ Stanford Cooperative Library Program; RLG. **Staff:** Marguerite Grady, Asst. Art Libn.

★12933★
STANFORD UNIVERSITY - BRANNER EARTH SCIENCES LIBRARY (Sci-Tech)
School of Earth Sciences Phone: (415) 497-2746
Stanford, CA 94305 Charlotte R.M. Derksen, Libn./Bibliog.
Founded: 1915. **Staff:** Prof 1; Other 4. **Subjects:** Geology, applied earth sciences, geophysics, petroleum engineering, micropaleontology, geochemistry. **Special Collections:** Hayden, King and Wheeler surveys; geothermal technical reports. **Holdings:** 74,500 books and bound periodical volumes; 82,000 maps; 800 Stanford dissertations; 500 Stanford student reports; 4700 microfiche. **Subscriptions:** 2450 journals and other serials. **Services:** Interlibrary loans; copying; library open to public for reference use only. **Automated Operations:** Computerized cataloging. **Computerized Information Services:** DIALOG, SDC, BRS, Questel, RLIN. **Networks/ Consortia:** Member of CLASS; University of California Berkeley/Stanford Cooperative Library Program; RLG. **Special Indexes:** Map series index (card); thesis series index (card).

★12934★
STANFORD UNIVERSITY - CENTRAL MAP COLLECTION (Geog-Map)
Cecil H. Green Library Phone: (415) 497-1811
Stanford, CA 94305 Karyl Tonge, Map Libn.
Founded: 1948. **Staff:** 1. **Holdings:** 77,000 maps. **Services:** Copying; circulation to authorized Stanford borrowers; library open to public with restrictions. **Networks/Consortia:** Member of CLASS; South Bay Cooperative Library System; University of California Berkeley/Stanford Cooperative Library Program; RLG. **Publications:** Selected Additions to the Central Map Collection, irregular; Map Collections (guides).

★12935★
STANFORD UNIVERSITY - CUBBERLEY EDUCATION LIBRARY (Educ)
Phone: (415) 497-2121
Stanford, CA 94305 Barbara Celone, Hd.Libn.
Founded: 1938. **Staff:** Prof 2; Other 6. **Subjects:** Education and related social sciences. **Special Collections:** 19th-century textbooks (2000); college catalogs (140,000). **Holdings:** 119,000 books and bound periodical volumes; 15,000 volumes of historical curriculum materials; 12,000 government documents (domestic and foreign); 13,000 textbooks (historical); 219,000 ERIC microfiche. **Subscriptions:** 1300 journals and other serials. **Services:** Interlibrary loans; copying; library use limited to library card holders. **Automated Operations:** Computerized cataloging and acquisitions. **Computerized Information Services:** DIALOG, SDC, BRS; Socrates (internal database). **Networks/Consortia:** Member of South Bay Cooperative Library System; CLASS; RLG; University of California Berkeley/Stanford Cooperative Library Program. **Publications:** Selected Acquisitions, monthly - distributed to faculty and interested individuals; Bibliographic and Guide series. **Staff:** Juanita McKinley, Asst.Hd.Libn.

★12936★
STANFORD UNIVERSITY - DEPARTMENT OF SPECIAL COLLECTIONS (Hum)
Cecil H. Green Library Phone: (415) 497-4054
Stanford, CA 94305 Michael Ryan, Chf.
Founded: 1938. **Staff:** Prof 4; Other 7. **Subjects:** British and American literature of the 19th and 20th centuries, John Steinbeck, book arts and the history of the book, 16th century continental books, history of science, music, theater, American history, California history and politics. **Special Collections:**

Charlotte Ashley Felton Memorial Library (British and American literature); Morgan A. and Aline D. Gunst Memorial Library of the Book Arts; Samuel I. and Cecile M. Barchas Collection on the History of Science and Ideas; Frederick E. Brasch Collection on Sir Isaac Newton and the History of Scientific Thought; Memorial Library of Music; Elmer E. Robinson Collection in American History; Antoine Borel Collection (manuscripts pertaining to California history and politics); James A. Healy Collection of Irish literature; Farm Labor and Chicano Experience Collection; Mary L. Schofield Collection of Children's Literature. **Holdings:** 100,000 books; 8.3 million manuscripts; 1600 maps; 50,000 photographs and prints. **Services:** Copying; department use limited to qualified readers. **Automated Operations:** Computerized cataloging, acquisitions and serials. **Computerized Information Services:** RLIN; Socrates (internal database). **Networks/Consortia:** Member of South Bay Cooperative Library System; CLASS; RLG; University of California Berkeley/Stanford Cooperative Library Program. **Publications:** Exhibition catalogs, irregular. **Staff:** Carol Rudisell, Mss.Libn.; Brenda Rueger, Rare Bk.Libn.; Mark Dimunation, Lib. for Sys. & Oper.

★12937★
STANFORD UNIVERSITY - ENGINEERING LIBRARY (Sci-Tech)
Stanford, CA 94305
Phone: (415) 497-1513
Michael V. Sullivan, Hd.
Founded: 1942. **Staff:** Prof 3; Other 4. **Subjects:** Engineering - civil, electrical, industrial, mechanical; aeronautics and astronautics; applied mechanics; electronics; materials science; operations research systems. **Special Collections:** Timoshenko Collection on applied mechanics (660 volumes); videotapes of class lectures. **Holdings:** 55,000 volumes; 3600 reels of microfilm; 400,000 microfiche; 150,000 technical reports; Visual Search Microfilm File Design Engineering Service. **Subscriptions:** 1640 journals and other serials. **Services:** Interlibrary loans; library use limited to library card holders. **Automated Operations:** Computerized cataloging and serials. **Computerized Information Services:** DIALOG, SDC, BRS, RLIN; Subject Interest Profile, Socrates (internal databases). **Networks/Consortia:** Member of South Bay Cooperative Library System; CLASS; University of California Berkeley/Stanford Cooperative Library Program; RLG. **Publications:** Selected New Titles, quarterly - distributed to faculty and students. **Special Indexes:** Subject Guide to Indexing and Abstracting Services in the Engineering Library (1st edition, 1973). **Staff:** Charles Early, Asst.Engr.Libn./Ref.; John Broadwin, Asst.Engr.Libn./Oper.

★12938★
STANFORD UNIVERSITY - FALCONER BIOLOGY LIBRARY (Sci-Tech)
Stanford, CA 94305
Phone: (415) 497-1528
Beth Weil, Hd.Libn.
Founded: 1926. **Staff:** Prof 1; Other 4. **Subjects:** Biochemistry, molecular biology, population genetics and ecology, organismal biology. **Holdings:** 73,000 books and bound periodical volumes. **Subscriptions:** 1300 journals and other serials. **Services:** Interlibrary loans; copying; library open to public for reference use only. **Computerized Information Services:** DIALOG, SDC, BRS; Socrates (internal database). **Networks/Consortia:** Member of South Bay Cooperative Library System; CLASS; RLG; University of California Berkeley/Stanford Cooperative Library Program. **Publications:** New Book List, monthly - available upon request. **Staff:** Claire Shoens, Oper.Mgr.

★12939★
STANFORD UNIVERSITY - FOOD RESEARCH INSTITUTE - LIBRARY (Agri; Food-Bev)
Stanford, CA 94305
Phone: (415) 497-3943
Charles C. Milford, Libn.
Founded: 1921. **Staff:** Prof 1; Other 1. **Subjects:** Economic aspects of agriculture, food supply, population, underdeveloped areas. **Special Collections:** Documents of foreign governments and international organizations. **Holdings:** 13,915 books; 25,000 pamphlets. **Subscriptions:** 1840 journals and other serials. **Services:** Interlibrary loans; copying; library open to public for reference use only. **Computerized Information Services:** RLIN. **Networks/Consortia:** Member of RLG.

★12940★
STANFORD UNIVERSITY - HOOVER INSTITUTION ON WAR, REVOLUTION AND PEACE - LIBRARY (Soc Sci)
Stanford, CA 94305
Phone: (415) 497-2058
Dr. John B. Dunlop, Assoc.Dir., Lib./Archv.
Founded: 1919. **Staff:** Prof 23; Other 41. **Subjects:** 20th century economic, political and social problems - special emphasis on World Wars I and II, and on the following geographical areas: Africa, China, Eastern Europe, U.S.S.R., Japan, Latin America, Middle East, United States, Western Europe. **Special Collections:** American Relief Administration records; military journals; international organizations; communist party materials; Paris Peace Conference records; propaganda and psychological warfare; underground movements. **Holdings:** 1.33 million volumes; 48,091 reels of microfilm; 18,231 microfiche; 4080 archives of national and international organizations, military government, political personnel; 32,259,148 manuscripts; 8029 maps; 262 videotapes; 255 computer tapes; pamphlets; photographs; posters; government documents; newspaper and periodical file in Slavic, Western and East Asian languages (27,600 titles). **Subscriptions:** 3164 journals and other serials; 394 newspapers. **Services:** Interlibrary loans; copying; library open to public, borrowing restricted. **Automated Operations:** Computerized cataloging and reference. **Computerized Information Services:** DIALOG, RLIN. Performs searches on cost recovery basis. Contact Person: David W. Heron, 497-2059. **Networks/Consortia:** Member of RLG. **Special Catalogs:** Book catalog; Middle East languages catalog; survey of area collection holdings. **Staff:** David W. Heron, Hd., Rd.Serv.; Joseph Kladko, Asst.Dir., Tech.Oper.; Robert Conquest, Cur., Russia & Europe; Peter Duignan, Cur., Africa Mid East; Ramon H. Myers, Cur., E. Asia Coll.; Joseph W. Bingaman, Cur., Latin Amer.Coll.; Agnes Peterson, Cur., W. Europe Coll.; Milorad M. Drachkovitch, Archv.; Charles Palm, Act.Archv.

★12941★
STANFORD UNIVERSITY - HOPKINS MARINE STATION - LIBRARY (Env-Cons)
Cabrillo Point
Pacific Grove, CA 93950
Phone: (408) 373-0460
Alan Baldridge, Hd.Libn.
Founded: 1920. **Staff:** Prof 1; Other 1. **Subjects:** Marine zoology and phycology, physiology and neurobiology, cell and developmental biology, biochemistry, immunology, ecology and population biology, oceanography. **Special Collections:** Mace MacFarland opisthobranchiate molluscan collection (800 items); G.M. Smith algae reprint collection (300 volumes). **Holdings:** 22,000 volumes; 132 maps; 1400 other materials. **Subscriptions:** 625 journals and other serials. **Services:** Interlibrary loans; copying; library open to public by appointment. **Automated Operations:** Computerized cataloging and acquisitions. **Computerized Information Services:** DIALOG. Performs searches on cost recovery basis. **Networks/Consortia:** Member of CLASS; RLG. **Publications:** List of faculty and student publications, annual. **Special Catalogs:** Bibliographies of common local marine invertebrates (card).

★12942★
STANFORD UNIVERSITY - INSTITUTE FOR ENERGY STUDIES - ENERGY INFORMATION CENTER (Energy)
Bldg. 500, Rm. 500C
Stanford, CA 94305
Phone: (415) 497-3237
Marian J. Rees, Dir.
Founded: 1974. **Staff:** Prof 1; Other 4. **Subjects:** Energy - policy, modeling; conservation. **Holdings:** 10,000 books; 112 bound periodical volumes; 200 videotapes; 200,000 microfiche; 25 annual reports and pamphlets; 20 boxes of clippings. **Subscriptions:** 150 journals and other serials. **Services:** Copying; SDI; center open to public with restrictions. **Computerized Information Services:** DIALOG, RLIN. **Networks/Consortia:** Member of Energy Librarians of the Bay Area; Western Information Network on Energy. **Special Catalogs:** Technical reports catalog (card).

★12943★
STANFORD UNIVERSITY - J. HUGH JACKSON LIBRARY (Bus-Fin)
Graduate School of Business
Stanford, CA 94305
Phone: (415) 497-2161
Bela Gallo, Dir.
Founded: 1932. **Staff:** Prof 11; Other 22. **Subjects:** Accounting, business economics, finance, international business, investment, management, marketing, quantitative analysis. **Special Collections:** Favre Collection (Pacific Northwest economics); Jackson Collection (accounting information files of former Dean of School). **Holdings:** 316,994 books and other cataloged items; government documents, pamphlets; 350,000 corporate reports; 3255 reels of microfilm; 590,027 microfiche. **Subscriptions:** 2247 periodicals; 97 newspapers. **Services:** Interlibrary loans (limited to faculty and graduate students); copying; library open to public with payment of fee. **Automated Operations:** Computerized serials. **Computerized Information Services:** RLIN. **Publications:** Selected Additions to the J. Hugh Jackson Library. **Special Catalogs:** Jackson Library Periodicals, annual (book); Jackson Library Annuals on Standing Order, annual (book). **Staff:** Evelyn Hu, Cat.Libn.; Janna Leffingwell, Cat.Libn.; Karen Wilson, Hd.Pub.Serv.Libn.; Robert Mayer, Asst.Dir./Hd., Tech.Serv.; Esther Pike, Acq.Libn.; Jean Robertson, Ser.Libn.; Henry Wang, Asst.Ref.Libn.

★12944★
STANFORD UNIVERSITY - LANE MEDICAL LIBRARY (Med)
Stanford University Medical Center
Stanford, CA 94305
Phone: (415) 497-6831
Peter Stangl, Dir.
Founded: 1906. **Staff:** Prof 9; Other 20. **Subjects:** Clinical medicine and its specialties, preclinical and basic sciences, public health, nursing and related fields. **Special Collections:** History of Medicine; Barkan Ophthalmology Collection. **Holdings:** 271,887 books and bound periodical volumes; 28,267

pamphlets and theses. **Subscriptions:** 2998 journals and other serials; 5 newspapers. **Services:** Interlibrary loans; copying; library open to public for reference use only. **Automated Operations:** Computerized cataloging and acquisitions. **Computerized Information Services:** MEDLARS, DIALOG, SDC, BRS, RLIN. Performs searches on cost recovery basis. Contact Person: Gloria Linder. **Networks/Consortia:** Member of Pacific Southwest Regional Medical Library Service (PSRMLS); CLASS; RLG. **Special Indexes:** Reference index. **Staff:** Valerie Su, Hd., Pub.Serv.; Gloria Linder, Hd., Ref.; Dick Miller, Hd., Tech.Serv.; Anne Davis, Hd., Lrng.Rsrc.Ctr.; Marcia Epelbaum, Hd., Circ.

★12945★
STANFORD UNIVERSITY - LAW LIBRARY (Law)
Stanford, CA 94305
Phone: (415) 497-2721
Prof. J. Myron Jacobstein, Law Libn.
Founded: 1894. **Staff:** Prof 7; Other 16. **Subjects:** Law, with particular emphasis on Anglo-American legislative and administrative materials. **Special Collections:** Maritime law; air law; French law; German law. **Holdings:** 300,000 volumes. **Subscriptions:** 5111 journals and other serials. **Services:** Interlibrary loans; library not open to public. **Automated Operations:** Computerized cataloging. **Networks/Consortia:** Member of CLASS; RLG. **Staff:** Rosalee Long, Assoc. Law Libn.; Iris Wildman, Pub.Serv.Libn.

★12946★
STANFORD UNIVERSITY - MATHEMATICAL AND COMPUTER SCIENCES LIBRARY (Sci-Tech; Comp Sci)
Bldg. 380, Sloan Mathematics Center
Stanford, CA 94305
Phone: (415) 497-4672
Harry P. Llull, Hd.Libn./Bibliog.
Founded: 1964. **Staff:** Prof 1; Other 3. **Subjects:** Mathematics, statistics, operations research, computer science. **Holdings:** 45,000 books and bound periodical volumes; 27,000 technical reports. **Subscriptions:** 1000 journals and other serials. **Services:** Interlibrary loans; copying; library open to public for reference use only. **Automated Operations:** Computerized cataloging and acquisitions. **Computerized Information Services:** DIALOG, SDC, BRS, RLIN; Socrates (internal database). **Networks/Consortia:** Member of CLASS; South Bay Cooperative Library System; RLG; University of California Berkeley/Stanford Cooperative Library Program. **Publications:** Recent Acquisitions, monthly; New Technical Reports List, semimonthly - both to faculty and researchers. **Special Indexes:** Index to technical reports.

STANFORD UNIVERSITY MEDICAL CENTER
See: Stanford University - Lane Medical Library

★12947★
STANFORD UNIVERSITY - MUSIC LIBRARY (Mus)
Braun Music Center
Stanford, CA 94305
Phone: (415) 497-1211
Jerry Persons, Hd.Libn.
Founded: 1948. **Staff:** Prof 3; Other 6. **Subjects:** Music. **Special Collections:** Stanford Archive of Recorded Sound (108,000 items); Stanford Memorial Library of Music. **Holdings:** 57,000 books and scores; 1600 reels of microfilm; 1000 microcards and microfiche; 16,000 phonograph records. **Subscriptions:** 475 journals and other serials. **Services:** Interlibrary loans; copying; listening facilitites for phonograph records, reel-to-reel tapes; library use limited to library card holders. **Automated Operations:** Computerized cataloging and acquisitions. **Computerized Information Services:** DIALOG, SDC, BRS; Socrates (internal database). **Networks/Consortia:** Member of South Bay Cooperative Library System; CLASS; University of California Berkeley/Stanford Cooperative Library Program; RLG. **Publications:** Stanford Archive of Recorded Sound (descriptive brochure). **Staff:** Barbara Eick, Archv.Mimi Tashiro, Asst. Music Libn.

★12948★
STANFORD UNIVERSITY - PHYSICS LIBRARY (Sci-Tech)
Stanford, CA 94305
Phone: (415) 497-4342
Virginia M. Kosanovic, Hd.Libn.
Staff: Prof 1. **Subjects:** Physics, astronomy, astrophysics, meteorology. **Special Collections:** Microwave and high-energy physics. **Holdings:** 38,000 books and bound periodical volumes; 1970 sky atlas photographs. **Subscriptions:** 595 journals and other serials. **Services:** Interlibrary loans; copying; library use limited to library card holders. **Automated Operations:** Computerized cataloging and acquisitions (through Green Library). **Computerized Information Services:** DIALOG, SDC, BRS; Socrates (internal database). **Networks/Consortia:** Member of South Bay Cooperative Library System; CLASS; University of California Berkeley/Stanford Cooperative Library Program; RLG.

★12949★
STANFORD UNIVERSITY - SWAIN LIBRARY OF CHEMISTRY AND CHEMICAL ENGINEERING (Sci-Tech)
Phone: (415) 497-9237
Stanford, CA 94305
Founded: 1901. **Staff:** Prof 1; Other 3. **Subjects:** Chemistry, chemical engineering. **Holdings:** 34,000 volumes; 900 microfiche; 360 reels of microfilm; 600 dissertations. **Subscriptions:** 1200 journals and other serials. **Services:** Interlibrary loans; copying; library use limited to library card holders. **Automated Operations:** Computerized cataloging and acquisitions. **Computerized Information Services:** DIALOG, RLIN, SDC, BRS; Socrates (internal database). **Networks/Consortia:** Member of CLASS; RLG; South Bay Cooperative Library System; University of California Berkeley/Stanford Cooperative Library Program. **Publications:** Selected Acquisitions List, monthly - distributed to department and industrial affiliates. **Staff:** Lynn Kaczor, Oper.Mgr.

★12950★
STANFORD UNIVERSITY - TANNER MEMORIAL PHILOSOPHY LIBRARY (Hum)
Department of Philosophy
Stanford, CA 94303
Phone: (415) 497-1539
Founded: 1960. **Staff:** Prof 1; Other 6. **Subjects:** Symbolic logic; philosophical logic; philosophy of mathematics, language and science; metaphysics and epistemology; ethics and philosophy of action; history of philosophy; aesthetics. **Special Collections:** Clarence Irving Lewis Memorial Collection (235 volumes). **Holdings:** 5000 books; 1000 bound periodical volumes; 150 dissertations (cataloged); 650 reprints and typescripts. **Subscriptions:** 67 journals and other serials. **Services:** Interlibrary loans; library open to public with approval of Stanford University Libraries. **Automated Operations:** Computerized cataloging and acquisitions.

★12951★
STANFORD UNIVERSITY - UNIVERSITY ARCHIVES (Hist)
Cecil H. Green Library
Stanford, CA 94305
Phone: (415) 497-4055
Roxanne-Louise Nilan, Univ.Archv.
Founded: 1965. **Staff:** Prof 2; Other 2. **Subjects:** University history. **Holdings:** Archives of the University, personal papers of faculty, trustees, staff, students, and Stanford family papers - includes 2500 Stanford technical reports; 300 3-dimensional objects; 5.3 million manuscripts; 510 reels of microfilm; 56,000 publications; 153,000 photographs; 3000 architectural drawings and maps; 2600 sound recordings and film; prints, posters and other ephemera. **Subscriptions:** 312 journals and other serials. **Services:** Limited copying; library open to public. **Publications:** Guide to the Manuscript and Archival Collections of the Stanford University Archives (1979). **Special Catalogs:** Descriptive guide to manuscript/archival collections; registers for each manuscript collection; special card catalogs for maps, photographs, posters, 3-dimensional objects, theses and dissertations.

★12952★
STANISLAUS COUNTY LAW LIBRARY (Law)
Rm. 223, Courthouse
Modesto, CA 95354
Phone: (209) 571-6967
Mindi E. Conley, Hd. Law Libn.
Founded: 1893. **Staff:** Prof 1. **Subjects:** Law. **Holdings:** 18,000 volumes. **Services:** Copying; library open to public for reference use only.

STANISLAUS COUNTY MEDICAL LIBRARY
See: Scenic General Hospital

★12953★
STANISLAUS COUNTY SCHOOLS - TEACHERS' PROFESSIONAL LIBRARY (Educ)
801 County Center No. 3 Ct.
Modesto, CA 95355
Phone: (209) 526-6593
V. Ruth Smith, Hd.
Staff: Prof 1; Other 1. **Subjects:** Education. **Holdings:** 9000 books. **Subscriptions:** 35 journals and other serials. **Services:** Library open to teachers only.

★12954★
STANLEY ASSOCIATES ENGINEERING, LTD. - LIBRARY (Env-Cons; Plan)
10512 169th St.
Edmonton, AB, Canada T5P 3X6
Phone: (403) 483-4777
Patricia Wilson, Libn.
Staff: Prof 1; Other 1. **Subjects:** Pollution control, transportation, environmental and municipal engineering, land development, water supply and distribution, urban and regional planning, structural engineering. **Holdings:** 2500 books; 300 bound periodical volumes; 4500 in-house reports and proposals; 20,000 engineering drawings on microfilm; 6000 original drawings; 1000 topographic maps. **Subscriptions:** 200 journals and other serials; 20 newspapers. **Services:** Interlibrary loans; copying; library open to public by

request. **Computerized Information Services:** DIALOG, QL Systems, CAN/OLE, National Ground Water Information Center.

★12955★
STANLEY CONSULTANTS - TECHNICAL LIBRARY (Sci-Tech; Plan)
Stanley Bldg.   Phone: (319) 264-6234
Muscatine, IA 52761   Kathy A. McNeal, Libn.
Staff: Prof 1; Other 2. **Subjects:** Engineering, architecture, urban and regional planning. **Holdings:** 12,500 books; 1000 bound periodical volumes; 4000 vendor catalogs; 115 videotapes of internal seminars; 24 cassettes. **Subscriptions:** 222 journals and other serials. **Services:** Interlibrary loans; copying; library open to public with restrictions. **Computerized Information Services:** DIALOG.

STANLEY (Edmund) LIBRARY
See: Friends University - Edmund Stanley Library

STANLEY LIBRARY
See: Franklin County Historical Society

★12956★
STAR OF THE REPUBLIC MUSEUM - LIBRARY (Hist)
Box 317   Phone: (409) 878-2461
Washington, TX 77880   D. Ryan Smith, Dir.
Subjects: Texas history, museums and museology, artifact identification. **Special Collections:** Showers-Brown Collection (Texana Collection). **Holdings:** 3000 books; 100 bound periodical volumes; 2000 manuscripts, documents; 300 maps; 100 newspapers, census documents and dissertations on microfilm. **Subscriptions:** 40 journals and other serials. **Services:** Copying; library open to public. **Publications:** Star of the Republic Museum Notes (newsletter), quarterly - free upon request. **Special Indexes:** Special Formats Index (booklet).

STARK COUNTY HISTORICAL SOCIETY LIBRARY
See: Mc Kinley Museum of History, Science and Education - Ralph K. Ramsayer, M.D. Library

★12957★
STARK COUNTY LAW LIBRARY ASSOCIATION - ALLIANCE BRANCH LAW LIBRARY (Law)*
City Hall
470 E. Market   Phone: (216) 823-6181
Alliance, OH 44601
Founded: 1930. **Subjects:** U.S. law. **Holdings:** 3500 volumes.

★12958★
STARK COUNTY LAW LIBRARY ASSOCIATION - LAW LIBRARY (Law)
Court House, Fourth Fl.   Phone: (216) 456-2330
Canton, OH 44702   Martha M. Cox, Dir.
Founded: 1890. **Staff:** Prof 1; Other 2. **Subjects:** U.S. and Ohio law. **Holdings:** 43,307 volumes; 37,678 fiche; 210 reels of microfilm. **Subscriptions:** 70 journals. **Services:** Copying; library open to public for reference use only. **Computerized Information Services:** Westlaw, DIALOG, Commerce Clearing House Electronic Legislative Search System (ELSS). Performs searches on cost recovery basis. **Staff:** Patti Bresnahan, Asst.Libn.

★12959★
STARK COUNTY LAW LIBRARY ASSOCIATION - MASSILLON BRANCH LAW LIBRARY (Law)*
City Hall   Phone: (216) 837-4271
Massillon, OH 44646
Founded: 1940. **Subjects:** Ohio law. **Holdings:** 2500 volumes.

STARK (Miriam Lutcher) LIBRARY
See: University of Texas, Austin - Harry Ransom Humanities Research Center

STARR (C.V.) EAST ASIAN LIBRARY
See: Columbia University - C.V. Starr East Asian Library

STARR (Dorothy C.S.) CIVIL WAR RESEARCH LIBRARY
See: Fort Ward Museum - Dorothy C.S. Starr Civil War Research Library

STARR KING SCHOOL FOR THE MINISTRY
See: Graduate Theological Union

★12960★
STATE BAR OF MICHIGAN - LIBRARY (Law)
306 Townsend St.   Phone: (517) 372-9030
Lansing, MI 48933   Douglas L. Sweet, Dir., R. & D.
Staff: 1. **Subjects:** Law. **Holdings:** 2000 books; 700 bound periodical volumes. **Subscriptions:** 10 journals and other serials; 5 newspapers. **Services:** Library open to lawyers only.

★12961★
STATE CAPITAL HISTORICAL ASSOCIATION - LIBRARY AND PHOTO ARCHIVES (Hist)
211 W. 21st Ave.   Phone: (206) 753-2580
Olympia, WA 98501   Derek R. Valley, Dir.
Founded: 1939. **Staff:** Prof 7. **Subjects:** Washington history, Victoriana, museology, art. **Special Collections:** Collection of Washington photographs, including early photos of pioneers, towns, industries, Indians, and state governments; archives of Northwest Indian art. **Holdings:** 3000 historical photographs. **Services:** Copying; archives open to public by arrangement.

★12962★
STATE FARM MUTUAL AUTOMOBILE INSURANCE COMPANY - LAW LIBRARY (Law)
One State Farm Plaza   Phone: (309) 766-5224
Bloomington, IL 61701   Laura Garrett, Libn.
Founded: 1962. **Staff:** 7. **Subjects:** Law, insurance, commerce, management. **Holdings:** 30,000 volumes. **Subscriptions:** 400 journals and other serials. **Services:** Interlibrary loans; library open to public for reference use only. **Computerized Information Services:** DIALOG, SDC, LEXIS, NEXIS. **Publications:** New Acquisitions, monthly. **Staff:** Sylvia Justice, Asst.Libn.

★12963★
STATE HISTORICAL SOCIETY OF IOWA - LIBRARY (Hist)
402 Iowa Ave.   Phone: (319) 338-5471
Iowa City, IA 52240   Peter H. Curtis, Hd.Libn.
Founded: 1857. **Staff:** Prof 7. **Subjects:** Iowa history and politics, regional Indians, genealogy, Iowa authors. **Special Collections:** Manuscript Collections - Robert Lucas Papers, Jonathon P. Dolliver Papers, Gilbert Haugen Papers, Cyrus Carpenter Papers; Iowa Industry House Organs. **Holdings:** 100,000 books; 10,000 bound periodical volumes; 15,000 pamphlets; 14,000 reels of microfilm; 10,000 bound newspapers; 25 VF drawers of newspaper clippings; 100,000 photographs; 2500 linear feet of manuscripts. **Subscriptions:** 575 journals and other serials; 26 newspapers. **Services:** Interlibrary loans; copying; library open to public. **Automated Operations:** Computerized cataloging. **Computerized Information Services:** OCLC. **Networks/Consortia:** Member of Bibliographic Center for Research, Rocky Mountain Region, Inc. (BCR). **Special Catalogs:** Newspaper Collection of the State Historical Society of Iowa compiled by L.O. Cheever, 1969; Bibliography of Iowa newspapers, 1831-1976 (book and online); manuscript catalog. **Staff:** David Kinnett, Mss.Libn.; Mary Bennett, Photographs Libn.; Karen Laughlin, Ref.Libn.; Susan Rogers, Acq.Libn.; Sharlane Grant, Preservation Libn.; Nancy Kraft, Cat.Libn.

★12964★
STATE HISTORICAL SOCIETY OF MISSOURI - LIBRARY (Hist)
1020 Lowry St.   Phone: (314) 882-7083
Columbia, MO 65201   Dr. Richard S. Brownlee, Dir.
Founded: 1898. **Staff:** Prof 13; Other 5. **Subjects:** Missouri and midwestern history; works by and about Missourians. **Special Collections:** J. Christian Bay rare book collection (5200 books and documents); special collection of Mark Twain and Eugene Field writings; Bishop William Fletcher McMurray Collection; Francis A. Sampson Collection. **Holdings:** 432,000 volumes; 700 reels of microfilmed manuscripts; 300,000 pages of original manuscripts; 1600 items in the map collection; Missouri newspapers on microfilm; 75,000 photographs; 6216 reels of microfilm of genealogical records. **Subscriptions:** 460 journals and other serials; 311 newspapers. **Services:** Interlibrary loans; copying; library open to public. **Publications:** Missouri Historical Review, issued quarterly to all members. **Remarks:** This library maintains a joint manuscript collection with the Western Historical Manuscript Collection of the University of Missouri.

STATE HISTORICAL SOCIETY OF MISSOURI MANUSCRIPTS
See: Western Historical Manuscript Collection/State Historical Society of Missouri Manuscripts Joint Collection

★12965★
STATE HISTORICAL SOCIETY OF NORTH DAKOTA - STATE ARCHIVES AND HISTORICAL RESEARCH LIBRARY (Hist)
Heritage Center   Phone: (701) 224-2668
Bismarck, ND 58505   Gerald Newborg, State Archv.
Founded: 1905. **Staff:** Prof 8; Other 3. **Subjects:** North Dakota state;

Northern Great Plains region; social, cultural, economic and political history; early exploration and travel; fur trade; plains military history; Northern Plains archeology, prehistory, ethnology, ethnohistory; historic preservation; genealogy. **Holdings:** 40,000 volumes; 2000 cubic feet of manuscripts; 7000 cubic feet of state and county archives; 40,000 photographs; 6200 reels of microfilm of newspapers; 800 titles of North Dakota newspapers; 2100 titles of periodicals; 1200 oral history interviews; sound recordings; maps; motion pictures. **Subscriptions:** 300 journals and other serials; 100 newspapers. **Services:** Interlibrary loans (limited); copying; library open to public for reference use only. **Automated Operations:** Computerized cataloging. **Computerized Information Services:** OCLC. **Networks/Consortia:** Member of MINITEX. **Publications:** North Dakota History: Journal of the Northern Plains, quarterly; Plains Talk, newsletter, quarterly. **Formerly:** Its Research and Reference Division. **Staff:** Dolores Vyzralek, Chf.Libn.; David Gray, Dp. State Archv.Todd Strand, Photo Archv.

★12966★
STATE HISTORICAL SOCIETY OF WISCONSIN - ARCHIVES DIVISION (Hist)
816 State St.   Phone: (608) 262-3338
Madison, WI 53706   F. Gerald Ham, State Archv. & Dir.
Staff: Prof 17; Other 9. **Subjects:** Wisconsin history; American frontier, 1750-1815; labor and industrial relations; socialism; mass communications; theater; agricultural history; civil rights; contemporary social action movements. **Special Collections:** Draper Collection (frontier); McCormick Collection (agriculture and agricultural manufacturing). **Holdings:** 38,000 cubic feet of Wisconsin state and local public records; 35,000 cubic feet of nongovernmental archives and manuscripts; 15,000 unbound maps; 2000 atlases; 500 audiotape titles on 3100 reels; 110 titles on 3500 phonograph records; 500,000 iconographic items; 50 machine-readable data files of state government records. **Services:** Interlibrary loans; copying; photo and film reproduction and dubbing of recordings for television. **Automated Operations:** Computerized cataloging. **Networks/Consortia:** Administers the Wisconsin Area Research Center Network. **Publications:** Accession reports in Wisconsin Magazine of History, quarterly; guides and inventories. **Remarks:** Includes the manuscript collections of the American Institute of the History of Pharmacy, the Mass Communications History Center, the Wisconsin Center for Film and Theatre Research and the Wisconsin Jewish Archives. **Staff:** Max J. Evans, Asst.Dir.; Harry Miller, Ref.Archv.; George A. Talbot, Archv. AV Coll.; Barbara J. Kaiser, Coll.Dev.

STATE HISTORICAL SOCIETY OF WISCONSIN - CIRCUS WORLD MUSEUM
See: Circus World Museum

★12967★
STATE HISTORICAL SOCIETY OF WISCONSIN - LIBRARY (Hist)
816 State St.   Phone: (608) 262-3421
Madison, WI 53706   James H. Sweetland, Hd.Libn.
Founded: 1846. **Staff:** Prof 19; Other 6. **Subjects:** History - American, Canadian, state, local, labor, U.S. church; radical/reform movements and groups in the U.S.; ethnic and minority groups in American life; genealogy; women's history. **Special Collections:** Labor history (John R. Commons Collection); labor newspapers; military history; radicalism. **Holdings:** 224,000 books and bound periodical volumes; 435,000 pamphlets; 152,000 reels of microfilm; 526,000 sheets of microforms; 368,000 government documents; 14,000 bound newspaper volumes. **Subscriptions:** 6500 periodicals; 280 newspapers. **Services:** Interlibrary loans; copying; library open to public. **Automated Operations:** Computerized cataloging. **Networks/Consortia:** Member of WILS; CRL. **Publications:** Wisconsin Public Documents Checklist, monthly with annual cumulations - free upon request; bibliographies, guides. **Special Indexes:** Index to names in Wisconsin federal census, 1820-1870, 1905 state census; Wisconsin necrology index; index of names in Wisconsin county histories. **Remarks:** This Library is a U.S. Federal Regional Depository, the official Wisconsin State Publications Depository, and a Canadian Federal Partial Depository. **Staff:** Herbert J. Tepper, Cat.Libn.; Ellen Burke, Circ.Libn.; John A. Peters, Govt.Pubn.Libn.; Gerald R. Eggleston, Acq.Libn.; James L. Hansen, Rd.Serv.Libn.; Karin Fox, Microforms Libn.

★12968★
STATE HISTORICAL SOCIETY OF WISCONSIN - WISCONSIN JEWISH ARCHIVES
816 State St.
Madison, WI 53706
Defunct. Archives merged with State Historical Society of Wisconsin - Archives Division.

★12969★
STATE LIBRARY OF FLORIDA (Info Sci)
R.A. Gray Bldg.   Phone: (904) 487-2651
Tallahassee, FL 32301   Barratt Wilkins, State Libn.
Founded: 1845. **Staff:** Prof 27; Other 38. **Subjects:** Florida, history, social sciences, library science. **Special Collections:** Floridana (20,000 items); genealogy (15,000 items). **Holdings:** 216,422 books; 6788 bound periodical volumes; 80,342 Florida public documents; 89,197 U.S. documents; 13,188 reels of microfilm; 136,852 microfiche; 3025 films. **Subscriptions:** 1251 journals and other serials; 11 newspapers. **Services:** Interlibrary loans; copying; SDI; library open to public. **Automated Operations:** Computerized cataloging, serials, circulation and film booking. **Computerized Information Services:** OCLC. **Networks/Consortia:** Member of SOLINET; Florida Library Information Network (FLIN); Florida COMCAT. **Publications:** Orange Seed (technical bulletin) - to libraries; Intercom (technical bulletin) - to trustees and friends; Keystone (technical bulletin) - to institutions; New Books, monthly - to state agency personnel; Florida Library Directory with Statistics, annual - free to libraries; Florida Public Documents, monthly; KWIC Index to Florida Public Documents, quarterly. **Remarks:** Includes the holdings of the Division of State Planning - Library. **Staff:** Jo Ann Ellingson, Asst. State Libn.; Darnell Pratt, Acq.Libn.; Kay Shy, Cat.Libn.; Ella Woodbury, Ref.Libn.; Virginia C. Grigg, Chf., Bur.Lib.Dev.; Helen Morgan Moeller, Pub.Lib.Cons.; Kathleen Mayo, Inst.Cons.; Susan Whittle, Pub.Lib.Cons.; Betty Ann Scott, Pub.Lib.Cons.Marvin Mounce, Pub.Lib.Cons.; Betty Miller, Pub.Lib.Cons.; Loretta Flowers, Pub.Lib.Cons.; William E. Paplinski, Chf., Bur.Lib.Serv.; Robert Gorin, ILL; Mary McRory, Florida Libn.; Patty Paul, Doc.Libn.; Freddie Ann Mellichamp, Chf., Lib.Sup.Serv.; Mary Moye, AV Libn.

★12970★
STATE LIBRARY OF OHIO (Info Sci)
65 S. Front St.   Phone: (614) 462-7061
Columbus, OH 43215   Richard M. Cheski, State Libn.
Founded: 1817. **Staff:** Prof 27; Other 98. **Subjects:** Management, education, social sciences, public administration, Ohio history. **Special Collections:** Genealogy (7000 items); Ohio and federal documents (869,067). **Holdings:** 622,238 books; 30,634 bound periodical volumes; 240,722 microforms. **Subscriptions:** 440 journals and other serials; 13 newspapers. **Services:** Interlibrary loans; copying; library open to public. **Automated Operations:** Computerized cataloging and circulation. **Computerized Information Services:** DIALOG, BRS, The Source, OCLC, LIBRIS. **Networks/Consortia:** Member of OHIONET; Greater Midwest Regional Medical Library Network (Region 3). **Publications:** Directory of Ohio Libraries, annual; News from the State Library, monthly; Ohio Documents, quarterly; Selected Publications, irregular; Information from the State Library, irregular. **Staff:** Susan Thomas, Dp. State Libn.; Catherine Mead, Hd., Ref. & Info.Serv.; Ira Phillips, Spec.Proj.Prog.Dev.; John Philip, Hd., Field Oper.; Floyd Dickman, Prog.Dev.Supv.

★12971★
STATE MUTUAL LIFE ASSURANCE COMPANY OF AMERICA - LIBRARY (Bus-Fin)
440 Lincoln St.   Phone: (617) 852-1000
Worcester, MA 01605   Mary F. Duffy, Assoc.Libn.
Founded: 1957. **Staff:** 2. **Subjects:** Insurance, actuarial science, business, law. **Holdings:** 16,000 books; 600 bound periodical volumes; 35 VF drawers of pamphlets and reports. **Subscriptions:** 500 journals and other serials. **Services:** Use of library may be requested.

★12972★
STATE PARK HEALTH CENTER - PATIENTS' AND MEDICAL LIBRARY
Box 115
State Park, SC 29147
Defunct

★12973★
STATE STREET CONSULTANTS, INC. - INFORMATION CENTER (Bus-Fin)
84 State St., Suite 905   Phone: (617) 720-2020
Boston, MA 02109   Denise Cloutier, Info.Mgr.
Staff: Prof 1. **Subjects:** Management, marketing, financial marketing, industry collections. **Holdings:** 1500 books; 100 VF drawers; 100 unbound reports; 150 cases of periodicals. **Subscriptions:** 72 journals and other serials. **Services:** SDI; center open to public with restrictions. **Computerized Information Services:** DIALOG; Sources Database (internal database). Performs searches on cost recovery basis.

★12974★
STATE TECHNICAL INSTITUTE AT MEMPHIS - GEORGE E. FREEMAN LIBRARY (Sci-Tech)
5983 Macon Cove　　　　　　　　　　　Phone: (901) 377-4111
Memphis, TN 38134　　　　　　　　　　Rosa S. Burnett, Libn.
Founded: 1968. **Staff:** Prof 3; Other 4. **Subjects:** Engineering - electrical/electronics, instrumentation, civil, architectural, mechanical, environmental, biomedical; chemical technology; data processing technologies. **Holdings:** 31,218 books; 4085 bound periodical volumes; 36 VF drawers; 9646 microforms. **Subscriptions:** 148 journals and other serials; 14 newspapers. **Services:** Interlibrary loans; copying; library open to public for reference use only. **Publications:** Library Handbook. **Staff:** Bettie Williams, Circ./Order Libn.; Mildred DeBois, Cat.Libn.

STATE UNIVERSITY OF NEW YORK
See: SUNY

★12975★
STATEN ISLAND COOPERATIVE CONTINUUM - EDUCATIONAL RESOURCE CENTER (Educ)
130 Stuyvesant Pl., Rm. 704　　　　　　Phone: (718) 390-7985
Staten Island, NY 10301　　　　　　　　John Gino, Prog.Dir.
Founded: 1973. **Staff:** Prof 1; Other 3. **Subjects:** Education, curriculum (K-12). **Holdings:** 9000 books; 50 bound periodical volumes; 1200 curriculum guides; 200 multimedia kits; 200 testing materials; 9 micro computers. **Services:** Interlibrary loans; copying; videotaping and editing for students and the educational community; center open to public. **Publications:** A/V Guide to ERC, irregular; ERC Newsletter, semiannual.

★12976★
STATEN ISLAND HISTORICAL SOCIETY - LIBRARY (Hist)
Court & Center Sts.　　　　　　　　　　Phone: (718) 351-1611
Staten Island, NY 10306　　　　　　　Stephen C. Barto, Res.Assoc.
Staff: Prof 1; Other 3. **Subjects:** History of Staten Island and neighboring communities, U.S. history. **Special Collections:** Rare books. **Holdings:** 5000 books; 350 bound periodical volumes; 30 VF drawers of Staten Island history; 8 VF drawers of Staten Island genealogy; 75 reels of microfilm; 400 cubic feet of manuscripts; 9000 uncataloged items. **Subscriptions:** 25 journals and other serials. **Services:** Copying; library open to public by appointment only.

★12977★
STATEN ISLAND HOSPITAL - MEDICAL STAFF LIBRARY (Med)
475 Seaview Ave.　　　　　　　　　　Phone: (718) 390-9000
Staten Island, NY 10305　　　　　　　　Song Ja Oh, Dir.
Founded: 1952. **Staff:** Prof 2; Other 2. **Subjects:** Internal medicine, surgery, pediatrics, obstetrics and gynecology. **Holdings:** 5000 books; 9000 bound periodical volumes; 920 Audio-Digest tapes. **Subscriptions:** 300 journals and other serials. **Services:** Interlibrary loans; copying; library open to public with restrictions. **Computerized Information Services:** MEDLINE.

★12978★
STATEN ISLAND INSTITUTE OF ARTS AND SCIENCES - ARCHIVES AND LIBRARY (Hist; Sci-Tech)
75 Stuyvesant Pl.　　　　　　　　　　Phone: (718) 727-1135
Staten Island, NY 10301　　　　　　　Eloise Beil, Archv./Libn.
Founded: 1881. **Staff:** Prof 2; Other 1. **Subjects:** Natural history, Staten Island history, archeology, black history, women's history, urban planning. **Special Collections:** Architecture; N.L. Britton; G.W. Curtis; J.P. Chapin; W.T. Davis (total, 1000 cubic feet); photographs and prints of old Staten Island; local black history; repository for U.S.Geological Survey publications; complete list of special collections available on request. **Holdings:** 12,000 books; 22,000 bound periodical volumes; 3000 maps; 1200 prints; 50,000 photographs; 1500 art museum and gallery catalogs; 1500 cubic feet of manuscripts, letters, and documents; 80 reels of microfilm of old newspapers. **Subscriptions:** 200 journals and other serials. **Services:** Interlibrary loans; copying; library open to public by appointment. **Publications:** Proceedings, 2/year - by subscription and exchange. **Special Catalogs:** Guide to Special Collections, 16 volumes; Guide to Institute Archives, 2 volumes. **Special Indexes:** Indexes to newspapers, science books, history books, special collections (all on cards). **Remarks:** Basic library has been divided into two sections, a Science Library and a History Library. **Staff:** Kristine K. Hogan, Asst.Archv./Libn.

★12979★
STATEN ISLAND INSTITUTE OF ARTS AND SCIENCES - HIGH ROCK PARK CONSERVATION CENTER - LIBRARY (Env-Cons)
200 Nevada Ave.　　　　　　　　　　Phone: (718) 987-6233
Staten Island, NY 10306　　　　　　　　Evelyn Hare, Libn.
Founded: 1964. **Staff:** Prof 1. **Subjects:** Environmental education,

mammalogy, salt and fresh water ecology, ornithology, botany, dendrology, geology, ichthyology, zoology, astronomy, energy, photography. **Holdings:** 2435 books; 4 boxes of Cornell Science leaflets; 2 boxes of Department of Agriculture leaflets; 2 boxes of Botanic Gardens pamphlets; 12 phonograph records of bird songs; filmstrips, audiovisual aids, Outdoor Biology Instructional Strategies (OBIS) materials. **Subscriptions:** 15 journals and other serials. **Services:** Videotape facilities; library open to public with restrictions.

★12980★
STATEN ISLAND ZOOLOGICAL SOCIETY - LIBRARY (Sci-Tech)
614 Broadway　　　　　　　　　　　Phone: (718) 442-3101
Staten Island, NY 10310　　　　　　　　Vincent Gattullo, Dir.
Founded: 1936. **Subjects:** Herpetology, mammals, invertebrates, fish, birds. **Holdings:** 781 books; 178 bound periodical volumes. **Subscriptions:** 22 journals and other serials.

STATES INFORMATION CENTER
See: Council of State Governments

STATISTICS CANADA
See: Canada - Statistics Canada

STATLER (Alice) LIBRARY
See: City College of San Francisco - Hotel and Restaurant Department - Alice Statler Library

STATUE OF LIBERTY NATL. MONUMENT
See: U.S. Natl. Park Service

★12981★
STAUFFER CHEMICAL COMPANY - CORPORATE LIBRARY (Sci-Tech)
Nyala Farm Rd.　　　　　　　　　　Phone: (203) 222-4371
Westport, CT 06881　　　　　　　　Jose G. Escarilla, Jr., Corp.Libn.
Staff: Prof 1; Other 1. **Subjects:** Business, chemistry. **Holdings:** 2150 books; 1000 annual reports; 500 reels of microfilm. **Subscriptions:** 100 journals and other serials; 10 newspapers. **Services:** Interlibrary loans; copying; SDI; library open to public by appointment. **Computerized Information Services:** DIALOG, Dow Jones News/Retrieval, BRS. **Networks/Consortia:** Member of Southwestern Connecticut Library Council (SWLC). **Publications:** Corporate Library Bulletin, bimonthly.

★12982★
STAUFFER CHEMICAL COMPANY - DE GUIGNE TECHNICAL CENTER - RESEARCH LIBRARY (Sci-Tech)
1200 S. 47th St.　　　　　　　　　　Phone: (415) 231-1018
Richmond, CA 94804　　　　　　　　　Linda Saylor, Lib.Supv.
Staff: Prof 4; Other 3. **Subjects:** Chemistry, chemical engineering, agriculture, biological sciences. **Holdings:** 8000 volumes; microforms; AV materials; patents. **Subscriptions:** 500 journals and other serials. **Services:** Library not open to public. **Automated Operations:** Computerized cataloging. **Computerized Information Services:** DIALOG, SDC, BRS, Pergamon InfoLine Ltd., CAS Online, Questel, MEDLINE, Hazardline, NIH-EPA Chemical Information System. **Networks/Consortia:** Member of SUNY/OCLC Library Network. **Staff:** Insoo Chu, Sr.Tech.Info.Spec.; Gretchen Peterson, Tech.Info.Spec.Frank Lopez, Assoc.Libn.

★12983★
STAUFFER CHEMICAL COMPANY - EASTERN RESEARCH CENTER INFORMATION SERVICES (Sci-Tech; Food-Bev)
Livingstone Ave.　　　　　　　　　　Phone: (914) 693-1200
Dobbs Ferry, NY 10522　　　Ramona C.T. Crosby, Supv.Info./Comp.Serv.
Founded: 1965. **Staff:** Prof 4; Other 2. **Subjects:** Phosphorous chemistry, food ingredients, polymers and plastics, lubricants, agricultural and specialty chemicals. **Holdings:** 12,500 books; 5700 reels of microfilm of periodicals and U.S. patent files; 3 VF drawers of pamphlets. **Subscriptions:** 774 journals and other serials. **Services:** Interlibrary loans; copying; services open to public with restrictions. **Automated Operations:** Computerized cataloging. **Computerized Information Services:** DIALOG, SDC, BRS, CDC, OCLC, NIH-EPA Chemical Information System; INQUIRE (internal database). **Publications:** Library Bulletin, monthly. **Staff:** Muriel Hogg, Sr.Libn.

★12984★
STAUFFER CHEMICAL COMPANY - MOUNTAIN VIEW RESEARCH CENTER LIBRARY (Agri)
Box 760　　　　　　　　　　　　Phone: (408) 739-0511
Mountain View, CA 94042　　　　　　　Martha L. Manion, Libn.
Staff: Prof 1; Other 1. **Subjects:** Agriculture, entomology, pesticide chemistry, weed science. **Holdings:** 6500 books; 5500 bound periodical

volumes; 25 VF drawers. **Subscriptions:** 280 journals and other serials. **Services:** Interlibrary loans; copying; reciprocal services with other libraries; library open to public by appointment. **Automated Operations:** Computerized cataloging. **Computerized Information Services:** OCLC, BRS, DIALOG, SDC, CAS Online.

★12985★
STAUFFER CHEMICAL COMPANY - SWS SILICONES - TECHNICAL LIBRARY (Sci-Tech)
3301 Sutton Rd.   Phone: (517) 263-5711
Adrian, MI 49221   Dr. George Wolf, Libn.
Subjects: Siloxanes, electronics, sealants, furniture, automotive products, petroleum, tire construction. **Holdings:** 400 books; 400 bound periodical volumes; 7 VF drawers of government publications and specifications; 3 VF drawers of reprints; 10 VF drawers of patents. **Subscriptions:** 90 journals and other serials; 10 newspapers. **Services:** Copying; library open to public with prior approval.

★12986★
STAUFFER CHEMICAL COMPANY - TECHNICAL INFORMATION CENTER (Sci-Tech; Med)
400 Farmington Ave.   Phone: (203) 674-6312
Farmington, CT 06032   Joanna W. Eickenhorst, Tech.Info.Spec.
Staff: Prof 1; Other 1. **Subjects:** Toxicology, environmental health, mutagenicity/genetics, inhalation toxicology, biochemistry, metabolism/pharmacokinetics. **Holdings:** 2000 books. **Subscriptions:** 140 journals and other serials. **Services:** Interlibrary loans; SDI. **Computerized Information Services:** NLM, SDC, DIALOG, OCLC, Occupational Health Services, Inc. **Networks/Consortia:** Member of Capitol Region Library Council. **Publications:** Acquisitions list, monthly; Journal Holdings List; style manual. **Special Indexes:** Technical Reports Index; Reprints Collection Index.

STEACIE SCIENCE LIBRARY
See: York University

★12987★
STEAMSHIP HISTORICAL SOCIETY OF AMERICA COLLECTION (Hist; Trans)
414 Pelton Ave.   Phone: (718) 727-9583
Staten Island, NY 10310   Alice S. Wilson, Sec./Libn.
Founded: 1940. **Staff:** Prof 1. **Subjects:** Marine transportation, steamship and steamboat history, naval history. **Special Collections:** Tracey Brook Collection; T.H. Franklin's collection of 19th century steamboats; B.M. Boyles' collection of Maine material; Hudson River Day Line Collection; R. Loren Graham marine photographs; Everett Viez ocean liner photographs. **Holdings:** 4000 books; 800 pamphlets; 20,000 ship photograph negatives; 50,000 pictures of ships; 1000 steamship company folders; 200 deck and cabin plans; 25,000 colored postcards. **Subscriptions:** 100 journals and other serials. **Services:** Copying; library open to public for reference use only. **Automated Operations:** Computerized cataloging. **Computerized Information Services:** OCLC. **Publications:** Steamboat Bill, quarterly; list of other publications - available on request. **Remarks:** Collection located at University of Baltimore Library, 1420 Maryland Ave., Baltimore, MD 21201.

★12988★
STEARNS CATALYTIC CORPORATION - PHILADELPHIA LIBRARY (Sci-Tech)
Centre Square West
1500 Market St.   Phone: (215) 864-8567
Philadelphia, PA 19102   Mary J. Kober, Dir.
Staff: Prof 1. **Subjects:** Engineering, chemical engineering. **Holdings:** 900 books; 703 bound periodical volumes; 200 vendors' catalogs; 2 VF drawers of vendors' bulletins; 35 VF drawers of standards, specifications, government publications. **Subscriptions:** 52 journals and other serials. **Services:** Interlibrary loans; library not open to public. **Formerly:** Catalytic, Inc.

★12989★
STEARNS-ROGER ENGINEERING CORPORATION - TECHNICAL LIBRARY (Sci-Tech)
4500 Cherry Creek, S.
Box 5888   Phone: (303) 692-2658
Denver, CO 80217   J.C. Hoover, Libn.
Founded: 1971. **Staff:** Prof 1; Other 3. **Subjects:** Engineering. **Holdings:** 11,000 books. **Subscriptions:** 289 journals and other serials. **Services:** Interlibrary loans; copying; library open to public by appointment. **Computerized Information Services:** DIALOG, SDC. **Special Indexes:** Index to vendor catalogs (card).

★12990★
STEEL FOUNDERS' SOCIETY OF AMERICA - LIBRARY
20611 Center Ridge Rd.
Rocky River, OH 44116
Defunct

★12991★
STEELE COUNTY HISTORICAL SOCIETY - ARCHIVES (Hist)
Box 144   Phone: (701) 945-2394
Hope, ND 58230   Helen Parkman, Cur.
Staff: 1. **Subjects:** Local history. **Holdings:** 400 books; 158 bound periodical volumes; 31 oral history tapes; old catalogs and magazines; photograph collection; town and school records. **Services:** Copying; archives open to public with restrictions.

STEEN LIBRARY
See: Stephen F. Austin State University

STEENBOCK MEMORIAL LIBRARY
See: University of Wisconsin, Madison

STEIN MEMORIAL LIBRARY
See: Agudas Achim Congregation

★12992★
STEIN ROE AND FARNHAM - LIBRARY (Bus-Fin)
150 S. Wacker Dr.   Phone: (312) 368-7840
Chicago, IL 60606   Nancy Marano, Libn.
Founded: 1932. **Staff:** Prof 2; Other 2. **Subjects:** Business, finance. **Holdings:** 4200 books; 110 bound periodical volumes; 111,000 microfiche. **Subscriptions:** 400 journals and other serials; 30 newspapers. **Services:** Interlibrary loans; copying; library open to public for reference use only on request. **Computerized Information Services:** DIALOG, Dow Jones News/Retrieval. **Staff:** Celeste Jannusch, Asst.Libn.

STEINBACH (Rabbi A. Alan) LIBRARY
See: Temple Ahavath Sholom - Rabbi A. Alan Steinbach Library

STEINBECK (John) LIBRARY
See: Salinas Public Library - John Steinbeck Library

STEINBECK (John) RESEARCH CENTER
See: San Jose State University - John Steinbeck Research Center

STEINBERG (David R.) INFORMATION CENTER
See: Corning Glass Works/Corning Medical & Scientific - David R. Steinberg Information Center

STEINBERG (Hedi) LIBRARY
See: Yeshiva University - Hedi Steinberg Library

STEINBERG (Sarah and Julius) MEMORIAL LIBRARY
See: Riverside Hospital - Sarah and Julius Steinberg Memorial Library

STEINER (Rudolph) LIBRARY
See: Anthroposophical Society in Canada - Rudolph Steiner Library

STEINER (Walter) MEMORIAL LIBRARY
See: Hartford Medical Society - Walter Steiner Memorial Library

STEINHEIMER COLLECTION OF SOUTHWESTERN CHILDREN'S LITERATURE
See: Tucson Public Library

STEINITZ (Kate Trauman) ARCHIVES
See: University of California, Los Angeles - Art Library - Elmer Belt Library of Vinciana

★12993★
STELCO INC. - CENTRAL LIBRARY
Stelco Tower
100 King St., W.
Hamilton, ON, Canada L8N 3T1
Defunct

★12994★
STELCO INC. - ENGINEERING SERVICES LIBRARY
100 King St., W.
Hamilton, ON, Canada L8N 3T1
Defunct

★12995★
STELCO INC. - RESEARCH AND DEVELOPMENT LIBRARY (Sci-Tech)
P.O. Box 2030   Phone: (416) 528-2511
Hamilton, ON, Canada L8N 3T1   David Rosenplot, Libn.
Staff: Prof 1; Other 2. Subjects: Ferrous metallurgy, engineering, pollution control. Holdings: 2200 books; 300 bound periodical volumes; microforms, patents, internal reports. Subscriptions: 250 journals and other serials. Services: Interlibrary loans; copying; library open to public by appointment. Computerized Information Services: Internal database. Networks/Consortia: Member of Sheridan Park Association. Publications: Current Awareness Bulletin, weekly. Special Indexes: Index of project and report files (computer print-out).

★12996★
STEP FAMILY FOUNDATION, INC. - LIBRARY (Soc Sci)
333 West End Ave.   Phone: (212) 877-3244
New York, NY 10023   Jeannette Lofas, Exec.Dir.
Staff: Prof 1; Other 2. Subjects: Self-awareness, the family, the stepfamily. Holdings: 1000 books; 100 audiotapes. Services: Seminars for professionals and people in step relationships; step family counseling services; library not open to public. Publications: Newsletter, quarterly; Step Family Foundation Digest, annual.

★12997★
STEPAN COMPANY - TECHNICAL INFORMATION CENTER (Sci-Tech)
Edens & Winnetka   Phone: (312) 446-7500
Northfield, IL 60093   Mary R. Davis, Supv.
Staff: Prof 1; Other 1. Subjects: Chemistry. Holdings: 3000 books; 6000 bound periodical volumes; 5000 technical reports; 1200 microfilm cartridges of patents. Subscriptions: 185 journals and other serials. Services: Interlibrary loans; center not open to public. Automated Operations: Computerized cataloging. Computerized Information Services: DIALOG, SDC, NLM, CompuServe. Publications: Current Literature. Special Catalogs: Special patent file (computer printout).

STEPHANSSON'S LIBRARY OF ICELANDIC CANADIAN POETRY
See: University of Manitoba - Archives and Special Collections

★12998★
STEPHEN F. AUSTIN STATE UNIVERSITY - STEEN LIBRARY - SPECIAL COLLECTIONS DEPARTMENT (Hist)
SFA Sta., Box 13055   Phone: (409) 569-4101
Nacogdoches, TX 75962   Linda Cheves Nicklas, Spec.Coll.Libn.
Staff: Prof 1; Other 2. Subjects: Local and East Texas history and literature; social, economic and religious life of East Texas; works by and about East Texans; forest history. Special Collections: Forest History Collection (1500 linear feet); university archives (210 linear feet); R.B. Blake Collection (93 volumes). Holdings: 13,582 books; 800 bound periodical volumes; 750 linear feet of manuscripts; 344 maps; 1728 photographs; 1550 microforms. Subscriptions: 80 journals and other serials. Services: Copying; library open to public. Publications: A Guide to Special Collections. Special Catalogs: Guides, inventories, calendars for manuscript collections; map, photograph and vertical file indexes (all card).

★12999★
STEPTOE AND JOHNSON - LIBRARY (Law)
1330 Connecticut Ave., N.W.   Phone: (202) 429-3000
Washington, DC 20036   Stephen G. Margeton, Libn.
Staff: Prof 4; Other 11. Subjects: Law. Holdings: 44,000 volumes. Services: Library not open to public.

★13000★
STEREO CLUB OF SOUTHERN CALIFORNIA - LIBRARY (Aud-Vis; Rec)
Box 35   Phone: (818) 357-8345
Duarte, CA 91010   David Starkman, Tech.Dir.
Founded: 1977. Staff: 3. Subjects: Stereoscopy; 3-D photography, movies and television; View-Master products and history. Holdings: 50 books; 6 VF drawers of articles, instruction manuals, pamphlets. Services: Copying (limited); library open to public with restrictions. Publications: 3-D News, monthly - by subscription. Formerly: Stereo Photographers, Collectors & Enthusiasts Club - Reel Three-D Enterprises.

STERLING CHEMISTRY LIBRARY
See: Yale University

★13001★
STERLING DRUG, INC. - HILTON-DAVIS CHEMICAL COMPANY DIVISION - LIBRARY (Sci-Tech)
2235 Langdon Farm Rd.   Phone: (513) 841-4074
Cincinnati, OH 45237   Carol Heusner, Libn.
Staff: Prof 1. Subjects: Pigments, chemical intermediates, optical brighteners, dyes, chromogenic compounds, antimicrobials. Holdings: 4500 books; 3788 bound periodical volumes; 7 VF drawers; 675 PB reports; 219 reels of microfilm; 340 microfiche; 11 audiotapes. Subscriptions: 100 journals and other serials. Services: Interlibrary loans; copying; library open to public on a limited schedule. Networks/Consortia: Member of Ohio-Kentucky Cooperating Libraries - Union List of Serials.

STERLING DRUG, INC. - LEHN & FINK PRODUCTS GROUP
See: Lehn & Fink Products Group

★13002★
STERLING DRUG, INC. STERLING-WINTHROP RESEARCH INSTITUTE - LIBRARY (Med)
Columbia Turnpike   Phone: (518) 445-8259
Rensselaer, NY 12144   Carol Bekar, Sr.Adm., Lib.Serv.
Staff: Prof 4; Other 5. Subjects: Biomedicine, chemistry, pharmacology, biology. Holdings: 20,000 books; 30,000 bound periodical volumes; 9218 microforms. Subscriptions: 782 journals and other serials. Services: Interlibrary loans; SDI; library open to public by appointment. Automated Operations: Computerized cataloging, serials and ILL. Computerized Information Services: SDC, DIALOG, MEDLINE. Networks/Consortia: Member of SUNY/OCLC Library Network; Capital District Library Council for Reference & Research Resources (CDLC). Publications: Library Bulletin, quarterly - to mailing list. Staff: Ann Marie Weis, Supv., Lib.Serv.; Patsy Schulenberg, Res.Spec.,Lib.Serv.; Patricia Carroll, ILL Libn.

★13003★
STERLING DRUG, INC. - WINTHROP LABORATORIES - MEDICAL LIBRARY (Med)
90 Park Ave.   Phone: (212) 972-6256
New York, NY 10016   Irene Frisch, Lib.Dir.
Founded: 1927. Staff: Prof 6; Other 2. Subjects: Drugs, pharmaceuticals, clinical medicine. Special Collections: Articles on drugs - abstracted and indexed. Holdings: 6000 books and bound periodical volumes; 115 VF drawers of articles; manuscripts, clippings, pamphlets, microfiche. Subscriptions: 400 journals and other serials. Services: Interlibrary loans; library open to public by appointment. Computerized Information Services: MEDLINE, CHEMLINE, TOXLINE, CANCERLINE, DIALOG; Inquire (indexed articles on products of interest; internal database). Networks/Consortia: Member of Greater Northeastern Regional Medical Library Program. Publications: Current References, semimonthly. Staff: Dorothy Kabakeris, Assoc.Libn.

★13004★
STERLING DRUG, INC. - ZIMPRO INC. - REFERENCE AND RESOURCE CENTER (Sci-Tech)
Military Rd.   Phone: (715) 359-7211
Rothschild, WI 54474
Subjects: Environmental control systems, sewage treatment. Holdings: 2000 books; 200 bound periodical volumes; 500 technical reports; 400 standards; 12 VF drawers of patents; 4 VF drawers of clippings. Subscriptions: 155 journals and other serials. Services: Interlibrary loans; copying; center open to public with restrictions. Networks/Consortia: Member of Wisconsin Library Network; Wisconsin Valley Library Service.

STERNBERG MEMORIAL MUSEUM
See: Fort Hays State University

★13005★
STETSON UNIVERSITY - ARCHIVES (Hist)
Box 1418   Phone: (904) 734-4121
DeLand, FL 32720   Joe I. Myers, Archv.
Subjects: Stetson University, 1883 to present. Special Collections: Stetson correspondence; catalogs and annuals. Holdings: 150 linear feet (5 file cabinets) of correspondence and letters from early DeLand settlers; campus photographs (including faculty, students, and athletics); biographies of all presidents and faculty members. Services: Interlibrary loans; copying; archives open to public.

★13006★
STETSON UNIVERSITY - CHEMISTRY LIBRARY (Sci-Tech)†
Box 1271   Phone: (904) 734-4121
De Land, FL 32720   James H. DeLap, Chem. Professor
Staff: 1. **Subjects:** Chemistry. **Holdings:** 2200 books; 4400 bound periodical volumes; 10 drawers of microfiche. **Subscriptions:** 28 journals and other serials. **Services:** Interlibrary loans; copying; library open to public.

★13007★
STETSON UNIVERSITY - COLLEGE OF LAW - CHARLES A. DANA LAW LIBRARY (Law)
1401 61st St., S.   Phone: (813) 345-1335
St. Petersburg, FL 33707   J. Lamar Woodard, Libn./Professor of Law
Founded: 1900. **Staff:** Prof 5; Other 4. **Subjects:** Law. **Holdings:** 200,000 volumes. **Subscriptions:** 700 journals and other serials. **Services:** Interlibrary loans; copying; library open to qualified persons. **Automated Operations:** Computerized cataloging. **Computerized Information Services:** Westlaw, LEXIS, OCLC. **Networks/Consortia:** Member of SOLINET; Tampa Bay Library Consortium. **Staff:** Roman Yoder, Asst.Libn.; Earlene Hurst, Ser.Libn.; Sally Ginsberg, Ref.Libn.; Pamela Burdett, Asst.Ref.Libn.

★13008★
STETSON UNIVERSITY - FLORIDA BAPTIST HISTORICAL COLLECTION (Hist; Rel-Theol)
Box 1353   Phone: (904) 734-2559
De Land, FL 32720   E. Earl Joiner, Cur.
Staff: 1. **Subjects:** History of Baptists, Southern Baptist and Florida Baptist Churches. **Holdings:** 1165 books and bound periodical volumes; 230 reels of microfilm; 122 boxes of Baptist Association minutes; vertical files. **Subscriptions:** 14 journals and other serials. **Services:** Interlibrary loans; copying; library open to public with restrictions. **Publications:** Florida Baptist Historical Society Newsletter. **Special Indexes:** Florida Baptist Historical Collection Index.

★13009★
STETSON UNIVERSITY - SCHOOL OF MUSIC LIBRARY (Mus)
Woodland Blvd.   Phone: (904) 734-4121
De Land, FL 32720   Janice Jenkins, Music Libn.
Founded: 1936. **Staff:** Prof 1; Other 8. **Subjects:** Music. **Special Collections:** Organ music recordings (370). **Holdings:** 5640 books; 906 bound periodical volumes; 7750 music scores; 5460 phonograph records; 740 pieces of old, popular sheet music; ensemble music for brass choir, band, orchestra and choir. **Subscriptions:** 36 journals and other serials. **Services:** Interlibrary loans; copying; library open to public for reference use only. **Computerized Information Services:** DIALOG. Performs searches on cost recovery basis.

STETTENHEIM (Ivan M.) LIBRARY
See: Congregation Emanu-El - Ivan M. Stettenheim Library

STEVENS (Charles E.) AMERICAN ATHEIST LIBRARY AND ARCHIVES INC.
See: Society of Separationists - Charles E. Stevens American Atheist Library and Archives Inc.

★13010★
STEVENS CLINIC HOSPITAL - LIBRARY (Med)
U.S. 52, East   Phone: (304) 436-3161
Welch, WV 24801   Karen Peery, Libn.
Staff: 2. **Subjects:** Medicine, surgery and related fields. **Holdings:** 800 volumes. **Services:** Copying; library open to public with restrictions.

STEVENS INSTITUTE OF TECHNOLOGY - PLASTICS INSTITUTE OF AMERICA
See: Plastics Institute of America

★13011★
STEVENS INSTITUTE OF TECHNOLOGY - SAMUEL C. WILLIAMS LIBRARY (Sci-Tech)
Castle Point Sta.   Phone: (201) 420-5198
Hoboken, NJ 07030   Richard P. Widdicombe, Dir.
Founded: 1890. **Staff:** Prof 5; Other 7. **Subjects:** Engineering, science, mathematics, scientific management. **Special Collections:** Leonardo da Vinci (Lieb Library); F.W. Taylor Collection (scientific management). **Holdings:** 100,000 books and bound periodical volumes; 2500 reels of microfilm; 8 VF drawers. **Subscriptions:** 1000 journals and other serials. **Services:** Interlibrary loans; copying; library open to public. **Automated Operations:** Computerized serials, circulation and accounting. **Computerized Information Services:** DIALOG, SDC, BRS, RLIN, NewsNet, Inc. Performs searches on cost recovery basis. Contact Person: Colleen Prezlock, 420-5423. **Staff:**

Colleen Prezlock, Info.Serv.Libn.; Barbara Laub, Info.Serv.Libn.; Jim Greaves, Info.Serv.Libn.; Ourida Oubraham, Info.Serv.Libn.

STEVENS (J.P.) AND CO., INC.
See: J.P. Stevens and Co., Inc.

STEVENS MEMORIAL MUSEUM
See: Washington County Historical Society - Library

STEVENSON (George B.) LIBRARY
See: Lock Haven State College - George B. Stevenson Library

STEVENSON (Marion) LIBRARY
See: Christian Board of Publication - Marion Stevenson Library

STEVENSON (Sara Shannon) SCIENCE LIBRARY
See: Vanderbilt University - Jean and Alexander Heard Library - Central Div. - Sara Shannon Stevenson Sci. Lib.

STEWART (David M.) LIBRARY
See: St. Helen's Island Museum Montreal - David M. Stewart Library

STEWART (Governor John W.) & MR. & MRS. CHARLES M. SWIFT RESEARCH CENTER
See: Sheldon Art Museum - Governor John W. Stewart & Mr. & Mrs. Charles M. Swift Research Center Library

STEWART RESOURCES CENTRE
See: Saskatchewan Teachers' Federation

STEWART ROOM
See: Glassboro State College - Savitz Library

STICKEL (William J.) MEMORIAL LIBRARY
See: American Podiatry Association - William J. Stickel Memorial Library

★13012★
STIEFEL LABORATORIES, INC. - RESEARCH INSTITUTE LIBRARY (Med)
                                           Phone: (518) 239-6901
Oak Hill, NY 12460   Loretta Lounsbury, Act.Libn.
Founded: 1967. **Staff:** 2. **Subjects:** Dermatology. **Holdings:** 300 books; 10 bound periodical volumes. **Subscriptions:** 40 journals and other serials. **Services:** Library not open to public.

STILL (A.T.) MEMORIAL LIBRARY
See: Kirksville College of Osteopathic Medicine - A.T. Still Memorial Library

STILL (Andrew Taylor) MEMORIAL LIBRARY
See: American Osteopathic Association - Andrew Taylor Still Memorial Library

★13013★
STILL WATERS FOUNDATION, INC. - STILL WATERS CENTRE LIBRARY (Soc Sci)
615 Stafford Ln.
Pensacola, FL 32506   Dana Faye Cobb
Staff: Prof 1; Other 3. **Subjects:** Metaphysics, parapsychology, comparative religions, earth science, space program, planetary discoveries, unexplained UFOs, astronomy, animal rights, anti-vivisection issues, animal care, preventive medicine, holistic health care theory, herbal medicine. **Special Collections:** Blavatsky; M.P. Hall; Edgar Cayce. **Holdings:** 5000 books; 2000 bound periodical volumes; 84 other cataloged items. **Subscriptions:** 23 journals and other serials. **Services:** Copying; library open to public for reference use only. **Publications:** Still Waters Digest, monthly.

STILLMAN LIBRARY
See: Tobey Hospital

★13014★
STILLWATER PUBLIC LIBRARY - ST. CROIX VALLEY ROOM (Hist)
223 N. 4th St.   Phone: (612) 439-1675
Stillwater, MN 55082   Sue Collins, Hist.
Founded: 1859. **Staff:** Prof 1. **Subjects:** Local history. **Special Collections:** John Runk pictures (700). **Holdings:** 800 books; newspaper clippings; manuscripts; scrapbooks; city directories. **Services:** Interlibrary loans; copying; room open to public for reference use only.

STIMSON LIBRARY
See: U.S. Army - Academy of Health Sciences

STIMSON (Russell L.) OPHTHALMIC REFERENCE LIBRARY
See: Canada College - Russell L. Stimson Ophthalmic Reference Library

STINE LABORATORY LIBRARY
See: Du Pont de Nemours (E.I.) & Company, Inc.

STITT (Edward Rhodes) LIBRARY
See: U.S. Navy - Edward Rhodes Stitt Library

STITT LIBRARY
See: Austin Presbyterian Theological Seminary

STOCK (Edith L.) MEMORIAL LIBRARY
See: Trinity United Church of Christ - Edith L. Stock Memorial Library

★13015★
STOCKBRIDGE LIBRARY ASSOCIATION - HISTORICAL ROOM (Hist)
Main & Elm Sts.   Phone: (413) 298-5501
Stockbridge, MA 01262   Pauline D. Pierce, Cur.
Founded: 1938. **Subjects:** Local and area history, genealogy, books by and about Stockbridge authors, Stockbridge imprints, Stockbridge Indians. **Special Collections:** Anson Clark, Jonathan Edwards, Field family, Daniel Chester French and Sedgwick Collections. **Holdings:** 1700 books and pamphlets; vital records and cemetery inscriptions; memorabilia and manuscripts; account books. **Services:** Interlibrary loans; room open to public.

★13016★
STOCKMEN'S MEMORIAL FOUNDATION - LIBRARY (Agri; Hist)
2116 27th Ave., N.E., No. 126   Phone: (403) 230-3338
Calgary, AB, Canada T2E 7A6   Helgi Leesment, Cons.Libn.
Founded: 1982. **Staff:** Prof 1; Other 1. **Subjects:** Alberta ranching history, beef cattle industry, Western art, ranching fiction. **Holdings:** 900 books; 50 bound periodical volumes; 25 pamphlet boxes of cattle breed organizations materials. **Subscriptions:** 70 journals and other serials; 5 newspapers. **Services:** Copying; library open to public for reference use only. **Publications:** Column in Home Quarter.

★13017★
STOCKPHOTOS, INC. - LIBRARY (Aud-Vis)*
275 Seventh Ave.
New York, NY 10001   Robert Werner, Dir.
Founded: 1967. **Staff:** 12. **Subjects:** Photographic collection of mood - romance, scenics, travel, families, girls, children; advertising photography. **Holdings:** 1 million photographs; catalogs of representative photos.

★13018★
STOCKTON NEWSPAPERS INC. - STOCKTON RECORD LIBRARY (Publ)
530 Market St.   Phone: (209) 943-6397
Stockton, CA 95201   Dorothy M. Frankhouse, Libn.
Founded: 1952. **Staff:** 3. **Subjects:** Local history. **Holdings:** 300 books; 200 VF drawers of newspaper clippings; 40 drawers of small pictures; 16 drawers of large pictures; 875 reels of microfilm; 150 microfiche. **Subscriptions:** 15 journals and other serials; 15 newspapers. **Services:** Library not open to public. **Staff:** Catherine Yanez, Asst.Libn.; Patricia Meyers, Asst.Libn.

★13019★
STOCKTON-SAN JOAQUIN COUNTY PUBLIC LIBRARY - CALIFORNIA ROOM (Hist)
603 N. El Dorado   Phone: (209) 944-8415
Stockton, CA 95202   Isabel Benson, Libn.
Subjects: Local and state history, 1850 to present; gold mining region of California. **Special Collections:** Writings of local pioneers concerning library development, theater, and government; early public documents; logbooks relating to library activities (1000 items total). **Holdings:** 2000 items. **Services:** Copying; room open to public for reference use only. **Automated Operations:** Computerized cataloging. **Computerized Information Services:** DIALOG.

★13020★
STOCKTON STATE HOSPITAL - PROFESSIONAL LIBRARY (Med)
510 El Magnolia   Phone: (209) 948-7181
Stockton, CA 95202   Walter Greening, Sr.Libn.
Staff: Prof 1. **Subjects:** Mentally handicapped, mentally ill, behavior therapy, child psychiatry, community mental health, psychiatric nursing. **Holdings:** 6700 books; 1200 bound periodical volumes; 158 reels of microfilm of

periodicals; 300 audiotapes. **Subscriptions:** 120 journals and other serials. **Services:** Interlibrary loans; copying; library open to public. **Networks/Consortia:** Member of Pacific Southwest Regional Medical Library Service (PSRMLS); Central Association of Libraries (CAL). **Publications:** Library News and Previews, quarterly. **Remarks:** Maintained by California State Department of Developmental Services.

★13021★
STOEL, RIVES, BOLEY, ET AL - LIBRARY (Law)
900 S.W. Fifth Ave.   Phone: (503) 224-3380
Portland, OR 97204   Larry W. Piper, Libn.
Staff: Prof 1; Other 4. **Subjects:** Law. **Holdings:** 33,000 books; 1200 bound periodical volumes. **Subscriptions:** 390 journals and other serials; 10 newspapers. **Services:** Interlibrary loans (limited); copying; library open to public with restrictions. **Computerized Information Services:** LEXIS, Westlaw, NewsNet, Inc., DIALOG, LEGI-SLATE.

STOLL MEMORIAL LIBRARY
See: Lancaster Bible College

STONE (Abraham) LIBRARY
See: Sanger (Margaret) Center-Planned Parenthood New York City - Abraham Stone Library

STONE (Edward Durell) LIBRARY
See: Boston Architectural Center - Alfred Shaw and Edward Durell Stone Library

STONE (Franz Theodore) LABORATORY
See: Ohio State University - Franz Theodore Stone Laboratory

STONE (George G.) CENTER FOR CHILDREN'S BOOKS
See: Claremont Graduate School - George G. Stone Center for Children's Books

★13022★
STONE, MARRACCINI & PATTERSON - RESEARCH & DEVELOPMENT LIBRARY (Plan)
455 Beach St.   Phone: (415) 775-7300
San Francisco, CA 94133   Ronnie Cadam, Libn.
Founded: 1965. **Staff:** Prof 1; Other 1. **Subjects:** Health planning, health care facilities design, medical facility planning, architecture, population statistics, urban planning. **Holdings:** 7280 books; 24 VF drawers of articles, clippings, pamphlets, reports and maps. **Subscriptions:** 140 journals and other serials. **Services:** Library not open to public.

STONE (Olive Clifford) LIBRARY
See: Butler County Historical Society - Olive Clifford Stone Library

★13023★
STONE AND WEBSTER ENGINEERING CORPORATION - TECHNICAL INFORMATION CENTER (Sci-Tech)
Box 5406   Phone: (303) 770-7700
Denver, CO 80217   Susan Newhams, Libn.
Founded: 1975. **Staff:** Prof 1; Other 1. **Subjects:** Engineering, energy resources, power plants. **Holdings:** 5000 books; 200 microfiche reports; plant engineering service microfilm cartridges; 506 computer program manuals. **Subscriptions:** 100 journals and other serials. **Services:** Interlibrary loans; library not open to public. **Automated Operations:** Computerized cataloging. **Computerized Information Services:** DIALOG, SDC. **Publications:** Acquisition list, monthly - for internal distribution only. **Special Catalogs:** Computer generated book catalog.

★13024★
STONE AND WEBSTER ENGINEERING CORPORATION - TECHNICAL INFORMATION CENTER (Sci-Tech)
245 Summer St.   Phone: (617) 589-8891
Boston, MA 02110   Nancy M. Pellini, Div.Mgr.
Staff: Prof 2; Other 5. **Subjects:** Engineering - chemical, civil, nuclear, electrical, environmental, mechanical, structural; petroleum and petroleum processing; electric power transmission and generation; geology and soils mechanics; gas processing and transmission; pulp and paper processing and manufacture; water desalination; synfuels. **Special Collections:** Visual Search microfilm file of documentation, commercial standards and International Organization for Standardization and IEC standards. **Holdings:** 10,000 books and bound periodical volumes; 15,000 reports. **Subscriptions:** 1200 journals and other serials. **Services:** Interlibrary loans; copying; library open to public by appointment. **Computerized Information Services:** DIALOG, SDC, DOE/RECON, NEXIS. **Publications:** Union List of Serials, annual; Guide to the

Technical Information Center.

★13025★
STONE AND WEBSTER MANAGEMENT CONSULTANTS, INC. -
INFORMATION CENTER/LIBRARY (Bus-Fin; Energy)
One Penn Plaza   Phone: (212) 290-6377
New York, NY 10119
Staff: Prof 1; Other 1. **Subjects:** Public utilities, power, engineering, business and finance, management and labor. **Holdings:** 3000 books; 400 bound periodical volumes; corporation records; microfiche for New York Stock Exchange, AME and selected OTC. **Subscriptions:** 400 journals and other serials; 15 newspapers. **Services:** Interlibrary loans; center not open to public.

★13026★
STONEHENGE STUDY GROUP - STONEHENGE VIEWPOINT LIBRARY (Hist)
2821 De La Vina St.   Phone: (805) 687-9350
Santa Barbara, CA 93105   Joan L. Cyr, Libn.
Staff: Prof 2; Other 2. **Subjects:** Archeoastronomy, astroarcheology, canopy theory, Hidden Halo hypothesis, Vailian canopy research, halo motifs. **Special Collections:** Unpublished manuscripts and published works of Isaac N. Vail, 1840-1912 (7000 pages). **Holdings:** 3400 books; 5000 pages on microfilm. **Subscriptions:** 32 journals and other serials. **Services:** Interlibrary loans; copying; library open to public by appointment. **Publications:** Stonehenge Viewpoint, 6/year. **Staff:** Donald L. Cyr, Ed.

★13027★
STONEHILL COLLEGE - ARNOLD B. TOFIAS INDUSTRIAL ARCHIVES (Bus-Fin)
Washington St.   Phone: (617) 238-1081
North Easton, MA 02356   Louise M. Kenneally, Archv.
Founded: 1973. **Staff:** Prof 1. **Subjects:** Business archives. **Special Collections:** O. Ames & Co. shovel papers; Union Pacific Railroad. **Holdings:** 1500 linear feet of manuscripts. **Services:** Archives open to public by appointment.

STONES RIVER NATL. BATTLEFIELD
See: U.S. Natl. Park Service

STONEWALL JACKSON HOUSE
See: Historic Lexington Foundation

★13028★
STONINGTON HISTORICAL SOCIETY - WHITEHALL LIBRARY (Hist)
Box 2D2
Stonington, CT 06378   Capt. Robert J. Ramsbotham, Pres.
Staff: Prof 1; Other 1. **Subjects:** Genealogy, local history, biography. **Holdings:** 500 books; manuscripts; photographs; ships' logs; biographies; maps; newspaper clippings; memorabilia. **Publications:** Historical Footnotes, quarterly.

STORED-PRODUCT INSECTS RESEARCH & DEVELOPMENT LABORATORY
See: U.S.D.A. - Agricultural Research Service

STOREY (Effie M.) LEARNING CENTER
See: Northwest Hospital - Effie M. Storey Learning Center

★13029★
STORMONT-VAIL REGIONAL MEDICAL CENTER AND SHAWNEE COUNTY MEDICAL SOCIETY - HEALTH SCIENCES LIBRARY (Med)
1500 S.W. 10th St.   Phone: (913) 354-6090
Topeka, KS 66606   Shirley Borglund, Hd.Libn.
Founded: 1889. **Staff:** Prof 3; Other 4. **Subjects:** Medicine, nursing, allied health sciences. **Holdings:** 8000 books; 13,500 bound periodical volumes. **Subscriptions:** 400 journals and other serials. **Services:** Interlibrary loans; copying; research; library open to public upon referral by a physician. **Networks/Consortia:** Member of Midcontinental Regional Medical Library Program. **Staff:** Carol Wadley, Nursing Sch.Libn.; Joan Ring, Acq./Cat.Libn.

STOTT EXPLORERS LIBRARY
See: Martin and Osa Johnson Safari Museum

★13030★
STOVE KING - LIBRARY (Rec)
1116 Capistrano Dr.   Phone: (801) 363-7143
Salt Lake City, UT 84116   Clarence Froman, Owner
Founded: 1976. **Staff:** Prof 2. **Subjects:** American antique stoves. **Holdings:** Old stove catalogs, stove trade cards dating from early 1800s to 1930; large album of photographs of restored antique stoves, with many unrestored "as

is" comparison photographs. **Services:** Library open to public with restrictions. **Staff:** Barry Froman, Co-Owner.

★13031★
STOWE-DAY FOUNDATION - LIBRARY (Hist)
77 Forest St.   Phone: (203) 522-9258
Hartford, CT 06105   Joseph S. Van Why, Dir.
Founded: 1964. **Staff:** Prof 2; Other 4. **Subjects:** Art, architecture, decorative arts, history, literature, slavery, women's suffrage. **Special Collections:** William H. Gillette papers, plays and photographs, 1853-1937; photographs; suffrage papers of Isabella Beecher Hooker; Katharine S. Day Collection; Saturday Morning Club Collection; literary manuscripts of Mark Twain and Harriet Beecher Stowe; 19th century wallpaper samples. **Holdings:** 15,000 books; 1500 bound periodical volumes; 150,000 manuscripts, especially Beecher family; 1500 pamphlets circa 1850, especially slavery; 3500 miscellaneous 19th century pamphlets. **Subscriptions:** 10 journals and other serials. **Services:** Interlibrary loans; copying; library open to public. **Networks/Consortia:** Member of Capitol Region Library Council. **Publications:** The Papers of Harriet Beecher Stowe (bibliography). **Special Catalogs:** Catalog of Nineteenth Century Chairs; American Artist Jared Flagg; William H. Gillette; microfiche of suffrage papers of Isabella Beecher Hooker. **Remarks:** The books of the Mark Twain Memorial, Hartford, Connecticut, are also cataloged and housed in the Stowe-Day Library. The Stowe-Day Foundation maintains an active publishing program, consisting of original and reprint works, which reflects the interests of the library. **Staff:** Diana Royce, Libn.; Roberta Bradford, Asst.Libn.

STOWE (Lyman Maynard) LIBRARY
See: University of Connecticut - Health Center - Lyman Maynard Stowe Library

STOXEN LIBRARY
See: Dickinson State College

★13032★
STRADLEY, RONON, STEVENS & YOUNG - LAW LIBRARY (Law)
1100 One Franklin Plaza   Phone: (215) 564-8190
Philadelphia, PA 19102   Linda-Jean Smith, Libn.
Founded: 1972. **Staff:** Prof 1; Other 1. **Subjects:** Law - corporate, Pennsylvania, tax, labor; securities. **Special Collections:** Pennsylvania Pamphlet Laws since the 1700s (500 volumes). **Holdings:** 4500 books; 500 bound periodical volumes; 4 VF drawers of annual reports; 5 VF drawers of memoranda files. **Subscriptions:** 150 journals and other serials. **Services:** Interlibrary loans; copying; library open to public by appointment. **Computerized Information Services:** LEXIS. **Networks/Consortia:** Member of Greater Philadelphia Law Library Association Union List. **Publications:** Information Items, monthly - for internal distribution only. **Special Catalogs:** Memoranda file (card).

STRASENBURGH PLANETARIUM
See: Rochester Museum and Science Center

★13033★
THE STRATEGIC CORPORATION - STRATEGIC MOVES LIBRARY (Soc Sci)
2165 S.W. Main St.   Phone: (503) 222-9028
Portland, OR 97205   Susan Limper, Staff Futurist
Founded: 1982. **Staff:** Prof 1; Other 3. **Subjects:** Public, social, economic, technological, political and strategic issues. **Holdings:** 59 environmental files; 10,000 other cataloged items. **Subscriptions:** 165 journals and other serials; 10 newspapers. **Services:** Library not open to public. **Automated Operations:** Computerized cataloging and serials. **Computerized Information Services:** MIKADO (internal database). **Publications:** Strategic Moves, monthly - by subscription.

STRATFORD GALLERY
See: Gallery/Stratford

★13034★
STRATFORD HALL PLANTATION - JESSIE BALL DUPONT MEMORIAL LIBRARY (Hist)
Stratford Post Office   Phone: (804) 493-8572
Stratford, VA 22558   Dr. Ralph Draughon, Jr., Libn./Hist.
Founded: 1980. **Staff:** Prof 2; Other 1. **Subjects:** Lee family in the political, social and economic life of the 18th-century; Virginia, 1763-1789; Robert E. Lee. **Special Collections:** Lee Family manuscripts (1200 items); Thomas Lee Shippen 1790 Inventory and Collection (600 volumes); Ditchley Collection of 16th, 17th and 18th-century books (2400 volumes). **Holdings:** 7500 books; 200 bound periodical volumes; 332 cubic feet of Stratford Hall archives; 125 reels of microfilm. **Services:** Copying; library open to public by appointment.

Staff: Margaret Elizabeth Gillie, Archv.

★13035★
STRATFORD HISTORICAL SOCIETY - LIBRARY (Hist)
967 Academy Hill
Box 382   Phone: (203) 378-0630
Stratford, CT 06497   Mrs. Einar M. Larson, Libn.
Founded: 1926. **Staff:** 2. **Subjects:** Stratford history and genealogy, Connecticut history. **Holdings:** 800 volumes; genealogical records and documents. **Services:** Library open to public by appointment only.

★13036★
STRATFORD SHAKESPEAREAN FESTIVAL FOUNDATION OF CANADA - STRATFORD FESTIVAL ARCHIVES (Theater)
Box 520   Phone: (519) 271-4040
Stratford, ON, Canada N5A 6V2   Daniel W. Ladell, Archv.
Staff: Prof 2. **Subjects:** The Stratford Festival. **Holdings:** 3000 cubic feet of original documents and artistic materials; 500 AV titles; 50,000 photographs; 1000 items of Shakespeareana; 1000 costumes, properties and models; 100 items of original art. **Subscriptions:** 10 journals and other serials. **Services:** Copying; archives open to qualified researchers only. **Staff:** Alexandra Cushing, Cur.

★13037★
STRATHY, ARCHIBALD AND SEAGRAM - LAW LIBRARY (Law)
3801 Commerce Court W.
Box 438   Phone: (416) 863-7525
Toronto, ON, Canada M5L 1J3   Alison J. Colvin, Libn.
Staff: Prof 1. **Subjects:** Law. **Holdings:** 5500 books and bound periodical volumes. **Services:** Interlibrary loans (limited); copying; library open to public with restrictions. **Publications:** Library bulletin, biweekly - for internal distribution only.

STRATTON (Leslie M.) NURSING LIBRARY
See: Methodist Hospital School of Nursing - Leslie M. Stratton Nursing Library

★13038★
STRAUB CLINIC & HOSPITAL, INC. - ARNOLD LIBRARY (Med)
888 S. King St.   Phone: (808) 544-0317
Honolulu, HI 96813   Frances P. Smith, Libn.
Founded: 1921. **Staff:** Prof 1. **Subjects:** Medicine - internal, nuclear, pediatric, adolescent, dermatology, surgery. **Special Collections:** Straub Clinic Proceedings; reprints of articles written and published by staff members. **Holdings:** 2500 books; 30 bound periodical volumes. **Subscriptions:** 160 journals and other serials. **Services:** Interlibrary loans; copying; SDI; library open to public. **Computerized Information Services:** MEDLINE, DIALOG, AMA/NET. Performs free searches. **Publications:** Straub Clinic Proceedings, quarterly - free upon request. **Special Indexes:** Reprint index (card; 1929 to present).

STRAUB (Lorenz G.) MEMORIAL LIBRARY
See: University of Minnesota - St. Anthony Falls Hydraulic Laboratory - Lorenz G. Straub Memorial Library

STRAUS (Nathan) YOUNG ADULT LIBRARY
See: New York Public Library - Donnell Library Center - Nathan Straus Young Adult Library

STRAUSS (Anna Lord) LIBRARY
See: Foundation for Citizen Education - Anna Lord Strauss Library

STRAUSS (Levi) & COMPANY
See: Levi Strauss & Company

★13039★
STRAWBERY BANKE, INC. - THAYER CUMINGS HISTORICAL REFERENCE LIBRARY (Hist)
454 Court St.   Phone: (603) 436-8010
Portsmouth, NH 03801   Nicole Osborn, Libn.
Staff: Prof 1. **Subjects:** Portsmouth history, decorative arts, architecture, archeology, horticulture. **Special Collections:** Business and family papers of Governor Ichabod and Sarah Parker Rice Goodwin, 1790s-1890s (8 cubic feet); Lowell Boat Shop Collection, 1881-1914 (5 boxes); papers of William and Charles Neil, Capt. John Hill, and Stephen Chase. **Holdings:** 2800 books; 30 bound periodical volumes; 25 reports; 24 cubic feet of manuscripts; 45 reels of microfilm. **Subscriptions:** 58 journals and other serials. **Services:** Copying; library open to public for reference use only.

★13040★
STRAYER COLLEGE - LEARNING RESOURCES CENTER (Bus-Fin; Comp Sci)
3045 Columbia Pike   Phone: (703) 892-5100
Arlington, VA 22204   David A. Moulton, Dir.
Staff: Prof 1; Other 1. **Subjects:** Data processing, computers, business and office administration, court and conference reporting. **Holdings:** 600 books; 1 VF drawer of pamphlets; 100 dictation cassettes. **Subscriptions:** 10 journals and other serials. **Services:** Interlibrary loans; center open to public. **Networks/Consortia:** Member of Consortium for Continuing Higher Education in Northern Virginia - Library Networking Committee. **Publications:** Library Handbook.

★13041★
STRAYER COLLEGE - WILKES LIBRARY (Bus-Fin)
1100 Vermont Ave., N.W.   Phone: (202) 861-5241
Washington, DC 20005   H. Barbara Krell, Dir. of Libs.
Staff: Prof 1; Other 2. **Subjects:** Business administration, data processing, accounting, health facilities administration, office administration. **Holdings:** 18,000 books; 12 drawers of pamphlets. **Subscriptions:** 120 journals and other serials; 10 newspapers. **Services:** Interlibrary loans; copying; library open to public. **Publications:** Library Handbook, annual.

STRECKER MUSEUM LIBRARY
See: Baylor University

★13042★
STROMBERG-CARLSON - TECHNICAL LIBRARY (Info Sci; Comp Sci)
1291 Hwy. 17-92
Box 700   Phone: (305) 339-1600
Longwood, FL 32750   Dolores Rosenbloom, Libn.
Staff: 1. **Subjects:** Telecommunications, electronics, computers. **Holdings:** 1000 books; 100 bound periodical volumes; 200 archival items; 100 reels of microfilm; reports. **Subscriptions:** 100 journals and other serials; 5 newspapers. **Services:** Interlibrary loans; library not open to public.

STROMBERG (Joseph G.) LIBRARY OF THE HEALTH SCIENCES
See: Swedish Covenant Hospital - Joseph G. Stromberg Library of the Health Sciences

STRONG (Kate) HISTORICAL LIBRARY
See: Museums at Stony Brook - Kate Strong Historical Library

★13043★
STRONG (Margaret Woodbury) MUSEUM - LIBRARY (Art; Hist)
One Manhattan Square   Phone: (716) 263-2700
Rochester, NY 14607   Elaine M. Challacombe, Libn.
Founded: 1972. **Staff:** Prof 3; Other 2. **Subjects:** U.S. social history, 19th-century decorative arts in the U.S., 19th-century woman in the home. **Special Collections:** Children's literature from late 19th and early 20th centuries (400 titles); Victorian publishers' bindings (600); miniature books (680); fore-edge paintings (47); Winslow Homer's library (20 volumes). **Holdings:** 20,000 books; 600 Parke-Bernet auction catalogs, 1938-1957; 4000 trade catalogs. **Subscriptions:** 114 journals and other serials. **Services:** Interlibrary loans; copying; library open to public. **Automated Operations:** Computerized cataloging. **Networks/Consortia:** Member of Rochester Regional Research Library Council (RRRLC); SUNY/OCLC Library Network. **Publications:** New Acquisitions list, monthly - for internal distribution only. **Staff:** Anna K. Wang, Asst.Libn./Cat.; Kathy Lazar, Asst.Libn./Ref.

STROSACKER LIBRARY
See: Northwood Institute

STROZIER (Robert Manning) LIBRARY
See: Florida State University

STRUGHOLD AEROMEDICAL LIBRARY
See: U.S. Air Force - Aerospace Medical Division - School of Aerospace Medicine

★13044★
STRYBING ARBORETUM SOCIETY - HELEN CROCKER RUSSELL LIBRARY (Sci-Tech)†
Golden Gate Pk.
9th Ave. & Lincoln Way   Phone: (415) 661-1316
San Francisco, CA 94122   M. Jane Gates, Hd.Libn.
Founded: 1972. **Staff:** Prof 2. **Subjects:** Horticulture, plant propagation, landscape gardening, flora of Mediterranean climates, plant hunting, history of gardening. **Holdings:** 8000 books, including 300 rare volumes; 550 bound periodical volumes; 8 scrapbooks of newspaper clippings; 1 scrapbook of

William Hammond Hall Archives; 3000 slide transparencies of plants; 6 VF drawers of brochures and pamphlets; nursery catalogs, old and current. **Subscriptions:** 90 journals and other serials. **Services:** Copying; library open to public for reference use only. **Special Catalogs:** Catalog of slide collection (card); catalog of old and current nursery catalog collections. **Remarks:** "The basic purpose of the library is to assist the home gardener and to provide information about the 5000 plants in the Strybing Arboretum." **Staff:** Barbara Pitschel, Asst.Libn.

STUART (John) RESEARCH LABORATORIES
See: Quaker Oats Company - John Stuart Research Laboratories

STUART LIBRARY OF WESTERN AMERICANA
See: University of the Pacific

STUART (Lyle) LIBRARY OF SEXUAL SCIENCE
See: Institute for Advanced Study of Human Sexuality

STUART MEMORIAL LIBRARY
See: Alta Bates Hospital

STUCK MEDICAL LIBRARY
See: Mount Clemens General Hospital

STUDENT STRUGGLE FOR SOVIET JEWRY
See: Center for Russian & East European Jewry/Student Struggle for Soviety Jewry

STUDENT VOLUNTEER MOVEMENT - ARCHIVES
See: Yale University - Divinity School Library

★13045★
STUDENTS' MUSEUM, INC. - LIBRARY (Sci-Tech)
516 Beaman St.
Chilhowee Pk., Box 6108   Phone: (615) 637-1121
Knoxville, TN 37914   David R. Sincerbox, Dir.
Founded: 1976. **Staff:** Prof 2; Other 5. **Subjects:** Science, history, nature, arts and crafts. **Special Collections:** Old tools (300); dolls (200); costumes (25); fossils (250); rocks and minerals (5000); Indian artifacts (20,000); man-made artifacts (20,000); shells (5000); stuffed animals (300); charts (300). **Holdings:** 2100 books; 200 manuscripts; 12,000 slides; 300 pamphlets; 2000 postcards. **Subscriptions:** 22 journals and other serials. **Services:** Library not open to public. **Automated Operations:** Computerized cataloging and acquisitions. **Computerized Information Services:** Internal database. **Publications:** World of Wonders, monthly newspaper; Guide to Museum Programs; Museum News; annual report; Special School - Summer Guide. **Staff:** Sylvia Gloeckner, Cur. of Educ.

STUDIO OF CONTEMPLATION
See: Arcane Order - Library

★13046★
STUDIO SUPPLIERS ASSOCIATION - BUSINESS LIBRARY (Bus-Fin)
548 Goffle Rd.   Phone: (201) 427-9384
Hawthorne, NJ 07506   Donald Franz, Exec.Sec.
Founded: 1975. **Staff:** 1. **Subjects:** Photography, optics, business. **Holdings:** 100 books; 250 bound periodical volumes; 50 market analysis reports; 2 16mm educational films. **Subscriptions:** 55 journals and other serials. **Services:** Copying; library open to public with restrictions.

STUHR MUSEUM
See: Hall County Museum Board

★13047★
STURDY MEMORIAL HOSPITAL - HEALTH SCIENCES LIBRARY (Med)
211 Park St.   Phone: (617) 222-5200
Attleboro, MA 02703   Juliet I. Mansfield, Libn.
Staff: Prof 1. **Subjects:** Medicine, nursing. **Special Collections:** Rare editions of medical and surgical books (82 volumes). **Holdings:** 1760 books; 450 bound periodical volumes; 8 VF drawers of articles, clippings, pamphlets. **Subscriptions:** 119 journals and other serials. **Services:** Interlibrary loans; copying; library open to public for reference use only. **Networks/Consortia:** Member of Association of Rhode Island Health Sciences Librarians (ARIHSL); Southeastern Massachusetts Consortium of Health Science Libraries (SEMCO).

STURGEON MUSIC LIBRARY
See: Mount Union College

STURGES (Gertrude E.) MEMORIAL LIBRARY
See: Rhode Island State Department of Health - Gertrude E. Sturges Memorial Library

STURGES (Gertrude) MEMORIAL LIBRARY
See: Group Health Association of America, Inc. - Gertrude Sturges Memorial Library

★13048★
STURGIS LIBRARY (Hist)†
Rte. 6A   Phone: (617) 362-6636
Barnstable, MA 02630   Susan R. Klein, Hd.Libn.
Founded: 1867. **Staff:** Prof 2; Other 2. **Subjects:** Genealogy, Barnstable County history, maritime history, 19th century English and American literature. **Special Collections:** Stanley W. Smith Collection of original Cape Cod documents and land deeds; Kittredge Collection of marine history. **Holdings:** 41,960 books; 200 bound periodical volumes; 250 sound recordings, tapes and cassettes; 87 reels of microfilm; 60 flat pictures; 1500 land deeds; 25 maps and charts. **Subscriptions:** 67 journals and other serials. **Services:** Interlibrary loans; copying; service to homebound and institutionalized; library open to public. **Publications:** Sturgis Library Newsletter, quarterly; A Short History of the Sturgis Library; 19th Century Literary Gentlemen. **Remarks:** This library has been declared the oldest library building in the U.S.; its original structure was built in 1644. **Staff:** Marilyn Kelley, Asst.Libn.

★13049★
STYLES (Mary Riley) PUBLIC LIBRARY - LOCAL HISTORY COLLECTION (Hist)
120 N. Virginia Ave.   Phone: (703) 241-5030
Falls Church, VA 22046   Anna Rups, Virginia Coll.Libn.
Subjects: Falls Church history. **Holdings:** 760 books; 225 public records; 105 manuscripts; 5000 photographs; 50,000 negatives; 228 maps; 221 oral history tapes; 6 reels of microfilm; 9 VF drawers of library archives; 5 VF drawers of other archival materials. **Subscriptions:** 26 journals and other serials. **Services:** Interlibrary loans; copying; collection open to public. **Remarks:** Library operates under the auspices of the City of Falls Church.

SUB-ARCTIC RESEARCH STATION LIBRARY
See: Mc Gill University

SUBBAROW MEMORIAL LIBRARY
See: American Cyanamid Company - Lederle Laboratories Division

★13050★
SUDBURY GENERAL HOSPITAL - HOSPITAL LIBRARY (Med)
700 Paris St., Station B   Phone: (705) 674-3181
Sudbury, ON, Canada P3E 3B5   D.M. Hawryliuk, Libn.
Founded: 1950. **Staff:** Prof 1. **Subjects:** Clinical medicine. **Special Collections:** Archival history of hospital (8 volumes of newspaper clippings). **Holdings:** 1200 books; 1120 bound periodical volumes. **Subscriptions:** 130 journals and other serials. **Services:** Interlibrary loans; copying; SDI; library open to public with restrictions.

★13051★
SUFFOLK ACADEMY OF MEDICINE - LIBRARY (Med)
850 Veterans Memorial Hwy.   Phone: (516) 724-7970
Hauppauge, NY 11787   Isabel V. Hathorn, Libn.
Founded: 1966. **Staff:** Prof 1; Other 1. **Subjects:** Medicine, dentistry, nursing. **Holdings:** 2950 books; 2600 periodicals; 90 bulletin collections; 125 cassette tapes; 24 shelves of pamphlets. **Subscriptions:** 390 journals and other serials. **Services:** Interlibrary loans; copying; library open to public for reference use only. **Automated Operations:** Computerized cataloging. **Computerized Information Services:** BRS, DIALOG, MEDLARS. Performs searches on cost recovery basis. **Networks/Consortia:** Member of Long Island Library Resource Council (LILRC); Greater Northeastern Regional Medical Library Program.

★13052★
SUFFOLK COOPERATIVE LIBRARY SYSTEM - AUDIOVISUAL DEPARTMENT (Aud-Vis)
Box 187   Phone: (516) 286-1600
Bellport, NY 11713   Philip Levering, AV Cons.
Staff: Prof 1; Other 5. **Subjects:** Films - children's, documentaries, nature study, feature length, old-time comedy classics; film as art. **Holdings:** 2500 16mm films; 500 VHS video cassettes. **Services:** Interlibrary loans; copying; library open to members of the library system. **Special Catalogs:** Film catalog, biennial - for a fee.

★13053★
SUFFOLK COUNTY HISTORICAL SOCIETY - LIBRARY (Hist)
300 W. Main St.   Phone: (516) 727-2881
Riverhead, NY 11901   Betty M. Carpenter, Libn.
Founded: 1886. **Staff:** 10. **Subjects:** Suffolk County history and genealogy;
Long Island history and genealogy. **Special Collections:** Revolutionary War
documents of Colonel Josiah Smith; Modern Times (Brentwood); Fullerton
negatives, circa 1900; E.T. Talmage weaving collection: Professional
Resources (Museum) Collection. **Holdings:** 15,000 volumes; microfilm;
manuscripts, clippings, records, documents, photographs, fiber swatch-books.
Subscriptions: 12 journals and other serials. **Services:** Copying; library open
to public with restrictions. **Networks/Consortia:** Member of Long Island
Library Resources Council (LILRC); Long Island Archives Conference.
Publications: Register. **Special Indexes:** Index to scrapbooks, glass
negatives (card); vital statistics (card); index to documents (card); abstracts
of documents (book). **Staff:** Alice W. Kappenberg, Archv.-Kpr.; Lois T. De
Wall, Res.Asst.

★13054★
SUFFOLK COUNTY WHALING MUSEUM - LIBRARY (Hist)
Main St.   Phone: (516) 725-0770
Sag Harbor, NY 11963   George A. Finckenor, Sr., Cur.
Staff: Prof 1; Other 3. **Subjects:** Whaling, fishing, antiques, shipping, Indians.
Special Collections: Log books of whaling ships; scrimshaw (on narwhal
tusks). **Holdings:** 300 books; ship models; oil paintings; furniture. **Services:**
Library open to public for reference use only on application.

★13055★
**SUFFOLK MARINE MUSEUM - HERVEY GARRETT SMITH RESEARCH
     LIBRARY (Hist)**
Montauk Hwy.
Box 144   Phone: (516) 567-1733
West Sayville, NY 11796   Ruth Dougherty Jennings, Libn.
Staff: Prof 1. **Subjects:** Boat building, yachting, racing, shipwrecks, U.S. Life
Saving Service, shellfishing, history of the America's Cup Race, the Merchant
Marine, U.S. Navy and U.S. Coast Guard. **Special Collections:** Ships' logs (4);
vessel construction plans; U.S. Life Saving Service records. **Holdings:** 1700
books; 50 bound periodical volumes; 2 slide programs; 40 navigational charts;
glass plate negatives. **Subscriptions:** 11 journals and other serials. **Services:**
Copying; library open to public for reference use only.

★13056★
SUFFOLK UNIVERSITY - LAW LIBRARY (Law)
41 Temple St.   Phone: (617) 723-4700
Boston, MA 02114   Edward Bander, Law Libn.
Founded: 1906. **Staff:** Prof 6; Other 8. **Subjects:** Law. **Holdings:** 175,000
books and bound periodical volumes; 42,000 volumes on microfiche; U.S.
Government documents depository. **Subscriptions:** 835 journals and other
serials; 18 newspapers. **Services:** Interlibrary loans; copying; library open to
public with restrictions. **Automated Operations:** Computerized cataloging and
serials. **Computerized Information Services:** LEXIS, Westlaw, OCLC. **Staff:**
Patricia I. Brown, Asst. Law Libn.; Nancy Bleakley, Govt.Docs.Libn.

★13057★
**SUFFOLK UNIVERSITY - MILDRED F. SAWYER LIBRARY - COLLECTION OF
     AFRO-AMERICAN LITERATURE (Area-Ethnic)**
8 Ashburton Pl.   Phone: (617) 723-4700
Boston, MA 02108   E.G. Hamann, Dir.
Staff: Prof 4; Other 8. **Subjects:** Afro-Americans - literature, bibliography,
history, biography, literary criticism. **Holdings:** 3800 books; 150 bound
periodical volumes. **Services:** Interlibrary loans; copying; library open to public
for reference use only. **Automated Operations:** Computerized cataloging.
Networks/Consortia: Member of NELINET; Fenway Library Consortium.
Publications: Acquisitions List, annual - free upon request. **Staff:** James R.
Coleman, Ref.Libn.; Mary Arthur, Ref.Libn.; Joseph Middleton, Ref.Libn.;
Martha McNamara, Ref.Libn.

★13058★
SUGAR ASSOCIATION, INC. - LIBRARY (Food-Bev)
1511 K St., N.W.   Phone: (202) 628-0189
Washington, DC 20005   Margaret E. Simon, Libn.
Founded: 1943. **Staff:** Prof 1. **Subjects:** Sugar, nutrition and health, food
technology. **Holdings:** 1500 books; 1000 bound periodical volumes; 50 VF
drawers of pamphlets, clippings, patents, miscellaneous documents.
Subscriptions: 104 journals and other serials. **Services:** Interlibrary loans;
copying; library open to public.

SUGARLANDS VISITOR CENTER
See: U.S. Natl. Park Service - Great Smoky Mountains Natl. Park

SUICIDE INFORMATION AND EDUCATION CENTRE
See: Canadian Mental Health Association

★13059★
SULLIVAN AND CROMWELL - LIBRARY (Law)†
125 Broad St.   Phone: (212) 558-4000
New York, NY 10004   Helene A. Weatherill, Libn.
Subjects: Law. **Holdings:** 29,500 volumes. **Services:** Library not open to
public. **Staff:** Barbara A. Clyne, Asst.Libn.

★13060★
SULLIVAN & CROMWELL - WASHINGTON D.C. LIBRARY (Law)
1775 Pennsylvania Ave., N.W.   Phone: (202) 857-1038
Washington, DC 20006   Stephannie K. Newton, Libn.
Founded: 1977. **Staff:** Prof 1; Other 1. **Subjects:** Law - antitrust, securities,
tax, energy, environmental; trade regulation. **Holdings:** 7500 books; 800
bound periodical volumes; documents; microforms. **Subscriptions:** 150
journals and other serials; 8 newspapers. **Services:** Interlibrary loans; copying;
SDI; library open to public with permission. **Computerized Information
Services:** LEXIS, NEXIS, DIALOG. **Special Catalogs:** Catalog of the book and
pamphlet collection (card); catalog of legislative materials (card).

SULLIVAN MEDICAL LIBRARY
See: St. Anne's Hospital

★13061★
SULPHUR INSTITUTE - LIBRARY (Sci-Tech)
1725 K St., N.W.   Phone: (202) 331-9660
Washington, DC 20006   J.S. Platou, Dir. of Info.
Subjects: Sulphur in industry and agriculture. **Holdings:** 500 books; 200
bound periodical volumes; 20 VF drawers. **Services:** Interlibrary loans; library
open to public by appointment.

SULZBACHER MEMORIAL LIBRARY
See: Spring Grove Hospital Center

SULZBERGER JOURNALISM LIBRARY
See: Columbia University

SUMMA CORPORATION - HUGHES HELICOPTERS
See: Hughes Helicopters

★13062★
**SUMMER INSTITUTE OF LINGUISTICS - DALLAS/NORMAN LIBRARY (Hum;
     Soc Sci)**
7500 W. Camp Wisdom Rd.   Phone: (214) 298-3331
Dallas, TX 75236   Melinda L. Lyons, Hd.Libn.
Staff: Prof 3; Other 2. **Subjects:** Linguistics, anthropology. **Special
Collections:** Summer Institute of Linguistics archives (9000 items on
microfiche). **Holdings:** 12,000 books; 1000 bound periodical volumes; 5000
vertical files. **Subscriptions:** 151 journals and other serials. **Services:**
Interlibrary loans; copying; library open to public for reference use only.
Publications: Acquisitions list, irregular. **Staff:** Dorothy L. White, Cat.; Susan
Demick, Off.Mgr.

SUMMERVILLE (W.W.) MEDICAL LIBRARY
See: Bethany Medical Center - W.W. Summerville Medical Library

SUMMIT COUNTY PUBLIC LIBRARY
See: Akron-Summit County Public Library

★13063★
SUMTER AREA TECHNICAL COLLEGE - LIBRARY (Sci-Tech)
506 N. Guignard Dr.   Phone: (803) 773-9371
Sumter, SC 29150   Fannie M. Davis, Libn.
Founded: 1963. **Staff:** Prof 1; Other 2. **Subjects:** Business, environmental
and civil engineering, secretarial science, radio broadcasting, marketing,
machine shop technology, automotive mechanics, criminal justice, accounting,
agricultural technology, electricity, natural resources management, nursing,
welding, climate control, electronics, paralegal science, fashion merchandising,
environmental quality control technology, drafting, tool and dye technology,
industrial maintenance. **Holdings:** 22,000 books; 618 bound periodical
volumes; 74 journal titles on microfiche; 250 VF drawers; 1934 AV items.
Subscriptions: 225 journals and other serials; 16 newspapers. **Services:**
Interlibrary loans; copying; library open to public for reference use only.
Automated Operations: Computerized cataloging. **Publications:** Workstudy

Handbook; Library Handbook; Policies and Procedures. **Special Catalogs:** Catalog to AV materials. **Staff:** Dianne Brandstadter, Dean, Lrng.Rsrcs.

SUN CHEMICAL CORPORATION - KOLLSMAN INSTRUMENT COMPANY
See: Kollsman Instrument Company

★13064★
SUN CHEMICAL CORPORATION - RESEARCH LIBRARY (Sci-Tech)
631 Central Ave.   Phone: (201) 933-4500
Carlstadt, NJ 07072   Kendal Funk, Libn.
Founded: 1938. **Staff:** Prof 1; Other 1. **Subjects:** Graphic arts, polymer chemistry, photochemistry, organic chemistry. **Holdings:** 2500 books; 3000 bound periodical volumes; 48 shelf feet of unbound official gazettes; 200 boxes of unbound periodicals; 7 VF drawers of reports. **Subscriptions:** 150 journals and other serials; 6 newspapers. **Services:** Library not open to public. **Computerized Information Services:** DIALOG, SDC, Pergamon InfoLine Ltd. **Publications:** Library Bulletin, weekly - for internal distribution only.

SUN COMPANY
See: Sun Tech, Inc.

★13065★
SUN EXPLORATION & PRODUCTION COMPANY - INFORMATION RESOURCES CENTER (Energy)
1201 Exchange
Box 936   Phone: (214) 699-3148
Richardson, TX 75080   Margaret Anderson, Libn.
Founded: 1966. **Staff:** Prof 1; Other 2. **Subjects:** Geology and geophysics, petroleum engineering, chemistry. **Holdings:** 20,000 volumes; 6000 dissertations, guidebooks and government documents; 6500 reports on microfiche. **Subscriptions:** 272 journals and other serials. **Services:** Interlibrary loans; copying; center open to public with restrictions. **Computerized Information Services:** DIALOG, SDC, Petroleum Data System.

★13066★
SUN LIFE ASSURANCE COMPANY OF CANADA - REFERENCE LIBRARY (Bus-Fin)
One Sun Life Executive Park   Phone: (617) 237-6030
Wellesley Hills, MA 02181   Pamela A. Mahaney, Libn.
Founded: 1973. **Staff:** Prof 2. **Subjects:** Insurance, management, data processing, law, labor, taxation. **Holdings:** 12,000 books; 29 VF drawers. **Subscriptions:** 667 journals and other serials; 14 newspapers. **Services:** Interlibrary loans; copying; library open to public with restrictions. **Publications:** Selected Articles of Interest, weekly; Book News, monthly; LIMRA Accessions, bimonthly. **Staff:** Carole Perla, Asst.Libn.

★13067★
SUN LIFE OF CANADA - INVESTMENT LIBRARY (Bus-Fin)
Box 4084, Sta. A   Phone: (416) 595-7894
Toronto, ON, Canada M5W 2K9   Elizabeth Gibson, Libn.
Founded: 1980. **Staff:** Prof 1; Other 2. **Subjects:** Investments, finance, economics, pensions, real estate, insurance. **Holdings:** 2000 books. **Subscriptions:** 620 journals and other serials; 20 newspapers. **Services:** Interlibrary loans; copying; library open to public. **Computerized Information Services:** DIALOG, Info Globe. **Publications:** List of new books, bimonthly - distributed internally and to selected libraries.

★13068★
SUN LIFE OF CANADA - REFERENCE LIBRARY (Bus-Fin)
200 University Ave.   Phone: (416) 595-7890
Toronto, ON, Canada M5H 3C7   Mrs. Trinidad B. Espiritu, Ref.Libn.
Founded: 1979. **Staff:** Prof 1; Other 5. **Subjects:** Life insurance, management, economics, government, health. **Holdings:** 1800 books. **Subscriptions:** 100 journals and other serials; 12 newspapers. **Services:** Interlibrary loans; library open to public for reference use only. **Computerized Information Services:** DIALOG, Info Globe. **Publications:** Acquisitions list, bimonthly.

★13069★
SUN LIFE OF CANADA - REFERENCE LIBRARY (Bus-Fin)
Box 6075, Sta. A   Phone: (514) 866-6411
Montreal, PQ, Canada H3C 3G5   France Payant, Libn.
Staff: Prof 1. **Subjects:** Insurance, actuarial research, finance. **Holdings:** 700 books. **Subscriptions:** 110 journals and other serials; 10 newspapers. **Services:** Interlibrary loans; library open to public with restrictions.

★13070★
SUN TECH, INC. - LIBRARY & INFORMATION SERVICE (Energy)
Box 1135   Phone: (215) 485-1121
Marcus Hook, PA 19061   Norman D. Morphet, Sect.Chf.
Staff: Prof 3; Other 7. **Subjects:** Petroleum, physics, chemistry, mathematics, chemical marketing, engineering, business, management. **Holdings:** 14,000 books; 14,000 bound periodical volumes; 65 VF drawers of pamphlets; 40 VF drawers of patents; 40 VF drawers of pamphlets (uncataloged); API project reports; 14,000 government documents; microfilm; microcards. **Subscriptions:** 800 journals and other serials; 19 newspapers. **Services:** Interlibrary loans; copying; library open to scholars for research by application. **Automated Operations:** Computerized serials. **Computerized Information Services:** Online systems. **Publications:** Book Accession List, monthly; Pamphlet Accession List, weekly - both for internal distribution only. **Special Indexes:** National Petroleum Refiners Association Question and Answer Sessions Index. **Formerly:** Sun Company. **Staff:** Phoebe Cassidy, Res.Libn.; Dale Rodenhaver, Bus.Libn.

★13071★
SUNBURY SHORES ARTS AND NATURE CENTRE, INC. - SUNBURY SHORES LIBRARY (Art; Env-Cons)
139 Water St.
P.O. Box 100   Phone: (506) 529-3386
St. Andrews, NB, Canada E0G 2X0   Mary Blatherwick, Prog.Dir./Art Cons.
Staff: 4. **Subjects:** Art history, crafts, natural science, ecology, photography. **Special Collections:** Kroenberger Memorial Collection (fine art); Vaughn Collection (fine art and natural science). **Holdings:** 800 books; 10 drawers of pictures; 15 sleeves of slides. **Subscriptions:** 10 journals and other serials. **Services:** Interlibrary loans; copying; library open to members and area schools.

★13072★
SUNCOR INC. - LIBRARY (Sci-Tech; Energy)
500 4th Ave., S.W.
P.O. Box 38   Phone: (403) 269-8128
Calgary, AB, Canada T2P 2V5   Pat Strong, Libn.
Founded: 1959. **Staff:** 2. **Subjects:** Petroleum industry, geology, geophysics, engineering, economics, office management, statistics. **Holdings:** 500 books; 700 government publications; 1000 pamphlets, reprints and clippings; 600 annual reports of other companies. **Subscriptions:** 72 journals and other serials. **Services:** Interlibrary loans; copying; library open to public for reference use only. **Publications:** Library Newsletter, monthly - for internal distribution only.

★13073★
SUNDSTRAND AVIATION - ENGINEERING LIBRARY (Sci-Tech)
4747 Harrison Ave.
Box 7002   Phone: (815) 226-6753
Rockford, IL 61125   Mrs. Fran Genrich, Libn.
Staff: Prof 2. **Subjects:** Design, research, manufacturing. **Holdings:** 3500 books; government and corporate reports; specifications and standards. **Subscriptions:** 110 journals and other serials. **Services:** Interlibrary loans; library not open to public. **Automated Operations:** Computerized cataloging. **Computerized Information Services:** DIALOG. **Networks/Consortia:** Member of Northern Illinois Library System. **Staff:** Adrian Freeman, Asst.Libn.

★13074★
SUNDSTRAND DATA CONTROL, INC. - LIBRARY (Sci-Tech)
Overlake Industrial Pk.   Phone: (206) 885-8420
Redmond, WA 98052   Peggy Lucero, Tech.Libn.
Founded: 1957. **Staff:** Prof 1. **Subjects:** Aerospace, electronics, avionics systems, instruments, passenger entertainment systems, industrial components. **Holdings:** 1200 books; military specifications and standards on microfilm; vendor catalogs. **Subscriptions:** 100 journals and other serials. **Services:** Interlibrary loans; library not open to public.

★13075★
SUNKIST GROWERS, INC. - CORPORATE LIBRARY (Bus-Fin; Food-Bev)
14130 Riverside Dr.   Phone: (818) 986-4800
Sherman Oaks, CA 91423   Claire H. Burday, Corp.Libn.
Founded: 1975. **Staff:** Prof 1; Other 2. **Subjects:** Business, management, marketing, citrus industry, agricultural economics, international trade. **Special Collections:** Media Library (3300 films; 100 videotapes; 6500 slides); archives (3000 citrus crate labels, early advertising, historical photographs). **Holdings:** 2000 books; 10,000 government documents; 30 VF drawers; 25,000 microfiche. **Subscriptions:** 350 journals and other serials; 15 newspapers. **Services:** Interlibrary loans; copying; library open to public by appointment only. **Computerized Information Services:** DIALOG, AGNET. **Publications:** Corporate Contents, irregular - for internal distribution only.

Special Catalogs: Media collection catalog (card). **Special Indexes:** Index to citrus crate labels by brand name (card).

★13076★
SUNKIST GROWERS, INC. - RESEARCH LIBRARY (Food-Bev)
760 E. Sunkist St.   Phone: (714) 983-9811
Ontario, CA 91761   Martha C. Nemeth, Tech.Libn.
Founded: 1939. **Staff:** Prof 1; Other 1. **Subjects:** Citrus and citrus products technology; chemistry - organic, analytical and food. **Holdings:** 1100 books; 1230 bound periodical volumes; 2000 reprints. **Subscriptions:** 117 journals and other serials. **Services:** Interlibrary loans; copying; library open to public by request. **Computerized Information Services:** DIALOG.

★13077★
SUNLAND CENTER AT GAINESVILLE - LIBRARY (Med)
Box 1150   Phone: (904) 395-1650
Gainesville, FL 32602   Susan L. Stephan, Libn.
Founded: 1954. **Staff:** Prof 1; Other 1. **Subjects:** High interest-low vocabulary picture books; professional materials; mental retardation; exceptional child education. **Holdings:** 4000 volumes; 2000 AV items. **Subscriptions:** 10 journals and other serials. **Services:** Interlibrary loans; library open to public with restrictions.

★13078★
SUNLAND CENTER AT ORLANDO - MEDICAL LIBRARY
7500 Silver Star Rd.
Orlando, FL 32818
Defunct

★13079★
SUNNYBROOK MEDICAL CENTRE - HEALTH SCIENCES LIBRARY (Med)
2075 Bayview Ave.   Phone: (416) 486-3880
Toronto, ON, Canada M4N 3M5   Linda McFarlane, Health Sci.Libn.
Staff: Prof 2; Other 10. **Subjects:** Medicine and nursing, hospital administration. **Holdings:** 8000 books; 16,000 bound periodical volumes; 2000 audiotapes; 200 videotapes; 15 drawers of pamphlets. **Subscriptions:** 640 journals and other serials. **Services:** Interlibrary loans; copying; SDI; library open to area medical practitioners. **Computerized Information Services:** MEDLINE, DIALOG. **Networks/Consortia:** Member of Toronto Medical Libraries Group.

★13080★
SUNNYVALE PATENT INFORMATION CLEARINGHOUSE (Law)
1500 Partridge Ave., Bldg. 7   Phone: (408) 738-5588
Sunnyvale, CA 94087   H. Maria Patermann, Dir. of Libs.
Founded: 1965. **Staff:** Prof 2; Other 7. **Subjects:** Patents from 1790 to present, federal trademark registrations, copyright reference information. **Holdings:** 1000 books; 2000 bound periodical volumes; 4 million patents; Federal Trademark Register; Official Gazette from 1790 to present. **Subscriptions:** 13 journals and other serials. **Services:** Copying; mail service of patent copies; clearinghouse open to public. **Computerized Information Services:** DIALOG. **Networks/Consortia:** Member of South Bay Cooperative Library System (SBCLS). **Publications:** Information brochures; Bibliography of Collection, annual. **Special Catalogs:** Guides for conducting a patent search and trademark search. **Remarks:** Maintained by the City of Sunnyvale, this library is a self-search center which is said to have the only subject-classified patent collection in the United States outside of Washington, DC. **Staff:** Mary-Jo Di Muccio, Adm.Libn.

SUNNYVALE PUBLIC LIBRARY - FRIENDS OF THE WESTERN PHILATELIC LIBRARY
See: Friends of the Western Philatelic Library

★13081★
SUNRAE LEARNING RESOURCES CENTER (Energy; Env-Cons)*
5679 Hollister Ave.   Phone: (805) 964-4483
Goleta, CA 93017   Kate Christensen, Libn.
Staff: Prof 1; Other 1. **Subjects:** Energy conservation and alternative energy sources; energy legislation in California. **Special Collections:** Department of Energy Abstracts, 1978-1979; Diablo Canyon research materials. **Holdings:** 700 books; 100 unbound periodicals; files and papers. **Subscriptions:** 20 journals and other serials. **Services:** Interlibrary loans; center open to public. **Publications:** Sunrae Newsletter, quarterly. **Remarks:** SUNRAE is an acronym for Solar Use Now for Resources and Employment.

★13082★
SUNRISE MUSEUMS, INC. - LIBRARY (Art; Sci-Tech)
746 Myrtle Rd.   Phone: (304) 344-8035
Charleston, WV 25314
Founded: 1961. **Staff:** 1. **Subjects:** Fine arts, natural sciences, anthropology. **Holdings:** 3000 volumes. **Subscriptions:** 40 journals and other serials. **Services:** Library open to public for reference use only.

SUNRISE HOSPITAL MEDICAL CENTER
See: Humana Hospital Sunrise

★13083★
SUNSET TRADING POST-OLD WEST MUSEUM - LIBRARY (Hist)
Rte. 1   Phone: (817) 872-2027
Sunset, TX 76270   Jack Glover, Owner
Subjects: Barbed wire, frontier, American Indian, cowboys and cattlemen, Civil War, Western painting, county history, guns and knives. **Special Collections:** Barbed Wire. **Holdings:** 2500 books; 200 pamphlets; clippings, drawings, Indian artifacts, Bronzes of the West by Jack Glover, unpublished stories, pictures, negatives. **Subscriptions:** 25 journals and other serials. **Services:** Library open to public with restrictions. **Publications:** International Barbed Wire Gazette, monthly; Barbed Wire Bible VI, 1980 - for sale.

★13084★
SUNY - AGRICULTURAL AND TECHNICAL COLLEGE AT ALFRED - WALTER C. HINKLE MEMORIAL LIBRARY (Agri; Sci-Tech)
                                            Phone: (607) 871-6313
Alfred, NY 14802   Barry Lash, Hd.Libn.
Founded: 1911. **Staff:** Prof 6; Other 6. **Subjects:** Agriculture, business, health and engineering technologies. **Special Collections:** Western New York History. **Holdings:** 52,864 books; 5988 bound periodical volumes; 58,000 pamphlets; 4730 reels of microfilm; 6922 microfiche. **Subscriptions:** 1469 journals and other serials; 12 newspapers. **Services:** Interlibrary loans; copying; library open to public. **Automated Operations:** Computerized cataloging and serials. **Computerized Information Services:** OCLC. **Networks/Consortia:** Member of South Central Research Library Council (SCRLC). **Publications:** Alfred Tech Periodicals - for local distribution only. **Staff:** Diana Hovorka, Asst.Ref.Libn.; Suzanne Wood, Tech.Serv.Libn.; Ellen Ehrig, Chf.Ref./ILL Libn.; Barbara Greil, Ser./Ref.Libn.; David Haggstrom, AV Libn.; Margaret Sands, Circ.Libn.

★13085★
SUNY - AGRICULTURAL AND TECHNICAL COLLEGE AT COBLESKILL - JARED VAN WAGENEN, JR. LEARNING RESOURCE CENTER (Agri)†
                                            Phone: (518) 234-5841
Cobleskill, NY 12043   Eleanor M. Carter, Dir.
Founded: 1920. **Staff:** Prof 11; Other 26. **Subjects:** Agriculture, business, education of young children, food service, applied biology, reference. **Special Collections:** Career and adult basic skills collection (604 items); Schoharie County history. **Holdings:** 64,347 books; 4600 bound periodical volumes; 4481 juvenile books; 64 VF drawers of pamphlets and documents; 4727 reels of microfilm; 20,192 AV items. **Subscriptions:** 726 journals and other serials; 16 newspapers. **Services:** Interlibrary loans; copying; media production; instructional design; center open to public. **Automated Operations:** Computerized cataloging and circulation. **Networks/Consortia:** Member of Capital District Library Council for Reference & Research Resources (CDLC); SUNY/OCLC Library Network. **Special Indexes:** Index to Times Journal (local newspaper) - book form; various slide-tape programs on library use. **Staff:** Norva Munford, Ser.Libn.; Mary Clist, Hd., Access Serv.; Anna Walsh, Supv.Ck. Staff; Linda Myers, Hd., Tech.Serv.; Elizabeth Tillapaugh, Circ. & Bibliog.Instr.; Gerald B. Kirsch, ILL Libn.

★13086★
SUNY - AGRICULTURAL AND TECHNICAL COLLEGE AT DELHI - LIBRARY (Agri; Sci-Tech)†
                                            Phone: (607) 746-4107
Delhi, NY 13753   Herbert J. Sorgen, Libn.
Founded: 1913. **Staff:** Prof 4; Other 4. **Subjects:** Agriculture and life sciences, engineering technologies, management, vocational education, nontraditional studies, liberal arts. **Holdings:** 47,000 books; 700 bound periodical volumes. **Subscriptions:** 550 journals and other serials. **Services:** Interlibrary loans; library open to public. **Automated Operations:** Computerized cataloging. **Networks/Consortia:** Member of SUNY/OCLC Library Network.

★13087★
SUNY - AGRICULTURAL AND TECHNICAL COLLEGE AT FARMINGDALE - THOMAS D. GREENLEY LIBRARY (Agri; Sci-Tech)
Melville Rd.   Phone: (516) 420-2040
Farmingdale, NY 11735   Michael G. Knauth, Chf.Libn.
Founded: 1912. **Staff:** Prof 12; Other 15. **Subjects:** Technology, business, agriculture, horticulture, dental hygiene, nursing, political science, liberal arts. **Holdings:** 114,343 books and bound periodical volumes; 22,000 pamphlets; 88,296 government documents; 10,554 reels of microfilm; 22,156 media units; 13,798 microfiche. **Subscriptions:** 1402 journals and other serials. **Services:** Interlibrary loans; copying for Long Island Resource Council; library open to public for reference use only. **Automated Operations:** Computerized cataloging. **Computerized Information Services:** OCLC. **Networks/Consortia:** Member of Long Island Library Resources Council; Long Island Media Consortium. **Publications:** Newsletter, irregular; bibliographic guides. **Staff:** Judi Bird, Hd., Acq.; Charlotte Schart, Hd., Ser.; Parker Van Hoogenstyn, Hd., Media/Spec. Project; Carol Greenholz, Hd., Tech.Serv./ Cat.; Sue Schapiro, Govt.Docs.; George LoPresti, Hd., Circ. & Reserve; Sylvia S. Ewen, Hd., Ref.

★13088★
SUNY - AGRICULTURAL AND TECHNICAL COLLEGE AT MORRISVILLE - LIBRARY (Agri; Sci-Tech)
                                      Phone: (315) 684-7055
Morrisville, NY 13408   Michael Gieryic, Hd.Libn.
Founded: 1910. **Staff:** Prof 5; Other 5. **Subjects:** Food processing, food service, agriculture, wood and automotive technology, natural resources conservation, nursing, horse husbandry, journalism. **Special Collections:** New York State Historical Collection. **Holdings:** 77,200 books; 4930 bound periodical volumes; 8922 reels of microfilm; 1800 recordings; 367 cassette tapes. **Subscriptions:** 510 journals and other serials; 27 newspapers. **Services:** Interlibrary loans; copying; library open to public. **Automated Operations:** Computerized cataloging. **Computerized Information Services:** OCLC. **Networks/Consortia:** Member of Central New York Library Resources Council (CENTRO). **Publications:** Periodicals Received Currently; Library Guide; Books, Bits and Basics (library newsletter). **Staff:** Colleen Stella, Ref./ILL Libn.; H. Red Fagan, Acq.Libn.; Phyllis Petersen, Hd. of Tech.Serv.

★13089★
SUNY AT ALBANY - GRADUATE LIBRARY FOR PUBLIC AFFAIRS AND POLICY (Soc Sci; Law)
Hawley Library
1400 Washington Ave.   Phone: (518) 455-6178
Albany, NY 12222   Ruth A. Fraley, Hd.Libn.
Founded: 1981. **Staff:** Prof 5; Other 10. **Subjects:** Public policy, criminal justice, social welfare, library and information science, law. **Special Collections:** Children's historical collection (9000 volumes); public policy archives. **Holdings:** 70,000 books; microfiche. **Services:** Interlibrary loans; library open to public. **Automated Operations:** Computerized cataloging and circulation. **Computerized Information Services:** BRS, Westlaw, OCLC. **Networks/Consortia:** Member of Capital District Library Council for Reference and Research Resources; Criminal Justice Information Exchange. **Staff:** Barbara Via, Ref.; Richard Irving, Bibliog.; H. Mendelsohn, Bibliog.; Mary Jane Brustman, Ref.

★13090★
SUNY AT BINGHAMTON - CENTER FOR MEDIEVAL AND EARLY RENAISSANCE STUDIES (Hum)
Binghamton, NY 13901   Paul E. Szarmach, Dir.
Founded: 1966. **Subjects:** Latin and Arabic paleography and codicology. **Remarks:** Supporting materials housed in Main Library include Vaticana Arabic manuscripts (1678 manuscripts on 425 reels of microfilm); Rare Books Collection; Manuscripta series (microfilm); Italian Archives, 13th-19th century (1000 pieces in Latin and Italian).

★13091★
SUNY AT BINGHAMTON - FINE ARTS LIBRARY (Art; Mus)
Vestal Pkwy. E.   Phone: (607) 798-4927
Binghamton, NY 13901   Marion Hanscom, Spec.Coll./Fine Arts Libn
Staff: Prof 4. **Subjects:** Art, music, theater history, cinema, costume, dance. **Holdings:** 56,000 books; 9500 bound periodical volumes; art exhibition catalogs; 14,200 recordings. **Subscriptions:** 416 journals and other serials. **Services:** Interlibrary loans; copying; library open to public; circulation with courtesy card. **Automated Operations:** Computerized cataloging, serials and circulation. **Networks/Consortia:** Member of South Central Research Library Council (SCRLC); CRL; RLG. **Staff:** George McKee, Bibliog./Ref.Libn.; Philip Conole, Music Record Cur.

★13092★
SUNY AT BINGHAMTON - SCIENCE LIBRARY (Sci-Tech)
Vestal Pkwy. E.   Phone: (607) 798-2528
Binghamton, NY 13901
Staff: Prof 4; Other 6. **Subjects:** Biological sciences, chemistry, geological sciences, health sciences, physics, psychology, nursing, general science, technology. **Special Collections:** Maps. **Holdings:** 110,000 books; 65,486 bound periodical volumes; 1500 technical reports; microforms. **Subscriptions:** 1835 journals; 1171 serials. **Services:** Interlibrary loans; copying; library open to public with courtesy card. **Computerized Information Services:** BRS, DIALOG, SDC. **Networks/Consortia:** Member of South Central Research Library Council (SCRLC); CRL; RLG. **Staff:** Erna Chamberlain, Sci.Ref.Libn.; Robin Eldridge, Sci.Ref.Libn.; Ronnie Goldberg, Search Spec.

★13093★
SUNY AT BINGHAMTON - SPECIAL COLLECTIONS (Rare Book; Hist)
Glenn G. Bartle Library
Vestal Pkwy. E.   Phone: (607) 798-4844
Binghamton, NY 13901   Marion Hanscom, Spec.Coll.Libn.
Staff: Prof 2. **Subjects:** History of books and printing; literary and historical collections. **Special Collections:** Padraic and Mary Colum papers (750 items); Max Reinhardt Library (theater); Max Reinhardt Archive (250,000 papers, letters, documents and original prompt books); photograph and negative collection (14,000 items); scene design materials; Tillie Losch Papers; Charles Monroe Dickinson Family Papers (2000 items relating to journalist and diplomat C.M. Dickinson, 1842-1924); Edwin Link (1904-1981) papers; Broome County Medical Society Collection; Arthur Schnitzler Archives on microfilm; Frances R. Conole Archive of Sound Recordings (45,000 phonograph records with a concentration of vocal/operatic recordings). **Holdings:** 20,000 volumes; 10,000 local and regional archives; 5000 publications, photographs and reports in University archives; 250 Mary Lavin papers; 5000 archival items of the Associated Colleges of Upper New York; 350 linear feet of archives and manuscripts. **Services:** Interlibrary loans; copying; collections open to public by appointment. **Publications:** Edwin Link Papers (pamphlet); Catalogue of the Colum Collection (pamphlet); Catalogue of the Lavin Collection (pamphlet); Lamony Montgomery Bowers Papers (pamphlet). **Special Catalogs:** Catalog of Reinhardt Library (card); manuscript catalog (card); supplementary rare book catalogs (card). **Staff:** Philip Conole, Cur., Conole Archv.

★13094★
SUNY AT BUFFALO - ARCHITECTURE & ENVIRONMENTAL DESIGN LIBRARY (Sci-Tech)
Hayes Hall
Main Street Campus   Phone: (716) 831-3505
Buffalo, NY 14214   Norma Segal, Hd.
Staff: Prof 2; Other 1. **Subjects:** Architecture, environmental design. **Special Collections:** Slide collection (15,000). **Holdings:** 11,232 volumes; product catalogs; VF drawers of pamphlets. **Subscriptions:** 160 journals and other serials. **Services:** Interlibrary loans; copying library open to public with restrictions. **Automated Operations:** Computerized cataloging and circulation. **Computerized Information Services:** DIALOG, BRS. Performs searches on cost recovery basis. **Networks/Consortia:** Member of SUNY/OCLC Library Network. **Publications:** AED Library Acquisitions List, monthly - to faculty and upon request.

★13095★
SUNY AT BUFFALO - CENTER FOR CURRICULUM PLANNING (Educ)
Faculty of Educational Studies
17 Baldy Hall   Phone: (716) 636-2488
Amherst, NY 14260   Dr. William Eller, Dir.
Founded: 1954. **Staff:** Prof 1; Other 3. **Subjects:** Education, textbooks and teacher guides (K-12), courses of study, curriculum guides. **Special Collections:** Gray Collection on Research in Reading. **Holdings:** 10,000 volumes; 10 VF drawers of publishers' catalogs; 3 VF drawers of Teaching Ideas files; 10 VF drawers of resource files; 5000 retrospective and historical textbooks; 350 tests; 200 supplementary instructional materials. **Subscriptions:** 40 journals and other serials. **Services:** Center open to public. **Publications:** In the Center, 3/year - free upon request. **Staff:** Norma Shatz, Lib.Coord.

★13096★
SUNY AT BUFFALO - CENTER FOR INTEGRATIVE STUDIES - LIBRARY (Soc Sci)
108 Hayes Hall
3435 Main St.   Phone: (716) 831-3727
Buffalo, NY 14214   Magda Cordell McHale, Dir.
Staff: Prof 2; Other 1. **Subjects:** Study of changes, futures and teaching. **Special Collections:** Futures research materials. **Holdings:** 2000 books; 300

periodicals; 1000 articles. **Subscriptions:** 89 journals and other serials. **Services:** Library open to public for reference use only. **Publications:** List of publications - available on request.

★13097★
SUNY AT BUFFALO - CHARLES B. SEARS LAW LIBRARY (Law)
O'Brian Hall, Amherst Campus　　　Phone: (716) 636-2048
Buffalo, NY 14260　　　　Professor Wade J. Newhouse, Dir.
Founded: 1887. **Staff:** Prof 9; Other 9. **Subjects:** Law. **Special Collections:** John Lord O'Brian Papers. **Holdings:** 283,995 volumes. **Subscriptions:** 2516 journals and other serials. **Services:** Interlibrary loans; copying; library open to public for reference use only. **Staff:** Marcia Zubrow, Hd.Ref.Libn.; Wayne Cardillo, Tech.Serv.Libn.; Mary Miller, Ser./Acq.Libn.; Nina Cascio, AV Libn.; Ellen M. Gibson, Assoc.Dir.; Sheila Fehlman, Ser.Cat.

★13098★
SUNY AT BUFFALO - HEALTH SCIENCES LIBRARY (Med)
Main St. Campus　　　　　Phone: (716) 831-3337
Buffalo, NY 14214　　　　　Mr. C.K. Huang, Dir.
Founded: 1846. **Staff:** Prof 17; Other 28. **Subjects:** Medicine, nursing, dentistry, pharmacy, allied health sciences, basic sciences. **Special Collections:** History of Medicine Collection (12,000 volumes). **Holdings:** 101,675 books; 120,433 bound periodical volumes; 1286 AV titles; 3000 pamphlets. **Subscriptions:** 3199 journals and other serials. **Services:** Interlibrary loans; copying; library open to public. **Automated Operations:** Computerized cataloging and circulation. **Computerized Information Services:** MEDLINE, BRS. **Networks/Consortia:** Member of Western New York Library Resources Council (WNYLRC); Greater Northeastern Regional Medical Library Program. **Publications:** Progress Report, annual - for exchange. **Staff:** Nancy Fabrizio, Assoc.Dir.; Remedios Silva, Hd.Cat.; Martha Manning, Hd., Info.Serv.; Amy Lyons, Hd., Circ.; Luella Allen, Hd., Media Rsrcs.Ctr.; Ruth Wheeler, Hd., Dissemination Serv.; Wilson Prout, Asst. to Dir.; Jane Day, Hd., Ser.; Steven Kovnat, Asst.Libn., Media Rsrcs.; Bradley Chase, Tech.Asst.; Lilli Sentz, Hist. of Med.Libn.; Richard Kaplan, Info.Serv.Libn.; Linda Lohr, Adm.Asst.; Karen Miller, Info.Serv./Libn.; Jean Silvester, Asst.Libn., Cat.

★13099★
SUNY AT BUFFALO - MUSIC LIBRARY (Mus)
Baird Hall　　　　　　Phone: (716) 636-2923
Buffalo, NY 14260　　　　　James Coover, Dir.
Staff: Prof 5; Other 3. **Subjects:** Music - history, theory, performance; jazz history; music education. **Special Collections:** Archives of the Center of the Creative and Performing Arts (10 linear meters); History of Music Librarianship in the U.S. (9 linear meters); Arnold Cornelissen Manuscript Collection (3 linear meters); Buffalo Musicians Collection (8 linear meters). **Holdings:** 19,500 books; 9500 bound periodical volumes; 46,500 scores and parts; 22,200 phonograph records and cassettes; 4800 microforms; 2100 slides and photographs. **Subscriptions:** 1000 journals and other serials. **Services:** Interlibrary loans; copying; library open to public. **Automated Operations:** Computerized cataloging and acquisitions (for phonograph records only). **Computerized Information Services:** RLIN. **Publications:** Current Acquisitions List, irregular; Newsletter, irregular; Evenings for New Music: A Catalogue, 1964-1977; Supplement, 1977-1980. **Staff:** Dr. Carol June Bradley, Assoc.Dir.; Diane Parr Walker, Music Cat./Ref.Libn.; Nancy Bren, Record Cat./Ref.Libn.; Gudrun Kilburn, Lit.Cat./Ref.Libn.

★13100★
SUNY AT BUFFALO - POETRY/RARE BOOKS COLLECTION (Hum; Rare Book)
University Libraries, 420 Capen Hall　　Phone: (716) 636-2918
Buffalo, NY 14260　　　　Robert J. Bertholf, Cur.
Founded: 1935. **Staff:** Prof 1; Other 2. **Subjects:** Twentieth-century poetry in English and in translation; rare books. **Special Collections:** Robert Graves; James Joyce; Wyndham Lewis; Dylan Thomas; William Carlos Williams. **Holdings:** 69,289 books and ephemera; 2825 periodical titles; 822 records; 450 tapes; photographs, paintings and sculpture; 35,421 manuscripts; 28,570 letters; microfilm. **Services:** Interlibrary loans; copying; collection open to public. **Automated Operations:** Computerized serials. **Networks/Consortia:** Member of SUNY/OCLC Library Network. **Publications:** Lockwood Memorial Library Christmas Broadsides, annual; Credences, 3/year - by subscription. **Special Catalogs:** James Joyce's Manuscripts and Letters at the University of Buffalo, 1962; The Personal Library of James Joyce; The Manuscripts and Letters of William Carlos Williams in the Poetry Collection, SUNYAB; A Descriptive Catalog of the Private Library of Thomas B. Lockwood.

★13101★
SUNY AT BUFFALO - SCIENCE AND ENGINEERING LIBRARY (Sci-Tech)
　　　　　　　　　Phone: (716) 636-2946
Buffalo, NY 14260　　　　Diane C. Parker, Dir.
Founded: 1949. **Staff:** Prof 7; Other 5. **Subjects:** Engineering, chemistry, environmental technology, physics, mathematics, geology. **Special Collections:** Rare books in chemistry and metallurgy. **Holdings:** 150,662 books; 89,886 bound periodical volumes; 2130 theses and dissertations; 90,035 technical reports; 160,000 maps; 855,137 microforms; 134 videotapes and audiotapes; 222 cassette tapes. **Subscriptions:** 2436 journals and other serials. **Services:** Interlibrary loans; copying; library open to public with restrictions. **Automated Operations:** Computerized cataloging and circulation. **Computerized Information Services:** DIALOG, BRS. Performs searches on cost recovery basis. **Networks/Consortia:** Member of Western New York Library Resources Council (WNYLRC); SUNY/OCLC Library Network. **Publications:** Subject bibliographies, occasional; New Books, monthly; Current Awareness Lists, occasional; audiovisual material list, occasional. **Staff:** Margaret Schenk, Hd., Coll.Dev.; P.J. Koshy, AV Libn.; J. Webster, Hd., Ref.

★13102★
SUNY AT BUFFALO - UNIVERSITY ARCHIVES (Hist)
420 Capen Hall　　　　Phone: (716) 636-2916
Buffalo, NY 14260　　　Shonnie Finnegan, Univ.Archv.
Subjects: Archives of the State University of New York at Buffalo and its predecessor, University of Buffalo, 1846 to present. **Special Collections:** Documents pertaining to the Darwin D. Martin House and other Buffalo buildings designed by Frank Lloyd Wright; records of local organizations. **Holdings:** 5480 linear feet of manuscripts, papers, and other archival materials. **Services:** Copying; archives open to public.

★13103★
SUNY - CENTRAL ADMINISTRATION RESEARCH LIBRARY (Educ)
State University Plaza, Rm. S540　　Phone: (518) 473-1070
Albany, NY 12246　　　　M. Joan Tauber, Libn.
Founded: 1967. **Staff:** Prof 1; Other 1. **Subjects:** Education (higher and professional), management, international education, finance, statistics. **Special Collections:** SUNY archival collection (300 items). **Holdings:** 19,000 books; 150 bound periodical volumes; 1000 VF items; 2000 government documents; 1000 microforms; 200 dissertations; 3000 ERIC research reports. **Subscriptions:** 250 journals and other serials. **Services:** Interlibrary loans; copying; SDI; library open to public with restrictions. **Computerized Information Services:** Online systems. **Publications:** Tables of Contents of Significant Journals, bimonthly; Acquisitions List, bimonthly; annotated lists of selected books, occasionally; listing of new microforms, occasionally.

★13104★
SUNY - COLLEGE AT BROCKPORT - DRAKE MEMORIAL LIBRARY (Educ)
　　　　　　　　　Phone: (716) 395-2141
Brockport, NY 14420　　　Dr. George W. Cornell, Dir. of Lib.Serv.
Founded: 1860. **Staff:** Prof 17; Other 23. **Subjects:** Nursing, physical and general education, U.S. history, criminal justice. **Special Collections:** Early American Imprints, 1639-1800 (Readex); Early English Books, 1475-1700 (Readex). **Holdings:** 335,121 books; 69,496 bound periodical volumes; 17,949 reels of microfilm; 229,962 microfiche; 850,669 micro-opaque cards. **Subscriptions:** 3500 journals and other serials; 50 newspapers. **Services:** Interlibrary loans; copying; library open to public. **Automated Operations:** Computerized cataloging, acquisitions and circulation. **Computerized Information Services:** OCLC. **Networks/Consortia:** Member of Rochester Regional Research Library Council (RRRLC); CRL. **Publications:** Faculty bibliography, annual; Drake Library Review, quarterly; subject bibliographies. **Special Indexes:** Indexes to New York State Museum Bulletins (numerical, author, subject); Index to U.S. Government Serials, 1953-1970. **Staff:** Steven F. Buckley, Hd. of Tech.Serv.

★13105★
SUNY - COLLEGE AT BUFFALO - BURCHFIELD CENTER-WESTERN NEW YORK FORUM FOR AMERICAN ART (Art)
1300 Elmwood Ave.　　　Phone: (716) 878-6011
Buffalo, NY 14222　　　Nancy M. Weekly, Libn./Archv.
Staff: Prof 1; Other 1. **Subjects:** American art, art education. **Special Collections:** Charles E. Burchfield Collection (1000 books and articles; 2500 slides; 10 VF drawers of journals); George William Eggers Archive (10 boxes of drawings and notes). **Holdings:** 1000 books; 10 VF drawers of clippings; 10 VF drawers of letters, manuscripts, original materials. **Services:** Library open to public by appointment.

★13106★
SUNY - COLLEGE AT BUFFALO - EDWARD H. BUTLER LIBRARY (Educ)
1300 Elmwood Ave.   Phone: (716) 878-6302
Buffalo, NY 14222   Dr. George C. Newman, Dir.
Founded: 1871. **Staff:** Prof 24; Other 33. **Subjects:** Education, sciences and humanities, fine and applied arts. **Special Collections:** Curriculum Laboratory Collection (22,924 volumes); Hertha Ganey Historical Children's Book Collection (310 volumes); Root-Kempke Historical Textbook Collection (676 volumes); Lois Lenski Collection (241 first edition autographed titles; 310 original illustrations, notes, research and dummies); Creative Studies Library (2500 volumes; 1700 microfilm dissertations); Independent Learning Center (8464 AV and nonprint items, educational games); Francis E. Fronczak Collection (18 linear feet); college archives (1384 linear feet); Paul G. Reilly Seneca Indian Hand Claims Collection (27 linear feet). **Holdings:** 396,008 books; 81,047 bound periodical volumes; 19,120 reels of microfilm; 452,466 microtext pieces; 465 maps. **Subscriptions:** 5753 journals and other serials; 42 newspapers. **Services:** Interlibrary loans; copying; library open to public for reference use only. **Automated Operations:** Computerized cataloging. **Computerized Information Services:** DIALOG, BRS. Contact Person: Maryruth Glogowski. **Networks/Consortia:** Member of Western New York Library Resources Council; SUNY/OCLC Library Network. **Publications:** Lois Lenski Children's Collection (booklet); Frances E. Fronczak Collection Inventory (booklet). **Staff:** Susan Besemer, Assoc.Dir.; Mary Karen Delmont, Asst. to Dir.; Paul Zadner, Hd., Circ./Per.; Carol Richards, Hd., Ref.; Shirley Posner, Hd., Acq.; Mary C. Hall, Hd., Cat.; Sr. Martin Joseph Jones, Hd.Archv./Spec.Coll.; Jerome Earley, Lrng.Sys.; Dr. Lucien E. Palmieri, Hd., Coll.Dev.; Marilyn Kihl, Curric.Lab.; Marjorie Lord, ILL; Al Riess, Microforms; Maryruth Glogowski, Coord., Search Serv.

★13107★
SUNY - COLLEGE AT BUFFALO - GREAT LAKES LABORATORY - LIMNOLOGY LIBRARY
1300 Elmwood Ave.
Buffalo, NY 14222
Subjects: Limnology, Great Lakes, water quality, benthos, plankton, waste treatment. **Holdings:** 35,000 government and university reports; 9300 reprints; 120 maps; unbound periodicals; 1 file drawer of microfiche. **Remarks:** Presently inactive.

★13108★
SUNY - COLLEGE AT CORTLAND - MEMORIAL LIBRARY (Educ)
Prospect Terrace
Box 2000   Phone: (607) 753-2221
Cortland, NY 13045   Selby U. Gration, Dir. of Libs.
Founded: 1869. **Staff:** Prof 14; Other 15. **Subjects:** Education, recreation, physical education, health education. **Special Collections:** Teaching Materials (21,314 books; 21,020 teaching materials); Cortland College Archives (8100 items); Knowlton Collection of Social Studies Textbooks (875 items); rare book collection (800). **Holdings:** 246,094 books; 41,547 bound periodical volumes; 388,701 microforms; 13,412 AV items; 271 VF drawers; 14,470 pictures; 10 files of pamphlets; 18,431 government documents. **Subscriptions:** 1568 journals and other serials; 8 newspapers. **Services:** Interlibrary loans; copying; SDI; library open to public with restrictions. **Automated Operations:** Computerized cataloging and ILL. **Computerized Information Services:** DIALOG, OCLC. Performs searches on cost recovery basis. Contact Person: Leonard Cohen, 753-2525. **Networks/Consortia:** Member of SUNY/OCLC Library Network; South Central Research Library Council (SCRLC). **Publications:** Facets; Setting the Book Straight on the Library; occasional publications - campus distribution to users. **Special Indexes:** Subject bibliographies; serials and periodicals list; lists of abstracts/indexes by subject. **Staff:** Mary Beilby, Coll.Dev.Libn.; Thomas Bonn, Media Libn.; Leonard Cohen, Hd., Rd.Serv.; Catherine Hanchett, Doc.Cat.Libn.; Gretchen Herrmann, Soc.Sci.Ref.-Bibliog.; David Kreh, Dir.Tchg.Mtls.Ctr.; Ellen Paterson, Sci.Ref.-Bibliog.; Johanna Bowen, Ser./Per.Libn.; Martha Atkins, Pub.Serv.Libn.; David Ritchie, Cat.Libn.; Rae Shepherd-Schlechter, Cat.Libn.; Lauren Stiles, Hum.Ref.-Bibliog.; Jacob Schuhle, Educ.Ref.-Bibliog.

★13109★
SUNY - COLLEGE OF ENVIRONMENTAL SCIENCE AND FORESTRY - F. FRANKLIN MOON LIBRARY (Env-Cons; Sci-Tech)
Phone: (315) 470-6716
Syracuse, NY 13210   Donald F. Webster, Libn.
Founded: 1911. **Staff:** Prof 8; Other 6. **Subjects:** Forests and forestry, environment, botany, zoology, polymer and cellulose chemistry, paper science, wildlife management, entomology, wood products engineering, soil science. **Holdings:** 52,846 books; 29,819 bound periodical volumes; 3765 bound theses; 59,994 microforms. **Subscriptions:** 2613 journals and other serials. **Services:** Interlibrary loans; copying; library open to public for reference use only. **Automated Operations:** Computerized cataloging. **Computerized**

Information Services: OCLC; SULIRS (internal database). **Publications:** New Accessions List; user guides. **Staff:** Elizabeth A. Elkins, Coord., Pub.Serv.Salvacion S. de la Paz, Coord., Bibliog.Oper.; Dianne Capritta, Coord., Coll.Dev.

★13110★
SUNY - COLLEGE OF ENVIRONMENTAL SCIENCE & FORESTRY - HUNTINGTON WILDLIFE FOREST LIBRARY (Env-Cons)
Phone: (518) 582-4551
Newcomb, NY 12852   Donald Webster, Dir. of Libs.
Staff: 1. **Subjects:** Wildlife, wildlife management, wildlife research, forestry, forest and wildlife, ecology. **Special Collections:** Collection of birds, mammals, insects, and plants indigenous to the area; local history, notes, photographs, and maps. **Holdings:** 370 books; 290 bound periodical volumes; 200 other cataloged items. **Subscriptions:** 18 journals and other serials. **Services:** Copying; library open to public with restrictions. **Staff:** Ray Masters, Res.Techn.

★13111★
SUNY - COLLEGE AT FREDONIA - MUSIC LIBRARY (Mus)
Phone: (716) 673-3183
Fredonia, NY 14063   Joseph Chouinard, Music Libn.
Founded: 1940. **Staff:** Prof 1; Other 1. **Subjects:** Music - education, performance and study, history, biography, criticism; monumenta. **Holdings:** 29,250 music scores; 13,500 music recordings; 2024 music titles in microformat; 10,600 music books; 800 cassettes. **Subscriptions:** 100 journals and other serials. **Services:** Interlibrary loans; copying; library open to public. **Automated Operations:** Computerized cataloging. **Computerized Information Services:** OCLC. **Networks/Consortia:** Member of Western New York Library Resources Council.

★13112★
SUNY - COLLEGE AT GENESEO - COLLEGE LIBRARIES (Educ)
Fraser Library   Phone: (716) 245-5591
Geneseo, NY 14454   Richard C. Quick, Dir. of Coll.Libs.
Founded: 1871. **Staff:** Prof 15; Other 16. **Subjects:** English and American literature, natural and physical sciences, music, computer science, education and special education, business management and accounting. **Special Collections:** Aldous Huxley (600 items); Genesee Valley Historical Collection (7500 items); Carl F. Schmidt Collection in American Architecture (5000 items); Wadsworth Family Papers, 1790-1952 (50,000 items); College Archives. **Holdings:** 375,000 books; 51,381 bound periodical volumes; 393,579 microforms, including 234,000 ERIC microfiche; 195,350 U.S. government documents. **Subscriptions:** 2410 journals and other serials; 19 newspapers. **Services:** Interlibrary loans; copying; library open to public with restrictions. **Automated Operations:** Computerized cataloging, acquisitions and serials. **Computerized Information Services:** BRS. **Networks/Consortia:** Member of Rochester Regional Research Library Council (RRRLC); SUNY/OCLC Library Network. **Publications:** Serials Holdings List (computer print-out). **Remarks:** Figures reflect the holdings of Milne Library and Fraser Library. **Staff:** William T. Lane, Hd., Info.Serv.; Janet A. Neese, Hd., Coll.Dev.; Paula M. Henry, Acq.Libn.; Adelaide L. LaVerdi, Hd.Cat.; Barbara Clarke, Libn., CRC; David W. Parish, Govt.Doc.Libn.; Diane Johnson, Ser.Libn.; Mary McGrath, Circ.Mgr.; Catherine Hughes, ILL Libn.; Paul MacLean, Mng.Libn., Fraser Lib.

★13113★
SUNY - COLLEGE AT ONEONTA - JAMES M. MILNE LIBRARY - SPECIAL COLLECTIONS (Hist)
Phone: (607) 431-2723
Oneonta, NY 13820   Martha Chambers, Spec.Coll.Libn.
Founded: 1889. **Staff:** Prof 1. **Special Collections:** New York State Historical Collection; 19th and Early 20th Century Popular Fiction; New York State Verse Collection; Early Textbooks and Early Educational Theory. **Holdings:** 6260 volumes; 300 masters' theses; 434 linear feet of archival material; 30 tapes. **Services:** Interlibrary loans; collections open to public with restrictions. **Automated Operations:** Computerized cataloging and serials. **Computerized Information Services:** OCLC. **Networks/Consortia:** Member of South Central Research Library Council.

★13114★
SUNY - COLLEGE OF OPTOMETRY - HAROLD KOHN MEMORIAL VISUAL SCIENCE LIBRARY (Med; Sci-Tech)
100 E. 24th St.   Phone: (212) 477-7965
New York, NY 10010-3677   Margaret Lewis, Libn.
Founded: 1956. **Staff:** Prof 2; Other 2. **Subjects:** Physiological optics, perception, developmental psychology, theory of optometry, public health, learning disabilities, ocular pathology, orthoptics. **Holdings:** 24,000 books; 4000 bound periodical volumes; 1200 tapes; 90 phonorecords; 22,000

slides; 400 reels of microfilm; 5000 pamphlets; 1200 indexed reprints on optics. **Subscriptions:** 500 journals and other serials. **Services:** Interlibrary loans; copying; library open to public for reference use only. **Automated Operations:** Computerized cataloging. **Computerized Information Services:** MEDLARS, OCLC. **Networks/Consortia:** Member of METRO. **Special Indexes:** Visual science articles, 1900-1947 (card). **Staff:** Rebecca Benet, Asst.Libn.

★13115★
SUNY - COLLEGE AT OSWEGO - PENFIELD LIBRARY - SPECIAL COLLECTIONS (Hist)

Phone: (315) 341-3122
Oswego, NY 13126
Founded: 1861. **Special Collections:** College archives; Oswego County history; rare books; President Millard Fillmore papers. **Holdings:** 6398 books; 560 linear feet of other cataloged items; 602 reels of microfilm; 15 microfiche; 511 audio cassettes; 4535 vertical files. **Services:** Interlibrary loans; copying; library open to public. **Computerized Information Services:** OCLC. **Networks/Consortia:** Member of North Country Reference and Research Resources Council. **Staff:** Nancy Osborne, Co-Coord.; Judith Wellman, Co-Coord.; Lois Stolp, Libn./Cat.

★13116★
SUNY - COLLEGE AT PLATTSBURGH - BENJAMIN F. FEINBERG LIBRARY - SPECIAL COLLECTIONS (Hist)

Phone: (518) 564-3180
Plattsburgh, NY 12901   Joseph G. Swinyer, Dir.
Founded: 1961. **Staff:** Prof 1; Other 4. **Subjects:** History of Upstate New York and Vermont; Canadiana; folklore of Adirondacks and Champlain Valley; recent environmental, industrial and demographic studies of the region; Rockwell Kent; University archives. **Special Collections:** History of Northern New York (7000 monographs; 15,000 ephemera and manuscripts); Marjorie Lansing Porter Folklore Collection (original discs and tapes); Kent-Delord papers; William Bailey papers; Truesdell Print Collection; Signor/Langlois Collection of architectural drawings and maps; Rockwell Kent Collection (1500 items); Feinberg Collection; 1980 Lake Placid Olympics. **Holdings:** 11,000 volumes; 65,000 manuscripts; 4000 maps and atlases; 5000 photographs; 1900 reels of microfilm; 400 recordings; 4000 pamphlets; 7200 clippings. **Subscriptions:** 36 journals and other serials. **Services:** Copying; collections open to public. **Special Catalogs:** Manuscripts for Research: Report of the Director, 1961-1974.

SUNY - COLLEGE AT PLATTSBURGH - MINER CENTER LIBRARY
See: Miner Center Library

★13117★
SUNY - COLLEGE AT POTSDAM - CRANE MUSIC LIBRARY (Mus)

Phone: (315) 268-3019
Potsdam, NY 13676   Sally Skyrm, Music Libn.
Staff: Prof 2; Other 2. **Subjects:** Music - education, performance, study, history, biography, criticism, monuments. **Special Collections:** Julia E. Crane School of Music Archives; Helen M. Hosmer Papers. **Holdings:** 10,887 books; 1670 bound periodical volumes; 20,323 scores; 11,831 phonograph records. **Subscriptions:** 136 journals and other serials. **Services:** Interlibrary loans; library open to public. **Networks/Consortia:** Member of Associated Colleges of the St. Lawrence Valley, Inc.; North Country Reference and Research Resources Council. **Staff:** David Ossenkop, Assoc.Libn.

★13118★
SUNY - COLLEGE AT POTSDAM - FREDERICK W. CRUMB MEMORIAL LIBRARY (Educ)
Pierrepont Ave.   Phone: (315) 268-4991
Potsdam, NY 13676   Dr. Thomas M. Peischl, Dir. of Libs.
Founded: 1880. **Staff:** Prof 12; Other 10. **Subjects:** Education and curriculum materials, art, 19th and 20th century German history, urban sociology, northern New York State history, Anglo-Irish literature. **Special Collections:** Bertrand A. Snell Collection (public and private papers); college archives. **Holdings:** 230,339 books; 47,694 bound periodical volumes; 7653 public school textbooks; 1080 phonograph records; 359,720 microforms; 56,093 government documents; 237 linear feet of archives, pamphlets and pictures; 4284 maps and charts. **Subscriptions:** 1665 journals and other serials; 27 newspapers. **Services:** Interlibrary loans; copying; library open to public. **Automated Operations:** Computerized cataloging and acquisitions. **Computerized Information Services:** OCLC. **Networks/Consortia:** Member of Associated Colleges of St. Lawrence Valley; North Country Reference and Research Resources Council. **Publications:** Subject bibliographies and library guides, irregular. **Staff:** Keith Compean, Asst. to Dir./Circ.; Selma V. Foster, OCLC Coord.;David Trithart, Ref.Libn.; Melba Gulick, Ref.Libn.; Nancy Edblom, Doc.Libn.; Kay Brown, Cat.Libn.; Frank Lepkowski, Cat.Libn.; Jane

Subramanian, Tech.Asst., Ser.; Margaret Weitzmann, Ref.Libn.; Rebecca Wilson, Ref.Libn.

★13119★
SUNY - DOWNSTATE MEDICAL CENTER - DEPARTMENT OF PSYCHIATRY LIBRARY (Med)
606 Winthrop St.   Phone: (718) 735-3915
Brooklyn, NY 11203   Patricia Tomasulo, Libn.
Founded: 1947. **Staff:** Prof 1. **Subjects:** Psychiatry, psychoanalysis, child psychiatry, psychology. **Holdings:** 2038 books; 1150 bound periodical volumes; 5 VF drawers of pamphlets and reprints. **Subscriptions:** 50 journals and other serials. **Services:** Interlibrary loans; library not open to public. **Also Known As:** Kings County Hospital - Psychiatry Library.

★13120★
SUNY - DOWNSTATE MEDICAL CENTER - MEDICAL RESEARCH LIBRARY OF BROOKLYN (Med)†
450 Clarkson Ave.
Box 14   Phone: (718) 270-1041
Brooklyn, NY 11203   Kenneth E. Moody, Dir.
Staff: Prof 14; Other 22. **Subjects:** Medicine, nursing, health related sciences. **Holdings:** 64,700 books; 175,300 bound periodical volumes; archives and memorabilia of various Brooklyn hospitals and medical societies. **Subscriptions:** 1600 journals and other serials. **Services:** Interlibrary loans; copying; SDI; library open to qualified scientists who need access to the collection. **Automated Operations:** Computerized cataloging, acquisitions and serials. **Computerized Information Services:** BRS, MEDLINE. **Networks/Consortia:** Member of Greater Northeastern Regional Medical Library Program; SUNY/OCLC Library Network; Medical Library Center of New York (MLCNY). **Staff:** Julie Semkow, Hd., AV;Martin Frum, Hd., Circ.; Rolfe DePuy, Hd., Tech.Serv.

★13121★
SUNY - EMPIRE STATE COLLEGE - CENTER FOR DISTANCE LEARNING (Educ)
2 Union Ave.   Phone: (518) 587-2100
Saratoga Springs, NY 12866   Daniel Granger, Dir.
Subjects: Reference collection of materials useful in locating/discovering learning resources for individual and independent study. **Holdings:** 2500 books; 500 AV catalogs; 1000 items in pamphlet file. **Special Indexes:** Audiovisual Distributers Catalogs Lists (computer print-out); Resources Information File (card). **Services:** Center open to public with restrictions.

★13122★
SUNY - MARITIME COLLEGE - STEPHEN B. LUCE LIBRARY (Sci-Tech)
Fort Schuyler   Phone: (212) 409-7231
Bronx, NY 10465   Richard H. Corson, Libn.
Founded: 1946. **Staff:** Prof 6; Other 6. **Subjects:** Marine transportation, maritime history, marine engineering, naval architecture, merchant marine. **Holdings:** 68,000 books and bound periodical volumes; 40,000 volumes of government documents; 10,105 microfiche; 5195 reels of microfilm; 263 titles of motion pictures. **Subscriptions:** 510 journals; 226 serials; 8 newspapers. **Services:** Interlibrary loans; copying; library open to public with identification. **Automated Operations:** Computerized cataloging and ILL. **Computerized Information Services:** OCLC. **Publications:** Maritima, 2/year - distributed to faculty and students; Stephen B. Luce Library Accessions, quarterly; bibliographic series, irregular. **Staff:** Filomena Magavero, Assoc.Libn.Rd.Serv.; Alvina Kalsch, Assoc.Libn.Tech.Serv.

★13123★
SUNY - SCHOOL OF PHARMACY - DRUG INFORMATION SERVICE - LIBRARY (Med)
Erie County Medical Center
462 Grider St.   Phone: (716) 898-3927
Buffalo, NY 14215   Dr. Sue Rozek
Founded: 1966. **Staff:** Prof 1. **Subjects:** Medicinals, pharmacology, therapeutics. **Holdings:** 70 books; 5 bound periodical volumes; microfilm. **Subscriptions:** 40 journals and other serials. **Services:** Library not open to public. **Publications:** Therapeutic Perspectives, bimonthly - to medical staff and other drug information centers.

★13124★
SUNY AT STONY BROOK - BIOLOGICAL SCIENCES LIBRARY (Sci-Tech)

Phone: (516) 246-5662
Stony Brook, NY 11794   Doris Williams, Libn.
Founded: 1975. **Staff:** Prof 1; Other 3. **Subjects:** Zoology, botany, general biology, biochemistry, microbiology, physiology, agriculture. **Special Collections:** Raymond Pearle Reprint Collection (625 volumes). **Holdings:** 30,828 books; 30,765 bound periodical volumes. **Subscriptions:** 785

journals. **Services:** Interlibrary loans; copying; library open to public for reference use only. **Computerized Information Services:** Online systems.

★13125★
SUNY AT STONY BROOK - CHEMISTRY LIBRARY (Sci-Tech)
Phone: (516) 246-5664
Stony Brook, NY 11794 Esther C. Linkletter, Hd.
Founded: 1965. **Staff:** Prof 1; Other 2. **Subjects:** Chemistry, biochemistry. **Holdings:** 18,494 books; 19,237 bound periodical volumes. **Subscriptions:** 350 journals and other serials. **Services:** Interlibrary loans; copying; library open to public for reference use only.

★13126★
SUNY AT STONY BROOK - DEPARTMENT OF SPECIAL COLLECTIONS (Rare Book)
Phone: (516) 246-3615
Stony Brook, NY 11794 Evert Volkersz, Libn.
Founded: 1969. **Staff:** Prof 1; Other 2. **Subjects:** Contemporary letters and literature, children's books, Ibero-Americana, Long Island, 20th century political and social movements, printing and publishing, SUNY at Stony Brook. **Special Collections:** Conrad Potter Aiken (60 volumes; 44 periodicals); Jorge Carrera Andrade (95 volumes; 7 linear feet of manuscripts); Children's Books, 1820-1950 (2200 volumes); Chilean Theater Pamphlets (57 bound volumes; 570 pamphlets); Robert Creeley (100 volumes, manuscripts); Fortune Press, London (100 volumes); Oakley Calvin Johnson Papers (10 volumes, 31 linear feet of manuscripts); Latin American Pamphlets (1215 items); Pablo Neruda (175 volumes); Robert Payne (160 volumes); Perishable Press, Ltd. (65 volumes, 10 linear feet of manuscripts); Juan and Eva Peron Pamphlets (380 items); Printing and Publishing Collection (750 volumes); Spanish-American Colonial Trade (103 sixteenth century unbound pamphlets); The Typophiles, New York (110 volumes); early 19th century Chilean newspapers and journals (41 titles); Irish political pamphlets, 1789-1829 (503 pamphlets bound in 78 volumes); Environmental Defense Fund, 1967-1975 (60 linear feet); Performing Arts Foundation Collection (60 linear feet); Senator Jacob K. Javits Collection (1500 linear feet). **Holdings:** 20,000 volumes; 3000 linear feet of manuscripts; 8000 pieces of ephemera and clippings; 48 linear feet of pamphlets. **Services:** Copying (limited); department open to public for reference use only. **Publications:** Information leaflets. **Special Catalogs:** Chronological imprints catalog (card).

★13127★
SUNY AT STONY BROOK - EARTH AND SPACE SCIENCES LIBRARY (Sci-Tech)
Phone: (516) 246-3616
Stony Brook, NY 11794 Rosalind Walcott, ESS Libn.
Founded: 1968. **Staff:** Prof 1; Other 2. **Subjects:** Geology, astronomy, oceanography, paleontology, meteorology, geomorphology. **Holdings:** 22,500 books; 12,900 bound periodical volumes; 3000 sheets of geological maps; 2500 Palomar Sky Survey and Southern Sky Survey photographic prints; film copies of seismograms for National Geophysical Data Center, 1964 to present (data from 20 stations). **Subscriptions:** 540 journals and other serials. **Services:** Interlibrary loans; copying; library open to public for reference use only. **Computerized Information Services:** Online systems.

★13128★
SUNY AT STONY BROOK - ENGINEERING LIBRARY (Sci-Tech)
Phone: (516) 246-7724
Stony Brook, NY 11794 Kenneth W. Furst, Libn.
Founded: 1964. **Staff:** Prof 1; Other 3. **Subjects:** Engineering, electrical sciences, mechanics and mechanical engineering, materials sciences, technology (including medical), computer science, mathematics and applied mathematics, chemical technology, applied physics, aerospace sciences. **Holdings:** 26,000 books; 21,000 bound periodical volumes. **Subscriptions:** 630 journals and other serials. **Services:** Interlibrary loans; copying; library open to public for reference use only.

★13129★
SUNY AT STONY BROOK - ENVIRONMENTAL INFORMATION SERVICE (Env-Cons)
Phone: (516) 246-5975
Stony Brook, NY 11794 David Allen, Libn.
Founded: 1970. **Staff:** Prof 1; Other 1. **Subjects:** Environment of Long Island; general environmental problems and energy issues. **Holdings:** 1500 titles of research and technical reports; 1600 titles of federal, state and local documents; 25 drawers of newspaper clippings; 6000 books and pamphlets. **Services:** Interlibrary loans; copying; library open to public for reference use only. **Computerized Information Services:** Online systems.

★13130★
SUNY AT STONY BROOK - HEALTH SCIENCES LIBRARY (Med)
Box 66 Phone: (516) 444-2512
East Setauket, NY 11733 Ruth Marcolina, Dir.
Founded: 1969. **Staff:** Prof 8; Other 13. **Subjects:** Medicine, dentistry, nursing, health and basic medical sciences, pharmacology, social welfare. **Special Collections:** History of medicine and dentistry. **Holdings:** 197,940 books and bound periodical volumes; microfilm. **Subscriptions:** 3941 journals and other serials; 7 newspapers. **Services:** Interlibrary loans; copying; SDI; library open to those involved in Nassau and Suffolk County health care. **Automated Operations:** Computerized cataloging and serials. **Computerized Information Services:** NLM, DIALOG, BRS. **Networks/Consortia:** Member of Union Catalog of Medical Periodicals (UCMP); Medical Library Center of New York; Long Island Library Resources Council; SUNY/OCLC Library Network. **Publications:** Guide to Health Sciences Library, annual - distributed to patrons. **Staff:** Antonija Prelec, Assoc.Dir./Coll.Dev.; Arlee May, Asst.Dir./Pub.Serv.; Helen Park, Cat.Libn.; Esther Wei, Hd., Ref.; Julitta Jo, Ser.Libn.; Jeanne Galbraith, Circ.Libn.; Betty Emilio, Lib.Tech.Asst.

SUNY AT STONY BROOK - INSTITUTE FOR ADVANCED STUDIES OF WORLD RELIGIONS
See: Institute for Advanced Studies of World Religions

★13131★
SUNY AT STONY BROOK - MAP LIBRARY (Geog-Map)
Phone: (516) 246-5975
Stony Brook, NY 11794 Barbara A. Shupe, Libn.
Founded: 1974. **Staff:** Prof 1. **Subjects:** U.S. topography, nautical information, Long Island, U.S. soil maps. **Holdings:** 1200 volumes; 43,000 U.S. Geological Survey topographic maps; 2000 Defense Mapping Agency depository items, 1975 to present; 3000 National Ocean Survey depository items; 1500 Suffolk County, NY tax maps; 9000 U.S. small scale sheet maps; 18,000 small scale maps of areas other than the United States. **Services:** Interlibrary loans; library open to public for reference use only.

★13132★
SUNY AT STONY BROOK - MATHEMATICS-PHYSICS LIBRARY (Sci-Tech)
Physics Bldg., C Fl. Phone: (516) 246-5666
Stony Brook, NY 11794 Sherry Chang, Libn.
Founded: 1964. **Staff:** Prof 1; Other 3. **Subjects:** Mathematics, physics, applied mathematics. **Holdings:** 32,000 books; 21,000 bound periodical volumes; 250 unbound lecture notes of academic organizations; 200 reels of microfilmed journals; 2000 unbound documents; 700 dissertations. **Subscriptions:** 600 journals and other serials. **Services:** Interlibrary loans; copying; library open to public for reference use only. **Computerized Information Services:** Online systems.

★13133★
SUNY AT STONY BROOK - MUSIC LIBRARY (Mus)
Phone: (516) 246-5660
Stony Brook, NY 11794 Judith Kaufman, Libn.
Founded: 1974. **Staff:** Prof 2; Other 4. **Subjects:** Music. **Holdings:** 45,000 books, scores and periodical volumes; 17,000 sound recordings; 6000 microforms. **Subscriptions:** 300 journals and other serials. **Services:** Interlibrary loans; copying; library open to public. **Automated Operations:** Computerized cataloging.

★13134★
SUNY AT STONY BROOK - POETRY COLLECTION (Hum)
Phone: (516) 246-5654
Stony Brook, NY 11794 Paul B. Wiener, AV Libn.
Staff: Prof 1; Other 1. **Subjects:** Poetry. **Holdings:** 85 video cassettes and 260 audio cassettes of poets reading and discussing their works. **Services:** Interlibrary loans; collection open to public. **Networks/Consortia:** Member of Long Island Media Consortium. **Publications:** Poetry Tapes at Stony Brook - available upon request.

★13135★
SUNY - SYRACUSE EDUCATIONAL OPPORTUNITY CENTER - PAUL ROBESON LIBRARY (Area-Ethnic; Educ)
100 New St. Phone: (315) 472-0130
Syracuse, NY 13202 Florence Beer, Libn.
Staff: Prof 3; Other 1. **Subjects:** Afro-Americans, job preparation, women, African fiction, business skills, minorities. **Special Collections:** Frazier Library of Afro-American Books (500 volumes); National Archives Collection of Afro-American Artists (23 trays of slides). **Holdings:** 9510 books and bound periodical volumes; 40 VF drawers. **Subscriptions:** 139 journals and other serials; 20 newspapers. **Services:** Interlibrary loans; copying; library open to public. **Networks/Consortia:** Member of Central New York Library Resources

Council. **Publications:** Periodical Holdings, annual - for internal distribution only; New Acquisitions Listings, semiannual. **Special Catalogs:** Catalog to audiovisual collection. **Staff:** Grace Lai, Asst.Libn.; Willa Green, Asst.Libn.

★13136★
SUNY - UPSTATE MEDICAL CENTER LIBRARY (Med)
766 Irving Ave.   Phone: (315) 473-4580
Syracuse, NY 13210   Evelyn L. Hoey, Dir.
Founded: 1834. **Staff:** Prof 8; Other 14. **Subjects:** Medicine, nursing, social and behavioral sciences. **Special Collections:** Americana (350 volumes); Geneva Medical College Library (300 volumes); Rare Books (1500 volumes); Medical School Archives and History of Medicine in Syracuse (3 VF cabinets). **Holdings:** 45,000 books; 90,500 bound periodical volumes. **Subscriptions:** 1800 journals and other serials. **Services:** Interlibrary loans; copying; library open to health professionals. **Automated Operations:** Computerized cataloging. **Computerized Information Services:** OCLC, MEDLINE, BRS. **Publications:** Library Bulletin, monthly; Library Guide, biennial; Annual Report; List of Currently Received Serials; Subject List of Currently Received Serials - all available on request. **Staff:** Peter Uva, Asst.Libn., Pub.Serv.; James Capodagli, Ref.Libn.; Catherine Seeley, Ref.Libn.; Patricia Onsi, Assoc.Libn., Tech.Serv; Linda Hulbert, Assoc.Libn., Coll.Dev.; Diane E. Hill, Media Libn.; Suzanne Murray, Assoc.Dir.

SUOMI SYNOD AND SUOMI COLLEGE ARCHIVES
See: Finnish-American Historical Archives

SUPREME COURT OF CANADA
See: Canada - Supreme Court of Canada

SUPREME COURT OF THE UNITED STATES
See: U.S. Supreme Court

★13137★
SURFACE MINING RESEARCH LIBRARY (Energy)
Box 5024   Phone: (304) 342-0717
Charleston, WV 25311   Norman Kilpatrick, Dir.
Founded: 1971. **Staff:** Prof 1; Other 1. **Subjects:** Surface coal mining, deep coal mining, utility reform, energy policy. **Holdings:** 700 volumes; 150 8x10 photos, 450 3x5 photos, and 700 slides of surface coal mining. **Services:** Copying; consulting. **Publications:** Basic Information Kit and Technical Information Kit - both free upon request; slide show on modern surface mining methods - available for purchase.

★13138★
SURGIKOS - TECHNICAL INFORMATION CENTER (Sci-Tech)
2500 Arbrook Blvd.
Box 130   Phone: (817) 465-3141
Arlington, TX 76010   W.B. Scroggs, Tech.Info.Coord.
Founded: 1970. **Staff:** Prof 1; Other 1. **Subjects:** Chemical and biological sciences. **Special Collections:** Antimicrobial chemistry (5000 reprints). **Holdings:** 1500 books; 1800 bound periodical volumes. **Subscriptions:** 275 journals and other serials. **Services:** Interlibrary loans; copying; center open to public by appointment. **Automated Operations:** Computerized cataloging. **Networks/Consortia:** Member of Dallas-Tarrant County Consortium of Health Science Libraries. **Publications:** Library information bulletin - for internal distribution only. **Remarks:** This is a subsidiary of Johnson and Johnson.

★13139★
SURREY MUSEUM - ARCHIVES (Hist)
Cloverdale
Box 1006   Phone: (604) 574-5744
Surrey, BC, Canada V3S 4P5   D.R. Hooser, Cur.
Founded: 1958. **Staff:** 3. **Subjects:** Local history. **Holdings:** 1000 books; school registers. **Services:** Copying; archives open to public.

★13140★
SUSQUEHANNA COUNTY HISTORICAL SOCIETY AND FREE LIBRARY ASSOCIATION (Hist)
Monument Square   Phone: (717) 278-1881
Montrose, PA 18801   Mary O. Garm, Libn.
Founded: 1907. **Staff:** Prof 2; Other 11. **Subjects:** Genealogy, natural science, art, music, humanities, religion. **Special Collections:** Gould Bird Books (38 volumes). **Holdings:** 74,377 volumes; 475 genealogical items. **Subscriptions:** 75 journals and other serials; 7 newspapers. **Services:** Interlibrary loans; copying; library open to public with restrictions. **Staff:** Elizabeth Smith, Cur., Hist.Dept.Susan Stone, Asst.Libn.; David Colwell, Ref.Libn.

★13141★
SUSSEX COUNTY HISTORICAL SOCIETY - LIBRARY (Hist)†
82 Main St.   Phone: (201) 383-6010
Newton, NJ 07860   Howard E. Case
Founded: 1904. **Subjects:** New Jersey and Sussex County history, archeology, genealogy, antiques. **Special Collections:** Roy Papers. **Holdings:** 2000 books; 10 bound periodical volumes; 600 genealogical files. **Services:** Library open to public for reference use only on a limited schedule.

★13142★
SUSSEX COUNTY LAW LIBRARY (Law)
Court House, 3 High St.   Phone: (201) 383-4590
Newton, NJ 07860   Barbara J. Smith, Ck. to Jury Comm.
Subjects: Law. **Holdings:** 45,000 books; 5000 bound periodical volumes. **Services:** Copying; library open to public.

★13143★
SUTHERLAND, ASBILL & BRENNAN - LIBRARY (Law)
1666 K St., N.W., Suite 800   Phone: (202) 887-3495
Washington, DC 20006   Nalini Rajguru, Libn.
Staff: Prof 3; Other 4. **Subjects:** Law - tax, energy, insurance, securities. **Special Collections:** Legislative histories of tax law, 1921 to present. **Holdings:** 20,000 books. **Subscriptions:** 169 journals and other serials. **Services:** Interlibrary loans; copying; library open to public with librarian's permission. **Computerized Information Services:** DIALOG, LEXIS. **Staff:** Ronald Pramberger, Leg.Libn.; Donna Bausch, Asst.Libn.

SUTHERLAND MEMORIAL LIBRARY
See: San Clemente Presbyterian Church

SUTRO LIBRARY
See: California State Library

★13144★
SUTTER COUNTY LAW LIBRARY (Law)
Court House   Phone: (916) 673-6544
Yuba City, CA 95991   Lillian R. Boss, Law Libn.
Staff: 1. **Subjects:** Law. **Holdings:** 7699 volumes. **Services:** Library open to public.

SUTTLE (William M.) MEDICAL LIBRARY
See: Hinds General Hospital - William M. Suttle Medical Library

SUZZALLO LIBRARY
See: University of Washington

SVERDRUP (George) LIBRARY AND MEDIA CENTER
See: Augsburg College - George Sverdrup Library and Media Center

★13145★
SVERDRUP & PARCEL AND ASSOCIATES, INC. - TECHNICAL LIBRARY (Sci-Tech)
801 N. 11th Blvd.   Phone: (314) 436-7600
St. Louis, MO 63101   R.A. Bodapati, Libn.
Founded: 1966. **Staff:** Prof 1. **Subjects:** Engineering - civil, structural, electrical, mechanical and environmental; architecture; urban and regional planning. **Holdings:** 8000 books. **Subscriptions:** 80 journals and other serials. **Services:** Interlibrary loans (with restrictions); library not open to public.

SWAIN HALL LIBRARY
See: Indiana University

SWAIN LIBRARY OF CHEMISTRY AND CHEMICAL ENGINEERING
See: Stanford University

★13146★
SWAIN SCHOOL OF DESIGN - LIBRARY (Art)
100 Madison St.   Phone: (617) 997-7831
New Bedford, MA 02740   Martha S. Maier, Lib.Dir.
Founded: 1882. **Staff:** Prof 2. **Subjects:** Fine arts, graphic arts and design. **Special Collections:** Local artists (pamphlets and clippings); slide collection (30,000 slides). **Holdings:** 17,000 books and bound periodical volumes. **Subscriptions:** 50 journals and other serials. **Services:** Interlibrary loans; copying; library open to public for reference use only. **Networks/Consortia:** Member of Southeastern Massachusetts Cooperating Libraries (SMCL); Southeastern Association for Cooperation in Higher Education in Massachusetts (SACHEM).

★13147★
SWAN WOOSTER CONSULTANTS LIMITED - LIBRARY (Sci-Tech)
202 Kensington House
1167 Bowness Rd., N.W.   Phone: (403) 283-3601
Calgary, AB, Canada T2N 3J6   W. Daunine Kemp, Libn.
Staff: 1. **Subjects:** Engineering. **Holdings:** 2800 books; 3500 bound periodical volumes; 40 VF drawers of papers and reports; 1500 other cataloged items. **Subscriptions:** 30 journals and other serials. **Services:** Interlibrary loans; library not open to public. **Special Indexes:** Index of periodicals. **Formerly:** Williams Brothers Canada Limited.

★13148★
SWANSBORO HISTORICAL ASSOCIATION, INC. - RESEARCH FILES (Hist)
Box 414   Phone: (919) 326-5361
Swansboro, NC 28584
Staff: 1. **Subjects:** Onslow County history, North Carolina maritime history, local genealogy. **Holdings:** 20,000 research note cards; 10 boxes of document copies; 2000 photographs. **Services:** Files open to public with restrictions.

SWANSON MEMORIAL LIBRARY
See: Kansas State University - Grain Science and Industry

★13149★
SWARTHMORE COLLEGE - CORNELL LIBRARY OF SCIENCE AND ENGINEERING (Sci-Tech)
                                                Phone: (215) 447-7261
Swarthmore, PA 19081   Emi K. Horikawa, Libn.
Founded: 1960. **Staff:** Prof 1; Other 2. **Subjects:** Mathematics, physics, chemistry, engineering, biology. **Holdings:** 35,600 books; 18,361 bound periodical volumes; 2100 government documents; 1270 periodicals on microfilm. **Subscriptions:** 625 journals and other serials. **Services:** Interlibrary loans; copying; library open to area researchers, fee charged in some cases. **Computerized Information Services:** DIALOG, BRS, OCLC. Performs searches free of charge and on cost recovery basis. **Networks/Consortia:** Member of PALINET & Union Library Catalogue of Pennsylvania. **Publications:** Current Periodicals List.

★13150★
SWARTHMORE COLLEGE - DANIEL UNDERHILL MUSIC LIBRARY (Mus)
                                                Phone: (215) 447-7232
Swarthmore, PA 19081   George K. Huber, Music Libn.
Founded: 1973. **Staff:** Prof 1. **Subjects:** Music and dance. **Holdings:** 4320 books; 800 bound periodical volumes; 8640 music scores; 10,462 phonograph records. **Subscriptions:** 73 journals and other serials. **Services:** Interlibrary loans; library open to area researchers, fee charged in some cases. **Computerized Information Services:** OCLC. **Networks/Consortia:** Member of PALINET & Union Library Catalogue of Pennsylvania.

★13151★
SWARTHMORE COLLEGE - FRIENDS HISTORICAL LIBRARY (Hist; Rel-Theol)
                                                Phone: (215) 447-7496
Swarthmore, PA 19081   J. William Frost, Dir.
Founded: 1871. **Staff:** Prof 2; Other 5. **Subjects:** Quaker faith, history and genealogy; Quaker social concerns - abolition of slavery, race relations, women's rights, peace, education, prison reform, mental health, Indian rights, temperance. **Special Collections:** Friends Meeting records (2000 volumes of manuscripts); Whittier (1700 books, 900 manuscripts); Quaker manuscripts (250 collections); Lucretia Mott manuscripts (7 boxes); Samuel Janney manuscripts (7 boxes); Elias Hicks manuscripts (12 boxes); journals of Quaker ministers (18 boxes); Charles F. Jenkins Autograph Collection (6 boxes). **Holdings:** 35,046 books; 1294 bound periodical volumes; 100 boxes of pictures; 81 chart case drawers of pictures, maps, broadsides, deeds, genealogical charts, marriage certificates; 2257 reels of microfilm. **Subscriptions:** 203 journals and other serials. **Services:** Interlibrary loans; copying; library open to public. **Computerized Information Services:** OCLC. **Networks/Consortia:** Member of PALINET & Union Library Catalogue of Pennsylvania. **Publications:** Descriptive leaflet. **Special Catalogs:** Guide to the Manuscript Collections of Friends Historical Library of Swarthmore College, 1982. **Special Indexes:** Quaker picture index (card); William Wade Hinshaw Index to Quaker Meeting Records (card); checklists for Quaker manuscript collections (loose-leaf); index to Whittier Collection (card). **Staff:** Albert W. Fowler, Assoc.Dir.

★13152★
SWARTHMORE COLLEGE - FRIENDS HISTORICAL LIBRARY - PEACE COLLECTION (Soc Sci)
McCabe Library   Phone: (215) 447-7557
Swarthmore, PA 19081   Jean R. Soderlund, Cur.
Founded: 1930. **Staff:** Prof 5; Other 1. **Subjects:** History of peace movement, nonviolence, pacifism, conscientious objection and conscription, disarmament, women and peace and justice. **Special Collections:** Jane Addams (350 books; 13,000 manuscripts; 170 document boxes of clippings and pictures); A.J. Muste (23 feet of manuscripts, correspondence and writings); Emily Greene Balch (36 feet of manuscripts, correspondence and writings); Fellowship of Reconciliation; Friends Committee on National Legislation; Clergy and Laity Concerned; Women's International League for Peace and Freedom; War Resister's League; SANE; National Interreligious Service Board for Conscientious Objectors; Women Strike for Peace; Central Committee for Conscientious Objectors; World Conference on Religion and Peace; World Peace Foundation; Business Executives Move (official depositors sending materials periodically). **Holdings:** 8300 books; 475 bound periodical volumes; 2100 peace posters and broadsides; 1000 reels of microfilm; 136 document groups. **Subscriptions:** 250 journals and other serials. **Services:** Interlibrary loans; copying; library open to public with restrictions on some collections. **Automated Operations:** Computerized cataloging and serials. **Computerized Information Services:** OCLC. **Networks/Consortia:** Member of PALINET & Union Library Catalogue of Pennsylvania. **Publications:** Guide to Swarthmore College Peace Collection. **Special Catalogs:** Checklists for major collections (loose-leaf). **Special Indexes:** Index for Jane Addams correspondence (card); index for archival collections (card). **Staff:** Eleanor M. Barr, Archv.; Barbara Addison, Cat.; Mary Ellen Clark, Asst. to Cur.; Martha P. Shane, Archv.

★13153★
SWARTHMORE COLLEGE - SPROUL OBSERVATORY LIBRARY (Sci-Tech)
                                                Phone: (215) 447-7261
Swarthmore, PA 19081   Emi K. Horikawa, Libn.
Staff: Prof 1; Other 1. **Subjects:** Astronomy. **Holdings:** 6500 books; 2300 bound periodical volumes; 2400 Observatory publications. **Subscriptions:** 42 journals and other serials. **Services:** Interlibrary loans. **Computerized Information Services:** DIALOG, BRS, OCLC. Performs searches free of charge and on cost recovery basis. **Networks/Consortia:** Member of PALINET & Union Library Catalogue of Pennsylvania.

SWARTHOUT (Glendon) ARCHIVE
See: Arizona State University - Special Collections

SWASEY (Ambrose) LIBRARY
See: Colgate Rochester/Bexley Hall/Crozer Theological Seminaries - Ambrose Swasey Library

★13154★
SWEDENBORG FOUNDATION - LIBRARY (Rel-Theol)
139 E. 23rd St.   Phone: (212) 673-7310
New York, NY 10010   Darrell Ruhl, Exec.Dir.
Staff: Prof 1; Other 4. **Subjects:** Works by and about Emanuel Swedenborg. **Special Collections:** Rare editions; image archive (slides, photographs, drawings). **Holdings:** 3000 books; 100 bound periodical volumes; engravings and prints; 10 paintings and drawings; 5 films. **Subscriptions:** 10 journals and other serials. **Services:** Library open to public with restrictions. **Publications:** LOGOS newsletter. **Staff:** Kristine Jordahl, Off.Mgr.

★13155★
SWEDENBORG LIBRARY AND BOOKSTORE (Rel-Theol)
79 Newbury St.   Phone: (617) 262-5918
Boston, MA 02116   Rafael Guiu, Mgr.
Founded: 1865. **Staff:** 3. **Subjects:** Swedenborg theological works, Swedenborgian Church (American and English), collateral works of Swedenborgian writers. **Special Collections:** First editions of Swedenborg's writings; photolithographic and photostatic copies of Swedenborg's manuscripts. **Holdings:** 2100 books; 210 bound periodical volumes; 1000 pamphlets. **Services:** Library open to public. **Remarks:** Maintained by the Massachusetts New Church Union. **Staff:** Howard Miller, Asst.Mgr.; Ann L. Sifneos .

SWEDENBORG MEMORIAL LIBRARY
See: Urbana College

★13156★
SWEDENBORG SCHOOL OF RELIGION - LIBRARY (Rel-Theol)
48 Sargent St.   Phone: (617) 244-0504
Newton, MA 02158   Marian Kirven, Libn.
Founded: 1866. **Staff:** 1. **Subjects:** Writings of Emanuel Swedenborg, theology. **Special Collections:** History and literature of the Swedenborgian Church (also known as the New Church or the Church of the New Jerusalem). **Holdings:** 32,600 books and bound periodical volumes; Swedenborgian Church archive materials - letters, manuscripts, committee reports, sermons. **Services:** Interlibrary loans; copying; library open to public by appointment.

Remarks: Incorporated as the New Church Theological School in 1881.

★13157★

SWEDISH AMERICAN HOSPITAL - HEALTH CARE LIBRARY (Med)†
1400 Charles St.   Phone: (815) 968-4400
Rockford, IL 61101   Peggy Fuller, Med.Libn.
Staff: Prof 1; Other 1. **Subjects:** Clinical medicine, hospital administration. **Holdings:** 1200 books; 300 video cassettes; 8 year backlog of periodicals. **Subscriptions:** 200 journals and other serials. **Services:** Interlibrary loans; copying; library open to public. **Computerized Information Services:** MEDLARS. **Networks/Consortia:** Member of Upstate Consortium of Medical and Allied Libraries in Northern Illinois; Northern Illinois Library System (NILS).

★13158★

SWEDISH CONSULATE GENERAL - SWEDISH INFORMATION SERVICE
(Area-Ethnic)
825 Third Ave.   Phone: (212) 751-5900
New York, NY 10022   Elisabeth Halvarsson-Stapen, Lib.Asst.
Founded: 1921. **Staff:** 2. **Subjects:** Contemporary Sweden. **Holdings:** 8000 books; 50 VF drawers of pamphlets and clippings. **Subscriptions:** 85 journals and other serials; 6 newspapers. **Services:** Copying; service open to public for reference use only. **Publications:** New accessions, semiannual - to users. **Staff:** Marna Feldt, Info.Off.

★13159★

SWEDISH CONSULATE - LIBRARY (Area-Ethnic)†
420 47th Ave., S.W.   Phone: (403) 243-1093
Calgary, AB, Canada T2S 1C4   R. Zoumer, Consul
Subjects: Sweden. **Special Collections:** History of Stockholm (in Swedish); old Swedish music (tape recordings). **Holdings:** 150 items, including films, maps and periodicals. **Subscriptions:** 39 journals and other serials. **Services:** Interlibrary loans; translations; library open to public with restrictions.

★13160★

SWEDISH COVENANT HOSPITAL - JOSEPH G. STROMBERG LIBRARY OF THE HEALTH SCIENCES (Med)
5145 North California Ave.   Phone: (312) 878-8200
Chicago, IL 60625   Jan Zibrat, Health Sci.Libn.
Staff: Prof 1; Other 1. **Subjects:** Family practice, medicine, nursing. **Holdings:** 1500 books; 2700 bound periodical volumes; audiovisual media. **Subscriptions:** 90 journals. **Services:** Interlibrary loans; library not open to public. **Computerized Information Services:** MEDLINE. **Networks/Consortia:** Member of Greater Midwest Regional Medical Library Network (Region 3); Metropolitan Consortium. **Publications:** Acquisitions List, quarterly - distributed to staff and other medical libraries in area.

★13161★

SWEDISH EMBASSY - LIBRARY-INFORMATION CENTER (Area-Ethnic)*
Watergate 600, Suite 1200
600 New Hampshire Ave., N.W.   Phone: (202) 298-3500
Washington, DC 20037   Larilyn Reitnauer, Libn.
Staff: 2. **Subjects:** Sweden - social policy, ethnology, government, history, education, literature. **Holdings:** 4000 books and bound periodical volumes; yearly publications by the Swedish government including the Yearbook of Nordic Statistics. **Services:** Library open to public with restrictions.

★13162★

SWEDISH HOSPITAL MEDICAL CENTER - REFERENCE LIBRARY (Med)
747 Summit Ave.   Phone: (206) 292-2484
Seattle, WA 98104   Jean C. Anderson, Chf.Libn.
Staff: Prof 1; Other 3. **Subjects:** Surgery, medicine, nursing, hospital administration. **Holdings:** 2000 volumes; 40 videotapes; 4 VF drawers of pamphlets. **Subscriptions:** 175 journals and other serials; 10 newspapers. **Services:** Interlibrary loans; library not open to public. **Networks/Consortia:** Member of Seattle Area Hospital Library Consortium; Washington Medical Librarians' Association.

★13163★

SWEDISH MEDICAL CENTER - LIBRARY (Med)
501 E. Hampden Ave.   Phone: (303) 786-6616
Englewood, CO 80110   Sandra Parker, Dir., Lib.Serv.
Founded: 1967. **Staff:** Prof 2; Other 1. **Subjects:** Neurosciences, medicine, nursing, health administration, rehabilitation, spinal cord/head injuries. **Holdings:** 1500 books; 2500 bound periodical volumes; 1110 unbound periodicals. **Subscriptions:** 350 journals and other serials. **Services:** Interlibrary loans; copying; library open to public by appointment. **Automated Operations:** Computerized cataloging. **Computerized Information Services:** NLM, DIALOG, BRS, SDC. Performs searches on contract basis. **Networks/Consortia:** Member of Denver Area Health Sciences Library Consortium.

Staff: Alice B. Smith, Asst.Libn.

★13164★

SWEDISH PIONEER HISTORICAL SOCIETY - SWEDISH-AMERICAN ARCHIVES OF GREATER CHICAGO (Area-Ethnic)
5125 N. Spaulding Ave.   Phone: (312) 583-5722
Chicago, IL 60625   Nancy Kahlich, Archv.
Founded: 1965. **Staff:** Prof 2; Other 4. **Subjects:** Swedish settlement in the U.S., Swedish culture, Swedish-American organizations, Swedish contributions to development of the U.S., outstanding Swedish-Americans. **Special Collections:** Contributions of Swedes to American life and culture; Swedish music; records of Swedish organizations in the U.S.; documents and papers of outstanding Swedish Americans; Henry Bengston; Carl Hjalmar Lundquist; Selma Jacobson; Swedish Royalty and Chicago; Sweden, the Land of Our Forefathers. **Holdings:** 5000 books (largely in Swedish language); 400 archive boxes of records; Swedish newspapers printed in Chicago, 1871-1981; 200 reels of Chicago Swedish organization records on microfilm. **Subscriptions:** 100 journals and other serials; 5 newspapers. **Services:** Copying; translations; archives open to public by appointment. **Automated Operations:** Computerized cataloging. **Publications:** Items in Swedish Pioneer Historical Society Quarterly. **Staff:** James M. Erickson, Exec.Dir.

★13165★

SWEETWATER COUNTY HISTORICAL MUSEUM - INFORMATION CENTER (Sci-Tech)
50 W. Flaming Gorge Ave.
Box 25   Phone: (307) 875-2611
Green River, WY 82935   Henry F. Chadey, Dir.
Founded: 1967. **Staff:** Prof 1; Other 1. **Subjects:** Coal mining. **Special Collections:** Pictures of coal mining in southwestern Wyoming (3000 items). **Holdings:** 300 books; 25 bound periodical volumes; 8 VF drawers of clippings and reports; 4 cubic feet of archival mining materials, including payroll, maps and contracts; 200 other publications; 20,000 photographs. **Services:** Copying; center open to public for research.

SWEM (Earl Gregg) LIBRARY
See: College of William and Mary - Earl Gregg Swem Library

★13166★

SWENSON SWEDISH IMMIGRATION RESEARCH CENTER (Area-Ethnic)
Augustana College
Box 175   Phone: (309) 794-7204
Rock Island, IL 61201   Joel W. Lundeen, Act.Dir.
Staff: Prof 2; Other 3. **Subjects:** Swedish immigration to the U.S., Swedish-American life and culture, biography of Swedes in the U.S. **Special Collections:** G.N. Swan Book Collection (6000 volumes); Oliver A. Linder Book Collection (600 volumes); Scandinaviana Book Collection (750 volumes); Swedish Topographical Map Collection (5 flat case drawers); Immigration Book Collection (2000 volumes). **Holdings:** 9000 books; 1000 bound periodical volumes; 200 uncataloged periodicals; 5.5 linear feet of Scandinavian-American Picture Collection; 120 linear feet of manuscripts; 8 linear feet of Oliver A. Linder clipping files; 1560 reels of microfilm of Swedish-American newspapers; 2000 reels of microfilm of Swedish-American church records; 160 reels of microfilm of records and papers of Swedish-American benevolent, fraternal and cultural organizations and their institutions. **Subscriptions:** 26 journals and other serials. **Services:** Copying; center open to public. **Automated Operations:** Computerized cataloging and acquisitions (through Augustana College Library). **Computerized Information Services:** OCLC (through Augustana College Library). **Publications:** Swedish-American Newspapers: A Guide to the Microfilms held by SSIRC at Augustana College, Rock Island, Illinois, compiled by Lilly Setterdahl, 1981. **Special Indexes:** Index to O.A. Linder clipping file; index to George M. Stephenson photostat collection; index to Scandinavian-American Picture Collection (all on cards). **Staff:** Kermit B. Westerberg, Archv./Libn.

SWETT (Morris) TECHNICAL LIBRARY
See: U.S. Army Field Artillery School - Morris Swett Technical Library

SWIFT (Mr. & Mrs. Charles M.) RESEARCH CENTER LIBRARY
See: Sheldon Art Museum - Governor John W. Stewart & Mr. & Mrs. Charles M. Swift Research Center Library

★13167★

SWIFT AND COMPANY - GENERAL OFFICE LIBRARY
115 W. Jackson Blvd.
Chicago, IL 60604
Defunct

★13168★
SWIFT AND COMPANY - RESEARCH AND DEVELOPMENT INFORMATION CENTER (Food-Bev; Sci-Tech)†
1919 Swift Dr.
Oak Brook, IL 60521
Phone: (312) 325-9320
Marcus Bornfleth, Hd., Info.Ctr.
Founded: 1905. **Staff:** Prof 1; Other 2. **Subjects:** Food, nutrition, fats and oils, chemistry, biochemistry, microbiology. **Holdings:** 7100 books; 6500 bound periodical volumes; 55,000 patents; 15,000 pamphlets; 100 reels of microfilm; 200 microfiche. **Subscriptions:** 620 journals and other serials. **Services:** Interlibrary loans; copying; SDI; library open to public with restrictions. **Automated Operations:** Computerized acquisitions and serials. **Computerized Information Services:** DIALOG. **Networks/Consortia:** Member of ILLINET; Midwest Medical Consortia. **Publications:** Patent Alert, weekly; Table of Contents - both for internal distribution only.

SWIFT (Sherman) REFERENCE LIBRARY
See: Canadian National Institute for the Blind - National Library Services - Sherman Swift Reference Library

★13169★
SWIGART MUSEUM - LIBRARY (Hist; Trans)
Museum Pk., Box 214
Huntingdon, PA 16652
Phone: (814) 643-3000
William E. Swigart, Jr., Exec.Dir.
Founded: 1927. **Staff:** Prof 1; Other 3. **Subjects:** Automotive history, transportation, automobiliana. **Special Collections:** Early transportation evolving into the automobile. **Holdings:** 1000 books; 612 bound periodical volumes; automobile literature; extensive uncataloged material; claims to have world's largest collection of license plates, emblems and nameplates. **Subscriptions:** 12 journals and other serials. **Services:** Copying; library open to public with restrictions. **Publications:** Museum Gazette, annual. **Staff:** Helen F. Swigart, Mgr.; Dolly M. Brennen, Off.Mgr.

★13170★
SWIMMER (Milton I.), PLANNING & DESIGN - LIBRARY
9100 Wilshire Blvd.
Beverly Hills, CA 90212
Defunct

SWRL
See: Southwest Regional Laboratory for Educational Research and Development

SYBRON CORPORATION - TAYLOR INSTRUMENT PROCESS CONTROL DIVISION
See: Combustion Engineering - Taylor Instrument

SYLVANIA
See: GTE Sylvania

★13171★
SYMES BUILDING LAW LIBRARY
820-16th St., Suite 800
Denver, CO 80202
Subjects: Law. **Holdings:** 20,000 volumes. **Remarks:** Sherman Agency, Inc. is agent for owner; library presently inactive.

★13172★
SYMMERS, FISH AND WARNER - RESEARCH LIBRARY (Law)
111 E. 50th St.
New York, NY 10022
Phone: (212) 751-6400
Eileen Finnegan, Libn.
Founded: 1956. **Staff:** Prof 1. **Subjects:** Law - insurance, transportation (marine and aviation). **Special Collections:** Admiralty and English Law Reports. **Holdings:** 12,500 volumes; pamphlets; maps. **Subscriptions:** 97 journals and other serials. **Services:** Interlibrary loans.

SYNAGOGUE ARCHITECTURAL AND ART LIBRARY
See: Union of American Hebrew Congregations

★13173★
SYNCRUDE CANADA, LTD. - LEARNING RESOURCE CENTRE
Mail Drop 0125, Bag 4009
Fort McMurray, AB, Canada T9H 3L1
Defunct. Holdings absorbed by its Operations Library.

★13174★
SYNCRUDE CANADA, LTD. - OPERATIONS LIBRARY (Sci-Tech; Energy)
Postal Bag 4009, Zone 3060
Fort McMurray, AB, Canada T9H 3L1
Phone: (403) 790-8773
Marcella Dankow, Lib.Techn.
Founded: 1977. **Staff:** Prof 1; Other 3. **Subjects:** Tar sands, synthetic crude production, petroleum, construction, plant and process design, process engineering, business and management. **Holdings:** 14,000 books; 100 bound periodical volumes; 13 lateral files of technical information; 800 microfiche; 150 videotapes; 100 16mm films; 50 other AV items. **Subscriptions:** 250 journals and other serials; 12 newspapers. **Services:** Interlibrary loans; library not open to public. **Automated Operations:** Computerized cataloging. **Computerized Information Services:** DIALOG, SDC, CAN/OLE. **Remarks:** Contains the holdings of its Learning Resource Centre.

★13175★
SYNCRUDE CANADA, LTD. - RESEARCH AND DEVELOPMENT LIBRARY (Sci-Tech; Energy)
P.O. Box 5790
Edmonton, AB, Canada T6C 4G3
Phone: (403) 464-8400
Peter J. Bates, Info.Spec.
Founded: 1960. **Staff:** Prof 1; Other 2. **Subjects:** Tar sands, chemistry, chemical engineering, petroleum, environment, mining. **Holdings:** 6000 books; 750 bound periodical volumes; 3000 patents; 1000 company reports; 1000 microfiche; reprints. **Subscriptions:** 150 journals and other serials; 5 newspapers. **Services:** Interlibrary loans; library not open to public. **Automated Operations:** Computerized cataloging. **Computerized Information Services:** Online systems. **Networks/Consortia:** Member of Alberta Information Association. **Publications:** Current awareness bulletin, monthly - for internal distribution only. **Special Indexes:** Index to company reports (computer print-out). **Staff:** B. Jordan, Lib.Techn.

★13176★
SYNERGY POWER INSTITUTE - LIBRARY (Soc Sci)
Box 9096
Berkeley, CA 94709
Phone: (415) 549-0839
James H. Craig, Dir.
Founded: 1968. **Staff:** Prof 1; Other 1. **Subjects:** Psychology, power, political science, sociology, U.S. history. **Holdings:** 4200 books. **Subscriptions:** 25 journals and other serials. **Services:** Library not open to public. **Publications:** Synergic Power: Beyond Domination and Permissiveness, 2nd edition, 1979; occasional papers. **Remarks:** Center founded in 1968 to do research and disseminate information about power and ways it can be used humanely and responsibly to change society. **Staff:** Marge Craig, Co-Dir.

SYNOD OF EVANGELICAL LUTHERAN CHURCHES ARCHIVES
See: Concordia Historical Institute

★13177★
SYNTEX, U.S.A. - CORPORATE LIBRARY/INFORMATION SERVICES (Med)
3401 Hillview Ave.
Palo Alto, CA 94304
Phone: (415) 855-5431
Gerry Seward, Mgr.
Founded: 1961. **Staff:** Prof 7; Other 5. **Subjects:** Organic chemistry, biochemistry, pharmacology, clinical medicine, veterinary medicine, physiology. **Special Collections:** Career/Management (300 items.) **Holdings:** 7000 books; 16,000 bound periodical volumes; 1400 microfilm cartridges; 22 volumes of bound reprints of papers authored by Syntex personnel. **Subscriptions:** 500 journals and other serials. **Services:** Interlibrary loans; copying; SDI; library open to public by application to librarian. **Automated Operations:** Computerized cataloging, acquisitions, serials and circulation. **Computerized Information Services:** DIALOG, NLM, SDC, BRS, CAS Online, Pergamon InfoLine Ltd., TEXTLINE, OCLC, RLIN; MEMIS (internal database). **Networks/Consortia:** Member of Pacific Southwest Regional Medical Library Service (PSRMLS); CLASS. **Publications:** Booklist, monthly; bibliographies; Periodicals List - all for internal distribution only. **Staff:** Vicki Garlow, Info.Spec.; Julie Pieprzyk, Info.Spec.; Kathy Westsik, Sr.Info.Spec.; Georgene Takato, Info.Spec.; Nam-Hee Im, Sr.Info.Spec.; Suja Choi, Cat.Libn.

SYRACUSE EDUCATIONAL OPPORTUNITY CENTER
See: SUNY

★13178★
SYRACUSE RESEARCH CORPORATION - LIBRARY (Sci-Tech; Energy)
Merrill Lane
Syracuse, NY 13210
Phone: (315) 425-5200
Mary E. O'Neill, Res.Libn.
Founded: 1968. **Staff:** Prof 1. **Subjects:** Environmental sciences, policy analysis, evaluation. **Holdings:** 2000 books; 1500 microforms; 1500 archival items. **Subscriptions:** 100 journals and other serials. **Services:** Interlibrary loans; library not open to public. **Computerized Information Services:** DIALOG, SDC. **Networks/Consortia:** Member of Central New York Library Resources Council.

★13179★

SYRACUSE UNIVERSITY - E.S. BIRD LIBRARY - AREA STUDIES DEPARTMENT (Area-Ethnic)

Syracuse, NY 13210

Phone: (315) 423-4176

Gurnek Singh, Hd./Asian Bibliog.

Staff: Prof 5; Other 5. **Subjects:** History; geography; anthropology; area studies - African, Asian, Latin American, Slavic. **Holdings:** 261,864 volumes; 12,500 documents and pamphlets; 125,000 maps; 1200 atlases; 1335 reels of microfilm; 22,510 microcards; 66,585 microfiche; 16,625 microprints. **Subscriptions:** 2300 journals and other serials. **Services:** Interlibrary loans; department open to public. **Automated Operations:** Computerized cataloging, acquisitions and circulation. **Computerized Information Services:** OCLC. **Networks/Consortia:** Member of SUNY/OCLC Library Network. **Staff:** Marcella Stark, History Bibliog.; Daniel Cordeiro, Latin Amer.Bibliog.; Mary Anne Waltz, Geog. & Map Bibliog.; Cheryl Kern-Simirenko, Slavic Bibliog.

★13180★

SYRACUSE UNIVERSITY - E.S. BIRD LIBRARY - FINE ARTS DEPARTMENT (Art; Mus)

Syracuse, NY 13210

Phone: (315) 423-2440

Donald Seibert, Dept.Hd./Music Bibliog.

Staff: Prof 4; Other 9. **Subjects:** Art, architecture, music, photography. **Special Collections:** Italian libretto collection (19th century Italian opera libretti, 1350); Liechtenstein Music Archive (microfilm collection of 17th century music preserved in Czechoslovakia); papers of Marcel Breuer and Pietro Belluschi; working drawings of a number of contemporary buildings; papers of American artists and critics including John Canaday, Richard Florsheim, John Singer Sargent, Eastman Johnson, Elihu Vedder, Jacob Lawrence, Edwin Dickinson, George Cruikshank and photographer Margaret Bourke White. **Holdings:** 58,727 volumes; 15,596 recordings; 21,106 scores; 949 tapes; 180,000 slides; 10,550 mounted photographs; 27,000 pictures; 7530 exhibition catalogs; 3685 pamphlets; 1421 microcards; 1323 microfiche. **Subscriptions:** 437 journals and other serials. **Services:** Interlibrary loans; copying; department open to public with restrictions on circulation. **Automated Operations:** Computerized cataloging, acquisitions and circulation. **Computerized Information Services:** OCLC. **Networks/Consortia:** Member of SUNY/OCLC Library Network. **Special Catalogs:** Catalog of art exhibition catalogs (card). **Staff:** Randall Bond, Art Bibliog.; Barbara Opar, Arch.Bibliog.; Johanna Prins, Slide Cur.

★13181★

SYRACUSE UNIVERSITY - E.S. BIRD LIBRARY - HUMANITIES DEPARTMENT (Hum)

Syracuse, NY 13210

Phone: (315) 423-4243

Staff: Prof 4; Other 4. **Subjects:** English and American literature, journalism, philosophy, religion, romance languages, classics. **Holdings:** 256,947 volumes. **Services:** Interlibrary loans; copying; department open to public with restrictions. **Automated Operations:** Computerized cataloging, acquisitions and circulation. **Computerized Information Services:** OCLC. **Networks/Consortia:** Member of SUNY/OCLC Library Network. **Staff:** Wendy Bousfield, Bibliog.; Rebecca Biefeld, Bibliog.; Elizabeth Gardiner, Bibliog.

SYRACUSE UNIVERSITY - E.S. BIRD LIBRARY - LAUBACH LITERACY INTERNATIONAL, INC.

See: Laubach Literacy International, Inc.

★13182★

SYRACUSE UNIVERSITY - E.S. BIRD LIBRARY - MEDIA SERVICES DEPARTMENT (Aud-Vis)

B101 Bird Library

Syracuse, NY 13210

Phone: (315) 423-2438

George Abbott, Hd.

Staff: Prof 2; Other 6. **Subjects:** Audiovisual materials. **Special Collections:** Broadcast Foundation of America audio recordings (5000 reels). **Holdings:** 16,000 items, including AV material and microforms. **Subscriptions:** 75 newspapers. **Services:** Department not open to public. **Computerized Information Services:** DIALOG, SDC, BRS, CIS, NLM, I.P. Sharp Associates, Ltd. **Staff:** James McPhee, Search Anl.

★13183★

SYRACUSE UNIVERSITY - E.S. BIRD LIBRARY - SOCIAL SCIENCES DEPARTMENT (Soc Sci; Bus-Fin)

Syracuse, NY 13210

Phone: (315) 423-3715

Carl Braun, Dept.Hd.

Staff: Prof 4; Other 5. **Subjects:** Business, economics, sociology, social work, education, political science, public administration. **Holdings:** 256,600 volumes; 15,500 pamphlets; ERIC microfiche collection; 34,000 microfiche reports of all corporations on the New York and American Stock Exchange.

Services: Interlibrary loans; copying; department open to public. **Automated Operations:** Computerized cataloging, acquisitions and circulation. **Computerized Information Services:** OCLC. **Networks/Consortia:** Member of SUNY/OCLC Library Network. **Staff:** Edward Goodman, Educ.Bibliog.; Cheryl Kern-Simirenko, Bibliog.; Roberta Palen, Bibliog.

SYRACUSE UNIVERSITY - ERIC CLEARINGHOUSE ON INFORMATION RESOURCES

See: ERIC Clearinghouse on Information Resources

★13184★

SYRACUSE UNIVERSITY - GEOLOGY LIBRARY (Sci-Tech)

300 Heroy Geology Lab

Syracuse, NY 13210

Phone: (315) 423-3337

Eileen Snyder, Libn.

Subjects: Geology, economic geology, geomorphology, geophysics, geochemistry. **Holdings:** 22,800 volumes. **Subscriptions:** 165 journals and other serials. **Services:** Interlibrary loans; copying; library open to public with restrictions. **Automated Operations:** Computerized cataloging and acquisitions. **Computerized Information Services:** OCLC. **Networks/Consortia:** Member of SUNY/OCLC Library Network.

★13185★

SYRACUSE UNIVERSITY - GEORGE ARENTS RESEARCH LIBRARY FOR SPECIAL COLLECTIONS (Rare Book)

E.S. Bird Library

Syracuse, NY 13210

Phone: (315) 423-2585

Metod M. Milac, Act.Hd.

Staff: Prof 7; Other 11. **Subjects:** Rare books, manuscripts, audio archives, university archives. **Holdings:** RARE BOOKS (120,000 volumes) - general collection of 15th-18th century imprints; early American imprints; finely printed and privately printed books; finely illustrated books; fine bindings; strong 19th and 20th century literature collections arranged by author; Spire Collection on Loyalists in the American Revolution; Novotny Library of Economic History; Stephen Crane Collection; William Hobart-Royce Balzac Collection; Mayfield Library; Leopold von Ranke Library. MANUSCRIPTS (30,000 linear feet) - Art (papers of artists, cartoonists, industrial designers, photographers, sculptors, architects); Business History (corporate records of various types of companies including forest industries, public utilities, publishing, printing, transportation, banking, voluntary associations, manufacturing); Government and Public Administration (papers of federal administrators, diplomats and military officers, federal and state judicial officers, state governors, department heads and administrators, federal legislators and statesmen); American Literature (papers of nonfiction authors, novelists, poets, playwrights, dramatists, historians, literary critics); Science Fiction (papers of science fiction writers, anthologists and publishers as well as documents related to societies, international meetings, science fiction art and radio and television programs and fantasy literature); Mass Communications (news photography, periodical and newspaper administration, editing and reporting, news commentators and columnists, foreign correspondants, personalities in music, entertainment, radio and television); Religion and Theology (papers of philosophers, missionaries, theologians, Christian church administrators and clergy); Social Science (documents relating to American military and naval history, local history, law, education, families, philanthropy, economics, explorations); Adult Education (papers of prominent adult educators and researchers and corporate records of international adult educational organizations). AUDIO ARCHIVES (250,000 recordings) - first eighty years of commercial sound recordings from the earliest of the Thomas Edison cylinder recordings to the most modern audiotapes; sound recordings of political leaders, poets, actresses, singers; transcriptions of audio broadcastings, musical and theatrical performances, folk music and contemporary compositions of the 20th century. UNIVERSITY ARCHIVES (10,500 linear feet) - History and development of Syracuse University; all relevant books, pamphlets, photographs, manuscripts; records of University faculty and staff; semiofficial papers of University life such as student publications, records of students clubs and organizations, files relating to student classes and activities, papers of faculty members; administrative records of University schools, colleges, offices and other units; records of University governing boards including Board of Trustees, University Senate, Board of Graduate Studies, and records of students groups. **Services:** Copying; library open to public. **Automated Operations:** Computerized cataloging. **Computerized Information Services:** OCLC. **Networks/Consortia:** Member of SUNY/OCLC Library Network. **Staff:** Mark F. Weimer, Rare Bk.Libn.; Carolyn A. Davis, Mss.Libn.; Walter L. Welch, Audio Archv.Cur.; William Storm, Dir., Audio Archv.; Amy S. Doherty, Univ.Archv.Libn.

★13186★

SYRACUSE UNIVERSITY - LAW LIBRARY (Law)

E.I. White Hall

Syracuse, NY 13210

Phone: (315) 423-2528

Thomas C. Kingsley, Libn.

Staff: Prof 4; Other 6. **Subjects:** Law. **Special Collections:** Depository for

U.S. government documents. **Holdings:** 140,000 volumes; 25,000 microforms of U.S. Supreme Court Records and Briefs; legislative histories. **Subscriptions:** 700 journals and other serials. **Services:** Library open to public. **Automated Operations:** Computerized cataloging. **Computerized Information Services:** LEXIS, Westlaw, OCLC. **Networks/Consortia:** Member of SUNY/OCLC Library Network. **Staff:** Brenda Adams, Assoc.Libn./Cat.; David L. Naylor, Assoc.Libn./Pub.Serv.; Louise Lantzy, Assoc.Libn./Acq.

★13187★
SYRACUSE UNIVERSITY - MATHEMATICS LIBRARY (Sci-Tech)
308 Carnegie Bldg.   Phone: (315) 423-2092
Syracuse, NY 13210   Mary Elling, Bibliog.
Staff: Prof 1. **Subjects:** Mathematics, history of mathematics, mathematical statistics, logic, algebra, numerical analysis, combinatorics, topology. **Special Collections:** Russian journals (translated). **Holdings:** 17,665 books; 13,415 bound periodical volumes; 1400 reports. **Subscriptions:** 400 journals and other serials. **Services:** Interlibrary loans; library open to public with restrictions. **Automated Operations:** Computerized cataloging and acquisitions. **Computerized Information Services:** OCLC. **Networks/Consortia:** Member of SUNY/OCLC Library Network.

★13188★
SYRACUSE UNIVERSITY - PHYSICS LIBRARY (Sci-Tech)
208 Physics Bldg.   Phone: (315) 423-2692
Syracuse, NY 13210   Eileen Snyder, Libn.
Staff: Prof 1; Other 1. **Subjects:** Physics, astronomy. **Holdings:** 19,600 volumes. **Subscriptions:** 215 journals and other serials. **Services:** Interlibrary loans; copying; library open to public. **Automated Operations:** Computerized cataloging and acquisitions. **Computerized Information Services:** OCLC. **Networks/Consortia:** Member of SUNY/OCLC Library Network.

★13189★
SYRACUSE UNIVERSITY - SCHOOL OF EDUCATION - EDUCATIONAL RESOURCE CENTER (Educ)
150 Marshall St.   Phone: (315) 423-3800
Syracuse, NY 13210   Dr. Tom Rusk Vickery, Dir.
Staff: Prof 5; Other 10. **Subjects:** Education. **Special Collections:** Diagnostic tests for school psychologists; collection of public school textbooks; children's books. **Holdings:** 19,000 books; multimedia material; curriculum material on microfiche; AV and production equipment; complete ERIC microfiche collection. **Services:** Center open to students and faculty.

★13190★
SYRACUSE UNIVERSITY - SCIENCE AND TECHNOLOGY LIBRARY (Sci-Tech)
105 Carnegie   Phone: (315) 423-2160
Syracuse, NY 13210   Pauline M. Miller, Hd., Sci. & Tech.Dept.
Staff: Prof 6; Other 6. **Subjects:** Engineering - chemical, civil, electrical, industrial, mechanical; computers and data processing; biology; botany; zoology; microbiology; biochemistry; chemistry; immunology; genetics; ecology; public health; general medicine; medicine and society; nursing; neuroscience; psychiatry; general science and technology; history and philosophy of science; nutrition; mining and metallurgy; physical geography. **Special Collections:** Zoological Record; microform reports from Atomic Energy Commission (AEC), Energy Research and Development Administration (ERDA), DOE, NASA and Society of Automotive Engineers (SAE). **Holdings:** 226,000 books and bound periodical volumes; 420,000 microforms. **Subscriptions:** 1600 journals and other serials. **Services:** Interlibrary loans; copying; library open to public. **Automated Operations:** Computerized cataloging, acquisitions, serials and circulation. **Computerized Information Services:** DIALOG, BRS, OCLC; SULIRS (internal database). **Networks/Consortia:** Member of SUNY/OCLC Library Network. **Staff:** Lockhart Russell, Engr.Bibliog.; Caroline C. Long, Health Sci.Bibliog.; Lee M. Murray, Pub.Serv.Libn.; H. Thomas Keays, Chem.Bibliog.

★13191★
SYSTEM DEVELOPMENT CORPORATION - ACOUSTIC RESEARCH CENTER LIBRARY
Unit 1
Moffett Field, CA 94035
Defunct

★13192★
SYSTEM DEVELOPMENT CORPORATION - LIBRARY (Info Sci; Comp Sci)
2500 Colorado Ave.   Phone: (213) 820-4111
Santa Monica, CA 90406   Ellen Sol, Supv., Lib.Oper.
Founded: 1956. **Staff:** Prof 1; Other 3. **Subjects:** Computers, data processing, information science, computer programming, system analysis and design, management, education, energy, behavioral science, military. **Special Collections:** Computer Manufacturers Documents Collection; SDC Computer Program Library. **Holdings:** 15,000 books; 1000 bound periodical volumes; 250,000 internal reports; 50,000 external reports. **Subscriptions:** 250 journals and other serials; 6 newspapers. **Services:** Interlibrary loans; library not open to public. **Automated Operations:** Computerized cataloging and serials. **Computerized Information Services:** DIALOG, SDC. **Staff:** Maurice Nicholson, Cat.

★13193★
SYSTEM PLANNING CORPORATION - TECHNICAL LIBRARY (Mil)
1500 Wilson Blvd.   Phone: (703) 841-3661
Arlington, VA 22209   Nicholas E. Mercury, Mgr.
Staff: Prof 3; Other 2. **Subjects:** Military science, international relations, computer science, radar. **Holdings:** 30,000 books. **Subscriptions:** 225 journals and other serials. **Services:** Interlibrary loans; library not open to public. **Automated Operations:** Computerized cataloging. **Computerized Information Services:** DTIC, DIALOG, DMS Online. **Staff:** Linda S. Glickman, Libn.; Barbara A. Mack, Acq.Libn.; Phyllis Moon, Libn.

★13194★
SYSTEMATICS GENERAL CORPORATION - LIBRARY (Sci-Tech; Mil)*
1606 Old Ox Rd.   Phone: (703) 471-2200
Sterling, VA 22170   Robin Posten, Libn.
Founded: 1948. **Staff:** 1. **Subjects:** Electronics, communications, aeronautics, energy, military specifications and standards. **Holdings:** 500 books; 210 bound periodical volumes; 300 other cataloged items; 60 volumes of International Convention Digests; 40 military handbooks; 45 American Standards Specifications. **Subscriptions:** 115 journals and other serials; 5 newspapers. **Services:** Interlibrary loans; library not open to public.

★13195★
SYSTEMS CONTROL GROUP - TECHNICAL LIBRARY (Comp Sci)
1801 Page Mill Rd.
Box 10025   Phone: (408) 494-1165
Palo Alto, CA 94303   Martha Liles, Libn.
Staff: Prof 1. **Subjects:** Computer software. **Holdings:** Figures not available. **Services:** Interlibrary loans; library open to public with approval of librarian. **Computerized Information Services:** DIALOG, NASA/RECON, DOE/RECON.

★13196★
SYVA COMPANY - LIBRARY/INFORMATION CENTER (Sci-Tech)
900 Arastradero Rd.   Phone: (415) 493-2200
Palo Alto, CA 94304   Louise Lohr, Mgr.
Founded: 1966. **Staff:** Prof 4; Other 4. **Subjects:** Organic chemistry, biochemistry, microbiology, medicine. **Holdings:** 6000 books. **Subscriptions:** 300 journals and other serials. **Services:** Interlibrary loans; library not open to public. **Computerized Information Services:** DIALOG, SDC, BRS, QUESTEL, OCLC, CAS Online, Pergamon InfoLine Ltd. **Networks/Consortia:** Member of CLASS. **Staff:** Paul S. Hanson, Tech.Info.Spec.; Kim Kubik, Tech.Info.Spec.; Meaghan Wheeler, Supv., Tech.Serv.

T

T.C.T. CHILDREN'S MEDICAL CENTER PEDIATRIC LIBRARY
See: Erlanger Medical Center - Medical Library

★13197★
TA ASSOCIATES - INFORMATION CENTER (Bus-Fin)
1801 McGill College Ave.   Phone: (514) 281-2753
Montreal, PQ, Canada H3A 2N4   Line St-Pierre, Libn.
Founded: 1975. **Staff:** Prof 1. **Subjects:** Employee benefits, pensions, tax laws and regulations. **Holdings:** 100 books; 200 government documents, 1975 to present; tax and pension guides, 1975 to present. **Subscriptions:** 25 journals and other serials. **Services:** Interlibrary loans; center not open to public. **Publications:** TA News and Views.

★13198★
TABOR OPERA HOUSE - LIBRARY
308 Harrison Ave.
Leadville, CO 80461
Founded: 1955. **Subjects:** History of Leadville, Colorado, Tabor Opera House history, Colorado history, paintings. **Remarks:** Presently inactive.

★13199★
TACKAPAUSHA MUSEUM - LIBRARY (Sci-Tech)
Washington Ave.   Phone: (516) 785-2802
Seaford, NY 11783   Richard D. Ryder, Cur.
Staff: 2. **Subjects:** Natural history, zoology, botany, ornithology, mammalogy, herpetology. **Holdings:** 1100 books. **Subscriptions:** 10 journals and other serials. **Services:** Library open for reference use by appointment. **Remarks:** Maintained by Nassau County Department of Recreation and Parks.

★13200★
TACOMA ART MUSEUM - LIBRARY (Art)
12th & Pacific Ave.   Phone: (206) 272-4258
Tacoma, WA 98402   Sally Norris, Libn.
Staff: 2. **Subjects:** Art. **Special Collections:** The Constance Lyon Collection of Japanese prints. **Holdings:** 1441 books; 3 vertical files. **Subscriptions:** 38 journals and other serials. **Services:** Copying; library open to public for reference use only. **Staff:** Sadie Uglow, Ref.Libn.

★13201★
TACOMA NEWS TRIBUNE - LIBRARY (Publ)
Box 11000   Phone: (206) 597-8626
Tacoma, WA 98411   Paula F. Stevens, Libn.
Founded: 1955. **Staff:** Prof 2; Other 1. **Subjects:** Newspaper reference topics. **Holdings:** 500 books; newspaper clippings; 5 VF drawers of pamphlets; 250 maps; News Tribune, 1909 to present, on microfilm. **Subscriptions:** 65 journals and other serials; 35 newspapers. **Services:** Library not open to public. **Automated Operations:** Computerized acquisitions and serials. **Special Indexes:** Roll Microfilm Index (book, online); Index to News Tribune (book, online); index to negatives (book); subject thesauri to files (book, online). **Staff:** Catherine Lord, Asst.Libn.

★13202★
TACOMA PUBLIC LIBRARY - SPECIAL COLLECTIONS (Hist)
1102 Tacoma Ave. S.   Phone: (206) 591-5622
Tacoma, WA 98402   Kevin Hegarty, Dir.
Staff: Prof 2; Other 1. **Subjects:** History - Northwest, Washington state. **Special Collections:** John B. Kaiser Collection (World War I posters and propaganda; 2000 volumes); Civil War and Abraham Lincoln (3000 volumes). **Holdings:** 20,000 books; 1500 bound periodical volumes; 300,000 photographs and photographic negatives; 900 linear feet of manuscripts; 750 linear feet of archives of local government; 15,000 slides; 35,000 maps; 65 VF drawers of clippings. **Subscriptions:** 35 journals and other serials. **Services:** Interlibrary loans; copying; collections open to public. **Automated Operations:** Computerized circulation. **Computerized Information Services:** DIALOG. **Networks/Consortia:** Member of WLN. **Special Indexes:** Northwest Note File (200,000 cards); Northwest Biography File (75,000 cards); Calendars of Manuscripts. **Staff:** Gary Fuller Reese, Mng.Libn.

TACTICAL TECHNOLOGY CENTER
See: Battelle-Columbus Laboratories

TAFT (Lorado) ARCHIVES
See: Northern Illinois University - Taft Field Campus - Instructional Materials Center

★13203★
TAFT MUSEUM - LIBRARY (Art)
316 Pike St.   Phone: (513) 241-0343
Cincinnati, OH 45202   Ruth K. Meyer, Dir.
Founded: 1932. **Subjects:** Art. **Holdings:** 1000 books; 900 bound periodical volumes; 800 slides of art collection. **Subscriptions:** 10 journals and other serials. **Services:** Library open to public by appointment. **Publications:** Taft Art Collection Catalogue, 1958.

TAFT (Robert A.) LABORATORY
See: U.S. Natl. Institute for Occupational Safety & Health - Technical Information Branch

★13204★
TAFT, STETTINIUS & HOLLISTER - LAW LIBRARY (Law)
First National Bank Ctr.   Phone: (513) 381-2838
Cincinnati, OH 45202   Maureen T. Willig, Libn.
Staff: Prof 1; Other 1. **Subjects:** Law. **Holdings:** 25,000 volumes. **Services:** Library not open to public. **Computerized Information Services:** LEXIS, DIALOG. **Networks/Consortia:** Member of Greater Cincinnati Library Consortium.

TAGGART (Jay P.) MEMORIAL LAW LIBRARY
See: Ohio Northern University - College of Law - Jay P. Taggart Memorial Law Library

TAICH
See: American Council of Voluntary Agencies for Foreign Service, Inc. - Tech. Assistance Info. Clearing House

★13205★
TALBOT COUNTY FREE LIBRARY - MARYLAND ROOM (Hist)
100 W. Dover St.   Phone: (301) 822-1676
Easton, MD 21601   Mrs. Kenneth Harvey, Hd.
Subjects: History - local and state, but with emphasis on Talbot County and other locations on the eastern shore; genealogy. **Special Collections:** H.L. Mencken (80 volumes); manuscripts and notes for James Michener's Chesapeake (25 boxes); manuscript of Dickson Preston's Young Frederick Douglass (1 box); manuscripts and notes for L.G. Shreve's Tench Tilghman, the Life and Times of Washington's Aide-de-Camp (3 boxes); history of the Society of Friends, 1773 to present (50 volumes). **Holdings:** 3700 books; unbound periodicals; 16 VF drawers; 60 boxes of manuscripts and ephemera; 69 boxes and bound volumes of newspapers; 86 reels of microfilm of newspapers; 32 reels of microfilm of census data; 26 reels of microfilm of church records. **Subscriptions:** 29 journals and other serials. **Services:** Copying; room open to public for reference use only. **Special Catalogs:** Catalog of subject headings (card); catalog to manuscript and ephemera collection (card); catalog of microfilm, newspapers, and maps.

TALBOTT LIBRARY
See: Westminster Choir College

★13206★
TALL TIMBERS RESEARCH STATION - LIBRARY (Env-Cons)
Rte. 1, Box 160   Phone: (904) 893-4153
Tallahassee, FL 32312   Sharri Moroshok, Libn.
Staff: Prof 1. **Subjects:** Fire ecology, wildlife management, ornithology, earthworms, botany, general ecology. **Special Collections:** Dr. Gordon E. Gates collection (earthworms; 5000 reprints; 52 drawers of index cards). **Holdings:** 2300 books; 2900 bound periodical volumes; 7000 reprints; 10,000 state, federal and international documents; 5 VF drawers of scientific research data; 150 maps. **Subscriptions:** 240 journals and other serials. **Services:** Interlibrary loans (limited); library not open to public.

★13207★
TALLADEGA COLLEGE - HISTORICAL COLLECTIONS (Area-Ethnic; Hist)
          Phone: (205) 362-0206
Talladega, AL 35160   Leon P. Spencer, Archv.
Subjects: American blacks; missions in Angola, Mozambique, and Zaire; the black church in South Africa; civil rights; education. **Special Collections:** College archives (includes the activities of Talladega alumni); Historical Collections (the black church, African missions, southern Africa, civil rights, education). **Holdings:** 120 linear feet of archival items. **Services:** Copying; collections open to serious researchers and noncampus undergraduates with letter from supervising faculty. **Publications:** A Guide to the Archives of

Talladega College, 1981; A Guide to the Collections, 1981.

★13208★
**TALLADEGA COUNTY LAW LIBRARY (Law)*
Judicial Bldg.   Phone: (205) 362-2050
Talladega, AL 35160   Jeffrey A. Willis, Hd.Libn.
Founded: 1951. **Staff:** Prof 1; Other 2. **Subjects:** Law. **Holdings:** 20,000 books; 3000 bound periodical volumes; 2000 pamphlets and documents. **Subscriptions:** 100 journals and other serials. **Services:** Copying; library open to public for research only.

★13209★
**TALLMADGE HISTORICAL SOCIETY - LIBRARY & ARCHIVES (Hist)*
One Tallmadge Circle   Phone: (216) 630-9760
Tallmadge, OH 44278   James B. Hillegas, Pres.
Founded: 1858. **Staff:** 1. **Subjects:** History of Tallmadge, Summit County, and Ohio. **Holdings:** Figures not available. **Services:** Library open to public by appointment. **Staff:** William Truex, Cur.

★13210★
TAM CERAMICS, INC. - LIBRARY
Hyde Park Blvd.
Niagara Falls, NY 14305
Defunct

TAMIMENT LIBRARY
See: New York University

TAMIR (Lt. David) LIBRARY AND READING ROOM
See: Consulate General of Israel - Lt. David Tamir Library and Reading Room

★13211★
TAMPA BAY REGIONAL PLANNING COUNCIL - RESEARCH & INFORMATION LIBRARY (Plan)
9455 Koger Blvd.   Phone: (813) 577-5151
St. Petersburg, FL 33702   Gertrude M. Bechtel, Asst.Libn.
Founded: 1962. **Staff:** Prof 1; Other 1. **Subjects:** Urban and regional planning, land use, housing, human resources, transportation, environment. **Special Collections:** Local and regional comprehensive plans; environmental impact statements; development of regional impacts. **Holdings:** 6000 books and technical documents; 600 maps. **Subscriptions:** 203 journals and other serials. **Services:** Interlibrary loans; copying; library open to public. **Networks/Consortia:** Member of Regional Economic Information Network. **Publications:** Bay Views, monthly; Info Brochure, annual.

★13212★
TAMPA ELECTRIC COMPANY - TECHNICAL REFERENCE CENTER (Energy)
702 N. Franklin St.   Phone: (813) 228-4547
Tampa, FL 33602   Patricia W. Boody, Tech.Libn.
Founded: 1982. **Staff:** Prof 1; Other 2. **Subjects:** Electric power generation, energy, environment, business and economics, management, data processing. **Holdings:** 1500 books; unbound periodicals; 2000 documents; 2500 microfiche; 680 computer manuals. **Subscriptions:** 450 journals and other serials; 15 newspapers. **Services:** Interlibrary loans; copying; SDI; center open to public. **Automated Operations:** Computerized cataloging, serials, and circulation. **Computerized Information Services:** DIALOG, The Source, Dun & Bradstreet Corporation. **Networks/Consortia:** Member of Tampa Bay Library Consortium. **Publications:** Information Resources Report, monthly - for internal distribution only.

★13213★
TAMPA GENERAL HOSPITAL - MEDICAL LIBRARY (Med)
Davis Islands   Phone: (813) 251-7328
Tampa, FL 33606   Loretta Holliday, Dir.
Founded: 1961. **Staff:** Prof 1; Other 1. **Subjects:** Medicine, otorhinolaryngology, pediatrics, obstetrics, gynecology, surgery, clinical medicine. **Special Collections:** Audio-Digest tapes on surgery, pediatrics, internal medicine, anesthesia, otolaryngology (750 tapes). **Holdings:** 1200 books; 1200 bound periodical volumes; 7 VF drawers of journals on microfiche. **Subscriptions:** 255 journals and other serials. **Services:** Interlibrary loans; copying; SDI; library open to public with authorization from administration. **Computerized Information Services:** MEDLINE. Performs searches on cost recovery basis. **Networks/Consortia:** Member of Tampa Bay Medical Library Network. **Publications:** TGH Medical Library Newsletter, quarterly - distributed to medical staff.

★13214★
TAMPA TRIBUNE & TAMPA TIMES - LIBRARY (Publ)
202 S. Parker St.   Phone: (813) 272-7665
Tampa, FL 33601   Louise N. LeGette, Chf.Libn.
Founded: 1895. **Staff:** Prof 8; Other 7. **Subjects:** Newspaper reference topics. **Holdings:** 1500 volumes; clippings; pamphlets; pictures; microfilm; reference books. **Services:** Library open to newspaper personnel only. **Staff:** Catherine Gess, Asst.Libn.

★13215★
TAMS ENGINEERS, ARCHITECTS & PLANNERS - LIBRARY (Sci-Tech)
655 Third Ave.   Phone: (212) 867-1777
New York, NY 10017
Founded: 1950. **Staff:** Prof 1. **Subjects:** Civil engineering, soil mechanics, water resources, traffic engineering, architecture, environmental planning, socioeconomics. **Holdings:** 6500 books; 300 bound periodical volumes; 3000 company reports; 3 VF drawers of pamphlets. **Subscriptions:** 200 journals and other serials. **Services:** Interlibrary loans; copying; library open to public by appointment.

TAMS-WITMARK ARCHIVES
See: Princeton University - William Seymour Theatre Collection

★13216★
TANDEM COMPUTERS, INC. - CORPORATE INFORMATION CENTER (Comp-Sci)
19333 Vallco Pkwy.   Phone: (408) 725-6000
Cupertino, CA 95014   Selma Zinker, Mgr., Lib.Serv.
Staff: Prof 3; Other 2. **Subjects:** Computer science, data processing, computer programming, marketing, business. **Holdings:** 4000 books; 1000 research reports; 200 microfiche; 500 technical reports. **Subscriptions:** 180 journals and other serials; 6 newspapers. **Services:** Interlibrary loans; center not open to public. **Automated Operations:** Computerized cataloging. **Computerized Information Services:** DIALOG, RLIN, The Source, Dow Jones News/Retrieval, OCLC, NEXIS, NewsNet. **Networks/Consortia:** Member of CLASS. **Staff:** Patty Bull, Bus.Libn.; Jane Differding, Ref.Libn.

TANGENT GROUP - HOMOSEXUAL INFORMATION CENTER
See: Homosexual Information Center - Tangent Group

TANNER MEMORIAL PHILOSOPHY LIBRARY
See: Stanford University

TANNER SCHOOL OF MANAGEMENT
See: Brigham Young University

TARLTON LAW LIBRARY
See: University of Texas, Austin - School of Law

★13217★
TARRANT COUNTY LAW LIBRARY (Law)
420 Courthouse   Phone: (817) 334-1481
Fort Worth, TX 76196   Frances Perry, Law Libn.
Founded: 1945. **Staff:** Prof 3; Other 2. **Subjects:** Law. **Holdings:** 27,000 books; 1050 bound periodical volumes; 580 cassette tapes. **Subscriptions:** 200 journals and other serials. **Services:** Interlibrary loans; copying (limited); library open to public for reference use only. **Special Indexes:** Index of Texas Law Review Articles.

TASKER SYSTEMS
See: Whittaker Corporation - Tasker Systems Division

TATE LABORATORY OF PHYSICS
See: University of Minnesota - Physics Library

★13218★
**TAUB (Ben) GENERAL HOSPITAL - DOCTOR'S MEDICAL LIBRARY (Med)*
1502 Taub Loop   Phone: (713) 791-7441
Houston, TX 77025   Angie Ortiz, Lib.Ck.
Founded: 1958. **Staff:** 1. **Subjects:** Medicine. **Holdings:** 1100 books; 110 bound periodical volumes; 12 VF drawers. **Subscriptions:** 110 journals and other serials; 8 newspapers. **Services:** Library not open to public. **Automated Operations:** Computerized cataloging and acquisitions.

TAUBMAN (Alfred) MEDICAL LIBRARY
See: University of Michigan - Alfred Taubman Medical Library

★13219★
TAUNTON STATE HOSPITAL - MEDICAL LIBRARY (Med)*
60 Hodges Ave.
Box 151   Phone: (617) 824-7551
Taunton, MA 02780
Staff: 1. **Subjects:** Psychiatry, psychology, medicine, social science. **Holdings:** 909 books; 1516 bound periodical volumes. **Subscriptions:** 81 journals and other serials; 10 newspapers. **Services:** Interlibrary loans; copying; library open to public for reference and overnight loan. **Networks/ Consortia:** Member of Southeastern Massachusetts Health Sciences Libraries (SEMCO).

TAX COURT OF CANADA
See: Canada - Tax Court of Canada

★13220★
TAX EXECUTIVES INSTITUTE, INC. - LIBRARY (Bus-Fin)
1300 N. 17th St., Suite 1300   Phone: (703) 522-3535
Arlington, VA 22209   Edward A. Sprague, Exec.Dir.
Founded: 1944. **Staff:** Prof 1; Other 1. **Subjects:** Taxation; tax - legislation, administration, management. **Holdings:** 750 books; 500 professional memoranda. **Subscriptions:** 15 journals and other serials. **Services:** Library open to TEI members and other tax professionals upon written request. **Publications:** Tax Executive (journal), quarterly - by subscription.

★13221★
TAX FOUNDATION - LIBRARY (Bus-Fin)
One Thomas Circle, N.W., Suite 500   Phone: (202) 328-4500
Washington, DC 20005   Marion Marshall, Libn.
Founded: 1937. **Staff:** Prof 1; Other 1. **Subjects:** Taxation, public finance, economics. **Special Collections:** Annual reports of the Secretary of the Treasury, 1852 to present; proceedings of the National Tax Association, 1907 to present; state tax studies. **Holdings:** 16,000 books; 85 VF drawers of clippings, documents and pamphlets. **Subscriptions:** 400 journals and other serials. **Services:** Interlibrary loans; copying; library open to public. **Publications:** Library Bulletin, monthly.

★13222★
TAYLOR (Bayard) MEMORIAL LIBRARY (Art)
216 E. State St.   Phone: (215) 444-2702
Kennett Square, PA 19348   Joseph A. Lordi, Dir.
Founded: 1895. **Staff:** Prof 1; Other 5. **Subjects:** Antiques, arts, social sciences, history, gardening. **Special Collections:** Harlan R. Cole Memorial Collection (reference collection on antiques); Bayard Taylor Collection (pre-1900 rare books); Pennsylvania Collection (local history); Society of Friends; Rare Books of the Union Library Company of Kennett Square (pre-1896); Botanica Collection of Trees, Shrubs and Wildflowers. **Holdings:** 40,000 books; 4 VF drawers of pamphlets, clippings, local history and maps. **Subscriptions:** 142 journals and other serials; 8 newspapers. **Services:** Interlibrary loans; copying; library open to public.

★13223★
TAYLOR BUSINESS INSTITUTE - LIBRARY (Bus-Fin)
One Penn Plaza   Phone: (212) 279-0510
New York, NY 10019   Roslyn Arnstein, Libn.
Founded: 1973. **Staff:** Prof 2. **Subjects:** Business administration, accounting, office management, secretarial studies, travel. **Holdings:** 3478 books; 13 VF drawers; 20 video cassettes. **Subscriptions:** 52 journals and other serials. **Services:** Library not open to public.

TAYLOR (David W.) NAVAL SHIP RESEARCH AND DEVELOPMENT CENTER
See: U.S. Navy - David W. Taylor Naval Ship Research and Development Center

TAYLOR (Edward P.) AUDIO-VISUAL CENTRE
See: Art Gallery of Ontario - Edward P. Taylor Audio-Visual Centre

TAYLOR (Edward P.) REFERENCE LIBRARY
See: Art Gallery of Ontario - Edward P. Taylor Reference Library

TAYLOR (Elizabeth Prewitt) MEMORIAL LIBRARY
See: Arkansas Arts Center - Elizabeth Prewitt Taylor Memorial Library

TAYLOR (Frederick W.) ARCHIVES
See: Hive Publishing Company - Management History Library

TAYLOR INSTRUMENT
See: Combustion Engineering, Inc.

TAYLOR (Ira J.) LIBRARY
See: Iliff School of Theology - Ira J. Taylor Library

★13224★
TAYLOR (Moses) HOSPITAL - LIBRARY (Med)
700 Quincy Ave.   Phone: (717) 969-4057
Scranton, PA 18411   Jo-Ann M. Babish, Dir., Lib.Serv.
Staff: Prof 1. **Subjects:** Medicine, health administration, nursing. **Holdings:** 1200 books; journals on microfilm. **Subscriptions:** 250 journals and other serials. **Services:** Interlibrary loans; copying; SDI; library open to public with restrictions. **Computerized Information Services:** DIALOG, MEDLARS. **Networks/Consortia:** Member of Health Information Library Network of Northeastern Pennsylvania. **Staff:** Belinda Carey, Lib.Asst.

TAYLOR MUSEUM LIBRARY
See: Colorado Springs Fine Arts Center - Reference Library and Taylor Museum Library

TAYLOR (Stanley) SOCIOLOGY READING ROOM
See: University of Alberta - Dept. of Sociology - Stanley Taylor Sociology Reading Room

TAYLOR (Abbot Vincent) LIBRARY
See: Belmont Abbey College - Abbot Vincent Taylor Library

★13225★
TAYLOR UNIVERSITY - AYRES ALUMNI MEMORIAL LIBRARY - SPECIAL COLLECTIONS (Rel-Theol)
                                           Phone: (317) 998-2751
Upland, IN 46989   David Dickey, Lib.Dir.
Staff: Prof 1. **Subjects:** Protestant theology. **Holdings:** 750 books. **Services:** Copying; library open to public. **Automated Operations:** Computerized cataloging. **Computerized Information Services:** DIALOG. Contact Person: Roger Phillips. **Networks/Consortia:** Member of INCOLSA.

★13226★
TCR SERVICE, INC. - COMMON LAW LIBRARY (Law)
One Prickly Pear Hill   Phone: (201) 461-7475
Croton-on-Hudson, NY 10520   Anne Dartnell, Supv.
Founded: 1967. **Staff:** Prof 1; Other 14. **Subjects:** Trademarks - registered and unregistered, active and inactive; patents; drugs; cosmetics; clothing; foods; transportation; chemicals; electronics. **Special Collections:** Thomas Register Catalog (60,000 trademarks). **Holdings:** 200 reels of microfilm; microfiche; Official Gazette of U.S. Patent Office, 1892 to present. **Subscriptions:** 269 journals and other serials. **Services:** Trademark research; depository for trademark information; library not open to public. **Publications:** Trademark Alert (pamphlet), weekly.

★13227★
TEACHERS COLLEGE - MILBANK MEMORIAL LIBRARY (Educ)
Columbia University
Box 307   Phone: (212) 678-3494
New York, NY 10027   Jane P. Franck, Dir.
Founded: 1887. **Staff:** Prof 29; Other 20. **Subjects:** Education, psychology, speech pathology and audiology, nursing, communications, computers, nutrition and related subjects. **Special Collections:** Harvey Darton Collection of English Children's Books before 1850; Annie E. Moore Collection of Illustrated Children's Books (18th and 19th centuries); Children's Village; Papers of Superintendents and Chancellors; rare education books of 15th century; historical manuscript collections in education, including Adelaide Nutting History of Nursing Collection; U.S. and foreign textbooks (K-12); Board of Education of the City of New York records; National Council of Social Studies records; National Kindergarten Association records; New York Juvenile Asylum records (300 feet); Nursing Archives (300 feet); Teachers College Archives. **Holdings:** 402,272 volumes; 254,269 microforms; 9492 AV and nonprint items; 450 cubic feet of manuscript material; 6467 book titles in microform. **Subscriptions:** 1858 journals and other serials. **Services:** Interlibrary loans (fee); copying; library open to public with special permits. **Computerized Information Services:** DIALOG, BRS, OCLC, RLIN. **Networks/Consortia:** Member of RLG; New York State Interlibrary Loan Network (NYSILL). **Publications:** Circulation and Borrowing Information; ILL Guide; Online Search Services; Special Collections; Photocopy Services; Current Awareness Series; Resource Center; Bulletin of New Titles. **Staff:** Susan Heintzelman, Asst.Dir., Coll.; Kay E. Vandergrift, Asst.Dir., Serv.; Andrew Sankowski, Hd., Rsrc.Ctr.; Maureen Horgan, Personnel/Fin.Coord.; Roger Wyatt, Hd., Lrng.Tech.Serv.; David Ment, Hd., Spec.Coll.; Heidi Hoerman, Hd., Tech.Sys. & Bibliog; Kathleen Murphy, Hd., Access Serv.; Larry Klein, Mss.Cur.; Fleurin Eshghi, Electronic Curric.Sys.; Elizabeth Coello, Ser.Cat.; Mary Rivera, Hd., Bibliog.Rec.Sect.; Carol Maus, Ref.Libn.; Jeanette

Perrussel, Hd., Cat. Maintenance; Vera Redl, Ref.Libn.; Katherine Sheng, Ref.Libn.; Roberta MacArthur, Hd., Pers./Microform Ctr.David Webster, Cons.; Mary Donovan, Pub.Serv.Libn.

★13228★
TEACHERS OF ENGLISH TO SPEAKERS OF OTHER LANGUAGES - TESOL LENDING LIBRARY (Educ)
201 D.C. Transit Bldg.
Georgetown University
Washington, DC 20057
Phone: (202) 625-4569
Ahmad Fassihian, Resource Spec.
Staff: 1. **Subjects:** English as a second language, linguistics, education, anthropology, bilingual education, culture. **Special Collections:** English as a Second Language texts (1500). **Holdings:** 3000 books. **Subscriptions:** 20 journals and other serials; 5 newspapers. **Services:** Interlibrary loans; library open to public by appointment for reference use. **Automated Operations:** Computerized cataloging and acquisitions.

★13229★
TEACHERS INSURANCE AND ANNUITY ASSOCIATION OF AMERICA - BUSINESS LIBRARY (Bus-Fin)
730 Third Ave.
New York, NY 10017
Phone: (212) 490-9000
Kathleen Kelleher, Libn.
Founded: 1959. **Staff:** Prof 2; Other 3. **Subjects:** Insurance, pensions and annuities, law, investment, higher education, old age. **Special Collections:** Carnegie Foundation reports. **Holdings:** 7500 books; 188 reels of microfilm; 45 VF drawers. **Subscriptions:** 385 journals and other serials; 8 newspapers. **Services:** Interlibrary loans; library open to SLA members by appointment only. **Automated Operations:** Computerized serials. **Computerized Information Services:** DIALOG. **Staff:** Mary-Lynne Bancone, Asst.Libn.

TEACHOUT-PRICE MEMORIAL LIBRARY
See: Hiram College

★13230★
TEAM FOUR INC. - LIBRARY (Plan)
14 N. Newstead Ave.
St. Louis, MO 63108
Phone: (314) 533-2200
Andrea Towell, Libn.
Staff: Prof 1; Other 1. **Subjects:** Planning, urban planning, master plans, architecture, landscape architecture. **Holdings:** 3300 books; 30 bound periodical volumes; 100 reports. **Subscriptions:** 30 journals and other serials; 5 newspapers. **Services:** Copying; library open to public with permission.

TEAMSTERS UNION
See: International Brotherhood of Teamsters, Chauffeurs, Warehousemen and Helpers of America

★13231★
TEANECK PUBLIC LIBRARY - ORAL AND LOCAL HISTORY PROJECT (Hist)
840 Teaneck Rd.
Teaneck, NJ 07666
Phone: (201) 837-4171
Hilda Lipkin, Dir.
Staff: Prof 13; Other 15. **Subjects:** Local history, early families, Jewish community, black community. **Holdings:** 100 cassettes; photographs; 4 notebooks; 1000 index cards. **Services:** Copying; collection open to public by appointment.

TEBEAU (Charlton W.) LIBRARY OF FLORIDA HISTORY
See: Historical Association of Southern Florida - Charlton W. Tebeau Library of Florida History

★13232★
TECHNIC INC. - LIBRARY (Sci-Tech)
1 Spectacle St.
Providence, RI 02910
Phone: (401) 781-6100
James V. Elliott, Jr., Pub.Rel.Off.
Staff: 1. **Subjects:** Electrochemistry, surface finishing, metallurgy, electronics, manufacturing, jewelry. **Special Collections:** Precious metals. **Holdings:** 250 shelves of books and bound periodical volumes. **Subscriptions:** 75 journals and other serials; 5 newspapers. **Services:** Copying; library open to public with restrictions. **Publications:** TechnicNews (newsletter).

TECHNICAL ASSISTANCE INFORMATION CLEARING HOUSE
See: American Council of Voluntary Agencies for Foreign Service, Inc.

★13233★
TECHNICAL ASSOCIATION OF THE PULP AND PAPER INDUSTRY - LIBRARY (Sci-Tech)
Box 105113
Atlanta, GA 30348
Phone: (404) 394-6130
Elizabeth A. Bibby, Info.Rsrc.Adm.
Founded: 1915. **Staff:** Prof 1. **Subjects:** Pulp, paper and related subjects. **Holdings:** 2000 books; 1500 bound periodical volumes. **Subscriptions:** 100

journals and other serials. **Services:** Copying; technical inquiries; library open to public. **Automated Operations:** Computerized serials. **Computerized Information Services:** DIALOG.

★13234★
TECHNICAL COLLEGE OF ALAMANCE - TECHNICAL LIBRARY (Sci-Tech)
Box 623
Haw River, NC 27265
Phone: (919) 578-2002
Founded: 1959. **Staff:** Prof 4; Other 3. **Subjects:** Applied arts, business and engineering technology, health and mechanical occupations. **Holdings:** 26,000 books; 2918 microforms. **Subscriptions:** 258 journals and other serials. **Services:** Interlibrary loans; copying; library open to public. **Networks/Consortia:** Member of Central Piedmont Consortium of Community Colleges and Technical Institutes - LRC Subsection; Area Health Consortium for Sharing Health Information.

TECHNICAL LIBRARY FOR TROPICAL AND HURRICANE METEOROLOGY
See: U.S. Natl. Oceanic & Atmospheric Administration - Coral Gables Library

★13235★
TECHNICAL UNIVERSITY OF NOVA SCOTIA - LIBRARY (Sci-Tech)
Barrington & Bishop St.
P.O. Box 1000
Halifax, NS, Canada B3J 2X4
Phone: (902) 429-8300
Mohammad Riaz Hussain, Libn.
Founded: 1949. **Staff:** Prof 4; Other 11. **Subjects:** Engineering - civil, chemical, mechanical, mineral, electrical, industrial; geology; mathematics; architecture. **Special Collections:** Fletcher Memorial Collection (geology and mining); Foulis Collection (environmental sciences). **Holdings:** 90,000 books and bound periodical volumes; 70,000 microfiche; 12,000 slides; 100 video cassettes. **Subscriptions:** 1250 journals and other serials. **Services:** Interlibrary loans; copying; microfilming; SDI; library open to public. **Computerized Information Services:** DIALOG, SDC, CAN/OLE, QL Systems. **Networks/Consortia:** Member of Association of Atlantic Universities Librarians' Council. **Publications:** Library Holdings of Serial Publications, annual. **Staff:** Tahira Hussain, Sr.Libn.; Sandra Scott, Pub.Serv.; Peggy D'Orsay, Tech.Serv.Libn.

★13236★
TECHNICON DATA SYSTEMS - TECHNICAL LIBRARY (Med; Comp Sci)
3255-1 Scott Blvd.
Santa Clara, CA 95051
Phone: (408) 727-9400
Margaret Yesso Watson, Libn.
Founded: 1982. **Staff:** Prof 1. **Subjects:** Hospital information systems, physicians and computers. **Special Collections:** Federal Information Processing Standards (FIPS) publications (complete set). **Holdings:** 200 books; 50 other cataloged items. **Subscriptions:** 63 journals and other serials. **Services:** Interlibrary loans; copying; SDI; library open to public by appointment. **Computerized Information Services:** DIALOG.

★13237★
TECHNICON INSTRUMENTS CORPORATION - LIBRARY (Med; Sci-Tech)
511 Benedict Ave.
Tarrytown, NY 10591
Phone: (914) 681-2338
Gitta Benglas, Libn.
Founded: 1962. **Staff:** Prof 1; Other 1. **Subjects:** Medicine, chemistry, computer science. **Holdings:** 15,000 books; archives of laboratory notebooks; dissertations; reports; microfilm; microfiche; 30 VF drawers; 200 audiotapes. **Subscriptions:** 290 journals and other serials. **Services:** Interlibrary loans; library not open to public. **Automated Operations:** Computerized acquisitions. **Computerized Information Services:** DIALOG.

★13238★
TECHNOLOGY APPLICATIONS, INC. - TECHNICAL LIBRARY (Sci-Tech)
5201 Leesburg Pike
Falls Church, VA 22041
Phone: (703) 931-2000
Frances M. Oliver, Tech.Libn.
Founded: 1984. **Staff:** Prof 1. **Subjects:** Naval engineering, automated information systems, industrial engineering, facilities management, logistics systems, civil engineering. **Holdings:** 253 books; 108 bound periodical volumes; 26 unbound reports. **Subscriptions:** 109 journals and other serials. **Services:** Interlibrary loans; library not open to public. **Computerized Information Services:** DIALOG; internal database.

★13239★
TECHNOLOGY & ECONOMICS, INC. - LIBRARY
2225 Massachusetts Ave.
Cambridge, MA 02140
Defunct

★13240★

TECHNOMIC INFORMATION SERVICES (Bus-Fin; Sci-Tech)
One N. Wacker Dr.   Phone: (312) 346-5900
Chicago, IL 60606   Robert W. Depke, II, Mgr., Info.Serv.
Founded: 1976. **Staff:** Prof 2; Other 2. **Subjects:** Management, agriculture, electronics, food/food service, packaging, telecommunications. **Special Collections:** Food Service Resource Center (500 books; 100 periodicals; 60 VF drawers). **Holdings:** 1500 books; 60 VF drawers of clippings. **Subscriptions:** 400 journals and other serials; 20 newspapers. **Services:** Interlibrary loans; copying; services open to public with approval. **Computerized Information Services:** DIALOG, NEXIS, Dow Jones News/ Retrieval, Dun & Bradstreet Corporation; Restaurant Concepts, Acquisition Database (internal databases). Performs searches on cost recovery basis. Contact Person: Robert Depke. **Networks/Consortia:** Member of Chicago Library System. **Publications:** TRA Foodservice Abstracts, monthly - by subscription; Restaurant Information Service (updates), monthly; Dynamics of the Chain Restaurant Market, annual. **Staff:** Ruth Corn, Info.Spec.

★13241★

TECHNOMIC PUBLISHING CO., INC. (TPC) - BUSINESS LIBRARY (Bus-Fin; Sci-Tech)
851 New Holland Ave.
Box 3535
Lancaster, PA 17604   Richard Dunn, Lib.Dir.
Staff: Prof 1. **Subjects:** Plastics, resins and urethane foam technology; health care; materials engineering. **Holdings:** 750 books; 40 bound periodical volumes. **Subscriptions:** 16 journals and other serials. **Services:** Library not open to public. **Formerly:** Located in Westport, CT.

★13242★

TECK MINING GROUP LTD. - LIBRARY (Sci-Tech)
1199 W. Hastings St.
Vancouver, BC, Canada V6E 2K5   Phone: (604) 687-1117
                                         Elizabeth Watson
Staff: Prof 1; Other 1. **Subjects:** Mining, geology. **Holdings:** 3000 books; 500 bound periodical volumes; 500 maps; 300 newspaper clippings. **Subscriptions:** 220 journals and other serials; 50 newspapers. **Services:** Library not open to public.

TEDESCHI (Cesare George) LIBRARY
See: Framingham Union Hospital - Cesare George Tedeschi Library

TEDROW TRANSPORTATION COLLECTION
See: University of Missouri, Kansas City

★13243★

TEHAMA COUNTY LAW LIBRARY (Law)
Court House, Rm. 20
Red Bluff, CA 96080   Jill Miller, Lib.Ck.
Staff: 1. **Subjects:** Law. **Holdings:** 8925 books; 200 bound periodical volumes; codes (annotated); reports and reporters; decennials; digests; U.S. Supreme Court reports. **Subscriptions:** 11 journals and other serials. **Services:** Library open to public.

★13244★

TEKTRONIX, INC. - CORPORATE LIBRARY (Sci-Tech; Comp Sci)
Box 500, MS 50-210   Phone: (503) 627-5388
Beaverton, OR 97077   Julianne Williams, Lib.Mgr.
Founded: 1958. **Staff:** Prof 1; Other 3. **Subjects:** Electronics, solid state physics, analytical chemistry, management, information display, computers, instrumentation, electron optics, materials science. **Holdings:** 10,000 books. **Subscriptions:** 400 journals and other serials. **Services:** Interlibrary loans; copying; library open to public by appointment only. **Computerized Information Services:** DIALOG, SDC. **Networks/Consortia:** Member of Washington County Cooperative Library Services.

★13245★

TEKTRONIX, INC. - WALKER ROAD BRANCH LIBRARY (Comp Sci)
MS 94-501
Box 4600
Beaverton, OR 97075   Phone: (503) 629-1062
                                         Yan Y. Soucie, Br.Libn.
Founded: 1980. **Staff:** Prof 1. **Subjects:** Computers, electronics, microprocessors, software engineering. **Holdings:** 1600 books. **Subscriptions:** 116 journals and other serials. **Services:** Interlibrary loans; library not open to public. **Computerized Information Services:** DIALOG. Performs searches both free of charge and on cost recovery basis. **Networks/Consortia:** Member of Washington County Cooperative Library Services.

★13246★

TEKTRONIX, INC. - WILSONVILLE BRANCH LIBRARY (Comp Sci)
Box 1000   Phone: (503) 685-3986
Wilsonville, OR 97070   Linda K. Appel, Br.Libn.
Staff: Prof 1; Other I. **Subjects:** Computer programming and graphics, electronics, business and management. **Holdings:** 1500 books; 250 literature searches. **Subscriptions:** 75 journals and other serials; 7 newspapers. **Services:** Interlibrary loans; copying; SDI; library open to public by appointment. **Computerized Information Services:** DIALOG, SDC. **Networks/Consortia:** Member of Washington County Cooperative Library Services; CLASS; WLN. **Publications:** Wilsonville Library Bulletin, biweekly - for internal distribution only. **Formerly:** Located in Beaverton, OR.

★13247★

TEL-MED HEALTH INFORMATION SERVICE (Med)
Fairview-Southdale Hospital
6401 France Ave. S.   Phone: (612) 924-5959
Minneapolis, MN 55435   Glad Schlossman, Dir.
Staff: 15. **Subjects:** Cancer; dental health; chemical dependency; eye, ear, nose and throat problems; child care; first aid; diseases - heart, venereal. **Holdings:** 288 tapes. **Services:** Service open to public. **Computerized Information Services:** Online systems. **Publications:** Listing of Tapes. **Remarks:** This is a telephone information service sponsored by the medical staffs of the Fairview Community Hospitals.

★13248★

TELE-UNIVERSITE - CENTRE DE DOCUMENTATION (Educ)
214, Ave. St-Sacrement   Phone: (418) 657-2262
Quebec, PQ, Canada G1N 4M6   Claude Tousignant, Hd.Libn.
Staff: Prof 2; Other 3. **Subjects:** Extension education, including education for adults and by correspondence; educational technology. **Holdings:** 8000 volumes; 139 films; 164 videotapes; 214 audiotapes; 7 records; 1105 transparencies; 23 dioramas; 75 educational games. **Subscriptions:** 240 journals and other serials; 5 newspapers. **Services:** Interlibrary loans; center open to public with restrictions. **Automated Operations:** Computerized cataloging. **Computerized Information Services:** DIALOG, BADADUQ. **Publications:** Les Nouveautes (a list of new acquisitions and abstracts of periodicals). **Staff:** Reine Belanger, Documentalist.

★13249★

TELECOM CANADA - INFORMATION RESOURCE CENTRE (Bus-Fin)
410 Laurier Ave., W.   Phone: (613) 560-3953
Ottawa, ON, Canada K1P 6H5   Joan Chinkiwsky, Mgr.
Founded: 1978. **Staff:** Prof 1; Other 2. **Subjects:** Telecommunications, telephone industry, business, marketing. **Holdings:** 1000 books. **Subscriptions:** 250 journals and other serials. **Services:** Interlibrary loans; center not open to public. **Automated Operations:** Computerized acquisitions and circulation. **Computerized Information Services:** SDC, DIALOG, QL Systems, CAN/OLE, BRS, Info Globe; internal databases. **Publications:** Acquisition lists, quarterly - for internal distribution only; Periodicals, annual - both annotated. **Formerly:** TransCanada Telephone System.

TELECOMMUNICATIONS INFORMATION CENTER
See: George Washington University

★13250★

TELEDYNE BROWN ENGINEERING - TECHNICAL LIBRARY (Sci-Tech)*
Cummings Research Pk.
300 Sparkman Dr. N.W.   Phone: (205) 532-1433
Huntsville, AL 35807   Peggy Shelton, Chf.Libn.
Founded: 1962. **Staff:** Prof 1; Other 2. **Subjects:** Research and development. **Holdings:** Figures not available for books; 200 bound periodical volumes; 50,000 documents; military specifications and standards; 3000 microfiche. **Subscriptions:** 200 journals and other serials. **Services:** Interlibrary loans; library not open to public. **Automated Operations:** Computerized circulation. **Staff:** Jettye McGehee, Circ.Libn.; Helga Williams, Adm.Libn.

★13251★

TELEDYNE CAE CORPORATION - ENGINEERING LIBRARY (Sci-Tech)
1330 Laskey Rd.   Phone: (419) 470-3027
Toledo, OH 43612   Marlene S. Dowdell, Dept.Hd., Data Mgt.
Founded: 1970. **Staff:** Prof 2. **Subjects:** Aeronautical engineering, aircraft gas turbine engines, jet engines, aerospace, metallurgy. **Special Collections:** National Advisory Committee for Aeronautics (NACA) Technical Memoranda and Technical Notes, 1920 to present. **Holdings:** 2900 books; 57 VF cabinets of reports; 2500 microfiche. **Subscriptions:** 100 journals and other serials. **Services:** Interlibrary loans; library not open to public. **Automated Operations:** Computerized cataloging and circulation. **Computerized**

Information Services: DIALOG, NASA/RECON, DTIC. **Networks/Consortia:** Ohio-Kentucky Cooperating Libraries - Union List of Serials. **Publications:** Acquisitions Bulletin, bimonthly - for internal distribution only. **Staff:** Lee Ann Hamel, Libn.

★13252★
TELEDYNE ENERGY SYSTEMS - LIBRARY (Energy)
110 W. Timonium Rd.   Phone: (301) 252-8220
Timonium, MD 21093   Cathy Layne, Libn.
Founded: 1976. **Staff:** Prof 1. **Subjects:** Energy conversion, aerospace engineering. **Holdings:** 2400 books; 101,000 technical reports. **Subscriptions:** 80 journals and other serials. **Services:** Interlibrary loans; copying; SDI; library open to public with restrictions. **Automated Operations:** Computerized cataloging. **Computerized Information Services:** DTIC.

★13253★
TELEDYNE ENGINEERING SERVICES - INFORMATION CENTER (Sci-Tech)
130 Second Ave.   Phone: (617) 890-3350
Waltham, MA 02254   Susan Fingerman, Mgr., Info.Serv.
Staff: Prof 1; Other 1. **Subjects:** Engineering - mechanical, civil; materials; stress analysis. **Holdings:** 1500 books; 2000 other cataloged items. **Subscriptions:** 84 journals and other serials. **Services:** Copying; SDI; center open to public with approval of manager. **Automated Operations:** Computerized cataloging. **Computerized Information Services:** OCLC, DIALOG. **Networks/Consortia:** Member of NELINET. **Publications:** Recent Acquisitions, bimonthly; Reports Received, irregular.

★13254★
TELEDYNE ISOTOPES - BUSINESS LIBRARY (Sci-Tech)
50 Vanburen Ave.   Phone: (201) 664-7070
Westwood, NJ 07675   Helen Principe, Res.Libn./Adm.Asst.
Founded: 1957. **Staff:** 2. **Subjects:** Oil recovery/TeleTrace, radiochemistry, health physics, waste disposal, thermoluminescent dosimetry, carbon, nuclear instruments, geochemistry, geology. **Special Collections:** Bound volumes of Science and Nature magazines. **Holdings:** Figures not available. **Subscriptions:** 55 journals and other serials. **Services:** Interlibrary loans, library open to public by appointment. **Automated Operations:** Computerized circulation. **Computerized Information Services:** Information on Demand (IOD). Performs free searches. **Staff:** Cora Starr, Circ.

★13255★
TELEDYNE RYAN AERONAUTICAL - TECHNICAL INFORMATION SERVICES (Sci-Tech)
2701 N. Harbor Dr.   Phone: (619) 291-7311
San Diego, CA 92101   William E. Ebner, Chf.
Founded: 1943. **Staff:** Prof 1; Other 2. **Subjects:** Aerodynamics, avionics, electronics. **Holdings:** 4000 books; 600 bound periodical volumes; 2400 other cataloged items; 120,000 Defense Documentation Center Technical Reports; 40,000 NASA Documentation items. **Subscriptions:** 150 journals and other serials. **Services:** Interlibrary loans; copying; SDI; services open to public for reference use only by appointment. **Computerized Information Services:** DIALOG. **Publications:** Library Bulletin, irregular - for internal distribution only.

★13256★
TELEDYNE SYSTEMS COMPANY - TECHNICAL LIBRARY (Comp Sci)
19601 Nordhoff St.   Phone: (818) 886-2211
Northridge, CA 91324   Linda Zazueta, Tech.Libn.
Staff: 1. **Subjects:** Communication systems, computers, microprocessors, digital signal processing. **Holdings:** 1000 books; 300 bound periodical volumes; 500 technical reports. **Subscriptions:** 63 journals and other serials. **Services:** Interlibrary loans; copying; library open to public with government clearance. **Special Catalogs:** Technical reports catalog; journal catalog (card and computer printout).

★13257★
TELEDYNE WATER PIK - INFORMATION CENTER
1730 E. Prospect St.
Fort Collins, CO 80553
Defunct

★13258★
TELEMEDIA, INC. - INFORMATION CENTER (Educ)
310 S. Michigan Ave.   Phone: (312) 987-4068
Chicago, IL 60604   Jane Gibson, Hd.
Staff: Prof 2. **Subjects:** Education-training, language instruction, English as a second language, petroleum industry, aviation, geography. **Holdings:** 1700 books; 500 military documents; 1000 inhouse publications; 14 VF drawers of corporate annual reports; 11 VF drawers; 2100 unbound periodicals.

Subscriptions: 72 journals and other serials; 5 newspapers. **Services:** Center not open to public. **Automated Operations:** Computerized cataloging. **Computerized Information Services:** DIALOG. **Staff:** Frank Drake, Info.Spec.

TELESAT CANADA
See: Canada - Telesat Canada

★13259★
TELEVISION INFORMATION OFFICE OF THE NATIONAL ASSOCIATION OF BROADCASTERS - RESEARCH SERVICES (Info Sci)†
745 Fifth Ave., 17th Fl.   Phone: (212) 759-6800
New York, NY 10151   James Poteat, Mgr., Res.Serv.
Founded: 1959. **Staff:** Prof 2; Other 6. **Subjects:** Television (except technical aspects). **Holdings:** 4500 books; 650 bound periodical volumes; 155 vertical files. **Subscriptions:** 265 journals and other serials; 10 newspapers. **Services:** Interlibrary loans; copying; services open to public by appointment only. **Publications:** Bibliography series. **Staff:** Leslie Slocum .

★13260★
TELSHE YESHIVA - RABBI A.N. SCHWARTZ LIBRARY (Rel-Theol)
28400 Euclid Ave.   Phone: (216) 943-5300
Wickliffe, OH 44092   Rabbi Binyomin Grunwald, Hd.Libn.
Founded: 1945. **Staff:** Prof 7; Other 2. **Subjects:** Talmud, Pentateuch, Jewish ethics and philosophy, Jewish law, Jewish history, Kabala, homiletics, Midrash. **Special Collections:** Hagaon Reb Eliezer Silver Collection; rare Sepharadic commentaries and Responsa; early printed volumes of Biblical commentaries (1500); Rabbi Elazari Collection; Rabbi Abramowitz Collection; Rabbi Schiff Library; Rabbi Levitan Collection. **Holdings:** 18,000 books; 1200 separate periodicals; 500 dissertations; 50 school publications; 25 manuscripts. **Subscriptions:** 10 journals and other serials. **Services:** Interlibrary loans; copying; library open to public but a security deposit is required. **Publications:** Kol Hayeshiva, quarterly; Pe'er Mordechai, annual; Pri Etz Chaim, annual. **Remarks:** A section of this library has been named the Rabbi Neuhaus Library. **Formerly:** Otzer Hasforim of Telshe Yeshiva.

★13261★
TEMPLE ADATH ISRAEL - RUBEN LIBRARY (Rel-Theol)
Old Lancaster Rd. & Highland Ave.   Phone: (215) 664-5150
Merion, PA 19066   Joan Furey, Libn.
Founded: 1955. **Staff:** Prof 1. **Subjects:** Judaica. **Holdings:** 5000 books; 8 drawers of clippings; 100 filmstrips. **Services:** Interlibrary loans; library open to area college students or by member sponsorship.

★13262★
TEMPLE AHAVATH SHOLOM - RABBI A. ALAN STEINBACH LIBRARY
1010 Ave. M
Brooklyn, NY 11230
Founded: 1938. **Subjects:** Jewish ethics, history, music; comparative religion; biography. **Holdings:** 4500 books; Rabbi Steinbach's manuscripts; Jewish antiquities. **Remarks:** Presently inactive.

★13263★
TEMPLE BETH EL - BILLIE DAVIS RODENBERG MEMORIAL LIBRARY (Rel-Theol)
1351 S. 14th Ave.   Phone: (305) 920-8225
Hollywood, FL 33020   Roslyn Kurland, Libn.
Staff: Prof 1; Other 4. **Subjects:** Judaica. **Holdings:** 6500 volumes. **Subscriptions:** 25 journals and other serials; 6 newspapers. **Services:** Interlibrary loans; copying; library open to public for reference use only.

★13264★
TEMPLE BETH EL - BUDDY BERMAN MEMORIAL LIBRARY (Rel-Theol)*
Broadway & Locust Ave.   Phone: (516) 569-2700
Cedarhurst, NY 11516   Mirel Touger, Libn.
Founded: 1937. **Staff:** Prof 1. **Subjects:** Judaica, Jewish history, theology. **Special Collections:** Cantorial Collection. **Holdings:** 5500 books. **Subscriptions:** 27 journals and other serials. **Services:** Copying; library open to public with restrictions.

★13265★
TEMPLE BETH-EL OF GREAT NECK - ARNOLD & MARIE SCHWARTZ LIBRARY (Rel-Theol)
5 Old Mill Rd.   Phone: (516) 487-0900
Great Neck, NY 11023   Linda Insler, Libn.
Founded: 1950. **Staff:** Prof 1. **Subjects:** Judaica - history, Holocaust, literature, biography; Israel. **Special Collections:** Children's collection. **Holdings:** 8000 books; records; reference books. **Subscriptions:** 25 journals and other serials. **Services:** Interlibrary loans; library open to students enrolled

in adult education at the temple and all congregants.

★13266★
TEMPLE BETH EL OF GREATER BUFFALO - LIBRARY (Rel-Theol)
2368 Eggert Rd.   Phone: (716) 836-3762
Tonawanda, NY 14150   Sandra Freed Gralnick, Libn.
Founded: 1920. **Staff:** Prof 1; Other 3. **Subjects:** Judaica. **Special Collections:** Samuel S. Luokin Memorial Music Reference Library; reference collection on Jewish art; large print books; children's collection; Holocaust collection. **Holdings:** 5000 books. **Services:** Library open to congregation, religious school and community.

★13267★
TEMPLE BETH EL - LIBRARY (Rel-Theol)†
225 E. Seventh St.   Phone: (201) 756-2333
Plainfield, NJ 07060   Irving Olian, Libn.
Founded: 1966. **Staff:** Prof 1; Other 1. **Subjects:** Judaica and Hebraica - juvenile and adult. **Holdings:** 3500 books. **Services:** Copying; library open to public.

★13268★
TEMPLE BETH EL - LIBRARY (Rel-Theol)
139 Winton Rd., S.   Phone: (716) 473-1770
Rochester, NY 14610   Anne Kirshenbaum, Libn.
Founded: 1946. **Staff:** Prof 1; Other 1. **Subjects:** Judaica - religion, philosophy, social science, history, art, literature, language, fiction, biography for adults and juveniles. **Holdings:** 5974 books; 7 file drawers of pamphlets and clippings. **Subscriptions:** 32 journals and other serials. **Services:** Interlibrary loans; library open to public with special permission.

★13269★
TEMPLE BETH EL - MAX & ANN GOLDBERG LIBRARY (Rel-Theol)
809 11th Ave., S.   Phone: (701) 232-0441
Fargo, ND 58103   Susan Plambeck, Libn.
Founded: 1953. **Staff:** 1. **Subjects:** Judaica, comparative religion. **Holdings:** 1500 books. **Services:** Library open to public.

★13270★
TEMPLE BETH EL - PRENTIS MEMORIAL LIBRARY (Rel-Theol)
7400 Telegraph Rd.   Phone: (313) 851-1100
Birmingham, MI 48010   Marilyn R. Brenner, Libn.
Founded: 1878. **Staff:** Prof 1. **Subjects:** Judaica, Christianity, philosophy, the arts, sociology, archeology, Bible, Jewish history, Jewish Americana. **Special Collections:** Leonard N. Simons Collection of rare Judaica; Irving I. Katz Collection of Jewish Americana. **Holdings:** 15,000 books; AV items; recordings; pamphlets. **Subscriptions:** 65 journals and other serials. **Services:** Copying; library open to public with restrictions.

★13271★
TEMPLE BETH-EL - WILLIAM G. BRAUDE LIBRARY (Rel-Theol)
70 Orchard Ave.   Phone: (401) 331-6070
Providence, RI 02906   Allan Metz, Libn.
Founded: 1894. **Staff:** Prof 1. **Subjects:** Judaica, Hebraica, Yiddish, Biblical studies, Holocaust, philosophy, folklore, music, rabbinics, anti-Semitism. **Special Collections:** Englander Collection. **Holdings:** 25,000 books; 258 bound periodical volumes; 432 pamphlets; clippings; programs of Rhode Island Jewish interest; Yiddish books; Hebrew books. **Subscriptions:** 73 journals and other serials; 10 newspapers. **Services:** Interlibrary loans; library open to public with deposit.

★13272★
TEMPLE BETH-EL - ZISKIND MEMORIAL LIBRARY (Rel-Theol)
385 High St.   Phone: (617) 674-3529
Fall River, MA 02720   Ida C. Pollock, Libn.
Staff: 1. **Subjects:** English Judaica. **Holdings:** 6000 books and bound periodical volumes; 200 phonograph records; 300 pamphlets and clippings. **Subscriptions:** 35 journals and other serials. **Services:** Library open to public.

★13273★
TEMPLE BETH ISRAEL - LIBRARY (Rel-Theol)*
3310 N. 10th Ave.   Phone: (601) 264-4428
Phoenix, AZ 85013   Mrs. Elliot Tempkin, Libn.
Staff: Prof 1. **Subjects:** Jewish history, Bible, literature, rabbinics, biography, art and music. **Special Collections:** Judaica Music Library (245 phonograph records, tapes and cassettes). **Holdings:** 16,221 books; 26 VF drawers of pamphlets, clippings and maps; 6 boxes of Temple archives. **Subscriptions:** 72 journals and other serials. **Services:** Interlibrary loans; copying; library open to public.

★13274★
TEMPLE BETH JOSEPH - ROSE BASLOE LIBRARY (Rel-Theol)
North Prospect St.   Phone: (315) 866-4270
Herkimer, NY 13350
Founded: 1957. **Subjects:** Judaica. **Holdings:** 2000 books. **Services:** Library open to public.

★13275★
TEMPLE BETH SHOLOM - HERBERT GOLDBERG MEMORIAL LIBRARY (Rel-Theol)†
Green St. & White Horse Pike
Haddon Heights, NJ 08035   Laura Olshan, Libn.
Staff: Prof 1. **Subjects:** Judaica. **Holdings:** 3000 books. **Subscriptions:** 12 journals and other serials.

★13276★
TEMPLE BETH SHOLOM - LIBRARY (Rel-Theol)
4144 Chase Ave.   Phone: (305) 538-7231
Miami Beach, FL 33140   Celia R. Huber, Libn.
Staff: Prof 1; Other 4. **Subjects:** Judaica (adult and juvenile), rabbinics. **Holdings:** 5000 books. **Subscriptions:** 60 journals and other serials. **Services:** Interlibrary loans; copying; library open to public with restrictions.

★13277★
TEMPLE BETH ZION - LIBRARY (Rel-Theol)
805 Delaware Ave.   Phone: (716) 886-7151
Buffalo, NY 14209   Donna J. Davidoff, Hd.Libn.
Founded: 1915. **Staff:** Prof 1. **Subjects:** Jewish religion, history, literature, art. **Special Collections:** Hasidism; Jewish mysticism; American Jewish history. **Holdings:** 11,500 books; 250 filmstrips and slides; 180 records and cassettes; archives. **Subscriptions:** 35 journals and other serials. **Services:** Interlibrary loans; library open to public. **Publications:** Lest We Forget: A Selected Annotated List of Books on the Holocaust; American Jewish Odyssey (annotated bibliography of the Jewish experience in America, as reflected in the library holdings); Jewish Children's Literature (annotated bibliography of books on Judaism and Jewish history for children up to age 14); Books on the Holocaust (list of library's holdings); Basic List for a Jewish Home Library.

★13278★
TEMPLE B'NAI ISRAEL - LASKER MEMORIAL LIBRARY (Rel-Theol)
3006 Ave. O   Phone: (409) 765-5796
Galveston, TX 77550   Mrs. Sidney R. Kay
Founded: 1956. **Staff:** 3. **Subjects:** Judaism, Jewish history, biblical history, Bible commentaries. **Holdings:** 2000 books. **Subscriptions:** 15 journals and other serials. **Services:** Library open to public. **Staff:** Sophie Nussenblatt; Rabbi Alan Greenbaum .

★13279★
TEMPLE B'RITH KODESH - LIBRARY (Rel-Theol)
2131 Elmwood Ave.   Phone: (716) 244-7060
Rochester, NY 14618   Bertha Cravets, Libn.
Staff: Prof 1; Other 1. **Subjects:** Judaica. **Holdings:** 8000 books. **Subscriptions:** 25 journals and other serials. **Services:** Library open to members of local congregations and students of local colleges and universities.

★13280★
TEMPLE DE HIRSCH SINAI - LIBRARY (Rel-Theol)
1511 E. Pike
Seattle, WA 98122   Kathryn K. Crane, Libn.
Staff: Prof 1. **Subjects:** Judaism, Jewish history, literature, biography, Holocaust, children's literature. **Holdings:** 4500 books. **Subscriptions:** 24 journals and other serials. **Services:** Interlibrary loans; copying (limited); library open to public with restrictions.

★13281★
TEMPLE EMANU-EL - ALEX F. WEISBERG LIBRARY (Rel-Theol)
8500 Hillcrest   Phone: (214) 368-3613
Dallas, TX 75225   Donna Berliner, Libn.
Founded: 1957. **Staff:** Prof 1; Other 2. **Subjects:** Judaica and related topics. **Holdings:** 8000 books. **Subscriptions:** 37 journals and other serials. **Services:** Programs for interfaith and senior citizens groups; library open to public.

★13282★
TEMPLE EMANU-EL - CONGREGATIONAL LIBRARY (Rel-Theol)
99 Taft Ave.   Phone: (401) 331-1616
Providence, RI 02906   Lillian Schwartz, Libn.
Founded: 1953. **Staff:** Prof 1. **Subjects:** Judaica, comparative religion.

Holdings: 6000 books. **Subscriptions:** 20 journals and other serials. **Services:** Interlibrary loans; copying; library open to public with required deposit. **Publications:** Booklists, occasional - for school use.

★13283★
TEMPLE EMANUEL - LIBRARY (Rel-Theol)
150 Derby Ave.   Phone: (203) 397-3000
Orange, CT 06477   Michael S. Chosak, Chm., Lib.Comm.
Subjects: Judaica. **Holdings:** 1000 books; 25 phonograph records. **Services:** Library open to public with permission.

★13284★
TEMPLE EMANU-EL - LIBRARY (Rel-Theol)
1701 Washington Ave.   Phone: (305) 538-2503
Miami Beach, FL 33139   Ruth M. Abelow, Libn.
Staff: Prof 1; Other 1. **Subjects:** Judaica including religion, Bible, Israel, biography, literature, history, sociology and education. **Special Collections:** Samuel Friedland Collection of Rare Books (600 volumes, mainly printed in Europe). **Holdings:** 7500 books; 55 cataloged periodicals; 250 pamphlets; 40 pamphlet boxes of uncataloged pamphlets on Israel and religion; 8 books of clippings. **Subscriptions:** 48 journals and other serials; 6 newspapers. **Services:** Library open to public (with refundable deposit). **Publications:** Temple Bulletin, weekly - distributed to Temple members; single copies available free upon request.

★13285★
TEMPLE EMANUEL - LIBRARY (Rel-Theol)†
Cooper River Pkwy. at Donahue   Phone: (609) 665-0669
Cherry Hill, NJ 08034   Rene Batterman, Libn.
Staff: Prof 1. **Subjects:** Judaism. **Special Collections:** Holocaust. **Holdings:** 5000 books; records; tapes. **Subscriptions:** 12 journals and other serials. **Services:** Copying; library open to public with restrictions.

★13286★
TEMPLE EMANU-EL - LIBRARY (Rel-Theol)
455 Neptune Blvd.   Phone: (516) 431-4060
Long Beach, NY 11561   Beth Moscowitz, Libn.
Founded: 1954. **Staff:** Prof 1. **Subjects:** Jewish religion and literature; Bible; Hebraica; current events in Israel. **Holdings:** 2876 books; 20 bound periodical volumes; 8 VF drawers; filmstrips; tapes; recordings. **Subscriptions:** 10 newspapers. **Services:** Library open to members. **Automated Operations:** Computerized cataloging and circulation. **Publications:** Temple Newsletter - to members only.

★13287★
TEMPLE EMANU-EL - WILLIAM P. ENGEL LIBRARY (Rel-Theol)
2100 Highland Ave.   Phone: (205) 933-8037
Birmingham, AL 35255   Adele Cohn, Libn.
Staff: Prof 2; Other 1. **Subjects:** Judaica, religion. **Holdings:** 3500 books. **Services:** Interlibrary loans; copying; library open to public as needed for research. **Staff:** Florence Goldstein, Asst.

★13288★
TEMPLE EMANU-EL OF YONKERS - LEVITAS LIBRARY (Rel-Theol)
306 Rumsey Rd.   Phone: (914) 963-0575
Yonkers, NY 10705   Irving Levitas, Libn.
Staff: Prof 1; Other 5. **Subjects:** Judaica, history, comparative religions, American literature, Asian studies. **Holdings:** 5000 volumes. **Subscriptions:** 12 journals and other serials. **Services:** Interlibrary loans; library open to students.

★13289★
TEMPLE ISRAEL OF GREATER MIAMI - LIBRARY (Rel-Theol)
137 N.E. 19th St.   Phone: (305) 573-5900
Miami, FL 33132   Beatrice T. Muskat, Libn.
Founded: 1944. **Staff:** Prof 2; Other 1. **Subjects:** Judaica. **Special Collections:** Biblical and juvenile collections; Haggadahs. **Holdings:** 10,000 books; pamphlets; American Jewish Archives; Near East reports; records; tapes; slides. **Subscriptions:** 30 journals and other serials. **Services:** Library open to public for reference use only. **Remarks:** Maintains a small branch library at 9990 N. Kendall Dr., Miami, FL 33176.

★13290★
TEMPLE ISRAEL OF HOLLYWOOD - JOSEPH H. CORWIN MEMORIAL LIBRARY (Rel-Theol)*
7300 Hollywood Blvd.   Phone: (213) 876-8330
Hollywood, CA 90046
Staff: Prof 1. **Subjects:** Judaica, children's books in Judaica only. **Holdings:** 8000 volumes. **Subscriptions:** 52 journals and other serials. **Services:**

Library not open to public.

★13291★
TEMPLE ISRAEL - LEONARD M. SANDHAUS MEMORIAL LIBRARY (Rel-Theol)
125 Pond St.   Phone: (617) 784-3986
Sharon, MA 02067   Janet Perlin, Libn.
Founded: 1953. **Staff:** Prof 1; Other 6. **Subjects:** Jewish religion, philosophy, history; American Jewish life; Israel and Zionism. **Special Collections:** Jewish literature. **Holdings:** 4350 books; 200 pamphlets; 50 tapes. **Subscriptions:** 30 journals and other serials; 5 newspapers. **Services:** Interlibrary loans; library open to public with restrictions. **Remarks:** Library serves students of Hebrew school, college students in the Boston area, members of the clergy of Sharon, teachers of religious schools in the community and members of the congregation.

★13292★
TEMPLE ISRAEL - LIBRARY (Rel-Theol)
1901 N. Flagler Dr.   Phone: (305) 833-8421
West Palm Beach, FL 33407   Elsie Leviton, Chm., Lib.Comm.
Founded: 1958. **Staff:** Prof 1; Other 5. **Subjects:** Judaica - history, literature, sociology, arts. **Special Collections:** Americana Judaica. **Holdings:** 6000 books; 12 bound periodical volumes; 1000 pamphlets, bibliographies, archives, clippings; 8 VF drawers; phonograph records; filmstrips. **Subscriptions:** 10 journals and other serials; 7 newspapers. **Services:** Library open to residents of Palm Beach county. **Staff:** Adele Sayles, Libn.

★13293★
TEMPLE ISRAEL - LIBRARY (Rel-Theol)
2324 Emerson Ave., S.   Phone: (612) 377-8680
Minneapolis, MN 55405   Georgia Kalman, Libn.
Founded: 1928. **Staff:** Prof 1. **Subjects:** Judaica, Jewish religion, philosophy. **Holdings:** 6000 books. **Subscriptions:** 20 journals and other serials; 6 newspapers. **Services:** Library open to public.

★13294★
TEMPLE ISRAEL - LIBRARY (Rel-Theol)
140 Central Ave.   Phone: (516) 239-1140
Lawrence, NY 11559   Donna Z. Lifland, Libn.
Founded: 1949. **Staff:** Prof 1; Other 6. **Subjects:** Judaica and affiliated subjects. **Holdings:** 5100 books; 20 bound periodical volumes; 225 filmstrips; 10 cassettes. **Subscriptions:** 19 journals and other serials. **Services:** Library open to public with permission.

★13295★
TEMPLE ISRAEL - RABBI LOUIS WITT MEMORIAL LIBRARY (Rel-Theol)
1821 Emerson Ave.   Phone: (513) 278-9621
Dayton, OH 45406   Jeanne B. Goldzwig, Libn.
Founded: 1925. **Subjects:** Judaica. **Holdings:** Figures not available. **Services:** Library not open to public.

★13296★
TEMPLE ISRAEL - MAX AND EDITH WEINBERG LIBRARY (Rel-Theol)
5725 Walnut Lake Rd.   Phone: (313) 661-5700
West Bloomfield, MI 48033   Bertha Wember, Libn.
Founded: 1962. **Staff:** Prof 1. **Subjects:** Judaism - history, biography, literature, arts; Holocaust; Bible study; Israel. **Holdings:** 7500 books; 8 VF drawers of clippings and pamphlets. **Subscriptions:** 30 journals and other serials. **Services:** Library open to public.

★13297★
TEMPLE ISRAEL - PAUL PELTASON LIBRARY (Rel-Theol)
10675 Ladue Rd.   Phone: (314) 432-8050
Creve Coeur, MO 63141   Mrs. Barry Katz
Founded: 1930. **Staff:** 1. **Subjects:** Judaica. **Holdings:** 4000 books. **Services:** Library open to public with restrictions.

★13298★
TEMPLE JUDEA - MEL HARRISON MEMORIAL LIBRARY (Rel-Theol)
5500 Granada Blvd.
Coral Gables, FL 33146   Zelda Harrison, Libn.
Founded: 1967. **Staff:** 5. **Subjects:** Judaica. **Holdings:** 4500 books. **Services:** Library not open to public.

★13299★
TEMPLE JUDEA MIZPAH - LIBRARY (Rel-Theol)
8610 Niles Center Rd.   Phone: (312) 676-1566
Skokie, IL 60077   Claire Alport, Lib.Chm.
Staff: Prof 3; Other 14. **Subjects:** Judaica. **Holdings:** 3700 books; 20 bound

periodical volumes. **Services:** Copying; library open to public with restrictions.

★13300★
TEMPLE LIBRARY (Rel-Theol)
University Circle & Silver Pk.   Phone: (216) 791-7755
Cleveland, OH 44106   Beth Dwoskin, Libn.
Founded: 1896. **Staff:** Prof 1. **Subjects:** Judaica. **Special Collections:** Abba
Hillel Silver Archives. **Holdings:** 23,000 books; pamphlets; maps; filmstrips;
slides. **Subscriptions:** 50 journals and other serials; 10 newspapers.
Services: Interlibrary loans; library open to public. **Remarks:** Branch library,
located at 26000 Shaker Blvd., contains mostly children's collection and adult
fiction.

★13301★
TEMPLE OHABAI SHALOM - LIBRARY (Rel-Theol)
5015 Harding Rd.   Phone: (615) 352-7620
Nashville, TN 37205   Annette R. Levy, Libn.
Staff: Prof 1; Other 1. **Subjects:** Bible commentary, Jewish history, children's
literature. **Holdings:** 5000 books. **Subscriptions:** 10 journals and other
serials. **Services:** Interlibrary loans; copying; library open to public.

★13302★
TEMPLE OHABEI SHALOM - SISTERHOOD LIBRARY (Rel-Theol)
1187 Beacon St.   Phone: (617) 277-6610
Brookline, MA 02146   Mary R. Rosen, Libn.
Founded: 1938. **Staff:** 1. **Subjects:** Bible, Judaism, biography, history,
Israel, religion, theology. **Holdings:** 3500 books. **Subscriptions:** 14 journals
and other serials. **Services:** Library open to public with restrictions.

★13303★
TEMPLE SHAAREY ZEDEK - LIBRARY (Rel-Theol)
Hartford & Getzville Rds.   Phone: (716) 838-3232
Amherst, NY 14226   Grace Stern, Libn.
Founded: 1959. **Staff:** Prof 2; Other 5. **Subjects:** Judaica. **Holdings:** 5400
volumes. **Subscriptions:** 10 journals and other serials. **Services:** Library open
to public. **Staff:** Ferne E. Mittleman, Asst.Libn.

★13304★
**TEMPLE SHAREY TEFILO-ISRAEL - EDWARD EHRENKRANTZ/ELCHANAN
ECHIKSON MEMORIAL LIBRARY** (Rel-Theol)
432 Scotland Rd.   Phone: (201) 763-4116
South Orange, NJ 07079   Ann R. Zeve, Libn.
Staff: Prof 1. **Subjects:** Bible; Jewish religion, history, customs, ceremonies,
holidays, practices; fiction. **Holdings:** 4500 volumes. **Services:** Library not
open to public. **Formed by the Merger of:** Temple Sharey Tefilo-Edward
Ehrenkrantz Library and Temple Israel Library.

★13305★
TEMPLE SINAI - JACK BALABAN MEMORIAL LIBRARY (Rel-Theol)
New Albany Rd.   Phone: (609) 829-0658
Cinnaminson, NJ 08077   Elaine Cohen, Libn.
Staff: Prof 1; Other 2. **Subjects:** Holocaust; Jewish history, religion, holidays,
and authors. **Special Collections:** Encyclopaedia Judaica. **Holdings:** 1000
books. **Services:** Library open to public with restrictions.

★13306★
TEMPLE SINAI - LIBRARY (Rel-Theol)
3100 Military Rd., N.W.   Phone: (202) 363-6394
Washington, DC 20015   Ellen Rosenberg Murphy, Libn.
Founded: 1960. **Staff:** Prof 1. **Subjects:** Judaism - philosophy, history; Bible;
theology; sociology of American Jews; Jewish traditions and folklore; Israeli
history; Holocaust. **Special Collections:** Celia B. Friedman Collection of
Hebrew Material (60 books); Selis Memorial Collection (comparative religion;
55 volumes); Bianka Zwick Memorial Collection (American-Jewish immigrant
experience). **Holdings:** 3500 volumes; 2 VF drawers of clippings, maps and
charts. **Subscriptions:** 30 journals and other serials; 6 newspapers. **Services:**
Library open to public with restrictions.

★13307★
TEMPLE SINAI - LIBRARY (Rel-Theol)†
50 Sewall Ave.   Phone: (617) 277-5888
Brookline, MA 02146   Jane Taubenfeld Cohen, Prin., Rel.Sch.
Staff: Prof 1. **Subjects:** Judaica, religion, Bible, Talmud. **Holdings:** 2200
books. **Services:** Library not open to public.

★13308★
**TEMPLE UNIVERSITY - CENTRAL LIBRARY SYSTEM - AMBLER CAMPUS
LIBRARY** (Educ)
Meetinghouse Rd.   Phone: (215) 643-1200
Ambler, PA 19002
Founded: 1958. **Staff:** Prof 3; Other 6. **Subjects:** Horticulture, education,
literature, history, landscape design, science, botany, sociology, business.
Special Collections: Horticulture and landscape design (3000 volumes);
Pennsylvania Affiliate Data Center (census materials). **Holdings:** 60,000
books; 3700 bound periodical volumes; 3500 recordings; 7000 pamphlets;
3000 reels of microfilm. **Subscriptions:** 600 journals and other serials; 20
newspapers. **Services:** Interlibrary loans; copying; library open to public for
reference use only. **Computerized Information Services:** OCLC, DIALOG,
BRS. **Networks/Consortia:** Member of Association of Research Libraries
(ARL); CRL; PALINET & Union Library Catalogue of Pennsylvania; RLG. **Staff:**
Veronica Miller, Asst.Libn./Rsrcs.

★13309★
**TEMPLE UNIVERSITY - CENTER FOR THE STUDY OF FEDERALISM -
LIBRARY** (Hist; Soc Sci)
Gladfelter Hall, 10th Fl.   Phone: (215) 787-1480
Philadelphia, PA 19122   Gail L. Charette, Hd.Libn.
Staff: Prof 1; Other 3. **Subjects:** American federalism, comparative federal
systems, federal theory, political culture, state and local governments,
environmental problems, covenants. **Holdings:** 1000 books; 1000 bound
periodical volumes; 1000 uncataloged items; 5 VF drawers. **Subscriptions:**
102 journals and other serials. **Services:** Library open to public. **Publications:**
CSF Notebook; Publius: The Journal of Federalism, quarterly; special reports
and books on key subject areas. **Remarks:** "The center is dedicated to the
study of federal principles, institutions, and processes as a practical means of
organizing political power in a free society. By initiating, sponsoring, and
conducting research projects and educational programs related to them, the
center seeks to increase and disseminate knowledge of federalism in general
and to develop specialists in the growing field of intergovernmental relations."

★13310★
TEMPLE UNIVERSITY - CENTRAL LIBRARY SYSTEM - AUDIO UNIT
Broad & Montgomery
Philadelphia, PA 19122
Subjects: Jazz, popular music, musical comedy, folk music, science fiction,
Latin America. **Special Collections:** Paley Presents Lecture Series (250 tape
recordings). **Holdings:** 14,707 phonograph records; 542 reel-to-reel tapes;
35 cassettes; 80 files of pictures. **Automated Operations:** Computerized
cataloging. **Computerized Information Services:** DIALOG, SDC, BRS, OCLC.
Special Catalogs: Individual Song Catalog for phonograph records in the
collection (card). **Remarks:** Presently inactive.

★13311★
TEMPLE UNIVERSITY - CENTRAL LIBRARY SYSTEM - BIOLOGY LIBRARY
(Sci-Tech)
248 Life Science Bldg.   Phone: (215) 787-8878
Philadelphia, PA 19122   Jocelyn McCrae, Bibliog.Asst.
Staff: 1. **Subjects:** Biology - cell, molecular, developmental; biochemistry;
genetics; physiology. **Holdings:** 1365 books; 11,408 bound periodical
volumes; 8 VF drawers of reprints; 50 volumes of dissertations and theses.
Services: Interlibrary loans; copying; library open to qualified users.
Automated Operations: Computerized cataloging. **Computerized
Information Services:** OCLC, DIALOG, BRS, SDC. **Networks/Consortia:**
Member of Association of Research Libraries (ARL); RLG; PALINET & Union
Library Catalogue of Pennsylvania; CRL.

★13312★
**TEMPLE UNIVERSITY - CENTRAL LIBRARY SYSTEM - CENTER CITY
LIBRARY** (Bus-Fin)
1619 Walnut St.   Phone: (215) 787-6950
Philadelphia, PA 19103   Cornelia Tucker, Hd.Libn.
Founded: 1978. **Staff:** Prof 1; Other 1. **Subjects:** Business administration,
real estate, liberal arts. **Holdings:** 5500 books. **Subscriptions:** 143 journals
and other serials. **Services:** Interlibrary loans; copying; library open to public
for reference use only. **Automated Operations:** Computerized cataloging.
Computerized Information Services: OCLC. **Networks/Consortia:** Member
of Association of Research Libraries (ARL); RLG; PALINET & Union Library
Catalogue of Pennsylvania; CRL.

★13313★
**TEMPLE UNIVERSITY - CENTRAL LIBRARY SYSTEM - CHARLES L.
BLOCKSON AFRO-AMERICAN HISTORICAL COLL.** (Hist; Area-Ethnic)
13th & Berks Sts.   Phone: (215) 787-6632
Philadelphia, PA 19122   Charles L. Blockson, Cur.
Founded: 1983. **Staff:** Prof 1; Other 2. **Subjects:** Afro-American history and

literature, African history, Caribbean, sociology, education. **Special Collections:** History of blacks in Pennsylvania; underground railroad. **Holdings:** 10,000 books; 10,000 other cataloged items. **Subscriptions:** 15 journals and other serials. **Services:** Copying; collection open to public for reference use only. **Publications:** Afro-Americana: An Exhibition of Selected Books, Manuscripts & Prints, 1984.

★13314★
TEMPLE UNIVERSITY - CENTRAL LIBRARY SYSTEM - CHEMISTRY LIBRARY (Sci-Tech)
Beury Hall, 1st Fl.   Phone: (215) 787-7120
Philadelphia, PA 19122   Dolores Michalak, Bibliog.Asst.
Founded: 1968. **Staff:** 1. **Subjects:** Chemistry - organic, inorganic, physical, analytical, theoreticaL; biochemistry. **Special Collections:** Guy F. Allen Memorial Collection in Chemical Education (100 volumes). **Holdings:** 1436 books; 10,481 bound periodical volumes; 2 VF of reprints; 125 volumes of theses and dissertations. **Subscriptions:** 200 journals and other serials. **Services:** Interlibrary loans; copying; library open to qualified users. **Automated Operations:** Computerized cataloging. **Computerized Information Services:** DIALOG, SDC, BRS, OCLC. **Networks/Consortia:** Member of Association of Research Libraries (ARL); RLG; PALINET & Union Library Catalogue of Pennsylvania; CRL.

★13315★
TEMPLE UNIVERSITY - CENTRAL LIBRARY SYSTEM - COLLEGE OF ENGINEERING AND ARCHITECTURE - LIBRARY (Sci-Tech)
12th & Norris Sts.   Phone: (215) 787-7828
Philadelphia, PA 19122   Raelaine Ballou, Libn.
Founded: 1921. **Staff:** Prof 1; Other 3. **Subjects:** Engineering - biomedical, civil, electrical, environmental, mechanical; architecture. **Holdings:** 15,000 books; 1100 bound periodical volumes. **Subscriptions:** 134 journals and other serials. **Services:** Interlibrary loans; copying; library open to public. **Computerized Information Services:** DIALOG, BRS, SDC, OCLC. **Networks/Consortia:** Member of Association of Research Libraries (ARL); CRL; PALINET & Union Library Catalogue of Pennsylvania; RLG. **Formerly:** Its College of Engineering - Technology Library.

★13316★
TEMPLE UNIVERSITY - CENTRAL LIBRARY SYSTEM - CONTEMPORARY CULTURE COLLECTION (Soc Sci)
13th & Berks Sts.   Phone: (215) 787-8667
Philadelphia, PA 19122   Patricia J. Case, Cur.
Founded: 1969. **Staff:** 1. **Subjects:** Social change, peace and disarmament, small press poetry, fringe politics, alternative life styles, feminism, gays. **Special Collections:** Counter culture and peace movement newspapers from the Vietnam era; early second wave feminist publications and literary chapbooks; Liberation News Service Archive (160 linear feet); Youth Liberation Archive (40 linear feet); Committee of Small Press Editors and Publishers Archive (32 linear feet); small presses archives (83 linear feet); personal papers of poet Lyn Lifshin (36 linear feet). **Holdings:** 7500 books and pamphlets; 3500 periodical, newspaper and newsletter titles; 600 reels of microfilm; 70 linear feet of ephemera. **Subscriptions:** 290 journals and other serials; 90 newspapers. **Services:** Copying; collection open to public for reference use only. **Automated Operations:** Computerized cataloging. **Computerized Information Services:** DIALOG, SDC, BRS, OCLC. **Networks/Consortia:** Member of Association of Research Libraries (ARL); CRL; PALINET & Union Library Catalogue of Pennsylvania; RLG. **Publications:** Periodical holdings lists, 1972, 1976; Alternative Press Periodicals: A Listing of Periodicals Microfilmed at The Collection, 1976; The Not in the New York Times Bibliography Series, monthly - free upon request.

★13317★
TEMPLE UNIVERSITY - CENTRAL LIBRARY SYSTEM - CONWELLANA-TEMPLANA COLLECTION (Hist)
13th & Berks Sts.   Phone: (215) 787-8240
Philadelphia, PA 19122   Miriam I. Crawford, Cur.
Founded: 1946. **Staff:** Prof 1; Other 2. **Subjects:** University archives; Russell Conwell - life and activities. **Special Collections:** Faculty and alumni publications (3800 volumes); sermons, manuscripts and publications of Russell Conwell (38 linear feet); personal library of Russell Conwell (1800 volumes); personal papers of faculty and alumni (125 linear feet); Barrows Dunham-Fred Zimring Collection (128 tapes and 66 transcriptions of oral history interviews and research materials related to dismissal of faculty members and academic freedom issues; 7 linear feet); Frank Ankenbrand papers, manuscript notebooks and publications (3 linear feet); Frank Brookhouser papers, correspondence, manuscripts and published columns (5 linear feet); Negley K. Teeters personal papers, correspondence, manuscripts and related files (3 linear feet); personal papers of Melville S. Green, statistical physicist (1950-1979; 14 linear feet); personal papers of David Swern,

1961-1982 (chemist and pioneer in plastics; 5 linear feet); personal papers of Henry Dexter Learned, linguistic scholar (1893-1978; 7 linear feet); Weiss-Karlen Collection (papers of novelist David Weiss and poet-playwright Stymean Karlen, 1940-1982; 20 linear feet); papers of William W. Tomlinson, 1950-1980 (including diaries of his travels; 50 linear feet); papers of Miriam Allen De Ford, 1903-1975 (mystery and historical writer; 2 linear feet). **Holdings:** 6425 books; 2106 bound periodical volumes; 1460 catalogs and reports; 8800 theses and dissertations; 500 linear feet of archives and manuscripts; 16 drawers of clippings, pictures and other items; 520 reels of microfilm; 600 reels of tape recordings; 2040 slides, posters, phonograph records and assorted memorabilia. **Subscriptions:** 121 journals and other serials. **Services:** Interlibrary loans; copying; collection open to public for reference use only. **Computerized Information Services:** DIALOG, SDC, OCLC, BRS. **Networks/Consortia:** Member of Association of Research Libraries (ARL); CRL; PALINET & Union Library Catalogue of Pennsylvania; RLG. **Publications:** Temple University Libraries Special Collections Newsletter, irregular. **Special Catalogs:** Inventories of manuscript and archives collections; General Guide to Archives and Manuscripts; Inventories of certain Record Groups and Personal Papers (in sheet form); Russell Herman Conwell: The Individual and His Influence, compiled by M.I. Crawford, 1977.

★13318★
TEMPLE UNIVERSITY - CENTRAL LIBRARY SYSTEM - MATHEMATICAL SCIENCES LIBRARY (Sci-Tech; Comp Sci)
407 Computer Sciences Bldg.   Phone: (215) 787-8434
Philadelphia, PA 19122   Sandra Thompson, Bibliog.Asst.
Founded: 1968. **Staff:** 1. **Subjects:** Pure and applied mathematics, statistics, computer and information sciences. **Holdings:** 2088 books; 9473 bound periodical volumes; 9 linear feet of technical reports. **Subscriptions:** 300 journals and other serials. **Services:** Interlibrary loans; copying; library open to qualified users. **Automated Operations:** Computerized cataloging. **Computerized Information Services:** DIALOG, SDC, BRS, OCLC. **Networks/Consortia:** Member of Association of Research Libraries (ARL); RLG; PALINET & Union Library Catalogue of Pennsylvania; CRL.

★13319★
TEMPLE UNIVERSITY - CENTRAL LIBRARY SYSTEM - NATIONAL IMMIGRATION ARCHIVES (Soc Sci)
Balch Institute Bldg.
18 S. 7th St.   Phone: (215) 922-3454
Philadelphia, PA 19106   Stephanie A. Morris, Cur.
Founded: 1978. **Staff:** 5. **Subjects:** Emigration from Europe, immigration, customs. **Special Collections:** U.S. Bureau of Customs records; Passenger Manifests, 1820-1906 (1500 cubic feet). **Holdings:** 50 books. **Services:** Archives not open to public. **Automated Operations:** Computerized cataloging. **Computerized Information Services:** OCLC, DIALOG, SDC, BRS; internal database. **Networks/Consortia:** Member of Association of Research Libraries (ARL); CRL; PALINET & Union Library Catalogue of Pennsylvania; RLG. **Special Indexes:** Index of 19th century passenger manifests (computer printout).

★13320★
TEMPLE UNIVERSITY - CENTRAL LIBRARY SYSTEM - PHOTO-JOURNALISM COLLECTION (Info Sci)
13th & Berks St.   Phone: (215) 787-8230
Philadelphia, PA 19122
Staff: Prof 2; Other 2. **Subjects:** Photo-journalism, news photography, news motion pictures, Philadelphia history in pictures. **Special Collections:** WPVI-TV News Film, 1947-1977; Philadelphia Inquirer Newspaper Photograph Archival Collection, 1937-1972; Philadelphia Evening Bulletin Library, 1847-1982 (clippings; photographs; index). **Holdings:** 50 books; 8000 canisters of news film; 500,000 sheet negatives (some glass); 200 cabinets and boxes of 8x10 prints. **Services:** Copying; collection open to public with restrictions. **Computerized Information Services:** OCLC, DIALOG, BRS, SDC, VU/TEXT. **Networks/Consortia:** Member of CRL; RLG; PALINET & Union Library Catalogue of Pennsylvania; Association of Research Libraries (ARL). **Publications:** News Photograph Collections: A Survey of Newspaper Practices and Archival Strategies, 1982 - free upon request. **Staff:** George D. Brightbill, Print Libn.; Elaine Clever, Film Libn.

★13321★
TEMPLE UNIVERSITY - CENTRAL LIBRARY SYSTEM - PHYSICS LIBRARY (Sci-Tech)
209A Barton Hall   Phone: (215) 787-7649
Philadelphia, PA 19122   Rhea Mihalisin, Bibliog.Asst.
Founded: 1968. **Staff:** 1. **Subjects:** Physics, astronomy. **Holdings:** 3087 books; 9315 bound periodical volumes; 1 VF drawer of reprints; 50 volumes of theses and dissertations; 1 VF drawer of preprints; 1 VF drawer of society newsletters. **Subscriptions:** 190 journals and other serials. **Services:**

Interlibrary loans; copying; library open to qualified users. **Automated Operations:** Computerized cataloging. **Computerized Information Services:** DIALOG, BRS, SDC, OCLC. **Networks/Consortia:** Member of Association of Research Libraries (ARL); RLG; PALINET & Union Library Catalogue of Pennsylvania; CRL.

★13322★

TEMPLE UNIVERSITY - CENTRAL LIBRARY SYSTEM - RARE BOOK & MANUSCRIPT COLLECTION (Rare Book)
13th & Berks St.   Phone: (215) 787-8230
Philadelphia, PA 19122   Thomas M. Whitehead, Hd., Spec.Coll.Dept.
Staff: Prof 2; Other 2. **Subjects:** English, French, American and Symbolist literature; business history; horticulture; lithography; printing, publishing and bookselling history. **Special Collections:** Charles Morice Papers; Constable & Company correspondence collection; Cochran History of Business Collection (500 volumes); Bush-Brown Horticulture Collection (500 volumes); Nordell 17th Century England Collection (150 volumes); Richard Ellis Library and Archive; Albert Caplan Limited Editions Club Collection; Sir Richard Owen correspondence collection; Walter de la Mare Collection. **Holdings:** 20,000 books; 2000 bound periodical volumes; 3000 war posters; 1000 linear feet of manuscripts. **Subscriptions:** 15 journals and other serials. **Services:** Copying; library open to public with restrictions. **Computerized Information Services:** OCLC, DIALOG, BRS, SDC. **Networks/Consortia:** Member of PALINET & Union Library Catalogue of Pennsylvania; Association of Research Libraries (ARL); CRL; RLG. **Special Catalogs:** Andre Girard (1970); Lithography· (1973); Richard Aldington (1973); 30 issued registers to manuscript collection. **Staff:** Sharon Fitzpatrick, Bibliog.Asst.; Cornelia King, Rare Book Bibliog.

★13323★

TEMPLE UNIVERSITY - CENTRAL LIBRARY SYSTEM - REFERENCE DEPARTMENT MAP UNIT (Geo-Map)
Paley Library
13th & Berks Sts.   Phone: (215) 787-8213
Philadelphia, PA 19122   Ida G. Ginsburgs, Map Libn.
Staff: Prof 1; Other 1. **Subjects:** Topography, geography, geology, hydrology. **Holdings:** 61,835 maps; 967 atlases. **Services:** Interlibrary loans; copying; collection open to public on a limited schedule. **Computerized Information Services:** BRS, SDC, DIALOG. Performs searches on cost recovery basis. Contact Person: James Hodson.

★13324★

TEMPLE UNIVERSITY - CENTRAL LIBRARY SYSTEM - SCHOOL OF SOCIAL ADMINISTRATION - LIBRARY
565 Ritter Hall Annex
Philadelphia, PA 19122
Defunct. Merged with the Zahn Instructional Materials Center to form Temple University - Central Library System - Zahn Instructional Materials Center/Social Administration Library.

★13325★

TEMPLE UNIVERSITY - CENTRAL LIBRARY SYSTEM - SCIENCE FICTION COLLECTION (Rec)
13th & Berks St.   Phone: (215) 787-8230
Philadelphia, PA 19122   Thomas M. Whitehead, Hd., Spec.Coll.Dept.
Founded: 1972. **Staff:** Prof 1; Other 1. **Subjects:** Science fiction, fantasy, Utopian literature. **Special Collections:** Paskow Science Fiction Library (5000 books; 2000 periodicals). **Holdings:** 8000 books; 600 bound periodical volumes; 1200 titles of fanzines; 100 linear feet of manuscripts; 2 linear feet of ephemera and brochures; 2 linear feet of movie scripts. **Subscriptions:** 25 journals and other serials. **Services:** Copying; library open to public. **Automated Operations:** Computerized cataloging. **Computerized Information Services:** DIALOG, SDC, OCLC, BRS. **Networks/Consortia:** Member of Association of Research Libraries (ARL); CRL; PALINET & Union Library Catalogue of Pennsylvania; RLG. **Publications:** Fanzines - Science Fiction and Fantasy Catalog, July, 1975.

★13326★

TEMPLE UNIVERSITY - CENTRAL LIBRARY SYSTEM - TYLER SCHOOL OF FINE ARTS - LIBRARY (Art)
Beech & Penrose Aves.   Phone: (215) 224-7575
Philadelphia, PA 19126   Mary Ivy Bayard, Libn.
Founded: 1935. **Staff:** 3. **Subjects:** Fine and applied arts. **Holdings:** 24,267 volumes; 6 VF drawers of pictures; 5 periodical titles on microfilm. **Subscriptions:** 118 journals and other serials. **Services:** Interlibrary loans; copying. **Computerized Information Services:** OCLC. **Networks/Consortia:** Member of Association of Research Libraries (ARL); CRL; RLG; PALINET & Union Library Catalogue of Pennsylvania.

★13327★

TEMPLE UNIVERSITY - CENTRAL LIBRARY SYSTEM - TYLER SCHOOL OF FINE ARTS - SLIDE LIBRARY (Art; Aud-Vis)
Beech & Penrose Aves.   Phone: (215) 224-7575
Philadelphia, PA 19126   Edith Zuckerman, Hd. Slide Cur.
Staff: Prof 2; Other 2. **Subjects:** Art history - prehistoric to contemporary; decorative arts; ceramics; graphics; photography; film. **Holdings:** 252,750 slides. **Services:** Copying; library open to faculty and graduate students. **Staff:** Patsy Dass, Slide Cur.

★13328★

TEMPLE UNIVERSITY - CENTRAL LIBRARY SYSTEM - URBAN ARCHIVES (Soc Sci)
13th & Berks Sts.   Phone: (215) 787-8257
Philadelphia, PA 19122   Dr. Fredric Miller, Cur.
Founded: 1967. **Staff:** Prof 2; Other 3. **Subjects:** Philadelphia area - housing, planning, social welfare, black studies, urban renewal, civil rights, politics, settlement houses, education, labor, criminal justice, business. **Holdings:** 474 books; 20,000 pamphlets; 150 collections of manuscripts; 750 maps; 5000 photographs. **Subscriptions:** 10 journals and other serials. **Services:** Copying; archives open to public. **Computerized Information Services:** DIALOG, OCLC, SDC, BRS. **Networks/Consortia:** Member of Association of Research Libraries (ARL); CRL; PALINET & Union Library Catalogue of Pennsylvania; RLG. **Publications:** Urban Archives Notes, biennial; Guides to Housing and Social Services Collections. **Special Catalogs:** Folder lists of manuscripts; catalog of pamphlets and photographs (card). **Staff:** Kenneth Fones-Wolf, Asst.Cur.

★13329★

TEMPLE UNIVERSITY - CENTRAL LIBRARY SYSTEM - ZAHN INSTRUCTIONAL MATERIALS CTR./SOCIAL ADM. LIB. (Educ; Soc Sci)
Ritter Annex 139
13th & Columbia Ave.   Phone: (215) 787-8481
Philadelphia, PA 19122   Linda Cotilla, Hd.Libn.
Staff: Prof 2; Other 3. **Subjects:** Instructional materials, education, social administration, welfare. **Special Collections:** Rena Slavin Epstein Memorial Collection in Mental Health (300 volumes). **Holdings:** 16,700 books; 600 bound periodical volumes; 450 volumes of masters' projects and theses; 20,000 nonprint curricular materials. **Subscriptions:** 106 journals and other serials. **Services:** Interlibrary loans; copying; library open to public. **Networks/Consortia:** Member of RLG; CRL; Association of Research Libraries (ARL). **Formed by the Merger of:** Zahn Instructional Materials Center and the School of Social Administration Library.

★13330★

TEMPLE UNIVERSITY - HEALTH SCIENCES CENTER - LIBRARY (Med)
N. Broad & Tioga Sts.   Phone: (215) 221-4032
Philadelphia, PA 19140   Ruth Y. Diamond, Dir.
Founded: 1901. **Staff:** Prof 9; Other 4. **Subjects:** Medicine, dentistry, pharmacy, basic sciences, nursing, allied health sciences. **Special Collections:** Medical History. **Holdings:** 87,500 volumes; microfilm; audiotapes. **Subscriptions:** 1072 journals and other serials. **Services:** Interlibrary loans; copying; library open to public. **Automated Operations:** Computerized cataloging. **Computerized Information Services:** MEDLINE, BRS, RLIN. **Networks/Consortia:** Member of RLG. **Publications:** Periodicals Holdings List, annual. **Remarks:** The Health Sciences Center comprises the Dental-Allied Health-Pharmacy Library and the Medical Library. Each is housed separately. **Staff:** Virginia Lampson, Dental Libn.; Marcelle Freyman, Asst. Dental Libn.; Hope Norcia, Dental Cat.; Ann Ludovici, Ref.Libn.; Toby Harke, Ref.Libn.; Maureen Smith, Cat.; Jean Choi, Cat.; Robert Rooney, Circ.Libn.

★13331★

TEMPLE UNIVERSITY HOSPITAL - HEALTH SCIENCES CENTER - DEPARTMENT OF DIAGNOSTIC IMAGING - LIBRARY (Med)
3401 N. Broad St.   Phone: (215) 221-4226
Philadelphia, PA 19140   Shirley T.L. Ding, Libn.
Founded: 1960. **Staff:** Prof 1. **Subjects:** Radiology, nuclear medicine. **Holdings:** 900 books; 561 bound periodical volumes; 3000 radiologic teaching cases; 18 department dissertations; 9 volumes of department publications; 5000 teaching slides; 1000 transparencies; 6 VF drawers of reprints. **Subscriptions:** 33 journals and other serials. **Services:** Library open to public for reference use only. **Formed by the Merger of:** Department of Radiology - Library and the Nuclear Medicine Department - Library.

★13332★

TEMPLE UNIVERSITY - LAW LIBRARY (Law)
N. Broad St. & Montgomery Ave.   Phone: (215) 787-7892
Philadelphia, PA 19122   John M. Lindsey, Law Prof./Law Libn.
Staff: Prof 7; Other 12. **Subjects:** Law, legal history. **Special Collections:**

Practice Books for the American States; Justice of the Peace Manuals; Hirst Free Law Library. **Holdings:** 320,534 books; 12,500 bound periodical volumes; microforms. **Subscriptions:** 2956 journals and other serials. **Services:** Interlibrary loans; copying; library open to public for reference use only. **Automated Operations:** Computerized cataloging. **Computerized Information Services:** Online systems. **Networks/Consortia:** Member of RLG. **Publications:** Acquisitions List, monthly. **Remarks:** This library is administered as an independent unit.

TEMPLE UNIVERSITY - NATIONAL ASSOCIATION OF SELF-INSTRUCTIONAL LANGUAGE PROGRAMS
See: National Association of Self-Instructional Language Programs

TENNECO CHEMICALS, INC.
See: Nuodex, Inc.

★13333★
TENNECO, INC. - CORPORATE LIBRARY (Bus-Fin; Sci-Tech)
1010 Milam St., Suite 2143
Box 2511   Phone: (713) 757-2788
Houston, TX 77001   Linda S. Shults, Libn.
Staff: Prof 2; Other 1. **Subjects:** Business, technology, oil, gas, engineering. **Holdings:** 5000 books; 1200 bound periodical volumes; government documents; corporate annual reports. **Subscriptions:** 176 journals and other serials; 5 newspapers. **Services:** Interlibrary loans; copying; library open to public by appointment. **Computerized Information Services:** DIALOG, SDC, Dow Jones News/Retrieval, NEXIS, New York Times Information Service, Hazardline. **Publications:** Library Bulletin, irregular - for internal distribution only. **Staff:** Marla E. Nickell, Libn.

★13334★
TENNECO MINERALS COMPANY - LIBRARY (Sci-Tech)
300 Union Blvd., Suite 300
Box 27F   Phone: (303) 692-6200
Lakewood, CO 80210   Sara E. Martin, Hd.Libn.
Founded: 1977. **Staff:** Prof 1; Other 1. **Subjects:** Geology, mining, business. **Holdings:** 20,000 books; 200 bound periodical volumes; 20 VF drawers and 5 flat case drawers of maps. **Subscriptions:** 105 journals and other serials. **Services:** Interlibrary loans; library not open to public. **Automated Operations:** Computerized cataloging. **Computerized Information Services:** DIALOG, SDC, LEXIS, NEXIS, Dow Jones News/Retrieval. **Publications:** Information Services Update, monthly - for internal distribution only. **Formerly:** Houston International Minerals Corporation.

★13335★
TENNECO OIL EXPLORATION AND PRODUCTION - GEOLOGICAL RESEARCH LIBRARY (Sci-Tech)
1100 Milam Bldg., Rm. 1460   Phone: (713) 757-8832
Houston, TX 77001
Founded: 1958. **Staff:** 2. **Subjects:** Geology, geophysics, oceanology, petroleum exploration and production, mineral exploration, mining, natural resources. **Holdings:** 23,000 volumes; 5000 maps. **Subscriptions:** 250 journals and other serials. **Services:** Interlibrary loans; copying; library open to petroleum and mineral company librarians. **Computerized Information Services:** DIALOG, SDC. **Publications:** Bi-monthly Library Bulletin - for internal distribution only. **Remarks:** Contains the holdings of the former Corporate Library. **Staff:** Olive Tyson, Libn.; Wilda Wiley, Libn.

★13336★
TENNECO, INC. - TENNECO OIL EXPLORATION AND PRODUCTION - CORPORATE LIBRARY
1100 Louisiana
Houston, TX 77002
Defunct. Holdings absorbed by Tenneco Oil Exploration and Production - Geological Research Library.

★13337★
TENNESSEAN NEWSPAPER - LIBRARY (Publ)
1100 Broadway   Phone: (615) 259-8007
Nashville, TN 37202   Annette Morrison, Hd.Libn.
Founded: 1940. **Staff:** Prof 1; Other 1. **Subjects:** Newspaper reference topics. **Holdings:** 1500 books; 75 bound periodical volumes; 566 VF drawers of pamphlets; 407 VF drawers of clippings; 148 VF drawers of photographs; 80 drawers of microfilm. **Subscriptions:** 30 journals and other serials. **Services:** Library open to journalists for serious research. **Special Indexes:** Files on people, reporter by-lines, criminals, lawsuit litigants and businesses (card). **Staff:** Vernice Nance, Asst.Libn.

★13338★
TENNESSEE BOTANICAL GARDENS & FINE ARTS CENTER - FINE ARTS CENTER LIBRARY (Art)
Cheekwood-Forrest Park Dr.   Phone: (615) 352-8632
Nashville, TN 37205
Subjects: Art, art history, decorative arts, contemporary American artists, photography. **Holdings:** 2000 volumes; 2000 slides. **Subscriptions:** 20 journals and other serials. **Services:** Library open to members and staff for reference use only.

★13339★
TENNESSEE BOTANICAL GARDENS & FINE ARTS CENTER - MINNIE RITCHEY & JOEL OWSLEY CHEEK LIBRARY (Sci-Tech)
Cheekwood-Forrest Park Dr.   Phone: (615) 356-3306
Nashville, TN 37205   Muriel H. Connell, Libn.
Founded: 1971. **Staff:** Prof 1; Other 1. **Subjects:** Horticulture, landscape architecture, plant science, ecology, wildflowers, garden design, decorative arts. **Holdings:** 4000 books; 200 bound periodical volumes; 220 pamphlets; 70 slide programs; 5000 slides; flower and seed catalogs. **Subscriptions:** 130 journals and other serials. **Services:** Interlibrary loans; copying; library open to public with restrictions.

TENNESSEE EASTMAN COMPANY
See: Eastman Kodak Company

TENNESSEE LESBIAN ARCHIVES
See: Okra Ridge Farm

★13340★
TENNESSEE STATE COMMISSION ON AGING - LIBRARY (Soc Sci)
700 Tennessee Bldg.
535 Church St.   Phone: (615) 741-2056
Nashville, TN 37219   Mason Rowe, Res.Anl.
Founded: 1963. **Staff:** 1. **Subjects:** Aging, geriatric psychology and sociology, retirement planning, community based health and social services. **Holdings:** 100 books; VF drawers; microfiche. **Subscriptions:** 10 journals and other serials. **Services:** Interlibrary loans; copying; library open to public for reference use only.

★13341★
TENNESSEE STATE COMMISSION FOR HUMAN DEVELOPMENT - RESOURCE LIBRARY (Soc Sci)
208 Tennessee Bldg.
535 Church St.   Phone: (615) 741-2424
Nashville, TN 37219
Staff: 1. **Subjects:** Race relations; discrimination in employment, housing and public accommodations; legislation and decisions rendered in discrimination cases. **Holdings:** 60 books; 500 bound periodical volumes; commission-related materials. **Subscriptions:** 10 journals and other serials. **Services:** Library open to public with restrictions. **Publications:** Annual Report.

★13342★
TENNESSEE STATE DEPARTMENT OF AGRICULTURE - LOU WALLACE LIBRARY (Agri)
Ellington Agricultural Center
Melrose Sta., Box 40627   Phone: (615) 741-1456
Nashville, TN 37204   Mark McBride, Adm.Asst., Pub.Aff.
Staff: Prof 1; Other 1. **Subjects:** Agriculture, statistics. **Holdings:** 1500 books. **Services:** Library open to public for reference use only.

★13343★
TENNESSEE STATE DEPARTMENT OF CONSERVATION - DIVISION OF GEOLOGY - CONSERVATION RESOURCE CENTER (Env-Cons)
701 Broadway   Phone: (615) 741-2726
Nashville, TN 37203   Robert A. Hershey, Dir./State Geologist
Subjects: Geology. **Holdings:** Figures not available. **Publications:** Annual list of publications - free upon request. **Remarks:** This center participates in a national and international exchange program. **Staff:** Doris E. Noble, Ed.

★13344★
TENNESSEE STATE DEPARTMENT OF ECONOMIC & COMMUNITY DEVELOPMENT - LIBRARY (Bus-Fin)
1014 Andrew Jackson Office Bldg. Phone: (615) 741-1995
Nashville, TN 37219   Edith Snider, Libn.
Founded: 1973. **Staff:** Prof 1; Other 1. **Subjects:** Industrial development, economics, minority business enterprise. **Special Collections:** Department Archives. **Holdings:** 3000 books; 300 documents; 750 file folios of corporation annual reports (Fortune 500 companies and major Tennessee companies). **Subscriptions:** 210 journals and other serials. **Services:**

Interlibrary loans; copying; library open to public with restrictions.

★13345★

TENNESSEE STATE DEPARTMENT OF EMPLOYMENT SECURITY - RESEARCH & STATISTICS SECTION (Soc Sci)
519 Cordell Hull Bldg.   Phone: (615) 741-2284
Nashville, TN 37219   Joe Cummings, Chf., Res. & Stat.
Staff: 1. **Subjects:** Data - labor market, census, economic. **Holdings:** Publications of the U.S. Bureau of Census, the U.S. Department of Labor, and the Department of Employment Security. **Services:** Copying; library open to public for reference use only. **Special Indexes:** Labor Market Information Directory.

★13346★

TENNESSEE STATE DEPARTMENT OF HEALTH AND ENVIRONMENT - FILM LIBRARY (Aud-Vis)
State Office Bldg.
Ben Allen Rd.   Phone: (615) 741-7276
Nashville, TN 37216   Randall Brady, Dir.
Founded: 1950. **Staff:** Prof 3; Other 2. **Subjects:** Health, safety, nutrition, drug abuse, allied health fields. **Special Collections:** Medical Self Help Series (24 sets). **Holdings:** 2500 films, filmstrips, slide series. **Services:** Materials available for free loan to Tennessee residents; library not open to public. **Publications:** The Film Catalog and supplements. **Formerly:** Tennesse State Department of Public Health - Film Library.

★13347★

TENNESSEE STATE DEPARTMENT OF PUBLIC HEALTH - MCH/HWP RESOURCE CENTER (Med)†
TDPH State Office Bldg.
Ben Allen Rd.   Phone: (615) 741-7276
Nashville, TN 37216   Randall Brady, Dir., Resource Ctr.
Staff: Prof 1. **Subjects:** Maternal and child health, nursing, public health, health education. **Holdings:** 500 books. **Subscriptions:** 100 journals and other serials. **Services:** Center open to public health professionals. **Networks/Consortia:** Member of Middle Tennessee Health Science Librarians (MTHSL). **Special Catalogs:** Media Resource Catalog (loose-leaf).

★13348★

TENNESSEE STATE DEPARTMENT OF TRANSPORTATION - LIBRARY (Trans)
James K. Polk Bldg., Suite 900   Phone: (615) 741-2330
Nashville, TN 37219   Ruth S. Letson, Libn.
Founded: 1973. **Staff:** Prof 1. **Subjects:** Transportation, Tennessee planning data, highways, road construction. **Special Collections:** Transportation Research Board publications. **Holdings:** 6500 books; 1000 local studies. **Subscriptions:** 80 journals and other serials. **Services:** Interlibrary loans; copying; library open to public for reference use only. **Publications:** New Books, monthly - for internal distribution only.

★13349★

TENNESSEE STATE ENERGY AUTHORITY - LIBRARY
707 Capitol Blvd. Bldg.
Nashville, TN 37219
Defunct

★13350★

TENNESSEE STATE LAW LIBRARY (Law)
Supreme Court Bldg.
401 Seventh Ave., N.   Phone: (615) 741-2016
Nashville, TN 37219   G. Alvis Winstead, Dir. & Libn.
Founded: 1937. **Staff:** Prof 2; Other 1. **Subjects:** Law. **Special Collections:** Depository Library. **Holdings:** 40,000 books; 1201 bound periodical volumes; 237 other cataloged items; 4 VF drawers; 200 cassettes of Supreme Court cases. **Subscriptions:** 116 journals and other serials. **Services:** Interlibrary loans; copying; library open to public. **Remarks:** The state also maintains law libraries at Jackson, Knoxville and Memphis.

★13351★

TENNESSEE STATE LEGISLATIVE LIBRARY (Soc Sci)
G-16 War Memorial Bldg.
Nashville, TN 37219   Phone: (615) 741-3091
                    Julie J. McCown, Leg.Libn.
Founded: 1977. **Staff:** Prof 1. **Subjects:** Tennessee law, legislative reference. **Holdings:** 12,000 volumes. **Subscriptions:** 70 journals and other serials. **Services:** Interlibrary loans; copying; library open to members of the legislature and open to public for reference use only. **Remarks:** Maintained by Office of Legal Services for the Tennessee General Assembly.

★13352★

TENNESSEE STATE LIBRARY AND ARCHIVES - ARCHIVES & MANUSCRIPTS SECTION (Hist)
403 Seventh Ave., N.   Phone: (615) 741-2561
Nashville, TN 37219   Jean B. Waggener, Dir.
Founded: 1853. **Staff:** Prof 7; Other 7. **Subjects:** History - Tennessee, U.S., Southern; genealogy. **Special Collections:** Papers of Jacob McGavock Dickinson, James Robertson, Andrew Jackson, George P. Buell, Henry Shelton Sanford (microfilm), Richard Ewell; land records, 1777-1903 (600 volumes); state agency and governors' papers, 1796 to present; legislative records and recordings, 1796 to present; state Supreme Court records, 1815-1955; ethics records, 1975-1976; county records on microfilm. **Holdings:** 2.7 million manuscript items; 800 volumes; 14,000 reels of microfilm; 3120 hours of recordings. **Services:** Interlibrary loans; copying; archives open to public. **Publications:** Registers of manuscript materials; checklist of microfilm; Guide to the Processed Manuscripts of the Tennessee Historical Society; Guide to Microfilm Holdings of the Manuscript Section. **Special Indexes:** Index to City Cemetery Records of Nashville; index to questionnaires of Civil War veterans. **Staff:** Tommy Adams, Archv.Proc.; John Thweatt, Hd., Mss.Proc.; Marylin Bell, Hd., Ref.

★13353★

TENNESSEE STATE LIBRARY - LIBRARY FOR THE BLIND AND PHYSICALLY HANDICAPPED (Aud-Vis)
403 Seventh Ave. N.   Phone: (615) 741-3915
Nashville, TN 37219   Miss Francis H. Ezell, Dir.
Founded: 1970. **Staff:** Prof 2; Other 11. **Subjects:** General reading material for the blind and physically handicapped. **Holdings:** 15,000 titles of books recorded on disc and cassette, transcribed into braille; large print books. **Subscriptions:** 83 journals and other serials (45 disc, 35 braille, 3 cassette). **Services:** Free service to citizens of Tennessee who cannot read, hold or turn the pages of a regular print book due to a visual or physical handicap. **Remarks:** WATS number is (800) 342-3308.

★13354★

TENNESSEE STATE LIBRARY - STATE LIBRARY DIVISION (Hist; Law)
403 7th Ave., N.   Phone: (615) 741-2764
Nashville, TN 37219   Miss Kendall Cram, Dir.
Founded: 1855. **Staff:** Prof 6; Other 17. **Subjects:** U.S. history, especially Jackson, Polk, Johnson administrations; wars in which Tennessee participated - War of 1812, Indian Wars, Mexican War, Civil War; political, social, cultural history of the Southeastern states; law and public administration; genealogy. **Special Collections:** Photographs, prints and cartoons of Tennessee subjects; popular sheet music; 19th century broadsides; Tennessee newspapers. **Holdings:** 250,000 volumes. **Subscriptions:** 1400 journals and other serials; 200 newspapers. **Services:** Interlibrary loans; copying; library open to public for reference use only. **Automated Operations:** Computerized cataloging. **Computerized Information Services:** OCLC. **Networks/Consortia:** Member of SOLINET. **Publications:** List of Tennessee State Publications, quarterly; Writings on Tennessee Counties; Tennessee Newspapers on Microfilm. **Staff:** Fran Schell, Ref.Libn.; Marvin Williams, Hd.Cat.

★13355★

TENNESSEE STATE PLANNING OFFICE - LIBRARY (Plan)
1800 Polk Bldg.
505 Deaderick St.   Phone: (615) 741-2363
Nashville, TN 37219-5082   Eleanor J. Burt, Libn.
Founded: 1935. **Staff:** Prof 1; Other 1. **Subjects:** Planning, Tennessee, public affairs. **Special Collections:** Tennessee planning studies; budget documents and state planning studies from other states; archives of planning office publications (4200 items); Tennessee state publications including departmental reports, Tennessee session laws and the Tennessee Code. **Holdings:** 9786 books and pamphlets; 1397 community planning color slides; 1980 Census Area Boundary Maps for Tennessee; 40 VF drawers; 8 cassettes; 1 film; 704 maps; 1455 microfiche; 37 binders of computer printouts. **Subscriptions:** 200 journals and other serials. **Services:** Interlibrary loans; copying; library open to public. **Publications:** Acquisitions List, bimonthly; periodical list, irregular - for internal distribution only. **Remarks:** Reference collections of 8340 items and selected journal and newspaper subscriptions are maintained in six sectional offices.

★13356★

TENNESSEE STATE PUBLIC SERVICE COMMISSION - LEGAL DEPARTMENT - LIBRARY (Law)
C1-103 Cordell Hull Bldg.   Phone: (615) 741-3191
Nashville, TN 37219   Henry Walker, Gen. Counsel
Founded: 1897. **Subjects:** Law, utility rates, transportation, tax assessments, railroads, transportation rates, utility service. **Holdings:** 2500 bound periodical volumes; docket files; transcripts; orders; court files.

Services: Copying; library open to public.

★13357★

TENNESSEE STATE SUPREME COURT - LAW LIBRARY (Law)
Supreme Court Bldg.
719 Locust St.   Phone: (615) 673-6128
Knoxville, TN 37902   Mamie H. Winstead, Libn.
Founded: 1937. **Staff:** Prof 1. **Subjects:** Law. **Holdings:** 38,000 volumes. **Subscriptions:** 150 journals and other serials. **Services:** Library open to public with restrictions. **Automated Operations:** Computerized cataloging.

★13358★

TENNESSEE VALLEY AUTHORITY - CONTRACT SERVICES (Geog-Map)
400 W. Summit Hill Dr., WPA3   Phone: (615) 632-2717
Knoxville, TN 37902   Mr. G.V. Rogers, Jr., Supv.
Founded: 1934. **Staff:** 2. **Subjects:** Tennessee Valley Region, planimetry, topography, water navigation, flood control, water power. **Special Collections:** National Geographic maps; raised relief maps. **Holdings:** 12,000 sheet maps; 300 atlases; 30,000 aerial photographs; navigation charts; geologic publications. **Services:** Reference and research services; sale of maps, charts, and engineering reproductions; services open to public. **Publications:** Price lists of selected maps and charts; list of publications - available upon request. **Formerly:** Its Map Sales Office. **Staff:** Harold Donahue, Mtls. Clerk.

★13359★

TENNESSEE VALLEY AUTHORITY - DIVISION OF LAND AND FOREST RESOURCES - NATURAL RESOURCES LIBRARY (Sci-Tech)†
Forestry Bldg.   Phone: (615) 494-7173
Norris, TN 37828   Janice P. McDonnell, Libn.
Founded: 1973. **Staff:** Prof 1; Other 2. **Subjects:** Forestry, fisheries, aquatic science, wildlife, waterfowl, recreation. **Holdings:** 8000 books; 15,000 documents. **Subscriptions:** 295 journals and other serials; 7 newspapers. **Services:** Interlibrary loans; copying; library open to public. **Computerized Information Services:** DIALOG, SDC, BRS, DOE/RECON, OCLC.

★13360★

TENNESSEE VALLEY AUTHORITY - LAW LIBRARY (Law)
400 W. Summit Hill Dr., E4A20   Phone: (615) 632-4391
Knoxville, TN 37902   Bonnie M. Holmes, Supv., Law Lib.Serv.
Staff: Prof 3; Other 4. **Subjects:** Law. **Holdings:** 20,000 books and bound periodical volumes. **Subscriptions:** 75 journals and other serials. **Services:** Interlibrary loans (limited); library not open to public.

★13361★

TENNESSEE VALLEY AUTHORITY - MAPS AND SURVEYS BRANCH - MAP INFORMATION AND RECORDS UNIT (Geog-Map)
101 Haney Bldg.   Phone: (615) 751-5404
Chattanooga, TN 37401   J.L. Dodd, Supv.
Founded: 1933. **Staff:** Prof 6; Other 1. **Subjects:** Land acquisition mapping, land sales mapping, special purpose mapping, navigation charts and maps, control data, aerial photography, topography. **Holdings:** 1.2 million maps, charts, photographs and control data. **Services:** Copying; unit open to public. **Special Catalogs:** Price Catalog of Selected Maps and Data (book).

★13362★

TENNESSEE VALLEY AUTHORITY - TECHNICAL LIBRARY (Sci-Tech)
National Fertilizer Development Ctr.   Phone: (205) 386-2871
Muscle Shoals, AL 35660   Shirley G. Nichols, Supv.Libn.
Founded: 1961. **Staff:** Prof 6; Other 5. **Subjects:** Agriculture, chemistry, chemical engineering, fertilizer, economics, environmental sciences, developing countries, occupational health. **Special Collections:** One of the most complete collections on fertilizer in U.S.; history of fertilizer and agriculture. **Holdings:** 32,600 books and bound periodical volumes; 1700 reels of microfilm; 400 VF drawers of pamphlets and documents. **Subscriptions:** 1190 journals and other serials; 8 newspapers. **Services:** Interlibrary loans; copying; bibliographies; reference services; library open to public. **Automated Operations:** Computerized cataloging and serials. **Computerized Information Services:** DIALOG, SDC, BRS, DOE/RECON, NLM, OCLC. **Networks/Consortia:** Member of FEDLINK. **Publications:** Current Awareness and New Acquisitions, weekly; Calendar of Events, monthly; Fertilizer Publications with quarterly supplement; Bibliographies, semiannual. **Remarks:** Main library in Knoxville, Tennessee is in charge of ordering and cataloging. **Staff:** Marcia M. Bystrom, Ref.Libn.; Drucilla Gambrell, Ref.Libn.; Wendolyn Clark, Ref.Libn.; Elizabeth Evans, Acq.Libn.

★13363★

TENNESSEE VALLEY AUTHORITY - TECHNICAL LIBRARY (Sci-Tech; Energy)
100-401 Bldg.   Phone: (615) 751-4913
Chattanooga, TN 37401   Dean Robinson, Supv., Lib.Serv.
Founded: 1957. **Staff:** Prof 3; Other 3. **Subjects:** Power, public utilities, environment, solar energy and alternate energy sources. **Holdings:** 26,862 books; 7000 government documents; 23,000 microfiche; 650 reels of microfilm; 100 audiotapes. **Subscriptions:** 343 journals and other serials. **Services:** Interlibrary loans; copying; library open to public. **Automated Operations:** Computerized cataloging. **Computerized Information Services:** DIALOG, DOE/RECON, OCLC. **Networks/Consortia:** Member of FEDLINK. **Publications:** Current Awareness, biweekly - for internal distribution only. **Remarks:** Main library in Knoxville, Tennessee is in charge of ordering and cataloging. **Staff:** Barbara Bazemore, Ref.; Francis Bishop, Acq.Libn.

★13364★

TENNESSEE VALLEY AUTHORITY - TECHNICAL LIBRARY (Sci-Tech)
400 Commerce Ave.   Phone: (615) 632-3464
Knoxville, TN 37902   Jesse C. Mills, Chf.Libn.
Founded: 1933. **Staff:** Prof 22; Other 18. **Subjects:** Administration and finance; agriculture; chemistry; engineering - civil, mechanical, electrical and nuclear; environmental sciences and education; flood control and navigation; forestry and wildlife; recreation; resource development; energy research development. **Special Collections:** History and development of TVA and Tennessee River Valley; TVA printed archives. **Holdings:** 107,000 books; 15,000 bound periodical volumes; 400,000 clippings; 50,000 documents; 700 reels of microfilm of newspapers. **Subscriptions:** 2500 journals and other serials; 106 newspapers. **Services:** Interlibrary loans; copying; bibliographies; reference services; library open to public. **Automated Operations:** Computerized cataloging. **Computerized Information Services:** DIALOG, SDC, BRS, DOE/RECON, OCLC. **Networks/Consortia:** Member of FEDLINK. **Remarks:** TVA maintains separate Technical Libraries in Knoxville, Norris and Chattanooga, Tennessee and Muscle Shoals, Alabama. The central staff in Knoxville handles acquisitions and cataloging of materials for all libraries; figures above include holdings of the three libraries.

★13365★

TENNESSEE WESTERN HISTORY AND FOLKLORE SOCIETY - LIBRARY (Hist)
Box 60072   Phone: (615) 226-1890
Nashville, TN 37206   Steve Eng, Cur.
Founded: 1979. **Staff:** Prof 1. **Subjects:** Tennessee and the Old West, Jesse and Frank James, the Seventh Cavalry (at Nashville), Ned Buntline, Clay Allison, Ambrose Bierce, Nat Love (black cowboy), J. Frank Dalton (Jesse James imposter), James Russell Davis (Cole Young imposter), John Wilkes Booth, Knights of the Golden Circle. **Special Collections:** Jesse James, 1847-1882 (275 items); Western imposters (200 items). **Holdings:** 200 books; 100 letters; 300 miscellaneous items; articles and news clippings; photographs; affidavits; artifacts; maps. **Services:** Copying (limited); research (limited); library open to serious scholars by appointment. **Remarks:** The society is interested in acquiring any information about Western events or persons with Tennessee connections. It is affiliated with the Friends of the James Farm (Kearney, MO), Friends of the Youngers (Los Angeles, CA), The Nashville Room of Nashville Public Library and The Tennessee State Library and Archive (Nashville, TN). The society library is located at 1406 Eastland Ave., Nashville, TN 37206.

★13366★

TERRA TEK RESEARCH - TECHNICAL LIBRARY (Energy)
420 Wakara Way
University Research Park   Phone: (801) 584-2400
Salt Lake City, UT 84108   Sharlene Ivie, Libn.
Founded: 1975. **Subjects:** Geothermal energy, rock mechanics, drilling, petroleum, materials testing. **Special Collections:** Technical reports. **Holdings:** Figures not available. **Services:** Interlibrary loans; copying; library open to public.

★13367★

TERRELL STATE HOSPITAL - STAFF LIBRARY (Med)
Box 70   Phone: (214) 563-6452
Terrell, TX 75160   Lillian Squires, Libn.
Founded: 1964. **Staff:** 2. **Subjects:** Psychiatry, neurology, medicine, nursing, psychology, mental health and allied sciences. **Holdings:** 4632 books; 240 bound periodical volumes; 1493 complete unbound periodical volumes; 1900 pamphlets and nonbook materials; 663 audio cassettes. **Subscriptions:** 129 journals and other serials; 8 newspapers. **Services:** Interlibrary loans; copying; library open to public for reference use only. **Networks/Consortia:** Member of TALON; Texas Department of Mental Health & Mental Retardation Library Association. **Publications:** Staff Library Handbook - distributed to professional

staff, hospital employees and students of affiliated schools.

TESZLER (Sandor) LIBRARY
See: Wofford College - Sandor Teszler Library

★13368★
TETRA TECH, INC. - LIBRARY (Env-Cons; Sci-Tech)†
630 N. Rosemead Blvd.					Phone: (818) 449-6400
Pasadena, CA 91107					Ella J. Jackson, Libn.
Staff: 1. **Subjects:** Environmental studies, engineering. **Holdings:** 1500 books; 4000 technical reports. **Subscriptions:** 150 journals and other serials. **Services:** Interlibrary loans; library not open to public. **Computerized Information Services:** Online systems.

★13369★
TEXACO CHEMICAL COMPANY, INC. - TECHNICAL LITERATURE SECTION (Sci-Tech)
Box 15730					Phone: (512) 459-6543
Austin, TX 78761					Mary E. Reese, Sr.Res.Libn.
Founded: 1946. **Subjects:** Chemistry and chemical engineering. **Holdings:** 4000 books; 3725 bound periodical volumes; 400 other cataloged items; patents; reports. **Subscriptions:** 300 journals and other serials.

★13370★
TEXACO INC. - ARCHIVES (Bus-Fin)
2000 Westchester Ave.					Phone: (914) 253-7129
White Plains, NY 10650					Stafford Acher, Hist.
Subjects: Texaco Incorporated. **Holdings:** 200 volumes; 1500 cubic feet of records; Texaco Incorporated photographs and publications. **Services:** Copying; archives open to public by appointment upon written request.

★13371★
TEXACO INC. - CORPORATE LIBRARY (Energy)
2000 Westchester Ave.					Phone: (914) 253-6382
White Plains, NY 10650					Holly J. Furman, Corp.Lib.Adm.
Founded: 1981. **Staff:** Prof 6; Other 3. **Subjects:** Business, energy, petroleum, area studies. **Holdings:** 8200 volumes; 129,000 microfiche; 1300 reels of microfilm. **Subscriptions:** 570 journals and other serials. **Services:** Interlibrary loans; copying; SDI; library open to public with restrictions. **Automated Operations:** Computerized cataloging, acquisitions, serials and circulation. **Computerized Information Services:** SDC, DIALOG, DOE/RECON, NEXIS, RUN, TEXTLINE, NewsNet, Inc., Dow Jones News/Retrieval, I.P. Sharp Associates, Ltd., EBSCO Subscription Services; DATALIB (internal database). **Networks/Consortia:** Member of Texaco Library Network; METRO. **Publications:** Update, monthly - for internal distribution only; Library brochures and bibliographies. **Staff:** Mary Addy, Info.Spec.; Susan Feir, Info.Spec.; Edith Palmer, Info.Spec.; Mitchell Feir, Info.Spec.; Susan Smith, Info.Spec.

TEXACO INC. - GETTY REFINING AND MARKETING COMPANY
See: Getty Refining and Marketing Company

★13372★
TEXARKANA HISTORICAL SOCIETY & MUSEUM - LIBRARY (Hist)
219 State Line Ave.
Box 2343					Phone: (214) 793-4831
Texarkana, TX 75501					Katy Caver, Cur.
Founded: 1971. **Staff:** Prof 2; Other 2. **Subjects:** Local history. **Special Collections:** Medical books of early local physicians; early school books and newspapers; local genealogy. **Holdings:** 1800 books; 15 scrapbooks of early residents; 40 Texarkana city directories; 44 annuals of local high schools. **Subscriptions:** 14 journals and newspapers. **Services:** Interlibrary loans; copying; library open to public by request. **Staff:** Louise Dillingham, Assoc.Cur.

★13373★
TEXAS A & M UNIVERSITY - ARCHIVES & MANUSCRIPTS COLLECTIONS (Hist)
Sterling C. Evans Library					Phone: (409) 845-1815
College Station, TX 77843					Dr. Charles R. Schultz, Univ.Archv.
Founded: 1950. **Staff:** Prof 2; Other 1. **Subjects:** Texas A & M University, Texas agriculture, technology, modern politics, education. **Special Collections:** Papers of Congressmen Olin E. Teague, Robert Casey, John Young and Graham Purcell; journalist Bascom N. Timmons; nuclear physicist Paul Aebersold; educator Tim M. Stinnett; author William A. Owens; Texas legislators Tom Creighton, Will L. Smith and Bill Presnel; real estate broker Owen Sherrill; animal scientist John McKinley Jones; engineer and highway administrator Thomas H. McDonald; records of the Texas Cotton Association; records of the Texas section of the American Society of Civil Engineers. **Holdings:** 7200 cubic feet of records of Texas A & M University and historical

manuscripts collections; photographs of campus; 150 hours of oral history interviews. **Services:** Copying; collections open to public. **Publications:** Inventories of individual manuscript and archival collections; guides to all holdings - both irregular. **Staff:** David L. Chapman, Assoc.Archv.

★13374★
TEXAS A & M UNIVERSITY - DEPARTMENTS OF OCEANOGRAPHY AND METEOROLOGY - WORKING COLLECTION (Sci-Tech)
Dept. of Oceanography					Phone: (409) 845-7327
College Station, TX 77843					Gloria Guffy, Resource Ctr.Supv.
Staff: Prof 1; Other 1. **Subjects:** Oceanography, meteorology. **Holdings:** 1100 books; 800 technical reports; 400 theses and dissertations; 400 external reports and publications. **Services:** Copying; collection open to public for reference use only. **Publications:** Contributions in Oceanography, annual - for exchange. **Special Catalogs:** Technical reports, 1947 to present.

TEXAS A & M UNIVERSITY - FOOD PROTEIN RESEARCH AND DEVELOPMENT CENTER
See: Food Protein Research and Development Center

★13375★
TEXAS A & M UNIVERSITY - MAP DEPARTMENT (Geog-Map)
Sterling C. Evans Library					Phone: (409) 845-1024
College Station, TX 77843					Judy Rieke, Map Libn.
Staff: Prof 1; Other 1. **Subjects:** Geology, soils, topography, energy resources, transportation. **Special Collections:** U.S. Geological Survey topographic maps for Texas, Arkansas, Colorado, New Mexico, Oklahoma, Louisiana; various Texas subjects (32 map drawers). **Holdings:** 1200 titles; 45 bound periodical volumes; 82,000 maps; 212 slides; 318 microfiche. **Services:** Interlibrary loans; department open to public.

★13376★
TEXAS A & M UNIVERSITY - MEDICAL SCIENCES LIBRARY (Med)
Veterinary Adm. Bldg., Rm. 101					Phone: (409) 845-7427
College Station, TX 77843					Virginia L. Algermissen, Dir.
Staff: Prof 8; Other 14. **Subjects:** Pre-clinical science, clinical medicine, veterinary medicine. **Holdings:** 22,000 books; 34,500 bound periodical volumes; 1015 microforms. **Subscriptions:** 1800 journals and other serials; 10 newspapers. **Services:** Interlibrary loans; copying; SDI; library open to public. **Automated Operations:** Computerized cataloging, acquisitions and serials. **Computerized Information Services:** BRS, DIALOG, SDC; internal database. **Networks/Consortia:** Member of TALON; TAMU Consortium of Medical Libraries; AMIGOS Bibliographic Council, Inc. **Publications:** Medical Sciences Library Newsletter. **Special Catalogs:** Union List of Serials (computer printout and microfiche). **Staff:** Charlotte Neill, Hd., Tech.Serv.; Rosa Botterill, Res.Asst.; Ann Duyka, Hd.Cat.; Barbara Thomas, Ref.; Gloria Sauceda, Academic Bus.Adm.; Esther Carrigan, Ser.Cat.; Kathrine MacNeil, Hd., Pub.Serv.

★13377★
TEXAS A & M UNIVERSITY - NAUTICAL ARCHAEOLOGY LIBRARY (Sci-Tech)
Dept. of Anthropology					Phone: (409) 845-6398
College Station, TX 77843-4352					Vicki Reid, Libn.
Staff: Prof 1. **Subjects:** Nautical archeology, maritime history, archeology, naval architecture, artifact conservation. **Special Collections:** G. Roger Edwards Collection (Greek and Roman Civilization, particularly Hellenistic Greece; 495 volumes). **Holdings:** 1300 books; 475 bound periodical volumes; 4000 other cataloged items; 2600 journal offprints, reports, and unpublished papers; 13 reels of microfilm; 13 microfiche. **Subscriptions:** 36 journals and other serials. **Services:** Library open to public for reference use only. **Remarks:** Library contains the holdings of the Institute of Nautical Archaeology.

★13378★
TEXAS A & M UNIVERSITY - REFERENCE DIVISION (Sci-Tech)
Sterling C. Evans Library					Phone: (409) 845-5741
College Station, TX 77843					Katherine M. Jackson, Hd., Ref.Div.
Founded: 1876. **Staff:** Prof 13; Other 9. **Subjects:** Agriculture, engineering and technology, physical sciences, biology, transportation, petroleum geology. **Holdings:** 9000 reference books. **Subscriptions:** 700 indexes and abstracts. **Services:** Interlibrary loans; copying; SDI; division open to public. **Automated Operations:** Computerized cataloging, acquisitions, serials and circulation. **Computerized Information Services:** Online systems. **Remarks:** Includes holdings of former Texas Engineers Library. **Staff:** John Abbott, Sci.Ref.Libn.; Judith Droessler, Sci.Libn.; Gayla Cloud, Sci.Libn.; Jane Dodd, Sci.Ref.Libn.; Charles Gilreath, Hd., Automated Info.Ret.; Vicki Anders, Hd., Bibliog.Instr.

★13379★
TEXAS A & M UNIVERSITY - SPECIAL COLLECTIONS DIVISION (Hum)
Sterling C. Evans Library   Phone: (409) 845-1951
College Station, TX 77843   Donald A. Dyal, Hd., Spec.Coll.Div.
Founded: 1968. **Staff:** Prof 2; Other 6. **Subjects:** Range livestock industry, science fiction, Texas, J. Frank Dobie, Western illustrators, Ku Klux Klan, W. Somerset Maugham, early printing. **Special Collections:** Jeff Dykes Range Livestock Collection; Science Fiction Research Collection; J. Frank Dobie Collection; Great Western Illustrators Collection. **Holdings:** 65,000 books; 8000 bound periodical volumes; 14,000 reprints on developmental biology. **Subscriptions:** 40 journals and other serials. **Services:** Copying (limited); collections open to public with restrictions. **Computerized Information Services:** OCLC. **Special Indexes:** Story index to science fiction anthologies.

★13380★
TEXAS A & M UNIVERSITY - TECHNICAL REPORTS DEPARTMENT (Sci-Tech)
Sterling C. Evans Library   Phone: (409) 845-2551
College Station, TX 77843   Lisa Abbott, Tech.Rpts.Libn.
Founded: 1972. **Staff:** Prof 2; Other 3. **Subjects:** Oceanography, transportation, water resources. **Holdings:** 23,000 technical reports; 525,000 NASA, DOE, NTIS and Atomic Energy Commission microfiche. **Services:** Interlibrary loans; copying; department open to public. **Staff:** Eugenia Tang, Cat.

TEXAS A & M UNIVERSITY - TEXAS (State) FOREST SERVICE
See: Texas (State) Forest Service

★13381★
TEXAS A & M UNIVERSITY - THERMODYNAMICS RESEARCH CENTER (Sci-Tech)
Texas Engineering Experiment Station   Phone: (409) 845-4940
College Station, TX 77843   Dr. Kenneth R. Hall, Dir.
Founded: 1942. **Staff:** Prof 10; Other 9. **Subjects:** Critical tables of physical and thermodynamic properties and spectral data in six categories (IR, UV, Raman, Mass, Proton NMR, C13 NMR) for hydrocarbons and related compounds and for other organic (nonhydrocarbon) and inorganic substances. **Holdings:** 1200 books; 1300 bound periodical volumes; 1000 sets of data; 500,000 data cards on physical and thermodynamic properties; 200 government documents on microfiche. **Subscriptions:** 10 journals and other serials. **Services:** Center open to public with permission. **Computerized Information Services:** DIALOG, CAS Online. **Publications:** Critically selected scientific data (loose-leaf), semiannual; Thermodynamics Research Center Hydrocarbon Project; T.R.C. Data Project; International Data Series - all by subcription; contributes to an annual bibliography on thermodynamics and thermochemistry; prepares the organic chemicals portion of "Bulletin of Chemical Thermodynamics." **Staff:** Randolph C. Wilhoit, Assoc.Dir.

★13382★
TEXAS A & M UNIVERSITY AT GALVESTON - LIBRARY (Sci-Tech)
Mitchell Campus
Pelican Island, Box 1675   Phone: (409) 766-3366
Galveston, TX 77553   Natalie W. Shipman, Lib.Dir.
Staff: Prof 3; Other 6. **Subjects:** Marine biology, ecology, systems engineering, maritime history, marine transportation and technology, maritime resources. **Holdings:** 32,000 books; 8000 bound periodical volumes; 28,000 titles on microfiche. **Subscriptions:** 700 journals and other serials; 9 newspapers. **Services:** Interlibrary loans; library open to public for reference use only. **Automated Operations:** Computerized cataloging, acquisitions and ILL. **Computerized Information Services:** OCLC. **Networks/Consortia:** Member of AMIGOS Bibliographic Council, Inc. **Publications:** Serials List, quarterly - free upon request. **Staff:** Kathleen Roberts, Pub.Serv.Libn.; Ellen Wong, Tech.Serv.Libn.

★13383★
TEXAS ADVISORY COMMISSION ON INTERGOVERNMENTAL RELATIONS - INFORMATION CENTER (Soc Sci)
Box 13206   Phone: (512) 475-3728
Austin, TX 78711   Catherine K. Harris, Libn.
Founded: 1972. **Staff:** Prof 1. **Subjects:** Intergovernmental relations, local government finance, public health, regional planning. **Special Collections:** U.S. Advisory Commission on Intergovernmental Relations reports. **Holdings:** 3000 books; 320 unbound titles; current set of Texas statutes. **Subscriptions:** 150 journals and other serials. **Services:** Center open to public for reference use only. **Publications:** List of publications - available on request.

★13384★
TEXAS BAPTIST HISTORICAL CENTER/MUSEUM - LIBRARY (Rel-Theol)
Rt. 5
Box 222   Phone: (409) 836-5117
Brenham, TX 77833   Jesse E. Bigbee, Dir.
Staff: Prof 1. **Subjects:** Baptist history. **Special Collections:** Annuals of the Baptist General Convention of Texas (60 volumes); Southern Baptist Annuals (58 volumes); Link's Letters (bound in two volumes). **Holdings:** 502 books; 12 VF drawers of other cataloged items. **Services:** Library open to public for reference use only.

★13385★
TEXAS BAPTIST INSTITUTE/SEMINARY - LIBRARY (Rel-Theol)
1300 Longview Dr.
Box 570   Phone: (214) 657-6543
Henderson, TX 75652   James A. Kirkland, Libn.
Staff: Prof 1. **Subjects:** Religion, Baptist theology and history. **Holdings:** 7094 books; 230 dissertations. **Subscriptions:** 50 journals and other serials. **Services:** Interlibrary loans; library open to public by special arrangement with librarian.

★13386★
TEXAS CATHOLIC HISTORICAL SOCIETY - CATHOLIC ARCHIVES OF TEXAS (Hist; Rel-Theol)
Capitol Sta., Box 13327   Phone: (512) 476-4888
Austin, TX 78711   Sr. M. Dolores Kasner, O.P., Dir.
Founded: 1923. **Staff:** Prof 1; Other 2. **Subjects:** Spanish exploration and missionary period (1519-1836), Catholic Church history in Texas, immigration and emigration, colonization. **Special Collections:** Ecclesiastical records of the Catholic Church in Texas, 1836-1950; Texas Catholic Conference Papers, 1958-1979; Charles S. Taylor papers, 1829-1868 (over 2000 items); Bishop Odin papers (over 400 letters of first Bishop of Texas, 1840-1870); Knights of Columbus Collection (106 boxes); Papers of Volunteers for Educational & Social Services, 1958-1979. **Holdings:** 950 volumes; 70,000 pages of Spanish and Mexican documents, 1519-1880; 50 VF drawers of ecclesiastical records; 50 document cases of private collections; 58 shelves of Catholic newspapers; 120 reels of microfilm; 26 boxes of pamphlets; 3 boxes of pictures. **Subscriptions:** 5 journals and other serials; 11 newspapers. **Services:** Interlibrary loans; copying; library open to public; some materials require special permits for use; service fee for reference work. **Publications:** Our Catholic Heritage in Texas, 1519-1950 (7 volumes).

★13387★
TEXAS CENTRAL COUNTIES CENTER FOR MENTAL HEALTH & MENTAL RETARDATION SERVICES - INFO. RESOURCE CENTER
Box 518
Temple, TX 76503
Subjects: Psychology, community mental health, psychiatry, sociology. **Holdings:** 3000 books; audiovisual films; 19 VF drawers of pamphlets, papers. **Remarks:** Presently inactive.

TEXAS CHILDREN'S HOSPITAL
See: St. Luke's Episcopal & Texas Children's Hospitals

★13388★
TEXAS CHIROPRACTIC COLLEGE - MAE HILTY MEMORIAL LIBRARY (Med)
5912 Spencer Hwy.   Phone: (409) 487-1170
Pasadena, TX 77505   Mara Umpierre, Hd.Libn.
Founded: 1954. **Staff:** Prof 3; Other 4. **Subjects:** Chiropractic, basic sciences, diagnosis, x-ray, public health, clinical sciences. **Special Collections:** C.S. Cooley and Carver Chiropractic College Collection; Willard Carver Collection. **Holdings:** 6500 books; 3500 bound periodical volumes; 4000 volumes of periodicals on microfiche; 8 VF drawers of pamphlets; 410 AV sets. **Subscriptions:** 203 journals. **Services:** Interlibrary loans; copying; library open to public for reference use only. **Computerized Information Services:** MEDLARS. Performs searches on cost recovery basis. Contact Person: Michelle M. Larson. **Networks/Consortia:** Member of Chiropractic Library Consortium; TALON. **Publications:** Learning Resources Center Newsletter, monthly. **Special Catalogs:** Subject Catalog of AV Collection (book). **Staff:** Michelle M. Larson, Ref.Libn.; Duffy Sharlach, AV Media Spec.

TEXAS CHRISTIAN UNIVERSITY - HYMN SOCIETY OF AMERICA, INC.
See: Hymn Society of America, Inc.

★13389★
TEXAS CHRISTIAN UNIVERSITY - INSTITUTE OF BEHAVIORAL RESEARCH - DRUG ABUSE COUNCIL LIBRARY
Fort Worth, TX 76129
Defunct

★13390★
TEXAS CHRISTIAN UNIVERSITY - INSTITUTE OF BEHAVIORAL RESEARCH - DRUG ABUSE EPIDEMIOLOGY DATA CENTER
Box 32902
Fort Worth, TX 76129
Defunct

★13391★
TEXAS CHRISTIAN UNIVERSITY - INSTITUTE OF BEHAVIORAL RESEARCH - TECHNICAL LIBRARY
Fort Worth, TX 76129
Defunct

★13392★
TEXAS CHRISTIAN UNIVERSITY - MARY COUTS BURNETT LIBRARY - BRITE DIVINITY SCHOOL COLLECTION (Rel-Theol)
Phone: (817) 921-7106
Fort Worth, TX 76129   Robert A. Olsen, Jr., Libn.
Founded: 1927. Staff: Prof 1; Other 1. Subjects: Religion, theology, biography, bibliography, literature by and about the Disciples of Christ. Holdings: 125,991 books; 15,202 bound periodical volumes; 12,711 volumes in microform. Subscriptions: 756 journals and other serials. Services: Interlibrary loans; copying. Computerized Information Services: OCLC, DIALOG, SDC, BRS, MEDLINE; Management Systems through Texas Christian University Computer Center (internal database). Networks/ Consortia: Member of Association for Higher Education of North Texas - Library Committee; AMIGOS Bibliographic Council, Inc.

★13393★
TEXAS CHRISTIAN UNIVERSITY - MARY COUTS BURNETT LIBRARY - MUSIC LIBRARY AND AUDIO CENTER (Mus)
Phone: (817) 921-7000
Fort Worth, TX 76129   Sheila Madden, Music Libn.
Founded: 1945. Staff: Prof 1; Other 2. Subjects: Music. Holdings: 12,660 books; 20,776 music scores; 8125 phonograph records; 3025 78 rpm records; 135 titles on microcards; 120 reels of microfilm; 2893 reel-to-reel and cassette tapes. Subscriptions: 72 journals and other serials. Services: Interlibrary loans; copying; library open to public with restrictions. Automated Operations: Computerized cataloging, serials and circulation. Computerized Information Services: OCLC, Automated Information Retrieval Service (AIRS). Networks/Consortia: Member of Association for Higher Education of North Texas - Library Committee; AMIGOS Bibliographic Council, Inc.

★13394★
TEXAS COLLEGE OF OSTEOPATHIC MEDICINE - HEALTH SCIENCES LIBRARY (Med)
Camp Bowie at Montgomery   Phone: (817) 735-2464
Fort Worth, TX 76107   Bobby R. Carter, Dir., Lib.Serv.
Founded: 1970. Staff: Prof 10; Other 17. Subjects: Health sciences, clinical and osteopathic medicine. Special Collections: Osteopathic medicine (600 volumes); oral history collection (15 items). Holdings: 27,162 books; 42,192 bound periodical volumes; 3019 AV programs; 4 VF drawers of pamphlets; 67 anatomical models. Subscriptions: 255 journals and other serials. Services: Interlibrary loans; copying; SDI; library open to public with restrictions. Automated Operations: Computerized cataloging and serials. Computerized Information Services: MEDLINE, DIALOG, BRS, OCLC. Performs searches on cost recovery basis. Contact Person: Richard C. Wood, 735-2591. Networks/Consortia: Member of AMIGOS Bibliographic Council, Inc.; Association for Higher Education of North Texas - Library Committee; Dallas-Tarrant County Consortium of Health Science Libraries; South Central Academic Libraries Consortium (SCAMEL). Staff: Craig Elam, Assoc.Dir., Tech.Serv.; Richard C. Wood, Assoc.Dir., Pub.Serv.; Moira McInroy-Hocevar, AV Libn.; John Taber, Ser./Acq.; Timothy Mason, Cat.Libn.; Adela O'Brien, Ref.Libn.; Ann Pfaffenberger, Ref.Libn.; Phyllis Muirhead, Ref.Libn.; Ray Stokes, Cur., Spec.Coll.

TEXAS CONFEDERATE MUSEUM LIBRARY
See: United Daughters of the Confederacy

★13395★
TEXAS EASTERN TRANSMISSION CORPORATION - LIBRARY (Bus-Fin; Energy)
1221 McKinney
Box 2521   Phone: (713) 759-3533
Houston, TX 77252   Kay Bailey, Libn.
Founded: 1958. Staff: Prof 1; Other 2. Subjects: Energy, oil and gas, finance, economics, management. Holdings: 6000 books; 450 bound periodical volumes; 32 periodicals on microfilm. Subscriptions: 400 journals and other serials; 17 newspapers. Services: Interlibrary loans; copying; library

available to public by telephone request. Automated Operations: Computerized acquisitions. Computerized Information Services: DIALOG, SDC, Dow Jones News/Retrieval.

TEXAS EASTMAN COMPANY
See: Eastman Kodak Company

★13396★
TEXAS EDUCATION AGENCY - RESOURCE CENTER LIBRARY (Educ)
201 E. 11th St.   Phone: (512) 834-4070
Austin, TX 78701   Linda Kemp, Libn.
Staff: Prof 1; Other 1. Subjects: Public school education. Special Collections: Complete ERIC microfiche collection; Texas state-adopted textbook collection. Holdings: 10,000 volumes. Subscriptions: 315 journals and other serials. Services: Library open to Texas educators and state government personnel only. Computerized Information Services: BRS. Remarks: Library is located at 1200 E. Anderson Lane, Austin, TX 78752.

★13397★
TEXAS ELECTRIC SERVICE COMPANY - LIBRARY (Bus-Fin; Sci-Tech)
115 W. 7th St.
Box 970   Phone: (817) 336-9454
Fort Worth, TX 76101   Melba Connelley, Libn.
Founded: 1954. Subjects: Business, management, electrical engineering. Holdings: 4500 books.

★13398★
TEXAS EMPLOYERS INSURANCE ASSOCIATION - ENGINEERING INFORMATION CENTER (Soc Sci)
Box 2759   Phone: (214) 653-8100
Dallas, TX 75221   Gay Bethel, Info.Res.Spec.
Founded: 1975. Staff: Prof 1. Subjects: Safety engineering, industrial hygiene, traffic safety. Holdings: 400 books; 3700 technical reports and pamphlets; 135 films, filmstrips, slides and cassettes. Subscriptions: 30 journals and other serials. Services: Interlibrary loans; copying; center open to public by appointment. Special Indexes: Index of in-house technical reports.

TEXAS ENGINEERING EXPERIMENT STATION
See: Texas A & M University - Thermodynamics Research Center

TEXAS FOREST PRODUCTS LABORATORY
See: Texas (State) Forest Service

★13399★
TEXAS GAS TRANSMISSION CORPORATION - LIBRARY (Sci-Tech; Bus-Fin)
Box 1160   Phone: (502) 926-8686
Owensboro, KY 42301   Frieda Rhodes, Libn.
Staff: Prof 1; Other 1. Subjects: Natural gas technology, finance, petroleum, geology, economics. Holdings: 2500 books; 27 bound periodical titles. Subscriptions: 225 journals and other serials. Services: Library not open to public.

TEXAS HERITAGE RESOURCE CENTER
See: San Antonio Conservation Society - Foundation Library

★13400★
TEXAS INSTRUMENTS, INC. - DATA SYSTEMS GROUP - SITE LIBRARY (Comp Sci)†
Box 2909, MS 2146   Phone: (512) 250-7421
Austin, TX 78769   James R. Neaves, Mgr., Site Lib.
Founded: 1978. Staff: Prof 1; Other 2. Subjects: Computer technology, electronics, market research. Holdings: 983 books; 69 bound periodical volumes; 1418 Underwriter's Laboratories standards; 124 consultant manuals; 655 marketing reports; 334 government abstracts; 7000 Bell System technical references. Subscriptions: 108 journals and other serials; 7 newspapers. Services: Interlibrary loans; searches from the sales field; library not open to public. Automated Operations: Computerized circulation. Computerized Information Services: DIALOG; IMS (internal database). Special Catalogs: Microfilm catalog.

★13401★
TEXAS INSTRUMENTS, INC. - HOUSTON SITE LIBRARY (Comp Sci)
Box 1443, MS 695   Phone: (713) 490-2981
Houston, TX 77001   Helen Manning, Libn.
Staff: Prof 1; Other 1. Subjects: Communications, electronics, marketing, electrical engineering. Holdings: 1600 books. Subscriptions: 180 journals and other serials; 10 newspapers. Services: Interlibrary loans; library not open to public. Automated Operations: Computerized cataloging, circulation and serials. Computerized Information Services: OCLC, DIALOG, SDC;

internal database. **Networks/Consortia:** Member of AMIGOS Bibliographic Council, Inc. **Publications:** New at the Library, monthly.

★13402★
TEXAS INSTRUMENTS, INC. - INFORMATION SYSTEMS & SERVICES LIBRARY (Comp Sci; Info Sci)
Box 226015, MS 3610   Phone: (214) 343-7954
Dallas, TX 75266   Cecilia Tung, Libn.
Staff: Prof 1. **Subjects:** Computer science and graphics, data processing, information science. **Holdings:** 800 books; 1000 IBM hardware and software manuals; industry reports. **Subscriptions:** 120 journals and other serials. **Services:** Interlibrary loans; library not open to public. **Automated Operations:** Computerized cataloging. **Computerized Information Services:** OCLC, DIALOG. **Networks/Consortia:** Member of AMIGOS Bibliographic Council, Inc. **Special Indexes:** Keyword Index of IBM hardware and software manuals.

★13403★
TEXAS INSTRUMENTS, INC. - LEWISVILLE TECHNICAL LIBRARY (Sci-Tech; Comp Sci)
Box 405, M/S 3411   Phone: (214) 462-5425
Lewisville, TX 75067   Stephanie S. Mutty, Libn.
Founded: 1980. **Staff:** Prof 1; Other 1. **Subjects:** Electronics; engineering - electrical, mechanical; computer science; aerospace; defense industry and technology. **Holdings:** 3500 books; 10,500 microforms. **Subscriptions:** 275 journals and other serials. **Services:** Interlibrary loans; library not open to public. **Automated Operations:** Computerized cataloging, serials and circulation. **Computerized Information Services:** DIALOG, BRS, OCLC; internal database.

★13404★
TEXAS INSTRUMENTS, INC. - NORTH BUILDING LIBRARY (Sci-Tech; Comp Sci)
Box 226015, MS 211   Phone: (214) 995-2803
Dallas, TX 75266   Frances Dort, Libn.
Founded: 1950. **Staff:** 1. **Subjects:** Electronic and mechanical engineering, mathematics, physics, manufacturing and production. **Holdings:** 5000 books; 3000 bound periodical volumes; 25,000 technical reports. **Subscriptions:** 200 journals and other serials. **Services:** Interlibrary loans; library not open to public. **Computerized Information Services:** DIALOG.

★13405★
TEXAS INSTRUMENTS, INC. - RESEARCH BUILDING LIBRARY (Sci-Tech; Comp Sci)
Box 225936, MS 135   Phone: (214) 995-2407
Dallas, TX 75265   Olga Paradis, Libn.
Staff: 1. **Subjects:** Physics, chemistry, mathematics, electronics. **Holdings:** 10,000 books; 6000 bound periodical volumes; 40 VF drawers of theses and pamphlets. **Subscriptions:** 230 journals and other serials. **Services:** Interlibrary loans; library not open to public. **Computerized Information Services:** OCLC, DIALOG. **Networks/Consortia:** Member of AMIGOS Bibliographic Council, Inc.

★13406★
TEXAS INSTRUMENTS, INC. - SEMICONDUCTOR BUILDING LIBRARY (Sci-Tech; Comp Sci)
Box 225012, MS 20   Phone: (214) 995-2511
Dallas, TX 75265   Kathy L. Nordhaus, Libn.
Founded: 1957. **Staff:** Prof 1. **Subjects:** Electronics, semiconductor technology, business management, computer science. **Holdings:** 8000 books; 3000 bound periodical volumes. **Subscriptions:** 200 journals and other serials; 9 newspapers. **Services:** Interlibrary loans; library not open to public. **Computerized Information Services:** OCLC, DIALOG. **Networks/Consortia:** Member of AMIGOS Bibliographic Council, Inc.

★13407★
TEXAS MEDICAL ASSOCIATION - MEMORIAL LIBRARY (Med)
1801 Lamar Blvd.   Phone: (512) 477-6704
Austin, TX 78701   Betty Afflerbach, Lib.Dir.
Staff: Prof 4; Other 7. **Subjects:** Medicine. **Holdings:** 53,000 books and bound periodical volumes; 100,000 reprints; 256 motion pictures; 1300 lecture tapes; 230 slide/tape programs; 170 video cassettes. **Subscriptions:** 1045 journals and other serials. **Services:** Interlibrary loans; copying; SDI; library open to nonmembers for fee. **Computerized Information Services:** MEDLARS. **Networks/Consortia:** Member of TALON. **Special Catalogs:** AV Catalog and supplements (book) - available for purchase; list of journals. **Staff:** Susan Michaelson; Susan Brock; Ellena Castaldi.

TEXAS MEDICAL CENTER LIBRARY
See: Houston Academy of Medicine

★13408★
TEXAS MEMORIAL MUSEUM - LIBRARY (Sci-Tech)†
24th & Trinity   Phone: (512) 471-1604
Austin, TX 78705   Terry Lee Morse, Libn.
Founded: 1938. **Staff:** Prof 1. **Subjects:** Anthropology, archeology, museology, natural history, Texas history, geology, paleontology, arms and armor, art and antiquities. **Special Collections:** Material on pictographs and petroglyphs. **Holdings:** 3000 books; 15 VF drawers of reprints and photographic files. **Subscriptions:** 150 journals and other serials. **Services:** Copying; library open to public by appointment for limited research. **Automated Operations:** Computerized cataloging. **Publications:** Publications on subject specialties, 3-4/year.

★13409★
TEXAS MID-CONTINENT OIL & GAS ASSOCIATION - LIBRARY (Sci-Tech)
United Bank Tower, Suite 500
400 W. 15th St.   Phone: (214) 478-6631
Dallas, TX 78701   Cheryl Stacy, Libn.
Staff: Prof 1. **Subjects:** Oil and gas. **Special Collections:** Bound issues of Oil and Gas Journal, early 1900s to present. **Holdings:** Figures not available. **Subscriptions:** 29 journals and other serials; 11 newspapers. **Services:** Library not open to public. **Automated Operations:** Computerized cataloging.

★13410★
TEXAS MUNICIPAL LEAGUE - LIBRARY (Soc Sci)
1020 Southwest Tower   Phone: (512) 478-6601
Austin, TX 78701   Ted Willis, Exec.Dir.
Founded: 1913. **Staff:** Prof 1. **Subjects:** Municipal government. **Holdings:** 300 books; 2000 articles. **Subscriptions:** 75 journals and other serials. **Services:** Interlibrary loans; library not open to public.

★13411★
TEXAS RESEARCH INSTITUTE OF MENTAL SCIENCES - LIBRARY (Med)
1300 Moursund   Phone: (713) 797-1976
Houston, TX 77030   Felicia S. Chuang, Libn.
Founded: 1959. **Staff:** Prof 2; Other 1. **Subjects:** Psychiatry, psychopharmacology, psychophysiology, neurochemistry, psychology. **Holdings:** 9400 books; 4000 bound periodical volumes; 64 dissertations on microfilm; 735 journal volumes on microfilm; 475 AV items. **Subscriptions:** 267 journals and other serials. **Services:** Interlibrary loans; copying (limited); library open to qualified professional personnel. **Computerized Information Services:** DIALOG, MEDLARS. **Networks/Consortia:** Member of TALON; Texas Department of Mental Health and Mental Retardation Library Association. **Staff:** Lester A. Goekler, Asst.Libn.

★13412★
TEXAS RESEARCH LEAGUE - LIBRARY (Soc Sci)
1117 Red River   Phone: (512) 472-3127
Austin, TX 78701   Claire Oxley, Res.Libn.
Staff: Prof 1. **Subjects:** Texas state government, government finance, demographics, transportation policy, education, health care delivery. **Special Collections:** League archives (300 volumes). **Holdings:** 3000 books. **Subscriptions:** 134 journals and other serials. **Services:** Interlibrary loans; library open to public with restrictions.

★13413★
TEXAS SCOTTISH RITE HOSPITAL FOR CRIPPLED CHILDREN - BRANDON CARRELL, M.D., MEDICAL LIBRARY (Med)
2222 Welborn St.   Phone: (214) 521-3168
Dallas, TX 75219-0567   Mary Peters, Med.Libn.
Staff: Prof 2. **Subjects:** Pediatric orthopedics and neurology. **Special Collections:** History of orthopedics. **Holdings:** 700 books; 525 bound periodical volumes. **Subscriptions:** 100 journals and other serials. **Services:** Interlibrary loans; library open to public for reference use only. **Networks/Consortia:** Member of Dallas-Tarrant County Consortium of Health Science Libraries. **Remarks:** Access to hospital departmental libraries can be requested through the Medical Librarian.

★13414★
TEXAS SOUTHERN UNIVERSITY - LAW LIBRARY (Law)†
3200 Cleburne   Phone: (713) 527-7125
Houston, TX 77004   David D. Melillo, Law Libn.
Founded: 1947. **Staff:** Prof 4; Other 6. **Subjects:** Law. **Holdings:** 80,000 books; 10,000 bound periodical volumes. **Subscriptions:** 360 journals and other serials. **Services:** Interlibrary loans; copying; library open to public. **Computerized Information Services:** Mead Data Central. **Staff:** Marguerite

Butler, Acq./Ref.Libn.; Mary E. Wanza, Assoc. Law Libn.

★13415★
TEXAS SOUTHERN UNIVERSITY - LIBRARY - HEARTMAN COLLECTION
(Hist; Area-Ethnic)
3201 Wheeler   Phone: (713) 527-7149
Houston, TX 77004   Dorothy H. Chapman, Cur.
Staff: Prof 1; Other 1. **Subjects:** Black culture and history, slavery. **Special Collections:** Barbara Jordan Archives (26 VF drawers); Texas Southern University Archives (8 VF drawers). **Holdings:** 25,000 books; 437 bound periodical volumes; 6000 pamphlets; 1 VF drawer of pictures; 1 VF drawer of sheet music. **Subscriptions:** 163 journals and other serials; 26 newspapers. **Services:** Interlibrary loans; copying; archives open to public. **Automated Operations:** Computerized cataloging and acquisitions. **Special Catalogs:** Heartman catalog. **Staff:** Margaret Tunstall, Acq.Libn.

★13416★
TEXAS SOUTHERN UNIVERSITY - PHARMACY LIBRARY (Med; Sci-Tech)
3201 Wheeler Ave.   Phone: (713) 527-7160
Houston, TX 77004   Norma Bean, Assoc.Dir.
Founded: 1949. **Staff:** 1. **Subjects:** Pharmacology. **Holdings:** 4500 books; 2500 bound periodical volumes. **Subscriptions:** 177 journals and other serials. **Services:** Interlibrary loans; copying; SDI; library open to public. **Computerized Information Services:** DIALOG. Performs searches on cost recovery basis. **Networks/Consortia:** Member of Houston Area Research Libraries Consortium.

★13417★
TEXAS STATE AERONAUTICS COMMISSION - LIBRARY & INFORMATION CENTER (Sci-Tech)
Capitol Sta., Box 12607   Phone: (512) 476-9262
Austin, TX 78711   Nonie Mitchel, Libn.
Founded: 1945. **Staff:** Prof 1. **Subjects:** Aviation, aircraft, airports, planning, aviation education, flight safety. **Holdings:** 170 films; reports; government documents; 40 feet of Federal Aviation Administration, Civil Aeronautics Board and National Transportation Safety Board regulations and publications; 2 bound volumes of clippings. **Subscriptions:** 50 journals and other serials. **Services:** Copying (limited); library open to public for reference use only. **Networks/Consortia:** Member of Texas State Library Communications Network. **Publications:** List of Texas Aeronautics Commission Publications. **Special Catalogs:** Aviation Film Library Catalog.

★13418★
TEXAS STATE AIR CONTROL BOARD - LIBRARY (Env-Cons)
6330 Hwy. 290 E.   Phone: (512) 451-5711
Austin, TX 78723   Kerry Williams, Libn.
Subjects: Air pollution, engineering, chemistry, physics, meteorology, law. **Special Collections:** Microfiche of technical subjects pertaining to air pollution (50,000). **Holdings:** 6000 books; 18 bound periodical volumes; 700 reprints. **Subscriptions:** 64 journals and other serials. **Services:** Interlibrary loans; copying; library open to public for reference use only. **Publications:** Technical reports on air pollution in Texas.

★13419★
TEXAS STATE BUREAU OF ECONOMIC GEOLOGY - WELL SAMPLE AND CORE LIBRARY (Sci-Tech)
Balcones Research Center
10100 Burnet Rd.   Phone: (512) 835-3042
Austin, TX 78758-4497   George Donaldson, Cur.
Founded: 1937. **Staff:** Prof 1; Other 10. **Subjects:** Well cores, borings and cuttings; oil scout tickets; drillers logs. **Special Collections:** John E. (Brick) Elliot Collection (geological information, well data, maps, aerial photographs; 5 VF drawers and 2 map cases). **Holdings:** 2900 cored wells; 65,000 cuttings wells; 750,000 drillers logs; 105,000 scout tickets. **Services:** Library open to public. **Automated Operations:** Computerized cataloging. **Special Indexes:** Computer printout listing of well holdings.

★13420★
TEXAS STATE - COURT OF APPEALS - 1ST SUPREME JUDICIAL DISTRICT - LAW LIBRARY (Law)
1307 San Jacinto, 10th Fl.   Phone: (713) 228-8311
Houston, TX 77002
Founded: 1892. **Subjects:** Law. **Holdings:** 10,000 volumes. **Services:** Library not open to public.

★13421★
TEXAS STATE - COURT OF APPEALS - 3RD SUPREME JUDICIAL DISTRICT - LAW LIBRARY (Law)
Capitol Sta., Box 12547   Phone: (512) 475-2441
Austin, TX 78711
Subjects: Law. **Holdings:** Figures not available. **Services:** Library not open to public.

TEXAS STATE - COURT OF APPEALS - 4th SUPREME JUDICIAL DISTRICT - LAW LIBRARY
See: Bexar County Law Library

★13422★
TEXAS STATE - COURT OF APPEALS - 5TH SUPREME JUDICIAL DISTRICT - LAW LIBRARY (Law)*
Dallas County Courthouse   Phone: (214) 749-8011
Dallas, TX 75202
Subjects: Law. **Holdings:** 8340 volumes.

★13423★
TEXAS STATE - COURT OF APPEALS - 6TH SUPREME JUDICIAL DISTRICT - LAW LIBRARY (Law)*
401 Texas City Hall
Third & Texas   Phone: (214) 794-2576
Texarkana, TX 75501
Subjects: Law. **Holdings:** 15,000 volumes.

★13424★
TEXAS STATE - COURT OF APPEALS - 7TH SUPREME JUDICIAL DISTRICT AND POTTER COUNTY - LAW LIBRARY (Law)
Potter County Courthouse   Phone: (806) 379-2470
Amarillo, TX 79101   Janis N. Thorne, Law Libn.
Founded: 1911. **Staff:** 3. **Subjects:** Law. **Holdings:** 16,240 volumes. **Services:** Copying; library open to public for reference use only. **Remarks:** Also serves the Amarillo Bar Association.

★13425★
TEXAS STATE - COURT OF APPEALS - 11TH SUPREME JUDICIAL DISTRICT - LAW LIBRARY (Law)
                                      Phone: (817) 629-2638
Eastland, TX 76448
Founded: 1925. **Subjects:** Law. **Holdings:** 7000 volumes. **Services:** Library open to public for reference use only.

TEXAS STATE - COURT OF CIVIL APPEALS - 10TH JUDICIAL DISTRICT - MC LENNAN COUNTY LAW LIBRARY
See: Mc Lennan County Law Library

★13426★
TEXAS STATE DEPARTMENT OF AGRICULTURE - LIBRARY (Agri)
Stephen F. Austin Bldg., Rm. 915
Box 12847   Phone: (512) 475-6467
Austin, TX 78711   Virginia Hall, Libn.
Founded: 1975. **Staff:** Prof 1. **Subjects:** Agriculture, livestock, gardening, international trade, cooking. **Special Collections:** U.S. Dept. of Agriculture Yearbook of Agriculture, 1897 to present. **Holdings:** 3000 books; 1000 bound periodical volumes; 200 pamphlets. **Subscriptions:** 300 journals and other serials; 40 newspapers. **Services:** Copying; library open to public.

★13427★
TEXAS STATE DEPARTMENT OF HEALTH - LIBRARY (Med)
1100 W. 49th St.   Phone: (512) 458-7559
Austin, TX 78756   John Burlinson, Libn.
Founded: 1958. **Staff:** Prof 1; Other 1. **Subjects:** Public health, infectious diseases, laboratory methods, dental health, pediatrics, nursing, hospitals and nursing homes, heart, cancer. **Holdings:** 10,305 volumes; 1500 unbound items. **Subscriptions:** 274 journals and other serials. **Services:** Interlibrary loans; copying; SDI; library open to public for reference use only. **Computerized Information Services:** DIALOG, MEDLARS, AMA/NET.

★13428★
TEXAS STATE DEPARTMENT OF HUMAN RESOURCES - LIBRARY (Soc Sci)
Box 2960   Phone: (512) 458-8568
Austin, TX 78769   Diana Boardman Houston, Libn.
Staff: Prof 1; Other 2. **Subjects:** Social work, child welfare, management, geriatrics, health services, human services. **Holdings:** 10,000 books; 600 AV materials. **Subscriptions:** 120 journals and other serials. **Services:** Interlibrary loans; copying; library open to public for reference use only. **Computerized Information Services:** DIALOG. **Publications:** DHR Library

Bulletin, quarterly - for internal distribution only.

★13429★
TEXAS STATE DEPARTMENT OF MENTAL HEALTH & MENTAL RETARDATION - CENTRAL OFFICE LIBRARY (Med)
Box 12668 Phone: (512) 465-4621
Austin, TX 78711 Becky S. Renfro, Libn.
Staff: Prof 1. **Subjects:** Mental health, mental retardation, alcoholism, drug abuse, rehabilitation. **Holdings:** 6000 books; 3000 bound periodical volumes; 20 file drawers of mental health files; 4 drawers of mental retardation files. **Subscriptions:** 50 journals and other serials. **Services:** Interlibrary loans; copying; library open to public for reference use only. **Computerized Information Services:** DIALOG. **Publications:** Library Services, annual. **Remarks:** Headquarters for the Texas Department of Mental Health and Mental Retardation Library Association.

★13430★
TEXAS STATE DEPARTMENT OF WATER RESOURCES - WATER RESOURCES RESEARCH LIBRARY (Env-Cons)
Stephen F. Austin Bldg., Rm. 511
Capitol Sta., Box 13087 Phone: (512) 475-3781
Austin, TX 78711 Sylvia Von Fange, Hd.Libn.
Founded: 1965. **Staff:** Prof 2; Other 3. **Subjects:** Water resources. **Special Collections:** Texas Department of Water Resources publications and those of predecessor agencies. **Holdings:** 55,000 books; 1700 bound periodical volumes; 8000 U.S. Geological Survey publications; 294 periodicals in microform; 2700 volumes of U.S. Environmental Protection Agency materials; 600 volumes of environmental impact statements; 3100 volumes of U.S. Army Corps of Engineers materials. **Subscriptions:** 555 journals and other serials. **Services:** Interlibrary loans; copying; library open to public with restrictions. **Automated Operations:** Computerized cataloging and circulation. **Computerized Information Services:** DIALOG, Water Resources Scientific Information Center (WRSIC), Texas Natural Resources Information System (TNRIS). **Publications:** Library Bulletin, monthly. **Special Catalogs:** Catalog of agency publications, annual. **Staff:** Greg Youngen, Asst.Libn.

★13431★
TEXAS STATE EMPLOYMENT COMMISSION - TEC LIBRARY (Soc Sci)
15th & Congress Phone: (512) 397-4987
Austin, TX 78778 Kaye Hanson, Libn.
Staff: 1. **Subjects:** Management, personnel management, human relations, communication, supervision. **Holdings:** 3500 books; 50 bound periodical volumes; TEC reports. **Services:** Interlibrary loans; library not open to public. **Publications:** TEC Catalog, annual.

★13432★
TEXAS (State) FOREST SERVICE - LIBRARY (Agri)
Texas A & M University Phone: (409) 845-2641
College Station, TX 77843
Founded: 1919. **Subjects:** Forestry. **Holdings:** 625 books; 325 bound periodical volumes; 6000 pamphlets and reports on microfiche. **Subscriptions:** 60 journals and other serials. **Services:** Library open to public for reference use only. **Automated Operations:** Computerized cataloging. **Networks/Consortia:** Member of SOUTHFORNET. **Special Catalogs:** Available publications of the Texas Forest Service (leaflet).

★13433★
TEXAS (State) FOREST SERVICE - TEXAS FOREST PRODUCTS LABORATORY - LIBRARY (Sci-Tech)
Box 310 Phone: (409) 632-6666
Lufkin, TX 75901 Kim Mericle, Libn.
Staff: Prof 1; Other 1. **Subjects:** Wood science, forest products technology and utilization. **Holdings:** 3025 books; 230 bound periodical volumes; 124,000 notebook articles; 36,400 articles in boxes. **Subscriptions:** 60 journals and other serials. **Services:** Interlibrary loans; copying; library open to public.

★13434★
TEXAS STATE INDUSTRIAL COMMISSION - RESEARCH LIBRARY (Soc Sci; Plan)
Capitol Sta., Box 12728 Phone: (512) 472-5059
Austin, TX 78711 Laura Koenig, Libn.
Staff: 1. **Subjects:** Industrial development, local demographics. **Special Collections:** Texas Metric System Advisory Council material. **Holdings:** 1500 books. **Subscriptions:** 42 journals and other serials. **Services:** Copying; library open to public.

★13435★
TEXAS STATE LAW LIBRARY (Law)
Supreme Court Bldg.
Box 12367 Phone: (512) 475-3807
Austin, TX 78711 James Hambleton, Dir.
Staff: Prof 3; Other 5. **Subjects:** Law. **Holdings:** 99,760 books; 3900 bound periodical volumes. **Subscriptions:** 215 journals and other serials. **Services:** Copying; library open to public. **Computerized Information Services:** Online systems. **Staff:** Barbara J. Serota, Assoc.Libn.; Kay Schlueter, Docs.Libn.

★13436★
TEXAS STATE LEGISLATIVE REFERENCE LIBRARY (Soc Sci; Law)
Capitol Sta., Box 12488 Phone: (512) 475-4626
Austin, TX 78711 James R. Sanders, Dir.
Founded: 1969. **Staff:** Prof 6; Other 4. **Subjects:** Law, Texas government and politics. **Holdings:** 30,000 volumes; 726 shelves of Texas documents; 150,000 newspaper clippings; 1586 reels of microfilm; Texas and out-of-state agency reports. **Subscriptions:** 620 journals and other serials; 32 newspapers. **Services:** Library open to public for reference use only. **Computerized Information Services:** Legislative bill status and history (internal database). **Publications:** Chief Elected Officials, biennial; bibliographies on state documents and new trade book acquisitions, monthly; Legislative Library Resources.

★13437★
TEXAS STATE LIBRARY (Hist; Law)
1201 Brazos
Capitol Sta., Box 12927 Phone: (512) 475-2996
Austin, TX 78711 Dr. Dorman H. Winfrey, Dir. & Libn.
Founded: 1909. **Staff:** Prof 57; Other 141. **Subjects:** Texas history and government, genealogy, librarianship, regional library for the blind. **Special Collections:** Texana Collection. **Holdings:** 1.2 million books and bound periodical volumes; 349,494 braille, large print, cassette and talking books; 196,394 microforms (newspapers, tax records). **Subscriptions:** 1314 journals and other serials; 30 newspapers. **Services:** Interlibrary loans; copying; library open to public with restrictions. **Automated Operations:** Computerized cataloging. **Computerized Information Services:** OCLC; centralized storage and retrieval program for Texas agency reports. **Networks/Consortia:** Member of AMIGOS Bibliographic Council, Inc. **Publications:** Texas Libraries, quarterly; Checklist of Texas State Government Publications, monthly; Division for the Blind and Physically Handicapped Newsletter, quarterly - all free upon request. **Special Catalogs:** Statewide Video Project (paper). **Special Indexes:** Index to state government publications, annual (book). **Staff:** William D. Gooch, Asst. State Libn.; William H. Carlton, Dir., Adm.Div.; Raymond W. Hitt, Dir., Lib.Dev.Div.; David B. Gracy, II, Dir., Archv.; Dale W. Propp, Dir., Blind Div.; Allan Quinn, Dir., Info.Serv.Div.; William Dyess, Dir., Rec.Mgt.Div.

★13438★
TEXAS STATE LIBRARY - INFORMATION SERVICES DIVISION (Hist; Info Sci)
Box 12927 Phone: (512) 475-2996
Austin, TX 78711 Allan S. Quinn, Div.Dir.
Staff: Prof 13; Other 21. **Subjects:** U.S. and Texas documents, genealogy, Texas history, biography, folklore. **Special Collections:** Texas State Publications Clearinghouse (the designated state office for the bibliographic control and distribution of Texas state documents). **Holdings:** 105,000 books; 1500 bound periodical volumes; 100,000 Texas state government documents; 900,000 U.S. government documents. **Subscriptions:** 1100 journals and other serials. **Services:** Interlibrary loans; copying; division open to public. **Automated Operations:** Computerized cataloging. **Computerized Information Services:** DIALOG, SDC, BRS. **Publications:** Public Documents Highlights for Texas, quarterly - free upon request; Texas State Documents, monthly. **Special Indexes:** Texas State Documents title and subject index. **Staff:** Bonnie Grobar, Mgr., Pub.Serv.Dept.; Rebecca Linton, Hd., Ref. & Doc. Unit; Nancy Ursery, Hd., State Docs. Unit; Robin Rader, Geneal. Unit.

★13439★
TEXAS STATE LIBRARY - LIBRARY SCIENCE COLLECTION (Info Sci)
Box 12927 Phone: (512) 475-3564
Austin, TX 78711 Anne Ramos, Libn.
Founded: 1956. **Staff:** Prof 1; Other 1. **Subjects:** Library science, librarianship, information science. **Holdings:** 4000 books; 250 bound periodical volumes; 43 VF drawers; 100 audio cassettes; 25 video cassettes. **Subscriptions:** 124 journals and other serials. **Services:** Interlibrary loans; copying; library open to public. **Computerized Information Services:** BRS, DIALOG, New York Times Information Service, SDC. **Publications:** Library Developments, bimonthly - free upon request. **Special Catalogs:** COM catalog of holdings.

★13440★
TEXAS STATE LIBRARY - LOCAL RECORDS DIVISION - SAM HOUSTON REGIONAL LIBRARY AND RESEARCH CENTER (Hist)
Farm Road 1011
Box 989   Phone: (409) 336-7097
Liberty, TX 77575   Robert L. Schaadt, Dir./Archv.
Founded: 1977. **Staff:** Prof 2; Other 2. **Subjects:** Texas history. **Special Collections:** Journal of Jean Laffite; Herbert Bolton's manuscript - Athanase de Mezieres & the Louisiana-Texas Frontier, 1768-1780; French Colony Champ D'Asile, 1819; Tidelands Papers; early Texas newspapers, 1846-1860; Congressman Martin Dies Papers, 1931-1960 (54 cubic feet); Jean Houston Baldwin Collection of Sam Houston (591 items); early Texas maps; Trinity River papers (8 feet); H.O. Compton Surveyors Books; Captain William M. Logan Papers; O'Brien Papers; Hardin Papers (52 feet); Julia Duncan Welder Collection (150 feet); family photograph collections; original and microfilm material from the 10 counties of the old Atascosito District - Southeast Texas, 1826-1960; Encino Press Collection; Carl Hertzog books; many individual family papers and collections. **Holdings:** 3324 books; county records; 2300 photographs; 6000 cubic feet of manuscripts, government records and archives. **Subscriptions:** 15 journals and other serials; 10 newspapers. **Services:** Interlibrary loans; copying; library open to public. **Special Indexes:** Llerena B. Friend card index on Sam Houston; inventories of collections in books. **Staff:** Sally Rogers, Asst.Dir./Cur.

★13441★
TEXAS STATE LIBRARY - REGIONAL HISTORICAL RESOURCES DEPOSITORIES & LOCAL RECORDS DIVISION (Hist)
Box 12927   Phone: (512) 475-2449
Austin, TX 78711   Marilyn von Kohl, Dir.
Staff: Prof 10; Other 4. **Subjects:** Texas - vital statistics, judicial proceedings, education, economic development, politics, family history/ biography. **Special Collections:** Tidelands Case Papers of Justice Price Daniel (130 cubic feet); early manuscripts and photographs of Sam Houston, David G. Burnet and others (400 cubic feet); early Texas furniture; American Indian artifacts. **Holdings:** 3000 books; vital statistics records of county and district clerk on microfilm. **Services:** Interlibrary loans; copying; division open to public. **Publications:** Texas County Records Manual; Texas Municipal Records Manual.

★13442★
TEXAS STATE LIBRARY - TEXAS ARCHIVES DIVISION (Hist)
1201 Brazos St.
Box 12927   Phone: (512) 475-2445
Austin, TX 78711   Dr. David B. Gracy, II, Dir.
Founded: 1876. **Staff:** Prof 10; Other 8. **Subjects:** Texas history. **Special Collections:** Archives of the Republic and State of Texas (25,000 linear feet). **Holdings:** 38,000 books; 3400 reels of microfilm; 2350 historical manuscript collections; 3500 maps; 70,000 photographic images. **Subscriptions:** 45 journals and other serials. **Services:** Copying; library open to public. **Publications:** Historical publications, irregular.

★13443★
TEXAS STATE PARKS & WILDLIFE DEPARTMENT - LIBRARY (Env-Cons)
4200 Smith School Rd.   Phone: (512) 479-4960
Austin, TX 78744
Staff: Prof 1; Other 1. **Subjects:** Natural resources, wildlife and fishery management, recreation, parks and historic sites, game laws of Texas. **Special Collections:** Complete sets of Pittman-Robertson Federal Aid in Wildlife Restoration and Dingell-Johnson Federal Aid in Fish Restoration Acts, both for Texas, 1939 to present. **Holdings:** 10,000 books. **Subscriptions:** 120 journals and other serials. **Services:** Interlibrary loans; library open to public. **Special Indexes:** Index to Pittman-Robertson and Dingell-Johnson federal aid research reports.

★13444★
TEXAS STATE PARKS & WILDLIFE DEPARTMENT - MARINE LABORATORY LIBRARY (Sci-Tech)
Box 1717   Phone: (512) 729-2328
Rockport, TX 78382   T.L. Heffernan, Lab.Supv.
Staff: 1. **Subjects:** Marine biology. **Holdings:** 300 books; 1400 bound periodical volumes; 44 VF boxes of unbound reprints. **Subscriptions:** 31 journals and other serials. **Services:** Library open to public for reference use only.

TEXAS STATE PUBLICATIONS CLEARINGHOUSE
See: Texas State Library - Information Services Division

★13445★
TEXAS STATE - RAILROAD COMMISSION OF TEXAS - CENTRAL RECORDS (Sci-Tech)
1124 South IH 35   Phone: (512) 445-1318
Austin, TX 78711   Mark Browning, Mgr.
Founded: 1963. **Staff:** 41. **Subjects:** Railroad Commission - Oil and Gas Division business. **Holdings:** 17,000 reels of microfilm. **Services:** Copying; research (limited); office open to public for reference use only. **Remarks:** The purpose of Central Records is to file division administrative decisions and all of the forms that the Railroad Commission requires for the drilling, operation and maintenance of all oil and gas wells in the State of Texas. Records are kept in either hard copy or microfilm. Holdings also consist of numerous plats, maps and logs.

★13446★
TEXAS STATE TECHNICAL INSTITUTE, HARLINGEN CAMPUS - LIBRARY (Sci-Tech; Educ)
                                                           Phone: (512) 425-4922
Harlingen, TX 78551-2628   David J. Diehl, Dir. of Lib.
Founded: 1970. **Staff:** Prof 2; Other 3. **Subjects:** Electronics, automotive mechanics, laser, instrumentation, dental laboratory, radio-TV repair, drafting and design, chemical technology, nuclear technology, data processing. **Holdings:** 17,000 books; 480 bound periodical volumes. **Subscriptions:** 420 journals and other serials; 20 newspapers. **Services:** Interlibrary loans; copying; library open to public for reference use only. **Staff:** Barbara Stewart, Libn.

★13447★
TEXAS STATE TECHNICAL INSTITUTE, MID-CONTINENT CAMPUS - LIBRARY (Sci-Tech; Educ)
Box 11117   Phone: (806) 335-2316
Amarillo, TX 79111   Cynthia Sadler, Hd.Libn.
Founded: 1970. **Staff:** Prof 1; Other 3. **Holdings:** 13,600 books; 1504 AV materials; 433 microfiche of journals. **Subscriptions:** 296 journals and other serials; 10 newspapers. **Services:** Interlibrary loans; copying; library open to public. **Computerized Information Services:** DIALOG.

★13448★
TEXAS STATE TECHNICAL INSTITUTE, WACO CAMPUS - LIBRARY (Sci-Tech; Educ)
                                                           Phone: (817) 799-3611
Waco, TX 76705   Linda S. Koepf, Dir., Lib.
Founded: 1967. **Staff:** Prof 5; Other 9. **Subjects:** Horticulture-floriculture, automotive mechanics, electronics, computer science, animal technology, commercial art and advertising, food service administration, welding. **Special Collections:** Industrial Standards Collection (587 volumes); Deaf and Sign Language Collection (400 volumes). **Holdings:** 50,384 books; 4212 bound periodical volumes; 297,523 microfiche of ERIC documents; 22,000 VF items; 1758 archival clippings. **Subscriptions:** 529 journals and other serials; 20 newspapers. **Services:** Interlibrary loans; copying; library open to public with restrictions on circulation. **Publications:** Library Newsletter, monthly - for internal distribution only. **Staff:** Jenny Mohundro, AV Libn.; Leora Kemp, Tech.Proc.Libn.; Mary Sexton, Ref.Libn.; Wilma Martin, Per.Libn.

★13449★
TEXAS TECH UNIVERSITY - HEALTH SCIENCES CENTER - LIBRARY OF THE HEALTH SCIENCES (Med)
                                                           Phone: (806) 743-2203
Lubbock, TX 79430   Charles W. Sargent, Ph.D., Dir.
Staff: Prof 14; Other 21. **Subjects:** Medicine, nursing, basic sciences. **Holdings:** 121,871 volumes; 100,000 slides, videotapes and other AV items. **Subscriptions:** 2405 journals and other serials. **Services:** Interlibrary loans; copying; SDI; library open to public with restrictions. **Automated Operations:** Computerized cataloging. **Computerized Information Services:** Online systems. **Networks/Consortia:** Member of TALON. **Publications:** LIPS, monthly - distributed to all full-time faculty and selected libraries. **Special Catalogs:** TALON Union List of Serials (microfiche); Media Catalog (computer). **Remarks:** Maintains branch libraries in Amarillo, Odessa and El Paso, TX. **Staff:** Neil Campbell, Asst.Dir./Tech.Serv.; Ann Gilmer, Assoc.Dir.; Donald Rose, Hd., Cat.; Mary Moore, Media Libn.; Anne Thorton-Tromp, Cat.; Ursula Scott, Info.Serv.; Peggy Edwards, Asst.Ref.Libn.; Teresa Knutt, Asst.Ref.Libn.; Debra Ward, Ext.Libn.; Dona Roush, Assoc.Dir., El Paso; Carolyn Patrick, Assoc.Dir., Amarillo.

★13450★
TEXAS TECH UNIVERSITY - HEALTH SCIENCES CENTER - REGIONAL ACADEMIC HEALTH CENTER LIBRARY (Med)
4800 Alberta Ave.   Phone: (915) 533-3020
El Paso, TX 79905   Dona Roush, Assoc.Dir.
Staff: Prof 1; Other 2. **Subjects:** Medicine. **Holdings:** 10,917 books; 12,169

bound periodical volumes. **Subscriptions:** 585 journals and other serials. **Services:** Interlibrary loans; copying. **Computerized Information Services:** Online systems. **Networks/Consortia:** Member of South Central Regional Medical Library Program. **Publications:** Bulletin, bimonthly - for internal distribution only. **Remarks:** This library is a branch of Texas Tech University - Library of the Health Sciences in Lubbock, TX.

★13451★
TEXAS TECH UNIVERSITY - LIBRARY (Sci-Tech; Hum)
Phone: (806) 742-2261
Lubbock, TX 79409 Dr. E. Dale Cluff, Dir. of Libs.
Founded: 1925. **Subjects:** Mathematics, biology, Spanish drama, Jewish and Hebrew literature. **Holdings:** 1.1 million books, bound periodical volumes and documents; 807,367 microforms. **Subscriptions:** 8283 journals and other serials; 70 newspapers. **Services:** Interlibrary loans; copying; library open to public. **Automated Operations:** Computerized cataloging, serials and circulation. **Computerized Information Services:** DIALOG, OCLC. **Networks/Consortia:** Member of AMIGOS Bibliographic Council, Inc. **Staff:** Connie Holland, Asst.Dir./Ref. & Instr.; Jennifer Cargill, Assoc.Dir./Tech.Proc.; Roberta Casella, Libn., Spec.Serv.; Margaret A. Dickson, Libn. & Chm., Cat.; Gloria Lyerla, Libn., ILL; Charlotte A. Hickson, Libn. & Chm., Acq.; Elma Fennell, Libn., Per. & Microforms; Mary Ann Higdon, Libn. & Chm., Doc.Dolores M. Maxwell, Bibliog.; Dr. Stewart W. Dyess, Asst.Dir./Lib.Adm.Serv.Gisela Webb, Asst.Dir./Personnel.

★13452★
TEXAS TECH UNIVERSITY - LIBRARY - DOCUMENTS DEPARTMENT (Info Sci)
Phone: (806) 742-2268
Lubbock, TX 79409 Mary Ann Higdon, Doc.Libn.
Founded: 1935. **Staff:** Prof 6; Other 4. **Subjects:** U.S. Government publications. **Holdings:** 75,100 bound volumes of U.S. documents; 424,200 unbound U.S. documents; 242,200 units of microtext. **Services:** Interlibrary loans; copying; library open to public. **Automated Operations:** Computerized cataloging and serials. **Computerized Information Services:** DIALOG, BRS, OCLC. **Networks/Consortia:** Member of AMIGOS Bibliographic Council, Inc. **Remarks:** This is a regional depository for U.S. Government publications. **Staff:** James A. Jacobs, Doc./Ref.Libn.; Thomas T. Rohrig, Ref.Libn.; Karen Hendrick, Ref.Libn.; Barbara Geyer, Ref.Libn.; Thomas K. Lindsey, Ref.Libn.

★13453★
TEXAS TECH UNIVERSITY - SCHOOL OF LAW LIBRARY (Law)
Phone: (806) 742-3794
Lubbock, TX 79409 Jane G. Olm, Dir.
Founded: 1966. **Staff:** Prof 5; Other 9. **Subjects:** Law. **Holdings:** 146,722 books and bound periodical volumes; 63,391 microfiche. **Subscriptions:** 2561 journals and other serials; 12 newspapers. **Services:** Interlibrary loans; copying; library open to public for reference use only. **Automated Operations:** Computerized cataloging. **Computerized Information Services:** OCLC, LEXIS. **Networks/Consortia:** Member of AMIGOS Bibliographic Council, Inc. **Staff:** Carolie R. Mullan, Assoc.Libn.; Grace Lee, Doc.Libn.; Louise Covington, Tech.Serv.Libn.; Sharon Blackburn, Automated Res.Coord.

★13454★
TEXAS TECH UNIVERSITY - SOUTHWEST COLLECTION (Hist)
Box 4090 Phone: (806) 742-3749
Lubbock, TX 79409 Dr. David Murrah, Dir.
Founded: 1955. **Staff:** Prof 6; Other 10. **Subjects:** Texas and Southwestern history and literature; history of Texas Tech University; social, economic and religious affairs of West Texas; socio-historical data pertaining to the area and its indigenous institutions; man-land confrontation in the arid and semi-arid Southwest including the struggle of the pioneer settlers (especially women); cattle industry; land colonization; mining; mechanized agriculture and the water problem. **Special Collections:** Ranching: Matador Land and Cattle Company, Spur Ranch, Pitchfork Land and Cattle Company, Bar S Ranch, Swenson Land and Cattle Company; Business: Itasca Cotton Manufacturing Company and Weavers Guild, Renfro Drug Company, Weatherby Motor Company, Cosden Petroleum Corporation, E.S. Graham Company, Higginbotham Brothers Company, John E. Morrison Company, records of the Quanah, Acme and Pacific, Fort Worth and Denver, Santa Fe railroads; Land Companies: Lone Star Land Company, Ripley Townsite Company, Yellow House Company, Texas Land and Development Company; Texas and Pacific Coal Company; Organizations: West Texas Chamber of Commerce, Texas Sheep and Goat Raisers Association, League of Women Voters; Individuals: R. Wright Armstrong, Clifford B. Jones, Carl Coke Rister, Ross Malone, William P. Soash, Preston Smith, Marvin Jones, George Mahon, Gordon McLendon. **Holdings:** 30,000 books; 16.5 million leaves of business and personal documents and university archives; 1500 maps; 3000 tape recordings; 6000 reels of microfilm; 1200 reels of movie film. **Subscriptions:** 424 journals and

other serials. **Services:** Interlibrary loans; copying; library open to public for reference use only. **Staff:** Dr. Doris Blaisdell, Assoc.Archv.; Jan Blodgett, Asst.Archv.; Janet Neugebauer, Asst.Archv.; Rebecca Herring, Asst.Archv.; Cindy Martin, Asst.Archv.

★13455★
TEXAS WOMAN'S UNIVERSITY - CENTER FOR THE STUDY OF LEARNING - LIBRARY (Educ)
Box 11300 Phone: (817) 382-3522
Denton, TX 76204 Dr. Mario C. Di Nello, Dir.
Subjects: Reading - methodology, teaching, testing. **Holdings:** 3000 books; 150 other cataloged items. **Services:** Library open to public by appointment for reference use.

★13456★
TEXAS WOMAN'S UNIVERSITY, DALLAS CENTER - F.W. AND BESSIE DYE MEMORIAL LIBRARY (Med)
1810 Inwood Rd. Phone: (214) 638-0084
Dallas, TX 75235 M. Virginia Kimzey, Coord., Health Sci.Lib.
Staff: Prof 1; Other 6. **Subjects:** Nursing, occupational therapy, medical records, health care administration, psychology, physical therapy. **Special Collections:** Nursing history collections. **Holdings:** 20,575 books; 6500 bound periodical volumes; 955 indices and theses; 304 professional papers; 41 reels of microfilm; 350 microfiche. **Subscriptions:** 333 journals and other serials. **Services:** Interlibrary loans; copying; library open to public for reference use only. **Automated Operations:** Computerized cataloging. **Computerized Information Services:** DIALOG, MEDLARS. **Networks/Consortia:** Member of Dallas-Tarrant County Consortium of Health Science Libraries; Association for Higher Education of North Texas - Library Committee (AHE); Metroplex Council of Health Science Librarians; TALON.

★13457★
TEXAS WOMAN'S UNIVERSITY - LIBRARY SCIENCE LIBRARY (Info Sci)
School of Library Science Phone: (817) 387-2418
Denton, TX 76204 James L. Thomas, Libn.
Founded: 1939. **Staff:** Prof 1; Other 6. **Subjects:** Library and information science, children's literature. **Holdings:** 17,594 books; 3787 bound periodical volumes; 291 reels of microfilm; 55 kits; 251 titles of library newsletters. **Subscriptions:** 128 journals and other serials. **Services:** Library open to public. **Computerized Information Services:** DIALOG, BRS. **Publications:** Occasional papers, irregular.

★13458★
TEXAS WOMAN'S UNIVERSITY - LIBRARY SCIENCE LIBRARY - PROYECTO LEER (Educ)
School of Library Science
Denton, TX 76204 Ali Mattei-Mejia, Coord.
Founded: 1967. **Subjects:** Spanish and bilingual (Spanish-English) materials. **Holdings:** 24,000 books, journals and nonprint materials. **Services:** Research collection and advisory service available to the public; materials evaluated and reviewed for dissemination; seminars, institutes and classes conducted for librarians and educators; traveling collection of selected titles available to librarians and educators. **Publications:** Proyecto LEER Bulletin, irregular.

★13459★
TEXAS WOMAN'S UNIVERSITY - SPECIAL COLLECTIONS (Hum)
Bralley Memorial Library
TWU Sta., Box 23715 Phone: (817) 566-6415
Denton, TX 76204 Metta Nicewarner, Spec.Coll.Libn.
Founded: 1932. **Staff:** Prof 1; Other 2. **Subjects:** Women's biography, history and literature; cookery. **Special Collections:** Woman's Collection (39,000 books and bound periodical volumes, including the Madeleine Henrey Collection and the LaVerne Harrell Clark Collection); Cookbook and Menu Collection (6500 books and bound periodical volumes, 1027 menus, including the Julie Bennell Cookbook Collection and the Margaret Scruggs Cookbook Collection); play collection (1800 books); Genevieve Dixon Collection (1051 books); university archives (7500 items). **Holdings:** 50,000 books and bound periodical volumes; 317,651 microforms; 450 media items. **Services:** Interlibrary loans; copying; library open to public. **Automated Operations:** Computerized cataloging. **Computerized Information Services:** DIALOG, OCLC, BRS, MEDLINE. **Networks/Consortia:** Member of Association for Higher Education of North Texas - Library Committee (AHE); AMIGOS Bibliographic Council, Inc.

★13460★
TEXASGULF, INC. - RESEARCH LIBRARY (Sci-Tech)†
High Ridge Park Phone: (203) 358-5135
Stamford, CT 06904 Patricia R. O'Shea, Corp.Libn.
Staff: Prof 1; Other 1. **Subjects:** Mining engineering, natural resources,

chemistry, metallurgy, chemical engineering. **Holdings:** 2000 books; bound U.S. patents. **Subscriptions:** 230 journals and other serials; 25 newspapers. **Services:** Interlibrary loans; copying; library open to public by appointment. **Computerized Information Services:** DIALOG, SDC, Copper Development Association.

★13461★
TEXTILE MUSEUM - ARTHUR D. JENKINS LIBRARY (Art; Hist)
2320 S St., N.W.   Phone: (202) 667-0442
Washington, DC 20008   Katherine T. Freshley, Libn.
Staff: Prof 1. **Subjects:** Oriental rugs; ancient textiles - Egyptian, Peruvian, Asian, Oriental, Central American and Southwest American. **Holdings:** 10,000 books and bound periodical volumes. **Subscriptions:** 144 journals and other serials. **Services:** Copying; library open to public.

★13462★
TEXTILE RESEARCH INSTITUTE - LIBRARY (Sci-Tech)
601 Prospect Ave.
Box 625   Phone: (609) 924-3150
Princeton, NJ 08540
Founded: 1945. **Staff:** 1. **Subjects:** Fibers, chemistry, textiles, polymers, physics, engineering, microscopy, cellulose. **Holdings:** 8000 books; 2000 bound periodical volumes; 50 VF drawers of reports, reprints, patents. **Subscriptions:** 153 journals and other serials. **Services:** Interlibrary loans (fee); copying; library open to public by arrangement. **Publications:** Books and journals received, semiannual.

★13463★
TEXTRON, INC. - BELL AEROSPACE TEXTRON - DALMO VICTOR OPERATIONS - TECHNICAL LIBRARY (Sci-Tech; Comp Sci)
1515 Industrial Way   Phone: (415) 595-1414
Belmont, CA 94002
Subjects: Antenna research, computers, electronics. **Holdings:** 800 books; 4000 technical documents. **Subscriptions:** 100 journals and other serials. **Services:** Library not open to public.

★13464★
TEXTRON, INC. - SPENCER KELLOGG DIVISION - RESEARCH CENTER LIBRARY (Sci-Tech)
4201 Genesee St.
Box 210   Phone: (716) 852-5850
Buffalo, NY 14225   Pamela G. Kobelski, Tech.Info.Supv.
Founded: 1955. **Staff:** Prof 1; Other 1. **Subjects:** Coatings technology; resins - epoxy, alkyd, urethane; vegetable oils. **Holdings:** 2500 books; 1500 bound periodical volumes; 40 VF drawers of technical literature; chemical patents on microfilm, 1967-1981; 6 VF drawers of foreign and domestic patents. **Subscriptions:** 128 journals and other serials. **Services:** Interlibrary loans; library not open to public, but information requests may be filled. **Computerized Information Services:** DIALOG. **Networks/Consortia:** Member of Western New York Library Resources Council (WNYLRC).

★13465★
THATCHER GLASS CORPORATION - RESEARCH CENTER LIBRARY (Sci-Tech)
Box 1505   Phone: (607) 737-3162
Elmira, NY 14902   Jenny C. Dean
Founded: 1952. **Staff:** Prof 1; Other 1. **Subjects:** Glass technology and science. **Holdings:** 1000 volumes; 132 bound periodical volumes; 2200 patents; 1000 pamphlets. **Subscriptions:** 87 journals and other serials. **Services:** Interlibrary loans; library not open to public. **Networks/Consortia:** Member of South Central Research Library Council.

★13466★
THEATRE HISTORICAL SOCIETY COLLECTION (Theater)
2215 W. North Ave.   Phone: (312) 252-7200
Chicago, IL 60647   William Benedict
Staff: Prof 1. **Subjects:** Theater architecture, theater. **Special Collections:** Chicago Architectural Photographing Co. (1000 negatives); Ben Hall Collection (photographs, clippings and memorabilia); blueprints. **Holdings:** Figures not available. **Services:** Copying; library open to public by appointment. **Publications:** Marquee, quarterly; annual publication on one theater or subject. **Formerly:** Located in Notre Dame, IN.

THEATRE RESEARCH INSTITUTE
See: Ohio State University

★13467★
THEDA CLARK REGIONAL MEDICAL CENTER - HEALTH SCIENCES LIBRARY (Med)
130 2nd St.   Phone: (414) 729-2190
Neenah, WI 54956   Nancy Berth Campbell, Supv., Lib.
Staff: Prof 1. **Subjects:** Medicine. **Holdings:** 1200 books and bound periodical volumes; 40 videotapes; 9 filmstrips; pamphlet file. **Subscriptions:** 350 journals and other serials. **Services:** Interlibrary loans; copying; library open to public. **Networks/Consortia:** Member of Fox River Valley Area Library Consortium; Fox Valley Library Council.

★13468★
THELEN, MARRIN, JOHNSON & BRIDGES - LAW LIBRARY (Law)
Two Embarcadero Center   Phone: (415) 392-6320
San Francisco, CA 94111   Marlene Weicht, Law Libn.
Staff: Prof 1; Other 3. **Subjects:** Law. **Holdings:** 30,000 volumes. **Subscriptions:** 240 journals and other serials. **Services:** Interlibrary loans; library not open to public. **Computerized Information Services:** DIALOG, BRS, LEXIS, New York Times Information Service. **Networks/Consortia:** Member of CLASS.

★13469★
THEOSOPHICAL BOOK ASSOCIATION FOR THE BLIND, INC. (Rel-Theol)
Krotona 54   Phone: (805) 646-2121
Ojai, CA 93023   Dennis Gottschalk, Pres.
Founded: 1910. **Staff:** 9. **Subjects:** Theosophy, science, healing, meditation, comparative religion, Yoga, philosophy, esoteric philosophy, spiritual awareness. **Holdings:** 1200 books; 600 tapes; magazines and pamphlets. **Services:** Library open to public by mail. **Publications:** Braille Star Theosophist, bimonthly. **Remarks:** Library holdings are in braille and on tape.

★13470★
THEOSOPHICAL SOCIETY IN AMERICA - OLCOTT LIBRARY & RESEARCH CENTER (Rel-Theol)
1926 N. Main St.
Box 270   Phone: (312) 668-1571
Wheaton, IL 60187   Mary Jo Schneider, Lib.Hd.
Founded: 1926. **Staff:** 3. **Subjects:** Theosophy (divine wisdom), comparative religions, healing, science, mysticism, Oriental philosophy and religion, philosophy, occult sciences. **Special Collections:** Rare works in subject areas; extensive holdings of late 19th and early 20th century occult and Theosophical periodicals. **Holdings:** 25,000 books; 500 bound periodical volumes; 400 Theosophical pamphlets; periodicals on microfilm. **Subscriptions:** 72 journals and other serials. **Services:** Interlibrary loans; copying; library open to public and research workers. **Special Catalogs:** Annotated reading lists of the library collection.

★13471★
THEOSOPHICAL SOCIETY IN MIAMI - LIBRARY (Rel-Theol)
119 N.E. 62nd St.   Phone: (305) 754-4331
Miami, FL 33138   Louise S. Ward, Libn.
Staff: Prof 1. **Subjects:** Theosophy; religion, especially eastern; yoga; philosophy; astrology; metaphysics. **Holdings:** 6000 books. **Services:** Library open to public. **Publications:** Free literature on theosophy.

★13472★
THEOSOPHICAL UNIVERSITY - LIBRARY (Rel-Theol)
2416 N. Lake Ave.   Phone: (818) 798-8020
Altadena, CA 91001   John P. Van Mater, Libn.
Founded: 1919. **Staff:** Prof 3; Other 3. **Subjects:** Theosophy, comparative religion and mythology, ancient and modern philosophy and science, occultism. **Special Collections:** Theosophical magazines, 1879 to present (nearly complete); first editions of Theosophical books. **Holdings:** 50,000 books; 5000 bound periodical volumes; 1000 pamphlets; 1000 Theosophical pamphlet files. **Subscriptions:** 30 journals and other serials. **Services:** Interlibrary loans (with reservations); library open to public for reference use only. **Remarks:** Maintained by the Theosophical Society of Pasadena. **Staff:** I. Manuel Oderberg, Res.Libn.; Sarah B. Van Mater, Asst.Libn.

THEOSOPHY HALL
See: United Lodge of Theosophists

★13473★
THERMARK CORPORATION - TECHNICAL INFORMATION SERVICES (Sci-Tech)†
650 W. 67th Pl.   Phone: (219) 322-5030
Schererville, IN 46375   Irene Ganas, Tech.Info.Serv.Mgr.
Founded: 1973. **Staff:** Prof 1. **Subjects:** Coatings technology. **Special Collections:** Radiation curing technology. **Holdings:** 237 books; 58 bound

periodical volumes; 450 other cataloged items; 2 VF drawers of technical reports; 66 audiotape cassettes; microfilm; patents. **Subscriptions:** 106 journals and other serials. **Services:** Services not open to public.

★13474★
THERMO KING CORPORATION - LIBRARY (Sci-Tech)
314 W. 90th St.   Phone: (612) 887-2336
Minneapolis, MN 55420   Mrs. Rougean Schoenborn, Corp.Libn.
Founded: 1973. **Staff:** Prof 1. **Subjects:** Refrigerated transport, air conditioning, refrigeration, heating, transportation, automotive engineering. **Special Collections:** International Institute of Refrigeration (61 volumes). **Holdings:** 1300 books; 2 VF drawers of patents; 10 VF drawers of documents; 1600 reports; 1900 vendor catalogs; 1 VF drawer of microfilm; 3 VF drawers of domestic and international standards. **Subscriptions:** 135 journals and other serials. **Services:** Interlibrary loans; library not open to public. **Automated Operations:** Computerized cataloging and acquisitions. **Computerized Information Services:** DIALOG, BRS.

THERMOPHYSICAL PROPERTIES RESEARCH CENTER
See: Purdue University - CINDAS

★13475★
THIELE KAOLIN COMPANY - RESEARCH & DEVELOPMENT LIBRARY (Sci-Tech)
Box 1056   Phone: (912) 552-3951
Sandersville, GA 31082   Barbara W. Goodman, Tech.Sec.-Libn.
Staff: Prof 1. **Subjects:** Clay beneficiation, kaolin, geology, mineralogy, applied chemistry. **Holdings:** 662 books; 47 bound periodical volumes; 13 VF drawers; 1116 patents. **Subscriptions:** 50 journals and other serials. **Services:** Interlibrary loans; copying; library open to public for reference use only. **Computerized Information Services:** DIALOG; Paperchem, Agricola, Claims Patents, CA Search (internal databases). Performs searches on cost recovery basis.

★13476★
THIOKOL CORPORATION - SPECIALTY CHEMICALS DIVISION LIBRARY
Box 8296
Trenton, NJ 08650
Defunct. Merged with Morton-Norwich Products, Inc. to form Morton Thiokol Inc. - Morton Chemical Division - Woodstock Research Information Center.

★13477★
THIRD BAPTIST CHURCH - LIBRARY (Rel-Theol)
620 N. Grand   Phone: (314) 533-7340
St. Louis, MO 63103
Founded: 1943. **Staff:** 10. **Subjects:** Bible, church doctrine, church history, church work, social sciences, literature, biography. **Holdings:** 6000 volumes; AV items. **Subscriptions:** 40 journals and other serials. **Services:** Library open to public with satisfactory references.

THIRD WORLD RESOURCE CENTRE
See: Windsor Coalition for Development

★13478★
THIRD WORLD WOMEN'S EDUCATIONAL RESOURCES, INC. - THIRD WORLD WOMEN'S ARCHIVES (Soc Sci)
Bush Terminal, Box 159   Phone: (718) 308-5389
Brooklyn, NY 11232
Staff: 9. **Subjects:** History and political philosophy of third world women, feminism, sexuality. **Holdings:** 3000 books; 1000 unbound periodical volumes; newsletters; flyers; posters; papers; tapes. **Services:** Archives open to public. **Publications:** Third World Women's Archives Newsletter, irregular - to mailing list. **Special Catalogs:** Bibliographies on women in Brazil, Cuba, Nicaragua. **Remarks:** Archives are located at 9 Second Ave., New York, NY. **Staff:** Mirtha Quintanales, Info.Dir.Sonia Alvarez, Info.Dir.

THIRTEEN RESEARCH LIBRARY
See: Educational Broadcasting Corporation

★13479★
THISTLETOWN REGIONAL CENTRE - LIBRARY (Soc Sci)
51 Panorama Court   Phone: (416) 741-1210
Rexdale, ON, Canada M9V 4L8   Joy Shanfield, Libn.
Founded: 1962. **Staff:** Prof 1; Other 1. **Subjects:** Child psychiatry and psychology, family therapy, special education. **Holdings:** 3000 books; 2000 bound periodical volumes; 200 audiotapes; 4 VF drawers; 1 drawer of government legislation. **Subscriptions:** 100 journals and other serials. **Services:** Interlibrary loans; copying; library open to public for reference use only. **Networks/Consortia:** Member of Toronto Health Libraries Association.

Remarks: Maintained by Ontario - Ministry of Community and Social Services.

THODE LIBRARY OF SCIENCE & ENGINEERING
See: Mc Master University

THOMAS (Carey S.) LIBRARY
See: Denver Conservative Baptist Seminary - Carey S. Thomas Library

★13480★
THOMAS COLLEGE - MARRINER LIBRARY (Bus-Fin)
W. River Rd.   Phone: (207) 873-0771
Waterville, ME 04901   Richard A. Boudreau, Libn.
Staff: Prof 1; Other 4. **Subjects:** Business. **Holdings:** 19,500 books and bound periodical volumes. **Subscriptions:** 215 journals and other serials; 12 newspapers. **Services:** Interlibrary loans; copying; library open to public with restrictions.

★13481★
THOMAS COUNTY HISTORICAL SOCIETY - LIBRARY (Hist)
1525 W. Fourth   Phone: (913) 462-6972
Colby, KS 67701   Helen L. Smith, Dir.
Founded: 1959. **Staff:** Prof 3; Other 3. **Subjects:** Local history. **Holdings:** 440 linear feet of microfilm, manuscripts, books, archives, photographs, slides, clippings, cassettes. **Subscriptions:** 42 journals and other serials. **Services:** Copying; library open to public for reference use only. **Publications:** Newsletter, quarterly - sent to members; Golden Jubilee, 1935 reprint; Land of the Windmills, 1976; Golden Heritage of Thomas County, Kansas, 1979 (all books). **Staff:** Miriam R. Beck, Sec.

THOMAS LIBRARY
See: Wittenberg University

★13482★
THOMAS, SNELL, JAMISON, RUSSELL, WILLIAMSON AND ASPERGER - LIBRARY (Law)
Fresno's Towne House, 10th Fl.
Box 1641   Phone: (209) 442-0600
Fresno, CA 93716   Susan Herzog, Libn.
Staff: Prof 1; Other 1. **Subjects:** Law. **Holdings:** 5000 books; 500 bound periodical volumes; 350 cassette tapes. **Subscriptions:** 140 journals and other serials. **Services:** Library not open to public.

★13483★
THOMPSON (Boyce) INSTITUTE - LIBRARY (Sci-Tech)
Cornell University
Tower Rd.   Phone: (607) 257-2030
Ithaca, NY 14853   Greta Colavito, Lib.Hd.
Staff: 1. **Subjects:** Plant science, environmental science, entomology, ecology. **Holdings:** 3500 books; 1500 bound periodical volumes. **Subscriptions:** 150 journals and other serials. **Services:** Copying; library open to public.

THOMPSON (C.Y.) LIBRARY
See: University of Nebraska, Lincoln - C.Y. Thompson Library

THOMPSON (David) UNIVERSITY CENTRE
See: David Thompson University Centre

THOMPSON (J.) PSYCHIATRY LIBRARY
See: Yeshiva University - Albert Einstein College of Medicine - Dept. of Psychiatry - J. Thompson Psychiatry Library

★13484★
THOMPSON (J. Walter) COMPANY - INFORMATION CENTER (Bus-Fin)
875 N. Michigan Ave.   Phone: (312) 951-4000
Chicago, IL 60611   Edward G. Strable, V.P., Dir., Info.Serv.
Founded: 1921. **Staff:** Prof 5; Other 5. **Subjects:** Advertising, advertising research, market research, marketing, consumer products and services, consumer behavior. **Holdings:** 4000 books; 225 VF drawers; 20,000 research reports; 1 million print advertisements; 1000 reels of microfilm. **Subscriptions:** 600 journals and other serials; 15 newspapers. **Services:** Interlibrary loans; center open to public by appointment. **Computerized Information Services:** DIALOG, BRS, NEXIS, Dun & Bradstreet Corporation; internal database (pop music). Performs free searches. **Networks/Consortia:** Member of ILLINET. **Staff:** Betty Dumbauld, Hd.Libn.; Margaret Opas, Asst.Libn.; Eric Halvorson, Ref.Libn.; Roberta Piccoli, Info.Spec.

★13485★
THOMPSON (J. Walter) COMPANY - INFORMATION CENTER (Bus-Fin)
466 Lexington Ave.   Phone: (212) 210-7000
New York, NY 10017   Nancy Terry Munger, Mgr., Info.Serv.
Founded: 1918. **Staff:** Prof 7; Other 4. **Subjects:** Advertising, marketing, industry. **Special Collections:** Picture and art; consumer print advertisements. **Holdings:** 7000 books; 300 bound periodical volumes; 265 VF drawers; 1351 reels of microfilm; 1500 microfiche. **Subscriptions:** 400 journals and other serials. **Services:** Interlibrary loans; center open to SLA members and others by appointment. **Computerized Information Services:** DIALOG, SDC, NEXIS, Dow Jones News/Retrieval, CYBERNET. **Staff:** Mary Gegelys, Dir., Info.Ctr.; Joan Goodsell, Cat.; Nadine Kasow, Ref.Libn.; Linda Rosen, Ref.Libn.; Meredith Olver, Ref.Libn.; Peggy Weiner, Ref.Libn.

★13486★
THOMPSON (J. Walter) COMPANY - RESEARCH LIBRARY (Bus-Fin)
10100 Santa Monica Blvd.   Phone: (213) 553-8383
Los Angeles, CA 90067   Suzanne Rampton, Assoc.Dir. of Res.
Founded: 1965. **Subjects:** Advertising, marketing, products and industry. **Holdings:** 400 books; 100 government census reports; 100 pamphlets; 10 drawers of product and industry files; 300 glass slides; 100 AV reels; 110 tapes; 25 phonograph records. **Subscriptions:** 400 journals and other serials; 20 newspapers. **Services:** Library not open to public.

★13487★
THOMPSON & KNIGHT - LIBRARY (Law)
3300 First City Ctr.   Phone: (214) 655-7568
Dallas, TX 75201   Jane Ward, Libn.
Staff: 3. **Subjects:** Law. **Holdings:** 20,000 volumes. **Subscriptions:** 75 journals and other serials. **Services:** Interlibrary loans; copying; library open only to Dallas area law librarians. **Computerized Information Services:** LEXIS.

THOMPSON LIBRARY
See: Ohio State University - Middle East/Islamica Reading Room

THOMPSON MEDICAL LIBRARY
See: U.S. Navy - Naval Hospital (CA-San Diego)

THOMPSON (Nancy) LIBRARY
See: Kean College of New Jersey - Nancy Thompson Library

THOMPSON (R.C.) LIBRARY
See: Maryland Rehabilitation Center - R.C. Thompson Library

THOMPSON (W.F.) MEMORIAL LIBRARY
See: U.S. Natl. Marine Fisheries Service - W.F. Thompson Memorial Library

★13488★
THOMSON, ROGERS, BARRISTERS & SOLICITORS - LIBRARY (Law)†
390 Bay St., Suite 3100   Phone: (416) 868-3100
Toronto, ON, Canada M5H 1W2   Dianne D. Sydij, Libn.
Staff: 1. **Subjects:** Law - commercial, motion picture, entertainment, copyright, insurance, aviation, taxation, real estate, municipal. **Holdings:** 10,000 books and bound periodical volumes. **Services:** Library not open to public.

★13489★
THOREAU LYCEUM - LIBRARY (Hum; Hist)
156 Belknap St.   Phone: (617) 369-5912
Concord, MA 01742   Anne McGrath, Cur.
Staff: Prof 1; Other 3. **Subjects:** Henry David Thoreau, American transcendentalism, natural history, Concord history, American literature. **Holdings:** 1500 volumes. **Services:** Library open to public with restrictions.

THOREK (Dr. Max) LIBRARY AND MANUSCRIPT ROOM
See: International College of Surgeons Hall of Fame - Dr. Joseph Montague Proctologic Library

THORMODSGARD (Olaf H.) LAW LIBRARY
See: University of North Dakota - Olaf H. Thormodsgard Law Library

★13490★
THORNDIKE, DORAN, PAINE AND LEWIS INC. - RESEARCH LIBRARY (Bus-Fin)
233 Peachtree St., N.E., Suite 700   Phone: (404) 688-2782
Atlanta, GA 30303   Linda Swann Austin, Libn.
Founded: 1970. **Staff:** Prof 1. **Subjects:** Investment information. **Holdings:**
100 volumes; 1000 company files on individual companies; 12 VF drawers of industry files. **Subscriptions:** 44 journals and other serials. **Services:** Library open to public by appointment with restrictions. **Special Catalogs:** Catalog of company files (card); catalog of analyst reports published in-house (card).

★13491★
THORNDIKE LIBRARY (Law)
1300 Court House   Phone: (617) 725-8078
Boston, MA 02108   Jean Roberts, Ed./Libn.
Founded: 1921. **Staff:** Prof 1. **Subjects:** Law. **Holdings:** 20,000 books; 525 bound periodical volumes. **Services:** Library is a private facility for Court use only. **Remarks:** Chartered as Judges Library Corporation in 1921. This library is part of the Massachusetts State Supreme Judicial Court.

★13492★
THORNTHWAITE (C.W.) ASSOCIATES LABORATORY OF CLIMATOLOGY - LIBRARY (Sci-Tech)
Rural Delivery 1
Elmer, NJ 08318   William J. Superior, Pres.
Subjects: Climatology, meteorology. **Holdings:** Figures not available. **Publications:** Publications in Climatology, irregular - for sale.

THORNTON (Harry) MEMORIAL LIBRARY
See: Pensacola Museum of Art - Harry Thornton Memorial Library

THORPE MUSIC LIBRARY
See: Illinois Wesleyan University

THORVALDSON LIBRARY
See: University of Saskatchewan

★13493★
THOUSAND ISLANDS MUSEUM, INC. - LIBRARY (Hist)
750 Mary St.   Phone: (315) 686-4104
Clayton, NY 13624   Frederick P. Schmitt, Asst.Dir.
Subjects: Fresh water nautical history, St. Lawrence River and Seaway history, boat building and restoration. **Holdings:** 500 volumes; 2000 periodicals, 1900 to present; 2000 photographs; 30 linear feet of vertical files. **Services:** Copying; library open to public by appointment.

★13494★
3D/INTERNATIONAL - CORPORATE LIBRARY
1900 West Loop South, Suite 200
Houston, TX 77027
Defunct

★13495★
THREE LIONS, INC. - LIBRARY (Aud-Vis)
145 E. 32nd St., 9th Fl.   Phone: (212) 725-2242
New York, NY 10016
Subjects: Geography, history, art, religion, human interest, education. **Holdings:** 200,000 pictorial items.

★13496★
3M - BUSINESS INFORMATION SERVICE (Bus-Fin)
3M Center, 220-1C-02   Phone: (612) 733-9057
St. Paul, MN 55144   Aletta Moore, Supv.
Founded: 1952. **Staff:** Prof 4; Other 2. **Subjects:** Marketing research and development, management, financial planning, personnel. **Special Collections:** U.S. General Services Administration Service containing federal supply schedules, contractor catalogs and price lists (on microfilm). **Holdings:** 3300 books; 10K reports for New York, American and over the counter exchanges, on microfiche. **Subscriptions:** 225 journals and other serials. **Services:** Interlibrary loans; serves public with advance notice and a 3M visitor's pass. **Computerized Information Services:** DIALOG, SDC, Mead Data Central, BRS, Dow Jones News/Retrieval, The Source, CompuServe, Inc., INVESTEXT. **Publications:** Abbreviations, bimonthly - for internal distribution only.

★13497★
3M CANADA - TECHNICAL INFORMATION CENTRE (Sci-Tech)
Box 5757   Phone: (519) 451-2500
London, ON, Canada N6A 4T1   Lorraine Busby, Tech.Libn.
Founded: 1973. **Staff:** Prof 1. **Subjects:** Polymer chemistry, plastics and rubber, adhesives, chemical technology. **Holdings:** 500 books; 200 items in vendor information file. **Subscriptions:** 150 journals and other serials. **Services:** Interlibrary loans; center not open to public. **Computerized Information Services:** DIALOG, Info Globe, CAN/OLE, Dow Jones News/Retrieval.

★13498★
3M - ENGINEERING INFORMATION SERVICES (Sci-Tech)
Bldg. 21-BW-02
St. Paul, MN 55144
Phone: (612) 778-4406
William T. Greene, Mgr.
Staff: Prof 3; Other 3. **Subjects:** Engineering. **Holdings:** 4000 books; 5000 vendor catalogs; 30,000 vendor catalogs on microfilm; 5 VF drawers of articles and pamphlets. **Subscriptions:** 180 journals and other serials. **Services:** Interlibrary loans; services open to public with advance notice and a 3M visitor's pass. **Computerized Information Services:** DIALOG, Mead Data Central, SDC, TECHNOTEC Data Base, BRS, OCLC, Faxon LINX, CAS Online, Dow Jones News/Retrieval, Questel, Pergamon InfoLine Ltd., International Patent Documentation Center (INPADOC), INVESTEXT, The Source, Official Airline Guides, Inc. (OAG), NLM. **Publications:** Engineering Spectrum, monthly - for internal distribution only. **Staff:** L.K. Hoekstra; A.E. Wardrop ;D.J. Willis .

★13499★
3M - LAW LIBRARY (Law)
Box 33428
St. Paul, MN 55133
Phone: (612) 733-1460
Virginia Groth, Libn.
Staff: 2. **Subjects:** Law. **Holdings:** 9000 volumes. **Services:** Library not open to public.

★13500★
3M - MERTLE LIBRARY
3M Center, Bldg. 235-1D
St. Paul, MN 55144
Founded: 1966. **Subjects:** Photomechanics, history of photography. **Special Collections:** Collection of Joseph S. Mertle. **Holdings:** 6000 volumes; 15 VF drawers of art material; 3 VF drawers of patents; 1 VF drawer of portraits; 8 VF drawers of subject files of clippings, reprints and pamphlets. **Special Catalogs:** Kardex catalog of art work. **Remarks:** Presently inactive.

★13501★
3M - PATENT AND TECHNICAL COMMUNICATIONS SERVICES (Sci-Tech)
3M Center, 201 2C-12
St. Paul, MN 55144
Phone: (612) 733-7670
Victoria K. Veach, Supv.
Staff: Prof 7; Other 6. **Subjects:** Patents, U.S. and foreign. **Special Collections:** Patents on imaging technology and temperature indicators. **Holdings:** 2700 bound periodical volumes; all U.S. patents, 1963 to present on microfilm, older patents in hard copy; foreign patents on aperture cards; 100,000 3M reports on microfilm. **Subscriptions:** 11 journals and other serials. **Services:** Executes patent searches and provides current awareness service which coordinates requests for information on continuing basis for 3M's technical, engineering and business staffs. Serves public with restrictions and advance notice only; 3M visitor's pass required. **Staff:** David R. Kaar; John M. Dudinyak; Nancy E. Lambert; Gus B. Culp; Kathy Jursik .

★13502★
3M - RIKER LABORATORIES, INC. - NORTHRIDGE LIBRARY
19901 Nordhoff St.
Northridge, CA 91324
Defunct

★13503★
3M - TECHNICAL COMMUNICATIONS CENTER
3M Center, 201-2C-12
St. Paul, MN 55144
Defunct. Merged with its Patent Information Center to form its Patent and Technical Communications Services.

★13504★
3M - 201 TECHNICAL LIBRARY (Sci-Tech)
3M Center, 201-2S
St. Paul, MN 55144
Phone: (612) 733-2447
Karen L. Flynn, Supv.
Founded: 1942. **Staff:** Prof 4; Other 2. **Subjects:** Chemistry, physics, polymer science, engineering, chemical technology, materials science. **Holdings:** 40,000 books; 50,000 bound periodical volumes; chemical trade literature and catalogs; government documents (microfiche). **Subscriptions:** 900 journals and other serials; 20 newspapers. **Services:** Interlibrary loans; library open to public with advance notice and a 3M visitor's pass. **Computerized Information Services:** DIALOG, SDC, NLM, BRS, CAS Online. **Networks/Consortia:** Member of Twin Cities Standards Cooperators. **Publications:** Alert, biweekly - for internal distribution only. **Special Catalogs:** Computerized List of Serials. **Special Indexes:** KWIC Index to literature searches, government documents and pamphlets. **Staff:** Mary E. Hansen; Paul Shrenka; Colleen Wall.

★13505★
3M - 209 LIBRARY (Sci-Tech)
3M Center, 209-BC-06
St. Paul, MN 55144
Phone: (612) 733-9794
Alice Bresnahan, Libn.
Staff: Prof 1; Other 1. **Subjects:** Coatings, photographic chemistry, ceramics, adhesion and adhesives, polymers. **Services:** Interlibrary loans; library open to public with advance notice and a 3M visitor's pass. **Computerized Information Services:** DIALOG, SDC, BRS. **Networks/Consortia:** Member of Twin Cities Standards Cooperators. **Publications:** 209 Library Bulletin (acquisitions list), monthly - for internal distribution only.

★13506★
3M - 230 LIBRARY (Sci-Tech)
3M Center, 230-1S-12
St. Paul, MN 55144
Phone: (612) 733-5017
Elizabeth Smith, Libn.
Founded: 1935. **Staff:** Prof 1; Other 1. **Subjects:** Elastomers, packaging, plastics, polymers, pressure sensitive adhesives, resins. **Holdings:** 2500 books; 700 reels of microfilm of periodicals; chemical trade literature. **Subscriptions:** 130 journals and other serials. **Services:** Interlibrary loans; library open to public with advance notice and a 3M visitor's pass. **Computerized Information Services:** DIALOG, SDC, BRS. **Publications:** 230 Library Choice, bimonthly - for internal distribution only.

★13507★
3M - 235 LIBRARY (Sci-Tech; Comp Sci)
3M Center, 234-1A-25
St. Paul, MN 55144
Phone: (612) 733-2592
Mariann Syr, Libn.
Founded: 1966. **Staff:** Prof 1; Other 1. **Subjects:** Reprographics, micrographics, paper technology, printing, electronics, computers. **Holdings:** 8700 volumes. **Subscriptions:** 215 journals and other serials. **Services:** Interlibrary loans; library open to public with advance notice and a 3M visitor's pass. **Computerized Information Services:** DIALOG, SDC, BRS. **Networks/Consortia:** Member of Twin Cities Standards Cooperators. **Publications:** Book Bin, monthly - for internal distribution only.

★13508★
3M - 236 LIBRARY (Sci-Tech)
3M Center, 236-1E-09
St. Paul, MN 55144
Phone: (612) 733-5751
Elaine L. Wardrop, Libn.
Founded: 1970. **Staff:** Prof 1; Other 1. **Subjects:** Chemistry, electronic engineering, textiles, packaging, polymers. **Holdings:** 6000 books; 2 VF drawers of annual reports; 5 VF drawers of house organs; 15 VF drawers of trade literature. **Subscriptions:** 265 journals and other serials; 5 newspapers. **Services:** Interlibrary loans; library open to public with advance notice and a 3M visitor's pass. **Computerized Information Services:** DIALOG, SDC, BRS. **Publications:** 236 Library Recorder, monthly - for internal distribution only. **Remarks:** Includes the holdings of the Benz Library.

★13509★
3M - 251 LIBRARY (Sci-Tech)
3M Center, 251-2A-06
St. Paul, MN 55144
Phone: (612) 733-5236
Ramona Huppert, Libn.
Founded: 1955. **Staff:** Prof 1; Other 1. **Subjects:** Abrasives, automotive technologies, chemistry, metallurgy, minerals, textiles, tribology. **Holdings:** 2800 titles. **Subscriptions:** 238 journals and other serials. **Services:** Interlibrary loans; library open to public with advance notice and a 3M visitor's pass. **Computerized Information Services:** DIALOG, SDC, BRS. **Publications:** Focus, bimonthly - for internal distribution only.

★13510★
3M - 270 LIBRARY (Med)
3M Center, 270-4A-06
St. Paul, MN 55144
Phone: (612) 733-3402
Eloise M. Jasken, Libn.
Founded: 1969. **Staff:** Prof 2; Other 1. **Subjects:** Biological sciences, medicine, biochemistry, pharmacology, biomedical engineering, biomaterials. **Holdings:** 6000 books; 7200 bound periodical volumes. **Subscriptions:** 431 journals and other serials. **Services:** Interlibrary loans; library open to public with advance notice and a 3M visitor's pass. **Computerized Information Services:** DIALOG, SDC, MEDLARS, BRS. **Publications:** Alembic, monthly - for internal distribution only. **Staff:** Judy Monroe .

THREE MILE ISLAND NUCLEAR GENERATING STATION
See: GPU Nuclear - TMI Technical Library

THUT (I.N.) WORLD EDUCATION CENTER
See: University of Connecticut - School of Education - I.N. Thut World Education Center

THYSSEN-BORNESMISZA, INC. - INFORMATION HANDLING SERVICES - GLOBAL ENGINEERING DOCUMENTS
See: Global Engineering Documents

TICE MEMORIAL LIBRARY
See: Cook County Hospital

★13511★
TICONDEROGA HISTORICAL SOCIETY - LIBRARY (Hist)
Hancock House
Moses Circle
Ticonderoga, NY 12883   Phone: (518) 585-7868
Subjects: Local history, 1609 to present. **Holdings:** 7000 pieces of correspondence, diaries, journals, logbooks, account books, business records, financial records, genealogical materials, public documents, maps, and photographs. **Services:** Library open to public.

TILDERQUIST MEMORIAL MEDICAL LIBRARY
See: Miller-Dwan Medical Center

★13512★
TILLAMOOK COUNTY PIONEER MUSEUM - LIBRARY (Hist)
2106 Second St.   Phone: (503) 842-4553
Tillamook, OR 97141   M. Wayne Jensen, Jr., Dir.
Founded: 1935. **Subjects:** Northwest history and natural history, local history, genealogy. **Holdings:** Genealogy and county records; reference books; Tillamook Indian material; Tillamook County cemetery records; county newspapers. **Services:** Copying; library open to public during museum hours.

★13513★
TIME, INC. - LIBRARY (Publ)
Time & Life Bldg.
Rockefeller Center   Phone: (212) 556-3746
New York, NY 10020   Benjamin Lightman, Chf.Libn.
Founded: 1930. **Staff:** Prof 31; Other 55. **Subjects:** News reference topics. **Special Collections:** Reporting of Time, Inc. newsgathering services throughout the world. **Holdings:** 87,000 books; 500,000 folders of clippings and reports. **Subscriptions:** 3000 journals and other serials; 9 newspapers. **Services:** Library not open to public. **Computerized Information Services:** DIALOG, Dow Jones News/Retrieval, Mead Data Central, BRS, INVESTEXT. **Special Indexes:** Indexes to company magazines (card). **Staff:** Jean Bodine, Hd. of Files; Patricia U. Rich, Hd. of Ref.; Margaret N. Kastner, Hd. of Index; Ellen Callahan, Hd. of Bk.Serv.; Lester Annenberg, Hd. of Sports Br.

★13514★
TIME-LIFE BOOKS INC. - REFERENCE LIBRARY (Hist; Rec)
777 Duke St.   Phone: (703) 960-5353
Alexandria, VA 22314   Louise D. Forstall, Hd.Libn.
Staff: Prof 2; Other 1. **Subjects:** History - United States Civil War, American West; photography; gardening; fantasy; culinary arts. **Special Collections:** Complete holdings of Time, Life and Fortune magazines. **Holdings:** 20,000 books; 350 bound periodical volumes. **Subscriptions:** 175 journals and other serials. **Services:** Interlibrary loans; library not open to public. **Staff:** Anne S. Heising, Libn.

★13515★
TIME, INC. - SPORTS LIBRARY (Rec)
Radio City Sta.
Box 614   Phone: (212) 841-3397
New York, NY 10019   Lester Annenberg, Hd.Libn.
Founded: 1960. **Staff:** Prof 3; Other 4. **Subjects:** Sports. **Special Collections:** Biographical folders (15,550). **Holdings:** 4000 books; 200 bound periodical volumes; 17,000 subject folders. **Subscriptions:** 160 journals and other serials; 9 newspapers. **Services:** Library not open to public. **Staff:** Harry Peckham, Asst.

★13516★
TIMEPLEX, INC. - ENGINEERING LIBRARY (Sci-Tech)
1 Communications Plaza
Rochelle Park, NJ 07662   Florence Gerardi, Libn.
Staff: Prof 1. **Subjects:** Data communications, telecommunications, electronic engineering. **Holdings:** 225 books. **Subscriptions:** 98 journals and other serials. **Services:** Interlibrary loans; library not open to public. **Computerized Information Services:** DIALOG. **Publications:** Monthly Acquisitions Bulletin.

★13517★
TIMES-WORLD CORPORATION - NEWSPAPER LIBRARY (Publ)
Box 2491   Phone: (703) 981-3279
Roanoke, VA 24010   Richard Hancock, Libn.
Founded: 1956. **Staff:** 3. **Subjects:** Newspaper reference topics. **Holdings:** 1500 books; newspaper clippings; pictures and biographical data; microfilm. **Subscriptions:** 18 journals and other serials. **Services:** Copying; library open to public for reference use only. **Also Known As:** Roanoke Times & World-News.

★13518★
TIMEX GROUP, LTD. - LEGAL & CORPORATE LIBRARY (Law; Bus-Fin)
Park Road Ext.   Phone: (203) 573-5268
Middlebury, CT 06762   Beth Abend, Libn.
Founded: 1979. **Staff:** Prof 1. **Subjects:** Corporate and tax law, general management. **Holdings:** 4000 books and bound periodical volumes. **Subscriptions:** 130 journals and other serials. **Services:** Interlibrary loans; library not open to public. **Computerized Information Services:** Online systems. **Networks/Consortia:** Member of Region One Cooperating Library Service Unit for Northwestern Connecticut.

★13519★
TIMKEN COMPANY - RESEARCH LIBRARY (Sci-Tech)
1835 Deuber Ave.   Phone: (216) 497-2049
Canton, OH 44706   Joellen A. Hadbavny, Info.Techn.
Staff: Prof 1. **Subjects:** Research management and planning, steel process research, bearing design, engineering research, materials handling. **Holdings:** 30,000 volumes; microfilm. **Services:** Interlibrary loans; copying; library open to public by appointment. **Automated Operations:** Computerized cataloging and acquisitions. **Computerized Information Services:** DIALOG, SDC, OCLC. **Networks/Consortia:** Member of OHIONET.

★13520★
TIMKEN MERCY HOSPITAL - MEDICAL LIBRARY (Med)
1320 Timken Mercy Dr.   Phone: (216) 489-1462
Canton, OH 44708   Jane L. Clark, Dir., Med.Lib.Serv.
Staff: Prof 1; Other 4. **Subjects:** Medicine, nursing, allied health sciences. **Holdings:** 4000 books; 4100 bound periodical volumes; 400 AV items. **Subscriptions:** 400 journals and other serials. **Services:** Interlibrary loans; copying; SDI; library open to public with restrictions. **Automated Operations:** Computerized cataloging. **Computerized Information Services:** Online systems. **Networks/Consortia:** Member of Northeastern Ohio Universities College of Medicine (NEOUCOM).

TIMPANOGOS CAVE NATL. MONUMENT
See: U.S. Natl. Park Service

★13521★
TIN RESEARCH INSTITUTE, INC. - LIBRARY & INFORMATION CENTER (Sci-Tech)
1353 Perry St.   Phone: (614) 424-6200
Columbus, OH 43201   Daniel J. Maykuth, Mgr.
Founded: 1949. **Staff:** Prof 3; Other 2. **Subjects:** Tin and its uses. **Special Collections:** Information File (28 subjects including tinplate, solders, bronze, bearings). **Holdings:** 350 volumes; 28 VF drawers of reports, manuscripts, patents; slides; films; photographs. **Subscriptions:** 45 journals and other serials. **Services:** Interlibrary loans; copying; library open to public. **Publications:** Tin and Its Uses, quarterly; research reports.

★13522★
TINGLEY (Carrie) CRIPPLED CHILDREN'S HOSPITAL - MEDICAL LIBRARY (Med)
1128 University Blvd., N.E.
Albuquerque, NM 87102   Dr. Charles F. Eberle, Med.Dir.
Staff: Prof 3. **Subjects:** Medicine and allied sciences. **Holdings:** 760 books; 250 bound periodical volumes; 140 resident papers. **Services:** Library not open to public. **Staff:** Dennis P. Grogan, Assoc.Med.Dir.Katherine L. Roberts, Dir., Med.Rec.

TINGLEY (Helen C.) MEMORIAL LIBRARY
See: University of Maryland - School of Medicine - Dept. of Psychiatry - Helen C. Tingley Memorial Library

TINKER AIR FORCE BASE (OK)
See: U.S. Air Force Hospital - Medical Library (OK-Tinker AFB)

★13523★
TINLEY PARK MENTAL HEALTH CENTER - INSTRUCTIONAL MEDIA LIBRARY (Med)†
7400 W. 183rd St.   Phone: (312) 532-7000
Tinley Park, IL 60477   Sally M. Cole, Libn.
Founded: 1962. **Staff:** Prof 1. **Subjects:** Psychiatry, psychology, community mental health, hospital administration. **Holdings:** 4100 books; 210 AV items; 8 files of pamphlets and reprints; 210 reels of microfilm of professional journals. **Subscriptions:** 174 journals and other serials; 12 newspapers. **Services:** Interlibrary loans; copying; library open to public for reference use only. **Networks/Consortia:** Member of Greater Midwest Regional Medical Library Network (Region 3); Chicago and South Consortium; Illinois Department of Mental Health and Development Disabilities Library Services Network. **Publications:** Serials Holdings List; Monthly List of Acquisitions. **Remarks:** Maintained by Illinois State Department of Mental Health and Developmental Disabilities.

★13524★
TIOGA COUNTY HISTORICAL SOCIETY MUSEUM - LIBRARY (Hist)
110-112 Front St.   Phone: (607) 687-2460
Owego, NY 13827   William Lay, Jr., Musm.Cur.
Founded: 1914. **Subjects:** Tioga County, Owego and Southern Tier (New York) history and genealogy. **Services:** Copying; library and museum open to public.

★13525★
TIPPECANOE COUNTY HISTORICAL ASSOCIATION - ALAMEDA MC COLLOUGH RESEARCH & GENEALOGY LIBRARY (Hist)
909 South St.   Phone: (317) 742-8411
Lafayette, IN 47901   John M. Harris, Dir.
Founded: 1970. **Staff:** Prof 3. **Subjects:** Genealogy; Indiana; Tippecanoe and local history. **Holdings:** 5000 books; 150 bound periodical volumes; 125 VF drawers of manuscripts and clippings; 40 scrapbooks; 575 reels of microfilm; 10,000 negatives; 2000 photographs. **Subscriptions:** 21 journals and other serials. **Services:** Copying; library open to public. **Publications:** Weatenotes (newsletter), monthly - distributed to membership; historical booklets and leaflets, one each annually - for sale. **Staff:** Carol N. Waddell, Asst.Dir.; Nancy Weirich, Libn.Sarah E. Cooke, Archv.; Rachel Road, Cur. of Photographs.

TIREMAN LEARNING MATERIALS LIBRARY
See: University of New Mexico

TISH ARCHIVES
See: University of Calgary - Special Collections Division

★13526★
TITANIUM METALS CORPORATION OF AMERICA - HENDERSON TECHNICAL LIBRARY (Sci-Tech)
Box 2128   Phone: (702) 564-2544
Henderson, NV 89015   Patricia A. Puckett, Tech.Libn.
Founded: 1952. **Staff:** 1. **Subjects:** Metallurgy, chemistry, physics, aerospace. **Holdings:** 1500 books; technical reports and papers. **Subscriptions:** 30 journals and other serials. **Services:** Library not open to public. **Automated Operations:** Computerized acquisitions.

TITUS (Paul) MEMORIAL LIBRARY AND SCHOOL OF NURSING LIBRARY
See: St. Margaret Memorial Hospital - Paul Titus Memorial Library and School of Nursing Library

TIU
See: The International University

★13527★
TOBACCO INSTITUTE - INFORMATION CENTER (Agri)
1875 Eye St., N.W., Suite 800   Phone: (202) 457-4800
Washington, DC 20006   Brenda B. Clark, Mgr., Info.Ctr.
Founded: 1958. **Staff:** Prof 3; Other 3. **Subjects:** Tobacco history, smoking/health controversy. **Holdings:** 2500 books; clippings; manuscripts; reports. **Subscriptions:** 200 journals and other serials; 5 newspapers. **Services:** Interlibrary loans; copying. **Computerized Information Services:** DIALOG, SDC, MEDLARS, New York Times Information Service. **Publications:** Tobacco state history series; Tobacco: Pioneer In American Industry; Tobacco Industry Profile; Cigarette Controversy; related smoking and health pamphlets. **Staff:** Dona McColloch, Ref.Libn.

TOBACCO LITERATURE SERVICE
See: North Carolina State University

★13528★
TOBACCO MERCHANTS ASSOCIATION OF THE U.S. - HOWARD S. CULLMAN LIBRARY (Agri)
1220 Broadway   Phone: (212) 239-4435
New York, NY 10001   R. Robert Sengstacken, Dir., Info.Serv.
Founded: 1915. **Staff:** Prof 1; Other 1. **Subjects:** Tobacco industry and products. **Special Collections:** Complete collections of Tobacco Leaf and U.S. Tobacco Journal; trademark and brand files of tobacco products; smokers' articles. **Holdings:** 2000 books; 296 bound periodical volumes; 150 VF drawers of pamphlets, archives and clippings; 18 shelves of government reports; 135 drawers of trademark file cards; 25 drawers of brand file cards. **Subscriptions:** 99 journals and other serials; 10 newspapers. **Services:** Copying; library open to public for reference use only by appointment only. **Publications:** List of publications - available upon request. **Special Indexes:** SYSTIM-INDEX (book); Cigarette Brand Directory (book). **Staff:** Farrell Delman, Exec.Dir.; Frank Lusardi, Asst.Libn.; Zoe Baylies, Res.Dir.

★13529★
TOBEY HOSPITAL - STILLMAN LIBRARY (Med)
High St.   Phone: (617) 295-0880
Wareham, MA 02571   Bonnie C. Hsu, Libn.
Staff: Prof 1. **Subjects:** Medicine, surgery, nursing, hospital administration, basic sciences. **Holdings:** 1000 books; vertical files. **Subscriptions:** 50 journals and other serials; 5 newspapers. **Services:** Interlibrary loans; copying; library open to public with restrictions. **Networks/Consortia:** Member of Southeastern Massachusetts Health Sciences Libraries. **Publications:** Newsletter, quarterly - for internal distribution only.

TOCANTINS MEMORIAL LIBRARY
See: Jefferson (Thomas) University - Cardeza Foundation

★13530★
TOCCOA FALLS COLLEGE - SEBY JONES LIBRARY (Rel-Theol)
Box 38   Phone: (404) 886-6831
Toccoa Falls, GA 30598   Ruth Good, Hd.Libn.
Staff: Prof 2; Other 1. **Subjects:** Religion, Bible, theology. **Holdings:** 62,000 books; 2500 bound periodical volumes; 3800 AV items; 1500 vertical files; 800 microforms. **Subscriptions:** 520 journals and other serials; 5 newspapers. **Services:** Interlibrary loans; copying; library open to public. **Staff:** Dawn Adams, Asst.Libn./Cat.

TOCH (Ernst) ARCHIVE
See: University of California, Los Angeles - Music Library

★13531★
TODAY NEWSPAPER - LIBRARY (Publ)†
308 Forrest Ave.
Box 1330   Phone: (305) 632-8700
Cocoa, FL 32922   Pamela P. Fortman, Lib.Dir.
Staff: Prof 1; Other 2. **Subjects:** Newspaper reference topics. **Special Collections:** Back copies of the Cocoa Tribune on microfilm, 1917 to present; Today on microfilm, 1966 to present. **Holdings:** 150 books; microfilm. **Services:** Interlibrary loans; library not open to public. **Publications:** Library Clips; Newsletter; Editorial Staff - all quarterly. **Special Indexes:** Index to Today articles from May 1, 1980 to present. **Remarks:** Today Newspaper published by Cape Publications Inc.

TODD LIBRARY
See: Rochester Museum and Science Center - Strasenburgh Planetarium

TOELLE MEMORIAL LIBRARY
See: Mount Carmel Spiritual Center

TOFIAS (Arnold B.) INDUSTRIAL ARCHIVES
See: Stonehill College - Arnold B. Tofias Industrial Archives

★13532★
TOLEDO BLADE - LIBRARY (Publ)
541 Superior St.   Phone: (419) 245-6188
Toledo, OH 43660   Mary E. Reddington, Hd.Libn.
Founded: 1926. **Staff:** Prof 2; Other 2. **Subjects:** Newspaper reference topics. **Special Collections:** Movie Stills, 1980 to present. **Holdings:** 4 drawers of clippings on microfiche; 1200 bound volumes of newspapers; newspapers on microfilm, 1835 to present; 500 drawers of clipping files. **Subscriptions:** 12 journals and other serials. **Services:** Library not open to public.

★13533★

TOLEDO EDISON COMPANY - LIBRARY (Bus-Fin; Sci-Tech)
Edison Plaza   Phone: (419) 259-5279
Toledo, OH 43652   Catherine Witker, Libn.Techn.
Founded: 1953. **Staff:** Prof 1. **Subjects:** Electricity, electrical engineering, mechanical engineering, accounting, business management, personnel and industrial relations, atomic energy. **Holdings:** 3000 books; 173 bound periodical volumes on microfilm; 10 VF drawers of pamphlets; 15 shelves of government documents; 26 shelves of reports; 101 audio cassettes. **Subscriptions:** 150 journals and other serials. **Services:** Interlibrary loans; copying; library open to public with permission. **Computerized Information Services:** DIALOG. **Publications:** News From the Library - for internal distribution only.

★13534★

TOLEDO HOSPITAL - LIBRARY (Med)
2142 N. Cove Blvd.   Phone: (419) 471-5437
Toledo, OH 43606   Linda Fankhauser Tillman, Dir.
Staff: Prof 2; Other 4. **Subjects:** Medicine, nursing, allied health sciences. **Holdings:** 5176 books; 16,000 bound periodical volumes; video cassettes; audio cassettes; slides; filmstrips. **Subscriptions:** 607 journals and other serials. **Services:** Interlibrary loans; copying; library open to public with restrictions. **Computerized Information Services:** BRS, OCLC, MEDLINE. **Networks/Consortia:** Member of Greater Midwest Regional Medical Library Network (Region 3); Health Science Librarians of Northwest Ohio. **Special Catalogs:** Catalog for audiovisual material (book). **Staff:** Susan Jacobs, Asst.Dir.

★13535★

TOLEDO LAW ASSOCIATION LIBRARY (Law)
Lucas County Court House   Phone: (419) 245-4747
Toledo, OH 43624   Brenda Woodruff, Libn./Dir.
Staff: Prof 1; Other 2. **Subjects:** Law. **Special Collections:** English and Canadian law. **Holdings:** 65,000 volumes. **Subscriptions:** 200 journals and other serials. **Services:** Interlibrary loans; library not open to public. **Computerized Information Services:** Westlaw, Auto-Cite. Performs searches on subscription basis.

★13536★

TOLEDO-LUCAS COUNTY PLAN COMMISSIONS - LIBRARY
One Government Ctr., Suite 1620
Jackson Street
Toledo, OH 43604
Subjects: Transportation, planning, urban renewal, ecology, conservation, census, public utilities, zoning. **Remarks:** Presently inactive.

★13537★

TOLEDO-LUCAS COUNTY PUBLIC LIBRARY - BUSINESS DEPARTMENT (Bus-Fin)
325 Michigan St.   Phone: (419) 255-7055
Toledo, OH 43624   Margaret Danziger, Dept.Hd.
Staff: Prof 5; Other 2. **Subjects:** Business, economics, investment, trade, consumerism. **Special Collections:** Phone directories (850 U.S.; 275 foreign); annual corporate reports representing 3500 companies; consumer index (540 headings). **Holdings:** 33,882 books; depository for federal documents; clippings on Toledo business in 120 scrapbooks and 5000 file envelopes; 1710 file envelopes of pamphlets; house organs. **Subscriptions:** 892 journals and other serials. **Services:** Interlibrary loans; copying; department open to public. **Automated Operations:** Computerized cataloging and acquisitions. **Computerized Information Services:** DIALOG, SDC, Dow Jones News/Retrieval, BRS. **Networks/Consortia:** Member of OHIONET.

★13538★

TOLEDO-LUCAS COUNTY PUBLIC LIBRARY - FINE ARTS AND AUDIO SERVICE DEPARTMENT (Art; Mus)
325 Michigan St.   Phone: (419) 255-7055
Toledo, OH 43624   Paula J. Baker, Dept.Hd.
Staff: Prof 5; Other 2. **Subjects:** Art, music, sports, costume, architecture, photography, theater, dance, entertainment. **Special Collections:** Framed prints for borrowing (331); sheet music (organ, 500; piano and voice, 4000; violin, 400); picture collection loan file (101,000). **Holdings:** 49,494 books; 10,202 phonograph records; 4937 audio cassettes; 101,000 flat pictures. **Subscriptions:** 186 journals and other serials. **Services:** Interlibrary loans; copying; department open to public. **Automated Operations:** Computerized cataloging and circulation. **Networks/Consortia:** Member of OHIONET. **Special Catalogs:** Catalog of local artists and art, theater and music (card; scrapbook).

★13539★

TOLEDO-LUCAS COUNTY PUBLIC LIBRARY - HISTORY-TRAVEL-BIOGRAPHY DEPARTMENT (Hist)
325 Michigan St.   Phone: (419) 255-7055
Toledo, OH 43624   Donald C. Barnette, Jr., Dept.Hd.
Staff: Prof 4; Other 1. **Subjects:** History, travel, geography, biography, archeology. **Holdings:** 93,116 books; 17,500 map sheets; duplicates of Toledo and northwest Ohio Collection for circulation; travel pamphlets. **Subscriptions:** 69 journals and other serials. **Services:** Interlibrary loans; copying; department open to public. **Automated Operations:** Computerized cataloging. **Networks/Consortia:** Member of OHIONET. **Publications:** Booklists, irregular - distributed to branches.

★13540★

TOLEDO-LUCAS COUNTY PUBLIC LIBRARY - LITERATURE/FICTION DEPARTMENT (Hum)
325 Michigan St.   Phone: (419) 255-7055
Toledo, OH 43624   William S. Granger, Dept.Hd.
Staff: Prof 4; Other 1. **Subjects:** Literature, language. **Special Collections:** Large print materials; foreign language materials; Adult Basic Education materials; criticism file. **Holdings:** 116,157 volumes. **Subscriptions:** 59 journals and other serials. **Services:** Interlibrary loans; copying; department open to public. **Automated Operations:** Computerized cataloging. **Networks/Consortia:** Member of OHIONET. **Publications:** Titles on Television, weekly - to local libraries.

★13541★

TOLEDO-LUCAS COUNTY PUBLIC LIBRARY - LOCAL HISTORY & GENEALOGY DEPARTMENT (Hist)
325 Michigan St.   Phone: (419) 255-7055
Toledo, OH 43624   James Marshall, Dept.Hd.
Founded: 1941. **Staff:** Prof 5; Other 2. **Subjects:** Genealogy, local history and regional materials - Ohio, Indiana, Michigan, Illinois and original 13 colonies. **Special Collections:** Manuscripts dealing with local urban history (80 boxes); local picture collection (10,000 items); map collection of Ohio and Toledo area, 1800 to present (300 items); oral history interviews (50). **Holdings:** 10,000 books; 1000 bound periodical volumes; 1500 reels of microfilm; 2000 microfiche; 300 scrapbooks relating to the local area; 600 reels of microfilm of Ohio census, at ten year intervals, 1820-1880, 1900; 438 reels of microfilm of Ohio Soundex census index, 1880 and 1900; 465 reels of microfilm of Toledo Blade, 1835 to present; Toledo City Council and Committee Minutes, 1837-1899. **Subscriptions:** 121 journals and other serials. **Services:** Copying; department open to public. **Automated Operations:** Computerized cataloging. **Networks/Consortia:** Member of OHIONET. **Special Indexes:** Toledo Blade Obituary Index, 1837 to present; manuscript index; map index; picture index; oral history index; architectural index (all on cards).

★13542★

TOLEDO-LUCAS COUNTY PUBLIC LIBRARY - SCIENCE AND TECHNOLOGY DEPARTMENT (Sci-Tech)
325 Michigan St.   Phone: (419) 255-7055
Toledo, OH 43624   Mary B. Hubbard, Dept.Hd.
Staff: Prof 6; Other 1. **Subjects:** Physical and natural sciences, applied science and technology. **Special Collections:** Glass and glass technology. **Holdings:** 80,083 books; depository for federal documents; 11,118 bound patent specifications plus microfilm, 1966 to present; 5 drawers of microforms; pamphlets and clippings. **Subscriptions:** 501 journals and other serials. **Services:** Interlibrary loans; copying; department open to public. **Automated Operations:** Computerized cataloging. **Computerized Information Services:** DIALOG, BRS. **Networks/Consortia:** Member of OHIONET.

★13543★

TOLEDO-LUCAS COUNTY PUBLIC LIBRARY - SOCIAL SCIENCE DEPARTMENT (Soc Sci)
325 Michigan St.   Phone: (419) 255-7055
Toledo, OH 43624   Marcia Learned Au, Dept.Hd.
Staff: Prof 8; Other 2. **Subjects:** Sociology, education, law, religion, philosophy. **Holdings:** 73,854 books; 15,785 bound periodical volumes; pamphlets; maps; federal and state documents; Toledo newspapers on microfilm. **Subscriptions:** 318 journals and other serials; 49 newspapers. **Services:** Interlibrary loans; copying; department open to public. **Automated Operations:** Computerized cataloging. **Computerized Information Services:** DIALOG, BRS. **Networks/Consortia:** Member of OHIONET.

★13544★
TOLEDO MUSEUM OF ART - ART REFERENCE LIBRARY (Art)†
Box 1013　　　　　　　　　　　　　Phone: (419) 255-8000
Toledo, OH 43697　　　　　　　　　　Anne O. Reese, Hd.Libn.
Founded: 1901. **Staff:** Prof 2. **Subjects:** History of art, decorative arts with special emphasis on glass, music. **Special Collections:** George W. Stevens Collection (history of writing). **Holdings:** 33,000 books; 5340 bound periodical volumes; 7540 collection catalogs; 100 VF drawers; sales catalogs; 55 reels of microfilm; 335 microfiche. **Subscriptions:** 295 journals and other serials. **Services:** Interlibrary loans; copying; library open to public. **Networks/Consortia:** Member of Art Research Libraries of Ohio (ARLO). **Staff:** Joan L. Sepessy, Asst.Libn.

TOLSON (Melvin B.) BLACK HERITAGE CENTER
See: Langston University - Melvin B. Tolson Black Heritage Center

★13545★
TOLSTOY FOUNDATION INC. - ALEXANDRA TOLSTOY MEMORIAL LIBRARY (Hum)
Lake Rd.　　　　　　　　　　　　　Phone: (914) 268-9208
Valley Cottage, NY 10989　　　　　　Tatiana Kalinin, Act.Libn.
Founded: 1950. **Staff:** Prof 1. **Subjects:** Russia - language, history, memoirs, literature. **Special Collections:** Definitive edition of Tolstoy's works, 1919-1958 (90 volumes, in Russian); translations of Tolstoy's works (including Japanese, Chinese, Arabic); criticism of Tolstoy's works in Russian and other languages; complete sets of the Chekhov Publishing House; rare items published before 1917, all in Russian; Prof. N. Arseniev Collection (2000 volumes); Goltsoff Collection (1500 volumes); Russian books on loan from Rockland Community College (2000). **Holdings:** 30,000 Russian books; 5000 English and French books. **Subscriptions:** 8 journals and other serials, all in Russian. **Services:** Library open to public with restrictions.

★13546★
TOM BAKER CANCER CENTER - LIBRARY (Med)
1331 - 29th St., N.W.　　　　　　　　Phone: (403) 270-1765
Calgary, AB, Canada T2N 4N2　　　　　Judy Flax, Libn.
Founded: 1982. **Staff:** Prof 1. **Subjects:** Oncology. **Holdings:** 1000 books; 500 bound periodical volumes; 50 audio cassettes; 19 video cassettes; 6 slide/tape programs. **Subscriptions:** 72 journals and other serials. **Services:** Interlibrary loans; copying; library open to area health professionals and patients and their families.

★13547★
TOMENSON SAUNDERS WHITEHEAD LTD./TA ASSOCIATES - RESOURCE CENTRE (Bus-Fin)
Toronto-Dominion Center
P.O. Box 439　　　　　　　　　　　Phone: (416) 361-6830
Toronto, ON, Canada M5K 1M3　　　　Glen Miller
Staff: 5. **Subjects:** Insurance, employee benefits, risk management, pensions, insurance law, actuarial science. **Special Collections:** Client reports and presentations (for internal use only). **Holdings:** 2000 monographs; 5 VF drawers of annual reports; 2 VF drawers of in-house reports; vertical file collection containing over 3000 subject files. **Subscriptions:** 104 journals and other serials; 6 newspapers. **Services:** Interlibrary loans; copying; center open to public by appointment. **Publications:** TSW National Information Bulletin; Information Update (newsletter), bimonthly - to clients. **Formed by the Merger of:** Tomenson Saunders Whitehead Ltd. Resource Centre and TA Associates Research Centre.

TOMLINSON EDUCATION CENTER
See: Pinellas County School Board - Mirror Lake/Tomlinson Education Center

TOMLINSON LIBRARY
See: Arkansas Tech University

★13548★
TOMPKINS COMMUNITY HOSPITAL - ROBERT BROAD MEDICAL LIBRARY (Med)
1285 Trumansburg Rd.　　　　　　　　Phone: (607) 274-4407
Ithaca, NY 14850　　　　　　　　　　Sally Van Idistine, Libn.
Subjects: Surgery, medicine, nursing. **Holdings:** 400 books; 800 bound periodical volumes. **Subscriptions:** 70 journals and other serials. **Services:** Copying.

★13549★
TOMPKINS (D.A.) MEMORIAL LIBRARY (Hist)
104 Courthouse Square
Box 468　　　　　　　　　　　　　　Phone: (803) 637-6480
Edgefield, SC 29824　　　　　　　　　Nancy C. Mims, Archv./Cur.
Founded: 1904. **Staff:** 1. **Subjects:** Antiquities of England, Ireland, Wales and Normandy; history - American Colonial, South Carolina, Confederate. **Special Collections:** Antebellum home library of James Madison Abney. **Holdings:** 9000 volumes; microfilm of Edgefield Advertiser, 1836-1902; 210 reels of microfilm of Edgefield County wills, probate records, equity and guardianships. **Services:** Copying; library open to public for reference use only.

TOMPKINS-MC CAW LIBRARY
See: Virginia Commonwealth University - Medical College of Virginia

★13550★
TONGASS HISTORICAL SOCIETY, INC. - ROBBIE BARTHOLOMEW MEMORIAL LIBRARY (Area-Ethnic)
629 Dock St.　　　　　　　　　　　Phone: (907) 225-5600
Ketchikan, AK 99901　　　　　　　　Virginia McGillvray, Dir.
Staff: 4. **Subjects:** Alaska - forestry, mining, fishing, Indians. **Special Collections:** Ketchikan Spruce Mills manuscript collection (425 cubic feet); regional photographs of Alaskan industries and Indians. **Holdings:** 1000 books; 346 reports; clippings of regional interest; 264 pamphlets of historical or ethnological interest. **Services:** Copying; library open to public for reference use only by request. **Remarks:** It cooperates with Alaska State Historical Library, Pouch G, Juneau, AK 99801.

TOOLE (K. Ross) ARCHIVES
See: University of Montana - Maureen & Mike Mansfield Library - K. Ross Toole Archives

TOPAZ MEMORIAL LIBRARY
See: Ohio State University

★13551★
TOPEKA STATE HOSPITAL - STAFF LIBRARY (Med)
2700 W. 6th St.　　　　　　　　　　Phone: (913) 296-4411
Topeka, KS 66606　　　　　　　　　　Laura E. Schafer, Libn.
Founded: 1950. **Staff:** Prof 1; Other 1. **Subjects:** Psychiatry, psychology, psychiatric nursing, social work, chaplaincy training. **Special Collections:** Rare books and journals on the history of psychiatry (150 volumes). **Holdings:** 6300 books; 2000 bound periodical volumes. **Subscriptions:** 50 journals and other serials. **Services:** Interlibrary loans; copying (limited); library open to public with approval of Director of Research and Training. **Networks/Consortia:** Member of Midcontinental Regional Medical Library Program.

TORAH VODAATH LIBRARY
See: Yeshiva Torah Vodaath and Mesifta

★13552★
TORONTO BOARD OF EDUCATION - EDUCATION CENTRE LIBRARY (Educ; Hist)
155 College St.　　　　　　　　　　Phone: (416) 591-8183
Toronto, ON, Canada M5T 1P6　　　　F. Eugene Gattinger, Coord., Lib.Serv.
Founded: 1961. **Staff:** Prof 14; Other 44. **Subjects:** Education, psychology, Canadian studies, literary criticism, Third World studies. **Special Collections:** Display Library (20,000 volumes); Historical Archives. **Holdings:** 47,000 volumes; 6000 subject vertical files; ERIC microfiche. **Subscriptions:** 1200 journals and other serials. **Services:** Interlibrary loans; copying; library open to public for reference use only. **Automated Operations:** Computerized cataloging. **Computerized Information Services:** DIALOG, SDC, Info Globe, BRS, UTLAS. **Networks/Consortia:** Member of Professional Education Libraries Cataloguing Network (PEL); Education Libraries Sharing of Resources Network (ELSOR). **Publications:** Additions and Accessions, 10/year; Conference Calendar, semiannual - both to all board personnel. **Staff:** Clare Bilsland, Supv., Lib.Res. & Tech.; Joy Thomas, Supv., Ref.; M. Cross, ILL; P. Harber, French Lib.Cons.; J. Kerrigan, Lib.Cons.; J. McGrath, Lib.Cons.

★13553★
TORONTO CITY PLANNING AND DEVELOPMENT DEPARTMENT - LIBRARY (Plan)
City Hall　　　　　　　　　　　　　Phone: (416) 947-7185
Toronto, ON, Canada M5H 2N2　　　　Georgina Moravec, Libn.
Founded: 1958. **Staff:** Prof 1; Other 2. **Subjects:** Planning, housing, urban design, transportation, civic administration, economy. **Special Collections:** Toronto collection of various reports (3000 volumes); Toronto Planning Board reports (microfiche). **Holdings:** 12,000 books; clippings (kept for two years). **Subscriptions:** 42 journals and other serials. **Services:** Interlibrary loans;

copying; library open to public with restrictions. **Special Catalogs:** Bibliography of Major Planning Publications.

TORONTO CITY RECORDS AND ARCHIVES DIVISION
See: City of Toronto Archives

★13554★
TORONTO DOMINION BANK - DEPARTMENT OF ECONOMIC RESEARCH - LIBRARY (Bus-Fin)
55 King St., W.   Phone: (416) 866-8068
Toronto, ON, Canada M5K 1A2   Ruth P. Smith, Libn.
Founded: 1960. **Staff:** Prof 2; Other 3. **Subjects:** Banking, finance, economics, trade, industry. **Holdings:** 7000 books; 5000 pamphlets; 24 VF drawers and 140 pamphlet boxes of weekly and monthly letters from financial institutions, associations and government; 11 VF drawers and 900 pamphlet boxes of Statistics Canada publications; 13 VF drawers of newspaper clippings; 250 pamphlet boxes of annual reports from companies and banks. **Subscriptions:** 220 journals and other serials; 29 newspapers. **Services:** Interlibrary loans; library open to public with librarian's permission. **Automated Operations:** Computerized serials. **Publications:** Recent Additions to the Library, monthly - for internal distribution only.

★13555★
TORONTO EAST GENERAL HOSPITAL - HEALTH SCIENCES LIBRARY (Med)
825 Coxwell Ave.   Phone: (416) 461-8272
Toronto, ON, Canada M4C 3E7   Roger Smithies, Libn.
Founded: 1960. **Staff:** Prof 1; Other 1. **Subjects:** Medicine, nursing, allied health fields. **Holdings:** 1200 books; 530 bound periodical volumes. **Subscriptions:** 160 journals and other serials. **Services:** Interlibrary loans; SDI; library open to staff only. **Networks/Consortia:** Member of Toronto Medical Libraries Group.

★13556★
TORONTO GENERAL HOSPITAL - FUDGER MEDICAL LIBRARY (Med)
101 College St.   Phone: (416) 595-3549
Toronto, ON, Canada M5G 1L7   Mrs. D. Cowper, Libn.
Founded: 1964. **Staff:** Prof 2; Other 7. **Subjects:** Medicine. **Special Collections:** History of medicine collections (1000 items). **Holdings:** 8000 books; 15,000 bound periodical volumes; cassettes; tapes; patient books. **Subscriptions:** 469 journals and other serials. **Services:** Interlibrary loans; copying; bibliographies; searches; library open to public with restrictions.

★13557★
TORONTO GLOBE AND MAIL, LTD. - LIBRARY (Publ)
444 Front St., W.   Phone: (416) 598-5075
Toronto, ON, Canada M5V 2S9   Amanda Valpy, Chf.Libn.
Staff: Prof 3; Other 10. **Subjects:** Newspaper reference topics. **Special Collections:** Galbraith Collection (500 photos of historical Toronto area). **Holdings:** 8000 books; 7 million newspaper clippings; one million photographs; 40 VF drawers of pamphlets; 5 million clippings on microfiche; 1242 reels of microfilm of The Globe and Mail; 200,000 photographic negatives. **Subscriptions:** 100 journals and other serials; 20 newspapers. **Services:** Interlibrary loans; library not open to public. **Automated Operations:** Computerized cataloging. **Computerized Information Services:** Info Globe. **Staff:** Marilyn Grad, Assoc.Libn.

TORONTO HARBOUR COMMISSIONERS - WORLD TRADE CENTRE TORONTO
See: World Trade Centre Toronto

★13558★
TORONTO INSTITUTE OF MEDICAL TECHNOLOGY - LIBRARY (Med; Sci-Tech)
222 St. Patrick St.   Phone: (416) 596-3123
Toronto, ON, Canada M5T 1V4   Patricia Fortin, Libn.
Staff: Prof 1; Other 3. **Subjects:** Medical technology - laboratory, radiological, nuclear medicine, respiratory; cytotechnology. **Holdings:** 15,000 books; 200 bound periodical volumes; 32,500 35mm slides (incorporating 250 slide/tape programs, 96 slide programs); 30 16mm films; 65 videotapes; 73 filmstrips; 12 diskettes. **Subscriptions:** 127 journals and other serials. **Services:** Interlibrary loans; copying; library open to public with restrictions. **Computerized Information Services:** MEDLINE. **Networks/Consortia:** Member of Toronto Health Libraries Association. **Publications:** AV teaching materials, biennial.

TORONTO JEWISH CONGRESS
See: Canadian Jewish Congress

TORONTO JEWISH CONGRESS - LATNER (ALBERT J.) JEWISH PUBLIC LIBRARY
See: Latner (Albert J.) Jewish Public Library

★13559★
TORONTO PUBLIC LIBRARY - CANADIANA COLLECTION OF CHILDREN'S BOOKS (Hum)
40 St. George St.
Boys and Girls House   Phone: (416) 593-5350
Toronto, ON, Canada M5S 2E4   Margaret Crawford Maloney, Hd.
Staff: Prof 3; Other 2. **Subjects:** Children's literature written or illustrated by Canadians or about Canadians or bearing a Canadian imprint. **Holdings:** 4000 books. **Services:** Copying; collection open to public for research use only. **Staff:** Jill Shefrin, Libn.; Dana Tenny, Libn.

★13560★
TORONTO PUBLIC LIBRARY - LILLIAN H. SMITH COLLECTION OF CHILDREN'S BOOKS (Hum)
40 St. George St.
Boys And Girls House   Phone: (416) 593-5350
Toronto, ON, Canada M5S 2E4   Margaret Crawford Maloney, Hd.
Founded: 1962. **Staff:** Prof 3; Other 2. **Subjects:** Children's literature in English, 1910 to present. **Holdings:** 4000 books; original art. **Services:** Copying; collection open to public for research use only. **Remarks:** Books in this collection represent a qualitative selection of twentieth century publications. **Staff:** Jill Shefrin, Libn.; Dana Tenny, Libn.

★13561★
TORONTO PUBLIC LIBRARY - MARGUERITE G. BAGSHAW COLLECTION (Theater)†
40 St. George St.
Boys and Girls House   Phone: (416) 593-5162
Toronto, ON, Canada M5S 2E4   Stephen Lee, Bagshaw Comm.Chm.
Founded: 1973. **Staff:** Prof 1; Other 1. **Subjects:** Puppetry, storytelling, creative drama, mime. **Holdings:** 850 books; 65 sets of puppets; 30 folders of reviews of Canadian groups; 35 posters on puppets; 12 toy theaters; 50 puppetry scripts. **Services:** Interlibrary loans; copying; collection open to public for reference use only. **Publications:** Marguerite Bagshaw Newsletter, annual - to friends of the theater and by request. **Staff:** R. Osler, Coord., Boys & Girls Serv; J. Graham, Libn.

★13562★
TORONTO PUBLIC LIBRARY - OSBORNE COLLECTION OF EARLY CHILDREN'S BOOKS (Rare Book)
40 St. George St.
Boys and Girls House   Phone: (416) 593-5350
Toronto, ON, Canada M5S 2E4   Margaret Crawford Maloney, Hd.
Founded: 1949. **Staff:** Prof 3; Other 2. **Subjects:** English children's literature, 14th century-1910; printing; book illustration; folklore; original art. **Special Collections:** Jean Thomson collection of original art; Queen Mary's collection of children's books; Florence Nightingale collection, G. A. Henty collection. **Holdings:** 14,000 books; 761 bound periodical volumes; manuscripts; 501 original pictures; original wood engravings. **Services:** Copying; collection open to public for research use only. **Publications:** Osborne Collection of Early Children's Books: A Catalogue (2 volumes, 1975). **Special Indexes:** Chronological index (book and card); illustrators and engravers index (book and card); publishers, booksellers and printers index (book and card). **Staff:** Jill Shefrin, Libn.; Dana Tenny, Libn.

★13563★
TORONTO PUBLIC LIBRARY - SPACED-OUT LIBRARY (Hum; Rec)
40 St. George St.   Phone: (416) 593-5351
Toronto, ON, Canada M5S 2E4   Doris Mehegan, Hd.
Founded: 1970. **Staff:** 2. **Subjects:** Science fiction and fantasy. **Holdings:** 14,500 books and bound periodical volumes; 8000 unbound periodicals; 750 vertical file folders, including manuscripts; 300 tapes and cassettes. **Subscriptions:** 50 journals and other serials. **Services:** Copying; library open to public for reference use only.

★13564★
TORONTO STAR NEWSPAPERS LTD. - LIBRARY (Publ)
One Yonge St.   Phone: (416) 367-2420
Toronto, ON, Canada M5E 1E6   Carol Lindsay, Chf.Libn.
Founded: 1923. **Staff:** Prof 3; Other 11. **Subjects:** Newspaper reference topics. **Special Collections:** Clipping files on subjects and personalities in the news. **Holdings:** 3000 books; 400,000 photographs; reports; government documents. **Subscriptions:** 50 journals and other serials; 8 newspapers. **Services:** Library open for staff use only.

★13565★
TORONTO STOCK EXCHANGE - LIBRARY (Bus-Fin)
The Exchange Tower
2 First Canadian Pl., 3rd Fl.   Phone: (416) 868-5326
Toronto, ON, Canada M5X 1J2   Shirley Foster, Libn.
Founded: 1970. **Staff:** 1. **Subjects:** Securities, investment, economics,
finance, stock options, commodities. **Special Collections:** Stock exchange
publications (Toronto, Canadian, U.S. and others); Toronto Stock Exchange
Policy Binders (70); archives (2 file drawers and 5 shelves). **Holdings:** 800
books; 2050 unbound reports, speeches and leaflets; 20 drawers of clippings;
2000 unbound publications. **Subscriptions:** 115 journals and other serials; 9
newspapers. **Services:** Interlibrary loans; copying; library open to public for
reference use only.

★13566★
TORONTO SUN - LIBRARY (Publ)
333 King St., E.   Phone: (416) 947-2257
Toronto, ON, Canada M5A 3X5   Julie Kirsh, Chf.Libn.
Staff: Prof 1; Other 7. **Subjects:** Newspaper reference topics. **Holdings:** 100
books; newspaper clippings; Toronto Sun on microfilm, 1971 to present;
Toronto Telegram on microfilm. **Subscriptions:** 10 journals and other serials.
Services: Library not open to public.

★13567★
**TORONTO TRANSIT COMMISSION - ENGINEERING & CONSTRUCTION
   LIBRARY (Sci-Tech)**
1900 Yonge St.   Phone: (416) 534-9511
Toronto, ON, Canada M4S 1Z2   Frances Villanti, Lib.Techn.
Staff: Prof 1. **Subjects:** Transportation, construction, design. **Holdings:**
3623 books; standards from the American Society for Testing and Materials,
Canadian Standards Association and Canadian Government Specifications
Board. **Subscriptions:** 63 journals and other serials. **Services:** Library open to
public with restrictions.

★13568★
TORONTO TRANSIT COMMISSION - HEAD OFFICE LIBRARY (Trans)†
1900 Yonge St.   Phone: (416) 481-4252
Toronto, ON, Canada M4S 1Z2   Adrian Gehring, Lib.Techn.
Staff: Prof 1. **Subjects:** Transportation. **Special Collections:** Photograph
collection; archival collection. **Holdings:** 1178 books. **Subscriptions:** 60
journals and other serials. **Services:** Interlibrary loans; library open to public
with restrictions.

★13569★
**TORONTO WESTERN HOSPITAL - R.C. LAIRD HEALTH SCIENCES LIBRARY
   (Med)**
399 Bathurst St.   Phone: (416) 369-5750
Toronto, ON, Canada M5T 2S8   Elizabeth A. Reid, Dir.
Founded: 1961. **Staff:** Prof 1; Other 4. **Subjects:** Medicine. **Holdings:** 2300
books; 7500 bound periodical volumes; 100 AV kits. **Subscriptions:** 325
journals and other serials. **Services:** Interlibrary loans; library not open to
public. **Publications:** Acquisitions list, quarterly - for internal distribution only.
Networks/Consortia: Member of Toronto Health Libraries Association.

★13570★
**TORRANCE MEMORIAL HOSPITAL MEDICAL CENTER - HEALTH SCIENCES
   LIBRARY (Med)**
3330 W. Lomita Blvd.   Phone: (213) 325-9110
Torrance, CA 90509   Anita N. Klecker, Dir. of Lib.Serv.
Founded: 1972. **Staff:** Prof 1; Other 1. **Subjects:** Medicine, surgery,
cardiology, pediatrics, nursing, oncology. **Holdings:** 461 books; 400
pamphlets; 257 Audio-Digest tapes; 44 videotapes. **Subscriptions:** 112
journals and other serials. **Services:** Interlibrary loans; copying; SDI; library
open only to health care professionals and students. **Computerized
Information Services:** MEDLARS, DIALOG. Performs searches on cost
recovery basis. **Networks/Consortia:** Member of Pacific Southwest Regional
Medical Library Service (PSRMLS).

★13571★
TORRINGTON HISTORICAL SOCIETY - LIBRARY (Hist)
192 Main St.   Phone: (203) 482-8260
Torrington, CT 06790   Catherine Calhoun, Exec.Dir.
Founded: 1944. **Staff:** Prof 2. **Subjects:** Town, county and State of
Connecticut history. **Holdings:** 5000 volumes. **Services:** Library open to
public.

TORT LIABILITY RESEARCH LIBRARY
See: Defense Research Institute, Inc. - Brief Bank

★13572★
TORY, TORY, DESLAURIERS & BINNINGTON - LIBRARY (Law)
Royal Bank Plaza, Suite 3400
P.O. Box 20   Phone: (416) 865-0040
Toronto, ON, Canada M5J 2K1   Janet Darby, Libn.
Staff: Prof 2; Other 1. **Subjects:** Canadian law. **Holdings:** 7000 books; 300
bound periodical volumes. **Subscriptions:** 70 journals; 30 law reports; 5
newspapers. **Services:** Interlibrary loans; copying; SDI (limited); library open
to public for reference use only, on request. **Computerized Information
Services:** QL Systems, Info Globe, DIALOG. Performs searches on cost
recovery basis. **Staff:** Laurel Murdoch, Leg.Libn.

TOSCANINI MEMORIAL ARCHIVES
See: New York Public Library - Performing Arts Research Center - Music
   Division

★13573★
TOSCO CORPORATION - INFORMATION CENTER
Box 2401
Santa Monica, CA 90406
Defunct

★13574★
TOSCO CORPORATION - TECHNICAL INFORMATION CENTER
18200 W. Hwy. 72
Golden, CO 80401
Defunct

★13575★
TOTAL PETROLEUM CANADA, LTD. - LIBRARY (Sci-Tech; Energy)
639 5th Ave., S.W., 12th Fl.   Phone: (403) 265-9080
Calgary, AB, Canada T2P 0M9   Cheryl Fishleigh, Libn.
Staff: Prof 1. **Subjects:** Geology, geophysics, petroleum engineering, business
management. **Holdings:** 800 books; 100 bound periodical volumes; 850
government documents; 240 research reports; 40 theses; 2 drawers of
pamphlets. **Subscriptions:** 86 journals and other serials. **Services:** Interlibrary
loans; copying; translations; library open to public by request. **Publications:**
Current News Bulletin, monthly - for internal distribution only. **Formerly:** Total
Petroleum (North America), Ltd.

★13576★
TOUCHE ROSS AND COMPANY - INFORMATION CENTER (Bus-Fin)
1633 Broadway   Phone: (212) 489-1600
New York, NY 10019   Harold W. Miller, Mgr., Info.Serv.
Staff: Prof 2; Other 3. **Subjects:** Accounting, business, management.
Holdings: 5000 books; 600 bound periodical volumes; 35,000 annual
reports; 1000 pamphlets; 250,000 microfiche. **Subscriptions:** 300 journals
and other serials; 10 newspapers. **Services:** Interlibrary loans; center open to
SLA members. **Computerized Information Services:** DIALOG, NEXIS,
TEXTLINE.

★13577★
TOUCHE ROSS AND COMPANY - LIBRARY (Bus-Fin)
700 2nd St., S.W., Suite 3500   Phone: (403) 263-4800
Calgary, AB, Canada T2P 0S7   L. Herman, Libn.
Staff: Prof 1; Other 1. **Subjects:** Accounting, auditing, taxation. **Holdings:**
3500 books; 900 bound periodical volumes. **Subscriptions:** 85 journals and
other serials; 6 newspapers. **Services:** Interlibrary loans; copying; SDI; library
open to public with restrictions on circulation. **Computerized Information
Services:** Info Globe, DIALOG, Infomart.

★13578★
TOUCHE ROSS AND COMPANY - LIBRARY (Bus-Fin)
715 5th Ave., S.W.   Phone: (403) 264-4441
Calgary, AB, Canada T2P 2X6   L. Herman, Libn.
Staff: Prof 1. **Subjects:** Accounting, auditing, taxation. **Holdings:** 1000
books; 100 bound periodical volumes. **Subscriptions:** 22 journals and other
serials. **Services:** Interlibrary loans; copying; library open to public with
restrictions on circulation.

★13579★
TOUCHE ROSS AND COMPANY - LIBRARY (Bus-Fin)
3700 Wilshire Blvd.   Phone: (213) 381-3251
Los Angeles, CA 90010   Kathy Tice, Libn.
Staff: Prof 2. **Subjects:** Auditing, taxation, management services. **Holdings:**
Figures not available. **Services:** Library not open to public. **Automated
Operations:** Computerized circulation. **Computerized Information Services:**
LEXIS, New York Times Information Service, OCLC, National Automated
Accounting Research System (NAARS). **Publications:** Newsletters; booklets.

Staff: Georgene Litten, Libn.

★13580★
TOUCHE, ROSS AND COMPANY - LIBRARY AND INFORMATION CENTER
(Bus-Fin)
Suite 700 Board of Trade
1177 W. Hastings   Phone: (604) 669-3343
Vancouver, BC, Canada V6E 2L2   C. Iona Douglas, Libn.
Staff: Prof 1. Subjects: Accounting, auditing, taxation, industry. Holdings: 2000 books; 2 VF drawers of clippings; annual reports; stock, exchange rate and dividend records. Subscriptions: 180 journals and other serials; 6 newspapers. Services: Interlibrary loans; library open to public with restrictions.

TOUCHE, ROSS & COMPANY (Montreal, PQ)
See: Charette, Fortier, Hawey/Touche, Ross

★13581★
TOUCHE, ROSS & COMPANY/TOUCHE ROSS & PARTNERS -
INFORMATION CENTRE (Bus-Fin)
100 King St. W.
Box 12, First Canadian Pl.   Phone: (416) 364-4242
Toronto, ON, Canada M5X 1B3   Barbara Dance, Libn.
Founded: 1975. Staff: Prof 1; Other 2. Subjects: Accounting, management consulting, marketing, taxation, electronic data processing, public administration. Holdings: 4000 books; Statistics Canada material. Subscriptions: 170 journals and other serials; 5 newspapers. Services: Interlibrary loans; copying; SDI; center open to public by appointment. Computerized Information Services: DIALOG, SDC, Info Globe, Dow Jones News/Retrieval. Performs searches on cost recovery basis. Publications: Newsletter, irregular.

TOUR (Sam) LIBRARY
See: American Standards Testing Bureau, Inc. - Sam Tour Library

★13582★
TOURO INFIRMARY - HOSPITAL LIBRARY SERVICES (Med)
1401 Foucher St., 10th Fl., M Bldg.   Phone: (504) 897-8102
New Orleans, LA 70115   Patricia J. Greenfield, Chf., Hosp.Lib.Serv.
Founded: 1947. Staff: Prof 2; Other 4. Subjects: Clinical medicine, nursing. Special Collections: Elsie Waldhorn Cohn Memorial Collection (medical history); Jonas Rosenthal Memorial Ophthalmology Collection. Holdings: 2000 books; 5000 bound periodical volumes; 300 videotapes; 5 VF drawers of pamphlets; 100 Audio-Digest tapes. Subscriptions: 220 journals and other serials. Services: Interlibrary loans; copying; library open to public for reference use only. Networks/Consortia: Member of TALON; New Orleans Area Health Science Libraries. Staff: Mary E. Hess, Asst.Libn.

★13583★
TOWERS, PERRIN, FORSTER & CROSBY, INC. - INFORMATION CENTER
(Bus-Fin)
600 Third Ave.   Phone: (212) 309-3482
New York, NY 10016   Joseph M. Simmons, Mgr.
Founded: 1925. Staff: Prof 3. Subjects: Pensions, profit-sharing, insurance, retirement, management, employee benefits. Holdings: 3000 books; 450 bound periodical volumes; 125 VF drawers of clippings, reports, pamphlets; company annual reports and proxy statements on microfiche. Subscriptions: 300 journals and other serials. Services: Interlibrary loans; copying; center open to public by appointment. Computerized Information Services: DIALOG, New York Times Information Service, NEXIS, INVESTEXT, NewsNet, Inc., Westlaw, Dow Jones News/Retrieval. Publications: Business News Notes, bimonthly; Databits. Special Indexes: Coordinate index for reports. Staff: Cynthia Gagen, Info.Spec.

★13584★
TOWERS, PERRIN, FORSTER & CROSBY - INFORMATION CENTRE (Bus-Fin)
800 Dorchester W., Suite 3010   Phone: (514) 866-7652
Montreal, PQ, Canada H3B 1X9   Amy L. Scowen, Info.Serv.Spec.
Staff: Prof 1; Other 1. Subjects: Employee benefits, compensation, actuarial science, taxation, labor, social security. Holdings: 1000 books; 100 internal reports; 8 VF drawers of pamphlets and clippings; 750 microfiche; AV materials. Subscriptions: 113 journals and other serials; 7 newspapers. Services: Center not open to public. Automated Operations: Computerized cataloging and acquisitions. Publications: Communique, weekly - for internal distribution only. Special Indexes: Internal reports index (computerized).

★13585★
TOWERS, PERRIN, FORSTER & CROSBY LTD. - INFORMATION CENTRE
(Bus-Fin)
250 Bloor St., E., Suite 1100
Toronto, ON, Canada M4W 3N3   Sari Bercovitch, Dir. of Info.Serv.
Staff: Prof 3. Subjects: Employee benefits, compensation, communications, human resource management, management. Holdings: 850 books; 200 salary surveys; 250 Conference Board publications; 550 annual reports; 500 vertical files; 4000 in-house reports on microfiche. Subscriptions: 100 journals and other serials. Services: Interlibrary loans; center not open to public. Automated Operations: Computerized cataloging. Computerized Information Services: DIALOG, Info Globe; internal database. Publications: Communique, weekly - for internal distribution only. Special Catalogs: Union catalog of company holdings in all offices (microfiche). Special Indexes: Index to in-house reports (online). Staff: Rosemary Lindsay, Info.Serv.Spec.; Laurie Mitchell, Info.Serv.Anl.

TOWLE (Charlotte) MEMORIAL LIBRARY
See: Spence-Chapin Services to Families and Children - Charlotte Towle Memorial Library

TOWNE LIBRARY
See: University of Pennsylvania - School of Engineering and Applied Science

★13586★
TOWNLEY & UPDIKE - LAW LIBRARY (Law)
405 Lexington Ave.   Phone: (212) 682-4567
New York, NY 10174   Josephine A. DiGiovanna, Libn.
Staff: Prof 1; Other 1. Subjects: Law - labor, product liability, antitrust, securities, patent, trademark and copyright. Holdings: 15,000 volumes. Subscriptions: 20 journals and other serials; 5 newspapers. Services: Interlibrary loans; library not open to public. Computerized Information Services: LEXIS, DIALOG.

★13587★
TOWNSEND-GREENSPAN & COMPANY, INC. - LIBRARY (Bus-Fin)
120 Wall St., 26th Fl.   Phone: (212) 943-9515
New York, NY 10005   Blanche Siegel, Libn.
Staff: Prof 1; Other 2. Subjects: National and international economic statistics, U.S. and foreign governments. Holdings: 1000 books; 1500 pamphlets. Subscriptions: 350 journals and other serials; 9 newspapers. Services: Interlibrary loans; library open to public with restrictions.

TOWNSEND (John Wilson) ROOM
See: Eastern Kentucky University - John Grant Crabbe Library - John Wilson Townsend Room

★13588★
TOWSON STATE UNIVERSITY - GERHARDT LIBRARY OF MUSICAL
INFORMATION (Mus)
Towson State University
Towson, MD 21204   Phone: (301) 321-2839
                                               Edwin L. Gerhardt, Cur.
Staff: Prof 2. Subjects: Music literature. Special Collections: Thomas A. Edison and the phonograph; John Philip Sousa and bands. Holdings: Figures not available for books; phonograph records; pictures; artifacts. Services: Copying, library open to public by appointment. Remarks: Library does not have a collection of scores or manuscripts. Direct all library correspondence to Edwin L. Gerhardt, 4926 Leeds Ave., Baltimore, MD 21227. Phone: (301) 242-0328. Staff: Dale E. Rauschenberg, Coord.

★13589★
TOWSON STATE UNIVERSITY - GERHARDT MARIMBA & XYLOPHONE
COLLECTION (Mus)
Towson State University
Towson, MD 21204   Phone: (301) 321-2839
                                               Edwin L. Gerhardt, Cur.
Staff: Prof 2. Subjects: Marimbas and xylophones. Holdings: Figures not available for books; VF drawers of materials on assorted marimbas, xylophones and artifacts. Services: Copying; library open to public by appointment. Remarks: The collection is a unique and comprehensive accumulation of marimba and xylophone lore. It includes literature, phonograph recordings, tape recordings, catalogs, music, methods, pictures, correspondence, miscellaneous information. It is not a collection of instruments. Direct all library correspondence to Edwin L. Gerhardt, 4926 Leeds Ave., Baltimore, MD 21227. Phone: (301) 242-0328. Staff: Dale E. Rauschenberg, Assoc.Prof., Music/Coord.

TOXICOLOGY DATA BANK
See: National Library of Medicine

TOXICOLOGY INFORMATION RESPONSE CENTER
See: Oak Ridge National Laboratory

TOY LIBRARY FOR SPECIAL CHILDREN
See: University Affiliated Cincinnati Center for Developmental Disorders - Research Library

★13590★
TOYS 'N THINGS, TRAINING & RESOURCE CENTER, INC. (Educ)
906 N. Dale   Phone: (612) 488-7284
St. Paul, MN 55103   Elizabeth Overstad, Toy Lib.Dir.
Staff: Prof 2; Other 12. **Subjects:** Toys, child development, day care, parenting, infant equipment. **Special Collections:** Toys appropriate for ages 6 weeks to 6 years (1500). **Holdings:** 1500 books; 600 films and filmstrips. **Subscriptions:** 30 journals and other serials. **Services:** Copying; center open to public with restrictions. **Publications:** List of publications - available on request; newsletter, monthly. **Special Indexes:** Toy Classification Index. **Staff:** Judy Kavanagh, Dir., Rsrc.Ctr.

TOZZER LIBRARY
See: Harvard University

★13591★
TRA ARCHITECTURE ENGINEERING PLANNING INTERIORS - LIBRARY (Plan)
215 Columbia   Phone: (206) 682-1133
Seattle, WA 98104   Dan Trefethen, Libn.
Founded: 1979. **Staff:** Prof 1; Other 1. **Subjects:** Architecture, engineering, airport planning and design, interior design, planning, graphic design. **Special Collections:** International Product File (4 VF drawers); Airport/Aircraft Data File (4 VF drawers). **Holdings:** 1500 books; 2000 reports; 2000 manufacturer's product catalogs; 10,000 slides. **Subscriptions:** 201 journals and other serials; 6 newspapers. **Services:** Interlibrary loans; library not open to public. **Computerized Information Services:** DIALOG.

★13592★
TRACOR JITCO, INC. - RESEARCH RESOURCES INFORMATION CENTER (Sci-Tech)
1776 E. Jefferson St.   Phone: (301) 881-4150
Rockville, MD 20852   Edward Post, Dir.
Staff: Prof 6; Other 3. **Subjects:** Research - biomedical, animal, biotechnological, clinical. **Holdings:** Figures not available. **Services:** Center not open to public. **Publications:** Research Resources Reporter, monthly; research resources directories, annual; DRR Program Highlights, annual. **Special Indexes:** Research Resources Reporter Index, annual. **Staff:** Gregory Freiherr, Asst.Dir.; Donald McKinstry, Sci. Adviser; Ron Cowen, Sci. Correspondent.

★13593★
TRACOR, INC. - TECHNICAL LIBRARY (Sci-Tech; Comp Sci)
6500 Tracor Ln.   Phone: (512) 926-2800
Austin, TX 78721   Sara Jane Lee, Libn.
Founded: 1962. **Staff:** Prof 1; Other 1. **Subjects:** Electronics, aerospace engineering, environmental science, acoustics, computer mathematics, physics. **Holdings:** 8000 books; 500 bound periodical volumes; 300 microfiche; 2500 technical reports. **Subscriptions:** 245 journals and other serials; 5 newspapers. **Services:** Interlibrary loans; copying; library open to public by appointment. **Automated Operations:** Computerized circulation. **Computerized Information Services:** DIALOG.

★13594★
TRACY-LOCKE/BBDO ADVERTISING - INFORMATION SERVICES DEPARTMENT (Bus-Fin)
Texas Commerce Bank Tower
Plaza of the Americas
Box 50129   Phone: (214) 742-3131
Dallas, TX 75250   Ellen Shapley, Mgr., Info.Serv.
Founded: 1967. **Staff:** Prof 1; Other 2. **Subjects:** Advertising, marketing, consumer products. **Holdings:** 1150 books; 700 titles of unbound periodicals; 120 reels of microfilm; 2 VF drawers of clippings on Texas subjects; 28 VF drawers for data on various subjects. **Subscriptions:** 400 journals and other serials. **Services:** Interlibrary loans; copying; department open to public by appointment. **Automated Operations:** Computerized serials. **Computerized Information Services:** DIALOG, Dow Jones News/Retrieval, NEXIS.

★13595★
TRADE RELATIONS COUNCIL OF THE UNITED STATES - LIBRARY (Bus-Fin)
1001 Connecticut Ave., N.W.
Washington, DC 20036   Eugene L. Stewart, Exec.Sec.
Subjects: Trade, tariff and related subjects. **Holdings:** Figures not available. **Services:** Library not open to public.

★13596★
TRAFFIC INJURY RESEARCH FOUNDATION OF CANADA (TIRF) - TECHNICAL INFORMATION CENTRE (Med)
171 Nepean St., 6th Fl.   Phone: (613) 238-5235
Ottawa, ON, Canada K2P 0B4   Joseph M. Grabetz, Libn.
Staff: Prof 1; Other 2. **Subjects:** Road safety - behavioral, medical, pharmacological and traffic health aspects. **Holdings:** 800 books; 100 bound periodical volumes; 4500 technical reports, statistics reports, government publications and newsletters. **Subscriptions:** 53 journals and other serials. **Services:** Interlibrary loans; copying; center open to researchers and specialists. **Publications:** Acquisition List, monthly.

TRAINING RESOURCES FOR EDUCATING EXCEPTIONAL STUDENTS
See: North Central Regional Center

★13597★
TRANET - LIBRARY (Sci-Tech; Soc Sci)
Box 567   Phone: (207) 864-2252
Rangeley, ME 04970   William N. Ellis, Exec.Dir.
Founded: 1976. **Staff:** 4. **Subjects:** Appropriate technology, alternative energy, alternative economics, social humanism, new ruralism. **Holdings:** 2000 books; 900 unbound magazines; 200 reports; 200 papers. **Subscriptions:** 50 journals and other serials. **Services:** Library open to public. **Publications:** Tranet, quarterly - distributed to members. **Staff:** Joanne Blythe, Ed.

TRANS-CANADA MEDICAL PLAN ARCHIVES
See: Ontario Medical Association - Library

★13598★
TRANS CANADA PIPELINES LTD. - LIBRARY (Sci-Tech; Energy)
530 8th Ave., S.W.
P.O. Box 500, Sta. M   Phone: (403) 269-5792
Calgary, AB, Canada T2P 3V6   Elizabeth A. Winter, Libn.
Staff: Prof 1; Other 1. **Subjects:** Geology; technology - petroleum, natural gas. **Holdings:** 600 books; 60 bound periodical volumes; 200 other cataloged items. **Subscriptions:** 118 journals and other serials. **Services:** Interlibrary loans; library open to public with librarian's permission. **Computerized Information Services:** DIALOG, SDC.

★13599★
TRANS CANADA PIPELINES LTD. - LIBRARY (Energy)
Box 54, Commerce Court West   Phone: (416) 869-2678
Toronto, ON, Canada M5L 1C2   Nancy L. Urbankiewicz, Sr.Libn.
Staff: Prof 1; Other 1. **Subjects:** Energy, pipelines, transmission, law. **Holdings:** 8000 books. **Subscriptions:** 300 journals and other serials; 10 newspapers. **Services:** Interlibrary loans; copying; library open to public with restrictions. **Computerized Information Services:** DIALOG, SDC, QL Systems, Info Globe, I.P. Sharp Associates. Performs searches on cost recovery basis. **Publications:** New Books in the Library, bimonthly - for internal distribution only.

★13600★
TRANS-PACIFIC GEOTHERMAL, INC. - LIBRARY (Energy)
1419 Broadway, Suite 415   Phone: (415) 763-7812
Oakland, CA 94612   Katherine Bertolucci, Libn.
Staff: Prof 1; Other 1. **Subjects:** Geothermal energy. **Holdings:** 3000 books; 2000 maps; unbound periodicals. **Subscriptions:** 33 journals and other serials. **Services:** Interlibrary loans; copying; library open to individuals with approval; parts of the collection are closed to the public. **Automated Operations:** Computerized cataloging. **Computerized Information Services:** DIALOG, The Source; internal database.

★13601★
TRANS QUEBEC & MARITIMES INC. - CENTRE DE DOCUMENTATION (Energy)
870 de Maisonneuve Blvd., E., 6th Fl.   Phone: (514) 286-5067
Montreal, PQ, Canada H2L 1Y6
Staff: Prof 2; Other 1. **Subjects:** Pipeline construction, regulation, natural gas. **Holdings:** 4000 books; 200 bound periodical volumes; 2000 clippings; 500 boxes of archival material. **Subscriptions:** 100 journals and other serials; 10 newspapers. **Services:** Interlibrary loans; copying; center open to public by

appointment. **Automated Operations:** Computerized cataloging, acquisitions and reference. **Computerized Information Services:** DIALOG, CAN/OLE, QL Systems, Questel. **Staff:** Chantale Dion; Colette Rajotte .

★13602★
TRANS WORLD AIRLINES, INC. - CORPORATE LIBRARY (Trans)
605 Third Ave.   Phone: (212) 557-6055
New York, NY 10158   Esther L. Giles, Corp.Libn.
Founded: 1965. **Staff:** Prof 1. **Subjects:** Air transportation. **Holdings:** 7000 books and bound periodical volumes; 1100 pamphlets; 7 VF drawers of annual reports; 350 volumes of company reports; Civil Aeronautics Board statistics; travel surveys. **Subscriptions:** 261 journals and other serials. **Services:** Interlibrary loans; copying; library open to public for reference use only on request. **Publications:** Library acquisitions list, monthly - for internal distribution only.

TRANSACTION TECHNOLOGY INC.
See: Citicorp/Transaction Technology Inc.

★13603★
TRANSALTA UTILITIES CORPORATION - LIBRARY (Energy; Bus-Fin)
110 12th Ave., S.W.
P.O. Box 1900   Phone: (403) 267-7388
Calgary, AB, Canada T2P 2M1   Shamim Kassam, Libn.
Staff: Prof 1; Other 2. **Subjects:** Electricity, management, reclamation. **Special Collections:** Electric Power Research Institute Research Reports. **Holdings:** 8000 books; 10 boxes of annual reports; 100 microfiche; 500 other cataloged items. **Subscriptions:** 600 journals and other serials; 50 newspapers. **Services:** Interlibrary loans; library open to public at librarian's discretion. **Computerized Information Services:** SDC, CAN/OLE, QL Systems, CANSIM, Info Globe.

★13604★
TRANSAMERICA DE LAVAL INC. - TECHNICAL LIBRARY (Sci-Tech)
Box 8788   Phone: (609) 890-5445
Trenton, NJ 08650   Ann C. Hunt, Libn.
Founded: 1943. **Staff:** 1. **Subjects:** Mechanical and marine engineering, compressors, gears, pumps, turbines. **Holdings:** 1200 books; 400 reports; 10 VF drawers of pamphlets and clippings; 6 VF drawers of archives. **Subscriptions:** 50 journals and other serials. **Services:** Interlibrary loans; copying; library open to public by referral.

★13605★
TRANSAMERICA OCCIDENTAL LIFE INSURANCE COMPANY - LAW LIBRARY (Law)
1150 S. Olive St., Suite T-2500   Phone: (213) 741-5083
Los Angeles, CA 90015   Susan Cuellar, Adm.Asst.
Staff: 1. **Subjects:** Insurance law, general law. **Holdings:** 9000 volumes. **Subscriptions:** 11 journals and other serials. **Services:** Library not open to public.

TRANSCANADA TELEPHONE SYSTEM
See: Telecom Canada

★13606★
TRANSCONTINENTAL GAS PIPE LINE CORPORATION - LIBRARY (Sci-Tech)
Box 1396   Phone: (713) 871-2321
Houston, TX 77251   Cheryl L. Watson, Libn.
Founded: 1951. **Staff:** Prof 2. **Subjects:** Natural gas industry, petroleum industry. **Holdings:** 1800 books; 700 bound periodical volumes; 10 VF drawers of information files. **Subscriptions:** 350 journals and other serials. **Services:** Interlibrary loans; copying; library open to public by appointment. **Computerized Information Services:** DIALOG, Dow Jones News/Retrieval. **Publications:** Library Lines (acquisitions list), monthly. **Remarks:** Library is located at 2800 S. Post Oak Rd., Houston, TX 77056. **Staff:** Jane Mascher, Asst.Libn.

TRANSLAB LIBRARY
See: California State Department of Transportation - Laboratory Library

★13607★
TRANSPORTATION INSTITUTE - LIBRARY (Trans)
5201 Auth Way   Phone: (301) 423-3335
Camp Springs, MD 20746   Chung-Tai Shen, Chf.Libn.
Founded: 1968. **Staff:** Prof 1; Other 1. **Subjects:** Merchant marine, transportation, economics, statistics, labor management, manpower. **Holdings:** 1400 volumes; 4000 documents; 3000 newspaper clippings; 1000 Congressional documents; 1300 documents on microfiche. **Subscriptions:** 90 journals and other serials; 8 newspapers. **Services:**

Interlibrary loans; library not open to public. **Publications:** Transportation Institute Library Bulletin, monthly - for internal distribution only. **Formerly:** Located in Washington, DC.

★13608★
TRANSPORTATION INSTITUTE - RESEARCH DOCUMENTATION CENTER (Trans)
301-303 Merrick Bldg.
North Carolina Agricultural & Tech. State Univ.   Phone: (919) 379-7745
Greensboro, NC 27411   Joyce H. Johnson, Adm.Off.
Staff: Prof 1. **Subjects:** Urban public transit, freight transportation, transportation for the elderly and handicapped, rural public transit, public transit finance. **Holdings:** 4000 books; 250 microfiche; unbound periodicals. **Services:** Interlibrary loans (through main university library); center open to public.

TRANSPORTATION RESEARCH BOARD LIBRARY
See: National Academy of Sciences - National Research Council

TRANSPORTATION RESEARCH INFORMATION CENTER
See: U.S. Dept. of Transportation - Urban Mass Transportation Adm.

TRANSPORTATION SYSTEMS CENTER
See: U.S. Dept. of Transportation

TRANSPORTATION TEST CENTER
See: U.S. Dept. of Transportation

★13609★
TRAPHAGEN SCHOOL OF FASHION - ETHEL TRAPHAGEN LEIGH MEMORIAL LIBRARY (Art)
257 Park Ave., S.   Phone: (212) 673-0300
New York, NY 10010   Allyn Rice Bloeme, Chf.Libn.
Founded: 1923. **Staff:** Prof 1; Other 2. **Subjects:** Fashion design and illustration, history of costume, art, interior design, architecture. **Special Collections:** Old and rare bound fashion periodicals of France, England, Germany and America; old German fine art books; Harper's Bazaar and Vogue, from their inception to the present; ethnic costumes (lithographs, original drawings). **Holdings:** 17,000 books; 716 bound periodical volumes; 40 VF drawers of clippings; 1130 lantern slides; 5000 color slides; black and white slides. **Subscriptions:** 14 journals and other serials. **Services:** Library open to public by appointment for publication research. **Publications:** Library Newsletter.

TRASANA TECHNICAL LIBRARY
See: U.S. Army - TRADOC Systems Analysis Activity

TRASK LIBRARY
See: Andover Newton Theological School

★13610★
TRAUB PLANT SCIENCE LIBRARY
2678 Prestwick Ct.
La Jolla, CA 92037
Defunct

TRAVAUX PUBLICS CANADA
See: Canada - Public Works Canada

★13611★
TRAVELERS INSURANCE COMPANIES - CORPORATE LIBRARY (Bus-Fin)
One Tower Square   Phone: (203) 277-5048
Hartford, CT 06115   Margaret Q. Orloske, Corp.Libn. & Hist.
Staff: Prof 3; Other 8. **Subjects:** Insurance, law, business management, data processing, actuarial science. **Special Collections:** Company history; mortality tables. **Holdings:** 65,000 books and unbound periodical volumes; 5 VF drawers of subject files. **Subscriptions:** 1200 journals and other serials; 6 newspapers. **Services:** Interlibrary loans; copying; library open to public by appointment. **Computerized Information Services:** DIALOG, SDC, LEGI-SLATE, Washington Service Bureau, Inc., NEXIS, TEXTLINE, Dow Jones News/Retrieval. **Networks/Consortia:** Member of Capitol Region Library Council. **Publications:** In short...in the Corporate Library, irregular - for internal distribution only. **Staff:** Mary T. Scott, Asst.Corp.Libn.; Jo Tonucci, Lib.Tech.Supv.; Harry Keiner, Archv.

★13612★
TRAVENOL LABORATORIES, INC. - HYLAND DIVISION - RESEARCH LIBRARY (Med)
1710 Flower Ave.   Phone: (213) 303-2491
Duarte, CA 91010   Monica Hermesch, Chf.Libn.
Founded: 1955. **Staff:** Prof 1; Other 1. **Subjects:** Immunology, biochemistry, hematology, virology, microbiology, clinical medicine and diagnosis. **Holdings:** 1457 books; 4675 bound periodical volumes; 150 technical reports; 10,000 reprints. **Subscriptions:** 100 journals and other serials. **Services:** Interlibrary loans; copying; library open to public by request. **Networks/Consortia:** Member of Pacific Southwest Regional Medical Library Service. **Publications:** What's Happening; Info to Go.

★13613★
TRAVENOL LABORATORIES, INC. - INFORMATION RESOURCE CENTER (Med; Sci-Tech)
6301 Lincoln Ave.   Phone: (312) 965-4700
Morton Grove, IL 60053   Diane H. Sherry, Mgr., Info.Rsrc.Ctr.
Founded: 1950. **Staff:** Prof 4; Other 6. **Subjects:** Medicine, pharmacology, chemistry, biomedical engineering, microbiology, enzymes. **Holdings:** 18,000 books; 24,000 bound and unbound periodicals; 72 VF drawers of manuscripts, reprints, documents; 11 VF drawers of pamphlets; 300 reels of microfilm. **Subscriptions:** 500 journals and other serials. **Services:** Interlibrary loans; copying; SDI; library open to public for reference use only on request. **Computerized Information Services:** DIALOG, SDC, BRS, NLM, OCLC, INVESTEXT, TEXTLINE, CAS Online, Dow Jones News/Retrieval, InfoLine, Westlaw, International Plastics Selectors, Inc., Questel, I.P. Sharp Associates, Ltd., Occupational Health Services, Inc., NIH-EPA Chemical Information System. **Networks/Consortia:** Member of North Suburban Library System; Lake County Consortium. **Publications:** Acquisitions List; Bibliographies, both monthly. **Staff:** Carol Worster, Supv.

★13614★
TRAVENOL LABORATORIES, INC. - INFORMATION RESOURCE CENTER (Med; Sci-Tech)
Route 120 and Wilson Rd.   Phone: (312) 546-6311
Round Lake, IL 60073   Barbara Petersen, Info.Spec.
Founded: 1975. **Staff:** Prof 2; Other 1. **Subjects:** Engineering - biomedical, pharmaceutical; plastics. **Holdings:** 1600 books; 6300 unbound periodical volumes; 900 government and industry specifications and standards; 200 reports; U.S. and foreign patents. **Subscriptions:** 186 journals and other serials. **Services:** Interlibrary loans; copying; SDI; center open to public for reference use only on request. **Computerized Information Services:** DIALOG, SDC, BRS, NLM, OCLC, CAS Online, International Plastics Selectors, Inc., InfoLine, Questel. **Networks/Consortia:** Member of North Suburban Library System; Lake County Consortium. **Staff:** Carol Worster, Supv.

★13615★
TRAVERSE CITY REGIONAL PSYCHIATRIC HOSPITAL - PROFESSIONAL RESOURCE LIBRARY (Med)
Elmwood & 11th Sts.   Phone: (616) 947-5550
Traverse City, MI 49684
Founded: 1885. **Staff:** Prof 1. **Subjects:** Psychiatry, psychology, neurology, medicine, nursing, social services. **Holdings:** 10,000 books; 3180 bound periodical volumes; 250 reprints; 41 films; 20 filmstrips; 26 tapes; 600 slides. **Subscriptions:** 53 journals and other serials. **Services:** Interlibrary loans; copying; library open to public with restrictions.

TRAVERTINE NATURE CENTER LIBRARY
See: U.S. Natl. Park Service - Chickasaw Natl. Recreation Area

TRAVIS AIR FORCE BASE (CA)
See: U.S. Air Force Hospital - David Grant Medical Center

★13616★
TRAVIS AVENUE BAPTIST CHURCH - MAURINE HENDERSON LIBRARY (Rel-Theol)
3041 Travis Ave.   Phone: (817) 924-4266
Fort Worth, TX 76110   Mrs. S.H. Henderson, Libn.
Founded: 1954. **Staff:** 4. **Subjects:** Religion, biography, history, literature. **Holdings:** 16,242 books; visual aid material. **Services:** Copying; library open to public with restrictions.

★13617★
TRC ENVIRONMENTAL CONSULTANTS, INC. - LIBRARY (Env-Cons)
800 Connecticut Blvd.   Phone: (203) 289-8631
East Hartford, CT 06108   Judith A. Douville, Info.Sci. & Mgr.
Staff: Prof 1. **Subjects:** Environmental science, hazardous wastes, air and water pollution, meteorology. **Holdings:** 1200 books; 900 documents,

conference proceedings, meteorological data, government documents, Environmental Protection Agency (EPA) documents, Air Pollution and Air Pollution Technical Data documents, and Environmental Protection Research Institute documents. **Subscriptions:** 120 journals and other serials. **Services:** Interlibrary loans; copying; library open to public by appointment. **Computerized Information Services:** DIALOG, SDC.

★13618★
TREAD OF PIONEERS MUSEUM - ROUTT COUNTY COLLECTION (Hist)
Box 772829   Phone: (303) 879-0240
Steamboat Springs, CO 80477   Diane Duquette, Chf.Libn.
Founded: 1981. **Staff:** Prof 1. **Subjects:** Local history and genealogy, skiing, ranching, mining. **Holdings:** 100 books; 3 file cabinets of manuscripts, photographs and clippings; 25 dissertations on microfilm; 1880 and 1890 census materials; photography; maps. **Services:** Copying; searches; library open to public with permission of librarian. **Remarks:** Maintained by East Routt Library District.

TRECKER (Harleigh B.) LIBRARY
See: University of Connecticut - School of Social Work - Harleigh B. Trecker Library

★13619★
TREE OF LIFE PRESS - LIBRARY AND ARCHIVES (Publ)
420 N.E. Blvd.
Gainesville, FL 32601   Reva Pachefsky, Libn.
Founded: 1971. **Staff:** Prof 1; Other 1. **Subjects:** Infant language development, child development, graphic arts. **Special Collections:** Archives of the Tree of Life Press; Collection of the Art of Robert (Ishmael) Grabb, Jr. **Services:** Interlibrary loans; library open to public by appointment. **Publications:** Newsletter; New Acquisitions; Listing of the Collection by Topic, all irregular.

TREES LIBRARY
See: North Central Regional Center

TRENDS PUBLISHING, INC.
See: Science Trends

★13620★
TRENTON FREE PUBLIC LIBRARY - ART & MUSIC DEPARTMENT (Art; Mus)
120 Academy St.
Box 2448   Phone: (609) 392-7188
Trenton, NJ 08608   Alice F. Fullam, Dept.Hd.
Staff: Prof 2; Other 2. **Subjects:** Fine arts, music, applied arts, antiques, dance, photography. **Special Collections:** Collection of original oil and water color paintings (22 items). **Holdings:** 6400 books; 2650 bound periodical volumes; 4500 phonograph records; 30 VF drawers of pictures; 4 VF cabinets of orchestral scores and parts; 1 VF cabinet of choral parts; 300 pieces of sheet music; 205 16mm films. **Subscriptions:** 90 journals and other serials. **Services:** Interlibrary loans; copying; department open to public. **Special Indexes:** Song index (card); paintings index (card); phonograph record index (card); dance index; arias index. **Staff:** Shirley Michael, Prin.Libn.

★13621★
TRENTON FREE PUBLIC LIBRARY - BUSINESS AND TECHNOLOGY DEPARTMENT (Bus-Fin; Sci-Tech)
120 Academy St.   Phone: (609) 392-7188
Trenton, NJ 08608   Richard D. Rebecca, Dept.Hd.
Founded: 1902. **Staff:** Prof 2; Other 2. **Subjects:** Business and finance, science and technology. **Holdings:** 9000 books; 2000 bound periodical volumes; 600 annual reports; 350 telephone directories; 300 trade directories; 25 VF drawers; loose-leaf financial services. **Subscriptions:** 200 journals and other serials. **Services:** Interlibrary loans; copying; department open to public. **Staff:** Nancy Leary, Sr.Libn.

★13622★
TRENTON FREE PUBLIC LIBRARY - GOVERNMENT DOCUMENTS COLLECTION (Info Sci)
120 Academy St.   Phone: (609) 392-7188
Trenton, NJ 08608   Nan Wright, Hd., Ref.Dept.
Founded: 1910. **Staff:** Prof 2; Other 1. **Special Collections:** Federal, state and local government documents; U.S. government periodicals and serial sets. **Holdings:** 25,000 books; 1000 bound periodical volumes; 250,000 other cataloged items. **Subscriptions:** 150 journals and other serials. **Services:** Interlibrary loans; copying; SDI; collection open to public. **Automated Operations:** Computerized cataloging. **Computerized Information Services:** OCLC. Performs free searches. **Contact Person:** James Kisthardt. **Networks/Consortia:** Member of PALINET & Union Library Catalogue of Pennsylvania.

Staff: James Kisthardt, Hd., Cat.Dept.; Nancy Leary, Sr.Libn.

★13623★
TRENTON FREE PUBLIC LIBRARY - TRENTONIANA COLLECTION (Hist)
120 Academy St.　　　　　　　　　　Phone: (609) 392-7188
Trenton, NJ 08608　　　　　　　　　Nan Wright, Hd., Ref.Dept.
Staff: Prof 6; Other 1. Subjects: Local history and genealogy. Special Collections: Early Trenton Fire Department minutes and records; New Jersey books and documents. Holdings: 4000 books; 403 bound periodical volumes; 26 VF drawers of photographs; 34 VF drawers of file materials; 175 maps and atlases; 5 VF drawers of manuscripts; 28 reels of film; 35 audiotapes; 47 oral histories; Trenton newspapers on microfilm; 5 pieces of Lenox china; 3 VF drawers of memorabilia; 30 boxes of unspecified materials. Subscriptions: 45 journals and other serials; 5 newspapers. Services: Copying; collection open to public. Staff: Richard Reeves, Sr.Asst.Libn.

★13624★
TRENTON PSYCHIATRIC HOSPITAL - MEDICAL LIBRARY (Med)
Box 7500　　　　　　　　　　　　Phone: (609) 396-8261
West Trenton, NJ 08628　　　　　　Elaine Scheuerer, Lib.Coord.
Founded: 1944. Staff: 1. Subjects: Psychiatry, psychotherapy, medicine, psychoanalysis, nursing. Holdings: 4000 books; 331 bound periodical volumes; 5 VF drawers of pamphlets; manuscripts; reports; clippings; 1 cabinet of phonograph records, tapes and filmstrips. Subscriptions: 80 journals and other serials. Services: Interlibrary loans; library open to public for reference use only. Networks/Consortia: Member of Central Jersey Health Science Libraries Association.

★13625★
TRENTON STATE COLLEGE - ROSCOE L. WEST LIBRARY - SPECIAL COLLECTIONS (Educ; Hist)
Hillwood Lakes CN550　　　　　　　Phone: (609) 771-2346
Trenton, NJ 08625　　　　　　Richard P. Matthews, Spec.Coll.Libn.
Founded: 1855. Staff: Prof 1. Special Collections: New Jersey; Trenton State College Archives (1000 items); historic textbooks (700 volumes); Trenton State faculty author collection (650 volumes); Trenton State College masters' theses (250 volumes); autograph collection (100 volumes); historic children's books (70 volumes); Feinstone Collection of the American Revolution (50 items); oral history collection (15 cassettes); Trenton State College alumni author collection (4 volumes); special illustrators collection (3 volumes). Holdings: 9500 books; 50 unbound reports; 35 manuscripts; 20 magnetic tapes. Services: Interlibrary loans; copying; collection open to public. Automated Operations: Computerized cataloging and circulation. Computerized Information Services: BRS, OCLC. Performs searches on cost recovery basis. Contact Person: Louise G. Fradlein, 771-2417. Networks/Consortia: Member of PALINET & Union Library Catalogue of Pennsylvania. Special Catalogs: Catalog of the Feinstone Collection of the American Revolution (typed list). Staff: Louise G. Fradlein .

★13626★
TRENTON TIMES - LIBRARY (Publ)
500 Perry St.　　　　　　　　　　Phone: (609) 396-3232
Trenton, NJ 08605　　　　　　　　Susan E. Connery, Dir.
Staff: Prof 2. Subjects: Newspaper reference topics. Holdings: Figures not available. Subscriptions: 10 journals and other serials; 5 newspapers. Services: Interlibrary loans; copying; SDI; library open to media and police. Staff: Debra Deamer, Res.

★13627★
TREVES (Ralph) WORKSHOP FEATURES - WORKSHOP PHOTOS (Aud-Vis)
311 Lake Evelyn Dr.　　　　　　　Phone: (305) 683-5167
West Palm Beach, FL 33411　　　　　Ralph Treves, Owner
Subjects: Manual crafts and skills, home improvements, hobby workshop projects, home security. Special Collections: Photographs illustrating manual skills and techniques related to shopwork, home construction and renovation. Holdings: 14,000 photographs available for reproduction by magazines, public relations agencies, newspapers, book publishers. Services: Feature articles and manuals written on assignment.

TREVOR (Elleston) ARCHIVE
See: Arizona State University - Special Collections

★13628★
TREXLER (Harry C.) MASONIC LIBRARY (Rec)
1524 Linden St.　　　　　　　　　Phone: (215) 432-2618
Allentown, PA 18102　　　　　　　Paul R. Breitenstein, Libn.
Staff: 1. Subjects: Freemasonry, Masonic history, Benjamin Franklin, George Washington. Holdings: 6000 books and bound periodical volumes. Services: Library open to public with restrictions. Remarks: Library is maintained by five Masonic lodges in Allentown. Staff: Myron P. Wehr, Pres.

TREXLER NURSES' LIBRARY
See: St. Luke's Hospital of Bethlehem, Pennsylvania - School of Nursing

TREXLER (Scott Andrew, II) MEMORIAL LIBRARY
See: Lehigh County Historical Society - Scott Andrew Trexler II Memorial Library

★13629★
TRI BROOK GROUP, INC. - LIBRARY (Med)
1100 Jorie Blvd., Suite 173　　　　　Phone: (312) 654-8070
Oak Brook, IL 60521　　　　　　Sandra Rumbyrt, Asst.Libn.
Staff: Prof 1. Subjects: Health care systems, health statistics. Holdings: 4000 volumes including government publications and reports. Subscriptions: 77 journals and other serials. Services: Library not open to public. Networks/Consortia: Member of Fox Valley Health Science Library Consortium.

★13630★
TRI-CITY JEWISH CENTER - JOSEPH AND BENJAMIN NEFF MEMORIAL LIBRARY (Rel-Theol)
2715 30th St.
Box 679　　　　　　　　　　　　Phone: (309) 788-3426
Rock Island, IL 61201
Founded: 1951. Subjects: Judaica. Holdings: 5500 books. Services: Library open to public with restrictions.

★13631★
TRI-COUNTY REGIONAL PLANNING COMMISSION - INFORMATION RESOURCE CENTER (Plan)
913 W. Holmes Rd., Suite 201　　　Phone: (517) 393-0342
Lansing, MI 48901　　　　　　Carrie Clinkscales, Exec.Asst.
Founded: 1956. Subjects: Urban and regional planning. Holdings: Figures not available. Services: Center open to public for reference use only. Computerized Information Services: DIALOG. Publications: Planning reports on Clinton, Eaton and Ingham counties, continual.

★13632★
TRI-COUNTY REGIONAL PLANNING COMMISSION - LIBRARY (Plan)
Box 2200　　　　　　　　　　　Phone: (309) 694-4391
East Peoria, IL 61611　　　　　Robert L. Pinkerton, Exec.Dir.
Founded: 1958. Subjects: Land use, housing, open space and recreation, environment, transportation. Special Collections: Environmental Protection Agency (EPA) Special Environmental Technical Studies. Holdings: 434 books; 252 bound periodical volumes; 120 items of census information; transportation documents; local development codes; maps (original of Standard Metropolitan Statistical Area). Subscriptions: 198 journals and other serials; 6 newspapers. Services: Interlibrary loans; copying; library open to public for in-office use. Publications: Annotated Bibliography of Agency Publications.

★13633★
TRI-COUNTY TECHNICAL COLLEGE - LEARNING RESOURCE CENTER (Sci-Tech; Educ)
Box 587　　　　　　　　　　　Phone: (803) 646-8361
Pendleton, SC 29670　　　　　Dr. Stephen B. Walter, Dir., L.R.C.
Founded: 1963. Staff: Prof 2; Other 6. Subjects: Animal industry, industrial electronics, business administration, paramedicine, automotive technology, secretarial science, machine shop, marketing, management, radio and television broadcasting, electronics engineering. Special Collections: Black studies (300 items); Child Development (3000 items); Medical Lab Technicians (200 items). Holdings: 35,695 books; 4565 bound periodical volumes; 4709 AV software items. Subscriptions: 158 journals and other serials; 16 newspapers. Services: Interlibrary loans; copying; comprehensive audiovisual production services; center open to residents of Anderson, Oconee or Pickens Counties, South Carolina. Publications: Quarterly and annual reports. Special Catalogs: Printed catalog of AV materials. Staff: Nancy C. Griese, Hd.Libn.

TRI-KAPPA COLLECTION OF AUBURN AUTOMOTIVE LITERATURE
See: Auburn-Cord-Duesenberg Museum

★13634★
TRI-STATE UNIVERSITY - PERRY T. FORD MEMORIAL LIBRARY (Sci-Tech; Educ)
S. Darling St.　　　　　　　　　Phone: (219) 665-3141
Angola, IN 46703　　　　　　Mrs. Enriqueta G. Taboy, Lib.Dir.
Staff: Prof 3; Other 3. Special Collections: NASA publications (29,648); Cameron Education Collection (elementary and secondary curriculum; 2129

items); industrial/commercial annual reports (1115). **Subscriptions:** 433 journals and other serials; 18 newspapers.

TRIANGLE CLUB ARCHIVES
See: Princeton University - William Seymour Theatre Collection

★13635★
TRIANGLE PUBLICATIONS, INC. - TV GUIDE MICROFILM LIBRARY (Publ)
Four Radnor Corporate Center Phone: (215) 293-8947
Radnor, PA 19088 Cathy Johnson, Microfilm Coord.
Staff: 2. **Subjects:** Television. **Holdings:** TV Guide on microfilm, 1953-1982. **Services:** Library not open to public. **Special Indexes:** TV Guide 25 Year Index, 1953-1977, with annual supplements.

★13636★
TRICO-KOBE, INC. - ENGINEERING LIBRARY (Sci-Tech)
3040 E. Slauson Ave. Phone: (213) 588-1271
Huntington Park, CA 90255 Zenny Mamdani, Engr.Adm.Asst.
Founded: 1952. **Staff:** 1. **Subjects:** Hydraulic oil well pumping, hydraulics, mechanical engineering, chemical engineering, petroleum production, acetylene manufacture. **Holdings:** 3000 volumes; 1500 patents; 7000 clippings. **Subscriptions:** 10 journals and other serials. **Services:** Library not open to public. **Formerly:** Kobe, Inc.

★13637★
TRIDENT TECHNICAL COLLEGE - NORTH CAMPUS LIBRARY (Sci-Tech; Educ)
Box 10367 Phone: (803) 572-6089
North Charleston, SC 29411 Marion L. Vogel, Dir., Lrng.Rsrcs.
Staff: Prof 1; Other 1. **Subjects:** Engineering technology, business and management, automotive and industrial crafts, horticulture, physical sciences. **Special Collections:** Sams Photofact Collection (Howard Sams Schematics for Radios and Televisions - entire collection). **Holdings:** 30,045 books; 39 bound periodical volumes; 325 government documents; 350 pamphlets in vertical file; 1064 reels of microfilm; 7579 microfiche; 51 realia; 134 phonograph records; 1712 audiotapes; 134 videotapes; 921 films; 26,857 slides; 539 overhead transparencies; 4 computer software programs. **Subscriptions:** 306 journals and other serials; 13 newspapers. **Services:** Interlibrary loans; copying; library open to public for reference use only. **Computerized Information Services:** DIALOG. Performs searches on cost recovery basis. Contact Person: Beverly Brooks, 572-6094. **Networks/Consortia:** Member of Charleston Consortium of Higher Education. **Publications:** Monthly Acquisition List - for internal distribution only; Audiovisual Bibliography, irregular. **Staff:** Beverly Brooks, Hd.Libn.; Rose Marie Huff, Acq.Libn.; Mack Lundy, III, AV Libn.

★13638★
TRIGOM - RESEARCH LIBRARY (Sci-Tech)*
Rampart Professional Complex
Rte. 302 Phone: (207) 846-3294
North Windham, ME 04062 Gregory M. Scott, Pres.
Staff: Prof 1. **Subjects:** Marine biology, marine environment and affairs, New England coastal ecology, socioeconomic data, fisheries. **Holdings:** 1500 reports. **Services:** Copying; library open to public by appointment.

TRIMBLE LIBRARY
See: Nazarene Bible College

★13639★
TRINITY BIBLE COLLEGE - GRAHAM LIBRARY (Rel-Theol)
Phone: (701) 349-3408
Ellendale, ND 58436 Esther Zink, Libn.
Staff: Prof 1; Other 3. **Subjects:** Bible, theology, church work, evangelism, Christian ministries, missions, elementary education. **Special Collections:** Pentecostal Works/Trinity Bible Institute archives. **Holdings:** 47,533 books; 6181 bound periodical volumes; 688 titles on microfiche; 20 VF drawers. **Subscriptions:** 348 journals and other serials. **Services:** Interlibrary loans; copying; library open to public. **Automated Operations:** Computerized cataloging. **Networks/Consortia:** Member of MINITEX. **Formerly:** Trinity Bible Institute.

★13640★
TRINITY COLLEGE - ARCHIVES (Hist)
Phone: (202) 269-2220
Washington, DC 20017 Sr. Columba Mullaly, Ph.D., Archv.
Founded: 1965. **Staff:** Prof 1. **Subjects:** Trinity College archives. **Holdings:** 550 cubic feet of records, minutes, photographs, artifacts, college catalogs (1899 to present) and student yearbooks (1911-1982). **Services:** Archives open to public with restrictions.

★13641★
TRINITY COLLEGE - WATKINSON LIBRARY (Hum)
300 Summit St. Phone: (203) 527-3151
Hartford, CT 06106 Dr. Jeffrey H. Kaimowitz, Cur.
Founded: 1857. **Staff:** Prof 3; Other 2. **Subjects:** Americana (especially 19th century), American Indians, black history, U.S. Civil War, caricature, folklore, witchcraft, graphic arts, history of printing, horology, medieval and European literature, philology (especially American Indian languages), jazz and blues, early voyages and travels, maritime history. **Special Collections:** Incunabula and other early printed books; private press books (especially Ashendene Press); English and American first editions (especially Frost, Millay, Marianne Moore, E.A. Robinson, Elinor Wylie); 18th and 19th century English and American periodicals; ornithology (6000 volumes); early psalm and hymn books and early secular song books; early American school books; W.C. Handy; manuscripts of Charles Dudley Warner, Frost, E.A. Robinson, Henry Barnard, Sibour, Nathan Allen, Watkinson family, Hartford families and other historical and literary figures. **Holdings:** 165,000 books and bound periodical volumes; atlases; 500 maps; 25,000 pieces of sheet music (mostly American); 1000 song sheets; printed ephemera including 80 indexed scrapbooks, advertisements, fashion plates, music and theater programs and valentines. **Subscriptions:** 40 journals and other serials. **Services:** Copying; library open to public for reference use only. **Automated Operations:** Computerized cataloging. **Computerized Information Services:** OCLC. **Networks/Consortia:** Member of NELINET. **Publications:** Bibliographies, irregular; exhibition catalogs. **Staff:** Margaret F. Sax, Assoc.Cur.; Karen B. Clarke, Asst.Cur., Ornithology.

★13642★
TRINITY COUNTY LAW LIBRARY (Law)*
Box R Phone: (916) 623-4000
Weaverville, CA 96093 Carol Rose, Sec.
Subjects: Law. **Holdings:** 3326 volumes. **Services:** Library open to public.

★13643★
TRINITY EPISCOPAL CHURCH - LIBRARY (Rel-Theol)*
1500 State St. Phone: (805) 965-7419
Santa Barbara, CA 93101 Edith P. Stickney, Libn.
Staff: Prof 2; Other 2. **Subjects:** Religion. **Holdings:** 2450 books. **Services:** Library open to public with restrictions. **Staff:** Marion Nydegger, Assoc.Libn.

★13644★
TRINITY EVANGELICAL DIVINITY SCHOOL - ROLFING MEMORIAL LIBRARY (Rel-Theol)
2065 Half Day Rd. Phone: (312) 945-8800
Deerfield, IL 60015 Dr. Brewster Porcella, Libn.
Staff: Prof 4; Other 12. **Subjects:** Biblical studies, evangelism and fundamentalism, theology, Christian education, church history. **Special Collections:** Evangelical Free Church of America Archives (books; periodicals; 8 VF drawers); Trinity Evangelical Divinity School Archives. **Holdings:** 96,000 books; 12,000 bound periodical volumes; 8632 microfiche; 2048 reels of microfilm. **Subscriptions:** 1150 journals and other serials; 5 newspapers. **Services:** Interlibrary loans; copying; library open to public. **Automated Operations:** Computerized cataloging. **Computerized Information Services:** OCLC. **Networks/Consortia:** Member of ILLINET; North Suburban Library System. **Staff:** William McKinley Yount, Ref.Libn.; Jacquelyn Allen, Cat.; Ruth Westerholm, Adm.Assoc.

★13645★
TRINITY LUTHERAN CHURCH - LIBRARY (Rel-Theol)
210 S. 7th St. Phone: (218) 236-1333
Moorhead, MN 56560 Rodney Erickson, Comm.Chm.
Founded: 1959. **Staff:** Prof 5; Other 3. **Subjects:** Biblical studies, personal growth, doctrine, missions, church history. **Special Collections:** Kittels Theological Dictionary (complete set); Interpreters Bible and Dictionary. **Holdings:** 4074 books. **Services:** Library open to public.

★13646★
TRINITY LUTHERAN CHURCH - LIBRARY (Rel-Theol)
1904 Winnebago St. Phone: (608) 249-8527
Madison, WI 53704 Sharon Kenyon, Libn.
Founded: 1946. **Staff:** 10. **Subjects:** Religion and related fields, home and family, missions, juvenile and adult literature. **Special Collections:** Bible Study Aids (600 items). **Holdings:** 4500 books; 2 VF drawers of clippings; 80 pamphlets and tapes. **Subscriptions:** Interlibrary loans; copying; library open to area residents. **Staff:** Mrs. Everette M. Jones, Asst.Libn.; Anna Ladd, Asst.Libn.; Francis Meyer, Asst.Libn.; Maxine Villand, Asst.Libn.

★13647★

TRINITY LUTHERAN HOSPITAL - FLORENCE L. NELSON MEMORIAL LIBRARY (Med)
31st & Wyandotte
Kansas City, MO 64108
Phone: (816) 753-4600
Cami L. Loucks, Dir.
Founded: 1970. **Staff:** Prof 2; Other 2. **Subjects:** Clinical medicine, preclinical medicine and nursing. **Special Collections:** Nelson Local History Collection (30 volumes). **Holdings:** 2762 books; 2387 bound periodical volumes; 12 VF drawers of pamphlets; 732 reels of microfilm; 14 microfiche; 5000 filmstrips, slides, audio cassettes and other AV equipment. **Subscriptions:** 362 journals and other serials. **Services:** Interlibrary loans; copying; library open to public for reference use only. **Computerized Information Services:** MEDLINE, DIALOG, SDC, Hazardline, EPA News, Occupational Health Services, Inc. **Networks/Consortia:** Member of Kansas City Library Network, Inc.; Kansas City Metropolitan Library Network. **Publications:** Medical Library Informat, bimonthly - for internal distribution only. **Special Catalogs:** AV union list; serials union list.

★13648★

TRINITY LUTHERAN SEMINARY - HAMMA LIBRARY (Rel-Theol)
2199 E. Main St.
Columbus, OH 43209
Phone: (614) 236-7116
Donald L. Huber, Libn.
Founded: 1830. **Staff:** Prof 2; Other 4. **Subjects:** Theology. **Special Collections:** Hymnals; catechisms. **Holdings:** 80,000 books; 6000 bound periodical volumes. **Subscriptions:** 450 journals and other serials. **Services:** Interlibrary loans; copying; library open to public for reference use only. **Automated Operations:** Computerized cataloging. **Networks/Consortia:** Member of OHIONET. **Staff:** Richard H. Mintel, Asst.Libn.

★13649★

TRINITY MEDICAL CENTER - ANGUS L. CAMERON MEDICAL LIBRARY (Med)†
Trinity Professional Bldg.
20 Fourth Ave., S.W.
Minot, ND 58701
Phone: (701) 857-5435
Frances E. Cockrum, AHEC Libn.
Founded: 1928. **Staff:** Prof 1. **Subjects:** Medicine. **Holdings:** 2500 books; 12,100 bound periodical volumes; 2000 AV programs. **Subscriptions:** 150 journals and other serials. **Services:** Interlibrary loans; copying; SDI; library open to public for reference use only. **Computerized Information Services:** MEDLINE. **Networks/Consortia:** Member of Greater Midwest Regional Medical Library (Region 3); Northwest Area Health Education Center Consortium. **Remarks:** This is the Northwest Area Health Education Library of the University of North Dakota School of Medicine Area Health Education Center Program.

★13650★

TRINITY MEDICAL CENTER - SCHOOL OF NURSING LIBRARY (Med)†
S. Main and 4th Ave.
Minot, ND 58701
Phone: (701) 857-5621
Mildred A. Morgan, Libn.
Founded: 1946. **Staff:** 1. **Subjects:** Nursing. **Holdings:** 5870 books; 271 bound periodical volumes. **Subscriptions:** 49 journals and other serials. **Services:** Interlibrary loans; library open to local students. **Networks/Consortia:** Member of Northwest Area Health Education Center Consortium.

★13651★

TRINITY MEMORIAL HOSPITAL - LIBRARY (Med)
5900 S. Lake Dr.
Cudahy, WI 53110
Phone: (414) 769-9000
Mrs. Pat Cameron, Libn.
Founded: 1967. **Subjects:** Medicine and nursing. **Holdings:** 1050 books; 2100 bound periodical volumes; 8 VF drawers of pamphlets; Audio-Digest tapes; 100 slides. **Subscriptions:** 140 journals and other serials. **Services:** Interlibrary loans; copying; library open to public for reference use only. **Computerized Information Services:** MEDLINE, BRS. **Networks/Consortia:** Member of Southeastern Wisconsin Health Sciences Library Consortium. **Publications:** Hospital Library Newsletter.

★13652★

TRINITY PRESBYTERIAN CHURCH - NORMAN S. HJORTH MEMORIAL LIBRARY (Rel-Theol)
Rte. 70 & W. Gate Dr.
Cherry Hill, NJ 08034
Phone: (609) 428-2050
Bernice Ahlquist, Chm., Lib.Comm.
Founded: 1961. **Staff:** Prof 1; Other 5. **Subjects:** Christian life and education, Bible study. **Holdings:** 2500 books; 25 phonograph records. **Services:** Library open to congregation members.

★13653★

TRINITY UNITED CHURCH OF CHRIST - EDITH L. STOCK MEMORIAL LIBRARY (Rel-Theol)
4700 S. Grand Blvd.
St. Louis, MO 63111
Phone: (314) 352-6645
Jean A. Allison, Chm., Lib.Comm.
Founded: 1960. **Holdings:** 2500 books; 60 records and 125 filmstrips. **Services:** Library open to public.

★13654★

TRINITY UNITED PRESBYTERIAN CHURCH - LIBRARY (Rel-Theol)
13922 Prospect Ave.
Santa Ana, CA 92705
Phone: (714) 544-7850
Patricia A. Veeh, Hd.Libn.
Founded: 1955. **Staff:** Prof 1; Other 6. **Subjects:** Bible, theology, psychology, church history, social concerns, missions, education, religions. **Holdings:** 6000 books; 55 bound periodical volumes; 300 cassettes. **Subscriptions:** 40 journals and other serials. **Services:** Library open to public with restrictions.

★13655★

TRINITY UNIVERSITY - DALLAS THEATER CENTER LIBRARY
3636 Turtle Creek Blvd.
Dallas, TX 75219
Founded: 1964. **Subjects:** Theater - acting, directing, dance and movement, art, costume and design, stage and set design, plays, children's theater; anthropology; psychology; history. **Special Collections:** Stecker Collection of Costume Books. **Holdings:** 12,000 books and plays; 8 noncirculating films of Dallas Theater Center productions; 25 recordings of plays; playbills and miscellaneous clippings; theater thesis. **Remarks:** Presently inactive.

★13656★

TRINITY UNIVERSITY - ELIZABETH COATES MADDUX LIBRARY - SPECIAL COLLECTIONS (Soc Sci)
715 Stadium Dr.
Box 56
San Antonio, TX 78284
Phone: (512) 736-8121
Richard Hume Werking, Lib.Dir.
Founded: 1869. **Holdings:** Paul A. Campbell Man and Space Collection (5000 items); 194,192 government documents; U.S. and selected Texas government document depository. **Services:** Interlibrary loans; copying. **Computerized Information Services:** DIALOG, BRS, OCLC, MARCIVE, Inc., Libs 100 System. **Networks/Consortia:** Member of Council of Research and Academic Libraries (CORAL); AMIGOS Bibliographic Council, Inc. **Staff:** Katherine D. Pettit, Spec.Coll.Libn.; Jane Mackay, Doc.Libn.

★13657★

TRIODYNE INC. CONSULTING ENGINEERS - INFORMATION CENTER (Sci-Tech)
5950 W. Touhy Ave.
Niles, IL 60648
Phone: (312) 677-4730
Beth A. Hamilton, Sr.Info.Sci.
Founded: 1979. **Staff:** Prof 4; Other 2. **Subjects:** Engineering - forensic, mechanical, automotive, civil; industrial safety; chemistry; materials science. **Holdings:** 6000 books; 40 VF drawers of technical reports; 6 VF drawers of engineering standards and specifications; 9 VF drawers of catalogs. **Subscriptions:** 255 journals and other serials. **Services:** Interlibrary loans; copying; SDI; center open to public by appointment. **Automated Operations:** Computerized cataloging. **Computerized Information Services:** SDC, OCLC, DIALOG; Safety Information System (internal database). **Networks/Consortia:** Member of North Suburban Library System; ILLINET. **Staff:** Aline M. Fairbanks, Engr.Ref.Libn.; Shirley W. Ruttenberg, Info.Anl.; Cheryl A. Hansen, Engr.Ref.Libn.

TRIPLER ARMY MEDICAL CENTER
See: U.S. Army Hospitals

★13658★

TRITON MUSEUM OF ART - LIBRARY (Art)
1505 Warburton Ave.
Santa Clara, CA 95050
Phone: (408) 248-4585
Jo Farb Hernandez, Dir.
Founded: 1965. **Subjects:** Contemporary art, international folk art, artists. **Special Collections:** Slide library of works of art in museum collection (400 slides). **Holdings:** 200 books; 300 exhibition catalogs and periodicals; 300 art newspapers; 300 art periodicals, 1919-1950; 12 volumes of news releases on Triton events. **Subscriptions:** 8 journals and other serials; 6 newspapers. **Services:** Library open to public with restrictions. **Staff:** Marc D'Estout, Asst.Dir.; David de la Torre, Dev.Dir.; Karen Shellhammer, Educ.Coord.; Lucretia Cerny, Publicist.

TROLLEY PARK
See: Oregon Electric Railway Historical Society, Inc.

★13659★
TROTTING HORSE MUSEUM - PETER D. HAUGHTON MEMORIAL LIBRARY (Rec)
240 Main St.   Phone: (914) 294-6330
Goshen, NY 10924   Philip A. Pines, Dir.
Founded: 1951. **Staff:** Prof 4. **Subjects:** History of standard bred horses, history of harness racing, training horses, horses in literature, veterinary medicine. **Holdings:** 400 books; 200 bound periodical volumes; 4400 record books, sale catalogs and racing records; videotapes; motion picture films. **Services:** Library open to public with permission.

TROWBRIDGE (Harry M.) RESEARCH LIBRARY
See: Wyandotte County Historical Society and Museum - Harry M. Trowbridge Research Library

★13660★
TROY STATE UNIVERSITY - LIBRARY - SPECIAL COLLECTIONS (Mus; Hist)
University Ave.   Phone: (205) 566-3000
Troy, AL 36082   Kenneth Croslin, Dir.
Founded: 1887. **Special Collections:** Paul Yoder Band Collection (492 scores; 17 books; 218 phonograph records); John Horry Dent Papers, 1851-1892 (Alabama and Georgia farmer; 25 volumes of manuscripts, farm journals and account books); Alabama history (110 manuscripts, historical papers, source material items); U.S. and Alabama documents (45,611 printed documents, 35,801 microforms); ERIC microfiche (334,836). **Services:** Interlibrary loans; copying; library open to public for reference use only. **Automated Operations:** Computerized cataloging. **Computerized Information Services:** OCLC, DIALOG. **Networks/Consortia:** Member of SOLINET.

★13661★
TROY TIMES RECORD - LIBRARY (Publ)
501 Broadway   Phone: (518) 272-2000
Troy, NY 12181   Ingrid Sharke, Libn.
Staff: Prof 1; Other 1. **Subjects:** Newspaper reference topics. **Holdings:** 100 books; newspapers, 1884 to present, on microfilm; clippings. **Services:** Library not open to public. **Special Indexes:** Index of clippings, 1977 to present.

★13662★
TRUDEAU INSTITUTE IMMUNOBIOLOGICAL RESEARCH LABORATORIES - LIBRARY (Med)
Algonquin Ave.
Box 59   Phone: (518) 891-3080
Saranac Lake, NY 12983   Joyce Ward, Libn.
Founded: 1900. **Staff:** 1. **Subjects:** Immunobiological research. **Holdings:** 13,000 books and bound periodical volumes. **Subscriptions:** 120 journals and other serials. **Services:** Interlibrary loans; copying; library open to public with permission. **Publications:** Trudeau Institute Annual Report.

★13663★
TRUE VINE MISSIONARY BAPTIST CHURCH - LIBRARY (Rel-Theol)†
831 Broadway Ave.
Box 1051   Phone: (318) 445-6730
Alexandria, LA 71301   Louise Humphrey, Libn.
Founded: 1947. **Staff:** Prof 3; Other 5. **Subjects:** Religion - philosophy, history, doctrine. **Holdings:** 2000 books; audiovisual aids. **Services:** Interlibrary loans; library open to other churches and the local community on a limited basis.

TRUETT (George W.) MEMORIAL LIBRARY
See: First Baptist Church of Dallas - First Baptist Academy - George W. Truett Memorial Library

TRUMAN (Harry S) LIBRARY
See: U.S. Presidential Libraries - Harry S Truman Library

★13664★
TRUMBULL MEMORIAL HOSPITAL - SCHOOL OF NURSING LIBRARY (Med)
1350 East Market St.   Phone: (216) 841-9371
Warren, OH 44484   Dorothy Stambaugh, Libn.
Staff: Prof 1. **Subjects:** Nursing. **Holdings:** 3486 books; 146 bound periodical volumes; 15 VF drawers of pamphlets and other items. **Subscriptions:** 117 journals and other serials. **Services:** Interlibrary loans; copying; library open to public for reference use only. **Networks/Consortia:** Member of Greater Midwest Regional Medical Library Network (Region 3); Northeastern Ohio Universities College of Medicine (NEOUCOM). **Publications:** List of New Acquisitions, bimonthly - for internal distribution only.

★13665★
TRUMBULL MEMORIAL HOSPITAL - WEAN MEDICAL LIBRARY (Med)
1350 E. Market St.   Phone: (216) 841-9379
Warren, OH 44482   Linda Bundy, Med.Libn.
Staff: Prof 1. **Subjects:** Medicine and allied health sciences. **Holdings:** 1441 books; 3439 bound periodical volumes. **Subscriptions:** 205 journals and other serials. **Services:** Interlibrary loans; copying; library open to college students. **Computerized Information Services:** MEDLINE. **Networks/Consortia:** Member of Northeastern Ohio Universities College of Medicine (NEOUCOM). **Publications:** Wean Library News, bimonthly - distributed to medical staff and dental service.

★13666★
TRUNKLINE GAS COMPANY - EMPLOYEE RESOURCE CENTER (Sci-Tech; Energy)
Box 1642   Phone: (713) 664-3401
Houston, TX 77001   Hershall Stair, Libn.
Staff: Prof 1. **Subjects:** Oil and gas industry, management, finance, public utility regulation, engineering. **Holdings:** 4000 books; 400 bound periodical volumes; 400 annual reports; 15 shelves of government documents; 18 shelves of oil and gas industry material. **Subscriptions:** 100 journals and other serials. **Services:** Interlibrary loans; copying; library open to industry employees. **Computerized Information Services:** SDC, NEXIS, DIALOG, Data Resources, Inc. (DRI).

TRUSTEE INFORMATION CENTER
See: Association of Governing Boards of Universities and Colleges

TRUTH (Sojourner) WOMEN'S RESOURCE LIBRARY
See: Women's Resource and Action Center - Sojourner Truth Women's Resource Library

TRUXTUN-DECATUR NAVAL MUSEUM LIBRARY
See: U.S. Navy - Department Library

★13667★
TRW, INC. - AIRCRAFT COMPONENTS GROUP LIBRARY (Sci-Tech)
23555 Euclid Ave.   Phone: (216) 383-3417
Cleveland, OH 44117   Sharon K. DeLong, Libn.
Founded: 1954. **Staff:** Prof 1; Other 1. **Subjects:** Metallurgy, nonmetallic materials, aerospace technology, mechanical engineering, nuclear engineering. **Holdings:** 5000 books; 4300 bound periodical volumes; 15,000 company reports; 40,000 contractor and government reports; 25,000 military specifications and standards. **Subscriptions:** 150 journals and other serials. **Services:** Interlibrary loans; library open to public by appointment. **Computerized Information Services:** DIALOG. **Formerly:** Its Engineering Library.

★13668★
TRW, INC. - BEARINGS DIVISION - RESEARCH & DEVELOPMENT TECHNICAL LIBRARY (Sci-Tech)
402 Chandler St.   Phone: (716) 661-2894
Jamestown, NY 14701   Harold E. Munson, Supv., Project Engr.
Founded: 1957. **Staff:** 2. **Subjects:** Ball bearings, roller bearings, lubrication, high temperature, cryogenic temperature, gas bearings, high vacuum, dry film, outer space applications. **Holdings:** 200 books; 2000 published articles; technical reports and patents. **Subscriptions:** 45 journals and other serials. **Services:** Library not open to public.

★13669★
TRW, INC. - DEFENSE SYSTEMS GROUP - SEAD TECHNICAL LIBRARY (Sci-Tech)
7600 Colshire Dr.   Phone: (703) 734-6243
McLean, VA 22102   Mary Drew, Lib.Mgr.
Founded: 1965. **Staff:** Prof 2; Other 2. **Subjects:** Underwater acoustics, systems engineering, sonar and radar systems. **Holdings:** 6000 books; 20,000 technical reports; 6000 technical reports in microform. **Subscriptions:** 203 journals and other serials. **Services:** Interlibrary loans; library open to public by arrangement. **Computerized Information Services:** DIALOG, BRS, DTIC, ESA-QUEST. **Networks/Consortia:** Member of Interlibrary Users Association; Metropolitan Washington Library Council. **Staff:** Jill Mercury, Doc.Libn.

TRW, INC. - ELECTROMAGNETIC SYSTEMS LABORATORIES
See: ESL/Subsidiary of TRW

★13670★
TRW, INC. - ELECTRONIC COMPONENTS - RESEARCH & DEVELOPMENT LIBRARY (Sci-Tech)
401 N. Broad St.   Phone: (215) 922-8900
Philadelphia, PA 19108   Barbara Welsh, Libn.
Founded: 1950. **Staff:** Prof 1. **Subjects:** Electronics, chemistry, physics. **Holdings:** 5200 books; 1600 bound periodical volumes; 17 VF drawers of patents; 5000 technical reports; 5200 technical notebooks. **Subscriptions:** 100 journals and other serials. **Services:** Library not open to public. **Computerized Information Services:** DIALOG. **Publications:** TIR lists, irregular - for internal distribution only.

★13671★
TRW, INC. - ENERGY DEVELOPMENT GROUP - LIBRARY
8301 Greensboro Dr.
McLean, VA 22102
Defunct

★13672★
TRW, INC. - INFORMATION CENTER/GOVERNMENT RELATIONS (Soc Sci)
1000 Wilson Blvd., Suite 2700   Phone: (703) 276-5016
Arlington, VA 22209   Kathleen Galiher Ott, Mgr.
Founded: 1973. **Staff:** Prof 1; Other 1. **Subjects:** Congressional legislation, public policy, international affairs. **Special Collections:** Company photo catalog. **Holdings:** 1000 books. **Subscriptions:** 32 journals and other serials. **Services:** Interlibrary loans; copying; center open to public. **Computerized Information Services:** Mead Data Central, LEGI-SLATE. **Publications:** Information Center Dataline, bimonthly - for internal distribution only.

★13673★
TRW, INC. - OPERATIONS & SUPPORT GROUP - ELECTRONICS & DEFENSE SECTOR - TECH. INFORMATION CENTER (Sci-Tech; Comp Sci)
One Space Park, Bldg. S., Rm. 1930   Phone: (213) 536-2631
Redondo Beach, CA 90278   Donna M. Mendenhall, Mgr.
Founded: 1954. **Staff:** Prof 15; Other 11. **Subjects:** Space systems, electronics, energy, computer technology. **Special Collections:** Records Center; American Institute of Aeronautics and Astronautics (AIAA) papers; SAE papers; NASA reports and microfiche. **Holdings:** 35,000 books; 9000 bound periodical volumes; 155,000 technical documents; 377,500 microfiche of documents. **Subscriptions:** 700 journals and other serials. **Services:** Interlibrary loans; copying; center open to public by appointment for use of unclassified material. **Computerized Information Services:** DOE/RECON, BRS, New York Times Information Service, DTIC, NASA/RECON, DIALOG, SDC, Mead Data Central, Ontyme II. **Staff:** Fumiko G. Oiye, Supv.; Patti Lee Jordan, Supv.; Gayle A. Seki, Supv.S.E. Singleton, Supv.

TRYON LIBRARY
See: University of Pittsburgh - Pymatuning Laboratory of Ecology

TRYON PALACE RESTORATION - LIBRARY
See: North Carolina State Department of Cultural Resources

★13674★
TUALITY COMMUNITY HOSPITAL - HEALTH SCIENCES LIBRARY (Med)
335 S.E. 8th Ave.   Phone: (503) 681-1121
Hillsboro, OR 97123   Robin Braun, Health Sci.Libn.
Founded: 1980. **Staff:** Prof 1. **Subjects:** Clinical medicine, pharmacology, nursing, therapeutics, cardiovascular medicine. **Special Collections:** Cardiovascular medicine (50 volumes). **Holdings:** 300 books; 109 bound periodical volumes. **Subscriptions:** 102 journals and other serials. **Services:** Interlibrary loans; copying; SDI; library open to local health professionals. **Computerized Information Services:** MEDLINE, DIALOG. Performs searches on cost recovery basis. **Networks/Consortia:** Member of Oregon Health Information Network (OHIN); Washington County Cooperative Library Services; Portland Area Health Sciences Librarians.

TUBA (Tubists Universal Brotherhood Association) RESOURCE LIBRARY
See: Ball State University - Music Library

TUCK MEMORIAL MUSEUM
See: Meeting House Green Memorial and Historical Association, Inc.

TUCKER (Gerald) MEMORIAL MEDICAL LIBRARY
See: National Jewish Hospital & Research Center/National Asthma Center - Gerald Tucker Memorial Medical Library

TUCKER LIBRARY OF THE HISTORY OF MEDICINE
See: University of Cincinnati - Medical Center Libraries - History of Health Sciences Library and Museum

★13675★
TUCSON CITIZEN - LIBRARY (Publ)
Box 26767   Phone: (602) 573-4570
Tucson, AZ 85726   Charlotte Kenan, Libn.
Staff: Prof 1; Other 5. **Subjects:** Newspaper reference topics. **Holdings:** 600 books; Tucson Citizen on microfilm (complete); 1 million clippings; 1200 microfilm jackets; 20 drawers of pamphlets, photographs and negatives; clipping files. **Subscriptions:** 70 journals and other serials; 10 newspapers. **Services:** Library not open to public. **Remarks:** The library is located at 4850 S. Park Ave., Tucson, AZ 85714.

★13676★
TUCSON CITY PLANNING DEPARTMENT - LIBRARY (Plan)
Box 27210   Phone: (602) 791-4234
Tucson, AZ 85726   Olya T. Tymciurak, Libn.
Founded: 1974. **Staff:** Prof 1. **Subjects:** Land use and development, planning, zoning, energy, environmental protection, economic development. **Special Collections:** City of Tucson planning reports, 1930 to present; local census reports, 1940 to present; zoning codes. **Holdings:** 5000 books; 150 bound periodical volumes; 300 microfiche; 3 VF drawers; slides; tapes. **Services:** Interlibrary loans; copying; SDI; library open to public for reference use only. **Publications:** PLAN (Planning Library Announcements and News), monthly. **Special Indexes:** Address list of city planning agencies in U.S. (card).

★13677★
TUCSON MEDICAL CENTER - MEDICAL LIBRARY (Med)
Box 42195   Phone: (602) 327-5461
Tucson, AZ 85733   Christee King, Mgr., Lib.Serv.
Founded: 1961. **Staff:** Prof 2; Other 1. **Subjects:** Clinical medicine and related sciences. **Holdings:** 2000 books; 8000 bound periodical volumes; 750 AV items. **Subscriptions:** 300 journals and other serials. **Services:** Interlibrary loans; library not open to public. **Computerized Information Services:** MEDLARS, BRS.

★13678★
TUCSON MUSEUM OF ART - LIBRARY (Art)
140 N. Main   Phone: (602) 623-4881
Tucson, AZ 85705   Dorcas Worsley, Libn.
Founded: 1974. **Staff:** Prof 6; Other 6. **Subjects:** Art - pre-Columbian, primitive, African and other ethnic groups, Spanish-Colonial, U.S., European, Western, Oriental, contemporary. **Special Collections:** Pre-Columbian art (2000 books; 1500 pamphlets; 15,000 slides). **Holdings:** 5700 books; 520 unbound periodical volumes; 3500 slides; 1 drawer archive of local galleries and museums; 25 VF drawers of scrapbooks, minutes and memorabilia of Tucson Museum archives, 1925 to present; 8 VF drawers of pamphlets by subject; 12 VF drawers of printed brochures, show announcements on artists; 2500 auction catalogs classified and arranged by subject; 4 drawers of archives on Arizona artists; 35 pamphlet boxes of publications from western states; 4300 mounted photographs. **Subscriptions:** 30 journals and other serials. **Services:** Interlibrary loans; copying; library open to public but materials circulate to museum members only. **Publications:** Brochure, 3rd edition, 1982. **Special Indexes:** Card index to Arizona and Southwestern magazines on art. **Staff:** Dorothy Siebecker, Cat.; Martha Lamont, Slide Libn.; Donald Powell, Bibliog.; Lucia Hu, Cat.

★13679★
TUCSON PUBLIC LIBRARY - STEINHEIMER COLLECTION OF SOUTHWESTERN CHILDREN'S LITERATURE (Hum)
200 S. 6th Ave.   Phone: (602) 791-4391
Tucson, AZ 85701   Karen Brown, Children's Libn.
Staff: Prof 1; Other 1. **Subjects:** Southwestern children's literature, folklore, and nonfiction. **Holdings:** 1200 books, filmstrips, posters, teaching aids, and phonograph records. **Services:** Copying; collection open to public. **Automated Operations:** Computerized cataloging, acquisitions, and circulation.

★13680★
TUCSON PUBLIC LIBRARY - TUCSON GOVERNMENTAL REFERENCE LIBRARY (Soc Sci)
City Hall, Local Government Info.Ctr.
Box 27210   Phone: (602) 791-4041
Tucson, AZ 85726   Ann T. Strickland, Libn.
Founded: 1974. **Staff:** Prof 1; Other 1. **Subjects:** Local government, inner city renewal, groundwater management, growth management. **Holdings:** 3200 books; 12,000 periodical volumes; 6000 technical documents; 1000 local documents. **Subscriptions:** 300 journals and other serials. **Services:** Copying; SDI; library open to public for reference use only. **Computerized Information Services:** DIALOG, SDC, Local Government Information Network (LOGIN), BRS, New York Times Information Service. **Networks/Consortia:** Member of Arizona Research Information Center (ARIC). **Publications:** New

Arrivals List, bimonthly - on request to other special libraries. **Special Indexes:** Subject index to local government articles in Tucson newspapers, 1976 to present.

★13681★

TUFTS UNIVERSITY - FLETCHER SCHOOL OF LAW & DIPLOMACY - EDWIN GINN LIBRARY (Law; Soc Sci)

Phone: (617) 628-5000

Medford, MA 02155   Natalie Schatz, Libn.

Founded: 1933. **Staff:** Prof 3; Other 7. **Subjects:** International law, world politics, economic development, foreign affairs, civilization. **Special Collections:** United Nations (45,000 microprint; 10,000 paper documents); Murrow Library (43,000 items of ephemera; 1600 books; 2 films; audiotapes); World Peace Foundation Library (27 VF drawers). **Holdings:** 100,000 books and bound periodical volumes. **Subscriptions:** 1320 journals and other serials; 37 newspapers. **Services:** Interlibrary loans; copying; library open to public. **Staff:** Henrietta Moore, Circ.Supv.

★13682★

TUFTS UNIVERSITY - HEALTH SCIENCES LIBRARY (Med)

136 Harrison Ave.   Phone: (617) 956-6706

Boston, MA 02111   Elizabeth K. Eaton, Dir.

Founded: 1906. **Staff:** Prof 7; Other 12. **Subjects:** Medicine, dentistry, veterinary medicine, nutrition, related health sciences. **Holdings:** 31,000 books; 60,000 bound periodical volumes; 851 audiotapes; 219 slide titles; 2812 reels of microfilm; 7 video discs; 21 audio journal titles; 653 videotapes; 52 AV kits; 24 phonograph records. **Subscriptions:** 1376 journals and other serials; 6 newspapers. **Services:** Interlibrary loans; copying; SDI; library open to public with restrictions. **Automated Operations:** Computerized cataloging, acquisitions and serials. **Computerized Information Services:** DIALOG, MEDLINE, BRS, Institute for Scientific Information (ISI), NEXIS, NIH-EPA Chemical Information System, OCLC. **Networks/Consortia:** Member of NELINET; Boston Library Consortium; Greater Northeastern Regional Medical Library Program; North Atlantic Health Sciences Libraries. **Publications:** Library Guide and Library Handbook, irregular. **Staff:** Cora C. Ho, Assoc.Libn.; Carolyn Waite, Hd., Tech.Serv.; Frances Faletra, Ser./Acq.Libn.; Linda VanHorn, Hd., Info.Serv.; Elizabeth J. Richardson, Info.Serv.Libn.; Drusilla Raidford, Info.Serv.Libn.

★13683★

TUFTS UNIVERSITY - MATHEMATICS-PHYSICS LIBRARY (Sci-Tech; Comp Sci)

Robinson Hall, Rm. 251   Phone: (617) 628-5000

Medford, MA 02155   Pauline A. Boucher, Asst.Sci.Libn.

Founded: 1955. **Staff:** Prof 1. **Subjects:** High energy physics, nuclear physics, solid state physics, quantum mechanics, electricity and magnetism, general relativity, astronomy, astrophysics, classical and functional analysis, algebra, group theory, topology, computer science. **Holdings:** 9000 books; 4700 bound periodical volumes; 135 dissertations; 1500 preprints. **Subscriptions:** 220 journals and other serials. **Services:** Interlibrary loans (through Wessell Library); library open to consortium members, others by permission. **Networks/Consortia:** Member of Boston Library Consortium. **Publications:** Tufts University Science Libraries Bulletin, every 6 weeks; Math-Physics Preprint List, monthly.

★13684★

TUFTS UNIVERSITY - RICHARD H. LUFKIN LIBRARY (Sci-Tech)

Anderson Hall   Phone: (617) 628-5000

Medford, MA 02155   Wayne B. Powell, Sci./Engr.Libn.

Founded: 1961. **Staff:** Prof 1; Other 1. **Subjects:** Civil, sanitary, mechanical and electrical engineering. **Holdings:** 12,000 books; 15,400 bound periodical volumes; 300 dissertations; 20,000 technical reports; 2800 microforms. **Subscriptions:** 400 journals and other serials. **Services:** Interlibrary loans (through Wessell Library); copying; library open to consortium members, others by permission. **Networks/Consortia:** Member of Boston Library Consortium. **Publications:** Tufts University Science Libraries Bulletin, every 6 weeks.

★13685★

TUFTS UNIVERSITY - ROCKWELL CHEMISTRY LIBRARY (Sci-Tech)

62 Talbot Ave.   Phone: (617) 628-5000

Medford, MA 02155   Pauline A. Boucher, Asst.Sci.Libn.

Staff: Prof 1. **Subjects:** Chemistry and chemical engineering. **Holdings:** 6500 books; 6600 bound periodical volumes; 550 dissertations; 230 microforms. **Subscriptions:** 170 journals and other serials. **Services:** Interlibrary loans (through Wessell Library); copying; library open to consortium members, others by permission. **Networks/Consortia:** Member of Boston Library Consortium. **Publications:** Tufts University Science Libraries Bulletin, every 6 weeks.

TUKEY (Harold B.) MEMORIAL LIBRARY

See: American Horticultural Society - Library

★13686★

TULANE UNIVERSITY OF LOUISIANA - ARCHITECTURE LIBRARY (Art; Sci-Tech)

Richardson Memorial Bldg.   Phone: (504) 865-4409

New Orleans, LA 70118   Frances E. Hecker, Hd.

Founded: 1948. **Staff:** 2. **Subjects:** Architecture, city planning, preservation, technology. **Holdings:** 7550 books; 673 bound periodical volumes. **Subscriptions:** 234 journals and other serials. **Services:** Interlibrary loans; copying; library open to public.

★13687★

TULANE UNIVERSITY OF LOUISIANA - DELTA REGIONAL PRIMATE RESEARCH CENTER - SCIENCE INFORMATION SERVICE (Sci-Tech; Med)

3 Rivers Rd.   Phone: (504) 892-2040

Covington, LA 70433   James L. Paysse, Ed.Asst.

Founded: 1963. **Staff:** 1. **Subjects:** Biochemistry, cancer, infectious diseases, neurobiology, pulmonary pathology, reproductive physiology, urology, veterinary science, immunology, parasitology, primatology, internal medicine. **Special Collections:** Reprints (20,100). **Holdings:** 6500 books; 5362 bound periodical volumes; 5 dissertations; 125 microforms. **Subscriptions:** 86 journals and other serials. **Services:** Interlibrary loans; copying; service open to students, scientists and researchers. **Automated Operations:** Computerized cataloging and ILL. **Computerized Information Services:** OCLC, MEDLINE, Louisiana Numerical Register (LNR). Performs searches on cost recovery basis. **Special Indexes:** Author indexes for reprints.

★13688★

TULANE UNIVERSITY OF LOUISIANA - HOWARD-TILTON MEMORIAL LIBRARY - LOUISIANA COLLECTION (Hist)

Phone: (504) 865-5643

New Orleans, LA 70118   Jane Stevens, Hd.

Staff: Prof 1; Other 3. **Subjects:** Louisiana - history and politics, art and architecture, literature, genealogy. **Holdings:** 21,000 books and bound periodical volumes; 64 VF drawers of clippings, pamphlets and other material; 18 VF drawers of pictures and portraits; 5 cases of maps; 42 volumes of Louisiana sheet music. **Services:** Copying; collection open to public with restrictions. **Automated Operations:** Computerized cataloging. **Computerized Information Services:** DIALOG, SDC, OCLC. **Special Indexes:** Indexes to books and periodicals, maps, sheet music (cards).

★13689★

TULANE UNIVERSITY OF LOUISIANA - LATIN AMERICAN LIBRARY (Area-Ethnic)

Howard-Tilton Memorial Library   Phone: (504) 865-5681

New Orleans, LA 70118   Thomas Niehaus, Dir.

Founded: 1924. **Staff:** Prof 1; Other 6. **Subjects:** Latin America - anthropology, archeology, art, history, economics, political science, sociology. **Special Collections:** Latin American Photographic Archive (11,760 photographs); Merle Greene Robertson Rubbings Collection (500 rubbings of stone relief sculpture); William E. Gates Collections of Mexicana; Lewis Hanke Papers (18 VF drawers); France V. Scholes Collection (copies and notes of materials from the Archivo General de Indias of Seville and Archivo General de la Nacion of Mexico; 76 VF drawers); Nicolas Leon Collection; Ephraim George Squier Papers; Francisco Morazan Papers; George H. Pepper Papers on Indians of the American Southwest; Viceregal and Ecclesiastical Mexican Collection (3000 dossiers); William Walker Papers; Central American Printed Ephemera Collection; other collections relating to colonial and 19th century Mexico, Yucatan and Chiapas. **Holdings:** 130,000 books; 110 cubic feet of manuscripts; 4000 pamphlets. **Subscriptions:** 1500 journals and other serials; 30 newspapers. **Services:** Interlibrary loans; copying; library open to public. **Automated Operations:** Computerized cataloging and circulation. **Computerized Information Services:** DIALOG, SDC, OCLC. **Networks/Consortia:** Member of SOLINET; CRL. **Services:** Catalog of Latin American Library, 1970 - 9 volumes; supplements, 1970, 1974, 1978. **Staff:** Ruth Olivera, Asst.Mss.Cat.

★13690★

TULANE UNIVERSITY OF LOUISIANA - LAW LIBRARY (Law)

School of Law   Phone: (504) 866-2751

New Orleans, LA 70118   David A. Combe, Libn.

Staff: Prof 8; Other 8. **Subjects:** Law - Roman, civil, maritime, comparative. **Holdings:** 280,000 volumes. **Subscriptions:** 2903 journals and other serials. **Services:** Interlibrary loans; copying; library open to public. **Computerized Information Services:** DIALOG, OCLC, SDC, LEXIS, NEXIS. **Networks/Consortia:** Member of SOLINET.

★13691★
TULANE UNIVERSITY OF LOUISIANA - MATHEMATICS RESEARCH LIBRARY (Sci-Tech)
Gibson Hall
Phone: (504) 865-5727
New Orleans, LA 70118
Dr. Terry Lawson, Prof., Mathematics
Founded: 1964. **Staff:** 1. **Subjects:** Graduate mathematics. **Holdings:** 10,400 books; 7500 bound periodical volumes; 133 Tulane math department dissertations. **Subscriptions:** 310 journals and other serials. **Services:** Interlibrary loans; copying; library open to public with permission of librarian. **Publications:** Lecture Notes in Mathematics - available for sale; conferences given by math department; list of lecture notes available on request.

★13692★
TULANE UNIVERSITY OF LOUISIANA - MAXWELL MUSIC LIBRARY (Mus)
Howard-Tilton Memorial Library
Phone: (504) 865-4527
New Orleans, LA 70118
Liselotte Andersson, Libn.
Staff: Prof 1; Other 3. **Subjects:** Music. **Holdings:** 24,350 volumes; 10,652 phonograph records and tapes. **Subscriptions:** 194 journals and other serials. **Services:** Interlibrary loans; copying; library open to public for reference use only. **Special Indexes:** Bach Index, anthologies containing music up to 1650 (for record collection); Song Index.

★13693★
TULANE UNIVERSITY OF LOUISIANA - SCHOOL OF BUSINESS ADMINISTRATION - NORMAN MAYER LIBRARY (Bus-Fin; Comp Sci)
Phone: (504) 865-6111
New Orleans, LA 70118
Dorothy Whittemore, Dir.
Founded: 1926. **Staff:** Prof 1; Other 3. **Subjects:** Accounting, finance, international business, marketing, computer science, behavioral analysis. **Special Collections:** Business and Financial History Collection (4000 corporate financial history folders of annual reports and other documents; 300 rare and/or historical books, pre-1930). **Holdings:** 42,000 volumes; 24 VF drawers of pamphlets. **Subscriptions:** 900 journals and other serials. **Services:** Interlibrary loans; copying; library open to public with restrictions.

★13694★
TULANE UNIVERSITY OF LOUISIANA - SCHOOL OF MEDICINE - RUDOLPH MATAS MEDICAL LIBRARY (Med)†
1430 Tulane Ave.
Phone: (504) 588-5155
New Orleans, LA 70112
William D. Postell, Jr., Med.Libn.
Founded: 1834. **Staff:** Prof 6; Other 8. **Subjects:** Medicine, biological sciences. **Special Collections:** Weinstein Collection (nonmedical books by and about doctors); Elizabeth Bass Collection (women in medicine). **Holdings:** 130,000 volumes. **Subscriptions:** 1350 journals and other serials. **Services:** Interlibrary loans; copying. **Computerized Information Services:** MEDLINE, DIALOG, SDC. **Networks/Consortia:** Member of TALON.

★13695★
TULANE UNIVERSITY OF LOUISIANA - SOUTHEASTERN ARCHITECTURAL ARCHIVE (Art)
7001 Freret St.
New Orleans, LA 70118
William R. Cullison, Cur.
Staff: Prof 1; Other 2. **Subjects:** Architecture - general, Louisiana, Southeastern U.S. **Holdings:** 2 million items, including 150,000 architectural drawings. **Services:** Copying; archive open to public.

★13696★
TULANE UNIVERSITY OF LOUISIANA - SPECIAL COLLECTIONS DIVISION - MANUSCRIPTS AND RARE BOOKS SECTION (Rare Book; Hist)
Howard-Tilton Memorial Library
Phone: (504) 865-5685
New Orleans, LA 70118
Wilbur E. Meneray, Ph.D., Hd.,Mss./Rare Bks.
Founded: 1941. **Staff:** Prof 3; Other 6. **Subjects:** New Orleans and southern Louisiana history, politics, economics and social history, 18th century to present; natural history; English county history; Romanov Russian history and travel; American Revolution; science fiction; 19th-20th century English language first editions. **Special Collections:** George W. Cable Collection; Favrot Family Papers (18th and early 19th century Louisiana); Charles Colcock Jones Papers (pre-Civil War minister and plantation owner in Georgia); Joseph Merrick Jones Steamboat Collection; Kuntz Collection (18th and early 19th century Louisiana); Albert Sidney and William Preston Johnston Papers; Louisiana Historical Association Collection (Civil War papers); papers of U.S. Representatives F. Edward Hebert and Dave Treen, Governor Sam Jones, Mayor deLesseps S. Morrison; Political Ephemera Collection; William B. Wisdom Collections of William Faulkner and 19th and 20th century first editions; Lafcadio Hearn Collection; Colonial Americana Collection; Tulane University (theses; dissertations; archives); Jules C. Alciatore Collections of Stendhal; Midlo Bookplate Collection; Rosel Brown Science Fiction Collection. **Holdings:** 3 million manuscripts; 37,700 rare book titles; 1000 titles of university archival materials. **Services:** Copying; library open to public with

identification. **Automated Operations:** Computerized cataloging. **Computerized Information Services:** OCLC. **Networks/Consortia:** Member of SOLINET. **Publications:** Favrot Papers transcriptions. **Special Catalogs:** Catalogs of the Kuntz, Faulkner and Hearn Collection; Favrot Library catalog; manuscript catalog; rare book catalog. **Staff:** Guillermo Nanez Falcon, Ph.D., Mss.Cat.; Sylvia V. Metzinger, Rare Books Cat.Archv.

★13697★
TULANE UNIVERSITY OF LOUISIANA - WILLIAM RANSOM HOGAN JAZZ ARCHIVE (Mus)
Howard-Tilton Memorial Library
Phone: (504) 865-5688
New Orleans, LA 70118
Curtis D. Jerde, Cur.
Founded: 1958. **Staff:** Prof 2; Other 4. **Subjects:** Classic New Orleans jazz, with related background material and a limited amount of material relating to later developments in jazz; blues; rhythm and blues; gospel music. **Special Collections:** Nick LaRocca Collection (2644 items); Al Rose Collection (6500 items); John Robichaux Collection (7219 items); Herbert A. Otto Collection (20 tapes); Robert W. Greenwood Collection (345 items); Robert Bradley Collection (1179 items); Roger Gulbrandsen Collection (4372 items); George Blanchin Collection (920 items); Genevieve Pitot Collection (1000 items); Ted Demuth Collection (370 items); Gospel Music Collection (600 items); George Bing Collection (116 items); William Russell notes; Henry Kmen notes; Edmond Souchon Collection; Ralston Crawford Collection. **Holdings:** 2000 books; 6000 photographs; 1700 oral history tapes; 10,000 pages of oral history summaries; 36,400 phonograph records; 63 piano rolls; 24 cylinder recordings; 14,000 pieces of sheet music; 2272 magnetic tapes; 32 motion picture reels; 6 reels of microfilm; 20 videotapes; 25,655 miscellaneous notes, clippings and posters. **Subscriptions:** 461 journals and other serials. **Services:** Interlibrary loans; copying (copies of taped summaries and digests available); archive open to public. **Automated Operations:** Computerized cataloging and circulation. **Computerized Information Services:** OCLC. **Publications:** List of publications - available upon request. **Special Catalogs:** Catalog of 78 rpm recordings (card); catalog of popular music in print (computerized catalog); name index of New Orleans musicians, past and present (card). **Staff:** Alma D. Williams, Asst. to Cur.

★13698★
TULARE COUNTY FREE LIBRARY - CALIFORNIA HISTORICAL RESEARCH COLLECTION - ANNIE R. MITCHELL ROOM (Hist)
200 W. Oak St.
Phone: (209) 733-8440
Visalia, CA 93277
Mary Anne Terstegge, Hist.Libn.
Staff: 1. **Subjects:** Tulare county history, San Joaquin Valley history, Sequoia National Park, Kaweah Commonwealth Colony, Sierra Nevada Mountains. **Special Collections:** George W. Stewart Manuscript Collection on Sequoia/Kings Canyon National Parks and the California National Guard. **Holdings:** 2863 books; 29 bound periodical volumes; 25 VF drawers of pamphlets and pictures; 35 boxes. **Services:** Copying; research collection open to public by appointment and on a limited schedule. **Networks/Consortia:** Member of San Joaquin Valley Library System.

★13699★
TULARE COUNTY LAW LIBRARY (Law)
County Civic Center, Rm. 1
Phone: (209) 733-6395
Visalia, CA 93291
Sharon Borbon, Law Lib.Coord.
Founded: 1892. **Staff:** 1. **Subjects:** Law and related subjects. **Holdings:** 17,000 volumes. **Services:** Copying; library open to public in presence of librarian.

★13700★
TULARE PUBLIC LIBRARY - INEZ L. HYDE MEMORIAL COLLECTION (Hist)
113 North F. St.
Tulare, CA 93274
Louise Longan, Libn.
Subjects: Genealogy, local history. **Special Collections:** Census records of Tulare County, 1860-1910. **Holdings:** 2932 volumes; 543 reels of microfilm; 11,847 microfiche. **Services:** Library open to public with restrictions. **Formerly:** Sequoia Genealogical Society - Inez L. Hyde Memorial Collection.

TULLIS RESOURCE CENTER
See: Kansas Technical Institute

TULLY (Alice) LIBRARY
See: New School of Music, Inc. - Alice Tully Library

★13701★
TULSA CITY-COUNTY LIBRARY SYSTEM - BUSINESS AND TECHNOLOGY DEPARTMENT (Sci-Tech)
400 Civic Ctr.
Phone: (918) 581-5211
Tulsa, OK 74103
J. Craig Buthod, Dept.Hd.
Founded: 1920. **Staff:** Prof 6; Other 5. **Subjects:** Earth and petroleum

sciences, energy technology, engineering, management, transportation, marketing. **Special Collections:** A.I. Levorsen Geology Collection (1600 books, serials and maps); General Land Office survey maps (18,000); C.R. Musgrave Transportation Library (700 items); documents pertaining to proposed nuclear power station (800); local floodplain maps (50). **Holdings:** 130,000 books; 21,000 bound periodical volumes; 51,000 geologic and topographic maps; 1500 local government documents; 160,000 federal government documents; 2000 telephone and city directories; 8000 periodicals and newspapers in microform. **Subscriptions:** 770 journals and other serials; 10 newspapers. **Services:** Interlibrary loans; copying; fee-based research; department open to public. **Automated Operations:** Computerized cataloging, acquisitions and circulation. **Computerized Information Services:** DIALOG, SDC. **Networks/Consortia:** Member of Tulsa Area Library Cooperative; Oklahoma Telecommunications Interlibrary System (OTIS). **Publications:** INFO, monthly except July and August. **Staff:** Robert Lieser, Libn.; Martha Mapes, Libn.; Kelly Jennings, Libn.; Karen Curtis, Libn.; Martha Gregory, Info. II Libn.

★13702★
TULSA COUNTY HISTORICAL SOCIETY - LIBRARY (Hist)
Tulsa City-County Library
400 Civic Ctr.   Phone: (918) 592-2595
Tulsa, OK 74103
Subjects: State and local history. **Holdings:** 600 cubic feet of reminiscences of pioneers, oral history tapes, diaries, business records, public documents, manuscript maps, and photographs. **Services:** Copying; library open to public.

★13703★
TULSA COUNTY LAW LIBRARY (Law)†
Tulsa County Court House, Rm. 242
500 S. Denver   Phone: (918) 584-0471
Tulsa, OK 74103   Rena C. Hanton, Libn.
Staff: Prof 1; Other 1. **Subjects:** Law. **Holdings:** 23,083 books and bound periodical volumes; 293 cassette tapes. **Services:** Copying; library open to public.

TULSA MEDICAL COLLEGE
See: University of Oklahoma

★13704★
TULSA WORLD-TULSA TRIBUNE - LIBRARY DEPARTMENT (Publ)
315 S. Boulder Ave.
Box 1770   Phone: (918) 583-2161
Tulsa, OK 74102   Lucy Towry, Libn.
Founded: 1941. **Staff:** Prof 2; Other 5. **Subjects:** Newspaper reference topics. **Holdings:** 700 books; 150,000 file envelopes of clippings; 50,000 file envelopes of photographs; 1125 reels of microfilm. **Services:** Copying (limited); library open to public by appointment only. **Staff:** Charles Cunningham, Asst.Libn.

★13705★
TULSA ZOOLOGICAL PARK - LIBRARY (Sci-Tech)
5701 E. 36th St., N.   Phone: (918) 835-8471
Tulsa, OK 74115   Carol Eames, Educ.Cur.
Founded: 1976. **Staff:** Prof 1. **Subjects:** Zoology, zoo animal husbandry. **Holdings:** 692 books; 1200 bound periodical volumes. **Subscriptions:** 14 journals and other serials. **Services:** Library open to members of zoo society.

TUNISON LABORATORY OF FISH NUTRITION
See: U.S. Fish & Wildlife Service

★13706★
TUOLUMNE COUNTY LAW LIBRARY (Law)
Court House
2 S. Green St.   Phone: (209) 533-5675
Sonora, CA 95370   Rose Engler, Law Libn.
Subjects: Law. **Holdings:** 17,115 volumes.

TURECK (Rosalyn) ARCHIVES
See: New York Public Library - Performing Arts Research Center - Rodgers & Hammerstein Archives of Recorded Sound

★13707★
TURKISH TOURISM AND INFORMATION OFFICE (Area-Ethnic)
821 United Nations Plaza   Phone: (212) 687-2194
New York, NY 10017   C. Kamil Muren, Dir.
Founded: 1960. **Subjects:** Travel in Turkey. **Holdings:** Figures not available for films, slides, posters, brochures, maps. **Publications:** Sales Planning Guide, annual.

★13708★
TURNER, COLLIE & BRADEN, INC. - LIBRARY AND INFORMATION SERVICES (Env-Cons; Sci-Tech)
Box 13089   Phone: (713) 780-4100
Houston, TX 77219   Jean Steinhardt, Libn.
Founded: 1973. **Staff:** Prof 1, Other 1. **Subjects:** Engineering - hydraulic, sanitary; water resources in Texas; transportation. **Special Collections:** Environmental Pollution and Control (2000 NTIS microfiche). **Holdings:** 10,000 books; 1500 bound periodical volumes; 2000 company reports. **Subscriptions:** 175 journals and other serials. **Services:** Interlibrary loans; copying; library open to public by appointment. **Automated Operations:** Computerized cataloging and serials. **Computerized Information Services:** DIALOG, SDC. **Remarks:** The firm's address is 5757 Woodway, Houston, TX 77057.

TURNER (J.A.) PROFESSIONAL LIBRARY
See: Peel County Board of Education - J.A. Turner Professional Library

TURNER MEMORIAL LIBRARY
See: Franklin Memorial Hospital

★13709★
TURTLE BAY MUSIC SCHOOL - LIBRARY (Mus)
244 E. 52nd St.   Phone: (212) 753-8811
New York, NY 10022   Lilien Weintraub, Libn.
Founded: 1925. **Staff:** 1. **Subjects:** Music. **Holdings:** Figures not available. **Services:** Library not open to public.

★13710★
TUSCARAWAS COUNTY GENEALOGICAL SOCIETY - LIBRARY (Hist)
Box 141
New Philadelphia, OH 44663   Marjorie Degen, Libn.
Staff: Prof 1; Other 10. **Subjects:** Genealogy, local history. **Special Collections:** Tuscarawas County records and history. **Holdings:** 318 books; 476 bound periodical volumes; 74 volumes of bound newsletters; 199 family histories; 38 cemetery records; 24 local histories; 43 city directories; 24 U.S. Census records; 78 reels of film of Tuscarawas County Probates; 8 Recordak film records; 13 Ohio histories; 17 maps and atlases; 10 ship lists; 20 out of state histories; 1 immigration record; 31 court records; 16 war records; 34 out of county histories; 9 research items and sources; 23 church histories; 16 deeds; 20 obituaries. **Services:** Interlibrary loans; copying; library open to public on a limited schedule. **Publications:** Tuscarawas County Pioneer Footprints, quarterly. **Special Indexes:** List of indexes - available upon request.

★13711★
TUSCARAWAS COUNTY LAW LIBRARY ASSOCIATION (Law)
Court House   Phone: (216) 364-3703
New Philadelphia, OH 44663   Diana L. Tripp, Libn.
Staff: 1. **Subjects:** Law. **Holdings:** 17,000 volumes. **Services:** Interlibrary loans; copying; library open to public. **Computerized Information Services:** Westlaw. Performs searches on cost recovery basis.

★13712★
TUSCULUM COLLEGE - INSTRUCTIONAL MATERIALS CENTER (Educ)
Box 88   Phone: (615) 639-3751
Greeneville, TN 37743   Dr. Shirley S. Beck, Chm., Div. of Prof.Educ.
Founded: 1973. **Subjects:** Education - special, elementary; school textbooks; children's literature; instructional materials. **Holdings:** 2400 books; 300 pamphlets; 75 filmstrips; 100 educational kits; 15 phonograph records; 15 film loops; 15 cassettes; 45 puzzles; 55 tests; 90 games; 30 charts; curriculum guides. **Services:** Center open to public. **Staff:** Virginia Pulley, Supv., IMC; Dr. Cynthia Suarez; William Smith.

★13713★
TUSKEGEE INSTITUTE - DEPARTMENT OF ARCHITECTURE LIBRARY (Art)
                                        Phone: (205) 727-8351
Tuskegee Institute, AL 36088   Luester Williams, Lib.Asst.
Staff: 1. **Subjects:** Architecture. **Holdings:** 5216 books; 500 bound periodical volumes. **Subscriptions:** 55 journals and other serials. **Services:** Library not open to public. **Automated Operations:** Computerized circulation.

★13714★
TUSKEGEE INSTITUTE - DIVISION OF BEHAVIORAL SCIENCE RESEARCH - RURAL DEVELOPMENT RESOURCE CENTER (Soc Sci)
Carnegie Hall, 4th Fl.   Phone: (205) 727-8575
Tuskegee Institute, AL 36088   Dr. Paul L. Wall, Dir.
Founded: 1904. **Staff:** Prof 1; Other 3. **Subjects:** Race relations and problems of the South; student attitudes and aspirations; problems related to

poverty and its alleviation; migration; informal adoption; gifted students; black oral history; patterns of individual and organizational adaptation; program evaluation; nutrition; sociocultural change; international rural development. **Holdings:** 5800 books; 400 bound journals; 14,000 pamphlets, brochures and reports. **Subscriptions:** 94 journals and other serials. **Services:** Copying; center open to public for reference use only. **Computerized Information Services:** DIALOG. **Publications:** Papers of George Washington Carver at Tuskegee Institute, 1864-1943 (1975, on microfilm); Tuskegee Institute News Clippings File, 1899-1966 (1978, on microfilm); Census News (newsletter), quarterly. **Staff:** Louise Riley, Libn.

★13715★
TUSKEGEE INSTITUTE - HOLLIS BURKE FRISSELL LIBRARY-ARCHIVES
(Area-Ethnic; Hist)
                                           Phone: (205) 727-8888
Tuskegee Institute, AL 36088   Daniel T. Williams, Archv.
Staff: Prof 1; Other 1. **Subjects:** African-American history, Tuskegee Institute history, civil rights, oral history. **Special Collections:** Washington Collection; Tuskegee Institute archives; Booker T. Washington papers (155 containers); George W. Carver papers (159 containers). **Holdings:** 25,000 books; 625 bound periodical volumes; 101 cabinets of Tuskegee Institute clipping files. **Subscriptions:** 39 journals and other serials; 19 newspapers. **Services:** Interlibrary loans; library open to public. **Computerized Information Services:** OCLC. **Networks/Consortia:** Member of Alabama Center for Higher Education (ACHE); CCLC. **Special Catalogs:** A Guide to the Special Collection and Archives of Tuskegee Institute (1974). **Staff:** Annie G. King, Hd.Libn.

★13716★
TUSKEGEE INSTITUTE - SCHOOL OF ENGINEERING LIBRARY (Sci-Tech)
                                           Phone: (205) 727-8901
Tuskegee Institute, AL 36088   Frances F. Davis, Libn.
Founded: 1962. **Staff:** Prof 1; Other 4. **Subjects:** Engineering - electrical, mechanical, nuclear, chemical. **Holdings:** 8549 books; 3700 bound periodical volumes; 19,000 pieces of material of Atomic Energy Commission; Energy Research Abstracts and Indexes. **Subscriptions:** 205 journals and other serials. **Services:** Library open to public with restrictions.

★13717★
TUSKEGEE INSTITUTE - VETERINARY MEDICINE LIBRARY (Med)†
                                           Phone: (205) 727-8307
Tuskegee Institute, AL 36088   Carolyn Ford, Libn.
Founded: 1949. **Staff:** Prof 2; Other 3. **Subjects:** Anatomy, physiology, microbiology, radiology, pharmacology, pathology. **Holdings:** 7667 books; 2014 bound periodical volumes. **Subscriptions:** 235 journals and other serials. **Services:** Interlibrary loans (fee); copying; library open to public. **Networks/Consortia:** Member of Cooperative College Library Center (CCLC); Alabama Center for Higher Education (ACHE). **Staff:** William E. Johnson, Dir., AT/AV Lab.

TUTT (Charles Leaming) LIBRARY
See: Colorado College - Charles Leaming Tutt Library

★13718★
TUTTLE (Lyle) TATTOOING - TATTOO ART MUSEUM - LIBRARY (Art)
30 Seventh St.   Phone: (415) 864-9798
San Francisco, CA 94103   Lyle Tuttle, Dir.
Subjects: Tattooing and related arts. **Holdings:** 200 books. **Services:** Copying; library open to public.

TUTWILER COLLECTION OF SOUTHERN HISTORY AND LITERATURE
See: Linn-Henley Library for Southern Historical Research

TV GUIDE MICROFILM LIBRARY
See: Triangle Publications, Inc.

★13719★
TV ONTARIO - LIBRARY (Educ; Info Sci)
P.O. Box 200, Station Q   Phone: (416) 484-2600
Toronto, ON, Canada M4T 2T1   Ms. Rechilde Volpatti, Supv.
Founded: 1970. **Staff:** Prof 1; Other 2. **Subjects:** Educational television, television production, education, communications. **Holdings:** 15,000 books. **Subscriptions:** 350 journals and other serials. **Services:** Interlibrary loans; copying; library open to public for reference use only. **Automated Operations:** Computerized cataloging. **Computerized Information Services:** DIALOG, SDC, Questel, Info Globe, QL Systems, BRC Associates, Inc.; MINISIS (internal database). **Publications:** Acquisition List, occasional - distributed to government and special libraries on request; journal articles and new acquisitions. **Remarks:** Distributes copies of its TV programs on

videotape through its VIPS services to school boards, colleges, universities and other educational institutions. **Formerly:** Ontario Educational Communications Authority.

TWA
See: Trans World Airlines, Inc.

TWAIN (Mark) ...
See: Mark Twain ...

★13720★
TWENTIETH CENTURY FOX FILM CORPORATION - RESEARCH LIBRARY
(Art; Hist)
10201 W. Pico Blvd.
Box 900   Phone: (213) 203-2782
Beverly Hills, CA 90213   Kenneth Kenyon, Hd. of Res.Dept.
Founded: 1924. **Staff:** Prof 2. **Subjects:** Architecture, house decoration, costume, travel, history, art. **Special Collections:** Wetzler and Tichy collections of World War II photographs (official U.S. and German Army photographs; 47 bound volumes). **Holdings:** 35,000 books; 5000 bound periodical volumes; 10,000 bound newspapers, pamphlets and plays; 345 VF drawers of photographs, clippings and maps; 600 research photographs bound in loose-leaf books. **Subscriptions:** 23 journals and other serials. **Services:** Interlibrary loans (fee); library not open to public. **Special Catalogs:** Catalog of magazine articles and pictures (card). **Staff:** Marti Pike, Res.Libn.

★13721★
TWENTIETH CENTURY FUND - LIBRARY (Soc Sci)
41 E. 70th St.   Phone: (212) 535-4441
New York, NY 10021   Nettie Gerduk, Libn.
Founded: 1935. **Staff:** Prof 1. **Subjects:** Economics, communications, international affairs, political science. **Holdings:** 1179 books. **Subscriptions:** 98 journals and other serials. **Services:** Interlibrary loans; library open to public on request.

★13722★
TWENTIETH CENTURY TRENDS INSTITUTE, INC. - SOURCE LIBRARY (Soc Sci)
c/o Darien High School
Nutmeg Ln.   Phone: (203) 655-3981
Darien, CT 06820   Norma Bellis, Libn.
Subjects: Government, politics, economics, sociology, communications media, psychology. **Holdings:** 3194 books. **Subscriptions:** 175 journals and other serials. **Services:** Copying; library open to public. **Special Indexes:** Articles index for subjects in library collection (card). **Staff:** ; Mrs. W. Cornwall, Pres.

★13723★
TWIRLY BIRDS - HELICOPTER ARCHIVE (Trans; Hist)
Box 18029   Phone: (301) 567-4407
Oxon Hill, MD 20745   John M. Slattery, Hist.
Subjects: Helicopter history. **Holdings:** Figures not available for books; 230 helicopter models. **Subscriptions:** 30 journals and other serials. **Publications:** Newsletter, 2/year - to members.

★13724★
TYLER COURIER-TIMES-TELEGRAPH - LIBRARY (Publ)
Box 2030   Phone: (214) 597-8111
Tyler, TX 75710   Leoma Pratt, Libn.
Staff: Prof 1. **Subjects:** Newspaper reference topics. **Holdings:** Bound monthly volumes of newspapers, December, 1910 to present. **Subscriptions:** 35 newspapers. **Services:** Copying; library open to public.

TYLER SCHOOL OF FINE ARTS
See: Temple University - Central Library System

★13725★
TYMSHARE, INC. - TECHNICAL LIBRARY (Info Sci; Comp Sci)
20705 Valley Green Dr.   Phone: (408) 446-6229
Cupertino, CA 95014   Dorothy Sands, Libn.
Founded: 1974. **Staff:** Prof 1; Other 1. **Subjects:** Computer science, communications, business. **Holdings:** 900 books; 2000 technical reports; 17 cases of manuals and archives. **Subscriptions:** 177 journals and other serials. **Services:** Interlibrary loans; library not open to public. **Computerized Information Services:** DIALOG. **Networks/Consortia:** Member of CLASS; South Bay Cooperative Library System.

★13726★
TYRE, KAMINS, KATZ & GRANOF - LIBRARY (Law)
1800 Century Park E., Suite 1000   Phone: (213) 553-6822
Los Angeles, CA 90067   Becky C. Davis, Libn.
Staff: 1. **Subjects:** Law - labor, tax, real estate, corporate; litigation.
Holdings: 12,000 volumes. **Subscriptions:** 163 journals and other serials.
Services: Library not open to public. **Formed by the Merger of:** Tyre &
Kamins and Katz, Granof & Palarz.

TYRRELL HISTORICAL LIBRARY
See: Beaumont Public Library System

TYRRELL (Sallie M., M.D.) MEMORIAL LIBRARY
See: St. Margaret Hospital - Sallie M. Tyrrell, M.D. Memorial Library

U

★13727★

U-HAUL INTERNATIONAL, INC. - CORPORATE LIBRARY (Bus-Fin)
2727 N. Central Ave.   Phone: (602) 263-6606
Phoenix, AZ 85036   Tom Schutter, Corp.Libn.
Staff: Prof 1; Other 2. **Subjects:** Management, marketing, transportation, engineering, personnel, insurance. **Holdings:** 1000 books; 43 bound periodical volumes; 55 VF drawers of corporate archives; 70 VF drawers of internal publications; 4 boxes of microfiche. **Subscriptions:** 179 journals and other serials. **Services:** Interlibrary loans; library not open to public. **Publications:** Information Center List of Publications, quarterly - for internal distribution only. **Special Indexes:** Publication Index, quarterly - for internal distribution only.

★13728★

U.P.E.C. CULTURAL CENTER - J.A. FREITAS LIBRARY (Hum; Area-Ethnic)
1120-24 E. 14th St.   Phone: (408) 483-7676
San Leandro, CA 94577   Carlos Almeida, Dir.
Staff: Prof 1; Other 2. **Subjects:** Portuguese literature, history of Portuguese in California. **Holdings:** 5010 books; newspapers and historical documents. **Services:** Copying; translations of works from Portuguese to English; library open to public. **Publications:** UPEC Life Magazine. **Staff:** Maria F. Almeida, Supv.; John Botelho, Ref.-Transl.

U.S.D.A.
Filed as if spelled out U.S. Dept. of Agriculture.

U.S.G.S.
See: U.S. Geological Survey

UAW
See: United Automobile, Aerospace & Agricultural Implement Workers of America

UCLA FILM ARCHIVES
See: University of California, Los Angeles

UCLA RADIO ARCHIVES
See: University of California, Los Angeles

★13729★

UFO INFORMATION RETRIEVAL CENTER, INC. (Sci-Tech)
Points West No. 158
3131 W. Cochise Dr.   Phone: (602) 997-1523
Phoenix, AZ 85021   Thomas M. Olsen, Pres.
Staff: Prof 1. **Subjects:** UFO sighting reports and related topics. **Special Collections:** Computer-machine-readable text and data. **Holdings:** 143 books; 140 bound periodical volumes; 50 volumes of unbound reports; 1100 Library of Congress cards on UFO topics; 50 purported photographs of UFO; 3 volumes of AV materials (lectures and symposia). **Services:** Center not open to public. **Computerized Information Services:** Computer search and referrals from internal databases for bibliographic and nonbibliographic information. **Publications:** The Reference for Outstanding UFO Sighting Reports, infrequent - by mail order request. **Special Indexes:** Verbatim text of anecdotal reports (magnetic tape); inverted index for 160 categories of reported characteristics.

UHLMAN (Robert) MEDICAL LIBRARY
See: Menorah Medical Center - Robert Uhlman Medical Library

★13730★

UKRAINIAN CULTURAL AND EDUCATIONAL CENTRE (Oserdok) - LIBRARY (Area-Ethnic)
184 Alexander Ave., E.   Phone: (204) 942-0218
Winnipeg, MB, Canada R3B 0L6   Orysia Tracz, Hd.Libn.
Founded: 1944. **Staff:** 3. **Subjects:** Ukrainian history, literature, language, art, ethnography; Ukrainian settlement in Canada. **Special Collections:** Rare book collection (17th-19th century; 75 volumes); Koshetz Music Collection. **Holdings:** 32,500 books; 12,000 periodicals; 300 music scores; 2000 slides. **Subscriptions:** 65 journals and other serials; 43 newspapers. **Services:** Interlibrary loans (limited); copying; library open to public for reference use only.

★13731★

UKRAINIAN ENGINEERS SOCIETY OF AMERICA - LIBRARY (Sci-Tech)
2 East 79th St.   Phone: (212) 535-7676
New York, NY 10021   Mr. E.B. Zmyj, Pres.
Subjects: Science and technology (in Ukrainian); development of the Ukraine. **Special Collections:** Engineering textbooks and handbooks in German and Russian; monographs, papers, reprints, theses and manuscripts authored by Ukrainian engineers and scientists in the U.S., Canada and Germany, 1950 to present. **Holdings:** 400 volumes. **Subscriptions:** 15 journals and other serials; 5 newspapers. **Services:** Copying; library not open to public. **Publications:** Ukrainian Engineering News, quarterly; Bulletin, quarterly. **Remarks:** Branches of the society are located in Philadelphia, Chicago and Detroit.

UKRAINIAN LIBRARY
See: St. Vladimir Institute

★13732★

UKRAINIAN MEDICAL ASSOCIATION OF NORTH AMERICA - UKRAINIAN MEDICAL ARCHIVES AND LIBRARY (Med)
2320 W. Chicago Ave.   Phone: (312) 235-8883
Chicago, IL 60622   Paul Pundy, M.D., Dir.
Staff: Prof 2. **Subjects:** Medicine. **Special Collections:** Russian Medical Encyclopedia (30 volumes); Ukrainian medical journals and books (originals, copies, microfilm); medical books and journals in English, Russian, German and Polish. **Holdings:** 1800 books; 200 bound periodical volumes; 8 VF drawers of clippings, pamphlets, unbound reports, photo albums. **Services:** Interlibrary loans; library open to public with written or telephone request. **Remarks:** An alternate telephone number is 559-3273. **Staff:** Dr. Marian Panczyszyn, Sec.

★13733★

UKRAINIAN MUSEUM - ARCHIVES, INC. (Area-Ethnic)
1202 Kenilworth Ave.   Phone: (216) 781-4329
Cleveland, OH 44113   Stepan Kikta, Pres.
Staff: 4. **Subjects:** Books in Ukrainian and about the Ukraine. **Special Collections:** Taras Shevchenko Collection (400 volumes). **Holdings:** 15,000 books; 1500 periodical volumes; archival materials in Ukrainian. **Subscriptions:** 15 journals and other serials; 30 newspapers. **Services:** Archives open to public with restrictions. **Remarks:** An alternate telephone number is 741-4537.

★13734★

UKRAINIAN MUSEUM OF CANADA - LIBRARY (Area-Ethnic)†
10611 110th Ave.   Phone: (403) 424-1530
Edmonton, AB, Canada T5H 1H7   Mrs. J. Verchomin, Dir.
Staff: 1. **Subjects:** Ukrainian embroidery, ceramics, woodcraft and Easter egg writing; folk art; historical costumes; music composers. **Special Collections:** Ukrainian literature. **Holdings:** 150 books; 100 bound periodical volumes; 100 handicraft magazines. **Services:** Library open to public by appointment.

★13735★

UKRAINIAN MUSEUM OF CANADA - LIBRARY (Area-Ethnic)
910 Spadina Crescent, E.   Phone: (306) 244-3800
Saskatoon, SK, Canada S7K 3H5   Albert Kachkowski, Dir.
Staff: Prof 3; Other 1. **Subjects:** Art, history, literature, ethnography. **Special Collections:** Archives. **Holdings:** 1200 volumes; 7000 slides. **Services:** Copying; library open to public by appointment. **Publications:** Pysanka: Icon of the Universe; Ukrainian Embroidery Designs and Stitches. **Formerly:** Ukrainian Women's Association of Canada - Ukrainian Museum of Canada.

★13736★

UKRAINIAN RESEARCH FOUNDATION - LIBRARY (Area-Ethnic)
6931 S. Yosemite   Phone: (303) 770-1220
Englewood, CO 80112   Bohdan Wynar, Pres.
Staff: Prof 1. **Subjects:** Ukraine - history, literature; economics; political science. **Holdings:** 7000 books; 2000 bound periodical volumes; manuscripts. **Subscriptions:** 150 journals and other serials; 15 newspapers. **Services:** Library not open to public.

UKRAINIAN WOMEN'S ASSOCIATION OF CANADA - UKRAINIAN MUSEUM OF CANADA
See: Ukrainian Museum of Canada

★13737★

ULRICH (Edwin A.) MUSEUM - LIBRARY/ARCHIVES (Art)
"Wave Crest" On-The-Hudson
Albany Post Rd.   Phone: (914) 229-7107
Hyde Park, NY 12583   Edwin A. Ulrich, Dir. and Owner
Staff: 1. **Subjects:** Art - three generations of the Waugh family of American

painters. **Special Collections:** Materials related to Samuel Bell Waugh (1814-1884), Frederick Judd Waugh (1861-1940), and Coulton Waugh (1896-1973). **Holdings:** 200 books; other cataloged items. **Services:** Library open to public.

★13738★
ULSTER COUNTY PLANNING BOARD - LIBRARY (Plan)
244 Fair St.
Box 1800
Kingston, NY 12401
Phone: (914) 331-9300
Dennis Doyle, Planner
Subjects: Planning, transportation, recreation, environmental management, energy conservation. **Holdings:** 500 books; 1000 bound periodical volumes; pamphlets; newsletters; maps. **Subscriptions:** 20 journals and other serials.

★13739★
UMSTEAD (John) HOSPITAL - LEARNING RESOURCE CENTER (Med)
Twelfth St.
Butner, NC 27509
Phone: (919) 575-7259
Brenda M. Ellis, Libn.
Founded: 1979. **Staff:** 3. **Subjects:** Psychiatry, neurology, nursing, medicine, sociology, psychology, geriatrics, child psychiatry. **Holdings:** 7528 books; 3000 bound periodical volumes; 350 other cataloged items; 4 VF drawers of staff publications and reports. **Subscriptions:** 60 journals and other serials. **Services:** Interlibrary loans; copying; AV production; center open to public. **Networks/Consortia:** Member of Resources for Health Information Consortium.

★13740★
UNCAP INTERNATIONAL, INC. - PROJECT COLLECTORS RESEARCH LIBRARY (Rec)
2613 Huron St.
Los Angeles, CA 90065
Phone: (213) 222-2012
James J. O'Connell, III, Cur.
Staff: 5. **Subjects:** Hobbies, history, culture. **Special Collections:** Numismatic and philatelic reference materials. **Holdings:** 6500 books; 500 bound periodical volumes; 32 books in microform; 10 slide sets; 200 periodicals and newsletters. **Services:** Library open to public for a fee. **Networks/Consortia:** Member of Southern California Answering Network (SCAN). **Publications:** Booklist, annual.

UNDERHILL (Caroline M.) RESEARCH LIBRARY
See: Andover Historical Society - Caroline M. Underhill Research Library

UNDERHILL (Daniel) MUSIC LIBRARY
See: Swarthmore College - Daniel Underhill Music Library

UNDERWOOD LAW LIBRARY
See: Southern Methodist University

★13741★
UNDERWOOD MC LELLAN LTD. - INFORMATION SERVICES (Comp Sci; Sci-Tech)
17007 107th Ave.
Edmonton, AB, Canada T5S 1G3
Phone: (403) 483-7722
Jacquie Fenton, Hd., Info.Serv.
Staff: Prof 1; Other 1. **Subjects:** Engineering and management consulting, information retrieval, computer systems. **Special Collections:** Shared logic word processing (manuals, tapes, and training documents). **Holdings:** 250 books; 2000 reports; 5000 proposals; government specifications; standards. **Subscriptions:** 92 journals and other serials. **Services:** Interlibrary loans; copying; library open to public with restrictions. **Automated Operations:** Computerized cataloging, serials and circulation. **Computerized Information Services:** DIALOG, CAN/OLE. Performs searches on cost recovery basis.

★13742★
UNDERWOOD-MEMORIAL HOSPITAL - MEDICAL LIBRARY (Med)
N. Broad St. & W. Redbank Ave.
Woodbury, NJ 08096
Phone: (609) 845-0100
Ellen K. Tiedrich, Libn.
Founded: 1951. **Staff:** Prof 1. **Subjects:** Medicine. **Holdings:** 3500 books; 1000 reels of microfilm. **Subscriptions:** 100 journals and other serials. **Services:** Interlibrary loans; copying; library open to public by appointment. **Computerized Information Services:** MEDLINE. **Networks/Consortia:** Member of Southwest New Jersey Consortium for Health Information Services; Greater Northeastern Regional Medical Library Program; Health Sciences Libraries of New Jersey.

★13743★
UNDERWOOD, NEUHAUS & COMPANY INC. - CORPORATE FINANCE LIBRARY (Bus-Fin)
724 Travis St.
Houston, TX 77002
Phone: (713) 221-2086
Founded: 1975. **Staff:** Prof 1; Other 1. **Subjects:** High technology

companies, savings and loan associations. **Special Collections:** Fortune 1000, selected foreign and Southwest Companies. **Holdings:** 140 books. **Subscriptions:** 14 journals and other serials; 9 newspapers. **Services:** Library open to affiliated companies.

★13744★
UNDERWOOD (William) COMPANY - LIBRARY
One Red Devil Lane
Westwood, MA 02090
Defunct. Holdings absorbed by Pet, Inc. - Corporate Information Center.

★13745★
UNDERWRITERS LABORATORIES INC. - STANDARDS REFERENCE CENTER (Sci-Tech)
333 Pfingsten Rd.
Northbrook, IL 60062
Phone: (312) 272-8800
A.N. Angonese, Sr.Assoc.Mng.Engr.
Staff: Prof 1; Other 1. **Holdings:** Standards - Underwriters' Laboratories, American Society for Testing and Materials, other national and international. **Subscriptions:** 42 journals and other serials. **Services:** Copying; center open to public.

UNESCO-INTERGOVERNMENTAL OCEANOGRAPHIC COMMISSION - INTERNATIONAL TSUNAMI INFORMATION CENTER
See: International Tsunami Information Center

★13746★
UNEXPECTED WILDLIFE REFUGE - LIBRARY (Env-Cons)
Unexpected Rd.
Newfield, NJ 08344
Hope Sawyer Buyukmihci, Sec.
Founded: 1968. **Staff:** 2. **Subjects:** Humane education, beavers, wildlife. **Special Collections:** Works of Grey Owl, Canadian naturalist. **Holdings:** Figures not available. **Services:** Library open to public for reference use only by appointment. **Publications:** The Beaver Defenders, quarterly - distributed to paid subscriber-members. **Also Known As:** The Beaver Defenders.

UNICEF
See: U.S. Committee for UNICEF

★13747★
UNIDYNAMICS/PHOENIX, INC. - LIBRARY
Box 2990
Phoenix, AZ 85062
Founded: 1963. **Subjects:** Chemistry, biology, pyrotechnics, aeronautical engineering. **Holdings:** 2000 books; 1500 technical reports; 800 patents; 400 technical abstracts. **Remarks:** Presently inactive.

★13748★
UNIDYNAMICS/ST. LOUIS, INC. - LIBRARY (Sci-Tech)
472 Paul Ave.
Box 11177
St. Louis, MO 63135
Phone: (314) 522-6700
Barbara Schulik, Libn.
Staff: Prof 1. **Subjects:** Basic and applied sciences and technologies. **Holdings:** 2200 books; 4500 reports, patents, documents. **Subscriptions:** 153 journals and other serials. **Services:** Interlibrary loans; copying; library open to public with approval of management.

★13749★
UNION OF AMERICAN HEBREW CONGREGATIONS - SYNAGOGUE ARCHITECTURAL AND ART LIBRARY (Art)†
838 Fifth Ave.
New York, NY 10021
Phone: (212) 249-0100
Myron E. Schoen, Dir.
Founded: 1950. **Staff:** Prof 1; Other 1. **Subjects:** History of synagogue architecture, contemporary synagogue art and architecture, art of Jewish interest, ceremonial objects. **Holdings:** 200 books; 50 bound periodical volumes; 3000 slides; 1000 photographs. **Services:** Interlibrary loans; copying; slide rental service; library open to public by appointment.

★13750★
UNION BANK - LIBRARY (Bus-Fin)
714 W. Olympic Blvd.
Los Angeles, CA 90015
Phone: (213) 236-6642
John D. Shea, Hd.Libn.
Staff: Prof 1. **Subjects:** Economics, banking. **Holdings:** 2500 books; 75 bound periodical volumes; 52 VF drawers of economic statistics, newsletters and government documents. **Subscriptions:** 75 journals and other serials; 5 newspapers. **Services:** Interlibrary loans; library open to public. **Computerized Information Services:** New York Times Information Service, NEXIS.

★13751★
UNION BIBLE SEMINARY - LIBRARY (Rel-Theol)
434 S. Union St.   Phone: (317) 896-9324
Westfield, IN 46074   Michael Williams, Academic Dean
Founded: 1951. Subjects: Bible, theology, Quaker history, general academic subjects. Holdings: 4000 volumes. Subscriptions: 32 journals and other serials.

★13752★
UNION CAMP CORP. - R & D DIVISION LIBRARY (Sci-Tech)†
Box 412   Phone: (609) 896-1200
Princeton, NJ 08540   Helen Lee, Libn.
Founded: 1963. Staff: Prof 1. Subjects: Pulp and paper, chemistry, engineering. Holdings: 3000 books; 4000 bound periodical volumes; 120 VF drawers of unbound reports. Subscriptions: 150 journals and other serials. Services: Interlibrary loans; copying; SDI; library open to public by request. Computerized Information Services: Online systems.

★13753★
UNION CARBIDE AGRICULTURAL PRODUCTS COMPANY, INC. - LIBRARY (Sci-Tech)
T.W. Alexander Dr.
Box 12014   Phone: (919) 549-2649
Research Triangle Park, NC 27709   Constance J. Lavoy, Lib.Serv.Supv.
Founded: 1981. Staff: Prof 2; Other 2. Subjects: Weed identification and control, insect identification and control, plant growth regulators, agricultural marketing, organic chemistry. Holdings: 8700 books; 4800 bound periodical volumes; 600 volumes of Agriculture Marketing Reports; 100 VF drawers of statistics, product information; crop reports; 364 reels of microfilm of agriculture patents. Subscriptions: 481 journals and other serials. Services: Interlibrary loans; copying; library open to public by appointment for reference use only. Computerized Information Services: DIALOG, SDC, CAS Online, National Pesticide Information Retrieval System (NPIRS), OCLC. Networks/Consortia: Member of SOLINET. Staff: Deborah K. Doerr, Cat.

★13754★
UNION CARBIDE CANADA, LTD. - REFERENCE LIBRARY (Sci-Tech)
123 Eglinton Ave., E.   Phone: (416) 488-1444
Toronto, ON, Canada M4P 1J3   K. Martha Nagata, Libn.
Founded: 1962. Staff: Prof 1; Other 1. Subjects: Chemistry, management, marketing. Holdings: 2000 books and current periodicals; 200 Canadian annual reports; 200 Statistics Canada publications. Subscriptions: 75 journals and other serials. Services: Interlibrary loans; copying; library open to public by appointment. Computerized Information Services: SDC, Info Globe.

★13755★
UNION CARBIDE CANADA, LTD. - TECHNICAL CENTRE LIBRARY (Sci-Tech)
10555 Metropolitan Blvd., E.
C.P. 700   Phone: (514) 645-5311
Pointe-Aux-Trembles, PQ, Canada H1B 5K8   A.M. de Jesus, Libn.
Founded: 1963. Staff: Prof 1. Subjects: Chemistry, plastics technology. Holdings: 1400 volumes; R&D reports. Subscriptions: 107 journals and other serials. Services: Interlibrary loans; library not open to public. Computerized Information Services: SDC, Pergamon InfoLine Ltd. Formerly: Its Plastics & Chemicals Technical Centre Library.

★13756★
UNION CARBIDE CORPORATION - BATTERY PRODUCTS DIVISION - TECHNICAL INFORMATION CENTER (Sci-Tech)
25225 Detroit Rd.   Phone: (216) 835-7631
Westlake, OH 44145   Claire Marie Langkau, Mgr., Tech.Info.
Founded: 1956. Staff: Prof 3; Other 4. Subjects: Batteries and related subjects, electrochemistry. Holdings: 6000 books; 10,000 documents; 30,000 patents. Subscriptions: 280 journals and other serials. Computerized Information Services: DIALOG, SDC; private online system covering patents of interest. Publications: Review of Literature, weekly - for internal distribution only. Staff: Michael F. Allan, Sr.Info.Spec.; Elaine M. Goldbach, Info.Spec.

★13757★
UNION CARBIDE CORPORATION - COATINGS SERVICE DEPARTMENT - LIBRARY (Sci-Tech)
1500 Polco St.
Box 24166   Phone: (317) 240-2520
Indianapolis, IN 46224   Mary Ann Brady, Libn.
Founded: 1945. Staff: Prof 1. Subjects: Metallurgy, mechanical engineering, advanced materials, high temperature coating technology. Holdings: 5800 books; 28,000 bound periodical volumes. Subscriptions: 275 journals and

other serials. Services: Interlibrary loans. Formerly: Its Engineering Products Division - Library.

★13758★
UNION CARBIDE CORPORATION - CORPORATE LIBRARY (Bus-Fin)
Section N2, Old Ridgebury Rd.   Phone: (203) 794-5314
Danbury, CT 06817   L. Arless Leve, Mgr.
Staff: Prof 4; Other 3. Subjects: Management; marketing; medicine; health, safety and environment; accounting; business; computers and information systems. Special Collections: Marketing Research reports; financial reports; government statistics. Holdings: 9000 books; 15 vertical files of pamphlets; 13 vertical files of statistics; 53 vertical files of financial reports. Subscriptions: 425 journals and other serials; 10 newspapers. Services: Interlibrary loans; library open to SLA and other selected library associations. Computerized Information Services: DIALOG, SDC, NEXIS, Dow Jones News/Retrieval, VU/TEXT, BRS, TEXTLINE, NLM. Staff: Mary McPherson, Ref.Libn.; Roger Miller, Bus.Info.Assoc.; Lorie Cecula, Marketing Info.Spec.

★13759★
UNION CARBIDE CORPORATION - ENGINEERING DEPARTMENT LIBRARY (Sci-Tech)
Box 8361   Phone: (304) 747-4608
South Charleston, WV 25303   Julia Adkins, Libn.
Founded: 1959. Staff: Prof 1; Other 1. Subjects: Engineering - chemical, mechanical, instrument, environmental, civil. Holdings: 8030 books; 815 bound periodical volumes; 48 reels of microfilm; 35 journal titles on microfilm. Subscriptions: 150 journals and other serials; 6 newspapers. Services: Interlibrary loans; copying; library open for limited access with permission. Publications: Acquisition list and Book Reviews, biweekly - for internal distribution only.

★13760★
UNION CARBIDE CORPORATION - FILMS-PACKAGING DIVISION - TECHNICAL LIBRARY (Sci-Tech)
6733 W. 65th St.   Phone: (312) 496-4286
Chicago, IL 60638   Mrs. Nijole K. Pupius, Tech.Libn.
Founded: 1945. Staff: Prof 1. Subjects: Natural and synthetic high polymers; food chemistry; chemistry - organic, physical, polymer; packaging; chemical engineering. Holdings: 4500 books; 4000 bound periodical volumes; 500 unbound periodical volumes; 150 boxes of patents; dissertations; translations; trade literature. Subscriptions: 250 journals and other serials. Services: Interlibrary loans; library not open to public.

★13761★
UNION CARBIDE CORPORATION - I.S. INFORMATION CENTER (Comp Sci)
Saw Mill River Rd.   Phone: (914) 789-2000
Tarrytown, NY 10591   Joan Schechtman, Mgr.
Founded: 1961. Staff: Prof 1. Subjects: Data processing, teleprocessing, time sharing, hardware, software, programming. Holdings: 1000 books; 150 government reports; 1000 manuals. Subscriptions: 60 journals and other serials; 5 newspapers. Services: Interlibrary loans; library not open to public. Automated Operations: Computerized cataloging, acquisitions and circulation. Computerized Information Services: Internal database. Publications: Library Bulletin, quarterly.

★13762★
UNION CARBIDE CORPORATION - LAW DEPARTMENT LIBRARY (Law)
Section N2, Old Ridgebury Rd.   Phone: (203) 794-6396
Danbury, CT 06817   Carolyn A. Lebl, Hd. Law Libn.
Founded: 1935. Staff: Prof 1; Other 2. Subjects: Law - antitrust, tax, patent, trademark, labor, corporation. Holdings: 30,000 volumes; 3 VF drawers; 7 titles in microform; Federal Register in microform, 1970 to present. Subscriptions: 75 journals and other serials. Services: Interlibrary loans; library not open to public. Computerized Information Services: LEXIS, DIALOG.

★13763★
UNION CARBIDE CORPORATION - LIBRARY & TECHNICAL INFORMATION SERVICE (Sci-Tech)
Tarrytown Technical Center   Phone: (914) 789-3700
Tarrytown, NY 10591   Joan Schechtman, Mgr.
Founded: 1971. Staff: Prof 4; Other 3. Subjects: Chemistry, chemical engineering, metals and materials, surface science, catalysis, industrial gases, physics. Holdings: 59,000 books and bound periodical volumes; 200 VF drawers of patents, internal reports, vendors bulletins and catalogs; 2800 reels of microfilm; 4000 microfiche; 5400 opaques. Subscriptions: 900 journals and other serials. Services: Interlibrary loans; library not open to public. Computerized Information Services: DIALOG, SDC. Publications: Newsletter, monthly; Union List, annual - both for internal distribution only.

Staff: Beulah C. Wood, Assoc.Libn.; Hannah V. Maslansky, Asst.Libn.; Iris J. Siewers, Info.Sci.

★13764★
UNION CARBIDE CORPORATION - LINDE DIVISION - COMMUNICATIONS LIBRARY (Sci-Tech)
Old Ridgebury Rd.   Phone: (203) 794-2000
Danbury, CT 06817   Marie Montgomery, Hd.Libn.
Founded: 1956. **Staff:** 3. **Subjects:** Cryogenics, gases, molecular sieves, welding, coating services, environmental systems, engineering products and processes, medical products. **Special Collections:** Historical material on Linde Division. **Holdings:** 100 books; 21 volumes of technical papers; 25 shelves and 4 drawers of data files, pictures, slides; 22 shelves of instruction literature. **Subscriptions:** 100 journals and other serials; 33 newspapers. **Services:** Library open to public for reference use only on request.

★13765★
UNION CARBIDE CORPORATION - LINDE DIVISION - TECHNICAL LIBRARY (Sci-Tech)
Box 44   Phone: (716) 879-2031
Tonawanda, NY 14151   Sandra C. Anderson, Tech.Libn.
Founded: 1939. **Staff:** Prof 1; Other 1. **Subjects:** Engineering - cryogenic, chemical, mechanical; chemistry. **Holdings:** 8000 books; 4500 bound periodical volumes; 950 reels of microfilm. **Subscriptions:** 252 journals and other serials. **Services:** Interlibrary loans. **Networks/Consortia:** Member of Western New York Library Resources Council (WNYLRC).

UNION CARBIDE CORPORATION - NUCLEAR DIVISION
See: Martin Marietta Energy Systems Inc.

★13766★
UNION CARBIDE CORPORATION - PARMA TECHNICAL CENTER - TECHNICAL INFORMATION SERVICE (Sci-Tech)
Box 6116   Phone: (216) 676-2120
Cleveland, OH 44101   Joan C. Long, Mgr.
Founded: 1945. **Staff:** Prof 2; Other 4. **Subjects:** Manufactured carbon and graphite, high temperature chemistry, metallurgy. **Holdings:** 12,000 books; 15,000 bound periodical volumes; 20,000 U.S. and foreign patents; 30,000 government documents and contract reports; 3000 proprietary reports. **Subscriptions:** 450 journals and other serials. **Services:** Interlibrary loans; SDI; collection open to public with special permission. **Automated Operations:** Computerized cataloging and patent indexes. **Computerized Information Services:** DIALOG, SDC; INDOC, ACCESS (internal databases). **Publications:** Weekly news bulletin; weekly abstract/title listing of references to carbon and graphite - for internal distribution only. **Special Indexes:** Literature of carbon and graphite; U.S. and foreign patent indexes; bibliography of carbon and graphite technology, 1945 to present. **Staff:** Linda Riffle, Asst.Mgr.

★13767★
UNION CARBIDE CORPORATION - RESEARCH AND DEVELOPMENT INFORMATION CENTER (Sci-Tech)
Bldg. 770
Box 8361   Phone: (304) 747-5119
South Charleston, WV 25303   Alice S. Behr, Tech.Libn.
Staff: Prof 1; Other 2. **Subjects:** Chemistry, chemical engineering, environmental sciences. **Holdings:** 45,000 books and bound periodical volumes. **Subscriptions:** 600 journals and other serials. **Services:** Interlibrary loans; copying; library open to public with restrictions.

★13768★
UNION CARBIDE CORPORATION - SOLVENTS & INTERMEDIATES DIVISION - PLANT LIBRARY (Sci-Tech)
3300 Fifth Ave., S.
Box 471   Phone: (409) 948-5562
Texas City, TX 77590   Jean Croix, Hd.
Staff: 1. **Subjects:** Science and technology. **Holdings:** 3500 books. **Subscriptions:** 40 journals and other serials. **Services:** Library not open to public.

★13769★
UNION CARBIDE CORPORATION - TECHNICAL INFORMATION SERVICE (Sci-Tech)
Bldg. 200
Box 670   Phone: (201) 356-8000
Bound Brook, NJ 08805   Carol B. Klemm, Staff Coord.
Staff: Prof 9; Other 7. **Subjects:** Polymers, plastics, organic chemistry. **Holdings:** 9000 books; 16,000 bound periodical volumes; U.S. patents on microfilm. **Subscriptions:** 500 journals and other serials. **Services:** Copying

(limited); SDI (for internal use only); service open to public by appointment. **Automated Operations:** Computerized cataloging and serials. **Computerized Information Services:** DIALOG, SDC, BRS, NEXIS, NLM, Pergamon InfoLine Ltd.; internal database. Performs searches on cost recovery basis. **Special Catalogs:** Serials and holdings locator (computer printout). **Special Indexes:** Literature Search Report Index (computer printout). **Staff:** Maria I.M. Lohse, Tech.Info.Spec./Patents.

★13770★
UNION CLUB - LIBRARY (Hist)
101 E. 69th St.   Phone: (212) 734-5400
New York, NY 10021   Helen M. Allen, Libn.
Founded: 1836. **Subjects:** New York City history. **Holdings:** Figures not available.

★13771★
UNION COLLEGE - ELLA JOHNSON CRANDALL MEMORIAL LIBRARY - SPECIAL COLLECTIONS (Rel-Theol)
3800 S. 48th St.   Phone: (402) 488-2331
Lincoln, NE 68506   Lawrence W. Onsager, Lib.Dir.
Staff: Prof 3; Other 4. **Special Collections:** Materials related to Seventh-Day Adventism (early denominational books and periodicals); college archives. **Holdings:** 2600 books; 1000 bound periodical volumes; 60 VF drawers. **Subscriptions:** 46 journals and other serials; 5 newspapers. **Services:** Library open to public with restrictions.

★13772★
UNION COLLEGE - SCHAFFER LIBRARY - SPECIAL COLLECTIONS (Hist; Sci-Tech)
                                    Phone: (518) 370-6278
Schenectady, NY 12308   Ann M. Seeman, Act.Dir.
Subjects: Humor, Unionana, microscopy, rare books and manuscripts. **Holdings:** 2800 volumes in Bailey Collection of North American Wit and Humor; 400 volumes in Kellert Microscopy Collection; 2000 volumes of rare books; manuscript collections; college archives; Schenectady Archives of Science and Technology. **Services:** Interlibrary loans; copying; collections open to public for reference use only. **Automated Operations:** Computerized cataloging, acquisitions, serials, and ILL. **Computerized Information Services:** DIALOG, OCLC, BRS; SINS-Serials Information System (internal database). Contact Person: David Gerhan, Hd., Info.Serv. **Networks/ Consortia:** Member of Capital District Library Council for Reference & Research Resources (CDLC). **Special Indexes:** Indexes to manuscripts in the Special Collections.

★13773★
UNION COUNTY HISTORICAL SOCIETY - JOHN B. DEANS MEMORIAL LIBRARY (Hist)
2nd & St. Louis Sts.   Phone: (717) 524-4461
Lewisburg, PA 17837   Gary W. Slear, Chm., Archv. & Musm.
Founded: 1963. **Staff:** 5. **Subjects:** Local history, genealogy. **Special Collections:** Oral traditions project (300 oral history tapes and transcripts; 5000 slides and photographs). **Holdings:** 1500 books, 250 bound periodical volumes; 40 cubic feet of clippings; tax records on microfilm. **Services:** Copying; library open to public. **Automated Operations:** Computerized cataloging and acquisitions. **Publications:** Biennial collection of manuscripts on local topics; regional studies of local crafts.

UNION DIME SAVINGS BANK
See: Goldome Bank

★13774★
UNION ELECTRIC COMPANY - LIBRARY (Sci-Tech)
1901 Gratiot St.
Box 149   Phone: (314) 621-3222
St. Louis, MO 63166   Constance Ford, Chf.Libn.
Founded: 1941. **Staff:** Prof 3; Other 1. **Subjects:** Engineering, public utility regulation, financing, general business, public and private power. **Holdings:** 12,000 volumes; 15 VF drawers of annual reports; 85 VF drawers of pamphlets and scientific society papers. **Subscriptions:** 542 journals and other serials. **Services:** Interlibrary loans; copying; library open to public (limited access). **Computerized Information Services:** DIALOG. **Publications:** What's New, monthly bulletin; Library Clipping Service, daily - both for internal distribution only. **Staff:** Patricia F. Gatlin, Supv. of Lib.Serv.

★13775★
UNION GAS, LTD. - LIBRARY SERVICE (Energy)†
50 Keil Dr., N.   Phone: (519) 352-3100
Chatham, ON, Canada N7M 5M1   Mrs. A. Steen
Staff: Prof 1; Other 1. **Subjects:** Natural gas industry, public utility regulation,

management, economics, energy, engineering. **Holdings:** 4500 books; 360 annual reports; 615 reels of microfilm; 220 microfiche. **Subscriptions:** 430 journals and other serials. **Services:** Interlibrary loans; copying; SDI; library open to public with restrictions. **Automated Operations:** Computerized cataloging. **Computerized Information Services:** Online systems. **Publications:** Library acquisitions, monthly - for internal distribution only. **Special Indexes:** KWIC index to engineering standards.

★13776★
UNION LEAGUE CLUB LIBRARY (Hist)
38 E. 37th St.　　　　　　　　　　Phone: (212) 685-3800
New York, NY 10016　　　　　　　　Jane Reed, Libn.
Founded: 1863. **Staff:** Prof 1. **Subjects:** Civil War; American history, art and biography; English literature. **Holdings:** 20,000 volumes. **Subscriptions:** 40 journals and other serials; 8 newspapers. **Services:** Library not open to public. **Publications:** ULC Club Bulletin, monthly. **Special Indexes:** Index of paintings in Union League Club.

★13777★
UNION LEAGUE OF PHILADELPHIA - LIBRARY (Hist)
140 S. Broad St.　　　　　　　　　　Phone: (215) 563-6500
Philadelphia, PA 19102　　　　　　　James G. Mundy, Jr., Libn.
Founded: 1862. **Staff:** Prof 1. **Subjects:** American Civil War; Lincoln; political history; Philadelphia and Pennsylvania history, biography. **Special Collections:** League archives (document cases). **Holdings:** 22,000 books. **Subscriptions:** 62 journals and other serials; 10 newspapers. **Services:** Library open to public with permission.

UNION LIBRARY CATALOGUE OF PENNSYLVANIA
See: Pennsylvania Area Library Network and Union Library Catalogue of Pennsylvania

★13778★
UNION MEMORIAL HOSPITAL - DR. JOHN M.T. FINNEY, JR. MEMORIAL MEDICAL LIBRARY (Med)†
201 E. University Pkwy.　　　　　　　Phone: (301) 235-7200
Baltimore, MD 21218　　　　　　　　Rena Snyder, Chf.Med.Libn.
Staff: Prof 1; Other 2. **Subjects:** Medicine, orthopedics. **Special Collections:** The hand (35 monographs; 11 journal subscriptions); sports medicine (25 monographs; 10 journal subscriptions). **Holdings:** 1450 books; 4000 bound periodical volumes; English articles on hand injuries and hand surgery published since 1966 (indexed). **Subscriptions:** 275 journals and other serials. **Services:** Interlibrary loans; copying; SDI; library open to health care professionals. **Computerized Information Services:** MEDLARS; Massachusetts General Hospital's computer-aided instruction programs in emergency medicine. **Networks/Consortia:** Member of Baltimore Consortia for Resource Sharing.

★13779★
UNION MEMORIAL HOSPITAL - NURSING LIBRARY (Med)
3301 N. Calvert St.　　　　　　　　　Phone: (301) 235-7200
Baltimore, MD 21218　　　　　　　　Carolyn M. Daugherty, Libn.
Founded: 1893. **Staff:** Prof 1; Other 7. **Subjects:** Nursing, medicine, sociology, psychology, life sciences. **Holdings:** 4000 books; 350 bound periodical volumes; 4 VF drawers of articles; 35 file boxes; 20 tapes; 50 cassettes; 100 pamphlets. **Subscriptions:** 120 journals and other serials. **Services:** Interlibrary loans; library not open to public. **Publications:** Monthly Lists of Acquisitions.

★13780★
UNION MUTUAL LIFE INSURANCE COMPANY - CORPORATE INFORMATION CENTER (Bus-Fin)
2211 Congress St.　　　　　　　　　Phone: (207) 780-2347
Portland, ME 04122　　　　　　　Phillip C. Kalloch, Jr., Supv., Info.Serv.
Founded: 1958. **Staff:** Prof 4; Other 2. **Subjects:** Life and health insurance, management, economics, business. **Special Collections:** Corporate archives; legal library; investments library. **Holdings:** 5000 books; 10 VF drawers. **Subscriptions:** 360 journals and other serials; 10 newspapers. **Services:** Interlibrary loans; center open to public by appointment. **Automated Operations:** Computerized serials. **Computerized Information Services:** DIALOG, SDC, Westlaw, Dow Jones News/Retrieval, INVESTEXT, Donnelly Marketing Information Services Division. **Publications:** CIC Review, weekly - for internal distribution only. **Staff:** Ellen Sottery, Bus.Info.Spec.; Sandra Hartford, Legal Info.Spec.; Sandra Shryock, Investment Info.Spec.

★13781★
UNION NATIONAL BANK AND TRUST COMPANY - LIBRARY (Bus-Fin)
14 Main St.　　　　　　　　　　　Phone: (215) 721-2400
Souderton, PA 18964　　　　　　　Gladys Detweiler, Libn.
Founded: 1966. **Staff:** 1. **Subjects:** Banking, audit controls, commercial and installment lending. **Holdings:** 250 books. **Subscriptions:** 50 journals and other serials. **Services:** Library open to public by appointment.

★13782★
UNION OIL COMPANY OF CALIFORNIA - INTERNATIONAL EXPLORATION LIBRARY (Sci-Tech)
461 S. Boylston St.　　　　　　　　Phone: (213) 977-6381
Los Angeles, CA 90017　　　　　　Ardis Weiss, Lib.Mgr.
Founded: 1960. **Staff:** Prof 1; Other 1. **Subjects:** Geology, petroleum geology, oceanography, geophysics. **Holdings:** 9000 books; 800 bound periodical volumes. **Subscriptions:** 100 journals and other serials. **Services:** Interlibrary loans; library not open to public. **Automated Operations:** Computerized cataloging, acquisitions, serials and circulation. **Computerized Information Services:** DIALOG. **Networks/Consortia:** Member of CLASS.

★13783★
UNION OIL COMPANY OF CALIFORNIA - LIBRARY-FILE ROOM (Sci-Tech)
2323 Knoll Dr.
Box 6176　　　　　　　　　　　　Phone: (805) 656-7600
Ventura, CA 93006　　　　　　　　Jeanne Gallagher, Libn.
Staff: Prof 1. **Subjects:** Geology, geophysics, paleontology. **Holdings:** 600 books; 200 maps; 180 linear feet of company reports; 550 reprints. **Subscriptions:** 10 journals and other serials. **Services:** Library not open to public.

★13784★
UNION OIL COMPANY OF CALIFORNIA - TECHNICAL INFORMATION CENTER (Sci-Tech; Energy)
376 S. Valencia Ave.
Box 76　　　　　　　　　　　　　Phone: (714) 528-7201
Placentia, CA 92621　　　　　　　Barbara J. Orosz, Hd.Libn.
Staff: Prof 3; Other 6. **Subjects:** Petroleum technology, chemistry, geosciences, oceanography, physics, chemical engineering, mathematics, agriculture, geology. **Holdings:** 22,000 books; 21,000 bound periodical volumes; 25 500 documents; 18,000 government documents; 35 shelves of maps. **Subscriptions:** 800 journals and other serials. **Services:** Interlibrary loans; copying; center open to students by appointment and for reference use only. **Computerized Information Services:** Internal database. **Publications:** List of books and documents, semimonthly - distributed to research center personnel. **Staff:** Gloria Okasako-Oshiro, Info.Chem.; Renee Robertson, Info.Chem.

★13785★
UNION OIL COMPANY OF CANADA, LTD. - LIBRARY (Sci-Tech; Energy)
335 8th Ave., S.W.
P.O. Box 999　　　　　　　　　　Phone: (403) 268-0303
Calgary, AB, Canada T2P 2K6　　　　Julie Graham, Libn.
Staff: Prof 1. **Subjects:** Geology, geophysics, law, mineralogy. **Holdings:** 1250 books; 300 bound periodical volumes; 1050 Geological Survey of Canada papers; 1050 reprints; 600 miscellaneous provincial papers; 100 microfiche. **Subscriptions:** 140 journals and other serials. **Services:** Interlibrary loans; copying; library open to employees and other libraries. **Computerized Information Services:** SDC.

UNION PACIFIC CORPORATION - ROCKY MOUNTAIN ENERGY
See: Rocky Mountain Energy

★13786★
UNION PACIFIC RAILROAD COMPANY - LAW LIBRARY (Law)
1515 S.W. 5th Ave., Suite 400　　　　Phone: (503) 249-2519
Portland, OR 97201　　　　　　L. James Bergmann, Gen. Solicitor
Staff: Prof 7; Other 8. **Subjects:** Law. **Holdings:** Figures not available. **Services:** Library open to corporation personnel and known attorneys; open to other legal professionals on request.

★13787★
UNION PACIFIC RAILROAD COMPANY - LIBRARY (Trans; Bus-Fin)
1416 Dodge St.　　　　　　　　　　Phone: (402) 271-4785
Omaha, NE 68179　　　　　　　　J.S. Boyer, Hd.Libn.
Founded: 1976. **Staff:** Prof 1; Other 1. **Subjects:** Transportation, business. **Holdings:** 7000 books; 1000 annual reports. **Subscriptions:** 600 journals and other serials. **Services:** Interlibrary loans; copying; library open to public with restrictions. **Automated Operations:** Computerized cataloging and serials. **Computerized Information Services:** DIALOG, SDC, NEXIS, Dow

Jones News/Retrieval. **Publications:** Track Talk, monthly.

★13788★
UNION SAINT-JEAN-BAPTISTE - MALLET LIBRARY (Hist)
One Social St.   Phone: (401) 769-0520
Woonsocket, RI 02895   Bro. Felician, S.C., Libn.
Founded: 1908. **Staff:** Prof 1. **Subjects:** Franco-American history and civilization, biography, genealogy, literature, religion, social sciences. **Special Collections:** Letters (600), 500 of which are addressed to Major Edmond Mallet; Ephemerides (33 volumes). **Holdings:** 4808 books; 42 bound periodical volumes; 350 pamphlets; 30 sets of manuscript notes; 50 maps; 1144 vertical file subject headings; 32 dissertations; 17 drawers of photographs; 112 reels of microfilm; 850 French-Canadian and French phonograph records. **Subscriptions:** 18 journals and other serials. **Services:** Library open to public with lending restrictions. **Also Known As:** Bibliotheque Mallet.

★13789★
UNION TEXAS PETROLEUM CORPORATION - LIBRARY (Sci-Tech)
Box 2120   Phone: (713) 960-7044
Houston, TX 77252   Betty J. Backus, Supv., Lib.
Staff: Prof 2. **Subjects:** Geology, chemical engineering, labor relations. **Holdings:** 4800 books. **Services:** Library open to public by appointment. **Remarks:** Union Texas Petroleum Corporation is an Allied Corporation company located at 1 Riverway, Houston, TX 77056.

★13790★
UNION THEOLOGICAL SEMINARY - BURKE LIBRARY (Rel-Theol)
3041 Broadway at Reinhold Niebuhr Place   Phone: (212) 662-7100
New York, NY 10027   Richard D. Spoor, Dir.
Founded: 1838. **Staff:** Prof 8; Other 13. **Subjects:** Bible, theology, sacred music, church history, missions, ecumenics. **Special Collections:** McAlpin Collection of British History and Theology; Van Ess Collection; sacred music collection (including hymnology); Bonhoeffer Collection; Auburn Collection; archives; Missionary Research Library Collection. **Holdings:** 585,000 volumes; 60,000 microforms. **Subscriptions:** 1500 journals. **Services:** Interlibrary loans; copying; library open to public upon application. **Computerized Information Services:** RLIN. **Networks/Consortia:** Member of New York State Interlibrary Loan Network (NYSILL); SUNY/OCLC Library Network; RLG; METRO.

★13791★
UNION THEOLOGICAL SEMINARY IN VIRGINIA - LIBRARY (Rel-Theol)
3401 Brook Rd.   Phone: (804) 355-0671
Richmond, VA 23227   Dr. John B. Trotti, Libn.
Founded: 1806. **Staff:** Prof 5; Other 21. **Subjects:** Bible, theology, church history. **Special Collections:** Presbyterian Church Archives (750 manuscript volumes); Human Relations Area Files (24,373 microfiche). **Holdings:** 228,993 volumes; 24,524 audio recordings (reel and cassette); 2206 films; 852 filmstrips; 58 videotapes; 22,129 slides; 484 kits and games. **Subscriptions:** 1249 journals and other serials and newspapers. **Services:** Interlibrary loans; copying; library open to public with restrictions on circulation. **Automated Operations:** Computerized cataloging. **Computerized Information Services:** OCLC, DIALOG, BRS. Performs searches on cost recovery basis. Contact Person: Martha B. Aycock. **Networks/Consortia:** Member of SOLINET. **Publications:** Scholar's Choice, semiannual - free. **Special Catalogs:** Reigner Recording Library Catalog. **Staff:** Dorothy Gilliam, Cat.; Linda Sue Quinn, Asst.Cat.; Martha Aycock, Ref.Libn.; Eleanor Godfrey, Media Rsrcs.Dir.

★13792★
UNION TRUST COMPANY OF MARYLAND - LIBRARY
Baltimore & St. Paul Sts.
Box 1077
Baltimore, MD 21203
Defunct

★13793★
UNION UNIVERSITY - ALBANY COLLEGE OF PHARMACY - LIBRARY (Med)
106 New Scotland Ave.   Phone: (518) 445-5217
Albany, NY 12208   John B. Hall, Libn.
Founded: 1927. **Staff:** Prof 1. **Subjects:** Pharmacy, medicine, physics, chemistry, biology, technology. **Holdings:** 10,000 books; 4000 bound periodical volumes; 150 periodicals; 600 pamphlets; de Haen and Iowa Drug Information Service; 25 linear feet of archival material. **Subscriptions:** 134 journals and other serials. **Services:** Interlibrary loans; copying; SDI; library open to public with restrictions. **Automated Operations:** Computerized cataloging. **Computerized Information Services:** BRS. Performs searches free of charge and on cost recovery basis. **Networks/Consortia:** Member of

Capital District Library Council for Reference & Research Resources (CDLC).

★13794★
UNION UNIVERSITY - ALBANY LAW SCHOOL - LIBRARY (Law)
80 New Scotland Ave.   Phone: (518) 445-2340
Albany, NY 12208   Robert T. Begg, Dir.
Founded: 1851. **Staff:** Prof 7; Other 8. **Subjects:** Law. **Special Collections:** English and government law. **Holdings:** 170,000 volumes. **Subscriptions:** 1040 journals and other serials. **Services:** Interlibrary loans; copying; library open to alumni, attorneys, college students, state and federal agencies. **Computerized Information Services:** LEXIS, Westlaw, OCLC. **Publications:** Directory; acquisitions list, monthly. **Staff:** Robert Emery, Ref.Libn.; Judith Westhuis, Tech.Serv.Libn.; Suzanne Ayer, Govt.Doc.Libn.; Lauren Pinseley, Asst.Cat.; Mary Wood, Circ./ILL; Barbara Norelli, Hd., Pub.Serv.

★13795★
UNION UNIVERSITY - ALBANY MEDICAL COLLEGE - SCHAFFER LIBRARY OF THE HEALTH SCIENCES (Med)
47 New Scotland Ave.   Phone: (518) 445-5586
Albany, NY 12208   Ursula H. Poland, Libn.
Founded: 1839. **Staff:** Prof 7; Other 10. **Subjects:** Medicine, pre-clinical sciences, nursing. **Holdings:** 25,500 books; 56,000 bound periodical volumes; 1132 AV items. **Subscriptions:** 1075 journals and other serials. **Services:** Interlibrary loans; copying; SDI; library open to allied health personnel. **Computerized Information Services:** BRS, NLM, OCLC, DIALOG. **Networks/Consortia:** Member of Capital District Library Council for Reference & Research Resources (CDLC); Greater Northeastern Regional Medical Library Program. **Publications:** Library Newsletter, irregular - for users and interested libraries. **Staff:** Eleanor McNutt, Assoc.Libn.; Sherry Hartman, Ref. & Database; Gail Botta, Coll.Dev.; Jill Stanton, AV & Ref.; Enid Geyer, Tech.Proc.; Charlene La Grange, Circ. & ILL.

★13796★
UNION UNIVERSITY - DUDLEY OBSERVATORY - LIBRARY (Sci-Tech)
69 Union Ave.   Phone: (518) 382-7583
Schenectady, NY 12308   Rita A. Spenser, Act.Libn.
Subjects: Astronomy, astrophysics, space science, physics, mathematics. **Special Collections:** Rare books in astronomy (250). **Holdings:** 5500 books; 10,000 bound periodical volumes; 8500 unbound serials; 6000 pamphlets, reports, specifications and standards; 13 VF drawers of star atlases; 2 VF drawers of astronomical pictures. **Subscriptions:** 250 journals and other serials. **Services:** Interlibrary loans; copying; library open to public. **Networks/Consortia:** Member of Capital District Library Council for Reference & Research Resources (CDLC). **Publications:** Dudley Observatory Reports, irregular - by exchange; Dudley Observatory Reprints - lists available, reprints may be requested.

★13797★
UNIONTOWN HOSPITAL ASSOCIATION - MEDICAL LIBRARY (Med)*
500 W. Berkeley St.   Phone: (412) 430-5178
Uniontown, PA 15401   Nina M. Stith, Med.Libn.
Staff: Prof 1. **Subjects:** Medicine and related health sciences. **Holdings:** 1848 books; 1062 bound periodical volumes; 12 VF drawers; 120 videotapes; 380 cassettes and reels of tape. **Subscriptions:** 163 journals and other serials. **Services:** Interlibrary loans; copying; library open to public with restrictions. **Networks/Consortia:** Member of Greater Northeastern Medical Library Program; Pittsburgh Regional Medical Library Group. **Staff:** Robert Mullen, Pres.

★13798★
UNIROYAL, INC. - CORPORATE LIBRARY (Bus-Fin)
World Headquarters   Phone: (203) 573-2000
Middlebury, CT 06749
Staff: Prof 1. **Subjects:** Business. **Holdings:** 1000 books; 200 bound periodical volumes; studies; annual reports; maps; Bureau of Census and Department of Commerce publications. **Subscriptions:** 200 journals and other serials; 25 newspapers. **Services:** Interlibrary loans; copying.

★13799★
UNIROYAL, LTD. - RESEARCH LABORATORIES LIBRARY (Sci-Tech)
120 Huron St.   Phone: (519) 822-3790
Guelph, ON, Canada N1H 6N3   Lorna P. Cole, Mgr., Info.Serv.
Founded: 1943. **Staff:** Prof 1; Other 2. **Subjects:** Organic chemistry, plastics, rubber, composite materials. **Holdings:** 5000 books; 2555 bound periodical volumes; 44 drawers of reports, trade catalogs, patents and pamphlets; 900 reels of microfilm. **Subscriptions:** 350 journals and other serials. **Services:** Interlibrary loans; copying; SDI; library open to public with restrictions. **Automated Operations:** Computerized serials. **Computerized Information Services:** DIALOG, SDC, QL Systems, CAS Online, Pesticide

Research Information System (PRIS), CAN/OLE, BRS, Info Globe, CANSIM; internal databases. **Publications:** Library Bulletin, biweekly; Accessions List, monthly; Reports List, quarterly; Library Notes, irregular. **Special Catalogs:** Company research reports; periodical holdings (both computerized).

★13800★
UNIROYAL, INC. - TECHNICAL LIBRARY (Sci-Tech)
Box 117   Phone: (203) 573-4509
Waterbury, CT 06720   D.H. Winslow, Mgr.
Staff: Prof 1; Other 1. **Subjects:** Chemistry, physics, rubber, plastics. **Holdings:** 8000 books; 10,000 bound periodical volumes; patents; clippings; pamphlets; dissertations; documents. **Subscriptions:** 200 journals and other serials. **Services:** Library not open to public. **Staff:** Doris Vork, Libn.

★13801★
UNIROYAL, INC. - UNIROYAL CHEMICAL DIVISION - MANAGEMENT & TECHNICAL INFORMATION SERVICES/LIBRARY (Sci-Tech)
Elm St.   Phone: (203) 723-3252
Naugatuck, CT 06770   Patricia Ann Harmon, Libn.
Staff: Prof 1; Other 2. **Subjects:** Agricultural chemicals, chemical engineering, organic chemistry, plastics and rubber technology. **Holdings:** 2000 books; 10,000 bound periodical volumes; 2200 reels of microfilm. **Subscriptions:** 450 journals and other serials. **Services:** Interlibrary loans; copying; library open to public with restrictions. **Automated Operations:** Computerized circulation. **Computerized Information Services:** DIALOG, SDC, NLM, Pergamon InfoLine Ltd., CAS Online, Dow Jones News/Retrieval. **Networks/Consortia:** Member of Region One Cooperating Libraries Service Unit for Northwestern Connecticut. **Staff:**

★13802★
UNITARIAN-UNIVERSALIST ASSOCIATION - ARCHIVES (Rel-Theol)
25 Beacon St.   Phone: (617) 742-2100
Boston, MA 02108   Carl Seaburg, Info.Off./Archv.
Subjects: History, religion, biography, churches and ministers. **Special Collections:** Records of Unitarian-Universalist Ministers and Churches. **Holdings:** Clippings; manuscripts; pictures; maps; correspondence. **Services:** Copying; library open to public for research and reference.

UNITARIAN-UNIVERSALIST ASSOCIATION - RELIGIOUS ARTS GUILD
See: Religious Arts Guild

★13803★
UNITARIAN AND UNIVERSALIST GENEALOGICAL SOCIETY - LIBRARY (Hist)
10605 Lakespring Way   Phone: (301) 628-2490
Cockeysville, MD 21030   Willis Clayton Tull, Jr., Libn.
Founded: 1971. **Staff:** Prof 1; Other 1. **Subjects:** Genealogical and biobibliographic records on Deists, Ethicists, Freethinkers, Hicksite Quakers, Humanists, Latitudinarian Anglicans, Pantheists, Reform Jews, Transcendentalists, and especially Unitarians and Universalists. **Holdings:** 1400 books; 9241 family records; 9241 ancestor charts; 9241 biobibliographic card files; 4 reels of census records on microfilm. **Subscriptions:** 14 journals and other serials. **Services:** Copying; library will exchange information by appointment or mail only. **Special Catalogs:** Ancestor catalog (card). **Special Indexes:** Query index (card). **Remarks:** This is the private library of Mr. Tull and is not affiliated with any denominational office, church, agency or organization. The earliest work in the collection was published in 1650, and the collection includes material in Hungarian, Japanese, Latin and Welsh.

★13804★
UNITED AIR LINES, INC. - ENGINEERING DEPARTMENT - LIBRARY (Sci-Tech)
San Francisco International Airport   Phone: (415) 876-3730
San Francisco, CA 94128   Josephine J. Whitney, Tech.Libn.
Founded: 1965. **Staff:** Prof 1. **Subjects:** Aeronautics, metals, electronics, mathematics, welding, meteorology, aircraft specifications and standards, computers, radio. **Special Collections:** Federal aviation regulations; aircraft (SAE) material specs; military specifications. **Holdings:** 7000 books and bound periodical volumes; 4000 technical reports; 240 reels of microfilm of vendor files; 180 reels of microfilm of United Air Lines, Boeing Aircraft and Douglas Aircraft manuals. **Subscriptions:** 50 journals and other serials. **Services:** Interlibrary loans; copying; library open to public. **Automated Operations:** Computerized cataloging. **Special Catalogs:** Catalog of United Air Lines annual reports from 1929 to present.

★13805★
UNITED AUTOMOBILE, AEROSPACE & AGRICULTURAL IMPLEMENT WORKERS OF AMERICA - RESEARCH LIBRARY (Soc Sci)
8000 E. Jefferson Ave.   Phone: (313) 926-5386
Detroit, MI 48214   Melba Kibildis, Libn.
Founded: 1947. **Staff:** Prof 2; Other 2. **Subjects:** Economics and collective bargaining in automobile, aerospace and agricultural implement industries; labor economics; industrial relations; United Automobile Workers. **Special Collections:** Automation; plant closings; UAW collective agreements; testimonies and speeches of UAW officers and staff. **Holdings:** Figures not available for books and periodicals; U.S., state and Canadian government documents; newspaper clippings; pamphlets; press releases; microforms. **Services:** Library not open to public. **Automated Operations:** Computerized cataloging. **Computerized Information Services:** DIALOG, SDC, LEXIS, Dow Jones News/Retrieval, Info Globe, Bureau of Labor Statistics; internal database. **Also Known As:** UAW; International Union, United Automobile, Aerospace & Agricultural Implement Workers of America. **Staff:** Jane C. Murphey, Asst.Libn.

★13806★
UNITED BANK OF DENVER, N.A. - INFORMATION CENTER LIBRARY (Bus-Fin)
1700 Broadway
Box 5247   Phone: (303) 861-8811
Denver, CO 80274   Nancy Ransier, Mktg.Res.Anl.
Founded: 1968. **Subjects:** Banking, finance, economics, management, business and industry. **Holdings:** 4000 books; 24 VF drawers of pamphlets; 300 theses; 600 internal reports; 100 videotapes on banking. **Subscriptions:** 250 journals and other serials; 11 newspapers. **Services:** Library open to public by special arrangement. **Automated Operations:** Computerized cataloging, subscription payment system and routing. **Computerized Information Services:** SDC. **Remarks:** Research, consulting, cataloging and searching are subcontracted from the Denver Public Library.

★13807★
UNITED BANK OF DENVER, N.A. - UNITED BANK CENTER - LAW LIBRARY (Law)
1700 Broadway
Tower Bldg., Suite 1215   Phone: (303) 861-4304
Denver, CO 80290   Breta M. Krodshen, Law Libn.
Staff: 1. **Subjects:** Law. **Special Collections:** U.S. government documents on taxes; U.S. Statutes at Large. **Holdings:** 14,784 books; 830 loose-leafs; 7863 unbound reports. **Subscriptions:** 13 journals and other serials. **Services:** Library open to in-house attorneys only.

★13808★
UNITED CATALYSTS, INC. - TECHNICAL LIBRARY (Sci-Tech)
Box 32370   Phone: (502) 637-9751
Louisville, KY 40232   Betty B. Simms, Tech.Libn.
Founded: 1943. **Staff:** Prof 1. **Subjects:** Catalysis, chemistry, physics, engineering, mathematics, management. **Special Collections:** Catalysis. **Holdings:** 4000 books; 3300 bound periodical volumes; 18,000 patents; 11,000 indexed documents; 18 VF drawers of indexed technical reports; microfilm. **Subscriptions:** 33 journals and other serials. **Services:** Interlibrary loans; reference service to comparable libraries; library open to public by appointment. **Computerized Information Services:** DIALOG, SDC. **Publications:** Acquisition Bulletin; Patent Awareness Bulletin; Articles of Interest Bulletin. **Special Indexes:** Indexes to documents, pamphlets and technical reports. **Remarks:** Library is located at 1227 S. 12th St., Louisville, KY 40210.

★13809★
UNITED CEREBRAL PALSY ASSOCIATION OF THE GREATER WATERBURY AREA - PROFESSIONAL RESOURCE CENTER (Med)
61 Bidwell St.   Phone: (203) 756-7843
Waterbury, CT 06770   Thomas R. Briggs, Ph.D., Principal
Subjects: Physically and severely handicapped, communication training, special education, parent training, therapeutic training. **Special Collections:** Severely physically handicapped. **Holdings:** 150 books; 100 other cataloged items. **Services:** Center open to public with restrictions.

★13810★
UNITED CEREBRAL PALSY OF NEW YORK CITY, INC. - LIBRARY (Med)
122 E. 23rd St.   Phone: (212) 677-7400
New York, NY 10010   Richard Gordon, Lib.Mgr.
Founded: 1959. **Staff:** Prof 2. **Subjects:** Cerebral palsy and related topics. **Holdings:** 524 books; 19 bound periodical volumes. **Subscriptions:** 13 journals and other serials; 5 newspapers. **Services:** Library open to public. **Publications:** Update, quarterly. **Staff:** Fanny L. Bluh, Adm.Asst.

★13811★
UNITED CHARITIES OF CHICAGO - LIBRARY (Soc Sci)
14 E. Jackson Blvd.   Phone: (312) 461-0800
Chicago, IL 60604   Marie T. Burns, Libn./Rec.Mgr.
Staff: Prof 1; Other 1. Subjects: Social work, law. Holdings: 6700 books;
3000 pamphlets. Subscriptions: 111 journals and other serials. Services:
Interlibrary loans; copying; library open to public by appointment. Networks/
Consortia: Member of Chicago Library System (CLS). Publications: New
Acquisitions, monthly - for internal distribution only.

★13812★
UNITED CHURCH BOARD FOR WORLD MINISTRIES - LIBRARY (Rel-Theol)
475 Riverside Dr., 16th Fl.
New York, NY 10115   Virginia Stowe, Libn.
Founded: 1820. Staff: Prof 2. Subjects: Missions of United Church Board
for World Ministries and its predecessors (especially American Board of
Commissioners for Foreign Ministries), third world areas. Holdings: 3000
books; 200 bound periodical volumes. Subscriptions: 50 journals and other
serials. Services: Library open to public by special permission. Remarks:
Archival records are located in Houghton Library, Harvard University,
Cambridge MA 02138, and in the library of Lancaster Theological Seminary,
Lancaster, PA 17603. Staff: Ithmer Wolfe, Asst.Libn.

★13813★
UNITED CHURCH OF CANADA - CENTRAL ARCHIVES (Hist)†
Birge-Carnegie Bldg., Victoria Univ.
73 Queen's Park Crescent, E.   Phone: (416) 978-3832
Toronto, ON, Canada M5S 2C4   Rev. Glenn Lucas, Archv./Hist.
Staff: Prof 6; Other 6. Subjects: History of United Church of Canada and
constituent churches (various Methodist, Presbyterian and Congregational
bodies established in Canada between 1749 and 1925); archival records.
Holdings: 6300 books; 4200 bound periodical volumes; 600 yearbooks;
9100 feet of manuscripts; 11,000 pamphlets; 1100 reels of microfilm; 350
tapes. Subscriptions: 140 journals and other serials; 5 newspapers.
Services: Copying; archives open to public with restrictions. Publications:
Bulletin, annual. Staff: Dr. N.E. Semple, Asst.Archv.; Mrs. M.A. Tyler,
Asst.Archv.; Mrs. E. Clapp, Libn.; Mrs. H. Michael, Libn.; Mrs. M. Tilley,
Bus.Mgr.

★13814★
UNITED CHURCH OF CANADA - ESSEX PRESBYTERY - RESOURCE CENTRE
(Rel-Theol)
208 Sunset Ave.   Phone: (519) 252-0353
Windsor, ON, Canada N9B 3A7   Jean Fanson
Staff: Prof 1; Other 1. Subjects: Religion. Holdings: Books; magazines;
church and Sunday School material; filmstrip; records; cassettes; posters.
Subscriptions: 14 journals and other serials. Services: Center open to public.

★13815★
UNITED CHURCH OF CANADA - MARITIME CONFERENCE ARCHIVES (Hist;
Rel-Theol)
Pine Hill Divinity Hall   Phone: (902) 429-4819
Halifax, NS, Canada B3H 3B5   Rev. Neil A. MacLeod, Archv.
Staff: Prof 1. Subjects: History of the Congregationalist, Methodist,
Presbyterian and United Churches in the Maritime provinces of Canada.
Special Collections: McGregor Papers; Black-McColl Papers; Geddie Letters.
Holdings: Several thousand books, pamphlets, manuscripts, pictures, letters.
Services: Interlibrary loans; copying; assistance with research; archives open
to public on a limited schedule.

UNITED CHURCH OF CHRIST - ARCHIVES
See: Evangelical and Reformed Historical Society - Lancaster Central
Archives and Library

★13816★
UNITED CHURCH OF CHRIST - CONNECTICUT CONFERENCE - ARCHIVES
(Hist; Rel-Theol)
125 Sherman St.   Phone: (203) 233-5564
Hartford, CT 06105   Rev. Wesley C. Ewert, Archv.
Staff: Prof 1. Subjects: United Church of Christ churches in Connecticut.
Special Collections: Historical records on its Connecticut churches;
correspondence and collections of Connecticut Missionary Society, 1798 to
present; file on Connecticut Congregational clergy. Holdings: 1500 books; 40
bound periodical volumes; uncataloged books and tracts. Services: Archives
open to public by arrangement with archivist.

★13817★
UNITED CHURCH OF CHRIST (Evangelical and Reformed) - CHURCH
LIBRARY (Rel-Theol)
Grand & Ohio Sts.   Phone: (216) 967-3559
Vermilion, OH 44089   Doris M. Feiszli, Lib.Chm.
Founded: 1954. Staff: Prof 1. Subjects: Religion, faith, devotions and
prayer, Bible, biography, missions. Holdings: 4000 books; AV materials.
Services: Library open to public for reference use only.

UNITED CHURCH OF CHRIST - PHILIP SCHAFF LIBRARY
See: Lancaster Theological Seminary of the United Church of Christ -
Philip Schaff Library

★13818★
UNITED CHURCH OF LOS ALAMOS - LIBRARY (Rel-Theol)
2525 Canyon Rd.
Box 1286   Phone: (505) 662-2971
Los Alamos, NM 87544   Martha C. MacMillan, Libn.
Founded: 1967. Staff: Prof 1; Other 3. Subjects: Religion, psychology,
family, social problems, health, philosophy. Holdings: 3350 books, pamphlets
and paperbacks. Subscriptions: 10 journals and other serials. Services:
Library open to public.

★13819★
UNITED CHURCH OF RELIGIOUS SCIENCE - LIBRARY ERNEST HOLMES
COLLEGE LIBRARY (Rel-Theol)
3251 W. Sixth St.
Box 75127   Phone: (213) 388-2181
Los Angeles, CA 90075   Albert T. Wickham, Hd.Libn.
Founded: 1974. Staff: Prof 1. Subjects: "New Thought," religion,
philosophy, science, mind science, psychology, occult. Special Collections:
Science of mind (200 items); Religions of the Far East (100 items); Manly P.
Hall Collection (25 items). Holdings: 8000 books; 300 audiotapes; 1000
metaphysical pamphlets and booklets; 4 VF drawers of clippings and archival
materials; 200 file boxes of past metaphysical, scientific and news
magazines. Subscriptions: 22 journals and other serials. Services:
Interlibrary loans; library open to public for reference use only. Special
Indexes: Index to Science of Mind Magazine.

★13820★
UNITED COOPERATIVES OF ONTARIO - HARMAN LIBRARY (Bus Fin)
Sta. A, P.O. Box 527   Phone: (416) 270-3560
Mississauga, ON, Canada L5A 3A4   Audrey Ferger, Libn.
Founded: 1964. Staff: 1. Subjects: History of cooperatives in Canada and
the United States, finance and credit, personnel, training and management
development, statistics. Holdings: 1800 books and bound periodical volumes;
2 VF drawers of archives; 150 pamphlets and annual reports. Subscriptions:
19 journals and other serials. Services: Interlibrary loans; copying (limited);
library open to public with restrictions.

★13821★
UNITED DAUGHTERS OF THE CONFEDERACY - CAROLINE MERIWETHER
GOODLETT LIBRARY (Hist)
U.D.C. Headquarters Bldg.
328 North Blvd.   Phone: (804) 355-1636
Richmond, VA 23220   Dorothy L. Barrett, Chm., Lib.Comm.
Founded: 1957. Staff: Prof 1; Other 1. Subjects: Civil War - causes and
Reconstruction. Holdings: 5000 books; diaries; letters; manuscripts; papers;
clippings; memorabilia; photographs. Services: Library open to members and
qualified historians by appointment.

★13822★
UNITED DAUGHTERS OF THE CONFEDERACY - TEXAS CONFEDERATE
MUSEUM LIBRARY (Hist)
112 E. 11th   Phone: (512) 472-2596
Austin, TX 78701   Florence Odom, Musm.Cur.
Founded: 1904. Staff: 1. Subjects: Southern history, Confederate States of
America military records. Holdings: 600 books. Services: Library open to
public. Staff: Mrs. L.J. Gittinger, Chm.

UNITED ELECTRICAL, RADIO AND MACHINE WORKERS OF AMERICA
ARCHIVES
See: University of Pittsburgh - Archives of Industrial Society

★13823★
UNITED ENGINEERS & CONSTRUCTORS INC. - BOSTON OFFICE - LIBRARY
(Sci-Tech)
100 Summer St.   Phone: (617) 338-6000
Boston, MA 02110   Rocco Piccinino, Jr., Libn.
Founded: 1908. Staff: Prof 2. Subjects: Engineering - power, mechanical,

civil, electrical, industrial, nuclear; environment; pollution - air, water; architecture. **Holdings:** 8000 books; 400 bound periodical volumes; 25,000 reports; 500 maps; vendor catalogs; 9000 standards; 5 VF drawers. **Subscriptions:** 175 journals and other serials. **Services:** Interlibrary loans; library open to public with permission. **Computerized Information Services:** DIALOG, SDC, NASA/RECON, DOE/RECON. **Staff:** Cleopatra Hondrodemos, Asst.Libn.

★13824★
UNITED ENGINEERS & CONSTRUCTORS INC. - LIBRARY (Sci-Tech; Energy)
30 S. 17th St.
Box 8223   Phone: (215) 422-3374
Philadelphia, PA 19101   Marie S. Knap, Hd.Libn.
Founded: 1928. **Staff:** Prof 2. **Subjects:** Heavy construction; design engineering and architecture; power plants; energy sources - nuclear, fossil fuels, solar, geothermal; wastewater; sanitary engineering; environmental protection; seismology; chemical process plants; iron and steel. **Special Collections:** Standards from voluntary standards organizations (10,000); Atomic Energy Commission, Nuclear Regulatory Commission, Energy Research and Development Administration, and Department of Energy contractor reports on microfiche (also includes AEC and NRC licensing dockets; over one million); government documents (20,000). **Holdings:** 7500 books; 16 VF drawers of technical material. **Subscriptions:** 600 journals and other serials; 10 newspapers. **Services:** Interlibrary loans (by prior arrangement). **Automated Operations:** Computerized cataloging and serials. **Computerized Information Services:** DIALOG, SDC, BRS, DOE/RECON, NASA/RECON. **Special Indexes:** KWOC Index. **Remarks:** A subsidiary of Raytheon Company. **Staff:** Janet S. Holly, Assoc.Libn.

★13825★
UNITED FARM WORKERS OF AMERICA, AFL-CIO - I.C. LIBRARY (Agri; Soc Sci)
La Paz   Phone: (805) 822-5571
Keene, CA 93531   Garland Taylor, Dir.
Founded: 1973. **Staff:** Prof 1. **Subjects:** Agriculture, agricultural research, agribusiness, food industry, economics, pesticide research, farm labor, union law. **Special Collections:** Books about Cesar Chavez and the United Farm Workers Union. **Holdings:** Figures not available.

★13826★
UNITED FOOD AND COMMERCIAL WORKERS INTERNATIONAL UNION - LIBRARY (Bus-Fin)†
1775 K St., N.W.   Phone: (202) 223-3111
Washington, DC 20006   Ellen Newton, Libn.
Founded: 1975. **Staff:** Prof 1; Other 1. **Subjects:** Labor and trade union history, business, economics, agriculture, food industry, retail industry. **Holdings:** 1300 books; 300 Bureau of Labor Statistics Reports; 25 U.S.D.A. periodicals; 24 VF drawers of clippings and pamphlets. **Subscriptions:** 500 journals and other serials; 100 newspapers. **Services:** Interlibrary loans; copying; SDI; library open to researchers by appointment. **Computerized Information Services:** DIALOG. **Networks/Consortia:** Member of Metropolitan Washington Library Council. **Publications:** Daily Hot Sheet - for internal distribution only.

★13827★
UNITED FRESH FRUIT AND VEGETABLE ASSOCIATION - LIBRARY (Food-Bev)
N. Washington at Madison   Phone: (703) 836-3410
Alexandria, VA 22314   Charles Magoon, Dir. of Res.
Subjects: Marketing of fresh fruits and vegetables, nutrition, crop statistics. **Holdings:** 40,000 items; 20 VF drawers. **Subscriptions:** 40 journals and other serials. **Staff:** Deborah A. Stapell, Mgr., Info.Serv.

★13828★
UNITED GRAIN GROWERS LTD. - LIBRARY (Agri)
433 Main St.
Box 6600   Phone: (204) 944-5572
Winnipeg, MB, Canada R3C 3A7   Carole Rogers, Libn.
Staff: 1. **Subjects:** Grain handling and production, agricultural history, company archives. **Holdings:** 2000 books; 150 vertical file boxes; 10 Statistics Canada publications. **Subscriptions:** 100 journals and other serials; 10 newspapers. **Services:** Interlibrary loans; library open to public for reference use only.

UNITED GRAND IMPERIAL COUNCIL
See: Red Cross of Constantine

★13829★
UNITED HEALTH SERVICES/WILSON HOSPITAL - LEARNING RESOURCES DEPARTMENT (Med)
33-57 Harrison St.   Phone: (607) 773-6030
Johnson City, NY 13790   Shirley Edsall, Mgr.
Staff: Prof 3; Other 5. **Subjects:** Medicine, nursing, health sciences administration. **Holdings:** 4000 books; 5400 bound periodical volumes; 1800 video cassettes, slide/tape programs, models, films, charts. **Subscriptions:** 305 journals and other serials. **Services:** Interlibrary loans; copying; SDI; self instructional learning lab; department open to public for reference use only. **Computerized Information Services:** MEDLINE, BRS, DIALOG. Performs free searches. **Networks/Consortia:** Member of South Central Research Library Council (SCRLC). **Formerly:** Wilson (Charles S.) Memorial Hospital. **Staff:** Gloria Restino, Media Libn.; Sue Hathaway, Circuit Libn.

★13830★
UNITED HOSPITAL CENTER INC. - MEDICAL LIBRARY (Med)
3 Hospital Plaza   Phone: (304) 624-2230
Clarksburg, WV 26301   Brenda J. Curry, Libn.
Staff: Prof 1. **Subjects:** Medicine, continuing education, hospital management, patient education. **Holdings:** 1900 books; 695 bound periodical volumes; 350 AV items; 124 video cassettes; 900 audio cassettes. **Subscriptions:** 189 journals and other serials. **Services:** Interlibrary loans; copying; SDI; library open to hospital staff and students. **Automated Operations:** Computerized serials. **Computerized Information Services:** MEDLARS, DIALOG. **Networks/Consortia:** Member of North-Central Area Consortium of Health Information Resources (NACHIR).

★13831★
UNITED HOSPITAL FUND OF NEW YORK - REFERENCE LIBRARY (Soc Sci)
3 E. 54th St.   Phone: (212) 754-1080
New York, NY 10022   Christine Bahr, Libn.
Founded: 1941. **Staff:** Prof 1; Other 1. **Subjects:** Hospital management, health services research, fund raising, volunteer services, public health. **Holdings:** 10,000 books; 20 VF drawers of reports, documents, pamphlets, clippings. **Subscriptions:** 100 journals and other serials. **Services:** Interlibrary loans; copying; library open to public by appointment. **Networks/Consortia:** Member of Manhattan-Bronx Health Sciences Library Group.

★13832★
UNITED HOSPITAL - LIBRARY (Med)
1200 S. Columbia Rd.   Phone: (701) 780-5187
Grand Forks, ND 58201   Janise Paulson Dorman, Libn.
Founded: 1952. **Staff:** Prof 1; Other 1. **Subjects:** Medicine, nursing, allied health sciences. **Holdings:** 525 books; 2 VF drawers of pamphlets and clippings. **Subscriptions:** 220 journals and other serials. **Services:** Interlibrary loans; copying; computer bibliographic searches; library open to public on request. **Networks/Consortia:** Member of Greater Midwest Regional Medical Library Network (Region 3).

★13833★
UNITED HOSPITALS MEDICAL CENTER OF NEWARK - LIBRARY/ INFORMATION SERVICES (Med)
15 S. Ninth St.   Phone: (201) 268-8774
Newark, NJ 07107   Rosary S. Gilheany, Dir./Lib. & Ref.Serv.
Founded: 1960. **Staff:** Prof 2; Other 2. **Subjects:** Medicine, nursing, ophthalmology, otorhinolaryngology, pediatrics, hospital administration. **Special Collections:** Orthopedics (2000 volumes in branch library at Orthopedic Hospital); Learning Resource Center Collection. **Holdings:** 4638 books; 6162 bound periodical volumes; tapes; 6 VF drawers of pamphlets, clippings, reprints; 2 VF drawers of archives; 3 shelves of archival materials; 655 AV programs; 7 audio cassette subscriptions (5 years). **Subscriptions:** 250 journals and other serials. **Services:** Interlibrary loans; copying; bibliographies for professionals; library open to public for reference use only by referral. **Computerized Information Services:** DIALOG, MEDLINE. **Networks/Consortia:** Member of Cosmopolitan Biomedical Library Consortium (CBLC); Health Sciences Libraries of New Jersey. **Publications:** Library Informer (newsletter and acquisitions list), quarterly. **Special Catalogs:** Children's Health Audiovisual Materials Project Catalog (pamphlet). **Staff:** Linda De Muro, Pub.Serv.Libn.

★13834★
UNITED ILLUMINATING COMPANY - LIBRARY (Sci-Tech; Energy)
80 Temple St.   Phone: (203) 787-7690
New Haven, CT 06506   Marie S. Richardson, Libn.
Founded: 1979. **Staff:** Prof 1. **Subjects:** Electricity - generation, distribution; energy resources; computer science; management; engineering. **Holdings:** 2200 books. **Subscriptions:** 445 journals and other serials; 5 newspapers. **Services:** Interlibrary loans; copying; library open to public by appointment.

Computerized Information Services: DIALOG, DOE/RECON. Publications: Something New at the UI Library (newsletter).

★13835★
UNITED LODGE OF THEOSOPHISTS - THEOSOPHY HALL - LIBRARY (Rel-Theol)
347 E. 72nd St.   Phone: (212) 535-2230
New York, NY 10021
Founded: 1922. Subjects: Theosophy, comparative religion, Buddhism, Hinduism, philosophy, psychology, psychic research, mythology and symbolism, Christian church history, the heretics. Special Collections: Original editions of writings of H.P. Blavatsky and W.Q. Judge. Holdings: 6500 books; 325 bound periodical volumes. Services: Library open to public.

UNITED MEDICAL STAFF OF BOULDER - BOULDER VALLEY MEDICAL LIBRARY
See: Boulder Valley Medical Library

★13836★
UNITED MERCHANTS AND MANUFACTURING COMPANY - RESEARCH CENTER LIBRARY (Sci-Tech)
Box 64   Phone: (803) 593-4461
Langley, SC 29834   Larry G. Smith, Mgr., Res.Serv.
Founded: 1962. Staff: Prof 1; Other 1. Subjects: Chemistry and chemical engineering, textiles. Holdings: 2500 books; 2200 bound periodical volumes; 500 other cataloged items. Subscriptions: 44 journals and other serials. Services: Library not open to public.

UNITED METHODIST CHURCH - ALABAMA-WEST FLORIDA CONFERENCE - DEPOSITORY OF ARCHIVAL AND HISTORICAL MATERIALS
See: Huntingdon College - Houghton Memorial Library

★13837★
UNITED METHODIST CHURCH - CENTRAL ILLINOIS CONFERENCE - CONFERENCE HISTORICAL SOCIETY LIBRARY (Rel-Theol)
1211 N. Park
Box 2050
Bloomington, IL 61702-2050
Staff: 2. Subjects: History of the Illinois Conference since 1824, Methodism in Illinois, United Brethren and Evangelical Churches. Holdings: 1200 books and bound periodical volumes; local church histories; biographies; early conference journals on microfilm. Services: Library open to public. Publications: Historical Messenger, quarterly.

★13838★
UNITED METHODIST CHURCH - GENERAL COMMISSION ON ARCHIVES AND HISTORY - LIBRARY AND ARCHIVES (Rel-Theol)
Box 127
Madison, NJ 07940   Kenneth E. Rowe, Libn.
Staff: Prof 3; Other 3. Subjects: Church records of Methodist Episcopal Church, Methodist Episcopal Church (South), Methodist Protestant Church, Methodist Church, Evangelical United Brethren Church, United Brethren in Christ Church, Evangelical Church, Evangelical Association, United Evangelical Church; United Methodist Church. Special Collections: Board of Mission Correspondence from missionaries and overseas conference journals; private papers of Methodist leaders and bishops. Holdings: 70,000 books; 600 bound periodical volumes; 4 million archival items; 100,000 feet of microfilm; 100 tubes of blueprints. Subscriptions: 200 journals and other serials. Services: Interlibrary loans; copying; library open to public with restrictions. Publications: Historians' Digest (newsletter), quarterly; Methodist History, quarterly. Remarks: Includes the holdings of the Association of Methodist Historical Societies and the former E.U.B. Historical Society. Staff: William C. Beal, Jr., Archv.

★13839★
UNITED METHODIST CHURCH - HISTORICAL SOCIETY OF THE EASTERN PENNSYLVANIA CONFERENCE - ARCHIVES ROOM (Rel-Theol)
Gossard Memorial Library
Lebanon Valley College   Phone: (717) 867-4411
Annville, PA 17003   Rev. Robert Curry, Archv.-Libn.
Founded: 1957. Subjects: Eastern Conference materials, general former Evangelical United Brethren Church materials. Holdings: 578 books; 42 bound periodical volumes; 463 conference proceedings; 53 VF drawers of unbound archival materials. Services: Archives Room open to public by appointment. Formerly: Evangelical United Brethren Church - Historical Society of the Eastern Conference. Staff: Carl Y. Ehrhart, Act.Libn.

UNITED METHODIST CHURCH - KANSAS EAST CONFERENCE - COMMISSION ON ARCHIVES AND HISTORY
See: Baker University - Archives and Historical Library

★13840★
UNITED METHODIST CHURCH - KANSAS WEST CONFERENCE - ARCHIVES AND HISTORY DEPOSITORY (Rel-Theol)
Southwestern College Library   Phone: (316) 221-4150
Winfield, KS 67156   Irene Lively, Archv.
Founded: 1928. Staff: 1. Subjects: Methodism, especially Kansas Methodism. Special Collections: Methodist conference journals and disciplines; unpublished histories of Central Kansas Conference Methodist churches (350). Holdings: 1000 volumes; church records; newspapers; manuscripts; memoirs; obituaries. Services: Copying; archives open to public by appointment.

★13841★
UNITED METHODIST CHURCH - NEBRASKA CONFERENCE - HISTORICAL CENTER (Rel-Theol)
Lucas Bldg.
Nebraska Wesleyan University
Box 4553   Phone: (402) 466-6769
Lincoln, NE 68504   Bernice Boilesen, Cur.
Founded: 1942. Staff: Prof 1. Subjects: United Methodist history, Nebraska Conference. Special Collections: Bible Collection (200); Conference Journals - Methodist, 1856 to present, Evangelical United Brethren, 1880 to present. Holdings: 15,000 volumes. Services: Copying; center open to public.

★13842★
UNITED METHODIST CHURCH - NORTHERN CALIFORNIA-NEVADA CONFERENCE - J.A.B. FRY RESEARCH LIBRARY (Rel-Theol)
University of the Pacific   Phone: (209) 946-2269
Stockton, CA 95211   Rev. William Bowler Jefferies, Dir. of Archv.
Staff: Prof 1. Subjects: Methodism, church history, Western Americana. Special Collections: Hymnbooks (900). Holdings: 2700 books; 400 bound periodical volumes; 5000 archival items. Subscriptions: 30 journals and other serials. Services: Interlibrary loans; copying; library open to public by appointment.

UNITED METHODIST CHURCH - PACIFIC AND SOUTHWEST CONFERENCE - ARCHIVES
See: School of Theology at Claremont - Theology Library

★13843★
UNITED METHODIST CHURCH - PHILADELPHIA ANNUAL CONFERENCE - HISTORICAL SOCIETY LIBRARY (Hist; Rel-Theol)
326 New St.   Phone: (215) 925-7788
Philadelphia, PA 19106   Brian McCloskey, Adm.
Subjects: Methodist history and related subjects. Special Collections: Annual Conference minutes, General Conference minutes of the United Methodist Church, 1784 to present. Holdings: 7000 books. Subscriptions: 20 journals and other serials. Services: Library open to students for reference.

★13844★
UNITED METHODIST CHURCH - SOUTH DAKOTA CONFERENCE - COMMITTEE ON ARCHIVES AND HISTORY - LIBRARY (Rel-Theol)
1331 W. University Ave.
Box 460   Phone: (605) 996-6552
Mitchell, SD 57301   Barbara Rich Sorenson, Archv.
Staff: Prof 1. Subjects: Religion, church history. Holdings: 2800 books; 300 bound periodical volumes; 350 slides and cassettes. Services: Copying; library open to public.

★13845★
UNITED METHODIST CHURCH - SOUTHERN NEW ENGLAND CONFERENCE - HISTORICAL SOCIETY LIBRARY (Rel-Theol)
745 Commonwealth Ave.   Phone: (617) 353-3034
Boston, MA 02215   William E. Zimpfer, Libn.
Subjects: New England Methodist history, Wesleyana. Holdings: 12,375 books; 300 bound periodical volumes; 200 other cataloged items; 1000 pamphlets; 8000 letters; 30 VF drawers on local churches. Subscriptions: 10 journals and other serials. Services: Interlibrary loans; copying; library open to public. Automated Operations: Computerized cataloging. Remarks: The library is housed in the library of the Boston University School of Theology and serviced by that staff on a contract basis.

UNITED METHODIST CHURCH - UPPER ROOM DEVOTIONAL LIBRARY, MUSEUM AND ARCHIVES
See: Upper Room Devotional Library, Museum and Archives

★13846★

UNITED METHODIST CHURCH - WESLEY THEOLOGICAL SEMINARY - LIBRARY (Rel-Theol)
4500 Massachusetts Ave., N.W.   Phone: (202) 363-0922
Washington, DC 20016   Roland E. Kircher, Dir.
Founded: 1882. **Staff:** Prof 3; Other 3. **Subjects:** Theology, religion, philosophy and related fields. **Special Collections:** Materials related to the former Methodist Protestant Church; Wesleyana. **Holdings:** 106,000 books; 13,000 bound periodical volumes; 2000 AV items; 825 tapes. **Subscriptions:** 525 journals; 10 newspapers. **Services:** Interlibrary loans; copying; library may be used by special arrangement with the librarian. **Automated Operations:** Computerized cataloging and ILL. **Computerized Information Services:** OCLC. **Networks/Consortia:** Member of Washington Theological Consortium; Consortium of Universities of the Washington Metropolitan Area; CAPCON.

★13847★

UNITED METHODIST CHURCH - WISCONSIN CONFERENCE - ARCHIVES (Hist; Rel-Theol)
750 Windsor St., Suite 302   Phone: (608) 837-7320
Sun Prairie, WI 53590   Mary E. Schroeder, Archv./Hist.Libn.
Staff: Prof 1. **Subjects:** Church history. **Holdings:** 2000 books; 50 bound periodical volumes; 20 VF drawers of archival materials; 15 boxes of newspapers. **Services:** Copying; archives open to public on a limited schedule. **Special Indexes:** Biographical indexes; church indexes.

★13848★

UNITED METHODIST CHURCH - YELLOWSTONE ANNUAL CONFERENCE - ARCHIVES (Rel-Theol)*
Box 297   Phone: (406) 745-3541
St. Ignatius, MT 59865   Rev. Ron Lang, Chm.
Subjects: Personal papers of Brother Van Orsdel (Methodist circuit rider in Montana); papers of other early-day Methodist ministers. **Holdings:** Books of historical value; microfilm; church materials of historical importance. **Services:** Archives open to public for reference use by appointment. **Special Catalogs:** List of United Methodist ministers who served within conference boundaries. **Remarks:** The archive is located in the library of Rocky Mountain College, Billings, MT 59102.

★13849★

UNITED METHODIST COMMN. ON ARCHIVES & HIST. - MINNESOTA ANNUAL CONFERENCE - ARCHIVES & HISTORICAL LIB. (Rel-Theol)
122 W. Franklin Ave., Rm. 400   Phone: (612) 870-3657
Minneapolis, MN 55404   Thelma Boeder, Archv./Exec.Sec.
Founded: 1856. **Staff:** Prof 1. **Subjects:** United Methodist Church and Evangelical United Brethren history, particularly in the Minnesota Conference; Methodism. **Special Collections:** Records of many discontinued churches in Minnesota Conference; Church Disciplines; annual conference minutes; journals. **Holdings:** 2000 books; 100 bound periodical volumes; archival records. **Services:** Copying; library open to public for reference use only.

★13850★

UNITED METHODIST COMMISSION ON ARCHIVES & HISTORY - NORTHWEST TEXAS ANNUAL CONFERENCE - ARCHIVES (Rel-Theol)
McMurry College
Jay-Rollins Library
Box 296   Phone: (915) 692-4130
Abilene, TX 79697   Jewell Posey, Archv.
Staff: Prof 1; Other 1. **Subjects:** Church history. **Special Collections:** J.O. Haymes (6 boxes); O.P. Clark (1 box); Cal C. Wright (21 linear feet); Alsie H. Carleton (10 linear feet). **Holdings:** 400 books; 100 bound periodical volumes; 200 membership minutes; 1 VF drawer of local church histories; 15 boxes of unbound reports and publicity; 48 cases of sermon manuscripts. **Services:** Copying; library open to public with restrictions.

★13851★

UNITED METHODIST COMMN. ON ARCHIVES & HISTORY - SOUTH CAROLINA CONFERENCE - HISTORICAL LIBRARY (Rel-Theol)
Wofford College
Spartanburg, SC 29301   Phone: (803) 585-4821
                                       Herbert Hucks, Jr., Cur.
Subjects: Methodist history with particular reference to South Carolina Methodism. **Holdings:** 1600 books and bound periodical volumes; minutes of the South Carolina conference; letters; notes; manuscripts. **Services:** Library open to public for reference use only.

★13852★

UNITED METHODIST HISTORICAL SOCIETY - BALTIMORE ANNUAL CONFERENCE - LOVELY LANE MUSEUM LIBRARY (Rel-Theol; Hist)
2200 St. Paul St.   Phone: (301) 889-4458
Baltimore, MD 21218   Rev. Edwin Schell, Exec.Sec./Libn.
Founded: 1855. **Staff:** Prof 2; Other 1. **Subjects:** Religion, Wesleyana, American church history, higher education, Methodism. **Special Collections:** Baltimore Conference Journal and papers; letters of Bishop Asbury; journals of early Methodist preachers; letters and notes of Bishop Coke; John F. Goucher papers; Maryland church records. **Holdings:** 4253 books; 280 bound periodical volumes; 16,000 reports, personal papers, church histories, clippings. **Subscriptions:** 25 journals and other serials; 10 newspapers. **Services:** Interlibrary loans; copying; library open to qualified researchers. **Publications:** Third Century Methodism, triennial; annual reports. **Special Catalogs:** United Methodist Clergy - Baltimore and Vicinity, 1773-1983 (card). **Staff:** Betty Ammons, Asst.Libn.

★13853★

UNITED METHODIST PUBLISHING HOUSE - LIBRARY (Publ; Rel-Theol)
201 Eighth Ave., S.   Phone: (615) 749-6335
Nashville, TN 37202   Rosalyn Lewis, Libn.
Staff: Prof 2; Other 2. **Subjects:** United Methodist Publishing House Archives, Methodist history, religion. **Special Collections:** Wesleyana (575 items). **Holdings:** 70,000 books; 14,000 bound periodical volumes; 60 VF drawers; 1100 reels of microfilm; 220 German language Methodistica; portraits; group pictures. **Subscriptions:** 263 journals and other serials; 62 newspapers. **Services:** Interlibrary loans; copying; library open to public for research use only. **Automated Operations:** Computerized cataloging. **Computerized Information Services:** OCLC. **Networks/Consortia:** Member of SOLINET. **Special Indexes:** Union List of United Methodist Ministers, 1773-1972 (150,000 cards). **Remarks:** An alternate telephone number is 749-6437. **Staff:** Agnes Fair, Tech.Serv.Libn.

★13854★

UNITED NATIONS ASSOCIATION OF THE UNITED STATES OF AMERICA - GREATER ST. LOUIS CHAPTER - LIBRARY (Soc Sci)
7359 Forsyth Blvd.   Phone: (314) 721-1961
St. Louis, MO 63105   Alice W. Dunlop, Libn.
Staff: 2. **Subjects:** International culture and history, political influence, United Nations, peace, conservation, nutrition. **Holdings:** 1200 books; 143 files on all U.N. member countries; U.N. publications; files on U.N. agencies. **Subscriptions:** 52 journals and other serials. **Services:** Interlibrary loans; copying; library open to public. **Networks/Consortia:** Member of St. Louis Regional Library Network. **Publications:** UN Center Newsletter.

★13855★

UNITED NATIONS - CENTRE FOR HUMAN SETTLEMENTS - INFORMATION OFFICE (Soc Sci)
University of British Columbia
2206 E. Mall   Phone: (604) 228-5095
Vancouver, BC, Canada V6T 1W5   James Carney, Info.Off.
Staff: Prof 1; Other 1. **Subjects:** Human settlements issues. **Special Collections:** Government documentation relating to the 1976 United Nations Conference on Human Settlements; over 200 films on human settlements issues produced by governments. **Holdings:** 50 published works on human settlements; documents; reports; information directories; videotapes; films. **Subscriptions:** 28 journals and other serials. **Services:** Interlibrary loans; copying; office open to public. **Publications:** Habitat News, 3/year; list of other publications - available on request. **Special Catalogs:** Film Catalog, English or French. **Remarks:** The centre's headquarters is in Nairobi, Kenya (Box 30030). There are additional information offices in Amman, Bangkok, Budapest, Geneva and Mexico City. **Also Known As:** Habitat.

★13856★

UNITED NATIONS - CENTRE ON TRANSNATIONAL CORPORATIONS - LIBRARY (Bus-Fin)
United Nations   Phone: (212) 754-3352
New York, NY 10017   Samuel K.B. Asante, Dir.,Adv./Info.Serv.Div.
Founded: 1976. **Subjects:** Transnational corporations, foreign direct investment. **Special Collections:** Company directories, corporate reports, United Nations documents. **Holdings:** Figures not available. **Services:** Library open to public by written or telephone application. **Automated Operations:** Computerized cataloging. **Computerized Information Services:** DIALOG, Dow Jones News/Retrieval, Dun & Bradstreet Corporation, SDC; internal databases. **Publications:** List of publications - available on request; library accessions lists, quarterly. **Staff:** Edith Ward, TNC Affairs Off.; Paul Dysenchuk, Res.Asst./Libn.

UNITED NATIONS COLLECTION
See: New York University

★13857★
UNITED NATIONS FUND FOR POPULATION ACTIVITIES - LIBRARY (Soc Sci)
220 E. 42nd St., Rm. DN-1710   Phone: (212) 850-5809
New York, NY 10017   Avi Green, Chf.
Staff: Prof 2; Other 2. **Subjects:** Population, family planning, economic development. **Holdings:** 4000 books; 2500 reprints. **Subscriptions:** 350 journals and other serials; 5 newspapers. **Services:** Interlibrary loans; copying; SDI; library open to graduate students and professional researchers. **Automated Operations:** Computerized cataloging. **Computerized Information Services:** DIALOG, MEDLINE, POPLINE; internal database. **Networks/Consortia:** Member of Association for Population/Family Planning Libraries and Information Centers - International (APLIC-International); Consortium of Foundation Libraries. **Publications:** Acquisitions list, bimonthly - available upon request; UNFPA Project Publications Abstracts - for internal distribution only. **Staff:** David P. Rose, Tech.Serv.Libn.

★13858★
UNITED NATIONS HEADQUARTERS - DAG HAMMARSKJOLD LIBRARY (Soc Sci)
United Nations   Phone: (212) 754-7412
New York, NY 10017   Vladimir Orlov, Dir.
Founded: 1946. **Staff:** Prof 65; Other 86. **Subjects:** Political affairs, economics, national and international law, social affairs, international relations, science and technology, statistics, transnational corporations, history and activities of the United Nations. **Special Collections:** U.N. and specialized agencies documents; League of Nations documents; Woodrow Wilson Memorial Library (international affairs, 1918-1945); official gazettes of member states. **Holdings:** 380,000 volumes; 70,000 maps; 12,300 reels of microfilm; 50,000 microcards; 180,000 microfiche. **Subscriptions:** 15,000 journals and other serials; 200 newspapers. **Services:** Interlibrary loans; copying (limited); library not open to public. **Automated Operations:** Computerized cataloging. **Computerized Information Services:** NEXIS; UNDOC Current Index, Current Bibliographic Information (internal databases). **Publications:** UNDOC: Current Index, 10/year - by subscription; Index to Proceedings, by session; Current Bibliographical Information, 12/year - available by subscription. **Staff:** Joseph L. Fuchs, Chf., Users' Serv.; Nathalie Dusoulier, Chf., Tech.Oper/Pubn.Serv.

★13859★
UNITED NEGRO COLLEGE FUND, INC. - DEPARTMENT OF ARCHIVES AND HISTORY (Educ)
500 E. 62nd St.   Phone: (212) 644-9672
New York, NY 10021   Gregory S. Hunter, Dir. of Archv.Prog.
Staff: Prof 3. **Subjects:** Higher education for blacks, history of philanthropy and fund raising. **Holdings:** 750 cubic feet of department. **Services:** Copying; department open to public with restrictions. **Staff:** Paula Williams, Asst.Archv.; Albert Palazzo, Proc.Archv.

UNITED OF OMAHA
See: Mutual of Omaha/United of Omaha

UNITED PRESBYTERIAN CHURCH OF THE ATONEMENT
See: Presbyterian Church of the Atonement

UNITED PRESBYTERIAN CHURCH IN THE U.S.A.
See: Presbyterian Church (U.S.A.)

UNITED PRESBYTERIAN CHURCH IN THE U.S.A. - PROGRAM AGENCY - GHOST RANCH CONFERENCE CENTER
See: Ghost Ranch Conference Center

UNITED PRESS INTERNATIONAL PHOTOGRAPH LIBRARY
See: Bettmann Archive

★13860★
UNITED SERVICES AUTOMOBILE ASSOCIATION - CORPORATE LIBRARY (Bus-Fin)
USAA Bldg.   Phone: (512) 690-2900
San Antonio, TX 78229   Frances Bethea Day, Mgr., Corp.Lib.
Founded: 1967. **Staff:** Prof 2; Other 2. **Subjects:** Insurance, business, management, computer science. **Holdings:** 3600 books; 8 drawers of pamphlets. **Subscriptions:** 300 journals and other serials. **Services:** Interlibrary loans; copying; SDI; library open to public by appointment. **Automated Operations:** Computerized cataloging. **Computerized Information Services:** DIALOG, SDC, OCLC, Dow Jones News/Retrieval, NEXIS; internal database. **Networks/Consortia:** Member of Council of Research and Academic Libraries (CORAL); AMIGOS Bibliographic Council, Inc. **Publications:** Reviews in Employee Newsletter - for internal distribution only. **Staff:** Barbara J. Schanzer, Libn.

★13861★
UNITED SOCIETY OF BELIEVERS - THE SHAKER LIBRARY (Rel-Theol)
Shaker Village, Sabbathday Lake   Phone: (207) 926-4865
Poland Spring, ME 04274   Bro. Theodore E. Johnson, Dir.
Staff: Prof 3; Other 2. **Subjects:** Shaker theology and history, biography, art, music, technology, herbology, historical agriculture, American communal societies. **Special Collections:** The Koreshan Unity; Christian Israelite Church; Religious Society of Friends. **Holdings:** 16,143 volumes; 8000 manuscripts; 20 VF drawers of catalogs, labels, broadsides; 8 VF drawers of tracts and pamphlets; 13 VF drawers of photographs, slides and maps; 385 reels of microfilm. **Subscriptions:** 106 journals and other serials. **Services:** Copying; library open to public by appointment. **Publications:** The Shaker Quarterly. **Staff:** Sr. R. Mildred Barker, Cur. of Mss.; Sr. Frances A. Carr, Archv.

★13862★
U.S. ADVISORY COMMISSION ON INTERGOVERNMENTAL RELATIONS - LIBRARY (Soc Sci)
1111 20th St., N.W.   Phone: (202) 653-5034
Washington, DC 20575   Patricia A. Koch, Libn.
Staff: Prof 1. **Subjects:** Intergovernmental relations, state and local government, metropolitan problems, taxation, federal and state aid, public administration, housing and development. **Holdings:** 15,000 books. **Subscriptions:** 300 journals and other serials. **Services:** Interlibrary loans; copying; library open to public. **Publications:** Periodical Index.

★13863★
U.S. AGENCY FOR INTERNATIONAL DEVELOPMENT - DEVELOPMENT INFORMATION CENTER (Soc Sci)
320 21st St., N.W., Rm. 105, SA-18   Phone: (703) 235-1000
Washington, DC 20523   Joanne M. Paskar, Hd.
Founded: 1978. **Staff:** Prof 6; Other 2. **Subjects:** Foreign assistance administration, agricultural and rural development, education, health and population planning, science and technology, engineering, transportation, irrigation, energy. **Holdings:** 100,000 books and reports; 4000 AID foreign assistance program documentation; 10,000 AID research reports on microfiche; FAO technical publications on microfiche. **Subscriptions:** 250 journals and other serials. **Services:** Interlibrary loans; library open to public. **Automated Operations:** Computerized cataloging. **Computerized Information Services:** DIALOG, SDC, OCLC, AID Development Information System (internal database). **Publications:** AID Research and Development Abstracts, quarterly - to government agencies, development organizations, research institutions, libraries. **Special Catalogs:** Research Literature for Development, Volume I: Food Production and Nutrition, December 1976; Volume II: Food Production and Nutrition; Development and Economics; Education and Human Resources; Health; Selected Development Areas, December 1977 (both book catalogs). **Remarks:** Library is located at 1601 N. Kent St., Arlington, VA.

U.S. AGENCY FOR INTERNATIONAL DEVELOPMENT - NITROGEN FIXATION BY TROPICAL AGRICULTURAL LEGUMES
See: Nitrogen Fixation by Tropical Agricultural Legumes

★13864★
U.S. AGENCY FOR INTERNATIONAL DEVELOPMENT - WATER & SANITATION FOR HEALTH PROJECT - INFORMATION CENTER (Env-Cons)
1611 N. Kent St., Rm. 1002   Phone: (703) 243-8200
Arlington, VA 22209   James E. Beverly, Info.Dir.
Staff: Prof 2. **Subjects:** Water supply, sanitation, environmental health, technology transfer. **Holdings:** 2500 reports and texts focusing on rural and near-urban areas in developing countries; reports on 66 least-developed countries. **Subscriptions:** 35 journals and other serials; 50 newsletters. **Services:** Center open to public. **Computerized Information Services:** DIALOG, SDC, BRS; internal database. **Also Known As:** WASH Information Center. **Staff:** Dan Campbell, Libn.

★13865★
U.S. AIR FORCE ACADEMY - LAW LIBRARY (Law)
                                      Phone: (303) 472-3680
Colorado Springs, CO 80840   Col. M.E. Kinevan, Prof. of Law
Subjects: Law - general, constitutional, governmental contract, international. **Holdings:** 5492 volumes. **Subscriptions:** 126 journals and other serials. **Services:** Library open to faculty and students only. **Staff:** Major Frank Dodge

★13866★
U.S. AIR FORCE ACADEMY - LIBRARY (Mil; Sci-Tech)
Phone: (303) 472-2590
Colorado Springs, CO 80840   Lt.Col. Reiner H. Schaeffer, Dir. of Libs.
Founded: 1955. **Staff:** Prof 16; Other 35. **Subjects:** Science, technology, humanities, social sciences, military art and science, aeronautics. **Special Collections:** Archival materials relating to the Air Force Academy; Colonel Richard Gimbel Aeronautics History Library (20,000 items); falconry. **Holdings:** 323251 books; 84,685 bound periodical volumes; 4522 phonograph records; 133,700 U.S. Government documents; 13,607 reels of microfilm; 395,554 reports on microfiche; 2000 maps. **Subscriptions:** 2719 journals and other serials; 101 newspapers. **Services:** Interlibrary loans; copying; library open to public with permission of the director. **Automated Operations:** Computerized cataloging. **Computerized Information Services:** DIALOG, SDC, BRS, OCLC, NASA/RECON, MEDLARS, DTIC. **Networks/Consortia:** Member of FEDLINK; Plains and Peaks Regional Library System; Bibliographical Center for Research, Rocky Mountain Region, Inc. (BCR). **Publications:** New Books List, bimonthly; Handbook; special bibliographies, irregular. **Staff:** Donald J. Barrett, Asst.Dir., Pub.Serv.; Capt. James A. Robb, Exec.Off.; Elisabeth J. Fleenor, Chf., Cat.Div.; Ms. Lee R. McLaughlin, Acq.Div.; Elizabeth Kysely, Chf., Ref.Div.; Duane Reed, Spec.Coll.Libn.

★13867★
U.S. AIR FORCE ACADEMY - MEDICAL LIBRARY (Med)
Phone: (303) 472-5107
Colorado Springs, CO 80840   Jeanne Entze, Libn.
Staff: 1. **Subjects:** Medicine. **Holdings:** 3223 books. **Subscriptions:** 285 journals and other serials. **Services:** Interlibrary loans; copying; library open to public for reference use only. **Automated Operations:** Computerized cataloging. **Computerized Information Services:** DIALOG. **Networks/Consortia:** Member of Colorado Council of Medical Librarians.

★13868★
U.S. AIR FORCE - ACCOUNTING AND FINANCE CENTER - TECHNICAL LIBRARY (Bus-Fin)
AFAFC/FL7040   Phone: (303) 370-7566
Denver, CO 80279   Alreeta Viehdorfer, Chf.Adm.Libn.
Founded: 1951. **Staff:** Prof 2; Other 1. **Subjects:** Accounting, data processing, business, management. **Holdings:** 8100 books; 148,500 Armed Forces and Defense Departments' directives and other government documents. **Subscriptions:** 340 journals and other serials; 10 newspapers. **Services:** Interlibrary loans; library open to federal employees. **Automated Operations:** Computerized cataloging. **Computerized Information Services:** OCLC, DIALOG, SDC. Performs searches on cost recovery basis. **Networks/Consortia:** Member of FEDLINK. **Staff:** Wilma A. Daane, Ref.Libn.

★13869★
U.S. AIR FORCE - AEROSPACE MEDICAL DIVISION - SCHOOL OF AEROSPACE MEDICINE - STRUGHOLD AEROMEDICAL LIBRARY (Med)
Phone: (516) 536-3322
Brooks AFB, TX 78235   Fred W. Todd, Chf.Libn.
Founded: 1918. **Staff:** Prof 12; Other 6. **Subjects:** Aerospace medicine, bioastronautics, bionucleonics, clinical medicine, dentistry, life sciences. **Holdings:** 33,296 books; 87,389 bound periodical volumes; 44,916 microfiche; 143,142 technical reports. **Subscriptions:** 2089 journals and other serials; 15 newspapers. **Services:** Interlibrary loans; copying; SDI; library open by special permission. **Automated Operations:** Computerized cataloging. **Computerized Information Services:** DIALOG, SDC, DTIC, MEDLARS, DOE/RECON, NASA/RECON, OCLC, BRS, NIH-EPA Chemical Information System; National Technical Information Service (NTIS), Institute for Scientific Information (ISI) Search Network, EBSCO Subscription Services, National Pesticide Information Retrieval System (NPIRS). **Networks/Consortia:** Member of TALON; Council of Research and Academic Libraries (CORAL); AMIGOS Bibliographic Council, Inc.; Health Oriented Libraries of San Antonio (HOLSA). **Publications:** Monthly Newsletter; Library Accessions List, monthly. **Special Indexes:** KWIC index to current serials titles; Indexes to Aeromedical Reviews and Technical Reports for the School of Aerospace Medicine (book). **Staff:** Bonnie Fridley, Chf., Pub.Serv.; Olive N. Brewster, Chf., Tech.Proc.; Diana Akins, Search Anl.; Dewey A. Goff, Jr., Chf., Docs.; Elsie Wagener, ILL Libn.; Kimmie Yu, Cat.; Marion Green, Chf.Med.Ed.; Mildred Bensinger, Med.Ed.; Ena Shaw, Med.Ed.; John Glowacz, Med.Ed.

★13870★
U.S. AIR FORCE - AIR FORCE MANPOWER & PERSONNEL CENTER - MORALE, WELFARE & RECREATION DIVISION - LIBRARY SERVICES BR.
AFMPC/MPCSOL   Phone: (512) 652-3037
Randolph AFB, TX 78150   Tony Dakan, Dir., USAF Libs.
Remarks: Section is administrative headquarters for Air Force library services

throughout the world with a total of 340 library facilities and a book stock of more than 5 million volumes.

★13871★
U.S. AIR FORCE - AIR FORCE SYSTEMS COMMAND - AIR FORCE GEOPHYSICS LABORATORY - RESEARCH LIBRARY (Sci-Tech; Comp Sci)
Hanscom Air Force Base   Phone: (617) 861-4895
Bedford, MA 01731   Ruth K. Seidman, Dir.
Staff: Prof 9; Other 8. **Subjects:** Physical and environmental sciences, geophysics, meteorology, math and computer science, astronomy and astrophysics, electronics and electrical engineering, chemical and materials sciences. **Special Collections:** Oriental Science Library (35,000 volumes); scientific manuscripts of 3rd and 4th Lords Rayleigh; early ballooning and aeronautics (200 volumes); rare books (2500 volumes). **Holdings:** 257,000 books and bound periodical volumes; 49,817 unbound technical reports; 1583 audio materials; 1548 reels of microfilm; 76,374 microfiche; 243 cassettes; 40 VF drawers of translations. **Subscriptions:** 2289 journals and other serials. **Services:** Interlibrary loans; copying; library open to public with restrictions. **Automated Operations:** Computerized cataloging and serials. **Computerized Information Services:** DIALOG, SDC, BRS, OCLC. **Networks/Consortia:** Member of FEDLINK. **Staff:** John W. Armstrong, Selection Libn.; Elfrieda L. Cavallari, Chf., Cat.; Ellen K. Dobi, Chf., Ref. & Circ.; Evano L. Cunha, Acq.Libn.

★13872★
U.S. AIR FORCE - AIR FORCE SYSTEMS COMMAND - LIBRARY DIVISION
AFSC/MPSL, Andrews Air Force Base   Phone: (301) 981-2598
Washington, DC 20334   Frances M. Quinn, Dir., Command Libs.
Staff: Prof 1; Other 1. **Remarks:** Director of Command Libraries is responsible for establishing plans and policies for library service in 22 Air Force Systems Command technical and base libraries.

★13873★
U.S. AIR FORCE - AIR FORCE SYSTEMS COMMAND - TECHNICAL INFORMATION CENTER (Mil)
Andrews AFB, MPSLT   Phone: (301) 981-3551
Washington, DC 20334   Yvonne A. Kinkaid, Chf.
Founded: 1952. **Staff:** Prof 1; Other 2. **Subjects:** Aerospace systems, management, energy, military affairs, operations research, government contracting, unconventional warfare, computer science. **Holdings:** 9900 books; 10,900 technical reports; 3000 reels of microfilm; 1400 audio cassettes; 250 video cassettes. **Subscriptions:** 500 journals and other serials; 40 newspapers. **Services:** Interlibrary loans; center not open to public. **Automated Operations:** Computerized cataloging. **Computerized Information Services:** DIALOG, The Source, DTIC, SDC, New York Times Information Service. **Networks/Consortia:** Member of FEDLINK.

★13874★
U.S. AIR FORCE - AIR FORCE SYSTEMS COMMAND - TECHNICAL INFORMATION CENTER (Sci-Tech)†
6585th Test Group/TSL   Phone: (505) 479-6511
Holloman AFB, NM 88330   Elizabeth Mohr, Libn.
Founded: 1954. **Staff:** Prof 1. **Subjects:** Electrical and electronic engineering, computer and data processing, physics, aerodynamics, mathematics. **Holdings:** 10,600 books; 8134 bound periodical volumes; 78 reels of microfilm. **Subscriptions:** 125 journals and other serials. **Services:** Interlibrary loans; copying; center open to public for reference use only. **Automated Operations:** Computerized cataloging. **Computerized Information Services:** DIALOG, OCLC. **Networks/Consortia:** Member of FEDLINK. **Publications:** List of Periodical Holdings.

★13875★
U.S. AIR FORCE - AIR TRAINING COMMAND - LIBRARY PROGRAM (Sci-Tech; Mil)
HQ ATC/DPSOL   Phone: (512) 652-3410
Randolph AFB, TX 78150   Duane A. Johnson, Command Libn.
Staff: Prof 32; Other 118. **Subjects:** Aeronautics, astronautics, engineering, leadership, military history, management, electronics. **Special Collections:** World War II; weather and instrument flying; survival training; education; vocational guidance; foreign affairs; foreign languages. **Holdings:** 433,917 books and bound periodical volumes; 4500 technical reports and documents; 168,580 microforms; 31,026 AV programs; 3910 maps. **Subscriptions:** 5673 journals and other serials; 551 newspapers. **Services:** Interlibrary loans; copying; library not open to public. **Automated Operations:** Computerized cataloging, acquisitions and ILL. **Computerized Information Services:** OCLC, DTIC, LIBS 100 System, New York Times Information Service. **Networks/Consortia:** Member of ILLINET, Council of Research and Academic Libraries (CORAL); Lincoln Trail Libraries System; Coastal Mississippi Library Cooperative (CMLC). **Remarks:** Command Librarian is responsible for

the administration, development and operation of 19 academic, technical and base libraries in Air Training Command. Information represents all 19 libraries.

★13876★
U.S. AIR FORCE - AIR UNIVERSITY - LIBRARY (Mil)
Phone: (205) 293-2606
Maxwell AFB, AL 36112
Robert B. Lane, Dir.
Founded: 1946. **Staff:** Prof 30; Other 40. **Subjects:** Military science, aeronautics, political science, military affairs. **Special Collections:** Air Force Authority materials. **Holdings:** 280,000 books; 95,000 bound periodical volumes; 495,000 cataloged military documents; 650,000 maps and charts; 6600 reels of microfilm of serials and newspapers; 120,000 regulations and manuals; 9000 clippings and pamphlets. **Subscriptions:** 2500 journals and other serials; 50 newspapers. **Services:** Interlibrary loans; SDI; library open to public with security restrictions. **Computerized Information Services:** DTIC, DIALOG, NEXIS, OCLC. **Networks/Consortia:** Member of SOLINET. **Publications:** Air University Library Index to Military Periodicals, quarterly; Air University Abstracts of Student Research Reports, annual - both for limited distribution; Guide to Library Services, occasional. **Staff:** Henry L. Sims, Exec.Off.; Helen N. Taliaferro, Chf., Rd.Serv.Div.; Donald B. Flournoy, Chf., Cartography; Regina A. Mayton, Chf., Sys.Div.

U.S. AIR FORCE - ALBERT F. SIMPSON HISTORICAL RESEARCH CENTER
See: U.S. Air Force - Historical Research Center

★13877★
U.S. AIR FORCE - ARMAMENT DIVISION, AIR FORCE ARMAMENT LABORATORY - TECHNICAL LIBRARY (Sci-Tech)
Phone: (904) 882-3212
Eglin AFB, FL 32542
June C. Stercho, Chf.
Founded: 1955. **Staff:** Prof 3; Other 4. **Subjects:** Aeronautics, electronics, physics, mathematics, biology, chemistry. **Holdings:** 10,575 books; 6052 bound periodical volumes; 172,000 technical reports; 12,200 reports on microfiche; 3322 reels of microfilm. **Subscriptions:** 731 journals and other serials. **Services:** Interlibrary loans; library open to qualified users. **Computerized Information Services:** DTIC, DIALOG, OCLC. **Networks/Consortia:** Member of FEDLINK. **Publications:** Accessions List, semimonthly - for internal distribution only. **Staff:** Mary A. Murphy, Open Lit.Libn.; Mary Weston, Doc.Libn.

★13878★
U.S. AIR FORCE BASE - ALTUS BASE LIBRARY (Mil)†
FL 4419
Phone: (405) 482-8670
Altus AFB, OK 73523
A. Lucille Lowrie, Libn.
Staff: Prof 1; Other 5. **Subjects:** Military. **Holdings:** 24,000 books; recordings; cassettes. **Subscriptions:** 128 journals and other serials; 16 newspapers. **Services:** Interlibrary loans; copying; library open to public with restrictions.

★13879★
U.S. AIR FORCE BASE - ANDREWS BASE LIBRARY (Mil)
FL 4425, Andrews AFB
Phone: (301) 981-6454
Washington, DC 20331
Staff: Prof 1; Other 3. **Subjects:** Aerospace, military history, ethnic literature. **Holdings:** 33,000 books; 180 bound periodical volumes; 2000 phonograph records, reels of microfilm and audio and video cassettes. **Subscriptions:** 300 journals and other serials; 15 newspapers. **Services:** Interlibrary loans; copying; library open to military public only.

★13880★
U.S. AIR FORCE BASE - BARKSDALE BASE LIBRARY (Mil)
FL 4608
Phone: (318) 869-4449
Barksdale AFB, LA 71110
Ronald J. Ferland, Libn.
Staff: Prof 3; Other 4. **Subjects:** Aviation, management, business, history. **Special Collections:** Louisiana history. **Holdings:** 30,174 books; 7200 microforms; 1300 phonograph records. **Subscriptions:** 168 journals and other serials; 17 newspapers. **Services:** Interlibrary loans; copying; library open to public. **Networks/Consortia:** Member of Green Gold Library System. **Staff:** Anita Dietzel, Lib.Techn.

★13881★
U.S. AIR FORCE BASE - BEALE BASE LIBRARY (Mil)
FL 4686
Phone: (916) 634-2706
Beale AFB, CA 95903
Sylvia J. Sefcik, Base Libn.
Staff: Prof 1; Other 2. **Special Collections:** Framed art works; AV Collection. **Holdings:** 35,163 books; 251 reels of microfilm; 2901 phonograph records and tapes. **Subscriptions:** 342 journals and other serials; 37 newspapers. **Services:** Interlibrary loans; copying; library open to public for reference use only. **Special Indexes:** Periodical Holdings.

★13882★
U.S. AIR FORCE BASE - BERGSTROM BASE LIBRARY (Mil)
FL 4857
Phone: (512) 479-4100
Bergstrom AFB, TX 78743
Louise St. John, Base Libn.
Staff: Prof 1; Other 4. **Subjects:** Aeronautics, social sciences, mathematics, U.S. wars, U.S. and foreign history and travel, languages. **Holdings:** 30,255 books; 3 files of pamphlets on foreign countries; 1 file of clippings on current history; 2104 phonograph records, tapes and filmstrips. **Subscriptions:** 260 journals and other serials; 23 newspapers. **Services:** Interlibrary loans; copying; library not open to public.

★13883★
U.S. AIR FORCE BASE - BLYTHEVILLE BASE LIBRARY (Mil)
FL 4634, Bldg. 555
Blytheville AFB, AR 72315
Bethey J. Johnson, Libn.
Staff: Prof 1; Other 3. **Subjects:** Fiction and nonfiction. **Holdings:** 20,000 books. **Subscriptions:** 180 journals and other serials; 18 newspapers. **Services:** Interlibrary loans not open to public.

★13884★
U.S. AIR FORCE BASE - BOLLING BASE LIBRARY (Mil)
Bolling AFB
Phone: (202) 767-4251
Washington, DC 20332
Gloria Guffey, Libn.
Staff: Prof 1; Other 3. **Subjects:** General collection. **Special Collections:** Resource material for the deaf and hearing impaired. **Holdings:** 23,000 books. **Subscriptions:** 101 journals and other serials. **Services:** Interlibrary loans; copying; library open to public on a limited basis. **Special Indexes:** Index to college catalogs and telephone books (microfiche); index to Monarch Notes (microfiche).

★13885★
U.S. AIR FORCE BASE - CANNON BASE LIBRARY (Mil)*
FL 4855
Phone: (505) 784-2786
Cannon AFB, NM 88101
M. Edith Pierce, Libn.
Staff: Prof 1; Other 3. **Subjects:** U.S. Air Force history, New Mexico History, Southwest. **Holdings:** 31,520 books; 1350 bound periodical volumes; 12,763 microfiche; 3030 AV items. **Subscriptions:** 382 journals and other serials; 59 newspapers. **Services:** Interlibrary loans; copying; library open to public with base commander's permission. **Networks/Consortia:** Member of New Mexico Information System (NEMISYS).

★13886★
U.S. AIR FORCE BASE - CARSWELL BASE LIBRARY (Mil)
FL 4689
Phone: (817) 735-5230
Carswell AFB, TX 76127
Christine R. Lain, Libn.
Founded: 1943. **Staff:** Prof 1; Other 3. **Subjects:** General and technical topics. **Holdings:** 21,000 books. **Services:** Interlibrary loans; library open to public with restrictions.

★13887★
U.S. AIR FORCE BASE - CASTLE BASE - BAKER LIBRARY (Mil)†
FL 4672, Bldg. 422
Phone: (209) 726-2630
Castle AFB, CA 95342
Enid L. Wilford, Base Libn.
Founded: 1956. **Staff:** Prof 1; Other 4. **Subjects:** Management, defense management, United States and military history, sociology, aeronautics. **Holdings:** 30,046 books; 30 bound theses; 3059 phonograph records and tapes; 1000 pamphlets; 196 reels of microfilm. **Subscriptions:** 255 journals and other serials; 20 newspapers. **Services:** Interlibrary loans; copying; library open to public for reference use only; affiliated students may borrow books. **Publications:** Minorities bibliographies - for internal distribution only.

★13888★
U.S. AIR FORCE BASE - CHANUTE BASE LIBRARY (Mil)†
FL 3018, Bldg. 95
Phone: (217) 495-3191
Chanute AFB, IL 61868
Founded: 1925. **Subjects:** General and technical subjects. **Holdings:** 25,000 volumes. **Subscriptions:** 308 journals and other serials. **Services:** Interlibrary loans; library open to active duty military and dependents, retired military and dependents, and civilians working at Chanute.

★13889★
U.S. AIR FORCE BASE - CHANUTE BASE TECHNICAL BRANCH LIBRARY (Sci-Tech; Mil)†
Bldg. 95
Phone: (217) 495-3191
Chanute AFB, IL 61868
Annette Gohlke, Libn.
Founded: 1964. **Staff:** Prof 1. **Subjects:** Aerospace, electronics, metallurgy. **Holdings:** 2500 books. **Subscriptions:** 63 journals and other serials. **Services:** Interlibrary loans; library open to military personnel and their dependents.

★13890★
U.S. AIR FORCE BASE - CHARLESTON BASE LIBRARY (Mil)
FL 4418   Phone: (803) 554-3134
Charleston AFB, SC 29404   William E. Darcy, Libn.
Staff: Prof 1; Other 4. **Holdings:** 24,210 books; 3776 photograph records.
Subscriptions: 448 journals and other serials; 94 newspapers. **Services:**
Interlibrary loans; library not open to public.

★13891★
U.S. AIR FORCE BASE - DOVER BASE LIBRARY (Mil)†
FL 4497   Phone: (302) 678-6246
Dover AFB, DE 19901   Linda Yorde, Lib.Techn.
Founded: 1953. **Staff:** Prof 1; Other 5. **Subjects:** History, aviation, general
topics. **Holdings:** 25,500 books; 10,000 microforms; college catalogs on
microfiche. **Subscriptions:** 248 journals and other serials; 18 newspapers.
Services: Interlibrary loans; copying; library open to public for reference use
only.

★13892★
U.S. AIR FORCE BASE - DYESS BASE LIBRARY (Mil)
FL 4661   Phone: (915) 696-2618
Dyess AFB, TX 79607   Edith V. Roebuck, Libn.
Founded: 1957. **Staff:** Prof 1; Other 3. **Subjects:** Social science, Air Force
history. **Special Collections:** Texas history and literature. **Holdings:** 21,000
books; 1500 phonograph records. **Subscriptions:** 225 journals and other
serials; 12 newspapers. **Services:** Interlibrary loans; library open to public for
reference use only. **Publications:** Book List, monthly.

★13893★
U.S. AIR FORCE BASE - EDWARDS BASE LIBRARY (Mil)†
6510th ABG/SSL STOP 115
FL 2805
Bldg. 2665   Phone: (805) 277-2375
Edwards AFB, CA 93523   Orin M. Moyer, Libn.
Founded: 1942. **Staff:** Prof 1; Other 2. **Subjects:** Recreation, education.
Holdings: 22,932 books; 319 bound periodical volumes; 608 phonograph
records; 24 tapes; 694 reels of microfilm; 83 8mm films; 150 cassettes.
Subscriptions: 350 journals and other serials. **Services:** Interlibrary loans;
library not open to public.

★13894★
U.S. AIR FORCE BASE - EGLIN BASE LIBRARY (Mil)
FL 2823   Phone: (904) 882-5088
Eglin AFB, FL 32542   F.P. Morgan, Chf., Lib.Br.
Founded: 1942. **Staff:** Prof 2; Other 5. **Subjects:** Aeronautics, military art
and science, counterinsurgency, aircraft and missile systems, mathematics,
management. **Holdings:** 49,663 books; 1638 bound periodical volumes;
4213 reels of microfilm; 14,245 microfiche; 3745 recordings and tapes;
1062 video cassettes; 14 films; 68 art prints; 7 sculptures; 1273 cassettes.
Subscriptions: 430 journals and other serials; 33 newspapers. **Services:**
Interlibrary loans; library not open to public. **Automated Operations:**
Computerized cataloging. **Computerized Information Services:** OCLC,
DIALOG. **Networks/Consortia:** Member of SOLINET. **Publications:**
Accessions list, bimonthly. **Staff:** Carole B. Steele, Asst.Libn.

★13895★
U.S. AIR FORCE BASE - EIELSON BASE LIBRARY (Mil)*
FL 5004, 5010 CSG/SSL   Phone: (907) 372-4184
Eielson AFB, AK 99702   Stella E. Ludwikowski, Adm.Libn.
Staff: Prof 1; Other 6. **Subjects:** Air Force professional and technical
material, fiction and nonfiction. **Special Collections:** Alaska (463 books);
black culture (160 books); drugs (52 books); children's collection. **Holdings:**
32,755 books and bound periodical volumes; 487 reels of microfilm; 4 VF
drawers. **Subscriptions:** 240 journals and other serials; 24 newspapers.
Services: Interlibrary loans; copying; library open to military and base
employees.

★13896★
U.S. AIR FORCE BASE - ENGLAND BASE LIBRARY (Mil)†
FL 4805   Phone: (318) 448-5760
England AFB, LA 71301   Rupert C. Thom, Libn.
Founded: 1952. **Staff:** Prof 1; Other 3. **Subjects:** Social and applied
sciences, American history and literature. **Special Collections:** Louisiana.
Holdings: 21,000 volumes; 2000 unbound periodicals; 200 microfiche.
Subscriptions: 115 journals and other serials; 12 newspapers. **Services:**
Interlibrary loans; library not open to public. **Publications:** Bibliographies, as
required - through Base Education Office.

★13897★
U.S. AIR FORCE BASE - FAIRCHILD BASE LIBRARY (Mil)
FL 4620   Phone: (509) 247-5556
Fairchild AFB, WA 99011   Nancy M. Bemis, Libn.
Staff: Prof 1; Other 6. **Subjects:** General and technical topics, military
science, Northwest, scouting, genealogy. **Special Collections:** Office
collections (47). **Holdings:** 32,301 books and bound periodical volumes;
3388 phonograph records and tapes; 673 microfiche; 657 reels of microfilm.
Subscriptions: 317 journals and other serials; 17 newspapers. **Services:**
Interlibrary loans; copying; library open to military personnel, dependents and
civilian base employees.

★13898★
U.S. AIR FORCE BASE - GEORGE BASE LIBRARY (Mil)†
FL 4812   Phone: (714) 269-3228
George AFB, CA 92392   Mrs. Frances Haysley, Base Libn.
Founded: 1941. **Staff:** Prof 1; Other 4. **Subjects:** Business and personnel
management, public administration, World War II, social problems, Air Force
history, California, foreign languages. **Holdings:** 26,407 books; 627 reels of
microfilm of periodicals; 55 art reproductions; 164 popular music cassettes;
98 phonograph records. **Subscriptions:** 240 journals and other serials; 9
newspapers. **Services:** Interlibrary loans; copying (limited); library open to
public for reference use only. **Networks/Consortia:** Member of San
Bernardino, Inyo, Riverside United Library Services (SIRCULS). **Publications:**
Booklists, irregular. **Staff:** Priscilla McGill, Lib.Techn.

★13899★
U.S. AIR FORCE BASE - GOODFELLOW BASE LIBRARY (Mil)†
FL 3030, Bldg. 712   Phone: (915) 653-3231
Goodfellow AFB, TX 76908   Elaine C. Penner, Libn.
Staff: Prof 1; Other 3. **Subjects:** Military science, foreign language, general
topics. **Holdings:** 28,000 books. **Subscriptions:** 113 journals and other
serials; 19 newspapers. **Services:** Interlibrary loans; library open to public
with restrictions.

★13900★
U.S. AIR FORCE BASE - GRISSOM BASE LIBRARY (Mil)
FL 4654, Bldg. 575   Phone: (317) 689-2056
Grissom AFB, IN 46971   David S. English, Libn.
Founded: 1956. **Staff:** Prof 1; Other 3. **Subjects:** Military science, business,
minorities. **Special Collections:** MacNaughton Booklease Plan (800 volumes).
Holdings: 24,346 books; 8772 AV items. **Subscriptions:** 212 journals and
other serials; 12 newspapers. **Services:** Interlibrary loans; copying; SDI;
library open to military personnel, dependents and civilians employed on base.
Automated Operations: Computerized cataloging. **Computerized
Information Services:** MARCIVE, Inc. **Publications:** Library Brochure,
irregular.

★13901★
U.S. AIR FORCE BASE - GUNTER BASE LIBRARY (Mil)
FL 3370   Phone: (205) 279-3179
Gunter AFS, AL 36114   Alta N. Hunt, Libn.
Founded: 1950. **Staff:** Prof 1; Other 8. **Subjects:** Recreational materials,
medicine, education, language, literature, history. **Holdings:** 23,000 books;
1500 recordings, 200 cassette recordings. **Subscriptions:** 100 journals and
other serials. **Services:** Library open to military personnel, their dependents,
and civilian employees only.

★13902★
U.S. AIR FORCE BASE - HANSCOM BASE LIBRARY (Mil)
FL 2835   Phone: (617) 861-2177
Hanscom AFB, MA 01731   Gerald T. Griffin, Chf., Lib.Br.
Staff: Prof 2. **Subjects:** Military, technical, educational and recreational
topics. **Holdings:** 23,571 books; records and tapes. **Subscriptions:** 405
journals and other serials; 38 newspapers. **Services:** Interlibrary loans;
copying; library open to authorized users and to public for specific research.
Automated Operations: Computerized cataloging. **Computerized
Information Services:** OCLC. **Networks/Consortia:** Member of FEDLINK.
Staff: Anne M. Duerell, Lib.Techn.; Susan L. Benzer, Hd., Circ.

★13903★
U.S. AIR FORCE BASE - HICKAM BASE LIBRARY (Mil)
FL 5260   Phone: (808) 449-2831
Hickam AFB, HI 96744   Stella K. Watanabe, Chf.Libn.
Staff: Prof 2; Other 7. **Subjects:** Military history, current foreign policy, U.S.
Air Force, management, investments. **Holdings:** 61,404 volumes.
Subscriptions: 450 journals and other serials; 47 newspapers. **Services:**
Interlibrary loans; copying; library open to public by appointment. **Staff:**
Joanne M. Okuma, Asst.Libn.

★13904★
U.S. AIR FORCE BASE - HOLLOMAN BASE LIBRARY (Mil)†
FL 4801   Phone: (505) 479-3939
Holloman AFB, NM 88310   Wanda M. Goecke, Libn.
Staff: Prof 2; Other 6. **Subjects:** Military aerospace history, contemporary issues, the Southwest, general topics. **Special Collections:** Southwest collection. **Holdings:** 25,000 books; 100 bound periodical volumes; 50 regional maps; 15,000 microfiche; 1500 phonograph records; 700 cassettes; 120 art prints; 3 VF drawers of pamphlets and clippings. **Subscriptions:** 310 journals and other serials; 28 newspapers. **Services:** Interlibrary loans; copying; library open to public for reference use only with base pass. **Automated Operations:** Computerized cataloging. **Staff:** Carol Austin, Lib.Techn.

★13905★
U.S. AIR FORCE BASE - HOMESTEAD BASE LIBRARY (Mil)†
FL 4829, 31 CSG/SSL   Phone: (305) 257-8184
Homestead AFB, FL 33039   Bettylou Rosen, Libn.
Staff: Prof 1; Other 8. **Subjects:** Aeronautics, Florida. **Holdings:** 31,000 books; 2000 records; 1004 audio and video cassettes; 11,000 microforms. **Subscriptions:** 388 journals and other serials; 33 newspapers. **Services:** Interlibrary loans; library not open to public. **Computerized Information Services:** DIALOG.

★13906★
U.S. AIR FORCE BASE - HOWARD BASE LIBRARY (Mil)
FL 4810
Howard AFB
APO Miami, FL 34001   S.K. Murdoch, Base Libn.
Staff: Prof 2; Other 7. **Subjects:** Military arts and sciences, Latin America. **Holdings:** 33,174 books; 1710 records and tapes. **Subscriptions:** 243 journals and other serials; 31 newspapers. **Services:** Interlibrary loans; copying; library open to persons with government identification.

★13907★
U.S. AIR FORCE BASE - KEESLER BASE - MC BRIDE LIBRARY (Mil; Comp Sci)
FL 3010
Bldg. 2222, Larchler Blvd., 3380 ABG/SSL   Phone: (601) 377-2181
Keesler AFB, MS 39534   Elizabeth A. DeCoux, Adm.Libn.
Staff: Prof 3; Other 15. **Subjects:** Telecommunications, computer science, military history, warfare, literature, management science. **Special Collections:** Professional military education and leadership. **Holdings:** 66,084 books; 1709 bound periodical volumes; 1447 AV materials; 931 technical reports and documents; 354 maps; 42,006 microforms. **Subscriptions:** 627 journals and other serials; 66 newspapers. **Services:** Interlibrary loans; copying; library open to public with commander's approval. **Publications:** Classified List of Periodicals; Guide to Use of Materials; Special bibliographies. **Staff:** Beth Meconitas, Ref.libn.

★13908★
U.S. AIR FORCE BASE - KELLY BASE - SPECIAL SERVICES LIBRARY (Mil)*
FL 2050   Phone: (512) 925-3214
Kelly AFB, TX 78241   Melvin P. McElfresh, Libn.
Founded: 1917. **Staff:** Prof 2; Other 3. **Subjects:** Aircraft, management, business, auto and home repair, logistics. **Holdings:** 27,716 books; 1363 reels of microfilm; 1271 phonograph records. **Subscriptions:** 75 journals and other serials; 9 newspapers. **Services:** Interlibrary loans; copying; library open to public for reference use only.

★13909★
U.S. AIR FORCE BASE - KIRTLAND BASE LIBRARY (Mil)
FL 4469   Phone: (505) 844-0795
Kirtland AFB, NM 87117   Alice R. Roy, Chf.Libn.
Founded: 1945. **Staff:** Prof 2; Other 6. **Subjects:** Military history and science, general education, Southwest. **Special Collections:** Southwest. **Holdings:** 49,701 books; 2000 reels of microfilm of periodicals; 348 tapes; 2604 phonograph records; 50 language records and tapes. **Subscriptions:** 569 journals and other serials; 28 newspapers. **Services:** Interlibrary loans; copying; Library open to active and retired military personnel and their families. **Computerized Information Services:** DIALOG (through New Mexico State Library). Performs free searches. **Publications:** New Acquisitions, monthly - for internal distribution only. **Staff:** Robert C. Mathews, Ref.Libn.

★13910★
U.S. AIR FORCE BASE - LANGLEY BASE LIBRARY (Mil)
FL 4800   Phone: (804) 764-3078
Langley AFB, VA 23665   David A.L. Smith, Base Libn.
Founded: 1942. **Staff:** Prof 2; Other 14. **Subjects:** Military history,

sociology, foreign affairs. **Holdings:** 65,000 books; 16 mm films; video cassettes; phonograph records; tapes. **Subscriptions:** 600 journals and other serials. **Services:** Copying; document delivery service. **Automated Operations:** Computerized cataloging and ILL. **Computerized Information Services:** OCLC, DIALOG.

★13911★
U.S. AIR FORCE BASE - LAUGHLIN BASE LIBRARY (Mil)*
FL 3099   Phone: (512) 298-5119
Laughlin AFB, TX 78840   William Darcy, Base Libn.
Staff: Prof 1; Other 4. **Subjects:** Aviation; military history, art, and science; management. **Holdings:** 11,592 books; 200 microfiche; 3 VF drawers of pamphlets. **Subscriptions:** 108 journals and other serials; 6 newspapers. **Services:** Interlibrary loans; library open to public with restrictions.

★13912★
U.S. AIR FORCE BASE - LITTLE ROCK BASE LIBRARY (Mil)
FL 4460, Bldg. 976   Phone: (501) 988-6979
Little Rock AFB, AR 72076   James Lee Clark, Base Libn.
Founded: 1956. **Staff:** Prof 1; Other 7. **Subjects:** Military science, aeronautics, management, social science. **Holdings:** 24,000 books. **Subscriptions:** 523 journals and other serials; 13 newspapers. **Services:** Interlibrary loans; copying.

★13913★
U.S. AIR FORCE BASE - LORING BASE LIBRARY (Mil)
FL 4678   Phone: (207) 999-2416
Loring AFB, ME 04751   Mary E. Bushey, Libn.
Founded: 1953. **Staff:** Prof 1; Other 4. **Special Collections:** Aeronautics. **Holdings:** 19,500 books; 2142 phonograph records; 951 tapes. **Subscriptions:** 225 journals and other serials; 20 newspapers. **Services:** Interlibrary loans; copying; library open to base personnel.

★13914★
U.S. AIR FORCE BASE - LOWRY BASE LIBRARY (Mil; Sci-Tech)†
Lowry Technical Training Ctr.
FL 3059, ABG/SSL   Phone: (303) 394-3093
Lowry AFB, CO 80230   Helen C. McClaughry, Base Libn.
Founded: 1939. **Staff:** Prof 1; Other 3. **Subjects:** Electronics, missiles, photography, nuclear weapons, intelligence, special instruments, aeronautics, logistics, general collection with emphasis on military subjects and education. **Holdings:** 50,000 books; 2000 recordings; 500 framed and unframed pictures. **Subscriptions:** 300 journals and other serials. **Services:** Interlibrary loans; copying; library not open to public. **Publications:** New Book List; Subject List.

★13915★
U.S. AIR FORCE BASE - LUKE BASE LIBRARY (Mil)†
FL 4887   Phone: (602) 856-6301
Luke AFB, AZ 85309   Betty L. Horn, Base Libn.
Founded: 1951. **Staff:** Prof 1; Other 7. **Subjects:** General collection with emphasis on aeronautics. **Special Collections:** Arizona history. **Holdings:** 34,546 books; 1057 phonograph records; 171 cassette tapes; 184 magnetic tapes; 11,207 microfiche. **Subscriptions:** 398 journals and other serials; 23 newspapers. **Services:** Interlibrary loans; library not open to public. **Staff:** Dulcie Geske, Lib.Techn.

★13916★
U.S. AIR FORCE BASE - MC CHORD BASE LIBRARY (Mil)
62 ABG/SSL   Phone: (206) 984-3454
McChord AFB, WA 98438   Margaret Ono, Base Libn.
Founded: 1940. **Staff:** Prof 1; Other 5. **Subjects:** Aeronautics, military history, fiction. **Holdings:** 25,000 books. **Subscriptions:** 115 journals and other serials. **Services:** Interlibrary loans; library not open to public.

★13917★
U.S. AIR FORCE BASE - MC CLELLAN BASE LIBRARY (Mil)
2852 ABG/SSL   Phone: (916) 643-4640
McClellan AFB, CA 95652   Weldon B. Champreys, Libn.
Founded: 1941. **Staff:** Prof 1; Other 5. **Subjects:** Aeronautics, psychology, literature, government. **Holdings:** 25,500 books; 3700 recordings; 157 reels of microfilm; 128 microfiche. **Subscriptions:** 230 journals and other serials; 20 newspapers. **Services:** Interlibrary loans; copying; library open to military and dependents and assigned civilians. **Publications:** New book list, bimonthly; bibliographies, monthly.

★13918★
U.S. AIR FORCE BASE - MC CONNELL BASE LIBRARY (Mil)
FL4621   Phone: (316) 681-5414
McConnell AFB, KS 67221   Mary E. Rinas, Libn.
Staff: Prof 1; Other 8. **Subjects:** General collection with emphasis on aeronautics. **Holdings:** 29,000 books; 350 bound periodical volumes; microforms; 5 VF drawers; art prints. **Subscriptions:** 399 journals and other serials; 30 newspapers. **Services:** Interlibrary loans; copying; library open to public if enrolled in education classes. **Networks/Consortia:** Member of South Central Kansas Library System (SCKLS).

★13919★
U.S. AIR FORCE BASE - MAC DILL BASE LIBRARY (Mil)
FL 4814   Phone: (813) 830-3607
MacDill AFB, FL 33608   Jacob Phillips, Base Libn.
Staff: Prof 1; Other 7. **Subjects:** Military history, Middle East and Latin America. **Holdings:** 23,377 books; 22,073 microforms; 1708 AV items; 104 framed art prints; 23 technical reports; 114 maps. **Subscriptions:** 400 journals and other serials; 22 newspapers. **Services:** Interlibrary loans; copying; library open to military personnel and to civilians attending on-base university classes. **Computerized Information Services:** DIALOG; NEXIS. Performs free searches. **Networks/Consortia:** Member of Tampa Bay Library Consortium.

★13920★
U.S. AIR FORCE BASE - MC GUIRE BASE LIBRARY (Mil)
FL 4484   Phone: (609) 724-2079
McGuire AFB, NJ 08641   Barbara-Ann Bomgardner, Base Libn.
Founded: 1948. **Staff:** Prof 1; Other 5. **Subjects:** General and technical subjects. **Holdings:** 25,500 books. **Subscriptions:** 276 journals and other serials. **Services:** Interlibrary loans; copying; library open to public for reference use only.

★13921★
U.S. AIR FORCE BASE - MALMSTROM BASE LIBRARY (Mil)
FL 4626   Phone: (406) 731-2748
Malmstrom AFB, MT 59402   Katherine V. Lex, Libn.
Founded: 1957. **Staff:** 5. **Subjects:** General, aviation, technical subjects. **Holdings:** 27,528 books; 14 VF drawers; 1006 government publications; 3632 AV programs; 35,336 microforms. **Subscriptions:** 710 journals and other serials; 49 newspapers. **Services:** Interlibrary loans; library not open to public.

★13922★
U.S. AIR FORCE BASE - MARCH BASE LIBRARY (Mil)
FL 4664   Phone: (714) 655-2203
March AFB, CA 92518   Marian M. Hamilton, Base Libn.
Staff: Prof 1; Other 3. **Subjects:** Aeronautics, education, political science, technology. **Special Collections:** California Collection (250 items); International Relations (318 items); Caldecott/Newbery; USC-SSMC Systems Management; Air War College. **Holdings:** 28,500 books; 203 maps; 604 reels of microfilm; 1686 phonograph records; 576 audiotapes; 100 video cassettes; 19 books on cassettes. **Subscriptions:** 180 journals and other serials; 13 newspapers. **Services:** Interlibrary loans (with other Armed Services libraries and the Inland Empire); library Open to military personnel and to civilian students enrolled in on-base education courses.

★13923★
U.S. AIR FORCE BASE - MATHER BASE LIBRARY (Mil)†
FL 3067   Phone: (916) 364-4759
Mather AFB, CA 95655   Mary Kay Briggs, Libn.
Founded: 1943. **Staff:** Prof 1; Other 3. **Subjects:** Aeronautics, electronics, weather. **Holdings:** 32,843 books. **Subscriptions:** 160 journals and other serials. **Services:** Interlibrary loans; library open to military (active duty and retired), dependents and Department of Defense civilians working on base.

★13924★
U.S. AIR FORCE BASE - MINOT BASE LIBRARY (Mil)*
91 CSG/SSL   Phone: (701) 727-4761
Minot AFB, ND 58705   Geraldine Y. Brosman, Libn.
Staff: Prof 1; Other 4. **Subjects:** Aeronautics, electronics, ethnic studies, art and crafts. **Holdings:** 28,648 books; 78 bound periodical volumes; 223 reels of microfilm; 2626 recordings; 4 VF drawers. **Subscriptions:** 672 journals and other serials; 41 newspapers. **Services:** Interlibrary loans; copying; library open to public with restrictions.

★13925★
U.S. AIR FORCE BASE - MOODY BASE LIBRARY (Mil)
                                         Phone: (912) 333-3539
Moody AFB, GA 31699   Madeleine A. Peyton, Libn.
Founded: 1951. **Staff:** Prof 1; Other 4. **Subjects:** Aeronautics, science, history, general topics. **Holdings:** 19,000 books; 2000 phonograph records; 7000 microfiche; 85 videotapes; 105 filmstrips. **Subscriptions:** 262 journals and other serials; 16 newspapers. **Services:** Interlibrary loans; copying; library open to military personnel and to civilians enrolled in on-base educational program.

★13926★
U.S. AIR FORCE BASE - MYRTLE BEACH BASE LIBRARY (Mil)*
FL 4806   Phone: (803) 238-7086
Myrtle Beach AFB, SC 29577   Jean L. Cady, Base Libn.
Founded: 1956. **Staff:** Prof 1; Other 5. **Subjects:** Aeronautics, military science, electronics, business, general topics. **Special Collections:** Air War College Seminar books (military and political science). **Holdings:** 18,000 books; 1000 phonograph records and cassette tapes. **Subscriptions:** 200 journals and other serials. **Services:** Interlibrary loans; library not open to public. **Remarks:** Maintains 43 office collections of 2500 books.

★13927★
U.S. AIR FORCE BASE - NELLIS BASE LIBRARY (Mil)
FL 4852, 554 CSG/SSL   Phone: (702) 643-2280
Nellis AFB, NV 89191   Dorothy Hart, Base Libn.
Founded: 1949. **Staff:** Prof 1; Other 7. **Subjects:** Aeronautics, business, management, military history, political science, general reference. **Holdings:** 38,500 books; 8668 tapes and phonograph records; 58 16mm films; 1800 video cassettes; 290 8mm films; 1378 slides; 253 art prints; 150 strategy games; 98 computer software items; 308 video games. **Subscriptions:** 458 journals and other serials; 11 newspapers. **Services:** Interlibrary loans; Dial-A-Story Program - 4 minute folktale (24 hour telephone service); library open to public for reference use only. **Computerized Information Services:** DIALOG.

★13928★
U.S. AIR FORCE BASE - NORTON BASE LIBRARY (Mil)
FL 4448   Phone: (714) 382-7119
Norton AFB, CA 92409   Robert R. DeBaun, Base Libn.
Founded: 1943. **Staff:** Prof 1; Other 3. **Subjects:** Aeronautics, management, political science. **Holdings:** 25,000 books; 20 VF drawers. **Subscriptions:** 455 journals and other serials; 17 newspapers. **Services:** Interlibrary loans; copying; library open to public for reference use only.

★13929★
U.S. AIR FORCE BASE - OFFUTT BASE LIBRARY (Mil)†
FL 4600   Phone: (402) 294-2533
Offutt AFB, NE 68113   Margaret A. Byrne, Libn.
Subjects: General collection. **Holdings:** 50,000 books and periodicals. **Services:** Library not open to public.

★13930★
U.S. AIR FORCE BASE - PATRICK BASE LIBRARY (Mil)†
FL 2829   Phone: (305) 494-6881
Patrick AFB, FL 32925   Marie D. Jennings, Adm.Libn.
Staff: Prof 2; Other 4. **Subjects:** Social science, engineering technology, history. **Holdings:** 37,000 books; 2500 audio cassettes; 110 video cassettes. **Subscriptions:** 460 journals and other serials; 17 newspapers. **Services:** Interlibrary loans; library not open to public.

★13931★
U.S. AIR FORCE BASE - PEASE BASE LIBRARY (Mil)
FL 4623   Phone: (603) 430-3734
Pease AFB, NH 03801
Subjects: Military science. **Holdings:** 28,000 volumes.

★13932★
U.S. AIR FORCE BASE - POPE BASE LIBRARY (Mil)
FL 4488   Phone: (919) 394-2791
Pope AFB, NC 28308   Jean L. Hort, Base Libn.
Staff: Prof 1; Other 4. **Subjects:** General and technical topics, music. **Holdings:** 20,000 books; 4 VF drawers of pamphlets and maps; 3500 phonograph records; 50 puzzles; book rental collection (500); 14,000 microfiche. **Subscriptions:** 270 journals and other serials; 24 newspapers. **Services:** Interlibrary loans; copying; preschool story service; library open to active duty and retired military and dependents and to civilians working on base.

★13933★
U.S. AIR FORCE BASE - RANDOLPH BASE LIBRARY (Mil)★
FL 3089   Phone: (512) 652-2617
Randolph AFB, TX 78150   Nova C. Maddox, Chf.Libn.
Staff: Prof 1; Other 7. **Subjects:** U.S. Air Force history, World War II, aeronautics, management, applied science, literature. **Special Collections:** Air War College Seminar Book Collection; Texas history. **Holdings:** 30,000 books. **Subscriptions:** 205 journals and other serials; 15 newspapers. **Services:** Interlibrary loans; copying; library open to public with restrictions. **Automated Operations:** Computerized cataloging.

★13934★
U.S. AIR FORCE BASE - REESE BASE LIBRARY (Mil)
Reese AFB
3060   Phone: (806) 885-4511
Lubbock, TX 79489
Founded: 1950. **Staff:** Prof 1; Other 5. **Subjects:** Aeronautics, management, travel, history, fiction. **Holdings:** 17,455 books. **Subscriptions:** 139 journals and other serials. **Services:** Interlibrary loans; library not open to public.

★13935★
U.S. AIR FORCE BASE - ROBINS BASE LIBRARY (Mil)
2853 ABG/SSL   Phone: (912) 926-5411
Robins AFB, GA 31098   Carolyn M. Covington, Chf., Lib.Br.
Staff: Prof 1; Other 9. **Subjects:** General and technical subjects. **Holdings:** 45,000 books. **Subscriptions:** 319 journals and other serials; 15 newspapers. **Services:** Interlibrary loans; library not open to public.

★13936★
U.S. AIR FORCE BASE - SHEPPARD BASE LIBRARY (Mil)
FL 3020   Phone: (817) 851-2687
Sheppard AFB, TX 76311   Linda Fryar, Libn.
Staff: Prof 2; Other 8. **Subjects:** General and technical topics. **Holdings:** 38,000 books; 5000 microforms; 3000 recordings. **Subscriptions:** 250 journals and other serials; 15 newspapers. **Services:** Interlibrary loans; copying; library open with approval of base commander. **Networks/Consortia:** Member of Texas State Library Communications Network.

★13937★
U.S. AIR FORCE BASE - TINKER BASE LIBRARY (Mil)
2854 ABG/SSL, Bldg. 5702   Phone: (405) 734-3083
Tinker AFB, OK 73145   Doris Haglund, Base Libn.
Founded: 1942. **Staff:** Prof 2; Other 6. **Subjects:** Aeronautics, engineering, management. **Special Collections:** Technical Mission Support publications. **Holdings:** 27,066 books; 1467 phonograph records. **Subscriptions:** 388 journals and other serials; 12 newspapers. **Services:** Interlibrary loans; library open to public with permission. **Staff:** Lucy Jamar, Asst.Libn.; Mary Burnside, Acq.; Melissa Cooper, Circ.libn.

★13938★
U.S. AIR FORCE BASE - TRAVIS BASE LIBRARY (Mil)
Mitchell Memorial Library
60 ABGp/SSL   Phone: (707) 438-5254
Travis AFB, CA 94535   Nina Jacobs, Libn.
Founded: 1956. **Staff:** Prof 1; Other 9. **Subjects:** Military science and aviation, general topics. **Holdings:** 48,236 books and bound periodical volumes; 4 VF drawers of pamphlets. **Subscriptions:** 473 journals and other serials; 14 newspapers. **Services:** Interlibrary loans; library not open to public. **Networks/Consortia:** Member of North Bay Cooperative Library System (NBCLS).

★13939★
U.S. AIR FORCE BASE - VANCE BASE LIBRARY (Mil)★
FL 3029   Phone: (405) 237-2121
Vance AFB, OK 73702   Tom L. Kirk, Chf.Libn.
Founded: 1941. **Staff:** Prof 1; Other 2. **Subjects:** General topics. **Holdings:** 14,500 books; 1300 volumes of American history/social life, pre-1900, on microfiche; 3200 phonograph records; 4500 microforms. **Subscriptions:** 118 journals and other serials; 9 newspapers. **Services:** Interlibrary loans; library not open to public. **Automated Operations:** Computerized cataloging.

★13940★
U.S. AIR FORCE BASE - VANDENBERG BASE LIBRARY (Mil)
Vandenberg AFB, Bldg. 10317   Phone: (805) 866-6414
Lompoc, CA 93437   Joseph L. Buelna, Base Libn.
Founded: 1952. **Staff:** Prof 2; Other 6. **Subjects:** Military and general topics. **Special Collections:** Military science; books for War College students. **Holdings:** 36,000 books; 4000 nonbook items; 3600 reels of microfilm of technical periodicals, 1970 to present; 2 VF drawers of pamphlets.

Subscriptions: 236 journals and other serials; 8 newspapers. **Services:** Interlibrary loans; copying; library open to public for reference use only.

★13941★
U.S. AIR FORCE BASE - WHEELER BASE LIBRARY (Mil)†
FL 5296, 15 Air Base Squadron (SSL)   Phone: (808) 655-1867
Wheeler AFB, HI 96854   Deborah A. Thompson, Base Libn.
Founded: 1960. **Staff:** Prof 1; Other 5. **Subjects:** Systems management, Air Force history, Hawaiiana, military history. **Holdings:** 28,000 books; 14 VF drawers; 1266 periodicals on microfilm; maps; phonograph records. **Subscriptions:** 195 journals and other serials; 39 newspapers. **Services:** Interlibrary loans; copying; library open to military and dependents.

★13942★
U.S. AIR FORCE BASE - WHITEMAN BASE LIBRARY (Mil)
FL 4625   Phone: (816) 687-3089
Whiteman AFB, MO 65305   Charlyne Van Oosbree, Base Libn.
Founded: 1951. **Staff:** Prof 1; Other 3. **Subjects:** Military interests, general fiction and nonfiction, children's literature. **Special Collections:** Military History. **Holdings:** 20,500 volumes; 600 audiotapes; 4000 microforms; 2500 phonograph records; 4 VF drawers of clippings and pamphlets. **Subscriptions:** 345 journals and other serials; 16 newspapers. **Services:** Interlibrary loans; library not open to public.

★13943★
U.S. AIR FORCE BASE - WRIGHT-PATTERSON GENERAL LIBRARY (Mil)★
FL 2300, Kittyhawk Ctr.   Phone: (513) 257-4815
Wright-Patterson AFB, OH 45433   Theresa J. Knasiak, Adm.Libn.
Staff: Prof 1; Other 3. **Subjects:** General and technical topics. **Holdings:** 40,000 books; AV materials. **Subscriptions:** 220 journals and other serials; 21 newspapers. **Services:** Interlibrary loans; copying; library open to public for reference use only.

★13944★
U.S. AIR FORCE COMMUNICATIONS COMMAND - TECHNICAL INFORMATION CENTER (Sci-Tech; Comp Sci)
HQ AFCC/DAPL
Bldg. 40, Fl 3114   Phone: (618) 256-4437
Scott AFB, IL 62225   Janet L. Schneider, Libn.
Staff: Prof 1; Other 3. **Subjects:** Communications, computers, electronics, engineering, mathematics, management. **Holdings:** 1400 technical reports; 3400 technical reports on microfilm. **Subscriptions:** 139 journals and other serials; 6 newspapers. **Services:** Center not open to public. **Computerized Information Services:** DTIC, OCLC. **Networks/Consortia:** Member of Kaskaskia Library System. **Publications:** Library News, monthly - for internal distribution only.

★13945★
U.S. AIR FORCE - ELECTRONIC SECURITY COMMAND - GENERAL LIBRARY (Sci-Tech; Comp Sci)
6923 SPTS/SSL   Phone: (512) 925-2617
San Antonio, TX 78243   Dale T. Ogden, Libn.
Staff: Prof 3; Other 1. **Subjects:** Engineering, telecommunications, computers, personnel management, recreation. **Holdings:** 18,000 books and bound periodical volumes; 3947 microforms; 2080 AV items. **Subscriptions:** 279 journals and other serials. **Services:** Interlibrary loans; library not open to public.

★13946★
U.S. AIR FORCE ENGINEERING AND SERVICES CENTER - TECHNICAL LIBRARY (Mil)
      Phone: (904) 283-6449
Tyndall AFB, FL 32403   Andrew D. Poulis, Chf.Tech.Libn.
Staff: Prof 1; Other 1. **Subjects:** Civil engineering, readiness, environmental protection, fire protection, runway repair, bird strikes. **Holdings:** 2500 books; 100 bound periodical volumes; 15,000 technical reports (10,000 on microfiche, 5000 manuscript volumes); 10,000 engineering reports on microfilm; 2000 slides; 300 magnetic tapes. **Subscriptions:** 425 journals and other serials; 10 newspapers. **Services:** Interlibrary loans; copying; SDI; library open to Air Force, Dept. of Defense, and other government agency personnel. **Automated Operations:** Computerized cataloging, serials, and circulation. **Computerized Information Services:** DIALOG, BRS, DOE/RECON, DTIC; internal databases. **Networks/Consortia:** Member of OCLC through FEDLINK.

★13947★

U.S. AIR FORCE ENVIRONMENTAL TECHNICAL APPLICATIONS CENTER - AIR WEATHER SERVICE TECHNICAL LIBRARY (Sci-Tech)
FL 4414
Scott AFB, IL 62225
Phone: (618) 256-2625
Col. Lawrence R. French, Commander
Founded: 1950. **Staff:** Prof 6; Other 9. **Subjects:** Meteorology, climatology. **Special Collections:** Meteorological and climatological data summarized for worldwide stations. **Holdings:** 4924 books; 2000 bound periodical volumes; technical reports - 105,140 hard copy and 62,064 microfiche. **Subscriptions:** 348 journals and other serials. **Services:** Interlibrary loans; center open to Army and Air Force agency personnel and their contractors. **Computerized Information Services:** SDC, DTIC, DIALOG, OCLC, BRS. **Networks/Consortia:** Member of FEDLINK; ILLINET. **Staff:** Walter S. Burgmann, Dir.; Kathryn E. Marshall, Chf., Lib.Serv.Sect.

★13948★

U.S. AIR FORCE - FLIGHT TEST CENTER - TECHNICAL LIBRARY (Sci-Tech)
6520 Test Group/Stop 238
Edwards AFB, CA 93523
Phone: (805) 277-3606
Carol Maples, Chf., Tech.Lib.
Founded: 1955. **Staff:** Prof 2; Other 2. **Subjects:** Aerodynamics, chemistry, physics, management, propulsion, mathematics. **Special Collections:** AFFTC technical reports; Air Force Rocket Propulsion Laboratory technical reports. **Holdings:** 27,000 books; 6000 bound periodical volumes; 10,000 Society Papers; 100,000 technical reports; audiotapes; periodicals on microfilm. **Subscriptions:** 800 journals and other serials. **Services:** Interlibrary loans; library not open to public. **Computerized Information Services:** DIALOG, OCLC. **Publications:** Accessions List of Unclassified Report Literature, weekly; List of Books Received, weekly - both restricted to center. **Staff:** Jolaine Lamb, Br.Libn.

★13949★

U.S. AIR FORCE - HISTORICAL RESEARCH CENTER (Hist)
Maxwell AFB, AL 36112
Phone: (205) 293-5958
Lloyd H. Cornett, Jr., Dir.
Founded: 1942. **Staff:** Prof 6; Other 6. **Subjects:** Army Air Force, U.S. Air Force history. **Special Collections:** Unit histories, 1942 to present; oral history tapes and transcripts; Air Corps Tactical School course materials (1920s and 1930s); materials relating to USAF activities in the Southeast Asian war; aircraft record card collection; End of Tour reports; Karlsruhe Collection on the German Air Force; papers of select Air Force personnel. **Holdings:** 3 million documents; 36,000 reels of microfilm; 1300 audiotapes. **Services:** Interlibrary loans (limited); copying; library open to public for reference use on request, with restrictions on classified and some other selected documents. **Special Catalogs:** Organizational catalogs reflecting the holdings by organization or special collection; bibliographies. **Formerly:** Its Albert F. Simpson Historical Research Center. Dr. Richard E. Morse, Chf., Ref.Div.; R. Cargill Hall, Chf., Res.Div.; Maurice Maryanow, Jr., Chf., Oral Hist.Div.; Barbara L. Hendry, Chf., Tech.Serv.Div.; Judy G. Endicott, Chf., Circ.

★13950★

U.S. AIR FORCE HOSPITAL - DAVID GRANT MEDICAL CENTER - MEDICAL LIBRARY (Med)
Travis AFB, CA 94535
Phone: (707) 438-3257
A. Peri Worthington, Med.Libn./Dir.
Founded: 1958. **Staff:** Prof 1; Other 2. **Subjects:** Medicine, family practice, dentistry, nursing. **Holdings:** 4500 books; 9400 bound periodical volumes. **Subscriptions:** 400 journals and other serials. **Services:** Interlibrary loans; library not open to public. **Computerized Information Services:** MEDLARS, BRS. Performs free searches. **Networks/Consortia:** Member of Pacific Southwest Regional Medical Library Service (PSRMLS). **Publications:** Quarterly newsletter - to staff.

★13951★

U.S. AIR FORCE HOSPITAL - EHRLING BERGQUIST REGIONAL HOSPITAL - MEDICAL LIBRARY (Med)
Offutt AFB, NE 68113
Phone: (402) 294-7301
Jan Hatcher, Lib.Mgr.
Founded: 1966. **Staff:** 1. **Subjects:** Surgery and allied health sciences. **Holdings:** 1650 books; 2000 unbound journals. **Subscriptions:** 140 journals and other serials. **Services:** Interlibrary loans; copying; library open to public for reference use only. **Computerized Information Services:** MEDLINE. Performs free searches.

★13952★

U.S. AIR FORCE HOSPITAL - MALCOLM GROW MEDICAL CENTER - LIBRARY (Med)
Andrews AFB
Washington, DC 20331
Phone: (202) 981-2354
Mary Alice Zelinka, Med.Libn.
Staff: Prof 1; Other 2. **Subjects:** internal medicine, nursing, cardiology,

surgery, dentistry, food service. **Holdings:** 13,000 books; 4500 bound periodical volumes; clippings; maps; bibliographies; dissertations; reprints; pamphlets; tapes; records; slides; 8 VF drawers of unbound materials. **Subscriptions:** 408 journals and other serials. **Services:** Interlibrary loans; library not open to public. **Computerized Information Services:** MEDLARS, OCLC. Performs free searches. **Networks/Consortia:** Member of FEDLINK.

★13953★

U.S. AIR FORCE HOSPITAL MEDICAL CENTER - MEDICAL LIBRARY (IL-Scott AFB) (Med)
Scott AFB, IL 62225
Phone: (618) 256-7437
Blanche A. Savage, Health Sci.Libn.
Staff: Prof 1; Other 1. **Subjects:** Medicine, nursing, dentistry, allied health sciences. **Holdings:** 8000 books; 4633 bound periodical volumes; 1500 pamphlets and tapes. **Subscriptions:** 325 journals and other serials; 5 newspapers. **Services:** Interlibrary loans; library not open to public. **Computerized Information Services:** Online systems. **Networks/Consortia:** Member of Areawide Hospital Library Consortium of Southwestern Illinois (AHLC).

★13954★

U.S. AIR FORCE HOSPITAL MEDICAL CENTER - MEDICAL LIBRARY (MS-Keesler AFB) (Med)
SGEL
Keesler AFB, MS 39534
Phone: (601) 377-2042
Rita F. Smith, Med.Libn.
Staff: Prof 1; Other 1. **Subjects:** Medicine, surgery, nursing. **Holdings:** 5000 books; 2900 bound periodical volumes; 1556 slides and tapes. **Subscriptions:** 380 journals and other serials. **Services:** Interlibrary loans; copying; SDI. **Computerized Information Services:** MEDLINE. **Networks/Consortia:** Member of Gulf Coast Biomedical Library Consortium.

★13955★

U.S. AIR FORCE HOSPITAL MEDICAL CENTER - MEDICAL LIBRARY (OH-Wright-Patterson AFB) (Med)
SGEL/Bldg. 830A
Wright-Patterson AFB, OH 45433
Phone: (513) 257-4506
Cheryl Harris, Biomed.Libn.
Staff: Prof 1; Other 4. **Subjects:** Clinical medicine, dentistry, veterinary medicine, hospital administration. **Special Collections:** Tropical medicine; plastic surgery; military and aerospace medicine. **Holdings:** 6500 books; 7000 bound periodical volumes; 4000 AV items; 45,000 microfiche. **Subscriptions:** 725 journals and other serials. **Services:** Interlibrary loans; copying; SDI; library open to members of affiliated institutions only. **Automated Operations:** Computerized cataloging, acquisitions, serials and circulation. **Computerized Information Services:** MEDLINE, DIALOG, BRS. **Networks/Consortia:** Member of Greater Midwest Regional Medical Library Network (Region 3); Southwest Ohio Council for Higher Education (SOC).

★13956★

U.S. AIR FORCE HOSPITAL - MEDICAL LIBRARY (AL-Montgomery) (Med)
Maxwell AFB
Montgomery, AL 36112
Phone: (205) 293-5852
Patricia A. Kuther, Med.Lib.Techn.
Founded: 1956. **Staff:** Prof 1. **Subjects:** General medicine, surgery, pathology, dentistry, nursing, veterinary medicine. **Holdings:** 4000 books and bound periodical volumes. **Subscriptions:** 180 journals and other serials. **Services:** Interlibrary loans; library not open to public.

★13957★

U.S. AIR FORCE HOSPITAL - MEDICAL LIBRARY (AK-Elmendorf AFB) (Med)
Elmendorf AFB, AK 99506
Phone: (907) 552-5325
Jeraldine J. Van den Top, Libn.
Founded: 1952. **Staff:** Prof 1; Other 3. **Subjects:** General and military medicine. **Holdings:** 4612 books; **Subscriptions:** 180 journals and other serials. **Services:** Interlibrary loans; copying; library open to health personnel for study. **Automated Operations:** Computerized cataloging. **Computerized Information Services:** MEDLINE. **Networks/Consortia:** Member of National Library of Medicine (NLM); Alaska Library Network. **Publications:** Holdings List, annual.

★13958★

U.S. AIR FORCE HOSPITAL - MEDICAL LIBRARY (CA-Mather AFB) (Med)
Mather AFB, CA 95655
Phone: (916) 364-3180
Carl Lord, Lib.Off.
Staff: 1. **Subjects:** Medicine. **Holdings:** 1000 books. **Subscriptions:** 107 journals and other serials. **Services:** Interlibrary loans; library not open to public.

★13959★

U.S. AIR FORCE HOSPITAL - MEDICAL LIBRARY (FL-Patrick AFB) (Med)
Phone: (305) 494-5501
Patrick AFB, FL 32925
Douglas M. Jackson, Libn.
Founded: 1968. **Staff:** Prof 1. **Subjects:** Medicine, psychiatry, nursing and allied health fields. **Holdings:** 774 books; 361 bound periodical volumes; 150 other items. **Subscriptions:** 82 journals and other serials. **Services:** Interlibrary loans; copying; library open to medical students.

★13960★

U.S. AIR FORCE HOSPITAL - MEDICAL LIBRARY (IL-Rantoul) (Med)
Chanute AFB
Phone: (217) 495-3068
Rantoul, IL 61868
R.M. Lucas, Med.Libn.
Staff: 1. **Subjects:** Medicine. **Holdings:** 2100 books; 116 bound periodical volumes; 480 audio cassettes. **Subscriptions:** 116 journals and other serials. **Services:** Interlibrary loans; library not open to public. **Networks/Consortia:** Member of Champaign-Urbana Consortium.

★13961★

U.S. AIR FORCE HOSPITAL - MEDICAL LIBRARY (NM-Kirtland AFB) (Med)
Phone: (505) 844-1086
Kirtland AFB, NM 87117
Alice T. Lee, Libn.
Founded: 1956. **Staff:** Prof 1. **Subjects:** Medicine, surgery, nursing, dentistry, veterinary medicine. **Holdings:** 2100 books; 465 bound periodical volumes; 3 VF drawers of audiotapes, pamphlets, reports, guides, monographs; 150 filmstrips, video cassettes and 16 mm films. **Subscriptions:** 103 journals and other serials. **Services:** Interlibrary loans; library not open to public. **Networks/Consortia:** Member of New Mexico Consortium of Biomedical Libraries.

★13962★

U.S. AIR FORCE HOSPITAL - MEDICAL LIBRARY (NY-Rome) (Med)*
Griffiss AFB
Phone: (315) 330-7713
Rome, NY 13441
Susan Ho, Med.Libn.
Staff: 1. **Subjects:** Nursing, internal medicine, dental services, mental and social health, surgery, veterinary medicine, food service. **Holdings:** 668 books; 90 bound periodical volumes. **Subscriptions:** 50 journals and other serials. **Services:** Interlibrary loans; library not open to public. **Publications:** Newsletter. **Special Catalogs:** Union list.

★13963★

U.S. AIR FORCE HOSPITAL - MEDICAL LIBRARY (OK-Tinker AFB) (Med)
Phone: (405) 734-8373
Tinker AFB, OK 73145
Mary B. Mills, Lib.Techn.
Staff: 1. **Subjects:** Pediatrics, internal medicine, surgery, nursing. **Holdings:** 1706 books; 370 bound periodical volumes. **Subscriptions:** 90 journals and other serials. **Services:** Interlibrary loans; copying; library open to public with restrictions. **Networks/Consortia:** Member of Greater Oklahoma City Area Health Sciences Library Consortium (GOAL).

★13964★

U.S. AIR FORCE HOSPITAL - MEDICAL LIBRARY (TX-Carswell AFB) (Med)*
Phone: (817) 735-7579
Carswell AFB, TX 76127
Jean Robbins, Med.Libn.
Founded: 1956. **Staff:** Prof 1. **Subjects:** Medicine, surgery, nursing, psychiatry, dentistry, orthopedics, veterinary medicine. **Holdings:** 2206 books; 1950 bound periodical volumes. **Subscriptions:** 154 journals and other serials. **Services:** Interlibrary loans; copying; library open to public for reference use only.

★13965★

U.S. AIR FORCE HOSPITAL - MEDICAL LIBRARY (TX-Reese AFB) (Med)
SGAS/35
Phone: (806) 885-4511
Reese AFB, TX 79489
Dorothy F. Haynes, Med.libn.
Staff: 2. **Subjects:** Medicine and medical specialties, dentistry. **Holdings:** 780 books; 1000 bound periodical volumes; 200 magnetic tapes. **Subscriptions:** 65 journals and other serials. **Services:** Library open to USAF personnel.

★13966★

U.S. AIR FORCE HOSPITAL - MEDICAL LIBRARY (WA - Fairchild AFB) (Med)
Phone: (509) 247-2801
Fairchild AFB, WA 99011
Linda M. Norton, Libn.
Staff: 1. **Subjects:** Medicine. **Holdings:** 1050 books; 70 medical journals (current year and past two years are kept). **Services:** Interlibrary loans; library not open to public.

★13967★

U.S. AIR FORCE HOSPITAL - SHEPPARD REGIONAL HOSPITAL - MEDICAL LIBRARY (Med)
Phone: (817) 851-6647
Sheppard AFB, TX 76311
Maxine Gustafson, Lib.Techn.
Staff: Prof 1. **Subjects:** Medicine, nursing, dentistry, pharmacy, hospital administration, veterinary medicine. **Holdings:** 3240 books; 2308 bound periodical volumes; 990 Audio-Digest tapes; 36 video cassette tapes; 1 VF drawer of pamphlets. **Subscriptions:** 148 journals and other serials. **Services:** Interlibrary loans; library open to public for reference use only. **Automated Operations:** Computerized cataloging. **Computerized Information Services:** Access to MEDLINE. **Networks/Consortia:** Member of TALON.

★13968★

U.S. AIR FORCE HOSPITAL - WILFORD HALL U.S.A.F. MEDICAL CENTER - MEDICAL LIBRARY (SGEL) (Med)*
Lackland AFB
Phone: (512) 670-7204
San Antonio, TX 78236
Royden R. Jones, Med.Libn.
Staff: Prof 2; Other 4. **Subjects:** Medicine, nursing, dentistry, hospital administration, veterinary medicine. **Holdings:** 9800 books; 13,800 bound periodical volumes; 4900 media units; 1825 reels of microfilmed journals. **Subscriptions:** 859 journals and other serials. **Services:** Interlibrary loans; library not open to public. **Computerized Information Services:** MEDLINE. **Publications:** Medical Library Letter of Information, monthly. **Staff:** Kyung H. Yu, Asst.Libn.

★13969★

U.S. AIR FORCE - HUMAN RESOURCES LABORATORY - LIBRARY (Soc Sci)
Phone: (512) 536-2651
Brooks AFB, TX 78235
Orrine L. Woinowsk, Adm.Libn.
Founded: 1948. **Staff:** Prof 1; Other 1. **Subjects:** Psychology, mathematical statistics. **Holdings:** 13,310 volumes; 11,689 technical reports; 1269 microforms. **Subscriptions:** 481 journals and other serials. **Services:** Interlibrary loans; copying; library open to public by appointment for reference use only. **Automated Operations:** Computerized cataloging, serials and ILL. **Computerized Information Services:** DIALOG. Performs free searches for laboratory personnel. **Networks/Consortia:** Member of Health Oriented Libraries of San Antonio (HOLSA); San Antonio Area Online Users Group; AMIGOS Bibliographic Council, Inc.; Council of Research & Academic Libraries (CORAL).

★13970★

U.S. AIR FORCE INSTITUTE OF TECHNOLOGY - LIBRARY (Sci-Tech; Mil)
Bldg. 640, Area B
Phone: (513) 255-5894
Wright-Patterson AFB, OH 45433
Virginia E. Eckel, Dir.
Founded: 1946. **Staff:** Prof 7; Other 8. **Subjects:** Aeronautics, astronautics, physics, engineering, mathematics, economics, chemistry, management, logistics. **Holdings:** 42,819 books; 29,286 bound periodical volumes; 645,720 technical reports on microfiche. **Subscriptions:** 1309 journals and other serials; 26 newspapers. **Services:** Interlibrary loans; library not open to public. **Automated Operations:** Computerized serials. **Networks/Consortia:** Member of Southwest Ohio Council for Higher Education (SOC). **Publications:** Computerized Journal Holdings List; Permuted Thesis Index - for internal distribution only. **Special Indexes:** Permuted Thesis Index print-out. **Remarks:** Includes the holdings of the School of Systems and Logistics Library. **Staff:** Helen Helton, Chf., Tech.Serv.; James T. Helling, Chf., Rd.Serv.; Linda Stoddart, Ref.Libn.; Mary L. Browning, Chf., Rd.Serv., Engr.Div.; Barry Boettcher, Chf., Rd.Serv., Logistics; Lynn Heinzeroth, Cat.

★13971★

U.S. AIR FORCE - KEESLER TECHNICAL TRAINING CENTER - ACADEMIC LIBRARY (Sci-Tech; Mil)
McClelland Hall, Bldg. 2818
Phone: (601) 377-4295
Keesler AFB, MS 39534
Verna Westerburg, Lib.Techn.
Founded: 1970. **Subjects:** Communications, electronics, management, military science, computer science, systems engineering. **Holdings:** 8500 books; 200 periodicals; 300 reports. **Services:** Interlibrary loans; library open to public with restrictions. **Computerized Information Services:** DTIC, Defense Logistics Studies Information Exchange (DLSIE).

★13972★

U.S. AIR FORCE MUSEUM - RESEARCH DIVISION LIBRARY (Hist)
Bldg. 489, Area B
Phone: (513) 255-3284
Wright-Patterson AFB, OH 45433
Charles G. Worman, Chf., Res.Div.
Staff: Prof 3; Other 3. **Subjects:** History and technology of the United States Air Force and its predecessor organizations. **Holdings:** 200,000 documents, including aircraft technical orders, manuscripts, photographs, and drawings. **Services:** Copying (documents); library open to public.

★13973★
U.S. AIR FORCE - OFFICE OF JUDGE ADVOCATE GENERAL - LEGAL REFERENCE LIBRARY (Law)
1900 Half St., S.W., Rm. 5113   Phone: (202) 693-5638
Washington, DC 20324   William J. Zschunke, Libn.
Founded: 1949. **Subjects:** Law. **Special Collections:** Criminal law. **Holdings:** 16,000 volumes. **Services:** Library open to public.

★13974★
U.S. AIR FORCE - OFFICE OF SCIENTIFIC RESEARCH - LIBRARY (Sci-Tech)
Bldg. 410   Phone: (202) 767-4910
Bolling AFB, DC 20332   Anthony G. Bialecki, Libn.
Founded: 1956. **Staff:** 1. **Subjects:** Physics, mathematics, solid state sciences, aerospace technology, chemistry, astronomy, life sciences, history and philosophy of science, information sciences. **Holdings:** 16,000 books; 2000 bound periodical volumes. **Subscriptions:** 280 journals and other serials; 5 newspapers. **Services:** Interlibrary loans; library open to researchers on a limited schedule.

U.S. AIR FORCE - OFFICE OF THE SURGEON GENERAL
See: U.S. Army/U.S. Air Force - Offices of the Surgeons General

★13975★
U.S. AIR FORCE - ROME AIR DEVELOPMENT CENTER - DATA & ANALYSIS CENTER FOR SOFTWARE (Comp Sci)
RADC/ISISI   Phone: (315) 336-0937
Griffiss AFB, NY 13441   Thomas Robbins, DACS Prog.Mgr.
Staff: Prof 5; Other 5. **Subjects:** Software - engineering, technology, reliability, maintenance, productivity, research. **Holdings:** 25 books; 2190 conference proceedings papers; 1567 journal articles; 32 standards and regulations; 693 theses, dissertations, and technical reports. **Subscriptions:** 15 journals and other serials; 5 newspapers. **Services:** Center open to public for reference use only. **Automated Operations:** Computerized cataloging and retrieval. **Computerized Information Services:** Software Engineering Bibliographic Database (internal database). **Publications:** Annual Annotated Bibliography of Acquisitions. **Staff:** Gineen Brement, Assoc.Prog.Tech.

★13976★
U.S. AIR FORCE - ROME AIR DEVELOPMENT CENTER - TECHNICAL LIBRARY (Sci-Tech)
RADC TST   Phone: (315) 330-7607
Griffiss AFB, NY 13441   Linda Evans, Chf., Tech.Lib.
Founded: 1942. **Staff:** Prof 3; Other 3. **Subjects:** Aeronautics, engineering, electronics, mathematics, science, electromagnetics, technology. **Holdings:** 17,300 books; 222,000 documents and technical reports. **Subscriptions:** 400 journals and other serials. **Services:** Interlibrary loans (limited); library open to public by appointment. **Computerized Information Services:** DIALOG, DTIC, OCLC. **Networks/Consortia:** Member of Central New York Library Resources Council (CENTRO). **Publications:** Accessions List.

★13977★
U.S. AIR FORCE SCHOOL OF HEALTH CARE SCIENCES - ACADEMIC LIBRARY (Med)
MSTL/114, Bldg. 1900   Phone: (817) 851-2256
Sheppard AFB, TX 76311   Theodore C. Kennedy, Supv.Libn.
Founded: 1956. **Staff:** Prof 1; Other 2. **Subjects:** General medicine, biological science, nursing, dentistry, pharmacy, hospital administration, management. **Holdings:** 12,000 books; 1200 technical reports; 3000 pamphlets. **Subscriptions:** 267 journals and other serials. **Services:** Interlibrary loans; copying; library open to public for reference use only.

★13978★
U.S. AIR FORCE - STRATEGIC AIR COMMAND - LIBRARY SERVICES SAC (DPSOL) (Mil)
Offutt AFB, NE 68113
Remarks: Command Library Services Headquarters is responsible for development and operation of all 25 base libraries within Strategic Air Command (SAC).

★13979★
U.S. AIR FORCE - STRATEGIC AIR COMMAND - 321 CSG/SS - LIBRARY (Mil)†
FL 4659   Phone: (701) 594-6725
Grand Forks AFB, ND 58205   Teresa M. Hathaway, Adm.Libn.
Staff: Prof 1; Other 5. **Subjects:** Military science. **Holdings:** 27,000 books; 14 bound periodical volumes; 182 reels of microfilm. **Subscriptions:** 514 journals and other serials; 52 newspapers. **Services:** Interlibrary loans; copying; library open to public.

★13980★
U.S. AIR FORCE - TACTICAL AIR COMMAND - LANGLEY BASE LIBRARY (Mil)
FL 4800   Phone: (804) 764-2906
Langley AFB, VA 23665   David A.L. Smith, Chf.Libn.
Staff: Prof 2; Other 5. **Subjects:** Aeronautics, management, military history, Virginia history, international relations. **Holdings:** 65,000 books. **Subscriptions:** 800 journals and other serials. **Services:** Interlibrary loans; library open to public by special arrangement. **Automated Operations:** Computerized circulation. **Computerized Information Services:** OCLC.

★13981★
U.S. AIR FORCE WEAPONS LABORATORY - TECHNICAL LIBRARY (Mil)
                                            Phone: (505) 844-7449
Kirtland AFB, NM 87117
Founded: 1947. **Staff:** Prof 7; Other 7. **Subjects:** Advanced weapons development, civil engineering, aeronautical systems, lasers, missile and space systems, electromagnetic pulse. **Holdings:** 26,000 books; 2100 bound periodical volumes; 6000 cartridges of microfilm of periodicals; 300,000 technical reports. **Subscriptions:** 800 journals and other serials. **Services:** Interlibrary loans; library open to public by permission of military authority. **Computerized Information Services:** DIALOG, SDC, DOE/RECON, NASA/RECON, OCLC. **Staff:** Keith R. Newsom, Supv.Libn., Open Lit.; Barbara Newton, Supv.Libn., Rpt.; Ann Klos, Ref.Libn.; Virginia King, Rpt.Cat.

★13982★
U.S. AIR FORCE - WESTERN SPACE AND MISSILE CENTER - WSMC/PMET TECHNICAL LIBRARY (Sci-Tech; Mil)
Western Space and Missile Center   Phone: (805) 866-9745
Vandenberg AFB, CA 93437   Paula Turley, Chf.Libn.
Founded: 1965. **Staff:** Prof 1; Other 2. **Subjects:** Aerospace vehicles, antennas, electronics, engineering, guided missiles, instrumentation, management, mathematics, propulsion. **Special Collections:** Radar; telemetry. **Holdings:** 12,500 books and bound periodical volumes; 2000 technical reports; 3400 maps; 41,000 microforms. **Subscriptions:** 394 journals and other serials; 35 newspapers. **Services:** Interlibrary loans; library not open to public. **Computerized Information Services:** DIALOG, SDC, NASA/RECON, DTIC. **Networks/Consortia:** Member of Total Interlibrary Exchange (TIE); CLASS. **Publications:** Periodicals Holdings; New Acquisitions - both for internal distribution only. **Staff:** Suzanne Stanton, Asst.Libn.

★13983★
U.S. AIR FORCE - WRIGHT AERONAUTICAL LABORATORIES - AEROSPACE STRUCTURES INFORMATION & ANALYSIS CENTER (Sci-Tech; Mil)
AFWAL/FIBRA/ASIAC   Phone: (513) 255-6688
Wright-Patterson AFB, OH 45433   Gordon R. Negaard, Dir.
Staff: Prof 4; Other 1. **Subjects:** Structures, computerized analysis, aircraft, stress (mechanics), mathematics, fatigue. **Special Collections:** Specialized and technical reports and publications dealing with aircraft structural design and analysis. **Holdings:** 10,000 technical reports; 30,000 reports on microfiche. **Services:** Interlibrary loans; copying; center open to government contractors. **Computerized Information Services:** DIALOG, DTIC, NASA/RECON. **Publications:** Newsletter, quarterly. **Staff:** Catherine Wolf, Info.Spec.

★13984★
U.S. AIR FORCE - WRIGHT-PATTERSON TECHNICAL LIBRARY (Mil; Sci-Tech)
Wright-Patterson AFB, Bldg. 22   Phone: (513) 255-3630
Dayton, OH 45433   Dorothy E. Siegfried, Chf.
Founded: 1918. **Staff:** Prof 7; Other 7. **Subjects:** Aeronautics, astronautics, physics, chemistry, mathematics, electronics, engineering, logistics, propulsion, aerospace medicine, human-factors engineering, management. **Special Collections:** Lahm & Chandler Collection (aeronautics). **Holdings:** 55,000 books; 68,000 bound journals; 650,000 technical reports; microforms; military specifications; industry standards. **Subscriptions:** 1500 journals and other serials. **Services:** Interlibrary loans; library open to public for reference use only. **Automated Operations:** Computerized cataloging, acquisitions and circulation. **Computerized Information Services:** DIALOG, NASA/RECON, DTIC, MEDLARS, SDC, NEXIS, Circa Library Circulation Systems. **Networks/Consortia:** Member of Southwest Ohio Council for Higher Education (SOC); Dayton Area MEDLINE Consortium. **Staff:** Gail Knudtson, Ref.; William Whalen, Online Searching; Willis Benson, Reports & ILL.

★13985★
UNITED STATES ANIMAL BANK, INC. - LIBRARY
Box 15426
San Francisco, CA 94115
Defunct

★13986★
U.S. ARCHITECTURAL AND TRANSPORTATION BARRIERS COMPLIANCE BOARD (ATBCB) - TECHNICAL RESOURCES LIBRARY (Plan)
330 C St., S.W.   Phone: (202) 472-2700
Washington, DC 20202   Judy Newton, Mgt.Anl.
Staff: Prof 1; Other 1. **Subjects:** Handicapped accessibility, barrier-free and accessible design, federal requirements for accessible design, transportation and communication barriers. **Holdings:** 1500 books; 500 documents. **Subscriptions:** 25 journals and other serials. **Services:** Interlibrary loans; copying; library open to public by appointment only. **Automated Operations:** Computerized cataloging.

★13987★
U.S. ARMED FORCES INSTITUTE OF PATHOLOGY - ASH LIBRARY (Med)†
Walter Reed Army Medical Ctr., Rm. 407
Stop 215   Phone: (202) 576-2983
Washington, DC 20306   Sally G. Allinson, Libn.
Founded: 1951. **Staff:** Prof 1; Other 1. **Subjects:** Pathology. **Holdings:** 21,000 books and bound periodical volumes; 10,000 documents, reports and pamphlets. **Subscriptions:** 375 journals and other serials. **Services:** Interlibrary loans; copying; library open to public.

★13988★
U.S. ARMED FORCES RADIOBIOLOGY RESEARCH INSTITUTE (AFRRI) - LIBRARY SERVICES (Med)
National Naval Medical Ctr., Bldg.42   Phone: (301) 295-0428
Bethesda, MD 20814   Nannette M. Pope, Hd., Lib.Serv.
Founded: 1962. **Staff:** Prof 2; Other 2. **Subjects:** Radiobiology, radiation physics, neurobiology, nuclear medicine, behavioral science, veterinary medicine. **Holdings:** 15,000 books; 20,000 bound periodical volumes; 6000 technical reports; Atomic Bomb Casualty Commission technical reports; 50,000 microfiche of U.S. government-funded technical reports. **Subscriptions:** 300 journals and other serials; 6 newspapers. **Services:** Interlibrary loans; copying; library open to outside users who must register at reception desk of institute. **Automated Operations:** Computerized cataloging, acquisitions and circulation. **Computerized Information Services:** BRS, MEDLINE, OCLC; Digital Datatrieve (internal database). **Networks/Consortia:** Member of FEDLINK; Bethesda Military Medical Library Group; Interlibrary Users Association (IUA); Southeastern/Atlantic Regional Medical Library Services. **Publications:** Current Awareness, monthly. **Special Catalogs:** Union List of Serials-National Naval Medical Center (book). **Staff:** Sandra S. Matthews, Ref.; Myron K. Allman, Circ.

★13989★
U.S. ARMED FORCES SCHOOL OF MUSIC - REFERENCE LIBRARY (Mus)
NAVPHI Base, Little Creek   Phone: (703) 464-7511
Norfolk, VA 23521
Founded: 1941. **Staff:** Prof 1; Other 1. **Subjects:** Music - analysis, conducting, composition, counterpoint, harmony, theory, instruments; jazz; military music. **Holdings:** 3600 books; 4800 scores; 5600 phonograph records; 8500 instrumental methods; 7000 solos; 900 song books. **Subscriptions:** 30 journals and other serials. **Services:** Library open to public with restrictions.

★13990★
U.S. ARMED FORCES STAFF COLLEGE - LIBRARY (Mil)
7800 Hampton Blvd.   Phone: (804) 444-5155
Norfolk, VA 23511   Margaret J. Martin, Libn.
Founded: 1947. **Staff:** Prof 7; Other 11. **Subjects:** Military science, national and international affairs, history. **Special Collections:** Military administrative publications (3500). **Holdings:** 7900 bound periodical volumes; 82,000 cataloged items; 10,000 microforms; 65 drawers and 716 boxes of archival items; 24 drawers of pamphlets. **Subscriptions:** 575 journals and other serials; 21 newspapers. **Services:** Interlibrary loans; bibliographic and reference services to other U.S. government libraries; library not open to public. **Computerized Information Services:** DIALOG, DTIC. Performs free searches. Contact Person: Gail Nicula. **Publications:** Library Accessions List, weekly; Current Periodical Review, weekly - both for internal distribution only. **Special Indexes:** Reference Index File; subject index to periodicals in defense area (card). **Staff:** Sandra Byrn, Chf., Tech.Serv.Br.; Gail Nicula, Chf., Rd.Serv.Br.

★13991★
U.S. ARMS CONTROL AND DISARMAMENT AGENCY - LIBRARY (Soc Sci)
Dept. of State Bldg., Rm. 5851
21st & C St., N.W.   Phone: (202) 632-1592
Washington, DC 20541   Diane A. Ferguson, Libn.
Staff: Prof 1; Other 1. **Subjects:** Arms control, disarmament, nuclear proliferation, international peacekeeping. **Holdings:** 5300 books; 900 U.N. documents; 1400 documents of the Committee on Disarmament; 500 Congressional documents; 300 ACDA research reports and publications. **Subscriptions:** 170 journals and other serials; 12 newspapers. **Services:** Interlibrary loans; copying; library open to public by advance arrangement. **Also Known As:** ACDA. **Remarks:** The library is located at 1700 N. Lynn St., Rm. 805, Rossyln, VA 22209. **Staff:** Carolyn S. Alford, Lib.Techn.

★13992★
U.S. ARMY - ACADEMY OF HEALTH SCIENCES - STIMSON LIBRARY (Med)
Bldg. 2840   Phone: (512) 221-2116
Ft. Sam Houston, TX 78234   Norma L. Sellers, Chf.Libn.
Founded: 1932. **Staff:** Prof 4; Other 6. **Subjects:** Military medicine, nursing, health care administration, management, psychiatry, veterinary medicine. **Holdings:** 55,000 books; 7970 bound periodical volumes; 2000 pamphlets; 10,000 technical reports; 2500 archival items; 3500 items on microfilm. **Subscriptions:** 457 journals and other serials. **Services:** Interlibrary loans; library not open to public. **Computerized Information Services:** MEDLINE. **Networks/Consortia:** Member of Council of Research & Academic Libraries (CORAL). **Publications:** List of periodical holdings. **Staff:** Bertha Huber, Ref.Libn.; Kay D. Livingston, Tech.Serv.; Helene T. Morrow, Serv.Libn.

★13993★
U.S. ARMY - AEROMEDICAL RESEARCH LABORATORY - SCIENTIFIC INFORMATION CENTER (Med)
Box 577   Phone: (205) 255-6907
Ft. Rucker, AL 36362   Sybil H. Bullock, Libn.
Founded: 1963. **Staff:** Prof 2; Other 5. **Subjects:** Aviation medicine, medicine, vision, audiology, aviation psychology, acoustics, optics. **Special Collections:** All Aeromedical Research Laboratory Reports. **Holdings:** 12,000 books; 5000 bound periodical volumes; 15,000 documents; 1500 reels of microfilm; 2000 opaque cards; 1500 VF items; 50 magnetic tapes. **Subscriptions:** 425 journals and other serials. **Services:** Interlibrary loans; copying; center open to public. **Computerized Information Services:** DIALOG. **Publications:** Monthly Acquisitions; Periodical List, annual; special bibliographies; union list; bibliography of USAARL technical reports and letter reports.

★13994★
U.S. ARMY AIR DEFENSE SCHOOL - LIBRARY (Mil)†
Bldg. 2, Wing E
Box 5040   Phone: (915) 568-5781
Ft. Bliss, TX 79916   Delfina C. Galloway, Chf.Libn.
Founded: 1924. **Staff:** Prof 2; Other 4. **Subjects:** Military art and science, air defense, military and world history, American history, education, human relations, psychology of management, technology, mathematics, science. **Special Collections:** Archives collection of military subjects; Southwest Collection; Battle Studies Collection. **Holdings:** 23,000 books; 500 bound periodical volumes; 36,000 reports and documents on microfiche; 3000 reels of microfilm; 20 VF drawers of pamphlets; 150 language recordings. **Subscriptions:** 345 journals and other serials; 24 newspapers. **Services:** Interlibrary loans; copying; SDI; library not open to public. **Computerized Information Services:** DIALOG. **Publications:** New books list. **Staff:** Norma M. Kudiesy, Pub.Serv.Libn.

★13995★
U.S. ARMY AND AIR FORCE EXCHANGE SERVICE - CENTRAL LIBRARY AD-M (Mil)
          Phone: (214) 330-3337
Dallas, TX 75222   Linda McVey, Lib.Tech.
Staff: Prof 1; Other 1. **Subjects:** Military regulations, business and management. **Special Collections:** Exchange Service manuals. **Holdings:** 600 books; 450 binders of regulations. **Subscriptions:** 40 journals and other serials; 6 newspapers. **Services:** Library not open to public.

★13996★
U.S. ARMY - ARMAMENT, MUNITIONS AND CHEMICAL COMMAND - TECHNICAL LIBRARY (Sci-Tech; Mil)
HDQ AMCCOM
SMCAR-ESP-L   Phone: (309) 794-4208
Rock Island, IL 61299-6000   Philip E. Krouse, Chf.
Founded: 1958. **Staff:** Prof 1; Other 4. **Subjects:** Weapons and ammunition, production engineering. **Holdings:** 20,000 books; 15,000 technical reports;

25,000 microfiche. **Subscriptions:** 120 journals and other serials. **Services:** Interlibrary loans; library open to public by appointment. **Computerized Information Services:** DIALOG, DTIC. **Formerly:** Its Armament Material Readiness Command.

★13997★
U.S. ARMY - ARMAMENT RESEARCH & DEVELOPMENT CENTER - BENET WEAPONS LABORATORY - TECHNICAL LIBRARY (Sci-Tech; Mil)
Watervliet Arsenal
Attn: DRSMC-LCB-TL   Phone: (518) 266-5613
Watervliet, NY 12189   Philip M. Casey, Chf., Sci./Tech.Info.
Staff: Prof 1; Other 6. **Subjects:** Metallurgy, physics, ordnance, artillery, cannon, mortars, composite materials, mechanics. **Holdings:** 9000 books; 5500 bound periodical volumes; 20,000 technical documents. **Subscriptions:** 400 journals and other serials. **Services:** Interlibrary loans; copying; library open to public on request subject to regulations. **Computerized Information Services:** DIALOG, BRS, DTIC. **Networks/Consortia:** Member of Capital District Library Council for Reference & Research Resources (CDLC). **Publications:** Library Bulletin; Library Accession List.

★13998★
U.S. ARMY - ARMAMENT RESEARCH & DEVELOPMENT CENTER - SCIENTIFIC AND TECHNICAL INFORMATION DIVISION (Sci-Tech)
ARRADCOM, Bldg. 59   Phone: (201) 724-2914
Dover, NJ 07801   Normand L. Varieur, Libn.
Founded: 1929. **Staff:** Prof 7; Other 13. **Subjects:** Chemistry, technology, engineering, ammunition, science, physics, explosives, fire control, optics, materials. **Special Collections:** Weapon Data Index; Fuze Catalog; Government-Industry Data Exchange Program Reports; Archive of Frankford Arsenal (Philadelphia, PA); Archive of Picatinny Arsenal; federal and military specifications and standards; commercial standards; vendor catalogs. **Holdings:** 70,000 books; 20,000 bound periodical volumes; 450,000 technical reports. **Subscriptions:** 1200 journals and other serials. **Services:** Interlibrary loans; copying (limited); division open to public for reference use only on request. **Automated Operations:** Computerized serials and circulation. **Computerized Information Services:** DIALOG, DTIC, BRS, OCLC. **Networks/Consortia:** Member of FEDLINK. **Publications:** Technical Information Bulletin, biweekly - for internal distribution only. **Staff:** Ismail Haznedari, Supv.Libn.; Ruth Meredith, Supv.Libn.

★13999★
U.S. ARMY - ARMED FORCES PEST MANAGEMENT BOARD - DEFENSE PEST MANAGEMENT INFORMATION ANALYSIS CENTER (Sci-Tech)
Walter Reed Army Medical Center
Forest Glen Section   Phone: (202) 427-5365
Washington, DC 20307   Cdr. Fred J. Santana, MSC, Hd.
Founded: 1963. **Staff:** Prof 5; Other 6. **Subjects:** Vectors of human disease, arthropods of economic importance, stored product insects, pesticides, pesticide application equipment, pest vertebrates, pest management, agronomy. **Holdings:** 954 books; 150,000 documents. **Subscriptions:** 168 journals and other serials. **Services:** Copying; center open to public with restrictions. **Automated Operations:** Computerized cataloging. **Computerized Information Services:** Internal database. **Publications:** Bibliographies.

★14000★
U.S. ARMY ARMOR SCHOOL - LIBRARY (Mil)
Gaffey Hall, 2369
Old Ironsides Ave.   Phone: (502) 624-6231
Ft. Knox, KY 40121   William H. Hansen, Chf.Libn.
Founded: 1941. **Staff:** Prof 2; Other 2. **Subjects:** Military science, history, political science, foreign affairs. **Holdings:** 20,000 books; 1000 bound periodical volumes; 14,092 Department of the Army publications; 138 reels of microfilm; 2432 student staff studies; 10,000 afteraction reports; 300,000 documents on microfiche. **Subscriptions:** 280 journals and other serials; 20 newspapers. **Services:** Interlibrary loans; library open to public with restrictions on defense information. **Automated Operations:** Computerized cataloging and acquisitions. **Computerized Information Services:** DTIC, DIALOG, BRS. **Networks/Consortia:** Member of TRALINET. **Staff:** Freeman E. Shell, Jr., Ref.Libn.

U.S. ARMY - ARMY MOBILITY EQUIPMENT RESEARCH & DEVELOPMENT CENTER
See: U.S. Army - Belvoir Research & Development Center

★14001★
U.S. ARMY - ARMY TRANSPORTATION MUSEUM - LIBRARY (Hist; Mil)
Drawer D   Phone: (804) 878-3603
Fort Eustis, VA 23604   Dennis P. Mroczkowski, Dir.
Subjects: History of transportation in the U.S. Army and the Transportation Corps, 1914 to present. **Holdings:** 1500 books; 250 films; 2000 photographs; 100 linear feet of noncurrent records of the U.S. Army Transportation Center and School, 1957 to present; 58 periodical titles. **Services:** Copying; library open to public.

★14002★
U.S. ARMY - AVIATION MUSEUM - LIBRARY (Mil)
Bldg. 6007   Phone: (205) 255-4507
Fort Rucker, AL 36362   Harford Edwards, Jr., Hist.
Subjects: U.S. Army aviation, 1942 to present; civilian aviation. **Holdings:** 500 documents, manuscripts, oral history tapes and manuscripts, and sound recordings. **Services:** Copying; library open to serious researchers only.

★14003★
U.S. ARMY AVIATION TRAINING LIBRARY (Mil; Sci-Tech)
Bldgs. 5906 & 5907
Drawer O   Phone: (205) 255-5014
Ft. Rucker, AL 36362   Anne P. Foreman, Chf.Libn.
Founded: 1955. **Staff:** Prof 3; Other 8. **Subjects:** Aviation, international affairs, sciences, military history and science, education, management. **Special Collections:** Documents on history and development of army aviation. **Holdings:** 32,641 books; 3786 bound periodical volumes; 107,714 documents, 6360 microforms of periodicals. **Subscriptions:** 445 journals and other serials; 9 newspapers. **Services:** Interlibrary loans; copying; SDI; library open to public with restrictions. **Automated Operations:** Computerized cataloging and acquisitions. **Computerized Information Services:** BRS, DTIC, NASA/RECON, NEXIS, LEXIS, DIALOG, OCLC. **Networks/Consortia:** Member of FEDLINK. **Publications:** Acquisitions lists; subject bibliographies; handbooks. **Special Indexes:** Periodical holdings lists; card indexes to periodicals and military publications.

★14004★
U.S. ARMY - BELVOIR RESEARCH & DEVELOPMENT CENTER - TECHNICAL LIBRARY (Sci-Tech; Mil)
Bldg. 315   Phone: (703) 664-5179
Ft. Belvoir, VA 22060   Gloria R. James, Chf., Tech.Lib.Div.
Staff: Prof 3; Other 9. **Subjects:** Vehicle drives, camouflage, amphibious vehicles, electric vehicles, detection and detectors, construction equipment, engineering, environmental control, gasahol, army equipment. **Holdings:** 15,000 books; 200 bound periodical volumes; 50,000 technical reports; 200 test reports. **Subscriptions:** 375 journals and other serials; 10 newspapers. **Services:** Interlibrary loans; library not open to public. **Automated Operations:** Computerized cataloging. **Computerized Information Services:** DTIC, DIALOG, BRS, OCLC, DTIC. Performs searches on cost recovery basis. Contact Person: Janice Pepper, 664-5339. **Formerly:** Its Army Mobility Equipment Research & Development Command. **Staff:** Janice Pepper, Ref.Libn., Doc.Sect.; Lois Carey, Ref.Libn. Open Lit.Sect.

U.S. ARMY - CENTER FOR MILITARY HISTORY
See: U.S. Army Museum, Presidio of Monterey

★14005★
U.S. ARMY CHEMICAL SCHOOL - FISHER LIBRARY (Sci-Tech; Mil)
Bldg. 2281   Phone: (205) 238-4414
Fort McClellan, AL 36205   Carla J. Pomager, Libn.
Founded: 1982. **Staff:** Prof 1; Other 3. **Subjects:** Chemical warfare, radiation protection, military history. **Special Collections:** Defense Department Technical Reports (2000); Defense Department documents (1500); rare books (150); Chemical School Archives (35 VF drawers). **Holdings:** 6500 books; 3150 documents; 77 periodical titles on microfilm (1977 to present). **Subscriptions:** 200 journals and other serials; 20 newspapers. **Services:** Interlibrary loans; copying; library open to public - documents may be used only by government agencies. **Computerized Information Services:** DIALOG, OCLC, BRS, DTIC. **Networks/Consortia:** Member of TRALINET.

★14006★
U.S. ARMY - CHEMICAL RESEARCH & DEVELOPMENT CENTER - INFORMATION SERVICES BRANCH - TECHNICAL LIBRARY (Sci-Tech)
                                            Phone: (301) 671-2934
Aberdeen Proving Ground, MD 21010   Edwin F. Gier, Chf., Tech.Lib.
Founded: 1919. **Staff:** Prof 4; Other 7. **Subjects:** Chemistry, ecology, pollution control. **Holdings:** 7000 books; 7950 bound periodical volumes; 265,000 government reports; 10,000 film cartridges. **Subscriptions:** 350

journals and other serials. **Services:** Interlibrary loans; copying; library not open to public. **Automated Operations:** Computerized cataloging and serials. **Computerized Information Services:** OCLC, DIALOG. **Networks/Consortia:** Member of FEDLINK. **Publications:** Periodical Holding List, irregular. **Formerly:** Its Chemical Systems Laboratory. **Staff:** C.R. Anaclerio, Chf., Info.Serv.Br.

★14007★
U.S. ARMY - COLD REGIONS RESEARCH & ENGINEERING LABORATORY - LIBRARY (Sci-Tech)
72 Lyme Rd.   Phone: (603) 646-4221
Hanover, NH 03755   Nancy C. Liston, Libn.
Founded: 1952. **Staff:** Prof 1; Other 2. **Subjects:** Physics, geology, hydrology, meteorology, geography, mathematics, engineering. **Special Collections:** Snow, ice and frozen ground; cold regions environment and materials. **Holdings:** 8000 books; 28,000 documents, reports, pamphlets, periodical articles; 460 reels of microfilm (30,000 articles); 350 map titles; 60,000 items on microfiche. **Subscriptions:** 350 journals and other serials. **Services:** Interlibrary loans; library open to other government agencies, government contractors, and scientists with related interests by appointment. **Computerized Information Services:** DIALOG, SDC. **Publications:** Library accession bulletin; CRREL publications list. **Special Catalogs:** Bibliography on Cold Regions Science and Technology. **Remarks:** An alternate telephone number is 646-4238.

★14008★
U.S. ARMY COMBAT DEVELOPMENTS EXPERIMENTATION COMMAND - TECHNICAL INFORMATION CENTER (Sci-Tech)†
HQ USACDEC
Bldg. 2925   Phone: (408) 242-3757
Ft. Ord, CA 93941   Carolyn I. Alexander, Chf.Libn.
Founded: 1966. **Staff:** Prof 2; Other 2. **Subjects:** Armor, behavioral sciences, experimental design, instrumentation, small arms, small unit organizations, helicopter warfare. **Holdings:** 5000 books and bound periodical volumes; 13,000 technical reports; 4000 publications; 50 pamphlets; 1000 microforms. **Subscriptions:** 400 journals and other serials; 10 newspapers. **Services:** Interlibrary loans; copying; center open for official use only. **Publications:** Acquisitions List; Serials List, annual.

★14009★
U.S. ARMY COMMAND AND GENERAL STAFF COLLEGE - COMBINED ARMS RESEARCH LIBRARY (Mil)
Bell Hall   Phone: (913) 684-3282
Ft. Leavenworth, KS 66027   Martha A. Davis, Libn.
Founded: 1906. **Staff:** Prof 10; Other 21. **Subjects:** Military art and science, military history, political science, management. **Holdings:** 105,000 books; 7000 bound periodical volumes; 140,000 documents; 400,000 microforms. **Subscriptions:** 650 journals and other serials; 32 newspapers. **Services:** Interlibrary loans; copying; library open to public with restrictions. **Automated Operations:** Computerized circulation. **Computerized Information Services:** DIALOG, SDC, BRS, NEXIS, OCLC, DTIC. **Networks/Consortia:** Member of TRALINET. **Staff:** Daniel Dorris, Chf., Ref.Serv.; Bertina Byers, Chf., Doc.Ctr.; Barbara T. Everidge, Sys.Libn.

★14010★
U.S. ARMY - COMMUNICATIONS-ELECTRONICS COMMAND - TECHNICAL LIBRARY (Sci-Tech)
DRSEL-ME-PSL   Phone: (201) 532-1298
Ft. Monmouth, NJ 07703
Founded: 1940. **Staff:** Prof 2; Other 2. **Subjects:** Mathematics, electrical engineering, personnel management, physics, electronic engineering, chemistry, photography, test engineering. **Special Collections:** Historical file of official Signal Corps literature; complete collection of Department of the Army literature on electronic equipment, cataloged by type designation. **Holdings:** 4000 books; 100,000 technical manuals and related publications; 1000 manufacturers' catalogs; 2500 pamphlets. **Subscriptions:** 300 journals and other serials. **Services:** Interlibrary loans; library not open to public. **Staff:** Marion Clinton, Libn.

★14011★
U.S. ARMY - COMMUNICATIONS SYSTEMS CENTER - ELECTRONICS MUSEUM (Mil)†
Myer Hall, Ave. of Memories   Phone: (201) 532-2445
Ft. Monmouth, NJ 07701   Edmond J. Norris, Dir.
Founded: 1942. **Staff:** Prof 2; Other 2. **Subjects:** U.S. Army Signal Corps history; development of American military communications. **Special Collections:** Brig. Gen. A.J. Myer documents (7000 pages). **Holdings:** 4000 volumes of out-of-print books, manuals and pamphlets. **Services:** Library open to qualified researchers. **Publications:** Fort Monmouth History and Place Names, 1917-1961.

★14012★
U.S. ARMY COMPUTER SYSTEMS COMMAND - TECHNICAL LIBRARY (Comp Sci)†
ACSC-DST (Annex), Stop H-9   Phone: (703) 756-5491
Ft. Belvoir, VA 22060   Grace Corbin, Tech.Info.Spec.
Founded: 1968. **Staff:** Prof 1; Other 1. **Subjects:** Data processing, computers, computer programming, operations research, functionally-oriented language, management information systems. **Holdings:** 2500 books; 3450 vendor manuals on computer hardware and programming; 1700 technical reports, part on microfiche; 1100 regulatory and standardization texts for federal and military ADP operations. **Subscriptions:** 190 journals and other serials. **Services:** Interlibrary loans; video self-study administration; library open to public for reference use only.

★14013★
U.S. ARMY - CONSTRUCTION ENGINEERING RESEARCH LABORATORY - H.B. ZACKRISON MEMORIAL LIBRARY (Sci-Tech)
Interstate Research Pk.
Box 4005   Phone: (217) 373-7217
Champaign, IL 61820   Martha A. Blake, Libn.
Founded: 1969. **Staff:** Prof 1; Other 1. **Subjects:** Environmental engineering, construction materials, construction management, structural engineering, architectural psychology, civil engineering. **Holdings:** 7000 books; 1000 bound periodical volumes; 10,000 technical reports. **Subscriptions:** 400 journals and other serials. **Services:** Interlibrary loans; copying; library open to public for reference use only. **Computerized Information Services:** SDC, DIALOG, OCLC, DTIC. **Networks/Consortia:** Member of ILLINET; FEDLINK. **Publications:** New Acquisitions - for internal distribution only; library brochure. **Special Catalogs:** Catalog of laboratory reports (card).

U.S. ARMY - CORPS OF ENGINEERS - COASTAL ENGINEERING RESEARCH CENTER
See: U.S. Army - Corps of Engineers - Humphrey's Engineering Center

★14014★
U.S. ARMY - CORPS OF ENGINEERS - DETROIT DISTRICT - TECHNICAL LIBRARY (Sci-Tech)
477 Federal McNamara Bldg., 6th Fl.
Box 1027   Phone: (313) 226-6231
Detroit, MI 48231   Monica Moffa, District Libn.
Staff: Prof 1; Other 1. **Subjects:** Engineering, water resources development, Great Lakes navigation, harbor structures, environmental and flood control. **Special Collections:** Detroit district technical reports and studies; district projects slide collection. **Holdings:** 3500 books; 5000 annual reports; government documents; climatological data. **Subscriptions:** 250 journals and other serials; 5 newspapers. **Services:** Interlibrary loans; library open to public. **Automated Operations:** Computerized cataloging. **Computerized Information Services:** OCLC, DIALOG. **Networks/Consortia:** Member of FEDLINK.

U.S. ARMY - CORPS OF ENGINEERS - ENGINEER WATERWAYS EXPERIMENT STATION
See: U.S. Army - Engineer Waterways Experiment Station

★14015★
U.S. ARMY - CORPS OF ENGINEERS - FORT WORTH DISTRICT - TECHNICAL LIBRARY (Sci-Tech)†
819 Taylor St.
Box 17300   Phone: (817) 334-2138
Fort Worth, TX 76102   Robin A. Osborne, Libn.
Founded: 1950. **Staff:** Prof 2; Other 2. **Subjects:** Law; engineering - civil, electrical, mechanical, safety; finance; nuclear science; ecology; environment. **Special Collections:** Air and water pollution, water resources development. **Holdings:** 15,000 books; 20,000 technical reports; army regulations; Congressional documents; industry standards and specifications on microfiche; Federal Register, 1969 to present. **Subscriptions:** 500 journals and other serials; 50 newspapers. **Services:** Interlibrary loans; library open to public for reference use only. **Automated Operations:** Computerized cataloging. **Computerized Information Services:** DIALOG, OCLC. **Networks/Consortia:** Member of FEDLINK. **Staff:** Cecilia Wetzbarger, Asst.Libn.

★14016★
U.S. ARMY - CORPS OF ENGINEERS - GALVESTON DISTRICT - LIBRARY (Sci-Tech)
Box 1229   Phone: (409) 766-3196
Galveston, TX 77553   Gail M. Henderson, Libn.
Founded: 1945. **Staff:** 2. **Subjects:** Civil engineering, construction and

operation of public works for navigation, flood control, environment, recreation, water resources, soil mechanics, law. **Special Collections:** Annual Reports of the Chief of Engineers, 1871-1980; Congressional documents, 1900-1978. **Holdings:** 8000 books; 2900 other cataloged items. **Subscriptions:** 158 journals and other serials; 19 newspapers. **Services:** Interlibrary loans; library open to public for reference use except for classified material. **Computerized Information Services:** DIALOG, OCLC. **Networks/ Consortia:** Member of FEDLINK.

★14017★
U.S. ARMY - CORPS OF ENGINEERS - HUMPHREY'S ENGINEERING CENTER - TECHNICAL LIBRARY (Sci-Tech)
Kingman Bldg., Rm. 3C02   Phone: (202) 325-7375
Ft. Belvoir, VA 22060   Bennie F. Maddox, Chf., Lib.Br.
Founded: 1940. **Staff:** Prof 3; Other 3. **Subjects:** Coastal engineering, hydraulics, shore protection, model studies, beach erosion, coastal ecology, navigation, coastal flood control. **Holdings:** 40,000 books; 60,000 technical reports; photographs; microforms; motion pictures. **Subscriptions:** 475 journals and other serials. **Services:** Interlibrary loans; copying; library open to public. **Automated Operations:** Computerized cataloging. **Computerized Information Services:** OCLC, DIALOG. **Formerly:** Its Coastal Engineering Research Center - Library.

★14018★
U.S. ARMY - CORPS OF ENGINEERS - HUNTINGTON DISTRICT - LIBRARY (Sci-Tech)
502 8th St.   Phone: (304) 529-5713
Huntington, WV 25721   Sandra V. Morris, Libn.
Staff: Prof 1; Other 2. **Subjects:** Water resource development, environmental science, civil engineering, hydrology. **Special Collections:** Oral history collection (75 hours). **Holdings:** 10,000 books; 260 bound periodical volumes. **Subscriptions:** 150 journals and other serials; 12 newspapers. **Services:** Interlibrary loans; copying; SDI; library open to public. **Automated Operations:** Computerized cataloging. **Computerized Information Services:** DIALOG, OCLC, LEXIS. **Networks/Consortia:** Member of FEDLINK.

★14019★
U.S. ARMY - CORPS OF ENGINEERS - HYDROLOGIC ENGINEERING CENTER - LIBRARY (Sci-Tech)
609 2nd St.   Phone: (916) 756-1104
Davis, CA 95616   Lynne L. Stevenson, Libn.
Staff: Prof 1. **Subjects:** Hydrology, hydrologic modeling, hydrologic engineering, water resources planning and management, hydraulics. **Holdings:** 500 books; 500 unbound reports; 1000 documents. **Subscriptions:** 15 journals and other serials. **Services:** Interlibrary loans; copying; SDI; library open to public with restrictions. **Computerized Information Services:** DIALOG, OCLC. **Networks/Consortia:** Member of FEDLINK.

★14020★
U.S. ARMY - CORPS OF ENGINEERS - JACKSONVILLE DISTRICT - TECHNICAL LIBRARY (Sci-Tech)
400 W. Bay St.
Box 4970   Phone: (904) 791-3643
Jacksonville, FL 32232   Oriana Brown West, District Libn.
Staff: Prof 2; Other 2. **Subjects:** Civil engineering, environmental resources, fish and wildlife, geology, coastal erosion, storms and hurricanes. **Special Collections:** Cross Florida Barge Canal; Central and Southern Florida Project for Flood Control and Other Purposes. **Holdings:** 4000 books; 8000 reports; Congressional documents, 1940-1970. **Subscriptions:** 150 journals and other serials. **Services:** Interlibrary loans; copying; library open to public for reference use only. **Automated Operations:** Computerized cataloging and acquisitions. **Computerized Information Services:** DIALOG, SDC, BRS, OCLC, Institute for Scientific Information (ISI). **Networks/Consortia:** Member of FEDLINK. **Publications:** Corps of Engineers Project Reports. **Staff:** Linda Smith, Cons./Cat.

★14021★
U.S. ARMY - CORPS OF ENGINEERS - LOWER MISSISSIPPI VALLEY DIV. - MISSISSIPPI RIVER COMMN. TECHNICAL LIB. (Sci-Tech)
Box 80   Phone: (601) 634-5880
Vicksburg, MS 39180   Sherrie L. Moran, Libn.
Founded: 1943. **Staff:** Prof 1; Other 1. **Subjects:** Flood control, navigation, hydraulics. **Holdings:** 47,500 books; 200 bound periodical volumes; 580 reels of microfilm; 3000 microfiche. **Subscriptions:** 420 journals and other serials; 15 newspapers. **Services:** Interlibrary loans; copying; library open to public with restrictions on loans. **Automated Operations:** Computerized cataloging. **Computerized Information Services:** DIALOG, OCLC, LEGI-SLATE. **Networks/Consortia:** Member of FEDLINK. **Publications:** List of publications received, monthly. **Staff:** Mary H. Hall, Lib.Techn.

★14022★
U.S. ARMY - CORPS OF ENGINEERS - MEMPHIS DISTRICT - LIBRARY (Sci-Tech)
B-314 Clifford Davis Federal Bldg.   Phone: (901) 521-3584
Memphis, TN 38103   Jacque Patterson, Libn.
Founded: 1932. **Staff:** Prof 1; Other 1. **Subjects:** Civil engineering, water resources, environmental concerns, transportation and economics. **Holdings:** 6000 books; 370 microforms. **Subscriptions:** 150 journals and other serials. **Services:** Interlibrary loans; copying; library open to public for reference use only. **Automated Operations:** Computerized cataloging. **Computerized Information Services:** DIALOG, OCLC. **Networks/Consortia:** Member of FEDLINK.

★14023★
U.S. ARMY - CORPS OF ENGINEERS - NEW ENGLAND DIVISION - TECHNICAL LIBRARY (Sci-Tech)
Bldg. 116N
424 Trapelo Rd.   Phone: (617) 647-8118
Waltham, MA 02254   Timothy P. Hays, Chf., Tech.Lib.
Staff: Prof 1; Other 2. **Subjects:** Water resources; hydrology; geotechnical, structural and civil engineering; ecology. **Special Collections:** New England River Basin Collection. **Holdings:** 10,000 books; 50 bound periodical volumes; 7000 reports; 5000 Corps of Engineers reports including reports on dredged materials; 1000 hydrology reports. **Subscriptions:** 300 journals and other serials; 20 newspapers. **Services:** Interlibrary loans; copying; SDI; library open to public with identification. **Automated Operations:** Computerized cataloging and acquisitions. **Computerized Information Services:** DIALOG, SDC, OCLC, LEXIS, NEXIS, ISI Search Network; internal database. Performs searches on cost recovery basis. **Networks/Consortia:** Member of FEDLINK.

U.S. ARMY - CORPS OF ENGINEERS - OFFICE OF THE CHIEF OF ENGINEERS See: U.S. Army - Office of the Chief of Engineers

★14024★
U.S. ARMY - CORPS OF ENGINEERS - OMAHA DISTRICT - LIBRARY (Sci-Tech)
215 N. 17th St.
6014 U.S. Post Office & Courthouse   Phone: (402) 221-3230
Omaha, NE 68102-4978   Valetta Sharp, Libn.
Staff: Prof 1; Other 2. **Subjects:** Engineering, water resources, law. **Holdings:** Agency regulations and directives. **Services:** Interlibrary loans; library open to public for reference use only. **Automated Operations:** Computerized cataloging. **Computerized Information Services:** DIALOG, OCLC. **Networks/Consortia:** Member of FEDLINK. **Remarks:** This library serves both the District Office and the Missouri River Division Office.

★14025★
U.S. ARMY - CORPS OF ENGINEERS - PHILADELPHIA DISTRICT - TECHNICAL LIBRARY (Sci-Tech)
2nd & Chestnut Sts.   Phone: (215) 597-3610
Philadelphia, PA 19106   Jeanne Marie Turner, Lib.Techn.
Founded: 1974. **Staff:** Prof 1. **Subjects:** Engineering - civil, environmental, coastal. **Special Collections:** U.S. Army Corps of Engineers - Philadelphia District technical reports; U.S. Army Corps of Engineers Laboratory technical reports (3500). **Holdings:** 5200 books; 2 VF drawers of standards; 200 microfiche; 2 VF drawers of information files. **Subscriptions:** 115 journals and other serials. **Services:** Interlibrary loans; library open to public with restrictions. **Automated Operations:** Computerized cataloging. **Computerized Information Services:** DIALOG, OCLC. **Networks/Consortia:** Member of FEDLINK. **Publications:** Accessions lists, monthly; bibliographies.

★14026★
U.S. ARMY - CORPS OF ENGINEERS - PORTLAND DISTRICT - LIBRARY (Sci-Tech)
Box 2946   Phone: (503) 221-6016
Portland, OR 97208   Christian P. Hurd, District Libn.
Founded: 1938. **Staff:** Prof 1; Other 2. **Subjects:** Engineering, law. **Holdings:** 10,000 books. **Subscriptions:** 135 journals and other serials; 10 newspapers. **Services:** Interlibrary loans; library open to public for reference use only. **Automated Operations:** Computerized cataloging and ILL. **Computerized Information Services:** DIALOG, SDC, BRS, OCLC.

★14027★
U.S. ARMY - CORPS OF ENGINEERS - ROCK ISLAND DISTRICT - TECHNICAL LIBRARY (Sci-Tech)
Clocktower Bldg.   Phone: (309) 788-6361
Rock Island, IL 61201
Staff: Prof 1; Other 1. **Subjects:** Civil engineering, hydraulics/locks and dams, flood and plain management, construction, soil mechanics,

environmental analysis. **Special Collections:** Hydraulics; Water Experiment Station technical reports; Water Resources Developments; construction. **Holdings:** 10,000 books; 20 bound periodical volumes; 15,000 technical reports; 5000 microfiche; 800 reels of microfilm; 25,000 slides. **Subscriptions:** 300 journals and other serials; 10 newspapers. **Services:** Interlibrary loans; copying; library open to public by appointment. **Automated Operations:** Computerized cataloging and ILL. **Computerized Information Services:** DIALOG, SDC, OCLC, DTIC. **Networks/Consortia:** Member of FEDLINK. **Publications:** Holdings List: Indices, Newspapers, Periodicals, annual; New Books and Reports List, monthly.

★14028★
U.S. ARMY - CORPS OF ENGINEERS - SACRAMENTO DISTRICT - TECHNICAL INFORMATION CENTER (Sci-Tech)
650 Capitol Mall   Phone: (916) 440-3404
Sacramento, CA 95814   Deborah A. Newton, District Libn.
Staff: Prof 1; Other 2. **Subjects:** Water, hydrology, hydraulics, environment, recreation planning, geology, architecture, construction. **Special Collections:** Annual Reports to the Chief of Engineers. **Holdings:** 25,000 volumes. **Subscriptions:** 213 journals and other serials; 5 newspapers. **Services:** Interlibrary loans (limited); copying; center open to public. Computerized cataloging. **Computerized Information Services:** DIALOG, SDC, BRS; Corps of Engineers Private File (internal database). Performs free searches. **Networks/Consortia:** Member of FEDLINK.

★14029★
U.S. ARMY - CORPS OF ENGINEERS - ST. LOUIS DISTRICT - LIBRARY (Sci-Tech)
210 Tucker Blvd., N.   Phone: (314) 263-5675
St. Louis, MO 63101   Katharine Hayes, District Libn.
Staff: Prof 1; Other 1. **Subjects:** Civil engineering, water resources, environment, wildlife management, recreation. **Holdings:** 9800 books; 6000 technical reports; microfilm. **Subscriptions:** 500 journals and other serials; 60 newspapers. **Services:** Interlibrary loans; copying; library open to public. **Automated Operations:** Computerized cataloging and serials. **Computerized Information Services:** OCLC, DIALOG, F.W. Faxon Company, Inc. **Networks/Consortia:** Member of FEDLINK. **Publications:** Periodical Holdings List, annual; Library Users Guide; New Books List, bimonthly. **Special Catalogs:** Microfiche catalog of book and report collection.

★14030★
U.S. ARMY - CORPS OF ENGINEERS - ST. PAUL DISTRICT - TECHNICAL LIBRARY (Sci-Tech)
1135 U.S. Post Office & Custom House   Phone: (612) 725-5921
St. Paul, MN 55101   Jean Marie Schmidt, Libn.
Staff: Prof 1. **Subjects:** Engineering, hydrology, water resources, dam construction, environmental studies, military history. **Special Collections:** Chief of Engineers Annual Reports, 1867 to present; Army Technical Manuals; Waterborne Commerce Statistics. **Holdings:** 8000 books; 1700 Waterway Experiment Station reports; 200 U.S. Geological Survey reports. **Subscriptions:** 210 journals and other serials. **Services:** Interlibrary loans; library open to public for reference use only. **Computerized Information Services:** DIALOG, OCLC. **Networks/Consortia:** Member of Metronet; FEDLINK.

★14031★
U.S. ARMY - CORPS OF ENGINEERS - SAVANNAH DISTRICT - TECHNICAL LIBRARY (Sci-Tech)
Box 889   Phone: (912) 944-5461
Savannah, GA 31402   James C. Dorsey, Chf., Tech.Lib.
Founded: 1968. **Staff:** Prof 1; Other 2. **Subjects:** Engineering, environmental studies, geology, hydrology. **Holdings:** 5600 books; 7000 technical reports; 16,920 microforms. **Subscriptions:** 360 journals and other serials. **Services:** Interlibrary loans; SDI; library open to public by appointment. **Automated Operations:** Computerized cataloging. **Computerized Information Services:** DIALOG, SDC, OCLC.

★14032★
U.S. ARMY - CORPS OF ENGINEERS - SEATTLE DISTRICT - LIBRARY (Sci-Tech)
Box C-3755   Phone: (206) 764-3728
Seattle, WA 98124   Pat J. Perry, District Libn.
Founded: 1940. **Staff:** Prof 2; Other 1. **Subjects:** Engineering, environment, hydraulics, marine construction, law. **Special Collections:** Army Field Law Library (7000 volumes); Eng/Tech Collection. **Holdings:** 15,000 books and reports; 15,000 technical reports on microfiche; 18,000 district slides; 5 drawers of pamphlets. **Subscriptions:** 350 journals and other serials; 30 newspapers. **Services:** Interlibrary loans; library open to public. **Automated Operations:** Computerized cataloging and circulation. **Computerized**

Information Services: DIALOG, SDC, BRS, DOE/RECON, DTIC, OCLC, Harris In-House Information System. **Publications:** New Titles, Periodical Holdings. **Special Indexes:** District slide file index. **Staff:** Mary E. Johnson, Asst.Libn.

★14033★
U.S. ARMY - CORPS OF ENGINEERS - SOUTH ATLANTIC DIVISION - LIBRARY & INFORMATION CENTER (Sci-Tech)
510 Title Bldg.
30 Pryor St., S.W.   Phone: (404) 221-6620
Atlanta, GA 30303   James D. Chestnut, Div.Libn.
Staff: Prof 1; Other 1. **Subjects:** Civil engineering, water resources, contract law. **Holdings:** 3400 books. **Subscriptions:** 202 journals and other serials. **Services:** Interlibrary loans; copying; center open to public for reference use only. **Automated Operations:** Computerized cataloging. **Computerized Information Services:** OCLC, DIALOG. **Networks/Consortia:** Member of FEDLINK; Georgia Library Information Network (GLIN).

★14034★
U.S. ARMY - CORPS OF ENGINEERS - SOUTH PACIFIC DIVISION - LIBRARY (Sci-Tech)
630 Sansome St., Rm. 1216   Phone: (415) 556-9727
San Francisco, CA 94111   Mary G. Anderson, Div.Libn.
Staff: Prof 1. **Subjects:** Civil and military engineering, water resources. **Special Collections:** Corps of Engineers annual reports; Waterways Experiment Station Reports. **Holdings:** 3026 books; 6000 bound reports. **Subscriptions:** 155 journals and other serials. **Services:** Interlibrary loans; library open to public for reference use only. **Automated Operations:** Computerized cataloging. **Computerized Information Services:** DIALOG, OCLC. **Networks/Consortia:** Member of OCLC Pacific Network. **Publications:** Accession lists, monthly; periodical lists, quarterly - both for internal distribution only.

★14035★
U.S. ARMY - CORPS OF ENGINEERS - SOUTHWESTERN DIVISION - LIBRARY (Sci-Tech)
1114 Commerce St.   Phone: (214) 767-2325
Dallas, TX 75242   Maxine C. Smith, Libn.
Staff: Prof 1; Other 2. **Subjects:** Engineering, science, law, economics. **Holdings:** 9000 volumes; 20,000 pamphlets; Visual Search Microfilm File; 16mm cassettes. **Subscriptions:** 180 journals and other serials. **Services:** Interlibrary loans; library open to public for reference use only. **Automated Operations:** Computerized cataloging and serials. **Computerized Information Services:** DIALOG, OCLC, LEGI-SLATE. Performs searches free of charge for up to 10 pages. **Networks/Consortia:** Member of FEDLINK. **Publications:** SWD Library Bookworm, bimonthly.

U.S. ARMY - DARCOM
See: U.S. Army - Materiel Development & Readiness Command (DARCOM)

★14036★
U.S. ARMY - DUGWAY PROVING GROUND - TECHNICAL LIBRARY (Mil; Sci-Tech)
                                                    Phone: (801) 522-3565
Dugway, UT 84022   Duane Williamson, Chf., Tech.Lib.
Founded: 1950. **Staff:** Prof 1; Other 2. **Subjects:** Chemistry, biology, chemical/biological warfare. **Special Collections:** Classified and unclassified documents related to chemical/biological testing (Access limited to U.S. government agencies and their contractors). **Holdings:** 6700 books; 2000 bound periodical volumes; 35,000 bound technical reports; 15,000 microforms. **Subscriptions:** 30 journals and other serials. **Services:** Interlibrary loans; library open to public by appointment. **Automated Operations:** Computerized acquisitions and circulation. **Computerized Information Services:** DIALOG, DTIC.

★14037★
U.S. ARMY - ELECTRONICS R & D COMMAND (ERADCOM) - HARRY DIAMOND LABORATORIES - TECHNICAL INFORMATION BRANCH (Sci-Tech)
2800 Powder Mill Rd. (DELHD-TA-L)   Phone: (202) 394-1010
Adelphi, MD 20783   Barbara L. McLaughlin, Chf.
Founded: 1959. **Staff:** Prof 4; Other 4. **Subjects:** Electronics, physics, engineering, chemistry, mathematics. **Holdings:** 34,900 books; 19,697 bound periodical volumes; 100,000 technical reports. **Subscriptions:** 726 journals and other serials. **Services:** Interlibrary loans; branch not open to public. **Automated Operations:** Computerized cataloging. **Computerized Information Services:** DIALOG, OCLC, SDC, DTIC. **Publications:** Accession List.

★14038★

U.S. ARMY - ELECTRONICS R & D COMMAND (ERADCOM) - TECHNICAL LIBRARY DIVISION (Sci-Tech)
Bldg. 2700, Attn: DELSD-L   Phone: (201) 544-2237
Ft. Monmouth, NJ 07703   William R. Werk, Chf.
Founded: 1942. **Staff:** Prof 3; Other 8. **Subjects:** Electronics, electrical engineering, chemistry, physics, computer science. **Holdings:** 48,000 books; 24,000 bound periodical volumes; 150,000 technical documents. **Subscriptions:** 350 journals and other serials. **Services:** Library not open to public. **Automated Operations:** Computerized cataloging and acquisitions. **Computerized Information Services:** DIALOG, OCLC. **Networks/Consortia:** Member of FEDLINK. **Staff:** Brenda W. Shanholtz, Libn.; Margaret Borden, Libn.

★14039★

U.S. ARMY ENGINEER SCHOOL - LIBRARY (Mil; Sci-Tech)
Bldg. 270   Phone: (703) 664-2524
Ft. Belvoir, VA 22060   Madge J. Busey, Lib.Dir.
Founded: 1935. **Staff:** Prof 2; Other 4. **Subjects:** Engineering, military history. **Special Collections:** Corps of Engineers history; rare books on engineering and military engineering from Revolutionary and Civil War periods. **Holdings:** 45,000 books; 65,000 training pamphlets and documents; 18,000 photographs; 15,000 military publications; documents and reports on microfiche; 20,000 AV items. **Subscriptions:** 348 journals and other serials. **Services:** Interlibrary loans; library not open to public. **Computerized Information Services:** DIALOG, DTIC, OCLC. **Networks/Consortia:** Member of TRALINET. **Publications:** Acquisition list, quarterly; periodicals list, annual. **Special Catalogs:** Military periodicals; special staff study research papers. **Special Indexes:** Index to The Engineer.

★14040★

U.S. ARMY - ENGINEER TOPOGRAPHIC LABORATORIES - SCIENTIFIC & TECHNICAL INFORMATION CENTER (Sci-Tech)
                                              Phone: (703) 664-3834
Ft. Belvoir, VA 22060   Mildred Stiger, Chf.
Staff: Prof 1; Other 2. **Subjects:** Geodesy, photogrammetry, remote sensing, robotics, mapping. **Holdings:** 6000 volumes; 190 bound periodical volumes; 2000 technical reports; 1000 microfiche. **Subscriptions:** 175 journals and other serials. **Services:** Interlibrary loans; copying; center open to government agencies, schools, industry. **Computerized Information Services:** DIALOG, Institute for Scientific Information (ISI), DTIC, OCLC. **Networks/Consortia:** Member of FEDLINK.

★14041★

U.S. ARMY - ENGINEER WATERWAYS EXPERIMENT STATION - COASTAL ENGINEERING INFORMATION ANALYSIS CENTER (Sci-Tech)
Box 631   Phone: (601) 634-2017
Vicksburg, MS 39180   Andre Szuwalski, Dir.
Subjects: Beach erosion, flood and storm protection, coastal and offshore structures, navigation structures. **Holdings:** Center acts as a central repository for the Corps of Engineers data collection under the field data collection program for coastal engineering. The data includes wave statistics, coastal currents, beach profiles and aerial photographs. Center is supported by holdings in the Technical Information Center. **Services:** Interlibrary loans. **Publications:** CERCular (information bulletin), quarterly; annotated bibliography of publications of the Coastal Engineering Research Center.

★14042★

U.S. ARMY - ENGINEER WATERWAYS EXPERIMENT STATION - CONCRETE TECHNOLOGY INFORMATION ANALYSIS CENTER (Sci-Tech)
Box 631   Phone: (601) 634-3264
Vicksburg, MS 39180   Bryant Mather, Dir.
Subjects: Concrete materials and properties, concrete tests and analysis, concrete construction, cements and pozzolans, reinforced concrete, waterstops and jointing materials, grouts and grouting, adhesives and coatings, corrosion in steel and concrete. **Holdings:** Center is supported by holdings of the Technical Information Center. **Services:** Interlibrary loans; copying. **Publications:** Published papers issued at irregular intervals - list available on request.

★14043★

U.S. ARMY - ENGINEER WATERWAYS EXPERIMENT STATION - HYDRAULIC ENGINEERING INFORMATION ANALYSIS CENTER (Sci-Tech)
Box 631   Phone: (601) 634-3368
Vicksburg, MS 39180   Bobby J. Brown, Dir.
Subjects: Hydraulics - river, harbor, tidal, closed conduit; flood control structures; navigation structures; harbor protective structures; underwater shock effects. **Holdings:** Center is supported by holdings in the Technical Information Center. **Services:** Interlibrary loans; copying.

★14044★

U.S. ARMY - ENGINEER WATERWAYS EXPERIMENT STATION - PAVEMENTS & SOIL TRAFFICABILITY INFO. ANALYSIS CTR. (Sci-Tech)
Box 631   Phone: (601) 634-2734
Vicksburg, MS 39180   Gerald W. Turnage, Dir.
Subjects: Soil trafficability, mobility, pavements, terrain evaluation. **Holdings:** Center is supported by the collection of holdings in the Technical Information Center. **Services:** Interlibrary loans; copying. **Publications:** Reports 1-5 - list available on request.

★14045★

U.S. ARMY - ENGINEER WATERWAYS EXPERIMENT STATION - SOIL MECHANICS INFORMATION ANALYSIS CENTER (Sci-Tech)
Box 631   Phone: (601) 634-3475
Vicksburg, MS 39180   Paul F. Hadala, Dir.
Subjects: Soil mechanics, soil dynamics, rock mechanics, foundation engineering, earthquake engineering, engineering geology, earth dams, subgrades. **Holdings:** Center is supported by holdings in the Technical Information Center. **Services:** Interlibrary loans; copying. **Publications:** Proceedings of Symposium on Applications of the Finite Element Method in Geotechnical Engineering; Microthesaurus of Soil Mechanics Terms; Evaluation Statements and Abstracts of Recent Acquisitions on Soil Mechanics and Related Subjects, bimonthly.

★14046★

U.S. ARMY - ENGINEER WATERWAYS EXPERIMENT STATION - TECHNICAL INFORMATION CENTER (Sci-Tech)
Box 631   Phone: (601) 634-2533
Vicksburg, MS 39180   Al Sherlock, Chf., Tech.Info.Ctr.
Founded: 1933. **Staff:** Prof 12; Other 20. **Subjects:** Hydraulics, soil mechanics, concrete, weapons effects, mobility of vehicles, environmental studies, explosive excavation, pavements, geology. **Holdings:** 300,000 volumes; 45,000 microforms. **Subscriptions:** 900 journals and other serials. **Services:** Interlibrary loans; copying; SDI; center open to public with restrictions. **Automated Operations:** Computerized circulation. **Computerized Information Services:** DTIC, DIALOG. **Publications:** Recent Acquisitions Lists, monthly - to government agencies; List of Post Authorization Reports, annual - to Corps of Engineers; List of Translations of Waterways Experiment Station, irregular - to Corps of Engineers; List of Publications of the U.S. Army Engineer Waterways Experiment Station, annual; List of Translations of Foreign Literature on Hydraulics, irregular; Bibliography on Tidal Hydraulics, irregular; WES Engineering Computer Programs Library Catalog, semiannual - to Corps of Engineers; bibliographies. **Remarks:** Supports the five Department of Defense Analysis Centers established at the Waterways Experiment Station, which do not have separate collections. **Staff:** Bernice Black, Chf., Lib.Br.; Alfrieda Clark, Chf., Spec. Projects; Hollis Landrum, Chf., Tech.Proc.Sect.; Don Kirby, Chf., Ref.Sect.; Jerry Griffith, Libn.; Terry Kiss, Ref.Libn.; Debbie Carpenter, Ref.Libn.; Carol McMillin, Ref.Libn.; Paul Taccarino, Libn.; Mary Dell Martin, Chf., Pub.Distr.Sect.; Katherine Kennedy, Tech.Info.Spec.

★14047★

U.S. ARMY - ENVIRONMENTAL HYGIENE AGENCY - LIBRARY (Med)
Bldg. E2100   Phone: (301) 671-4236
Aberdeen Proving Ground, MD 21010   Krishan S. Goel, Libn.
Founded: 1955. **Staff:** Prof 1; Other 2. **Subjects:** Occupational medicine, safety and health; chemistry and toxicology; audiology; medical entomology; laser, microwave and radiological safety and health; air and water pollution; sanitary engineering. **Holdings:** 12,000 books; 18,000 bound periodical volumes; 8400 R&D reports; 3000 microfiche. **Subscriptions:** 450 journals and other serials. **Services:** Interlibrary loans; copying; SDI; library open to agency guests and researchers from accredited institutions. **Automated Operations:** Computerized serials. **Computerized Information Services:** OCLC, DIALOG, MEDLINE.

★14048★

U.S. ARMY IN EUROPE (USAREUR) - LIBRARY AND RESOURCE CENTER (Mil)
HQ USAREUR and Seventh Army
APO New York, NY 09403   Duane G. Nahley, Supv.Libn.
Founded: 1948. **Staff:** Prof 5; Other 8. **Subjects:** Military affairs, business, international relations, current events, political science, education. **Special Collections:** World War II, unit histories, campaigns. **Holdings:** 70,000 books; 75,000 microforms; 3500 video cassettes; ERIC documents. **Subscriptions:** 950 journals and other serials; 20 newspapers. **Services:** Interlibrary loans; copying; SDI; center open to public. **Automated Operations:** Computerized cataloging and circulation. **Computerized Information Services:** CIS. **Publications:** Subject bibliographies, irregular; periodical holdings, annual. **Staff:** George Patail, Ref.Libn.; Jane Cohen,

Ref.Libn.; Ann Parham, Ref.Libn.; Jewell Player, Tech.Serv.Libn.

★14049★
U.S. ARMY FIELD ARTILLERY SCHOOL - MORRIS SWETT TECHNICAL LIBRARY (Mil)
Snow Hall, Rm. 16   Phone: (405) 351-4525
Ft. Sill, OK 73503   Lester L. Miller, Jr., Supv.Libn.
Founded: 1911. **Staff:** Prof 2; Other 4. **Subjects:** Military science and history, history of field artillery, political science, technology, management. **Special Collections:** U.S. Field Artillery Unit Histories; rare book collection. **Holdings:** 89,531 books and bound periodical volumes; 22,000 other cataloged items; 126,270 microforms; 31,000 Department of the Army and Department of Defense publications. **Subscriptions:** 381 journals and other serials; 35 newspapers. **Services:** Interlibrary loans; copying; SDI; library open to public for reference use only. **Computerized Information Services:** DTIC, BRS, DIALOG, OCLC. **Networks/Consortia:** Member of Oklahoma Teletype Information Service (OTIS); Oklahoma Special Collections and Archives Network (OSCAN); Oklahoma Health Sciences Library Association (OHSLA). **Publications:** Special bibliographies, indexes and checklists, irregular; subject headings and "U" Military Science Classification List. **Special Indexes:** Card index to military periodicals dating to mid-1800s; in-house military science and subject indexes; century series bibliographies. **Staff:** Matha H.C. Relph, Libn.

★14050★
U.S. ARMY - FORT MEADE MUSEUM - LIBRARY (Mil)
                                        Phone: (301) 677-6966
Ft. George G. Meade, MD 20755   David C. Cole, Cur.
Founded: 1963. **Subjects:** Military history, history of 1st U.S. Army, history of Ft. Meade. **Special Collections:** Photographs of World Wars I and II; weapons, uniforms and accoutrements and other memorabilia of the army. **Holdings:** 1000 books; 3000 artifacts. **Services:** Interlibrary loans; copying; library open to public for reference use only.

★14051★
U.S. ARMY - HEADQUARTERS TRADOC/FORT MONROE LIBRARY & INTERN TRAINING CENTER (Mil)
Bldg. 133   Phone: (804) 727-2821
Ft. Monroe, VA 23651   Frances M. Doyle, Supv.Libn.
Staff: Prof 2; Other 4. **Subjects:** Military science, management, training and education. **Special Collections:** Department of the Army publications (60,000). **Holdings:** 11,000 books; 375 bound periodical volumes; 3000 technical documents. **Subscriptions:** 350 journals and other serials; 10 newspapers. **Services:** Interlibrary loans; library open to Department of Defense personnel. **Computerized Information Services:** DIALOG, BRS, DTIC, OCLC, OPTIMIS, Circa Library Circulation System. **Networks/Consortia:** Member of TRALINET. **Publications:** Selected Acquisitions List; A Guide to Professional Reading, quarterly - to headquarters staff offices. **Formed by the Merger of:** U.S. Army - Training and Doctrine Command - Technical Library and U.S. Army Post - Fort Monroe - Library. **Staff:** Patricia W. Henry, Supv. of Intern Trng.

★14052★
U.S. ARMY HOSPITALS - BASSETT ARMY HOSPITAL - MEDICAL LIBRARY (Med)
                                        Phone: (907) 353-5194
Ft. Wainwright, AK 99703   Mary Heidel, Lib.Techn.
Staff: Prof 1. **Subjects:** Surgery, obstetrics/gynecology, pediatrics, nursing, internal medicine, radiology. **Holdings:** 1800 books; 40 bound periodical volumes. **Subscriptions:** 204 journals and other serials. **Services:** Interlibrary loans; library open to public for reference use only.

★14053★
U.S. ARMY HOSPITALS - BAYNE JONES ARMY COMMUNITY HOSPITAL - MEDICAL LIBRARY (Med)
                                        Phone: (318) 535-3725
Ft. Polk, LA 71459   Mary K. Bradford, Med.Lib.Techn.
Staff: Prof 1. **Subjects:** Medicine, pathology, hospital administration, dentistry. **Holdings:** 6000 volumes; 200 bound periodical volumes. **Subscriptions:** 200 journals and other serials. **Services:** Interlibrary loans; library not open to public. **Networks/Consortia:** Member of TALON. **Formerly:** Its Fort Polk Army Hospital.

★14054★
U.S. ARMY HOSPITALS - BLANCHFIELD ARMY COMMUNITY HOSPITAL - MEDICAL LIBRARY (Med)
                                        Phone: (502) 798-8014
Ft. Campbell, KY 42223   Ina L. Nesbitt, Med.Libn.
Founded: 1959. **Staff:** Prof 1; Other 1. **Subjects:** Medicine and related

topics. **Special Collections:** Ciba slide collection. **Holdings:** 3416 books; 2610 bound periodical volumes; video cassettes; Audio-Digest tapes. **Subscriptions:** 360 journals and other serials. **Services:** Interlibrary loans; copying; library open to medical personnel on limited basis. **Computerized Information Services:** MEDLARS. **Networks/Consortia:** Member of Greater Midwest Regional Medical Library Network (Region 3).

★14055★
U.S. ARMY HOSPITALS - BLISS ARMY HOSPITAL - MEDICAL LIBRARY (Med)
                                        Phone: (602) 538-5668
Ft. Huachuca, AZ 85613   Thomasa J. Martin, Lib.Off.
Staff: Prof 1. **Subjects:** Clinical medicine, nursing, hospital administration. **Special Collections:** Medicine in World War II (especially surgery). **Holdings:** 1238 books; unbound and bound periodical volumes; 500 audiovisual cassettes; 100 audio cassettes. **Subscriptions:** 163 journals and other serials. **Services:** Interlibrary loans; copying; library open to public with approval of Library Officer. **Publications:** Quarterly Report - for internal distribution only. **Staff:** Ann E. Nichols, Libn.

★14056★
U.S. ARMY HOSPITALS - BROOKE ARMY MEDICAL CENTER - MEDICAL LIBRARY (Med)
Bldg. 1001   Phone: (512) 221-4119
Ft. Sam Houston, TX 78234   Ida E. Davis, Adm.Libn.
Staff: Prof 2; Other 3. **Subjects:** Medicine, dentistry, nursing and allied health sciences, religion, social work. **Special Collections:** Institute of Surgical Research on Burns (7600 volumes). **Holdings:** 17,310 books; 26,050 bound periodical volumes; 3030 paperback books. **Subscriptions:** 675 journals and other serials. **Services:** Interlibrary loans; copying; library open to members of health professions for reference. **Computerized Information Services:** MEDLINE, OCLC.

★14057★
U.S. ARMY HOSPITALS - CUTLER ARMY HOSPITAL - MEDICAL LIBRARY (Med)
                                        Phone: (617) 796-6750
Ft. Devens, MA 01433   Mrs. Leslie R. Seidel, Med.Libn.
Staff: Prof 1; Other 1. **Subjects:** Medicine, surgery, nursing, dentistry. **Holdings:** 1800 books; 2500 bound periodical volumes. **Subscriptions:** 180 journals and other serials. **Services:** Interlibrary loans; copying; library open to public with borrowing limited to professional medical U.S. Army personnel. **Networks/Consortia:** Member of Northeastern Consortium for Health Information (NECHI).

★14058★
U.S. ARMY HOSPITALS - D.D. EISENHOWER ARMY MEDICAL CENTER - MEDICAL LIBRARY (Med)†
                                        Phone: (404) 791-6765
Ft. Gordon, GA 30905   Judy M. Krivanek, Med.Libn.
Staff: Prof 1; Other 2. **Subjects:** Surgery, psychiatry, internal medicine, dentistry, nursing. **Holdings:** 4680 books; 2968 bound periodical volumes. **Subscriptions:** 300 journals and other serials. **Services:** Interlibrary loans; library not open to public.

★14059★
U.S. ARMY HOSPITALS - DARNALL ARMY HOSPITAL - MEDICAL LIBRARY (Med)
                                        Phone: (817) 288-8368
Ft. Hood, TX 76544   Frank M. Norton, Adm.Libn.
Staff: Prof 2; Other 1. **Subjects:** Medicine and related topics. **Holdings:** 2600 books; 3500 bound periodical volumes; 400 audiotapes; 209 videotapes. **Subscriptions:** 450 journals and other serials. **Services:** Interlibrary loans; copying; library open to medical professionals. **Automated Operations:** Computerized cataloging, acquisitions, serials and circulation. **Computerized Information Services:** MEDLINE, BRS, DIALOG, Birth Defects Information System, AMA/NET. **Staff:** Jonella B. Lein, Tech.Info.Spec.

★14060★
U.S. ARMY HOSPITALS - FITZSIMONS ARMY MEDICAL CENTER - MEDICAL-TECHNICAL LIBRARY (Med)
                                        Phone: (303) 361-3378
Aurora, CO 80045-5000   Sharon Johnson, Adm.Libn.
Founded: 1947. **Staff:** Prof 2; Other 3. **Subjects:** Medicine and allied sciences. **Holdings:** 13,400 books; 24,500 bound periodical volumes. **Subscriptions:** 700 journals and other serials. **Computerized Information Services:** DIALOG, OCLC.

★14061★
U.S. ARMY HOSPITALS - FORT CARSON ARMY HOSPITAL - MEDICAL LIBRARY (Med)
Bldg. 6235
Ft. Carson, CO 80913
Phone: (303) 579-3209
Alfreda H. Hanna, Med.Libn.
Staff: 2. **Subjects:** Medicine, nursing and related topics. **Holdings:** 5000 books; 6500 bound periodical volumes; 660 AV items. **Subscriptions:** 280 journals and other serials. **Services:** Interlibrary loans; copying; library open to public with restrictions. **Computerized Information Services:** MEDLARS, OCLC, Octanet, DIALOG. Performs free searches for libraries providing free services. **Networks/Consortia:** Member of Colorado Council of Medical Librarians; Peaks and Valleys (Medical) Library Consortium; FEDLINK.

U.S. ARMY HOSPITALS - FORT POLK ARMY HOSPITAL
See: U.S. Army Hospitals - Bayne Jones Army Community Hospital

★14062★
U.S. ARMY HOSPITALS - IRWIN ARMY HOSPITAL - MEDICAL LIBRARY (Med)
Bldg. 485
Ft. Riley, KS 66442
Phone: (913) 239-7874
Phyllis J. Whiteside, Med.Libn.
Staff: Prof 1. **Subjects:** Medicine, surgery, dentistry, nursing. **Holdings:** 1406 books; 1619 bound periodical volumes. **Subscriptions:** 207 journals and other serials. **Services:** Interlibrary loans; copying; library open to public with restrictions. **Networks/Consortia:** Member of Midcontinental Regional Medical Library Program. **Publications:** Newsletter, monthly.

★14063★
U.S. ARMY HOSPITALS - KENNER ARMY HOSPITAL - MEDICAL LIBRARY (Med)*
Ft. Lee, VA 23801
Phone: (804) 734-1339
Betty K. Lewis, Libn.
Subjects: Medicine. **Holdings:** 2200 volumes.

★14064★
U.S. ARMY HOSPITALS - GENERAL LEONARD WOOD ARMY COMMUNITY HOSPITAL - MEDICAL LIBRARY (Med)
Ft. Leonard Wood, MO 65473
Phone: (314) 368-9110
Mrs. Marian B. Strang, Med.Libn.
Founded: 1950. **Staff:** Prof 1. **Subjects:** Medicine. **Holdings:** 3500 books; 3000 bound periodical volumes. **Subscriptions:** 200 journals and other serials. **Services:** Interlibrary loans; library not open to public.

★14065★
U.S. ARMY HOSPITALS - LETTERMAN ARMY MEDICAL CENTER - MEDICAL LIBRARY (Med)
Bldg. 1100, Rm. 338
Presidio of San Francisco, CA 94123
Phone: (415) 561-2465
William Koch, Adm.Libn.
Founded: 1918. **Staff:** Prof 2; Other 3. **Subjects:** Medicine, nursing, psychology, hospital administration, military medical history. **Holdings:** 5000 books; 20,000 bound periodical volumes. **Subscriptions:** 650 journals and other serials. **Services:** Interlibrary loans; library not open to public. **Automated Operations:** Computerized cataloging and ILL. **Computerized Information Services:** DIALOG, BRS, MEDLARS, OCLC. **Networks/Consortia:** Member of San Francisco Biomedical Library Network. **Staff:** Dixie Meagher, Libn.

★14066★
U.S. ARMY HOSPITALS - LYSTER ARMY COMMUNITY HOSPITAL - MEDICAL LIBRARY (Med)
Bldg. 301
U.S. Army Aeromedical Center
Ft. Rucker, AL 36362
Phone: (205) 255-4504
Jeanette A. Chambers, Lib.Techn.
Staff: 1. **Subjects:** Medicine, nursing, veterinary medicine, aviation medicine, dentistry. **Holdings:** 2600 books; 2031 bound periodical volumes; 430 audiovisual cassettes; 10 subscriptions for audio cassettes (24 tapes/year); 75 other cassettes. **Subscriptions:** 100 journals and other serials. **Services:** Interlibrary loans; copying; library open to public for reference use only.

★14067★
U.S. ARMY HOSPITALS - MC DONALD USA COMMUNITY HOSPITAL - MEDICAL LIBRARY (Med)†
Ft. Eustis, VA 23604
Phone: (804) 878-2897
Helen O. Hearn, Lib.Mgr.
Staff: 1. **Subjects:** Medicine, dentistry, nursing. **Holdings:** 1500 books; 1100 bound periodical volumes. **Subscriptions:** 100 journals and other serials. **Services:** Interlibrary loans; library not open to public.

★14068★
U.S. ARMY HOSPITALS - MADIGAN ARMY MEDICAL CENTER - MEDICAL LIBRARY (Med)
Box 375
Tacoma, WA 98431
Phone: (206) 967-6782
Elizabeth C. Bolden, Libn.
Founded: 1944. **Staff:** Prof 2; Other 2. **Subjects:** Medicine, dentistry, nursing, hospital administration, pharmacology. **Holdings:** 25,000 books; 6900 bound periodical volumes; 4 VF drawers of pamphlets and reprints. **Subscriptions:** 535 journals and other serials. **Services:** Interlibrary loans; library not open to public. **Computerized Information Services:** NLM, OCLC. **Publications:** Information Sources and Resources, irregular - to personnel at the center and local medical libraries.

★14069★
U.S. ARMY HOSPITALS - MADIGAN ARMY MEDICAL CENTER - MORALE SUPPORT LIBRARY (Mil)
Tacoma, WA 98431
Phone: (206) 967-6198
Marganne Weathers, Adm.Libn.
Founded: 1944. **Staff:** Prof 1. **Special Collections:** Military affairs, patient education. **Holdings:** 20,000 books; 1800 phonograph records; 6 VF drawers of pamphlets. **Subscriptions:** 135 journals and other serials; 10 newspapers. **Services:** Interlibrary loans; copying; library open to public for reference use only; borrowers need military identification. **Automated Operations:** Computerized cataloging. **Networks/Consortia:** Member of WLN. **Publications:** List of new books, monthly; annotated bibliographies of special collections subjects, irregular.

★14070★
U.S. ARMY HOSPITALS - MARTIN ARMY COMMUNITY HOSPITAL - MEDICAL LIBRARY (Med)
Ft. Benning, GA 31905
Phone: (404) 544-1341
E.A. Tate, Med.Libn.
Founded: 1958. **Staff:** Prof 1; Other 1. **Subjects:** Medicine and allied health sciences. **Holdings:** 2300 books; 1700 bound periodical volumes; 500 audio cassette tapes. **Subscriptions:** 317 journals and other serials. **Services:** Interlibrary loans; library open to health care professionals for reference use only. **Computerized Information Services:** MEDLINE. **Networks/Consortia:** Member of Southeastern/Atlantic Regional Medical Library Services; Atlanta Health Science Libraries Consortium; Health Science Libraries of Central Georgia (HSLCG). **Publications:** Library Acquisitions; Internal News Bulletin, quarterly.

★14071★
U.S. ARMY HOSPITALS - NOBLE ARMY HOSPITAL - MEDICAL LIBRARY (Med)
Ft. McClellan, AL 36205
Phone: (205) 238-2411
Pauline Mayhall, Lib.Mgr.
Founded: 1951. **Staff:** 1. **Subjects:** Medicine and allied sciences. **Holdings:** 3500 books; 3350 bound periodical volumes; 2500 pamphlets, papers, bibliographies. **Subscriptions:** 150 journals and other serials. **Services:** Interlibrary loans; copying; library open to public for reference use only.

★14072★
U.S. ARMY HOSPITALS - TRIPLER ARMY MEDICAL CENTER - MEDICAL LIBRARY (Med)
Tripler AMC, HI 96859
Linda Requena, Chf., Med.Lib.
Staff: Prof 2; Other 2. **Subjects:** Medicine, paramedical sciences, dentistry, nursing. **Holdings:** 15,000 books; 25,000 bound periodical volumes. **Subscriptions:** 500 journals and other serials. **Services:** Interlibrary loans; copying; SDI; library open to public with restrictions. **Computerized Information Services:** MEDLINE.

★14073★
U.S. ARMY HOSPITALS - WALSON ARMY HOSPITAL - MEDICAL LIBRARY (Med)
Ft. Dix, NJ 08640
Phone: (609) 562-5741
Alice H. Gadsden, Med.Libn.
Founded: 1959. **Staff:** Prof 1; Other 1. **Subjects:** Medicine, dentistry, nursing, psychiatry. **Holdings:** Figures not available. **Services:** Interlibrary loans. **Networks/Consortia:** Member of Greater Northeastern Regional Medical Library Program; Pinelands Consortium for Health Information.

★14074★
U.S. ARMY HOSPITALS - WALTER REED ARMY MEDICAL CENTER - MEDICAL LIBRARY (Med)
Bldg. 2, Rm. 2G
Washington, DC 20307
Phone: (202) 576-1238
Beth E. Smith, Chf.Libn.
Staff: Prof 3; Other 6. **Subjects:** Medicine and allied fields. **Special Collections:** History of science and medicine (Fred C. Ainsworth Endowment

Library). **Holdings:** 15,000 books; 10,000 bound periodical volumes. **Subscriptions:** 508 journals and other serials. **Subscriptions:** 723 journals and other serials. **Services:** Interlibrary loans; library not open to public. **Computerized Information Services:** MEDLINE; OCLC, AMA/NET. **Networks/Consortia:** Member of FEDLINK.

★14075★
U.S. ARMY HOSPITALS - WILLIAM BEAUMONT ARMY MEDICAL CENTER - MEDICAL LIBRARY (Med)†
Bldg. 7777
El Paso, TX 79920
Phone: (915) 569-3121
Merle I. Alexander, Med.Libn.
Founded: 1931. **Staff:** Prof 3; Other 2. **Subjects:** Surgery, medicine, nursing, dentistry, hospital administration. **Holdings:** 17,000 books; 12,000 bound periodical volumes; 20,000 periodical volumes on microfilm; 630 AV titles. **Subscriptions:** 600 journals and other serials. **Services:** Interlibrary loans; library not open to public. **Computerized Information Services:** MEDLINE, DIALOG, OCLC. **Networks/Consortia:** Member of TALON. **Special Catalogs:** Catalog of Audiovisual Holdings (book). **Staff:** Holbrook W. Yorke, Med.Libn.

★14076★
U.S. ARMY HOSPITALS - WOMACK ARMY COMMUNITY HOSPITAL - MEDICAL LIBRARY (Med)
Ft. Bragg, NC 28307
Phone: (919) 396-1819
Cecilia C. Edwards, Med.Libn.
Founded: 1958. **Staff:** 3. **Subjects:** Medicine, dentistry and allied health sciences. **Holdings:** 2800 books; 4000 bound periodical volumes; 2 VF drawers of clippings, pamphlets, documents. **Subscriptions:** 310 journals and other serials. **Services:** Interlibrary loans; copying; library open to public with restrictions. **Automated Operations:** Computerized cataloging. **Computerized Information Services:** MEDLINE. Performs free searches. **Networks/Consortia:** Member of Cape Fear Health Sciences Information Consortium; FEDLINK; Southeastern/Atlantic Regional Medical Library Service.

★14077★
U.S. ARMY INFANTRY SCHOOL - DONOVAN TECHNICAL LIBRARY (Mil)
Infantry Hall, Bldg. 4
Ft. Benning, GA 31905
Phone: (404) 544-4053
Vivian S. Dodson, Chf., Lrng.Rsrcs.Div.
Founded: 1919. **Staff:** Prof 3; Other 4. **Subjects:** Military history, military art and science, political science, social science, national defense, foreign affairs, management, education. **Special Collections:** Map collection (10,000); rare military books (10,000). **Holdings:** 55,000 books and bound periodical volumes; 50,000 classified and unclassified documents. **Subscriptions:** 326 journals and other serials; 24 newspapers. **Services:** Interlibrary loans; copying; library use limited to military community. **Computerized Information Services:** DIALOG, DTIC. **Networks/Consortia:** Member of TRALINET.

★14078★
U.S. ARMY - THE INSTITUTE OF HERALDRY - LIBRARY (Mil)
Cameron Station
5010 Duke St., Bldg. 15
Alexandria, VA 22314
Phone: (202) 274-6544
Herbert M. Pastan, Libn.
Founded: 1962. **Staff:** Prof 1. **Subjects:** Heraldry, arts, colors, flags, lettering and decorations, history, medals, military history (chiefly U.S.), military insignia, military uniforms, seals, signs, symbolisms, weapons. **Special Collections:** Looseleaf notebooks (1500) comprised of materials on uniforms, flags, and decorations of the U.S. Army from 1776 to the present. **Holdings:** 12,000 volumes; 8 VF drawers. **Services:** Library open to public by appointment.

U.S. ARMY INSTITUTE FOR MILITARY ASSISTANCE
See: U.S. Army - JFK Special Warfare Center

★14079★
U.S. ARMY INTELLIGENCE CENTER & SCHOOL - ACADEMIC LIBRARY (Mil)
Alvarado Hall
Ft. Huachuca, AZ 85613
Phone: (602) 538-5930
Sylvia J. Webber, Chf.
Founded: 1970. **Staff:** Prof 2; Other 4. **Subjects:** Military intelligence, military history, foreign affairs, political science, military geography, area studies of countries of the world. **Holdings:** 9000 books; 2500 items in VF drawers; 2000 student research papers. **Subscriptions:** 200 journals and other serials; 5 newspapers. **Services:** Interlibrary loans; copying; SDI; library open to public by appointment. **Computerized Information Services:** DIALOG, DTIC, OCLC. **Staff:** Pauline Spanabel, Ref./Rd.Serv.Libn.

★14080★
U.S. ARMY INTELLIGENCE SCHOOL, DEVENS - LIBRARY (Mil)†
Ft. Devens, MA 01433
Phone: (617) 796-3413
Ornella L. Pensyl, Chf.
Founded: 1951. **Staff:** Prof 4; Other 4. **Subjects:** Military science, electronics, education. **Special Collections:** Electronic warfare. **Holdings:** 7000 books and bound periodical volumes; 22,000 microfiche; 17,400 classified documents; 13,000 military publications. **Subscriptions:** 318 journals and other serials; 22 newspapers. **Services:** Interlibrary loans; library not open to public. **Automated Operations:** Computerized cataloging and acquisitions. **Computerized Information Services:** DIALOG, OCLC, BRS, DTIC; internal database. **Networks/Consortia:** Member of TRALINET; FEDLINK. **Publications:** Monthly Acquisitions list - free upon request. **Special Catalogs:** Learning Center Catalog, quarterly (book).

★14081★
U.S. ARMY - INTELLIGENCE AND THREAT ANALYSIS CENTER - TECHNICAL INFORMATION CENTER (Mil)
Bldg. A, Rm. 2204
Arlington Hall Station
Arlington, VA 22212
Phone: (202) 692-1428
Dean A. Burns, Chf.
Staff: Prof 6; Other 7. **Subjects:** Military intelligence. **Special Collections:** Army threat documents. **Holdings:** Figures not available. **Services:** Interlibrary loans (limited); center not open to public. **Automated Operations:** Computerized cataloging. **Computerized Information Services:** DIALOG, NEXIS, SDC. **Remarks:** Requests for documents should be submitted through channels. Contractors must submit requests through their contract monitors. All requests must include certification of need to know. **Staff:** Anne E. Bert, Tech.Info.Spec.; Barbara G. Williams, Tech.Info.Spec.; Deane Pinckard, Tech.Info.Spec.

★14082★
U.S. ARMY - JFK SPECIAL WARFARE CENTER - MARQUAT MEMORIAL LIBRARY (Mil)
Rm. 140, Kennedy Hall
Ft. Bragg, NC 28307
Phone: (919) 396-9383
Frank M. London, Supv.Libn.
Founded: 1952. **Staff:** Prof 2. **Subjects:** Military assistance, international studies, unconventional warfare, political science. **Holdings:** 45,000 books and bound periodical volumes; pamphlets and documents; Human Relations Area Files (microfilm). **Subscriptions:** 350 journals and other serials; 20 newspapers. **Services:** Interlibrary loans; copying; library open to public for reference use only. **Automated Operations:** cataloging AND circulation. **Computerized Information Services:** BRS, DIALOG, OCLC, DTIC. **Networks/Consortia:** Member of FEDLINK. **Publications:** Accession List, Periodical Holdings List, Library guide. **Formerly:** U.S. Army Institute for Military Assistance. **Staff:** Jim Moore, Ref.Libn.

★14083★
U.S. ARMY - JUDGE ADVOCATE GENERAL'S SCHOOL - LIBRARY (Law; Mil)
Phone: (804) 293-9824
Charlottesville, VA 22903-1781
R. Vivian Hebert, Law Libn.
Founded: 1951. **Staff:** Prof 1; Other 1. **Subjects:** Military and federal law, military science. **Holdings:** 12,844 volumes. **Subscriptions:** 382 journals and other serials; 5 newspapers. **Services:** Interlibrary loans; copying; library open to public for reference use only.

★14084★
U.S. ARMY - LANGUAGE TRAINING FACILITY - LIBRARY (Hum)
Bldg. 2509
USA Education Ctr.
Ft. George G. Meade, MD 20755
Phone: (301) 677-7255
Dorothy R. Kimball, Chf.
Staff: Prof 1; Other 1. **Subjects:** Foreign languages. **Holdings:** 8000 books; foreign language tapes, workbooks, dictionaries, encyclopedias. **Services:** Interlibrary loans; library open to reservists, dependents and staff. **Also Known As:** Fort Meade Army Education Center, Language Laboratory. **Staff:** Margret Kightlinger, Libn./Techn.

★14085★
U.S. ARMY - LANGUAGE TRAINING FACILITY - LIBRARY (Hum)
Bldg. 4404
Ft. Hood, TX 76544
Phone: (817) 287-7506
Else B. d'Emery, Libn.
Founded: 1958. **Staff:** Prof 2. **Subjects:** Books and texts in 40 foreign languages, area studies of foreign nations. **Special Collections:** Bible collection in 56 languages and dialects. **Holdings:** 8000 books; 2000 magnetic tapes; 4 VF drawers of pamphlets, articles. **Subscriptions:** 50 international journals and other serials. **Services:** Interlibrary loans; library open to military personnel, dependents, retirees and Department of Army civilians. **Staff:** Martine Pinney, Libn.

★14086★
U.S. ARMY - LOGISTICS LIBRARY (Mil)
Attn: ATSM - OSL
Bldg. P-12500
Ft. Lee, VA 23801
Phone: (703) 734-4286
Raymon Trisdale, Chf.Libn.
Founded: 1971. **Staff:** Prof 3; Other 4. **Subjects:** Logistics, military history, management, computer science, social sciences, business and finance, food and nutrition. **Holdings:** 93,279 books; 425 bound periodical volumes; 2 million U.S. Government serial publications; 131,612 unbound periodicals; 16,547 periodicals in microform; 20,000 reports. **Subscriptions:** 600 journals and other serials; 9 newspapers. **Services:** Interlibrary loans; copying; library open to public for reference use only. **Automated Operations:** Computerized cataloging and acquisitions. **Computerized Information Services:** BRS, DIALOG, DTIC, OPTIMIS, OCLC. Performs free searches. **Networks/Consortia:** Member of FEDLINK; TRALINET. **Publications:** Acquisitions list, quarterly; Library Handbook. **Staff:** Kenneth A. Grabach, Ref.Libn.; Lucy R. Greene, Asst.Libn.

U.S. ARMY - MATERIALS & MECHANICS RESEARCH CENTER - NONDESTRUCTIVE TESTING INFORMATION ANALYSIS CENTER
See: Southwest Research Institute - Nondestructive Testing Information Analysis Center

★14087★
U.S. ARMY - MATERIALS & MECHANICS RESEARCH CENTER - TECHNICAL LIBRARY (Sci-Tech; Mil)
Phone: (617) 923-5460
Watertown, MA 02172
Margaret M. Murphy, Chf., Tech.Lib.
Founded: 1920. **Staff:** Prof 3; Other 3. **Subjects:** Materials science, mechanics, composite materials, metallurgy, nondestructive testing, chemistry, engineering, ceramics, polymer chemistry, military science, physics. **Holdings:** 25,000 books; 20,000 bound periodical volumes; 33,000 documents (hard copy); 47,000 documents (microfiche); 913 volumes on microfiche/microfilm. **Subscriptions:** 650 journals and other serials; 15 newspapers. **Services:** Interlibrary loans; copying; library not open to public. **Computerized Information Services:** DIALOG, BRS, DTIC, OCLC. **Networks/Consortia:** Member of FEDLINK; NELINET. **Publications:** Monographs, annotated bibliographies, both irregular. **Staff:** Susan A. Macksey, Libn.; Robert C. Seidel, Libn.

U.S. ARMY - MATERIEL DEVELOPMENT & READINESS COMMAND - AUTOMATED LOGISTIC MANAGEMENT SYSTEMS AGENCY
See: Automated Logistic Management Systems Agency

★14088★
U.S. ARMY - MATERIEL DEVELOPMENT & READINESS COMMAND (DARCOM) - INTERN TRAINING CENTER LIBRARY (Sci-Tech; Mil)
Red River Army Depot
Texarkana, TX 75507
Phone: (214) 838-3430
Lelia K. Vollman, Lib.Tech.Supv.
Staff: Prof 1; Other 2. **Subjects:** Management; logistics; engineering - mechanical, electrical, safety, production, maintainability, quality and reliabilty. **Special Collections:** U.S. Military Regulations (2000); Intern Training Center Research Reports (600). **Holdings:** 16,000 books; 280 periodical volumes; 400 technical reports. **Subscriptions:** 266 journals and other serials; 10 newspapers. **Services:** Interlibrary loans; copying; library open to public with restrictions. **Computerized Information Services:** DTIC, U.S. National Technical Information Service (NTIS). **Networks/Consortia:** Member of Defense Logistics Studies Information Exchange. **Publications:** Accessions list, monthly.

★14089★
U.S. ARMY - MATERIEL DEVELOPMENT & READINESS COMMAND - HEADQUARTERS - TECHNICAL LIBRARY (Mil)
5001 Eisenhower Ave.
Alexandria, VA 22333
Phone: (202) 274-8152
Phyllis Ortutay, Chf.
Founded: 1973. **Staff:** Prof 2; Other 3. **Subjects:** Management, technology, mathematics and statistics, military affairs, data processing, social sciences and economics. **Holdings:** 17,000 volumes. **Services:** Interlibrary loans; library not open to public. **Automated Operations:** Computerized cataloging. **Computerized Information Services:** DIALOG, BRS, DTIC, OCLC. **Networks/Consortia:** Member of FEDLINK. **Also Known As:** U.S. Army - DARCOM.

★14090★
U.S. ARMY MEDICAL BIOENGINEERING RESEARCH & DEVELOPMENT LABORATORY - TECHNICAL REFERENCE LIBRARY (Sci-Tech; Med)
Fort Detrick, Bldg. 568
Frederick, MD 21701
Phone: (301) 663-2502
Edna M. Snyder, Libn.
Founded: 1964. **Staff:** 2. **Subjects:** Field medical equipment; pest management systems; entomology; environmental protection in air, land, and water pollution; solid waste and pesticide disposal. **Holdings:** 5500 books; 1500 bound periodical volumes; 6100 technical reprints, patents, and reports; 1000 photographs; 2200 slides. **Subscriptions:** 200 journals and other serials. **Services:** Interlibrary loans (limited); copying; library open to public on special request. **Publications:** Reprints of journal publications - available on request; technical reports - available at Defense Technical Information Center.

★14091★
U.S. ARMY MEDICAL RESEARCH INSTITUTE OF CHEMICAL DEFENSE - WOOD TECHNICAL LIBRARY (Med)
Bldg. E3100
Aberdeen Proving Ground, MD 21010-5425
Phone: (301) 671-4135
Patricia M. Pepin, Chf., Lib.Br.
Staff: Prof 2; Other 2. **Subjects:** Pharmacology, biomedicine, psychology, biochemistry, medicine, toxicology. **Holdings:** 4000 books; 4416 bound periodical volumes; 10,956 microfilm. **Subscriptions:** 832 journals and other serials. **Services:** Interlibrary loans; copying; SDI; library open to public for reference use only. **Automated Operations:** Computerized cataloging. **Computerized Information Services:** OCLC. **Networks/Consortia:** Member of FEDLINK. **Publications:** New Acquisitions List, monthly - to each branch.

★14092★
U.S. ARMY MEDICAL RESEARCH INSTITUTE OF INFECTIOUS DISEASES - MEDICAL LIBRARY (Med)
Fort Detrick
Frederick, MD 21701
Phone: (301) 663-2720
Ruth S. Janssen, Libn.
Staff: Prof 1. **Subjects:** Medicine, microbiology, biochemistry. **Holdings:** 7600 books; 6500 bound periodical volumes; 6 shelves of contract reports; 22 shelves of miscellaneous reports. **Subscriptions:** 190 journals and other serials. **Services:** Interlibrary loans; library open to public with access to Fort Detrick.

★14093★
U.S. ARMY - MILITARY ACADEMY - ARCHIVES (Hist)
Phone: (914) 938-2017
West Point, NY 10996
Founded: 1954. **Staff:** Prof 1; Other 1. **Subjects:** History of the U.S. Military Academy and the Post of West Point; cadet personnel records from 1802; alumni data on graduates, 1802-1894. **Holdings:** 27 cubic meters of archives, including 10 feet of sound recordings; print/negative collection; official registers; yearbooks; catalogs. **Services:** Copying; archives open to public by permission.

★14094★
U.S. ARMY - MILITARY ACADEMY - LIBRARY (Mil)
Phone: (914) 938-3833
West Point, NY 10966
Egon A. Weiss, Libn.
Founded: 1802. **Staff:** Prof 23; Other 39. **Subjects:** Military arts and sciences, military history, history of the U.S. Army, history of U.S. Military Academy, engineering and technology, social sciences, modern American literature. **Special Collections:** Chess (350 items); early astronomy (170 items); military art and science (23,000 items); early atlases (200 items); Orientalia (3600 items); West Pointiana (3800 items); William Faulkner (600 first editions and criticisms). **Holdings:** 370,000 books; 47,000 bound periodical volumes; 27,000 other items; 135,000 documents; 375,000 microforms; 2600 college catalogs; 25,700 manuscripts; 8000 sound recordings. **Subscriptions:** 2000 journals; 56 newspapers. **Services:** Interlibrary loans; library open to public by appointment. **Automated Operations:** Computerized cataloging and circulation. **Computerized Information Services:** DIALOG, OCLC. **Networks/Consortia:** Member of SUNY/OCLC Library Network; Southeastern New York Library Resources Council (SENYLRC). **Publications:** USMA Library Handbook/Reference Supplement, biannual; New Books, monthly; Periodical and Selective Serial Holdings; Selected Educational Media, annual; USMA Library Bulletin, occasional; Art Show Display Catalogs, irregular. **Special Catalogs:** Subject index to USMA serial publications; subject index to selected military periodicals, 1916-1960; Subject Catalog of the Military Art and Science Collection in the Library of the United States Military Academy with Selected Author and Added Entries, including a Preliminary Guide to the Manuscript Collection, 1969 (4 volumes); Official Records of the American Civil War: a researcher guide, 1977; Catalog of the Orientalia Collection of the USMA Library, 1977; bibliography of military history, 1978. **Staff:** Donald M. Koslow, Assoc.Libn.; Georgiana Watson, User Serv.Libn.; Robert E. Schnare, Spec.Coll.Libn; Joseph M. Barth, Coll.Dev.Libn.; Larry Randall, Sys.Libn; Angela H. Kao, Orientalia Libn.; Alan C. Aimone, Military Hist.Libn.; Nicholas S. Battipaglia, Jr., Math/Sci.Libn.; Elaine B. Eatroff, Cur. of Rare Books;Kevin Jones, AV Libn.; Marie T. Capps, Maps & Mss.Libn.; Charles A. Ralston, Tech.Serv.Libn.

★14095★
U.S. ARMY MILITARY HISTORY INSTITUTE (Mil; Hist)
Phone: (717) 245-4139
Carlisle Barracks, PA 17013-5008 Col. Donald P. Shaw, Dir.
Founded: 1967. **Staff:** Prof 21; Other 24. **Subjects:** Military history, U.S. and foreign history. **Special Collections:** Dyer Institute of Interdisciplinary Studies; Military Order of the Loyal Legion of the United States - Massachusetts Commandery Library. **Holdings:** 350,000 books; 12,000 bound periodical volumes; 700,000 military publications; 150,000 reports and studies; 5000 military unit histories; 2000 hours of oral history taped interviews; 4 million manuscripts; 500,000 photographs; 10 slide collections; 6700 audiotapes; 700 phonograph records; 37 Edison cylinders; 700 motion pictures; 5000 reels of microfilm. **Subscriptions:** 125 journals and other serials. **Services:** Interlibrary loans; copying; institute open to public. **Automated Operations:** Computerized cataloging and ILL. **Computerized Information Services:** OCLC. **Networks/Consortia:** Member of FEDLINK. **Publications:** Newsletter, semiannual; subject bibliographies; Vignettes of Military History, biweekly. **Staff:** John F. Votaw, Dp.Dir.; Nancy L. Gilbert, Asst.Dir./Lib.Serv.; Dr. Edward J. Drea, Asst.Dir./Hist.Serv.; Mary Lou Harris, Asst.Dir./Adm.Serv.; LTC Martin W. Andresen, Chf., Oral Hist.Br.

★14096★
U.S. ARMY MILITARY POLICE SCHOOL - LIBRARY (Mil; Law)
Bldg. 3181, Rm. 10 Phone: (205) 238-3737
Ft. McClellan, AL 36201 Sybil P. Parker, Supv.Libn.
Staff: Prof 1; Other 1. **Subjects:** Police science, education, military affairs, criminology, penology, military history. **Holdings:** 17,500 books; 750 bound periodical volumes; 6500 paperbacks; 3000 reports; 1500 pamphlets; 30,000 military publications; 1550 microforms. **Subscriptions:** 270 journals and other serials; 25 newspapers. **Services:** Interlibrary loans; copying; library open to public with restrictions. **Computerized Information Services:** DIALOG. **Networks/Consortia:** Member of TRALINET. **Publications:** New book list. **Remarks:** The library now includes the holdings of the Women's Army Corps School Library.

★14097★
U.S. ARMY - MISSILE COMMAND & MARSHALL SPACE FLIGHT CENTER - REDSTONE SCIENTIFIC INFORMATION CENTER (Sci-Tech)
Phone: (205) 876-3251
Redstone Arsenal, AL 35898 James P. Clark, Dir.
Founded: 1949. **Staff:** Prof 19; Other 14. **Subjects:** Astronautics, astronomy, chemistry, engineering, management, mathematics, meteorology, physics. **Special Collections:** Rockets; missiles; space technology; lasers. **Holdings:** 185,000 books; 75,000 bound periodical volumes; 1.4 million documents and reports. **Subscriptions:** 3300 journals and other serials. **Services:** Interlibrary loans; copying; translations; literature surveys; Center open to public with restrictions on classified material. **Automated Operations:** Computerized cataloging, acquisitions and circulation. **Computerized Information Services:** DTIC, NASA/RECON, BRS, DIALOG, SDC, New York Times Information Service. **Networks/Consortia:** Member of Alabama Library Exchange, Inc. (ALEX). **Publications:** Literature surveys; data compilations; Periodicals Catalog, semiannual - as requested. **Special Catalogs:** COM Book Catalog. **Staff:** Joyce Plaster, Chf., Rd.Serv.; Jane Cooney, Chf., Oper.; Dorothy I. Ward, Acq.Libn.; Cecelia Thorn, Ser.Libn.

★14098★
U.S. ARMY MISSILE & MUNITIONS CENTER & SCHOOL - MMCS TECHNICAL LIBRARY (Sci-Tech)
Bldg. 3323 Phone: (205) 876-7425
Redstone Arsenal, AL 35897-6280 Eva M. Cathey, Adm.Libn.
Founded: 1959. **Staff:** Prof 3; Other 4. **Subjects:** Guided missiles, electrical engineering, mathematics, physics, management, education. **Holdings:** 15,000 books; 420 bound periodical volumes; 20,000 reports; 720 AV items; 3000 microfiche; 84,800 documents; 78,720 military publications. **Subscriptions:** 260 journals and other serials. **Services:** Interlibrary loans (limited); copying; library open to public. **Computerized Information Services:** DIALOG, DTIC. **Networks/Consortia:** Member of TRALINET. **Publications:** Acquisitions Listings, bimonthly; Library Guide. **Staff:** Eleanore Zeman, Cat./Ref.

★14099★
U.S. ARMY MUSEUM OF HAWAII - REFERENCE LIBRARY (Mil)
Box 8064 Phone: (808) 543-2639
Honolulu, HI 96830 Thomas M. Fairfull, Musm.Dir.
Subjects: Military history and technology, World War II, Hawaiiana. **Holdings:** 3000 books; 2000 photographs; published unit histories; general miliary history reference publications. **Services:** Library open to public by appointment.

★14100★
U.S. ARMY MUSEUM, PRESIDIO OF MONTEREY - LIBRARY (Mil)
Ewing Rd., Bldg. 113
AFZW - POM - Museum Phone: (408) 242-8414
Monterey, CA 93944 Margaret B. Adams, Cur.
Staff: Prof 1. **Subjects:** Monterey County - local and military history, archeology; Presidio of Monterey history; U.S. Army - history, equipment. **Holdings:** 100 books; 150 microfiche; 8 VF drawers of clippings and reports. **Services:** Library open to public by appointment for reference use. **Remarks:** The library is operated by the U.S. Army's Center for Military History located in Washington, DC.

★14101★
U.S. ARMY - NATICK RESEARCH AND DEVELOPMENT CENTER - TECHNICAL LIBRARY (Sci-Tech)
Phone: (617) 651-4542
Natick, MA 01760 Carol J. Bursik, Chf.
Founded: 1946. **Staff:** Prof 6; Other 3. **Subjects:** Food sciences and engineering, textile technology, environmental medicine, chemistry, packaging technology, physics. **Special Collections:** Bibliography on Physiological Effects of High Altitude (4000 references); U.S. Army Quartermaster research on clothing, 1942 to present (269 technical reports). **Holdings:** 31,500 books; 14,500 bound periodical volumes; 44,500 technical reports; 280 reels of microfilm. **Subscriptions:** 1260 journals and other serials; 10 newspapers. **Services:** Interlibrary loans; library open to public for reference use only. **Automated Operations:** Computerized circulation. **Computerized Information Services:** DIALOG, SDC, DTIC. **Publications:** Technical Library Accessions List, monthly - for internal distribution only. **Special Catalogs:** Periodical holdings (punched cards). **Staff:** Patricia B. Olstead, Chf., Lib.Serv.; Bianca G. D'Atri, Acq.Libn.; M. Eileen Collins, Doc.Libn.; Mary A. Auer, Cat.; Margaret H. Coletti, Ref.Libn.

★14102★
U.S. ARMY - OFFICE OF THE ADJUTANT GENERAL - MORALE SUPPORT DIRECTORATE - LIBRARY ACTIVITIES DIVISION (Mil; Info Sci)
Hoffman Bldg. I, Rm. 1450 Phone: (703) 325-9700
Alexandria, VA 22331 Nellie B. Strickland, Div.Chf.
Staff: Prof 4; Other 2. **Computerized Information Services:** OCLC. **Networks/Consortia:** Member of FEDLINK. **Publications:** Monthly booklist; army regulations and directives pertaining to the Army Library Program. **Remarks:** Division is administrative headquarters for the U.S. Army Morale Support Library Program, and establishes overall policy and procedures for the administration of over 278 general libraries, branches, bookmobiles and technical processing centers. It also selects and purchases books for post libraries to supplement local acquisitions, and provides reading materials for isolated troop units and maneuver areas. **Staff:** Una D. Huggins, Chf.Acq.Libn.; Kathryn L. Earnest, Field Serv.Libn.; Anita Parins, Asst.Acq.Libn.

★14103★
U.S. ARMY - OFFICE OF THE CHIEF OF ENGINEERS - LIBRARY (Sci-Tech)
20 Massachusetts Ave., N.W. Phone: (202) 272-0455
Washington, DC 20314 Sarah A. Mikel, Chf., Tech.Info.Div.
Founded: 1941. **Staff:** Prof 4; Other 5. **Subjects:** Engineering - civil, environmental, military, mechanical; management. **Special Collections:** Early documents and reports of the Corps of Engineers; army explorations and surveys in the Middle and Far West, 1820-1890. **Holdings:** 40,000 books; 2000 bound periodical volumes; 22,000 Corps of Engineers reports; microforms; Congressional documents. **Subscriptions:** 750 journals and other serials; 5 newspapers. **Services:** Interlibrary loans; copying; SDI; library open to public for reference use only. **Automated Operations:** Computerized cataloging. **Computerized Information Services:** DIALOG, SDC, New York Times Information Service, LEXIS, DTIC, OCLC, LEGI-SLATE. **Networks/Consortia:** Member of FEDLINK. **Publications:** Acquisitions List, monthly - available on request; Periodicals Holdings List, annual; library brochure. **Special Indexes:** Index to Annual Report of the Chief of Engineers, 1775-1972 (book). **Staff:** Ann P. Crumpler, Chf., Ref.Sec.; Harriet Teffeau, Congressional Ref.

U.S. ARMY - OFFICE OF THE SURGEON GENERAL
See: U.S. Army/U.S. Air Force - Offices of the Surgeons General

★14104★
U.S. ARMY OPERATIONAL TEST & EVALUATION AGENCY (OTEA) - TECHNICAL LIBRARY (Sci-Tech; Mil)
5600 Columbia Pike Phone: (202) 756-2234
Falls Church, VA 22041 Ava Dell Headley, Libn.
Staff: Prof 2; Other 1. **Subjects:** Test methodology, experimental/statistical design, instrumentation, reliability engineering, human engineering, combat arms/combat support weapon systems of U.S. Army. **Special Collections:**

Army military publications (150 feet). **Holdings:** 3000 books; 1000 documents; 2000 microforms. **Subscriptions:** 225 journals and other serials; 9 newspapers. **Services:** Interlibrary loans; library not open to public. **Computerized Information Services:** DTIC. **Publications:** Library accessions lists.

★14105★
U.S. ARMY ORDNANCE CENTER & SCHOOL - LIBRARY (Mil)
Attn: ATSL-SE-LI, Bldg. 3071　　　Phone: (301) 278-4991
Aberdeen Proving Ground, MD 21005　　Janice C. Weston, Chf.Libn.
Founded: 1940. **Staff:** Prof 1; Other 3. **Subjects:** Military science, ordnance, management, educational technology, military history. **Special Collections:** U.S. Department of the Army publications (135,167). **Holdings:** 16,640 books; 368 bound periodical volumes; 8674 reports; 14 classified documents; 125 tape recordings; 1100 microfiche; 900 reels of microfilm of back periodicals. **Subscriptions:** 279 journals and other serials; 9 newspapers. **Services:** Interlibrary loans; copying; library open to public for reference use only and with prior approval. **Automated Operations:** Computerized cataloging and acquisitions. **Computerized Information Services:** DIALOG, OCLC, DTIC. **Networks/Consortia:** Member of TRALINET. **Publications:** Monthly Acquisitions List; periodical listing, annual.

★14106★
U.S. ARMY - PATTON MUSEUM OF CAVALRY & ARMOR - EMERT L. DAVIS MEMORIAL LIBRARY (Hist)
4554 Fayette Ave.
Box 208　　　　　　　　　Phone: (502) 624-6350
Ft. Knox, KY 40121　　　　　Phyllis S. Cassler, Libn.
Founded: 1975. **Staff:** Prof 1. **Subjects:** Armored fighting vehicles, arms and military equipment, armor warfare, uniforms and insignia, unit histories. **Holdings:** 5845 books; 100 bound periodical volumes; 128 volumes of photographs; 15 drawers of maps; 16 drawers of pamphlets; 20 boxes of archives; Fort Knox photographs and maps. **Subscriptions:** 15 journals and other serials. **Services:** Interlibrary loans; library open to qualified researchers. **Publications:** Selected Bibliography: George S. Patton (materials in library collection). **Staff:** John Campbell, Musm.Dir.

★14107★
U.S. ARMY - PENTAGON LIBRARY (Mil)
The Pentagon, Rm. 1 A 518　　　Phone: (202) 695-5346
Washington, DC 20310　　　　Dorothy A. Cross, Dir.
Founded: 1850. **Staff:** Prof 17; Other 21. **Subjects:** Military science, law, political science, history, computer science, international affairs, technology, social science, management, administration. **Special Collections:** Army studies; regulatory publications; legislative histories; army unit histories. **Holdings:** 200,000 volumes; 1.5 million documents. **Subscriptions:** 2000 journals and other serials. **Services:** Interlibrary loans; copying; SDI; library open to Department of Defense personnel only. **Automated Operations:** Computerized cataloging, acquisitions, serials and circulation. **Computerized Information Services:** BRS, LEXIS, NEXIS, DTIC, LEGI-SLATE, OCLC; PAILS, OPTIMIS, Integrated Library System (ILS) (internal databases). Performs free searches. Contact Person: Mary Bob Vick, 697-1951. **Networks/Consortia:** Member of FEDLINK. **Publications:** Selected Current Acquisitions List, monthly; subject bibliographies, irregular; briefing guides, irregular; Checklist of Periodical Holdings, annual. **Staff:** Ruth Mullane, Chf., Info.Serv.Br.; Mary Bob Vick, Tech./Automated Serv.Br.; Gene Kubal, Chf., Gen.Ref.Sect.; Irene Miner, Chf., Per.Sect.; Dexter Fox, Chf./Tech.Serv.Sect.; Marcia Stone, Chf./Army Stud.Sect.; Al Hardin, Chf., Law Sect.; Loche McLean, Chf., ADP Sect.

★14108★
U.S. ARMY - PLASTICS TECHNICAL EVALUATION CENTER - LIBRARY (Sci-Tech)
Armament Research and Development Center　　Phone: (201) 724-2778
Dover, NJ 07801　　　　　　Alfred M. Anzalone, Lib.Cons.
Founded: 1960. **Staff:** Prof 3; Other 4. **Subjects:** Plastics, composites, adhesives, material degradation, chemical agents, compatibility of plastics with energetic materials. **Special Collections:** PLASTEC reports archives. **Holdings:** 1500 books; 200 bound periodical volumes; 40,000 technical reports; microfilm library of military specifications and standards, commercial and foreign standards. **Subscriptions:** 65 journals and other serials; 5 newspapers. **Services:** Interlibrary loans; copying (limited); SDI; services to all paying customers, Department of Defense agencies and their contractors; library open to public on request. **Automated Operations:** Computerized cataloging. **Computerized Information Services:** SDC, DIALOG, OCLC, DTIC, BRS, NASA/RECON, DOE/RECON, Gale Research Company; PLASTEC, COMPAT, MADPAC (internal databases). Performs searches on cost recovery and subscription bases. Contact Person: Harry Pebly, 724-4222. **Networks/Consortia:** Member of FEDLINK. **Publications:** State-of-the Art reports; technical reports; technical notes, special bibliographies; evaluation reports -

all released through the National Technical Information Service. **Staff:** Len Silver, On-site Contract Mgr.

★14109★
U.S. ARMY POST - ABERDEEN PROVING GROUND - MORALE SUPPORT ACTIVITIES DIVISION - POST LIBRARY (Mil)
Bldg. 3320　　　　　　　Phone: (301) 278-3221
Aberdeen Proving Ground, MD 21005　　Rose Marie Serbu, Adm.Libn.
Staff: Prof 1; Other 3. **Subjects:** Biography, English and American literature, auto repair, military history. **Holdings:** 42,596 books; 4 drawers of information files; 28 drawers of microfilm. **Subscriptions:** 300 journals and other serials; 31 newspapers. **Services:** Interlibrary loans; copying; library open to public with restrictions.

★14110★
U.S. ARMY POST - FORT BELVOIR - VAN NOY LIBRARY (Mil)
Bldg. 1024　　　　　　　Phone: (703) 664-1045
Ft. Belvoir, VA 22060　　　　Madge J. Busey, Dir.
Founded: 1939. **Staff:** Prof 3; Other 9. **Subjects:** Military science, social sciences, management. **Holdings:** 116,590 books; 6527 pamphlets; 4943 phonograph records and tapes; 3243 periodical volumes on microfilm; 21,000 books in microform. **Subscriptions:** 530 journals and other serials; 43 newspapers. **Services:** Interlibrary loans; copying; library open to public for reference use only. **Automated Operations:** Computerized cataloging. **Computerized Information Services:** DIALOG, OCLC, DTIC. **Networks/Consortia:** Member of FEDLINK; TRALINET. **Publications:** Monthly acquisitions list; annual Christmas Book - both distributed upon request. **Special Catalogs:** Catalog of periodical holdings. **Staff:** Carolyn Graves, Chf., Tech.Serv.; Barbara Grochowski, Chf., Ref.Dept.; Delores Ostraco, Chf., Circ.Serv.

★14111★
U.S. ARMY POST - FORT BENNING - RECREATION SERVICES LIBRARY BRANCH (Mil)†
Bldg. 93　　　　　　　　Phone: (404) 544-4911
Ft. Benning, GA 31905　　　Gwendolyn I. Lewis, Supv.Libn.
Founded: 1920. **Staff:** Prof 3; Other 6. **Subjects:** Military science, art, education, business and general reference. **Holdings:** 112,000 books; 5000 bound and unbound periodicals; 1077 periodical volumes on microfilm; 24,000 pamphlets and clippings; 10,752 AV items. **Subscriptions:** 452 journals and other serials; 75 newspapers. **Services:** Interlibrary loans; copying; library open to military and civilian personnel employed on the post. **Networks/Consortia:** Member of Georgia Library Information Network (GLIN). **Staff:** Harriet Pitchford, Cat.; Lois Booth, Ref.Libn.

★14112★
U.S. ARMY POST - FORT BRAGG - LIBRARY (Mil)
HQ, XVIII Airborne Corps & Fort Bragg
AFZA-PA-MS　　　　　　　Phone: (919) 396-1691
Ft. Bragg, NC 28307　　　　Barbara A. Eller, Chf.Libn.
Founded: 1941. **Subjects:** Military science, military history. **Holdings:** 89,600 books; 600,000 microforms (including periodicals and special collections). **Subscriptions:** 700 journals and other serials; 32 newspapers. **Services:** Interlibrary loans; copying.

★14113★
U.S. ARMY POST - FORT CARSON - LIBRARY (Mil)
　　　　　　　　　　　　Phone: (303) 579-2350
Ft. Carson, CO 80913　　　　Roger M. Miller, Lib.Dir.
Staff: Prof 2; Other 9. **Subjects:** Military science, black literature, career and vocational guidance. **Special Collections:** Colorado Book Collection. **Holdings:** 45,362 books; 1500 phonograph records; 5400 pamphlets; 8168 microforms; 140 framed art prints. **Subscriptions:** 259 journals and other serials; 20 newspapers. **Services:** Interlibrary loans; copying; library open to employees and military families. **Networks/Consortia:** Member of Plains and Peaks Regional Library Service System. **Remarks:** A bookmobile is also part of the Fort Carson library system. **Staff:** Marcia Mohn, Tech.Serv.Libn.

★14114★
U.S. ARMY POST - FORT CLAYTON - MORALE SUPPORT ACTIVITIES - LIBRARY (Mil)
P.O. Drawer 933
APO Miami, FL 34004　　　　Pamela A. Shelton, Post Libn.
Staff: Prof 3; Other 6. **Subjects:** Military sciences, Latin America, Panama. **Holdings:** 60,000 books; 20,000 bound periodical volumes; 25,000 AV and microfilm materials. **Subscriptions:** 290 journals and other serials; 30 newspapers. **Services:** Interlibrary loans; copying; library not open to public. **Publications:** Library Abstracts, bimonthly; local military commands. **Staff:** Ruby O. Woods-Robinson, Ref.Libn.; Helen G. Hopkins, Ref.Libn.

★14115★
U.S. ARMY POST - FORT DIX - LIBRARY (Mil)
Pennsylvania Ave., Bldg. 6501   Phone: (609) 562-4858
Fort Dix, NJ 08640   Valerie D. Fashion, Act.Dir.
Staff: Prof 2; Other 3. Subjects: History, military science, management. Holdings: 54,610 books; 1535 reels of microfilm. Subscriptions: 280 journals and other serials. Services: Interlibrary loans; library open to public for reference use only. Computerized Information Services: BRS, DIALOG, DTIC, OCLC. Performs free searches.

★14116★
U.S. ARMY POST - FORT GREELY - LIBRARY (Mil)
Bldg. 663   Phone: (907) 873-3217
APO Seattle, WA 98733   Bonnie Ricks, Lib.Dir.
Staff: Prof 1; Other 3. Subjects: Arctic region, war and history, technology, hunting, fishing, general fiction. Holdings: 20,000 volumes; 2050 AV items. Subscriptions: 100 journals and other serials; 8 newspapers. Services: Interlibrary loans; copying; library open to public with restrictions.

★14117★
U.S. ARMY POST - FORT HAMILTON - LIBRARY (Mil)
Bldg. 404   Phone: (718) 836-4100
Brooklyn, NY 11252   Amelia K. Sefton, Libn. I
Founded: 1942. Staff: Prof 1; Other 1. Subjects: Military history, science and tactics. Special Collections: Newyorkana Collection. Holdings: 27,000 volumes; phonograph records. Services: Interlibrary loans; library not open to public. Computerized Information Services: DIALOG, OCLC. Networks/Consortia: Member of TRALINET.

★14118★
U.S. ARMY POST - FORT HOOD - MSA DIVISION - CASEY MEMORIAL LIBRARY (Mil; Comp Sci)
Bldg. 18000   Phone: (817) 685-5202
Ft. Hood, TX 76544   M.F. Hardin, Chf.Libn.
Staff: Prof 5; Other 18. Subjects: General collection with emphasis on computer science, business, history, English; military science. Holdings: 69,000 books; 600 phonograph recordings; 300 video cassettes; 32,000 microforms. Subscriptions: 300 journals and other serials; 30 newspapers. Services: Interlibrary loans; copying; library open to military and Fort Hood employees. Automated Operations: Computerized cataloging and ILL. Computerized Information Services: OCLC. Networks/Consortia: Member of FEDLINK. Publications: Selected Subject Bibliographies, irregular. Staff: Annette Thorpe, Post Libn.; Mary F. Rogerson, Ref.Libn.; Pam Shelton, Cat.

★14119★
U.S. ARMY POST - FORT HUACHUCA LIBRARY DIVISION - TECHNICAL LIBRARY (Sci-Tech; Comp Sci)
Greely Hall, Rm. 2102   Phone: (602) 538-6304
Fort Huachuca, AZ 85613   Dorothy C. Tompkins, Chf.Libn.
Staff: Prof 2; Other 5. Subjects: Telecommunication, electronic engineering, computer science, electrical engineering, mathematics, optics. Special Collections: Army technical manuals; field manuals; research and development documents; vendors' catalogs, engineering design file, standards, regulations (on microfilm). Holdings: 7000 books; 2000 bound periodical volumes; 110,000 hard copy reports; 200,000 documents in microform; 2550 VSMF (Visual Search Microfilm File) microfilms; 3000 periodicals on microfilm. Subscriptions: 350 journals and other serials; 5 newspapers. Services: Interlibrary loans; copying; library open to current and retired military and Department of Defense personnel. Automated Operations: Registered patron roster. Publications: Weekly acquisition list - to interested patrons. Staff: Hildegard Currie, Ref. & Rd.Serv.

★14120★
U.S. ARMY POST - FORT JACKSON - LIBRARY (Mil)
Bldg. 4679   Phone: (803) 751-4816
Ft. Jackson, SC 29207   Marilyn E. Mize, Adm.Libn.
Founded: 1946. Staff: Prof 3; Other 8. Subjects: Military science, history, business and management, human relations. Holdings: 79,730 books; 100 framed art prints; 1719 unbound periodicals; 1046 recordings and cassettes. Subscriptions: 324 journals and other serials; 15 newspapers. Services: Interlibrary loans; copying; library open to public for reference use only. Remarks: An alternate telephone number is 751-5589. Staff: Dorothy P. Ackerman, Per.; Iris W. Richardson, Post Libn.

★14121★
U.S. ARMY POST - FORT LEONARD WOOD - MAIN POST LIBRARY (Mil)
Bldg. 1607   Phone: (314) 368-7169
Ft. Leonard Wood, MO 65473   Christine M. Reser, Chf.Libn.
Founded: 1941. Staff: Prof 2; Other 8. Subjects: Military affairs,

government, history, social sciences, sports and recreation. Special Collections: Children's collection; framed art reproductions; war games. Holdings: 44,000 books; magazines on microfilm; college catalogs on microfiche; 1979-1982 NewBank on microfiche. Subscriptions: 211 journals and other serials; 14 newspapers. Services: Copying; library open to public for reference use only. Automated Operations: Computerized cataloging and acquisitions. Computerized Information Services: BRS, DTIC, OCLC, DIALOG. Networks/Consortia: Member of Springfield Green County Library Network; TRALINET.

★14122★
U.S. ARMY POST - FORT LEWIS - LIBRARY SYSTEM (Mil)
Bldg. 2109   Phone: (206) 967-7736
Ft. Lewis, WA 98433-5000   Patricia A. Louderback, Chf.Libn.
Founded: 1944. Staff: Prof 5; Other 11. Subjects: Military science, social sciences, psychology, mathematics, languages, education, literature. Special Collections: Military affairs (8000 titles). Holdings: 110,000 books; 11,880 microforms; 12,671 phonograph records, cassettes, maps and art prints. Subscriptions: 425 journals and other serials. Services: Interlibrary loans; library not open to public. Networks/Consortia: Member of WLN. Remarks: Fort Lewis Library System consists of 1 main library, 3 branch libraries and 1 field library. Staff: Bonnie Tucker, Main Post Libn.; Fay Robinson, Br.Libn.; Elsa Largen, Proc.Ctr.; Ute Jarasitis, ILL; Patrice Balliet, Children's Serv.

★14123★
U.S. ARMY POST - FORT MC PHERSON - LIBRARY SYSTEM (Mil)
Bldg. T-44   Phone: (404) 752-3218
Ft. McPherson, GA 30330   Terri Kiss, Chf.Libn.
Staff: Prof 3; Other 5. Subjects: Military history. Special Collections: Department of Defense documents. Holdings: 30,000 books; 15,000 army documents. Subscriptions: 450 journals and other serials; 15 newspapers. Services: Interlibrary loans; library not open to public. Computerized Information Services: DTIC, OCLC. Networks/Consortia: Member of Georgia Library Information Network (GLIN). Staff: Lorna Andrle, Libn.; Dawn Fuller, Libn.

★14124★
U.S. ARMY POST - FORT RICHARDSON - LIBRARY (Mil)
Bldg. 636   Phone: (907) 862-9188
Ft. Richardson, AK 99505   Virginia Chaney, Lib.Dir.
Staff: Prof 2; Other 3. Subjects: Military science, Arctic regions, foreign languages. Special Collections: Military science (633 volumes); military history (952 volumes); Arctic region (875 volumes). Holdings: 39,638 books; 3776 microfiche; 4986 pamphlets. Subscriptions: 197 journals and other serials; 23 newspapers. Services: Interlibrary loans; copying; reader's advisory; library open to public for reference use only. Networks/Consortia: Member of WLN. Staff: Doris A. Sheible, Asst.Libn.

★14125★
U.S. ARMY POST - FORT RILEY - LIBRARIES (Mil)†
Bldg. 6   Phone: (913) 239-2460
Ft. Riley, KS 66442   Dan W. Viergever, Main Post Libn.
Staff: Prof 4. Subjects: Military science. Holdings: 50,000 books; 3000 phonograph records; periodicals on microfilm; telephone books and college catalogs on microfiche. Subscriptions: 200 journals and other serials; 25 newspapers. Services: Interlibrary loans; copying. Staff: Jeanette Hoel, Cat.

★14126★
U.S. ARMY POST - FORT STEWART/HUNTER AAF LIBRARY SYSTEM (Mil)
Box 3179   Phone: (912) 767-2828
Ft. Stewart, GA 31314   Richard D. Boyce, Morale Sup.Lib.Coord.
Founded: 1942. Staff: Prof 4; Other 15. Subjects: Military science, military history. Special Collections: Library of American Civilization (microfiche); Newsbank and Names in News; Korean language books and magazines; Library of English Literature (microfiche). Holdings: 62,584 books; 1736 bound periodical volumes; 53,396 microforms; 2000 phonograph records and cassettes; VF drawers (3040 items); magnetic tapes. Subscriptions: 774 journals and other serials; 56 newspapers. Services: Interlibrary loans; copying; library open to military personnel and dependents. Automated Operations: Computerized cataloging and acquisitions. Computerized Information Services: EBSCO Subscription Services, OCLC. Networks/Consortia: Member of Georgia Library Information Network (GLIN); FEDLINK. Remarks: The library system consists of the main post library, a branch library and two bookmobiles. Staff: M. Malinda Johnson, Post Libn.; Patricia Vanderburg, Ref.Libn.; Fawn Walker, Tech.Serv.Libn.

★14127★

U.S. ARMY POST - FORT STORY - LIBRARY (Mil)
Bldg. T-530   Phone: (804) 422-7548
Ft. Story, VA 23459   Patricia L. Alderman, Libn.
Staff: Prof 1; Other 1. **Subjects:** Military science, history. **Holdings:** 15,000 books; 6 war games; 2 VF drawers of clippings. **Subscriptions:** 100 journals and other serials; 10 newspapers. **Services:** Interlibrary loans; SDI; library open to military personnel, retirees, and dependents. **Computerized Information Services:** BRS. Performs free searches. **Networks/Consortia:** Member of TRALINET.

★14128★

U.S. ARMY POST - FORT WAINWRIGHT - LIBRARY (Mil)
Bldg. 3717   Phone: (907) 353-6114
Ft. Wainwright, AK 99703   Isabelle Mudd, Adm.Libn.
Founded: 1961. **Staff:** Prof 2; Other 2. **Subjects:** General. **Special Collections:** Alaska and the Arctic; military. **Holdings:** 26,000 books; 2150 pamphlets, posters, paintings; 3823 disc and cassette recordings; 2352 video cassettes. **Subscriptions:** 217 journals and other serials and newspapers. **Services:** Interlibrary loans; copying; library open to active and retired military personnel and dependents; open to public for reference use only. **Networks/Consortia:** Member of Alaska Library Network; WLN. **Staff:** Alfred Preston, Libn.

★14129★

U.S. ARMY POST - PRESIDIO OF SAN FRANCISCO - POST LIBRARY SYSTEM (Mil)
Bldg. 386   Phone: (415) 561-3448
Presidio of San Francisco, CA 94129   Juanita Taylor, Chf.Libn.
Founded: 1944. **Staff:** Prof 4; Other 4. **Subjects:** Military science, military history, international relations, area studies. **Special Collections:** History of the Presidio of San Francisco; California and San Francisco history. **Holdings:** 50,000 volumes; 25 VF drawers of documents, pamphlets and clippings. **Subscriptions:** 200 journals and other serials. **Services:** Interlibrary loans; copying; library open to public for reference use only. **Staff:** Carolyn A. Garrett, Cat.Libn.; Joan R. Keller, Ext.Serv.Libn.; Andrew Minjiras, Post Libn.

★14130★

U.S. ARMY RESEARCH OFFICE - TECHNICAL LIBRARY (Sci-Tech)
Box 12211   Phone: (919) 549-0641
Research Triangle Park, NC 27709   Brenda Mann, Tech.Libn.
Staff: Prof 1; Other 1. **Subjects:** Physical sciences, engineering, materials, mathematics, geosciences, biology. **Holdings:** 2300 books. **Subscriptions:** 225 journals and other serials; 10 newspapers. **Services:** Library open to other government agencies. **Automated Operations:** Computerized cataloging.

★14131★

U.S. ARMY - RESEARCH AND TECHNOLOGY LABS (AVRADCOM) - APPLIED TECH. LABORATORY - TECHNICAL LIB. (Sci-Tech)
    Phone: (804) 878-2963
Ft. Eustis, VA 23604   Mrs. Lealer M. Hughes, Libn.
Founded: 1945. **Staff:** Prof 2; Other 1. **Subjects:** Aeronautical engineering, Army aircraft, composite structures, low speed aeronautics, aircraft flight control systems, flight safety and research, V/STOL aircraft, rotary wing aircraft. **Holdings:** 11,000 books and bound periodical volumes; 82,000 technical reports (hard copy and microfiche); 900,000 engineer drawings and technical data on Army aircraft. **Subscriptions:** 200 journals and other serials. **Services:** Interlibrary loans; copying; SDI; library open to public with restrictions. **Computerized Information Services:** Online systems. **Staff:** Edwin Knihnicki, Asst.Libn.

★14132★

U.S. ARMY SCHOOL OF THE AMERICAS - LIBRARY/LEARNING CENTER (Mil)
Bldg. 400, MOLASC-SS
APO Miami, FL 34008   Rafael E. Coulson, Lib.Dir.
Founded: 1961. **Staff:** Prof 1; Other 2. **Subjects:** Military science, military history, national development of Latin America, general management, foreign relations. **Special Collections:** Irregular warfare (guerilla warfare and jungle warfare); terrorism (450 volumes). **Holdings:** 16,500 books; 15 VF drawers of pamphlets; 30 drawers of maps; 50 pamphlet files of Rand Studies. **Subscriptions:** 133 journals and other serials; 15 newspapers. **Services:** Interlibrary loans; library open to members of all armed forces and Panama Canal employees.

★14133★

U.S. ARMY SERGEANTS MAJOR ACADEMY - OTHON O. VALENT LEARNING RESOURCES CENTER (Mil)
Bldg. 11203   Phone: (915) 568-8176
Ft. Bliss, TX 79918   Marijean Murray, Supv.Libn.
Founded: 1972. **Staff:** Prof 3; Other 3. **Subjects:** Management, psychology, human relations, leadership, military studies. **Special Collections:** Collection of rare books on military history and the history of the Non-Commissioned Officer Corps (500 items). **Holdings:** 35,000 books; 1200 bound periodical volumes; 20 academy archives; 900 AV items; 10,518 microfiche; 4192 reels of microfilm. **Subscriptions:** 430 journals and other serials; 26 newspapers. **Services:** Interlibrary loans; copying; center open to public for reference use only. **Computerized Information Services:** DIALOG. **Networks/Consortia:** Member of TRALINET. **Staff:** Marion Brown, Libn.; Virginia Atwater, Libn.

★14134★

U.S. ARMY SIGNAL CENTER & FORT GORDON - CONRAD TECHNICAL LIBRARY (Mil; Sci-Tech; Comp Sci)
Bldg. 29807   Phone: (404) 791-3922
Ft. Gordon, GA 30905   Margaret H. Novinger, Adm.Libn.
Staff: Prof 1; Other 3. **Subjects:** Communications-electronics, computer science, technology, military art and science, leadership, educational technology. **Holdings:** 10,350 books; 108 bound periodical volumes; 16,000 documents; 2285 periodical volumes on microfilm; 5898 microfiche; 20 VF drawers of pamphlets and monographs. **Subscriptions:** 320 journals and other serials; 6 newspapers. **Services:** Interlibrary loans; library not open to public. **Computerized Information Services:** DIALOG, DTIC, OCLC. **Networks/Consortia:** Member of Georgia Library Information Network (GLIN); TRALINET.

★14135★

U.S. ARMY SOLDIER SUPPORT CENTER - MAIN LIBRARY (Mil)†
Bldg. 400, Rm. 205   Phone: (317) 542-3891
Ft. Benjamin Harrison, IN 46216   Mrs. Marina Griner, Supv.Libn.
Founded: 1957. **Staff:** Prof 4; Other 3. **Subjects:** Mass communications; journalism; management; military history, art and science; business; public relations. **Special Collections:** Silver Anvils; Department of Defense publications; law collection. **Holdings:** 55,000 volumes; 425 AV items; 2000 reports; 210,000 documents; 2000 microforms; 151 VF drawers. **Subscriptions:** 450 journals and other serials; 100 newspapers. **Services:** Interlibrary loans; copying; SDI; library open to public for reference use only. **Automated Operations:** Computerized cataloging, acquisitions and ILL. **Computerized Information Services:** DIALOG, OCLC. **Networks/Consortia:** Member of FEDLINK; TRALINET. **Publications:** Library Guide; acquisition lists; newsletter, monthly. **Special Catalogs:** Bibliographies; current awareness files. **Remarks:** Library serves U.S. Institute of Administration and Defense Information School. **Staff:** Thelma Shutt, Hd., Ref.Serv.; Eula Mallery, Hd., Tech.Serv.; Geneva Murphy, Hd., Pub.Serv.

★14136★

U.S. ARMY - SPECIAL SERVICES DIVISION - SHARPE ARMY DEPOT - LIBRARY (Mil; Geog-Map)
    Phone: (209) 982-2404
Lathrop, CA 95331   Donna Eaton, Lib.Techn.
Staff: Prof 1. **Subjects:** Maps. **Holdings:** 5000 books; 500 Department of the Army publications. **Subscriptions:** 15 journals and other serials. **Services:** Interlibrary loans; copying; library open to active and retired servicemen and civilians working at the depot.

★14137★

U.S. ARMY - TACOM SUPPORT ACTIVITY-SELFRIDGE - RECREATION SERVICES LIBRARY (Mil)
Bldg. 169   Phone: (313) 466-5238
Selfridge Air Natl. Guard Base, MI 48045   JoAnn Bonnett, Chf., Lib.Br.
Founded: 1971. **Staff:** Prof 2. **Subjects:** History, military affairs, management. **Holdings:** 20,000 books; cassettes; phonograph records; 5 VF drawers of pamphlets, maps and clippings. **Subscriptions:** 114 journals and other serials; 11 newspapers. **Services:** Interlibrary loans; copying; library serves military personnel and their dependents, retirees and civilians employed on base.

★14138★

U.S. ARMY - TANK-AUTOMOTIVE COMMAND - TECHNICAL LIBRARY SERVICE BRANCH (Mil; Sci-Tech)
28251 Van Dyke   Phone: (313) 573-2470
Warren, MI 48090   Louis X. Barbalas, Chf.
Staff: Prof 2; Other 5. **Subjects:** Automotive mechanics, materials science, physical science, military science, engineering. **Holdings:** 6000 books;

administrative military publications; 25,000 technical reports; 45 drawers of microfiche. **Subscriptions:** 105 journals and other serials. **Services:** Interlibrary loans; library open to government contractors on special request. **Computerized Information Services:** DTIC.

★14139★
U.S. ARMY - TRADOC SYSTEMS ANALYSIS ACTIVITY - TRASANA TECHNICAL LIBRARY (Mil; Sci-Tech)
Attn: ATOR-TSL
White Sands Missile Range, NM 88002
Phone: (505) 678-3135
Julie A. Gibson, Adm.Libn.
Founded: 1977. **Staff:** Prof 1; Other 6. **Subjects:** Military science, ordnance, operations research, computer science, modelling. **Special Collections:** Defense Mapping Agency map collection. **Holdings:** 3000 books and bound periodical volumes; 35,000 technical reports. **Subscriptions:** 220 journals and other serials. **Services:** Interlibrary loans; library not open to public. **Automated Operations:** Computerized cataloging and circulation. **Computerized Information Services:** DIALOG, BRS, NASA/RECON, DTIC, OCLC; Technical Library Information System database. Performs free searches. **Networks/Consortia:** Member of TRALINET. **Publications:** Up for Grabs.

U.S. ARMY - TRAINING AND DOCTRINE COMMAND - TECHNICAL LIBRARY
See: U.S. Army - Headquarters TRADOC/Fort Monroe Library & Intern Training Center

★14140★
U.S. ARMY TRANSPORTATION - TECHNICAL INFORMATION AND RESEARCH CENTER (Mil; Trans)
Bldg. 705
Ft. Eustis, VA 23604
Phone: (804) 878-5563
Jo An I. Stolley, Chf.Libn.
Founded: 1944. **Staff:** Prof 3; Other 3. **Subjects:** Military transportation, military history, instructional technology. **Special Collections:** U.S. Army Transportation School Materials. **Holdings:** 45,397 books, bound periodical volumes and documents; 26,163 unbound periodicals and newspapers; 54,107 official publications; 22,251 miscellaneous items. **Subscriptions:** 250 journals and other serials; 5 newspapers. **Services:** Interlibrary loans; copying; center open to public for reference use only. **Computerized Information Services:** DIALOG, BRS, DTIC, OCLC. **Networks/Consortia:** Member of TRALINET. **Special Indexes:** Indexing Service for military transportation journals. **Staff:** Marion H. Knihnicki, Supv.Libn.; Nancy B. Michael, Tech.Serv.Libn.

★14141★
U.S. ARMY - TROOP SUPPORT AND AVIATION MATERIEL READINESS COMMAND - STINFO AND REFERENCE LIBRARY (Mil)†
4300 Goodfellow Blvd.
St. Louis, MO 63120
Phone: (314) 263-2345
Grace C. Feng, Supv.Libn.
Founded: 1954. **Staff:** Prof 3; Other 12. **Subjects:** Aircraft systems and components, aircraft procurements, aircraft/helicopter services, aircraft performance, aeronautical engineering. **Holdings:** 7000 books; 1300 bound periodical volumes; 2900 other cataloged items; 18,000 federal administrative publications; 109,000 federal technical publications (specifications and standards, manuals and bulletins); 500 classified publications; 150,000 specifications, standards and cross reference lists on microfilm. **Subscriptions:** 430 journals and other serials. **Services:** Interlibrary loans (fee); copying; mechanized Lektrievers; library open to public with government authorization. **Publications:** Library bulletin. **Staff:** Thomas Tipsword, Cat./Ref.Libn.

★14142★
U.S. ARMY - TROPIC TEST CENTER - TECHNICAL INFORMATION CENTER (Sci-Tech)
Fort Clayton
Drawer 942
APO Miami, FL 34004
Ann B. Guerriers, Tech.Info.Spec.
Founded: 1969. **Staff:** Prof 1. **Subjects:** Tropical material research; scientific, engineering and corrosion testing; meteorology; physics; chemistry. **Special Collections:** Tropical material test documents (6000); Tropical Test Center reports (500); Panama Canal area meteorological reports (1000); material testing in the tropics (300). **Holdings:** 800 books; 40 VF drawers of maps; 1500 microfiche; 44 volumes of test operations procedures (1200 documents); 2000 tropical testing documents; 2000 tropical regions reports; 15,000 microfiche. **Subscriptions:** 50 journals and other serials; 5 newspapers. **Services:** Interlibrary loans; copying; center open to public with restrictions. **Automated Operations:** Computerized cataloging, serials and circulation. **Computerized Information Services:** TICARS (Technical Information Center Automated Retrieval System; internal database). **Remarks:** The Technical Information Center is located in the Republic of Panama. The telephone number is 85-5910.

★14143★
U.S. ARMY/U.S. AIR FORCE - OFFICES OF THE SURGEONS GENERAL - JOINT MEDICAL LIBRARY (Med)
The Pentagon, Rm. 1B - 473
Washington, DC 20310
Phone: (202) 695-5752
Donna K. Griffitts, Adm.Libn.
Founded: 1969. **Staff:** Prof 1; Other 2. **Subjects:** Military and general medicine, hospital administration. **Holdings:** 12,000 books; 8000 bound periodical volumes; 500 microfiche cards; 200 boxes of pamphlets. **Subscriptions:** 412 journals and other serials. **Services:** Interlibrary loans; library not open to public. **Computerized Information Services:** Online systems. **Special Indexes:** Index to annual reports of army and air force surgeons general.

★14144★
U.S. ARMY - WALTER REED ARMY INSTITUTE OF RESEARCH - LIBRARY (Med)
Walter Reed Army Medical Center
Washington, DC 20307
Phone: (202) 576-3314
V. Lynn Gera, Adm.Libn.
Founded: 1946. **Staff:** Prof 2; Other 4. **Subjects:** Communicable diseases, immunology, dentistry, veterinary sciences, biochemistry, internal medicine, physiology, psychiatry, surgery. **Holdings:** 17,222 books; 13,000 bound periodical volumes. **Subscriptions:** 1000 journals and other serials. **Services:** Interlibrary loans; library open to public for reference use only by authorization. **Computerized Information Services:** DIALOG, Integrated Library System (ILS). **Publications:** Union List of Biomedical Periodicals in the libraries of WRAIR, WRAMC and AFIP (Armed Forces Institute of Pathology), annual.

★14145★
U.S. ARMY WAR COLLEGE - LIBRARY (Mil)
Carlisle Barracks, PA 17013
Phone: (717) 245-3660
Barbara E. Stevens, Dir.
Founded: 1951. **Staff:** Prof 11; Other 18. **Subjects:** Military science, international relations, political science, management, economics, behavioral science. **Holdings:** 55,669 books; 6831 bound periodical volumes; 70,000 documents and paperbound books; 40,762 maps; 750 audio cassettes; 331 audiotapes; 45 video cassettes; 47 VF drawers; 344,334 microforms (uncataloged). **Subscriptions:** 1245 journals and other serials; 42 newspapers. **Services:** Interlibrary loans; library not open to public. **Automated Operations:** Computerized cataloging and serials. **Computerized Information Services:** DIALOG, DTIC, OPTIMIS, OCLC; internal database. Performs free searches. **Networks/Consortia:** Member of FEDLINK. **Publications:** Key References; Periodicals Directory; annotated bibliographies; Library Acquisitions Bulletin, biweekly. **Special Indexes:** U.S. Army War College Research Papers and Other Published Writing (brochure). **Staff:** Joan M. Hench, Chf., Coll.Dev.Br.; Margaret E. MacGregor, Chf., Course Coord./Circ.Bohdan I. Kohutiak, Chf., Serv.Br.; Lidwina J. Gole, Chf., Preparations Br.; Kathryn E. Davis, Selection/Acq.Libn.; Dorothy S. Kriete, Ref.Libn.; Kathleen Miller, Cat.; Richard L. Weary, Maps/Micrographics Libn.; Albert G. West, Cat.

★14146★
U.S. ARMY - WHITE SANDS MISSILE RANGE - TECHNICAL LIBRARY DIVISION (Sci-Tech; Mil)
Phone: (505) 678-1317
White Sands Missile Range, NM 88002
Laurel B. Saunders, Chf.
Founded: 1955. **Staff:** Prof 5; Other 10. **Subjects:** Optics, guided missiles, electronics, mathematics, physics, computers. **Special Collections:** Military specifications and industrial standards. **Holdings:** 4000 books; 2000 bound periodical volumes; 80,000 microforms; 20,000 research and development reports; 2.5 million engineering drawings. **Subscriptions:** 400 journals and other serials. **Services:** Interlibrary loans; library not open to public. **Automated Operations:** Computerized cataloging. **Computerized Information Services:** DIALOG, DTIC, OCLC, Government-Industry Data Exchange Program (GIDEP), NASA/RECON; internal databases. **Publications:** Acquisitions of open literature and documents, annual; Bulletin, monthly; Periodical Holdings. **Staff:** Ralph Austin, Chf., Lit.; Amelia Sutton, Chf., Doc.

U.S. ARMY - WOMEN'S ARMY CORPS SCHOOL - LIBRARY
See: U.S. Army Military Police School - Library

★14147★
U.S. ARMY - YUMA PROVING GROUND - FOREIGN INTELLIGENCE, SCIENTIFIC & TECHNICAL INFO.DIV. - TECHNICAL LIB. (Sci-Tech)
Attn: STEYP-FIO-TL
Yuma, AZ 85364
Phone: (602) 328-2527
Jean McCall, Chf.
Founded: 1965. **Staff:** Prof 1. **Subjects:** Research and development, test and evaluation, engineering and technology, U.S. Army materiel. **Holdings:** 4000 books; 400 bound periodical volumes; 35,000 other cataloged items; 200,000 documents in microform, including 16mm visual search microfilm

service. **Subscriptions:** 140 journals and other serials. **Services:** Interlibrary loans (for material with limited control); library not open to public. **Computerized Information Services:** DTIC.

U.S. ATTORNEY
See: U.S. Dept. of Justice

★14148★
U.S. BANCORP - RESOURCE LIBRARY (Bus-Fin)
555 S.W. Oak St.   Phone: (503) 225-5816
Portland, OR 97204
Staff: 1. **Subjects:** Banking and finance, management, personnel administration and supervision, education and training, psychology and sociology. **Special Collections:** History of U.S. National Bank of Oregon (books and photographs). **Holdings:** 2500 books; 455 AV cassettes; 200 programmed instruction courses; 300 theses, speeches and reports. **Subscriptions:** 63 journals and other serials. **Services:** Library not open to public. **Publications:** Resource Guide, annual update; Organization Directory, annual - both for internal distribution only. **Staff:** Carol Daley, Rsrc.Libn.; Kathleen CannCasciato, Rsrc.Libn.

★14149★
UNITED STATES BEET SUGAR ASSOCIATION - LIBRARY
1156 Fifteenth St., N.W.
Washington, DC 20005
Defunct

★14150★
UNITED STATES BORAX RESEARCH CORPORATION - RESEARCH LIBRARY (Sci-Tech)
412 Crescent Way   Phone: (714) 774-2670
Anaheim, CA 92801   Betty J. Robson, Res.Libn.
Founded: 1956. **Staff:** Prof 2; Other 3. **Subjects:** Chemistry, agriculture, mining, metallurgy, glass, ceramics. **Holdings:** 1600 books; 2200 bound periodical volumes; 2800 other bound volumes; 1500 government research reports; 6 VF drawers of patents; 1500 company research reports; 12 drawers of microcards; 120 reels of microfilm. **Subscriptions:** 200 journals and other serials. **Services:** Interlibrary loans; copying; library open to public for reference use only, on request. **Computerized Information Services:** DIALOG, DTIC. **Publications:** Library Bulletin, weekly - for internal distribution only. **Special Indexes:** KWIC indexes to internal reports and patents.

★14151★
U.S. BUREAU OF ALCOHOL, TOBACCO AND FIREARMS - NATIONAL LABORATORY LIBRARY (Sci-Tech)
1401 Research Blvd.   Phone: (301) 443-1195
Rockville, MD 20850
Staff: 1. **Subjects:** Alcohol, chromatography, forensic sciences and photography, firearms, tobacco. **Special Collections:** Alcohol, Tobacco and Firearms regulations. **Holdings:** 6000 books; 4000 bound periodical volumes; 25 volumes of laboratory reports; government documents. **Subscriptions:** 50 journals and other serials. **Services:** Interlibrary loans; library not open to public. **Automated Operations:** Computerized cataloging. **Computerized Information Services:** BRS, DIALOG, OCLC. **Networks/Consortia:** Member of FEDLINK. **Special Catalogs:** Union List of Periodicals of Treasury Libraries. **Remarks:** This is a branch of the U.S. Department of the Treasury.

★14152★
U.S. BUREAU OF ALCOHOL, TOBACCO AND FIREARMS - REFERENCE LIBRARY (Sci-Tech)
1200 Pennsylvania Ave., N.W.   Phone: (202) 566-7602
Washington, DC 20226   Vicki R. Herrmann, Libn.
Staff: Prof 1. **Subjects:** Alcohol, tobacco, firearms, explosives. **Special Collections:** Tax and regulation history of the alcohol and tobacco industries in the United States (200 volumes). **Holdings:** 400 books; 100 bound periodical volumes; 300 linear feet of indexed hearings, projects, tasks, and correspondence. **Subscriptions:** 90 journals and other serials. **Services:** Interlibrary loans; copying; SDI; library open to public with written permission. **Special Indexes:** Index of correspondence (card); indexes of in-house and bureau publications, rulings and procedures, relevant Treasury Decisions, archival projects, and legal memoranda (books).

★14153★
U.S. BUREAU OF THE CENSUS - INFORMATION SERVICES PROGRAM - ATLANTA REGIONAL OFFICE (Soc Sci)
1365 Peachtree St., N.E., Rm. 523   Phone: (404) 881-3312
Atlanta, GA 30309   Joseph T. Reilly, Data User Serv.Off.
Subjects: U.S. census reports. **Holdings:** Figures not available. **Services:** Office open to public.

★14154★
U.S. BUREAU OF THE CENSUS - INFORMATION SERVICES PROGRAM - BOSTON REGIONAL OFFICE - LIBRARY (Soc Sci)
441 Stuart St., 10th Fl.   Phone: (617) 223-2327
Boston, MA 02116   Arthur G. Dukakis, Regional Dir.
Staff: 4. **Subjects:** U.S. census reports. **Holdings:** 4000 books; 8 VF drawers; 1977 economic censuses, 1980 census reports (both on microfiche); census maps. **Subscriptions:** 16 journals and other serials. **Services:** Copying; library open to public.

★14155★
U.S. BUREAU OF THE CENSUS - INFORMATION SERVICES PROGRAM - CHARLOTTE REGIONAL OFFICE - LIBRARY (Soc Sci)
230 S. Tryon St., Suite 800   Phone: (704) 371-6144
Charlotte, NC 28202   Frank Ambrose, Info.Serv.Spec.
Founded: 1977. **Staff:** Prof 2; Other 1. **Subjects:** U.S. census reports. **Holdings:** 4000 books; 60 bound periodical volumes; 4 drawers of microfiche. **Services:** Copying; library open to public for reference use only. **Staff:** Ken Wright, Info.Serv.Spec.

★14156★
U.S. BUREAU OF THE CENSUS - INFORMATION SERVICES PROGRAM - CHICAGO REGIONAL OFFICE - REFERENCE CENTER (Soc Sci)
55 E. Jackson Blvd., Rm. 1306   Phone: (312) 353-0980
Chicago, IL 60604   Stanley D. Moore, Reg.Dir.
Founded: 1975. **Staff:** Prof 4; Other 1. **Subjects:** U.S. census - population, housing, manufacturers, retail trade, agriculture, wholesale/service trades. **Holdings:** 3500 books; 350 bound periodical volumes; 200 series; Census Bureau computer tape technical documentation; 1980 census data on microfiche; census tract maps; block maps (Illinois, Indiana). **Services:** Copying (limited); assistance with census data through telephone access services; free census data access and use workshops; consultations; staff available for on-site workshops and presentations as well as conference seminars, panels and convention exhibits; center open to public. **Networks/Consortia:** Member of Illinois State Data Center Cooperative (ISDCC); Indiana State Data Center. **Publications:** Census Information Digest - for regional users of census data (Illinois and Indiana). **Staff:** Mary F. Grady, Info.Serv.Spec.; Crystal M. Hudson, Info.Serv.Spec.; Stephen Laue, Info.Serv.Spec.; Norma Marti, Info.Serv.Spec.

★14157★
U.S. BUREAU OF THE CENSUS - INFORMATION SERVICES PROGRAM - DALLAS REGIONAL OFFICE - LIBRARY (Soc Sci)
Earle Caball Federal Bldg.
1100 Commerce St.   Phone: (214) 767-0625
Dallas, TX 75242   Brooks Sitton, Coord.
Founded: 1976. **Staff:** Prof 3; Other 1. **Subjects:** U.S. census reports. **Holdings:** 3500 volumes; 1980 census reports on microfiche. **Subscriptions:** 12 journals and other serials. **Services:** Copying; library open to public. **Staff:** Lionel Rawlins, Community Serv.Spec.; Alfonso Mirabal, Info.Serv.Spec.

★14158★
U.S. BUREAU OF THE CENSUS - INFORMATION SERVICES PROGRAM - DENVER REG. OFFICE - CENSUS PUBLICATION CENTER (Soc Sci)
7655 W. Mississippi Ave.
Box 26750   Phone: (303) 234-5825
Denver, CO 80226   Gerald O'Donnell, Info.Serv.
Staff: Prof 3; Other 1. **Subjects:** U.S. census reports. **Holdings:** Figures not available. **Services:** Copying; center open to public. **Staff:** Gina Valdez, Info.Serv.Spec.; Kendrick J. Ellwanger, Supervisory Statistician.

★14159★
U.S. BUREAU OF THE CENSUS - INFORMATION SERVICES PROGRAM - DETROIT REGIONAL OFFICE - INFORMATION CENTER (Soc Sci)
231 W. Lafayette St., Rm. 565   Phone: (313) 226-4675
Detroit, MI 48226   Susan Hardy, Coord., Info.Serv.
Staff: Prof 4; Other 1. **Subjects:** U.S. census reports. **Special Collections:** 1980 Census for Michigan and Ohio (microfiche). **Holdings:** 2550 volumes. **Services:** Copying; center open to public. **Publications:** Great Lakes Data Highlights Bimonthly; Census Users in Ohio and Michigan. **Staff:** Sandra Lucas, Community Serv.Spec.; Kurt Metzger, Info.Serv.Spec.; Karen Henry, Community Serv.Spec.

★14160★
U.S. BUREAU OF THE CENSUS - INFORMATION SERVICES PROGRAM - KANSAS CITY REGIONAL OFFICE - LIBRARY (Soc Sci)
One Gateway Center, Suite 500   Phone: (816) 374-4601
Kansas City, KS 66101   John W. Dale, Prog.Coord.
Staff: Prof 4; Other 1. **Subjects:** U.S. census reports. **Holdings:** Figures not

available. **Services:** Interlibrary loans; copying; library open to public. **Staff:** Bernard Arzu; Dennis Johnson

★14161★
U.S. BUREAU OF THE CENSUS - INFORMATION SERVICES PROGRAM - LOS ANGELES REGIONAL OFFICE - LIBRARY (Soc Sci)
11777 San Vincente Blvd., 8th Fl.   Phone: (213) 209-6612
Los Angeles, CA 90049
Staff: Prof 5; Other 1. **Subjects:** U.S. census reports - population, housing, economic, construction. **Holdings:** Figures not available. **Services:** Library open to public. **Publications:** Data News, quarterly. **Staff:** John Ramirez, Info.Serv.Spec.; Eva Gay, Info.Serv.Spec.; Bud Steinfeld, Info.Serv.Spec.; John Hernandez, Info.Serv.Spec.; Jerry Wong, Info.Serv.Spec.

★14162★
U.S. BUREAU OF THE CENSUS - INFORMATION SERVICES PROGRAM - NEW YORK REGIONAL OFFICE - LIBRARY (Soc Sci)
26 Federal Plaza, Rm. 37-100   Phone: (212) 264-4730
New York, NY 10278   William F. Hill, Regional Dir.
Founded: 1976. **Staff:** 5. **Subjects:** U.S. census reports. **Holdings:** 15,000 volumes. **Services:** SDI (selective); library open to public.

★14163★
U.S. BUREAU OF THE CENSUS - INFORMATION SERVICES PROGRAM - PHILADELPHIA REGIONAL OFFICE - LIBRARY (Soc Sci)
Federal Bldg., Rm. 9244
600 Arch St.   Phone: (215) 597-8314
Philadelphia, PA 19106   David C. Lewis, Chf.
Subjects: U.S. census reports. **Holdings:** Census publications and 1980 census on microfiche for Delaware, Maryland, New Jersey, Pennsylvania and West Virginia. **Services:** Library open to public.

★14164★
U.S. BUREAU OF THE CENSUS - INFORMATION SERVICES PROGRAM - SEATTLE REGIONAL OFFICE - LIBRARY (Soc Sci)
1700 Westlake Ave., N.   Phone: (206) 442-7080
Seattle, WA 98174   Betty J. Owens, Libn.
Staff: Prof 4. **Subjects:** U.S. census reports. **Special Collections:** Bureau of the Census Block Statistics and Census Tract Reports. **Holdings:** 5000 books; 100 bound periodical volumes; microfiche. **Services:** Interlibrary loans; copying; library open to public. **Staff:** Larry Hartke, Info.Spec.; Alice Salomon, Info.Spec.; George Whitaker, Info.Spec.

★14165★
U.S. BUREAU OF THE CENSUS - LIBRARY & INFORMATION SERVICES BRANCH (Soc Sci)
Federal Bldg. No. 3   Phone: (301) 763-5040
Washington, DC 20233   Betty Baxtresser, Chf.
Founded: 1952. **Staff:** Prof 9; Other 14. **Subjects:** Economics, population, public finance with emphasis on state and local governments, statistical methodology, urban studies, data processing. **Special Collections:** U.S. Census publications, 1790-1980 (45,457); microfiche (21,160); census volumes, statistical yearbooks and bulletins of foreign governments (21,101); publications on electronic data processing (1326). **Holdings:** 127,132 books; 803 bound periodical volumes; 11,500 microfiche; 2245 annual corporation reports; 28 drawers of Congressional materials; census staff papers; 590 college catalogs. **Subscriptions:** 3128 journals and other serials; 19 newspapers. **Services:** Interlibrary loans; copying; SDI; library open to public. **Automated Operations:** Computerized cataloging and serials (partial). **Computerized Information Services:** DIALOG, SDC, NEXIS, OCLC, Institute for Scientific Information (ISI). **Networks/Consortia:** Member of FEDLINK. **Publications:** Library Notes, monthly - available on request.

★14166★
U.S. BUREAU OF INDIAN AFFAIRS - OFFICE OF FIELD OPERATIONS - DIVISION OF LAW ENFORCEMENT - LAW LIBRARY
Box 399
Brigham City, UT 84302
Defunct

U.S. BUREAU OF LAND MANAGEMENT - ALASKA OUTER-CONTINENTAL SHELF OFFICE - LIBRARY
See: **U.S. Dept. of the Interior - Minerals Management Service - Alaska Outer-Continental Shelf Regional Library**

★14167★
U.S. BUREAU OF LAND MANAGEMENT - CALIFORNIA STATE OFFICE - LIBRARY (Env-Cons)
2800 Cottage Way   Phone: (916) 484-4253
Sacramento, CA 95825   Louise Tichy, Mgt.Asst.
Staff: 2. **Subjects:** Land resources, recreation, environmental statements, U.S. statutes, interior land decisions. **Holdings:** 2500 books; unbound periodicals; newspaper clippings. **Subscriptions:** 41 journals and other serials. **Services:** Interlibrary loans; copying; library open to public for reference use only. **Computerized Information Services:** Raptor Management Research System (internal database). Performs searches on cost recovery basis. Contact Person: Dr. Richard Olendorff, 484-4541.

★14168★
U.S. BUREAU OF LAND MANAGEMENT - CASPER DISTRICT OFFICE - LIBRARY (Env-Cons)
951 Rancho Rd.   Phone: (307) 261-5591
Casper, WY 82601   Trudy Closson, Rec.Mgr.
Staff: 1. **Subjects:** Mines, environment. **Holdings:** Mine plans; environmental statements; 100 cubic feet of Bureau of Land Management publications. **Subscriptions:** 20 journals and other serials. **Services:** Library open to public for reference use only.

★14169★
U.S. BUREAU OF LAND MANAGEMENT - DENVER LIBRARY (Env-Cons)
Denver Federal Ctr.
Bldg. 50 - D245   Phone: (303) 234-4578
Denver, CO 80225   Ora Wagoner, Libn.
Subjects: Forestry, range and wildlife management. **Holdings:** 30,000 volumes. **Subscriptions:** 500 journals and other serials. **Services:** Interlibrary loans; copying; library open to public for reference use only. **Automated Operations:** Computerized cataloging. **Computerized Information Services:** DIALOG, SDC, BRS.

★14170★
U.S. BUREAU OF LAND MANAGEMENT - EASTERN STATES OFFICE LIBRARY (Env-Cons)
350 S. Pickett St.
Alexandria, VA 22304   M. Willette Proctor, Mgt.Asst.
Founded: 1975. **Staff:** Prof 1. **Subjects:** Land management and environmental assessment. **Holdings:** 10,000 books; BLM manuals; public lands law books; U.S. Department of the Interior manuals. **Subscriptions:** 50 journals and other serials. **Services:** Interlibrary loans; copying; library open to public.

★14171★
U.S. BUREAU OF LAND MANAGEMENT - MONTANA STATE OFFICE LIBRARY (Env-Cons)
222 N. 32nd St.
Box 36800   Phone: (406) 657-6671
Billings, MT 59107   Carolyn M. Nelson, Libn.
Founded: 1972. **Staff:** Prof 1; Other 1. **Subjects:** Water resources, land use, range management, wildlife, coal, minerals. **Special Collections:** Missouri River Basin Reports. **Holdings:** 9000 books. **Subscriptions:** 280 journals and other serials; 8 newspapers. **Services:** Interlibrary loans; copying; library open to public with restrictions. **Automated Operations:** Computerized cataloging and ILL. **Computerized Information Services:** OCLC. **Networks/Consortia:** Member of National Natural Resources Library and Information System (NNRLIS); FEDLINK.

★14172★
U.S. BUREAU OF LAND MANAGEMENT - NEW MEXICO STATE OFFICE LIBRARY (Env-Cons)
Box 1449   Phone: (505) 988-6047
Santa Fe, NM 87501   M. Ferne Bridgford, Supv.Mgt.Asst.
Founded: 1967. **Staff:** 1. **Subjects:** Management - land resource, wildlife, recreation, minerals, range; environmental protection. **Special Collections:** U.S. Statutes at Large; Interior Board of Land Appeals decisions. **Holdings:** 6000 books; 500 bound periodical volumes. **Subscriptions:** 100 journals and other serials. **Services:** Copying; library open to public for reference use only.

★14173★
U.S. BUREAU OF MINES - ALASKA FIELD OPERATIONS CENTER LIBRARY (Energy; Sci-Tech)
Box 550   Phone: (907) 364-2111
Juneau, AK 99802   Helen Jacobson, Lib.Techn.
Staff: 1. **Subjects:** Mining, geology, engineering in Northern Regions, permafrost construction, mineral deposits of Alaska. **Special Collections:** U.S. Geological Survey publications on Alaska; U.S. Bureau of Mines

publications; extensive publications on permafrost; state and territory of Alaska publications on mining and minerals. **Holdings:** 3600 volumes; 4600 documents; 5500 titles on microfilm; 5000 maps; 36 VF drawers. **Subscriptions:** 40 journals and other serials. **Services:** Interlibrary loans; copying; library open to public. **Special Indexes:** Index of Bureau of Mines Publications on Alaska.

★14174★
U.S. BUREAU OF MINES - ALBANY TECHNICAL LIBRARY (Sci-Tech)
Box 70   Phone: (503) 967-5864
Albany, OR 97321   Eleanor Abshire, Libn.
Staff: Prof 1; Other 1. **Subjects:** Metallurgy, chemistry, physics, chemical engineering, thermodynamics, materials, environmental science. **Holdings:** 10,000 books; 17,000 bound periodical volumes; 16,000 technical reports; 11,000 microfiche. **Subscriptions:** 152 journals and other serials. **Services:** Interlibrary loans; library open to public for reference use only. **Computerized Information Services:** DIALOG.

★14175★
U.S. BUREAU OF MINES - AVONDALE RESEARCH CENTER LIBRARY (Sci-Tech)
4900 La Salle Rd.   Phone: (301) 436-7552
Avondale, MD 20782   Paul F. Moran, Libn.
Founded: 1943. **Staff:** Prof 1; Other 1. **Subjects:** Chemistry, mineral industries, chemical engineering, corrosion, metallurgy, x-ray spectroscopy, recycling of solid wastes, asbestos. **Holdings:** 6646 books; 3835 bound periodical volumes; 163 reels of microfilm. **Subscriptions:** 160 journals and other serials. **Services:** Interlibrary loans; library open to public for reference use only. **Computerized Information Services:** DIALOG.

★14176★
U.S. BUREAU OF MINES - BOEING SERVICES INTERNATIONAL - LIBRARY (Sci-Tech; Energy)
4800 Forbes Ave.   Phone: (412) 621-4500
Pittsburgh, PA 15213   Kathleen M. Stabryla, Lead Libn.
Staff: Prof 4; Other 2. **Subjects:** Coal research, fossil fuels, mining, geology, chemistry. **Special Collections:** U.S. Bureau of Mines publications (complete set). **Holdings:** 165,000 books; 54,000 bound periodical volumes; 182 VF drawers; 72 microfilm drawers. **Subscriptions:** 237 journals and other serials. **Services:** Interlibrary loans; copying (limited); library open to public for reference use only. **Computerized Information Services:** DIALOG. **Staff:** Bernard Kenney, Br.Libn.; Chia-ling Wu, Libn.

★14177★
U.S. BUREAU OF MINES - BOULDER CITY RESEARCH LIBRARY
500 Date St.
Boulder City, NV 89005
Defunct

★14178★
U.S. BUREAU OF MINES - BRANCH OF OPERATIONS & SUPPORT - LIBRARY (Sci-Tech)
2401 E St., N.W.   Phone: (202) 634-1116
Washington, DC 20241   Judy C. Jordan, Lib.Techn.
Founded: 1965. **Staff:** Prof 1; Other 2. **Subjects:** Mineral industry, statistics and economics. **Special Collections:** Mineral yearbooks, 1925-1982. **Holdings:** 22 VF drawers of clippings; 600 reels of microfilm. **Subscriptions:** 233 journals and other serials. **Services:** Library open to public for reference use only, on request. **Formerly:** U.S. Bureau of Mines - Administrative Services - Library.

★14179★
U.S. BUREAU OF MINES - CHARLES W. HENDERSON MEMORIAL LIBRARY (Sci-Tech)
Denver Federal Center, Bldg. 20   Phone: (303) 234-2817
Denver, CO 80225   Ann Elizabeth Chapel, Libn.
Founded: 1963. **Staff:** Prof 1. **Subjects:** Mining, engineering, economics, research, geology. **Holdings:** 20,000 books; 700 bound periodical volumes; 1870 maps and charts; 7670 bulletins; 2000 water supply papers. **Subscriptions:** 150 journals and other serials; 6 newspapers. **Services:** Interlibrary loans; copying; library open to public with restrictions. **Computerized Information Services:** DIALOG, OCLC. **Networks/Consortia:** Member of FEDLINK.

★14180★
U.S. BUREAU OF MINES - RENO RESEARCH CENTER - LIBRARY (Sci-Tech)†
1605 Evans Ave.   Phone: (702) 784-5348
Reno, NV 89512   Janice Behers, Lib.Techn.
Staff: 1. **Subjects:** Chemistry, metallurgy, chemical engineering, physics,

geology. **Holdings:** 3279 books; 1775 bound periodical volumes; 2112 reports, manuscripts, documents. **Subscriptions:** 117 journals and other serials. **Services:** Interlibrary loans; copying; library open to public for reference use only. **Automated Operations:** Computerized cataloging. **Computerized Information Services:** DIALOG (for internal use only).

★14181★
U.S. BUREAU OF MINES - ROLLA RESEARCH CENTER - LIBRARY (Sci-Tech)
1300 Bishop Ave.
Box 280   Phone: (314) 364-3169
Rolla, MO 65401
Founded: 1921. **Staff:** 1. **Subjects:** Metallurgy and mining research. **Holdings:** 2000 books; 200 bound periodical volumes; 2000 reports; U.S. Bureau of Mines publications. **Subscriptions:** 33 journals and other serials. **Services:** Interlibrary loans; library open to public for reference use only.

★14182★
U.S. BUREAU OF MINES - SALT LAKE CITY RESEARCH CENTER - LIBRARY (Env-Cons)
729 Arapeen Dr.   Phone: (801) 524-6112
Salt Lake City, UT 84108   W.I. Nissen, Tech.Supv.
Staff: 1. **Subjects:** Metallurgy research, natural resources conservation, environmental pollution, engineering, physical sciences. **Special Collections:** Bureau of Mines publications (1311 bound volumes). **Holdings:** 5108 books; 2199 bound periodical volumes; 15 shelves of state publications (California, Colorado, Idaho, Montana); 39 notebooks of patents. **Subscriptions:** 56 journals and other serials. **Services:** Interlibrary loans; library open to public for reference use only. **Staff:** Jean B. Beckstead, Libn.

★14183★
U.S. BUREAU OF MINES - TUSCALOOSA RESEARCH CENTER - REFERENCE LIBRARY (Sci-Tech; Energy)
Box L   Phone: (205) 758-0491
University, AL 35486   Susan D. Markham, Lib.Techn.
Founded: 1938. **Staff:** Prof 1; Other 1. **Subjects:** Chemistry, metallurgy, thermodynamics, physical chemistry, ceramics. **Holdings:** Bureau of Mines publications. **Subscriptions:** 100 journals and other serials. **Services:** Interlibrary loans; library open to public with restrictions. **Computerized Information Services:** DIALOG.

★14184★
U.S. BUREAU OF MINES - TWIN CITIES RESEARCH CENTER - LIBRARY (Sci-Tech; Energy)
5629 Minnehaha Ave., S.   Phone: (612) 725-4503
Minneapolis, MN 55417   Merle Bernstein, Libn.
Staff: Prof 1; Other 1. **Subjects:** Metallurgy, mining. **Special Collections:** Oil shale data bank; diesel motor exhaust gases. **Holdings:** 6800 books; 2000 bound periodical volumes; 73 VF drawers of reports, documents, patents. **Subscriptions:** 160 journals and other serials. **Services:** Interlibrary loans; library open to public for reference use only. **Automated Operations:** Computerized ILL. **Computerized Information Services:** DIALOG, OCLC. **Networks/Consortia:** Member of FEDLINK. **Publications:** Accession list, monthly - for internal distribution only.

★14185★
U.S. BUREAU OF RECLAMATION - LIBRARY (Sci-Tech)
2800 Cottage Way   Phone: (916) 484-4404
Sacramento, CA 95825   Margaret Elder, Lib.Techn.
Founded: 1946. **Staff:** Prof 1; Other 1. **Subjects:** Water and water resources, power, agriculture. **Holdings:** 12,000 volumes. **Subscriptions:** 150 journals and other serials. **Services:** Interlibrary loans; copying; library open to public for reference use only. **Publications:** Accession list, quarterly; magazine list, annual.

★14186★
U.S. BUREAU OF RECLAMATION - LIBRARY (Sci-Tech)†
Engineering & Research Center
Denver Federal Center
Box 25007   Phone: (303) 234-3019
Denver, CO 80225   Paul F. Mulloney, Chf., Lib.Br.
Founded: 1930. **Staff:** Prof 5; Other 5. **Subjects:** Water resources development; design, construction and operation of dams, power plants, pumping plants, canals, transmission lines. **Holdings:** 65,000 books; 14,000 bound periodical volumes; 80,000 archival items; 20,000 specifications; 20,000 internal reports; 10,000 reports on microfilm; 30,000 external reports. **Subscriptions:** 900 journals and other serials. **Services:** Interlibrary loans; library open to public for reference use only. **Automated Operations:** Computerized cataloging. **Computerized Information Services:** Online systems. **Publications:** Library Accession List - for internal distribution only.

Special Catalogs: Subject catalog of internal and external reports (book). **Staff:** Gertrude E. Schalow, Asst.Libn.; Suzanne Shepherd, Bk.Cat.; Margaret Watson, Libn.; Sandra Bowers, Hd.Ref.Libn.

★14187★
U.S. BUREAU OF RECLAMATION - TECHNICAL LIBRARY (Sci-Tech)
1404 Colorado St.
Box 427   Phone: (702) 293-8570
Boulder City, NV 89005   Cretha L. Riggle, Lib.Techn.
Staff: 4. **Subjects:** Water and resources development, hydrology, canals and other hydraulic structures, flood control, hydroelectric power, ecology, soils. **Special Collections:** Project histories for the lower Colorado region. **Holdings:** 5000 volumes. **Subscriptions:** 49 journals and other serials. **Services:** Interlibrary loans; library open to public. **Computerized Information Services:** Online systems.

★14188★
U.S. CAVALRY MUSEUM - LIBRARY (Mil)
Bldg. 30   Phone: (913) 239-2737
Fort Riley, KS 66442   Terry Van Meter, Dir.
Staff: 4. **Subjects:** United States cavalry. **Special Collections:** Complete black/white 16mm sound set of 12 cavalry training films, 1940. **Holdings:** Annual reports of Secretary of War; Cavalry Journal; photographs. **Services:** Library open to researchers with restrictions.

★14189★
U.S. CENTERS FOR DISEASE CONTROL - CDC LIBRARY (Med)
1600 Clifton Rd., N.E.   Phone: (404) 329-3396
Atlanta, GA 30333   Mary Alice Mills, Dir.
Founded: 1947. **Staff:** Prof 7; Other 10. **Subjects:** Communicable diseases, epidemiology, laboratory medicine, medical entomology, microbiology, biochemistry, public health, veterinary medicine, virology. **Holdings:** 81,600 books and bound periodical volumes; 124 theses; 2500 U.S. Department of Health and Human Services publications; 55 serial titles on microfilm. **Subscriptions:** 953 journals and other serials. **Services:** Interlibrary loans; copying; SDI; library open to public with restrictions. **Automated Operations:** Computerized cataloging and serials. **Computerized Information Services:** BRS, DIALOG, LEXIS, NEXIS, MEDLINE; internal database. **Networks/ Consortia:** Member of FEDLINK; Atlanta Health Science Library Consortium. **Publications:** Library Up-Date, quarterly; Serial Holdings, annual. **Remarks:** The center is maintained by the U.S. Public Health Service. **Staff:** Carole Dean, Asst.Dir./Chf.,Tech.Serv.; Susan Gould, Chf., Cat.Serv.; Louise Lewis, Chf., Pub.Serv.; Betty Cardell, Acq.; Harriette Morgan, Ser.

★14190★
U.S. CENTERS FOR DISEASE CONTROL - CHAMBLEE FACILITY LIBRARY (Env-Cons; Med)
1600 Clifton Rd., N.E., 30/35   Phone: (404) 452-4167
Atlanta, GA 30333
Staff: Prof 1; Other 2. **Subjects:** Toxicology, clinical chemistry, vector biology and control, parasitic diseases, endocrinology, chronic diseases. **Holdings:** 3000 books; 900 bound periodical volumes; 175 volumes of journals on microfilm. **Subscriptions:** 300 journals and other serials. **Services:** Interlibrary loans; library open to public by appointment. **Automated Operations:** Computerized cataloging, serials and circulation. **Staff:** Delburna Anderson, Tech.Info.Spec.; Pamela Martin, Tech.Info.Spec.

U.S. CENTERS FOR DISEASE CONTROL - NATL. INSTITUTE FOR OCCUPATIONAL SAFETY AND HEALTH
See: U.S. Natl. Institute for Occupational Safety and Health

UNITED STATES CHAMBER OF COMMERCE
See: Chamber of Commerce of the United States of America

★14191★
U.S. CIVIL AERONAUTICS BOARD - LIBRARY (Trans)
Universal Bldg., Rm. 912
Connecticut & Florida Aves., N.W.   Phone: (202) 673-5101
Washington, DC 20428   Mary Louise Ransom, Supv.libn.
Founded: 1941. **Staff:** Prof 2. **Subjects:** Air law, administrative law, air carrier statistics, aeronautics, economics, transportation. **Holdings:** 25,000 books; 700 bound periodical volumes. **Subscriptions:** 85 journals and other serials. **Services:** Library open to public for reference use only.

★14192★
U.S. COAST GUARD ACADEMY - LIBRARY (Mil)
                                            Phone: (203) 444-8510
New London, CT 06320   Paul H. Johnson, Hd.Libn.
Founded: 1876. **Staff:** Prof 5; Other 4. **Subjects:** Coast Guard and Naval

history, seafaring, piracy, marine subjects. **Special Collections:** U.S. documents depository. **Holdings:** 134,000 books. **Subscriptions:** 630 journals and other serials. **Services:** Interlibrary loans; library not open to public. **Automated Operations:** Computerized cataloging and ILL. **Computerized Information Services:** DIALOG. Performs free searches. **Networks/Consortia:** Member of NELINET. **Staff:** Mary A. McKenzie, Hd., Pub.Serv.; Patricia A. Daragan, Hd., Tech.Serv.; Pamela A. McNulty, Ref. & Docs.Libn.; Sheila Lamb, Asst.Tech.Serv./Ref.Libn.

★14193★
U.S. COAST GUARD/AIR STATION - BASE LIBRARY (Mil)
Otis AFB   Phone: (617) 968-5062
Cape Cod, MA 02542   Evelyn L. Norton, Act.Libn.
Founded: 1974. **Staff:** 2. **Subjects:** U.S. and European history, American literature, military engineering, social sciences, aeronautics, children's literature. **Special Collections:** Air Forces (600 volumes); aeronautics (900 volumes); World War II history (2000 volumes). **Holdings:** 35,000 books; 200 bound periodical volumes; 600 paperbacks; 3 VF drawers of pamphlets; maps. **Subscriptions:** 110 journals and other serials; 10 newspapers. **Services:** Interlibrary loans; copying; library open to public. **Publications:** New Books, monthly - for internal distribution only.

★14194★
U.S. COAST GUARD - RESEARCH AND DEVELOPMENT CENTER - TECHNICAL INFORMATION CENTER (Sci-Tech)*
Avery Point   Phone: (203) 445-8501
Groton, CT 06340   Dorothy E. Siegfried, Tech.Info.Spec.
Founded: 1979. **Staff:** Prof 1. **Subjects:** Navigation, marine pollution technology, fire research, ice technology, search and rescue. **Holdings:** 1000 books; 1000 reports. **Subscriptions:** 150 journals and other serials; 10 newspapers. **Services:** Interlibrary loans; copying; SDI; center open to public with permission. **Automated Operations:** Computerized cataloging. **Computerized Information Services:** DIALOG, SDC, DTIC. **Publications:** Library Update, bimonthly.

★14195★
U.S. COAST GUARD - SUPPORT CENTER LIBRARY (Mil)
Governors Island, Bldg. S251   Phone: (212) 264-8694
New York, NY 10004   Bessie Seymour, Libn.
Founded: 1966. **Staff:** Prof 2; Other 1. **Subjects:** Military history, seamanship, U.S. Coast Guard. **Holdings:** 30,000 volumes; phonograph records. **Subscriptions:** 105 journals and other serials. **Services:** Interlibrary loans; library open to public for reference use only. **Formerly:** Its Tampa Memorial Library. **Staff:** Anson Huang, Asst.Libn.

★14196★
U.S. COMMISSION ON CIVIL RIGHTS - NATL. CLEARINGHOUSE LIBRARY (Soc Sci)
1121 Vermont Ave., N.W.   Phone: (202) 254-6636
Washington, DC 20425   Lenora W. McMillan, Chf.Libn.
Founded: 1957. **Staff:** Prof 3; Other 4. **Subjects:** Civil rights, economics, education, sex discrimination, sociology, law. **Special Collections:** The aged and the handicapped. **Holdings:** 50,000 books; 1100 bound periodical volumes; 1200 state and federal codes and statutes; 110 legal periodical titles; 500 reels of microfilm of minority periodicals; 300 journals on microfiche. **Subscriptions:** 440 journals and newspapers. **Services:** Interlibrary loans; copying; library open to public for reference use only. **Automated Operations:** Computerized cataloging. **Computerized Information Services:** DIALOG, OCLC. **Publications:** Monthly acquisitions list; bibliographies. **Staff:** David Tsuneishi, Rd.Serv.; Michael L. Williams, Cat.

★14197★
UNITED STATES COMMITTEE FOR REFUGEES - LIBRARY (Soc Sci)
20 W. 40th St.   Phone: (212) 398-9142
New York, NY 10018   Roger Winter, Dir.
Subjects: Refugee matters. **Holdings:** Figures not available for books. **Services:** Telephone referral and response to inquiries; library not open to public. **Publications:** Refugee Reports (newsletter), bimonthly - by subscription; World Refugee Survey, annual; periodic issue papers - free upon request. **Remarks:** United States Committee for Refugees is the publications and public information program of American Council for Nationalities Service, a private, nonprofit organization.

★14198★
U.S. COMMITTEE FOR UNICEF - INFORMATION CENTER ON CHILDREN'S CULTURES (Soc Sci)
331 E. 38th St.   Phone: (212) 686-5522
New York, NY 10016   Melinda Greenblatt, Chf.Libn.
Founded: 1968. **Staff:** Prof 2; Other 2. **Subjects:** Children in Asia, Africa,

the Caribbean, the Pacific, the Middle East and Latin America and their primary school texts, literature, education, social life, customs, festivals, games. **Holdings:** 17,000 books; 100 boxes of reports, booklists, pamphlets; 3500 pictures by children; 15,200 photographs of children; 445 phonograph records; 445 filmstrips; 110 films. **Subscriptions:** 50 journals and other serials. **Services:** Interlibrary loans; copying; center open to public. **Publications:** Bibliographies of children's books about countries in Asia, Africa, Latin America, the Pacific, the Caribbean and the Middle East. **Staff:** Jacqueline Doganges, Ref.Libn.

★14199★
U.S. COMPTROLLER OF THE CURRENCY - LIBRARY (Bus-Fin)
490 L'Enfant Plaza, S.W., 5th Fl.   Phone: (202) 447-1843
Washington, DC 20219   Audrey L. Ruge, Libn.
Founded: 1974. **Staff:** Prof 2; Other 4. **Subjects:** Law, banking, economics. **Holdings:** 43,500 volumes. **Subscriptions:** 500 journals and other serials; 10 newspapers. **Services:** Interlibrary loans; library open to public with restrictions. **Automated Operations:** Computerized cataloging. **Computerized Information Services:** DIALOG, OCLC. **Networks/Consortia:** Member of FEDLINK. **Publications:** Recent Acquisitions and Journal Articles, monthly - distributed to other banking libraries. **Staff:** Mary K. Wilson, Asst.Libn.

U.S. CONGRESS - HOUSE OF REPRESENTATIVES
See: U.S. House of Representatives

U.S. CONGRESS - OFFICE OF TECHNOLOGY ASSESSMENT
See: U.S. Office of Technology Assessment

U.S. CONGRESS - SENATE
See: U.S. Senate

U.S. CONGRESSIONAL BUDGET OFFICE
See: Congressional Budget Office

U.S. CONN LIBRARY
See: Wayne State College

U.S. CONSUMER PRODUCT SAFETY COMMISSION
See: Consumer Product Safety Commission

★14200★
U.S. COURT OF APPEALS, DISTRICT OF COLUMBIA CIRCUIT - LIBRARY (Law)
5518 U.S. Court House
3rd & Constitution Ave., N.W.   Phone: (202) 535-3401
Washington, DC 20001   Nancy Lazar, Circuit Libn.
Staff: Prof 3. **Subjects:** Law. **Holdings:** 90,000 volumes. **Subscriptions:** 200 journals and other serials; 7 newspapers. **Services:** Copying; library open to public with permission of librarian. **Staff:** Theresa Santella, Dp. Circuit Libn.; Laura Kimberly, Asst.Libn. for Tech.Serv.; Christine Pembroke, Asst.Libn.

★14201★
U.S. COURT OF APPEALS FOR THE FEDERAL CIRCUIT - NATIONAL COURTS' LIBRARY (Law)
717 Madison Pl., N.W., Rm. 218   Phone: (202) 633-5871
Washington, DC 20439   Patricia M. McDermott, Libn.
Staff: Prof 2; Other 1. **Subjects:** Law, taxation, government contracts, patents and trademarks, customs, international trade. **Holdings:** 30,500 books. **Subscriptions:** 91 journals and other serials. **Services:** Interlibrary loans; copying; library open to members of the Courts' Bar. **Computerized Information Services:** Westlaw. **Publications:** New in the National Courts' Library, bimonthly - free upon request. **Staff:** David J. Lockwood, Asst.Libn.

★14202★
U.S. COURT OF APPEALS, 1ST CIRCUIT - LIBRARY (Law)
1208 McCormack P.O. & Court House   Phone: (617) 223-2891
Boston, MA 02109   Karen M. Moss, Circuit Libn.
Staff: Prof 3; Other 1. **Subjects:** State and federal law and administrative material; slip onions from all circuits. **Special Collections:** Selective depository items, 1979 to present. **Holdings:** 40,000 books; 125 bound periodical volumes; Code of Federal Regulations; Federal Register and Congressional Record in microform. **Subscriptions:** 101 journals and other serials. **Services:** Interlibrary loans to Boston area libraries; library open to members of the bar. **Automated Operations:** Computerized cataloging. **Computerized Information Services:** Westlaw, OCLC. **Staff:** Judith Lavine, Asst.Libn.; Sharen Leonard, Asst.Libn., Tech.Serv.

★14203★
U.S. COURT OF APPEALS, 2ND CIRCUIT - LIBRARY (Law)
U.S. Court House, Rm. 2501, Foley Sq.   Phone: (212) 791-1052
New York, NY 10007   Margaret J. Evans, Chf.Libn.
Founded: 1917. **Staff:** Prof 6; Other 3. **Subjects:** Law, legislative history. **Holdings:** 40,000 books; 4500 bound periodical volumes. **Subscriptions:** 138 journals and other serials. **Services:** Library open to public with librarian's permission. **Automated Operations:** Computerized cataloging. **Computerized Information Services:** LEXIS, Westlaw. **Networks/Consortia:** Member of FEDLINK. **Publications:** Acquisitions List and Comments; Library Report Letter. **Special Indexes:** Index to Second Circuit Slip Opinions. **Staff:** Jean Clark, Asst.Libn.; Mary J. Washburn, Asst.Libn.; Sally C. Hand, Asst.Libn.; Jacqueline Stanford .

★14204★
U.S. COURT OF APPEALS, 3RD CIRCUIT - BRANCH LIBRARY (Law)
U.S. Post Office & Court House
Box 1068   Phone: (201) 645-3034
Newark, NJ 07101   Gerry Saletta, Libn.
Founded: 1975. **Staff:** Prof 1; Other 1. **Subjects:** Law. **Holdings:** 17,000 volumes. **Subscriptions:** 26 journals and other serials. **Services:** Interlibrary loans; copying; library open to public. **Computerized Information Services:** Online systems. **Special Catalogs:** Case name files for slip opinions from the U.S. Court of Appeals, 3rd Circuit and the U.S. District Court for the District of New Jersey.

★14205★
U.S. COURT OF APPEALS, 3RD CIRCUIT - LIBRARY (Law)
22409 U.S. Court House
601 Market St.   Phone: (215) 597-2009
Philadelphia, PA 19106   Dorothy A. Cozzolino, Chf.Libn.
Staff: Prof 3; Other 3. **Subjects:** Law, political science. **Holdings:** 45,000 books; 4000 bound periodical volumes. **Subscriptions:** 80 journals and other serials. **Services:** Interlibrary loans (limited); copying; library open to public with approval of librarian. **Staff:** Marsha Frederick, Asst.Libn.

★14206★
U.S. COURT OF APPEALS, 3RD CIRCUIT - PITTSBURGH BRANCH LIBRARY (Law)
512 U.S. Courthouse   Phone: (412) 644-6485
Pittsburgh, PA 15219   Linda Schneider, Libn.
Staff: Prof 2; Other 1. **Subjects:** Law - U.S., Pennsylvania, New Jersey, Virgin Islands, Delaware. **Holdings:** 14,000 books; 465 bound periodical volumes. **Subscriptions:** 45 journals and other serials; 6 newspapers. **Services:** Interlibrary loans; copying; library open to public. **Computerized Information Services:** Westlaw. **Special Indexes:** Western District of Pennsylvania Opinions (by case name, by subject; card); Middle District of Pennsylvania Opinions (by case name, by subject; card). **Staff:** Barbara Alexander, Asst.Libn.

★14207★
U.S. COURT OF APPEALS, 4TH CIRCUIT - LIBRARY (Law)
U.S. Courthouse, Rm. 424
Tenth & Main Sts.   Phone: (804) 771-2219
Richmond, VA 23219   Iris C. Stevenson, Circuit Libn.
Founded: 1891. **Staff:** Prof 3; Other 4. **Subjects:** Law. **Holdings:** 52,000 volumes. **Services:** Interlibrary loans; copying; library open to judiciary and members of the bar. **Computerized Information Services:** Westlaw. **Staff:** Peter A. Frey, Asst.Libn.; Elaine H. Woodward, Tech.Serv.Libn.; Patricia L. Hargis, Asst.Libn.

★14208★
U.S. COURT OF APPEALS, 5TH CIRCUIT - LIBRARY (Law)
600 Camp St., Rm. 106   Phone: (504) 589-6510
New Orleans, LA 70130   Max G. Dodson, Circuit Libn.
Staff: Prof 1; Other 5. **Subjects:** Law. **Holdings:** 45,000 books; 190 bound periodical volumes; microfiche. **Services:** Interlibrary loans; copying; library open to public with restrictions.

★14209★
U.S. COURT OF APPEALS, 6TH CIRCUIT - LIBRARY (Law)
617 U.S. Court House & Post Office Bldg.   Phone: (513) 684-2678
Cincinnati, OH 45202   Kathy Joyce Welker, Circuit Libn.
Founded: 1894. **Staff:** Prof 2; Other 2. **Subjects:** Law. **Holdings:** 60,000 volumes. **Services:** Library not open to public. **Computerized Information Services:** Westlaw.

★14210★
U.S. COURT OF APPEALS, 8TH CIRCUIT - BRANCH LIBRARY (Law)
Post Office and Courthouse
600 W. Capitol, Rm. 220   Phone: (501) 378-5039
Little Rock, AR 72201   Allison Pitcock, Libn.
Founded: 1981. **Staff:** Prof 1; Other 1. **Subjects:** Law. **Holdings:** 8000 books; 200 bound periodical volumes; 100 other cataloged items. **Subscriptions:** 50 journals and other serials. **Services:** Interlibrary loans; copying; library open to members of the federal bar. **Computerized Information Services:** Westlaw.

★14211★
U.S. COURT OF APPEALS, 8TH CIRCUIT - LIBRARY (Law)
U.S. Court House
811 Grand Ave., Rm. 845   Phone: (816) 842-9450
Kansas City, MO 64106   Margaret Tranne Pearce, Libn.
Subjects: Law. **Holdings:** 13,000 volumes. **Services:** Library open to members of the bar.

★14212★
U.S. COURT OF APPEALS, 8TH CIRCUIT - LIBRARY (Law)
U.S. Court & Customs House, Rm. 503   Phone: (314) 425-4930
St. Louis, MO 63101   David K. Brennan, Circuit Libn.
Staff: Prof 4; Other 2. **Subjects:** Law. **Holdings:** 23,000 books; 838 bound periodical volumes. **Subscriptions:** 91 journals and other serials. **Services:** Interlibrary loans; library open to government attorneys, members of the federal bar and to the public by permission. **Computerized Information Services:** Westlaw. **Publications:** Book catalog, annual. **Special Indexes:** Index-Digest of Eighth Circuit Opinions. **Remarks:** Branch libraries are located in Little Rock, AR; St. Paul, MN; Omaha, NE; Des Moines, IA; Kansas City, MO.

★14213★
U.S. COURT OF APPEALS, 8TH CIRCUIT - RESEARCH LIBRARY (Law)
590 Federal Bldg.
316 N. Robert St.   Phone: (612) 725-7177
St. Paul, MN 55101   Kathryn C. Kratz, Br.Libn.
Staff: 1. **Subjects:** Legal research topics. **Holdings:** 14,000 volumes. **Services:** Copying; library open to public. **Computerized Information Services:** Westlaw.

★14214★
U.S. COURT OF APPEALS, 9TH CIRCUIT - LIBRARY (Law)
709 W. 9th St.
Box 3-4000   Phone: (907) 586-7458
Juneau, AK 99802
Subjects: Law. **Holdings:** 7000 volumes. **Services:** Library open to attorneys and law students. **Formerly:** U.S. District Court.

★14215★
U.S. COURT OF APPEALS, 9TH CIRCUIT - LIBRARY (Law)
U.S. Courthouse, Rm. 6434
230 N. First Ave.   Phone: (602) 261-3879
Phoenix, AZ 85025-0074   Delores E. Daniels, Libn.
Staff: Prof 2; Other 2. **Subjects:** Law. **Holdings:** 17,000 books; 815 bound periodical volumes. **Subscriptions:** 642 journals and other serials; 5 newspapers. **Services:** Interlibrary loans; library not open to public. **Computerized Information Services:** Westlaw. **Publications:** Library Guide, annual - for internal distribution only. **Staff:** Richard Wiebelhaus, Asst.Libn.

★14216★
U.S. COURT OF APPEALS, 9TH CIRCUIT - LIBRARY (Law)
1702 U.S. Courthouse   Phone: (213) 688-3636
Los Angeles, CA 90012   Joanne Mazza, Libn.
Staff: Prof 2; Other 2. **Subjects:** Law. **Holdings:** 27,000 books. **Services:** Copying; library open to public for reference use only. **Computerized Information Services:** Westlaw.

★14217★
U.S. COURT OF APPEALS, 9TH CIRCUIT - LIBRARY (Law)
Box 5731   Phone: (415) 556-6129
San Francisco, CA 94101   Edward Chichura, Chf.Libn.
Staff: Prof 3; Other 3. **Subjects:** Law. **Holdings:** 46,512 volumes; 13,415 documents; 65,536 microforms. **Subscriptions:** 419 journals and other serials. **Services:** Interlibrary loans; library open to public. **Computerized Information Services:** LEXIS, Westlaw. **Publications:** For the Record, weekly - for internal distribution only. **Special Indexes:** Index to current 9th Circuit opinions. **Staff:** Sue Welsh, Asst. Circuit Libn.; Deborah Celle, Asst.Libn., Tech.Serv.

★14218★
U.S. COURT OF APPEALS, 9TH CIRCUIT - LIBRARY (Law)
Pioneer Courthouse   Phone: (503) 221-6042
Portland, OR 97204   Scott M. McCurdy, Libn.
Staff: Prof 2. **Subjects:** Law. **Holdings:** 10,000 books; 400 bound periodical volumes. **Services:** Interlibrary loans; copying; library open to attorneys on day of court proceedings. **Computerized Information Services:** Westlaw. **Staff:** Dianne Schauer, Asst.Libn.; Nancy Hoover, Asst.Libn.

★14219★
U.S. COURT OF APPEALS, 10TH CIRCUIT - LIBRARY (Law)
U.S. Court House, Rm. C 411   Phone: (303) 837-3591
Denver, CO 80294   J. Terry Hemming, Chf.Libn.
Staff: Prof 3; Other 2. **Subjects:** Law. **Holdings:** 28,000 volumes. **Services:** Interlibrary loans; copying; library open to public. **Automated Operations:** Computerized cataloging. **Computerized Information Services:** Westlaw. **Networks/Consortia:** Member of Colorado Consortium of Law Libraries. **Staff:** Loretta Nolin, Asst.Libn.; Catherine Eason, Ref.Libn.; Carol Minor, Cat.

★14220★
U.S. COURT OF APPEALS, 10TH CIRCUIT - OKLAHOMA CITY GENERAL LIBRARY (Law)
200 N.W. 4th St.   Phone: (405) 232-7441
Oklahoma City, OK 73102   Sharon Ware, Sec.
Staff: Prof 1. **Subjects:** Law. **Special Collections:** Unpublished opinions of the Tenth Circuit. **Holdings:** U.S. code and statutes at large; law reviews and digests. **Services:** Library open to public for reference use only.

★14221★
U.S. COURT OF APPEALS, 11TH CIRCUIT - LIBRARY (Law)
56 Forsyth St., N.W.   Phone: (404) 221-2510
Atlanta, GA 30303   Elaine P. Fenton, Circuit Libn.
Staff: Prof 3; Other 2. **Subjects:** Law. **Holdings:** 25,000 books; 5000 bound periodical volumes; 8 cabinets of microforms. **Subscriptions:** 150 journals and other serials; 6 newspapers. **Services:** Interlibrary loans; library open to attorneys only. **Automated Operations:** Computerized cataloging. **Computerized Information Services:** Westlaw, OCLC. **Networks/Consortia:** Member of FEDLINK. **Staff:** Sara M. Straub, Asst.Libn.; Sue T. Lee, Asst.Libn.

★14222★
U.S. COURT OF INTERNATIONAL TRADE - LAW LIBRARY (Law)
One Federal Plaza   Phone: (212) 264-2816
New York, NY 10007   Abraham Montekio, Libn.
Founded: 1926. **Staff:** Prof 2; Other 3. **Subjects:** Law, customs, international trade, science and technology. **Special Collections:** Customs laws and procedures (3000 volumes); legislative histories of custom and trade laws; tariff schedules. **Holdings:** 36,000 volumes; government documents; 12 VF drawers of pamphlets; microfiche. **Subscriptions:** 28 journals and other serials; 5 newspapers. **Services:** Interlibrary loans; copying; library open to public by appointment. **Computerized Information Services:** Westlaw. **Networks/Consortia:** Member of Law Library Association of Greater New York. **Publications:** Official court reporter; contributions to Custom Bulletin. **Staff:** Bruce Liebman, Asst.Libn.

★14223★
U.S. COURT OF MILITARY APPEALS - LIBRARY (Law; Mil)
450 E St., N.W.   Phone: (202) 693-7573
Washington, DC 20442   Mary S. Kuck, Libn.
Founded: 1952. **Staff:** Prof 1. **Subjects:** Law - military, criminal, evidence, international. **Special Collections:** Air Force, Army, Navy and Marine Corps regulations. **Holdings:** 19,000 volumes. **Subscriptions:** 60 journals and other serials. **Services:** Interlibrary loans; library open to public for reference use only, on request. **Publications:** Bibliography on Military Law.

★14224★
U.S. CUSTOMS SERVICE - LIBRARY AND INFORMATION CENTER (Soc Sci; Law)
1301 Constitution Ave., N.W., Rm. 3340   Phone: (202) 566-5642
Washington, DC 20229   Patricia M. Dobrosky, Dir.
Founded: 1975. **Staff:** Prof 5; Other 4. **Subjects:** Economics, law, social sciences, physical sciences, law enforcement, drugs. **Holdings:** 42,000 volumes. **Subscriptions:** 500 journals and other serials. **Services:** Interlibrary loans; copying; SDI; library open to public for reference use only. **Automated Operations:** Computerized cataloging and acquisitions. **Computerized Information Services:** DIALOG, LEXIS, NEXIS, LEGI-SLATE, OCLC. **Networks/Consortia:** Member of FEDLINK. **Publications:** U.S. Customs Service Bulletin, monthly - distributed in-house and mailed on request; Media Varia. **Staff:** Susan J. Arrington, Spec. Projects Libn.; Martha Glock, User

Serv.Libn.; Cecilia Hlatshwayo, Bus. & Econ.Libn.; Linda S. Dobb, Tech.Serv.Libn.

★14225★
U.S. CUSTOMS SERVICE - REGION II - LAW LIBRARY (Law)*
6 World Trade Ctr., Rm. 732   Phone: (212) 466-4579
New York, NY 10048   Ann Marie D'Ambrosio, Lib.Techn.
Founded: 1965. **Staff:** Prof 1. **Subjects:** Customs, federal statutes and regulations, New York and New Jersey statutes and cases. **Holdings:** 12,000 books; 2000 bound periodical volumes; 500 other cataloged items. **Subscriptions:** 66 journals and other serials. **Services:** Library open to public.

★14226★
U.S. DEFENSE AUDIOVISUAL AGENCY - DEPOSITORY ACCESSIONS BRANCH (DAVA-N-OAA) (Aud-Vis)
Norton Activity   Phone: (714) 382-6315
Norton AFB, CA 92409   John Faibisy, Br.Chf.
Staff: 6. **Subjects:** Army, Navy, Air Force and Marine Corps documentary film, 1950 to present; U.S. Department of Defense film productions, 1949 to present; World Wars I and II; Korean War. **Special Collections:** Wright Field Collection, 1920-1949. **Holdings:** 125 million feet of motion picture and video records. **Services:** Depository open to public with clearance through appropriate Department of Defense public affairs office. **Remarks:** The depository branch is the office of record for all motion pictures or video materials created or acquired by the U.S. military.

★14227★
U.S. DEFENSE AUDIOVISUAL AGENCY - NAVAL PHOTO CENTER
Anacostia Naval Sta., Bldg. 168
Washington, DC 20374
Defunct. Holdings absorbed by its Still Picture Library.

★14228★
U.S. DEFENSE AUDIOVISUAL AGENCY - STILL PHOTO DEPOSITORY - ARMY COLLECTION
The Pentagon, Rm. 5A486
Washington, DC 20310
Defunct. Holdings absorbed by its Still Picture Library.

★14229★
U.S. DEFENSE AUDIOVISUAL AGENCY - STILL PICTURE LIBRARY (Aud-Vis; Mil)
Bldg. 168, NDW   Phone: (202) 433-2166
Washington, DC 20374   Roy K. Heitman
Founded: 1943. **Staff:** Prof 12; Other 4. **Subjects:** Military activities, equipment, weapons, operations, personalities, history of military aviation, aircraft, ships, World War II, Korean War, Vietnam. **Holdings:** Over two million color and black and white photographs. **Services:** Copying; reprints available for fee to unofficial requestors, free of charge to government agencies; library open to public. **Remarks:** Absorbed the holdings of its former Naval Photo Center and Still Photo Depository - Army Collection. **Staff:** Michael Rusnak, Activity Chf.

★14230★
U.S. DEFENSE COMMUNICATIONS AGENCY - NATL. MILITARY COMMAND SYSTEM SUPPORT CENTER - TECHNICAL LIBRARY
BF 679, The Pentagon
Washington, DC 20301
Defunct. Holdings absorbed by its Technical and Management Information Center.

★14231★
U.S. DEFENSE COMMUNICATIONS AGENCY - TECHNICAL AND MANAGEMENT INFORMATION CENTER (Sci-Tech; Comp Sci)
Headquarters, DCA, Code H308C   Phone: (202) 692-2468
Washington, DC 20305   Donald A. Guerriero, Lib.Dir.
Founded: 1974. **Staff:** Prof 4; Other 6. **Subjects:** Telecommunications, computer science, systems analysis, operations research, management. **Holdings:** 10,000 books; 1500 technical reports. **Subscriptions:** 500 journals and other serials. **Services:** Interlibrary loans (limited); center not open to public. **Computerized Information Services:** OCLC, DIALOG, DTIC, SDC, BRS. **Networks/Consortia:** Member of FEDLINK. **Remarks:** Serves the headquarters and field agencies of the Defense Communications Agency (DCA). Center is located in Arlington, VA with a branch in Reston, VA. Absorbed the holdings of its Natl. Military Command System Support Center - Technical Library. **Staff:** Paul A. Tolovi, Info.Spec.; William Mills, Libn.; Grace Aitel, Libn.

★14232★
U.S. DEFENSE CONTRACT ADMINISTRATION SERVICES OF MILWAUKEE AREA - LIBRARY (Mil)
310 W. Wisconsin Ave., Suite 340   Phone: (414) 291-4327
Milwaukee, WI 53204   Nancy Slowinski, QA Data Ck.
Founded: 1965. **Staff:** 2. **Holdings:** Microfilm library of military and federal specifications and standards; QPL qualified products lists; manufacturers' code books and miscellaneous publications. **Services:** Library open to public for reference use only. **Automated Operations:** Computerized cataloging. **Computerized Information Services:** Online systems. Performs free searches.

★14233★
U.S. DEFENSE INTELLIGENCE AGENCY - LIBRARY RTS-2A (Mil)
          Phone: (202) 692-5311
Washington, DC 20301   H. Holzbauer, Chief Libn.
Founded: 1963. **Staff:** Prof 23; Other 26. **Subjects:** Intelligence - armed forces, transportation, environmental, scientific and technical, economic, sociological; communications and electronics. **Special Collections:** Intelligence reports, documents, periodicals. **Holdings:** 63,000 books; 80,000 reports; 45,000 translations; 1 million microfiche; 2.5 million unbound reports. **Subscriptions:** 3000 journals and other serials. **Services:** Interlibrary loans; library not open to public but public information act requests are satisfied. **Automated Operations:** Computerized cataloging, acquisitions, serials and circulation; COM generated catalog. **Computerized Information Services:** DIALOG, New York Times Information Service, SDC, Mead Data Central, OCLC. **Networks/Consortia:** Member of FEDLINK.

★14234★
U.S. DEFENSE LOGISTICS AGENCY - DEFENSE CONSTRUCTION SUPPLY CTR. - TECH. DATA PROCESSING BRANCH - LIBRARY (Sci-Tech)
3990 E. Broad St.   Phone: (614) 238-3549
Columbus, OH 43216-5000   Joseph S. Cohen, Chf.
Staff: 16. **Holdings:** Specifications, manufacturers' catalogs, government specifications and standards. **Services:** Library not open to public.

★14235★
U.S. DEFENSE LOGISTICS AGENCY - DEFENSE ELECTRONICS CENTER - LIBRARY
1507 Wilmington Pike
Dayton, OH 45444
Defunct

★14236★
U.S. DEFENSE LOGISTICS AGENCY - DEFENSE GENERAL SUPPLY CENTER - CENTER LIBRARY (Mil)
          Phone: (804) 275-3215
Richmond, VA 23297   Yvonne H. Oakley, Ctr.Libn.
Staff: Prof 1. **Subjects:** Management, military science, economics, political science. **Holdings:** 6259 volumes; 280 boxes of unbound magazines; operating regulations and manuals. **Subscriptions:** 72 journals and other serials; 13 newspapers. **Services:** Interlibrary loans; library open to public with restrictions. **Special Catalogs:** Library shelf list handbook.

★14237★
U.S. DEFENSE LOGISTICS AGENCY - DEFENSE INDUSTRIAL SUPPLY CENTER - TECHNICAL DATA MANAGEMENT OFFICE (Sci-Tech)
700 Robbins Ave.   Phone: (215) 697-2757
Philadelphia, PA 19111   William Helkowski, Chf.Tech. Data Mgr.
Founded: 1961. **Staff:** 43. **Subjects:** Steels and their finishes, engineering, management, general hardware. **Holdings:** 2000 books; 800,000 aperture cards (manufacturers' drawings); 20,000 manufacturers' catalogs; 35,000 government specifications and standards; cartridge film file. **Services:** Office not open to public.

★14238★
U.S. DEFENSE LOGISTICS AGENCY - DEFENSE LOGISTICS SERVICES CENTER - LIBRARY (Mil; Comp Sci)
Federal Ctr.
50 N. Washington St.   Phone: (616) 962-6511
Battle Creek, MI 49016   Anna K. Winger, Libn.
Founded: 1962. **Staff:** Prof 1. **Subjects:** Electronic data processing, adult education, management. **Holdings:** 3400 books; 275 government documents. **Subscriptions:** 244 journals and other serials. **Services:** Interlibrary loans; library open to public for reference use only.

★14239★
U.S. DEFENSE LOGISTICS AGENCY - DEFENSE PERSONNEL SUPPORT CTR. - DIRECTORATE OF MED. MATERIEL TECH. LIBRARY (Med)
2800 S. 20th St., Bldg. 9-3-F   Phone: (215) 952-2110
Philadelphia, PA 19101   Gerald J. Ziccardi, Med.Libn.
Founded: 1952. **Staff:** Prof 1. **Subjects:** Medicine, pharmacy, engineering. **Holdings:** 5875 books; 1500 bound periodical volumes; 1500 manufacturers' catalogs; 300 documents; 45 reels of microfilm of periodicals; titles; 40 pharmaceutical tapes. **Subscriptions:** 128 journals and other serials; 12 newspapers. **Services:** Interlibrary loans; library not open to public. **Publications:** Directorate of Medical Materiel, monthly - for internal distribution only. **Special Catalogs:** Document file holdings; manufacturers' catalogs holdings (both on cards).

★14240★
U.S. DEFENSE LOGISTICS AGENCY - HEADQUARTERS LIBRARY (Mil; Comp Sci)
Cameron Sta.   Phone: (202) 274-6055
Alexandria, VA 22304-6100   Barbara Ralston, Chf.Libn.
Founded: 1962. **Subjects:** Management, automatic data processing. **Special Collections:** Military regulations (5000 items). **Holdings:** 8300 books; 100,000 microforms. **Subscriptions:** 425 journals and other serials. **Services:** Interlibrary loans; library open to public by permission. **Automated Operations:** Computerized cataloging, serials and circulation. **Computerized Information Services:** OCLC. **Networks/Consortia:** Member of FEDLINK. **Staff:** Barbara Sable, Asst.Libn.

★14241★
U.S. DEFENSE MAPPING AGENCY - AEROSPACE CENTER - TECHNICAL LIBRARY (Sci-Tech)
3200 S. Second St.   Phone: (314) 263-4267
St. Louis, MO 63118   Russell E. Kappesser, Chf., Tech.Lib.
Founded: 1943. **Staff:** Prof 5; Other 4. **Subjects:** Earth sciences, astronomy, mathematics, lithography, maps and map projections, management. **Holdings:** 12,100 books; 1000 bound periodical volumes; 17,100 unbound volumes; 24,200 scientific-technical reports; 750 microtexts; 150 AV items. **Subscriptions:** 480 journals and other serials; 20 newspapers. **Services:** Interlibrary loans; library not open to public. **Publications:** Acquisitions List, semimonthly - limited distribution; Technical Library Users' Guide, irregular. **Special Catalogs:** DMAAC Technical Library Serials Catalog, annual - limited distribution. **Staff:** Margaret A. Mechanic, Ref.Libn.; N. Louise Hildebrand, Tech.Info.Spec./Acq.; R. Emerson, Tech.Info.Spec.

★14242★
U.S. DEFENSE MAPPING AGENCY - HYDROGRAPHIC/TOPOGRAPHIC CENTER- SUPPORT DIVISION - SCIENTIFIC DATA DEPARTMENT (Geog-Map)
6500 Brookes Lane   Phone: (301) 227-2080
Washington, DC 20315   Frank Lozupone, Chf., Sup.Div.
Founded: 1871. **Staff:** Prof 65; Other 30. **Subjects:** Topography, cartography, hydrography, bathymetry, geodesy, toponomy. **Special Collections:** Department of Defense libraries of maps, geodetic data, foreign place names, nautical charts, bathymetric data. **Holdings:** 80,000 books, periodicals and documents; 500,000 maps; 25,000 charts; 4.5 million place names; 50,000 bathymetric surveys. **Services:** Interlibrary loans (limited); copying; map mounting and laminating; library open to U.S. government agencies only. **Automated Operations:** Computerized cataloging. **Computerized Information Services:** DIALOG, SDC; internal databases. **Publications:** Biweekly accessions listings. **Staff:** Maurice S. Stuckey, Chf., Sci. Data Dept.

U.S. DEFENSE NUCLEAR AGENCY - ARMED FORCES RADIOBIOLOGY RESEARCH INSTITUTE
See: U.S. Armed Forces Radiobiology Research Institute (AFRRI)

★14243★
U.S. DEFENSE NUCLEAR AGENCY - TECHNICAL LIBRARY (Sci-Tech)
          Phone: (202) 325-7780
Washington, DC 20305   Betty L. Fox, Info. Programs Mgr.
Founded: 1947. **Staff:** Prof 3; Other 4. **Subjects:** Nuclear science and technology, nuclear weapons effects. **Holdings:** 8000 volumes; 70,000 technical reports. **Subscriptions:** 300 journals and other serials. **Services:** Interlibrary loans; library not open to public. **Automated Operations:** Computerized cataloging and circulation. **Computerized Information Services:** NEXIS, DIALOG, DTIC. **Staff:** Ethel D. Scaccio, Hd., Cat. and Clas.; Sandra E. Young, Hd., Ref./Info.Serv.

★14244★
U.S. DEFENSE TECHNICAL INFORMATION CENTER (Sci-Tech; Info Sci)
Cameron Sta.   Phone: (202) 274-7633
Alexandria, VA 22314   Hubert E. Sauter, Adm.
Staff: 460. **Subjects:** All areas of science and technology. **Holdings:** 1.2 million reports of Department of Defense research, development, test and evaluation. **Services:** Document announcement; secondary distribution of full-size and microform copies of documents; bibliographies; cumulated indexes; defense management information data banks (current work and program planning summaries); referrals. **Computerized Information Services:** Operates the Defense RDT&E online system. **Publications:** Technical Abstract Bulletin; Defense Technical Information Center Digest. **Remarks:** Services of the Defense Technical Information Center are available only to Department of Defense activities, other federal government organizations, their contractors, sub-contractors and grantees. Further information available from Reference Services Branch, Defense Technical Information Center.

★14245★
U.S. DEFENSE TECHNICAL INFORMATION CENTER - DTIC ON-LINE SERVICE FACILITY (Info Sci; Sci-Tech)
11099 S. LaCienega Blvd.   Phone: (213) 643-1108
Los Angeles, CA 90045   Carol D. Finney, Mgr.
Staff: Prof 2. **Subjects:** Research and development funded by the U.S. Department of Defense. **Special Collections:** Information Analysis Center collections. **Holdings:** 2 million documents. **Services:** Facility open to government agencies and U.S. Department of Defense registered and potential registered contractors. **Computerized Information Services:** DTIC. **Publications:** Technical Abstract Bulletin (TAB), bimonthly. **Special Indexes:** TAB Indexes, monthly and annual. **Staff:** L.A. Ames, Tech.Info.Spec.

★14246★
U.S. DEFENSE TECHNICAL INFORMATION CENTER - TECHNICAL LIBRARY (Sci-Tech; Comp Sci)
Cameron Sta., Bldg. 5   Phone: (202) 274-6833
Alexandria, VA 22314   Robert Billingsley, Libn.
Founded: 1958. **Staff:** Prof 1; Other 1. **Subjects:** Computer and information sciences, physical sciences, engineering, life sciences. **Holdings:** 5000 books. **Subscriptions:** 301 journals and other serials. **Services:** Interlibrary loans; library not open to public. **Automated Operations:** Computerized cataloging and serials. **Computerized Information Services:** DIALOG, SDC, BRS, NASA/RECON, OCLC; internal database. **Networks/Consortia:** Member of FEDLINK. **Remarks:** An internal support library primarily for DTIC personnel.

★14247★
U.S.D.A. - AGRICULTURAL RESEARCH SERVICE - CENTRAL GREAT PLAINS RESEARCH STATION - LIBRARY (Agri)
Box K   Phone: (303) 345-2259
Akron, CO 80720   Dr. D.E. Smika, Location Leader
Founded: 1907. **Staff:** Prof 6; Other 11. **Subjects:** Agronomy, soils, water, plants, hydrology. **Holdings:** 250 books. **Subscriptions:** 26 journals and other serials. **Services:** Library open to public.

★14248★
U.S.D.A. - AGRICULTURAL RESEARCH SERVICE - EASTERN REGIONAL RESEARCH CENTER LIBRARY (Sci-Tech; Food-Bev)
600 E. Mermaid Lane   Phone: (215) 233-6602
Philadelphia, PA 19118   Wendy H. Kramer, Adm.Libn.
Founded: 1940. **Staff:** Prof 1; Other 3. **Subjects:** Chemistry, biochemistry, chemical engineering, food sciences, leather research, plant sciences, microbiology. **Holdings:** Figures not available. **Subscriptions:** 500 journals and other serials. **Services:** Interlibrary loans; copying (limited); library open to public for reference use only. **Automated Operations:** Computerized cataloging. **Computerized Information Services:** DIALOG, SDC, OCLC. **Networks/Consortia:** Member of FEDLINK; Interlibrary Delivery Service of Pennsylvania (IDS); Greater Northeastern Regional Medical Library Program. **Publications:** Accession List, monthly.

★14249★
U.S.D.A. - AGRICULTURAL RESEARCH SERVICE - HONEY BEE PESTICIDES/ DISEASES RESEARCH LABORATORY - LIBRARY (Agri)
University of Wyoming
University Sta., Box 3168   Phone: (307) 766-2281
Laramie, WY 82071   W.T. Wilson, Res. Entomologist
Staff: Prof 3; Other 6. **Subjects:** Apiculture, pesticides, beekeeping, honey bees, bee diseases, insect pathology, entomology. **Holdings:** 480 books and bound periodical volumes; bulletins and reprints. **Services:** Library open to graduate students in apiculture research.

★14250★

U.S.D.A. - AGRICULTURAL RESEARCH SERVICE - HORTICULTURAL CROPS RESEARCH LABORATORY - LIBRARY (Sci-Tech; Agri)
5578 E. Air Terminal Dr.   Phone: (209) 487-5310
Fresno, CA 93727   J. Steven Tebbets, Biol.Techn./Libn.
Staff: 1. **Subjects:** Stored-product entomology, insect pathology. **Holdings:** 250 books; 360 issues of periodicals. **Subscriptions:** 12 journals and other serials. **Services:** Copying; library open to public for reference use only. **Computerized Information Services:** Internal database. **Publications:** 20 scientific articles/year. **Formerly:** Its Stored-Product Insects Research Laboratory.

★14251★

U.S.D.A. - AGRICULTURAL RESEARCH SERVICE - HORTICULTURAL RESEARCH LABORATORY LIBRARY (Agri)
2120 Camden Rd.   Phone: (305) 898-6791
Orlando, FL 32803   Joyce S. Darr, Libn.
Founded: 1970. **Staff:** 1. **Subjects:** Citrus culture, citrus breeding, citrus processing, citrus insects, nematology, plant pathology, plant physiology, biochemistry, transportation, storage and marketing of fruits and vegetables. **Special Collections:** Publications and reprints on citrus and related topics. **Holdings:** 1500 books; 1000 bound periodical volumes; reprints; slides and photographs. **Subscriptions:** 100 journals and other serials. **Services:** Interlibrary loans; copying; library open to the staff and students of nearby universities and experimental stations.

★14252★

U.S.D.A. - AGRICULTURAL RESEARCH SERVICE - MEAT ANIMAL RESEARCH CENTER (Sci-Tech)
Box 166   Phone: (402) 762-3241
Clay Center, NE 68933   Patricia L. Sheridan, Libn.
Staff: Prof 1. **Subjects:** Animal - science, breeding and reproduction, nutrition; agricultural engineering; meats; production systems. **Holdings:** 782 books; 1700 bound periodical volumes. **Subscriptions:** 153 journals and other serials. **Services:** Interlibrary loans; copying; center open to public with restrictions. **Computerized Information Services:** DIALOG. **Networks/Consortia:** Member of FEDLINK. **Also Known As:** Roman L. Hruska U.S. Meat Animal Research Center.

★14253★

U.S.D.A. - AGRICULTURAL RESEARCH SERVICE - NATL. ANIMAL DISEASE CENTER LIBRARY (Sci-Tech; Med)
Box 70   Phone: (515) 239-8200
Ames, IA 50010   Janice K. Eifling, Libn.
Founded: 1961. **Staff:** Prof 1; Other 1. **Subjects:** Biomedicine, microbiology, veterinary science. **Holdings:** 8000 books; 18,000 bound periodical volumes. **Subscriptions:** 450 journals and other serials. **Services:** Interlibrary loans; copying; ARS Current Awareness Literature Service; library open to qualified researchers. **Computerized Information Services:** DIALOG. **Publications:** Library Notes, monthly - for internal distribution only; Periodical Holdings List, annual. **Special Catalogs:** Card Catalog of literature references on animal diseases, 1800-1940.

★14254★

U.S.D.A. - AGRICULTURAL RESEARCH SERVICE - NATL. TILLAGE MACHINERY LABORATORY LIBRARY (Agri)
Box 792   Phone: (205) 887-8596
Auburn, AL 36830   Robert L. Schafer, Dir.
Staff: 1. **Subjects:** Tillage, traction, soil-machine relations, soil reactions, earth-moving. **Special Collections:** Foreign translations of technical publications. **Holdings:** 300 books; 500 bound periodical volumes; 7000 other cataloged items; 18,000 theses, reports; 50 technical films; 5000 slides; 5000 photographs. **Subscriptions:** 20 journals and other serials. **Services:** Interlibrary loans; library open to public.

★14255★

U.S.D.A. - AGRICULTURAL RESEARCH SERVICE - NORTH CENTRAL REGION - MARKET PATHOLOGY RESEARCH LIBRARY
536 S. Clark St., Rm. 183
Chicago, IL 60605
Defunct. Holdings absorbed by its National Agricultural Library in Beltsville, MD.

★14256★

U.S.D.A. - AGRICULTURAL RESEARCH SERVICE - NORTHERN REGIONAL RESEARCH CENTER LIBRARY (Sci-Tech)
1815 N. University St.   Phone: (309) 685-4011
Peoria, IL 61604   Donald L. Blevins, Libn.
Founded: 1940. **Staff:** Prof 1; Other 2. **Subjects:** Organic chemistry,

chemical engineering, biochemistry, microbiology, fermentation. **Holdings:** 10,000 books; 32,000 bound periodical volumes; 200 reels of microfilm. **Subscriptions:** 320 journals and other serials. **Services:** Interlibrary loans; copying; SDI; library open to public. **Automated Operations:** Computerized cataloging. **Computerized Information Services:** DIALOG, SDC, OCLC. **Networks/Consortia:** Member of FEDLINK; Heart of Illinois Consortium (HILC); Illinois Valley Library System. **Publications:** Accession List, quarterly - distributed on request.

★14257★

U.S.D.A. - AGRICULTURAL RESEARCH SERVICE - PLUM ISLAND ANIMAL DISEASE CENTER LIBRARY (Agri)
Box 848   Phone: (516) 323-2500
Greenport, NY 11944   Stephen Perlman, Libn.
Founded: 1954. **Staff:** Prof 1; Other 1. **Special Collections:** Foreign animal diseases. **Holdings:** 10,000 books; 12,000 bound periodical volumes; 11,565 reprints; 85 VF drawers of pamphlets and reprints. **Subscriptions:** 288 journals and other serials. **Services:** Interlibrary loans; copying; library open to public with clearance from the librarian. **Special Catalogs:** Card catalog on foreign animal diseases; subject catalog on computerized tape.

★14258★

U.S.D.A. - AGRICULTURAL RESEARCH SERVICE - SNAKE RIVER CONSERVATION RESEARCH CENTER - LIBRARY (Agri)
Route 1, Box 186   Phone: (208) 423-5582
Kimberly, ID 83341   A. Smith, Libn.
Staff: Prof 2; Other 1. **Subjects:** Agriculture, agronomy, entomology, computers, plant and crop science, soil science, meteorology, ecology and environment, water and hydrology. **Holdings:** 1150 books; 1100 bound periodical volumes; 2300 reprints. **Subscriptions:** 45 journals and other serials. **Services:** Interlibrary loans; library open to public for reference use only. **Publications:** New Book List - for internal distribution only.

★14259★

U.S.D.A. - AGRICULTURAL RESEARCH SERVICE - SOUTH ATLANTIC AREA - RICHARD B. RUSSELL AGRI. RESEARCH CTR. LIB. (Agri)
College Station Rd., Box 5677   Phone: (404) 546-3314
Athens, GA 30613   Benna Brodsky Thompson, Libn.
Staff: Prof 1; Other 2. **Subjects:** Agriculture, toxicology, food safety. **Holdings:** 6000 books and bound periodical volumes. **Subscriptions:** 340 journals and other serials. **Services:** Interlibrary loans; copying; SDI; library open to public. **Automated Operations:** Computerized cataloging and ILL. **Computerized Information Services:** DIALOG, OCLC, DOE/RECON, CAS Online, MEDLARS, Pergamon InfoLine Ltd. **Networks/Consortia:** Member of FEDLINK. **Publications:** Newsletter.

★14260★

U.S.D.A. - AGRICULTURAL RESEARCH SERVICE - SOUTHERN REGIONAL RESEARCH CENTER (Sci-Tech; Food-Bev)
1100 Robert E. Lee Blvd.
Box 19687   Phone: (504) 589-7072
New Orleans, LA 70179   Dorothy B. Skau, Libn.
Founded: 1941. **Staff:** Prof 2; Other 2. **Subjects:** Chemistry, textiles, food processing, plant sciences, mechanical and chemical engineering, microscopy - including electron microscopy, vegetable fats and oils, microbiology, statistics. **Special Collections:** Trade literature; U.S. and foreign patents in laboratory's fields of interest. **Holdings:** 40,000 volumes; 59 VF drawers of pamphlets, foreign patents, trade literature, reprints, translations and manuscripts; 68 shelves of U.S. patents. **Subscriptions:** 2111 journals and other serials. **Services:** Interlibrary loans; center open to public for reference use only. **Automated Operations:** Computerized cataloging. **Computerized Information Services:** DIALOG, OCLC. **Networks/Consortia:** Member of FEDLINK. **Publications:** Accession List, monthly. **Special Indexes:** Bibliography on Aflatoxin and Byssinosis (card).

★14261★

U.S.D.A. - AGRICULTURAL RESEARCH SERVICE - SOUTHWEST RANGELAND WATERSHED RESEARCH CENTER (Env-Cons)
442 E. 7th St.   Phone: (602) 792-6381
Tucson, AZ 85705-8599   E. Sue Anderson, Libn.
Staff: 1. **Subjects:** Water and soil conservation, sediment, runoff, erosion, rainfall. **Holdings:** 300 books; 100 bound periodical volumes; 1600 theses and papers. **Subscriptions:** 23 journals and other serials. **Services:** Interlibrary loans; center open to public with restrictions. **Publications:** Bibliography of abstracts and papers, annual - to mailing list.

★14262★

U.S.D.A. - AGRICULTURAL RESEARCH SERVICE - STORED-PRODUCT INSECTS RESEARCH & DEVELOPMENT LAB. - LIB. (Sci-Tech; Agri)
Box 22909   Phone: (912) 233-7981
Savannah, GA 31403   Charlene F. Davis, Lib.Techn.
Staff: Prof 1. **Subjects:** Stored-product insect control, entomology, chemistry, biology, insect-resistant packaging, mothproofing, insect rearing. **Holdings:** 4000 books; 8000 bound periodical volumes; 7 VF drawers of U.S.D.A. publications; 2000 slides; 4000 unbound journals; 17,000 reprints; 200 microfiche. **Subscriptions:** 220 journals and other serials. **Services:** Interlibrary loans; library open with director's permission. **Publications:** Psocoptera, irregular - for internal distribution only.

★14263★

U.S.D.A. - AGRICULTURAL RESEARCH SERVICE - WATER CONSERVATION LABORATORY LIBRARY (Sci-Tech; Agri)†
4331 E. Broadway Rd.   Phone: (602) 261-4356
Phoenix, AZ 85040   Frieda Bell, Libn.
Founded: 1961. **Staff:** Prof 1. **Subjects:** Agricultural and irrigation engineering, hydraulics, hydrology, soils, plant physiology, chemistry, meteorology, instrumentation, wastewater renovation, infrared remote sensing, plant stress. **Holdings:** 1200 books; 200 bound periodical volumes; laboratory annual reports; reports of Geological Survey and ARS Series. **Subscriptions:** 85 journals and other serials. **Services:** Library open to public for reference use only. **Publications:** Listing of publications of laboratory staff members, annual.

★14264★

U.S.D.A. - AGRICULTURAL RESEARCH SERVICE - WESTERN REGIONAL RESEARCH CENTER LIBRARY (Agri)
                                                              Phone: (415) 486-3351
Berkeley, CA 94710   Rena Schonbrun, Libn.
Founded: 1940. **Staff:** Prof 1; Other 2. **Subjects:** Cereals, fruits and vegetables, field crops, food technology, pharmacology, chemistry, nutrition. **Holdings:** 32,000 books, bound periodical volumes and pamphlets. **Subscriptions:** 550 journals. **Services:** Interlibrary loans; copying; SDI; library open to public by appointment. **Automated Operations:** Computerized cataloging. **Computerized Information Services:** DIALOG, OCLC. **Networks/Consortia:** Member of FEDLINK. **Publications:** Library Accessions and Notes - for internal distribution only.

★14265★

U.S.D.A. - ECONOMIC RESEARCH SERVICE - ERS REFERENCE CENTER (Agri)
500 12th St., S.W., Rm. 147   Phone: (202) 447-4382
Washington, DC 20250   Cynthia Kenyon, Dir.
Staff: Prof 2. **Subjects:** Agricultural economics. **Special Collections:** Comprehensive collection of the U.S.D.A. - Economic Research Service and U.S.D.A. - Economics and Statistics Service publications (unbound and/or on microfiche). **Holdings:** 350 bound periodical volumes. **Subscriptions:** 400 journals and other serials. **Services:** Interlibrary loans; copying (limited); SDI; center open to public for reference use only, by appointment. **Computerized Information Services:** DIALOG. **Publications:** Journal Holdings, irregular; News from ERS Reference Center, irregular - both for internal distribution only. **Special Catalogs:** Quick Bibliographies on timely subjects in agricultural economics (pamphlet). **Staff:** Dorothy Heise, Tech.Info.Spec.

U.S.D.A. - FOREST SERVICE
See: U.S. Forest Service

★14266★

U.S.D.A. - NATIONAL AGRICULTURAL LIBRARY (Agri; Sci-Tech)
10301 Baltimore Blvd.   Phone: (301) 344-3755
Beltsville, MD 20705   Joseph H. Howard, Dir.
Founded: 1862. **Staff:** Prof 70; Other 83. **Subjects:** Plant science, chemistry, animal industry, veterinary medicine, biology, agricultural engineering, rural sociology, forestry, entomology, law, food and nutrition, soils and fertilizers, agricultural products, economic science, farm machinery. **Special Collections:** Foreign and domestic nursery and seed trade catalogs; flock, herd and stud books; rare book collection; AV collection on food and nutrition; apiculture; James M. Gwin Collection (poultry); Charles E. North Collection (milk sanitation). **Holdings:** 1.8 million volumes; 10,000 microforms, reports and maps. **Subscriptions:** 24,000 journals and newspapers. **Services:** Interlibrary loans; copying; SDI; library open to public. **Automated Operations:** Computerized cataloging and serials. **Computerized Information Services:** DIALOG, BRS, OCLC, New York Times Information Service; internal databases. **Networks/Consortia:** Member of FEDLINK. **Publications:** Agricultural Libraries Information Notes, monthly; AGRICOLA (computerized tape service), monthly - for sale. **Special Catalogs:** National

Agricultural Library Catalog, monthly. **Special Indexes:** Bibliographies and Literature of Agriculture, irregular. **Remarks:** Holdings given include material in U.S.D.A. - National Agricultural Library, agency field and branch libraries. **Staff:** Samuel T. Waters, Assoc.Dir.;Philip Turner, Act.Chf., Info.Sys.Div.

★14267★

U.S.D.A. - NATIONAL AGRICULTURAL LIBRARY - FOOD AND NUTRITION INFORMATION CENTER (Food-Bev)
10301 Baltimore Blvd., Rm. 304   Phone: (301) 344-3719
Beltsville, MD 20705   Robyn Frank, Dir.
Founded: 1971. **Staff:** Prof 2; Other 1. **Subjects:** Human nutrition research and education, food service management and food technology. **Special Collections:** Audiovisual materials. **Holdings:** 7500 books; 1700 AV items; 2 drawers of pamphlets; games; posters. **Subscriptions:** 150 journals and other serials. **Services:** Interlibrary loans; copying. **Automated Operations:** Computerized cataloging. **Computerized Information Services:** Online systems. **Formerly:** Part of its Human Nutrition Information Service.

U.S.D.A. - NATIONAL AGRICULTURAL LIBRARY - NATIONAL ARBORETUM
See: U.S. Natl. Arboretum

★14268★

U.S.D.A. - OFFICE OF GENERAL COUNSEL - LAW LIBRARY (Law)
Independence Ave. at 12th St., S.W.
Rm. 1406, S Bldg.   Phone: (202) 447-7751
Washington, DC 20250   Edward S. Billings, Law Libn.
Founded: 1910. **Staff:** Prof 3; Other 3. **Subjects:** Law; legislative histories of federal acts of interest to the Department of Agriculture; federal administrative decisions (selective). **Holdings:** 116,277 books; 2404 bound periodical volumes; 49 16mm reels of microfilm of Congressional Globe (complete); 192,748 microfiche cards of the CIS microfiche library of the working papers of the U.S. Congress; 328 16mm reels of microfilm of Federal Register, March 1936-December 1979; 484 reels of 35mm microfilm; 131 reels of 16mm microfilm. **Subscriptions:** 115 journals and other serials. **Services:** Interlibrary loans (within metropolitan area); copying; library open to public for reference use only. **Computerized Information Services:** LEXIS, Westlaw, OCLC. **Staff:** Adya Skmay, Asst. Law Libn.

★14269★

U.S.D.A. - PHOTOGRAPHY DIVISION - PHOTOGRAPH LIBRARY (Aud-Vis; Agri)
14th & Independence Ave., S.W.   Phone: (202) 447-6633
Washington, DC 20250
Staff: Prof 2; Other 4. **Subjects:** Agriculture, food production and marketing, land use. **Holdings:** 70,000 black and white photographs; 20,000 color slides. **Services:** Library open to public. **Publications:** Catalog of USDA Photos; Filmstrips and Slide Sets of the USDA - both free upon request. **Staff:** Dave Warren, Pict.Ed.; Thedosia Thomas, Color Slide Ed.

U.S.D.A. - SOIL CONSERVATION SERVICE
See: U.S. Soil Conservation Service

U.S. DEPT. OF THE AIR FORCE
See: U.S. Air Force

U.S. DEPT. OF THE ARMY
See: U.S. Army

U.S. DEPT. OF COMMERCE - BUREAU OF THE CENSUS
See: U.S. Bureau of the Census

★14270★

U.S. DEPT. OF COMMERCE - COMMERCE PRODUCTIVITY CENTER (Soc Sci)
14th St. & Constitution Ave., N.W., Rm. 7413   Phone: (202) 377-0940
Washington, DC 20230   States Clawson, Mgr.
Founded: 1978. **Staff:** Prof 2; Other 1. **Subjects:** Technology and innovation, productivity, quality of working life, economics, management, labor relations, public administration. **Holdings:** 5580 books and bound periodical volumes; 2000 microfiche; 2000 clippings. **Subscriptions:** 60 journals and other serials. **Services:** Interlibrary loans; copying (both limited); center open to public. **Publications:** Publications on productivity and quality of working life. **Staff:** Carol Ann Meares, Asst.Mgr./Info.Spec.

★14271★

U.S. DEPT. OF COMMERCE - INTERNATIONAL TRADE ADMINISTRATION - ALBUQUERQUE DISTRICT OFFICE LIBRARY (Bus-Fin)★
505 Marquette Ave., N.W., Suite 1015   Phone: (505) 766-2386
Albuquerque, NM 87102   William E. Dwyer, Dir.
Staff: 2. **Subjects:** Census Bureau publications, foreign country directories.

Services: Interlibrary loans; copying; library open to public.

★14272★
U.S. DEPT. OF COMMERCE - INTERNATIONAL TRADE ADMINISTRATION - ANCHORAGE DISTRICT OFFICE LIBRARY (Bus-Fin)
701 C St.
Box 32
Anchorage, AK 99513
Phone: (907) 271-5041
Richard M. Lenahan, Act.Dir.
Subjects: Census Bureau publications, Alaska and international commerce reference files. Holdings: 1000 volumes. Services: Library open to public.

★14273★
U.S. DEPT. OF COMMERCE - INTERNATIONAL TRADE ADMINISTRATION - ATLANTA DISTRICT OFFICE LIBRARY (Bus-Fin)*
1365 Peachtree St., N.E., Suite 600
Atlanta, GA 30032
Phone: (404) 881-4873
Christine B. Brown, Trade Ref.Asst.
Staff: Prof 1. Subjects: Demographic and economic statistics, foreign trade lead publications, patents, copyrights. Holdings: 600 books; 32 bound periodical volumes. Subscriptions: 31 journals and other serials. Services: Copying; library open to public. Computerized Information Services: DIALOG, SDC, BRS. Publications: Census and foreign trade publications.

★14274★
U.S. DEPT. OF COMMERCE - INTERNATIONAL TRADE ADMINISTRATION - BALTIMORE DISTRICT OFFICE LIBRARY (Bus-Fin)
415 U.S. Customhouse
Gay & Lombard Sts.
Baltimore, MD 21202
Phone: (301) 962-3560
Mary T. Conrad, Trade Spec.
Staff: Prof 3; Other 2. Subjects: International trade, export expansion, domestic economic growth. Holdings: 50 VF drawers; 4 bookcases; trade directories for 20 countries. Services: Library open to public.

★14275★
U.S. DEPT. OF COMMERCE - INTERNATIONAL TRADE ADMINISTRATION - BIRMINGHAM DISTRICT OFFICE LIBRARY (Bus-Fin)*
908 S. 20th St., Suites 200-201
Birmingham, AL 35205
Phone: (205) 254-1331
Gayle C. Shelton, Jr., Dir.
Subjects: Department and Census Bureau publications. Holdings: 170 books; reports. Services: Library open to public.

★14276★
U.S. DEPT. OF COMMERCE - INTERNATIONAL TRADE ADMINISTRATION - BOSTON DISTRICT OFFICE LIBRARY (Bus-Fin)
441 Stuart St., 10th Fl.
Boston, MA 02116
Phone: (617) 223-2312
Frank J. O'Connor, Dir.
Founded: 1930. Staff: 14. Subjects: Business, commerce, foreign and domestic trade. Holdings: 960 linear feet of reference files. Services: Library open to public. Publications: Commerce New England Newsletter, irregular.

★14277★
U.S. DEPT. OF COMMERCE - INTERNATIONAL TRADE ADMINISTRATION - BUFFALO DISTRICT OFFICE LIBRARY (Bus-Fin)*
1312 Federal Bldg.
111 W. Huron St.
Buffalo, NY 14202
Phone: (716) 846-4191
Robert F. Magee, Dir.
Subjects: Census Bureau and department publications. Holdings: 3000 volumes. Services: Library open to public.

★14278★
U.S. DEPT. OF COMMERCE - INTERNATIONAL TRADE ADMINISTRATION - CHARLESTON DISTRICT OFFICE LIBRARY (Bus-Fin)
3000 New Federal Office Bldg.
500 Quarrier St.
Charleston, WV 25301
Phone: (304) 347-5123
Roger L. Fortner, Dir.
Subjects: Department publications, International Trade Administration directories, West Virginia state pamphlets and studies, exporting information, economic statistics, patent and copyright information. Holdings: 4400 volumes. Services: Library open to public.

★14279★
U.S. DEPT. OF COMMERCE - INTERNATIONAL TRADE ADMINISTRATION - CHEYENNE DISTRICT OFFICE LIBRARY
Federal O'Mahoney Ctr., Rm. 8007
2120 Capitol Ave.
Cheyenne, WY 82001
Defunct

★14280★
U.S. DEPT. OF COMMERCE - INTERNATIONAL TRADE ADMINISTRATION - CHICAGO DISTRICT OFFICE LIBRARY (Bus-Fin)
Mid-Continental Plaza Bldg., Rm. 1406
55 E. Monroe
Chicago, IL 60603
Phone: (312) 353-4450
Bernadine C. Roberson, Libn.
Founded: 1940. Staff: 1. Subjects: Business economics, population (census), foreign trade statistics. Special Collections: Census materials; foreign trade directories. Holdings: 5000 books; 5000 pamphlets; 500 bibliographies. Subscriptions: 30 journals and other serials. Services: Library open to public.

★14281★
U.S. DEPT. OF COMMERCE - INTERNATIONAL TRADE ADMINISTRATION - CINCINNATI DISTRICT OFFICE LIBRARY (Bus-Fin)*
10504 Federal Office Bldg.
550 Main St.
Cincinnati, OH 45202
Phone: (513) 684-2944
Gordon B. Thomas, Dir.
Subjects: Domestic and international trade, statistical data, catalogs, trade journals, industry reports, department publications, directories, Census Bureau materials. Holdings: 33 bookcase sections; 88 VF drawers. Services: Library open to public.

★14282★
U.S. DEPT. OF COMMERCE - INTERNATIONAL TRADE ADMINISTRATION - CLEVELAND DISTRICT OFFICE LIBRARY (Bus-Fin)
666 Euclid Ave., Rm. 600
Cleveland, OH 44114
Phone: (216) 522-4750
Zelda W. Milner, Dir.
Founded: 1947. Staff: Prof 1; Other 1. Subjects: International trade, marketing, economic trends, business. Holdings: 5700 volumes; 100 VF drawers. Services: Professional consultations by international trade specialists; library open to public with registration required. Publications: Business America - Ohio, bimonthly.

★14283★
U.S. DEPT. OF COMMERCE - INTERNATIONAL TRADE ADMINISTRATION - DALLAS DISTRICT OFFICE LIBRARY (Bus-Fin)
1110 Commerce St., Rm. 7A5
Dallas, TX 75242
Phone: (214) 767-0542
C. Carmon Stiles, Dir.
Subjects: Domestic and foreign commerce. Holdings: 3725 volumes. Services: Library open to public.

★14284★
U.S. DEPT. OF COMMERCE - INTERNATIONAL TRADE ADMINISTRATION - DES MOINES DISTRICT OFFICE LIBRARY (Bus-Fin)*
817 Federal Bldg.
210 Walnut St.
Des Moines, IA 50309
Phone: (515) 284-4222
Jesse N. Durden, Dir.
Subjects: Department publications and selected items from other agencies; foreign trade statistics; census statistics. Holdings: Figures not available. Services: Copying; library open to public.

★14285★
U.S. DEPT. OF COMMERCE - INTERNATIONAL TRADE ADMINISTRATION - DETROIT DISTRICT OFFICE LIBRARY (Bus-Fin)
445 Federal Bldg.
231 W. Lafayette
Detroit, MI 48226
Phone: (313) 226-3650
George R. Campbell, Act.Dir.
Subjects: Economics, marketing, trade, census. Holdings: 600 volumes; 4 drawers of international trade statistics on microfiche. Subscriptions: 30 journals and other serials. Services: Library open to public. Computerized Information Services: DIALOG; internal database. Publications: Business America - Michigan Newsletter, monthly.

★14286★
U.S. DEPT. OF COMMERCE - INTERNATIONAL TRADE ADMINISTRATION - GREENSBORO DISTRICT OFFICE LIBRARY (Bus-Fin)
203 Federal Bldg., West Market St.
Greensboro, NC 27402
Phone: (919) 378-5345
Jack F. Whiteley, Dp.Dir.
Subjects: Domestic and foreign commerce. Holdings: 1400 volumes. Subscriptions: 15 journals and other serials. Services: Library open to public. Computerized Information Services: DIALOG; Automatic Information Transfer System (internal database).

★14287★
U.S. DEPT. OF COMMERCE - INTERNATIONAL TRADE ADMINISTRATION - HARTFORD DISTRICT OFFICE LIBRARY (Bus-Fin)*
Federal Office Bldg., Rm. 610-B
450 Main St.
Hartford, CT 06103
Phone: (203) 244-3530
Richard C. Kilbourn, Dir.
Subjects: Department publications including Census statistics. Holdings:

Figures not available. **Services:** Library open to public.

★14288★
U.S. DEPT. OF COMMERCE - INTERNATIONAL TRADE ADMINISTRATION - HOUSTON DISTRICT OFFICE LIBRARY (Bus-Fin)†
515 Rusk Ave., Rm. 2625   Phone: (713) 226-4231
Houston, TX 77002   Felicito C. Guerrero, Dir.
Subjects: Commerce Department and general business publications.
Holdings: 600 volumes. **Services:** Library open to public.

★14289★
U.S. DEPT. OF COMMERCE - INTERNATIONAL TRADE ADMINISTRATION - MIAMI DISTRICT OFFICE LIBRARY (Bus-Fin)
Federal Bldg., Rm. 224
51 S.W. First Ave.   Phone: (305) 350-5267
Miami, FL 33130   Ivan A. Cosimi, Dir.
Subjects: Business, foreign and domestic trade. **Special Collections:** Foreign directories; government reports. **Services:** Library open to public.

★14290★
U.S. DEPT. OF COMMERCE - INTERNATIONAL TRADE ADMINISTRATION - MILWAUKEE DISTRICT OFFICE LIBRARY (Bus-Fin)★
Federal Bldg.
517 E. Wisconsin Ave.   Phone: (414) 291-3473
Milwaukee, WI 53202   Russell H. Leitch, Dir.
Subjects: Economic and market research materials, technology, foreign trade statistics and directories. **Holdings:** 6000 volumes. **Services:** Library open to public.

★14291★
U.S. DEPT. OF COMMERCE - INTERNATIONAL TRADE ADMINISTRATION - MINNEAPOLIS DISTRICT OFFICE LIBRARY (Bus-Fin)
108 Federal Bldg.
110 S. Fourth St.   Phone: (612) 349-3338
Minneapolis, MN 55401   Mary Hobbs, Trade Spec.
Staff: Prof 1. **Subjects:** Census data, marketing information, government statistics, foreign trade, area development. **Special Collections:** Directories. **Holdings:** Figures not available. **Services:** Interlibrary loans; library open to public.

★14292★
U.S. DEPT. OF COMMERCE - INTERNATIONAL TRADE ADMINISTRATION - NASHVILLE DISTRICT OFFICE LIBRARY (Bus-Fin)
One Commerce Pl., Suite 1427   Phone: (615) 251-5161
Nashville, TN 37239   Martha Broadway, Trade Ref.Asst.
Founded: 1930. **Staff:** Prof 2. **Subjects:** International trade, economic studies, foreign trade regulations, customs procedures. **Holdings:** 1000 books; 77 bound periodical volumes; 3000 other cataloged items. **Subscriptions:** 27 journals and other serials; 6 newspapers. **Services:** Interlibrary loans; copying; library open to public for reference use only. **Computerized Information Services:** DIALOG, Foreign Traders Index; internal database. Performs searches on cost recovery basis. Contact Person: Jim Charlet. **Formerly:** Its Memphis District Office Library. **Staff:** Jim Charlet, Dist.Dir.

★14293★
U.S. DEPT. OF COMMERCE - INTERNATIONAL TRADE ADMINISTRATION - NEW ORLEANS DISTRICT OFFICE LIBRARY (Bus-Fin)
International Trade Mart, Rm. 432
2 Canal St.   Phone: (504) 589-6546
New Orleans, LA 70130   Raymond E. Eveland, Dir.
Subjects: Publications of Department of Commerce. **Holdings:** Foreign trade statistics on microfilm and microfiche; domestic census statistics; foreign phone books and commerical directories. **Services:** Library open to public.

★14294★
U.S. DEPT. OF COMMERCE - INTERNATIONAL TRADE ADMINISTRATION - NEW YORK DISTRICT OFFICE LIBRARY (Bus-Fin)
26 Federal Plaza   Phone: (212) 264-0630
New York, NY 10278   Stuart Werner, Tech.Info.Spec.
Founded: 1925. **Staff:** Prof 2. **Subjects:** Census, economics, business, technology, foreign trade, marketing. **Special Collections:** Foreign and domestic trade directories. **Holdings:** 4500 books; 65 VF drawers of economic and business information. **Subscriptions:** 75 journals and other serials; 10 newspapers. **Services:** Copying; library open to public. **Computerized Information Services:** DIALOG. **Staff:** Elisa Colas, Tech.Info.Spec.

★14295★
U.S. DEPT. OF COMMERCE - INTERNATIONAL TRADE ADMINISTRATION - PHILADELPHIA DISTRICT OFFICE LIBRARY (Bus-Fin)★
9448 Federal Bldg.
600 Arch St.   Phone: (215) 597-2850
Philadelphia, PA 19106   Robert Kistler, Dir.
Subjects: Department publications, state industrial directories, foreign business directories, international marketing information. **Holdings:** 800 volumes; Department of Commerce publications. **Services:** Library open to public.

★14296★
U.S. DEPT. OF COMMERCE - INTERNATIONAL TRADE ADMINISTRATION - PHOENIX DISTRICT OFFICE LIBRARY (Bus-Fin)
Valley Bank Center
201 N. Central Ave., Suite 2750   Phone: (602) 261-3285
Phoenix, AZ 85073   Donald W. Fry, Dir.
Founded: 1946. **Staff:** Prof 6. **Subjects:** Technology, census, agriculture, business, education, transportation, Indians, importing and exporting, Arizona statistics. **Holdings:** 6000 books; 1500 other volumes. **Services:** Library open to public.

★14297★
U.S. DEPT. OF COMMERCE - INTERNATIONAL TRADE ADMINISTRATION - PITTSBURGH DISTRICT OFFICE LIBRARY (Bus-Fin)
2002 Federal Bldg.
1000 Liberty Ave.   Phone: (412) 644-2850
Pittsburgh, PA 15222   William M. Bradley, Dir.
Subjects: Domestic and foreign commerce, census publications. **Holdings:** 1000 volumes; 140 VF drawers of government pamphlets, reports and statistics. **Subscriptions:** 30 journals and other serials. **Services:** Library open to public.

★14298★
U.S. DEPT. OF COMMERCE - INTERNATIONAL TRADE ADMINISTRATION - PORTLAND DISTRICT OFFICE LIBRARY
1220 S.W. 3rd Ave., Rm. 618
Portland, OR 97204
Defunct

★14299★
U.S. DEPT. OF COMMERCE - INTERNATIONAL TRADE ADMINISTRATION - RICHMOND DISTRICT OFFICE LIBRARY (Bus-Fin)
8010 Federal Bldg.
400 N. 8th St.   Phone: (804) 771-2246
Richmond, VA 23240   Philip A. Ouzts, Dir.
Subjects: Census publications, business economics, foreign trade. **Holdings:** 1300 volumes. **Services:** Library open to public.

★14300★
U.S. DEPT. OF COMMERCE - INTERNATIONAL TRADE ADMINISTRATION - ST. LOUIS DISTRICT OFFICE LIBRARY (Bus-Fin)
120 S. Central Ave., Suite 400   Phone: (314) 425-3302
St. Louis, MO 63105
Subjects: Export information, foreign trade materials. **Holdings:** 1500 volumes. **Services:** Interlibrary loans; library open to public.

★14301★
U.S. DEPT. OF COMMERCE - INTERNATIONAL TRADE ADMINISTRATION - SALT LAKE CITY DISTRICT OFFICE LIBRARY (Bus-Fin)
340 U.S. Post Office Bldg.
350 S. Main St.   Phone: (801) 524-5116
Salt Lake City, UT 84101   Stephen P. Smoot, Dir.
Founded: 1945. **Subjects:** Business economics. **Holdings:** 200 books. **Services:** Library open to public.

★14302★
U.S. DEPT. OF COMMERCE - INTERNATIONAL TRADE ADMINISTRATION - SAN JUAN DISTRICT OFFICE LIBRARY (Bus-Fin)
Federal Office Bldg., Rm. 659   Phone: (809) 753-4555
Hato Rey, PR 00918   Enrique Vilella, Dir.
Staff: 4. **Subjects:** Market statistics, international economic and marketing information, export/import information. **Holdings:** 1000 volumes; international manufacturers' directories. **Services:** Copying; library open to public.

★14303★
**U.S. DEPT. OF COMMERCE - INTERNATIONAL TRADE ADMINISTRATION -
SAVANNAH DISTRICT OFFICE LIBRARY (Bus-Fin)**
222 U.S. Courthouse & P.O. Bldg.
125-29 Bull St.
Box 9746   Phone: (912) 944-4204
Savannah, GA 31412   James W. McIntire, Dir.
Subjects: Census and other department publications, foreign and domestic
trade directories, market research, foreign trade and tariff regulations.
Holdings: 1800 volumes. **Services:** Library open to public.

★14304★
U.S. DEPT. OF COMMERCE - LAW LIBRARY (Law)
14th & Pennsylvania Ave., N.W., Rm. 1894   Phone: (202) 377-5517
Washington, DC 20230   Thomas B. Fleming, Chf. Law Libn.
Staff: Prof 2; Other 1. **Subjects:** International law, antitrust, government
procurement. **Special Collections:** Congressional documents, circa 1930 to
present. **Holdings:** 30,000 books; 10,000 bound periodical volumes;
100,000 other cataloged items. **Subscriptions:** 202 journals and other
serials. **Services:** Interlibrary loans; library open to public. **Automated
Operations:** Computerized cataloging. **Computerized Information Services:**
LEXIS, Legi-Slate, Westlaw, DIALOG, OCLC, NEXIS. **Networks/Consortia:**
Member of FEDLINK. **Remarks:** Library is accessible to the deaf through TTY
at (202) 377-5588. **Staff:** William Alan Fulton, Asst.Chf.

★14305★
U.S. DEPT. OF COMMERCE - LIBRARY (Bus-Fin)
14th & Constitution Ave., N.W.   Phone: (202) 377-3611
Washington, DC 20230   Stanley J. Bougas, Dir.
Founded: 1913. **Staff:** Prof 11; Other 7. **Subjects:** Economics, foreign
trade, business, law, economic theory, economic conditions, statistics,
marketing, industry, finance, legislation, management, merchant marine,
navigation, marine engineering, shipping, shipbuilding, nuclear propulsion.
Special Collections: U.S. Census; Department of Commerce publications;
maritime law; E.D.A. Technical Assistance Program Studies; law and
legislation; international law. **Holdings:** 385,000 books and bound periodical
volumes; 75,000 law books; 4000 reels of microfilm; 200,000 volumes of
microfiche. **Subscriptions:** 1600 journals and other serials. **Services:**
Interlibrary loans; copying; Public Information; library open to public for
reference use only. **Automated Operations:** Computerized cataloging.
Computerized Information Services: DIALOG, OCLC, SDC, BRS, LEXIS,
LEGI-SLATE, New York Times Information Service. **Networks/Consortia:**
Member of FEDLINK. **Publications:** Directory of Libraries in the U.S. Dept. of
Commerce (COM 72-11147); Library Bulletin. **Special Catalogs:** Law catalog.
Remarks: Contains the holdings of the U.S. Dept. of Commerce - National
Telecommunications and Information Administration Library. **Staff:** Joan
Taylor, Act.Chf., Rd.Serv.; Willene J. Gaines, Chf., Tech.Serv.; Marie Scroggs,
Adm.Asst; Joan R. Taylor, Ref.Libn.; Barbara Howenstine, Ref.Libn.; Mary S.
Hardison, Acq.Libn.; Uko Villemi, Cat.;William A. Fulton, Asst.Chf., Law Br.

U.S. DEPT. OF COMMERCE - NATL. BUREAU OF STANDARDS
See: U.S. Natl. Bureau of Standards

**U.S. DEPT. OF COMMERCE - NATL. OCEANIC & ATMOSPHERIC
ADMINISTRATION**
See: U.S. Natl. Oceanic & Atmospheric Administration

★14306★
**U.S. DEPT. OF COMMERCE - NATL. TECHNICAL INFORMATION SERVICE
(Sci-Tech)**
5285 Port Royal Rd.   Phone: (703) 487-4600
Springfield, VA 22161
Holdings: 1.2 million titles of U.S. government-sponsored research,
development and engineering reports and other analyses prepared by federal
agencies, their contractors or grantees. **Services:** Current abstracts of NTIS
documents and other records of interest; copies of reports sold in paper or
microform copy; microfiche service; magnetic tapes are available.
Computerized Information Services: Online bibliographic searches.
Publications: Abstract newsletters; journals, biweekly; **Special Catalogs:**
Annual catalog of holdings. **Special Indexes:** Indexes to current abstracts
published in weekly journals. **Remarks:** The service is a central source for the
public sale of government-sponsored reports, software and database
services. NTIS has agreements with several hundred federal research-
sponsoring organizations to provide the most complete list of publications
possible.

**U.S. DEPT. OF COMMERCE - NATL. TELECOMMUNICATIONS AND
INFORMATION ADMINISTRATION LIBRARY**
See: U.S. Dept. of Commerce - Library

U.S. DEPT. OF COMMERCE - PATENT & TRADEMARK OFFICE
See: U.S. Patent & Trademark Office

**U.S. DEPT. OF DEFENSE - DEFENSE ADVANCED RESEARCH PROJECTS
AGENCY - TACTICAL TECHNOLOGY CENTER**
See: Battelle-Columbus Laboratories - Tactical Technology Center

U.S. DEPT. OF DEFENSE - DEFENSE AUDIOVISUAL AGENCY
See: U.S. Defense Audiovisual Agency

U.S. DEPT. OF DEFENSE - DEFENSE COMMUNICATIONS AGENCY
See: U.S. Defense Communications Agency

U.S. DEPT. OF DEFENSE - DEFENSE CONTRACT ADMINISTRATION
See: U.S. Defense Contract Administration

★14307★
**U.S. DEPT. OF DEFENSE - DEFENSE INDUSTRIAL PLANT EQUIPMENT
CENTER - TECHNICAL DATA REPOSITORY & LIBRARY (Sci-Tech)★**
Airways Blvd.   Phone: (901) 744-5549
Memphis, TN 38114   Johnny F. Murray, Chf., Lib.
Founded: 1963. **Staff:** Prof 1; Other 1. **Holdings:** 580 books and bound
periodical volumes; 20,000 administrative, manufacturers' and military
technical publications; 2050 feet of manufacturers' commercial technical
data. **Subscriptions:** 23 journals and other serials. **Services:** Interlibrary
loans; library not open to public. **Automated Operations:** Computerized
serials. **Special Indexes:** Data location (online). **Staff:** Peggy B. Goolsby,
Lib.Techn.

U.S. DEPT. OF DEFENSE - DEFENSE INTELLIGENCE AGENCY
See: U.S. Defense Intelligence Agency

U.S. DEPT. OF DEFENSE - DEFENSE LOGISTICS AGENCY
See: U.S. Defense Logistics Agency

U.S. DEPT. OF DEFENSE - DEFENSE MAPPING AGENCY
See: U.S. Defense Mapping Agency

U.S. DEPT. OF DEFENSE - DEFENSE NUCLEAR AGENCY
See: U.S. Defense Nuclear Agency

U.S. DEPT. OF DEFENSE - DEFENSE TECHNICAL INFORMATION CENTER
See: U.S. Defense Technical Information Center

**U.S. DEPT. OF DEFENSE - ELECTROMAGNETIC COMPATIBILITY ANALYSIS
CENTER**
See: IIT Research Institute - Electromagnetic Compatibility Analysis
Center

★14308★
**U.S. DEPT. OF DEFENSE - LANGUAGE INSTITUTE - ACADEMIC LIBRARY
(Area-Ethnic)★**
Presidio, Bldg. 618   Phone: (408) 242-8206
Monterey, CA 93940   Gary D. Walter, Libn.
Founded: 1944. **Staff:** Prof 4; Other 6. **Subjects:** Foreign languages,
linguistics, history and culture of foreign countries. **Holdings:** 75,000 books;
650 bound periodical volumes; 8 VF drawers of pamphlets and clippings; 65
reels of microfilm; 1400 video cassettes. **Subscriptions:** 600 journals and
other serials; 150 newspapers. **Services:** Interlibrary loans; copying; library
open to public for reference use only, on request. **Computerized Information
Services:** DIALOG. **Staff:** Nancy I. Hill, Lib.Techn.

U.S. DEPT. OF DEFENSE - NATL. DEFENSE UNIVERSITY
See: U.S. Natl. Defense University

U.S. DEPT. OF DEFENSE - RELIABILITY ANALYSIS CENTER
See: IIT Research Institute - Reliability Analysis Center

U.S. DEPT. OF DEFENSE - U.S. ARMED FORCES STAFF COLLEGE
See: U.S. Armed Forces Staff College

U.S. DEPT OF EDUCATION - EAST CENTRAL NETWORK
See: Sangamon State University - East Central Network

**U.S. DEPT. OF EDUCATION - INTER AMERICA RESEARCH ASSOCIATES -
CONSUMER EDUCATION RESOURCE NETWORK**
See: Consumer Education Resource Network

U.S. DEPT. OF EDUCATION - NATL. INSTITUTE FOR HANDICAPPED RESEARCH - UNIV. CENTER FOR INTERNATIONAL REHABILITATION
See: Michigan State University - University Center for International Rehabilitation

★14309★
U.S. DEPT. OF EDUCATION - REFUGEE MATERIALS CENTER (Educ)
324 E. 11th St., 9th Fl.   Phone: (816) 374-2276
Kansas City, MO 64106   Bud Tumy, Dir.
Staff: Prof 1. **Subjects:** English as a second language: Vietnamese/English, Laotian/English, Cambodian/English, Chinese/English, and Spanish/English. **Special Collections:** Collection of ESL texts, workbooks, tapes (1100 titles); collections of materials in Vietnamese, Cambodian, Lao, Chinese, and other languages (400 titles). **Holdings:** 1100 books; 400 other cataloged items. **Services:** Library open to public.

U.S. DEPT OF EDUCATION - WESTERN CURRICULUM COORDINATION CENTER (WCCC)
See: Western Curriculum Coordination Center (WCCC)

★14310★
U.S. DEPT. OF ENERGY - ALASKA POWER ADMINISTRATION - LIBRARY (Energy)
Box 50   Phone: (907) 586-7405
Juneau, AK 99802   Linda F. Peele, Plan.Div.Asst.
Subjects: Water and power resources, Alaska natural resources, engineering. **Special Collections:** Alaskan utilities. **Holdings:** Figures not available. **Subscriptions:** 34 journals and other serials. **Services:** Interlibrary loans; copying; library open to public with restrictions.

★14311★
U.S. DEPT. OF ENERGY - ALBUQUERQUE OPERATIONS OFFICE - LIBRARY AND PUBLIC DOCUMENT ROOM (Energy; Sci-Tech)
Box 5400   Phone: (505) 844-4378
Albuquerque, NM 87115   Philip Larragoite, Libn.
Founded: 1975. **Staff:** Prof 1; Other 1. **Subjects:** Nuclear waste management, nuclear weapons history. **Special Collections:** Waste Isolation Pilot Project (400 items). **Holdings:** 1,000 books; 3725 reports and microfiche. **Subscriptions:** 22 journals and other serials. **Services:** Interlibrary loans; copying; library open to public for reference use only. **Computerized Information Services:** DOE/RECON. Performs searches on cost recovery basis.

U.S. DEPT. OF ENERGY - AMES LABORATORY
See: Ames Laboratory

U.S. DEPT. OF ENERGY - ARGONNE NATL. LABORATORY
See: Argonne National Laboratory

U.S. DEPT. OF ENERGY - BARTLESVILLE ENERGY TECHNOLOGY CENTER LIBRARY
See: National Institute for Petroleum & Energy Research (NIPER) - Library

U.S. DEPT. OF ENERGY - BENDIX FIELD ENGINEERING CORPORATION
See: Bendix Field Engineering Corporation

U.S. DEPT. OF ENERGY - BIOMEDICAL COMPUTING TECHNOLOGY INFORMATION CENTER
See: Biomedical Computing Technology Information Center

★14312★
U.S. DEPT. OF ENERGY - BONNEVILLE POWER ADMINISTRATION - LIBRARY (Energy; Sci-Tech)
1002 N.E. Holladay St.
Box 3621   Phone: (503) 234-3361
Portland, OR 97208   Karen L. Hadman, Chf., Lib.Br.
Founded: 1939. **Staff:** Prof 5; Other 5. **Subjects:** Electrical engineeering, law, conservation, natural resources, mathematics, basic sciences, mechanical and civil engineering, personnel administration. **Special Collections:** Western SUN (Solar Utilization Network) Collection (5000 volumes); U.S. Department of Energy Region 10 Information Resource Center Collection (8000 volumes); Bonneville Power Administration publications and reports. **Holdings:** 27,200 volumes. **Subscriptions:** 900 journals and other serials. **Services:** Interlibrary loans; library open to public. **Computerized Information Services:** DOE/RECON, DIALOG, BRS, LEXIS, NEXIS. **Publications:** Library Bulletin, quarterly; new book list, quarterly; research guides, irregular - all distributed internally and by request. **Staff:** Johannes S. Schimmelbusch, Engr.Libn.; Jean Connors, Law Libn.; Brenda E. Bonnell, Energy Conserv.Libn.; Monte V. Gittings, Cat.Libn.; Roberto Urzua, Oper./Tech.Serv.Libn.

U.S. DEPT. OF ENERGY - BROOKHAVEN NATL. LABORATORY
See: Brookhaven National Laboratory

U.S. DEPT. OF ENERGY - CONSERVATION AND RENEWABLE ENERGY INQUIRY AND REFERRAL SERVICE
See: Conservation and Renewable Energy Inquiry and Referral Service

★14313★
U.S. DEPT. OF ENERGY - ENERGY INFORMATION ADMINISTRATION - NATIONAL ENERGY INFORMATION CENTER (Energy)
Forrestal Bldg., Rm. 1F-048   Phone: (202) 252-8800
Washington, DC 20585   John E. Daniels, Dir.
Staff: Prof 34; Other 3. **Subjects:** Energy and energy statistics. **Services:** Center open to public; also responds to telephone and letter inquiries. **Computerized Information Services:** DIALOG, SDC, BRS, DOE/RECON; Federal Energy Data Index (internal database). **Publications:** New Releases; Energy Data Contacts Finder. **Special Catalogs:** EIA Publications: A User's Guide; Energy Information Directory. **Staff:** Neal Moerschel, Dir., Info.Ref.Serv.; John Weiner, Dir., Pubns.Serv.Div.

★14314★
U.S. DEPT. OF ENERGY - ENERGY LIBRARY (Energy)
MA 232   Phone: (202) 252-5955
Washington, DC 20585   Ronald R. Turner, Act.Chf.
Founded: 1947. **Staff:** Prof 11; Other 9. **Subjects:** Energy resources and technologies; economic, environmental and social effects of energy; energy regulation; water resources; management. **Special Collections:** Legislative histories relating to Atomic Energy Commission (AEC) and Energy Research and Development Administration (ERDA); ERDA, Federal Energy Administration (FEA) and DOE technical reports. **Holdings:** 885,000 volumes of books, journals, technical reports and government documents. **Subscriptions:** 1600 journals and other serials. **Services:** Interlibrary loans; copying; SDI; library open to public by appointment. **Automated Operations:** Computerized cataloging, acquisitions, serials and circulation. **Computerized Information Services:** DIALOG, SDC, NEXIS, DOE/RECON, MEDLARS, Chase Econometrics, OCLC, RLIN, BRS, NASA/RECON. **Networks/Consortia:** Member of RLG. **Publications:** Data Bases Available at the Energy Library, irregular. **Remarks:** The Energy Library is formed from the libraries of the former Atomic Energy Commission and Energy Research and Development Administration. **Staff:** Denise B. Diggin, Germantown Libn.; Maria E. Vignone, Forrestal Bldg.Libn.

★14315★
U.S. DEPT. OF ENERGY - ENVIRONMENTAL MEASUREMENTS LABORATORY LIBRARY (Sci-Tech; Energy)
376 Hudson St.   Phone: (212) 620-3606
New York, NY 10014   Michael P. Durso, Libn.
Founded: 1947. **Staff:** Prof 1. **Subjects:** Physics, chemistry, environmental science, radiation physics. **Holdings:** 5800 books; 1800 bound periodical volumes; 30,000 technical reports; 35,000 reports in microform. **Subscriptions:** 125 journals and other serials. **Services:** Interlibrary loans; library not open to public. **Computerized Information Services:** DIALOG.

U.S. DEPT. OF ENERGY - FEDERAL ENERGY REGULATORY COMMISSION
See: Federal Energy Regulatory Commission

U.S. DEPT. OF ENERGY - GRAND FORKS ENERGY TECHNOLOGY CENTER LIBRARY
See: University of North Dakota - Energy Research Center - Energy Library

U.S. DEPT OF ENERGY - IDAHO NATL. ENGINEERING LABORATORY
See: EG&G, Inc. - Idaho National Engineering Laboratory

U.S. DEPT OF ENERGY - KNOLLS ATOMIC POWER LABORATORY
See: Knolls Atomic Power Laboratory

U.S. DEPT. OF ENERGY - LABORATORY OF BIOMEDICAL AND ENVIRONMENTAL SCIENCES
See: University of California, Los Angeles - Laboratory of Biomedical and Environmental Sciences

★14316★
U.S. DEPT. OF ENERGY - LARAMIE PROJECTS LIBRARY (Energy)
University Sta., Box 3395   Phone: (307) 721-2201
Laramie, WY 82071   B.J. Davidson, Libn.
Founded: 1947. **Staff:** Prof 1; Other 1. **Subjects:** In-situ recovery research - oil shale, tar sands, coal gasification; geology; chemistry; physics. **Special**

Collections: In-house publications. **Holdings:** 3000 monographs; U.S. Bureau of Mines collection on microfiche; reports. **Subscriptions:** 128 journals and other serials. **Services:** Interlibrary loans; library open to public. **Computerized Information Services:** DOE/RECON, DIALOG.

U.S. DEPT. OF ENERGY - LAWRENCE BERKELEY LABORATORY
See: Lawrence Berkeley Laboratory

U.S. DEPT OF ENERGY - LAWRENCE LIVERMORE NATL. LABORATORY
See: Lawrence Livermore National Laboratory

★14317★
U.S. DEPT. OF ENERGY - MORGANTOWN ENERGY TECHNOLOGY CENTER
LIBRARY (Energy)†
Box 880   Phone: (304) 599-7183
Morgantown, WV 26505   S. Elaine Pasini, Libn.
Founded: 1953. **Staff:** Prof 2; Other 1. **Subjects:** Coal and fossil fuel, petroleum, chemistry, chemical engineering, geology, coal gasification. **Special Collections:** U.S. Office of Coal Research reports (100); U.S. Dept. of Energy publications; U.S. Bureau of Mines publications (complete). **Holdings:** 10,000 books; 7000 bound periodical volumes; 1500 reports; 20 VF drawers of patents. **Subscriptions:** 300 journals and other serials. **Services:** Interlibrary loans; copying; library open to public. **Computerized Information Services:** DOE/RECON, SDC, DIALOG. **Publications:** Library Accession List, semiannual.

U.S. DEPT. OF ENERGY - NATIONAL INSTITUTE FOR PETROLEUM &
ENERGY RESEARCH
See: National Institute for Petroleum & Energy Research

★14318★
U.S. DEPT. OF ENERGY - NEVADA OPERATIONS OFFICE - TECHNICAL
LIBRARY (Sci-Tech; Energy)
Box 14100   Phone: (702) 295-1274
Las Vegas, NV 89114   Cynthia Ortiz, Libn.
Founded: 1969. **Staff:** Prof 2; Other 1. **Subjects:** Nuclear explosives, radiation bioenvironmental effects, geology, hydrology, alternate energy sources, radioactive waste storage. **Special Collections:** Peaceful uses of nuclear explosions. **Holdings:** 2240 books; 48,000 technical reports; 60,000 microfiche of technical reports; 5 file drawers of clippings; 275 maps. **Subscriptions:** 220 journals and other serials. **Services:** Interlibrary loans; copying; library open to public by prior arrangement. **Computerized Information Services:** DOE/RECON, DIALOG, LEXIS, NEXIS.

U.S. DEPT. OF ENERGY - OAK RIDGE NATL. LABORATORY
See: Oak Ridge National Laboratory

★14319★
U.S. DEPT. OF ENERGY - OFFICE OF GENERAL COUNSEL LAW LIBRARY
(Law)
1000 Independence Ave., S.W., Rm. 6A 156   Phone: (202) 252-4848
Washington, DC 20585   Oscar E. Strothers, Chf. Law Libn.
Founded: 1975. **Staff:** Prof 3. **Subjects:** Law - energy, environmental, contract, administrative, patents; statutes. **Holdings:** 40,000 volumes; microfiche. **Subscriptions:** 130 journals and other serials. **Services:** Interlibrary loans; copying (limited); library open to public for reference use only. **Computerized Information Services:** LEXIS, JURIS, Westlaw. **Staff:** Paula Lipman, Asst.Libn.

★14320★
U.S. DEPT. OF ENERGY - OFFICE OF SCIENTIFIC AND TECHNICAL
INFORMATION (OSTI) - TECHNICAL INFORMATION CENTER (Energy)
Box 62   Phone: (615) 576-6837
Oak Ridge, TN 37831   Nancy Hardin
Founded: 1947. **Subjects:** Energy. **Special Collections:** Information science (4000 items). **Holdings:** 8000 books; 100 bound periodical volumes; 600,000 technical reports; 5000 conference proceedings; 2500 engineering drawing packages. **Subscriptions:** 1000 journals and other serials. **Services:** Center open to public with restrictions. **Automated Operations:** Computerized cataloging. **Computerized Information Services:** DOE/RECON, DIALOG, SDC, BRS. **Publications:** Energy Research Abstracts, semimonthly; Nuclear Safety, bimonthly; Energy Abstracts for Policy Analysis, Fossil Energy Update, Fusion Energy Update, Geothermal Energy Update, Solar Energy Update, Current Energy Patents, Energy Meetings, Synthetic Fuels Update, Energy and the Environment, all monthly; Direct Energy Conversion, Nuclear Fuel Cycle, Nuclear Reactor Safety, Radioactive Waste Management, Acid Precipitation, Coal-Based Synfuels, Coal Preparation and Pollution Control, Laser Research, Nuclear Fuel Cycle, Solar Thermal Energy Technology, Unconventional Petroleum, all semimonthly; Energygrams,

quarterly. **Remarks:** This is a centralized R&D Information Management center for the U.S. Dept. of Energy. Requests for information and publications, including interlibrary loan, should be directed to Request Section, (615) 576-1305. An in-house microfiche contractor supplies DOE-funded organizations with microfiche or hard copies of all DOE technical reports on demand or through standard distribution. **Staff:** Bonnie C. Carroll, Asst.Mgr.

U.S. DEPT. OF ENERGY - PACIFIC NORTHWEST LABORATORY
See: Battelle-Northwest - Pacific Northwest Laboratory

U.S. DEPT. OF ENERGY - REYNOLDS ELECTRICAL AND ENGINEERING
COMPANY, INC. - COORDINATION AND INFORMATION CENTER
See: Reynolds Electrical and Engineering Company, Inc. - Coordination and Information Center

U.S. DEPT. OF ENERGY - SANDIA NATL. LABORATORIES
See: Sandia National Laboratories

U.S. DEPT. OF ENERGY - SAVANNAH RIVER PLANT
See: Savannah River Plant

U.S. DEPT. OF ENERGY - SOLAR ENERGY RESEARCH INSTITUTE
See: Solar Energy Research Institute

U.S. DEPT. OF ENERGY - STANFORD LINEAR ACCELERATOR CENTER
See: Stanford Linear Accelerator Center

U.S. DEPT. OF ENERGY - WESTINGHOUSE ELECTRIC CORPORATION-
BETTIS ATOMIC POWER LABORATORY
See: Westinghouse Electric Corporation - Bettis Atomic Power Laboratory

U.S. DEPT. OF HEALTH AND HUMAN SERVICES - ARTHRITIS
INFORMATION CLEARINGHOUSE
See: Arthritis Information Clearinghouse

★14321★
U.S. DEPT. OF HEALTH AND HUMAN SERVICES - DEPARTMENT LIBRARY
(Soc Sci; Educ)†
330 Independence Ave., S.W., Rm 1436 N.   Phone: (202) 245-6791
Washington, DC 20201   Charles F. Gately, Dir.
Founded: 1953. **Staff:** Prof 10; Other 11. **Subjects:** Social welfare, social sciences, education, health, medicine, law and legislation, administration and management. **Special Collections:** Departmental archival collection. **Holdings:** 565,000 books and bound periodical volumes; 350,000 microforms; vertical file of pamphlets and clippings. **Subscriptions:** 5000 journals and other serials. **Services:** Interlibrary loans; copying; library open to public. **Computerized Information Services:** OCLC, BRS, MEDLINE, JURIS, Mead Data Central, DIALOG, New York Times Information Service, LEGI-SLATE. **Staff:** James Arrington, Chf., Circ. & ILL; Violet L. Carter, Adm.Off.; John Boyle, Dp.Dir.

★14322★
U.S. DEPT. OF HEALTH AND HUMAN SERVICES - EVALUATION
DOCUMENTATION CENTER (EDC) (Soc Sci)
200 Independence Ave., S.W.   Phone: (202) 245-6833
Washington, DC 20201   Carolyn G. Solomon, Tech.Info.Spec.
Staff: Prof 2. **Subjects:** Health, social security, income maintenance, education. **Special Collections:** Department of Health and Human Services Program Evaluation Reports. **Holdings:** 1850 books; Executive Summaries. **Services:** Copying; center open to public. **Automated Operations:** Computerized cataloging and acquisitions. **Computerized Information Services:** Internal database. **Publications:** Compendium of Health and Human Services Evaluations, annual; Users Guide to the EDC. **Special Indexes:** Index of program names, sponsoring agencies and subject names. **Remarks:** Evaluation reports are made available to the public through the National Technical Information Service (NTIS), U.S. Dept. of Commerce, Springfield, VA.

U.S. DEPT. OF HEALTH AND HUMAN SERVICES - NATL. CENTER ON CHILD
ABUSE AND NEGLECT
See: Clearinghouse on Child Abuse and Neglect Information

U.S. DEPT. OF HEALTH AND HUMAN SERVICES - NATIONAL CENTER FOR
HEALTH STATISTICS - CLEARINGHOUSE ON HEALTH INDEXES
See: National Center for Health Statistics - Clearinghouse on Health Indexes

U.S. DEPT. OF HEALTH AND HUMAN SERVICES - NATIONAL INSTITUTE OF ENVIRONMENTAL HEALTH SCIENCES
See: National Institute of Environmental Health Sciences

U.S. DEPT. OF HEALTH AND HUMAN SERVICES - NATL. LIBRARY OF MEDICINE
See: National Library of Medicine

U.S. DEPT. OF HEALTH AND HUMAN SERVICES - NEW ENGLAND RESOURCE CENTER FOR CHILDREN AND FAMILIES
See: New England Resource Center for Children and Families

U.S. DEPT. OF HEALTH AND HUMAN SERVICES - OFFICE OF THE ASSISTANT SECRETARY FOR PLANNING & EVALUATION - PROJECT SHARE
See: Aspen Systems Corporation - Project SHARE

U.S. DEPT. OF HEALTH AND HUMAN SERVICES - PUBLIC HEALTH SERVICE
See: U.S. Public Health Service

U.S. DEPT. OF HEALTH AND HUMAN SERVICES - PUBLIC HEALTH SERVICE - NATIONAL HEALTH INFORMATION CLEARINGHOUSE
See: National Health Information Clearinghouse

★14323★
U.S. DEPT. OF HEALTH AND HUMAN SERVICES - REGION I INFORMATION CENTER (Soc Sci)
John F. Kennedy Bldg., Rm. 2411   Phone: (617) 223-7291
Boston, MA 02203   Robert Castricone, Info.Spec.
Staff: 2. **Subjects:** Health, welfare, human development, civil rights. **Holdings:** Figures not available. **Services:** Center open to public.

U.S. DEPT. OF HEALTH AND HUMAN SERVICES - SOCIAL SECURITY ADMINISTRATION
See: U.S. Social Security Administration

★14324★
U.S. DEPT. OF HOUSING AND URBAN DEVELOPMENT - LIBRARY (Soc Sci; Plan)
451 Seventh St., S.W., Rm. 8141   Phone: (202) 755-6376
Washington, DC 20410   Carol A. Johnson, Proj.Mgr.
Founded: 1934. **Staff:** Prof 12; Other 4. **Subjects:** Housing, community development, urban planning, sociology, law, mortgage and construction finance, architecture, land use, intergovernmental relations. **Special Collections:** HUD publications; HUD-sponsored reports including Comprehensive Planning (701) and Model Cities (50,000 reports). **Holdings:** 600,000 items. **Subscriptions:** 2200 journals and other serials. **Services:** Interlibrary loans; copying (limited); SDI; library open to public for reference use only. **Automated Operations:** Computerized cataloging and acquisitions. **Computerized Information Services:** DIALOG, SDC, NEXIS, BRS, Westlaw, RLIN, DOE/RECON, OCLC. **Networks/Consortia:** Member of FEDLINK. **Publications:** Recent Library Acquisitions; Library Periodicals List; special bibliographies. **Special Catalogs:** Computer printout for Comprehensive Planning Reports. **Remarks:** The HUD Library is operated under contract for the U.S. Department of Housing and Urban Development by Aspen Systems Corporation.

★14325★
U.S. DEPT. OF HOUSING & URBAN DEVELOPMENT - PHOTOGRAPHY LIBRARY (Aud-Vis; Plan)
451 7th St., S.W., Rm. B-120   Phone: (202) 755-7305
Washington, DC 20410   David A. Murdock, Visual Info.Spec.
Staff: Prof 1. **Subjects:** Housing, urban development, housing for the elderly, housing renewal. **Special Collections:** Instant Rehab (Core) in New York City (500 color slides; 150 black and white negatives); Operation Breakthrough; Johnstown Flood Disaster. **Holdings:** 200,000 black and white negatives; 40,000 color slides; 10,000 black and white prints. **Services:** Interlibrary loans; library open to public by appointment only.

★14326★
U.S. DEPT. OF HOUSING AND URBAN DEVELOPMENT - REGION I - LIBRARY (Plan)†
J.F.K. Federal Bldg.   Phone: (617) 223-4674
Boston, MA 02203   Christine A. Fraser, Libn.
Staff: Prof 1. **Subjects:** Housing, planning, urban development, law. **Holdings:** 1500 books; 3500 microfiche. **Subscriptions:** 100 journals and other serials; 10 newspapers. **Services:** Interlibrary loans; copying; SDI; library open to public. **Automated Operations:** Computerized cataloging. **Computerized Information Services:** OCLC, JURIS, HUD USER, U.S. Department of Housing

and Urban Development Library Division. **Networks/Consortia:** Member of FEDLINK. **Publications:** Information-Information, monthly - free to mailing list.

★14327★
U.S. DEPT. OF HOUSING AND URBAN DEVELOPMENT - REGION II - LIBRARY (Soc Sci; Plan)
26 Federal Plaza, Rm. 1304   Phone: (212) 264-8175
New York, NY 10278   Susan J. Heller, Regional Libn.
Founded: 1966. **Staff:** Prof 2. **Subjects:** Housing, planning, urban development, architecture, laws pertaining to building codes, construction, building industry. **Holdings:** 900 books; 5 VF drawers of pamphlets; HUD-subsidized planning and research reports; microfiche. **Subscriptions:** 100 journals and other serials and newspapers. **Services:** Interlibrary loans; SDI; library open to public. **Staff:** Bernard H. Taylor, Libn.

★14328★
U.S. DEPT. OF HOUSING AND URBAN DEVELOPMENT - REGION III - LIBRARY (Plan)†
6th and Walnut St.
Curtis Bldg., Rm. 989   Phone: (215) 597-2608
Philadelphia, PA 19106   Beverly R. Taplinger, Lib.Techn.
Founded: 1962. **Staff:** 1. **Subjects:** Housing, law, urban sociology, city planning, political science, building technology. **Special Collections:** Housing and Urban Affairs, 1965-1979 microform collection (5000 items). **Holdings:** 6000 books and bound periodical volumes; 600 Federal Register System items; 600 Congressional Records; 1100 legislative materials; 3 VF drawers; 3000 microfiche. **Subscriptions:** 50 journals and other serials; 5 newspapers. **Services:** Interlibrary loans; copying; SDI; library open to public with restricted borrowing privileges. **Computerized Information Services:** New York Times Information Service, SDC, DIALOG, OCLC. **Publications:** Regional Library: New, Novel and Noteworthy (bibliographies), monthly. **Staff:** Russell J. Harrison, Dir.

★14329★
U.S. DEPT. OF HOUSING AND URBAN DEVELOPMENT - REGION IV - LIBRARY (Soc Sci)*
Richard B. Russell Fed. Bldg., Rm. 722
75 Spring St., S.W.   Phone: (404) 221-3367
Atlanta, GA 30303   Mrs. Davide B. Williams, Regional Libn.
Founded: 1968. **Staff:** Prof 1; Other 2. **Subjects:** Housing, planning, urban development, economic analysis, law, statistics. **Special Collections:** Housing and Urban Affairs (2700 microfiche; 1000 titles). **Holdings:** 17,000 books; 87 bound periodical volumes; Federal Register, 1967 to present, on microfilm; 12 drawers of VF items. **Subscriptions:** 83 journals and other serials. **Services:** Interlibrary loans; copying; library open to public. **Publications:** Instructions on maintaining field collections - for internal distribution only.

★14330★
U.S. DEPT. OF HOUSING AND URBAN DEVELOPMENT - REGION VI - LIBRARY (Soc Sci; Plan)
221 W. Lancaster, 8th Fl.
Box 2905   Phone: (817) 870-5431
Fort Worth, TX 76113   Susan M. Hayes, Regional Libn.
Founded: 1966. **Staff:** Prof 1. **Subjects:** Law (for Arkansas, Texas, Oklahoma, Louisiana and New Mexico), housing, economics, community development, management. **Holdings:** 6500 books; city charters for states listed above. **Subscriptions:** 129 journals and other serials. **Services:** Interlibrary loans; library open to public with restrictions. **Publications:** New titles list, irregular.

★14331★
U.S. DEPT. OF HOUSING AND URBAN DEVELOPMENT - REGION VIII - LIBRARY
Executive Tower Bldg.
1405 Curtis St.
Denver, CO 80202
Defunct

★14332★
U.S. DEPT. OF HOUSING AND URBAN DEVELOPMENT - REGION IX - LIBRARY (Soc Sci; Plan)
450 Golden Gate Ave.
Box 36003   Phone: (415) 556-6484
San Francisco, CA 94102   Joanne Lee, Libn.
Founded: 1969. **Subjects:** Housing, regional planning (city, county and state), metropolitan area problems, land use, minority groups. **Special Collections:** Comprehensive planning reports (701) prepared by local communities under

grants from the Department of Housing and Urban Development in California, Nevada and Arizona. **Holdings:** 5000 books and bound periodical volumes; 9000 microfiche. **Services:** Library open to public on a limited schedule.

★14333★

U.S. DEPT. OF THE INTERIOR - ALASKA RESOURCES LIBRARY (Env-Cons)
701 C St.
Box 36   Phone: (907) 271-5025
Anchorage, AK 99513   Martha L. Shepard, Libn.
Founded: 1972. **Staff:** Prof 4; Other 2. **Subjects:** Alaska - resources, wildlife, land management, forestry/vegetation; Arctic environment; pipelines; outer continental shelf; hydrology; pollution; engineering and geology. **Special Collections:** Alaskan map collection of original overlays; microfiche library of CRREL bibliography. **Holdings:** 20,000 volumes; 7000 maps. **Subscriptions:** 800 journals and other serials. **Services:** Interlibrary loans; copying; library open to public. **Computerized Information Services:** DIALOG, OCLC, SDC, LEXIS. **Networks/Consortia:** Member of National Natural Resources Library and Information System (NNRLIS).

U.S. DEPT. OF THE INTERIOR - BUREAU OF LAND MANAGEMENT
See: U.S. Bureau of Land Management

U.S. DEPT. OF THE INTERIOR - BUREAU OF MINES
See: U.S. Bureau of Mines

U.S. DEPT. OF THE INTERIOR - BUREAU OF RECLAMATION
See: U.S. Bureau of Reclamation

★14334★

U.S. DEPT. OF THE INTERIOR - DIVISION OF INFORMATION AND LIBRARY SERVICES - LAW BRANCH (Law)
18th & C Sts., N.W., Rm. 7100W   Phone: (202) 343-4571
Washington, DC 20240   Carl Kessler, Chf.
Founded: 1975. **Staff:** Prof 2; Other 2. **Subjects:** Law - public land, Indian, natural resources, administrative and environmental. **Special Collections:** Pre-Federal Register regulations of the Department of the Interior (1000 pieces); Native American Legal Materials (500 microfiche). **Holdings:** 30,000 books; 2000 bound periodical volumes; 10,000 microfiche; 1000 reels of microfilm; 3000 microfiche of Indian Claims Commission materials; 10 reels of microfilm of executive orders; 1000 microfiche of Council of State Governments publications; 150 legislative histories. **Subscriptions:** 801 journals and other serials. **Services:** Library open to public for reference use only. **Automated Operations:** Computerized cataloging. **Computerized Information Services:** Online systems; Public Land Order Status System (internal database). **Networks/Consortia:** Member of National Natural Resources Library and Information System (NNRLIS); FEDLINK. **Publications:** Law Library Update, monthly - for internal distribution only; Law Library Guide, annual - free upon request; Selected List of Federal Register Items of Interest to the Department of the Interior. **Special Indexes:** Statutory Index to the Legislative History Collection; Index to Microfilmed Public Lands Withdrawal Orders; Index to the Files on the Passage of PL96-487, Alaska National Interest Lands Conservation Act. **Staff:** Ocedell Barnes, Ref.Libn.

U.S. DEPT. OF THE INTERIOR - FISH & WILDLIFE SERVICE
See: U.S. Fish & Wildlife Service

U.S. DEPT. OF THE INTERIOR - GEOLOGICAL SURVEY
See: U.S. Geological Survey

★14335★

U.S. DEPT. OF THE INTERIOR - INDIAN ARTS AND CRAFTS BOARD (Art)
Rm. 4004, 18th & C Sts., N.W.   Phone: (202) 343-2773
Washington, DC 20240   Robert G. Hart, Gen.Mgr.
Founded: 1935. **Subjects:** Contemporary Native American arts and crafts. **Services:** Prepares answers or makes referrals for inquiries concerning contemporary Native American arts and crafts of the U.S.; no facilities maintained for researchers. **Publications:** Source Directory of Native American Owned and Operated Arts and Crafts Businesses. **Remarks:** The Indian Arts and Crafts Board serves Indians, Eskimos, Aleuts and the general public as an information, promotional and advisory clearinghouse for all matters pertaining to the development of authentic Native American arts and crafts. **Staff:** Myles Libhart, Dir. of Pubn.; Geoffrey Stamm, Dir., Advisory Serv.

★14336★

U.S. DEPT. OF THE INTERIOR - MINERALS MANAGEMENT SERVICE - ALASKA OUTER CONTINENTAL SHELF REGIONAL LIBRARY (Env-Cons)
Box 101159   Phone: (907) 261-2409
Anchorage, AK 99510   Christine R. Huffaker, Rec.Mgr.
Founded: 1976. **Staff:** 3. **Subjects:** Environmental science, geophysics,

geology, socioeconomic assessment. **Holdings:** 5000 books; 1500 bound periodical volumes. **Subscriptions:** 100 journals and other serials; 10 newspapers. **Services:** Library not open to public. **Automated Operations:** Computerized cataloging. **Computerized Information Services:** LEXIS, NEXIS, OCLC. **Formerly:** U.S. Bureau of Land Management - Alaska Outer-Continental Shelf Office - Library.

U.S. DEPT. OF THE INTERIOR - NATL. PARK SERVICE
See: U.S. Natl. Park Service

★14337★

U.S. DEPT. OF THE INTERIOR - NATURAL RESOURCES LIBRARY (Env-Cons; Energy)
18th & C Sts., N.W.   Phone: (202) 343-5815
Washington, DC 20240   Phillip M. Haymond, Chf., Info./Lib.Serv.Dir.
Founded: 1949. **Staff:** Prof 23; Other 28. **Subjects:** Conservation, energy and power, land use, parks, American Indians, fish and wildlife, mining, law, management. **Special Collections:** Archival collection of materials published by Department of Interior (150,000 items). **Holdings:** 600,000 books; 100,000 bound periodical volumes; 8000 reels of microfilm; 50,000 volumes of unbound periodicals; 300,000 microfiche. **Subscriptions:** 17,000 journals and other serials. **Services:** Interlibrary loans; copying; library open to public with restrictions. **Automated Operations:** Computerized cataloging, acquisitions, serials and ILL. **Computerized Information Services:** DIALOG, SDC, BRS, New York Times Information Service, OCLC. **Networks/Consortia:** Headquarters of National Natural Resources Library and Information System; member of FEDLINK. **Publications:** Accession List; Directory of Libraries and Information Centers in the Department of the Interior; Library Alert; Law Library Update; Selected List of Federal Register Items of Interest to the Department of Interior. **Staff:** Ellen Cook, Chf., Info.Sys.; Robert Uskavitch, Chf., Info.Serv.; Sue Ellen Sloca, Chf., Info. Products.

★14338★

U.S. DEPT. OF THE INTERIOR - OFFICE OF REGIONAL SOLICITOR - LAW LIBRARY (Law)*
Bldg. 67, Rm. 1400
Denver Federal Center   Phone: (303) 234-3175
Denver, CO 80225   Sally Raines, Libn.
Staff: 1. **Subjects:** Law. **Special Collections:** Environment Reporter (complete set); all public laws; extensive contract textbooks and Comptroller General decisions. **Holdings:** 6750 books; 274 notebooks containing Interior Decisions, IBCA, IBIA, IBLA Memo Decisions; Gower Service for oil, gas, minerals; state statutes and session laws for Colorado, South and North Dakota, Wyoming, Montana and Kansas. **Services:** Interlibrary loans; copying; library open to public with restrictions.

★14339★

U.S. DEPT. OF JUSTICE - ANTITRUST DIVISION LIBRARY (Law)
10th & Pennsylvania Ave., N.W., Rm. 3310   Phone: (202) 633-2431
Washington, DC 20530   Roger N. Karr, Libn.
Staff: Prof 3; Other 2. **Subjects:** Antitrust law, administrative law, business. **Special Collections:** Legislative histories (110). **Holdings:** 18,000 volumes. **Subscriptions:** 350 journals and other serials. **Services:** Interlibrary loans; library not open to public. **Computerized Information Services:** DIALOG, SDC, MEDLINE, NEXIS, LEXIS, JURIS, LEGI-SLATE, Dow Jones News/Retrieval, Dun & Bradstreet Corporation, Westlaw.

★14340★

U.S. DEPT. OF JUSTICE - CIVIL DIVISION LIBRARY (Law)
10th & Pennsylvania Ave., N.W., Rm. 3344   Phone: (202) 633-3523
Washington, DC 20530   Evangeline Mastriani, Libn.
Staff: Prof 2; Other 2. **Subjects:** Law, customs, bankruptcy, government contracts, commercial law, admiralty, aviation, patents, trademarks, copyright. **Special Collections:** Legislative histories (90). **Holdings:** 45,000 books; 1200 bound periodical volumes. **Subscriptions:** 500 journals and other serials. **Services:** Interlibrary loans; library not open to public. **Computerized Information Services:** DIALOG, SDC, LEXIS, NEXIS, JURIS, LEGI-SLATE, Dow Jones News/Retrieval, Westlaw, MEDLINE.

★14341★

U.S. DEPT. OF JUSTICE - CIVIL RIGHTS DIVISION - LIBRARY (Soc Sci; Law)
10th & Pennsylvania Ave., N.W., Rm. 7618   Phone: (202) 633-4098
Washington, DC 20530   Kathleen T. Larson, Libn.
Staff: Prof 2; Other 2. **Subjects:** Civil rights, constitutional law, demographics. **Holdings:** 6600 books. **Subscriptions:** 136 journals and other serials. **Services:** Interlibrary loans; library not open to public. **Computerized Information Services:** JURIS, Westlaw, LEXIS, NEXIS, DIALOG, SDC, LEGI-SLATE, Dow Jones News/Retrieval, MEDLINE.

★14342★
U.S. DEPT. OF JUSTICE - CRIMINAL DIVISION - LIBRARY (Law)
10th & Pennsylvania Ave., N.W., Rm. 2420   Phone: (202) 633-2383
Washington, DC 20530   Winifred M. Hart, Libn.
Staff: Prof 2; Other 1. **Subjects:** Criminal law, evidence. **Holdings:** 15,000 books. **Subscriptions:** 12 journals and other serials. **Services:** Interlibrary loans; library not open to public. **Computerized Information Services:** JURIS, LEXIS, NEXIS, Westlaw, DIALOG, SDC, LEGI-SLATE, Dow Jones News/Retrieval, MEDLINE.

U.S. DEPT. OF JUSTICE - DRUG ENFORCEMENT ADMINISTRATION
See: U.S. Drug Enforcement Administration

★14343★
U.S. DEPT. OF JUSTICE - FEDERAL BUREAU OF INVESTIGATION - F.B.I. ACADEMY - LIBRARY (Law)
    Phone: (703) 640-6131
Quantico, VA 22135   Robert L. Keadle, Unit Chf.
Founded: 1973. **Staff:** Prof 3; Other 11. **Subjects:** Law enforcement, police, criminal justice. **Holdings:** 30,000 books; 1200 bound periodical volumes; 10,250 government documents; 5225 vertical file materials; 11,680 items in law library; 2350 AV materials; 15,500 microfiche. **Subscriptions:** 485 journals and other serials; 6 newspapers. **Services:** Interlibrary loans; SDI; library open to public by special permission only. **Computerized Information Services:** DIALOG, NEXIS, MEDLARS, JURIS, Westlaw; RCMP Forensic Science Data Base (internal database). **Publications:** Subject bibliographies - available upon request. **Special Catalogs:** Periodicals holdings list, annual; training films catalog, annual. **Staff:** Sandra Coupe, Libn.; Melinda Cavis, Libn.

★14344★
U.S. DEPT. OF JUSTICE - FEDERAL PRISON SYSTEM - LIBRARY (Soc Sci)
320 First St., N.W.   Phone: (202) 724-3029
Washington, DC 20534   Lloyd W. Hooker, Libn.
Founded: 1960. **Staff:** Prof 1; Other 1. **Subjects:** Criminology, corrections, criminal psychology. **Special Collections:** Archival material of the bureau (100 items). **Holdings:** 2523 books and bound periodical volumes; 65 periodicals; 1200 items in information file; 98 research papers; 250 annual reports. **Subscriptions:** 81 journals and other serials. **Services:** Interlibrary loans; library open to those in correctional work and related fields, including graduate students doing research in corrections. **Publications:** Correctional Bookshelf, a bibliography, 1977.

★14345★
U.S. DEPT. OF JUSTICE - LAND AND NATURAL RESOURCES DIVISION LIBRARY (Law)
10th & Pennsylvania Ave., N.W., Rm. 2333   Phone: (202) 633-2768
Washington, DC 20530   Adelaide Loretta Brown, Libn.
Staff: Prof 2; Other 1. **Subjects:** Civil cases regarding lands, titles, water rights, Indian claims, hazardous waste, public works, pollution control, marine resources, fish and wildlife, environment. **Special Collections:** Legislative histories (55). **Holdings:** 13,300 volumes; 900 records and briefs. **Subscriptions:** 160 journals and other serials. **Services:** Interlibrary loans; library not open to public. **Computerized Information Services:** JURIS, DIALOG, SDC, LEXIS, NEXIS, LEGI-SLATE, Dow Jones News/Retrieval, Westlaw, MEDLINE.

★14346★
U.S. DEPT. OF JUSTICE - MAIN LIBRARY (Law)
10th & Pennsylvania Ave., N.W., Rm. 5400   Phone: (202) 633-3775
Washington, DC 20530   Dee Sampson, Chf., Rd.Serv.
Founded: 1831. **Staff:** Prof 12; Other 11. **Subjects:** Law, business and allied subjects. **Special Collections:** Legislative histories (54); Department of Justice publications. **Holdings:** 200,000 volumes; 1 million volumes in microform. **Subscriptions:** 1600 journals and other serials. **Services:** Interlibrary loans; copying; library open to public with permission. **Automated Operations:** Computerized cataloging, acquisitions, serials and circulation. **Computerized Information Services:** DIALOG, OCLC, SDC, LEXIS, JURIS, NEXIS, LEGI-SLATE, Dow Jones News/Retrieval, MEDLINE, Westlaw. **Networks/Consortia:** Member of FEDLINK. **Publications:** Library Bulletin, monthly; Library Handbook, annual.

★14347★
U.S. DEPT. OF JUSTICE - NATIONAL INSTITUTE OF CORRECTIONS - NIC INFORMATION CENTER (Soc Sci)
1790 30th St., Suite 130   Phone: (303) 444-1101
Boulder, CO 80301   Coralie Whitmore, Dir.
Subjects: Prisons, jails, probation, parole, community corrections. **Holdings:** 10,000 documents. **Services:** Interlibrary loans; copying; center open to public. **Automated Operations:** Computerized cataloging, acquisitions, serials

and circulation. **Computerized Information Services:** DIALOG; internal database. **Networks/Consortia:** Member of Criminal Justice Information Exchange. **Publications:** Corrections Information Series. **Staff:** Eileen Conway, Rsrc.Coord.; Larry Linke, Info.Serv.Coord.; Barbara Sudol, Libn.; Jane Perlmutter, Libn.

★14348★
U.S. DEPT. OF JUSTICE - NATIONAL INSTITUTE OF JUSTICE - LIBRARY (Soc Sci; Law)
633 Indiana Ave., N.W., Rm. 900   Phone: (202) 724-5884
Washington, DC 20531   Kyle Kramer, Libn.
Founded: 1970. **Staff:** 1. **Subjects:** Law enforcement, police science, juvenile delinquency, courts, corrections, white-collar crime, spouse and child abuse, victims. **Holdings:** 3000 books; 1000 U.S. government documents. **Subscriptions:** 150 journals and other serials. **Services:** Library open to public.

★14349★
U.S. DEPT. OF JUSTICE - NATIONAL INSTITUTE OF JUSTICE - NATL. CRIMINAL JUSTICE REF. SERVICE (Soc Sci; Law)
Box 6000   Phone: (301) 251-5500
Rockville, MD 20850   Harvey C. Byrd, III, Prog.Dir.
Founded: 1972. **Subjects:** Law enforcement, criminal and juvenile justice, white-collar crime, public corruption, courts, corrections, crime prevention/security, evaluations and research, criminology, victim/witness assistance, dispute resolution. **Holdings:** 75,000 books, research reports, articles and AV materials; 20,000 documents on microfiche. **Subscriptions:** 200 journals and other serials. **Services:** Interlibrary loans; dissemination of NIJ published documents and microfiched documents; referrals; service open to public. **Computerized Information Services:** DIALOG, JURIS; computer retrieval from abstract file. Performs searches on cost recovery basis. **Networks/Consortia:** Member of Criminal Justice Information Exchange. **Publications:** NIJ Reports (research and abstract bulletin), bimonthly; Selected Bibliographies, Microfiche Packages, Current Awareness Materials, irregular; Directory of Criminal Justice Information Sources. **Special Indexes:** Document Retrieval Index (microfiche); index to microfiche collection. **Staff:** Anthony Cain, Asst. Mgr., Ref.Serv.; Susan LaPerla, Libn.

★14350★
U.S. DEPT. OF JUSTICE - TAX DIVISION LIBRARY (Bus-Fin; Law)
10th & Pennsylvania Ave., N.W., Rm. 4335   Phone: (202) 633-2819
Washington, DC 20530   Michael Rahill, Libn.
Staff: Prof 2; Other 2. **Subjects:** Taxation, bankruptcy. **Holdings:** 30,000 volumes. **Services:** Interlibrary loans; library not open to public. **Computerized Information Services:** JURIS, LEXIS, NEXIS, Westlaw, DIALOG, SDC, LEGI-SLATE, Dow Jones News/Retrieval, MEDLINE.

★14351★
U.S. DEPT. OF JUSTICE - UNITED STATES ATTORNEY, CENTRAL DISTRICT OF CALIFORNIA - LIBRARY (Law)*
1214 U.S. Court House
312 N. Spring St.   Phone: (213) 688-2419
Los Angeles, CA 90012
Staff: Prof 1; Other 1. **Subjects:** Law. **Holdings:** 13,000 volumes. **Services:** Library not open to public.

★14352★
U.S. DEPT. OF JUSTICE - UNITED STATES ATTORNEY, DISTRICT OF NEW JERSEY - LAW LIBRARY (Law)†
970 Broad St.   Phone: (201) 645-2387
Newark, NJ 07102   Martha Bomgardner, Libn.
Staff: Prof 1. **Subjects:** Law. **Holdings:** 5800 volumes. **Services:** Interlibrary loans; library not open to public. **Computerized Information Services:** JURIS.

★14353★
U.S. DEPT. OF JUSTICE - UNITED STATES ATTORNEY, DISTRICT OF PENNSYLVANIA - LIBRARY (Law)
3310 U.S. Courthouse
601 Market St.   Phone: (215) 597-2161
Philadelphia, PA 19106   Pamela M. Ward, Law Libn.
Staff: Prof 1; Other 2. **Subjects:** Criminal law. **Holdings:** 7600 books; 40 bound periodical volumes. **Subscriptions:** 12 journals and other serials; 10 newspapers. **Services:** Interlibrary loans; copying; library open to public with restrictions. **Computerized Information Services:** JURIS. **Special Indexes:** Briefs of the Third Circuit.

★14354★

U.S. DEPT. OF JUSTICE - UNITED STATES ATTORNEY, NORTHERN DISTRICT OF ILLINOIS - LIBRARY (Law)
1500 Dirksen Federal Bldg.
219 S. Dearborn St.   Phone: (312) 353-5338
Chicago, IL 60604   Mary Alice Stack, Libn.
Staff: Prof 1. **Subjects:** Federal law. **Holdings:** 12,000 volumes. **Services:** Library not open to public.

★14355★

U.S. DEPT. OF JUSTICE - UNITED STATES ATTORNEY, SOUTHERN DISTRICT OF NEW YORK - LIBRARY (Law)
One St. Andrew's Plaza, 6th Fl.   Phone: (212) 791-0029
New York, NY 10007   Barbara J. Zelenko, Hd.Libn.
Staff: Prof 1; Other 3. **Subjects:** Law. **Holdings:** 20,000 books; law memoranda; manuscripts; 12 VF drawers of clippings; sample indictment file; 6 VF drawers of sample charge files. **Subscriptions:** 6 newspapers. **Services:** Interlibrary loans; library not open to public. **Computerized Information Services:** JURIS, LEXIS.

★14356★

U.S. DEPT. OF LABOR - BUREAU OF LABOR STATISTICS - INFORMATION AND ADVISORY SECTION (Soc Sci)
1515 Broadway, Rm. 3400   Phone: (212) 944-3121
New York, NY 10036   Martin Karlin, Chf.
Founded: 1949. **Subjects:** Labor force, employment, productivity, industrial relations, occupational outlook, occupational health and safety statistics, consumer and producer price indexes. **Holdings:** 500 books; 1500 bound periodical volumes; 5000 pamphlets. **Subscriptions:** 100 journals and other serials. **Services:** Copying; special 24-hour number providing latest Consumer Price Index: (212) 944-3125; 24-hour number providing data on unemployment: (212) 944-2923; 24-hour number providing weekly Bureau of Labor Statistics update on recent research findings: (212) 944-3149; library open to public. **Staff:** Patricia Bommicino; Lillian Kohlrieser; Robert Okell; Paul Sekscenski.

★14357★

U.S. DEPT. OF LABOR - BUREAU OF LABOR STATISTICS - NORTH CENTRAL REGIONAL OFFICE REFERENCE LIBRARY (Soc Sci)
230 S. Dearborn St., 9th Fl.   Phone: (312) 353-1880
Chicago, IL 60604   Ronald M. Guzicki, Supv. Economist
Staff: Prof 3; Other 6. **Subjects:** Labor force, prices, productivity, occupational safety and health, compensation, industrial relations. **Holdings:** Bureau of Labor Statistics bulletins, reports and monthly labor reviews. **Services:** Library open to public for reference use only. **Computerized Information Services:** LABSTAT (internal database).

★14358★

U.S. DEPT. OF LABOR - EMPLOYMENT & TRAINING ADMINISTRATION - REGION IV RESOURCE CENTER (Soc Sci)*
1371 Peachtree St., N.E., Suite 434   Phone: (404) 881-3534
Atlanta, GA 30367   Toussaint Hayes, Training Dir.
Staff: Prof 1; Other 1. **Subjects:** Employment and training programs, labor statistics, training packages, management development. **Holdings:** 3500 volumes. **Services:** Interlibrary loans; center open to public. **Automated Operations:** Computerized cataloging and acquisitions. **Computerized Information Services:** Internal database.

★14359★

U.S. DEPT. OF LABOR - EMPLOYMENT & TRAINING ADMINISTRATION - REGION VIII TECHNICAL RESOURCE LIBRARY (Soc Sci)*
1617 Federal Office Bldg.
1961 Stout St.   Phone: (303) 837-4571
Denver, CO 80294   Larry Wieland, Libn.
Founded: 1976. **Staff:** Prof 1. **Subjects:** Employment, training, labor. **Special Collections:** Comprehensive Employment and Training Act history (150 volumes). **Holdings:** 3500 books; 180 bound periodical volumes; 150 films; 5 VF drawers of pamphlets; 5 VF drawers of newsletters and in-house publications. **Subscriptions:** 27 journals and other serials. **Services:** Interlibrary loans; copying; library open to public with restrictions. **Automated Operations:** Computerized cataloging. **Computerized Information Services:** DIALOG; internal database. **Publications:** Library news bulletin, monthly - for internal distribution only.

★14360★

U.S. DEPT. OF LABOR - EMPLOYMENT & TRAINING ADMINISTRATION - REGION X RESOURCE CENTER (Soc Sci)*
909 First Ave., No. 1145   Phone: (206) 442-1078
Seattle, WA 98174   Ellen Kampel, Info.Dir.
Staff: Prof 1. **Subjects:** Employment and training, CETA, labor markets.

Holdings: Figures not available. **Subscriptions:** 23 journals and other serials. **Services:** Interlibrary loans; copying (limited); center open to public. **Automated Operations:** Computerized cataloging. **Computerized Information Services:** Internal database. **Publications:** New Acquisitions List, bimonthly.

★14361★

U.S. DEPT. OF LABOR - LIBRARY (Soc Sci)†
200 Constitution Ave., N.W.   Phone: (202) 523-6988
Washington, DC 20210
Founded: 1917. **Staff:** Prof 15; Other 16. **Subjects:** Economics, labor. **Special Collections:** Trade union constitutions, proceedings and journals. **Holdings:** 535,000 volumes; labor papers on microfilm. **Subscriptions:** 3200 journals; 9 newspapers. **Services:** Interlibrary loans (limited); copying; library open for reference purposes. **Automated Operations:** Computerized cataloging, acquisitions and circulation. **Computerized Information Services:** OCLC, DIALOG, New York Times Information Service, BRS, SDC. **Networks/Consortia:** Member of FEDLINK. **Publications:** Periodicals Currently Received by the U.S. Department of Labor Library, irregular. **Staff:** Natalie G. Morton, Asst.Libn., Rd.Serv.; Sabina Jacobson, Asst.Libn., Tech.Proc.

★14362★

U.S. DEPT. OF LABOR - LIBRARY - LAW LIBRARY DIVISION (Law)
200 Constitution Ave., N.W., Rm. N-2439   Phone: (202) 523-7991
Washington, DC 20210   Donald L. Martin, Law Libn.
Founded: 1940. **Staff:** Prof 2; Other 2. **Subjects:** Labor law and related fields. **Holdings:** 25,000 volumes. **Services:** Library open to public. **Automated Operations:** Computerized acquisitions.

★14363★

U.S. DEPT. OF LABOR - MINE SAFETY & HEALTH ADMINISTRATION - INFORMATIONAL SERVICES LIBRARY (Sci-Tech)
Box 25367   Phone: (303) 234-4961
Denver, CO 80225   James A. Greenhalgh, Libn.
Founded: 1979. **Staff:** Prof 1; Other 1. **Subjects:** Mine safety and health, mining industry. **Special Collections:** Federal standards. **Holdings:** 883 books and bound periodical volumes; 2112 government documents on microfiche; 3500 Bureau of Mine reports; 1215 Mine Safety & Health Administration reports; vendor catalogs. **Subscriptions:** 157 journals and other serials. **Services:** Interlibrary loans; copying; library open to public. **Automated Operations:** Computerized cataloging and serials. **Computerized Information Services:** DIALOG, NLM, OCLC. **Publications:** New Publications List, monthly; occasional bibliographies.

U.S. DEPT. OF LABOR - OCCUPATIONAL SAFETY AND HEALTH ADMINISTRATION
See: U.S. Dept. of Labor - OSHA

★14364★

U.S. DEPT. OF LABOR - OSHA - IDAHO AREA OFFICE - LIBRARY (Med; Sci-Tech)
550 W. Fort St., Rm. 324   Phone: (208) 334-1867
Boise, ID 83703   David M. Bernard, Area Dir.
Staff: 2. **Subjects:** Safety, health, industrial hygiene, chemistry, fire codes. **Holdings:** 500 books; 90 bound periodical volumes. **Services:** Library not open to public.

★14365★

U.S. DEPT. OF LABOR - OSHA - REGION III LIBRARY (Med; Sci-Tech)
3535 Market St.   Phone: (215) 596-1201
Philadelphia, PA 19104   Barbara Goodman, Libn.
Staff: Prof 1. **Subjects:** Occupational health and safety, industrial hygiene, toxic substances. **Special Collections:** National Institute of Occupational Safety and Health (NIOSH) documents; OSHA standards. **Holdings:** 1500 books. **Services:** Interlibrary loans; copying; library open to public for reference use only. **Computerized Information Services:** MEDLARS, NIOSHTIC. **Networks/Consortia:** Member of National Library of Medicine (NLM).

★14366★

U.S. DEPT. OF LABOR - OSHA - REGIONAL LIBRARY (Med; Sci-Tech)
6003 Federal Office Bldg.
909 First Ave.   Phone: (206) 442-5930
Seattle, WA 98174   Donna M. Hoffman, Libn.
Staff: Prof 1. **Subjects:** Industrial hygiene, toxic substances, industrial safety. **Special Collections:** ANSI Standards; NIOSH documents. **Holdings:** 1000 titles. **Subscriptions:** 30 journals and other serials. **Services:** Interlibrary loans; copying; library open to public. **Computerized Information Services:** NLM, DIALOG; NIOSHTIC (internal database).

★14367★

U.S. DEPT. OF LABOR - OSHA - TECHNICAL DATA CENTER (Med; Sci-Tech)
200 Constitution Ave., N.W.
Rm. N-2439 Rear Phone: (202) 523-9700
Washington, DC 20210 Thomas A. Towers, Dir.
Founded: 1972. **Staff:** Prof 7; Other 5. **Subjects:** Occupational safety, industrial hygiene, toxicology, hazardous materials, fire safety, electrical safety, noise, carcinogens. **Holdings:** 8000 books and bound periodical volumes; 105,000 microfiche; 2000 technical documents; 3000 standards and codes. **Subscriptions:** 280 journals and other serials. **Services:** Interlibrary loans; copying; center open to public for reference use only. **Computerized Information Services:** DIALOG, SDC, BRS, NIH-EPA Chemical Information System, NLM; NIOSHTIC, TIRS (internal databases). **Networks/ Consortia:** Member of FEDLINK. **Publications:** TDC User Reference Guide; Information and Insight Bulletin, quarterly - for internal and limited external distribution. **Staff:** Shirley Marshall, Tech.Info.Spec.; Denise E. Hayes, Tech.Info.Spec.; Daniel Marsick, Tech.Info.Spec.Elaine C. Johnson, Tech.Info.Spec.; James Towles, Tech.Info.Spec.; Robert Turnage, Tech.Info.Spec.

U.S. DEPT. OF THE NAVY
See: U.S. Navy

U.S. DEPT. OF STATE - AGENCY FOR INTERNATIONAL DEVELOPMENT
See: U.S. Agency for International Development

★14368★

U.S. DEPT. OF STATE - LIBRARY (Soc Sci; Hist)
Phone: (202) 632-0372
Washington, DC 20520 Conrad P. Eaton, Libn.
Founded: 1789. **Staff:** Prof 12; Other 10. **Subjects:** International relations, diplomatic history, international law, treaties and agreements, political history, economic conditions, social and cultural developments, ideologies and trends, law. **Holdings:** 650,000 books. **Subscriptions:** 1100 journals and other serials. **Services:** Interlibrary loans; library may be consulted by special arrangement. **Automated Operations:** Computerized cataloging and circulation. **Computerized Information Services:** DIALOG, SDC, BRS, NEXIS, Dow Jones News/Retrieval, RLIN, Data Resources, Inc. (DRI). **Staff:** Dan O. Clemmer, Chf., Rd.Serv.; Doris R. Mosley, Chf., Tech.Serv.Br.

★14369★

U.S. DEPT. OF STATE - OFFICE OF THE LEGAL ADVISER - LAW LIBRARY (Law)
Rm. 6422, Dept. of State Phone: (202) 632-4130
Washington, DC 20520 Helena P. von Pfeil, Law Libn.
Founded: 1920. **Staff:** Prof 1; Other 1. **Subjects:** Law - international, comparative, foreign and U.S. **Holdings:** 60,000 volumes. **Subscriptions:** 200 journals and other serials. **Services:** Library not open to public. **Automated Operations:** Computerized cataloging AND serials. **Computerized Information Services:** LEXIS, Westlaw, OCLC. Performs searches on cost recovery basis.

U.S. DEPT. OF TRANSPORTATION - COAST GUARD
See: U.S. Coast Guard

U.S. DEPT. OF TRANSPORTATION - FEDERAL AVIATION ADMINISTRATION
See: U.S. Federal Aviation Administration

U.S. DEPT. OF TRANSPORTATION - FEDERAL HIGHWAY ADMINISTRATION
See: U.S. Federal Highway Administration

★14370★

U.S. DEPT. OF TRANSPORTATION - LIBRARY AND DISTRIBUTION SERVICES DIVISION (Trans)
400 7th St., S.W. Phone: (202) 426-1792
Washington, DC 20590 Lawrence E. Leonard, Lib.Dir.
Founded: 1969. **Staff:** Prof 20; Other 12. **Subjects:** Highways, aviation, marine transportation, law, urban mass transit, railroads. **Special Collections:** Aviation reports (50,000 volumes); aviation technical publications (4600 titles). **Holdings:** 365,000 books; 48,500 bound periodical volumes; 80 pamphlet boxes of state highway department maps; 40,000 pamphlets in VF drawers; 509,580 microforms. **Subscriptions:** 2100 journals and other serials; 5 newspapers. **Services:** Interlibrary loans; copying; division open to public for limited reference use. **Automated Operations:** Computerized cataloging, acquisitions, serials and ILL. **Computerized Information Services:** DIALOG, BRS, New York Times Information Service, JURIS, NEXIS, LEXIS, OCLC, LEGI-SLATE, Westlaw, DOE/RECON, DTIC. Performs searches for departmental staff. **Networks/Consortia:** Member of FEDLINK. **Publications:** Selected Library Acquisitions, quarterly - for official distribution.

Special Indexes: Periodicals Index File on transportation, 1921-1982 (card). **Remarks:** The 10-A Services Section, M-493.2, library is located at 800 Independence Ave., S.W., Washington, DC 20591 and the phone number is (202) 426-3611. The library director can be reached at (202) 426-2565. The phone number for general reference is 426-1792 and 426-2563 for law. Subject scope of the 10-A library stresses air transportation and aviation and related subjects. There is also a Coast Guard law collection located at 2100 2nd St., S.W., Washington, DC 20593, telephone (202) 755-7610. **Staff:** Dorothy Poehlman, Chf., Info.Serv.Br.; Frances E. Loar, Chf., Tech.Serv.Br.; William Mills, Chf., Acq.Sect.; Mon-hua Mona Kuo, Chf., Cat.Sect.; Loretta A. Norris, Chf., Law Serv.Sect.; Thomas M. Haggerty, Chf., 10A Serv.Sect.; Mary Jo Burke, Chf., HQ Serv.Sect.

U.S. DEPT. OF TRANSPORTATION - MARITIME ADMINISTRATION
See: U.S. Maritime Administration

U.S. DEPT. OF TRANSPORTATION - MARITIME ADMINISTRATION - MERCHANT MARINE ACADEMY
See: U.S. Merchant Marine Academy

U.S. DEPT. OF TRANSPORTATION - NATL. HIGHWAY TRAFFIC SAFETY ADMINISTRATION
See: U.S. Natl. Highway Traffic Safety Administration

★14371★

U.S. DEPT. OF TRANSPORTATION - TRANSPORTATION SYSTEMS CENTER - TECHNICAL REFERENCE CENTER (Trans)
Kendall Sq. Phone: (617) 494-2783
Cambridge, MA 02142 Hadassah Linfield, Dir.
Founded: 1970. **Staff:** Prof 7; Other 2. **Subjects:** Transportation - all aspects. **Holdings:** 69,000 books and reports; 650 bound periodical volumes; 250,000 microfiche; 36 VF drawers of maps. **Subscriptions:** 150 journals and other serials. **Services:** Interlibrary loans; center open to public with restrictions. **Automated Operations:** Computerized cataloging. **Computerized Information Services:** Transportation Research Information Service (TRIS), OCLC, DIALOG, LEGI-SLATE. **Networks/Consortia:** Member of FEDLINK. **Staff:** Robert Perrault, ILL.

★14372★

U.S. DEPT. OF TRANSPORTATION - TRANSPORTATION TEST CENTER - TECHNICAL LIBRARY (Sci-Tech)
Box 11130 Phone: (303) 545-5660
Pueblo, CO 81001 Georgeann Guagliardo, Sec./Libn.
Founded: 1978. **Staff:** 1. **Subjects:** Railroad research, engineering sciences, track/train dynamics. **Special Collections:** Association of American Railroads technical reports (200); Urban Mass Transportation Administration technical reports (90); Federal Railroad Administration technical documents (400); Office for Research & Experiments of the International Union of Railways, Utrecht, reports (127). **Holdings:** 3667 books, technical articles and technical reports; conference and symposium proceedings; bibliographic material containing abstracts of technical articles and reports on railroad research. **Subscriptions:** 15 journals and other serials. **Services:** Interlibrary loans; copying (limited); library open to public with restrictions. **Automated Operations:** Computerized cataloging, acquisitions and serials. **Networks/ Consortia:** Member of Department of Transportation Library Network. **Publications:** New Acquisitions, monthly. **Special Indexes:** Supplements to Index of Technical Library Holdings. **Remarks:** This is a field library of the U.S. Department of Transportation, Washington, D.C., established to assist research and development activities at the Test Center, which is administered by the Federal Railroad Administration.

★14373★

U.S. DEPT. OF TRANSPORTATION - URBAN MASS TRANSPORTATION ADM. - TRANSPORTATION RESEARCH INFO. CENTER (TRIC) (Trans)
400 7th St., S.W. Phone: (202) 426-9157
Washington, DC 20590 Ronald J. Fisher, Chf., Info.Serv.Div.
Staff: Prof 3. **Subjects:** Urban transportation - bus and paratransit systems, rail and construction technology, new systems and technology, service and methods, planning and analysis, management resources. **Holdings:** 4000 reports. **Services:** Copying; SDI; center open to public by appointment; responds to inquiries. **Computerized Information Services:** DIALOG. **Publications:** UMTA Abstracts, bimonthly. **Remarks:** The Urban Mass Transportation Administration sponsors the Urban Mass Transportation Research Information Service (UMTRIS), a computer-based information system operated by the Transportation Research Board (TRB) and the National Academy of Sciences. UMTRIS contains transportation information from domestic and international sources and is available as DIALOG File 63. **Staff:** Winnie Muse, Tech.Info.Spec.; Marina Drancsak, Tech.Info.Spec.

U.S. DEPT. OF THE TREASURY - BUREAU OF ALCOHOL, TOBACCO AND FIREARMS
See: U.S. Bureau of Alcohol, Tobacco and Firearms

U.S. DEPT. OF THE TREASURY - COMPTROLLER OF THE CURRENCY
See: U.S. Comptroller of the Currency

★14374★
U.S. DEPT. OF THE TREASURY - INFORMATION SERVICES DIVISION - TREASURY DEPT. LIBRARY (Bus-Fin; Law)
Main Treasury Bldg., Rm. 5030   Phone: (202) 566-2777
Washington, DC 20220   Elisabeth S. Knauff, Mgr., Info.Serv.Div.
Founded: 1789. **Staff:** Prof 6; Other 5. **Subjects:** Taxation, public finance, law, domestic and international economics and economic conditions. **Holdings:** 78,000 books and bound periodical volumes; 265,000 microfiche; 6600 reels of microfilm. **Services:** Interlibrary loans; copying; library open to public for reference use only. **Automated Operations:** Computerized cataloging, acquisitions (partial), serials (limited) and circulation. **Computerized Information Services:** DIALOG, LEXIS, NEXIS, OCLC. **Networks/Consortia:** Member of FEDLINK; Metropolitan Washington Library Council. **Staff:** Christine R. Rudy, Chf., Rd.Serv.Br.; Tina Kelley, Legal Ref.Libn.; Betty Elmore, Ser.Cat.; Mary Pope, Chf., Tech.Serv.Br.; Edmund Csetalvay, Acq.Libn.

U.S. DEPT. OF THE TREASURY - INTERNAL REVENUE SERVICE
See: U.S. Internal Revenue Service

★14375★
U.S. DISTRICT COURT - DISTRICT OF OREGON - LIBRARY (Law)
529 U.S. Courthouse
620 S.W. Main   Phone: (503) 221-6042
Portland, OR 97219   Scott McCurdy, Libn.
Staff: Prof 2. **Subjects:** Law. **Holdings:** 11,000 volumes. **Services:** Interlibrary loans; library open to attorneys on day of hearing. **Computerized Information Services:** Westlaw. **Staff:** Diane Schauer, Asst.Libn.; Nancy Hoover, Asst.Libn.

★14376★
U.S. DISTRICT COURT - EASTERN DISTRICT OF NEW YORK - LIBRARY (Law)
225 Cadman Plaza E.   Phone: (718) 330-7483
Brooklyn, NY 11201   Lillian B. Garrell, Law Libn.
Founded: 1965. **Staff:** Prof 1; Other 1. **Subjects:** Federal and state law. **Holdings:** 21,500 books; 500 bound periodical volumes; 600 other cataloged items; 3500 items of Congressional Record; 3000 items of Federal Register; 85 reels of microfilm. **Subscriptions:** 110 journals and other serials. **Services:** Library not open to public. **Computerized Information Services:** Westlaw.

★14377★
U.S. DISTRICT COURT - LAW LIBRARY (Law)
701 C St.
Box 4   Phone: (907) 271-5655
Anchorage, AK 99513   Laura Bunnell, Libn.
Staff: Prof 1; Other 1. **Subjects:** Law. **Holdings:** 13,240 books; 590 bound periodical volumes; 530 pamphlets. **Subscriptions:** 72 journals and other serials. **Services:** Library open to attorneys. **Computerized Information Services:** Westlaw.

★14378★
U.S. DISTRICT COURT - LEGAL LIBRARY (Law)*
Box 3671   Phone: (809) 725-9229
San Juan, PR 00904   Ana Milagros Rodriguez, Libn.
Staff: 1. **Subjects:** Law. **Holdings:** 15,000 volumes. **Subscriptions:** 250 journals and other serials. **Services:** Copying; library open to public with written permission.

★14379★
U.S. DISTRICT COURT - LIBRARY (Law)*
U.S. Court House
Box 50128   Phone: (808) 546-3163
Honolulu, HI 96850   Isabel T. Anduha, Court Libn.
Staff: 1. **Subjects:** Law. **Holdings:** 22,700 volumes; Nita Younger Cassette Series (14 tapes). **Services:** Library serves U.S. Court personnel, supporting staff, federal and state agencies and attorneys practicing before the court.

★14380★
U.S. DISTRICT COURT - NORTHERN CALIFORNIA DISTRICT - LOUIS E. GOODMAN MEMORIAL LIBRARY (Law)
450 Golden Gate Ave.
Box 36060   Phone: (415) 556-7979
San Francisco, CA 94102   Lynn Lundstrom, Libn.
Founded: 1964. **Staff:** Prof 2; Other 1. **Subjects:** Federal and state law. **Holdings:** 25,000 books; 2000 bound periodical volumes. **Subscriptions:** 265 journals and other serials; 6 newspapers. **Services:** Library serves attorneys before the court and judges. **Computerized Information Services:** Westlaw. **Staff:** Gayle Goedde, Asst.Libn.

★14381★
U.S. DRUG ENFORCEMENT ADMINISTRATION - LIBRARY (Law)
1405 Eye St., N.W.   Phone: (202) 633-1369
Washington, DC 20537   Morton S. Goren, Libn.
Staff: Prof 1; Other 3. **Subjects:** Narcotic addiction, dangerous drug abuse, law and legislation, law enforcement, drug abuse education, international control. **Holdings:** 10,000 books; 24 VF drawers. **Subscriptions:** 300 journals and other serials. **Services:** Interlibrary loans; copying; library open to public. **Publications:** Accession list, monthly.

U.S. ELECTROMAGNETIC COMPATIBILITY ANALYSIS CENTER
See: IIT Research Institute - Electromagnetic Compatibility Analysis Center

U.S. ENVIRONMENTAL PROTECTION AGENCY
See: Environmental Protection Agency

★14382★
U.S. EQUAL EMPLOYMENT OPPORTUNITY COMMISSION - LIBRARY (Soc Sci; Law)
2401 E St., N.W.   Phone: (202) 634-6990
Washington, DC 20507   Susan D. Taylor, Lib.Dir.
Founded: 1964. **Staff:** Prof 2; Other 3. **Subjects:** Employment discrimination, minorities, women, testing, labor law, civil rights. **Special Collections:** Equal Employment Opportunity Commission Publications. **Holdings:** 12,500 books; 400 bound periodical volumes; 250 EEOC publications; 24 VF drawers; 311 reels of microfilm; 37 linear inches of microfiche; 4000 monographs. **Subscriptions:** 300 journals and other serials; 5 newspapers. **Services:** Interlibrary loans; copying; SDI; library open to public for reference use only. **Computerized Information Services:** LEXIS, DIALOG, OCLC. **Networks/Consortia:** Member of FEDLINK. **Publications:** Monthly Acquisitions List. **Staff:** Minnie Sue Ripy, Res.Libn.

★14383★
U.S. EXECUTIVE OFFICE OF THE PRESIDENT - LIBRARY (Soc Sci)
726 Jackson Place, N.W., Rm. G-102   Phone: (202) 395-3654
Washington, DC 20503   Adrienne Kosciusko, Dir., Lib. & Info.Serv.
Founded: 1978. **Staff:** Prof 7; Other 5. **Subjects:** Public administration, political science, Presidency, economics, federal legislation, policymaking. **Special Collections:** Federal government reorganization; World War II administrative history; federal government appropriations. **Holdings:** 132,000 books; 4000 bound periodical volumes; 717,200 sheets of Congressional material on microfiche; 16,000 sheets of periodicals on microfiche; 4200 reels of microfilm of periodicals. **Subscriptions:** 710 journals and other serials. **Services:** Copying; SDI; library open to public with special permission. **Automated Operations:** Computerized cataloging, acquisitions, serials and circulation. **Computerized Information Services:** DIALOG, SDC, NEXIS, BRS, LEGI-SLATE, Dialcom, Inc., OCLC, CompuServe, Inc. Contact Person: Robert Updegrove. **Networks/Consortia:** Member of FEDLINK; Metropolitan Washington Library Council. **Staff:** Robert Updegrove, Libn.

★14384★
U.S. EXECUTIVE OFFICE OF THE PRESIDENT - OFF. OF MANAGEMENT & BUDGET/OFPP - FEDERAL ACQUISITION INST. LIB.
726 Jackson Place, N.W.
Washington, DC 20503
Defunct. Holdings absorbed by the U.S. General Services Administration - GSA Library.

★14385★
U.S. FEDERAL AVIATION ADMINISTRATION - AERONAUTICAL CENTER LIBRARY, AAC-64D (Sci-Tech)
6500 S. MacArthur
Box 25082   Phone: (405) 686-4709
Oklahoma City, OK 73125   Virginia C. Hughes, Libn.
Staff: Prof 2. **Subjects:** Aeronautics, airplanes, mathematics, avionics,

electronics, management, aviation medicine, human factors. **Holdings:** Figures not available for books, periodicals and technical reports. **Services:** Interlibrary loans; library open to public. **Remarks:** Includes its Civil Aeromedical Institute Library; telephone number is (405) 686-4398. **Staff:** Darrell R. Goulden, Med.Libn.

★14386★
U.S. FEDERAL AVIATION ADMINISTRATION - CENTRAL REGION LIBRARY (Trans)
Federal Bldg., Rm. 1556
601 E. 12th St.   Phone: (816) 374-5486
Kansas City, MO 64106   Judy Shifrin, Chf., Lib.Serv.
Founded: 1965. **Staff:** Prof 1; Other 1. **Subjects:** Aeronautics, management, environment, engineering, science. **Special Collections:** Law (2700 bound volumes and loose-leaf materials). **Holdings:** 5000 books; 450 bound periodical volumes; 50,000 agency reports; 9 VF drawers; 500 reels of microfilm; 55,000 microfiche; 2000 specifications and standards. **Subscriptions:** 245 journals and other serials. **Services:** Interlibrary loans; copying; library open to public for reference use only.

★14387★
U.S. FEDERAL AVIATION ADMINISTRATION - EASTERN REGION LIBRARY (Trans)
Federal Bldg.
J.F. Kennedy Intl. Airport   Phone: (718) 995-3325
Jamaica, NY 11430   Shirley Sheard, Libn.
Founded: 1965. **Staff:** Prof 1. **Subjects:** Aeronautics, aviation, transportation, management. **Holdings:** 2000 books; 800 pamphlets; 15,000 NASA reports on microfiche; 8000 National Advisory Committee for Aeronautics (NACA) and NASA reports; 1500 Federal Aviation Administration (FAA) research and development reports; 8 VF drawers of clippings and pamphlets; 217 reels of microfilm. **Subscriptions:** 50 journals and other serials. **Services:** Interlibrary loans; library open to public.

★14388★
U.S. FEDERAL AVIATION ADMINISTRATION - LAW LIBRARY (Trans; Law)
800 Independence Ave., S.W.   Phone: (202) 426-3604
Washington, DC 20591   Jane Braucher, Libn.
Staff: Prof 2; Other 3. **Subjects:** Law and legislation - aviation, medical, labor, administrative, international, environmental. **Holdings:** 50,000 books; 50,000 films; 50,000 congressional documents. **Services:** Library open to public with permission. **Computerized Information Services:** DIALOG, LEXIS, NEXIS, LEGI-SLATE, OCLC.

★14389★
U.S. FEDERAL AVIATION ADMINISTRATION - SOUTHERN REGION LIBRARY (Trans)†
3400 Norman Berry Dr.   Phone: (404) 763-7276
East Point, GA 30344   Doris P. Little, Libn.
Staff: Prof 1. **Subjects:** Aeronautics and its related literature, engineering and technology, aviation law and medicine, science, environment, safety, transportation, management and personnel, administration. **Holdings:** 14,000 books; 355 bound periodical volumes; 25 VF drawers of pamphlets; 1800 equipment instruction manuals; 600 reels of microfilm; 5900 reports on microfiche; 15,000 unbound research reports; 1110 documents. **Subscriptions:** 404 journals and other serials. **Services:** Interlibrary loans; copying; library open to public for reference use only. **Automated Operations:** Computerized serials. **Networks/Consortia:** Member of Transportation Research Information Services Network (TRISNET); CCLC; Georgia Library Information Network (GLIN). **Publications:** Library Acquisitions and Services List, monthly.

★14390★
U.S. FEDERAL AVIATION ADMINISTRATION - TECHNICAL INFORMATION RESEARCH FACILITY (ACT 624) (Trans)
                                     Phone: (609) 484-5772
Atlantic City Airport, NJ 08405   Harry Kemp, Mgr.
Founded: 1958. **Staff:** Prof 5; Other 7. **Subjects:** Air traffic control, collision avoidance, aviation safety, radar, navigation, configuration management. **Special Collections:** National Airspace System Documentation Archives; Addison B. Johnson Air Traffic Control Resource Center. **Holdings:** 7000 books; 3500 bound periodical volumes; 2000 technical reports; 80,000 unbound, uncataloged technical reports. **Subscriptions:** 400 journals and other serials. **Services:** Interlibrary loans; copying; SDI; custom bibliographies; facility open to public. **Automated Operations:** Computerized cataloging, acquisitions, serials and circulation. **Computerized Information Services:** DIALOG, DTIC, NASA/RECON, OCLC; internal database. Performs searches free of charge and on cost recovery basis. **Publications:** Acquisitions List. **Special Catalogs:** NAS Documents Catalog.

★14391★
U.S. FEDERAL COMMUNICATIONS COMMISSION - LIBRARY (Sci-Tech)†
1919 M St., N.W.   Phone: (202) 632-7100
Washington, DC 20554   Sheryl A. Segal, Lib.Dir.
Founded: 1934. **Staff:** Prof 3; Other 4. **Subjects:** Telecommunications, electrical engineering, law, economics, public utility regulation, public administration, management, statistics. **Special Collections:** Legislative histories of Communications Act of 1934 and related statutes; Congressional hearings in the area of telecommunications. **Holdings:** 45,000 books; 123 bound periodical volumes; 6200 VF items; 3000 reels of microfilm. **Subscriptions:** 305 journals and other serials. **Services:** SDI; library open to public for reference use only. **Automated Operations:** Computerized cataloging, serials and circulation. **Computerized Information Services:** DIALOG, SDC, OCLC. **Publications:** Acquisitions list, bimonthly. **Staff:** Gloria Thomas, Ref.; Phyllis B. Shocket, Ref./Leg.Hist.

★14392★
U.S. FEDERAL DEPOSIT INSURANCE CORPORATION - LIBRARY (Bus-Fin)
550 Seventeenth St., N.W.   Phone: (202) 389-4314
Washington, DC 20429   Carole Cleland, Chf.Libn.
Founded: 1935. **Staff:** Prof 4; Other 5. **Subjects:** Banking, finance, economics, law. **Special Collections:** State banking commissioners annual reports. **Holdings:** 80,000 volumes. **Subscriptions:** 1200 journals and other serials. **Services:** Interlibrary loans; copying; library open to public with restrictions. **Computerized Information Services:** DIALOG, Westlaw, New York Times Information Service, BRS, LEXIS, NEXIS, Dow Jones News/ Retrieval, Dun and Bradstreet Corporation, OCLC. **Networks/Consortia:** Member of FEDLINK. **Publications:** Recent Acquisitions, monthly. **Special Indexes:** Banking index (KWIC, KWOC computer printout). **Also Known As:** FDIC.

U.S. FEDERAL ELECTION COMMISSION
See: Federal Election Commission

★14393★
U.S. FEDERAL HIGHWAY ADMINISTRATION - OFFICE OF THE CHIEF COUNSEL - LEGISLATIVE/REFERENCE LIBRARY (Trans; Law)
400 Seventh St., S.W., Rm. 4205   Phone: (202) 426-0754
Washington, DC 20590   Sherie A. Abbasi, Law Libn.
Staff: Prof 1. **Subjects:** Highways and roads. **Special Collections:** Legislative histories of highways, 1909 to present. **Holdings:** Figures not available. **Services:** Library open to public by appointment. **Computerized Information Services:** LEXIS, NEXIS; internal databases. Performs searches on subscription basis. **Publications:** Federal laws and material relating to the Federal Highway Administration, biennial.

★14394★
U.S. FEDERAL HOME LOAN BANK BOARD - LAW LIBRARY (Law)
1700 G St., N.W.   Phone: (202) 377-6470
Washington, DC 20552   Joyce A. Potter, Libn.
Founded: 1933. **Staff:** 3. **Subjects:** Law, savings and loan associations. **Holdings:** 20,000 volumes. **Services:** Interlibrary loans; library not open to public.

★14395★
U.S. FEDERAL HOME LOAN BANK BOARD - RESEARCH LIBRARY (Bus-Fin)
1700 G St., N.W.   Phone: (202) 377-6296
Washington, DC 20552   Janet B. Smith, Libn.
Founded: 1935. **Staff:** Prof 2; Other 1. **Subjects:** Real estate, finance, banking, savings and loan, business, economics. **Special Collections:** Files of annual reports of savings and loan supervisory authorities. **Holdings:** 22,000 volumes; 12 VF drawers of pamphlets and statistical reports. **Subscriptions:** 450 journals and other serials; 11 newspapers. **Services:** Interlibrary loans; copying; use of library may be requested. **Automated Operations:** Computerized cataloging. **Computerized Information Services:** DIALOG, OCLC. **Publications:** Library Handbook; Library Bulletin, monthly; Acquisition List, monthly - limited distribution.

★14396★
U.S. FEDERAL JUDICIAL CENTER - INFORMATION SERVICE (Soc Sci)†
1520 H St., N.W.   Phone: (202) 633-6365
Washington, DC 20005   Jane M. Gafvert, Info.Spec.
Staff: Prof 2; Other 2. **Subjects:** Judicial administration, court management, crime and criminals, probation, constitutional law. **Special Collections:** Dolley Madison Collection (life of Mrs. Madison; 60 volumes). **Holdings:** 4500 books; 60 bound periodical volumes; 80 volumes of seminar materials; 9 drawers of article files; 3 file drawers of court rules and local rules of federal courts; 150 volumes of Federal Reporter 2d on ultrafiche. **Subscriptions:** 70 journals and other serials. **Services:** Interlibrary loans; copying; service open to public.

Computerized Information Services: DIALOG, New York Times Information Service; internal database. **Publications:** Catalog of Publications. **Staff:** Lindsey Hundt, Asst.Info.Spec.

★14397★
U.S. FEDERAL MARITIME COMMISSION - LIBRARY (Law)
1100 L St., N.W.   Phone: (202) 523-5762
Washington, DC 20573   Mary Ellen Daffron, Libn.
Founded: 1961. **Staff:** Prof 1; Other 1. **Subjects:** Law, maritime law, marine transportation, economics, oil pollution. **Special Collections:** Containerization (intermodal transportation); shipping; legislation. **Holdings:** 10,300 books; 176 bound periodical volumes; 9 VF drawers of legislative histories, Congressional hearings, reports (uncataloged); 1100 Congressional hearings and reports; 75 pamphlet boxes of port news and statistical information. **Subscriptions:** 200 journals and other serials; 8 newspapers. **Services:** Interlibrary loans; copying; library open to public. **Publications:** Library Acquisitions, monthly - for internal distribution only.

★14398★
U.S. FEDERAL TRADE COMMISSION - LIBRARY (Bus-Fin)
6th St. & Pennsylvania Ave., N.W.   Phone: (202) 523-3871
Washington, DC 20580   Susanne B. Hendsey, Lib.Dir.
Founded: 1915. **Staff:** Prof 7; Other 19. **Subjects:** Antitrust, consumerism, advertising, economics, law, business, accounting. **Holdings:** 115,000 volumes, 200,000 microforms. **Subscriptions:** 1500 journals and other serials. **Services:** Interlibrary loans; copying; library open to public. **Automated Operations:** Computerized cataloging, acquisitions and serials. **Computerized Information Services:** DIALOG, SDC, LEXIS, Dow Jones News/Retrieval, NEXIS, OCLC, Westlaw. **Networks/Consortia:** Member of FEDLINK. **Publications:** Monthly Library Bulletin; Bibliography Series; Periodicals Holdings List; Legislative Histories Holdings List.

★14399★
U.S. FISH & WILDLIFE SERVICE - ABERNATHY SALMON CULTURAL DEVELOPMENT CENTER - RESEARCH & INFO. CENTER (Sci-Tech; Agri)
1440 Abernathy Rd.   Phone: (206) 425-6072
Longview, WA 98632   David A. Leith, Dir.
Founded: 1942. **Staff:** 8. **Subjects:** Fish culture, feeding salmonids, water reuse, diseases of fish, temperature, hatchery techniques. **Holdings:** 125 books; 175 bound periodical volumes; 2125 other cataloged items; 5 drawers of reprints. **Services:** Interlibrary loans; library not open to public.

★14400★
U.S. FISH & WILDLIFE SERVICE - COLUMBIA NATIONAL FISHERIES RESEARCH LABORATORY LIBRARY (Env-Cons; Agri)
Route 1   Phone: (314) 875-5399
Columbia, MO 65201   Dr. Richard Shoettger, Dir.
Founded: 1959. **Staff:** Prof 2. **Subjects:** Pesticides, agricultural chemicals, pollution, environmental contaminants. **Holdings:** 2000 books; 1000 bound periodical volumes; 2000 monographs; 13,000 reprints. **Subscriptions:** 200 journals and other serials. **Services:** Interlibrary loans; copying; library open to public. **Computerized Information Services:** Online systems. **Staff:** Ell-Piret Multer, Tech.Info.Spec.; Axie Hindman, Libn.

★14401★
U.S. FISH & WILDLIFE SERVICE - EAST CENTRAL RESERVOIR INVESTIGATIONS LIBRARY
Federal Bldg.
Bowling Green, KY 42101
Defunct

★14402★
U.S. FISH & WILDLIFE SERVICE - FISH FARMING EXPERIMENTAL STATION - LIBRARY (Sci-Tech; Agri)
Box 860   Phone: (501) 673-8761
Stuttgart, AR 72160   Harry K. Dupree, Dir.
Founded: 1962. **Subjects:** Fisheries (freshwater), parasites and diseases, physiology, nutrition, aquaculture. **Holdings:** 850 volumes; 7500 reprints. **Subscriptions:** 146 journals and other serials. **Services:** Interlibrary loans; library open to public. **Staff:** Joyce Cooper, Libn.

★14403★
U.S. FISH & WILDLIFE SERVICE - JOHN VAN OOSTEN GREAT LAKES FISHERY RESEARCH LIBRARY (Sci-Tech; Env-Cons)
Great Lakes Fishery Laboratory
1451 Green Rd.   Phone: (313) 994-3331
Ann Arbor, MI 48105   Cynthia McCauley, Libn.
Staff: Prof 1. **Subjects:** Fishery biology, aquatic ecology, pesticide, mercury and water pollution, Great Lakes. **Holdings:** 3000 books; 1800 bound periodical volumes; 40,000 reprints. **Subscriptions:** 163 journals and other serials. **Services:** Interlibrary loans; library open to public. **Automated Operations:** Computerized cataloging and ILL. **Computerized Information Services:** DIALOG, MEDLINE. **Networks/Consortia:** Member of FEDLINK.

★14404★
U.S. FISH & WILDLIFE SERVICE - LIBRARY (Sci-Tech; Env-Cons)
1011 E. Tudor Rd.   Phone: (907) 786-3358
Anchorage, AK 99503   Sharon Palmisano, Libn.
Staff: Prof 1. **Subjects:** Alaska fisheries and wildlife. **Special Collections:** U.S. Fish and Wildlife Service publications; Alaska Department of Fish and Game publications. **Holdings:** 1600 books; 2700 monographs. **Subscriptions:** 80 journals and other serials. **Services:** Interlibrary loans; copying; library open to public. **Computerized Information Services:** OCLC.

★14405★
U.S. FISH & WILDLIFE SERVICE - NATIONAL FISHERIES CENTER - TECHNICAL INFORMATION SERVICES (Sci-Tech; Agri)
Box 700   Phone: (304) 725-8461
Kearneysville, WV 25430   Joyce A. Mann-Grim, Tech.Info.Off.
Founded: 1959. **Staff:** Prof 3; Other 2. **Subjects:** Aquaculture; fish - diseases, nutrition, pathology, physiology, bacteriology, virology, parasitology, culture, immunology, chemotherapy, freshwater biology. **Special Collections:** Fish diseases (16,000 reprints); benthic organisms and plankton, water quality monitoring and biological assessment methodology (3000 reports and reprints); fish culture (8000 reports and reprints); clearinghouse for all Fish & Wildlife Service aquacultural materials. **Holdings:** 25,000 books; 27,000 reprints; government depository for Fish Disease Leaflets; 9 VF drawers of publications by staff members. **Subscriptions:** 786 journals and other serials. **Services:** Interlibrary loans; copying; services open to public with restrictions. **Automated Operations:** Computerized cataloging. **Computerized Information Services:** DIALOG, BRS, OCLC; FISH (internal database). **Networks/Consortia:** Member of FEDLINK. **Publications:** Fish Health News, quarterly. **Remarks:** Statistics include the holdings of the Fish Farming Experimental Station in Stuttgart, Arkansas; the National Fishery Research and Development Laboratory in Wellsboro, Pennsylvania; the Southeastern Fish Cultural Laboratory in Marion, Alabama; the Tunison Laboratory of Fish Nutrition in Cortland, New York and its Field Station in Hagerman, Idaho.

★14406★
U.S. FISH & WILDLIFE SERVICE - NATIONAL FISHERY RESEARCH LABORATORY LIBRARY (Sci-Tech)
Box 818   Phone: (608) 783-6451
La Crosse, WI 54602-0818   Rosalie A. Schnick, Tech.Info.Spec.
Founded: 1959. **Staff:** Prof 1; Other 1. **Subjects:** Fish management, toxicology, pharmacology, fish culture and physiology, limnology. **Special Collections:** Complete sets of volumes of early studies on fish culture, fish diseases and fishery biology. **Holdings:** 3500 books; 300 bound periodical volumes; 15,000 reprints; 10,000 leaflets and pamphlets. **Subscriptions:** 200 journals and other serials. **Services:** Interlibrary loans; library open to public for reference use only on request. **Computerized Information Services:** DIALOG, OCLC. **Publications:** List of Serials - available on request. **Remarks:** Contains the holdings of the U.S. Fish & Wildlife Service - Natl. Reservoir Research Library.

★14407★
U.S. FISH & WILDLIFE SERVICE - NATL. RESERVOIR RESEARCH LIBRARY
100 W. Rock St.
Fayetteville, AR 72701
Defunct. Holdings absorbed by U.S. Fish & Wildlife Service - National Fishery Research Laboratory Library.

★14408★
U.S. FISH & WILDLIFE SERVICE - NORTHERN PRAIRIE WILDLIFE RESEARCH CENTER LIBRARY (Sci-Tech; Env-Cons)
Box 1747   Phone: (701) 252-5363
Jamestown, ND 58401   Angie Kokott, Libn.
Founded: 1965. **Staff:** Prof 1. **Subjects:** Wildlife management and research, avian biology, plant and animal ecology. **Holdings:** 2500 books; 700 bound periodical volumes; 5000 color slides; 1000 black/white photographs. **Subscriptions:** 150 journals and other serials. **Services:** Interlibrary loans; copying; library open to qualified persons by permission. **Computerized Information Services:** DIALOG, JOURNALINK, OCLC. **Networks/Consortia:** Member of MINITEX; FEDLINK.

★14409★

U.S. FISH & WILDLIFE SERVICE - OFFICE OF AUDIO-VISUAL - LIBRARY (Aud-Vis)

Dept. of the Interior, Rm. 8070
Washington, DC 20240
Phone: (202) 343-8770
Craig A. Koppie, Visual Info.Spec.
Staff: 1. **Subjects:** Wildlife, primarily birds and endangered species. **Holdings:** 15,000 still photographs and color transparencies. **Services:** Photographs may be consulted by authors, editors, publishers and conservationists.

★14410★

U.S. FISH & WILDLIFE SERVICE - PATUXENT WILDLIFE RESEARCH CENTER LIBRARY (Sci-Tech; Env-Cons)

Phone: (301) 498-0235
Laurel, MD 20708
Lynda Garrett, Libn.
Founded: 1942. **Staff:** Prof 1; Other 3. **Subjects:** Wildlife, especially birds; environmental pollution - pesticides, heavy metals, oil; biostatistics. **Holdings:** 8000 books; 35,000 reprints and pamphlets; 16,000 topographic maps. **Subscriptions:** 400 journals and other serials. **Services:** Interlibrary loans; copying; library open to public for reference use only. **Automated Operations:** Computerized cataloging and ILL. **Computerized Information Services:** OCLC. **Networks/Consortia:** Member of National Natural Resources Library & Information System; Maryland Interlibrary Loan Organization (MILO).

★14411★

U.S. FISH & WILDLIFE SERVICE - SCIENCE REFERENCE LIBRARY (Sci-Tech; Env-Cons)

Federal Bldg., Fort Snelling
Twin Cities, MN 55111
Phone: (612) 725-3576
Veronica Siedle, Libn.
Founded: 1964. **Staff:** Prof 1. **Subjects:** Wildlife, fish, river basin development and water pollution, environmental quality, forestry, outdoor recreation, soils, engineering. **Special Collections:** U.S. Fish and Wildlife Service publications (5000 items). **Holdings:** 15,000 books; 450 bound periodical volumes; 2000 reprints and reports. **Subscriptions:** 111 journals and other serials. **Services:** Interlibrary loans; library open to public for reference use only on request. **Automated Operations:** Computerized cataloging. **Computerized Information Services:** DIALOG, NTIS, OCLC. **Networks/Consortia:** Member of MINITEX; FEDLINK.

★14412★

U.S. FISH & WILDLIFE SERVICE - TUNISON LABORATORY OF FISH NUTRITION - LIBRARY (Sci-Tech)

28 Gracie Rd.
Cortland, NY 13045
Phone: (607) 753-9391
Gary L. Rumsey, Dir.
Staff: 1. **Subjects:** Fish nutrition, fish physiology, fishery biology, general nutrition, general physiology. **Holdings:** 650 books; 300 bound periodical volumes; 4500 reprints. **Services:** Interlibrary loans; copying; library open to public for reference use only.

★14413★

U.S. FISH & WILDLIFE SERVICE - WILDLIFE RESEARCH CENTER LIBRARY (Sci-Tech; Env-Cons)

Federal Center, Bldg. 16
Denver, CO 80225
Phone: (303) 234-4919
Diana L. Dwyer, Libn.
Staff: Prof 1; Other 2. **Subjects:** Wildlife biology, zoology, ornithology, mammalogy, ecology, pesticides, analytical chemistry, statistics, land use and energy in relation to wildlife. **Special Collections:** Fish and Wildlife Service publications; wildlife reprints and technical reports. **Holdings:** 9000 books; 600 bound periodical volumes; 1500 technical reports and reprints; 500 unbound periodical volumes. **Subscriptions:** 200 journals and other serials. **Services:** Interlibrary loans; copying; library open to public with restrictions. **Automated Operations:** Computerized cataloging and ILL. **Computerized Information Services:** DIALOG, NIH-EPA Chemical Information System (CIS), OCLC; Predator Database (internal database). **Networks/Consortia:** Member of FEDLINK. **Publications:** Acquisitions list, quarterly; Serials Holdings, irregular; publications list, annual.

★14414★

U.S. FOOD & DRUG ADMINISTRATION - BUREAU OF RADIOLOGICAL HEALTH - LIBRARY (Med)†

12720 Twinbrook Pkwy.
Rockville, MD 20857
Phone: (301) 443-1038
Mary G. Berkey, Libn.
Founded: 1962. **Staff:** Prof 2; Other 3. **Subjects:** Radiology, radiobiology, radiation, nuclear medicine, radiological health, radiation hazards, emission, microwaves, ultrasonics, lasers. **Special Collections:** Radiological health; radiation protection; x-rays medical usage. **Holdings:** 4500 books; 2500 bound periodical volumes. **Subscriptions:** 400 journals and other serials. **Services:** Interlibrary loans; information retrieval; library open to qualified users for research in subject field. **Automated Operations:** Computerized

cataloging. **Publications:** Acquisitions List, quarterly - to other libraries.

★14415★

U.S. FOOD & DRUG ADMINISTRATION - CENTER FOR FOOD SAFETY & APPLIED NUTRITION - LIBRARY (Food-Bev)

200 C St., S.W., Rm. 3321, HFF-37
Washington, DC 20204
Phone: (202) 245-1235
Robert F. Clarke, Ph.D., Dir.
Subjects: Chemistry, analytical chemistry, toxicology, food technology, nutrition, medicine, biology, cosmetics. **Holdings:** 18,000 books; 10,000 bound periodical volumes; 1500 reports, documents and pamphlets; 40,000 volumes in microform. **Subscriptions:** 800 journals and other serials. **Services:** Interlibrary loans; library open to public. **Automated Operations:** Computerized cataloging. **Computerized Information Services:** OCLC, JOURNALINK. **Networks/Consortia:** Member of FEDLINK. **Special Catalogs:** Union List of Periodicals in conjunction with other federal libraries. **Formerly:** Its Bureau of Foods. **Staff:** Frances Tersillo, User Serv.Libn.

★14416★

U.S. FOOD & DRUG ADMINISTRATION - FISHERY RESEARCH BRANCH - LIBRARY (Sci-Tech)

Box 158
Dauphin Island, AL 36528
Phone: (205) 861-2962
Patsy C. Purvis
Staff: Prof 8; Other 6. **Subjects:** Microbiology, marine biology, chemistry. **Holdings:** 400 books. **Subscriptions:** 20 journals and other serials. **Services:** Library open to public with special arrangement. **Formerly:** Its Gulf Coast Technical Services Unit.

★14417★

U.S. FOOD & DRUG ADMINISTRATION - NATIONAL CENTER FOR DEVICES & RADIOLOGICAL HEALTH - LIBRARY (Med)

8757 Georgia Ave., HFK-45
Silver Spring, MD 20910
Phone: (301) 427-7755
Harriet Albersheim, Libn.
Staff: Prof 1; Other 2. **Subjects:** Medicine, medical devices, biomedical engineering, biomaterials, polymer science. **Special Collections:** Medical Equipment Devices and Supplies Service (MEDS) collection (5000 medical and in vitro diagnostic manufacturers catalogs on microfilm). **Holdings:** 6000 books; 100 bound periodical volumes. **Subscriptions:** 300 journals and other serials. **Services:** Interlibrary loans; copying; library open to public for reference use only. **Automated Operations:** Computerized cataloging. **Computerized Information Services:** DIALOG, MEDLINE. **Networks/Consortia:** Member of FEDLINK. **Publications:** Recent Additions, quarterly - for internal distribution only. **Formerly:** Bureau of Medical Devices Library.

★14418★

U.S. FOOD & DRUG ADMINISTRATION - NATIONAL CENTER FOR DRUGS AND BIOLOGIES - MEDICAL LIBRARY/HFN-630 (Med)

5600 Fishers Lane, Rm. 11B-40
Rockville, MD 20857
Phone: (301) 443-3180
Elizabeth C. Kelly, Dir., Med.Lib.
Staff: Prof 11; Other 10. **Subjects:** Drug therapy and adverse effects, biologies, chemistry, veterinary medicine, pharmacology, toxicology, pharmacy, biostatistics, clinical medicine, health laws of the U.S., consumer affairs. **Special Collections:** FDA Archives Collection (6200 items). **Holdings:** 23,000 books; 30,000 bound periodical volumes; 210 VF drawers of drug literature card services; 325 journal titles on microfilm; 1500 folders of pamphlets and reprints. **Subscriptions:** 1950 journals and other serials. **Services:** Interlibrary loans; copying; SDI; translations; library open to nongovernment personnel for official study or research. **Automated Operations:** Computerized cataloging. **Computerized Information Services:** NLM, BRS, SDC, DIALOG, OCLC, NIH-EPA Chemical Information System (CIS), JOURNALINK, CAS Online. **Networks/Consortia:** Member of FEDLINK; Southeastern/Atlantic Regional Medical Library Services. **Publications:** FDA Medical Library Recent Additions; List of Periodicals and Selected Serial Publications in the FDA Medical Library. **Formerly:** Its Bureau of Drugs.

★14419★

U.S. FOOD & DRUG ADMINISTRATION - NATIONAL CENTER FOR TOXICOLOGICAL RESEARCH - LIBRARY (Sci-Tech)

Jefferson, AK 72079
Susan Laney-Sheehan, Supv.Libn.
Founded: 1972. **Staff:** Prof 2; Other 3. **Subjects:** Toxicology, chemistry, teratogenesis, carcinogenesis, mutagenesis, biochemistry. **Special Collections:** Bacteriology. **Holdings:** 15,000 books; 500 bound periodical volumes. **Subscriptions:** 216 journals and other serials. **Services:** Interlibrary loans; copying; SDI; library open to public. **Automated Operations:** Computerized cataloging and serials. **Computerized Information Services:** SDC, BRS, MEDLARS, OCLC. **Networks/Consortia:** Member of FEDLINK; AMIGOS Bibliographic Council, Inc. **Staff:** Judy Emde, Ref.Libn.

★14420★
U.S. FOOD & DRUG ADMINISTRATION - NATL. CLEARINGHOUSE FOR POISON CONTROL CENTERS (Sci-Tech)
5600 Fishers Lane
HDF 240, Rm. 1345   Phone: (301) 443-6260
Rockville, MD 20857   Mark I. Fow, Act.Dir.
Staff: Prof 7. **Subjects:** Poisons, toxicology, pharmacology, detoxification. **Holdings:** Figures not available. **Services:** Clearinghouse open to public with restrictions.

★14421★
U.S. FOOD AND DRUG ADMINISTRATION - WINCHESTER ENGINEERING & ANALYTICAL CENTER - LIBRARY (Med)
109 Holton St.   Phone: (617) 729-5700
Winchester, MA 01890   Lisa A. Leone, Ck.
Founded: 1961. **Staff:** 1. **Subjects:** Radiology, medical roentgenology, chemistry, physics, nuclear science, oceanography, statistics, medicine, electronics. **Holdings:** 1000 books; 710 bound periodical volumes; technical documents and miscellaneous reports; 20 VF drawers of unbound materials. **Subscriptions:** 109 journals and other serials. **Services:** Interlibrary loans; copying; library open to public for reference use only upon request.

U.S. FOREIGN CLAIMS SETTLEMENT COMMISSION
See: Foreign Claims Settlement Commission of the United States

★14422★
U.S. FOREST SERVICE - APACHE-SITGREAVES NATL. FOREST - ARCHIVES (Env-Cons; Hist)
Box 640   Phone: (602) 333-4301
Springerville, AZ 85938
Subjects: Apache-Sitgreaves National Forest - history from 1906 to present, management and use of the forest's resources including timber, range lands, soil, water, and recreational facilities. **Holdings:** 9 cubic feet of correspondence, diaries, logbooks, account books, business records, maps, charts, and aerial photographs. **Services:** Copying; archives open to public by appointment.

★14423★
U.S. FOREST SERVICE - FLATHEAD NATL. FOREST CENTER (Sci-Tech)
Box 147   Phone: (406) 755-5401
Kalispell, MT 59901
Subjects: Timber, engineering. **Holdings:** 100 books. **Services:** Center open to public with restrictions.

★14424★
U.S. FOREST SERVICE - FOREST PRODUCTS LABORATORY LIBRARY (Sci-Tech; Agri)
Box 5130   Phone: (608) 264-5712
Madison, WI 53705   Roger Scharmer, Libn.
Founded: 1910. **Staff:** Prof 2; Other 5. **Subjects:** Forest products utilization, energy from wood, paper and pulp, wood engineering, wood process and protection, timber, wood products economics. **Special Collections:** Forest products utilization. **Holdings:** 56,300 books and bound periodical volumes; 30,300 technical reports; 20,000 bulletins, reports, reprints; 6100 patents; 5900 microforms. **Subscriptions:** 550 journals. **Services:** Interlibrary loans; copying (limited); library open to public. **Publications:** Accession list, monthly - sent to Forest Service, National Agricultural Library, forestry schools, foreign forest products laboratories. **Special Indexes:** KWIC Index of FPL reports (book); Centralized Title Service from Forestry Bureau, Oxford, England (card and microfilm). **Staff:** Judy Kessenich, Ref.Libn.

U.S. FOREST SERVICE - GILA NATL. FOREST
See: U.S. Natl. Park Service - Gila Cliff Dwellings Natl. Monument

★14425★
U.S. FOREST SERVICE - INSTITUTE OF NORTHERN FORESTRY - LIBRARY (Agri)
308 Tanana Dr.   Phone: (907) 474-7443
Fairbanks, AK 99701
Founded: 1963. **Subjects:** Forestry research, entomology, silviculture, fire research, fire ecology, wildlife habitat research. **Holdings:** 750 books; 300 bound periodical volumes; 2500 research notes and reprints. **Subscriptions:** 120 journals and other serials. **Services:** Library open to public.

★14426★
U.S. FOREST SERVICE - INSTITUTE OF TROPICAL FORESTRY - LIBRARY (Env-Cons)
Box AQ   Phone: (809) 763-3939
Rio Piedras, PR 00928   JoAnne Feheley, Lib.Techn.
Subjects: Tropical forestry and ecology, wildlife management. **Holdings:**

50,000 cataloged items. **Services:** Interlibrary loans; copying; library open to public for reference use only. **Automated Operations:** Computerized mailing list for dissemination of Institute's publications. **Computerized Information Services:** DIALOG, CAB, SDC. **Publications:** ITF Annual Letter.

★14427★
U.S. FOREST SERVICE - INTERMOUNTAIN FOREST & RANGE EXPERIMENT STATION - LIBRARY (Agri)
Forest Service Bldg.
507 25th St.   Phone: (801) 625-5444
Ogden, UT 84401   Elizabeth G. Close, Tech.Info.Off.
Founded: 1962. **Staff:** Prof 2; Other 2. **Subjects:** Forest management, range management, watershed management, forest fire, wildlife, forest disease, forest economics, forest utilization, forest insects. **Holdings:** 7000 books; 2500 bound periodical volumes; 29,000 reprints, pamphlets, translations; 6 files of microfiche; 4 drawers of microfilm. **Subscriptions:** 450 journals and other serials. **Services:** Interlibrary loans; library open to public. **Computerized Information Services:** DIALOG, SDC, BRS, RLIN, OCLC. **Networks/Consortia:** Member of FEDLINK; WESTFORNET. **Publications:** WESTFORNET Monthly Alert.

★14428★
U.S. FOREST SERVICE - INYO NATL. FOREST - INFORMATION CENTER (Agri; Env-Cons)
873 N. Main St.   Phone: (714) 873-5841
Bishop, CA 93514   Ray Schaaf, Pub.Aff.Off.
Subjects: Forestry, environment. **Holdings:** 300 books. **Subscriptions:** 20 journals and other serials; 6 newspapers. **Services:** Copying (limited); center open to public with restrictions. **Networks/Consortia:** Member of WESTFORNET.

★14429★
U.S. FOREST SERVICE - NATL. FORESTS IN FLORIDA - LIBRARY (Env-Cons; Hist)
227 N. Brorough St., Suite 4061   Phone: (904) 681-7266
Tallahassee, FL 32301
Subjects: National Forests in Florida, 1900 to present. **Holdings:** 10 cubic feet (300 items) of diaries, land transactions, agency correspondence, and aerial photographs. **Services:** Copying; library open to public during business hours.

★14430★
U.S. FOREST SERVICE - NORTH CENTRAL FOREST EXPERIMENT STATION LIBRARY (Agri)
1992 Folwell Ave.   Phone: (612) 642-5257
St. Paul, MN 55108   Floyd L. Henderson, Libn.
Founded: 1923. **Staff:** Prof 1; Other 3. **Subjects:** Forestry, forest management, forest botany, silviculture, forest protection, forest economics, watershed management, forest recreation, associated use of forests. **Holdings:** 800 books; 1800 bound periodical volumes; 20,000 pamphlets; 27 drawers of maps. **Subscriptions:** 270 journals and other serials. **Services:** Interlibrary loans; copying; library open to public. **Computerized Information Services:** DIALOG, OCLC. **Networks/Consortia:** Member of MINITEX; FEDLINK. **Publications:** Accessions to the Reference Collection, irregular - for station and field unit personnel.

★14431★
U.S. FOREST SERVICE - NORTHEASTERN FOREST EXPERIMENT STATION LIBRARY (Agri; Env-Cons)
370 Reed Rd.   Phone: (215) 461-3105
Broomall, PA 19008   Thomas L. Baucom, Pub.Aff.Off.
Founded: 1961. **Staff:** 1. **Subjects:** Economics, forest botany, silviculture, forest mensuration, forest utilization, forest management, forest entomology and pathology, forest resources and conservation, watershed management. **Holdings:** Figures not available.

★14432★
U.S. FOREST SERVICE - PACIFIC NORTHWEST FOREST & RANGE EXPERIMENT STATION - FORESTRY SCI. LAB. LIB. (Agri; Env-Cons)
653 Federal Bldg.
Box 909   Phone: (907) 586-7301
Juneau, AK 99802   Carol A. Ayer, Libn.
Founded: 1961. **Staff:** 2. **Subjects:** Boreal forestry, fisheries, wildlife, engineering, recreation. **Holdings:** 2500 books; 3000 bound periodical volumes; 24,000 pamphlets, reprints and reports; 8000 government serial documents; 250 maps and charts; 150 photographs; 30 reels of microfilm and microfiche. **Subscriptions:** 224 journals and other serials. **Services:** Interlibrary loans; library open to public but circulation of material is limited. **Computerized Information Services:** DIALOG. **Networks/Consortia:**

Member of WESTFORNET. **Publications:** Accession Lists, bimonthly; Periodicals and Serials Holdings Lists; Station Publication Lists; special subject bibliographies - all irregular.

★14433★
U.S. FOREST SERV. - PACIFIC SOUTHWEST FOREST & RANGE EXPERIMENT STA. - WESTFORNET-BERKELEY SERV.CTR. (Agri; Env-Cons)
1960 Addision St.
Box 245   Phone: (415) 486-3686
Berkeley, CA 94701   Theodor B. Yerke, WESTFORNET Prog.Mgr.
Founded: 1960. **Staff:** Prof 5; Other 7. **Subjects:** Forest management, silviculture, watershed management, computers and statistics, wildlife management, environmental protection. **Holdings:** 32,000 volumes, documents, offprints, reprints, preprints, bulletins, research notes. **Subscriptions:** 602 journals and other serials. **Services:** Interlibrary loans; copying; SDI; library open to public. **Automated Operations:** Computerized cataloging. **Computerized Information Services:** DIALOG, SDC, BRS, RLIN, OCLC; internal databases. **Networks/Consortia:** Member of WESTFORNET. **Publications:** WESTFORNET Monthly Alert. **Special Indexes:** FAMULUS-based indexes and abstract collections. **Staff:** Vincent P. Aitro, Tech.Proc.Anl.; Dennis Galvin, Supv., Serv.Ctr.; Andrea Gabriel, Cat.Libn.

★14434★
U.S. FOREST SERVICE - PERMANENT PHOTOGRAPHIC COLLECTION (Aud-Vis)
Box 2417, Rm. 51-RPE   Phone: (703) 235-8215
Washington, DC 20013   William G. Hauser, Visual Info.Off.
Founded: 1896. **Staff:** Prof 1; Other 3. **Subjects:** National Forests, trees and other vegetation, fire, timber, grazing, people using public lands, recreation, portraits, Mount St. Helens. **Holdings:** 60,000 photographs in browsing collection; 600,000 negatives; 20,000 color transparencies; 100,000 color slides. **Services:** Interlibrary loans; copying; photographs supplied on request; library open to public. **Automated Operations:** Computerized cataloging and acquisitions; Ft. Collins Computer Center-Forest Service negative number listing. **Special Indexes:** Alphabetical subject listing (computer printout); microfilm positives of the earliest 300,000 images in collection; microfilm of forms listing images (first 60 years of collection). **Remarks:** The collection is located at 1621 N. Kent St., Lower Lobby Rm. 51, Rosslyn, Arlington, VA.

★14435★
U.S. FOREST SERVICE - RECREATION RESOURCE MGT. - CULTURAL RESOURCE MGT. - RES. & ARCHV. CTR. (Env-Cons; Hist)
630 Sansome St.   Phone: (415) 556-4175
San Francisco, CA 94111
Subjects: History of the National Forests in California - logging, mining, grazing, forestry, recreation, subsistence uses; history of California Indians, Euro-Americans, Chinese, and other cultural and ethnic groups in the National Forests, 1800 to present. **Holdings:** 1700 manuscripts, records, and oral history materials. **Services:** Copying; center open to public during business hours.

★14436★
U.S. FOREST SERVICE - ROCKY MOUNTAIN FOREST & RANGE EXPERIMENT STATION - LIBRARY (Agri)
240 W. Prospect St.   Phone: (303) 221-4390
Fort Collins, CO 80526   Frances J. Barney, Libn.
Founded: 1966. **Staff:** Prof 2; Other 2. **Subjects:** Forest management, shelterbelts, snow avalanches, watershed management, forest entomology and pathology, forest fire ecology, nematology, ecology of arid lands, history of forestry in Rocky Mountains. **Special Collections:** World Mistletoe Literature (on Famulus retrieval system; 7000 references); Boyce Index to Forest Pathology Literature (30 card file drawers). **Holdings:** 10,000 books; 3000 bound periodical volumes; 18,000 unbound serials; 10 VF drawers of reprints; 150 reels of microfilm (Oxford Catalog and periodicals); 500 dissertations; 2 VF drawers of Rocky Mountain Station historical material. **Subscriptions:** 650 journals and other serials. **Services:** Interlibrary loans; copying; library open to public for reference use only. **Computerized Information Services:** DIALOG, SDC, BRS, RLIN, OCLC. **Networks/Consortia:** Member of WESTFORNET. **Staff:** Robert W. Dano, Tech.Info.Spec.

★14437★
U.S. FOREST SERVICE - SOUTHERN FOREST EXPERIMENT STATION LIBRARY (Agri; Env-Cons)
Rm. T-10210 Postal Service Bldg.
701 Loyola Ave.   Phone: (504) 589-6798
New Orleans, LA 70113   Linda A. Korb, Libn.
Founded: 1921. **Staff:** Prof 1; Other 1. **Subjects:** Forest management,

forest economics, forest utilization, range management, watershed management, forest disease, forest fire, forest insects, wildlife habitat. **Holdings:** 5000 books; 8000 bound periodical volumes; 38,000 pamphlets; 1200 translations; 15 VF drawers of publications of the Southern Forest Experiment Station. **Subscriptions:** 250 journals and other serials. **Services:** Interlibrary loans; copying; library open to public. **Computerized Information Services:** DIALOG, BRS, OCLC. **Networks/Consortia:** Member of FEDLINK.

★14438★
U.S. GENERAL ACCOUNTING OFFICE - BOSTON REGIONAL OFFICE - TECHNICAL LIBRARY (Bus-Fin)
100 Summer St., Suite 1907   Phone: (617) 223-6536
Boston, MA 02110   Jennifer Arns, Tech.Info.Spec.
Staff: Prof 1. **Subjects:** Auditing, accounting, public administration, federally sponsored or assisted health programs, law enforcement, environmental protection, procurement of major systems. **Special Collections:** All GAO publications (20 VF drawers); Comptroller General Decisions (published and unpublished). **Holdings:** Public laws and legislative histories; appropriation hearings for current Congress; technical reports; Congressional documents; U.S. Code; statutes at large. **Subscriptions:** 29 journals and other serials. **Services:** Interlibrary loans; library open to public for reference use only. **Computerized Information Services:** Library of Congress (LOCIS), NEXIS, DIALOG; internal database. **Networks/Consortia:** Member of FEDLINK.

★14439★
U.S. GENERAL ACCOUNTING OFFICE - OFFICE OF LIBRARY SERVICES (Law; Bus-Fin)
441 G St., N.W.   Phone: (202) 275-5180
Washington, DC 20548   Phyllis Christenson, Dir.
Founded: 1949. **Staff:** Prof 23; Other 32. **Subjects:** Law, accounting and auditing, management, policy analysis, program evaluation, energy. **Special Collections:** Federal departmental regulatory material; legislative history collection; GAO Historical Collection. **Holdings:** 80,000 volumes; 1 million microfiche. **Subscriptions:** 1700 journals and other serials; 7 newspapers. **Services:** Interlibrary loans; library open to public for reference use only. **Automated Operations:** Computerized cataloging and serials. **Computerized Information Services:** DIALOG, SDC, New York Times Information Service, Library of Congress (LOCIS), MEDLARS, DOE/RECON, BRS, JURIS, LEXIS, LEGIS, Westlaw, OCLC; internal database. **Networks/Consortia:** Member of FEDLINK. **Publications:** Library Focus, monthly; Library & Information Services Handbook. **Staff:** Maureen Canick, Mgr., Tech.Lib.; Larry Boyer, Mgr., Law Lib.; Bonita Mueller, Mgr., Tech.Serv.

★14440★
U.S. GENERAL ACCOUNTING OFFICE - PHILADELPHIA REGIONAL RESOURCE CENTER (Bus-Fin)
434 Walnut St., 11th Fl.   Phone: (215) 597-7360
Philadelphia, PA 19106   Linda Carnevale Skale, Tech.Info.Spec.
Founded: 1979. **Staff:** Prof 1. **Subjects:** Accounting; U.S. legislation, government decisions and regulations. **Special Collections:** Decisions of the U.S. Comptroller General, 1921 to present. **Holdings:** 500 books; 22 General Accounting Office annual reports, 1961 to present; complete set of Public Laws from 90th Congress to present; General Accounting Office documents, 1977 to present. **Subscriptions:** 52 journals and other serials. **Services:** Interlibrary loans; copying; SDI; center open to public by appointment. **Computerized Information Services:** DIALOG, Library of Congress Information System (LOCIS), OCLC, VU/TEXT; internal database.

★14441★
U.S. GENERAL ACCOUNTING OFFICE - SAN FRANCISCO REGIONAL OFFICE - LIBRARY (Bus-Fin)
1275 Market St.   Phone: (415) 556-6200
San Francisco, CA 94103   Linda F. Sharp, Tech.Info.Spec.
Founded: 1976. **Staff:** Prof 1; Other 1. **Subjects:** Auditing, program evaluation, legislation. **Special Collections:** U.S. General Accounting Office Audit Reports, annual reports. **Holdings:** 10 VF drawers of reports on microfiche. **Subscriptions:** 30 journals and other serials. **Services:** Interlibrary loans; SDI; library open to public by appointment. **Computerized Information Services:** Online systems.

★14442★
U.S. GENERAL SERVICES ADMINISTRATION - CONSUMER INFORMATION CENTER (Soc Sci)
18th & F St., N.W.   Phone: (202) 566-1794
Washington, DC 20405   Teresa Nasif, Director
Founded: 1970. **Subjects:** Automobiles, budget and money management, child care, employment and education, health, food, diet and nutrition, gardening, housing and home maintenance. **Holdings:** 200 pamphlets. **Services:** News release and script service available to the media and

interested educators; center not open to public. **Publications:** Consumer Information Catalog, quarterly - free of charge. **Remarks:** The mailing address for publications is Consumer Information Center, Pueblo, CO 81009. **Staff:** Mary M. Arsenoff, Br.Chf.; Kathryn Brown, Catalog Ed.

★14443★
U.S. GENERAL SERVICES ADMINISTRATION - GSA LIBRARY (Law; Sci-Tech)
General Services Bldg., Rm. 1033
18th & F Sts., N.W.   Phone: (202) 535-7788
Washington, DC 20405   Gail L. Kohlhorst, Chf.
Founded: 1961. **Staff:** Prof 6; Other 5. **Subjects:** Law, engineering, management, architecture, data processing, procurement, emergency preparedness. **Special Collections:** Legislative histories of public laws of interest to General Services Administration; historic and official documents dealing with U.S. public buildings; Federal Acquisition Institute Library (historic and current materials on federal procurement). **Holdings:** 100,000 books; 3000 bound periodical volumes; 12,000 government documents; 2000 microforms; 8000 unbound reports, theses, handbooks and periodicals. **Subscriptions:** 450 journals and other serials; 12 newspapers. **Services:** Interlibrary loans; copying; SDI; library open to public for reference use only. **Automated Operations:** Computerized cataloging and acquisitions. **Computerized Information Services:** DIALOG, Dow Jones News/Retrieval, NEXIS, Westlaw, OCLC, Auto-Cite. **Networks/Consortia:** Member of FEDLINK. **Publications:** Current Literature, quarterly - for internal distribution only. **Special Catalogs:** Catalog of federal procurement and contracting (card). **Staff:** Helen Bradley, Asst.Chf.; Darwin Koester, Gen.Ref.Libn.; Susan Harlem, Law Libn.; Caroline Ladeira, Procurement Ref.Libn.

U.S. GENERAL SERVICES ADMINISTRATION - NATL. ARCHIVES & RECORDS SERVICE
See: **U.S. Natl. Archives & Records Service**

★14444★
U.S. GEOLOGICAL SURVEY - DENVER LIBRARY (Sci-Tech)
Denver Federal Ctr.
Stop 914, Box 25046   Phone: (303) 236-1000
Denver, CO 80225   Robert A. Bier, Jr., Chf.Libn.
Founded: 1948. **Staff:** Prof 6; Other 15. **Subjects:** Geology, mineral and water resources, mineralogy, physics, paleontology, petrology, chemistry, soil and environmental sciences. **Special Collections:** Photographic Library (300,000 items); Field Records Library (80,000 items). **Holdings:** 175,000 books; 60,000 bound periodical volumes; 75,000 other cataloged items; 15,000 microforms; 65,000 topographic maps of U.S.; 1500 geologic world maps; 7000 USGS maps in series (complete); 20,000 reports and pamphlets. **Subscriptions:** 1600 journals and other serials. **Services:** Interlibrary loans; library open to public for reference use only. **Automated Operations:** Computerized cataloging and circulation. **Computerized Information Services:** DIALOG, SDC. **Networks/Consortia:** Member of Denver Regional Libraries Courier Service. **Staff:** Jane Bonn, Ref./Circ.Libn.; Caryl L. Shields, ILL Libn.; Marjorie E. Dalechek, Photo Libn.; Deborah F. Rowen, Field Rec.Libn.

★14445★
U.S. GEOLOGICAL SURVEY - EROS DATA CENTER - TECHNICAL REFERENCE UNIT (Sci-Tech)
EROS Data Center   Phone: (605) 594-6511
Sioux Falls, SD 57198   Karen Tramp, Customer Serv.Techn.
Founded: 1974. **Staff:** 1. **Subjects:** Remote sensing, natural resources. **Special Collections:** ERTS reports (microfiche). **Holdings:** 3000 books; 200 bound periodical volumes; 6000 microfiche; 200 NASA technical letters; 12,000 reports; 2000 periodicals. **Subscriptions:** 55 journals and other serials. **Services:** Interlibrary loans; unit open to public. **Automated Operations:** Computerized cataloging. **Computerized Information Services:** DIALOG. **Publications:** EROS Program Reprints, distributed on request (subject); New Acquisitions List, quarterly. **Special Catalogs:** Remote Sensing Bibliographies. **Formerly:** Its Don L. Kulow Memorial Library. **Also Known As:** Earth Resources Observation Systems Data Center.

★14446★
U.S. GEOLOGICAL SURVEY - FLAGSTAFF FIELD CENTER - BRANCH LIBRARY (Sci-Tech)
2255 N. Gemini Dr.   Phone: (602) 779-3311
Flagstaff, AZ 86001   James R. Nation, Libn.
Founded: 1964. **Staff:** Prof 1; Other 2. **Subjects:** Earth sciences, space sciences. **Holdings:** 23,361 volumes; 26,500 maps. **Subscriptions:** 315 journals and other serials. **Services:** Interlibrary loans; library open to public for reference use only.

★14447★
U.S. GEOLOGICAL SURVEY - LIBRARY (Sci-Tech)
345 Middlefield Rd., MS955   Phone: (415) 323-8111
Menlo Park, CA 94025   Eleanore E. Wilkins, Libn.
Founded: 1953. **Staff:** Prof 4; Other 12. **Subjects:** Geology and related sciences. **Holdings:** 250,000 volumes. **Services:** Interlibrary loans; library open to public for reference use only.

★14448★
U.S. GEOLOGICAL SURVEY - LIBRARY (Sci-Tech)
Federal Bldg.
300 E. 8th St.   Phone: (512) 482-5520
Austin, TX 78701   Patricia Tenner, Libn.
Staff: Prof 1; Other 1. **Subjects:** Hydrology, hydrogeology, hydrologic and environmental engineering, water quality. **Special Collections:** U.S.G.S Professional Papers (complete collection); U.S.G.S. Water Supply Papers (complete collection). **Holdings:** 3000 books; 5000 technical reports. **Subscriptions:** 15 journals and other serials. **Services:** Interlibrary loans; library open to public for reference use only. **Automated Operations:** Computerized cataloging. **Computerized Information Services:** DIALOG.

★14449★
U.S. GEOLOGICAL SURVEY - LIBRARY (Sci-Tech)
National Ctr., Mail Stop 950   Phone: (703) 860-6671
Reston, VA 22092   George H. Goodwin, Jr., Chf.Libn.
Founded: 1882. **Staff:** Prof 23; Other 32. **Subjects:** Geology, mineralogy, mineral resources, water resources, petrology, paleontology. **Special Collections:** George F. Kunz Collection of Gems and Precious Stones; Douglas C. Alverson Collection of Russian Geological Books. **Holdings:** 730,000 volumes; 296,000 maps; 265,000 pamphlets; 290,000 microforms; doctoral dissertations on microfilm and microfiche; NTIS report literature on microfiche. **Subscriptions:** 10,000 journals and other serials. **Services:** Interlibrary loans; copying; SDI; library open to public with borrowing restricted to interlibrary loan. **Automated Operations:** Computerized cataloging, serials and circulation. **Computerized Information Services:** DIALOG, SDC, DOE/RECON, OCLC. **Networks/Consortia:** Member of FEDLINK. **Special Catalogs:** Catalog of the U.S. Geological Survey Library - available for purchase. **Staff:** Edward H. Liszewski, Asst.Chf.Libn.; Barbara A. Chappell, Hd., Ref./Circ.; Bobby M. Reed, Hd., Cat.Sect.; Michael J. Kubisiak, Hd., Acq.Sect.

★14450★
U.S. GEOLOGICAL SURVEY - NATL. CARTOGRAPHIC INFORMATION CENTER (NCIC) (Geog-Map)
Federal Ctr., Stop 511
Box 25046   Phone: (303) 234-4388
Denver, CO 80225   Rudolph Hildebrandt, Cartographer
Founded: 1947. **Staff:** 15. **Subjects:** Topographic maps, aerial photography, space imagery, orthophotoquads, digital data, land use. **Special Collections:** Out of print topographic quadrangles (266 reels of microfilm). **Holdings:** 480 VF drawers of maps; 1 million aerial photographs. **Services:** Copying; center open to public for reference use only. **Computerized Information Services:** Internal database. **Publications:** NCIC Newsletter. **Special Indexes:** Topographic and orthophotoquad advance material index (map indexes available for each state).

★14451★
U.S. GEOLOGICAL SURVEY - NATL. CARTOGRAPHIC INFORMATION CENTER (NCIC) (Geog-Map)
507 National Center   Phone: (703) 860-6045
Reston, VA 22092   Alan R. Stevens, Chf.
Founded: 1974. **Staff:** 47. **Subjects:** Maps and charts, aerial photos and space imagery, geodetic control, digital cartographic/geographic data (tapes), related cartographic data. **Holdings:** Cartographic Catalog (50,000 entries); Aerial Photo Summary Record System (1.3 million airphoto quadrangles); Map and Chart Information System (165,000 map records). **Publications:** NCIC Newsletter, irregular; technical user guides, as needed. **Special Catalogs:** Catalogs of U.S. aerial photography coverage, U.S. map coverage and cartographic references (microfiche), semiannual. **Remarks:** NCIC provides information on cartographic data produced by federal agencies, states and commercial organizations. **Staff:** John T. Wood, Dp.Chf.; Lyle Kemper, Chf., User Serv.Br.;Donald Arries, Chf., Data Acq.Br.; John Wilson, Chf., Sys.Anl.

★14452★
U.S. GEOLOGICAL SURVEY - NATL. CARTOGRAPHIC INFORMATION CENTER (NCIC) - WESTERN BRANCH (Geog-Map)
345 Middlefield Rd., M.S. 32   Phone: (415) 323-8111
Menlo Park, CA 94025   William J. Johnson, Chf., NCIC - W.
Staff: 29. **Subjects:** Maps and charts, aerial photography, geodetic control,

satellite imagery. **Holdings:** 25 million photographs and images. **Services:** Copying; photograph reproduction; center open to public. **Automated Operations:** Computerized cataloging and acquisitions. **Publications:** Brochures (topographic, geologic, water resources, conservation). **Special Indexes:** Published map and advanced materials indexes. **Staff:** Gerald Greenberg, Chf., Data Acq.; Richard Zorker, Chf., User Serv.

★14453★
U.S. GEOLOGICAL SURVEY - NATIONAL MAPPING DIVISION ASSISTANCE FACILITY - LIBRARY (Sci-Tech)
National Space Technology Labs   Phone: (601) 688-3541
NSTL Station, MS 39529   Frank Beatty, Libn.
Founded: 1973. **Staff:** Prof 1; Other 1. **Subjects:** Remote sensing, mapping, platforms and sensors, electromagnetic energy, cultural features and other man-related aspects of remote sensing, animal and plant life, geology and meteorology, hydrology and astronomy, data processing and management. **Special Collections:** Photo interpretation keys (87 items). **Holdings:** 850 books; 183 bound periodical volumes; 13,000 microfiche documents; 4000 maps. **Subscriptions:** 41 journals and other serials. **Services:** Interlibrary loans; copying; microfiche loan service; library open to public. **Publications:** Remote Sensing and Mapping Source List. **Staff:** Marti Larkin, Asst.Libn.

★14454★
U.S. GEOLOGICAL SURVEY - WATER RESOURCES DIVISION - COLORADO DISTRICT LIBRARY (Sci-Tech)
Federal Center
Box 25046, Stop 415   Phone: (303) 234-3487
Denver, CO 80225   Barbara J. Condron, Libn.
Founded: 1973. **Staff:** Prof 1. **Subjects:** Water resources, limnology, coal, oil shale. **Special Collections:** Annual reports of the Colorado River Basin, Arkansas River Basin, Missouri River and Rio Grande River; U.S. Geological Survey Water Supply Papers (complete); oil shale material. **Holdings:** 1000 books; 5000 pamphlets and serials; 2000 microfiche; 10 videotapes; 5 VF drawers of clippings and small pamphlets. **Subscriptions:** 35 journals and other serials. **Services:** Interlibrary loans; copying (limited); library open to public for reference use only. **Automated Operations:** Computerized cataloging. **Computerized Information Services:** OCLC. **Remarks:** Branch libraries are located at Lakewood, Pueblo, Grand Junction and Meeker, Colorado.

★14455★
U.S. GEOLOGICAL SURVEY - WATER RESOURCES DIVISION - INFORMATION RESOURCE CENTER (Sci-Tech)
6023 Guion Rd., Suite 201   Phone: (317) 927-8640
Indianapolis, IN 46254   Sharon S. Kuhnlein, IRC Supv.
Founded: 1977. **Subjects:** Hydrology, water resources in Indiana, geology, water pollution. **Holdings:** 7000 books; 225 reports on microfiche; 600 maps; 1000 reprints. **Subscriptions:** 30 journals and other serials. **Services:** Interlibrary loans; center open to public with restrictions. **Networks/ Consortia:** Member of Central Indiana Area Library Services Authority. **Publications:** New Acquisitions, monthly - for internal distribution only.

★14456★
U.S. GEOLOGICAL SURVEY - WATER RESOURCES DIVISION - LIBRARY (Sci-Tech)
1815 University Ave.   Phone: (608) 262-2488
Madison, WI 53705-4042   Rachel Lansing, Adm.Oper.Asst.
Staff: 1. **Subjects:** Surface and ground water, water quality. **Special Collections:** Complete set of WRD Wisconsin publications. **Holdings:** 2000 books; 530 water supply papers; 450 professional papers; 136 bulletins; 170 circulars. **Services:** Library open to public for reference use only.

★14457★
U.S. GEOLOGICAL SURVEY - WATER RESOURCES DIVISION - NATL. WATER DATA STORAGE & RETRIEVAL SYSTEM (Sci-Tech)
National Ctr., Mail Stop 437   Phone: (703) 860-6871
Reston, VA 22092   Philip Cohen, Chf. Hydrologist
Founded: 1889. **Staff:** Prof 16; Other 9. **Subjects:** Surface water stage and discharge, chemical quality parameters, radiochemistry, sedimentology, pesticide and biological concentrations in water, ground and surface water levels, flood frequency and flood inundation mapping. **Holdings:** Observations from 16,600 streamflow gauging stations, 6230 water quality measuring stations, 800,000 wells and springs; historical data dating to 1890. **Services:** Data collection and analysis; data from computerized files is available on magnetic tape or cards; system open to public, fee charged for services. **Publications:** List of publications - available on request. **Also Known As:** WATSTORE.

★14458★
U.S. GEOLOGICAL SURVEY - WATER RESOURCES DIVISION - NEW YORK DISTRICT - LIBRARY (Sci-Tech)
343 Court House
Box 1350   Phone: (518) 472-3107
Albany, NY 12201   Denise A. Wiltshire, Libn.
Staff: Prof 1; Other 1. **Subjects:** Geochemistry, hydrology, geology, climatology. **Special Collections:** Acid Precipitation Collection (reprints and documents). **Holdings:** 6500 books; 250 pamphlet boxes of periodicals; 1000 maps; climatological data; 950 hydrologic investigations; atlases. **Subscriptions:** 50 journals and other serials. **Services:** Library open to public for reference use only. **Computerized Information Services:** DIALOG, SDC, OCLC, BRS, Chemical Substances Information Network (CSIN). **Networks/ Consortia:** Member of National Natural Resources Library and Information System; FEDLINK. **Publications:** Activities brochure, annual; Water Resources Activities in New York (U.S. Geological Survey open-file report series).

★14459★
U.S. GEOLOGICAL SURVEY - WATER RESOURCES DIVISION - NEW YORK SUBDISTRICT - LIBRARY (Sci-Tech)
5 Aerial Way   Phone: (516) 938-8830
Syosset, NY 11791   Joan M. Bachmann, Adm.Asst.
Staff: 1. **Subjects:** Water resources, geology of Long Island. **Special Collections:** U.S. Geological Survey's professional papers; water supply papers; water resources investigations. **Holdings:** 300 books; 27 bound periodical volumes. **Subscriptions:** 19 journals and other serials. **Services:** Library open to public for reference use only.

★14460★
U.S. GEOLOGICAL SURVEY - WATER RESOURCES DIVISION - READING ROOM (Sci-Tech)
Western Bank, Rm. 714
505 Marquette N.W.   Phone: (505) 766-2810
Albuquerque, NM 87102   Janie S. Jones, Libn.
Founded: 1958. **Staff:** Prof 1. **Subjects:** Hydrology, geology of New Mexico. **Special Collections:** Topographic and geologic maps. **Holdings:** 10,000 books; 25,000 unbound periodicals and paper items. **Subscriptions:** 45 journals and other serials. **Services:** Room open to public for reference use only.

★14461★
U.S. GEOLOGICAL SURVEY - WATER RESOURCES LIBRARY (Sci-Tech)
Aspinall Federal Bldg., Rm. 223
Box 2027   Phone: (303) 245-5257
Grand Junction, CO 81502   D.L. Collins, Subdistrict Chf.
Staff: 2. **Subjects:** Water resources. **Holdings:** 900 books; 700 bound periodical volumes; 50 volumes of basic data reports; 75 maps; 75 decisions on names in the U.S.; 50 reels of microfilm of well log data for Colorado. **Services:** Interlibrary loans; library open to public with restrictions.

★14462★
U.S. GEOLOGICAL SURVEY - WESTERN MINERAL RESOURCES LIBRARY (Sci-Tech)
656 U.S. Court House
920 W. Riverside Ave.   Phone: (509) 456-4677
Spokane, WA 99201   Anita W. Tarbert, Lib.Techn.
Founded: 1948. **Staff:** 1. **Subjects:** Geology and related sciences. **Special Collections:** U.S. Geological Survey publications (almost complete run). **Holdings:** Figures not available for books and bound periodical volumes; 1200 feet of shelving including topographic maps of Pacific Northwest states and Alaska; state publications related to geology of Idaho, Washington, Montana and Oregon. **Services:** Library open to public with restrictions.

★14463★
UNITED STATES GOLF ASSOCIATION - GOLF HOUSE LIBRARY (Rec)
Golf House   Phone: (201) 234-2300
Far Hills, NJ 07931   Janet Seagle, Libn./Musm.Cur.
Staff: Prof 1. **Subjects:** Golf. **Holdings:** 7000 books; 440 bound periodical volumes; 35 scrapbooks of newspaper clippings. **Subscriptions:** 25 journals and other serials. **Services:** Library open to public for reference use only.

★14464★
UNITED STATES GYPSUM COMPANY - CORPORATE LIBRARY (Sci-Tech)
101 S. Wacker Dr.   Phone: (312) 321-5810
Chicago, IL 60606   Patricia A. Julien, Libn.
Staff: Prof 1; Other 1. **Subjects:** Business, building materials, nonmetallic minerals, mining, architecture, building construction. **Holdings:** 1550 books; 30 VF drawers. **Subscriptions:** 250 journals and other serials. **Services:**

Interlibrary loans; copying; library open to public for reference use only. **Networks/Consortia:** Member of ILLINET. **Publications:** Off the Shelf, bimonthly - for internal distribution only.

★14465★
UNITED STATES GYPSUM COMPANY - GRAHAM J. MORGAN RESEARCH LIBRARY (Sci-Tech)
700 N. Hwy. 45   Phone: (312) 362-9797
Libertyville, IL 60048   Marie Ehrmann, Res.Libn.
Founded: 1961. **Staff:** Prof 2; Other 1. **Subjects:** Building materials, gypsum products, engineering, plastics and adhesives, lime, coatings, chemistry, mineral fibers, wood and paper, fertilizers, acoustical products. **Holdings:** 5007 books; 2450 bound periodical volumes; 1528 pamphlets; 30,227 laboratory reports; 952 reels of microfilm; 782 microfiche; 5 VF drawers of unbound reports, articles, documents. **Subscriptions:** 338 journals and other serials. **Services:** Library open to public with the approval of the director of research. **Automated Operations:** Computerized serials. **Computerized Information Services:** DIALOG, SDC, BRS. Performs searches for staff. **Networks/Consortia:** Member of North Suburban Library System (NSLS). **Publications:** For Your Information, monthly - for internal distribution only. **Special Indexes:** Gypsum references (index generated by computer). **Staff:** Sylvia Beardsley, Info.Spec.

★14466★
U.S. HOCKEY HALL OF FAME - LIBRARY (Rec)
Hat Trick Ave.
Box 657   Phone: (218) 749-5167
Eveleth, MN 55734   Earl Berglund, Exec.Dir.
Founded: 1973. **Subjects:** Ice hockey. **Special Collections:** College hockey rulebooks. **Holdings:** Unbound periodicals; newspapers; guide books; programs; scrapbooks. **Services:** Library open to serious researchers only.

★14467★
U.S. HOUSE OF REPRESENTATIVES - LIBRARY (Soc Sci; Law)
B-18 Cannon Bldg.   Phone: (202) 225-0462
Washington, DC 20515   E. Raymond Lewis, Libn.
Founded: 1792. **Staff:** 4. **Subjects:** Legislation, law. **Special Collections:** Congressional documents from the Continental Congress to present. **Holdings:** 225,000 volumes. **Services:** Use of library restricted to members and committees of Congress and their staffs, except by special permission. **Publications:** Index to Congressional Committee Hearings in the House.

★14468★
U.S. INDUSTRIAL CHEMICALS COMPANY - RESEARCH DEPARTMENT LIBRARY (Sci-Tech)
1275 Section Rd.   Phone: (513) 761-4130
Cincinnati, OH 45237   Michelle M. Rudy, Tech.Libn.
Staff: Prof 1. **Subjects:** Organometallic chemistry, catalysis, polymers and polymerization. **Holdings:** 5000 books; 5000 bound periodical volumes; U.S. chemical patents in microform, 1966 to present. **Subscriptions:** 140 journals and other serials; 10 newspapers. **Services:** Interlibrary loans; library not open to public. **Automated Operations:** Computerized serials. **Computerized Information Services:** DIALOG, Pergamon InfoLine Ltd., CAS Online. Performs searches for staff only. **Publications:** New Acquisitions, monthly - for internal distribution only. **Special Indexes:** Research Library Journals (computer printout). **Remarks:** Company is a subsidiary of National Distillers and Chemicals Corporation.

★14469★
U.S. INDUSTRIAL CHEMICALS COMPANY - TUSCOLA PLANT TECHNICAL LIBRARY AND INFORMATION CENTER (Sci-Tech)
Box 218   Phone: (217) 253-3311
Tuscola, IL 61953   Lois C. Bodoh, Tech.Libn.
Founded: 1960. **Staff:** Prof 1. **Subjects:** Engineering, chemistry, plastics. **Holdings:** 5500 books; 2000 bound periodical volumes; 1000 patents; 15 VF drawers of pamphlets; 300 reels of microfilm and microfiche. **Subscriptions:** 40 journals and other serials. **Services:** Interlibrary loans; copying; limited searches for information on plastics, alcohols and certain industrial chemicals and processes. **Publications:** Restricted company reports, monthly.

★14470★
U.S. INFORMATION AGENCY - LIBRARY (Soc Sci)†
400 C St., S.W.   Phone: (202) 655-4000
Washington, DC 20024   Jeanne R. Zeydel, Agency Libn.
Founded: 1955. **Staff:** Prof 18; Other 17. **Subjects:** International affairs, Americana, area studies, communication. **Special Collections:** Russian (17,000 volumes); agency historical collection (5000 volumes). **Holdings:** 74,000 books; 26,200 bound periodical volumes; 775 VF drawers of

clippings and documents; 465 VF drawers of classified documents; 90,500 microforms. **Subscriptions:** 430 journals and other serials; 14 newspapers. **Services:** Interlibrary loans; library not open to public. **Automated Operations:** Computerized cataloging. **Computerized Information Services:** DIALOG, OCLC, SDC, New York Times Information Service, NEXIS. **Publications:** Acquisition list (3) - for internal distribution only. **Special Indexes:** Index to Agency Program Materials.

★14471★
U.S. INFORMATION AGENCY - LIBRARY PROGRAM DIVISION (Info Sci)
301 4th St., S.W., Rm. 324   Phone: (202) 485-2932
Washington, DC 20547   Robert Murphy, Dir.
Holdings: 828,255 books; periodicals, documents, microforms and AV materials. **Remarks:** Agency functions as service headquarters for 131 I.A. libraries in 81 countries abroad, and also provides support to library programs in 27 Binational Centers. Holdings listed above represent combined resources. **Formerly:** Its Office of the Associate Directorate for Educational & Cultural Affairs.

U.S. INFORMATION CENTER FOR THE UNIVERSAL DECIMAL CLASSIFICATION
See: University of Maryland, College Park

★14472★
UNITED STATES INFORMATION SERVICE - LIBRARY SERVICE (Soc Sci)
150 Wellington St., 3rd Fl.   Phone: (613) 238-5335
Ottawa, ON, Canada K1P 5A4   Brenda Brady, Supv.Libn.
Founded: 1960. **Staff:** Prof 2. **Subjects:** United States - politics and government, legislation and policy; Canadian/American relations. **Special Collections:** United States Code Annotated; Code of Federal Regulations; selected U.S. Government publications; current speeches. **Holdings:** 3000 books and government documents; 14 VF drawers of clippings; telephone directories of major U.S. cities. **Subscriptions:** 93 journals and other serials. **Services:** Interlibrary loans; locates addresses and backgrounds of U.S. departments and institutions; provides information on U.S. laws, legislation and documents; service open to public. **Computerized Information Services:** DIALOG. Performs free searches for selected users. **Staff:** Kyle Malone, Ref.Libn.

U.S. INSTITUTE OF ADMINISTRATION AND DEFENSE INFORMATION SCHOOL
See: U.S. Army Soldier Support Center - Main Library

★14473★
U.S. INTERAGENCY ADVANCED POWER GROUP - POWER INFORMATION CENTER (Sci-Tech; Energy)
Franklin Research Center
20th & Race Sts.   Phone: (215) 448-1034
Philadelphia, PA 19103   Joyce E. Michelfelder, Dp.Dir.
Founded: 1960. **Staff:** Prof 4; Other 4. **Subjects:** Electrochemistry; electromagnetics; mechanics; thermoelectrics; chemical, nuclear and solar energy; magnetohydrodynamics; superconductivity. **Holdings:** 3800 project briefs and project reports. **Services:** Center open to public with agency approval. **Automated Operations:** Mechanized retrieval. **Publications:** Project Briefs. **Special Indexes:** Indexes to briefs, quarterly and annual indexes.

★14474★
U.S. INTERNAL REVENUE SERVICE - LAW LIBRARY (Law)†
Internal Revenue Service Bldg., Rm. 4324
1111 Constitution Ave., N.W.   Phone: (202) 566-6342
Washington, DC 20224   Anne B. Scheer, Libn.
Founded: 1917. **Staff:** Prof 8; Other 9. **Subjects:** Federal tax law, international taxation, accounting, management, economics. **Special Collections:** Historical collection of Internal Revenue publications and tax returns; legislative histories of all Internal Revenue acts and related statutes. **Holdings:** 100,000 volumes. **Subscriptions:** 300 journals and other serials; 8 newspapers. **Services:** Interlibrary loans (to government agencies only); library open to government employees only on official business. **Automated Operations:** Computerized cataloging. **Computerized Information Services:** LEXIS, OCLC. **Networks/Consortia:** Member of FEDLINK. **Publications:** Library Bulletin, monthly. **Also Known As:** IRS.

★14475★
U.S. INTERNATIONAL TRADE COMMISSION - LIBRARY (Soc Sci)
701 E St., N.W.   Phone: (202) 523-0013
Washington, DC 20436   Barbara J. Pruett, Chf., Lib.Div.
Founded: 1917. **Staff:** Prof 6; Other 7. **Subjects:** U.S. trade policy, international trade, foreign trade statistics, tariffs. **Holdings:** 77,500

volumes. **Subscriptions:** 2200 journals and other serials. **Services:** Interlibrary loans except for legislative histories; copying (fee); library open to public. **Computerized Information Services:** OCLC, DIALOG, LEGI-SLATE, New York Times Information Service. **Networks/Consortia:** Member of FEDLINK. **Publications:** Selected current acquisitions, monthly - to staff and by request. **Staff:** Hennie R. Schneider, Ref.Libn.; Beth Root, Tech.Serv.

★14476★
U.S. INTERSTATE COMMERCE COMMISSION - LIBRARY (Soc Sci)†
Twelfth & Constitution Ave., N.W., Rm. 3392   Phone: (202) 275-7328
Washington, DC 20423   Doris E. Watts, Libn.
Founded: 1894. **Staff:** Prof 2; Other 1. **Subjects:** Transportation, U.S. transportation history, finance, law, federal regulation, economics, valuation, administrative law, accounting, statistics. **Holdings:** 94,000 books and bound periodical volumes; 18 files of pamphlets and unbound materials; 46 files of Congressional materials. **Subscriptions:** 95 journals and other serials. **Services:** Interlibrary loans; library open to public for reference use only. **Publications:** Acquisitions bulletin, bimonthly.

★14477★
U.S. LEAGUE OF SAVINGS INSTITUTIONS - LIBRARY (Bus-Fin)
1709 New York Ave., N.W.   Phone: (202) 637-8920
Washington, DC 20006   Katherine Harahan, Libn.
Staff: Prof 1; Other 2. **Subjects:** Savings and loans, economics. **Special Collections:** Savings and loan congressional items; general historical data. **Holdings:** 8000 books. **Subscriptions:** 200 journals and other serials; 15 newspapers. **Services:** Interlibrary loans; library open to public with librarian's permission. **Computerized Information Services:** LEGI-SLATE.

U.S. LIBRARY OF CONGRESS
See: Library of Congress

★14478★
UNITED STATES LIFESAVING ASSOCIATION - LIBRARY & INFORMATION CENTER (Med)
3650 5th Ave.   Phone: (619) 291-2620
San Diego, CA 92103   Byron Wear, Natl.Exec.Dir.
Founded: 1964. **Staff:** Prof 1. **Subjects:** Open-water lifeguarding, rescue procedures, first aid and resuscitation, ocean environment, marine safety, flood rescue procedures. **Special Collections:** Films and photographs of open-water lifeguard subjects; lifeguard manuals from United States and World Lifesaving. **Holdings:** 500 books; 50 bound periodical volumes; 2000 other cataloged items; 500 emergency services pamphlets; 1000 U.S. Lifesaving Magazines; 1000 lifesaving photographs; 100 reports. **Subscriptions:** 15 journals and other serials. **Services:** Interlibrary loans; copying; library open to public. **Automated Operations:** Computerized acquisitions. **Publications:** Annual Reports; Emergency Services, annual; Lifeguarding and Marine Safety; Beach Information. **Remarks:** Sponsors the American Lifesaving Emergency Response Team (A.L.E.R.T.) to respond to floods and water disasters throughout the United States.

★14479★
U.S. MARINE CORPS - CAMP H.M. SMITH LIBRARY (Mil)
Bldg. 27   Phone: (808) 477-6348
Honolulu, HI 96861   Evelyn Mau, Libn.
Founded: 1966. **Staff:** Prof 1; Other 2. **Subjects:** Marine Corps. **Special Collections:** Military Occupational Specialty Instruction Courses. **Holdings:** 10,000 books; cassette tapes; phonograph records. **Subscriptions:** 60 journals and other serials; 8 newspapers. **Services:** Interlibrary loans; library not open to public.

★14480★
U.S. MARINE CORPS - CAMP PENDLETON LIBRARY SYSTEM (Mil)
Marine Corps Base
1122 E St.   Phone: (619) 725-5104
Camp Pendleton, CA 92055   Patrick J. Carney, Lib.Dir.
Founded: 1950. **Staff:** Prof 3; Other 14. **Subjects:** Military art and science. **Holdings:** 98,378 books and bound periodical volumes; 22 VF drawers of pamphlets; 49,058 microforms; 115 films; 1897 phonograph records. **Subscriptions:** 636 journals and other serials; 27 newspapers. **Services:** Interlibrary loans; copying; library open to public for reference use only on request. **Automated Operations:** Computerized cataloging. **Networks/Consortia:** Member of San Diego Greater Metropolitan Area Library Council (METRO). **Publications:** Library Bulletin, irregular - for internal distribution only. **Remarks:** Maintains 3 base branch libraries and a bookmobile. **Staff:** Raul P. Fernandez, Asst.Dir; Mrs. Vernese B. Thompson, Cons.

★14481★
U.S. MARINE CORPS - EDUCATION CENTER - JAMES CARSON BRECKINRIDGE LIBRARY & AMPHIBIOUS WARFARE RESEARCH FACILITY (Mil)
Marine Corps Development &
Education Command   Phone: (703) 640-2248
Quantico, VA 22134   David C. Brown, Adm.Libn.
Founded: 1928. **Staff:** Prof 3; Other 5. **Subjects:** Military art and science, history, naval art and science, political and social science. **Special Collections:** Amphibious operations; Marine Corps; federal documents depository, 1967 to present. **Holdings:** 60,000 books and bound periodical volumes; 4500 unbound periodicals; 3700 serial publications in microform; 4000 documents; 7000 other printed materials; 100 tapes and phonograph records. **Subscriptions:** 380 journals and other serials; 10 newspapers. **Services:** Interlibrary loans; copying; library open to public by permission. **Automated Operations:** Computerized cataloging. **Computerized Information Services:** OCLC. **Networks/Consortia:** Member of FEDLINK. **Publications:** New Acquisitions List, bimonthly; Current Contents of Selected Military Periodicals, monthly - both limited official distribution. **Staff:** Mary J. Porter, Ref.Libn.; Patricia Salchert, Acq.; JoAnn H. Payne, Cat.

★14482★
U.S. MARINE CORPS - EL TORO AIR STATION LIBRARY (Mil)
Bldg. 280   Phone: (714) 651-3474
Santa Ana, CA 92709-5007   Marianna Clark, Hd.Libn.
Staff: Prof 1; Other 5. **Subjects:** History, military science, biography, social science. **Special Collections:** Early California history; Marine Corps and military aviation history. **Holdings:** 55,000 books and bound periodical volumes; 1 file cabinet of maps; 2 file cabinets of pamphlets; 19,000 volumes in microform; microfiche. **Subscriptions:** 340 journals and other serials; 13 newspapers. **Services:** Interlibrary loans; copying; library open to military personnel and families and to Civil Service personnel on base.

★14483★
U.S. MARINE CORPS - HISTORICAL CENTER LIBRARY (Hist; Mil)†
Washington Navy Yard, Bldg. 58   Phone: (202) 433-4253
Washington, DC 20374   Lt.Col. P.A. Forbes, Hd.Sup.Br.
Staff: Prof 1; Other 1. **Subjects:** U.S. Marine Corps history, history of amphibious warfare, general naval and military history. **Special Collections:** Marine-published periodicals and newspapers; Marine Corps doctrinal publications; personal papers of famous figures in Marine Corps history. **Holdings:** 25,000 books; 500 bound periodical volumes; 6500 pamphlets; 5000 maps; 500 reels of microfilm; 1987 shelf feet of miscellaneous research papers. **Services:** Interlibrary loans; copying; library open to public. **Special Catalogs:** Marine Corps Historical Publications Catalog. **Staff:** Evelyn A. Englander, Libn.; Patricia Morgan, Lib.Asst.

★14484★
U.S. MARINE CORPS - KANEOHE AIR STATION LIBRARY (Mil)
Bldg. 219   Phone: (808) 257-3583
Kaneohe Bay, HI 96863   Murray R. Visser, Supv.Libn.
Founded: 1951. **Staff:** Prof 3; Other 6. **Subjects:** Military history, U.S. Marine Corps. **Special Collections:** Hawaiiana; children's literature (1271 volumes). **Holdings:** 30,000 books; 26,480 microforms; 8854 paperback books; 10,131 miscellaneous items in VF drawers; 1166 phonograph records. **Subscriptions:** 154 journals and other serials; 11 newspapers. **Services:** Interlibrary loans; copying; library open to military dependents and to civilians who work on base. **Special Catalogs:** Leatherneck index, 1962-1980; Marine Corps Gazette Index, 1952-1980. **Staff:** Kerstin Fien, Lib.Techn.; Cindy Smith, Lib.Techn.

★14485★
U.S. MARINE CORPS - LOGISTICS BASE, ALBANY, GA - TECHNICAL LIBRARY (Sci-Tech; Mil)
                                                     Phone: (912) 439-6470
Albany, GA 31704   John Larry Nesmith, Libn.
Founded: 1966. **Staff:** 1. **Subjects:** Physical science, engineering, ordnance, electronics, military science. **Special Collections:** Marine Corps publications. **Holdings:** 25,000 books; 40,000 military specifications and standards on microfilm; 200 Army handbooks and bulletins. **Subscriptions:** 40 journals and other serials. **Services:** Interlibrary loans; library not open to public. **Automated Operations:** Computerized acquisitions.

★14486★
U.S. MARINE CORPS - MARINE BAND LIBRARY (Mus)
Marine Barracks
Eighth & Eye Sts., S.E.   Phone: (202) 433-4298
Washington, DC 20390   Frank P. Byrne, Jr., Chf.Libn.
Staff: Prof 6. **Subjects:** Band music, orchestra music, instrumental

ensembles, national anthems, piano music, dance band. **Special Collections:** Band archives; The John Philip Sousa Collection. **Holdings:** 600 books; 36,000 pieces of sheet music. **Services:** Library open to public with director's approval.

★14487★

U.S. MARITIME ADMINISTRATION - NATL. MARITIME RESEARCH CENTER - STUDY CENTER (Sci-Tech; Trans)

Kings Point, NY 11024   Phone: (516) 482-8200
                                         Rayma Feldman, Sr.Info.Spec.
Founded: 1973. **Staff:** Prof 2; Other 3. **Subjects:** Ship operations and structures, ship simulation, navigation safety, maritime training, mariner performance, bridge design, shipping economics. **Holdings:** 1200 books; 2700 periodical volumes; 9000 reports and serials. **Subscriptions:** 250 journals and other serials. **Services:** SDI; center open to public by appointment. **Publications:** Acquisitions List, irregular. **Staff:** Elinor Haber, Info.Spec.

★14488★

U.S. MERCHANT MARINE ACADEMY - SCHUYLER OTIS BLAND MEMORIAL LIBRARY (Trans)

Kings Point, NY 11024   Phone: (516) 482-8200
                                         George J. Billy, Libn.
Founded: 1942. **Staff:** Prof 3; Other 4. **Subjects:** Merchant marine, nautical science, maritime history, marine engineering. **Holdings:** 125,000 books; 12 VF drawers of maritime research reports; 300 maps; 2300 microforms. **Subscriptions:** 1000 journals and other serials. **Services:** Interlibrary loans; copying (limited); library open to public. **Automated Operations:** Computerized cataloging. **Computerized Information Services:** DIALOG. **Networks/Consortia:** Member of Long Island Library Resources Council (LILRC). **Publications:** Acquisitions List, monthly; Library Information Bulletins and Subject Bibliographies, irregular. **Staff:** Stephen R. Wiist, Tech.Serv.Libn.; Marcia Goldberg, Ref.Libn.

★14489★

U.S. NASA - AMES RESEARCH CENTER - DRYDEN FLIGHT RESEARCH FACILITY - LIBRARY (Sci-Tech)

Box 273   Phone: (805) 258-3311
Edwards, CA 93523
Staff: Prof 2. **Subjects:** Flight research, aerodynamics, flight testing and systems, aerospace medicine and human factors, instrumentation, aerostructures, propulsion, data systems. **Holdings:** 3500 books; 2400 bound periodical volumes; audio cassettes, microfiche and film; reports. **Services:** Interlibrary loans; copying; library open to public with restrictions. **Networks/Consortia:** Member of NASA Library Network (NALNET). **Publications:** Accessions list, weekly - on request. **Staff:** Carolyn J. Reese, Libn.; James F. Maher, Libn.

★14490★

U.S. NASA - AMES RESEARCH CENTER - LIBRARY (Sci-Tech)

Moffett Field, Mail Stop 202-3   Phone: (415) 965-5157
Mountain View, CA 94035   Sarah C. Dueker, Chf., Lib.Br.
Founded: 1940. **Staff:** Prof 4; Other 4. **Subjects:** Aeronautics, astrophysics, geophysics, aerospace sciences, life sciences, fluid mechanics and dynamics, computers and simulation, navigation and control, mathematics, physics. **Special Collections:** NACA and NASA documents on microfilm, 1915-1962; Biogenesis and Origin of Life Collection. **Holdings:** 57,000 books; 75,000 bound periodical volumes; 60,000 technical reports; 90,000 technical reports on microfiche. **Subscriptions:** 1045 journals and other serials. **Services:** Interlibrary loans; copying; library open to public. **Automated Operations:** Computerized cataloging. **Computerized Information Services:** NASA/RECON, DIALOG, MEDLINE, RLIN; internal database. **Networks/Consortia:** Member of NASA Library Network (NALNET). **Publications:** Ames Bibliography. **Special Catalogs:** Catalog of NACA and NASA documents on 16mm microfilm, 1915-1962. **Remarks:** Includes the holdings of the Life Sciences Library. **Staff:** Kitty Foutty, Ref.Libn.; Lesley Whitaker, Ref.Libn.; Betty Sherwood, ILL Libn./Bibliog.

★14491★

U.S. NASA - GODDARD INSTITUTE FOR SPACE STUDIES - LIBRARY (Sci-Tech)

2880 Broadway   Phone: (212) 678-5613
New York, NY 10025   Sarah Scott, Lib.Mgr.
Staff: Prof 2; Other 1. **Subjects:** Physics, astronomy, astrophysics, meteorology, remote sensing. **Holdings:** 12,000 books; 7500 bound periodical volumes; 700 technical reports. **Subscriptions:** 250 journals and other serials. **Services:** Library open to institute scientists and staff. **Automated Operations:** Computerized circulation. **Computerized Information Services:** NASA/RECON, DIALOG. **Staff:** Barbara Palmer, Libn.

★14492★

U.S. NASA - GODDARD SPACE FLIGHT CENTER - LIBRARY (Sci-Tech; Comp Sci)†

Greenbelt, MD 20771   Phone: (301) 344-6244
                                Adelaide A. DelFrate, Hd., Lib.Br.
Founded: 1959. **Staff:** Prof 11; Other 14. **Subjects:** Astronomy, physics, climatology, mathematics, computers, communication. **Holdings:** 70,000 books; 40,000 bound periodical volumes; 450,000 NASA reports on microfiche. **Subscriptions:** 900 journals and other serials. **Services:** Interlibrary loans; copying; library open to public. **Automated Operations:** Computerized cataloging and circulation. **Computerized Information Services:** OCLC, DIALOG, SDC, NASA/RECON. **Networks/Consortia:** Member of NASA Library Network (NALNET). **Staff:** John Boggess, Dp.Br.Hd.

★14493★

U.S. NASA - HEADQUARTERS LIBRARY (Sci-Tech)

600 Independence Ave., S.W.
Code NHS-4, Rm. A39   Phone: (202) 453-8545
Washington, DC 20546   Mary Elizabeth Anderson, Libn.
Staff: Prof 6; Other 2. **Subjects:** Aerospace science, technology and policy-related social science, management. **Holdings:** 24,000 books; 5000 bound periodical volumes; 2000 bound volumes of reports; 3000 unbound reports; 800,000 NASA microfiche. **Subscriptions:** 600 journals and other serials. **Services:** Interlibrary loans; library open to public subject to security regulations. **Automated Operations:** Computerized circulation. **Computerized Information Services:** NASA/RECON, OCLC, DIALOG. Performs searches for NASA staff only. **Networks/Consortia:** Member of FEDLINK; NASA Library Network (NALNET). **Staff:** Eleanor Burdette, Ref.Serv.; Barbara Williams, Site Supv.

★14494★

U.S. NASA - JOHN F. KENNEDY SPACE CENTER - LIBRARY (Sci-Tech)

SAN 302 - 9905   Phone: (305) 867-3600
Kennedy Space Center, FL 32899   M. Konjevich, Lib.Mgr.
Founded: 1962. **Staff:** Prof 8; Other 6. **Subjects:** Aerospace sciences. **Special Collections:** Kennedy Space Center Reports; archives; photograph collection. **Holdings:** 26,931 books; 6291 bound periodical volumes; 103,000 technical reports; 900,000 microfiche; 250,310 specifications and standards; 20 VF drawers of pamphlets. **Subscriptions:** 1289 journals and other serials. **Services:** Interlibrary loans (limited); copying (limited); NASA SDI program; library open to public with approval of proper KSC/NASA authority. **Computerized Information Services:** DIALOG, NIH-EPA Chemical Information System, CAS Online, Hazardline, MEDLARS, Chemical Substances Information Network. **Networks/Consortia:** Member of NASA Library Network (NALNET). **Special Indexes:** Shuttle and Cargo Indexes for the Space Transportation System; KSC Index of Specifications and Standards; Index to the Spaceport News. **Staff:** V.A. Rapetti, Chf.Libn.D. Guelzow, Hd., Proc.; M. Rawls, Hd., Rd./Ref.Serv.; W. Cooper, Hd., Docs.; K. Nail, Archv.; L. Lee, Specifications.

★14495★

U.S. NASA - LANGLEY RESEARCH CENTER - TECHNICAL LIBRARY MS 185 (Sci-Tech)†

Hampton, VA 23665   Phone: (804) 827-2786
                              Jane S. Hess, Hd., Tech.Lib.Br.
Founded: 1920. **Staff:** Prof 9; Other 12. **Subjects:** Aerodynamics, aeronautics, physics and chemistry, materials, structural mechanics, mathematics, fluid mechanics, astronomy and astrophysics, electrical and electronic equipment and theory, instrumentation. **Holdings:** 60,000 books; 28,000 bound periodical volumes; 750,000 microfiche; 286,000 reports; 150 audiotapes. **Subscriptions:** 825 journals and other serials. **Services:** Interlibrary loans; library open to public. **Automated Operations:** Computerized cataloging. **Computerized Information Services:** NASA/RECON. **Publications:** New Books and Documents, monthly - for internal distribution only. **Staff:** Sue Seward, Hd., Ref.; Vickie Sweet, Circ./Acq.; Sue Miller, ILL.

★14496★

U.S. NASA - LEWIS RESEARCH CENTER - LIBRARY (Sci-Tech)†

21000 Brookpark Rd.   Phone: (216) 433-4000
Cleveland, OH 44135   Dorothy Morris, Chf., Lib.
Founded: 1942. **Staff:** Prof 4; Other 7. **Subjects:** Aeronautics, energy, space technology. **Holdings:** 50,000 books; 20,000 bound periodical volumes; 180,000 research reports; 95,000 military and federal specifications; 800,000 microfiche; 304 theses on microfilm; 1500 microcards. **Subscriptions:** 1000 journals and other serials; 6 newspapers. **Services:** Interlibrary loans; copying; translation; literature searching; SDI literature program (all except interlibrary loan are for employees only); library open to qualified persons. **Computerized Information Services:** Mechanized

retrieval. **Staff:** Susanne Oberc, Ref.Libn.; Leona Jarabek, Ref.Libn.; Sandra Crowley, Ref.Libn.

★14497★
U.S. NASA - LYNDON B. JOHNSON SPACE CENTER - TECHNICAL LIBRARY (Sci-Tech)
Houston, TX 77058
Phone: (713) 483-4048
Martin P. McDonough, Lead Libn.
Founded: 1962. **Staff:** Prof 4; Other 4. **Subjects:** Space sciences, space vehicles, life sciences, astronomy, astrophysics, navigation and guidance, telemetry, mathematics, physics. **Holdings:** 59,000 books; 15,000 bound periodical volumes; 220,000 technical reports; 530,000 microfiche. **Subscriptions:** 436 journals and other serials. **Services:** Interlibrary loans; library not open to public. **Automated Operations:** Computerized circulation and reference. **Computerized Information Services:** NASA/RECON, OCLC. **Publications:** User's Guide - available upon request. **Staff:** Robert L. Phelps, Ref.Libn.; Barbara Middlebrook, Ref.Libn.; Laura Chiu, Cat./Ser.Libn.

★14498★
U.S. NASA - MSFC LIBRARY (Sci-Tech)
Code AS24L
Marshall Space Flight Ctr., AL 35812
Phone: (205) 453-1880
Annette K. Tingle, Lib.Mgr.
Founded: 1960. **Staff:** Prof 1; Other 2. **Subjects:** Space flight, astronautics, solar energy, space processing, engineering, science. **Holdings:** 3000 books; 500 bound periodical volumes; 80,000 documents (paper); 1 million NASA microfiche; NASA Information Center (Freedom of Information). **Subscriptions:** 170 journals and other serials. **Services:** Library not open to public. **Computerized Information Services:** DIALOG, NASA/RECON, SDC. **Networks/Consortia:** Member of NASA Library Network (NALNET).

★14499★
U.S. NASA - NATL. SPACE TECHNOLOGY LABORATORIES - RESEARCH LIBRARY (Sci-Tech)
NSTL Station, MS 39529
Phone: (601) 688-3244
Mary Meighen, Chf.Libn.
Founded: 1964. **Staff:** Prof 2; Other 2. **Subjects:** Remote sensing, computers, cryogenics, electronics, environmental science and technology, marine science, space technology. **Holdings:** 10,000 books; 3000 reports. **Subscriptions:** 160 journals and other serials. **Services:** Interlibrary loans; copying; library open to public on request. **Automated Operations:** Computerized book catalog. **Computerized Information Services:** BRS, NASA/RECON, DIALOG, OCLC. **Networks/Consortia:** Member of FEDLINK.

★14500★
U.S. NASA - WALLOPS FLIGHT CENTER - TECHNICAL LIBRARY (Sci-Tech)
Wallops Island, VA 23337
Phone: (804) 824-3411
Jane N. Foster, Lib.Adm.
Founded: 1959. **Staff:** Prof 2; Other 2. **Subjects:** Aerospace, electronics, mathematics, engineering, technology, physics. **Holdings:** 20,200 books; 4290 bound periodical volumes; 642,190 microfiche; 26,000 full size copies of technical reports. **Subscriptions:** 423 journals and other serials. **Services:** Interlibrary loans; library open to public by appointment. **Computerized Information Services:** NASA/RECON. **Publications:** Booster (new books list), 4/year - for internal distribution only.

★14501★
U.S. NATL. ARBORETUM - LIBRARY (Sci-Tech)
3501 New York Ave., N.E.
Washington, DC 20002
Phone: (202) 475-4815
Staff: Prof 1; Other 1. **Subjects:** Botany, taxonomy, floristics, horticulture, gardening, genetics, plant breeding. **Special Collections:** Nursery and seed trade catalogs (15 VF drawers); floral prints; early photographs of U.S. Department of Agriculture Plant Exploration trips; U.S. Department of Agriculture photographs of agricultural practices of early 20th century; Bonsai; Ikebana; U.S. Plant Patent File (4500); Carlton R. Ball Collection on Salix (25 volumes); Arie F. den Boer manuscripts on crabapples (967 folders). **Holdings:** 5500 books; 1500 bound periodical volumes; 15 VF drawers of pamphlets and clippings. **Subscriptions:** 200 journals and other serials. **Services:** Interlibrary loans to National Agricultural Library only; SDI; library open to public for on-site research. **Automated Operations:** Computerized cataloging. **Computerized Information Services:** DIALOG, OCLC. **Remarks:** Library is a branch of the National Agricultural Library of the U.S. Department of Agriculture.

★14502★
U.S. NATL. ARCHIVES & RECORDS SERVICE - FEDERAL ARCHIVES AND RECORDS CENTER, REGION 1 (Hist)
380 Trapelo Rd.
Waltham, MA 02154
Phone: (617) 647-8100
Clifford Amsler, Jr., Dir.
Staff: Prof 2; Other 2. **Subjects:** Noncurrent permanent federal government

records for agencies located in Vermont, New Hampshire, Massachusetts, Connecticut, Rhode Island and Maine. **Holdings:** 14,000 cubic feet of records of federal agencies in New England, 1789-1962. Records include those of U.S. District and Circuit Courts, U.S. Court of Appeals, customs and Coast Guard activities, Naval Shore Establishments inclding Boston and Portsmouth, NH naval shipyards, Bureau of Public Roads, U.S. Army Corps of Engineers and War Manpower Commission (World War II), 35,000 reels of National Archives microfilm publications; U.S. Census reports for 1790-1910 (microfilm). **Services:** Copying; center open to public. **Publications:** Research Opportunities at the Federal Archives and Records Center - Archives Branch. **Staff:** James K. Owens, Chf.Archv.; Stanley Tozeski, Archv.

★14503★
U.S. NATL. ARCHIVES & RECORDS SERVICE - FEDERAL ARCHIVES AND RECORDS CENTER, REGION 2 (Hist)
Bldg. 22-MOT Bayonne
Bayonne, NJ 07002
Phone: (201) 858-7251
O.R. Whitelock, Dir.
Founded: 1950. **Subjects:** Permanently valuable records of federal agencies in New York State, New Jersey, Puerto Rico and The Virgin Islands (1790-1978). **Holdings:** 50,000 cubic feet of archives; 35,000 reels of National Archives microfilm. **Services:** Copying; center open to public for research. **Staff:** Joel Buckwald, Chf., Archv.Br.; Anthony J. Fantozzi, Archv.

★14504★
U.S. NATL. ARCHIVES & RECORDS SERVICE - FEDERAL ARCHIVES AND RECORDS CENTER, REGION 3 (Hist)
5000 Wissahickon Ave.
Philadelphia, PA 19144
Phone: (215) 951-5588
Charles T. Glessner, Dir.
Founded: 1952. **Staff:** Prof 36. **Subjects:** Archives and records of federal agencies located in Pennsylvania, Delaware, Maryland, Virginia and West Virginia. **Special Collections:** Regional Archives Holdings (26,000 cubic feet of records of U.S. District Court, U.S. Court of Appeals for 3rd and 4th Circuit, U.S. Corps of Engineers, Bureau of Census, National Park Service, Bureau of Mines, U.S. Attorneys and Marshals, Bureau of Customs and Internal Revenue Service). **Holdings:** 564,330 cubic feet of federal government archives and records; 12,500 reels of microfilm. **Services:** Copying; center open to public with restrictions, dependent on agency regulations. **Special Catalogs:** List of microfilm holdings; list of textual record holdings. **Staff:** Dr. Robert J. Plowman, Regional Archv.; Joseph J. Sheehan, Archv.

★14505★
U.S. NATL. ARCHIVES & RECORDS SERVICE - FEDERAL ARCHIVES AND RECORDS CENTER, REGION 4 (Hist)
1557 St. Joseph Ave.
East Point, GA 30344
Phone: (404) 763-7474
Thomas G. Hudson, Dir.
Founded: 1950. **Staff:** Prof 7; Other 35. **Subjects:** Inactive records (1716-1978) of the Federal Government from field offices and courts in North Carolina, South Carolina, Tennessee, Kentucky, Georgia, Florida, Alabama, Mississippi. **Special Collections:** Records of World War I Selective Service System for the entire United States; Regional Archives (35,000 cubic feet and 28,000 reels of microfilm); records of the Corps of Engineers, the Office of Price Administration and the War Manpower Commission. **Holdings:** 950,000 cubic feet of records. **Services:** Copying; center open to public. **Publications:** Research Opportunities and list of microfilm available, biennial - distributed to mailing list. **Special Catalogs:** Catalog of Federal Court records; shelf list finding aids on material in regional archives and in Records Center. **Staff:** Gayle P. Peters, Regional Archv.; Charles R. Reeves, Archv.; Mary Ann Hawkins, Archv.

★14506★
U.S. NATL. ARCHIVES & RECORDS SERVICE - FEDERAL ARCHIVES AND RECORDS CENTER, REGION 5 (Hist)
7358 S. Pulaski Rd.
Chicago, IL 60629
Phone: (312) 581-7816
Peter W. Bunce, Chf., Archv.Br.
Founded: 1969. **Staff:** Prof 2; Other 2. **Subjects:** Inactive and noncurrent Federal Government records for Illinois, Wisconsin, Michigan, Indiana, Ohio and Minnesota. **Special Collections:** U.S. Circuit and District Court records, 1806-1963; Army Corps of Engineers, 1833-1951; records from the Bureau of Indian Affairs field offices, 1870-1952; Internal Revenue Service field office records, 1890-1917; Immigration and Naturalization Service; index to Chicago-area naturalizations, 1840-1950; records of the Argonne National Laboratory, 1946-1970; U.S. Circuit Court of Appeals, 6th and 7th circuits, 1891-1955; War Manpower Commission field office records, 1941-1945; Bureau of Fish and Wildlife field office records, 1880-1969; Soil Conservation Service field office records, 1953-1959; U.S. Attorneys precedent case files, 1905-1971; Chinese immigration case files, 1894-1940; duplicate copies of naturalizations in Chicago municipal courts, 1871-1906; War Assets Administration records, 1945-1952; U.S. Coast Guard

unit logs, 1959-1981; Federal Highway Administration records, 1920-1960; Bureau of Marine Inspection and Navigation, 1850-1968; U.S. Public Health Service, Cleveland Marine Hospital, 1878-1922; Agricultural Research Service records, 1937-1966. **Holdings:** 44,400 cubic feet of records; 35,000 reels of microfilm. **Services:** Copying; center open to public with restrictions. **Computerized Information Services:** NARS A-1 (internal database). **Publications:** Research Opportunities; Microfilm List No. 3 - both available on request. **Staff:** W. Kenneth Shanks, Archv.

★14507★
U.S. NATL. ARCHIVES & RECORDS SERVICE - FEDERAL ARCHIVES AND RECORDS CENTER, REGION 6 (Hist)
2306 E. Bannister Rd.   Phone: (816) 926-7271
Kansas City, MO 64131   Patrick Borders, Ctr.Dir.
Founded: 1951. **Staff:** Prof 21; Other 25. **Subjects:** Noncurrent administrative and program records accessioned from Federal Agencies in the states of Iowa, Nebraska, Kansas and Missouri, including pre-1900 records from the Bureau of Customs, Geological Survey, Internal Revenue Service, the Forest Service, U.S. Coast Guard, U.S. Attorneys and Marshals, and the Weather Bureau; Bureau of Indian Affairs Reservations located in the present states of North and South Dakota, Minnesota, Nebraska, and Kansas (1850-1965); United States District and Territorial Courts (1824-1965). **Holdings:** 625,800 cubic feet. **Services:** Copying; microfilming; reference service; center open to genealogical researchers. **Special Catalogs:** In-house archives inventories and shelf lists. **Staff:** Linda M. Stubbs, Chf., Operations Br.; R. Reed Whitaker, Chf., Archv.Br.

★14508★
U.S. NATL. ARCHIVES & RECORDS SERVICE - FEDERAL ARCHIVES AND RECORDS CENTER, REGION 7 (Hist)
501 Felix at Hemphill, Bldg. 1
Box 6216   Phone: (817) 334-5525
Fort Worth, TX 76115   Kent Carter, Chf., Archv.Br.
Founded: 1951. **Staff:** Prof 3; Other 2. **Subjects:** Inactive records of U.S. government agencies in Texas, Oklahoma, Arkansas, New Mexico, and Louisiana. **Special Collections:** U.S. census reports, 1790-1900; index to civil war records; passenger records from various ports; Bureau of Indian Affairs records from the state of Oklahoma. **Holdings:** 24,000 cubic feet of records; 30,000 reels of microfilm. **Services:** Copying; archives open to public except for restricted records. **Staff:** Overnice C. Wilks, Archv.Techn.

★14509★
U.S. NATL. ARCHIVES & RECORDS SERVICE - FEDERAL ARCHIVES AND RECORDS CENTER, REGION 8 (Hist)
Denver Federal Center, Bldg. 48   Phone: (303) 234-3187
Denver, CO 80225
Founded: 1951. **Staff:** Prof 5; Other 30. **Subjects:** Inactive and archival records of the federal government for Arizona, Colorado, Montana, Wyoming, North Dakota, South Dakota, New Mexico, and Utah. **Holdings:** 625,000 cubic feet of noncurrent records; 13,000 cubic feet of archives. **Services:** Copying; reference service to federal agencies and researchers; center open to public.

★14510★
U.S. NATL. ARCHIVES & RECORDS SERVICE - FEDERAL ARCHIVES AND RECORDS CENTER, REGION 9 (Hist)
24000 Avila Rd.   Phone: (714) 831-4220
Laguna Niguel, CA 92677   Kenneth F. Rossman, Dir.
Staff: Prof 3; Other 3. **Subjects:** Inactive and noncurrent Federal Government records for Arizona, Clark County, Nevada and Southern California. **Special Collections:** Pre-presidential materials of Richard Nixon; National Archives microfilm publications of national significance; records of Bureau of Indian Affairs, Bureau of Land Management, Bureau of Customs, U.S. District Courts. **Holdings:** 10,011 cubic feet. **Services:** Copying; center open to public with restrictions. **Staff:** Fred W. Klose, Archv.

★14511★
U.S. NATL. ARCHIVES & RECORDS SERVICE - FEDERAL ARCHIVES AND RECORDS CENTER, REGION 9 (Hist)
1000 Commodore Dr.   Phone: (415) 876-9009
San Bruno, CA 94066   Michael Anderson, Chf., Archv.Br.
Founded: 1969. **Staff:** Prof 2; Other 3. **Subjects:** Archival records of the Federal Government in Nevada (except Clark County), Northern California, Hawaii, and the Pacific Ocean areas. **Special Collections:** Records of the government of American Samoa; records of the Bureau of Indian Affairs (California and Nevada). **Holdings:** 16,000 cubic feet of archives (original records); 20,000 reels of microfilm. **Services:** Copying; center open to public. **Publications:** Research Opportunities, Chinese Studies in Federal Records, and Microfilm Publications Concerning Spanish Private Land Grant Claims.

★14512★
U.S. NATL. ARCHIVES & RECORDS SERVICE - FEDERAL ARCHIVES AND RECORDS CENTER, REGION 10 (Hist)
6125 Sand Point Way   Phone: (206) 442-4502
Seattle, WA 98115   David Piff, Chf., Archv.Br.
Founded: 1969. **Staff:** 4. **Subjects:** Inactive records of agencies of the Federal Government for Washington, Oregon, Idaho, Alaska, and Montana; Bureau of Customs; Bureau of Land Management; Bureau of Indian Affairs; U.S. Army Corps of Engineers; U.S. District Courts. **Special Collections:** Sir Henry S. Wellcome Papers (Metlakahtla, Alaska controversy). **Holdings:** 20,000 cubic feet of records; 40,000 reels of microfilm. **Services:** Copying; center open to public with restrictions. **Publications:** Preliminary Inventories; Special Lists; Guide to Seattle Archives Branch (1977). **Staff:** Joyce Justice, Archv.

★14513★
U.S. NATL. ARCHIVES & RECORDS SERVICE - LIBRARY AND PRINTED ARCHIVES BRANCH (Hist)
Eighth & Pennsylvania Ave., N.W.   Phone: (202) 523-3049
Washington, DC 20408   Nancy V. Menan, Chf.
Founded: 1934. **Staff:** Prof 8; Other 9. **Subjects:** United States and federal administrative history; archival administration; records management. **Special Collections:** Archival administration and records management collection (158 linear feet). **Holdings:** Containing over 180,000 items, it is composed of three major collections. The first consists of commercially published books and periodicals primarily on the subject of United States history. The second is a special collection of archival administration and records management materials which are shelved in boxes and arranged according to a classification scheme specially designed for use in the National Archives Library. The third collection consists of Federal Government Publications housed in a closed stack area and arranged by the Superintendent of Documents classification system. A limited number of genealogical materials owned by the library are housed in the microfilm research room for use along with census microfilms. These items are identified in the library's main card catalog by a red strip across the top of the catalog card. Printed archive holdings consist of the Publications of the U.S. Government (Record Group 287) dating from 1789 (2.4 million items). **Subscriptions:** 451 journals and other serials. **Services:** Interlibrary loans (on library holdings only); copying; library open to public with research pass. **Automated Operations:** Computerized cataloging and acquisitions. **Computerized Information Services:** OCLC. **Networks/ Consortia:** Member of FEDLINK. **Remarks:** A reference telephone number is (202) 523-3286.

★14514★
U.S. NATL. ARCHIVES & RECORDS SERVICE - NATL. ARCHIVES (Hist)
Eighth & Constitution Ave., N.W.   Phone: (202) 523-3218
Washington, DC 20408   Dr. Robert M. Warner, U.S. Archv.
Founded: 1934. **Subjects:** Permanently valuable records of the Federal Government of the United States (1774 to present) consisting of 2 million cubic feet. **Special Collections:** 6 million still pictures including Mathew C. Brady Collection; Printed Archives Branch; cartographic records consisting of 5 million items. **Holdings:** 100,000 reels of motion picture film; 200,000 reels of microfilm; 80,000 sound recordings; 2 million books and pamphlets. **Services:** Interlibrary loans; copying; archives open to public. **Publications:** Publications of the National Archives and Records Service. **Special Catalogs:** Finding aids, guides, exhibition catalogs, instructional materials.

★14515★
U.S. NATL. ARCHIVES & RECORDS SERVICE - NATL. ARCHIVES - CARTOGRAPHIC & ARCHITECTURAL BRANCH (Geog-Map)
8th & Pennsylvania Ave., N.W.   Phone: (703) 756-6700
Washington, DC 20408   William H. Cunliffe, Chf.
Staff: Prof 9; Other 15. **Subjects:** Maps, charts, aerial photographs, architectural drawings, engineering plans and related records produced or acquired by federal agencies as part of their official activities, including material relating to military operations, explorations, public land surveys, and various civil works. **Holdings:** 2 million maps and charts; 10 million aerial photographs; 250,000 architectural drawings and engineering plans; 500 cubic feet of survey field notebooks and census enumeration district descriptions. **Services:** Copying; information relating to holdings is provided in response to written requests; persons wishing to examine records are admitted to search room after obtaining a card of admission. **Publications:** Guides, inventories and lists - limited supply is available for free distribution to libraries. **Remarks:** Library is located at 841 S. Pickett St., Alexandria, VA. **Staff:** Charles E. Taylor, Supv., Projects; John Dwyer, Supv., Ref.Serv.

★14516★

U.S. NATL. ARCHIVES & RECORDS SERVICE - NATL. ARCHIVES - MOTION PICTURE, SOUND, & VIDEO BRANCH (Aud-Vis)

7th St. & Pennsylvania Ave., N.W.   Phone: (202) 523-3063
Washington, DC 20408   William Murphy, Br.Chf.

Staff: Prof 1; Other 5. **Special Collections:** Ford Film Collection; Universal Newsreel; March of Time newsreel; National Public Radio Collection; Mile Ryan Phonoarchive; League of Nations; American Town Meeting of the Air; Longines Chronoscope; Harmon Foundation; Country Music Time; ABC Radio Collection. **Holdings:** Figures not available for motion pictures, sound recordings, and videotapes. **Services:** Copying; branch open to public by appointment for reference use. **Computerized Information Services:** INFOCEN (internal database). **Staff:** Charles De Arman, Supv.Libn.

★14517★

U.S. NATL. ARCHIVES & RECORDS SERVICE - NATL. AUDIOVISUAL CENTER - INFORMATION SERVICES SECTION (Aud-Vis)

                                                Phone: (301) 763-1896
Washington, DC 20409   John McLean, Dir.

Subjects: Alcohol, drugs, business and government management, career education, environment, energy conservation, foreign language instruction, industrial safety, information science, nursing, science, special and vocational education, consumer education, engineering, dentistry, medicine, emergency medical services, fire/law enforcement, flight/meteorology, social sciences, space. **Holdings:** 13,000 titles of slide sets, audiotapes, filmstrips, multimedia kits, video cassettes, 16mm films. **Subscriptions:** 60 journals and other serials. **Services:** Center open to public by appointment. **Automated Operations:** Computerized cataloging. **Computerized Information Services:** DAVIS system. **Publications:** Selected Audiovisuals Produced by the U.S. Government, 1984; information lists in 20 areas - free upon request. **Remarks:** Requests for loan information should be sent to the Information Services Section. **Staff:** Diana M. Wade, Hd., Info.Serv.

★14518★

U.S. NATL. ARCHIVES & RECORDS SERVICE - NATL. PERSONNEL RECORDS CENTER (Mil)

9700 Page Blvd.   Phone: (314) 263-7201
St. Louis, MO 63132   David L. Petree, Dir.

Subjects: Service and medical records of persons who have served in the Armed Forces, records of noncurrent organizations which have been a part of the military establishment, personnel and medical records of former federal employees. **Holdings:** 1.5 million cubic feet of military personnel records (MPR); 1.5 million cubic feet of civilian personnel records (CPR). **Remarks:** The National Personnel Records Center (MPR) maintains and services the records of separated military personnel of the Army dating from 1912; Navy dating from 1885; Air Force dating from 1947; Marine Corps dating from 1893; Coast Guard dating from 1906. The National Personnel Records Center (CPR) maintains and services the personnel and medical records of former federal employees; it is located at 111 Winnebago St., St. Louis, MO 63118. **Staff:** Paul D. Gray, Asst.Dir., MPR; Delbert A. Bishop, Asst.Dir., CPR.

U.S. NATL. ARCHIVES & RECORDS SERVICE - PRESIDENTIAL LIBRARIES
See: U.S. Presidential Libraries

★14519★

U.S. NATL. ARCHIVES & RECORDS SERVICE - STILL PICTURE BRANCH (Aud-Vis; Hist)

Pennsylvania Ave. at 8th St., N.W.   Phone: (202) 523-3236
Washington, DC 20408   Joe D. Thomas, Chf.

Staff: Prof 3. **Subjects:** Archival photograph files of U.S. Federal Government agencies. Includes American and world cultural, social, environmental, economic, technological and political history of a nongovernmental nature, as well as activities of military and civilian government agencies; historical photographs of precursors of contemporary government activity. **Special Collections:** Included in the wide-ranging files are historical photographs from such agencies as: American Commission for the Protection and Salvage of Artistic and Historic Monuments in War Areas, 1943-1946 (German destruction of monuments; vandalism of historic buildings; architectural damage caused by war activities in Europe and Japan; works of art); Department of Defense, 1775-1957 (Army, Navy, Air Force, and Marine Corps personnel, activities, installations, ordnance and transport; includes Revolutionary War, Mathew Brady Civil War photographs, western exploration, surveys, settlement, minor military expeditions, Spanish-American War, World War I, history of flight, scenic photographs, recruiting and war loan posters, effects of atomic bombing of Japan, occupation of Germany and Japan and U.S. Navy photographs of World War II and the Korean War); Harmon Foundation Collection of Photographs, 1922-1966 (art works by black American and African artists; prominent black Americans; foreign art objects; activities of blacks on campuses of southern colleges; exhibits of black artists'

works and art workshops); Department of the Interior, 1850-1973 (geological surveys; western land development; coastal fishing; wildlife; power, irrigation and soil conservation projects; national parks and recreation; U.S. territories; Indian affairs; Antarctic exploration; Bureau of Mines activities and Russell Lee photographs of coal mining activities in 1946); NASA, 1920-1965 (history of aviation and rocketry research and development; lunar surface photographs); Tennessee Valley Authority, 1933-1941 (dams, scenery, and recreational areas; Lewis Hine photographs of families forced to leave their land); Department of the Treasury, 1917-1977 (posters for war bonds and E bonds campaigns; stills from World War I promotional movies; Bureau of Engraving and printing activities); Office of War Information, 1940-1950 (World War II military operations and U.S. home front; U.S. and foreign posters; international conferences and personalities; views of American life and culture for foreign distribution). **Holdings:** 5 million black and white original and copy photographs, glass negatives, unprinted film negatives, color photograph prints, color transparencies and negatives, stereograms, posters, postcards, artworks, and photographs of artworks and graphics. **Services:** Copying; most material available for editorial reproduction (some copyrighted, some restricted), some for advertising purposes; branch open to public for reference use only. **Publications:** List of government agencies with photographic holdings in the Still Picture Branch - available upon request. **Staff:** Barbara Burger, Archv.; Betty Hill, Archv.; Ed McCarter, Archv.; Jonathan Heller, Archv.

★14520★

U.S. NATL. ARCHIVES & RECORDS SERVICE - WASHINGTON NATL. RECORDS CENTER (Hist)

4205 Suitland   Phone: (301) 763-7000
Suitland, MD 20409   Ferris E. Stovel, Dir.

Founded: 1950. **Subjects:** Records of U.S. Government agencies in the District of Columbia, Maryland, Virginia and West Virginia. **Holdings:** 3 million cubic feet of records.

★14521★

U.S. NATL. BUREAU OF STANDARDS - ALLOY PHASE DIAGRAM DATA CENTER (Sci-Tech)

Bldg. 223, Rm. B-150   Phone: (301) 921-2917
Washington, DC 20234   K.J. Bhansali, Dir.

Staff: Prof 5; Other 2. **Subjects:** Alloy phase stability and phase diagrams, metallurgy, metal physics, magnetism, electronic structures, density of states, physical properties of alloys. **Holdings:** Collection of alloy phase diagram evaluations and related compilations. **Subscriptions:** 20 journals and other serials. **Services:** Center open to public with restrictions. **Publications:** NBS Alloy Data Center, NBS Tech Note 464, 1968; NBS ADC Permuted Materials Index, NBS Special Publication 324, 1971; NBS ADC Author Index, NBS-OSRDB-70-2, 1971; Soft X-ray Spectra of Metallic Solids: Critical Review of Selected Systems and Annotated Spectral Index, NBS Special Publication 369, 1974; Alloy Phase Diagram Data, Materials Science Engineering: 24, 1, 1976; Metallic Shifts in NMR, Progress in Materials Science 20, parts 1, 2, 3 and 4, 1977; Applications of Phase Diagrams in Metallurgy and Ceramics (proceedings of workshop); NBS Special Publication 496, 1978; Numerical Physical Property Data for Metal Hydrides Utilized for Hydrogen Storage, Hydrogen Energy System, 1978; Bulletin of Alloy Phase Diagrams, bimonthly. **Special Indexes:** Compilations of Binary Ti- Al- and Fe-based alloy phase diagrams. **Staff:** Dr. Joanne L. Murray, Metallurgist; D.J. Kahan, Metallurgist; M.E. Read, Metallurgist; Dr. L.H. Bennet, Metallurgist.

★14522★

U.S. NATL. BUREAU OF STANDARDS - ATOMIC ENERGY LEVELS DATA CENTER (Energy)

Physics Bldg., Rm. A155   Phone: (301) 921-2011
Washington, DC 20234   Dr. William C. Martin, Physicist

Staff: Prof 3. **Subjects:** Atomic energy levels and spectra. **Holdings:** 7000 reprints of pertinent papers on atomic energy levels and spectra. **Services:** Copying; center open to public. **Automated Operations:** Computerized cataloging. **Publications:** Bibliography on Atomic Energy Levels and Spectra, quadrennial - to users of the Data Center; Compilations of Atomic Energy Levels, 1-2/year. **Special Catalogs:** Current card catalog on atomic spectra which covers information not yet published in bibliographies. **Staff:** Dr. J. Sugar, Physicist; Arlene F. Musgrove, Tech.Info.Spec.

★14523★

U.S. NATL. BUREAU OF STANDARDS - CHEMICAL THERMODYNAMICS DATA CENTER (Sci-Tech)

Chemistry Bldg., Rm. A158
Washington, DC 20234   David Garvin, Mgr.

Subjects: Chemical thermodynamics, molecular parameters, correlation of physical properties. **Holdings:** 250 books; 117 bound periodical volumes; 33 reels of microfilm; 26.5 meters of unbound journals; microfilm file of papers on experiments (96,000). **Services:** Center open to public. **Automated Operations:** Computerized acquisitions. **Computerized Information Services:** DIALOG, SDC. **Publications:** NBS Tables of Chemical Thermodynamic Properties. **Special Indexes:** Index to thermochemical measurements coded by substance and property measured (card, 250,000 entries, with computer tape backup); bibliography of papers on thermochemical and related measurements (60,000 entries). **Staff:** Vivian B. Parker, Sr. Data Anl.; R.L. Nuttall, Data Anl.; R.H. Schumm, Data Anl.; D. Neumann, Data Anl.

★14524★

U.S. NATL. BUREAU OF STANDARDS - DATA CENTER ON ATOMIC LINE SHAPES AND SHIFTS
Bldg. 221, Rm. A267
Washington, DC 20234
Subjects: Spectral line broadening, atomic line shifts, line shifts and line shapes. **Holdings:** 3000 papers on line broadening and shifts (1889 to 1981). **Remarks:** Presently inactive.

★14525★

U.S. NATL. BUREAU OF STANDARDS - DATA CENTER ON ATOMIC TRANSITION PROBABILITIES (Sci-Tech)
A267 Physics Bldg.   Phone: (301) 921-2071
Washington, DC 20234   Dr. W.L. Wiese, Dir.
Founded: 1960. **Staff:** Prof 3. **Subjects:** Atomic transition probabilities. **Holdings:** Complete and up-to-date files on publications on atomic transition probabilities (4000 articles). **Services:** Numerical data and bibliographies provided on atomic transition probabilities; center open to public. **Automated Operations:** Computerized cataloging. **Networks/Consortia:** Member of National Standard Reference Data System (NSRDS). **Publications:** Bibliographies and critically-evaluated data tables. **Staff:** G.A. Martin, Physicist; J.R. Fuhr, Physicist.

★14526★

U.S. NATL. BUREAU OF STANDARDS - FIRE RESEARCH INFORMATION SERVICES (Sci-Tech)
Bldg. 224, Rm. A252
Natl. Bureau of Standards   Phone: (301) 921-3249
Washington, DC 20234   Nora H. Jason, Project Ldr.
Founded: 1971. **Staff:** 2. **Subjects:** Fire research and safety, combustion, combustion toxicology, arson, fabric flammability, fire modeling, fire suppression, building fires. **Holdings:** 400 books and bound periodical volumes; 25,000 technical reports and conference proceedings. **Subscriptions:** 115 journals and other serials. **Services:** Interlibrary loans; services open to public. **Computerized Information Services:** Online systems. **Publications:** Fire Research Publications, annual.

★14527★

U.S. NATL. BUREAU OF STANDARDS - FUNDAMENTAL CONSTANTS DATA CENTER (Sci-Tech)
Bldg. 220, Rm. B258   Phone: (301) 921-2701
Washington, DC 20234   Dr. Barry N. Taylor, Chf.
Founded: 1970. **Staff:** Prof 1. **Subjects:** Fundamental constants, precision measurement. **Holdings:** 7500 journal article reprints dating to late 1960s. **Services:** Center not open to public. **Publications:** Preprints on Precision Measurement and Fundamental Constants (listing of preprints and published papers), quarterly.

★14528★

U.S. NATL. BUREAU OF STANDARDS - ION KINETICS AND ENERGETICS DATA CENTER (Sci-Tech)
A265 - Chemistry   Phone: (301) 921-2783
Washington, DC 20234   Dr. Sharon G. Lias, Dir.
Founded: 1963. **Staff:** 2. **Subjects:** Ionization potentials, appearance potentials, heats of formation of positive ions, proton affinity, electron affinity, ion-molecule reaction rate constants. **Holdings:** 6000 reprints. **Services:** Center open to public. **Publications:** A Bibliography on Ion-Molecule Reactions, NBS Technical Note 291; Ionization Potentials, Appearance Potentials, and Heats of Formation of Gaseous Positive Ions, NSRDS-NBS 26; Energetics of Gaseous Ions, J. Phys. Chem. Ref. 6, Suppl. 1 (1977); The Measurement of Ionization and Appearance Potentials, International J. Mass Spectro. Ion Phys 20, 139 (1976); Ionization Potential and Appearance Potential Measurements, NSRDS-NBS 71 (1971-1981); Evaluated Gas Basicities and Proton Affinities (1984).

★14529★

U.S. NATL. BUREAU OF STANDARDS - LIBRARY (Sci-Tech)
E106 Administration Bldg.   Phone: (301) 921-3451
Washington, DC 20234   Patricia W. Berger, Chf.Info.Rsrcs./Serv.Dir.
Founded: 1901. **Staff:** Prof 11; Other 19. **Subjects:** Physical sciences, metrology, engineering, technology, mathematics. **Special Collections:** Museum collection of scientific apparatus and other memorabilia of the past work of the National Bureau of Standards; oral history collection; energy conservation; history of metrology and standardization; intergovernmental affairs. **Holdings:** 200,000 books and bound periodical volumes; scientific artifacts and historical files, AV collection. **Subscriptions:** 2500 journals and other serials. **Services:** Interlibrary loans; copying (limited); library open to public for reference use only. **Automated Operations:** Computerized cataloging, acquisitions, serials and circulation. **Computerized Information Services:** DIALOG, SDC, BRS, NLM, LEXIS, NEXIS, NIH-EPA Chemical Information System, NASA/RECON, DOE/RECON, ISI, New York Times Information Service, OCLC, Government-Industry Data Exchange Program (GIDEP). **Networks/Consortia:** Member of FEDLINK; Metropolitan Washington Library Council; Interlibrary Users Association. **Publications:** NBS Library Abstract and Index Collection, biennial updates; Data Bases available at NBS Library, biennial updates; NBS Serial Holdings, annual; NBS Library Handbook, biennial updates; An Annotated List of Historically and Scientifically Important Works Published Before 1900 in the Library of the National Bureau of Standards; Foundations of Metrology: Important Early Works on Weights and Measures in the Library of the National Bureau of Standards. **Special Catalogs:** Catalog to literature in the standard reference data field. **Remarks:** Contains the holdings of the defunct National Weights and Measures Library and partial holdings of the Office of Standard Reference Data. **Staff:** Walter Weinstein, Hist.Info.Spec.; Marvin A. Bond, Chf., Lib.Res.Dev.; Sami Klein, Chf., Lib.Info.Serv.

★14530★

U.S. NATL. BUREAU OF STANDARDS - METALLURGY DIVISION - DIFFUSION IN METALS DATA CENTER (Sci-Tech)
Bldg. 223, Rm. A153   Phone: (301) 921-3356
Washington, DC 20234   John R. Manning, Task Leader
Staff: Prof 2; Other 1. **Subjects:** Solid-state diffusion, liquid diffusion, diffusion coatings, oxidation, permeation, electromigration, thermomigration. **Special Collections:** Atomic motion in solids (25,000 documents). **Holdings:** 500 books; 10,000 reports on microfilm. **Services:** Center open to public for reference use only. **Automated Operations:** Computerized cataloging and acquisitions. **Networks/Consortia:** Member of National Standard Reference Data System. **Publications:** Diffusion in Copper and Copper Alloys; The Metallurgy of Copper. **Staff:** Daniel B. Butrymowicz, Dir.

★14531★

U.S. NATL. BUREAU OF STANDARDS - NATIONAL CENTER FOR STANDARDS AND CERTIFICATION INFORMATION (Sci-Tech)
Rm. 617, Administration   Phone: (301) 921-2587
Washington, DC 20234   Sophie J. Chumas, NCSCI Supv.
Founded: 1965. **Staff:** Prof 3; Other 2. **Subjects:** Engineering and product standards, specifications, test methods, analytical methods, codes and recommended practices; certification rules and programs; standardization; international, foreign, state and U.S. Government standards and regulations. **Holdings:** 300 reference books; 30,000 U.S. national and industry standards; 40,000 U.S. Government standards; 3000 state standards; 150,000 foreign national standards; 8000 international standards; 100 unbound articles, pamphlets, reports and monographs; microform files. **Subscriptions:** 120 journals and other serials. **Services:** Referral services; center open to public for reference use only. **Automated Operations:** Computerized indexing. **Computerized Information Services:** BRS; internal databases. **Publications:** List of publications - available on request. **Special Indexes:** KWIC Index of the U.S. voluntary engineering standards. **Remarks:** This collection of standards is the largest and most comprehensive of its kind in the United States. It is located at Quince Orchard Rd. & Rte. 270, Gaithersburg, MD. **Staff:** Sara Wimsatt, Tech.Info.Spec.; Ethelene Lewis, Tech.Info.Spec.

★14532★

U.S. NATL. BUREAU OF STANDARDS - OFFICE OF STANDARD REFERENCE DATA - REFERENCE CENTER (Sci-Tech)
A-320 Physics Bldg.   Phone: (301) 921-2228
Washington, DC 20234   Cynthia A. Goldman, Libn.
Founded: 1963. **Staff:** Prof 2; Other 2. **Subjects:** Physical chemical properties data of substances and systems, thermodynamics and transport data, chemical kinetics, colloid and surface properties, mechanical properties, solid state data, atomic and molecular data, nuclear data. **Holdings:** 2800 books, bound periodical volumes and loose-leaf services; 2000 other cataloged items; 150 volumes of Russian materials. **Subscriptions:** 25 journals and other serials. **Services:** Copying (limited); center open to public.

Networks/Consortia: Member of National Standard Reference Data System (NSRDS). **Publications:** Journal of Physical and Chemical Reference Data (JPCRD), quarterly; NSRDS Reference Data Report, irregular - free upon request; US NSRDS-NBS Series, NBS Special Publications, Technical Notes, Handbooks, Monographs, Russian Translations - all available for government and private publishers; NSRDS Publications List, 1964-1980 - free upon request. **Staff:** Gertrude Sherwood, Info.Spec.

★14533★
U.S. NATL. BUREAU OF STANDARDS - PHASE DIAGRAMS FOR CERAMISTS - DATA CENTER (Sci-Tech)

Washington, DC 20234

Phone: (301) 921-2844
Lawrence P. Cook, Dir.

Staff: Prof 3. **Subjects:** Chemical phase equilibria data (phase diagrams of nonmetallic, inorganic substances). **Services:** Inquiries about phase diagrams are answered. **Publications:** Phase Diagrams for Ceramists, irregular - for sale by American Ceramic Society. **Remarks:** A data collection center sponsored jointly by the U.S. National Bureau of Standards and the American Ceramic Society.

★14534★
U.S. NATL. BUREAU OF STANDARDS - PHOTON AND CHARGED PARTICLE DATA CENTER (Sci-Tech)

Rm. 311, Radiation Physics Bldg., NBS
Gaithersburg, MD 20899

Phone: (301) 921-2685
Martin J. Berger, Mgr.

Founded: 1952. **Staff:** Prof 4. **Subjects:** Electrons, positrons, protons and other charged particles; stopping power and range tables; photon cross sections: Compton scattering atomic and nuclear photoeffect, pair production and atomic form factors; x-ray attenuation coefficients; critical evaluations; radiation dosimetry. **Holdings:** 5 VF drawers of x-ray and Gamma ray total cross section reprints and reports; 20 VF drawers of partial cross sections, applications to shielding, radiometric gauging, x-ray crystallography and other related reprints; 5 VF drawers of photonuclear data reprints. **Services:** Will answer inquiries; library open to public with professional interest in the field. **Networks/Consortia:** Member of National Standard Reference Data System (NSRDS). **Publications:** Evaluation of Collision Stopping Power of Elements and Compounds for Electrons and Positrons (1982); Pair, Triplet and Total Atomic Cross Sections (and Mass Attenuation Coefficients) for 1 MeV - 100 GeV Photons in Elements $Z=1-100$ (1980); Photonuclear Data-Abstract Sheets, 1955-1982 ($Z=1-95$). **Special Indexes:** Photonuclear Data Index (1955-1972, 1973-1981). **Staff:** H.M. Gerstenberg; J.H. HubbellS.M. Seltzer .

★14535★
U.S. NATL. CAPITAL PLANNING COMMISSION - LIBRARY
1325 G St., N.W., Rm. 1018
Washington, DC 20576
Defunct

★14536★
U.S. NATL. DEFENSE UNIVERSITY - DEPARTMENT OF DEFENSE COMPUTER INSTITUTE - DODCI TECHNICAL LIBRARY (Mil; Comp Sci)
Bldg. 175, Rm. 37
Washington Navy Yard
Washington, DC 20374

Phone: (202) 433-3653
Penelope F. Moore, Lib.Techn.

Staff: 1. **Subjects:** Automated information systems, computer hardware and software management. **Holdings:** 1550 books; 150 other cataloged items. **Subscriptions:** 100 journals and other serials; 9 newspapers. **Services:** Interlibrary loans; copying; library open to public. **Computerized Information Services:** Internal database. Performs free searches.

★14537★
U.S. NATL. DEFENSE UNIVERSITY - LIBRARY (Mil)
Fort Lesley J. McNair
4th & P Sts., S.W.
Washington, DC 20319

Phone: (202) 693-8437
J. Thomas Russell, Lib.Dir.

Founded: 1976. **Staff:** Prof 17; Other 17. **Subjects:** Military history and science, industrial mobilization, political science, national security affairs, international relations. **Special Collections:** Papers of Maxwell D. Taylor, Lyman L. Lemnitzer, Andrew J. Goodpaster and Paul D. Adams; speeches on industrial mobilization by J. Carlton Ward, Jr.; early edition of Marshal de Saxe; Libraries of Arthur W. Radford and Hoffman Nickerson (both on military history), and Ralph L. Powell (China). **Holdings:** 205,000 books and bound periodical volumes; 15 VF drawers; 600 linear feet of local history materials. **Subscriptions:** 1100 journals and newspapers. **Services:** Interlibrary loans; library open to public by appointment. **Automated Operations:** Computerized cataloging. **Computerized Information Services:** DIALOG, SDC, NEXIS, OCLC, DTIC. **Networks/Consortia:** Member of FEDLINK. **Publications:** New acquisitions listing, bimonthly - distributed locally and on request; Handbook,

biennial; subject pathfinders and bibliographies, irregular. **Staff:** Howard Hume, Dp.Dir.; John Cornelius, Cat.Libn.; Patricia Altner, Ref.Libn.; Julia Mayo, Chf., Ref.Serv.; Johanna de Onis, Ref.Libn.; Elmer Long, Doc.Libn.; Janice Haines, Acq.Libn.; Alta Davis, Automation Libn.; Elizabeth Slawson, Chf., Acq.; Jane Petitmermet, Ref.Libn.; Susan Lemke, Chf., Spec.Coll.; Mary-Stuart Taylor, Chf., Cat.; Marcia Whipple, Ref.Libn.

U.S. NATIONAL FOUNDATION ON THE ARTS AND THE HUMANITIES
See: National Endowment for the Arts; National Endowment for the Humanities

★14538★
U.S. NATL. HIGHWAY TRAFFIC SAFETY ADMINISTRATION - TECHNICAL REFERENCE DIVISION (Sci-Tech; Trans)
400 7th St., S.W., Rm. 5108
Washington, DC 20590

Phone: (202) 426-2768
Jerome A. Holiber, Chf.

Founded: 1967. **Staff:** Prof 9; Other 2. **Subjects:** Motor vehicle safety, highway safety, alcohol countermeasures for driving safety, automobile occupant protection, emergency medical services. **Special Collections:** NHTSA Research Reports; Federal Motor Vehicle Standards Docket; Compliance Test Reports; Defects Investigation Reports; Recall Campaigns; Crash Test Reports. **Holdings:** 2100 books; 35,000 reports; 500,000 microfiche. **Subscriptions:** 100 journals and other serials. **Services:** Interlibrary loans (limited); copying; division open to public for reference use only. **Computerized Information Services:** DIALOG; Manufacturer's Service Bulletins, Consumer Complaints, Recall Campaigns (internal databases). Performs searches on cost recovery basis plus fee for staff time. **Publications:** Highway Safety Literature, quarterly - by subscription. **Staff:** Dawn Gordy, Tech.Info.Spec.; Clara Wampler, Tech.Info.Spec.; Paulette Twine, Tech.Info.Spec.; Frances Bean, Tech.Info.Spec.; Grace Ogden, Tech.Info.Spec.; Mary Lou Engel, Tech.Info.Spec.; Robert Hornickle, Tech.Info.Spec.; Sylvia Gilbard, Tech.Info.Spec.

★14539★
U.S. NATL. INSTITUTE FOR OCCUPATIONAL SAFETY AND HEALTH - REFERENCE ROOM
5600 Fishers Ln., Rm. 17-50
Rockville, MD 20857
Defunct

★14540★
U.S. NATL. INSTITUTE FOR OCCUPATIONAL SAFETY & HEALTH - TECHNICAL INFORMATION BRANCH (Med)
Robert A. Taft Laboratory
4676 Columbia Pkwy.
Cincinnati, OH 45226

Phone: (513) 684-8321
Vivian Morgan, Sect.Chf.

Founded: 1960. **Staff:** Prof 3; Other 2. **Subjects:** Occupational safety and health, industrial hygiene and toxicology. **Holdings:** 10,000 books; 10,000 bound periodical volumes; 1000 other cataloged items. **Subscriptions:** 800 journals and other serials. **Services:** Interlibrary loans; branch open to public. **Computerized Information Services:** OCLC. **Remarks:** Institute is a branch of U.S. Centers for Disease Control. **Formerly:** Its Clearinghouse for Occupational Safety & Health Information. **Staff:** Roberta Andrews, Libn.; Helen Stafford, Asst.Libn.

U.S. NATL. INSTITUTES OF HEALTH - ARTHRITIS INFORMATION CLEARINGHOUSE
See: Arthritis Information Clearinghouse

★14541★
U.S. NATL. INSTITUTES OF HEALTH - DIVISION OF COMPUTER RESEARCH & TECHNOLOGY - LIBRARY (Comp Sci)
9000 Rockville Pike
Bldg. 12A, Rm. 3018
Bethesda, MD 20205

Phone: (301) 496-1658
Ellen M. Chu, Libn.

Founded: 1966. **Staff:** Prof 1; Other 2. **Subjects:** Computer science, mathematics, statistics, medical information systems, information science. **Holdings:** 6000 books and reports; 800 bound periodical volumes. **Subscriptions:** 200 journals and other serials. **Services:** Interlibrary loans; SDI; library open to public by special permission. **Automated Operations:** Computerized cataloging and circulation. **Computerized Information Services:** DIALOG, MEDLARS, BRS, OCLC. **Networks/Consortia:** Member of FEDLINK; Metropolitan Washington Library Council; Interlibrary Users Association. **Remarks:** Institutes are a part of the U.S. Public Health Service.

U.S. NATL. INSTITUTES OF HEALTH - HIGH BLOOD PRESSURE INFORMATION CENTER
See: High Blood Pressure Information Center

★14542★
U.S. NATL. INSTITUTES OF HEALTH - LIBRARY (Med; Sci-Tech)
9000 Rockville Pike
Bldg. 10, Rm. 1L-25   Phone: (301) 496-2447
Bethesda, MD 20205   Carolyn P. Brown, Chf.
Founded: 1903. **Staff:** Prof 25; Other 37. **Subjects:** Medicine, health
sciences, chemistry, pathology, physiology, biology, physics. **Holdings:**
81,867 books; 194,604 bound periodical volumes; 6869 microforms.
Subscriptions: 3637 journals and other serials. **Services:** Interlibrary loans;
copying; SDI; library open to public for reference use only. **Automated
Operations:** Computerized cataloging, acquisitions, serials and circulation.
Computerized Information Services: DIALOG, BRS, NLM, OCLC, PHILSOM,
SDC. **Networks/Consortia:** Member of FEDLINK. **Publications:** Recent
Additions to the NIH Library, monthly. **Remarks:** Institutes are a part of the
U.S. Public Health Service. **Staff:** Maxine Hanke, Dp.Chf.; Jennylind C.
Boggess, Staff Libn.; Rosalie H. Stroman, Chf., Rd.Serv.Sect.; Lisa C. Wu,
Chf., Tech.Serv.; Jean Soong, Hd., Monographs Proc.; Elsie Cerutti, Chf., Ref.
& Bibliog.Serv; Arthur Wade, Hd., Jnl.Proc.; Patricia A. Barnes, ILL Libn.; Joan
Daghita, Hd., Circ.

★14543★
**U.S. NATL. INSTITUTES OF HEALTH - NATIONAL CANCER INSTITUTE -
CANCER INFORMATION CLEARINGHOUSE** (Med)
Bldg. 31, Rm. 10A18   Phone: (301) 496-4070
Bethesda, MD 20205   Joseph Bangiolo, Dir.
Staff: Prof 2; Other 1. **Subjects:** Cancer - public and patient educational
materials. **Holdings:** 200 books; 200 programs; 800 brochures; 800 AV
items. **Services:** Clearinghouse open to public by request. **Computerized
Information Services:** Cancer Information Clearinghouse database (internal
database).

**U.S. NATL. INSTITUTES OF HEALTH - NATIONAL CANCER INSTITUTE -
FLORIDA STATE COMPREHENSIVE CANCER CENTER**
See: Florida State Comprehensive Cancer Center

★14544★
**U.S. NATL. INSTITUTES OF HEALTH - NATIONAL CANCER INSTITUTE -
FREDERICK CANCER RES. FACILITY - SCIENTIFIC LIB.** (Med)
Box B - Bldg. 426   Phone: (301) 663-7261
Frederick, MD 21701   Michele M. Sansbury, Mgr.
Founded: 1972. **Subjects:** Cancer biology, chemotherapy and allied fields.
Holdings: 15,000 books; 21,000 bound periodical volumes; 3500 periodical
volumes on microfilm. **Subscriptions:** 702 journals and other serials.
Services: Interlibrary loans; library open to public with restrictions.
Automated Operations: Computerized serials. **Computerized Information
Services:** OCLC. **Publications:** Accessions list, monthly; Serial holdings list,
annual.

U.S. NATL. INSTITUTES OF HEALTH - NATIONAL INSTITUTE ON AGING
See: National Institute on Aging

★14545★
**U.S. NATL. INSTITUTES OF HEALTH - NATL. INSTITUTE OF ALLERGY &
INFECTIOUS DISEASES - ROCKY MOUNTAIN LAB. LIB.** (Med)
                                             Phone: (406) 363-3211
Hamilton, MT 59840   Liza Serha Hamby, Libn./Med.Sci.
Founded: 1932. **Staff:** Prof 1. **Subjects:** Medicine, virology, bacteriology,
immunology, entomology, chemistry, parasitology, pathology, microbiology,
biochemistry, biology, sexually transmitted disease. **Holdings:** 11,000 books;
16,000 bound periodical volumes. **Subscriptions:** 266 journals and other
serials. **Services:** Interlibrary loans (limited); copying; library not open to
public. **Computerized Information Services:** MEDLARS.

**U.S. NATL. INSTITUTES OF HEALTH - NATL. INSTITUTE OF ARTHRITIS,
DIABETES, & DIGESTIVE & KIDNEY DISEASES**
See: National Institute of Arthritis, Diabetes, & Digestive & Kidney
Diseases

**U.S. NATL. INSTITUTES OF HEALTH - NATIONAL INSTITUTE OF DENTAL
RESEARCH**
See: National Institute of Dental Research

**U.S. NATL. INSTITUTES OF HEALTH - NATL. INSTITUTE OF
ENVIRONMENTAL HEALTH SCIENCES**
See: National Institute of Environmental Health Sciences

★14546★
**U.S. NATL. INSTITUTES OF HEALTH - NATL. INST. OF NEUROLOGICAL &
COMMUNICATIVE DISORDERS & STROKE - EPILEPSY LIB.** (Med)
Federal Bldg., Rm. 114   Phone: (301) 496-6830
Bethesda, MD 20205   Judith L. Kirsch, Tech.Info.Spec.
Staff: Prof 1; Other 4. **Subjects:** Epilepsy, neurological disorders, anti-
convulsants. **Holdings:** 400 books; 100 bound periodical volumes; 65,000
journal articles. **Subscriptions:** 40 journals and other serials. **Services:**
Interlibrary loans; copying; SDI; library open to public for reference use only.
Computerized Information Services: DIALOG, BRS, NLM. **Special Indexes:**
Epilepsy index, volumes 1-5 (microfiche and hard copy).

U.S. NATL. INSTITUTES OF HEALTH - NATL. LIBRARY OF MEDICINE
See: National Library of Medicine

★14547★
U.S. NATL. LABOR RELATIONS BOARD - LAW LIBRARY (Soc Sci; Law)
1717 Pennsylvania Ave., N.W., Rm. 900   Phone: (202) 254-9055
Washington, DC 20570   Barbara W. Hazelett, Adm.Libn.
Founded: 1937. **Staff:** Prof 3; Other 5. **Subjects:** Law, labor law, labor
relations, labor history, economics, political science. **Special Collections:** The
library is a national resource for the literature of the U.S. primary labor
relations law and related subjects. It includes nearly everything published by
and about the National Labor Relations Board and the National Labor Relations
Act, as amended. **Holdings:** 45,000 volumes. **Subscriptions:** 300 journals
and other serials. **Services:** Interlibrary loans; SDI; library open to public for
reference use only on request. **Automated Operations:** Computerized
cataloging. **Publications:** New Books & Current Labor Articles, bimonthly;
Bibliography of the Labor Management Relations Act, 1947, as amended,
biennial supplements; Recommended Publications for the National Labor
Relations Board Regional Office Libraries, irregular. **Staff:** Julie McCartney,
Tech.Serv.Libn.; Susan H. Simon, Ref.Libn.

★14548★
**U.S. NATL. MARINE FISHERIES SERVICE - AUKE BAY FISHERIES
LABORATORY - FISHERIES RESEARCH LIBRARY** (Sci-Tech; Env-Cons)
Box 210155   Phone: (907) 789-7231
Auke Bay, AK 99821   Paula Johnson, Libn.
Founded: 1960. **Staff:** Prof 1. **Subjects:** Biological sciences, fisheries,
oceanography, water pollution. **Special Collections:** Scandinavian fisheries
periodicals; International North Pacific Fisheries Commission documents;
Pribiloff Island Log Books. **Holdings:** 11,500 books; 2700 bound periodical
volumes; 500 manuscripts; 1500 reprints; 2000 translations; 105 reels of
microfilm; 40 microfiche and microcard titles; 1500 slides. **Subscriptions:**
202 journals and other serials. **Services:** Interlibrary loans; copying; library
open to public. **Computerized Information Services:** DIALOG. **Publications:**
Accession List, quarterly.

★14549★
**U.S. NATL. MARINE FISHERIES SERVICE - FISHERIES LABORATORY -
LIBRARY**
Drawer 1207
Pascagoula, MS 39567
Subjects: Marine resources and research, microbiology, chemistry, fisheries,
fishing gear. **Holdings:** 4000 books; 1800 bound periodical volumes; 60
separates. **Remarks:** Presently inactive.

★14550★
**U.S. NATL. MARINE FISHERIES SERVICE - HONOLULU LABORATORY -
LIBRARY** (Sci-Tech)*
2750 Dole St.
Box 3830   Phone: (808) 946-2181
Honolulu, HI 98612   Hazel S. Nishimura, Libn.
Founded: 1950. **Staff:** Prof 1. **Subjects:** Marine biology, ichthyology
(especially tuna); oceanography. **Holdings:** 3800 books. **Subscriptions:** 200
journals and other serials. **Services:** Interlibrary loans; copying; library open to
qualified researchers for reference only.

★14551★
**U.S. NATL. MARINE FISHERIES SERVICE - MILFORD LABORATORY
LIBRARY** (Sci-Tech; Env-Cons)
212 Rogers Ave.   Phone: (203) 783-4234
Milford, CT 06460
Staff: Prof 1. **Subjects:** Fisheries, marine biology, aquaculture, cytology,
genetics, ecology, microbiology, physiology, biochemistry, microscopy,
statistics, marine pollution. **Special Collections:** Reprints (primarily fisheries
and related subjects); Contributions - Scripps Institution of Oceanography;
Woods Hole Oceanographic Institution Collected Reprints; U.S. Bureau of
Fisheries and NOAA/NMFS documents, 1874 to present. **Holdings:** 2000

books; 1500 bound periodical volumes; 1800 slides. **Subscriptions:** 100 journals and other serials; 7 abstracting services. **Services:** Interlibrary loans; library open to public for reference use only with permission. **Computerized Information Services:** DIALOG.

★14552★
U.S. NATL. MARINE FISHERIES SERVICE - NATIONAL MARINE MAMMAL LABORATORY - LIBRARY (Sci-Tech)*
7600 Sand Point Way N.E., Bldg. 32   Phone: (206) 442-4580
Seattle, WA 98115   Sherry Pearson, Tech.Info.Spec.
Staff: 1. **Subjects:** Marine mammals. **Holdings:** 975 books and bound periodical volumes; 32 VF drawers of reprints. **Subscriptions:** 41 journals and other serials. **Services:** Interlibrary loans.

★14553★
U.S. NATL. MARINE FISHERIES SERVICE - NORTHEAST FISHERIES CENTER - LIBRARY (Sci-Tech; Env-Cons)
                              Phone: (617) 548-5123
Woods Hole, MA 02543   Judith Brownlow, Libn.
Founded: 1893. **Staff:** Prof 2; Other 1. **Subjects:** Fishery biology, marine biology, oceanography, management and law of fisheries. **Special Collections:** Research documents of the former International Commission for the Northwest Atlantic Fisheries (ICNAF) and the current Northwest Atlantic Fisheries Organization (NAFO); annual meeting documents of the International Council for the Exploration of the Sea (I.C.E.S.). **Holdings:** 15,500 books; 16,000 bound periodical volumes; 7000 other cataloged items; 50 films; 2000 slides; scrapbooks of newspaper clippings and photographs (1940-1967); archives. **Subscriptions:** 64 journals and other serials. **Services:** Interlibrary loans; copying; library open to public. **Automated Operations:** Computerized cataloging and serials. **Computerized Information Services:** DIALOG, BRS. **Networks/Consortia:** Member of FEDLINK. **Publications:** Quarterly acquisitions lists. **Special Catalogs:** Collected Reprints of the Northeast Fisheries Center, 1977 to present. **Staff:** Susan P. Rockwell, Lib.Techn.

★14554★
U.S. NATL. MARINE FISHERIES SERVICE - NORTHEAST FISHERIES CENTER - OXFORD LAB. LIBRARY (Sci-Tech; Env-Cons)
                              Phone: (301) 226-5193
Oxford, MD 21654   Susie K. Hines, Libn.
Founded: 1961. **Staff:** Prof 1. **Subjects:** Marine shellfish and fish pathology, marine resource investigations. **Special Collections:** U.S. government publications on fisheries. **Holdings:** 3000 books; 4700 bound periodical volumes; 20,000 reprints and pamphlets. **Subscriptions:** 200 journals and other serials. **Services:** Interlibrary loans; copying; library open to public for reference use only. **Computerized Information Services:** DIALOG, OCLC. **Networks/Consortia:** Member of FEDLINK. **Special Catalogs:** Serials Holding List, annual.

★14555★
U.S. NATL. MARINE FISHERIES SERVICE - NORTHWEST & ALASKA FISHERIES CENTER - LIBRARY (Sci-Tech; Env-Cons)
2725 Montlake Blvd., E.   Phone: (206) 442-7795
Seattle, WA 98112   Patricia Cook, Libn.
Staff: Prof 2. **Subjects:** Fisheries, oceanography, chemistry, biochemistry, food technology, statistics. **Holdings:** 16,000 books and bound periodical volumes; 4000 files of reprints; 3000 files of translations. **Subscriptions:** 220 journals and other serials. **Services:** Interlibrary loans; library open to public for reference use only. **Computerized Information Services:** Online systems. **Staff:** Eleanor Uhlinger, Lib.Techn.

★14556★
U.S. NATL. MARINE FISHERIES SERVICE - SANDY HOOK LABORATORY - LIONEL A. WALFORD LIBRARY (Sci-Tech; Env-Cons)
                              Phone: (201) 872-0200
Highlands, NJ 07732   Claire L. Steimle, Libn.
Founded: 1961. **Staff:** Prof 1; Other 1. **Subjects:** Fisheries, environmental problems, marine invertebrates, biological and chemical oceanography, plankton behavior, microbiology, New York Bight. **Special Collections:** Fishery Bulletins and Reports to Commissioner of Fisheries; Benedict Collection of Sportfishing (131 volumes); Special Pollution Collection (150 volumes). **Holdings:** 6000 books; 4500 bound periodical volumes; 14,000 documents. **Subscriptions:** 300 journals and other serials. **Services:** Interlibrary loans; copying (limited); bibliographies; library open to public by appointment.

★14557★
U.S. NATL. MARINE FISHERIES SERVICE - SOUTHEAST FISHERIES CENTER - BEAUFORT LABORATORY LIBRARY (Sci-Tech)†
                              Phone: (919) 728-4595
Beaufort, NC 28516   Ann Bowman Hall, Libn.
Founded: 1949. **Staff:** Prof 1. **Subjects:** Fishes, fisheries, marine biology, radioecology, oceanography. **Holdings:** 13,000 books and bound periodical volumes; 100 linear feet of unbound materials. **Subscriptions:** 380 journals and other serials. **Services:** Interlibrary loans; library open to public with restrictions. **Automated Operations:** Computerized cataloging. **Computerized Information Services:** DIALOG, SDC, BRS. **Networks/Consortia:** Member of U.S. Natl. Oceanic & Atmospheric Administration - Southeastern Area Resources Cooperative (NOAASARC). **Publications:** List of Serials.

★14558★
U.S. NATL. MARINE FISHERIES SERVICE - SOUTHEAST FISHERIES CENTER - GALVESTON LABORATORY LIBRARY (Sci-Tech; Env-Cons)
4700 Avenue U   Phone: (409) 766-3506
Galveston, TX 77550   Patricia Torrefranca, Libn.
Founded: 1950. **Staff:** Prof 1. **Subjects:** Shrimp research, aquaculture, fishery biology, marine science, oceanography, environmental research and marine ecology. **Holdings:** 4475 books; 883 bound periodical volumes; 33,000 unbound journals; 6475 reprints; 1600 microcards; 13,500 technical abstracts on 3x5 cards; 462 translations. **Subscriptions:** 275 journals and other serials. **Services:** Interlibrary loans; copying (limited); library open to public by appointment. **Publications:** List of Acquisitions.

★14559★
U.S. NATL. MARINE FISHERIES SERVICE - SOUTHEAST FISHERIES CENTER - MIAMI LAB. LIBRARY (Sci-Tech)
75 Virginia Beach Dr.   Phone: (305) 361-4229
Miami, FL 33149   Julianne Josiek, Hd.Libn.
Founded: 1965. **Staff:** Prof 1. **Subjects:** Marine biology, fish, fisheries. **Special Collections:** Reprint collection (7000 concerning fish, fish eggs and larvae). **Holdings:** 15,719 books and bound periodical volumes. **Subscriptions:** 350 journals and other serials. **Services:** Interlibrary loans; copying; library open to public for reference use only on request. **Automated Operations:** Computerized cataloging. **Computerized Information Services:** DIALOG, BRS, OCLC.

★14560★
U.S. NATL. MARINE FISHERIES SERVICE - SOUTHEAST FISHERIES CENTER - PANAMA CITY LAB. - LIBRARY (Sci-Tech; Env-Cons)
3500 Delwood Beach Rd.   Phone: (904) 234-6541
Panama City, FL 32407   Rosalie Vaught, Libn.
Founded: 1962. **Staff:** Prof 1. **Subjects:** Fishery science, marine and fresh water biology, oceanography, zoology, ecology. **Holdings:** 2500 books and bound periodical volumes; 8500 technical reports; 10,000 unbound periodicals and technical reports; 85 dissertations; 8000 reprints. **Subscriptions:** 300 journals and other serials. **Services:** Interlibrary loans; copying; library open to public. **Computerized Information Services:** DIALOG. **Networks/Consortia:** Member of U.S. National Oceanic & Atmospheric Administration Library and Information Network. **Publications:** List of contributions, annual; serials holdings list.

★14561★
U.S. NATL. MARINE FISHERIES SERVICE - SOUTHWEST FISHERIES CENTER - LIBRARY (Sci-Tech; Env-Cons)
Box 271   Phone: (619) 453-2820
La Jolla, CA 92038   Dan Gittings, Libn.
Founded: 1965. **Staff:** Prof 1; Other 1. **Subjects:** Fisheries, oceanography, marine biology. **Holdings:** 2500 books; 12,000 periodical volumes; 9000 pamphlets. **Subscriptions:** 280 journals and other serials. **Services:** Interlibrary loans; copying; library open to public. **Computerized Information Services:** DIALOG, BRS; OCLC. **Remarks:** Figures include Inter-American Tropical Tuna Commission Collection.

★14562★
U.S. NATL. MARINE FISHERIES SERVICE - TIBURON LABORATORY LIBRARY (Sci-Tech; Env-Cons)
3150 Paradise Dr.   Phone: (415) 435-3149
Tiburon, CA 94920   Maureen Woods, Libn.
Founded: 1962. **Staff:** Prof 1. **Subjects:** Marine biology, fishery science, commercial fishing, sport fisheries, oceanography. **Special Collections:** Collection of W.H. Rich on Salmon; Dr. Victor L. Loosanoff Reprint Collection on commercial mollusks; Susumu Kato Shark Reprint Collection on shark taxonomy. **Holdings:** 2800 books; 2700 bound periodical volumes; 12,000 reprints. **Subscriptions:** 250 journals and other serials. **Services:** Interlibrary

loans; library open to public for reference use only. **Automated Operations:** Computerized cataloging and ILL. **Computerized Information Services:** DIALOG, SDC, BRS; OCLC. **Networks/Consortia:** Member of FEDLINK. **Publications:** Occasional reprints.

★14563★
U.S. NATL. MARINE FISHERIES SERVICE - W.F. THOMPSON MEMORIAL LIBRARY (Sci-Tech; Env-Cons)
Box 1638   Phone: (907) 486-3298
Kodiak, AK 99615   Patricia Branson, Libn.
Founded: 1971. **Staff:** 1. **Subjects:** Fisheries, biology, chemistry, fishery food science, Alaska fishing research. **Special Collections:** Collection of W.F. Thompson, leader in Alaska fishery research. **Holdings:** 2500 books; 3300 bound periodical volumes; leaflets, circulars, reports and biological reports. **Subscriptions:** 90 journals and other serials; 5 newspapers. **Services:** Interlibrary loans; copying; library open to public by permission. **Remarks:** The Service may also be reached at (907) 487-4961.

★14564★
U.S. NATIONAL MINE HEALTH AND SAFETY ACADEMY - LEARNING RESOURCE CENTER (Sci-Tech; Educ)
Airport Rd.
Box 1166   Phone: (304) 255-0451
Beckley, WV 25801   Dr. Leslie E. Woelflin, Chf., Lrng.Res.Ctr.
Staff: Prof 2; Other 3. **Subjects:** Mine and industrial safety, industrial health, management, education. **Special Collections:** Audiovisual materials on mine safety. **Holdings:** 8300 books; 705 films; 460 video cassettes; 115,000 microfiche; 729 reels of microfilm; 247 audio cassettes; 326 slide/tape sets; 153 slide sets. **Subscriptions:** 211 journals and other serials; 5 newspapers. **Services:** Copying; SDI; center open to public for reference use only. **Automated Operations:** Computerized cataloging. **Computerized Information Services:** Online systems. **Publications:** Acquisitions list, weekly. **Staff:** Helen B. Caraway, Libn.

U.S. NATIONAL OCEAN SERVICE
See: U.S. Natl. Oceanic and Atmospheric Administration - National Ocean Service

★14565★
U.S. NATL. OCEANIC & ATMOSPHERIC ADMINISTRATION - ASSESSMENT AND INFORMATION SERVICES CENTER (Sci-Tech)
Federal Bldg., Rm. 212   Phone: (314) 875-5263
Columbia, MO 65201   Rita Terry
Staff: 1. **Subjects:** Climatology, ecology, crop production, world food supply, energy consumption. **Holdings:** 100 volumes; raw climatological data; reprint/report file. **Subscriptions:** 75 journals and other serials. **Services:** Center open to public for reference use only. **Automated Operations:** Computerized cataloging.

★14566★
U.S. NATL. OCEANIC & ATMOSPHERIC ADMINISTRATION - ATMOSPHERIC TURBULENCE & DIFFUSION LABORATORY - LIBRARY (Sci-Tech)
Box E   Phone: (615) 576-1236
Oak Ridge, TN 37830   Ruth A. Green
Staff: 1. **Subjects:** Energy production, air pollution, forest meteorology, climatic studies. **Holdings:** 2500 volumes; 6000 technical reports and reprints. **Subscriptions:** 60 journals and other serials. **Services:** Library open to public for reference use only. **Remarks:** The Laboratory is operated for the Department of Energy as a division of the National Oceanic & Atmospheric Administration's Air Resources Laboratory.

★14567★
U.S. NATL. OCEANIC & ATMOSPHERIC ADMINISTRATION - CAMP SPRINGS CENTER
5200 Auth Rd.
Camp Springs, MD 20233
Defunct. Holdings absorbed by its Library and Information Services Division - Main Library.

★14568★
U.S. NATL. OCEANIC & ATMOSPHERIC ADMINISTRATION - CORAL GABLES LIBRARY (Sci-Tech)
Gables 1 Tower, 6th Fl.   Phone: (305) 666-0413
Coral Gables, FL 33146   Robert Ting, Chf.Libn.
Staff: Prof 1. **Subjects:** Tropical meteorology, hurricane meteorology, satellite meteorology. **Special Collections:** Films of clouds and rainband as planes penetrate hurricanes. **Holdings:** 5000 volumes; contractor reports; college, government and private meteorological reports; microfilmed maps and hemispheric information; films of reconnaissance and research flights into

hurricanes; films of clouds and rainband in hurricanes; photopanel films of instrument panel of planes in hurricane flight; film of radar in planes; printouts of processed data on information from hurricane flights. **Subscriptions:** 30 journals and other serials. **Services:** Interlibrary loans; copying; library open to public for reference use only. **Also Known As:** Technical Library for Tropical and Hurricane Meteorology.

U.S. NATL. OCEANIC & ATMOSPHERIC ADMINISTRATION - ENVIRONMENTAL RESEARCH LABORATORIES
See: U.S. Natl. Oceanic & Atmospheric Administration - Mountain Administrative Support Center

★14569★
U.S. NATL. OCEANIC & ATMOSPHERIC ADMINISTRATION - GEOPHYSICAL FLUID DYNAMICS LABORATORY - LIBRARY (Sci-Tech)
Box 308   Phone: (609) 452-6550
Princeton, NJ 08542   Philip Fraulino, Libn.
Founded: 1968. **Staff:** Prof 1. **Subjects:** Meteorology, climatology, oceanography, fluid dynamics. **Special Collections:** Russian monographs on meteorology and climatology (200 volumes); atmospheric sciences collection. **Holdings:** 7500 books; 1500 bound periodical volumes; 3000 technical reports; 50 atlases; 30 films. **Subscriptions:** 100 journals and other serials. **Services:** Interlibrary loans; copying; library open to public. **Automated Operations:** Computerized cataloging and serials. **Computerized Information Services:** DIALOG, OCLC; internal database. **Networks/Consortia:** Member of FEDLINK. **Publications:** GFDL Activities and Plans, annual. **Special Catalogs:** Bibliography of the works of L.S. Gantin, Russian scientist.

★14570★
U.S. NATL. OCEANIC & ATMOSPHERIC ADMINISTRATION - GEORGETOWN CENTER (Sci-Tech)
3300 Whitehaven   Phone: (202) 634-7346
Washington, DC 20235   Ida Lewis
Founded: 1971. **Staff:** Prof 1; Other 1. **Subjects:** Fisheries, marine biology, oceanography. **Holdings:** 9600 books. **Subscriptions:** 600 journals and other serials. **Services:** Interlibrary loans; copying; SDI; center open to public for reference use only. **Automated Operations:** Computerized cataloging. **Computerized Information Services:** Online systems.

★14571★
U.S. NATL. OCEANIC & ATMOSPHERIC ADMINISTRATION - GREAT LAKES ENVIRONMENTAL RESEARCH LABORATORY LIBRARY (Sci-Tech)†
2300 Washtenaw Ave.   Phone: (313) 668-2242
Ann Arbor, MI 48104   Barbara J. Carrick, Libn.
Staff: Prof 1; Other 2. **Subjects:** Great Lakes - hydraulics, hydrology, limnology, limnologic systems, meteorological weather data, physical oceanography, water characteristics, modeling, water quality control; information analysis. **Holdings:** 9000 books; 200 bound periodical volumes; 217 reels of microfilm of Great Lakes Archives, 1841-1952; 12 VF drawers of pamphlets; 124 titles of agency publications in print for sale or interlibrary loan. **Subscriptions:** 210 journals and other serials. **Services:** Interlibrary loans; copying; library open to public for reference use only. **Computerized Information Services:** Online systems. **Publications:** List of publications - available on request.

★14572★
U.S. NATL. OCEANIC & ATMOSPHERIC ADMINISTRATION - LIBRARY AND INFORMATION SERVICES DIVISION - MAIN LIBRARY (Sci-Tech)
6009 Executive Blvd.   Phone: (301) 443-8330
Rockville, MD 20852   Elizabeth J. Yeates, Chf., LISD
Founded: 1846. **Staff:** Prof 15; Other 16. **Subjects:** Geodesy, surveying, oceanography, geophysics, geodetic and hydrographic surveying, photogrammetry, nautical and aeronautical cartography, fisheries, geodetic astronomy, meteorology, climatology, hydrology, atmospheric physics, ocean engineering, mathematics, computer science. **Special Collections:** Rare book collection which includes scientific treatises dating from the 16th and 17th centuries. **Holdings:** 654,000 volumes; 100,100 bound periodical volumes; 100,400 bound documents; 19,500 microfiche; 34,000 reports, maps, charts and data publications. **Subscriptions:** 9040 journals and other serials. **Services:** Interlibrary loans; copying; SDI; provides consultative and technical guidance to 37 NOAA libraries and information centers with highly specialized collections in meteorology, climatology, hydrology, marine biology and fisheries science located throughout the U.S.; library open to public for reference use only. **Automated Operations:** Computerized cataloging, serials and acquisitions. **Computerized Information Services:** DIALOG, SDC, BRS, NEXIS, NLM, LEGI-SLATE, Institute for Scientific Information (ISI), OCLC. **Networks/Consortia:** Member of FEDLINK; U.S. Natl. Oceanic and Atmospheric Administration Library and Information Network. **Publications:** Acquisitions list; list of publications - available on request. **Special Catalogs:**

COM catalog for U.S. Natl. Oceanic and Atmospheric Administration Library and Information Network. **Remarks:** Maintains 4 branches in the Washington, D.C. area, Miami, FL and Seattle, WA. **Staff:** Frances F. Swim, Regional Libs.Coord; Laurie E. Stackpole, Chf., Lib.Serv.Br.

★14573★
U.S. NATL. OCEANIC & ATMOSPHERIC ADMINISTRATION - MIAMI LIBRARY (Sci-Tech)
4301 Rickenbacker Causeway   Phone: (305) 361-4428
Miami, FL 33149   Robert N. Ting, Chf.Libn.
Founded: 1970. **Staff:** Prof 2; Other 1. **Subjects:** Oceanography, tropical meteorology, marine geology, ocean engineering/chemistry, applied mathematics, physics. **Special Collections:** U.S. Coast and Geodetic Survey Report, 1866 to present. **Holdings:** 12,000 volumes; 19,000 technical reports; 750 atlases and symposia; 12,000 microforms; 4000 charts and maps. **Subscriptions:** 180 journals and other serials. **Services:** Interlibrary loans; copying; SDI; library open to public for reference use only. **Automated Operations:** Computerized cataloging. **Computerized Information Services:** Online systems. **Networks/Consortia:** Member of U.S. Natl. Oceanic & Atmospheric Administration - Southeastern Area Resources Cooperative (NOAASARC). **Publications:** New acquisitions list, monthly.

★14574★
U.S. NATL. OCEANIC & ATMOSPHERIC ADMINISTRATION - MOUNTAIN ADMINISTRATIVE SUPPORT CTR. - LIBRARY (Sci-Tech; Comp Sci)
325 Broadway, RAS/MC5   Phone: (303) 497-3271
Boulder, CO 80303   Joan Maier McKean, Chf., Lib.Serv.
Founded: 1954. **Staff:** Prof 8; Other 8. **Subjects:** Mathematics, electronics engineering, atmospheric science, aeronomy, computer science, telecommunications, radio physics, oceanography, marine sciences, astrophysics, cryogenics, radio engineering, physics, astronomy. **Holdings:** 39,070 books; 23,009 bound periodical volumes; 30,337 technical reports; 326,669 titles on microfiche; 175 audio cassettes; 50 video cassettes. **Subscriptions:** 1403 journals and other serials. **Services:** Interlibrary loans; copying; telefacsimile; library open to public for reference use only. **Automated Operations:** Computerized cataloging, acquisitions and circulation. **Computerized Information Services:** DIALOG, SDC, BRS, DOE/RECON, NASA/RECON, DTIC, OCLC. **Networks/Consortia:** Member of FEDLINK; Bibliographic Center for Research, Rocky Mountain Region, Inc. (BCR). **Publications:** TRAC Sheet, monthly; Library Notes, weekly - both for internal distribution only; Periodicals Handbook, every 18 months - available to libraries. **Special Catalogs:** Card catalog for reports acquired before January, 1971; TRACY Catalog (computer printout of technical reports received from January, 1971 to present). **Formerly:** Its Environmental Research Laboratories. **Staff:** Jean Bankhead, Hd., Ref.Serv./ILL; Clara Steele, Cat.Libn.; Jane Watterson, Hd., Circ.Serv.; John Welsh, Sys.Anl.

★14575★
U.S. NATL. OCEANIC & ATMOSPHERIC ADMINISTRATION - NATIONAL CLIMATIC DATA CENTER LIBRARY (Sci-Tech)
Federal Bldg., OA/D542x2   Phone: (704) 258-2850
Asheville, NC 28801   R.L. Money, Chf., User Serv.Br.
Founded: 1962. **Staff:** 1. **Subjects:** Climatology, meteorology, oceanography, mathematics, physics, weather records. **Special Collections:** Past weather records. **Holdings:** 10,455 books; 700 bound periodical volumes; 29 reels of microfilm; 2000 microfiche; 94,000 pamphlets; 8 atmosphere models. **Subscriptions:** 300 journals and other serials. **Services:** Interlibrary loans; copying; library open to public with restrictions. **Computerized Information Services:** DIALOG, SDC, BRS, OCLC. **Networks/Consortia:** Member of U.S. Natl. Oceanic & Atmospheric Administration - Southeastern Area Resources Cooperative (NOAASARC). **Remarks:** Center is part of the National Environmental Satellite Data & information Services. **Staff:** Linda D. Preston, Libn.

U.S. NATL. OCEANIC & ATMOSPHERIC ADMINISTRATION - NATL. MARINE FISHERIES SERVICE
See: U.S. Natl. Marine Fisheries Service

★14576★
U.S. NATL. OCEANIC & ATMOSPHERIC ADMINISTRATION - NATL. OCEAN SERVICE - MAP LIBRARY (Geog-Map)
6501 Lafayette Ave.   Phone: (301) 436-6978
Riverdale, MD 20737   Gordon Allen, Tech.Info.Spec.
Staff: Prof 1; Other 5. **Subjects:** U.S. nautical and aeronautical charts, U.S. and Canadian topographical maps, special maps. **Special Collections:** Retrospective chart products of N.O.S. and its predecessor agencies. **Holdings:** 500,000 cataloged items. **Services:** Copying; library open to public. **Publications:** Lists of new source materials - for internal use. **Special Catalogs:** Book cartobibliographies.

★14577★
U.S. NATL. OCEANIC & ATMOSPHERIC ADM. - NATL. OCEAN SERVICE - PHYSICAL SCIENCE SERVICES SECT. - MAP LIB. (Geog-Map)
    Phone: (301) 436-5766
Riverdale, MD 20737   Henry L. Carter, Act.Chf.
Founded: 1938. **Staff:** Prof 9; Other 5. **Subjects:** Cartographic information. **Special Collections:** Civil War maps (800); early city plans; 19th century nautical charts; 16th, 17th and 18th century historical expedition maps; Great Lakes nautical charts (6500). **Holdings:** 138,000 cartographic publications of the 19th century; 8000 charts in aeronautical chart file, 1927 to present; 22 atlases; 214 American Revolution maps. **Services:** Copying; limited search by written request; library open to public for reference use only. **Publications:** Original and Facsimile Cartographic Treasures; Cartobibliography of Civil War Maps, 1980 - both available on request; Cartobibliography Age of Exploration, 1982. **Special Catalogs:** Summary of National Ocean Service Technical Publications and Charts, 1982. **Staff:** Charles Chettle, Res.Asst.

★14578★
U.S. NATL. OCEANIC & ATMOSPHERIC ADMINISTRATION - NATIONAL OCEANOGRAPHIC DATA CENTER (Sci-Tech)
    Phone: (202) 634-7500
Washington, DC 20235   Edward L. Ridley, Dir.
Founded: 1961. **Staff:** 95. **Subjects:** Oceanography - physical, chemical, biological. **Holdings:** Standard oceanographic data: Nansen cast and bathythermograph data covering the world's oceans; multidisciplinary data from environmental surveys in selected off-shore areas of the U.S.; surface current data and data from environmental buoys off-shore U.S.; and data from special programs such as the Ocean Thermal Energy Conversion (OTEC) and the Nearshore Sediment Transport Study (NSTS). **Subscriptions:** 155 journals and other serials. **Services:** Data from automated data files and information requests; center open to public. **Automated Operations:** Computerized data retrieval and presentation. **Publications:** List of publications available on request. User's Guide to NODC Services (which describes specialized services and products) - free upon request. **Remarks:** Library is located at 2001 Wisconsin Ave. N.W., Page Bldg. One., Washington, DC 20007. Center is part of the National Environmental Satellite Data & Information Services. **Staff:** Irving Perlroth, Data PreparationJames Churgin, Data Serv.

★14579★
U.S. NATL. OCEANIC & ATMOSPHERIC ADMINISTRATION - SEATTLE CENTER (Sci-Tech)
7600 Sand Point Way, N.E., Bin C15700, Bldg. 3   Phone: (206) 527-6241
Seattle, WA 98115   Bruce Keck, Libn.
Founded: 1980. **Staff:** Prof 1; Other 1. **Subjects:** Physical and coastal oceanography, marine pollution, geochemistry, marine meteorology. **Holdings:** 4000 books. **Subscriptions:** 150 journals and other serials. **Services:** Interlibrary loans; copying; SDI; center open to public for reference use only. **Automated Operations:** Computerized cataloging and acquisitions. **Computerized Information Services:** DIALOG, BRS, SDC, NIH-EPA Chemical Information System, NEXIS, LEGI-SLATE, OCLC, Institute for Scientific Information (ISI). **Networks/Consortia:** Member of FEDLINK; U.S. Natl. Oceanic and Atmospheric Administration Library and Information Network.

★14580★
U.S. NATL. OCEANIC & ATMOSPHERIC ADMINISTRATION - SUITLAND CENTER
Federal Bldg. 4, Rm. 3216
Suitland, MD 20233
Defunct

U.S. NATL. OCEANIC & ATMOSPHERIC ADMINISTRATION - WORLD DATA CENTER A
See: World Data Center A

★14581★
U.S. NATL. PARK SERVICE - ABRAHAM LINCOLN BIRTHPLACE NATL. HISTORIC SITE - LIBRARY (Hist)
Rte. 1   Phone: (502) 358-3874
Hodgenville, KY 42748   Gary V. Talley, Chf., Interpretation
Founded: 1916. **Staff:** 4. **Subjects:** Abraham Lincoln. **Special Collections:** Thomas Lincoln Land Records (microfilm and photostats); Lincoln Farm Association Collection (photographs and documents). **Holdings:** 200 books and bound periodical volumes. **Services:** Library open to public with restrictions.

★14582★
U.S. NATL. PARK SERVICE - ALASKA AREA OFFICE - LIBRARY
540 W. 5th Ave.
Anchorage, AK 99501
Defunct. Holdings absorbed by U.S. Dept. of the Interior - Alaska Resources Library.

★14583★
U.S. NATL. PARK SERVICE - ALLEGHENY PORTAGE RAILROAD NATL. HISTORIC SITE - LIBRARY (Trans; Hist)
Lemon House
Box 247
Cresson, PA 16630
Phone: (814) 886-8176
Dean R. Garrett, Chf.
Founded: 1964. **Staff:** Prof 3; Other 3. **Subjects:** Railroad, 1834-1854; transportation and canals of Pennsylvania, 1830-1850; Johnstown Flood of 1889. **Holdings:** 120 volumes; 12 rare documents; old newspaper files. **Services:** Library open to public for reference use only. **Staff:** Lawrence Trombello, Chf.; Joe Nicholson, Park Ranger.

★14584★
U.S. NATL. PARK SERVICE - ANDREW JOHNSON NATL. HISTORIC SITE - LIBRARY (Hist)
College & Depot Sts.
Box 1088
Greeneville, TN 37744-1088
Phone: (615) 474-2006
Edward G. Speer, Park Tech.
Special Collections: Andrew Johnson (65 volumes); The Presidency (21 volumes); Tennessee history (50 volumes); Civil War and Reconstruction history (22 volumes). **Holdings:** 200 books, periodicals, pamphlets and Park Service documents and publications. **Services:** Library open to public for reference use only.

★14585★
U.S. NATL. PARK SERVICE - ANTIETAM NATL. BATTLEFIELD - VISITOR CENTER LIBRARY (Hist)
Box 158
Sharpsburg, MD 21782
Phone: (301) 432-5124
Betty J. Otto, Libn./Cur.
Staff: 1. **Subjects:** Civil War; several regimental histories; Battles of Antietam, South Mountain, September, 1862 and Monocacy, June, 1864. **Special Collections:** Henry Kyd Douglas Collection; NPS and local Washington County publications. **Holdings:** 900 books; 3 VF drawers of periodicals; 6 VF drawers of reports, manuscripts, transcripts and copies of diaries, slides, photographs, news articles and park history; 33 motion pictures; maps. **Services:** Library open to public for reference use only, by appointment.

★14586★
U.S. NATL. PARK SERVICE - APPOMATTOX COURT HOUSE NATL. HISTORICAL PARK - LIBRARY (Hist)
Box 218
Appomattox, VA 24522
Phone: (703) 352-8987
Ronald G. Wilson, Pk.Hist.
Staff: Prof 2; Other 2. **Subjects:** Civil War, history of Park and Village of Appomattox. **Holdings:** 1000 books; 3700 artifacts and maps. **Services:** Library open to public for reference use only. **Special Indexes:** Confederate enlisted men who surrendered at Appomattox (card). **Staff:** Jon Montgomery, Supt.

★14587★
U.S. NATL. PARK SERVICE - ARLINGTON HOUSE, THE ROBERT E. LEE MEMORIAL - LIBRARY (Hist)
Turkey Run Park
McLean, VA 22101
Phone: (703) 557-0613
Agnes D. Mullins, Cur.
Staff: 1. **Subjects:** Robert E. Lee, George W.P. Custis, Arlington House. **Special Collections:** 19th century sheet music. **Holdings:** 500 books; 100 pamphlets; 70 Custis and Lee family and associated family manuscripts. **Services:** Library open to public by appointment. **Remarks:** Library is located at the Arlington National Cemetery, Arlington, VA.

★14588★
U.S. NATL. PARK SERVICE - ASSATEAGUE ISLAND NATL. SEASHORE - LIBRARY (Env-Cons)
Rte. 2, Box 294
Berlin, MD 21811
Phone: (301) 641-1441
Larry G. Points, Chf., Interp.
Staff: 2. **Subjects:** Marine biology, botanical sciences, zoological sciences, geography. **Special Collections:** Research documents and reprint abstracts of seashore environments (150). **Holdings:** 450 books; 5800 color slides of Assateague Island and environs. **Services:** Library open to public with restrictions.

★14589★
U.S. NATL. PARK SERVICE - AZTEC RUINS NATL. MONUMENT - LIBRARY (Hist)
Box U
Aztec, NM 87410
Phone: (505) 334-6174
Founded: 1923. **Staff:** Prof 1. **Subjects:** Archeology, natural history, National Park Service history. **Holdings:** 500 books; 5 VF drawers of maps; pamphlets; 16 volumes of ruins stabilization reports. **Services:** Interlibrary loans; library open to public with restrictions.

★14590★
U.S. NATL. PARK SERVICE - BADLANDS NATL. PARK - LIBRARY (Hist)
Box 6
Interior, SD 57750
Phone: (605) 433-5361
Midge Johnston, Bus.Mgr.
Founded: 1961. **Staff:** 1. **Subjects:** Badlands, Indians of South Dakota, South Dakota. **Holdings:** 1000 books; 500 bound periodical volumes. **Services:** Interlibrary loans; copying; library open to public with restrictions. **Remarks:** Maintained by Badlands Natural History Association.

★14591★
U.S. NATL. PARK SERVICE - BANDELIER NATL. MONUMENT - LIBRARY (Hist)
Phone: (505) 672-3861
Los Alamos, NM 87544
Edward J. Greene, Supv.Pk.Ranger
Staff: 2. **Subjects:** Bandelier National Monument excavations and stabilization; archeology, ethnology and natural history of the Southwest. **Holdings:** 1400 books; 100 pamphlets; 11 VF drawers of early correspondence; 1 box of cassette tapes of guest speakers and oral history; annual and monthly reports of Southwest monuments, 1933-1940; monthly report of superintendent, 1941-1978; unpublished excavation and stabilization reports; excavation maps. **Subscriptions:** 25 journals and other serials; 7 newspapers. **Services:** Library open to researchers by request. **Publications:** Trail Guides for Frijoles Canyon and Tsankawi - for sale.

★14592★
U.S. NATL. PARK SERVICE - BIG HOLE NATL. BATTLEFIELD - LIBRARY (Hist)
Box 237
Wisdom, MT 59761
Phone: (406) 689-3155
Alfred W. Schulmeyer, Supt.
Subjects: Nez Perce War of 1877. **Holdings:** 100 books. **Services:** Library open to researchers.

★14593★
U.S. NATL. PARK SERVICE - BIGHORN CANYON NATL. RECREATION AREA - LIBRARY (Hist)*
Box 458
Fort Smith, MT 59035
Phone: (406) 666-2412
Theo D. Hugs, Park Techn.
Founded: 1967. **Staff:** Prof 1. **Subjects:** Local history, Crow Indian history, ethnology, wildlife, geology, botany, archeology. **Special Collections:** Government reports on Crow Indians of Montana. **Holdings:** 986 books. **Subscriptions:** 31 journals and other serials. **Services:** Interlibrary loans; copying; library open to public.

★14594★
U.S. NATL. PARK SERVICE - BOOKER T. WASHINGTON NATL. MONUMENT - LIBRARY (Hist)
Rte. 1, Box 195
Hardy, VA 24101
Phone: (703) 721-2094
Richard Saunders, Chf.Interp. & Rsrcs.Mgt.
Subjects: Booker T. Washington, black history, local agriculture in the mid-19th century, Appalachian culture. **Special Collections:** Correspondence and documents relating to Burroughs plantation, birthplace of Booker T. Washington. **Holdings:** 600 books; photographs. **Services:** Interlibrary loans; copying (limited); library open to public.

★14595★
U.S. NATL. PARK SERVICE - CABRILLO NATL. MONUMENT - LIBRARY & INFORMATION CENTER (Hist; Env-Cons)†
Box 6670
San Diego, CA 92106
Phone: (714) 293-5450
Founded: 1966. **Subjects:** History - California, Mexico, San Diego; conservation; ecology; lighthouses; marine life; California gray whale. **Holdings:** 1500 books; photographs and slides. **Subscriptions:** 10 journals and other serials. **Services:** Library open for on-site reference use only.

★14596★
U.S. NATL. PARK SERVICE - CAPE COD NATL. SEASHORE - LIBRARY (Env-Cons; Hist)
Marconi Station Site
South Wellfleet, MA 02663
Phone: (617) 349-3785
G. Franklin Ackerman, Chf., Interp.
Founded: 1961. **Staff:** 1. **Subjects:** Ecology, local history, botany, earth

sciences. **Special Collections:** U.S. Life Saving Service annual reports, 1879-1914; Rhodora Journal of the New England Botanical Club (26 volumes). **Holdings:** 2300 books. **Subscriptions:** 33 journals and other serials. **Services:** Interlibrary loans; library open to public for reference use only.

★14597★
U.S. NATL. PARK SERVICE - CAPE HATTERAS NATL. SEASHORE LIBRARY
(Hist; Env-Cons)
Rte. 1, Box 675
Manteo, NC 27954
Phone: (919) 473-2111
Sue Swanson, Sec./Libn.
Founded: 1955. **Staff:** Prof 1. **Subjects:** History and natural history of North Carolina Outer Banks. **Special Collections:** Records and annual reports of U.S. Life-Saving Service. **Holdings:** 3500 books; 100 bound periodical volumes; 4000 items in technical reference file; 200 microforms. **Subscriptions:** 30 journals and other serials. **Services:** Interlibrary loans; library open to public by appointment.

★14598★
U.S. NATL. PARK SERVICE - CAPE LOOKOUT NATL. SEASHORE - LIBRARY
(Env-Cons)
415 Front St.
Box 378
Beaufort, NC 28516
Phone: (919) 728-2121
William T. Springer, Chf., Park Oper.
Founded: 1976. **Staff:** 2. **Subjects:** Seashore ecology, geology, Outer Banks history, marine natural history, barrier island ecology, lighthouses and life-saving, local history. **Holdings:** 2000 volumes. **Subscriptions:** 18 journals and other serials. **Services:** Library open to public for reference use only with permission of park superintendent. **Remarks:** Library located at the District Office, Harken Island, NC. **Staff:** Robert Patton, Interp.Spec.

★14599★
U.S. NATL. PARK SERVICE - CARL SANDBURG HOME NATL. HISTORIC SITE - MUSEUM/LIBRARY (Hist)
Box 395
Flat Rock, NC 28731
Phone: (704) 693-4178
Benjamin Davis, Supt.
Founded: 1969. **Staff:** Prof 2. **Holdings:** 9000 books. **Services:** Library open to public as a museum only. **Remarks:** This historic house contains part of Carl Sandburg's personal working library. **Staff:** Warren R. Weber, Cur.

★14600★
U.S. NATL. PARK SERVICE - CARLSBAD CAVERNS NATL. PARK - LIBRARY
(Sci-Tech)
3225 National Parks Hwy.
Carlsbad, NM 88220
Phone: (505) 885-8884
Robert W. Peters, Interp.Spec.
Staff: 1. **Subjects:** Geology, botany, zoology, paleontology, parks and conservation, regional history. **Holdings:** 3500 books; 100 bound periodical volumes; 850 reprints; 63 boxes. **Subscriptions:** 25 journals and other serials. **Services:** Library open to public for reference use only on request.

★14601★
U.S. NATL. PARK SERVICE - CASTILLO DE SAN MARCOS NATL. MONUMENT & FORT MATANZAS NATL. MONUMENT - LIBRARY (Hist)
1 Castillo Dr.
St. Augustine, FL 32084
Phone: (904) 829-6506
Subjects: Florida's colonial history, 1518-1833, especially the construction and repair of Castillo de San Marcos and Fort Matanzas. **Special Collections:** Spanish and British records concerning Florida's colonial history; East Florida Papers (Spanish military, administrative, ecclesiastical, financial, and personal records of the territory; 175 reels of microfilm total). **Services:** Library open to public by appointment.

★14602★
U.S. NATL. PARK SERVICE - CHACO CANYON NATL. MONUMENT - STUDY LIBRARY (Sci-Tech)
Chaco Star Rte. 4
Box 6500
Bloomfield, NM 87413
Phone: (505) 786-5384
Ellen Boling, Pk.Techn.
Subjects: Chaco and Southwest archeology, Southwest ethnology, geology, botany, zoology. **Special Collections:** Unpublished records of exploration, research, and preservation of the Chaco area. **Holdings:** 1250 books; 300 bound periodical volumes. **Services:** Library not open to public.

★14603★
U.S. NATL. PARK SERVICE - CHACO CENTER - LIBRARY (Sci-Tech)
Box 26176
Albuquerque, NM 87125
Phone: (505) 766-3545
Thomas C. Windes, Supv.Archeo.
Staff: Prof 1; Other 1. **Subjects:** Archeology - North American, Southwestern, Chaco Canyon, U.S. **Special Collections:** R.G. Vivian Archive (3047 professional papers, manuscripts, field notes and other materials).

Holdings: 865 books; 1300 institutional publications; 32,356 photographs and negatives; 4192 color slides; 775 maps. **Services:** Library open to public for reference use only. **Networks/Consortia:** Member of Department of Interior Libraries and Information Service. **Special Indexes:** Subject and proper name indexes to archive.

★14604★
U.S. NATL. PARK SERVICE - CHAMIZAL NATL. MEMORIAL - LIBRARY (Hist)
109 N. Oregon, Suite 1316
Box 722
El Paso, TX 79944
Phone: (915) 541-7780
Richard Razo, Interp.Spec.
Founded: 1967. **Staff:** 1. **Subjects:** Border disputes between U.S. and Mexico, Mexican and Spanish drama, political evolution in Mexico, U.S. and Mexican history, biology. **Holdings:** 1200 books; historic documents and manuscripts (border disputes). **Subscriptions:** 10 journals and other serials. **Services:** Library open to public for reference use only.

★14605★
U.S. NATL. PARK SERVICE - CHEROKEE STRIP LIVING MUSEUM - DOCKING RESEARCH CENTER ARCHIVES LIBRARY (Hist)
S. Summit Street Rd.
Box 230
Arkansas City, KS 67005
Phone: (316) 442-6750
Cheryl Voigtlander, Libn.
Founded: 1981. **Staff:** Prof 1; Other 1. **Subjects:** Local history, genealogy. **Special Collections:** Speeches and pictures of Governor Robert Docking (5 filing cabinets). **Holdings:** 325 books; 1018 bound periodical volumes; 50 pamphlets on historical events; 20 unbound reports; newspapers; 15 patents; maps; pictures; letters; manuscripts; clippings; dissertations; 6 reels of microfilm; 10 tapes. **Services:** Copying; research upon request; library open to public for reference use only. **Remarks:** Library contains the holdings of the Cowley County Genealogical Society.

★14606★
U.S. NATL. PARK SERVICE - CHICKASAW NATL. RECREATION AREA - TRAVERTINE NATURE CENTER LIBRARY (Env-Cons)
Box 201
Sulphur, OK 73086
Phone: (405) 622-3165
Bert L. Speed, Chf.Pk. Interpreter
Staff: 4. **Subjects:** Biological sciences, botany, zoology, American Indians, U.S. history, astronomy, geology, natural resources. **Holdings:** 800 books; 5 boxes of pamphlets; 80 boxes of periodicals. **Subscriptions:** 31 journals and other serials. **Services:** Library open to public.

★14607★
U.S. NATL. PARK SERVICE - COULEE DAM NATL. RECREATION AREA - FORT SPOKANE VISITOR CENTER (Mil; Hist)*
Star Rte., Box 51
Davenport, WA 99122-0051
Phone: (509) 725-2715
Steve Shrader, District Ranger
Founded: 1966. **Staff:** 2. **Subjects:** Military history, 1880-1900; Colville Indian Agency, 1900-1930; history and natural sciences of the Upper Columbia River Valley. **Special Collections:** Artifactual study collection of Fort Spokane. **Holdings:** 5 volumes of copies of historical news articles and diaries; 9 volumes of professional research reports. **Services:** Center open to public for reference use only. **Automated Operations:** Computerized cataloging.

★14608★
U.S. NATL. PARK SERVICE - CRATER LAKE NATL. PARK - LIBRARY (Sci-Tech)
Box 7
Crater Lake, OR 97604
Henry M. Tanski, Jr., Asst.Interp.
Staff: 1. **Subjects:** Geology, botany, zoology, human history. **Holdings:** 1300 books; 100 bound periodical volumes; 6 VF drawers of journal articles and similar material. **Subscriptions:** 17 journals and other serials. **Services:** Library open to researchers in the park who have special need for materials.

★14609★
U.S. NATL. PARK SERVICE - CUMBERLAND GAP NATL. HISTORICAL PARK - LIBRARY (Hist)
Box 840
Middlesboro, KY 40965
Phone: (606) 248-2817
Wes Leishman, Interpretation Chf.
Founded: 1959. **Staff:** 1. **Subjects:** History, folklife, natural history, transportation. **Special Collections:** Hensly Settlement Oral History Collection (on local Appalachian culture; 87 tapes). **Holdings:** 1250 books; 200 bound periodical volumes; 50 documents. **Services:** Library open to public by appointment for research.

★14610★
**U.S. NATL. PARK SERVICE - CUSTER BATTLEFIELD NATL. MONUMENT -
    LIBRARY** (Hist)
Box 39   Phone: (406) 638-2622
Crow Agency, MT 59022   Neil C. Mangum, Park Hist.
Founded: 1952. **Staff:** 2. **Subjects:** Battle of Little Big Horn, George Custer,
Western history, Indian wars. **Special Collections:** Elizabeth B. Custer
Correspondence Collection. **Holdings:** 500 books; 500 bound periodical
volumes; 8000 artifacts, relics and correspondences. **Subscriptions:** 10
journals and other serials. **Services:** Copying; library open to public for
reference use only. **Staff:** Mardell Irene Plainfeather, Park Techn./Hist.

★14611★
U.S. NATL. PARK SERVICE - DE SOTO NATL. MEMORIAL - LIBRARY (Hist)
75th St., N.W.   Phone: (813) 792-0458
Bradenton, FL 33529   Guy L. LaChine, Supv. Park Ranger
Staff: 2. **Subjects:** Spanish exploration, general exploration, American history.
Holdings: 1116 volumes. **Services:** Library open to public for reference use
only by appointment.

★14612★
**U.S. NATL. PARK SERVICE - DEATH VALLEY NATL. MONUMENT -
    REFERENCE AND RESEARCH LIBRARY** (Sci-Tech; Env-Cons)
                                                          Phone: (714) 786-2331
Death Valley, CA 92328   Shirley A. Harding, Cur./Libn.
Founded: 1933. **Staff:** Prof 1; Other 2. **Subjects:** Death Valley geology,
history and research; biological sciences. **Special Collections:** Graduate
theses in the natural sciences prepared from Death Valley data (50 volumes).
Holdings: 3500 books; 50 bound periodical volumes; 60 boxes of pamphlets
and reprints; 55 boxes of unbound periodicals; 3 VF drawers of folders on
National Park System areas. **Subscriptions:** 14 journals and other serials; 7
newspapers. **Services:** Interlibrary loans; copying; library open to public on
written request.

★14613★
U.S. NATL. PARK SERVICE - DENALI NATL. PARK - LIBRARY (Env-Cons)
Box 9   Phone: (907) 683-2294
McKinley Park, AK 99755   Doug Cuillard, Chf. Naturalist
Subjects: Natural history, history. **Holdings:** 1400 books. **Subscriptions:** 10
journals and other serials. **Services:** Library open to public by appointment.

★14614★
**U.S. NATL. PARK SERVICE - DINOSAUR NATL. MONUMENT - QUARRY
    VISITOR CENTER - LIBRARY** (Sci-Tech)†
Box 128   Phone: (801) 789-2115
Jensen, UT 84035   Dennis B. Davies, Chf. Naturalist-Dir.
Founded: 1962. **Staff:** 1. **Subjects:** Paleontology, geology, American history,
zoology, botany, agriculture, range and wildlife management, natural history.
Holdings: 2900 books; 330 bound periodical volumes; 300 reprints.
Subscriptions: 30 journals and other serials. **Services:** Library open to public
on request. **Remarks:** Funding and maintenance costs donated by Dinosaur
Nature Association. **Staff:** Linda L. West, Libn.

★14615★
U.S. NATL. PARK SERVICE - EDISON NATL. HISTORIC SITE - ARCHIVES
    (Sci-Tech; Hist)
Main St. and Lakeside Ave.   Phone: (201) 736-0550
West Orange, NJ 07052   Mary Bowling, Archv.
Founded: 1887. **Subjects:** Invention, science, electricity, botanic research,
chemistry, geology. **Holdings:** 10,000 volumes; 3 million pages of Edison's
personal and laboratory correspondence and documents; business records of
Edison Industries and Thomas Alva Edison, Inc.; 3000 notebooks kept by
Edison and his workers; 9000 photographic negatives. **Services:** Copying
(limited); archives may be consulted by special arrangement only.

★14616★
**U.S. NATL. PARK SERVICE - EFFIGY MOUNDS NATL. MONUMENT -
    LIBRARY** (Sci-Tech)
Box K   Phone: (319) 873-2356
McGregor, IA 52157   Thomas A. Munson, Supt.
Staff: Prof 1. **Subjects:** Archeology, anthropology, ethnology, local history,
natural sciences. **Holdings:** 2100 books. **Subscriptions:** 17 journals and
other serials. **Services:** Library open to public for reference use only.

★14617★
**U.S. NATL. PARK SERVICE - EVERGLADES NATL. PARK - REFERENCE
    LIBRARY** (Env-Cons)†
Box 279   Phone: (305) 245-5266
Homestead, FL 33030
Founded: 1964. **Staff:** Prof 1. **Subjects:** Birds, botany, ecology, national

parks, South Florida area - natural history and water resources. **Holdings:**
6525 books and bound periodical volumes; 10,500 pamphlets and reprints;
635 maps; 945 microforms. **Subscriptions:** 170 journals and other serials.
Services: Interlibrary loans; library open to public for reference use only.

★14618★
**U.S. NATL. PARK SERVICE - FIRE ISLAND NATL. SEASHORE -
    HEADQUARTERS LIBRARY** (Hist; Sci-Tech)
120 Laurel St.   Phone: (516) 289-4810
Patchogue, NY 11772   Neal Bullington, Asst.Chf. Ranger
Staff: 1. **Subjects:** Barrier Island geology, marine biology, oceanography,
history. **Holdings:** 5000 books; 1000 other cataloged items. **Services:**
Copying; library open to public for reference use only.

★14619★
**U.S. NATL. PARK SERVICE - FLORISSANT FOSSIL BEDS NATIONAL
    MONUMENT - LIBRARY** (Hist)
Box 185   Phone: (303) 748-3253
Florissant, CO 80816   Walt Saenger, Chf., Visitor Serv.
Subjects: Geology, paleontology, natural history. **Holdings:** 500 books.
Services: Library open to public upon request.

★14620★
U.S. NATL. PARK SERVICE - FORT DAVIS NATL. HISTORIC SITE - LIBRARY
    (Mil; Hist)
Box 1456   Phone: (915) 426-3225
Fort Davis, TX 79734   Douglas C. McChristian, Supt.
Founded: 1963. **Subjects:** Frontier military history. **Special Collections:**
Colonel Benjamin H. Grierson Manuscript Collection (7000 letters and
documents on microfilm, covering the period 1850-1890). **Holdings:** 1300
books; 100 pamphlets and magazines; 30 frontier military maps (copies); 10
manuscripts and theses; 100 reels of microfilm (records of Fort Davis, papers
of B.H. Grierson). **Services:** Library open to public for reference use only.

★14621★
**U.S. NATL. PARK SERVICE - FORT LARAMIE NATL. HISTORIC SITE -
    LIBRARY** (Hist)
Box 178   Phone: (307) 837-2221
Fort Laramie, WY 82212   Phillip J. Gomez, Park Techn.
Founded: 1955. **Staff:** 1. **Subjects:** Western history, Oregon-California-
Mormon trails, Plains Indians. **Holdings:** 3500 books; 150 reels of microfilm.
Services: Copying; library open to scholars for reference use only.

★14622★
**U.S. NATL. PARK SERVICE - FORT LARNED NATL. HISTORIC SITE -
    LIBRARY** (Hist; Mil)
Rte. 3   Phone: (316) 285-3571
Larned, KS 67550   John B. Arnold, Supt.
Founded: 1966. **Staff:** 1. **Subjects:** Fort Larned, 1859-1878, Plains Indians,
Santa Fe Trail, military history, Indian Wars 1848-1890, museum
conservation and preservation. **Holdings:** 775 books; 75 reels of microfilm;
10 binders of national archives. **Subscriptions:** 10 journals and other serials.
Services: Library open to public by appointment.

★14623★
**U.S. NATL. PARK SERVICE - FORT MC HENRY NATL. MONUMENT -
    LIBRARY** (Mil; Hist)
End of Fort Ave.   Phone: (301) 962-4290
Baltimore, MD 21230   Paul E. Plamann, Hist.
Subjects: Military history of the War of 1812, Battle of Baltimore, history of
Fort McHenry. **Holdings:** 425 volumes; original documents; photostats;
microfilms. **Services:** Library open to public on special request.

★14624★
**U.S. NATL. PARK SERVICE - FORT NECESSITY NATL. BATTLEFIELD -
    LIBRARY** (Hist)
The National Pike   Phone: (412) 329-5512
Farmington, PA 15437   Robert Warren, Supt.
Founded: 1962. **Staff:** 2. **Subjects:** Battle of Great Meadows (July 3, 1754),
French and Indian War, 19th century transportation in western Pennsylvania,
fauna and flora of the region. **Holdings:** 800 books. **Services:** Library open to
public by appointment.

★14625★
U.S. NATL. PARK SERVICE - FORT PULASKI NATL. MONUMENT - LIBRARY
    (Mil; Hist)
Box 98   Phone: (912) 786-5787
Tybee Island, GA 31328   Talley Kirkland, Hist.
Founded: 1924. **Staff:** Prof 1. **Subjects:** Military history, history of Fort

Pulaski, Georgia history, Civil War. **Special Collections:** Complete set of the official records (including Navy records) of the War of the Rebellion. **Holdings:** 400 books; 100 other cataloged items; 500 Civil War photographs of Fort Pulaski and soldiers in it; 200 photographs of 1930s restoration; 100 photographs of other forts and historic sites. **Services:** Interlibrary loans; copying (limited); library open to public with restrictions.

★14626★
U.S. NATL. PARK SERVICE - FORT SUMTER NATL. MONUMENT - LIBRARY (Hist)
1214 Middle St.   Phone: (803) 883-3123
Sullivan's Island, SC 29482   Brien Varnado, Supt.
Founded: 1948. **Staff:** 2. **Subjects:** Civil War, Revolutionary War, Fort Sumter, Fort Moultrie, U.S. Seacoast fortifications, artillery, South Carolina, firearms, conservation. **Special Collections:** War of the Rebellion, Official Records of the Union and Confederate Armies (128 volumes); Naval Records (30 volumes); American Revolution naval documents. **Holdings:** 700 books; 200 bound periodical volumes; 250 maps; 650 pamphlets. **Subscriptions:** 10 journals and other serials. **Services:** Library open to public for reference use only, by reservation. **Staff:** David R. Ruth, Hist.

★14627★
U.S. NATL. PARK SERVICE - FORT UNION NATL. MONUMENT - LIBRARY (Hist; Mil)
                                   Phone: (505) 425-8025
Watrous, NM 87753   Carol M. Kruse, Unit Mgr.
Founded: 1956. **Subjects:** Santa Fe Trail and Fort Union history, military history, Western Americana. **Special Collections:** Fort Union documents on microcards and microfilm. **Holdings:** 1300 books. **Subscriptions:** 10 journals and other serials. **Services:** Library open to public for reference use only.

★14628★
U.S. NATL. PARK SERVICE - FORT VANCOUVER NATL. HISTORIC SITE - LIBRARY (Hist)
1501 E. Evergreen Blvd.   Phone: (206) 696-7655
Vancouver, WA 98661   Kent J. Taylor, Supv./Pk. Ranger
Subjects: Fur trade; Hudson's Bay Company; Pacific Northwest - history, flora and fauna, Indians; National Park Service; 19th century daily life; archeology and reconstruction of Fort Vancouver. **Special Collections:** Artifacts dealing with the structure of old Fort Vancouver and U.S. military barracks of 1850s (3000 items). **Holdings:** 800 books; 177 bound periodical volumes; historical pamphlets; 60 historic documents. **Services:** Library open to public for reference use only. **Remarks:** Pacific Northwest National Parks Association cooperates in maintaining library, which is primarily for use of park service staff.

★14629★
U.S. NATL. PARK SERVICE - FREDERICK DOUGLASS HOME AND VISITOR CENTER - LIBRARY (Hist)
1411 W St., S.E.   Phone: (202) 426-5962
Washington, DC 20020   Tyra Walker
Founded: 1850. **Staff:** 1. **Subjects:** History, biography, science, geography, philosophy. **Special Collections:** History of Women's Suffrage (4 volumes); Executive Documents, 1820-1895. **Holdings:** 2000 books. **Subscriptions:** 14 journals and other serials. **Services:** Library not open to public. **Also Known As:** National Capital Park-East, Douglass Private Collection.

★14630★
U.S. NATL. PARK SERVICE - FREDERICK LAW OLMSTED NATL. HISTORIC SITE - ARCHIVES (Plan; Hist)
99 Warren St.   Phone: (617) 566-1689
Brookline, MA 02146   Elizabeth S. Banks, Coll.Mgr.
Staff: Prof 1; Other 2. **Subjects:** Landscape architecture, urban design, city planning. **Special Collections:** 19th and early 20th century photographic prints of parks, landscapes, estates, urban design in European cities and towns (25 linear feet). **Holdings:** 1000 books; 650 bound periodical volumes; 1500 landscape architectural drawings from 1860 to 1979; 60,000 photographic prints of Olmsted landscape jobs in the U.S. and Canada; 30 linear feet of landscape job planting lists. **Services:** Copying; archives open to public by appointment to scholars.

★14631★
U.S. NATL. PARK SERVICE - FREDERICKSBURG & SPOTSYLVANIA NATL. MILITARY PARK - LIBRARY (Hist)
Box 679   Phone: (703) 373-4461
Fredericksburg, VA 22401   Robert K. Krick, Chf.Hist.
Founded: 1927. **Staff:** 3. **Subjects:** Civil War in Virginia. **Holdings:** 5000 books; 250 bound periodical volumes; 1000 manuscript items; 1000 reels of microfilm; 10 drawers of maps. **Services:** Copying; library open to public by

appointment. **Staff:** D.A. Lilley, Hist.; E.J. Raus, Hist.

★14632★
U.S. NATL. PARK SERVICE - GEORGE WASHINGTON CARVER NATL. MONUMENT - LIBRARY (Hist)
Box 38   Phone: (417) 325-4151
Diamond, MO 64840   Gentry Davis, Supt.
Subjects: George Washington Carver, black history, national parks. **Special Collections:** Carver Collection (3019 archives and artifacts); original Carver letters (97 items). **Holdings:** 246 books; 130 documents and technical reports; 50 maps and charts; 1505 pictures and study prints; 16 VF drawers of park administrative records. **Subscriptions:** 14 journals and other serials. **Services:** Copying; SDI; library open to public for reference use only. **Special Catalogs:** Carver Collection.

★14633★
U.S. NATL. PARK SERVICE - GETTYSBURG NATL. MILITARY PARK - CYCLORAMA CENTER LIBRARY (Hist)
                                   Phone: (717) 334-1124
Gettysburg, PA 17325   Kathleen R. Georg, Coord.
Staff: 2. **Subjects:** Battle of Gettysburg, Civil War, Lincoln, Eisenhower at Gettysburg, 19th century life, environment. **Special Collections:** Eisenhower oral history (70 tapes); William H. Tipton photographs (1800). **Holdings:** 3300 books; 20 VF drawers; 1700 maps and plans; 172 reels of microfilm. **Subscriptions:** 20 journals and other serials. **Services:** Copying (limited); library open to public for reference use only. **Staff:** John S. Heiser, Asst.Hist.

★14634★
U.S. NATL. PARK SERVICE - GILA CLIFF DWELLINGS NATL. MONUMENT - VISITOR CENTER LIBRARY (Sci-Tech; Area-Ethnic)*
Rte. 11, Box 100   Phone: (505) 534-9461
Silver City, NM 88061
Subjects: Archeology, natural history, Mogollon Indians. **Special Collections:** Mogollon Indian artifacts. **Holdings:** 300 books. **Services:** Library open to public. **Remarks:** Consolidated with U.S. Forest Service to also serve Gila National Forest.

★14635★
U.S. NATL. PARK SERVICE - GLACIER NATL. PARK - GEORGE C. RUHLE LIBRARY (Env-Cons)
                                   Phone: (406) 888-5441
West Glacier, MT 59936   Beth Ladeau, Pk.Libn.
Founded: 1975. **Staff:** 1. **Subjects:** Environment, geology, glaciology, mammals, Plains Indians. **Special Collections:** Schultz books on the Plains Indians. **Holdings:** 8000 books; 2000 reprints; 4000 museum specimens. **Subscriptions:** 27 journals and other serials; 6 newspapers. **Services:** Library open to public for reference use only.

U.S. NATL. PARK SERVICE - GOLDEN GATE NATL. RECREATION AREA - NATIONAL MARITIME MUSEUM
See: National Maritime Museum

★14636★
U.S. NATL. PARK SERVICE - GRAND CANYON RESEARCH LIBRARY (Env-Cons)†
Grand Canyon Natl. Park   Phone: (602) 638-2411
Grand Canyon, AZ 86023   Louise M. Hinchliffe, Lib.Techn.
Founded: 1931. **Staff:** 1. **Subjects:** Grand Canyon region - geology, zoology, botany, ethnology, archeology, anthropology, history. **Holdings:** 7300 books and bound periodical volumes; river journals; clippings; reprints. **Subscriptions:** 42 journals and other serials. **Services:** Library open to public for reference use only by appointment.

★14637★
U.S. NATL. PARK SERVICE - GRAND PORTAGE NATL. MONUMENT - LIBRARY (Hist)
Box 666   Phone: (218) 387-2788
Grand Marais, MN 55604   Donald W. Carney, Supv. Park Ranger
Staff: 1. **Subjects:** American-Canadian fur trade, Chippewa Indian culture, Canadian-Minnesota exploration and history. **Special Collections:** Wisconsin Historical Collection (21 volumes); journals of the Hudson's Bay Company (24 volumes); works of Samuel De Champlain (6 volumes). **Holdings:** 700 books; 100 bound periodical volumes. **Services:** Library open to public with restrictions.

★14638★
U.S. NATL. PARK SERVICE - GRAND TETON NATL. PARK - LIBRARY (Env-Cons)
Drawer 170   Phone: (307) 733-2880
Moose, WY 83012
Founded: 1929. Subjects: Grand Teton National Park - fauna, flora, history, geology; Western history. Holdings: 1500 books; pamphlets; 1030 historic photographs. Subscriptions: 15 journals and other serials. Services: Library open to public for reference use only. Remarks: Library is primarily for the use of park employees.

★14639★
U.S. NATL. PARK SERVICE - GRANT-KOHRS RANCH NATL. HISTORIC SITE (Hist)
Box 790   Phone: (406) 846-2070
Deer Lodge, MT 59722   Neysa Dickey, Lead Park Techn.
Staff: Prof 1. Subjects: History - ranching, local, Western U.S., natural; interpretation. Special Collections: Frontier cattle era collection; oral histories. Holdings: 1000 volumes. Services: Library open to public for reference use only.

★14640★
U.S. NATL. PARK SERVICE - GREAT SMOKY MOUNTAINS NATL. PARK - SUGARLANDS VISITOR CENTER (Env-Cons; Hist)
                                        Phone: (615) 436-5615
Gatlinburg, TN 37738   Claryse D. Myers, Libn.
Staff: Prof 1. Subjects: Natural sciences, area history, pioneer and oral history, environment, geology, history of park. Special Collections: Journals of naturalists; historic maps; memorabilia of early settlers; archival collection (18,000 black and white photographs; 250 linear feet of files); Research/Resource Management Report Series (66). Holdings: 2800 books; 22 bound periodical volumes; 125 theses and dissertations; 38 VF drawers of technical papers and clippings; 123 tapes and transcriptions; records; films. Subscriptions: 45 journals and other serials. Services: Interlibrary loans (limited); center open to public for reference use only.

★14641★
U.S. NATL. PARK SERVICE - HALEAKALA NATL. PARK - LIBRARY (Sci-Tech)
Box 369   Phone: (808) 572-9306
Makawao, HI 96768   Carol Beadle, Pk.Techn., Interp.
Staff: 1. Subjects: Botany, zoology, Hawaiiana, geology, ecology, parks, archeology. Special Collections: IBP-Island Ecosystems (all of Hawaii, 75). Holdings: 560 books; 18 file boxes of pertinent subject material. Services: Library open to public for reference use only on request.

★14642★
U.S. NATL. PARK SERVICE - HARPERS FERRY CENTER - BRANCH OF GRAPHICS RESEARCH - PICTURE LIBRARY (Aud-Vis)
5508 Port Royal Rd.   Phone: (703) 756-6138
Springfield, VA 22151-2393   Thomas A. DuRant, Pict.Libn.
Founded: 1982. Staff: Prof 1. Subjects: National Park Service. Special Collections: George A. Grant Collection (ca. 1929-1954); E.B. Thompson Collection (ca. 1900-1940); George Wright/Joseph Dixon Collection (natural science, ca. 1930-1950). Holdings: 3000 books; 1.5 million images, including 39 file cabinets of prints, 12 file cabinets of negatives, and 1200 3-ring binders of prints and slides. Services: Interlibrary loans; library open to public with restrictions. Automated Operations: Computerized cataloging.

★14643★
U.S. NATL. PARK SERVICE - HARPERS FERRY CENTER LIBRARY (Hist)
                                        Phone: (304) 535-6371
Harpers Ferry, WV 25425   David Nathanson, Chf.Libn.
Staff: Prof 2; Other 3. Subjects: American history, natural history, museology, decorative arts. Special Collections: U.S. National Park Service Research Reports (11,000 items); Harry Wandrus collection of technical books (500 volumes); Harold L. Peterson collection of works on military art and science, and firearms (2500 volumes); Vera Craig Pictorial Archive of American Interiors (250 items); National Park Service History Collection (2000 books; 200 bound periodical volumes; 500 boxes of documents; 100 films; 600 museum artifacts; 1000 hours of oral history tapes). Holdings: 14,000 books; 400 bound periodical volumes; 120 shelf feet of unbound periodicals; 20 VF drawers of pamphlets; 190 reels of microfilm; 12,000 microfiche; 960 trade catalogs. Subscriptions: 175 journals and other serials. Services: Interlibrary loans; copying; library open to public for reference use only. Automated Operations: Computerized cataloging and ILL. Computerized Information Services: DIALOG, OCLC. Networks/Consortia: Member of FEDLINK; National Natural Resources Library and Information System (NNRLIS); West Virginia Library Commission Union

Catalog. Publications: New Accessions at HFC Library, monthly. Special Catalogs: Guide to the Trade Catalog Collection (1983); Guide to the NPS Reports Collection; Guide to the Reprint File; NPS Oral History Survey (1981); NPS Union Catalog of Civil War Regimental Histories and Personal Narratives (1984). Staff: Ruthanne Heriot, Spec.Coll.Libn.; Nancy Potts, Lib.Techn.

★14644★
U.S. NATL. PARK SERVICE - HARPERS FERRY NATL. HISTORICAL PARK - LIBRARY (Hist)
Box 65   Phone: (304) 535-6371
Harpers Ferry, WV 25425   Hilda E. Staubs, Musm.Techn.
Founded: 1962. Staff: 1. Subjects: John Brown, Armory, Civil War, Negro education, local and general history, natural science, military science. Holdings: 1846 books; 230 historical newspapers; 209 research reports on historic structures, sites, archeology and related histories; 53 college catalogs; 58 binders of unpublished correspondence and papers; booklet and document file; historic and modern photographs; 136 reels of microfilm. Services: Interlibrary loans; library open to public for reference use only.

★14645★
U.S. NATL. PARK SERVICE - HAWAII VOLCANOES NATL. PARK - LIBRARY (Sci-Tech)
                                        Phone: (808) 967-7311
Hawaii National Park, HI 96718
Founded: 1916. Staff: 1. Subjects: Volcanology, zoology, botany, ancient culture of Hawaiians. Holdings: 2000 books; 460 bound periodical volumes; 977 pamphlets; 2000 black and white pictures; 3000 slides. Subscriptions: 17 journals and other serials. Services: Library open to public for reference use only.

★14646★
U.S. NATL. PARK SERVICE - HOMESTEAD NATL. MONUMENT - RESEARCH LIBRARY (Hist)
R.R. 3, Box 47   Phone: (402) 223-3514
Beatrice, NE 68310-9416   Randall K. Baynes, Supt.
Founded: 1939. Staff: Prof 1; Other 5. Subjects: U.S. public lands policy and Western expansion, U.S. agricultural history, Nebraska history, ecology and natural history. Special Collections: Museum Study Collection on the homesteading experience and the local area of Nebraska (189 books). Holdings: 380 books; 60 bound periodical volumes; 40 park archives. Services: Library open to public for reference use only.

★14647★
U.S. NATL. PARK SERVICE - HOPEWELL VILLAGE NATL. HISTORIC SITE - LIBRARY (Hist)
R.D. 2, Box 345   Phone: (215) 582-8773
Elverson, PA 19520   Elizabeth E. Disrude, Supt.
Founded: 1938. Staff: 1. Subjects: 18th- and 19th-century ironmaking. Special Collections: Hopewell Furnace Records (80 items); name file for persons associated with the Hopewell Furnace during its 113 years of operation. Holdings: 500 books; 100 unpublished reports; 10,000 furnace documents; microfilm. Services: Interlibrary loans; library open to public for reference use only during park hours. Special Indexes: Hopewell Source Material Index.

★14648★
U.S. NATL. PARK SERVICE - INDEPENDENCE NATL. HISTORICAL PARK - LIBRARY (Hist)†
313 Walnut St.   Phone: (215) 597-8047
Philadelphia, PA 19106   David C. Dutcher, Chf.Pk.Hist.
Founded: 1951. Staff: Prof 1. Subjects: American history, Philadelphia and Pennsylvania history, arts and crafts. Special Collections: Independence Hall Association Papers; Judge Edwin O. Lewis Papers. Holdings: 6000 books; 710 bound periodical volumes; 200 manuscripts; 540 reels of microfilm; 150 resource studies reports; 150,000 research note cards; 12,000 photographs; 30,000 slides; 60 films; 35 training videotapes. Subscriptions: 34 journals and other serials. Services: Photographic reference and duplication; film loan service; library open to public. Remarks: Library is located at 120 S. Third St., Philadelphia, PA.

★14649★
U.S. NATL. PARK SERVICE - INFORMATION CLEARINGHOUSE (Env-Cons; Rec)*
75 Spring St., S.W., Suite 1092   Phone: (404) 221-3889
Atlanta, GA 30303   Linda Hall, Libn.
Founded: 1974. Staff: Prof 1. Subjects: Recreation planning, historic preservation, conservation, activity planning, bicycling. Special Collections: Statewide Comprehensive Outdoor Recreation Plan (SCORP) and related materials (500 items). Holdings: 1200 books; 258 subject files; 400 general

use handout materials. **Subscriptions:** 32 journals and other serials. **Services:** Clearinghouse open to public with supervision.

★14650★
U.S. NATL. PARK SERVICE - INTERAGENCY ARCHEOLOGICAL SERVICE LIBRARY
655 Parfet St.
Box 25287
Denver, CO 80225
Defunct

★14651★
U.S. NATL. PARK SERVICE - JEFFERSON NATL. EXPANSION MEMORIAL - LIBRARY (Hist)
11 N. Fourth St.   Phone: (314) 425-6023
St. Louis, MO 63102
Founded: 1959. **Staff:** 1. **Subjects:** Westward expansion, St. Louis, Thomas Jefferson, Lewis & Clark. **Holdings:** 3100 books; 450 other cataloged items; research reports. **Subscriptions:** 15 journals and other serials. **Services:** Copying; library open to public for reference use only by appointment.

★14652★
U.S. NATL. PARK SERVICE - KENNESAW MOUNTAIN NATL. BATTLEFIELD PARK - LIBRARY (Hist)
Box 1167   Phone: (404) 427-4686
Marietta, GA 30061   Emmet A. Nichols, Chf. Interpreter
Founded: 1939. **Staff:** 3. **Subjects:** Civil War, 19th century American history, ecology and natural history, Georgia history. **Holdings:** 1000 books; 20 diaries; 25 reels of microfilm; 20 manuscripts and letters; 6 films. **Services:** Library open to public for serious research.

★14653★
U.S. NATL. PARK SERVICE - KINGS MOUNTAIN NATL. MILITARY PARK - LIBRARY (Hist)
Box 31   Phone: (803) 936-7921
Kings Mountain, NC 28086   James J. Anderson, Chf.Interp. & Rsrcs.Mgt.
Founded: 1941. **Subjects:** Revolutionary War history. **Holdings:** Figures not available. **Services:** Library open to public with restrictions.

★14654★
U.S. NATL. PARK SERVICE - LAKE MEAD NATL. RECREATION AREA - LIBRARY (Env-Cons)
601 Nevada Hwy.   Phone: (702) 293-4041
Boulder City, NV 89005   John S. Mohlenrich, Chf. Park Interp.
Founded: 1962. **Staff:** 2. **Subjects:** History, geology, water resources, natural history. **Holdings:** 1400 books; 250 bound periodical volumes. **Services:** Library open to public for reference use only. **Staff:** Gwen Davidson, Libn.

★14655★
U.S. NATL. PARK SERVICE - LAVA BEDS NATL. MONUMENT - LIBRARY (Sci-Tech)
          Phone: (916) 667-2282
Tulelake, CA 96134   Gary Hathaway, Chf., Div. of Interp.
Staff: 1. **Subjects:** History of Modoc War (1872-1873), geology and volcanology, natural history, Indian ethnography, archeology. **Holdings:** 1500 books; 5 VF drawers. **Services:** Library open to public by appointment.

★14656★
U.S. NATL. PARK SERVICE - LIBRARY (Env-Cons; Hist)
655 Parfet St.
Box 25287   Phone: (303) 234-4443
Denver, CO 80225   Ruth A. Larison, Libn.
Founded: 1971. **Staff:** Prof 1; Other 1. **Subjects:** National parks and monuments, outdoor recreation, ecology, landscape and historic architecture, American history. **Special Collections:** Brochures and pamphlets on individual national parks and monuments (2000 items). **Holdings:** 15,000 books, reports, documents and dissertations. **Subscriptions:** 300 journals and other serials; 10 newspapers. **Services:** Interlibrary loans; copying; library open to public for reference use only. **Automated Operations:** Computerized cataloging and ILL. **Computerized Information Services:** OCLC. **Networks/Consortia:** Member of FEDLINK; National Natural Resources Library and Information System (NNRLIS).

★14657★
U.S. NATL. PARK SERVICE - LINCOLN BOYHOOD NATL. MEMORIAL - LIBRARY (Hist)
          Phone: (812) 937-4757
Lincoln City, IN 47552   Norman D. Hellmers, Supt.
Founded: 1962. **Staff:** 1. **Subjects:** Abraham Lincoln, pioneer life, state and

local history. **Special Collections:** Interpretive Museum 1816-1830 period of Lincoln's life. **Holdings:** 1000 books; 25 bound periodical volumes; pamphlets; maps; documents. **Subscriptions:** 16 journals and other serials. **Services:** Copying; library open to public for reference use only. **Publications:** Handout copies of information about Lincoln.

★14658★
U.S. NATL. PARK SERVICE - LONGFELLOW NATL. HISTORIC SITE - LIBRARY (Hum)
105 Brattle St.   Phone: (617) 876-4491
Cambridge, MA 02138   Kathleen Catalano, Cur.
Staff: Prof 1; Other 1. **Subjects:** European literature and languages, American literature, H.W. Longfellow's works, Dante, Scandinavian literature. **Holdings:** 10,000 books, bound periodical volumes and pamphlets; 175 linear feet of family papers of Longfellow-Wadsworth-Appleton-Dana. **Services:** Library open to public for bona fide scholarly use only.

★14659★
U.S. NATL. PARK SERVICE - LYNDON B. JOHNSON NATL. HISTORICAL PARK - LIBRARY (Hist)
Box 329   Phone: (512) 868-7128
Johnson City, TX 78636   John T. Tiff, Hist.
Founded: 1970. **Staff:** Prof 1; Other 1. **Subjects:** Lyndon B. Johnson and his family, Texas Hill Country history, local natural history. **Special Collections:** Oral history collection on life and times of LBJ (500 tapes). **Holdings:** 2000 books; 750 slides; 20 VF drawers of pamphlets; artifacts; 125 reels of 35mm microfilm of historic newspapers. **Subscriptions:** 15 journals and other serials. **Services:** Copying (limited); library open to public for reference use only for approved research.

★14660★
U.S. NATL. PARK SERVICE - MANASSAS NATL. BATTLEFIELD PARK - LIBRARY (Hist)
Box 1830   Phone: (703) 754-7107
Manassas, VA 22110   Haywood S. Harrell, Chf.Hist.
Founded: 1940. **Staff:** Prof 4. **Subjects:** Civil War history, campaigns and battles of First and Second Manassas (Bull Run), general military works, Civil War biographies. **Special Collections:** Fitz-John Porter Collection; James Brewerton Ricketts Collection; T.C.H. Smith Papers; unpublished journal of Abner Doubleday, 1862. **Holdings:** 2000 books, bound periodical volumes, and pamphlets; 500 contemporary photographs; 200 photostats of Civil War related newspapers; 1000 photostats of documents, diaries and memoirs; 100 maps; bibliography files on First and Second Manassas. **Services:** Copying; library open to public by appointment. **Staff:** Mike Andrus, Archv.; Jim Burgress, Cur.

★14661★
U.S. NATL. PARK SERVICE - MESA VERDE NATL. PARK - MUSEUM LIBRARY (Env-Cons; Hist)
Box 38   Phone: (303) 529-4475
Mesa Verde Natl. Park, CO 81330   Wanda L. Padilla, Park Lib.Techn.
Staff: Prof 1. **Subjects:** Archeology, ethnology, anthropology, history. **Special Collections:** Early historical and archeological documents of Mesa Verde Natl. Park. **Holdings:** 5557 books; 150 bound periodical volumes; 42 filing boxes of unbound documents. **Subscriptions:** 51 journals and other serials. **Services:** Interlibrary loans; library not open to public. **Networks/Consortia:** Member of Southwest Regional Library Service System.

★14662★
U.S. NATL. PARK SERVICE - MIDWEST ARCHEOLOGICAL CENTER - RESEARCH LIBRARY (Hist; Env-Cons)*
Federal Bldg., Rm. 474
100 Centennial Mall N.   Phone: (402) 471-5392
Lincoln, NE 68508   Lynn M. Mitchell, Lib.Techn.
Founded: 1969. **Staff:** Prof 1. **Subjects:** Archeology of the mid-continental United States, National Park Service, American Indians. **Holdings:** 400 books; 5600 bound periodical volumes; 1900 volumes of manuscripts; 100 volumes of government publications. **Subscriptions:** 45 journals and other serials. **Services:** Library not open to public.

★14663★
U.S. NATL. PARK SERVICE - MIDWEST REGIONAL OFFICE LIBRARY (Hist)†
1709 Jackson St.   Phone: (402) 221-3471
Omaha, NE 68102   Emily Bolton, Pub.Info.Asst.
Founded: 1935. **Staff:** 1. **Subjects:** Western Americana, ethnology and anthropology. **Special Collections:** Pacific railroad surveys; early Western travel; Westerners brand book. **Holdings:** 6000 books; special reports (historical research, interpretive planning, historic structures, salvage archeology). **Subscriptions:** 15 journals and other serials. **Services:** Library

open to public for limited use.

★14664★
U.S. NATL. PARK SERVICE - MOORES CREEK NATL. BATTLEFIELD -
LIBRARY (Hist)
Box 69   Phone: (919) 283-5591
Currie, NC 28435   John W. Stockert, Supt.
Founded: 1960. **Staff:** 1. **Subjects:** North Carolina history, American
Revolution, national parks, environment, Highland Scots. **Holdings:** 200
books; 100 bound volumes of periodicals and historical papers. **Services:**
Library open to public for reference use only.

★14665★
U.S. NATL. PARK SERVICE - MORRISTOWN NATL. HISTORICAL PARK -
LIBRARY (Hist)
Washington Place   Phone: (201) 539-2017
Morristown, NJ 07960   Thomas O.C. Smith, Libn.
Founded: 1955. **Staff:** Prof 1. **Subjects:** History of the American Revolution,
Colonial Americana, New Jersey local history. **Holdings:** 20,000 books; 300
bound periodical volumes; 500 pamphlets; 46,000 manuscripts; 252 reels of
microfilm. **Subscriptions:** 50 journals and other serials. **Services:** Interlibrary
loans; copying; library open to public. **Special Catalogs:** Guide to the
Manuscript Collection.

★14666★
U.S. NATL. PARK SERVICE - MOUND CITY GROUP NATL. MONUMENT -
LIBRARY (Hist)
16062 State Route 104   Phone: (614) 774-1125
Chillicothe, OH 45601   Kenneth Apschnikat, Supt.
Subjects: Archeology, Hopewell and other prehistoric Indian cultures of Ohio,
environment and environmental education, Ohio history. **Special Collections:**
Reports of archeological research on Hopewell and Adena cultures conducted
at Monument; Hopewell Archeological Conference papers, 1978. **Holdings:**
1800 books; 650 magazines, reports, unbound articles. **Services:** Library
open to public by request. **Staff:** John A. Mangimeli, Park Techn.

★14667★
U.S. NATL. PARK SERVICE - MUIR WOODS NATL. MONUMENT - LIBRARY*
Mill Valley, CA 94941
Founded: 1972. **Subjects:** Redwood ecology, northern California plants,
salmon, national parks, John Muir. **Special Collections:** Natural resource
studies of the Muir Woods. **Holdings:** 200 books; 25 bound periodical
volumes; 320 slides; 15 special reports; maps. **Remarks:** Presently inactive.

★14668★
U.S. NATL. PARK SERVICE - NATCHEZ TRACE PARKWAY - LIBRARY &
VISITOR CENTER (Hist)
R.R. 1, NT-143   Phone: (601) 842-1572
Tupelo, MS 38801
Founded: 1963. **Staff:** 1. **Subjects:** History, natural history, national parks.
Special Collections: Papers and letters related to Choctaw and Chickasaw
Indians (200 items). **Holdings:** 2300 books; 200 bound periodical volumes;
3500 color slides; 10,000 negatives. **Subscriptions:** 10 journals and other
serials. **Services:** Interlibrary loans; copying; library open to public.

★14669★
U.S. NATL. PARK SERVICE - NATL. CAPITAL REGION - ROCK CREEK
NATURE CENTER LIBRARY (Env-Cons)
5200 Glover Rd., N.W.   Phone: (202) 426-6829
Washington, DC 20015   Lurrie V. Pope, Supv. Park Ranger
Subjects: Birds, mammals, reptiles, astronomy, park and milling history,
environment and environmental education. **Holdings:** 1000 books; 32 boxes
of clippings and photographs; unbound journals. **Services:** Library open to
public for reference use only. **Publications:** Mimeographed nature leaflets.

★14670★
U.S. NATL. PARK SERVICE - NEZ PERCE NATL. HISTORICAL PARK -
LIBRARY (Area-Ethnic; Hist)
Box 93   Phone: (208) 843-2261
Spalding, ID 83551   Fahy C. Whitaker, Supt.
Founded: 1965. **Staff:** 4. **Subjects:** Nez Perce Indians, Nez Perce War,
Indian ethnology, history of the Northwest and Idaho, Western history.
Holdings: 850 books; 300 historical photographs; 1000 photographs.
Services: Library open to public with restrictions on reference and archival
materials.

★14671★
U.S. NATL. PARK SERVICE - OLYMPIC NATL. PARK - PIONEER MEMORIAL
MUSEUM - LIBRARY (Env-Cons)
3002 Mount Angeles Rd.   Phone: (206) 452-4501
Port Angeles, WA 98362   Henry C. Warren, Chf.Pk. Naturalist
Staff: 1. **Subjects:** Natural history, Northwest Indians, Olympic National Park.
Special Collections: Letters and published material relating to establishment
of Olympic National Park. **Holdings:** 2000 books; 4 VF drawers of clippings,
memoranda and letters relating to natural and human history of Olympic
National Park. **Subscriptions:** 18 journals, serials and newspapers. **Services:**
Library open to public with restrictions on some material.

★14672★
U.S. NATL. PARK SERVICE - ORGAN PIPE CACTUS NATL. MONUMENT -
LIBRARY (Hist)
Rte. 1, Box 100
Ajo, AZ 85321   Caroline Wilson, Interp.
Staff: 1. **Subjects:** Natural and cultural history, ecology of the Sonora Desert
and the Southwest, U.S. Natl. Park Service history and policies. **Holdings:**
1368 books and bound periodical volumes; research reports and manuscripts.
Services: Library open to park employees and approved researchers.

★14673★
U.S. NATL. PARK SERVICE - PEA RIDGE NATL. MILITARY PARK - LIBRARY
(Mil; Hist)
                                          Phone: (501) 451-8122
Pea Ridge, AR 72751   Billy D. Stout, Hist.
Founded: 1960. **Subjects:** Battle of Pea Ridge, Civil War west of the
Mississippi, regimental histories, Indians of the Civil War, arms and
equipment, medicine. **Special Collections:** Battle of Pea Ridge (30 units of
microfilm and 15 reports). **Holdings:** 450 books; letters and clippings.
Services: Library open to public for reference use only.

★14674★
U.S. NATL. PARK SERVICE - PERRY'S VICTORY & INTERNATIONAL PEACE
MEMORIAL - LIBRARY (Hist)
Box 549   Phone: (419) 285-2184
Put-In-Bay, OH 43456   Harry C. Myers, Supt.
Subjects: Naval victory of Oliver H. Perry over British at the Battle of Lake
Erie, War of 1812; Lake Erie Islands. **Special Collections:** Construction of
memorial designed by Freedlander and Seymour. **Holdings:** 250 books; 2 VF
drawers of reports and correspondence from Centennial Commission and
subsequent organizations; 2 VF drawers of pamphlets; 1200 photographs.
Services: Library open to public by appointment.

★14675★
U.S. NATL. PARK SERVICE - PETERSBURG NATL. BATTLEFIELD - LIBRARY
(Hist)
Box 549   Phone: (804) 732-3531
Petersburg, VA 23803   Christopher M. Calkins, Hist./Park Ranger
Founded: 1926. **Staff:** Prof 2. **Subjects:** Civil War, Petersburg. **Holdings:**
1800 books; 200 bound periodical volumes; 500 maps; 200 letters and
documents. **Subscriptions:** 10 journals and other serials. **Services:** Copying
(limited); library open to public by appointment. **Staff:** John R. Davis, Chf.,
Interp.

★14676★
U.S. NATL. PARK SERVICE - PETRIFIED FOREST NATL. PARK - LIBRARY
(Sci-Tech; Hist)
                                          Phone: (602) 524-6228
Petrified Forest Natl. Park, AZ 86028   Terry E. Maze, Interp.Spec.
Subjects: Petrified wood, geology, natural and cultural history. **Holdings:**
2190 books and bound periodical volumes. **Subscriptions:** 19 journals and
other serials. **Services:** Library open to public by appointment.

★14677★
U.S. NATL. PARK SERVICE - PIPESTONE NATL. MONUMENT - LIBRARY &
ARCHIVES (Hist)
Box 727   Phone: (507) 825-5463
Pipestone, MN 56164   David L. Lane, Supt.
Subjects: Archeology, history, ethnology - as related to early Indian
occupation of the Northern Plains; white exploration and settlement of the
region. **Special Collections:** Publications relating to ceremonial pipes and
Indian smoking customs. **Holdings:** 430 volumes; manuscripts; reports;
clippings; microfilms; photographs; slides. **Services:** Library open to public for
reference use only.

★14678★
U.S. NATL. PARK SERVICE - POINT REYES NATL. SEASHORE - LIBRARY
(Sci-Tech)
Phone: (415) 663-1092
Point Reyes, CA 94956
Subjects: Natural history, Indians, environmental education, geology, California history, sea life, mammals, botany, National Park Service. **Holdings:** 1000 books; reports. **Services:** Library open to public for reference use only by special arrangement.

★14679★
U.S. NATL. PARK SERVICE - PU'UHONUA O HONAUNAU NATL. HISTORICAL PARK - LIBRARY (Area-Ethnic)
Box 129
Phone: (808) 328-2326
Honaunau, HI 96726
Blossom Sapp, Libn.
Founded: 1961. **Staff:** 2. **Subjects:** Hawaiian culture and history, National Park Service. **Holdings:** 291 books; 87 manuscripts. **Services:** Library open to public for reference use only.

★14680★
U.S. NATL. PARK SERVICE - RICHMOND NATL. BATTLEFIELD PARK - LIBRARY (Hist)
3215 E. Broad St.
Phone: (804) 226-1981
Richmond, VA 23223
Keithel C. Morgan, Chf.Interp.
Founded: 1966. **Staff:** 3. **Subjects:** Civil War, national parks, museums. **Holdings:** 600 books. **Services:** Library open to public for reference use only by appointment.

★14681★
U.S. NATL. PARK SERVICE - ROCKY MOUNTAIN NATIONAL PARK - LIBRARY (Hist)
Phone: (303) 586-2371
Estes Park, CO 80517
Helen M. Burgener, Libn.
Staff: Prof 1. **Subjects:** Rocky Mountain National Park - history, geology, plant and animal ecology; Western history. **Special Collections:** Enos Mills collection; William Allen White collection. **Holdings:** 1300 books; 150 bound periodical volumes; 98 theses; 50 boxes of clippings and reports; 4 volumes of maps; 50 oral history tapes and cassettes. **Subscriptions:** 39 journals and other serials. **Services:** Copying; library open to public with restrictions.

★14682★
U.S. NATL. PARK SERVICE - ROOSEVELT-VANDERBILT NATL. HISTORIC SITES - MUSEUMS (Hist)
Phone: (914) 229-9115
Hyde Park, NY 12538
Franceska Macsali, Site Libn./Park Ranger
Staff: 1. **Subjects:** Franklin and Eleanor Roosevelt, National Park Service, environment, Vanderbilt families, architecture, antiques, historic houses. **Holdings:** 835 books and bound periodical volumes. **Services:** Museums not open to public. **Remarks:** There are three historic house museums, consisting of the homes of Franklin D. Roosevelt, Eleanor Roosevelt and the Vanderbilt Mansion. The small library in the park headquarters is for staff use only.

★14683★
U.S. NATL. PARK SERVICE - RUSSELL CAVE NATL. MONUMENT - LIBRARY
(Sci-Tech)
Rte. 1, Box 175
Phone: (205) 495-2672
Bridgeport, AL 35740
Dorothy Marsh, Unit Mgr.
Staff: 4. **Subjects:** Archeology of Russell Cave. **Special Collections:** Miscellaneous points and shards (1500). **Holdings:** 80 books; 4 unbound manuscripts. **Services:** Library open to public for reference use only.

★14684★
U.S. NATL. PARK SERVICE - SALEM MARITIME NATL. HISTORIC SITE - LIBRARY (Hist)
Custom House, Derby St.
Phone: (617) 744-4323
Salem, MA 01970
John M. Frayler, Cur.
Founded: 1937. **Staff:** 1. **Subjects:** Maritime history, Essex County and local history, recreation and conservation. **Holdings:** 500 books; 150 periodicals; 3 VF drawers of Custom House records; pamphlets and clippings. **Services:** Copying (limited); library open to public by appointment.

★14685★
U.S. NATL. PARK SERVICE - SARATOGA NATL. HISTORICAL PARK - LIBRARY (Hist)
R.D. 2, Box 33
Phone: (518) 664-9821
Stillwater, NY 12170
S. Paul Okey, Pk.Hist.
Founded: 1941. **Subjects:** Battles of Saratoga, military campaign of 1777, American Revolution, National Park System. **Special Collections:** Microfilm collection of primary participant accounts of the battles. **Holdings:** 800 books; 900 maps; 1200 photographs; 1000 slides; 100 unbound reports and primary source transcript groupings. **Services:** Library open to public by appointment.

★14686★
U.S. NATL. PARK SERVICE - SAUGUS IRON WORKS NATL. HISTORIC SITE - LIBRARY (Sci-Tech; Hist)
244 Central St.
Phone: (617) 233-0050
Saugus, MA 01906
Frank Studinski, Supv. Park Ranger
Founded: 1969. **Staff:** Prof 2; Other 1. **Subjects:** Early iron technology, 17th century life, natural history, Americana. **Holdings:** 500 books. **Services:** Library open to public for reference use only.

★14687★
U.S. NATL. PARK SERVICE - SCOTTS BLUFF NATL. MONUMENT - LIBRARY
(Hist)
Box 427
Phone: (308) 436-4340
Gerling, NE 69341
Russell Osborn, Chf. Ranger
Staff: 1. **Subjects:** Westward movement, Oregon Trail. **Holdings:** 850 books, diaries. **Services:** Library open to members.

★14688★
U.S. NATL. PARK SERVICE - SHILOH NATL. MILITARY PARK - LIBRARY
(Hist)
Box 61
Phone: (901) 689-5275
Shiloh, TN 38376
George A. Reaves, Chf.Interp. & Rsrcs.Mgt.
Founded: 1894. **Subjects:** Battle of Shiloh, American Civil War, military arms and equipment. **Holdings:** 1000 books; 200 unbound periodicals; 150 monographs; 200 letters from Civil War personnel. **Services:** Library open to public for reference use only.

★14689★
U.S. NATL. PARK SERVICE - SITKA NATL. HISTORICAL PARK - LIBRARY
(Area-Ethnic; Hist)
Box 738
Phone: (907) 747-6281
Sitka, AK 99835
Gary Candelaria, Chf. Park Ranger
Founded: 1965. **Staff:** Prof 1. **Subjects:** Pacific Northwest Coast Indians, arts and crafts, ethnology, archeology, Southeast Alaska history, natural history, Russian American history. **Holdings:** 1150 books; 200 clippings and special papers; 55 tapes; 14 films. **Services:** Library open to public with permission and advance request.

★14690★
U.S. NATL. PARK SERVICE - STATUE OF LIBERTY NATL. MONUMENT - AMERICAN MUSEUM OF IMMIGRATION - LIBRARY (Hist)
Liberty Island
Phone: (212) 732-1236
New York, NY 10004
Paul J. Kinney, Musm.Cur.
Founded: 1972. **Staff:** Prof 1; Other 4. **Subjects:** Immigration, Statue of Liberty, Ellis Island. **Special Collections:** Augustus F. Sherman Collection of Ellis Island photographs; immigrant oral history tapes, with transcripts; Holland-American Lines passenger lists. **Holdings:** 1000 books; 3000 photographs; 9000 photographic slides; aperture cards and microfiche of Statue of Liberty, Ellis Island, and American Museum of Immigration drawings and reports. **Services:** Copying; tape duplication; photo duplication; library open to public by appointment. **Staff:** Won H. Kim, Libn.

★14691★
U.S. NATL. PARK SERVICE - STONES RIVER NATL. BATTLEFIELD - LIBRARY (Hist)
Old Nashville Hwy.
Rte. 10, Box 401
Phone: (615) 893-9501
Murfreesboro, TN 37130
Donald E. Magee, Pk.Supt.
Founded: 1932. **Staff:** 2. **Subjects:** American history, Civil War history, environmental education, National Park Service. **Holdings:** 400 books; 124 bound periodical volumes; 10 Civil War manuscripts. **Services:** Library not open to public. **Staff:** Elizabeth C. Cook, Park Techn.; Daniel Brown, Hist.

★14692★
U.S. NATL. PARK SERVICE - THEODORE ROOSEVELT NATL. PARK - LIBRARY (Hist)
Phone: (701) 623-4466
Medora, ND 58645
Michele Hellickson, Interpretation Chf.
Founded: 1947. **Staff:** 2. **Subjects:** Theodore Roosevelt, open range cattle industry, environment and ecology, natural sciences of the area, Fort Union, Knife River Indian Villages. **Holdings:** 1900 books; 45 boxes of unbound pamphlets and manuscripts; 57 boxes of unbound periodicals. **Subscriptions:** 30 journals and other serials. **Services:** Library open to public for reference use only. **Staff:** Susan W. Snow, Libn.

★14693★
U.S. NATL. PARK SERVICE - TIMPANOGOS CAVE NATL. MONUMENT - LIBRARY (Env-Cons)
R.R. 3, Box 200
American Fork, UT 84003
Phone: (801) 756-4497
James Boll, Supv.Pk. Ranger
Staff: 1. **Subjects:** Speleology, environmental conservation, geology, botany, zoology, entomology. **Holdings:** 350 books; 300 unbound periodicals. **Services:** Library open to public for reference use only.

★14694★
U.S. NATL. PARK SERVICE - VICKSBURG NATL. MILITARY PARK - LIBRARY (Mil; Hist)
Box 349
Vicksburg, MS 39180-0349
Phone: (601) 636-0583
David F. Riggs, Musm.Cur.
Staff: 1. **Subjects:** Vicksburg campaign, U.S.S. Cairo. **Special Collections:** 100 manuscript collections on the Vicksburg campaign. **Holdings:** 600 books; 300 folders of other cataloged items. **Services:** Interlibrary loans; library open to public by appointment for reference use.

★14695★
U.S. NATL. PARK SERVICE - WALNUT CANYON NATL. MONUMENT - LIBRARY (Sci-Tech)
Rte. 1, Box 25
Flagstaff, AZ 86001
Phone: (602) 526-3367
Founded: 1935. **Staff:** 1. **Subjects:** National parks, archeology and natural history of the Southwest. **Holdings:** 700 books. **Services:** Library open to public for reference use only. **Remarks:** Serves primarily as a staff development library.

★14696★
U.S. NATL. PARK SERVICE - WESTERN ARCHEOLOGICAL AND CONSERVATION CENTER - LIBRARY (Sci-Tech)
1415 N. 6th Ave.
Box 41058
Tucson, AZ 85717
Phone: (602) 629-6995
W. Richard Horn, Libn.
Founded: 1953. **Staff:** Prof 2; Other 2. **Subjects:** Archeology, ethnology, and history of the Southwest; natural history - geology, botany, biology. **Special Collections:** Ruins Stabilization reports; unpublished archeological reports. **Holdings:** 17,000 books; 350 bound periodical volumes; 100 VF drawers of reports, manuscripts, clippings, pamphlets, documents; 170,000 photographic images. **Subscriptions:** 300 journals and other serials. **Services:** Interlibrary loans; copying; library open to public for reference use only. **Automated Operations:** Computerized cataloging. **Computerized Information Services:** DIALOG, OCLC. **Networks/Consortia:** Member of FEDLINK. **Staff:** Lynn M. Mitchell, Asst.Libn.

★14697★
U.S. NATL. PARK SERVICE - WESTERN REGIONAL OFFICE - REGIONAL RESOURCES LIBRARY (Hist; Env-Cons)
450 Golden Gate Ave., Rm. 14009
Box 36063
San Francisco, CA 94102
Phone: (415) 556-4165
Gordon Chappell, Regional Hist.
Subjects: History, archeology, historic architecture, natural history (all limited to National Park Service areas in California, Nevada, Arizona, Hawaii and Guam). **Holdings:** 3500 books; 30 VF drawers of manuscripts, research files, clippings and archival materials. **Services:** Copying; library open to public for reference use only.

★14698★
U.S. NATL. PARK SERVICE - WUPATKI-SUNSET CRATER LIBRARY (Sci-Tech)
HC 33, Box 444A
Flagstaff, AZ 86001
Phone: (602) 527-7040
Jan S. Ryan, Park Techn./Libn.
Staff: 1. **Subjects:** Archeology, ethnology, natural history. **Holdings:** 1000 books; 200 bound periodical volumes; 800 pamphlets. **Services:** Library open to public for reference use only.

★14699★
U.S. NATL. PARK SERVICE - YELLOWSTONE LIBRARY AND MUSEUM ASSOCIATION (Hist; Sci-Tech)*
Yellowstone National Park, WY 82190
Phone: (307) 344-7381
Geri Hape, Bus.Mgr.
Founded: 1931. **Staff:** 2. **Subjects:** History of Yellowstone area, science. **Special Collections:** Haynes Guides to Yellowstone, 1894-1966; superintendents' reports, 1872 to present. **Holdings:** 9760 books; 15,000 reprints; 4 drawers of manuscripts; 36 drawers of reprint material and clippings; maps. **Subscriptions:** 65 journals and other serials. **Services:** Interlibrary loans; copying; library open to public with restrictions. **Staff:** Beverly Whitman, Lib.Techn.

★14700★
U.S. NATL. PARK SERVICE - YOSEMITE NATL. PARK - RESEARCH LIBRARY (Env-Cons)
Box 577
Yosemite National Park, CA 95389
Phone: (209) 372-4461
Mary Vocelka, Lib.Techn.
Founded: 1923. **Staff:** 2. **Subjects:** History and natural history of Yosemite National Park. **Holdings:** 8000 books; 900 bound periodical volumes; 36 VF drawers; 150 boxes of historical documents; maps; black and white photographs. **Subscriptions:** 80 journals and other serials. **Services:** Interlibrary loans; library open to public. **Staff:** David Forgang, Cur.

★14701★
U.S. NATL. PARK SERVICE - ZION NATL. PARK - LIBRARY (Env-Cons)
Springdale, UT 84767
Phone: (801) 772-3256
Marion Hilkey, Libn.
Founded: 1930. **Staff:** 1. **Subjects:** History, geology, plants, wildlife. **Special Collections:** USGS Surveys 1878 (7 volumes). **Holdings:** 2700 books; 36 periodicals. **Subscriptions:** 22 journals and other serials; 5 newspapers. **Services:** Interlibrary loans; library open to public with restrictions. **Publications:** Nature trail leaflets and natural science books published through the Zion Natural History Association; list of publications available upon request. **Remarks:** The interpretive, scientific and historical programs of the park are assisted by the Zion Natural History Association.

★14702★
U.S. NATL. WEATHER SERVICE - CENTRAL REGION HEADQUARTERS - LIBRARY (Sci-Tech)
601 E. 12th St., Rm. 1844
Kansas City, MO 64106
Phone: (816) 374-5672
Dorothy Babich
Staff: 1. **Subjects:** Meteorology, climatology, hydrology. **Holdings:** 1708 volumes. **Services:** Library open to public for reference use only.

★14703★
U.S. NATL. WEATHER SERVICE - WEATHER SERVICE NUCLEAR SUPPORT OFFICE - LIBRARY (Sci-Tech)
Box 14985
Las Vegas, NV 89114
Phone: (702) 734-3515
Linda Schmith
Staff: 1. **Subjects:** Nuclear science, meteorology, radioactivity, pollution. **Holdings:** 300 volumes. **Subscriptions:** 17 journals and other serials. **Services:** Library not open to public.

U.S. NAVAL...
See: U.S. Navy - Naval...

★14704★
U.S. NAVY - CENTER FOR NAVAL ANALYSES - LIBRARY (Mil)
2000 N. Beauregard St.
Alexandria, VA 22311
Phone: (703) 998-3580
Jill C. Hanna, Chf.Libn.
Staff: Prof 2; Other 2. **Subjects:** Systems analysis, statistics, mathematics, military science, operations research, economics. **Holdings:** 13,000 books; 1000 bound periodical volumes; 2000 Congressional documents. **Subscriptions:** 400 journals and other serials; 8 newspapers. **Services:** Interlibrary loans; library not open to public. **Computerized Information Services:** DIALOG, NEXIS, OCLC. **Networks/Consortia:** Member of Interlibrary Users Association; Metropolitan Washington Library Council; CAPCON; Consortium for Continuing Higher Education in Northern Virginia - Library Networking Committee. **Publications:** Library Information Bulletin, monthly. **Special Indexes:** List of Journal Holdings.

★14705★
U.S. NAVY - DAVID W. TAYLOR NAVAL SHIP RESEARCH AND DEVELOPMENT CENTER - TECHNICAL INFORMATION CENTER (Sci-Tech)
Code 522
Bethesda, MD 20084
Phone: (202) 227-1309
Dr. Michael Dankewych, Libn.
Subjects: Naval architecture; hydromechanics; structural mechanics; acoustics and vibration; mathematics; underwater ballistics; pure and applied physics; marine, electrical, mechanical and civil engineering; environmental protection and safety; fabrication technology; energy; aerodynamics. **Special Collections:** DTNSRDC reports. **Holdings:** 35,000 books; 18,000 bound periodical volumes; 100,000 technical reports; 23,000 classified documents; 280,000 microfiche. **Subscriptions:** 900 journals and other serials. **Services:** Interlibrary loans to other government agencies; copying; SDI; center is open for staff use only and for other government employees by special arrangement. **Automated Operations:** Computerized cataloging, serials and circulation. **Computerized Information Services:** DIALOG, Institute for Scientific Information (ISI), DOE/RECON, DTIC, GIDEP, NASA/RECON, SDC. **Publications:** Accession Bulletin, biweekly - for internal distribution only. **Special Indexes:** DTNSRDC Report index. **Remarks:** Includes Ship Design Plans Collection and Classified Vault and Annapolis

Technical Information Center. **Staff:** Alvetta D. Smythe, Hd., Annapolis TIC.

★14706★
U.S. NAVY - DEPARTMENT LIBRARY (Mil)
Bldg. 44
Washington Navy Yard   Phone: (202) 433-2386
Washington, DC 20374   Stanley Kalkus, Dir.
Founded: 1800. **Staff:** Prof 5; Other 3. **Subjects:** Naval history, naval art and science, polar studies, naval and military biography, maritime law, naval ordnance, voyages. **Special Collections:** Congressional documents; Reports of the Secretary of the Navy; manuscripts; American Revolution maps and charts; rare books (10,000); Truxtun-Decatur Naval Museum Library. **Holdings:** 200,000 books; 32,000 bound periodical volumes; 10,000 pamphlets; 10,000 reels of microfilm. **Subscriptions:** 400 journals and other serials. **Services:** Interlibrary loans; copying; library open to public. **Automated Operations:** Computerized cataloging. **Computerized Information Services:** DIALOG, DTIC, SDC, OCLC. **Networks/Consortia:** Member of FEDLINK; Metropolitan Washington Library Council. **Publications:** Accession List; Subject Bibliographies, both monthly. **Staff:** John E. Vajda, Asst.Libn.; Barbara Lynch, Ref.Libn.

★14707★
U.S. NAVY - EDWARD RHODES STITT LIBRARY (Med)
Naval Hospital   Phone: (202) 295-1184
Bethesda, MD 20814-5011   Jerry Meyer, Adm.Libn.
Founded: 1902. **Staff:** Prof 2; Other 3. **Subjects:** Medicine and related sciences. **Special Collections:** Pastoral Counseling Collection (500 volumes); Video Cassette Collection (950 tapes). **Holdings:** 65,000 volumes; 800 audiotapes. **Subscriptions:** 730 journals and other serials. **Services:** Interlibrary loans; library not open to public. **Automated Operations:** Computerized cataloging. **Computerized Information Services:** MEDLINE, BRS.

★14708★
U.S. NAVY - FLEET ANALYSIS CENTER (FLTAC) - LIBRARY (Sci-Tech; Comp Sci)*
Naval Weapons Sta.
Seal Beach
Corona Annex   Phone: (714) 736-4467
Corona, CA 91720   Daysi Hollingsworth, Libn.
Founded: 1953. **Staff:** Prof 1; Other 1. **Subjects:** Electronics, computers, mathematics, management. **Holdings:** 6000 books; 1400 bound periodical volumes; 450 microfilms. **Subscriptions:** 120 journals and other serials; 5 newspapers. **Services:** Interlibrary loans; library not open to public. **Computerized Information Services:** Online systems. **Publications:** Accessions List, biweekly - for internal distribution only.

★14709★
U.S. NAVY - FLEET ANTI-SUBMARINE WARFARE TRAINING CENTER, ATLANTIC - TACTICAL LIBRARY (Sci-Tech)
      Phone: (804) 444-1660
Norfolk, VA 23511   Elizabeth H. Evans, Libn.
Founded: 1956. **Staff:** Prof 1; Other 2. **Subjects:** Anti-submarine warfare, equipments, vehicles, oceanography, tactics, anti-submarine warfare foreign capabilities. **Holdings:** 10,000 books; 200 bound periodical volumes. **Subscriptions:** 22 journals and other serials. **Services:** Maintains operation orders and post exercise results on major ASW exercises; maintains retrieval system compatible with similar library in San Diego; U.S. government clearance for secret and cognizant, bureau "Need to Know" certification for individual user within the Department of Defense only. **Automated Operations:** Mechanized retrieval. **Publications:** Quarterly Accession List to military commands - distributed.

★14710★
U.S. NAVY - FLEET COMBAT DIRECTION SYSTEMS SUPPORT ACTIVITY, SAN DIEGO - TECHNICAL INFO. SERVICES OFFICE (Comp Sci)
200 Catalina Blvd.   Phone: (619) 225-2950
San Diego, CA 92147   Marilyn Soldwisch, Tech.Info.Serv.Spec.
Founded: 1961. **Staff:** 1. **Subjects:** Computer technology, software, hardware, tactical data systems. **Holdings:** 9165 documents and technical reports; 1400 microfiche. **Subscriptions:** 23 journals and other serials. **Automated Operations:** Computerized cataloging. **Publications:** Accessions list.

U.S. NAVY - MARINE CORPS
See: U.S. Marine Corps

★14711★
U.S. NAVY - NAVAL ACADEMY - NIMITZ LIBRARY (Mil)
      Phone: (301) 267-2194
Annapolis, MD 21402   Professor Richard A. Evans, Lib.Dir.
Founded: 1845. **Staff:** Prof 20; Other 31. **Subjects:** Naval science, naval history, history, international relations, biography, technology, science. **Special Collections:** Benjamin Collection (1150 volumes of early works on electricity); Weidorn Collection (900 volumes containing colorplates); Guggenheim Collection (2950 volumes, including literary first editions); Steichen Collection (10,000 photographs). **Holdings:** 310,000 books; 78,000 bound periodical volumes; 15,100 reels of microfilm; 88,000 government documents; 12,500 technical reports. **Subscriptions:** 1785 journals and other serials; 38 newspapers. **Services:** Interlibrary loans; copying; library open to public with restrictions. **Automated Operations:** Computerized cataloging. **Computerized Information Services:** DIALOG, SDC, OCLC. **Networks/Consortia:** Member of FEDLINK. **Publications:** Nimitz Library Newsletter and Guide to the Nimitz Library - both irregular; Serials Holdings List, biennial. **Staff:** Assoc.Prof. John P. Cummings, Assoc.Dir.; Asst.Prof.Robert A. Lambert, Asst.Libn., Tech.Serv.; Alice S. Creighton, Asst.Libn., Spec.Coll.

★14712★
U.S. NAVY - NAVAL AEROSPACE MEDICAL INSTITUTE - LIBRARY (Med)
Bldg. 1953, Code 012   Phone: (904) 452-2256
Pensacola, FL 32508   Ruth T. Rogers, Adm.Libn.
Founded: 1940. **Staff:** Prof 1; Other 2. **Subjects:** Aviation and aerospace medicine, medical specialties, basic sciences. **Holdings:** 10,000 books; 10,000 bound periodical volumes. **Subscriptions:** 300 journals and other serials. **Services:** Interlibrary loans; library not open to public.

★14713★
U.S. NAVY - NAVAL AIR DEVELOPMENT CENTER - TECHNICAL INFORMATION BRANCH (Sci-Tech)
Technical Services Dept.   Phone: (215) 441-2429
Warminster, PA 18974   Dora Huang, Br.Hd.Libn.
Founded: 1944. **Subjects:** Naval aviation, air and ship navigation, aerospace medicine, systems engineering, computer science, crew systems. **Special Collections:** Defense reports; NASA reports. **Holdings:** 30,000 books; 20,000 bound periodical volumes; 400,000 technical reports including microfiche. **Subscriptions:** 650 journals. **Services:** Interlibrary loans; library open to Department of Defense personnel and approved government contractors. **Automated Operations:** Computerized cataloging. **Computerized Information Services:** DIALOG, DTIC, NASA/RECON, OCLC. **Networks/Consortia:** Member of FEDLINK.

★14714★
U.S. NAVY - NAVAL AIR ENGINEERING CENTER - TECHNICAL LIBRARY, CODE 1115 (Sci-Tech)
Naval Air Engineering Center   Phone: (201) 323-2893
Lakehurst, NJ 08733   Deloris J. Swan, Lib.Off.
Founded: 1917. **Staff:** 2. **Subjects:** Aerodynamics, aeronautics, astronautics, aviation medicine, electronics, mechanical engineering, guided missiles, ground support equipment, mathematics. **Special Collections:** NASA reports. **Holdings:** 10,000 books; 4000 unbound periodical volumes; 56,000 technical reports. **Subscriptions:** 207 journals and other serials. **Services:** Interlibrary loans; library not open to public. **Publications:** List of Accessions Received by NAEC Library, bimonthly - for internal distribution only. **Staff:** Roberta Graves .

★14715★
U.S. NAVY - NAVAL AIR PROPULSION CENTER - TECHNICAL LIBRARY (Sci-Tech)
Box 7176   Phone: (609) 896-5600
Trenton, NJ 08628   Robert Malone, Libn.
Founded: 1955. **Staff:** Prof 1. **Subjects:** Aircraft engines and fuels. **Holdings:** 1000 books; 1000 unbound periodical volumes; 7500 technical reports; 1000 government specifications; 1000 microcards. **Subscriptions:** 100 journals and other serials; 2 newspapers. **Services:** Interlibrary loans; library open to outside users with security clearance. **Publications:** Accessions list, 5/year - limited distribution.

★14716★
U.S. NAVY - NAVAL AIR STATION (CA-Alameda) - LIBRARY (Mil)
Bldg. 2, Wing 3   Phone: (415) 869-2519
Alameda, CA 94501   Barbara A. Arnott, Adm.Libn.
Founded: 1940. **Staff:** Prof 1; Other 6. **Subjects:** Navy and other military branches, California, careers and education, women and minorities. **Holdings:** 23,500 volumes; 200 bound periodical volumes; 10 VF drawers of pamphlets and clippings; 20 shelves of periodicals; 1200 phonograph records/tapes

(mainly popular music). **Subscriptions:** 88 journals and other serials; 8 newspapers. **Services:** Interlibrary loans; copying; library open to public with visitor permit. **Staff:** Robert Shannon, Educ.Serv.Off., Supv.

★14717★
U.S. NAVY - NAVAL AIR STATION (CA-Lemoore) - LIBRARY (Mil)
Bldg. 821   Phone: (209) 998-3144
Lemoore, CA 93245   Lois C. Gruntorad, Libn.
Founded: 1961. **Staff:** 2. **Subjects:** U.S. Navy, biography, history, science. **Holdings:** 22,000 books. **Subscriptions:** 65 journals and other serials; 10 newspapers. **Services:** Interlibrary loans; copying; library open to students and civil employees. **Networks/Consortia:** Member of San Joaquin Valley Library System (SJVLS).

★14718★
U.S. NAVY - NAVAL AIR STATION (CA-North Island) - LIBRARY (Mil; Sci-Tech)
Bldg. 650   Phone: (619) 437-7041
San Diego, CA 92135   Sharon Nelson, Adm.Libn.
Staff: Prof 1; Other 3. **Subjects:** Naval aviation and history. **Holdings:** 25,000 books; 12 drawers of pamphlets. **Subscriptions:** 114 journals and other serials; 8 newspapers. **Services:** Interlibrary loans; copying; library open to public by appointment.

★14719★
U.S. NAVY - NAVAL AIR STATION (FL-Jacksonville) - LIBRARY (Mil)
Bldg. 930, Box 52   Phone: (904) 772-3415
Jacksonville, FL 32212   Patricia C. Doyle, Adm.Libn.
Staff: Prof 1; Other 2. **Subjects:** World War II; naval history and aviation. **Holdings:** 200 bound periodical volumes; 1200 records. **Subscriptions:** 100 journals and other serials; 12 newspapers. **Services:** Copying; library not open to public.

★14720★
U.S. NAVY - NAVAL AIR STATION (FL-Key West) - LIBRARY (Mil)*
Bldg. 623A   Phone: (305) 296-3561
Key West, FL 33040   LCDR M. Gore, Lib.Off.
Staff: 1. **Subjects:** Naval air history, naval history, sailing and cruising. **Holdings:** 22,303 books; 21 bound periodical volumes; 861 phonograph records. **Subscriptions:** 6 newspapers. **Services:** Interlibrary loans; library not open to public. **Staff:** Ardina M. McClain, Lib.Techn.

★14721★
U.S. NAVY - NAVAL AIR STATION (FL-Pensacola) - LIBRARY (Mil; Sci-Tech)
Bldg. 633   Phone: (904) 452-4362
Pensacola, FL 32508   C. R. Moreland, Hd.Libn.
Staff: Prof 2; Other 4. **Subjects:** Aviation, Navy, military training. **Special Collections:** Historical archives for naval installations in the area. **Holdings:** 110,000 books; 500 bound periodical volumes; 500 reels of microfilm of periodical backfiles; 8 VF drawers of clippings and pamphlets on local history. **Subscriptions:** 120 journals and other serials; 18 newspapers. **Services:** Interlibrary loans (limited); library open to active and retired military personnel and their dependents, Civil Service employees and open to public by special appointment. **Staff:** Marie Baxter, Lib.Supv.

★14722★
U.S. NAVY - NAVAL AIR STATION (ME-Brunswick) - LIBRARY (Mil)
Box 21   Phone: (207) 921-2639
Brunswick, ME 04011   Judy A. Hoshaw, Libn.
Staff: Prof 1; Other 1. **Subjects:** Navy, World War II. **Holdings:** 14,500 books; 283 phonograph records; 67 films. **Subscriptions:** 66 journals and other serials; 13 newspapers. **Services:** Interlibrary loans; library open to public for reference use only.

★14723★
U.S. NAVY - NAVAL AIR STATION (TN-Memphis) - LIBRARY (Mil; Sci-Tech)
S-78   Phone: (901) 872-5683
Millington, TN 38054   Relda D. Hale, Libn.
Staff: Prof 1; Other 7. **Subjects:** Electronics, avionics, aeronautics, navigation, military history and biography, geography. **Special Collections:** "Welcome Aboard" - packets from world-wide military installations. **Holdings:** 49,000 books; 450 bound periodical volumes; 400 phonograph records. **Subscriptions:** 110 journals and other serials; 9 newspapers. **Services:** Interlibrary loans; library open to active and retired military personnel and dependents and civilian employees.

★14724★
U.S. NAVY - NAVAL AIR STATION (TX-Corpus Christi) - LIBRARY (Mil)
Station Library, Bldg. 5   Phone: (512) 939-3574
Corpus Christi, TX 78419   Eugene V. Lopez, Libn.
Founded: 1941. **Staff:** 4. **Subjects:** U.S. Navy, World War II, aeronautics. **Holdings:** 22,000 books; 8 VF drawers of clippings, pamphlets, pictures, and maps. **Subscriptions:** 140 journals and other serials. **Services:** Interlibrary loans; copying; library open to public by permission.

★14725★
U.S. NAVY - NAVAL AIR STATION - TECHNICAL LIBRARY (Sci-Tech)†
Code 6860   Phone: (805) 982-8156
Point Mugu, CA 93042   I.K. Burtnett, Hd.Libn.
Founded: 1948. **Staff:** Prof 3; Other 6. **Subjects:** Aeronautics, mathematics, electronics, astronautics, meteorology, oceanography, naval history, physics, radar technology. **Holdings:** 40,000 books; 9000 bound periodical volumes; 135,000 reports; 1000 reels of microfilm. **Subscriptions:** 350 journals and other serials. **Services:** Interlibrary loans; library open to Department of Defense personnel and others with requisite security clearance. **Special Indexes:** Bibliographies and indexes.

★14726★
U.S. NAVY - NAVAL AIR SYSTEMS COMMAND - TECHNICAL LIBRARY AIR-7226 (Sci-Tech)
    Phone: (202) 692-9006
Washington, DC 20361   Pat Stone, Hd.Libn.
Founded: 1922. **Staff:** Prof 5; Other 5. **Subjects:** Aeronautics, weapon systems, management, mathematics, materials, electronics. **Special Collections:** Technical manuals; naval aviation including airships. **Holdings:** 14,000 books; 1600 bound periodical volumes; 500,000 technical reports. **Subscriptions:** 300 journals and other serials. **Services:** Interlibrary loans; copying; library serves government agencies and contractors only. **Automated Operations:** Computerized cataloging. **Computerized Information Services:** DIALOG, DTIC, OCLC. **Networks/Consortia:** Member of FEDLINK. **Publications:** Accessions list, monthly. **Remarks:** The Naval Air Systems Command Technical Library was formerly a part of the Bureau of Naval Weapons Technical Library and the Bureau of Aeronautics Technical Library. The aeronautics collection dates back to 1922. **Staff:** Marilyn Harned, Ref.Libn.

★14727★
U.S. NAVY - NAVAL AIR TEST CENTER - NAVAL AIR STATION - PATUXTENT RIVER CENTRAL LIBRARY (Mil; Sci-Tech)
Bldg. 407   Phone: (301) 863-3686
Patuxent River, MD 20670   Suzanne M. Ryder, Dir.
Founded: 1943. **Staff:** Prof 2; Other 4. **Subjects:** Engineering, aviation, military science and history, management, computer science, science. **Holdings:** 60,000 books; 15,000 government documents. **Subscriptions:** 400 journals and other serials; 25 newspapers. **Services:** Interlibrary loans; copying; library open only to base personnel and retired military with the exception of a government documents depository that serves all residents of Southern Maryland. **Automated Operations:** Computerized cataloging. **Computerized Information Services:** DIALOG. **Formerly:** Its Engineering & Technical Library. **Staff:** Pamela M. Hilton, Libn.

★14728★
U.S. NAVY - NAVAL AMPHIBIOUS BASE (CA-Coronado) - LIBRARY (Mil)
    Phone: (619) 437-2473
San Diego, CA 92155   Nadine Bangsberg, Adm. Libn.
Founded: 1950. **Staff:** Prof 1; Other 2. **Subjects:** Naval history, amphibious operations, general nonfiction, guerrilla warfare, Vietnam, World War II. **Holdings:** 25,000 books; 159 bound periodical volumes; 2600 tapes and phonograph records; 1500 paperbacks. **Subscriptions:** 125 journals and other serials; 8 newspapers. **Services:** Interlibrary loans; library not open to public. **Publications:** Subject bibliographies; Book List, monthly - for internal distribution only.

★14729★
U.S. NAVY - NAVAL AMPHIBIOUS SCHOOL - JOHN SIDNEY MC CAIN AMPHIBIOUS WARFARE LIBRARY (Mil)
Bldg. 3504   Phone: (804) 464-7467
Norfolk, VA 23521   Carolyn G. Jones, Dir., Lib.Serv.
Founded: 1965. **Staff:** 1. **Subjects:** Amphibious warfare, military arts and sciences. **Holdings:** 1200 books; 2000 documents. **Subscriptions:** 77 journals and other serials. **Services:** Interlibrary loans; library open to qualified researchers.

★14730★
U.S. NAVY - NAVAL AVIONICS CENTER - TECHNICAL LIBRARY (Sci-Tech)
21st & Arlington Ave.   Phone: (317) 353-7765
Indianapolis, IN 46218   Louise Boyd, Supv.
Founded: 1945. **Subjects:** Mathematics, electronics, electrical engineering, physics, metallurgy, avionics equipment. **Holdings:** 11,000 books; 2000 microfiche; 30,000 technical reports. **Subscriptions:** 450 journals and other serials. **Services:** Interlibrary loans; library not open to public.

U.S. NAVY - NAVAL BIOSCIENCES LABORATORY
See: University of California, Berkeley - Naval Biosciences Laboratory

★14731★
U.S. NAVY - NAVAL COASTAL SYSTEMS CENTER - TECHNICAL INFORMATION SERVICES BRANCH (Sci-Tech; Mil)†
                                         Phone: (904) 234-4381
Panama City, FL 32407   Myrtle J. Rhodes, Supv.Libn.
Founded: 1945. **Staff:** Prof 2; Other 3. **Subjects:** Mine and ordnance countermeasures, acoustic countermeasures, amphibious operations support, naval diving and salvage support, inshore warfare, coastal technology. **Holdings:** 21,000 books; 5000 bound periodical volumes; 45,000 technical reports. **Subscriptions:** 475 journals and other serials; 5 newspapers. **Services:** Interlibrary loans; copying; library open to outside users cleared by Security Office. **Automated Operations:** Computerized cataloging, serials and circulation. **Computerized Information Services:** Online systems. **Publications:** OFFLINE, bimonthly. **Special Catalogs:** Computer-generated subject catalogs. **Staff:** B. Householder, Bk.Cat./Ref.; Gwyn Stewart, Acq./Ser.; Laura Thompson, DTIC Oper.

★14732★
U.S. NAVY - NAVAL CONSTRUCTION BATTALION CENTER - LIBRARY (Sci-Tech; Mil)
Code 31L   Phone: (805) 982-4411
Port Hueneme, CA 93043   Betty M. Smith, Libn.
Staff: Prof 1; Other 2. **Subjects:** Naval history, construction, building trades, guerilla warfare, engineering, survival. **Holdings:** 25,000 books; 1000 disc records; 52 8mm films. **Subscriptions:** 100 journals and other serials. **Services:** Interlibrary loans; copying; library open to public with restrictions. **Special Catalogs:** Bibliographies on ethnic groups and women.

★14733★
U.S. NAVY - NAVAL DENTAL RESEARCH INSTITUTE - LIBRARY (Med)
Naval Base, Bldg. 1-H   Phone: (312) 688-5647
Great Lakes, IL 60088   Myra J. Rouse, Libn.
Staff: Prof 1; Other 1. **Subjects:** Clinical dentistry, basic sciences, oral biology and dental research. **Holdings:** 450 books; 1550 bound periodical volumes. **Subscriptions:** 74 journals and other serials. **Services:** Interlibrary loans; library not open to public.

★14734★
U.S. NAVY - NAVAL EDUCATION AND TRAINING CENTER - LIBRARY SYSTEM (Mil)
Main Library Bldg. 114   Phone: (401) 841-3044
Newport, RI 02841   James F. Aylward, Adm.
Founded: 1973. **Staff:** Prof 2; Other 4. **Subjects:** Military and naval science, naval history, technology, curriculum background. **Holdings:** 70,000 books; 250 bound periodical volumes; 10 VF drawers; 1200 microforms; 2500 NAV manuals; 1700 audio materials. **Subscriptions:** 280 journals and other serials; 28 newspapers. **Services:** Interlibrary loans; copying; library open to public with Naval Command permission. **Computerized Information Services:** DTIC, Defense Logistics Study Information Exchange (DLSIE). **Remarks:** The NETC Library System includes the main library plus the Curriculum Support Library, Chaplains School Library, Correctional Center Library and the Naval Regional Medical Center Library. An additional telephone number is (401) 841-4352. **Staff:** Robert S. Wessells, Asst.Libn.; Paul Cotsoridis, Hd., Circ. Control.

★14735★
U.S. NAVY - NAVAL ELECTRONICS SYSTEMS ENGINEERING CENTER - SAN DIEGO LIBRARY (Sci-Tech)
4297 Pacific Hwy.
Box 80337   Phone: (619) 260-2482
San Diego, CA 92138
Founded: 1967. **Staff:** Prof 1; Other 2. **Subjects:** Electronics, engineering, antennas, finance, computers, business administration. **Special Collections:** U.S. Navy Electronic Equipment, DOD Electronic Equipment. **Holdings:** 6000 books; 5000 reports; 11,000 other cataloged items. **Subscriptions:** 123 journals and other serials. **Services:** Interlibrary loans; library open to Department of Defense contractors. **Special Catalogs:** Subject, Equipment

nomenclature.

★14736★
U.S. NAVY - NAVAL ENVIRONMENTAL PREDICTION RESEARCH FACILITY - TECHNICAL LIBRARY (Sci-Tech)
Naval Postgraduate School
Annex Bldg. 22   Phone: (408) 646-2813
Monterey, CA 93943   Joanne M. May, Libn.
Founded: 1971. **Staff:** Prof 1. **Subjects:** Meteorology. **Holdings:** 2900 books; 3000 bound periodical volumes; 7560 technical reports; 30,000 microfiche. **Subscriptions:** 125 journals and other serials. **Services:** Interlibrary loans; copying; SDI; library open to Department of Defense only. **Computerized Information Services:** DIALOG. **Publications:** Library Bulletin, biweekly - for internal distribution only.

★14737★
U.S. NAVY - NAVAL EXPLOSIVE ORDNANCE DISPOSAL TECHNOLOGY CENTER - TECHNICAL LIBRARY (Sci-Tech)
                                         Phone: (301) 743-4738
Indian Head, MD 20640   Bonnie D. Davis, Adm.Libn.
Staff: Prof 3; Other 4. **Subjects:** U.S. ordnance, foreign ordnance, explosives, underwater equipment, diving. **Special Collections:** Explosive ordnance disposal procedures, tools and equipment. **Holdings:** 10,000 books; 95,000 documents; 32,000 engineering drawings; 500 photographs; 12,000 microfiche; 60 reels of microfilm. **Subscriptions:** 250 journals and other serials. **Services:** Interlibrary loans; copying; library open to outside users with permission of the head librarian. **Publications:** Accession List, monthly. **Staff:** Annie L. Dudley, Asst.Libn.

★14738★
U.S. NAVY - NAVAL FACILITIES ENGINEERING COMMAND - HISTORICAL INFORMATION OFFICE (Hist; Mil)
Naval Construction Batalion Ctr.   Phone: (805) 982-5563
Port Hueneme, CA 93043
Subjects: History of the Naval Facilities Engineering Command, the Naval Construction Force (Seabees), and the Navy's Civil Engineering Corps, 1940 to present. **Special Collections:** Records of the Naval Facilities Engineering Command (acquisition, construction, and maintenance of the Naval shore establishment in the U.S. and abroad); Naval Construction Force records (operational accomplishments of the combat construction branch of the U.S. Navy); Civil Engineers Corps records (the evolving role of the civil engineer in the U.S. Navy). **Holdings:** 12,000 cubic feet of records. **Services:** Copying; office open to public during business hours.

★14739★
U.S. NAVY - NAVAL FACILITIES ENGINEERING COMMAND - NORTHERN DIVISION - DESIGN DIVISION LIBRARY (Mil; Sci-Tech)
Bldg. 77-L
Philadelphia Naval Base   Phone: (215) 897-6043
Philadelphia, PA 19112   Mary Crum, Engr.Libn.
Staff: Prof 1; Other 2. **Subjects:** Civil engineering, architectural design, mechanical and electrical engineering, management. **Special Collections:** Navy manuals (200). **Holdings:** 2000 books; 500 unbound reports and documents. **Subscriptions:** 64 journals and other serials. **Services:** Copying; library not open to public. **Automated Operations:** Computerized cataloging. **Computerized Information Services:** Internal database. **Publications:** Design Library Newsletter, quarterly - for internal distribution only.

★14740★
U.S. NAVY - NAVAL FACILITIES ENGINEERING COMMAND - TECHNICAL LIBRARY (Sci-Tech)
Hoffman Bldg. 2, 200 Stovall St.   Phone: (202) 325-8507
Alexandria, VA 22332   Cynthia K. Neyland, Libn.
Founded: 1941. **Staff:** Prof 1. **Subjects:** Engineering, architecture, management, general science and mathematics. **Holdings:** 15,000 books; 5000 technical reports. **Subscriptions:** 200 journals and other serials. **Services:** Interlibrary loans (excludes NAVFAC publications); copying; library open to Department of Defense personnel. **Automated Operations:** Computerized cataloging. **Computerized Information Services:** DIALOG, OCLC. **Networks/Consortia:** Member of FEDLINK.

★14741★
U.S. NAVY - NAVAL HEALTH RESEARCH CENTER - WALTER L. WILKINS BIO-MEDICAL LIBRARY (Med)
Box 85122   Phone: (619) 225-6640
San Diego, CA 92138   Mary Aldous, Libn.
Founded: 1959. **Staff:** Prof 1; Other 1. **Subjects:** Environmental and stress medicine, psychiatry, work physiology, biological sciences, social medicine. **Special Collections:** Prisoners of War studies. **Holdings:** 7755 books; 3969

bound periodical volumes; 7113 technical reports; 195 audiotapes. **Subscriptions:** 214 journals and other serials. **Services:** Interlibrary loans; library open to public with restrictions. **Computerized Information Services:** DIALOG, BRS, MEDLARS. **Publications:** Periodicals holding list.

★14742★
U.S. NAVY - NAVAL HISTORICAL CENTER - OPERATIONAL ARCHIVES (Mil; Hist)
Bldg. 210, Washington Navy Yard   Phone: (202) 433-3170
Washington, DC 20374   Dr. Dean C. Allard, Dir.
Staff: Prof 7; Other 3. **Subjects:** U.S. Naval history, naval operations, naval archives, naval biography. **Special Collections:** CNO records; oral history interview transcripts; China repository; aviation histories; materials relating to World War II and post-war operations. **Holdings:** 9500 feet of records and documents, including 1200 feet of action and operational reports, 1941-1953; 900 feet of naval command war diaries, 1941-1953; 570 feet of miscellaneous records and publications, 1931-1950. **Services:** Interlibrary loans; copying (both limited); reading room open to public. **Publications:** List of open collections and publications - available on request. **Staff:** Bernard F. Cavalcante, Asst.Hd.

★14743★
U.S. NAVY - NAVAL HISTORICAL CENTER - PHOTOGRAPHIC SECTION (Hist; Aud-Vis)
Washington Navy Yard   Phone: (202) 433-2765
Washington, DC 20374
Staff: Prof 2. **Subjects:** Visual aspects of naval history, including weapons, wars, U.S. and foreign naval ships and others. **Holdings:** 200,000 photographs, prints, drawings and posters. **Services:** Copying; section open to public.

★14744★
U.S. NAVY - NAVAL HOSPITAL (CA-Camp Pendleton) - MEDICAL LIBRARY (Med)
                                                 Phone: (714) 725-1322
Camp Pendleton, CA 92055   Deborah G. Batey, Med.Libn.
Founded: 1949. **Staff:** Prof 1; Other 1. **Subjects:** General medicine, nursing, family practice, patient education. **Holdings:** 1000 books; 4800 bound periodical volumes; 350 AV programs. **Subscriptions:** 200 journals and other serials. **Services:** Interlibrary loans; copying; library open to public for reference use only. **Networks/Consortia:** Member of Pacific Southwest Regional Medical Library Service (PSRMLS); San Diego County Federal Medical Libraries. **Publications:** Medical Library News, bimonthly - for internal distribution only; Patient Learning Center Catalog, irregular.

★14745★
U.S. NAVY - NAVAL HOSPITAL (CA-Oakland) - MEDICAL LIBRARY (Med)
8750 Mountain Blvd.   Phone: (415) 639-2031
Oakland, CA 94627   Jane C. O'Sullivan, Adm.Libn.
Staff: Prof 2; Other 2. **Subjects:** Medicine, nursing, paramedical sciences, psychiatry. **Special Collections:** Preventive medicine (300 volumes). **Holdings:** 8000 books; 10,000 bound periodical volumes. **Subscriptions:** 475 journals and other serials. **Services:** Interlibrary loans; library not open to public. **Computerized Information Services:** MEDLINE, BRS. **Networks/Consortia:** Member of Pacific Southwest Regional Medical Library Service (PSRMLS). **Publications:** Serials List, annual; New Book List, monthly - to department heads. **Staff:** Harriet V. Cohen, Med.Libn.

★14746★
U.S. NAVY - NAVAL HOSPITAL (CA-San Diego) - THOMPSON MEDICAL LIBRARY (Med)
                                                 Phone: (619) 233-2367
San Diego, CA 92134
Founded: 1923. **Staff:** Prof 2; Other 2. **Subjects:** Medicine, nursing, dentistry, hospital administration. **Special Collections:** Meyer Wiener Collection on Ophthalmology. **Holdings:** 13,792 books; 13,198 bound periodical volumes. **Subscriptions:** 573 journals. **Services:** Interlibrary loans; copying; SDI; library open to military personnel. **Computerized Information Services:** DIALOG, MEDLINE, BRS. **Networks/Consortia:** Member of Pacific Southwest Regional Medical Library Service (PSRMLS). **Publications:** List of journal titles (subscription), annual; recent acquisitions, quarterly; Library Newsletter, quarterly. **Staff:** Jan B. Dempsey, Ref.Libn.

★14747★
U.S. NAVY - NAVAL HOSPITAL (FL-Jacksonville) - MEDICAL LIBRARY (Med)
                                                 Phone: (904) 772-3439
Jacksonville, FL 32214   Bettye W. Stilley, Med.Libn.
Founded: 1942. **Staff:** Prof 1. **Subjects:** Medicine. **Holdings:** 1500 books;

2400 bound periodical volumes; 500 other cataloged items; 1500 cassette tapes. **Subscriptions:** 162 journals and other serials. **Services:** Interlibrary loans; library not open to public.

★14748★
U.S. NAVY - NAVAL HOSPITAL (FL-Orlando) - MEDICAL LIBRARY (Med)†
                                                 Phone: (305) 646-4959
Orlando, FL 32813   Alice Crownfield, Med.Libn.
Staff: Prof 1. **Subjects:** Clinical medicine. **Holdings:** 800 books; 500 bound periodical volumes. **Subscriptions:** 86 journals and other serials. **Services:** Interlibrary loans; library not open to public.

★14749★
U.S. NAVY - NAVAL HOSPITAL (FL-Pensacola) - MEDICAL LIBRARY (Med)
                                                 Phone: (904) 453-6635
Pensacola, FL 32512   Juan E. Terry, Med.Libn.
Staff: Prof 1; Other 1. **Subjects:** Medicine, allied health sciences. **Holdings:** 5000 books; 15,000 bound periodical volumes. **Subscriptions:** 228 journals and other serials. **Services:** Interlibrary loans; copying; library open to public.

★14750★
U.S. NAVY - NAVAL HOSPITAL (Guam) - MEDICAL LIBRARY (Med)
Box 7747   Phone: (671) 344-9250
FPO San Francisco, CA 96630
Founded: 1954. **Staff:** Prof 1. **Subjects:** Medicine, nursing, dentistry, surgery, obstetrics. **Holdings:** 1800 books; 1300 bound periodical volumes. **Subscriptions:** 150 journals and other serials. **Services:** Interlibrary loans; copying; library open to medical profession.

★14751★
U.S. NAVY - NAVAL HOSPITAL (IL-Great Lakes) - MEDICAL LIBRARY (Med)
Bldg. 200-H   Phone: (312) 688-4601
Great Lakes, IL 60088   Phyllis A. Gibbs, Med.Libn.
Founded: 1945. **Staff:** Prof 1. **Subjects:** Medicine, surgery, dentistry, nursing. **Holdings:** 2100 books; 4100 bound periodical volumes. **Subscriptions:** 150 journals and other serials. **Services:** Interlibrary loans; library not open to public. **Networks/Consortia:** Member of Lake County Consortium; Greater Midwest Regional Medical Library Network (Region 3).

★14752★
U.S. NAVY - NAVAL HOSPITAL (NC-Camp Lejeune) - MEDICAL LIBRARY (Med)
                                                 Phone: (919) 451-4076
Camp Lejeune, NC 28542   Betty Frazelle, Lib.Techn.
Founded: 1941. **Staff:** 1. **Subjects:** Medicine and related sciences. **Holdings:** 2130 books; 4771 bound periodical volumes. **Subscriptions:** 185 journals and other serials. **Services:** Interlibrary loans; library not open to public.

★14753★
U.S. NAVY - NAVAL HOSPITAL (PA-Philadelphia) - MEDICAL LIBRARY (Med)
17th & Pattison Aves.   Phone: (215) 755-8314
Philadelphia, PA 19145   Giovina Cavacini, Libn.
Founded: 1917. **Staff:** Prof 1. **Subjects:** Medicine and allied sciences. **Holdings:** 6000 books; 8000 bound periodical volumes; Audio-Digest tapes. **Subscriptions:** 275 journals and other serials. **Services:** Interlibrary loans; copying; library open to public with restrictions. **Computerized Information Services:** NLM. **Networks/Consortia:** Member of Greater Northeastern Regional Medical Library Program.

★14754★
U.S. NAVY - NAVAL HOSPITAL (RI-Newport) - MEDICAL LIBRARY (Med)
Cypress & Third Sts.   Phone: (401) 841-1180
Newport, RI 02840   Winifred M. Jacome, Lib.Techn.
Staff: 1. **Subjects:** Medicine and related subjects, dentistry. **Holdings:** 2600 books; Audio-Digest tapes, 1968 to present. **Subscriptions:** 100 journals and other serials. **Services:** Interlibrary loans; library open to public for reference use only.

★14755★
U.S. NAVY - NAVAL HOSPITAL (TN-Memphis) - GENERAL AND MEDICAL LIBRARY (Med)
                                                 Phone: (901) 872-5846
Millington, TN 38054   Virginia C. Masner, Libn.
Founded: 1942. **Staff:** Prof 1. **Subjects:** Dentistry, medicine, nursing. **Holdings:** 5511 volumes. **Subscriptions:** 110 journals and other serials. **Services:** Interlibrary loans; copying. **Automated Operations:** Access to online systems. **Networks/Consortia:** Member of Association of Memphis

Area Health Science Libraries (AMAHSL). **Publications:** Lists of new books posted on hospital bulletin boards.

★14756★
U.S. NAVY - NAVAL HOSPITAL (TX-Corpus Christi) - MEDICAL LIBRARY (Med)
Phone: (512) 939-3863
Corpus Christi, TX 78419   Dorothy Reichenstein, Med.Libn.
Founded: 1941. **Staff:** 2. **Subjects:** Medicine, surgery, nursing, and allied health sciences. **Holdings:** 1261 books; 734 bound periodical volumes; 184 other cataloged items; pamphlets. **Subscriptions:** 74 journals and other serials. **Services:** Interlibrary loans; library not open to public. **Networks/Consortia:** Member of Coastal Bend Health Sciences Library Consortium.

★14757★
U.S. NAVY - NAVAL HOSPITAL (VA-Portsmouth) - MEDICAL LIBRARY (Med)
Phone: (804) 398-5386
Portsmouth, VA 23708   Suad Jones, Med.Libn.
Staff: Prof 1; Other 2. **Subjects:** Medicine and allied sciences. **Holdings:** 4705 books; 13,155 bound periodical volumes. **Subscriptions:** 547 journals and other serials. **Services:** Interlibrary loans; copying; library open to public for reference use only on request. **Computerized Information Services:** MEDLINE, OCLC, BRS. Performs searches for a fee.

★14758★
U.S. NAVY - NAVAL HOSPITAL (WA-Bremerton) - MEDICAL LIBRARY (Med)
Phone: (206) 478-9316
Bremerton, WA 98314   Jane Easley, Libn.
Founded: 1947. **Staff:** 1. **Subjects:** Medicine, nursing, administration. **Holdings:** 1300 books; 2700 bound periodical volumes. **Subscriptions:** 145 journals and other serials. **Services:** Interlibrary loans; copying; bibliographic service; library open to qualified medical personnel. **Computerized Information Services:** NLM.

★14759★
U.S. NAVY - NAVAL INSTITUTE - ORAL HISTORY OFFICE (Hist; Mil)
Phone: (301) 268-6110
Annapolis, MD 21402   Paul Stillwell, Oral Hist.Dir.
Founded: 1969. **Staff:** Prof 1; Other 6. **Subjects:** Naval biography, Coast Guard biography, naval aviation. **Special Collections:** Admiral Nimitz Collection; POLARIS interviews; WAVE interviews. **Holdings:** 140 bound volumes containing 80,000 pages of transcripts; tapes of 200 individual memoirs. **Services:** Library open to researchers by appointment. **Remarks:** Copies of all bound volumes are also available in the special collections at the Nimitz Library of the U.S. Naval Academy, Annapolis, MD and the Naval History Center, Washington Navy Yard, Washington, DC.

★14760★
U.S. NAVY - NAVAL INSTITUTE - REFERENCE & PHOTOGRAPHIC LIBRARY (Mil)
Phone: (301) 268-6110
Annapolis, MD 21402   Patty M. Maddocks, Dir.
Staff: 4. **Subjects:** U.S. Navy - ships, aircraft, personalities; American Revolution; Vietnam War; foreign ships and personalities. **Special Collections:** James C. Fahey Ship and Aircraft Collection of U.S. Navy; "Our Navy" collection. **Holdings:** 4000 books; 100 bound periodical volumes; 100 oral history materials; 100 bound volumes of proceedings. **Subscriptions:** 103 journals and other serials. **Services:** Copying; library open to public. **Publications:** U.S. Naval Institute Proceedings. **Special Indexes:** Proceedings Index; Navy Oral History Index.

★14761★
U.S. NAVY - NAVAL INTELLIGENCE SUPPORT CENTER - INFORMATION SERVICES DIVISION (Mil)
4301 Suitland Rd.
Code 63   Phone: (202) 763-1606
Washington, DC 20390   Alice T. Cranor, Hd., Info.Serv.Div.
Founded: 1944. **Staff:** Prof 5; Other 20. **Subjects:** Military intelligence, science and technology. **Special Collections:** Russian Language technical book and manual collection (4500). **Holdings:** 5000 books; 50,000 reports; 50,000 documents. **Subscriptions:** 1000 journals and other serials; 30 newspapers. **Services:** Interlibrary loans; division not open to public. **Automated Operations:** Computerized cataloging, acquisitions, serials and circulation. **Computerized Information Services:** DIALOG, SDC, BRS. **Publications:** Weekly Accession Bulletin; Library Happenings, irregular; Periodicals Collection, updated annually. **Staff:** Stephanie V. Williams, Hd., Ref.Br.; D.Janean Garrett, Hd., Tech.Serv.Br.

★14762★
U.S. NAVY - NAVAL MEDICAL COMMAND - NAVAL DENTAL CLINIC - NATIONAL CAPITAL REGION - WILLIAM L. DARNALL LIBRARY (Med)
Phone: (202) 295-0080
Bethesda, MD 20814   Patricia A. Evans, Chr., Lrng.Rsrcs.
Staff: 1. **Subjects:** Dentistry, medicine. **Holdings:** 8500 books. **Subscriptions:** 71 journals and other serials. **Services:** Interlibrary loans; copying (limited); library open to public.

★14763★
U.S. NAVY - NAVAL MEDICAL RESEARCH INSTITUTE - INFORMATION SERVICES BRANCH (Med)
Phone: (202) 295-2186
Bethesda, MD 20814   Rosemary B. Spitzen, Adm.Libn.
Founded: 1942. **Staff:** Prof 1; Other 2. **Subjects:** Infectious diseases, casualty care, hyperbaric medicine, experimental surgery, transplantation, military medicine. **Special Collections:** Naval Medical Research Institute Reports, 1943 to present. **Holdings:** 5000 books. **Subscriptions:** 250 journals and other serials. **Services:** Interlibrary loans; copying; SDI; library open to public for reference use only. **Automated Operations:** Computerized cataloging. **Computerized Information Services:** DIALOG, OCLC, BRS; internal database. **Networks/Consortia:** Member of Interlibrary Users Association; FEDLINK. **Publications:** Summaries of Research, annual; Union List of Serials, annual.

★14764★
U.S. NAVY - NAVAL MILITARY PERSONNEL COMMAND - TECHNICAL LIBRARY (Soc Sci)
Arlington Annex, Rm. 1403   Phone: (202) 694-2073
Washington, DC 20370   Joyce A. Lane, Libn.
Founded: 1946. **Staff:** Prof 1; Other 1. **Subjects:** Education, psychology, personnel administration, statistics, management. **Holdings:** 4000 books; 125 VF drawers of technical reports. **Subscriptions:** 350 journals and other serials. **Services:** Interlibrary loans; library serves Bureau and other government agencies only.

★14765★
U.S. NAVY - NAVAL OBSERVATORY - MATTHEW FONTAINE MAURY MEMORIAL LIBRARY (Sci-Tech)
34th and Massachusetts Ave., N.W.   Phone: (202) 653-1499
Washington, DC 20390   Brenda G. Corbin, Libn.
Founded: 1843. **Staff:** Prof 1; Other 1. **Subjects:** Astronomy, astrophysics, celestial mechanics, geophysics, mathematics and physics. **Special Collections:** Rare books (1482-1800; astronomy, navigation and mathematics; 800 volumes). **Holdings:** 75,000 volumes; slides; microfiche; maps; manuscripts; archives. **Subscriptions:** 200 journals and other serials. **Services:** Interlibrary loans; copying (both limited); library open to graduate students. **Automated Operations:** Computerized cataloging. **Computerized Information Services:** OCLC, DIALOG. **Networks/Consortia:** Member of FEDLINK. **Publications:** Naval Observatory Publications - restricted distribution; Acquisitions List, quarterly.

★14766★
U.S. NAVY - NAVAL OCEAN SYSTEMS CENTER - TECHNICAL LIBRARY (Sci-Tech)
Phone: (619) 225-6171
San Diego, CA 92152   Joan Ingersoll, Hd.
Founded: 1977. **Staff:** Prof 5; Other 10. **Subjects:** Electronics, physics, ocean engineering, underwater ordnance, communications, oceanography, artificial intelligence, robotics. **Holdings:** 60,000 books; 60,000 bound periodical volumes; 100,000 technical reports. **Subscriptions:** 1200 journals. **Services:** SDI; library open to Department of Defense employees. **Automated Operations:** Computerized cataloging. **Computerized Information Services:** DIALOG, BRS, SDC, OCLC, DTIC; LMARS (internal retrieval system for technical reports). **Publications:** List of periodical holdings, annual; New Publications, biweekly; Current Alert biweekly; Current Awareness, monthly. **Remarks:** The Technical Library maintains two branches: the Topside Technical Library Branch and the Bayside Technical Library Branch. Staff: Kathy Wright, Hd., Bayside Br.

★14767★
U.S. NAVY - NAVAL OCEANOGRAPHIC OFFICE - NAVY LIBRARY (Sci-Tech)
NSTL   Phone: (601) 688-4597
Bay St. Louis, MS 39522   Katharine Wallace, Supv.Libn.
Founded: 1871. **Staff:** Prof 2; Other 2. **Subjects:** Oceanography - biological, chemical, geological and physical; ocean engineering; cartography; photogrammetry; meteorology. **Special Collections:** Domestic and foreign sailing directions; International Hydrographic Bureau publications and oceanographic expeditions; Naval Oceanographic Office publications.

Holdings: 100,000 books, bound periodical volumes, documents, translations and pamphlets; 10,000 microforms. **Subscriptions:** 550 journals and other serials. **Services:** Interlibrary loans; copying; library open to qualified research workers. **Automated Operations:** Computerized cataloging. **Computerized Information Services:** DIALOG. **Networks/Consortia:** Member of FEDLINK. **Publications:** Accessions List, monthly - for internal distribution only. **Staff:** Ann Loomis, Libn.

★14768★

U.S. NAVY - NAVAL ORDNANCE STATION - TECHNICAL LIBRARY (Sci-Tech; Mil)
50 D, MDS 50   Phone: (502) 367-5667
Louisville, KY 40214   Elizabeth T. Miles, Lib.Techn.
Staff: 2. **Subjects:** Naval ordnance, engineering. **Holdings:** 1900 books; 27 bound periodical volumes; 1945 technical reports; 45,500 government specifications. **Services:** Interlibrary loans; library open to public with restrictions.

★14769★

U.S. NAVY - NAVAL ORDNANCE STATION - TECHNICAL LIBRARY (5246) (Sci-Tech; Mil)
     Phone: (301) 743-4742
Indian Head, MD 20640   Charles F. Gallagher, Supv.Libn.
Staff: Prof 1; Other 3. **Subjects:** Explosives and propellants, missiles and rockets, aerospace technology, chemistry, chemical engineering, management. **Holdings:** 24,000 books; 5500 bound periodical volumes; 60,000 domestic and foreign research reports; 7400 microcards, several thousand microfiche. **Subscriptions:** 400 journals and other serials. **Services:** Interlibrary loans; library not open to public. **Automated Operations:** Computerized cataloging and serials. **Computerized Information Services:** DTIC, DIALOG. **Publications:** Accessions Bulletin - for internal distribution only.

★14770★

U.S. NAVY - NAVAL POSTGRADUATE SCHOOL - DUDLEY KNOX LIBRARY (Sci-Tech; Mil)
     Phone: (408) 646-2341
Monterey, CA 93943   Paul Spinks, Dir. of Libs.
Staff: Prof 15; Other 18. **Subjects:** Engineering, physical sciences, naval science, operations research, administrative sciences, international affairs. **Special Collections:** Christopher Buckley, Jr. Library (naval and maritime history, 8000 volumes). **Holdings:** 155,000 books; 70,000 bound periodical volumes; 1000 AV materials; 182,000 research reports (paper); 16,000 pamphlets; 356,000 microforms. **Subscriptions:** 1760 journals and other serials; 20 newspapers. **Services:** Interlibrary loans; copying; SDI; library open to public, but some facilities limited to authorized personnel. **Automated Operations:** Computerized serials. **Computerized Information Services:** DIALOG, BRS, RLIN, NEXIS, CIRC II, DTIC; SABIRS III (internal database). **Networks/Consortia:** Member of CLASS; Monterey Bay Area Cooperative Library System (MOBAC); South Bay Cooperative Library System (SBCLS). **Publications:** New on the Shelf, monthly; Library Periodicals: Current Subscriptions and Earlier Holdings, annual; This is Your Library, annual - all for internal distribution only. **Staff:** Terry Britt, Assoc.Dir. of Libs.; Sharon Serzan, Hd., Acq.Div.; Bobbie Carr, Hd., Cat.Div.; Roger Martin, Hd., Rd.Serv.Div.; Kenneth Lauderdale, Hd., Res. Reports Div.

★14771★

U.S. NAVY - NAVAL REGIONAL MEDICAL CLINIC - MEDICAL LIBRARY (Med)
     Phone: (703) 640-2887
Quantico, VA 22134   Mrs. F.B. Starr, Libn.
Staff: 2. **Subjects:** Medicine. **Holdings:** 54 books; 63 medical and nursing journals. **Subscriptions:** 45 journals and other serials. **Services:** Library not open to public.

★14772★

U.S. NAVY - NAVAL RESEARCH LABORATORY - RUTH H. HOOKER TECHNICAL LIBRARY (Sci-Tech)
Code 2620   Phone: (202) 767-2357
Washington, DC 20375   Peter H. Imhof, Libn.
Founded: 1927. **Staff:** Prof 10; Other 20. **Subjects:** Physics, chemistry, electronics. **Holdings:** 145,000 books and bound periodical volumes; 175,000 reports on microfiche and 375,000 paper reports. **Subscriptions:** 2000 journals and other serials. **Services:** Interlibrary loans; copying; library open with prior arrangement. **Publications:** Your Library as a Research Tool. **Staff:** J. Patrick McConnel, Dp.Libn.; Fred Rettenmaier, Ref.Libn.; Eileen Pickenpaugh, Res.Cons.; Doris Folen, Hd., Doc.Sect.; Patricia Cook, ILL.

★14773★

U.S. NAVY - NAVAL RESEARCH LABORATORY - SHOCK AND VIBRATION INFORMATION CENTER (Sci-Tech)
Code 5804   Phone: (202) 767-3306
Washington, DC 20375   J. Gordan Showalter, Hd.
Founded: 1949. **Staff:** Prof 2; Other 3. **Subjects:** Vibrations, shocks, acoustics, structures, test facilities and results, environmental testing. **Special Collections:** Institute of Environmental Science Proceedings (50); Shock and Vibration Digest; Shock and Vibration Bulletins; shock and vibration monographs. **Services:** Center open to public with a fee for services. **Publications:** Yearly Digest; Bulletin Index; catalog of all previous publications. **Staff:** Rudolph H. Volin, Mechanical Engr.

★14774★

U.S. NAVY - NAVAL RESEARCH LABORATORY - UNDERWATER SOUND REFERENCE DETACHMENT - TECHNICAL LIBRARY (Sci-Tech)
755 Gatlin Ave.
Box 8337   Phone: (305) 859-5120
Orlando, FL 32856   Marge Tarnowski, Libn.
Founded: 1954. **Staff:** 1. **Subjects:** Underwater sound, electroacoustics, electronics, mathematics. **Holdings:** 4500 books; 1200 bound periodical volumes; 10,165 documents in paper copy; 1500 documents on microfiche. **Subscriptions:** 70 journals and other serials. **Services:** Library not open to public. **Publications:** USRD Library Bulletin - for internal distribution only.

★14775★

U.S. NAVY - NAVAL SCHOOL - CIVIL ENGINEER CORPS OFFICERS - MOREELL LIBRARY (Sci-Tech)
     Phone: (805) 982-3241
Port Hueneme, CA 93043   Dianne G. Thompson, Lib.Dir.
Founded: 1946. **Staff:** Prof 1; Other 2. **Subjects:** Engineering and construction management, economic analysis, PERT and CPM, civil engineering. **Special Collections:** Admiral Ben Moreell Collection (1100 volumes and correspondence). **Holdings:** 7982 books; 370 bound periodical volumes; 7468 reports and 7500 texts; 4500 course materials; 300 microfiche. **Subscriptions:** 209 journals and other serials; 8 newspapers. **Services:** Interlibrary loans; copying; literature searches and bibliographies for staff; library open to public upon written request. **Networks/Consortia:** Member of Total Interlibrary Exchange (TIE).

★14776★

U.S. NAVY - NAVAL SCHOOL OF HEALTH SCIENCES - LIBRARY (Bus-Fin)
Bethesda, MD 20014   Phyllis R. Blum, Libn.
Subjects: Accounting, business management, health care administration, personnel management, medical sociology. **Holdings:** 4000 books; 1000 bound periodical volumes; 165 American Hospital Association publications. **Subscriptions:** 130 journals and other serials. **Services:** Interlibrary loans; library not open to public. **Computerized Information Services:** MEDLINE, BRS, OCLC.

★14777★

U.S. NAVY - NAVAL SEA SYSTEMS COMMAND - LIBRARY DOCUMENTATION BRANCH (SEA 09B31) (Sci-Tech)
Rm. 1S28, National Center, Bldg. 3   Phone: (202) 692-3349
Washington, DC 20362   Alan M. Lewis, Hd., Lib.Doc.Br.
Founded: 1976. **Staff:** Prof 7; Other 8. **Subjects:** Engineering - marine, electrical, mechanical, nuclear; naval architecture and ordnance; marine propulsion; acoustics; shipbuilding. **Special Collections:** Complete sets of RINA Transactions and U.S. Naval Institute Proceedings. **Holdings:** 25,000 books; 7000 bound periodical volumes; 500,000 research and development reports; 110,000 technical manuals; 60,000 microforms. **Subscriptions:** 500 journals and other serials. **Services:** Interlibrary loans; copying; SDI; library open to navy contractors, authorized Department of Defense components and federal libraries. **Automated Operations:** Computerized cataloging. **Computerized Information Services:** OCLC, DIALOG, SDC, NEXIS; Ships Analysis and Retrieval Program (SHARP; internal database). **Networks/Consortia:** Member of FEDLINK. **Publications:** FOCUS (list of acquisitions), monthly - circulated to authorized Department of Defense components.

★14778★

U.S. NAVY - NAVAL SHIP SYSTEMS ENGINEERING STATION HEADQUARTERS - TECHNICAL LIBRARY (Sci-Tech)
Bldg. 619, Naval Base   Phone: (215) 952-7078
Philadelphia, PA 19112   Pearl O. Robinson, Libn.
Founded: 1979. **Staff:** Prof 1; Other 6. **Subjects:** Engineering - marine, mechanical, electrical; chemistry; metallurgy. **Holdings:** 125,000 books and Navy manuals; microforms. **Subscriptions:** 162 journals and other serials. **Services:** Interlibrary loans; library open to public with clearance from security

manager. **Computerized Information Services:** Information Handling Services (IHS). **Publications:** List of agency reports, monthly.

★14779★
U.S. NAVY - NAVAL SHIPYARD (CA-Long Beach) - TECHNICAL LIBRARY
(Sci-Tech)
Code 202.4, Bldg. 300, Rm. 358   Phone: (213) 547-6515
Long Beach, CA 90822   Mari S. Zeoli, Libn.
Staff: Prof 1; Other 5. **Subjects:** Naval architecture, ship repair and maintenance, electronic equipment, mechanical equipment, industrial management, occupational safety. **Special Collections:** Naval Sea Command Technical Publications. **Holdings:** 8000 books; 110,000 technical manuals and reports; 150,000 microfilm copies of military specifications and standards; 1000 microfiche; 10,000 manufacturers' catalogs and 4000 American Society for Testing and Materials (ASTM) specifications; government reports relating to U.S. Fleet. **Subscriptions:** 107 journals and other serials. **Services:** Interlibrary loans; library open to Department of Defense contractors. **Publications:** Acquisitions list, irregular.

★14780★
U.S. NAVY - NAVAL SHIPYARD (CA-Mare Island) - TECHNICAL LIBRARY
(Sci-Tech)
Code 202.13, Stop T-4   Phone: (707) 646-4306
Vallejo, CA 94592-5100   Layne Huseth, Hd., Shipyard Tech.Lib.
Founded: 1945. **Staff:** Prof 3; Other 3. **Subjects:** Naval shipbuilding; occupational safety and health; chemistry; engineering - nuclear, civil, mechanical, chemical. **Holdings:** 40,000 books; 1500 bound periodical volumes; 3000 technical reports; 12,000 specifications and standards. **Subscriptions:** 285 journals and other serials. **Services:** Interlibrary loans; copying (limited); library open to public by appointment. **Publications:** Accessions list, monthly; periodical list, annual.

★14781★
U.S. NAVY - NAVAL SHIPYARD (HI-Pearl Harbor) - TECHNICAL LIBRARY
(Sci-Tech)
Code 250.4, Box 400   Phone: (808) 471-3408
Pearl Harbor, HI 96860   Lincoln H.S. Yu, Libn.
Founded: 1951. **Staff:** Prof 1; Other 9. **Subjects:** Engineering, naval shipbuilding. **Holdings:** 40,000 volumes. **Services:** Library not open to public.

★14782★
U.S. NAVY - NAVAL SHIPYARD (NH-Portsmouth) - TECHNICAL LIBRARY
(Sci-Tech)
Code 863   Phone: (603) 439-1000
Portsmouth, NH 03801   Josephine Rafferty, Tech.Libn.
Founded: 1947. **Staff:** Prof 1; Other 1. **Subjects:** Submarines, naval architecture, marine engineering, nuclear engineering, mathematics, noise and vibration, electrical engineering, materials, management. **Special Collections:** Society of Naval Architects and Marine Engineers Transactions (complete set, 1893 to present). **Holdings:** 20,000 books and bound periodical volumes; 13,000 technical reports; 4 VF drawers of reprints and pamphlets; 350 reels of microfilm; videotapes. **Subscriptions:** 180 journals and other serials. **Services:** Interlibrary loans; copying; library open to public with restrictions.

★14783★
U.S. NAVY - NAVAL SHIPYARD (PA-Philadelphia) - TECHNICAL LIBRARY
(Sci-Tech)
Philadelphia Naval Base   Phone: (215) 897-3657
Philadelphia, PA 19112   Alice R. Murray, Dir.
Founded: 1946. **Staff:** Prof 1; Other 2. **Subjects:** Naval science and architecture; engineering - marine, electrical, mechanical; electronics; mathematics. **Special Collections:** Shipbuilding, naval engineering. **Holdings:** 10,000 books; 100 bound periodical volumes; 61,000 technical reports; 5000 microfiche; 2000 cartridges of microfilm. **Subscriptions:** 203 journals and other serials. **Services:** Interlibrary loans (limited to the Department of Defense); library not open to public.

★14784★
U.S. NAVY - NAVAL SHIPYARD (SC-Charleston) - TECHNICAL LIBRARY
(Sci-Tech)
Naval Base   Phone: (803) 743-3843
Charleston, SC 29408   D.C. Woody, Act.Techn.
Founded: 1946. **Staff:** 5. **Subjects:** Naval engineering and architecture, electronics, management, ordnance, mathematics. **Holdings:** 1000 books; 100,000 technical manuals; 4000 reports and pamphlets. **Subscriptions:** 60 periodicals. **Services:** Interlibrary loans; library not open to public.

★14785★
U.S. NAVY - NAVAL SHIPYARD (VA-Norfolk) - TECHNICAL LIBRARY (Sci-Tech; Comp Sci)†
Code 202.3, Bldg. 29, 2nd Fl.   Phone: (703) 393-5580
Portsmouth, VA 23709   Carolyn B. Orr, Libn.
Staff: 14. **Subjects:** Engineering, mathematics, mechanical trades, nuclear physics, computers, physics, chemistry. **Holdings:** 5000 books; 1500 reports; 25,000 technical manuals; 40 reels of magnetic tape. **Subscriptions:** 200 journals and other serials. **Services:** Interlibrary loans; library not open to public.

★14786★
U.S. NAVY - NAVAL STATION LIBRARY (CA-San Diego) (Mil)
Naval Station, Box 15   Phone: (619) 235-1403
San Diego, CA 92136   Christine E. Larsen, Dir./Adm.Libn.
Staff: Prof 2; Other 2. **Subjects:** Naval history, World War II, general fiction and nonfiction. **Special Collections:** Auxiliary Library Service Collection for Naval Officers (professional reading). **Holdings:** 24,000 books; 400 bound periodical volumes. **Subscriptions:** 154 journals and other serials; 18 newspapers. **Services:** Interlibrary loans; copying; library open to public for reference use only, circulation limited to active military or Department of Defense civilians, dependents or retirees. **Publications:** Current Subscriptions & Periodicals Holdings List, annual; Classified List of Periodicals, annual; Selected Acquistions List/Naval Station General Library Bulletin, bimonthly; bibliographies; reading lists. **Staff:** Marion N. Steele, Asst.Libn.

★14787★
U.S. NAVY - NAVAL STATION LIBRARY (FL-Mayport) (Mil)
Box 235   Phone: (904) 246-5393
Mayport, FL 32228   Ron Argentati, Libn.
Staff: Prof 1; Other 2. **Subjects:** Naval history, military art and science, navigation, World War II, naval architecture. **Holdings:** 11,500 books. **Subscriptions:** 72 journals and other serials; 6 newspapers. **Services:** Interlibrary loans; library not open to public.

★14788★
U.S. NAVY - NAVAL STATION LIBRARY (Guam) (Mil)
Box 174
FPO San Francisco, CA 96630   Beverly J. Endsley, Lib.Techn.
Staff: Prof 1; Other 2. **Subjects:** General collection. **Special Collections:** Auxiliary Library Service Collection (Far East Area); World War II. **Holdings:** 23,400 volumes. **Subscriptions:** 90 journals and other serials. **Services:** Interlibrary loans; library open to military personnel and their dependents. **Remarks:** Library is located in Barracks 4, U.S. Naval Station, Guam.

★14789★
U.S. NAVY - NAVAL SUBMARINE MEDICAL RESEARCH LABORATORY - MEDICAL LIBRARY (Med)
Naval Submarine Base New London
Box 900   Phone: (203) 449-3629
Groton, CT 06340   Elaine M. Gaucher, Libn.
Founded: 1945. **Staff:** Prof 1; Other 1. **Subjects:** Submarine medicine, diving, physiology, psychology. **Holdings:** 5032 books; 5800 bound periodical volumes; 6000 documents; 1300 microforms; 1000 in-house reports. **Subscriptions:** 150 journals and other serials. **Services:** Interlibrary loans; copying; library open to doctors, hospital staff, corpsmen and researchers. **Publications:** Submarine Medical Research Laboratory Reports.

★14790★
U.S. NAVY - NAVAL SUPERVISOR OF SHIPBUILDING, CONVERSION AND REPAIR - TECHNICAL LIBRARY (Sci-Tech; Mil)
U.S. Naval Station, Code 253
Box 119   Phone: (619) 235-2455
San Diego, CA 92136   Pat Merritt, Libn.
Founded: 1960. **Staff:** 2. **Subjects:** Ship systems, ordnance, electronics, engineering. **Holdings:** 27,000 books and bound periodical volumes; 500 reels of microfilm of military and federal specifications; 300 reels of microfilm of design information files; manuals and textbooks. **Subscriptions:** 10 journals and other serials. **Services:** Interlibrary loans; library open to federal personnel and government contractors.

★14791★
U.S. NAVY - NAVAL SUPPLY CENTER - TECHNICAL DIVISION - TECHNICAL LIBRARY (Sci-Tech; Mil)
937 North Harbor Dr.   Phone: (619) 235-3237
San Diego, CA 92132   Ivy Seaberry, Lib.Techn.
Founded: 1950. **Staff:** 1. **Subjects:** Electronics; ordnance; weapons; fire control systems; automotive, electrical, and mechanical engineering. **Holdings:** 25,355 books and bound periodical volumes; 3136 reels of

microfilm; 550,600 aperture cards; 35,700 microfiche. **Subscriptions:** 10 journals and other serials. **Services:** Library open to public.

★14792★
U.S. NAVY - NAVAL SUPPLY SYSTEMS COMMAND - LIBRARY (Mil)
Rm. 509, Bldg. 3, Crystal Mall   Phone: (202) 695-4704
Washington, DC 20376   James Crouch, Libn.
Founded: 1926. **Staff:** 1. **Subjects:** Management, supply management, naval logistics. **Holdings:** 10,000 books. **Subscriptions:** 50 journals and other serials. **Services:** Interlibrary loans; library open to public with librarian's permission.

★14793★
U.S. NAVY - NAVAL SUPPORT ACTIVITY - LIBRARY
Bldg. 47   Phone: (206) 526-3577
Seattle, WA 98115   Bob Kinsedahl, Libn.
Founded: 1932. **Staff:** Prof 1. **Subjects:** Nonfiction, fiction, science, art, mystery, science fiction. **Holdings:** 10,000 volumes; pamphlets. **Subscriptions:** 22 journals and other serials. **Services:** Library serves Station personnel and retired military personnel and their dependents.

★14794★
U.S. NAVY - NAVAL SURFACE WEAPONS CENTER - CENTER LIBRARY (Sci-Tech; Mil)
Mail Code E43   Phone: (703) 663-8994
Dahlgren, VA 22448   Dr. J. Marshal Hughes, II, Ctr.Libn.
Founded: 1953. **Staff:** Prof 8; Other 6. **Subjects:** Mathematics, electronics, physics, weapons systems, management, chemistry, materials. **Special Collections:** Independent Research and Development Navy/Industry Collection; general library with academic collection to support university center on grounds. **Holdings:** 130,000 books; 7000 bound periodical volumes; 9500 periodical volumes on microfilm; 250,000 documents. **Subscriptions:** 800 journals and other serials; 10 newspapers. **Services:** Interlibrary loans; copying; SDI; translations; library open to government agencies and contractors. **Automated Operations:** Computerized cataloging. **Computerized Information Services:** DIALOG, NASA/RECON, DOE/RECON, DTIC; internal database. **Publications:** Accession Lists, biweekly; SDI, daily. **Remarks:** The Center Library is composed of the Dahlgren and White Oak libraries. Figures represent the combined holdings of the libraries.

★14795★
U.S. NAVY - NAVAL SURFACE WEAPONS CENTER - WHITE OAK LIBRARY (Sci-Tech; Mil)†
White Oak   Phone: (202) 394-1922
Silver Spring, MD 20910   Mary Jane Brewster, Hd.
Founded: 1944. **Staff:** Prof 8; Other 8. **Subjects:** Naval ordnance, explosives, aerodynamics, plastics, magnetic materials, optics, mathematics. **Holdings:** 49,000 books; 12,000 bound periodical volumes; 160 periodical titles on microfilm. **Services:** Interlibrary loans; copying (limited); library open to other government agencies and contractors. **Automated Operations:** Computerized cataloging. **Computerized Information Services:** DIALOG, SDC, NASA/RECON, DOE/RECON, DTIC; internal database. **Staff:** Charlotte Mullinix, Libn.; Elizabeth Tucker, Libn.

★14796★
U.S. NAVY - NAVAL TEST PILOT SCHOOL - RESEARCH LIBRARY (Sci-Tech; Mil)
Naval Air Test Ctr.   Phone: (301) 863-4411
Patuxent River, MD 20670   Robert B. Richards, Hd. of Academics
Founded: 1950. **Staff:** Prof 1; Other 1. **Subjects:** Aeronautical engineering, aircraft flight testing, propulsion, aircraft systems, space engineering. **Special Collections:** Aero engineering; flight testing; atmospheric propulsion. **Holdings:** 700 books; 2300 reports. **Subscriptions:** 10 journals and other serials. **Services:** Library open to U.S. government agencies.

★14797★
U.S. NAVY - NAVAL TRAINING EQUIPMENT CENTER - TECHNICAL INFORMATION CENTER (Mil; Sci-Tech; Comp Sci)
TIC, Bldg. 2068   Phone: (305) 646-4797
Orlando, FL 32813   Marcia Davidoff, Chf.Libn.
Founded: 1946. **Staff:** Prof 2; Other 3. **Subjects:** Training simulation technology, military training methodology, human factors, engineering, equipment and systems, mathematics and computers, ordnance, physics. **Special Collections:** Technical reports and handbooks for simulators and training devices (13,000); human factors reports relating to theory, design and use of training devices. **Holdings:** 4700 books; 1100 bound periodical volumes; 26,000 documents and manuals; 2700 microforms; specifications; standards. **Subscriptions:** 300 journals and other serials; 8 newspapers. **Services:** Interlibrary loans (limited); center not open to public. **Publications:**

Technical Spotlight, monthly; Annual periodical list - both for internal use only. **Special Catalogs:** KROS-TERM Ready Reference Engineering Data System (training device technology). **Remarks:** The center is operated by the University of Central Florida. **Staff:** T.R. Pfarrer, Asst.Libn.

★14798★
U.S. NAVY - NAVAL UNDERWATER SYSTEMS CENTER - NEW LONDON TECHNICAL LIBRARY (Sci-Tech; Mil)†
Bldg. 80   Phone: (203) 447-4276
New London, CT 06320   David L. Hanna, Hd.Libn.
Founded: 1970. **Staff:** Prof 2; Other 3. **Subjects:** Underwater - acoustics, ordnance, surveillance; antisubmarine warfare. **Holdings:** 20,000 volumes; 400,000 technical documents; 425,000 government reports on microfiche. **Subscriptions:** 505 journals and other serials. **Services:** Interlibrary loans; library not open to public. **Automated Operations:** Computerized cataloging. **Computerized Information Services:** DIALOG, SDC, DTIC, BRS, Library Management & Retrieval System (LMARS). **Publications:** Periodical holding list. **Staff:** J. Ned Shaw, Libn.; Charles Logan, Cat.

★14799★
U.S. NAVY - NAVAL UNDERWATER SYSTEMS CENTER - NEWPORT TECHNICAL LIBRARY (Sci-Tech; Mil)†
    Phone: (401) 841-4338
Newport, RI 02840   Mary Barravecchia, Hd.Libn.
Staff: Prof 3. **Subjects:** Antisubmarine warfare, undersea warfare and surveillance, underwater ordnance, target detection. **Holdings:** 14,000 books; 425,000 technical documents. **Subscriptions:** 525 journals and other serials. **Services:** Interlibrary loans; literature surveys; library not open to public. **Automated Operations:** Computerized cataloging. **Computerized Information Services:** DIALOG, SDC, DTIC, BRS, Library Management & Retrieval System (LMARS). **Publications:** Technical reports. **Remarks:** An associated library is maintained at New London, CT 06320. **Staff:** Philip Tomposki, Ref.Libn.; Robert Aspry, Libn.

★14800★
U.S. NAVY - NAVAL WAR COLLEGE - LIBRARY (Mil; Educ)
    Phone: (401) 841-2641
Newport, RI 02841   Earl R. Schwass, Dir.
Founded: 1884. **Staff:** Prof 15; Other 17. **Subjects:** Military art and science; naval art and science; international relations; international law; economics; history. **Holdings:** 157,788 books and bound periodical volumes; 83,477 classified documents; 15,954 periodical volumes in microform. **Subscriptions:** 511 journals and other serials. **Services:** Interlibrary loans; library open to public with permission. **Automated Operations:** Computerized cataloging and ILL. **Computerized Information Services:** OCLC, DIALOG. **Networks/Consortia:** Member of NELINET; Consortium of Rhode Island Academic and Research Libraries; FEDLINK. **Publications:** Faculty Guide, Research Guide, both annual - for internal distribution only. **Staff:** Marilyn D. Curtis, Hd., Tech.Serv.; Murray L. Bradley, Hd., Rd.Serv.

★14801★
U.S. NAVY - NAVAL WEAPONS CENTER - LIBRARY DIVISION (Sci-Tech; Mil)
Mail Code 3433   Phone: (619) 939-2507
China Lake, CA 93555   Joseph M. Burge, Hd., Lib.Div.
Founded: 1946. **Staff:** Prof 8; Other 14. **Subjects:** Rockets, missiles, propellants, explosives, chemistry, physics, electronics, aerodynamics, parachutes. **Holdings:** 30,000 books; 50,000 bound periodical volumes; 180,000 reports; 600,000 microfiche copies of technical reports. **Subscriptions:** 750 journals and other serials. **Services:** Interlibrary loans; restricted access to library. **Automated Operations:** Computerized document retrieval and catalog production. **Computerized Information Services:** DIALOG, SDC, DTIC, RLIN, OCLC. **Networks/Consortia:** Member of FEDLINK; CLASS. **Publications:** Accession List of Technical Reports, bimonthly; Periodicals Table of Contents List, weekly; Periodicals List, annual; Guide to the Use of NWC Technical Library; Accession List of Books, monthly. **Staff:** Margaret O'Drobinak, Hd., Info.Serv.Br.; Elizabeth Wilkie, Hd., Center Lib.; Mary Coraggio, Hd., Tech.Serv.Br.

★14802★
U.S. NAVY - NAVAL WEAPONS STATION - LIBRARY (Sci-Tech; Mil)
Bldg. 705   Phone: (804) 887-4726
Yorktown, VA 23691   Eleanor Lacy Sorokatch, Libn.
Founded: 1961. **Staff:** Prof 1; Other 2. **Subjects:** Naval mines, missiles, torpedoes, corrosion, depth charges, explosives, underwater weapons, engineering. **Holdings:** 10,000 books; 7000 technical reports; 5000 pamphlets, documents and catalogs. **Subscriptions:** 188 journals and other serials. **Services:** Interlibrary loans; copying; library open to qualified persons by permission. **Publications:** Accession Lists, monthly.

★14803★
U.S. NAVY - NAVAL WEAPONS SUPPORT CENTER - LIBRARY (Sci-Tech)†
Code 016   Phone: (812) 854-1615
Crane, IN 47522   Peggy Curran, Supv.Libn.
Founded: 1958. Staff: Prof 1; Other 5. Subjects: Explosives, ammunition, pyrotechnics, engineering, military science, electronics. Special Collections: History file (2000). Holdings: 21,000 books; 1775 bound periodical volumes; 360,000 aperture cards; 1500 reels of microfilm; 1350 technical reports. Subscriptions: 520 journals and other serials; 15 newspapers. Services: Interlibrary loans; library not open to public. Computerized Information Services: Government-Industry Data Exchange Program (GIDEP). Networks/Consortia: Member of Four Rivers Area Library Services Authority.

★14804★
U.S. NAVY - NAVY PERSONNEL RESEARCH & DEVELOPMENT CENTER - TECHNICAL LIBRARY (Soc Sci; Mil; Comp Sci)
Code P22L   Phone: (619) 225-7971
San Diego, CA 92152   Marie D. McDowell, Libn.
Founded: 1953. Staff: Prof 2; Other 2. Subjects: Industrial and social psychology, education, computer technology, human engineering, management science. Holdings: 6000 books; 3300 bound periodical volumes; 28,200 technical reports; 5000 microfiche. Subscriptions: 300 journals and other serials. Services: Interlibrary loans; copying; SDI; library open to public with restrictions. Computerized Information Services: DIALOG, OCLC. Networks/Consortia: Member of FEDLINK. Publications: Acquisitions List, biweekly; Periodical Holdings List, annual.

★14805★
U.S. NAVY - OFFICE OF THE GENERAL COUNSEL - LAW LIBRARY (Law; Mil)
Crystal Plaza 5, Rm. 450   Phone: (202) 692-7378
Washington, DC 20360   Mary E. Williams, Hd.Libn.
Founded: 1949. Staff: Prof 2. Subjects: Government contracts, contract claims, procurement, taxation, civil personnel law. Holdings: 20,000 books; 1400 bound periodical volumes; 6 VF cabinets of reports, documents, hearings; 3 VF drawers of newspaper clippings; 3 VF drawers of reprints; 8 VF drawers of Congressional documents. Subscriptions: 72 journals and other serials. Services: Interlibrary loans; copying (limited); library open to public. Computerized Information Services: Justice Retrieval and Inquiry System (JURIS). Remarks: The library is located at 2211 Jefferson Davis Hwy., Arlington, VA 22202. Staff: Sharyl Wernick, Libn.

★14806★
U.S. NAVY - OFFICE OF THE JUDGE ADVOCATE GENERAL - LAW LIBRARY (Law; Mil)
Hoffman Bldg. No. 2
200 Stovall St.   Phone: (202) 325-9565
Alexandria, VA 22332   Richard S. Barrows, Libn.
Staff: Prof 4; Other 2. Subjects: Law - military, international, criminal. Special Collections: Opinions of the Judge Advocate General (unpublished); Decisions of the U.S. Navy Court of Military Review (unpublished). Holdings: 45,000 volumes; 23 VF drawers. Subscriptions: 95 journals and other serials. Services: Interlibrary loans; library open to public. Remarks: Supports two hundred field libraries. Staff: Sue Roach, Hd., Ref./Tech.Serv.

★14807★
U.S. NAVY - OFFICE OF NAVAL RESEARCH - LIBRARY (Sci-Tech; Mil)
633 Ballston Tower, No. 1
800 N. Quincy St.   Phone: (202) 696-4415
Arlington, VA 22217   Mrs. Dorcas E. Tabor, Lib.Techn.
Founded: 1948. Staff: 2. Subjects: Biological and medical sciences, physical and chemical sciences, naval and marine sciences, social sciences. Holdings: 20,000 periodicals; reference books. Subscriptions: 483 journals and other serials; 5 newspapers. Services: Interlibrary loans; copying; library open to public by permission. Computerized Information Services: DIALOG, OCLC. Networks/Consortia: Member of FEDLINK.

★14808★
U.S. NAVY - REGIONAL DATA AUTOMATION CENTER - TECHNICAL LIBRARY (Sci-Tech; Mil; Comp Sci)
Bldg. 143, Washington Navy Yard   Phone: (202) 433-5700
Washington, DC 20374   William H. Hagen, Libn.
Founded: 1964. Staff: 2. Subjects: Electronic data processing, management, data communications, mathematics, naval science. Holdings: 5400 books; 218 bound periodical volumes; 3006 technical documents (hardcover); 113 microfiche. Subscriptions: 186 journals and other serials. Services: Interlibrary loans; copying; library open to Defense Department employees. Automated Operations: Computerized circulation. Special Catalogs: Catalog of project documentation (computer printout).

★14809★
U.S. NAVY - STRATEGIC SYSTEMS PROJECT OFFICE - TECHNICAL LIBRARY (Sci-Tech; Mil)
                                          Phone: (202) 697-2852
Washington, DC 20376   June R. Gable, Tech.Lib.Br.Hd.
Staff: Prof 1; Other 2. Subjects: Missile technology, mathematics, electronics, solid propellants, management. Holdings: 2500 books; 40,000 technical reports; 4 VF drawers of pamphlets. Subscriptions: 175 journals and other serials. Services: Interlibrary loans; library open to persons with appropriate security clearance and need-to-know. Automated Operations: Computerized cataloging. Computerized Information Services: DIALOG, OCLC. Networks/Consortia: Member of FEDLINK.

★14810★
U.S. NAVY - SUBMARINE BASE - SUBMARINE FORCE LIBRARY AND MUSEUM (Mil)
Code 340, Box 16   Phone: (203) 449-3174
Groton, CT 06349   Robert J. Zollars, Dir.
Founded: 1964. Staff: Prof 2. Subjects: Submarine history and memorabilia. Special Collections: Submarines and their inventors prior to 1900; U.S. Navy and foreign submarines; biographical file of submariners; U.S. submarine patrol reports of WW II and the Korean War; German submarine patrol reports and war diaries of WW II; histories of General Dynamics/Electric Boat (1915-1964) and Naval Submarine Base, Groton (1868 to present); J.P. Holland, Simon Lake, Admiral James Fife, Captain William Quigley, Captain John Canoose and Gunner Owen Hill papers; U.S. submarine cachets, submarine paintings and photographs. Holdings: 8000 books; 50,000 photographs; blueprints; technical manuals; memorabilia. Subscriptions: 20 journals and other serials. Services: Library open to public by appointment through director. Publications: Museum brochure. Remarks: Museum open through Public Affairs Officer (Box 44, SUBASE, New London, Groton, CT 06349). Staff: Richard B. Dominguez, Adm. Asst.

★14811★
U.S. NEWS & WORLD REPORT - LIBRARY (Publ)
2400 N St., N.W.   Phone: (202) 955-2350
Washington, DC 20037   Kathleen Trimble, Lib.Dir.
Staff: Prof 10; Other 5. Subjects: Government, politics, history, economics, law. Holdings: 10,000 books; 4000 volumes of congressional hearings and reports; 10,000 vertical files; 6600 newspaper clipping files; 9000 biographical files. Services: Interlibrary loans; copying; SDI; library open to public with restrictions. Computerized Information Services: NEXIS. Special Indexes: Card index with abstracts of U.S. News & World Report. Formerly: United States News Publishing, Inc. Staff: Rose Marie Atkinson, Asst.Dir.

★14812★
U.S. NUCLEAR REGULATORY COMMISSION - LAW LIBRARY (Law)
STOP 555   Phone: (301) 492-7584
Washington, DC 20555   Charlotte David, Chf., Legal Info.Serv.
Staff: Prof 3. Subjects: Law - nuclear energy, environmental, administrative. Special Collections: Publications of the Joint Committee on Atomic Energy, 1945-1975 (complete set); AEC and NRC Reports, 1956 to present. Holdings: 10,000 books; 1500 bound periodical volumes; 500 technical documents; 10 drawers of the Federal Register, the Congressional Record and law journals in microform. Subscriptions: 113 journals and other serials. Services: Interlibrary loans; library open to public when librarian is present. Computerized Information Services: LEXIS; TERA (internal database). Networks/Consortia: Member of D.C. Area Law Libraries. Publications: Law Library News, monthly - for internal distribution only. Special Catalogs: Administrative Law Article File (card and loose-leaf); Law Review Articles & Speeches (loose-leaf). Special Indexes: Significant Federal Court Case File - AEC and NRC issues (loose-leaf). Remarks: Library is located at 7735 Old Georgetown Rd., Bethesda, MD 20014. Staff: Sauci S. Churchill, Law Libn.; Anna Fotias, Leg.Spec.

U.S. OFFICE OF DISEASE PREVENTION AND HEALTH SERVICES - NATIONAL HEALTH INFORMATION CLEARINGHOUSE
See: National Health Information Clearinghouse

U.S. OFFICE OF EDUCATION - REGION VI - RESEARCH INFORMATION CENTER
See: Dallas Public Library - History and Social Sciences Division

★14813★
U.S. OFFICE OF PERSONNEL MANAGEMENT - LIBRARY (Soc Sci)
1900 E St., N.W.   Phone: (202) 632-4432
Washington, DC 20415   Betty B. Guerin, Supv.Libn.
Founded: 1940. Staff: Prof 5; Other 4. Subjects: Personnel administration,

public administration, civil service, law, legislative reference, social science, political science, management. **Special Collections:** Baruch Collection (personal papers of Ismar Baruch, expert in position classification and salary administration); civil service history. **Holdings:** 95,000 books; 500 bound periodical volumes; 4000 other cataloged items. **Subscriptions:** 500 journals and other serials. **Services:** Interlibrary loans; library open to public for reference use only. **Computerized Information Services:** DIALOG, BRS. **Publications:** Personnel Literature, monthly with annual index - for sale by U.S. Government Printing Office. **Staff:** Catherine Tashjean, Ref.Libn.; Leon Brody, Ref.Libn; Stephen Palincsar, Ref.Libn.

U.S. OFFICE OF PRESIDENTIAL LIBRARIES
See: U.S. Presidential Libraries

★14814★
U.S. OFFICE OF TECHNOLOGY ASSESSMENT - INFORMATION CENTER (Sci-Tech)
Congress of the United States
Washington, DC 20510
Phone: (202) 226-2160
Martha M. Dexter, Mgr., Info.Serv.
Staff: Prof 2; Other 3. **Subjects:** Technology assessment, future, science policy. **Holdings:** 6000 books; 1000 documents in VF drawers. **Subscriptions:** 700 journals and other serials; 9 newspapers. **Services:** Interlibrary loans; copying; SDI; center open to public with restrictions. **Automated Operations:** Computerized circulation. **Computerized Information Services:** DIALOG, SDC, BRS, MEDLINE, NASA/RECON, DOE/RECON, DTIC, Library of Congress Information System (LOCIS); House Information Systems (HIS). **Networks/Consortia:** Member of FEDLINK. **Publications:** FOCUS, biweekly newsletter. **Staff:** Gail M. Kouril, Asst.Mgr., Info.Serv.

★14815★
U.S. OLYMPIC COMMITTEE - SPORTS MEDICINE INFORMATION CENTER (Med)
Sports Medicine Div.
Dept. of Education Services
1750 E. Boulder St.
Colorado Springs, CO 80909
Phone: (303) 632-5551
Mary Margaret Newsom, Coord. of Educ.Serv.
Staff: Prof 1; Other 1. **Subjects:** Sports medicine - exercise physiology, biomechanics, sports psychology, vision and dental screening, athletic training, injury prevention and treatment, health maintenance and conditioning, coaching science. **Holdings:** 1000 books; unbound periodicals; reprints; sports rulebooks; U.S. Olympic Committee central files of photographs, slides, and 16mm films; N.G.B. constitutions and by-laws. **Subscriptions:** 280 journals and other serials; 5 newspapers. **Services:** Interlibrary loans; copying; SDI; center open to public for reference use only. **Automated Operations:** Computerized cataloging, serials, and indexes. **Computerized Information Services:** SDC, DIALOG, BRS; SMILE (internal database). **Networks/Consortia:** Member of Bibliographical Center for Research, Rocky Mountain Region, Inc. (BRS). **Publications:** SportsMediscope (newsletter), bimonthly.

★14816★
U.S. PATENT & TRADEMARK OFFICE - SCIENTIFIC LIBRARY (Sci-Tech)†
Crystal Plaza Bldg. 3
2021 Jefferson Davis Hwy.
Arlington, VA 22202
Phone: (703) 557-2955
Henry Rosicky, Prog.Mgr.
Founded: 1836. **Staff:** Prof 17; Other 26. **Subjects:** Technology, applied science. **Special Collections:** Foreign patents (12 million in numerical arrangement). **Holdings:** 250,000 books; 87,800 bound periodical volumes; 58,790 titles on microfiche; 350 titles on microfilm. **Subscriptions:** 1600 journals and other serials. **Services:** Interlibrary loans; copying; library open to public for reference use only. **Computerized Information Services:** DIALOG, OCLC, SDC, BRS, MEDLINE, DOE/RECON, DTIC. **Networks/Consortia:** Member of FEDLINK. **Staff:** Dora D. Weinstein, Hd., User Serv.; Barry Balthrop, Hd., Foreign Patents.

★14817★
U.S. PEACE CORPS - INFORMATION SERVICES DIVISION (Soc Sci; Sci-Tech)
806 Connecticut Ave., N.W., Rm. M-407
Washington, DC 20526
Phone: (202) 254-3307
Rita C. Warpeha, Chf.Libn.
Founded: 1966. **Staff:** Prof 2; Other 2. **Subjects:** Developing countries (Asia, Africa, Latin America, the South Pacific Islands, Caribbean); economic development; cross-cultural studies; community development; appropriate technology. **Special Collections:** Peace Corps; foreign language learning materials. **Holdings:** 35,000 books; 54 shelves of folder materials. **Subscriptions:** 300 journals and other serials. **Services:** Interlibrary loans; library open to public with restrictions. **Computerized Information Services:** DIALOG, OCLC. **Networks/Consortia:** Member of FEDLINK; Metropolitan Washington Library Council. **Publications:** List of Acquisitions, monthly - for in-house use. **Staff:** Victoria Fries, Ref.Libn.; Vernell Womack, Lib.Techn.

U.S. PHILLIPS CORPORATION - SIGNETICS CORPORATION
See: Signetics Corporation

★14818★
U.S. POSTAL SERVICE - LIBRARY (Bus-Fin)
475 L'Enfant Plaza, S.W.
Washington, DC 20260
Phone: (202) 245-4021
Jane F. Kennedy, Gen.Mgr.
Founded: 1955. **Staff:** Prof 5; Other 6. **Subjects:** Management, law, engineering, economics, marketing, electronic data processing. **Special Collections:** History and operation of U.S. Postal Service. **Holdings:** 56,000 volumes; 8000 microforms; 35,000 government documents; pictures on 263 subjects; VF material on 673 subjects. **Subscriptions:** 850 journals and other serials. **Services:** Interlibrary loans; copying; library open to public for reference use only. **Computerized Information Services:** DIALOG, LEXIS, BRS, RLIN, NEXIS, Dun & Bradstreet Corporation, Dow Jones News/Retrieval. **Staff:** Harold E. Stark, Info.Serv.Spec.; Catherine East, Info.Serv.Spec.

★14819★
U.S. POSTAL SERVICE - TRAINING & DEVELOPMENT INSTITUTE - TECHNICAL TRAINING CENTER LIBRARY (Sci-Tech)
Box 1400
Norman, OK 73070-7810
Phone: (405) 366-2121
Founded: 1970. **Staff:** Prof 1; Other 1. **Subjects:** Electronics, plant maintenance, automobiles, mathematics. **Special Collections:** Publications of the U.S. Postal Service. **Holdings:** 2500 volumes. **Subscriptions:** 200 journals and other serials; 10 newspapers. **Services:** Library open only to staff, students and contract personnel. **Publications:** Monthly, quarterly, annual Activities Report and Acquisitions List - for internal distribution only.

★14820★
U.S. PRESIDENTIAL LIBRARIES - CARTER PRESIDENTIAL MATERIALS PROJECT (Hist)
77 Forsyth St., S.W.
Atlanta, GA 30303
Phone: (404) 221-3942
Dr. Donald B. Schewe, Dir.
Founded: 1981. **Staff:** Prof 6; Other 9. **Subjects:** Presidency of Jimmy Carter. **Holdings:** Papers of Jimmy Carter during his presidency (27 million pages). **Services:** Not open to the public. **Automated Operations:** Computerized cataloging and acquisitions. **Computerized Information Services:** DIALOG. **Networks/Consortia:** Member of FEDLINK. **Staff:** Dr. David E. Alsobrook, Supv.Archv.; Dr. Martin I. Elzy, Supv.Archv.; Robert Bohanan, Libn.

★14821★
U.S. PRESIDENTIAL LIBRARIES - DWIGHT D. EISENHOWER LIBRARY (Hist)
S.E. Fourth St.
Abilene, KS 67410
Phone: (913) 263-4751
Dr. John E. Wickman, Dir.
Founded: 1961. **Staff:** Prof 25; Other 10. **Subjects:** Dwight D. Eisenhower - his life, presidency and military career; World War II. **Special Collections:** Papers of Dwight D. Eisenhower and his associates. **Holdings:** 24,000 books; 19 million pages of manuscripts; 12,000 government documents; 23,000 items in VF drawers; 250,000 photographs; 2205 hours of sound recordings; 4055 reels of microfilm; 675,000 feet of motion picture film. **Subscriptions:** 75 journals and other serials. **Services:** Interlibrary loans (limited); copying; library open to public on written application to the director. **Publications:** Overview (newsletter), quarterly - available on request; Dwight D. Eisenhower: A Selected Bibliography of Periodical and Dissertation Literature. **Special Catalogs:** List of Holdings, biennial - available on request; registers to manuscript collections. **Remarks:** Maintained by the U.S. National Archives & Records Service. **Staff:** James W. Leyerzapf, Supv.Archv.

★14822★
U.S. PRESIDENTIAL LIBRARIES - FRANKLIN D. ROOSEVELT LIBRARY (Hist)
259 Albany Post Rd.
Hyde Park, NY 12538
Phone: (914) 229-8114
William R. Emerson, Dir.
Founded: 1941. **Staff:** Prof 10; Other 18. **Subjects:** The New Deal (1933-1940), World War II, Franklin D. Roosevelt, American naval history (1775 to present), American political and social history (1900-1950). **Special Collections:** Papers of Franklin and Eleanor Roosevelt and various associates; American children's books, 18th-19th centuries; Franklin D. Roosevelt's naval history library, manuscripts, and ship models; Americana and Hudson Valley local history books and manuscripts; Archives of the Livingston Family, 1680-1880. **Holdings:** 45,000 books; 87,000 pamphlets and serials; 16 million manuscripts; 126,000 photographs; 21,000 museum objects; 1300 reels of microfilm; 200 microfiche; 300,000 feet of motion picture film; 1100 phonograph records; 1000 audiotapes. **Subscriptions:** 23 journals and other serials. **Services:** Interlibrary loans; copying; library open to public upon application. **Networks/Consortia:** Member of Southeastern New York Library Resources Council. **Publications:** Franklin D. Roosevelt and Conservation,

1911-1945, 2 volumes, 1957; Calendar of Speeches and other Published Statements of Franklin D. Roosevelt, 1910-1920; Franklin D. Roosevelt and Foreign Affairs, 10 volumes, 1979; Era of Franklin D. Roosevelt: A Selected Bibliography of Periodical, Essay, and Dissertation Literature, 1945-1971; The Roosevelt-Churchill Messages (microfilm); The Press Conferences of Franklin D. Roosevelt, 1933-1945 (microfilm). **Remarks:** Maintained by U.S. National Archives & Records Service. **Staff:** Sheryl Griffith, Act.Supv.Libn.; Frances M. Seeber, Sr.Supv.Archv.Marguerite B. Hubbard, Musm.Cur.; Raymond Teichman, Supv.Archv.; Mark Renovitch, AV Archv.

★14823★
U.S. PRESIDENTIAL LIBRARIES - GERALD R. FORD LIBRARY (Hist)
1000 Beal Ave.   Phone: (313) 668-2218
Ann Arbor, MI 48109   Dr. Don W. Wilson, Dir.
Founded: 1981. **Staff:** Prof 11; Other 3. **Subjects:** Gerald R. Ford; U.S. Presidency, government and politics, 1974-1976; U.S. Congress, 1948-1977. **Special Collections:** Papers of Gerald R. Ford, 1948 to present; papers of individuals and records of agencies and organizations associated with Gerald Ford's career. **Holdings:** 7500 books; 50 bound periodical volumes; 8000 linear feet of archival records; 300,000 photographs; 900 hours of audiotapes; 65,000 feet of film; 950 hours of videotapes. **Subscriptions:** 34 journals and other serials. **Services:** Copying; library open to public. **Publications:** Newsletter, annual; List of holdings, revised monthly - both free upon request. **Special Indexes:** Inventory of each archivally processed collection (typescript); keyword index to public statements by President Ford (card). **Remarks:** Maintained by the U.S. National Archives and Records Service. **Staff:** David A. Horrocks, Supv.Archv.; Richard Holzhausen, Supv.Archv., AV; William Stewart, Dp.Dir.

★14824★
U.S. PRESIDENTIAL LIBRARIES - HARRY S TRUMAN LIBRARY (Hist)
                                                        Phone: (816) 833-1400
Independence, MO 64050   Dr. Benedict K. Zobrist, Dir.
Founded: 1957. **Staff:** Prof 12; Other 32. **Subjects:** Career and administration of former President Harry S Truman; nature and history of the presidency of the United States. **Holdings:** 44,567 books; 2264 bound periodical volumes; 12.7 million manuscripts on paper; 72,391 other printed items; 371 oral history interviews; 25 VF drawers. **Subscriptions:** 87 journals and other serials. **Services:** Interlibrary loans; copying; library open to public by written application. **Publications:** Harry S Truman Library/Institute Newsletter; Whistlestop, quarterly. **Special Catalogs:** Historical Materials in the Harry S Truman Library (book). **Remarks:** Maintained by U.S. National Archives & Records Service. **Staff:** Dr. George H. Curtis, Asst.Dir.

★14825★
U.S. PRESIDENTIAL LIBRARIES - HERBERT HOOVER LIBRARY (Hist)
                                                        Phone: (319) 643-5301
West Branch, IA 52358   Robert Wood, Dir.
Staff: 19. **Subjects:** Herbert Hoover, 20th century history with special emphasis on the period 1920-1960. **Special Collections:** Manuscripts of George Akerson, American Child Health Association, Arthur A. Ballantine, Delph E. Carpenter, William R. Castle, Colorado River Commission, George Hastings, Hoover Commissions (1947 and 1953), Herbert Hoover, Irwin B. Laughlin, Nathan W. MacChesney, William P. MacCracken, Hanford MacNider, Verne Marshall, Bradley Nash, Gerald Nye, Westbrook Pegler, John F. Shafroth, Truman Smith, French Strother, Charles C. Tansill, Walter Trohan, Robert E. Wood, Herbert D. Brown, George C. Drescher, Ralph Evans, Harold R. Gross, Bourke B. Hickenlooper, Robert H. Lucas, Ferdinand L. Mayer, Maurice Pate, Lewis H. Strauss, Henry J. Taylor, Hugh R. Wilson. **Holdings:** 24,442 volumes; 30,320 photographs; 147,641 feet of motion picture film; 2717 reels of microfilm; 81 microfiche; 10,838 pages of oral history transcripts; 227 hours of sound recordings. **Subscriptions:** 46 journals and other serials. **Services:** Interlibrary loans; copying; library open to researchers who apply in writing. **Special Catalogs:** Book catalog; still photographs; finding aids and selected indexes for manuscript collections; Historical Materials in the Herbert Hoover Presidential Library (copies available upon request). **Remarks:** Maintained by U.S. National Archives & Records Service. **Staff:** Mildred Mather, Archv.-Libn.

★14826★
U.S. PRESIDENTIAL LIBRARIES - JOHN F. KENNEDY LIBRARY (Hist)
Columbia Point on Dorchester Bay   Phone: (617) 929-4500
Boston, MA 02125   Dan H. Fenn, Jr., Dir.
Staff: Prof 19; Other 29. **Subjects:** John F. Kennedy and his administration, mid-20th century American politics and government. **Special Collections:** Oral history; Robert Kennedy papers; Ernest Hemingway papers; Seymour Harris Economics Collection. **Holdings:** 25,000 volumes; 25 million manuscript pages; 2.2 million pages of records of the Democratic National Committee; 500,000 pages of collections of personal papers; 40,000 pages

of oral history interviews; 12,500 museum objects; 2500 reels of records and papers; 100,000 still photographs; 4500 sound recordings; 6.5 million feet of motion picture film. **Subscriptions:** 22 journals and other serials. **Services:** Interlibrary loans; copying; library open to public. **Special Catalogs:** Historical Materials in the John F. Kennedy Library; The Kennedy Collection: A Subject Guide. **Remarks:** Maintained by U.S. National Archives & Records Service. **Staff:** E. William Johnson, Chf.Archv.; Ronald E. Whealan, Libn.; David F. Powers, Musm.Cur.

★14827★
U.S. PRESIDENTIAL LIBRARIES - LYNDON B. JOHNSON LIBRARY (Hist)
2313 Red River   Phone: (512) 482-5137
Austin, TX 78705   Harry J. Middleton, Dir.
Founded: 1971. **Staff:** Prof 20; Other 10. **Subjects:** Lyndon B. Johnson - career, administration, family, and papers; U.S. Presidency; American political, social, and economic history, 1937 to present. **Special Collections:** Oral history interviews; individual personal papers. **Holdings:** 14,176 books; 2986 unbound periodicals; 4926 Congressional hearings; 34.5 million archives-manuscript pages; 593,743 photographs; 5758 video recordings; 11,589 sound recordings; 37,776 museum items; 824,076 feet of motion picture film; 5 VF drawers of periodical articles; 2 VF drawers of papers and dissertations; 8 VF drawers of newspaper clippings. **Subscriptions:** 11 journals and other serials. **Services:** Interlibrary loans (limited); copying; library open to public. **Publications:** "The Lyndon B. Johnson Library" - distributed to visitors. **Special Catalogs:** Finding Aids to papers of Lyndon B. Johnson as President, Congressman, Senator, and Vice President (notebook form); finding aids to oral histories. **Remarks:** Maintained by U.S. National Archives & Records Service. **Staff:** Charles W. Corkran, Asst.Dir.; Christina Lawson, Supv., Archv.; Gary Yarrington, Musm.Cur.; Michael Gillette, Chf., Oral Hist.Sect.; Frank Wolfe, Chf., Tech.Serv.; Barbara Jensen, Adm.Off.

★14828★
U.S. PRESIDENTIAL MUSEUM - LIBRARY OF THE PRESIDENTS (Hist)
622 N. Lee   Phone: (915) 332-7123
Odessa, TX 79761
Subjects: Presidents of the United States and presidential candidates. **Holdings:** 3500 volumes; unbound periodicals. **Services:** Library open to public.

★14829★
U.S. PUBLIC HEALTH SERVICE - ALASKA NATIVE HEALTH SERVICE - HEALTH SCIENCES LIBRARY (Med)
Mt. Edgecumbe Hospital
Box 4577   Phone: (907) 966-2411
Sitka, AK 99835   Frank Sutton, Adm.Off.
Staff: 2. **Subjects:** Medicine, dentistry, nursing, health education. **Holdings:** 433 books. **Subscriptions:** 38 journals and other serials. **Services:** Interlibrary loans; copying; library open to public with restrictions.

U.S. PUBLIC HEALTH SERVICE - CENTERS FOR DISEASE CONTROL
See: U.S. Centers for Disease Control

U.S. PUBLIC HEALTH SERVICE - FOOD & DRUG ADMINISTRATION
See: U.S. Food & Drug Administration

★14830★
U.S. PUBLIC HEALTH SERVICE HOSPITAL - NATIONAL HANSEN'S DISEASE CENTER - MEDICAL LIBRARY (Med)
                                                        Phone: (504) 642-7771
Carville, LA 70721   Anna Belle Steinbach, Med.Libn.
Staff: Prof 1. **Subjects:** Hansen's disease, dermatology, ophthalmology, bone and joint surgery, plastic surgery, rehabilitation, physical therapy, dentistry, nursing. **Special Collections:** Leprosy Archives (all material published in English about leprosy from 1958 to present). **Holdings:** 8000 books; 10,000 unbound items; films; slides; tapes. **Subscriptions:** 130 journals and other serials. **Services:** Interlibrary loans; copying; library open to qualified users. **Networks/Consortia:** Member of TALON.

U.S. PUBLIC HEALTH SERVICE - NATL. INSTITUTE ON ALCOHOL ABUSE & ALCOHOLISM - NATL. CLEARINGHOUSE FOR ALCOHOL INFO.
See: National Clearinghouse for Alcohol Information

U.S. PUBLIC HEALTH SERVICE - NATL. INSTITUTE ON DRUG ABUSE
See: National Institute on Drug Abuse

★14831★

U.S. PUBLIC HEALTH SERVICE - NATL. INSTITUTE OF MENTAL HEALTH - COMMUNICATION CENTER - LIBRARY (Med)†
Parklawn Bldg., Rm. 15C-05
5600 Fishers Lane   Phone: (301) 443-4506
Rockville, MD 20857   Angela Sirrocco, Chf.
Founded: 1972. **Staff:** Prof 1; Other 5. **Subjects:** Mental health, psychopharmacology, behavioral sciences, child development, psychiatry, crime and delinquency. **Special Collections:** National Institute of Mental Health publications. **Holdings:** 5500 books; 150 bound periodical volumes. **Subscriptions:** 600 journals and other serials. **Services:** Interlibrary loans; library open to public for reference use only. **Automated Operations:** Computerized cataloging and acquisitions. **Publications:** Acquisitions list, monthly. **Remarks:** The National Institute of Mental Health Communication Center is a section of the National Clearinghouse for Mental Health Information.

★14832★

U.S. PUBLIC HEALTH SERVICE - NATL. INSTITUTE OF MENTAL HEALTH - MENTAL HEALTH STUDY CENTER LIBRARY (Med)†
2340 University Blvd., E.   Phone: (301) 436-6340
Adelphi, MD 20783   Ina Micas, Libn.
Founded: 1962. **Subjects:** Community mental health, psychiatry, psychology, sociology, applied anthropology, social work, public health, education, child development. **Special Collections:** Archives file of staff papers and publications (1500 items). **Holdings:** 5000 books; 1000 bound periodical volumes. **Subscriptions:** 200 journals and other serials. **Services:** Interlibrary loans; copying; library open to MHSC staff only. **Publications:** Publications and Papers of the Mental Health Study Center Staff and Bibliography 1948-1979.

★14833★

U.S. PUBLIC HEALTH SERVICE - NATL. INSTITUTE OF MENTAL HEALTH - SCIENCE COMMUNICATION BRANCH - MENTAL HEALTH LIB. (Med)
5600 Fishers Lane, Rm. 15-99   Phone: (301) 443-4533
Rockville, MD 20857   Anne H. Rosenfeld, Chf.
Founded: 1983. **Staff:** Prof 6; Other 5. **Subjects:** Mental health and mental illness, psychiatry, psychopharmacology, psychology, crime and delinquency, social work, aging, child and minority mental health. **Special Collections:** Archival file of National Institute of Mental Health (NIMH) publications, 1950 to present. **Holdings:** 7000 books; 2000 unbound reports; 6.5 cabinets of microfilm of journals. **Subscriptions:** 800 journals and other serials. **Services:** Interlibrary loans; consultation; library open to public for reference use only; borrowing privileges reserved for staff. **Computerized Information Services:** DIALOG, MEDLINE. **Networks/Consortia:** Member of Mid-Atlantic Regional Medical Library Program (MARMLP); Maryland Interlibrary Loan Organization (MILO). **Publications:** NIMH Science Reports; NIMH Science Reporter; NIMH Publications List; Library Monthly Acquisitions list - all available on request. **Remarks:** Library is a branch of the U.S. Public Health Service - National Institute of Mental Health - Division of Communications and Education. **Formerly:** National Clearinghouse for Mental Health Information. **Staff:** Joan Abell, Chf., Pub. Inquiries Sect.

U.S. PUBLIC HEALTH SERVICE - NATL. INSTITUTES OF HEALTH
See: U.S. Natl. Institutes of Health

U.S. PUBLIC HEALTH SERVICE - OFFICE ON SMOKING AND HEALTH
See: Office on Smoking and Health

★14834★

U.S. PUBLIC HEALTH SERVICE - PARKLAWN HEALTH LIBRARY (Med; Soc Sci)
5600 Fishers Ln., Rm. 13-12   Phone: (301) 443-2665
Rockville, MD 20857   Salvador B. Waller, Lib.Dir.
Founded: 1969. **Staff:** Prof 5; Other 9. **Subjects:** Delivery of health services, health planning, health care statistics, health services research, social aspects of health care, emergency medical services. **Special Collections:** Public Health Service Numbered Report Series; Vital Statistics of the U.S.; Public Health Service Contract Reports. **Holdings:** 15,000 books; 2000 bound periodical volumes; 10,000 NTIS reports on microfiche. **Subscriptions:** 1000 journals and other serials; 5 newspapers. **Services:** Interlibrary loans; copying; SDI; library open to public for reference use only. **Automated Operations:** Computerized cataloging. **Computerized Information Services:** DIALOG, MEDLINE, OCLC, New York Times Information Service; Emergency Medical Services Database (internal database). Performs free searches. **Publications:** Parklawn Health Library Bulletin, monthly - to mailing list; Periodical List - free upon request. **Special Indexes:** KWIC index to books. **Staff:** Bruce Yamasaki, Dp./Chf., PGC Br.; Sophia Yang, Acq.Libn.; Terry Freeman, Ref.Libn.; Karen Myers, Ref.Libn.

★14835★

U.S. RAILROAD RETIREMENT BOARD - LIBRARY (Soc Sci)
844 Rush St.   Phone: (312) 751-4928
Chicago, IL 60611   Kay Collins, Libn.
Founded: 1940. **Staff:** Prof 1; Other 1. **Subjects:** Law, legislation, social sciences. **Holdings:** 100,000 volumes; 83 VF drawers of legislative materials; 28 VF drawers of miscellaneous unbound materials. **Subscriptions:** 179 journals and other serials. **Services:** Interlibrary loans; library open to public by appointment. **Networks/Consortia:** Member of Chicago Library System.

★14836★

UNITED STATES RAILWAY ASSOCIATION - USRA DOCUMENT CENTER (Trans)
955 L'Enfant Plaza North, S.W.   Phone: (202) 488-8777
Washington, DC 20595   James R. Gasser, Mgr., Doc.Ctr.
Staff: Prof 1. **Subjects:** Transportation-railroad economics, law, government, finance. **Holdings:** 5000 boxes of archival material; 1700 reels of microfilm; 2900 computer tapes. **Subscriptions:** 10 journals and other serials; 10 newspapers. **Services:** Center open to public for reference use only. **Remarks:** Document Center consists of a library, archives and depository.

U.S. REFRACTORIES DIVISION
See: General Refractories Company

★14837★

U.S. SECURITIES AND EXCHANGE COMMISSION - LIBRARY (Bus-Fin)
450 5th St., N.W.   Phone: (202) 272-2618
Washington, DC 20549   Charlene C. Derge, Libn.
Founded: 1934. **Staff:** Prof 4; Other 5. **Subjects:** Accounting, corporations, economics, finance, government, investments, law, public utilities, securities, statistics, stock exchanges. **Special Collections:** Legislative histories of statutes administered by agency. **Holdings:** 60,000 books; 5000 bound periodical volumes. **Subscriptions:** 400 journals and other serials. **Services:** Interlibrary loans to other government agencies only; copying; library open to public by appointment. **Computerized Information Services:** LEXIS, OCLC. **Publications:** Library Bulletin, biweekly; Congressional Record Digest, daily. **Staff:** Raymond J. Kramer, Asst.Libn.

★14838★

U.S. SECURITIES AND EXCHANGE COMMISSION - PUBLIC REFERENCE LIBRARY (Bus-Fin)
219 S. Dearborn, Rm. 1242   Phone: (312) 353-7433
Chicago, IL 60604   Donald J. Evers, Chf.Ref.Libn.
Founded: 1940. **Staff:** Prof 1; Other 3. **Subjects:** Securities laws, SEC releases and special studies. **Holdings:** 500 bound periodical volumes; financial statements; corporate annual reports; 20,000 files of reports by publicly owned companies on microfiche; registration statements, applications and financial data for regional broker/dealers and investment advisors; annual reports for registered investment companies. **Services:** Copying; library open to public. **Remarks:** Other repositories of this same information are located in SEC headquarters in Washington, DC and regional offices in New York City and Los Angeles. Requests for copies of documents should be sent to U.S. Securities and Exchange Commission, Washington, DC 20549.

★14839★

U.S. SENATE - LIBRARY (Soc Sci)
Capitol Bldg., Suite S-332   Phone: (202) 224-7106
Washington, DC 20510   Roger K. Haley, Senate Libn.
Founded: 1871. **Staff:** Prof 6; Other 15. **Subjects:** Legislation, government, political science, history, biography, economics. **Special Collections:** House and Senate bills and resolutions; committee hearings; proceedings and debates. **Holdings:** 100,000 volumes; 500,000 microforms. **Subscriptions:** 180 journals and other serials; 10 newspapers. **Services:** Library not open to public. **Automated Operations:** Computerized cataloging. **Computerized Information Services:** NEXIS, LEXIS, DIALOG, OCLC, House Information System (HIS), Library of Congress Information System (LOCIS); SLCC (internal database). Performs free searches. **Networks/Consortia:** Member of FEDLINK. **Publications:** Presidential Vetoes. **Staff:** Ann C. Womeldorf, Asst.Libn.; Gregory C. Harness, Hd.Ref.Libn.; Thea Koehler, Ref.Libn.; Leona Pfund, Automated Sys.Coord.

★14840★

U.S.S. MASSACHUSETTS MEMORIAL COMMITTEE, INC. - ARCHIVES & TECHNICAL LIBRARY (Sci-Tech; Hist)
Battleship Cove   Phone: (617) 678-1100
Fall River, MA 02721   Mark Newton, Educ.Coord./Cur.
Founded: 1982. **Staff:** Prof 1. **Subjects:** Naval engineering and ordnance, naval radio and radar, shipboard ephemera, World War II naval history,

battleship systems. **Holdings:** 300 books; 200 bound periodical volumes; films; 75 shelf feet of blueprints; 5 reels of microfilm; voice recordings of first U.S. fleet raids on Japan; 250 pages of correspondence. **Services:** Copying; library open to public by appointment with one-time research fee. **Publications:** Bibliographies.

★14841★
U.S. SMALL BUSINESS ADMINISTRATION - REFERENCE LIBRARY (Bus-Fin)
1441 L St., N.W.   Phone: (202) 653-6914
Washington, DC 20416   Margaret Hickey, Libn.
Founded: 1958. **Staff:** Prof 1; Other 1. **Subjects:** Business, finance, management. **Holdings:** 5000 volumes; 80 VF drawers of reports, pamphlets, documents. **Subscriptions:** 160 journals and other serials. **Services:** Interlibrary loans; library open to public for reference use only.

★14842★
U.S. SOCIAL SECURITY ADMINISTRATION - BRANCH LIBRARY (Soc Sci)
Universal N. Bldg., Rm. 320-0
1875 Connecticut Ave. N.W.   Phone: (202) 673-5624
Washington, DC 20009   Octavio Alvarez, Libn.
Founded: 1972. **Staff:** Prof 1; Other 2. **Subjects:** Social Security programs, disability insurance, income maintenance, pension benefits, health insurance, medical care. **Special Collections:** Research Grant Reports and Contract Reports of SSA and Office of Research and Statistics. **Holdings:** 9000 books; 100 bound periodical volumes; 200 pamphlets; 500 microforms. **Subscriptions:** 260 journals and other serials. **Services:** Interlibrary loans; copying; library open to public with permission. **Automated Operations:** Computerized circulation.

★14843★
U.S. SOCIAL SECURITY ADMINISTRATION - COMPARATIVE STUDIES STAFF REFERENCE ROOM (Law)
1875 Connecticut Ave., N.W.
Universal North Bldg., Rm. 940   Phone: (202) 673-5713
Washington, DC 20009   Ilene Zeitzer, Tech.Info.Spec.
Staff: Prof 1; Other 1. **Subjects:** Social security, disability, work injuries and health care laws in foreign countries. **Special Collections:** Foreign annual yearbooks, 1965 to present; publications of the International Labor Organization, the Organization for Economic Cooperation and Development (OECD) and the International Social Security Association. **Holdings:** 25,000 books and bound periodical volumes; 38 VF drawers of clippings on international subjects. **Subscriptions:** 153 journals and other serials. **Services:** Library open to public by appointment. **Publications:** Social Security Bulletin; Social Security Programs throughout the World, biennial.

★14844★
U.S. SOCIAL SECURITY ADMINISTRATION - LIBRARY INFORMATION & GRAPHICS SERVICES BRANCH (Soc Sci)
6401 Security Blvd.
Altmeyer Bldg., Rm. 570   Phone: (301) 594-1650
Baltimore, MD 21235   Rowena S. Sadler, Chf., Lib.Info. & Br.
Founded: 1942. **Staff:** Prof 8; Other 8. **Subjects:** Social insurance, medical and hospital economics, operations research, management, personnel administration, supervision and training, electronic data processing, law, health insurance, business and management. **Holdings:** 86,762 books; 8250 bound periodical volumes; 520,000 microfiche; 3200 ultrafiche. **Subscriptions:** 739 journals and other serials. **Services:** Interlibrary loans; copying (limited); library open to public for reference use only on request. **Automated Operations:** Computerized cataloging and acquisitions. **Computerized Information Services:** DIALOG, BRS, LEXIS, NEXIS, REG-ULATE, LEGI-SLATE, Justice Retrieval and Inquiry System (JURIS), OCLC. **Publications:** SSA Library Notes, monthly; Bibliographic Quick Lists; Legislative Notes (guide to particular Social Security laws) - all free upon request. **Special Indexes:** Index to legislative information (card). **Remarks:** Maintains a Washington, DC branch. **Staff:** Gertrude Culverhouse, Chf., Ref./Pub.Serv.; Leo Hollenbeck, Ref.Libn.; Dorothy Dougherty, Ref.Libn.; Joyce Donohue, Law Libn.; Eris Roth, Chf., Tech.Serv.; Celeste Huecker, Cat.Libn.; Eugene Malkowski, Acq.Libn.; Octavio Alvarez, Br.Libn.

★14845★
U.S. SOIL CONSERVATION SERVICE - NATIONAL PHOTOGRAPHIC LIBRARY (Aud-Vis)
Box 2890   Phone: (202) 447-7547
Washington, DC 20013   E. Joseph Larson, Chf., AV Br.
Founded: 1935. **Staff:** 6. **Subjects:** Soil erosion, conservation practices, agricultural scenes. **Holdings:** 10,000 photographs. **Services:** Library open to public with restrictions. **Remarks:** The Soil Conservation Service operates under the jurisdiction of the U.S. Department of Agriculture.

★14846★
UNITED STATES SPACE EDUCATION ASSOCIATION - G.L. BORROWMAN ASTRONAUTICS LIBRARY (Sci-Tech)
P.O. Box 1032
Weyburn, SK, Canada S4H 2L3   Gerald L. Borrowman, Chf.Libn.
Staff: Prof 2. **Subjects:** Astronautics, American and Soviet space programs, Apollo and Gemini projects, space shuttle. **Holdings:** 2000 books; 2000 bound periodical volumes; press kits and photographs. **Subscriptions:** 32 journals and other serials. **Services:** Library not open to public.

★14847★
UNITED STATES SPACE EDUCATION ASSOCIATION - USSEA MEDIA CENTER (Sci-Tech)
746 Turnpike Rd.   Phone: (717) 367-3265
Elizabethtown, PA 17022   Stephen M. Cobaugh, Intl.Pres.
Founded: 1973. **Staff:** 7. **Subjects:** NASA space program, space sciences, solar power, UFOs, science fiction. **Special Collections:** NASA Technical Publications (1000 documents); Solar Power Abstracts (250 documents). **Holdings:** 1000 books; 500 bound periodical volumes; 2100 slides, photographs and cassettes; 1000 brochures and reports; 3000 clippings. **Subscriptions:** 30 journals and other serials. **Services:** Copying; center open to public with restrictions. **Publications:** Space Age Times, bimonthly; USSEA Update, monthly.

★14848★
UNITED STATES SPORTS ACADEMY - LIBRARY (Rec)
124 University Blvd.
Box 8650   Phone: (205) 343-7700
Mobile, AL 36605   Judy Burnham, Act.Libn.
Staff: 2. **Subjects:** Sports, including medicine and management; fitness; coaching. **Holdings:** 2191 books; 8 VF drawers of clippings; 71 cassette tapes; films; slides; periodicals on microfiche. **Subscriptions:** 185 journals and other serials. **Services:** Interlibrary loans Copying; library open to public for reference use only. **Computerized Information Services:** SDC, MEDLARS. Performs searches on cost recovery basis. **Publications:** Handbook; Shelflist, monthly acquisitions list. **Special Catalogs:** Books by discipline (computer printout).

★14849★
UNITED STATES STEEL CORPORATION - INFORMATION CENTER (Sci-Tech)
600 Grant St.   Phone: (412) 433-3459
Pittsburgh, PA 15230   Nancy J. Suvak, Supv.
Founded: 1938. **Staff:** Prof 1; Other 1. **Subjects:** Business, finance, economics, trade statistics for steel and steel consuming industries, chemicals. **Holdings:** 5000 volumes; 200 VF drawers of pamphlets, government publications and releases, annual reports, internal reports, and studies. **Subscriptions:** 200 journals and other serials. **Services:** Interlibrary loans; center open to public with restrictions. **Automated Operations:** Computerized cataloging. **Computerized Information Services:** DIALOG, NEXIS, I.P. Sharp Associates, Ltd., Dow Jones News/Retrieval, Dun & Bradstreet Corporation.

★14850★
UNITED STATES STEEL CORPORATION - TECHNICAL INFORMATION CENTER (Sci-Tech)
MS 88   Phone: (412) 825-2344
Monroeville, PA 15146   Angela R. Pollis, Staff Supv.
Founded: 1928. **Staff:** Prof 4; Other 2. **Subjects:** Metallurgy, materials science, steel manufacture and finishing, chemistry and physics, coal and coke technology, physical chemistry. **Holdings:** 50,000 books; 2000 periodicals; 1500 dissertations; 30,000 translations (commercial and others); 15,000 government and university reports; chemical abstracts on microfilm. **Subscriptions:** 700 journals and other serials; 5 newspapers. **Services:** Interlibrary loans; center not open to public. **Automated Operations:** Computerized cataloging and serials. **Computerized Information Services:** DIALOG, NEXIS, Inforonics, Inc; mechanized retrieval for internal technical reports. **Special Indexes:** Listings of technical reports, KWIC and KWOC. **Staff:** L.W. Berger, Sr.Res.Info.Spec.; J.A. Richardson, Res.Libn.

★14851★
UNITED STATES STUDENT ASSOCIATION - INFORMATION SERVICES (Soc Sci)
One Dupont Circle, Suite 300   Phone: (202) 775-8943
Washington, DC 20036   Gregory Moore, Pres.
Staff: Prof 1. **Subjects:** PSE governance, student activism (history), women and minorities, collective bargaining, educational innovation, funding PSE. **Special Collections:** National Student Association Publications, 1947 to present. **Holdings:** 1200 books; 250 file sleeves of data; 500 unbound

reports and periodicals. **Subscriptions:** 30 journals and other serials; 200 newspapers. **Services:** Copying; library open to members with restrictions depending on nature of request. **Publications:** Research Periodicals on topics of member interest - for sale.

★14852★
U.S. SUPREME COURT - LIBRARY (Law)
One First St., N.E.   Phone: (202) 252-3000
Washington, DC 20543   Roger F. Jacobs, Libn.
Staff: Prof 7; Other 16. **Subjects:** Law, legislative histories. **Special Collections:** Records and briefs of the Supreme Court since 1832; Gerry Collection (26,000 volumes). **Holdings:** 250,000 books; 50,000 microforms; 15,000 bound periodical volumes. **Subscriptions:** 4050 journals and other serials. **Services:** Copying; library open to members of Supreme Court Bar and government attorneys. **Automated Operations:** Computerized cataloging. **Computerized Information Services:** DIALOG, NEXIS, OCLC, LEXIS, Westlaw, Justice Retrieval and Inquiry System (JURIS); Library of Congress Information System (LOCIS). **Networks/Consortia:** Member of FEDLINK. **Staff:** Penny A. Hazelton, Asst.Libn., Res.; Rosalie Sherwin, Asst.Libn., Tech.Serv.

★14853★
U.S. TAX COURT - LIBRARY (Law)
400 Second St., N.W.   Phone: (202) 376-2707
Washington, DC 20217   Jeanne R. Bonynge, Libn.
Founded: 1924. **Staff:** Prof 2; Other 3. **Subjects:** Federal tax law - income, estate and gift. **Holdings:** 36,000 books; 7800 bound periodical volumes; 375,000 Index-Digest card file of federal tax cases; 1000 reels of microfilm of Congressional Record and Federal Register; 5000 cards of tax legislation (microfiche). **Subscriptions:** 85 journals and other serials. **Services:** Interlibrary loans (limited); library not open to public. **Computerized Information Services:** LEXIS, OCLC, Westlaw. **Publications:** Library Memorandum, monthly - to Tax Court personnel. **Special Indexes:** File of tax cases arranged by case name, Internal Revenue code section and subjects (card). **Staff:** Elsa B. Silverman, Asst.Libn.

★14854★
U.S. TEAM HANDBALL FEDERATION - ADMINISTRATIVE OFFICE LIBRARY (Rec)
1750 E. Boulder   Phone: (303) 632-5551
Colorado Springs, CO 80909   Dr. Peter Buehning, Pres.
Staff: 1. **Subjects:** Team handball - rules, equipment, technique. **Holdings:** Films and videotapes. **Services:** Library open to public with restrictions. **Publications:** Team Handball USA.

U.S. TENNESSEE VALLEY AUTHORITY
See: Tennessee Valley Authority

★14855★
UNITED STATES TESTING COMPANY, INC. - LIBRARY (Sci-Tech)†
1415 Park Ave.   Phone: (201) 792-2400
Hoboken, NJ 07030   Dorothy M. Campbell, Libn.
Founded: 1930. **Staff:** Prof 1; Other 1. **Subjects:** Biology; chemistry; consumer research; engineering - materials, physical, electronics, product and nuclear; environmental testing; paper; plastics; textiles. **Holdings:** 6000 books and bound periodical volumes; 5000 military and government specifications. **Subscriptions:** 150 journals and other serials. **Services:** Library not open to public.

★14856★
UNITED STATES TRADEMARK ASSOCIATION - LAW LIBRARY (Law)
6 E. 45th St.   Phone: (212) 986-5880
New York, NY 10017   Charlotte Jones, Mng.Ed./Libn.
Founded: 1878. **Staff:** 13. **Subjects:** Trademarks. **Holdings:** 1800 books; 73 bound periodical volumes; 8 VF drawers of clippings. **Subscriptions:** 40 journals and other serials. **Services:** Library open to public.

★14857★
U.S. TRAVEL DATA CENTER - LIBRARY (Bus-Fin)
1899 L St., N.W.   Phone: (202) 293-1040
Washington, DC 20036   Dr. Douglas Frechtling, Dir.
Founded: 1973. **Staff:** 10. **Subjects:** Travel and tourism. **Holdings:** 3000 research documents; 3800 government documents; 250 unpublished travel research reports; 15,000 clippings; 20 tapes. **Subscriptions:** 27 journals and other serials. **Services:** Library open only to members of U.S. Travel Data Center. **Publications:** Publications Catalog, annual - free upon request. **Staff:** Ida Simmons, Mgr. of Commun.

★14858★
UNITED STATES TRUST COMPANY - INVESTMENT LIBRARY (Bus-Fin)
45 Wall St.   Phone: (212) 806-4500
New York, NY 10005   Trudy Daley, Chf.Libn.
Founded: 1961. **Staff:** Prof 1; Other 3. **Subjects:** Investments, banking, finance. **Holdings:** 2500 volumes; 300 unbound periodicals; 3000 corporation files. **Subscriptions:** 300 journals and other serials; 25 newspapers. **Services:** Interlibrary loans; copying; library open to clients and members of Special Libraries Association.

★14859★
U.S. UNIFORMED SERVICES UNIVERSITY OF THE HEALTH SCIENCES - LEARNING RESOURCE CENTER (Med; Mil)
4301 Jones Bridge Rd.   Phone: (301) 295-3356
Bethesda, MD 20814   Chester J. Pleztke, Assoc.Prof. & Dir.
Staff: Prof 5; Other 15. **Subjects:** Medicine, military medicine. **Holdings:** 72,818 books and journals; 50,000 bound periodical volumes. **Subscriptions:** 1470 journals and other serials; 10 newspapers. **Services:** Interlibrary loans; copying; center open to public. **Automated Operations:** Computerized cataloging, acquisitions, serials and circulation. **Computerized Information Services:** DIALOG, NLM, OCLC; USUHS Information System (internal database). **Networks/Consortia:** Member of FEDLINK; Southeastern/ Atlantic Regional Medical Library Services. **Publications:** Research Series Guide; Exhibit Bibliographies - both irregular and for internal distribution only. **Staff:** Janice Powell Muller, Hd., Tech.Serv.; Judith Torrence, Hd., Ref. & Info.Serv.

★14860★
U.S. VETERANS ADMINISTRATION (AL-Birmingham) - HOSPITAL MEDICAL LIBRARY (Med)
700 S. 19th St.   Phone: (205) 933-8101
Birmingham, AL 35233   Mary Ann Knotts, Chf., Lib.Serv.
Founded: 1953. **Staff:** Prof 4; Other 1. **Subjects:** Medicine, dentistry, nursing, hospital administration. **Holdings:** 1000 books; 2487 bound periodical volumes; 800 AV items. **Subscriptions:** 200 journals and other serials. **Services:** Interlibrary loans; library open to public with restrictions. **Computerized Information Services:** NLM, DIALOG. **Networks/Consortia:** Member of VALNET; Jefferson County Hospital Librarian's Association. **Staff:** Henrietta Mims, Med.Libn.; Beth Owens, Med.libn.; Gail Frey, Med.Libn.; Jennifer Burt, Lib.Techn.

★14861★
U.S. VETERANS ADMINISTRATION (AL-Montgomery) - MEDICAL CENTER LIBRARY (142D) (Med)
215 Perry Hill Rd.   Phone: (205) 272-4670
Montgomery, AL 36193   M. Johnette Cummins, Chf., Lib.Serv.
Founded: 1940. **Staff:** Prof 2. **Subjects:** Medicine and allied health subjects. **Holdings:** 700 books; 839 bound periodical volumes; 156 audio cassettes; 50 AV items. **Subscriptions:** 100 journals. **Services:** Interlibrary loans; bibliographies; library open to public for reference use only. **Automated Operations:** Computerized cataloging. **Computerized Information Services:** MEDLINE. **Networks/Consortia:** Member of VALNET. **Staff:** Susan Helms, Asst.Libn.

★14862★
U.S. VETERANS ADMINISTRATION (AL-Tuscaloosa) - HOSPITAL MEDICAL LIBRARY (Med)
                                             Phone: (205) 553-3760
Tuscaloosa, AL 35404   Olivia S. Maniece, Chf.Libn.
Founded: 1932. **Staff:** Prof 2; Other 2. **Subjects:** Medicine and allied sciences. **Special Collections:** Psychiatry; geriatrics and gerontology; community mental health. **Holdings:** 4774 books; 1460 bound periodical volumes; 150 other cataloged items; 200 manuscripts, reports and clippings. **Subscriptions:** 185 journals and other serials; 24 newspapers. **Services:** Interlibrary loans; copying; SDI; library open to those affiliated with the medical center. **Computerized Information Services:** MEDLINE. Performs free searches. **Networks/Consortia:** Member of VALNET. **Publications:** The News-O-Gram. **Staff:** Betsy S. Pertzog, Med.Libn.

★14863★
U.S. VETERANS ADMINISTRATION (AL-Tuskegee) - MEDICAL CENTER LIBRARY (Med)
                                             Phone: (205) 727-0550
Tuskegee, AL 36083   Artemisia J. Junier, Chf., Lib.Serv.
Founded: 1948. **Staff:** Prof 3; Other 2. **Subjects:** Medicine, patient education. **Holdings:** 28,000 books; 9500 bound periodical volumes; 2300 pieces of AV software. **Subscriptions:** 586 journals and other serials. **Services:** Interlibrary loans; copying; library open to public with restrictions. **Computerized Information Services:** NLM. **Networks/Consortia:** Member

of VALNET. **Staff:** Inez C. Pinkard, Med.Libn.; Elaine P. McGee, Libn.

★14864★
U.S. VETERANS ADMINISTRATION (AZ-Phoenix) - HOSPITAL LIBRARY
(Med)
Seventh St. & Indian School Rd.   Phone: (602) 277-5551
Phoenix, AZ 85012   Diane Wiesenthal, Chf., Lib.Serv.
Founded: 1946. **Staff:** Prof 2; Other 1. **Subjects:** Medicine, nursing, allied
health sciences. **Special Collections:** Staff development, patient education.
Holdings: 3161 books; 2953 bound periodical volumes; AV materials.
Subscriptions: 300 journals and other serials. **Services:** Interlibrary loans;
copying; library open to public for reference use only. **Computerized
Information Services:** MEDLINE, TOXLINE, International Cancer Research
Data Bank Program. **Networks/Consortia:** Member of VALNET.
Publications: Acquisitions List, quarterly; Journal Holdings, annual - distributed
to staff and other libraries. **Remarks:** Patients' library contains additional
volumes. **Staff:** Oma Jean Crosier; Loraine Yeske .

★14865★
**U.S. VETERANS ADMINISTRATION (AZ-Prescott) - HEALTH SCIENCES
LIBRARY** (Med)
          Phone: (602) 445-4860
Prescott, AZ 86313   Carol Mills, Chf., Lib.Serv.
Staff: Prof 1; Other 1. **Subjects:** Medicine, nursing, surgery, dentistry, allied
health sciences, administration. **Holdings:** 1200 books; 3000 bound
periodical volumes; 300 AV items; 10 titles on microfilm. **Subscriptions:** 140
journals and other serials; 10 newspapers. **Services:** Interlibrary loans;
copying; library open to public but materials circulate only by special
arrangement. **Networks/Consortia:** Member of VALNET. **Remarks:** Patients'
library contains an additional 7500 volumes.

★14866★
**U.S. VETERANS ADMINISTRATION (AZ-Tucson) - MEDICAL CENTER
LIBRARY** (Med)
S. 6th Ave.   Phone: (602) 792-1450
Tucson, AZ 85723   Mark Peterson, Chf., Lib.Serv.
Staff: 2. **Subjects:** Medicine, nursing, surgery, neurology, psychiatry,
radiology. **Holdings:** 2775 books; 8366 bound periodical volumes; 630
volumes on microfilm. **Subscriptions:** 280 journals and other serials.
Services: Interlibrary loans; copying; library open to qualified reseachers.
Computerized Information Services: MEDLINE. **Networks/Consortia:**
Member of VALNET.

★14867★
**U.S. VETERANS ADMINISTRATION (AR-Fayetteville) - MEDICAL CENTER
LIBRARY** (Med)
1100 N. College   Phone: (501) 443-4301
Fayetteville, AR 72701   Jeanine Brown, Chf., Lib.Serv.
Founded: 1946. **Staff:** Prof 2; Other 1. **Subjects:** Medicine, nursing, allied
health subjects. **Holdings:** 2300 books; 1700 bound and unbound periodical
volumes. **Subscriptions:** 200 journals and other serials. **Services:** Interlibrary
loans; copying; SDI; library open to public for reference use only.
Computerized Information Services: MEDLARS, BRS. Performs free
searches. Contact Person: Mary Fran Prottsman. **Networks/Consortia:**
Member of VALNET; Northwest Arkansas Shared Audio-Visual Medical Library.
Remarks: Patients' library contains an additional 3500 volumes.

★14868★
U.S. VETERANS ADMINISTRATION (AR-Little Rock) - HOSPITAL LIBRARIES
(Med)
300 E. Roosevelt Rd.   Phone: (501) 372-8361
Little Rock, AR 72206   George M. Zumwalt, Chf., Lib.Serv.
Founded: 1950. **Staff:** Prof 3; Other 2. **Subjects:** Medicine, surgery, nursing,
psychiatry, psychology, social work, dietetics. **Holdings:** 4000 books; 6822
bound periodical volumes; 44 16mm motion pictures; 234 video cassettes;
230 audio cassettes; 509 slides and filmstrips. **Subscriptions:** 390 journals
and other serials. **Services:** Interlibrary loans; copying; library open to
professionals or health science students. **Computerized Information
Services:** BRS, MEDLINE. **Remarks:** Above data includes the holdings of the
U.S. Veterans Administration Hospital Library in North Little Rock, which has
consolidated its library service with the Little Rock Hospital Library. Patients'
libraries contain an additional 5000 volumes. **Staff:** Jack W. Griffith, Libn.,
NLR Div.; Michael M. Blarton, Health Sci.Libn., LR Div.

★14869★
**U.S. VETERANS ADMINISTRATION (CA-Fresno) - HOSPITAL MEDICAL
LIBRARY** (Med)
2615 E. Clinton Ave.   Phone: (209) 225-6100
Fresno, CA 93703   Cynthia K. Meyer, Chf., Lib.Serv.
Founded: 1950. **Staff:** Prof 2; Other 2. **Subjects:** Medicine, nursing, allied

sciences. **Special Collections:** Bound reprints on valley fever published from
1892 to present. **Holdings:** 4000 books; 4500 bound periodical volumes.
Subscriptions: 340 journals and other serials. **Services:** Interlibrary loans;
copying; SDI; library open to public for reference use only. **Computerized
Information Services:** MEDLARS, DIALOG. **Networks/Consortia:** Member of
VALNET; Areawide Library Network (AWLNET). **Staff:** Paul L. Connor,
Med.Libn.

★14870★
U.S. VETERANS ADMINISTRATION (CA-Livermore) - MEDICAL LIBRARY
(Med)
Arroyo Rd.   Phone: (415) 447-2560
Livermore, CA 94550   Jane H. Levie, Chf.Libn.
Founded: 1925. **Staff:** Prof 1; Other 1. **Subjects:** Medicine, nursing, allied
health subjects. **Holdings:** 1203 books; 1774 bound periodical volumes;
cassette tapes. **Subscriptions:** 150 journals and other serials. **Services:**
Interlibrary loans; copying; library open to public for reference use only.
Networks/Consortia: Member of VALNET.

★14871★
**U.S. VETERANS ADMINISTRATION (CA-Loma Linda) - HOSPITAL LIBRARY
SERVICE** (Med)
11201 Benton St.   Phone: (714) 825-7084
Loma Linda, CA 92357   Kathleen M. Puffer, Chf.
Staff: Prof 2; Other 2. **Subjects:** Medicine. **Holdings:** 2500 books.
Subscriptions: 400 journals and other serials. **Services:** Interlibrary loans;
copying; SDI; library open to public. **Automated Operations:** Computerized
cataloging. **Computerized Information Services:** DIALOG, MEDLINE, BRS,
GTE. **Networks/Consortia:** Member of VALNET; SIRCULS; Inland Empire
Medical Library Cooperative. **Staff:** Jean Leonard, Clinical Libn.

★14872★
**U.S. VETERANS ADMINISTRATION (CA-Long Beach) - MEDICAL CENTER
LIBRARY** (Med)
5901 E. Seventh St.   Phone: (213) 498-1313
Long Beach, CA 90822   Betty F. Connolly, Chf., Lib.Serv.
Founded: 1946. **Staff:** Prof 5; Other 2. **Subjects:** Medicine and allied fields,
patient education. **Holdings:** 6100 books; 9000 bound periodical volumes;
1141 other volumes; AV materials. **Subscriptions:** 550 journals and other
serials. **Services:** Interlibrary loans; copying; library open to public for
reference use only. **Automated Operations:** Computerized serials and AV
holdings. **Computerized Information Services:** DIALOG, MEDLARS.
Networks/Consortia: Member of VALNET; Consumer Health Information
Cooperative (CHIC). **Remarks:** Patients' library contains an additional 3050
volumes. **Staff:** Karen Vogel, Med.Libn.; Irene Lovas, AV Libn.; Patti Flynn,
Patient Libn.; Meredith Mitchell, Med.Libn.

★14873★
**U.S. VETERANS ADMINISTRATION (CA-Los Angeles) - MEDICAL
RESEARCH LIBRARY** (Med)
Wilshire & Sawtelle Blvds.   Phone: (213) 478-3711
Los Angeles, CA 90073   Christine Anderson, Chf., Med.Res.Lib.
Staff: Prof 1; Other 1. **Subjects:** Biochemistry, immunology, microbiology,
molecular biology, physiology, ultrastructural research, metabolism. **Holdings:**
3400 books; 6200 bound periodical volumes; 17 VF drawers of pamphlets.
Subscriptions: 125 journals and other serials. **Services:** Interlibrary loans;
library not open to public. **Automated Operations:** Computerized acquisitions
and serials. **Computerized Information Services:** MEDLARS, Checkmate
(internal database). **Networks/Consortia:** Member of VALNET; CLASS;
Pacific Southwest Regional Medical Library Service (PSRMLS). **Publications:**
Library Bulletin, bimonthly; Library Acquisitions List - for internal distribution
only; Quarterly Newsletter - for internal distribution only.

★14874★
**U.S. VETERANS ADMINISTRATION (CA-Los Angeles) - WADSWORTH
MEDICAL LIBRARY 691W/142D (Med)**
Wilshire & Sawtelle Blvds.   Phone: (213) 824-3102
Los Angeles, CA 90073   Christa Buswell, Chf., Lib.Serv.
Staff: Prof 5; Other 4. **Subjects:** Clinical medicine, surgery, dentistry, nursing,
epilepsy, geriatrics, nutrition, social work. **Special Collections:** Patient
Education Resource Library (500 volumes); AV collection (400 items in all
media). **Holdings:** 6044 books; 12,557 bound periodical volumes; pamphlet
file of monographs. **Subscriptions:** 480 journals and other serials; 12
newspapers. **Services:** Interlibrary loans; SDI; library open to public for
reference use only. **Automated Operations:** Computerized cataloging.
Computerized Information Services: MEDLINE; Checkmate (internal
database). **Networks/Consortia:** Member of VALNET; CLASS; Pacific
Southwest Regional Medical Library Service (PSRMLS); Metropolitan
Cooperative Library System (MCLS); Consumer Health Information

Cooperative (CHIC). **Publications:** Library Newsletter, quarterly - for internal distribution only and VALNET members. **Staff:** Marianne Davis, Chf., Med.Lib.; Susan Harker, Chf., Patient Educ.Lib.; Sandra Schonlaw, Med.Libn.

★14875★
U.S. VETERANS ADMINISTRATION (CA-Martinez) - HOSPITAL LIBRARY (Med)
150 Muir Rd.   Phone: (415) 228-6800
Martinez, CA 94553   Dorothea E. Bennett, Chf., Lib.Serv.
Founded: 1947. **Staff:** Prof 2; Other 1. **Subjects:** Medicine. **Holdings:** 5407 books; 7221 bound periodical volumes; 945 audiotapes. **Subscriptions:** 478 journals and other serials. **Services:** Interlibrary loans; library open to health care personnel for reference use only. **Networks/Consortia:** Member of VALNET. **Staff:** R.W. Phillips, Asst.Libn.

★14876★
U.S. VETERANS ADMINISTRATION (CA-Palo Alto) - MEDICAL CENTER - MEDICAL LIBRARIES (Med)
3801 Miranda Ave.   Phone: (415) 493-5000
Palo Alto, CA 94304   C.R. Gallimore, Chf., Lib.Serv.
Founded: 1922. **Staff:** Prof 4; Other 2. **Subjects:** Medicine and behavioral sciences. **Holdings:** 13,000 books; 13,000 bound periodical volumes; 5000 recreational books. **Subscriptions:** 690 journals and other serials; 6 newspapers. **Services:** Interlibrary loans; copying; library open to public by appointment. **Networks/Consortia:** Member of VALNET.

★14877★
U.S. VETERANS ADMINISTRATION (CA-San Diego) - MEDICAL CENTER LIBRARY (Med)
3350 La Jolla Village Dr.   Phone: (619) 453-7500
San Diego, CA 92161   Connie Baker, Chf.Libn.
Staff: Prof 4. **Subjects:** Internal medicine, surgery, nursing, dentistry, biomedical research, allied health sciences. **Holdings:** 6000 books; 8000 bound periodical volumes; 9 VF drawers of pamphlets; 427 reels of microfilm; 500 AV materials. **Subscriptions:** 520 journals and other serials. **Services:** Interlibrary loans; library not open to public. **Computerized Information Services:** DIALOG, MEDLARS. **Networks/Consortia:** Member of VALNET; CLASS. **Publications:** Medical Library Bulletin, quarterly - agency distribution only; Journal Holdings List, annual - in-house and Southern California VA hospitals; AV Holdings List, annual - selective distribution. **Remarks:** Patients' Health Information Collection contains an additional 2000 items.

★14878★
U.S. VETERANS ADMINISTRATION (CA-San Francisco) - MEDICAL CENTER LIBRARY (Med)
42nd Ave. & Clement St.   Phone: (415) 221-4810
San Francisco, CA 94121   Cynthia A. Avallone, Chf.Libn.
Founded: 1947. **Staff:** Prof 3; Other 1. **Subjects:** Health sciences. **Special Collections:** Patient education. **Holdings:** 4500 books; 12,000 bound periodical volumes. **Subscriptions:** 300 journals and other serials. **Services:** Interlibrary loans; copying; SDI; library open to public. **Computerized Information Services:** MEDLINE. **Networks/Consortia:** Member of VALNET; San Francisco Biomedical Library Network. **Remarks:** Includes a Patient Education Resource Center. **Staff:** Sen Yee, Patient Educ.Libn.; Sara Gouveia, Med.Libn.

★14879★
U.S. VETERANS ADMINISTRATION (CA-Sepulveda) - BIOMEDICAL ENGINEERING & COMPUTING CENTER - LIBRARY (Med; Comp Sci)
V.A. Hospital   Phone: (213) 891-7711
Sepulveda, CA 91343   William R. West, Chf., Lib.Serv.
Founded: 1972. **Subjects:** Biomedical instrumentation, engineering, computers, data processing, electronics, electrical safety. **Holdings:** 400 books; 50 bound periodical volumes.

★14880★
U.S. VETERANS ADMINISTRATION (CO-Denver) - HOSPITAL LIBRARY (Med)
1055 Clermont St.
Denver, CO 80220   Ruth E. Gilbert, Chf., Lib.Serv.
Founded: 1947. **Staff:** Prof 2. **Subjects:** Medicine and allied clinical sciences. **Holdings:** 3000 books; 5000 bound periodical volumes; 200 pamphlets. **Subscriptions:** 250 journals and other serials. **Networks/Consortia:** Member of VALNET. **Remarks:** Patients' library contains an additional 4000 volumes.

★14881★
U.S. VETERANS ADMINISTRATION (CO-Grand Junction) - MEDICAL CENTER MEDICAL LIBRARY (Med)
2121 North Ave.   Phone: (303) 242-0731
Grand Junction, CO 81501   Lynn L. Bragdon, Chf., Lib.Serv.
Founded: 1948. **Staff:** Prof 1. **Subjects:** Medicine and surgery. **Holdings:** 1200 books; 900 bound periodical volumes. **Subscriptions:** 130 journals and other serials. **Services:** Interlibrary loans; library not open to public. **Networks/Consortia:** Member of VALNET; Midcontinental Regional Medical Library Program. **Remarks:** Patients' library contains an additional 1600 volumes.

★14882★
U.S. VETERANS ADMINISTRATION (CT-Newington) - HOSPITAL HEALTH SCIENCES LIBRARY (Med)
555 Willard Ave.   Phone: (203) 666-6951
Newington, CT 06111   Julie A. Lueders, Chf., Lib.Serv.
Founded: 1938. **Staff:** Prof 1; Other 1. **Subjects:** Medicine, surgery, psychiatry, nursing, hospital administration. **Holdings:** 2279 books; 1700 bound periodical volumes. **Subscriptions:** 210 journals and other serials. **Services:** Interlibrary loans; copying; library open to public for reference use only. **Computerized Information Services:** MEDLINE, BRS. **Networks/Consortia:** Member of VALNET; Connecticut Association of Health Science Libraries (CAHSL); Capital Area Association of Medical Library Directors. **Remarks:** Patients' library contains an additional 4550 volumes.

★14883★
U.S. VETERANS ADMINISTRATION (CT-West Haven) - MEDICAL CENTER LIBRARY (Med)
West Spring St.   Phone: (203) 932-5711
West Haven, CT 06516   William J. Preston, Chf., Lib.Serv.
Staff: Prof 2; Other 1. **Subjects:** Medicine, psychiatry, psychology. **Holdings:** 6000 books; 8700 bound periodical volumes; AV materials. **Subscriptions:** 325 journals and other serials. **Services:** Interlibrary loans; copying; library open to area health professionals for reference use only. **Automated Operations:** Computerized cataloging and serials. **Computerized Information Services:** DIALOG, MEDLARS, BRS. **Networks/Consortia:** Member of VALNET; Connecticut Association of Health Science Libraries (CAHSL). **Remarks:** Patients' library contains an additional 5426 volumes. **Staff:** Fran Bernstein, Med.Libn.

★14884★
U.S. VETERANS ADMINISTRATION (DE-Wilmington) - CENTER MEDICAL LIBRARY (Med)
1601 Kirkwood Hwy.   Phone: (302) 994-2511
Wilmington, DE 19805   Donald A. Passidomo, Chf.Libn.
Founded: 1940. **Staff:** Prof 2; Other 1. **Subjects:** General medicine, surgery, dentistry, nursing. **Holdings:** 3600 books; 5500 bound periodical volumes; 2000 AV programs and other AV materials; medical journals on microfilm. **Subscriptions:** 300 journals and other serials. **Services:** Interlibrary loans; copying (for ILL); SDI; library open to medical staff and affiliated students only. **Automated Operations:** Computerized cataloging. **Computerized Information Services:** MEDLINE. **Networks/Consortia:** Member of VALNET; Wilmington Area Biomedical Library Consortium (WABLC). **Special Catalogs:** AV Holdings List (cataloged by title and subject); Acquisitions List, quarterly - to hospital staff. **Staff:** Helen Post, Med.Libn.

★14885★
U.S. VETERANS ADMINISTRATION (DC-Washington) - GENERAL COUNSEL'S LAW LIBRARY (026H) (Law)
810 Vermont Ave., N.W., Rm. 1039   Phone: (202) 389-2159
Washington, DC 20420   Nina Kahn, Law Libn.
Staff: Prof 2; Other 3. **Subjects:** Law, with emphasis on veterans' laws. **Holdings:** 25,000 volumes. **Services:** Interlibrary loans; library is for official use of the Veterans Administration and other government agencies. **Computerized Information Services:** Westlaw, Justice Retrieval and Inquiry System (JURIS). **Staff:** Dorothy Foreman, Asst. Law Libn.

★14886★
U.S. VETERANS ADMINISTRATION (DC-Washington) - HEADQUARTERS CENTRAL OFFICE LIBRARY (142D1) (Med)
Veterans Administration
810 Vermont Ave., N.W.   Phone: (202) 389-2430
Washington, DC 20420   Karen Renninger, Chf., Lib.Div.
Founded: 1930. **Staff:** Prof 8; Other 3. **Subjects:** Medicine, dentistry, veterans affairs, management, aging. **Special Collections:** Historical material relating to Veterans Administration. **Holdings:** 15,000 books; 13,000 bound periodical volumes; 650 audio- and videotapes; slides. **Subscriptions:** 600 journals and other serials. **Services:** Interlibrary loans; copying; library open to

public. **Computerized Information Services:** DIALOG, SDC, BRS, MEDLARS, Mead Data Central. **Networks/Consortia:** Member of VALNET; District of Columbia Health Sciences Information Network (DOCHSIN). **Publications:** Acquistion List, bimonthly; Pathfinders in geriatrics, herbicides. **Staff:** Doris Doran, Asst./Network Dev.; Harry D. Weitkemper, Asst./Lib.Oper.Wendy N. Carter, Rd.Serv.Spec.; Cicely P. Marks, Tech.Serv.Spec.; Jean McVoy, Rsrcs.Coord./Spec.; Mary Ann Tatman, AV Prog.Spec.; Michael Green, AV Lib.Techn.

★14887★
U.S. VETERANS ADMINISTRATION (DC-Washington) - HEADQUARTERS LIBRARY DIVISION (142D) (Med)
Veterans Administration Bldg.
810 Vermont Ave., N.W. Phone: (202) 389-2781
Washington, DC 20420 Karen Renninger, Chf., Lib.Div.
Subjects: Clinical medicine, allied health sciences, hospital administration, veterans benefits, medical education. **Special Collections:** Veterans Administration publications. **Holdings:** 2.75 million books; 545,620 bound periodical volumes; 500,000 AV software items; pamphlets, microforms and government documents. **Subscriptions:** 5000 journals and other serials; 500 newspapers. **Services:** Interlibrary loans; copying; SDI; library open to public with restrictions. **Automated Operations:** Computerized cataloging. **Computerized Information Services:** Online systems. **Networks/Consortia:** Headquarters of VALNET which is involved in 30 consortia. **Publications:** VALNET Bulletin, monthly - distributed to VA hospital libraries and others; ADP Directory; ILL Directory; Online Centers Directory. **Special Catalogs:** Union List of Periodicals in the Medical Libraries of the Veterans Administration; Union List of Audiovisuals in the Libraries of the Veterans Administration; Union List of Monographs in the Libraries of the Veterans Administration. **Remarks:** The division administers the libraries in VA facilities throughout the U.S. with a combined staff of 428 library professionals and 278 nonprofessionals. The network includes 175 hospital libraries. Figures given represent combined holdings. **Staff:** Doris Doran, Asst./Network Dev.; Harry Weitkemper, Asst.Chf./Lib.Oper.; Wendy Carter, Rd.Serv.Spec.; Jean McVoy, Rsrcs.Coord./Spec.; Cicely Marks, Tech.Serv.Spec.; Mary Ann Tatman, AV Prog.Spec.; Michael Green, AV lib.Techn.

★14888★
U.S. VETERANS ADMINISTRATION (DC-Washington) - MEDICAL CENTER LIBRARY (Med)
50 Irving St., N.W. Phone: (202) 745-8262
Washington, DC 20422 Mary Netzow, Chf.Libn.
Staff: Prof 3. **Subjects:** General medicine, surgery. **Holdings:** 2000 books; 4300 bound periodical volumes. **Subscriptions:** 200 journals and other serials. **Services:** Interlibrary loans. **Computerized Information Services:** Online systems. **Staff:** Ginny DuPont, Med.Libn.; Linda Steele, Libn.

★14889★
U.S. VETERANS ADMINISTRATION (FL-Bay Pines) - CENTER LIBRARY (Med)
Phone: (813) 391-9644
Bay Pines, FL 33504 Ann A. Conlan, Chf., Lib.Serv.
Staff: Prof 3; Other 1. **Subjects:** Medicine, surgery, psychiatry, nursing, radiology, dentistry. **Special Collections:** Gerontology. **Holdings:** 5000 books; 2000 bound periodical volumes. **Subscriptions:** 339 journals and other serials. **Services:** Interlibrary loans; library not open to public. **Computerized Information Services:** BRS, MEDLINE. **Networks/Consortia:** Member of VALNET; Tampa Bay Medical Library Network. **Staff:** Arnold Jasen, AV Libn.; Jacqueline Rahman, PHE Libn.

★14890★
U.S. VETERANS ADMINISTRATION (FL-Gainesville) - HOSPITAL LIBRARY (Med)
Phone: (904) 376-1611
Gainesville, FL 32602 Marylyn E. Gresser, Chf., Lib.Serv.
Founded: 1967. **Staff:** Prof 2; Other 1. **Subjects:** Health education, neurology, surgery, internal medicine, nursing, pathology, pharmacology, ophthalmology, psychiatry, radiology. **Holdings:** 6657 books; 2500 periodical volumes; journal volumes on microfilm. **Subscriptions:** 358 journals and other serials; 9 newspapers. **Services:** Interlibrary loans; copying; library open to those involved in the medical or paramedical fields. **Computerized Information Services:** BRS, MEDLINE. **Networks/Consortia:** Member of VALNET. **Publications:** New Books List, quarterly; Medical Library Policies & Journal Holdings, annual.

★14891★
U.S. VETERANS ADMINISTRATION (FL-Lake City) - MEDICAL CENTER - LEARNING RESOURCE CENTER (Med)
Baya & Marion Sts. Phone: (904) 752-1400
Lake City, FL 32055 Shirley Mabry, Chf., Lib.Serv.
Staff: Prof 2; Other 2. **Subjects:** Medicine, surgery, nursing and allied health sciences; hospital administration. **Holdings:** 2500 books; 3000 bound periodical volumes; 1050 AV items; 600 patient education pamphlet titles; 8 VF drawers; 2000 volumes in microform; 300 talking books. **Subscriptions:** 205 journals and other serials. **Services:** Interlibrary loans; copying; transparencies; center open for reference use to professionals and lay persons requiring health information. **Computerized Information Services:** MEDLINE. **Networks/Consortia:** Member of VALNET. **Publications:** Medical Books Acquisition Bulletin, bimonthly; Audiovisual Bulletin, semiannual; Annual Journal List. **Remarks:** Patients' library contains an additional 5000 volumes and 3000 paperbacks.

★14892★
U.S. VETERANS ADMINISTRATION (FL-Miami) - MEDICAL CENTER LIBRARY (Med)
1201 N.W. 16th St. Phone: (305) 324-3187
Miami, FL 33125 Raissa Maurin, Chf.Libn.
Founded: 1946. **Staff:** Prof 3; Other 2. **Subjects:** Medicine, nursing, psychology, related fields. **Holdings:** 2699 books; 5328 bound periodical volumes; Audio-Digest tapes; 599 audiovisual. **Subscriptions:** 644 journals and other serials. **Services:** Interlibrary loans; library not open to public. **Computerized Information Services:** NLM. **Networks/Consortia:** Member of VALNET. **Publications:** Serials Holding List. **Staff:** Jeff Kager, Med.Libn.; Thomas Cummins, Patients' Libn.

★14893★
U.S. VETERANS ADMINISTRATION (FL-Tampa) - MEDICAL LIBRARY (Med)
James A. Haley Veterans Hospital
13000 N. 30th St. Phone: (813) 971-4500
Tampa, FL 33612 Iris A. Renner, Chf., Lib.Serv.
Staff: Prof 2; Other 1. **Subjects:** Internal medicine, psychiatry, nursing. **Holdings:** 5290 books; 5122 bound periodical volumes. **Subscriptions:** 350 journals and other serials. **Services:** Interlibrary loans; copying; SDI; library open to public. **Computerized Information Services:** MEDLARS, BRS. **Networks/Consortia:** Member of VALNET; Tampa Bay Medical Library Network. **Staff:** Nancy Van Buskirk, Med.Libn.

★14894★
U.S. VETERANS ADMINISTRATION (GA-Atlanta) - HOSPITAL MEDICAL LIBRARY (Med)
1670 Clairmont Rd. Phone: (404) 321-6111
Decatur, GA 30033 Eugenia H. Abbey, Chf.Libn.
Founded: 1945. **Staff:** Prof 2; Other 2. **Subjects:** Medicine, health and social sciences. **Holdings:** 4638 books; 7000 bound periodical volumes; 150 AV items. **Subscriptions:** 420 journals and other serials. **Services:** Interlibrary loans; copying; SDI; library open to public for reference use only. **Computerized Information Services:** MEDLINE. **Networks/Consortia:** Member of VALNET; Atlanta Health Science Libraries Consortium; Georgia Library Information Network (GLIN). **Remarks:** Hospital serves Atlanta area. Patients' library contains an additional 5000 volumes.

★14895★
U.S. VETERANS ADMINISTRATION (GA-Augusta) - HOSPITAL LIBRARY (Med)
Phone: (404) 724-5116
Augusta, GA 30910 Dorothy K. Jones, Chf., Lib.Serv.
Founded: 1937. **Staff:** Prof 4; Other 3. **Subjects:** Medicine, nursing, psychiatry and related fields. **Holdings:** 4801 books; 2497 bound periodical volumes; 3 VF drawers. **Subscriptions:** 299 journals and other serials; 30 newspapers. **Services:** Interlibrary loans; library not open to public. **Computerized Information Services:** OCLC, MEDLINE. **Networks/Consortia:** Member of VALNET. **Remarks:** Patients' library contains an additional 17,706 volumes. **Staff:** Anita Bell, Med.Libn.; Lillie A. Lockwood, Libn.; Elizabeth Northington, Med.Libn.

★14896★
U.S. VETERANS ADMINISTRATION (GA-Dublin) - CENTER LIBRARY (Med)
Phone: (912) 272-1210
Dublin, GA 31021 Mrs. Kodell M. Thomas, Chf., Lib.Serv.
Founded: 1948. **Staff:** Prof 1; Other 1. **Subjects:** Medicine, nursing and allied health sciences. **Holdings:** 3800 books; 750 bound periodical volumes; 65 unbound journals; audiovisual software; microfilm. **Subscriptions:** 245 journals and other serials. **Services:** Interlibrary loans; copying; library open to medical professionals only. **Computerized Information Services:** MEDLINE.

Networks/Consortia: Member of VALNET; Health Science Libraries of Central Georgia. **Remarks:** Patients' library contains an additional 8800 volumes.

★14897★
U.S. VETERANS ADMINISTRATION (ID-Boise) - MEDICAL CENTER LIBRARY (142D) (Med)
500 W. Fort St.   Phone: (208) 338-7206
Boise, ID 83702-4598   Gordon Carlson, Chf.Libn.
Founded: 1929. **Staff:** Prof 1; Other 1. **Subjects:** Clinical medicine. **Holdings:** 2000 books; 2894 bound periodical volumes; 450 AV programs. **Subscriptions:** 240 journals and other serials. **Services:** Interlibrary loans; library open to health science professionals and students. **Computerized Information Services:** BRS. **Networks/Consortia:** Member of VALNET; Boise Valley Health Sciences Library Consortium. **Publications:** New Acquisitions List, quarterly - distributed on request.

★14898★
U.S. VETERANS ADMINISTRATION (IL-Chicago) - LAKESIDE HOSPITAL MEDICAL LIBRARY (Med)
333 E. Huron St.   Phone: (312) 943-6600
Chicago, IL 60611   Lydia Tkaczuk, Chf., Lib.Serv.
Founded: 1954. **Staff:** Prof 2; Other 1. **Subjects:** Medicine and allied health sciences. **Special Collections:** Patient education; management/employee development collection. **Holdings:** 5000 books; 3500 bound periodical volumes; 200 other cataloged items; 2 VF drawers of pamphlets. **Subscriptions:** 250 journals and other serials. **Services:** Interlibrary loans; copying. **Computerized Information Services:** MEDLINE. **Networks/Consortia:** Member of VALNET; Metropolitan Consortium; Greater Midwest Regional Medical Library Network (Region 3). **Publications:** Medical Library Quarterly. **Staff:** Cheryl Potthast, Med.Libn.

★14899★
U.S. VETERANS ADMINISTRATION (IL-Chicago) - WESTSIDE HOSPITAL LIBRARY (Med)
820 S. Damen Ave.   Phone: (312) 666-6500
Chicago, IL 60612   Lynne D. Morris, Chf., Lib.Serv.
Founded: 1953. **Staff:** Prof 3; Other 3. **Subjects:** Medicine and allied sciences. **Holdings:** 6000 books; 3497 bound periodical volumes; 9 linear feet of VF materials; 2300 AV materials. **Subscriptions:** 350 journals and other serials. **Services:** Interlibrary loans; SDI; library open to public. **Computerized Information Services:** MEDLINE, BRS. **Networks/Consortia:** Member of VALNET; Illinois Health Libraries Consortium; Chicago Library System. **Remarks:** Patients' library contains an additional 2000 volumes. **Staff:** John R. Cline, Med.Libn.; Bryan Parhad, Patients' Libn.; Susan Koval, AV Techn.

★14900★
U.S. VETERANS ADMINISTRATION (IL-Danville) - MEDICAL CENTER LIBRARY (Med)
                                        Phone: (217) 442-8000
Danville, IL 61832   Betsy Taylor, Chf., Lib.Serv.
Staff: Prof 3; Other 2. **Subjects:** Psychiatry, psychology, medicine and related fields. **Holdings:** 2900 books; 2275 bound periodical volumes; 342 reels of microfilm. **Subscriptions:** 190 journals and other serials. **Services:** Interlibrary loans; library open to health care community for reference use. **Networks/Consortia:** Member of VALNET; Lincoln Trail Libraries System. **Publications:** New Titles List, quarterly - for internal distribution only. **Remarks:** Patients' library contains an additional 3000 volumes.

★14901★
U.S. VETERANS ADMINISTRATION (IL-Hines) - LIBRARY SERVICES (142D) (Med)
Edward Hines, Jr. Medical Center   Phone: (312) 343-7200
Hines, IL 60141   Bill Leavens, Chf.Libn.
Staff: Prof 2; Other 4. **Subjects:** Hospital administration, medicine, nursing and allied fields. **Holdings:** 10,300 books; 16,200 bound periodical volumes. **Subscriptions:** 750 journals and other serials. **Services:** Interlibrary loans; copying; library open to public. **Automated Operations:** Computerized acquisitions. **Networks/Consortia:** Member of VALNET; Suburban Library System (SLS); Greater Midwest Regional Medical Library Network (Region 3). **Remarks:** Patients' libraries contain an additional 9000 volumes. **Staff:** Mary Ellen Klupping, Med.libn.; Ann Novacich, Libn.; Marian Daley, Libn.

★14902★
U.S. VETERANS ADMINISTRATION (IL- Marion) - HOSPITAL LIBRARY (Med)
W. Main St.   Phone: (618) 997-5311
Marion, IL 62959   Joy E. Zuger, Chf., Lib.Serv.
Staff: Prof 1; Other 1. **Subjects:** Medicine and surgery. **Services:** Interlibrary

loans; library open to public with restrictions. **Automated Operations:** Computerized cataloging. **Networks/Consortia:** Member of VALNET; Shawnee Library System. **Remarks:** Affiliated with Southern Illinois University Medical School at Carbondale, IL.

★14903★
U.S. VETERANS ADMINISTRATION (IL-North Chicago) - HOSPITAL LIBRARY (Med)
                                        Phone: (312) 689-1900
North Chicago, IL 60064   Carl Worstell, Chf.Libn.
Staff: Prof 3; Other 1. **Subjects:** Psychiatry, psychology, medicine and related fields. **Holdings:** 4600 books; 4100 bound periodical volumes; 2 VF drawers; 700 AV items. **Subscriptions:** 450 journals and other serials; 5 newspapers. **Services:** Interlibrary loans; copying; library open to health science professionals. **Computerized Information Services:** BRS, MEDLINE. **Networks/Consortia:** Member of VALNET; Lake County Consortium. **Publications:** Newsletter; New Book List; bibliographies. **Staff:** Lou Ann Moore, Med.Libn.; Sylvia Thoele, Media Libn.

★14904★
U.S. VETERANS ADMINISTRATION (IN-Fort Wayne) - HOSPITAL LIBRARY (Med)
1600 Randalia Dr.   Phone: (219) 743-5431
Fort Wayne, IN 46805   Enolia L. Stalnaker, Chf., Lib.Serv.
Founded: 1950. **Staff:** Prof 1. **Subjects:** Medicine, nursing, pre-clinical sciences. **Holdings:** 750 books; 100 bound periodical volumes; 100 volumes of unbound periodicals; 210 AV items; 138 microforms. **Subscriptions:** 132 journals and other serials; 10 newspapers. **Services:** Interlibrary loans; copying; library open to community health professionals. **Networks/Consortia:** Member of VALNET; Tri-ALSA; Northeast Indiana Health Sciences Libraries. **Remarks:** Patients' library contains an additional 2442 volumes.

★14905★
U.S. VETERANS ADMINISTRATION (IN-Indianapolis) - MEDICAL CENTER LIBRARY (Med)
1481 W. Tenth St.   Phone: (317) 635-7401
Indianapolis, IN 46202   Judith Alfred, Lib.Serv.
Founded: 1952. **Staff:** Prof 3; Other 2. **Subjects:** General medicine, surgery, nursing, psychiatry, allied health sciences. **Holdings:** 3200 books; 4400 bound periodical volumes; 3000 reels of microfilm; 800 AV programs. **Subscriptions:** 375 journals and other serials. **Services:** Interlibrary loans; copying; SDI library open to public. **Automated Operations:** Computerized cataloging. **Computerized Information Services:** MEDLINE, BRS. Performs free searches. Contact Person: Janet Harouny. **Networks/Consortia:** Member of VALNET; Central Indiana Health Science Library Consortium. **Publications:** New Book List, quarterly; AV list; serials list. **Staff:** Parm Weedman, Med.Libn.; Janet Harouny, Med.Libn.

★14906★
U.S. VETERANS ADMINISTRATION (IN-Marion) - HOSPITAL MEDICAL LIBRARY (Med)
E. 38th St. at Home Ave.   Phone: (317) 674-3321
Marion, IN 46952   Joy E. Zuger
Founded: 1930. **Staff:** Prof 2; Other 3. **Subjects:** Medicine, with special emphasis on psychiatry and psychology. **Special Collections:** NCME video cassette library. **Holdings:** 2400 books; 6500 bound periodical volumes (also in microform); 300 government documents; slides; audio and video cassettes; microforms. **Subscriptions:** 548 journals and other serials; 40 newspapers. **Services:** Interlibrary loans; copying; library open to local health care community with special permission. **Automated Operations:** Computerized cataloging and serials. **Computerized Information Services:** MEDLINE. **Networks/Consortia:** Member of VALNET; Eastern Indiana Area Library Services Authority. **Special Catalogs:** AV holdings (card). **Remarks:** Patients' library contains an additional 6123 volumes, with emphasis on patient health education.

★14907★
U.S. VETERANS ADMINISTRATION (IA-Des Moines) - HOSPITAL LIBRARY (Med)
30th & Euclid Ave.   Phone: (515) 255-2173
Des Moines, IA 50310   Clare M. Jergens, Chf., Lib.Serv.
Founded: 1934. **Staff:** Prof 2; Other 2. **Subjects:** Medicine, nursing, psychology, audiology, patient education. **Holdings:** 3824 books; 4227 bound periodical volumes. **Subscriptions:** 405 journals and other serials. **Services:** Interlibrary loans; copying; library open to public for reference use only. **Computerized Information Services:** MEDLINE. **Networks/Consortia:** Member of VALNET; Polk County Biomedical Consortium (PCBC); Greater Midwest Regional Medical Library Network (Region 3). **Publications:** Source (newsletter), quarterly - ID; periodicals holdings list, annual - for internal

distribution, consortia and VALNET members. **Staff:** Charles Huelsbeck, Libn.

★14908★
U.S. VETERANS ADMINISTRATION (IA-Iowa City) - HOSPITAL LIBRARY
(Med)
Phone: (319) 338-0581
Iowa City, IA 52241 Marilyn J. Kraus, Med.Libn.
Founded: 1952. **Staff:** Prof 1. **Subjects:** Medicine, allied health sciences. **Holdings:** 2331 books; 2585 bound periodical volumes; 477 AV materials. **Subscriptions:** 247 journals and other serials. **Services:** Interlibrary loans. **Computerized Information Services:** NLM. **Networks/Consortia:** Member of VALNET.

★14909★
U.S. VETERANS ADMINISTRATION (IA-Knoxville) - MEDICAL CENTER LIBRARY (Med)
Phone: (515) 842-3101
Knoxville, IA 50138
Founded: 1921. **Staff:** Prof 2; Other 2. **Subjects:** Psychiatry, psychology, medicine. **Holdings:** 10,000 books; 1183 bound periodical volumes. **Subscriptions:** 400 journals and other serials; 20 newspapers. **Services:** Interlibrary loans; library not open to public. **Networks/Consortia:** Member of VALNET.

★14910★
U.S. VETERANS ADMINISTRATION (KS-Leavenworth) - CENTER MEDICAL LIBRARY (Med)
Phone: (913) 682-2000
Leavenworth, KS 66048 Bennett F. Lawson, Chf., Lib.Serv.
Staff: Prof 2; Other 1. **Subjects:** Medicine and allied health sciences. **Holdings:** 3535 books; 4743 bound periodical volumes; 1400 periodical volumes on microfilm. **Subscriptions:** 230 journals and other serials. **Services:** Interlibrary loans; copying; library open to public for reference use only. **Computerized Information Services:** MEDLINE, BRS, DIALOG. **Networks/Consortia:** Member of VALNET. **Remarks:** Patients' library contains an additional 15,006 volumes. **Staff:** Judith Guttshail, Med.Libn.

★14911★
U.S. VETERANS ADMINISTRATION (KS-Topeka) - DR. KARL A. MENNINGER MEDICAL LIBRARY (Med)
2200 Gage Blvd. Phone: (913) 272-3111
Topeka, KS 66622 Norma R. Godfrey, Chf., Lib.Serv.
Founded: 1946. **Staff:** Prof 3; Other 3. **Subjects:** Psychiatry, internal medicine, pathology, neurology, surgery, rehabilitation medicine, psychology, social service, fine arts. **Holdings:** 19,000 books; 5800 bound periodical volumes; 13 VF drawers of clippings, reprints and original papers. **Subscriptions:** 340 journals and other serials. **Services:** Interlibrary loans; library open to public for reference use only. **Computerized Information Services:** MEDLINE, BRS. **Networks/Consortia:** Member of VALNET. **Publications:** Recent Acquisitions, quarterly - free upon request. **Remarks:** Holdings include patients' library of approximately 9200 volumes. **Staff:** Nancy Vaughn, Med.Libn.; Rosemarie Adkins, Tech.Serv.Libn.

★14912★
U.S. VETERANS ADMINISTRATION (KS-Wichita) - MEDICAL CENTER LIBRARY (Med)
5500 E. Kellogg St. Phone: (316) 685-2221
Wichita, KS 67208
Founded: 1933. **Staff:** Prof 2; Other 1. **Subjects:** Medicine, nursing and allied health sciences; social sciences; hospital administration. **Holdings:** 2750 books; 3500 bound periodical volumes; 4 VF drawers of pamphlets; 500 AV items. **Subscriptions:** 185 journals and other serials. **Services:** Interlibrary loans; copying; SDI; library open to public for reference use only. **Automated Operations:** Computerized cataloging. **Computerized Information Services:** MEDLARS, OCTANET. **Networks/Consortia:** Member of VALNET. **Remarks:** Patients' library contains an additional 5000 volumes.

★14913★
U.S. VETERANS ADMINISTRATION (KY-Lexington) - MEDICAL CENTER LIBRARY (Med)
Phone: (606) 233-4511
Lexington, KY 40511 Ethel F. Mullins, Chf., Lib.Serv.
Staff: Prof 3; Other 3. **Subjects:** Psychiatry, psychology, nursing, social sciences, medicine, surgery. **Holdings:** 6180 books; 4241 bound periodical volumes. **Subscriptions:** 260 journals and other serials. **Services:** Interlibrary loans; copying; library open to public with permission. **Computerized Information Services:** MEDLINE. **Networks/Consortia:** Member of VALNET; Kentucky Health Sciences Library Consortium. **Staff:** Diane Gelarden-Cooper, Med.Libn.; Deborah Kessler, Libn.

★14914★
U.S. VETERANS ADMINISTRATION (KY-Louisville) - HOSPITAL LIBRARY
(Med)
800 Zorn Ave. Phone: (502) 895-3401
Louisville, KY 40202 James F. Kastner, Chf.Libn.
Founded: 1946. **Staff:** Prof 3; Other 1. **Subjects:** Clinical medicine, surgery, nursing, psychiatry, social work. **Special Collections:** American Military History Collection (300 volumes). **Holdings:** 2500 books; 7000 bound periodical volumes; 2000 volumes of journals in microform; 1250 AV programs. **Subscriptions:** 400 journals and other serials; 35 newspapers. **Services:** Interlibrary loans; copying; library open to public with restrictions. **Computerized Information Services:** MEDLINE, BRS. **Networks/Consortia:** Member of VALNET; Kentucky Health Sciences Library Consortium; Kentucky Union List of Serials (KULS). **Remarks:** Patients' library contains an additional 2000 volumes. **Staff:** Gene M. Haynes, Med.Libn.; Janna Smith, Libn.

★14915★
U.S. VETERANS ADMINISTRATION (LA-Alexandria) - MEDICAL CENTER MEDICAL LIBRARY (Med)
Phone: (318) 473-0010
Alexandria, LA 71301 Nancy M. Guillet, Chf.Libn.
Founded: 1930. **Staff:** Prof 1; Other 2. **Subjects:** General medicine. **Holdings:** 1214 books; 2475 bound periodical volumes; 61 maps and atlases; 425 AV items. **Subscriptions:** 117 journals and other serials; 10 newspapers. **Services:** Interlibrary loans; copying (limited); library open to public with restrictions. **Networks/Consortia:** Member of VALNET; TALON; Health Sciences Library Association of Louisiana. **Remarks:** Patients' library contains an additional 3763 volumes.

★14916★
U.S. VETERANS ADMINISTRATION (LA-New Orleans) - MEDICAL CENTER LIBRARY (Med)
1601 Perdido St. Phone: (504) 589-5272
New Orleans, LA 70146 Wilma B. Neveu, Chf., Lib.Serv.
Founded: 1945. **Staff:** Prof 2; Other 1. **Subjects:** Medicine, nursing, dentistry, surgery and allied health sciences. **Holdings:** 3966 books; 2482 bound periodical volumes. **Subscriptions:** 163 journals and other serials; 12 newspapers. **Services:** Interlibrary loans; library not open to public. **Computerized Information Services:** MEDLINE. **Networks/Consortia:** Member of VALNET. **Remarks:** Patients' library contains an additional 4190 volumes. **Staff:** Charles Bagnerise, Asst.Libn.

★14917★
U.S. VETERANS ADMINISTRATION (LA-Shreveport) - MEDICAL CENTER LIBRARY (Med)
510 E. Stoner Phone: (318) 424-6036
Shreveport, LA 71130 Shirley B. Hegenwald, Chf., Lib.Serv.
Founded: 1950. **Staff:** Prof 2. **Subjects:** General medicine. **Holdings:** 1943 books; 1237 bound periodical volumes; 2 VF drawers of pamphlets. **Subscriptions:** 208 journals and other serials; 10 newspapers. **Services:** Interlibrary loans; copying; library open to qualified persons. **Networks/Consortia:** Member of VALNET. **Remarks:** Patients' library contains an additional 3600 volumes.

★14918★
U.S. VETERANS ADMINISTRATION (ME-Augusta) - CENTER LIBRARY (Med)
Togus Br. (402/142D) Phone: (207) 623-8411
Augusta, ME 04330 Melda W. Page, Chf.Libn.
Staff: Prof 4; Other 5. **Subjects:** Medicine, surgery, psychiatry, nursing, alcoholism, health administration. **Holdings:** 4000 books; 3800 bound periodical volumes; 2000 AV items; 400 serial titles in microform; 6 VF drawers of Togus historical collection. **Subscriptions:** 650 journals and other serials; 50 newspapers. **Services:** Interlibrary loans; copying; SDI; library open to public. **Computerized Information Services:** MEDLINE, DIALOG, BRS, Brodart Book Express. **Networks/Consortia:** Member of VALNET; Health Science Library and Information Cooperative of Maine. **Publications:** Medical Library Newsletter, bimonthly. **Special Catalogs:** Patient Health Education Subject Brochures; AV Holdings List. **Staff:** Judy Littlefield, Supv.Lib.Techn.; June Roullard, AV Libn.; Christopher Bovie, Med.Libn.; Gary Pelletier, ILL Techn.

★14919★
U.S. VETERANS ADMINISTRATION (ME-Togus) - MEDICAL & REGIONAL OFFICE CENTER (Med)
Phone: (207) 623-8411
Augusta, ME 04330 Melda W. Page, Chf.Libn.
Founded: 1933. **Staff:** Prof 3; Other 4. **Subjects:** Social sciences/psychiatry, medicine, alcoholism, nursing, dentistry, hospital administration. **Special Collections:** Patient health education (100 items). **Holdings:** 4500

books; 2000 AV items; 3100 other cataloged items. **Subscriptions:** 650 journals and other serials; 50 newspapers. **Services:** Interlibrary loans; copying; SDI; center open to public. **Automated Operations:** Computerized cataloging. **Computerized Information Services:** DIALOG, MEDLINE, BRS, OnTyme. Performs free searches. **Networks/Consortia:** Member of VALNET; Health Science Library and Information Cooperative of Maine (HSLIC). **Publications:** Medical Library Newsletter, quarterly; Patients' Library Newssheet, weekly. **Staff:** June C. Roullard, Med.Sci.Libn.; Chris Bovie, Med.Libn.

★14920★
U.S. VETERANS ADMINISTRATION (MD-Baltimore) - MEDICAL CENTER LIBRARY SERVICE (142D) (Med)
3900 Loch Raven Blvd.   Phone: (301) 467-9932
Baltimore, MD 21218   Deborah A. Gustin, Chf., Lib.Serv.
Staff: Prof 1; Other 1. **Subjects:** Medicine, surgery, nursing. **Holdings:** 3000 books; 4000 bound periodical volumes; 200 AV items; staff and VA publications; pamphlets. **Subscriptions:** 280 journals and other serials. **Services:** Interlibrary loans; copying; SDI; library open to public for reference use only. **Computerized Information Services:** BRS, NLM. **Networks/Consortia:** Member of VALNET. **Publications:** Acquisitions List, monthly - for internal distribution only. **Remarks:** Patients' library contains an additional 3000 volumes including AV materials and vocational and patient health education collections.

★14921★
U.S. VETERANS ADMINISTRATION (MD-Fort Howard) - HOSPITAL LIBRARY (Med)
                                             Phone: (301) 477-1800
Fort Howard, MD 21052   Jacqueline Bird, Chf.Libn.
Founded: 1941. **Staff:** Prof 2; Other 1. **Subjects:** Medicine. **Holdings:** 2071 books; 2262 bound periodical volumes. **Subscriptions:** 160 journals and other serials. **Services:** Interlibrary loans; copying; library open to public by permission. **Computerized Information Services:** MEDLINE. Performs free searches. **Networks/Consortia:** Member of VALNET. **Remarks:** Patients' library contains an additional 6785 volumes. **Staff:** Betty A. Withrow, Med.Libn.

★14922★
U.S. VETERANS ADMINISTRATION (MD-Perry Point) - HOSPITAL MEDICAL LIBRARY (Med)
                                             Phone: (301) 642-2411
Perry Point, MD 21902   Mr. Lynn F. Delozier, Chf.Libn.
Founded: 1947. **Staff:** Prof 3; Other 5. **Subjects:** Psychiatry, psychology, social work, physical medicine. **Holdings:** 4803 books; 4298 bound periodical volumes; 1323 cassettes; 8 VF drawers of clippings, pamphlets and reprints. **Subscriptions:** 153 journals and other serials. **Services:** Interlibrary loans; copying; library open to public for reference use only. **Computerized Information Services:** BRS. **Networks/Consortia:** Member of VALNET; Maryland Association of Health Science Librarians. **Remarks:** Patients' library contains an additional 10,763 volumes. **Staff:** Elizabeth McMillan, Med.Libn.; Margaret Orman, Ref.Libn.

★14923★
U.S. VETERANS ADMINISTRATION (MA-Bedford) - EDITH NOURSE ROGERS MEMORIAL VETERANS HOSPITAL - MEDICAL LIBRARY (Med)
200 Springs Rd.   Phone: (617) 275-7500
Bedford, MA 01730   Sanford S. Yagendorf, Libn.
Founded: 1928. **Staff:** Prof 4; Other 2. **Subjects:** Psychology, medicine, nursing, social work. **Holdings:** 4938 books; 2497 bound periodical volumes; 18 AV items. **Subscriptions:** 261 journals and other serials. **Services:** Interlibrary loans; library open to qualified users by permission. **Publications:** Acquisition list, monthly - distributed to hospital staff. **Remarks:** Patients' library contains an additional 10,000 volumes.

★14924★
U.S. VETERANS ADMINISTRATION (MA-Boston) - HOSPITAL MEDICAL LIBRARY (Med)
150 S. Huntington Ave.   Phone: (617) 739-3434
Boston, MA 02130   Patricia J. McGrath, Chf., Lib.Serv.
Founded: 1952. **Staff:** Prof 3; Other 3. **Subjects:** General medicine and surgery. **Holdings:** 5000 books; 5000 bound periodical volumes. **Subscriptions:** 400 journals and other serials. **Services:** Interlibrary loans; copying; library open to qualified users. **Computerized Information Services:** MEDLINE, BRS. **Networks/Consortia:** Member of VALNET; Boston Biomedical Library Consortium. **Remarks:** Patients' library contains an additional 5344 volumes. **Staff:** Naomi Michalak, Patients' Libn.

★14925★
U.S. VETERANS ADMINISTRATION (MA-Boston) - OUTPATIENT CLINIC LIBRARY SERVICE (142D) (Med)
17 Court St.   Phone: (617) 223-2082
Boston, MA 02108   Carolyn B. Mathes, Chf., Lib.Serv.
Founded: 1975. **Staff:** Prof 2; Other 3. **Subjects:** Health sciences, consumer health, U.S. military, management. **Holdings:** 2500 books; 1836 periodical volumes (on microfilm); 1000 patient education pamphlets. **Subscriptions:** 180 journals and other serials; 6 newspapers. **Services:** Interlibrary loans; copying; SDI; library open to public. **Computerized Information Services:** DIALOG, BRS, CLASS. Performs free searches. **Networks/Consortia:** Member of VALNET; Greater New England Regional Medical Library Program; New England Online Users Group (NENON). **Publications:** Newsletter, 4/year; bibliographies; new acquisitions list, monthly. **Staff:** Olga Lycamanenko, Libn.

★14926★
U.S. VETERANS ADMINISTRATION (MA-Brockton) - MEDICAL CENTER LIBRARY (Med)
Belmont St.   Phone: (617) 583-4500
Brockton, MA 02401   Suzanne Noyes, Chf., Lib.Serv.
Founded: 1953. **Staff:** Prof 2; Other 2. **Subjects:** Psychiatry, psychology, hospital administration, nursing, medicine, alcoholism, drug abuse. **Holdings:** 6200 books; 8000 bound periodical volumes; 400 other cataloged items. **Subscriptions:** 450 journals and other serials. **Services:** Interlibrary loans; copying; library open to public. **Computerized Information Services:** MEDLINE. **Networks/Consortia:** Member of VALNET; Greater Northeastern Regional Medical Library Program; Southeastern Massachusetts Cooperating Libraries (SMCL); Southeastern Massachusetts Health Sciences Libraries. **Publications:** Medical Library Newsletter, monthly. **Remarks:** Patients' library contains an additional 15,000 volumes. **Staff:** Bruce Thornlow, Ref./AV Libn.; Donald Carter, Supv., LRC.

★14927★
U.S. VETERANS ADMINISTRATION (MA-Northampton) - MEDICAL CENTER LIBRARY (Med)
N. Main St.   Phone: (413) 584-4040
Northampton, MA 01060   Marjorie E. Sullivan, Chf., Lib.Serv.
Founded: 1935. **Staff:** Prof 3; Other 3. **Subjects:** Neurology, psychiatry, psychology, medicine. **Holdings:** 2833 books; 696 bound periodical volumes; 1350 volumes on microfilm; 511 unbound journal volumes. **Subscriptions:** 190 journals and other serials. **Services:** Interlibrary loans; library open to public for reference use only. **Computerized Information Services:** BRS. **Networks/Consortia:** Member of VALNET; Western Massachusetts Health Information Consortium; Massachusetts Health Sciences Library Network. **Remarks:** Patients' library contains an additional 7454 volumes.

★14928★
U.S. VETERANS ADMINISTRATION (MI-Allen Park) - MEDICAL CENTER LIBRARY SERVICE (142D) (Med)
                                             Phone: (313) 562-6000
Allen Park, MI 48101   Arlene Devlin, Chf., Lib.Serv.
Founded: 1939. **Staff:** Prof 3; Other 3. **Subjects:** Surgery, oncology, internal medicine, psychiatry, psychology, health management. **Special Collections:** Health information for patients; patient record slide collection; complete works of Sigmund Freud; Armed Forces Institute of Pathology (AFIP) Pathology Series. **Holdings:** 5500 books; 2500 bound periodical volumes; 900 AV items. **Subscriptions:** 400 journals and other serials; 8 newspapers. **Services:** Interlibrary loans; library not open to public. **Automated Operations:** Computerized cataloging. **Computerized Information Services:** OCLC, DIALOG, BRS, MEDLINE. **Networks/Consortia:** Member of VALNET; Health Instructional Resources Association (HIRA); Metropolitan Detroit Medical Library Group (MDMLG). **Publications:** Book list, quarterly; journal list, annual. **Staff:** Mary Jo Durivage, Med.Libn.

★14929★
U.S. VETERANS ADMINISTRATION (MI-Ann Arbor) - HOSPITAL LIBRARY (Med)
2215 Fuller Rd.   Phone: (313) 769-7100
Ann Arbor, MI 48105   Vickie Smith, Lib.Techn.
Founded: 1953. **Subjects:** Medicine. **Holdings:** 3404 books; 3610 bound periodical volumes. **Services:** Interlibrary loans; SDI; library open to public with restrictions. **Networks/Consortia:** Member of VALNET.

★14930★
U.S. VETERANS ADMINISTRATION (MI-Battle Creek) - MEDICAL CENTER LIBRARY (Med)
                                             Phone: (616) 966-5600
Battle Creek, MI 49016   Thomas Pyles, Jr., Chf., Lib.Serv.
Founded: 1925. **Staff:** Prof 2; Other 3. **Subjects:** Psychiatry and neurology.

Holdings: 2554 books; 913 bound periodical volumes; 1655 volumes of journals on microfilm. **Subscriptions:** 423 journals and other serials; 21 newspapers. **Services:** Interlibrary loans; copying; library open to public. **Networks/Consortia:** Member of VALNET. **Remarks:** Patients' library contains an additional 9380 books and 138 bound periodical volumes. **Staff:** Barbara C. Burhans, Biomed.Libn.

★14931★
U.S. VETERANS ADMINISTRATION (MI-Iron Mountain) - MEDICAL CENTER LIBRARY (Med)
East H St.
Iron Mountain, MI 49801
Phone: (906) 774-3300
Phyllis E. Goetz, Chf., Lib.Serv.
Founded: 1950. **Staff:** Prof 1; Other 1. **Subjects:** Internal medicine, surgery, nursing. **Holdings:** 1474 books; 2318 bound periodical volumes; 15 files of patient education materials; 87 video cassettes; 365 audio cassettes; 592 filmstrips and slide/tape kits. **Subscriptions:** 253 journals and other serials; 29 newspapers. **Services:** Interlibrary loans; copying; library open to professionals. **Automated Operations:** Computerized cataloging. **Computerized Information Services:** MEDLINE. **Networks/Consortia:** Member of VALNET; UP Health Sciences Libraries Consortium; Michigan Health Sciences Libraries Association; Mid-Peninsula Library Cooperative. **Remarks:** Patients' library contains an additional 5700 volumes.

★14932★
U.S. VETERANS ADMINISTRATION (MI-Saginaw) - MEDICAL CENTER LIBRARY (Med)
1500 Weiss St.
Saginaw, MI 48602
Phone: (517) 793-2340
Nancy R. Dingman, Chf.Libn.
Founded: 1950. **Staff:** Prof 2; Other 1. **Subjects:** Medicine, surgery, nursing, health education. **Special Collections:** Respiratory, coronary and intensive care; computer information and management. **Holdings:** 3000 books; periodicals in microform; 1000 AV materials; health education pamphlets. **Subscriptions:** 150 journals and other serials; 6 newspapers. **Services:** Interlibrary loans; copying; SDI; library open to hospital personnel only. **Automated Operations:** Access to computerized cataloging, acquisitions and serials. **Computerized Information Services:** MEDLINE, DIALOG, BRS; internal databases. **Networks/Consortia:** Member of VALNET; Valley Regional Health Science Librarians; Greater Midwest Regional Medical Library Network (Region 3); Health Instructional Resources Association. **Remarks:** Patients' library contains an additional 2500 volumes and a large collection of health educational AV, print and pamphlet materials.

★14933★
U.S. VETERANS ADMINISTRATION (MN-Minneapolis) - MEDICAL CENTER LIBRARY SERVICE (Med)
54th St. & 48th Ave., S.
Minneapolis, MN 55417
Phone: (612) 725-6767
Lionelle Elsesser, Chf., Lib.Serv.
Founded: 1946. **Staff:** Prof 3; Other 6. **Subjects:** General medicine, psychology, pre-clinical sciences. **Holdings:** 5500 books; 11,000 bound periodical volumes; 1500 volumes on microfilm; 1500 AV programs. **Subscriptions:** 500 journals and other serials; 5 newspapers. **Services:** Interlibrary loans; patient education; library not open to public. **Automated Operations:** Computerized cataloging. **Computerized Information Services:** MEDLINE, DIALOG, BRS. **Networks/Consortia:** Member of VALNET; Greater Midwest Regional Medical Library (Region 3); Twin Cities Biomedical Consortium (TCBC). **Publications:** Acquisitions list, quarterly; special bibliographies; list of journal holdings, annual; patient education publications. **Remarks:** Patients Education Center/Library has print and nonprint collections in health care field for patients, families and staff. **Staff:** Margery MacNeill, Med.Libn.; Marie Nelson, Libn., Patient Educ.Ctr.; Kathy Mackay, AV Libn.; Linda Lindsey, ILL Techn.

★14934★
U.S. VETERANS ADMINISTRATION (MN-St. Cloud) - MEDICAL CENTER LIBRARY (Med)
St. Cloud, MN 56301
Phone: (612) 252-1670
Sanford J. Banker, Chf., Lib.Serv.
Founded: 1924. **Staff:** Prof 3; Other 1. **Subjects:** General medicine, psychology, nursing, geriatrics. **Holdings:** 2000 books; 1000 bound periodical volumes; microfilm. **Subscriptions:** 250 journals and other serials. **Networks/Consortia:** Member of VALNET. **Remarks:** Patients' library contains an additional 8000 volumes.

★14935★
U.S. VETERANS ADMINISTRATION (MS-Jackson) - CENTER LIBRARY (Med)
1500 E. Woodrow Wilson
Jackson, MS 39216
Phone: (601) 362-4471
Carol Sistrunk, Chf.Libn.
Founded: 1946. **Staff:** Prof 2; Other 1. **Subjects:** Medicine and related subjects. **Holdings:** 1800 books; 2750 bound periodical volumes; 2000

volumes of journals on microfilm; 275 AV software items. **Subscriptions:** 200 journals and other serials; 15 newspapers. **Services:** Interlibrary loans; copying (limited); library open to public by permission. **Computerized Information Services:** MEDLINE. **Networks/Consortia:** Member of VALNET; Central Mississippi Council of Medical Libraries; Mississippi Biomedical Library Consortium. **Remarks:** Patients' library contains an additional 5000 volumes.

★14936★
U.S. VETERANS ADMINISTRATION (MO-Columbia) - HOSPITAL LIBRARY (Med)
800 Stadium Rd.
Columbia, MO 65201
Phone: (314) 443-2511
Ray Starke, Chf., Lib.Serv.
Founded: 1972. **Staff:** Prof 2; Other 3. **Subjects:** Medicine, surgery. **Special Collections:** Patient education (267 books; 67 AV materials). **Holdings:** 4400 books; 2000 bound periodical volumes. **Subscriptions:** 300 journals and other serials; 14 newspapers. **Services:** Interlibrary loans; copying; SDI; library open to public for reference use only. **Automated Operations:** Computerized cataloging and serials. **Computerized Information Services:** MEDLARS, BRS, DIALOG. **Networks/Consortia:** Member of VALNET; Mid-Missouri Library Network. **Staff:** Linda Dagley, Med.Libn.; Joyce Homan, Lib.Techn.

★14937★
U.S. VETERANS ADMINISTRATION (MO-Kansas City) - MEDICAL CENTER LIBRARY (Med)
4801 Linwood Blvd.
Kansas City, MO 64128
Phone: (816) 861-4700
Shirley C. Ting, Chf., Lib.Serv.
Founded: 1952. **Staff:** Prof 2; Other 1. **Subjects:** Medicine, surgery, neurology, nursing, psychology, psychiatry. **Holdings:** 4730 books; 6278 bound periodical volumes; 550 AV materials. **Subscriptions:** 360 journals and other serials; 10 newspapers. **Services:** Interlibrary loans; copying; SDI; library open to public for reference use only. **Automated Operations:** Computerized serials and circulation. **Computerized Information Services:** MEDLINE, BRS, Octanet; internal database. **Networks/Consortia:** Member of VALNET; Midcontinental Regional Medical Library Program. **Remarks:** Patients' library contains an additional 4669 volumes. **Staff:** Margaret A. Brennan, Med.Libn.

★14938★
U.S. VETERANS ADMINISTRATION (MO-Poplar Bluff) - MEDICAL CENTER LIBRARY (142D) (Med)
Highway 67 North
Poplar Bluff, MO 63901
Phone: (314) 686-4151
Kwang Hee Streiff, Chf., Lib.Serv.
Staff: Prof 1; Other 7. **Subjects:** Medicine. **Holdings:** 877 books; AV equipment and software. **Subscriptions:** 96 journals and other serials; 24 newspapers. **Services:** Interlibrary loans; copying; library open to community health care personnel. **Computerized Information Services:** MEDLINE. **Networks/Consortia:** Member of VALNET; Midcontinental Regional Medical Library Program. **Remarks:** Patients' library contains an additional 4101 books and 84 periodicals.

★14939★
U.S. VETERANS ADMINISTRATION (MO-St. Louis) - HOSPITAL LIBRARY (Med)
St. Louis, MO 63125
Phone: (314) 652-4100
Larry Weitkemper, Chf., Lib.Serv.
Staff: Prof 5. **Subjects:** Medicine and allied health sciences. **Holdings:** 5868 books; 6960 bound periodical volumes; AV collection. **Subscriptions:** 400 journals and other serials. **Services:** Library not open to public. **Networks/Consortia:** Member of VALNET. **Remarks:** Patients' library contains an additional 8000 volumes and 3000 volumes of journals on microfilm. **Staff:** Helen H. Henderson, Libn.; Robert Klein, Libn.; Katie W. Deberry, Libn.; Alfreida Keeling, Libn.

★14940★
U.S. VETERANS ADMINISTRATION (MT-Fort Harrison) - MEDICAL CENTER LIBRARY (Med)
Fort Harrison, MT 59636
Phone: (406) 442-6410
Maurice C. Knutson, Chf., Lib.Serv.
Staff: Prof 1. **Subjects:** Medicine, particularly internal medicine and surgery. **Holdings:** 1484 books; 1631 bound periodical volumes. **Subscriptions:** 268 journals and other serials; 10 newspapers. **Services:** Interlibrary loans; library open to public with restrictions. **Computerized Information Services:** MEDLARS. **Networks/Consortia:** Member of VALNET; Montana Health Sciences Information Network; Helena Area Health Sciences Library Consortia. **Remarks:** Patients' library contains an additional 6013 volumes.

★14941★

U.S. VETERANS ADMINISTRATION (MT-Miles City) - MEDICAL CENTER LIBRARY (Med)

Miles City, MT 59301

Phone: (406) 232-3060
Donna B. Sweeney, Act.Chf., Lib.Serv.

Founded: 1951. **Staff:** 1. **Subjects:** Medicine. **Holdings:** 1189 books; 18 bound periodical volumes. **Subscriptions:** 219 journals and other serials; 33 newspapers. **Services:** Interlibrary loans; library not open to public. **Remarks:** Patients' library contains an additional 1573 volumes.

★14942★

U.S. VETERANS ADMINISTRATION (NE-Grand Island) - HOSPITAL LIBRARY (Med)

2201 N. Broadwell St.
Grand Island, NE 68801

Phone: (308) 382-3660

Founded: 1950. **Staff:** Prof 1. **Subjects:** Medicine, surgery and nursing. **Holdings:** 1074 books; 487 bound periodical volumes; talking books, cassette books and large print books. **Subscriptions:** 110 journals and other serials. **Services:** Interlibrary loans; copying; loan services from Library of Congress and regional libraries for blind and physically handicapped; library open to public by permission. **Remarks:** Patients' library contains an additional 2985 volumes and 67 journal subscriptions.

★14943★

U.S. VETERANS ADMINISTRATION (NE-Lincoln) - MEDICAL CENTER LIBRARY (Med)

600 S. 70th St.
Lincoln, NE 68510

Phone: (402) 489-3802
Jean Landfield, Chf.Libn.

Staff: Prof 1; Other 1. **Subjects:** Medicine and allied sciences. **Holdings:** 2400 books; 3800 bound periodical volumes; 700 journals on microfilm; 700 AV items. **Subscriptions:** 180 journals and other serials; 4 newspapers. **Services:** Interlibrary loans; copying; library open to qualified medical personnel. **Computerized Information Services:** NLM. **Networks/Consortia:** Member of Lincoln Health Science Library Group; VALNET. **Remarks:** Patients' library contains an additional 3000 volumes.

★14944★

U.S. VETERANS ADMINISTRATION (NE-Omaha) - HOSPITAL LIBRARY (Med)

4101 Woolworth Ave.
Omaha, NE 68105

Phone: (402) 346-8800
Lois J. Inskeep, Chf., Lib.Serv.

Founded: 1950. **Staff:** Prof 1; Other 1. **Subjects:** Medicine and allied health sciences. **Holdings:** 2000 books; 3800 bound periodical volumes; 2000 AV items. **Subscriptions:** 250 journals and other serials; 25 newspapers. **Services:** Interlibrary loans; copying; library open to public by request. **Networks/Consortia:** Member of VALNET.

★14945★

U.S. VETERANS ADMINISTRATION (NV-Reno) - MEDICAL CENTER - LEARNING CENTER (Med)

1000 Locust St.
Reno, NV 89509

Phone: (702) 786-7200
Janet F. Monk, Chf., Lib.Serv.

Staff: Prof 3; Other 1. **Subjects:** Clinical medicine, gerontology. **Holdings:** 2300 books. **Subscriptions:** 210 journals and other serials. **Services:** Interlibrary loans; copying; SDI; library open to public with referral. **Automated Operations:** Computerized cataloging. **Computerized Information Services:** DIALOG, MEDLARS. Performs free searches. **Networks/Consortia:** Member of VALNET; Northern California and Nevada Medical Library Group. **Staff:** Ester Robles, Libn.; Louise Papile-Miller, AV Spec.

★14946★

U.S. VETERANS ADMINISTRATION (NH-Manchester) - MEDICAL CENTER LIBRARY (Med)

718 Smyth Rd.
Manchester, NH 03104

Phone: (603) 624-4366
Joan McGinnis, Chf.Libn.

Founded: 1950. **Staff:** Prof 1; Other 1. **Subjects:** Medicine, surgery, nursing. **Holdings:** 1650 books; 1500 bound periodical volumes. **Subscriptions:** 130 journals and other serials; 12 newspapers. **Services:** Interlibrary loans; copying; library open to public with restrictions. **Computerized Information Services:** BRS, NLM. **Networks/Consortia:** Member of VALNET; Hospital Library Development Services. **Remarks:** Patients' library contains an additional 2500 volumes.

★14947★

U.S. VETERANS ADMINISTRATION (NJ-East Orange) - MEDICAL CENTER LIBRARY (Med)

East Orange, NJ 07019

Phone: (201) 676-1000
Calvin A. Zamarelli, Chf.Libn.

Founded: 1952. **Staff:** Prof 3; Other 3. **Subjects:** General medicine.

Holdings: 10,000 books; 9000 bound periodical volumes; 2000 AV items. **Subscriptions:** 400 journals and other serials. **Services:** Interlibrary loans; copying; library open to public. **Computerized Information Services:** MEDLINE. **Networks/Consortia:** Member of VALNET. **Remarks:** Patients' library contains an additional 6500 volumes. **Staff:** David Madden, Med.Libn.; Judith Grace, AV Libn.

★14948★

U.S. VETERANS ADMINISTRATION (NJ-Lyons) - HOSPITAL LIBRARY (Med)

Knollcroft Rd.
Lyons, NJ 07939

Phone: (201) 647-0180
James G. Delo, Chf./Med.Libn.

Founded: 1930. **Staff:** Prof 2; Other 1. **Subjects:** Psychiatry, neurology, psychology, medicine, nursing. **Holdings:** 9000 books; 5200 bound periodical volumes; 500 AV items. **Subscriptions:** 400 journals and other serials; 14 newspapers. **Services:** Interlibrary loans; copying; library open to public for reference use only. **Networks/Consortia:** Member of VALNET; Medical Resources Consortium of Central New Jersey (MEDCORE). **Remarks:** Patients' library contains an additional 13,329 volumes. **Staff:** Marian Krugman, Patients' Libn.

★14949★

U.S. VETERANS ADMINISTRATION (NM-Albuquerque) - MEDICAL CENTER LIBRARY (Med)

2100 Ridgecrest Dr., S.E.
Albuquerque, NM 87108

Phone: (505) 265-1711
Nancy Myer, Chf., Lib.Serv.

Founded: 1932. **Staff:** Prof 2; Other 1. **Subjects:** Medicine, surgery, nursing, psychiatry. **Holdings:** 1530 books; 8537 bound periodical volumes. **Subscriptions:** 393 journals and other serials; 10 newspapers. **Services:** Interlibrary loans; copying; library open to public by special permission. **Computerized Information Services:** MEDLINE, DIALOG. **Networks/Consortia:** Member of VALNET. **Remarks:** Patients' library contains an additional 1225 volumes. **Staff:** Phyllis L. Kregstein, Biomed.Libn.

★14950★

U.S. VETERANS ADMINISTRATION (NY-Albany) - MEDICAL CENTER LIBRARY (500/142-D) (Med)

113 Holland Ave.
Albany, NY 12208

Phone: (518) 462-3311
John F. Connors, Adm.Libn.

Founded: 1951. **Staff:** Prof 2; Other 1. **Subjects:** Medicine, surgery, psychiatry, psychology, nursing, social work. **Holdings:** 1850 books; 7600 bound periodical volumes; 45 AV items; 1200 reels of microfilm; 150 talking and large print books. **Subscriptions:** 360 journals and other serials; 8 newspapers. **Services:** Interlibrary loans; copying; library open to public. **Automated Operations:** Computerized cataloging. **Computerized Information Services:** MEDLINE, BRS. **Networks/Consortia:** Member of VALNET; Capital District Library Council for Reference & Research Resources (CDLC); Greater Northeastern Regional Medical Library Program. **Publications:** Acquisitions lists, irregular. **Remarks:** Patients' library contains an additional 1000 volumes. **Staff:** Denise Watlington, Med.Libn.

★14951★

U.S. VETERANS ADMINISTRATION (NY-Batavia) - MEDICAL CENTER LIBRARY (Med)

Redfield Pkwy.
Batavia, NY 14020

Phone: (716) 343-7500
Madeline A. Coco, Chf.Libn.

Founded: 1934. **Staff:** Prof 1; Other 1. **Subjects:** General medicine, surgery, nursing, pathology, radiology. **Holdings:** 1700 books; 1700 bound periodical volumes. **Subscriptions:** 99 journals and other serials. **Services:** Interlibrary loans; copying; library open to medical professionals and students. **Computerized Information Services:** MEDLINE. **Networks/Consortia:** Member of VALNET; Western New York Library Resources Council. **Remarks:** Patients' library contains an additional 4500 volumes.

★14952★

U.S. VETERANS ADMINISTRATION (NY-Bath) - MEDICAL CENTER LIBRARY (Med)

Bath, NY 14810

Phone: (607) 776-2111
Norma W. Haskins, Chf., Lib.Serv.

Founded: 1930. **Staff:** Prof 2; Other 1. **Subjects:** Geriatrics, chronic diseases, general internal medicine. **Special Collections:** Dental education (125 8mm cartridges). **Holdings:** 1479 books; 1000 bound periodical volumes; 482 video cassettes; 53 16mm films. **Subscriptions:** 123 journals and other serials; 23 newspapers. **Services:** Interlibrary loans; SDI; AV materials for professional education shown by arrangement; library open to public with permission for reference use only. **Automated Operations:** Computerized cataloging. **Computerized Information Services:** MEDLINE. Contact Person: Sally Hillegas. **Networks/Consortia:** Member of VALNET; Three R's Council, Ithaca. **Publications:** Quarterly Newsletter. **Remarks:** Patients' library contains an additional 12,521 volumes. **Staff:** Sally Ann

Hillegas, Med.Libn.

★14953★
U.S. VETERANS ADMINISTRATION (NY-Bronx) - MEDICAL CENTER LIBRARY (Med)
130 W. Kingsbridge Rd.
Bronx, NY 10468   Margaret M. Kinney, Chf.Libn.
Staff: Prof 3; Other 3. **Subjects:** Medicine and related subjects. **Holdings:** 20,244 volumes. **Services:** Interlibrary loans; library open to public with restrictions. **Computerized Information Services:** Online systems. **Networks/Consortia:** Member of VALNET. **Remarks:** Patients' library contains an additional 9126 volumes.

★14954★
U.S. VETERANS ADMINISTRATION (NY-Brooklyn) - MEDICAL CENTER LIBRARY (Med)
800 Poly Place   Phone: (718) 836-6600
Brooklyn, NY 11209   Barbara B. Goldberg, Chf.Libn.
Founded: 1947. **Staff:** Prof 5; Other 3. **Subjects:** Medicine, surgery, psychiatry, psychology, social work. **Holdings:** 6685 books; 7226 bound periodical volumes; 106 video cassettes; 138 slide sets; 6 films. **Subscriptions:** 500 journals and other serials. **Services:** Interlibrary loans; library not open to public. **Automated Operations:** Computerized cataloging. **Computerized Information Services:** MEDLARS, DIALOG, BRS. **Networks/Consortia:** Member of VALNET; Medical Library Center of New York; Brooklyn-Queens-Staten Island Health Science Librarians (BQSI); METRO. **Staff:** Ruth Levine, Patients Libn.; Francine Tidona, Med.Libn.; Jeff Nicholas, Staff Libn.

★14955★
U.S. VETERANS ADMINISTRATION (NY-Buffalo) - MEDICAL CENTER LIBRARY SERVICE (Med)
3495 Bailey Ave.   Phone: (716) 834-9200
Buffalo, NY 14215   Joyce Kaupa, Libn.
Founded: 1950. **Staff:** Prof 3; Other 1. **Subjects:** Medicine, surgery, nursing, management, patient education. **Holdings:** 3000 books; 8000 bound periodical volumes; 1000 AV items. **Subscriptions:** 361 journals and other serials. **Services:** Interlibrary loans; copying; SDI; library open to public for reference use only. **Computerized Information Services:** BRS, NLM, DIALOG. Performs free searches for staff and undergraduate students. Contact Person: James Mendola. **Networks/Consortia:** Member of VALNET; Western New York Library Resources Council (WNYLRC); Greater Northeastern Regional Medical Library Program; Library Consortium of Health Institutions in Buffalo (LCHIB). **Publications:** Newsletter, quarterly; Serial Holdings List. **Special Catalogs:** Patient Education Bibliography; Management Bibliography; Nursing Bibliography. **Remarks:** Patients' library contains an additional 7947 volumes. **Staff:** James Mendola, Med.Libn.; Russell Hall, Med.Libn.; Barbara Kunkel, Techn.

★14956★
U.S. VETERANS ADMINISTRATION (NY-Canandaigua) - MEDICAL CENTER LIBRARY (142D) (Med)
          Phone: (315) 394-2000
Canandaigua, NY 14424   Peter Fleming, Chf., Lib.Serv.
Founded: 1933. **Staff:** Prof 2; Other 3. **Subjects:** Psychiatry, psychology, nursing, medicine. **Holdings:** 4000 books; 612 bound periodical volumes; 2488 other volumes. **Subscriptions:** 200 journals and other serials. **Services:** Interlibrary loans. **Automated Operations:** Computerized cataloging. **Computerized Information Services:** NLM, BRS. **Networks/Consortia:** Member of Rochester Regional Research Library Council (RRRLC). **Remarks:** Patients' library contains an additional 7270 volumes. **Staff:** Vikki Cecere, Libn.

★14957★
U.S. VETERANS ADMINISTRATION (NY-Castle Point) - MEDICAL CENTER LIBRARY (Med)
          Phone: (914) 831-2000
Castle Point, NY 12511   William E. Kane, Chf., Lib.Serv.
Staff: Prof 1; Other 1. **Subjects:** Internal medicine, surgery, spinal cord injury. **Holdings:** 1701 books; 649 bound periodical volumes; 262 audio cassettes; 27 video cassettes. **Subscriptions:** 124 journals and other serials; 10 newspapers. **Services:** Interlibrary loans; copying; library open to public with restrictions. **Networks/Consortia:** Member of VALNET; Southeastern New York Library Resources Council (SENYLRC). **Remarks:** Patients' library contains an additional 923 volumes.

★14958★
U.S. VETERANS ADMINISTRATION (NY-Montrose) - HOSPITAL LIBRARY (Med)
          Phone: (914) 737-4400
Montrose, NY 10548   Eileen J. Liberty, Chf., Lib.Serv.
Founded: 1950. **Staff:** Prof 4; Other 2. **Subjects:** Medicine, psychiatry, psychology. **Special Collections:** Patient Education Collection. **Holdings:** 3876 books; 3134 bound periodical volumes; 15 VF drawers of pamphlets and clippings; 350 AV units. **Subscriptions:** 386 journals and other serials. **Services:** Interlibrary loans; library open to public by request. **Networks/Consortia:** Member of VALNET; Health Information Libraries of Westchester (HILOW). **Publications:** Medical Library News, bimonthly - distributed to staff members and VA hospitals. **Remarks:** Patients' library contains an additional 5067 volumes. **Staff:** Norma Goldstein, Patients' Libn.; Robert Mohrman, Med.Libn.Karl Yung, ILL Libn.

★14959★
U.S. VETERANS ADMINISTRATION (NY-New York) - MEDICAL LIBRARY (Med)
408 First Ave.   Phone: (212) 686-7500
New York, NY 10010   Malvin Vitriol, Chf.Libn.
Founded: 1955. **Staff:** Prof 4; Other 5. **Subjects:** Medicine, surgery, neurology, psychiatry and nursing. **Holdings:** 3100 books; 5684 bound periodical volumes. **Subscriptions:** 350 journals and other serials; 10 newspapers. **Services:** Interlibrary loans; library open to affiliated medical professionals. **Computerized Information Services:** MEDLINE. **Networks/Consortia:** Member of VALNET; Medical Library Center of New York (MLCNY); Manhattan-Bronx Health Sciences Library Group. **Remarks:** Patients' library contains an additional 5344 volumes. **Staff:** Irene Lovas, Med.Libn.; Karin Wiseman, Libn.

★14960★
U.S. VETERANS ADMINISTRATION (NY-New York) - OFFICE OF TECHNOLOGY TRANSFER - REFERENCE COLLECTION (Med)
252 Seventh Ave., 3rd Fl.   Phone: (212) 620-6670
New York, NY 10001   Lily W. Hom, Tech.Info.Spec.
Founded: 1949. **Staff:** Prof 2; Other 1. **Subjects:** Prosthetics, sensory aids, orthotics, spinal cord injury, rehabilitation, automotive adaptive equipment, biomechanics. **Holdings:** 3500 books; 8000 patents; 80 motion pictures; 35 video cassettes; 13,800 articles and reprints; 2500 technical and contractor reports. **Subscriptions:** 130 journals and other serials. **Services:** Interlibrary loans; copying; collection open to public for reference use only with permission. **Networks/Consortia:** Member of Rehabilitation Information Round Table. **Special Indexes:** Index to Journal of Rehabilitation Research and Development.

★14961★
U.S. VETERANS ADMINISTRATION (NY-Northport) - HEALTH SCIENCE LIBRARY (Med)
          Phone: (516) 261-4400
Northport, NY 11768   Deborah Lewek, Chf., Lib.Serv.
Staff: Prof 6; Other 2. **Subjects:** Medicine and allied health sciences; psychiatry; dentistry. **Special Collections:** Geriatrics; hospital administration. **Holdings:** 5000 books; 8500 bound periodical volumes; 2000 AV programs. **Subscriptions:** 600 journals and other serials. **Services:** Interlibrary loans; library open to public for reference use only. **Computerized Information Services:** MEDLINE, BRS, DIALOG. **Networks/Consortia:** Member of VALNET; Medical & Scientific Libraries of Long Island (MEDLI). **Publications:** Library Line, quarterly. **Staff:** Caryl Kazan, Asst.Chf; Marc Horowitz, AV Libn.; Robert Toronto, Libn.; Magdelene Aquilino, ILL Libn.; Henry Nietzschmann, Libn.

★14962★
U.S. VETERANS ADMINISTRATION (NY-Syracuse) - MEDICAL CENTER LIBRARY (Med)
Irving Ave. & University Pl.   Phone: (315) 476-7461
Syracuse, NY 13210   June M. Mitchell, Chf., Lib./LRC Serv.
Founded: 1953. **Staff:** Prof 3. **Subjects:** Clinical medicine, surgery, nursing, psychology, social work. **Holdings:** 4000 books; 2595 bound periodical volumes; 800 pamphlets. **Subscriptions:** 185 journals and other serials. **Services:** Library open to public for reference use only. **Computerized Information Services:** MEDLINE. **Networks/Consortia:** Member of VALNET; Central New York Library Resources Council (CENTRO). **Remarks:** Patients' library contains an additional 10,000 volumes, including management collection. Learning Resources Center, established in 1975, adds many AV resources for patient education and staff instruction and training. **Staff:** Kay A.W. Root, Med.Libn.E. Nancy Hellwig, AV Libn.

★14963★

U.S. VETERANS ADMINISTRATION (NC-Asheville) - MEDICAL CENTER LIBRARY (Med)

Asheville, NC 28805

Phone: (704) 298-7911
Richard Haver, Chf.Libn.

Staff: Prof 1; Other 1. **Subjects:** General medicine, cardiopulmonary medicine, thoracic surgery, nursing. **Holdings:** 2000 books; 3000 bound periodical volumes. **Subscriptions:** 240 journals and other serials. **Services:** Interlibrary loans; copying; library open to medical professionals. **Computerized Information Services:** NLM, DIALOG. **Networks/Consortia:** Member of VALNET.

★14964★

U.S. VETERANS ADMINISTRATION (NC-Durham) - MEDICAL CENTER LIBRARY (Med)

508 Fulton St.
Durham, NC 27705

Phone: (919) 286-0411
Leola H. Jenkins, Chf.Libn.

Founded: 1953. **Staff:** Prof 2; Other 1. **Subjects:** Medicine, basic sciences. **Holdings:** 6094 books and bound periodical volumes; 1256 AV items. **Subscriptions:** 428 journals and other serials; 10 newspapers. **Services:** Interlibrary loans; library open to public with restrictions. **Computerized Information Services:** MEDLINE, BRS. **Networks/Consortia:** Member of VALNET. **Staff:** Margaret F. Clifton, Med.Libn.; Sheila H. Thompson, Per./ILL Libn.

★14965★

U.S. VETERANS ADMINISTRATION (NC-Fayetteville) - HOSPITAL LIBRARY (Med)

Fayetteville, NC 28301

Phone: (919) 488-2120
Nancy A. Clark, Chf., Lib.Serv.

Founded: 1940. **Staff:** Prof 1; Other 1. **Subjects:** Medicine, nursing, dentistry. **Holdings:** 2577 books; 3978 periodicals. **Subscriptions:** 410 journals and other serials. **Services:** Interlibrary loans; copying; SDI; library open to public with restrictions. **Computerized Information Services:** MEDLINE. **Networks/Consortia:** Member of VALNET; Cape Fear Health Sciences Information Consortium. **Remarks:** Patients' library contains an additional 3900 volumes.

★14966★

U.S. VETERANS ADMINISTRATION (NC-Salisbury) - MEDICAL CENTER LIBRARY (Med)

1601 Brenner Ave.
Salisbury, NC 28144

Phone: (704) 636-2351
Mara R. Wilhelm, Chf., Lib.Serv.

Founded: 1953. **Staff:** Prof 3; Other 3. **Subjects:** Psychology, psychiatry, nursing, internal medicine, surgery, gerontology, dentistry. **Holdings:** 2165 books; 1375 AV items. **Subscriptions:** 353 journals and other serials. **Services:** Interlibrary loans; library open to health science professionals. **Computerized Information Services:** MEDLINE. **Networks/Consortia:** Member of VALNET. **Publications:** Newsletter, monthly - for internal distribution only. **Remarks:** Patients' library contains an additional 2998 volumes. **Staff:** Christine Simpson, Libn.; Lucile Owsley, Libn.

★14967★

U.S. VETERANS ADMINISTRATION (ND-Fargo) - CENTER LIBRARY (Med)

Phone: (701) 232-3241

Fargo, ND 58102

Founded: 1945. **Staff:** Prof 3. **Subjects:** Medicine, dentistry, nursing, social work, hospital administration. **Holdings:** 2001 books; 5605 bound periodical volumes; 2 VF drawers of reprints, pamphlets and bibliographies. **Subscriptions:** 380 journals and other serials. **Services:** Interlibrary loans; copying; library open to southeastern area of North Dakota. **Computerized Information Services:** MEDLINE, BRS. **Networks/Consortia:** Member of VALNET; Valley Medical Network. **Remarks:** Patients' library services and patient education material available.

★14968★

U.S. VETERANS ADMINISTRATION (OH-Brecksville) - HOSPITAL LIBRARY (Med)

10000 Brecksville Rd.
Brecksville, OH 44141

Phone: (216) 526-3030
Nancy S. Tesmer, Chf., Lib.Serv.

Founded: 1961. **Staff:** Prof 3; Other 3. **Subjects:** Psychology, nursing, psychiatry, social work, neurology. **Special Collections:** Suicide file (5000 references). **Holdings:** 4807 volumes; 20 dissertations; 1600 AV units of software. **Subscriptions:** 250 journals and other serials. **Services:** Interlibrary loans; SDI; library open to public. **Computerized Information Services:** MEDLINE, DIALOG, BRS. **Networks/Consortia:** Member of VALNET. **Publications:** Library Newsletter, bimonthly. **Special Catalogs:** Subject coded reference catalog on Suicide Collection (card). **Remarks:** Patients' library contains an additional 8759 volumes. **Staff:** Mary Conway,

Med.Libn.; John C. White, AV Libn.

★14969★

U.S. VETERANS ADMINISTRATION (OH-Chillicothe) - HOSPITAL LIBRARY (Med)

Chillicothe, OH 45601

Phone: (614) 773-1141
Barbara A. Schultz, Chf., Lib.Serv.

Founded: 1947. **Staff:** Prof 2; Other 2. **Subjects:** Psychiatry, medicine and allied health sciences. **Holdings:** 4525 volumes; 4 VF drawers. **Subscriptions:** 220 journals and other serials. **Services:** Interlibrary loans; copying; SDI. **Computerized Information Services:** MEDLARS, BRS. **Networks/Consortia:** Member of VALNET. **Remarks:** Patients' library contains an additional 7050 volumes.

★14970★

U.S. VETERANS ADMINISTRATION (OH-Cincinnati) - MEDICAL CENTER LIBRARY (Med)

3200 Vine St.
Cincinnati, OH 45220

Cynthia R. Sterling, Libn.

Staff: Prof 1; Other 3. **Subjects:** Medicine, mental health, nursing, surgery. **Holdings:** 10,036 volumes. **Subscriptions:** 218 journals and other serials. **Services:** Interlibrary loans; SDI; library open to public. **Automated Operations:** Computerized cataloging. **Computerized Information Services:** NLM, BRS. **Networks/Consortia:** Member of Cincinnati Online Consortium for Life Sciences (COCLS); Miami Valley Union List.

★14971★

U.S. VETERANS ADMINISTRATION (OH-Cleveland) - HOSPITAL LIBRARY (Med)

10701 East Blvd.
Cleveland, OH 44106

Phone: (216) 791-3800
Nancy S. Tesmer, Chf.Libn.

Founded: 1946. **Staff:** Prof 4; Other 4. **Subjects:** Clinical and pre-clinical medicine. **Holdings:** 9664 books; 7915 bound periodical volumes. **Subscriptions:** 485 journals and other serials. **Services:** Interlibrary loans; copying; library open to public by permission. **Computerized Information Services:** DIALOG, BRS, MEDLINE. **Networks/Consortia:** Member of VALNET. **Remarks:** Patients' library contains an additional 7495 volumes. The library also serves the Brecksville unit, 10000 Brecksville Rd., Brecksville, OH 44141. **Staff:** Mary Nourse, Med.Libn.Mary Conway, Med.Libn.; John C. White, AV Libn.

★14972★

U.S. VETERANS ADMINISTRATION (OH-Dayton) - CENTER LIBRARY (Med)

4100 W. Third St.
Dayton, OH 45428

Phone: (513) 268-6511
Lendell Beverly, Chf., Lib.Serv.

Founded: 1867. **Staff:** Prof 4; Other 5. **Subjects:** Medicine, nursing, hospital administration, patient education, military history. **Special Collections:** U.S. Military History (1200 volumes); patient education. **Holdings:** 7000 books; 4840 bound periodical volumes. **Subscriptions:** 460 journals and other serials; 22 newspapers. **Services:** Interlibrary loans; copying; library open to public for reference use only. **Automated Operations:** Computerized cataloging. **Computerized Information Services:** BRS, NLM. **Networks/Consortia:** Member of VALNET; Miami Valley Association of Health Sciences Libraries. **Publications:** Fact Sheet; new book list, monthly. **Remarks:** Patients' library contains an additional 19,875 volumes. **Staff:** Cheryl Harris, Health Sci.Libn.

★14973★

U.S. VETERANS ADMINISTRATION (OK-Muskogee) - MEDICAL CENTER LIBRARY (Med)

1101 Honor Height Dr.
Muskogee, OK 74401

Phone: (918) 683-3261
Larry L. Shea, Chf., Lib.Serv.

Staff: Prof 2; Other 1. **Subjects:** Medicine, nursing and allied sciences. **Holdings:** 2463 books; 4584 bound periodical volumes; 1288 AV items. **Subscriptions:** 263 medical journals and 37 administrative serials; 12 newspapers. **Services:** Interlibrary loans; copying; SDI; library open to hospital staff and medical professionals in the community. **Computerized Information Services:** MEDLARS. **Networks/Consortia:** Member of VALNET; TALON; Oklahoma Health Science Libraries Association (OHSLA). **Publications:** Library Newsletter, monthly. **Special Catalogs:** AV Catalog. **Remarks:** Patients' library contains an additional 3400 volumes and 172 patient education programs. **Staff:** Dawn Williams, Med.Libn.

★14974★

U.S. VETERANS ADMINISTRATION (OK-Oklahoma City) - MEDICAL CENTER LIBRARY (Med)

921 N.E. 13th St.
Oklahoma City, OK 73104

Phone: (405) 272-9876
Verlean Delaney, Chf.Libn.

Founded: 1946. **Staff:** 3. **Subjects:** Medicine, patient health education, consumer information. **Holdings:** 2248 books; 4372 bound periodical volumes; 380 AV items. **Subscriptions:** 379 journals and other serials. **Services:** Interlibrary loans; SDI; library open to public for reference use only. **Computerized Information Services:** NLM. **Networks/Consortia:** Member of VALNET; Greater Oklahoma City Area Health Sciences Library Consortium (GOAL). **Publications:** Medical Media Newsbreak, biweekly - for in-house and VA Medical District 20 distribution.

★14975★
U.S. VETERANS ADMINISTRATION (OR-Portland) - MEDICAL LIBRARY (Med)
3710 S.W. U.S. Veterans Hospital Rd.
Box 1035   Phone: (503) 222-9221
Portland, OR 97207   Mrs. Nymah L. Trued, Chf., Lib.Serv.
Staff: Prof 2; Other 2. **Subjects:** Medicine, nursing and allied sciences. **Holdings:** 2386 books; 6010 bound periodical volumes. **Subscriptions:** 310 journals and other serials. **Services:** Interlibrary loans; copying; library open to public for reference use only. **Networks/Consortia:** Member of VALNET.

★14976★
U.S. VETERANS ADMINISTRATION (OR-Roseburg) - MEDICAL CENTER LIBRARY SERVICE (Med)
Garden Valley Blvd.   Phone: (503) 672-4411
Roseburg, OR 97470
Staff: Prof 1; Other 1. **Subjects:** Medicine, patient education, management, nursing. **Holdings:** 3000 books; 1090 bound periodical volumes; large-print materials. **Subscriptions:** 210 journals and other serials; 15 newspapers. **Services:** Interlibrary loans; copying; SDI; library open to public when referred by another librarian. **Computerized Information Services:** NLM, MEDLARS, DIALOG. **Networks/Consortia:** Member of VALNET; Oregon Health Information Network (OHIN).

★14977★
U.S. VETERANS ADMINISTRATION (OR-White City) - LIBRARY (Med)
VA Domiciliary   Phone: (503) 826-2111
White City, OR 97503   Sarah Fitzpatrick, Chf., Lib.Serv.
Staff: Prof 2; Other 1. **Subjects:** Medicine. **Holdings:** 11,637 books; 101 bound periodical volumes. **Subscriptions:** 322 journals and other serials; 22 newspapers. **Services:** Interlibrary loans; library not open to public. **Networks/Consortia:** Member of VALNET.

★14978★
U.S. VETERANS ADMINISTRATION (PA-Altoona) - JAMES E. VAN ZANDT MEDICAL CENTER LIBRARY (Med)
                                            Phone: (814) 943-8164
Altoona, PA 16603   Rose Altberg, Chf.Libn.
Founded: 1950. **Staff:** Prof 1. **Subjects:** Medicine, general topics. **Holdings:** 5817 books; 1065 periodical volumes; AV materials and microforms. **Subscriptions:** 95 journals and other serials; 7 newspapers. **Services:** Interlibrary loans; library open to public with restrictions. **Publications:** Orientation booklets for patients and medical staff.

★14979★
U.S. VETERANS ADMINISTRATION (PA-Butler) - MEDICAL CENTER LIBRARY (Med)
                                            Phone: (412) 287-4781
Butler, PA 16001   Dianne Hohn, Chf., Lib.Serv.
Founded: 1946. **Staff:** Prof 2; Other 1. **Subjects:** Nursing, general medicine. **Holdings:** 2000 books; 3000 periodical volumes, bound and in microform. **Subscriptions:** 100 journals and other serials; 10 newspapers. **Services:** Interlibrary loans; copying; library open to public for reference use only. **Computerized Information Services:** BRS. Performs searches on subscription basis. **Networks/Consortia:** Member of VALNET. **Remarks:** Patients' library contains an additional 5623 volumes. **Staff:** Donna D. Blose, Libn.

★14980★
U.S. VETERANS ADMINISTRATION (PA-Coatesville) - MEDICAL CENTER LIBRARY (Med)
                                            Phone: (215) 384-7711
Coatesville, PA 19320   Alice M. VonderLindt, Chf., Lib.Serv.
Founded: 1930. **Staff:** Prof 3; Other 3. **Subjects:** Psychiatry, neurology, medicine, nursing, psychology. **Holdings:** 7200 books; 8000 bound periodical volumes; information file (10 VF drawers); 1500 AV items. **Subscriptions:** 400 journals and other serials; 20 newspapers. **Services:** Interlibrary loans; copying; library open to health service personnel only. **Computerized Information Services:** DIALOG, MEDLINE, BRS. **Networks/Consortia:** Member of VALNET; Consortium for Health Information and Library Services (CHI). **Remarks:** Patients' library contains an additional 10,500 volumes.

Staff: Barbara E. Stranick, Libn.

★14981★
U.S. VETERANS ADMINISTRATION (PA-Lebanon) - MEDICAL CENTER LIBRARY (Med)
State Drive   Phone: (717) 272-6621
Lebanon, PA 17042   David E. Falger, Chf., Lib.Serv.
Founded: 1947. **Staff:** Prof 3; Other 3. **Subjects:** Medicine, aging and geriatrics, psychiatry. **Holdings:** 1625 books; 800 periodical volumes on microfilm. **Subscriptions:** 272 journals and other serials; 37 newspapers. **Services:** Interlibrary loans; copying (limited); library open to public with restrictions. **Computerized Information Services:** MEDLINE, BRS. **Networks/Consortia:** Member of VALNET; Greater Northeastern Regional Medical Library Program; Central Pennsylvania Health Sciences Library Association (CPHSLA). **Publications:** Quarterly newsletter. **Remarks:** Patients' library contains an additional 5600 books. **Staff:** Barbara E. Deaven, Med.Libn.

★14982★
U.S. VETERANS ADMINISTRATION (PA-Philadelphia) - MEDICAL CENTER LIBRARY (Med)
University & Woodland Aves.   Phone: (215) 823-5860
Philadelphia, PA 19104   Robert S. Lyle, Chf., Lib.Serv.
Founded: 1953. **Staff:** Prof 2; Other 1. **Subjects:** Medicine and allied subjects. **Holdings:** 3010 books; 7100 bound periodical volumes. **Subscriptions:** 415 journals and other serials. **Services:** Interlibrary loans; copying; SDI; library open to public by permission. **Computerized Information Services:** BRS, MEDLINE. **Networks/Consortia:** Member of VALNET. **Remarks:** Patients' library contains an additional 4000 volumes. **Staff:** Danute Muraska Gedeika, Libn.

★14983★
U.S. VETERANS ADMINISTRATION (PA-Pittsburgh) - HOSPITAL LIBRARY (Med)
Highland Dr.   Phone: (412) 363-4900
Pittsburgh, PA 15206   Pauline M. Mason, Chf., Lib.Serv.
Founded: 1953. **Staff:** Prof 2; Other 2. **Subjects:** General medicine, psychiatry, neurology, nursing. **Holdings:** 4420 books; 2812 bound periodical volumes; 8 VF drawers of pamphlets. **Subscriptions:** 220 journals and other serials. **Services:** Interlibrary loans; library not open to public. **Computerized Information Services:** MEDLINE. **Networks/Consortia:** Member of VALNET. **Publications:** Bibliographies. **Remarks:** Patients' library contains an additional 6310 volumes.

★14984★
U.S. VETERANS ADMINISTRATION (PA-Pittsburgh) - MEDICAL CENTER LIBRARY SERVICE (142D) (Med)
University Dr. C   Phone: (412) 683-3000
Pittsburgh, PA 15240   Tuula Beazell, Chf., Lib.Serv.
Founded: 1946. **Staff:** Prof 2; Other 2. **Subjects:** Medicine and related subjects. **Holdings:** 3100 books; 10,000 bound periodical volumes. **Subscriptions:** 400 journals and other serials. **Services:** Interlibrary loans. **Networks/Consortia:** Member of VALNET. **Staff:** Sandra Mason, Med.Libn.

★14985★
U.S. VETERANS ADMINISTRATION (PA-Wilkes-Barre) - MEDICAL CENTER LIBRARY (Med)
1111 E. End Blvd.   Phone: (717) 824-3521
Wilkes-Barre, PA 18711   Bruce D. Reid, Chf., Lib.Serv.
Founded: 1950. **Staff:** Prof 2; Other 1. **Subjects:** Medicine and allied health sciences. **Holdings:** 5895 books; 4366 bound periodical volumes. **Subscriptions:** 215 journals and other serials. **Services:** Interlibrary loans; library open to public with restrictions. **Computerized Information Services:** Online systems. **Networks/Consortia:** Member of VALNET; Northeastern Pennsylvania Bibliographic Center (NEPBC); Health Information Library Network of Northeastern Pennsylvania. **Remarks:** Patients' library contains an additional 5000 volumes.

★14986★
U.S. VETERANS ADMINISTRATION (PR-San Juan) - HOSPITAL LIBRARY (Med)
VA Medical & Regional Office Center
Box 4867   Phone: (809) 765-3185
San Juan, PR 00936   Raquel A. Walters, Chf., Lib.Serv.
Founded: 1947. **Staff:** Prof 2; Other 2. **Subjects:** Medicine and specialties, nursing, surgery and specialties, dietetics and nutrition. **Holdings:** 8598 books and bound periodical volumes; AV materials. **Subscriptions:** 610 journals and other serials. **Services:** Interlibrary loans; bibliographic search; library open to public through sharing agreements with community institutions.

Computerized Information Services: NLM. Networks/Consortia: Member of RMEC Medical District 3. Publications: Annual Periodical Holding List; Quarterly New Medical Books List; Annual Library Orientation Guide. Remarks: Patients' library contains an additional 8745 volumes with special collections on the Caribbean, management, talking books. Staff: Virginia E. Budet, Patients Libn.

★14987★
U.S. VETERANS ADMINISTRATION (RI-Providence) - HEALTH SCIENCES LIBRARY (Med)
Davis Park
Providence, RI 02908
Phone: (401) 273-7100
Lynn A. Lloyd, Chf., Lib.Serv.
Founded: 1949. Staff: Prof 2. Subjects: Medicine, nursing, psychology, allied health sciences, social work, management. Holdings: 3500 books; 4000 bound periodical volumes; AV materials. Subscriptions: 280 journals and other serials; 18 newspapers. Services: Interlibrary loans; copying; SDI; library open to public for reference use only. Automated Operations: Computerized bibliographies. Computerized Information Services: MEDLINE, BRS. Networks/Consortia: Member of Association of Rhode Island Health Sciences Librarians (ARIHSL). Remarks: Patients' library contains consumer health education collection.

★14988★
U.S. VETERANS ADMINISTRATION (SC-Columbia) - WILLIAM JENNINGS BRYAN-DORN VETERANS HOSPITAL - LIBRARY (Med)
Garners Ferry Rd.
Columbia, SC 29201
Phone: (803) 776-4000
Charletta P. Felder, Chf., Lib.Serv.
Founded: 1933. Staff: Prof 2. Subjects: Medicine, surgery, nursing, dentistry, psychiatry. Holdings: 3300 books; 2900 bound periodical volumes; 1300 AV items. Subscriptions: 225 journals and other serials; 35 newspapers. Services: Interlibrary loans; copying; library open to public with restrictions. Networks/Consortia: Member of VALNET; Columbia Area Medical Librarians Association (CAMLA). Remarks: Patients' library contains an additional 6500 volumes. Staff: Emily E. Clyburn, Staff Libn.

★14989★
U.S. VETERANS ADMINISTRATION (SD-Fort Meade) - MEDICAL CENTER LIBRARY (Med)
Fort Meade, SD 57741
Phone: (605) 347-2511
Eugene A. Stevens, Chf., Lib.Serv.
Founded: 1945. Staff: Prof 1; Other 1. Subjects: Medicine and allied health sciences. Holdings: 1200 books; 1001 volumes of journals on microfilm; 142 AV titles. Subscriptions: 114 journals and other serials; 20 newspapers. Services: Interlibrary loans; copying; library open to public. Computerized Information Services: MEDLINE. Networks/Consortia: Member of VALNET. Remarks: Patients' library contains an additional 1700 volumes.

★14990★
U.S. VETERANS ADMINISTRATION (SD-Hot Springs) - CENTER LIBRARY (Med)
Hot Springs, SD 57747
Phone: (605) 745-4101
Carole W. Miles, Med.Libn.
Staff: Prof 1; Other 1. Subjects: Geriatrics, surgery. Holdings: 845 books; 781 bound periodical volumes. Subscriptions: 108 journals and other serials. Services: Interlibrary loans; library open to the medical community. Remarks: Patients' library contains an additional 10,135 volumes.

★14991★
U.S. VETERANS ADMINISTRATION (SD-Sioux Falls) - HOSPITAL LIBRARY (Med)
2501 W. 22nd St.
Sioux Falls, SD 57101
Phone: (605) 336-3230
Lori Klein, Chf., Lib.Serv.
Staff: Prof 2; Other 2. Subjects: General medicine and allied health sciences. Special Collections: AV medical collection (1200 programs). Holdings: 4600 books; 4631 bound periodical volumes; 4968 reels of microfilm; 1168 AV items. Subscriptions: 400 journals and other serials; 50 newspapers. Services: Interlibrary loans; library open to members of medical community. Computerized Information Services: MEDLINE. Networks/Consortia: Member of VALNET. Remarks: Patients' library contains an additional 2984 volumes.

★14992★
U.S. VETERANS ADMINISTRATION (TN-Johnson City) - MEDICAL CENTER LIBRARY (Med)
Mountain Home, TN 37684
Phone: (615) 926-1171
Mary Jane Crutchfield, Chf., Lib.Serv.
Staff: Prof 3; Other 3. Subjects: Medicine and related subjects. Holdings: 3206 books; 3681 bound periodical volumes. Subscriptions: 200 journals and other serials. Services: Interlibrary loans; library open to public with

restrictions. Computerized Information Services: MEDLARS. Networks/Consortia: Member of VALNET; Tri-Cities Area Health Sciences Libraries Consortium. Remarks: Patients' library contains an additional 19,839 volumes. Staff: Emory Boone, Libn.; Nancy Dougherty, Libn.

★14993★
U.S. VETERANS ADMINISTRATION (TN-Memphis) - MEDICAL CENTER LIBRARY (Med)
1030 Jefferson Ave.
Memphis, TN 38104
Phone: (901) 523-8990
Mary Virginia Taylor, Chf., Lib.Serv.
Founded: 1941. Staff: Prof 3; Other 1. Subjects: Medicine, dentistry, nursing. Holdings: 4650 books; 3377 bound periodical volumes; microfilm. Subscriptions: 250 journals and other serials. Services: Interlibrary loans; library open to outsiders in health related fields for reference use only. Computerized Information Services: MEDLINE. Networks/Consortia: Member of VALNET; Association of Memphis Area Health Science Libraries. Remarks: Patients' library contains an additional 13,055 volumes. Staff: Mari Lyn Melin, MEDLINE Libn.; Marcia Schuldt, ILL Libn.

★14994★
U.S. VETERANS ADMINISTRATION (TN-Murfreesboro) - MEDICAL CENTER LIBRARY (Med)
Murfreesboro, TN 37130
Phone: (615) 893-1360
Joy W. Hunter, Chf., Lib.Serv.
Staff: Prof 3; Other 1. Subjects: Psychiatry, medicine. Holdings: 2500 books; 2320 bound periodical volumes. Subscriptions: 190 journals and other serials. Services: Interlibrary loans; library not open to public. Automated Operations: Computerized cataloging. Computerized Information Services: MEDLINE. Networks/Consortia: Member of VALNET. Publications: Libragram, quarterly - for internal distribution only. Remarks: Patients' library contains an additional 5600 volumes. Staff: Marie Eubanks, Med.Libn.; Ruby H. Nichols, Patients' Libn.; Phyllis A. Jenkins, Lib.Techn.

★14995★
U.S. VETERANS ADMINISTRATION (TN-Nashville) - MEDICAL CENTER LIBRARY SERVICE (Med)
1310 24th Ave., S.
Nashville, TN 37203
Phone: (615) 327-4751
Barbara A. Meadows, Chf., Lib.Serv.
Founded: 1946. Staff: Prof 2; Other 1. Subjects: Medicine, nursing, psychology, nuclear medicine, hospital administration, dentistry. Holdings: 2050 books; 4202 bound periodical volumes; 294 AV programs. Subscriptions: 263 journals and other serials. Services: Interlibrary loans; copying; library open to public for reference use only. Automated Operations: Computerized cataloging and serials. Computerized Information Services: MEDLINE. Networks/Consortia: Member of VALNET; Middle Tennessee Health Science Librarians (MTHSL).

★14996★
U.S. VETERANS ADMINISTRATION (TX-Amarillo) - HOSPITAL LIBRARY (Med)
Amarillo, TX 79106
Phone: (806) 355-9703
Cheryl A. Latham, Chf., Lib.Serv.
Founded: 1941. Staff: Prof 1; Other 1. Subjects: General medicine, surgery, nursing, dentistry. Special Collections: Staff and patient education collection (550 AV materials; 150 pamphlet titles). Holdings: 3894 books; periodicals on microfilm; 500 pamphlets and VA publications. Subscriptions: 235 journals and other serials. Services: Interlibrary loans; copying; library open to area medical personnel only. Networks/Consortia: Member of VALNET. Publications: Medical Newsletter, quarterly. Special Catalogs: Serials listing; Patient Education Materials Catalog. Remarks: Patients' library contains an additional 2957 volumes.

★14997★
U.S. VETERANS ADMINISTRATION (TX-Big Spring) - HOSPITAL LIBRARY (Med)
2400 S. Gregg St.
Big Spring, TX 79720
Phone: (915) 263-7361
Donald D. Fortner
Founded: 1950. Staff: Prof 1. Subjects: General medicine, surgery. Holdings: 947 books; 1149 bound periodical volumes. Subscriptions: 63 journals and other serials. Services: Interlibrary loans; library open to qualified health personnel only. Remarks: Patients' library contains an additional 3112 volumes.

★14998★
U.S. VETERANS ADMINISTRATION (TX-Bonham) - SAM RAYBURN MEMORIAL VETERANS CENTER MEDICAL LIBRARY (Med)
9th & Lipscomb Sts.
Bonham, TX 75418
Phone: (214) 583-2111
Dorothea C. Linn, Chf., Lib.Serv.
Founded: 1951. Staff: Prof 1; Other 1. Subjects: Medicine, surgery and

allied health subjects. **Holdings:** 713 books; 248 bound periodical volumes; 110 Audio-Digest tapes. **Subscriptions:** 152 journals and other serials. **Services:** Interlibrary loans; copying (limited); library open to public with restrictions. **Computerized Information Services:** MEDLINE, DIALOG. **Networks/Consortia:** Member of VALNET. **Remarks:** Patients' library contains an additional 4819 books.

★14999★

U.S. VETERANS ADMINISTRATION (TX-Dallas) - MEDICAL CENTER LIBRARY (142D) (Med)
4500 S. Lancaster Rd.   Phone: (214) 372-7025
Dallas, TX 75080   Barbara W. Huckins, Chf., Lib.Serv.
Founded: 1940. **Staff:** Prof 3; Other 2. **Subjects:** Medicine, surgery, allied health sciences and management. **Special Collections:** Patient health information training pamphlets (25 VF drawers). **Holdings:** 4000 books; 10,000 bound periodical volumes; 4500 volumes on microfilm; 800 AV items. **Subscriptions:** 470 journals and other serials. **Services:** Interlibrary loans; SDI; library open to health care personnel. **Automated Operations:** Computerized cataloging. **Computerized Information Services:** MEDLARS, BRS; internal database. **Networks/Consortia:** Member of VALNET; Dallas-Tarrant County Consortium of Health Science Libraries; Metroplex Council of Health Science Librarians. **Remarks:** Patients' library contains an additional 6124 volumes. **Staff:** Shirley A. Campbell, Med.Libn.; Linda J. Knerr, Med.Libn.

★15000★

U.S. VETERANS ADMINISTRATION (TX-Houston) - MEDICAL CENTER LIBRARY (Med)
2002 Holcombe Blvd.   Phone: (713) 795-4411
Houston, TX 77211   Jerry E. Barrett
Staff: Prof 3; Other 2. **Subjects:** Medicine. **Holdings:** 2864 books; 7500 periodical volumes. **Subscriptions:** 235 journals and other serials. **Services:** Interlibrary loans; library open to qualified users. **Computerized Information Services:** MEDLINE. **Networks/Consortia:** Member of VALNET. **Remarks:** The center maintains a Patient Library.

★15001★

U.S. VETERANS ADMINISTRATION (TX-Kerrville) - HEALTH SCIENCES LIBRARY (Med)
Memorial Blvd.   Phone: (512) 896-2020
Kerrville, TX 78028   Lawrence M. Larimer, Chf., Lib.Serv.
Founded: 1922. **Staff:** Prof 1; Other 1. **Subjects:** Medicine and allied health sciences. **Holdings:** 2300 books; journals on microfilm, 1967 to present; 400 video cassettes and 16mm films. **Subscriptions:** 125 journals and other serials. **Services:** Interlibrary loans; copying; SDI; AV loans; library open to public for reference use only. **Computerized Information Services:** MEDLINE. **Networks/Consortia:** Member of VALNET; Kerrville Area Health Sciences Libraries. **Publications:** Library Newsletters; Guide to New Media Titles; New Book List, all quarterly; Annual Periodical Subscription List; Guide to the Use of the Health Sciences Library.

★15002★

U.S. VETERANS ADMINISTRATION (TX-Marlin) - MEDICAL CENTER LIBRARY SERVICE (142D) (Med)
1016 Ward St.   Phone: (817) 883-3511
Marlin, TX 76661   Lewis Koster, Chf., Lib.Serv.
Founded: 1950. **Staff:** Prof 1. **Subjects:** Medicine, nursing, allied health sciences, health care administration. **Holdings:** 3500 books; 1000 bound periodical volumes; 40 unbound reports; 50 pamphlets. **Subscriptions:** 186 journals and other serials. **Services:** Interlibrary loans; library open to public. **Networks/Consortia:** Member of VALNET. **Remarks:** Patients' collection included in above figures.

★15003★

U.S. VETERANS ADMINISTRATION (TX-San Antonio) - MEDICAL CENTER LIBRARY SERVICE (142D) (Med)
7400 Merton Minter Blvd.   Phone: (512) 696-9660
San Antonio, TX 78284   Elosia Mitchell, Chf.
Founded: 1973. **Staff:** Prof 2; Other 2. **Subjects:** Medicine and allied health sciences. **Holdings:** 4790 books; 4500 bound periodical volumes; 250 AV items. **Subscriptions:** 400 journals and other serials; 21 newspapers. **Services:** Interlibrary loans; library not open to public. **Computerized Information Services:** NLM, BRS. **Networks/Consortia:** Member of CLASS; VALNET; Health Oriented Libraries of San Antonio (HOLSA); Council of Research & Academic Libraries (CORAL). **Publications:** Library Newsletter, quarterly; Library Handbook, annual; subject bibliographies - for internal distribution only. **Staff:** Robert Schnick, Med.Libn.

★15004★

U.S. VETERANS ADMINISTRATION (TX-Temple) - MEDICAL CENTER MEDICAL LIBRARY (Med)
Olin E. Teague Veterans Adm. Ctr.
1901 S. First St.   Phone: (817) 778-4811
Temple, TX 76501   Mary E. Curtis-Kellett, Chf., Lib.Serv.
Founded: 1942. **Staff:** Prof 3; Other 3. **Subjects:** Medicine, surgery, nursing, dentistry. **Special Collections:** Patient education. **Holdings:** 3224 books; 9038 bound periodical volumes; 8 VF drawers of clippings and pamphlets; 17 VF drawers of audio cassettes; 260 video cassette tapes. **Subscriptions:** 500 journals and other serials; 12 newspapers. **Services:** Interlibrary loans; copying; library open to health care professionals for reference use only. **Automated Operations:** Computerized circulation and serials. **Computerized Information Services:** NLM. **Networks/Consortia:** Member of VALNET. **Remarks:** Patients' library contains an additional 17,000 volumes. **Staff:** Barbara Coronado, Med.Libn.; Donna Meadows, Med.Libn.

★15005★

U.S. VETERANS ADMINISTRATION (TX-Waco) - MEDICAL CENTER LIBRARY (Med)
Memorial Dr.   Phone: (817) 752-6581
Waco, TX 76703   Barbara H. Hobbs, Chf., Lib.Serv.
Founded: 1932. **Staff:** Prof 4; Other 2. **Subjects:** Psychiatry, neurology, psychology, nursing, gerontology. **Holdings:** 4475 volumes; 1219 volumes on microfilm; 760 AV items; 8 VF drawers. **Subscriptions:** 272 journals and other serials. **Services:** Interlibrary loans; copying; library open to public with restrictions. **Computerized Information Services:** MEDLINE. **Networks/Consortia:** Member of VALNET; TALON. **Publications:** Medical Library Newsletter, bimonthly - for internal distribution only. **Staff:** Barbara Ann Pascavage, Libn.

★15006★

U.S. VETERANS ADMINISTRATION (UT-Salt Lake City) - HOSPITAL MEDICAL LIBRARY (Med)
500 Foothill Dr.   Phone: (801) 582-1209
Salt Lake City, UT 84148   Cherryi M. Povey, Chf., Lib.Serv.
Staff: Prof 3; Other 3. **Subjects:** Medicine, surgery, psychiatry, related fields. **Holdings:** 3995 books; 10,917 bound periodical volumes; 1696 reels of microfilm; 85 video cassettes; 240 pamphlets. **Subscriptions:** 342 journals and other serials. **Services:** Interlibrary loans; copying; library open to public for reference use only. **Computerized Information Services:** Online systems. **Networks/Consortia:** Member of VALNET; Midcontinental Regional Medical Library Program; Utah Health Sciences Library Consortium. **Publications:** Book, journal, microfilm holdings lists, annual. **Remarks:** Patients' library contains an additional 5699 volumes.

★15007★

U.S. VETERANS ADMINISTRATION (VT-White River Junction) - ALLIED HEALTH SCIENCES LIBRARY (Med)
                                   Phone: (802) 295-9369
White River Junction, VT 05001   John A. Package, Chf.Libn.
Staff: Prof 2. **Subjects:** Medicine. **Holdings:** 1345 books; 323 bound periodical volumes; 962 reels of microfilm. **Subscriptions:** 240 journals and other serials. **Services:** Interlibrary loans; copying; library open to public with permission of chief librarian. **Automated Operations:** Computerized cataloging and acquisitions. **Networks/Consortia:** Member of VALNET. **Remarks:** Patients' library contains an additional 2479 volumes.

★15008★

U.S. VETERANS ADMINISTRATION (VA-Hampton) - MEDICAL CENTER LIBRARY (Med)
                                   Phone: (804) 722-9961
Hampton, VA 23667   Nancy J. Smith, Chf., Lib.Serv.
Staff: Prof 4; Other 2. **Subjects:** Surgery, medicine, nursing, psychology, patient education. **Holdings:** 6000 books; 500 bound periodical volumes. **Subscriptions:** 540 journals and other serials; 8 newspapers. **Services:** Interlibrary loans; library open to public by request. **Computerized Information Services:** BRS, MEDLINE. **Networks/Consortia:** Member of VALNET; Tidewater Health Sciences Libraries (THSL). **Publications:** Book lists, quarterly; special bibliographies; Medical Library News. **Remarks:** Patients' library contains an additional 10,100 volumes. **Staff:** Matilda N. Young, Med.Libn.; Elois Morgan, Coll.Mgmt.Libn.; Maggie Demchuk, Patient Educ.Libn.

★15009★

U.S. VETERANS ADMINISTRATION (VA-Richmond) - HOSPITAL LIBRARY (Med)
1201 Broad Rock Blvd.   Phone: (804) 231-9011
Richmond, VA 23249   Eleanor Rollins, Chf., Lib.Serv.
Founded: 1945. **Staff:** Prof 2; Other 1. **Subjects:** Medicine, psychology and

sociology. **Holdings:** 4000 books; 6000 bound periodical volumes; 1000 AV materials; 1000 volumes on microfilm. **Subscriptions:** 304 journals and other serials. **Services:** Interlibrary loans; copying; library open to public with restrictions. **Remarks:** Patients' library contains an additional 9500 volumes.

★15010★
U.S. VETERANS ADMINISTRATION (VA-Salem) - MEDICAL CENTER LIBRARY (Med)
Salem, VA 24153
Phone: (703) 982-2463
Jean A. Kennedy, Chf.Libn.
Staff: Prof 3; Other 3. **Subjects:** Medicine, psychiatry, nursing, allied health subjects. **Holdings:** 4567 books; 3527 bound periodical volumes; 2070 AV items. **Subscriptions:** 259 journals and other serials. **Services:** Interlibrary loans; copying; SDI; library open to community health professionals. **Computerized Information Services:** MEDLARS. **Networks/Consortia:** Member of VALNET. **Publications:** Medical Library Bulletin and AV Bulletin, both quarterly. **Remarks:** Patients' library contains an additional 9009 volumes. **Staff:** Jacqueline S. Cahill, Med.Libn.; Susan B. DuGrenier, Patients' Libn.

★15011★
U.S. VETERANS ADMINISTRATION (WA-Seattle) - HOSPITAL MEDICAL LIBRARY (Med)
4435 Beacon Ave., S.
Phone: (206) 762-1010
Seattle, WA 98108
Martha Leredu, Chf., Lib.Serv.
Staff: Prof 2; Other 2. **Subjects:** Medicine. **Special Collections:** Patient education program. **Holdings:** 1620 books; 4000 bound periodical volumes; 850 AV items. **Subscriptions:** 405 journals and other serials. **Services:** Interlibrary loans; SDI; library open to public for reference use only. **Computerized Information Services:** MEDLINE, BRS. Performs free searches. **Networks/Consortia:** Member of VALNET; Seattle Area Hospital Library Consortium. **Publications:** Medical Library Newsletter, irregular - for internal distribution only. **Staff:** Jeanyce Roden, Med.Libn.

★15012★
U.S. VETERANS ADMINISTRATION (WA-Spokane) - MEDICAL CENTER LIBRARY (Med)
N. 4815 Assembly St.
Phone: (509) 328-4521
Spokane, WA 99205
Ruth A. Jones, Chf.Libn.
Founded: 1950. **Staff:** Prof 1; Other 1. **Subjects:** Medicine and allied health sciences. **Special Collections:** Health Information Center. **Holdings:** 153 books; 924 bound periodical volumes; 113 video cassettes; 15 models; pamphlets; patient teaching charts. **Subscriptions:** 323 journals and other serials. **Services:** Interlibrary loans; copying; SDI; library open to public for reference use only. **Networks/Consortia:** Member of VALNET. **Remarks:** Patients' library contains an additonal 2069 volumes.

★15013★
U.S. VETERANS ADMINISTRATION (WA-Tacoma) - MEDICAL CENTER LIBRARY (Med)
American Lake
Phone: (206) 582-8440
Tacoma, WA 98493
Dennis L. Levi, Chf., Lib.Serv.
Founded: 1924. **Staff:** Prof 2; Other 1. **Subjects:** Psychiatry, psychology, general medicine, nursing. **Holdings:** 1980 books; 2 VF drawers of pamphlets. **Subscriptions:** 314 journals and other serials; 33 newspapers. **Services:** Interlibrary loans; SDI; library open to public for reference use only. **Computerized Information Services:** MEDLARS, BRS. **Networks/Consortia:** Member of VALNET. **Remarks:** Patients' library contains an additional 4631 volumes.

★15014★
U.S. VETERANS ADMINISTRATION (WA-Vancouver) - HOSPITAL LIBRARY (Med)
Fourth Plain & O Sts.
Phone: (206) 696-4061
Vancouver, WA 98661
Mrs. Nymah L. Trued, Chf., Lib.Serv.
Founded: 1946. **Staff:** Prof 2; Other 1. **Subjects:** Medicine. **Special Collections:** Patient Health Information. **Holdings:** 1300 books; 976 bound periodical volumes; AV materials; 116 records. **Subscriptions:** 330 journals and other serials. **Services:** Interlibrary loans; library open to public for reference use only. **Networks/Consortia:** Member of VALNET. **Remarks:** Patients' library contains an additional 4500 volumes. All inquiries about the hospital library should be sent to Box 1035, Portland, OR 97201.

★15015★
U.S. VETERANS ADMINISTRATION (WA-Walla Walla) - HOSPITAL LIBRARY (Med)
77 Wainwright Dr.
Phone: (509) 525-5200
Walla Walla, WA 99362
Max J. Merrell, Chf.Libn.
Staff: Prof 1; Other 1. **Subjects:** Medicine, surgery, nursing and related fields.

Holdings: 900 books; 700 volumes of journals. **Subscriptions:** 130 journals and other serials. **Services:** Interlibrary loans; copying; SDI; library open to public for reference use only; borrowing by special permission of librarian. **Computerized Information Services:** MEDLINE. **Networks/Consortia:** Member of VALNET; WLN. **Remarks:** Patients' library contains an additional 1000 volumes. **Special Catalogs:** VA Medical District Union List of Audiovisuals in Walla Walla.

★15016★
U.S. VETERANS ADMINISTRATION (WV-Beckley) - MEDICAL CENTER LIBRARY (Med)
200 Veterans Ave.
Phone: (304) 255-2121
Beckley, WV 25801
Shelley C. Doman, Chf., Lib.Serv.
Founded: 1951. **Staff:** Prof 1. **Subjects:** Medicine, nursing, surgery. **Holdings:** 1004 volumes; 973 volumes of journals; 2 VF drawers of patient education pamphlets; Audio-Digest tapes; microfilm. **Subscriptions:** 117 journals and other serials. **Services:** Interlibrary loans; copying; library open to public with restrictions. **Networks/Consortia:** Member of VALNET. **Remarks:** Patients' library contains an additional 1911 volumes.

★15017★
U.S. VETERANS ADMINISTRATION (WV-Clarksburg) - MEDICAL CENTER LIBRARY SERVICE (Med)
Clarksburg, WV 26301
Phone: (304) 623-3461
Edward J. Poletti, Chf., Lib.Serv.
Founded: 1950. **Staff:** Prof 1; Other 1. **Subjects:** Medicine. **Holdings:** 1181 books; 2301 bound periodical volumes. **Subscriptions:** 138 journals and other serials; 25 newspapers. **Services:** Interlibrary loans; copying; library open to public for reference use only. **Computerized Information Services:** NLM, BRS. **Networks/Consortia:** Member of VALNET; North Central Area Consortium for Health Information Resources (NACHIR). **Remarks:** Patients' library contains an additional 3448 volumes.

★15018★
U.S. VETERANS ADMINISTRATION (WV-Huntington) - MEDICAL CENTER LIBRARY (Med)
1540 Spring Valley Dr.
Phone: (304) 429-6741
Huntington, WV 25704
Founded: 1931. **Staff:** Prof 1; Other 1. **Subjects:** Clinical medicine, surgery, nursing. **Holdings:** 3900 books; 2539 bound periodical volumes; Audio-Digest tapes; microfilm. **Subscriptions:** 250 journals and other serials; 10 newspapers. **Services:** Interlibrary loans; copying; SDI; library open to public with restrictions. **Automated Operations:** Computerized cataloging. **Computerized Information Services:** OCLC, MEDLINE, DIALOG, BRS. **Networks/Consortia:** Member of VALNET; West Virginia Biomedical Information Network; Huntington Health Science Library Consortium. **Remarks:** Patients' library contains an additional 50 books.

★15019★
U.S. VETERANS ADMINISTRATION (WV-Martinsburg) - CENTER MEDICAL LIBRARY (Med)
Martinsburg, WV 25401
Phone: (304) 263-0811
Barbara S. Adams, Chf.Libn.
Founded: 1945. **Staff:** Prof 2; Other 2. **Subjects:** Medicine, surgery and allied health sciences. **Holdings:** 3000 books; 5435 bound periodical volumes; 996 AV items; 53 titles on microfilm. **Subscriptions:** 300 journals and other serials. **Services:** Interlibrary loans; copying. **Networks/Consortia:** Member of VALNET. **Remarks:** Patients' library contains an additional 6400 volumes. **Staff:** Geraldine Meyer, Med.Lib.Techn.

★15020★
U.S. VETERANS ADMINISTRATION (WI-Madison) - WILLIAM S. MIDDLETON MEMORIAL VETERANS HOSPITAL - LIBRARY (Med)
2500 Overlook Terrace
Phone: (608) 256-1901
Madison, WI 53705
Anne M. Taylor, Chf., Lib.Serv.
Founded: 1951. **Staff:** Prof 1. **Subjects:** General medicine. **Holdings:** 3000 books; 12,000 bound periodical volumes. **Subscriptions:** 271 journals and other serials. **Services:** Interlibrary loans; library not open to public. **Computerized Information Services:** MEDLINE. **Networks/Consortia:** Member of South Central Wisconsin Health Planning Area Cooperative.

★15021★
U.S. VETERANS ADMINISTRATION (WI-Tomah) - HOSPITAL LIBRARY (Med)
Tomah, WI 54660
Phone: (608) 372-3971
William E. Nielsen, Chf., Lib.Serv.
Founded: 1947. **Staff:** Prof 4; Other 1. **Subjects:** Psychiatry, neurology, general medicine, psychology, nursing, aging. **Holdings:** 1600 books; 505 bound periodical volumes; 100 volumes of unbound journals; AV materials.

Subscriptions: 150 journals and other serials. Services: Interlibrary loans; copying; library open to public. Computerized Information Services: MEDLINE. Performs free searches. Networks/Consortia: Member of VALNET; Western Wisconsin Consortium. Publications: Acquisitions List; special bibliographies. Remarks: Patients' library contains an additional 7182 volumes. Staff: Xena Kenyon, Libn.

★15022★
U.S. VETERANS ADMINISTRATION (WI-Wood) - MEDICAL CENTER LIBRARY (Med)
Wood, WI 53193
Phone: (414) 384-2000
Maureen Farmer, Med.Libn.
Founded: 1946. Staff: Prof 2; Other 2. Subjects: Medicine, nursing, dentistry and allied health sciences. Holdings: 5100 books; 5000 bound periodical volumes; 1300 AV items. Subscriptions: 387 journals and other serials. Services: Interlibrary loans; SDI; library open to public with restrictions. Computerized Information Services: MEDLINE. Networks/Consortia: Member of VALNET; Southeastern Wisconsin Health Sciences Library Consortium. Remarks: Patients' library contains an additional 20,000 volumes.

★15023★
U.S. VETERANS ADMINISTRATION (WY-Cheyenne) - CENTER LIBRARY (Med)
2360 E. Pershing Blvd.
Cheyenne, WY 82001
Phone: (307) 778-7550
Edwina M. Hubbard, Libn.
Staff: Prof 1. Subjects: Medicine, nursing. Holdings: 759 books; 2063 volumes of journals, bound and on microfilm. Subscriptions: 55 journals and other serials; 15 newspapers. Services: Interlibrary loans; copying; library open to public with restrictions. Networks/Consortia: Member of VALNET. Remarks: Patients' library contains an additional 2577 volumes.

★15024★
U.S. VETERANS ADMINISTRATION (WY-Sheridan) - MEDICAL CENTER LIBRARY (Med)
Sheridan, WY 82801
Phone: (307) 672-3473
Donna Homewood, Chf., Lib.Serv.
Staff: Prof 1; Other 2. Subjects: Psychiatry, psychology, medicine, nursing, administration. Holdings: 2250 books; 200 bound periodical volumes; 1615 periodical volumes on microfilm; 2000 AV items. Subscriptions: 300 journals and other serials. Services: Interlibrary loans; copying; library open to public. Computerized Information Services: MEDLARS. Networks/Consortia: Member of VALNET; Health Sciences Information Network (HSIN); Northeastern Wyoming Medical Library Consortium. Remarks: Patients' library contains an additional 5000 volumes.

UNITED TECHNOLOGIES CORPORATION - CARRIER CORPORATION
See: Carrier Corporation

★15025★
UNITED TECHNOLOGIES CORPORATION - CHEMICAL SYSTEMS DIVISION - LIBRARY (Sci-Tech)
Box 50015
San Jose, CA 95150-0015
Phone: (408) 778-4784
Harold E. Wilcox, Supv.
Founded: 1959. Staff: Prof 2. Subjects: Chemical propulsion, chemical technology, mechanical engineering, aeronautical engineering. Special Collections: National Advisory Committee for Aeronautics (NACA) Annual Reports, 1915-1959. Holdings: 5500 books; 2000 bound periodical volumes; 1850 microfilm cartridges; 6700 microfiche; 25,000 other cataloged items. Subscriptions: 153 journals and other serials. Services: Interlibrary loans; library not open to public. Computerized Information Services: NASA/RECON, DIALOG, DTIC. Networks/Consortia: Member of CLASS. Publications: Library Bulletins, irregular - for internal distribution only. Staff: Eric Kristofferson, Ref./Info.Spec.

★15026★
UNITED TECHNOLOGIES CORPORATION - ELLIOTT COMPANY - LIBRARY (Sci-Tech)
N. Fourth St.
Jeannette, PA 15644
Phone: (412) 527-8054
Geri K. Keitzer, Libn.
Staff: Prof 1. Subjects: Turbines, compressors. Holdings: 2300 books; 4200 pamphlets; 900 company technical reports and memoranda; 300 microfiche. Subscriptions: 90 journals and other serials. Services: Interlibrary loans; library not open to public.

★15027★
UNITED TECHNOLOGIES CORPORATION - INMONT - LIBRARY (Sci-Tech)
1255 Broad St.
Clifton, NJ 07015
Phone: (201) 365-3400
Joanne Freeman, Libn.
Staff: Prof 1; Other 2. Subjects: Polymer chemistry, printing inks, automotive paints and coatings, adhesives. Holdings: 4000 books; 3000 bound periodical volumes; corporate archives. Subscriptions: 183 journals and other serials. Services: Interlibrary loans; library not open to public. Computerized Information Services: DIALOG, NEXIS, SDC, Pergamon InfoLine Ltd. Networks/Consortia: Member of United Technologies Library System. Publications: Journal of Contents, biweekly; New Additions, quarterly - both for internal distribution only.

★15028★
UNITED TECHNOLOGIES CORPORATION - LIBRARY (Sci-Tech)
United Technologies Research Center
East Hartford, CT 06108
Phone: (203) 727-7120
Irving H. Neufeld, Chf., UTC Lib.Sys.
Founded: 1939. Staff: Prof 16; Other 24. Subjects: Aerospace sciences and engineering, power plants and energy conversion, metals and materials, electronics, lasers, physics, chemistry. Holdings: 32,000 book titles; 15,000 bound periodical volumes; 105,000 technical reports and preprint titles; 500,000 microfiche. Subscriptions: 1000 journals and other serials. Services: Interlibrary loans (limited); library not open to public. Computerized Information Services: DIALOG, SDC, Dow Jones News/Retrieval, BRS, DTIC, NEXIS, NASA/RECON, DOE/RECON, Electronic Materials Information Service (EMIS). Networks/Consortia: Member of United Technologies Library System. Publications: Library Bulletin; Microfiches/Reports, both biweekly; Business Contents, semimonthly - all for internal distribution only.

UNITED TECHNOLOGIES CORPORATION - NORDEN SYSTEMS, INC.
See: Norden Systems, Inc.

★15029★
UNITED TECHNOLOGIES CORPORATION - PRATT & WHITNEY AIRCRAFT GROUP - MATERIALS ENGINEERING RESEARCH LIB. (Sci-Tech)
Aircraft Rd.
Middletown, CT 06457
Phone: (203) 344-5138
Noreen O. Steele, Libn.
Founded: 1961. Staff: Prof 1. Subjects: Materials, metals, chemistry, physics, mechanics. Holdings: 3000 books; 1000 bound periodical volumes; 3000 technical reports. Subscriptions: 100 journals and other serials. Services: Interlibrary loans; library not open to public. Computerized Information Services: DIALOG, NEXIS, SDC. Networks/Consortia: Member of United Technologies Library System.

★15030★
UNITED TECHNOLOGIES CORPORATION - SIKORSKY AIRCRAFT DIVISION - DIVISION LIBRARY (Sci-Tech)
N. Main St.
Stratford, CT 06601
Phone: (203) 386-4713
Robert M. Knapik, Lib.Supv.
Founded: 1945. Staff: Prof 1; Other 1. Subjects: Aeronautics, engineering, management. Special Collections: Helicopter and vertical takeoff and landing (VTOL) aircraft data. Holdings: 3300 books; 90,000 technical government reports. Subscriptions: 85 journals and other serials. Services: Interlibrary loans; copying; library open to public with restrictions. Automated Operations: Computerized cataloging and circulation. Computerized Information Services: DIALOG, SDC. Networks/Consortia: Member of Southwestern Connecticut Library Council; United Technologies Library System. Publications: Library Bulletin of new materials, semimonthly; Technical Data Received, weekly - both for internal distribution only. Special Indexes: KWOC Index in COM format.

★15031★
UNITED THEOLOGICAL SEMINARY - LIBRARY (Rel-Theol)
1810 Harvard Blvd.
Dayton, OH 45406
Phone: (513) 278-5817
Elmer J. O'Brien, Libn.
Founded: 1872. Staff: Prof 2; Other 3. Subjects: Theology. Special Collections: Evangelical United Brethren Church Collection (8000 items). Holdings: 98,270 volumes. Subscriptions: 365 journals and other serials; 5 newspapers. Services: Interlibrary loans; copying; library open to public by application with references. Automated Operations: Computerized cataloging and serials. Computerized Information Services: OCLC. Networks/Consortia: Member of Southwest Ohio Council for Higher Education (SOC). Staff: Richard R. Berg, Asst.Libn.

★15032★
UNITED THEOLOGICAL SEMINARY OF THE TWIN CITIES - LIBRARY (Rel-Theol)
3000 Fifth St., N.W.
New Brighton, MN 55112
Phone: (612) 633-4311
Arthur L. Merrill, Dir.
Founded: 1962. Staff: Prof 3; Other 4. Subjects: Theology, the church,

history, education, sociology, psychology, philosophy. **Holdings:** 59,000 volumes; 318 films and filmstrips; 491 microforms; 92 videotapes; 772 cassettes and tapes. **Subscriptions:** 282 journals and other serials. **Services:** Interlibrary loans; copying; library open to public. **Computerized Information Services:** Joint consortium catalog (internal database). **Networks/Consortia:** Member of Minnesota Consortium of Theological Schools. **Staff:** Harriet Kruse, Libn./Circ.; Janet Weiss, Cat.

★15033★
UNITED VIRGINIA BANK - INFORMATION CENTER (Bus-Fin)
Box 26665   Phone: (804) 782-7452
Richmond, VA 23261   Marion D. George, V.P., Info.Serv/Corp.Rec.
Founded: 1970. **Staff:** Prof 2; Other 2. **Subjects:** Banking, finance, economics, statistics, accounting, management, economic statistics of Southeastern U.S., international banking and economic data. **Holdings:** 10,000 books; 50 VF drawers of annual reports of banks and bank holding companies; 5 drawers of international economic and financial data; 20 drawers of banking-related subjects. **Subscriptions:** 500 journals and other serials; 10 newspapers. **Services:** Interlibrary loans; copying; center open to students and customers by appointment. **Automated Operations:** Computerized cataloging and serials. **Computerized Information Services:** DIALOG, Dow Jones News/Retrieval, TEXTLINE, NEXIS. **Publications:** Books 'n Things (informational sheet), monthly - to banks and holding company management personnel.

★15034★
UNITED WAY OF AMERICA - INFORMATION CENTER (Soc Sci)
701 N. Fairfax St.   Phone: (703) 836-7100
Alexandria, VA 22314-2088   Henry M. Smith, Dir.
Founded: 1934. **Staff:** Prof 2; Other 2. **Subjects:** History and management of social and human services, fund raising, information and referral, voluntarism. **Special Collections:** United Way of America archival collection. **Holdings:** 600 books; 60 bound periodical volumes; 10,000 monographs and research reports; 80 specialized loan folders. **Subscriptions:** 170 journals and other serials (including 20 titles on microfilm); 5 newspapers. **Services:** Interlibrary loans; copying; center open to area researchers, social work students and human service professionals. **Automated Operations:** Computerized cataloging. **Computerized Information Services:** DIALOG, SDC; internal database. **Publications:** Digest of Selected Reports, semiannual; Let's Share (brochure). **Staff:** Barbara L. Owen, Libn.

★15035★
UNITED WAY OF CHICAGO - LIBRARY (Soc Sci)
125 S. Clark St.   Phone: (312) 580-2697
Chicago, IL 60603-4012   Sally J. Barnum, Mgr.
Founded: 1977. **Staff:** Prof 1; Other 1. **Subjects:** Social services, fund raising, social statistics, nonprofit management, child welfare, gerontology. **Special Collections:** United Way of Chicago and predecessor agency archives (Welfare Council of Metropolitan Chicago, Community Fund of Chicago, Council for Community Services, Crusade of Mercy; 225 titles). **Holdings:** 10,000 books; 300 reports on microfiche. **Subscriptions:** 150 journals and other serials; 5 newspapers. **Services:** Interlibrary loans; SDI; library open to public by appointment. **Automated Operations:** Computerized cataloging. **Computerized Information Services:** OCLC. **Networks/Consortia:** Member of ILLINET; Chicago Library System; Greater Midwest Regional Medical Library Network (Region 3). **Publications:** Recent Acquisitions, monthly - for staff and requesting local libraries.

★15036★
UNITED WAY, INC., LOS ANGELES - LIBRARY (Soc Sci)
621 S. Virgil Ave.   Phone: (213) 736-1300
Los Angeles, CA 90005   Jim Pursley, Coord., Proj.Oper.
Founded: 1970. **Staff:** Prof 1. **Subjects:** Community organization, social service, fund raising, demographics, management. **Special Collections:** Publications of the Welfare Planning Council, 1922-1972. **Holdings:** 5500 books; 3000 pamphlets. **Subscriptions:** 125 journals and other serials. **Services:** Interlibrary loans; copying; library open to public for reference use only. **Computerized Information Services:** DIALOG. **Publications:** Special Report - for internal distribution only.

★15037★
UNITED WAY OF THE LOWER MAINLAND - SOCIAL PLANNING AND RESEARCH DEPARTMENT LIBRARY (Soc Sci)
1625 W. 8th Ave.   Phone: (604) 731-7781
Vancouver, BC, Canada V6J 1T9   Jeanette Hall, Asst.Libn.
Founded: 1965. **Staff:** 1. **Subjects:** Family violence, income assistance, housing, social problems, child abuse and child sexual abuse, social services planning. **Special Collections:** United Way of the Lower Mainland publications (100 titles). **Holdings:** 3000 books and bound reports; 2500 unbound

reports, pamphlets and ephemera. **Subscriptions:** 25 journals and other serials. **Services:** Interlibrary loans; copying; library open to public for reference use only.

UNITED WORLD COLLEGES - LESTER B. PEARSON COLLEGE OF THE PACIFIC
See: Pearson (Lester B.) College of the Pacific

★15038★
UNITY OF FAIRFAX - LIBRARY (Rel-Theol)
2854 Hunter Mill Rd.
Oakton, VA 22124   Lorna Barnes, Libn.
Staff: Prof 1; Other 2. **Subjects:** Religion, metaphysics. **Holdings:** 1000 books. **Services:** Library open to public.

★15039★
UNITY MEDICAL CENTER - LIBRARY (Med)
550 Osborne Rd.   Phone: (612) 786-2200
Fridley, MN 55432   Michael F. Winter, Med.Libn.
Founded: 1973. **Staff:** Prof 1. **Subjects:** Medicine, nursing and allied health sciences. **Holdings:** 800 books; 3000 bound periodical volumes. **Subscriptions:** 99 journals and other serials. **Services:** Interlibrary loans to network members; copying; library open to public by special arrangement. **Automated Operations:** Computerized cataloging. **Computerized Information Services:** MEDLINE, BRS. **Networks/Consortia:** Member of Twin Cities Biomedical Consortium.

★15040★
UNIVERSAL CITY STUDIOS - RESEARCH DEPARTMENT LIBRARY (Art; Hist)
100 Universal City Plaza   Phone: (213) 985-4321
Universal City, CA 91608   Robert A. Lee, Hd., Res.Dept.
Founded: 1916. **Staff:** Prof 4; Other 2. **Subjects:** American West, Americana, costume, literature, art and architecture, wars, film history, history, biography. **Holdings:** 22,000 books; 700 bound periodical volumes; 6000 files of clippings, stills, brochures, pictures, illustrations, slides and transparencies for background research on film and television projects. **Subscriptions:** 90 journals and other serials. **Services:** Library not open to public. **Special Indexes:** Clipping file index; pictorial magazine index. **Staff:** Sherri Seeling, Res.Spec.; Margaret Ross, Res.Spec.; Jane Marshall, Res.Spec.

★15041★
UNIVERSAL-CYCLOPS SPECIALTY STEEL DIVISION - TECHNICAL INFORMATION CENTER
Mayer St.
Bridgeville, PA 15017
Founded: 1954. **Subjects:** Metallurgy, specialty steels, stainless steels, high temperature metals, refractory metals. **Holdings:** 1700 books; 3000 bound periodical volumes. **Remarks:** Presently inactive.

★15042★
UNIVERSAL FOODS CORPORATION - TECHNICAL INFORMATION CENTER (Sci-Tech; Food-Bev)
6143 N. 60th St.   Phone: (414) 535-4307
Milwaukee, WI 53218   Aileen Mundstock, Tech.Info.Spec.
Founded: 1951. **Staff:** Prof 1; Other 1. Fermentation industry, biotechnology, biochemistry, microbiology, chemistry, quality control, product development, engineering. **Holdings:** 4000 books and bound periodical volumes; patents; in-house reports. **Subscriptions:** 60 journals and other serials. **Services:** Serves corporate technical staff; copying (limited); center open to public with restrictions. **Automated Operations:** Computerized cataloging, acquisitions and serials. **Computerized Information Services:** DIALOG, SDC. **Networks/Consortia:** Member of Library Council of Metropolitan Milwaukee, Inc. (LCOMM).

★15043★
UNIVERSAL POSTAL UNION COLLECTORS - LIBRARY
740 Wiggins Circle
Pascagoula, MS 39567
Defunct

★15044★
UNIVERSAL SERIALS & BOOK EXCHANGE, INC. - DUPLICATE EXCHANGE CLEARINGHOUSE & INFORMATION CENTER (Info Sci)
3335 V St., N.E.   Phone: (202) 636-8723
Washington, DC 20018   Mary W. Ghikas, Exec.Dir.
Founded: 1948. **Staff:** Prof 6; Other 36. **Subjects:** Exchange of publications, library science. **Holdings:** 100,000 books and government documents; 4 million journal issues. **Subscriptions:** 25 journals and other serials. **Services:** Interlibrary loans; center open to member libraries, nonmembers charged fee.

Automated Operations: Computerized cataloging. **Computerized Information Services:** DIALOG, BRS, UTLAS, OCLC; internal database. Performs searches on cost recovery basis. Contact Person: Pat Emerson. **Networks/Consortia:** Member of CAPCON. **Publications:** USBE/News (newsletter and catalog), monthly - by subscription. **Special Indexes:** Most Available Titles (microfiche), annual. **Remarks:** Center functions as a cooperative world-wide agency for redistribution of duplicates among libraries. Distribution also serves as substitute for interlibrary loan. **Staff:** Patricia R. Emerson, Dir., Member Serv.; Robert Hodges, Bus.Mgr.; Claude Hooker, Dir., Oper.; Henry Reid, Br.Mgr.; Lothar Mueller, Facilities Mgr.

★15045★
UNIVERSITE LAVAL - BIBLIOTHEQUE (Area-Ethnic; Hum; Sci-Tech)
Cite Universitaire
Ste. Foy, PQ, Canada G1K 7P4
Phone: (418) 656-3343
Celine R. Cartier, Dir.
Founded: 1852. **Staff:** Prof 82; Other 221. **Subjects:** French Canadian and Quebec studies; French Canadian folklore; Quebec geography; ethnic groups from Quebec and Canada; French and French Canadian literature; 19th century French musical press; law; philosophy of science; philosophy - Aristotelian, Thomist and French modern; food and nutrition; wood science technology and forest ecology (mycories); animal science; soils; phytopathology; electrochemistry and corrosion; noise pollution; wind energy. **Holdings:** 1 million books; 378,832 bound periodical volumes; 91,128 maps; 126,194 aerial photographs; 158,376 transparencies; 13,942 phonograph records; 4978 films; 563,537 microforms. **Subscriptions:** 36,3ll journals and other serials; 111 newspapers. **Services:** Interlibrary loans; SDI; Miracode system. **Automated Operations:** Computerized cataloging, acquisitions, serials and circulation. **Computerized Information Services:** DIALOG, SDC, QL Systems, CAN/OLE, MEDLINE, BRS, Questel, SABINE, UTLAS, CANSIM, New York Times Information Service, Info Globe, Infoline. **Publications:** Guides bibliographiques; Repertoire de vedettes-matieres; Guide du lecteur; Liste de periodiques par sujet; Liste des commandes permanentes; Liste de nouvelles acquisitions. **Special Catalogs:** Film catalog. **Staff:** Claude Bonnelly, Dir. Adjoint; Philippe Houyoux, Chf., Soc.Sci./Hum.Coll.; Gilles Deschatelets, Chf., Sci.Coll.; Agathe Garon, Chf., Circ.; Jean-Marie Scantland, Chf., Spec.Coll.; Doris Dufour, Online/SDI Serv.; Helene Genest, Online/SDI Serv.

★15046★
UNIVERSITE LAVAL - CENTRE D'ETUDES NORDIQUES (CEN) - CENTRE DE DOCUMENTATION
Pavillon de la Tour des Arts
Ste. Foy, PQ, Canada G1K 7P4
Defunct

★15047★
UNIVERSITE LAVAL - INTERNATIONAL CENTRE FOR RESEARCH ON BILINGUALISM (Soc Sci)
Pavillon Casault, 6th Fl.
Ste. Foy, PQ, Canada G1K 7P4
Phone: (418) 656-3232
Guy Teasdale, Lib.Techn.
Founded: 1967. **Staff:** 3. **Subjects:** Bilingualism, bilingual education, sociolinguistics, psycholinguistics, language rights and contact. **Special Collections:** Commission on Bilingualism and Biculturalism; Commission Gendron; Commission Bibeau; Commission Laurendeau-Dunton; Report of the Bilingual Districts Advisory Board. **Holdings:** 5000 books; 30,000 documents; 250 reels of microfilm. **Subscriptions:** 140 journals and other serials. **Services:** Copying; center open to public. **Automated Operations:** Computerized cataloging and acquisitions. **Publications:** List of publications - available upon request.

★15048★
UNIVERSITE DE MONCTON - BIBLIOTHEQUE DE DROIT (Law)
Phone: (506) 858-4569
Moncton, NB, Canada E1A 3E9
Simonne Clermont, Law Libn.
Founded: 1978. **Staff:** Prof 2; Other 7. **Subjects:** Law. **Holdings:** 26,000 books; 35,500 bound periodical volumes; 3771 AV items; 5000 dissertations. **Subscriptions:** 503 journals and other serials. **Services:** Interlibrary loans; copying; library open to public for reference use only. **Computerized Information Services:** QL Systems. Performs searches on cost recovery basis. Contact Person: Simonne Clermont. **Publications:** Liste selective des nouvelles acquisitions. **Staff:** Carmel Allain, Cat.

★15049★
UNIVERSITE DE MONCTON - CENTRE D'ETUDES ACADIENNES (Area-Ethnic)
Phone: (506) 858-4085
Moncton, NB, Canada E1A 3E9
Ronald Leblanc, Libn.
Staff: Prof 5; Other 3. **Subjects:** Acadian history, genealogy, and folklore. **Holdings:** 9014 books and pamphlets; 3500 reels of microfilm; 432 feet of manuscripts; 2000 reels of magnetic tape of Acadian folk tales and songs. **Services:** Interlibrary loans (limited); copying; center open to public.

Publications: Contact-Acadie, irregular. **Staff:** Muriel Roy, Dir.

★15050★
UNIVERSITE DE MONCTON - FACULTE DES SCIENCES DE L'EDUCATION - CENTRE DE RESSOURCES PEDAGOGIQUES (Educ)
Phone: (506) 858-4356
Moncton, NB, Canada E1A 3E9
Berthe Boudreau, Dir.
Founded: 1973. **Staff:** Prof 1; Other 3. **Subjects:** Education (instructional material on the subject studies in public schools). **Holdings:** 17,732 books, kits and tests; 28,172 slides; 1052 filmstrips; 1577 pictures; 1992 transparencies. **Services:** Copying; center open to public with restrictions on loans. **Staff:** Henri Nowlan, Documentalist.

★15051★
UNIVERSITE DE MONTREAL - AMENAGEMENT-BIBLIOTHEQUE (Art; Plan)
C.P. 6128, Succursale A
Montreal, PQ, Canada H3C 3J7
Phone: (514) 343-7177
Jacqueline Pelletier, Libn.
Founded: 1964. **Staff:** Prof 3; Other 6. **Subjects:** Architecture, landscape architecture, design, city planning, urbanism, sociology. **Holdings:** 49,000 books; 7390 bound periodical volumes; 32,600 slides; 360 microforms. **Subscriptions:** 640 journals and other serials. **Services:** Interlibrary loans; copying; library open to public with restrictions. **Automated Operations:** Computerized cataloging. **Computerized Information Services:** DIALOG, SDC, CAN/OLE, Questel, QL Systems. **Publications:** Acquisitions list, monthly - limited distribution.

UNIVERSITE DE MONTREAL - ASSOCIATION DES UNIVERSITES PARTIELLEMENT OU ENTIEREMENT DE LANGUE FRANCAISE
See: Association des Universites Partiellement ou Entierement de Langue Francaise

★15052★
UNIVERSITE DE MONTREAL - AUDIOVIDEOTHEQUE (Aud-Vis)
C.P. 6128, Succursale A
Montreal, PQ, Canada H3C 3J7
Phone: (514) 343-7344
Ginette Gagnier, Libn.
Staff: Prof 2; Other 5. **Holdings:** 10,000 AV items. **Services:** Interlibrary loans; library open to public with restrictions. **Automated Operations:** Computerized cataloging.

★15053★
UNIVERSITE DE MONTREAL - BIBLIOTHECONOMIE-BIBLIOTHEQUE (Info Sci)
C.P. 6128, Succursale A
Montreal, PQ, Canada H3C 3J7
Phone: (514) 343-6047
Georges Clonda, Libn.
Founded: 1961. **Staff:** Prof 1; Other 3. **Subjects:** Library science. **Holdings:** 21,795 books; 8270 bound periodical volumes; 1275 microforms. **Subscriptions:** 750 journals and other serials. **Services:** Interlibrary loans; copying; library open to public with restrictions. **Automated Operations:** Computerized cataloging and circulation. **Publications:** Acquisitions list, monthly - limited distribution. **Special Catalogs:** Periodicals list (book).

★15054★
UNIVERSITE DE MONTREAL - BIBLIOTHEQUE PARA-MEDICALE (Med)
C.P. 6128, Succursale A
Montreal, PQ, Canada H3C 3J7
Phone: (514) 343-7490
Johanne Hopper, Libn.
Founded: 1963. **Staff:** Prof 2; Other 8. **Subjects:** Nursing, health administration, nutrition, dietetics, epidemiology, environmental health, audiology, ergotherapy, orthophonics, physiotherapy, social and preventive medicine. **Holdings:** 38,100 books; 12,700 bound periodical volumes; 160 microforms. **Subscriptions:** 1300 journals and other serials. **Services:** Interlibrary loans; copying; library open to public with restrictions. **Automated Operations:** Computerized cataloging. **Computerized Information Services:** DIALOG, SDC, BRS, MEDLINE, CAN/OLE, Questel, QL Systems. **Publications:** Acquisitions list, monthly - limited distribution.

★15055★
UNIVERSITE DE MONTREAL - BIBLIOTHEQUE DE LA SANTE (Med)
C.P. 6128, Succursale A
Montreal, PQ, Canada H3C 3J7
Phone: (514) 343-6826
Therese Peternell, Libn.
Founded: 1962. **Staff:** Prof 6; Other 28. **Subjects:** Medicine, dentistry, pharmacy. **Holdings:** 70,000 books; 92,671 bound periodical volumes; 2200 microforms; 10,770 slides. **Subscriptions:** 2640 journals and other serials. **Services:** Interlibrary loans; copying; library open to public with restrictions. **Automated Operations:** Computerized cataloging. **Computerized Information Services:** DIALOG, SDC, BRS, CAN/OLE, MEDLINE, Questel, QL Systems. **Publications:** Acquisitions list - limited distribution. **Special Catalogs:** Periodicals list.

★15056★

UNIVERSITE DE MONTREAL - BIOLOGIE-BIBLIOTHEQUE (Sci-Tech)
C.P. 6128, Succursale A   Phone: (514) 343-6801
Montreal, PQ, Canada H3C 3J7   Vesna Blazina, Libn.
Founded: 1962. **Staff:** Prof 2; Other 5. **Subjects:** Biology, zoology.
Holdings: 14,800 books; 16,700 bound periodical volumes; 1925
microforms. **Subscriptions:** 664 journals and other serials. **Services:**
Interlibrary loans; copying; library open to public with restrictions. **Automated
Operations:** Computerized cataloging. **Computerized Information Services:**
DIALOG, BRS, SDC, CAN/OLE, MEDLINE, Questel, QL Systems. **Publications:**
Acquisitions list, irregular - limited distribution.

★15057★

UNIVERSITE DE MONTREAL - BOTANIQUE-BIBLIOTHEQUE (Sci-Tech)
4101 Est, Rue Sherbrooke   Phone: (514) 256-9441
Montreal, PQ, Canada H1X 2B2   Nicole Taillefer-Witty, Libn.
Founded: 1925. **Staff:** 1. **Subjects:** General botany, taxonomy, genetics,
evolution, paleobotany, ecology, plant physiology, mycology, algology,
bryology. **Holdings:** 25,850 books; 12,700 bound periodical volumes;
10,640 microforms. **Subscriptions:** 290 journals and other serials. **Services:**
Interlibrary loans; copying; library open to public with restrictions.
Publications: Acquisitions list, monthly - limited distribution.

★15058★

**UNIVERSITE DE MONTREAL - CENTRE D'ETUDES ET DE DOCUMENTATION
    EUROPEENNES** (Soc Sci)
3150 Rue Jean-Brillant
C.P. 6128, Succursale A   Phone: (514) 343-7870
Montreal, PQ, Canada H3C 3J7   Lucie Bouchard, Documentaliste
Founded: 1967. **Subjects:** European integration studies and the implications
for Canada, law. **Special Collections:** European Economic Communities
Publications. **Holdings:** 500 books; 20 drawers of newspaper clippings.
Subscriptions: 103 journals and other serials. **Services:** Center open to
public.

★15059★

**UNIVERSITE DE MONTREAL - CENTRE INTERNATIONAL DE CRIMINOLOGIE
    COMPAREE - DOCUMENTATION CENTRE** (Soc Sci)
C.P. 6128, Succursale A   Phone: (514) 343-6534
Montreal, PQ, Canada H3C 3J7   Jacqueline DePlaen, Hd., Doc.
Founded: 1964. **Staff:** Prof 2; Other 1. **Subjects:** Criminology. **Holdings:**
1000 books; 6000 documents, theses, research reports, government reports
and statistics. **Subscriptions:** 80 journals and other serials. **Services:**
Copying; center open to public with restrictions. **Publications:** List of
publications - free upon request. **Also Known As:** International Centre for
Comparative Criminology. **Staff:** Aniela Belina, Documentaliste.

★15060★

**UNIVERSITE DE MONTREAL - CENTRE DE RECHERCHE SUR LES
    TRANSPORTS - DOCUMENTATION CENTRE** (Trans)
C.P. 6128, Succursale A   Phone: (514) 343-6949
Montreal, PQ, Canada H3C 3J7   Sylvie Hetu, Libn.
Founded: 1971. **Staff:** Prof 1; Other 1. **Subjects:** Transportation, urban and
regional planning. **Holdings:** 200 books; 30 bound periodical volumes; 5300
technical reports; 17 microfiche. **Subscriptions:** 40 journals and other serials.
Services: Interlibrary loans; copying; SDI; center open to public for reference
use only. **Automated Operations:** Computerized cataloging. **Computerized
Information Services:** DIALOG, Questel, CAN/OLE. **Publications:** Bulletin du
C.R.T., quarterly - free upon request.

★15061★

**UNIVERSITE DE MONTREAL - CENTRE DE RECHERCHES CARAIBES -
    BIBLIOTHEQUE** (Area-Ethnic)*
C.P. 6128   Phone: (514) 343-5807
Montreal, PQ, Canada H3C 3J7   Michelle Cote, Documentaliste
Founded: 1968. **Staff:** Prof 1. **Subjects:** West Indies - anthropology,
sociology, history, geography, languages, literature, social and economic
studies, natural sciences. **Holdings:** 3000 books and bound periodical
volumes; 2000 reprints; 90 dissertations and theses; 100 maps.
Subscriptions: 25 journals and other serials. **Services:** Copying; library open
to public. **Publications:** List of publications - distributed on request. **Remarks:**
A branch of the centre is located in Fond St-Jacques, Ste-Marie, Martinique,
F.W.I.

★15062★

UNIVERSITE DE MONTREAL - CHIMIE-BIBLIOTHEQUE (Sci-Tech)
C.P. 6128, Succursale A   Phone: (514) 343-6459
Montreal, PQ, Canada H3C 3J7   Corinne Haumont, Libn.
Founded: 1963. **Staff:** Prof 1; Other 2. **Subjects:** Chemistry. **Holdings:**

6000 books; 13,400 bound periodical volumes; 7545 microforms.
Subscriptions: 280 journals and other serials. **Services:** Interlibrary loans;
copying; library open to public with restrictions. **Automated Operations:**
Computerized cataloging. **Computerized Information Services:** DIALOG,
SDC, BRS, CAN/OLE, Questel, QL Systems. **Publications:** Acquisitions list,
monthly - limited distribution. **Special Catalogs:** Periodicals catalog (book).

**UNIVERSITE DE MONTREAL - CLINICAL RESEARCH INSTITUTE OF
    MONTREAL**
See: Clinical Research Institute of Montreal

★15063★

UNIVERSITE DE MONTREAL - COLLECTIONS SPECIALES (Hist)
C.P. 6128, Succursale A   Phone: (514) 343-7753
Montreal, PQ, Canada H3C 3J7   Genevieve Bazin, Libn.
Founded: 1984. **Staff:** Prof 2; Other 1. **Subjects:** Canadian history. **Special
Collections:** The Louis Melzack Collection of Canadian Books (4000 volumes);
The L.F. Georges Baby Collection of Canadian Books (1250 volumes).
Services: Copying; collection open to public. **Automated Operations:**
Computerized cataloging.

★15064★

**UNIVERSITE DE MONTREAL - DEPARTEMENT DE DEMOGRAPHIE - SERVICE
    DE LA RECHERCHE DOCUMENTATION** (Soc Sci)
C.P. 6128, Succursale A   Phone: (514) 343-7567
Montreal, PQ, Canada H3C 3J7   Isabelle Laperle, Documentaliste
Founded: 1965. **Staff:** Prof 1. **Subjects:** Census, vital statistics, mortality,
marriages, fertility, population theory and policy, migration, geographical
distribution and ethnic groups, historical demography. **Special Collections:**
Census of Canada, 1850 to present; vital statistics of Canada, 1921 to
present; Canadian Yearbook, 1900 to present. **Holdings:** 3889 books; 2000
bound periodical volumes; 3611 reprints, dissertations and unbound reports.
Subscriptions: 225 journals and other serials. **Services:** Interlibrary loans;
copying; library open to public. **Special Catalogs:** Catalog on Canadian
demography, 1935-73 (edge-notched cards).

★15065★

UNIVERSITE DE MONTREAL - DROIT-BIBLIOTHEQUE (Law)
C.P. 6206, Succursale A   Phone: (514) 343-6132
Montreal, PQ, Canada H3C 3T6   Paquerette Ranger, Libn.
Founded: 1942. **Staff:** Prof 5; Other 17. **Subjects:** Law. **Special
Collections:** Public law, civil law, history of law. **Holdings:** 58,000 books;
61,300 bound periodical volumes; 10,900 microforms. **Subscriptions:** 1670
journals and other serials. **Services:** Interlibrary loans; copying; library open to
public with restrictions. **Automated Operations:** Computerized cataloging.
Computerized Information Services: DIALOG, SDC, BRS, CAN/OLE,
Questel, QL Systems. **Publications:** Reader's Guide.

**UNIVERSITE DE MONTREAL - ECOLE DES HAUTES ETUDES
    COMMERCIALES DE MONTREAL**
See: Ecole des Hautes Etudes Commerciales de Montreal

UNIVERSITE DE MONTREAL - ECOLE POLYTECHNIQUE
See: Ecole Polytechnique

★15066★

UNIVERSITE DE MONTREAL - EDUCATION PHYSIQUE-BIBLIOTHEQUE
    (Educ)
C.P. 6128, Succursale A   Phone: (514) 343-6765
Montreal, PQ, Canada H3C 3J7   Lise Mayrand, Libn.
Founded: 1966. **Staff:** Prof 1; Other 3. **Subjects:** Physical education, sports,
physiology, psychology, education. **Holdings:** 15,060 books; 5530 bound
periodical volumes; 14,000 microforms. **Subscriptions:** 440 journals and
other serials. **Services:** Interlibrary loans; copying; library open to public with
restrictions. **Automated Operations:** Computerized cataloging. **Publications:**
Acquisitions list, periodicals list - both have limited distribution.

★15067★

**UNIVERSITE   DE   MONTREAL   -   EDUCATION/PSYCHOLOGIE/
    COMMUNICATION-BIBLIOTHEQUE** (Educ)
C.P. 6128, Succursale A   Phone: (514) 343-6638
Montreal, PQ, Canada H3C 3J7   Marielle Durand, Libn.
Founded: 1965. **Staff:** Prof 5; Other 23. **Subjects:** Education, pedagogy,
psychology, communication, audiovisuals, school administration. **Special
Collections:** Rey-Herme Collection (3500 volumes); Villeneuve Collection
(8150 volumes). **Holdings:** 62,820 books; 24,480 bound periodical volumes;
236,000 microforms. **Subscriptions:** 1630 journals and other serials.
Services: Interlibrary loans; copying; library open to public with restrictions.
Automated   Operations: Computerized   cataloging.   **Computerized**

Information Services: DIALOG, BRS, SDC, CAN/OLE, Questel, QL Systems. **Publications:** Acquisitions list; list of serials; list of reference works - limited distribution. **Special Catalogs:** Rey-Herme Collection Catalog.

★15068★
UNIVERSITE DE MONTREAL - GEOGRAPHIE-BIBLIOTHEQUE (Sci-Tech)
C.P. 6128, Succursale A   Phone: (514) 270-3727
Montreal, PQ, Canada H3C 3J7   Francine Caplette, Hd.
Staff: 1. **Subjects:** Geography. **Holdings:** 2275 books; 2740 bound periodical volumes; 552 microforms. **Subscriptions:** 420 journals and other serials. **Services:** Interlibrary loans; copying; library open to public with restrictions. **Automated Operations:** Computerized cataloging and circulation. **Publications:** Acquisitions list, monthly - limited distribution.

★15069★
UNIVERSITE DE MONTREAL - GEOLOGIE-BIBLIOTHEQUE (Sci-Tech)
C.P. 6128, Succursale A   Phone: (514) 343-6831
Montreal, PQ, Canada H3C 3J7   Clement Arwas, Libn.
Founded: 1965. **Staff:** Prof 1; Other 1. **Subjects:** Geology. **Holdings:** 9300 books; 14,130 bound periodical volumes; 900 microforms. **Subscriptions:** 320 journals and other serials. **Services:** Interlibrary loans; copying; library open to public with restrictions. **Automated Operations:** Computerized cataloging. **Publications:** Acquisitions list; periodicals list - both have limited distribution.

★15070★
UNIVERSITE DE MONTREAL - INFORMATIQUE-BIBLIOTHEQUE (Info Sci; Comp Sci)
C.P. 6128, Succursale A   Phone: (514) 343-6819
Montreal, PQ, Canada H3C 3J7   Louis Sarrasin, Libn.
Founded: 1966. **Staff:** Prof 1; Other 1. **Subjects:** Computer science, applied linguistics, operations research, systems theory. **Holdings:** 17,300 books; 3800 bound periodical volumes; 1450 microforms. **Subscriptions:** 290 journals and other serials. **Services:** Interlibrary loans; copying; library open to public with restrictions. **Computerized Information Services:** DIALOG, SDC, BRS, CAN/OLE, Questel, QL Systems. **Publications:** Acquisitions list, monthly - limited distribution; periodicals list.

UNIVERSITE DE MONTREAL - INSTITUT DE DIAGNOSTIC ET DE RECHERCHES CLINIQUES DE MONTREAL
See: Clinical Research Institute of Montreal

UNIVERSITE DE MONTREAL - INSTITUT DE MEDECINE ET DE CHIRURGIE EXPERIMENTALES
See: International Institute of Stress - Library and Documentation Center

★15071★
UNIVERSITE DE MONTREAL - MATHEMATIQUES-BIBLIOTHEQUE (Sci-Tech)
C.P. 6128, Succursale A   Phone: (514) 343-6703
Montreal, PQ, Canada H3C 3J7   Rita Paquette, Libn.
Founded: 1966. **Staff:** Prof 1; Other 3. **Subjects:** Mathematics. **Holdings:** 18,660 books; 11,440 bound periodical volumes; 4080 microforms. **Subscriptions:** 350 journals and other serials. **Services:** Interlibrary loans; copying; library open to public with restrictions. **Computerized Information Services:** DIALOG, BRS, SDC, CAN/OLE, Questel, QL Systems. **Publications:** Reports of Higher Mathematics Seminars, 3/year; acquisitions list, monthly - limited distribution.

★15072★
UNIVERSITE DE MONTREAL - MEDECINE VETERINAIRE-BIBLIOTHEQUE (Med)
C.P. 5000   Phone: (514) 773-8521
St-Hyacinthe, PQ, Canada J2S 7C6   Jean-Paul Jette, Dir.
Founded: 1948. **Staff:** Prof 1; Other 4. **Subjects:** Veterinary medicine, animal science. **Special Collections:** French veterinary theses (10,000). **Holdings:** 13,100 books; 38,000 bound periodical volumes. **Subscriptions:** 600 journals and other serials. **Services:** Interlibrary loans; copying; library open to public. **Automated Operations:** Computerized cataloging. **Computerized Information Services:** DIALOG, MEDLINE; TELUM (internal database). Performs limited free searches. **Publications:** Liste de Nouvelles Acquisitions, irregular - limited distribution.

★15073★
UNIVERSITE DE MONTREAL - MUSIQUE-BIBLIOTHEQUE (Mus)
C.P. 6128, Succursale A   Phone: (514) 343-6432
Montreal, PQ, Canada H3C 3J7   Monique Lecavalier, Libn.
Founded: 1952. **Staff:** Prof 2; Other 4. **Subjects:** Music. **Holdings:** 7800 books; 1810 bound periodical volumes; 6780 phonograph records; 2400 slides; 11,950 scores; 3770 microforms; 4050 audiotapes. **Subscriptions:**

290 journals and other serials. **Services:** Interlibrary loans; copying; library open to public with restrictions. **Automated Operations:** Computerized cataloging. **Publications:** Acquisitions list - for internal distribution only. **Special Catalogs:** Periodicals list.

★15074★
UNIVERSITE DE MONTREAL - OPTOMETRIE-BIBLIOTHEQUE (Med)
C.P. 6128, Succursale A   Phone: (514) 343-7674
Montreal, PQ, Canada H3C 3J7   Denise Lacroix, Libn.
Founded: 1964. **Staff:** 1. **Subjects:** Optometry. **Holdings:** 2930 books; 4280 bound periodical volumes. **Subscriptions:** 135 journals and other serials. **Services:** Interlibrary loans; copying; library open to public with restrictions. **Automated Operations:** Computerized cataloging. **Publications:** Acquisitions list, monthly - limited distribution.

★15075★
UNIVERSITE DE MONTREAL - PHYSIQUE-BIBLIOTHEQUE (Sci-Tech)
C.P. 6128, Succursale A   Phone: (514) 343-6613
Montreal, PQ, Canada H3C 3J7   Janine Cadet, Libn.
Founded: 1966. **Staff:** Prof 1; Other 2. **Subjects:** Physics, astrophysics, astronomy, biophysics. **Holdings:** 12,330 books; 14,360 bound periodical volumes. **Subscriptions:** 260 journals and other serials. **Services:** Interlibrary loans; copying; library open to public with restrictions. **Automated Operations:** Computerized cataloging. **Computerized Information Services:** DIALOG, BRS, SDC, CAN/OLE, Questel, QL Systems. **Publications:** Acquisitions list, monthly - limited distribution. **Special Catalogs:** Periodicals list.

★15076★
UNIVERSITE DE MONTREAL - PSYCHO-EDUCATION-BIBLIOTHEQUE (Educ)
750 Est, Boul. Gouin   Phone: (514) 382-2977
Montreal, PQ, Canada H2C 1A6   Yolande Beaudoin, Libn.
Founded: 1970. **Staff:** Prof 1; Other 1. **Subjects:** Child psychology, rehabilitation of maladjusted children. **Holdings:** 8900 books; 2000 bound periodical volumes; 25 microforms. **Subscriptions:** 190 journals and other serials. **Services:** Interlibrary loans; library open to public with restrictions. **Automated Operations:** Computerized cataloging. **Publications:** Acquisitions list - for internal distribution only.

★15077★
UNIVERSITE DE MONTREAL - SCIENCES HUMAINES ET SOCIALES-BIBLIOTHEQUE (Hum; Soc Sci)
C.P. 6202, Succursale A   Phone: (514) 343-7424
Montreal, PQ, Canada H3C 3T2   Richard Greene, Libn.
Founded: 1968. **Staff:** Prof 15; Other 42. **Subjects:** Anthropology, criminology, demography, history, French studies, geography, linguistics, philosophy, industrial relations, political science, economics, social service, sociology, science history, science policy, comparative literature, art history, African studies. **Holdings:** 475,900 books; 117,200 bound periodical volumes; 202,000 microforms; 17,700 AV items (Mediatheque). **Subscriptions:** 3230 journals and other serials. **Services:** Interlibrary loans; copying; library open to public with restrictions. **Automated Operations:** Computerized cataloging and circulation. **Computerized Information Services:** DIALOG, BRS, SDC, CAN/OLE, Questel, QL Systems. **Publications:** Bibliographic guides; acquisitions list, monthly - limited distribution. **Special Catalogs:** Journals and periodicals list (on microfilm); Preliminary Inventory of Landmarks of Science Collection. **Staff:** Alexandre Jonynas, Asst.Dir.

★15078★
UNIVERSITE DE MONTREAL - THEOLOGIE-PHILOSOPHIE BIBLIOTHEQUE (Rel-Theol)
C.P. 6128, Succursale A   Phone: (514) 343-6592
Montreal, PQ, Canada H3C 3J7   Francoise Beaudet, Libn.
Founded: 1974. **Staff:** Prof 1; Other 5. **Subjects:** Theology, Jewish studies, philosophy. **Holdings:** 56,300 books; 19,100 bound periodical volumes; 5600 microforms. **Subscriptions:** 550 journals and other serials. **Services:** Interlibrary loans; copying; library open to public with restrictions. **Automated Operations:** Computerized cataloging. **Computerized Information Services:** DIALOG, SDC, BRS, CAN/OLE, Questel, QL Systems. **Publications:** Acquisitions list, monthly - limited distribution.

UNIVERSITE D'OTTAWA
See: University of Ottawa

★15079★
UNIVERSITE DU QUEBEC - ECOLE NATIONALE D'ADMINISTRATION PUBLIQUE - CENTRE DE DOCUMENTATION (Soc Sci)
945 Ave. Wolfe   Phone: (418) 657-2485
Ste. Foy, PQ, Canada G1V 3J9   Michel Gelinas, Libn.
Founded: 1969. **Staff:** Prof 1; Other 9. **Subjects:** Public administration,

management, economics, political science. **Holdings:** 17,000 books; 3765 pamphlets; 380 dissertations; 159 theses. **Subscriptions:** 719 journals and other serials; 7 newspapers. **Services:** Interlibrary loans; copying; center open to public. **Automated Operations:** Computerized cataloging. **Computerized Information Services:** DIALOG, Questel, MINISIS, iNET GATEWAY, BADADUQ. Contact Person: Michel Gelinas. **Publications:** Vient de paraitre; Bulletin signaletique des acquisitions; Les cahiers de l'ENAP; Guide bibliographique en administration publique; Administration publique Canadienne, bibliographie; Thesaurus multilingue en administration publique.

★15080★
UNIVERSITE DU QUEBEC - MEDIATHEQUE (Educ)†
2875, Boul. Laurier   Phone: (418) 657-2578
Ste. Foy, PQ, Canada G1V 2M3   Yvon Isabel, Directeur
Founded: 1972. **Staff:** Prof 2; Other 1. **Subjects:** Higher education, administration, information processing. **Holdings:** 2000 books; 1000 Quebec and federal publications; 200 Quebec statutes. **Subscriptions:** 153 journals and other serials. **Services:** Interlibrary loans; copying; library open to public on request. **Automated Operations:** Computerized cataloging and serials. **Computerized Information Services:** Online systems. **Staff:** Jean-Pierre Roy, Libn.

★15081★
UNIVERSITE DU QUEBEC EN ABITIBI-TEMISCAMINGUE - BIBLIOTHEQUE
(Educ)
446, rue Gagne
Box 8000   Phone: (819) 762-0971
Rouyn, PQ, Canada J9X 5M5   Serge Allard, Dir.
Founded: 1971. **Staff:** Prof 3; Other 14. **Subjects:** Education, administration. **Special Collections:** Northwest Quebec (Abitibi-Temiscamingue; 6608 documents; 4 newspaper titles; 10,622 slides and AV items). **Holdings:** 39,479 books; 191,615 microforms; 8549 AV documents. **Subscriptions:** 523 journals and other serials. **Services:** Interlibrary loans; copying; library open to public with restrictions. **Computerized Information Services:** DIALOG, BADADUQ. **Publications:** Liste des nouveaux titres catalogues et classifies. **Remarks:** Includes part of the holdings of College d'Abitibi-Temiscamingue Library. **Staff:** Levis Tremblay, Tech.Serv.; Andre Beland, Ref.Libn.

★15082★
UNIVERSITE DU QUEBEC A HULL - BIBLIOTHEQUE (Educ)
C.P. 1250, Succursale B   Phone: (819) 776-8381
Hull, PQ, Canada J8X 3X7   Andre Chenier, Directeur
Founded: 1972. **Staff:** Prof 4; Other 10. **Subjects:** Administration, education, nursing, social sciences, visual arts, literature, linguistics. **Holdings:** 54,000 books; 7532 bound periodical volumes. **Subscriptions:** 1000 journals and other serials; 5 newspapers. **Services:** Interlibrary loans; copying; SDI; library open to public with restrictions. **Automated Operations:** Computerized cataloging and serials. **Computerized Information Services:** DIALOG, BRS, INFORMATECH, CAN/OLE, QL Systems, BADADUQ. **Staff:** Gilles Bergeron, Rd.Serv.Libn.; Danielle Boisvert, Ref.Libn.; Louise Grondines, Cat.Libn.; Jacques Cloutier, Acq.

★15083★
UNIVERSITE DU QUEBEC A MONTREAL - AUDIOVIDEOTHEQUE (Aud-Vis)
C.P. 8889   Phone: (514) 282-4332
Montreal, PQ, Canada H3C 3P3   Huquette Tanguay, Audiovideothecaire
Staff: Prof 1; Other 1. **Subjects:** Sexology, administration, earth sciences, psychology. **Holdings:** 800 films and videotapes. **Services:** Interlibrary loans; library open to public with restrictions.

★15084★
UNIVERSITE DU QUEBEC A MONTREAL - BIBLIOTHEQUE DES ARTS (Art)
C.P. 8889, Succursale A   Phone: (514) 282-6134
Montreal, PQ, Canada H3C 3P3   Daphne Dufresne, Chf.Libn.
Founded: 1944. **Staff:** Prof 1; Other 8. **Subjects:** Painting, sculpture, art history, Canadian art, design, engraving. **Holdings:** 50,000 books; 3500 bound periodical volumes; 112,000 slides; 1000 microforms; 11 drawers of clippings on Canadian art. **Subscriptions:** 273 journals and other serials. **Services:** Interlibrary loans; copying; library open to university students. **Automated Operations:** Computerized cataloging, circulation and acquisitions. **Computerized Information Services:** BADADUQ. **Networks/Consortia:** Member of CREPUQ.

★15085★
UNIVERSITE DU QUEBEC A MONTREAL - BIBLIOTHEQUE DE MUSIQUE
(Mus)
C.P. 8889, Succursale A   Phone: (514) 282-3934
Montreal, PQ, Canada H3C 3P3   Renald Beaumier, Dir.
Staff: Prof 2; Other 3. **Subjects:** Music education and therapy, musicology.

Special Collections: Canadian Broadcasting Corporation (CBC) Music Program archives, 1940-1983. **Holdings:** 4662 books; 234 bound periodical volumes; 7825 scores; 5047 phonograph records; 6000 tape records. **Subscriptions:** 68 journals and other serials. **Services:** Interlibrary loans; copying; library open to public. **Automated Operations:** Computerized cataloging, circulation and acquisitions. **Computerized Information Services:** BADADUQ. **Networks/Consortia:** Member of CREPUQ.

★15086★
UNIVERSITE DU QUEBEC A MONTREAL - BIBLIOTHEQUE DES SCIENCES
(Sci-Tech)
C.P. 8889, Succursale A   Phone: (514) 282-6164
Montreal, PQ, Canada H3C 3P3   Conrad Corriveau, Dir.
Staff: Prof 3; Other 8. **Subjects:** Chemistry, biology, mathematics, physics, geology, technology, psychology. **Holdings:** 47,000 books; 28,000 bound periodical volumes; 186 AV items; 2000 microforms. **Subscriptions:** 950 journals and other serials. **Services:** Interlibrary loans; copying; library open to public for reference use only. **Automated Operations:** Computerized cataloging, acquisitions and circulation. **Computerized Information Services:** DIALOG, CAN/OLE, BRS, SDC, MEDLINE, INFO/tek, QL Systems, International Development Research Centre (IDRC), BADADUQ. **Networks/Consortia:** Member of CREPUQ. **Special Catalogs:** Lists of periodical and monograph holdings (computer printout). **Staff:** Jean Juneau, Ref.Libn.; Mychelle Boulet, Ref.Libn.

★15087★
UNIVERSITE DU QUEBEC A MONTREAL - BIBLIOTHEQUE DES SCIENCES DE
L'EDUCATION (Educ)
C.P. 8889, Succursale A   Phone: (514) 282-6174
Montreal, PQ, Canada H3C 3P3   Denis Rousseau, Dir.
Staff: Prof 3; Other 8. **Subjects:** Continuing teacher education, elementary and secondary education, physical education, disadvantaged and exceptional child education, hearing and learning disabilities, professional and vocational information. **Special Collections:** ERIC documents. **Holdings:** 39,000 books; 6000 bound periodical volumes; 153,000 ERIC microfiche; 3900 microcards; 677 reels of microfilm; 225 film loops; 1550 slides. **Subscriptions:** 385 journals and other serials. **Services:** Interlibrary loans; copying. **Automated Operations:** Computerized cataloging, acquisitions and circulation. **Computerized Information Services:** BRS, DIALOG, SDC, INFO/tek, MEDLINE, CAN/OLE, BADADUQ, International Development Research Centre (IDRC). **Networks/Consortia:** Member of CREPUQ. **Special Catalogs:** Lists of periodical holdings (computer printout). **Staff:** J.-Etienne Favreau, Ref.Libn.; Danielle Mallette, Ref.Libn.; Monique Gaucher, Libn.

★15088★
UNIVERSITE DU QUEBEC A MONTREAL - BIBLIOTHEQUES DES SCIENCES
JURIDIQUES (Law)
C.P. 8889, Succursale A   Phone: (514) 282-6184
Montreal, PQ, Canada H3C 3P3   Micheline Drapeau, Dir.
Founded: 1974. **Staff:** Prof 3; Other 7. **Subjects:** Jurisprudence; social security; consumer and environmental protection; law - constitutional, family, fiscal, health, housing, labor, poverty, public education, social; immigration and civil rights. **Holdings:** 28,049 volumes; 9 VF drawers of microfiche; 103 magnetic tapes; 189 reels of microfilm. **Subscriptions:** 246 journals and other serials. **Services:** Interlibrary loans; copying; library open to public with restrictions. **Automated Operations:** Computerized cataloging, acquisitions and circulation. **Computerized Information Services:** BADADUQ. **Networks/Consortia:** Member of CREPUQ. **Staff:** Claudio Antonelli, Ref.Libn.; Jean-Paul Reid, Ref.Libn.

★15089★
UNIVERSITE DU QUEBEC A MONTREAL - CARTOTHEQUE (Geog-Map)
C.P. 8889, Succursale A   Phone: (514) 282-3133
Montreal, PQ, Canada H3C 3P8   Leon-Pierre Sciamma, Responsable
Staff: Prof 2; Other 2. **Subjects:** Cartography, aerial photography. **Holdings:** 7000 books; 500 bound periodical volumes; 400,000 aerial photographs; 68,000 maps. **Services:** Interlibrary loans; library open to public. **Computerized Information Services:** BADADUQ. **Networks/Consortia:** Member of CREPUQ.

★15090★
UNIVERSITE DU QUEBEC A MONTREAL - CENTRE DE DOCUMENTATION
ECONOMIE-ADMINISTRATION (Soc Sci)
C.P. 8889, Succursale A   Phone: (514) 282-6136
Montreal, PQ, Canada H3C 3P8   Monique Cote, Libn.
Founded: 1971. **Staff:** Prof 1; Other 1. **Subjects:** Economics, administration, urban studies. **Holdings:** 5300 books; 882 feet of brokerage publications, public documents and university studies; 18 drawers of reports; 7523 microfiche; 339 reels of microfilm. **Subscriptions:** 26 journals and other

serials. **Services:** Center open to public. **Automated Operations:** Computerized acquisitions. **Computerized Information Services:** BADADUQ, MINISIS. **Networks/Consortia:** Member of CREPUQ. **Publications:** Nouveautes and periodical highlights, monthly.

★15091★
UNIVERSITE DU QUEBEC A MONTREAL - CENTRE DE DOCUMENTATION EN SCIENCES HUMAINES (Soc Sci)
C.P. 8889, Succursale A　　　　　　Phone: (514) 282-6138
Montreal, PQ, Canada H3C 3P3　　　Louis LeBorgne, Documentaliste
Staff: Prof 1; Other 1. **Subjects:** Political parties, labor unions, feminism, urban movements, Latin America, ethnic studies. **Special Collections:** Quebec labor union archives; Quebec and Canadian political party archives; Quebec feminist movement archives. **Holdings:** 820 books; 72 boxes of archives; 365 linear feet of bound periodical volumes; 25 VF drawers; 320 reels of microfilm; 12 linear feet of microfilm, 900 maps. **Subscriptions:** 58 journals and other serials. **Services:** Interlibrary loans; copying; library open to public. **Automated Operations:** Computerized cataloging and acquisitions. **Computerized Information Services:** BADADUQ. **Networks/Consortia:** Member of CREPUQ.

★15092★
UNIVERSITE DU QUEBEC A RIMOUSKI - CARTOTHEQUE (Geog-Map)
300, Avenue des Ursulines　　　　　Phone: (418) 724-1669
Rimouski, PQ, Canada G5L 3A1　　　Yves Michaud, Map Libn.
Founded: 1971. **Staff:** Prof 1. **Subjects:** Cartography, aerial photography. **Special Collections:** Canadian, Quebec, East Quebec, lower St. Lawrence and Gaspesia region maps. **Holdings:** 700 books; 700 atlases; 25,000 maps; 20,000 aerial photographs; 100 other cataloged items. **Services:** Library open to public. **Publications:** Information cartologigue, irregular.

★15093★
UNIVERSITE DU QUEBEC A TROIS-RIVIERES - CARTOTHEQUE (Geog-Map)
Pavillon Leon-Provancher
C.P. 500　　　　　　　　　　　Phone: (819) 376-5351
Trois-Rivieres, PQ, Canada G9A 5H7　Marie Lefebvre, Cartothecaire
Staff: Prof 1; Other 1. **Subjects:** Cartography, aerial photography, statistics. **Special Collections:** Maps of the Trois-Rivieres region. **Holdings:** 1372 books and bound periodical volumes; 33,413 maps; 186 atlases; 3 globes; 5 relief models; 44,615 aerial photographs. **Services:** Library open to public. **Networks/Consortia:** Member of Association des Cartotheques Canadiennes. **Remarks:** The map collection is administered by the Department of Humanities.

★15094★
UNIVERSITE ST-PAUL - BIBLIOTHEQUE (Rel-Theol)
223 Main　　　　　　　　　　　Phone: (613) 236-1393
Ottawa, ON, Canada K1S 1C4　　Gaston Rioux, O.M.I., Chf.Libn.
Founded: 1937. **Staff:** Prof 2; Other 13. **Subjects:** Religious sciences, philosophy, canon law, medieval sciences, theology, Bible, church history. **Holdings:** 335,000 books; 62,000 bound periodical volumes; 3000 reels of microfilm; 32,000 microfiche. **Subscriptions:** 1100 journals and other serials. **Services:** Interlibrary loans; copying; library open to public with restrictions. **Remarks:** Maintained by Oblate Fathers.

★15095★
UNIVERSITE DE SHERBROOKE - FACULTE DE MEDECINE - BIBLIOTHEQUE DES SCIENCES DE LA SANTE (Med)
Centre Hospitalier Universitaire　　Phone: (819) 565-2096
Sherbrooke, PQ, Canada J1H 5N4　　Germain Chouinard, Dir.
Founded: 1965. **Staff:** Prof 1; Other 6. **Subjects:** Health sciences. **Holdings:** 75,337 volumes. **Subscriptions:** 1300 journals and other serials. **Services:** Interlibrary loans; copying; SDI; library open to public with restrictions. **Automated Operations:** Computerized cataloging and circulation. **Computerized Information Services:** NLM, DIALOG, BRS, SDC, CAN/OLE. Performs searches on cost recovery and subscription basis.

UNIVERSITE DE SUDBURY
See: University of Sudbury

★15096★
UNIVERSITY AFFILIATED CINCINNATI CENTER FOR DEVELOPMENTAL DISORDERS - RESEARCH LIBRARY (Med; Educ)
Pavilion Bldg.
3300 Elland Ave.　　　　　　　Phone: (513) 559-4626
Cincinnati, OH 45229　　　Dorothy A. Gilroy, Chf.Res.Libn.
Founded: 1960. **Staff:** Prof 2; Other 1. **Subjects:** Developmental disabilities, mental retardation, learning disabilities, special education, pediatrics, neurology, nutrition, rehabilitation, psychology, social work, vocational counseling. **Special Collections:** Library for parents of exceptional children (800 books and 500 pamphlet titles for distribution); Toy Library for Special Children; bibliography collection. **Holdings:** 13,000 books; 1850 bound periodical volumes; 400 AV items; 100,000 reprint articles relating to developmental disorders and pediatrics; 3 VF drawers of staff publications; 10,000 slides. **Subscriptions:** 200 journals and other serials. **Services:** Interlibrary loans; copying; SDI; library open to public with restrictions and for reference only. **Computerized Information Services:** BRS, MEDLINE, Birth Defects Information System (BDIS). **Networks/Consortia:** Member of Cincinnati Area Health Sciences Library Association (CAHSLA); Greater Midwest Regional Medical Library Network (Region 3); Cincinnati Online Consortium for Life Sciences (COCLS); U.S. Toy Library Association. **Publications:** Library Bulletin, quarterly - for internal distribution and limited outside distribution. **Special Indexes:** Card index to reprint file. **Remarks:** Affiliated with University of Cincinnati and Cincinnati Children's Hospital. **Staff:** Barbarie Hill; Joanne Jeffrey .

★15097★
UNIVERSITY OF AKRON - ARCHIVES OF THE HISTORY OF AMERICAN PSYCHOLOGY (Soc Sci)
　　　　　　　　　　　　　Phone: (216) 375-7285
Akron, OH 44325　　　　　　John A. Popplestone, Dir.
Founded: 1965. **Staff:** Prof 2; Other 10. **Subjects:** American psychology. **Special Collections:** Papers of E.A. Doll, H.H. Goddard, H.S. Hollingworth, Leta Hollingworth, K. Koffka, A. Maslow, M. Scheerer, W. Shipley, E.C. Tolman; historical laboratory equipment (600 items). **Holdings:** 2000 linear feet of documents. **Services:** Copying; archives open to scholars. **Staff:** Marion White McPherson, Assoc.Dir.

UNIVERSITY OF AKRON - BIERCE LIBRARY
See: American Chemical Society, Inc. - Rubber Division - John H. Gifford Memorial Library & Information Ctr.

★15098★
UNIVERSITY OF AKRON - CENTER FOR PEACE STUDIES - LIBRARY (Soc Sci)
　　　　　　　　　　　　　Phone: (216) 375-7008
Akron, OH 44325　　　　　　Warren F. Kuehl, Dir.
Staff: 1. **Subjects:** Peace movements and their history; internationalism; human rights; peace education. **Special Collections:** Library of World Peace Studies (3013 microfiche). **Holdings:** 350 books; 2 VF drawers of peace societies and organizations; 2 VF drawers of academic peace programs. **Subscriptions:** 13 journals and other serials. **Services:** Copying; library open to public. **Publications:** International Peace Studies Newsletter - 3/year, free to mailing list. **Special Indexes:** Human Rights bibliography (card).

★15099★
UNIVERSITY OF AKRON - SCHOOL OF LAW - C. BLAKE MC DOWELL LAW LIBRARY (Law)
Law Center　　　　　　　　　Phone: (216) 375-7447
Akron, OH 44325　　　　　　Paul Richert, Law Libn.
Founded: 1965. **Staff:** Prof 5; Other 6. **Subjects:** Anglo-American law. **Holdings:** 162,000 volumes. **Subscriptions:** 867 periodicals. **Services:** Interlibrary loans; copying; library open to public. **Computerized Information Services:** LEXIS, OCLC, Westlaw. **Publications:** Acquisition List, monthly - for internal distribution only.

★15100★
UNIVERSITY OF ALABAMA - BUSINESS LIBRARY (Bus-Fin)
Box S　　　　　　　　　　Phone: (205) 348-6096
University, AL 35486　　　Dorothy Eady Brown, Sr.Libn.
Founded: 1925. **Staff:** Prof 2; Other 4. **Subjects:** Accounting, banking, economics, finance, human resource management, marketing, international business, real estate, transportation, business law, insurance. **Special Collections:** Corporate reports (82,000). **Holdings:** 107,607 books; 26,500 bound periodical volumes; 1040 reels of microfilm; 179,630 microfiche. **Subscriptions:** 2400 journals and other serials. **Services:** Interlibrary loans; copying; library open to public. **Computerized Information Services:** DIALOG, SDC, BRS, OCLC. Performs searches on cost recovery basis. **Special Catalogs:** Corporate catalog (card).

★15101★
UNIVERSITY OF ALABAMA - COLLEGE OF COMMUNITY HEALTH SCIENCES - HEALTH SCIENCES LIBRARY (Med)
Box 6331　　　　　　　　　Phone: (205) 348-4950
University, AL 35486　　　Lisa Rains, Chf.Med.Libn.
Founded: 1973. **Staff:** Prof 2; Other 11. **Subjects:** Medicine, nursing, pharmacy, medical sociology. **Special Collections:** AV programs on clinical medicine (2000). **Holdings:** 9000 books; 15,000 bound periodical volumes;

16 VF drawers of pamphlets and clippings. **Subscriptions:** 475 journals and other serials. **Services:** Interlibrary loans; copying; library open to health care professionals. **Computerized Information Services:** MEDLARS. **Special Catalogs:** Computer-produced catalog of AV software programs. **Remarks:** Includes the holdings of the Druid City Hospital - Medical Library, 809 University Blvd., E., Tuscaloosa, AL. **Staff:** Barbara P. Doughty, Med.Ref.Libn.; Bobby Selwyn, Mgr., Circ./AV.

★15102★
UNIVERSITY OF ALABAMA - ENGINEERING LIBRARY (Sci-Tech; Comp Sci)
Box S   Phone: (205) 348-6551
University, AL 35486   Aydan Kalyoncu, Sr.Libn.
Founded: 1963. **Staff:** Prof 1; Other 2. **Subjects:** Engineering, technology, computer science. **Special Collections:** NASA documents. **Holdings:** 70,000 books, bound periodical volumes, and technical reports; 4000 microforms. **Subscriptions:** 500 journals and other serials. **Services:** Interlibrary loans; bibliographic instruction; copying; library open to public. **Computerized Information Services:** DIALOG, SDC, BRS, OCLC, CAS Online. Performs searches on cost recovery basis. **Networks/Consortia:** Member of Association of Research Libraries (ARL).

★15103★
UNIVERSITY OF ALABAMA - JONES LAW INSTITUTE - LIBRARY (Law)*
1500 East Fairview Ave.   Phone: (205) 832-5588
Montgomery, AL 36106   John R. Huthnance, Dir.
Founded: 1928. **Staff:** Prof 1; Other 1. **Subjects:** Law. **Holdings:** 5000 books. **Subscriptions:** 24 journals and other serials. **Services:** Library is open to local students and attorneys only.

★15104★
UNIVERSITY OF ALABAMA - MC LURE EDUCATION LIBRARY (Educ)
Box S   Phone: (205) 348-6055
University, AL 35486   Sharon Lee Stewart, Act.Sr.Libn.
Founded: 1928. **Staff:** Prof 2; Other 4. **Subjects:** Higher education; special education; curriculum and instruction; health, physical education and recreation; behavioral studies; fine arts education; vocational and adult education. **Special Collections:** Curriculum Laboratory; Children's and Young Adult Collection; history of education in America. **Holdings:** 110,000 books; 6000 bound periodical volumes; 350,000 microforms; 3 VF drawers of newsletters; 6 VF drawers of additional material. **Subscriptions:** 901 journals and other serials. **Services:** Interlibrary loans; copying and microfiche-to-microfiche copying; library open to public. **Computerized Information Services:** DIALOG, OCLC, BRS, SDC. **Networks/Consortia:** Member of SOLINET; Association of Research Libraries (ARL). **Publications:** Education Library Resources. **Staff:** Helga Visscher, Ref.Libn.

★15105★
UNIVERSITY OF ALABAMA - OFFICE OF PLANNING AND OPERATIONS - ADMINISTRATIVE RESEARCH LIBRARY
222 Rose Administration Bldg.
Box 6156
University, AL 35486
Defunct

★15106★
UNIVERSITY OF ALABAMA - SCHOOL OF LAW - ALABAMA LAW REVIEW - LIBRARY (Law)
Box 1976   Phone: (205) 348-7191
University, AL 35486   Deborah Fisher, Res.Ed.
Staff: 1. **Subjects:** Federal and state law. **Holdings:** 3366 books; 361 bound periodical volumes. **Subscriptions:** 25 journals and other serials. **Services:** Library not open to public. **Publications:** Alabama Law Review, 4/year - by subscription.

★15107★
UNIVERSITY OF ALABAMA - SCHOOL OF LAW LIBRARY (Law)
Box 6205   Phone: (205) 348-5925
University, AL 35486-6205   Cherry L. Thomas, Act. Law Libn.
Founded: 1872. **Staff:** Prof 6; Other 5. **Subjects:** Law. **Special Collections:** U.S. Supreme Court Justice Hugo L. Black Collection. **Holdings:** 178,000 books; 24,500 bound periodical volumes; 40,000 microforms. **Subscriptions:** 3400 journals and other serials; 16 newspapers. **Services:** Interlibrary loans; copying; library open to public. **Computerized Information Services:** LEXIS, DIALOG, Westlaw. **Staff:** David Lowe, Computer Serv./Docs.; Ruth Weeks, Cat.; Paul Birch, Ref.; Jeanette Yackle, Ref./Coll.Dev.; Virginia Hare, Pub.Serv.Libn.

★15108★
UNIVERSITY OF ALABAMA - SCIENCE LIBRARY (Sci-Tech)
Box S   Phone: (205) 348-5959
University, AL 35486   John S. Langen, Sr.Libn.
Founded: 1963. **Staff:** Prof 1; Other 1. **Subjects:** Chemistry, physics, biology, geology, astronomy, mathematics, microbiology. **Special Collections:** Alabama Museum of Natural History (1500 volumes). **Holdings:** 80,000 books and bound periodical volumes; 850 theses; 315 science dissertations; 168 reels of microfilm. **Subscriptions:** 1300 journals and other serials. **Services:** Interlibrary loans; copying; library open to public. **Computerized Information Services:** DIALOG, SDC, BRS, OCLC.

★15109★
UNIVERSITY OF ALABAMA - WILLIAM STANLEY HOOLE SPECIAL COLLECTIONS LIBRARY (Hum; Rare Book)
Box S   Phone: (205) 348-5512
University, AL 35486   Joyce H. Lamont, Cur.
Staff: Prof 5; Other 2. **Subjects:** Alabamiana, travels in the South East, southern Americana, early imprints, state documents. **Special Collections:** Rare books (12,500); manuscripts (14 million); university archives (4 million items); Alabamiana (35,000 volumes); black folk music (250 magnetic tapes); oral history (875 magnetic tapes); maps (15,000). **Holdings:** 46,000 books; 10,000 theses, dissertations and pamphlets. **Subscriptions:** 135 journals and other serials. **Services:** Interlibrary loans; copying; library open to public. **Computerized Information Services:** OCLC; VTLS (internal database). **Networks/Consortia:** Member of SOLINET. **Special Indexes:** Finding aids for manuscripts and archival collections.

★15110★
UNIVERSITY OF ALABAMA IN BIRMINGHAM - LISTER HILL LIBRARY OF THE HEALTH SCIENCES (Med)
University Sta.   Phone: (205) 934-5460
Birmingham, AL 35294   Richard B. Fredericksen, Dir.
Founded: 1945. **Staff:** Prof 12; Other 26. **Subjects:** Medicine, dentistry, nursing, public health, optometry, allied health fields. **Special Collections:** Lawrence Reynolds Collection (rare medical books and manuscripts; 9202 items); Alabama Museum of the Health Sciences (medical history; 10,700 items). **Holdings:** 56,151 books; 90,296 bound periodical volumes; 7759 microtexts; 2674 slides; 30 phonograph records. **Subscriptions:** 2300 journals and other serials. **Services:** Interlibrary loans; copying; library open to public. **Automated Operations:** Computerized serials. **Computerized Information Services:** OCLC, MEDLINE, BRS. **Networks/Consortia:** Member of Consortium of Southern Biomedical Libraries (CONSOBIL); SOLINET. **Publications:** Rare Books and Collections of the Reynolds Historical Library: A Bibliography, 1968; Alabama Medicus (newsletter); Reynolds Library Associates Newsletter. **Special Catalogs:** Alabama Bibliography File; Biography File; Faculty Publications File; serials holdings list. **Staff:** Lynn M. Fortney, Assoc.Dir./Pub.Serv.; Rick B. Forsman, Assoc.Dir./Tech.Serv.

★15111★
UNIVERSITY OF ALABAMA IN BIRMINGHAM - SCHOOL OF MEDICINE - ANESTHESIOLOGY LIBRARY (Med)
Kracke - 5
Dept. of Anesthesiology
University Sta.   Phone: (205) 934-6500
Birmingham, AL 35294   A.J. Wright, Clinical Libn.
Staff: Prof 1; Other 1. **Subjects:** Anesthesia. **Holdings:** 603 books; 371 bound periodical volumes; 100 cassettes; 80 videotapes; 1111 slides; 2107 reprints. **Subscriptions:** 48 journals and other serials. **Services:** Interlibrary loans; copying; SDI; library open to public with restrictions. **Automated Operations:** Computerized cataloging. **Computerized Information Services:** NLM, DIALOG. **Networks/Consortia:** Member of Jefferson County Hospital Librarians' Association. **Publications:** BI-WEEKLY: A Selection of Recent Anesthesia Articles in Non-Specialty Journals, biweekly.

★15112★
UNIVERSITY OF ALABAMA AT HUNTSVILLE - ARCHIVES AND SPECIAL COLLECTIONS (Hist)
The Library
Box 1247   Phone: (205) 895-6540
Huntsville, AL 35807
Subjects: University history and records, northern Alabama history. **Special Collections:** Congressman Robert E. Jones papers (correspondence and office files); university archives, 1947 to present; Willy Ley papers (space science; manuscripts and personal papers). **Holdings:** 320 linear feet of papers and manuscripts. **Services:** Copying; collections open to public during business hours.

★15113★

UNIVERSITY OF ALASKA - ALASKA AGRICULTURAL EXPERIMENT STATION - LIBRARY (Agri)
Box AE   Phone: (907) 745-3257
Palmer, AK 99645   Dr. Winston M. Laughlin, Soil Sci.
Founded: 1950. **Staff:** Prof 1. **Subjects:** Agriculture, soil science, statistics, chemistry, entomology, plant pathology. **Holdings:** 1800 books; 3000 bound periodical volumes; 40,500 abstracts on cards. **Subscriptions:** 138 journals and other serials. **Services:** Interlibrary loans; copying (limited); library open to public.

★15114★

UNIVERSITY OF ALASKA - ALASKA NATIVE LANGUAGE CENTER - RESEARCH LIBRARY (Area-Ethnic)
302 Chapman Bldg.   Phone: (907) 474-7874
Fairbanks, AK 99701
Subjects: Alaskan native languages, Eskimo languages, Athabaskan languages, Amerindian linguistics. **Holdings:** 5000 books, journals, unpublished papers, field notes, and archival materials. **Subscriptions:** 15 journals and other serials. **Services:** Library open to public with permission. **Special Catalogs:** Annotated catalog available for purchase.

★15115★

UNIVERSITY OF ALASKA - ALASKA AND POLAR REGIONS DEPARTMENT (Hist)
Elmer E. Rasmuson Library   Phone: (907) 479-7261
Fairbanks, AK 99701   Paul H. McCarthy, Archv./Hd.
Founded: 1965. **Staff:** Prof 8; Other 39. **Subjects:** Alaska - history, business, anthropology, sciences, university; Arctic; Antarctic. **Special Collections:** Alaska historical photograph collection (109,000 items); rare books (3200); rare maps (450); oral history; Alaska Book Collection; Alaska Congressional papers of Anthony Dimond (1933-1945); Ernest Gruening (1959-1974); Ralph J. Rivers (1959-1966); E.L. Bartlett (1944-1968); Howard Pollock (1966-1970); Nick Begich (1970-1972); Senator Mike Gravel (1968-1980). **Holdings:** 75,000 books and bound periodical volumes; 10,982 microforms; 2400 Alaska historical and university audiotapes; 300 reels of videotape; 730 reels of archival movie film; 2000 cubic feet of university archives; 4200 cubic feet of manuscripts; 158,350 U.S. government documents. **Subscriptions:** 935 journals and other serials; 50 newspapers. **Services:** Copying; department open to public. **Networks/Consortia:** Member of WLN. **Publications:** Published Guide to the Holdings in the University Archives and Manuscript Collections (microfiche). **Special Catalogs:** Bibliography of Alaskana (microfiche). **Special Indexes:** Alaska Commercial Co. Records, 1868-1911; Anthony J. Dimond Papers, 1933-1945, an inventory; Ralph J. Rivers Papers, 1959-1966; an inventory; Howard W. Pollock Papers, 1967-1971, an inventory; unpublished indexes for all processed collections; translations of historic Alaskan documents in foreign languages.

★15116★

UNIVERSITY OF ALASKA - BIO-MEDICAL LIBRARY (Med)
    Phone: (907) 479-7442
Fairbanks, AK 99701   Dwight Ittner, Libn.
Staff: Prof 1; Other 3. **Subjects:** Health sciences, veterinary medicine, fish biology and fisheries, animal physiology, microbiology. **Holdings:** 17,006 books; 14,723 bound periodical volumes; 2000 volumes in microform. **Subscriptions:** 536 journals and other serials. **Services:** Interlibrary loans; copying; library open to public. **Automated Operations:** Computerized cataloging. **Computerized Information Services:** DIALOG, BRS. **Networks/Consortia:** Member of Pacific Northwest Regional Health Sciences Library Service; WLN; Alaska Library Network.

★15117★

UNIVERSITY OF ALASKA - COLLEGE OF HUMAN & RURAL DEVELOPMENT - RESOURCE CENTER (Educ)
Gruening Bldg., Rm. 50A   Phone: (907) 474-6634
Fairbanks, AK 99701   Jim Stricks, Coord.
Founded: 1974. **Staff:** 3. **Subjects:** Cross-cultural education (emphasizing Alaska), Alaska native cultures and their socioeconomic context. **Special Collections:** Alaska student- and community-produced materials; Small High School Project curriculum materials; course materials from cross-cultural degree programs. **Holdings:** 3000 books; 2000 vertical file items; complete publications of Center for Cross-Cultural Studies. **Subscriptions:** 15 journals and other serials; 10 newspapers. **Services:** Interlibrary loans; copying; center open to public with restrictions.

★15118★

UNIVERSITY OF ALASKA - GEOPHYSICAL INSTITUTE LIBRARY (Sci-Tech)†
    Phone: (907) 479-7503
Fairbanks, AK 99701   Julia H. Tryslehorn, Libn.
Founded: 1949. **Staff:** Prof 1; Other 1. **Subjects:** Physics, astronomy, geophysics, geology, mathematics, electronic engineering, meteorology, solar terrestrial science, geothermal energy, glaciology, solid earth sciences, oceanography, remote sensing, polar phenomena. **Holdings:** 18,000 books and bound periodical volumes; technical reports and data. **Subscriptions:** 500 journals and other serials. **Services:** Interlibrary loans; copying; library open to public. **Computerized Information Services:** DIALOG, SDC. **Publications:** Bibliography of publications, biennial - by request.

★15119★

UNIVERSITY OF ALASKA - INSTITUTE OF MARINE SCIENCE - LIBRARY (Sci-Tech)
    Phone: (907) 474-7740
Fairbanks, AK 99701   Robert C. Williams, Libn.
Founded: 1965. **Staff:** Prof 1; Other 1. **Subjects:** Oceanography - general, chemical, biological, geological, physical; aquaculture; marine biology; fisheries biology; fisheries oceanography; limnology; marine ecology; pollution. **Holdings:** 6500 books; 2000 bound periodical volumes; 5660 reprints; 200 microfiche titles; 550 in-house reprints for gifts and exchange; 1507 hydrographic charts; 16 films; 4 videotapes; 13,000 technical reports. **Subscriptions:** 490 journals and other serials. **Services:** Interlibrary loans; copying; library open to public. **Automated Operations:** Computerized cataloging, acquisitions and serials. **Computerized Information Services:** DIALOG, SDC, OnTyme; internal database. **Publications:** I.M.S. Library New Books List, monthly; I.M.S. Library New Reports List, monthly - both for faculty, staff, students and for exchange. **Special Indexes:** KWIC Index to Marine Science Bibliography; Index to Reprints.

★15120★

UNIVERSITY OF ALASKA - INSTITUTE OF MARINE SCIENCE - SEWARD MARINE STATION LIBRARY (Sci-Tech)
Box 617   Phone: (907) 224-5261
Seward, AK 99664   Robert C. Williams, Inst.Libn.
Staff: 2. **Subjects:** Physical and chemical oceanography, aquaculture, marine biology, marine botany. **Special Collections:** Aquaculture reprint collection. **Holdings:** 1300 books; 400 bound periodical volumes; 10,200 reprints; 2300 technical reports; 2000 hydrographic charts. **Subscriptions:** 120 journals and other serials. **Services:** Interlibrary loans; copying; reference; library open to public with restrictions. **Special Indexes:** Key Word Index to 6500 references to Alaska Marine Organisms. **Staff:** Jan Trettner, Asst.Libn.

★15121★

UNIVERSITY OF ALASKA - WILDLIFE LIBRARY (Sci-Tech)
Division of Life Sciences   Phone: (907) 474-7672
Fairbanks, AK 99701   Dr. Frederick C. Dean, Supv.
Staff: Prof 1; Other 1. **Subjects:** Wildlife management, animal ecology, mammalogy, plant ecology, wildlife economics, outdoor recreation, Arctic ecology. **Special Collections:** Government reports. **Holdings:** 300 volumes; 10,000 reprints. **Subscriptions:** 31 journals and other serials. **Services:** Copying, library open to public. **Computerized Information Services:** Reprint collection emphasizing Alaskan, arctic-sub-arctic birds and mammals (internal database). **Special Catalogs:** Termatrex cataloging of reprints (taxonomic, geographic area, date). **Staff:** Carol J. Button .

★15122★

UNIVERSITY OF ALASKA, ANCHORAGE - ALASKA HEALTH SCIENCES LIBRARY (Med)
3211 Providence Dr.   Phone: (907) 786-1870
Anchorage, AK 99508   Stanley Truelson, Dir.
Founded: 1968. **Staff:** Prof 3; Other 5. **Subjects:** Medicine and related health sciences. **Services:** Interlibrary loans; copying; SDI; Table of Contents; library open to public with restrictions on services. **Automated Operations:** Computerized cataloging. **Computerized Information Services:** MEDLINE. **Networks/Consortia:** Member of WLN. **Remarks:** Administered by Alaska State Division of State Libraries & Museums. **Staff:** Patricia A. Yenney, Libn. I; Loretta Andress, Libn. I.

★15123★

UNIVERSITY OF ALASKA, ANCHORAGE - ANCHORAGE URBAN OBSERVATORY - LIBRARY (Soc Sci)
3210 Providence Dr.   Phone: (907) 786-1760
Anchorage, AK 99508   Susan Gorski
Staff: Prof 1. **Subjects:** Alaska socioeconomic and cultural studies; oil and gas development; public opinion. **Holdings:** 30 books; 2500 reports; 10,000 clippings; 250,000 card images of data. **Services:** Copying; library open to

public.

★15124★

UNIVERSITY OF ALASKA, ANCHORAGE - ARCTIC ENVIRONMENTAL INFORMATION AND DATA CENTER (Env-Cons)
707 A St.   Phone: (907) 279-4523
Anchorage, AK 99501   Barbara J. Sokolov, Supv., Info.Sci. Group
Founded: 1972. **Staff:** Prof 2; Other 5. **Subjects:** Alaska - environment, geology, fisheries, glaciology, land use planning, oil pollution, energy resources, coastal zone management; Arctic research; Alaska climate records. **Special Collections:** Depository for Arctic Petroleum Operators Association Reports. **Holdings:** 4700 books; reports and pamphlets; maps; 1500 photos on Alaska; 4500 microfiche. **Subscriptions:** 66 journals and other serials. **Services:** Copying; center open to public. **Automated Operations:** Current research profile for Alaska; Alaska bibliographies, searchable by region and/or subject. **Computerized Information Services:** Internal databases. **Publications:** Current Research Profile for Alaska, annual. **Special Indexes:** Comprehensive Bibliography and Index of Environmental Information: a) Along the Three Alternative Gas Pipeline Routes, 1978/79 (one volume and supplement); b) For the Beluga-Susitna, Nenana and Western Arctic Coal Fields, 1978/79 (three volumes); c) For the Northwest and Lower Yukon-Kuskokwim Areas of Alaska, 1979 (one volume); Prince William Sound: Annotated Bibliography and Index, 1979; Alaska Coastal Bibliography and Index: Statewide, 1982.

★15125★

UNIVERSITY OF ALASKA, ANCHORAGE - LIBRARY - ARCHIVES & MANUSCRIPTS DEPARTMENT (Hist; Rare Book)
3211 Providence Dr.   Phone: (907) 786-1849
Anchorage, AK 99508   Dennis F. Walle, Archv./Mss.Cur.
Founded: 1979. **Staff:** Prof 1; Other 3. **Special Collections:** University archives and historical manuscripts (200 items); social, political and cultural organizations, business records, papers of individuals and families (1000 cubic feet). **Services:** Department open to public with restrictions. **Publications:** Annual Report; Guide to R.T. Harris Collection; occasional guides to specific collections. **Special Catalogs:** Unpublished inhouse guide containing collection inventories.

★15126★

UNIVERSITY OF ALASKA, ANCHORAGE - LIBRARY - GOVERNMENT DOCUMENTS (Info Sci)
3211 Providence Dr.   Phone: (907) 786-1874
Anchorage, AK 99508   Alden Rollins, Gov.Docs.Libn.
Founded: 1973. **Special Collections:** Government documents. **Holdings:** 121,972 volumes. **Services:** Interlibrary loans; copying; library open to public. **Computerized Information Services:** DIALOG, SDC; University of Alaska Computer Network (internal database). **Networks/Consortia:** Member of Alaska Library Network; WLN. **Publications:** Census Alaska: Number of Inhabitants, 1792-1970. **Special Indexes:** Anchorage Documents File, 1970 to present.

★15127★

UNIVERSITY OF ALASKA, ANCHORAGE - LIBRARY - SPECIAL COLLECTIONS (Hist; Music)
3211 Providence Dr.   Phone: (907) 786-1873
Anchorage, AK 99508   John Summerhill, Supv., Spec.Coll.
Founded: 1973. **Special Collections:** Alaskana Collection; sheet music collection; rare books; maps. **Holdings:** Figures not available. **Services:** Interlibrary loans; copying; collections open to public. **Computerized Information Services:** DIALOG, SDC; University of Alaska Computer Network (internal database). **Networks/Consortia:** Member of Alaska Library Network; WLN. **Special Catalogs:** Catalog of Sheet Music at the UAA Library.

★15128★

UNIVERSITY OF ALBERTA - BOREAL INSTITUTE FOR NORTHERN STUDIES - LIBRARY (Geog-Map)
CW 401 Biological Sciences Bldg.   Phone: (403) 432-4409
Edmonton, AB, Canada T6G 2E9   Mrs. G.A. Cooke, Libn.
Founded: 1960. **Staff:** Prof 2; Other 15. **Subjects:** All subjects (including fiction) as they relate to the arctic and cold regions of the world, with particular emphasis on Canada's boreal forest and northern regions, Alaska, and other circumpolar countries; biological, physiological and physical science coverage of Antarctica. **Special Collections:** Boreal Institute Vertical Files on Northern Affairs (newspaper clippings); native and northern newspapers; consultant reports on pipelines, MacKenzie Highway and community development in Northwest Territories; Hudson Bay Factor (Louis Romanet) papers; documents used in the compilation of the Peace Athabasca Delta Project. **Holdings:** 44,000 volumes (including pamphlets); 11,000 maps; 27 films; 47 filmstrips; 190 sound recordings; 1000 reels of microfilm; 15,000 microfiche. **Subscriptions:** 808 journals and other serials. **Services:**

Interlibrary loans; copying; library open to public. **Automated Operations:** Computerized cataloging. **Computerized Information Services:** DIALOG, SDC, CAN/OLE, QL Systems; Boreal (internal database). **Publications:** Boreal Institute Vertical Files on Northern Affairs (a microfiche clipping service with KWIC index on paper), monthly - by subscription; Library Bulletin, monthly - by subscription or exchange; Northern Titles KWIC Index, monthly - by exchange or subscription, also available online through QL Systems; Yukon Bibliography Update, irregular - for purchase, also available online through QL Systems; BINS bibliographic series, monthly - by exchange or subscription; occasional publications; annual report. **Special Indexes:** KWIC Index to newspaper clippings; Northern Titles KWIC index. **Staff:** Robin Minion, Asst.Libn.

★15129★

UNIVERSITY OF ALBERTA - BRUCE PEEL SPECIAL COLLECTIONS LIBRARY (Rare Book; Hum; Hist)
Rutherford South   Phone: (403) 432-5998
Edmonton, AB, Canada T6G 2J8   John W. Charles, Spec.Coll.Libn.
Founded: 1964. **Staff:** Prof 2; Other 4. **Subjects:** Western Canadiana; English literature, 1600-1930; Canadian drama; European drama, 17th and 18th century; California history; European history, 1500-1900. **Special Collections:** John Bunyan (early editions; 245 volumes); Milton (early editions; 165 volumes); Salzburg (16th-18th century editions of canon law and ecclesiastical works; 700 volumes); Cuala Press (250 items including broadsides); D.H. Lawrence (early editions; 290 volumes); Grabhorn Press (600 volumes); 19th century English theater playbills (900); Curwen Press (in-house collection of their publications, 1920-1956; 1000 volumes, 3000 ephemera, scrapbooks, posters); Gregory Javitch Collection on North American Indians (ceremonial dances, documents relating to the acquisition of Indian territory; 600 volumes). **Holdings:** 48,650 books; 11,400 volumes of University of Alberta dissertations and theses (complete collection); 700 volumes of Rutherford pamphlets (Canadiana); 44 boxes of various Canadian manuscripts and documents; 48 boxes and volumes of notes on Alberta folklore and local history; 39 boxes and photocopies of manuscripts in Georg Kaiser Archiv; Black Sparrow Press archives, 1966-1970 (archives for first 94 publications); 10 volumes and 350 manuscripts in Ariel Bension Collection (Sephardic manuscripts and texts); 153 volumes of Wordsworth (facsimiles of Dove Cottage manuscripts). **Services:** Interlibrary loans; copying (both restricted); library open to public. **Automated Operations:** Computerized circulation. **Computerized Information Services:** DIALOG, SDC, QL Systems, CAN/OLE, UTLAS. **Publications:** News from the Rare Book Room, irregular; University of Alberta Theses, semiannual - both available on request. **Staff:** Jeannine Green, Spec.Coll.libn.

★15130★

UNIVERSITY OF ALBERTA - CENTRE FOR THE STUDY OF MENTAL RETARDATION - LIBRARY (Med)
6-123A Education II   Phone: (403) 432-4439
Edmonton, AB, Canada T6G 2E1   Heidi Julien, Sec.
Founded: 1967. **Subjects:** Biology, medicine, neurology, psychology, education. **Holdings:** 250 books and bound periodical volumes; 50 other cataloged items. **Services:** Interlibrary loans; library not open to public.

★15131★

UNIVERSITY OF ALBERTA - COMPUTING SCIENCE READING ROOM (Sci-Tech);Comp Sci)
604 General Services Bldg.   Phone: (403) 432-3977
Edmonton, AB, Canada T6G 2H1   Jennifer Penny, Libn.
Founded: 1968. **Staff:** Prof 1; Other 6. **Subjects:** Computing science, mathematics, statistics, engineering. **Holdings:** 4500 books; 500 bound periodical volumes; 3500 technical reports; 1000 IBM manuals; 200 theses. **Subscriptions:** 200 journals and other serials. **Services:** Interlibrary loans; room open to public with special borrower's card. **Automated Operations:** Computerized cataloging.

UNIVERSITY OF ALBERTA - DEPT. OF COMPARATIVE LITERATURE - AFRICAN LITERATURE ASSOCIATION
See: African Literature Association

★15132★

UNIVERSITY OF ALBERTA - DEPT. OF SOCIOLOGY - STANLEY TAYLOR SOCIOLOGY READING ROOM (Soc Sci)
Dept. of Sociology   Phone: (403) 439-1604
Edmonton, AB, Canada T6G 2H4   Kerri Calvert, Lib.Asst.
Staff: Prof 1; Other 1. **Subjects:** Demography, criminology, statistics and methodology. **Special Collections:** Canada, U.S. and International census. **Holdings:** 7537 books; 521 bound periodical volumes; 250 dissertations; 10 unbound reports; 2000 reprints and conference papers; 300 maps. **Subscriptions:** 182 journals and other serials. **Services:** Room open to public for reference use only. **Publications:** List of publications - available upon

request. **Formerly:** Its Population Research Library.

★15133★
UNIVERSITY OF ALBERTA - DIVISION OF EDUCATIONAL RESEARCH - TECHNICAL LIBRARY (Educ; Comp Sci)
3-104 Education North   Phone: (403) 432-3762
Edmonton, AB, Canada T6G 2G5   Dr. Steve Hunka, Coord.
Staff: 1. **Subjects:** Computers, computer-based instruction, statistics and research design. **Holdings:** 4824 books and bound periodical volumes; 40 VF drawers. **Subscriptions:** 50 journals and other serials; 10 newspapers. **Services:** Interlibrary loans; copying; library open to students for reference use. **Automated Operations:** Computerized cataloging. **Staff:** Anna Hammond, Libn.

★15134★
UNIVERSITY OF ALBERTA - FACULTE ST-JEAN - BIBLIOTHEQUE (Area-Ethnic)
8406 91st St.   Phone: (403) 468-1254
Edmonton, AB, Canada T6C 4G9   Juliette J. Henley, Act.Hd.Libn.
Founded: 1910. **Staff:** Prof 2; Other 4. **Subjects:** History - French-Canadian, Western Canadian; ethnology; literature - French, French-Canadian; French language resources in education, arts, humanities, social sciences and science. **Special Collections:** French government documents (1500 items). **Holdings:** 35,000 books (mainly in French); 1106 bound periodical volumes; 1 filing drawer of microfilm; 1 filing box of microfiche. **Subscriptions:** 200 journals and other serials; 12 newspapers. **Services:** Interlibrary loans; library open to public for reference use only. **Staff:** Usha Prasada-Kole, Cat.

★15135★
UNIVERSITY OF ALBERTA - H.T. COUTTS LIBRARY (Educ)
Faculty of Education Bldg.   Phone: (403) 432-2371
Edmonton, AB, Canada T6G 2G5   Madge MacGown, Hd.
Founded: 1945. **Staff:** Prof 9; Other 33. **Subjects:** Education, teaching materials, children's literature. **Special Collections:** Historical Textbook Collection; William Gray Reading Collection (on microfiche). **Holdings:** 209,479 volumes; 228,287 titles on microfiche; 6214 reels of microfilm; 27,920 titles of nonbook materials; 5844 newspaper clippings; 2508 theses; ERIC, ONTERIS and MICROLOG education collection microfiche. **Subscriptions:** 930 journals. **Services:** Interlibrary loans; copying; library open to public for reference use only. **Automated Operations:** Computerized cataloging, acquisitions and circulation. **Computerized Information Services:** DIALOG, SDC, BRS, SPIRES. **Special Indexes:** Alberta Education Index; Index to Faculty of Education theses held by library (computer printout); picture and art slide indexes; index to record collection; index to curriculum guides. **Staff:** Josie Tong, Tech.Serv.Libn.; Maryon McClary, Cat.; Deborah Dancik, Educ.Libn.; Kathleen De Long, Asst.Educ.Libn.; John White, Asst.Educ.Libn.; Leslie LaFleur, Curric.Libn.; Faye Maxwell, Asst.Curric.Libn.; Frances Mielke, Asst.Curric.Libn.

★15136★
UNIVERSITY OF ALBERTA - HUMANITIES AND SOCIAL SCIENCES LIBRARY (Hum; Soc Sci)
Rutherford North   Phone: (403) 432-3794
Edmonton, AB, Canada T6G 2J4   B.J. Busch, Area Coord.
Founded: 1972. **Staff:** Prof 11; Other 47. **Subjects:** Humanities, social sciences, business and commerce, physical education, library science. **Holdings:** 1 million volumes; 120,000 bound periodical volumes; 1 million microforms. **Subscriptions:** 4149 journals and other serials; 131 newspapers. **Services:** Interlibrary loans; copying; SDI; library open to public for reference use only. **Automated Operations:** Computerized cataloging, acquisitions, serials and circulation. **Computerized Information Services:** DIALOG, SDC, BRS, International Development Research Centre (IDRC), Info Globe; internal database. Performs searches on cost recovery basis for outside users. **Publications:** Library Guide. **Special Indexes:** Business Annual Reports Index. **Staff:** Mrs. G. Lewis, Coll.Coord.; D. Poff, Ref.Coord.; B. Champion, Ref.Libn.; G. Olson, Ref.Libn.; W. Quoika-Stanka, Ref.Libn.; D. Sharplin, Ref.Libn.; K. West, Ref.Libn.; K. Wikeley, Ref.Libn.; L. Moffat, Per./Microforms Libn.

★15137★
UNIVERSITY OF ALBERTA - HUMANITIES AND SOCIAL SCIENCES LIBRARY - GOVERNMENT PUBLICATIONS (Soc Sci)
    Phone: (403) 432-3776
Edmonton, AB, Canada T6G 2J8   Sally Manwaring, Hd., Govt.Pubn.Lib.
Staff: Prof 2; Other 5. **Subjects:** Economics, political science, business, history, sociology. **Holdings:** 290,000 books and bound periodical volumes; 335,000 microforms. **Services:** Interlibrary loans; copying; library open to public. **Automated Operations:** Computerized serials. **Publications:** Statistical sources in the library, a selected bibliography, 1974; Descriptive

guide to government publications of Canada, Great Britain, the United States and international bodies, 1977; Selected Accessions List, bimonthly - for internal distribution and by request. **Special Indexes:** KWOC index to current acquisitions, 1981 to present. **Remarks:** Contains the holdings of the former Periodicals and Microforms Centre. **Staff:** Suzan Hebditch, Asst.Govt.Pubns.Libn.

UNIVERSITY OF ALBERTA - INSTITUTE OF LAW RESEARCH AND REFORM
See: Institute of Law Research and Reform

UNIVERSITY OF ALBERTA - INTERNATIONAL OMBUDSMAN INSTITUTE
See: International Ombudsman Institute

★15138★
UNIVERSITY OF ALBERTA - JOHN W. SCOTT HEALTH SCIENCES LIBRARY (Med)
    Phone: (403) 432-3791
Edmonton, AB, Canada T6G 2B7   Sylvia R. Chetner, Act. Area Coord.
Staff: Prof 5; Other 7. **Subjects:** Medicine, nursing, dentistry, pharmacy, rehabilitation medicine, health services administration. **Special Collections:** Rawlinson Historical Collection (1000 volumes). **Holdings:** 142,178 books and bound periodical volumes; 2230 microfiche. **Subscriptions:** 2017 journals and other serials. **Services:** Interlibrary loans; copying; SDI; library open to public with restrictions. **Automated Operations:** Computerized cataloging, acquisitions and circulation. **Computerized Information Services:** DIALOG, SDC, BRS, CAN/OLE, MEDLINE. **Special Indexes:** Index to Alberta Medical Bulletin (card). **Staff:** Lea K. Starr, Ref.Libn.; J. Buckingham, Ref.Libn.

★15139★
UNIVERSITY OF ALBERTA - LAW LIBRARY (Law)
Law Centre   Phone: (403) 432-5560
Edmonton, AB, Canada T6G 2H5   Lillian MacPherson, Law Libn.
Founded: 1951. **Staff:** Prof 5; Other 12. **Subjects:** Anglo-American law. **Holdings:** 200,000 volumes. **Subscriptions:** 3479 journals and other serials. **Services:** Interlibrary loans; copying; library open to public with restrictions. **Automated Operations:** Computerized cataloging and acquisitions. **Computerized Information Services:** DIALOG, QL Systems. **Staff:** Lillian MacPherson, Law Libn.; S. Patricia Rempel, Ref.; Christine Ewaskiw, Tech.Serv./Ref.; Audrey Eikeland, Ref.

★15140★
UNIVERSITY OF ALBERTA - NUCLEAR PHYSICS LIBRARY (Sci-Tech)
Nuclear Research Center   Phone: (403) 432-3637
Edmonton, AB, Canada T6G 2N5   G.M.T. Tratt, Sec.
Staff: 2. **Subjects:** Nuclear physics. **Holdings:** 757 books; 1645 bound periodical volumes; 102 theses; 543 preprints and reprints of internal research reports; 1222 external reports. **Subscriptions:** 33 journals and other serials. **Services:** Library open to public. **Publications:** Progress Report, annual.

★15141★
UNIVERSITY OF ALBERTA - PERIODICALS AND MICROFORMS CENTRE
Rutherford South, 2nd Fl.
Edmonton, AB, Canada T6G 2J8
Defunct. Absorbed by the University of Alberta - Humanities & Social Science Library.

UNIVERSITY OF ALBERTA - ST. STEPHEN'S COLLEGE
See: St. Stephen's College

★15142★
UNIVERSITY OF ALBERTA - SCIENCE AND TECHNOLOGY LIBRARY (Sci-Tech)
    Phone: (403) 432-2728
Edmonton, AB, Canada T6G 2J8   Margo Young, Area Coord.
Founded: 1963. **Staff:** Prof 6; Other 8. **Subjects:** Pure sciences, engineering, agriculture, forestry, household economics. **Holdings:** 400,000 books and bound periodical volumes. **Subscriptions:** 5000 journals and other serials. **Services:** Interlibrary loans; copying; SDI; library open to public. **Automated Operations:** Computerized acquisitions, serials and circulation. **Computerized Information Services:** DIALOG, SDC, CAN/OLE, QL Systems, BRS, Info Globe. Performs searches on a flat fee basis for outside users. **Special Indexes:** KWOC Index for Government Documents (microfiche). **Staff:** David Jones, Coll.Coord.; Vera Kunda, Ref.Coord.; Susan Moysa, Ref.Libn.; John Miletich, Ref.Libn.; Sandra Campbell, Ref.Libn.; Marianne Jamieson, Ref.Libn.

★15143★

UNIVERSITY OF ALBERTA - UNIVERSITY MAP COLLECTION (Geog-Map)
B-7 H.M. Tory Bldg.   Phone: (403) 432-4760
Edmonton, AB, Canada T6G 2H4   Ron Whistance-Smith, Univ. Map Curator
Staff: Prof 1; Other 2. **Subjects:** Topography, cartography. **Holdings:** 2200 atlases; 334 gazetteers; 950 reference books; 40 titles of bound periodical volumes; 2150 technical reports; 200,000 maps; 700,000 air photographs; historical maps of Western Canada; 165 reels of microfilm of air photos; 992 air photo indexes on microfiche. **Subscriptions:** 173 journals and other serials. **Services:** Interlibrary loans; collection open to public with restrictions. **Publications:** Accessions list, bimonthly - available upon request.

★15144★

UNIVERSITY OF ARIZONA - ARID LANDS INFORMATION CENTER (Sci-Tech)
845 N. Park Ave.   Phone: (602) 621-7897
Tucson, AZ 85719   Deirdre Campbell, Libn.
Staff: Prof 2; Other 3. **Subjects:** Deserts of the world - international research, economic crops, remote sensing. **Special Collections:** Consortium for International Development (moisture utilization; 25,000 documents). **Holdings:** 6000 volumes; 100 environmental impact statements; 350 serial publications. **Services:** Copying; SDI; center open to public with restrictions. **Computerized Information Services:** DIALOG, DOE/RECON. Performs searches on fee basis. **Publications:** List of publications - available on request.

★15145★

UNIVERSITY OF ARIZONA - ARIZONA BUREAU OF GEOLOGY & MINERAL TECHNOLOGY LIBRARY (Sci-Tech; Energy)
845 N. Park Ave.   Phone: (602) 621-7906
Tucson, AZ 85719   Thomas G. McGarvin, Res.Asst.
Founded: 1915. **Staff:** 1. **Subjects:** Geology, mining. **Special Collections:** Mining Company and Mine Collection (20 VF drawers of newspaper clippings); geology of Arizona (20 VF drawers of newspaper clippings and other materials); Arizona Bureau of Geology and Mineral Technology (open file reports; 5 VF drawers). **Holdings:** 300 books; 500 bound periodical volumes; 400 open file reports of the U.S. Geological Survey and the U.S.Bureau of Mining; 125 dissertations and theses; 8000 government documents; 15 VF drawers and 4 map cases of maps. **Subscriptions:** 10 journals and other serials. **Services:** Copying; SDI; library open to public for reference use only.

★15146★

UNIVERSITY OF ARIZONA - ARIZONA COOPERATIVE WILDLIFE RESEARCH UNIT - RESEARCH COLLECTION (Env-Cons)
218 Biological Sciences Bldg.   Phone: (602) 621-7297
Tucson, AZ 85721   Valery Catt, Unit Sec.
Founded: 1951. **Staff:** Prof 4. **Subjects:** Mammals, birds, plants, wildlife, soils, water. **Holdings:** 125 volumes; 482 boxes of reports, manuscripts, pamphlets, reprints.

★15147★

UNIVERSITY OF ARIZONA - ARIZONA HEALTH SCIENCES CENTER LIBRARY (Med)
1501 N. Campbell Ave.   Phone: (602) 626-6121
Tucson, AZ 85724   Thomas D. Higdon, Libn.
Founded: 1967. **Staff:** Prof 14; Other 20. **Subjects:** Medicine and allied health sciences; preclinical sciences. **Special Collections:** Hugh H. Smith Collection/Public Health (300 volumes). **Holdings:** 59,538 books; 78,082 bound periodical volumes; 2905 titles of media software; 20 drawers of microforms. **Subscriptions:** 3332 journals and other serials. **Services:** Interlibrary loans; copying; library open to public. **Automated Operations:** Computerized cataloging and circulation. **Computerized Information Services:** DIALOG, BRS. Performs searches on cost recovery basis. Contact Person: Fred Heidenreich, 626-7724. **Networks/Consortia:** Member of AMIGOS Bibliographic Council, Inc.; Pacific Southwest Regional Medical Library Service (PSRMLS). **Publications:** Media Software Titles (subject list) 1983, annual supplement; Serials Holdings, 1983, annual supplement; Bulletin, bimonthly. **Staff:** Bertha R. Almagro, Asst.Libn./Proc.; Anita T. Glassmeyer, Media Libn.; Jeanette C. McCray, Assoc.Libn/Hd., Pub.Serv.; Fred Heidenreich, Hd., Ref.Serv.; Marilyn Martam, Hd., Loan Serv.

★15148★

UNIVERSITY OF ARIZONA - ARIZONA STATE MUSEUM LIBRARY (Soc Sci; Art)
                    Phone: (602) 626-4695
Tucson, AZ 85721   Hans Bart, Musm.Libn.
Founded: 1958. **Staff:** Prof 1; Other 3. **Subjects:** Southwestern anthropology and museology. **Special Collections:** Kelemen Collection of Latin American art and architecture (1000 items). **Holdings:** 35,000 volumes; 500 bound periodical volumes; 2000 folders of archival material. **Subscriptions:**

100 journals and other serials. **Services:** Interlibrary loans; copying; library open to public.

★15149★

UNIVERSITY OF ARIZONA - CENTER FOR CREATIVE PHOTOGRAPHY (Art)
843 E. University Blvd.   Phone: (602) 626-4636
Tucson, AZ 85719   Terence Pitts, Cur., Photo Archv.
Founded: 1975. **Staff:** Prof 5; Other 9. **Subjects:** Photography. **Holdings:** 8000 books; 1000 bound periodical volumes; 600 reels of microfilm; 36 feet of biographical files; 300 tapes of video oral history; photographic archives, including those of Ansel Adams. **Subscriptions:** 50 journals and other serials. **Services:** Interlibrary loans; copying; center open to public. **Automated Operations:** Computerized cataloging. **Computerized Information Services:** OCLC. **Publications:** The Archive, irregular. **Staff:** Amy Stark, Archv.Libn.; Nancy Solomon, Pubns.Coord.; James Engeart, Dir.; Lawrence Fong, Registrar.

★15150★

UNIVERSITY OF ARIZONA - COLLEGE OF ARCHITECTURE LIBRARY (Art; Plan)
                    Phone: (602) 626-2498
Tucson, AZ 85721   Kathryn Wayne, Libn.
Founded: 1961. **Staff:** Prof 1; Other 4. **Subjects:** Architecture, urban planning, building technology, historic preservation. **Special Collections:** Arizona Architectural Archives (12,000 original drawings of early Arizona buildings). **Holdings:** 10,000 books; 1600 bound periodical volumes; 24,500 slides. **Subscriptions:** 140 journals and other serials. **Services:** Copying; library open to public for reference use only. **Publications:** College of Architecture Library Newsletter/Booklist, bimonthly - free.

★15151★

UNIVERSITY OF ARIZONA - COLLEGE OF LAW LIBRARY (Law)†
                    Phone: (602) 626-1413
Tucson, AZ 85721   Ronald L. Cherry, Dir.
Founded: 1915. **Staff:** Prof 7; Other 6. **Subjects:** Law. **Special Collections:** Natural resources; law relating to American Indians; Latin American law. **Holdings:** 142,879 volumes; 48,223 volumes in microform. **Subscriptions:** 2715 journals and other serials; 5 newspapers. **Services:** Interlibrary loans; copying; library open to public. **Automated Operations:** Computerized cataloging. **Staff:** Jean Humphrey, Asst.Libn., Tech.Serv.; Edward White, Asst.Libn., Pub.Serv.; Eugenio Revilla, Asst.Libn., Foreign; Carol G. Elliott, Cat.; Patricia Misaghi, Acq.; Bruce Palmer, Cat.

★15152★

UNIVERSITY OF ARIZONA - DIVISION OF ECONOMIC AND BUSINESS RESEARCH - LIBRARY (Bus-Fin)
College of Business
& Public Administration   Phone: (602) 621-2109
Tucson, AZ 85721   Holly A. Penix, Lib.Asst.
Staff: Prof 1; Other 3. **Subjects:** Economic, demographic and industrial data for Arizona; energy; employment; labor and productivity; travel and tourism. **Special Collections:** Regional econometric models for Pima and Maricopa counties and state of Arizona. **Holdings:** 7300 items. **Subscriptions:** 359 journals and other serials; 6 newspapers. **Services:** Library open to public for reference use only. **Computerized Information Services:** Arizona Economic Indicators Database (internal database).

★15153★

UNIVERSITY OF ARIZONA - DIVISION OF MEDIA & INSTRUCTIONAL SERVICES - FILM LIBRARY (Aud-Vis)
Audiovisual Bldg.   Phone: (602) 621-3282
Tucson, AZ 85721   Katherine Holsinger, Mgr.
Founded: 1919. **Staff:** Prof 1; Other 6. **Special Collections:** Archive Film Collection (2500 16mm film titles); archive collection of television commercials; Gallagher Memorial Film Collection. **Holdings:** 7500 16mm motion pictures in active collection. **Services:** Films available for rental; library open to public. **Networks/Consortia:** Member of Consortium of University Film Centers (CUFC). **Publications:** Catalog; Newsletter. **Special Catalogs:** Film rental catalog.

★15154★

UNIVERSITY OF ARIZONA ENVIRONMENTAL PSYCHOLOGY PROGRAM - LIBRARY (Soc Sci)
Dept. of Psychology   Phone: (602) 626-2921
Tucson, AZ 85721   Robert B. Bechtel, Dir., Env.Psych.
Founded: 1980. **Staff:** Prof 2; Other 1. **Subjects:** Environmental psychology, behavior and environment, post occupancy evaluations. **Special Collections:** Edward T. Hall Library (2529 items). **Holdings:** 1200 books; 100 bound periodical volumes; 3500 other items. **Subscriptions:** 7 journals and other serials. **Services:** Interlibrary loans; copying; library open to public with

permission from psychology office. **Special Catalogs:** Environmental Research and Development Foundation and Hall Library card catalogs.

★15155★
UNIVERSITY OF ARIZONA - ENVIRONMENTAL RESEARCH LABORATORY - LIBRARY (Env-Cons)
Tucson International Airport Phone: (602) 621-7962
Tucson, AZ 85706 Susan Morales, Info.Spec.
Staff: Prof 1. **Subjects:** Aquaculture, salt tolerant crops, controlled environment agriculture, solar energy. **Holdings:** 900 books. **Subscriptions:** 92 journals and other serials. **Services:** Interlibrary loans; copying; library open to public for reference use only. **Automated Operations:** Computerized cataloging. **Computerized Information Services:** DIALOG. **Networks/Consortia:** Member of Arizona Online Users Group.

★15156★
UNIVERSITY OF ARIZONA - GOVERNMENT DOCUMENTS DEPARTMENT (Info Sci)
University Library Phone: (602) 621-4871
Tucson, AZ 85721 Cynthia E. Bower, Hd.Doc.Libn.
Founded: 1907. **Staff:** Prof 2; Other 6. **Subjects:** U.S. business and economics, environmental studies, American history, politics and government, foreign relations, health care, education, law enforcement and criminal justice. **Special Collections:** Selected holdings of National Archives microfilm (5000 reels); U.S. Congressional hearings and committee prints, 1869-1969 (75,000 microfiche). **Holdings:** 795,000 printed documents; 250,000 ERIC microfiche; 500,000 other microfiche; 6200 reels of microfilm. **Subscriptions:** 3200 journals and other serials. **Services:** Interlibrary loans; copying; department open to public. **Automated Operations:** Computerized circulation. **Computerized Information Services:** DIALOG, OCLC, BRS. Performs free searches. **Publications:** Documents Despatch, bimonthly - free upon request. **Special Indexes:** Geographic index to environmental impact statements (card file). **Staff:** Robert P. Mitchell, Intl.Doc.Libn.

★15157★
UNIVERSITY OF ARIZONA - INSTITUTE OF ATMOSPHERIC PHYSICS LIBRARY (Sci-Tech)
PAS Bldg., Rm. 542
Tucson, AZ 85721 Christine Hanrahan, Libn.
Staff: Prof 1. **Subjects:** Physical and dynamical meteorology, cloud physics, atmospheric dynamics, thunderstorm electricity, micrometeorology. **Special Collections:** Manuscripts, publications and library of Dr. James E. McDonald. **Holdings:** 3000 volumes. **Subscriptions:** 55 journals and other serials. **Services:** Copying; library open to public for reference use only.

★15158★
UNIVERSITY OF ARIZONA - LIBRARY SCIENCE COLLECTION (Info Sci)
Graduate Library School
1515 E. First Phone: (602) 621-3383
Tucson, AZ 85721 Cecil W. Wellborn, Hd.Libn.
Staff: Prof 1; Other 3. **Subjects:** Libraries, library organization, books, book binding and printing, cataloging, children's literature. **Special Collections:** Historical Children's Collection. **Holdings:** 12,680 books; 1931 bound periodical volumes; 7 drawers of pamphlets and newsletters; 1 drawer of library school catalogs, library guides and handbooks, masters' theses. **Subscriptions:** 568 journals and other serials. **Services:** Interlibrary loans; copying; collection open to public.

★15159★
UNIVERSITY OF ARIZONA - MAP COLLECTION (Geog-Map)
University Library Phone: (602) 621-2596
Tucson, AZ 85721 James Minton, Hd. Map Libn.
Founded: 1955. **Staff:** Prof 3; Other 1. **Subjects:** Geology, mines and mineral resources, history, topography, climate, water resources. **Special Collections:** Frank A. Schilling Military Collection (military post of the Southwest; 60 maps); Maurice Garland Fulton Collection (history of the Southwest; 59 maps). **Holdings:** 4608 books; 288 bound periodical volumes; 165,000 sheet maps; 16,381 aerial photographs and 13 globes; 7 drawers of pamphlets; 930 microfiche; 60 relief models; 11 reels of microfilm of sheet maps. **Subscriptions:** 39 journals and other serials. **Services:** Interlibrary loans; copying; collection open to public. **Automated Operations:** Computerized cataloging. **Computerized Information Services:** OCLC. **Publications:** UA Map News Monthly - free upon request. **Special Indexes:** A Guide for Purchasing Maps of Arizona (book); listing of place names in Arizona counties (book). **Staff:** Linda D. Cottrell, Map Cat.Libn.; Dale Steele, Map Ref.Libn.

★15160★
UNIVERSITY OF ARIZONA - MEDIA CENTER (Aud-Vis)
Library Phone: (602) 621-3441
Tucson, AZ 85721 Bonnie L. Woollet, Hd. Media Libn.
Founded: 1977. **Staff:** Prof 1; Other 6. **Subjects:** Nonprint materials for elementary through college levels, school textbooks. **Holdings:** 19,000 juvenile trade books; 11,700 textbooks; 9000 nonprint titles; 450 reference books and serials. **Services:** Center open to public. **Automated Operations:** Computerized cataloging and circulation. **Publications:** VISUALS, quarterly newsletter - free upon request.

★15161★
UNIVERSITY OF ARIZONA - MUSIC COLLECTION (Mus)
Phone: (602) 626-2140
Tucson, AZ 85721 Dorman H. Smith, Hd. Music Libn.
Founded: 1959. **Staff:** Prof 2; Other 4. **Subjects:** Music - classical, ethnic, folk, popular. **Special Collections:** National Flute Association Collection; International Trombone Association Resource Library; Arizona and Southwest; historical popular sheet music. **Holdings:** 85,000 scores; 25,000 phonograph records and tapes; microforms. **Subscriptions:** 205 journals and other serials. **Services:** Interlibrary loans; copying; collection open to public. **Automated Operations:** Computerized circulation. **Special Indexes:** Song, piano and jazz indexes (card). **Remarks:** Music books and journals housed separately.

★15162★
UNIVERSITY OF ARIZONA - OFFICE OF ARID LANDS STUDIES - BIORESOURCES RESEARCH LIBRARY (Energy)
250 E. Valencia Phone: (602) 621-7928
Tucson, AZ 85706 Pamela Portwood, Lib.Asst.
Staff: Prof 1; Other 2. **Subjects:** Energy - resource development, research, biomass production and conversion, solar. **Holdings:** 100 books; 700 other cataloged items. **Subscriptions:** 12 journals and other serials. **Services:** Copying; library open to public for reference use only. **Computerized Information Services:** DIALOG. Performs searches on cost recovery basis. Contact Person: Deirdre Campbell, 621-7897. **Staff:** Deirdre Campbell, Libn.

★15163★
UNIVERSITY OF ARIZONA - OPTICAL SCIENCES CENTER - READING ROOM (Sci-Tech)†
Phone: (602) 626-3143
Tucson, AZ 85721 Dr. Hyatt Gibbs, Supv.
Founded: 1968. **Staff:** Prof 2. **Subjects:** Optics, optical physics, optical engineering. **Holdings:** 3100 books; 400 bound periodical volumes; 175 theses and dissertations. **Subscriptions:** 48 journals and other serials. **Services:** Copying; room open to public with the approval of the supervisor. **Staff:** Michele Phillips, Documentarian.

★15164★
UNIVERSITY OF ARIZONA - ORIENTAL STUDIES COLLECTION (Area-Ethnic)
University Library Phone: (602) 621-6380
Tucson, AZ 85721 Mary J. McWhorter, Act.Hd.Libn.
Founded: 1964. **Staff:** Prof 2; Other 5. **Subjects:** Social studies and humanities of China, Japan, S. Asia and Middle East; vernacular language materials - Chinese, Japanese, Arabic, Hindi, Urdu, Panjabi, Persian, Turkish. **Holdings:** 102,000 books and bound periodical volumes; 1141 reels of microfilm. **Subscriptions:** 870 journals and other serials; 75 newspapers. **Services:** Interlibrary loans; copying; collection open to public by permission. **Automated Operations:** Computerized circulation. **Staff:** John B. Liu, Oriental Stud.Libn.Gene Hsiao, Cat.Libn.

★15165★
UNIVERSITY OF ARIZONA - POETRY CENTER (Hum)
1086 N. Highland Ave. Phone: (602) 621-2462
Tucson, AZ 85719 Lois Shelton, Dir.
Founded: 1960. **Staff:** Prof 1; Other 1. **Subjects:** Poetry. **Holdings:** 11,000 books and periodicals; 500 phonograph records and tapes. **Subscriptions:** 190 journals and other serials. **Services:** Center open to public; sponsors a series of poetry readings annually. **Publications:** Creative Writing Newsletter, 4/year.

★15166★
UNIVERSITY OF ARIZONA - SCIENCE-ENGINEERING LIBRARY (Sci-Tech)
Phone: (602) 621-6394
Tucson, AZ 85721 Shelley E. Phipps, Hd.Libn.
Founded: 1963. **Staff:** Prof 7; Other 7. **Subjects:** Agriculture, astronomy, biology, chemistry, computer science, engineering, forestry, geology, hydrology, mathematics, mining and metallurgy, optical science, physics. **Special Collections:** Arid lands. **Holdings:** 350,000 volumes; 1 million microforms; 25,000 U.S. government documents (hard copy); 1700

pamphlets. **Subscriptions:** 9000 journals and other serials. **Services:** Interlibrary loans; copying; SDI; library open to public. **Automated Operations:** Computerized circulation. **Computerized Information Services:** DIALOG, BRS, Pergamon InfoLine Ltd., OCLC, Questel. Performs searches on cost recovery basis. **Networks/Consortia:** Member of AMIGOS Bibliographic Council, Inc. **Publications:** SEL News; New Accessions List - for distribution to interested faculty. **Remarks:** An additional telephone number is 621-6384. **Staff:** Charlene B. Morse, Sci.Engr.Ref.Libn.; Robert W. Mautner, Sci.Engr.Ref.Libn.; Douglas E. Jones, Sci.Engr.Ref.Libn.; Susanne Redalje, Sci.Engr.Ref.Libn.; Jeanne J. Pfander, Sci.Engr.Ref.Libn.; Christine Sherratt, Sci.Engr.Ref.Libn.

★15167★

UNIVERSITY OF ARIZONA - SPACE IMAGERY CENTER (Sci-Tech)
Lunar & Planetary Laboratory　　　Phone: (602) 621-4861
Tucson, AZ 85721　　　Gail S. Georgenson, Res.Libn.
Founded: 1977. **Staff:** Prof 1; Other 2. **Subjects:** Space photography, planetary sciences. **Holdings:** 750,000 images of planets and satellites taken from earth-based telescopes and from spacecraft; 1000 maps; 23 atlases; 3000 35mm slides. **Services:** Center open to public with restrictions. **Automated Operations:** Computerized cataloging; videodisc retrieval system.

★15168★

UNIVERSITY OF ARIZONA - SPECIAL COLLECTIONS DEPARTMENT (Hist; Hum)†
University Library　　　Phone: (602) 621-6423
Tucson, AZ 85721　　　Louis A. Hieb, Hd.Libn.
Founded: 1959. **Staff:** Prof 3; Other 3. **Subjects:** Arizona, University of Arizona archives, Southwest, science fiction, history of science. **Special Collections:** Frank Holme Collection; Thomas Wood Stevens Collection; Lewis W. Douglas Papers; War Relocation Authority Papers; Hubbell Trading Post Papers; Bukowski and Wakoski Poetry Collections. **Holdings:** 70,000 volumes; 500 manuscript collections. **Services:** Copying; department open to public.

★15169★

UNIVERSITY OF ARKANSAS, FAYETTEVILLE - CHEMISTRY LIBRARY (Sci-Tech; Comp Sci)
Chemistry Bldg.　　　Phone: (501) 575-4601
Fayetteville, AR 72701　　　Carolyn DeLille, Libn.
Staff: Prof 1; Other 4. **Subjects:** Chemistry, mathematics, physics, chemical technology, computer science. **Holdings:** 8997 books; 11,532 bound periodical volumes. **Subscriptions:** 253 journals and other serials. **Services:** Interlibrary loans; copying; library open to public.

★15170★

UNIVERSITY OF ARKANSAS, FAYETTEVILLE - FINE ARTS LIBRARY (Art)
　　　Phone: (501) 575-4708
Fayetteville, AR 72701　　　Joyce M. Clinkscales, Libn.
Staff: Prof 1; Other 16. **Subjects:** Art, architecture, music, city planning, interior design, landscape architecture. **Special Collections:** Edward Durrell Stone papers; William Grant Still papers. **Holdings:** 38,500 books; 5000 bound periodical volumes; 138 reels of microfilm; 15 slide sets. **Subscriptions:** 200 journals and other serials. **Services:** Interlibrary loans; copying; SDI; library open to public. **Computerized Information Services:** OCLC. **Networks/Consortia:** Member of AMIGOS Bibliographic Council, Inc. **Remarks:** The special collections, recordings, and some rare books are housed in Mullins Library.

★15171★

UNIVERSITY OF ARKANSAS, FAYETTEVILLE - LAW LIBRARY (Law)
　　　Phone: (501) 575-5604
Fayetteville, AR 72701　　　George E. Skinner, Dir.
Founded: 1924. **Staff:** Prof 4; Other 4. **Subjects:** Law. **Special Collections:** Selective government depository. **Holdings:** 177,000 books; 30,000 bound periodical volumes. **Subscriptions:** 550 journals and other serials. **Services:** Interlibrary loans; copying; library open to public. **Computerized Information Services:** LEXIS, Westlaw.

★15172★

UNIVERSITY OF ARKANSAS, FAYETTEVILLE - SPECIAL COLLECTIONS DIVISION (Hist)
　　　Phone: (501) 575-4101
Fayetteville, AR 72701　　　Michael J. Dabrishus, Cur.
Staff: Prof 3; Other 6. **Subjects:** Arkansas - history, politics, culture and folklore; Ozark folklore. **Special Collections:** John Gould Fletcher Collection (1983 volumes); Otto Ernest Rayburn Library of Folklore (838 volumes); Dime Novel Collection (1630 items); Haldeman-Julius Little Blue Books (2404 items). **Holdings:** 40,299 books; 11,980 bound periodical volumes; 6500

linear feet of manuscripts; 200 linear feet of university archives; 4150 photographs; 250 rare maps. **Subscriptions:** 425 journals and other serials. **Services:** Interlibrary loans; copying; library open to public with restrictions. **Computerized Information Services:** OCLC. **Networks/Consortia:** Member of AMIGOS Bibliographic Council, Inc. **Special Catalogs:** A Guide to Selected Manuscripts Collections in the University of Arkansas Library, 1976; card catalog of published titles; unpublished finding aids to manuscript collections. **Special Indexes:** Index to Arkansas periodicals (card). **Staff:** Deborah K. McAnallen, Asst.Libn.Ethel C. Simpson, Asst.Libn.

★15173★

UNIVERSITY OF ARKANSAS, FAYETTEVILLE - TECHNOLOGY CAMPUS LIBRARY (Sci-Tech; Comp Sci)
1201 McAlmont St.
Box 3017　　　Phone: (501) 373-2754
Little Rock, AR 72203　　　Brent A. Nelson, Libn.
Founded: 1958. **Staff:** Prof 1; Other 1. **Subjects:** Electronics, engineering, chemistry, physics. **Holdings:** 14,178 books; 5283 bound periodical volumes; 7 VF drawers of pamphlets, documents and clippings. **Subscriptions:** 308 journals and other serials. **Services:** Interlibrary loans; copying; library open to public.

★15174★

UNIVERSITY OF ARKANSAS AT LITTLE ROCK - CENTER FOR LIBRARY & INFORMATION SCIENCE EDUCATION & RES. (CLISER) (Info Sci)
Library Suite 507
33rd & University　　　Phone: (501) 569-3421
Little Rock, AR 72204　　　Donald D. Foos, Dir.
Founded: 1982. **Staff:** Prof 2; Other 1. **Subjects:** Information - marketing, retrieval; systems - analysis, design. **Holdings:** 4000 books; 1000 bound periodical volumes; 500 other cataloged items. **Subscriptions:** 20 journals and other serials. **Services:** Interlibrary loans; copying; library open to public. **Automated Operations:** Computerized cataloging, acquisitions, and serials. **Computerized Information Services:** BRS, DIALOG, Educational Resources Information Center, OCLC. Performs searches on cost recovery basis. **Networks/Consortia:** Member of AMIGOS. **Publications:** CLISER occasional papers. **Staff:** Dr. Ed Howie, Res.Assoc.

★15175★

UNIVERSITY OF ARKANSAS AT LITTLE ROCK - PULASKI COUNTY LAW LIBRARY (Law)
400 W. Markham　　　Phone: (501) 371-1071
Little Rock, AR 72201　　　Ruth H. Brunson, Dir.
Founded: 1965. **Staff:** Prof 6; Other 5. **Subjects:** Law. **Holdings:** 112,000 books; 900 cassettes. **Subscriptions:** 1074 journals and other serials. **Services:** Interlibrary loans; copying; library open to public. **Staff:** Melanie Nelson, Acq.; Linda Cross, Cat.; Dana Davis, Ref.Libn.;Pauline Ghidotti, Asst.Dir.

★15176★

UNIVERSITY OF ARKANSAS FOR MEDICAL SCIENCES - MEDICAL SCIENCES LIBRARY (Med)
4301 W. Markham　　　Phone: (501) 661-5980
Little Rock, AR 72205　　　Rose Hogan, Dir.
Founded: 1879. **Staff:** Prof 13; Other 25. **Subjects:** Medical sciences. **Holdings:** 128,000 books and bound periodical volumes; 1800 AV materials. **Subscriptions:** 2700 journals and other serials. **Services:** Interlibrary loans; copying; library open to public for reference use only. **Automated Operations:** Computerized cataloging and serials. **Computerized Information Services:** OCLC, MEDLINE. **Networks/Consortia:** Member of AMIGOS Bibliographic Council, Inc.; TALON. **Staff:** Neil Kelley, Coord., Pub.Serv.; Mary Ryan, Coord., Tech.Serv.; Sally Kasalko, Ref.Libn.; Jean Ann Moles, Ser.Libn.; Jeffrey Baskin, AV Libn.; Edwina Walls, Hist. of Med.Libn.; Margaret Ann Johnson, ILL Libn.; Amanda Saar, Circ.Libn.; Nancy Turpentine, Assoc.Ref.Libn.; Jan North, Monographs Libn.; Janet Mitcham, Assoc. Monographs Libn.; Leo Clougherty, Assoc.Ref.Libn.

★15177★

UNIVERSITY OF ARKANSAS FOR MEDICAL SCIENCES - NORTHWEST ARKANSAS HEALTH EDUCATION CENTER - LIBRARY (Med)
1125 N. College　　　Phone: (501) 521-7615
Fayetteville, AR 72701　　　Connie M. Wilson, Libn.
Founded: 1975. **Staff:** Prof 1; Other 1. **Subjects:** Medicine, nursing, and allied health sciences. **Holdings:** 1500 books; 3260 bound periodical volumes. **Subscriptions:** 168 journals and other serials. **Services:** Interlibrary loans; copying; SDI; library open to public for reference use only. **Automated Operations:** Computerized cataloging. **Computerized Information Services:** MEDLINE, BRS, OCLC. **Networks/Consortia:** Member of Northwest Arkansas Shared Audio-Visual Medical Library; Arkansas AHEC Consortium.

Publications: From the Shelf, irregular - mailing list basis. **Special Catalogs:** Library Guide. **Remarks:** Library has been designated as the regional information center for the Northwest Arkansas area and serves health professionals in an eleven county area. It is located at Washington Regional Medical Center where it provides services to hospital staff, family practice residents and medical students. **Staff:** Carol Martin, Asst.Libn.

★15178★
UNIVERSITY OF ARKANSAS, MONTICELLO - LIBRARY - SPECIAL COLLECTIONS (Hist; Info Sci)
Box 3599   Phone: (501) 367-6811
Monticello, AR 71655   William F. Droessler, Libn.
Special Collections: Arkansas Collection (1000 items and miscellaneous pamphlets); government documents (75,000). **Services:** Interlibrary loans; copying; library open to public. **Automated Operations:** Computerized cataloging and ILL.

★15179★
UNIVERSITY OF ARKANSAS, PINE BLUFF - JOHN BROWN WATSON MEMORIAL LIBRARY (Educ; Hum)†
N. Cedar St.
U.S. Hwy. 79   Phone: (501) 541-6825
Pine Bluff, AR 71601   E.J. Fontenette, Libn.
Founded: 1938. **Staff:** 1. **Subjects:** History and biography, emigration, sociology, literature, slavery and emancipation, education, music, religion, economics. **Special Collections:** Afro-American Literature; Paul Laurence Dunbar Papers (9 reels of microfilm). **Holdings:** 4615 books; 65 bound periodical volumes; 73 reels of microfilm of the Pittsburgh Courier; 4 recordings; 4 films; 18 overhead transparencies; periodicals on microfilm. **Subscriptions:** 41 journals and other serials; 10 newspapers. **Services:** Interlibrary loans; copying; library open to public. **Computerized Information Services:** OCLC. **Networks/Consortia:** Member of AMIGOS Bibliographic Council, Inc.

★15180★
UNIVERSITY OF BALTIMORE - LANGSDALE LIBRARY (Bus-Fin; Soc Sci)
1420 Maryland Ave.   Phone: (301) 625-3067
Baltimore, MD 21201   William Newman, Lib.Dir.
Staff: Prof 12; Other 17. **Subjects:** Business, public administration, political science, psychology. **Special Collections:** Herwood Accounting Collection (1200 volumes); Current Urban Documents (microfiche); U.S. Government Documents Depository. **Holdings:** 200,000 books; 10,000 bound periodical volumes; 25,000 items in microform; 5000 photographs; 1500 cubic feet of archival material. **Subscriptions:** 800 journals and other serials; 20 newspapers. **Services:** Interlibrary loans; copying; library open to public. **Automated Operations:** Computerized cataloging and circulation. **Computerized Information Services:** DIALOG, SDC, OCLC. **Networks/Consortia:** Member of CAPCON.

★15181★
UNIVERSITY OF BALTIMORE - LANGSDALE LIBRARY - SPECIAL COLLECTIONS DEPARTMENT (Plan; Soc Sci)
1304 St. Paul St.   Phone: (301) 625-3135
Baltimore, MD 21202   Dr. W. Theodore Durr, Dir.
Staff: Prof 2; Other 2. **Subjects:** Planning and urban renewal, housing and community development, social welfare, family planning, business, church related activity. **Special Collections:** Oral histories; 55 collections of records received from organizations and associations important to the economic, political and social development of the Baltimore region. **Holdings:** 5500 linear feet of manuscripts and archives. **Services:** Copying; center open to public. **Automated Operations:** Computerized cataloging. **Computerized Information Services:** Online systems. **Publications:** Urban Information Thesaurus; The Records of Baltimore's Private Organizations. **Formerly:** University of Baltimore - Baltimore Region Institutional Studies Center (BRISC). **Staff:** Adele Newburger, Archv.; Sherry Watkins, Archv.

★15182★
UNIVERSITY OF BALTIMORE - LAW LIBRARY (Law)
1415 Maryland Ave.   Phone: (301) 625-3400
Baltimore, MD 21201   Emily R. Greenberg, Dir.
Founded: 1925. **Staff:** Prof 5; Other 7. **Subjects:** Anglo-American law. **Holdings:** 100,000 books; 37,000 microforms. **Subscriptions:** 1700 journals and other serials. **Services:** Interlibrary loans; copying; SDI; library open to members of Maryland Bar. **Computerized Information Services:** OCLC. **Networks/Consortia:** Member of CAPCON. **Staff:** Ann Wiley Van Hassel, Assoc.Libn.; Patricia Behles, Govt.Doc.Libn.Dwight King, Ref.Libn.; Jane Cupit, Ref.Libn.; Nancy Quental, Tech.Serv.Libn.

★15183★
UNIVERSITY OF BRIDGEPORT - MAGNUS WAHLSTROM LIBRARY - SPECIAL COLLECTIONS (Hum)
126 Park Ave.   Phone: (203) 576-4740
Bridgeport, CT 06601   Judith Lin Hunt, Univ.Libn.
Holdings: McKew Parr Memorial Collection (exploration); Starr Collection (English literature); graphic arts; Socialist-Labor Movement; Lincolniana (manuscripts; clippings; photographs); health sciences. **Services:** Interlibrary loans; collections open to public. **Automated Operations:** Computerized cataloging and ILL. **Computerized Information Services:** BRS, OCLC. Performs searches on cost recovery basis. Contact Person: Carol Harker, 576-4747. **Networks/Consortia:** Member of NELINET; Southwestern Connecticut Library Council. **Staff:** Carol Harker, Hd., Database Serv.

★15184★
UNIVERSITY OF BRIDGEPORT - SCHOOL OF LAW - LAW LIBRARY (Law)
126 Park Ave.   Phone: (203) 576-4056
Bridgeport, CT 06601   Madeleine J. Wilken, Prof./Dir.,Law Info.Serv.
Staff: Prof 6; Other 8. **Subjects:** Law - federal, state and international. **Holdings:** 175,000 volumes; legal treatises; journals; government documents. **Services:** Interlibrary loans; library open to public with restrictions. **Automated Operations:** Computerized cataloging and acquisitions. **Computerized Information Services:** LEXIS, NEXIS, DIALOG, Auto-Cite. **Networks/Consortia:** Member of NELINET; New England Law Library Consortium (NELLC). **Staff:** Ann DeVeaux, Asst.Libn., Pub.Serv.; Ana Tulumello, Ref.Libn.; Theresa Fu, Cat.Libn.; Beth Mobley, Asst.Libn., Tech.Serv.

★15185★
UNIVERSITY OF BRITISH COLUMBIA - ASIAN STUDIES LIBRARY (Area-Ethnic)
1871 W. Mall   Phone: (604) 228-2427
Vancouver, BC, Canada V6T 1W5   Tung-King Ng, Hd.
Founded: 1960. **Staff:** Prof 3; Other 3. **Subjects:** East Asia (mainly Chinese and Japanese) - history, classics, language, literature, philosophy, Buddhism, fine arts, archeology, economics, political science, sociology, anthropology, education. **Special Collections:** P'u-pan Collection (45,000 volumes in Chinese, including 320 editions of the 12th-17th centuries; 270 gazetteers). **Holdings:** 226,840 volumes in East Asian languages; 27,897 volumes in Indic languages; 2463 periodical titles of Japanese government publications; 3634 reels of microfilm; 7243 microfiche. **Subscriptions:** 703 Chinese and Japanese journals and other serials; 22 Chinese and Japanese newspapers. **Services:** Interlibrary loans; copying; library open to public for reference use only; annual fee required for circulation. **Automated Operations:** Computerized cataloging, acquisitions and serials. **Computerized Information Services:** UTLAS. **Publications:** Reference lists, irregular. **Special Catalogs:** A descriptive catalog of valuable manuscripts and rare books from China (P'u-pan Collection) by Dr. Yi-t'ung Wang (book form, mimeographed, 1959); title index to P'u-pan Collection (vernacular, on cards); Bibliography on the History of the Chinese Book and Calligraphy (book form, 1970); Periodicals in Asian Studies (book form, revised edition 1971; 3rd edition, 1979). **Staff:** Tsuneharu Gonnami, Japanese Ref.Libn.; Shui-Yim Tse, Chinese Ref.Libn.

★15186★
UNIVERSITY OF BRITISH COLUMBIA - BIOMEDICAL BRANCH LIBRARY (Med)
Vancouver General Hospital
700 W. 10th Ave.   Phone: (604) 875-4505
Vancouver, BC, Canada V5Z 1L5   George C. Freeman, Hd., Biomed.Br.
Founded: 1952. **Staff:** Prof 2; Other 5. **Subjects:** Clinical medicine. **Holdings:** 10,306 books; 16,533 bound periodical volumes. **Subscriptions:** 580 journals and other serials. **Services:** Interlibrary loans (through the university's Woodward Biomedical Library); copying; library open to public for reference use only. **Automated Operations:** Computerized circulation. **Computerized Information Services:** NLM, BRS, DIALOG. **Staff:** Nancy Forbes, Ref.Libn.

★15187★
UNIVERSITY OF BRITISH COLUMBIA - CENTRE FOR HUMAN SETTLEMENTS - AV LIBRARY
Vancouver, BC, Canada V6T 1W5
Defunct

★15188★
UNIVERSITY OF BRITISH COLUMBIA - CHARLES CRANE MEMORIAL LIBRARY (Aud-Vis)
1874 East Mall   Phone: (604) 228-6111
Vancouver, BC, Canada V6T 1W5   Paul E. Thiele, Libn. & Hd.
Founded: 1968. **Subjects:** University and college texts, reference materials,

literature, research and reports for the blind, visually impaired and handicapped nonprint readers. **Special Collections:** Electronic, optical and mechanical reading aids for the blind; Crane ABC - Alternate Book Centre. **Holdings:** 40,000 talking books on cassette and reel, 25,000 braille volumes; 300 large print books; 500 printed books on blindness and disability. **Subscriptions:** 12 journals and other serials (recorded, braille, large print and ordinary print). **Services:** Interlibrary loans; search and location service of books and materials for the blind and handicapped; sales of duplicate copies of talking books; recordings of books on demand (Crane Library Recording Centre has nine sound studios, high speed duplicating and mixing facilities). **Computerized Information Services:** BRS, ABLEDATA, DOBIS. **Publications:** Crane Works in Progress, monthly (computer-produced); FUNSTUFF: Recreational and Leisure Materials in the Crane Collection (1982). **Special Catalogs:** Crane Library Microfiche Catalogue. **Staff:** Judith C. Thiele, Ref. & Coll.Libn.

★15189★

UNIVERSITY OF BRITISH COLUMBIA - CURRICULUM LABORATORY (Educ)
Scarfe Bldg., 2125 Main Mall   Phone: (604) 228-5378
Vancouver, BC, Canada V6T 1Z5   Howard Hurt, Hd.
Staff: Prof 3; Other 11. **Subjects:** Educational theory and methods, children's literature. **Holdings:** 80,000 books; 6000 bound periodical volumes; 500 slide sets; 28 drawers of pamphlets; 1000 kits; 10,000 pictures; 200 jackdaws; 1500 posters; 2000 transparencies; 100 maps; 3000 filmstrips; 3000 audiotapes; 430 videotapes. **Subscriptions:** 600 journals and other serials. **Services:** Interlibrary loans; copying; SDI; open to public for reference use only. **Automated Operations:** Computerized acquisitions, serials and circulation. **Publications:** Orientation brochure; bibliographies. **Staff:** Pat Dunn, Ref.Libn.; Jeanne Naslund, Ref.Libn.

★15190★

UNIVERSITY OF BRITISH COLUMBIA - DATA LIBRARY (Info Sci; Comp Sci)
6356 Agricultural Rd., Rm. 206   Phone: (604) 228-5587
Vancouver, BC, Canada V6T 1W5   Ms. Laine Ruus, Hd., Data Lib.
Founded: 1972. **Staff:** Prof 2; Other 1. **Subjects:** Social sciences, humanities, sciences. **Special Collections:** Canada census, 1961, 1966, 1971, 1976, 1981; Canadian Institute of Public Opinion surveys (300 sub-files of data). **Holdings:** 1000 books; 2500 files and sub-files of machine-readable data; 1500 codebooks. **Subscriptions:** 31 journals and other serials. **Services:** Copying of data files where contracts allow; library open to public with restrictions on some files. **Computerized Information Services:** Internal databases. **Networks/Consortia:** Member of Roper Center. **Special Catalogs:** Data Library Catalogue (COM) - free upon request. **Remarks:** The Data Library, jointly operated by the UBC Library and the UBC Computing Centre, acquires, organizes and services a collection of nonbibliographic data in machine-readable form. **Staff:** Ms. S. Adach, Data Lib. Programmer.

★15191★

UNIVERSITY OF BRITISH COLUMBIA - DEPARTMENT OF GEOGRAPHY - MAP AND AIR PHOTO CENTRE (Geog-Map)
2075 Wesbrook Pl.   Phone: (604) 228-3048
Vancouver, BC, Canada V6T 1W5   Rosemary J. Hadley, Map Libn.
Staff: Prof 1. **Subjects:** Maps, air photography. **Special Collections:** Tri-Met air photo coverage of British Columbia; provincial/federal air photo indexes for British Columbia. **Holdings:** 165,643 air photos; 10,735 air photo index maps; 79,483 maps. **Services:** Interlibrary loans (limited); center open to public. **Staff:** Dr. A.L. Farley, Assoc.Prof. & Supv.

★15192★

UNIVERSITY OF BRITISH COLUMBIA - ERIC W. HAMBER LIBRARY (Med)
Children's Hospital
4480 Oak St.   Phone: (604) 875-2154
Vancouver, BC, Canada V6H 3V4   Ann M.A. Nelson, Libn.
Founded: 1982. **Staff:** Prof 1; Other 5. **Subjects:** Clinical medicine, pediatrics, obstetrics and gynecology. **Holdings:** 3000 books. **Subscriptions:** 430 journals and other serials. **Services:** Interlibrary loans; copying; SDI; library open to public. **Automated Operations:** Computerized cataloging, acquisitions and circulation. **Computerized Information Services:** DIALOG, BRS, NLM. **Networks/Consortia:** Member of Health Sciences Library Network.

★15193★

UNIVERSITY OF BRITISH COLUMBIA - FINE ARTS DIVISION (Art)
University Library, 1956 Main Mall   Phone: (604) 228-2720
Vancouver, BC, Canada V6T 1Y3   Melva J. Dwyer, Hd.
Founded: 1948. **Staff:** Prof 3; Other 7. **Subjects:** Fine arts, architecture, community and regional planning, history of costume and dance, artistic photography, fashion design. **Holdings:** 78,000 books; 22,000 bound periodical volumes; 26,000 pamphlets; 3793 photographs; 46,078 pictures;

20,000 exhibition catalogs; 25,000 clippings; 7242 microforms. **Subscriptions:** 425 journals and other serials. **Services:** Interlibrary loans; copying; division open to public with restrictions. **Automated Operations:** Computerized cataloging, serials and circulation. **Computerized Information Services:** DIALOG, Infomart, UTLAS, BRS, Info Globe, New York Times Information Service, MEDLINE. **Publications:** Theses relating to planning and fine arts - free upon request. **Special Catalogs:** Card catalogs of exhibitions, pictures, planning pamphlets and clippings; Canadian art and artists, fashion design and designers. **Staff:** Diana Cooper, Fine Arts Ref.Libn.; Peggy McBride, Planning Ref.Libn.

★15194★

UNIVERSITY OF BRITISH COLUMBIA - GOVERNMENT PUBLICATIONS & MICROFORMS DIVISIONS (Info Sci)
University Library   Phone: (604) 228-2584
Vancouver, BC, Canada V6T 1Y3   Suzanne Dodson, Hd.
Founded: 1964. **Staff:** Prof 5; Other 8. **Subjects:** Publications from all levels of government and from all parts of the world, varied subjects on microforms. **Holdings:** 2.6 million microforms; 550,000 uncataloged government publications. **Subscriptions:** 10,000 journals and other serials (government publications). **Services:** Interlibrary loans; copying; division open to public. **Automated Operations:** Computerized acquisitions, serials and processing. **Special Catalogs:** Union list of all government publications in the library system. **Remarks:** Although the Microforms Division is administered by the same staff as the Government Publications Division, the microform collection covers every possible subject and is not limited to government publications. **Staff:** Theresa Iverson, Proc.Libn.; Constance Fitzpatrick, Ref.Libn.; Mary Luebbe, Ref.Libn.; Susan Mathew, Ref.Libn.

★15195★

UNIVERSITY OF BRITISH COLUMBIA - HUMANITIES AND SOCIAL SCIENCES DIVISION (Hum)
University Library   Phone: (604) 228-2411
Vancouver, BC, Canada V6T 1Y3   Charles F. Forbes, Hd.
Founded: 1984. **Staff:** Prof 10; Other 5. **Subjects:** Religion, language and literature, philosophy, history, linguistics, classical studies, theater, film, sociology, business administration, anthropology, commerce, economics, psychology, geography, political science, education, physical education, library science. **Special Collections:** Slavonic studies; Canadiana (including French Canadiana); Australian literature; Canadian Indians and Eskimos (22,000 VF items). **Holdings:** 42,000 books and bound periodical volumes; annual reports of 800 companies; 21 VF drawers of reports and information on associations. **Subscriptions:** 7700 journals and other serials. **Services:** Interlibrary loans; copying; division open to public. **Computerized Information Services:** DIALOG, SDC, BRS; SDIProfiles (internal database). **Publications:** Reference bibliographies and "Start Here" guides, irregular - distributed on request. **Formed by the Merger of:** Humanities Division Library and the Social Sciences Division Library. **Staff:** Leszek M. Karpinski, Libn.; Helene Redding, Libn.; Elizabeth Caskey, Libn.; Seonaid Lamb, Libn.; Lois Carrier, Libn.; Marilyn Dutton, Libn.; Iza Laponce, Libn.; Dorothy Martin, Libn.; Pia Christensen, Libn.; Joseph Jones, Libn.

★15196★

UNIVERSITY OF BRITISH COLUMBIA - LAW LIBRARY (Law)
1822 East Mall   Phone: (604) 228-2275
Vancouver, BC, Canada V6T 1W5   Thomas J. Shorthouse, Law Libn.
Founded: 1945. **Staff:** Prof 3; Other 12. **Subjects:** Law. **Holdings:** 130,000 books and bound periodical volumes; law reports; statutes; legal journals; monographs. **Subscriptions:** 2900 journals and other serials. **Services:** Interlibrary loans; copying; library open to public with restrictions. **Automated Operations:** Computerized acquisitions and circulation. **Computerized Information Services:** QL Systems. **Staff:** Allen H. Soroka, Asst.Libn., Ref.; Mary E. Mitchell, Ref.Libn.

★15197★

UNIVERSITY OF BRITISH COLUMBIA - MAC MILLAN FORESTRY/ AGRICULTURE LIBRARY (Agri; Sci-Tech)
MacMillan Bldg., 2357 Main Mall   Phone: (604) 228-3445
Vancouver, BC, Canada V6T 2A2   Mary W. Macaree, Hd.
Founded: 1967. **Staff:** Prof 2; Other 4. **Subjects:** Agricultural sciences, aquaculture, food science, forestry and forest products. **Holdings:** 52,000 books and bound periodical volumes; 65,000 unbound government publications; 200 annual reports; 12,060 microfiche; 281 reels of microfilm; 189 slides; 1600 maps. **Subscriptions:** 2100 journals and other serials. **Services:** Interlibrary loans; copying; SDI; library open to public. **Automated Operations:** Computerized serials and circulation. **Computerized Information Services:** CAN/SDI, CAN/OLE, DIALOG; Document Retrieval System (internal database). Performs searches on cost recovery basis. **Staff:** Lore Brongers, Ref.Libn.

★15198★

UNIVERSITY OF BRITISH COLUMBIA - MAP DIVISION (Geog-Map)
University Library
Vancouver, BC, Canada V6T 1Y3   Phone: (604) 228-2231
    Maureen F. Wilson, Hd.
Founded: 1964. **Staff:** Prof 1; Other 3. **Subjects:** Maps, cartography, map librarianship. **Holdings:** 2040 books; 2606 atlases; 376 gazetteers; 125,683 maps; 116 pamphlet boxes of tourist literature and city guides; 226 microfiche. **Services:** Copying; division open to public. **Publications:** Acquisitions list, quarterly; bibliographies, occasional; guide to collections.

★15199★

UNIVERSITY OF BRITISH COLUMBIA - MARJORIE SMITH LIBRARY (Soc Sci)
School of Social Work
6201 Cecil Green Pk. Rd.
Vancouver, BC, Canada V6T 1W5   Phone: (604) 228-2242
    Judith Frye, Hd.
Founded: 1965. **Staff:** Prof 1; Other 2. **Subjects:** Social work, public welfare, social policy, community organization, human behavior. **Holdings:** 16,000 books; 1300 bound periodical volumes; 28 VF drawers of pamphlets and annual reports. **Subscriptions:** 125 journals and other serials. **Services:** Interlibrary loans; copying; library open to public.

★15200★

UNIVERSITY OF BRITISH COLUMBIA - MATHEMATICS LIBRARY (Comp Sci; Sci-Tech)
1984 Main Mall
Vancouver, BC, Canada V6T 1W5   Phone: (604) 228-2667
    Rein J. Brongers, Hd.
Founded: 1966. **Staff:** Prof 1; Other 2. **Subjects:** Mathematics, computer science. **Holdings:** 25,000 books and bound periodical volumes. **Subscriptions:** 350 journals and other serials. **Services:** Interlibrary loans; library open to public.

★15201★

UNIVERSITY OF BRITISH COLUMBIA - MINING & METALLURGICAL READING ROOM (Sci-Tech)
6350 Stores Rd.
Vancouver, BC, Canada V6V 1E4   Phone: (604) 228-2540
    A.E. Hall, Asst.Prof.
Subjects: Mining, mineral processing, geology, physics, chemistry, mathematics. **Holdings:** Figures not available. **Services:** Room open to public for reference use only. **Remarks:** Enquiries should be directed to University Library, 1956 Main Mall, Vancouver, BC V6T 1Y3.

★15202★

UNIVERSITY OF BRITISH COLUMBIA - MUSIC LIBRARY (Mus)
6361 Memorial Rd.
Vancouver, BC, Canada V6T 1W5   Phone: (604) 228-3589
    Hans Burndorfer, Hd.
Staff: Prof 2; Other 2. **Subjects:** Music. **Holdings:** 50,000 books and scores; 3000 reels of microfilm; 10,000 recordings. **Subscriptions:** 150 journals and other serials. **Services:** Interlibrary loans; copying; library open to public. **Staff:** Kirsten Walsh, Music Ref.Libn.

★15203★

UNIVERSITY OF BRITISH COLUMBIA - ST. PAUL'S HOSPITAL HEALTH SCIENCES LIBRARY (Med)
1081 Burrard St.
Vancouver, BC, Canada V6Z 1Y6   Phone: (604) 682-2344
    Barbara J. Saint, Hd.
Founded: 1950. **Staff:** Prof 1; Other 5. **Subjects:** Health sciences. **Holdings:** 3000 books; 200 unbound periodical volumes. **Subscriptions:** 275 journals and other serials. **Services:** Interlibrary loans; copying; SDI; library open to public. **Automated Operations:** Computerized cataloging, acquisitions, serials and circulation. **Computerized Information Services:** DIALOG, BRS, SDC, NLM, CAN/OLE, QL Systems, Institute for Scientific Information (ISI). Performs searches on cost recovery basis. **Publications:** Newsletter, irregular - for internal distribution only. **Special Catalogs:** Periodical holdings (book), annual. **Remarks:** Library was previously a department of the hospital but is now under the administration of University of British Columbia.

★15204★

UNIVERSITY OF BRITISH COLUMBIA - SCHOOL OF LIBRARIANSHIP READING ROOM (Info Sci)
1956 Main Mall, Rm. 831
Vancouver, BC, Canada V6T 1Y3   Phone: (604) 228-2446
    Margaret Burke, Libn.
Founded: 1961. **Staff:** Prof 1. **Subjects:** Librarianship, publishing and book trade. **Holdings:** 5478 books and bound periodical volumes; 20 filing drawers of annual reports, newsletters and publishers' catalogs; 90 pamphlet boxes of course materials. **Subscriptions:** 150 journals and other serials. **Services:** Interlibrary loans; room open to public with restrictions.

★15205★

UNIVERSITY OF BRITISH COLUMBIA - SCIENCE DIVISION (Sci-Tech)
University Library
Vancouver, BC, Canada V6T 1Y3   Phone: (604) 228-3295
    Rein J. Brongers, Hd.
Staff: Prof 4; Other 2. **Subjects:** Chemistry, physics, engineering, mathematics, geology, astronomy. **Special Collections:** Rand Corporation Depository, 1970 to present. **Holdings:** 150,000 volumes. **Subscriptions:** 3000 journals and other serials. **Services:** Interlibrary loans; copying; division open to public. **Computerized Information Services:** CAN/OLE, DIALOG, QL Systems, BRS. **Staff:** Helen Mayoh, Ref.Libn.; Sundaram Venkataraman, Ref.Libn.; Jack McIntosh, Ref.Libn.

★15206★

UNIVERSITY OF BRITISH COLUMBIA - SOCIAL SCIENCES DIVISION
University Library
Vancouver, BC, Canada V6T 1Y3
Defunct. Merged with the University of British Columbia - Humanities Division to form the University of British Columbia - Humanities & Social Sciences Division.

★15207★

UNIVERSITY OF BRITISH COLUMBIA - SPECIAL COLLECTIONS DIVISION (Hist)
University Library
1956 Main Mall
Vancouver, BC, Canada V6T 1Y3   Phone: (604) 228-2521
    Anne Yandle, Hd.
Founded: 1960. **Staff:** Prof 5; Other 4. **Subjects:** Canadian history, travel and literature; Pacific Northwest; early children's literature; historical cartography; 19th century English and Anglo-Irish literature; University of British Columbia; labor and business history. **Special Collections:** Colbeck Collection (English and Anglo-Irish belles lettres; 20,000 books); Robert Burns Collection (700 books); Thomas J. Wise Collection (200 books); University Archives and Historical Manuscripts Collections (5500 linear feet). **Holdings:** 63,000 books and bound periodical volumes; 6000 pamphlets; 7744 maps; 50,000 photographs; 1200 audiotapes; 72 films. **Subscriptions:** 150 journals and other serials. **Services:** Copying; division open to public. **Automated Operations:** Computerized cataloging and serials. **Staff:** Joan Selby, Colbeck Libn.; Laurenda Daniells, Univ.Archv.; George Brandak, Mss.Cur.; Frances Woodward, Ref.Libn.

★15208★

UNIVERSITY OF BRITISH COLUMBIA - SPENCER ENTOMOLOGICAL MUSEUM - LIBRARY (Sci-Tech)
Dept. of Zoology
Vancouver, BC, Canada V6T 2A9   Phone: (604) 228-3379
    G.G.E. Scudder, Dir.
Founded: 1953. **Staff:** Prof 2. **Subjects:** Entomology. **Holdings:** 300 books; 8000 reprints; 50 series of unbound journals. **Services:** Copying; library open to public at the discretion of the director. **Special Catalogs:** Subject catalog for reprints. **Staff:** S. Cannings, Cur.

★15209★

UNIVERSITY OF BRITISH COLUMBIA - WILSON RECORDINGS COLLECTION (Mus)
1958 Main Mall
Vancouver, BC, Canada V6T 1W5   Phone: (604) 228-2534
    Doug Kaye, Hd.
Staff: Prof 1; Other 4. **Subjects:** Literature, music. **Holdings:** 35,000 phonograph records. **Automated Operations:** Computerized cataloging and circulation. **Special Indexes:** Author/composer, title, performer and class indexes on microfiche.

★15210★

UNIVERSITY OF BRITISH COLUMBIA - WOODWARD BIOMEDICAL LIBRARY (Med; Sci-Tech)
2198 Health Sciences Mall
Vancouver, BC, Canada V6T 1W5   Phone: (604) 228-2762
    Anna R. Leith, Hd.
Founded: 1950. **Staff:** Prof 12; Other 35. **Subjects:** Medicine, zoology, botany, dentistry, pharmacy, nursing, rehabilitation medicine, nutrition. **Special Collections:** Historical Collection in Science and Medicine (5000 volumes; pictures; manuscripts; letters; reprints; artifacts). **Holdings:** 140,000 books; 120,000 bound periodical volumes; 18,000 microforms. **Subscriptions:** 4700 journals and other serials. **Services:** Interlibrary loans; copying; SDI; library open to public for reference use only. **Automated Operations:** Computerized acquisitions, serials and circulation. **Computerized Information Services:** NLM, DIALOG, CAN/OLE, BRS, QL Systems. **Staff:** Elsie de Bruijn, Assoc.Libn.; Lynne Hallonquist, Life Sci.Bibliog.; Lee Perry, Historical Coll.; Stephanie Dykstra, Ser.Libn.; Diana Kent, Ref.Libn.; John Cole, Ref.Libn.; Pat Lysyk, Ref.Libn.; William Parker, Ref.Libn.; Florence Doidge, Circ.Libn.; Jim Henderson, Ref.Libn.; Margaret Price, Ref.Libn.

UNIVERSITY OF CALGARY - ARCTIC INSTITUTE OF NORTH AMERICA
See: Arctic Institute of North America

★15211★
UNIVERSITY OF CALGARY - ARTS AND HUMANITIES LIBRARY (Hum)†
2500 University Dr., N.W.   Phone: (403) 284-5976
Calgary, AB, Canada T2N 1N4   Kathy Zimon, Asst. Area Hd./Arts Libn.
Founded: 1966. Staff: Prof 8; Other 13. Subjects: Literature; art; drama; philosophy; religious studies; Germanic, Slavic and Romance languages. Holdings: Figures not available. Services: Interlibrary loans; copying; SDI; library open to public. Automated Operations: Computerized cataloging, acquisitions and circulation. Computerized Information Services: DIALOG, CAN/OLE, QL Systems. Staff: Nora Robbins, Hum.Libn.; Rita Vine, Mus.Libn.; Jan Rosenender; Saundra Lipton; Carolyn Ryder .

★15212★
UNIVERSITY OF CALGARY - CANADIAN INSTITUTE OF RESOURCES LAW - LIBRARY (Law; Energy)
BioSciences Bldg., Rm. 430M   Phone: (403) 282-2569
Calgary, AB, Canada T2N 1N4   Evangeline S. Case, Pubn.Off.
Subjects: Canadian energy regulation, oil and gas law. Holdings: 75 books; 5 book shelves and 2 VF drawers of Canadian regulatory tribunal publications. Subscriptions: 25 journals and other serials. Services: Copying; library open to public with permission.

★15213★
UNIVERSITY OF CALGARY - EDUCATION MATERIALS CENTER (Educ)*
2500 University Dr., N.W.   Phone: (403) 284-5637
Calgary, AB, Canada T2N 1N4   Dr. Philomena Hauck, Dir.
Founded: 1963. Staff: Prof 3; Other 5. Subjects: Teaching methods, elementary and secondary curriculum, school libraries, children's literature. Special Collections: Archive collection of Alberta curriculum guides and texts. Holdings: 55,000 books; 5000 pictures; 1500 phonograph records; 300 video cassettes; 4000 filmstrips; 2500 kits; 3000 slides. Subscriptions: 130 journals and other serials. Services: Copying; center open to public for reference use only. Remarks: Center is maintained by the university's Faculty of Education. Staff: Gudrun Wight, Media Spec.; David Brown, Ref. & Cat.

★15214★
UNIVERSITY OF CALGARY - ENVIRONMENT-SCIENCE-TECHNOLOGY LIBRARY (Sci-Tech; Env-Cons)†
2500 University Dr., N.W.   Phone: (403) 284-5966
Calgary, AB, Canada T2N 1N4   Hazel Fry, Area Hd.
Staff: Prof 6; Other 17. Subjects: Physical and biological sciences, engineering, geology and geophysics, northern studies, environment and architecture, urban and regional planning, mathematics and computing science, nursing. Special Collections: Canadian Architectural Archives. Holdings: Figures not available for books and bound periodical volumes; architectural drawings; maps; air photos; microforms. Subscriptions: 3170 journals and other serials. Services: Interlibrary loans (fee); copying; library open to public. Automated Operations: Computerized cataloging, acquisitions and circulation. Computerized Information Services: DIALOG, CAN/OLE, QL Systems, Stanford Public Information Retrieval System (SPIRES), SDC; NOMADS, Surveying Engineering Database (internal databases). Staff: Valorie Orr, Asst. Area Hd.; Lynda Hall; Yvonne Hinks; Flora Grabowska; Sharon Neary ; Robert Batchelder, Map/Airphoto Libn.; Annalise Walker, Canadian Arch.Archv.

★15215★
UNIVERSITY OF CALGARY - KANANASKIS ENVIRONMENTAL SCIENCES CENTRE - LIBRARY (Env-Cons)
                                             Phone: (403) 284-5355
Seebe, AB, Canada T0L 1X0   Grace LeBel, Libn.
Staff: 1. Subjects: Chemistry, biology, environmental research. Special Collections: Environmental collection. Holdings: 4000 books; 3000 unpublished reports and theses. Subscriptions: 40 journals and other serials. Services: Library not open to public.

★15216★
UNIVERSITY OF CALGARY - LAW LIBRARY (Law)†
2500 University Dr., N.W.   Phone: (403) 284-5090
Calgary, AB, Canada T2N 1N4   Georgia Macrae, Law Libn.
Founded: 1975. Staff: Prof 4; Other 12. Subjects: Law. Holdings: 85,000 books and bound periodical volumes. Subscriptions: 2849 journals and other serials. Services: Interlibrary loans; copying; library open to public. Computerized Information Services: QL Systems; Alberta Statute Citator (internal database). Staff: Don Sanders; Umesh VyasJune Vermeulen .

★15217★
UNIVERSITY OF CALGARY - MEDIA UTILIZATION UNIT & FILM LIBRARY (Aud-Vis)*
2500 University Dr., N.W.   Phone: (403) 284-6146
Calgary, AB, Canada T2N 1N4   Jennie Paine, Mgr.
Founded: 1969. Staff: Prof 2; Other 4. Subjects: Social sciences. Special Collections: Film study collection (243 titles); University of Calgary Public Service programs (183 titles). Holdings: 2050 16mm film titles; 700 videotape titles; 25 slide sets; 8 VF drawers of distributors' catalogs. Subscriptions: 65 journals and other serials. Services: Interlibrary loans; rental service; library open to public with restrictions. Automated Operations: Computerized cataloging. Publications: Media Methods, bimonthly - distributed to faculty members. Special Catalogs: Catalog of film and videotape holdings (book). Staff: Douglas Coughlin, Film Libn.

★15218★
UNIVERSITY OF CALGARY - MEDICAL LIBRARY (Med)†
Health Sciences Centre   Phone: (403) 284-6858
Calgary, AB, Canada T2N 1N4   Andras Kirchner, Med.Libn.
Founded: 1968. Staff: Prof 4; Other 16. Subjects: Health sciences with special emphasis on family practice. Holdings: 71,000 books and bound periodical volumes; 350 microforms; 56 films; 193 videotapes; 105 slide/ tape programs; 2134 cassettes. Subscriptions: 1696 journals and other serials. Services: Interlibrary loans; copying; SDI; library open to public. Automated Operations: Computerized cataloging and acquisitions. Computerized Information Services: DIALOG, MEDLARS. Publications: Recent Acquisition List, quarterly. Staff: Pamela Griffin, Asst.Med.Libn.; M.L. Chan, Hd.Cat.; William Maes, Hd., Pub.Serv.

★15219★
UNIVERSITY OF CALGARY - SOCIAL SCIENCES LIBRARY (Soc Sci)†
2500 University Dr., N.W.   Phone: (403) 284-5965
Calgary, AB, Canada T2N 1N4   Gretchen Ghent, Area Hd.
Founded: 1966. Staff: Prof 9; Other 12. Subjects: History, archeology and classics, management and economics, education, sociology and anthropology, social welfare, psychology, physical education, geography. Holdings: Figures not available. Subscriptions: 2400 journals and other serials; 50 newspapers. Services: Interlibrary loans; copying; SDI; library open to public. Automated Operations: Computerized cataloging, acquisitions and circulation. Computerized Information Services: DIALOG, SDC, CAN/OLE, QL Systems, Info Globe, Dow Jones News/Retrieval, SPIRES; NOMADS (internal database). Remarks: Library maintains the Government Publications Division and newspapers for the entire University of Calgary Libraries. Staff: Shelagh Mikulak, Asst. Area Hd.; Lynn Hendrie; Maurice Lepper; Pauline Mathezer; Margot Millard; Noel Owens; Rhys Williams .

UNIVERSITY OF CALGARY - SPECIAL COLLECTIONS - ANGLICAN ARCHIVES
See: Anglican Church of Canada - Diocese of Calgary - Anglican Archives

★15220★
UNIVERSITY OF CALGARY - SPECIAL COLLECTIONS DIVISION (Hum)†
2500 University Dr., N.W.   Phone: (403) 284-5972
Calgary, AB, Canada T2N 1N4   Apollonia Steele, Spec.Coll.Libn.
Founded: 1966. Staff: Prof 3; Other 3. Subjects: Canadian literature. Special Collections: Papers of Hugh MacLennan, Alice Munro, Mordecai Richler, Brian Moore, W.O. Mitchell, Christie Harris, Robert Kroetsch, Rudy Weibe, George Ryga, Gwen Ringwood, Len Peterson, Michael Cook, Joanna Glass, Earle Birney, George Bowering, Red Lane, Grant MacEwan, James Gray, Bruce Hutchison, Alden Nowlan, Clark Blaise, John Metcalf, Lois Kerr; Morris Surdin (papers; musical scores; Canadian Broadcasting Corporation scripts); archives of Tish, Image and Ariel (literary periodicals); archives of Coach House Press; E.C.W. Press. Holdings: 30,000 books and bound periodical volumes; 875 meters of manuscripts and archives. Subscriptions: 10 journals and other serials. Services: Copying; collections open to public. Automated Operations: Computerized cataloging and acquisitions. Publications: Occasional papers. Staff: Jan Roseneder, Bibliog.; Jean Tener, Archv.; Carolyn Ryder.

★15221★
UNIVERSITY OF CALIFORNIA - KEARNEY AGRICULTURAL CENTER (Agri)
9240 S. Riverbend Ave.   Phone: (209) 646-2794
Parlier, CA 93648   Fred H. Swanson, Act.Dir.
Staff: Prof 30; Other 60. Subjects: Agronomy, agricultural economics, entomology, nematology, plant pathology, pomology, viticulture, vegetable crops, water science, biological control. Holdings: 2000 books; 10,000 reprints. Services: Center open to public by permission. Staff: Kathyrn L. Montanez, Adm.Asst.; Dr. Robert F. Brewer, Chm., Lib.Comm.

★15222★

UNIVERSITY OF CALIFORNIA - LOS ALAMOS NATIONAL LABORATORY - LIBRARY (Sci-Tech; Comp Sci)
MS-P362, Box 1663   Phone: (505) 667-4448
Los Alamos, NM 87545   J. Arthur Freed, Hd.Libn.
Founded: 1943. Staff: Prof 14; Other 26. Subjects: Military and peaceful uses of nuclear energy, physics, chemistry, materials science, engineering, energy, mathematics and computers, astronomy, geology. Special Collections: Biomedicine (40,000 volumes). Holdings: 110,000 books; 200,000 bound periodical volumes; 650,000 technical reports; 500 reels of motion picture film. Subscriptions: 8500 journals and other serials. Services: Interlibrary loans; copying; in-house translation; library open to public on limited schedule. Automated Operations: Computerized serials. Computerized Information Services: DIALOG, SDC, BRS, DOE/RECON, RLIN, NLM, NASA/RECON, DTIC, NEXIS. Publications: What's New; Publications of Los Alamos Research. Special Catalogs: Card catalog for technical reports; computer listing of laboratory sponsored unclassified publications. Staff: Karen Stoll, Dp.Hd.Libn.; Lois Godfrey, Asst.Hd.Libn.; Carol Nielson, Ref.Libn.; Marilyn Treiman, Ref.Libn.; Ann Beyer, Ref.Libn.; Jean Furnish, Ref.Libn.; Carroll Sue Wagner, Ref.Libn.; Betty Burnett, Supv., Main Lib.; Viola Salazar, Asst.Supv., Main Lib.; Dan Baca, Supv., Rpt.Lib.; Judy Young, Asst.Rpt.Libn.; Connie Sheridan, Supv., Tech.Proc.; Theresa Connaughton, Asst.Supv., Tech.Proc.

★15223★

UNIVERSITY OF CALIFORNIA, BERKELEY - ANTHROPOLOGY LIBRARY (Soc Sci)
230 Kroeber Hall   Phone: (415) 642-2400
Berkeley, CA 94720   Dorothy A. Koenig, Libn.
Founded: 1956. Staff: Prof 1; Other 2. Subjects: Anthropology. Holdings: 55,278 volumes; 548 microforms; 10,930 pamphlets. Subscriptions: 1191 journals and other serials. Services: Interlibrary loans (through 307 General Library); copying; library open for reference with restrictions on circulation.

★15224★

UNIVERSITY OF CALIFORNIA, BERKELEY - ASIAN AMERICAN STUDIES LIBRARY (Area-Ethnic)
3407 Dwinelle Hall   Phone: (415) 642-2218
Berkeley, CA 94720   Mrs. Wei Chi Poon, Hd.Libn.
Founded: 1970. Staff: Prof 1; Other 4. Subjects: Asians in the U.S. past and present. Special Collections: Chinese American Research Collection (archival materials in English and Chinese; 20,000 items). Holdings: 35,000 volumes; 3000 slides; 106 videotapes; 16 16mm films. Subscriptions: 123 journals and other serials; 93 newspapers. Services: Library open to public with restrictions on circulation.

★15225★

UNIVERSITY OF CALIFORNIA, BERKELEY - ASTRONOMY-MATHEMATICS-STATISTICS-COMPUTER SCIENCES LIBRARY (Sci-Tech; Comp Sci)
100 Evans Hall   Phone: (415) 642-3381
Berkeley, CA 94720   Kimiyo T. Hom, Libn.
Founded: 1959. Staff: Prof 1; Other 2. Subjects: Astronomy, mathematics (pure and applied), statistics, computer science. Holdings: 54,279 volumes; 2634 photographic plates; 53 manuscripts; 32 maps; 69 microforms; 2932 pamphlets; 3 sound recordings. Subscriptions: 1264 journals and other serials. Services: Interlibrary loans (through 307 General Library); copying; library open to public for reference with restricted circulation.

★15226★

UNIVERSITY OF CALIFORNIA, BERKELEY - BANCROFT LIBRARY (Hist; Rare Book)
  Phone: (415) 642-3781
Berkeley, CA 94720   James D. Hart, Dir.
Founded: 1859. Staff: Prof 19; Other 27. Special Collections: Bancroft Collection (history of western North America, particularly western plains states to the Pacific Coast and from Panama to Alaska with greatest emphasis on California and Mexico); Rare Books (incunabula, 403 items); rare European, English, U.S. and South American imprints; fine printing of all periods and places (emphasis on modern English and American typography, medieval manuscript books and documents, papyri); University Archives; Regional Oral History Office (recollections of persons who have contributed to the development of the West and the nation); Mark Twain Papers (collection of the author's manuscripts, correspondence, related documentary material and the editorial program to publish it); history of science and technology, particularly in California. Holdings: 293,009 volumes; 35.1 million manuscripts; 21,000 maps and atlases; 2.27 million pictures and portraits; 39,932 microforms; 5826 recordings; 72,667 pamphlets; 968 motion pictures. Subscriptions: 1577 journals and other serials. Services: Interlibrary loans (limited to microfilm; through 307 General Library); copying

(limited); library open to public. Automated Operations: Computerized cataloging. Publications: A Guide to the Manuscripts of the Bancroft Library, Volumes 1 and 2, Berkeley, 1963 and 1972; Bancroftiana (newsletter issued for the Friends of the Bancroft Library), 3/year. Special Catalogs: A Catalog of the Bancroft Collection, 1964, and supplements (book).

★15227★

UNIVERSITY OF CALIFORNIA, BERKELEY - BIOCHEMISTRY LIBRARY (Sci-Tech)
430 Biochemistry Bldg.   Phone: (415) 642-5112
Berkeley, CA 94720   Rebecca Martin, Hd.Libn.
Founded: 1950. Staff: 1. Subjects: Biochemistry. Holdings: 8500 volumes. Subscriptions: 165 journals and other serials. Services: Copying; library open for reference with limited circulation.

★15228★

UNIVERSITY OF CALIFORNIA, BERKELEY - BIOLOGY LIBRARY (Sci-Tech)
3503 Life Sciences Bldg.   Phone: (415) 642-2531
Berkeley, CA 94720   Rebecca Martin, Hd.Libn.
Founded: 1930. Staff: Prof 4; Other 8. Subjects: Anatomy, bacteriology, biochemistry, botany, physiology, biology, immunology, medicine, zoology. Special Collections: Rare Book Collection (17th-19th century natural history; 20,000 volumes). Holdings: 215,000 volumes; 44,432 pamphlets and reprints; 8547 reels of microfilm; 5072 microfiche. Subscriptions: 4000 journals and other serials. Services: Interlibrary loans (through 307 General Library); copying; library open to public for reference with restricted circulation. Computerized Information Services: DIALOG, SDC, BRS, NLM, RLIN.

★15229★

UNIVERSITY OF CALIFORNIA, BERKELEY - BOTANICAL GARDEN - LIBRARY (Sci-Tech)
Centennial Dr.   Phone: (415) 642-3343
Berkeley, CA 94720   Dr. James Affolter, Cur.
Staff: Prof 1. Subjects: Horticulture, plant taxonomy, botanical gardens. Holdings: 1000 books; 30 feet of other cataloged items. Subscriptions: 20 journals and other serials. Services: Library not open to public.

★15230★

UNIVERSITY OF CALIFORNIA, BERKELEY - CENTER FOR CHINESE STUDIES - LIBRARY (Area-Ethnic)
12 Barrows Hall, Rm. 64   Phone: (415) 642-6510
Berkeley, CA 94720   Chi-Ping Chen, Libn.
Founded: 1959. Staff: Prof 1; Other 2. Subjects: Social sciences and humanities of Peoples' Republic of China. Special Collections: KEIO Collection (10 drawers of microfilm); Documents of Contemporary China, 1949-1975 (650 microfiche); Chen Cheng Collection (10 drawers of microfilm). Holdings: 31,718 volumes; 40 drawers of microfilm; 3631 items in VF drawers; newspaper clippings. Subscriptions: 210 journals and other serials; 40 newspapers. Services: Interlibrary loans (through 307 General Library); copying; library open to public.

UNIVERSITY OF CALIFORNIA, BERKELEY - CENTER FOR THE STUDY, EDUCATION & ADVANCEMENT OF WOMEN
See: Center for the Study, Education & Advancement of Women

★15231★

UNIVERSITY OF CALIFORNIA, BERKELEY - CHEMISTRY LIBRARY (Sci-Tech)
100 Hildebrand Hall   Phone: (415) 642-3753
Berkeley, CA 94720   George Vdovin, Libn.
Founded: 1948. Staff: Prof 1; Other 1. Subjects: Chemistry - inorganic, organic, physical; chemical kinetics; chemical thermodynamics; chemical engineering; electrochemistry; transport and mass transfer; polymer chemistry. Special Collections: Russian monographs and serials obtained on exchange; U.S. chemical patents (20,000). Holdings: 40,000 volumes; 31,300 microforms; 322 pamphlets. Subscriptions: 700 journals and other serials. Services: Interlibrary loans (through 307 General Library); copying; library open for reference with restricted circulation. Computerized Information Services: DIALOG, BRS.

★15232★

UNIVERSITY OF CALIFORNIA, BERKELEY - CHICANO STUDIES LIBRARY (Area-Ethnic)†
110 Wheeler Hall   Phone: (415) 642-3859
Berkeley, CA 94720   Francisco Garcia-Ayvens, Coord.
Founded: 1970. Staff: 6. Subjects: Chicano, Mexican American, Spanish speaking/surname people in U.S.; Raza; farmworkers; bilingual/bicultural groups. Special Collections: Retrospective Newspaper Collection, 1844-1943; Chicano Art Color Transparencies (4000); Chicano Posters (800).

Holdings: 4300 volumes; 150 bound periodical volumes; 4300 other cataloged items; 1500 microforms; 350 audiotapes; 10 videotapes; 5 films; 5000 slides; 20 maps; 1000 noncurrent journal titles; 150 linear feet of archives. **Subscriptions:** 400 journals and other serials; 75 newspapers. **Services:** Interlibrary loans; library open to public. **Networks/Consortia:** Member of University of California Chicano Information Management Consortium. **Publications:** List of publications - available on request.

★15233★
UNIVERSITY OF CALIFORNIA, BERKELEY - EARTH SCIENCES LIBRARY (Sci-Tech)
230 Earth Sciences Bldg.   Phone: (415) 642-2997
Berkeley, CA 94720   Julie Rinaldi, Act.Hd.
Founded: 1961. **Staff:** Prof 1; Other 2. **Subjects:** Geology, geophysics, seismology, physical geography, paleontology. **Holdings:** 83,202 volumes; 8272 microforms; 2508 pamphlets; 6 sound recordings; 46,579 maps. **Subscriptions:** 2842 journals and other serials. **Services:** Interlibrary loans (through 307 General Library); copying; library open for reference with limited circulation.

★15234★
UNIVERSITY OF CALIFORNIA, BERKELEY - EARTHQUAKE ENGINEERING RESEARCH CENTER LIBRARY (Sci-Tech)
1301 S. 46th St.   Phone: (415) 231-9403
Richmond, CA 94804   S. Joy Svihra, Hd.
Founded: 1972. **Staff:** Prof 2; Other 2. **Subjects:** Engineering - earthquake, civil, geotechnical, structural; geology; seismology; natural hazard mitigation. **Holdings:** 21,000 items including 2050 nonbook materials. **Subscriptions:** 283 journals and other serials. **Services:** Interlibrary loans; copying; SDI; library open to public. **Computerized Information Services:** DIALOG, OCLC; MELVYL (internal database). Performs searches on cost recovery basis. Contact Person: Helen Tseng, 231-9401. **Publications:** Abstract Journal in Earthquake Engineering, annual - by subscription; UCB/EERC reports, irregular - by subscription or single issues; Library Acquisitions Alert, bimonthly - free upon request; EERC News, quarterly - free upon request. **Special Catalogs:** Printed catalog (to 1975). **Remarks:** Library materials are in English, Asian and other Indo-European languages. **Staff:** Helen Tseng, Asst.Libn.

★15235★
UNIVERSITY OF CALIFORNIA, BERKELEY - EAST ASIATIC LIBRARY (Area-Ethnic)
208 Durant Hall   Phone: (415) 642-2556
Berkeley, CA 94720   Donald H. Shively, Hd.
Founded: 1947. **Staff:** Prof 11; Other 14. **Subjects:** Publications in Chinese, Korean and Japanese languages, primarily in the humanities and social sciences. **Special Collections:** Asami Library of Yi dynasty Korean books and manuscripts; Murakami Library of Meiji literature, 1868-1911; Chohyo-kaku collection of Chinese stone and bronze rubbings; Japanese woodblock and lithograph maps (17th to early 20th centuries); Doi Gakken collection of Chinese poetry and prose by Japanese writers; Soshin and Motoori collections of xylographic editions of Tokugawa and early Meiji periods and the Kihon section containing publications of the 100 years prior to World War II; Rare Books Room collection devoted to pre-1644 Chinese and pre-1660 Japanese imprints. **Holdings:** 481,387 volumes; 6892 manuscripts; 2104 Chinese rubbings; 5373 microforms; 1700 old maps; 5050 prints and photographs. **Subscriptions:** 4217 journals and other serials; 36 newspapers. **Services:** Interlibrary loans (through 307 General Library); copying; library open to public with restrictions. **Networks/Consortia:** Member of RLG. **Publications:** Newly Cataloged Books in the East Asiatic Library, monthly. **Special Catalogs:** Book Catalog, 1968, first supplement, 1973; Asami Library, 1969.

★15236★
UNIVERSITY OF CALIFORNIA, BERKELEY - EDUCATION/PSYCHOLOGY LIBRARY (Educ)
2600 Tolman Hall   Phone: (415) 642-4208
Berkeley, CA 94720   Barbara Kornstein, Hd., Lib.
Founded: 1924. **Staff:** Prof 3; Other 5. **Subjects:** Education, psychology and related subjects. **Special Collections:** ERIC microfiche collection; children's and young adult collection. **Holdings:** 110,000 volumes; 297,000 microforms. **Subscriptions:** 2200 journals and other serials. **Services:** Interlibrary loans (through 307 General Library); copying; library open to public. **Computerized Information Services:** DIALOG, BRS, NLM. **Staff:** Sonya Kaufman, Hd., Ref.Serv.

★15237★
UNIVERSITY OF CALIFORNIA, BERKELEY - ENERGY AND RESOURCES PROGRAM - ENERGY INFORMATION CENTER (Energy)†
Rm. 100, Bldg. T-4   Phone: (415) 642-1004
Berkeley, CA 94720   Mari Wilson, Assoc.Libn.
Founded: 1975. **Staff:** Prof 1; Other 1. **Subjects:** Energy policy - U.S. and international, comparative environmental impacts of energy technologies, resource economics, renewable resources, energy conservation - policy and analysis, energy and developing countries, community energy planning, arms control and disarmament. **Special Collections:** NTIS Microfiche, 1975-1978 (energy; 6 VF drawers); U.S. Department of Energy reports (selected titles; 6000). **Holdings:** 3000 books; 2000 pamphlets, articles, charts and graphs. **Subscriptions:** 80 journals and other serials. **Services:** Copying; SDI (for staff only); center open to public for reference use only. **Computerized Information Services:** DOE/RECON. **Networks/Consortia:** Member of Energy Librarians of the Bay Area; Western Information Network on Energy (WINE). **Publications:** Energy Classification Scheme; bibliographies; acquisitions list.

★15238★
UNIVERSITY OF CALIFORNIA, BERKELEY - ENTOMOLOGY LIBRARY (Sci-Tech)
Wellman Hall, Rm. 210   Phone: (415) 642-2030
Berkeley, CA 94720   Nancy Axelrod, Unit Hd.
Founded: 1943. **Staff:** 1. **Subjects:** Entomology, parasitology, helminthology, biological control, insect pathology and related subjects. **Holdings:** 14,500 volumes; 17,050 pamphlets and reprints; 4 sound recordings. **Subscriptions:** 360 journals and other serials. **Services:** Interlibrary loans (through 307 General Library); copying; library open to public for reference with restricted circulation.

★15239★
UNIVERSITY OF CALIFORNIA, BERKELEY - ENVIRONMENTAL DESIGN LIBRARY (Art; Plan)
210 Wurster Hall   Phone: (415) 642-4818
Berkeley, CA 94720   James R. Burch, Act.Hd.
Founded: 1964. **Staff:** Prof 3; Other 3. **Subjects:** Architecture, city and regional planning, landscape architecture. **Holdings:** 150,570 volumes; 6105 microforms; 26,500 pamphlets. **Subscriptions:** 1714 journals and other serials. **Services:** Interlibrary loans (through 307 General Library); copying; library open to public for reference with restricted circulation.

★15240★
UNIVERSITY OF CALIFORNIA, BERKELEY - EXTENSION MEDIA CENTER (Aud-Vis)
2223 Fulton St.   Phone: (415) 642-0460
Berkeley, CA 94720   Olga Knight, Dir.
Founded: 1915. **Staff:** Prof 2; Other 14. **Subjects:** Anthropology, sciences, social studies and social issues, futures studies, education, arts. **Special Collections:** Documentaries; anthropology; education; ecology; ethnic studies; film studies; women. **Holdings:** 4000 films in rental collection; 350 films for sale; 250 videotapes for sale. **Services:** Film rental and preview before purchase; center open to public; rental film distribution limited to continental U.S. **Automated Operations:** Semi-automated film reservation system (CPT); Computerized cataloging. **Networks/Consortia:** Member of Consortium of University Film Centers; Educational Film Library Association. **Publications:** Brochures; newsletters; books; study guides. **Special Catalogs:** Rental catalogs; sales catalogs.

★15241★
UNIVERSITY OF CALIFORNIA, BERKELEY - FOREST PRODUCTS LIBRARY (Sci-Tech)
47th & Hoffman Blvd.   Phone: (415) 231-9549
Richmond, CA 94804   Peter A. Evans, Libn.
Founded: 1963. **Staff:** Prof 1; Other 1. **Subjects:** Wood chemistry, pulp and paper technology, adhesives, wood preservation, timber physics, identification and anatomy of wood. **Holdings:** 8018 books and bound periodical volumes; 4429 pamphlets; 668 microforms. **Subscriptions:** 322 journals and other serials. **Services:** Interlibrary loans (through 307 General Library); copying; SDI; library open to public. **Computerized Information Services:** DIALOG; MELVYL (internal database). **Special Catalogs:** List of FPL staff publications, biennial.

★15242★
UNIVERSITY OF CALIFORNIA, BERKELEY - FORESTRY LIBRARY (Env-Cons)
260 Mulford Hall   Phone: (415) 642-2936
Berkeley, CA 94720   Esther Johnson, Libn.
Founded: 1948. **Staff:** Prof 2; Other 2. **Subjects:** Forestry, conservation, wildlife management and related subjects. **Special Collections:** Metcalf-Fritz Photograph Collection (6400 photographs of western forestry, 1910-1960). **Holdings:** 28,500 volumes; 85 manuscripts; 1800 maps; microforms; 8000 unbound pamphlets. **Subscriptions:** 1370 journals and other serials. **Services:** Interlibrary loans (through 307 General Library); copying; library open to public for reference with restricted circulation. **Computerized Information Services:** DIALOG; MELVYL (internal database). **Staff:** Peter Evans, Ref.Libn.

★15243★

UNIVERSITY OF CALIFORNIA, BERKELEY - GIANNINI FOUNDATION OF AGRICULTURAL ECONOMICS - RESEARCH LIBRARY (Agri)
248 Giannini Hall Phone: (415) 642-7121
Berkeley, CA 94720 Grace Dote, Libn.
Founded: 1930. **Staff:** Prof 1; Other 2. **Subjects:** Agriculture - economics, labor, land utilization, valuation and tenure, marketing and transportation problems, cost of production and marketing studies; water resources economics; conservation of natural resources. **Special Collections:** Federal state market news reports from most major U.S. cities, 1920-1982. **Holdings:** 18,000 volumes; 120,000 pamphlets; 3500 microforms; 140 maps. **Subscriptions:** 3000 journals and other serials. **Services:** Copying; library open to qualified researchers for reference only. **Publications:** Economic research of interest to agriculture, triennial - distributed to mailing list; Material added to the Giannini Foundation Library, 10/year - by subscription.

★15244★

UNIVERSITY OF CALIFORNIA, BERKELEY - GOVERNMENT DOCUMENTS DEPARTMENT (Soc Sci; Info Sci)
General Library Phone: (415) 642-3287
Berkeley, CA 94720 Elizabeth Myers, Hd.
Founded: 1938. **Staff:** Prof 7; Other 14. **Subjects:** National and state government and politics, international government organizations. **Holdings:** 313,000 volumes; 13,000 uncataloged monographs; 294,000 microforms. **Subscriptions:** 31,085 journals and other serials. **Services:** Interlibrary loans (through 307 General Library); copying; department open to public. **Automated Operations:** Computerized acquisitions. **Computerized Information Services:** DIALOG, SDC. **Staff:** Suzanne Gold, Libn./Asst.Hd.; Gail Nichols, Libn.; Deborah Sommer, Assoc.Libn.; Philip Hoehn, Libn./Map Rm.; Jo Ann Brock, Assoc.Libn.; Susan Huff, Asst.Libn.

★15245★

UNIVERSITY OF CALIFORNIA, BERKELEY - GRADUATE SCHOOL OF JOURNALISM - LIBRARY (Info Sci)†
140 North Gate Hall Phone: (415) 642-0415
Berkeley, CA 94720 David W. Brown, Libn.
Founded: 1977. **Staff:** Prof 1; Other 1. **Subjects:** Print journalism, photojournalism, broadcasting. **Special Collections:** Major authors collection (225 volumes). **Holdings:** 2225 books; 300 bound periodical volumes; 250 theses; 4 VF drawers of pamphlets; unbound periodicals; newspapers. **Subscriptions:** 75 journals and other serials; 25 newspapers. **Services:** Copying; library open to public with restrictions.

★15246★

UNIVERSITY OF CALIFORNIA, BERKELEY - INSTITUTE OF GOVERNMENTAL STUDIES - LIBRARY (Soc Sci)
Moses Hall, Rm. 109 Phone: (415) 642-5659
Berkeley, CA 94720 Jack Leister, Hd.Libn.
Founded: 1920. **Staff:** Prof 4; Other 8. **Subjects:** Administration, metropolitan problems, planning, finance, taxation, welfare, criminology, personnel, transportation, local government. **Holdings:** 392,235 pamphlets and documents; 10,168 microforms. **Subscriptions:** 1966 journals and other serials. **Services:** Interlibrary loans; library open to public for reference use only. **Computerized Information Services:** OCLC. **Networks/Consortia:** Member of CLASS.

★15247★

UNIVERSITY OF CALIFORNIA, BERKELEY - INST. OF INDUSTRIAL RELATIONS - LABOR OCCUPATIONAL HEALTH PROGRAM LIB. (Sci-Tech)
2521 Channing Way Phone: (415) 642-5507
Berkeley, CA 94720 Susan Salisbury, Staff Libn.
Staff: 1. **Subjects:** Chemical and physical occupational hazards, medical and industrial hygiene, standards and regulations, workers' compensation and education. **Special Collections:** Papers and pamphlets on occupational health topics; resource center for information on the hazards of video display terminals. **Holdings:** 1500 books; 150 unbound periodicals; newspaper clipping file. **Subscriptions:** 40 journals and other serials; 110 newspapers. **Services:** Copying; library open to public for reference use only. **Publications:** Labor Occupational Health Program Monitor (newsletter), bimonthly - by subscription; Getting the Facts (guidebook on setting up a health and safety library, includes an extensive occupational health bibliography) - available by request. **Special Indexes:** Occupational health and safety and labor-related issues index (card).

★15248★

UNIVERSITY OF CALIFORNIA, BERKELEY - INSTITUTE OF INDUSTRIAL RELATIONS LIBRARY (Soc Sci)
2521 Channing Way, Rm. 110 Phone: (415) 642-1705
Berkeley, CA 94720 Nanette O. Sand, Libn.
Founded: 1948. **Staff:** Prof 2; Other 2. **Subjects:** Industrial relations, labor and allied social science topics. **Special Collections:** Tenth Regional War Labor Board Collection (World War II). **Holdings:** 40,000 cataloged items; 3000 uncataloged items. **Subscriptions:** 800 journals and other serials. **Services:** Interlibrary loans; library open for reference with restricted circulation.

★15249★

UNIVERSITY OF CALIFORNIA, BERKELEY - INSTITUTE OF INTERNATIONAL STUDIES LIBRARY (Soc Sci)
340 Stephens Hall Phone: (415) 642-3633
Berkeley, CA 94720 Colette G. Myles, Hd.
Founded: 1919. **Staff:** Prof 2. **Subjects:** International politics; international organization; economic integration in Africa, Europe and Latin America; methodology of comparative studies in political science and sociology; economic development and political change; technology and society; area studies. **Special Collections:** Current political and economic newsletters from Latin America, Africa and the Middle East; collection of journals on Francophone Africa. **Holdings:** 11,300 volumes; 9700 pamphlets. **Subscriptions:** 225 journals and other serials; 5 newspapers. **Services:** Interlibrary loans; library open to public. **Staff:** Serge Millan .

★15250★

UNIVERSITY OF CALIFORNIA, BERKELEY - INSTITUTE OF TRANSPORTATION STUDIES LIBRARY (Trans)
412 McLaughlin Hall Phone: (415) 642-3604
Berkeley, CA 94720 Michael C. Kleiber, Hd.Libn.
Founded: 1948. **Staff:** Prof 3; Other 4. **Subjects:** Transportation. **Holdings:** 94,000 books; 11,500 bound periodical volumes; 15 VF drawers of newspaper clippings; visual aids; 775 maps; 24,000 microfiche. **Subscriptions:** 2456 journals and other serials. **Services:** Interlibrary loans; copying; library open to public for reference use only. **Automated Operations:** Computerized cataloging. **Computerized Information Services:** DIALOG, OCLC; MELVYL (internal database). **Networks/Consortia:** Member of TRISNET. **Publications:** Selected list of recent acquisitions, monthly; Library References, irregular. **Special Indexes:** Index to 40,000 articles (card). **Staff:** Daniel Krummes, Tech.Serv.Libn.; Catherine Cortelyou, Pub.Serv.Libn.

★15251★

UNIVERSITY OF CALIFORNIA, BERKELEY - LAW LIBRARY (Law)
230 Law Bldg. Phone: (415) 642-4044
Berkeley, CA 94720 Robert Berring, Law Libn.
Founded: 1907. **Staff:** Prof 11; Other 24. **Subjects:** Law - Anglo-American, foreign, international. **Special Collections:** Robbins Collection of canon and ecclesiastical law; Colby Collection of mining law; Robbins Collection of civil and medieval law. **Holdings:** 450,000 volumes; 52,229 microforms; 857 sound recordings; 120 manuscripts; 284,000 court briefs and theses. **Subscriptions:** 7801 journals and other serials. **Services:** Interlibrary loans; library open to public for reference use only. **Computerized Information Services:** LEXIS, RLIN, OCLC, INNOVACQ, Westlaw. **Networks/Consortia:** Member of RLG. **Remarks:** The Graduate Theological Union Library works cooperatively with the Canon Law Collection. **Also Known As:** Garret W. McEnerney Law Library.

UNIVERSITY OF CALIFORNIA, BERKELEY - LAWRENCE BERKELEY LABORATORY
See: Lawrence Berkeley Laboratory

★15252★

UNIVERSITY OF CALIFORNIA, BERKELEY - LIBRARY SCHOOL LIBRARY (Info Sci)
2 South Hall Phone: (415) 642-2253
Berkeley, CA 94720 Virginia Pratt, Libn.
Founded: 1946. **Staff:** Prof 1; Other 1. **Subjects:** Library science and history of libraries; printing, publishing and book trade; information - storage, retrieval, policy, services; archives and records management; bibliographical organization, theory and methods; bibliography, history and criticism of children's literature. **Holdings:** 41,215 volumes; 1833 microforms; 4347 pamphlets; 58 sound recordings. **Subscriptions:** 1790 journals and other serials. **Services:** Interlibrary loans (through 307 General Library); copying; library open to public. **Publications:** Selected Additions to the Library School Library, bimonthly - free.

★15253★

UNIVERSITY OF CALIFORNIA, BERKELEY - MAP ROOM (Geog-Map)
137 General Library
Berkeley, CA 94720
Phone: (415) 642-4940
Philip Hoehn, Map Libn.
Founded: 1917. **Staff:** Prof 1; Other 2. **Subjects:** Worldwide maps, national and regional atlases. **Holdings:** 2300 volumes; 240,000 maps; 22,000 aerial photographs; 700 pamphlets; 6900 microforms. **Subscriptions:** 200 journals and other serials. **Services:** Interlibrary loans (through 307 General Library); copying; room open to public. **Automated Operations:** Computerized cataloging. **Networks/Consortia:** Member of RLG.

★15254★

UNIVERSITY OF CALIFORNIA, BERKELEY - MUSIC LIBRARY (Mus)
240 Morrison Hall
Berkeley, CA 94720
Phone: (415) 642-2623
Michael A. Keller, Hd.
Founded: 1947. **Staff:** Prof 4; Other 6. **Subjects:** History of Western music; history of opera; 18th century instrumental music; contemporary American and European music; ethnomusicology; Afro-American, Indic, Indonesian and Japanese music; historiography of music. **Special Collections:** Connick and Romberg Opera Collections (10,000 scores); music manuscripts of the 11th-15th centuries (1200 titles); music manuscripts of the 20th century (200 titles); Chambers Campanology Collection; archival collections (135 items); Cortot Opera Collection (400 scores); Italian instrumental music (1000 manuscripts); opera libretti (5000). **Holdings:** 115,092 volumes, including 69,000 musical scores; 30,000 sound recordings; 5191 early music manuscripts; 5100 microforms; 6531 pamphlets; 508 slides. **Subscriptions:** 929 journals and other serials. **Services:** Interlibrary loans (through 307 General Library); copying; library open to public for reference use only. **Automated Operations:** Computerized cataloging. **Computerized Information Services:** DIALOG, RLIN; internal database. **Networks/Consortia:** Member of RLG. **Publications:** Duckles and Elmer Thematic Catalog of a Manuscript Collection of Italian Instrumental Music of the 18th century, 1963; Cum Nutis Variorum (newsletter), 10/year. **Special Catalogs:** Early Music Printing in Music Library. **Staff:** Ruth Tucker, Hd., Tech.Proc.; Ann P. Basart; John A. Emerson.

★15255★

UNIVERSITY OF CALIFORNIA, BERKELEY - NATIVE AMERICAN STUDIES LIBRARY (Area-Ethnic)
3415 Dwinelle Hall
Berkeley, CA 94720
Phone: (415) 642-2793
Rosalie McKay, Libn.
Staff: 3. **Subjects:** Native Americans. **Special Collections:** Bureau of American Ethnology Annual Reports and Bulletins (complete); Bancroft's works (39 volumes); Curtis' North American Indians (16 volumes); University of California publications (2 file drawers); Papers of Indian Rights Association and National Archives tribal census on microfilm; Indian art (3500 slides). **Holdings:** 7800 monographs; dissertations on microfilm; 150 phonograph records; 100 cassettes; 67 reel-to-reel tapes; 90 videotapes. **Subscriptions:** 200 Indian newsletters and journals. **Services:** Library open to public for reference use only; limited circulation to faculty and students.

★15256★

UNIVERSITY OF CALIFORNIA, BERKELEY - NATURAL RESOURCES LIBRARY (Agri; Env-Cons)
40 Giannini Hall
Berkeley, CA 94720
Phone: (415) 642-4493
Norma Kobzina, Hd.
Founded: 1963. **Staff:** Prof 2; Other 3. **Subjects:** Agriculture, environmental sciences, pest management, nutrition. **Holdings:** 100,591 volumes; 10,941 pamphlets; 745 microforms. **Subscriptions:** 4300 journals and other serials. **Services:** Interlibrary loans (through 307 General Library); copying; library open to public for reference with restricted circulation. **Computerized Information Services:** DIALOG, BRS, SDC, NTIS, RLIN.

★15257★

UNIVERSITY OF CALIFORNIA, BERKELEY - NAVAL BIOSCIENCES LABORATORY - LIBRARY (Med)
Bldg. 844, Naval Supply Ctr.
Oakland, CA 94625
Phone: (415) 832-5217
Theresa Dundon, Libn.
Founded: 1950. **Staff:** Prof 1. **Subjects:** Recombinant DNA, hybrydoma research, microbiology, virology, bacteriology, immunology, cancer research. **Holdings:** 3005 books. **Subscriptions:** 88 journals and other serials. **Services:** Interlibrary loans; library not open to public. **Remarks:** Library is maintained jointly by the University of California, Berkeley and the U.S. Navy.

★15258★

UNIVERSITY OF CALIFORNIA, BERKELEY - OPTOMETRY LIBRARY (Sci-Tech)
490 Minor Hall
Berkeley, CA 94720
Phone: (415) 642-1020
Alison Howard, Hd.
Founded: 1949. **Staff:** Prof 1; Other 1. **Subjects:** Optometry, physiological optics, ophthalmology. **Holdings:** 7462 volumes; 668 pamphlets; 414 microforms; 251 sound recordings; 3300 slides; 120 video recordings; 30 motion pictures. **Subscriptions:** 182 journals and other serials. **Services:** Interlibrary loans (through 307 General Library); copying; library open for reference. **Computerized Information Services:** DIALOG, BRS. **Publications:** Acquisition lists, monthly - distributed to local and related libraries.

★15259★

UNIVERSITY OF CALIFORNIA, BERKELEY - PHYSICS LIBRARY (Sci-Tech)
Phone: (415) 642-3122
Berkeley, CA 94720
Camille Wanat, Hd.
Founded: 1948. **Staff:** Prof 1; Other 3. **Subjects:** Physics and related sciences. **Holdings:** 32,988 volumes; 405 microforms; 323 pamphlets; 20 sound recordings. **Subscriptions:** 492 journals and other serials. **Services:** Interlibrary loans (through 307 General Library); copying; library open to public. **Automated Operations:** Computerized cataloging and acquisitions. **Computerized Information Services:** DIALOG, BRS; MELVYL (internal database). Performs searches on cost recovery basis. **Networks/Consortia:** Member of RLG. **Publications:** Acquisitions List, monthly.

★15260★

UNIVERSITY OF CALIFORNIA, BERKELEY - PUBLIC HEALTH LIBRARY (Med)
42 Earl Warren Hall
Berkeley, CA 94720
Phone: (415) 642-2511
Thomas J. Alexander, Hd.
Founded: 1947. **Staff:** Prof 4; Other 4. **Subjects:** Public health, epidemiology, biostatistics, hospital administration, environmental health, maternal and child health, biomedical science (laboratory), occupational health, toxicology. **Holdings:** 70,000 volumes; 6197 pamphlets; 60 microforms. **Subscriptions:** 2080 journals and other serials. **Services:** Interlibrary loans (through 307 General Library); copying; library open to public for reference use only. **Computerized Information Services:** DIALOG, BRS, SDC, NLM. **Staff:** Cristina Fowler, Ref.Libn.; Charleen Kubota, Ref.Libn.; Joan Friedman, Ref.Libn.

★15261★

UNIVERSITY OF CALIFORNIA, BERKELEY - SCIENCE & MATHEMATICS EDUCATION LIBRARY (Educ; Sci-Tech)
Lawrence Hall of Science
Centennial Dr.
Berkeley, CA 94720
Phone: (415) 642-1334
Ann M. Jensen, Libn.
Founded: 1970. **Staff:** Prof 1. **Subjects:** Teaching aids in math, science, and environmental education; teacher education; curriculum development; science, math and environmental education trade books (juvenile and adult). **Holdings:** 8000 volumes. **Subscriptions:** 60 journals and other serials. **Services:** Interlibrary loans; copying; library open to public.

★15262★

UNIVERSITY OF CALIFORNIA, BERKELEY - SEBASTIAN S. KRESGE ENGINEERING LIBRARY (Sci-Tech; Comp Sci)
Stephen D. Bechtel Engineering Center
Berkeley, CA 94720
Phone: (415) 642-3339
Patricia Davitt Maughan, Libn.
Staff: Prof 2; Other 8. **Subjects:** Engineering - civil, mineral, mechanical, nuclear, electrical, industrial; computer science; operations research; naval architecture; materials science; mining and metallurgy. **Special Collections:** IHS industry standard reports. **Holdings:** 118,000 books; 494,000 technical reports on paper and in microform. **Subscriptions:** 3914 journals and other serials. **Services:** Interlibrary loans (through 307 General Library); copying; library open to public for reference use only. **Automated Operations:** Computerized cataloging and acquisitions. **Computerized Information Services:** DIALOG, RLIN, OCLC; MELVYL (internal database). Performs searches on cost recovery basis. Contact Person: Saundra Lormand, 642-3532. **Staff:** Saundra Lormand, Online Serv.Libn.; Diane Brown, Pub.Serv.Libn.

★15263★

UNIVERSITY OF CALIFORNIA, BERKELEY - SOCIAL SCIENCE LIBRARY (Soc Sci)
30 Stephens Hall
Berkeley, CA 94720
Phone: (415) 642-0370
Geraldine Scalzo, Hd.
Founded: 1964. **Staff:** Prof 3; Other 8. **Subjects:** Economics, business administration, labor, political science, sociology, public policy. **Special Collections:** Labor union publications. **Holdings:** 94,000 volumes; 743,000 microforms; 37,218 pamphlets. **Subscriptions:** 2861 journals and other serials. **Services:** Interlibrary loans (through 307 General Library); copying; library open to public, special borrowers' card required. **Computerized Information Services:** DIALOG. **Publications:** Berkeley Business Guides, 1-14 - local distribution.

★15264★

UNIVERSITY OF CALIFORNIA, BERKELEY - SOCIAL WELFARE LIBRARY (Soc Sci)

216 Haviland Hall — Phone: (415) 642-4432
Berkeley, CA 94720 — Geraldine Scalzo, Hd.
Founded: 1963. **Staff:** 2. **Subjects:** Social welfare. **Holdings:** 19,776 volumes; 1095 pamphlets; 9 microforms. **Subscriptions:** 275 journals and other serials. **Services:** Interlibrary loans (through 307 General Library); copying; library open to public for reference use only.

★15265★

UNIVERSITY OF CALIFORNIA, BERKELEY - SOUTH/SOUTHEAST ASIA LIBRARY SERVICE (Area-Ethnic)

438 General Library — Phone: (415) 642-3095
Berkeley, CA 94720 — Peter Ananda, Hd.
Staff: Prof 2; Other 4. **Subjects:** South and southeast Asia - history, political science, language and literature (especially strong in Hindi, Urdu, Tamil, Sanskrit, Nepal, Indonesian, Malay, Thai and Vietnamese), art and art history, sociology, education, music, environmental design, philosophy and religion, anthropology, geography. **Special Collections:** Ghadar Party Collection; Nepal Collection; Thai Collection; modern Hindi, Indonesian and Malay literature; government publications on India and Indonesia. **Holdings:** 300,000 books; 60,000 bound periodical volumes; 5000 other cataloged items; 2500 dissertations; 1000 reels of microfilm; pamphlets; manuscripts; videotapes; sound recordings; maps; monographs. **Subscriptions:** 1550 journals and other serials; 75 newspapers. **Services:** Interlibrary loans; copying; library open to public. **Automated Operations:** Computerized cataloging, acquisitions and serials. **Computerized Information Services:** DIALOG, OCLC, BRS, RLIN; GLADIS (internal database). Performs searches on cost recovery basis. **Special Catalogs:** Catalog of South Asia by language (card); catalog of Southeast Asia by country (card). **Staff:** Kenneth R. Logan, Asst.Hd.

★15266★

UNIVERSITY OF CALIFORNIA, BERKELEY - STATE DATA PROGRAM LIBRARY (Soc Sci)

Survey Research Center
2538 Channing Way — Phone: (415) 642-6571
Berkeley, CA 94720 — Ilona Einowski, Archv.
Founded: 1958. **Staff:** 1. **Subjects:** Sociology, political science, psychology, survey research methods, statistics, opinion polls, U.S. Census. **Special Collections:** Unpublished reports on social science, topics employing survey research methods. **Holdings:** 1000 volumes; 2000 studies on computer tapes; questionnaires, interview forms, codebooks and data sets of past U.S. and foreign surveys; news releases of Gallup, Harris, Canadian Gallup, L.A. Times and California polls. **Subscriptions:** 40 journals and other serials. **Services:** Copying; magnetic tape reproduction of data sets from past surveys; library open to public for reference use only. **Special Catalogs:** Catalog of available material, annual - by subscription.

★15267★

UNIVERSITY OF CALIFORNIA, BERKELEY - UNIVERSITY EXTENSION - CONTINUING EDUCATION OF THE BAR - LIBRARY (Law)

2300 Shattuck Ave. — Phone: (415) 642-5343
Berkeley, CA 94704 — Virginia Polak, Libn.
Founded: 1960. **Staff:** Prof 1; Other 2. **Subjects:** Law. **Holdings:** 15,000 books and bound periodical volumes. **Subscriptions:** 221 journals and other serials; 7 newspapers. **Services:** Library not open to public. **Publications:** Recent Acquisitions, bimonthly - for internal distribution only.

★15268★

UNIVERSITY OF CALIFORNIA, BERKELEY - UNIVERSITY HERBARIUM - LIBRARY (Sci-Tech)

Department of Botany — Phone: (415) 642-2465
Berkeley, CA 94720
Subjects: Botany. **Special Collections:** History of the University Herbarium, 1870s to present (field books kept by collectors; correspondence; transactions information; photographs of persons and events related to the Herbarium). **Holdings:** 100 linear feet of archival materials. **Services:** Copying; library open to public during business hours.

★15269★

UNIVERSITY OF CALIFORNIA, BERKELEY - WATER RESOURCES CENTER ARCHIVES (Env-Cons)

410 O'Brien Hall — Phone: (415) 642-2666
Berkeley, CA 94720 — Gerald J. Giefer, Libn.
Founded: 1956. **Staff:** Prof 1; Other 2. **Subjects:** Water as a natural resource, water resources development and management, municipal and industrial water uses and problems, reclamation and irrigation, flood control, waste disposal, coastal engineering, water quality, water law. **Special**

Collections: Ocean engineering (20,000 pieces); manuscript collection of papers of men prominent in western water development (4290). **Holdings:** 83,055 volumes; 5131 maps; 637 microforms; 7821 manuscripts. **Subscriptions:** 1607 journals and other serials. **Services:** Interlibrary loans; copying; archives open to public for reference use only. **Computerized Information Services:** OCLC. **Publications:** Selected Recent Accessions, bimonthly; Archives series (monographs), irregular; list of other publications available.

★15270★

UNIVERSITY OF CALIFORNIA, DAVIS - AGRICULTURAL ECONOMICS BRANCH LIBRARY (Agri)

Voorhies Hall — Phone: (916) 752-1540
Davis, CA 95616 — Susan Casement, Libn.
Founded: 1950. **Staff:** Prof 1; Other 1. **Subjects:** Agricultural economics; agricultural business; land, resource and consumer economics; international agriculture. **Holdings:** 6192 volumes; 221,873 pamphlets. **Services:** Copying; library open to public for reference use only.

★15271★

UNIVERSITY OF CALIFORNIA, DAVIS - ENVIRONMENTAL TOXICOLOGY LIBRARY (Env-Cons)

— Phone: (916) 752-2562
Davis, CA 95616 — Dr. Ming-Yu Li, Doc.Spec.
Founded: 1966. **Staff:** Prof 1; Other 2. **Subjects:** Pesticides, environmental pollutants, toxic metals, PCB, air and water pollutants, food additives and toxicants, hazardous wastes management. **Special Collections:** Pesticide chemicals and subject files. **Holdings:** 5000 books; 3500 bound periodical volumes; 65,000 abstract cards (classified); 36,000 items on pesticides in VF drawers; 41,000 items in subject files on environmental pollutants, toxic metals and elements, hazardous substances and waste management. **Subscriptions:** 100 journals and other serials. **Services:** Copying; library open to public with special permission - for reference use only. **Computerized Information Services:** NLM, BRS, DIALOG, SDC; Pesticide Data Bank (internal database). **Publications:** Chlorinated Hydrocarbon Pesticides (1974-1978); Pesticides: A Selected Bibliography, 1975.

★15272★

UNIVERSITY OF CALIFORNIA, DAVIS - F. HAL HIGGINS LIBRARY OF AGRICULTURAL TECHNOLOGY

Shields Library
Davis, CA 95616
Defunct. Holdings absorbed by the University of California, Davis - University Libraries.

★15273★

UNIVERSITY OF CALIFORNIA, DAVIS - HEALTH SCIENCES LIBRARY (Med)

— Phone: (916) 752-1214
Davis, CA 95616 — Marjan Merala, Libn.
Founded: 1966. **Staff:** Prof 8; Other 26. **Subjects:** Medicine, veterinary medicine, experimental biology, primatology. **Special Collections:** Veterinary historical collection. **Holdings:** 46,571 books; 139,714 bound periodical volumes; 7554 microforms; 3881 foreign veterinary theses; 16,532 slides; 6837 other AV materials. **Subscriptions:** 5527 journals and other serials. **Services:** Interlibrary loans; copying; SDI; library open to public with fee card for outside users. **Automated Operations:** Computerized cataloging, serials and circulation. **Computerized Information Services:** NLM, BRS, DIALOG, SDC, NIH-EPA Chemical Information System. Performs searches on cost recovery basis. Contact Person: Peter J. Vigil, 752-6204. **Networks/Consortia:** Member of Pacific Southwest Regional Medical Library Service (PSRMLS). **Publications:** HSL News, monthly - distributed to library clientele. **Staff:** Winifred E. Kistler, Pub.Serv.Libn.; David C. Anderson, Tech.Serv.Libn.; May E. Price, Cat.; Peter Vigil, Online Search Coord.; Lynne Apostle, Ref.Libn.;Terri L. Malmgren, Libn., UCDMC; Carolyn S. Kopper, Asst.Libn., UCDMC.

★15274★

UNIVERSITY OF CALIFORNIA, DAVIS - INSTITUTE OF GOVERNMENTAL AFFAIRS - LIBRARY (Soc Sci; Plan)

— Phone: (916) 752-2045
Davis, CA 95616 — Katherine Bruce Bostock, Hd.Libn.
Founded: 1962. **Staff:** Prof 1. **Subjects:** Administration, city, regional and state planning, decision-making in environmental quality control; public policy; police administration; personnel; politics, political parties, elections and campaign literature; conservation and recreation; regulatory agencies. **Holdings:** 5000 books; 130,000 clippings; 95,000 other cataloged items. **Subscriptions:** 700 journals and other serials. **Services:** Interlibrary loans; library open to researchers, students and public. **Publications:** Accessions list, monthly - distributed within the university system.

★15275★

UNIVERSITY OF CALIFORNIA, DAVIS - MEDICAL CENTER LIBRARY (Med)
4301 X St.   Phone: (916) 453-3529
Sacramento, CA 95817   Terri L. Malmgren, Libn.
Staff: Prof 2; Other 4. **Subjects:** Medicine, nursing. **Holdings:** 8980 books; 13,470 bound periodical volumes; 5031 AV materials. **Subscriptions:** 652 journals and other serials. **Services:** Copying; library open to public for reference use only. **Computerized Information Services:** MEDLINE, DIALOG. **Networks/Consortia:** Member of Pacific Southwest Regional Medical Library Service (PSRMLS); Mountain Valley Library System. **Publications:** Monthly Newsletter/Acquisitions List - for internal distribution only.

★15276★

UNIVERSITY OF CALIFORNIA, DAVIS - MICHAEL AND MARGARET B. HARRISON WESTERN RESEARCH CENTER (Hist)
Department of Special Collections
Shields Library   Phone: (916) 752-1621
Davis, CA 95616   Michael Harrison, Dir.
Founded: 1981. **Staff:** Prof 1. **Subjects:** History and development of the trans-Mississippi West, mid-19th century to present; American Indians; ethnic studies; military, local and economic history; sociology; folklore; exploration and travel; geography; religious studies, especially the Catholic and Mormon churches; literature; art and architecture; history of printing. **Special Collections:** Books from Western fine presses; correspondence with 20th-century artists, writers and enthusiasts of the American West; original works of art. **Holdings:** 61,000 titles. **Services:** Center open to public by appointment only.

★15277★

UNIVERSITY OF CALIFORNIA, DAVIS - PHYSICAL SCIENCES LIBRARY (Sci-Tech)
University Library   Phone: (916) 752-1627
Davis, CA 95616   Marlene Tebo, Hd.Libn.
Founded: 1971. **Staff:** Prof 4; Other 11. **Subjects:** Chemistry, physics, mathematics, statistics, engineering, geology. **Special Collections:** Depository for DOE documents and selected NASA documents. **Holdings:** 80,000 books; 110,000 bound periodical volumes; 700,000 DOE microforms; 7300 maps; 35,000 NASA microforms; 100,000 additional microforms; 29,184 research reports; 1181 vertical files. **Subscriptions:** 2269 journals and other serials. **Services:** Interlibrary loans; copying; SDI; library open to public. **Computerized Information Services:** DIALOG, SDC, BRS, CAS Online. **Staff:** Johanna Ross, Libn.; Glee Willis, Asst.Libn.; Edward Jestes, Libn.

★15278★

UNIVERSITY OF CALIFORNIA, DAVIS - SCHOOL OF LAW - LAW LIBRARY (Law)
                Phone: (916) 752-3322
Davis, CA 95616   Mortimer D. Schwartz, Law Libn.
Founded: 1963. **Staff:** Prof 7; Other 13. **Subjects:** Law - U.S. and California; common law countries; international, comparative and foreign law. **Special Collections:** Depository for federal and California documents. **Holdings:** 191,824 volumes; 41,390 volumes in microform. **Subscriptions:** 6278 journals and other serials. **Services:** Interlibrary loans; copying; library open to public. **Computerized Information Services:** LEXIS, RLIN, Westlaw; MELVYL (internal database). **Staff:** Mrs. Pat B. Piper, Assoc. Law Libn.; Alfred J. Lewis, Assoc. Law Libn.; Judy C. Janes, Asst. Law Libn.

★15279★

UNIVERSITY OF CALIFORNIA, DAVIS - UNIVERSITY LIBRARIES - SPECIAL COLLECTIONS (Sci-Tech; Agri; Hum)
                Phone: (916) 752-2110
Davis, CA 95616   Donald Kunitz, Hd., Spec.Coll.
Special Collections: American literature (18th, 19th and early 20th centuries); animal and fish culture (50,200 volumes); apiculture (6250 volumes; 55,000 archival records and ephemera); Avant-Garde Poetry, Gary Snyder Papers (15,000 pieces); botany (17,500 volumes); brewing and fermentation (2500 volumes); California artists and architecture (9300 pieces); California citrus industry-advertising art (3400 pieces); California historical manuscripts-pioneering and mining (6500 pieces); California promotional materials (2430 pieces); contemporary issues (14,200 pieces); energy and space research (Atomic Energy Commission, DOE, NASA and National Research Council technical reports on microfiche; 749,178 pieces); English history, literature and religion (16th, 17th and 19th centuries); enology, viticulture and wine (13,100 volumes; 54,000 archival records and ephemera); entomology and nematology (17,500 volumes); Ferry-Morse Archive (5535 pieces); fine printing (1000 volumes); food and agriculture organization of the U.N. (publications in microfiche, 1975 to present); foods and food science and industry (22,500 volumes; 4100 archival records and ephemera); genetics (6200 volumes); Agricultural Technology (375,000 pieces); performing arts collection (177,100 pieces); plant culture and pomology (31,900 volumes; 21,500 archival records, nursery catalogs, photographs and ephemera); radical groups (8000 pamphlets); zoology (25,000 volumes). **Holdings:** 1.83 million books; 725,285 bound periodical volumes; 589,286 government documents; 119,082 manuscripts; 105,374 maps; 1.83 million microforms; 538,560 pamphlets; 14,473 sound recordings; 46,480 current serial titles. **Services:** Interlibrary loans; copying; library open to public with fee card for outside users. **Automated Operations:** Computerized cataloging, acquisitions, serials and circulation. **Computerized Information Services:** DIALOG, SDC, BRS. **Networks/Consortia:** Member of Mountain Valley Library System; North Bay Cooperative Library System; North State Cooperative Library System; Pacific Southwest Regional Medical Library Service (PSRMLS); RLG. **Staff:** Linda Hoffmann, Hd., Gov.Docs.

★15280★

UNIVERSITY OF CALIFORNIA, DAVIS - WOMEN'S RESOURCES & RESEARCH CENTER - LIBRARY (Soc Sci)
Women's Center   Phone: (916) 752-3372
Davis, CA 95616   Joy Fergoda, Lib.Coord.
Staff: 1. **Subjects:** Women's issues, concerns and research. **Special Collections:** Native and Pioneer Women in Yolo and Solano Counties, California (oral history collection; 28 tapes and 2 photograph albums). **Holdings:** 2000 books; 5500 vertical file materials; 470 audiotapes. **Subscriptions:** 130 journals and other serials; 14 newspapers. **Services:** Copying; library open to public for reference use only, second copies may circulate to university students, staff and faculty.

★15281★

UNIVERSITY OF CALIFORNIA, IRVINE - BIOLOGICAL SCIENCES LIBRARY (Sci-Tech)
                Phone: (714) 856-6730
Irvine, CA 92717   Margaret Aguirre, Lib.Asst.
Staff: 7. **Subjects:** Biological sciences. **Holdings:** 26,000 volumes. **Subscriptions:** 1100 journals and other serials. **Services:** Interlibrary loans; copying; library open to public with restrictions. **Automated Operations:** Computerized serials. **Remarks:** The Biological Sciences Library is a branch of the Biomedical Library.

★15282★

UNIVERSITY OF CALIFORNIA, IRVINE - BIOMEDICAL LIBRARY (Med)
Box 19556   Phone: (714) 856-6652
Irvine, CA 92713   F. Raymond Long, Asst.Univ.Libn.
Founded: 1969. **Staff:** Prof 7; Other 7. **Subjects:** Medicine. **Special Collections:** Bibliotheca Neurologica Courville (special book collection featuring aspects of medical history and research in neurology). **Holdings:** 120,000 books and bound periodical volumes; 5000 audio cassettes; 475 microfiche; pamphlet file. **Subscriptions:** 1677 journals and other serials. **Services:** Interlibrary loans; copying; SDI; library open to public for reference use only. **Automated Operations:** Computerized cataloging, serials and circulation. **Computerized Information Services:** MEDLINE, BRS, DIALOG, SDC. **Networks/Consortia:** Member of Pacific Southwest Regional Medical Library Service (PSRMLS); Nursing Information Consortium of Orange County (NICOC). **Publications:** Biomedical Library News and New Books, monthly. **Special Catalogs:** Catalog of Works in the Neurological Sciences Collected by Cyril Brian Courville, M.D., Representative of Clinical Neurology, Neuroanatomy, and Neuropathology with Particular Reference to Head Trauma (book); Serial Holdings, 1980, with periodic updates (book). **Staff:** Herbert Ahn, Ref.Libn.; Rochelle Bock, Sr.Ref.Libn.; Judith Bube, Acq.Libn.Cynthia Butler, Hd., Pub.Serv.; Stephen Clancy, Ref.Libn.; Joyce Loepprich, Ser.Libn.; Jae Hwi Myong, Cat.Libn.

★15283★

UNIVERSITY OF CALIFORNIA, IRVINE - INSTITUTE OF TRANSPORTATION STUDIES - RESOURCE CENTER (Trans)
Rm. 150 SST   Phone: (714) 856-6564
Irvine, CA 92717   Lyn Wong, Libn.
Staff: Prof 2. **Subjects:** Urban transportation. **Holdings:** 3000 books; 200 bound periodical volumes; 6000 NTIS technical reports on microfiche; 500 dissertations. **Subscriptions:** 30 journals and other serials. **Services:** Interlibrary loans; copying; SDI; center open to public. **Computerized Information Services:** Online systems. **Networks/Consortia:** Member of Transportation Research Services Information Network (TRISNET). **Staff:** Deborah Smith, Asst.Rsrcs.Spec.

★15284★

UNIVERSITY OF CALIFORNIA, IRVINE - MEDICAL CENTER LIBRARY (Med)
101 City Dr., S.   Phone: (714) 634-5798
Orange, CA 92668   Susan Russell, Hd.Libn.
Staff: Prof 2; Other 2. **Subjects:** Clinical medicine. **Holdings:** 28,000 books and bound periodical volumes; 4 VF drawers; 10 filmstrips; 100 slide and cassette programs; 130 videotapes. **Subscriptions:** 743 journals and other serials. **Services:** Interlibrary loans; copying; SDI; library open to public. **Automated Operations:** Computerized serials and circulation. **Computerized Information Services:** DIALOG, SDC, BRS, MEDLINE. **Networks/Consortia:** Member of Nursing Information Consortium of Orange County (NICOC). **Remarks:** The Medical Center Library is a branch of the Biomedical Library. **Staff:** Emiko Samard, Ref.Libn.

★15285★

UNIVERSITY OF CALIFORNIA, LOS ANGELES - ACADEMY OF TELEVISION ARTS & SCIENCES - TELEVISION ARCHIVES (Aud-Vis)
Theater Arts Dept.
1438 Melnitz Hall   Phone: (213) 206-8013
Los Angeles, CA 90024   Dan Einstein, Archv.
Founded: 1965. **Staff:** Prof 3; Other 2. **Subjects:** Commercial television programs and production material, kinescopes, films and tapes. **Special Collections:** Hallmark Hall of Fame television series; Alcoa Collection; Jack Benny, Loretta Young, Ann Sothern Collections. **Holdings:** 20,000 films and tapes of programs. **Services:** Archives open to researchers, students and the public by appointment only. **Publications:** Catalog of holdings. **Also Known As:** ATAS/UCLA Television Archives. **Staff:** Robert Rosen, Dir.; Eleanore Tanin, Broadcast Supv.

★15286★

UNIVERSITY OF CALIFORNIA, LOS ANGELES - AFRICAN STUDIES CENTER - LIBRARY (Area-Ethnic)
10367 Bunche Hall   Phone: (213) 825-2944
Los Angeles, CA 90024   Dr. Michael Lofchie, Dir.
Founded: 1959. **Staff:** 1. **Subjects:** Africa. **Holdings:** 100 bound periodical volumes; 100 pamphlets; 100 monographs; 75 bibliographies. **Subscriptions:** 20 journals and other serials. **Services:** Library open to public for reference use only.

★15287★

UNIVERSITY OF CALIFORNIA, LOS ANGELES - AMERICAN INDIAN STUDIES CENTER - LIBRARY (Area-Ethnic)
3220 Campbell Hall   Phone: (213) 825-4591
Los Angeles, CA 90024   Velma S. Salabiye, Libn.
Staff: Prof 1; Other 2. **Subjects:** American Indians including government relations, history, literature, art, language, Indians in California, works of Indian authorship. **Special Collections:** Dissertations and theses by and about American Indians; Indian newspapers and journals. **Holdings:** 6000 volumes; 9 VF drawers of pamphlets and clippings. **Services:** Copying; library open to public with restrictions.

★15288★

UNIVERSITY OF CALIFORNIA, LOS ANGELES - ARCHITECTURE & URBAN PLANNING LIBRARY (Art; Plan)
1302 Architecture Bldg.   Phone: (213) 825-2747
Los Angeles, CA 90024   Jon S. Greene, Libn.
Staff: Prof 1; Other 2. **Subjects:** Architecture, urban planning. **Holdings:** 17,278 books and bound periodical volumes; 66 reels of microfilm; 124 microfiche; 9 sound recordings. **Subscriptions:** 350 journals and other serials. **Services:** Interlibrary loans; copying; library open to public. **Automated Operations:** Computerized cataloging, acquisitions and serials. **Computerized Information Services:** Internal database.

★15289★

UNIVERSITY OF CALIFORNIA, LOS ANGELES - ART DEPARTMENT - VISUAL RESOURCE COLLECTION & SERVICES (Art)
3239 Dickson Art Center
405 Hilgard Ave.   Phone: (213) 825-3725
Los Angeles, CA 90024   Sandra Ducoff Garber, Slide Cur.
Founded: 1958. **Staff:** Prof 3; Other 2. **Subjects:** Painting, sculpture, applied art and architecture - European, Islamic, Japanese, Indian, American, Chinese, African; Pre-Columbian, Oceanic and American Indian art; contemporary art forms. **Holdings:** 240,000 slides. **Services:** Collection not open to public. **Special Indexes:** Artists and architects index to slide collection and manuscript index by title and location (both punched cards). **Staff:** Susan Rosenfeld, Asst. Slide Curator; Ron Reimers, Photographer.

★15290★

UNIVERSITY OF CALIFORNIA, LOS ANGELES - ART LIBRARY (Art)
2250 Dickson Art Center   Phone: (213) 825-3817
Los Angeles, CA 90024   Joyce P. Ludmer, Art Libn.
Founded: 1952. **Staff:** Prof 2; Other 4. **Subjects:** Art, art and architectural history, design. **Holdings:** 75,569 volumes; 149 VF drawers of uncataloged serials, clippings, museum catalogs, one-person exhibition catalogs and announcements; 65 manuscripts; 599 reels of microfilm; 8018 microfiche; 63,466 pamphlets. **Subscriptions:** 1457 journals and other serials. **Services:** Interlibrary loans; copying; library open to public for reference use only. **Automated Operations:** Computerized acquisitions and serials. **Special Indexes:** Princeton Index of Christian Art; Decimal Index to the Art of the Low Countries (DIAL); Index of Jewish Art; Marburger Index. **Staff:** Patricia Moore, Hd., Tech.Serv./Acq.

★15291★

UNIVERSITY OF CALIFORNIA, LOS ANGELES - ART LIBRARY - ELMER BELT LIBRARY OF VINCIANA (Art)
Dickson Art Center   Phone: (213) 825-3817
Los Angeles, CA 90024   Joyce Ludmer, Art Libn./Dir.
Founded: 1971. **Subjects:** Italian Renaissance, Leonardo da Vinci, Renaissance technology. **Special Collections:** Archives of Dr. Elmer Belt and Kate Trauman Steinitz; graphics collection; Renaissance furniture and objects. **Holdings:** 15,000 books; 500 unbound and bound periodical volumes; 8 VF drawers of pamphlets and clippings; 22 file boxes of clippings; documents; 19 file boxes of articles arranged by author; 30 file boxes of magazines. **Services:** Copying; library open to public by appointment. **Special Catalogs:** Catalogue of the Incunabula in the Elmer Belt Library of Vinciana, 1971 (book). **Special Indexes:** Leonardo Subject Index (card).

★15292★

UNIVERSITY OF CALIFORNIA, LOS ANGELES - ASIAN AMERICAN STUDIES CENTER READING ROOM (Area-Ethnic)
2230 Campbell Hall   Phone: (213) 825-5043
Los Angeles, CA 90024   Marjorie Lee, Coord.
Staff: 3. **Subjects:** Asian American studies. **Holdings:** 5000 volumes. **Services:** Room open to public. **Publications:** Asian American Library Resources at University of California, Los Angeles - available upon request.

★15293★

UNIVERSITY OF CALIFORNIA, LOS ANGELES - BIOMEDICAL LIBRARY (Med; Sci-Tech)
Center for Health Sciences   Phone: (213) 825-5781
Los Angeles, CA 90024   Alison Bunting, Act.Hd.Libn.
Founded: 1947. **Staff:** Prof 20; Other 40. **Subjects:** Medicine, dentistry, nursing, public health, biology, microbiology, botany, zoology. **Special Collections:** Japanese medical books and prints; classics in ornithology and mammalogy from the Donald R. Dickey Library of Vertebrate Zoology; S. Weir Mitchell Collection (history of medical science); Dr. M.N. Beigelman Collection (classics in ophthalmology); Florence Nightingale Collection; John A. Benjamin Collection of Medical History. **Holdings:** 398,186 volumes; 40 manuscripts; 411 maps; 1142 reels of microfilm; 11,494 microfiche; 3591 sound recordings; 7215 pamphlets. **Subscriptions:** 6891 journals and other serials. **Services:** Interlibrary loans; copying; SDI. **Automated Operations:** Computerized cataloging, acquisitions, serials and circulation. **Computerized Information Services:** NLM, BRS, SDC, DIALOG. **Networks/Consortia:** Base for Pacific Southwest Regional Medical Library Service (PSRMLS). **Publications:** Recent Acquisitions in the Biomedical Library, monthly - for sale; Serials Holdings List, annual - for sale; Brief Guide to the Biomedical Library, annual - free upon request. **Special Catalogs:** Book Catalog, 1972-1977, microfiche - for sale.

★15294★

UNIVERSITY OF CALIFORNIA, LOS ANGELES - BRAIN INFORMATION SERVICE (Med)
Center for Health Sciences   Phone: (213) 825-6011
Los Angeles, CA 90024   Michael H. Chase, Dir.
Founded: 1964. **Staff:** Prof 1. **Subjects:** Neurosciences, alcohol and driving, sleep. **Holdings:** Figures not available. **Remarks:** This is a specialized information center to serve the neuroscience research community.

★15295★

UNIVERSITY OF CALIFORNIA, LOS ANGELES - CHEMISTRY LIBRARY (Sci-Tech)
4238 Young Hall   Phone: (213) 825-3342
Los Angeles, CA 90024   Marion C. Peters, Libn.
Founded: 1947. **Staff:** Prof 1; Other 2. **Subjects:** Chemistry - organic, inorganic, analytical, physical; biochemistry. **Special Collections:** Morgan Memorial Collection (history of chemistry). **Holdings:** 55,111 books and

bound periodical volumes; U.S. chemical patents in microform, 1952 to present. **Subscriptions:** 764 journals and other serials. **Services:** Interlibrary loans; copying; SDI; library open to public. **Automated Operations:** Computerized cataloging, acquisitions and serials. **Computerized Information Services:** DIALOG, SDC, BRS, CAS Online, Institute for Scientific Information (ISI); ORION (internal database). **Networks/Consortia:** Member of California Library Network (CALINET).

★15296★
UNIVERSITY OF CALIFORNIA, LOS ANGELES - CHICANO STUDIES RESEARCH LIBRARY (Area-Ethnic)
3121 Campbell Hall
405 Hilgard Ave.   Phone: (213) 206-6052
Los Angeles, CA 90024   Richard Chabran, Assoc.Libn./Coord.
Founded: 1969. **Staff:** Prof 1; Other 2. **Subjects:** Immigration, labor, higher education, school desegregation, Raza women, Chicano literature, U.S.-Mexico relations. **Special Collections:** Ron Lopez papers; Latino Community Development Archive; Casa Collection; Mexico-U.S. Relations Archive; Magdalena Mora Archive; Jose Ortiz papers; Grace Montanas Davis Papers. **Holdings:** 7000 books; 200 bound periodical volumes; 1680 theses and dissertations; 51 16mm films; 9000 clippings and pamphlets; 100 student papers; 1525 microforms; 136 posters; 3 multimedia kits; 275 pictures; 124 phonograph records; 140 cassettes; 54 audiotapes; 6 filmstrips; 22 realia; 25 maps; 20 videotapes; 262 slides. **Subscriptions:** 55 journals and other serials; 20 newspapers. **Services:** Interlibrary loans; copying; library open to public for reference use only. **Automated Operations:** Computerized cataloging. **Computerized Information Services:** ORION (internal database). **Publications:** Early Childhood Education: A Selected Bibliography (1972); The Chicana: A Comprehensive Bibliographic Study (1976); Quien Sabe? A Preliminary List of Chicano Reference Materials (1981).

★15297★
UNIVERSITY OF CALIFORNIA, LOS ANGELES - COMPUTER SCIENCE DEPARTMENT - ARCHIVES (Comp Sci)
3440 Boelter Hall   Phone: (213) 825-4317
Los Angeles, CA 90024   Doris Sublette, Libn.
Staff: Prof 1. **Subjects:** Computer science. **Special Collections:** Institute of Electrical and Electronics Engineers Repository Collection. **Holdings:** 3000 books; 181 bound periodical volumes; 10,000 technical reports; 3000 dissertations, theses and microfiche. **Subscriptions:** 150 journals. **Services:** Interlibrary loans; archives not open to public. **Automated Operations:** Computerized circulation. **Publications:** CSD Newsletter, monthly.

★15298★
UNIVERSITY OF CALIFORNIA, LOS ANGELES - DEPARTMENT OF SPECIAL COLLECTIONS (Hist; Hum)
University Research Library, Fl. A   Phone: (213) 825-4988
Los Angeles, CA 90024   David Zeidberg, Hd.
Founded: 1946. **Staff:** Prof 5; Other 10. **Subjects:** Californiana; motion pictures; radio; television; dance; blacks in entertainment and literature; Japanese in America; history of photography; folklore, including broadside ballads, songsters, hymnals, American almanacs; university archives; popular culture, including pulp magazines and comic books. **Special Collections:** Michael Sadleir Collection of 19th century English fiction; Ahmanson-Murphy Collection of Aldines; Sir Maurice Holmes Collection of Captain Cook; English and American auction catalogs; early children's books; Bodoni imprints; Spinoza Collection; manuscripts of William Starke Rosecrans, Franz Werfel, Henry Stevens, John Houseman, Ralph Bunche; oral history interviews; Near Eastern manuscripts (Arabic, Turkish, Persian, Armenian); books and manuscripts of Henry Miller, Norman Douglas, Aldous Huxley, Edward Gordon Craig, Gertrude Stein, Maria Edgeworth, Raymond Chandler. **Holdings:** 149,392 volumes; 18,663,403 manuscripts; 552 volumes of newspapers; 95,000 pieces of ephemera and clippings; 44,753 pamphlets; 300,000 pictorial items; 2515 historical maps; 7931 reels of microfilm; 3003 sound recordings. **Subscriptions:** 279 journals and other serials. **Services:** Copying (limited); department open to public for reference use only. **Automated Operations:** Computerized cataloging, acquisitions, serials and circulation. **Computerized Information Services:** OCLC. **Special Catalogs:** Bibliographies of Henry Miller, Kenneth Rexroth and Lawrence Durrell. **Staff:** James Davis, Rare Bks.Libn.Anne Caiger, Univ.Archv.; Hilda Bohem, Pub.Serv.Libn.

★15299★
UNIVERSITY OF CALIFORNIA, LOS ANGELES - EDUCATION & PSYCHOLOGY LIBRARY (Educ)
390 Powell Library Bldg.   Phone: (213) 825-4081
Los Angeles, CA 90024   Barbara Duke, Hd.
Founded: 1965. **Staff:** Prof 4; Other 5. **Subjects:** Education; general, experimental, abnormal, social and developmental psychology; English as a second language; kinesiology. **Special Collections:** Teaching English as a

Second Language (10,000 volumes). **Holdings:** 133,653 volumes; 1517 ephemeral materials; 445,999 microforms; 300 cassettes. **Subscriptions:** 2553 journals and other serials. **Services:** Interlibrary loans; copying; library open to public. **Automated Operations:** Computerized cataloging, acquisitions and serials. **Computerized Information Services:** DIALOG, BRS. **Publications:** Information Leaflets, numbers 1-3, annual. **Staff:** Mrs. San Oak Kim, Asst.Hd.; Diane Pezzullo, Ref./Circ.Libn.; Diana Fitzgerald, Ref./Res.Libn.

★15300★
UNIVERSITY OF CALIFORNIA, LOS ANGELES - ENGINEERING & MATHEMATICAL SCIENCES LIBRARY (Sci-Tech)
8270 Boelter Hall   Phone: (213) 825-3982
Los Angeles, CA 90024   Karen L. Andrews, Hd.Libn.
Founded: 1945. **Staff:** Prof 3; Other 6. **Subjects:** Astronomy; atmospheric science; mathematics; computer science; engineering - aeronautical, biomedical, chemical, civil, electrical, electronics, environmental, industrial; materials science; mechanical, nuclear and systems science. **Special Collections:** Technical Reports Collection (including depository items from DOE, NASA, NTIS, Rand Corporation; meteorology report collection). **Holdings:** 178,119 books and bound periodical volumes; 1,290,478 microforms; 70,000 technical reports; 136 maps. **Subscriptions:** 6790 journals and other serials. **Services:** Interlibrary loans; copying; library open to public. **Automated Operations:** Computerized cataloging, acquisitions and serials. **Computerized Information Services:** DIALOG, SDC, BRS; ORION (internal database). **Networks/Consortia:** Member of CALINET. **Staff:** B. June Armstrong, Ref.Libn.; Bruce E. Pelz, Coll.Mgt.Libn.

★15301★
UNIVERSITY OF CALIFORNIA, LOS ANGELES - ENGLISH READING ROOM (Hum)
1120 Rolfe Hall   Phone: (213) 825-4511
Los Angeles, CA 90024   Tim Strawn, Hd.
Founded: 1950. **Staff:** 1. **Subjects:** English literature, American literature, composition. **Holdings:** 21,427 books; 733 recordings; 200 slides. **Subscriptions:** 129 journals and other serials.

★15302★
UNIVERSITY OF CALIFORNIA, LOS ANGELES - ENVIRONMENTAL SCIENCE AND ENGINEERING - LIBRARY (Env-Cons)
2066 Engineering I Bldg.   Phone: (213) 825-7332
Los Angeles, CA 90024
Founded: 1970. **Staff:** 1. **Subjects:** Environmental sciences, air quality, energy sources, ecology, urban studies. **Holdings:** 2000 technical, governmental and environmental impact reports and monographs; 500 periodicals. **Subscriptions:** 25 journals and other serials. **Services:** Library not open to public. **Staff:** Dr. Richard L. Perrine, Prof.

UNIVERSITY OF CALIFORNIA, LOS ANGELES - ERIC CLEARINGHOUSE FOR JUNIOR COLLEGES
See: ERIC Clearinghouse for Junior Colleges

★15303★
UNIVERSITY OF CALIFORNIA, LOS ANGELES - GEOLOGY-GEOPHYSICS LIBRARY (Sci-Tech)
Geology Bldg., Rm. 4697   Phone: (213) 825-1055
Los Angeles, CA 90024   Sarah E. How, Hd.
Founded: 1940. **Staff:** Prof 1; Other 1. **Subjects:** Geology, geophysics, planetary sciences, paleontology, economic geology, mining. **Special Collections:** California geology; UCLA geology theses and dissertations. **Holdings:** 86,624 books and bound periodical volumes; 151 reels of microfilm; 8815 microfiche. **Subscriptions:** 2091 journals and other serials. **Services:** Interlibrary loans; copying; library open to public. **Automated Operations:** Computerized acquisitions and serials. **Computerized Information Services:** DIALOG, RLIN, SDC, BRS; ORION (internal database). **Networks/Consortia:** Member of CALINET.

★15304★
UNIVERSITY OF CALIFORNIA, LOS ANGELES - HOUSING, REAL ESTATE & URBAN LAND STUDIES PROGRAM COLLECTION (Plan)
405 Hilgard
Graduate School of Management 4274   Phone: (213) 825-3977
Los Angeles, CA 90024   Frank G. Mittelbach, Dir./Prof.
Founded: 1952. **Staff:** Prof 2; Other 2. **Subjects:** Transportation, housing and real estate, land use, environment, planning, urban sociology. **Special Collections:** Reprints; journals; articles; Council of Planning Libraries bibliographies 1-130; Housing and Urban Development (miscellaneous reports). **Holdings:** 2800 books; 16,000 pamphlets and monographs; 6000 government pamphlets and census materials; clippings. **Subscriptions:** 75

journals and other serials. **Services:** Interlibrary loans; copying; collection open to public. **Publications:** Real Estate Indicators, quarterly.

★15305★
UNIVERSITY OF CALIFORNIA, LOS ANGELES - INSTITUTE FOR SOCIAL SCIENCE RESEARCH - SOCIAL SCIENCE DATA ARCHIVE (Soc Sci)
405 Hilgard Ave.   Phone: (213) 825-0711
Los Angeles, CA 90024   Elizabeth Stephenson, Data Archv.
Staff: Prof 1; Other 1. **Subjects:** Social science. **Special Collections:** California Polls; Los Angeles Metropolitan Area Surveys; National Center for Health Statistics data repository. **Holdings:** 1000 studies and their accompanying documentation. **Services:** Interlibrary loans; archive open to public with restrictions. **Automated Operations:** Computerized cataloging. **Computerized Information Services:** ORION (internal database). **Publications:** ISSR - SSDA Newsletter, monthly.

★15306★
UNIVERSITY OF CALIFORNIA, LOS ANGELES - LABORATORY OF BIOMEDICAL AND ENVIRONMENTAL SCIENCES - LIBRARY (Med)
900 Veteran Ave.   Phone: (213) 825-8741
Los Angeles, CA 90024
Founded: 1955. **Staff:** Prof 1; Other 1. **Subjects:** Biochemistry, nuclear medicine, environmental science, energy, cell biology. **Special Collections:** Depository for USAEC reports. **Holdings:** 7000 books; 7000 bound periodical volumes; 1200 government reports; 100,000 reports on microfiche; 500 technical reports. **Subscriptions:** 200 journals and other serials. **Services:** Interlibrary loans; copying; library open to public with restrictions. **Computerized Information Services:** DOE/RECON, MEDLINE, DIALOG, SDC, BRS. **Publications:** Annual reports. **Remarks:** The Laboratory of Biomedical and Environmental Sciences operates under contract to the U.S. Department of Energy.

★15307★
UNIVERSITY OF CALIFORNIA, LOS ANGELES - LAW LIBRARY (Law)
School of Law Bldg.
405 Hilgard Ave.   Phone: (213) 825-7826
Los Angeles, CA 90024   Frederick E. Smith, Law Libn.
Founded: 1949. **Staff:** Prof 8; Other 14. **Subjects:** Law. **Special Collections:** Anglo-American legal materials; David Bernard Memorial Aviation Law Library. **Holdings:** 283,808 volumes; 70,506 microforms; 1019 sound recordings; 37,459 government documents. **Subscriptions:** 5092 journals and other serials. **Services:** Interlibrary loans; copying; library open to public for reference use only with limited schedule and limited access on weekends. **Automated Operations:** Computerized cataloging. **Computerized Information Services:** LEXIS. **Staff:** Myra Saunders, Pub.Serv.; Adrienne Alan, Tech.Proc.

★15308★
UNIVERSITY OF CALIFORNIA, LOS ANGELES - MANAGEMENT LIBRARY (Bus-Fin)
Graduate School of Management   Phone: (213) 825-3138
Los Angeles, CA 90024   Robert Bellanti, Hd.
Founded: 1961. **Staff:** Prof 5; Other 7. **Subjects:** All fields of management and business administration, accounting-information systems, business economics, computers and information systems, finance and investments, personnel and industrial relations, international and comparative management studies, arts management, marketing, operations research, socio-technical systems/behavioral science, urban land economics. **Special Collections:** Robert E. Gross Collection of Rare Books in Business and Economics; James R. Pattillo Library of Banking and Finance; Dean Emeritus Neil H. Jacoby Collection (his publications); annual and 10K reports of major American and foreign corporations. **Holdings:** 130,844 volumes; 243,800 hard copy, microcards, and microfiche of annual and 10K reports of corporations; 6270 reels of microfilm of journals, newspapers and the Goldsmiths'-Kress Collection of Rare Books in Business and Economics. **Subscriptions:** 4660 journals and other serials. **Services:** Interlibrary loans; copying; library open to public for reference use only. **Automated Operations:** Computerized cataloging, acquisitions and circulation. **Computerized Information Services:** SDC, DIALOG, OCLC, BRS; ORION (internal database). **Networks/Consortia:** Member of CLASS. **Publications:** GSM Library Guides. **Staff:** Eloisa G. Yeargain, Ref.Libn.; Tracey Miller, Coll.Dev./Ref.; Alvis Price, Ref.Libn.; Lerleen Costa, Tech.Serv.Sect.; Arturo Esparza, Circ.Sect.

★15309★
UNIVERSITY OF CALIFORNIA, LOS ANGELES - MAP LIBRARY (Geog-Map)
Bunche Hall, Rm. A-253   Phone: (213) 825-3526
Los Angeles, CA 90024   Carlos B. Hagen, Hd.
Founded: 1957. **Staff:** Prof 1; Other 3. **Subjects:** Nautical and aeronautical charts, map intelligence materials, topographic maps (world coverage), city

plans. **Special Collections:** Latin America and Pacific Ocean materials. **Holdings:** 6059 books; 423,563 maps; 1200 technical reports; 30,578 VF of city plans and road maps; 2450 atlases; 12,330 aerial photographs. **Subscriptions:** 311 journals and other serials. **Services:** Interlibrary loans; copying; library open to public for reference use only. **Publications:** Newsletter & Selected Acquisitions, irregular; technical reports.

★15310★
UNIVERSITY OF CALIFORNIA, LOS ANGELES - MATHEMATICS READING ROOM (Sci-Tech)
Mathematics Science Bldg., Rm. 5379   Phone: (213) 825-4930
Los Angeles, CA 90024   Sharon Marcus, Libn.
Founded: 1948. **Staff:** Prof 1; Other 2. **Subjects:** Mathematics. **Holdings:** 8105 books; 7700 bound periodical volumes; reports and reprints; preprints of faculty and students; 202 department dissertations. **Subscriptions:** 133 journals and other serials. **Services:** Reading room open to public for reference use only.

UNIVERSITY OF CALIFORNIA, LOS ANGELES - MEDICAL CENTER
See: Los Angeles County Harbor-UCLA Medical Center

★15311★
UNIVERSITY OF CALIFORNIA, LOS ANGELES - MUSIC LIBRARY (Mus)
1102 Schoenberg Hall
405 Hilgard Ave.   Phone: (213) 825-4881
Los Angeles, CA 90024   Stephen M. Fry, Music Libn.
Founded: 1942. **Staff:** Prof 3; Other 50. **Subjects:** Music, musicology, ethnomusicology, music education. **Special Collections:** Ethnomusicology Archive (telephone: 825-1695); Ernst Toch Archive; Erich Zeisl Archive; Archive of Popular American Music (450,000 popular song sheets; telephone: 825-1665); John Vincent Archive; Clarence V. Mader Archive; 17th- and 18th-century Venetian libretti (11,000); film and TV recordings and manuscript score collection. **Holdings:** 42,000 books and bound periodical volumes; 53,000 music scores; 150,000 manuscripts; 2500 reels of microfilm; 5500 microforms; 34,552 sound recordings 1717 slides; 35 reels of motion picture film; 385 glossy prints; 65 cartons of manuscripts and documents of American composers; 10,162 pamphlets. **Subscriptions:** 1100 journals and other serials. **Services:** Interlibrary loans; copying; library open to public. **Automated Operations:** Computerized acquisitions and text editing. **Publications:** UCLA Music Library Bibliography Series, irregular; UCLA Music Library Discography Series, irregular; Guide to UCLA Music Library, annual; exhibit catalogs - all publications free upon request. **Special Indexes:** Tunedex/song-dex (10,000 song cards). **Staff:** Marsha Berman, Assoc. Music Libn.; Gordon Theil, Asst. Music Libn.; Ann Briegleb, Ethnomusicology Archv.

UNIVERSITY OF CALIFORNIA, LOS ANGELES - NEUROPSYCHIATRIC INSTITUTE
See: Neuropsychiatric Institute - Mental Health Information Service

★15312★
UNIVERSITY OF CALIFORNIA, LOS ANGELES - ORAL HISTORY PROGRAM LIBRARY (Hist)
136 Powell Library   Phone: (213) 825-4932
Los Angeles, CA 90024   Dale Treleven, Dir.
Staff: Prof 3; Other 7. **Subjects:** Arts in southern California, architecture, civil liberties, printing and bookselling, politics and government, university history. **Holdings:** 275 volumes of tape transcriptions. **Services:** Copying; library open to public. **Special Catalogs:** Catalog of holdings (bound). **Staff:** Richard Candida Smith, Prin.Ed.; Rebecca Torres, Adm.Asst.

★15313★
UNIVERSITY OF CALIFORNIA, LOS ANGELES - ORIENTAL LIBRARY (Area-Ethnic)
21617 University Research Library   Phone: (213) 825-4836
Los Angeles, CA 90024   Mr. Ik-Sam Kim, Hd.
Founded: 1956. **Staff:** Prof 3; Other 2. **Subjects:** Books on art, archeology, history, literature, Buddhism, linguistics, political science, religion, sociology, humanities and social science of East Asia in the Chinese, Japanese and Korean languages. **Holdings:** 197,623 volumes of books and bound periodical volumes; 2223 reels of microfilm; 719 pamphlets. **Subscriptions:** 1154 journals and other serials; 45 newspapers. **Services:** Interlibrary loans; copying; library open to public.

★15314★
UNIVERSITY OF CALIFORNIA, LOS ANGELES - PHYSICAL SCIENCES & TECHNOLOGY LIBRARIES (Sci-Tech; Info Sci)
8251 Boelter Hall   Phone: (213) 825-6515
Los Angeles, CA 90024   Alan R. Benenfeld, Coord.
Founded: 1975. **Staff:** Prof 5; Other 3. **Remarks:** Administrative unit for

Chemistry, Engineering and Mathematical Sciences, Geology/Geophysics and Physics Libraries including centralized cataloging and interlibrary loan service. **Staff:** Dorothy McGarry, Hd.Cat.; Carole Kochevar, Hd., ILL.

★15315★
UNIVERSITY OF CALIFORNIA, LOS ANGELES - PHYSICS LIBRARY (Sci-Tech)
213 Kinsey Hall   Phone: (213) 825-4792
Los Angeles, CA 90024   J. Wally Pegram, Libn.
Founded: 1947. **Staff:** Prof 1; Other 2. **Subjects:** Physics - solid state, high energy and particle, mathematical; elementary particles; acoustics; astrophysics and applied fields. **Special Collections:** SLAC High Energy Preprint Library. **Holdings:** 37,670 books and bound periodical volumes; 2000 preprints (High Energy); 66 microforms. **Subscriptions:** 623 journals and other serials. **Services:** Interlibrary loans; copying; library open to public for reference use only. **Automated Operations:** Computerized acquisitions and serials. **Computerized Information Services:** DIALOG, SDC, BRS. **Networks/Consortia:** Member of CALINET.

★15316★
UNIVERSITY OF CALIFORNIA, LOS ANGELES - PUBLIC AFFAIRS SERVICE (Soc Sci; Plan)
405 Hilgard   Phone: (213) 825-3135
Los Angeles, CA 90024   Eugenia Eaton, Hd.
Staff: Prof 6; Other 9. **Subjects:** Government, social and economic problems and development, local and regional planning, industrial relations, ethnic studies, social welfare, politics and political parties. **Services:** Interlibrary loans; copying; service open to public for reference use only. **Automated Operations:** Computerized acquisitions and serials. **Computerized Information Services:** DIALOG, SDC, BRS. **Staff:** Eudora Loh, Foreign Docs.Libn.; Roberta Medford, State Docs.Libn.; Barbara Silvernail, Intl./U.S.Docs.Libn.;Joyce Toscan, Non-Govt.Org.Libn.; Dorothy Wells, Local Docs.Libn.

UNIVERSITY OF CALIFORNIA, LOS ANGELES - REED NEUROLOGICAL INSTITUTE - ROSE READING ROOM
See: Neuropsychiatric Institute - Mental Health Information Service

★15317★
UNIVERSITY OF CALIFORNIA, LOS ANGELES - THEATER ARTS LIBRARY (Theater)
22478 University Research Library   Phone: (213) 825-4880
Los Angeles, CA 90024   Mrs. Audree Malkin, Libn.
Founded: 1947. **Staff:** Prof 1; Other 2. **Subjects:** Motion pictures, television, radio. **Special Collections:** Jessen Collection (2169 stills and 901 portraits from the silent era through 1940); Twentieth Century-Fox Motion Picture Still Collection (3 million production stills; 3178 proof sheets; 658 proof sheet books; 71 keysets and 164 color transparencies from the 1950-1960 period); Universal Studios Keybooks (645); Papers of Mark Robson, William Wyler, Allan Joslyn, Stanley Kramer; Columbia Pictures Still Collection (80,000 production stills; 188 keysets from the 1950-1960 period); Metro-Goldwyn-Mayer Screenplay Collection (1270 screenplays covering the period 1924-1960); Film Poster Collection (2500 rare and early posters of American, Polish and Czechoslovakian productions, 1915 to present); Richard Dix Collection (5217 stills). **Holdings:** 12,754 volumes; 3.08 million production stills and portraits, 1905 to present; 12,000 screenplays, television and radio scripts; 8347 slides; 102,000 clippings; 2500 motion picture programs; 670 film festival programs. **Subscriptions:** 270 journals and other serials. **Services:** Copying (limited); library open to public. **Automated Operations:** Computerized cataloging. **Special Catalogs:** Motion Pictures: A Catalog of Books, Periodicals, Screen Plays, and Productions, 1 volume, 1976.

★15318★
UNIVERSITY OF CALIFORNIA, LOS ANGELES - UCLA FILM ARCHIVES (Aud-Vis; Hist)
Department of Theater Arts   Phone: (213) 206-8013
Los Angeles, CA 90024   Charles Hopkins, Film Archv.
Founded: 1968. **Staff:** Prof 4; Other 4. **Subjects:** U.S. commercial films since the development of sound, European features, animation films. **Special Collections:** Paramount Collection (740 prints); Twentieth Century-Fox Collection (620); Warner Brothers Collection (600 prints); National Telefilms Associates Collection (2000); animated film collection (300); Sonney Amusement Enterprises Collection of Early Exploitation Films (300); Hearst-Metrotone Newsreel Library. **Holdings:** 25,000 35mm and 16mm prints and pre-print materials. **Services:** Archives open to public. **Networks/Consortia:** Member of Archives Advisory Committee (ACC). **Staff:** Robert Gitt, Film Preservation; Robert Rosen, Dir.; Blaine Bartell, Newsreel Archv.; Martha Yee, Cat.

★15319★
UNIVERSITY OF CALIFORNIA, LOS ANGELES - UCLA RADIO ARCHIVES (Hist; Aud-Vis)
Department of Theater Arts   Phone: (213) 206-8013
Los Angeles, CA 90024   Ronald Staley, Radio Archv.
Founded: 1975. **Staff:** Prof 3; Other 1. **Subjects:** Comedy and dramatic programs; news and public affairs. **Special Collections:** Jack Benny Collection (1932-1955); Carnation Collection (1941-1952); Hallmark Cards Collection (1939-1955); Edward R. Murrow broadcasts (1950-1953, 110 broadcasts); Screen Guild Players Collection (1939-1949); Nelson Collection (1944-1954, includes a complete set of the Adventures of Ozzie and Harriet series). **Holdings:** 40,000 transcriptions on discs, master tapes and wire. **Services:** Library open to public. **Staff:** Eleanore Tanin, Broadcast Supv.; Robert Rosen, Dir.

★15320★
UNIVERSITY OF CALIFORNIA, LOS ANGELES - UNIVERSITY ELEMENTARY SCHOOL LIBRARY (Educ)
405 Hilgard Ave.   Phone: (213) 825-4928
Los Angeles, CA 90024   Judith Kantor, Hd.Libn.
Founded: 1920. **Staff:** Prof 1; Other 1. **Subjects:** Children's literature. **Special Collections:** Folk literature; poetry collection. **Holdings:** 16,787 books; 512 bound periodical volumes. **Subscriptions:** 35 journals and other serials. **Services:** Interlibrary loans; library open to public with restrictions. **Automated Operations:** Computerized cataloging and acquisitions.

★15321★
UNIVERSITY OF CALIFORNIA, LOS ANGELES - WATER RESOURCES CENTER ARCHIVES (Env-Cons)
2081 Engineering I   Phone: (213) 825-7734
Los Angeles, CA 90024   Beth R. Willard, Assoc.Libn.
Founded: 1967. **Staff:** Prof 1; Other 1. **Subjects:** Water - resources, reclamation, pollution, supply, quality and economics; wastes disposal; irrigation; flood control; water law; environment; energy; soils; water-based recreation. **Holdings:** Figures not available. **Services:** Interlibrary loans; archives open to public with restrictions on circulation. **Computerized Information Services:** DOE/RECON.

★15322★
UNIVERSITY OF CALIFORNIA, LOS ANGELES - WAYLAND D. HAND LIBRARY OF FOLKLORE AND MYTHOLOGY (Hum)
                                         Phone: (213) 825-4242
Los Angeles, CA 90024   Inkeri Rank, Libn.
Staff: Prof 1; Other 2. **Subjects:** Folklore and folk literature, mythology, folk music and folk song, folklife, material culture, folk arts, ethnology. **Special Collections:** Western European folklore atlases; Ralph Steele Boggs Collection of Latin American folklore. **Holdings:** 3060 books; 867 bound periodical volumes; 173 boxes and 3 VF drawers of reprints, pamphlets and clippings; 946 reels of microfilm; 222 cassettes; 2046 tapes; 6000 phonograph records. **Subscriptions:** 108 journals and other serials. **Services:** Library open to visiting scholars. **Special Catalogs:** American Ethnic Bibliography (card); Bibliography of Games and Other Play Activities (card); Ralph Steele Boggs Collection of Latin American Folklore (card). **Remarks:** Library is maintained by the Center for the Study of Comparative Folklore and Mythology.

★15323★
UNIVERSITY OF CALIFORNIA, LOS ANGELES - WILLIAM ANDREWS CLARK MEMORIAL LIBRARY (Hum)
2520 Cimarron St.   Phone: (213) 731-8529
Los Angeles, CA 90018-2098   Norman J.W. Thrower, Dir.
Staff: Prof 4; Other 6. **Subjects:** English civilization, 1640-1750; Eric Gill; John Dryden; Oscar Wilde; Montana history; modern graphic arts. **Holdings:** 78,000 volumes; 14,500 manuscripts. **Services:** Copying; library open to public for research purposes. **Computerized Information Services:** ORION, MELVYL (internal databases). **Publications:** Seminar papers, 3 or 4/year - by subscription; Augustan Reprint Society, 6/year - by subscription. **Staff:** Thomas F. Wright, Libn.; John Bidwell, Ref.Libn.

★15324★
UNIVERSITY OF CALIFORNIA, RIVERSIDE - BIO-AGRICULTURAL LIBRARY (Agri)
                                         Phone: (714) 787-3238
Riverside, CA 92521   Barbara Montanary, Hd.Libn.
Staff: Prof 4; Other 9. **Subjects:** Biochemistry, biology, biomedical sciences, citrus and desert horticulture, entomology, environmental sciences, nematology, pest management, plant pathology, plant sciences, soil sciences-agricultural engineering, statistics. **Special Collections:** Avocado Collection (new and historical books, clippings, notes, manuscripts); Citrus Collection (citrus fruits and citrus industry in California); desert ecology; arid land

research; collections on jojoba, guayule and dates. **Holdings:** 130,000 volumes. **Subscriptions:** 2000 journals and other serials. **Services:** Interlibrary loans; copying; SDI; library open to public. **Automated Operations:** Computerized circulation. **Computerized Information Services:** DIALOG, SDC, BRS, NLM. **Networks/Consortia:** Member of Inland Empire Academic Libraries Cooperative (IEALC).

★15325★
UNIVERSITY OF CALIFORNIA, RIVERSIDE - CALIFORNIA MUSEUM OF PHOTOGRAPHY (Art)
Phone: (714) 787-4787
Riverside, CA 92521   Charles Desmarais, Dir.
Staff: Prof 4; Other 3. **Subjects:** Photography, art. **Special Collections:** Keystone-Mast Collection (major world events and sites, 1880-1930; 350,000 stereo photographs); University Print Collection (10,000 photographs of extraordinary artistic and historical value); Bingham Collection (4000 cameras, 1851 to present). **Services:** Copying; museum open to public by appointment. **Computerized Information Services:** Internal database. **Publications:** CMP Bulletin, 5/year - to members. **Staff:** Edward W. Earle, Cur., Keystone-Mast Coll.; Katherine V. Diage, Cur.; Dan Meinwald, Registrar/Cur.

★15326★
UNIVERSITY OF CALIFORNIA, RIVERSIDE - DEEP CANYON DESERT RESEARCH CENTER - LIBRARY (Sci-Tech)
Box 1738   Phone: (619) 341-3655
Palm Desert, CA 92261   Allan Muth, Ph.D., Resident Dir.
Staff: Prof 1. **Subjects:** Desert - biology, climatology, archeology, geology; ecology; hydrology. **Special Collections:** Rare books about the desert. **Holdings:** 350 books; 392 bound periodical volumes; 65 dissertations and theses; 20 reports; 30 maps; 20 aerial photographs; 150 slides. **Services:** Library open to scientists.

★15327★
UNIVERSITY OF CALIFORNIA, RIVERSIDE - DEPARTMENT OF ENTOMOLOGY - LIBRARY (Sci-Tech)
Phone: (714) 787-4315
Riverside, CA 92521   Saul I. Frommer, Sr.Musm.Sci.
Staff: 2. **Subjects:** Entomology with emphasis on systematic entomology, biological control and insect biology. **Special Collections:** Specialized collections maintained by various departmental members. **Holdings:** Dissertations (stored in the main entomology building, under care of departmental secretary). **Services:** Copying; holdings may be viewed by the public by appointment. **Remarks:** An alternate phone number is 787-3677. **Staff:** Jack C. Hall, Sr.Musm.Sci.

★15328★
UNIVERSITY OF CALIFORNIA, RIVERSIDE - EDUCATION SERVICES LIBRARY (Educ)
Box 5900   Phone: (714) 787-3715
Riverside, CA 92517   Marie Genung, Hd., Educ.Serv.
Founded: 1970. **Staff:** 2. **Subjects:** Education. **Holdings:** 25,000 volumes (includes textbooks, children's literature, kits with cassettes and tapes, curriculum guides, study prints and educational tests). **Services:** Library open to public. **Special Catalogs:** Children's literature collection, textbook collection, curriculum guides, nonbook materials and test collection. **Staff:** Lois Malloy .

★15329★
UNIVERSITY OF CALIFORNIA, RIVERSIDE - ENGLISH DEPARTMENT LIBRARY (Hum)
Humanities Bldg.   Phone: (714) 787-5301
Riverside, CA 92521   Elizabeth Lang, Hd.
Founded: 1965. **Staff:** 1. **Subjects:** English literary bibliography, literary reference and criticism. **Special Collections:** Olga W. Vickery Collection of Southern Literature (100 volumes); Mortimer Proctor Memorial Collection (700 volumes). **Holdings:** 3600 volumes; 300 pamphlets; 60 recordings; 100 offprints. **Subscriptions:** 45 journals and other serials. **Services:** Library open to the university community.

★15330★
UNIVERSITY OF CALIFORNIA, RIVERSIDE - GOVERNMENT PUBLICATIONS DEPARTMENT - LIBRARY (Info Sci; Law)
Box 5900   Phone: (714) 787-3226
Riverside, CA 92517   James Rothenberger, Dept.Hd.
Staff: Prof 2; Other 6. **Subjects:** U.S. and California governments, international organizations. **Special Collections:** Law Collection (National Reporter System; federal and California statutory and administrative law). **Holdings:** 20,000 volumes; 350,000 government documents; 100,000

microforms. **Services:** Interlibrary loans; copying; library open to public. **Computerized Information Services:** DIALOG, BRS, SDC. Performs searches on cost recovery basis. Contact Person: Margaret Mooney. **Staff:** Margaret Mooney, Asst.Libn.

★15331★
UNIVERSITY OF CALIFORNIA, RIVERSIDE - MAP SECTION - LIBRARY (Geog-Map)
Box 5900   Phone: (714) 787-3226
Riverside, CA 92517   James Rothenberger, Dept.Hd.
Founded: 1963. **Staff:** Prof 1; Other 1. **Subjects:** All areas of the world with emphasis on the western hemisphere. **Special Collections:** U.S. Geological Survey topographic maps (depository); Defense Mapping Agency Topographic Center maps (depository). **Holdings:** 65,000 sheet maps; 1500 folded maps; 900 atlases. **Subscriptions:** 10 journals and other serials. **Services:** Interlibrary loans; library open to public. **Automated Operations:** Computerized cataloging. **Staff:** Richard Beaumont .

★15332★
UNIVERSITY OF CALIFORNIA, RIVERSIDE - MUSIC LIBRARY (Mus)
Phone: (714) 787-3137
Riverside, CA 92521   John W. Tanno, Assoc.Univ.Libn.
Founded: 1963. **Staff:** Prof 1; Other 3. **Subjects:** Musicology, composition and theory, organology, performance practice. **Special Collections:** Books on bells and carillons (200 titles); Niels Wilhelm Gade Collection (all editions and arrangements of his works); Oswald Jonas Memorial Archive, incorporating the Heinrich Schenker Archive; Harry and Grace James Recorded Sound Archive (10,000 78s); Works Progress Administration (WPA) Southern California Music Project Collection (750 scores and parts). **Holdings:** 17,000 volumes; 16,000 scores; 9500 phonograph records; 200 reels of microfilm. **Subscriptions:** 300 journals and other serials. **Services:** Interlibrary loans; copying; library open to public.

★15333★
UNIVERSITY OF CALIFORNIA, RIVERSIDE - OFFICE OF TECHNICAL INFO. - STATEWIDE AIR POLLUTION RESEARCH CTR.
Riverside, CA 92521
Founded: 1971. **Subjects:** Air pollution, air quality, atmospheric transformations, effects on vegetation. **Special Collections:** San Francisco Bay Area Pollution Control District's Library (16,000 entries on microfilm); Biological Effects of Air Pollution on Plants (9000 copies of articles). **Holdings:** 200 books; 3000 unbound technical reports; 4 shelves of newspaper clippings; 13 shelves of research staff reprints; 20 shelves of other material. **Special Catalogs:** Catalog of Research Center staff publications, 1950-1982. **Special Indexes:** TRIM computerized index of unbound reports. **Remarks:** Presently inactive.

★15334★
UNIVERSITY OF CALIFORNIA, RIVERSIDE - PHYSICAL SCIENCES LIBRARY (Sci-Tech)
Phone: (714) 787-3511
Riverside, CA 92517   Richard W. Vierich, Hd.Libn.
Founded: 1961. **Staff:** Prof 2; Other 4. **Subjects:** Chemistry, physics, energy science, geology, geophysics, geography, mathematics and computer science, soil and environmental science, pre-engineering. **Special Collections:** Weaver and Putnam collections in geology; geologic maps (15,000); Sadtler, Coblentz & API/MCA spectra; U.S. Geological Survey open file reports microfiche collection. **Holdings:** 88,000 books and bound periodical volumes; 10,503 microforms; 260 reels of microfilm. **Subscriptions:** 1800 journals and other serials. **Services:** Interlibrary loans; copying; SDI; library open to public. **Automated Operations:** Computerized circulation. **Computerized Information Services:** LIBS 100 System. **Networks/Consortia:** Member of Inland Empire Academic Libraries Cooperative (IEALC); San Bernardino, Inyo, Riverside Counties United Library Services (SIRCULS). **Special Indexes:** Index to Maps in the Physical Sciences Library (microfiche). **Staff:** Vernal Norris, Chf.Lib.Asst.; Carol Resco, Ref.Libn./Comp. Searching.

★15335★
UNIVERSITY OF CALIFORNIA, RIVERSIDE - SPECIAL COLLECTIONS (Hum)
Box 5900   Phone: (714) 787-3233
Riverside, CA 92517   Clifford R. Wurfel, Hd., Spec.Coll.
Staff: Prof 2; Other 1. **Special Collections:** 20th century English literature; Ezra Pound (700 volumes); Juan Silvano Godoi Collection (45 volumes; 57 boxes); Eaton Collection of Fantasy and Science Fiction (30,000 volumes; 4500 periodicals); historical collection of children's literature (2000 volumes); Thomas Hardy Theater Collection; Skinner-Ropes Collection (7000 manuscripts, 1843-1917, including 5 Civil War diaries and extensive Californiana); Sadakichi Hartmann Collection (47 boxes); Oswald Jonas/Heinrich Schenker Collection (71 boxes); Jack Hirschman poetry (2700 sheets

of manuscripts); William Blake Collection (900 volumes); Niels Gade Collection (600 volumes); German National Socialism (5000 volumes); photography (3000 volumes); utopias (500 volumes); women (5000 volumes); history of citriculture; date growing. **Holdings:** 50,000 books; 100 bound periodical volumes; university archives (1200 items and 52 tapes); 2300 volumes of dissertations. **Services:** Interlibrary loans; copying; library open to public.

★15336★
UNIVERSITY OF CALIFORNIA, SAN DIEGO - BIOMEDICAL LIBRARY (Med)
La Jolla, CA 92093
Phone: (619) 452-3253
Mary Horres, Libn.
Founded: 1963. **Staff:** Prof 8; Other 30. **Subjects:** Clinical and pre-clinical medicine, biology. **Holdings:** 156,563 books and bound periodical volumes. **Subscriptions:** 3527 journals and other serials. **Services:** Interlibrary loans; copying; library open to public. **Automated Operations:** Computerized cataloging and serials. **Computerized Information Services:** NLM, BRS, OCLC, DIALOG. Performs searches on cost recovery basis. **Networks/Consortia:** Member of Pacific Southwest Regional Medical Library Service (PSRMLS). **Staff:** Susan Starr, Hd., Pub.Serv.; Thomas Morton, Hd., Tech.Serv.

★15337★
UNIVERSITY OF CALIFORNIA, SAN DIEGO - MEDICAL CENTER LIBRARY (Med)
225 Dickinson St.
Phone: (619) 294-6520
San Diego, CA 92103
Sue Ann M. Johnson, Hd.Libn.
Staff: Prof 1; Other 6. **Subjects:** Medicine, nursing. **Holdings:** 22,864 books and bound periodical volumes; 7315 slides; 1298 cassettes. **Subscriptions:** 719 journals and other serials. **Services:** Interlibrary loans; copying; library open to public for limited reference service but materials do not circulate. **Automated Operations:** Computerized serials. **Computerized Information Services:** NLM, BRS, DIALOG. **Networks/Consortia:** Member of Pacific Southwest Regional Medical Library Service (PSRMLS). **Remarks:** Library is a branch of the Biomedical Library.

★15338★
UNIVERSITY OF CALIFORNIA, SAN DIEGO - SCIENCE & ENGINEERING LIBRARY (Sci-Tech; Comp Sci)
C-075E
Phone: (619) 452-3257
La Jolla, CA 92093
Beverlee French, Libn.
Founded: 1965. **Staff:** Prof 3; Other 10. **Subjects:** Mathematics, chemistry, physics, computer science, engineering, astronomy. **Holdings:** 131,201 volumes. **Subscriptions:** 2273 journals and other serials. **Services:** Interlibrary loans; copying; library open to public. **Computerized Information Services:** DIALOG, SDC, BRS. **Staff:** Karen Feeney, Ref.Libn.

★15339★
UNIVERSITY OF CALIFORNIA, SAN DIEGO - SCRIPPS INSTITUTION OF OCEANOGRAPHY LIBRARY (Sci-Tech)
Phone: (619) 452-3274
La Jolla, CA 92093
William J. Goff, Libn.
Founded: 1913. **Staff:** Prof 4; Other 15. **Subjects:** Physical oceanography, marine biology, geological sciences. **Special Collections:** Expedition literature. **Holdings:** 180,803 volumes; 102,363 reports and reprints; 51,171 maps and charts; 20,171 microforms. **Subscriptions:** 3555 journals and other serials. **Services:** Interlibrary loans; copying; library open to public for reference use only. **Automated Operations:** Computerized cataloging. **Computerized Information Services:** DIALOG, SDC, BRS, OCLC. **Staff:** Barbara Tillett, Tech.Serv.Libn.; Diana Lane, Ref.Libn.; Deborah Day, Archv.

★15340★
UNIVERSITY OF CALIFORNIA, SAN DIEGO - UNIVERSITY LIBRARIES (Hum)
Phone: (619) 452-3336
La Jolla, CA 92093
Millicent D. Abell, Univ.Libn.
Staff: Prof 55; Other 159. **Subjects:** Oceanography, marine biology, marine geology, mathematics, physics, chemistry, earth sciences, Spanish literature, philosophy, medicine. **Special Collections:** D.H. Lawrence Collection; Ernest Hemingway Collection; Baja California Collection; Renaissance; Pacific voyages; Spanish Civil War; Archive for New Poetry; Ira Wolff Mystery Collection. **Holdings:** 1,613,656 volumes. **Subscriptions:** 29,662 journals and other serials. **Services:** Interlibrary loans; copying; library open to public for reference use only. **Automated Operations:** Computerized cataloging and serials. **Computerized Information Services:** DIALOG, OCLC, SDC, BRS. **Networks/Consortia:** Member of CRL; Association of Research Libraries (ARL); San Diego Greater Metropolitan Area Library & Information Agency Council (METRO); CLASS. **Remarks:** Figures given include holdings of the Central University Library and five branch libraries. **Staff:** Phyllis S. Mirsky, Asst.Univ.Libn.George J. Soete, Asst.Univ.Libn.; Carol A. Mandel, Asst.Univ.Libn.; Garrett Bowles, Music Libn.; I. Marc Gittelsohn,

Undergraduate Libn.; M. Sharon Anderson, Doc.Dept.Libn.; Marilyn J. Wilson, Acq.Libn.; Suzanne Metzger, Act.Cat.Libn.; Judith Herschman, Ref.Libn.; Joanne Donovan, Act.Circ.Libn.; Lynda Claasen, Spec.Coll.Libn.

★15341★
UNIVERSITY OF CALIFORNIA, SAN FRANCISCO - HASTINGS COLLEGE OF THE LAW - LEGAL INFORMATION CENTER (Law)
200 McAllister St.
Phone: (415) 557-1354
San Francisco, CA 94102-4978
Dan F. Henke, Dir.
Founded: 1878. **Staff:** Prof 9; Other 22. **Subjects:** Law. **Special Collections:** Sutro Room (collection of trials and legal biographies); U.S. and California Documents Depository. **Holdings:** 348,361 volumes. **Subscriptions:** 4690 journals and other serials; 30 newspapers. **Services:** Interlibrary loans; copying; center open to public with restrictions. **Automated Operations:** Computerized cataloging. **Computerized Information Services:** OCLC, DIALOG, Westlaw, LEXIS, NEXIS. Performs searches on cost recovery basis. Contact Person: Laura Peritore, 557-8413. **Networks/Consortia:** Member of LAWNET. **Publications:** Monthly Acquisitions List; Hastings Law Library Guide. **Staff:** Gail Winson, Assoc.Libn.; Robert Berger, Asst.Libn.; Linda Weir, Ref.Libn.; Karen Toran, Circ.Libn.; Mary Glennon, Cat.; Laura Peritore, Ser./Ref.Libn.; Veronica Maclay, Govt.Doc.Libn.

★15342★
UNIVERSITY OF CALIFORNIA, SAN FRANCISCO - LIBRARY (Med)
Parnassus Ave., 257-S
Phone: (415) 666-2334
San Francisco, CA 94143
David Bishop, Univ.Libn.
Founded: 1864. **Staff:** Prof 19; Other 49. **Subjects:** Health sciences, medicine, dentistry, pharmacy, nursing. **Special Collections:** History of Health Sciences; Oriental Medicine; homeopathy; Osleriana; California medicine. **Holdings:** 597,341 volumes. **Subscriptions:** 3923 journals and other serials. **Services:** Interlibrary loans; copying; library open to public with restricted circulation. **Automated Operations:** Computerized cataloging. **Computerized Information Services:** MEDLINE, OCLC, SDC. **Networks/Consortia:** Member of San Francisco Consortium; Pacific Southwest Regional Medical Library Service (PSRMLS). **Publications:** Serials Titles List. **Staff:** Richard S. Cooper, Assoc.Univ.Libn.; Mary P. Barr, Hd., Pub.Serv.; Steven I. Tarczy, Hd., Tech.Serv.

★15343★
UNIVERSITY OF CALIFORNIA, SANTA BARBARA - ARTS LIBRARY (Art; Mus)
Phone: (805) 961-3613
Santa Barbara, CA 93106
William R. Treese, Hd./Art Libn.
Staff: Prof 4; Other 9. **Subjects:** Art, music, history of photography. **Special Collections:** Art Exhibition Catalog Collection (40,000); Archive of Art Auction Catalogs (35,000); Archive of Recorded Vocal Music (20,000 78 rpm discs). **Holdings:** 115,000 books and bound periodical volumes; 26,000 LP phonograph records; 11,500 microforms; 68 videotapes; 2000 audiotapes. **Subscriptions:** 704 journals and other serials. **Services:** Interlibrary loans; copying; library open to public. **Automated Operations:** Computerized cataloging and circulation. **Computerized Information Services:** DIALOG, BRS, OCLC, RLIN; internal database. **Networks/Consortia:** Member of RLG. **Special Indexes:** Art Exhibition Catalog Subject Index (1978); computerized catalog of Archive of Recorded Vocal Music. **Staff:** Martin Silver, Asst.Hd./Music Libn.; Susan Sonnet, Asst. Music Libn.

★15344★
UNIVERSITY OF CALIFORNIA, SANTA BARBARA - BLACK STUDIES LIBRARY UNIT (Area-Ethnic)
Phone: (805) 961-2922
Santa Barbara, CA 93106
Sylvia Y. Curtis, Act.Libn.
Founded: 1971. **Staff:** Prof 1; Other 1. **Subjects:** Afro-American studies, African area studies, Caribbean studies, black literature and history. **Holdings:** 4000 books; 5 VF drawers of newspaper clippings; 5 VF drawers of pamphlets; catalogs from black colleges and universities. **Subscriptions:** 101 journals and other serials. **Services:** Interlibrary loans; SDI; library open to public. **Automated Operations:** Computerized cataloging, acquisitions, serials and circulation. **Computerized Information Services:** DIALOG, BRS, SDC. **Publications:** The AfroAmerican, quarterly - to staff, patrons and on request.

★15345★
UNIVERSITY OF CALIFORNIA, SANTA BARBARA - DEPARTMENT OF SPECIAL COLLECTIONS (Rare Book; Hum)
University Library
Phone: (805) 961-3420
Santa Barbara, CA 93106
Christian Brun, Dept.Hd.
Staff: Prof 1; Other 2. **Special Collections:** Printing; Abraham Lincoln; Civil War; antislavery; U.S. westward expansion; Aldous Huxley; Samuel Beckett; Henry James; Robinson Jeffers; Charles Bukowski; W. Somerset Maugham; avante-garde literature; illustrated books; birth control; circus; Californiana;

Bibles; Colombian novels; Mauritius; Spanish Inquisition; French revolutionary pamphlets; Christmas books; press books; trade catalogs; evolution; Edmund Burke; Pear Tree Press; Rudge Press; Mme. Lotte Lehman Archive; Pearl Chase Collection; Donald Culross Peattie Collection; George Tebbetts Collection; Stuart L. Bernath Collection; Morris Ernst Banned Book Collection. **Holdings:** 94,000 books; 301,756 manuscripts; 2400 theses; 1600 reels of microfilm; 12,000 microcards. **Subscriptions:** 63 journals and other serials. **Services:** Interlibrary loans; copying; collections open to qualified individuals.

★15346★
UNIVERSITY OF CALIFORNIA, SANTA BARBARA - GOVERNMENT PUBLICATIONS DEPARTMENT (Info Sci)
University Library   Phone: (805) 961-2863
Santa Barbara, CA 93106   Herbert Linville, Hd.
Staff: Prof 5; Other 6. **Subjects:** Federal, state and international government publications. **Holdings:** 519,087 government publications (paper copy); 261,717 government publications in microform. **Subscriptions:** 5838 journals and other serials. **Services:** Interlibrary loans; copying; department open to public. **Staff:** Gary Peete, Foreign Doc.Libn.Joan Pursell, Local Doc.Libn.Lucia Snowhill, U.S. Doc.Libn.

★15347★
UNIVERSITY OF CALIFORNIA, SANTA BARBARA - LIBRARY - CHICANO STUDIES COLLECTION (Area-Ethnic)
University Library   Phone: (805) 961-2756
Santa Barbara, CA 93106   Sal Guerena, Assoc.Libn./Unit Hd.
Staff: Prof 1; Other 1. **Subjects:** Chicano literature and history, social sciences, bibliography, bilingual education. **Special Collections:** Chicano Studies Serial Collection (300 titles on microfilm); Chicano Studies Literary Videotape Series (38 videotapes). **Holdings:** 6500 books; 200 bound periodical volumes; 6500 files of pamphlets, clippings; 200 posters. **Subscriptions:** 65 journals and other serials. **Services:** Interlibrary loans; copying; library open to public for reference use only. **Automated Operations:** Computerized cataloging. **Computerized Information Services:** OCLC. **Networks/Consortia:** Member of CRL; University of California Chicano Information Management Consortium. **Publications:** Chicanos: A Checklist of Current Materials, biennial - free upon request; list of additional publications - free upon request. **Also Known As:** Coleccion Tloque Nahuaque.

★15348★
UNIVERSITY OF CALIFORNIA, SANTA BARBARA - MAP AND IMAGERY LABORATORY - LIBRARY (Geog-Map)
                                     Phone: (805) 961-2779
Santa Barbara, CA 93106   Larry Carver, Dept.Hd.
Founded: 1967. **Staff:** Prof 1; Other 5. **Subjects:** Remotely sensed imagery, topographic maps, physical and biological science mapping, land use mapping, nautical charts. **Special Collections:** Remotely sensed imagery (1.4 million aerial photographs/satellite imagery); U.S. Geological Survey historic backfiles of topographic maps; Corps of Engineers historic backfiles of topographic mapping. **Holdings:** 2400 atlases and gazetteers; 287,000 maps; EROS microforms. **Services:** Interlibrary loans (limited); training on cartographic/remote sensing interpretation/information transfer lab equipment by prior arrangement. **Computerized Information Services:** Earth Resources Observation System (EROS), OCLC; internal database. **Networks/Consortia:** Member of Total Interlibrary Exchange (TIE); Joint University of California Map Library Management Group. **Special Catalogs:** EROS Data Center's MicroCatalog.

★15349★
UNIVERSITY OF CALIFORNIA, SANTA BARBARA - ORIENTAL COLLECTION (Area-Ethnic)
University Library   Phone: (805) 961-2365
Santa Barbara, CA 93106   Henry H. Tai, Oriental Libn.
Staff: Prof 2; Other 1. **Subjects:** East Asia - humanities, social sciences. **Holdings:** 60,000 books; 9000 bound periodical volumes; 360 microforms. **Subscriptions:** 297 journals and other serials; 17 newspapers. **Services:** Interlibrary loans; collection open to public. **Computerized Information Services:** OCLC. **Networks/Consortia:** Member of RLG. **Staff:** Sung In Horton, Asst.Libn.

★15350★
UNIVERSITY OF CALIFORNIA, SANTA BARBARA - SCIENCES-ENGINEERING LIBRARY (Sci-Tech)
                                     Phone: (805) 961-2765
Santa Barbara, CA 93106   Alfred J. Hodina, Hd.
Founded: 1966. **Staff:** Prof 6; Other 9. **Subjects:** Geography; physical sciences; life sciences; geology; military science; marine science; mathematics; computer science; linguistics; speech and communication; environmental studies; engineering - chemical, nuclear, electrical, mechanical.

Special Collections: Oil Spill Information Center Archives (contains materials of the Santa Barbara oil spill of January 24, 1969; 3000 documents). **Holdings:** 344,500 books and bound periodical volumes; 603,000 technical and contract reports; 3500 pamphlets; 2000 uncataloged items. **Subscriptions:** 5900 journals and other serials. **Services:** Interlibrary loans; copying; library open to public. **Computerized Information Services:** DIALOG, SDC, BRS, MEDLINE, NIH-EPA Chemical Information System, RLIN, NLM, Earth Resources Observation System (EROS); Instructional Improvement Information Data Base (internal database). **Publications:** Laboratory workbook on information resources in science and engineering; literature guides in chemistry, geography, botany, ergonomics and in general biology - distributed through office of University Librarian. **Staff:** Robert Sivers, Asst.Hd.; Norma Claussen, Engr./Math Libn.; Virginia Weiser, Life Sci.Libn.;Albert Krichmar, Linguistics/Commun.Libn.

★15351★
UNIVERSITY OF CALIFORNIA, SANTA CRUZ - DEAN E. MC HENRY LIBRARY (Hum)
                                     Phone: (408) 429-2801
Santa Cruz, CA 95064   Allan J. Dyson, Univ.Libn.
Staff: Prof 27; Other 65. **Subjects:** Literature, local history. **Special Collections:** Thomas Carlyle; Kenneth Patchen; Gregory Bateson; Robert Heinlein; South Pacific; Santa Cruz local history including pre-statehood and Mexican local government archives; Trianon Press Archive; fine printing; Californiana. **Services:** Interlibrary loans; copying; library open to public. **Automated Operations:** Computerized cataloging and circulation. **Computerized Information Services:** DIALOG, BRS, OCLC. **Special Catalogs:** Catalog of the South Pacific Collection. **Staff:** Margaret Robinson, Hd., Ref.; Rita Bottoms, Hd., Spec. Coll.; Gary Carlton, Hd., Circ.; Marion Taylor, Hd., Coll.Plan.

★15352★
UNIVERSITY OF CALIFORNIA, SANTA CRUZ - MAP COLLECTION (Geog-Map)
McHenry Library Bldg.   Phone: (408) 429-2364
Santa Cruz, CA 95064   Stanley D. Stevens, Map Libn.
Staff: Prof 1; Other 1. **Subjects:** Cartography and aerial photography. **Special Collections:** Sanborn maps on color film of Monterey Bay area cities; historical maps of Santa Cruz County and the four adjacent counties; depository library for complete topographical coverage of Canada and the United States. **Holdings:** 128,000 maps; 19,000 aerial photographs; 1500 microfiche of nautical charts; 4000 Sanborn maps on film mounted into slides. **Services:** Interlibrary loans (limited); copying; collection open to public. **Automated Operations:** Computerized cataloging. **Computerized Information Services:** OCLC. **Special Catalogs:** Catalog of Aerial Photos in the Map Collection of the University Library (May, 1979; loose-leaf binder).

★15353★
UNIVERSITY OF CALIFORNIA, SANTA CRUZ - REGIONAL HISTORY PROJECT (Hist)
Dean E. McHenry Library   Phone: (408) 429-2847
Santa Cruz, CA 95064   Randall Jarrell, Dir.
Founded: 1965. **Staff:** Prof 1; Other 1. **Subjects:** California and central California Coast area: social, economic, agricultural and governmental history, transportation, principal industries. **Holdings:** Transcripts of interviews, photographs of interviewees. **Services:** Library open to researchers on request, for reference use only. **Publications:** Bibliography - available on request. **Special Indexes:** Master regional history index. **Remarks:** Transcripts are also on deposit in the Bancroft Library of University of California, Berkeley, and some are available on microfilm through the New York Times Oral History Program.

★15354★
UNIVERSITY OF CALIFORNIA, SANTA CRUZ - SCIENCE LIBRARY (Sci-Tech)
                                     Phone: (408) 429-2050
Santa Cruz, CA 95064   Carolyn Miller, Sci.Libn.
Founded: 1969. **Staff:** Prof 5; Other 3. **Subjects:** Astronomy, biology, chemistry, earth sciences, mathematics, physics. **Special Collections:** Lick Observatory Library (33,000 volumes; 750 serials). **Holdings:** 165,000 volumes. **Subscriptions:** 3500 journals and other serials. **Services:** Interlibrary loans; copying; library open to public. **Computerized Information Services:** Online systems. **Staff:** George Keller, Sci.Ref.Libn.; Jacqualin Manss, Hd., Circ.

★15355★
UNIVERSITY OF CAPE BRETON - BEATON INSTITUTE ARCHIVES (Hist)
Box 5300   Phone: (902) 564-6343
Sydney, NS, Canada B1P 6L2   Dr. R.J. Morgan, Dir.
Founded: 1957. **Staff:** Prof 3; Other 3. **Subjects:** Cape Breton Island -

history, labor history, Gaelic literature, folklore, political history; traditional Scottish music of Cape Breton Island; genealogy. **Special Collections:** John Parker Nautical Collection (8.7 meters); Gaelic and Scottish collection (3000 volumes); political papers. **Holdings:** 5000 books; 200 bound periodical volumes; 200 unbound reports; 20,000 photographs; 800 maps; 115 meters of manuscripts; 5 VF drawers of clippings; 600 reels of microfilm; 150 large scrapbooks; 3500 tapes; 600 slides; 50 videotapes. **Subscriptions:** 10 journals and other serials. **Services:** Copying; archives open to public. **Formerly:** College of Cape Breton. **Staff:** Dr. Mary K. Macleod, Asst.Dir.; Elizabeth Planetta, Cur.

UNIVERSITY CENTER FOR INTERNATIONAL REHABILITATION
See: Michigan State University

UNIVERSITY OF CENTRAL FLORIDA - FLORIDA SOLAR ENERGY CENTER
See: Florida Solar Energy Center

UNIVERSITY OF CENTRAL FLORIDA - NAVAL TRAINING EQUIPMENT CENTER
See: U.S. Navy - Naval Training Equipment Center

★15356★
UNIVERSITY OF CHICAGO - ART LIBRARY (Art)
Joseph Regenstein Library
1100 E. 57th St.　　　　　　　　　　Phone: (312) 962-8439
Chicago, IL 60637　　　　　　　　　Hans Lenneberg, Art Libn.
Founded: 1938. **Staff:** Prof 1; Other 6. **Subjects:** Art - ancient through modern; photography. **Holdings:** 56,500 volumes; sales catalogs; pamphlets. **Services:** Interlibrary loans; copying; library open to public with restrictions. **Automated Operations:** Computerized cataloging, acquisitions and circulation. **Networks/Consortia:** Member of CRL; RLG; ILLINET. **Special Catalogs:** Union Art Catalog (includes the holdings of major Chicago art libraries, through 1980).

★15357★
UNIVERSITY OF CHICAGO - BUSINESS/ECONOMICS LIBRARY (Bus-Fin)
Joseph Regenstein Library
1100 E. 57th St.　　　　　　　　　　Phone: (312) 753-3428
Chicago, IL 60637　　　　　　Jennette S. Rader, Bus./Econ.Libn.
Staff: Prof 2; Other 1. **Subjects:** Economics, economic and business history, finance, accounting. **Holdings:** 375,000 books. **Subscriptions:** 4000 journals and other serials. **Services:** Interlibrary loans; copying; library open to public with restrictions. **Automated Operations:** Computerized cataloging, acquisitions and circulation. **Networks/Consortia:** Member of CRL; RLG; ILLINET. **Staff:** Ralph Rohrer, Ref.Libn.

★15358★
UNIVERSITY OF CHICAGO - CHEMISTRY LIBRARY
5747 S. Ellis Ave.
Chicago, IL 60637
Defunct. Merged with Crerar (John) Library, University of Chicago - Eckhart Library and University of Chicago - Dr. Frank Billings Library to form University of Chicago - John Crerar Library.

UNIVERSITY OF CHICAGO COMPUTATION CENTER
See: Merriam Center Library

★15359★
UNIVERSITY OF CHICAGO - DEPARTMENT OF ART - MAX EPSTEIN ARCHIVE (Art)
Regenstein Library, Rm. 420
1100 E. 57th St.
Chicago, IL 60637　　　　　　　　Phone: (312) 962-7080
Founded: 1938. **Staff:** Prof 1; Other 4. **Subjects:** General art. **Special Collections:** Photographs of medals in the Courtauld Institute and the British Museum; Armenian Architectural Collection. **Holdings:** 550,000 photographs. **Services:** Archive open to public with restrictions. **Special Indexes:** Decimal Index of Arts in the Lowlands (DIAL); iconographic index; Illustrated Bartsch Index; Marburger Microfiche Index.

★15360★
UNIVERSITY OF CHICAGO - ECKHART LIBRARY
Eckhart Hall, Second Fl.
Chicago, IL 60637
Defunct. Merged with Crerar (John) Library, University of Chicago - Chemistry Library and University of Chicago - Dr. Frank Billings Library to form University of Chicago - John Crerar Library.

★15361★
UNIVERSITY OF CHICAGO - FAR EASTERN LIBRARY (Area-Ethnic)
Joseph Regenstein Library
1100 E. 57th St.　　　　　　　　　　Phone: (312) 962-8436
Chicago, IL 60637　　　　　　　　James K.M. Cheng, Cur.
Founded: 1936. **Staff:** Prof 6; Other 12. **Subjects:** Chinese classics, philosophy, history, archeology, biography, social sciences, literature and art; Japanese history, social sciences and literature. **Special Collections:** Chinese classics; Chinese local gazetteers; rare books. **Holdings:** 258,000 volumes (Chinese); 112,000 volumes (Japanese); 2700 volumes (Korean); 6400 volumes (Tibetan, Mongol, Manchu and other Far Eastern languages); 5000 pamphlets; 6200 volumes (Western language reference works); 18,000 microforms. **Subscriptions:** 2900 journals and other serials. **Services:** Interlibrary loans; copying; library open to qualified visitors. **Networks/Consortia:** Member of CRL; ILLINET; RLG. **Publications:** Reference List: Chinese Local Histories, 1969; Far Eastern Serials, 1977; Daisaku Ikeda Collection of Japanese Religion and Culture, 1977. **Special Catalogs:** Author-title catalog of Chinese Collection (8 volumes); author-title catalog of Japanese Collection (4 volumes); classified catalog and subject index of the Chinese and Japanese Collections (6 volumes), 1974; 12 volume First Supplement to above catalogs, 1981. **Staff:** Wen-Pai Tai, Chinese Libn.; Eizaburo Okuizumi, Japanese Libn.; Tai-loi Ma, Hd., Cat.

★15362★
UNIVERSITY OF CHICAGO - DR. FRANK BILLINGS LIBRARY
Billings Hospital, 950 E. 59th St.
Box 406
Chicago, IL 60637
Defunct. Merged with Crerar (John) Library, University of Chicago - Chemistry Library and University of Chicago - Eckhart Library to form University of Chicago - John Crerar Library.

★15363★
UNIVERSITY OF CHICAGO HOSPITALS & CLINICS - PHARMACEUTICAL SERVICES - DRUG INFORMATION CENTER (Med)
5841 S. Maryland Ave.　　　　　　　Phone: (312) 947-6046
Chicago, IL 60637　　　　Jeannell M. Mansur, Pharm.D., Dir.
Founded: 1975. **Staff:** Prof 2. **Subjects:** Pharmacy, biopharmaceutics, clinical pharmacology. **Holdings:** 300 books; 50 bound periodical volumes; 100 boxes of journals; Iowa Drug Information System. **Subscriptions:** 28 journals and other serials. **Services:** Center not open to public. **Automated Operations:** Computerized formulary maintenance. **Computerized Information Services:** NLM. **Publications:** Topics in Drug Therapy, monthly - by subscription. **Special Indexes:** Formulary. **Staff:** Donna J. Clay, Drug Info. Pharmacist.

★15364★
UNIVERSITY OF CHICAGO - JOHN CRERAR LIBRARY (Sci-Tech; Med)
5730 S. Ellis　　　　　　　　　　　Phone: (312) 962-7715
Chicago, IL 60637　　　Patricia K. Swanson, Asst.Dir. for Sci.Libs.
Staff: Prof 8; Other 24. **Subjects:** Astronomy; astrophysics; biological sciences, including botany, physiology and zoology; chemistry; clinical medicine; computer science; geophysical sciences, including geology, meteorology and oceanography; history of medicine; history of science; mathematics; physics; statistics; technology. **Holdings:** 350,000 books; 550,000 bound periodical volumes. **Subscriptions:** 10,000 journals and other serials. **Services:** Interlibrary loans; copying; library open to public with restrictions. **Automated Operations:** Computerized cataloging, acquisitions and circulation. **Computerized Information Services:** BRS, DIALOG, NIH-EPA Chemical Information System, MEDLARS, Questel, SDC, OCLC; internal database. Performs searches on cost recovery basis plus service fee. Contact Person: Ammiel Prochovnik. **Networks/Consortia:** Member of ILLINET; RLG; CRL; Greater Midwest Regional Medical Library Network (Region 3). **Publications:** Translations Register Index, monthly - by subscription. **Special Indexes:** Index to scientific translations into English (card). Formed by the **Merger of:** Crerar (John) Library, University of Chicago - Chemistry Library, University of Chicago - Eckhart Library and University of Chicago - Dr. Frank Billings Library. **Staff:** James Vaughan, Hd., Access Serv.; Kathleen Zar, Hd., Ref. & Subj.Serv.; Ammiel Prochovnik, Asst.Libn.; J. Walter Shelton, Assoc.Libn.

★15365★
UNIVERSITY OF CHICAGO - LAW SCHOOL LIBRARY (Law)
1121 E. 60th St.　　　　　　　　　　Phone: (312) 753-3425
Chicago, IL 60637　　　　　　　Judith M. Wright, Law Libn.
Founded: 1902. **Staff:** Prof 8; Other 14. **Subjects:** Anglo-American, foreign and international law. **Special Collections:** U.S. Supreme Court Briefs and Records. **Holdings:** 424,000 volumes. **Subscriptions:** 5952 journals and other serials. **Services:** Interlibrary loans; library not open to public.

Automated Operations: Computerized cataloging and acquisitions. Computerized Information Services: LEXIS, Westlaw; internal database. Networks/Consortia: Member of CRL; ILLINET. Publications: Selected List of Recent Publications Added to the Library, bimonthly; Law Library Handbook, annual. Staff: Camille Riley, Hd.Ref.Libn.; Judith G. Gecas, Hd., Pub.Serv.; Lorna Tang, Hd.Cat.; Gayle S. Edelman, Hd., Tech.Serv.; Jane Strable, Docs.Libn.; Adolf Sprudz, For. Law Libn.

★15366★
UNIVERSITY OF CHICAGO - MAP COLLECTION (Geog-Map)
Joseph Regenstein Library
1100 E. 57th St.   Phone: (312) 962-8761
Chicago, IL 60637
Founded: 1931. Staff: Prof 1; Other 2. Subjects: Maps, atlases, charts and aerial photographs. Special Collections: 19th-century county atlases (500); 19th- and early 20th-century urban plans (American and foreign); depository for maps of the U.S. Geological Survey, the U.S. Defense Mapping Agency, the Superintendent of Documents and U.S. National Ocean Survey. Holdings: 5000 books; 280,000 maps; 9000 aerial photographs. Subscriptions: 10 journals and other serials. Services: Interlibrary loans (contingent on condition of materials); copying; collection open to public with restrictions. Automated Operations: Computerized cataloging, acquisitions and circulation. Computerized Information Services: DIALOG, SDC, MEDLINE. Networks/Consortia: Member of CRL; RLG; ILLINET.

★15367★
UNIVERSITY OF CHICAGO - MUSIC COLLECTION (Mus)
Joseph Regenstein Library
1100 E. 57th St.   Phone: (312) 962-8451
Chicago, IL 60637   Hans Lenneberg, Music Libn.
Founded: 1940. Staff: Prof 3; Other 4. Subjects: Music, musicology, theory. Special Collections: Chicago Jazz Archive (200 hours of recordings). Holdings: 81,500 books; 6000 reels of microfilm; 8300 recordings. Subscriptions: 300 journals and other serials. Services: Interlibrary loans; copying; collection open to public with restrictions. Automated Operations: Computerized cataloging, acquisitions and circulation. Networks/Consortia: Member of CRL; RLG; ILLINET. Staff: Dena Epstein, Asst. Music Libn.; Edna Christopher, Cat.

★15368★
UNIVERSITY OF CHICAGO - NATIONAL OPINION RESEARCH CENTER - LIBRARY AND DATA ARCHIVES (Soc Sci)
6030 S. Ellis Ave.   Phone: (312) 962-1213
Chicago, IL 60637   Patrick Bova, Libn.
Founded: 1941. Staff: Prof 1; Other 2. Subjects: Sociology, public opinion research, statistics, political science, education, health and medicine. Special Collections: Current domestic and foreign public opinion polls; U.S. International Communication Agency Research Reports. Holdings: 3000 books; 24 VF drawers; NORC numbered research reports; data and materials from NORC studies; NORC field materials. Subscriptions: 100 journals and other serials. Services: Interlibrary loans; copying; library open to qualified users. Networks/Consortia: Member of Chicago Library System. Publications: Bibliography of publications, annual - gratis to mailing list.

★15369★
UNIVERSITY OF CHICAGO - ORIENTAL INSTITUTE - ARCHIVES (Area-Ethnic; Hist)
1155 E. 58th St.   Phone: (312) 962-9520
Chicago, IL 60637-1569   John A. Larson, Archv.
Staff: Prof 1; Other 4. Subjects: Ancient Near East, Near Eastern archeology, Egyptology, Assyriology, Syro-Palestinian archeology, Achaemenid Persian art. Special Collections: The Director's Files (1919 to present); the personal papers of Jens Henry Breasted, Harold H. Nelson, William F. Edgerton, Keith C. Seele, Nabia Abbot, Wilhelm Spiegelberg, W. Max Muller, and Raymond O. Bowman; field records and publication materials of the Institute's archeological field expeditions in the Near East: The Epigraphic and Architectural Survey in Egypt, The Anatolian Expedition (Alishar Huyuk), The Megiddo Expedition, The Persepolis Expedition, The Nippur Expedition, The Iraq Expedition (Khorsabab, Tell Asmar, Tell Agrab, Khafajah), and The Prehistoric Expedition. Holdings: 200 VF drawers; 100,000 black and white photographic images (1905 to present). Services: Copying; archives open to qualified scholars by appointment. Special Catalogs: The 1905-1907 Breasted Expeditions to Egypt and the Sudan: A Photographic Study (2 volumes); Persepolis and Ancient Iran; The 1919/1920 Expedition to the Near East; Ptolemais Cyrenaica - all on microfiche.

★15370★
UNIVERSITY OF CHICAGO - ORIENTAL INSTITUTE - DIRECTOR'S LIBRARY (Area-Ethnic)
1155 E. 58th St.   Phone: (312) 962-9537
Chicago, IL 60637   Charles E. Jones, Res.Archv.
Staff: Prof 1; Other 2. Subjects: Egyptology, Assyriology, Northwest Semitic languages, Near Eastern archeology, Hittitology, general ancient Near Eastern studies. Holdings: 10,139 books; 5562 bound periodical volumes; 9000 other cataloged items; 1700 maps. Subscriptions: 616 journals and other serials. Services: Library open to members of the Institute.

★15371★
UNIVERSITY OF CHICAGO - SOCIAL SERVICES ADMINISTRATION LIBRARY (Soc Sci)
969 E. 60th St.   Phone: (312) 753-3426
Chicago, IL 60637   Eileen Libby, Libn.
Founded: 1965. Staff: Prof 1; Other 3. Subjects: Social services, American and foreign social work, social problems, child welfare, health care, psychotherapy. Holdings: 17,518 books; 1883 bound periodical volumes; 5100 pamphlets; 6555 microforms. Subscriptions: 400 journals and other serials. Services: Interlibrary loans (through main university library); copying; library open to public with restrictions. Automated Operations: Computerized cataloging and acquisitions. Computerized Information Services: Access to DIALOG, SDC. Networks/Consortia: Member of ILLINET; CRL; RLG. Publications: Selected List of New Acquisitions, monthly.

★15372★
UNIVERSITY OF CHICAGO - SOUTH ASIA COLLECTION (Area-Ethnic)
1100 E. 57th St.   Phone: (312) 962-8430
Chicago, IL 60637   Maureen L.P. Patterson, Bibliog./Hd.
Founded: 1959. Staff: Prof 1; Other 3. Subjects: Humanities and social sciences in thirty South Asian and many Western languages; Indology; regional history and culture; economics; geography; art history. Special Collections: Albert Mayer papers; Gitel Steed papers; Bhubaneshwar Archive on Modern Orissa. Holdings: 175,000 books; 35,000 bound periodical volumes; 50 VF drawers of pamphlets and ephemera. Subscriptions: 5500 journals and other serials; 15 newspapers. Services: Interlibrary loans (through main university library); copying; collection open to public with restrictions. Automated Operations: Computerized cataloging, acquisitions and circulation. Computerized Information Services: DIALOG, SDC. Networks/Consortia: Member of CRL; RLG; ILLINET. Publications: Guide to the Albert Mayer Papers. Special Catalogs: Pamphlet Collection Card Catalog.

★15373★
UNIVERSITY OF CHICAGO - SPECIAL COLLECTIONS (Rare Book; Hum)
Joseph Regenstein Library
1100 E. 57th St.   Phone: (312) 962-8705
Chicago, IL 60637   Robert Rosenthal, Cur.
Special Collections: Ludwig Rosenberger Collection of Judaica; Donnelley Collection of fine printing and the history of printing; Grant Collection of English Bibles; William E. Barton Collection of Lincolniana; Frank Collection of anatomical illustration; Durrett Collection of the history of Kentucky and the Ohio River Valley; Encyclopaedia Britannica Collection of books for children, particularly of the nineteenth century; the Croue Collection of Balzac's works; American Bible Union and Hengstenberg Collections of early theology and Biblical criticism; Littlefield Collection of early American schoolbooks; Samuel Harper Collection of Russian political pamphlets, 1902-1946; Lincke Collection of German fiction, 1790-1850; Hirsch-Bernays Collection of Continental literature; Celia and Delia Austrian Collection of English drama to 1800; Eckels Collection of Cromwelliana; Heinemann Goethe Collection; Helen and Ruth Regenstein Collection of Rare Books (English and American Literature); personal papers of William Beaumont, Saul Bellow, Stephen A. Douglas, William H. English, Elijah Grant, John Gunther, Salmon O. Levinson, Fielding Lewis, Frank O. Lowden, Wyndham Robertson, Julius Rosenwald, Joel T. Hart, Joshua Lacy Wilson, George Nicholas, Michael Polanyi and others; Sir Nicholas Bacon Collection of papers and manorial records relating to estates in Norfolk and Suffolk; office files of Poetry: A Magazine of Verse, including the personal papers of Harriet Monroe; life records of Geoffrey Chaucer; The Canterbury Tales transcripts and photostats of manuscripts; ethno-history collection including reproductions of source material about the first contact of the white man and Indian in the Mississippi Valley; Wieboldt-Rosenwald Collection of photostats of German folksongs; Edgar J. Goodspeed Collection of New Testament manuscripts; Archive of the Czechs and Slovaks abroad; University of Chicago archives, including papers of Enrico Fermi, Robert Herrick, William Vaughn Moody, Howard Taylor Ricketts, Thomas C. Chamberlin, Hermann E. von Holst, William F. Ogburn, Ernest W. Burgess, Charles E. Merriam, James Franck and other members of the faculty. Holdings: 200,000 volumes; 6 million pieces of manuscript and archival materials. Networks/Consortia: Member of CRL; RLG; ILLINET. Staff: Daniel

Meyer, Asst.Univ.Archv.; Margaret Fusco, Mss.Spec./Adm.Asst.

★15374★
UNIVERSITY OF CHICAGO - YERKES OBSERVATORY LIBRARY (Sci-Tech)
Williams Bay, WI 53191
Phone: (414) 245-5555
J.A. Lola, Asst. in Chg.
Founded: 1897. **Staff:** 1. **Subjects:** Astronomy, astrophysics. **Holdings:** 15,000 books; 10,000 bound periodical volumes. **Subscriptions:** 250 journals and other serials. **Services:** Interlibrary loans; copying; library open to public by appointment.

★15375★
UNIVERSITY OF CINCINNATI - ARCHIVES AND RARE BOOKS DEPARTMENT (Hum; Rare Book)
Carl Blegen Library, 8th Fl.
Cincinnati, OH 45221
Phone: (513) 475-6459
Alice M. Vestal, Hd.
Founded: 1973. **Staff:** Prof 2; Other 1. **Subjects:** University of Cincinnati, Southwestern Ohio, 18th-century English literature, travel and exploration, North American Indian. **Special Collections:** Rare Book Collection (10,000); University Archives (4600 linear feet); Urban Studies Collection (1100 linear feet); Ohio Network Collection (1100 linear feet); Medical History Collection (700 linear feet); History of Design Collection; University Biographical File (40 linear feet); university theses and dissertations; Southwest Ohio Public Records (151 reels of microfilm). **Services:** Copying; department open to public with restrictions. **Networks/Consortia:** Member of Greater Cincinnati Library Consortium (GCLC); Ohio Network of American History Research Centers.

★15376★
UNIVERSITY OF CINCINNATI - COLLEGE CONSERVATORY OF MUSIC - GORNO MEMORIAL MUSIC LIBRARY (Mus)
Carl Blegen Library, Rm. 417
Cincinnati, OH 45221
Phone: (513) 475-4471
Robert O. Johnson, Hd.
Founded: 1967. **Staff:** Prof 3; Other 2. **Subjects:** Music performance, history and theory; musicology; dance; broadcasting; theater arts; music education. **Special Collections:** Everett Helm Collection (1500 items); Leigh Harline Collection (500 items); Anatole Chujoy Memorial Dance Collection (700 items). **Holdings:** 23,000 books and bound periodical volumes; 26,000 music scores; 19,000 phonograph records; 4500 microforms. **Subscriptions:** 600 journals and other serials. **Services:** Interlibrary loans; copying; library open to public for reference use only. **Automated Operations:** Computerized cataloging. **Networks/Consortia:** Member of Greater Cincinnati Library Consortium (GCLC); OHIONET. **Staff:** Mark Palkovic, Rec.Libn.; Susan Lundell, Music Cat.

★15377★
UNIVERSITY OF CINCINNATI - DEPARTMENT OF ENVIRONMENTAL HEALTH LIBRARY (Sci-Tech; Env-Cons)
Kettering Laboratory Library
3223 Eden Ave.
Cincinnati, OH 45267
Phone: (513) 872-5771
Evelyn M. Widner, Sr.Res.Assoc.
Founded: 1930. **Staff:** Prof 5; Other 4. **Subjects:** Environmental health, toxicology, physiology, analytical chemistry, statistics. **Special Collections:** Industrial health. **Holdings:** 6700 books; 3000 bound periodical volumes; 78 VF drawers of reprints, reports, translations; 800 microfiche and reels of microfilm; technical abstracts on cards; 530 unpublished reports. **Subscriptions:** 200 journals and other serials. **Services:** Interlibrary loans; copying; library open to professional personnel. **Computerized Information Services:** BRS, DIALOG, SDC, MEDLARS, DOE/RECON, NIH-EPA Chemical Information System. **Networks/Consortia:** Member of Cincinnati Area Health Sciences Library Association (CAHSLA); Cincinnati Online Consortium for Life Sciences (COCLS); Biomedical Communications Network. **Special Indexes:** Trace metals index (card). **Staff:** Ruth P. Trosset, Assoc.Prof.; Geraldine L. Krueger, Sr.Res.Assoc.Theodore A. Morris, Sr.Lib.Assoc./Spec.; Carol A. Warren, Res.Assoc.

★15378★
UNIVERSITY OF CINCINNATI - DESIGN, ARCHITECTURE, ART & PLANNING LIBRARY (Art)
800 Alms Bldg.
Cincinnati, OH 45221-0016
Phone: (513) 475-3238
Elizabeth D. Byrne, Hd.
Founded: 1929. **Staff:** Prof 1; Other 2. **Subjects:** Architecture, art history, art education, planning, interior design, industrial design, fine arts, fashion, urban studies, health planning, graphic design. **Special Collections:** Ladislas Segoe Collection (200 volumes on city planning). **Holdings:** 32,731 books; 8483 serial volumes; 160 reels of microfilm. **Subscriptions:** 400 journals and other serials. **Services:** Interlibrary loans; copying; library open to public with fee card required for nonuniversity persons to check out materials. **Automated Operations:** Computerized cataloging. **Networks/Consortia:**

Member of Greater Cincinnati Library Consortium (GCLC); OHIONET.

★15379★
UNIVERSITY OF CINCINNATI - ENGINEERING LIBRARY (Sci-Tech)
880 Baldwin Hall
Cincinnati, OH 45221
Phone: (513) 475-3761
Dorothy F. Byers, Hd.
Staff: Prof 2; Other 3. **Subjects:** Engineering - environmental, nuclear, civil, mechanical, aerospace, chemical, metallurgical, electrical, industrial; computers; material science; applied mechanics; metallurgy. **Special Collections:** Transportation Collection (1500 documents and other items). **Holdings:** 23,000 books; 27,000 bound periodical volumes; technical reports; DOE and NASA microfiche. **Subscriptions:** 750 journals and other serials. **Services:** Interlibrary loans; copying; library open to public. **Automated Operations:** Computerized cataloging. **Computerized Information Services:** DIALOG, SDC. Performs searches on cost recovery basis. Contact Person: Linda Tafel. **Networks/Consortia:** Member of Greater Cincinnati Library Consortium (GCLC); OHIONET. **Staff:** Ann Ridgway, Lib.Assoc.; Linda Tafel, Ref.Libn.

★15380★
UNIVERSITY OF CINCINNATI - GEOLOGY LIBRARY (Sci-Tech; Geog-Map)
103 Old Tech Bldg.
ML 13
Cincinnati, OH 45221
Phone: (513) 475-4332
Richard A. Spohn, Hd.
Staff: Prof 1; Other 1. **Subjects:** Geology. **Special Collections:** S.V. Hrabar - Exxon Guidebook Collection (1200 guidebooks of U.S. and Canada). **Holdings:** 26,262 books; 6642 bound periodical volumes; 78,000 maps. **Subscriptions:** 500 journals and other serials. **Services:** Interlibrary loans; library open to public. **Automated Operations:** Computerized cataloging. **Networks/Consortia:** Member of OHIONET; Greater Cincinnati Library Consortium (GCLC).

★15381★
UNIVERSITY OF CINCINNATI - GEORGE ELLISTON POETRY COLLECTION (Hum)
646 Central Library
Cincinnati, OH 45221
Phone: (513) 475-4709
James Cummins, Cur.
Staff: Prof 1. **Subjects:** 20th century poetry. **Special Collections:** Rare book collection (300 titles). **Holdings:** 7264 books; 434 bound periodical volumes; 413 phonograph records. **Subscriptions:** 88 journals and other serials. **Services:** Collection open to public for reference use only. **Publications:** Calendar of events, 3/year.

★15382★
UNIVERSITY OF CINCINNATI - JOHN MILLER BURNAM CLASSICAL LIBRARY (Hum)
Carl Blegen Library, Rm. 320
Cincinnati, OH 45221
Phone: (513) 475-6724
Jean Susorney Wellington, Hd.
Founded: 1900. **Staff:** Prof 1; Other 1. **Subjects:** Classical and bronze age Greek archeology, Greek and Latin languages and literature, Greek and Latin paleography and epigraphy, Byzantine and modern Greece, modern Greek language and literature, ancient history. **Special Collections:** Paleography Collection (1500 volumes); Modern Greek Collection (30,000 volumes). **Holdings:** 110,000 volumes; 15,000 foreign dissertations; 1500 items in the offprint collection; 515 reels of microfilm; 2356 microfiche. **Subscriptions:** 1800 journals and other serials. **Services:** Interlibrary loans; copying; library open to public for reference use only. **Automated Operations:** Computerized cataloging. **Networks/Consortia:** Member of OHIONET; Greater Cincinnati Library Consortium (GCLC). **Special Catalogs:** Catalog of the Modern Greek Collection, University of Cincinnati, 5 volumes (1980); The Modern Greek Collection in the Library of the University of Cincinnati, by Niove Kyparissiotis (1960). **Staff:** Eugenia Foster, Cur.

★15383★
UNIVERSITY OF CINCINNATI - MATHEMATICS LIBRARY (Sci-Tech; Comp Sci)
840 Old Chemistry Bldg.
Cincinnati, OH 45221
Phone: (513) 475-4449
Joyce Pons, Hd.
Founded: 1973. **Staff:** Prof 1. **Subjects:** Pure and applied mathematics (especially complex analysis, functional analysis, mathematical logic, topology, differential geometry, probability and statistics); computer science. **Holdings:** 10,180 books; 9716 bound periodical volumes. **Subscriptions:** 268 journals and other serials. **Services:** Interlibrary loans; copying; library open to public. **Automated Operations:** Computerized cataloging. **Networks/Consortia:** Member of OHIONET; Greater Cincinnati Library Consortium (GCLC).

★15384★

UNIVERSITY OF CINCINNATI - MEDICAL CENTER LIBRARIES - COLLEGE OF NURSING & HEALTH - LEVI MEMORIAL LIBRARY (Med)

Vine St. & St. Clair Ave.   Phone: (513) 872-5543
Cincinnati, OH 45219   Ava Fried, Dir.
Staff: Prof 1; Other 2. **Subjects:** Nursing, clinical medicine, gerontology, education, sociology. **Special Collections:** Phoebe Kandel Historical Collection (history of nursing). **Holdings:** 10,500 volumes. **Subscriptions:** 400 journals and other serials. **Services:** Interlibrary loans; library open to public by permission. **Computerized Information Services:** Online systems.

★15385★

UNIVERSITY OF CINCINNATI - MEDICAL CENTER LIBRARIES - HEALTH SCIENCES LIBRARY (Med)†

231 Bethesda Ave.   Phone: (513) 872-5627
Cincinnati, OH 45267   Richard Lucier, Dir., Media/Lib.Serv.
Founded: 1974. **Staff:** Prof 7; Other 10. **Subjects:** Medicine, pharmacy, ophthalmology, pharmacology. **Holdings:** 45,000 books; 90,000 bound periodical volumes; 3500 AV materials. **Subscriptions:** 2710 journals and other serials. **Services:** Interlibrary loans; copying; SDI; library open to public. **Automated Operations:** Computerized ILL. **Computerized Information Services:** DIALOG, BRS, SDC, NLM. **Networks/Consortia:** Member of Greater Midwest Regional Medical Library Network (Region 3); Cincinnati Area Health Sciences Library Association (CAHSLA); Biomedical Communication Network (BCN). **Publications:** MCL Newsletter, quarterly - to library patrons. **Special Catalogs:** Media Resources Center Catalog; Serials Holdings of the Health Sciences Library; Tucker Library of the History of Medicine (all book form). **Staff:** Susan Anthony, Dir., Info.Serv.; Stephena Harmony, Libn.; Ruth Epstein, Ref.Libn.; Alice Hurlebaus, Acq.Libn.; Jane Gorsky, Ref.Libn.

★15386★

UNIVERSITY OF CINCINNATI - MEDICAL CENTER LIBRARIES - HISTORY OF HEALTH SCIENCES LIBRARY AND MUSEUM (Hist; Med)

Eden & Bethesda Aves., Wherry Hall   Phone: (513) 872-5120
Cincinnati, OH 45267   Billie Broaddus, Dir.
Staff: Prof 2. **Subjects:** History of medicine and pharmacy. **Special Collections:** Tucker Library of the History of Medicine (1500 items); Mussey Collection (19th century medicine; 4000 items); Daniel Drake Historical Collection (60 items). **Holdings:** 26,000 books; 3555 bound periodical volumes; 10,000 pamphlets; 100 linear feet of archives; 2000 photographs; 21 oral history videotapes; 150 diplomas and certificates; 2000 medical instruments; 109 pharmacy jars (Cantagalli 15th century replicas produced in 1890s). **Subscriptions:** 15 journals and other serials. **Services:** Interlibrary loans; copying; library open to public with restrictions. **Computerized Information Services:** NLM, BRS. **Special Catalogs:** Tucker Library of the History of Medicine (book); Guide to the Mussey Medical and Scientific Library. **Staff:** Susanne Gilliam, Cat.; Cory Oysler, Conservation.

★15387★

UNIVERSITY OF CINCINNATI - OBSERVATORY LIBRARY (Sci-Tech)

Observatory Pl.
High Park   Phone: (513) 475-2331
Cincinnati, OH 45208   Marianne Wells, Hd., Physics Lib.
Subjects: Astronomy. **Special Collections:** Rare books. **Holdings:** 13,000 volumes. **Services:** Library open to public by appointment. **Remarks:** Library is maintained by University of Cincinnati - Physics Library.

★15388★

UNIVERSITY OF CINCINNATI - OESPER CHEMISTRY-BIOLOGY LIBRARY (Sci-Tech)

Brodie A-3, Rm. 503 (151)   Phone: (513) 475-4524
Cincinnati, OH 45221   Dorice Des Chene, Hd.
Staff: Prof 1; Other 2. **Subjects:** Chemistry, biology. **Holdings:** 30,000 books; 32,000 bound periodical volumes; 216 reels of microfilm; 1865 microfiche. **Subscriptions:** 908 journals and other serials. **Services:** Interlibrary loans; copying; library open to public, ID card required for check out of materials. **Automated Operations:** Computerized cataloging. **Computerized Information Services:** DIALOG, NLM, SDC, BRS, OCLC. **Networks/Consortia:** Member of Greater Cincinnati Library Consortium (GCLC); OHIONET.

★15389★

UNIVERSITY OF CINCINNATI - OMI COLLEGE OF APPLIED SCIENCE - TIMOTHY C. DAY TECHNICAL LIBRARY (Sci-Tech)

100 E. Central Pkwy.   Phone: (513) 475-6553
Cincinnati, OH 45210   John P. Hiestand, Libn.
Founded: 1828. **Staff:** Prof 1; Other 2. **Subjects:** Technology - electrical, mechanical and civil engineering, chemical, building construction. **Holdings:** 34,584 books; 4000 bound periodical volumes; 1700 microforms.

Subscriptions: 164 journals and other serials. **Services:** Interlibrary loans; copying; library open to public for reference use only. **Networks/Consortia:** Member of Greater Cincinnati Library Consortium (GCLC).

★15390★

UNIVERSITY OF CINCINNATI - PHYSICS LIBRARY (Sci-Tech)

406 Braunstein Hall   Phone: (513) 475-2331
Cincinnati, OH 45221   Marianna Wells, Hd.
Founded: 1929. **Staff:** 2. **Subjects:** Classical and modern physics (all fields), solid state physics, biophysics, geophysics, nuclear physics, atmospheric and terrestrial physics. **Holdings:** 39,262 books; 10,550 bound periodical volumes; 217 dissertations. **Subscriptions:** 318 journals and other serials. **Services:** Interlibrary loans; copying; library open to public. **Automated Operations:** Computerized cataloging. **Networks/Consortia:** Member of Greater Cincinnati Library Consortium (GCLC); OHIONET. **Remarks:** Maintains the University of Cincinnati - Observatory Library.

★15391★

UNIVERSITY OF CINCINNATI - RAYMOND WALTERS COLLEGE - LIBRARY (Med)

9555 Plainfield Rd.   Phone: (513) 745-4313
Cincinnati, OH 45236   Lucy Wilson, Coll.Libn.
Staff: Prof 4; Other 6. **Subjects:** Dental hygiene. **Special Collections:** Local suburban newspapers. **Holdings:** 39,321 books; 2500 government documents; 12,000 microforms; 1500 pamphlets. **Subscriptions:** 671 journals and other serials; 16 newspapers. **Services:** Interlibrary loans; copying; SDI; library open to public. **Automated Operations:** Computerized cataloging. **Computerized Information Services:** DIALOG. Contact Person: Gerald Nidich, (513) 745-4314. **Networks/Consortia:** Member of OHIONET; Greater Cincinnati Library Consortium (GCLC). **Publications:** New & Novel, quarterly - to college faculty. **Staff:** Susan Falgner, Evening Ref.Libn.

★15392★

UNIVERSITY OF CINCINNATI - ROBERT S. MARX LAW LIBRARY (Law)

Law School   Phone: (513) 472-3016
Cincinnati, OH 45221   Jorge L. Carro, Hd.Libn.
Founded: 1832. **Staff:** Prof 4; Other 4. **Subjects:** Law - general, comparative, international; government documents. **Special Collections:** Morgan Collection on Human Rights (800 volumes). **Holdings:** 185,000 volumes. **Subscriptions:** 650 journals and other serials; 12 newspapers. **Services:** Interlibrary loans; copying; library open to public for reference use only. **Automated Operations:** Computerized cataloging. **Computerized Information Services:** LEXIS, Westlaw, NEXIS. **Staff:** Steve Perkins, Act.Ref.Libn.; Janet Wardlaw, Ser.; Pat Keller, Acq.; Janice Platt, Cat.; Mark Dinkelacker, Circ.; Charles Parsons, Govt.Doc.

UNIVERSITY OF CINCINNATI - UNIVERSITY AFFILIATED CINCINNATI CENTER FOR DEVELOPMENTAL DISORDERS
See: University Affiliated Cincinnati Center for Developmental Disorders

★15393★

UNIVERSITY CITY PUBLIC LIBRARY - RECORD COLLECTION (Mus)

6701 Delmar
University City, MO 63130   Robert L. Miller, Libn.
Subjects: Music - classical, popular, jazz, folk. **Holdings:** 12,300 music and spoken word phonograph records; 190 art prints; 200 8mm films; scores. **Services:** Collection open to public.

★15394★

UNIVERSITY CLUB LIBRARY (Hum)

1 W. 54th St.   Phone: (212) 572-3418
New York, NY 10019   Guy St. Clair, Dir.
Founded: 1879. **Staff:** Prof 3; Other 4. **Subjects:** Literature; history - New York, American, world; collegiana; biography. **Special Collections:** Tinker, Darrow, Rudge Collections on printing and printing history; Bicklehaupt Collection of Sporting Books; Southern Society Collection of Books about the South. **Holdings:** 135,000 books; 1500 bound periodical volumes; 150 VF drawers of New York newspapers in microform; 25 VF drawers of University Club Archives. **Subscriptions:** 150 journals and other serials; 20 newspapers. **Services:** Interlibrary loans; copying; library open to serious scholars with written application. **Staff:** Andrew J. Berner, Asst.Libn.; Ali Zarabi, Tech.Serv.Libn.

★15395★

UNIVERSITY OF COLORADO, BOULDER - ACADEMIC MEDIA SERVICES (Aud-Vis)

Stadium Bldg., Rm. 361
Campus Box 455   Phone: (303) 492-7341
Boulder, CO 80309   Dr. Elwood E. Miller, Dir.
Founded: 1923. **Staff:** Prof 3; Other 16. **Subjects:** Social studies, science,

arts and humanities, language, general areas. **Special Collections:** 16mm educational films covering most subject areas for primary, elementary, junior, senior and adult groups; Alternative Energy Motion Pictures. **Holdings:** 6000 16mm films; 14,000 audiotapes; 100 videotapes. **Services:** Interlibrary loans; audio- and videotape duplication; services open to public. **Special Catalogs:** University of Colorado Educational Motion Picture Catalog. **Formerly:** Its Educational Media Center. **Staff:** Dan Niemeyer, Prod.Supv.; Jan Sichel, Supv., Film & Video Lib.

★15396★
UNIVERSITY OF COLORADO, BOULDER - ART AND ARCHITECTURE LIBRARY (Art)
Norlin Library
Campus Box 184   Phone: (303) 492-7955
Boulder, CO 80309   Liesel Nolan, Libn.
Founded: 1966. **Staff:** Prof 1; Other 2. **Subjects:** Art, architecture, environmental design, filmmaking, photography. **Special Collections:** Major art exhibition catalogs, 1962 to present (4438 items). **Holdings:** 57,647 volumes; 13,000 bound periodical volumes; artists files; museum files; picture files. **Subscriptions:** 320 journals and other serials. **Services:** Interlibrary loans; copying; library open to public.

★15397★
UNIVERSITY OF COLORADO, BOULDER - AUDIOVISUAL/MICROFORMS DEPARTMENT (Aud-Vis)
Norlin Library
Campus Box 184   Phone: (303) 492-6930
Boulder, CO 80309   Sharon Gause, Libn.
Founded: 1968. **Staff:** Prof 1; Other 2. **Subjects:** Literature, social science, art, science. **Holdings:** 1865 audiotapes; 4319 phonograph records; 341 filmstrips; 126 film loops; 121 videotapes; 6246 slides; 475,371 microforms. **Services:** Library open to public.

★15398★
UNIVERSITY OF COLORADO, BOULDER - BUSINESS RESEARCH DIVISION - BUSINESS & ECONOMIC COLLECTION (Bus-Fin)
Campus Box 420   Phone: (303) 492-8227
Boulder, CO 80309   C.R. Goeldner, Dir.
Founded: 1915. **Subjects:** National and Colorado economic data, finance, marketing, real estate, insurance, management. **Holdings:** 4500 volumes. **Subscriptions:** 65 journals and other serials. **Services:** Copying; library open to public.

★15399★
UNIVERSITY OF COLORADO, BOULDER - BUSINESS RESEARCH DIVISION - TRAVEL REFERENCE CENTER (Rec)
Campus Box 420   Phone: (303) 492-8227
Boulder, CO 80309   C.R. Goeldner, Dir.
Founded: 1969. **Staff:** 2. **Subjects:** Travel, tourism, recreation, leisure. **Holdings:** 40 books; 2 VF drawers of travel papers, speeches and miscellaneous publications; 5000 other items. **Subscriptions:** 20 journals and other serials. **Services:** Copying; center open to public. **Staff:** Karen Duca, Economist.

★15400★
UNIVERSITY OF COLORADO, BOULDER - CENTER FOR ECONOMIC ANALYSIS - LIBRARY (Bus-Fin)
Economics Bldg. 208
Campus Box 257   Phone: (303) 492-7413
Boulder, CO 80309   Michael Greenwood
Founded: 1964. **Staff:** Prof 1; Other 1. **Subjects:** Economics. **Holdings:** 500 volumes. **Subscriptions:** 40 journals and other serials. **Services:** Interlibrary loans (limited); library not open to public. **Formerly:** Its Bureau of Economic Research.

★15401★
UNIVERSITY OF COLORADO, BOULDER - CENTER FOR PUBLIC POLICY RESEARCH LIBRARY
125 Ketchum Hall
Campus Box 330
Boulder, CO 80309
Defunct

★15402★
UNIVERSITY OF COLORADO, BOULDER - EARTH SCIENCES LIBRARY (Sci-Tech)
Campus Box 184   Phone: (303) 492-6133
Boulder, CO 80309   Terrie O'Neal, Lib.Techn.
Founded: 1876. **Staff:** 1. **Subjects:** Physical geology, historical geology,

mineralogy, paleontology, stratigraphy, geophysics, geochemistry, oceanography, structural geology. **Holdings:** 25,522 volumes. **Subscriptions:** 318 journals and other serials. **Services:** Interlibrary loans; copying; library open to public.

★15403★
UNIVERSITY OF COLORADO, BOULDER - EDUCATIONAL MEDIA CENTER - NATIONAL CENTER FOR AUDIO TAPES
Stadium Bldg.
Campus Box 379
Boulder, CO 80309
Defunct

★15404★
UNIVERSITY OF COLORADO, BOULDER - ENGINEERING LIBRARY (Sci-Tech)
Campus Box 184   Phone: (303) 492-5396
Boulder, CO 80309   Jean D. Messimer, Libn.
Founded: 1965. **Staff:** Prof 1; Other 2. **Subjects:** Engineering. **Holdings:** 83,000 volumes; 400 titles on microfilm and microfiche. **Subscriptions:** 750 journals. **Services:** Interlibrary loans; copying; library open to public. **Publications:** Weekly acquisitions list.

★15405★
UNIVERSITY OF COLORADO, BOULDER - GOVERNMENT PUBLICATIONS DIVISION (Info Sci)
Norlin Library
Campus Box 184   Phone: (303) 492-8834
Boulder, CO 80309   Catharine J. Reynolds, Hd., Govt.Pubn.
Staff: Prof 2; Other 4. **Subjects:** Government publications - federal, state, foreign, international. **Holdings:** 171,901 volumes; 9360 reels of microfilm; 1.7 million microcards and microfiche; 164,700 microprints. **Services:** Interlibrary loans; copying; division open to public. **Remarks:** Includes the holdings of the Regional Technical Reports Center.

★15406★
UNIVERSITY OF COLORADO, BOULDER - INSTITUTE OF ARCTIC & ALPINE RESEARCH - READING ROOM (Sci-Tech)
Rose M. Litman Research Lab.
Campus Box 450   Phone: (303) 492-6387
Boulder, CO 80309   Martha Andrews, Prof.Res.Asst.
Staff: 1. **Subjects:** Arctic and Alpine environments (past and present), meteorology, climatology, geomorphology, hydrology, palynology, Quaternary geology, glaciology, plant and animal ecology. **Holdings:** 2000 books; 250 bound periodical volumes; 300 reprints; 3000 reports; 300 maps; 200 microfiche; 180 theses. **Subscriptions:** 60 journals and other serials. **Services:** Room open to serious researchers for reference use only.

★15407★
UNIVERSITY OF COLORADO, BOULDER - INSTITUTE OF BEHAVIORAL SCIENCE - IBS RESEARCH LIBRARY (Soc Sci)
IBS Bldg. 1
Campus Box 483   Phone: (303) 492-8340
Boulder, CO 80309   Diana Oldsen, Lib.Techn.
Founded: 1969. **Staff:** 1. **Subjects:** Social science. **Holdings:** 300 volumes; 200 departmental publications. **Subscriptions:** 15 journals and other serials. **Services:** Interlibrary loans; copying; SDI; library open to public. **Computerized Information Services:** DIALOG.

★15408★
UNIVERSITY OF COLORADO, BOULDER - JOINT INSTITUTE FOR LABORATORY ASTROPHYSICS - DATA CENTER (Sci-Tech)
Campus Box 440   Phone: (303) 492-7801
Boulder, CO 80309   J.W. Gallagher, Mgr.
Founded: 1963. **Staff:** Prof 3; Other 1. **Subjects:** Low-energy atomic collision; collisions of low-energy electrons and photons with atoms and simple molecules; low-energy heavy-particle collisions. **Holdings:** 19,000 documents on microfiche; data files of atomic cross-sections; 12 magnetic tapes. **Services:** Center open to public for reference use only. **Networks/Consortia:** Member of National Standard Reference Data System. **Publications:** Articles in the Journal of Physical and Chemical Reference Data. **Special Indexes:** Annotated bibliographies on time-share disk files and hard copies. **Also Known As:** The Atomic Collision Cross Section Data Center.

★15409★
UNIVERSITY OF COLORADO, BOULDER - LAW LIBRARY (Law)
Fleming Law Bldg.   Phone: (303) 492-7534
Boulder, CO 80309   Oscar J. Miller, Law Libn.
Founded: 1892. **Staff:** Prof 4; Other 2. **Subjects:** Law, international law. **Holdings:** 166,000 volumes. **Subscriptions:** 400 journals and other serials.

★15410★

UNIVERSITY OF COLORADO, BOULDER - MAP LIBRARY (Geog-Map)
Norlin Library
Campus Box 184
Boulder, CO 80309   Phone: (303) 492-7578
Holdings: General map collection (125,000 sheets). **Services:** Library open to public for reference use only.

★15411★

UNIVERSITY OF COLORADO, BOULDER - MATHEMATICS & PHYSICS LIBRARY (Sci-Tech)
Duane Physical Laboratories G140
Campus Box 184   Phone: (303) 492-8231
Boulder, CO 80309   Allen Wynne, Dept.Hd.
Founded: 1963. **Staff:** Prof 1; Other 2. **Subjects:** Mathematics, astrogeophysics, physics, computer science, astrophysics. **Special Collections:** High Energy Physics (5000 preprints and reports). **Holdings:** 62,500 volumes; 120 linear feet of government publications. **Subscriptions:** 750 journals and other serials. **Services:** Interlibrary loans; copying; library open to public. **Computerized Information Services:** DIALOG, SDC, BRS, New York Times Information Service. **Publications:** Bi-weekly Acquisitions - distributed on request. **Special Indexes:** Index to physics, astrophysics, and atmospheric sciences book reviews; index to the library's reference collection; index to the library's documents collection (all punched card).

★15412★

UNIVERSITY OF COLORADO, BOULDER - MUSIC LIBRARY (Mus)
N-290 Warner Imig Music Bldg.
Campus Box 184   Phone: (303) 492-8093
Boulder, CO 80309   Karl Kroeger, Music Libn.
Founded: 1959. **Staff:** Prof 2; Other 3. **Subjects:** Music scores and books. **Special Collections:** Lumpkin Folk Song Collection (research collection). **Holdings:** 46,000 volumes; 26,000 phonograph records and phonotapes; 40,000 scores. **Subscriptions:** 250 journals and other serials. **Services:** Interlibrary loans; copying; library open to public.

★15413★

UNIVERSITY OF COLORADO, BOULDER - SCHOOL OF LAW - ROCKY MOUNTAIN MINERAL LAW FOUNDATION - RESEARCH LIBRARY
Fleming Law Bldg.
Box 405   Phone: (303) 449-0943
Boulder, CO 80309
Defunct

★15414★

UNIVERSITY OF COLORADO, BOULDER - SCIENCE LIBRARY (Sci-Tech)
Norlin Library
Campus Box 184   Phone: (303) 492-5136
Boulder, CO 80302   David Fagerstrom, Libn.
Founded: 1939. **Staff:** Prof 2; Other 2. **Subjects:** Chemistry; biology - molecular, cellular, developmental, environmental, organismic, population; psychology; pharmacy; speech pathology; audiology; artificial intelligence; exercise physiology. **Holdings:** 143,000 volumes; 5000 microforms. **Subscriptions:** 2000 journals and other serials. **Services:** Interlibrary loans; copying; library open to public.

★15415★

UNIVERSITY OF COLORADO, BOULDER - SPECIAL COLLECTIONS DEPARTMENT (Rare Book)
Norlin Library
Campus Box 184   Phone: (303) 492-6144
Boulder, CO 80309   Nora Quinlan, Hd.
Founded: 1940. **Staff:** Prof 2; Other 2. **Special Collections:** American photography; Bibles in many languages; children's literature (Epsteen Collection); 18th-century pamphlets; Aileen Fisher Manuscripts; Gene Fowler Manuscripts; French Revolution (Bowen Collection); Aldous Huxley; David Lavender Manuscripts; Hugh McDiarmid; John Masefield; Florence Crannell Means Manuscripts; History of Metallurgy (Tour Collection); Mountaineering (Hart Collection); Samuel French Plays; silver money (Dickson Leavens Collection); Edward Young (Pettit Collection); 18th-century English literature; 20th-century English and American literature; Ashendene Press; Doves Press; Kelmscott Press; Limited Editions Club; Nonesuch Press. **Holdings:** 33,000 volumes. **Services:** Interlibrary loans; department open to public.

★15416★

UNIVERSITY OF COLORADO, BOULDER - THERAPEUTIC RECREATION INFORMATION CENTER (TRIC)
Dept. of Physical Educ. & Recreation
Box 354
Boulder, CO 80309
Defunct

★15417★

UNIVERSITY OF COLORADO, BOULDER - WESTERN HISTORICAL COLLECTION & UNIVERSITY ARCHIVES (Hist)
Norlin Library
Campus Box 184   Phone: (303) 492-7242
Boulder, CO 80309   Dr. John A. Brennan, Cur.
Founded: 1918. **Staff:** Prof 1; Other 2. **Subjects:** Colorado history, 19th- and 20th-century American West, political leadership, organized labor, professional organizations, business and industry. **Special Collections:** Women's International League for Peace and Freedom Papers; National Farmers Union Archives; Edward P. Costigan Papers; Western Federation of Miners Archives; James G. Patton Papers; Herrick Roth Papers; Elwood Brooks Papers; Western History Association Papers. **Holdings:** 14,000 linear feet of historical manuscripts; 3000 linear feet of university archives; 2000 linear feet of newspapers; 12,000 volumes; pamphlets; maps; photographs; microfilm. **Services:** Copying; collection open to public. **Publications:** A Guide to Manuscript Collections (1982); guides to individual manuscript collections - available by request (fee charged).

★15418★

UNIVERSITY OF COLORADO, BOULDER - WILLIAM M. WHITE BUSINESS LIBRARY (Bus-Fin; Comp Sci)
Business Bldg.
Campus Box 184   Phone: (303) 492-8367
Boulder, CO 80309   Carol Krismann, Bus.Libn.
Founded: 1970. **Staff:** Prof 2; Other 2. **Subjects:** Information systems, management and organization, finance, accounting, marketing, transportation, management science, banking, real estate, insurance. **Special Collections:** Douglas H. Buck Financial Records Collection (66,700 annual and 10K reports on microfiche). **Holdings:** 57,000 volumes; 1700 serials on microfilm. **Subscriptions:** 600 journals; 12 newspapers. **Services:** Interlibrary loans; copying; library open to public. **Automated Operations:** Computerized cataloging. **Computerized Information Services:** DIALOG, BRS, SDC. **Publications:** Acquisitions list, monthly.

UNIVERSITY OF COLORADO, BOULDER - WORLD DATA CENTER A - GLACIOLOGY INFORMATION CENTER
See: World Data Center A - Glaciology Information Center

★15419★

UNIVERSITY OF COLORADO HEALTH SCIENCES CENTER - DENISON MEMORIAL LIBRARY (Med)†
4200 E. 9th Ave.   Phone: (303) 394-7469
Denver, CO 80262   Charles Bandy, Dir.
Founded: 1924. **Staff:** Prof 10; Other 25. **Subjects:** Medicine, nursing, dentistry, allied health sciences. **Holdings:** 71,719 books; 100,306 bound periodical volumes. **Subscriptions:** 2001 journals and other serials. **Services:** Interlibrary loans (fee); copying; SDI; library open to public. **Automated Operations:** Computerized cataloging and circulation. **Computerized Information Services:** OCLC, New York Times Information Service, DIALOG, SDC, BRS. **Networks/Consortia:** Member of Midcontinental Regional Medical Library Program. **Staff:** Margaret Butkovich, Assoc.Dir.; Irene Ogura, Hd.Cat.Libn.; Janice Butler, Hd., Coll.Dev.; Sharon Davis, Asst.Dir., Info.Serv.; Vicki Milam, Hd., Acq.; Kristin Louden, Hd., Circ.; Susan McCarthy, Ref.Libn.; Connie Wethey, Ref.Libn.; Sandi Julias, Ref.Libn.

★15420★

UNIVERSITY OF COLORADO HEALTH SCIENCES CENTER - RENE A. SPITZ PSYCHIATRIC LIBRARY (Med)
4200 E. 9th Ave., C-249   Phone: (303) 394-7039
Denver, CO 80262   Irwin Berry, Libn.
Founded: 1967. **Staff:** Prof 1. **Subjects:** Psychiatry, psychoanalysis. **Holdings:** 2900 books; 350 bound periodical volumes; 2550 unbound journals; 100 cassettes. **Subscriptions:** 15 journals and other serials. **Services:** Interlibrary loans; copying; library open to public with restrictions. **Networks/Consortia:** Member of Colorado Council of Medical Librarians.

★15421★

UNIVERSITY COMMUNITY HOSPITAL - MEDICAL LIBRARY (Med)
3100 E. Fletcher Ave.   Phone: (813) 971-6000
Tampa, FL 33612   Gwen E. Walters, Lib.Mgr.
Staff: Prof 3; Other 1. **Subjects:** Medicine, nursing, allied health, management. **Holdings:** 1750 books; 525 bound periodical volumes; 160 periodicals in microform; 21 file drawers of microfilm; 2 file drawers of microfiche; slides. **Subscriptions:** 375 journals and other serials. **Services:** Interlibrary loans; copying; SDI; library open to public for reference use only. **Automated Operations:** Computerized cataloging and acquisitions. **Computerized Information Services:** DIALOG, MEDLARS. **Networks/Consortia:** Member of Tampa Bay Medical Library Network. **Staff:** Jo Ann W.

Tibbs, Med.Libn.; M.J. Bradley, Tech.Serv.Libn.

★15422★

UNIVERSITY CONGREGATIONAL CHURCH - LIBRARY (Rel-Theol)
4515 16th Ave., N.E.   Phone: (206) 524-2322
Seattle, WA 98105   Gertrude Wulfekoetter, Libn.
Staff: Prof 6; Other 7. **Subjects:** Religion, Bible, theology, social affairs,
philosophy, biography. **Special Collections:** Children's library (1500 volumes).
Holdings: 5800 books; 500 cassettes. **Subscriptions:** 14 journals and other
serials. **Services:** Interlibrary loans; copying; library open to public. **Staff:**
Laurel Hufford, Children's Libn.; Claire Marston, Lib.Asst.; Heli Gray, Lib.Asst.;
Alice Nugent, Lib.Asst.; Donna Hoffman, Lib.Asst.

★15423★

**UNIVERSITY OF CONNECTICUT - CENTER FOR REAL ESTATE & URBAN
ECONOMIC STUDIES - REFERENCE & DOCUMENTS ROOM (Soc Sci)**
U-41-RE   Phone: (203) 486-3227
Storrs, CT 06268   Judith B. Paesani, Asst.Dir.
Staff: Prof 6; Other 4. **Subjects:** Real estate, urban studies, housing, finance,
land use. **Holdings:** 4000 volumes. **Subscriptions:** 65 journals and other
serials. **Services:** Interlibrary loans; room open to public with restrictions.
Publications: Real estate reports, general series and working papers, irregular
- list available on request.

★15424★

**UNIVERSITY OF CONNECTICUT - HEALTH CENTER - LYMAN MAYNARD
STOWE LIBRARY (Med)**
                                        Phone: (203) 674-2547
Farmington, CT 06032-9984   Ralph Arcari, Dir. of Lib.
Founded: 1966. **Staff:** Prof 10; Other 23. **Subjects:** Medicine, dentistry,
allied health sciences. **Special Collections:** Learning Resources Center
collection of audiovisuals (4250 items in health sciences). **Holdings:** 43,437
books; 90,161 bound periodical volumes; 6 drawers of pamphlets.
Subscriptions: 3228 journals and other serials. **Services:** Interlibrary loans;
copying; SDI; library open to public. **Automated Operations:** Computerized
cataloging, acquisitions, serials and circulation. **Computerized Information
Services:** MEDLINE, DIALOG, BRS. **Networks/Consortia:** Member of Capitol
Region Library Council; NELINET; Greater Northeastern Regional Medical
Library Program; Association of Medical Library Directors. **Publications:** New
Acquisitions, monthly; Newsletter, monthly; Serials Holdings, annual; Health
Sciences Audiovisual Resources List, annual. **Staff:** Marion Levine, Asst.Dir.;
Malcolm Brantz, AV Libn.; John McGinty, Circ./ILL Libn.; Sandra Millard,
Hd.Ref.Libn.;James Estrada, Cat.Libn.; Eugene Cseh, Coll.Mgt.Libn.

★15425★

**UNIVERSITY OF CONNECTICUT - HOMER BABBIDGE LIBRARY - SPECIAL
COLLECTIONS (Soc Sci; Hum)**
                                        Phone: (203) 486-2524
Storrs, CT 06268   Richard H. Schimmelpfeng, Dir., Spec.Coll.
Founded: 1881. **Staff:** Prof 4; Other 2. **Special Collections:** Charles Olson
Archives; Turkish language collection; Puerto Rican Collection; Madrid
Collection; Spanish periodicals and newspapers; Gaines Americana Collection;
Kays Horse Collection; Alternative Press Collection; little magazines; Edwin
Way Teale archives; Chilean history and literature; Jose Toribio Medina
Collection; modern German drama; French language and dialects; Luis
Camoens; Powys Brothers; American socialist and communist pamphlets and
periodicals. **Holdings:** Figures not available. **Services:** Interlibrary loans;
copying; collections open to public. **Automated Operations:** Computerized
circulation. **Computerized Information Services:** BRS, OCLC. **Publications:**
Bibliography series, irregular; HARVEST, irregular.

★15426★

**UNIVERSITY OF CONNECTICUT - INSTITUTE OF MATERIALS SCIENCE -
READING ROOM (Sci-Tech)**
                                        Phone: (203) 486-3637
Storrs, CT 06268   Mary Roche, Adm.Asst.
Staff: 1. **Subjects:** Metallurgy, polymer science, materials science. **Holdings:**
50 books; 200 bound periodical volumes. **Subscriptions:** 95 journals and
other serials. **Services:** Copying; room open to public.

★15427★

**UNIVERSITY OF CONNECTICUT - INSTITUTE FOR SOCIAL INQUIRY (Soc
Sci)**
Box U-164   Phone: (203) 486-4440
Storrs, CT 06268   Everett C. Ladd, Jr., Exec.Dir.
Founded: 1968. **Staff:** Prof 24; Other 6. **Subjects:** Public opinion surveys,
election data, census data (U.S. and foreign). **Special Collections:** Roper
Center Archive. **Holdings:** Over 10,000 surveys. **Subscriptions:** Poll releases,
journals and serials. **Services:** Provides instruction in the use of social data;

engages in original data collection, including the Connecticut Poll; conducts
workshops and seminars; assists in the administration of special research
projects involving social data for public-service agencies in Connecticut.
Remarks: The institute is a local archive of survey and aggregate data in
machine readable form and serves as a multipurpose research and teaching
facility for the social sciences. It also hosts the archival development
component, user services and Office of the Executive Director of the Roper
Center (see the description of the Roper Center for further information).
Staff: Marilyn Potter, Asst.Dir./User Serv.; Anne-Marie Mercure, Mgr./
Archv.; Jack Davis, Asst.Dir./Tech.Serv.; G. Donald Ferree, Assoc.Dir.

★15428★

**UNIVERSITY OF CONNECTICUT - INSTITUTE OF URBAN RESEARCH -
LIBRARY (Soc Sci)**
                                        Phone: (203) 486-4518
Storrs, CT 06268   Jean W. Gosselin, Educ.Asst.
Staff: Prof 1; Other 1. **Subjects:** Urban affairs. **Special Collections:**
Connecticut town and city materials; special reports from Connecticut
agencies. **Holdings:** 300 books; 25 bound periodical volumes; 2500
pamphlets; 150 newsletters; newspaper clipping file. **Subscriptions:** 16
journals and other serials. **Services:** Library open to public with restrictions.

★15429★

**UNIVERSITY OF CONNECTICUT - LABOR EDUCATION CENTER -
INFORMATION CENTER (Soc Sci)**
Bishop Bldg., Rm. 213   Phone: (203) 486-3417
Storrs, CT 06268   George E. O'Connell, Dir.
Founded: 1946. **Subjects:** Labor studies, industrial relations. **Holdings:** 300
volumes. **Subscriptions:** 20 journals and other serials. **Services:** Center open
to public with restrictions.

★15430★

UNIVERSITY OF CONNECTICUT - LAW SCHOOL LIBRARY (Law)
120 Sherman St.   Phone: (203) 523-4841
Hartford, CT 06105-2289   Dennis J. Stone, Law Libn.
Founded: 1942. **Staff:** Prof 6; Other 11. **Subjects:** Law. **Holdings:** 200,000
books; AV materials; microfiche. **Subscriptions:** 980 journals and other
serials. **Services:** Interlibrary loans; copying; library open to public for
reference use only. **Automated Operations:** Computerized cataloging.
Computerized Information Services: LEXIS, Westlaw, OCLC. **Networks/
Consortia:** Member of NELINET; New England Law Library Consortium
(NELLC). **Staff:** Judith F. Anspach, Assoc.Libn.; Robert Connell, Asst.Law
Libn./Tech.Serv.; Randall Snyder, Asst.Libn./Pub.Serv.

★15431★

**UNIVERSITY OF CONNECTICUT - LEARNING RESOURCES DIVISION -
CENTER FOR INSTRUCTIONAL MEDIA & TECHNOLOGY (Educ)**
249 Glenbrook Rd., Rm. 3
Box U-1   Phone: (203) 486-2530
Storrs, CT 06268
Founded: 1947. **Staff:** Prof 2; Other 6. **Subjects:** Education and related
areas. **Holdings:** 14,000 books, pamphlets and bound periodical volumes;
8000 children's books; 1000 curriculum guides; 1600 instructional media
units. **Subscriptions:** 200 journals and other serials. **Services:** Interlibrary
loans; copying; center open to public with restrictions.

★15432★

UNIVERSITY OF CONNECTICUT - MAP LIBRARY (Geog-Map)
                                        Phone: (203) 486-4589
Storrs, CT 06268   Thornton P. McGlamery, Map Libn.
Founded: 1976. **Staff:** Prof 1; Other 1. **Subjects:** Maps, cartography.
Special Collections: Petersen Collection; New England town maps of the 19th
century. **Holdings:** 1700 books; 100,000 maps; 4 VF drawers of aerial
photographs of Connecticut; 10 VF drawers of U.S. Geological Survey papers
and reports; 5 VF drawers of international tourist information; 4 VF drawers
of map publisher and dealer catalogs. **Services:** Interlibrary loans; copying;
library open to public. **Automated Operations:** Computerized cataloging,
acquisitions, serials and circulation. **Computerized Information Services:**
National Cartographic Information Center (NCIC). **Special Indexes:** Index of
maps and cartographic information in books, periodicals and government
publications (card).

★15433★

UNIVERSITY OF CONNECTICUT - MUSIC LIBRARY (Mus)
U-12   Phone: (203) 486-2502
Storrs, CT 06268   Dorothy McAdoo Bognar, Hd.
Staff: Prof 2; Other 2. **Subjects:** Music. **Holdings:** 8100 books; 1400 bound
periodical volumes; 10,000 scores; 14,900 phonograph records; 360 reels of
microfilm. **Subscriptions:** 80 journals and other serials. **Services:** Interlibrary

loans; library open to public for reference use only; circulation limited to university community. **Automated Operations:** Computerized cataloging. **Computerized Information Services:** OCLC. **Networks/Consortia:** Member of NELINET. **Publications:** Guide to the Music Library, irregular - for internal distribution only. **Special Catalogs:** Catalog of piano music and vocal music in collections (card). **Staff:** Joseph Scott .

★15434★
UNIVERSITY OF CONNECTICUT - PHARMACY LIBRARY AND LEARNING CENTER (Med)
Box U-92   Phone: (203) 486-2218
Storrs, CT 06268   Georgia Scura, Dir.
Staff: Prof 2. **Subjects:** Pharmaceutics, pharmacology, pharmacognosy, pharmaceutical chemistry, health care services. **Holdings:** 5000 books; 4000 bound periodical volumes; 5 VF drawers of pamphlets and clippings; 332 AV units; 158 reels of microfilm of periodicals. **Subscriptions:** 267 journals and other serials. **Services:** Interlibrary loans; copying; library open to public for reference use only; borrowing limited to university personnel. **Computerized Information Services:** BRS, NLM. **Staff:** David Keighley, Media Spec.

★15435★
UNIVERSITY OF CONNECTICUT - PUERTO RICAN CENTER - ROBERTO CLEMENTE LIBRARY (Area-Ethnic)
Univ. Box 188   Phone: (203) 486-2204
Storrs, CT 06268   Ino Rios, Dir.
Founded: 1974. **Staff:** 1. **Subjects:** Puerto Rico - history, literature, anthropology, economics, art. **Holdings:** 500 volumes, including videotape set of the Puerto Rican Debate at the University of Connecticut, 1977. **Subscriptions:** 27 journals and other serials. **Services:** Library open to public.

★15436★
UNIVERSITY OF CONNECTICUT - ROPER CENTER (Soc Sci)
Box U-164R   Phone: (203) 486-4440
Storrs, CT 06268   Everett C. Ladd, Exec.Dir.
Founded: 1946. **Staff:** Prof 24; Other 4. **Subjects:** Survey data contributed by the world's major survey organizations. **Special Collections:** Gallup opinion surveys, 1936 to present; Yankelovich, Skelly and White surveys for Time magazine; CBS/New York Times; ABC/Washington Post; NBC/Associated Press; National Opinion Research Center (NORC); Roper Organization; United States Information Agency Surveys; International Research Associates surveys; Gallup Affiliates surveys. **Holdings:** Over 10,000 surveys. **Services:** Data set reproduction; data analysis; search and retrieval; duplication of questionnaires and codebooks; copying; center open to public with restrictions. **Publications:** Study listings organized by country; under contract, produces the "Opinion Roundup" section for the magazine Public Opinion; Data Set News (announcements of data sets of special interest to the research community). **Remarks:** Since 1977, the Roper Center operates through a formal partnership of the University of Connecticut, Yale University and Williams College. The University of Connecticut branch of the Roper Center - which has primary operating responsibilities - is housed administratively within the Institute for Social Inquiry.

★15437★
UNIVERSITY OF CONNECTICUT - SCHOOL OF BUSINESS ADMINISTRATION LIBRARY (Bus-Fin)
39 Woodland St.   Phone: (203) 241-4905
Hartford, CT 06105   Patricia A. Slevinsky, Libn.
Founded: 1960. **Staff:** Prof 2; Other 5. **Subjects:** Business, insurance, data processing, economics. **Holdings:** 17,000 books; 400 bound periodical volumes; 8 drawers of pamphlets; 50 drawers of annual reports and company history; 2500 reels of microfilm of business and insurance periodicals and newspapers. **Subscriptions:** 540 journals and other serials; 17 newspapers. **Services:** Interlibrary loans; copying; library open to public. **Automated Operations:** Computerized cataloging. **Computerized Information Services:** OCLC. **Networks/Consortia:** Member of NELINET; Capitol Region Library Council. **Staff:** Ken Kerr, Asst.Libn.

★15438★
UNIVERSITY OF CONNECTICUT - SCHOOL OF EDUCATION - I.N. THUT WORLD EDUCATION CENTER (Educ)
Box U-32   Phone: (203) 486-3321
Storrs, CT 06268   Dr. Frank A. Stone, Dir.
Staff: Prof 2; Other 2. **Subjects:** Education - multicultural, international, global, bilingual-bicultural, urban; education for development. **Special Collections:** The Peoples of Connecticut oral histories (150); artifacts collection for teaching about other cultures and nations. **Holdings:** 600 books; 800 documents; 60 sets of slides. **Subscriptions:** 20 journals and other serials. **Services:** Interlibrary loans; copying; center open to public. **Automated Operations:** Computerized cataloging, acquisitions, serials and

circulation. **Computerized Information Services:** Online systems. **Publications:** Communique, irregular. **Special Catalogs:** Catalog of Asian and Middle Eastern Studies resources in Connecticut; annotated bibliography on Peace Studies; curriculum guides for the Peoples of Connecticut, World Education Monograph Series, Multicultural Educational Research Methodologies Series. **Staff:** Dr. Patricia Snyder Weibust, Assoc.Dir.; Dr. Byungchai Cora Hahn, Media Coord.; Dr. Richard H. Pfau, Coord.

★15439★
UNIVERSITY OF CONNECTICUT - SCHOOL OF SOCIAL WORK - HARLEIGH B. TRECKER LIBRARY (Soc Sci)
Greater Hartford Campus   Phone: (203) 241-4722
West Hartford, CT 06117
Founded: 1946. **Staff:** Prof 3; Other 1. **Subjects:** Child study, psychoanalysis, psychology, social work, sociology, social security, social welfare, psychiatry, social research, criminology and correction, recreation. **Holdings:** 38,000 volumes; 1200 microforms. **Subscriptions:** 300 journals and other serials. **Services:** Interlibrary loans; copying; library open to public.

★15440★
UNIVERSITY OF DAYTON - LAW SCHOOL LIBRARY (Law)
300 College Park   Phone: (513) 229-2314
Dayton, OH 45469   Prof. Thomas L. Hanley, Dir.
Founded: 1974. **Staff:** Prof 4; Other 9. **Subjects:** Law, political science, social sciences. **Holdings:** 165,000 volumes; government documents. **Subscriptions:** 605 journals and other serials; 15 newspapers. **Services:** Interlibrary loans; copying; library open to public for reference use only. **Automated Operations:** Computerized cataloging and ILL. **Computerized Information Services:** LEXIS, Westlaw, OCLC. **Networks/Consortia:** Member of Southwest Ohio Council for Higher Education (SOC); Ohio Regional Association of Law Libraries. **Publications:** Recent Acquisitions List, monthly; Table of Contents of Law Reviews Received; Annual Report. **Staff:** Theodora Artz, Hd., Acq.Dept.; Geraldine Wernersbach, Hd., Ref./Circ.Dept.; Michael Krieger, Hd., Cat.Dept.

★15441★
UNIVERSITY OF DAYTON - MARIAN LIBRARY (Rel-Theol)
300 College Park   Phone: (513) 229-4214
Dayton, OH 45469   Rev. Theodore Koehler, S.M., Dir.
Founded: 1943. **Staff:** Prof 4; Other 4. **Subjects:** Virgin Mary in theology, devotions, belles lettres, art, music. **Special Collections:** Clugnet Collection (Marian shrines; 8000 items); religious art (300 volumes). **Holdings:** 65,000 volumes; 48,000 clippings; 200 reels of microfilm; 2 boxes of American bishops' pastoral letters; 2200 slides; 4 manuscripts; 5000 pictures; 10,000 holy cards; postcards of Marian shrine and art; 10 albums of postage stamps; 1000 photographs; 300 medals; 80 phonograph records; 100 cassettes. **Subscriptions:** 110 journals and other serials; 10 newspapers. **Services:** Interlibrary loans; copying; library open to public. **Publications:** Marian Library Studies, annual - available by subscription; Marian Library Newsletter, 2/year - free upon request. **Special Catalogs:** Union catalog of Marian holdings in selected North American libraries. **Special Indexes:** Author/title indexes to proceedings of International Mariological Congresses: 1950, 1954, 1958, 1965, 1971, 1975; indexes to selected journals. **Staff:** William Fackovec, S.M., Cat./Bibliog.; Helen Nykolyshyn, Cat.

★15442★
UNIVERSITY OF DAYTON - ROESCH LIBRARY - SPECIAL COLLECTIONS/ RARE BOOKS (Hum)
300 College Park Ave.   Phone: (513) 229-4221
Dayton, OH 45469   Cecilia Mushenheim, Archv./Spec.Coll.Libn.
Founded: 1970. **Staff:** Prof 2. **Subjects:** 20th-century English and American first editions, science fiction, Dayton Performing Arts, Paul Lawrence Dunbar. **Special Collections:** Jacobs Collection; Science Fiction Writers of America Collection; Urban Schnurr Collection; Victory Theatre Papers; Catholic Council on Civil Liberties Papers; Association for Creative Change Papers. **Holdings:** 3750 books; 60 document boxes. **Services:** Copying; collections open to public by appointment. **Automated Operations:** Computerized cataloging and circulation. **Computerized Information Services:** DIALOG, BRS. **Networks/ Consortia:** Member of Southwestern Ohio Council for Higher Education (SOC). **Special Catalogs:** Card catalog of rare books, Jacobs, and science fiction collections; Inventory of Urban Schnurr Collection. **Staff:** Linda Keir Hinrichs, Rare Bk.Libn.

★15443★
UNIVERSITY OF DAYTON - SCHOOL OF EDUCATION - CURRICULUM MATERIALS CENTER (Educ)
300 College Park, Chaminade Hall   Phone: (513) 229-3140
Dayton, OH 49469   Sr. Catherine Rudolph, O.S.F., Dir.
Founded: 1955. **Staff:** Prof 2; Other 3. **Subjects:** Elementary and secondary

textbooks, children's literature, teacher education. **Holdings:** 13,500 books; 250 bound periodical volumes; 74 sets of transparencies; 2200 filmstrips; 595 records; 57 models; 386 material kits; 223 cartridges; 454 sets of charts and posters; 650 other teaching aids; 60 VF drawers. **Subscriptions:** 64 journals and other serials. **Services:** Center open to public for reference use only. **Publications:** Monthly News Bulletin, bimonthly during school months - distributed to faculty and students. **Special Catalogs:** Book catalogs provided for student teachers. **Staff:** Eileen Thomas, Cat.

UNIVERSITY OF DAYTON - SOCIETY OF MARY
See: Society of Mary

★15444★
UNIVERSITY OF DELAWARE, NEWARK - AGRICULTURE LIBRARY (Agri)
002 Agricultural Hall   Phone: (302) 451-2530
Newark, DE 19711   Frederick B. Getze, Assoc.Libn.
Founded: 1888. **Staff:** Prof 1; Other 1. **Subjects:** Agriculture and related areas in biology and chemistry, veterinary medicine. **Special Collections:** State agricultural experiment station documents; Unidel History of Horticultural Landscape Architecture (housed at Morris Library). **Holdings:** 15,000 books; 17,200 bound periodical volumes; 350 reels of microfilm; 700 other cataloged items. **Subscriptions:** 505 journals and other serials. **Services:** Interlibrary loans; copying; library open to public. **Automated Operations:** Computerized cataloging, acquisitions, circulation, serials and ILL. **Computerized Information Services:** DIALOG, SDC, BRS, OCLC. **Networks/ Consortia:** Member of Association of Research Libraries (ARL); CRL; PALINET & Union Library Catalogue of Pennsylvania. **Staff:** Elizabeth Shenk, Lib.Anl.

★15445★
UNIVERSITY OF DELAWARE, NEWARK - ARCHIVES (Hist)
78 E. Delaware Ave.   Phone: (302) 451-2750
Newark, DE 19711   John M. Clayton, Jr., Archv./Dir., Rec.Mgt
Founded: 1969. **Staff:** Prof 2; Other 2. **Subjects:** University of Delaware history. **Holdings:** 9250 theses and dissertations; 320 bound periodical volumes; 3000 cubic feet of records; 950 reels of AV materials; 8000 photographs and negatives. **Services:** Copying; archives open to public for approved research projects. **Automated Operations:** Computerized cataloging. **Staff:** Jean K. Crary, Rec.Mgt.Adm.

★15446★
UNIVERSITY OF DELAWARE, NEWARK - CENTER FOR COMPOSITE MATERIALS - COMPOSITE MATERIALS REFERENCE ROOM (Sci-Tech)
201 Spencer Laboratory   Phone: (302) 738-8149
Newark, DE 19716
Staff: 1. **Subjects:** Engineering mechanics, materials science, polymer science. **Special Collections:** Composite materials (2000 volumes). **Holdings:** 400 books; 100 bound periodical volumes; 1500 other cataloged items. **Subscriptions:** 22 journals and other serials. **Services:** Copying; room open to public for reference use only.

★15447★
UNIVERSITY OF DELAWARE, NEWARK - CHEMISTRY/CHEMICAL ENGINEERING LIBRARY (Sci-Tech)
202 Brown Laboratory   Phone: (302) 451-2993
Newark, DE 19711   Grace Vattilano, Chem.Lib.Supv.
Founded: 1938. **Staff:** 1. **Subjects:** Chemistry and chemical engineering. **Special Collections:** Unidel History of Chemistry Collection (housed at Morris Library). **Holdings:** 8780 books; 9180 bound periodical volumes; 1013 reels of microfilm; Sadtler Spectra. **Subscriptions:** 376 journals and other serials. **Services:** Interlibrary loans; copying; library open to public. **Automated Operations:** Computerized cataloging, acquisitions, circulation, serials and ILL. **Computerized Information Services:** BRS, OCLC. **Networks/Consortia:** Member of Association of Research Libraries (ARL); CRL; PALINET & Union Library Catalogue of Pennsylvania.

★15448★
UNIVERSITY OF DELAWARE, NEWARK - COLLEGE OF EDUCATION - COMPUTER BASED EDUCATION RESEARCH LIBRARY (Educ; Comp Sci)
Willard Hall Education Bldg., Rm. 105   Phone: (302) 451-2927
Newark, DE 19711   Gary A. Feurer, Coord.
Staff: 2. **Subjects:** Council for Basic Education research materials and applications; lesson design; research design and analysis. **Holdings:** 1000 books. **Subscriptions:** 10 journals and other serials. **Services:** Library open to faculty and students of the university. **Automated Operations:** Computerized cataloging. **Also Known As:** Center for Interdisciplinary Research in Computer Based Education (CIRCLE).

★15449★
UNIVERSITY OF DELAWARE, NEWARK - COLLEGE OF MARINE STUDIES - MARINE STUDIES COMPLEX LIBRARY (Sci-Tech)
Harry L. Cannon Marine Studies Laboratory   Phone: (302) 645-4290
Lewes, DE 19958   Dorothy Allen, Marine Stud.Lib.Supv.
Founded: 1973. **Staff:** 1. **Subjects:** Marine biology and geology, physical and chemical oceanography. **Special Collections:** All publications of Delaware College of Marine Studies; Sea Grant publications. **Holdings:** 7088 books; 4230 bound periodical volumes; 5300 reprints. **Subscriptions:** 136 journals and other serials. **Services:** Interlibrary loans; copying; library open to public. **Automated Operations:** Computerized cataloging, acquisitions, serials, circulation and ILL. **Computerized Information Services:** DIALOG, SDC, BRS. **Networks/Consortia:** Member of Association of Research Libraries (ARL); CRL; PALINET & Union Library Catalogue of Pennsylvania.

★15450★
UNIVERSITY OF DELAWARE, NEWARK - COLLEGE OF URBAN AFFAIRS - LIBRARY (Soc Sci)*
Willard Hall Bldg.   Phone: (302) 451-2394
Newark, DE 19711   Mary Helen Callahan, Accounts Adm.
Staff: 1. **Subjects:** Government, economics and sociology (primarily Delaware); census information on all school districts in New Castle County. **Holdings:** 2000 books. **Subscriptions:** 40 journals and other serials. **Services:** Students and others may borrow items with special permission. **Publications:** Bibliography of staff publications.

UNIVERSITY OF DELAWARE, NEWARK - DELAWARE STATE GEOLOGICAL SURVEY
See: Delaware State Geological Survey

★15451★
UNIVERSITY OF DELAWARE, NEWARK - DISASTER RESEARCH CENTER - LIBRARY (Soc Sci)
                                                  Phone: (302) 451-2581
Newark, DE 19716
Founded: 1963. **Staff:** Prof 3; Other 10. **Subjects:** Disaster research, sociology of disaster and mass emergencies. **Holdings:** 3000 books; 12,000 reports and articles; 200 dissertations and theses; 7500 interview transcripts; documents; newspapers. **Subscriptions:** 70 journals and other serials. **Services:** Copying; library open to public by appointment. **Publications:** Publications List, semiannual - free upon request. **Formerly:** Ohio State University - Disaster Research Center, located in Columbus, OH.

★15452★
UNIVERSITY OF DELAWARE, NEWARK - EDUCATION RESOURCE CENTER (Educ)
013 Willard Hall Education Bldg.   Phone: (302) 451-2335
Newark, DE 19716   Janet Hill Dove, Dir.
Founded: 1972. **Staff:** Prof 2; Other 3. **Subjects:** Curriculum materials in elementary science and mathematics, elementary language arts, occupational education, music, art, special education, elementary social studies and reading. **Holdings:** 25,000 books; 700 AV materials and kits. **Subscriptions:** 80 education journals. **Services:** Center open to public. **Computerized Information Services:** Special Education Mini Center (internal database). **Networks/Consortia:** Member of Delaware Learning Resource System (DLRS). **Special Catalogs:** Computerized book catalog.

★15453★
UNIVERSITY OF DELAWARE, NEWARK - HUGH M. MORRIS LIBRARY - PHYSICS BRANCH LIBRARY (Sci-Tech)
221 Sharp Laboratory   Phone: (302) 451-2323
Newark, DE 19711   Joseph W. Bradley, Physics Lib.Supv.
Staff: 1. **Subjects:** Physics, astronomy, astrophysics, mathematics, engineering. **Holdings:** 3050 books; 2125 bound periodical volumes. **Subscriptions:** 66 journals and other serials. **Services:** Interlibrary loans; library open to public. **Automated Operations:** Computerized cataloging, acquisitions, serials, circulation and ILL. **Computerized Information Services:** DIALOG, SDC, BRS, OCLC. **Networks/Consortia:** Member of Association of Research Libraries (ARL); CRL; PALINET & Union Library Catalogue of Pennsylvania.

UNIVERSITY OF DELAWARE, NEWARK - JEAN PIAGET SOCIETY
See: Piaget (Jean) Society

UNIVERSITY OF DENVER - CENTER FOR JUDAIC STUDIES
See: Rocky Mountain Jewish Historical Society - Ira M. Beck Memorial Library

★15454★

UNIVERSITY OF DENVER - COLLEGE OF LAW - WESTMINSTER LAW LIBRARY (Law)
1900 Olive St. - LTLB   Phone: (303) 753-3406
Denver, CO 80220   Alfred J. Coco, Libn.
Founded: 1898. **Staff:** Prof 4; Other 8. **Subjects:** Law. **Holdings:** 188,143 books, bound periodical volumes, microforms, government documents. **Subscriptions:** 2091 journals and other serials. **Services:** Interlibrary loans; copying; library open to lawyers on payment of annual fee. **Computerized Information Services:** Westlaw. **Staff:** Sue Weinstein, Assoc.Libn./Hd.Pub.Serv.; Barbara Allen, Cat.Libn.; Barbara Bintliff, Ref.Libn.

★15455★

UNIVERSITY OF DENVER AND DENVER RESEARCH INSTITUTE - INDUSTRIAL ECONOMICS AND MANAGEMENT DIVISION LIBRARY (Soc Sci)
2455 E. Asbury   Phone: (303) 753-3206
Denver, CO 80208   Judith Farris, Info.Spec.
Staff: Prof 1; Other 1. **Subjects:** Socioeconomic impacts, energy policy, water resources policy, technology transfer, international development. **Holdings:** 3000 books. **Subscriptions:** 150 journals and other serials; 5 newspapers. **Services:** Library not open to public. **Computerized Information Services:** DIALOG, SDC, BRS.

★15456★

UNIVERSITY OF DENVER AND DENVER RESEARCH INSTITUTE - LABORATORY FOR APPLIED MECHANICS - LIBRARY (Energy; Sci-Tech)
2360 S. Gaylord   Phone: (303) 753-3623
Denver, CO 80208
Staff: Prof 1. **Subjects:** Oil shale, geothermal energy, terminal ballistics, ordnance, structural mechanics, atmospheric sciences. **Holdings:** 1000 books. **Subscriptions:** 20 journals and other serials; 5 newspapers. **Services:** Library not open to public.

★15457★

UNIVERSITY OF DENVER AND DENVER RESEARCH INSTITUTE - SOCIAL SYSTEMS RESEARCH AND EVALUATION LIBRARY (Soc Sci)
2135 E. Wesley   Phone: (303) 871-3381
Denver, CO 80208   Bonnie Moul, Info.Spec.
Founded: 1978. **Staff:** Prof 1; Other 1. **Subjects:** Human services, communication, program evaluation, information and database management, education. **Special Collections:** Social Systems Research and Evaluation project reports; material on deinstitutionalization of the mentally ill, mentally retarded and the elderly. **Holdings:** 250 technical reports; 50 file boxes of reprints, clippings and documents. **Subscriptions:** 60 journals and other serials. **Services:** Library not open to public. **Remarks:** The SSRE library serves the professional research staff in the division. The Denver Research Institute is a nonprofit contract research organization.

★15458★

UNIVERSITY OF DENVER - PENROSE LIBRARY - SPECIAL COLLECTIONS (Hist)
2150 E. Evans Ave.   Phone: (303) 871-3428
Denver, CO 80208   Steven Fisher, Spec.Coll.Libn.
Founded: 1864. **Special Collections:** Judaica (17,000 volumes); Husted Culinary Collection (8000 items); Miller Civil War Collection (1000 items); Davidson Folklore Collection (1000 items). **Services:** Interlibrary loans; copying; collections open to public with fee. **Automated Operations:** Computerized cataloging, acquisitions, serials and circulation. **Computerized Information Services:** Online systems. **Networks/Consortia:** Member of Colorado Alliance of Research Libraries (CARL).

UNIVERSITY OF DENVER - ROCKY MOUNTAIN JEWISH HISTORICAL SOCIETY
See: Rocky Mountain Jewish Historical Society

★15459★

UNIVERSITY OF DETROIT - EVENING COLLEGE OF BUSINESS AND ADMINISTRATION - LIBRARY (Bus-Fin)
651 E. Jefferson   Phone: (313) 927-1525
Detroit, MI 48226   JoAnn Chalmers, Libn.
Founded: 1961. **Staff:** Prof 1; Other 1. **Subjects:** Accounting, economics, finance, management, marketing, statistics. **Holdings:** 11,000 books; 1700 bound periodical volumes; 500 corporate annual reports. **Subscriptions:** 100 journals and other serials. **Services:** Interlibrary loans; copying; library open to public for reference. **Computerized Information Services:** OCLC. **Networks/Consortia:** Member of Michigan Library Consortium (MLC).

★15460★

UNIVERSITY OF DETROIT - LIBRARY MEDIA CENTER (Aud-Vis; Educ)
4001 W. McNichols Rd.   Phone: (313) 927-1075
Detroit, MI 48221   Maris L. Cannon, Adm.Asst.
Founded: 1961. **Staff:** 4. **Subjects:** History, literature, language arts, fine arts, education, business and management, sociology, psychology, science, mathematics, religious studies, philosophy, economics, political science. **Holdings:** 1097 phonograph records and sets; 1510 filmstrips and filmstrip sets with sound; 129 slides and slide sets with sound; 634 models and games; 61 video cassettes and 16mm films; 278 audio cassettes and sets; 1740 transparencies and sets; 224 vertical file subject entries; 275 testing materials titles; reference materials. **Services:** Interlibrary loans; copying; AV equipment pool; AV aids for the visually impaired; projection rooms; group study rooms; photography; AV software production; audio cassette duplication; graphic design, production and duplication; punch binding; center open to public for reference use only. **Networks/Consortia:** Member of Michigan Library Consortium (MLC). **Publications:** Bibliography of Recent Acquisitions, annual.

★15461★

UNIVERSITY OF DETROIT - SCHOOL OF DENTISTRY LIBRARY (Med)
2931 E. Jefferson Ave.   Phone: (313) 446-1817
Detroit, MI 48207   Victor DeSchryver, Dir.
Founded: 1932. **Staff:** Prof 2; Other 4. **Subjects:** Dentistry. **Holdings:** 13,000 books; 15,700 bound periodical volumes. **Subscriptions:** 350 journals and other serials. **Services:** Interlibrary loans; copying; library open to public for reference use only. **Computerized Information Services:** MEDLINE, DIALOG. **Networks/Consortia:** Member of Michigan Library Consortium (MLC). **Publications:** Acquisitions, bimonthly. **Staff:** Mary Agnes Shoup, Asst.Libn.

★15462★

UNIVERSITY OF DETROIT - SCHOOL OF LAW LIBRARY (Law)
651 E. Jefferson Ave.   Phone: (313) 961-5444
Detroit, MI 48226   Byron D. Cooper, Dir.
Founded: 1912. **Staff:** Prof 5; Other 4. **Subjects:** Law - United States, Canada, England. **Holdings:** 180,000 volumes; 50,000 volumes in microform. **Subscriptions:** 1800 journals and other serials; 10 newspapers. **Services:** Interlibrary loans; copying; library open to public. **Automated Operations:** Computerized cataloging. **Computerized Information Services:** LEXIS, OCLC. **Networks/Consortia:** Member of Michigan Library Consortium (MLC). **Publications:** Law Library Guide, annual - distributed to students; Current Acquisitions List, monthly. **Staff:** Colleen M. Hickey, S.S.J., Assoc.Dir.; Mary E. Hayes, Ref.Libn.; Kathy P. Krisciunas, Tech.Serv.Libn.; Gene P. Moy, Docs./Circ.Libn.; Katherine A. Cooper, Res.Spec.

★15463★

UNIVERSITY OF THE DISTRICT OF COLUMBIA - HARVARD STREET LIBRARY (Educ)†
1100 Harvard St., N.W.   Phone: (202) 673-7018
Washington, DC 20009   Lottie Wright, Supv.
Staff: Prof 3; Other 1. **Subjects:** Education, human ecology. **Special Collections:** Library of American Civilization (20,000 microfiche); Trevor Arnett Library of Black Culture (8000 reels of microfilm); Miner-Wilson Collection (2000 rare books); legislative history of Federal City College. **Holdings:** 111,000 books; 10,000 bound periodical volumes; 150,000 microforms; archives. **Subscriptions:** 500 journals and other serials; 6 newspapers. **Services:** Interlibrary loans; copying; library open to public with restrictions. **Networks/Consortia:** Member of Consortium of Universities of the Washington Metropolitan Area. **Special Catalogs:** Catalog of Miner-Wilson Collection; District of Columbia Teachers College Library (book catalog). **Staff:** William Crawford, Lib.Techn.; Taro G. Gehani, Acq.Libn.; Elizabeth M. Thompson, Media Serv.Libn.; Anne Robinson, Media Serv.Libn.

★15464★

UNIVERSITY OF THE DISTRICT OF COLUMBIA - LEARNING RESOURCES DIVISION (Soc Sci; Hist)†
4200 Connecticut Ave., N.W.   Phone: (202) 282-7536
Washington, DC 20008   Albert J. Casciero, Dir.
Special Collections: Human Relations Area File (65 cabinets of 5" x 8" slips); African/Afro-Hispanic/American Media Collection (25 films; 97 books; 2 VF drawers of clippings); Atlanta University Black Culture Collection; water resources (625 items); 513 linear feet of University of D.C. archives; 962 microfiche on slavery source materials. **Services:** Interlibrary loans; copying; division open to public with restrictions. **Automated Operations:** Computerized cataloging and circulation. **Computerized Information Services:** DIALOG, OCLC, SDC. **Networks/Consortia:** Member of CAPCON; Consortium of Universities of the Washington Metropolitan Area.

★15465★

UNIVERSITY OF FLORIDA - AGRICULTURAL RESEARCH CENTER - LIBRARY
(Agri)*
Box 728
Hastings, FL 32045
Phone: (904) 692-1792
R.B. Workman, Assoc. Professor
Staff: Prof 1. **Subjects:** Agriculture, vegetable production. **Holdings:** 300 books; 240 bound periodical volumes; 100 unbound periodicals; 1400 unbound agricultural bulletins and pamphlets. **Subscriptions:** 28 journals and other serials. **Services:** Library open to public for reference use only.

★15466★

UNIVERSITY OF FLORIDA - AGRICULTURAL RESEARCH CENTER - LIBRARY
(Agri; Sci-Tech)
Inst. of Food & Agricultural Sciences
Box 388
Leesburg, FL 32748
Phone: (904) 787-3423
Dr. Gary W. Elmstrom, Ctr.Dir.
Founded: 1930. **Staff:** 2. **Subjects:** Plant pathology, vegetable crops, fruit crops, entomology. **Holdings:** 1267 volumes; 5335 indexed reprints; 109 unbound journals; 4250 abstract cards; 21,345 index cards. **Subscriptions:** 51 journals and other serials. **Services:** Library not open to public.

★15467★

UNIVERSITY OF FLORIDA - AGRICULTURAL RESEARCH & EDUCATION CENTER - BELLE GLADE LIBRARY (Agri; Sci-Tech)
Inst. of Food & Agricultural Sciences
Drawer A
Belle Glade, FL 33430
Phone: (305) 996-3062
Dr. Myers, Lib.Comm.Chm.
Staff: 1. **Subjects:** Agriculture, soils science, rice, vegetables, sugarcane, tropical botany, animal science, crops science, horticulture science. **Holdings:** 5000 books; 3700 bound periodical volumes. **Subscriptions:** 171 journals and other serials. **Services:** Interlibrary loans; copying; library open to public for reference use only. **Publications:** AREC Research Reports EES.

★15468★

UNIVERSITY OF FLORIDA - AGRICULTURAL RESEARCH & EDUCATION CENTER - FORT LAUDERDALE LIBRARY (Agri; Sci-Tech)
Inst. of Food & Agricultural Sciences
3205 S.W. 70th Ave.
Fort Lauderdale, FL 33314
Phone: (305) 475-8990
Dr. William B. Ennis, Jr., Ctr.Dir.
Staff: Prof 1. **Subjects:** Ornamental horticulture, entomology, turf science, plant pathology, soils, aquatic weeds science, environmental quality. **Holdings:** 1200 books; 360 bound periodical volumes. **Subscriptions:** 65 serials. **Services:** Library open to public with restrictions. **Computerized Information Services:** Access to online systems. **Publications:** Conference proceedings; Library Bulletin. **Staff:** Iris J. Caldwell, Libn.

★15469★

UNIVERSITY OF FLORIDA - AGRICULTURAL RESEARCH & EDUCATION CENTER - LAKE ALFRED LIBRARY (Agri; Sci-Tech)
Inst. of Food & Agricultural Sciences
700 Experiment Station Rd.
Lake Alfred, FL 33850
Phone: (813) 956-1151
Pamela K. Russ, Assoc.Univ.Libn.
Founded: 1935. **Staff:** Prof 1. **Subjects:** Chemistry, botany, entomology, nematology, agronomy. **Special Collections:** Yothers Rare Book Collection (citrus). **Holdings:** 4375 books; 7258 bound periodical volumes; 850 documents; 24 VF drawers of citrus reprints; 1595 Florida Geological Survey maps. **Subscriptions:** 180 journals and other serials. **Services:** Copying; library open to public for reference use only. **Automated Operations:** Computerized ILL. **Computerized Information Services:** DIALOG. **Special Indexes:** Citrus card file (author and subject).

★15470★

UNIVERSITY OF FLORIDA - AGRICULTURAL RESEARCH & EDUCATION CENTER - QUINCY LIBRARY
Rte. 3, Box 638
Quincy, FL 32351
Subjects: Agriculture. **Holdings:** Figures not available. **Remarks:** Presently inactive.

★15471★

UNIVERSITY OF FLORIDA - AQUATIC WEED PROGRAM - INFORMATION AND RETRIEVAL CENTER (Env-Cons)
2183 McCarty Hall
Gainesville, FL 32611
Phone: (904) 392-1799
Victor Ramey, Info.Spec.
Staff: Prof 2; Other 1. **Subjects:** Aquatic plants - biology, control, utilization, ecology. **Holdings:** 500 books; 15,000 other cataloged items. **Services:** Interlibrary loans; copying; center open to public for reference use only; bibliographic current-awareness service (computer printout); retrospective database searches (computer printout). **Automated Operations:**

Computerized cataloging, acquisitions, and document indexing. **Computerized Information Services:** DIALOG; Aquatic Weed Program (internal database). Performs free searches. **Publications:** Aquaphyte, biennial - free upon request. **Staff:** Karen Brown, Lib.Tech.Asst.

★15472★

UNIVERSITY OF FLORIDA - ARCHITECTURE & FINE ARTS LIBRARY (Art)
201 FAA
Gainesville, FL 32611
Phone: (904) 392-0222
Edward H. Teague, AFA Libn.
Staff: Prof 2; Other 2. **Subjects:** Architecture, fine arts, interior design, building construction, landscape architecture, urban design. **Holdings:** 56,639 books and bound periodical volumes; 12 VF drawers; 20 drawers of Historic American Buildings Survey drawings and pictures; 656 microforms. **Subscriptions:** 431 journals and other serials. **Services:** Interlibrary loans; copying; library open to public. **Publications:** New Books Received, monthly. **Staff:** Howard W. Huseman, Assoc.Univ.Libn.

★15473★

UNIVERSITY OF FLORIDA - BALDWIN LIBRARY (Hum)
308 Library East
Gainesville, FL 32611
Dr. Ruth Baldwin
Staff: Prof 1; Other 1. **Subjects:** Children's literature. **Holdings:** 76,000 books.

★15474★

UNIVERSITY OF FLORIDA - BELKNAP COLLECTION FOR THE PERFORMING ARTS (Mus; Theater)
512 Library W.
Gainesville, FL 32611
Phone: (904) 392-0322
Sidney Ives, Libn.
Founded: 1953. **Staff:** Prof 1; Other 3. **Subjects:** Dance, opera, music, theater, film. **Special Collections:** Ringling Collection of early playbills, engravings, prints and photographs; 20th-century American playbills; Florida performing arts files; popular sheet music collection; Sarah Belknap Correspondence and Guide to the Performing Arts. **Holdings:** 1800 books; 200 bound periodical volumes; 200,000 souvenir programs, prints and photographs, clippings, correspondence and posters. **Subscriptions:** 60 journals and other serials. **Services:** Copying; library open to public.

★15475★

UNIVERSITY OF FLORIDA - CENTER FOR CLIMACTERIC STUDIES - ROBERT B. GREENBLATT LIBRARY (Med)
901 N.W. 8th Ave., Suite B1
Gainesville, FL 32601
Phone: (904) 392-3184
Morris Note Lovitz, M.D., Dir.
Staff: Prof 1. **Subjects:** Biological, psychological and sociological aspects of the climacteric years. **Holdings:** 100 books; 50 booklets; 3000 professional journal reprints. **Services:** Copying; library open to public for reference use only. **Publications:** Menopause Update, quarterly - available through membership or by subscription.

★15476★

UNIVERSITY OF FLORIDA - CENTER FOR WETLANDS REFERENCE LIBRARY (Env-Cons)
Phelps Laboratory
Gainesville, FL 32611
Phone: (904) 392-2424
G. Ronnie Best, Assoc.Dir.
Staff: 1. **Subjects:** Wetlands research, ecosystems modeling, energy analysis. **Holdings:** 800 books; 16 VF drawers of unbound reports; 84 dissertations; 48 hard copy technical reports; 7 paperback technical reports. **Services:** Library open to public during specified hours.

★15477★

UNIVERSITY OF FLORIDA - CHEMISTRY LIBRARY (Sci-Tech)
216 Leigh Hall
Gainesville, FL 32611
Phone: (904) 392-0573
Carol Drum, Univ.Libn.
Founded: 1940. **Staff:** Prof 1; Other 1. **Subjects:** Chemistry - general, quantum theory, physical, organic, inorganic, analytical. **Holdings:** 10,000 books; 20,000 bound periodical volumes; 635 dissertations and theses; 2150 microforms. **Subscriptions:** 200 journals. **Services:** Interlibrary loans; copying; library open to public. **Computerized Information Services:** DIALOG, SDC, NIH-EPA Chemical Information System, OCLC. **Networks/Consortia:** Member of SOLINET.

★15478★

UNIVERSITY OF FLORIDA - COASTAL & OCEANOGRAPHIC ENGINEERING DEPARTMENT - COASTAL ENGINEERING ARCHIVES (Sci-Tech)
433 Weil Hall
Gainesville, FL 32611
Phone: (904) 392-2710
Lucile Lehmann, Archv.
Staff: Prof 1; Other 1. **Subjects:** Coastal engineering, beach erosion, Florida beaches, estuarine hydrodynamics, hurricanes, storm surge, tidal inlets, water waves. **Special Collections:** Army Corps of Engineers documents on the

Florida coast and tidal hydraulics (900 items). **Holdings:** 316 books; 6640 technical reports; 990 nautical charts; 500 maps; 740 aerial photographs of the Florida coast; 2200 drawings. **Subscriptions:** 100 journals and other serials. **Services:** Interlibrary loans; archives open to public for reference use only. **Publications:** Lists of laboratory publications (indexed), annual updates; acquisitions lists. **Staff:** Helen Twedell, ILL, Acq.

★15479★
UNIVERSITY OF FLORIDA - DOCUMENTS LIBRARY (Info Sci)
254 Library West   Phone: (904) 392-0367
Gainesville, FL 32611   Sally Cravens, Libn.
Staff: Prof 4; Other 4. **Subjects:** Government publications - United States, foreign, international, Florida and other states. **Holdings:** 603,043 documents; 305,472 microfiche; 19 reels of microfilm; 19 VF drawers of Florida material. **Services:** Interlibrary loans; copying; library open to public. **Automated Operations:** Computerized cataloging. **Computerized Information Services:** OCLC, DIALOG, SDC; Focus (internal database). **Staff:** Gary Cornwell, Asst.Libn./U.S., Fed.Docs; Bonnie Konop, Asst.Libn./State Docs.

★15480★
UNIVERSITY OF FLORIDA - EDUCATION LIBRARY (Educ)
1500 Norman Hall   Phone: (904) 392-0707
Gainesville, FL 32611   Myra Suzanne Brown, Act.Chm./Assoc.Libn.
Staff: Prof 3; Other 2. **Subjects:** Education, child development, higher education, psychology, counseling. **Holdings:** 64,464 books; 7486 bound periodical volumes; 215,000 ERIC microfiche. **Services:** Interlibrary loans; copying; library open to public. **Automated Operations:** Online systems. **Staff:** Linda Sparks, Assoc.Libn.

★15481★
UNIVERSITY OF FLORIDA - ENGINEERING & PHYSICS LIBRARY (Sci-Tech; Comp Sci)
410 Weil Hall   Phone: (904) 392-0987
Gainesville, FL 32611   Roger V. Krumm, Libn.
Founded: 1948. **Staff:** Prof 3; Other 5. **Subjects:** Engineering, physics, astronomy, applied chemistry, computer science, materials, energy, general science. **Special Collections:** Atomic Energy Commission, Energy Research and Development Administration and DOE reports; NASA publications; Rand Corporation publications. **Holdings:** 40,000 books; 51,000 bound periodical volumes; 10,000 technical reports; 250,000 Atomic Energy Commission-DOE reports (mostly on microfiche). **Subscriptions:** 1015 journals and other serials. **Services:** Interlibrary loans; copying; library open to public with restrictions. **Computerized Information Services:** DIALOG, SDC, OCLC, Tech-Net. **Networks/Consortia:** Member of SOLINET. **Publications:** News & Booklist, monthly - for internal distribution only. **Staff:** Barry Hartigan, Assoc.Libn.; Alice Primack, Assoc.Libn.

UNIVERSITY OF FLORIDA - FLORIDA STATE MEDICAL ENTOMOLOGY LABORATORY LIBRARY
See: Florida State Medical Entomology Laboratory Library

★15482★
UNIVERSITY OF FLORIDA - FLORIDA STATE MUSEUM LIBRARY (Sci-Tech)
Museum Rd.   Phone: (904) 392-1721
Gainesville, FL 32611   F. Wayne King, Dir.
Founded: 1917. **Subjects:** Natural history, anthropology. **Holdings:** 20,000 volumes and separates. **Services:** Library not open to public. **Staff:** Graig D. Shaak, Assoc.Dir.

★15483★
UNIVERSITY OF FLORIDA - GULF COAST RESEARCH & EDUCATION CENTER - BRADENTON LIBRARY (Agri; Sci-Tech)
Inst. of Food & Agricultural Sciences
5007 60th St., E.   Phone: (813) 755-1568
Bradenton, FL 34203
Staff: 1. **Subjects:** Plant pathology, entomology, vegetable crops, horticulture. **Holdings:** 550 books; 900 bound periodical volumes. **Subscriptions:** 40 journals and other serials. **Services:** Library not open to public.

★15484★
UNIVERSITY OF FLORIDA - HUME LIBRARY (Agri)
Inst. of Food & Agricultural Sciences
McCarty Hall   Phone: (904) 392-1934
Gainesville, FL 32611   Albert C. Strickland, Libn.
Founded: 1900. **Staff:** Prof 7; Other 11. **Subjects:** Agriculture, botany, horticulture, entomology, bacteriology, animal science, statistics, biological science. **Special Collections:** Botanical classics and early agricultural journals,

especially those published in Florida. **Holdings:** 45,000 books; 82,000 bound periodical volumes; 6600 bound documents; 187,000 unbound documents; 4650 microfiche sheets of botanical classics; 105,000 microfiche; 23,000 reels of microfilm. **Subscriptions:** 2300 journals and other serials; 10 newspapers. **Services:** Interlibrary loans (fee); copying; library open to public. **Automated Operations:** Computerized cataloging, acquisitions and serials. **Computerized Information Services:** DIALOG, SDC, OCLC. **Networks/Consortia:** Member of SOLINET. **Publications:** Hume Library List of Serials, irregular - selected distribution. **Staff:** William B. Weaver, Ref.Libn.; Gustave T. Kovalik, Assoc.Ref.Libn.; Siew Phek Su, Asst.Cat.Libn.; Ann H. King, Asst.Ref.Libn.; Lawan Orser, Cat.Libn.; Anita L. Battiste, Asst.Ref.Libn.

★15485★
UNIVERSITY OF FLORIDA - ISSER AND RAE PRICE LIBRARY OF JUDAICA (Hist; Rel-Theol)
18 Library East   Phone: (904) 392-0308
Gainesville, FL 32611   Robert Singerman, Hd. & Assoc.Libn.
Founded: 1977. **Staff:** Prof 1. **Subjects:** Judaism, Jewish history, Hebrew and Yiddish literature, Israel and Zionism, Rabbinic literature, Old Testament. **Special Collections:** Mishkin Collection (40,000 volumes). **Holdings:** 52,500 books; 1500 bound periodical volumes; 430 reels of microfilm. **Subscriptions:** 160 journals and other serials. **Services:** Interlibrary loans; copying; library open to public for reference use only. **Automated Operations:** Computerized cataloging. **Computerized Information Services:** OCLC. **Networks/Consortia:** Member of SOLINET. **Publications:** Isser and Rae Price Library of Judaica Report, semiannual - free upon request. **Special Catalogs:** Catalog to pre-1881 Hebrew and Yiddish imprints (card).

★15486★
UNIVERSITY OF FLORIDA - J. HILLIS MILLER HEALTH CENTER LIBRARY (Med)
Box J-206   Phone: (904) 392-4016
Gainesville, FL 32611   Ted F. Srygley, Dir.
Founded: 1956. **Staff:** Prof 11; Other 30. **Subjects:** Medicine, basic medical sciences, nursing, pharmacy, veterinary medicine, health-related sciences, dentistry. **Holdings:** 38,000 books; 154,000 bound periodical volumes; 1200 films, tapes, phonograph records; Ciba collection (slides). **Subscriptions:** 1900 journals and other serials. **Services:** Interlibrary loans (fee); copying; library open to public by permission. **Computerized Information Services:** MEDLINE, DIALOG, SDC, OCLC. **Networks/Consortia:** Member of SOLINET. **Publications:** New Book List; annual periodical list. **Staff:** Esther Jones, Pub.Serv.Libn.Leonard Rhine, Tech.Serv.Libn.

★15487★
UNIVERSITY OF FLORIDA - LATIN AMERICAN COLLECTION (Area-Ethnic)
4th Fl., Library East   Phone: (904) 392-0360
Gainesville, FL 32611   Dr. Rosa Q. Mesa, Dir.
Founded: 1967. **Staff:** Prof 2; Other 10. **Subjects:** Latin America, Caribbean and Circum-Caribbean, Brazil. **Special Collections:** Caribbean Collection (45,880 books; 203 current periodicals; 13,494 reels of microfilm); Latin American Collection (179,517 books; 1103 periodicals; 16,982 reels of microfilm; 6808 microcards; 12,200 microfiche). **Holdings:** 6200 dissertations on microfilm; Latin American vertical file. **Subscriptions:** 1068 journals and other serials; 38 newspapers. **Services:** Interlibrary loans; collection open to public. **Special Catalogs:** Latin American Collection printed catalog, 1973 (13 volumes); First Supplement, 1980 (7 volumes). **Staff:** Jean Romeo, Asst.Libn.

★15488★
UNIVERSITY OF FLORIDA - LAW LIBRARY (Law)
                                          Phone: (904) 392-0418
Gainesville, FL 32611   Betty W. Taylor, Dir.
Founded: 1909. **Staff:** Prof 9; Other 10. **Subjects:** Law - tax, labor, statutory, water resources, property and public, international, admiralty, Latin American. **Holdings:** 230,824 volumes; 114,156 volumes in microform. **Subscriptions:** 5000 journals and other serials. **Services:** Interlibrary loans; copying; library open to public by permission. **Automated Operations:** Computerized cataloging and serials. **Computerized Information Services:** LEXIS, Westlaw, Control Data Corporation, OCLC. **Networks/Consortia:** Member of SOLINET. **Staff:** Robert Munro, Law Libn.; Carol Felts, Assoc.Libn.; Pamela D. Williams, Assoc.Libn.; Carole Grooms, Assoc.Libn.; Susy B. Gilman, Asst.Libn.; A.R. Donnelly, Asst.Libn.

★15489★
UNIVERSITY OF FLORIDA - MAP LIBRARY (Geog-Map)
Library East   Phone: (904) 392-0803
Gainesville, FL 32611   Dr. HelenJane Armstrong, Map Libn.
Staff: Prof 1; Other 4. **Subjects:** Maps, aerial photographs and remote

sensing images including the specialized areas of Latin America, Africa and Southeastern United States. **Special Collections:** Erwin Raisz Collection of Maps and Cartographic Papers; Sanborn Historical Maps of Florida Cities (5000). **Holdings:** 317,800 maps; 146,300 aerial photographs and remote sensing images; 110 relief models. **Services:** Library open to public. **Automated Operations:** Computerized cataloging. **Computerized Information Services:** OCLC. **Publications:** Acquisitions List, irregular.

★15490★
UNIVERSITY OF FLORIDA - MUSIC LIBRARY (Mus)
231 Music Bldg.   Phone: (904) 392-6678
Gainesville, FL 32611   Robena Eng Cornwell, Asst.Univ.Libn.
Founded: 1972. **Staff:** Prof 1; Other 1. **Subjects:** Music. **Special Collections:** Claude Murphree Collection (10 VF drawers). **Holdings:** 15,500 books; 6500 scores; 1350 bound periodical volumes; 6000 phonograph records and tapes; 775 titles of VF material; 205 reels of microfilm. **Subscriptions:** 95 journals and other serials. **Services:** Interlibrary loans; copying; library open to public with restrictions. **Automated Operations:** Computerized cataloging.

★15491★
UNIVERSITY OF FLORIDA - MUSIC LIBRARY - THE AMERICAN LISZT SOCIETY, INC. - ARCHIVES (Mus)
                                          Phone: (904) 392-6674
Gainesville, FL 32611
Subjects: Franz Liszt - life, works, professional career. **Special Collections:** Records of the annual American Liszt Society festival, 1967 to present (8 linear feet of programs, tape recordings of festival performances, and papers read at the festivals); Liszt's Don Sanche (copy of manuscript). **Services:** Copying; archives open to public with advance permission.

★15492★
UNIVERSITY OF FLORIDA - P.K. YONGE LABORATORY SCHOOL - MEAD LIBRARY (Educ)
1080 S.W. 11th Ave.   Phone: (904) 392-1506
Gainesville, FL 32611   Thelma B. Larche, Hd.Libn.
Founded: 1934. **Staff:** Prof 2; Other 2. **Subjects:** Curriculum materials (grades K-12). **Holdings:** 19,000 volumes; 100 bound periodical volumes; 253 maps; 441 recordings; 867 filmstrips; 124 tapes; 55 cassettes; 107 film loops; 12 games; 193 kits; 10 reels of microfilm; 192 posters; 635 slides; 343 transparencies; 411 books in professional collection. **Subscriptions:** 78 journals and other serials. **Services:** Interlibrary loans; library open to qualified persons.

★15493★
UNIVERSITY OF FLORIDA - P.K. YONGE LIBRARY OF FLORIDA HISTORY (Hist)
4th Fl., Library West   Phone: (904) 392-0319
Gainesville, FL 32611   Elizabeth Alexander, Libn.
Founded: 1944. **Staff:** Prof 1; Other 3. **Subjects:** Florida history. **Special Collections:** Stetson Collection (photostats from the colonial archives in Spain, 1500-1821; 100,000). **Holdings:** 25,000 books; 700 newspapers on microfilm; 700 major manuscript collections; 3000 miscellaneous manuscripts; 2300 reels of microfilm; 2355 maps. **Services:** Copying; library open to public.

★15494★
UNIVERSITY OF FLORIDA - PHYSICS AND ASTRONOMY READING ROOM (Sci-Tech)
261 Williamson Hall   Phone: (904) 392-6686
Gainesville, FL 32611   Dorothy Patterson Lisca, Supv./Lib.Tech.Asst.
Staff: Prof 1; Other 5. **Subjects:** Physics, astronomy, atmospheric sciences. **Holdings:** 10,000 books; 15,000 bound periodical volumes; dissertations; preprints. **Subscriptions:** 149 journals and other serials. **Services:** Interlibrary loans; copying; library open to public with consent of the University.

★15495★
UNIVERSITY OF FLORIDA - RARE BOOKS & MANUSCRIPTS (Rare Book)
531 Library West   Phone: (904) 392-0321
Gainesville, FL 32611   Sidney Ives, Libn.
Staff: Prof 2; Other 3. **Subjects:** 17th-, 18th- and 19th-century English and American literature; English theology (especially 17th century); modern English and American poetry; history of science; Irish literary revival. **Special Collections:** Printing and graphic arts; Rochambeau papers; John Wilson Croker papers; papers of Margaret Dreier Robins; Bromsen-Medina and Harrisse collections of Latin American bibliography; Jeremie papers (Haiti); Sir Walter Scott; Florida authors: papers of Alden Hatch, Zora Neale Hurston, John D. MacDonald, Edith Pope, Marjorie Kinnan Rawlings and Lillian Smith;

manuscripts of Lady Gregory; P.D. Howe Collection of New England authors' first printings and manuscripts; Kohler Collection of Victorian theology. **Holdings:** 58,700 books; 350 unbound periodical volumes; 515 linear feet of manuscripts; 99 linear feet of pamphlets. **Subscriptions:** 74 journals and other serials. **Services:** Copying (limited); library open to public. **Computerized Information Services:** OCLC. **Networks/Consortia:** Member of SOLINET. **Special Indexes:** Manuscript collection index (loose-leaf).

★15496★
UNIVERSITY OF FLORIDA - TRANSPORTATION RESEARCH CENTER (Trans)
Civil Engineering Dept.
245 Weil Hall   Phone: (904) 392-6656
Gainesville, FL 32611   Deborah Reaves, Asst. in Engr.
Subjects: Transportation engineering and planning, traffic engineering. **Holdings:** 100 books; 1800 government and private reports. **Subscriptions:** 10 journals and other serials. **Services:** Copying; center open to public by appointment. **Publications:** Research publications, 12/year.

★15497★
UNIVERSITY OF FLORIDA - TROPICAL RESEARCH & EDUCATION CENTER - HOMESTEAD LIBRARY (Agri; Sci-Tech)
Inst. of Food & Agricultural Sciences
18905 S.W. 280th St.   Phone: (305) 247-4624
Homestead, FL 33031   R.T. McSorley, Act.Dir.
Staff: 14. **Subjects:** Plant pathology, entomology, plant nutrition, horticulture, tropical foliage plants, soil science, tropical exotics, tissue culture. **Special Collections:** Collection on all aspects of mango culture and tropical and subtropical fruits. **Holdings:** 3200 books; 750 bound periodical volumes. **Subscriptions:** 75 journals and other serials. **Services:** Library not open to public. **Staff:** C.M. Sullivan, Libn.

★15498★
UNIVERSITY OF FLORIDA - UNIVERSITY ARCHIVES AND UNIVERSITY COLLECTION (Hist)
303 Library East   Phone: (904) 392-6547
Gainesville, FL 32611   Carla Kemp, Univ.Archv.
Founded: 1951. **Staff:** Prof 1; Other 1. **Subjects:** University history. **Holdings:** 25,000 volumes; 1300 cubic feet of manuscripts (from faculty, staff, alumni); 1566 linear feet of university publications, theses, dissertations, newspapers, yearbooks, ephemera and photographs. **Services:** Copying; archives open to public.

★15499★
UNIVERSITY OF FLORIDA - URBAN AND REGIONAL PLANNING DOCUMENTS COLLECTION (Plan)
Library West   Phone: (904) 392-0317
Gainesville, FL 32611   Margaret S. LeSourd, Assoc.Univ.Libn.
Staff: Prof 1; Other 1. **Subjects:** Planning. **Special Collections:** HUD 701 planning reports. **Holdings:** 29,500 documents. **Services:** Interlibrary loans; collection open to public, courtesy card required for borrowing.

★15500★
UNIVERSITY OF GEORGIA - DEPARTMENT OF RECORDS MANAGEMENT & UNIVERSITY ARCHIVES (Hist)
4th Fl., Old Section
Ilah Dunlap Little Memorial Library   Phone: (404) 542-8151
Athens, GA 30602   Dr. John Carver Edwards, Rec.Off./Archv.
Founded: 1972. **Staff:** 4. **Subjects:** Presidential papers, administrative records, student records, fiscal records. **Special Collections:** Ecological Society of America Collection. **Holdings:** 7000 cubic feet of university archival material. **Services:** Archives open to public. **Staff:** G. Wilson Page, Asst.Rec.Off.

★15501★
UNIVERSITY OF GEORGIA - GEORGIA AGRICULTURAL EXPERIMENT STATION LIBRARY (Agri)
                                          Phone: (404) 228-7238
Experiment, GA 30212   Carole L. Ledford, Libn.
Staff: Prof 1; Other 2. **Subjects:** Agriculture and related sciences. **Holdings:** 36,000 volumes. **Subscriptions:** 557 journals and other serials. **Services:** Interlibrary loans; library open to public with restrictions. **Computerized Information Services:** DIALOG, BRS.

★15502★
UNIVERSITY OF GEORGIA - GEORGIA COASTAL PLAIN EXPERIMENT STATION LIBRARY (Agri)
                                          Phone: (912) 386-3447
Tifton, GA 31793   Emory Cheek, Lib.Assoc.
Founded: 1924. **Staff:** 2. **Subjects:** Agricultural research. **Holdings:** 16,500

volumes; 300 theses and dissertations; 20 VF drawers of reprints and pamphlets. **Subscriptions:** 300 journals and other serials. **Services:** Interlibrary loans; copying; library primarily for use of research personnel at the station.

★15503★
UNIVERSITY OF GEORGIA - GOVERNMENT DOCUMENTS DEPARTMENT
(Soc Sci; Info Sci)
University of Georgia Libraries   Phone: (404) 542-8949
Athens, GA 30602   Susan C. Field, Docs.Libn.
Founded: 1907. **Staff:** Prof 4; Other 4. **Subjects:** U.S. Government publications; Georgia state documents; United Nations documents; Canadian, British and French documents. **Holdings:** 1 million volumes; 700,000 microfiche; 160 reels of microfilm. **Subscriptions:** 10,387 journals and other serials. **Services:** Interlibrary loans; copying; department open to public. **Automated Operations:** Computerized cataloging, acquisitions and serials. **Computerized Information Services:** DIALOG, BRS, SDC, OCLC. **Networks/ Consortia:** Member of SOLINET. **Publications:** List of publications - available upon request. **Special Indexes:** U.S. agency, U.S. shelflist; Georgia shelflist, Georgia keyword, Georgia title; U.N. shelflist and series title; Canada shelflist and series title; Great Britain shelflist; France shelflist (all on cards).

★15504★
UNIVERSITY OF GEORGIA - LAW LIBRARY (Law)
                                        Phone: (404) 542-8480
Athens, GA 30602   Erwin C. Surrency, Prof./Libn.
Staff: Prof 7; Other 11. **Subjects:** Law. **Holdings:** 293,048 volumes; 4017 reels of microfilm; 190,029 microfiche. **Subscriptions:** 939 journals and other serials; 13 newspapers. **Services:** Interlibrary loans; copying; library open to public. **Computerized Information Services:** LEXIS, Westlaw, OCLC. **Publications:** List of Acquisitions. **Special Indexes:** Index to legal publications in the state of Georgia (cards). **Staff:** Jose R. Pages, Acq.Libn.; Carol Ramsey, Cat.Libn.; Martha N. Hampton, Law Ser.Libn.; Jose F. Rodriguez, Circ. & Ref.Libn.; Diana Duderwicz, Asst.Cat.Libn.; Margaret M.R. Durkin, Asst.Pub.Serv.Libn.

★15505★
UNIVERSITY OF GEORGIA - MANUSCRIPTS COLLECTION (Hum)
University of Georgia Libraries   Phone: (404) 542-2972
Athens, GA 30602   Larry Gulley, Mss.Libn.
Staff: Prof 1; Other 2. **Subjects:** Georgia (1732 to present), Civil War, literature, music, social history, education. **Special Collections:** Egmont Papers; Charles C. Jones Collection; Telamon Cuyler Collection; Olin Downs Collection; Charles Coburn Collection; Ward Morehouse Collection; Paris Music Hall Collection; Keith Read Collection; Margaret Mitchell Marsh Papers; Lillian Smith Papers. **Holdings:** 2.5 million manuscripts. **Services:** Collection open to public. **Special Catalogs:** Unpublished guides.

★15506★
UNIVERSITY OF GEORGIA - RARE BOOKS DEPARTMENT (Rare Book)
                                        Phone: (404) 542-2972
Athens, GA 30602   Robert M. Willingham, Rare Bks.Cur.
Staff: Prof 2; Other 2. **Subjects:** Georgiana, Confederate imprints, theater, fine printing, American and English literature, photography, historical maps. **Special Collections:** De Renne Collection of Georgiana. **Holdings:** 53,000 volumes. **Services:** Department open to public. **Staff:** Nancy Stamper, Cat.; Mary Ellen Brooks, Bibliog.

★15507★
UNIVERSITY OF GEORGIA - RICHARD B. RUSSELL MEMORIAL LIBRARY
(Hist)
University of Georgia Libraries   Phone: (404) 542-5788
Athens, GA 30602   Sheryl Vogt, Hd.
Founded: 1974. **Staff:** 4. **Subjects:** 20th century Georgia politics, U.S. Congress, civil rights, agricultural legislation, defense and armed services legislation. **Holdings:** 8000 linear feet. **Services:** Interlibrary loans; copying; library open to public; visiting scholars should write for application to do research. **Staff:** Orlean Castronis, Archv.Assoc.; James Cross, Libn.

UNIVERSITY OF GEORGIA - SCHOOL OF VETERINARY MEDICINE LIBRARY
See: University of Georgia - Science Library

★15508★
UNIVERSITY OF GEORGIA - SCIENCE LIBRARY (Sci-Tech)
                                        Phone: (404) 542-4535
Athens, GA 30602   Arlene E. Luchsinger, Hd.
Staff: Prof 2; Other 22. **Subjects:** Science, technology, agriculture, home economics, medicine. **Holdings:** 435,000 volumes; maps. **Subscriptions:** 5500 journals. **Services:** Interlibrary loans; copying; library open to public.

Automated Operations: Computerized acquisitions. **Computerized Information Services:** DIALOG, BRS, OCLC, SDC. **Networks/Consortia:** Member of SOLINET. **Remarks:** Includes the holdings of the School of Veterinary Medicine Library.

★15509★
UNIVERSITY OF GEORGIA - SCIENCE LIBRARY - MAP COLLECTION (Geog-Map)
University of Georgia Libraries   Phone: (404) 542-4535
Athens, GA 30602   John Sutherland, Map Cur.
Staff: Prof 2; Other 2. **Subjects:** Topography, geology, natural resources, climate, population. **Special Collections:** Sanborn Atlas Sheets of Georgia (7100). **Holdings:** 190,000 aerial photographs; 290,000 maps; 900 atlases. **Services:** Interlibrary loans; copying; library open to public. **Computerized Information Services:** OCLC. **Publications:** Selected Acquisitions, quarterly; Sanborn Fire Insurance Maps of Georgia Held by the Map Collection; Atlases in the Map Collection; Aerial Photograph coverage of Georgia Held by the Map Collection.

★15510★
UNIVERSITY OF GEORGIA - SKIDAWAY INSTITUTE OF OCEANOGRAPHY -
LIBRARY (Sci-Tech)
Box 13687   Phone: (912) 356-2474
Savannah, GA 31406-0687   Teri Lynn Herbert, Libn.
Staff: Prof 1. **Subjects:** Oceanography, marine resources, fisheries, marine pollution, geochemistry, marine research. **Special Collections:** Climatological data for Georgia and adjacent states; sea surface isotherm records, 1960 to 1979; Gulf Stream data, 1966 to present; marine science reprints (11,000). **Holdings:** 3500 books; 6000 bound periodical volumes; 8000 reports, documents and unbound serials. **Subscriptions:** 260 journals and other serials; 35 newsletters. **Services:** Interlibrary loans; copying; library open to public with restrictions. **Automated Operations:** Computerized cataloging, acquisitions and serials (through University of Georgia Libraries). **Computerized Information Services:** DIALOG, OCLC. **Networks/Consortia:** Member of SOLINET; CRL; Association of Research Libraries (ARL). **Publications:** Serials holdings list - available upon request and for a fee; Skidaway Institute Staff Publications List, 1969-1981 - free upon request. **Remarks:** The library is a branch of the University of Georgia Libraries but the Skidaway Institute of Oceanography is a separate research unit of the University System of Georgia.

★15511★
UNIVERSITY OF GUAM - MICRONESIAN AREA RESEARCH CENTER -
PACIFIC COLLECTION (Area-Ethnic)
U.O.G. Sta.   Phone: (717) 734-2921
Mangilao, GU 96913   Albert L. Williams, Libn.
Founded: 1967. **Staff:** Prof 3; Other 3. **Subjects:** Micronesia - history, marine biology, anthropology, missions, languages, World War II. **Special Collections:** Spanish manuscripts; South Pacific Commission depository; Guam Constitutional Convention Papers. **Holdings:** 15,000 books and bound periodical volumes; 80 VF drawers of clippings and pamphlets; 1000 slides; 30 VF drawers containing 12,000 photographs; 58 boxes of microfiche; 1300 reels of microfilm; 150 boxes of archives; 2000 sheets of maps and charts; 220 tapes. **Subscriptions:** 300 journals and other serials. **Services:** Copying (limited); collection open to public for reference use only. **Publications:** Bibliographies; special publications; MARC Working Papers; Newsletter. **Special Indexes:** Indexes for photographs, Pacific Islands, ships, personalities; tables of contents and subject indexes for manuscripts. **Staff:** Marjorie G. Driver, Spanish Period Spec.

★15512★
UNIVERSITY OF GUELPH - HUMANITIES AND SOCIAL SCIENCES DIVISION -
MAP COLLECTION (Geog-Map)†
McLaughlin Library   Phone: (519) 824-4120
Guelph, ON, Canada N1G 2W1   Mrs. F. Francis, Ref.Libn.
Staff: 4. **Subjects:** Cartography, including agriculture, climatology, economics, geology, historiology, hydrology, land use, population, soils, topography, transportation. **Holdings:** 55,000 maps; 975 atlases; 80 gazetteers; indexes; cartobibliographies; cartographic equipment. **Services:** Interlibrary loans (limited); collection open to public. **Automated Operations:** Computerized cataloging, acquisitions, serials and circulation. **Special Catalogs:** COM map catalogs.

★15513★
UNIVERSITY OF GUELPH - LIBRARY (Soc Sci; Agri; Hum)
McLaughlin Library   Phone: (519) 824-4120
Guelph, ON, Canada N1G 2W1   Margaret L. Beckman, Chf.Libn.
Founded: 1964. **Staff:** Prof 38; Other 118. **Subjects:** Agriculture, veterinary medicine, humanities, social sciences, natural and applied sciences. **Holdings:**

2 million volumes. **Subscriptions:** 9000 journals and other serials; 48 newspapers. **Services:** Interlibrary loans; copying; SDI; library open to public. **Automated Operations:** Computerized cataloging, acquisitions, serials, circulation, documents and maps. **Computerized Information Services:** QL Systems, CAN/OLE, BRS, SDC, DIALOG; internal databases. **Networks/ Consortia:** Member of Ontario Council of University Libraries (OCUL). **Publications:** Reports, irregular; bibliography series, irregular; Collection Update, semiannual. **Staff:** Dr. J. Black, Assoc.Libn.; Ellen M. Pearson, Asst.Libn.; Mr. L. Porter, Asst.Libn.

★15514★

UNIVERSITY OF HARTFORD - ANNE BUNCE CHENEY LIBRARY (Art)
200 Bloomfield Ave.   Phone: (203) 243-4397
West Hartford, CT 06117   Jean J. Miller, Libn.
Founded: 1963. **Staff:** Prof 1; Other 1. **Subjects:** Art history, art education, applied art, decorative arts, crafts, photography, typography. **Holdings:** 10,964 books; 1262 bound periodical volumes; 12,011 mounted reproductions; 2977 pamphlets; 8 VF drawers of exhibition catalogs. **Subscriptions:** 98 journals and other serials. **Services:** Interlibrary loans; copying; library open to public. **Computerized Information Services:** OCLC. **Networks/Consortia:** Member of NELINET; Capitol Region Library Council; Hartford Consortium for Higher Education.

★15515★

UNIVERSITY OF HARTFORD - DANA SCIENCE & ENGINEERING LIBRARY (Sci-Tech)
200 Bloomfield Ave., Dana Bldg.   Phone: (203) 243-4404
West Hartford, CT 06117   Frances T. Libbey, Sci./Engr.Libn.
Founded: 1967. **Staff:** Prof 2; Other 15. **Subjects:** Chemistry, biology, physiological psychology, mathematics, physics, earth sciences, engineering. **Special Collections:** History of Science (300 volumes). **Holdings:** 15,000 books; 16,000 bound periodical volumes; microforms; 30 masters' theses. **Subscriptions:** 750 journals and other serials. **Services:** Interlibrary loans; copying; library open to public for reference use only. **Automated Operations:** Computerized cataloging. **Computerized Information Services:** DIALOG. **Networks/Consortia:** Member of Hartford Consortium for Higher Education. **Publications:** Listing of Periodical Holdings - for consortium members.

★15516★

UNIVERSITY OF HARTFORD - HARTT SCHOOL OF MUSIC - ALLEN MEMORIAL LIBRARY (Mus)
200 Bloomfield Ave.   Phone: (203) 243-4491
West Hartford, CT 06117   Ethel Bacon, Libn.
Staff: Prof 2; Other 3. **Subjects:** Music and performing arts. **Special Collections:** Robert E. Smith Record Collection (30,000 phonograph records); Kalmen Opperman Collection (clarinet). **Holdings:** 11,000 books; 1050 bound periodical volumes; 24,000 pieces of music; 16,000 phonograph records; 2000 audiotapes; 160 reels of microfilm. **Subscriptions:** 100 journals and other serials. **Services:** Interlibrary loans; copying; library open to public for reference use only. **Automated Operations:** Computerized cataloging. **Computerized Information Services:** OCLC. **Networks/Consortia:** Member of NELINET; Hartford Consortium for Higher Education.

★15517★

UNIVERSITY OF HAWAII - ASIA COLLECTION (Area-Ethnic)
Hamilton Library, 2550 The Mall   Phone: (808) 948-8116
Honolulu, HI 96822   Joyce Wright, Hd., Asia Coll.
Founded: 1962. **Staff:** Prof 10; Other 2. **Subjects:** East, Southeast and South Asia. **Special Collections:** Sakamaki Collection (Ryukyus). **Holdings:** 268,342 volumes; 24,910 reels of microfilm; 14,000 microfiche; 10,000 uncataloged monographs. **Services:** Interlibrary loans; copying; library open to public. **Publications:** List of publications - available upon request. **Staff:** Masato Matsui, Hd., E. Asia Vernacular.

★15518★

UNIVERSITY OF HAWAII - CENTER FOR KOREAN STUDIES - LIBRARY (Area-Ethnic)
1881 East-West Rd.   Phone: (808) 948-7041
Honolulu, HI 96822   Charlotte Oser, Adm.Off.
Staff: Prof 1; Other 1. **Subjects:** Korea. **Holdings:** 5500 titles, including 775 serial titles; 726 reels of microfilm of doctoral dissertations; 27 16mm films; 223 reels of microfilm of newspapers; 51 lectures and 7 conference/ workshops on audio cassette; 13 cassette-slide sets. **Subscriptions:** 105 journals and other serials; 11 newspapers. **Services:** Copying; film showings; library open to public with restrictions. **Publications:** Informal acquisitions lists.

★15519★

UNIVERSITY OF HAWAII - DEPARTMENT OF HISTORY - PACIFIC REGIONAL ORAL HISTORY PROGRAM - LIBRARY (Hist; Area-Ethnic)
2530 Dole St.   Phone: (808) 948-8486
Honolulu, HI 96822   Edward Beechert, Dir.
Staff: Prof 1; Other 1. **Subjects:** Hawaiian labor, agricultural and ethnic history. **Holdings:** 126 interview transcripts. **Services:** Copying; library open to public with restrictions. **Special Catalogs:** Catalog of interviews.

UNIVERSITY OF HAWAII - HAWAII INSTITUTE OF GEOPHYSICS
See: Hawaii Institute of Geophysics

★15520★

UNIVERSITY OF HAWAII - INSTITUTE FOR ASTRONOMY - MAUNA KEA OBSERVATORY - LIBRARY (Sci-Tech)
177 Makaala   Phone: (808) 935-3371
Hilo, HI 96720   Sara Thompson, Libn.
Staff: Prof 1. **Subjects:** Astronomy, astrophysics. **Holdings:** 400 books; 300 bound periodical volumes; 2 VF drawers of preprints and reprints; 20 map drawers of sky surveys. **Subscriptions:** 52 journals and other serials. **Services:** Interlibrary loans; library not open to public.

UNIVERSITY OF HAWAII - INSTITUTE OF CULTURE AND COMMUNICATION
See: Institute of Culture and Communication

UNIVERSITY OF HAWAII - NITROGEN FIXATION BY TROPICAL AGRICULTURAL LEGUMES
See: Nitrogen Fixation by Tropical Agricultural Legumes

★15521★

UNIVERSITY OF HAWAII - PACIFIC BIO-MEDICAL RESEARCH CENTER - LIBRARY (Med)
41 Ahui St.   Phone: (808) 531-3538
Honolulu, HI 96813   Dr. Barbara H. Gibbons, Res.
Founded: 1967. **Staff:** 1. **Subjects:** Biochemistry, cell biology, developmental morphology, molecular biology. **Special Collections:** Reprints of papers by C.F.W. McClure. **Holdings:** 700 bound periodical volumes. **Subscriptions:** 15 journals and other serials. **Services:** Copying; library open to public with restrictions.

★15522★

UNIVERSITY OF HAWAII - PUBLIC SERVICES - GOVERNMENT DOCUMENTS, MAPS & MICROFORMS (Info Sci; Geog-Map)
Hamilton Library, 2550 The Mall   Phone: (808) 948-8230
Honolulu, HI 96822   Janet Morrison, Hd.
Founded: 1945. **Staff:** Prof 3; Other 5. **Holdings:** 62,624 volumes; public documents of official U.S. agencies (regional depository), state agricultural departments and experiment stations, League of Nations, United Nations and its affiliated agencies (UNESCO, Food and Agriculture Organization, World Health Organizations), European Economic Community (EEC) and selected British, Australian and New Zealand documents; 530,094 unbound parts; 730,536 microforms; maps. **Services:** Interlibrary loans; copying; collection open to public.

★15523★

UNIVERSITY OF HAWAII - SCHOOL OF PUBLIC HEALTH - LIBRARY (Med)
1960 East-West Rd.
Court D., Rm. 207   Phone: (808) 948-8666
Honolulu, HI 96822   Carol W. Arnold, Hd.Libn.
Founded: 1968. **Staff:** Prof 2; Other 2. **Subjects:** Public health, health services planning and administration, environmental health, population studies, quantitative health sciences, health education, maternal and child health, public health nutrition, international health, population and family planning studies. **Special Collections:** Kaiser-Hawaii Health Care Microfiche Collection (organization and delivery of health care; 22,000 microfiche). **Holdings:** 14,000 books; 1200 bound periodical volumes; 750 theses and dissertations; 1000 VF items. **Subscriptions:** 427 journals and other serials. **Services:** Interlibrary loans; copying; library open to public with permission of librarian. **Networks/Consortia:** Member of Pacific Southwest Regional Medical Library Service (PSRMLS). **Special Indexes:** Index to the School of Public Health Collection of Student Papers (book).

★15524★

UNIVERSITY OF HAWAII - SOCIAL SCIENCE RESEARCH INSTITUTE (Soc Sci)
Porteus Hall 704, Maile Way   Phone: (808) 948-8930
Honolulu, HI 96822   Donald M. Topping, Dir.
Founded: 1974. **Subjects:** Research in the social sciences with emphasis on Hawaii and the Pacific; anthropology; language acquisition; geography;

linguistics; political science; communications; sociology; development studies; cognitive studies. **Holdings:** Figures not available. **Publications:** Asian Perspectives, semiannual; Oceanic Linguistics, semiannual; Asian and Pacific Archeology Series; Hawaii Series (annotated bibliographies); Oceanic Linguistics: Special Publications (monographs); PALI Language Texts - all distributed by University Press of Hawaii. **Remarks:** SSRI is one of eight research institutes of the University of Hawaii, Manoa, that are administratively housed in the Office of Research Administration. The primary goal is to conduct research funded by state, federal and private agencies.

★15525★
UNIVERSITY OF HAWAII - SPECIAL COLLECTIONS - ARCHIVES (Hist)
Sinclair Library, 2425 Campus Rd.   Phone: (808) 948-6673
Honolulu, HI 96822   David Kittelson, Assoc.Lib.Spec.
Founded: 1968. **Staff:** Prof 1. **Special Collections:** Hawaii War Records Depository (200 feet of transcripts, photocopies, microfilm, letters, memoranda, diaries, narratives, books, pamphlets, articles, federal, territorial and municipal documents relating to Hawaii in World War II). **Holdings:** Noncurrent official records of the university, including publications; nonofficial records of faculty and staff, and miscellaneous historical material about the university. **Services:** Copying; archives open to public. **Special Catalogs:** Guides to holdings, specialized finding aids.

★15526★
UNIVERSITY OF HAWAII - SPECIAL COLLECTIONS - HAWAIIAN COLLECTION (Area-Ethnic)
Hamilton Library, 2550 The Mall   Phone: (808) 948-8264
Honolulu, HI 96822   Dr. Chieko Tachihata, Asst.Lib.Spec.
Founded: 1927. **Staff:** Prof 1. **Subjects:** Hawaiian Islands, Captain Cook, state and county government documents, children's literature, Hawaiian language materials. **Special Collections:** Rare Hawaiiana; 19th century Hawaiian business and literary manuscripts (15 feet). **Holdings:** 75,000 volumes; microfilm; 19 file cabinets of newspaper clippings. **Subscriptions:** 1743 journals and other serials. **Services:** Interlibrary loans; copying; collection open to public. **Publications:** Current Hawaiiana, quarterly; Dissertations and Theses, University of Hawaii at Manoa, annual. **Special Catalogs:** Union catalog of Hawaiian holdings of several Honolulu libraries (card); file of theses by fields of study (card).

★15527★
UNIVERSITY OF HAWAII - SPECIAL COLLECTIONS - JEAN CHARLOT COLLECTION (Art; Hum)
Hamilton Library, Rm. 501
2550 The Mall   Phone: (808) 948-8473
Honolulu, HI 96822   Eleanor Au, Hd., Spec.Coll.
Staff: 1. **Subjects:** French artist and writer Jean Charlot (1898-1979). **Holdings:** Art works, documents and working papers of and relating to Charlot: Oil paintings, mural drawings, sketchbooks, and prints by Charlot; published and unpublished writings by Charlot; private documents, including Charlot's daily journal; tape-recorded interviews; correspondence; reminiscences; Charlot's personal library of over 1500 items; works by other artists, including Orozco, Siquieros, Rivera, Edward Weston, Ben Shahn, Louis Elshemius and Hawaiian artists; prints by Posada and Daumier; Mexican folk art; documents by or relating to other artists and scholars.

★15528★
UNIVERSITY OF HAWAII - SPECIAL COLLECTIONS - PACIFIC COLLECTION (Area-Ethnic)
Hamilton Library, 2550 The Mall   Phone: (808) 948-8264
Honolulu, HI 96822   Renee Heyum, Cur.
Founded: 1959. **Staff:** Prof 3. **Subjects:** Pacific Islands - government, economics, law, linguistics, vernacular texts, literature, anthropology, history; Melanesia; Micronesia; Polynesia. **Special Collections:** Depository for microfilm issued by PAMBU (Pacific Manuscripts Bureau), Canberra; out-of-state theses; depository for South Pacific Commission; rare Pacific materials. **Holdings:** 46,000 volumes. **Subscriptions:** 995 journals and other serials. **Services:** Interlibrary loans; copying; collection open to public. **Publications:** Acquisitions List.

★15529★
UNIVERSITY OF HAWAII - SPECIAL COLLECTIONS - RARE BOOKS (Rare Book)
Hamilton Library, 2550 The Mall   Phone: (808) 948-8230
Honolulu, HI 96822   Eleanor C. Au, Hd., Spec.Coll.
Staff: Prof 1. **Special Collections:** Authors - Jack London, Mark Twain, Herman Melville, C.W. Stoddard; Book Arts Collection; juvenile books; historical text books; Social Movement Collection. **Services:** Collection open to public for reference use only.

★15530★
UNIVERSITY OF HAWAII - WAIKIKI AQUARIUM - LIBRARY (Sci-Tech)
2777 Kalakaua Ave.   Phone: (808) 923-9741
Honolulu, HI 96815   Denise M. Davies, Libn.
Founded: 1980. **Staff:** Prof 1; Other 1. **Subjects:** Marine aquarium technology, zoology, oceanography, vertebrata, invertebrata, mollusca, ichthyology, with specialty in the Hawaii-South Pacific region. **Special Collections:** Collection of out-of-print aquarium magazines. **Holdings:** 1000 books; 75 journals and newsletters; 10 VF drawers of reprints; reports. **Services:** Copying; SDI; library open to public for reference use only by request. **Publications:** Directory of Public Aquaria of the World; Directory of Aquarium Specialists; nature pamphlets; Kilo i'a Looking at the Sea, monthly newsletter; acquisitions list and "Current Contents" (contains tables of contents of journals of professional interest to the staff) - both distributed to staff. **Special Catalogs:** Subject catalog (selected subjects only) for reprints, journals and newsletters received (card).

★15531★
UNIVERSITY HEALTH CENTER OF PITTSBURGH - CENTER FOR EMERGENCY MEDICINE - LIBRARY (Med)
190 Lothrop St., Suite 113   Phone: (412) 624-2858
Pittsburgh, PA 15213   R.D. Stewart, M.D., Dir.
Staff: Prof 2; Other 5. **Subjects:** Emergency medicine, pre-hospital care, critical care medicine. **Holdings:** 300 books; 500 bound periodical volumes. **Subscriptions:** 50 journals and other serials. **Services:** Library open to public with restrictions. **Staff:** G.W. Porter, Adm.

★15532★
UNIVERSITY OF HEALTH SCIENCES/CHICAGO MEDICAL SCHOOL - LIBRARY (Med)
3333 Green Bay Rd.   Phone: (312) 578-3655
North Chicago, IL 60064   Nancy W. Garn, Dir.
Founded: 1912. **Staff:** Prof 5; Other 15. **Subjects:** Medicine and related health sciences. **Holdings:** 15,000 books; 25,000 bound periodical volumes; 2800 reels of microfilm (20,000 volumes); 4 drawers of residency files. **Subscriptions:** 1237 journals and other serials; 7 newspapers. **Services:** Interlibrary loans; copying; library open to public with letter of introduction. **Automated Operations:** Computerized cataloging. **Computerized Information Services:** BRS, OCLC. **Networks/Consortia:** This is a supplemental resource institute of Greater Midwest Regional Medical Library Network (Region 3). **Publications:** New Acquisitions List, monthly; UHS/CMS Subject Listing of Journals; Library Fact Sheet, annual. **Staff:** Robert Schmid, Assoc.Dir.; Sharyn Fradin, Asst.Libn.; Ramune Kubilius, Ref. & Ser.Libn.; Gary Dandurand, AV Libn.; Kevin Robertson, Circ. & ILL Libn.

★15533★
UNIVERSITY OF HEALTH SCIENCES - LIBRARY (Med)
2105 Independence Blvd.   Phone: (816) 283-2451
Kansas City, MO 64124   Marilyn J. DeGeus, Dir. of Libs.
Staff: Prof 4; Other 4. **Subjects:** Medicine, osteopathy. **Holdings:** 44,500 books; 14,850 bound periodical volumes; 1721 cassette tape titles; 2291 slide titles; 50 pamphlets; 2750 videotapes; 26 filmstrips; 2 microfiche; 54 transparencies; 4 teaching models; 24 three-dimensional disc titles. **Subscriptions:** 1870 journals and other serials. **Services:** Interlibrary loans; copying; library open to public for reference use only. **Automated Operations:** Computerized cataloging. **Computerized Information Services:** MEDLINE, TOXLINE, OCLC. **Networks/Consortia:** Member of Kansas City Library Network, Inc. (KCLN); Missouri Library Network Corporation. **Publications:** The Library and You. **Staff:** Mary Kralicek, Ser. & Ref.Libn.; Eleanor Sanders, Cat.; Terri Alexander, AV.

★15534★
UNIVERSITY HOSPITAL AND CLINIC - HERBERT L. BRYANS MEMORIAL LIBRARY (Med)
1200 West Leonard St.   Phone: (904) 436-9187
Pensacola, FL 32501   Ms. Sammie Campbell, Libn.
Staff: Prof 1. **Subjects:** Medicine, dentistry, nursing, dietetics, hospital administration. **Holdings:** 2000 books; 2635 bound periodical volumes; 4 VF drawers. **Subscriptions:** 160 journals and other serials. **Services:** Interlibrary loans; copying; library open to public with restrictions. **Remarks:** Audiovisual materials are available through the Pensacola Education Program.

★15535★
UNIVERSITY HOSPITAL - HEALTH SCIENCES LIBRARY (Med)
1350 Walton Way   Phone: (404) 722-9011
Augusta, GA 30910   Jane B. Wells, Libn.
Staff: Prof 1; Other 1. **Subjects:** Medicine, nursing, allied health fields. **Holdings:** 4500 books; 350 bound periodical volumes. **Subscriptions:** 225 journals and other serials. **Services:** Interlibrary loans; library not open to

public.

UNIVERSITY HOSPITAL (Louisville General)
See: Humana Hospital University

★15536★
UNIVERSITY HOSPITALS OF CLEVELAND & CASE WESTERN RESERVE UNIVERSITY - DEPT. OF PATHOLOGY - LIBRARY (Med)
2085 Adelbert Rd.   Phone: (216) 368-2482
Cleveland, OH 44106   Jeanette W. Nagy, Dir.
Founded: 1930. **Staff:** Prof 1. **Subjects:** Pathology, biochemistry, obstetrics/gynecology, surgery, neuropathology, immunology, histology-cytology. **Holdings:** 2000 books; 7000 bound periodical volumes; reprints; theses; dissertations. **Subscriptions:** 75 journals and other serials. **Services:** Library open to public with restrictions.

★15537★
UNIVERSITY OF HOUSTON - AUDIOVISUAL SERVICES (Aud-Vis)
University Park Campus   Phone: (713) 749-2361
Houston, TX 77004   Joseph R. Schroeder, Dir.
Founded: 1927. **Staff:** Prof 6; Other 12. **Holdings:** 1000 films, videotapes and AV modules. **Services:** Full audiovisual services to administration and instructional programs: television, photographic, audio and graphic production; media distribution; media supplies; electronic maintenance; instruction development. **Remarks:** Includes holdings of the Education Learning Resource Center. **Staff:** James Joplin, Asst.Dir., Prod.Serv.; Umesh Kapur, Asst.Dir., Tech.Serv.; Betty Bishop, Coord., Educ. LRC.

UNIVERSITY OF HOUSTON - COLLEGE OF LAW - NATIONAL COLLEGE OF DISTRICT ATTORNEYS
See: National College of District Attorneys

★15538★
UNIVERSITY OF HOUSTON - COLLEGE OF OPTOMETRY LIBRARY (Med)
                                         Phone: (713) 749-2411
Houston, TX 77004   Suzanne Ferimer, Dir., Lrng.Rsrcs.
Staff: Prof 1; Other 3. **Subjects:** Ocular diagnosis, public health services, contact lenses, history of optometry, pediatric optometry, optics, physiological optics. **Holdings:** 5208 books and bound periodical volumes; 300 audio cassettes; 3 drawers of vertical files, bibliographies, reports; 60 video cassettes; 40 slide-tape presentations; 310 pamphlets. **Subscriptions:** 119 journals and other serials. **Services:** Interlibrary loans; copying; library open to public with restrictions. **Automated Operations:** Computerized cataloging, acquisitions and circulation. **Computerized Information Services:** DIALOG, SDC, NLM, BRS. **Networks/Consortia:** Member of AMIGOS Bibliographic Council, Inc.; Houston Area Research Libraries Consortium (HARLIC).

★15539★
UNIVERSITY OF HOUSTON - COLLEGE OF PHARMACY LIBRARY (Med)
University Park Campus   Phone: (713) 749-1566
Houston, TX 77004   Derral Parkin, Libn.
Founded: 1947. **Staff:** Prof 1; Other 4. **Subjects:** Chemistry, pharmacy, pharmaceuticals, toxicology, pharmacognosy, pharmacology. **Special Collections:** History and biography of pharmacy and medicine. **Holdings:** 10,788 books and bound periodical volumes; 50 pharmaceutical catalogs; College of Pharmacy catalogs. **Subscriptions:** 170 journals and other serials. **Services:** Interlibrary loans; copying; library open to public with permission. **Automated Operations:** Computerized cataloging, acquisitions and circulation. **Computerized Information Services:** SDC, BRS, DIALOG, NLM. **Networks/Consortia:** Member of Houston Area Research Libraries Consortium (HARLIC); AMIGOS Bibliographic Council, Inc. **Publications:** Quarterly acquisitions list - for internal distribution only.

★15540★
UNIVERSITY OF HOUSTON - FRANZHEIM ARCHITECTURE LIBRARY (Art)
University Park Campus   Phone: (713) 749-1193
Houston, TX 77004   Margaret Culbertson, Libn.
Founded: 1961. **Staff:** 2. **Subjects:** Architecture, history of architecture, urban design. **Holdings:** 14,585 books and bound periodical volumes; 600 city planning pamphlets; 4 drawers of master plans and planning reports for universities, elementary and secondary schools. **Subscriptions:** 150 journals and other serials. **Services:** Interlibrary loans; library open to public for reference use only. **Automated Operations:** cataloging, acquisitions and circulation. **Computerized Information Services:** DIALOG, SDC, BRS. **Networks/Consortia:** Member of Houston Area Research Libraries Consortium (HARLIC); AMIGOS Bibliographic Council, Inc.

★15541★
UNIVERSITY OF HOUSTON - LAW LIBRARY (Law)
University Park Campus   Phone: (713) 749-3191
Houston, TX 77004   Jon S. Schultz, Dir.
Staff: Prof 7; Other 8. **Subjects:** Law. **Holdings:** 169,000 volumes; 5000 Texas Supreme Court briefs; 5000 microcards; 260,000 microfiche. **Subscriptions:** 2159 journals and other serials. **Services:** Interlibrary loans; copying; library open to public with permission. **Automated Operations:** Computerized cataloging, acquisitions and circulation. **Computerized Information Services:** SDC, BRS, LEXIS, Westlaw, LIBS 100 System. **Networks/Consortia:** Member of AMIGOS Bibliographic Council, Inc.; TALON-LAW; LAWNET.

★15542★
UNIVERSITY OF HOUSTON - LIBRARIES - SPECIAL COLLECTIONS (Hist; Hum)
University Park Campus   Phone: (713) 749-2725
Houston, TX 77004   Dr. David Farmer, Cur. of Spec.Coll.
Staff: Prof 1; Other 1. **Subjects:** Texana; Western history; Houston, British, and American authors; Latin drama. **Special Collections:** George Fuerman Collection of City of Houston; W.B. Bates Collection of Western Americana (100 volumes); Jones Drama Collection (1500 volumes); Israel Shreve papers (25); James V. Allred papers (100 linear feet); Larry McMurtry manuscripts (60 boxes); Beverly Lowry manuscripts (5 boxes); Ian de Hartog manuscripts (19 boxes); Aldous Huxley manuscripts (3 boxes); historical railroad and Western hemisphere maps; Kenneth Patchen ephemera (188 items). **Holdings:** 20,000 books; 2000 bound periodical volumes. **Subscriptions:** 11 journals and other serials. **Services:** Collections open to public with supervision. **Special Catalogs:** W.B. Bates Collection Catalog; Robinson Jeffers Collection Catalog.

★15543★
UNIVERSITY OF HOUSTON - MUSIC LIBRARY (Mus)
University Park Campus   Phone: (713) 749-2534
Houston, TX 77004   Samuel R. Hyde, Libn.
Founded: 1975. **Staff:** 1 Prof 1; Other 2. **Subjects:** Music. **Holdings:** 28,085 books, bound periodical volumes and musical scores. **Subscriptions:** 109 journals and other serials. **Services:** Interlibrary loans; copying; library open to public for reference use only. **Automated Operations:** Computerized cataloging, acquisitions and circulation. **Computerized Information Services:** DIALOG. **Networks/Consortia:** Member of Houston Area Research Libraries Consortium (HARLIC); AMIGOS Bibliographic Council, Inc.

UNIVERSITY OF HOUSTON, VICTORIA
See: Victoria College/University of Houston, Victoria

★15544★
UNIVERSITY OF IDAHO - ARCHIVE OF PACIFIC NORTHWEST ARCHAEOLOGY (Sci-Tech)
Dept. of Sociology/Anthropology   Phone: (208) 885-6123
Moscow, ID 83843   Roderick Sprague, Dir.
Staff: Prof 1; Other 1. **Subjects:** Pacific Northwest - archeology, historical archeology, physical anthropology. **Holdings:** 3500 complete photocopies of all materials relating to the archeology and physical anthropology of the Pacific Northwest. **Services:** Copying; archive open to public.

★15545★
UNIVERSITY OF IDAHO - THE BOYD AND GRACE MARTIN INSTITUTE OF HUMAN BEHAVIOR - LIBRARY (Soc Sci)
                                         Phone: (208) 885-6527
Moscow, ID 83843   Boyd A. Martin, Dir.
Staff: Prof 1; Other 1. **Subjects:** Causes of war, violence and terrorism; conditions of peace; conflict resolution and prevention; conflicts which lead to war. **Special Collections:** Nuclear war, armament, disarmament, and arms races (films). **Holdings:** 1000 books. **Services:** Interlibrary loans; copying; library open to public for reference use only. **Automated Operations:** Computerized cataloging and acquisitions. **Computerized Information Services:** Online systems. **Networks/Consortia:** Member of WLN.

★15546★
UNIVERSITY OF IDAHO - BUREAU OF PUBLIC AFFAIRS RESEARCH - LIBRARY (Soc Sci)
                                         Phone: (208) 885-6563
Moscow, ID 83843   Sid Duncombe, Dir.
Founded: 1959. **Staff:** Prof 2; Other 1. **Subjects:** State and local politics and administration. **Holdings:** Current library of reference books, pamphlets, reports, periodicals, newsletters and other publications of governmental research bureaus and state and local agencies throughout the nation. **Services:** Research, training and consulting services for state and local

government agencies in Idaho.

★15547★
UNIVERSITY OF IDAHO - HUMANITIES LIBRARY (Hum)
Phone: (208) 885-6584
Moscow, ID 83843   Margaret Snyder, Libn.
Staff: Prof 1; Other 2. **Subjects:** Literature, music, language, art, philosophy, architecture. **Holdings:** 110,808 books; 29,326 bound periodical volumes; 118,315 volumes in microform. **Subscriptions:** 1781 journals and other serials; 110 newspapers. **Services:** Interlibrary loans; copying; library open to public. **Networks/Consortia:** Member of WLN.

★15548★
UNIVERSITY OF IDAHO - IDAHO WATER RESOURCES RESEARCH INSTITUTE - TECHNICAL INFO. CENTER & READING ROOM (Env-Cons)
Phone: (208) 885-6429
Moscow, ID 83843   John R. Busch
Staff: Prof 1; Other 2. **Subjects:** Water resources, resource economics, outdoor recreation, groundwater, irrigation, wild and scenic rivers, water seepage, agriculture, water law, precipitation distribution, small hydroelectric developments. **Holdings:** 7000 books and bound periodical volumes. **Services:** Center open to public. **Publications:** Newsletter and information bulletins; Scenic Rivers series; Completion Report series.

★15549★
UNIVERSITY OF IDAHO - LAW LIBRARY (Law)
College of Law   Phone: (208) 885-6521
Moscow, ID 83843   James Heller, Libn.
Founded: 1911. **Staff:** Prof 3; Other 4. **Subjects:** Law. **Holdings:** 95,675 volumes. **Subscriptions:** 1611 journals and other serials. **Services:** Interlibrary loans; copying. **Networks/Consortia:** Member of WLN.

★15550★
UNIVERSITY OF IDAHO - SCIENCE AND TECHNOLOGY LIBRARY (Sci-Tech)
Phone: (208) 885-6235
Moscow, ID 83843   Donna Hanson, Libn.
Staff: Prof 2; Other 1. **Subjects:** Forestry, agriculture, mining and geology, entomology, engineering, physical sciences, biological sciences. **Holdings:** 117,432 books; 97,499 bound periodical volumes; 4050 microforms. **Subscriptions:** 6198 journals and other serials. **Services:** Interlibrary loans; copying; library open to public. **Networks/Consortia:** Member of WLN.

★15551★
UNIVERSITY OF IDAHO - SOCIAL SCIENCE LIBRARY (Soc Sci)
Phone: (208) 885-6344
Moscow, ID 83843   Dennis Baird, Libn.
Staff: Prof 3; Other 2. **Subjects:** History, education, political science, sociology, business and economics. **Holdings:** 144,478 books; 35,116 bound periodical volumes; 407,747 government publications; 60,948 volumes in microform (including ERIC reports on microfiche); 126,173 sheet maps. **Subscriptions:** 3082 journals and other serials. **Services:** Interlibrary loans; copying; library open to public. **Networks/Consortia:** Member of WLN.

★15552★
UNIVERSITY OF IDAHO - SPECIAL COLLECTIONS LIBRARY (Hum)
Phone: (208) 885-7951
Moscow, ID 83843   Stanley A. Shepard, Libn.
Staff: Prof 1; Other 2. **Subjects:** Pacific Northwest, Idaho publications, University of Idaho archives, Sir Walter Scott, Basques, Ezra Pound. **Holdings:** 33,166 volumes; 54,486 prints and photographs. **Subscriptions:** 656 journals and other serials. **Services:** Interlibrary loans; copying; library open to public for reference use only. **Networks/Consortia:** Member of WLN.

★15553★
UNIVERSITY OF ILLINOIS - AGRICULTURE LIBRARY (Agri)
226 Mumford Hall
1301 W. Gregory   Phone: (217) 333-2416
Urbana, IL 61801   Nancy Davis, Asst.Libn.
Founded: 1915. **Staff:** Prof 2; Other 3. **Subjects:** Agricultural economics, animal science, agricultural engineering, horticulture, food science and technology, agricultural history, forestry. **Holdings:** 69,000 books and bound periodical volumes; 600 microforms. **Subscriptions:** 2850 journals and other serials. **Services:** Interlibrary loans; copying; library open to public. **Automated Operations:** Computerized cataloging, acquisitions, serials and circulation. **Computerized Information Services:** BRS, DIALOG. **Publications:** Selected New Acquisitions List, bimonthly.

★15554★
UNIVERSITY OF ILLINOIS - APPLIED LIFE STUDIES LIBRARY (Educ)
Main Library, Rm. 146
1408 W. Gregory Dr.   Phone: (217) 333-3615
Urbana, IL 61801   Patricia McCandless, Libn.
Founded: 1949. **Staff:** Prof 1; Other 2. **Subjects:** Leisure studies; education - physical, health, safety, driver; sport science (including biomechanics, medicine, psychology, sociology, history); dance. **Special Collections:** Avery Brundage Collection (1600 volumes). **Holdings:** 19,500 books and bound periodical volumes; 1100 theses; 6 VF drawers of pamphlets; 10,536 microcards; 4300 microfiche. **Subscriptions:** 525 journals and other serials. **Services:** Interlibrary loans; copying. **Automated Operations:** Computerized circulation. **Publications:** Acquisition list, bimonthly - distributed to faculty, students and others on request.

★15555★
UNIVERSITY OF ILLINOIS - ASIAN LIBRARY (Area-Ethnic)
325 Main Library
1408 W. Gregory Dr.   Phone: (217) 333-1501
Urbana, IL 61801   William S. Wong, Asst.Dir.
Founded: 1965. **Staff:** Prof 5; Other 6. **Subjects:** East Asia, South Asia and the Middle East - history, literature, linguistics, economics, sociology. **Holdings:** 200,000 books. **Subscriptions:** 700 journals and other serials. **Services:** Interlibrary loans; copying; library open to public. **Remarks:** The University of Illinois Rare Book Room contains a collection of Japanese rare books. **Staff:** Robert G. Sewell, Japanese Bibliog.; Yasuko Makino, East Asian Cat.; Narindar Aggarwal, Asst. Asian Libn.; Karen Wei, Chinese Cat.

★15556★
UNIVERSITY OF ILLINOIS - ASIAN LIBRARY - SOUTH AND WEST ASIAN DIVISION (Area-Ethnic)
329 Main Library
1408 W. Gregory Dr.   Phone: (217) 333-2492
Urbana, IL 61801   Narindar K. Aggarwal, Asst. Asian Libn.
Founded: 1964. **Staff:** Prof 1; Other 2. **Subjects:** South and West Asia - languages, literature, history, culture. **Holdings:** 71,000 books; 150 bound periodical volumes. **Services:** Interlibrary loans; library open to public.

★15557★
UNIVERSITY OF ILLINOIS - BIOLOGY LIBRARY (Sci-Tech)
101 Burrill Hall
407 S. Goodwin   Phone: (217) 333-3654
Urbana, IL 61801   Elisabeth B. Davis, Libn.
Founded: 1884. **Staff:** Prof 2; Other 12. **Subjects:** Biology, botany, entomology, biophysics, genetics, ecology, microbiology, physiology, zoology. **Special Collections:** Oberholser reprint collection on ornithology. **Holdings:** 110,978 volumes. **Subscriptions:** 2058 journals and other serials. **Services:** Interlibrary loans; copying; SDI; library open to public by permit. **Automated Operations:** Computerized cataloging, acquisitions and circulation. **Computerized Information Services:** DIALOG, BRS. **Publications:** List of New Acquisitions, monthly; Guides to the Literature Held in the Biology Library. **Staff:** Mitsuko Williams, Asst.Libn.

★15558★
UNIVERSITY OF ILLINOIS - CHEMISTRY LIBRARY (Sci-Tech)
257 Noyes Laboratory
505 S. Matthews   Phone: (217) 333-3737
Urbana, IL 61801   Dr. Lucille Wert, Chem.Libn.
Founded: 1892. **Staff:** Prof 2; Other 3. **Subjects:** Chemistry - analytical, inorganic, organic, physical; biochemistry; chemical engineering. **Holdings:** 70,000 books and bound periodical volumes; 925 films and microfiche. **Subscriptions:** 1147 journals and other serials. **Services:** Interlibrary loans; copying; library open to public. **Automated Operations:** Computerized circulation. **Computerized Information Services:** DIALOG, BRS, NIH-EPA Chemical Information System. **Publications:** List of Acquisitions, monthly; Chemistry Library Communications.

★15559★
UNIVERSITY OF ILLINOIS - CITY PLANNING AND LANDSCAPE ARCHITECTURE LIBRARY (Plan)
203 Mumford Hall
1301 W. Gregory Dr.   Phone: (217) 333-0424
Urbana, IL 61801   Mary D. Ravenhall, Libn.
Founded: 1912. **Staff:** Prof 1; Other 1. **Subjects:** City and regional planning, landscape architecture, urban studies. **Holdings:** 19,383 books and bound periodical volumes; 10,000 pamphlets. **Subscriptions:** 587 journals and other serials. **Services:** Interlibrary loans; copying; library open to public by permit from Main Library. **Publications:** Acquisitions List, irregular - mailing list.

★15560★

UNIVERSITY OF ILLINOIS - CLASSICS LIBRARY (Hum)
419A Main Library
1408 W. Gregory Dr.   Phone: (217) 333-1124
Urbana, IL 61801   Suzanne Griffiths, Libn.
Subjects: Classical languages and literatures, Roman and Greek history and civilizations, classical archeology. **Special Collections:** Dittenberger-Vahlen Collection. **Holdings:** 41,988 books and bound periodical volumes. **Subscriptions:** 362 journals and other serials. **Services:** Library open to public for reference use only.

★15561★

UNIVERSITY OF ILLINOIS - COLLEGE OF ENGINEERING - ENGINEERING DOCUMENTS CENTER (Sci-Tech)
208 Engineering Hall
1308 W. Green St.   Phone: (217) 333-1510
Urbana, IL 61801   Mu-chin Cheng, Doc.Libn.
Staff: Prof 1. **Subjects:** Engineering. **Holdings:** 8000 technical reports. **Services:** Interlibrary loans; copying; center not open to public. **Automated Operations:** Computerized cataloging. **Special Indexes:** Engineering Documents Center Index, annual.

★15562★

UNIVERSITY OF ILLINOIS - COLLEGE OF MEDICINE AT ROCKFORD - LIBRARY OF THE HEALTH SCIENCES (Med)
1601 Parkview Ave.   Phone: (815) 987-7377
Rockford, IL 61107   Stuart J. Kolner, Br.Libn.
Founded: 1941. **Staff:** Prof 2; Other 13. **Subjects:** Medicine, nursing, biomedical sciences, consumer health. **Holdings:** 23,500 books; 19,100 bound periodical volumes; 1500 pamphlets; 7283 slides; 512 reels of microfilm; 1900 magnetic tapes. **Subscriptions:** 620 journals and other serials. **Services:** Interlibrary loans; copying; SDI; library open to public. **Automated Operations:** Computerized cataloging, serials and circulation. **Computerized Information Services:** NLM, BRS, DIALOG; Library Computer System (LCS; internal database). Performs searches on cost recovery basis. **Networks/Consortia:** Member of Greater Midwest Regional Medical Library Network (Region 3); Northern Illinois Library System. **Publications:** Library Guide, annual; Offshoots (newsletter) - both free upon request. **Also Known As:** Woodruff L. Crawford Branch Library of the Health Sciences.

★15563★

UNIVERSITY OF ILLINOIS - COMMERCE LIBRARY (Bus-Fin)
Rm. 101, Main Library
1408 W. Gregory Dr.   Phone: (217) 333-3619
Urbana, IL 61801   M. Balachandran, Libn.
Staff: Prof 3; Other 4. **Subjects:** Economics, business administration, accounting, finance. **Holdings:** 46,855 books and bound periodical volumes; 90,360 company annual reports and 10K reports on microfiche. **Subscriptions:** 2205 journals and other serials. **Services:** Interlibrary loans; library open to public by permit. **Automated Operations:** Computerized circulation. **Publications:** Acquisitions List, 10/year - for internal distribution only. **Staff:** T. Parks .

★15564★

UNIVERSITY OF ILLINOIS - COMMUNICATIONS LIBRARY (Info Sci)
122 Gregory Hall   Phone: (217) 333-2216
Urbana, IL 61801   Nancy Allen, Libn.
Founded: 1933. **Staff:** Prof 1; Other 2. **Subjects:** Advertising, broadcasting, magazines, newspapers, public relations, communication theory, mass communications, photography, publishing, typography, motion pictures. **Holdings:** 16,000 books and bound periodical volumes. **Subscriptions:** 774 journals and other serials; 30 newspapers. **Services:** Interlibrary loans; library open to public with permit from Main Library. **Automated Operations:** Computerized circulation. **Publications:** Acquisition List (annotated), quarterly.

★15565★

UNIVERSITY OF ILLINOIS - COMMUNITY RESEARCH CENTER - INFORMATION RESOURCE CENTER (Soc Sci; Law)
505 E. Green St., Suite 210   Phone: (217) 333-0443
Champaign, IL 61820   James W. Brown, Dir.
Staff: Prof 2; Other 1. **Subjects:** Jail removal, deinstitutionalization, alternative services and programs, detention, corrections, architecture. **Special Collections:** National Institute of Juvenile Justice and Delinquency Prevention - Assessment Center Reports (15); Institute of Judicial Administration/American Bar Association, Juvenile Justice Standards (21 volumes). **Holdings:** 2400 books; 3000 technical assistance files; slides; architectural drawings; data tapes; vertical files. **Subscriptions:** 35 journals and other serials. **Services:** Copying; library open to public by appointment. **Automated Operations:** Computerized cataloging. **Computerized**

Information Services: Internal database. Performs searches on cost recovery basis. **Formerly:** National Clearinghouse for Criminal Justice Planning and Architecture. **Staff:** Brandt W. Pryor, Res.Assoc.

★15566★

UNIVERSITY OF ILLINOIS - COORDINATED SCIENCE LABORATORY LIBRARY (Sci-Tech)
1101 W. Springfield, Rm. 269 A   Phone: (217) 333-4368
Urbana, IL 61801
Founded: 1951. **Staff:** Prof 1. **Subjects:** Electrical engineering, computers and control, physics, systems theory. **Holdings:** 2000 books; 2100 bound periodical volumes; 500 technical reports. **Subscriptions:** 132 journals and other serials. **Services:** SDI; library open to public for reference use only.

★15567★

UNIVERSITY OF ILLINOIS - DEPARTMENT OF COMPUTER SCIENCE LIBRARY (Comp Sci)
260 Digital Computer Laboratory   Phone: (217) 333-6777
Urbana, IL 61801   Prof. S. Muroga, Chm., Lib.Comm.
Founded: 1961. **Staff:** Prof 1; Other 2. **Subjects:** Computer science, electrical engineering, applied mathematics. **Holdings:** 10,300 books; 2700 bound periodical volumes; 6600 technical reports; 2040 departmental reports. **Subscriptions:** 100 journals and other serials. **Services:** Library not open to public.

★15568★

UNIVERSITY OF ILLINOIS - DOCUMENTS LIBRARY (Info Sci)
200d Main Library   Phone: (217) 333-1056
Urbana, IL 61801   Paula Watson, Hd.
Founded: 1980. **Staff:** Prof 4; Other 3. **Subjects:** U.S. government and Illinois state publications. **Holdings:** 10,000 volumes; 100,000 microforms. **Services:** Interlibrary loans; copying; library open to public for reference use only. **Automated Operations:** Computerized cataloging and circulation. **Computerized Information Services:** BRS, OCLC, DIALOG. **Networks/Consortia:** Member of ILLINET. **Staff:** John Littlewood, Doc.Libn.; Susan Bekiares, Doc.Libn.

★15569★

UNIVERSITY OF ILLINOIS - EDUCATION AND SOCIAL SCIENCE LIBRARY (Educ; Soc Sci)
100 Main Library
1408 W. Gregory Dr.   Phone: (217) 333-2305
Urbana, IL 61801   Barton M. Clark, Libn.
Staff: Prof 6; Other 13. **Subjects:** Education, anthropology, psychology, political science, social work, sociology, speech and hearing science. **Special Collections:** C.W. Odell Test Collection (7000 educational and psychological tests); children's literature collection; Human Relations Area Files; U.N. official records; parapsychology and the occult; curriculum collection. **Holdings:** 110,000 books and bound periodical volumes; ERIC microfiche. **Subscriptions:** 1900 journals and other serials. **Services:** Interlibrary loans; copying; library open to public on a limited basis. **Automated Operations:** Computerized circulation. **Computerized Information Services:** DIALOG, BRS. **Publications:** Bibliographies, occasional.

★15570★

UNIVERSITY OF ILLINOIS - ENGINEERING LIBRARY (Sci-Tech)
221 Engineering Hall
1308 W. Green St.   Phone: (217) 333-3576
Urbana, IL 61801   William Mischo, Engr.Libn.
Staff: Prof 2; Other 5. **Subjects:** Engineering - civil, electrical, mechanical, aeronautical, nuclear, ceramics, agricultural, materials, metallurgy; bioengineering; theoretical and applied mechanics. **Special Collections:** U.S. National Advisory Committee for Aeronautics (NACA) Depository Sets, 1915-1958; U.S. NASA Depository Sets, 1978 to present. **Holdings:** 175,000 books and bound periodical volumes. **Subscriptions:** 3500 journals and other serials. **Services:** Interlibrary loans; copying; library open to public by permit from Main Library. **Automated Operations:** Computerized circulation.

★15571★

UNIVERSITY OF ILLINOIS - ENGLISH LIBRARY (Hum)
321 Library
1408 W. Gregory Dr.   Phone: (217) 333-2220
Urbana, IL 61801   Melissa Cain, Libn.
Founded: 1908. **Staff:** Prof 1. **Subjects:** English literature - early, medieval, Renaissance, 17th-20th centuries; American literature; philology; theater; folk tales. **Holdings:** 24,676 books and bound periodical volumes. **Subscriptions:** 514 journals and other serials. **Services:** Interlibrary loans; copying.

UNIVERSITY OF ILLINOIS - ERIC CLEARINGHOUSE ON ELEMENTARY AND EARLY CHILDHOOD EDUCATION
See: ERIC Clearinghouse on Elementary and Early Childhood Education

★15572★
UNIVERSITY OF ILLINOIS - GEOLOGY LIBRARY (Sci-Tech)
223 Natural History Bldg.
1301 W. Green St.　　　　　　　　　Phone: (217) 333-1266
Urbana, IL 61801　　　　　　　　　Dederick C. Ward, Libn.
Founded: 1959. **Staff:** Prof 1; Other 3. **Subjects:** Geology, mineralogy, paleontology, geomorphology, geophysics, geochemistry, oceanography, stratigraphy, petrology. **Special Collections:** History of Geology (early rare items in geology); biographies of geologists; popular works in geological science (works for the layperson). **Holdings:** 77,400 books and bound periodical volumes; 54,000 geological maps; 1650 microforms. **Subscriptions:** 2432 journals and other serials. **Services:** Interlibrary loans; copying; library open to public by permit from Main Library. **Automated Operations:** Computerized circulation. **Publications:** Acquisition list, monthly - to mailing list.

★15573★
UNIVERSITY OF ILLINOIS - HIGHWAY TRAFFIC SAFETY CENTER - LIBRARY (Trans)*
404 Engineering Hall　　　　　　　Phone: (217) 333-1270
Urbana, IL 61801　　　　Dr. John Baerwald, Dir., Coll. of Engr.
Staff: 1. **Subjects:** Traffic engineering, accident reports and statistics, mass transit, safety education. **Special Collections:** Uppsala Psychological Reports (250); National Road and Traffic Research Institute Reports, Sweden (200). **Holdings:** 5000 books; 6000 unbound periodical volumes; 6 boxes of pamphlets; 5 VF drawers of newsletters; 6 notebooks of clippings; 30 cases of slides. **Subscriptions:** 95 journals and other serials. **Services:** Copying; library open to public with restrictions. **Publications:** Research Reports, irregular. **Staff:** Lynn A. Miller, Libn.

★15574★
UNIVERSITY OF ILLINOIS - HISTORY AND PHILOSOPHY LIBRARY (Hist)
424 Main Library
1408 W. Gregory Dr.　　　　　　　Phone: (217) 333-1091
Urbana, IL 61801　　　　　　　　　Martha Friedman, Libn.
Founded: 1918. **Staff:** Prof 1; Other 2. **Subjects:** Medieval and modern philosophy; political theory; history - American, European, Far Eastern, Latin American. **Special Collections:** Horner Lincoln Collection including the R.T. Lincoln Collection of Lincoln papers, the Lincoln presidential papers and the Herndon-Weik manuscript collection (all on microfilm). **Holdings:** 21,311 books and bound periodical volumes. **Subscriptions:** 585 journals and other serials. **Services:** Interlibrary loans (through Main Library). **Automated Operations:** Computerized circulation.

★15575★
UNIVERSITY OF ILLINOIS - HOME ECONOMICS LIBRARY (Soc Sci)
905 S. Goodwin Ave.　　　　　　　Phone: (217) 333-0748
Urbana, IL 61801　　　　　　　　　Barbara C. Swain, Libn.
Founded: 1957. **Staff:** Prof 1; Other 1. **Subjects:** Foods and nutrition, textiles and clothing, interior decoration and home furnishings, institution management, child development, family relationships, family and consumer economics, home economics education, food science. **Holdings:** 17,710 books and bound periodical volumes; 2608 slides. **Subscriptions:** 256 journals and other serials. **Services:** Interlibrary loans; library open to public by permit from Main Library. **Publications:** Selected List of New Books, quarterly.

★15576★
UNIVERSITY OF ILLINOIS - HOUSING RESEARCH & DEVELOPMENT PROGRAM - LIBRARY (Soc Sci)
1204 W. Nevada　　　　　　　　　Phone: (217) 333-7330
Urbana, IL 61801　　　　　Trudy Patton, Libn./Res.Assoc.
Staff: Prof 1. **Subjects:** Housing design, community development, housing for the elderly, low-income housing, environmental psychology, government programs. **Holdings:** 2000 books; 20 bound periodical volumes; 4 VF drawers of clippings, reports, pamphlets, brochures and maps. **Subscriptions:** 37 journals and other serials. **Services:** Library open to public.

★15577★
UNIVERSITY OF ILLINOIS - ILLINOIS HISTORICAL SURVEY LIBRARY (Hist)
1A Main Library
1408 W. Gregory Dr.　　　　　　　Phone: (217) 333-1777
Urbana, IL 61801　　　　　　　　　John Hoffman, Libn.
Founded: 1910. **Staff:** Prof 2; Other 1. **Subjects:** Regional history - Mississippi Valley and subsidiary areas. **Special Collections:** Religious Society

of Friends; communitarianism; Illinois labor; German immigration. **Holdings:** 9580 books and bound periodical volumes; 1600 maps; 551 linear feet of archives and manuscripts; 693 reels of microfilm of manuscripts; 3145 VF items. **Subscriptions:** 54 journals and other serials. **Services:** Interlibrary loans; copying; library open to public for reference and research only. **Publications:** Manuscripts guide to collections at the University of Illinois at Urbana-Champaign; Guide to the Heinrich A. Ratterman Collection of German-American Manuscripts; Guide to the Papers in the John Hunter Walker Collection, 1911-1953.

★15578★
UNIVERSITY OF ILLINOIS - ILLINOIS STATE NATURAL HISTORY SURVEY - LIBRARY (Sci-Tech)
196 Natural Resources Bldg.
607 E. Peabody　　　　　　　　　Phone: (217) 333-6892
Champaign, IL 61820　　　　　　　Carla G Heister, Libn.
Founded: 1858. **Staff:** Prof 1; Other 1. **Subjects:** Economic entomology, faunistic survey and insect identification, aquatic biology, applied botany and plant pathology, wildlife research, environmental quality. **Holdings:** 36,000 books and bound periodical volumes. **Subscriptions:** 651 journals and other serials. **Services:** Interlibrary loans; copying; library open to public for reference use only. **Automated Operations:** Computerized cataloging, acquisitions and circulation. **Computerized Information Services:** BRS, DIALOG, OCLC. Performs searches on cost recovery basis. **Networks/Consortia:** Member of ILLINET.

★15579★
UNIVERSITY OF ILLINOIS - INSTITUTE OF LABOR AND INDUSTRIAL RELATIONS LIBRARY (Soc Sci)
504 E. Armory　　　　　　　　　　Phone: (217) 333-2380
Champaign, IL 61820　　　　　　　Margaret A. Chaplan, Libn.
Founded: 1947. **Staff:** Prof 1; Other 2. **Subjects:** Labor and industrial relations. **Holdings:** 9720 books and bound periodical volumes; 30,000 VF items; 809 reels of microfilm; 1500 microfiche; 53 audio cassettes. **Subscriptions:** 421 journals and other serials. **Services:** Interlibrary loans; copying; library open to public. **Automated Operations:** Computerized circulation. **Computerized Information Services:** DIALOG, BRS, SDC. Performs searches on cost recovery basis.

★15580★
UNIVERSITY OF ILLINOIS - LAW LIBRARY (Law)
104 Law Bldg.
504 E. Pennsylvania Ave.　　　　　Phone: (217) 333-2914
Champaign, IL 61820　　　　　　　Richard Surles, Dir.
Founded: 1897. **Staff:** Prof 8; Other 10. **Subjects:** Law and related social sciences. **Special Collections:** Depository for U.S. documents, Illinois State documents and European Economic Community documents; Archives of the American Association of Law Libraries. **Holdings:** 400,000 volumes; 33,586 microcards; 1139 reels of microfilm; 150,294 microfiche; 2957 pamphlets. **Subscriptions:** 6766 journals and other serials. **Services:** Interlibrary loans; copying; library open to public. **Computerized Information Services:** LEXIS, Westlaw; LCS (internal database). **Special Catalogs:** Research Aids. **Staff:** Fred Mansfield, Bibliog.; Timothy Kearley, Foreign Law Libn.; Cheryl Nyberg, Docs./Ref.Libn.; Kathryn Webster, Tech.Serv.Libn.; Carol Boast, Hd., Ref.; Maria Porta, Circ./Ref.Libn.

★15581★
UNIVERSITY OF ILLINOIS - LIBRARY AND INFORMATION SCIENCE LIBRARY (Info Sci)
306 Main Library
1408 W. Gregory Dr.　　　　　　　Phone: (217) 333-3804
Urbana, IL 61801　　　　　　　　　Patricia Stenstrom, Libn.
Founded: 1906. **Staff:** Prof 1; Other 2. **Subjects:** Library and information science. **Holdings:** 13,259 volumes; 1293 microfiche. **Subscriptions:** 1181 journals and other serials. **Services:** Interlibrary loans; copying; library open to public by permit from Main Library. **Automated Operations:** Computerized circulation.

★15582★
UNIVERSITY OF ILLINOIS - MAP AND GEOGRAPHY LIBRARY (Geog-Map)
418 Main Library
1408 W. Gregory Dr.　　　　　　　Phone: (217) 333-0827
Urbana, IL 61801　　　　　　　　　David A. Cobb, Libn.
Founded: 1944. **Staff:** Prof 1; Other 1. **Subjects:** Maps, geography, Illinois aerial photography, atlases, gazetteers. **Special Collections:** Sanborn fire insurance maps for Illinois cities; Cavagna Library of 16th-19th century maps of Italy; 19th century U.S. coastal charts. **Holdings:** 15,000 books and bound periodical volumes; 135,000 aerial photographs; 330,000 maps; 475 reels of microfilm. **Subscriptions:** 700 journals and other serials. **Services:**

Interlibrary loans; copying; library open to public. **Automated Operations:** Computerized cataloging. **Computerized Information Services:** OCLC. **Networks/Consortia:** Member of ILLINET. **Publications:** Biblio, bimonthly; Acquisition Policy Statement. **Special Catalogs:** Catalog of Aerial Photographs in the Map and Geography Library; Sanborn Maps; State Atlases in the University of Illinois Library; List of Illinois County Atlases.

★15583★

UNIVERSITY OF ILLINOIS - MATHEMATICS LIBRARY (Sci-Tech; Comp Sci)
216 Altgeld Hall
1409 W. Green St.   Phone: (217) 333-0258
Urbana, IL 61801   Nancy D. Anderson, Libn.
Staff: Prof 2; Other 2. **Subjects:** Pure and applied mathematics, mathematical physics, statistics, computer sciences. **Holdings:** 57,000 books and bound periodical volumes; 400 microforms. **Subscriptions:** 850 journals and other serials. **Services:** Interlibrary loans; copying; library open to public with permit from Main Library. **Automated Operations:** Computerized circulation. **Publications:** List of Acquisitions, monthly - to mailing list.

★15584★

UNIVERSITY OF ILLINOIS - MODERN LANGUAGES AND LINGUISTICS LIBRARY (Hum)
425 Main Library
1408 W. Gregory Dr.   Phone: (217) 333-0076
Urbana, IL 61801   Sara de Mundo Lo, Libn.
Founded: 1911. **Staff:** Prof 2; Other 2. **Subjects:** Romance and Germanic language and literature, linguistics. **Special Collections:** Linguistic atlases; International Cinema Collection; Proust Collection; Chicano Collection. **Holdings:** 17,000 books; 800 bound periodical volumes. **Subscriptions:** 400 journals and other serials; 40 newspapers. **Services:** Interlibrary loans; copying; library open to public. **Automated Operations:** Computerized circulation. **Publications:** The Stentor, irregular - distributed to faculty; user's guide - free upon request.

★15585★

UNIVERSITY OF ILLINOIS - MUSIC LIBRARY (Mus)
Music Bldg.   Phone: (217) 333-1173
Urbana, IL 61801   William M. McClellan, Music Libn.
Founded: 1943. **Staff:** Prof 3; Other 5. **Subjects:** Music - performance and research. **Special Collections:** Pre-1800 music manuscripts and editions on microfilm (emphasis on medieval and Renaissance vocal music, lute and keyboard music sources; 2000 titles); American popular sheet music issued 1830-1970 (vocal; 100,000 titles); Rafael Joseffy Collection of 19th-century piano music (2000 titles); Joseph Szigeti Collection of violin music, 19th-20th century (manuscripts and editions; 700 titles); choral reference collection (single copies of octavos; 40,000 titles); recorded concerts and programs, School of Music, 1950 to present (2500 reels of tape). **Holdings:** 28,000 books and bound periodical volumes; 120,000 scores and parts; 9000 reels of microfilm; 2422 microcards; 169 microfiche; 45,000 phonograph records; cassettes; 4 VF drawers of pamphlets. **Subscriptions:** 1175 journals and other serials. **Services:** Interlibrary loans; copying; library open to public. **Automated Operations:** Computerized circulation. **Staff:** Jean Geil, Assoc. Music Libn.

★15586★

UNIVERSITY OF ILLINOIS - NEWSPAPER LIBRARY (Info Sci)
Main Library, Rm. 1
1408 W. Gregory Dr.   Phone: (217) 333-1509
Urbana, IL 61801
Staff: 2. **Holdings:** 10,661 volumes; 66,000 reels of microfilm; 8810 microcards. **Subscriptions:** 50 journals and other serials; 629 newspapers. **Services:** Interlibrary loans; copying; library open to public. **Publications:** Holdings of Subject Classified Newspapers; general newspapers in microform - backfiles; Foreign Newspapers Currently Received; U.S. Newspapers Currently Received; Labor Newspapers Currently Received; Labor Newspapers on Microfilm and Other Special Listings, revised and reissued biennially.

★15587★

UNIVERSITY OF ILLINOIS - PHYSICS/ASTRONOMY LIBRARY (Sci-Tech)
204 Loomis Laboratory
1110 W. Green St.   Phone: (217) 333-2101
Urbana, IL 61801   Bernice Lord Hulsizer, Libn.
Founded: 1948. **Staff:** Prof 1; Other 2. **Subjects:** Physics - solid state, nuclear, theoretical, medical; astronomy and astrophysics; magnetism; optics. **Holdings:** 34,300 books and bound periodical volumes; 360,000 microforms of Atomic Energy Commission-DOE materials. **Subscriptions:** 815 journals and other serials. **Services:** Interlibrary loans; copying; library open to public with permit. **Automated Operations:** Computerized circulation. **Computerized Information Services:** BRS. **Publications:** Acquisitions list, irregular; dedicated issues of journals list. **Special Catalogs:** Conference file keyword index (card).

★15588★

UNIVERSITY OF ILLINOIS - RARE BOOK ROOM (Rare Book)
346 Main Library
1408 W. Gregory Dr.   Phone: (217) 333-3777
Urbana, IL 61801   N. Frederick Nash, Libn.
Staff: Prof 2; Other 1. **Subjects:** Sixteenth- and seventeenth-century editions of classical authors, Bibles, catechisms and sermons, grammars and dictionaries; English and American literature and history; Italian drama, history, and biography; history of science. **Special Collections:** Milton Collection (3000 volumes); Ingold Shakespeare Collection; Clayton Papers, 1579-1744 (3020 original letters and documents); Cobbett Collection; 17th-century newsletters; Proust correspondence; Meine Collection of American Humor; Harwell Collection of Confederate Imprints; Hollander Collection on Economics; Baskette Collection on Freedom of Expression; Nickell Collection of 18th-Century English Literature; Winston S. Churchill Collection; Carl Sandburg Collection; H.G. Wells Collection; emblem books of Germany and low countries, 16th and 17th centuries; Japanese rare books. **Holdings:** 141,535 books, manuscripts, pamphlets and early periodicals; 26,870 reels of microfilm. **Subscriptions:** 55 journals and other serials. **Services:** Interlibrary loans; copying (limited); room open to public. **Special Catalogs:** Book catalog (1972, 11 volumes; Supplement, 1978, 2 volumes). **Staff:** Mary Ceibert, Asst.Libn.

★15589★

UNIVERSITY OF ILLINOIS - RICKER LIBRARY OF ARCHITECTURE AND ART (Art)
208 Architecture Bldg.   Phone: (217) 333-0224
Urbana, IL 61801   Dee Wallace, Libn.
Founded: 1873. **Staff:** Prof 3; Other 3. **Subjects:** Architecture, fine arts, applied arts, art education, art history, history of photography, industrial design, graphic design. **Holdings:** 42,000 volumes. **Subscriptions:** 540 journals and other serials. **Services:** Interlibrary loans; library open to public. **Automated Operations:** Computerized circulation.

★15590★

UNIVERSITY OF ILLINOIS - SLAVIC AND EAST EUROPEAN LIBRARY (Aera-Ethnic)
225 Main Library   Phone: (217) 333-1349
Urbana, IL 61801   Marianna Choldin, Asst.Dir. of Gen.Serv.
Staff: Prof 9; Other 7. **Subjects:** Slavic languages, literature, history. **Holdings:** 463,000 books and bound periodical volumes; 2325 other cataloged items. **Subscriptions:** 2000 journals and other serials. **Services:** Interlibrary loans; copying; library open to public with permit from Main Library. **Automated Operations:** Computerized circulation. **Remarks:** Maintains Slavic Reference Service which handles bibliographic and reference questions in the humanities and social sciences. **Staff:** Robert H. Burger, Slavic Cat; Darinka Craft, Slavic Cat.; Petro Kolesnyk, Slavic Cat.; Harold M. Leich, Slavic Acq.; June E. Pachuta, Slavic Bibliog.Dmytro Shtohryn, Slavic Cat.Libn.; Mary Stuart, Slavic Bibliog.

★15591★

UNIVERSITY OF ILLINOIS - SURVEY RESEARCH LABORATORY - SRL DATA ARCHIVE
1005 W. Nevada St.
Urbana, IL 61801
Defunct

★15592★

UNIVERSITY OF ILLINOIS - SURVEY RESEARCH LABORATORY - SURVEY AND CENSUS DATA LIBRARY (Soc Sci)
1005 W. Nevada St.   Phone: (217) 333-7109
Urbana, IL 61801   Mary A. Spaeth, Survey Res.Info.Coord.
Founded: 1967. **Staff:** Prof 1. **Subjects:** Survey research, U.S. Census data, consumer behavior. **Holdings:** 1200 books; 2000 unbound periodicals; 65 VF drawers of government publications, reprints, newsletters, reports, pamphlets, catalogs. **Subscriptions:** 20 journals and other serials. **Services:** Library open to researchers for reference use only. **Computerized Information Services:** SRLLIST (internal database; keyword file to SRL studies).

★15593★

UNIVERSITY OF ILLINOIS - UNIVERSITY ARCHIVES (Hist)
University Library, Rm. 19
1408 W. Gregory Dr.   Phone: (217) 333-0798
Urbana, IL 61801   Maynard Brichford, Univ.Archv.
Founded: 1963. **Staff:** Prof 2; Other 1. **Subjects:** Higher education, graduate

education, teaching, research, public service, science and technology, humanities, extracurricular activities, business archives, agriculture, fraternities, library science, librarianship, athletics, physical education. **Holdings:** 5671 cubic feet of office records; 2426 cubic feet of faculty papers; 901 cubic feet of publications; 896 cubic feet of American Library Association (ALA) archives; scrapbooks; clippings; pamphlets; microfilm; photographs; sound recordings; 9.3 million historical manuscripts. **Services:** Copying; archives open to public. **Publications:** Annual Report; Manuscripts Guide to Collections at the University of Illinois at Urbana-Champaign; Guide to ALA Archives. **Special Catalogs:** Recorded series control (4192 cards); supplementary finding aids (lists, publications, narrative descriptions, file guides); PARADIGM online series and subject control and data processing listings. Series are arranged by source and record groups and subgroups are listed in the University Archives Classification Guide.

★15594★

UNIVERSITY OF ILLINOIS - VETERINARY MEDICINE LIBRARY (Med)
1257 Vet. Med. Basic Sciences Bldg.
2001 S. Lincoln Ave.   Phone: (217) 333-2193
Urbana, IL 61801   David Self, Libn.
Founded: 1952. **Staff:** Prof 2; Other 2. **Subjects:** Pathology, physiology, pharmacology, bacteriology, veterinary science, parasitology. **Holdings:** 20,884 volumes; 10 VF drawers of pamphlets. **Subscriptions:** 673 journals and other serials. **Services:** Interlibrary loans; copying; library open to public. **Automated Operations:** Computerized circulation. **Computerized Information Services:** DIALOG, BRS, NLM.

★15595★

UNIVERSITY OF ILLINOIS AT CHICAGO - ENERGY RESOURCES CENTER - DOCUMENTS CENTER (Energy)
412 S. Peoria St.
Box 4348   Phone: (312) 996-4490
Chicago, IL 60680   Donald R. Bless, Res.Libn.
Staff: Prof 1; Other 1. **Subjects:** Energy - resources, policy, conservation, technology; alternative energy technologies; electric utility statistics. **Special Collections:** Heat and mass transfer (225 monographs; 15 journal subscriptions). **Holdings:** 4000 books; 100 bound periodical volumes; 2 VF drawers of clippings; 2 VF drawers of pamphlets; 100 maps; 100 reports on microfiche. **Subscriptions:** 120 journals and other serials. **Services:** Interlibrary loans; copying; SDI; center open to public. **Computerized Information Services:** DIALOG, BRS. **Networks/Consortia:** Member of Midwest Universities Energy Consortium. **Publications:** Quarterly Selected Acquisitions List - free upon request.

★15596★

UNIVERSITY OF ILLINOIS AT CHICAGO - HEALTH SCIENCES CENTER - LIBRARY OF THE HEALTH SCIENCES (Med)
1750 W. Polk St.   Phone: (312) 996-8974
Chicago, IL 60612   Irwin H. Pizer, Univ.Libn.
Founded: 1890. **Staff:** Prof 32; Other 65. **Subjects:** Medicine, dentistry, nursing, pharmacy, public health, behavioral sciences, allied health professions. **Special Collections:** Kiefer Collection (urology; 2000 volumes); herbals and pharmacopoeias (500 volumes); Bailey Collection (neurology and psychiatry; 1000 volumes); medical center archives; archives of the Medical Library Association (65 VF drawers). **Holdings:** 165,622 books; 179,751 bound periodical volumes; 46,581 documents; 38,403 multimedia items; 552 cubic feet of archives. **Subscriptions:** 4585 journals and other serials. **Services:** Interlibrary loans; SDI; library open to public for reference use only. **Automated Operations:** Computerized cataloging, serials and circulation; online regional catalog of monographs and AV material. **Computerized Information Services:** MEDLINE, BRS, SDC, DIALOG, OCLC. **Networks/Consortia:** Member of ILLINET; Greater Midwest Regional Medical Library Network (Region 3). **Publications:** Serial Holdings List, Illinois Health and Science Libraries, annual - available for purchase; News Notes, monthly; Annual Report; Library Guides for Chicago, Peoria, Rockford, and Urbana branches, annual; Information Services Department guides to various special segments of the literature of the health sciences; Media Software Holdings catalog; Proceedings of the Dedication of the Library; Subject List of Current Serials; Bibliographiti, quarterly. **Special Catalogs:** Percival Bailey Catalog of Neurology and Psychiatry; Joseph Kiefer Catalog of Urology; Dental Literature Collection; Pharmacopoeias, Formularies, and Dispensatories; Warren Henry Cole - a bibliography; Catalog of pre-fire Chicago imprints (1844-1871). (All catalogs available for purchase.) **Remarks:** Library is the Region VII Medical Library of the National Library of Medicine. **Staff:** Barbara Millar, Assoc.Univ.Libn.Tech.Serv; John N. Theall, Assoc.Univ.Libn.Pub.Serv.; Robert Adelsperger, Hd., Spec.Coll./Archv.; Anna Treimanis, Hd.Cat.; Margaret Ovitsky, Hd., Info.Serv.; Michael Felice, Hd., Ser.; Lorraine Lazouskas, Hd., Circ.; James Parrish, Extramural Prog.; Kathryn Hammell, Hd., Acq.; Kimberly Goldman, ILL Libn.; Ruby S. May, Assoc.Dir.; Dana Van Loo, Prog.Coord.;

Patricia Pinkowski, Prog.Coord.

★15597★

UNIVERSITY OF ILLINOIS AT CHICAGO - HEALTH SCIENCES CENTER - LIBRARY OF THE HEALTH SCIENCES (Med)
Box 1649   Phone: (309) 671-3095
Peoria, IL 61656   Michele Johns, Br.Libn.
Founded: 1971. **Staff:** Prof 2; Other 6. **Subjects:** Medicine, basic sciences, nursing. **Holdings:** 19,365 books; 17,273 bound periodical volumes; 1964 AV programs; 3242 government documents. **Subscriptions:** 693 journals and other serials. **Services:** Interlibrary loans; SDI for faculty; library open to public with restrictions. **Automated Operations:** Computerized circulation. **Computerized Information Services:** NLM, BRS, DIALOG; Library Computer System (internal database). **Networks/Consortia:** Member of Greater Midwest Regional Medical Library Network (Region 3); Heart of Illinois Library Consortium (HILC); Illinois Valley Library System. **Publications:** Annual Report; Library Guide; Current List of Serials; Subject List of Current Serials. **Special Catalogs:** Subject Guide to Audiovisual Holdings (book). **Remarks:** Library is located at One Illini Dr., Peoria, IL 61605. **Staff:** Melanie Wilson, Ref.Libn.

★15598★

UNIVERSITY OF ILLINOIS AT CHICAGO - HEALTH SCIENCES CENTER - LIBRARY OF THE HEALTH SCIENCES (Med)
506 S. Mathews
102 Medical Sciences Bldg.   Phone: (217) 333-4893
Urbana, IL 61801   Phyllis C. Self, Health Sci.Libn.
Founded: 1971. **Staff:** Prof 2; Other 4. **Subjects:** Medicine, nursing, basic sciences, gerontology, rehabilitation. **Holdings:** 16,438 books; 5500 bound periodical volumes; 5000 pamphlets; 5000 AV items. **Subscriptions:** 616 journals and other serials. **Services:** Interlibrary loans; copying; library open to public. **Automated Operations:** Computerized circulation. **Computerized Information Services:** MEDLINE, BRS, DIALOG, OCLC. **Networks/Consortia:** Member of Greater Midwest Regional Medical Library Network (Region 3); ILLINET. **Staff:** Francesca Anstine, Asst.Libn.

★15599★

UNIVERSITY OF ILLINOIS AT CHICAGO - SCIENCE LIBRARY (Sci-Tech)
Science & Engineering South Bldg.
Box 7565   Phone: (312) 996-5396
Chicago, IL 60680   Cynthia A. Steinke, Sci.Libn.
Founded: 1970. **Staff:** Prof 3; Other 6. **Subjects:** Chemistry, biology, geology, astronomy, physics. **Special Collections:** Sadtler Research Laboratories Standard Collections of Spectra; industry standards and codes. **Holdings:** 44,000 books; 55,000 bound periodical volumes; 71,000 technical reports (paper and microform). **Subscriptions:** 1738 journals and other serials. **Services:** Interlibrary loans; copying; library open to public for reference use only. **Automated Operations:** Computerized cataloging. **Computerized Information Services:** OCLC, DIALOG, BRS; LCS (internal database). **Publications:** New Books in Science and Technology, monthly.

★15600★

UNIVERSITY OF ILLINOIS AT CHICAGO - UNIVERSITY LIBRARY - MAP SECTION (Geog-Map)
Box 8198   Phone: (312) 996-5277
Chicago, IL 60680   Marsha L. Selmer, Map Libn.
Staff: Prof 1; Other 1. **Subjects:** Maps, atlases. **Special Collections:** Historic Urban Plans (complete set); 16th-19th century maps of the Russian Empire and Eastern Europe; 19th century maps of Illinois; 17th-18th century maps of the Great Lakes; aerial photograph maps of Chicago and northeastern Illinois. **Holdings:** 121,631 maps; 589 atlases. **Services:** Interlibrary loans; library open to public.

★15601★

UNIVERSITY OF IOWA - ART LIBRARY (Art)
Art Bldg.   Phone: (319) 353-4440
Iowa City, IA 52242   Harlan Sifford, Libn.
Staff: Prof 1; Other 1. **Subjects:** Art. **Holdings:** 60,000 volumes. **Services:** Interlibrary loans; copying; library open to public for reference use only.

★15602★

UNIVERSITY OF IOWA - BOTANY-CHEMISTRY LIBRARY (Sci-Tech)
                                        Phone: (319) 353-3707
Iowa City, IA 52242   Sally Fry, Libn.
Staff: Prof 1; Other 1. **Subjects:** Botany, chemistry and related fields. **Holdings:** 66,000 volumes. **Services:** Interlibrary loans; copying; library open to public for reference use only.

★15603★

UNIVERSITY OF IOWA - BUSINESS LIBRARY (Bus-Fin)
College of Business Administration
Phillips Hall
Iowa City, IA 52242
Phone: (319) 353-5803
Patricia H. Foley, Bus.Lbn.
Founded: 1965. **Staff:** Prof 2; Other 1. **Subjects:** Management, labor relations, labor unions, accounting, finance. **Special Collections:** Major labor union periodicals. **Holdings:** 22,000 volumes. **Services:** Interlibrary loans; copying; library open to public for reference use only.

★15604★

UNIVERSITY OF IOWA - COLLEGE OF EDUCATION - CURRICULUM RESOURCES LABORATORY (Educ)
N140 Lindquist Center
Iowa City, IA 52242
Phone: (319) 353-4515
Paula O. Brandt, Coord.
Staff: Prof 2; Other 3. **Subjects:** Children's books; adolescent novels; special, elementary and secondary education curriculum materials. **Special Collections:** K-12 textbooks (17,000) and curriculum guides (5000). **Holdings:** 28,000 books; 3200 AV items, games, computer diskettes, picture sets and other nonprint items. **Services:** Copying; laboratory open to public. **Publications:** Newsletter, irregular. **Staff:** Carol Vogt, Ref.Lbn.

★15605★

UNIVERSITY OF IOWA - COLLEGE OF PHARMACY - IOWA DRUG INFORMATION SERVICE (Med)
Westlawn, Box 330
Iowa City, IA 52242
Phone: (319) 353-4639
Hazel H. Seaba, Dir.
Staff: Prof 9; Other 15. **Subjects:** Drugs and drug therapy. **Holdings:** 182,000 articles on microfilm; Drug and Disease Indexes, 1966 to present on microfilm. **Subscriptions:** 156 journals and other serials. **Services:** SDI; service open to subscribers. **Automated Operations:** Drug Literature Microfilm File (internal database). **Publications:** Procedure Manual, annual; Cross Reference Index, annual; Drug Literature Microfilm File, annual with monthly updates.

★15606★

UNIVERSITY OF IOWA - ENGINEERING LIBRARY (Sci-Tech)
106 Engineering Bldg.
Iowa City, IA 52242
Phone: (319) 353-5224
John W. Forys, Lbn.
Staff: Prof 1; Other 1. **Subjects:** Engineering, science, technology. **Holdings:** 61,000 volumes. **Services:** Interlibrary loans; copying; library open to public for reference use only.

★15607★

UNIVERSITY OF IOWA - GEOLOGY LIBRARY (Sci-Tech)
136 Trowbridge Hall
Iowa City, IA 52242
Phone: (319) 353-4225
Louise Zipp, Lbn.
Staff: Prof 1; Other 1. **Subjects:** Sedimentology, crystallography, mineralogy, structural geology, petrology, geochemistry, geophysics, engineering geology. **Holdings:** 35,000 volumes. **Services:** Interlibrary loans; library open to public for reference use only.

★15608★

UNIVERSITY OF IOWA - HEALTH SCIENCES LIBRARY (Med)
Health Sciences Library Bldg.
Iowa City, IA 52242
Phone: (319) 353-5382
David S. Curry, Lbn.
Founded: 1870. **Staff:** Prof 8; Other 7. **Subjects:** Medicine, speech pathology, dentistry, nursing, pharmacy. **Special Collections:** John Martin History of Medicine Collection. **Holdings:** 185,000 volumes. **Services:** Interlibrary loans; copying; library open to public for reference use only. **Automated Operations:** Computerized cataloging and serials. **Computerized Information Services:** MEDLINE. **Networks/Consortia:** Member of Greater Midwest Regional Medical Library Network (Region 3).

★15609★

UNIVERSITY OF IOWA - INSTITUTE OF URBAN AND REGIONAL RESEARCH - LIBRARY (Trans; Plan)
N222 Oakdale Campus
Iowa City, IA 52242
Phone: (319) 353-3862
John W. Fuller, Dir.
Founded: 1968. **Staff:** 1. **Subjects:** Transportation, planning, development, energy, environment, land use. **Holdings:** 4000 books; 1500 vertical file materials; 150 microfiche. **Subscriptions:** 95 journals and other serials. **Services:** Interlibrary loans; copying; library open to public with director's permission. **Publications:** List of publications - available upon request.

★15610★

UNIVERSITY OF IOWA - IOWA URBAN COMMUNITY RESEARCH CENTER - REFERENCE LIBRARY (Soc Sci)
W170 Seashore Hall
Iowa City, IA 52242
Phone: (319) 353-4119
Lyle W. Shannon, Dir.
Founded: 1958. **Subjects:** U.S. Census, vital statistics and public health, population and demography, minority groups, juvenile delinquency and crime. **Special Collections:** Selected series of U.S. Census since 1910. **Holdings:** 1000 books; 25 drawers of reprints, publications; punched cards and tapes on all studies conducted since 1958. **Subscriptions:** 30 journals and other serials. **Services:** Library open to public. **Publications:** Monograph series - available for purchase.

★15611★

UNIVERSITY OF IOWA - LABORATORY FOR POLITICAL RESEARCH (Soc Sci)
345A Schaeffer Hall
Iowa City, IA 52242
Phone: (319) 353-3103
Prof. Greg Caldeira, Dir.
Founded: 1968. **Staff:** Prof 3; Other 1. **Subjects:** Political science, sociology, history, geography, economics, law. **Special Collections:** Des Moines Register and Tribune public opinion polls; machine-readable bibliographies on legislative behavior and communist political systems. **Holdings:** 450 data sets. **Services:** Copying; library open to public. **Publications:** Laboratory for Political Research Report Series; Reprint Series; SSDA Codebooks. **Special Indexes:** Listing of archive holdings; index of survey items on legislative behavior; Annual Report. **Remarks:** Includes the Social Science Data Archive. **Staff:** John Kolp, Prog.Assoc.; C.H. Lu, Tech.Dir.; James R. Grifhorst, Data Archv.Mgr.

★15612★

UNIVERSITY OF IOWA - LAW LIBRARY (Law)
Law Center
Iowa City, IA 52242
Phone: (319) 353-5968
George A. Strait, Dir.
Founded: 1865. **Staff:** Prof 11; Other 12. **Subjects:** Anglo-American law. **Holdings:** 118,440 books; 251,685 bound periodical volumes; microform holdings of U.S. Supreme Court records and briefs. **Subscriptions:** 6221 journals and other serials; 10 newspapers. **Services:** Interlibrary loans; copying; library open to public. **Computerized Information Services:** LEXIS, Westlaw, RLIN. **Networks/Consortia:** Member of RLG. **Staff:** Katherine Belgum, Assoc. Law Libn.; Donna Hirst, Tech.Serv.; Virginia Melroy, Cat.; Thomas Eicher, Ref.; Mary Ertl, Acq.; Sandra Lockett, Docs.; Rene Chapman, Hd.Cat.; John Bengstrom; Karen Nobbs, Cat.

★15613★

UNIVERSITY OF IOWA - LIBRARY SCIENCE LIBRARY (Info Sci)
Main Library
Iowa City, IA 52242
Phone: (319) 353-3946
Sandra S. Ballasch, Libn.
Founded: 1967. **Staff:** Prof 1. **Subjects:** Library science. **Holdings:** 11,000 volumes. **Services:** Interlibrary loans; copying; library open to public for reference use only.

★15614★

UNIVERSITY OF IOWA - MATHEMATICS LIBRARY (Sci-Tech)
MacLean Hall
Iowa City, IA 52242
Phone: (319) 353-5939
Sally Fry, Libn.
Staff: Prof 1; Other 1. **Subjects:** Mathematics. **Holdings:** 34,000 volumes. **Services:** Interlibrary loans; copying; library open to public for reference use only.

★15615★

UNIVERSITY OF IOWA - MUSIC LIBRARY (Mus)
Music Bldg.
Iowa City, IA 52242
Phone: (319) 353-3797
Founded: 1957. **Staff:** Prof 1; Other 2. **Subjects:** Music. **Holdings:** 62,000 volumes. **Services:** Interlibrary loans; copying; library open to public. **Special Catalogs:** F.K. Gable: Annotated catalog of rare music items in the libraries of the University of Iowa.

★15616★

UNIVERSITY OF IOWA - OFFICE OF THE STATE ARCHAEOLOGIST - DOCUMENT COLLECTION (Sci-Tech)
317 Eastlawn
Iowa City, IA 52242
Phone: (319) 353-5175
Ruth Von Dracek, Docs.Cur.
Staff: Prof 1. **Subjects:** Archeology, anthropology, geomorphology, soil surveys, ethnology, physical anthropology. **Special Collections:** All published and unpublished archeological surveys and excavations performed in Iowa; office archives. **Holdings:** 1000 books; 10,000 other cataloged items. **Subscriptions:** 34 journals and other serials. **Services:** Copying; SDI; collection open to public for reference use only. **Computerized Information**

Services: DIALOG, SDC, BRS (through Iowa State Library); internal database. **Special Catalogs:** Bibliography on Mesquakie Indians. **Special Indexes:** Index to the Journal of the Iowa Archeological Society and Newsletter.

★15617★
UNIVERSITY OF IOWA - PHYSICS LIBRARY (Sci-Tech)
Physics Research Center   Phone: (319) 353-4762
Iowa City, IA 52242   Jack W. Dickey, Libn.
Staff: Prof 1; Other 1. **Subjects:** Physics. **Holdings:** 36,000 volumes.
Services: Interlibrary loans; copying; library open to public for reference use only.

★15618★
UNIVERSITY OF IOWA - PSYCHOLOGY LIBRARY (Soc Sci)
    Phone: (319) 353-5345
Iowa City, IA 52242   Dorothy M. Persson, Libn.
Staff: Prof 1; Other 2. **Subjects:** Psychology. **Holdings:** 41,000 volumes.
Services: Interlibrary loans; copying; library open to public for reference use only.

★15619★
UNIVERSITY OF IOWA - SPECIAL COLLECTIONS DEPARTMENT (Rare Book)
Main Library   Phone: (319) 353-4854
Iowa City, IA 52242   Frank Paluka, Hd.
Staff: Prof 4; Other 3. **Subjects:** Rare books, university archives. **Special Collections:** Brewer-Leigh Hunt Collection (2200 volumes; 3520 leaves of manuscript; 1635 manuscript letters); Iowa Authors Collection (6000 volumes; 3000 manuscripts); Bollinger-Lincoln Collection (4600 volumes; 480 pamphlets); History of Hydraulics Collection (550 volumes); general rare books collection (26,000 volumes); general manuscript collections (430 collections of personal or corporate records); map collection (190,000 maps and aerial photographs; 3300 atlases); university archives (4000 linear feet of papers; 4000 volumes); French medals, 1848 (842); original Ding Darling cartoons (6000); right-wing ephemeral publications (1000 titles). **Services:** Department open to public. **Publications:** Books at Iowa, semiannual - to members of the Friends of the University of Iowa Libraries. **Special Indexes:** The Wallace Papers: An Index to the Microfilm Editions of the Henry A. Wallace Papers (1975), 2 volumes; A Guide for the Study of the Recent History of the U.S. (1977). **Staff:** Robert A. McCown, Mss.Libn.; Earl M. Rogers, Cur. of Archv.; Richard Green, Map Libn.

★15620★
UNIVERSITY OF IOWA - ZOOLOGY LIBRARY (Sci-Tech)
301 Zoology Bldg.   Phone: (319) 353-5419
Iowa City, IA 52242   Jack W. Dickey, Libn.
Staff: Prof 1; Other 1. **Subjects:** Zoology. **Holdings:** 30,000 volumes.
Services: Interlibrary loans; copying; library open to public for reference use only.

★15621★
UNIVERSITY OF KANSAS - CENTER FOR PUBLIC AFFAIRS (Soc Sci)
607 Blake Hall   Phone: (913) 864-3701
Lawrence, KS 66045   Thelma Helyar, Libn.
Founded: 1965. **Staff:** Prof 1; Other 1. **Subjects:** Survey research, urban studies, census data, evaluation, data processing, Indians of North America, education, personnel management, environmental studies, housing, population, social science, statistics. **Holdings:** 9000 volumes. **Subscriptions:** 200 journals and other serials. **Services:** Interlibrary loans; copying; center open to public. **Publications:** Kansas Statistical Abstract and Kansas Voters Guide, annual - available by subscription; Center for Public Affairs Monograph Series.

★15622★
UNIVERSITY OF KANSAS - DEPARTMENT OF SPECIAL COLLECTIONS (Hum)
Spencer Research Library   Phone: (913) 864-4334
Lawrence, KS 66045   Alexandra Mason, Spencer Libn.
Founded: 1953. **Staff:** Prof 7; Other 3. **Subjects:** 17th- and 18th-century English history, economics, literature; history of ornithology; European Renaissance and early modern history, economics, politics; discovery and exploration; Latin America; history of botany; Anglo-Irish literature. **Special Collections:** Summerfield Collection of Renaissance and Early Modern Books (7400 volumes including 130 incunabula); Roger Clubb Memorial Collection of Books in Anglo-Saxon Types (300 books); Brodie of Brodie Collection of 17th- to 19th-century pamphlets (1200 items); Edmund Curll Collection (750 books); English Poetical Miscellanies, 18th century (475 books); Melvin French Revolutionary Collection (9000 items); Realey Collection of Walpoliana (500 items); Robert Horn Collection of Panegyrics on the Duke of Marlborough (200 items); 18th-century English Pamphlet Collection (15,000 items); James Joyce Collection (900 books); Rainer Maria Rilke Collection (1700 items);

W.B. Yeats Collection (650 items); New American Poetry Collection (6000 items); Ellis Ornithology Collection (15,000 volumes, pamphlets, letters, drawings and manuscripts); Linnaeus Collection (1750 volumes); Children's Literature, 18th to 20th century (6500 volumes); H.L. Mencken (780 volumes, scrapbooks, manuscripts); Science Fiction (7000 items); O'Hegarty Anglo-Irish Literature and History (12,000 volumes); manuscripts and documents in medieval, early modern and modern literature, history and science (480,000 items); Bond Collection of 18th-century English newspapers and periodicals; paleography and manuscript studies; Frank Lloyd Wright Collection (books; blueprints; clippings; photographs; manuscripts); Griffith Collection on Guatemala; W.D. Paden Collection of Tennyson; World Science Fiction Collection Depository; Howey Collection of Economics and Economic History to 1850 (3000 volumes). **Holdings:** 171,751 books and periodicals; 884 rare maps; 2092 photographs; 1032 linear feet of manuscripts. **Services:** Copying; department open to public for reference use only. **Automated Operations:** Computerized cataloging and serials. **Computerized Information Services:** OCLC. **Networks/Consortia:** Member of Bibliographical Center for Research, Rocky Mountain Region, Inc. (BCR). **Publications:** Exhibit catalogs, irregular - available on request; A Guide to the Collections, 1972. **Special Catalogs:** Catalog of manuscripts (loose-leaf). **Special Indexes:** Indexes of provenance, printers, 15th-17th century woodcuts and engravings (card); Boys-Mizener first-line index to English poetical miscellanies (card); chronological indexes to books and manuscripts. **Staff:** William L. Mitchell, Consrv.Libn.; Ann Hyde, Mss.Libn.; Sarah H. Hocker, Botany Libn.;L.E.J. Helyar, Cur. in Graphics; Joseph Springer, Asst.Libn.

★15623★
UNIVERSITY OF KANSAS - DOCUMENTS COLLECTION (Info Sci)
117 Spencer Research Library   Phone: (913) 864-4662
Lawrence, KS 66045   Marion L. Howey, Doc.Libn.
Founded: 1869. **Staff:** Prof 1; Other 3. **Subjects:** Census, statistics, official publications (domestic, foreign); United Nations. **Special Collections:** Regional depository of U.S. documents; depository of United Nations documents; British documents published by Her Majesty's Stationery Office; UNESCO, International Monetary Fund (IMF), Food and Agriculture Organization and Organization for Economic Cooperation and Development publications; Kansas State census on microfilm; U.S. Dept. of Commerce, Joint Publications Research Service (JPRS) publications on microfilm. **Holdings:** 701,239 documents; 353,610 microforms. **Subscriptions:** 1590 journals and other serials. **Services:** Interlibrary loans; copying; collection open to public. **Computerized Information Services:** OCLC. **Networks/Consortia:** Member of Bibliographical Center for Research, Rocky Mountain Region, Inc. (BCR); Kansas Library Network. **Publications:** Duplicate List of Regional Depository, monthly - to other depository libraries. **Special Catalogs:** SuDOC shelf list.

★15624★
UNIVERSITY OF KANSAS - EAST ASIAN LIBRARY (Area-Ethnic)
Watson Library   Phone: (913) 864-4669
Lawrence, KS 66045   Eugene Carvalho, Libn.
Founded: 1964. **Staff:** Prof 2; Other 2. **Subjects:** Chinese and Japanese history, literature, language, culture; contemporary China; contemporary Japan. **Holdings:** 90,770 books and bound periodical volumes. **Subscriptions:** 400 journals and other serials; 15 newspapers. **Services:** Interlibrary loans; copying; library open to public. **Automated Operations:** Computerized cataloging, serials and circulation. **Computerized Information Services:** OCLC. **Networks/Consortia:** Member of Bibliographical Center for Research, Rocky Mountain Region, Inc. (BCR); Kansas Library Network. **Remarks:** Materials primarily in Chinese, Japanese and Korean languages. **Staff:** Gary Bjorge, Assoc.Libn.

★15625★
UNIVERSITY OF KANSAS - ENGINEERING LIBRARY (Sci-Tech)
1012 Learned Hall   Phone: (913) 864-3866
Lawrence, KS 66045
Staff: Prof 1; Other 3. **Subjects:** Engineering. **Holdings:** 35,237 books and bound periodical volumes. **Subscriptions:** 800 journals and other serials. **Services:** Interlibrary loans; copying; library open to public. **Automated Operations:** Computerized cataloging and serials. **Computerized Information Services:** DIALOG, SDC, OCLC, BRS. **Networks/Consortia:** Member of Bibliographical Center for Research, Rocky Mountain Region, Inc. (BCR); Kansas Library Network.

★15626★
UNIVERSITY OF KANSAS - JOURNALISM LIBRARY (Info Sci)
William Allen White School of Journalism
210 Flint Hall   Phone: (913) 864-4755
Lawrence, KS 66045   Ethel Stewart, Libn.
Founded: 1955. **Staff:** Prof 1. **Subjects:** Newspaper journalism, mass communications, broadcasting, graphic arts, advertising. **Holdings:** Figures

not available. **Services:** Interlibrary loans; copying; library open to public. **Computerized Information Services:** OCLC. **Networks/Consortia:** Member of Bibliographical Center for Research, Rocky Mountain Region, Inc. (BCR); Kansas Library Network.

★15627★
UNIVERSITY OF KANSAS - KANSAS COLLECTION (Hist)
220 Spencer Research Library   Phone: (913) 864-4274
Lawrence, KS 66045   Sheryl K. Williams, Cur.
Founded: 1892. **Staff:** Prof 2; Other 3. **Subjects:** Kansas and Great Plains - social movements, business and economic history, social and cultural history, politics, travel. **Special Collections:** Overland diaries; depository of Kansas State Printer; J.J. Pennell Collection of photographs and negatives, 1886-1923 (32,000 items). **Holdings:** 93,262 volumes; 4616 linear feet of manuscripts; 1,010,304 photographs; 60,773 glass negatives; 9332 sheets and volumes of maps; 4259 cartoons. **Subscriptions:** 1575 journals and other serials; 50 newspapers. **Services:** Interlibrary loans; copying; collection open to public. **Automated Operations:** Computerized cataloging and serials. **Computerized Information Services:** OCLC. **Networks/Consortia:** Member of Bibliographical Center for Research, Rocky Mountain Region, Inc. (BCR); Kansas Library Network. **Publications:** Guide to Manuscript Holdings. **Staff:** Jean Skipp, Asst.Cur.

★15628★
UNIVERSITY OF KANSAS - MAP LIBRARY (Geog-Map)
110 Spencer Library   Phone: (913) 864-4420
Lawrence, KS 66045   Richard Embers, Map Lib.Assoc.
Founded: 1950. **Staff:** 1. **Subjects:** Geology, geography, vegetation, city plans, cartography. **Holdings:** 2447 volumes; 224,195 maps. **Subscriptions:** 25 journals and other serials. **Services:** Interlibrary loans; copying; library open to public. **Automated Operations:** Computerized cataloging and serials. **Computerized Information Services:** OCLC. **Networks/Consortia:** Member of Bibliographical Center for Research, Rocky Mountain Region, Inc. (BCR); Kansas Library Network. **Publications:** New Acquisitions List, monthly - available on request.

★15629★
UNIVERSITY OF KANSAS MEDICAL CTR. - COLLEGE OF HEALTH SCI. AND HOSPITAL - ARCHIE R. DYKES LIB. OF THE HEALTH SCI. (Med)
2100 W. 39th   Phone: (913) 588-7166
Kansas City, KS 66103   Earl Farley, Dir.
Founded: 1906. **Staff:** Prof 10; Other 29. **Subjects:** Basic and clinical medicine, allied health sciences, nursing, social work. **Special Collections:** Educational Resource Center. **Holdings:** 48,054 books; 71,063 bound periodical volumes. **Subscriptions:** 1955 journals and other serials. **Services:** Interlibrary loans; copying; library open to public. **Automated Operations:** Computerized cataloging, serials and circulation. **Computerized Information Services:** BRS, NLM, OCLC, DIALOG. **Networks/Consortia:** Member of Midcontinental Regional Medical Library Program; Kansas City Metropolitan Library Network. **Publications:** New Titles, monthly - for internal distribution only. **Formerly:** Its Clendening Library. **Staff:** Darlene Gaetano, Tech.Serv.; D.A. Thomas, Info.Serv.; Judy L. Allyn, Rd.Serv.

★15630★
UNIVERSITY OF KANSAS - MURPHY LIBRARY OF ART HISTORY (Art)
Helen Foresman Spencer Museum of Art Phone: (913) 864-3020
Lawrence, KS 66045   Susan V. Craig, Art Libn.
Founded: 1970. **Staff:** Prof 1; Other 3. **Subjects:** Art, design, photography, architecture, art history. **Special Collections:** Ephemeral collection of museum and gallery publications. **Holdings:** 57,801 volumes; 14 drawers of pamphlet files on artists. **Subscriptions:** 460 journals and other serials. **Services:** Interlibrary loans; copying; library open to public. **Automated Operations:** Computerized cataloging, serials and circulation. **Computerized Information Services:** OCLC, DIALOG (through Watson Library). **Networks/Consortia:** Member of Bibliographical Center for Research, Rocky Mountain Region, Inc. (BCR); Kansas Library Network.

★15631★
UNIVERSITY OF KANSAS REGENTS CENTER - LIBRARY (Educ)
9900 Mission Rd.   Phone: (913) 341-4554
Shawnee Mission, KS 66206   Nancy J. Burich, Libn.
Founded: 1976. **Staff:** Prof 1; Other 4. **Subjects:** Education, business, American history, literature, engineering management, urban planning, public administration. **Holdings:** 10,453 books; 2234 multimedia curriculum materials; 3439 microforms. **Subscriptions:** 407 journals and other serials; 8 newspapers. **Services:** Interlibrary loans; copying; library open to public with restrictions. **Automated Operations:** Computerized serials. **Computerized Information Services:** DIALOG, BRS. **Networks/Consortia:** Member of Kansas City Metropolitan Library Network (KCMLN). **Publications:** Library

Lines, monthly.

★15632★
UNIVERSITY OF KANSAS - SCHOOL OF LAW LIBRARY (Law)
New Green Hall   Phone: (913) 864-3025
Lawrence, KS 66045   Peter C. Schanck, Dir.
Founded: 1904. **Staff:** Prof 5; Other 7. **Subjects:** Law. **Special Collections:** Basic collection in the law of Great Britain, Canada and other common law countries; Russian law (includes complete code of the Russian Empire, 1801-1894). **Holdings:** 215,000 volumes; selected government documents; microforms. **Subscriptions:** 3400 journals and other serials. **Services:** Interlibrary loans; copying; library open to public. **Automated Operations:** Computerized cataloging. **Computerized Information Services:** LEXIS, Westlaw, NEXIS, DIALOG. **Networks/Consortia:** Member of Kansas Library Network; Northeast Kansas Library System (NEKL); Mid-America Law School Library Consortium. **Publications:** Weekly List of Acquisitions - for internal distribution only. **Staff:** Fritz Snyder, Ref. & Acq.Libn.; Martin E. Wisneski, Ser. & Docs.Libn.; Mary D. Burchill, Pub.Serv.Libn; Mon Yin Lung, Cat.Libn.

★15633★
UNIVERSITY OF KANSAS - SCIENCE LIBRARY (Sci-Tech)
6040 Malott Hall   Phone: (913) 864-4928
Lawrence, KS 66045   Jeanne Richardson, Sci.Libn.
Founded: 1954. **Staff:** Prof 3; Other 5. **Subjects:** Chemistry, physics, pharmacy, biology, geology, medicine, astronomy, history of science, general science. **Holdings:** 211,992 volumes; 23,964 government documents; 104,617 microforms. **Subscriptions:** 6000 journals and other serials. **Services:** Interlibrary loans; library open to public. **Automated Operations:** Computerized cataloging, serials and circulation. **Computerized Information Services:** DIALOG, SDC, BRS, NLM, OCLC. **Networks/Consortia:** Member of Bibliographical Center for Research, Rocky Mountain Region, Inc. (BCR); Kansas Library Network. **Staff:** Kathleen Neeley, Asst.Sci.Libn.

★15634★
UNIVERSITY OF KANSAS - SLAVIC COLLECTION (Area-Ethnic)
Watson Library   Phone: (913) 864-3957
Lawrence, KS 66045   George Jerkovich, Dir./Cur.
Founded: 1954. **Staff:** Prof 3; Other 2. **Subjects:** Slavic literature, languages, linguistics, history, politics, geography, philosophy, religion, law. **Special Collections:** Pre-revolutionary Russian/Soviet (92,000 volumes in Russian); Polish history and politics (31,000 volumes in Polish); South-Slavic (35,000 volumes); 17th-century Polonica; Slavic language history (13,000 volumes); related area studies holdings (165,000 volumes in English, German, French and other languages). **Holdings:** 171,000 volumes in original/vernacular language; 165,000 volumes in translation. **Services:** Interlibrary loans; collection open to public. **Automated Operations:** Computerized cataloging, serials and circulation. **Computerized Information Services:** OCLC. **Networks/Consortia:** Member of Bibliographical Center for Research, Rocky Mountain Region, Inc. (BCR); Kansas Library Network. **Staff:** Kermit R. Sewell, Exchange Lib.

★15635★
UNIVERSITY OF KANSAS - THOMAS GORTON MUSIC LIBRARY (Mus)
448 Murphy Hall   Phone: (913) 864-3496
Lawrence, KS 66045   Earl Gates, Libn.
Founded: 1953. **Staff:** Prof 2; Other 1. **Subjects:** Music. **Holdings:** 34,899 books and scores; 49,106 sound recordings; 4899 microforms. **Services:** Interlibrary loans; copying; library open to public. **Automated Operations:** Computerized cataloging and serials. **Computerized Information Services:** OCLC. **Networks/Consortia:** Member of Bibliographical Center for Research, Rocky Mountain Region, Inc. (BCR); Kansas Library Network. **Staff:** Ellen Johnson, Assoc.Libn.

★15636★
UNIVERSITY OF KANSAS - UNIVERSITY ARCHIVES (Hist)
422 Spencer Library   Phone: (913) 864-4188
Lawrence, KS 66045   John M. Nugent, Univ.Archv.
Founded: 1969. **Staff:** Prof 2; Other 1. **Subjects:** University of Kansas. **Special Collections:** University records, 1866 to present; faculty papers; D'Ambra photographs, 1925-1970. **Holdings:** 19,440 volumes; 341,998 negatives; 90,267 photographs; 2234 tapes; 11,991 linear feet of university records; 3543 reels of 16mm film; 528 reels of microfilm; 673 videotapes. **Services:** Interlibrary loans; copying; archives open to public with restrictions. **Computerized Information Services:** OCLC. **Networks/Consortia:** Member of Bibliographical Center for Research, Rocky Mountain Region, Inc. (BCR); Kansas Library Network. **Staff:** Edward Kehde, Archv.

★15637★
UNIVERSITY OF KANSAS - WEALTHY BABCOCK MATHEMATICS LIBRARY
(Sci-Tech; Comp Sci)
209 Strong Hall   Phone: (913) 864-3440
Lawrence, KS 66045   Ruth D. Fauhl, Lib.Asst.
Staff: 1. Subjects: Mathematics and computer science. Holdings: 25,999
volumes. Subscriptions: 300 journals and other serials. Services: Interlibrary
loans; copying; library open to public. Automated Operations: Computerized
cataloging and serials. Computerized Information Services: OCLC.
Networks/Consortia: Member of Bibliographical Center for Research, Rocky
Mountain Region, Inc. (BCR); Kansas Library Network.

★15638★
UNIVERSITY OF KANSAS - WILCOX COLLECTION OF CONTEMPORARY
    POLITICAL MOVEMENTS (Soc Sci)
Kansas Collection, Spencer Library   Phone: (913) 864-4274
Lawrence, KS 66045   Sheryl K. Williams, Cur., Kansas Coll.
Founded: 1965. Staff: Prof 1. Subjects: Conservative organizations,
Socialism and Communism, anti-Communist movements, radical student
movements, political ideology, propaganda. Special Collections: Radical
student movements of the 1960s; right-wing political literature, 1960 to
present. Holdings: 3500 books; 3 feet of manuscripts; 26,000 pieces of
ephemera (2000 pieces cataloged); 32 phonograph records. Subscriptions:
45 journals and other serials; 36 newspapers. Services: Interlibrary loans
(limited); copying; collection open to public. Automated Operations:
Computerized serials. Computerized Information Services: OCLC.
Networks/Consortia: Member of Bibliographical Center for Research, Rocky
Mountain Region, Inc. (BCR); Kansas Library Network. Publications: Brochure.

★15639★
UNIVERSITY OF KENTUCKY - AGRICULTURE LIBRARY (Agri)
N 24 Agricultural Science Ctr., N.   Phone: (606) 258-2758
Lexington, KY 40546-0091   Antoinette P. Powell, Libn.
Founded: 1905. Staff: Prof 3; Other 5. Subjects: Agriculture, forestry,
veterinary medicine, food nutrition, entomology, horticulture, botany,
landscape architecture. Holdings: 29,800 books; 54,109 bound periodical
volumes; 1862 reels of microfilm; 7003 microfiche; 7845 U.S. Department
of Agriculture publications; 3078 unbound materials; 18,000 cards containing
nutrition abstracts on microfilm; 6243 microfiche. Subscriptions: 2530
journals and other serials; 10 newspapers. Services: Interlibrary loans;
copying; library open to public. Automated Operations: Computerized
cataloging. Computerized Information Services: OCLC, DIALOG, BRS;
ANSER NETWORK - College of Agriculture (internal database). Performs
searches on cost recovery basis. Networks/Consortia: Member of SOLINET.
Publications: Monthly Acquisitions List - available upon request. Special
Indexes: Index of Kentucky Agricultural Experiment Station Publications
(card). Staff: Agnes McDowell, Selection; Lillian Mesner, Cat.

★15640★
UNIVERSITY OF KENTUCKY - BIOLOGICAL SCIENCES LIBRARY (Sci-Tech)
313 Thomas Hunt Morgan Bldg.   Phone: (606) 258-5889
Lexington, KY 40506-0225   Mildred A. Moore, Biological Sci.Libn.
Founded: 1963. Staff: Prof 1; Other 1. Subjects: Microbiology, biology,
botany, zoology, virology, endocrinology. Holdings: 17,089 books; 20,203
bound periodical volumes; 965 microforms. Subscriptions: 385 journals and
other serials. Services: Interlibrary loans; copying; library open to public.
Automated Operations: Computerized cataloging. Computerized
Information Services: OCLC. Networks/Consortia: Member of SOLINET.
Publications: Acquisitions List, 8/year.

★15641★
UNIVERSITY OF KENTUCKY - CHEMISTRY-PHYSICS LIBRARY (Sci-Tech)
150 Chemistry-Physics Bldg.   Phone: (606) 258-5954
Lexington, KY 40506-0055
Founded: 1963. Staff: Prof 1; Other 1. Subjects: Chemistry, physics,
astronomy. Special Collections: American Chemical Society's Men and
Molecules series (371 tapes). Holdings: 8583 books; 33,042 bound
periodical volumes; 230 reels of microfilm. Subscriptions: 469 journals and
other serials. Services: Interlibrary loans; copying; library open to public with
special borrowers card.

★15642★
UNIVERSITY OF KENTUCKY - EDUCATION LIBRARY (Educ)
205 Dickey Hall   Phone: (606) 258-4939
Lexington, KY 40506-0017   Larry Greenwood, Educ.Libn.
Staff: Prof 1; Other 2. Subjects: Education. Special Collections: Juvenile
and young adult collection (13,010 volumes). Holdings: 61,982 volumes;
306,784 ERIC microfiche; curriculum guides on microfiche. Subscriptions:
300 journals and other serials. Services: Interlibrary loans; copying; library

open to public with restrictions. Computerized Information Services:
DIALOG, BRS.

★15643★
UNIVERSITY OF KENTUCKY - GEORGE W. PIRTLE GEOLOGY LIBRARY (Sci-
    Tech; Energy)
100 Bowman Hall   Phone: (606) 258-5730
Lexington, KY 40506-0059   Vivian S. Hall, Libn.
Founded: 1923. Staff: Prof 1; Other 4. Subjects: Petroleum geology and
paleontology, mining geology, mineralogy, petrology, geochemistry, all aspects
of geology including regional and economic. Special Collections: Depository
for all U.S. Geological Survey publications; paleontology; Repository of Black
Shale Documents by U.S. Department of Energy researchers. Holdings:
11,179 books; 27,493 bound periodical volumes; 99,845 maps; 396 reels of
microfilm; 7176 microfiche. Subscriptions: 1116 journals and other serials.
Services: Interlibrary loans; copying; library open to public. Automated
Operations: Computerized cataloging and acquisitions. Computerized
Information Services: DIALOG, SDC, New York Times Information Service,
OCLC, Info-Ky News Retrieval System. Networks/Consortia: Member of
SOLINET. Publications: Acquisition list, monthly; theses listing. annual.

★15644★
UNIVERSITY OF KENTUCKY - HUNTER M. ADAMS ARCHITECTURE
    LIBRARY (Art; Plan)
College of Architecture
200 Pence Hall   Phone: (606) 257-1533
Lexington, KY 40506-0041   Harry Gilbert, Libn.
Founded: 1962. Staff: Prof 1; Other 1. Subjects: Architecture, landscape
architecture, city and urban planning, historic preservation, alternative energy
sources, photography, interior design. Special Collections: Rare books; Le
Corbusier (175 volumes); Kentucky architecture. Holdings: 18,009 books;
7175 bound periodical volumes; 232 sheets of architectural plans and
drawings; 150 reels of microfilm; 666 microfiche; 6950 VF items; 48
cassettes. Subscriptions: 150 journals and other serials. Services:
Interlibrary loans; copying; library open to public. Automated Operations:
Computerized cataloging and acquisitions. Computerized Information
Services: DIALOG, SDC, OCLC. Networks/Consortia: Member of SOLINET.
Publications: Periodic Acquisitions List; Library Guide.

★15645★
UNIVERSITY OF KENTUCKY - INSTITUTE FOR MINING AND MINERALS
    RESEARCH - IMMR LIBRARY (Energy)
Kentucky Energy Res. Laboratory
Iron Works Pike, Box 13015   Phone: (606) 252-5535
Lexington, KY 40512-3015   Theresa K. Wiley, Lib.Mgr.
Founded: 1974. Staff: Prof 1; Other 1. Subjects: Coal, oil shale, energy.
Holdings: 8200 books; 846 bound periodical volumes; 44,000 technical
reports in microform. Subscriptions: 150 journals and other serials.
Services: Interlibrary loans; library open to public for reference use only.
Automated Operations: Computerized cataloging. Computerized
Information Services: DIALOG, OCLC, SDC. Performs searches on cost
recovery basis. Publications: Research Reports - for sale.

★15646★
UNIVERSITY OF KENTUCKY - LAW LIBRARY (Law)
College of Law   Phone: (606) 258-8686
Lexington, KY 40506-0048   William James, Dir.
Founded: 1908. Staff: Prof 4. Subjects: Law. Special Collections:
Kocourek Collection on Jurisprudence; Records and Briefs on U.S. Supreme
Court (full opinions 1917 to present. Holdings: 181,937 books; 151,610
U.S. Government publications (partial depository). 361,956 microforms;
1693 audiotapes and cassettes. Subscriptions: 1340 journals and other
serials; 10 newspapers. Services: Interlibrary loans; copying; Kentucky Legal
Information; library open to public. Computerized Information Services:
OCLC, LEXIS, Westlaw. Networks/Consortia: Member of CRL; SOLINET.
Publications: Acquisitions List, monthly; table of contents for periodicals
received, weekly; Users Manual, annual. Staff: Cheryl Jones, Pub.Serv.Libn.;
JoEllen McComb, Circ./Ref.Libn.; Catherine Penberthy, Circ.Libn.; Ebba Jo
Sexton, Tech.Serv.Libn.

★15647★
UNIVERSITY OF KENTUCKY - MARGARET I. KING LIBRARY - ART LIBRARY
    (Art; Theater)
                                                 Phone: (606) 257-3938
Lexington, KY 40506-0039   Meg Shaw, Art Libn.
Staff: Prof 1; Other 1. Subjects: Art and theater arts. Holdings: 20,973
books; 5669 bound periodical volumes; 68 reels of microfilm; 812
microfiche; 36 VF drawers of pamphlets and catalogs. Subscriptions: 168
journals and other serials. Services: Interlibrary loans; copying; library open to

public.

★15648★

UNIVERSITY OF KENTUCKY - MARGARET I. KING LIBRARY - GOVERNMENT PUBLICATIONS/MAP DEPARTMENT (Info Sci)

Lexington, KY 40506

Phone: (602) 257-3139
Sandra McAnich, Hd., Govt.Pubns.

Staff: Prof 2; Other 5. **Subjects:** Government publications - U.S., Canada, Great Britain, Kentucky and other states of the U.S., United Nations documents, European Communities documents. **Holdings:** 750,000 books; 250,000 unbound reports; 2000 linear feet of microfiche; 300 linear feet of microfilm; 700 linear feet of microprint; 120 linear feet of microcards. **Subscriptions:** 11,000 journals and other serials. **Services:** Interlibrary loans; copying; department open to public. **Publications:** Let's Talk Documents. **Staff:** Barbara Hale, Assoc.Docs.Libn.

★15649★

UNIVERSITY OF KENTUCKY - MARGARET I. KING LIBRARY - GOVERNMENT PUBLICATIONS/MAP DEPARTMENT - MAP COLLECTION (Geog-Map)

Lexington, KY 40506-0039

Phone: (606) 257-1853
Gwen Curtis, Hd.

Staff: 4. **Subjects:** Cartography. **Special Collections:** Kentucky maps, 1875 to present; Southeastern U.S. maps, 1800 to present; Sanborn Insurance Maps of Kentucky cities (7895 sheets); Defense Mapping Agency Depository (21,000 sheets). **Holdings:** 465 books; 7870 maps; 62,100 uncataloged maps and aerial photographs; 780 atlases. **Services:** Interlibrary loans; copying; collections open to public with limited circulation. **Automated Operations:** Computerized cataloging. **Computerized Information Services:** OCLC. **Networks/Consortia:** Member of SOLINET. **Publications:** Selected Acquisitions Bulletin, quarterly - to faculty and other libraries. **Remarks:** Kentucky maps published before 1875 are housed in the Special Collections Department of the King Library; geology and hydrology maps are housed in the Geology Library.

★15650★

UNIVERSITY OF KENTUCKY - MARGARET I. KING LIBRARY - SPECIAL COLLECTIONS AND ARCHIVES (Hist)

11 King Library N.
Lexington, KY 40506-0039

Claire McCann, Mss.Libn.

Staff: Prof 7; Other 5. **Subjects:** Kentuckiana, 20th century politics, Appalachia, English romantic literature. **Holdings:** 80,000 volumes; 12,000 cubic feet of manuscripts. **Subscriptions:** 850 journals and other serials. **Services:** Interlibrary loans; copying; collections open to public. **Automated Operations:** Computerized cataloging. **Computerized Information Services:** OCLC. **Networks/Consortia:** Member of SOLINET. **Special Catalogs:** Applied Anthropology Documentation Project; catalogs to Dime Novel collection, Science Fiction Collection, Milton Collection, Cortot Collection, Kentucky Imprint Collection; theses catalog; catalogs to photographic archives, microfilm, and manuscripts (all on cards).

★15651★

UNIVERSITY OF KENTUCKY - MATHEMATICAL SCIENCES LIBRARY (Sci-Tech; Comp sci)

OB-9 Patterson Office Tower
Lexington, KY 40506-0027

Phone: (606) 257-8365
Karen S. Croneis, Libn.

Staff: Prof 1. **Subjects:** Mathematics, computer science (software), statistics. **Holdings:** 15,000 books; 11,600 bound periodical volumes. **Subscriptions:** 425 journals and other serials. **Services:** Interlibrary loans; copying; library open to public. **Publications:** Monthly acquisitions list.

★15652★

UNIVERSITY OF KENTUCKY - MEDICAL CENTER LIBRARY (Med)

Lexington, KY 40536-0084

Phone: (606) 233-5300
Omer Hamlin, Jr., Dir.

Founded: 1957. **Staff:** Prof 10; Other 17. **Subjects:** Medicine, dentistry, nursing, pharmacy, allied health professions. **Special Collections:** Harvey Collection; Servetus Collection. **Holdings:** 70,380 books; 91,777 bound periodical volumes; 945 reels of microfilm; 1976 AV items. **Subscriptions:** 1792 journals and other serials. **Services:** Interlibrary loans (fee); copying; SDI; library open to health science personnel. **Automated Operations:** Computerized cataloging. **Computerized Information Services:** MEDLINE, DIALOG, BRS, SDC; OCLC. **Networks/Consortia:** Member of Greater Midwest Regional Medical Library Network (Region 3). **Staff:** Sara Leech, Assoc.; Janet Stith, Asst.; Edna Pray, Pharmacy Libn.; Karl Heinz-Boewe, Ref.Libn.; Bev Hilton, AV Libn.; Lynn Barnett, Cat.Libn.; Florence Jones, Order Libn.; Bernadette Baldini, Tech.Serv.; Stephanie Allen, Ref.Libn.

★15653★

UNIVERSITY OF KENTUCKY - MUSIC LIBRARY/LISTENING CENTER (Mus)

116 Fine Arts Bldg.
Lexington, KY 40506-0022

Phone: (606) 258-2800
Cathy S. Hunt, Music Libn.

Staff: Prof 1; Other 2. **Subjects:** Music - history, theory, education; applied music. **Special Collections:** Alfred Cortot Collection of early theory books (265 books). **Holdings:** 38,800 books and scores; 3200 bound periodical volumes; 9200 phonograph records; 6400 microforms; 1550 cassettes. **Subscriptions:** 210 journals and other serials. **Services:** Interlibrary loans; copying; library open to public with check-out privileges for residents of Kentucky. **Automated Operations:** Computerized cataloging and acquisitions. **Computerized Information Services:** OCLC. **Networks/Consortia:** Member of SOLINET.

★15654★

UNIVERSITY OF KENTUCKY - ROBERT E. SHAVER LIBRARY OF ENGINEERING (Sci-Tech)

355 Anderson Hall
Lexington, KY 40506-0046

Phone: (606) 258-2965
Russell H. Powell, Libn.

Founded: 1965. **Staff:** Prof 1; Other 1. **Subjects:** Environment; coal mining and processing; transportation; engineering mechanics; energy; engineering - civil, mechanical, electrical, chemical, metallurgical. **Holdings:** 48,549 volumes; 1658 reels of microfilm; 51,477 microfiche. **Subscriptions:** 950 journals and other serials. **Services:** Interlibrary loans; copying; library open to public with restrictions on borrowing. **Computerized Information Services:** DIALOG, SDC, DOE/RECON, OCLC. **Networks/Consortia:** Member of SOLINET.

★15655★

UNIVERSITY OF KING'S COLLEGE - KING'S COLLEGE LIBRARY (Rel-Theol; Hum)

Halifax, NS, Canada B3H 2A1

Phone: (902) 423-8428
Dr. W.J. Hankey, Chf.Libn.

Staff: Prof 2; Other 3. **Subjects:** Theology, Canadiana, philosophy, history, classics, journalism. **Special Collections:** Incunabula and rare books (10,000 volumes); William Inglis Morse Canadiana Collection; Journalism Resource Collection; Weldon China Collection. **Holdings:** 75,000 books and bound periodical volumes; college archives. **Subscriptions:** 220 journals and other serials; 30 newspapers. **Services:** Interlibrary loans; library open to public with restrictions. **Special Catalogs:** Incunabula. **Staff:** Janet Hunt, Asst.Libn.

★15656★

UNIVERSITY OF LA VERNE - COLLEGE OF LAW - LIBRARY (Law)

1950 3rd St.
La Verne, CA 91750

Phone: (714) 593-7184
Suzanne Miller, Law Libn.

Founded: 1978. **Staff:** Prof 1; Other 2. **Subjects:** Law. **Special Collections:** Juvenile Law (3080 volumes). **Holdings:** 75,000 volumes; 2500 reels of microfilm; 240,903 microfiche; 333 cassette tapes. **Subscriptions:** 337 journals and other serials. **Services:** Interlibrary loans; copying; library open to public. **Automated Operations:** Computerized cataloging. **Computerized Information Services:** Westlaw.

★15657★

UNIVERSITY OF LOUISVILLE - ALLEN R. HITE ART INSTITUTE - MARGARET M. BRIDWELL ART LIBRARY (Art)

Belknap Campus
Louisville, KY 40292

Phone: (502) 588-6741
Gail R. Gilbert, Hd., Art Lib.

Founded: 1956. **Staff:** Prof 1; Other 1. **Subjects:** Art - Renaissance, medieval, ancient, American; modern architecture; German sculpture; art history; city planning. **Special Collections:** Robert J. Doherty typography collection; Ainslie Hewett bookplate collection. **Holdings:** 38,700 books; 7700 bound periodical volumes; 29 museum bulletins; 700 posters; artists' files (6000 folders); information files (4000 folders). **Subscriptions:** 213 journals and other serials. **Services:** Interlibrary loans; library open to public for reference use only.

★15658★

UNIVERSITY OF LOUISVILLE - DEPARTMENT OF RARE BOOKS AND SPECIAL COLLECTIONS (Rare Book)

Belknap Campus
Louisville, KY 40292

Phone: (502) 588-6762
George T. McWhorter, Cur.

Founded: 1837. **Staff:** Prof 2. **Subjects:** Astronomy-mathematics, World War I, literary first editions, Irish Literary Renaissance literature, American humor, Louisvilliana. **Special Collections:** Bullitt Collection of rare astronomy and mathematics (400 items); Arthur Rackham Collection of books, manuscripts, original art (500 items); Edgar Rice Burroughs Collection (5000 items); H.L. Mencken Collection (500 items); Graham Greene Collection (250 items); Lawrence Durrell Collection (200 items); J.D. Salinger Collection (200 items); American Humor (3000 items); Lafcadio Hearn Collection (200 items);

World War I Collection (2000 items); Mosher Press (1000 volumes); Roger Manvell Collection of Theater & Film History (20,000 items); Irish Literary Renaissance Collection (2000 volumes, manuscripts and ephemera). **Holdings:** 70,000 books and periodicals; 84 linear feet of manuscripts. **Services:** Interlibrary loans; copying; library open to public for reference use only. **Also Known As:** University of Louisville - John L. Patterson Room. **Staff:** Delinda Stephens Buie, Asst.Cur., Rare Bks.

★15659★
UNIVERSITY OF LOUISVILLE - DWIGHT ANDERSON MEMORIAL MUSIC LIBRARY (Mus)†
2301 S. 3rd St.　　　　　　　　　　　　Phone: (502) 588-5659
Louisville, KY 40292　　　　　　　　　　Marion Korda, Libn.
Founded: 1947. **Staff:** Prof 2; Other 4. **Subjects:** Music. **Special Collections:** Early American Sheet Music; Kentucky imprints; Kentucky composers; music archival collection; Louisville Orchestra Commissioning Project materials; Jean Thomas "Traipsin' Woman" Collection; Isidore Phillip Archive and Memorial Library. **Holdings:** 15,523 books; 3600 bound periodical volumes; 18,275 scores; 617 titles of microtexts and microfilms; 2000 music tapes; 15,000 sound recordings; 22,000 uncataloged items. **Subscriptions:** 500 journals and other serials. **Services:** Interlibrary loans; copying; library open to public, registration required for borrowing purposes. **Automated Operations:** Computerized cataloging and circulation. **Computerized Information Services:** OCLC. **Networks/Consortia:** Member of SOLINET.

UNIVERSITY OF LOUISVILLE - J.B. SPEED SCIENTIFIC SCHOOL - LIBRARY
See: University of Louisville - Kersey Library

UNIVERSITY OF LOUISVILLE - JOHN L. PATTERSON ROOM
See: University of Louisville - Department of Rare Books and Special Collections

★15660★
UNIVERSITY OF LOUISVILLE - KERSEY LIBRARY (Sci-Tech)
Belknap Campus　　　　　　　　　　　　Phone: (502) 588-6297
Louisville, KY 40292　　　　　　　　　　Carol S. Brinkman, Dir.
Staff: Prof 2; Other 4. **Subjects:** Applied mathematics; computer science; engineering - chemical, electrical, mechanical, civil, industrial, nuclear, environmental; physics; chemistry; mathematics; statistics; astronomy; history of science and technology; general science. **Holdings:** 87,322 volumes; 26,525 microforms. **Subscriptions:** 837 journals and other serials. **Services:** Interlibrary loans; copying; library open to public. **Computerized Information Services:** Online systems. **Formed by the Merger of:** University of Louisville - J.B. Speed Scientific School - Library and University of Louisville - Sebastian S. Kresge Natural Science Library.

★15661★
UNIVERSITY OF LOUISVILLE - KORNHAUSER HEALTH SCIENCES LIBRARY (Med)
　　　　　　　　　　　　　　　　Phone: (502) 588-5771
Louisville, KY 40292　　　　　　　　　　Leonard M. Eddy, Dir.
Staff: Prof 9; Other 14. **Subjects:** Medicine, dentistry, nursing, allied health sciences. **Holdings:** 46,428 books; 91,131 bound periodical volumes; 3541 AV items. **Subscriptions:** 1031 journals. **Services:** Interlibrary loans; copying; library open to public. **Automated Operations:** Computerized cataloging and circulation. **Computerized Information Services:** BRS, MEDLINE, OCLC. **Networks/Consortia:** Member of Greater Midwest Medical Library Network (Region 3). **Publications:** Bio-Echo, every 6 weeks. **Staff:** Nancy Craig Lee, Hd., Tech.Serv.; Parthenia Durrett, Circ.; Mary S. Barber, Asst. to Dir.; Mark Plaiss, Ref.Libn.; Diane Nichols, Ref.Libn.; Nancy Utterback, Hd., Pub.Serv.; Virginia Leightly, Acq.; Mary Grant, ILL; Sherrill McConnell, Archv.; Neal Nixon, Cat.

UNIVERSITY OF LOUISVILLE - NATIONAL CRIME PREVENTION INSTITUTE
See: National Crime Prevention Institute

★15662★
UNIVERSITY OF LOUISVILLE - PHOTOGRAPHIC ARCHIVES (Aud-Vis; Hist)
Belknap Campus　　　　　　　　　　　　Phone: (502) 588-6752
Louisville, KY 40292　　　　　　　　　　James C. Anderson, Cur.
Staff: Prof 3; Other 2. **Subjects:** History of Louisville; 20th century social history; American industry; oil industry; photography - historic, artistic, documentary and commercial. **Special Collections:** Antique media and equipment; Lou Block Collection; Will Bowers Collection; Bradley Studio/Georgetown Collection; Theodore M. Brown/Robert J. Doherty Collection; Caldwell Tank Company Collection; Cooper Collection; erotic photography; Fine Print Collection; Arthur Y. Ford albums; Forensic Photography Collection; Vida Hunt Francis Collection; Mary D. Hill Collection; Joseph Krementz

Collection; Clarence John Laughlin Collection; Macauley Collection; Manvell Collection (film stills); Boyd Martin Collection; Kate Matthews Collection; Metropolitan Sewer District Collection; R.G. Potter Collection; J.C. Rieger Collection; Jean Thomas Collection; World Wars I and II photographs; Caufield and Shook of Louisville Collection; Roy E. Stryker (Farm Security Administration) Collection. **Holdings:** 750,000 photographs and photograph-related items (special collections); 500 books; 10,000 pages of manuscripts. **Services:** Interlibrary loans; copying; photographic print service; library open to public with restrictions. **Automated Operations:** Computerized cataloging. **Special Catalogs:** Exhibition catalogs; illustrated brochure of holdings - available for purchase. **Staff:** David Horvath, Asst.Cur./Cat.

★15663★
UNIVERSITY OF LOUISVILLE - SCHOOL OF LAW LIBRARY (Law)
Belknap Campus　　　　　　　　　　　　Phone: (502) 588-6392
Louisville, KY 40292　　　　　　　　　　Gene W. Teitelbaum, Law Libn.
Founded: 1926. **Staff:** Prof 3; Other 4. **Subjects:** Law. **Special Collections:** Correspondence of Mr. Justice Brandeis (150,000 items) and Mr. Justice Harlan, 1833-1911 (1500 items). **Holdings:** 130,000 volumes. **Subscriptions:** 904 journals and other serials. **Services:** Interlibrary loans; library open to public with restrictions.

★15664★
UNIVERSITY OF LOUISVILLE - SEBASTIAN S. KRESGE NATURAL SCIENCE LIBRARY
Belknap Campus
Louisville, KY 40208
Defunct. Merged with University of Louisville - J.B. Speed Scientific School Library to form its Kersey Library.

★15665★
UNIVERSITY OF LOUISVILLE - UNIVERSITY ARCHIVES AND RECORDS CENTER (Hist)
Ekstrom Library　　　　　　　　　　　　Phone: (502) 588-6674
Louisville, KY 40292　　　　　　　William J. Morison, Dir./Univ.Archv.
Founded: 1973. **Staff:** Prof 5; Other 4. **Subjects:** History of the university and its predecessor schools; political, social, economic and cultural history of Louisville and the geographic region; regional business. **Special Collections:** Louis D. Brandeis Papers (184 reels of microfilm); Louisville and Nashville Railroad Company Records (155 linear feet; 39 reels of microfilm; 46 oral history interviews); Louisville Orchestra records (125 linear feet); Simmons University Records (5 linear feet). **Holdings:** 5000 linear feet of archives, including personal papers; 1500 linear feet of local government archives; 1700 linear feet of Kentuckiana Historical Collections, including records of local organizations and personal papers of area individuals and families; 904 reels of microfilm. **Services:** Copying; microfilming; archives open to public with restrictions. **Publications:** A Place Where Historical Research May Be Pursued: Selected Primary Sources in the University of Louisville Archives; Papers of Louis D. Brandeis at the University of Louisville, Microfilm Edition, 1981; D.W. Griffith Papers 1897-1954: Guide to the Microfilm Edition, 1982. **Staff:** Thomas Owen, Asst.Dir.; Dwayne Cox, Assoc.Univ.Archv.; Sherrill McConnell, Dir., Hist.Coll.; Deborah Skaggs, Access Archv.; Larry Raymond, Hd., Microform Lab.

★15666★
UNIVERSITY OF LOUISVILLE - UNIVERSITY ARCHIVES AND RECORDS CENTER - ORAL HISTORY CENTER (Hist)
Belknap Campus　　　　　　　　　　　　Phone: (502) 588-6674
Louisville, KY 40292
Founded: 1968. **Staff:** Prof 3. **Subjects:** History of Louisville, Kentucky, including the Louisville Orchestra; prominent citizens; the university; the Courier-Journal; the Louisville Times; the Louisville and Nashville Railroad; photography; Jewish history. **Holdings:** 1000 tape cassettes. **Services:** Copying; copies of tapes and finding aids available; center open to public. **Staff:** Dwayne Cox, Co-Dir.; Carl G. Ryant, Co-Dir.

★15667★
UNIVERSITY OF LOUISVILLE - URBAN STUDIES CENTER - LIBRARY (Soc Sci)
College of Urban and Public Affairs　　　　　Phone: (502) 588-6626
Louisville, KY 40292　　　　　　　Shirley Demos, Dir., Info.Rsrcs.
Staff: Prof 1; Other 1. **Subjects:** Demography of Kentucky, housing needs assessment, public opinion surveys, public administration, municipal planning. **Special Collections:** Census maps for Kentucky, 1970 and 1980 (1000). **Holdings:** 5000 books; 168 computer tapes; 150 computer printouts; maps; microfiche. **Subscriptions:** 37 journals and other serials. **Services:** Copying; library open to public. **Computerized Information Services:** Internal database. **Remarks:** The Urban Studies Center operates the State Data Center of Kentucky which answers questions concerning census data with

information from the population, housing and economic censuses.

★15668★

UNIVERSITY OF LOWELL, NORTH CAMPUS - ALUMNI/LYDON LIBRARY (Sci-Tech)†
1 University Ave.　　　　　　　　Phone: (617) 452-5000
Lowell, MA 01854　　　　　　　　Joseph V. Kopycinski, Dir.
Founded: 1897. **Staff:** Prof 6; Other 10. **Subjects:** Engineering, plastics chemistry, physics, business management, electronics. **Holdings:** 125,168 books; 20,435 bound periodical volumes; 4900 reels of microfilm; 250,000 government publications (depository). **Subscriptions:** 775 journals and other serials; 8 newspapers. **Services:** Interlibrary loans; copying; library open to public for reference use only. **Automated Operations:** Computerized cataloging. **Computerized Information Services:** OCLC. **Networks/Consortia:** Member of NELINET; New England On-line Users Group (NENON); Massachusetts Conference of Chief Librarians of Public Higher Educational Institutions (MCCLPHEI); Merrimack Interlibrary Cooperative (MILC). **Publications:** Media Services Film and Video Catalog; Union List of Periodicals. **Staff:** Patricia Noreau, Per.Libn.; Joan Ellis, Coord.Ref.Serv.; Martha Mayo, Spec.Coll.Libn.; Leslie Kaplan, Media Serv.

★15669★

UNIVERSITY OF LOWELL, NORTH CAMPUS - UNIVERSITY LIBRARIES - SPECIAL COLLECTIONS (Hist)
1 University Ave.　　　　　　　　Phone: (617) 454-7811
Lowell, MA 01854　　　　　　　Martha Mayo, Hd., Spec.Coll.
Founded: 1971. **Staff:** Prof 1; Other 2. **Subjects:** Middlesex Canal; Lowell, Massachusetts, hydraulics, women in industry, textile manufacturing, Warren H. Manning. **Special Collections:** Lowell Historical Society Collection; Middlesex Canal Association Collection; Locks & Canals Collection; Manning Family Collection; University Archives; Olney Collection (textile books); Boston & Maine Railroad Historical Society Collection; Lowell Museum Collection; Greater Lowell Chapter of the American Association of University Women Records. **Holdings:** 24,000 volumes; 75 VF drawers and 300 linear feet of records and manscripts; 1500 architectural and engineering drawings; 300 maps; 15,000 photographs; 25 paintings; 900 reels of microfilm. **Services:** Copying; collections open to public. **Special Catalogs:** Locks & Canals Collection (printout); Manning Family Collection (printout). **Special Indexes:** Index of VF material; index of photographs; inventories of some records and manuscript collections.

★15670★

UNIVERSITY OF LOWELL, SOUTH CAMPUS - DANIEL H. O'LEARY LIBRARY - SPECIAL COLLECTIONS (Educ)
Wilder St.　　　　　　　　　　Phone: (617) 452-5000
Lowell, MA 01854　　　　Rosanna Kowalewski, Act.Dir. of Univ.Libs.
Founded: 1894. **Staff:** Prof 6; Other 10. **Subjects:** Health, education, criminal justice, music. **Holdings:** ERIC microfiche collection; U.S. Geological Survey maps of New England; music collection (8000 scores; 7000 phonograph records); film-video collection (600 items). **Services:** Interlibrary loans; copying; SDI; collections open to public for reference use only. **Automated Operations:** Computerized cataloging, acquisitions and circulation. **Computerized Information Services:** DIALOG, BRS, OCLC. Performs searches on cost recovery basis with a service fee for outside users. Contact Person: John Callahan. **Networks/Consortia:** Member of NELINET; Northeast Consortium of Colleges and Universities in Massachusetts (NECCUM). **Staff:** John Callahan, Ref.Libn.; Lawrence Caylor, Acq.Libn.; Paul Coppens, Hd., Media Serv.; Mitchell Shuldman, Mus.Libn.; Leslie Kaplan, Media Prod.Libn.

★15671★

UNIVERSITY OF MAINE, FARMINGTON - MANTOR LIBRARY (Educ)†
　　　　　　　　　　　　　　　　Phone: (207) 778-3501
Farmington, ME 04938　　　　　　John P. Burnham, Hd.Libn.
Founded: 1933. **Staff:** Prof 4; Other 5. **Subjects:** Special education - exceptional children, behavioral disorders, mental retardation, gifted children, sensory disorders, speech defects and physical handicaps. **Holdings:** 90,000 books; 4900 bound periodical volumes; 6500 VF materials; 8700 reels of microfilm; 12,300 microfiche. **Subscriptions:** 700 journals and other serials. **Services:** Interlibrary loans; copying; library open to public. **Automated Operations:** Computerized cataloging. **Computerized Information Services:** OCLC. **Networks/Consortia:** Member of NELINET. **Staff:** Shirley A. Martin, Ref.Libn.; Vincent Courtney, Tech.Serv.

★15672★

UNIVERSITY OF MAINE, ORONO - IRA C. DARLING CENTER LIBRARY (Sci-Tech)
　　　　　　　　　　　　　　　　Phone: (207) 563-3146
Walpole, ME 04573　　　　　　　Louise M. Dean, Libn.
Founded: 1967. **Staff:** Prof 1. **Subjects:** Marine biology; oceanography -

biological, physical, Gulf of Maine, chemical and geological; fisheries; aquaculture. **Holdings:** 5700 books; 2000 bound periodical volumes; 8000 reprints; 1500 microforms. **Subscriptions:** 180 journals and other serials. **Services:** Interlibrary loans; copying; library open to public.

★15673★

UNIVERSITY OF MAINE, ORONO - NORTHEAST ARCHIVES OF FOLKLORE AND ORAL HISTORY (Hist)
Dept. of Anthropology
S. Stevens Hall　　　　　　　　Phone: (207) 581-1891
Orono, ME 04469　　　　　　　　Edward D. Ives, Dir.
Founded: 1964. **Staff:** Prof 1; Other 1. **Subjects:** Folklore, oral history. **Special Collections:** Folksong; lumbering and river driving; folklife of Maine and the Maritime Provinces. **Holdings:** 1700 cataloged accessions; 5600 photographs of lumbering and other aspects of folklife. **Services:** Copying; archives open to public. **Publications:** Northeast Folklore, annual. **Special Indexes:** Place names, personal names, song titles, subjects.

★15674★

UNIVERSITY OF MAINE, ORONO - RAYMOND H. FOGLER LIBRARY - SPECIAL COLLECTIONS DEPARTMENT (Hist)
　　　　　　　　　　　　　　Phone: (207) 581-1686
Orono, ME 04469　　　　　　Eric S. Flower, Dept.Hd.
Founded: 1970. **Staff:** Prof 2; Other 2. **Subjects:** State of Maine, maritime history. **Special Collections:** State of Maine Collection (12,000 volumes); Maine State Documents Collection (6500 items); University Collection (11,500 items); Clinton L. Cole Marine Library (4000 volumes); O'Brien Collection of American Negro History and Culture (600 items); Philip H. Taylor Collection of Modern History, War, and Diplomacy (500 volumes); Thoreau Fellowship Papers. **Holdings:** 30,000 books; 400 bound periodical volumes; 1140 archive boxes of manuscripts on Maine; 2000 maps of Maine; 5000 reels of microfilm relating to Maine. **Subscriptions:** 75 journals and other serials; 36 Maine newspapers. **Services:** Interlibrary loans; copying; library open to public. **Automated Operations:** Computerized acquisitions and serials. **Special Catalogs:** A Catalog of the Clinton L. Cole Collection (1972). **Special Indexes:** Maine Times Index; Down East Magazine Index; Maine Campus Index; Maine Townsman Index; Maine Teacher Index; Elderberry Times Index (each in card or book form); Shaker Quarterly Index; Maine Life Index; **Staff:** Muriel A. Sanford, Spec.Coll.Libn.

★15675★

UNIVERSITY OF MAINE, PRESQUE ISLE - LIBRARY AND LEARNING RESOURCES CENTER - SPECIAL COLLECTIONS (Hist)
181 Main St.　　　　　　　　　Phone: (207) 764-0311
Presque Isle, ME 04769　　　　　John Vigle, Dir.
Staff: Prof 5; Other 3. **Holdings:** Aroostook County, Maine Collection (1000 volumes); Maine Collection (690 volumes); 12,650 government documents; 4 VF drawers; scrapbooks. **Services:** Interlibrary loans; copying; collections open to public. **Automated Operations:** Computerized cataloging. **Computerized Information Services:** The Source, BRS, OCLC, DIALOG. Performs free searches. Contact Person: Dennis Frank. **Networks/Consortia:** Member of NELINET. **Staff:** Anna McGrath, Tech.Serv.Libn.; Dennis Frank, Ref.Libn.; Nancy Roe, Cat.

★15676★

UNIVERSITY OF MAINE SCHOOL OF LAW - DONALD L. GARBRECHT LAW LIBRARY (Law)
246 Deering Ave.　　　　　　　Phone: (207) 780-4350
Portland, ME 04102　　　　　　Dan J. Freehling, Law Libn.
Founded: 1961. **Staff:** Prof 8; Other 5. **Subjects:** Law. **Holdings:** 185,000 books and books in microform. **Subscriptions:** 2600 journals and other serials. **Services:** Interlibrary loans; copying; library open to public with restrictions. **Automated Operations:** Computerized cataloging and ILL. **Computerized Information Services:** Westlaw, DIALOG, RLIN. **Networks/Consortia:** Member of CLASS; New England Law Library Consortium (NELLC) **Staff:** Elizabeth Ginkel, Asst. Law Libn.; Ramona L. Moore, Ser.Libn.; Kathie K. Tibbetts, Asst. Law Libn.; Patricia M. Milligan, Sr.Cat.; Maureen Kays, Circ./Ref.Libn.; Suzanne I. Pellitier, Acq.Libn.; Isa Lang, Lawyer Libn.

★15677★

UNIVERSITY OF MANITOBA - ADMINISTRATIVE STUDIES LIBRARY (Bus-Fin)
　　　　　　　　　　　　　　　Phone: (204) 474-8440
Winnipeg, MB, Canada R3T 2N2　　　Judith Head, Hd.Libn.
Founded: 1971. **Staff:** Prof 1; Other 6. **Subjects:** Accounting, finance, marketing, business administration, actuarial and business mathematics, public policy, business law, industrial relations. **Holdings:** 14,500 books and bound periodical volumes; annual reports for 800 companies (past 5 years). **Subscriptions:** 380 journals and other serials. **Services:** Interlibrary loans;

copying; library open to public. **Computerized Information Services:** DIALOG, MEDLINE, CAN/OLE, Infomart, QL Systems, InfoGlobe, UTLAS.

★15678★
UNIVERSITY OF MANITOBA - AGRICULTURE LIBRARY (Agri)
Phone: (204) 474-9457
Winnipeg, MB, Canada R3T 2N2   Judith Harper, Hd.
Founded: 1906. **Staff:** Prof 1; Other 2. **Subjects:** Agriculture, animal science, plant science, entomology, agricultural economics, soil science, food science. **Holdings:** 15,750 books and bound periodical volumes. **Subscriptions:** 340 journals and other serials. **Services:** Interlibrary loans; copying; SDI; library open to public. **Automated Operations:** Computerized circulation. **Computerized Information Services:** DIALOG, CAN/OLE, UTLAS.

★15679★
UNIVERSITY OF MANITOBA - ARCHITECTURE & FINE ARTS LIBRARY (Art)
206 Architecture Bldg.   Phone: (204) 474-9216
Winnipeg, MB, Canada R3T 2N2   Peter Anthony, Hd.Libn.
Founded: 1916. **Staff:** Prof 2; Other 8. **Subjects:** Architecture, interior design, fine arts, city planning, photography, graphics, design, landscape architecture, environmental studies. **Holdings:** 54,500 books and bound periodical volumes; 1200 maps; 28 VF drawers of art reproductions; 600 large art reproductions; 500 student projects; 1100 product catalogs; 40 VF drawers of miscellaneous material. **Subscriptions:** 500 journals and other serials. **Services:** Interlibrary loans; copying. **Automated Operations:** Computerized circulation. **Computerized Information Services:** DIALOG, UTLAS. **Staff:** Michele Laing, Ref.Libn.

★15680★
UNIVERSITY OF MANITOBA - ARCHIVES AND SPECIAL COLLECTIONS (Rare Book; Hum)
331 Elizabeth Dafoe Library   Phone: (204) 474-9986
Winnipeg, MB, Canada R3T 2N2   Richard E. Bennett, Hd.
Staff: Prof 4; Other 1. **Subjects:** Western Canadiana, Iceland, Manitoba literary manuscripts, university archives and publications, antiquarian books. Icelandic collection (23,500 volumes); **Holdings:** University of Manitoba theses and dissertations (5000); Winnipeg Tribune Collection of Photographs and Newsclippings, 1920-1980 (500 cubic feet); Dysart Memorial Collection of Rare Books and Incunabula (69 titles); Frederick Philip Grove Collection of Literary Manuscripts (4 linear feet); Bertram R. Brooker Collection of Literary Manuscripts and Private Library (4 linear feet); Dorothy Livesay Collection of Literary Manuscripts (40 linear feet); Marshall Gauvin Library of Free Thought and Rationalist Literature (200 linear feet); Bruce Chown, M.D. Collection of Medical Research (3 linear feet); T. Glendenning Hamilton, M.D. Collection of Psychic Phenomena (5 linear feet); Photograph Collection of Selkirk, Manitoba (15 linear feet); University Administrative Office Archives (271 linear feet); Rudyard Kipling Library Collection; Charles G.D. Roberts and Bliss Carman Literature Collection; Stephan G. Stephansson's Private Library (Icelandic Canadian poetry); Guttormur J. Guttormsson Private Library (Icelandic Canadian poetry); John W. Dafoe Collection; Oscar Brand collection; papers of Isaac Pitblado, Jack Murta. **Services:** Copying; collections open to public. **Automated Operations:** Computerized cataloging. **Computerized Information Services:** UTLAS. **Publications:** Published registers available for the following collections: John W. Dafoe, Frederick Philip Grove, T.G. Hamilton, Bruce Chown, Bertram Brooker, Margaret Konantz and the University of Manitoba Financial Administration Papers. **Special Indexes:** KWIC Index of the University Publications Collection. **Staff:** Kathryn Dean, Cur. of Mss.; Sigrid Johnson, Icelandic Libn.; Corrado Santoro, Ref.Archv.

★15681★
UNIVERSITY OF MANITOBA - D.S. WOODS EDUCATION LIBRARY (Educ)
228 Education Bldg.   Phone: (204) 474-9976
Winnipeg, MB, Canada R3T 2N2   Doreen Shanks, Hd.Libn.
Staff: Prof 3; Other 10. **Subjects:** Education, child development, guidance, physical education. **Special Collections:** Manitoba school textbooks (21,000 volumes). **Holdings:** 57,000 books and bound periodical volumes; 325,000 ERIC microfiche. **Subscriptions:** 675 journals and other serials. **Services:** Interlibrary loans; copying; library open to public. **Automated Operations:** Computerized circulation. **Computerized Information Services:** UTLAS. **Staff:** Richard Ellis, Ref.Libn.; David Thirlwall, Ref.Libn.

★15682★
UNIVERSITY OF MANITOBA - DENTAL LIBRARY (Med)
780 Bannatyne Ave.   Phone: (204) 786-3635
Winnipeg, MB, Canada R3E 0W3   Doris Pritchard, Hd.Libn.
Founded: 1958. **Staff:** Prof 2; Other 4. **Subjects:** Dentistry. **Holdings:** 20,000 books and bound periodical volumes; 1500 pamphlets. **Subscriptions:** 425 journals and other serials. **Services:** Interlibrary loans;

copying; library open to medical and dental professionals. **Automated Operations:** Computerized circulation. **Computerized Information Services:** UTLAS.

★15683★
UNIVERSITY OF MANITOBA - E.K. WILLIAMS LAW LIBRARY (Law)
Robson Hall   Phone: (204) 474-9995
Winnipeg, MB, Canada R3T 2N2   Denis Marshall, Hd.Libn.
Founded: 1922. **Staff:** Prof 3; Other 12. **Subjects:** Law. **Holdings:** 112,500 books and bound periodical volumes. **Subscriptions:** 850 journals and other serials. **Services:** Interlibrary loans; copying; bibliographic and reference service for members of legal profession residing in Manitoba. **Automated Operations:** Computerized circulation. **Computerized Information Services:** QL Systems, UTLAS. **Staff:** Debra Bedford Benson, Cat.; John Davis, Ref.Libn.

★15684★
UNIVERSITY OF MANITOBA - ENGINEERING LIBRARY (Sci-Tech)
351 Engineering Bldg.   Phone: (204) 474-9445
Winnipeg, MB, Canada R3T 2N2   Patricia Routledge, Act.Hd.
Founded: 1907. **Staff:** Prof 2; Other 5. **Subjects:** Engineering - civil, electrical, agricultural, geological, mechanical. **Holdings:** 37,500 books and bound periodical volumes. **Subscriptions:** 600 journals and other serials. **Services:** Interlibrary loans; copying; SDI; library open to public. **Automated Operations:** Computerized circulation. **Computerized Information Services:** CAN/OLE, Infomart, DIALOG, QL Systems, MEDLINE, UTLAS.

★15685★
UNIVERSITY OF MANITOBA - MEDICAL LIBRARY (Med)
Medical College Bldg.
770 Bannatyne Ave.   Phone: (204) 786-4342
Winnipeg, MB, Canada R3T 0W3   Audrey M. Kerr, Hd.Med.Libn.
Founded: 1895. **Staff:** Prof 5; Other 17. **Subjects:** Medicine and basic medical sciences. **Special Collections:** History of Medicine. **Holdings:** 86,000 books and bound periodical volumes. **Subscriptions:** 1475 journals and other serials. **Services:** Interlibrary loans; bibliographic and reference services for members of the medical profession residing in Manitoba; library open to qualified users. **Automated Operations:** Computerized circulation. **Computerized Information Services:** UTLAS, MEDLINE. **Staff:** Michael Tennenhouse, Pub.Serv.Libn; Love Negrych, Cat.; Natalia Pohorecky, Ref.Libn.

★15686★
UNIVERSITY OF MANITOBA - MUSIC LIBRARY (Mus)
223 Music Bldg.   Phone: (204) 474-9567
Winnipeg, MB, Canada R3T 2N2   Vladimir Simosko, Adm.Hd.
Founded: 1965. **Staff:** Prof 1; Other 2. **Subjects:** Music reference and research, historical musicology, instruments and voice, theory and analysis of music, ethnomusicology. **Holdings:** 15,000 books and bound periodical volumes; 6000 phonograph records; 27,000 items of performance music; composers' works and scores. **Subscriptions:** 150 journals and other serials. **Services:** Interlibrary loans; library open to public with restrictions on borrowing. **Automated Operations:** Computerized circulation. **Computerized Information Services:** UTLAS. **Special Catalogs:** Phonorecord and performance music catalogs (computerized and on cards). **Staff:** Bruce Carlson, Supv.

★15687★
UNIVERSITY OF MANITOBA - ST. JOHN'S COLLEGE - LIBRARY (Rel-Theol)
400 Dysart Rd.   Phone: (204) 474-8542
Winnipeg, MB, Canada R3T 2M5   Patrick D. Wright, Libn.
Founded: 1849. **Staff:** Prof 1; Other 2. **Subjects:** Religion, Canadian studies, humanities. **Holdings:** 45,000 volumes. **Subscriptions:** 150 journals and other serials. **Services:** Interlibrary loans; copying; library open to public. **Automated Operations:** Computerized circulation. **Computerized Information Services:** UTLAS.

★15688★
UNIVERSITY OF MANITOBA - ST. PAUL'S COLLEGE - LIBRARY (Rel-Theol)
Phone: (204) 474-8585
Winnipeg, MB, Canada R3T 2M6   Fr. Harold Drake, Hd.
Founded: 1931. **Staff:** Prof 1; Other 4. **Subjects:** Religion, theology. **Special Collections:** Vatican archives on microfilm (transactions and correspondence pertaining to Canada, 1668 to present; in progress). **Holdings:** 61,000 books and bound periodical volumes. **Subscriptions:** 240 journals and other serials. **Services:** Interlibrary loans; copying; library open to public. **Automated Operations:** Computerized circulation. **Computerized Information Services:** UTLAS.

★15689★

UNIVERSITY OF MANITOBA - SCIENCE LIBRARY (Sci-Tech)
Phone: (204) 474-8171
Winnipeg, MB, Canada R3T 2N2 Yong Cha Jo, Hd.
Founded: 1906. **Staff:** Prof 2; Other 10. **Subjects:** Physical, mathematical and biological sciences; computer science; pharmacy; statistics. **Holdings:** 112,500 books and bound periodical volumes. **Subscriptions:** 1500 journals and other serials. **Services:** Interlibrary loans; copying; library open to public with restrictions. **Automated Operations:** Computerized circulation. **Computerized Information Services:** CAN/OLE, Infomart, DIALOG, UTLAS. **Staff:** W. Westelaken, Ref.Libn.; C. Brault, Ref.Libn.

★15690★

UNIVERSITY OF MARYLAND - SCHOOL OF MEDICINE - DEPT. OF PSYCHIATRY - HELEN C. TINGLEY MEMORIAL LIBRARY (Med)
Maryland Psychiatric Research Ctr.
Box 3235
Catonsville, MD 21228 Phone: (301) 747-1071
Edward D. French, Libn.
Staff: Prof 1. **Subjects:** Psychiatry and related fields. **Holdings:** 400 volumes; 50 bound periodical volumes; 50 audio cassettes; 50 reference works. **Subscriptions:** 15 journals and other serials. **Services:** Interlibrary loans; library not open to public.

★15691★

UNIVERSITY OF MARYLAND, BALTIMORE - HEALTH SCIENCES LIBRARY (Med)
111 S. Greene St.
Baltimore, MD 21201 Phone: (301) 528-7545
Cyril C.H. Feng, Libn.
Founded: 1813. **Staff:** Prof 26; Other 36. **Subjects:** Medicine, dentistry, pharmacy, nursing, social work. **Special Collections:** Crawford Medical Historical Collection; Cordell Medical Historical Collection; Grieves Dental Historical Collection; historical book collections in pharmacy, social work and nursing. **Holdings:** 119,454 books; 123,739 bound periodical volumes; University of Maryland archives. **Subscriptions:** 2792 journals and other serials. **Services:** Interlibrary loans; copying; library open to qualified public for reference use only. **Automated Operations:** Computerized cataloging, serials and circulation. **Computerized Information Services:** OCLC, DIALOG, BRS, MEDLINE. Performs searches on cost recovery basis. **Networks/Consortia:** Member of PALINET & Union Library Catalogue of Pennsylvania; Southeastern/Atlantic Regional Medical Library Services; Maryland Interlibrary Loan Organization (MILO). **Staff:** Patricia Knudsen, Dp.Dir.

★15692★

UNIVERSITY OF MARYLAND, BALTIMORE - SCHOOL OF LAW - MARSHALL LAW LIBRARY (Law)
20 N. Paca St.
Baltimore, MD 21201 Phone: (301) 528-7270
Barbara S. Gontrum, Dir.
Founded: 1843. **Staff:** Prof 6; Other 16. **Subjects:** Law. **Special Collections:** U.S. Government document depository. **Holdings:** 207,751 volumes; microforms. **Subscriptions:** 3507 journals and other serials. **Services:** Interlibrary loans; copying; library open to public. **Automated Operations:** Computerized cataloging. **Computerized Information Services:** LEXIS, OCLC, DIALOG, Westlaw. **Networks/Consortia:** Member of PALINET & Union Library Catalogue of Pennsylvania. **Staff:** Pamela Bluh, Asst.Libn., Tech.Serv.; Maxine Grosshans, Sr.Ref.Libn.; Dennis Guion, Ref.Libn.; Beverly. Rubenstein, Ref./Cat.Libn.; Ann Suh, Asst.Libn., Rd.Serv.

★15693★

UNIVERSITY OF MARYLAND, COLLEGE PARK - COLLEGE OF LIBRARY & INFORMATION SERVICES - LIBRARY (Info Sci)
College Park, MD 20742 Phone: (301) 454-6003
William G. Wilson, Libn.
Founded: 1965. **Staff:** Prof 2; Other 5. **Subjects:** Organization of knowledge, bibliography, administration, information science, computer applications for libraries, juvenile books, communication. **Holdings:** 39,000 books; 4600 bound periodical volumes; 2300 pamphlets; 154 VF drawers of pamphlets and reports; 17,600 microforms; 1600 nonprint items (570 titles). **Subscriptions:** 500 journals and other serials. **Services:** Interlibrary loans; copying; library open to public with limited circulation. **Automated Operations:** Computerized cataloging, acquisitions and serials. **Publications:** Accession Lists, monthly; orientation handouts. **Staff:** William B. Pitt, Assoc.Libn.

UNIV. OF MARYLAND, COLLEGE PARK - COLL. OF LIB. & INFO. SERV. - U.S. INFO. CTR. FOR THE UNIVERSAL DECIMAL CLASSIFICATION
See: University of Maryland, College Park - U.S. Information Center for the Universal Decimal Classification

★15694★

UNIVERSITY OF MARYLAND, COLLEGE PARK - COMPUTER SCIENCE CENTER - PROGRAM LIBRARY (Comp Sci; Info Sci)
Phone: (301) 454-4261
College Park, MD 20742 Barbara Rush, Program Libn.
Founded: 1963. **Staff:** Prof 2; Other 2. **Subjects:** Computer science, information science, mathematics, statistics. **Special Collections:** System Reference Libraries for UNIVAC 1100 series; reference manuals for IBM 4300; Maryland State Data Center (500 U.S. census publications and magnetic tapes of census statistics). **Holdings:** 3500 books; 750 bound periodical volumes; 5000 technical reports; 1000 computer usage reports; 1450 computer programs on magnetic tape; 30 computer newsletters from universities. **Subscriptions:** 125 journals and other serials. **Services:** Copying; library open to public for reference use only. **Automated Operations:** Computerized cataloging. **Publications:** Program Library Bulletin, monthly. **Special Indexes:** KWOC Index for all computer programs; KWOC Index of library's holdings of proceedings. **Staff:** Luella Murch, Asst. Program Libn.

★15695★

UNIVERSITY OF MARYLAND, COLLEGE PARK - LIBRARIES - ARCHITECTURE LIBRARY (Art; Plan)
Phone: (301) 454-4316
College Park, MD 20742 Berna E. Neal, Libn.
Founded: 1967. **Staff:** Prof 1; Other 2. **Subjects:** Architecture, urban design. **Special Collections:** Library of Dr. Robert Branner, medieval architecture historian (1000 volumes); collection on world expositions, 1851-1937 (500 volumes, pamphlets, clippings, engravings and memorabilia). **Holdings:** 20,000 books; 5000 bound periodical volumes. **Subscriptions:** 150 journals and other serials. **Services:** Interlibrary loans; copying; library open to public for reference use only. **Automated Operations:** Computerized circulation.

★15696★

UNIVERSITY OF MARYLAND, COLLEGE PARK - LIBRARIES - ART LIBRARY (Art)
Phone: (301) 454-2065
College Park, MD 20742 Courtney A. Shaw, Hd.
Founded: 1979. **Staff:** Prof 2; Other 2. **Subjects:** Art history, studio art, art education, decorative or applied arts. **Special Collections:** Decimal Index to the Art of the Low Countries; Index photographique d'art de France; emblem books. **Holdings:** 55,000 books; 10 VF drawers; 25,000 art reproduction files. **Subscriptions:** 190 journals and other serials. **Services:** Interlibrary loans; copying; library open to public for reference use only. **Automated Operations:** Computerized cataloging, acquisitions and serials. **Computerized Information Services:** DIALOG, SDC. **Staff:** Patricia Lynagh, Ref.Libn.

★15697★

UNIVERSITY OF MARYLAND, COLLEGE PARK - LIBRARIES - CHARLES E. WHITE MEMORIAL LIBRARY (Sci-Tech)
Phone: (301) 454-2609
College Park, MD 20742 Elizabeth W. McElroy, Libn.
Staff: Prof 2; Other 2. **Subjects:** Chemistry, biochemistry, spectroscopy, microbiology, bacteriology, nuclear chemistry. **Holdings:** 26,000 books; 22,000 bound periodical volumes; 2000 cartridges of microfilm; 1250 dissertations. **Subscriptions:** 440 journals and other serials. **Services:** Interlibrary loans; copying; library open to public for reference use only. **Automated Operations:** Computerized cataloging, acquisitions and serials. **Computerized Information Services:** DIALOG, SDC, MEDLARS. Performs searches on cost recovery basis.

★15698★

UNIVERSITY OF MARYLAND, COLLEGE PARK - LIBRARIES - EAST ASIA COLLECTION (Area-Ethnic)
Phone: (301) 454-5459
College Park, MD 20742 Frank Joseph Shulman, Cur.
Founded: 1963. **Staff:** Prof 3; Other 2. **Subjects:** Social sciences (Japanese, Chinese and Korean languages); modern Japanese, Chinese and Korean history and literature; World War II (Pacific area). **Special Collections:** Gordon W. Prange Collection: Allied Occupation of Japan, 1945-1952 (35,000 Japanese-language monographs; 10,000 titles of Japanese magazines; 12,000 titles of Japanese newspapers; 20 file cabinets of unique censored materials from Supreme Commander, Allied Powers' Censorship Detachment); papers of Justin Williams, Sr. (69 filing boxes of material relating to political aspects of the Allied Occupation of Japan). **Holdings:** 50,000 books; 4000 bound periodical volumes; 1492 reels of microfilm; 232 filing boxes of U.S. Army, Allied Translator and Interpreter Service documents and transcripts of International Military Tribunal for the Far East; 100 photograph albums relating to Japanese history and naval affairs; U.S. Office of Strategic Bombing Survey materials on the interrogation of Japanese officials.

Subscriptions: 400 journals and other serials; 29 newspapers. Services: Interlibrary loans; collection open to public for reference use only. Automated Operations: Computerized cataloging, acquisitions, serials and circulation. Publications: Microfilm Edition of Censored Periodicals, 1945-1949; User's Guide to the Gordon W. Prange Collection, I. Special Catalogs: Newspapers and periodicals from period of Allied Occupation of Japan - card files (in preparation); extensive guide to Justin Williams papers.

★15699★
UNIVERSITY OF MARYLAND, COLLEGE PARK - LIBRARIES - ENGINEERING & PHYSICAL SCIENCES LIBRARY (Sci-Tech)
College Park, MD 20742
Phone: (301) 454-3037
Herbert N. Foerstel, Hd.Libn.
Founded: 1953. Staff: Prof 6; Other 13. Subjects: Astronomy, computer science, engineering, geology, mathematics, oceanography, physics. Special Collections: Patent Depository Library (20 year backfile of patents); R. von Mises Collection (1100 titles; 217 boxes of reprints); Max Born Collection (650 titles and 6 boxes of reprints in theoretical mathematics and physics). Holdings: 94,358 books; 90,031 bound periodical volumes; 95,961 hard copy reports; 613,610 microfiche; 2842 reels of microfilm; 112,228 reports on microcard. Subscriptions: 1559 journals and other serials. Services: Copying; library open to public for reference use only. Automated Operations: Computerized cataloging, serials, acquisitions and circulation. Computerized Information Services: DIALOG, SDC, MEDLARS, OCLC. Publications: New Books, monthly - to departments and library representatives.

★15700★
UNIVERSITY OF MARYLAND, COLLEGE PARK - LIBRARIES - HISTORICAL MANUSCRIPTS AND ARCHIVES DEPARTMENT (Hist)
College Park, MD 20742
Phone: (301) 454-2318
Lauren R. Brown, Cur.
Staff: Prof 2; Other 1. Special Collections: Personal and organizational papers relating to Maryland (Greenbelt Homes, Inc. Collection; papers of Millard Tydings); archives of trade unions (Tobacco Workers and Cigar Makers); university archives and publications; papers of faculty members; University of Maryland, College Park theses and dissertations. Holdings: 1000 cubic feet of archival material. Services: Department open to public for reference use only. Publications: Personal and Organizational Papers Relating to Maryland; Greenbelt, Maryland: A Guide to Further Sources; University Fact Book.

★15701★
UNIVERSITY OF MARYLAND, COLLEGE PARK - LIBRARIES - KATHERINE ANNE PORTER ROOM (Hum)
College Park, MD 20742
Phone: (301) 454-4020
Donald Farren, Assoc.Dir., Spec.Coll.
Staff: Prof 1; Other 1. Subjects: The personal library and memorabilia of the author, Katherine Anne Porter. Holdings: 2000 books. Services: Room open to public for reference use only.

★15702★
UNIVERSITY OF MARYLAND, COLLEGE PARK - LIBRARIES - MARYLANDIA DEPARTMENT (Rare Book)
McKeldin Library
College Park, MD 20742
Phone: (301) 454-3035
Peter H. Curtis, Cur.
Staff: Prof 2; Other 3. Subjects: Maryland history - political, social, economic, industrial, agricultural. Special Collections: Maryland state, county and municipal documents (400 cubic feet). Holdings: 50,000 volumes; 50 drawers of maps. Subscriptions: 300 journals and other serials. Services: Department open to public for reference use only.

★15703★
UNIVERSITY OF MARYLAND, COLLEGE PARK - LIBRARIES - MUSIC LIBRARY (Mus)
College Park, MD 20742
Phone: (301) 454-3036
Neil Ratliff, Fine Arts Libn.
Founded: 1958. Staff: Prof 4; Other 4. Subjects: Music, dance. Special Collections: American Bandmasters Association Research Center; Music Educators National Conference Historical Center; College Band Directors National Association Archives; National Association of College Wind and Percussion Instructors Research Center; Jacob Coopersmith Library of Handeliana; Wallenstein Collection of Orchestra Music (29,628 items); Contemporary Music Project (CMP) Lending Service; Archives of the Music Library Association. Holdings: 22,000 books and bound periodical volumes; 27,216 music scores 19,307 phonograph records; 5292 Special Collections; 671 VF drawers. Subscriptions: 324 journals and other serials. Services: Interlibrary loans; copying; library open to public for reference use only. Automated Operations: Computerized cataloging, acquisitions, serials and

circulation. Computerized Information Services: DIALOG, SDC.

★15704★
UNIVERSITY OF MARYLAND, COLLEGE PARK - LIBRARIES - MUSIC LIBRARY - INTERNATIONAL PIANO ARCHIVES AT MARYLAND (Mus)
Hornbake Library
College Park, MD 20742
Neil Ratliff, Fine Arts Lib.
Founded: 1965. Subjects: Music, performance practice, piano and harpsichord. Holdings: 400 books and pamphlets; 15,000 phonograph records; 1100 recorded tapes; 2300 piano roll records; 4000 scores; 2 historic instruments; music manuscripts.

★15705★
UNIVERSITY OF MARYLAND, COLLEGE PARK - LIBRARIES NONPRINT MEDIA SERVICES (Aud-Vis)
Hornbake Library
College Park, MD 20742
Phone: (301) 454-4723
Allan C. Rough, Hd., Nonprint Media Serv.
Founded: 1972. Staff: Prof 2; Other 8. Subjects: Physical sciences, sociology, history, English literature and theater, women's studies, business & management. Special Collections: Video cassettes of Watergate hearings (162); NOVA (series) video cassettes (135); BBC Shakespeare Series (complete plays on videocassette); U.S. Air Force Film Collection (600); USDA Food and Nutrition Information Center's Deposit AV Collection (3250 items). Holdings: 12 laser videodiscs; 40 slide sets; 980 16mm films; 1954 video cassettes. Services: Services open to public by arrangement with department head. Automated Operations: Computerized circulation and media booking system. Special Catalogs: Subject "Mediagraphies" (media bibliographies, 102). Staff: Jack Lattimore, Nonprint Libn.; Angela Domanico, Oper.Supv.; Paul Malec, Electronic Media Sys.Mgr.; Philip Fryer, Film Unit Supv.

★15706★
UNIVERSITY OF MARYLAND, COLLEGE PARK - LIBRARIES - RARE BOOKS AND LITERARY MANUSCRIPTS DEPARTMENT (Rare Book)
College Park, MD 20742
Phone: (301) 454-3035
Staff: Prof I. Subjects: Rare books in a wide range of scholarly fields, American and English authors of the modern period. Special Collections: Katherine Anne Porter papers; Djuna Barnes papers; modern first editions; mazarinades; Ralph D. Remley collection on the Book Arts; type specimen books; French plays. Holdings: 25,000 books; 500 cubic feet of manuscripts.

★15707★
UNIVERSITY OF MARYLAND, COLLEGE PARK - LIBRARIES - WOMEN'S STUDIES PAMPHLET COLLECTION (Soc Sci)
Reference Department
McKeldin Library
College Park, MD 20742
Phone: (301) 454-5704
Susan Cardinale, Coord.
Staff: 1. Subjects: Women's studies, feminism, women's liberation movement. Holdings: 1000 items. Services: Collection open to public for reference use only.

★15708★
UNIVERSITY OF MARYLAND, COLLEGE PARK - M. LUCIA JAMES CURRICULUM LABORATORY (Educ)
College of Education
College Park, MD 20742
Phone: (301) 454-5466
Dr. Charles Brand, Dir.
Staff: Prof 2; Other 2. Subjects: Education - elementary, secondary, teacher, special, art, early childhood, curriculum development; guidance and counseling. Special Collections: Curriculum guides from all states and major cities of U.S.; special subject collections by subject/name. Holdings: 25,000 volumes; reports of curriculum projects; microfiche; 60 filmstrips; 184 slides; 140 transparencies; 800 multimedia kits and manipulative teaching aids; 44 maps; 150 tapes; 76 VF drawers; 44 VF drawers of resource materials; 350 standardized test specimen sets. Subscriptions: 125 journals and other serials. Services: Copying; transparency making; laboratory open to public for reference use only. Publications: Bibliographies; recent acquisitions and special reports on curriculum materials - distributed to students, staff and faculty of the College of Education; Tabs on the Lab, bimonthly newsletter. Staff: Janice Newman, Asst.Dir.

★15709★
UNIVERSITY OF MARYLAND, COLLEGE PARK - MARYLAND CENTER FOR PRODUCTIVITY AND QUALITY OF WORKING LIFE - LIB. (Soc Sci)
College of Business and Management
College Park, MD 20742
Phone: (301) 454-6688
Jan R. Lawrence, Commun.Mgr.
Founded: 1977. Staff: Prof 3; Other 2. Subjects: Productivity, productivity measurement, management development, participative management, labor-management cooperation, gainsharing. Holdings: 1100 books. Subscriptions:

30 journals and other serials. **Services:** library open to public. **Publications:** Maryland Workplace (newsletter), bimonthly - free upon request.

★15710★

UNIVERSITY OF MARYLAND, COLLEGE PARK - NATIONAL CLEARINGHOUSE FOR COMMUTER PROGRAMS (Trans)
1195 Adele H. Stamp Union   Phone: (301) 454-5274
College Park, MD 20742   Dr. Barbara Jacoby, Dir.
Staff: Prof 1; Other 1. **Subjects:** Student commuters, housing, transportation, tenant/landlord relations, energy, orientation. **Holdings:** 8 VF drawers of manuscripts, reports, handbooks. **Services:** Copying; clearinghouse open to public by appointment. **Publications:** The Commuter, quarterly - to members.

★15711★

UNIVERSITY OF MARYLAND, COLLEGE PARK - U.S. INFORMATION CENTER FOR THE UNIVERSAL DECIMAL CLASSIFICATION (Info Sci)
College of Library & Info.Serv.   Phone: (301) 454-3785
College Park, MD 20742   Hans H. Wellisch, Dir.
Staff: Prof 1. **Subjects:** Universal Decimal Classification (UDC). **Special Collections:** UDC schedules in English and in the major languages of Europe and Asia. **Holdings:** 500 books. **Services:** Interlibrary loans; copying; center open to public.

★15712★

UNIVERSITY OF MARYLAND, SOLOMONS - CTR. FOR ENVIRONMENT & ENVIRONMENTAL STUD. - CHESAPEAKE BIOL. LAB. - LIB. (Sci-Tech)
Box 38   Phone: (301) 326-4281
Solomons, MD 20688   Kathleen Heil-Zampier, Libn.
Staff: Prof 1. **Subjects:** Marine research, biology, and zoology; oceanography; aquatic microbiology. **Special Collections:** Freshwater sponge reprints; shellfish reprints (1200); larvel fishes (7000 reprints). **Holdings:** 4000 books; 4100 bound periodical volumes; 3500 reports and documents; 2000 manuscripts; 1000 archival items; 17,000 reprints; 55 VF drawers of laboratory publications. **Subscriptions:** 103 journals and other serials. **Services:** Interlibrary loans; library open to public. **Networks/Consortia:** Member of Maryland Interlibrary Loan Organization (MILO). **Publications:** Newsletter, monthly; annual bibliography of serials - both for internal distribution only.

★15713★

UNIVERSITY OF MASSACHUSETTS, AMHERST - LABOR RELATIONS & RESEARCH CENTER LIBRARY (Soc Sci)
Draper Hall   Phone: (413) 545-2884
Amherst, MA 01003   Janice Tausky, Libn.
Founded: 1965. **Staff:** 2. **Subjects:** Industrial relations. **Holdings:** 3000 books; 10,000 pamphlets. **Subscriptions:** 400 journals and other serials. **Services:** Interlibrary loans; copying; library open to public with restrictions. **Staff:** Shameem Syed, Asst.Libn.

★15714★

UNIVERSITY OF MASSACHUSETTS, AMHERST - LIBRARY - DEPARTMENT OF ARCHIVES (Hist; Area-Ethnic)
                                         Phone: (413) 545-2780
Amherst, MA 01003   John Kendall, Act.Archv.
Staff: Prof 1; Other 3. **Subjects:** University of Massachusetts, Afro-American studies. **Special Collections:** Records of the University of Massachusetts; faculty and student theses and papers; papers of W.E.B. Du Bois, Joseph Obrebski, Harvey Swados, Robert Francis, Horace Mann Bond, Erasmus Darwin Hudson, Maurice A. Donahue; Linguistic Atlas of New England; Samizdat (Soviet underground writings); Renaissance diplomatic documents (unique microfilm, 1850 reels); Thurber-Woolson collection of botanical manuscripts, 1803-1918. **Holdings:** 4000 linear feet of records, manuscripts, clippings, photographs, maps, building plans, microfilm, audiotapes and books. **Services:** Copying; department open to public. **Special Catalogs:** The Papers of W.E.B. Du Bois: A Guide; The Horace Mann Bond Papers: A Guide; A Summary Guide to the Archives and Manuscripts Collection.

★15715★

UNIVERSITY OF MASSACHUSETTS, AMHERST - LIBRARY - SPECIAL COLLECTIONS AND RARE BOOKS (Rare Book)
                                         Phone: (413) 545-0274
Amherst, MA 01003   John D. Kendall, Hd.
Staff: Prof 1; Other 1. **Subjects:** History of botany and entomology to 1900, historical geography and cartography of Northeastern United States to 1900; history of Massachusetts and New England; antislavery movement in New England. **Holdings:** Alspach Yeats Collection (600 items); Federal Land Bank Collection (270 items); Robert Francis Collection (100 items); Binet's French

Revolution Collection (1524 items); Massachusetts Pamphlet Collection (985); 12,000 books. **Services:** Copying; collections open to public. **Automated Operations:** Computerized cataloging, acquisitions, serials, and circulation (through main library). **Computerized Information Services:** OCLC. **Networks/Consortia:** Member of CRL; NELINET; HILC, Inc.

★15716★

UNIVERSITY OF MASSACHUSETTS, AMHERST - MORRILL BIOLOGICAL & GEOLOGICAL SCIENCES LIBRARY (Sci-Tech)
214 Morrill Science Ctr.   Phone: (413) 545-2674
Amherst, MA 01003   James L. Craig, Libn.
Founded: 1963. **Staff:** Prof 3; Other 6. **Subjects:** Botany, zoology, geology, microbiology. **Special Collections:** Arthur Cleveland Bent (ornithology); Guy Chester Crampton (entomology and evolutionary biology). **Holdings:** 97,000 volumes; 100,000 maps. **Subscriptions:** 1000 journals and other serials. **Services:** Interlibrary loans; copying; library open to public for reference use only; borrowing privileges upon application. **Networks/Consortia:** Member of Boston Library Consortium. **Publications:** New Acquisitions List, weekly, internal and limited external distribution; Literature Guides, irregular - for internal distribution only. **Staff:** Laurence Feldman, Br.Libn.; Alena Chadwick, Ref.Libn.

★15717★

UNIVERSITY OF MASSACHUSETTS, AMHERST - MUSIC LIBRARY (Mus)
Fine Arts Center, Rm. 149   Phone: (413) 545-2870
Amherst, MA 01003   Pamela Juengling, Mus.Libn.
Staff: Prof 1; Other 3. **Subjects:** Music. **Special Collections:** Alma Werfel Collection; Howard LeBow Collection; Philp Bezanson papers. **Holdings:** 13,000 books; 3000 bound periodical volumes; 9000 music scores; 11,000 phonograph records; 600 other items. **Subscriptions:** 250 journals and other serials. **Services:** Interlibrary loans; copying; library open to public. **Automated Operations:** Computerized cataloging and acquisitions. **Computerized Information Services:** DIALOG, OCLC. Performs searches on cost recovery basis. Contact Person: Jean Haley, 545-0150. **Networks/Consortia:** Member of NELINET. **Special Catalogs:** Catalog of recording analytics (card).

★15718★

UNIVERSITY OF MASSACHUSETTS, AMHERST - PHYSICAL SCIENCES LIBRARY (Sci-Tech)
Graduate Research Ctr.   Phone: (413) 545-1370
Amherst, MA 01003   Eric Esau, Libn.
Founded: 1971. **Staff:** Prof 3; Other 6. **Subjects:** Engineering - chemical, civil, electrical, industrial, mechanical; chemistry; physics and astronomy; mathematics and statistics; aeronautics and astronautics; computer science; food technology; polymer science; wood technology. **Holdings:** 85,000 books; 50,000 bound periodical volumes; 600,000 technical reports on microfiche. **Subscriptions:** 1700 journals and other serials. **Services:** Interlibrary loans; copying; library open to public for reference use only; borrowing privileges on application. **Automated Operations:** Computerized cataloging and acquisitions. **Computerized Information Services:** DIALOG. **Networks/Consortia:** Member of Boston Library Consortium. **Staff:** Linda Ray Arny, Ref./Asst.Br.Libn.; Alena Chadwick, Ref.Libn.

★15719★

UNIVERSITY OF MASSACHUSETTS MEDICAL SCHOOL & WORCESTER DISTRICT MEDICAL SOCIETY - LIBRARY (Med)
55 N. Lake Ave.   Phone: (617) 856-2511
Worcester, MA 01605   Donald J. Morton, Dir.
Founded: 1966. **Staff:** Prof 9; Other 11. **Subjects:** Medicine, health sciences, human biology. **Special Collections:** Scientific government publications depository; history of medicine. **Holdings:** 25,000 books; 80,000 bound periodical volumes. **Subscriptions:** 2350 journals and other serials. **Services:** Interlibrary loans; copying; SDI; library open to public. **Automated Operations:** Computerized cataloging and serials. **Computerized Information Services:** MEDLINE, BRS, DIALOG, SDC, MEDLARS, OCLC. **Networks/Consortia:** Member of Worcester Area Cooperating Libraries (WACL); Boston Library Consortium; Central Massachusetts Consortium of Health Related Libraries (CMCHRL); Greater Northeastern Regional Medical Library Program; Massachusetts Conference of Chief Librarians in Public Higher Educational Institutions. (MCCLPHEI). **Staff:** Beverly Shattuck, Asst.Dir., Pub.Serv.; Jean M. Conelley, Asst.Dir., Tech.Serv.

★15720★

UNIVERSITY OF MEDICINE AND DENTISTRY OF NEW JERSEY AT NEWARK - GEORGE F. SMITH LIBRARY (Med)
100 Bergen St.   Phone: (201) 456-4580
Newark, NJ 07103   Philip Rosenstein, Dir. of Libs.
Staff: Prof 15; Other 15. **Subjects:** Health sciences. **Special Collections:**

Rare book collection; archival collection. **Holdings:** 35,000 books; 70,000 bound periodical volumes; audiovisual aids. **Subscriptions:** 2252 journals and other serials. **Services:** Interlibrary loans; copying; SDI; bibliographic retrieval; library open to public for reference use only. **Automated Operations:** Computerized cataloging, acquisitions, serials and circulation. **Computerized Information Services:** DIALOG, SDC, BRS, NLM, OCLC. **Networks/Consortia:** Member of Greater Northeastern Regional Medical Library Program. **Publications:** Periodicals holdings, biennial; Library Newsletter, 4/year. **Special Catalogs:** Media Catalog (book format); Rare Book Catalog (book). **Staff:** Reginald W. Smith, Assoc.Dir. of Libs.Victor Basile, Asst.Libn., Tech.Proc.; Madeline Taylor, Ser.Libn.; George Sprung, Ref.Libn.; Esther Meiboom, Hosp.Libn.; Sushila Kapadia, Info.Sys.Libn.; Melvin White, Chf., Circ.; Stuart Sammis, Archv.; Valentine Allen, ILL; Laura Barrett, AV Libn.; Janice Rettino, Mgr., Lib.Dev.; Robert Cupryk, Ref.Libn.; Daria Gorman, Cat.; Barbara Packard, Chf.Cat.

★15721★

UNIVERSITY OF MEDICINE AND DENTISTRY OF NEW JERSEY - RUTGERS MEDICAL SCHOOL - MEDIA LIBRARY (Med; Aud-Vis)
University Heights   Phone: (201) 463-4460
Piscataway, NJ 08854   Adrienne Berenbaum, Libn.
Staff: Prof 1. **Subjects:** Medicine and related fields. **Holdings:** 1500 books; 2000 AV items. **Services:** Interlibrary loans; library open to public for reference use only. **Networks/Consortia:** Member of Medical Resources Consortium of Central New Jersey (MEDCORE).

★15722★

UNIV. OF MEDICINE & DENTISTRY OF NJ - RUTGERS MED. SCHOOL - MIDDLESEX GENERAL-UNIV. HOSPITAL - HEALTH SCI.LIB. (Med)
CN 19   Phone: (201) 937-7606
New Brunswick, NJ 08903   Mary R. Scanlon, Libn.
Founded: 1982. **Staff:** Prof 2; Other 5. **Subjects:** Clinical medicine, hospital administration, nursing. **Holdings:** 2754 books; 7000 bound periodical volumes; 300 AV items. **Subscriptions:** 336 journals and other serials. **Services:** Interlibrary loans; copying; library open to public for reference use only. **Computerized Information Services:** MEDLINE, DIALOG. Performs free searches. Contact Person: Kerry O'Rourke, 937-7604. **Networks/Consortia:** Member of Medical Resources Consortium of Central New Jersey (MEDCORE). **Publications:** Library Notes, bimonthly - available upon request. **Staff:** Kerry O'Rourke, Ref.Libn.

★15723★

UNIV. OF MEDICINE AND DENTISTRY OF NEW JERSEY - SCHOOL OF OSTEOPATHIC MED. - DR. JERROLD S. SCHWARTZ MEM. LIB. (Med)
Kennedy Memorial Hospital
University Medical Ctr. - Stratford Div.
18 E. Laurel Rd.   Phone: (609) 784-4000
Stratford, NJ 08084   Judith Schuback, Libn.
Staff: Prof 2; Other 2. **Subjects:** Medicine, nursing, hospital administration, allied health sciences. **Special Collections:** Osteopathy. **Holdings:** 2500 books; 6000 bound periodical volumes; 200 AV programs; 250 government documents; 2 vertical files; 200 reels of microfilm. **Subscriptions:** 450 journals and other serials. **Services:** Interlibrary loans; copying; SDI; library open to public by appointment. **Automated Operations:** Computerized cataloging. **Computerized Information Services:** MEDLARS, BRS. Performs free searches for staff. Contact Person: Janice Skica, 435-2421. **Networks/Consortia:** Member of Southwest New Jersey Consortium for Health Information Services; Health Sciences Library Association of New Jersey. **Publications:** Selected Acquisitions, quarterly; newsletter, quarterly - both for internal distribution only. **Formerly:** New Jersey School of Osteopathic Medicine. **Staff:** Janice Skica, Med.Libn.

★15724★

UNIVERSITY OF MIAMI - DOROTHY & LEWIS ROSENSTIEL SCHOOL OF MARINE & ATMOSPHERIC SCIENCES - LIBRARY (Sci-Tech)
4600 Rickenbacker Causeway   Phone: (305) 361-4007
Miami, FL 33149   Kay K. Hale, Libn.
Staff: Prof 1; Other 4. **Subjects:** Marine sciences (especially tropical), biology, fisheries, marine geology and geophysics, ocean engineering, physical and chemical oceanography, atmospheric sciences. **Holdings:** 39,000 volumes; 25,000 reprints; 600 reels of microfilm; 600 microfiche; 1242 microcards; 45 sets of oceanographic expedition reports; 250 atlases. **Subscriptions:** 1000 journals and other serials. **Services:** Interlibrary loans; copying; library open to public for reference use only. **Computerized Information Services:** DIALOG, OCLC. **Networks/Consortia:** Member of SOLINET.

★15725★

UNIVERSITY OF MIAMI - LOWE ART MUSEUM LIBRARY (Art)
1301 Stanford Dr.   Phone: (305) 284-3535
Coral Gables, FL 33146   Ms. Zan Gay, Libn.
Founded: 1971. **Subjects:** Art history. **Holdings:** 3000 books; 1500 unbound periodical volumes; 3500 museum exhibition catalogs. **Subscriptions:** 14 journals and other serials. **Services:** Library open to public by appointment. **Staff:** Lucile Ball, Libn.

★15726★

UNIVERSITY OF MIAMI - MORTON COLLECTANEA (Sci-Tech)
Box 8204   Phone: (305) 284-3741
Coral Gables, FL 33124   Dr. Julia F. Morton, Dir.
Founded: 1932. **Staff:** Prof 1; Other 2. **Subjects:** Economic botany. **Special Collections:** Tropical fruits and vegetables; poisonous plants; medicinal plants; edible wild plants; aquatic plants; honeybee plants; horticulture. **Holdings:** 5800 books; 3000 unbound journals; 186 VF drawers of plant species subject files. **Subscriptions:** 25 journals and other serials. **Services:** Copying; consultations; library open to scientists and students from other institutions. **Publications:** Communications.

★15727★

UNIVERSITY OF MIAMI - RICHTER LIBRARY - ARCHIVES DIVISION (Hist)
    Phone: (305) 284-3247
Coral Gables, FL 33124
Subjects: University history, 1926 to present; Florida. **Holdings:** 362 linear feet of records and correspondence of the founders and first presidents of the university, noncurrent faculty personnel records; tape recordings of campus events; basketball game films; 55 literary manuscripts. **Services:** Copying; archives open to public.

★15728★

UNIVERSITY OF MIAMI - SCHOOL OF LAW LIBRARY (Law)
Box 248087   Phone: (305) 284-2250
Coral Gables, FL 33124   Westwell R. Daniels, Law Libn.
Staff: Prof 6; Other 18. **Subjects:** Law - Anglo-American, Latin American, Caribbean area, European. **Holdings:** 280,000 books and bound periodical volumes; 32,000 microforms. **Subscriptions:** 4100 journals and other serials. **Services:** Interlibrary loans; library open to those doing legal research. **Automated Operations:** Computerized cataloging. **Computerized Information Services:** LEXIS, Westlaw, OCLC. **Networks/Consortia:** Member of SOLINET. **Staff:** Kathryne B. Stokes, Assoc.Libn.; Leila S. Glenn, Cat.Helen M. Rogers, Ref.

★15729★

UNIVERSITY OF MIAMI - SCHOOL OF MEDICINE - BASCOM PALMER EYE INSTITUTE - LIBRARY (Med)
Ann Bates Leach Eye Hospital
900 N.W. 17th St.
Box 016880   Phone: (305) 326-6078
Miami, FL 33101   Reva Hurtes, Libn.
Founded: 1962. **Staff:** Prof 1; Other 2. **Subjects:** Ophthalmology, visual optics, visual physiology and anatomy. **Special Collections:** Historical and rare books (600 volumes). **Holdings:** 8000 volumes; AV materials. **Subscriptions:** 158 journals and other serials. **Services:** Interlibrary loans; copying; SDI; library open to public on a limited basis. **Computerized Information Services:** BRS.

★15730★

UNIVERSITY OF MIAMI - SCHOOL OF MEDICINE - LOUIS CALDER MEMORIAL LIBRARY (Med)
Box 016950   Phone: (305) 547-6441
Miami, FL 33101   Henry L. Lemkau, Jr., Dir.
Founded: 1952. **Staff:** Prof 10; Other 25. **Subjects:** Medicine, nursing. **Special Collections:** Weinstein Collection containing paramedical literature (461 volumes); Ophthalmology Collection (6770 volumes); History of Medicine Collection (3584 volumes); Florida Collection (273 volumes); rare books (501 volumes). **Holdings:** 52,781 books; 76,237 bound periodical volumes; 620 Florida pamphlets; 152 linear feet of archives; 20 linear feet of clipping files; 1821 illustrations; 212 medallions; 1151 portraits; 256 dissertations; 296 volumes of faculty publications; 1000 classics. **Subscriptions:** 1884 journals and other serials. **Services:** Interlibrary loans; copying; SDI; library open to health science personnel and institutions of Southern Florida. **Computerized Information Services:** MEDLINE, DIALOG, BRS, SDC, OCLC. **Networks/Consortia:** Member of Consortium of Southern Biomedical Libraries; Southeastern/Atlantic Regional Medical Library Services; Miami Health Sciences Library Consortium (MHSLC); SOLINET. **Publications:** Bulletin; guide; Fee Structure; Periodicals Currently Received. **Staff:** Flora H. Wellington, Coll.Spec.; August La Rocco, Spec. Projects Libn.; Dorian Martyn,

Hd.Tech.Serv.; Teresita D. Sayus, Circ.Libn.David Olson, Ref.Libn.; Arlene Volz, Ref.Libn.; Lauri Chait, Asst.Cat.; Isabel S. Caballero, Hist. of Med.Libn.; Rosa Gomez, Per.Coord.; Amalia de la Vega, ILL Coord.; Suzetta C. Burrows, Assoc.Dir./Media Prog.; Mary P. Dillon, Assoc.Dir./Lib.Prog.

★15731★
UNIVERSITY OF MIAMI - SCHOOL OF MUSIC - ALBERT PICK MUSIC LIBRARY (Mus)
Coral Gables, FL 33124
Phone: (305) 284-2429
Nancy Kobialka, Music Libn.
Founded: 1957. **Staff:** Prof 2; Other 3. **Subjects:** Music scores and recordings. **Special Collections:** Autographed recordings (composers and performers); ethnic recordings, especially Latin American, Yiddish, Jazz; Inter-American Music Archive; Handleman Institute of Recorded Sound Archives (25,000 uncataloged recordings); Yiddish music scores and recordings. **Holdings:** 26,000 music scores; 16,700 recordings. **Subscriptions:** 180 journals and other serials. **Services:** Interlibrary loans; library open to public for reference use only. **Automated Operations:** Computerized cataloging. **Computerized Information Services:** OCLC. **Networks/Consortia:** Member of SOLINET. **Special Catalogs:** Inter-American Music Archive (card). **Staff:** Holly Oberle, Music Cat.

★15732★
UNIVERSITY OF MICHIGAN - AEROSPACE ENGINEERING DEPARTMENTAL LIBRARY (Sci-Tech)
221 Aerospace Engineering Bldg.
Ann Arbor, MI 48109
Phone: (313) 764-7200
Jackie Kuczborski, Sec./Libn.
Staff: 1. **Subjects:** Aerospace science, plasma physics, fluid mechanics, aerodynamics, mathematics, structures and elasticity. **Holdings:** 1000 books; 6000 NASA reports, departmental dissertations. **Subscriptions:** 20 journals and other serials. **Services:** Library open to public with permission of the department chairman.

★15733★
UNIVERSITY OF MICHIGAN - ALFRED TAUBMAN MEDICAL LIBRARY (Med)
1135 E. Catherine
Ann Arbor, MI 48109
Phone: (313) 764-1210
L. Yvonne Wulff, Hd.
Founded: 1920. **Staff:** Prof 9; Other 26. **Subjects:** Basic medical sciences, clinical medicine, nursing, pharmacy, history of medicine. **Special Collections:** Crummer Collection (History of Medicine); Warthin Collection (Dance of Death). **Holdings:** 260,334 books and bound periodical volumes. **Subscriptions:** 2480 journals and other serials. **Services:** Interlibrary loans; copying; SDI. **Automated Operations:** Computerized cataloging, acquisitions and circulation. **Computerized Information Services:** DIALOG, BRS, SDC, OCLC, NLM, RLIN. **Networks/Consortia:** Member of Greater Midwest Regional Medical Library Network (Region 3). **Staff:** Betty A. Peck, Adm.Asst.; Helen F. Meranda, Rare Bks.Coord.; Diane G. Schwartz, Ref.Hd.; Sandra C. Dow, Ref.Libn.; Whitney K. Field, Circ.Hd.; Nancy J. Rosenzweig, Reserve Supv.; Doris M. Mahony, Ref.Libn.; Dottie Eakin, Pub.Serv.Coord.; Barbara L. Shipman, Database Coord.; Marilynn Simpson, ILL Hd.

★15734★
UNIVERSITY OF MICHIGAN - ART & ARCHITECTURE LIBRARY (Art; Plan)
2106 Art & Architecture Bldg.
Ann Arbor, MI 48109
Phone: (313) 764-1303
Peggy Ann Kusnerz, Libn.
Staff: Prof 2; Other 4. **Subjects:** Architecture, art history, urban and regional planning, landscape architecture, applied art, art education, photography. **Special Collections:** Jens Jensen landscape drawings. **Holdings:** 45,000 books; 82 VF drawers of pamphlets; 1500 photographs; 35,000 slides; 650 maps; 477 prints; 2000 drawings. **Subscriptions:** 450 journals and other serials; 5 newspapers. **Services:** Interlibrary loans; copying; library open to public with restrictions. **Automated Operations:** Computerized cataloging and acquisitions. **Computerized Information Services:** RLIN. **Networks/Consortia:** Member of RLG. **Publications:** Guide Series - available upon request. **Staff:** Dorothy Shields, Asst.Libn.

★15735★
UNIVERSITY OF MICHIGAN - ASIA LIBRARY (Area-Ethnic)
Hatcher Graduate Library, 4th Fl.
Ann Arbor, MI 48109
Phone: (313) 764-0406
Weiying Wan, Hd.
Founded: 1947. **Staff:** Prof 7; Other 6. **Subjects:** East Asian humanities and the social sciences, including anthropology, archeology, calligraphy, communism, drama, theater, economics, education, ethics, fine arts, geography, history, journalism, linguistics, phonology, library science, military history, military science, music, political science, religion, sociology. **Special Collections:** Union Research Institute Classified Files on China; Red Guards materials, classified files on the Cultural Revolution; rare editions of Chinese fiction in Japanese collections; Ming local gazetteers and literary collections; National Peking Library Rare Book Collection on microfilm; British Public

Record Office Archives on China; non-Buddhist Tun-huang materials from the British Museum and the Bibliotheque Nationale; Japanese local history; materials on the Occupation of Japan; Japanese literature; Japanese Diet Proceedings; Bartlett Collection of Botanical Works and Materia Medica; Kamada Collection of Pre-war Japanese Works. **Holdings:** 200,825 volumes in Chinese; 168,117 volumes in Japanese; 1612 volumes in Korean; 15,554 reels of microfilm and 12,239 sheets of microfiche in Chinese; 5636 reels of microfilm and 5041 sheets of microfiche in Japanese. **Subscriptions:** 1654 journals and other serials; 29 newspapers. **Services:** Interlibrary loans; copying. **Publications:** Selective List of New Acquisitions, bimonthly. **Staff:** Masaei Saito, Asst.Hd.; Choo Suh, Sr. Japanese Libn.; Sharon Ying, Chinese Cat.Supv.; Wei-Yi Ma, Chinese Bibliog.; Mei-Ying Lin, Chinese Cat.; Takaharu Yamakawa, Japanese Cat.

★15736★
UNIVERSITY OF MICHIGAN - BIOLOGICAL STATION LIBRARY (Sci-Tech)
Pellston, MI 49769
Phone: (616) 539-8048
Patricia B. Yocum, Hd.
Subjects: Zoology, botany, ichthyology, parisitology, limnology, ornithology. **Holdings:** 11,500 volumes; 1700 station papers. **Subscriptions:** 69 journals and other serials. **Services:** Library open only during summer. **Remarks:** Telephone number in Ann Arbor, MI is (313) 764-1494.

★15737★
UNIVERSITY OF MICHIGAN - BUREAU OF GOVERNMENT LIBRARY (Soc Sci)
100A Rackham Bldg.
Ann Arbor, MI 48109
Phone: (313) 763-3185
Founded: 1914. **Staff:** 2. **Subjects:** Administration, finance, taxation, public policy, personnel. **Holdings:** 59,499 volumes; 91 VF drawers of pamphlets and newspaper clippings; 247 reels of microfilm. **Subscriptions:** 145 journals and other serials. **Services:** Interlibrary loans; library open to public. **Remarks:** Includes Institute of Public Policy Studies materials.

★15738★
UNIVERSITY OF MICHIGAN - BURN CENTER - LIBRARY (Med)
200 N. Ingalls
Ann Arbor, MI 48104
Phone: (313) 763-0555
Julia L. Case, Libn.
Staff: Prof 1. **Subjects:** Burns - research, care, prevention; rehabilitation; reconstructive surgery. **Holdings:** 125 books; 27,000 articles; 4 films. **Services:** Interlibrary loans; copying; library open to public by appointment. **Publications:** International Bibliography on Burns, 1969 with annual supplements - for sale.

★15739★
UNIVERSITY OF MICHIGAN - BUSINESS ADMINISTRATION LIBRARY - INDUSTRIAL RELATIONS SECTION
330 Graduate School of Business Adm.
Ann Arbor, MI 48109
Defunct. Absorbed by its Kresge Business Administration Library.

★15740★
UNIVERSITY OF MICHIGAN - CENTER FOR CONTINUING EDUCATION OF WOMEN - LIBRARY (Educ; Soc Sci)
350 S. Thayer
Ann Arbor, MI 48109
Phone: (313) 764-6555
Patricia Padala, Libn.
Staff: Prof 1; Other 1. **Subjects:** Women - employment, education, status, counseling. **Holdings:** 400 books; 2500 dissertations, manuscripts, unpublished papers, articles and government publications; 200 bibliographies classified by subject; 3 drawers of vocational files; 1 drawer of clippings; Michigan Occupational Information System microfiche. **Subscriptions:** 65 journals and other serials. **Services:** Copying; library open to public. **Publications:** Acquisition List, monthly; Current Periodicals Bibliography; The Job Search, a selected annotated bibliography; Part Time, a selected bibliography - all free upon request.

★15741★
UNIVERSITY OF MICHIGAN - CENTER FOR RESEARCH ON ECONOMIC DEVELOPMENT (Soc Sci)
240 Lorch Hall
Ann Arbor, MI 48109
Phone: (313) 763-6609
Carol R. Wilson, Libn.
Founded: 1965. **Staff:** Prof 2; Other 4. **Subjects:** Economic development, agricultural economics, health economics. **Special Collections:** African government documents (9500 items); Asian and Latin American government documents (2500 items); Livestock in Africa documentation (500 items). **Holdings:** 250 books; 300 series of research working papers; socioeconomic development plans for 85 countries on microfiche. **Subscriptions:** 260 journals and other serials. **Services:** Interlibrary loans; copying; center open to public for reference use only. **Publications:** Recent Working Papers Acquisition Bulletin, monthly- for internal distribution only; CRED Discussion

Papers series, irregular - by subscription; CREDITS, semiannual newsletter - free upon request; Project Reports, irregular - for sale. **Special Indexes:** Index to Livestock in Africa (card). **Remarks:** An alternate telephone number is 764-9490. **Staff:** Cynthia G. Manley, Asst.Libn.

★15742★
UNIVERSITY OF MICHIGAN - CHEMISTRY LIBRARY (Sci-Tech)
2000 Chemistry Bldg.　　　　　　　　Phone: (313) 764-7337
Ann Arbor, MI 48109-1055　　　　　　Jack W. Weigel, Libn.
Staff: Prof 1; Other 2. **Subjects:** Chemistry. **Special Collections:** Friedrich Konrad Beilstein; Gmelin; Landolt-Bornstein; Sadtler Spectra. **Holdings:** 50,000 books and bound periodical volumes; chemical abstracts. **Subscriptions:** 400 journals and other serials. **Services:** Interlibrary loans; copying; library open to public for reference use only. **Computerized Information Services:** DIALOG, SDC, CAS Online. **Publications:** Acquisitions List, bimonthly; serials list, annual.

★15743★
UNIVERSITY OF MICHIGAN - COOPERATIVE INFORMATION CENTER FOR HOSPITAL MANAGEMENT STUDIES (Med)
M3039 School of Public Health　　　　Phone: (313) 764-1394
Ann Arbor, MI 48109　　　　　　　　Gene Regenstreif, Libn.
Founded: 1959. **Staff:** Prof 1; Other 2. **Subjects:** Hospital management, manpower, health insurance, nursing homes and extended care, mental health services, ambulatory care, legal aspects and planning of health care. **Holdings:** 8 VF drawers of pamphlets; 480 theses; 74 VF drawers of Information Center documents; 8 VF drawers of serials and reports; 16 VF drawers of reserve articles; 1224 reels of microfilm. **Subscriptions:** 100 journals and other serials. **Services:** Interlibrary loans; annotated bibliographies; center open to public by appointment. **Publications:** Abstracts of Health Care Management Studies, annual - available by subscription. **Special Indexes:** Index to Volumes I-V Abstracts of H.M.C.S., book form.

★15744★
UNIVERSITY OF MICHIGAN - DENTISTRY LIBRARY (Med)
1100 Dentistry　　　　　　　　　　Phone: (313) 764-1526
Ann Arbor, MI 48109-1078　　　　　　Susan I. Seger, Hd.Libn.
Founded: 1908. **Staff:** Prof 2; Other 6. **Subjects:** Dentistry. **Special Collections:** Rare Book Collection (850 items). **Holdings:** 44,000 books and bound periodical volumes; 25 VF drawers of pamphlets. **Subscriptions:** 615 journals and other serials. **Services:** Interlibrary loans; copying; library open to public for reference use only. **Automated Operations:** Computerized cataloging and acquisitions. **Networks/Consortia:** Member of Greater Midwest Regional Medical Library Network (Region 3); RLG. **Publications:** Library Information Guide; Special Subject Bibliographies. **Special Indexes:** Index of M.S. theses (card). **Staff:** Ruth Cressman, Asst.Libn.

★15745★
UNIVERSITY OF MICHIGAN - DEPARTMENT OF GEOLOGICAL SCIENCES - SUBSURFACE LABORATORY LIBRARY (Sci-Tech)
1009 C.C. Little Bldg.　　　　　　　Phone: (313) 764-2434
Ann Arbor, MI 48109　　　　　　　　Joyce M. Budai, Dir.
Staff: 2. **Subjects:** Geology, stratigraphy, sedimentary rocks, sedimentation. **Special Collections:** Michigan well history central system file; subsurface geology materials and information. **Holdings:** Figures not available. **Services:** Interlibrary loans; copying; library open to public. **Computerized Information Services:** MICRO Data Management System (internal database). Performs searches on cost recovery basis. **Special Catalogs:** Core, mounted strip log, electric log and descriptive log catalogs.

★15746★
UNIVERSITY OF MICHIGAN - DEPARTMENT OF RARE BOOKS AND SPECIAL COLLECTIONS - LIBRARY (Rare Book)
711 Hatcher Graduate Library　　　　Phone: (313) 764-9377
Ann Arbor, MI 48109　　　　　　　　Robert J. Starring, Hd.
Staff: Prof 6; Other 5. **Subjects:** Rare books on all branches of knowledge. **Special Collections:** Worcester Philippine Collection; imaginary voyages; history of science; English and American drama; incunabula; manuscripts - biblical, medieval, renaissance, modern, oriental; papyri (7000 items); theater collections; Shakespeare; Labadie Collection on social protest movements (148,000 items). **Holdings:** 420,000 items including books, bound periodical volumes, pamphlets, manuscripts and nonbook materials. **Services:** Interlibrary loans; copying (both limited); collection open to qualified researchers. **Publications:** Occasional exhibition catalogs. **Staff:** Helen S. Butz, Rare Bk.Libn.; Mary Ann Sellers, Rare Bk.Libn.; Kathryn L. Beam, Ms.Libn.; Edward C. Weber, Labadie Coll.Libn.; R. Anne Okey, Labadie Coll.Libn.

★15747★
UNIVERSITY OF MICHIGAN - ENGINEERING-TRANSPORTATION LIBRARY (Sci-Tech; Trans)
Undergraduate Library Bldg.　　　　　Phone: (313) 764-7494
Ann Arbor, MI 48109　　　　　　　　Maurita P. Holland, Libn.
Founded: 1903. **Staff:** Prof 3; Other 10. **Subjects:** All divisions and aspects of engineering except nuclear engineering; all divisions and aspects of transportation. **Special Collections:** Early U.S. canals and railroads; Currier and Ives prints. **Holdings:** 400,000 books and bound periodical volumes. **Subscriptions:** 2600 journals and other serials. **Services:** Interlibrary loans; copying. **Computerized Information Services:** DIALOG, SDC, DOE/RECON, NASA/RECON, QL Systems, NIH-EPA Chemical Information System, BRS; internal database. **Publications:** Library News, monthly - free upon request. **Staff:** Sharon Balius, Hd., Ref./Spec.Coll.

★15748★
UNIVERSITY OF MICHIGAN - ENGLISH LANGUAGE INSTITUTE - LIBRARY (Hum)
1013 North University Bldg.　　　　　Phone: (313) 764-2413
Ann Arbor, MI 48109　　　　　　　　Patricia M. Aldridge, Libn.
Founded: 1960. **Staff:** 1. **Subjects:** Teaching English as a foreign language, teaching modern foreign language, English grammar, linguistics, psycholinguistics, sociolinguistics, bilingual education, language laboratories, foreign students in the U.S. **Holdings:** 6750 books and pamphlets; 400 boxed volumes of periodicals; 28 VF drawers; 15 series of Working Papers; 30 videotapes; audiotapes; microfiche; microfilm. **Subscriptions:** 105 journals and other serials. **Services:** Interlibrary loans; copying; library open to public for reference use only on request. **Remarks:** Includes the holdings of the Linguistics Department Library.

UNIVERSITY OF MICHIGAN - ERIC CLEARINGHOUSE ON COUNSELING AND PERSONNEL SERVICES
See: ERIC Clearinghouse on Counseling and Personnel Services

★15749★
UNIVERSITY OF MICHIGAN - FINE ARTS LIBRARY (Art)
103 Tappan Hall　　　　　　　　　Phone: (313) 764-5405
Ann Arbor, MI 48109　　　　　　　　Margaret P. Jensen, Hd.
Staff: Prof 1; Other 2. **Subjects:** History of art and architecture. **Holdings:** 53,554 volumes; 10,000 pamphlets; 20 VF drawers. **Subscriptions:** 220 journals and other serials. **Services:** Interlibrary loans; library open to public for reference use only.

UNIVERSITY OF MICHIGAN - GUILD OF CARILLONNEURS IN NORTH AMERICA
See: Guild of Carillonneurs in North America

UNIVERSITY OF MICHIGAN - HIGHWAY SAFETY RESEARCH INSTITUTE
See: University of Michigan - Transportation Research Institute

★15750★
UNIVERSITY OF MICHIGAN - HISTORY OF ART DEPARTMENT - ARCHIVES OF ASIAN ART (Art)
519 S. State
4 Tappan Hall　　　　　　　　　　Phone: (313) 764-5555
Ann Arbor, MI 48109　　　　　　　　Wendy Holden, Cur.
Staff: Prof 1; Other 6. **Subjects:** Chinese, Japanese, South and Southeast Asian art. **Special Collections:** Photographs of paintings from the National Palace Museum, Taiwan; Indian Buddhist cave sites; Thai art. **Holdings:** 80,000 photographs and mounted reproductions. **Services:** Slides and photographs of Chinese painting available for sale to institutions.

★15751★
UNIVERSITY OF MICHIGAN - HISTORY OF ART DEPARTMENT - COLLECTION OF SLIDES AND PHOTOGRAPHS (Art)
107 Tappan Hall　　　　　　　　　Phone: (313) 764-5404
Ann Arbor, MI 48109　　　　　　　　Joy Alexander, Cur.
Founded: 1946. **Staff:** Prof 6; Other 35. **Subjects:** History of art. **Holdings:** 220,000 35mm transparencies; 30,000 lantern slides; 170,000 photographs and mounted reproductions. **Services:** Illustrative material provided to history of art faculty for lectures and research.

★15752★
UNIVERSITY OF MICHIGAN - HOPWOOD ROOM (Hum)
1006 Angell Hall　　　　　　　　　Phone: (313) 764-6296
Ann Arbor, MI 48109　　　　　　　　Andrea Beauchamp, Prog.Coord.
Subjects: Contemporary literature. **Special Collections:** Hopwood Awards manuscripts. **Holdings:** Figures not available.

★15753★
UNIVERSITY OF MICHIGAN - HUMAN PERFORMANCE CENTER - LIBRARY
330 Packard Rd.
Ann Arbor, MI 48104
Defunct

UNIVERSITY OF MICHIGAN - INSTITUTE OF GERONTOLOGY
See: Institute of Gerontology

★15754★
UNIVERSITY OF MICHIGAN - INST. FOR SOCIAL RESEARCH - INTER-UNIVERSITY CONSORTIUM FOR POLITICAL & SOC. RES. (Info Sci)
Box 1248   Phone: (313) 764-2570
Ann Arbor, MI 48106   Maia I. Bergman, Archv.Libn.
Staff: Prof 12; Other 13. **Subjects:** International and national social, economic and political data: elections, census; international relations; aging and the aging process; crime, deviance and criminal justice; recreation and leisure; recreational land use. **Holdings:** 900 collections of machine-readable data containing 15,000 discrete data files. **Services:** Services open to public for a fee. **Computerized Information Services:** Online systems. **Publications:** Guide to Resources and Services, annual; annual report; ICPSR's Bulletin, quarterly; codebooks. **Also Known As:** ICPSR.

★15755★
UNIVERSITY OF MICHIGAN - INSTITUTE FOR SOCIAL RESEARCH - LIBRARY (Soc Sci)
426 Thompson St.
Box 1248   Phone: (313) 764-8513
Ann Arbor, MI 48109   Mrs. Adye Bel Evans, Libn.
Staff: Prof 1; Other 1. **Subjects:** Social psychology, industrial psychology, mental health, economic behavior. **Holdings:** 3000 books, monographs, unpublished papers and research reports comprising publications of institute staff; 1000 research reports produced by other survey institutions. **Subscriptions:** 100 journals and other serials. **Services:** Interlibrary loans; copying; library open to public for reference use only. **Publications:** Bibliography of institute-authored publications, issued annually with five-year cumulations.

★15756★
UNIVERSITY OF MICHIGAN - KRESGE BUSINESS ADMINISTRATION LIBRARY (Bus-Fin)
Graduate School of Business Adm.
Tappan & Monroe Sts.   Phone: (313) 764-1375
Ann Arbor, MI 48109-1234   Carol Holbrook, Dir.
Founded: 1925. **Staff:** Prof 6; Other 8. **Subjects:** General business, accounting, finance, marketing, statistics, international banking and finance, human resource management, organizational behavior. **Special Collections:** Historic and current files of 85 U.S. unions including newspapers, constitutions, proceedings, histories and collective agreements; historic files of 275 U.S. companies related to personnel administration and labor-management relations. **Holdings:** 200,000 books and bound periodical volumes; government documents; corporate financial reports; 10K reports; looseleaf services. **Subscriptions:** 1500 journals and other serials. **Services:** Copying; SDI; library open to public. **Automated Operations:** Computerized cataloging. **Computerized Information Services:** DIALOG, BRS, Dow Jones News/Retrieval, RLIN; internal databases. RLG. **Remarks:** Includes holdings of its former Industrial Relations Section.

★15757★
UNIVERSITY OF MICHIGAN - LAW LIBRARY (Law)
Legal Research Bldg.   Phone: (313) 764-9322
Ann Arbor, MI 48109   Beverley J. Pooley, Dir.
Founded: 1859. **Staff:** Prof 13; Other 24. **Subjects:** Anglo-American law, foreign law, international law, international organizations, Roman law, legal bibliography. **Holdings:** 580,000 volumes. **Subscriptions:** 9285 journals and other serials. **Services:** Interlibrary loans; copying; library open to public. **Automated Operations:** Computerized cataloging and circulation. **Computerized Information Services:** LEXIS, Westlaw. **Networks/Consortia:** Member of RLG. **Staff:** Margaret A. Leary, Assoc.Dir.Bruce S. Johnson, Chf.Ref.Libn.; Bobbie Snow, Chf.Circ.Libn.; Evelyn L. Smith, Chf.Cat.Libn.; Leah M. Gunn, Chf. Order Libn.

★15758★
UNIVERSITY OF MICHIGAN - LIBRARY EXTENSION SERVICE
2360 Bonisteel Blvd.
Ann Arbor, MI 48109
Defunct

★15759★
UNIVERSITY OF MICHIGAN - LIBRARY SCIENCE LIBRARY (Info Sci)
300 Hatcher Graduate Library   Phone: (313) 764-9375
Ann Arbor, MI 48109   James E. Crooks, Libn.
Staff: Prof 1; Other 2. **Subjects:** Library science, history of libraries, history of publishing, history of bookselling, history of the book, bibliography, children's literature, online information services, information storage and retrieval. **Holdings:** 46,575 books; 27 VF drawers of pamphlets; 460 dissertations; 421 reels of microfilm; 2608 sheets of microfiche; 100 AV items. **Subscriptions:** 474 journals and other serials. **Services:** Interlibrary loans; library open to university students and staff. **Automated Operations:** Computerized cataloging, acquisitions and circulation. **Computerized Information Services:** DIALOG, BRS, SDC.

UNIVERSITY OF MICHIGAN - LINGUISTICS DEPARTMENT LIBRARY
See: University of Michigan - English Language Institute - Library

★15760★
UNIVERSITY OF MICHIGAN - MAP ROOM (Geog-Map)
825 Hatcher Graduate Library   Phone: (313) 764-0407
Ann Arbor, MI 48109
Staff: Prof 1; Other 5. **Subjects:** Topographic maps, political maps, nautical charts, thematic maps, history of cartography. **Holdings:** 280,000 sheet maps; 5000 monographs and serial titles; 3000 aerial photographs; atlases; gazetteers; cartobibliographies. **Services:** Interlibrary loans; copying; map-o-graph; library open to public for reference use only. **Staff:** Mary Lou Westin, Supv.; Jerry Thornton, Cat.

★15761★
UNIVERSITY OF MICHIGAN - MATHEMATICS LIBRARY (Sci-Tech)
3027 Angell Hall   Phone: (313) 764-7266
Ann Arbor, MI 48109   Jack W. Weigel, Libn.
Founded: 1930. **Staff:** Prof 1; Other 2. **Subjects:** Mathematics, statistics, history of mathematics. **Holdings:** 48,000 books and bound periodical volumes; 300 reels of microfilm; 490 dissertations. **Subscriptions:** 670 journals and other serials. **Services:** Interlibrary loans; library open to public for reference use only. **Computerized Information Services:** DIALOG. Performs searches on cost recovery basis.

★15762★
UNIVERSITY OF MICHIGAN - MATTHAEI BOTANICAL GARDENS - LIBRARY (Sci-Tech)
1800 N. Dixboro Rd.   Phone: (313) 764-1168
Ann Arbor, MI 48105   Laurianne L. Hannan, Coll. Botanist
Staff: Prof 1. **Subjects:** Botany, horticulture. **Holdings:** 1700 volumes; 5 VF drawers of brochures and clippings. **Subscriptions:** 28 journals and other serials. **Services:** Library open to public for reference use only.

★15763★
UNIVERSITY OF MICHIGAN - MEDICAL SCHOOL - LEARNING RESOURCE CENTER (Med)
1135 E. Catherine St.
Box 38   Phone: (313) 763-6770
Ann Arbor, MI 48109-0010   Judith G. Calhoun, Ph.D., Coord., LRC
Staff: Prof 9; Other 15. **Subjects:** Education - medical, nursing, allied health. **Special Collections:** National Center for Health Statistics Microdata tapes (15). **Holdings:** 3000 books. **Services:** Interlibrary loans; copying; center open to public. **Computerized Information Services:** DIALOG, AVLINE; Stanford Public Information Retrieval Spires System (internal database). Contact Person: Patricia Martin. **Networks/Consortia:** Member of HIRA. **Publications:** Audiovisual Resources for Hypertension Education, 1981; Audiovisual Resources for Diabetes Education, 1982; Audiovisual Resources for Teaching Physical Examination Techniques, 1983 - all available for purchase; Media Messenger, newsletter. **Special Catalogs:** Instructional Materials Catalog. **Special Indexes:** Curriculum Indices. **Formerly:** Furstenberg Student Study Center - Library. **Staff:** Achla B. Karnani, Media Consultant; Patricia W. Martin, AV Consultant; Elaine M. Hockman, Prog.Anl.

★15764★
UNIVERSITY OF MICHIGAN - MENTAL HEALTH RESEARCH INSTITUTE - LIBRARY (Med)
205 Washtenaw Pl.   Phone: (313) 764-4202
Ann Arbor, MI 48109   Anne C. Davis, Libn.
Founded: 1956. **Staff:** Prof 1. **Subjects:** Psychiatry, epidemiology of mental illness, mental health care systems analysis, neurology, neurochemistry. **Holdings:** 4000 books; 2000 periodical volumes; 100 government documents; 300 communications; annual reports; preprints. **Subscriptions:** 34 journals and other serials. **Services:** Interlibrary loans; document delivery; SDI; library open to public for reference use only. **Automated Operations:**

Computerized cataloging. **Computerized Information Services:** DIALOG, MEDLARS. **Networks/Consortia:** Member of RLG. **Publications:** MHRI Library News - for internal distribution only.

★15765★
UNIVERSITY OF MICHIGAN - MICHIGAN HISTORICAL COLLECTIONS - BENTLEY HISTORICAL LIBRARY (Hist)
1150 Beal   Phone: (313) 764-3482
Ann Arbor, MI 48109   Francis X. Blouin, Jr., Dir.
Staff: Prof 9; Other 6. **Subjects:** History of the State of Michigan, churches of Michigan, education in Michigan, Michigan business, University of Michigan, politics and government of Michigan and United States, ethnic groups. **Special Collections:** Philippine Islands; Sino-American relations; printed and manuscript holdings on temperance and prohibition in the U.S. **Holdings:** 35,000 volumes; 40 million manuscript items; 1700 maps; 350 reels of microfilmed newspapers; 32 VF drawers; 400,000 photographs. **Subscriptions:** 176 journals and other serials. **Services:** Copying; library open to public. **Publications:** Annual Report; Bulletins, annual; Michigan Gazette, annual; Bibliographical series, irregular; Guide to the Michigan Historical Collections. **Staff:** William K. Wallach, Asst.Dir.; Thomas Powers, Archv.; May Davis Hill, Assoc.Archv.; Mary Jo Pugh, Ref.Archv.; James Craven, Consrv.; Kenneth Scheffel, Assoc.Archv.; Leonard Coombs, Asst.Archv.; Marjorie Barritt, Asst.Archv.; Frank Boles, Asst.Archv.

★15766★
UNIVERSITY OF MICHIGAN - MICHIGAN INFORMATION TRANSFER SOURCE (MITS) (Info Sci)
205 Harlan Hatcher Graduate Library   Phone: (313) 763-5060
Ann Arbor, MI 48109-1205   Anne K. Beaubien, Dir.
Founded: 1980. **Staff:** Prof 1; Other 3. **Services:** Interlibrary loans; copying; SDI; bibliography preparation; organization of materials, patents. **Computerized Information Services:** DIALOG, BRS, OCLC, SDC. **Networks/Consortia:** Member of RLG. **Publications:** Brochure. **Remarks:** MITS provides research and information services to business, industry and individuals on a cost recovery basis. Fee schedule is available upon request.

UNIVERSITY OF MICHIGAN - MUSEUM OF ZOOLOGY - WILSON ORNITHOLOGICAL SOCIETY
See: Wilson Ornithological Society

★15767★
UNIVERSITY OF MICHIGAN - MUSEUMS LIBRARY (Sci-Tech)
2500 Museums Bldg.   Phone: (313) 764-0467
Ann Arbor, MI 48109   Patricia B. Yocum, Hd.
Founded: 1928. **Staff:** Prof 1; Other 2. **Subjects:** Natural history with emphasis on systematic and taxonomic works. **Special Collections:** Anthropology; paleontology; botany; birds; herpetology; fish; insects; mammals; mollusca. **Holdings:** 100,000 books and bound periodical volumes; 658 maps. **Subscriptions:** 1400 journals and other serials. **Automated Operations:** Computerized acquisitions. **Networks/Consortia:** Member of RLG. **Remarks:** Includes the holdings of the museum's Herbarium Library.

★15768★
UNIVERSITY OF MICHIGAN - MUSIC LIBRARY (Mus)
3250 Earl V. Moore Bldg., N. Campus   Phone: (313) 764-2512
Ann Arbor, MI 48109   Peggy E. Daub, Music Libn.
Founded: 1942. **Staff:** Prof 2; Other 4. **Subjects:** Music and books on music. **Special Collections:** Rare book collection; Women's music collection (1800 scores) **Holdings:** 70,000 books; 2000 reels of microfilm; 20,000 phonograph records. **Subscriptions:** 400 journals and other serials. **Services:** Interlibrary loans; copying; library open to public for reference use only. **Networks/Consortia:** Member of RLG.

★15769★
UNIVERSITY OF MICHIGAN - NATURAL SCIENCE/NATURAL RESOURCES LIBRARY (Sci-Tech)
3140 Natural Science Bldg.   Phone: (313) 764-1494
Ann Arbor, MI 48109   Patricia B. Yocum, Hd.
Founded: 1953. **Staff:** Prof 3; Other 4. **Subjects:** Biology, geology, natural resources. **Special Collections:** Alaska Pipeline File. **Holdings:** 155,000 books and bound periodical volumes; 2100 masters' theses. **Subscriptions:** 1800 journals and other serials. **Services:** Copying; library open to public for reference use only. **Automated Operations:** Computerized cataloging, acquisitions and circulation. **Computerized Information Services:** DIALOG, BRS. **Networks/Consortia:** Member of RLG.

★15770★
UNIVERSITY OF MICHIGAN - NORTH ENGINEERING LIBRARY (Sci-Tech)
1002 I.S.T. Bldg.   Phone: (313) 764-5298
Ann Arbor, MI 48109   Maurita Petersen Holland, Hd.
Founded: 1974. **Staff:** Prof 1; Other 2. **Subjects:** Nuclear power, reactor design and construction, radiation utilization and effects, natural science aspect of the Great Lakes, limnology, biophysics, biochemistry. **Holdings:** 70,000 books and bound periodical volumes; 40,000 full size Atomic Energy Commission and DOE reports; 80,000 AEC microcards; 350,000 AEC and DOE microfiche. **Subscriptions:** 300 journals and other serials. **Services:** Interlibrary loans; copying; library open to public. **Computerized Information Services:** DIALOG, BRS, SDC, DOE/RECON, NASA/RECON, QL Systems, NIH-EPA Chemical Information System. **Special Catalogs:** Computer printout on microfiche of 4000 technical reports in Great Lakes collection by authors, issuing agency, subject and report series.

★15771★
UNIVERSITY OF MICHIGAN - PHYSICS-ASTRONOMY LIBRARY (Sci-Tech)
290 Dennison Bldg.   Phone: (313) 764-3442
Ann Arbor, MI 48109   Jack W. Weigel, Libn.
Founded: 1924. **Staff:** Prof 1; Other 2. **Subjects:** Astronomy, physics, applied mathematics. **Holdings:** 54,000 books and bound periodical volumes; 108 reels of microfilm; 578 technical reports; 700 dissertations. **Subscriptions:** 880 journals and other serials. **Services:** Interlibrary loans; library open to public for reference use only. **Computerized Information Services:** DIALOG. **Special Catalogs:** Union List of Selected Serials in the University of Michigan Library, annual.

★15772★
UNIVERSITY OF MICHIGAN - SCHOOL OF EDUCATION & SCHOOL OF LIB. SCI. - INSTR. STRATEGY SERV. (Educ; Aud-Vis; Comp Sci)
3001 School of Education
Corner East and South University Avenues   Phone: (313) 764-0519
Ann Arbor, MI 48109   Elaine K. Didier, Ph.D., Dir.
Founded: 1979. **Staff:** Prof 6; Other 35. **Subjects:** Elementary and secondary education, library science, higher education, microcomputers, media services. **Special Collections:** Instructional Resources (microcomputers, textbooks, curriculum guides, teaching aids, AV materials); AV/TV/Photography; Media Production Laboratory; graphics design and production. **Holdings:** 1000 books; 6500 textbooks; 2300 dissertations; 1200 AV materials; 2000 microcomputer programs; 36 VF drawers of curriculum guides; 32 VF drawers of information files; 1500 tests. **Services:** Copying; demonstration and evaluation of curriculum materials, microcomputers and software; consultation; workshops; services open to public. **Computerized Information Services:** Internal databases. **Special Catalogs:** Software catalog (computerized). **Staff:** Jennifer Marquardt, Instr.Rsrcs.; Margaret Schmidt, Instr.Rsrcs.; Claire Sandler, AV; Ed Saunders, AV; Claudia Berg, Media Prod./Graphics Serv.

★15773★
UNIVERSITY OF MICHIGAN - SCHOOL OF PUBLIC HEALTH - CENTER FOR POPULATION PLANNING - REFERENCE COLLECTION (Soc Sci)
                                         Phone: (313) 763-5732
Ann Arbor, MI 48109   Ellen Katzer, Libn.
Staff: Prof l. **Subjects:** National and international polulation policy and family planning; educational and medical aspects of family planning; family planning systems; demography. **Holdings:** 500 books; 6000 unbound reports; 600 country files representing 70 countries; family planning program data; reprints; documents; conference proceedings. **Subscriptions:** 100 journals and other serials; 20 newspapers. **Services:** Collection open to public for reference use only. **Networks/Consortia:** Member of Association for Population/Family Planning Libraries and Information Centers - International (APLIC - International). **Special Catalogs:** Holdings lists of country files, journals and serials.

★15774★
UNIVERSITY OF MICHIGAN - SCHOOL OF PUBLIC HEALTH - PUBLIC HEALTH LIBRARY (Med)
M2030 School of Public Health   Phone: (313) 764-5473
Ann Arbor, MI 48109   Mary Townsend, Libn.
Founded: 1943. **Staff:** Prof 2; Other 4. **Subjects:** Community public health, environmental and industrial health, biostatistics, toxicology, gerontology, preventive medicine. **Holdings:** 56,000 books and bound periodical volumes; 581 pamphlet boxes. **Subscriptions:** 500 journals and other serials. **Services:** Interlibrary loans; library is open to other state university faculty and students in Michigan. **Automated Operations:** Computerized cataloging and acquisitions. **Networks/Consortia:** Member of RLG.

★15775★
UNIVERSITY OF MICHIGAN - SOCIAL WORK LIBRARY (Soc Sci)
1548 Frieze Bldg.   Phone: (313) 764-5169
Ann Arbor, MI 48109   Christina W. Neal, Hd.
Staff: Prof 1; Other 3. **Subjects:** Social work. **Special Collections:** Minority content in the curriculum; National Assessment of Juvenile Corrections (NAJEC); reprints; case studies. **Holdings:** 34,000 books; 200 boxes of pamphlets; 10 cassettes. **Subscriptions:** 500 journals and other serials. **Services:** Interlibrary loans; copying; consultation; library open to public with restrictions. **Computerized Information Services:** BRS. **Publications:** Accessions list, semiannual - for internal distribution only; information leaflets, annual - available on request.

★15776★
UNIVERSITY OF MICHIGAN - TRANSPORTATION RESEARCH INSTITUTE - LIBRARY (Trans)
2901 Baxter Rd.   Phone: (313) 764-2171
Ann Arbor, MI 48109-2150   Ann C. Grimm, Libn.
Founded: 1966. **Staff:** Prof 2; Other 3. **Subjects:** Highway safety, accident investigation, biomechanics, driver behavior and characteristics, vehicle dynamics, shipbuilding. **Subscriptions:** 220 journals and other serials. **Services:** Interlibrary loans; copying (limited); library open to public for reference use only. **Computerized Information Services:** DIALOG. **Publications:** Transportation Research Information (acquisitions list), weekly - available on exchange basis. **Formerly:** Its Highway Safety Research Institute. **Staff:** R. Guy Gattis, Asst.Libn.

★15777★
UNIVERSITY OF MICHIGAN - TRANSPORTATION RESEARCH INSTITUTE - PUBLIC INFORMATION MATERIALS CENTER (Trans)
2901 Baxter Rd.   Phone: (313) 764-2171
Ann Arbor, MI 48109-2150   Ann C. Grimm, Libn.
Founded: 1972. **Staff:** Prof 1; Other 1. **Subjects:** Public information campaigns, program evaluation. **Holdings:** 900 journal articles/research reports; 200 radio and television spots (commercials); 400 radio and television scripts; 700 pamphlets; 30 films and filmstrips; 350 print advertisements; 50 posters; 450 promotional gimmicks used in advertising campaigns. **Services:** Interlibrary loans; copying (limited); bibliographic searches (limited); center open to public by appointment. **Special Catalogs:** Materials Catalog - free mailing list distribution.

★15778★
UNIVERSITY OF MICHIGAN - WILLIAM L. CLEMENTS LIBRARY (Hist)
S. University Ave.   Phone: (313) 764-2347
Ann Arbor, MI 48109   John C. Dann, Dir.
Founded: 1923. **Staff:** Prof 5; Other 3. **Subjects:** Rare Americana to 1877 - discovery and exploration, early settlement, Indian relations, colonial wars, American Revolution, beginnings of federal government, Northwest Territory, War of 1812, early reforms, Westward movement, Civil War, arts and crafts. **Holdings:** 60,000 books and bound periodical volumes; 350 manuscript collections, 1740-1900; 36,000 printed and manuscript maps; 40,000 pieces of sheet music, 1790-1920. **Subscriptions:** 6 journals and other serials. **Services:** Library open by permission only; readers must be interviewed. **Special Catalogs:** Guide to Manuscript Collections; Division of Maps; Guide to Manuscript Maps; Author/Title Catalog of Americana 1493-1860 in The William L. Clements Library (book, 7 volumes). **Staff:** Richard W. Ryan, Cur. of Bks.; Galen Wilson, Mss.Libn.; Arlene P. Shy, Hd., Rd.Serv.

UNIVERSITY MICROFILMS INTERNATIONAL
See: Xerox Corporation

★15779★
UNIVERSITY OF MINNESOTA - AGRICULTURAL EXTENSION SERVICE - DIAL-U INSECT AND PLANT INFORMATION CLINIC (Sci-Tech)
155 Alderman Hall
1970 Folwell   Phone: (612) 376-3380
St. Paul, MN 55108   Dr. Mark Ascerno, Dial-U Coord.
Founded: 1983. **Staff:** Prof 4; Other 8. **Subjects:** Horticulture, plant pathology, entomology, insect control. **Holdings:** 200 books; 400 extension fact sheets and bulletins. **Subscriptions:** 15 journals and other serials. **Remarks:** This is a telephone information service that can be reached by area residents calling 1-975-0200. Caller is automatically charged a special fee when information number is used. **Staff:** Deborah Brown, Horticulture Ext.Spec.; Jerry Heaps, Entomology Ext. Fellow; Jill Pokorny, Plant Pathology Fellow.

★15780★
UNIVERSITY OF MINNESOTA - AGRICULTURAL EXTENSION SERVICE - EXTENSION HOME ECONOMICS - INFO. CTR.
1985 Buford Ave.
St. Paul, MN 55108
Defunct

★15781★
UNIVERSITY OF MINNESOTA - AGRICULTURAL EXTENSION SERVICE - MINNESOTA ANALYSIS & PLANNING SYSTEM (Soc Sci)
475 Coffey Hall
1420 Eckles Ave.   Phone: (612) 376-7003
St. Paul, MN 55108   David M. Nelson, Dir.
Staff: Prof 3; Other 12. **Subjects:** U.S. census of population, 1960-1980; Minnesota demographics; surveys - all on computer database. **Holdings:** 500 computer tapes; 200 other items. **Services:** System open to public by appointment. **Computerized Information Services:** Online systems. Performs searches on cost recovery basis. **Publications:** MAPS Newsletter, bimonthly - free upon request. **Special Indexes:** Data File Inventory. **Also Known As:** MAPS. **Staff:** Patricia Kovel-Jarboe, Census Info.Spec.

★15782★
UNIVERSITY OF MINNESOTA - AMES LIBRARY OF SOUTH ASIA (Area-Ethnic)
Wilson Library s-10
309 19th Ave. S.   Phone: (612) 373-2890
Minneapolis, MN 55455   Henry Scholberg, Libn.
Founded: 1908. **Staff:** Prof 1. **Subjects:** South Asia - history, economics, political science, art, literature, philology, philosophy, religion, music. **Special Collections:** French India (400 volumes); Portuguese India (500 volumes); Sanskrit series (4000 volumes). **Holdings:** 101,529 books and bound periodical volumes; 8921 microforms; 18 feet of manuscripts; 560 AV items; 147 maps. **Subscriptions:** 1948 journals and other serials. **Services:** Interlibrary loans; copying; library open to public for reference use only. **Networks/Consortia:** Member of Southeast Asia Microform Project (SEAM); MINITEX; RLG. **Special Indexes:** Author-subject index of the Journal of Indian History; author-subject index of 19th century pamphlet collection.

★15783★
UNIVERSITY OF MINNESOTA - ARCHITECTURE LIBRARY (Art; Plan)
160 Architecture Bldg.
89 Church St., S.E.   Phone: (612) 373-2203
Minneapolis, MN 55455   A. Kristine Johnson, Hd.
Founded: 1913. **Staff:** Prof 1; Other 1. **Subjects:** Architecture, planning, landscape architecture, design methodology, energy conservation, interior design, environmental psychology. **Holdings:** 29,870 books and bound periodical volumes; pamphlets and theses; 231 AV items; 30 microforms. **Subscriptions:** 226 journals and other serials. **Services:** Interlibrary loans; copying; library open to public for reference use only. **Networks/Consortia:** Member of MINITEX; RLG. **Special Catalogs:** Thesis and pamphlet catalogs (card).

★15784★
UNIVERSITY OF MINNESOTA - ART COLLECTION (Art)
Wilson Library
309 19th Ave., S.   Phone: (612) 373-2875
Minneapolis, MN 55455   Herbert Scherer, Art Libn.
Founded: 1951. **Staff:** Prof 1; Other 1. **Subjects:** Painting, sculpture, architecture, art history, art philosophy, art criticism, decorative arts, crafts, photography, Scandinavian art and architecture. **Special Collections:** Hylton Thomas Collection; baroque and rococo art and architecture in Italy, France, Germany and Central Europe (3000 books and exhibition catalogs). **Holdings:** 63,694 books and bound periodical volumes (including 6530 exhibition catalogs); 2633 microforms. **Subscriptions:** 421 journals and other serials. **Services:** Interlibrary loans; library open to public for reference use only. **Computerized Information Services:** DIALOG, BRS, SDC. **Networks/Consortia:** Member of MINITEX; RLG.

UNIVERSITY OF MINNESOTA - ASSOCIATED COLLEGIATE PRESS/ NATIONAL SCHOLASTIC PRESS ASSOCIATION
See: Associated Collegiate Press/National Scholastic Press Association

★15785★
UNIVERSITY OF MINNESOTA - AUDIO VISUAL LIBRARY SERVICE (Aud-Vis)
3300 University Ave., S.E.   Phone: (612) 373-5452
Minneapolis, MN 55414   Judith A. Gaston, Dir.
Founded: 1913. **Staff:** Prof 2; Other 16. **Subjects:** Education, training, entertainment, health, film study. **Holdings:** 9750 16mm films; 13,500 prints. **Subscriptions:** 20 journals and other serials. **Services:** Library open to

public. **Automated Operations:** Computerized circulation.

★15786★
UNIVERSITY OF MINNESOTA - BELL MUSEUM OF NATURAL HISTORY - LIBRARY (Sci-Tech)
10 Church St., S.E.   Phone: (612) 373-7771
Minneapolis, MN 55455   Tom English, Libn.
Staff: Prof 1. **Subjects:** Ornithology, ethology, mammalogy, herpetology, animal behavior, taxonomy. **Holdings:** 10,416 volumes; 56 AV items. **Subscriptions:** 268 journals and other serials. **Services:** Interlibrary loans; library open to public for reference only. **Networks/Consortia:** Member of MINITEX; RLG.

★15787★
UNIVERSITY OF MINNESOTA - BIOMEDICAL LIBRARY (Med; Sci-Tech)
Diehl Hall
505 Essex St., S.E.   Phone: (612) 373-5584
Minneapolis, MN 55455   Sherrilynne Fuller, Dir.
Founded: 1892. **Staff:** Prof 10; Other 15. **Subjects:** Medicine and allied fields, nursing, dentistry, pharmacy, public health, biology. **Special Collections:** Owen H. Wangensteen Historical Library of Biology and Medicine (40,131 volumes). **Holdings:** 304,782 books and bound periodical volumes; 1432 AV programs; 545 microforms. **Subscriptions:** 3511 journals and other serials. **Services:** Interlibrary loans; copying; library open to public for reference use only. **Automated Operations:** Computerized cataloging, acquisitions and serials. **Computerized Information Services:** BRS, MEDLARS, SDC, DIALOG, Biomedical Information Service. Performs searches on cost recovery basis. **Networks/Consortia:** Member of Greater Midwest Regional Medical Library Network (Region 3); MINITEX; RLG. **Publications:** Bio-Medical Library Bulletin. **Remarks:** Contains the holdings of the former Pharmacy Library.

★15788★
UNIVERSITY OF MINNESOTA - BUSINESS REFERENCE SERVICE (Bus-Fin)
Wilson Library, 2nd Fl.
309 19th Ave., S.   Phone: (612) 373-4109
Minneapolis, MN 55455   Judy Wells, Bus.Libn.
Staff: Prof 2; Other 1. **Subjects:** Business, finance, investments, marketing, accounting, management information systems, insurance, transportation. **Special Collections:** Corporation Annual Reports (43,142); 10K SEC reports (15,751 on microfiche). **Holdings:** 19,600 books and bound periodical volumes; 27,659 microforms. **Subscriptions:** 528 journals and other serials. **Services:** Interlibrary loans; copying; service open to public for reference use only. **Computerized Information Services:** DIALOG, SDC, BRS. **Networks/Consortia:** Member of MINITEX; RLG.

★15789★
UNIVERSITY OF MINNESOTA - CENTER FOR YOUTH DEVELOPMENT AND RESEARCH - RESOURCE ROOM (Soc Sci)
386 McNeal Hall
1985 Buford Ave.   Phone: (612) 376-7624
St. Paul, MN 55108   Paula Simon, Resource Rm.Coord.
Subjects: Youth. **Holdings:** 1000 books; 1000 clippings; 100 county reports. **Subscriptions:** 18 journals and other serials. **Services:** Center open to public. **Publications:** Occasional papers and reports. **Special Catalogs:** Youth-related materials in the University of Minnesota libraries (card).

★15790★
UNIVERSITY OF MINNESOTA - CHARLES BABBAGE INSTITUTE COLLECTION (Comp Sci)
104 Walter Library
117 Pleasant St., S.E.   Phone: (612) 376-9336
Minneapolis, MN 55455   Bruce Bruemmer, Archv.
Staff: Prof 1. **Subjects:** History of information processing. **Holdings:** 200 books; 100 bound periodical volumes; 150 linear feet of oral interview transcripts, records, papers, computer manuals and reports; AV items. **Subscriptions:** 13 journals and other serials. **Services:** Copying; Collection open to serious researchers by appointment. **Publications:** Newsletter, quarterly - free upon request. **Staff:** Arthur Norberg, Dir.

★15791★
UNIVERSITY OF MINNESOTA - CHEMISTRY LIBRARY (Sci-Tech)
4 Walter Library
117 Pleasant St., S.E.   Phone: (612) 373-2375
Minneapolis, MN 55455   Beverly A. Lee, Libn.
Founded: 1918. **Staff:** Prof 1; Other 1. **Subjects:** Chemistry - physical, analytical, organic, general; spectroscopy. **Holdings:** 84,150 books and bound periodical volumes; 66 feet of manuscripts; 1190 microforms. **Subscriptions:** 895 journals and other serials. **Services:** Interlibrary loans;

copying; library open to public for reference use only. **Computerized Information Services:** BRS. **Networks/Consortia:** Member of MINITEX; RLG.

★15792★
UNIVERSITY OF MINNESOTA - CHILDREN'S LITERATURE RESEARCH COLLECTIONS (Hum)
109 Walter Library
117 Pleasant St., S.E.   Phone: (612) 373-9731
Minneapolis, MN 55455   Karen Nelson Hoyle, Cur.
Founded: 1949. **Staff:** Prof 1; Other 1. **Subjects:** Children's books - first editions, manuscripts, illustrations; children's periodicals; American and British dime novels, periodicals, story papers, pulps; Big Little Books; comic books. **Special Collections:** Kerlan Collection (35,835 books; manuscript materials for 2202 titles; illustration materials for 2509 titles; correspondence); Hess Collection (47,583 dime novels; 25,000 periodicals, story papers, pulps; 561 Big Little Books; 1200 comic books); Wanda Gag Collection (33 books; manuscript and illustration materials for 8 titles); Children's Periodicals Collection (64 19th-century American titles; 26 19th-century British titles); Series Books Collection (7859 books); Beulah Counts Rudolph Collection of Figurines, Wall Hangings and Book Marks (400 figurines; 68 wall hangings; 700 book marks); Paul Bunyan Collection (138 books; 8 linear feet of related materials); Ethnicity in Children's Literature; The Immigration Experience; Translations to English; Non-English Language books (3600 titles). **Holdings:** 44,914 books and bound periodical volumes; 452.4 feet of manuscripts; 127 microforms. **Subscriptions:** 21 journals and other serials. **Services:** Copying (limited); Collections open for research upon application. **Networks/Consortia:** Member of RLG. **Publications:** List of brochures and bibliographies - available on request.

★15793★
UNIVERSITY OF MINNESOTA - CLASSICS DEPARTMENT - SEMINAR LIBRARY (Hum)
311 Folwell Hall
9 Pleasant St., S.E.   Phone: (612) 373-3924
Minneapolis, MN 55455   Prof. Jackson Hershbell, Libn.
Staff: Prof 1. **Subjects:** Latin, Greek, classical civilization. **Special Collections:** Classics Curriculum Library of elementary and intermediate texts. **Holdings:** 2000 volumes. **Services:** Copying; library open to public with restrictions.

★15794★
UNIVERSITY OF MINNESOTA - DELOITTE HASKINS & SELLS TAX RESEARCH ROOM (Bus-Fin)
Wilson Library, 2nd Fl.
309 19th Ave., S.   Phone: (612) 373-4109
Minneapolis, MN 55455   Judy Wells, Bus.Libn.
Founded: 1978. **Subjects:** Taxation. **Holdings:** 966 volumes; 252 tax pamphlets. **Services:** Copying; room open to public for reference use only. **Networks/Consortia:** Member of RLG.

★15795★
UNIVERSITY OF MINNESOTA - DEPARTMENT OF LINGUISTICS - LINGUISTICS LIBRARY (Educ)
146 Klaeber Court
320 16th Ave., S.E.   Phone: (612) 373-5769
Minneapolis, MN 55455   Karen Frederickson, Sr.Sec.
Subjects: Linguistics. **Holdings:** 400 books. **Subscriptions:** 67 journals and other serials. **Services:** Library not open to public.

★15796★
UNIVERSITY OF MINNESOTA - DRUG INFORMATION SERVICES (Soc Sci)
3-106 Health Science Unit F
308 Harvard St., S.E.   Phone: (612) 376-7190
Minneapolis, MN 55455   Gary R. Gallo, Dir.
Founded: 1970. **Staff:** Prof 3; Other 1. **Subjects:** Social aspects and research findings of drugs of abuse, alternatives to drug abuse, school curricula, drug abuse in business, treatment and prevention of drug abuse. **Holdings:** 16,000 books, bound periodical volumes and reprints; pamphlets; AV materials. **Subscriptions:** 23 journals and other serials. **Services:** Interlibrary loans; copying; services open to public. **Computerized Information Services:** BRS. **Networks/Consortia:** Member of Twin Cities Biomedical Consortium (TCBC). **Publications:** DIS Newsletter, 6/year. **Special Catalogs:** Thesaurus for Drug Info database (from BRS); Updated Word List. **Remarks:** The Center is part of the College of Pharmacy and the University of Minnesota Hospital's Department of Pharmacy. **Also Known As:** DIS. **Staff:** Gail B. Weinberg, Libn.

★15797★

UNIVERSITY OF MINNESOTA - EAST ASIAN LIBRARY (Area-Ethnic)
Wilson Library, S-30
309 19th Ave., S.   Phone: (612) 373-3737
Minneapolis, MN 55455   Richard Wang, Hd.
Staff: Prof 1; Other 1. **Subjects:** China and Japan - language and literature, history and politics, philosophy and religion; Asian art history. **Holdings:** 81,294 books and bound periodical volumes; 1049 microforms; 6 maps. **Subscriptions:** 321 journals and other serials. **Services:** Interlibrary loans; copying; library open to public for reference use only. **Networks/Consortia:** Member of MINITEX; RLG.

★15798★

UNIVERSITY OF MINNESOTA - ECONOMICS RESEARCH LIBRARY (Bus-Fin)
525 Science Classroom Bldg.
222 Pleasant St., S.E.   Phone: (612) 373-5958
Minneapolis, MN 55455   Wendy Williamson, Lib.
Founded: 1969. **Staff:** 1. **Subjects:** Economics, econometrics, mathematics. **Holdings:** 2700 books; 11,000 working papers; 250 documents; 3500 reprints. **Subscriptions:** 50 journals and other serials. **Services:** Library open to state and university employees and students on a limited schedule. **Publications:** Recent Acquisitions, monthly.

★15799★

UNIVERSITY OF MINNESOTA - EDUCATION-PSYCHOLOGY-LIBRARY SCIENCE COLLECTION (Educ; Info Sci)
Walter Library, Rm. 206
117 Pleasant St., S.E.   Phone: (612) 376-4100
Minneapolis, MN 55455   Patricia Stark, Educ.Libn.
Founded: 1962. **Staff:** Prof 3; Other 1. **Subjects:** Education, psychology, library science. **Special Collections:** Educational Testing Service; tests (microfiche); psychological tests. **Holdings:** 154,546 books and bound periodical volumes; 386,184 microforms; college catalogs on microfiche; ERIC microfiche; annual reports from college and university libraries. **Subscriptions:** 1976 journals and other serials. **Services:** Interlibrary loans; copying; SDI; collection open to public for reference use only. **Computerized Information Services:** DIALOG, BRS, SDC. **Networks/Consortia:** Member of MINITEX; RLG. **Staff:** Kathleen Gorman, Ref./Lib.Sci.Bibliog.; Susan Gangl, Psych./Lib.Sci.Bibliog.

★15800★

UNIVERSITY OF MINNESOTA - ENGINEERING LIBRARY (Sci-Tech; Energy)
128 Lind Hall
207 Church St., S.E.   Phone: (612) 373-2957
Minneapolis, MN 55455   Raymond A. Bohling, Hd.
Founded: 1913. **Staff:** Prof 2; Other 2. **Subjects:** Engineering - civil, aerospace, chemical, mechanical, electrical, mining; metallurgy; material science; computer science; energy. **Holdings:** 132,710 volumes; 3596 government publications; 168 AV items; 6547 microforms. **Subscriptions:** 1633 journals and other serials. **Services:** Interlibrary loans; copying; library open to public for reference use only. **Computerized Information Services:** DIALOG, BRS, SDC. **Networks/Consortia:** Member of MINITEX; RLG. **Staff:** Carol Baldwin, Ref./Bibliog.

★15801★

UNIVERSITY OF MINNESOTA - ERIC SEVAREID JOURNALISM LIBRARY (Info Sci)
121 Murphy Hall
206 Church St., S.E.   Phone: (612) 373-3174
Minneapolis, MN 55455   Kathleen Hansen, Prof./Libn.
Founded: 1941. **Staff:** Prof 1; Other 1. **Subjects:** Mass communications, newspaper journalism, broadcasting, magazine journalism, graphic arts, advertising, international communication, public relations, behavioral research. **Special Collections:** Thomas Heggen Memorial Library (creative writing, 1000 items); Eric Sevareid Papers (29 reels of microfilm). **Holdings:** 4800 books; 1300 bound periodical volumes; 1000 pamphlets; 120 theses. **Subscriptions:** 135 journals and other serials; 40 newspapers. **Services:** Interlibrary loans; copying; library open to public. **Automated Operations:** Computerized cataloging. **Computerized Information Services:** DIALOG. Performs searches on cost recovery basis. **Networks/Consortia:** Member of RLG.

★15802★

UNIVERSITY OF MINNESOTA - FIRE CENTER (Sci-Tech)
33 North Hall
2005 Buford Ave.   Phone: (612) 376-3535
St. Paul, MN 55108   Esther C.D. Doughty, Libn.
Founded: 1968. **Staff:** Prof 1. **Subjects:** Fire protection, prevention, and training; fire safety education; fire department management; disaster planning; emergency medical and rescue services; hazardous materials. **Special Collections:** National Fire Protection Association standards; state fire marshal fire equipment certificates. **Holdings:** 3000 books; 11 VF drawers; 50 AV items. **Subscriptions:** 120 journals and other serials. **Services:** Interlibrary loans; copying; center open to public with restrictions. **Networks/Consortia:** Member of Metronet. **Publications:** Holdings lists - arson and firesetting; fire safety and fire prevention public education. **Special Catalogs:** Subject headings list; film catalog; indexes and abstracts of selected periodical articles.

★15803★

UNIVERSITY OF MINNESOTA - GEOLOGY LIBRARY (Sci-Tech)
Pillsbury Hall, Rm. 204
310 Pillsbury Dr., S.E,   Phone: (612) 373-4052
Minneapolis, MN 55455   Marie Dvorzak, Hd.
Founded: 1911. **Staff:** Prof 1; Other 1. **Subjects:** Geology - structural, economic, surficial, marine, environmental; geophysics; geochemistry; mineralogy; petrology; stratigraphy; hydrology; limnology; paleontology. **Special Collections:** United States Geological Survey Depository; Minnesota Geological Survey publications. **Holdings:** 36,724 books and bound periodical volumes; 77,099 maps; 7514 microforms. **Subscriptions:** 894 journals and other serials. **Services:** Interlibrary loans; copying; library open to public for reference use only. **Computerized Information Services:** GeoRef Information Systems; Geosystems. **Networks/Consortia:** Member of MINITEX; RLG. **Also Known As:** Winchell Library of Geology.

★15804★

UNIVERSITY OF MINNESOTA - GOVERNMENT PUBLICATIONS LIBRARY (Info Sci)
409 Wilson Library
309 19th Ave., S.   Phone: (612) 373-7813
Minneapolis, MN 55455   William LaBissoniere, Libn.
Staff: Prof 1; Other 4. **Subjects:** All government publications. **Special Collections:** Regional depository for U.S. and Minnesota state documents. **Holdings:** 1.87 million documents; 655,218 microforms. **Subscriptions:** 6947 journals and other serials. **Services:** Interlibrary loans; copying; library open to public for reference use only; loans made with acceptable identification. **Networks/Consortia:** Member of MINITEX; RLG.

★15805★

UNIVERSITY OF MINNESOTA - HAROLD SCOTT QUIGLEY CENTER OF INTERNATIONAL STUDIES LIBRARY
1246 Social Sciences Bldg.
267 19th Ave., S.
Minneapolis, MN 55455
Staff: 1. **Subjects:** Foreign policy; international studies - politics, organizations, law, economics. **Holdings:** 1200 books; 600 bound periodical volumes. **Automated Operations:** Computerized cataloging. **Remarks:** Presently inactive.

★15806★

UNIVERSITY OF MINNESOTA - HORMEL INSTITUTE - LIBRARY (Sci-Tech)
801 16th Ave., N.E.   Phone: (507) 433-8804
Austin, MN 55912   Jacqueline Budde, Libn.
Founded: 1948. **Staff:** Prof 1. **Subjects:** Lipid chemistry, lipid biochemistry, lipid microbiology. **Holdings:** 1800 books; 7400 bound periodical volumes. **Subscriptions:** 110 journals and other serials. **Services:** Interlibrary loans; copying; library open to public with permission. **Automated Operations:** Computerized cataloging. **Computerized Information Services:** DIALOG, OCLC. **Networks/Consortia:** Member of MINITEX.

★15807★

UNIVERSITY OF MINNESOTA - IMMIGRATION HISTORY RESEARCH CENTER COLLECTION (Area-Ethnic)
826 Berry St.   Phone: (612) 373-5581
St. Paul, MN 55114   Susan Grigg, Cur.
Staff: Prof 1; Other 1. **Subjects:** East, Central and South European and Near Eastern immigration and ethnic groups in the United States, 1880 to present with emphasis on Finns, Italians and Slavic peoples; ethnic labor and political movement; ethnic churches, presses and fraternal organizations; resettlement of refugees after World War II; immigrant welfare agencies; Ukraine and Ukrainians. **Special Collections:** Records of the American Council for Nationalities Service, Jugoslav Socialist Federation, Latvian Chorus Shield of Songs, Minnesota Finnish-American Historical Society, National Slovak Society, United Ukrainian American Relief Committee and other ethnic organizations; papers of Anthony Capraro, Philip K. Hitti, Karol T. Jaskolski, Joseph C. Roucek and other ethnic scholars and leaders; publications of ethnic presses and organizations. **Holdings:** 41,502 books and bound periodical volumes (including 3000 serial titles; files of 900 newspapers); 1654 AV

items; 65 maps; 3078 feet of manuscripts; 5234 microforms. **Subscriptions:** 12 journals and other serials. **Services:** Interlibrary loans (microfilm only); copying (limited); collection open for research upon application. **Networks/Consortia:** Member of RLG. **Publications:** IHRC Ethnic Collections Series (9 volumes) - for sale; Spectrum (IHRC newsletter), 3/year - by subscription; conference proceedings; reprints; preservation manuals; survey guides; microfilm guides - all for sale; publications brochure - available upon request. **Staff:** Rudolph J. Vecoli, Dir.

★15808★
UNIVERSITY OF MINNESOTA - INDUSTRIAL RELATIONS CENTER - REFERENCE ROOM (Soc Sci)
309 Management & Economics, West Campus
271 19th Ave., S.   Phone: (612) 373-3681
Minneapolis, MN 55455   Georgianna Herman, Libn. & Supv.
Founded: 1945. **Staff:** Prof 2; Other 2. **Subjects:** Personnel administration, labor relations, human resource management, collective bargaining, management theory, industrial sociology, labor economics, industrial psychology. **Special Collections:** Publications from industrial relations centers in the U.S. (5000). **Holdings:** 11,000 books; 3600 bound periodical volumes; 120 VF drawers of subject files; 5500 government documents; 570 volumes of court cases, labor arbitration awards and other loose-leaf reporting services. **Subscriptions:** 130 journals and other serials; 60 labor union newspapers. **Services:** Copying; reference room open to public. **Staff:** Mariann Nelson, Ref.Anl.

★15809★
UNIVERSITY OF MINNESOTA - INFORM (Info Sci)
179 Wilson Library
309 19th Ave., S.   Phone: (612) 373-5938
Minneapolis, MN 55455
Staff: Prof 1; Other 2. **Services:** INFORM is a service unit which provides fee-based research for business, industry and individuals. Services include copying, book loans, bibliography preparation and database searching. Fee schedule available on request.

★15810★
UNIVERSITY OF MINNESOTA - JAMES FORD BELL LIBRARY (Hist)
Wilson Library 462
309 19th Ave., S.   Phone: (612) 373-2888
Minneapolis, MN 55455   John Parker, Cur.
Founded: 1953. **Staff:** Prof 2. **Subjects:** History of European overseas expansion to 1800. **Holdings:** 10,032 books and bound periodical volumes; 200 AV items; 200 reels of microfilm. **Services:** Copying; collection open to public for reference use only. **Networks/Consortia:** Member of RLG. **Publications:** The Merchant Explorer, annual - distributed on request and to selected libraries. **Special Catalogs:** The James Ford Bell Library: an annotated catalog of original source materials relating to the history of European expansion, 1400-1800, 1981. **Staff:** Carol Urness, Asst.Cur.

★15811★
UNIVERSITY OF MINNESOTA - LANDSCAPE ARBORETUM - ELMER L. & ELEANOR J. ANDERSEN HORTICULTURAL LIBRARY (Sci-Tech)
3675 Arboretum Dr.   Phone: (612) 443-2460
Chaska, MN 55318   June Rogier, Libn.
Founded: 1973. **Staff:** Prof 1. **Subjects:** Horticulture, botany, natural science, landscape architecture. **Special Collections:** Wildflowers - botanical illustrations; Frances R. Williams Collection (publications on the genus Hosta); seed and nursery catalogs. **Holdings:** 8007 books and bound periodical volumes; 555 AV items; 9 manuscripts; 27 microforms. **Subscriptions:** 286 journals and other serials. **Services:** Library open to public for reference use only; Arboretum plant locater. **Networks/Consortia:** Member of RLG.

★15812★
UNIVERSITY OF MINNESOTA - LAW LIBRARY (Law)
229 19th Ave. S.   Phone: (612) 373-2737
Minneapolis, MN 55455   Kathleen Price, Dir.
Founded: 1888. **Staff:** Prof 10; Other 12. **Subjects:** Law - Anglo-American, foreign. **Special Collections:** American Indians; British Commonwealth legal materials, including Indian and Pakistani legal materials. **Holdings:** 445,718 volumes; 269,093 microforms. **Subscriptions:** 8700 journals and other serials. **Services:** Interlibrary loans; copying; library open to public for reference use only. **Automated Operations:** Computerized cataloging. **Computerized Information Services:** LEXIS, Westlaw, Commerce Clearing House Electronic Legislative Search System (ELSS), RLIN, OCLC. **Networks/Consortia:** Member of MINITEX. **Publications:** Newsletter, monthly; Law Library Guide, irregular. **Staff:** Phyllis Marion, Asst. Dir.; Vera R. Carlsson, Hd. of Acq.; Gail M. Daly, Hd. of Cat.; Joseph Levstik, Foreign Law Libn.; Mary Ann Nelson, Ref.; Milagros R. Rush, Hd. of Ser.;Tom Woxland, Hd. of Pub.Serv.;

Susanne Nevin, Cat.; Nancy McCormick, Circ.

★15813★
UNIVERSITY OF MINNESOTA - LEARNING RESOURCES CENTER - NON-PRINT LIBRARY (Educ; Aud-Vis)
111 Walter Library
117 Pleasant St., S.E.   Phone: (612) 373-2538
Minneapolis, MN 55455   Daniel Donnelly, Act.Hd.
Staff: Prof 1; Other 3. **Subjects:** Foreign languages, liberal arts, science, agriculture, ethnic materials, graphic materials. **Holdings:** 12,000 sound recordings; 1000 video programs. **Services:** Center open to public for reference use only. **Staff:** Susan Gangle, Libn.

★15814★
UNIVERSITY OF MINNESOTA - LITZENBERG-LUND LIBRARY (Med)
Box 395, Mayo Memorial Bldg.
420 Delaware St., S.E.   Phone: (612) 373-8851
Minneapolis, MN 55455   Sandra Morrison, Libn.
Founded: 1977. **Staff:** 1. **Subjects:** Obstetrics, gynecology, endocrinology, oncology. **Special Collections:** Historical medical and obstetrics-gynecology books; population studies materials. **Holdings:** 578 books; 585 bound periodical volumes; World Fertility Survey Depository. **Subscriptions:** 28 journals and other serials. **Services:** Interlibrary loans; copying; library open to public with restrictions. **Special Indexes:** Index of obstetrics-gynecology journals. **Remarks:** The Litzenberg-Lund Library is sponsored by the University of Minnesota Obstetrics & Gynecology Associates and donations.

★15815★
UNIVERSITY OF MINNESOTA - MANUSCRIPTS DIVISION (Hist)
826 Berry St.   Phone: (612) 376-7271
St. Paul, MN 55114   Alan K. Lathrop, Cur.
Founded: 1970. **Staff:** Prof 1. **Special Collections:** Literary Manuscripts Collections - papers of Gordon R. Dickson (36 linear feet), Clifford D. Simak (580 linear feet), John Berryman (50 linear feet), Frederick Manfred (35 linear feet), H.P. Lovecraft (87 items), Thomas Disch (6 linear feet), Arthur Motley (195 linear feet); Performing Arts Archives - records of Guthrie Theater (200 linear feet), Minnesota Orchestra (250 linear feet); Northwest Architectural Archives - records of American Terra Cotta Company, Purcell and Elmslie, architects (100,000 items), Morrel and Nichols Landscape Architects (48 linear feet), Ellerbe Architects (20 linear feet), Liebenberg and Kaplan Architects (840 linear feet), L.S. Buffington Drawings Collection (2200 items). **Holdings:** 2900 books; 15,000 posters; 34,000 photographs; 6521 feet of manuscripts; 388 microforms; 24,633 AV items. **Services:** Copying; division open for research upon application. **Networks/Consortia:** Member of RLG. **Publications:** Newsletter, 5/year. **Special Indexes:** Index to architectural archives by building name, identifying media and type of documentation (card).

★15816★
UNIVERSITY OF MINNESOTA - MAP LIBRARY (Geog-Map)
Wilson Library, S-76
309 19th Ave. S.   Phone: (612) 373-2825
Minneapolis, MN 55455   J. Mai Treude, Libn.
Founded: 1940. **Staff:** Prof 1; Other 1. **Special Collections:** Ames Library of South Asia map collection of India; early maps of Minnesota. **Holdings:** 3913 books and bound periodical volumes; 214,377 maps; 16 microforms; atlases; pamphlets; 154,519 AV items. **Subscriptions:** 33 journals and other serials. **Services:** Interlibrary loans (limited); copying; library open to public with restrictions. **Networks/Consortia:** Member of MINITEX, RLG. **Publications:** Maps of Minnesota, an annotated list of sources (out of print). **Special Catalogs:** Catalog of Aerial Photography in the Map Library. **Special Indexes:** Address file of map and atlas publishers and dealers, by subject (card).

★15817★
UNIVERSITY OF MINNESOTA - MATHEMATICS LIBRARY (Sci-Tech)
Vincent Hall, Rm. 310
206 Church St. S.E.   Phone: (612) 376-7207
Minneapolis, MN 55455   Margie L. Voelker, Libn.
Staff: Prof 1; Other 1. **Subjects:** Pure mathematics, theoretical statistics. **Holdings:** 25,465 books and bound periodical volumes; 3 feet of manuscripts. **Subscriptions:** 348 journals and other serials. **Services:** Interlibrary loans; copying; library open to public for reference use only. **Computerized Information Services:** DIALOG, SDC, BRS. **Networks/Consortia:** Member of MINITEX; RLG.

★15818★
UNIVERSITY OF MINNESOTA - MIDDLE EAST LIBRARY (Area-Ethnic)
S50 Wilson Library
309 19th Ave., S.   Phone: (612) 373-7804
Minneapolis, MN 55455   Nassif Youssif, Hd.
Founded: 1967. **Staff:** Prof 1; Other 1. **Subjects:** Arabic, Hebrew, Persian and Turkish languages, literature and history. **Special Collections:** Middle Eastern vernaculars (32,000 volumes). **Holdings:** 33,992 books and bound periodical volumes; 45 government publications; 111 AV items; 18 microforms. **Subscriptions:** 197 journals and other serials; 32 newspapers. **Services:** Interlibrary loans; library open to public for reference use only. **Networks/Consortia:** Member of MINITEX; RLG.

UNIVERSITY OF MINNESOTA - MINITEX
See: MINITEX

★15819★
UNIVERSITY OF MINNESOTA - MINNESOTA CENTER FOR PHILOSOPHY OF SCIENCE - DEPARTMENTAL LIBRARY (Sci-Tech)
309 Ford Hall
224 Church St., S.E.   Phone: (612) 373-2845
Minneapolis, MN 55455   Philip Kitcher, Dir.
Subjects: Philosophy of science, physics, psychology; theoretical physics; psychology; logic (mathematical). **Holdings:** 1000 books; reprints; manuscripts. **Services:** Interlibrary loans; library open to instructors and graduate students.

UNIVERSITY OF MINNESOTA - MINNESOTA GEOLOGICAL SURVEY
See: Minnesota Geological Survey

★15820★
UNIVERSITY OF MINNESOTA - MUSIC LIBRARY (Mus)
204a Walter Library
117 Pleasant St., S.E.   Phone: (612) 373-3438
Minneapolis, MN 55455   Katharine Holum, Music Libn.
Founded: 1947. **Staff:** Prof 2; Other 1. **Subjects:** Musicology, music history, opera, theory and composition, vocal, instrumental and orchestra music, ethnomusicology, folk music, music therapy, music education, keyboard music. **Special Collections:** Donald N. Ferguson Collection of Rare Books and Scores (336 volumes); Operas of 18th & early 19th centuries (160 volumes); Ritzen Collection of Sound Recordings (2200 phonograph records); Latin American music scores (450 volumes); Berger Band Library (335 volumes). **Holdings:** 50,064 books, bound periodical volumes and music scores; 24,880 AV items; 780 microforms. **Subscriptions:** 246 journals and other serials. **Services:** Interlibrary loans; copying; library open to public for reference use only. **Computerized Information Services:** DIALOG, BRS, SDC. **Networks/Consortia:** Member of MINITEX; RLG.

★15821★
UNIVERSITY OF MINNESOTA - NEWMAN CENTER LIBRARY (Rel-Theol)
1701 University Ave., S.E.   Phone: (612) 331-3437
Minneapolis, MN 55414   Christine Cundall, Libn.
Staff: Prof 1; Other 1. **Subjects:** Theology, philosophy, humanities, ethics, medical ethics. **Special Collections:** Third World Library; Newman Center history. **Holdings:** 7500 books and bound periodical volumes; 195 tapes; 6 VF drawers of pamphlets and clippings; 1 box of materials about Pierre Teilhard de Chardin; 1 box of Newman publications. **Subscriptions:** 26 journals and other serials. **Services:** Interlibrary loans; library open to public.

★15822★
UNIVERSITY OF MINNESOTA - OCCUPATIONAL INFORMATION LIBRARY (Educ)
101 Eddy Hall
192 Pillsbury Dr., S.E.   Phone: (612) 373-4193
Minneapolis, MN 55455   Dr. Ellen Betz, Supv. of Lib.
Staff: 2. **Subjects:** Educational and career opportunities. **Holdings:** 200 books; 2000 school catalogs; 300 occupational files based on Dictionary of Occupational Titles; 36 cassette tapes on careers. **Subscriptions:** 12 journals and other serials. **Services:** Library open to public.

★15823★
UNIVERSITY OF MINNESOTA - PHYSICS LIBRARY (Sci-Tech)
260 Tate Lab. of Physics
116 Church St. S.E.   Phone: (612) 373-3362
Minneapolis, MN 55455   Donald Marion, Libn.
Founded: 1971. **Staff:** Prof 1; Other 1. **Subjects:** Physics, experimental and theoretical - high energy, nuclear, solid state, atmospheric, astrophysics; history of physics with emphasis on 19th and 20th centuries; astronomy. **Holdings:** 26,431 books and bound periodical volumes; 11 feet of manuscripts; 35 audio cassettes; 1033 microforms; depository for the Archive for History of Quantum Physics (AHQP). **Subscriptions:** 251 journals and other serials. **Services:** Interlibrary loans; microform copying; library open to public for reference use only; AHQP open by prior application only. **Networks/Consortia:** Member of MINITEX; RLG.

★15824★
UNIVERSITY OF MINNESOTA - PUBLIC ADMINISTRATION LIBRARY (Soc Sci)
365 Blegen Hall
269 19th Ave. S.   Phone: (612) 373-2892
Minneapolis, MN 55455   Eunice Bisbee Johnson, Sr.Lib.Asst.
Founded: 1936. **Staff:** 2. **Subjects:** Public administration, local government, policy analysis and evaluation, human services, land use. **Holdings:** 47,281 books and bound periodical volumes; 18 AV items; 750 microforms. **Subscriptions:** 460 journals and other serials. **Services:** Interlibrary loans (limited); library open to public for reference use only. **Computerized Information Services:** DIALOG, BRS, SDC. **Networks/Consortia:** Member of MINITEX; RLG.

★15825★
UNIVERSITY OF MINNESOTA - ST. ANTHONY FALLS HYDRAULIC LABORATORY - LORENZ G. STRAUB MEMORIAL LIBRARY (Sci-Tech)
Mississippi River at Third Ave., S.E.   Phone: (612) 373-2782
Minneapolis, MN 55414   Diana Dalbothen, Libn.
Founded: 1964. **Staff:** 1. **Subjects:** Hydraulics, hydrology, fluid mechanics, water resources. **Holdings:** 2000 books; 10,000 other cataloged items. **Subscriptions:** 15 journals and other serials. **Services:** Copying; library open to public.

★15826★
UNIVERSITY OF MINNESOTA - SCANDINAVIAN COLLECTION (Area-Ethnic)
Wilson Library
309 19th Ave. S.   Phone: (612) 376-2550
Minneapolis, MN 55455   Mariann Tiblin, Bibliog.
Subjects: Scandinavian literature, history, travel, geography. **Special Collections:** Jeppe Aakjaer Collection (110 volumes); Scandinavian Children's Literature Collection (700 volumes); Scandinavian Government Documents Collection; Par Lagerkvist Collection (158 volumes); Finnish-American Collection; Scandinavian maps; Scandinavian Travels Collection; August Strindberg Collection (800 volumes); Swedish Royal Decrees (1649-1824). **Holdings:** 150,000 volumes (in general Wilson Library collection). **Services:** Interlibrary loans; copying; collection open to public for reference use only. **Computerized Information Services:** DIALOG, BRS, SDC. **Networks/Consortia:** Member of MINITEX; RLG. **Remarks:** Materials in the Scandinavian Collection are located in various departments of the university libraries.

★15827★
UNIVERSITY OF MINNESOTA - SOCIAL AND ADMINISTRATIVE PHARMACY READING ROOM (Med)
7-159 Health Sciences Unit F
308 Harvard St., S.E.   Phone: (612) 376-5326
Minneapolis, MN 55455   Dr. Albert I. Wertheimer, Dir.
Staff: 2. **Subjects:** Pharmacy, drugs, health service. **Holdings:** 260 books; 290 bound periodical volumes; 3100 NTIS reports on microfiche; government publications; Ph.D. dissertations. **Subscriptions:** 51 journals and other serials. **Services:** Collection open to public with permission.

★15828★
UNIVERSITY OF MINNESOTA - SOCIAL WELFARE HISTORY ARCHIVES (Soc Sci)
109 Walter Library
117 Pleasant St., S.E.   Phone: (612) 373-4420
Minneapolis, MN 55455   David Klaassen, Cur.
Staff: Prof 2; Other 1. **Subjects:** Social welfare, settlement movement, professional social work, voluntary associations, recreation, health. **Special Collections:** Records and files of Survey Associates, National Federation of Settlements, National Association of Social Workers, United Neighborhood Houses of New York and others; social service organization materials (600 linear feet); contemporary feminist periodicals and pamphlets (100 linear feet). **Holdings:** 1130 books; 4008 feet of manuscripts; 1410 microforms; 144 AV items. **Subscriptions:** 73 journals and other serials. **Services:** Interlibrary loans (limited); copying; archives open for research upon application. **Publications:** Guide to Holdings, 1979; Descriptive Inventories of Collections in the Social Welfare History Archives. **Networks/Consortia:** Member of RLG. **Staff:** Clarke Chambers, Dir.

★15829★

UNIVERSITY OF MINNESOTA - SPECIAL COLLECTIONS AND RARE BOOKS LIBRARY (Rare Book)
Wilson Library 466
309 19th Ave. S.   Phone: (612) 373-2897
Minneapolis, MN 55455   Austin J. McLean, Cur., Spec.Coll.
Staff: Prof 2. **Subjects:** History, literature, philosophy, astronomy, 17th century England and Holland, private press books, fortification, Scandinavian travel. **Special Collections:** Walter De La Mare; Henry Miller; John Galsworthy; Franklin Delano Roosevelt; August Strindberg; Sinclair Lewis; John Steinbeck; Sherlock Holmes; Charles Dickens - Edwin Drood; Modern Greek literature; Par Lagerquist; Thomas Wolfe; World War I pamphlets (6000); Swedish Royal Decrees (2655). **Holdings:** 80,344 books and bound periodical volumes. **Subscriptions:** 23 journals and other serials. **Services:** Copying; library open to public for reference use only. **Networks/Consortia:** Member of RLG. **Special Indexes:** Card indexes to places, dates, printers of books before 1700; card index to private press books by press, printer, designers; card indexes of provenance, manuscripts, signed bindings.

★15830★

UNIVERSITY OF MINNESOTA - STATISTICS LIBRARY (Sci-Tech)
270a Vincent Hall
206 Church St., S.E.   Phone: (612) 373-3035
Minneapolis, MN 55455   Seymour Geisser, Dir.
Staff: 4. **Subjects:** Statistics. **Holdings:** 175 books; 151 bound periodical volumes; 14 bound theses; 900 School of Statistics technical reports. **Subscriptions:** 10 journals and other serials. **Services:** Copying; library open to public for reference use only.

★15831★

UNIVERSITY OF MINNESOTA - UNDERGROUND SPACE CENTER - LIBRARY (Sci-Tech; Plan)
790 Civil and Mineral Engr.Bldg.
500 Pillsbury Dr., S.E.   Phone: (612) 376-5341
Minneapolis, MN 55455   Arlene R. Bennett, Adm.Sec.
Founded: 1977. **Staff:** Prof 1. **Subjects:** Earth sheltered housing, energy, underground space use, rock and soil mechanics, alternative energy financing and legislation, building codes. **Holdings:** 150 books; 200 technical papers; 600 documents; 900 clippings. **Subscriptions:** 20 journals and other serials. **Services:** Library open to public for reference use only. **Publications:** Underline (newsletter), quarterly - by subscription. **Special Indexes:** Professionals involved in underground construction (computer listings). **Staff:** Dr. Ray Sterling, Dir.

★15832★

UNIVERSITY OF MINNESOTA - UNIVERSITY ARCHIVES (Hist)
10 Walter Library
117 Pleasant St. S.E.   Phone: (612) 373-2891
Minneapolis, MN 55455
Staff: Prof 2; Other 1. **Subjects:** University archives. **Special Collections:** Personal papers of people connected with the University. **Holdings:** 63,739 books, bound periodical volumes and dissertations; 10,029 linear feet of manuscripts; 40 VF drawers of ready reference material; 903 microforms; 38,292 AV items. **Subscriptions:** 430 journals and other serials. **Subscriptions:** 1740 journals and other serials. **Services:** Copying; archives open for research upon application. **Networks/Consortia:** Member of RLG. **Special Indexes:** Indexes for 7 major University publications (card).

★15833★

UNIVERSITY OF MINNESOTA, CROOKSTON - KIEHLE LIBRARY - MEDIA RESOURCES (Agri; Bus-Fin)
                                                   Phone: (218) 281-6510
Crookston, MN 56716   Harold J. Opgrand, Dir., Media Rsrcs.
Staff: Prof 3; Other 8. **Subjects:** Agriculture, horsemanship, business, foods. **Special Collections:** Minnesota State Depository materials. **Holdings:** 21,115 books; 97 periodicals on microfilm; 1695 AV programs. **Subscriptions:** 704 journals and other serials; 40 newspapers. **Services:** Interlibrary loans; copying; library open to public, AV materials may be used in-house only. **Automated Operations:** Computerized cataloging and ILL. **Computerized Information Services:** OCLC. **Networks/Consortia:** Member of MINITEX. **Staff:** Berneil C. Nelson, Sr.Lib.Asst.; Patricia Carlson, Libn.

★15834★

UNIVERSITY OF MINNESOTA, DULUTH - HEALTH SCIENCE LIBRARY (Med)
2400 Oakland Ave.   Phone: (218) 726-8585
Duluth, MN 55812   Diane C.P. Ebro, Dir.
Founded: 1971. **Staff:** Prof 3; Other 2. **Subjects:** Medicine, dentistry, veterinary medicine, forensic medicine, nursing, biology, behavioral science. **Holdings:** 13,621 books; 50,022 bound periodical volumes; 500 pamphlets;

4467 reels of microforms. **Subscriptions:** 430 journals and other serials. **Services:** Interlibrary loans; copying; SDI; library open to public. **Automated Operations:** Computerized cataloging and serials. **Computerized Information Services:** DIALOG, SDC, NLM, BRS, OCLC. **Networks/Consortia:** Member of Greater Midwest Regional Medical Library Network (Region 3); MINITEX; Arrowhead Professional Libraries Association (APLA). **Special Catalogs:** Serials Holding List. **Staff:** Jeanette Mueller, Ref./Online Serv.; Laureen Ross, ILL.

★15835★

UNIVERSITY OF MINNESOTA, DULUTH - LAKE SUPERIOR BASIN STUDIES CENTER - LAKE SUPERIOR REFERENCE LIBRARY
217 Research Lab. Bldg., Lower Campus
Duluth, MN 55812
Subjects: Environment, Lake Superior, hydrology, wildlife, limnology, recreation. **Special Collections:** Minnesota Ornithological Collection. **Holdings:** 600 books; 7000 bound periodical volumes; 1500 slides; 50 unbound reports; 30 manuscripts; 2500 reprints; 1000 pieces of data. **Remarks:** Presently inactive.

UNIVERSITY OF MINNESOTA, DULUTH - NORTHEAST MINNESOTA HISTORICAL CENTER
See: Northeast Minnesota Historical Center

UNIVERSITY OF MINNESOTA, MORRIS - WEST CENTRAL MINNESOTA HISTORICAL CENTER
See: West Central Minnesota Historical Center

★15836★

UNIVERSITY OF MINNESOTA, ST. PAUL - BIOCHEMISTRY LIBRARY (Sci-Tech)
406 Biological Sciences Ctr.
1445 Gortner Ave.   Phone: (612) 373-1582
St. Paul, MN 55108   Jeffrey Dains, Lib.Asst.
Staff: 1. **Subjects:** Biochemistry, plant biochemistry, animal biochemistry, chemistry of cereals and cereal products, genetics, cell biology. **Holdings:** 16,878 books and bound periodical volumes; 8188 microforms. **Subscriptions:** 233 journals and other serials. **Services:** Interlibrary loans (through Central Library, St. Paul Campus); copying; library open to public for reference use. **Networks/Consortia:** Member of MINITEX; RLG.

★15837★

UNIVERSITY OF MINNESOTA, ST. PAUL - CENTRAL LIBRARY (Agri; Sci-Tech)
1984 Buford Ave.   Phone: (612) 373-0904
St. Paul, MN 55108   Richard L. Rohrer, Dir.
Founded: 1890. **Staff:** Prof 7; Other 13. **Subjects:** Agricultural economics and engineering, agricultural and home economics education, home economics, agronomy and plant genetics, animal science, horticultural sciences, biological sciences, applied statistics, food science and nutrition, plant pathology, soil science. **Special Collections:** U.S.D.A. Depository materials; agricultural experiment station, extension, and international agricultural exchange publications. **Holdings:** 124,475 books and bound periodical volumes; 260,945 documents; 2470 maps; 4 AV items; 26,297 microforms. **Subscriptions:** 2570 journals and other serials. **Services:** Interlibrary loans; copying; BASIS (fee-based services); library open to public for reference use only. **Computerized Information Services:** BRS, DIALOG, SDC. **Networks/Consortia:** Member of MINITEX; RLG. **Staff:** Margaret Johnson, Hd., Tech.Serv.; John Beecher, Hd., Pub.Serv.

★15838★

UNIVERSITY OF MINNESOTA, ST. PAUL - DEPARTMENT OF VOCATIONAL & TECHNICAL EDUCATION - LEARNING RESOURCE CENTER (Educ)
Vocational & Technical Educ. Bldg.
1954 Buford Ave.   Phone: (612) 373-3838
St. Paul, MN 55108   Dr. Jerome Moss, Dir.
Founded: 1965. **Staff:** 2. **Subjects:** Vocational and technical education, research and development materials, SOM instructional materials. **Special Collections:** All documents available on microfiche from AIM and ARM. **Holdings:** 20,000 documents; 10 drawers of microfiche; 7 drawers of microfilm; 5000 hard copy items. **Services:** Center open to public for reference use only. **Automated Operations:** Computer-compiled bibliographies; microfiche to microfiche duplication.

★15839★

UNIVERSITY OF MINNESOTA, ST. PAUL - ENTOMOLOGY, FISHERIES AND WILDLIFE LIBRARY (Sci-Tech; Env-Cons)
1980 Folwell Ave.
375 Hodson Hall   Phone: (612) 373-1741
St. Paul, MN 55108   Katherine S. Chiang, Hd.
Founded: 1905. **Staff:** Prof 1; Other 1. **Subjects:** Entomology, fisheries,

wildlife, pesticides, water pollution, limnology, aquatic biology. **Special Collections:** Bee collection (800 monographs; 87 journal titles). **Holdings:** 30,785 books and bound periodical volumes; 32,701 documents; 82 maps; 813 AV items; 2764 microforms. **Subscriptions:** 856 journals and other serials. **Services:** Interlibrary loans; copying; library open to public for reference use only. **Computerized Information Services:** DIALOG. **Networks/Consortia:** Member of MINITEX; RLG.

★15840★
UNIVERSITY OF MINNESOTA, ST. PAUL - FORESTRY LIBRARY (Sci-Tech; Env-Cons)
Green Hall
1530 N. Cleveland Ave.   Phone: (612) 373-1407
St. Paul, MN 55108   Jean Albrecht, Libn.
Founded: 1899. **Staff:** Prof 1; Other 1. **Subjects:** Forestry, forest products, outdoor recreation, conservation of natural resources, hydrology, range management, aerial photogrammetry, remote sensing, pulp and paper. **Holdings:** 20,591 books and bound periodical volumes; 52,714 documents; 2836 maps; 537 AV items; 1870 microforms. **Subscriptions:** 979 journals and other serials. **Services:** Interlibrary loans (through Central Library, St. Paul Campus); copying; library open to public for reference use only. **Computerized Information Services:** SDC, DIALOG. **Networks/Consortia:** Member of MINITEX; RLG.

★15841★
UNIVERSITY OF MINNESOTA, ST. PAUL - HERBARIUM COLLECTION (Sci-Tech)
St. Paul Campus Library
1984 Buford Ave.
St. Paul, MN 55108
Special Collections: Special subject collection of botanical taxonomic materials (2130 volumes; 1500 reprints and pamphlets). **Holdings:** Figures not available. **Subscriptions:** 12 journals and other serials. **Services:** Collection open to faculty and graduate students only.

★15842★
UNIVERSITY OF MINNESOTA, ST. PAUL - PLANT PATHOLOGY LIBRARY (Sci-Tech)
202 Stakman Hall
1519 Gortner Ave.   Phone: (612) 373-1669
St. Paul, MN 55108   Erik Biever, Lib.Asst.
Founded: 1909. **Staff:** 1. **Subjects:** Phytopathology, mycology, air pollution effects on vegetation. **Holdings:** 6938 books and bound periodical volumes; 6525 government publications; 66 AV items; 92 microforms. **Subscriptions:** 115 journals and other serials. **Services:** Interlibrary loans (through Central Library, St. Paul Campus); copying; library open to public for reference use. **Networks/Consortia:** Member of MINITEX; RLG.

★15843★
UNIVERSITY OF MINNESOTA, ST. PAUL - VETERINARY MEDICAL LIBRARY (Med)
450 Veterinary Science Bldg.
1971 Commonwealth Ave.   Phone: (612) 373-1455
St. Paul, MN 55108   Livija Carlson, Libn.
Staff: Prof 1; Other 1. **Subjects:** Veterinary medicine. **Special Collections:** German veterinary theses. **Holdings:** 32,118 books and bound periodical volumes; 10,894 documents; 606 microforms; dissertations. **Subscriptions:** 771 journals and other serials. **Services:** Interlibrary loans; copying; library open to public for reference use only. **Networks/Consortia:** Member of MINITEX; RLG. **Special Catalogs:** Pamphlet and documents catalogs.

★15844★
UNIVERSITY OF MINNESOTA TECHNICAL COLLEGE, WASECA - LEARNING RESOURCES (Agri)
                                                 Phone: (507) 835-1000
Waseca, MN 56093   Nan Wilhelmson, Dir.
Founded: 1971. **Staff:** Prof 3; Other 1. **Subjects:** Agricultural business, production, industries and services; animal health technology; food industry and technology; home and family services; horticulture technology. **Holdings:** 20,000 books; 490 bound periodical volumes; 3500 AV items; 5800 government documents; 1700 microforms; 12,000 pamphlets. **Subscriptions:** 650 journals and other serials; 40 newspapers. **Services:** Interlibrary loans; copying; center open to public. **Automated Operations:** Computerized cataloging. **Computerized Information Services:** DIALOG, OCLC. **Networks/Consortia:** Member of MINITEX; Southcentral Minnesota Inter-Library Exchange (SMILE); Waseca Interlibrary Resource Exchange (WIRE). **Special Indexes:** Monthly Bibliography - free upon request. **Staff:** Kathryn Rynders, Ref.Libn.; Kathleen Ashe, Tech.Serv.Libn.

★15845★
UNIVERSITY OF MISSISSIPPI - ARCHIVES & SPECIAL COLLECTIONS/ MISSISSIPPIANA (Hist)
                                                 Phone: (601) 232-7408
University, MS 38677   Dr. Thomas M. Verich, Hd. of Archv. & Spec.Coll
Founded: 1975. **Staff:** Prof 2; Other 3. **Subjects:** Mississippi subjects and authors. **Special Collections:** Lumber archives of lumber industry of southern Mississippi (268 linear feet); William Faulkner Collection (2000 volumes); Wynn Collection of Faulkner editions; Senator Pat Harrison Collection (51 linear feet including photographs); Arthur Palmer Hudson Folklore Collection (5 linear feet); David L. Cohn Collection (12 linear feet); Stark Young Collection (3.5 linear feet); Revolutionary War Letters (1 linear foot); Goldstein Folklore Collection (12,000 volumes; 4000 phonograph records); Rayburn Collection of Paper Americana and blues phonodiscs (20 linear feet); Gorove Space Law Collection (100 linear feet); B.B. King Collection (147 linear feet; 7300 phonograph records); Herschel Brickell Collection (4000 manuscript items; 3400 volumes; 150 linear feet); William Faulkner Rowan Oak Literary Manuscript Collection. **Holdings:** 32,000 books; 3000 bound periodical volumes; 2000 manuscripts; 525 linear feet of University of Mississippi archival materials; 221 linear feet of Thomas G. Abernathy papers; 67 linear feet of Carroll Gartin papers, 1913-1966; 485 linear feet of John E. Rankin papers, 1882-1960; 164 linear feet of William M. Whittington papers, 1878-1962; 180 linear feet of William M. (Fishbait) Miller papers (all papers are unprocessed); 9.5 linear feet of Henry H. Bellamann papers, 1882-1945; 80 linear feet of James W. Garner papers. **Subscriptions:** 150 journals and other serials. **Services:** Interlibrary loans; copying; archives open to public; some materials do not circulate. **Staff:** Robert A. Linder, Sr.Libn.

★15846★
UNIVERSITY OF MISSISSIPPI - BUREAU OF BUSINESS & ECONOMIC RESEARCH LIBRARY (Bus-Fin)
School of Business Administration   Phone: (601) 232-7481
University, MS 38677
Subjects: Economics, business, public finance, government. **Holdings:** 5000 documents; Mississippi documents. **Subscriptions:** 300 journals and other serials. **Services:** Interlibrary loans; library open to public for reference use only.

★15847★
UNIVERSITY OF MISSISSIPPI - BUREAU OF GOVERNMENTAL RESEARCH LIBRARY (Soc Sci)
                                                 Phone: (601) 232-7401
University, MS 38677   Dorothy I. Wilson, Ed.Asst.
Founded: 1945. **Staff:** Prof 1. **Subjects:** State, local and national government; public administration and regional governance. **Special Collections:** Mississippi Collection (500 volumes). **Holdings:** 5500 volumes; 10 VF drawers of publications and clippings; 78 dissertations and masters' theses. **Subscriptions:** 200 journals and other serials. **Services:** Library open to qualified researchers.

★15848★
UNIVERSITY OF MISSISSIPPI - SCHOOL OF EDUCATION LIBRARY (Educ)
School of Education Bldg.   Phone: (601) 232-7040
University, MS 38677   Joyce Taylor, Educ.Libn.
Founded: 1976. **Staff:** Prof 1; Other 10. **Subjects:** Education. **Holdings:** 11,900 books; 165 bound periodical volumes; 728 dissertations; 900 AV items; 110 linear feet of curriculum guides, standardized tests and resource materials; 8 global maps. **Subscriptions:** 81 journals and other serials. **Services:** Interlibrary loans; copying; SDI; library open to public. **Computerized Information Services:** Online systems. **Publications:** Bibliography of Doctoral Dissertations in Education Completed at the University of Mississippi, 1953-1976.

★15849★
UNIVERSITY OF MISSISSIPPI - SCHOOL OF LAW LIBRARY (Law)
                                                 Phone: (601) 232-7361
University, MS 38677   Thomas M. Steele, Law Libn.
Founded: 1854. **Staff:** Prof 6; Other 6. **Subjects:** Law - American and international. **Special Collections:** Papers of Senator Eastland (1600 linear feet); Senator Cochran (75 linear feet); Congressman Lott (40 linear feet); Judge Smith (20 linear feet). **Holdings:** 113,000 volumes; 55,000 microforms. **Subscriptions:** 1898 journals and other serials. **Services:** Interlibrary loans; copying; library open to public with restrictions. **Automated Operations:** Computerized cataloging. **Computerized Information Services:** LEXIS, Westlaw, DIALOG, OCLC. **Networks/Consortia:** Member of SOLINET. **Publications:** Brief case, monthly. **Staff:** Chet Bunnell, Pub.Serv.Libn.; Ann Fessenden, Tech.Serv.Libn.; John Sobotka, Archv.; Ellis Tucker, Sys.Libn.; Pencie Latham, Cat./Circ.Libn.

★15850★

UNIVERSITY OF MISSISSIPPI - SCHOOL OF PHARMACY - AUSTIN A. DODGE PHARMACY LIBRARY (Med)

University, MS 38677

Phone: (601) 232-7381
Nancy F. Fuller, Libn.

Founded: 1965. **Staff:** Prof 1; Other 1. **Subjects:** Pharmacy, medicine, organic chemistry, health care administration, botany (pharmacognosy). **Holdings:** 25,083 books, bound periodical volumes, reels of microfilm and AV items; 29 VF drawers of pamphlets; 127 dissertations and graduate theses from School of Pharmacy. **Subscriptions:** 412 journals and other serials; 5 newspapers. **Services:** Interlibrary loans; copying; library open to public for reference use only. **Computerized Information Services:** BRS, DIALOG, SDC, OCLC.

UNIVERSITY OF MISSOURI - COLLEGE OF VETERINARY MEDICINE -OFA HIP DYSPLASIA REGISTRY
See: Orthopedic Foundation for Animals - OFA Hip Dysplasia Registry

★15851★

UNIVERSITY OF MISSOURI - COLUMBIA MISSOURIAN - NEWSPAPER REFERENCE LIBRARY (Publ)

9th & Elm
Columbia, MO 65201

Phone: (314) 882-4876
Robert Stevens, Newspaper Ref.Libn.

Staff: Prof 1; Other 6. **Subjects:** Columbia, Boone County, Missouri. **Holdings:** 77 books; 37,800 biographical clippings files; 10,800 subject clippings files; 13,200 photograph and illustration files; 560 pamphlet files. **Services:** Copying; library open to public for reference use only. **Special Indexes:** Subject index to file cards and clippings.

★15852★

UNIVERSITY OF MISSOURI - ENGINEERING LIBRARY (Sci-Tech)

2017 Engineering Bldg.
Columbia, MO 65211

Phone: (314) 882-2379
Alfred H. Jones, Libn.

Founded: 1906. **Staff:** Prof 1; Other 2. **Subjects:** Engineering - chemical, civil, electrical, industrial, mechanical, agricultural, nuclear. **Holdings:** 58,056 volumes. **Subscriptions:** 562 journals and other serials. **Services:** Interlibrary loans; copying; library open to public with restrictions on borrowing. **Automated Operations:** Computerized cataloging and acquisitions. **Computerized Information Services:** DIALOG, SDC, BRS, OCLC. **Networks/Consortia:** Member of CRL. **Publications:** New Book List, monthly - distributed to engineering faculty.

★15853★

UNIVERSITY OF MISSOURI - FREEDOM OF INFORMATION CENTER (Info Sci)

223 Walter Williams Hall
Box 858
Columbia, MO 65205

Phone: (314) 882-4856
Dr. Paul L. Fisher, Dir.

Founded: 1959. **Subjects:** Access to information at all levels of government, censorship, legal issues related to the activities of the communications media, First Amendment. **Holdings:** 600 volumes; journals; pamphlets; clippings; reprints; government documents; dissertations. **Subscriptions:** 200 journals and other serials. **Services:** Copying; copying and research from files on access to information. **Publications:** FoI Center Report, 18/year; FoI Digest, bimonthly - both by subscription.

UNIVERSITY OF MISSOURI - FREEDOM OF INFORMATION CENTER - INVESTIGATIVE REPORTERS AND EDITORS, INC.
See: Investigative Reporters and Editors, Inc.

★15854★

UNIVERSITY OF MISSOURI - GEOLOGY LIBRARY (Sci-Tech)

201 Geology Bldg.
Columbia, MO 65211

Phone: (314) 882-4860
Robert Heidlage, Lib.Asst.

Staff: 5. **Subjects:** Paleontology, stratigraphy, sedimentology, geochemistry, geomorphology, hydrology. **Holdings:** 37,689 volumes; 100,000 maps. **Subscriptions:** 500 journals and other serials. **Services:** Interlibrary loans; copying; library open to public for reference use; materials circulate to library card holders only. **Automated Operations:** Computerized cataloging and acquisitions. **Computerized Information Services:** OCLC, DIALOG, SDC, BRS. **Networks/Consortia:** Member of CRL.

★15855★

UNIVERSITY OF MISSOURI - HEALTH CARE TECHNOLOGY CENTER & INFORMATION SCIENCE GROUP - INFORMATION CENTER (Med)

605 Lewis Hall
Columbia, MO 65211

Phone: (314) 882-4906
Arjun Reddy, Hd.

Founded: 1977. **Staff:** Prof 3; Other 2. **Subjects:** Health care technology, health services research, computer applications in medicine. **Special Collections:** Medical Information Systems (2600 entries), includes Drug Information Systems (290 entries) and Hospital Information Systems (600 entries); Microprocessors (200 entries); Medical Imaging (2000 entries), including Computerized Tomography (1200 entries) and Ultrasound (600 entries); End-Stage Renal Disease (460 entries); Medical Competency Examination (290 entries); Hospital Technology Costs (500 entries); Mental Health Information Systems (1200 entries). **Holdings:** 1200 books; 2000 unbound periodicals; 6000 reprints; 800 pamphlets, clippings, manuscripts and reports. **Subscriptions:** 70 journals and other serials. **Services:** Copying; center open to public through HCTC Project Staff. **Computerized Information Services:** DIALOG, MEDLARS; database for HSRC/HCTC Special Collections. **Staff:** Beatrice Engley, Info.Spec.; Jody Neikirk, Info.Asst.

★15856★

UNIVERSITY OF MISSOURI - HEALTH SCIENCES LIBRARY (Med)

Health Sciences Center
Columbia, MO 65212

Phone: (314) 882-8086
Dean Schmidt, Libn.

Founded: 1903. **Staff:** Prof 7; Other 10. **Subjects:** Medicine, nursing, hospital administration. **Holdings:** 143,487 books and bound periodical volumes; 230 microforms; 500 tapes; 150 motion pictures; 200 AV kits; 25 phonograph records; 2000 slides. **Subscriptions:** 1857 journals and other serials. **Services:** Interlibrary loans; copying; library open to public for reference use only. **Automated Operations:** Computerized cataloging, acquisitions and serials. **Computerized Information Services:** MEDLINE, BRS, DIALOG, SDC. **Staff:** Emma Jean McKinin, Hd., Pub.Serv.; Richard Rexroat, Hd., Ser.Sect.; Alice Edwards, Ref.Libn.; Diane Johnson, Hd., ILL; Jane Mongeon, Hd., Acq.; Wilma Gulstad, Hd., Cat.

★15857★

UNIVERSITY OF MISSOURI - JOURNALISM LIBRARY (Info Sci)

117 Walter Williams Hall
Columbia, MO 65202

Phone: (314) 882-7502
Robert C. Hahn, Libn.

Founded: 1908. **Staff:** Prof 2; Other 2. **Subjects:** Advertising, broadcasting, journalism, magazines, news writing and management, newspaper publishing, photography, public relations, semantics, typography, linotype. **Holdings:** 19,000 books; 3000 bound periodical volumes. **Subscriptions:** 370 journals and other serials.

★15858★

UNIVERSITY OF MISSOURI - MATH SCIENCES LIBRARY (Sci-Tech; Comp Sci)

206 Math Sciences Bldg.
Columbia, MO 65211

Phone: (314) 882-7286
Alfred H. Jones, Libn.

Founded: 1968. **Staff:** 2. **Subjects:** Mathematics, computer science, statistics. **Holdings:** 26,616 books and bound periodical volumes. **Subscriptions:** 401 journals and other serials. **Services:** Interlibrary loans; library open to public with restrictions. **Automated Operations:** Computerized cataloging, acquisitions and circulation. **Computerized Information Services:** DIALOG, SDC, BRS, OCLC. **Networks/Consortia:** Member of CRL.

★15859★

UNIVERSITY OF MISSOURI - MUSEUM LIBRARY (Art)

Pickard Hall
Columbia, MO 65211

Phone: (314) 882-3591
Forrest McGill, Dir. of Musm.

Subjects: Art history, archeology. **Holdings:** 500 books; 5000 exhibition and sales catalogs. **Services:** Library open to public with restrictions.

★15860★

UNIVERSITY OF MISSOURI - RESEARCH PARK LIBRARY (Sci-Tech)

132 Dalton Research Ctr.
Columbia, MO 65211

Phone: (314) 882-3527
Janice Dysart, Research Park Libn.

Founded: 1968. **Staff:** Prof 1. **Subjects:** Life sciences, nuclear sciences. **Special Collections:** AEC/ERDA/DOE Administrative Reports (700,000 microforms). **Holdings:** 2766 books; 460 bound periodical volumes; 34 theses and dissertations. **Subscriptions:** 60 journals and other serials. **Services:** Interlibrary loans; copying; library open to public. **Automated Operations:** Computerized cataloging, acquisitions and circulation. **Computerized Information Services:** DIALOG, SDC, BRS, OCLC. **Networks/Consortia:** Member of CRL.

★15861★

UNIVERSITY OF MISSOURI - SCHOOL OF LAW LIBRARY (Law)

Tate Hall
Columbia, MO 65211

Phone: (314) 882-4597
Susan D. Csaky, Prof./Law Libn.

Staff: Prof 5; Other 6. **Subjects:** Law. **Special Collections:** Lawson Collection (criminal law and criminology); U.S. and state government document depository. **Holdings:** 160,496 volumes; 138,671 microforms. **Subscriptions:** 2206 journals and other serials. **Services:** Interlibrary loans; copying; library open to public with restrictions. **Automated Operations:**

Computerized cataloging. **Computerized Information Services:** LEXIS, OCLC, Westlaw. **Networks/Consortia:** Member of Mid-America Law School Library Consortium; Libraries of the University of Missouri Information Network (LUMIN); Missouri Library Network Corporation; CLASS. **Publications:** Law Library Guide; Selected Acquisitions List; Information Services; bibliographies. **Staff:** Jo Ann Humphreys, Pub.Serv. Law Libn.; David G. Cowan, Instr.Serv. Law Libn.; Connie Fennewald, Acq. Law Libn.; Bruce Frost, Cat. Law Libn.

★15862★

UNIVERSITY OF MISSOURI - VETERINARY MEDICAL LIBRARY (Med)
W218 Veterinary Medicine   Phone: (314) 882-2461
Columbia, MO 65211   Trenton Boyd, Libn.
Founded: 1951. **Staff:** Prof 1; Other 2. **Subjects:** Veterinary medicine. **Holdings:** 32,302 volumes; 712 microforms. **Subscriptions:** 598 journals and other serials. **Services:** Interlibrary loans; copying; library open to public. **Automated Operations:** Computerized cataloging, acquisitions and serials. **Computerized Information Services:** MEDLINE, DIALOG, SDC, BRS.

UNIVERSITY OF MISSOURI - WESTERN HISTORICAL MANUSCRIPT COLL./ STATE HIST. SOCIETY OF MISSOURI MANUSCRIPTS JOINT COLL.
See: Western Historical Manuscript Collection/State Historical Society of Missouri Manuscripts Joint Collection

★15863★

UNIVERSITY OF MISSOURI, KANSAS CITY - CONSERVATORY LIBRARY (Mus)
General Library
5100 Rockhill Rd.   Phone: (816) 276-1675
Kansas City, MO 64110
Founded: 1906. **Staff:** Prof 1; Other 1. **Subjects:** Music. **Special Collections:** Archives of the Institute for Studies in American Music; manuscripts from MacDowell Colony and regional composers; Virgil Thomson Room (77,000 pieces of correspondence; articles; published music). **Holdings:** 46,337 volumes; 16,702 recordings; 54,460 music sheets. **Subscriptions:** 276 journals and other serials. **Services:** Interlibrary loans; copying; library open to public for reference use only. **Special Catalogs:** Bibliography in American music (card).

★15864★

UNIVERSITY OF MISSOURI, KANSAS CITY - HEALTH SCIENCES LIBRARY (Med)
2411 Holmes   Phone: (816) 474-4100
Kansas City, MO 64108   Marilyn Sullivan, Chf.Libn.
Founded: 1967. **Staff:** Prof 7; Other 8. **Subjects:** Medicine, nursing. **Holdings:** 14,419 books; 46,387 bound periodical volumes; 2019 AV titles. **Subscriptions:** 953 journals and other serials. **Services:** Interlibrary loans; copying; SDI; library open to members of the health sciences community. **Computerized Information Services:** DIALOG, BRS, SDC, MEDLARS; current references on patient care management. **Networks/Consortia:** Member of Kansas City Library Network, Inc. (KCLN); Kansas City Metropolitan Library Network (KCMLN). **Publications:** Current References, monthly - free to UMKC School of Medicine and affiliated institutions. **Remarks:** Contains the archives of the American Nurses' Association. **Staff:** Susan Case, Sr. Clinical Med.Libn.; Sally Chu, AV Med.Libn.Jeanne Sarkis, Sr. Clinical Med.Libn.; Randy Morris, Ill.

★15865★

UNIVERSITY OF MISSOURI, KANSAS CITY - LAW LIBRARY (Law)
School of Law
5100 Rockhill Rd.   Phone: (816) 276-1650
Kansas City, MO 64110   Charles R. Dyer, Law Libn.
Staff: Prof 5; Other 4. **Subjects:** Law. **Holdings:** 116,121 volumes; 107,805 microfiche; 54 reels of microfilm. **Subscriptions:** 3876 journals and other serials. **Services:** Interlibrary loans; copying; library open to public. **Automated Operations:** Computerized cataloging. **Computerized Information Services:** LEXIS, OCLC. **Networks/Consortia:** Member of Mid-America Association of Law Libraries (MAALL). **Staff:** Shelley Dowling, Asst.Libn.; Linda Stephenson, Asst.Libn.; Michele Finerty, Asst.Libn.; Annabelle Beach, Asst.Libn.

★15866★

UNIVERSITY OF MISSOURI, KANSAS CITY - SCHOOL OF DENTISTRY LIBRARY (Med)
650 E. 25th St.   Phone: (816) 234-0494
Kansas City, MO 64108   Ann Marie Corry, Dental Libn.
Founded: 1920. **Staff:** Prof 2; Other 3. **Subjects:** Dentistry. **Holdings:** 10,289 books; 9280 bibliographic volumes of periodicals. **Subscriptions:** 394 journals and other serials. **Services:** Interlibrary loans; copying; library

open to public for reference use only. **Computerized Information Services:** BRS, MEDLINE, OCTANET. **Networks/Consortia:** Member of Kansas City Library Network, Inc. (KCLN). **Staff:** Carolyn M. Ruby, Asst. Dental Libn.

★15867★

UNIVERSITY OF MISSOURI, KANSAS CITY - SNYDER COLLECTION OF AMERICANA (Hist)
General Library
5100 Rockhill Rd.   Phone: (816) 276-1534
Kansas City, MO 64110
Founded: 1937. **Subjects:** Political campaign literature; Civil War; Indians of North America; Kansas and Missouri - history, travel, biography, fiction, poetry; 19th-century Americana; early Missouri and Kansas imprints. **Holdings:** 25,000 volumes; 28 VF drawers of clippings. **Services:** Interlibrary loans (limited); copying.

★15868★

UNIVERSITY OF MISSOURI, KANSAS CITY - TEDROW TRANSPORTATION COLLECTION (Trans)
General Library
5100 Rockhill Rd.   Phone: (816) 276-1534
Kansas City, MO 64110
Founded: 1950. **Subjects:** Transportation - railroad, motor, water, air. **Holdings:** 1250 books and bound periodical volumes. **Services:** Interlibrary loans; copying.

★15869★

UNIVERSITY OF MISSOURI, ROLLA - CURTIS LAWS WILSON LIBRARY (Sci-Tech)
    Phone: (314) 341-4227
Rolla, MO 65401   Ronald Bohley, Libn.
Founded: 1871. **Staff:** Prof 8; Other 19. **Subjects:** Mining, metallurgy, engineering, geology, earth sciences. **Special Collections:** U.S. Atomic Energy Commission reports; U.S. Geological Survey publications; U.S. Bureau of Mines publications. **Holdings:** 350,000 volumes. **Subscriptions:** 2000 journals and other serials; 20 newspapers. **Services:** Interlibrary loans; copying; library open to public. **Automated Operations:** Computerized cataloging. **Computerized Information Services:** DIALOG, SDC, OCLC; internal database. **Networks/Consortia:** Member of Missouri Library Network Corporation. **Special Catalogs:** Catalog of microfilm held by all University of Missouri Libraries. **Staff:** Jean Eisenman, Asst.Dir., Pub.Serv.; James Cubit, Asst.Dir., Tech.Serv.

★15870★

UNIVERSITY OF MISSOURI, ST. LOUIS - EDUCATION LIBRARY (Educ)
8001 Natural Bridge Rd.   Phone: (314) 553-5571
St. Louis, MO 63121   Virginia R. Workman, Hd., Educ.Lib.
Founded: 1976. **Staff:** Prof 1; Other 14. **Subjects:** Education, children's literature. **Special Collections:** Test collection (1013); K-12 textbooks (10,386). **Holdings:** 45,082 books; 4613 bound periodical volumes; 4400 curriculum guides; 297,444 ERIC microfiche and indexes; 6021 curriculum guides on microfiche. **Subscriptions:** 400 journals and other serials. **Services:** Interlibrary loans; library not open to public. **Computerized Information Services:** BRS. **Networks/Consortia:** Member of St. Louis Regional Library Network. **Staff:** Leta Webster, Tech.Serv.Supv.; Sharon Mohme, Pub.Serv.Supv.

★15871★

UNIVERSITY OF MISSOURI, ST. LOUIS - HEALTH SCIENCES LIBRARY (Med)
8001 Natural Bridge Rd.   Phone: (314) 553-5909
St. Louis, MO 63121   Cheryle J. Cann, Health Sci.Libn.
Founded: 1981. **Staff:** Prof 1; Other 1. **Subjects:** Optometry, ophthalmology, nursing, public health, medicine. **Holdings:** 2500 books; 1000 bound periodical volumes; 255 AV materials; 172 reels of microfilm; 982 microfiche. **Subscriptions:** 190 journals and other serials. **Services:** Interlibrary loans; SDI (upon written request); library open to public. **Computerized Information Services:** BRS. Performs searches on cost recovery basis. **Networks/Consortia:** Member of St. Louis Medical Librarian's Association. **Publications:** Self-Guided Tour of the Health Sciences Library-UMSL - to new students, faculty and staff in nursing and optometry.

★15872★

UNIVERSITY OF MISSOURI, ST. LOUIS - THOMAS JEFFERSON LIBRARY - SPECIAL COLLECTIONS (Soc Sci; Hum)
8001 Natural Bridge Rd.   Phone: (314) 553-5053
St. Louis, MO 63121   Ron Krash, Dir.
Holdings: Colonial Latin American history; Utopian literature and science fiction; U.S. Government Depository Library. **Services:** Interlibrary loans; copying; collections open to public with special permit. **Automated**

Operations: Computerized cataloging. **Computerized Information Services:** DIALOG, BRS, OCLC; internal database. Performs searches on cost recovery basis. Contact Person: Mark Scheu, 553-5060. **Networks/Consortia:** Member of St. Louis Regional Library Network.

★15873★
UNIVERSITY OF MISSOURI, ST. LOUIS - WOMEN'S CENTER (Soc Sci)
107A Benton Hall
8001 Natural Bridge Rd.   Phone: (314) 553-5380
St. Louis, MO 63121   Cathy Burack, Dir.
Staff: 3. **Subjects:** Women - politics, psychology, medicine; male sex roles. **Holdings:** 450 books; 500 unbound periodicals; 8 VF drawers of clippings and reports. **Subscriptions:** 6 newspapers. **Services:** Center not open to public.

UNIVERSITY OF MONCTON
See: Universite de Moncton

★15874★
UNIVERSITY OF MONTANA - BUREAU OF BUSINESS AND ECONOMIC RESEARCH - LIBRARY (Bus-Fin)
School of Business Administration   Phone: (406) 243-5113
Missoula, MT 59812
Staff: 1. **Subjects:** Economic indicators in the United States and Montana; regional economics with emphasis on Montana and northern Rocky Mountain area; wood products industry. **Special Collections:** Montana, Idaho, and Wyoming Forest Industry Data Systems. **Holdings:** Figures not available. **Subscriptions:** 52 journals and other serials. **Services:** Copying; library open to public with restrictions. **Publications:** List of publications - available on request. **Staff:** James Sylvester, Res.Asst.

★15875★
UNIVERSITY OF MONTANA - MAUREEN & MIKE MANSFIELD LIBRARY - K. ROSS TOOLE ARCHIVES (Hist)
                                     Phone: (406) 243-2053
Missoula, MT 59812   Dale L. Johnson, Archv.
Staff: Prof 1. **Subjects:** Montana - business history, forest industries; politics and government. **Special Collections:** James W. Gerard Collection; Mike Mansfield Collection; James E. Murray Collection; Joseph M. Dixon Collection. **Holdings:** 800 oral histories; 30,000 photographs; 8000 feet of manuscripts. **Services:** Copying; archives open to public.

UNIVERSITY OF MONTANA - MONTANA ENVIRONMENTAL LIBRARY
See: Western Montana Scientists' Committee for Public Information - Montana Environmental Library

★15876★
UNIVERSITY OF MONTANA - OFFICE OF CAREER SERVICES - CAREER PLANNING & RESOURCE CENTER (Soc Sci)
Center for Student Development, Lodge 148   Phone: (406) 243-5460
Missoula, MT 59802   Richard McDonough, Career Counselor
Founded: 1974. **Staff:** Prof 1; Other 4. **Subjects:** Career information. **Holdings:** 200 books; 1200 reports, monographs, pamphlet files; state and national job vacancy listings; state and federal government career information; corporate literature; undergraduate and graduate school information. **Subscriptions:** 12 journals and other serials. **Services:** Center open to public for reference use only.

★15877★
UNIVERSITY OF MONTANA - SCHOOL OF FORESTRY - OXFORD COLLECTION (Env-Cons)
Science Division, Mansfield Library   Phone: (406) 243-6411
Missoula, MT 59812   Robert Schipf, Sci.Libn.
Staff: Prof 1; Other 1. **Subjects:** Forestry sciences, conservation, range management, public administration, wildlife management, wood science and technology, recreation. **Holdings:** 36,431 cataloged items; 379 boxes of government bulletins and circulars; 761 boxes of state materials; 443 boxes and 100 VF drawers of reprints and government publications; 30 unbound journals; 300,000 technical abstracts on cards. **Subscriptions:** 43 journals and other serials. **Services:** Collection open to public by appointment. **Staff:** Irene Evers, Asst.Sci.Libn.

★15878★
UNIVERSITY OF MONTANA - SCHOOL OF LAW - LAW LIBRARY (Law)
                                     Phone: (406) 243-6171
Missoula, MT 59801   Maurice M. Michel, Libn.
Founded: 1911. **Staff:** Prof 1; Other 3. **Subjects:** Law. **Special Collections:** Indian law (135 treatises). **Holdings:** 104,241 books. **Subscriptions:** 642 journals and other serials. **Services:** Interlibrary loans; copying; library open to public for reference use only. **Computerized Information Services:** Westlaw.

UNIVERSITY OF MONTREAL
See: Universite de Montreal

★15879★
UNIVERSITY OF NEBRASKA, LINCOLN - ARCHITECTURE LIBRARY (Art; Plan)
104 Architectural Hall   Phone: (402) 472-1208
Lincoln, NE 68588-0410   Kathleen A. Johnson, Assoc.Prof.
Staff: Prof 1; Other 2. **Subjects:** Architecture, community and regional planning. **Holdings:** 16,603 books; 8386 bound periodical volumes; 487 volumes on microfilm; 2788 volumes on microfiche; 48 VF drawers. **Subscriptions:** 229 journals and other serials. **Services:** Interlibrary loans; library open to public. **Automated Operations:** Computerized circulation. **Computerized Information Services:** DIALOG, SDC, BRS (through Love Library).

★15880★
UNIVERSITY OF NEBRASKA, LINCOLN - BIOLOGICAL SCIENCES LIBRARY (Sci-Tech)
Manter Hall 402   Phone: (402) 472-2756
Lincoln, NE 68588-0118   Richard E. Voeltz, Assoc. Professor
Founded: 1895. **Staff:** Prof 1; Other 2. **Subjects:** Botany, zoology, microbiology. **Holdings:** 28,232 books; 33,265 bound periodical volumes; 527 microforms. **Subscriptions:** 946 journals and other serials. **Services:** Interlibrary loans; copying; library open to public. **Automated Operations:** Computerized cataloging, acquisitions and circulation. **Computerized Information Services:** DIALOG. **Publications:** Acquisitions list, biweekly - for internal distribution only.

★15881★
UNIVERSITY OF NEBRASKA, LINCOLN - C.Y. THOMPSON LIBRARY (Agri; Sci-Tech)
East Campus   Phone: (402) 472-2802
Lincoln, NE 68583-0717   Lyle Schreiner, Professor
Staff: Prof 4; Other 4. **Subjects:** Agriculture, home economics, textiles, wildlife conservation, human development, nutrition, applied sciences. **Special Collections:** Entomology collection containing many rare volumes. **Holdings:** 107,512 books; 104,160 bound periodical volumes; 7058 microforms. **Subscriptions:** 4611 journals and other serials; 7 newspapers. **Services:** Interlibrary loans; copying; library open to public. **Automated Operations:** Computerized cataloging, acquisitions and circulation. **Computerized Information Services:** DIALOG, SDC, BRS. **Publications:** Acquisitions list, biweekly - for internal distribution only.

★15882★
UNIVERSITY OF NEBRASKA, LINCOLN - CENTER FOR GREAT PLAINS STUDIES (Hist)
205 Love Library   Phone: (402) 472-6220
Lincoln, NE 68588-0475   Jon Nelson, Cur.
Founded: 1980. **Staff:** Prof 1; Other 3. **Subjects:** History and art of the American West. **Holdings:** 2000 books; 500 photographs; 225 paintings; 200 sculptures; 100 drawings and graphics. **Automated Operations:** Computerized cataloging. **Publications:** Great Plains Quarterly.

★15883★
UNIVERSITY OF NEBRASKA, LINCOLN - CHEMISTRY LIBRARY (Sci-Tech)
Hamilton Hall 427   Phone: (402) 472-2739
Lincoln, NE 68588-0305   Richard E. Voeltz, Assoc. Professor
Founded: 1930. **Staff:** Prof 1; Other 1. **Subjects:** Chemistry and chemical engineering. **Holdings:** 13,185 books; 19,869 bound periodical volumes; 969 microforms. **Subscriptions:** 450 journals and other serials. **Services:** Interlibrary loans; copying; library open to public. **Automated Operations:** Computerized cataloging, acquisitions and circulation. **Computerized Information Services:** DIALOG, SDC, BRS. **Publications:** Acquisitions list, monthly - for internal distribution only.

★15884★
UNIVERSITY OF NEBRASKA, LINCOLN - COLLEGE OF LAW LIBRARY (Law)
East Campus   Phone: (402) 472-3548
Lincoln, NE 68583   John D. Nelson, Law Libn.
Founded: 1891. **Staff:** Prof 4; Other 4. **Subjects:** Anglo-American law. **Special Collections:** U.S. taxation. **Holdings:** 55,405 books; 78,485 bound periodical volumes; 21,401 volumes in microform; 20,971 volumes on microfiche. **Subscriptions:** 3558 journals and other serials; 5 newspapers. **Services:** Interlibrary loans; copying; library open to public for reference use only. **Automated Operations:** Computerized cataloging. **Computerized Information Services:** LEXIS, Westlaw. Performs searches on subscription basis. Contact Person: Robert B. Voelker. **Staff:** Patricio Aranda-Coddou, Assoc.Libn., Ref./Res.; Brian D. Striman, Asst.Libn., Tech.Serv.; Robert B.

Voelker, Asst.Libn., Pub.Serv.

★15885★

UNIVERSITY OF NEBRASKA, LINCOLN - DENTISTRY LIBRARY (Med)
College of Dentistry, East Campus, Rm. 8   Phone: (402) 472-1323
Lincoln, NE 68583-0740   Lyle Schreiner, Professor
Staff: Prof 1; Other 1. **Subjects:** Dentistry, dental hygiene. **Holdings:** 4514
books; 4749 bound periodical volumes. **Subscriptions:** 184 journals and other
serials. **Services:** Interlibrary loans; copying; library open to public.
Automated Operations: Computerized cataloging, acquisitions and
circulation. **Computerized Information Services:** DIALOG. **Publications:**
Acquisitions list, monthly - for internal distribution only.

★15886★

UNIVERSITY OF NEBRASKA, LINCOLN - ENGINEERING LIBRARY (Sci-Tech)
Nebraska Hall, 2nd Fl. W.   Phone: (402) 472-3411
Lincoln, NE 68588-0516   Alan V. Gould, Asst. Professor
Founded: 1973. **Staff:** Prof 1; Other 2. **Subjects:** Engineering. **Special
Collections:** Government Printing Office depository; U.S. Department of
Energy depository; patent depository. **Holdings:** 32,772 books; 41,121
bound periodical volumes; 88,597 microfiche; 1490 reels of microfilm.
Subscriptions: 1057 journals and other serials. **Services:** Interlibrary loans;
copying; library open to public. **Automated Operations:** Computerized
cataloging, acquisitions and circulation. **Computerized Information Services:**
DIALOG. **Publications:** Acquisitions list, monthly - for internal distribution
only.

★15887★

UNIVERSITY OF NEBRASKA, LINCOLN - GEOLOGY LIBRARY (Sci-Tech)
Morrill Hall, Rm. 303   Phone: (402) 472-2653
Lincoln, NE 68588-0341   Agnes Adams, Asst. Professor
Founded: 1895. **Staff:** Prof 1; Other 1. **Subjects:** Geology. **Special
Collections:** Geological maps (70,000). **Holdings:** 10,847 books; 22,772
bound periodical volumes. **Subscriptions:** 1421 journals and other serials.
Services: Interlibrary loans; copying; library open to public. **Automated
Operations:** Computerized cataloging, acquisitions and circulation.
Computerized Information Services: DIALOG. **Publications:** Acquisitions
list, monthly - for internal distribution only.

★15888★

UNIVERSITY OF NEBRASKA, LINCOLN - INSTRUCTIONAL MEDIA CENTER
(Aud-Vis; Educ)
421 Nebraska Hall   Phone: (402) 472-1910
Lincoln, NE 68583-0900
Staff: Prof 4; Other 10. **Subjects:** Educational curriculum (primary through
college), agriculture, business, nursing education. **Special Collections:** Great
Plains Trilogy Series; Nine to Get Ready Series; Nebraska Television Council
for Nursing Education films. **Holdings:** 5462 films (4424 titles); filmstrips;
audiotapes. **Subscriptions:** 12 journals and other serials. **Services:** Copying;
center open to public. **Networks/Consortia:** Member of Consortium of
University Film Centers (CUFC). **Publications:** Educational Film Catalog and
supplement, 1983; What's Available in the Reel World of Business and
Industry? (business films). **Staff:** James L. Titterington, Coord., Film Lib.; Jan
Wacker, Staff Asst.; Mary Klika, Film Libn.

★15889★

UNIVERSITY OF NEBRASKA, LINCOLN - MATHEMATICS LIBRARY (Sci-
Tech)
Oldfather Hall, Rm. 907   Phone: (402) 472-3731
Lincoln, NE 68588-0361   Agnes Adams, Asst. Professor
Founded: 1966. **Staff:** Prof 1; Other 1. **Subjects:** Mathematics. **Holdings:**
6462 books; 7553 bound periodical volumes. **Subscriptions:** 350 journals
and other serials. **Services:** Interlibrary loans; copying; library open to public.
Automated Operations: Computerized cataloging, acquisitions and
circulation. **Computerized Information Services:** DIALOG.

★15890★

UNIVERSITY OF NEBRASKA, LINCOLN - MUSIC LIBRARY (Mus)†
30 Westbrook Music Bldg.   Phone: (402) 472-6300
Lincoln, NE 68588-0101   Susan Messerli, Music Libn.
Founded: 1980. **Staff:** Prof 1; Other 3. **Subjects:** Music - history, literature,
theory, performance. **Special Collections:** Guenther Collection of Passion
Music (313 items). **Holdings:** 13,779 journals and other serials; 2237 bound
periodical volumes; 8000 sound recordings; 7450 microforms.
Subscriptions: 143 journals and other serials. **Services:** Interlibrary loans;
copying; library open to public. **Automated Operations:** Computerized
cataloging. **Computerized Information Services:** DIALOG, SDC, OCLC.
Networks/Consortia: Member of NEBASE.

★15891★

UNIVERSITY OF NEBRASKA, LINCOLN - PHYSICS LIBRARY (Sci-Tech)
Behlen Laboratory, Rm. 263   Phone: (402) 472-1209
Lincoln, NE 68588-0112   Agnes Adams, Asst. Professor
Founded: 1965. **Staff:** Prof 1; Other 1. **Subjects:** Physics, astronomy.
Holdings: 7034 books; 11,301 bound periodical volumes; 20 microforms.
Subscriptions: 485 journals and other serials. **Services:** Interlibrary loans;
copying; library open to public. **Automated Operations:** Computerized
cataloging, acquisitions and circulation. **Computerized Information Services:**
DIALOG. **Publications:** Acquisitions list, weekly - for internal distribution only.

★15892★

**UNIVERSITY OF NEBRASKA, LINCOLN - STATE MUSEUM - HAROLD W.
MANTER LABORATORY - LIBRARY** (Sci-Tech)
W-529 Nebraska Hall
16th and W Sts.   Phone: (402) 472-3334
Lincoln, NE 68588-0514   Mary Hanson Pritchard, Prof. & Cur.
Staff: 2. **Subjects:** Parasitology. **Special Collections:** Collection of articles on
parasitology (45,000 reprints). **Holdings:** 800 books; 525 bound periodical
volumes; 1750 other cataloged items. **Services:** Library open to public by
appointment for reference use. **Publications:** Contributions from the Harold
W. Manter Laboratory, irregular; University Library exchange list and request;
Technical Bulletins, irregular. **Remarks:** The Laboratory is a research unit
encompassing specimen collections as well as a specialized library for
parasitological research.

★15893★

**UNIVERSITY OF NEBRASKA, LINCOLN - UNIVERSITY ARCHIVES AND
SPECIAL COLLECTIONS** (Hist; Hum)
303 Love Library   Phone: (402) 472-2531
Lincoln, NE 68588   Joseph G. Svoboda, Professor
Staff: Prof 2; Other 1. **Subjects:** Nebraskana, World Wars I and II, ethnicity,
French Revolution, railroads, American folklore, university archives. **Special
Collections:** Mari Sandoz Collection (210 feet); Benjamin A. Botkin Collection
(500 feet; 10,000 volumes); Charles E. Bessey Papers (45 feet); Charles M.
Russell Collection (50 feet; 500 volumes); Czech-American Collection (250
feet; 4000 volumes); Christlieb Collection of Western Americana (3000
volumes); Mazour Collection of Russian History and Culture (5200 volumes).
Holdings: 44,000 books; 1000 bound periodical volumes; 4800 cubic feet of
university archives; 17,700 volumes of university theses and dissertations.
Services: Interlibrary loans; copying; library open to public.

★15894★

**UNIVERSITY OF NEBRASKA MEDICAL CENTER - MC GOOGAN LIBRARY OF
MEDICINE** (Med)
42nd & Dewey Ave.   Phone: (402) 559-4006
Omaha, NE 68105   Robert M. Braude, Dir.
Founded: 1902. **Staff:** Prof 14; Other 30. **Subjects:** Medicine, nursing,
pharmacy, allied health sciences. **Special Collections:** History of medicine;
Nebraska Archives of Medicine; H. Winnett Orr Historical Collection (American
College of Surgeons). **Holdings:** 65,922 books; 125,559 bound periodical
volumes; 965 microforms; 25 VF drawers of archives. **Subscriptions:** 3071
journals and other serials. **Services:** Interlibrary loans (fee); copying; SDI;
library open to public. **Automated Operations:** Computerized cataloging,
circulation and serials. **Computerized Information Services:** DIALOG, NLM,
BRS, SDC. **Networks/Consortia:** Headquarters for Midcontinental Regional
Medical Library Program. **Remarks:** Contains the holdings of Eppley Institute
for Research in Cancer & Allied Diseases - Library. **Staff:** Audrey A. Powderly,
Assoc.Dir., Tech.Serv.; Carolyn G. Weaver, Assoc.Dir., Pub.Serv.; Carolyn A.
Reid, Assoc.Dir., MCRMLP; Georgene E. Fawcett, Hd., Acq./Ser.; Mark E.
Funk, Hd., Coll.Dev.; Marie A. Reidelbach, Hd., Ref.; Robert A. Pisciotta, Hd.,
Cat.; Joan E. Latta, Ref.; Helen Yam, Hist. of Med.; Bernice M. Hetzner, Hist.
of NE Med.; Claire E. Gadzikowski, Spec.Proj.Coord., MCRMLP; Dorothy B.
Willis, Reg.Dev.Coord., MCRMLP.

★15895★

UNIVERSITY OF NEVADA, LAS VEGAS - GAMING RESEARCH CENTER (Rec)
4505 Maryland Pkwy.   Phone: (702) 739-3252
Las Vegas, NV 89154   Susan Dolin, Spec.Coll.Libn.
Founded: 1966. **Staff:** Prof 2; Other 1. **Subjects:** Gambling, horse racing,
lotteries, cards. **Holdings:** 5000 books; 250 bound periodical volumes; 600
clippings. **Subscriptions:** 205 journals and other serials; 10 newspapers.
Services: Copying; center open to public. **Automated Operations:**
Computerized cataloging, acquisitions, serials and circulation. **Publications:** A
Gambling Bibliography, 1972 (based on the collection, listing over 1700
items). **Special Catalogs:** Gambling Catalog, a list of monographs from the
research collection at the University of Nevada, Las Vegas, 1978.

★15896★

UNIVERSITY OF NEVADA, RENO - BASQUE STUDIES PROGRAM (Area-Ethnic)
Library
Reno, NV 89557
Phone: (702) 784-4854
William A. Douglass, Coord.
Staff: Prof 2; Other 2. **Subjects:** Basque culture and authors. **Holdings:** 15,000 books; 1400 bound periodical volumes; 51 boxes of archives; 140 reels of microfilm; 15,000 slides; 400 cassettes and phonograph records. **Subscriptions:** 80 journals and other serials; 6 newspapers. **Services:** Interlibrary loans; copying; library open to public. **Publications:** Basque Studies Program Newsletter, semiannual - free upon request.

★15897★

UNIVERSITY OF NEVADA, RENO - DESERT RESEARCH INSTITUTE - DANDINI PARK LIBRARY (Env-Cons)
7010 Dandini Blvd.
Reno, NV 89512
Roberta K. Orcutt, D.R.I. Libn.
Staff: Prof 1; Other 2. **Subjects:** Water resources. **Holdings:** 800 books; 130 bound periodical volumes; 7400 government publications; 5500 technical reports. **Subscriptions:** 60 journals and other serials. **Services:** Interlibrary loans; collection open to public. **Computerized Information Services:** DIALOG, BRS, DOE/RECON. **Publications:** Publications Received, monthly. **Special Catalogs:** Catalog of technical reports. **Formerly:** Its Water Resources Collection.

★15898★

UNIVERSITY OF NEVADA, RENO - DESERT RESEARCH INSTITUTE - LIBRARY (Sci-Tech)
Box 60220
Reno, NV 89506
Phone: (702) 972-1676
Roberta K. Orcutt, D.R.I./Phys.Sci.Libn.
Staff: Prof 1; Other 1. **Subjects:** Atmospheric physics, meteorology, weather modification, Antarctic studies, air pollution. **Holdings:** 5794 books; 2347 bound periodical volumes; 2156 bound government publications; 18,616 unbound government publications; 940 technical reports; 3098 microforms. **Subscriptions:** 214 journals and other serials. **Services:** Interlibrary loans; copying; library open to public. **Computerized Information Services:** DIALOG, BRS. **Networks/Consortia:** Member of CLASS.

★15899★

UNIVERSITY OF NEVADA, RENO - ENGINEERING LIBRARY (Sci-Tech)
Scrugham Engineering Bldg., Rm. 228
Reno, NV 89557
Phone: (702) 784-6945
Mary B. Ansari, Libn.
Founded: 1962. **Staff:** Prof 2; Other 2. **Subjects:** Civil, electrical and mechanical engineering; engineering technology; computer science. **Holdings:** 17,738 books; 9409 bound periodical volumes; 1266 government reports; 479 pamphlets. **Subscriptions:** 442 journals. **Services:** Interlibrary loans; copying; library open to public. **Automated Operations:** Computerized cataloging, acquisitions and serials. **Computerized Information Services:** DIALOG, BRS. Performs searches on cost recovery basis. Contact Person: Anne Amaral. **Networks/Consortia:** Member of Information Nevada. **Publications:** New Book List, monthly - available on request. **Staff:** Anne Amaral, Info.Spec.

★15900★

UNIVERSITY OF NEVADA, RENO - LIFE AND HEALTH SCIENCES LIBRARY (Sci-Tech)
Fleischmann College of Agriculture Bldg.
Reno, NV 89557
Phone: (702) 784-6616
Mary B. Ansari, Libn.
Founded: 1958. **Staff:** Prof 2; Other 2. **Subjects:** Biology, agriculture, health resources, nursing, speech pathology and audiology, medical technology. **Special Collections:** Bankofier Collection on horses. **Holdings:** 24,588 books; 22,076 bound periodical volumes; 108,097 bound USDA documents; FAO and WHO documents; state experiment station and extension documents; technical translations. **Subscriptions:** 511 journals. **Services:** Interlibrary loans; copying; SDI; library open to public. **Automated Operations:** Computerized cataloging, acquisitions and serials. **Computerized Information Services:** DIALOG, BRS. Performs searches on cost recovery basis. Contact Person: Anne Amaral, 784-6617. **Networks/Consortia:** Member of Information Nevada; U.S. Department of Agriculture Document Delivery Service. **Publications:** New Book List, quarterly - free upon request. **Staff:** Anne Amaral, Info.Spec.

★15901★

UNIVERSITY OF NEVADA, RENO - MACKAY SCHOOL OF MINES LIBRARY (Sci-Tech)
Phone: (702) 784-6596
Reno, NV 89557
Mary B. Ansari, Libn.
Founded: 1908. **Staff:** Prof 3; Other 3. **Subjects:** Earth science; engineering - mining, chemical and metallurgical; geography. **Special Collections:** Theses on the geology of Nevada. **Holdings:** 12,042 books; 12,657 bound periodical volumes; 657 reels of microfilm; 92,321 maps; 17,900 microfiche; 7807 bound government reports; 10,564 unbound government reports. **Subscriptions:** 301 journals. **Services:** Interlibrary loans; copying; library open to public with restrictions on borrowing. **Automated Operations:** Computerized cataloging, acquisitions and serials. **Computerized Information Services:** DIALOG, BRS. Performs searches on cost recovery basis. Contact Person: Anne Amaral. **Networks/Consortia:** Member of Information Nevada. **Publications:** New Book List, quarterly - on request; Mackay School of Mines Thesis List, annual - on request; Mineral Waste and Recovery Bibliography. **Special Indexes:** Nevada Mining and Geology File (28,000 cards). **Staff:** Linda P. Newman, Asst. Mines & Map Libn.; Anne Amaral, Info.Spec.

UNIVERSITY OF NEVADA, RENO - NATIONAL JUDICIAL COLLEGE
See: National Judicial College

★15902★

UNIVERSITY OF NEVADA, RENO - PHYSICAL SCIENCES LIBRARY (Sci-Tech)
New Chemistry Bldg., Rm. 316
Reno, NV 89557
Phone: (702) 784-6716
Roberta K. Orcutt, Physical Sci.Libn.
Founded: 1965. **Staff:** Prof 1; Other 1. **Subjects:** Chemistry, physics. **Holdings:** 9289 books; 14,396 bound periodical volumes; 75 reels of microfilm; 1572 microfiche. **Subscriptions:** 238 journals and other serials. **Services:** Interlibrary loans; copying; library open to public. **Automated Operations:** Computerized cataloging and acquisitions. **Computerized Information Services:** DIALOG, BRS.

★15903★

UNIVERSITY OF NEVADA, RENO - RESEARCH AND EDUCATIONAL PLANNING CENTER (Educ)
College of Education, Rm. 201
Reno, NV 89557
Phone: (702) 784-4921
Daniel Cline, Dir.
Staff: Prof 5; Other 2. **Subjects:** Legal education; Nevada and world history; school facility planning; bilingual education; Western community studies; risk reduction. **Special Collections:** ERIC publications; M-X publications. **Holdings:** 2000 books, documents, journals, unbound fugitive material. **Services:** Interlibrary loans; center open to public. **Publications:** REPC Annual Report; Governor's Youth Conference Report, 1979; final report, Governor's Drug Abuse Prevention Program, 1971-1978.

★15904★

UNIVERSITY OF NEVADA, RENO - SAVITT MEDICAL LIBRARY (Med)
Savitt Medical Sciences Bldg.
Reno, NV 89557
Phone: (702) 784-4625
Joan S. Zenan, Libn.
Founded: 1978. **Staff:** Prof 3; Other 6. **Subjects:** Medicine and allied health sciences. **Special Collections:** Medical archives of Nevada. **Holdings:** 28,000 volumes. **Subscriptions:** 497 journals and other serials. **Services:** Interlibrary loans; copying; library open to public. **Automated Operations:** Computerized cataloging. **Computerized Information Services:** Online systems. **Networks/Consortia:** Member of Pacific Southwest Regional Medical Library Service (PSRMLS). **Staff:** Debbie Ketchell, Outreach Libn.; Joan Burkett, ILL & Online Searching

★15905★

UNIVERSITY OF NEVADA, RENO - SPECIAL COLLECTIONS DEPARTMENT/ UNIVERSITY ARCHIVES (Hist)
University Library
Reno, NV 89557
Phone: (702) 784-6538
Robert E. Blesse, Hd.
Founded: 1963. **Staff:** Prof 1; Other 4. **Subjects:** Nevada history, 20th-century poetry and fiction, anthropology, ethnography, architecture, women in the trans-Mississippi West, magic, witchcraft, history of printing, university archives, mining, water and land use. **Special Collections:** Nevada Collection; Great Basin Anthropological Collection; Women in the West; Modern Authors Collection (170 English and American writers, prominent after 1910); University of Nevada, Reno archives; History of Printing and the Book Arts Collection; Nevada Architectural Archives; Senator Alan Bible papers; Virginia & Truckee Railroad Collection; Samuel Johnson; Robert Burns; George Stewart. **Holdings:** 42,000 books; 600 bound periodical volumes; 3000 linear feet of manuscripts; 25,000 photographs; 1400 maps. **Subscriptions:** 120 journals and other serials. **Services:** Copying; department open to public for reference use only. **Special Catalogs:** Specialized subject and form catalogs (card); guides to manuscript collections.

★15906★

UNIVERSITY OF NEW BRUNSWICK - EDUCATION RESOURCE CENTRE (Educ)
D'Avray Hall
P.O. Box 7500
Fredericton, NB, Canada E3B 5H5
Phone: (506) 453-3516
Andrew Pope, Educ.Libn.
Founded: 1973. **Staff:** Prof 2; Other 4. **Subjects:** Education, home

economics. **Special Collections:** Micmac-Maliseet Institute (525 volumes). **Holdings:** 26,973 books; 1770 bound periodical volumes; 287,855 microfiche; 28 VF drawers of pamphlets; 16,341 AV and instructional items. **Subscriptions:** 305 journals and other serials. **Services:** Interlibrary loans; copying; center open to public. **Automated Operations:** Computerized cataloging. **Computerized Information Services:** InfoMart, DIALOG; PHOENIX (internal database). Performs free searches on PHOENIX; DIALOG searches on cost recovery basis. **Staff:** Helen Craig, Asst.Libn.

★15907★

UNIVERSITY OF NEW BRUNSWICK - ENGINEERING LIBRARY (Sci-Tech)
Sir Edmund Head Hall
P.O. Box 7500   Phone: (506) 453-4747
Fredericton, NB, Canada E3B 5H5   Everett R. Dunfield, Engr.Libn.
Founded: 1967. **Staff:** Prof 2; Other 5. **Subjects:** Engineering - civil, mechanical, geological, electrical, forest, survey, chemical; computer science; transportation; bioengineering. **Holdings:** 23,500 books; 12,000 bound periodical volumes; 23,500 reports on microfiche and microfilm; 1225 theses; 100 films and slide sets; 10,000 reports, pamphlets and clippings. **Subscriptions:** 975 journals and other serials. **Services:** Interlibrary loans; copying; SDI; library open to public. **Automated Operations:** CAN/OLE, DIALOG; ENLIST III, PHOENIX (internal databases). **Publications:** Bibliographies and manuals - for inhouse and patron use only.

★15908★

UNIVERSITY OF NEW BRUNSWICK - LAW LIBRARY (Law)
Ludlow Hall
Bag Service No. 44999   Phone: (506) 453-4669
Fredericton, NB, Canada E3B 6C9   Anne Crocker, Law Libn.
Founded: 1933. **Staff:** 8. **Subjects:** Law and common law. **Special Collections:** Lord Beaverbrook Legal Collection. **Holdings:** 80,000 books and bound periodical volumes; 3103 volumes in microform; 127 AV titles. **Subscriptions:** 1497 journals and other serials. **Services:** Interlibrary loans; copying; library open to public. **Automated Operations:** Computerized cataloging. **Computerized Information Services:** QL Systems, UTLAS; PHOENIX (internal database). **Publications:** Acquisitions List, monthly - available on exchange basis. **Staff:** Patti Jill Collins, Doc./Cat.Libn.; Michael McGuire, Ref.Libn./Comp.Serv.Coord.

★15909★

UNIVERSITY OF NEW BRUNSWICK - SCIENCE LIBRARY (Sci-Tech)
P.O. Box 7500   Phone: (506) 453-4601
Fredericton, NB, Canada E3B 5H5   Eszter L.K. Schwenke, Hd.
Staff: Prof 1; Other 5. **Subjects:** Forestry, biology, chemistry, geology, physics. **Special Collections:** Forestry Collection (9730 pamphlets). **Holdings:** 33,594 books; 35,190 bound periodical volumes; 732 theses; 311 reels of microfilm; 11,620 microcards; 6950 microfiche. **Subscriptions:** 1040 journals and other serials. **Services:** Interlibrary loans; copying; SDI; library open to public. **Computerized Information Services:** DIALOG, CAN/OLE, QL Systems, Information Retrieval System for the Sociology of Leisure and Sport (SIRLS), MEDLINE; PHOENIX (internal database). **Special Indexes:** ENLIST, forestry pamphlet file (online and printout); GEOSCAN, New Brunswick mineral assessment file (microfiche). **Remarks:** An alternate phone number is 453-4602.

★15910★

UNIVERSITY OF NEW ENGLAND - COLLEGE OF OSTEOPATHIC MEDICINE - NECOM LIBRARY (Med)†
11 Hills Beach Rd.   Phone: (207) 283-0171
Biddeford, ME 04005   Rosemary G. Kelley, Med.Libn.
Founded: 1978. **Staff:** Prof 3; Other 3. **Subjects:** Medicine, preclinical sciences, family practice. **Special Collections:** Osteopathic medicine (114 titles). **Holdings:** 3072 books; 2398 bound periodical volumes; 1114 audio cassettes; 69 slide/tape programs; 2655 slides; 28 video cassettes; 46 motion pictures. **Subscriptions:** 261 journals and other serials. **Services:** Interlibrary loans; copying; library open to public. **Networks/Consortia:** Member of Health Sciences Library and Information Cooperative of Maine (HSLIC). **Staff:** Katherine de Zengotita, Ref.Lib./Cat.; Priscilla L. Smith-Toth, Asst. to the Med.Libn.

★15911★

UNIVERSITY OF NEW HAMPSHIRE - BIOLOGICAL SCIENCES LIBRARY (Sci-Tech; Agri)
Kendall Hall
Durham, NH 03824   Phone: (603) 862-1018
       Lloyd H. Heidgerd, Br.Libn.
Staff: Prof 1; Other 2. **Subjects:** General biology, agriculture, botany, zoology, entomology, animal science, plant science, physiology, biochemistry. **Holdings:** 15,000 books; 15,000 bound periodical volumes; 50,000 bulletins and circulars (agricultural). **Subscriptions:** 800 journals and other serials.

Services: Interlibrary loans; library open to limited public use. **Automated Operations:** Computerized serials list; Computerized cataloging. **Computerized Information Services:** DIALOG, OCLC. **Networks/Consortia:** Member of NELINET; New Hampshire College & University Council, Library Policy Committee (NHCUC); New England On-Line Users Group (NENON).

★15912★

UNIVERSITY OF NEW HAMPSHIRE - CHEMISTRY LIBRARY (Sci-Tech)
Parsons Hall   Phone: (603) 862-1083
Durham, NH 03824   Edward Dauphinais, Libn.
Staff: Prof 1; Other 1. **Subjects:** Chemistry. **Holdings:** 17,334 volumes. **Subscriptions:** 170 journals and other serials. **Services:** Interlibrary loans; copying; library open to public. **Automated Operations:** Computerized serials. **Computerized Information Services:** OCLC, DIALOG, SDC. **Networks/Consortia:** Member of New England On-Line Users Group (NENON); NELINET; New Hampshire College & University Council, Library Policy Committee (NHCUC).

★15913★

UNIVERSITY OF NEW HAMPSHIRE - DAVID G. CLARK MEMORIAL PHYSICS LIBRARY (Sci-Tech)
DeMeritt Hall   Phone: (603) 862-2348
Durham, NH 03824   Edward Dauphinais, Libn.
Founded: 1965. **Staff:** Prof 1; Other 1. **Subjects:** Physics. **Holdings:** 13,321 books; 11,382 bound periodical volumes; 120 theses; 70 film loops. **Subscriptions:** 180 journals and other serials. **Services:** Interlibrary loans; copying; library open to public. **Automated Operations:** Computerized cataloging and acquisitions. **Computerized Information Services:** DIALOG, SDC, OCLC. **Networks/Consortia:** Member of NELINET; New Hampshire College & University Council, Library Policy Committee (NHCUC); New England On-Line Users Group (NENON).

★15914★

UNIVERSITY OF NEW HAMPSHIRE - DEPARTMENT OF MEDIA SERVICES - FILM LIBRARY (Aud-Vis)
Dimond Library   Phone: (603) 862-2240
Durham, NH 03824   John D. Bardwell, Dir.
Staff: Prof 10; Other 8. **Holdings:** 3000 educational films for all ages. **Services:** Films available for rent; library open to New England area residents. **Special Catalogs:** Instructional Film Catalog (book); New England Health Resource Center Catalog; Radio Quebec films and videotapes catalog (French). **Staff:** Joann Brady, Graphic Designer; Frederick Littlefield, TV Producer-Dir.; John Adams, Univ. Photographer; Gary Samson, Filmmaker; Marsha Kennedy, Coord., Film Distr.

★15915★

UNIVERSITY OF NEW HAMPSHIRE - ENGINEERING-MATH LIBRARY (Sci-Tech; Comp Sci)
Kingsbury Hall   Phone: (603) 862-1196
Durham, NH 03824   Edward Dauphinais, Libn.
Staff: Prof 1; Other 1. **Subjects:** Engineering - mechanical, civil, electrical, chemical; mathematics; materials science; computer science. **Holdings:** 35,264 volumes; 663 reels of microfilm of journals. **Subscriptions:** 600 journals and other serials. **Services:** Interlibrary loans; copying; library open to public. **Automated Operations:** Computerized serials. **Computerized Information Services:** DIALOG, SDC, OCLC. **Networks/Consortia:** Member of New England On-Line Users Group (NENON); NELINET; New Hampshire College & University Council, Library Policy Committee (NHCUC).

★15916★

UNIVERSITY OF NEW HAMPSHIRE - NEW HAMPSHIRE WATER RESOURCE RESEARCH CENTER - LIBRARY (Sci-Tech)
108 Pettee Hall   Phone: (603) 862-2144
Durham, NH 03824   Gayle J. Dorsey, Libn./Res.
Founded: 1965. **Staff:** 1. **Subjects:** Chemical and biological analysis of water, evaporation and transpiration, watershed management, groundwater, water law and economics, interbasin transfers, water conservation. **Holdings:** 520 books and bound periodical volumes; 6361 pamphlets; 7500 reports and documents. **Subscriptions:** 15 journals and newsletters. **Services:** Interlibrary loans; library open to public. **Publications:** Research reports and associated publications. **Special Catalogs:** Keyterm and title catalogs; shelf list.

★15917★

UNIVERSITY OF NEW HAMPSHIRE - SPECIAL COLLECTIONS (Hist; Hum)
Dimond Library   Phone: (603) 862-2714
Durham, NH 03824   Barbara A. White, Spec.Coll.Libn.
Staff: Prof 1; Other 1. **Subjects:** New Hampshire. **Special Collections:** Archives of the University of New Hampshire, including dissertations (10,000

volumes); Robert Frost (250 volumes); angling (2500 volumes); New Hampshire (21,000 volumes); Early New Hampshire Imprints (850 volumes); historical juvenile books (1200). **Holdings:** 45,000 books; 1900 cubic feet of manuscripts. **Services:** Copying; collections open to public. **Publications:** Friends of the University of New Hampshire Library Notes, annual - distributed to Friends of the Library. **Special Catalogs:** Robert Frost New Hampshire, 1976, printed catalog; Guide to Special Collections, 1983.

★15918★
UNIVERSITY OF NEW MEXICO - BUNTING MEMORIAL SLIDE LIBRARY (Aud-Vis**)**
Fine Arts Center
Albuquerque, NM 87131
Phone: (505) 277-6415
A. Zelda Richardson, Dir.
Staff: Prof 3. **Subjects:** Art, architecture. **Holdings:** 275,000 slides. **Services:** Library serves faculty only.

★15919★
UNIVERSITY OF NEW MEXICO - BUREAU OF BUSINESS & ECONOMIC RESEARCH DATA BANK (Bus-Fin**)**
1920 Lomas Blvd., N.E.
Albuquerque, NM 87131
Phone: (505) 277-6626
Betsie Kasner, Hd., Info.Serv.
Founded: 1945. **Staff:** Prof 2; Other 3. **Subjects:** New Mexico, economics, income, employment, demographics, census. **Special Collections:** Census of Population and Housing for New Mexico, 1940-1980. **Holdings:** 12,000 cataloged publications. **Subscriptions:** 400 journals and other serials. **Services:** Copying; library open to public. **Automated Operations:** Computerized cataloging. **Publications:** New Mexico Business, monthly; Southwestern Review of Management and Economics, quarterly - both by subscription. **Special Catalogs:** Computerized list of holdings. **Staff:** Kevin Kargacin, Asst. Economist.

★15920★
UNIVERSITY OF NEW MEXICO - DEPARTMENT OF ANTHROPOLOGY - CLARK FIELD ARCHIVES AND LIBRARY (Soc Sci**)**
Roma & University, N.E.
Albuquerque, NM 87131
Phone: (505) 277-4524
E. Mickel, Off.Mgr.
Staff: 3. **Subjects:** Anthropology, archeology, ethnology, linguistics, biological anthropology, history. **Holdings:** 5000 books; 10,000 bound periodical volumes; 1000 reprints; 50 dissertations. **Subscriptions:** 20 journals and other serials. **Services:** Archives open to public for reference use only.

★15921★
UNIVERSITY OF NEW MEXICO - FINE ARTS LIBRARY (Art; Mus**)**
Phone: (505) 277-2357
Albuquerque, NM 87131
James B. Wright, Hd.
Founded: 1963. **Staff:** Prof 2; Other 3. **Subjects:** Art, music, architecture, photography. **Special Collections:** Archives of Southwestern Music; art exhibition catalogs. **Holdings:** 93,000 books; 21,000 records and tapes. **Subscriptions:** 350 journals and other serials. **Services:** Listening center; copying; library open to public. **Staff:** Nancy Pistorius, Asst.Libn.

UNIVERSITY OF NEW MEXICO - HARWOOD FOUNDATION LIBRARY
See: Harwood Foundation Library of the University of New Mexico

★15922★
UNIVERSITY OF NEW MEXICO - JONSON GALLERY - LIBRARY (Art**)**
1909 Las Lomas Rd., N.E.
Albuquerque, NM 87106
Phone: (505) 243-4667
Subjects: Artist Raymond Jonson, 1910 to present. **Holdings:** 13,000 items including correspondence, diaries, photographs, typescripts of lectures, and manuscripts. **Services:** Library open to public with permission of director.

★15923★
UNIVERSITY OF NEW MEXICO - MEDICAL CENTER LIBRARY (Med**)**
North Campus
Albuquerque, NM 87131
Phone: (505) 277-2548
Erika Love, Dir.
Founded: 1963. **Staff:** Prof 10; Other 31. **Subjects:** Medicine, basic sciences, nursing, pharmacy, allied health sciences. **Special Collections:** History of medicine. **Holdings:** 37,266 books; 71,303 bound periodical volumes; 6369 AV programs. **Subscriptions:** 2260 journals and other serials. **Services:** Interlibrary loans; SDI; outreach programs for New Mexico health personnel; borrowing privileges extended to all students enrolled full-time at UNM Medical Center Campus, UNM faculty and graduate students, and UNM health care personnel; library open to public for reference use only. **Automated Operations:** Computerized cataloging and circulation. **Computerized Information Services:** OCLC, NLM, BRS, DIALOG, SDC. **Networks/Consortia:** Member of TALON; AMIGOS Bibliographic Council, Inc. **Publications:** Adobe Medicus; New Books, both bimonthly - both distributed to user community and selected U.S. medical libraries; Medical Center Faculty

Publications list. **Special Indexes:** Serials List (computer printout) - distributed on-campus and locally only. **Staff:** Cecile C. Quintal, Assoc.Dir.; Sandra Spurlock, Asst.Dir.

★15924★
UNIVERSITY OF NEW MEXICO - SCHOOL OF LAW LIBRARY (Law**)**
1117 Stanford, N.E.
Albuquerque, NM 87131
Phone: (505) 277-6236
Myron Fink, Libn.
Founded: 1950. **Staff:** Prof 6; Other 23. **Subjects:** Law. **Special Collections:** American Indian law; Community Land Grant law; Mexican and Latin American legal materials. **Holdings:** 179,350 volumes; 449,000 microforms (69,000 volume equivalents); 12,000 New Mexico Supreme Court records and briefs. **Subscriptions:** 2700 journals and other serials; 21 newspapers. **Services:** Interlibrary loans; copying; library open to public. **Automated Operations:** Computerized cataloging, acquisitions and circulation. **Computerized Information Services:** LEXIS, OCLC, Westlaw. **Networks/Consortia:** Member of AMIGOS Bibliographic Council, Inc. **Publications:** A Guide to the School of Law Library; Annual New Acquisitions List - both distributed to members of the New Mexico State Bar, judicial offices, patrons; New Titles Received. **Special Catalogs:** Catalog of American Indian Law. **Staff:** Richard Bowler, Assoc.Libn./Ref.Serv.; Lorraine Lester, Sys. & Mgt.Libn.; Jerry C. Phillips, Asst.Tech.Serv.Libn.; Thaddeus Bejnar, Legal Res.Libn.

★15925★
UNIVERSITY OF NEW MEXICO - SPECIAL COLLECTIONS DEPARTMENT (Hist**)**
General Library
Albuquerque, NM 87131
Phone: (505) 277-6451
William E. Tydeman, Hd.
Staff: Prof 2; Other 6. **Subjects:** New Mexico history, Mexicana, Indians of North America, southwestern architectural history. **Special Collections:** Doris Duke Collection of oral history (982 tapes); Pioneer Foundation (527 tapes). **Holdings:** 35,000 volumes; 2000 tape recordings; 3000 linear feet of manuscript material; 17,000 photographs. **Subscriptions:** 121 journals and other serials. **Services:** Copying; library open to public. **Publications:** Annual report. **Remarks:** The Special Collections Department consists of five divisions - the Anderson Room, containing Western Americana; the Coronado Room collection on the history and culture of New Mexico; the Bell Room, housing the rare book collection; and the manuscript and architectural records, which are also separately housed. **Staff:** Tim Wehrkamp, Asst.Hd.

★15926★
UNIVERSITY OF NEW MEXICO - TECHNOLOGY APPLICATION CENTER (Sci-Tech**)**
Phone: (505) 277-3622
Albuquerque, NM 87131
Stanley A. Morain, Dir.
Founded: 1965. **Staff:** Prof 10; Other 5. **Subjects:** Remote sensing, earth photography, geographic information systems. **Special Collections:** Remote sensing bibliography (citations). **Holdings:** 10K slides of earth-oriented photography. **Services:** Image processing; short courses; visiting scientist program; photograph search service. **Computerized Information Services:** NASA/RECON, EROS Data Center. Performs searches on cost recovery and subscription bases. **Publications:** Remote Sensing of Natural Resources Quarterly Literature Review. **Also Known As:** TAC. **Staff:** Mike Inglis, Assoc.Dir.; Amy Budge, Photograph Search Serv.

★15927★
UNIVERSITY OF NEW MEXICO - TIREMAN LEARNING MATERIALS LIBRARY (Educ**)**
Phone: (505) 277-3854
Albuquerque, NM 87131
Eileen E. Schroeder, Hd.
Founded: 1965. **Staff:** Prof 1; Other 1. **Subjects:** Children's and young adult's literature; textbooks for kindergarten through high school. **Special Collections:** Anita Osuna Carr Bicultural Bilingual Collection. **Holdings:** 12,000 books; 80 bound periodical volumes; 825 filmstrips, sound filmstrips, kits and games; 516 cassette tapes; 74 film loops; 72 study prints; 309 phonograph records; 20 VF drawers; 5 VF drawers of curriculum guides; 4 VF drawers of pictures; curriculum microfiche. **Services:** Interlibrary loans; library open to public. **Automated Operations:** Computerized cataloging and acquisitions. **Remarks:** Library is a regional evaluation center for state textbooks.

★15928★
UNIVERSITY OF NEW MEXICO - WILLIAM J. PARISH MEMORIAL LIBRARY (Bus-Fin**)**
Phone: (505) 277-5912
Albuquerque, NM 87131
Judith Bernstein, Bus.Adm.Libn.
Founded: 1969. **Staff:** Prof 1; Other 3. **Subjects:** Accounting, finance, personnel, marketing, international management, management information systems. **Holdings:** 31,000 books; 14,000 unbound periodicals; 20,000 10K

and annual reports. **Subscriptions:** 1200 journals and other serials. **Services:** Interlibrary loans; copying; library open to public with limited circulation. **Automated Operations:** Computerized cataloging and acquisitions. **Computerized Information Services:** DIALOG, SDC, BRS, New York Times Information Service, OCLC. **Networks/Consortia:** Member of AMIGOS Bibliographic Council, Inc. **Publications:** Annual report; monthly new books list - for internal distribution only.

★15929★

UNIVERSITY OF NEW ORLEANS - EARL K. LONG LIBRARY - ARCHIVES & MANUSCRIPTS/SPECIAL COLLECTIONS DEPT. (Law; Bus-Fin)
Lake Front   Phone: (504) 286-7273
New Orleans, LA 70148   D. Clive Hardy, Archv.
Founded: 1958. **Staff:** Prof 4. **Subjects:** Ethnic groups of New Orleans, New Orleans labor unions, Orleans Parish School Board, Chamber of Commerce of New Orleans. **Special Collections:** Crabites Collection of Egyptology; Frank Von der Haar Collection of William Faulkner (3000 items); Louisiana Supreme Court records, 1813-1929; local business, educational and architectural records; Marcus Christian Collection. **Holdings:** 8000 books; 2000 bound periodical volumes; 100,000 manuscripts. **Subscriptions:** 40 journals and other serials. **Services:** Interlibrary loans; copying; department open to public. **Automated Operations:** Computerized cataloging, acquisitions and circulation. **Special Catalogs:** Special Collections at the University of New Orleans; Faulkner: The Frank A. Von der Haar Collection. **Staff:** Dr. Raymond O. Nussbaum, Lib.Asst. II; Marie E. Windell, Lib.Asst. II; Beatrice R. Oswley, Lib.Asst. I.

★15930★

UNIVERSITY OF NORTH CAROLINA - INSTITUTE OF MARINE SCIENCES - LIBRARY (Sci-Tech)
3407 Arendell St.   Phone: (919) 726-6841
Morehead City, NC 28557   Brenda B. Bright, Libn.
Founded: 1948. **Staff:** Prof 1; Other 1. **Subjects:** Biological oceanography, marine ecology, malacology, ichthyology, mycology, carcinology. **Holdings:** 1284 books; 2501 bound periodical volumes; 22,850 reprints; 90 dissertations. **Subscriptions:** 293 journals and other serials. **Services:** Interlibrary loans; copying; library open to public for reference use only. **Publications:** Separates of staff publications. **Staff:** Charles H. Peterson, Bk.Chm.

★15931★

UNIVERSITY OF NORTH CAROLINA, ASHEVILLE - SOUTHERN HIGHLANDS RESEARCH CENTER (Hist)
                                          Phone: (704) 258-6414
Asheville, NC 28814   Dr. Milton Ready, Dir.
Subjects: Western North Carolina, 1833 to present; Appalachia. **Special Collections:** Asheville and Buncombe County photograph collection; papers of U.S. Representative Roy A. Taylor concerning the proposed Mount Mitchell National Park; oral history recordings of mountaineers (200); collections of black, Jewish, Greek, and other ethnic groups in Appalachia; Tom Wolfe Collection. **Holdings:** 50 linear feet of records and photographs. **Services:** Copying; center open to public.

★15932★

UNIVERSITY OF NORTH CAROLINA, CHAPEL HILL - ALFRED T. BRAVER LIBRARY (Sci-Tech; Comp Sci)
Phillips Hall 039A   Phone: (919) 962-2323
Chapel Hill, NC 27514   Dana M. Sally, Math/Physics Libn.
Founded: 1920. **Staff:** Prof 1; Other 3. **Subjects:** Mathematics, physics, statistics, computer science, operations research, astronomy. **Holdings:** 67,000 books and bound periodical volumes; 571 technical reports; 167 microfiche; 96 audiotapes. **Subscriptions:** 814 journals and other serials. **Services:** Interlibrary loans; copying; library open to public. **Automated Operations:** Computerized cataloging. **Computerized Information Services:** OCLC, DIALOG. **Networks/Consortia:** Member of SOLINET. **Publications:** List of new books received, monthly; special subject bibliographies, irregular - both available on request.

★15933★

UNIVERSITY OF NORTH CAROLINA, CHAPEL HILL - ART LIBRARY (Art)
Art Classroom Studio Bldg.   Phone: (919) 933-2397
Chapel Hill, NC 27514   Philip A. Rees, Art Libn.
Founded: 1958. **Staff:** Prof 1; Other 1. **Subjects:** Art. **Holdings:** 47,000 volumes; 11,100 microfiche; 280 reels of microfilm. **Subscriptions:** 330 journals and other serials. **Services:** Interlibrary loans; copying; library open to public with limited circulation.

★15934★

UNIVERSITY OF NORTH CAROLINA, CHAPEL HILL - CENTER FOR ALCOHOL STUDIES - LIBRARY (Med)
Wing B Medical School 207-H   Phone: (919) 966-5678
Chapel Hill, NC 27514   Myra A. Carpenter, Soc.Res.Asst.
Staff: Prof 1. **Subjects:** Alcohol research, alcoholism. **Holdings:** 550 books; 36 bound periodical volumes; 3000 reprints; clippings. **Subscriptions:** 30 journals and other serials. **Services:** Interlibrary loans; copying; library open to public. **Publications:** Activities Report, annual - free upon request.

★15935★

UNIVERSITY OF NORTH CAROLINA, CHAPEL HILL - CENTER FOR EARLY ADOLESCENCE - INFORMATION SERVICES DIVISION (Soc Sci)
Carr Mill Mall, Suite 223   Phone: (919) 966-1148
Carrboro, NC 27510   Susan Rosenzweig, Info.Mgr.
Staff: Prof 1; Other 1. **Subjects:** Young adolescents - biological, cognitive, psychological and social development; middle schools and junior high schools; youth advocacy/services; sexuality and sex education; nutrition; after-school care. **Holdings:** 7000 books and articles; statistics. **Subscriptions:** 150 journals and other serials. **Services:** Phone and mail reference; copying; center open to public. **Publications:** Common Focus (newsletter), irregular - free upon request; assorted bibliographies and resource lists on early adolescence - for sale; thesaurus of subject descriptors. **Remarks:** The center is part of the School of Public Health, Department of Maternal and Child Health.

★15936★

UNIVERSITY OF NORTH CAROLINA, CHAPEL HILL - GEOLOGY LIBRARY (Sci-Tech)
Mitchell Hall 029-A   Phone: (919) 962-2386
Chapel Hill, NC 27514   Miriam L. Sheaves, Libn.
Staff: Prof 1; Other 1. **Subjects:** Geology, geophysics, paleontology, oceanography. **Holdings:** 40,817 volumes; 102,948 mapsheets; 7148 microforms; depository of U.S. Geological Survey topographic and geologic maps. **Subscriptions:** 700 journals and other serials. **Services:** Interlibrary loans; copying; library open to public. **Computerized Information Services:** DIALOG.

★15937★

UNIVERSITY OF NORTH CAROLINA, CHAPEL HILL - HEALTH SCIENCES LIBRARY (Med)
                                          Phone: (919) 966-2111
Chapel Hill, NC 27514   Samuel Hitt, Dir.
Founded: 1952. **Staff:** Prof 23; Other 36. **Subjects:** Medicine, nursing, dentistry, public health, pharmacy, allied health sciences. **Special Collections:** History of Health Sciences. **Holdings:** 66,504 books; 135,023 bound periodical volumes; 1853 pamphlets; 3322 AV units. **Subscriptions:** 3926 journals and other serials. **Services:** Interlibrary loans; copying; SDI; library open to public. **Automated Operations:** Computerized cataloging. **Computerized Information Services:** BRS, DIALOG, SDC, NLM, OCLC. Performs searches on cost recovery basis. **Networks/Consortia:** Member of Southeastern/Atlantic Regional Medical Library Services; SOLINET; North Carolina Area Health Education Centers Program (AHEC) - Library and Information Services Network. **Publications:** Recent Acquisitions, monthly; Annual Report; News & Views, semimonthly - by mail. **Staff:** Gary Byrd, Assoc.Dir.; Kathryn Mendenhall, Hd., Sys. & Res.; Marjory Waite, Hd., Acq./ Ser.Serv.; Jo Anne Boorkman, Hd., Coll.Dev.; Wallace McLendon, Hd., Circ.Serv.; April Wreath, Hd., Cat.Serv.; Diane Foxman, Hd., AV Serv.; Nidia Scharlock, Hd., Info.Serv.; Ellen Brassil, Hd., Info.Mgt.Educ.; Nancy Bruce, Hd., Rare Bks.Serv.; James Shedlock, Coord. Online Search; Carolyn Lipscomb, Coord., Staff Dev./Pubn.

★15938★

UNIVERSITY OF NORTH CAROLINA, CHAPEL HILL - HIGHWAY SAFETY RESEARCH CENTER - LIBRARY (Trans)
Trailer 13, CTP, 197 A   Phone: (919) 933-2202
Chapel Hill, NC 27514   Beth A. Boone, Libn.
Founded: 1970. **Staff:** Prof 1. **Subjects:** Highway safety, accident and investigation analysis, driver education and licensing, restraint systems usage and effectiveness, traffic records, evaluation of highway safety programs. **Special Collections:** Material on North Carolina, including data on traffic accidents, arrest/disposition reports, driver licensing and driver improvement programs. **Holdings:** 12,800 books, documents, technical reports; 575 bound periodical volumes; 26,647 research reports on microfiche. **Subscriptions:** 125 journals and other serials. **Services:** Interlibrary loans; copying; library open to public for reference use only. **Computerized Information Services:** DIALOG.

★15939★

UNIVERSITY OF NORTH CAROLINA, CHAPEL HILL - INSTITUTE OF GOVERNMENT - LIBRARY (Soc Sci; Law)
Knapp Bldg. 059A   Phone: (919) 966-5381
Chapel Hill, NC 27514   Rebecca S. Ballentine, Libn.
Founded: 1930. **Staff:** Prof 2; Other 1. **Subjects:** Public administration, state and local government, public law. **Holdings:** 1805 books; 3125 bound periodical volumes; 25,707 pamphlets. **Subscriptions:** 488 journals and other serials; 12 newspapers. **Services:** Interlibrary loans; copying; library open to public. **Computerized Information Services:** LEXIS. Performs searches on subscription basis. **Networks/Consortia:** Member of Triangle Research Libraries Network (TRLN). **Publications:** Acquisitions List, monthly. **Special Catalogs:** Publications of the Institute of Government, biennial. **Staff:** Lois G. Best, Asst.Libn.

★15940★

UNIVERSITY OF NORTH CAROLINA, CHAPEL HILL - INSTITUTE OF OUTDOOR DRAMA - ARCHIVES (Theater)
202 Graham Memorial Hall   Phone: (919) 962-1328
Chapel Hill, NC 27514   Mark R. Sumner, Dir.
Founded: 1963. **Staff:** Prof 1; Other 2. **Subjects:** Architecture, lighting, scripts, organization, finance, personnel, promotion and publicity, production, planning. **Holdings:** 21 VF drawers of documents, souvenir programs, articles, manuscripts, dissertations, photographs, theses, clippings. **Services:** Archives not open to public. **Publications:** Newsletter, quarterly; assorted bulletins on phases of outdoor drama.

★15941★

UNIVERSITY OF NORTH CAROLINA, CHAPEL HILL - INSTITUTE FOR RESEARCH IN SOCIAL SCIENCE - DATA LIBRARY (Soc Sci)
Manning Hall 026A, Rm. 10   Phone: (919) 966-3346
Chapel Hill, NC 27514   Diana McDuffee, Dir.
Founded: 1969. **Staff:** Prof 5; Other 2. **Subjects:** Census data, election data, student attitude data, mass political behavior, political systems, socioeconomic data, social systems/socialization, international/cross-national public opinion polls. **Special Collections:** Public Opinion Poll conducted by Louis Harris & Associates, Inc., 1963 to present. **Holdings:** 2000 machine-readable data files. **Services:** Data sets can be disseminated for a fee; library open to public. **Automated Operations:** Computerized cataloging. **Computerized Information Services:** DIALOG; Harris Question Retrieval System (internal database). **Publications:** List of publications - available upon request. **Also Known As:** Louis Harris Data Center. **Staff:** Sue A. Dodd, Libn.; Ann Gray, Libn.; Josephine Marsh, Data. Proc.; Judy Poole, Census Cons.; David Sheaves, Libn.

★15942★

UNIVERSITY OF NORTH CAROLINA, CHAPEL HILL - JOHN N. COUCH LIBRARY (Sci-Tech)
301 Coker Hall 010-A   Phone: (919) 962-3783
Chapel Hill, NC 27514   William R. Burk, Botany Libn.
Founded: 1926. **Staff:** Prof 1; Other 1. **Subjects:** Mycology, plant physiology, genetics, economic botany, algae, world floras, horticulture, cytology, ecology, plant taxonomy, paleobotany. **Special Collections:** Rare books in mycology (1000 volumes); collected papers of university botanists (reprints and photocopies; 16 volumes of 589 published works). **Holdings:** 23,002 books; 12,100 bound periodical volumes; 1462 maps; 10,162 microforms; 7000 mycological reprints. **Subscriptions:** 718 journals and other serials. **Services:** Interlibrary loans; copying; library open to public. **Computerized Information Services:** DIALOG. **Publications:** Library Literature Guides on botanical topics, irregular - for internal distribution only. **Special Indexes:** Index to mycological reprints (in preparation).

★15943★

UNIVERSITY OF NORTH CAROLINA, CHAPEL HILL - KENAN CHEMISTRY LIBRARY (Sci-Tech)
269 Venable Hall 045-A   Phone: (919) 933-1188
Chapel Hill, NC 27514   Jimmy Dickerson, Chem.Libn.
Staff: Prof 1; Other 2. **Subjects:** All branches of chemistry. **Special Collections:** Venable History of Science Collection (850 volumes). **Holdings:** 36,587 volumes; 2391 microforms. **Subscriptions:** 278 journals and other serials. **Services:** Interlibrary loans; copying; library open to public with restrictions. **Computerized Information Services:** DIALOG, CAS Online, NIH-EPA Chemical Information System. **Publications:** Monthly new book list - free upon request.

★15944★

UNIVERSITY OF NORTH CAROLINA, CHAPEL HILL - LAW LIBRARY (Law)
Van Hecke-Wettach Bldg.   Phone: (919) 933-1321
Chapel Hill, NC 27514   Mary W. Oliver, Law Libn.
Staff: Prof 7; Other 11. **Subjects:** Law. **Special Collections:** Native American law. **Holdings:** 221,511 volumes; 247,155 microforms. **Subscriptions:** 4666 journals and other serials. **Services:** Copying; library open to public for reference use only. **Computerized Information Services:** Westlaw. **Staff:** Kathleen Cheape, Asst. Law Libn.; Patricia Wall, Acq.Libn.; Carol Avery, Cat.; Timothy Coggins, Hd., Rd.Serv.; Deborah Webster, Asst.Hd.; Martha Barefoot, Rd.Serv.

★15945★

UNIVERSITY OF NORTH CAROLINA, CHAPEL HILL - MAPS COLLECTION (Geog-Map)
Wilson Library 024A   Phone: (919) 933-3028
Chapel Hill, NC 27514   Celia D. Poe, Map Libn.
Staff: Prof 1. **Subjects:** Cartography. **Holdings:** 93,000 maps (including maps of Defense Mapping Agency, National Ocean Survey and U.S. Geological Survey); 1200 atlases; 600 reference works and cartobibliographies; 310 gazetteers. **Subscriptions:** 12 journals and other serials. **Services:** Interlibrary loans (limited); copying; collection open to public.

★15946★

UNIVERSITY OF NORTH CAROLINA, CHAPEL HILL - MUSIC LIBRARY (Mus)
Hill Hall   Phone: (919) 933-1030
Chapel Hill, NC 27514
Founded: 1935. **Staff:** Prof 3; Other 3. **Subjects:** Music, music literature, musicology. **Special Collections:** Opera; history of music theory; North Carolina folk music archive; early American music collection; American shape-note tunebook collection. **Holdings:** 32,000 books and bound periodical volumes; 52,000 volumes of music; 22,000 phonograph records; 2400 reels of microfilm; 2300 microcards; 500 microfiche. **Subscriptions:** 600 journals and other serials. **Services:** Interlibrary loans; copying. **Computerized Information Services:** OCLC. **Networks/Consortia:** Member of SOLINET. **Special Indexes:** Song anthology index; early American music index; American shape-note tunebook collection index; place/date/publisher index for rare materials. **Staff:** Kathryn P. Logan, Asst. Music Libn. Alan Gregory, Music Cat.

★15947★

UNIVERSITY OF NORTH CAROLINA, CHAPEL HILL - NORTH CAROLINA COLLECTION (Hist; Rare Book)
Wilson Library 024-A   Phone: (919) 933-1172
Chapel Hill, NC 27514   H.G. Jones, Cur.
Founded: 1844. **Staff:** Prof 3; Other 4. **Subjects:** North Caroliniana; books by and about North Carolinians. **Special Collections:** Sir Walter Raleigh Collection (by and about Raleigh); Thomas Wolfe Collection (by and about Wolfe); Bruce Cotton Collection (fine and rare North Caroliniana). **Holdings:** 163,852 volumes; 4218 maps; 3717 broadsides; 12,664 manuscripts; 10,884 reels of microfilm; 33,815 pictures; 150,000 mounted newspaper clippings. **Subscriptions:** 3000 journals and other serials. **Services:** Copying; collection open to public with identification. **Publications:** North Caroliniana Society Imprints, annual. **Staff:** Alice R. Cotten, Asst.Cur.

★15948★

UNIVERSITY OF NORTH CAROLINA, CHAPEL HILL - RARE BOOK COLLECTION (Rare Book)
Wilson Library 024A   Phone: (919) 962-1143
Chapel Hill, NC 27514   Paul S. Koda, Cur.
Staff: Prof 3; Other 3. **Subjects:** History of the book, incunabula, English and American literature, French history, Americana. **Special Collections:** George Baer Collection of Fine Bindings; Jacques Barzun and Wendell Hertig Taylor Collection of Crime and Detection; Mary Shore Cameron Collection of Sherlock Holmes; Confederate Imprint Collection; Preston Davie Collection of Early Americana; Annette Duchein Collection of Ornithology; Burton Emmett Collection of First Editions and Fine Typography; Eton College Collection; Bowman Gray Collection Relating to World Wars I and II; Hanes Foundation for the Study of the Origin and Development of the Book; Dannie N. Heineman Collection of Hebraica and Judaica; Archibald Henderson Collection of George Bernard Shaw; Roland Holt Collection of American Theater; Walter Hooper Collection of C.S. Lewis; William Henry Hoyt Collection of French History; Richard Jente Collection of Proverbs; Kellam Collection of "The Night Before Christmas"; Clifford and Glady Lyons Collection of Robert Frost; Mazarinades Collection; Reference Collection for Rare Books; Shedd Collection of Aphorisms; Southern Pamphlets Collection; Samuel A. Tannenbaum Collection of William Shakespeare; Leslie Weil Collection of Science; William A. Whitaker Collections of Charles Dickens, Costume Plate Books, George Cruikshank, Grolier Club First Editions, Samuel Johnson and His Circle and William Makepeace Thackeray; Victorian Bindings; Richard H. Wilmer, Jr. Collection of

Civil War Novels. **Holdings:** 70,000 books. **Subscriptions:** 20 journals and other serials. **Services:** Interlibrary loans; copying; collection open to public with restrictions. **Automated Operations:** Computerized cataloging. **Staff:** Roberta A. Engleman, Assoc.Cur./Cat.; Elizabeth Lansing, Cat.; Margaret Bell, Coll.Asst.; Imre Kalanyos, Rd.Rm.Supv.

★15949★
UNIVERSITY OF NORTH CAROLINA, CHAPEL HILL - SCHOOL OF LIBRARY SCIENCE LIBRARY (Info Sci)
114 Manning Hall   Phone: (919) 962-8361
Chapel Hill, NC 27514   Ellen D. Sutton, Interim Libn.
Founded: 1931. **Staff:** 2. **Subjects:** Librarianship, documentation, communication, publishing, management, education. **Special Collections:** Historical collection of children's literature in the United States; annual reports and newsletters of libraries and related institutions. **Holdings:** 61,038 books and bound periodical volumes; 1252 reels of microfilm; 1483 microcards and microfiche; 1476 documents in report literature collection. **Subscriptions:** 1000 journals and other serials. **Services:** Copying; library open to public with restrictions. **Publications:** Acquisitions list, monthly - primarily for internal distribution.

UNIVERSITY OF NORTH CAROLINA, CHAPEL HILL - SCHOOL OF PUBLIC HEALTH - CENTER FOR EARLY ADOLESCENCE
See: University of North Carolina, Chapel Hill - Center for Early Adolescence

★15950★
UNIVERSITY OF NORTH CAROLINA, CHAPEL HILL - SOUTHERN HISTORICAL COLLECTION & MANUSCRIPTS DEPARTMENT (Hist)
Wilson Library 024A   Phone: (919) 933-1345
Chapel Hill, NC 27514   Carolyn A. Wallace, Dir./Cur.
Founded: 1930. **Staff:** Prof 5; Other 3. **Subjects:** Southern history and culture, university history, American and English literature. **Holdings:** Over 8 million manuscript items organized in over 4300 groups; University of North Carolina archives (1.1 million items); 2271 microforms; 363 AV items; 1815 audiotapes. **Services:** Copying; library open to public for reference use only. **Publications:** The Southern Historical Collection: A Guide to Manuscripts, 1970 (Supplement, 1976). **Staff:** Michael G. Martin, Jr., Asst.Cur./Archv.; Richard A. Shrader, Ref.Archv.; Tim West, Tech.Serv.Archv.; Frances A. Weaver, Asst.Univ.Archv.

★15951★
UNIVERSITY OF NORTH CAROLINA, CHAPEL HILL - ZOOLOGY LIBRARY (Sci-Tech)
213 Wilson Hall 046A   Phone: (919) 962-2264
Chapel Hill, NC 27514   John B. Darling, Libn.
Founded: 1940. **Staff:** Prof 1; Other 1. **Subjects:** Invertebrate and vertebrate zoology, cell biology, genetics, physiology, evolution, molecular biology, embryology, behavior, ecology. **Holdings:** 33,168 volumes. **Subscriptions:** 590 journals and other serials. **Services:** Interlibrary loans; copying; library open to public.

★15952★
UNIVERSITY OF NORTH CAROLINA, GREENSBORO - DANCE COLLECTION (Hum)
Jackson Library, Special Collections   Phone: (919) 379-5246
Greensboro, NC 27412   Emilie Mills, Spec.Coll.Libn.
Staff: Prof 1; Other 2. **Subjects:** History of the dance; modern dance; dance notation. **Special Collections:** Early dance books, 16th-18th centuries (100 volumes). **Holdings:** 3000 volumes. **Subscriptions:** 40 journals and other serials. **Services:** Collection open to public for research purposes.

★15953★
UNIVERSITY OF NORTH CAROLINA, GREENSBORO - EUGENIE SILVERMAN BAIZERMAN ARCHIVE (Art)
Jackson Library, Special Collections   Phone: (919) 379-5246
Greensboro, NC 27412
Staff: Prof 1; Other 2. **Subjects:** Art. **Special Collections:** Eugenie Silverman Baizerman Archive. **Holdings:** 2000 items. **Services:** Archive open to public but manuscript materials are not available. **Special Catalogs:** Catalog of Special Collections' Manuscripts and Archives.

★15954★
UNIVERSITY OF NORTH CAROLINA, GREENSBORO - GEORGE HERBERT COLLECTION (Hist)
Jackson Library, Special Collections   Phone: (919) 379-5246
Greensboro, NC 27412
Staff: Prof 2; Other 1. **Special Collections:** George Herbert Collection of books, dating from the 17th to 20th centuries; Cross-Bias Newsletter, 1975

to present; Friends of Bemerton miscellanea (50 items). **Holdings:** 100 books; dissertations on Herbert (4 titles on microfilm). **Services:** Copying; collection open to public for research.

★15955★
UNIVERSITY OF NORTH CAROLINA, GREENSBORO - GIRLS BOOKS IN SERIES (Hum)
Jackson Library, Special Collections   Phone: (919) 379-5246
Greensboro, NC 27412   Emilie Mills, Spec.Coll.Libn.
Staff: Prof 1; Other 2. **Subjects:** Children's literature. **Holdings:** 200 books. **Services:** Collection open to serious researchers.

★15956★
UNIVERSITY OF NORTH CAROLINA, GREENSBORO - LOIS LENSKI COLLECTION (Hum; Rare Book)
Jackson Library, Special Collections   Phone: (919) 379-5246
Greensboro, NC 27412
Subjects: Children's literature. **Special Collections:** Lois Lenski Collection (5000 books, manuscripts, original drawings, correspondence, photographs, clippings and ephemera); early children's books, 18th-19th centuries (1500). **Services:** Copying (limited); collection open to public for serious research.

★15957★
UNIVERSITY OF NORTH CAROLINA, GREENSBORO - LUIGI SILVA COLLECTION (Mus)
Jackson Library, Special Collections   Phone: (919) 379-5246
Greensboro, NC 27412
Staff: Prof 1; Other 2. **Subjects:** History and teaching of the cello. **Special Collections:** Luigi Silva Library of the History and Teaching of the Cello. **Holdings:** 200 books; 20 bound periodical volumes; 73 boxes of manuscripts and printed scores; 80 bound volumes of chamber music. **Services:** Copying; collection open to public for reference use only. **Special Catalogs:** Catalog of the cello collections at University of North Carolina at Greensboro: Part I: The Luigi Silva Collection (1978).

★15958★
UNIVERSITY OF NORTH CAROLINA, GREENSBORO - PHYSICAL EDUCATION HISTORY COLLECTION (Educ)
Jackson Library, Special Collections   Phone: (919) 379-5246
Greensboro, NC 27412
Subjects: Physical activity, training, theory; gymnastics; dance history. **Special Collections:** Gymnastics books dating from the 16th century; early dance books and landmark works on all types of physical activity, training and theory, from the 16th century to the early 1900s in English and several foreign languages. **Holdings:** 1500 books and pamphlets. **Services:** Collection open to the public for serious research.

★15959★
UNIVERSITY OF NORTH CAROLINA, GREENSBORO - PRINTING COLLECTION (Rare Book)
Jackson Library, Special Collections   Phone: (919) 379-5246
Greensboro, NC 27412
Staff: Prof 1; Other 2. **Subjects:** Private presses, history of printing, 20th-century illustrated books. **Special Collections:** Modern fine printing and the art of the book; 19th-century American publishers' trade bindings; American publishers' cloth, early period. **Holdings:** 1000 books and bound periodical volumes. **Services:** Copying; collection open to public for research only.

★15960★
UNIVERSITY OF NORTH CAROLINA, GREENSBORO - RANDALL JARRELL COLLECTION (Hum)
Jackson Library, Special Collections   Phone: (919) 379-5246
Greensboro, NC 27412
Staff: Prof 1; Other 2. **Subjects:** Randall Jarrell. **Holdings:** 300 books; over 3000 manuscript items; 10 films and tapes; 6 recordings. **Services:** Copying; collection open to public for research only.

★15961★
UNIVERSITY OF NORTH CAROLINA, GREENSBORO - SAUL BAIZERMAN ARCHIVE (Art)
Jackson Library, Special Collections   Phone: (919) 379-5246
Greensboro, NC 27412
Staff: Prof 2; Other 1. **Special Collections:** Saul Baizerman (1889-1957), sculptor. **Holdings:** Drawings, sketches, photographs of sculptures completed and in progress; exhibition catalogs, reviews, journals, personal memorabilia (2100 items). **Services:** Archive open to public with restrictions on unpublished material. **Special Indexes:** Special Collections' Manuscripts and Archives - description with box listings.

★15962★

UNIVERSITY OF NORTH CAROLINA, GREENSBORO - WAY & WILLIAMS COLLECTION (Publ; Rare Book)
Jackson Library, Special Collections   Phone: (919) 379-5246
Greensboro, NC 27412
Holdings: Way & Williams Collection (200 books, manuscripts, correspondence and original drawings of a Chicago literary publishing firm from 1895-1898). Important associations include Will Bradley, Maxfield Parrish, William Allen White. **Services:** Collection open to public for serious research.

★15963★

UNIVERSITY OF NORTH CAROLINA, GREENSBORO - WOMAN'S COLLECTION (Soc Sci)
Jackson Library, Special Collections   Phone: (919) 379-5246
Greensboro, NC 27412
Staff: Prof 1; Other 2. **Subjects:** Women - education, history, suffrage; history of costume; women authors; manners and morals; child raising and family life. **Special Collections:** Women in the 17th-19th centuries. **Holdings:** 4000 books; 254 bound periodical volumes. **Services:** Copying; collection open to public for research purposes. **Publications:** The Woman's Collection, A Check-list of Holdings, 1975.

★15964★

UNIVERSITY OF NORTH CAROLINA, GREENSBORO - WOMEN DETECTIVES FICTION COLLECTION (Hum)
Jackson Library, Special Collections   Phone: (919) 379-5246
Greensboro, NC 27412
Staff: Prof 2; Other 1. **Subjects:** Women detectives in American fiction, 1890 to present. **Holdings:** 300 books. **Services:** Copying (limited); library open to public for research.

★15965★

UNIVERSITY OF NORTH CAROLINA, WILMINGTON - WILLIAM MADISON RANDALL LIBRARY - HELEN HAGAN RARE BOOK ROOM (Rare Book)
Box 3725   Phone: (919) 791-4330
Wilmington, NC 28401
Subjects: History of the lower Cape Fear area of North Carolina (includes Brunswick, Columbus, New Hanover, and Pender counties), 1700 to present. **Special Collections:** Papers of Congressman Alton Lennon and Thomas J. Armstrong; local history collection (includes land grants from George II and property documents); collection of ephemera about North Carolina artists and art institutions. **Holdings:** 130 linear feet of archival material. **Services:** Copying; room open to public. **Publications:** Descriptive inventory of the Armstrong papers.

★15966★

UNIVERSITY OF NORTH DAKOTA - CHEMISTRY LIBRARY (Sci-Tech)
224 Abbott Hall   Phone: (701) 777-2741
Grand Forks, ND 58202   Evelyn Cole, Sec.
Staff: 1. **Subjects:** Chemistry - electrochemistry, environmental, inorganic, organometallic, medicinal. **Holdings:** 3600 books; 6800 bound periodical volumes; 611 microfiche; 21,510 microcards; 24 reels of microfilm. **Subscriptions:** 150 journals and other serials. **Services:** Interlibrary loans; library open to public. **Networks/Consortia:** Member of MINITEX; North Dakota Network for Knowledge.

★15967★

UNIVERSITY OF NORTH DAKOTA - DEPARTMENT OF SPECIAL COLLECTIONS (Hist)
Chester Fritz Library   Phone: (701) 777-4625
Grand Forks, ND 58202   Dan Rylance, Coord. of Spec.Coll.
Founded: 1963. **Staff:** Prof 2; Other 2. **Subjects:** North and South Dakota history and genealogy, Northern Great Plains, Plains Indians, agrarian radicalism, Nonpartisan League (North Dakota), oral history, women's history, environment. **Special Collections:** Depository of North Dakota State Documents; Orin G. Libby Manuscript Collection (5000 linear feet); University Archives (800 linear feet); Fred Aandahl Collection of Books on Great Plains (1200 volumes); North Dakota material (4000 volumes); Norwegian and German newspapers; genealogy and family history (1500 volumes; 2000 reels of microfilm). **Holdings:** 5700 books; 25,000 state documents. **Services:** Copying; library open to public. **Automated Operations:** Computerized acquisitions. **Publications:** University of North Dakota Theses and Dissertations on North Dakota; Reference Guide to North Dakota History and Literature, 1979; Guide to Orin G. Libby Manuscript Collection, 1975 (volume 2, 1983). **Special Catalogs:** Subject Guide to Orin G. Libby Manuscript Collection, 1979. **Special Indexes:** Index to the Dakota Student (newspaper). **Staff:** Colleen Oihus, Asst.Cur.

★15968★

UNIVERSITY OF NORTH DAKOTA - EDUCATIONAL RESOURCES INFORMATION CENTER
Chester Fritz Library
Grand Forks, ND 58202
Defunct

★15969★

UNIVERSITY OF NORTH DAKOTA - ENERGY RESEARCH CENTER - ENERGY LIBRARY (Energy)
University Sta., Box 8213   Phone: (701) 777-5132
Grand Forks, ND 58202   Mary W. Scott, Libn.
Founded: 1951. **Staff:** Prof 1; Other 1. **Subjects:** Fossil energy conversion, coal, lignite. **Holdings:** 3000 books; 760 bound periodical volumes; U.S. Dept. of Energy reports; 211 periodical titles. **Subscriptions:** 90 journals and other serials. **Services:** Interlibrary loans (through Chester Fritz Library); copying; SDI; library open to public. **Automated Operations:** Computerized cataloging. **Computerized Information Services:** DIALOG, SDC, BRS, OCLC. Performs searches on cost recovery basis. **Networks/Consortia:** Member of MINITEX. **Formerly:** U.S. Dept. of Energy - Grand Forks Energy Technology Center Library.

★15970★

UNIVERSITY OF NORTH DAKOTA - ENGINEERING LIBRARY (Sci-Tech)
Harrington Hall, University Sta.   Phone: (701) 777-3040
Grand Forks, ND 58202   Ruth Peterson, Libn.
Staff: 1. **Subjects:** Engineering - chemical, civil, electrical, and mechanical. **Holdings:** 10,741 books; 8440 bound periodical volumes; 4600 microfiche; 715 reels of microfilm. **Subscriptions:** 380 journals and other serials. **Services:** Interlibrary loans; copying; library open to public. **Computerized Information Services:** DIALOG, SDC. **Networks/Consortia:** Member of MINITEX; North Dakota Network for Knowledge.

★15971★

UNIVERSITY OF NORTH DAKOTA - GEOLOGY LIBRARY (Sci-Tech)
Leonard Hall, University Sta.   Phone: (701) 777-3221
Grand Forks, ND 58202   Holly Gilbert, Ref.Libn.
Staff: 1. **Subjects:** Geology, paleontology, petroleum engineering, North Dakota geology. **Special Collections:** Depository for state geological surveys publications; U.S. Geological Survey publications and U.S. Bureau of Mines publications; U.S.G.S. open-file reports for North Dakota. **Holdings:** 10,212 books; 18,622 bound periodical volumes; 86 microfiche; 210 reels of microfilm; 130,000 U.S. Geological Survey topographic maps; 7700 other maps; air photograph collection for North Dakota. **Subscriptions:** 756 journals and other serials. **Services:** Interlibrary loans; copying; library open to public. **Computerized Information Services:** DIALOG, SDC. **Networks/Consortia:** Member of MINITEX; North Dakota Network for Knowledge.

★15972★

UNIVERSITY OF NORTH DAKOTA - INSTITUTE FOR ECOLOGICAL STUDIES - ENVIRONMENTAL RESOURCE CENTER - LIBRARY (Env-Cons)
Box 8278   Phone: (701) 777-2851
Grand Forks, ND 58202   Rod Sayler, Dir.
Founded: 1972. **Staff:** 2. **Subjects:** Ecology, land use, water and air pollution, chemical and biological contaminants, wildlife, environmental education, energy, nonrenewable resources. **Holdings:** 1000 books; 600 research reports; 1000 environmental impact statements; 12 drawers of pamphlets; 600 maps. **Services:** Interlibrary loans; copying; SDI; center open to public.

★15973★

UNIVERSITY OF NORTH DAKOTA - MATH-PHYSICS LIBRARY (Sci-Tech)
211 Witmer Hall   Phone: (701) 777-2911
Grand Forks, ND 58202   Monica Bednarz, Sec.
Staff: 1. **Subjects:** Field theory, solid state physics, mathematical physics, thin films, mathematical analysis, mathematical models. **Holdings:** 7000 books. **Subscriptions:** 230 journals and other serials. **Services:** Interlibrary loans; library open to public. **Networks/Consortia:** Member of MINITEX; North Dakota Network for Knowledge.

★15974★

UNIVERSITY OF NORTH DAKOTA - MUSIC LIBRARY (Mus)
Hughes Fine Arts Center
Grand Forks, ND 58202   Julie Reiman, Libn.
Staff: 2. **Subjects:** Music. **Holdings:** 4000 phonograph records; 4000 scores. **Services:** Interlibrary loans; copying; library open to public, phonograph records do not circulate.

★15975★

UNIVERSITY OF NORTH DAKOTA - OLAF H. THORMODSGARD LAW LIBRARY (Law)
Phone: (701) 777-2204
Grand Forks, ND 58201　　　Rita T. Reusch, Dir.
Founded: 1899. **Staff:** Prof 5; Other 3. **Subjects:** Law. **Holdings:** 112,996 books; 16,849 bound periodical volumes; 92,365 volumes in microform; 152 audio cassettes. **Subscriptions:** 3369 journals and other serials. **Services:** Interlibrary loans; copying; library open to public. **Automated Operations:** Computerized cataloging. **Computerized Information Services:** LEXIS. **Networks/Consortia:** Member of MINITEX. **Staff:** Donald D. Olson, Tech.Serv.Libn.; Patricia Folkestad, Ser.Libn.; Dennis Fossum, Monograph Libn.; Donald Hughes, Pub.Serv./Ref.Libn.

★15976★

UNIVERSITY OF NORTH DAKOTA - SCHOOL OF MEDICINE - HARLEY E. FRENCH MEDICAL LIBRARY (Med)
Phone: (701) 777-3993
Grand Forks, ND 58202　　　David Boilard, Dir.
Founded: 1949. **Staff:** Prof 5; Other 5. **Subjects:** Medicine, nursing, physical therapy. **Special Collections:** Dr. French Collection (books by and about doctors; history of medicine). **Holdings:** 20,000 books; 32,000 bound periodical volumes; 1200 AV programs; 7300 microfiche. **Subscriptions:** 1090 journals and other serials. **Services:** Interlibrary loans; SDI; library open to public for reference use only. **Automated Operations:** Computerized cataloging and ILL. **Computerized Information Services:** OCLC, MEDLINE, TOXLINE, BRS. Performs free MEDLINE and TOXLINE searches; BRS searches on cost recovery basis. Contact Person: Lorraine Ettl. **Networks/Consortia:** Member of Greater Midwest Regional Medical Library Network (Region 3); MINITEX. **Publications:** Biomedia Report, bimonthly. **Special Catalogs:** Audiovisual catalog (book). **Staff:** Lila Pedersen, Asst.Dir./Coll.Dev.; Lorraine Ettl, Pub.Serv.; Nancy Austin, Cat.

UNIVERSITY OF NORTH DAKOTA SCHOOL OF MEDICINE - NORTHWEST AREA HEALTH EDUCATION LIBRARY
See: Trinity Medical Center - Angus L. Cameron Medical Library

★15977★

UNIVERSITY OF NORTHERN COLORADO - UNIVERSITY ARCHIVES (Hist)
James A. Michener Library　　　Phone: (303) 351-2632
Greeley, CO 80639　　　Dr. Robert P. Markham, Coord. of Archv.
Staff: Prof 1; Other 1. **Special Collections:** University and faculty publications; papers of important community leaders; papers and manuscripts of James A. Michener. **Holdings:** 2000 books; 100 bound periodical volumes; 500 other cataloged items; 200 boxes of papers and manuscripts. **Services:** Interlibrary loans; copying; SDI; archives open to public. **Automated Operations:** Computerized cataloging, acquisitions, serials, circulation, and holdings. **Networks/Consortia:** Member of Colorado Alliance of Research Libraries (CARL). **Publications:** List of publications - available on request. **Special Indexes:** Index of old slides; faculty index.

★15978★

UNIVERSITY OF NORTHERN IOWA - LIBRARY - SPECIAL COLLECTIONS (Educ; Hist)
Phone: (319) 273-6307
Cedar Falls, IA 50613　　　Gerald L. Peterson, Spec.Coll.Libn.
Staff: Prof 1; Other 1. **Subjects:** Education, Iowa history. **Special Collections:** American fiction first editions, proofs and manuscripts (4000 volumes); university archives. **Holdings:** 5500 books; 750 cubic feet of manuscripts. **Services:** Interlibrary loans; copying; collections open to public.

★15979★

UNIVERSITY OF NOTRE DAME - ARCHITECTURE LIBRARY (Art; Plan)
210 Architectural Bldg.　　　Phone: (219) 239-6654
Notre Dame, IN 46556　　　Anton Masin, Libn.
Staff: Prof 1; Other 1. **Subjects:** Architecture, related art and design, city planning, environment, landscape architecture. **Holdings:** 17,000 books and bound periodical volumes; 8 VF drawers; 25,000 slides. **Subscriptions:** 91 journals and other serials. **Services:** Interlibrary loans; copying; library open to public for reference use only.

★15980★

UNIVERSITY OF NOTRE DAME - ARCHIVES (Hist)
607 Memorial Library　　　Phone: (219) 239-6447
Notre Dame, IN 46556　　　Dr. Wendy Clauson Schlereth, Univ.Archv.
Founded: 1875. **Staff:** Prof 5; Other 12. **Subjects:** American Catholicism, University of Notre Dame. **Holdings:** 4000 linear feet of manuscripts and archival material. **Services:** Copying; archives open to public. **Publications:** Guides to microfilmed collections - available for purchase.

★15981★

UNIVERSITY OF NOTRE DAME - CENTER FOR THE STUDY OF HUMAN RIGHTS - READING ROOM (Soc Sci)
Law School, Rm. 301
Notre Dame, IN 46556　　　Rita Kopezynski
Founded: 1974. **Staff:** Prof 1. **Subjects:** Black studies, civil rights, international human rights, amnesty. **Special Collections:** Theodore M. Hesburgh Civil Rights Collection (14,000 documents); Mexican American Collection (40 reels of microfilm). **Holdings:** 1100 books; 40 bound periodical volumes; 100 documents of the U.S. Civil Rights Commission. **Services:** Room open to public for reference use only.

★15982★

UNIVERSITY OF NOTRE DAME - CHEMISTRY/PHYSICS LIBRARY (Sci-Tech)
231 Nieuwland Science Hall　　　Phone: (219) 239-7203
Notre Dame, IN 46556　　　Karla P. Goold, Libn.
Founded: 1963. **Staff:** Prof 1; Other 2. **Subjects:** Chemistry - analytical, biochemistry, environmental, inorganic, organic, photochemistry, polymer, solid-state, stereo, theoretical; physics - acoustical, astrophysics, biophysics, computer, cryogenics, elementary particle, high energy, mathematical, nuclear, radio, solid-state, technical. **Holdings:** 55,604 volumes. **Subscriptions:** 950 journals and other serials. **Services:** Interlibrary loans; copying; library open to public for reference use only. **Computerized Information Services:** DIALOG, BRS.

★15983★

UNIVERSITY OF NOTRE DAME - ENGINEERING LIBRARY (Sci-Tech)
149 Fitzpatrick Hall of Engineering　　　Phone: (219) 239-6665
Notre Dame, IN 46556　　　Robert J. Havlik, Engr.Libn.
Staff: Prof 1; Other 2. **Subjects:** Engineering - civil, aerospace, mechanical, electrical, environmental, metallurgical, chemical. **Holdings:** 24,500 books; 17,500 bound periodical volumes; 12,500 microfiche. **Subscriptions:** 625 journals and other serials. **Services:** Interlibrary loans; copying; library open to public for reference use only. **Computerized Information Services:** DIALOG, BRS.

★15984★

UNIVERSITY OF NOTRE DAME - INTERNATIONAL DOCUMENTATION CENTER (Soc Sci)
213 Memorial Library　　　Phone: (219) 239-6587
Notre Dame, IN 46556　　　Theodore B. Ivanus, Hd.
Staff: Prof 1; Other 1. **Subjects:** International relations, foreign policy, diplomacy. **Holdings:** 850 boxes of newspaper clippings; 140 files of pamphlets. **Subscriptions:** 30 newspapers. **Services:** Center open to public.

★15985★

UNIVERSITY OF NOTRE DAME - LAW SCHOOL LIBRARY (Law)
221 Memorial Library
Box 535　　　Phone: (219) 239-7024
Notre Dame, IN 46556　　　Kathleen Farmann, Law Libn.
Founded: 1869. **Staff:** Prof 5; Other 3. **Subjects:** Law. **Holdings:** 123,350 volumes. **Subscriptions:** 697 journals and 3000 other serials. **Services:** Interlibrary loans; copying; library open to public. **Computerized Information Services:** LEXIS, Westlaw. Performs searches on subscription basis. Contact Person: James Gates. **Staff:** Stanley Farmann, Assoc. Law Libn.; Granville Cleveland, Asst. Law Libn.; James Gates, Staff Libn.

★15986★

UNIVERSITY OF NOTRE DAME - LIFE SCIENCES RESEARCH LIBRARY (Sci-Tech)
Galvin Life Sciences Bldg.　　　Phone: (219) 239-7209
Notre Dame, IN 46556　　　Dorothy Coil, Libn.
Founded: 1938. **Staff:** Prof 1; Other 2. **Subjects:** Biology, genetics, microbiology, entomology, parasitology, gnotobiology. **Holdings:** 22,500 volumes. **Subscriptions:** 580 journals and other serials. **Services:** Interlibrary loans; copying; library open to public for reference use only. **Computerized Information Services:** DIALOG, BRS.

★15987★

UNIVERSITY OF NOTRE DAME - MATHEMATICS LIBRARY (Sci-Tech)
200 Computing Center　　　Phone: (219) 239-7278
Notre Dame, IN 46556　　　Jennifer Helman, Supv.
Founded: 1962. **Staff:** 1. **Subjects:** Pure mathematics. **Holdings:** 26,560 volumes. **Subscriptions:** 250 journals and other serials. **Services:** Interlibrary loans; copying; library open to public for reference use only.

★15988★

UNIVERSITY OF NOTRE DAME - MEDIEVAL INSTITUTE LIBRARY (Hist)
715 Memorial Library   Phone: (219) 239-7420
Notre Dame, IN 46556   Dr. Louis Jordan, Hd.
Staff: Prof 1; Other 1. **Subjects:** Medieval studies. **Special Collections:**
Frank M. Folsom Ambrosiana; Microfilm & Photograph Collection; medieval
education; medieval manuscripts; medieval seals. **Holdings:** 50,000 volumes;
15,000 microforms; 12 VF drawers. **Subscriptions:** 300 journals and other
serials. **Services:** Interlibrary loans; copying; library open to public for
reference use only.

★15989★

**UNIVERSITY OF NOTRE DAME - RADIATION LABORATORY - RADIATION
CHEMISTRY DATA CENTER (Sci-Tech)**
                                              Phone: (219) 239-6527
Notre Dame, IN 46556   Dr. Alberta B. Ross, Supv.
Founded: 1965. **Staff:** Prof 4; Other 3. **Subjects:** Radiation chemistry,
photochemistry. **Holdings:** 73,000 journal articles, reports. **Services:** Center
open to scientists on request. **Computerized Information Services:** RCDC
Bibliographic Database (internal database). **Publications:** Biweekly List of
Papers on Radiation Chemistry and Photochemistry and annual indexed
cumulation; critical reviews and data compilations in NSRDS report series;
Thesaurus for Radiation Chemistry. **Staff:** Dr. W.P. Helman; Dr. Gordon Hug;
Dr. Ian Carmichael.

★15990★

**UNIVERSITY OF NOTRE DAME - RARE BOOKS AND SPECIAL COLLECTIONS
DEPARTMENT (Hum; Rare Book)**
102 Memorial Library   Phone: (219) 239-6489
Notre Dame, IN 46556   David E. Sparks, Hd.
Staff: Prof 1; Other 2. **Subjects:** Theology, philosophy, language and
literature, sports and games, botany. **Special Collections:** John Augustine
Zahm Collection on Dante (5000 items); John Bennett Shaw Collection on
Chesterton (2000 items); Rare Books Collection (25,000 items);
International Sports/Games Research Collection (500,000 items); Jeremiah
D.M. Ford Collection on Romance Languages and Literature (3000 items);
Edward L. Greene Collection on Botany (4000 items); Notre Dame Collection
(8000 items). **Subscriptions:** 150 journals and other serials. **Services:**
Interlibrary loans (limited); copying; department open to public. **Special
Catalogs:** Exhibit catalogues; Incunabula Typographica, 1979; Catalogue of
Medieval and Renaissance Manuscripts, 1978.

★15991★

UNIVERSITY OF NOTRE DAME - SNITE MUSEUM OF ART - LIBRARY (Art)
                                              Phone: (219) 239-5466
Notre Dame, IN 46556   Lisa M. Stanczak, Libn.
Staff: Prof 1. **Subjects:** Art. **Holdings:** 2500 books; 3000 unbound
periodicals. **Services:** Copying; library open to public with restrictions.

★15992★

UNIVERSITY OF OKLAHOMA - ART LIBRARY (Art)†
Jacobson Hall, Rm. 203   Phone: (405) 325-2841
Norman, OK 73019   Donald E. Koozer, Supv.
Founded: 1939. **Staff:** Prof 1. **Subjects:** Painting, sculpture, design, art
history, drawing, printmaking. **Holdings:** 11,508 books; 562 microfiche.
Subscriptions: 52 journals and other serials. **Services:** Interlibrary loans;
copying; library open to public with restrictions.

★15993★

UNIVERSITY OF OKLAHOMA - BIOLOGICAL STATION LIBRARY (Sci-Tech)
Star Route B
Kingston, OK 73439   Loren G. Hill, Dir.
Founded: 1947. **Staff:** Prof 3. **Subjects:** Aquatic ecology, fisheries,
limnology, population ecology, biology. **Special Collections:** Lake Texoma
Collection (1200 items); Riggs Collection (fishes and fisheries; 5550 items);
Greenbank Collection (fishes and fisheries; 2081 items). **Holdings:** 3238
volumes; 4927 reprints. **Subscriptions:** 300 journals and other serials.
Services: Library open to qualified persons. **Special Indexes:** Indexes to Lake
Texoma Collection and reprints. **Staff:** Marian McCarley, Asst.Libn.; Catherine
Hubbs, Asst.Libn.

★15994★

**UNIVERSITY OF OKLAHOMA - CENTER FOR ECONOMIC AND
MANAGEMENT RESEARCH (Bus-Fin)***
307 W. Brooks St., Rm. 4   Phone: (405) 325-2931
Norman, OK 73019
Staff: 1. **Subjects:** Statistics on Oklahoma business and economic conditions;
economic aspects of energy. **Holdings:** 500 books; 25 bound periodical
volumes; 1500 government documents; 24 VF drawers of reports.

Subscriptions: 150 journals and other serials; 6 newspapers. **Services:**
Copying; center open to students and researchers; restricted lending to
noncenter employees. **Publications:** Oklahoma Business Bulletin, monthly;
Statistical Abstract of Oklahoma, biennial; Review of Regional Economics,
semiannual.

★15995★

**UNIVERSITY OF OKLAHOMA - CHEMISTRY-MATHEMATICS LIBRARY (Sci-
Tech)**
Physical Sciences Center, 207   Phone: (405) 325-5628
Norman, OK 73019   Jeanne G. Howard, Libn.
Founded: 1921. **Staff:** Prof 1; Other 1. **Subjects:** Chemistry, mathematics.
Holdings: 50,000 volumes; 12,787 microforms. **Subscriptions:** 586
journals and other serials. **Services:** Interlibrary loans; copying; library open to
public for reference use only. **Computerized Information Services:** DIALOG,
SDC, BRS, OCLC. Performs searches on cost recovery basis. **Networks/
Consortia:** Member of AMIGOS Bibliographic Council, Inc.; RLG.

★15996★

UNIVERSITY OF OKLAHOMA - ENGINEERING LIBRARY (Sci-Tech)
                                              Phone: (405) 325-2941
Norman, OK 73019   Jean Poland, Libn.
Staff: 3. **Subjects:** Engineering - electrical, mechanical, chemical, geological,
industrial, nuclear, petroleum, civil, aerospace, metallurgy; computer science;
environmental science. **Holdings:** 45,000 books and bound periodical
volumes; 1800 uncataloged pamphlets and reprints; 540 microfiche; 73 reels
of microfilm. **Subscriptions:** 600 journals and other serials. **Services:**
Interlibrary loans; copying; library open to public. **Automated Operations:**
Computerized circulation. **Computerized Information Services:** DIALOG,
SDC, BRS, OCLC. **Networks/Consortia:** Member of AMIGOS Bibliographic
Council, Inc.; RLG.

★15997★

UNIVERSITY OF OKLAHOMA - GEOLOGY LIBRARY (Sci-Tech; Energy)
830 Van Vleet Oval, Rm. 103   Phone: (405) 325-6451
Norman, OK 73019   Claren M. Kidd, Libn.
Staff: Prof 1; Other 1. **Subjects:** Geology, paleontology, mineralogy,
palynology, petroleum geology, geochemistry, geophysics, oceanography,
hydrology. **Special Collections:** Herndon Map Service (Oklahoma); theses on
Oklahoma geology. **Holdings:** 70,101 volumes; 90,111 maps; 180,322 PI
completion cards; 366,579 Oklahoma Corporation drillers logs. **Subscriptions:**
1000 journals and other serials. **Services:** Interlibrary loans; copying; library
open to public.

★15998★

**UNIVERSITY OF OKLAHOMA - HARRY W. BASS COLLECTION IN BUSINESS
HISTORY (Bus-Fin; Hist)**
401 W. Brooks   Phone: (405) 325-3941
Norman, OK 73019   Dr. Daniel A. Wren, Cur.
Founded: 1955. **Staff:** Prof 1; Other 3. **Subjects:** History - business,
economic, management. **Special Collections:** Sears Roebuck catalogs on
microfilm; rare books in economic history. **Holdings:** 17,000 books; 650
bound periodical volumes; 1750 pamphlets. **Subscriptions:** 15 journals and
other serials. **Services:** Collection open to public. **Publications:** Catalogs of
the Collection, irregular.

★15999★

**UNIVERSITY OF OKLAHOMA - HEALTH SCIENCES CENTER - DEAN A. MC
GEE EYE INSTITUTE - LIBRARY (Med)**
Department of Ophthalmology
608 Stanton L. Young Blvd.   Phone: (405) 271-6085
Oklahoma City, OK 73104   Sheri Taylor, Libn.
Staff: Prof 1. **Subjects:** Ophthalmology. **Holdings:** 1200 books; 1000 bound
periodical volumes; 30 slide sets; 84 video cassettes. **Subscriptions:** 34
journals and other serials. **Services:** Interlibrary loans; SDI; library open to
medical personnel only. **Computerized Information Services:** MEDLARS,
BRS; University of Oklahoma internal database. **Networks/Consortia:**
Member of Greater Oklahoma City Area Health Sciences Library Consortium
(GOAL).

★16000★

**UNIVERSITY OF OKLAHOMA - HEALTH SCIENCES CENTER - DEPARTMENT
OF SURGERY LIBRARY (Med)**
Oklahoma Memorial Hospital
Box 26307   Phone: (405) 271-5506
Oklahoma City, OK 73126   Linda R. O'Rourke, Med.Libn.
Staff: Prof 1. **Subjects:** Surgery - general, plastic, neurosurgery, thoracic and
cardiovascular, oral; emergency medicine and trauma. **Holdings:** 3349 books
and bound periodical volumes. **Subscriptions:** 90 journals and other serials.

Services: Interlibrary loans; copying; SDI; library open to affiliated surgical personnel. **Computerized Information Services:** DIALOG, MEDLARS. **Networks/Consortia:** Member of Greater Oklahoma City Area Health Sciences Library Consortium (GOAL). **Special Indexes:** 10-year Key Word Index to Current Problems in Surgery (updated each December, beginning with 1978).

★16001★
UNIVERSITY OF OKLAHOMA - HEALTH SCIENCES CENTER LIBRARY (Med)
1000 Stanton L. Young Blvd.
Box 26901   Phone: (405) 271-2285
Oklahoma City, OK 73190   C.M. Thompson, Dir.
Founded: 1928. **Staff:** Prof 10; Other 25. **Subjects:** Medicine, dentistry, nursing, public health, pharmacy, allied health subjects. **Holdings:** 67,000 books; 88,000 bound periodical volumes. **Subscriptions:** 2304 journals and other serials. **Services:** Interlibrary loans; copying; library open to public for reference use only. **Automated Operations:** Computerized cataloging. **Computerized Information Services:** DIALOG, SDC, MEDLARS, OCLC. **Networks/Consortia:** Member of AMIGOS Bibliographic Council, Inc.; TALON; Oklahoma Telecommunications Interlibrary System (OTIS). **Publications:** Guide, annual; Footnote, bimonthly. **Staff:** Barbara B. Peshel, Monograph Serv.; Ruth W. Wender, Assoc. to Dir.; Virgil L. Jones, Ref.Libn.; Dana D. Testa, AV Serv.; Ilse Von Brauchitsch, Ref.Libn.; Joanne Callard, General Serv.; Phyllis Lansing, Ref.Serv.; Sally Shrout, Ser.Serv.; Jack Wagner, Cat.

★16002★
UNIVERSITY OF OKLAHOMA - HISTORY OF SCIENCE COLLECTIONS (Sci-Tech; Hist)
401 W. Brooks, Rm. 339   Phone: (405) 325-2741
Norman, OK 73019   Duane H.D. Roller, Cur.
Founded: 1951. **Staff:** Prof 2; Other 4. **Subjects:** History of science and technology. **Special Collections:** DeGolyer, Klopsteg, Crew, Sally Hall, Nielsen, Lacy, ADF and Harlow Collections. **Holdings:** 62,000 volumes; 2500 volumes of uncataloged pamphlets and reprints; 850 photographs; 25,000 volumes in microform; 22 cubic feet of manuscripts. **Subscriptions:** 130 journals and other serials. **Services:** Copying; collections open to public by permission. **Automated Operations:** Computerized cataloging and circulation. **Computerized Information Services:** DIALOG, SDC, OCLC, BRS. **Networks/Consortia:** Member of Association of Research Libraries (ARL); RLG; AMIGOS Bibliographic Council, Inc. **Special Catalogs:** Card, book and computerized catalogs. **Special Indexes:** Index to journal articles (card). **Staff:** Marcia M. Goodman, Libn.

★16003★
UNIVERSITY OF OKLAHOMA - LAW LIBRARY (Law)
300 Timberdell Rd.   Phone: (405) 325-4311
Norman, OK 73019   Laura N. Gasaway, Dir.
Founded: 1909. **Staff:** Prof 7; Other 7. **Subjects:** Law. **Special Collections:** Law - Indian, water, space; Indian land titles. **Holdings:** 146,905 volumes; 71,318 volumes in microform. **Subscriptions:** 2651 journals and other serials; 25 newspapers. **Services:** Interlibrary loans; copying; library open to legal researchers, law students, faculty. **Automated Operations:** Computerized cataloging and acquisitions. **Computerized Information Services:** LEXIS, Westlaw. **Networks/Consortia:** Member of Mid-America Law School Library Consortium; AMIGOS Bibliographic Council, Inc. **Publications:** Law Library Newsletter, monthly; Acquisitions List, monthly; User's Guide; Research Guide; annual report. **Staff:** John D. Edwards, Assoc.Libn.; Marilyn K. Nicely, Tech.Serv.Libn.; Amber Lee Smith, Pub.Serv.Libn.; Christine Corcos, Acq.Libn.; Margie Wait, Circ.Libn.

★16004★
UNIVERSITY OF OKLAHOMA - LIMITED ACCESS COLLECTION (Rare Book)
401 W. Brooks, Rm. 440   Phone: (405) 325-2048
Norman, OK 73019   Duane H.D. Roller, Cur.
Staff: Prof 2; Other 1. **Special Collections:** Lois Lenski Children's Literature Collection; Bizzell Bible Collection. **Holdings:** 11,850 volumes. **Services:** Copying; collection open to public by permission. **Automated Operations:** Computerized cataloging and circulation. **Computerized Information Services:** DIALOG, SDC, OCLC. **Networks/Consortia:** Member of Association of Research Libraries (ARL); RLG; CRL; AMIGOS Bibliographic Council, Inc. **Staff:** Marcia M. Goodman, Libn.

★16005★
UNIVERSITY OF OKLAHOMA - MUSIC LIBRARY (Mus)
                                             Phone: (405) 325-4243
Norman, OK 73019   Jan Seifert, Fine Arts Libn.
Staff: Prof 1; Other 4. **Subjects:** Music - education, history, theory, performance; composers' bibliographies; history of instruments. **Special

Collections: Spencer Norton Collection (12,937 volumes); Joseph Benton Collection (100 items); **Holdings:** 22,000 books; 1640 bound periodical volumes; 10,325 phonograph records; 13,000 music scores; 64 reels of microfilm; 420 tape recordings; 108 micro opaque cards; 342 microfiche. **Subscriptions:** 76 journals and other serials. **Services:** Interlibrary loans; copying; SDI; library open to public. **Computerized Information Services:** OCLC. **Networks/Consortia:** Member of RLG.

★16006★
UNIVERSITY OF OKLAHOMA - PHYSICS-ASTRONOMY LIBRARY (Sci-Tech)
219 Neilsen Hall   Phone: (405) 325-3961
Norman, OK 73019   Jeanne Howard, Libn.
Staff: Prof 1; Other 3. **Subjects:** Quantum mechanics, high energy physics, astronomy, astrophysics, classical physics. **Special Collections:** Atlases of the northern and southern skies. **Holdings:** 9000 books; 11,000 bound periodical volumes; 1448 AEC reports; 220 uncataloged pamphlets. **Subscriptions:** 205 journals and other serials. **Services:** Interlibrary loans; library open to public. **Automated Operations:** Computerized and acquisitions.

★16007★
UNIVERSITY OF OKLAHOMA - SCHOOL OF ARCHITECTURE LIBRARY (Art; Plan)
                                             Phone: (405) 325-5521
Norman, OK 73019   Ilse Davis, Lib.Techn.
Founded: 1929. **Subjects:** Architecture, landscape architecture, urban, environmental and interior design. **Special Collections:** Lt. Orville S. Witt Memorial Collection. **Holdings:** 10,422 books; 398 manufacturers' catalogs. **Subscriptions:** 87 journals and other serials. **Services:** Interlibrary loans.

★16008★
UNIVERSITY OF OKLAHOMA - SCHOOL OF DRAMA LIBRARY
Norman, OK 73019
Defunct

★16009★
UNIVERSITY OF OKLAHOMA - SCIENCE AND PUBLIC POLICY PROGRAM - LIBRARY (Env-Cons; Sci-Tech)
601 Elm Ave., Rm. 431   Phone: (405) 325-2554
Norman, OK 73019   Emily T. Terrell, Libn.
Staff: Prof 1. **Subjects:** Energy policy, impact assessment, environmental policy, regional studies, technology assessment, science policy. **Holdings:** 5000 books; unbound periodicals; 3 file cabinets of clippings. **Subscriptions:** 24 journals and other serials. **Services:** Copying; library open to public for reference use only. **Computerized Information Services:** DIALOG.

★16010★
UNIVERSITY OF OKLAHOMA - TULSA MEDICAL COLLEGE - LIBRARY (Med)
2808 S. Sheridan   Phone: (918) 838-3464
Tulsa, OK 74129   Janet Minnerath, Hd.Libn.
Staff: Prof 1; Other 5. **Subjects:** Medicine. **Holdings:** 5090 books; 15,073 bound periodical volumes. **Subscriptions:** 600 journals and other serials. **Services:** Interlibrary loans; copying; SDI; library open to public. **Computerized Information Services:** NLM, BRS, DIALOG. **Networks/Consortia:** Member of Tulsa Area Library Cooperative (TALC); AMIGOS Bibliographic Council, Inc.; South Central Academic Medical Libraries Consortium (SCAMEL).

★16011★
UNIVERSITY OF OKLAHOMA - WESTERN HISTORY COLLECTIONS (Hist)
630 Parrington Oval, Rm. 452   Phone: (405) 325-3641
Norman, OK 73019   John S. Ezell, Cur.
Founded: 1927. **Staff:** Prof 7; Other 2. **Subjects:** American Indian, Oklahoma, American Southwest, American Trans-Mississippi West, recent U.S. **Special Collections:** Cherokee Nation Papers; Patrick J. Hurley Papers; E.E. Dale Papers; Helen G. Douglas, Robert S. Kerr, Carl Albert, and other Congressional papers. **Holdings:** 30 million items in manuscript collection; 500,000 items in Photographic Archives; 20,000 microforms; 12,000 maps; 6000 transcripts, tapes and discs of oral history; 700,000 University of Oklahoma archives; newspapers, posters, broadsides. **Services:** Copying (limited); collections open to public with restrictions. **Automated Operations:** Computerized cataloging. **Computerized Information Services:** OCLC. **Networks/Consortia:** Member of RLG. **Publications:** Guide to Regional Manuscripts in Division of Manuscripts of University of Oklahoma Library, 1960. **Special Catalogs:** Calendars and catalogs of individual collections; catalog of microform holdings; University of Oklahoma Congressional Record Series, Numbers 1-15; University of Oklahoma Western History Collections: Manuscripts Records Series, Numbers 1-3. **Staff:** Jack D. Haley, Assoc.Cur.; Daryl Morrison, Libn.; John Caldwell, Congressional Archv.; Judith D. Day,

Asst. Congressional Archv; Shelley Arlen, Photo Archv.; Wayne Donica, Congressional Rec.Spec.

★16012★
UNIVERSITY OF OKLAHOMA - WESTERN HISTORY COLLECTIONS - LIBRARY DIVISION (Hist)
Monnet Hall, Rm. 300
630 Parrington Oval   Phone: (405) 325-3641
Norman, OK 73019   John S. Ezell, Cur.
Founded: 1927. Staff: Prof 3. Subjects: American Indian, Oklahoma, American Southwest, American Trans-Mississippi West, ethnic and minority groups of the American West, energy conservation. Special Collections: Edward E. Dale Collection; Alan Farley Collection; Walter Ferguson Collection; Henry B. Bass Collection; Fred Schonwald Collection; John W. Morris Collection; Norman Brillhart Collection; other smaller collections. Holdings: 90,000 books; 15,000 bound periodical volumes; 25,000 pamphlets and documents; 15,000 microforms. Subscriptions: 250 journals and other serials; 50 newspapers. Services: Copying; mail reference research; library open to public with restrictions. Staff: Jack D. Haley, Assoc.Cur.; Daryl Morrison, Libn.

★16013★
UNIVERSITY OF OREGON - ARCHITECTURE AND ALLIED ARTS BRANCH LIBRARY (Art; Plan)
                                             Phone: (503) 686-3637
Eugene, OR 97403   Rayburn R. McCready, Hd.Libn.
Staff: Prof 2; Other 4. Subjects: Architecture, fine arts, interior design, landscape design, urban planning, art history and education, historic preservation. Holdings: 35,000 volumes; 46,500 prints and photographs; 161,500 slides; 3900 pamphlets. Subscriptions: 250 journals and other serials. Services: Interlibrary loans (through Main Library); copying; library open to public.

★16014★
UNIVERSITY OF OREGON - BUREAU OF GOVERNMENTAL RESEARCH AND SERVICE LIBRARY (Soc Sci)
Box 3177   Phone: (503) 686-3048
Eugene, OR 97403   Katherine G. Eaton, Libn.
Staff: Prof 1; Other 5. Subjects: Public administration - finance, planning, lands; intergovernmental relations; social services; transportation; environment; welfare. Holdings: 30,000 books and reports. Subscriptions: 200 journals and other serials. Services: Interlibrary loans; copying; library open to public. Publications: Monthly accessions list. Special Indexes: Index to thesis projects of School of Community Service & Public Affairs and Department of Planning, Public Policy and Management.

★16015★
UNIVERSITY OF OREGON - CAREER INFORMATION CENTER (Educ)
221 Hendricks Hall
Box 3257   Phone: (503) 686-3235
Eugene, OR 97403   Lawrence H. Smith, Dir.
Founded: 1972. Staff: 1. Subjects: Career awareness and planning, job search, interview techniques, resume and cover-letter writing. Holdings: 200 books; 70 feet and shelves of pamphlets from professional organizations; 1 VF drawer of training information sources. Services: Center not open to public but will answer mail or phone questions from others interested in career planning.

★16016★
UNIVERSITY OF OREGON - CAREER INFORMATION SYSTEM (Educ)
1787 Agate St.   Phone: (503) 686-3872
Eugene, OR 97403   Bruce McKinlay, Dir.
Founded: 1971. Staff: Prof 12; Other 10. Subjects: Occupations, study and training programs, education, computer systems for guidance. Holdings: 3000 volumes; occupational information in 260 areas; 130 programs of study and training; information on 200 Oregon schools. Subscriptions: 30 journals and other serials. Services: Copying; open to public. Networks/Consortia: Headquarters of Oregon Career Information System (CIS - a statewide consortium of schools and agencies involved in occupational counseling and education with affiliates in other states). Publications: Updated issues of printouts - annual subscription basis; Oregon Occupations; Oregon Schools. Special Catalogs: Research bibliographies; directories.

★16017★
UNIVERSITY OF OREGON - COLLEGE OF BUSINESS ADMINISTRATION - DIVISION OF RESEARCH†
140 Gilbert Hall
Eugene, OR 97403
Subjects: Business. Holdings: 100 volumes. Remarks: Presently inactive.

★16018★
UNIVERSITY OF OREGON - DEPARTMENT OF ENGLISH - RANDALL V. MILLS ARCHIVES OF NORTHWEST FOLKLORE (Hist)
                                             Phone: (503) 686-3925
Eugene, OR 97403   Janet M. Cliff, Archv.
Staff: Prof 1. Subjects: Folklore and folklife, oral history. Special Collections: Robert Winslow Gordon Collection; Randall V. Mills Collection. Holdings: 300 books; 3000 unpublished field research projects. Subscriptions: 10 journals and other serials. Services: Copying; library open to public.

★16019★
UNIVERSITY OF OREGON - ENVIRONMENTAL STUDIES CENTER (Env-Cons; Energy)
                                             Phone: (503) 686-5006
Eugene, OR 97403   Pamela Vorachek, Libn.
Founded: 1971. Staff: 5. Subjects: Ecology, environmental issues, energy. Holdings: 5200 books; 100 bound periodical volumes; environmental impact statements; 250 clipping and article folders; maps. Subscriptions: 100 journals and other serials. Services: Center open to public with restrictions. Publications: Resource Lists, irregular - free upon request; bibliographies and reading lists. Special Catalogs: Catalog of Environmental Studies of University.

UNIVERSITY OF OREGON - ERIC CLEARINGHOUSE ON EDUCATIONAL MANAGEMENT
See: ERIC Clearinghouse on Educational Management

★16020★
UNIVERSITY OF OREGON - GOVERNMENT DOCUMENTS SECTION (Publ)
University Library   Phone: (503) 686-3070
Eugene, OR 97403   John A. Shuler, Act.Hd.
Staff: Prof 2; Other 2. Subjects: U.S., Canadian and British government documents; intergovernmental organizations. Holdings: 250,000 documents; 282,000 microforms. Subscriptions: 2900 journals and other serials. Services: Interlibrary loans; copying; section open to public. Computerized Information Services: DIALOG, BRS.

★16021★
UNIVERSITY OF OREGON - INSTITUTE OF RECREATION RESEARCH AND SERVICE (Rec)
180 Esslinger Hall   Phone: (503) 686-3602
Eugene, OR 97403   Larry L. Neal, Dir.
Subjects: Therapeutic recreation, park and recreation areas, theory and philosophy of leisure, outdoor education and recreation. Special Collections: L.S. Rodney Library of Recreation Administration. Holdings: 200 books; 2000 bound periodical volumes; 600 studies; 1000 park and recreation materials; clippings. Subscriptions: 10 journals and other serials. Services: institute open to public. Formerly: Its Center of leisure Studies.

★16022★
UNIVERSITY OF OREGON - INSTRUCTIONAL MEDIA CENTER (Aud-Vis)
University Library   Phone: (503) 686-3091
Eugene, OR 97403   George E. Bynon, Dir.
Staff: Prof 2; Other 14. Subjects: Instructional media. Holdings: 1320 films and film loops; 816 filmstrips; 242 media kits; 140 videotapes. Services: Center open to public for reference use only. Networks/Consortia: Member of Consortium of University Film Centers (CUFC). Publications: IMC Newsletter, quarterly - to faculty and staff. Special Catalogs: IMC Film catalog. Staff: Bill Leonard, Hd., Graphic Arts Serv.

★16023★
UNIVERSITY OF OREGON - LAW LIBRARY (Law)
                                             Phone: (503) 686-3088
Eugene, OR 97403   Dennis R. Hyatt, Libn.
Founded: 1884. Staff: Prof 4; Other 5. Subjects: Law. Holdings: 119,235 volumes; 57,063 volumes in microform. Subscriptions: 1981 journals and other serials. Services: Interlibrary loans; copying. Automated Operations: Computerized cataloging and acquisitions. Computerized Information Services: OCLC, LEXIS, DIALOG, Westlaw, Oregon Legislative Information Service (OLIS).

★16024★
UNIVERSITY OF OREGON - MAP LIBRARY (Geog-Map)
165 Condon Hall   Phone: (503) 686-3051
Eugene, OR 97403   Peter L. Stark, Hd.
Staff: Prof 1; Other 1. Subjects: Cartographic materials, geography, aerial photography. Holdings: 800 volumes; 247,000 maps; 315,000 aerial photographs; 2500 atlases. Services: Interlibrary loans; copying; library open

to public for reference use only. **Publications:** Acquisitions list, semiannual - by exchange. **Special Indexes:** Index to maps (card).

★16025★
UNIVERSITY OF OREGON - MATHEMATICS LIBRARY (Sci-Tech; Comp Sci)
University Library   Phone: (503) 686-3023
Eugene, OR 97403   Isabel A. Stirling, Hd.Libn.
Staff: 1. **Subjects:** Mathematics, computer science. **Holdings:** 20,000 volumes. **Subscriptions:** 400 journals and other serials.

★16026★
UNIVERSITY OF OREGON - MICROFORMS AND RECORDINGS DEPARTMENT (Aud-Vis)
University Library   Phone: (503) 686-3080
Eugene, OR 97403   Rory Funke, Hd.
Founded: 1980. **Staff:** 5. **Holdings:** 1 million microforms; 25,500 phonograph records; 2000 tapes. **Services:** Interlibrary loans; copying; department open to public. **Publications:** Oregon Newspapers on Microfilm, 1980.

UNIVERSITY OF OREGON - NEPAL/USAID PROJECT
See: American-Nepal Education Foundation

★16027★
UNIVERSITY OF OREGON - OREGON INSTITUTE OF MARINE BIOLOGY - LIBRARY (Sci-Tech)
     Phone: (503) 888-5534
Charleston, OR 97420   Jean Hanna, Libn.
Staff: 1. **Subjects:** Marine biology, ecology, environmental research, comparative physiology of blood pigments of vertebrates and invertebrates. **Special Collections:** Student reports inventory of Coos Bay (database of 600 reports). **Holdings:** 3000 books; 300 maps; 150 topographic maps; 2500 reprints; 2000 slides; herbarium collection of local flora. **Subscriptions:** 30 journals and other serials. **Services:** Interlibrary loans; copying; library open to public for reference use only.

★16028★
UNIVERSITY OF OREGON - ORIENTALIA COLLECTION (Hist; Area-Ethnic)
University Library   Phone: (503) 686-3114
Eugene, OR 97403   Wen-Kai Kung, Bibliog.
Staff: Prof 2. **Subjects:** East Asia - history, language, literature, religion, humanities, social sciences. **Holdings:** 40,000 volumes. **Subscriptions:** 495 journals and other serials. **Services:** Interlibrary loans; copying; library open to public. **Staff:** Michiko Banman, Bibliog.

UNIVERSITY OF OREGON - SCHOOL OF LAW - OCEAN AND COASTAL LAW CENTER
See: Ocean and Coastal Law Center

★16029★
UNIVERSITY OF OREGON - SCIENCE LIBRARY (Sci-Tech)
University Library   Phone: (503) 686-3075
Eugene, OR 97403   Isabel A. Stirling, Hd.Libn.
Staff: Prof 2; Other 5. **Subjects:** Basic sciences, physics, chemistry, biological sciences, neuroscience, geology. **Holdings:** 200,000 volumes; 18,000 microforms. **Subscriptions:** 3000 journals and other serials. **Services:** Interlibrary loans (through Main Library); copying. **Computerized Information Services:** DIALOG, BRS.

★16030★
UNIVERSITY OF OREGON - SPECIAL COLLECTIONS DIVISION (Hist)
University Library   Phone: (503) 686-3068
Eugene, OR 97403   Kenneth Duckett, Cur.
Staff: Prof 3; Other 2. **Subjects:** Political, social, economic, and literary history of the United States in the 19th and 20th centuries, with emphasis on Oregon and the Pacific Northwest. **Special Collections:** Manuscript Collection (materials of political conservatives, authors and illustrators of children's literature, writers of western fiction, missionaries to the Far East, 20th-century artists and illustrators; Pacific Northwest authors, architects, politicians and business figures); Photograph Collection (largely negatives, Pacific Northwest, Alaska, Appalachia, and the Far East); Rare Book Collection (western Americana, travels and voyages, pulp magazines, Esperanto language books and journals); Oregon Collection (circulating collection of books and journals on all phases and periods of Oregon history, life and letters). **Holdings:** 60,000 volumes; 2 million manuscripts; 125,000 photographic images; 75,000 architectural drawings. **Subscriptions:** 880 journals and other serials. **Services:** Interlibrary loans from the Oregon Collection; limited copying of manuscripts. **Special Catalogs:** Catalog of Manuscripts in the University of Oregon Library, 1971 (book); Catalog of the George Alan Connor

Esperanto Collection, 1978 (pamphlet); Inventory of the Papers of Senator Wayne L. Morse, 1974 (book); Inventory of the Papers of T. Coleman Andrews, 1967 (pamphlet); Catalog of the Louis Conrad Rosenberg Collection, 1978 (pamphlet).

UNIVERSITY OF ORIENTAL STUDIES
See: American University of Oriental Studies

★16031★
UNIVERSITY OF OSTEOPATHIC MEDICINE AND HEALTH SCIENCES - LIBRARY (Med)†
3200 Grand Ave.   Phone: (515) 271-1430
Des Moines, IA 50312   Mrs. Krishna Sahu, Dir.
Founded: 1900. **Staff:** Prof 1; Other 3. **Subjects:** Medicine, surgery, osteopathy, podiatry, allied health sciences. **Holdings:** 26,200 volumes. **Subscriptions:** 450 journals and other serials. **Services:** Interlibrary loans; library open to public for reference use only. **Networks/Consortia:** Member of Polk County Biomedical Consortium (PCBC); Greater Midwest Regional Medical Library Network (Region 3). **Publications:** Annual report - for internal distribution only.

★16032★
UNIVERSITY OF OTTAWA - HEALTH SCIENCES LIBRARY (Med)
451 Smyth Rd.   Phone: (613) 737-6521
Ottawa, ON, Canada K1H 8M4   Myra Owen, Dir.
Staff: Prof 4; Other 7. **Subjects:** Medicine, nursing, kinanthropology. **Holdings:** 38,000 books; 39,000 bound periodical volumes; 600 filmstrips; 90 video cassettes; 544 audio cassettes. **Subscriptions:** 1270 journals and other serials. **Services:** Interlibrary loans; copying; library open to public with limited borrowing privileges. **Automated Operations:** Computerized circulation. **Computerized Information Services:** Infomart, BRS, MEDLINE, CAN/OLE. **Staff:** Helena Wybenga, Ref./Tech.Serv.; Fleurette Gregoire, Ref.; Michelle LeBlanc, Ref.

★16033★
UNIVERSITY OF OTTAWA - INSTITUTE FOR INTERNATIONAL COOPERATION - DOCUMENTATION CENTRE
14 Henderson
Ottawa, ON, Canada K1N 6N5
Defunct. Holdings absorbed by University of Ottawa - Morisset Library.

★16034★
UNIVERSITY OF OTTAWA - LAW LIBRARY (Law)
Fauteux Hall
57 Copernicus St.   Phone: (613) 231-4943
Ottawa, ON, Canada K1N 6N5   Raymond Dicaire, Act.Libn.
Staff: Prof 4; Other 16. **Subjects:** Civil law (Quebec), common law. **Holdings:** 133,320 books; 8458 microfiche (1623 titles); 292 reels of microfilm; 367 cassettes. **Subscriptions:** 1468 journals and other serials; 12 newspapers. **Services:** Interlibrary loans; copying; library open to public for reference use only. **Staff:** Mr. Chin-Shih Tang, Ref. (Common Law); Marcel Joanisse, Cat.

★16035★
UNIVERSITY OF OTTAWA - MAP LIBRARY (Geog-Map)
Morisset Library
65 Hastey St., Rm. 353   Phone: (613) 231-6830
Ottawa, ON, Canada K1N 9A5   Aileen Desbarats, Hd.
Founded: 1968. **Staff:** Prof 2; Other 4. **Subjects:** Geography (especially physical and urban); urban planning; map coverage of Ottawa and the national capital region, Northern Canada, Bolivia, Chile, Colombia, Ecuador, Peru, French-speaking Africa. **Holdings:** 122,762 sheet maps; 456 wall maps; 1665 atlases; 14 globes; 244,142 aerial photographs; 1099 diapositive mapping plates; 6694 reference books; 375 bound periodical volumes. **Subscriptions:** 58 journals and other serials. **Services:** Interlibrary loans; copying; library open to public.

★16036★
UNIVERSITY OF OTTAWA - MORISSET LIBRARY (Hum; Soc Sci)
65 Hastey St.   Phone: (613) 231-6880
Ottawa, ON, Canada K1N 9A5   Yvon Richer, Univ.Chf.Libn.
Founded: 1904. **Staff:** Prof 35; Other 150. **Subjects:** Humanities and social sciences. **Special Collections:** Rare book collection. **Holdings:** 796,000 volumes; 3100 dissertations; 591,089 microfiche; 112,463 slides; 1192 films. **Subscriptions:** 9250 journals and other serials. **Services:** Interlibrary loans; copying; library open to public. **Automated Operations:** Computerized cataloging and circulation. **Computerized Information Services:** DIALOG, QL Systems, Infomart, CAN/OLE, BRS, MEDLINE, UTLAS. **Publications:** Subject bibliographies. **Remarks:** The library is a depository for publications of the Canadian federal government, the province of Ontario, and for the United

Nations and its affiliates. **Staff:** Jean LeBlanc, Dir.; Dorothy Thomson, Asst.Libn., Coll.; Suzanne St-Jacques, Hd., Ref.Serv.; Agnes Sulyok, Hd., Circ.; Frank Di Trolio, Coll.; Krystyna Miedzinska, Ser.Marie Duhamel, Govt.Pubn.

★16037★
UNIVERSITY OF OTTAWA - MUSIC LIBRARY (Mus)
One Stewart St.   Phone: (613) 231-5717
Ottawa, ON, Canada K1N 6H7   Debra Begg, Libn.
Founded: 1970. **Staff:** Prof 1; Other 2. **Subjects:** Music. **Holdings:** 16,000 scores; 6000 phonograph records; 755 tapes. **Services:** Interlibrary loans (through Morisset Library). **Remarks:** Book collection and journals housed at Morisset Library.

★16038★
UNIVERSITY OF OTTAWA - TEACHER EDUCATION LIBRARY (Educ)
651 Cumberland St.   Phone: (613) 231-5986
Ottawa, ON, Canada K2P 1L3   Jan Kolaczek, Libn.
Staff: Prof 2; Other 3. **Subjects:** Teacher education, elementary and secondary teaching in both French and English languages, education theory. **Holdings:** 40,000 volumes; 1500 filmstrips and film loops; 80 slide carousels; 450 multimedia kits; 3500 mounted photographs; 949 sound recordings; 200 video cassettes; 100 videotapes. **Subscriptions:** 190 journals and other serials. **Services:** Interlibrary loans; copying; SDI; library open to public with restrictions on borrowing. **Also Known As:** Bibliotheque de la Formation a l'Enseignement.

★16039★
UNIVERSITY OF OTTAWA - VANIER SCIENCE & ENGINEERING LIBRARY
(Sci-Tech)
11 Somerset St., E.   Phone: (613) 231-2324
Ottawa, ON, Canada K1N 9A4   Blanca Stead, Act.Dir.
Staff: Prof 4; Other 8. **Subjects:** Science, engineering. **Special Collections:** Academic dissertations in science and technology accepted by the university. **Holdings:** 55,500 books; 65,500 bound periodical volumes. **Subscriptions:** 1700 journals and other serials. **Services:** Interlibrary loans; copying; library open to public with restrictions on borrowing. **Computerized Information Services:** Online systems. **Staff:** Maurice Alarie, Ref.; Edith Arbach, Ref.

UNIVERSITY OF THE PACIFIC - MC GEORGE SCHOOL OF LAW
See: Mc George School of Law

UNIVERSITY OF THE PACIFIC - SCHOOL OF DENTISTRY
See: Pacific Medical Center & University of the Pacific School of Dentistry

★16040★
UNIVERSITY OF THE PACIFIC - SCIENCE LIBRARY (Sci-Tech)†
751 Brookside Rd.   Phone: (209) 946-2568
Stockton, CA 95207   Judith K. Andrews, Sci.Libn.
Founded: 1955. **Staff:** Prof 1; Other 1. **Subjects:** Pharmacy, drug information, medicine, biology, chemistry, physics. **Holdings:** 19,941 books; 14,676 bound periodical volumes; 990 reels of microfilm; 625 microcards and microfiche. **Subscriptions:** 625 journals and other serials. **Services:** Interlibrary loans; copying; library open to public with restrictions. **Automated Operations:** Computerized cataloging. **Computerized Information Services:** DIALOG, RLIN.

★16041★
UNIVERSITY OF THE PACIFIC - STUART LIBRARY OF WESTERN
AMERICANA (Hist)
                                           Phone: (209) 946-2404
Stockton, CA 95211   John Porter Bloom, Dir.
Founded: 1947. **Staff:** 4. **Subjects:** Californiana, Western Americana, Western authors. **Special Collections:** Early California exploration; fur trade; John Muir papers; Jack London family collection. **Holdings:** 40,000 volumes; 5000 pamphlets; 8000 photographs; 500 maps; 1000 linear feet of manuscripts. **Subscriptions:** 116 journals and other serials. **Services:** Interlibrary loans; copying; library open to public. **Publications:** Monographs; Pacific Historian, quarterly - by subscription. **Special Indexes:** Bibliographic Guides to Archives. **Also Known As:** Holt-Atherton Pacific Center for Western Studies.

UNIVERSITY OF THE PACIFIC - UNITED METHODIST CHURCH - NORTHERN
CALIFORNIA-NEVADA CONFERENCE
See: United Methodist Church - Northern California-Nevada Conference

★16042★
UNIVERSITY OF PENNSYLVANIA - ANNENBERG SCHOOL OF
COMMUNICATIONS - LIBRARY (Info Sci)†
3620 Walnut St./C5   Phone: (215) 898-7027
Philadelphia, PA 19104   Sandra B. Grilikhes, Hd.Libn.
Founded: 1962. **Staff:** Prof 3; Other 3. **Subjects:** Theory and research of communications; public communications; mass media communication; interpersonal communications; social psychology of communication; communications economics; sound communication; history and technology of communication. **Special Collections:** Annenberg Faculty Publications; 16mm film catalogs; alternative press collection; Sol Worth Ethnographic Film Archive; television script archive. **Holdings:** 18,600 books and bound periodical volumes; 40 VF drawers of pamphlets and clippings; 350 theses and dissertations; 600 Colloquium tapes and disc recordings; 625 annual reports of large communication companies; 75 annual reports of U.S. public television stations; 581 reels of microfilm; 3270 microfiche. **Subscriptions:** 426 journals and other serials; 8 newspapers. **Services:** Interlibrary loans; library open to public for reference use only. **Computerized Information Services:** RLIN. **Publications:** Selected New Acquisitions, quarterly; Selected Reference Sources in Communications - free on request. **Staff:** Joan Bernstein, Asst.Libn.

★16043★
UNIVERSITY OF PENNSYLVANIA - ARCHIVES AND RECORDS CENTER (Hist)
North Arcade, Franklin Field   Phone: (215) 898-7024
Philadelphia, PA 19104   Mark Frazier Lloyd, Univ.Archv.
Staff: Prof 2; Other 2. **Subjects:** University history. **Holdings:** 135 linear feet of books; 200 linear feet of bound periodical volumes; 8017 cubic feet of manuscripts; 22,000 photographs, drawings, prints and paintings; 79 cubic feet of memorabilia. **Subscriptions:** 12 journals and other serials. **Services:** Interlibrary loans; copying; archives open to public. **Computerized Information Services:** Access to online systems. **Publications:** Report, biennial. **Special Indexes:** Guide to the Archives of the University of Pennsylvania from 1740 to 1820. **Staff:** Hamilton Elliott, Asst.Univ.Archv.

★16044★
UNIVERSITY OF PENNSYLVANIA - BIDDLE LAW LIBRARY (Law)
3400 Chestnut St./I4   Phone: (215) 898-7478
Philadelphia, PA 19104   Elizabeth S. Kelly, Libn.
Founded: 1886. **Staff:** Prof 9; Other 14. **Subjects:** Legislation - American, foreign; reports of judicial decisions - Anglo-American and others; administrative regulations and decisions; law - Anglo-American, foreign, canon, Roman, international. **Holdings:** 351,255 volumes. **Subscriptions:** 953 journals and other serials. **Services:** Interlibrary loans; copying; library open to public for reference use only. **Computerized Information Services:** LEXIS, Westlaw, OCLC. **Networks/Consortia:** Member of RLG; PALINET & Union Library Catalogue of Pennsylvania. **Staff:** Cynthia Arkin, Assoc.Libn.Marta Tarnawsky, Asst.Libn., Intl. Law; Ronald Day, Ref.; Patricia Callahan, Hd.Cat.; Susan L. Hengel, Cat.; Jeanne Williams, Circ.Supv.; Merle Slyhoff, Acq.Libn.

★16045★
UNIVERSITY OF PENNSYLVANIA - BIOMEDICAL LIBRARY (Med)
Johnson Pavilion/G2
36th & Hamilton Walk   Phone: (215) 898-4223
Philadelphia, PA 19104   Eleanor Goodchild, Biomed.Libn.
Founded: 1916. **Staff:** Prof 11; Other 14. **Subjects:** Medicine, biology, nursing, health care, basic sciences. **Holdings:** 139,330 volumes; 1992 AV items. **Subscriptions:** 2300 journals and other serials. **Services:** Interlibrary loans; copying; orientations; workshops; library open to public for reference use only. **Automated Operations:** Computerized cataloging, acquisitions and ILL. **Computerized Information Services:** DIALOG, BRS, NLM, OCLC. **Networks/Consortia:** Member of RLG; Greater Northeastern Regional Medical Library Program; PALINET & Union Library Catalogue of Pennsylvania. **Staff:** Judie Malamud, Asst.Libn., Pub.Serv.; Linda Rosenstein, Asst.Libn., Tech.Serv.

★16046★
UNIVERSITY OF PENNSYLVANIA - CENTER FOR THE HISTORY OF
CHEMISTRY (Sci-Tech)
Van Pelt Library, 6th Fl.   Phone: (215) 898-7553
Philadelphia, PA 19104   Dr. Arnold W. Thackray, Dir.
Staff: Prof 2; Other 1. **Subjects:** Chemistry, chemical engineering, chemical industry. **Holdings:** Figures not available. **Services:** Copying; center open to public. **Computerized Information Services:** RLIN, OCLC. **Networks/Consortia:** Member of RLG. **Publications:** CHOC News. **Remarks:** The purpose of this center is to locate, preserve, catalog and make available records of American chemistry, chemical engineering and the chemical industry. It is jointly sponsored by the University of Pennsylvania and the

American Chemical Society, and is located in the Edgar Fahs Smith Memorial Collection. **Staff:** Dr. Eleanor Maass, Act.Asst.Dir.

★16047★

UNIVERSITY OF PENNSYLVANIA - DEPARTMENT OF FOLKLORE & FOLKLIFE - ARCHIVE (Hist)
417 Logan Hall
Philadelphia, PA 19104
Phone: (215) 898-7352
Dr. Kenneth Goldstein, Hd.
Subjects: New Foundland folksong, West Indies, Virginia and Pennsylvania, American Folklore Society. **Special Collections:** Mac Edward Leach Collections from New Foundland and Jamaica; Kenneth Goldstein Collection (New Foundland); Jacob Elder Collection (Trinidad); American Folklore Society letters (1918-1943). **Holdings:** 251 volumes; 600 phonograph records; 30 dissertations; 2 VF drawers of student papers. **Subscriptions:** 28 journals and other serials; 10 newspapers. **Services:** Copying; archive open to public. **Remarks:** Archives are not open during the summer months.

★16048★

UNIVERSITY OF PENNSYLVANIA - EDGAR FAHS SMITH MEMORIAL COLLECTION IN THE HISTORY OF CHEMISTRY (Sci-Tech)
Van Pelt Library/CH
Philadelphia, PA 19104
Phone: (215) 898-7088
Dr. Arnold W. Thackray, Cur.
Founded: 1931. **Subjects:** History of chemistry, alchemy, chemical biography, chemical engineering, chemical industry, early medicine, metallurgy, mineralogy, pharmacy, pyrotechnics. **Special Collections:** Photographs, prints and engravings (3000); commemorative stamps (55); oral history transcripts (25). **Holdings:** 15,000 books; 550 bound periodical volumes; 74 bound manuscripts; 26 VF drawers of unbound material; 300 late 19th-century German chemical dissertations; 8 boxes of Archives of the Division of Chemical Education, American Chemical Society. **Subscriptions:** 18 journals and other serials. **Services:** Interlibrary loans; copying; collection open to public. **Computerized Information Services:** OCLC. **Networks/Consortia:** Member of RLG; PALINET & Union Library Catalogue of Pennsylvania. **Special Catalogs:** Catalog of the Edgar Fahs Smith Memorial Collection in the History of Chemistry (book); Catalog of Manuscripts in the Libraries of the University of Pennsylvania to 1800 (book). **Remarks:** The Collection is associated with the Center for History of Chemistry.

★16049★

UNIVERSITY OF PENNSYLVANIA - FINE ARTS LIBRARY (Art; Plan)
Furness Bldg./CK
Philadelphia, PA 19104
Phone: (215) 898-8325
Alan E. Morrison, Libn.
Founded: 1890. **Staff:** Prof 2; Other 9. **Subjects:** Architecture, city planning, history of art, landscape architecture, regional planning, urban design. **Special Collections:** City Planning Pamphlet Collection; rare architectural books, 16th to 20th century. **Holdings:** 79,000 books and bound periodical volumes; 11,000 pamphlets; 58,000 mounted photographs; 243,000 35mm slides. **Subscriptions:** 700 journals and other serials. **Services:** Interlibrary loans; copying; library open to public for reference use only. **Computerized Information Services:** OCLC. **Networks/Consortia:** Member of RLG; PALINET & Union Library Catalogue of Pennsylvania.

★16050★

UNIVERSITY OF PENNSYLVANIA - GEOLOGY MAP LIBRARY (Geog-Map)
Hayden Hall
240 S. 33rd St.
Philadelphia, PA 19104
Phone: (215) 898-5630
Carol Faul, Map Libn.
Staff: Prof 1; Other 1. **Subjects:** Topographic and geologic maps. **Holdings:** 100,000 maps; oceanographic charts. **Services:** Copying; library open to public.

★16051★

UNIVERSITY OF PENNSYLVANIA - HENRY CHARLES LEA LIBRARY (Hist)
Van Pelt Library
3420 Walnut St.
Philadelphia, PA 19104
Phone: (215) 898-7088
Founded: 1924. **Subjects:** Medieval and Renaissance history, church history, canon law, inquisition, witchcraft. **Special Collections:** Text manuscripts, 12th-18th centuries (600 volumes). **Holdings:** 18,000 volumes. **Services:** Library open to qualified scholars. **Computerized Information Services:** OCLC. **Networks/Consortia:** Member of RLG; PALINET & Union Library Catalogue of Pennsylvania. **Special Catalogs:** Catalog of Manuscripts in the Libraries of the University of Pennsylvania to 1800 (book). **Remarks:** Holdings available through the staff of the Rare Book Collection, Van Pelt Library.

★16052★

UNIVERSITY OF PENNSYLVANIA - HORACE HOWARD FURNESS MEMORIAL LIBRARY (Hum)
Van Pelt Library
3420 Walnut St./CH
Philadelphia, PA 19104
Phone: (215) 898-7552
Georgiana Ziegler, Cur.
Founded: 1932. **Staff:** Prof 1. **Subjects:** Shakespeare, medieval to 17th-century English drama. **Special Collections:** Playbills, promptbooks and pictures; dissertations on Shakespeare and his contemporaries (2000 reels of microfilm); STC Collection. **Holdings:** 19,000 volumes. **Services:** Library open to qualified scholars. **Computerized Information Services:** OCLC. **Networks/Consortia:** Member of RLG; PALINET & Union Library Catalogue of Pennsylvania.

UNIVERSITY OF PENNSYLVANIA HOSPITAL - SAMUEL BELLET LIBRARY OF LAW, MEDICINE AND BEHAVIORAL SCIENCE
See: Bellet (Samuel) Library of Law, Medicine and Behavioral Science

★16053★

UNIVERSITY OF PENNSYLVANIA - JOHN PENMAN WOOD LIBRARY OF NATIONAL DEFENSE (Mil)
3000 South St.
Philadelphia, PA 19104
Phone: (215) 898-7757
Margaret Brinkley, Adm.Asst.
Founded: 1928. **Staff:** 1. **Subjects:** Officer education and production; leadership, organization and management; operations, tactics and strategy; logistics, supply and transportation; military biography and history; principles of war, weaponry and war gaming; medical services. **Holdings:** 2432 books; 66 bound periodical volumes. **Services:** Interlibrary loans; library open to public for reference use only.

★16054★

UNIVERSITY OF PENNSYLVANIA - JOHNSON RESEARCH FOUNDATION LIBRARY (Sci-Tech)
Richards Bldg.
37th & Hamilton Walk
Philadelphia, PA 19104
Phone: (215) 898-4387
Founded: 1949. **Staff:** 1. **Subjects:** Biochemistry, biophysics, physiology. **Holdings:** 600 books; 1000 bound periodical volumes. **Subscriptions:** 40 journals and other serials. **Services:** Library open to public.

★16055★

UNIVERSITY OF PENNSYLVANIA - LIPPINCOTT LIBRARY (Bus-Fin)
3420 Walnut St./CH
Philadelphia, PA 19104
Phone: (215) 898-5924
Michael Halperin, Hd.Libn.
Founded: 1927. **Staff:** Prof 9; Other 13. **Subjects:** Applied economics, econometrics, business, management, finance, multinational enterprises, marketing, accounting, insurance, labor, industrial relations, transportation, statistics, regional science, operations research, real estate. **Holdings:** 185,500 volumes; 90 VF drawers of pamphlets; 71,000 reports from 29,000 corporations; 2900 reels of microfilm; 159 linear feet of trade union journals; 79,000 microfiche and microcards. **Subscriptions:** 4800 journals and other serials. **Services:** Interlibrary loans; copying; library open to public. **Automated Operations:** Computerized cataloging and circulation. **Computerized Information Services:** DIALOG, BRS, OCLC, VU/TEXT, Dow Jones News/Retrieval. Performs searches on cost recovery basis. **Networks/Consortia:** Member of RLG; PALINET & Union Library Catalogue of Pennsylvania. **Publications:** The Pilot, Guide to the Lippincott Library. **Staff:** Martha Lightwood, Asst.Libn.; Geraldine E. McCulley, Asst.Libn., Tech.Proc.

UNIVERSITY OF PENNSYLVANIA - MARRIAGE COUNCIL OF PHILADELPHIA
See: Marriage Council of Philadelphia

★16056★

UNIVERSITY OF PENNSYLVANIA - MATHEMATICS-PHYSICS-ASTRONOMY LIBRARY (Sci-Tech)
Rittenhouse Laboratory/E1
Philadelphia, PA 19104
Phone: (215) 898-8173
Marion A. Kreiter, Libn.
Founded: 1948. **Staff:** Prof 1; Other 1. **Subjects:** Astronomy, mathematics, physics. **Holdings:** 47,750 volumes. **Subscriptions:** 510 journals and other serials. **Services:** Interlibrary loans; copying; library open to public for reference use only. **Computerized Information Services:** DIALOG, OCLC, BRS. **Networks/Consortia:** Member of RLG; PALINET & Union Library Catalogue of Pennsylvania.

★16057★

UNIVERSITY OF PENNSYLVANIA - MORRIS ARBORETUM LIBRARY (Sci-Tech)
9414 Meadowbrook Ave.
Philadelphia, PA 19118
Phone: (215) 247-5777
Founded: 1932. **Subjects:** Ornamental horticulture, basic floras of the world,

plant pathology, urban forestry and silviculture, exploration. **Holdings:** 5000 books; 2500 bound periodical volumes. **Subscriptions:** 100 journals and other serials. **Services:** Interlibrary loans; library open to public for reference use only. **Staff:** Timothy R. Tomlinson, Assoc.Dir.; Ann F. Rhoads, Asst.Dir., Botany.

★16058★

UNIVERSITY OF PENNSYLVANIA - MUSEUM LIBRARY (Soc Sci)
33rd & Spruce Sts./F1   Phone: (215) 898-7840
Philadelphia, PA 19104   Jean S. Adelman, Libn.
Founded: 1887. **Staff:** Prof 1; Other 2. **Subjects:** Archeology, anthropology, ethnology. **Special Collections:** Brinton Collection of 19th-century American Indian linguistics and ethnology (4000 titles). **Holdings:** 80,000 books and bound periodical volumes; 4500 cataloged pamphlets; 50 reels of microfilm. **Subscriptions:** 850 journals and other serials. **Services:** Interlibrary loans; copying (for ILL only); library open to public for reference use only. **Computerized Information Services:** OCLC, BRS. **Networks/Consortia:** Member of RLG; PALINET & Union Library Catalogue of Pennsylvania.

★16059★

UNIVERSITY OF PENNSYLVANIA - NEW BOLTON CENTER - JEAN AUSTIN DU PONT LIBRARY (Med)
382 W. Street Rd.   Phone: (215) 444-5800
Kennett Square, PA 19348   Alice K. Holton, Lib.Serv.Asst.
Founded: 1963. **Staff:** 1. **Subjects:** Veterinary medicine - emphasis on large animal medicine. **Special Collections:** Fairman Rogers Rare Book Collection on Horsemanship (1075 volumes). **Holdings:** 820 books; 2300 bound periodical volumes. **Subscriptions:** 75 journals and other serials. **Services:** Interlibrary loans; copying; library open to public for reference use only. **Computerized Information Services:** DIALOG. **Networks/Consortia:** Member of Greater Northeastern Regional Medical Library Program. **Special Catalogs:** Catalog of Fairman Rogers Collection (book).

★16060★

UNIVERSITY OF PENNSYLVANIA - POPULATION STUDIES CENTER - DEMOGRAPHY LIBRARY (Soc Sci)
3718 Locust Walk   Phone: (215) 898-5375
Philadelphia, PA 19174   Cindi S. Posner, Res.Bibliog.
Staff: 1. **Subjects:** Foreign and United States census, population organizations, demographic surveys, statistics. **Special Collections:** Foreign censuses for 50 countries (varying years); statistical materials for 113 countries; United Nations repository; World Fertility Survey repository; John D. Durand Collection (historical demography). **Holdings:** 5000 books; 39 bound periodical volumes; reprints; dissertations. **Subscriptions:** 53 journals and other serials. **Services:** Interlibrary loans; copying; library not open to public, but special requests will be taken from related interest institutions. **Networks/Consortia:** Member of Association for Population/Family Planning Libraries and Information Centers-International (APLIC-International). **Publications:** Acquisitions List, quarterly - to related interest institutions.

★16061★

UNIVERSITY OF PENNSYLVANIA - RARE BOOK COLLECTION (Rare Book)†
Van Pelt Library, 3420 Walnut St.   Phone: (215) 898-7088
Philadelphia, PA 19104   Lyman W. Riley, Asst.Dir. of Libs.
Staff: Prof 4. **Subjects:** English and American literature, Spanish drama. **Special Collections:** Jonathan Swift (1400 volumes); English novel to 1820 (3000 volumes); Torquato Tasso (16th and 17th centuries; 350 volumes); Aristotle (800 volumes published before 1700). **Holdings:** 90,000 books; 2500 linear feet of manuscripts. **Services:** Interlibrary loans; copying; collection open to public. **Automated Operations:** Computerized cataloging. **Networks/Consortia:** Member of RLG. **Special Catalogs:** Catalogs to: manuscripts to 1800, 1965; sixteenth-century imprints, 1976; English seventeenth-century imprints, 1978; Spanish drama of the Golden Age, 1971; Aristotle collection, 1961 (all in book form). **Staff:** Neda M. Westlake, Cur., Rare Bk.Coll.; Daniel Traister, Asst.Cur., Spec.Coll.; Marjory Fraser, Supv., Rd.Rm.

UNIVERSITY OF PENNSYLVANIA - ROBERT DUNNING DRIPPS LIBRARY OF ANESTHESIA
See: Hospital of the University of Pennsylvania - Robert Dunning Dripps Library of Anesthesia

UNIVERSITY OF PENNSYLVANIA - S.S. HUEBNER FOUNDATION FOR INSURANCE EDUCATION
See: Huebner (S.S.) Foundation for Insurance Education

★16062★

UNIVERSITY OF PENNSYLVANIA - SCHOOL OF DENTAL MEDICINE - LEON LEVY LIBRARY (Med)
4001 Spruce St./A1   Phone: (215) 898-8969
Philadelphia, PA 19104   John M. Whittock, Jr., Libn.
Founded: 1914. **Staff:** Prof 2; Other 3. **Subjects:** Dentistry, oral biology, history of dentistry. **Special Collections:** S.S. White Collection of U.S. dental patents, 1798-1967; S.S. White Collection of dental catalogs; foreign dental dissertations, 1880-1965 (5000); rare, early dental books and dental history books; Thomas W. Evans' letters and manuscripts. **Holdings:** 18,500 books; 27,000 bound periodical volumes; dissertations; pictures; clippings. **Subscriptions:** 700 journals and other serials. **Services:** Interlibrary loans; copying; library open to public for reference use only. **Computerized Information Services:** OCLC. **Networks/Consortia:** Member of RLG; PALINET & Union Library Catalogue of Pennsylvania. **Staff:** Elizabeth Jendryk, Asst.Libn.

★16063★

UNIVERSITY OF PENNSYLVANIA - SCHOOL OF ENGINEERING AND APPLIED SCIENCE - MOORE LIBRARY (Sci-Tech)
200 South 33rd St./D2   Phone: (215) 898-8135
Philadelphia, PA 19104   Charles J. Myers, Libn.
Founded: 1926. **Staff:** Prof 1; Other 2. **Subjects:** Electrical engineering, electronics, computers, information science, optics, systems engineering. **Special Collections:** Robotics. **Holdings:** 21,000 volumes. **Subscriptions:** 419 journals and other serials. **Services:** Interlibrary loans; copying; library open to public for reference use only. **Computerized Information Services:** OCLC, DIALOG, BRS. **Networks/Consortia:** Member of RLG; PALINET & Union Library Catalogue of Pennsylvania.

★16064★

UNIVERSITY OF PENNSYLVANIA - SCHOOL OF ENGINEERING AND APPLIED SCIENCE - TOWNE LIBRARY (Sci-Tech)
220 S. 33rd St./D3   Phone: (215) 898-7266
Philadelphia, PA 19104   Charles J. Myers, Libn.
Founded: 1947. **Staff:** Prof 1; Other 2. **Subjects:** Engineering - chemical, civil, metallurgical, mechanical, aeronautical, transportation and environmental; engineering science; materials science; bioengineering. **Special Collections:** Depository for NASA reports; robotics; heat transfer; fluid mechanics. **Holdings:** 73,695 books and bound periodical volumes; 165,500 microfiche; 357 videotapes. **Subscriptions:** 700 journals and other serials. **Services:** Interlibrary loans; copying; library open to public for reference use only. **Computerized Information Services:** DIALOG, BRS, OCLC. **Networks/Consortia:** Member of RLG; PALINET & Union Library Catalogue of Pennsylvania.

★16065★

UNIVERSITY OF PENNSYLVANIA - SCHOOL OF SOCIAL WORK - SMALLEY LIBRARY OF SOCIAL WORK (Soc Sci)†
Caster Bldg./C3
3701 Locust Walk   Phone: (215) 898-5508
Philadelphia, PA 19104   Evelyn Butler, Libn.
Founded: 1911. **Staff:** Prof 2; Other 1. **Subjects:** Social work, child welfare, crime and criminology. **Holdings:** 40,000 books; 3100 bound periodical volumes; 5200 masters' theses, doctoral dissertations and research projects; 60 VF drawers of pamphlets. **Subscriptions:** 333 journals and other serials. **Services:** Interlibrary loans; copying; library open to public with restrictions. **Computerized Information Services:** OCLC. **Networks/Consortia:** Member of RLG; PALINET & Union Library Catalogue of Pennsylvania. **Publications:** Accession Book, 3/year - distributed to faculty and all graduate schools of social work. **Staff:** Mary B. Sparhawk, Cat./Ref.Libn.

★16066★

UNIVERSITY OF PENNSYLVANIA - SCHOOL OF VETERINARY MEDICINE - C.J. MARSHALL MEMORIAL LIBRARY (Med)
3800 Spruce St./H1   Phone: (215) 898-8874
Philadelphia, PA 19104   Lillian Bryant, Libn.
Founded: 1908. **Staff:** Prof 1; Other 1. **Subjects:** Veterinary medicine, comparative medicine, animal husbandry. **Special Collections:** Fairman Rogers Collection - horsemanship and equitation. **Holdings:** 33,000 books and bound periodical volumes; 18 VF drawers of pamphlets, circulars and reprints. **Subscriptions:** 515 journals and other serials. **Services:** Interlibrary loans; copying; library open to public for reference use only. **Computerized Information Services:** DIALOG, OCLC. **Networks/Consortia:** Member of Greater Northeastern Regional Medical Library Program; RLG; PALINET & Union Library Catalogue of Pennsylvania.

★16067★

UNIVERSITY OF PENNSYLVANIA - UNIVERSITY HOSPITAL LIBRARY (Med)†
3400 Spruce St./G1   Phone: (215) 662-2571
Philadelphia, PA 19104   Susan Cleveland, Dir.
Founded: 1952. **Staff:** Prof 2; Other 2. **Subjects:** Clinical medicine, surgery.
Holdings: 13,000 books and bound periodical volumes. **Subscriptions:** 275
journals and other serials. **Services:** Interlibrary loans; copying; SDI; library
open to public for reference use only.

★16068★

**UNIVERSITY OF PENNSYLVANIA - WISTAR INSTITUTE OF ANATOMY &
     BIOLOGY - LIBRARY (Med)**
36th & Spruce Sts.   Phone: (215) 898-3508
Philadelphia, PA 19104   J.A. Hunter, Libn.
Founded: 1892. **Staff:** Prof 1; Other 1. **Subjects:** Cancer, virus diseases,
cytology, immunology, genetics, biochemistry. **Special Collections:** Personal
library of General Isaac J. Wistar (including English and scientific classics,
Americana and history; 1000 volumes). **Holdings:** 5000 books; 9000 bound
periodical volumes. **Subscriptions:** 162 journals and other serials. **Services:**
Interlibrary loans; library open to public for reference use only. **Computerized
Information Services:** NLM, BRS, DIALOG, SDC, Institute for Scientific
Information (ISI).

★16069★

UNIVERSITY OF PITTSBURGH - AFRO-AMERICAN LIBRARY (Area-Ethnic)
Hillman Library   Phone: (412) 624-4447
Pittsburgh, PA 15260   Arthur C. Gunn, Libn.
Founded: 1969. **Staff:** Prof 1; Other 1. **Subjects:** History; political science;
literature; literary criticism; social sciences; culture - including the arts; blacks
in Western Pennsylvania. **Special Collections:** Atlanta University Black Culture
Collection (microfilm); W.E.B. Dubois Papers (microfilm); papers of the
Congress of Racial Equity (microfilm); black history and landmarks in Western
Pennsylvania (80 slides). **Holdings:** 11,077 volumes; 6 VF drawers of
clippings, pamphlets; 31 periodical reprints on microfilm. **Subscriptions:** 70
journals and other serials; 29 newspapers. **Services:** Interlibrary loans; library
open to public for reference use only. **Automated Operations:** Computerized
cataloging. **Computerized Information Services:** DIALOG, BRS, New York
Times Information Service. **Networks/Consortia:** Member of Pittsburgh
Regional Library Center (PRLC).

★16070★

**UNIVERSITY OF PITTSBURGH - ALLEGHENY OBSERVATORY - LIBRARY
     (Sci-Tech)**
159 Riverview Airway   Phone: (412) 321-2400
Pittsburgh, PA 15260
Founded: 1868. **Staff:** 1. **Subjects:** Astronomy, mathematics, spectroscopic
subjects, physics, general science. **Special Collections:** British and French
Astronomical Association publications (1800 to present); exchange
publications from over 500 observatories throughout the world. **Holdings:**
7000 volumes. **Subscriptions:** 115 journals and other serials. **Services:**
Interlibrary loans; library open to public for reference use only. **Publications:**
Allegheny Observatory reports, irregular - sent to other observatories as
exchange item and free to libraries upon request. **Remarks:** All inquiries
concerning this library should be directed to Paul Kobulnicky, Physics Library,
208 Engineering Hall. Telephone number is 624-4482.

★16071★

UNIVERSITY OF PITTSBURGH - ARCHIVES (Hist)
363 Hillman Library   Phone: (412) 624-4428
Pittsburgh, PA 15260   Dr. Marilyn P. Whitmore, Univ.Archv.
Founded: 1966. **Staff:** Prof 2; Other 1. **Subjects:** University of Pittsburgh
history and records. **Holdings:** 15,663 books; 310 bound periodical volumes;
2085 linear feet of manuscripts; 24,396 microforms; 1437 films; 3902
photographs; 318 sound recordings; 718 slides; 286 drawings and prints.
Services: Copying; archives open to public. **Staff:** Leila Jamison, Asst.Archv.

★16072★

**UNIVERSITY OF PITTSBURGH - ARCHIVES OF INDUSTRIAL SOCIETY (Soc
     Sci)**
363-H., Hillman Library
Univ. of Pittsburgh
Pittsburgh, PA 15260   Phone: (412) 624-4429
                                            Frank A. Zabrosky, Cur.
Founded: 1963. **Staff:** 5. **Subjects:** History - urban, labor and ethnic.
Special Collections: 412 collections (primarily manuscripts) of individuals,
businesses, churches, institutions, organizations, labor unions, ethnic groups;
municipal records of Pittsburgh, Allegheny, Allegheny County; United Electrical,
Radio and Machine Workers of America Archives; Pittsburgh City
Photographer Collection; oral history tapes. **Holdings:** 752 volumes; 8890
linear feet of manuscripts; 1357 reels of microfilm; 82 phonograph records;

642 tape cassettes; maps; architectural drawings, plans, sketches; 70,000
photographic images (glass plates, negatives, prints). **Services:** Copying;
copies of inventories to specific collections available upon request at cost; use
of collections subject to conditions of owner/donor if such imposed; access
to archives is conditional. **Special Catalogs:** Resources on the Ethnic and the
Immigrant in the Pittsburgh Area (book; 1979). **Staff:** Mark McColloch,
Archv.; Frank Kurtik, Proj.Archv.

★16073★

UNIVERSITY OF PITTSBURGH - BEVIER ENGINEERING LIBRARY (Sci-Tech)
126 Benedum Hall   Phone: (412) 624-4484
Pittsburgh, PA 15261   Sandra S. Kerbel, Libn.
Founded: 1956. **Staff:** Prof 1; Other 2. **Subjects:** Engineering - chemical,
civil, electrical, industrial, mechanical, metallurgical, petroleum, aeronautical,
environmental, mining, bioengineering and materials; energy resources.
Special Collections: Selected depository for U.S. Department of Energy,
Environmental Protection Agency and selected National Bureau of Standards
documents; Advisory Group for Aerospace Research and Development
depository set. **Holdings:** 45,239 volumes; 32,768 microfiche; 2877 reels
of microfilm; 3854 U.S. documents; 100 nonprint items. **Subscriptions:** 930
journals and other serials. **Services:** Interlibrary loans; copying; library open to
public. **Computerized Information Services:** DIALOG, OCLC, DOE/RECON;
internal database. **Networks/Consortia:** Member of Pittsburgh Regional
Library Center (PRLC); CRL.

★16074★

**UNIVERSITY OF PITTSBURGH - BIOLOGICAL SCIENCES AND PSYCHOLOGY
     LIBRARY (Sci-Tech)**
A-217 Langley Hall   Phone: (412) 624-4489
Pittsburgh, PA 15260   D.L. Johnston, Hd.
Founded: 1961. **Staff:** Prof 1; Other 2. **Subjects:** Biological sciences,
biophysics, biochemistry, psychology. **Holdings:** 30,000 books; 22,000
bound periodical volumes. **Subscriptions:** 560 journals and other serials.
Services: Interlibrary loans; copying; library open to public for reference use
only. **Automated Operations:** Computerized circulation. **Computerized
Information Services:** DIALOG. Performs free searches for students and
faculty; performs searches on cost recovery basis to others. **Networks/
Consortia:** Member of Pittsburgh Regional Library Center (PRLC).

★16075★

UNIVERSITY OF PITTSBURGH - CHEMISTRY LIBRARY (Sci-Tech)
200 Alumni Hall   Phone: (412) 624-5026
Pittsburgh, PA 15260   Paul J. Kobulnicky, Libn.
Staff: Prof 1; Other 1. **Subjects:** Chemistry - organic, physical, analytical;
chemistry of natural products; spectroscopy. **Holdings:** 12,000 books;
13,000 bound periodical volumes; spectral files and indices. **Subscriptions:**
165 journals and other serials. **Services:** Interlibrary loans; copying; library
open to public. **Computerized Information Services:** OCLC, DIALOG.
Performs searches free of charge to faculty and students; on cost recovery
basis to others. **Publications:** Monthly Acquisitions List.

★16076★

UNIVERSITY OF PITTSBURGH - CIOCCO LIBRARY (Med)
130 De Soto St.   Phone: (412) 624-3016
Pittsburgh, PA 15261   Suzanne O. Paul, Dir.
Founded: 1949. **Staff:** Prof 2; Other 2. **Subjects:** Public health, industrial
hygiene, biostatistics, epidemiology, microbiology, public health
administration, radiation health, toxicology. **Special Collections:** Parran
Collection; Wilson G. Smillie Collection. **Holdings:** 50,000 volumes.
Subscriptions: 200 journals and other serials. **Services:** Interlibrary loans;
copying; SDI; library open to public for reference use only. **Computerized
Information Services:** DIALOG, BRS, NLM. Performs searches on cost
recovery basis. **Networks/Consortia:** Member of Pittsburgh Regional Library
Center (PRLC). **Publications:** Monthly List of Books Acquired. **Formerly:** Its
Graduate School of Public Health Library. **Staff:** Mary M. Dolinar, Asst.Libn.

★16077★

UNIVERSITY OF PITTSBURGH - COMPUTER SCIENCE LIBRARY (Comp Sci)
200 Alumni Hall   Phone: (412) 624-6699
Pittsburgh, PA 15260   Paul Kobulnicky, Libn.
Founded: 1956. **Staff:** Prof 1; Other 1. **Subjects:** Programming techniques
and languages, data processing, computer-assisted instruction, numerical
analysis, artificial intelligence, automata theory, information storage and
retrieval, computer management. **Holdings:** 7000 books; 3000 bound
periodical volumes; machine and systems manuals. **Subscriptions:** 125
journals and other serials. **Services:** Interlibrary loans; copying; library open to
public. **Computerized Information Services:** OCLC, DIALOG. **Special
Indexes:** KWIC index to technical report literature.

★16078★

UNIVERSITY OF PITTSBURGH - DARLINGTON MEMORIAL LIBRARY (Hist)
Cathedral of Learning Phone: (412) 624-4491
Pittsburgh, PA 15260 Dennis Lambert, Libn.
Founded: 1918. **Staff:** Prof 1; Other 1. **Subjects:** Colonial Americana, Pennsylvania and Ohio Valley history (pre-1870). **Special Collections:** O'Hara Darlington Collection (first editions of 19th-century English novels). **Holdings:** 15,293 books; 1507 bound periodical volumes; 273 bound volumes of newspapers; 4570 pamphlets; 290 prints; 901 maps; 5799 manuscripts. **Services:** Copying; library open to public for reference use only. **Publications:** Guide to Manuscripts Collection; Women in Historical Perspective: Guide to the Resources in the Darlington Memorial Library - for sale.

★16079★

UNIVERSITY OF PITTSBURGH - EAST ASIAN LIBRARY (Area-Ethnic)
234 Hillman Library Phone: (412) 624-4457
Pittsburgh, PA 15260 Dr. Thomas Kuo, Cur.
Founded: 1960. **Staff:** Prof 4; Other 2. **Subjects:** Chinese, Japanese and Korean humanities and social sciences. **Special Collections:** Complete Sets of Ku chin t'u shu chi ch'eng (800 volumes - 1934 photolithographic edition of 1728 original collection); Yuan chien lei han (Imperial Palace block print edition of 1710); Shigaku zasshi, 1889 to present and Rekishi-Gaku Kenkyu, 1928 to present. **Holdings:** 120,510 volumes; 3505 reels of microfilm; 3000 miscellaneous items. **Subscriptions:** 1519 journals and other serials; 71 newspapers. **Services:** Interlibrary loans; copying; library open to public. **Automated Operations:** Computerized circulation. **Networks/Consortia:** Member of Pittsburgh Regional Library Center (PRLC). **Publications:** A Selected List of Outstanding New Acquisitions, quarterly. **Special Catalogs:** East Asian Periodicals and Serials (1970); Catalog of Microfilms of the East Asian Library of the University of Pittsburgh (1971); The Chinese Local History - Descriptive Holding List (1969). **Staff:** Paul J. Ho, Dp.Cur.; Joseph Chang, Bibliog./Cat. (Japanese); Lisa Woo, Bibliog./Cat. (Chinese).

★16080★

UNIVERSITY OF PITTSBURGH - ECONOMICS/COLLECTION IN REGIONAL ECONOMICS (Soc Sci)
Mervis Hall, Rm. 430
139 University Pl.
Pittsburgh, PA 15260 Phone: (412) 624-4492
Patricia Suozzi, Econ.Libn.
Staff: Prof 1; Other 1. **Subjects:** Regional economics, econometrics, economic theory, international trade and finance, money and banking, demography and statistics. **Holdings:** 17,200 books; 6000 bound periodical volumes; 4580 working papers; 150 doctoral dissertations. **Subscriptions:** 245 journals and other serials. **Services:** Interlibrary loans; collection open to public for reference use only. **Computerized Information Services:** I.P. Sharp Associates Limited, DIALOG, OCLC, VU/TEXT. Performs searches free of charge to faculty and students; on cost recovery basis to others. **Networks/Consortia:** Member of Pittsburgh Regional Library Center (PRLC). **Publications:** Economics Books: Current Selections, quarterly - available on subscription basis; Bimonthly Acquisitions Letter - free upon request. **Staff:** Elizabeth Hubbard, Lib.Assoc.

★16081★

UNIVERSITY OF PITTSBURGH - FALK LIBRARY OF THE HEALTH SCIENCES (Med)
Scaife Hall, 2nd Fl. Phone: (412) 624-2521
Pittsburgh, PA 15261 Laurabelle Eakin, Dir.
Founded: 1957. **Staff:** Prof 11; Other 15. **Subjects:** Medicine, biology, dentistry, nursing, pharmacy and allied health professions. **Special Collections:** History of medicine and dental medicine (12,000 items); history of anesthesia (400 items). **Holdings:** 211,194 books and bound periodical volumes; 7300 unbound and bound reports; 1680 AV materials. **Subscriptions:** 2526 journals and other serials. **Services:** Interlibrary loans; copying; library open to public for reference use only. **Computerized Information Services:** MEDLINE, BRS, DIALOG. **Networks/Consortia:** Member of Greater Northeastern Regional Medical Library Program. **Publications:** Recent List of Acquisitions and Newsletter, monthly. **Special Catalogs:** Title and subject list of serials; Union list of serials. **Staff:** June Bandemer, Asst.Dir./Hd., Rd.Serv.; Julia D'Andrea, Cat.; Esther Waldron, Hd., Cat.Dept.; Margaret Norden, Ref.Libn.; Madlynne Harris, Ref.Libn.; Jonathon Erlen, Ph.D., Cur., Hist.Coll.; Sally Wilson, Ser.Libn.; Robert Sherman, Acq.Libn.; Elizabeth Geltz, Nursing Libn.; Amy Korman, LRC Libn.

★16082★

UNIVERSITY OF PITTSBURGH - FOSTER HALL COLLECTION (Mus)
Stephen Foster Memorial
Forbes Ave. Phone: (412) 624-4100
Pittsburgh, PA 15260 Dr. Deane L. Root, Cur.
Founded: 1931. **Staff:** Prof 1; Other 2. **Subjects:** Life and works of Stephen Collins Foster. **Holdings:** 500 books; 100 bound periodical volumes; 1000 pieces of 19th-century sheet music; 3000 uncataloged pieces; 2000 20th-century scores and collections for vocal and instrumental ensembles; 1000 magazine and newspaper articles; 100 manuscripts; 1000 pictures and photographs; 300 broadsides; 800 78 rpm phonograph records; 500 songbooks; foster instruments and artifacts. **Services:** Interlibrary loans; copying; collection open to public by appointment. **Publications:** Songs of Stephen Foster; research monographs - both for sale. **Special Catalogs:** Dictionary catalog with index files for arrangers, broadsides, derivata, magazines, recordings, pictures, scores and songbooks (card).

★16083★

UNIVERSITY OF PITTSBURGH - GRADUATE SCHOOL OF BUSINESS LIBRARY (Bus-Fin)
1501 Cathedral of Learning Phone: (412) 624-6408
Pittsburgh, PA 15260 Susan Neuman, Dir.
Founded: 1961. **Staff:** Prof 2; Other 4. **Subjects:** Econometrics, economics, business, management, accounting, industrial labor relations, behavioral science in business, business and society, marketing, finance. **Holdings:** 34,000 books; 4000 bound periodical volumes; New York and American Stock Exchange - listed companies' annual reports on microfiche; 12 VF drawers of pamphlets. **Subscriptions:** 600 journals and other serials; 10 newspapers. **Services:** Interlibrary loans; copying; library open to public for reference use only. **Computerized Information Services:** DIALOG, BRS, I.P. Sharp Associates, Ltd., NEXIS, VU/TEXT. **Networks/Consortia:** Member of Pittsburgh Regional Library Center (PRLC). **Publications:** Bimonthly Acquisitions List. **Staff:** Maureen Lambert, Ref.Libn.

UNIVERSITY OF PITTSBURGH - GRADUATE SCHOOL OF PUBLIC HEALTH LIBRARY
See: University of Pittsburgh - Ciocco Library

★16084★

UNIVERSITY OF PITTSBURGH - GRADUATE SCHOOL OF PUBLIC & INTERNATIONAL AFFAIRS LIBRARY (Soc Sci)
Forbes Quadrangle, 1st Fl. West Phone: (412) 624-4738
Pittsburgh, PA 15260 Nicholas C. Caruso, Libn.
Founded: 1958. **Staff:** Prof 3; Other 1. **Subjects:** Public administration, urban affairs, economic and social development, international affairs. **Holdings:** 94,834 books; 4785 bound periodical volumes; 2781 pamphlets; 3964 government documents. **Subscriptions:** 887 journals and other serials. **Services:** Interlibrary loans; library open to public for reference use only. **Automated Operations:** Computerized cataloging. **Computerized Information Services:** DIALOG, SDC; internal databases. **Networks/Consortia:** Member of Pittsburgh Regional Library Center (PRLC). **Publications:** Accessions list. **Staff:** Lucy Thomas, Libn.; Mary Lois Kepes, Libn.

★16085★

UNIVERSITY OF PITTSBURGH - HENRY CLAY FRICK FINE ARTS LIBRARY (Art)
Phone: (412) 624-4124
Pittsburgh, PA 15260 Anne W. Gordon, Hd.
Founded: 1927. **Staff:** Prof 2; Other 3. **Subjects:** Art of the Western World, with special strength in Byzantine, early Christian, Medieval, Renaissance and modern periods; Oriental art; studio arts. **Special Collections:** Medieval illuminated manuscript facsimiles. **Holdings:** 55,000 volumes; 66,000 mounted photographs; 89 Oriental scrolls (facsimiles). **Subscriptions:** 320 journals and other serials. **Services:** Interlibrary loans; library open to public. **Networks/Consortia:** Member of Pittsburgh Regional Library Center (PRLC). **Special Catalogs:** Exhibitions Catalog File; Art Sales Catalog File.

★16086★

UNIVERSITY OF PITTSBURGH - HUMAN RELATIONS AREA FILES (Soc Sci)
G16 Hillman Library Phone: (412) 624-4449
Pittsburgh, PA 15260 Jean R. Aiken, Info.Libn.
Staff: Prof 1; Other 1. **Subjects:** Anthropology and related behavioral sciences. **Holdings:** Figures not available. **Services:** Files open to public for reference use only.

★16087★

UNIVERSITY OF PITTSBURGH - LATIN AMERICAN COLLECTION (Area-Ethnic)
171 Hillman Library Phone: (412) 624-4425
Pittsburgh, PA 15260 Eduardo Lozano, Bibliog.
Staff: Prof 3; Other 1. **Subjects:** Latin America - humanities, social sciences. **Special Collections:** Cuban Collection (11,500 volumes); Bolivian Collection (8500 volumes); Human Relations Area File (650 sources). **Holdings:** 172,000 books; 34,000 bound periodical volumes; 4116 reels of microfilm;

19,545 microfiche; 13,157 microcards; 1000 Bolivian political pamphlets; 1350 maps; 500 dissertations. **Subscriptions:** 4250 journals and other serials; 10 newspapers. **Services:** Interlibrary loans; copying; collection open to public. **Automated Operations:** Computerized cataloging, acquisitions, serials and circulation. **Computerized Information Services:** DIALOG, BRS, NEXIS, VU/TEXT, OCLC. Performs searches free of charge to faculty and students; on cost recovery basis to others. Contact Person: Fern Brody, 624-4438. **Publications:** Cuban Periodicals in the University of Pittsburgh Libraries, 3rd edition, 1981. **Special Catalogs:** Catalog of Latin American Periodicals (indexes by country and subject); Catalog of the Bolivian Collection (author and subject indexes).

★16088★

UNIVERSITY OF PITTSBURGH - LAW LIBRARY (Law)
3900 Forbes Ave.   Phone: (412) 624-6213
Pittsburgh, PA 15260   Jenni Parrish, Dir.
Founded: 1895. **Staff:** Prof 5; Other 11. **Subjects:** Law. **Holdings:** 170,000 volumes. **Subscriptions:** 2934 journals and other serials. **Services:** Interlibrary loans; copying; library open to public for reference use only. **Automated Operations:** Computerized cataloging. **Computerized Information Services:** LEXIS, BRS, Westlaw, DIALOG. **Networks/Consortia:** Member of Pittsburgh Regional Library Center (PRLC); Mid-Atlantic Law Library Cooperative (MALLCO). **Staff:** Linda Drago, Assoc. Law Libn.; Cynthia Larter, Asst. Law Libn.; Patricia Horvath, Asst. Law Libn.; Marc Silverman, Asst. Law Libn.

★16089★

UNIVERSITY OF PITTSBURGH - MATHEMATICS LIBRARY (Sci-Tech)
809 William Pitt Union   Phone: (412) 624-4488
Pittsburgh, PA 15260   Sandra S. Kerbel, Hd.
Founded: 1963. **Staff:** Prof 1. **Subjects:** Mathematics - pure, applied, numerical; statistics. **Holdings:** 15,190 volumes; 83 reels of microfilm; 868 microfiche. **Subscriptions:** 218 journals and other serials. **Services:** Interlibrary loans; copying; library open to public. **Computerized Information Services:** DIALOG; internal database. **Networks/Consortia:** Member of Pittsburgh Regional Library Center (PRLC); CRL.

★16090★

UNIVERSITY OF PITTSBURGH - NASA INDUSTRIAL APPLICATIONS CENTER (NIAC) (Sci-Tech; Info Sci; Comp Sci)
8th Fl., William Pitt Union   Phone: (412) 624-5212
Pittsburgh, PA 15260   Paul A. McWilliams, Exec.Dir.
Founded: 1963. **Staff:** Prof 12; Other 13. **Subjects:** Science and technology, business and marketing, computer and information sciences. **Services:** Center provides full consulting and information brokerage activities; computer retrieval services; engineering services; database system development; database creation; special multidisciplinary studies and international projects; document procurement; center open to public for reference use only. **Computerized Information Services:** DIALOG, SDC, NASA/RECON; internal databases. **Publications:** United States Political Science Documents (USPSD) annual reference guide (hard copy and online). **Staff:** Mark Cromie, Sr.Mgr., Mktg.; Rosalind Haw, Sr.Mgr., Adm.; Jan P. Miller, Sr.Mgr., Sys. & Oper.

★16091★

UNIVERSITY OF PITTSBURGH - PENNSYLVANIA ETHNIC HERITAGE STUDIES CENTER (Area-Ethnic)†
4G31 Forbes Quad   Phone: (412) 624-4936
Pittsburgh, PA 15260   Frank Zabrosky, Archv./Libn.
Staff: Prof 5. **Subjects:** Ethnic and social history of Pittsburgh and western Pennsylvania. **Holdings:** Figures not available. **Services:** Copying; center open to public. **Publications:** Newsletter.

★16092★

UNIVERSITY OF PITTSBURGH - PHYSICS LIBRARY (Sci-Tech)
208 Engineering Hall   Phone: (412) 624-4482
Pittsburgh, PA 15260   Paul J. Kobulnicky, Libn.
Founded: 1953. **Staff:** Prof 1; Other 1. **Subjects:** Physics, nuclear physics, high energy, atomic and molecular solid state, quantum optics, relativity, atmospheric physics, low temperature physics, earth and planetary sciences. **Holdings:** 15,000 books; 15,000 bound periodical volumes. **Subscriptions:** 240 journals and other serials. **Services:** Interlibrary loans; copying; library open to public. **Computerized Information Services:** OCLC, DIALOG. Performs searches free of charge to faculty and students; on cost recovery basis to others. **Networks/Consortia:** Member of Pittsburgh Regional Library Center (PRLC). **Publications:** Monthly Acquisitions List.

★16093★

UNIVERSITY OF PITTSBURGH - PRESBYTERIAN-UNIVERSITY HOSPITAL - MEDICAL STAFF LIBRARY (Med)
DeSoto at O'Hara Sts.   Phone: (412) 647-3287
Pittsburgh, PA 15213   Mrs. Bianka M. Hesz, Med.Libn.
Founded: 1943. **Staff:** Prof 1; Other 3. **Subjects:** Clinical medicine, cancer, hematology, neurology, surgery. **Holdings:** 1407 books; 2514 bound periodical volumes; 322 Audio-Digest tapes. **Subscriptions:** 152 journals and other serials. **Services:** Interlibrary loans; copying; library open to public. **Publications:** Newsletter, 2/year.

★16094★

UNIVERSITY OF PITTSBURGH - PYMATUNING LABORATORY OF ECOLOGY - TRYON LIBRARY (Sci-Tech)
R.R. 1, Box 7   Phone: (814) 683-5813
Linesville, PA 16424   Dr. Richard T. Hartman, Dir.
Founded: 1949. **Staff:** 1. **Subjects:** Ecology, field biology, limnology, animal behavior. **Holdings:** 1900 books; 200 bound periodical volumes. **Subscriptions:** 11 journals and other serials. **Services:** Copying; library open to public with restrictions. **Publications:** Special publications of Pymatuning Laboratory, irregular.

★16095★

UNIVERSITY OF PITTSBURGH - READING/COMMUNICATIONS RESOURCE CENTER
Forbes Quadrangle
Pittsburgh, PA 15260
Defunct

★16096★

UNIVERSITY OF PITTSBURGH - SCHOOL OF EDUCATION - INTERNATIONAL & DEVELOPMENT EDUCATION PROGRAM CLEARINGHOUSE (Educ)
5A01 Forbes Quadrangle   Phone: (412) 624-1281
Pittsburgh, PA 15260   Carmelita Lavayna-Portugal, Dir.
Founded: 1963. **Staff:** Prof 1; Other 2. **Subjects:** Development, international and comparative education, educational planning, social sciences and education, adult and literacy education, evaluation, nonformal education, minority programs. **Special Collections:** Latin America, Southeast Asia, United Nations, Peace Corps, Agency for International Development (AID), Europe, Africa, North America, Oceania, Organization for Economic Cooperation and Development (OECD), Women's Studies (9000 total items). **Holdings:** 500 books; 200 unbound serials; 5000 ephemera; 250 proceedings of conferences; 200 reports; unpublished papers; 250 theses, bulletins, organizations and newsletters; U.N. materials; student papers. **Services:** Interlibrary loans; library open to public for research, exchange and reference. **Publications:** IDEP Network News (includes new acquisitions); occasional papers. **Remarks:** Alternate phone numbers are 624-5574 and 624-5575.

★16097★

UNIVERSITY OF PITTSBURGH - SCHOOL OF LIBRARY & INFORMATION SCIENCE - INTERNATIONAL LIB. INFO. CTR. (Info Sci)
135 N. Bellefield Ave.   Phone: (412) 624-3394
Pittsburgh, PA 15260   Dr. Richard Krzys, Dir.
Founded: 1964. **Holdings:** 23,000 volumes. **Services:** Library open to public. **Remarks:** This library maintains a special collection of materials relating to libraries, librarianship, documentation and book production and distribution abroad. Resources are primarily of a nonbook nature including library reports, studies resulting from assignments by American librarians and data on overseas book and library activities of government, philanthropic and industrial agencies. Noteworthy collections within the center include those relating to Australia, Canada, Germany, Great Britain, India, Italy, Latin America and Pakistan. **Staff:** Jean Kindlin, Dir., Lib. & Media Serv.

★16098★

UNIVERSITY OF PITTSBURGH - SCHOOL OF LIBRARY & INFORMATION SCIENCE - LIBRARY (Info Sci)†
135 N. Bellefield Ave.
LIS Bldg., 3rd Fl.   Phone: (412) 624-5238
Pittsburgh, PA 15260   Jean Kindlin, Dir., Lib. & Media Serv.
Founded: 1962. **Staff:** Prof 4; Other 2. **Subjects:** Library and information science, history of the book, printing, publishing, communication, information retrieval, documentation, model collection of children's and young adult literature. **Special Collections:** Historical collection of children's literature, including the Fred Rogers Archives; rare book collection of titles primarily in the field of history of books and printing. **Holdings:** 53,215 books; 7375 bound periodical volumes; doctoral dissertations on microfilm; 7111 pamphlets; 3033 microforms. **Subscriptions:** 877 journals and other serials. **Services:** Interlibrary loans; copying; library open to public. **Computerized Information Services:** DIALOG, SDC. **Networks/Consortia:** Member of

Pittsburgh Regional Library Center (PRLC).

★16099★

UNIVERSITY OF PITTSBURGH - SCHOOL OF SOCIAL WORK - BUHL LIBRARY (Soc Sci)
Hillman Library
Pittsburgh, PA 15260
Phone: (412) 624-4456
Patricia Miles Carle
Founded: 1938. **Staff:** Prof 1; Other 1. **Subjects:** Social work, community studies, family interaction, child welfare, gerontology, juvenile justice. **Special Collections:** Classified Abstract Archive of Alcohol Literature (19,000 cards). **Holdings:** 13,645 volumes; 22 VF drawers. **Subscriptions:** 90 journals and other serials; 68 newsletters. **Services:** Interlibrary loans; library open to public with restrictions. **Automated Operations:** Computerized cataloging. **Computerized Information Services:** DIALOG, BRS, OCLC. **Networks/ Consortia:** Member of Pittsburgh Regional Library Center (PRLC).

★16100★

UNIVERSITY OF PITTSBURGH - SPECIAL COLLECTIONS DEPARTMENT (Rare Book)
363 Hillman Library
Pittsburgh, PA 15260
Phone: (412) 624-4430
Charles E. Aston, Jr., Coord.
Founded: 1968. **Staff:** Prof 3; Other 3. **Subjects:** Incunabula, early printed books, little presses, 20th-century poetry, early American textbooks, 20th-century Spanish literature, theater programs and playbills, detective and mystery stories, modern dance, popular culture, science fiction, history and philosophy of science. **Special Collections:** Hervey Allen Collection; Mary Roberts Rinehart Collection; Ramon Gomez de la Serna Collection; Curtis Theater Collection; Nietz Textbook Collection; Bernard S. Horne Memorial-Izaak Walton Compleat Angler Collection; Anna Pavlowa-Karl G. Heinrich Collection; Archive of Popular Culture; William Steinberg Collection; Rudolf Carnap Collection; Hans Reichenbach papers; Frank P. Ramsey Papers; Walter and Martha Leuba Collection. **Holdings:** 48,457 volumes; 199 broadsides and dealer catalogs; 11,615 photographs; 278 posters; 502,984 theater programs; 52,750 theater history clippings; 442 sheet music scores; 1335 pamphlets; 1635 microforms. **Subscriptions:** 30 journals and other serials; 15 newspapers. **Services:** Copying; department open to public for reference use only. **Computerized Information Services:** Internal database. **Special Catalogs:** Card files on printers, book designers, typography, paper, book illustration. **Staff:** Jean Blanco, Cur./Bibliog.; Pat Gladis, Cons.Libn.; Richard Nolan, Cur.

★16101★

UNIVERSITY OF PITTSBURGH - THEODORE M. FINNEY MUSIC LIBRARY (Mus)
Music Bldg.
Pittsburgh, PA 15260
Phone: (412) 624-4130
Norris L. Stephens, Libn.
Founded: 1966. **Staff:** Prof 1; Other 3. **Subjects:** Music. **Special Collections:** Pre-1800 music and music literature (1000 items); Fidelis Zitterbart (1000 manuscripts); Adolph Foerster (290 manuscripts and printed music); Ethelbert Nevin (100 manuscripts and printed music); William Steinberg (800 items). **Holdings:** 45,000 books, music scores and sheet music; 1500 bound periodical volumes; 1500 microforms; 20,000 phonograph records. **Subscriptions:** 75 journals and other serials. **Services:** Interlibrary loans; copying; library open to public. **Automated Operations:** Computerized cataloging, acquisitions and serials. **Computerized Information Services:** DIALOG, BRS, OCLC. Performs searches free of charge to students and faculty, on cost recovery basis to others. **Networks/Consortia:** Member of Pittsburgh Regional Library Center (PRLC).

★16102★

UNIVERSITY OF PITTSBURGH - UNIVERSITY CENTER FOR INSTRUCTIONAL RESOURCES (Soc Sci; Aud-Vis)
G-20 Hillman Library
Pittsburgh, PA 15260
Phone: (412) 624-4468
Dr. J. Fred Gage, Dir.
Founded: 1968. **Staff:** Prof 18; Other 17. **Subjects:** Education, psychology, anthropology, history, life sciences, sociology, women's studies, black studies, film studies, administration of justice, labor history. **Special Collections:** Faces of Change, 25 film series produced by American Universities' field staff, anthropological films on five countries; Maurice Falk Medical Fund (15 films); Ascent of Man series; Civilisation series; Europe the Mighty Continent series; World at War series (4 films); growing collections of films on aging, labor history and film studies. **Holdings:** 1300 16mm films; various reference books on nonprint media; 79 games; 39 kits; 16 transparencies; 77 slide sets; 206 filmstrips; 244 video recordings; 580 audio recordings; 27 manipulatives. **Subscriptions:** 27 journals and other serials. **Services:** Free loan for university classroom use; video duplication; center open to public with restrictions. **Automated Operations:** Computerized cataloging. **Computerized Information Services:** OCLC. **Networks/Consortia:** Member of Consortium of University Film Centers (CUFC). **Special Catalogs:**

University of Pittsburgh Film Catalog, 1978, supplement, 1979, 1981, 1982; various mediagraphies; video recording catalog, November 1983. **Staff:** Kathleen Matesic, Asst.Dir., Media Serv.; Scott Koziol, Non-print cat.

★16103★

UNIVERSITY OF PITTSBURGH - WESTERN PSYCHIATRIC INSTITUTE AND CLINIC - LIBRARY (Med)
3811 O'Hara St.
Pittsburgh, PA 15213
Phone: (412) 624-2378
Lucile S. Stark, Dir.
Founded: 1942. **Staff:** Prof 5; Other 5. **Subjects:** Psychiatry, behavioral science, neurology, marriage and family, clinical psychology, child development. **Special Collections:** Rare books in the History of Psychiatry (2300 volumes housed in Falk Library, School of Medicine, University of Pittsburgh). **Holdings:** 45,000 books and bound periodical volumes; 1300 audio- and videotapes; 8 VF drawers of ephemera. **Subscriptions:** 500 journals and other serials. **Services:** Interlibrary loans; copying; SDI; library open to public for reference use only; borrowers must be affiliated with a university hospital or mental health center. **Computerized Information Services:** MEDLINE, DIALOG, SDC, BRS. **Publications:** Booklist of New Books Cataloged - general distribution; Current Awareness Series - for internal distribution only; Media Resources Catalog. **Staff:** Barbara A. Epstein, Ref.Libn.; Elizabeth Barclay, Ref. & Cat.Libn.; Patricia Reavis, AV Libn.; Meliza Jackson, Patients' Libn.

★16104★

UNIVERSITY OF PRINCE EDWARD ISLAND - ROBERTSON LIBRARY (Area-Ethnic)
Charlottetown, PE, Canada C1A 4P3
Phone: (902) 892-1243
M.C. Crockett, Chf.Libn.
Founded: 1975. **Staff:** Prof 8; Other 17. **Special Collections:** Prince Edward Island collection. **Holdings:** 4500 books; 104 bound periodical volumes; clippings; pamphlets; government documents; microforms. **Subscriptions:** 18 journals and other serials; 6 newspapers. **Services:** Library open to public for reference use only. **Staff:** F.L. Pigot, Ref.Libn.

★16105★

UNIVERSITY OF PUERTO RICO - AGRICULTURAL EXPERIMENT STATION - LIBRARY (Agri; Food-Bev)★
Box H
Rio Piedras, PR 00928
Phone: (809) 767-9705
Joan P. Hayes, Libn.
Founded: 1915. **Staff:** Prof 1; Other 2. **Subjects:** Agriculture, biology, chemistry, food technology, rum research. **Holdings:** 11,796 books; 19,737 bound periodical volumes; 273,413 pamphlets, technical reports, annual reports. **Subscriptions:** 895 journals and other serials. **Services:** Interlibrary loans; copying; library open to public for reference use only. **Publications:** Book List, irregular; Monthly Library List - distributed to staff members and government libraries. **Special Indexes:** Index to the Journal of Agriculture of the University of Puerto Rico (book and card); indexes to Revista de Agricultura de Puerto Rico (card) and Caribbean Journal of Science (card).

UNIVERSITY OF PUERTO RICO - CARIBBEAN REGIONAL LIBRARY
See: Caribbean Regional Library

★16106★

UNIVERSITY OF PUERTO RICO - COLLEGE OF EDUCATION - SELLES SOLA MEMORIAL COLLECTION (Educ)†
Rio Piedras, PR 00931
Phone: (809) 764-0000
Lina B. Morales, Hd.Libn.
Staff: Prof 2; Other 1. **Subjects:** Education, psychology, educational philosophy. **Special Collections:** Public school textbook collection, 1900 to present. **Holdings:** 17,229 books; 1677 bound periodical volumes; 500 pamphlets; 28 VF drawers of clippings; 200 unbound reports; 2488 textbooks; 425 pictures. **Subscriptions:** 45 journals and other serials. **Services:** Interlibrary loans; copying; collection open to public for reference use only. **Special Indexes:** Indexes to local educational periodicals. **Remarks:** The Selles Sola documents were sent to the university's General Library. **Staff:** Rafael Melendez, Libn.

★16107★

UNIVERSITY OF PUERTO RICO - GENERAL LIBRARY - SPECIAL COLLECTIONS (Hum; Soc Sci)†
Jose M. Lazaro Memorial Library
Box C
San Juan, PR 00931
Phone: (809) 764-0000
Raquel Sarraga, Hd., Spec.Coll.
Founded: 1903. **Special Collections:** Juan Ramon Jimenez Collection (89,788 items); Caribbean collection (115,668 items); documents depository for the U.S. Government, United Nations, Organization of American States, AEC; Army map serial collection (1,479,540 items); Room for the Blind (872 items). **Services:** Interlibrary loans; copying; library open to public by

permission. **Automated Operations:** Computerized cataloging, acquisitions, serials and circulation. **Computerized Information Services:** Internal database. **Publications:** Anuario Bibliografico Puertorriqueno, annual. **Special Catalogs:** Union Catalog of University Libraries of Puerto Rico. **Special Indexes:** Index of Spanish poetry (card). **Remarks:** Houses Caribbean Regional Library.

★16108★

UNIVERSITY OF PUERTO RICO - GRADUATE SCHOOL OF LIBRARIANSHIPS - LIBRARY (Info Sci)
Box 21906   Phone: (809) 764-0000
San Juan, PR 00931   Vilma Rivera Bayron, Libn.
Staff: Prof 1; Other 3. **Subjects:** School and university libraries - administration; history of books and libraries; cataloging and classification; juvenile literature. **Special Collections:** Juvenile collection. **Holdings:** 23,886 books; 4459 bound periodical volumes; 919 other cataloged items; 1547 AV items. **Subscriptions:** 596 journals and other serials. **Services:** Interlibrary loans; copying; library open to public. **Automated Operations:** Computerized acquisitions. **Computerized Information Services:** DIALOG. **Special Indexes:** Boletin de la UNESCO para las Bibliotecas (book); SALALM Working Papers (card); Indice de Articulos de Periodicos de Bibliotecologia Puertorriquena (book); Bibliografia Bibliotecologia Puertorriquena (book); EGEBIANA, irregular.

★16109★

UNIVERSITY OF PUERTO RICO - GRADUATE SCHOOL OF PLANNING - LIBRARY (Plan)†
UPR Sta., Box BE   Phone: (809) 764-0000
Rio Piedras, PR 00931   Martha Torres-Irizarry, Libn.
Founded: 1965. **Staff:** Prof 1; Other 1. **Subjects:** Planning - general, urban, regional, agricultural, educational, environmental; economics; sociology. **Holdings:** 13,935 books; 1931 bound periodical volumes; 5148 volumes of Puerto Rican and Latin American government publications; 11,061 pamphlets; 474 maps; 113 microfiche; 5 reels of microfilm; 456 student monographs. **Subscriptions:** 261 journals and other serials. **Services:** Interlibrary loans; copying; library open to public for reference use only on request, circulation with special permit. **Special Indexes:** Author, title, subject index to PLERUS (journal published by the school), volume 1 to present (card); index to Revista Interamericana de Planificacion, volume 1 to present (card); author and title index to planning periodicals in Spanish (card).

★16110★

UNIVERSITY OF PUERTO RICO - HISTORICAL RESEARCH CENTER (Hist)★
University Sta., Box 22802   Phone: (809) 764-0000
Rio Piedras, PR 00931   Dr. Aida R. Caro Costas, Dir.
Staff: Prof 3; Other 2. **Subjects:** Puerto Rico, the Caribbean, Spain. **Holdings:** 3837 books; 4862 bound periodical volumes; 76 theses; 7122 reprints; 6472 translations; 14,210 reels of microfilm; 11,563 microfiche. **Subscriptions:** 47 journals and other serials. **Services:** Copying; center open to public with restrictions.

★16111★

UNIVERSITY OF PUERTO RICO - HUMACAO UNIVERSITY COLLEGE - LIBRARY (Sci-Tech; Hum)
Bo. Tejas, CUH-Sta.   Phone: (809) 852-2525
Humacao, PR 00661   Ileana D. Martinez, Dir.
Founded: 1962. **Staff:** Prof 8; Other 18. **Subjects:** Natural sciences, applied sciences, electronics, social sciences, social welfare, special education. **Special Collections:** Puerto Rican collection (4227 books; 121 periodicals). **Holdings:** 66,527 volumes; 3257 bound periodical volumes; 6108 unbound periodicals; 752 phonograph records; 1495 reels of microfilm; 68 cassettes; 4375 documents; 128 maps. **Subscriptions:** 672 journals and other serials; 21 newspapers. **Services:** Interlibrary loans; copying; library open to public. **Publications:** List of New Acquisitions; Desde la Biblioteca, irregular; Mundo Bibliografico, quarterly. **Staff:** Laura C. Garcia, Pub.Serv.Coord.; Ramon Budet, Ref.Libn.; Carlos Perez, CPR Libn.; Violeta Guzman, Per.Libn.; Angela M. Ruiz de Nieves, Cat.

★16112★

UNIVERSITY OF PUERTO RICO - LAW SCHOOL LIBRARY (Law)
Box L   Phone: (809) 764-0000
Rio Piedras, PR 00931   Carmelo Delgado Cintron, Law Libn.
Founded: 1913. **Staff:** Prof 8; Other 22. **Subjects:** Law - common, civil, international. **Special Collections:** Rare Puerto Rican Law Books Collection. **Holdings:** 115,893 volumes. **Subscriptions:** 1114 journals and other serials. **Services:** Interlibrary loans; copying; library open to public. **Staff:** Altagracia Miranda, Hd., Ref.; Marta E. Perez, Hd., Doc.Dept.; Enriqueta Marcano, Hd.Cat.; Idalia Chinea, Cat.; Josefina Bulerin, Hd., Circ. & Ref.; Carmen M. Melendez, Circ.; Miguel A. Rivera, Circ.; Orietta Ayala, Hd., Acq.Dept.

★16113★

UNIVERSITY OF PUERTO RICO - MAYAGUEZ CAMPUS LIBRARY - MARINE SCIENCES COLLECTION (Sci-Tech)
                                                      Phone: (809) 832-3150
Mayaguez, PR 00708   Sheila Dunstan, Libn.
Founded: 1954. **Staff:** Prof 1; Other 1. **Subjects:** Marine biology; marine invertebrates; fish biology; marine botany; aquaculture; chemical, physical, geological and biological oceanography. **Special Collections:** Reprints on Marine Sciences (10,026). **Holdings:** 1169 books; 3671 bound and unbound periodicals; 6248 documents; 130 theses; 14 reels of microfilm; 510 microfiche; 2 tapes. **Subscriptions:** 208 journals and other serials. **Services:** Interlibrary loans; copying; library open to public for reference use only on request. **Computerized Information Services:** DIALOG. Performs searches on cost recovery basis. Contact Person: Ada C. Ramoglam or Iraida O. Padovani. **Networks/Consortia:** Member of Sociedad de Bibliotecarios de Puerto Rico (SBPR); Marine Sciences Library Association. **Publications:** Contributions, annual - available on exchange basis. **Staff:** Bertha Cutress, Res.Assoc.

★16114★

UNIVERSITY OF PUERTO RICO - MAYAGUEZ CAMPUS LIBRARY - SPECIAL COLLECTIONS (Sci-Tech; Hum)
Main Library   Phone: (809) 834-4040
Mayaguez, PR 00708   Grace Quinones, Spec.Coll.Libn.
Founded: 1911. **Special Collections:** Theses (627) and books written by professors and alumni; Nuclear Science Collection; Puerto Rican Collection; government documents (236,520). **Services:** Interlibrary loans; copying; library open to public for external use of material with special permission. **Publications:** Documents holdings, monthly; list of theses, semiannual. **Staff:** Margarita M. Sanchez, Doc.Libn.

★16115★

UNIVERSITY OF PUERTO RICO - MEDICAL SCIENCES CAMPUS - LIBRARY (Med)
Box 5067   Phone: (809) 767-9626
Rio Piedras, PR 00936   Aura J. Panepinto, Dir.
Founded: 1950. **Staff:** Prof 5; Other 23. **Subjects:** Medicine, dentistry, public health, nursing, tropical medicine, pharmacy, allied health professions. **Special Collections:** History of Medicine; Puerto Rican Medical Collection; Dr. Bailey K. Ashford Collection. **Holdings:** 47,450 books; 56,920 bound periodical volumes; 5000 clippings; 700 reprints; 1000 pamphlets. **Subscriptions:** 1215 journals and other serials. **Services:** Interlibrary loans; copying; library open to public with restrictions. **Computerized Information Services:** MEDLINE. **Special Indexes:** Author index to Boletin de la Asociacion Medica de Puerto Rico (card). **Staff:** Iris Ribera De Cambre, Dir., Tech.Serv.; Ana Moscoso, Ref.Dept.; Maritza Garcia, Ser.Libn.; Margarita Jimenez, ILL Libn.

★16116★

UNIVERSITY OF PUERTO RICO - NATURAL SCIENCE LIBRARY (Sci-Tech)★
Box 22446   Phone: (809) 764-0000
Rio Piedras, PR 00931   Giovanna Del Pilar Barber, Hd.
Founded: 1954. **Staff:** Prof 6; Other 2. **Subjects:** Chemistry, biology, mathematics, physics, technology, geology, astronomy, physiology, anatomy. **Special Collections:** Environmental Management Program (567 volumes). **Holdings:** 32,900 books; 27,339 bound periodical volumes; 113 videotapes; 88 motion pictures; 254 pamphlets; 28,749 microforms. **Subscriptions:** 1256 journals and other serials. **Services:** Interlibrary loans; copying; library open to public for reference use only. **Publications:** List of Periodicals, List of Serials - both annual; bibliographies, monthly. **Special Catalogs:** Card catalog of Environmental Management Program. **Staff:** Mariano Maura, Libn.; Carmen A. Gonzalez, Libn.; Lydia Aulf; Francisco Feliciano; Miriam J. Santiago; Aura S. Cordero; Celia de De Leon .

★16117★

UNIVERSITY OF PUERTO RICO - PUERTO RICAN COLLECTION (Area-Ethnic)†
UPR Sta., Box C   Phone: (809) 764-0000
Rio Piedras, PR 00931   Denise Perez
Founded: 1929. **Staff:** Prof 5; Other 6. **Subjects:** Puerto Rican humanities, social sciences, natural sciences, applied sciences. **Special Collections:** Rare books (2700 19th-century books printed in or dealing with Puerto Rico); 19th-century newspapers; Puerto Rican posters (690); manuscripts. **Holdings:** 51,347 books; 44,197 bound periodical volumes; 71,155 government documents and pamphlets; 1465 reels of microfilm; 237 maps; 1981 posters; 109 tapes. **Services:** Interlibrary loans; copying; collection open to public for reference use only. **Publications:** Indice de Revistas Puertorriquenas. **Special Indexes:** Indexes of Puerto Rican short stories, illustrations, San Juan Star (Sunday Magazine), El Mundo (newspaper),

reviews, biographies, manuscripts, posters, theses and periodicals. **Staff:** Luz M. Lajara, Libn.Maria E. Ordonez, Libn.; Ada M. Felicie, Libn.; Eric Omar; Juan R. Bigas; Elsie Colon.

★16118★

UNIVERSITY OF PUERTO RICO - SCHOOL OF PUBLIC ADMINISTRATION - LIBRARY (Soc Sci)†

Rio Piedras, PR 00931

Phone: (809) 764-0000
Perfecto Camacho, Libn.

Founded: 1949. **Staff:** Prof 1; Other 3. **Subjects:** Government personnel administration, organization and management, budgeting, public administration, administrative law, human relations, public relations, government. **Holdings:** 10,626 books; 1226 bound periodical volumes; 1129 government documents of Puerto Rico; 398 readings. **Subscriptions:** 20 journals and other serials. **Services:** Interlibrary loans; library open to public for reference use only. **Special Catalogs:** Bibliography of the Municipios of Puerto Rico (to be published). **Staff:** Roxana Ruiz; Daniel Ortiz; Lucrecia Beltran.

★16119★

UNIVERSITY OF PUGET SOUND - SCHOOL OF LAW LIBRARY (Law)

950 Broadway Plaza
Tacoma, WA 98402

Phone: (206) 756-3326
Anita M. Steele, Dir.

Staff: Prof 6; Other 7. **Subjects:** Law. **Holdings:** 90,900 books; 11,770 bound periodical volumes; 94,600 volumes in microform. **Subscriptions:** 2990 journals and other serials; 17 newspapers. **Services:** Interlibrary loans; copying; library open to public with limited circulation. **Automated Operations:** Computerized cataloging, acquisitions and serials. **Computerized Information Services:** Online systems. **Networks/Consortia:** Member of WLN. **Staff:** Lei Seeger, Assoc. Law Libn.; Betty Warner, Acq.Libn.; Suzanne Harvey, Cat.Libn.; Bob Menanteaux, Ref.Libn.; Roger Becker, Sys.Anl.Libn.

UNIVERSITY OF QUEBEC
See: Universite du Quebec

★16120★

UNIVERSITY OF REGINA - BILINGUAL CENTRE - LIBRARY (Soc Sci)

College West No. 218
Regina, SK, Canada S4S 0A2

Phone: (306) 584-4177

Subjects: Bilingualism, translation. **Holdings:** 500 books. **Subscriptions:** 10 journals and other serials; 10 newspapers. **Services:** Library open to public.

UNIVERSITY OF REGINA - CAMPION COLLEGE
See: Campion College

★16121★

UNIVERSITY OF REGINA - CANADIAN PLAINS RESEARCH CENTER INFORMATION SYSTEM (Area-Ethnic; Env-Cons)

Regina, SK, Canada S4S 0A2

Phone: (306) 584-4758
Carol MacDonald, Coord., Info.Serv.

Staff: 7. **Subjects:** Plains research and researchers, information sources on Plains area, North American prairies (all aspects), Western Canadian history, native and ethnic studies, environmental studies. **Special Collections:** Moose Mountain Local Studies Project (180 photographs; 12 cassette tapes); Plains Cree Conference (audio cassettes; 12 videotapes). **Holdings:** Reference collection for staff use. **Services:** Copying; center open to public with restrictions. **Computerized Information Services:** QL Systems. **Publications:** Directories on computer - Researchers and Research Projects; Canadian Plains Bulletin, quarterly - to mailing list and by request.

★16122★

UNIVERSITY OF REGINA - EDUCATION BRANCH LIBRARY (Educ)

Regina, SK, Canada S4S 0A2

Phone: (306) 584-4642
Del Affleck, Hd.

Staff: Prof 3; Other 7. **Subjects:** Education, children's literature. **Holdings:** 112,900 books; 13,500 bound periodical volumes; 313,600 microfiche (ERIC, CANEDEX); 20,500 AV items; 20,100 study prints; 16,500 VF items; 31,600 games and kits. **Subscriptions:** 480 journals and other serials. **Services:** Interlibrary loans; copying; library open to public with restrictions. **Automated Operations:** Computerized cataloging, acquisitions and serials. **Staff:** Marianne Thauberger, Libn.; Sharon Stevelman, Libn.

★16123★

UNIVERSITY OF REGINA - MAP LIBRARY (Geog-Map)

Regina, SK, Canada S4S 0A2

Phone: (306) 584-4401

Founded: 1968. **Staff:** Prof 1; Other 2. **Subjects:** Cartography. **Special Collections:** Historical urban plans and air photos (15,000 items). **Holdings:** 5000 books and bound periodical volumes; 65,000 maps; 15,000 air photos;

800 microforms; 15 globes. **Subscriptions:** 28 journals and other serials. **Services:** Copying; library open to public with restrictions. **Publications:** List of special acquisitions; list of atlases; list of wall maps; list of class-sets; Map Library Resources; Map Library Brochure.

UNIVERSITY OF REGINA - SASKATCHEWAN ARCHIVES BOARD
See: Saskatchewan Archives Board

UNIVERSITY OF REGINA - SASKATCHEWAN INDIAN FEDERATED COLLEGE
See: Saskatchewan Indian Federated College

★16124★

UNIVERSITY RESEARCH CORPORATION - LIBRARY (Soc Sci)

5530 Wisconsin Ave.
Chevy Chase, MD 20815

Phone: (301) 654-8338
Patricia Place, Libn.

Subjects: International health, criminal justice, housing rehabilitation, management and evaluation. **Special Collections:** Alcohol and drug abuse (300 volumes and VF materials). **Holdings:** 6500 books; 3500 other cataloged items; 30 VF drawers. **Subscriptions:** 62 journals and other serials; 68 newspapers. **Services:** Interlibrary loans; library open to public by appointment. **Computerized Information Services:** DIALOG, MEDLARS. Performs searches for internal staff only.

★16125★

UNIVERSITY OF RHODE ISLAND - ART DEPARTMENT - SLIDE LIBRARY (Art; Aud-Vis)

Fine Arts Center
Kingston, RI 02881

Subjects: Arts - fine, graphic, applied; architecture; photography. **Holdings:** 50,000 slides.

★16126★

UNIVERSITY OF RHODE ISLAND - INTERNATIONAL CENTER FOR MARINE RESOURCE DEVELOPMENT - LIBRARY (Sci-Tech)

Main Library
Kingston, RI 02881

Phone: (401) 792-2938
Mary Jane Beardsley, Libn.

Founded: 1973. **Staff:** Prof 1; Other 1. **Subjects:** Fisheries, aquaculture, developing countries. **Holdings:** 13,000 books and documents. **Subscriptions:** 200 journals and other serials. **Services:** Interlibrary loans; copying (limited); library open to public. **Computerized Information Services:** DIALOG, BRS. **Publications:** Titles on artisanal fisheries; list of publications - available on request.

★16127★

UNIVERSITY OF RHODE ISLAND - RHODE ISLAND ORAL HISTORY PROJECT (Hist)

Library - Special Collections
Kingston, RI 02881

Phone: (401) 792-2594
David C. Maslyn, Hd., Spec.Coll.

Founded: 1972. **Subjects:** Millworkers of Rhode Island and their social milieu, 1900 to present; Narragansett Indians; university history; local Franco-American community; state jewelry industry. **Holdings:** 200 tapes of interviews; typescripts of some taped interviews; 70 tapes and transcripts of 1938 hurricane. **Services:** Library open to public.

★16128★

UNIVERSITY OF RHODE ISLAND - SPECIAL COLLECTIONS (Rare Book)

Library
Kingston, RI 02881

Phone: (401) 792-2594
David C. Maslyn, Hd.

Founded: 1966. **Staff:** Prof 1; Other 1. **Special Collections:** Rare books (6200 volumes); Rhode Island Collection (2645 volumes); Whitman (245 volumes); Pound (390 volumes); Millay (105 volumes); Robinson (150 volumes); herbals; fine press books; printing presses, 1830-1840; working presses - Albion, Adams, Washington. **Holdings:** 9585 volumes; theses; 900 linear feet of university archives; 2115 linear feet of personal papers; 11,570 maps; 16 VF drawers of ephemera. **Services:** Copying; collections open to public with restrictions. **Computerized Information Services:** OCLC. **Networks/Consortia:** Member of Rhode Island Interrelated Library Network; NELINET; Consortium of Rhode Island Academic and Research Libraries, Inc. (CRIARL). **Publications:** Internal finding aids; New Leaves Press - Library Keepsakes.

★16129★

UNIVERSITY OF RHODE ISLAND, NARRAGANSETT BAY - DIVISION OF MARINE RESOURCES - MARINE AWARENESS CENTER

Graduate School of Oceanography
Narragansett Bay, RI 02882

Defunct

★16130★

UNIVERSITY OF RHODE ISLAND, NARRAGANSETT BAY - PELL MARINE SCIENCE LIBRARY (Sci-Tech)†

Narragansett, RI 02882

Phone: (401) 792-6161
Kenneth T. Morse, Chf.Libn.

Founded: 1959. **Staff:** Prof 2; Other 3. **Subjects:** Oceanography, marine biology and technology, fisheries. **Special Collections:** Marine and polar expeditional reports (123 shelf feet); Paul S. Galtsoff Reprint Collection on the American Oyster (230 pamphlet boxes). **Holdings:** 8075 books; 10,324 bound periodical volumes; 1342 sheets of U.S. nautical charts; 16,000 reprints of scientific papers. **Subscriptions:** 970 journals and other serials. **Services:** Interlibrary loans; copying; library open to public for reference use only. **Publications:** Graduate School of Oceanography, University of Rhode Island, Collected Reprints, annual - by exchange. **Staff:** Judith B. Barnett, Asst.Libn.

★16131★

UNIVERSITY OF RICHMOND - E. CLAIBORNE ROBINS SCHOOL OF BUSINESS LIBRARY (Bus-Fin)

Boatwright Library
Richmond, VA 23173

Phone: (804) 285-6394
Littleton M. Maxwell, Libn.

Staff: Prof 1; Other 2. **Subjects:** Business administration, accounting, economics, finance, management, marketing. **Holdings:** 26,500 books; 5000 bound periodical volumes; 200 cassettes; 20 file cabinets of annual reports; 5 file cabinets of vertical files. **Subscriptions:** 1000 journals and other serials; 12 newspapers. **Services:** Interlibrary loans; copying; library open to public. **Automated Operations:** Computerized cataloging. **Computerized Information Services:** DIALOG, SDC, BRS, OCLC, Dow Jones News/ Retrieval. **Networks/Consortia:** Member of SOLINET; Richmond Area Libraries Cooperative. **Special Indexes:** Business and Economic update (card).

★16132★

UNIVERSITY OF RICHMOND - MUSIC LIBRARY (Mus)

Richmond, VA 23173

Phone: (804) 285-6398
Bonlyn G. Hall, Libn.

Founded: 1955. **Staff:** Prof 1; Other 5. **Subjects:** Music scores and recordings. **Holdings:** 255 books; 6850 phonograph records; 5980 scores. **Subscriptions:** 35 journals and other serials. **Services:** Interlibrary loans; copying; library open to public. **Automated Operations:** Computerized cataloging.

★16133★

UNIVERSITY OF RICHMOND - WILLIAM T. MUSE MEMORIAL LAW LIBRARY (Law)

Richmond, VA 23173

Phone: (804) 285-6239
Susan B. English, Law Libn.

Staff: Prof 5; Other 7. **Subjects:** Law. **Special Collections:** Environmental law. **Holdings:** 62,787 books; 10,031 bound periodical volumes; 31,254 volumes in microform. **Subscriptions:** 1500 journals and other serials; 10 newspapers. **Services:** Interlibrary loans; library open to public for reference use only. **Automated Operations:** Computerized cataloging. **Computerized Information Services:** LEXIS, OCLC. **Networks/Consortia:** Member of SOLINET. **Publications:** The Museletter, quarterly newsletter; Selected List of Recent Acquisitions, quarterly - both for internal distribution only. **Staff:** Joyce Manna Janto, Acq.Libn.; William H. Grady, Ref.Libn.; Sally H. Wambold, Cat.Libn.; Anne H. Cresap, Cat.Libn.

★16134★

UNIVERSITY OF ROCHESTER - ASIA LIBRARY (Area-Ethnic)

Rush Rhees Library, River Campus
Rochester, NY 14627

Phone: (716) 275-4489
Datta S. Kharbas, Libn.

Staff: Prof 1; Other 1. **Subjects:** Chinese, Japanese and Indian history and philosophy; Japanese and Chinese language and literature; Sanskrit language and literature; Hindi language and literature; Marathi language and literature. **Special Collections:** Asahi Shinbun on microfilm; Times of India, 1861-1889 (Indian gazetteers on microfilm); India census, 1881-1971. **Holdings:** 95,000 books; 11,000 bound periodical volumes. **Subscriptions:** 420 journals and other serials; 12 newspapers. **Services:** Interlibrary loans; copying; library open to public on written request. **Computerized Information Services:** DIALOG, BRS. **Special Catalogs:** Catalog of the East Asia Collection.

★16135★

UNIVERSITY OF ROCHESTER - CARLSON LIBRARY (Sci-Tech)

Hutchison Hall, River Campus
Rochester, NY 14627

Phone: (716) 275-4465
Michael Poulin, Libn.

Founded: 1972. **Staff:** Prof 1; Other 3. **Subjects:** Chemistry, biology, mathematics, statistics, computer science. **Holdings:** 29,955 books; 27,005 bound periodical volumes. **Subscriptions:** 951 journals. **Services:** Interlibrary

loans; copying; library open to public for reference use only. **Computerized Information Services:** DIALOG, SDC, BRS, NIH-EPA Chemical Information System; internal database.

★16136★

UNIVERSITY OF ROCHESTER - CHARLOTTE WHITNEY ALLEN LIBRARY (Art)

Memorial Art Gallery
490 University Ave.
Rochester, NY 14607

Phone: (716) 275-4765
Stephanie Frontz, Libn.

Staff: Prof 1; Other 1. **Subjects:** Art history, museology. **Holdings:** 16,000 books; 2000 bound periodical volumes; 2600 unbound museum bulletins and annual reports; 24 VF drawers of clippings, exhibition catalogs, pamphlets; Sotheby Parke-Bernet auction sales catalogs, 1952 to present; historical scrapbooks of Memorial Art Gallery. **Subscriptions:** 85 journals and other serials. **Services:** Interlibrary loans; copying; library open to public.

★16137★

UNIVERSITY OF ROCHESTER - DEPARTMENT OF ENERGY LIBRARY

400 Elmwood Ave.
Rochester, NY 14642

Defunct. Absorbed by University of Rochester - School of Medicine & Dentistry - Edward G. Miner Library.

★16138★

UNIVERSITY OF ROCHESTER - DEPARTMENT OF RARE BOOKS AND SPECIAL COLLECTIONS (Rare Book)

River Campus
Rochester, NY 14627

Phone: (716) 275-4477
Peter Dzwonkoski, Hd.

Founded: 1930. **Staff:** Prof 4; Other 3. **Subjects:** Rare books; literary and historical manuscripts; university archives; local history; Restoration and 19th-century British theatre and drama; history of law and political theory; 19th-century American political history. **Special Collections:** Thomas E. Dewey Papers; William Henry Seward Papers; Thomas Weed Papers; Guzzetta Collection of Leonardo da Vinci; Ellwanger & Barry Horticultural Library; Up-State New York Historical Collection; Susan B. Anthony; Lewis Henry Morgan; Robert Southey; Henry James; John Masefield; Christopher Morley; John Ruskin Collection (400 volumes); Frederick Exley archive; Thomas McGuane manuscripts; books illustrated with mounted photographs; 19th- and 20th-century trade-bindings; local imprints through 1860. **Holdings:** 60,000 volumes; 2.5 million manuscripts; 500,000 archival items; 8 VF drawers of ephemera. **Subscriptions:** 20 journals and other serials. **Services:** Copying; department open to qualified scholars. **Publications:** Library Bulletin, irregular - distributed to friends and institutions. **Staff:** Karl S. Kabelac, Mss.Libn.; Mary Huth, Asst.Hd.

★16139★

UNIVERSITY OF ROCHESTER - EASTMAN SCHOOL OF MUSIC - SIBLEY MUSIC LIBRARY (Mus)

44 Swan St.
Rochester, NY 14604

Phone: (716) 275-3018
Mary Wallace Davidson, Libn.

Founded: 1904. **Staff:** Prof 11; Other 10. **Subjects:** Music scores and books about music. **Special Collections:** Pougin Collection (books on music and theater); Krehbiel Collection (folk music); Gordon Collection (chamber music). **Holdings:** 375,000 volumes; 60,000 phonograph records; 1400 manuscripts, autograph letters; 56,000 pieces of early American sheet music; 22,000 items in the choral octavo collection; 750 volumes of clippings. **Subscriptions:** 500 journals and other serials. **Services:** Interlibrary loans; copying; library open to public for reference use only. **Automated Operations:** Computerized cataloging and ILL. **Networks/Consortia:** Member of SUNY/OCLC Library Network. **Publications:** The Sibley Muse (newsletter), quarterly - free upon request. **Special Indexes:** Pre-1949 Periodical Index (card). **Staff:** Charles Lindahl, Assoc.Libn.; Joan Swanekamp, Hd., Tech.Proc.; Iva Buff, Acq.Libn.; Ross Wood, Ref.Libn.; Dr. Louise Goldberg, Rare Books Libn.Stuart Milligan, Circ.Libn.; Neil Bunker, Bibliog.Spec.

★16140★

UNIVERSITY OF ROCHESTER - EDUCATION LIBRARY (Educ)

Rush Rhees Library
Rochester, NY 14627

Phone: (716) 275-4481
Kathleen McGowan, Ref.Libn.

Founded: 1962. **Staff:** Prof 1; Other 2. **Subjects:** Education - theory and practice, general, history, research, evaluation. **Special Collections:** Children's books (2500); masters' theses (700); test specimen sets (2600); curriculum materials (3500). **Holdings:** 34,000 books; complete set of ERIC microfiche; 3500 pamphlets. **Subscriptions:** 533 journals and other serials. **Services:** Interlibrary loans; library open to public with restrictions. **Computerized Information Services:** BRS, DIALOG. **Publications:** Accession List of Selected Education Titles, quarterly - to faculty and local libraries. **Remarks:** The Education Library is part of the Reference Department of Rush

Rhees Library.

★16141★
UNIVERSITY OF ROCHESTER - ENGINEERING LIBRARY (Sci-Tech)
Gavett Hall   Phone: (716) 275-4486
Rochester, NY 14627   Isabel Kaplan, Libn.
Founded: 1960. **Staff:** Prof 1; Other 1. **Subjects:** Engineering - electrical, nuclear, chemical; mechanical and aerospace sciences; laser fusion; alternative energy. **Holdings:** 25,000 books; 13,000 bound periodical volumes. **Subscriptions:** 500 journals and other serials. **Services:** Interlibrary loans; copying; library open to public for reference use only. **Computerized Information Services:** DIALOG, SDC, BRS, DOE/RECON. Performs searches on cost recovery basis to university affiliates; service charge to others. **Publications:** Engineering Library Newsletter, monthly - to faculty and selected staff and administrators.

★16142★
UNIVERSITY OF ROCHESTER - FINE ARTS LIBRARY (Art)
Rush Rhees Library, River Campus   Phone: (716) 275-4476
Rochester, NY 14627   Stephanie Frontz, Libn.
Staff: Prof 1; Other 1. **Subjects:** Architecture, sculpture, painting, photography, graphic arts, decorative arts. **Holdings:** 35,000 books; 8500 bound periodical volumes; 3000 exhibition catalogs and pamphlets; 28 VF drawers of clippings and ephemera. **Subscriptions:** 220 journals and other serials. **Services:** Interlibrary loans; copying; library open to public for reference use only. **Computerized Information Services:** OCLC. **Networks/Consortia:** Member of Rochester Regional Research Library Council (RRRLC).

★16143★
UNIVERSITY OF ROCHESTER - GEOLOGY/MAP LIBRARY (Geog-Map)
Rush Rhees Library
Rochester, NY 14627   Arleen Somerville, Libn.
Founded: 1960. **Staff:** Prof 1; Other 1. **Subjects:** Environment, geological sciences, paleontology, mineralogy, sedimentation, geochemistry, maps and atlases. **Holdings:** 13,000 books; 10,000 bound periodical volumes; U.S. Geological Survey microfiche; 30,000 maps. **Subscriptions:** 300 journals and other serials. **Services:** Interlibrary loans; copying; library open to public for reference use only. **Computerized Information Services:** DIALOG, SDC, BRS, GEAC, OCLC, RLIN.

★16144★
UNIVERSITY OF ROCHESTER - LABORATORY FOR LASER ENERGETICS - LIBRARY (Sci-Tech)
250 E. River Rd.   Phone: (716) 275-5768
Rochester, NY 14623   Loretta Caren, Libn.
Founded: 1976. **Staff:** Prof 1; Other 1. **Subjects:** Plasma physics, inertial confinement fusion. **Holdings:** 850 books; 4500 technical reports. **Subscriptions:** 41 journals and other serials. **Services:** Interlibrary loans; copying; SDI; library open to public by appointment. **Computerized Information Services:** DIALOG, SDC, BRS, DOE/RECON, NEXIS. **Networks/Consortia:** Member of New York State Interlibrary Loan Network (NYSILL); Rochester Regional Research Library Council (RRRLC).

★16145★
UNIVERSITY OF ROCHESTER - MANAGEMENT LIBRARY (Bus-Fin)
Rush Rhees Library, River Campus   Phone: (716) 275-4482
Rochester, NY 14627   Edward P. Wass, Libn.
Founded: 1962. **Staff:** Prof 3; Other 1. **Subjects:** Management, accounting, economics, finance, marketing, operations research and management, quantitative business methods, computer and information science, behavioral science in industry. **Holdings:** Annual reports of 5000 companies (hard copy and microform); 56 VF drawers of pamphlets on industry statistics and economic conditions; 3500 working papers; 18,000 microforms. **Services:** Interlibrary loans; library open to public. **Computerized Information Services:** DIALOG, NEXIS, TEXTLINE, Dow Jones News/Retrieval, BRS, SDC. **Publications:** Bulletin and list of recent acquisitions, 10/year; Rochester Management Bibliographies, irregular. **Staff:** Janet Prentice, Libn.; Datta Kharbas, Libn.

★16146★
UNIVERSITY OF ROCHESTER - PHYSICS-OPTICS-ASTRONOMY LIBRARY (Sci-Tech)
374 Bausch & Lomb Bldg.   Phone: (716) 275-4469
Rochester, NY 14627   Loretta Caren, Hd.
Founded: 1960. **Staff:** Prof 1; Other 3. **Subjects:** Physics, optics, astronomy. **Holdings:** 10,000 books; 10,000 bound periodical volumes; 2000 preprints and reports. **Subscriptions:** 366 journals and other serials. **Services:** Interlibrary loans; copying; library open to public for reference use only. **Computerized Information Services:** DIALOG, SDC, BRS. **Publications:**

Newsletter, quarterly; New Books List.

★16147★
UNIVERSITY OF ROCHESTER - SCHOOL OF MEDICINE & DENTISTRY - EDWARD G. MINER LIBRARY (Med)
601 Elmwood Ave.   Phone: (716) 275-3364
Rochester, NY 14642   Lucretia McClure, Med.Libn.
Founded: 1923. **Staff:** Prof 9; Other 15. **Subjects:** Medicine, nursing, psychiatry, dental research. **Special Collections:** Edward W. Mulligan History of Medicine Collection; Edward G. Miner Yellow Fever Collection. **Holdings:** 185,000 volumes. **Subscriptions:** 2900 journals and other serials. **Services:** Interlibrary loans; copying. **Automated Operations:** Computerized cataloging. **Computerized Information Services:** DIALOG, BRS, OCLC, MEDLINE. **Networks/Consortia:** Member of Rochester Regional Research Library Council (RRRLC); Greater Northeastern Regional Medical Library Program. **Publications:** Bulletin, monthly - distributed to medical personnel and institutions. **Remarks:** Also serves the School of Nursing and Strong Memorial Hospital.

★16148★
UNIVERSITY OF SAN DIEGO - MARVIN & LILLIAN KRATTER LAW LIBRARY (Law)
Alcala Pk.   Phone: (619) 293-4541
San Diego, CA 92110   Joseph S. Ciesielski, Dir.
Founded: 1954. **Staff:** Prof 7; Other 9. **Subjects:** Law. **Special Collections:** Selective government documents depository. **Holdings:** 207,000 volumes. **Subscriptions:** 1150 journals and other serials; 30 newspapers. **Services:** Interlibrary loans; copying; library open to public for reference use only. **Automated Operations:** Computerized cataloging. **Computerized Information Services:** LEXIS, Westlaw, OCLC. **Staff:** Marguerite Most, Assoc. Law Libn.; Georgia Briscoe, Hd., Tech.Serv./Doc.; Peggy Strand, Cat.;Mary Lynn Hyde, Govt.Doc./ILL.

★16149★
UNIVERSITY OF SAN FRANCISCO - SCHOOL OF LAW LIBRARY (Law)
Kendrick Hall   Phone: (415) 666-6679
San Francisco, CA 94117   Virginia Kelsh, Law Libn./Assoc.Prof.
Founded: 1912. **Staff:** Prof 4; Other 4. **Subjects:** Law. **Holdings:** 99,796 volumes; 358,024 microforms; 292 audio cassettes. **Subscriptions:** 2206 journals and other serials; 9 newspapers. **Services:** Interlibrary loans; library open to public for reference use only on request. **Automated Operations:** Computerized cataloging. **Computerized Information Services:** LEXIS, Westlaw. **Networks/Consortia:** Member of CLASS. **Staff:** Eleanor Covalesky, Cat.Libn.; Mary M. FitzGerald, Acq. & Ser.Libn.; Marian Shostrom, Ref.Libn.

★16150★
UNIVERSITY OF SAN FRANCISCO - SPECIAL COLLECTIONS DEPARTMENT/ DONOHUE RARE BOOK ROOM (Rare Book)
Richard A. Gleeson Library
2130 Fulton St.   Phone: (415) 666-6718
San Francisco, CA 94117   D. Steven Corey, Spec.Coll.Libn.
Staff: Prof 1. **Subjects:** 16th- and 17th-century English religious history; graphic arts; San Francisco area private press books; English and American literature of the 19th and 20th century. **Special Collections:** St. Thomas More and English Contemporaries; recusant literature; Robert Graves (first editions; translations; manuscripts; letters); Charles Carroll of Carrollton (books; letters; account books; ephemera); Robinson Jeffers (first editions; manuscripts; letters); Madeline Gleason Poetry Archive and Collection of San Francisco Poets; A.E. Housman (first editions); Laurence Housman (first editions and letters); 1890s collection, including Arthur Symons, Oscar Wilde, Norman Gale, George Moore and William Watson; Max Beerbohm collection; Norman and Charlotte Strouse Collection of Richard Le Gallienne (first editions; manuscripts; letters); Mr. and Mrs. S. Gale Herrick Collection of the Gregynog Press; William P. Barlow, Jr. Collection of the Daniel Press; M. Wallace Friedman Collection of L. Frank Baum and Oziana; Norman and Charlotte Strouse Collections of: The Book Club of California, Allen Press, Victor Hammer, Hammer Creek Press, John Henry Nash and the Peregrine Press; Theodore M. and Frances B. Lilienthal Grabhorn Press Collection; R.S. Speck Collection of the Kennedy Press; Overbrook Press; Kenneth Ball Collection of Christmas Literature; Albert Sperisen Collection of Eric Gill (books; prints; woodblocks; drawings; letters; ephemera); The Colt Press and James McNeill Whistler; William Everson (books; letters; ephemera); Tamalpais Press of Roger Levenson (complete archive); Scholartis Press; Cranium Press (complete archive); Black Stone Press (complete); Two Windows Press (complete); Mallette Dean Archive; Clark Pamphlet File of political, social and military literature, 1914-1939; Van Houten Collection of Spanish manuscripts, correspondence of Jose de Piedade (1784-1818) and Marie Guadalupe de Lencastre (1679-1691) relating to missions in Mexico and South America; Adolph Sutro Archive-Sutro Baths and Sutro Tunnel (6

boxes); George Poultney Theatre typescripts, 19th- and 20th-century drama (273 items); George Tyrell-Modernist controversy (1890-1910); Winterburn Bookplate Collection; Eidenmuller Collection of American Women's Suffrage. **Holdings:** 15,000 volumes; photographs; prints; letters; manuscripts. **Services:** Copying; library open to public. **Computerized Information Services:** OCLC. **Publications:** Occasional keepsakes; announcements of exhibitions; brochure briefly describing collections is available upon request. **Special Catalogs:** Files of presses, prints, manuscripts, letters, provenance, bindings, bookplates, chronology (card). **Remarks:** The special collections were started in 1951; the Donohue Room was dedicated in 1972. **Also Known As:** University of San Francisco - Countess Bernardine Murphy Donohue Rare Book Room.

★16151★
UNIVERSITY OF SANTA CLARA - ARCHIVES (Hist; Rel-Theol)
Santa Clara, CA 95053   Gerald McKevitt, S.J., Dir.
Staff: Prof 2; Other 3. **Subjects:** Mission Santa Clara, University of Santa Clara, Jesuits, higher education. **Special Collections:** John J. Montgomery Aviation Collection; Bernard J. Reid Papers; Bernard R. Hubbard Collection; Mission Santa Clara sacramental registers, 1777-1851. **Holdings:** 1000 books and bound periodical volumes; university archives; all University of Santa Clara publications and newspapers. **Services:** Copying; archives open to public by appointment. **Staff:** Julie O'Keefe, Asst.Archv.

★16152★
UNIVERSITY OF SANTA CLARA - EDWIN A. HEAFEY LAW LIBRARY (Law)†
University of Santa Clara Law School   Phone: (408) 984-4451
Santa Clara, CA 95053   Mary B. Emery, Libn.
Founded: 1963. **Staff:** Prof 6; Other 5. **Subjects:** Law. **Special Collections:** Collection on the development of water and power legislation in the U.S. and California (joint collection with the city of Santa Clara). **Holdings:** 104,114 volumes; 473 AV items; 2650 volumes on ultrafiche; 47,346 volumes on microfiche. **Subscriptions:** 7498 journals and other serials; 17 newspapers. **Services:** Interlibrary loans; copying; library open to law alumni, to public with permission. **Automated Operations:** Computerized cataloging and acquisitions. **Computerized Information Services:** LEXIS, RLIN. **Networks/Consortia:** Member of South Bay Cooperative Library System (SBCLS); CLASS. **Publications:** Acquisitions List, irregular. **Staff:** Regina T. Wallen, Hd., Tech.Serv.; Dee Ann Dugan, Ref.; Mary D. Hood, Hd., Pub.Serv.; Martha Mille, Circ.; Marilyn Earhart, Acq.

★16153★
UNIVERSITY OF SASKATCHEWAN - EDUCATION BRANCH LIBRARY (Educ)
                                     Phone: (306) 343-3793
Saskatoon, SK, Canada S7N 0W0   Margaret Baldock, Libn.
Founded: 1920. **Staff:** Prof 2; Other 6. **Subjects:** Education, practice teaching materials, social foundations, physical education, health, science, juvenile and adult fiction. **Holdings:** 72,492 volumes; 175,908 microforms; 46,149 AV items; 19,805 clippings; 7715 pamphlets; 214 maps. **Subscriptions:** 663 journals and other serials. **Services:** Interlibrary loans; copying; library open to public with courtesy card. **Computerized Information Services:** DIALOG, SDC, BRS. **Staff:** Pat Parnell, Ref.Libn.

★16154★
UNIVERSITY OF SASKATCHEWAN - ENGINEERING BRANCH LIBRARY (Sci-Tech)
                                     Phone: (306) 343-2062
Saskatoon, SK, Canada S7N 0W0   David Salt, Engr. & Sci.Libn.
Staff: 3. **Subjects:** Engineering - mechanical, electrical, civil, agricultural. **Holdings:** 38,281 volumes; 1950 pamphlets; 272 documents; 2301 microforms. **Subscriptions:** 933 journals and other serials. **Services:** Library open to public with courtesy card. **Automated Operations:** Computerized circulation. **Computerized Information Services:** DIALOG, SDC, BRS.

★16155★
UNIVERSITY OF SASKATCHEWAN - GEOLOGY BRANCH LIBRARY (Sci-Tech)
                                     Phone: (306) 343-4358
Saskatoon, SK, Canada S7N 0W0   Marilyn Lapp, Lib.Asst.
Staff: 1. **Subjects:** Geological sciences. **Holdings:** 30,913 volumes. **Subscriptions:** 400 journals and other serials. **Services:** Library open to public with courtesy card.

★16156★
UNIVERSITY OF SASKATCHEWAN - HEALTH SCIENCES LIBRARY (Med)
                                     Phone: (306) 343-3168
Saskatoon, SK, Canada S7N 0W0   Dr. Wilma Sweaney, Libn.
Founded: 1951. **Staff:** Prof 2; Other 6. **Subjects:** Medicine, clinical and basic sciences, nursing, biochemistry, cancer research. **Holdings:** 88,128 volumes;

12,655 slides; 130 cassettes; 45 kits; 20 realia. **Subscriptions:** 1454 journals and other serials. **Services:** Interlibrary loans; copying; library open to medical professionals. **Computerized Information Services:** MEDLARS, BRS, DIALOG, QL Systems, SDC. **Staff:** Lorraine Smith, Libn.

★16157★
UNIVERSITY OF SASKATCHEWAN - LAW LIBRARY (Law)
                                     Phone: (306) 343-4273
Saskatoon, SK, Canada S7N 0W0   E. Stanek, Law Libn.
Founded: 1915. **Staff:** Prof 2; Other 6. **Subjects:** Law. **Holdings:** 115,325 volumes; 12,048 microforms; 16,199 documents; 34,364 pamphlets; 118 AV items. **Subscriptions:** 1392 journals and other serials. **Services:** Interlibrary loans; copying; library open to public with courtesy card. **Computerized Information Services:** QL Systems. **Staff:** Ken Whiteway, Rd.Serv.Libn.

★16158★
UNIVERSITY OF SASKATCHEWAN - LUTHERAN THEOLOGICAL SEMINARY - OTTO OLSON MEMORIAL LIBRARY (Rel-Theol)
114 Seminary Crescent   Phone: (306) 343-8204
Saskatoon, SK, Canada S7N 0X3   Mary Mitchell, Libn.
Staff: 1. **Subjects:** Religion, mythology, free thought, Judaism, Christianity, Bible, doctrinal theology, practical theology, church history. **Holdings:** 38,000 volumes. **Subscriptions:** 150 journals and other serials. **Services:** Interlibrary loans; copying; library open to public. **Remarks:** The Lutheran Theological Seminary is an autonomous affiliate of the university.

★16159★
UNIVERSITY OF SASKATCHEWAN - PHYSICS BRANCH LIBRARY (Sci-Tech)
                                     Phone: (306) 343-4934
Saskatoon, SK, Canada S7N 0W0   Lori Nizinkevitch, Lib.Asst.
Staff: 1. **Subjects:** Physics. **Holdings:** 20,715 volumes. **Subscriptions:** 183 journals and other serials. **Services:** Library open to public with courtesy card.

★16160★
UNIVERSITY OF SASKATCHEWAN - ST. ANDREW'S COLLEGE - LIBRARY (Rel-Theol)
1121 College Dr.   Phone: (306) 343-6631
Saskatoon, SK, Canada S7N 0W3   Jo-Anne Coulic, Asst.Libn.
Staff: 2. **Subjects:** Religion and theology. **Holdings:** 25,400 books; 850 bound periodical volumes; 110 tapes; dissertations. **Subscriptions:** 80 journals and other serials. **Services:** Interlibrary loans; copying; library open to public with restrictions. **Automated Operations:** Computerized cataloging and serials. **Remarks:** St. Andrew's College is an autonomous affiliate of the university.

★16161★
UNIVERSITY OF SASKATCHEWAN - ST. THOMAS MORE COLLEGE - SHANNON LIBRARY (Rel-Theol; Soc Sci)
1437 College Dr.   Phone: (306) 343-4561
Saskatoon, SK, Canada S7N 0W6   Dr. Margot King, Libn.
Staff: Prof 1; Other 2. **Subjects:** Theology, women in monasticism, church history, Christian sociology, history, English, philosophy, psychology, sociology, economics, political science, Biblical literature. **Special Collections:** St. Thomas More (all books and all editions); complete holdings of Chesterton, Belloc, Wells, and Christopher Dawson. **Holdings:** 35,000 volumes. **Subscriptions:** 175 journals and other serials. **Services:** Interlibrary loans; library open to public. **Remarks:** St. Thomas More College is an autonomous affiliate of the university. **Staff:** Jane Brown, Assoc.Libn.

★16162★
UNIVERSITY OF SASKATCHEWAN - SPECIAL COLLECTIONS - SHORTT LIBRARY OF CANADIANA (Hist)
University Library   Phone: (306) 343-4514
Saskatoon, SK, Canada S7N 0W0   Shirley Perkins, Hd.
Staff: Prof 1; Other 1. **Subjects:** Prairie provinces, pre-Confederation history, Canadian Church history. **Special Collections:** Morton Manuscripts on Rupert's Land and North-West Territories to 1940 (45 linear feet). **Holdings:** 33,945 volumes; 2502 pamphlets; 3500 photographs. **Subscriptions:** 45 journals and other serials. **Services:** Interlibrary loans; copying.

★16163★
UNIVERSITY OF SASKATCHEWAN - THORVALDSON LIBRARY (Sci-Tech)
Thorvaldson Bldg.   Phone: (306) 343-2956
Saskatoon, SK, Canada S7N 0W0   Connie Fendelet, Lib.Asst.
Staff: 1. **Subjects:** Chemistry, pharmacy, chemical engineering, home economics. **Holdings:** 24,817 volumes. **Subscriptions:** 436 journals and other serials. **Services:** Library open to public with courtesy card.

★16164★
UNIVERSITY OF SASKATCHEWAN - WESTERN COLLEGE OF VETERINARY MEDICINE - LIBRARY (Med)
Saskatoon, SK, Canada S7N 0W0
Phone: (306) 343-3249
John V. James, Libn.
Founded: 1965. Staff: Prof 1; Other 2. Subjects: Veterinary medicine, animal science. Holdings: 33,175 books; 15,127 bound periodical volumes; 309 microforms. Subscriptions: 802 journals and other serials. Services: Interlibrary loans; copying; SDI; library open to veterinarians of Western Canada. Automated Operations: Computerized cataloging and circulation. Computerized Information Services: DIALOG, SDC, BRS, CAN/OLE. Publications: New Acquisitions, monthly; Bulletin, quarterly.

UNIVERSITY OF SHERBROOKE
See: Universite de Sherbrooke

★16165★
UNIVERSITY OF THE SOUTH - ARCHIVES (Hist)
duPont Library
Sewanee, TN 37375
Phone: (615) 598-5931
Gertrude Mignery, Univ.Archv.
Staff: Prof 1; Other 1. Subjects: University history, Protestant Episcopal Church in the South, local and regional history. Special Collections: Manuscripts and correspondence with authors published in Sewanee Review (10,000 items). Holdings: 1500 books; 500,000 manuscripts and photographs. Services: Interlibrary loans; copying; archives open to public. Automated Operations: Computerized cataloging. Computerized Information Services: OCLC. Networks/Consortia: Member of SOLINET.

★16166★
UNIVERSITY OF THE SOUTH - SCHOOL OF THEOLOGY LIBRARY (Rel-Theol)
Sewanee, TN 37375
Phone: (615) 598-5931
Thomas E. Camp, Libn.
Staff: Prof 2; Other 2. Subjects: Theology, Biblical studies, church music and art, church history, religious biography, liturgy and ritual, Episcopal Church in the U.S.A. Special Collections: Bayard Hale Jones Liturgical Library. Holdings: 86,000 books; 5500 bound periodical volumes; 2000 pamphlets. Subscriptions: 494 journals and other serials. Services: Interlibrary loans; copying; library open to qualified applicants. Automated Operations: Computerized cataloging and acquisitions. Networks/Consortia: Member of SOLINET. Staff: Thomas F. Gilbert, Cat.Libn.

★16167★
UNIVERSITY OF SOUTH ALABAMA - COLLEGE OF MEDICINE - BIOMEDICAL LIBRARY (Med)
Library 312
Mobile, AL 36688
Phone: (205) 460-7043
Robert Donnell, Hd.
Founded: 1972. Staff: Prof 7; Other 13. Subjects: Medicine, nursing. Holdings: 24,302 books; 40,786 bound periodical volumes; AV items; 600 reels of microfilm of periodicals. Subscriptions: 2460 journals and other serials. Services: Interlibrary loans (fee); copying; SDI; library open to public with restrictions. Automated Operations: Computerized cataloging, acquisitions, serials and ILL. Computerized Information Services: BRS, NLM, OCLC, Northwestern On-Line Total Integrated System (NOTIS). Networks/Consortia: Member of SOLINET. Publications: Acquisitions & Information Letter, quarterly - free upon request. Staff: Patricia Rodgers, Coord., Tech.Serv.; Geneva Bush, Sr.Hosp.Libn.; Patricia Ramage, Ser.Libn.; Judy Johnston, Coord., Online Searches; Sr. Mary Giles Peresich, Cat.Libn.

★16168★
UNIVERSITY OF SOUTH ALABAMA - LIBRARY - SPECIAL COLLECTIONS (Hist)
Mobile, AL 36688
Phone: (205) 460-7028
Founded: 1964. Subjects: Local history, Alabama authors. Holdings: 921 books; university archival materials; masters' theses. Services: Library open to public for reference use only. Computerized Information Services: OCLC, Northwestern On-Line Total Integrated System (NOTIS), DIALOG, BRS.

UNIVERSITY OF SOUTH CAROLINA - BELLE W. BARUCH LIBRARY IN MARINE SCIENCE
See: Baruch (Belle W.) Institute for Marine Biology and Coastal Research

★16169★
UNIVERSITY OF SOUTH CAROLINA - BUREAU OF GOVERNMENTAL RESEARCH AND SERVICE - LIBRARY (Soc Sci)
Columbia, SC 29208
Phone: (803) 777-8156
Sandra T. Cowen, Chf., Info.Serv.
Founded: 1947. Staff: Prof 1. Subjects: State and local government, public finance, public personnel administration. Holdings: 300 books; 1500 South Carolina documents; 5000 federal and state documents. Subscriptions: 203 journals and other serials. Services: Library open to public for reference use only. Automated Operations: Computerized cataloging. Special Catalogs: Bibliography of Bureau publications.

★16170★
UNIVERSITY OF SOUTH CAROLINA - COLEMAN KARESH LAW LIBRARY (Law)
Law Center
Columbia, SC 29208
Phone: (803) 777-5942
Joseph R. Cross, Jr., Act.Hd. Law Lib.
Founded: 1867. Staff: Prof 6; Other 7. Subjects: Law. Holdings: 175,776 volumes; 426,460 microfiche; 1953 reels of microfilm; 1290 audio cassettes; 71 video cassettes. Subscriptions: 3127 journals and other serials; 11 newspapers. Services: Interlibrary loans; copying; library open to public. Automated Operations: Computerized cataloging. Computerized Information Services: LEXIS, Westlaw, OCLC. Networks/Consortia: Member of SOLINET. Staff: Steve Huang, Assoc. Law Libn.; Paula G. Benson, Ref.Libn.; Melissa M. Surber, Acq./Ser.Libn.Diana Osbaldiston, Cat.Libn.; Cassandra S. Gissendanner, Cat.Libn.

★16171★
UNIVERSITY OF SOUTH CAROLINA - MAP LIBRARY (Geog-Map)
James F. Byrnes Ctr.
Columbia, SC 29208
Phone: (803) 777-2802
David C. McQuillan, Map Libn.
Staff: Prof 1. Subjects: Maps. Holdings: 183,000 maps; 1160 atlases; 41,965 aerial photographs; U.S. Geological Survey depository. Services: Copying; library open to public for reference use only.

UNIVERSITY OF SOUTH CAROLINA - NATIONAL ASSOCIATION FOR SPORT & PHYSICAL EDUCATION (NASPE)
See: National Association for Sport & Physical Education (NASPE)

★16172★
UNIVERSITY OF SOUTH CAROLINA - SCHOOL OF MEDICINE LIBRARY (Med)
Columbia, SC 29208
Phone: (803) 733-3344
R. Thomas Lange, Chf.Med.Libn.
Founded: 1975. Staff: Prof 5; Other 14. Subjects: Medicine. Holdings: 9000 books; 41,500 bound periodical volumes; 550 media programs; 3900 reels of microfilm. Subscriptions: 1207 journals and other serials. Services: Interlibrary loans; copying; SDI; library open to public with services to medical professionals only. Automated Operations: Computerized cataloging, acquisitions and serials. Computerized Information Services: OCLC, DIALOG, SDC, BRS, MEDLARS. Networks/Consortia: Member of SOLINET; Columbia Area Medical Librarians Association. Publications: Southeastern Medical Periodicals Union List; South Carolina Union List of Medical Periodicals, annual - free to participating libraries, for sale to individuals. Staff: Julie Johnson McGowan, Assoc.Med.Libn.; Ruth Hempel, Cat.Libn.; Karen Warren, Ser.Libn.; Sarah Gable, Ref.Libn.

★16173★
UNIVERSITY OF SOUTH CAROLINA - SOUTH CAROLINIANA LIBRARY (Hist)
Columbia, SC 29208
Phone: (803) 777-3131
Allen H. Stokes, Libn.
Staff: Prof 4; Other 5. Subjects: South Caroliniana. Holdings: 76,000 books and pamphlets; 2.1 million manuscripts; 500,000 issues of South Carolina newspapers; 2200 maps; 10,500 reels of microfilm; 14,000 pictures; 400 pieces of sheet music. Subscriptions: 307 journals and other serials; 63 newspapers. Services: Interlibrary loans; copying; library open to public for reference use only. Staff: Eleanor Richardson, Ref.Libn.; Herbert Hartsook, Mss.Libn.; Thomas L. Johnson, Asst.Libn.

★16174★
UNIVERSITY OF SOUTH CAROLINA - THOMAS COOPER LIBRARY - RARE BOOKS & SPECIAL COLLECTIONS DEPARTMENT (Rare Book)
Columbia, SC 29208
Phone: (803) 777-8154
Roger Mortimer, Hd., Spec.Coll.
Staff: Prof 1; Other 2. Subjects: English and American literature, ornithology, history of science, travel, theology. Special Collections: American Civil War; Left Book Club Collection; Papers of Lord Allen of Hurtwood (2000 manuscripts). Holdings: 30,000 books; 1000 bound periodical volumes. Services: Interlibrary loans; copying; department open to public for reference use only. Publications: Rare Book Collections in the McKissick Memorial Library.

★16175★
UNIVERSITY OF SOUTH CAROLINA - UNIVERSITY ARCHIVES (Hist)
McKissick Museums
Columbia, SC 29208
Phone: (803) 777-7251
George D. Terry, Dir./Archv.
Founded: 1976. Staff: Prof 2; Other 2. Subjects: University history. Special

Collections: 19th-century library records; personal papers of James F. Brynes (4 cubic feet); photographs (20 cubic feet). **Holdings:** 3500 cubic feet of archives; complete set of student yearbooks, 1899 to present; minutes of meetings of faculty senate and board of trustees, 1803-1962. **Services:** Copying; archives open to public. **Special Catalogs:** University Archives Preliminary Guide; Guide to University Archives Photographic Collection.

UNIVERSITY OF SOUTH DAKOTA - AMERICAN INDIAN RESEARCH PROJECT
See: American Indian Research Project

★16176★

UNIVERSITY OF SOUTH DAKOTA - BUSINESS RESEARCH BUREAU (Bus-Fin)
School of Business   Phone: (605) 677-5287
Vermillion, SD 57069   Dr. Jerry Johnson, Dir.
Founded: 1937. **Staff:** Prof 4; Other 14. **Subjects:** Clearinghouse for information on research pertaining to business, industrial development, health planning, tourism and recreation and vocational education. **Subscriptions:** 20 journals and other serials. **Services:** Bureau open to public except for classified matter. **Publications:** South Dakota Business Review, quarterly publication of Bureau; Bulletin series of special research projects, 4/year.

UNIVERSITY OF SOUTH DAKOTA - CENTER FOR STUDY OF THE HISTORY OF MUSICAL INSTRUMENTS
See: Shrine to Music Museum

★16177★

UNIVERSITY OF SOUTH DAKOTA - CHEMISTRY LIBRARY (Sci-Tech)
Pardee Laboratory   Phone: (605) 677-5487
Vermillion, SD 57069
Subjects: Chemistry, chemical physics, history of science, philosophy of science. **Special Collections:** A.M. Pardee historical book collection (420 volumes). **Holdings:** 710 books; 3038 bound periodical volumes. **Subscriptions:** 103 journals and other serials. **Services:** Interlibrary loans; copying; library open to public, journals do not circulate.

★16178★

UNIVERSITY OF SOUTH DAKOTA - CHRISTIAN P. LOMMEN HEALTH SCIENCES LIBRARY (Med)
School of Medicine   Phone: (605) 677-5347
Vermillion, SD 57069   David A. Hulkonen, Dir.
Founded: 1907. **Staff:** Prof 4; Other 10. **Subjects:** Anatomy, physiology, pharmacology, microbiology, pathology, biochemistry, nursing, dental hygiene, medical technology, clinical medicine. **Special Collections:** History of Medicine; medical school archives. **Holdings:** 34,894 books; 34,144 bound periodical volumes; 1100 AV software programs. **Subscriptions:** 1200 journals and other serials. **Services:** Interlibrary loans; copying; bibliographic and reference services; consultation services for hospitals; library open to public. **Automated Operations:** Computerized cataloging and serials. **Computerized Information Services:** OCLC, BRS, MEDLINE, PHILSOM. Performs searches on cost recovery basis. Contact Person: Rita Sieracki. **Networks/Consortia:** Member of Greater Midwest Regional Medical Library Network (Region 3); MINITEX. **Special Catalogs:** AV Union Catalog (online). **Special Indexes:** Index to faculty publications (computer printout). **Staff:** Mary Helms, Hd., Tech.Serv.; Gene Sederstrom, Tech.Serv.Libn.Rita Sieracki, Ref.Libn.; Kimberly Elliot, ILL.

★16179★

UNIVERSITY OF SOUTH DAKOTA - GOVERNMENTAL RESEARCH LIBRARY (Soc Sci)
       Phone: (605) 677-5242
Vermillion, SD 57069   Russell L. Smith, Dir.
Founded: 1939. **Subjects:** State and local government, public administration, South Dakota government, political behavior, public finance, Missouri Valley development, American Indians, public law, legislative apportionment. **Special Collections:** Missouri River Basin Commission publications (complete set). **Holdings:** 6000 books; 400 bound periodical volumes; 20,000 newspaper clippings from South Dakota dailies, 1950 to present. **Subscriptions:** 47 journals and other serials. **Services:** Copying; library open to public for reference use only. **Publications:** Public Affairs, quarterly; Reports, irregular; Special Projects, irregular.

★16180★

UNIVERSITY OF SOUTH DAKOTA - I.D. WEEKS LIBRARY - RICHARDSON ARCHIVES (Hist)
       Phone: (605) 677-5371
Vermillion, SD 57069   Elizabeth Lang, Archv.
Staff: Prof 1; Other 1. **Subjects:** History - Western U.S., frontier, South

Dakota; American Indians. **Special Collections:** Herman P. Chilson Western Americana Collection. **Holdings:** 10,500 books; 3100 feet of manuscripts. **Services:** Copying; archives open to public with permission. **Automated Operations:** Computerized cataloging. **Computerized Information Services:** OCLC. **Networks/Consortia:** Member of MINITEX.

★16181★

UNIVERSITY OF SOUTH DAKOTA - MC KUSICK LAW LIBRARY (Law)
       Phone: (605) 677-5259
Vermillion, SD 57069   Eileen Collier Bouniol, Hd. Law Libn.
Founded: 1901. **Staff:** Prof 6; Other 2. **Subjects:** U.S., English and Canadian law. **Special Collections:** Law - agricultural, Indian, family, water, tax, professional responsibility; arts and the law; South Dakota Supreme Court briefs (50 VF drawers drawers); U.S. Circuit Court, 8th Circuit slip opinions. **Holdings:** 99,642 books; 11,034 bound periodical volumes; 3 VF drawers of pamphlets; 10,104 volumes in microform; 4 VF drawers of archives. **Subscriptions:** 1366 journals and other serials; 10 newspapers. **Services:** Interlibrary loans (fee); copying; SDI; library open to public. **Automated Operations:** Computerized cataloging. **Computerized Information Services:** Westlaw. Performs searches on subscription basis. **Networks/Consortia:** Member of MINITEX. **Publications:** Selective list of acquisitions, quarterly; surveys of library holdings in specialized areas of law, 3/year - distributed to South Dakota Clerks of Court, legal services, selected South Dakota attorneys and libraries. **Special Indexes:** List of Periodicals; Survey of Bibliographies and Indexes; Guide to the Law Library; Locator Guide. **Staff:** Candice Spurlin, Circ.Libn.Delores Jorgenson, Cat./ILL Libn.; Shirley Bridge, Acq.Libn./Accounting; Karyl Knodel, Ser.Libn.; Sam Huang, Legal Ref.Libn.

UNIVERSITY OF SOUTH DAKOTA - W.H. OVER MUSEUM
See: Over (W.H.) Museum

★16182★

UNIVERSITY OF SOUTH DAKOTA, SPRINGFIELD - CARL G. LAWRENCE LIBRARY (Educ)†
       Phone: (605) 369-2296
Springfield, SD 57062
Staff: Prof 2; Other 3. **Subjects:** Vocational-technical subjects. **Holdings:** 85,000 books; 17,000 bound periodical volumes. **Services:** Interlibrary loans; library open to public.

★16183★

UNIVERSITY OF SOUTH FLORIDA - DIVISION OF EDUCATIONAL RESOURCES - FILM LIBRARY (Aud-Vis)
4202 Fowler Ave.   Phone: (813) 974-2874
Tampa, FL 33620   Delma Rodriguez, AV Media Dir.
Staff: Prof 2; Other 6. **Subjects:** Education, special education, social studies, literature, fine arts, management. **Special Collections:** Physical Education for the Handicapped (19 titles); Mid-Life and Pre-Retirement (30 titles); Protocol Materials for Teacher Training (76 titles). **Holdings:** 3000 16mm films; 100 video cassettes. **Services:** Library open to public - rental fee for film usage. **Networks/Consortia:** Member of Consortium of University Film Centers (CUFC). **Special Catalogs:** Triennial book catalog of currently available film titles, updated with annual supplements - catalog sent upon request. **Staff:** Charles L. Gordon, Film Lib.Coord.

UNIVERSITY OF SOUTH FLORIDA - FLORIDA HISTORICAL SOCIETY
See: Florida Historical Society

★16184★

UNIVERSITY OF SOUTH FLORIDA - LIBRARY - SPECIAL COLLECTIONS DEPARTMENT (Hum; Hist)
       Phone: (813) 974-2732
Tampa, FL 33620   Mr. J.B. Dobkin, Spec.Coll.Libn.
Staff: Prof 2; Other 4. **Subjects:** Floridiana, 19th- and early 20th-century American literature. **Special Collections:** Florida Collection (20,000 volumes; maps; photographs; other items); Hudson Collection of Hard Cover Boys and Girls Series Books (8000 volumes); Dime Novel Collection (9000 items); Early American Textbook Collection (1000 volumes); 19th-Century American Literature Collection (20,000 volumes). **Services:** Interlibrary loans (limited); copying; collections open to public. **Automated Operations:** Computerized cataloging and serials. **Computerized Information Services:** OCLC. **Networks/Consortia:** Member of SOLINET. **Publications:** Ex Libris, irregular - distributed internally and to other libraries. **Staff:** Paul Eugen Camp, Assoc.Libn.

★16185★
UNIVERSITY OF SOUTH FLORIDA - MEDICAL CENTER LIBRARY (Med)
Box 31
Tampa, FL 33612
Phone: (813) 974-2399
Maxyne M. Grimes, Act.Dir.
Founded: 1971. **Staff:** Prof 6; Other 13. **Subjects:** Medicine, nursing, public health. **Holdings:** 20,948 books; 54,317 bound periodical volumes. **Subscriptions:** 1641 journals and other serials. **Services:** Interlibrary loans; copying; SDI; library open to public for health related research. **Computerized Information Services:** Online systems. **Networks/Consortia:** Member of Tampa Bay Medical Library Network. **Publications:** Occasional papers. **Staff:** Ada M. Seltzer, Asst.Dir., Pub.Serv.; Margot Horacek, Ref.Libn.; James S. Tillman, Cat.; Sarah Harmon, Network Coord.

★16186★
UNIVERSITY OF SOUTHERN CALIFORNIA - ARCHITECTURE & FINE ARTS LIBRARY (Art)
University Park - MC 0182
Los Angeles, CA 90089-0182
Phone: (213) 743-2798
Alson Clark, Libn.
Founded: 1925. **Staff:** Prof 1; Other 3. **Subjects:** Art history, history of architecture, city planning, ceramics, photography. **Holdings:** 49,336 books; 28 VF drawers on architecture and fine arts; 8 VF drawers on city planning; 150,000 slides; 10 VF drawers of exhibition catalogs. **Subscriptions:** 200 journals and other serials. **Services:** Interlibrary loans; copying; library open to public for reference use only. **Staff:** Lindy Narver, Slide Cur.

UNIVERSITY OF SOUTHERN CALIFORNIA - ARNOLD SCHOENBERG INSTITUTE
See: Arnold Schoenberg Institute

★16187★
UNIVERSITY OF SOUTHERN CALIFORNIA - CATALINA MARINE SCIENCE CENTER - LIBRARY (Sci-Tech)
Big Fisherman Cove
Box 398
Avalon, CA 90704
Phone: (213) 743-6792
Dr. Ann M. Muscat, Asst.Dir.
Founded: 1969. **Staff:** 1. **Subjects:** Marine biology, oceanography, marine ecology. **Holdings:** 700 books; 100 bound periodical volumes. **Subscriptions:** 30 journals and other serials. **Services:** Interlibrary loans; copying; library open to public by permission. **Remarks:** Alternate phone numbers are 743-6793 and 743-7882.

UNIVERSITY OF SOUTHERN CALIFORNIA - CITIZENS' RESEARCH FOUNDATION
See: Citizens' Research Foundation

★16188★
UNIVERSITY OF SOUTHERN CALIFORNIA - CROCKER BUSINESS LIBRARY (Bus-Fin)
University Park - MC 1421
Los Angeles, CA 90089-1421
Phone: (213) 743-7348
Judith A. Truelson, Dir.
Staff: Prof 3; Other 4. **Subjects:** Accounting and taxation, finance, marketing, decision sciences, organizational behavior, business economics, management, investments, multinational business. **Holdings:** 60,050 books; 9356 bound periodical volumes; 13,074 reels of microfilm; 36,289 microfiche; 12,039 annual reports. **Subscriptions:** 1650 journals and other serials; 50 newspapers. **Services:** Library open to public. **Computerized Information Services:** DIALOG, SDC. **Publications:** Selected subject bibliographies - for internal distribution only; Top Fifty Acquisitions, monthly - for internal distribution only. **Staff:** Lillian Yang, Pub.Serv./Ref.Libn.; Janet Lundgren, Tech.Serv./Ref.Libn.

UNIVERSITY OF SOUTHERN CALIFORNIA - DENTISTRY LIBRARY
See: University of Southern California - Health Sciences Campus - Dentistry Library

★16189★
UNIVERSITY OF SOUTHERN CALIFORNIA - EDUCATION & INFORMATION STUDIES LIBRARY (Educ)
University Park - MC 0182
Los Angeles, CA 90089-0182
Phone: (213) 743-6249
Mae L. Furbeyre, Interim Hd.Libn.
Staff: Prof 2; Other 6. **Subjects:** Education and related subjects, instructional technology, educational psychology, international education, sociology of education, higher education, early childhood education, library and information sciences. **Special Collections:** Curriculum Collection (7839 texts and 6532 courses); juvenile books (6500 volumes); Chen Collection in Asian Education (2500 items); tests (1815); Wilson Collection of old textbooks (200 volumes); Dorothy Snyder Early Childhood Education Collection. **Holdings:** 117,000 books; 7000 bound periodical volumes; 140 AV materials; 31 films; 300,000 microfiche; 9 VF drawers of pamphlets; 5000 reels of microfilm.

Subscriptions: 466 journals and other serials. **Services:** Interlibrary loans; copying; library open to public for reference use only. **Publications:** New Book List, quarterly. **Staff:** Chris Cockcroft, Asst.Educ.Libn.

★16190★
UNIVERSITY OF SOUTHERN CALIFORNIA - ETHEL PERCY ANDRUS GERONTOLOGY CENTER - GERONTOLOGICAL INFO. CENTER (Soc Sci)
3715 McClintock Ave.
Los Angeles, CA 90007
Phone: (213) 743-5990
Jean E. Mueller, Libn.
Founded: 1966. **Staff:** Prof 3; Other 4. **Subjects:** Gerontology. **Special Collections:** Doctoral dissertations on aging and gerontology, 1934-1976, on microfilm; Archives of Gerontology Center. **Holdings:** 9276 books; 637 bound periodical volumes; 2000 reprint files; 500 pamphlet files; 100 newsletters. **Subscriptions:** 105 journals and other serials. **Services:** Copying; library open to public for reference use only. **Automated Operations:** Computerized cataloging and serials. **Computerized Information Services:** DIALOG, SDC, BRS, New York Times Information Service; AGEX (internal database). **Networks/Consortia:** Member of CALINET; CLASS. **Publications:** A Bibliography of Doctoral Dissertations on Aging from American Institutions of Higher Learning, 1934-1969 through 1976-1978; Journal of Gerontology, 1971 - annual. **Staff:** Margaret L. Kronauer, Info.Spec.; Stewart R. Greathouse, Info.Spec.

UNIVERSITY OF SOUTHERN CALIFORNIA - GREENE AND GREENE LIBRARY
See: Greene and Greene Library

UNIVERSITY OF SOUTHERN CALIFORNIA - HANCOCK LIBRARY OF BIOLOGY & OCEANOGRAPHY
See: Hancock (Allan) Foundation - Hancock Library of Biology & Oceanography

★16191★
UNIVERSITY OF SOUTHERN CALIFORNIA - HEALTH SCIENCES CAMPUS - DENTISTRY LIBRARY (Med)
Norris Medical Library
2025 Zonal Ave.
Los Angeles, CA 90033
Phone: (213) 224-7231
Frank O. Mason, Libn.
Founded: 1897. **Staff:** Prof 2; Other 2. **Subjects:** Dentistry, medicine, allied sciences. **Special Collections:** History of Dentistry (400 volumes). **Holdings:** 30,000 books; 11,500 bound periodical volumes; 1839 test files; 2519 AV items and filmstrips; 781 reading files. **Subscriptions:** 425 journals and other serials. **Services:** Interlibrary loans (fee); copying; SDI; library open to public with library card. **Computerized Information Services:** DIALOG, MEDLARS, MEDLINE. **Networks/Consortia:** Member of CALINET; Pacific Southwest Regional Medical Library Service (PSRMLS). **Publications:** List of Recently Acquired Titles, bimonthly - for internal distribution only; The Mouthpiece, bimonthly - restricted. **Staff:** John P. Glueckert, Asst.Libn.

★16192★
UNIVERSITY OF SOUTHERN CALIFORNIA - HEALTH SCIENCES CAMPUS - NORRIS MEDICAL LIBRARY (Med)
2025 Zonal Ave.
Los Angeles, CA 90033
Phone: (213) 224-7231
Nelson J. Gilman, Libn./Dir.
Founded: 1928. **Staff:** Prof 17; Other 21. **Subjects:** Medicine, pharmacy and allied fields. **Special Collections:** History of Medicine; Ethnopharmacology of American Indians. **Holdings:** 44,410 books; 72,405 bound periodical volumes; 34,010 slides; 4447 microfiche; 105 reels of microfilm; 2308 audio cassettes; 663 video cassettes; 53 motion picture reels; 44 filmstrips; 26 discs. **Subscriptions:** 2147 journals and other serials. **Services:** Interlibrary loans; copying; library open to public for reference use only. **Computerized Information Services:** DIALOG, MEDLARS, SDC, BRS, OCLC. **Networks/Consortia:** Member of Pacific Southwest Regional Medical Library Service (PSRMLS); CALINET; CLASS. **Publications:** Learning Resources Newsletter, bimonthly; Library Newsletter, bimonthly; Information, irregular; Union List of Health Science Serials, annual; occasional papers. **Staff:** Sherrilynne Fuller, Assoc.Dir.; Michele DeVoe, Ref.Libn.; Elva Yanez, Ref.Libn.; Bill Clintworth, Pub.Serv.Libn.; Diane Glunz, Ref.Libn.; Janice Contini, Ref.Libn.; Ruth Monahon, Ref.Libn.; Janis Brown, LRC Coord.; Elizabeth Wood, Acq./Ser.Libn.; Margaret Wineburgh-Freed, Cat.Libn.; David Morse, Tech.Serv.Libn.; Alice Karasick, Circuit-Rider Libn.; Louise Adams, Circuit-Rider Libn.

★16193★
UNIVERSITY OF SOUTHERN CALIFORNIA - INFORMATION SCIENCES INSTITUTE - LIBRARY (Comp Sci)
4676 Admiralty Way
Marina Del Rey, CA 90292
Phone: (213) 822-1511
Alicia Sabatine Drake, Tech.Libn.
Founded: 1972. **Staff:** 2. **Subjects:** Computer science, mathematics, electronics, cognitive psychology, linguistics. **Holdings:** 1000 books; 200

bound periodical volumes; 4000 technical reports. **Subscriptions:** 100 journals and other serials. **Services:** Interlibrary loans; library not open to public. **Automated Operations:** Computerized cataloging, acquisitions, serials and circulation. **Computerized Information Services:** DIALOG, SDC.

★16194★

UNIVERSITY OF SOUTHERN CALIFORNIA - INSTITUTE OF SAFETY & SYSTEMS MANAGEMENT - LIBRARY (Sci-Tech)
University Park - MC 0021   Phone: (213) 743-6253
Los Angeles, CA 90089-0021   Monir Ziaian, Hd.Libn.
Founded: 1966. **Staff:** Prof 2; Other 7. **Subjects:** Accident prevention, safety, occupational safety, human factors, organizational management and behavior, systems management. **Holdings:** 8000 books; 1100 bound periodical volumes; annual reports, proceedings, indexes, abstracts, newsletters. **Subscriptions:** 373 journals and other serials; 10 newspapers. **Services:** Interlibrary loans; copying (fee); library open to public for reference use only. **Automated Operations:** Computerized cataloging. **Computerized Information Services:** DIALOG, OCLC. Performs searches on subscription and fee bases. **Publications:** List of acquisitions, bimonthly - for internal distribution only. **Remarks:** The library serves 67 ISSM study centers in the U.S., Japan and West Germany in addition to the USC campus.

★16195★

UNIVERSITY OF SOUTHERN CALIFORNIA - LAW LIBRARY (Law)
University Park - MC 0072   Phone: (213) 743-6487
Los Angeles, CA 90089-0072   Albert Brecht, Dir.
Founded: 1896. **Staff:** Prof 9; Other 10. **Subjects:** Anglo-American law, legal history, legal literature, taxation, labor law, entertainment law, environmental law. **Special Collections:** Legislative history of Internal Revenue Acts; depository of Copyright Office publications. **Holdings:** 190,830 books and bound periodical volumes; 230,676 microforms; 230 shelves of documents; 643 audiotapes and video cassettes. **Subscriptions:** 3336 journals and other serials. **Services:** Interlibrary loans; copying; SDI; library open to public with restrictions. **Automated Operations:** Computerized cataloging. **Computerized Information Services:** LEXIS, Westlaw, DIALOG, NEXIS, RLIN. Performs searches on subscription basis. Contact Person: John Hasko. **Publications:** Acquisition list, monthly; library guide, irregular; newsletter, semiannual; subject guide to secondary sources, irregular. **Staff:** Frank Houdek, Assoc.Dir.; Victoria K. Trotta, Hd., Tech.Serv.; R. Paul Burton, Cur.; Fannie Fishlyn, Circ.; John Hasko, Ref.; Stephanie Owaki, Cat.; Leonette Williams, Acq.

★16196★

UNIVERSITY OF SOUTHERN CALIFORNIA - LIBRARY - CINEMA LIBRARY (Theater)
University Park - MC 0182   Phone: (213) 743-6058
Los Angeles, CA 90089-0182   Robert Knutson, Hd., Dept.Spec.Coll.
Founded: 1964. **Staff:** Prof 1; Other 3. **Subjects:** Motion pictures, television, radio. **Special Collections:** MGM Collection (1918-1958; 1900 titles, including screenplay drafts, synopses and treatments); Warner Brothers Collection (all files from Burbank studio through 1967); Twentieth Century-Fox Script Collection (1919-1967; 900 titles); Universal Pictures Collection (800 boxes); motion picture clippings and ephemera (175 feet); U.S. theater programs (50 feet); motion picture stills (135 feet); over 150 collections of memorabilia from directors, writers, producers, actors. **Holdings:** 18,000 books and bound periodical volumes; 250 reels of microfilm; 427 cartridges of videotape (David Wolper productions); teleplay collection; screenplay collection; 1700 reels and cartridges of audiotape; 1200 phonograph records (soundtracks and original cast recordings). **Subscriptions:** 220 journals and other serials. **Services:** Interlibrary loans; copying; library open to public for reference use only. **Networks/Consortia:** Member of CALINET. **Special Catalogs:** Catalog of Screenplays; Catalog of Audiotapes; Catalog of Theater Programs (all on cards). **Special Indexes:** Index of Collections (loose-leaf); An Index to Screenplays, Interviews and Special Collections (1975); An Index to Warner Bros. Collection; An Index to Universal Pictures Collection.

★16197★

UNIVERSITY OF SOUTHERN CALIFORNIA - LIBRARY - DEPARTMENT OF SPECIAL COLLECTIONS (Hist; Hum)
University Park - MC 0182   Phone: (213) 743-6058
Los Angeles, CA 90089-0182   Robert Knutson, Hd.
Founded: 1940. **Staff:** Prof 2; Other 3. **Subjects:** Western history, aeronautical history. **Special Collections:** Admiral William H. Standley Collection (47 document boxes); Southern California Congressmen; Library of Aeronautical History (100 document boxes). **Holdings:** 51,000 volumes; 50,000 manuscripts; 12,000 clippings. **Subscriptions:** 54 journals and other serials. **Services:** Interlibrary loans; department open to public for reference use only. **Networks/Consortia:** Member of CALINET. **Special Catalogs:** Guide to Special Collections (loose-leaf).

★16198★

UNIVERSITY OF SOUTHERN CALIFORNIA - LIBRARY - DEPARTMENT OF SPECIAL COLLECTIONS - AMERICAN LITERATURE COLLECTION (Hum)
University Park - MC 0182   Phone: (213) 743-6058
Los Angeles, CA 90089-0182   William Jankos, Cur.
Founded: 1940. **Staff:** Prof 1. **Subjects:** American literature since 1850 (first editions, association items, manuscripts). **Special Collections:** Hamlin Garland Papers (12,000 items); Jack London Collection (300 items); Willard S. Morse Collections of Ambrose Bierce, William Dean Howells, Sinclair Lewis, and Frank Norris; Paul Bowles Collection; Kenneth Rexroth Collection. **Holdings:** 37,000 books; 19,000 manuscripts; 10,000 clippings. **Subscriptions:** 20 journals and other serials. **Services:** Interlibrary loans; copying; collection open to public for reference use only. **Special Catalogs:** American Literature Letter catalog (card); calendar of Jack London Collection (loose-leaf). **Special Indexes:** Index to Hamlin Garland Collection (book).

UNIVERSITY OF SOUTHERN CALIFORNIA MEDICAL CENTER
See: Los Angeles County/University of Southern California Medical Center

★16199★

UNIVERSITY OF SOUTHERN CALIFORNIA - MUSIC LIBRARY (Mus)
University Park - MC 0182   Phone: (213) 743-2525
Los Angeles, CA 90089-0182   Rodney D. Rolfs, Music Libn.
Staff: Prof 1; Other 2. **Subjects:** Music. **Holdings:** 2000 books; 4 VF drawers of pamphlets; clippings on 260 subjects; 465 librettos; 15,000 phonograph records; 32,000 scores; 3000 cassettes. **Subscriptions:** 145 journals and other serials. **Services:** Interlibrary loans; library open to public for reference use only.

★16200★

UNIVERSITY OF SOUTHERN CALIFORNIA - NASA INDUSTRIAL APPLICATION CENTER (NIAC) (Sci-Tech)
Denney Research Bldg., 3rd Fl.
University Park   Phone: (213) 743-6132
Los Angeles, CA 90007   Radford G. King, Dir.
Founded: 1967. **Staff:** 15. **Subjects:** Aerodynamics, aircraft, auxiliary systems, biosciences, biotechnology, chemistry, communications, computers, electronic equipment, electronics, facilities research and support, fluid mechanics, geophysics, instrumentation and photography, machine elements and processes, masers, metallic and nonmetallic materials, mathematics, meteorology, navigation, nuclear engineering, physics (general, atomic, molecular, nuclear, plasma, solid state), propellants, propulsion systems, space radiation, space sciences, space vehicles, structural mechanics, thermodynamics and combustion. **Holdings:** Figures not available. **Computerized Information Services:** NASA/USC has at its disposal the data banks of NASA, the Department of Defense, DIALOG, SDC, New York Times Information Service, Dow Jones News/Retrieval and MEDLINE. Technology services include Current Awareness Information Services (current awareness search; standard interest profile; monthly manual search of any source) and Retrospective Information Services (retrospective search; one time search of any source for period desired). **Remarks:** NASA/USC is a nonprofit organization whose purpose is to disseminate technological information to U.S. industry and to implement NASA's Technology Utilization Program in the Western U.S. **Staff:** Robert Mixer, Asst.Dir.; Herbert Asbury, Prog.Mgr., NASA; David T. Komoto, Database Dev.Coord.; Becky Jensen, Mgr., Info.Serv.; Patti Brown, Info.Spec.; Dan Haley, Info.Spec.; Suzanne Mull, Doc.Ret.Libn.; Sandra Tung, Info.Spec.

★16201★

UNIVERSITY OF SOUTHERN CALIFORNIA - PHILOSOPHY LIBRARY (Hum)
University Park - MC 0182   Phone: (213) 743-2634
Los Angeles, CA 90089-0182   Bridget Molloy, Libn.
Founded: 1930. **Staff:** Prof 1; Other 1. **Subjects:** Philosophy. **Special Collections:** W.T. Harris Collection; Gomperz Collection (11,000 volumes; 2000 pamphlets). **Holdings:** 58,000 books; 4200 bound periodical volumes. **Subscriptions:** 160 journals and other serials. **Services:** Interlibrary loans; copying; library open to public for reference use only.

★16202★

UNIVERSITY OF SOUTHERN CALIFORNIA - POPULATION RESEARCH LABORATORY - LIBRARY (Soc Sci)
University Pk., Research Annex 385   Phone: (213) 743-2950
Los Angeles, CA 90007   Prof. David M. Heer, Assoc.Dir.
Founded: 1960. **Subjects:** Population, demography, census, human ecology, urban sociology. **Special Collections:** U.S. Census of Population and Housing - 1940, 1950, 1960, 1970; Latin American census. **Holdings:** 6000 items including U.S. Bureau of Census reports, vital statistics reports, United Nations reports, maps, computer tapes, journals, books, reprints, dissertations,

newsletters, pamphlets, bibliographies. **Subscriptions:** 30 journals and other serials. **Services:** Library open to public upon request.

★16203★

UNIVERSITY OF SOUTHERN CALIFORNIA - SCIENCE & ENGINEERING LIBRARY (Sci-Tech)
University Park - MC 0481   Phone: (213) 743-2118
Los Angeles, CA 90089-0481   A. Albert Baker, Hd.
Founded: 1970. **Staff:** Prof 3; Other 6. **Subjects:** Chemistry, physics, biological sciences, engineering, mathematics, geology, astronomy, computer science. **Special Collections:** David Spence Library (rubber technology). **Holdings:** 89,000 books; 74,000 bound periodical volumes; 25,000 technical reports; 1200 pamphlets; 14,000 microforms; rubber formulary on 15,000 punched cards. **Subscriptions:** 2500 journals. **Services:** Interlibrary loans; copying; library open to public for reference use only. **Computerized Information Services:** DIALOG. **Staff:** Hazel Wetts, Libn.; Linda Weber, Circ.Libn.

★16204★

UNIVERSITY OF SOUTHERN CALIFORNIA - SOCIAL WORK LIBRARY (Soc Sci)
University Park - MC 0411   Phone: (213) 743-7932
Los Angeles, CA 90089-0411   Ruth Britton, Libn.
Founded: 1971. **Staff:** Prof 1; Other 2. **Subjects:** Social work, social welfare, child welfare, community organizations. **Holdings:** 29,000 books; 500 unpublished masters' theses; 100 AV items and games; uncataloged collection of the Regional Research Institute in Social Welfare. **Subscriptions:** 152 journals and other serials. **Services:** Interlibrary loans; copying; library open to public for reference use only. **Publications:** New Book list, bimonthly.

★16205★

UNIVERSITY OF SOUTHERN CALIFORNIA - VON KLEINSMID LIBRARY (Soc Sci)
University Park - MC 0182   Phone: (213) 743-7347
Los Angeles, CA 90089-0182   Mr. Lynn Sipe, Libn.
Founded: 1928. **Staff:** Prof 3; Other 4. **Subjects:** International relations, political science, public administration, urban and regional planning, economic development, international economic relations. **Special Collections:** International documents collection. **Holdings:** 200,000 volumes. **Subscriptions:** 1500 journals and other serials. **Services:** Interlibrary loans; copying; library open to public for reference use only. **Automated Operations:** Computerized circulation. **Computerized Information Services:** DIALOG. **Publications:** Newsletter; Selected Recent Acquisitions, monthly - local distribution. **Special Indexes:** International & Public Affairs Index (card). **Staff:** Janice Hanks, Asst.Libn.; Annelore Stern, Asst.Libn.

★16206★

UNIVERSITY OF SOUTHERN CALIFORNIA - VON KLEINSMID LIBRARY - ORIENTALIA COLLECTION (Area-Ethnic)
University Park - MC 0182   Phone: (213) 743-7347
Los Angeles, CA 90089-0182   Ken Kline, Libn.
Staff: Prof 3; Other 3. **Subjects:** Social sciences, humanities. **Holdings:** 20,000 volumes. **Subscriptions:** 100 journals and other serials. **Services:** Interlibrary loans; copying; library open to public for reference use only.

★16207★

UNIVERSITY OF SOUTHERN COLORADO - LIBRARY - SPECIAL COLLECTIONS (Area-Ethnic; Info; Sci)
2200 Bonforte Blvd.   Phone: (303) 549-2361
Pueblo, CO 81001   Beverly A. Moore, Dir.
Founded: 1933. **Staff:** Prof 9; Other 7. **Special Collections:** Slavic Heritage Collection (1200 volumes and uncataloged items); U.S. Government publications depository (196,000 documents). **Services:** Interlibrary loans; copying; library open to public with restrictions. **Automated Operations:** Computerized cataloging, acquisitions, serials, circulation and interlibrary loan. **Computerized Information Services:** DIALOG. **Networks/Consortia:** Member of Arkansas Valley Regional Library Service System; Bibliographic Center for Research, Rocky Mountain Region, Inc. (BCR). **Staff:** Tony Moffeit, Hd., Pub. & Tech.Serv.; Kirstine Stjernholm, Ref.Libn.; Daniel Sullivan, Hd.Cat.Libn.; Janina Janes, Per.Libn.; Robert Cain, Docs.Libn.; Elaine Jurries, ILL Libn.; Ruth Burnham, Asst.Ref.Libn.

★16208★

UNIVERSITY OF SOUTHERN MAINE - CENTER FOR RESEARCH & ADVANCED STUDY - RESEARCH CENTER LIBRARY (Soc Sci)
246 Deering Ave.   Phone: (207) 780-4411
Portland, ME 04102   Janet F. Brysh, Libn.
Founded: 1973. **Staff:** Prof 1. **Subjects:** Maine - state, county, economic and social data; economic and environmental resources; health/social welfare;

energy; transportation; population/housing; manpower; taxes; education. **Special Collections:** Port Authority of Portland (450 items); regional collection for Foundation Center of New York (open collection). **Holdings:** 900 books; 75 bound periodical volumes; 300 other items; 44 VF drawers of state and federal agency reports and documents, data compilations; 95 newsletters and bulletins; microfiche aperture cards of IRS tax exempt foundations for Maine; 24 cassette and reel tapes. **Subscriptions:** 65 journals and other serials; 5 newspapers. **Services:** Interlibrary loans; copying; library open to public. **Publications:** A Directory of Foundations in the State of Maine, annual. **Remarks:** "In the Center for Research and Advanced Study there are four institutes, namely, Marine Law, Economic, Human Services Development and The New Enterprise which includes the Small Business Development Center. The Research teams publish the results of their studies and these are bound and become part of the Research Center Library. Copies of these reports are also sent to the University libraries on the Portland-Gorham campuses."

★16209★

UNIVERSITY OF SOUTHERN MAINE - NEW ENTERPRISE INSTITUTE - ENTERPRISE INFORMATION SERVICE (Bus-Fin)
246 Deering Ave.   Phone: (207) 780-4420
Portland, ME 04102   Janet F. Brysh, Libn.
Subjects: Business. **Special Collections:** Starting a Business collection (books; pamphlets). **Holdings:** 650 books; 12 VF drawers of clippings; telephone directories for Maine, Massachusetts, and major U.S. cities). **Subscriptions:** 104 journals and other serials. **Services:** Copying; service open to public.

★16210★

UNIVERSITY OF SOUTHERN MISSISSIPPI - GEOLOGY DEPARTMENT - LIBRARY (Sci-Tech)
Southern Sta., Box 5044   Phone: (601) 266-7196
Hattiesburg, MS 39406   Dr. Daniel A. Sundeen, Assoc.Prof.
Founded: 1972. **Staff:** 2. **Subjects:** Geology. **Special Collections:** State geological publications; government geological publications; road logs for field trips; oil well logs. **Holdings:** 20,000 volumes. **Subscriptions:** 10 journals and other serials. **Services:** Library open to public with permission of Geology Department.

★16211★

UNIVERSITY OF SOUTHERN MISSISSIPPI - MC CAIN LIBRARY (Educ; Hist)
Southern Sta., Box 5148   Phone: (601) 266-4347
Hattiesburg, MS 39406-5148   Claude E. Fike, Dir.
Founded: 1976. **Staff:** Prof 7; Other 3. **Subjects:** Mississippiana, genealogy, Civil War, children's literature, political cartoons. **Special Collections:** Papers of Theodore G. Bilbo, William M. Colmer, Governor Paul B. Johnson; Cleanth Brooks Literature Collection, Lena Y. de Grummond Collection of Children's Literature; Ernest A. Walen Collection of Confederate Literature and Imprints; Sam Woods Collection of Rare Books; Association of American Editorial Cartoonists Collection; University Archives; Association of American Railroads Collection; Gulf, Mobile & Ohio Railroad Collection. **Holdings:** 46,000 volumes; 6000 linear feet of manuscripts and illustrations. **Subscriptions:** 220 journals and other serials; 64 newspapers. **Services:** Interlibrary loans; copying (limited); library open to public for reference use only. **Automated Operations:** Computerized cataloging and serials. **Computerized Information Services:** OCLC. **Networks/Consortia:** Member of SOLINET (via USM Cook Library). **Publications:** Juvenile Miscellany, quarterly - by subscription. **Staff:** John Kelly, Cur.; Terry Latour, Cur.; Henry Simmons, Cur.; Frank Walker, Asst.Archv.; Betty Drake, Libn.; Delores Jones, Libn.

★16212★

UNIVERSITY OF SOUTHWESTERN LOUISIANA - CENTER FOR LOUISIANA STUDIES (Hist)
Box 4-0831   Phone: (318) 231-6027
Lafayette, LA 70504   Glenn R. Conrad, Dir.
Staff: Prof 5; Other 2. **Subjects:** Louisiana history. **Special Collections:** Louisiana Colonial Records; Women in Louisiana Collection; folklore and folklife. **Holdings:** Photographs; magnetic tapes; documents; microfilm. **Services:** Copying; center open to public with restrictions. **Publications:** USL History Series; USL Architecture Series; Louisiana Language and Life Series. **Staff:** Carl A. Brasseaux, Asst.Dir.; Vaughn Baher-Simpon; Barry Jean Ancelet; Gertrude Taylor, Ed.

★16213★

UNIVERSITY OF SOUTHWESTERN LOUISIANA - JEFFERSON CAFFERY LOUISIANA ROOM (Hist)
Dupre Library
302 E. St. Mary   Phone: (318) 231-6031
Lafayette, LA 70504   Cynthia J. Rice, Ref.Libn.
Founded: 1962. **Staff:** Prof 2; Other 1. **Subjects:** Cajun and Creole culture,

state and local history, colonial records, agriculture, petroleum, genealogy. **Special Collections:** Acadiana; Louisiana state documents; Zimmer Papers (uncataloged reports and orders of the State Conservation Commission relative to oil production of Louisiana: 252 single files; 100 packages; 6 boxes; 204 volumes); Caffery Collection; Freeland Collection of Photographic Plates; Archives of Louisiana Folklore (500 taped interviews); university archives; Colonial Records program. **Holdings:** 20,000 books and bound periodical volumes; 36 VF drawers of clippings and pamphlets; 600 theses; 1 million archival items in 113 collections; microforms; tape recordings. **Services:** Copying; microfilming; library open to public.

★16214★
UNIVERSITY OF SOUTHWESTERN LOUISIANA - ORNAMENTAL HORTICULTURE LIBRARY (Sci-Tech; Agri)
Dept. of Agricultural Sciences
Box 44333   Phone: (318) 231-6064
Lafayette, LA 70504   Brenda Kosiba, Libn.
Founded: 1960. **Staff:** 1. **Subjects:** Ornamental horticulture, agronomy, vegetable culture, pomology. **Special Collections:** Ornamental and native herbarium (10,000 specimens). **Holdings:** 5719 volumes; 390 VF drawers. **Subscriptions:** 100 journals and other serials. **Services:** Interlibrary loans; library open to public with restrictions. **Networks/Consortia:** Member of Bayouland Library System.

★16215★
UNIVERSITY OF SUDBURY - JESUIT ARCHIVES (Hist)
                                                   Phone: (705) 673-5661
Sudbury, ON, Canada P3E 2C6   Robert Toupin, S.J., Dir.
Founded: 1913. **Staff:** Prof 1. **Subjects:** History - Sudbury city, area villages, Manitoulin Island, Indians, Jesuit missionaries. **Special Collections:** Societe historique du Nouvel-Ontario (80 volumes); College du Sacre-Coeur, Sudbury. **Holdings:** 350 books; 200 bound periodical volumes; 150 pamphlets; 18 cassettes; 33 maps; 300 photographic portraits; 450 boxes of archival material. **Subscriptions:** 15 journals and other serials. **Services:** Interlibrary loans; copying; archives open to public with restrictions.

★16216★
UNIVERSITY OF SUDBURY - LIBRARY (Rel-Theol; Area-Ethnic)
                                                   Phone: (705) 673-5661
Sudbury, ON, Canada P3E 2C6   Stanislaw Chojnacki, Dir. of Lib.
Founded: 1960. **Staff:** 3. **Subjects:** Religion, philosophy, American Indian studies, folklore. **Holdings:** 32,803 books; 4400 bound periodical volumes. **Subscriptions:** 153 journals and other serials; 10 newspapers. **Services:** Interlibrary loans; copying; library open to public.

★16217★
UNIVERSITY OF TENNESSEE - AGRICULTURE-VETERINARY MEDICINE LIBRARY (Agri; Med)
Veterinary Medicine Teaching Hospital   Phone: (615) 974-7338
Knoxville, TN 37996-4500   Don Jett, Libn.
Staff: Prof 2; Other 4. **Subjects:** Agriculture, veterinary medicine. **Holdings:** 95,229 volumes. **Subscriptions:** 2948 journals and other serials. **Services:** Interlibrary loans; library open to public for reference use only. **Computerized Information Services:** DIALOG, MEDLINE, DOE/RECON, SDC, BRS.

★16218★
UNIVERSITY OF TENNESSEE - ARBORETUM SOCIETY - LIBRARY (Sci-Tech)
Univ. of Tenn. Experiment Station & Arboretum
901 Kerr Hollow Rd.   Phone: (615) 483-3571
Oak Ridge, TN 37830   Richard M. Evans, Supv., Forestry Sta.
Staff: 2. **Subjects:** Botany, horticulture, trees and shrubs, landscaping, floriculture. **Holdings:** 200 books; bulletins, journals, and plant lists from all major arboreta in the United States and abroad. **Services:** Copying (limited); library open to public for reference use only.

★16219★
UNIVERSITY OF TENNESSEE - CENTER FOR THE HEALTH SCIENCES LIBRARY (Med)
800 Madison Ave.   Phone: (901) 528-5638
Memphis, TN 38163   Jess A. Martin, Dir.
Founded: 1913. **Staff:** Prof 11; Other 23. **Subjects:** Medicine, dentistry, nursing, pharmacy, allied health sciences. **Special Collections:** Wallace Collection (books authored by University of Tennessee personnel). **Holdings:** 34,693 books; 103,200 bound periodical volumes; 129 microforms; 306 slide programs; 387 filmstrips; 220 films; 981 video and audio cassettes. **Subscriptions:** 2145 journals and other serials. **Services:** Interlibrary loans; copying; library open to public for reference use only. **Automated Operations:** Computerized cataloging. **Computerized Information Services:** OCLC, DIALOG, MEDLINE; internal database. **Networks/Consortia:** Member

of SOLINET. **Publications:** Library Guide, annual; Periodicals Holdings List, annual; Library Bulletin, bimonthly. **Staff:** Karen J. Graves, Hd., Educ.Serv.Dept.; Anne Carroll Bunting, Hd., Tech.Serv.Dept.; Gail Findlay, Acq.Libn.; Wilma R. Lasslo, Circ.Libn.; Frances Verble, Cat.; Mary K. Givens, ILL Libn./Hd.Ref.Libn.; Glenda Perry, Ser.Libn.; Ronald R. Sommer, Hd., Rd.Serv.Dept.Ellen McDonell, Ref.Libn.; Louann Hurst, Educ.Serv.Libn.; Susan Selig, Br.Libn.

★16220★
UNIVERSITY OF TENNESSEE - COLLEGE OF LAW LIBRARY (Law)
1505 W. Cumberland Ave.   Phone: (615) 974-4381
Knoxville, TN 37996-1800   D. Cheryl Picquet, Act.Dir.
Founded: 1890. **Staff:** Prof 4; Other 10. **Subjects:** Law. **Special Collections:** Depository of U.S. documents (10,000); constitutional law books and materials in braille (948 volumes). **Holdings:** 75,500 books; 122,500 bound periodical volumes. **Subscriptions:** 2593 journals and other serials; 16 newspapers. **Services:** Interlibrary loans; copying; library open to public. **Automated Operations:** Computerized cataloging. **Computerized Information Services:** Westlaw. Performs searches on cost recovery basis. **Staff:** Terry Campbell, Act.Ref.Libn.; Reba A. Best, Hd., Cat.

★16221★
UNIVERSITY OF TENNESSEE - ENERGY, ENVIRONMENT & RESOURCES CENTER - JOINT RESEARCH CENTERS' LIBRARY (Env-Cons; Trans)
327 S. Stadium Hall   Phone: (615) 974-4251
Knoxville, TN 37996-0710   Alan B. Johns, Libn.
Founded: 1981. **Staff:** Prof 1; Other 1. **Subjects:** Energy conservation, solar energy, coal, waste management, transportation, water resources. **Holdings:** 5000 books; 10,000 technical reports. **Subscriptions:** 100 journals and other serials. **Services:** Interlibrary loans; copying; library open to public. **Publications:** Quarterly acquisitions list.

UNIVERSITY OF TENNESSEE - INSTITUTE FOR PUBLIC SERVICE - MUNICIPAL TECHNICAL ADVISORY SERVICE
See: Municipal Technical Advisory Service

★16222★
UNIVERSITY OF TENNESSEE - MEMORIAL RESEARCH CENTER AND HOSPITAL - PRESTON MEDICAL LIBRARY (Med)
1924 Alcoa Hwy.   Phone: (615) 971-3305
Knoxville, TN 37920   Martha C. Childs, Libn.
Founded: 1966. **Staff:** Prof 2; Other 3. **Subjects:** Medicine, hematology, biochemistry, immunology. **Holdings:** 2600 books; 20,000 bound periodical volumes. **Subscriptions:** 400 journals and other serials. **Services:** Interlibrary loans; copying; library open to public with limited circulation. **Computerized Information Services:** MEDLARS. Performs searches on cost recovery basis. **Networks/Consortia:** Member of Knoxville Area Health Sciences Library Consortium (KAHSLC). **Formerly:** Its Center for the Health Sciences. **Staff:** Lynn Yeomans Gard, Libn.

★16223★
UNIVERSITY OF TENNESSEE - MUSIC LIBRARY (Mus)
Music Bldg., Rm. 301   Phone: (615) 974-3474
Knoxville, TN 37796-2600   Pauline S. Bayne, Libn.
Founded: 1971. **Staff:** Prof 1; Other 2. **Subjects:** Music. **Special Collections:** Galston-Busoni music collection (manuscripts; photographs; memorabilia; 2000 scores for piano); Grace Moore memorabilia, photographs, autographed and annotated scores. **Holdings:** 22,535 volumes; 8950 audio cassettes. **Subscriptions:** 260 journals and other serials. **Services:** Interlibrary loans; copying; library open to public. **Computerized Information Services:** DIALOG, SDC (through Main Library).

★16224★
UNIVERSITY OF TENNESSEE - SPACE INSTITUTE LIBRARY (Sci-Tech)
                                                   Phone: (615) 455-0631
Tullahoma, TN 37388   Helen B. Mason, Libn.
Founded: 1965. **Staff:** Prof 2; Other 1. **Subjects:** Physics, mathematics, electrical and metallurgical engineering, aerodynamics, MHD power generation, propulsion, aerospace science, computer science. **Holdings:** 14,486 books and bound periodical volumes; 552 theses ; 31,400 reports; 149,000 microfiche. **Subscriptions:** 170 journals and other serials. **Services:** Interlibrary loans; copying; unrestricted loan to staff of Arnold Engineering Development Center; limited loans to local citizens and Junior College. **Computerized Information Services:** DOE/RECON, DIALOG, OCLC. **Networks/Consortia:** Member of SOLINET. **Staff:** Mary Lo, Libn.; Marjorie Joseph, Libn.

★16225★
UNIVERSITY OF TENNESSEE - SPECIAL COLLECTIONS
Phone: (615) 974-4480
Knoxville, TN 37996-1000   John Dobson, Spec.Coll.Libn.
Founded: 1959. **Staff:** Prof 1; Other 3. **Subjects:** Tennesseana, 19th-century American fiction, Southern Indians, early imprints. **Special Collections:** Estes Kefauver Collection, political papers and memorabilia (1204 feet); Radiation Biology Archives (70,000 items); William Congreve Collection; University of Tennessee Archives (600 feet). **Holdings:** 27,557 books; 2.27 million manuscripts. **Services:** Copying; collection open to public with restrictions. **Publications:** Occasional publication. **Special Catalogs:** Rare books catalog (card); unpublished registers and calendars to manuscript collections.

★16226★
UNIVERSITY OF TEXAS - INSTITUTE OF TEXAN CULTURES AT SAN ANTONIO - LIBRARY (Area-Ethnic)
801 S. Bowie St.
Box 1226   Phone: (512) 226-7651
San Antonio, TX 78294   Deborah S. Large, Dir.Lib.Serv.
Founded: 1968. **Staff:** Prof 2; Other 4. **Subjects:** Texas ethnic history and regional folklore. **Special Collections:** Photograph collection (35,000 indexed copy negatives on Texas subjects); San Antonio Light negative collection (60,000 negatives made from 1920 to 1940 and retired from the newspaper morgue). **Holdings:** 4500 books; 80 bound periodical volumes; 100 VF drawers. **Services:** Interlibrary loans; copying; reproduction of photographs; library open to public for reference use only, by appointment. **Networks/Consortia:** Member of Council of Research and Academic Libraries (CORAL). **Publications:** The Texians and the Texans - series of ethnic pamphlets; slide and filmstrips useful for teaching; books on Texas history and Institute exhibits; photograph catalog. **Special Indexes:** Subject index to photographs.

★16227★
UNIVERSITY OF TEXAS - M.D. ANDERSON HOSPITAL AND TUMOR INSTITUTE - RESEARCH MEDICAL LIBRARY (Med)
Texas Medical Center   Phone: (713) 792-2282
Houston, TX 77030   Marie Harvin, Res.Med.Libn.
Founded: 1945. **Staff:** Prof 6; Other 6. **Subjects:** Cancer, radiological physics, cell biology. **Special Collections:** Rare books and early treatises on cancer (375 volumes). **Holdings:** 17,500 books; 28,000 bound periodical volumes. **Subscriptions:** 1100 journals and other serials. **Services:** Interlibrary loans; copying; library open to public for reference use only. **Automated Operations:** Computerized serials and circulation. **Computerized Information Services:** OCLC, MEDLINE. **Networks/Consortia:** Member of TALON; AMIGOS Bibliographic Council, Inc. **Publications:** Current Articles on Neoplasia, weekly - free upon request to physicians and other scientific libraries. **Also Known As:** University of Texas System Cancer Center.

★16228★
UNIVERSITY OF TEXAS - PORT ARANSAS MARINE LABORATORY - LIBRARY (Sci-Tech)
Phone: (512) 749-6723
Port Aransas, TX 78373   Ruth Grundy, Libn.
Founded: 1941. **Staff:** Prof 1; Other 2. **Subjects:** Marine science in the areas of botany, chemistry, ecology, geology, zoology. **Holdings:** 8000 books; 35,000 bound periodical volumes; documents; maps; 400 exchange journals. **Subscriptions:** 140 journals and other serials. **Services:** Interlibrary loans; copying; library open to public. **Computerized Information Services:** DIALOG. **Publications:** Contributions in Marine Science, irregular.

★16229★
UNIVERSITY OF TEXAS, ARLINGTON - LIBRARY - DIVISION OF SPECIAL COLLECTIONS AND ARCHIVES (Hist)
Box 19497   Phone: (817) 273-3393
Arlington, TX 76019   Dr. Charles C. Colley, Dir.
Founded: 1974. **Staff:** Prof 3; Other 9. **Subjects:** Mexican war, Texas history, cartographic history, Texas labor archives, Yucatan history, printing arts in Texas. **Special Collections:** Jenkins Garrett Collection (12,000 items); Cartographic History Library (3500 items); Robertson Colony Collection of historic Texana. **Holdings:** 11,000 books; 134 bound periodical volumes; 3500 maps, sheet music, lithographs; 400 linear feet of manuscript materials; 1000 folders of newspapers; historic photographs; 4 VF drawers of clippings. **Subscriptions:** 27 journals and other serials. **Services:** Copying; library open to public for reference use only. **Networks/Consortia:** Member of AMIGOS Bibliographic Council, Inc. **Staff:** Dr. Malcolm D. McLean, Dir., Robertson Coll.; Robert Gamble, Univ.Archv.

★16230★
UNIVERSITY OF TEXAS, AUSTIN - ARCHITECTURE & PLANNING LIBRARY (Art; Plan)
General Libraries, BTL 200   Phone: (512) 471-1844
Austin, TX 78712-7330   Eloise E. McDonald, Arch. & Plan.Libn.
Staff: Prof 1; Other 2. **Subjects:** Architecture, architectural history, landscape architecture, city and regional planning. **Special Collections:** Architectural Drawings Collection (40,000 drawings). **Holdings:** 18,354 books; 6525 bound periodical volumes; 17,810 HUD 701 depository items; 219 reels of microfilm; 561 microfiche. **Subscriptions:** 333 journals and other serials. **Services:** Interlibrary loans; copying; library open to public. **Publications:** Library Guide.

★16231★
UNIVERSITY OF TEXAS, AUSTIN - ASIAN COLLECTION (Area-Ethnic)
General Libraries, MAI 316   Phone: (512) 471-3135
Austin, TX 78712-7330   Kevin Lin, Libn.
Staff: Prof 2; Other 2. **Subjects:** China and Japan; art; history, especially of Meiji Period in Japan; politics; economics and statistics; anthropology; philosophy; literature; linguistics (in Chinese and Japanese); India, Bangladesh and Sri Lanka - language, literature, history, philosophy, religion, economics, government, education (in Hindi, Pali, Prakrit, Sanskrit, Urdu). **Special Collections:** Selected South Asian research materials in English - census of India, 1872-1951 on microfiche; bound censuses of India and Pakistan, and district gazetteers. **Holdings:** 72,000 books and bound periodical volumes; 10,546 microfiche; 711 reels of microfilm. **Subscriptions:** 366 journals and other serials; 15 newspapers. **Services:** Interlibrary loans; copying; library open to public. **Publications:** Library Guide. **Remarks:** Materials in Indian languages other than those stated above are in the Collection Deposit Library. **Staff:** Merry Burlingham, South Asian Libn.

★16232★
UNIVERSITY OF TEXAS, AUSTIN - BENSON LATIN AMERICAN COLLECTION (Area-Ethnic)
General Libraries, SRH 1.108   Phone: (512) 471-3818
Austin, TX 78712-7330   Laura Gutierrez-Witt, Libn.
Staff: Prof 5; Other 19. **Subjects:** Latin American anthropology, economics, education, geography, government, history, law, literature, music, philology, philosophy, religion, science; Mexican American history, social sciences and literature; studies on Hispanics in the U.S. **Special Collections:** Genaro Garcia; Joaquin Garcia Icazbalceta; Luis Garcia Pimentel; Alejandro Prieto; W.B. Stephens; Diego Munoz; Manuel Gondra; Hernandez y Davalos; Sanchez Navarro family; Simon Lucuix Rio de La Plata Library (21,000 volumes); Arturo Taracena Flores Library (Guatemala; 10,000 titles); Pedro Martinez Reales Gaucho Collection; Pablo Salce Arredondo Collection of Mexican Manuscripts and Imprints; Julio Cortazar Literary Papers; St. John del Rey Mining Company Archives from Brazil; Chicano Writers Manuscript Collection (21 linear feet); Archive of the League of United Latin American Citizens (70 linear feet); Raza Unida Party Archive (5 linear feet); Economy Furniture Company Strike Collection (3 linear feet); Carlos Castaneda Collection (35 linear feet); Eleuterio Escobar Collection (15 linear feet); Carlos Villalongin Dramatic Company Archives (247 playscripts; 32 photographs; 15 playbills and notices). **Holdings:** 453,800 volumes; 4 million pages of manuscripts; 18,000 reels of microfilm; 15,000 maps; 11,431 microfiche; 20,086 pages of broadsides; 22,100 prints and photographs; 10,000 volumes of newspapers; 1273 phonograph records; 2595 slides. **Subscriptions:** 18,774 journals and other serials. **Services:** Interlibrary loans; copying; library open to public for reference use only. **Publications:** Catalog of the Benson Latin American Collection; Bibliographic Guide to Latin American Studies; Mexican American Archives in the Benson Collection: A Supplement for Educators; Chicano Film Guide, 2nd edition; Archives and Manuscripts on Microfilm in the Nettie Lee Benson Latin American Collection: A Checklist; Mexican American Archives in the Benson Collection: A Guide for Users; Inventory of the Records of the Cuban Consulate, Key West, Florida, 1886-1961 (microfilm); Revolution and Counterrevolution in Guatemala, 1944-1983: An Annotated Bibliography of Materials in the Benson Latin American Collection. **Remarks:** Includes the holdings of University of Texas, Austin - Mexican American Library Program. **Staff:** Ann Hartness-Kane, Asst.Hd.Libn.; Jane Garner, Archv.; Donald Gibbs, Bibliog.; Anne Jordan, Rare Bks.Libn.

★16233★
UNIVERSITY OF TEXAS, AUSTIN - BUREAU OF BUSINESS RESEARCH - INFORMATION SERVICES (Bus-Fin)
Box 7459, University Sta.   Phone: (512) 471-1616
Austin, TX 78713   Rita J. Wright, Libn.
Founded: 1926. **Staff:** Prof 1; Other 2. **Subjects:** Texas - demographics, economics, industries. **Holdings:** 1000 books; Texas and U.S. government documents; publications from other bureaus of business research. **Subscriptions:** 300 journals and other serials. **Services:** Copying; services

are primarily for use of research staff of Bureau, faculty of Graduate School of Business and graduate students; inquiries for information from the public are answered; library open to public. **Computerized Information Services:** Directory of Texas Manufacturers (internal database). Performs searches on fee basis. Contact Person: Laurie Gamel. **Publications:** Texas Trade and Professional Associations, biennial; Texas Fact Book, annual.

★16234★
UNIVERSITY OF TEXAS, AUSTIN - BUREAU OF ECONOMIC GEOLOGY READING ROOM/DATA CENTER (Sci-Tech)
Balcones Research Center
10100 Burnet Road
Austin, TX 78758-4497   Kay Forward, Mgr.
Staff: 3. **Subjects:** Texas geology, mineral data, Texas water resources. **Special Collections:** Maps (56 VF drawers); open file reports (32 VF drawers). **Holdings:** 5000 volumes. **Services:** Reading room open to public for reference use only.

★16235★
UNIVERSITY OF TEXAS, AUSTIN - CENTER FOR ENERGY STUDIES - ENERGY INFORMATION SERVICE (Energy)
ENS 143   Phone: (512) 471-4946
Austin, TX 78712   Carol J. Wallin, Res.Assoc.
Founded: 1974. **Staff:** Prof 1; Other 1. **Subjects:** Energy resources - petroleum, natural gas, solar, geothermal, electric, nuclear, coal; energy conservation, policy and technology. **Holdings:** 2500 books; 150 bound periodical volumes; 4 VF drawers of clippings; 33,000 reports on microfiche; 300 pamphlets. **Subscriptions:** 126 journals and other serials. **Services:** Copying; service open to public. **Publications:** Recent Acquisitions, monthly - for internal distribution only.

★16236★
UNIVERSITY OF TEXAS, AUSTIN - CENTER FOR INTERCULTURAL STUDIES IN FOLKLORE AND ETHNOMUSICOLOGY - LIBRARY (Soc Sci)
Student Services Bldg., Rm. 3.106   Phone: (512) 471-1288
Austin, TX 78712   Dr. Richard Bauman, Dir.
Founded: 1970. **Staff:** 1. **Subjects:** Folklore, anthropology, sociology, ethnomusicology. **Holdings:** 900 books; 540 bound periodical volumes; 600 articles. **Subscriptions:** 18 journals and other serials.

★16237★
UNIVERSITY OF TEXAS, AUSTIN - CENTER FOR TRANSPORTATION RESEARCH (Trans)
ECJ 2.510   Phone: (512) 471-1414
Austin, TX 78712   Betty Hudman, Libn.
Staff: Prof 1; Other 1. **Subjects:** Transportation planning, transportation and highway engineering. **Special Collections:** NTIS Technical Reports on microfiche. **Holdings:** 300 books; 7500 reports; 430 unbound periodical volumes; 13,250 microforms. **Subscriptions:** 25 journals and other serials. **Services:** Interlibrary loans; copying; SDI; center open to public. **Computerized Information Services:** DIALOG. **Publications:** Selected Acquisitions List, semimonthly.

★16238★
UNIVERSITY OF TEXAS, AUSTIN - CHEMISTRY LIBRARY (Sci-Tech)
General Libraries, WEL 2.132   Phone: (512) 471-1303
Austin, TX 78712-7330   Aubrey E. Skinner, Libn.
Staff: Prof 1; Other 1. **Subjects:** Chemistry, biochemistry, nutrition, chemical engineering. **Holdings:** 21,956 books; 22,113 bound periodical volumes; 144 reels of microfilm; 2548 microfiche. **Subscriptions:** 623 journals and other serials. **Services:** Interlibrary loans; copying; library open to public. **Publications:** Library Guide. **Also Known As:** John W. Mallet Chemistry Library.

★16239★
UNIVERSITY OF TEXAS, AUSTIN - CLASSICS LIBRARY (Hum)
General Libraries, WAG 1   Phone: (512) 471-5742
Austin, TX 78712-7330   Bernice M. Dawson, Lib.Asst.
Staff: 1. **Subjects:** Greek literature, Latin literature, classical civilization, Greek and Latin language, classical archaeology, Greek and Roman history, epigraphy and numismatics. **Holdings:** 15,674 books; 1901 bound periodical volumes; 77 reels of microfilm. **Subscriptions:** 161 journals and other serials. **Services:** Interlibrary loans; copying; library open to public. **Publications:** Library Guide.

★16240★
UNIVERSITY OF TEXAS, AUSTIN - DOCUMENTS COLLECTION (Info Sci)
General Libraries, PCL 2.400   Phone: (512) 471-3813
Austin, TX 78712-7330   Kathleen Eisenbeis, Libn.
Staff: Prof 2; Other 5. **Subjects:** U.S. government documents, U.N. documents. **Holdings:** 197,345 U.S. documents; 78,727 U.N. documents. **Services:** Interlibrary loans; copying; library open to public.

★16241★
UNIVERSITY OF TEXAS, AUSTIN - ENGINEERING LIBRARY (Sci-Tech)
General Libraries, ECJ 1.300   Phone: (512) 471-1610
Austin, TX 78712-7330   Susan B. Ardis, Libn.
Staff: Prof 2; Other 4. **Subjects:** Aerospace, civil, electrical, mechanical and petroleum engineering; engineering mechanics; meteorology; applied mathematics. **Holdings:** 46,164 books; 54,602 bound periodical volumes; 466,433 microfiche (including DOE technical reports); 1322 reels of microfilm; 82,015 microcards; 27,849 hardcopy earlier AEC technical reports; U.S. Patent Depository Library. **Subscriptions:** 2301 journals and other serials. **Services:** Interlibrary loans; copying; library open to public. **Publications:** Library Guide. **Also Known As:** Richard W. McKinney Library. **Staff:** Charlotte Eisman, Asst.Engr.Libn.

★16242★
UNIVERSITY OF TEXAS, AUSTIN - EUGENE C. BARKER TEXAS HISTORY CENTER (Hist)
General Libraries, SRH 2.109   Phone: (512) 471-5961
Austin, TX 78712-7330   Dr. Don E. Carleton, Hd.Libn./Archv.
Staff: Prof 8; Other 15. **Subjects:** Texas history, literature and folklore; Texas state documents; University of Texas publications and history; Southern and Western history. **Special Collections:** Dime novel collection; Kell Frontier Collection; Austin papers; Bexar Archives; Bryan papers; T.S. Henderson papers; James S. Hogg papers; Ashbel Smith papers; Jesse Jones papers; James Wells papers; Martin M. Crane papers; Luther M. Evans Collection; James Harper Starr papers; True West archives. **Holdings:** 127,000 volumes; 3000 linear feet of university records; 22,500 linear feet of non-university records; 20,000 items in cartographic collection; 2000 titles of historic Texas newspapers; 100 VF drawers of clippings; 1500 scrapbooks; 8335 reels of microfilm; 605 tapes of oral recordings; sound archives. **Subscriptions:** 424 journals and other serials. **Services:** Interlibrary loans; copying; center open to public. **Publications:** Archives Guide; Library Guide. **Staff:** Katherine Adams, Asst.Hd.Libn./Archv.; Ralph Elder, Pub.Serv.; Mary Beth Fleischer, Asst.Libn.

★16243★
UNIVERSITY OF TEXAS, AUSTIN - FILM LIBRARY (Aud-Vis)
General Libraries, EDA G-12
Box W   Phone: (512) 471-3572
Austin, TX 78712-7448   Jane Hazelton, Media Coord.
Staff: Prof 1; Other 6. **Special Collections:** Films of University of Texas football games, 1937 to present. **Holdings:** 3464 16mm educational films; 206 slide/tape programs; 12 video cassettes. **Services:** Interlibrary loans; rentals; library open to public. **Networks/Consortia:** Member of Consortium of University Film Centers. **Publications:** Bridges for Ideas (media handbook series). **Special Catalogs:** Learning Resource Guide (film catalog); selected film listings on various subjects.

★16244★
UNIVERSITY OF TEXAS, AUSTIN - FINE ARTS LIBRARY (Art; Mus)
General Libraries, FAB 3.200   Phone: (512) 471-4777
Austin, TX 78712-7330   Carole Cable, Fine Arts Libn.
Staff: Prof 4; Other 8. **Subjects:** Art history, aesthetics, studio art, philosophy of art, art education, play production, drama education, theatrical designing, playwriting, dance, applied music, composition, ethnomusicology, music education, music theory, musicology. **Holdings:** 110,276 books; 10,380 bound periodical volumes; prints and mounted photographs; VF drawers of pamphlets, clippings; 13,706 phonograph records; 922 tapes; cassettes; 977 slides; 2941 reels of microfilm; 16,458 microfiche; 992 microcards. **Subscriptions:** 1104 journals and other serials. **Services:** Interlibrary loans; copying; library open to public. **Publications:** Library Guide. **Staff:** Joyce Hess, Art; Olga Buth, Music; Karl F. Miller, AV Libn.

★16245★
UNIVERSITY OF TEXAS, AUSTIN - GEOLOGY LIBRARY (Sci-Tech)
General Libraries, GEO 302   Phone: (512) 471-1257
Austin, TX 78712   Chestalene Pintozzi, Libn.
Staff: Prof 1; Other 2. **Subjects:** Geology, paleontology, mineralogy, geophysics, petroleum geology, oceanography, volcanology. **Holdings:** 59,349 books and bound periodical volumes; 148 reels of microfilm; 1817 microfiche; 29,540 maps. **Subscriptions:** 1334 journals and other serials.

Services: Interlibrary loans; copying; library open to public. Publications: Library Guide. Also Known As: Joseph C. Walter, Jr. and Elizabeth C. Walter Geology Library.

★16246★
UNIVERSITY OF TEXAS, AUSTIN - HARRY RANSOM HUMANITIES RESEARCH CENTER (Hum)
Box 7219　　　　　　　　　　　Phone: (512) 471-1833
Austin, TX 78712　　　　　　　　　Decherd Turner, Dir.
Staff: Prof 18; Other 37. Subjects: American literature, English literature, French literature, photography, theater arts, book arts. Special Collections: Norman Bel Geddes (250,000 items); Alfred A. and Blanche Knopf Library and Publishing Archives (100,000 items); David O. Selznick film archives (1 million items); Miriam Lutcher Stark Library (10,000 items); John Henry Wrenn Library (6000 items). Holdings: 9 million pages of manuscripts; 800,000 volumes; 4 million photographic images; 3000 linear feet of clippings, playbills and miscellaneous files; 80,000 other items, including art. Services: Copying; use of unique materials requires approval of faculty committee. Computerized Information Services: OCLC. Networks/Consortia: Member of AMIGOS Bibliographic Council, Inc. Publications: University of Texas Library Chronicle, 4/year; exhibition catalogs; catalogs of collections; bibliographies; bibliographical monographs. Staff: Carlton Lake, Exec.Cur., French Coll.Don Etherington, Asst.Dir./Consrv.Off.; Sally Leach, Asst. to the Dir.; Catherine Henderson, Res.Libn.; John Chalmers, Libn.W.H. Crain, Cur., Theater Arts; Roy Flukinger, Cur., Photog.; Maria X. Wells, Cur., Italian Coll.

★16247★
UNIVERSITY OF TEXAS, AUSTIN - HOGG FOUNDATION FOR MENTAL HEALTH - LIBRARY (Soc Sci)
W.C. Hogg Bldg., Rm. 301　　　　　Phone: (512) 471-5041
Austin, TX 78712　　　　　　　　　Anita Faubion, Libn.
Staff: 2. Subjects: Psychology, psychiatry, gerontology, learning disabilities, parenting, social work, sociology, education, family life. Special Collections: Regional Foundation Library, depository of the Foundation Center in N.Y. (Internal Revenue Service tax returns from foundations in Texas); collection on foundations and philanthropy, grant seeking, proposal writing and fund-raising information. Holdings: 1500 books; 300 Foundation annual reports. Subscriptions: 16 journals and newsletters. Services: Library open to public.

★16248★
UNIVERSITY OF TEXAS, AUSTIN - HUMANITIES RESEARCH CENTER - THEATRE ARTS COLLECTIONS (Theater)
Box 7219　　　　　　　　　　　Phone: (512) 471-9122
Austin, TX 78712
Staff: Prof 2; Other 5. Special Collections: Gloria Swanson Collection (500,000 items, 20,000 photographs); David O. Selznick Collection; Ernest Lehman Collection; M-G-M Matte Drawings; Maurice Zolotow Collection; Alfred Junge Collection; King Vidor Collection. Holdings: 15,000 books; 40,000 bound periodical volumes; 100 films and videotapes; stills; manuscripts; screenplays; TV scripts; contracts; legal documents; clippings; posters; advertising materials; financial records; set designs and set models. Subscriptions: 53 journals and other serials. Services: Copying; library open to public by appointment for reference use. Staff: Dr. William H. Crain, Cur.; Dr. Raymond W. Daum, Cur.

★16249★
UNIVERSITY OF TEXAS, AUSTIN - INSTITUTE FOR GEOPHYSICS - LIBRARY (Sci-Tech)
4920 North IH 35
Austin, TX 78751　　　　　　　　Josefa A. York, Libn.
Founded: 1973. Staff: Prof 1. Subjects: Geophysics, marine geology, seismology, earth sciences, planetary science, oceanography. Holdings: 3029 books; 1602 bound periodical volumes; 77 dissertations; 61 VF drawers of reprints, pamphlets and documents; 1959 maps; 18,000 tapes of marine seismic profiling data; 14,000 tapes and 33,000 seismograms of lunar and martian seismograph data; Central American seismograph network data, 1974 to present; World Seismograph Network microfilm library, 1972-1975; ocean bottom seismograph data. Subscriptions: 269 journals and other serials. Services: Interlibrary loans; copying; library open to public for reference use only. Computerized Information Services: DIALOG. Publications: List of publications - available upon request.

UNIVERSITY OF TEXAS, AUSTIN - LYNDON B. JOHNSON SCHOOL OF PUBLIC AFFAIRS LIBRARY
See: University of Texas, Austin - Wasserman Public Affairs Library

★16250★
UNIVERSITY OF TEXAS, AUSTIN - MAP COLLECTION (Geog-Map)
General Libraries, PCL 1.306　　　　Phone: (512) 471-5944
Austin, TX 78712-7330　　　　　　Dennis Dillon, Map Libn.
Staff: Prof 1; Other 1. Subjects: Maps. Special Collections: Depository for U.S. Geological Survey topographic quadrangles; maps from U.S. Defense Mapping Agency, Special Foreign Currency Program, U.S. Air Force and U.S. National Ocean Survey. Holdings: 339 volumes; 172,139 maps. Services: Interlibrary loans; copying; library open to public.

★16251★
UNIVERSITY OF TEXAS, AUSTIN - MEXICAN AMERICAN LIBRARY PROGRAM
Austin, TX 78712
Defunct. Holdings absorbed by University of Texas, Austin - Benson Latin American Collection.

★16252★
UNIVERSITY OF TEXAS, AUSTIN - MIDDLE EAST COLLECTION (Area-Ethnic)
General Libraries, MAI 316　　　　Phone: (512) 471-4675
Austin, TX 78712-7330　　　　　　Abazar Sepehri, Libn.
Staff: Prof 1; Other 4. Subjects: Arabic and Persian language and literature; general Middle East studies in the vernacular. Holdings: 40,790 books; 2755 bound periodical volumes; 551 reels of microfilm; 3766 microfiche. Subscriptions: 439 journals and other serials. Services: Interlibrary loans; copying; collection open to public. Publications: Library Guide (introductory brochure); Middle East Collection: A Guide for Faculty and Students.

★16253★
UNIVERSITY OF TEXAS, AUSTIN - NATURAL FIBERS INFORMATION CENTER (Agri)*
University Sta., Box 8180　　　　　Phone: (512) 471-1063
Austin, TX 78712　　　　　　　　Mary P. Green, Act.Dir.
Staff: 3. Subjects: Agricultural and economic statistics, export and import statistics, natural fibers (cotton, wool, mohair), oilseeds, production, climatological data. Holdings: 1600 books; 2000 bound periodical volumes; 140,000 pamphlets, circulars; 200 manuscripts; 12 VF drawers of climatological summaries and meteorological charts; 400 fiber and fabric samples; 2 VF drawers of photographs and negatives. Subscriptions: 231 journals and other serials. Services: Minor statistical searches; abstract service; center open to public for reference use only. Publications: Abstracts, 12/year; climatological summaries and meteorological drought charts, irregular.

★16254★
UNIVERSITY OF TEXAS, AUSTIN - ORAL BUSINESS HISTORY PROJECT
BEB 454C
Austin, TX 78712
Defunct

★16255★
UNIVERSITY OF TEXAS, AUSTIN - PHYSICS-MATHEMATICS-ASTRONOMY LIBRARY (Sci-Tech)
General Libraries, RLM 4.200　　　　Phone: (512) 471-7539
Austin, TX 78712-7330　　　　　　John H. Sandy, Libn.
Staff: Prof 1; Other 2. Subjects: Astronomy, physics, mathematics. Holdings: 28,174 books; 28,035 bound periodical volumes; 193 reels of microfilm; 15 microfiche; 1500 35mm microfilm strips. Subscriptions: 739 journals and other serials. Services: Interlibrary loans; copying; library open to public. Publications: Library Guide. Also Known As: John M. Kuehne Library.

★16256★
UNIVERSITY OF TEXAS, AUSTIN - POPULATION RESEARCH CENTER LIBRARY (Soc Sci)
1800 Main Bldg.　　　　　　　　Phone: (512) 471-5514
Austin, TX 78712　　　　　　　　Doreen S. Goyer, Dir., Lib. Core
Founded: 1960. Staff: Prof 2; Other 1. Subjects: Population and census data, human ecology, human fertility. Special Collections: International census publications (covers 80% of all bona fide national population censuses taken; 25,000 items). Holdings: 7000 books; 27 file drawers of reprints, unbound reports and other ephemera; 440 linear feet of periodicals; 200 microfiche; 1042 reels of microfilm. Subscriptions: 80 journals and other serials. Services: Interlibrary loans; copying; library open to qualified researchers. Computerized Information Services: NLM. Performs searches on cost recovery basis. Networks/Consortia: Member of APLIC Census Network. Publications: International Population Census Bibliography, Handbook of National Population Censuses (1983).

★16257★

UNIVERSITY OF TEXAS, AUSTIN - SCHOOL OF LAW - TARLTON LAW LIBRARY (Law)
727 E. 26th St.   Phone: (512) 471-7726
Austin, TX 78705   Roy M. Mersky, Dir. of Res.
Founded: 1885. **Staff:** Prof 22; Other 20. **Subjects:** Anglo-American law, international law. **Special Collections:** U.S. government depository; AEI depository; European communities depository; U.N. documents; briefs of U.S. Supreme Court, 5th Circuit Court of Appeals (Texas cases) and Texas courts. **Holdings:** 620,000 books and bound periodical volumes; 19,600 microcards; 6296 reels of microfilm; 294,754 microfiche. **Subscriptions:** 7443 journals and other serials. **Services:** Interlibrary loans; SDI; library open to public. **Automated Operations:** Computerized cataloging, acquisitions and ILL. **Computerized Information Services:** LEXIS, Westlaw, DIALOG, BRS, Commerce Clearing House Electronic Legislative Search System (ELSS), OCLC, ALANET, RLIN. **Publications:** Tarlton Law Library Legal Bibliography Series, irregular; Notes from the Tarlton Law Library, bimonthly; Contents Pages of Legal Periodicals, weekly. **Special Indexes:** Index to Periodical Articles Related to Law. **Staff:** Gary Gott, Assoc.Libn., Tech.Serv.; Mickie A. Voges, Dir., Info.Serv.; Dan Dabney, Ref.Libn.; Eleanor DeLashmitt, Ref.Libn.; Leslie Prather-Forbis, Ref.Libn.; Pierrette Moreno, Circ.; Barbara Bridges, Govt.Doc.Libn.; John H. Petesch, Cat.Libn.; Adrienne deVergie, Cat.Libn.; Andrew Barnes, Cat.Libn.; Susan L. More, Acq.Libn.; Carole W. Knobil, Assoc.Libn., Spec.Coll.; Daniel Martin, Asst.Adm.Libn.; Mary Menke, Ser.Libn.

★16258★

UNIVERSITY OF TEXAS, AUSTIN - SCIENCE LIBRARY (Sci-Tech)
General Libraries, MAI 220   Phone: (512) 471-1475
Austin, TX 78712-7330   Nancy Elder, Libn.
Staff: Prof 2; Other 3. **Subjects:** Botany, microbiology, zoology, genetics, ecology, marine biology, pharmacy, pharmacology, pharmacognosy, pharmaceutical administration, pharmaceutical chemistry. **Special Collections:** Gray Herbarium Index. **Holdings:** 53,130 volumes; 50,008 bound periodical volumes; 1381 reels of microfilm; 8424 microfiche; 1032 microcards. **Subscriptions:** 1821 journals and other serials. **Services:** Interlibrary loans; copying; library open to public. **Publications:** Library Guide.

★16259★

UNIVERSITY OF TEXAS, AUSTIN - WASSERMAN PUBLIC AFFAIRS LIBRARY (Soc Sci)
General Libraries
Sid Richardson Hall, 3.243   Phone: (512) 471-4486
Austin, TX 78712-7330   Olive Forbes, Hd.Libn.
Staff: Prof 2; Other 10. **Subjects:** Politics and government, public administration, public finance, social problems and policy, civil rights, discrimination, public welfare, pollution and environmental policy, education, regional and municipal planning, public health, evaluation research. **Special Collections:** Budgets and financial reports for selected cities, counties and states; Henry David Manpower Policy Collection; state documents; selective U.S. documents depository since 1968 (45,000 documents). **Holdings:** 45,000 volumes; 90 VF drawers of pamphlets; 1900 reels of microfilm; 38,900 microfiche. **Subscriptions:** 1690 journals and other serials. **Services:** Copying; library open to public and to state and local government officials and employees. **Formerly:** Its Lyndon B. Johnson School of Public Affairs Library.

UNIVERSITY OF TEXAS, AUSTIN - WINEDALE HISTORICAL CENTER
See: Winedale Historical Center

★16260★

UNIVERSITY OF TEXAS, DALLAS - CALLIER CENTER FOR COMMUNICATIONS DISORDERS - LIBRARY (Educ; Aud-Vis)
1966 Inwood Rd.   Phone: (214) 783-3143
Dallas, TX 75235   Edward James Earle, Libn.
Founded: 1969. **Staff:** Prof 1; Other 1. **Subjects:** Education of the deaf, language development, communication disorders. **Holdings:** 2200 professional books; 1000 bound periodical volumes; 800 children's books; 10 AV kits; 30 videotapes; 370 kits; 80 sets of study prints and pictures. **Subscriptions:** 85 journals and other serials. **Services:** Library open to public with restrictions on borrowing.

UNIVERSITY OF TEXAS, DALLAS - GEOLOGICAL INFORMATION LIBRARY OF DALLAS
See: Geological Information Library of Dallas (GILD)

★16261★

UNIVERSITY OF TEXAS, EL PASO - INSTITUTE OF ORAL HISTORY (Hist)
Liberal Arts 339   Phone: (915) 747-5488
El Paso, TX 79968   Vicki L. Ruiz, Ph.D., Dir.
Staff: Prof 2; Other 2. **Subjects:** History - El Paso and Ciudad Juarez,

Chihuahua; history of University of Texas, El Paso; Mexican Americans; the Border; the Mexican Revolution; Border Labor History. **Holdings:** 550 manuscripts; 900 magnetic tapes. **Services:** Institute open to public. **Special Catalogs:** Catalog of Oral History Program; interviewee and subject files (card).

★16262★

UNIVERSITY OF TEXAS, EL PASO - LIBRARY - DOCUMENTS/MAPS LIBRARY (Soc Sci; Geog-Map)
Library Annex   Phone: (915) 747-5685
El Paso, TX 79968   Brenda McDonald, Hd.
Founded: 1974. **Staff:** Prof 1; Other 4. **Subjects:** Economics and business, political science, geology, history, sociology, sciences. **Special Collections:** U.S. documents depository (110,492 items); Texas documents depository (9571 items); U.S. Geological Survey maps depository; National Oceanic and Atmospheric Administration maps; Defense Mapping Agency (total map collection 76,040 items). **Holdings:** 592,202 volumes; 12,724 reels of microfilm; 160,206 microfiche; 4600 microprints. **Services:** Interlibrary loans; copying; SDI; library open to public with restrictions. **Computerized Information Services:** DIALOG, BRS, OCLC through University Library). **Networks/Consortia:** Member of AMIGOS Bibliographic Council, Inc. **Publications:** Government Documents (newsletter), bimonthly - campus distribution; Carto-points, quarterly - to map libraries in the U.S. and to interested faculty. **Special Indexes:** Subject index to microforms (card); subject and area index to maps (card).

★16263★

UNIVERSITY OF TEXAS, EL PASO - LIBRARY - S.L.A. MARSHALL MILITARY HISTORY COLLECTION (Mil; Hist)
Rm. 139   Phone: (915) 747-5697
El Paso, TX 79968-0582   Thomas B. Burdett, Cur.
Founded: 1974. **Staff:** 1. **Subjects:** Military history from antiquity to the present with emphasis on World Wars I and II, British colonial wars, Vietnamese conflict, Israeli wars, Korean War. **Special Collections:** Brigadier General S.L.A. Marshall papers (67 linear feet of papers; 42 linear feet of memorabilia); Rear Admiral Edwin C. Parsons papers (10 linear feet); Major General Frank S. Ross papers (2 linear feet); Major Edward F. Hinkle papers (1 linear foot). **Holdings:** 7000 books; 33 bound periodical volumes; miscellaneous collections of military papers. **Services:** Copying; collection open to public for reference use only. **Publications:** Newsletter of the S.L.A. Marshall Military History Collection, semiannual - to mailing list.

★16264★

UNIVERSITY OF TEXAS, EL PASO - LIBRARY - SPECIAL COLLECTIONS (Hum)
                                                        Phone: (915) 747-5684
El Paso, TX 79968   Fred W. Hanes, Dir. of Libs.
Founded: 1913. **Special Collections:** Southwest and Border Studies (8440 books); rare books (5865); western fiction (1680 books); art (6225 books); Judaica (1730 books); Hertzog (1370 books); Mexican Archives on microfilm (2047 reels); oral history (391 reels; 227 transcripts); manuscripts (458 collections); military history (7000 books); Chicano studies (1300 books; 40 films and other AV items). **Services:** Interlibrary loans (limited); copying; collections open to public. **Automated Operations:** Computerized cataloging. **Computerized Information Services:** DIALOG, BRS, OCLC. **Networks/Consortia:** Member of AMIGOS Bibliographic Council, Inc. **Special Catalogs:** Mexico and the Southwest: Microfilm Holdings of Historical Documents and Rare books at the University of Texas at El Paso Library. **Staff:** Cesar Caballero, Hd.Spec.Coll.Dept.; Juan A. Sandoval, Hd. Chicano Serv.

★16265★

UNIVERSITY OF TEXAS, EL PASO - NURSING/MEDICAL LIBRARY (Med)
                                                        Phone: (915) 533-6094
El Paso, TX 79968   Esperanza A. Moreno, Hd.Libn.
Founded: 1892. **Staff:** Prof 1; Other 3. **Subjects:** Nursing, medicine, allied health sciences. **Special Collections:** Lois J. Wikoff, R.N., Memorial Historical Nursing Collection. **Holdings:** 16,491 books; 11,179 bound periodical volumes; 14 VF drawers of pamphlets. **Subscriptions:** 354 journals and other serials. **Services:** Interlibrary loans; copying; library open to non-professionals for reference only. **Automated Operations:** Computerized cataloging, acquisitions and serials. **Computerized Information Services:** BRS, MEDLARS. **Networks/Consortia:** Member of Del Norte Biosciences Library Consortium. **Publications:** Journal holdings list, biennial; Union List of Serials, 1984 (2nd edition; computerized). **Staff:** Alice M. Chavez, Libn. I.

★16266★

UNIVERSITY OF TEXAS, EL PASO - SCIENCE/ENGINEERING/ MATHEMATICS LIBRARY (Sci-Tech)

Library Annex
El Paso, TX 79968
Phone: (915) 747-5138
Fletcher C. Newman, Hd.
Staff: Prof 1; Other 3. Subjects: Science, engineering, mathematics. Special Collections: Landmarks of Science (10,000 volumes on microcard). Holdings: 75,000 books; 40,000 bound periodical volumes; 1400 reels of microfilm; 22,000 other microforms. Subscriptions: 1100 journals and other serials. Services: Interlibrary loans; copying; library open to public for reference use only.

★16267★

UNIVERSITY OF TEXAS, EL PASO - TEACHING MATERIALS CENTER (Educ)

College of Education
El Paso, TX 79968
Phone: (915) 747-5417
Jean Stevens, Hd.
Founded: 1972. Staff: Prof 1; Other 2. Subjects: Education - elementary, secondary, special and physical; educational psychology and administration. Holdings: 42,915 books; 5000 bound periodical volumes; 2600 curriculum guides; 350 subject folders of pamphlets. Subscriptions: 243 journals and other serials. Services: Interlibrary loans; copying; center open to public with restrictions. Automated Operations: Computerized cataloging. Computerized Information Services: OCLC. Networks/Consortia: Member of AMIGOS Bibliographic Council, Inc. Formerly: Its Education Library.

★16268★

UNIVERSITY OF TEXAS HEALTH SCIENCE CENTER, DALLAS - LIBRARY (Med)

5323 Harry Hines Blvd.
Dallas, TX 75235
Phone: (214) 688-3368
Jean K. Miller, Dir.
Founded: 1943. Staff: Prof 19; Other 35. Subjects: Medicine, biochemistry, biological science, medical specialities. Special Collections: Medical history. Holdings: 174,227 volumes; 2543 AV titles; 22,782 microforms. Subscriptions: 2425 journals and other serials; 5 newspapers. Services: Interlibrary loans; copying; SDI; library open to public. Automated Operations: Computerized cataloging, serials and circulation. Computerized Information Services: DIALOG, SDC, OCLC, BRS, Informatics, Inc., PHILSOM. Networks/Consortia: Member of TALON; Association for Higher Education of North Texas - Library Committee (AHE); AMIGOS Bibliographic Council, Inc. Publications: Library Acquisitions newsletter, monthly - to faculty and by request; Annual Report - by request. Staff: Patricia Armes, Assoc.Dir.; Carmel Bush, Hd., Cat.; William Maina, Asst.Dir., Pub.Serv.; Patricia McKeown, Hd., Comp.Ref.; James Craig, Assoc.Dir., TALON;Mary Rydesky, Hd., LRC; Helen Mayo, Hd., Ref.; Robert Want, Search Anl.; Linda Kondraske, Search Anl.; Gay Langston, Hd., Circ.; Brenda Mahar, Hd., ILL; Marianne Babitch, Ref.; Susan Bader, Ref.; Sherry Porter, Ser.; Paula Galbraith, Online Serv., TALON; Sue Ramond, Ref.

★16269★

UNIVERSITY OF TEXAS HEALTH SCIENCE CENTER, HOUSTON - DENTAL BRANCH LIBRARY (Med)

Box 20068
Houston, TX 77225
Phone: (713) 792-4094
Lorrayne B. Webb, Libn.
Founded: 1943. Staff: Prof 2; Other 3. Subjects: Dentistry. Special Collections: History of dentistry. Holdings: 11,800 books; 12,400 bound periodical volumes; theses. Subscriptions: 343 journals and other serials. Services: Interlibrary loans; copying; library open to public for reference use only. Automated Operations: Computerized circulation. Publications: Current Awareness of Periodicals. Staff: Ann T. Williams, Asst.Libn.

★16270★

UNIVERSITY OF TEXAS HEALTH SCIENCE CENTER, SAN ANTONIO - BRADY/GREEN EDUCATIONAL RESOURCES CENTER (Med)

4502 Medical Dr.
San Antonio, TX 78284
Phone: (512) 223-6361
Rajia C. Tobia, Libn.
Founded: 1958. Staff: Prof 1; Other 2. Subjects: Obstetrics, pediatrics, psychiatry, family practice, general medicine. Holdings: 1228 books; 3529 bound periodical volumes. Subscriptions: 148 journals and other serials. Services: Interlibrary loans; copying; center open to public. Computerized Information Services: DIALOG, SDC, BRS, MEDLARS. Networks/Consortia: Member of Health Oriented Libraries of San Antonio (HOLSA).

★16271★

UNIVERSITY OF TEXAS HEALTH SCIENCE CENTER, SAN ANTONIO - LIBRARY (Med)

7703 Floyd Curl Dr.
San Antonio, TX 78284
Phone: (512) 691-6271
Dr. David A. Kronick, Libn.
Founded: 1968. Staff: Prof 8; Other 31. Subjects: Health related sciences, nursing, dentistry. Special Collections: History of medicine (5000 volumes).

Holdings: 71,000 books; 70,000 bound periodical volumes; 2700 AV titles. Subscriptions: 2600 journals and other serials. Services: Interlibrary loans; copying; SDI; film booking; library open to public for reference use only. Automated Operations: Computerized cataloging, serials and circulation. Computerized Information Services: DIALOG, OCLC, Library Information Services (LIS), SDC, BRS, NLM; Networks/Consortia: Member of PHILSOM; AMIGOS Bibliographic Council, Inc.; Council of Research and Academic Libraries (CORAL). Publications: Library Acquisitions; Library Bibliography Series; UTHSCSA Publications; Library News. Special Catalogs: Videotape Catalog; Multimedia Catalog. Staff: Virginia Bowden, Assoc.Dir.; Sally Bethea, Asst.Dir.Pub.Serv.; Sallieann Swanner, Asst.Dir.Tech.Serv.; Ellen Todd Hanks, Coll.Dev.; Joyce Ray, Spec.Coll.Daniel Jones, ILL; Evelyn Olivier, Spec.Proj.; Barbara Greene, Asst.Dir., Tchg.Lrng.Ctr.; Martha Knott, Tchg.Lrng.Ctr.; Geraldine Eisenberg, Cat.; Rajia Tobia, Ref.; Patricia Riley, Ref.; Dan Taylor, Ref.; Ruth Uhlhorn, Ref./ILL; Ruth Bierschenk, Ref.; Anne Comeaux, Ref.

★16272★

UNIVERSITY OF TEXAS MEDICAL BRANCH - MOODY MEDICAL LIBRARY (Med)

Phone: (409) 765-1971
Galveston, TX 77550
Emil F. Frey, Dir.
Founded: 1891. Staff: Prof 18; Other 54. Subjects: Medicine, nursing, history of medicine, allied health sciences. Special Collections: History of medicine; medical prints and portraits. Holdings: 69,228 books; 151,626 bound periodical volumes; 33,200 other cataloged items; 1109 AV items. Subscriptions: 3509 journals and other serials; 15 newspapers. Services: Interlibrary loans; copying; SDI; library open to public. Automated Operations: Computerized cataloging, acquisitions, serials and circulation. Computerized Information Services: MEDLINE, OCLC. Networks/ Consortia: Member of AMIGOS Bibliographic Council, Inc.; TALON. Publications: The Bookman, 6/year. Special Catalogs: Rare books catalog (card and computer). Staff: Larry J. Wygant, Assoc.Dir., Pub.Serv.; John M. Smith, Assoc.Dir., Tech.Serv.; Pauline V. Power, Asst.Dir., Tech.Serv.; Mary M. Asbell, Ext.Libn.; Alexander C. Bienkowski, AV Libn.; Dr. Inci A. Bowman, Cur., Hist./Med.; Judith Rosenthal, Clin.Med.Libn.; Sheila Ross-Carter, ILL Libn.; Carol B. Phillips, Chf.Ref.Libn.Mary Ann Perussina, Ref.Libn.; Richard R. Rasche, Cat.,Hist.; Gary C. Rasmussen, Assoc.Dir., Auto.Serv.; William F. Sherwood, Systems Anl.; Katherine C. Odom, Clinical Med.Libn.; Alice C. Wygant, Ref.Libn.; Patricia Lee, Ref.Libn.; Patricia A. Ciejka, Clinical Med.Libn.

UNIVERSITY OF TEXAS SYSTEM CANCER CENTER
See: University of Texas - M.D. Anderson Hospital and Tumor Institute

★16273★

UNIVERSITY OF TOLEDO - COLLEGE OF LAW LIBRARY (Law)

2801 W. Bancroft St.
Toledo, OH 43606
Phone: (419) 537-2733
Janet L. Wallin, Law Libn.
Staff: Prof 5; Other 6. Subjects: Law. Special Collections: Josef L. Kunz Collection (international and comparative law; 1000 volumes). Holdings: 140,936 books and bound periodical volumes; 30,842 volumes in microform. Subscriptions: 2808 journals and other serials. Services: Interlibrary loans; library open to public. Automated Operations: Computerized cataloging and ILL. Computerized Information Services: LEXIS, OCLC. Publications: Recent Acquisitions List, monthly - distributed on request. Staff: P. Michael Whipple, Assoc. Law Libn.; Diane S. Bitter, Cat.; Theodore A. Potter, Acq.; Clara Smith, Circ.; Joseph Fugere, Evening Supv.

★16274★

UNIVERSITY OF TOLEDO - WARD M. CANADAY CENTER (Hum)

William S. Carlson Library
Toledo, OH 43606
Phone: (419) 537-2443
David J. Martz, Jr., Dir.
Staff: Prof 2; Other 2. Subjects: 20th century American poetry, 20th century Southern authors, 20th century black American literature, university history, history of books and printing. Special Collections: Ezra Pound Collection (300 volumes); William Faulkner Collection (480 volumes); William Dean Howells Collection (140 volumes); Herbert W. Martin Collection (15 feet); Etheridge Knight Collection (10 feet); Richard T. Gosser Collection (20 feet); Jean Gould Collection (11 feet); university archives (900 feet); Manuscript Collection (8 feet). J.H. Leigh Hunt (100 volumes); Scott Nearing (50 volumes); T.S. Eliot (200 volumes); William Carlos Williams (75 volumes); Marianne Moore (75 volumes); Broadside Press (200 items). Services: Copying; center open to public. Automated Operations: Computerized cataloging. Computerized Information Services: OCLC. Publications: Friends of The University of Toledo Libraries; exhibition catalogs. Special Catalogs: Card catalogs to 20th Century Black Authors Collection, William Faulkner Collection, University of Toldeo Theses and Dissertations Collection and 20th century American poetry. Staff: Joel F. Wurl, Archv.

★16275★

UNIVERSITY OF TORONTO - A.E. MAC DONALD OPHTHALMIC LIBRARY (Med)

1 Spadina Crescent   Phone: (416) 978-2635
Toronto, ON, Canada M5S 2J5   Amy Reszczynski, Sec.
Staff: 1. **Subjects:** Ophthalmology. **Special Collections:** Historical collection. **Holdings:** 1000 bound periodical volumes; reprints of publications by Ophthalmology Department members (1950 to present). **Subscriptions:** 25 journals and other serials. **Services:** Interlibrary loans; library not open to public.

★16276★

UNIVERSITY OF TORONTO - ANTHROPOLOGY READING ROOM (Soc Sci)

Sidney Smith Hall, Rm. 560A
100 St. George St.   Phone: (416) 978-3296
Toronto, ON, Canada M5S 1A1   Tessa J. Ireland, Sec.
Founded: 1967. **Staff:** 1. **Subjects:** Archeology; physical, social and cultural anthropology; linguistics. **Special Collections:** Human Relations Area Files. **Holdings:** 2478 volumes; 61,900 microforms. **Services:** Reading room open to public with restrictions. **Publications:** Accession list, monthly - for internal distribution only. **Special Catalogs:** Department of Anthropology publications; International Biological Program reports.

★16277★

UNIVERSITY OF TORONTO - ASTRONOMY LIBRARY (Sci-Tech)

60 St. George St., Rm. 1306   Phone: (416) 884-2112
Toronto, ON, Canada M5S 187   Lynda Colbeck, Libn.
Founded: 1933. **Staff:** Prof 1. Other 1. **Subjects:** Astronomy, astrophysics, radio astronomy. **Holdings:** 20,000 books, bound periodical volumes, observatory publications. **Subscriptions:** 480 journals and other serials. **Services:** Interlibrary loans; copying; library open to public for reference use only. **Publications:** Acquisitions list, weekly. **Special Indexes:** Preprint index. **Formerly:** Its David Dunlap Observatory - Library.

★16278★

UNIVERSITY OF TORONTO - AUDIO-VISUAL LIBRARY (Aud-Vis)

                    Phone: (416) 978-6084
Toronto, ON, Canada M5S 2E8   Liz Avison, Hd.Libn.
Staff: Prof 3; Other 6. **Subjects:** Media, broadcasting. **Holdings:** 603 books; 911 films; 1379 video cassettes; 380 sound recordings. **Subscriptions:** 96 journals and other serials. **Services:** Interlibrary loans; copying; videotape dubbing; library open to public. **Staff:** Lynette Mannion, Film Libn.

★16279★

UNIVERSITY OF TORONTO - CENTRE OF CRIMINOLOGY - LIBRARY (Law; Soc Sci)

130 St. George St., Suite 8055   Phone: (416) 978-7068
Toronto, ON, Canada M5S 1A5   Catherine J. Matthews, Libn.
Founded: 1963. **Staff:** Prof 2; Other 1. **Subjects:** Criminology. **Holdings:** 18,347 volumes; 250 files of newspaper clippings (by subject); 2100 reprints. **Subscriptions:** 275 journals and other serials. **Services:** Interlibrary loans; copying; library open to public with deposit required for borrowing. **Publications:** Criminology Library Acquisitions List, 3/year.

★16280★

UNIVERSITY OF TORONTO - CENTRE FOR INDUSTRIAL RELATIONS - INFORMATION SERVICE (Bus-Fin)

                    Phone: (416) 978-2928
Toronto, ON, Canada M5S 2E8   Elizabeth Perry, Libn.
Founded: 1968. **Staff:** Prof 2; Other 1. **Subjects:** Labor relations, labor economics, personnel administration, industrial psychology, industrial sociology, labor law, manpower training. **Special Collections:** Labor union archives (constitutions, newspapers, proceedings and clippings). **Holdings:** 7885 books and bound periodical volumes; 806 linear feet of clippings, reprints, photocopies, reports, pamphlets, statistics and documents. **Subscriptions:** 495 journals and other serials. **Services:** Copying; service open to public for reference use only. **Staff:** Susan Western, Subject Spec.

★16281★

UNIVERSITY OF TORONTO - CENTRE FOR URBAN AND COMMUNITY STUDIES - RESOURCE ROOM (Soc Sci; Hist)

455 Spadina Ave.   Phone: (416) 978-4478
Toronto, ON, Canada M5S 2G8   Judith Kjellberg, Info.Off.
Staff: 1. **Subjects:** Urban studies. **Holdings:** 500 books; 4000 documents, manuscripts, and research papers. **Subscriptions:** 44 journals and other serials. **Services:** Interlibrary loans; library open to public with restrictions. **Publications:** Newsletter, 5/year.

UNIVERSITY OF TORONTO - DAVID DUNLAP OBSERVATORY - LIBRARY
See: University of Toronto - Astronomy Library

★16282★

UNIVERSITY OF TORONTO - DEPARTMENT OF BOTANY LIBRARY (Sci-Tech)

Botany Bldg., Rm. 202
6 Queen's Pk.   Phone: (416) 978-3538
Toronto, ON, Canada M5S 1A1   Ellen Chamberlain, Sec.
Founded: 1932. **Staff:** 1. **Subjects:** Botany, bacteriology, biology, agriculture, paleobotany, horticulture, biochemistry. **Holdings:** 12,129 volumes; 5550 slides and transparencies. **Subscriptions:** 209 journals and other serials. **Services:** Interlibrary loans.

★16283★

UNIVERSITY OF TORONTO - DEPARTMENT OF CHEMISTRY LIBRARY (Sci-Tech)

Lash-Miller Bldg., Rms. 429-433
Willcocks & St. George Sts.   Phone: (416) 978-3587
Toronto, ON, Canada M5S 2T4   Donna Allen, Sec.
Founded: 1938. **Staff:** 2. **Subjects:** Chemistry - analytical, inorganic, organic, physical. **Holdings:** 26,215 volumes; 2180 microforms. **Subscriptions:** 396 journals and other serials. **Services:** Interlibrary loans; copying.

★16284★

UNIVERSITY OF TORONTO - DEPARTMENT OF COMPUTER SCIENCE LIBRARY (Comp Sci)

McLennan Physical Labs.
60 St. George St.   Phone: (416) 978-2987
Toronto, ON, Canada M5S 2E7   Stephanie Johnston, Libn.
Founded: 1950. **Staff:** Prof 1; Other 1. **Subjects:** Computing machines, information retrieval, numerical analysis, automatic translation. **Special Collections:** Abstracts on cards. **Holdings:** 9924 volumes; 440 microforms. **Subscriptions:** 147 journals and other serials. **Services:** Interlibrary loans. **Special Catalogs:** Punched card title listings.

★16285★

UNIVERSITY OF TORONTO - DEPARTMENT OF GEOLOGY - COLEMAN LIBRARY (Sci-Tech)

Mining Bldg., Rm. 316
170 College St.   Phone: (416) 978-3024
Toronto, ON, Canada M5S 1A1   L.A. Eschenauer, Sec.
Staff: Prof 1. **Subjects:** Geology. **Holdings:** 25,794 volumes; 936 microforms. **Subscriptions:** 181 journals and other serials.

★16286★

UNIVERSITY OF TORONTO - DEPARTMENT OF MEDICAL RESEARCH LIBRARY (Med)

Banting & Best Institute, Rm. 304
112 College St.   Phone: (416) 978-2588
Toronto, ON, Canada M5G 1L6   Colin Savage
Founded: 1953. **Staff:** 1. **Subjects:** Medicine, physiology, diabetes, insulin, anticoagulants, lipid metabolism. **Holdings:** 6728 volumes. **Subscriptions:** 46 journals and other serials.

★16287★

UNIVERSITY OF TORONTO - DEPARTMENT OF PHYSICS LIBRARY (Sci-Tech)

McLennan Physical Labs., Rm. 211
Russell & Huron Sts.   Phone: (416) 978-5788
Toronto, ON, Canada M5S 1A7   B. Chu, Libn.
Founded: 1910. **Staff:** Prof 1; Other 1. **Subjects:** Physics, geophysics. **Holdings:** 23,153 volumes. **Subscriptions:** 296 journals and other serials. **Services:** Interlibrary loans.

★16288★

UNIVERSITY OF TORONTO - DEPARTMENT OF ZOOLOGY LIBRARY (Sci-Tech)

Ramsey-Wright Bldg., Rm. 225
St. George & Harbord Sts.   Phone: (416) 978-3515
Toronto, ON, Canada M5S 1A1   R. O'Grady, Sec.
Staff: 2. **Subjects:** Zoology, aquatic biology. **Holdings:** 14,633 volumes; 70,790 indexed reprints and articles. **Subscriptions:** 246 journals and other serials.

★16289★
UNIVERSITY OF TORONTO - EAST ASIAN LIBRARY (Area-Ethnic)
280 Huron St.   Phone: (416) 928-3300
Toronto, ON, Canada M5S 1A1   Anna U, Libn.
Staff: Prof 3. **Subjects:** East Asia. **Special Collections:** Mu Collection (Chinese rare books); Chinese local histories; modern Japanese literature (13,000 volumes). **Holdings:** 150,892 volumes; 8764 reels of microfilm. **Subscriptions:** 600 journals and other serials. **Services:** Interlibrary loans; copying; library open to public for reference use only. **Remarks:** Library's Indic and Western language materials have been transferred to the general stack. **Staff:** Teresa Hsieh, Instr.-Libn.; S. Uyenaka, Japanese Bibliog.

★16290★
UNIVERSITY OF TORONTO - FACULTY OF APPLIED SCIENCE AND ENGINEERING - CENTRE FOR BUILDING SCIENCE - LIBRARY (Sci-Tech)
35 St. George St.   Phone: (416) 978-5053
Toronto, ON, Canada M5S 1A4   Mr. A. Seskus, Res.Off.
Subjects: Air infiltration, moisture movement, materials, energy conservation, retrofit, construction. **Holdings:** 250 books; 1000 other cataloged items. **Subscriptions:** 10 journals and other serials. **Services:** Library open to public with chairman's approval.

★16291★
UNIVERSITY OF TORONTO - FACULTY OF DENTISTRY LIBRARY (Med)
124 Edward St., Rm. 202   Phone: (416) 978-2796
Toronto, ON, Canada M5G 1G6   Susan Goddard, Faculty Libn.
Founded: 1925. **Staff:** Prof 2; Other 2. **Subjects:** Dentistry, medicine, health sciences. **Special Collections:** Phyllis M. Smith Collection (rare books and catalogs). **Holdings:** 22,000 books and bound periodical volumes; 44 microforms; 12 linear feet of clippings, pamphlets and other vertical file materials. **Subscriptions:** 225 journals and other serials. **Services:** Interlibrary loans; copying; library open to public with restrictions. **Computerized Information Services:** MEDLINE, CAN/OLE. Performs searches on cost recovery basis. **Publications:** Current journal title page lists, monthly; Filling the Gap, quarterly - to faculty and dental libraries. **Special Catalogs:** The Rare Books Collection of the Dental Library, University of Toronto and the Harry R. Abbott Memorial Library, 1978; staff articles file (cards). **Staff:** Susan Murray, Libn.

★16292★
UNIVERSITY OF TORONTO - FACULTY OF EDUCATION LIBRARY (Educ)
371 Bloor St., W.   Phone: (416) 978-3224
Toronto, ON, Canada M5S 2R7   Mary Shortt, Chf.Libn.
Founded: 1906. **Staff:** Prof 3; Other 6. **Subjects:** Education - history, philosophy, psychology, administration and general methodology. **Special Collections:** Authorized school textbooks from the 19th century. **Holdings:** 34,723 books and bound periodical volumes; 2457 microforms; government documents; picture collection. **Subscriptions:** 325 journals and other serials. **Services:** Interlibrary loans; copying; library open to public. **Publications:** Bibliographic aids for teachers.

★16293★
UNIVERSITY OF TORONTO - FACULTY OF ENGINEERING LIBRARY (Sci-Tech)
Sandford Fleming Bldg., Rm 2402
10 King's College Rd.   Phone: (416) 978-6109
Toronto, ON, Canada M5S 1A4   E.S. Brown
Staff: Prof 2; Other 6. **Subjects:** Engineering - civil, mechanical, industrial, chemical and electrical; engineering science and technology; metallurgy; aerospace science. **Holdings:** 97,510 books and bound periodical volumes; 1348 microforms. **Subscriptions:** 1304 journals and other serials. **Services:** Interlibrary loans; copying.

★16294★
UNIVERSITY OF TORONTO - FACULTY OF FORESTRY LIBRARY (Sci-Tech)
Forestry Bldg., Rm. 102
45 St. George St.   Phone: (416) 978-6016
Toronto, ON, Canada M5S 1A1   Jean Bohne, Libn.
Founded: 1907. **Staff:** 2. **Subjects:** Forestry. **Holdings:** 22,916 volumes; 5913 microforms; 909 maps; 130 slides and transparencies. **Subscriptions:** 383 journals and other serials. **Services:** Interlibrary loans; copying.

★16295★
UNIVERSITY OF TORONTO - FACULTY OF LAW LIBRARY (Law)
78 Queen's Park   Phone: (416) 978-3719
Toronto, ON, Canada M5S 1A1   Christine Attalai, Act.Chf.Libn.
Staff: Prof 3; Other 9. **Subjects:** Law. **Special Collections:** Raoul Collection in International Law (4500 volumes). **Holdings:** 101,159 books and bound periodical volumes. **Subscriptions:** 1497 journals and other serials. **Services:**

Interlibrary loans; library open to public, borrowing on application.

★16296★
UNIVERSITY OF TORONTO - FACULTY OF LIBRARY SCIENCE LIBRARY (Info Sci)
140 St. George St.   Phone: (416) 978-7060
Toronto, ON, Canada M5S 1A1   Diane Henderson, Chf.Libn.
Founded: 1928. **Staff:** Prof 4; Other 6. **Subjects:** Library science, Canadian bibliography, printing, history of libraries and publishing. **Special Collections:** Library-related annual reports and calendars. **Holdings:** 88,457 books and bound periodical volumes; 96 linear feet of pamphlets and newspaper clippings; 16,923 microforms; 25 drawers of reprint files. **Subscriptions:** 1529 journals and other serials. **Services:** Interlibrary loans; copying; library open to public, only those in library field may borrow. **Automated Operations:** Automated indexes; automated serials list and check-in system. **Special Indexes:** Automated index to ERIC and NTIS reports; KWOC index to reprint files.

★16297★
UNIVERSITY OF TORONTO - FACULTY OF MANAGEMENT STUDIES LIBRARY (Bus-Fin)
246 Bloor St., W.   Phone: (416) 978-3421
Toronto, ON, Canada M5S 1V4   Margaret McKay, Libn.
Founded: 1950. **Staff:** Prof 1; Other 5. **Subjects:** Accounting, marketing, finance, organizational behavior, statistics, management science, administration, industrial relations, business mathematics. **Special Collections:** Working papers of North American and European business schools. **Holdings:** 48,929 books and bound periodical volumes; 203 microforms; 17,540 government documents; 12 drawers of Canadian company annual reports; 12 drawers of reprint files. **Subscriptions:** 440 journals and other serials. **Services:** Interlibrary loans; copying; library open to public for reference use only. **Publications:** Business Research: Basic Reference Sources; Selected List of Recent Acquisitions, every six weeks. **Special Indexes:** Index to working paper collection (list file). **Remarks:** The Faculty of Management Studies Library is affiliated with the University's Centre for Industrial Relations Information Service.

★16298★
UNIVERSITY OF TORONTO - FACULTY OF MUSIC LIBRARY (Mus)
Edward Johnson Bldg.   Phone: (416) 978-3734
Toronto, ON, Canada M5S 1A1   Kathleen McMorrow, Libn.
Founded: 1945. **Staff:** Prof 4; Other 10. **Subjects:** Music - theory, history, biography. **Special Collections:** Creighton Collection of Violin Recordings; rare book room; Cobbett Chamber Music Collection; Fisher Collection (historical books, music and instruments). **Holdings:** 94,612 volumes; 25,353 items of sheet music; 133,845 sound recordings. **Subscriptions:** 795 journals and other serials. **Services:** Interlibrary loans; copying; library open to public for music-related research. **Staff:** Jean Lavender, Asst.Libn.; Steven Pallay, Cat.Libn.; James Creighton, Recordings Archv.

★16299★
UNIVERSITY OF TORONTO - FACULTY OF PHARMACY - R.O. HURST LIBRARY (Med)
25 Russell St.   Phone: (416) 978-2870
Toronto, ON, Canada M5S 1A1   Barbara A. Gallivan, Libn.
Staff: Prof 1; Other 1. **Subjects:** Pharmacy, chemistry, history of pharmacy and medicine. **Special Collections:** R.O. Hurst Collection of Pharmacopoeias; history of pharmacy. **Holdings:** 7909 volumes. **Subscriptions:** 118 journals and other serials. **Services:** Interlibrary loans.

★16300★
UNIVERSITY OF TORONTO - FINE ARTS LIBRARY (Art)
100 St. George St.   Phone: (416) 978-3290
Toronto, ON, Canada M5S 1A1   Andrea Retfalvi, Libn.
Founded: 1934. **Staff:** Prof 1; Other 1. **Subjects:** History and techniques of fine arts. **Special Collections:** Photographs of illustrated Bibles of the 12th and 13th centuries (8500); exhibition and sales catalogs. **Holdings:** 17,469 books; 2200 mounted reproductions; 87,981 photographs. **Subscriptions:** 21 journals and other serials. **Services:** Library not open to public. **Special Indexes:** Subject index to Bible illustrations.

★16301★
UNIVERSITY OF TORONTO - GENERAL LIBRARY - SCIENCE AND MEDICINE DEPARTMENT (Sci-Tech; Med; Food-Bev)
    Phone: (416) 978-2284
Toronto, ON, Canada M5S 1A5   Ms. G. Heaton, Hd.
Staff: Prof 12; Other 29. **Subjects:** Technology (excluding engineering), science, medicine, nursing, anatomy, food sciences, bacteriology, industrial hygiene. **Holdings:** 379,169 books and bound periodical volumes; 82,674

technical reports; 46,219 microforms. **Subscriptions:** 3274 journals and other serials. **Services:** Interlibrary loans; copying; department open to public with restrictions.

★16302★

UNIVERSITY OF TORONTO - INSTITUTE FOR AEROSPACE STUDIES - LIBRARY (Sci-Tech)
4925 Dufferin St.   Phone: (416) 667-7712
Downsview, ON, Canada M3H 5T6   Asta Luik, Libn.
Founded: 1950. **Staff:** Prof 1; Other 1. **Subjects:** Aerophysics, aeronautical engineering. **Holdings:** 5700 books and bound periodical volumes; 437 dissertations; 67,000 reports. **Subscriptions:** 103 journals and other serials. **Services:** Interlibrary loans (fee); copying; library open to public for research.

★16303★

UNIVERSITY OF TORONTO - INSTITUTE OF CHILD STUDY - LIBRARY (Soc Sci; Educ)
45 Walmer Rd.   Phone: (416) 978-5086
Toronto, ON, Canada M5R 2X2   Miriam Herman, Lib.Techn.
Staff: 1. **Subjects:** Child psychology and development, assessment and counselling, early childhood education. **Holdings:** 5568 volumes; 1200 pamphlets. **Subscriptions:** 40 journals and other serials. **Services:** Library open to public for reference use only.

★16304★

UNIVERSITY OF TORONTO - INSTITUTE FOR POLICY ANALYSIS - LIBRARY (Soc Sci)
150 St. George St.   Phone: (416) 928-8623
Toronto, ON, Canada M5S 2E9   U. Gutenburg, Lib.Techn.
Staff: 1. **Subjects:** Economics. **Holdings:** 6151 reports; 300 working reports of the institute and reports from other libraries. **Services:** Copying; library open to public.

★16305★

UNIVERSITY OF TORONTO - KNOX COLLEGE - CAVEN LIBRARY (Rel-Theol)
59 St. George St.   Phone: (416) 979-2532
Toronto, ON, Canada M5S 2E6   A. Burgess, Libn.
Founded: 1845. **Staff:** Prof 2; Other 1. **Subjects:** Theology (Presbyterian), philosophy, social ethics, Church history (Reformation era). **Special Collections:** Reproductions of Biblical codices; early editions of Bibles and commentaries; reproductions of medieval illuminated manuscripts; John Calvin Collection. **Holdings:** 63,516 volumes; 383 microforms. **Subscriptions:** 164 journals and other serials. **Services:** Interlibrary loans; copying; library open to public.

★16306★

UNIVERSITY OF TORONTO - MAP LIBRARY (Geog-Map)
130 St. George St., Rm. 1001   Phone: (416) 978-3372
Toronto, ON, Canada M5S 1A5   Joan Winearls, Map Libn.
Staff: Prof 2; Other 3. **Subjects:** Geography, cartography. **Holdings:** 9621 books and atlases; 169,945 maps; 193,641 aerial photographs. **Subscriptions:** 40 journals and other serials. **Services:** Interlibrary loans; copying; library open to public. **Publications:** Accessions list, bimonthly.

★16307★

UNIVERSITY OF TORONTO - MATHEMATICS LIBRARY (Sci-Tech)
Sidney Smith Hall, Rm. 2124
100 St. George St.   Phone: (416) 978-8624
Toronto, ON, Canada M5S 1A1   Chibeck Graham, Libn.
Founded: 1970. **Staff:** Prof 1; Other 1. **Subjects:** Mathematics. **Holdings:** 16,393 volumes. **Subscriptions:** 500 journals and other serials. **Services:** Interlibrary loans; library not open to public.

★16308★

UNIVERSITY OF TORONTO - PATHOLOGY LIBRARY (Med)
Banting Institute, Rms. 108-109
100 College St.   Phone: (416) 978-2558
Toronto, ON, Canada M5G 1L5   Sophia Duda, Libn.
Founded: 1923. **Staff:** 1. **Subjects:** Pathology, immunology, bacteriology. **Holdings:** 3829 volumes. **Subscriptions:** 77 journals and other serials. **Services:** Interlibrary loans; copying.

★16309★

UNIVERSITY OF TORONTO - PONTIFICAL INSTITUTE OF MEDIAEVAL STUDIES - LIBRARY (Hist)
113 St. Joseph   Phone: (416) 926-7146
Toronto, ON, Canada M5S 1J4   Rev. D.F. Finlay, Libn.
Founded: 1929. **Staff:** Prof 3; Other 2. **Subjects:** Medieval life and thought. **Special Collections:** Gordon Taylor Microfilm Collection; Etienne Gilson

Collection; Gerald B. Phelan Archives. **Holdings:** 56,000 books; 11,600 bound periodical volumes; 2.5 million pages on microfilm. **Subscriptions:** 150 journals and other serials. **Services:** Interlibrary loans; copying; library open to bona fide scholars with letters of introduction.

★16310★

UNIVERSITY OF TORONTO - ST. MICHAEL'S COLLEGE - JOHN M. KELLY LIBRARY (Rel-Theol)
113 St. Joseph St.   Phone: (416) 926-7111
Toronto, ON, Canada M5S 1J4   Rev. J. Bernard Black, Libn.
Founded: 1929. **Staff:** Prof 9; Other 14. **Subjects:** Humanities, medieval studies, theology. **Special Collections:** Counter Reformation; G.K. Chesterton; J.H. Newman; Roy Campbell; Stathas Collection (Spain); Etienne Gilson Archive. **Holdings:** 236,000 books and bound periodical volumes; 6 linear feet of VF material; 7250 microforms; 16,417 slides. **Subscriptions:** 1600 journals and other serials; 25 newspapers. **Services:** Interlibrary loans; copying; library open to public. **Automated Operations:** Computerized cataloging. **Computerized Information Services:** UTLAS. **Publications:** Pamphlets on the Counter Reformation and Newman collections. **Special Catalogs:** Catalog of the Pontifical Institute Library (book). **Remarks:** St. Michael's College Library is affiliated with the University of Toronto's Pontifical Institute of Mediaeval Studies Library. **Staff:** Louise H. Girard, Hd., Tech.Serv.; Mrs. M. McGrath, Hd., Ref.; Mrs. E. Collins, Hd., Circ.

★16311★

UNIVERSITY OF TORONTO - SCHOOL OF ARCHITECTURE AND PLANNING LIBRARY (Plan)
230 College St.   Phone: (416) 978-2649
Toronto, ON, Canada M5S 1A1   Pamela Manson-Smith, Libn.
Founded: 1922. **Staff:** Prof 1; Other 1. **Subjects:** Architecture, urban and regional planning. **Holdings:** 20,334 books and bound periodical volumes; 20 VF drawers of pamphlets. **Subscriptions:** 150 journals and other serials. **Services:** Interlibrary loans; copying; library open to public for reference use only.

★16312★

UNIVERSITY OF TORONTO - THOMAS FISHER RARE BOOK LIBRARY (Rare Book; Hist; Hum)
120 St. George St.   Phone: (416) 978-5285
Toronto, ON, Canada M5S 1A5   Richard G. Landon, Dept.Hd.
Founded: 1955. **Staff:** Prof 9; Other 11. **Subjects:** English literature, Canadian literature, European literature, theater history, history, Canadian history, philosophy and theology, science, history of medicine, art, book arts and bibliography, rare books. **Special Collections:** Fisher Collection of Shakespeare editions and Shakespeareana (3000 volumes); Endicott Collection of works by British authors whose careers fall between 1880 and 1930 (4500 volumes); DeLury Collection of Anglo-Irish literature (5000 volumes); Duncan Collection of editions of D.H. Lawrence, Richard Aldington, Max Beerbohm, Norman Douglas and Aldous Huxley (800 volumes); Yellowback Collection of popular Victorian reading (fiction and nonfiction; 400 volumes); manuscript collections of Canadian authors, including Earle Birney, Margaret Atwood, Mazo De La Roche, Duncan Campbell Scott, Ernest Buckler, Leonard Cohen, Mavis Gallant, Dennis Lee, Gwendolyn McEwan, John Newlove, Raymond Souster, Josef Skvorecky, W.A. Deacon; Canadian literary periodicals; Rousseau Collection (700 volumes); Voltaire Collection (900 volumes); Italian play collection (especially Renaissance period; 6500 volumes); Rime Collection of Italian lyric verse (700 volumes); Buchanan Collection of Spanish and Italian literature and historical works (1700 volumes); Petlice Collection of Czechoslovakian works not allowed to be published in Czechoslovakia (200 volumes); Bagnani Collection of editions of Petronius Arbiter (200 volumes); Juvenile Drama Collection (6000 sheets; 150 volumes); papers of Dora Mavor Moore, Canadian director and founder of the New Play Society; French Revolution pamphlets (900); Spanish Civil War Collection (650 volumes); Shelden Collection of Australiana (1500 volumes); Czechoslovakia '68 Collection and Czechoslovakian History and Politics Collection (2500 volumes); Radio Free Europe Collection (3000 items); 17th- and 18th-century British history; Canadian history, discovery and exploration (30,000 manuscripts; 1200 maps, plans and insurance plans of Canadian towns); Kenny Collection of socialist and radical Canadian material (2500 volumes); Woodsworth Collection of Co-operative Commonwealth Federation material (700 items); Maclean Hunter and Southam Press Collections of periodicals and trade journals (310 titles); papers of Mark Gayn, Canadian foreign correspondent, 1909-1981; historical manuscript collections and papers of eminent Canadians, including J.B. Tyrrell, James Mavor, Sir Alan MacNab, Sir Edmund Walker; James Forbes Collection of 17th-century theological works (1600 volumes); Aristotle Collection (300 volumes); Bacon Collection (250 volumes); Hobbes Collection (500 volumes); Locke Collection (170 volumes); Science Collection, with emphasis on Renaissance astronomy, physics, mechanics, and on English experimental science of the 17th and 18th

centuries (4500 volumes); Galileo Collection (300 volumes); James L. Baillie Collection of ornithological works (3000 items); Darwin Collection (2000 volumes); Einstein Collection (300 volumes); Bronowski Collection (books and papers); Simcoe Collection of works on military science (360 volumes); Victorian Natural History Collection (1700 volumes); Jason A. Hannah Collection of first and significant editions of medical works from classical times to the 20th century (6000 volumes); Sir Frederick Banting books and manuscripts, including records of experiments leading to insulin; Fisher Hollar Collection of etchings by Wenceslaus Hollar, 1607-1677 (100 volumes; 3500 etchings); John E. Langdon Collection on silver and silversmiths (1000 volumes); G.M. Miller Collection of architectural plans for buildings in Toronto region, 1888-1952 (1300 plans); L.B. Duff Collection and reference collections of works on the arts of the books, on collectors and on bibliography (1500 volumes); Stanbrook Abbey Press Collection (125 volumes); Middle Hill Press Collection (325 volumes); Thoreau MacDonald Collection (illustrator; 300 volumes); Birdsall Collection of binders' finishing tools, 18th and 19th centuries (3000 tools); booksellers' catalogs. **Holdings:** 200,000 books; 3020 linear feet and 375 volumes of other cataloged items. **Subscriptions:** 300 journals and other serials. **Services:** Interlibrary loans; copying (both limited); library open to public. **Automated Operations:** Computerized cataloging. **Computerized Information Services:** UTLAS. **Publications:** A Brief Guide to the Collections; exhibition catalogs, 5-6/year - both free upon request. **Special Catalogs:** Manuscript collection finding aids; chronological file for Canadiana holdings (card); autograph, bookplate, association, binding and printers' files (all card). **Staff:** Katharine Martyn, Asst.Hd.; Rachel Grover, Mss.Libn.; E. Anne Jocz, Hd.Cat.; Emrys Evans, Conservator & Binder.

★16313★
UNIVERSITY OF TORONTO - UNIVERSITY ARCHIVES (Hist)
Fisher Library
120 St. George St.   Phone: (416) 978-2277
Toronto, ON, Canada M5S 1A5   Harold A. Averill, Act.Univ.Archv.
Founded: 1965. **Staff:** Prof 2; Other 3. **Subjects:** University of Toronto, higher education. **Holdings:** 9000 linear feet of publications of and about the university, theses, manuscripts, clippings, photographs, plans, tape recordings, motion picture films. **Services:** Interlibrary loans; copying; archives open to public. **Special Catalogs:** Finding aids in typescript.

★16314★
UNIVERSITY OF TORONTO - UNIVERSITY OF TRINITY COLLEGE - LIBRARY (Rel-Theol; Hum)
6 Hoskin Ave.   Phone: (416) 978-2653
Toronto, ON, Canada M5S 1H8   Linda Wilson Corman, Hd.Libn.
Staff: Prof 3; Other 7. **Subjects:** Anglican theology, English Literature, classics, philosophy, French and German literature. **Special Collections:** Bishop Strachan Collection (500 volumes); S.P.C.K. Collection (400 volumes). **Holdings:** 107,000 books and bound periodical volumes. **Subscriptions:** 200 journals and other serials. **Services:** Interlibrary loans; copying; library open to public for reference use only. **Automated Operations:** Computerized cataloging. **Computerized Information Services:** BRS. **Staff:** Lesie Del Bianco, Asst.Libn.

★16315★
UNIVERSITY OF TORONTO - VICTORIA UNIVERSITY - LIBRARY (Hum; Soc Sci)
71 Queen's Park Crescent, E.   Phone: (416) 978-3821
Toronto, ON, Canada M5S 1K7   Dr. Robert C. Brandeis, Chf.Libn.
Staff: Prof 5; Other 12. **Subjects:** Humanities, social sciences, theology. **Special Collections:** E.J. Pratt Manuscript Collection; Coleridge Collection (350 books and manuscripts); Tennyson Collection (500 books and periodical articles); Wesleyana Collection (800 books); Woolf/Bloomsbury/Hogarth Press Collection (500 books); Church of Christ Disciples Archives; Hymnology (500 hymn books). **Holdings:** 200,300 volumes; 150 Emmanuel College theses. **Subscriptions:** 793 journals and other serials. **Services:** Interlibrary loans; copying; library open to public registration. **Automated Operations:** Computerized cataloging. **Remarks:** Victoria University Library houses its Arts College Collection in the E.J. Pratt Library, which also houses the Centre for Reformation and Renaissance Studies Collection (14,000 volumes). Victoria's Theological Collection is housed in the Emmanuel College Library.

★16316★
UNIVERSITY OF TORONTO - WYCLIFFE COLLEGE - LEONARD LIBRARY (Rel-Theol)
Hoskin Ave.   Phone: (416) 979-2870
Toronto, ON, Canada M5S 1H7   Adrienne Taylor, Coll.Libn.
Founded: 1880. **Staff:** Prof 1; Other 1. **Subjects:** Theology. **Special Collections:** Cody Memorial Library (mainly homiletics). **Holdings:** 43,337 books and bound periodical volumes; 2200 pamphlets; maps. **Subscriptions:** 105 journals and other serials. **Services:** Interlibrary loans; copying; library

open to public by permission. **Automated Operations:** Computerized cataloging.

UNIVERSITY OF TRINITY COLLEGE
See: University of Toronto

★16317★
UNIVERSITY OF TULSA - COLLEGE OF LAW LIBRARY (Law)
3120 E. Fourth Pl.   Phone: (918) 592-6000
Tulsa, OK 74104   Marian Parker, Dir./Asst.Prof.
Founded: 1923. **Staff:** Prof 5; Other 6. **Subjects:** Law. **Special Collections:** American Indian law; Energy Law and Policy Collection. **Holdings:** 163,000 volumes; 65,700 microfiche; 10 VF drawers. **Subscriptions:** 600 journals and other serials. **Services:** Interlibrary loans; copying; library open to public. **Automated Operations:** Computerized cataloging, acquisitions and ILL. **Computerized Information Services:** LEXIS, NEXIS, OCLC. Performs searches on subscription basis. Contact Person: William R. Varga. **Networks/Consortia:** Member of AMIGOS Bibliographic Council, Inc. **Remarks:** Includes holdings of the University of Tulsa Law Research Center. **Staff:** Sue Sark, Coll.Dev.; Katherine J. Tooley, Tech.Serv.; William R. Varga, Pub.Serv.; Jeanne Rehberg, Ref.

★16318★
UNIVERSITY OF TULSA - DIVISION OF INFORMATION SERVICES (Comp Sci; Info Sci)
600 S. College Ave.   Phone: (918) 592-6000
Tulsa, OK 74104   John Dowgray, Dir.
Founded: 1961. **Staff:** Prof 15; Other 5. **Services:** Division does abstracting and information retrieval for the petroleum industry.

★16319★
UNIVERSITY OF TULSA - MC FARLIN LIBRARY - RARE BOOKS AND SPECIAL COLLECTIONS (Hum; Hist)
600 S. College Ave.   Phone: (918) 592-6000
Tulsa, OK 74120   Dr. David Farmer, Dir., Rare Bks./Spec.Coll
Staff: Prof 3; Other 4. **Subjects:** 20th century British and American literature; Indian history, law, and policy; World War I; Proletarian literature; American fiction regarding Vietnam; performing arts. **Special Collections:** Cyril Connolly library; Edmund Wilson library; Schleppey Indian Collection; Indian Claims Commission Archives. **Holdings:** 80,000 books; 1000 bound periodical volumes; 14 VF drawers of Alice Robertson papers; 50,000 British and American 20th century literary manuscripts; 300 pieces of 20th century American Indian art; 150 territorial maps. **Subscriptions:** 20 journals and other serials; 25 newspapers. **Services:** Interlibrary loans; copying; collections open to public with written permission. **Automated Operations:** Computerized cataloging and acquisitions. **Computerized Information Services:** DIALOG. **Networks/Consortia:** Member of Tulsa Area Library Cooperative (TALC); Oklahoma Special Collections and Archives Network (OSCAN). **Publications:** Tracings, weekly Newsletter - for internal distribution only. **Special Catalogs:** Finding aids. **Staff:** Caroline Seydell Swinson, Cur. of Mss.; Toby Murray, Archv.

★16320★
UNIVERSITY OF TULSA - SIDNEY BORN TECHNICAL LIBRARY (Sci-Tech)
600 S. College
Tulsa, OK 74104
Defunct. Holdings absorbed by University of Tulsa - Mc Farlin Library.

★16321★
UNIVERSITY OF UTAH - AUDIO-VISUAL SERVICES (Aud-Vis)
Marriott Library, 4th Fl.   Phone: (801) 581-6283
Salt Lake City, UT 84112   Ralph E. Kranz, AV Libn.
Staff: Prof 1; Other 9. **Subjects:** Music, drama, poetry, art, dance, social sciences, sciences, architecture. **Holdings:** 2054 audio cassettes; 15,408 phonograph records; 21,118 slides; 491 filmstrips; 121 films; 7361 audiotapes; 2797 video cassettes; 124 videotapes. **Services:** Audio-Visual Services open to public for reference use only. **Computerized Information Services:** OCLC. **Networks/Consortia:** Member of Bibliographic Center for Research, Rocky Mountain Region, Inc. (BCR).

★16322★
UNIVERSITY OF UTAH - CENTER FOR PUBLIC AFFAIRS AND ADMINISTRATION - RESEARCH LIBRARY (Soc Sci)
214 Orson Spencer Hall   Phone: (801) 581-6781
Salt Lake City, UT 84112   Bryna Pocock, Libn.
Founded: 1947. **Staff:** I. **Subjects:** Public administration, political science, planning, budgeting. **Holdings:** 2700 books; 700 bound periodical volumes; 60 VF drawers; 520 boxes of pamphlets; 420 volumes of national and international documents; 2000 reports. **Subscriptions:** 135 journals,

newsletters and other serials. **Services:** Library open to public for reference use only. **Publications:** Occasional papers and reports - price list available.

★16323★

UNIVERSITY OF UTAH - DOCUMENTS DIVISION (Energy; Bus-Fin)
Marriott Library   Phone: (801) 581-8394
Salt Lake City, UT 84112   Julianne P. Hinz, Doc.Libn.
Staff: Prof 3; Other 5. **Subjects:** Energy research and development, business and economics, statistics, geological and earth sciences, legislative documents, presidential materials, patents. **Special Collections:** Energy research and development reports, 1950 to present; congressional committee prints on microfiche (15,100 prints); congressional committee hearings on microfiche (29,400 hearings); American Statistics Index Nondepository Collection on microfiche (complete set); United Nations Depository Collection. **Holdings:** 350,000 volumes. **Subscriptions:** 1050 journals and other serials. **Services:** Interlibrary loans; copying; division open to public. **Computerized Information Services:** DIALOG, SDC, BRS. **Staff:** Maxine R. Haggerty, Doc.Acq.Libn.; Juri Stratford, Intl.Doc.Libn.

★16324★

UNIVERSITY OF UTAH - HUMAN RELATIONS AREA FILES (Soc Sci)
Marriott Library   Phone: (801) 581-7024
Salt Lake City, UT 84112   Mark W. Emery, Ref.Libn.
Founded: 1950. **Staff:** Prof 1. **Subjects:** Anthropology, behavioral sciences, geography, history, psychology, sociology, political science. **Holdings:** 5000 books; 3.5 million slips. **Services:** Files open to public for reference use only.

★16325★

UNIVERSITY OF UTAH - INSTRUCTIONAL MEDIA SERVICES (Aud-Vis)
207 Milton Bennion Hall   Phone: (801) 581-6112
Salt Lake City, UT 84112   Stephen H. Hess, Dir.
Founded: 1952. **Staff:** 29. **Subjects:** Social and behavioral sciences, literature, history, science, mathematics. **Holdings:** 5000 film titles. **Services:** T.V. distribution/production; photography and graphics; AV equipment service; instructional design; fee charged to outside users. **Special Catalogs:** University of Utah Film Library Catalog and Supplement. **Staff:** Jan Bruckman, Supv., Film Lib.

★16326★

UNIVERSITY OF UTAH - LAW LIBRARY (Law)
College of Law   Phone: (801) 581-6438
Salt Lake City, UT 84112   Ms. Lane Wilkins, Dir.
Staff: Prof 7; Other 8. **Subjects:** Law. **Holdings:** 229,648 volumes; 221,807 microfiche; 1685 reels of microfilm; 163 cassettes. **Subscriptions:** 5224 journals and other serials; 10 newspapers. **Services:** Interlibrary loans; copying; library open to public. **Computerized Information Services:** RLIN, Westlaw. **Networks/Consortia:** Member of RLG. **Publications:** Acquisitions, monthly; miscellaneous bibliographies. **Staff:** Terry Beckwith, Pub.Serv.Libn.; Ellen Ouyang, Tech.Serv.Libn.; Nancy Cheng, Govt.Docs.; William Sanderson, Non-Print; Martha Byrnes, Asst.Libn.

★16327★

UNIVERSITY OF UTAH - MAP LIBRARY (Geog-Map)
158 Marriott Library   Phone: (801) 581-7533
Salt Lake City, UT 84112   Barbara Cox, Map Libn.
Staff: Prof 1; Other 1. **Subjects:** Maps. **Holdings:** 400 books; 120,000 maps; 100 photographs. **Services:** Interlibrary loans; copying; library open to public. **Automated Operations:** Computerized cataloging and circulation.

★16328★

UNIVERSITY OF UTAH - MATHEMATICS LIBRARY (Sci-Tech)
121 JWB   Phone: (801) 581-6208
Salt Lake City, UT 84112   Christine Zeidner, Sci. & Engr.Libn.
Founded: 1965. **Staff:** Prof 1; Other 2. **Subjects:** Mathematics. **Holdings:** 5800 books; 8100 bound periodical volumes; 1400 technical reports. **Subscriptions:** 210 journals and other serials. **Services:** Interlibrary loans; copying; library open to public.

★16329★

UNIVERSITY OF UTAH - MIDDLE EAST LIBRARY (Area-Ethnic)
Marriott Library   Phone: (801) 581-6311
Salt Lake City, UT 84112   Ragai N. Makar, Libn.
Staff: Prof 1; Other 3. **Subjects:** Language and literature, history, religious studies, sociology, politics, archeology. **Special Collections:** Papyrus and paper documents; Arabic, Persian and Turkish manuscripts (250 items); Abushady Collection; Martin Levy Collection on the History of Arabic Science (10,000 items); microfilm collection of Arabic and Greek manuscripts (2255 reels); illustrated history of Rashid al-Din; manuscript Korans; paleography manuscripts; U.S. Department of State, Affairs of Turkey

documents, 1910-1929 (125 reels of microfilm); Hebrew journals. **Holdings:** 103,559 books; 10,900 periodical volumes; 465 reels of microfilm of Middle Eastern newspapers. **Subscriptions:** 504 journals and other serials; 54 newspapers. **Services:** Interlibrary loans; copying (except vault material); library open to students and faculty. **Automated Operations:** Computerized cataloging, acquisitions, serials and circulation. **Computerized Information Services:** OCLC. **Networks/Consortia:** Member of Utah College Library Council; Association of Research Libraries (ARL); Bibliographic Center for Research, Rocky Mountain Region, Inc. **Publications:** Aziz S. Atiya Library for Middle East Studies; Arabic Collection, 1968 (Supplement I, 1971 and Supplement II, 1979); Middle East Bibliographic Bulletin, triennial.

★16330★

UNIVERSITY OF UTAH - SPECIAL COLLECTIONS DEPARTMENT (Hist)
Marriott Library   Phone: (801) 581-8863
Salt Lake City, UT 84112   Gregory C. Thompson, Asst.Dir., Spec.Coll.
Staff: Prof 3; Other 20. **Subjects:** Utah, Mountain West, Mormons, Indians. **Holdings:** 63,550 books; 5389 periodical titles; 1665 linear feet of archives; 26,128 theses and dissertations; 1679 federal documents; 4146 folders of clippings; 6245 folders of pamphlets; 4000 linear feet of manuscripts; 62,000 photographs. **Subscriptions:** 1710 journals and other serials; 239 newspapers. **Services:** Interlibrary loans; copying (both limited); department open to public for reference use only. **Automated Operations:** Computerized cataloging, acquisitions, serials and circulation. **Publications:** Registers - distributed to other libraries and historical societies; Annie Clark Tanner Memorial Trust Fund, Utah, the Mormons and the West Series, semiannual. **Special Indexes:** Analytical index; Arizona index; chronicle index; review index; university contracts index; manuscript index (all of cards). **Staff:** Ruth Yeaman, Libn.; Walter Jones, Libn.; Clint Bailey, Archv.; F.T. Johnson, Rec.Mgr.; Margery Ward, Pubn.

★16331★

UNIVERSITY OF UTAH - SPENCER S. ECCLES HEALTH SCIENCES LIBRARY (Med)
Bldg. 89
10 N. Medical Dr.   Phone: (801) 581-8771
Salt Lake City, UT 84112   Priscilla M. Mayden, Dir.
Founded: 1906. **Staff:** Prof 9; Other 27. **Subjects:** Medicine, pharmacy, nursing, basic medical sciences, health. **Special Collections:** University Hospital Clinical Reference Library (300 books; 1250 bound periodical volumes); Documents depository for health publications (15,300 items). **Holdings:** 38,000 books; 60,000 bound periodical volumes; 4000 AV items. **Subscriptions:** 1700 journals and other serials. **Services:** Interlibrary loans; copying; SDI; film programs; library open to public with annual permit. **Automated Operations:** Computerized cataloging, acquisitions, serials, circulation and ILL. **Computerized Information Services:** BRS, MEDLINE, OCLC, PHILSOM. **Networks/Consortia:** Member of Midcontinental Regional Medical Library Program; headquarters of Utah Health Sciences Library Consortium. **Publications:** Synapse (acquisitions list), bimonthly; IMS Newsletter; consortium newsletter, quarterly. **Special Catalogs:** Media Services Catalog and Supplement (computer produced). **Special Indexes:** MEDOC: Index to U.S. Government Publications in the Health Sciences (cumulated and published quarterly). **Remarks:** Co-depository for Midcontinental Audiovisual Resource Sharing Project (MARS). **Staff:** Elena Eyzaguirre, Asst.Dir.; Wayne Peay, Computer & Media Serv.; Valerie Florance, Docs.; Joan Stoddart, Clinical Libn.; Nina Doughtery, Info.Serv.; Joyce Lounberg, Tech.Serv.; Karen Butter, Pub.Serv.

★16332★

UNIVERSITY OF VERMONT - CHEMISTRY/PHYSICS LIBRARY (Sci-Tech)
        Phone: (802) 656-2268
Burlington, VT 05405   Craig A. Robertson, Chem./Physics Libn.
Staff: Prof 1; Other 1. **Subjects:** Chemistry, physics. **Holdings:** 8524 books; 14,534 bound periodical volumes; 350 reels of microfilm; 1635 microfiche. **Subscriptions:** 425 journals and other serials. **Services:** Interlibrary loans; copying; library open to public, circulation limited to University of Vermont community. **Computerized Information Services:** DIALOG, BRS, CAS Online. **Publications:** Library Handbook; acquisitions list, monthly - both for internal distribution only.

★16333★

UNIVERSITY OF VERMONT - DIVISION OF HEALTH SCIENCES - CHARLES A. DANA MEDICAL LIBRARY (Med)
Given Bldg.   Phone: (802) 656-2200
Burlington, VT 05405   Ellen Nagle, Med.Libn.
Founded: 1917. **Staff:** Prof 5; Other 16. **Subjects:** Medicine and related fields. **Special Collections:** Historical items. **Holdings:** 21,985 books; 51,014 bound periodical volumes; 6896 AV items. **Subscriptions:** 1391 journals and other serials. **Services:** Interlibrary loans; copying; library open to

public. **Computerized Information Services:** DIALOG, BRS, MEDLINE, OCLC; internal database. Performs searches on cost recovery basis. Contact Person: Sara Andrews. **Networks/Consortia:** Member of Greater Northeastern Regional Medical Library Program; Hospital Library Development Services (HLDS). **Publications:** HLDS News, bimonthly - to participating hospital librarians; Dana Medical Library Newsletter, monthly - to user groups. **Staff:** Sara Andrews, Ref.Hd.; Amy Cooper, Hd., Tech.Serv.; Bob Sekerak, Plan.Off.; Carolyn Fox, Ref.Libn.; Joanne Weinstock, Ref.Libn.

★16334★
UNIVERSITY OF VERMONT - PRINGLE HERBARIUM - LIBRARY (Sci-Tech)
Botany Dept.
Burlington, VT 05405
Phone: (802) 656-3221
David S. Barrington, Cur.
Subjects: Plant taxonomy, botany, genetics. **Special Collections:** Memorabilia and collection of Cyrus Guernsey Pringle and Nellie Flynn. **Holdings:** 500 books; 120 bound periodical volumes; 6000 reprints; 331,000 dried plants. **Services:** Interlibrary loans; library open to public. **Publications:** Pringle Herbarium Newsletter.

★16335★
UNIVERSITY OF VERMONT - WILBUR COLLECTION OF VERMONTIANA (Hist)
Bailey/Howe Library
Burlington, VT 05405
Phone: (802) 656-2138
John Buechler, Asst.Dir., Spec.Coll.
Staff: Prof 3; Other 2. **Subjects:** Vermontiana - history, literature, steamboat transportation, manufacturing, education, labor, religion, agriculture, politics, state and local government. **Special Collections:** Manuscripts of Dorothy Canfield Fisher, Warren Austin, John Spargo, Ira Allen, Champlain Transportation Company, Roswell Farnham (Vermont Governor), James Hartness (Vermont Governor), General William Wells, Henry Stevens and family, George P. Marsh; papers of Senator Winston Prouty, Senator George D. Aiken, Governor Philip H. Hoff, Congressmen Richard Mallary, William Meyer and several other Vermont public figures and companies. **Holdings:** 15,000 books; 3000 linear feet of manuscripts; 900 maps; census reports on microfilm, 1810-1880, 1900; 75,000 photographs. **Subscriptions:** 110 journals and other serials. **Services:** Interlibrary loans; copying; library open to public on limited basis. **Publications:** Liber, Friends of the Library Newsletter, irregular - to members only. **Special Catalogs:** Guides to Manuscripts Collection (card and loose leaf). **Staff:** J.K. Graffagnino, Cur.; Connell Gallagher, Mss.

★16336★
UNIVERSITY OF VICTORIA - KATHARINE MALTWOOD COLLECTION (Art)
P.O. Box 1700
Victoria, BC, Canada V8W 2Y2
Phone: (604) 477-6911
Martin Segger, Cur.
Founded: 1944. **Staff:** Prof 1; Other 1. **Subjects:** Art. **Special Collections:** Personal papers and writings of Katharine Maltwood (3000 items); 19th and 20th century architectural plans of regional significance (5000 sheets). **Holdings:** 1000 books; 50 bound periodical volumes. **Services:** Library open to public. **Special Indexes:** Client index to architectural plans; index to Maltwood papers; index to artifact collection.

★16337★
UNIVERSITY OF VICTORIA - LAW LIBRARY (Law)
P.O. Box 2300
Victoria, BC, Canada V8W 3B1
Phone: (604) 477-6911
Diana M. Priestly, Law Libn.
Staff: Prof 3; Other 13. **Subjects:** Law - Canada, U.S., England, Ireland, Scotland, Australia, New Zealand. **Holdings:** 120,000 books and bound periodical volumes; 2750 reels of microfilm; 32,500 microfiche.

★16338★
UNIVERSITY OF VICTORIA - MC PHERSON LIBRARY - CURRICULUM LABORATORY (Educ)
P.O. Box 1800
Victoria, BC, Canada V8W 3H5
Phone: (604) 477-6911
Donald E. Hamilton, Educ.Libn.
Founded: 1964. **Staff:** Prof 2; Other 5. **Subjects:** Curriculum-support material, education. **Holdings:** 30,000 books and bound periodical volumes; 4500 AV items; 9 VF drawers of pamphlets; elementary and secondary school textbooks. **Subscriptions:** 90 journals and other serials. **Services:** Interlibrary loans; copying; laboratory open to public with restrictions. **Automated Operations:** Computerized circulation. **Publications:** Annual information sheets; resource guide to community for teachers. **Special Catalogs:** Multi-media catalog (card).

★16339★
UNIVERSITY OF VICTORIA - MC PHERSON LIBRARY - MUSIC & AUDIO COLLECTION (Mus)
P.O. Box 1800
Victoria, BC, Canada V8W 3H5
Phone: (604) 477-6911
Sandra Benet, Music Libn.
Staff: Prof 1; Other 4. **Subjects:** Music history and literature, music performance, recorded sound. **Special Collections:** William F. Tickle Collection (theatre and dance orchestra music, 1919-1960). **Holdings:** 30,000 books and scores; 30,000 sound recordings; music publisher's catalogues; unbound sheet music. **Subscriptions:** 272 journals and other serials. **Services:** Interlibrary loans; copying; listening facilities; collection open to public for reference use only. **Automated Operations:** Computerized cataloging, serials and circulation. **Networks/Consortia:** Member of Computerized Information Services: UTLAS. British Columbia Union Catalogue. **Publications:** Information sheet. **Special Indexes:** Index to record collection by manufacturer's number (card); index to music publishers and dealers and their specialties (card and worksheet); index to ethnic recordings (card). **Staff:** Judith White, Sr.Supv.

★16340★
UNIVERSITY OF VICTORIA - MC PHERSON LIBRARY - SPECIAL COLLECTIONS (Hum; Hist)
Box 1800
Victoria, BC, Canada V8W 3H5
Phone: (604) 477-6911
Howard B. Gerwing, Rare Bks.Libn.
Staff: Prof 2; Other 2. **Subjects:** Modern British literature, Vancouver Island studies, Western Canadiana, North American anthropology, Canadian military history, Pacific Rim studies. **Special Collections:** Sir Herbert Read Archives (400 books; 6 drawers of manuscripts); Sir John Betjeman (250 books; 38 drawers of manuscripts); Robert Graves Archives (300 books; 3 drawers of manuscripts). **Holdings:** 38,000 books and bound periodical volumes; 300 pieces of sheet music; 10 VF drawers of military maps; 70 drawers of literary manuscripts; University of Victoria Archives (300 books; 12 drawers). **Subscriptions:** 30 journals and other serials. **Services:** Interlibrary loans; copying; SDI; library open to public for reference use only. **Automated Operations:** Computerized cataloging and serials. **Computerized Information Services:** Online systems. **Special Indexes:** Indexes to Sir Herbert Read and Robert Graves Archives. **Staff:** Christopher Petter, Archv.

★16341★
UNIVERSITY OF VICTORIA - MC PHERSON LIBRARY - UNIVERSITY MAP COLLECTION (Geog-Map)
P.O. Box 1800
Victoria, BC, Canada V8W 3H5
Phone: (604) 477-6911
M.A. Brian Turnbull, Map Cur.
Founded: 1967. **Staff:** 1. **Subjects:** General reference map collection, with emphasis on Western North America, the Pacific Basin, Oceania, East Asia, Western Europe; aerial photographs mainly of Vancouver Island. **Holdings:** 315 atlases; 55,000 maps; 83,000 aerial photographs. **Services:** Interlibrary loans; copying; collection open to persons engaged in scholarly research.

★16342★
UNIVERSITY OF VIRGINIA - ARTHUR J. MORRIS LAW LIBRARY (Law)
School of Law
Charlottesville, VA 22901
Phone: (804) 924-3384
Larry B. Wenger
Staff: Prof 11; Other 20. **Subjects:** Law - Anglo-American, international, foreign. **Special Collections:** John Bassett Moore Collection of International Law; Oceans Law and Policy Collection. **Holdings:** 125,550 books; 243,714 bound periodical volumes; 128,290 other cataloged items (microform equivalencies); 51,064 government documents. **Subscriptions:** 6213 journals and other serials; 17 newspapers. **Services:** Interlibrary loans; copying; library open to public with restrictions. **Automated Operations:** Computerized cataloging. **Computerized Information Services:** LEXIS, Westlaw, OCLC. **Networks/Consortia:** Member of SOLINET. **Staff:** Barbara G. Murphy, Assoc. Law Libn.; Mary L. Cooper, Tech.Serv.Libn.; Susan Tulis, Docs.Libn.Anne Mustain, Cat.Libn.; Michael Klepper, Media Serv.Libn.; Margaret Aycock, Oceans/Intl. Law Libn.; Jacqueline Lichtman, Rd.Serv.Libn.

★16343★
UNIVERSITY OF VIRGINIA - BIOLOGY/PSYCHOLOGY LIBRARY (Sci-Tech)
Gilmer Hall
Charlottesville, VA 22901
Phone: (804) 924-0678
Sandra Dulaney, Libn.
Staff: 2. **Subjects:** Biological sciences, psychology. **Holdings:** 17,600 volumes. **Subscriptions:** 391 journals and other serials. **Services:** Interlibrary loans; copying; library open to public.

★16344★
UNIVERSITY OF VIRGINIA - BLANDY EXPERIMENTAL FARM LIBRARY (Sci-Tech)
Box 175
Boyce, VA 22620
Phone: (703) 837-1758
Thomas E. Ewert, Dir.
Founded: 1926. **Staff:** Prof 1. **Subjects:** Plant science, genetics, botany, plant taxonomy, plant collecting, horticulture. **Special Collections:** Manuals of plants of the world; genetic reprint collection. **Holdings:** 2000 books; 1400 bound periodical volumes; 6000 reprints. **Subscriptions:** 50 journals and other serials. **Services:** Interlibrary loans; library open to public with prior permission.

★16345★

UNIVERSITY OF VIRGINIA - CHEMISTRY LIBRARY (Sci-Tech)
Chemistry Bldg.   Phone: (804) 924-3159
Charlottesville, VA 22901   Robert LaRue, Libn.
Staff: 1. **Subjects:** Chemistry. **Holdings:** 19,526 volumes. **Subscriptions:** 320 journals and other serials. **Services:** Interlibrary loans; copying; library open to public.

★16346★

UNIVERSITY OF VIRGINIA - CLIFTON WALLER BARRETT LIBRARY (Hum)
Alderman Library   Phone: (804) 924-3366
Charlottesville, VA 22901   Joan S. Crane, Cur.Amer.Lit.
Subjects: American literature from American Revolution to present. **Holdings:** 40,770 books; 180,000 manuscripts. **Services:** Copying; library open to public for advanced research only. **Publications:** Exhibition Catalogs, occasional.

★16347★

UNIVERSITY OF VIRGINIA - COLGATE DARDEN GRADUATE SCHOOL OF BUSINESS ADMINISTRATION - LIBRARY (Bus-Fin)
Box 6550   Phone: (804) 924-7321
Charlottesville, VA 22906   Henry Wingate, Libn.
Founded: 1957. **Staff:** Prof 1; Other 5. **Subjects:** Business, management, finance, accounting, economics, marketing, organization behavior. **Special Collections:** Corporation annual reports and 10K reports (200,000 microfiche). **Holdings:** 50,000 books; 5000 bound periodical volumes; 2000 reels of microfilm of periodicals. **Subscriptions:** 900 journals and other serials; 10 newspapers. **Services:** Interlibrary loans; copying; library open to public. **Computerized Information Services:** DIALOG, SDC, BRS, New York Times Information Service, Dow Jones News/Retrieval.

★16348★

UNIVERSITY OF VIRGINIA - EDUCATION LIBRARY (Educ)
Ruffner Hall
405 Emmet St.
Charlottesville, VA 22903   Betsy Anthony, Libn.
Staff: Prof 1; Other 3. **Subjects:** Education. **Holdings:** 25,000 books; 1300 bound periodical volumes; ERIC microfiche. **Subscriptions:** 600 journals and other serials. **Services:** Interlibrary loans; copying.

★16349★

UNIVERSITY OF VIRGINIA - ENGINEERING LIBRARY
Thornton Hall
Charlottesville, VA 22901
Defunct. Merged with Science/Technology Information Center to form its Science & Engineering Library.

★16350★

UNIVERSITY OF VIRGINIA - FISKE KIMBALL FINE ARTS LIBRARY (Art)
Bayly Dr.   Phone: (804) 924-7024
Charlottesville, VA 22903   Mary C. Dunnigan, Libn.
Founded: 1970. **Staff:** Prof 3; Other 5. **Subjects:** Architecture, art, archeology, city planning, theater, landscape architecture, film, photography, costume. **Special Collections:** Frances Benjamin Johnson Photograph Collection of Virginia Architecture (1000); William Morris Library on Forgery of Works of Art, 15th century to present (700 items); drawings of Charles F. Gillette (landscape architect). **Holdings:** 84,000 books and bound periodical volumes; 135,282 architecture slides; 7995 microforms. **Subscriptions:** 787 journals and other serials. **Services:** Interlibrary loans; copying; library open to public with circulation restrictions on some holdings. **Automated Operations:** Computerized cataloging. **Computerized Information Services:** OCLC. **Networks/Consortia:** Member of SOLINET. Christie D. Stephenson, Asst. Fine Arts Libn.; Marika S. Simms, Slide Libn.; Lynda S. White, Asst. Fine Arts Libn.

UNIVERSITY OF VIRGINIA - INSTITUTE OF CHARTERED FINANCIAL ANALYSTS
See: Institute of Chartered Financial Analysts

★16351★

UNIVERSITY OF VIRGINIA - LIBRARY - MANUSCRIPTS DEPARTMENT & UNIVERSITY ARCHIVES (Hist)
                                                  Phone: (804) 924-3025
Charlottesville, VA 22901   Edmund Berkeley, Jr., Cur. of Archv.
Subjects: Virginia history and literature, American literature, Afro-Americans. **Holdings:** 10 million manuscripts; 1 million archival items. **Services:** Interlibrary loans (limited); copying; archives open to public.

★16352★

UNIVERSITY OF VIRGINIA - LIBRARY - RARE BOOK DEPARTMENT (Rare Book; Hum; Hist)
                                                  Phone: (804) 924-3366
Charlottesville, VA 22901   Julius P. Barclay, Cur. of Rare Bks.
Staff: Prof 5; Other 5. **Subjects:** American literature and history, voyages and travels, typography, Gothic novel in British literature, railroads, evolution. **Special Collections:** Stone Collection of Typography; Sadleir-Black Gothic Novel Collection; Streeter Railroad Collection; Victorius Evolution Collection. **Holdings:** 200,000 volumes; 30 VF drawers of Virginiana; 115 drawers of maps; 65 boxes of broadsides; 950 bound volumes of newspapers; 30 drawers of posters. **Subscriptions:** 126 journals and other serials. **Services:** Copying; department open to public with restrictions. **Automated Operations:** Computerized cataloging and circulation. **Computerized Information Services:** DIALOG, BRS, SDC, Questel, RLIN (access through the main library). Performs searches for half of cost. Contact Person: Carol M. Pfeiffer, Dir. of Adm.Serv., (804) 924-0502. **Networks/Consortia:** Member of OCLC. **Publications:** Chapter and Verse, irregular - to members of the Library Associates and other libraries in the U.S. and Canada. **Staff:** Clinton Sisson, Asst. to Cur.; Mildred K. Abraham, Libn., Rd.Serv.; Joan St.C. Crane, Cur., Amer.Lit.Coll.; William H. Runge, Cur., McGregor Lib.

★16353★

UNIVERSITY OF VIRGINIA - MATHEMATICS-ASTRONOMY LIBRARY (Sci-Tech)
Mathematics-Astronomy Bldg.   Phone: (804) 924-7806
Charlottesville, VA 22901   Roma Reed, Libn.
Staff: 1. **Subjects:** Mathematics, astronomy. **Holdings:** 28,705 volumes. **Subscriptions:** 337 journals and other serials. **Services:** Interlibrary loans; copying; library open to public.

★16354★

UNIVERSITY OF VIRGINIA - MEDICAL CENTER - CLAUDE MOORE HEALTH SCIENCES LIBRARY (Med)
Box 234   Phone: (804) 924-5464
Charlottesville, VA 22908   Terry A. Thorkildson, Dir. & Assoc.Prof.
Founded: 1825. **Staff:** Prof 11; Other 21. **Subjects:** Biological and medical sciences, nursing and allied health subjects. **Special Collections:** Walter Reed Archives. **Holdings:** 141,150 books and bound periodical volumes; 2692 AV programs. **Subscriptions:** 1806 journals and other serials. **Services:** Interlibrary loans; copying; SDI; library open to public with restrictions. **Computerized Information Services:** DIALOG, SDC, BRS, NLM. Performs searches on cost recovery basis. **Publications:** Claude Moore Health Sciences Library News, monthly; **Special Catalogs:** Virginia Union List of Biomedical Serials, annual; HSIRC Catalog. **Staff:** Elaine C. Alligood, Asst.Dir., Pub.Serv.; John Patruno, Jr., Assoc.Dir.; George P. Paul, Ref.Libn.; Richard A. Peterson, Ref.Libn.; Steven M. Sanders, Hd., Instr.Rsrcs.; Marylin James, Act.Hd.Cat.Libn.; Carolyn Taylor, Coll.Dev.Libn.; Joan Echtenkamp, Hist.Coll.Libn.

★16355★

UNIVERSITY OF VIRGINIA - MEDICAL CENTER - DEPARTMENT OF NEUROLOGY - ELIZABETH J. OHRSTROM LIBRARY (Med)
Box 394   Phone: (804) 924-2676
Charlottesville, VA 22908   Janice Reynolds, Libn.
Staff: Prof 2. **Subjects:** General neurology, pediatric neurology, cardiovascular systems. **Holdings:** 3000 books; 1500 bound periodical volumes. **Subscriptions:** 50 journals and other serials. **Services:** Library not open to public. **Staff:** Lawrence H. Phillips, II, Chm., Lib.Comm.

★16356★

UNIVERSITY OF VIRGINIA - MID ATLANTIC CENTER FOR COMMUNITY EDUCATION - LIBRARY
School of Education
217 Ruffner Hall, 405 Emmet St.
Charlottesville, VA 22903
Subjects: Community education, citizens involvement, interagency relations, community organization, community schools, lifelong learning. **Holdings:** 1800 books; 300 bound periodical volumes; 75 films and AV materials; 125 dissertations and research reports. **Automated Operations:** Computerized cataloging and acquisitions. **Remarks:** Presently inactive.

★16357★

UNIVERSITY OF VIRGINIA - MUSIC LIBRARY (Mus)
Old Cabell Hall   Phone: (804) 924-7041
Charlottesville, VA 22901   Evan Bonds, Music Libn.
Staff: Prof 2; Other 3. **Subjects:** Music. **Special Collections:** Mackay-Smith Collection of 18th century imprints; Monticello Music Collection; printed and manuscript collection of the music of John Powell; 19th-century American

sheet music. **Holdings:** 36,768 volumes; 2573 microfiche; 875 reels of microfilm; 3120 microcards; 650 magnetic tapes; 10,000 recordings. **Subscriptions:** 436 journals and other serials. **Services:** Interlibrary loans; copying; library open to public. **Special Catalogs:** Computer Catalog of Nineteenth-Century American-Imprint Sheet Music (microfiche). **Staff:** Karen Edge, Asst. Music Libn.

★16358★
UNIVERSITY OF VIRGINIA - PHYSICS LIBRARY (Sci-Tech)
Physics Bldg.   Phone: (804) 924-6589
Charlottesville, VA 22901   Violetta Mercado, Libn.
Staff: 2. **Subjects:** Physics. **Holdings:** 21,278 volumes. **Subscriptions:** 273 journals and other serials. **Services:** Interlibrary loans; copying; library open to public.

★16359★
UNIVERSITY OF VIRGINIA - SCIENCE & ENGINEERING LIBRARY (Sci-Tech)
Clark Hall   Phone: (804) 924-7209
Charlottesville, VA 22901   Edwina H. Pancake, Dir.
Staff: Prof 4; Other 12. **Subjects:** General science and technology including reference materials. **Special Collections:** Government technical reports from Atomic Energy Commission, Department of Defense, and NASA. **Holdings:** 197,000 volumes; 213,382 titles of paper-copy technical reports; 800,000 technical reports on microfiche. **Subscriptions:** 1461 journals and other serials. **Services:** Interlibrary loans; library open to public. **Formed by the Merger of:** Its Engineering Library and its Science/Technology Information Center. **Staff:** Jean L. Cooper, Tech.Serv.Libn.; Douglas P. Hurd, Pub.Serv.Libn.; J.F. O'Bryant, Sci.Bibliog.

★16360★
UNIVERSITY OF VIRGINIA - TRACY W. MC GREGOR LIBRARY (Hist)
Alderman Library   Phone: (804) 924-3366
Charlottesville, VA 22901   William H. Runge, Cur.
Subjects: American history, especially Southeastern United States, from 1607 through the 19th century. **Holdings:** 21,000 books; 10,000 manuscripts. **Services:** Copying; library open to public for advanced research only. **Publications:** Exhibition catalogs, occasional.

★16361★
UNIVERSITY OF WASHINGTON - ARCHITECTURE-URBAN PLANNING LIBRARY (Art; Plan)
334 Gould Hall, JO-30   Phone: (206) 543-4067
Seattle, WA 98195   Betty L. Wagner, Libn.
Founded: 1923. **Staff:** Prof 1; Other 2. **Subjects:** Architecture, urban planning, landscape architecture, building construction. **Holdings:** 26,085 books and bound periodical volumes; 7360 pamphlets; 3258 reports. **Subscriptions:** 310 journals and other serials. **Services:** Interlibrary loans; copying; library open to public for reference use only. **Computerized Information Services:** OCLC. **Networks/Consortia:** Member of WLN.

★16362★
UNIVERSITY OF WASHINGTON - ART LIBRARY (Art)
101 Art Bldg., DM-10   Phone: (206) 543-0648
Seattle, WA 98195   Connie T. Okada, Libn.
Founded: 1949. **Staff:** Prof 1; Other 2. **Subjects:** Painting, ceramics, printmaking, sculpture, industrial design, fiber arts, fiber arts, metal design, graphics design, photography, history of art. **Holdings:** 33,595 books and bound periodical volumes; 25 drawers of pamphlets and clippings; 7500 mounted reproductions. **Subscriptions:** 379 journals and other serials. **Services:** Interlibrary loans; copying; library open to public for reference use only. **Computerized Information Services:** OCLC. **Networks/Consortia:** Member of WLN.

★16363★
UNIVERSITY OF WASHINGTON - ART SLIDE COLLECTION (Art; Aud-Vis)
120 Art Bldg., DM-10   Phone: (206) 543-0649
Seattle, WA 98195   Marietta S. Foubert, Preparator
Staff: 2. **Subjects:** Fine arts and related material. **Holdings:** 200,000 slides. **Services:** Open to other campus departments and museum personnel.

★16364★
UNIVERSITY OF WASHINGTON - BUSINESS ADMINISTRATION LIBRARY (Bus-Fin)
100 Balmer Hall, DJ-10   Phone: (206) 543-4360
Seattle, WA 98195   Anne B. Passarelli, Hd.Libn.
Founded: 1951. **Staff:** Prof 2; Other 5. **Subjects:** Management, marketing, personnel and labor, accounting, finance, international business, transportation, insurance, real estate, business law. **Holdings:** 41,491 books and bound periodical volumes; 6736 pamphlets and research reports; 43,894

annual reports of corporations; 173,157 microfiche of U.S. corporation records. **Subscriptions:** 1034 journals and other serials; 15 newspapers. **Services:** Interlibrary loans; copying; library open to public for reference use only. **Computerized Information Services:** DIALOG, SDC, BRS, OCLC. **Networks/Consortia:** Member of WLN. **Publications:** Bibliographies, irregular. **Staff:** Grace H. Malson, Asst.Libn.

★16365★
UNIVERSITY OF WASHINGTON - CENTER FOR LAW & JUSTICE - CLJ/NCADBIP INFORMATION SERVICE (Law; Soc Sci)
1107 N.E. 45th St., Suite 505   Phone: (206) 543-1485
Seattle, WA 98105   Janette H. Schueller, Info.Spec.
Staff: Prof 1; Other 1. **Subjects:** Juvenile delinquency and its prevention, juvenile justice, school-based delinquency prevention strategies, criminal justice, social science methodology, violent behavior. **Special Collections:** Juvenile delinquency prevention program questionnaire responses, descriptions, and evaluations. **Holdings:** 3000 books; 1000 evaluative reports; 300 microfiche. **Subscriptions:** 89 journals and other serials. **Services:** Interlibrary loans; copying; SDI; library open to public for reference use only. **Automated Operations:** Computerized cataloging. **Computerized Information Services:** DIALOG; NCADBIP literature database, Prevention Programs (internal databases). **Networks/Consortia:** Member of Criminal Justice Information Exchange. **Publications:** New Acquisitions List, monthly - to staff and interested parties. **Remarks:** NCADBIP stands for National Center for the Assessment of Delinquency Behavior and Its Prevention, which is a federally funded project at the center.

★16366★
UNIVERSITY OF WASHINGTON - CENTER FOR STUDIES IN DEMOGRAPHY AND ECOLOGY - LIBRARY (Soc Sci)
102 Savery Hall, DK-40   Phone: (206) 543-5035
Seattle, WA 98195   Thomas W. Pullum, Dir.
Staff: 1. **Subjects:** Census, vital statistics, demography, ecology. **Holdings:** 2000 books; 1000 U.S. Government periodicals; 200 publications on family planning.

★16367★
UNIVERSITY OF WASHINGTON - CHEMISTRY-PHARMACY LIBRARY (Sci-Tech)
192 Bagley Hall, BG-10   Phone: (206) 543-1603
Seattle, WA 98195   Heidi Mercado
Staff: Prof 1; Other 2. **Subjects:** Chemistry, chemical engineering, pharmacy. **Holdings:** 47,500 volumes. **Subscriptions:** 955 journals and other serials. **Services:** Interlibrary loans; copying; library open to public for reference use only. **Computerized Information Services:** DIALOG, SDC, CAS Online, NIH/EPA Chemical Information System, OCLC. Performs searches on cost recovery basis. **Networks/Consortia:** Member of WLN.

★16368★
UNIVERSITY OF WASHINGTON - COMPUTING INFORMATION CENTER (Comp Sci)
3737 Brooklyn N.E., HG-45   Phone: (206) 543-8519
Seattle, WA 98105   Myers Hildebrandt, Mgr.
Founded: 1967. **Staff:** Prof 3; Other 5. **Subjects:** Computing, programming languages, hardware, software, programming, electronic music, data communications. **Special Collections:** Collection of computer produced art; conferences/symposia in the computer science field. **Holdings:** 5000 books; 1350 bound periodical volumes; 7000 technical reports; computer manuals. **Subscriptions:** 600 journals and other serials. **Services:** Interlibrary loans; copying; SDI; center open to public with restrictions. **Computerized Information Services:** CIRIX (internal database). **Publications:** Computing Resources for the Professional, bimonthly - by subscription; list of additional publications - available upon request. **Staff:** Richard Oberg, Lib.Spec.; Jan Gorden, Lib.Spec.

★16369★
UNIVERSITY OF WASHINGTON - CURRICULUM MATERIALS SECTION (Educ)
Suzzallo Library, FM-25   Phone: (206) 543-2725
Seattle, WA 98195
Founded: 1960. **Staff:** Prof 1; Other 2. **Subjects:** Children's literature, elementary and secondary curriculum and instruction, educational and psychological testing, curriculum development projects, educational games/simulations. **Special Collections:** Children's Literature Archive; Resource Center for Gifted Education. **Holdings:** 51,079 books, including textbooks and curriculum guides; 200 bound periodical volumes; 8000 children's literature book jackets, 1920-1965, arranged by author; 3080 standardized tests; 277 games and simulations; 6264 curriculum guides on microfiche. **Subscriptions:** 58 journals and other serials. **Services:** Interlibrary loans (limited); copying;

section open to public for reference use only. **Computerized Information Services:** OCLC. **Networks/Consortia:** Member of WLN.

★16370★
UNIVERSITY OF WASHINGTON - DRAMA LIBRARY (Theater)
25 Drama-TV Bldg., BH-20   Phone: (206) 543-5148
Seattle, WA 98195   Liz Fugate, Libn.
Founded: 1931. **Staff:** Prof 1; Other 1. **Subjects:** Drama history, dramatic literature, theatre history, acting, children's theatre, costume, make-up, scene design, creative dramatics, directing, lighting, playwriting, mime, theatre buildings and architecture. **Special Collections:** 19th Century Acting Editions (2807). **Holdings:** 17,731 books and bound periodical volumes; unbound play collection (21,000 acting editions); 85 phonograph records; 116 tapes. **Subscriptions:** 94 journals and other serials. **Services:** Interlibrary loans; copying; library open to public for reference use only. **Computerized Information Services:** OCLC. **Networks/Consortia:** Member of WLN. **Special Catalogs:** Catalog of 19th Century Acting Editions and theses (card). **Special Indexes:** Index of anthologies; sound effects.

★16371★
UNIVERSITY OF WASHINGTON - EAST ASIA LIBRARY (Area-Ethnic)
322 Gowen Hall, DO-27   Phone: (206) 543-4490
Seattle, WA 98195   Karl Lo, Hd.
Founded: 1947. **Staff:** Prof 5; Other 10. **Subjects:** Social sciences, humanities, natural sciences, literature and language, history, religion and philosophy, arts. **Special Collections:** Works in Chinese, Japanese, Korean, Tibetan, Thai, Vietnamese, Mongolian, Manchu and Indonesian. **Holdings:** 270,897 books and bound periodical volumes; 1043 reels of microfilm; 6529 microfiche; 3882 pamphlets. **Subscriptions:** 2157 journals and other serials; 88 newspapers. **Services:** Interlibrary loans; copying; library open to public for reference use only. **Computerized Information Services:** OCLC. **Networks/Consortia:** Member of WLN. **Staff:** Yeen-Mei Wu Chang, China Libn.; Elise Chin, Hd., Cat.Sect.; Teruko Kyuma Chin, Japan Libn.; Yoon-Whan Choe, Korea Libn.

★16372★
UNIVERSITY OF WASHINGTON - ENGINEERING LIBRARY (Sci-Tech)
Engineering Library Bldg., FH-15   Phone: (206) 543-0740
Seattle, WA 98195   Harold N. Wiren, Hd.Libn.
Founded: 1947. **Staff:** Prof 2; Other 5. **Subjects:** Applied mathematics, applied physics, computer science, energy, engineering, environment, social management of technology, theoretical and applied mechanics. **Holdings:** 103,112 volumes; 44,447 paper copy technical reports; 1 million technical reports in microform; patent specifications, 1966 to present, on microfilm. **Subscriptions:** 2359 journals and other serials. **Services:** Interlibrary loans; copying; library open to public for reference use only. **Computerized Information Services:** DIALOG, SDC, BRS, OCLC. **Networks/Consortia:** Member of WLN. **Special Catalogs:** Technical report catalog (card). **Staff:** Carol Green, Asst.Libn.

★16373★
UNIVERSITY OF WASHINGTON - FISHERIES-OCEANOGRAPHY LIBRARY (Sci-Tech)
151 Oceanography Teaching Bldg., WB-30   Phone: (206) 543-4279
Seattle, WA 98195   Thomas D. Moritz, Hd.Libn.
Founded: 1950. **Subjects:** Fisheries science, marine biology, oceanography, food science and technology, marine policy. **Special Collections:** Canadian translations of fisheries and aquatic sciences on microfiche; Pacific Salmon Literature Compilation. **Holdings:** 48,970 books and bound periodical volumes; 58,049 reprints, translations, reports; 314 reels of microfilm; 6009 microcards; 5278 microfiche; 1737 maps. **Subscriptions:** 1052 journals and other serials. **Services:** Interlibrary loans; copying; library open to public for reference use only. **Computerized Information Services:** DIALOG, SDC, BRS, OCLC. **Networks/Consortia:** Member of WLN. **Special Catalogs:** Selected References to Literature on Marine Expeditions, 1700-1960, published 1972. **Staff:** Kathy Carr, Asst.Libn.

★16374★
UNIVERSITY OF WASHINGTON - FISHING VESSEL SAFETY CENTER - LIBRARY (Sci-Tech)
326 Mechanical Engineering Bldg.
Mail Stop FU-10
Seattle, WA 98195   Phone: (206) 543-7446
                                          Bruce H. Adee, Dir.
Staff: 1. **Subjects:** Fishing vessels and their safety. **Holdings:** 100 books; 500 other cataloged items. **Subscriptions:** 12 journals and other serials. **Services:** Library open to public. **Publications:** Occasional reports.

★16375★
UNIVERSITY OF WASHINGTON - FOREST RESOURCES LIBRARY (Sci-Tech)
60 Bloedel Hall, AQ-15   Phone: (206) 543-2758
Seattle, WA 98195   Barbara B. Gordon, Hd.
Founded: 1947. **Staff:** Prof 1; Other 3. **Subjects:** Forestry, forest management, wood science and technology, paper and pulp technology, logging engineering, forest economics, forest soils, forest pathology, forest entomology, fire control, silvics and silviculture, pulp and paper, forest hydrology, recreation, wood chemistry, wood anatomy. **Holdings:** 46,697 books and bound periodical volumes. **Subscriptions:** 1178 journals and other serials. **Services:** Interlibrary loans; copying; library open to public for reference use only. **Computerized Information Services:** DIALOG, SDC, BRS, OCLC. **Networks/Consortia:** Member of WLN.

★16376★
UNIVERSITY OF WASHINGTON - FRIDAY HARBOR LABORATORIES - LIBRARY (Sci-Tech)
NJ-22   Phone: (206) 378-2501
Friday Harbor, WA 98250   Kathy M. Carr, Libn.
Founded: 1921. **Staff:** Prof 1. **Subjects:** Marine biology, invertebrate embryology, invertebrate zoology, marine algology, fish biology. **Holdings:** 15,552 volumes. **Subscriptions:** 174 journals and other serials. **Services:** Interlibrary loans; copying; library open to public by permission. **Computerized Information Services:** DIALOG, SDC, BRS. **Remarks:** Librarian is available at the Friday Harbor Library only during summer quarter; September through May contact Assistant Librarian, Fisheries-Oceanography Library at (206) 543-4279.

★16377★
UNIVERSITY OF WASHINGTON - GEOGRAPHY LIBRARY (Geog-Map)
415 Smith Hall, DP-10   Phone: (206) 543-5244
Seattle, WA 98195   Joan E. Christ, Libn.
Founded: 1952. **Staff:** Prof 1; Other 1. **Subjects:** Geography, cartography, regional science. **Holdings:** 15,701 books and bound periodical volumes. **Subscriptions:** 355 journals and other serials. **Services:** Interlibrary loans; library open to public for reference use only. **Computerized Information Services:** OCLC. **Networks/Consortia:** Member of WLN.

★16378★
UNIVERSITY OF WASHINGTON - GOVERNMENT PUBLICATIONS DIVISION (Info Sci)
Suzzalo Library, FM-25   Phone: (206) 543-1937
Seattle, WA 98195   Eleanor L. Chase, Hd.Libn.
Founded: 1890. **Staff:** Prof 4; Other 3. **Subjects:** Demography and population, energy resources, international trade, natural resources, water resources, U.S. Government. **Special Collections:** Depository for U.S. documents; United Nations, Food and Agriculture Organization, UNESCO, European Communities; Canada; Washington; Alaska. **Holdings:** 960,481 government publications; 14,064 volumes in microform. **Services:** Interlibrary loans; copying; division open to public. **Computerized Information Services:** DIALOG, SDC, BRS, OCLC. **Networks/Consortia:** Member of WLN. **Staff:** Andrew F. Johnson, State/Local Docs.Libn.; David Maack, Intl./Foreign Docs.Libn.; Cynthia Fugate, Docs.Ser.Libn.

★16379★
UNIVERSITY OF WASHINGTON - GRADUATE SCHOOL - JOINT CENTER FOR GRADUATE STUDY - LIBRARY (Bus-Fin; Sci-Tech)
100 Sprout Rd.   Phone: (509) 943-3176
Richland, WA 99352   Beverly Jane Cooper, Libn.
Staff: Prof 1; Other 1. **Subjects:** Business, science, technology, education. **Holdings:** 10,000 volumes. **Subscriptions:** 300 journals and other serials. **Services:** Interlibrary loans; copying; library open to public. **Computerized Information Services:** DIALOG. Performs searches on cost recovery basis for outside users. **Networks/Consortia:** Member of WLN.

★16380★
UNIVERSITY OF WASHINGTON - HEALTH SCIENCES LIBRARY (Med)
T-231 Health Sciences, SB-55   Phone: (206) 543-5530
Seattle, WA 98195   Gerald J. Oppenheimer, Dir.
Founded: 1949. **Staff:** Prof 16; Other 30. **Subjects:** Medicine, dentistry, nursing, pharmacy, public health, psychology. **Special Collections:** Biomedical history (2000 volumes). **Holdings:** 75,000 books; 157,500 bound periodical volumes; 25,250 microcards; 11,500 microfiche. **Subscriptions:** 4800 journals and other serials. **Services:** Interlibrary loans; copying; SDI; library open to public for reference use only. **Computerized Information Services:** DIALOG, SDC, NLM, BRS, AMA/NET, OCLC. **Networks/Consortia:** Headquarters of Pacific Northwest Regional Health Sciences Library Service (PNRHSLS); member of WLN. **Publications:** The Supplement (newsletter of the Pacific Northwest Regional Health Sciences Library Service), quarterly -

distributed to the libraries of the Pacific Northwest. **Staff:** Muriel Wood, Asst.Dir.; Kay Denfeld, Online Coord.; Colleen Weum, Coll.Dev.Libn.; Lorraine Raymond, Pub.Serv.Libn.; Ellen Howard, Ref.Coord.; Leroy Chadwick, Ser.Libn.; Dale Middleton, Assoc.Dir., PNRHSLS; Carole Stock, Online Coord./ PNRHSLS; Linda Milgrom, Ref./PNRHSLS; Nancy Press, Educ.Coord./ PNRHSLS; Randy Erickson, Sys.Spec./PNRHSLS.

★16381★
UNIVERSITY OF WASHINGTON - HEALTH SCIENCES LIBRARY - K.K. SHERWOOD LIBRARY (Med)
Harborview Medical Ctr.
325 9th Ave., ZA-43
Seattle, WA 98104
Phone: (206) 223-3360
Sharon Babcock, Lib.Supv.
Staff: 2. **Subjects:** Core medical collection. **Holdings:** 1050 books; 3210 bound periodical volumes. **Subscriptions:** 175 journals and other serials. **Services:** Interlibrary loans; copying; library open to public for reference use only. **Remarks:** The K.K. Sherwood Library is a sub-branch of the Health Sciences Library.

★16382★
UNIVERSITY OF WASHINGTON - HENRY ART GALLERY TEXTILE COLLECTION (Art)
51 Drama-TV Bldg., DL-10
Seattle, WA 98195
Phone: (206) 543-1739
Judy Sourakli, Registrar
Founded: 1982. **Subjects:** Textiles, garments and tools from around the world, 1500 B.C. to present, including folk and period costumes, embroidery, laces, tapestries and church garments and cloths. **Special Collections:** Ethnic Doll Collection; Western Textile and Dress Collection (1000 lace pieces, 17th-20th centuries; European brocades, velvets and church pieces, 14th-19th centuries; tapestries, 17th and 18th centuries; 19th- and 20th-century women's and children's clothing; 20th-century designer fashions). **Holdings:** 12,136 items. **Services:** Collection open to researchers. **Formed by the Merger of:** Its Costume and Textile Study Center, Drama Costume Collection and Henry Art Gallery Textile Collection.

★16383★
UNIVERSITY OF WASHINGTON - MAP SECTION (Geog-Map)
Suzzallo Library, FM-25
Seattle, WA 98195
Phone: (206) 543-9392
Steven Z. Hiller, Hd.
Staff: Prof 1; Other 1. **Subjects:** Geologic and topographic maps, nautical charts, aerial photographs. **Special Collections:** Braille maps and atlases (300). **Holdings:** 1406 books; 217,012 maps; 39,164 aerial photographs; 253 reels of microfilm; 2116 microfiche. **Services:** Interlibrary loans; copying; section open to public for reference use only. **Computerized Information Services:** OCLC. **Networks/Consortia:** Member of WLN.

★16384★
UNIVERSITY OF WASHINGTON - MARIAN GOULD GALLAGHER LAW LIBRARY (Law)
School of Law
1100 N.E. Campus Pkwy., JB-20
Seattle, WA 98105
Phone: (206) 543-4089
Elizabeth R. Wilkins, Law Libn.
Founded: 1899. **Staff:** Prof 11; Other 19. **Subjects:** Law. **Special Collections:** Japanese legal material; biography - Washington State Bench and Bar (15 file drawers of pictures and biographical sketches). **Holdings:** 402,700 volumes; 135 bound volumes of clippings. **Subscriptions:** 3500 journals and 5000 serials. **Services:** Interlibrary loans; copying; distribution of catalog cards for legal materials in Japanese; library open to public for reference use only. **Automated Operations:** Computerized cataloging. **Networks/Consortia:** Member of WLN. **Publications:** Current Index to Legal Periodicals, weekly; List of Books Cataloged, monthly; Legal Research Guide, annual - all are available on an exchange basis. **Staff:** J. Wesley Cochran, Assoc. Law Libn.; Reba Turnquist, Asst. Law Libn.; Takika Lee, Comparative Law Libn.

★16385★
UNIVERSITY OF WASHINGTON - MATHEMATICS RESEARCH LIBRARY (Sci-Tech)
C306 Padelford, GN-50
Seattle, WA 98195
Phone: (206) 543-7296
Martha Tucker Murdoch, Hd.
Staff: Prof 1; Other 1. **Subjects:** Pure and theoretical mathematics and statistics. **Holdings:** 25,388 books and bound periodical volumes. **Subscriptions:** 449 journals and other serials. **Services:** Interlibrary loans; copying; library open to public for reference use only. **Computerized Information Services:** DIALOG, SDC, BRS, OCLC. Performs searches on cost recovery basis. **Networks/Consortia:** Member of WLN.

★16386★
UNIVERSITY OF WASHINGTON - MUSIC LIBRARY (Mus)
113 Music Bldg., DN-10
Seattle, WA 98195
Phone: (206) 543-1168
David A. Wood, Hd.Libn.
Founded: 1950. **Staff:** Prof 3; Other 2. **Subjects:** Music. **Special Collections:** American music center (Kinscella Collection); opera scores, 17th-19th century; Eric Offenbacher Mozart Collection (recordings); Melvin Harris Collection of Wind Recordings. **Holdings:** 46,212 books, scores, and bound periodical volumes; 30,541 scores; 1368 reels of microfilm; 36,697 sound recordings. **Subscriptions:** 512 journals and other serials. **Services:** Interlibrary loans; copying; library open to public for reference use only. **Computerized Information Services:** OCLC. **Networks/Consortia:** Member of WLN. **Staff:** John R. Gibbs, Asst.Libn.; Deborah L. Pierce, Music Cat.

★16387★
UNIVERSITY OF WASHINGTON - NATURAL SCIENCES LIBRARY (Sci-Tech)
Suzzallo Library, FM-25
Seattle, WA 98195
Phone: (206) 543-1243
Nancy G. Blase, Hd.
Founded: 1935. **Staff:** Prof 2; Other 3. **Subjects:** Zoology, geology, geophysics, botany, atmospheric sciences, general science, history of science, biology, nutrition, textile sciences. **Holdings:** 192,353 volumes. **Subscriptions:** 2670 journals and other serials. **Services:** Interlibrary loans; copying; library open to public for reference use only. **Computerized Information Services:** DIALOG, SDC, BRS, OCLC. Performs searches on cost recovery basis. **Networks/Consortia:** Member of WLN. **Staff:** Pamela A. Mofjeld, Asst.Libn.

★16388★
UNIVERSITY OF WASHINGTON - PACIFIC NORTHWEST LONG-TERM CARE CENTER - INFORMATION CLEARINGHOUSE
University of Washington JM-20
Seattle, WA 98195
Subjects: Aging, long-term care, gerontology. **Holdings:** 2000 reports, documents and unpublished papers; 60 newsletters. **Automated Operations:** Computerized cataloging. **Computerized Information Services:** NLM, DIALOG. **Remarks:** Presently inactive.

★16389★
UNIVERSITY OF WASHINGTON - PHILOSOPHY LIBRARY (Hum)
331 Savery, DK-50
Seattle, WA 98195
Phone: (206) 543-5856
Joan E. Christ, Libn.
Founded: 1948. **Staff:** Prof 1. **Subjects:** Philosophy, aesthetics, political and legal philosophy. **Holdings:** 18,302 books and bound periodical volumes. **Subscriptions:** 204 journals and other serials. **Services:** Interlibrary loans; copying; library open to public for reference use only. **Computerized Information Services:** OCLC. **Networks/Consortia:** Member of WLN.

★16390★
UNIVERSITY OF WASHINGTON - PHYSICS-ASTRONOMY LIBRARY (Sci-Tech)
219 Physics Bldg., FM-15
Seattle, WA 98195
Phone: (206) 543-2988
Martha Austin, Hd.Libn.
Founded: 1935. **Staff:** Prof 1. **Subjects:** Physics, astronomy. **Holdings:** 23,350 books and bound periodical volumes; sky atlases. **Subscriptions:** 325 journals and other serials. **Services:** Interlibrary loans; copying; library open to public for reference use only. **Computerized Information Services:** DIALOG, SDC, BRS, OCLC. **Networks/Consortia:** Member of WLN.

★16391★
UNIVERSITY OF WASHINGTON - POLITICAL SCIENCE LIBRARY (Soc Sci)
220 Smith Hall, DP 25
Seattle, WA 98195
Phone: (206) 543-2389
Al Fritz, Libn.
Founded: 1945. **Staff:** Prof 1; Other 3. **Subjects:** Political science. **Holdings:** 57,344 books and bound periodical volumes. **Subscriptions:** 635 journals and other serials; 5 newspapers. **Services:** Interlibrary loans; copying; library open to public for reference use only. **Computerized Information Services:** DIALOG, SDC, BRS, OCLC. **Networks/Consortia:** Member of WLN.

★16392★
UNIVERSITY OF WASHINGTON - REGIONAL PRIMATE RESEARCH CENTER - PRIMATE INFORMATION CENTER (Sci-Tech; Med)
SJ-50
Seattle, WA 98195
Phone: (206) 543-4376
Benella Caminiti, Mgr.
Founded: 1963. **Subjects:** Nonhuman primates, biomedical research, behavioral sciences. **Services:** SDI. **Publications:** Current Primate References, monthly listing of citations - available by subscription; retrospective bibliographies from extensively indexed reference files - available for purchase; recurrent bibliographies, monthly - available by subscription; list of miscellaneous publications available on request. **Remarks:**

The Primate Information Center is an indexing service providing literature-based information to scientists throughout the world. Its staff offers special assistance to those with information needs not met by its services.

★16393★

UNIVERSITY OF WASHINGTON - SOCIAL WORK LIBRARY (Soc Sci)
Social Work/Speech-Hearing Bldg., JH-30　　　　Phone: (206) 545-2180
Seattle, WA 98195　　　　　　　　　　　　　Guela G. Johnson, Libn.
Founded: 1954. **Staff:** Prof 1; Other 2. **Subjects:** Social work; health care; social welfare, policy and service; human growth and behavior; case services; community organizations; social research. **Holdings:** 22,089 books and bound periodical volumes; 4757 pamphlets. **Subscriptions:** 212 journals and other serials. **Services:** Interlibrary loans; copying; reading room for disabled persons with adaptive equipment; library open to public for reference use only. **Computerized Information Services:** DIALOG, SDC, BRS, OCLC. **Networks/Consortia:** Member of WLN.

★16394★

UNIVERSITY OF WASHINGTON - SPECIAL COLLECTIONS DIVISION - PACIFIC NORTHWEST COLLECTION (Area-Ethnic; Hist)
Suzzallo Library, FM-25　　　　　　　　　Phone: (206) 543-1929
Seattle, WA 98195　　　　　　　　　　　　Carla Rickerson, Hd.
Founded: 1905. **Staff:** Prof 2; Other 2. **Subjects:** Northwest Coast Indians; journals of exploration; state and local history; regional economics and business; regional culture; contemporary issues; Pacific Northwest - Washington, Oregon, Idaho, western Montana, Yukon, British Columbia, Alberta and Alaska. **Special Collections:** Journals of 18th and 19th century explorers in region; Japanese internment camp newspapers; Mount St. Helen's eruption. **Holdings:** 45,000 books and bound periodical volumes; 12,449 pamphlets; 4305 regional maps, 1700-1930; 250 scrapbooks (indexed); 122 VF drawers of uncataloged clippings. **Subscriptions:** 351 journals and other serials; 25 newspapers. **Services:** Interlibrary loans (limited); copying; library open to public for reference use only. **Computerized Information Services:** DIALOG, SDC, BRS, OCLC. Performs searches on cost recovery basis. **Networks/Consortia:** Member of WLN. **Special Indexes:** Pacific Northwest Regional Newspaper and Periodical Index (649,000 entries); Klondike Nugget Index, 1898-1903 (card); Index of Contacts with Native Americans from Explorers' Journals (card).

★16395★

UNIVERSITY OF WASHINGTON - SPECIAL COLL.DIV. - PACIFIC NORTHWEST COLLECTION - ARCHITECTURAL HISTORY COLL. (Art; Hist)
Suzzallo Library, FM-25　　　　　　　　　Phone: (206) 543-0742
Seattle, WA 98195　　　　　　　　Richard H. Engeman, Asst.Libn.
Staff: Prof 1. **Subjects:** History and development of architecture and landscape; architecture in Pacific Northwest, 1880 to present. **Holdings:** 25,000 architectural plans, drawings, renderings and ephemera. **Services:** Copying; collection open to public for reference use only. **Computerized Information Services:** OCLC. **Networks/Consortia:** Member of WLN.

★16396★

UNIVERSITY OF WASHINGTON - SPECIAL COLL.DIV. - PACIFIC NORTHWEST COLLECTION - HISTORICAL PHOTOGRAPHY COLL. (Aud-Vis)
Suzzallo Library, FM-25　　　　　　　　　Phone: (206) 543-1929
Seattle, WA 98195　　　　　　　　Richard H. Engeman, Asst.Libn.
Staff: Prof 1. **Subjects:** History in photography of Pacific Northwest and Alaska. **Holdings:** 350,000 photographic negatives and prints. **Services:** Copying; library open to public for reference use only. **Computerized Information Services:** OCLC. **Networks/Consortia:** Member of WLN. **Special Catalogs:** Pacific Northwest Native American photographs and graphic materials (microfiche); Timber industry photographs by Clark Kinsey (microfiche). **Remarks:** The collections document the history of photography in the Pacific Northwest since 1860 and in Alaska and the Yukon Territory of Canada during the Gold Rush and after. Collection includes works of individual photographers in addition to topical assemblies of native American images and portraits, totem culture and carving, regional architectural history, urban visual elements of Seattle and western Washington, minorities and social issues, transportation, industries, regional theater history, cultural resources, landscape. The J. Willis Sayre collection includes 40,000 studio and stage portraits of American theatrical and vaudeville performers and personalities of the recital and concert stage.

★16397★

UNIVERSITY OF WASHINGTON - UNIVERSITY ARCHIVES & MANUSCRIPT DIVISION - MANUSCRIPT COLLECTION (Hist)
Suzzallo Library, FM-25　　　　　　　　　Phone: (206) 543-1879
Seattle, WA 98195　　　　　　　　　　Richard Berner, Hd.Libn.
Staff: Prof 2; Other 2. **Subjects:** Washington politics and government, congressional papers, public power, forest products, fisheries and mining, American literature, urban affairs, ethnic history, education. **Holdings:** 15,538 linear feet of manuscripts. **Services:** Interlibrary loans (limited); copying; collection open to researchers with some restrictions. **Computerized Information Services:** State Historical Records Advisory Board (statewide database). **Publications:** Guide to the Wilbert McLeod Chapman Collection; Manual for Accessioning, Arrangement and Description of Manuscripts and Archives. **Special Catalogs:** Comprehensive Guide to the Manuscripts Collections and to the Personal Papers in the University Archives. **Special Indexes:** Inventories for each accession; indexed for inclusion in cumulative name and subject indexes. **Staff:** Karyl Winn, Mss.Libn.

★16398★

UNIVERSITY OF WASHINGTON - UNIVERSITY ARCHIVES & MANUSCRIPT DIVISION - UNIVERSITY ARCHIVES (Hist)
3902 Cowlitz Rd., HO-10　　　　　　　　Phone: (206) 543-6509
Seattle, WA 98195　　　　　　　　Richard C. Berner, Univ.Archv.
Founded: 1967. **Staff:** Prof 1; Other 1. **Subjects:** University history and administration. **Holdings:** 6900 linear feet of archives; records of major administrative offices and academic departments; personal papers of faculty and administrators, students and faculty organizations, university publications. **Services:** Copying; archives open to public; private papers open to researchers with restrictions. **Computerized Information Services:** State Historical Records Advisory Board (statewide database). **Special Indexes:** Inventories of individual accessions which are indexed in Manuscript Section for nonuniversity names, and in University Archives a cumulative name index for all university offices and departments.

UNIVERSITY OF WATERLOO - CANADIAN INDUSTRIAL INNOVATION CENTRE/WATERLOO
See: Canadian Industrial Innovation Centre/Waterloo

★16399★

UNIVERSITY OF WATERLOO - DANA PORTER ARTS LIBRARY (Hum; Soc Sci)
　　　　　　　　　　　　　　　　　　Phone: (519) 885-1211
Waterloo, ON, Canada N2L 3G1　　　Murray C. Shepherd, Univ.Libn.
Staff: Prof 44; Other 112. **Subjects:** Humanities, social and behavioral sciences, human kinetics and leisure studies, environmental studies. **Special Collections:** Works of Eric Gill; Euclid's Elements and History of Mathematics; private presses (Dolmen, Nonesuch, Golden Cockerel); Santayana Collection; D.R. Davis "Southey" Collection; rare materials from Lady Aberdeen Library of the History of Women; Crapo Dance Collection. **Holdings:** 1.06 million books and bound periodical volumes; 605,904 government publications; 447,329 microforms. **Subscriptions:** 10,518 journals and other serials. **Services:** Interlibrary loans; copying; facilities for the visually handicapped. **Automated Operations:** Computerized circulation. **Computerized Information Services:** Online systems. **Publications:** Focus, Aids, Research Guide, irregular - for internal distribution only; bibliographies and occasional papers, irregular - external distribution; Library Handbook, annual - for internal distribution only. **Staff:** Bruce MacNeil, Assoc.Libn./Pub.Serv.; C. David Emery, Assoc.Libn./Coll.; Lorraine Beattie, Asst.to the Libn., Adm.; Carolynne Presser, Assoc.Libn./Plan. & Sys.; Lois Claxton, Coord./Info.Serv.

★16400★

UNIVERSITY OF WATERLOO - ENGINEERING, MATHEMATICS & SCIENCE DIVISIONAL LIBRARY (Sci-Tech)
　　　　　　　　　　　　　　　　　　Phone: (519) 885-1211
Waterloo, ON, Canada N2L 3G1
Staff: Prof 6; Other 26. **Subjects:** Engineering, mathematics, sciences, optometry, architecture. **Holdings:** 288,053 books and bound periodical volumes; 40,000 technical reports; 27,083 microforms; 7235 maps; 85,958 government publications. **Subscriptions:** 4246 journals and other serials. **Services:** Interlibrary loans; copying; library open to public. **Automated Operations:** Computerized circulation. **Computerized Information Services:** Online systems; internal database. **Publications:** Focus, Aids, Research Guide & Checklist Series, irregular - for internal distribution only. **Special Indexes:** KWOC Index to IEEE and ACM Conference proceedings (card). **Staff:** F. Abrams, Hd., Ref./Coll.Dev.; D. Morton, Coord., Online Ref.; C. McDonald, Coord./User Serv.

★16401★

UNIVERSITY OF WATERLOO - ONLINE INFO. RETRIEVAL SYSTEM FOR THE SOCIOLOGY OF LEISURE & SPORT (SIRLS) (Soc Sci; Rec)
　　　　　　　　　　　　　　　　　　Phone: (519) 885-1211
Waterloo, ON, Canada N2L 3G1　　　Betty Smith, Database Mgr./Cons.
Founded: 1971. **Staff:** Prof 1; Other 2. **Subjects:** Sociology and social psychology of leisure and sport. **Holdings:** 11,000 documents, articles, conference papers, theses, dissertations, unpublished papers and reports

(hardcopy and microfiche). **Services:** Online access by external users; user-request searches; document duplication. **Publications:** SIRLS Brochure - free upon request; Sociology of Leisure and Sport Abstracts (journal). **Remarks:** Maintained by the University's Faculty of Human Kinetics and Leisure Studies, SIRLS provides online access to 13,000 abstracted citations.

★16402★
UNIVERSITY OF WATERLOO - UNIVERSITY MAP AND DESIGN LIBRARY (Env-Cons; Geog-Map)
Environmental Studies Bldg., Rm. 246   Phone: (519) 885-1211
Waterloo, ON, Canada N2L 3G1   Richard Hugh Pinnell, Map Libn.
Founded: 1965. **Staff:** Prof 2; Other 3. **Subjects:** Cartography. **Special Collections:** Environmental Studies Honours Essays (1351). **Holdings:** 5781 books, atlases and bound periodical volumes; 69,286 maps; 20,863 aerial photographs; 275 gazetteers. **Subscriptions:** 65 journals and other serials. **Services:** Copying; library open to public. **Automated Operations:** Computerized circulation. **Staff:** Ann Naese, Map Cur.

★16403★
UNIVERSITY OF WEST FLORIDA - JOHN C. PACE LIBRARY - CURRICULUM MATERIALS LIBRARY (Educ)
        Phone: (904) 474-2439
Pensacola, FL 32504   Ron Toifel, Dir.
Staff: Prof 1; Other 1. **Subjects:** Elementary, secondary and special education textbooks; teaching aides; nonprint media for all subjects, K-12. **Holdings:** 11,000 books; 500 filmstrips; 2500 slides; 300 transparencies; 1100 kits and games; 3100 cassette tapes and phonograph records; 270 publishers' catalogs; 7 VF drawers of pamphlets and ephemera; 2700 curriculum guides; 1400 curricula on microfiche; 85 education reference books; 7 global maps; 990 prints, photographs, posters and charts. **Services:** Library open to public with restrictions. **Computerized Information Services:** DIALOG.

★16404★
UNIVERSITY OF WEST FLORIDA - JOHN C. PACE LIBRARY - SPECIAL COLLECTIONS (Hist)
        Phone: (904) 474-2213
Pensacola, FL 32504   Dean DeBolt, Spec.Coll.Libn.
Staff: Prof 1; Other 2. **Subjects:** West Florida, 1559 to present, including Florida under Spanish, British, American and Confederate governments; Pensacola, 1559 to present; university archives. **Special Collections:** George Washington Sully watercolors, 1833-1839; Governor Sidney Catts papers (5000 items). **Holdings:** 3500 rare books and monographs; 500,000 manuscript and archival documents; 3000 maps; 5000 photographs; 200 newspapers. **Services:** Copying; library open to public. **Special Catalogs:** Separate collection inventories; Guide to the Manuscripts, 1979.

★16405★
UNIVERSITY OF WEST LOS ANGELES - LAW LIBRARY (Law)*
10811 W. Washington Blvd.   Phone: (213) 204-4603
Culver City, CA 90230   Dinah Granifei, Hd.Libn.
Founded: 1967. **Staff:** Prof 1; Other 12. **Subjects:** Law. **Holdings:** 19,000 books; 2116 bound periodical volumes; 2553 volumes on microfiche. **Subscriptions:** 254 journals and other serials. **Services:** Copying; library open to public for reference use only.

★16406★
UNIVERSITY OF WESTERN ONTARIO - CPRI LIBRARY (Med)
Box 2460, Terminal A   Phone: (519) 471-2540
London, ON, Canada N6A 4G6   Asta Hansen, Libn.
Staff: Prof 1; Other 1. **Subjects:** Administration; audiology; behavior modification; biochemistry; clinical chemistry; cytogenetics; electroencephalography; therapy - music, physical, occupational and speech; neurology; nursing; pathology; nutrition; pediatrics; psychiatry; psychology; public health; recreation; social work; sociology; special education. **Holdings:** 2200 books; 3000 bound periodical volumes; 300 staff papers; 5000 reprints; 50 reports; 50 government directories and acts. **Subscriptions:** 173 journals and other serials. **Services:** Interlibrary loans; copying; library open to professionals and university students. **Publications:** Current Research Programmes and Papers Published, annual (from 1960); CPRI Annual Symposium Monographs (from no. 1, 1970). **Special Indexes:** Index to reprints (card). **Also Known As:** Children's Psychiatric Research Institute.

★16407★
UNIVERSITY OF WESTERN ONTARIO - D.B. WELDON LIBRARY - DEPARTMENT OF SPECIAL COLLECTIONS (Hist)
        Phone: (519) 679-6289
London, ON, Canada N6A 3K7   Beth Miller, Libn.
Staff: Prof 1. **Subjects:** Canadiana - literature, pre-1867 to present, history,

voyages and travel, black studies; Edwardian writers, 1889-1918; British history, 16th and 17th centuries; history of science and medicine; Napoleonic era and the French Revolution. **Special Collections:** G. William Stuart Collection of Milton and Miltonia (825 titles); 19th century plays of manners and morals (578 titles); John Galt Collection (150 volumes); Richard Maurice Bucke Collection (personal library: 850 volumes; 21 linear feet of scrapbooks and pamphlets; diaries, letters, documents). **Holdings:** 21,000 books; 1100 bound periodical volumes; 400 British and American pamphlets of Edwardian era; 250 contemporary Canadian pamphlets. **Services:** Interlibrary loans; copying (both limited); department open to public. **Automated Operations:** Computerized cataloging and acquisitions. **Special Catalogs:** G.W. Stuart Collection of Milton and Miltonia; Canadian Chronological Imprints; Private Press Holdings; British/American Pamphlets; Canadian Pamphlets; Juvenialia.

★16408★
UNIVERSITY OF WESTERN ONTARIO - D.B. WELDON LIBRARY - REGIONAL COLLECTION (Hist)
        Phone: (519) 679-6213
London, ON, Canada N6A 3K7   Edward Phelps, Libn.
Founded: 1942. **Staff:** Prof 1; Other 2. **Subjects:** Canadiana, Ontario regional and local history, historical geography, archives. **Special Collections:** County records (local public archives, business archives, private papers); Ontario textbook collection. **Holdings:** 3000 books; 300 bound periodical volumes; 2600 U.W.O. dissertations; 4500 boxes and 3000 volumes of manuscripts and archives; 800 reels of microfilm; 5000 pictures, broadsides, newspapers; 3000 textbooks; 10,000 sheets of maps and fire insurance plans. **Subscriptions:** 10 journals and other serials. **Services:** Interlibrary loans; copying; collection open to public with restrictions. **Automated Operations:** Computerized cataloging. **Publications:** Western Ontario Historical Notes, annual - free to libraries. **Remarks:** Genealogical inquiries are forwarded to the London, ON Genealogical Society.

★16409★
UNIVERSITY OF WESTERN ONTARIO - DEPARTMENT OF GEOGRAPHY - MAP LIBRARY (Geog-Map)
        Phone: (519) 679-3424
London, ON, Canada N6A 5C2   Serge A. Sauer, Map Cur.
Founded: 1966. **Staff:** Prof 2; Other 1. **Subjects:** Canadiana, geography, planning, natural resources. **Holdings:** 195,000 maps; 20,000 air photographs; 1630 atlases; 1180 theses. **Services:** Interlibrary loans; copying; library open to public. **Publications:** Theses Bibliography, annual; Newsletter, irregular. **Special Catalogs:** Atlas listing (automated). **Remarks:** This is regarded as the largest university map collection in Canada. The Great Lakes Cartographic Resource Centre is located in the Map Library.

★16410★
UNIVERSITY OF WESTERN ONTARIO - ENGINEERING LIBRARY (Sci-Tech)
        Phone: (519) 679-6120
London, ON, Canada N6A 5B9   Bogdana Brajsa, Libn.
Founded: 1959. **Staff:** Prof 1; Other 4. **Subjects:** Engineering - chemical, civil, electrical, materials, mechanical. **Holdings:** 23,600 books; 17,700 bound periodical volumes; 3050 research reports; 2053 government documents; 767 pamphlets; 1420 microforms. **Subscriptions:** 715 journals and other serials. **Services:** Interlibrary loans; copying; SDI; library open to public. **Automated Operations:** Computerized cataloging, acquisitions, serials and circulation.

★16411★
UNIVERSITY OF WESTERN ONTARIO - FACULTY OF EDUCATION LIBRARY (Educ)
Althouse College
1137 Western Rd.   Phone: (519) 679-3488
London, ON, Canada N6G 1G7   Anna Holman, Libn.
Founded: 1965. **Staff:** Prof 2; Other 6. **Subjects:** Education. **Holdings:** 80,886 books; 10,458 bound periodical volumes; 325,982 microfiche; 35,476 AV items; 246 pamphlets; 1050 government documents; 439 reels of microfilm; 8 VF drawers of clippings; 2089 computer programs; 900 curriculum guidelines. **Subscriptions:** 521 journals and other serials. **Services:** Interlibrary loans; copying; library open to public excluding school and community college students. **Automated Operations:** Computerized cataloging, acquisitions, serials and circulation. **Special Catalogs:** Audiovisual catalog (card). **Staff:** Sally McCrae, Coll.Libn.; Jean Colhoun, Hd., Circ.

★16412★
UNIVERSITY OF WESTERN ONTARIO - LAW LIBRARY (Law)
        Phone: (519) 679-2857
London, ON, Canada N6A 3K7   Dr. Margaret A. Banks, Libn.
Staff: Prof 3; Other 7. **Subjects:** Law. **Holdings:** 127,733 volumes; 398 cassettes; 8766 microforms. **Subscriptions:** 3297 journals and other serials.

Services: Interlibrary loans; copying; library open to public with restrictions. **Automated Operations:** Computerized cataloging, acquisitions, serials and circulation. **Staff:** Eleanor Jones, Hd., Proc. Unit; Marianne Welch, Ref./ Coll.Libn.

★16413★
UNIVERSITY OF WESTERN ONTARIO - MUSIC LIBRARY (Mus)
London, ON, Canada N6A 3K7
Phone: (519) 679-2466
William Guthrie, Libn.
Founded: 1963. **Staff:** Prof 4; Other 6. **Subjects:** Music theory, music history, applied music, music education. **Special Collections:** Opera, 1597-1900 (1100 manuscripts and scores); letters written by or to Gustav Mahler (500). **Holdings:** 82,785 volumes and scores; 157,000 choral, band and orchestral music scores; 21,500 sound recordings; 7600 microforms; 1350 pamphlets. **Subscriptions:** 620 journals and other serials. **Services:** Interlibrary loans; copying; disc and tape recording listening facilities; library open to public. **Automated Operations:** Computerized cataloging, acquisitions, serials and circulation. **Staff:** Sr. Louise Smith, Coll.Libn.; Cynthia Leive, Music Cat.; Jane Baldwin, Music Ref.Libn.

★16414★
UNIVERSITY OF WESTERN ONTARIO - SCHOOL OF BUSINESS ADMINISTRATION - BUSINESS LIBRARY & INFORMATION CENTRE (Bus-Fin)
London, ON, Canada N6A 3K7
Phone: (519) 679-3255
Jerry Mulcahy, Libn.
Founded: 1960. **Staff:** Prof 1; Other 4. **Subjects:** International business, finance, marketing, operations research, labor relations, accounting. **Special Collections:** Microfiche collection of Canadian and U.S. company data (15,800 items). **Holdings:** 43,000 books; 9500 bound periodical volumes; 7200 government documents (coded); 1500 microforms; 400 pamphlets; 120 cassettes; 16,600 items on companies, industries and business conditions in Canada. **Subscriptions:** 1930 journals and other serials. **Services:** Interlibrary loans; copying; reference service to academic and business community; library open to public with borrowing restrictions. **Automated Operations:** Computerized cataloging, acquisitions, serials and circulation. **Computerized Information Services:** QL Systems, BRS, DIALOG, Info Globe. **Staff:** Elsie Brown, Ref.Supv.

★16415★
UNIVERSITY OF WESTERN ONTARIO - SCHOOL OF LIBRARY & INFORMATION SCIENCE - LIBRARY (Info Sci)
London, ON, Canada N6A 1H1
Phone: (519) 679-3542
Victoria Ripley, Academic Sup.Serv.Coord.
Founded: 1967. **Staff:** Prof 5; Other 5. **Subjects:** Library and information science, computers and electronic data processing, children's literature, Slavic studies, communications. **Special Collections:** Pre-1800 handprinted books (10,000 volumes); dictionaries (500); private press books (600). **Holdings:** 68,000 books; 14,500 bound periodical volumes; 10,000 microforms; 300 tapes. **Subscriptions:** 817 journals and other serials. **Services:** Interlibrary loans; copying; library open to public. **Automated Operations:** Computerized cataloging, circulation and serials. **Publications:** Guide to the Library, annual - free upon request. **Special Catalogs:** COM catalogs: classified catalog with author-title index; serials list; special collections catalog. **Special Indexes:** KWOC index to technical reports and ERIC documents on microfiche. **Staff:** Hanna Marti, Spec.Coll.Libn.John Fracasso, Automated Sys. & Serv.; Martie Grof-Ianelli, Asst.Libn.

★16416★
UNIVERSITY OF WESTERN ONTARIO - SCIENCES LIBRARY (Med)
Natural Sciences Centre
London, ON, Canada N6A 5B7
Phone: (519) 679-6601
Larry C. Lewis, Sci.Libn.
Founded: 1881. **Staff:** Prof 6; Other 22. **Subjects:** Anesthesia, anatomy, applied mathematics, astronomy, biochemistry, biology, biophysics, chemistry, clinical neurological sciences, communicative disorders, computer science, dentistry, epidemiology, family medicine, genetics, geology, geophysics, history of medicine and science, mathematics, medicine, microbiology, nursing, obstetrics and gynecology, occupational therapy, ophthalmology, otolaryngology, pediatrics, pathology, pharmacology, physical medicine, physical therapy, physics, physiology, plant sciences, psychiatry, radiation oncology, radiology, statistics, surgery, zoology. **Holdings:** 279,751 books and bound periodical volumes; 29,650 microforms; 7008 AV materials. **Subscriptions:** 5045 journals and other serials. **Services:** Interlibrary loans; copying; library open to public with restrictions. **Automated Operations:** Computerized cataloging, acquisitions, serials and circulation. **Computerized Information Services:** BRS, CAN/OLE, DIALOG, NLM, SDC; internal database. **Staff:** Anne Walker, Coll./Ref.Libn.; Vijay Kumar, Hd., Proc.Serv.; Eva Borda, Coll./Ref.Libn.; Linda Voelker, Coll./Ref.Libn.; Jean Vitai, Coll./ Ref.Libn.

UNIVERSITY OF WESTERN ONTARIO - SCIENCES LIBRARY - COLLEGE OF FAMILY PHYSICIANS OF CANADA
See: College of Family Physicians of Canada

UNIVERSITY OF WESTERN ONTARIO - WESTMINSTER INSTITUTE FOR ETHICS AND HUMAN VALUES
See: Westminster Institute for Ethics and Human Values

★16417★
UNIVERSITY OF WINDSOR - FACULTY OF EDUCATION LIBRARY (Educ)
600 Third Concession Rd.
Windsor, ON, Canada N9E 1A5
Phone: (519) 969-0520
Thomas J. Robinson, Educ.Libn.
Founded: 1962. **Staff:** Prof 1; Other 2. **Subjects:** Education. **Special Collections:** School texts; children's literature; Montessori Memorial Collection. **Holdings:** 50,000 books; 2116 bound periodical volumes; 1162 filmstrips; 7500 mounted pictures; 700 unmounted pictures and charts; 346 cassettes; 566 kits; 262 records; 12 drawers of pamphlets; 3139 government documents; ERIC microfiche, 1966 to date; ONTERIS microfiche, 1972 to date. **Subscriptions:** 190 journals and other serials. **Services:** Interlibrary loans; copying; library open to public for reference use only. **Automated Operations:** Computerized cataloging and serials. **Computerized Information Services:** Online systems (through Leddy Library).

★16418★
UNIVERSITY OF WINDSOR - PAUL MARTIN LAW LIBRARY (Law)
Windsor, ON, Canada N9B 3P4
Phone: (519) 253-4232
Paul T. Murphy, Law Libn.
Staff: Prof 3; Other 9. **Subjects:** Law. **Holdings:** 62,947 books; 113,522 bound periodical volumes. **Subscriptions:** 2150 journals and other serials. **Services:** Interlibrary loans; copying; library open to public with restrictions. **Computerized Information Services:** QL Systems, DIALOG, CAN/OLE, UTLAS, Westlaw, Eurolex. **Staff:** Daniel K.L. Boen, Cat.Libn.; Huey-Min Soong, Ref.Libn.

★16419★
UNIVERSITY OF WINNIPEG - LIBRARY - SPECIAL COLLECTIONS (Area-Ethnic; Rel-Theol)
515 Portage Ave.
Winnipeg, MB, Canada R3B 2E9
Phone: (204) 786-7811
Dr. W.R. Converse, Chf.Libn.
Special Collections: Ashdown Collection of Canadian Studies; Newcombe Collection of Theology; Canadian Council on Urban and Regional Research (CCURR); Conference of Manitoba and Northwestern Ontario Archives; United Church of Canada. **Holdings:** Figures not available. **Services:** Interlibrary loans; copying; SDI; collections open to public for reference use only. **Automated Operations:** Computerized cataloging, acquisitions, serials, and circulation. **Computerized Information Services:** DIALOG, Info Globe, QL Systems, SDC, International Development Research Centre (IDRC). Performs searches on cost recovery basis. Contact Person: William Pond, 786-7811, extension 538. **Staff:** William Pond .

★16420★
UNIVERSITY OF WISCONSIN, EAU CLAIRE - AREA RESEARCH CENTER AND UNIVERSITY ARCHIVES (Hist)
McIntyre Library
Eau Claire, WI 54701
Phone: (715) 836-2739
Richard L. Pifer, Archv.
Staff: Prof 1; Other 2. **Subjects:** History of western Wisconsin, lumbering history, genealogy, university history. **Special Collections:** Historical atlases and plat books of Wisconsin (44 reels of microfilm). **Holdings:** 1000 linear feet and 40 reels of microfilm of historical manuscripts; 330 maps and atlases; 620 linear feet and 350 reels of microfilm of university records; 19,000 photographs/negatives. **Services:** Interlibrary loans; copying; center open to public for reference use only. **Networks/Consortia:** Member of Historical Society of Wisconsin - Area Research Center Network.

★16421★
UNIVERSITY OF WISCONSIN, EAU CLAIRE - SIMPSON GEOGRAPHIC RESEARCH CENTER - MAP LIBRARY (Geog-Map)
Department of Geography
Eau Claire, WI 54701
Phone: (715) 836-3244
Adam Cahow, Cur., Geographic Mtls.
Staff: Prof 1; Other 5. **Subjects:** Maps of North America. **Holdings:** 120,000 maps; Eau Claire weather data for last 30 years; 200 atlases; 1500 aerial photographs. **Services:** Interlibrary loans; copying; library open to public. **Publications:** New Listings - for interested faculty.

★16422★
UNIVERSITY OF WISCONSIN, GREEN BAY - AREA RESEARCH CENTER (Hist; Soc Sci)
2420 Nicolet Dr.
Green Bay, WI 54301-7001
Phone: (414) 465-2539
Marian A. Gould, Act.Dir., Spec.Coll.
Staff: Prof 1; Other 1. **Subjects:** Local history, communism, socialism and

anarchy. **Special Collections:** Leon Kramer Collection of Communist, Socialist and Anarchist literature (10,000 pamphlets). **Holdings:** 7500 books; 3500 linear feet of local governmental records and private papers. **Services:** Interlibrary loans; copying; center open to public. **Networks/Consortia:** Member of State Historical Society of Wisconsin - Area Research Center Network. **Special Indexes:** Belgian American Research Materials; Guide to Archives and Manuscripts in the University of Wisconsin, Green Bay Area Research Center.

★16423★

UNIVERSITY OF WISCONSIN, GREEN BAY - WOMEN'S EDUCATIONAL PROGRAMS - WOMEN'S STUDIES RESOURCE LIBRARY (Soc Sci)
LC 750
Green Bay, WI 54302
Phone: (414) 465-2136
Patricia Maguire, Spec.
Staff: Prof 1; Other 2. **Subjects:** Women's history, women's movement, biography, resources available to women. **Holdings:** 200 books; 50 bound periodical volumes; information files. **Subscriptions:** 15 journals and other serials. **Services:** Library open to public. **Formerly:** Its Lucy Stone Center - Resource Library.

★16424★

UNIVERSITY OF WISCONSIN, LA CROSSE - AUDIOVISUAL CENTER - FILM LIBRARY (Aud-Vis)
1705 State St.
La Crosse, WI 54601
Phone: (608) 785-8040
Gary Goorough, Coord., Film Lib.
Founded: 1961. **Staff:** Prof 5; Other 23. **Holdings:** 6889 film titles. **Services:** Television services; library open to public. **Automated Operations:** Computerized cataloging, acquisitions and circulation. **Networks/Consortia:** Member of Consortium of University Film Centers (CUFC). **Special Catalogs:** 1982 Film Rental catalog. **Staff:** Dale Montgomery, Dir.

★16425★

UNIVERSITY OF WISCONSIN, LA CROSSE - CENTER FOR CONTEMPORARY POETRY (Hum)
Murphy Library
1631 Pine St.
La Crosse, WI 54601
Phone: (608) 785-8511
Edwin L. Hill, Spec.Coll.Libn.
Founded: 1970. **Staff:** Prof 1; Other 1. **Subjects:** Contemporary poetry, with emphasis on Midwestern poetry. **Special Collections:** August Derleth (107 volumes); private presses - Prairie, Trovillion, Sumac, Perishable Press, Bieler Press, Penumbra Press, Sea Pen Press, Meadow Press, Toothpaste Press, Crepuscular Press, Arkham House (112 volumes); Skeeters Collection of Gothic, Fantasy and Science Fiction (1046 volumes). **Holdings:** 4000 books. **Subscriptions:** 65 journals and other serials. **Services:** Copying (limited); center open to public; persons seeking particular information should call in advance. **Special Indexes:** Index to manuscripts (card).

★16426★

UNIVERSITY OF WISCONSIN, LA CROSSE - CURRICULUM AND INSTRUCTION CENTER (Educ)
College of Education
Morris Hall
La Crosse, WI 54601
Phone: (608) 785-8651
Ed Zeimet, Libn.
Founded: 1972. **Staff:** Prof 1; Other 1. **Subjects:** Literature for children and young adults; education - English, mathematics, social studies, science. **Holdings:** 31,444 books, bound periodical volumes and nonprint items; 10 curriculum files; 2 standard test files; 24 vertical files. **Subscriptions:** 45 journals and other serials. **Services:** Center open to area teachers.

★16427★

UNIVERSITY OF WISCONSIN, LA CROSSE - MURPHY LIBRARY (Educ)
1631 Pine St.
La Crosse, WI 54601
Phone: (608) 785-8505
Dale Montgomery, Dir., Instr.Serv.
Founded: 1909. **Staff:** Prof 9; Other 17. **Subjects:** Humanities, business administration, education, physical education, science, medical technology. **Special Collections:** Local and regional history (3000 volumes; 750 tapes; 35,000 photographs; maps); Steamboats (15,000 photographs and data files). **Holdings:** 328,823 books; 43,206 bound periodical volumes; 130,566 government documents; 28,034 reels of microfilm; 493,258 microforms. **Subscriptions:** 2390 journals and other serials; 43 newspapers. **Services:** Interlibrary loans; copying; library open to students, faculty and local community. **Computerized Information Services:** OCLC. **Networks/Consortia:** Member of Wisconsin Interlibrary Services (WILS). **Remarks:** Local cooperative lending with Viterbo College and Western Wisconsin Technical Institute. **Staff:** S. Sechrest, Doc.; Christine Berg, Circ.Susan Klein, Lib.Instr.;E. Millich, ILL; C. Marx, Cat.; O. Thompson, Microforms; Dale Gresseth, Ser.; Karin Sandvik, Acq.

★16428★

UNIVERSITY OF WISCONSIN, MADISON - AFRICAN STUDIES INSTRUCTIONAL MATERIALS CENTER (Area-Ethnic)†
Teachers Education Bldg.
225 N. Mills St.
Madison, WI 53706
Phone: (608) 263-4178
Dr. Joseph Adjaye, Outreach Coord.
Founded: 1971. **Staff:** Prof 1; Other 3. **Subjects:** Social studies, music, literature, French, art, anthropology, science, economics, African languages, mathematics, education, history, geography, global issues. **Special Collections:** Life in African countries slide collection (5000). **Holdings:** 2700 books; 200 maps; cassettes; discs; filmstrips; transparencies; 73 vertical files. **Subscriptions:** 30 journals and other serials. **Services:** Center open to public. **Networks/Consortia:** Member of Madison Area Library Council (MALC). **Special Catalogs:** Catalog of 35mm slide collection, 1977. **Remarks:** Maintained by University of Wisconsin, Madison - African Studies Program. The slide collection is located at 1334 Van Hise Hall, 1220 Linden Drive, Madison, WI 53706. An additional phone number is 263-2171.

★16429★

UNIVERSITY OF WISCONSIN, MADISON - ARCHIVES (Hist)
B134 Memorial Library
728 State St.
Madison, WI 53706
Phone: (608) 262-3290
J. Frank Cook, Dir.
Staff: Prof 6. **Subjects:** University archives. **Holdings:** 1000 books; 18,000 cubic feet of archival materials. **Services:** Interlibrary loans; copying; archives open to public with restrictions. **Staff:** Bernard Schermetzler, Archv./Iconographer; Nancy Kunde, Archv./Rec.Mgr.; James Liebig, Archv./Assoc.Dir.; Steve Masar, Archv./Processor; Laura Smail, Spec./Oral Hist.

★16430★

UNIVERSITY OF WISCONSIN, MADISON - BIOLOGY LIBRARY (Sci-Tech)
Birge Hall
430 Lincoln Dr.
Madison, WI 53706
Phone: (608) 262-2740
Silvia Watson, Act.Libn.
Founded: 1907. **Staff:** Prof 1; Other 1. **Subjects:** Botany, zoology. **Holdings:** 39,000 volumes. **Subscriptions:** 700 journals and other serials. **Services:** Library open to public for reference use. **Publications:** Acquisitions list, quarterly; library use aids. **Special Catalogs:** Serials file (card).

★16431★

UNIVERSITY OF WISCONSIN, MADISON - BOTANY DEPARTMENT - HERBARIUM LIBRARY (Sci-Tech)
158 Birge Hall
Madison, WI 53706
Phone: (608) 262-2792
H.H. Iltis, Dir. of Herbarium
Founded: 1849. **Subjects:** Taxonomy of flowering plants, corn, lichens, mosses; Wisconsin and United States flora; biogeography; evolution. **Special Collections:** Specimens of pressed dried plants from all over the world (750,000); C.R. Huskins and D.C. Cooper reprint collections on cyptology; man's need for nature; topographic and vegetation maps. **Holdings:** 2000 volumes; 490 bound periodical volumes; 40,000 reprints; 67 dissertations; 155 boxes of microcards. **Subscriptions:** 13 journals and other serials. **Services:** Copying; library open to public with restrictions. **Publications:** Atlas of the Vascular Flora of Wisconsin Plants; 60 papers on selected Wisconsin plant families; books on lichens.

★16432★

UNIVERSITY OF WISCONSIN, MADISON - BUREAU OF AUDIOVISUAL INSTRUCTION - LIBRARY (Aud-Vis)
1327 University Ave.
Box 2093
Madison, WI 53701
Phone: (608) 262-1644
Dr. Hal F. Riehle, Dir.
Staff: Prof 5; Other 16. **Holdings:** 15,100 prints of 16mm motion picture films (8440 titles). **Services:** Library open to public. **Automated Operations:** Computerized cataloging, acquisitions and circulation. **Networks/Consortia:** Member of Consortium of University Film Centers (CUFC). **Special Catalogs:** Bound book catalog printed every 2-3 years; interim catalog, annual; special catalogs and lists periodically. **Staff:** Joel D. Larson, Coord., Film Lib.Serv.

★16433★

UNIVERSITY OF WISCONSIN, MADISON - CARTOGRAPHIC LABORATORY - ARTHUR H. ROBINSON MAP LIBRARY (Geog-Map)
310 Science Hall
550 N. Park St.
Madison, WI 53706
Phone: (608) 262-1471
Mary Galneder, Map Libn.
Staff: Prof 1; Other 2. **Subjects:** Worldwide coverage of topographic, thematic and general maps; aerial photographs; nautical charts. **Holdings:** 500 books; 207,500 maps; 133,545 aerial photographs; 2468 air photo mosaic indexes. **Services:** Interlibrary loans; library open to public for reference use only. **Formerly:** Its Map and Air Photo Library.

★16434★

UNIVERSITY OF WISCONSIN, MADISON - CENTER FOR DEMOGRAPHY - LIBRARY (Soc Sci)
4457 Social Science Bldg.   Phone: (608) 262-2182
Madison, WI 53706   Ruth Sandor, Libn.
Founded: 1962. **Staff:** Prof 1. **Subjects:** Demography. **Holdings:** 10,000 books; 200 bound periodical volumes; 200 U.S. census reports; international population censuses on microfilm, 1945-1967; reprints; documents. **Subscriptions:** 200 journals and other serials. **Services:** Library open to public with restrictions. **Networks/Consortia:** Member of Association for Population/Family Planning Libraries and Information Centers - International (APLIC-International). **Publications:** Acquisition List, monthly - free upon request; List of Periodical Holdings.

★16435★

UNIVERSITY OF WISCONSIN, MADISON - CENTER FOR HEALTH SCIENCES LIBRARIES (Med)†
1305 Linden Dr.   Phone: (608) 262-6594
Madison, WI 53706   Virginia Holtz, Dir.
Staff: Prof 16; Other 18. **Subjects:** Health sciences and health care administration. **Special Collections:** History of medicine (15,000 volumes). **Holdings:** 90,000 books; 110,000 bound periodical volumes; 3500 audiovisual materials; 3660 pamphlets and government documents. **Subscriptions:** 4500 journals and other serials. **Services:** Interlibrary loans; copying; SDI; library open to public. **Automated Operations:** Computerized cataloging. **Computerized Information Services:** MEDLINE, BRS, TOXLINE. **Networks/Consortia:** Member of Wisconsin Interlibrary Services (WILS); Greater Midwest Regional Medical Library Network (Region 3). **Remarks:** The Center for Health Sciences Libraries includes the holdings of the William S. Middleton Health Sciences Library at the above address and the Weston Clinical Science Center Library, 600 Highland Ave., Rm. J5120, Madison, WI 53792. **Staff:** Dorothy Whitcomb, Hist.Coll.Libn.; Ruth Swanson, Weston Lib.; Dorothy Kanter, Coll.Dev.; Lowell Ransom, Cat.; Kay Cimpl, Weston Lib.; Judith Hathway, Cat.Terrance Jones, Cat.; Susan Kirkbride, Ref.Libn.; Wanda Auerbach, Ref.Libn.; Blanche Singer, ILL; Diane Slater, AV Libn.; Barbara Schmiechen, Ref./Ext.Libn.; Rose Mosigien, Circ./Ref.Libn.; Phyllis Kauffman, Cat.; Patricia Wilcox, Ref.Libn.

★16436★

UNIVERSITY OF WISCONSIN, MADISON - CENTER FOR LIMNOLOGY - LIBRARY (Sci-Tech)
680 N. Park   Phone: (608) 262-3304
Madison, WI 53706   Jane Colwin, Libn.
Staff: Prof 1. **Subjects:** Limnology, ecology, zoology, fishes, oceanography, environmental studies. **Holdings:** 2700 books; 400 bound periodical volumes; 43 volumes of periodicals on microfiche; 724,000 reprints; 1600 government documents; 172 microfiche; 293 unbound journals. **Subscriptions:** 150 journals and other serials. **Services:** Library open to public for reference use only with permission of director of laboratory.

★16437★

UNIVERSITY OF WISCONSIN, MADISON - CHEMISTRY LIBRARY (Sci-Tech)
Chemistry Bldg.   Phone: (608) 262-2942
Madison, WI 53706   Kendall Rouse, Chem.Libn.
Founded: 1947. **Staff:** Prof 1; Other 1. **Subjects:** Chemistry - analytical, inorganic, organic, physical, theoretical. **Holdings:** 12,948 books; 18,424 bound periodical volumes; Chemical Abstracts on microfilm, 1907-1983. **Subscriptions:** 400 journals and other serials. **Services:** Interlibrary loans; copying; library open to public. **Computerized Information Services:** CAS Online, Institute for Scientific Information (ISI). **Publications:** New Acquisitions List, monthly.

★16438★

UNIVERSITY OF WISCONSIN, MADISON - COLLEGE OF ENGINEERING - TECHNICAL REPORTS CENTER (Sci-Tech)
Kurt F. Wendt Library
215 N. Randall Ave.   Phone: (608) 262-6845
Madison, WI 53706   Jean Gilbertson, Libn.
Founded: 1965. **Staff:** Prof 1; Other 1. **Subjects:** Engineering - nuclear, aerospace, environmental; computer science; standards and specifications; science and technology. **Special Collections:** Department of Energy Reports (320,000); National Aeronautics and Space Administration Reports (280,000); U.S. Patent Collection (4 million). **Holdings:** 101,000 paper copy reports; 1.2 million microforms. **Services:** Interlibrary loans; copying; center open to public.

★16439★

UNIVERSITY OF WISCONSIN, MADISON - COOPERATIVE CHILDREN'S BOOK CENTER (CCBC) (Educ)
Helen C. White Hall, Rm. 4289-4290
600 N. Park St.   Phone: (608) 263-3721
Madison, WI 53706   Ginny Moore Kruse, Dir.
Founded: 1963. **Staff:** Prof 3; Other 4. **Subjects:** Children's literature - current trade titles, recommended titles in print, 19th- and early 20th-century titles, children's books by Wisconsin authors and illustrators, aids in book selection, children's book exhibits; publishing of juvenile books; intellectual freedom and book censorship; book reviewing and evaluation; book illustration. **Special Collections:** Edgar Rice Burroughs Collection (60 titles); Mother Goose Collection (80 titles); Thornton Burgess Collection (150 titles); Alternative Press Collection (483 titles); Newbery and Caldecott Medal books, including first printings and significant editions; historical and contemporary pop-up books. **Holdings:** 25,000 volumes; 12 VF drawers of material on children's literature; 3 manuscripts. **Subscriptions:** 44 journals; 22 newsletters. **Services:** Offers lectures, workshops, conferences, speeches, courses and special events; open to adult public for reference use only; circulating resources for professional use. **Publications:** Bibliographies; Alternative Press Publishers of Children's Books: a Directory - both free to Wisconsin residents and for sale to nonresidents. **Remarks:** Supported by the Wisconsin Department of Public Instruction through the Division for Library Services and by the University of Wisconsin, Madison through the School of Education and the Library School. **Staff:** Kathleen Horning, Spec.Coll.Coord.; Gloria Waity, Outreach Libn.

★16440★

UNIVERSITY OF WISCONSIN, MADISON - DATA AND PROGRAM LIBRARY SERVICE (Soc Sci)
4452 Social Science Bldg.   Phone: (608) 262-7962
Madison, WI 53706   Alice Robbin, Hd.
Founded: 1966. **Staff:** Prof 3. **Subjects:** Political science, sociology, economics, history, census-demography. **Special Collections:** Slave trade to the Americas; Florentine census and property survey of 1428; american fertility surveys; occupational and social mobility. **Holdings:** 300 books; 80 bound periodical volumes; 1280 codebooks for data; 70 guides to data archival holdings; 100 programs of statistical software; 2000 magnetic tapes. **Subscriptions:** 32 journals and other serials. **Services:** Interlibrary loans; copying; service open to public. **Publications:** Directory of the Machine Readable Data and Program Holdings of the Data and Program Library Service. **Staff:** Tom Flory, Data Libn.

★16441★

UNIVERSITY OF WISCONSIN, MADISON - DEPARTMENT OF PSYCHIATRY - LITHIUM INFORMATION CENTER (Med)
600 Highland Ave.   Phone: (608) 263-6171
Madison, WI 53792   Margaret G. Baudhuin, Libn./Info.Spec.
Founded: 1975. **Staff:** Prof 5; Other 3. **Subjects:** Medical uses of lithium. **Holdings:** 11,000 articles, books, abstracts and miscellaneous items (computer storage). **Services:** Copying; SDI; center open to public; direct access to holdings through a compatible computer terminal. **Automated Operations:** Computerized cataloging. **Computerized Information Services:** Lithium Library. Performs searches on fee basis. **Publications:** Lithium and Manic Depression: A Guide; Lithium and the Kidney: A Bibliography. **Staff:** James W. Jefferson, M.D., Co-Dir.; John H. Greist, M.D., Co-Dir.; Judith A. Carroll, Res.Spec.; Bette L. Hartley, Libn.

★16442★

UNIVERSITY OF WISCONSIN, MADISON - DEPARTMENT OF RURAL SOCIOLOGY - APPLIED POPULATION LAB. - LIBRARY (Soc Sci)
Agriculture Hall, Rm. 316   Phone: (608) 262-3029
Madison, WI 53706   Stephen J. Tordella, Spec.
Staff: Prof 1. **Subjects:** Demographic material on fertility, mortality, migration. **Holdings:** 2000 books; 24 VF drawers of pamphlets. **Subscriptions:** 10 journals and other serials. **Services:** Copying; library open to public by appointment. **Automated Operations:** WISPOP (demographic database for Wisconsin).

★16443★

UNIVERSITY OF WISCONSIN, MADISON - DEPARTMENT OF URBAN AND REGIONAL PLANNING - GRADUATE RESEARCH CENTER (Plan)
Music Hall
925 Lathrop Dr.   Phone: (608) 262-1004
Madison, WI 53706   Irwin Weintraub, Libn.
Founded: 1965. **Staff:** Prof 1; Other 1. **Subjects:** Urban and regional planning, land and water resources, zoning, social services planning, planning in developing areas. **Holdings:** 5000 books; 25,000 reports and pamphlets; 100 theses and dissertations. **Subscriptions:** 65 journals and other serials.

Services: Interlibrary loans; copying; center open to public.

★16444★

UNIVERSITY OF WISCONSIN, MADISON - F.B. POWER PHARMACEUTICAL LIBRARY (Med)
School of Pharmacy
425 N. Charter St.   Phone: (608) 262-2894
Madison, WI 53706   Dolores Nemec, Libn.
Founded: 1883. **Staff:** Prof 1; Other 1. **Subjects:** Pharmacy and related subjects. **Special Collections:** Catalogs of drugs and pharmaceutical equipment, 1860 to present; Kremers Reference Files, 1870 to present (pamphlets; correspondence; manuscripts; pictures; broadsides; clippings); Iowa Drug Information Service. **Holdings:** 11,995 books; 21,296 bound periodical volumes. **Subscriptions:** 400 journals and 308 serials. **Services:** Interlibrary loans; copying (fee); library open to public for reference use only.

★16445★

UNIVERSITY OF WISCONSIN, MADISON - GEOGRAPHY LIBRARY (Geog-Map)
280 Science Hall   Phone: (608) 262-1706
Madison, WI 53706   Miriam E. Kerndt, Geog.Libn.
Staff: Prof 1; Other 1. **Subjects:** Geography, cartography. **Holdings:** 45,000 books and bound periodical volumes. **Subscriptions:** 400 journals and other serials. **Services:** Interlibrary loans; library open to public. **Automated Operations:** Computerized cataloging. **Computerized Information Services:** OCLC. **Networks/Consortia:** Member of Wisconsin Interlibrary Services (WILS). **Publications:** Acquisitions list, 3/year.

★16446★

UNIVERSITY OF WISCONSIN, MADISON - GEOLOGY-GEOPHYSICS LIBRARY (Sci-Tech)
440 Weeks Hall   Phone: (608) 262-8956
Madison, WI 53706   Nancy L. Crossfield, Libn.
Staff: Prof 1. **Subjects:** Geology, geophysics, oceanography. **Holdings:** 15,000 books; 31,000 bound periodical volumes; 700 department theses, 1970 to present; 2300 maps. **Subscriptions:** 2500 journals and other serials. **Services:** Interlibrary loans; copying; library open to public. **Automated Operations:** Computerized serials and acquisitions. **Computerized Information Services:** DIALOG. **Publications:** Acquisitions list, monthly.

★16447★

UNIVERSITY OF WISCONSIN, MADISON - GERALD G. SOMERS GRADUATE REFERENCE ROOM (Soc Sci)
8432 Social Science Bldg.
1180 Observatory Dr.   Phone: (608) 262-6195
Madison, WI 53706   Mary L. Crompton, Libn.
Founded: 1964. **Staff:** Prof 1; Other 10. **Subjects:** Sociology, economics, industrial relations, anthropology. **Special Collections:** Institute for Research on Poverty Collection; economic history. **Holdings:** 11,360 books; 3310 bound periodical volumes; 6750 pamphlets. **Subscriptions:** 170 journals and other serials. **Services:** Interlibrary loans; room open to public. **Publications:** Acquisitions list, monthly.

★16448★

UNIVERSITY OF WISCONSIN, MADISON - INSTITUTE FOR RESEARCH IN THE HUMANITIES - LIBRARY (Hum)
Old Observatory   Phone: (608) 262-3855
Madison, WI 53706   Loretta Freiling, Prog.Asst.
Founded: 1959. **Staff:** 1. **Subjects:** Humanities - Ancient to Renaissance. **Special Collections:** Works by Benedetto Croce (500 volumes). **Holdings:** 1100 books. **Services:** Library open to public with restrictions.

★16449★

UNIVERSITY OF WISCONSIN, MADISON - KOHLER ART LIBRARY (Art)
Elvehjem Museum of Art
800 University Ave.   Phone: (608) 263-2256
Madison, WI 53706   William C. Bunce, Dir. & Hd.Libn.
Founded: 1970. **Staff:** Prof 2; Other 4. **Subjects:** Art, architecture, decorative arts. **Holdings:** 91,158 books, bound periodical volumes and serials; 32 VF drawers of exhibition and sales catalogs; theses and dissertations; 12,240 microforms. **Subscriptions:** 621 journals and other serials. **Services:** Copying; library open to public, but some materials do not circulate. **Staff:** Louise Henning, Asst.Libn.

★16450★

UNIVERSITY OF WISCONSIN, MADISON - LAND TENURE CENTER - LIBRARY (Agri)
434 Steenbock Memorial Library
550 Babcock Dr.   Phone: (608) 262-1240
Madison, WI 53706   Teresa J. Anderson, Libn.
Founded: 1962. **Staff:** Prof 2; Other 1. **Subjects:** Land tenure, agrarian reform, agricultural economics, Latin America, Asia, Africa, rural development, underdeveloped areas. **Holdings:** 22,000 books; 1200 bound periodical volumes; 34,000 unbound reports, manuscripts, clippings, pamphlets, documents; 8 VF drawers of microfilm; 100 titles of Economic Development Plans; 250 titles of dissertations. **Subscriptions:** 400 journals and other serials. **Services:** Interlibrary loans; copying; library open to public. **Publications:** Accessions List, irregular - free upon request; irregular bibliographies; annotated bibliography on land tenure and reform in Latin America, Africa and Asia. **Special Indexes:** Many journal articles indexed in the catalog. **Staff:** Beverly R. Phillips, Libn.

★16451★

UNIVERSITY OF WISCONSIN, MADISON - LAW SCHOOL LIBRARY (Law)
                                                       Phone: (608) 262-1128
Madison, WI 53706   Anita Morse, Dir.
Founded: 1868. **Staff:** Prof 9; Other 5. **Subjects:** Law, criminal justice, foreign law. **Holdings:** 253,803 books and bound periodical volumes; 108,184 microform titles. **Subscriptions:** 3822 serials; 20 newspapers. **Services:** Interlibrary loans; copying; library open to public. **Automated Operations:** Computerized cataloging. **Computerized Information Services:** OCLC, LEXIS. **Networks/Consortia:** Member of Wisconsin Interlibrary Services (WILS). **Publications:** Selected recent acquisitions; current corrections literature. **Staff:** Nancy Paul, Asst.Dir., Tech.Serv.; Cindy May, Cat.Libn.; Gloria Holz, Circ./Reserve Libn.; William Ebbott, Asst.Dir., Rd.Serv.; Vera Page, Foreign Law Libn.; Marcia Griskavich, Cat.Libn.; Barbara Meyer, Pub.Serv.Libn.

★16452★

UNIVERSITY OF WISCONSIN, MADISON - LAW SCHOOL LIBRARY - CRIMINAL JUSTICE REFERENCE & INFORMATION CENTER (Soc Sci)
L140 Law Library   Phone: (608) 262-1499
Madison, WI 53706   Sue L. Center, Asst.Dir.
Founded: 1969. **Staff:** Prof 3; Other 2. **Subjects:** Criminal justice system, police science, corrections, drug abuse, delinquency, alcoholism. **Special Collections:** Penal Press Publications. **Holdings:** 29,000 books and bound periodical volumes. **Subscriptions:** 1000 journals and other serials. **Services:** Interlibrary loans; copying; center open to public with restrictions. **Publications:** Current Criminal Justice Literature, bimonthly - distributed to agencies in Wisconsin. **Staff:** Marcia Griskavich, Libn.; Barbara Meyer, Libn.

★16453★

UNIVERSITY OF WISCONSIN, MADISON - LIBRARY SCHOOL LIBRARY (Info Sci)
600 N. Park St.   Phone: (608) 263-2960
Madison, WI 53706   Sally Davis, Libn.
Founded: 1906. **Staff:** Prof 2; Other 2. **Subjects:** Library science, information science, children's literature, young adult literature. **Holdings:** 48,000 books; 3965 bound periodical volumes; 8800 pamphlets; 1700 microforms; 2500 AV materials. **Subscriptions:** 450 journals and other serials. **Services:** Interlibrary loans; copying; library open to public. **Networks/Consortia:** Member of Wisconsin Interlibrary Services (WILS). **Staff:** Peggy Green, Asst.Libn.

★16454★

UNIVERSITY OF WISCONSIN, MADISON - MARINE ENVIRONMENT READING ROOM
1225 W. Dayton St., Room 1229
Madison, WI 53706
Defunct

★16455★

UNIVERSITY OF WISCONSIN, MADISON - MATHEMATICS LIBRARY (Sci-Tech)
B224 Van Vleck Hall   Phone: (608) 262-3596
Madison, WI 53706   Shirley Tan Shen, Libn.-Spec.
Founded: 1938. **Staff:** Prof 1. **Subjects:** Mathematics, statistics, computer sciences, mathematical physics. **Holdings:** 34,776 volumes. **Subscriptions:** 373 journals and other serials. **Services:** Interlibrary loans; copying; library open to public for reference use only.

★16456★

UNIVERSITY OF WISCONSIN, MADISON - MEMORIAL LIBRARY - DEPARTMENT OF RARE BOOKS & SPECIAL COLLECTIONS (Hum; Rare Book)
728 State St.   Phone: (608) 262-3243
Madison, WI 53706   John Tedeschi, Cur.
Staff: Prof 2; Other 2. **Subjects:** History of science, 19th- and 20th-century American literature, English literature, Socialistica, Russian history, 17th- and 18th-century European social and political history. **Special Collections:** Thordarson Collection (history of science; 5000 volumes); Bassett-Brownell Mark Twain Collection (500 volumes; periodicals; manuscripts); Sukov Collection of Little Magazines (4500 titles); Russian Underground Collection (1800 items); French pamphlet collection (2500 titles); Cairns Collection (American women writers; 2800 titles). **Holdings:** 55,000 books; 29,000 periodical volumes. **Subscriptions:** 1200 journals and other serials. **Services:** Department open to public with restrictions. **Publications:** Exhibit catalogs, 2/year. **Special Indexes:** Chronological files (book and card); literature in translation and interview indexes. **Staff:** Deb Reilly, Asst.Cur.

★16457★

UNIVERSITY OF WISCONSIN, MADISON - MILLS MUSIC LIBRARY (Mus)
B162 Memorial Library
728 State St.   Phone: (608) 263-1884
Madison, WI 53706   Arne J. Arneson, Music Libn.
Staff: Prof 2; Other 7. **Subjects:** Music. **Special Collections:** American music before 1900 (1200 items); Wisconsin folk songs (Stratman-Thomas Collection); Civil War band books; American musical theater (Thomas-Witmark Collection). **Holdings:** 41,000 scores; 32,800 books and bound periodical volumes; 33,000 recordings; 745 reels of microfilm. **Subscriptions:** 418 journals and other serials. **Services:** Interlibrary loans; library open to public for reference use only. **Automated Operations:** Computerized cataloging. **Special Catalogs:** Catalog of American music collection (card).

★16458★

UNIVERSITY OF WISCONSIN, MADISON - NIEMAN-GRANT JOURNALISM READING ROOM (Info Sci)
2130 Vilas Communication Hall
821 University Ave.   Phone: (608) 263-3387
Madison, WI 53706   Mary Kay Nagel, Libn.
Founded: 1953. **Staff:** Prof 2. **Subjects:** Journalism and reporting, law of mass communications, mass communications methodology and research, mass media in the U.S., public opinion and propaganda, public relations, international communications, advertising, photojournalism and photography. **Special Collections:** Thayer Law of Mass Communications Collection (350). **Holdings:** 5000 books; 1500 bound periodical volumes; 3 VF drawers of pamphlets; 20 boxes of reports. **Subscriptions:** 150 journals and other serials; 90 newspapers. **Services:** Room open to public for research projects. **Networks/Consortia:** Member of Special Campus Libraries Group. **Remarks:** Reading Room is part of the School of Journalism and Mass Communications. **Staff:** Diane Kenna, Asst.Libn.

★16459★

UNIVERSITY OF WISCONSIN, MADISON - PHYSICS LIBRARY (Sci-Tech)
1150 University Ave.   Phone: (608) 262-9500
Madison, WI 53706   Sandra Moline, Libn.
Founded: 1974. **Staff:** Prof 1; Other 3. **Subjects:** Experimental and theoretical physics. **Special Collections:** Photograph collection of Nobel Prize winners in physics. **Holdings:** 13,000 books; 15,000 bound periodical volumes. **Subscriptions:** 500 journals and other serials. **Services:** Interlibrary loans; library open to public. **Publications:** Acquisitions List and Information Letter, monthly.

★16460★

UNIVERSITY OF WISCONSIN, MADISON - PLANT PATHOLOGY MEMORIAL LIBRARY (Sci-Tech)
1630 Linden Dr.   Phone: (608) 262-1410
Madison, WI 53706   Helen H. Kuntz, Libn.
Subjects: Phytopathology, plant virology, plant physiology. **Special Collections:** Johnson-Hoggan Memorial Collection of Plant Virus Literature. **Holdings:** 2646 books; 2301 bound periodical volumes; 65,000 reprints; 400 theses and dissertations. **Subscriptions:** 90 journals and other serials. **Services:** Interlibrary loans; library open to public for reference use only. **Special Catalogs:** Catalogs of abstracts of virus materials and of reprint materials in all branches of plant pathology (card).

★16461★

UNIVERSITY OF WISCONSIN, MADISON - POULTRY SCIENCE DEPARTMENT - HALPIN MEMORIAL LIBRARY (Agri)
Animal Science Bldg., Rm. 214
1675 Observatory Dr.   Phone: (608) 262-1243
Madison, WI 53706   Louis C. Arrington, Prof.
Founded: 1960. **Staff:** 2. **Subjects:** Poultry science. **Special Collections:** Radford Collection of poultry literature. **Holdings:** 840 books; 600 bound periodical volumes; 12,000 reprints and pamphlets. **Subscriptions:** 30 journals and other serials. **Services:** Library open to public.

★16462★

UNIVERSITY OF WISCONSIN, MADISON - SCHOOL OF EDUCATION - INSTRUCTIONAL MATERIALS CENTER (Educ)
Teacher Education Bldg.
225 N. Mills St.   Phone: (608) 263-4750
Madison, WI 53706   Deane W. Hill, Dir.
Founded: 1950. **Staff:** Prof 3; Other 13. **Subjects:** Education, print and non-print instructional materials, children's literature. **Special Collections:** Standardized tests; curriculum guides on microfiche. **Holdings:** 50,000 books and media items; 1460 bound periodical volumes; microfiche; ERIC microfiche with indexes. **Subscriptions:** 300 journals and other serials. **Services:** Interlibrary loans; copying; center open to public with borrower's card. **Automated Operations:** Computerized cataloging. **Computerized Information Services:** DIALOG, BRS. **Networks/Consortia:** Member of Wisconsin Interlibrary Services (WILS). **Special Catalogs:** Bibliographies on topics of current interest in education. **Remarks:** Includes the holdings of its former Historical Materials Collection. **Staff:** Jane Magee, Tech.Serv.; Jo Ann Carr, Pub.Serv., Instr.Prog.

★16463★

UNIVERSITY OF WISCONSIN, MADISON - SCHOOL OF SOCIAL WORK - VIDEO RESOURCE LIBRARY (Soc Sci; Aud-Vis)
425 Henry Mall, Suite 163   Phone: (608) 263-3663
Madison, WI 53706   Rebecca Roberts, Supv.
Founded: 1978. **Staff:** Prof 1; Other 20. **Subjects:** Addiction, child abuse, mental illness and therapy. **Holdings:** 500 videotapes. **Services:** Copying; library open to public. **Publications:** VRL Connection newsletter, semiannual. **Special Catalogs:** Video Resource Library Catalog, annual.

★16464★

UNIVERSITY OF WISCONSIN, MADISON - SCHOOL OF SOCIAL WORK - VIRGINIA L. FRANKS MEMORIAL LIBRARY (Soc Sci)
425 Henry Mall, Rm. 230   Phone: (608) 263-3840
Madison, WI 53706   Thurston Davini, Libn.
Founded: 1972. **Staff:** Prof 1. **Subjects:** Social work - education and administration, psychotherapy and behavior modification, corrections, alcoholism and drug abuse, adoption and foster care. **Special Collections:** Unpublished theses and research projects (500); social gerontology books; pamphlets; periodicals; VF drawers; AV materials. **Holdings:** 11,102 books; 1065 bound periodical volumes; VF items. **Subscriptions:** 217 journals and other serials. **Services:** Interlibrary loans; copying; library open to public with restrictions. **Computerized Information Services:** BRS, DIALOG.

★16465★

UNIVERSITY OF WISCONSIN, MADISON - SEMINARY OF MEDIEVAL SPANISH STUDIES - LIBRARY (Area-Ethnic)
1120 Van Hise Hall   Phone: (608) 262-2529
Madison, WI 53706   Lloyd Kasten, Prof.
Founded: 1931. **Subjects:** Alfonso X of Castile, Old Spanish and Aragonese, Old Spanish literature. **Special Collections:** Photostatic reproduction of works of Alfonso X; Vocabulary files of works of Alfonso X and of Juan Fernandez de Heredia; Old Spanish dictionaries. **Holdings:** 8500 books; 550 bound periodical volumes; 274 volumes of photostats; 4500 pamphlets and reprints; 38 drawers of notes and research materials; 50 dissertations; 450 reels of microfilm. **Subscriptions:** 25 journals and other serials. **Services:** Copying; library open to public with restrictions.

★16466★

UNIVERSITY OF WISCONSIN, MADISON - SMALL BUSINESS DEVELOPMENT & RECREATION CENTER - LIBRARY (Bus-Fin; Rec)
602 State St.   Phone: (608) 263-3166
Madison, WI 53703   Susan Awe, Info.Coord.
Staff: Prof 2. **Subjects:** Small business, recreation, tourism/hospitality. **Holdings:** 300 books; 1000 reports, documents, and clippings; 35 VF drawers of hospitality industry information. **Subscriptions:** 23 journals and other serials. **Services:** Interlibrary loans; copying; library open to public. **Computerized Information Services:** DIALOG; UW WITS (internal database). **Contact Person:** Wes Mott, (608) 263-7900. **Publications:** Small Business

Development Center Newsletter, bimonthly; Wisconsin Small Business Forum, 3/year - subscription basis.

★16467★
UNIVERSITY OF WISCONSIN, MADISON - STEENBOCK MEMORIAL LIBRARY
(Agri; Sci-Tech)
550 Babcock Dr.   Phone: (608) 262-9990
Madison, WI 53706   Daisy T. Wu, Dir.
Founded: 1904. **Staff:** Prof 8; Other 8. **Subjects:** Agriculture, life sciences, home economics, natural resources, veterinary medicine. **Special Collections:** Miller Bee Collection (5000 volumes); Swanton Cooperative Collection; Levitan Cookbook Collection. **Holdings:** 109,740 books; 76,553 bound periodical volumes; 24,466 bound documents; 10,540 units of microforms; 325 programs on videotapes, audiotapes and slide-sets. **Subscriptions:** 3995 journals and other serials. **Services:** Interlibrary loans; copying; SDI; library open to public. **Automated Operations:** Computerized cataloging and serials. **Computerized Information Services:** DIALOG, BRS. **Networks/Consortia:** Member of CRL. **Publications:** New Booklist, monthly; bibliographic series and library guide series, both irregular. **Staff:** Emily Wixson, Ref.Libn; Kathi Gilbertson, Hd., Tech.Serv.; Ken Frazier, Hd., Info.Serv.; Lois Komai, Ref.Libn.; Robert Sessions, Ref.Libn./Vet.Med.; Marylou Stursa, Hd., Doc.

★16468★
UNIVERSITY OF WISCONSIN, MADISON - THEORETICAL CHEMISTRY INSTITUTE - LIBRARY (Sci-Tech)
1101 University Ave., Rm. 8326   Phone: (608) 262-1511
Madison, WI 53706   Barbara Kelly, Prog.Asst./Supv.
Founded: 1962. **Staff:** 1. **Subjects:** Quantum mechanics, statistical mechanics, scattering theory, transport phenomena, thermodynamics. **Special Collections:** University of Wisconsin Naval Research Laboratory Reports; Theoretical Chemistry Institute Reports. **Holdings:** 2264 books; 12,273 bound periodical volumes; 65,000 other cataloged items. **Services:** Library open to public by permission. **Special Indexes:** Complete index of University of Wisconsin Theoretical Chemistry Institute Reports and complete index of publications of the Theoretical Chemistry Institute.

★16469★
UNIVERSITY OF WISCONSIN, MADISON - TRACE R & D CENTER - LIBRARY
(Soc Sci)
314 Waisman
1500 Highland Ave.   Phone: (608) 262-6966
Madison, WI 53706   Mary Brady, Proj.Dir.
Staff: Prof 1; Other 1. **Subjects:** Nonvocal communication. **Holdings:** 12 linear feet and 2 filing cabinets of research materials. **Subscriptions:** 10 journals and other serials.

★16470★
UNIVERSITY OF WISCONSIN, MADISON - UNIVERSITY CENTER FOR COOPERATIVES - COOPERATIVE LIBRARY (Soc Sci)
Lowell Hall, Rm. 514
610 Langdon St.   Phone: (608) 262-3251
Madison, WI 53706   MaryJean McGrath, Act.Libn.
Founded: 1962. **Staff:** Prof 1; Other 1. **Subjects:** Cooperatives. **Special Collections:** Rochdale Collection (900 items of early U.S., English co-op books, European cooperative federations' annual reports); Shaars Collection. **Holdings:** 5300 books; 16 VF drawers of research working papers of Works Progress Administration (WPA) research on cooperatives; 45 VF drawers of information on all aspects and types of cooperatives, worldwide. **Subscriptions:** 235 journals and other serials. **Services:** Interlibrary loans; copying; library open to public with restrictions.

★16471★
UNIVERSITY OF WISCONSIN, MADISON - WASHBURN OBSERVATORY - WOODMAN ASTRONOMICAL LIBRARY (Sci-Tech)
6521 Sterling Hall
475 N. Charter St.   Phone: (608) 262-1320
Madison, WI 53706   Marcia Lynn Cooke, Libn.
Founded: 1882. **Staff:** Prof 1. **Subjects:** Astronomy, astrophysics. **Special Collections:** Noncommercial astronomical (Society and/or Observatory) publications (800 titles). **Holdings:** 5000 books; 3000 bound periodical volumes; 3000 volumes of noncommercial serials; 4670 charts, plates and photographs; 1065 microfiche. **Subscriptions:** 45 journals and other serials. **Services:** Interlibrary loans; copying; SDI; library open to public for reference use only. **Networks/Consortia:** Member of Madison Area Library Council (MALC); Wisconsin Interlibrary Services (WILS).

★16472★
UNIVERSITY OF WISCONSIN, MADISON - WATER RESOURCES CENTER - LIBRARY (Env-Cons)
1975 Willow Dr.   Phone: (608) 262-3069
Madison, WI 53706   Sarah L. Calcese, Libn.
Founded: 1965. **Staff:** Prof 1; Other 2. **Subjects:** Water resources - pollution sources, abatement and control, waste water treatment, limnology, resources management, research and planning. **Special Collections:** Eutrophication (7000 reprints and documents); Water Resources Economics Collection (800 reprints). **Holdings:** 16,000 books and technical reports. **Subscriptions:** 19 journals and other serials; 80 newsletters. **Services:** Interlibrary loans; library open to public. **Automated Operations:** Computerized cataloging. **Networks/Consortia:** Member of Madison Area Library Council (MALC). **Publications:** Monthly Acquisitions List - available upon request.

★16473★
UNIVERSITY OF WISCONSIN, MADISON - WILLIAM A. SCOTT BUSINESS LIBRARY (Bus-Fin)
Bascom Hall   Phone: (608) 262-5935
Madison, WI 53706   Marilyn Hicks, Bus.Libn.
Founded: 1955. **Staff:** Prof 1; Other 1. **Subjects:** Accounting, finance, marketing, real estate, insurance, international business. **Special Collections:** Corporate annual reports; Johnson Foundation Collection (productivity). **Holdings:** 18,404 books; 6000 periodical volumes; 21,000 microfiche; 213 reels of microfilm; 900 masters' papers. **Subscriptions:** 400 journals and other serials; 6 newspapers. **Services:** Interlibrary loans; copying; library open to public. **Networks/Consortia:** Member of Wisconsin Interlibrary Services (WILS).

★16474★
UNIVERSITY OF WISCONSIN, MADISON - WISCONSIN CENTER FOR FILM AND THEATER RESEARCH (Theater)
6039 Vilas Communication Hall   Phone: (608) 262-9706
Madison, WI 53706   Russell Merritt, Dir.
Founded: 1960. **Staff:** Prof 2; Other 3. **Subjects:** Film, television, theater, radio. **Holdings:** Over 200 manuscript collections of individuals and organizations in the performing arts, including scripts, correspondence, production and promotional materials, legal files, financial records; 12,000 films; 2 million photographs. The largest collection is the United Artists Corporation Collection which contains the corporate records of United Artists from its founding in 1919 through 1951, and includes: 1750 feature films from Warner Brothers, RKO and Monogram film libraries with related manuscripts; 2000 episodes from the ZIV Library of Television Programs with related manuscripts; 1500 Vitaphone short subjects and 600 Warner and Popeye cartoons with related manuscripts. **Services:** Copying and photoduplication of stills; center open to public; original material does not circulate; film archive open to qualified researchers by appointment only. **Publications:** Brochure; guide to collections; feature film list. **Special Catalogs:** Detailed inventories available for each processed collection. **Special Indexes:** Production title index for films, stills and scripts (card). **Staff:** Maxine Fleckner, Film Archv.

★16475★
UNIVERSITY OF WISCONSIN, MADISON - WISCONSIN REGIONAL PRIMATE RESEARCH CENTER - PRIMATE CENTER LIBRARY (Sci-Tech)
1223 Capitol Court   Phone: (608) 263-3512
Madison, WI 53706   Lawrence Jacobsen, Hd.Libn.
Founded: 1973. **Staff:** Prof 2; Other 2. **Subjects:** Primatology, neurosciences, reproductive physiology, behavioral endocrinology, animal behavior. **Special Collections:** Primate vocalizations and other nonprint media; Neurosciences Research Program Collection; rare books. **Holdings:** 4000 books; 9000 bound periodical volumes; 500 unbound volumes; topical reprint file (3000 items); 100 masters' and Ph.D. theses (center research). **Subscriptions:** 181 journals and other serials. **Services:** Interlibrary loans; copying; SDI; library open to public. **Automated Operations:** Computerized cataloging and serials. **Computerized Information Services:** MEDLINE, OCLC, BRS. Performs searches on cost recovery basis. **Networks/Consortia:** Member of Wisconsin Interlibrary Services (WILS). **Publications:** Primate Library Report: Print Acquisitions, bimonthly.

★16476★
UNIVERSITY OF WISCONSIN, MADISON - ZOOLOGICAL MUSEUM LIBRARY
(Sci-Tech)
L.E. Noland Bldg.
250 N. Mills St.   Phone: (608) 262-3766
Madison, WI 53706   John A.W. Kirsch, Dir.
Founded: 1849. **Staff:** Prof 1. **Subjects:** Zoology. **Holdings:** 1500 volumes; monographs; 8000 reprints; original field data. **Services:** Interlibrary loans;

copying; library open to public with restrictions.

UNIVERSITY OF WISCONSIN, MILWAUKEE - AMERICAN GEOGRAPHICAL SOCIETY
See: American Geographical Society Collection of the University of Wisconsin, Milwaukee - Golda Meir Library

★16477★
UNIVERSITY OF WISCONSIN, MILWAUKEE - AREA RESEARCH CENTER (Hist)
2311 E. Hartford Ave.   Phone: (414) 963-5402
Milwaukee, WI 53201   Allan Kovan, Cur.
Founded: 1965. **Staff:** Prof 1; Other 1. **Subjects:** Private papers, county documents of Milwaukee, Ozaukee, Sheboygan, Washington and Waukesha counties; local history, business and association papers, church papers. **Holdings:** 404 manuscript collections; 132 state, county and local government record series. **Services:** Copying; center open to public. **Networks/Consortia:** Member of State Historical Society of Wisconsin - Area Research Center Network. **Publications:** John A. Fleckner and Stanley Mallach, Guide to Historical Resources in Milwaukee Area Archives, 1976.

★16478★
UNIVERSITY OF WISCONSIN, MILWAUKEE - FEMINIST CENTER - LIBRARY (Soc Sci)*
Student Union Box 189
P.O. Box 413   Phone: (414) 963-5683
Milwaukee, WI 53201   Julie A. Jorgensen, Dir.
Staff: 4. **Subjects:** Abortion, homosexuality, feminism, politics of women, rape and sexual assault. **Holdings:** 200 books; 5 bound periodical volumes; 1 slide show; 6 cassettes; 1 film; 300 subject files. **Subscriptions:** 13 journals and other serials; 5 newspapers. **Services:** Library open to public.

★16479★
UNIVERSITY OF WISCONSIN, MILWAUKEE - GOLDA MEIR LIBRARY - CURRICULUM COLLECTION (Educ; Aud-Vis)
Box 604   Phone: (414) 963-4074
Milwaukee, WI 53201   Julie Czisny, Educ.Libn.
Founded: 1956. **Staff:** Prof 1; Other 4. **Subjects:** Children's and young adult literature, elementary and secondary AV media, reference collection for AV media and children's literature. **Special Collections:** Children's Literature Historical Collection (727). **Holdings:** 17,749 books; 398 bound periodical volumes; 2335 curriculum guides; 8810 K-12 textbooks; 2606 AV items; 698 seminar papers; 242 tests; ERIC microfiche collection. **Subscriptions:** 29 journals and other serials. **Services:** Interlibrary loans (limited); copying; library open to public under rules and regulations of the University Library. **Automated Operations:** Computerized cataloging. **Networks/Consortia:** Member of Wisconsin Interlibrary Services (WILS); Library Council of Metropolitan Milwaukee, Inc. (LCOMM). **Publications:** Selected Materials List; Pathfinders.

★16480★
UNIVERSITY OF WISCONSIN, MILWAUKEE - GRADUATE SCHOOL - OFFICE OF RESEARCH - INFORMATION LIBRARY (Soc Sci)
Box 340   Phone: (414) 963-4063
Milwaukee, WI 53201   Victor J. Larson, Info.Spec.
Founded: 1967. **Staff:** Prof 1; Other 2. **Special Collections:** Federal and foundation extramural support program information - program announcements, guideline documents, general information items, reference books relating to sources of funds, information and proposal writing guides. **Holdings:** 10,000 documents; 2 VF drawers of Senate and House bills; 9 VF drawers of federal program information; 4 VF drawers of foundation and corporate program information; 100 program application kits. **Subscriptions:** 125 journals and other serials. **Services:** Copying; computer and manual searches for funding sources; center open to public by appointment. **Publications:** Acquisitions List, quarterly; Application Deadline List, bimonthly.

★16481★
UNIVERSITY OF WISCONSIN, MILWAUKEE - GREENE MEMORIAL MUSEUM - LIBRARY
3367 N. Downer Ave.
Milwaukee, WI 53201
Founded: 1913. **Subjects:** Paleontology, mineralogy, geology. **Holdings:** 300 volumes. **Remarks:** This is the personal reference library of Thomas A. Greene, a 19th century collector whose fossil and mineral collections make up the bulk of the museum collection. Presently inactive.

★16482★
UNIVERSITY OF WISCONSIN, MILWAUKEE - INSTITUTE OF WORLD AFFAIRS - RESOURCE CENTER (Soc Sci)
Bolton 659
Box 413   Phone: (414) 963-4251
Milwaukee, WI 53201   David Garnham, Coord.
Founded: 1960. **Staff:** Prof 1. **Subjects:** United States foreign policy, United Nations, regional organizations, international relations, current world problems, international trade and finance, international energy, arms control. **Holdings:** 300 books; 100 bound periodical volumes; 50 other cataloged items. **Subscriptions:** 13 journals and other serials. **Services:** Center not open to public.

★16483★
UNIVERSITY OF WISCONSIN, MILWAUKEE - MORRIS FROMKIN MEMORIAL COLLECTION (Soc Sci)
2311 E. Hartford Ave.   Phone: (414) 963-5402
Milwaukee, WI 53201   Stanley Mallach, Bibliog.
Founded: 1969. **Staff:** Prof 1. **Subjects:** Socialism in the U.S., 1890-1940; communism in the U.S., 1920-1940; labor movement in the U.S., 1865-1940; social insurance in the U.S. to 1940; reform movements in the U.S., 1865-1940; housing and city planning in the U.S., 1890-1940; materials on European movements and events that affected American Left and reform movements. **Holdings:** 3900 books; 1700 pamphlets. **Services:** Copying; library open to public for reference use only.

★16484★
UNIVERSITY OF WISCONSIN, MILWAUKEE - MUSIC COLLECTION (Mus)
2311 E. Hartford Ave.
Box 604   Phone: (414) 963-5529
Milwaukee, WI 53201   Richard E. Jones, Music Libn.
Staff: Prof 1; Other 2. **Subjects:** Music - history, criticism, theory, instruction and study; music bibliography; music librarianship; music sociology; chamber music. **Special Collections:** American Arriaga Archive (52 items); Slovenian Music Collection (1500 items). European-Tradition Music Catalog & Bibliography Collection (4000 items); John Dale Owen Jazz Recordings Collection (10,000 items). **Holdings:** 14,500 books; 1740 bound periodical volumes; 11,000 scores and parts; 36,000 recordings and tapes; 4000 catalogs, pamphlets and bibliographies; 3900 microforms. **Subscriptions:** 100 journals and other serials. **Services:** Interlibrary loans; copying; collection open to public with restrictions. **Automated Operations:** Computerized cataloging, serials, circulation. **Computerized Information Services:** OCLC. **Networks/Consortia:** Member of Wisconsin Interlibrary Services (WILS); Library Council of Metropolitan Milwaukee, Inc. (LCOMM); OCLC Musical Recordings Analytics Consortium (OMRAC). **Staff:** Patricia Wiese, Dir., Audio Ctr.; Elly Johnson, Music Cat.

★16485★
UNIVERSITY OF WISCONSIN, OSHKOSH - UNIVERSITY LIBRARIES AND LEARNING RESOURCES - SPECIAL COLLECTIONS (Educ)
800 Algoma Blvd.   Phone: (414) 424-3333
Oshkosh, WI 54901   J. Daniel Vann, Exec.Dir.
Founded: 1871. **Special Collections:** Rowland Collection (Limited Editions Club); Pare Lorentz Collection (16mm films); archives of the Wisconsin Area Research Center. **Holdings:** Figures not available. **Services:** Interlibrary loans; copying; collections open to public for reference use only. **Automated Operations:** Computerized cataloging, acquisitions and circulation. **Computerized Information Services:** OCLC, DIALOG, BRS, SDC; PULL (internal database). **Networks/Consortia:** Member of Wisconsin Interlibrary Services (WILS); Council of Wisconsin Libraries, Inc. (COWL); Fox Valley Library Council.

★16486★
UNIVERSITY OF WISCONSIN, PARKSIDE - UNIVERSITY ARCHIVES AND AREA RESEARCH CENTER (Hist)
Box 2000   Phone: (414) 553-2411
Kenosha, WI 53141   Nicholas C. Burckel, Dir.
Staff: Prof 2; Other 1. **Subjects:** History - local, state, university; genealogy. **Special Collections:** Irving Wallace; Norman Mailer; David Kherdian; H.O. Teisberg; Collection of American Plays; Black Sparrow Collection; Perishable Press Collection. **Holdings:** 1234 books; 36 bound periodical volumes; 2300 cubic feet of manuscripts and archives; 2000 reels of microfilm censuses and local newspapers. **Subscriptions:** 26 journals and other serials. **Services:** Copying; archives open to public. **Special Catalogs:** Guide to Archives and Manuscripts in the University of Wisconsin-Parkside Area Research Center. **Staff:** Luella Vines .

★16487★
UNIVERSITY OF WISCONSIN, PLATTEVILLE - KARRMANN LIBRARY - SPECIAL COLLECTIONS (Hist)
725 W. Main St.　　　　　　　　　　Phone: (608) 342-1688
Platteville, WI 53818　　　　　　　　　Jerome P. Daniels, Dir.
Founded: 1866. Special Collections: Southwest Wisconsin History, including specialization in the history of the upper Mississippi Valley lead-zinc mining region (books; microforms; archival materials); Southwestern Wisconsin Area Research Center (archives and manuscripts). Holdings: Figures not available. Services: Interlibrary loans; copying; library open to public. Automated Operations: Computerized cataloging and acquisitions. Computerized Information Services: OCLC, ERIC. Performs searches on partial cost recovery basis. Contact Person: Bryan L. Schwark. Networks/Consortia: Member of Wisconsin Interlibrary Services (WILS); State Historical Society of Wisconsin-Area Research Center Network. Staff: Bryan L. Schwark .

★16488★
UNIVERSITY OF WISCONSIN, RIVER FALLS - CHALMER DAVEE LIBRARY (Educ)
120 E. Cascade Ave.　　　　　　　　Phone: (715) 425-3321
River Falls, WI 54022　　　　　　　　Richard A. Cooklock, Dir.
Founded: 1875. Staff: Prof 7; Other 9. Subjects: Education. Special Collections: Western Americana and frontier history; Pierce and St. Croix county history. Holdings: 185,706 books; 27,988 bound periodical volumes; 8095 AV items; 142,387 government documents; 337,641 microforms including 279,951 ERIC microfiche. Subscriptions: 1455 journals and other serials; 47 newspapers. Services: Interlibrary loans; copying; library open to public but deposit is required for borrowing. Automated Operations: Computerized cataloging, acquisitions and serials. Computerized Information Services: BRS, OCLC. Networks/Consortia: Member of Wisconsin Interlibrary Services (WILS). Staff: Herman Storm, Tech.Serv.; Jane Peirce, Ref. & ILL.

★16489★
UNIVERSITY OF WISCONSIN, RIVER FALLS - CHALMER DAVEE LIBRARY - AREA RESEARCH CENTER (Hist)
　　　　　　　　　　　　　　Phone: (715) 425-3567
River Falls, WI 54022　　　　　　　　Timothy L. Ericson, Archv.
Founded: 1875. Staff: Prof 1; Other 6. Subjects: History of Western Wisconsin (Pierce County, Polk County, St. Croix County, Washburn County, Burnett County); Civil War history; genealogy. Special Collections: Oral History (250 tapes); Wisconsin Census Records, 1832-1910. Holdings: 1000 books; newspaper collection; 1075 linear feet in manuscript collection; 1300 reels of microfilm; 2000 pamphlets; 10,000 photographs. Subscriptions: 10 journals and other serials. Services: Interlibrary loans; copying; library open to public for reference use only. Networks/Consortia: Member of State Historical Society of Wisconsin - Area Research Center Network. Special Indexes: Voices of the St. Croix Valley, bound index to Oral History Collections; vital statistics index for Burnett, Pierce, Polk and St. Croix counties, 1850-1910 (60,000 card entries); university alumni index (25,000 card entries).

★16490★
UNIVERSITY OF WISCONSIN, STEVENS POINT - JAMES H. ALBERTSON CENTER FOR LEARNING RESOURCES (Educ)
　　　　　　　　　　　　　　Phone: (715) 346-2540
Stevens Point, WI 54481　　　　　　　Allen F. Barrows, Dir. of Pub.Serv.
Staff: Prof 17; Other 18. Subjects: Natural resources, communicative disorders, home economics, education, communication. Special Collections: Federal government depository; Wisconsin State depository. Holdings: 285,328 books; 50,682 bound periodical volumes; 125,241 microforms; 14,141 audiovisual materials; 500,000 volumes of government documents. Subscriptions: 1780 journals and other serials; 22 newspapers. Services: Interlibrary loans; copying; center open to public. Automated Operations: Computerized cataloging. Computerized Information Services: OCLC. Networks/Consortia: Member of Wisconsin Interlibrary Services (WILS). Staff: Fred M. Buehler, Asst.Ref.Libn.; Theresa Chao, Per.Libn.; Arthur M. Fish, Doc.Libn.; John D. Gillesby, Hd.Ref.Libn.; Kathleen Halsey, Asst.Ref.Libn.; Linette Schuler, Lib.Instr.; Lois Huizar, Instr.Mtls.Ctr.Libn.; Keith F. Lea, Dir., Tech.Serv.; Patricia Paul, Hd.Cat.; Zofia A. Soroka, Hd.Bibliog.; Alice L. Randlett, Acq.Libn.

★16491★
UNIVERSITY OF WISCONSIN, STEVENS POINT - UNIVERSITY ARCHIVES & PORTAGE COUNTY HISTORICAL SOCIETY COLLECTION (Hist)
012 Old Main Bldg.　　　　　　　　Phone: (705) 346-2586
Stevens Point, WI 54481　　　　　　　William G. Paul, Univ.Archv.
Subjects: History and development of the University of Wisconsin, Stevens Point, 1894 to present; individuals and institutions of Stevens Point and central Wisconsin. Holdings: 800 linear feet of manuscripts, photographs, tapes, catalogs, bulletins, tapes of events and activities, faculty committee minutes, yearbooks, administrative correspondence and reports, and personnel records; Portage County Historical Society records, papers, and photographs. Services: Copying; archives open to public.

UNIVERSITY OF WYOMING - AMERICAN HERITAGE CENTER ARCHIVES
See: American Public Works Association - Information Service

★16492★
UNIVERSITY OF WYOMING - ANIMAL SCIENCE DIVISION - WOOL LIBRARY (Sci-Tech)
University Sta.
Box 3354　　　　　　　　　　　　Phone: (307) 766-5212
Laramie, WY 82071　　　　　　　　Robert Stobart, Dir.
Founded: 1908. Staff: Prof 1; Other 2. Subjects: Wool science, wool textiles, sheep husbandry. Special Collections: W.T. Ritch Collection. Holdings: 830 books; 275 bound periodical volumes; 9850 bulletins, articles, and reprints; 900 containers of various specimens of animal and other textile fibers. Subscriptions: 18 journals and other serials. Services: Library open to public upon request.

★16493★
UNIVERSITY OF WYOMING - COLLEGE OF HUMAN MEDICINE - FAMILY PRACTICE RESIDENCY PROGRAM - LEARNING RESOURCES CENTER (Med)
1522 East A St.　　　　　　　　　　Phone: (307) 266-3076
Casper, WY 82601　　　　　　　　　Naomi Lange, Med.Libn.
Staff: Prof 1; Other 1. Subjects: Medicine - clinical, family practice, behavioral. Holdings: 800 books; 300 video cassettes; 675 audio cassettes; 42 slide/tape programs; 16 slide programs. Subscriptions: 26 journals and other serials. Services: Interlibrary loans; copying; SDI; center open to public - with limited borrowing privileges. Computerized Information Services: MEDLARS. Networks/Consortia: Member of Muddy Mountain Health Sciences Library Consortium.

★16494★
UNIVERSITY OF WYOMING - GEOLOGY LIBRARY (Sci-Tech)†
S.H. Knight Geology Bldg.　　　　　　Phone: (307) 766-3374
Laramie, WY 82071　　　　　　　　Josephine Battisti, Libn.
Founded: 1956. Staff: 3. Subjects: Geology, paleontology, geophysics, remote sensing, geomorphology, petrology. Holdings: 23,458 books; 9852 bound periodical volumes; 22,551 documents; 25,113 maps; 100 microforms. Subscriptions: 1620 journals and other serials. Services: Interlibrary loans; copying; library open to public.

UNIVERSITY OF WYOMING - HONEY BEE PESTICIDES/DISEASES RESEARCH LABORATORY
See: U.S.D.A. - Agricultural Research Service - Honey Bee Pesticides/ Diseases Research Laboratory

★16495★
UNIVERSITY OF WYOMING - LAW LIBRARY (Law)
College of Law　　　　　　　　　　Phone: (307) 766-5175
Laramie, WY 82071　　　　　　　　Catherine Mealey, Law Libn./Prof.
Founded: 1920. Staff: Prof 4; Other 5. Subjects: Law. Special Collections: Roman Law (Blume Collection). Holdings: 86,000 volumes; 43,000 microfiche. Subscriptions: 2700 journals and other serials. Services: Interlibrary loans; copying; library open to public for reference use. Computerized Information Services: LEXIS, Westlaw, DIALOG, OCLC; internal database. Staff: M.F. Blackstone, Assoc. Law Libn.; Janet Weir, Asst. Law Libn.; Nancy Greene, Asst.Libn./Tech.Serv.

★16496★
UNIVERSITY OF WYOMING - PETROLEUM HISTORY AND RESEARCH CENTER LIBRARY (Hist; Sci-Tech)*
William Robertson Coe Library
Univ. Sta., Box 3334　　　　　　　　Phone: (307) 766-4114
Laramie, WY 82071　　　　　　　　Dr. Gene M. Gressley, Dir.
Founded: 1956. Subjects: Petroleum history. Holdings: Figures not available. Services: Library open to public.

★16497★
UNIVERSITY OF WYOMING - SCIENCE AND TECHNOLOGY LIBRARY (Sci-Tech)
University Sta., Box 3262　　　　　　Phone: (307) 766-5165
Laramie, WY 82071　　　　　　　　Linda S. Keiter, Asst. Dir., Sci.Libs.
Founded: 1970. Staff: Prof 6; Other 13. Subjects: Psychology, chemistry, physics, mathematics, engineering, agriculture, health and natural sciences.

Holdings: 190,000 volumes. **Subscriptions:** 4000 journals. **Services:** Interlibrary loans; copying; library open to public. **Automated Operations:** Computerized serials. **Computerized Information Services:** DIALOG, BRS, MEDLARS, NIH-EPA Chemical Information System (CIS), SDC, DOE/RECON. Performs searches on cost recovery basis. **Contact Person:** Larry Jonsen, 766-4263. **Networks/Consortia:** Member of Bibliographical Center for Research, Rocky Mountain Region, Inc. (BCR). **Remarks:** Houses Wyoming Health Sciences Information Network, representing Region IV in the National Library of Medicine's Biomedical Communications Network. **Staff:** Diana Shelton, Hd., Ref.; A. James Bothmer, Hd., HSIN; Barbara Volpi-Stagner, Hd., Circ.; Larry Jonsen, Hd., BDS.

★16498★

UNIVERSITY OF WYOMING - WATER RESEARCH CENTER - LIBRARY
Laramie, WY 82071
Subjects: Water resources, evaporation, snow and ice, conservation, irrigation, water law, river basins and water planning, sanitary and civil engineering. **Special Collections:** U.S. Geological Survey water supply papers relating to Wyoming. **Holdings:** 500 books; 14,000 pamphlets, reports and articles; 100 maps. **Automated Operations:** Internal database. **Remarks:** Presently inactive.

★16499★

UNIVERSITY OF WYOMING - WESTERN HISTORY RESEARCH CENTER LIBRARY (Hist)*
William Robertson Coe Library
Univ. Sta., Box 3334   Phone: (307) 766-4114
Laramie, WY 82071   Dr. Gene M. Gressley, Dir.
Founded: 1945. **Staff:** Prof 3; Other 26. **Subjects:** Western Americana. **Special Collections:** Range cattle industry history; business; conservation; petroleum; mining; performing arts; mountaineering; water resources; transportation history. **Holdings:** 26,000 books; 1500 bound periodical volumes; 64 file cases of clippings and pamphlets; 6000 linear feet of manuscripts; 1500 reels of microfilm; 39,485 maps; 110,000 photographs. **Subscriptions:** 62 journals and other serials; 53 newspapers. **Services:** Interlibrary loans; copying; library open to public. **Publications:** News releases.

★16500★

UNIVERSITY OF WYOMING - WYOMING CAREER INFORMATION SYSTEM (Educ)
Div. of Student Educational Opportunity
Box 3808, University Sta.   Phone: (307) 766-6189
Laramie, WY 82701   Karen P. Scott, Dir.
Staff: Prof 3; Other 2. **Subjects:** National and Wyoming labor market information, training programs, Wyoming school information, career information. **Subscriptions:** 35 journals and other serials. **Automated Operations:** Computerized cataloging, acquisitions, serials, and circulation. **Computerized Information Services:** Performs searches free of charge for individuals and on cost recovery basis for institutions. **Networks/Consortia:** Member of Career Information System (CIS). **Publications:** List of publications - available on request. **Staff:** Diane Latos, Info.Anl.; Juanita Rodriguez, Info.Anl.

UOP INC.
See: Signal UOP Research Center

★16501★

UOP INC. - PATENT LIBRARY
Ten UOP Plaza
Des Plaines, IL 60016
Defunct. Absorbed by Signal UOP Research Center - Technical Information Center.

★16502★

UP FRONT, INC. - LIBRARY (Med)
Coconut Grove Sta.
Box 330589
Miami, FL 33233-0589   Phone: (305) 446-3585
                                         James N. Hall, Dir.
Founded: 1973. **Subjects:** Drug information. **Holdings:** 1000 books; 900 unbound periodicals; 9 VF drawers and 100 pamphlet files of drug information. **Subscriptions:** 27 journals and other serials; 5 newspapers. **Services:** Copying; library open to public for reference use only. **Networks/Consortia:** Member of Miami Health Sciences Library Consortium (MHSLC). **Publications:** Street Pharmacologist, monthly - by subscription.

★16503★

UPDATA PUBLICATIONS, INC. - LIBRARY (Publ)
1746 Westwood Blvd.   Phone: (213) 474-5900
Los Angeles, CA 90024   Judy Harrington, Libn.
Founded: 1973. **Staff:** Prof 1. **Subjects:** Micropublishing, publishing, videodiscs, information retrieval. **Special Collections:** National Advisory Committee for Aeronautics Collection, 1915-1958 (13,914 microfiche); U.S. Bureau of Mines Collection, 1910 to present (15,000 microfiche); Mine Safety and Health (400 microfiche); Central Intelligence Agency (1275 microfiche); U.S. Army Area Handbooks (527 microfiche); U.S. Geological Survey Water Supply Papers (7000 microfiche); U.S. Department of Agriculture (30,000 microfiche); U.S. Department of Labor Statistics (5000 microfiche); U.S. Bureau of Fisheries (3000 microfiche); U.S. Government Indexes of various departments (400 microfiche). **Holdings:** 2000 books; 76,000 microfiche; 60 reels of microfilm. **Subscriptions:** 40 journals and other serials. **Services:** SDI; library open to public on request. **Computerized Information Services:** DIALOG, SDC.

UPJOHN COMPANY - ASGROW SEED COMPANY
See: Asgrow Seed Company

★16504★

UPJOHN COMPANY - BUSINESS LIBRARY 88-91 (Bus-Fin; Med)
                                         Phone: (616) 323-6351
Kalamazoo, MI 49001   Valerie Noble, Hd.
Founded: 1960. **Staff:** Prof 1; Other 3. **Subjects:** Business and finance, management and supervision, marketing, microcomputer applications, clinical medicine, pharmaceuticals and drugs. **Holdings:** 5000 books; 800 SRI International reports; 100 annual reports; 500 microfiche; 300 cassettes; telephone directories and road maps to major U.S. cities. **Subscriptions:** 250 journals and other serials. **Services:** Interlibrary loans; copying; SDI; library open to public by appointment. **Automated Operations:** Computerized subscriptions systems and acquisitions. **Computerized Information Services:** DIALOG, SDC, New York Times Information Service, MEDLINE, Dow Jones News/Retrieval, Tymshare Inc., OCLC. **Networks/Consortia:** Member of Kalamazoo Et Al (KETAL); Southwest Michigan Library Cooperative (SMLC). **Publications:** Monthly List of New Materials. **Special Catalogs:** Selective author-subject catalog, biennial. **Special Indexes:** KWIC index to Corporate Archives. **Staff:** Jill Hankison, Libn.

★16505★

UPJOHN COMPANY - CORPORATE TECHNICAL LIBRARY (Sci-Tech; Med)
                                         Phone: (616) 385-6414
Kalamazoo, MI 49001   Lorraine Schulte, Mgr.
Founded: 1941. **Staff:** Prof 13; Other 18. **Subjects:** Chemistry, biochemistry, pharmacology, biomedical sciences, mathematics, computer science. **Holdings:** 20,000 books; 35,000 bound periodical volumes. **Subscriptions:** 1300 journals and other serials. **Services:** Interlibrary loans; copying; SDI; library open to public with prior approval. **Automated Operations:** Computerized cataloging and subscription control system. **Computerized Information Services:** DIALOG, SDC, BRS, NLM, OCLC, CAS Online, Institute for Scientific Information (ISI), NIH-EPA Chemical Information System (CIS); internal databases. **Networks/Consortia:** Member of Kalamazoo Et Al (KETAL); Michigan Library Consortium (MLC); Southwest Michigan Library Cooperative (SMLC). **Publications:** Library Additions, weekly; CTL News, bimonthly; Brief Guide to the Corporate Technical Library, annual. **Special Catalogs:** Upjohn Scientific Publications, annual. **Staff:** Liga Greenfield, Hd., Tech.Doc.Serv.; Ruth Morris, Tech.Serv.Libn.; Michael Homan, Hd., Info.Serv.Susan Fierke, Info.Spec.; Julie Macksey, Info.Sci.; Janet Everitt, Info.Spec.; Rein Virkhaus, Info.Sci.; Lydia Hines, Staff Sci.; James Powell, Info.Sci.; June Slach, Lib.Sys.Spec.

★16506★

UPJOHN COMPANY - D.S. GILMORE RESEARCH LABORATORIES - LIBRARY (Sci-Tech)†
410 Sackett Point Rd.   Phone: (203) 281-2782
North Haven, CT 06473   A. Munim Nashu, EPA Coord./Libn.
Founded: 1964. **Staff:** Prof 1. **Subjects:** Chemistry - organic, polymer. **Holdings:** 1600 books; 3500 bound periodical volumes; 100 DSG scientist publication; 25 DSG technical reports and bulletins. **Subscriptions:** 110 journals and other serials. **Services:** Interlibrary loans; copying; library open with permission of the management.

★16507★

UPJOHN COMPANY - PATENT LAW DEPARTMENT - LIBRARY (Law)
Bldg. 32-1   Phone: (616) 385-7569
Kalamazoo, MI 49001   Doreen B. Canton, Patent Law Libn.
Founded: 1950. **Staff:** Prof 1. **Subjects:** U.S. patents, copyright law, company reprints, medicine and pharmaceuticals. **Special Collections:** U.S.

chemical patents; U.S. Official Gazette (microform). **Holdings:** 2000 books; 1500 bound periodical volumes. **Subscriptions:** 75 journals and other serials. **Services:** Interlibrary loans and copying within the UpJohn Company; library open to doctors and company employees on site. **Computerized Information Services:** LEXIS, DIALOG. Performs free searches. **Special Indexes:** Patent index (card).

UPJOHN LIBRARY
See: Kalamazoo College

UPLANDS FARM ENVIRONMENTAL CENTER
See: Nature Conservancy - Long Island Chapter

★16508★
UPPER CANADA RAILWAY SOCIETY, INC. - LIBRARY (Trans)
Box 122, Sta. A
Toronto, ON, Canada M5W 1A2
Founded: 1941. **Subjects:** Canadian railways and Canadian street railways. **Special Collections:** Railroad club publications - Canadian, U.S., British, Belgian, Australian. **Holdings:** Books; maps; timetables; artifacts. **Services:** Library open to public by prior arrangement.

★16509★
UPPER COLORADO RIVER COMMISSION - LIBRARY (Env-Cons)
355 S. Fourth East St.   Phone: (801) 531-1150
Salt Lake City, UT 84111   Gerald R. Zimmerman, Exec.Dir.
Staff: 3. **Subjects:** Water and related resource development. **Holdings:** 6000 volumes. **Services:** Library open to public.

UPPER GREAT PLAINS TRANSPORTATION INSTITUTE
See: North Dakota State University

★16510★
UPPER ROOM DEVOTIONAL LIBRARY, MUSEUM AND ARCHIVES (Rel-Theol)
1908 Grand Ave.
Box 189   Phone: (615) 327-2700
Nashville, TN 37202   Julie L. Julian, Libn./Res.Asst.
Founded: 1955. **Staff:** Prof 1. **Subjects:** Devotions, prayers, meditations, spiritual formation, hymns, Methodism. **Special Collections:** Manuscripts of John Wesley's works and letters. **Holdings:** 14,000 books; 200 other cataloged items; 150 feet of archival materials of The Upper Room. **Subscriptions:** 30 journals and other serials. **Services:** Interlibrary loans; copying.

★16511★
UPPER SAVANNAH AREA HEALTH EDUCATION CONSORTIUM - LIBRARY (Med)
Self Memorial Hospital
Spring St.   Phone: (803) 227-4851
Greenwood, SC 29646   Nancy Morrow, Libn.
Founded: 1977. **Staff:** Prof 1; Other 1. **Subjects:** Medicine. **Holdings:** 1000 books. **Subscriptions:** 117 journals and other serials. **Services:** Interlibrary loans; copying; library open to public. **Computerized Information Services:** NLM. Performs searches on cost recovery basis.

★16512★
UPPER SNAKE RIVER VALLEY HISTORICAL SOCIETY - LIBRARY (Hist)
49 North Center
Box 244
Rexburg, ID 83440   Jerry Glenn, Libn.
Founded: 1965. **Staff:** Prof 1; Other 3. **Subjects:** Idaho history. **Holdings:** 100 books; 50 tapes; 18 videotapes; 12 maps. **Subscriptions:** 10 journals and other serials. **Services:** Copying; library open to public by appointment. **Publications:** Snake River Echoes, quarterly.

URANIUM INFORMATION CENTRE
See: British Columbia Research Council

★16513★
URBAN INSTITUTE - LIBRARY (Soc Sci)
2100 M St., N.W.   Phone: (202) 223-1950
Washington, DC 20037   Camille A. Motta, Dir. of Lib./Archv.
Founded: 1968. **Staff:** Prof 3; Other 2. **Subjects:** Public policy and economics, housing and urban development, health policy, public finance, human resources research, productivity and economic development, income security. **Special Collections:** Urban Institute archival materials. **Holdings:** 26,000 books and documents; 700 periodical titles; 3500 reels of microfilm. **Subscriptions:** 600 journals. **Services:** Interlibrary loans (fee); SDI; library

open to public by appointment. **Computerized Information Services:** DIALOG, BRS. **Networks/Consortia:** Member of Metropolitan Washington Library Council; Interlibrary Users Association (IUA). **Staff:** Susan Dow, Pub.Serv.Libn.; Marla Schwartz, Tech.Serv.Libn.

★16514★
URBAN INVESTMENT AND DEVELOPMENT COMPANY - INFORMATION CENTER (Plan)
333 N. Wacker Dr.   Phone: (312) 845-3596
Chicago, IL 60606   Charles LaGrutta, Info./Rec.Mgr..
Founded: 1973. **Staff:** Prof 1. **Subjects:** City planning, real estate, urban development. **Holdings:** 3000 books; 25 VF drawers of pamphlets. **Subscriptions:** 180 journals and other serials; 33 newspapers. **Services:** Interlibrary loans; copying; SDI; center open to public by arragement. **Networks/Consortia:** Member of Chicago Library System; ILLINET.

★16515★
URBAN LAND INSTITUTE - LIBRARY (Plan)†
1090 Vermont Ave., N.W., Suite 300   Phone: (202) 289-8500
Washington, DC 20005   Elizabeth Baker, Libn.
Founded: 1958. **Staff:** Prof 1. **Subjects:** Land use, real estate, urban planning, housing, environment. **Holdings:** 6000 books; U.S. census publications, 1960; ULI publications. **Subscriptions:** 300 journals and other serials. **Services:** Interlibrary loans; copying; library open to public.

URBAN MASS TRANSPORTATION ADMINISTRATION
See: U.S. Dept. of Transportation

★16516★
URBAN TRANSPORTATION DEVELOPMENT CORPORATION - METRO CANADA LIBRARY (Trans)
Box 70, Sta. A.   Phone: (613) 384-3100
Kingston, ON, Canada K7M 6P9   Theresa Brennan, Mgr., Rec./Off.Sys.
Founded: 1974. **Staff:** Prof 1; Other 1. **Subjects:** Urban transportation, engineering, marketing, business. **Special Collections:** Engineering standards and specifications (150 items). **Holdings:** 2000 books; 1200 technical reports; 200 documents. **Subscriptions:** 100 journals and other serials. **Services:** Interlibrary loans; library open to public by appointment and with restrictions. **Networks/Consortia:** Member of Canadian Transportation Research Information System (CTRIS). **Publications:** Accession List, quarterly; Annual Report.

URBAN WILDLIFE RESEARCH CENTER, INC.
See: National Institute for Urban Wildlife

★16517★
URBANA COLLEGE - SWEDENBORG MEMORIAL LIBRARY - SPECIAL COLLECTIONS (Rel-Theol)
College Way   Phone: (513) 652-1301
Urbana, OH 43078   Connie Salyers, Libn.
Staff: Prof 1; Other 2. **Special Collections:** Swedenborgian Collection (1839 titles). **Services:** Interlibrary loans; copying; library open to public. **Automated Operations:** Computerized cataloging. **Networks/Consortia:** Member of Dayton-Miami Valley Consortium; OHIONET.

URBANA FREE LIBRARY - CHAMPAIGN COUNTY HISTORICAL ARCHIVES
See: Champaign County Historical Archives

★16518★
URBANA FREE LIBRARY - URBANA MUNICIPAL DOCUMENTS PROJECT (Soc Sci)
201 S. Race St.   Phone: (217) 384-0092
Urbana, IL 61801-3283   Jean E. Koch, Dir.
Founded: 1979. **Staff:** Prof 1; Other 2. **Subjects:** Urbana city government. **Holdings:** 20,400 documents on 3700 microfiche. **Services:** Copying; library open to public with restrictions. **Automated Operations:** Computerized indexing. **Networks/Consortia:** Member of Lincoln Trail Libraries System. **Special Indexes:** Alphabetical, geographical, numerical and citation indexes (COM).

URIS LIBRARY AND RESOURCE CENTER
See: Metropolitan Museum of Art

USAREUR
See: U.S. Army in Europe

★16519★

UTAH INTERNATIONAL, INC. - INFORMATION SERVICES/LIBRARY (Env-Cons)
550 California St.   Phone: (415) 981-1515
San Francisco, CA 94104   Jerry McWilliams, Mgr.
Founded: 1973. **Staff:** Prof 2; Other 2. **Subjects:** Mining, geology, business. **Special Collections:** Early history of construction in the West (photographs). **Holdings:** 15,000 books. **Subscriptions:** 600 journals and other serials. **Services:** Interlibrary loans; library open to public by appointment. **Automated Operations:** Computerized cataloging. **Computerized Information Services:** DIALOG, SDC, RLIN. **Networks/Consortia:** Member of CLASS. **Staff:** Karen Kiefer, Info.Spec.

★16520★

UTAH STATE ARCHIVES (Hist)
Archives Bldg.
Capitol Hill   Phone: (801) 533-5250
Salt Lake City, UT 84114   M. Liisa Fagerlund, State Archv.
Founded: 1956. **Staff:** Prof 9; Other 31. **Subjects:** Public records of the State of Utah and its political subdivisions. **Special Collections:** Military burial records. **Holdings:** 60,000 cubic feet of semi-active and historically valuable records; 60,000 cubic feet of records in paper copy; 68,000 reels of microfilm; 90,000 microfiche. **Services:** Copying; archives open to public. **Networks/Consortia:** Member of Conference of Intermountain Archivists (CIA). **Publications:** Utah State Bulletin; laws and administrative rules of state; Records Retention Schedule; State Roster. **Special Catalogs:** Preliminary Inventory of County Microfilm (microfiche); Guide to Official Records of Genealogical Value in the State of Utah; Inventory - Military Department, Record Group 027. **Staff:** Loretta L. Hefner, Bur.Archv./Rec.Anl.; Yan A. Neiswender, Bur.Archv./Tech.Serv.

★16521★

UTAH STATE BOARD OF EDUCATION - UTAH INFORMATION TECHNICAL DEMONSTRATION CENTER (Educ)
Curriculum and Instruction Program
250 E. Fifth, S.   Phone: (801) 533-5061
Salt Lake City, UT 84111   Robert Olson, Mgr.
Staff: Prof 3; Other 4. **Subjects:** All school subjects. **Special Collections:** ERIC collection. **Holdings:** Figures not available. **Services:** Interlibrary loans; copying; SDI; center open to public for a fee. **Computerized Information Services:** CompuServe, Inc., DIALOG, BRS, SDC, Dow Jones News/Retrieval; Project Resources (internal database). **Publications:** Newsletter, monthly.

★16522★

UTAH STATE HISTORICAL SOCIETY - RESEARCH LIBRARY (Hist)
300 Rio Grande   Phone: (801) 533-5808
Salt Lake City, UT 84105   Jay M. Haymond, Libn.
Founded: 1952. **Staff:** Prof 6; Other 1. **Subjects:** Utah history, Mormon history, Western history. **Special Collections:** Utah water records (200 linear feet); Works Progress Administration records (124 linear feet). **Holdings:** 21,000 books; 18,000 bound periodical volumes; 300,000 photographs; 21,000 pamphlets; 10,000 maps; 1500 oral history tapes; 3500 linear feet of manuscripts; 1200 reels of microfilm; 160 feet of clippings files. **Subscriptions:** 320 journals and other serials. **Services:** Copying; library open to public. **Automated Operations:** Computerized cataloging. **Computerized Information Services:** OCLC; internal database. **Publications:** Oral History Guide, annual; Guide to Unpublished Materials - to members. **Special Indexes:** Utah History Index (card). **Staff:** Steven R. Wood, Ref.Libn.; Linda Thatcher, Acq.Libn.Gary Topping, Mss.Cur.; Susan Mortenson, Map & Photo.Libn.

★16523★

UTAH STATE HOSPITAL - LIBRARY (Med)
East Center St.
Box 270   Phone: (801) 373-4400
Provo, UT 84601   Janina Chilton, Libn.
Staff: Prof 1. **Subjects:** Medicine, psychology. **Holdings:** 900 volumes; records and tapes. **Subscriptions:** 54 journals and other serials. **Services:** Library not open to public. **Computerized Information Services:** DIALOG. **Remarks:** Also maintains a patients' collection of 1500 volumes and 14 journal subscriptions.

★16524★

UTAH STATE LAW LIBRARY (Law)
332 State Capitol Bldg.   Phone: (801) 533-5280
Salt Lake City, UT 84114   Geoffrey J. Butler, Law Libn.
Staff: Prof 2; Other 1. **Subjects:** Law. **Holdings:** 42,000 volumes. **Services:** Copying. **Staff:** Russell E. Van Allen, Asst. Law Libn.

★16525★

UTAH STATE LIBRARY (Info Sci)
2150 South 300 West, Suite 16   Phone: (801) 533-5875
Salt Lake City, UT 84115   Russell L. Davis, Dir.
Founded: 1957. **Staff:** Prof 15; Other 20. **Subjects:** State and federal government. **Holdings:** 32,882 volumes; 28,383 reference materials; 36,798 federal documents; 20,470 state documents. **Subscriptions:** 105 journals and other serials. **Services:** Interlibrary loans; copying; library open to public with restrictions. **Automated Operations:** Computerized cataloging and acquisitions. **Computerized Information Services:** DIALOG, SDC, BRS, New York Times Information Service. Performs free searches. Contact Person: Sue Holmes. **Networks/Consortia:** Member of Bibliographic Center for Research, Rocky Mountain Region, Inc. (BCR). **Publications:** Horsefeathers, monthly - free upon request. **Staff:** Amy Owen, Deputy Dir.; Douglas Abrams, Tech.Serv.Dir.; Mary Southwell, Spec. Projects.; Edith Blankenship, Cat.; Douglas Hindmarsh, Ref.Serv.Dir.; Sue Holmes; Sandra Long, Acq.

★16526★

UTAH STATE LIBRARY - BLIND AND PHYSICALLY HANDICAPPED PROGRAM - REGIONAL LIBRARY (Aud-Vis)
2150 South 300 West, Suite 16   Phone: (801) 533-5855
Salt Lake City, UT 84115   Gerald Buttars, Dir.
Founded: 1934. **Staff:** Prof 6; Other 10. **Holdings:** 384,771 talking books and braille books; cassettes; open reel; large print books. **Subscriptions:** 100 journals and other serials. **Services:** Interlibrary loans; copying; radio reading service; library open to blind and physically handicapped. **Automated Operations:** Computerized circulation. **Networks/Consortia:** Member of National Library Service for the Blind & Physically Handicapped (NLS). **Publications:** The Ensign, monthly. **Remarks:** This Regional Library for the Blind is the Multi-State Center for 13 Western states. **Staff:** Karnell Parry, Multi-State Libn.; Sharon Steglich, Circ.Libn.; Bessie Oakes, Braille Libn.; Rex Wallgren, Radio Prog.Mgr.

★16527★

UTAH STATE LIBRARY - FILM PROGRAM (Aud-Vis)
2150 South 300 West, Suite 9   Phone: (801) 533-5875
Salt Lake City, UT 84115   David Mann, Hd.
Staff: Prof 1. **Subjects:** Health and general subjects. **Holdings:** 2102 items. **Services:** Health collection open to public; general collection open to public libraries.

UTAH STATE - 3RD JUDICIAL DISTRICT - SALT LAKE COUNTY LAW LIBRARY
See: Salt Lake County Law Library

UTAH VALLEY BRANCH GENEALOGICAL LIBRARY
See: Brigham Young University

★16528★

UTAH VALLEY HOSPITAL - MEDICAL LIBRARY (Med)
1034 N. 500 W.   Phone: (801) 373-7850
Provo, UT 84601   Gregory R. Patterson, Dir., Med.Lib.
Staff: Prof 2. **Subjects:** Medicine. **Special Collections:** Pediatrics (150 volumes). **Holdings:** 2100 books; 20,000 bound periodical volumes; 3 drawers of manuscripts. **Subscriptions:** 425 journals and other serials; 25 newspapers. **Services:** Interlibrary loans; copying; library open to public. **Automated Operations:** Computerized serials. **Computerized Information Services:** NLM. Performs searches on cost recovery basis. **Networks/Consortia:** Member of Midcontinental Regional Medical Library Program; Utah Health Sciences Library Consortium. **Publications:** Exchange List, free upon request. **Staff:** Alan Grosbeck, Media Spec.

★16529★

UTAH WATER RESEARCH LABORATORY - LIBRARY (Sci-Tech)
Utah State Univ.   Phone: (801) 752-4100
Logan, UT 84322   Tammy Bachman-Gabbert, Libn.
Founded: 1965. **Staff:** Prof 1; Other 2. **Subjects:** Water and water related subjects. **Special Collections:** UWRL Project Report Series, occasional papers and proceedings. **Holdings:** 20,000 books. **Subscriptions:** 21 journals and other serials. **Services:** Interlibrary loans; copying; library open to public. **Publications:** List of books cataloged into the library, monthly. **Special Catalogs:** Special catalog of UWRL publications. **Staff:** Donna Falkenborg, Ed.

★16530★

UTICA/MARCY PSYCHIATRIC CENTER - MARCY CAMPUS PROFESSIONAL LIBRARY (Med)
1213 Court St.   Phone: (315) 736-3301
Utica, NY 13502   Janina Strife, Sr.Libn.
Founded: 1964. **Staff:** Prof 1. **Subjects:** Psychiatry, nursing, social welfare.

Holdings: 2500 books; 650 bound periodical volumes; 3 VF drawers of pamphlets, clippings, reprints. **Subscriptions:** 54 journals and other serials. **Services:** Interlibrary loans; copying; SDI; literature searches; library open to public for reference use only. **Networks/Consortia:** Member of Central New York Library Resources Council (CENTRO); Library Exchange & Resource Network (LEARN); Health Resources Council of Central New York (HRCCNY).

★16531★
**UTICA/MARCY PSYCHIATRIC CENTER - UTICA CAMPUS LIBRARY
  SERVICES (Med)**
1213 Court St.   Phone: (315) 797-6800
Utica, NY 13502   Toms E. Smith, Sr.Libn.
Founded: 1961. **Staff:** Prof 1. **Subjects:** Psychiatry, neurology, medicine, nursing. **Special Collections:** Historical medical books and journals (1000 volumes). **Holdings:** 2382 books; 725 bound periodical volumes; 1089 unbound periodical volumes. **Subscriptions:** 157 journals and other serials. **Services:** Interlibrary loans; copying; library open to health personnel; others by appointment. **Networks/Consortia:** Member of Central New York Library Resources Council (CENTRO); Greater Northeastern Regional Medical Library Program; Library Exchange & Resource Network (LEARN).

★16532★
UTICA MUTUAL INSURANCE COMPANY - RESOURCE CENTER (Bus-Fin)
180 Genesee St.   Phone: (315) 735-3321
New Hartford, NY 13413   Therese C. Kinney, Rsrcs.Coord.
Staff: Prof 1. **Subjects:** Law, insurance, business management, history. **Holdings:** 9200 books. **Subscriptions:** 89 journals and other serials. **Services:** Interlibrary loans; copying; center open to public with approval. **Automated Operations:** Computerized cataloging. **Computerized Information Services:** DIALOG; internal database.

★16533★
UTICA OBSERVER DISPATCH & UTICA DAILY PRESS - LIBRARY (Publ)†
221-3 Oriskany Plaza   Phone: (315) 797-9150
Utica, NY 13502   Virginia Malecki, Libn.
Founded: 1922. **Staff:** Prof 1. **Subjects:** Newspaper reference topics. **Holdings:** 172 VF drawers of clippings; microfilm, 1946 to present. **Subscriptions:** 12 newspapers. **Services:** Copying; library open to public with restrictions.

V

★16534★
VALDEZ HISTORICAL SOCIETY, INC. N-P - VALDEZ HERITAGE ARCHIVES ALIVE (Hist)
Royal Center Egan Drive
Box 6   Phone: (907) 835-4367
Valdez, AK 99686   Dorothy I. Clifton, Dir.
Founded: 1959. **Staff:** 2. **Subjects:** Alaska, Valdez, poetry, philately, religion. **Holdings:** 4000 square feet of archival materials; films; slides. **Services:** Copying; archives open to public; free film and slide showings.

VALENT (Othon O.) LEARNING RESOURCES CENTER
See: U.S. Army Sergeants Major Academy - Othon O. Valent Learning Resources Center

VALENTINE (H.A.) MEMORIAL LIBRARY
See: High Street Christian Church - H.A. Valentine Memorial Library

★16535★
VALENTINE MUSEUM - LIBRARY (Hist)
1015 E. Clay St.   Phone: (804) 649-0711
Richmond, VA 23219   Sarah Shields, Cur.
Staff: Prof 1. **Subjects:** Life and history of Richmond, fine arts and photography. **Special Collections:** Cook Collection of Photographs (10,000); advertising - chromolithographs, especially tobacco; Hibb's Collection (580 prints); maps and atlases; greeting cards; correspondence of Edgar Allan Poe, Daniel Call, George S. Cook, James Chaffin, the Valentine family and others. **Holdings:** 7000 books; 104 bound periodical volumes; 10,000 documents; 32 VF drawers; 77 volumes of manuscripts; 40,000 photographs. **Subscriptions:** 10 journals and other serials. **Services:** Copying; library open to public by appointment. **Staff:** Edie Jeter, Libn.

★16536★
VALERO ENERGY CORPORATION - CORPORATE RESOURCE CENTER (Sci-Tech; Bus-Fin)
530 McCullough
Box 500   Phone: (512) 246-2869
San Antonio, TX 78292   Mary S. Woods, Supv.
Staff: Prof 2; Other 2. **Subjects:** Natural gas, petroleum refining, exploration, management, business. **Holdings:** 1500 books; 1000 bound periodical volumes; 250 reports on microfiche; 15 VF drawers. **Subscriptions:** 354 journals and other serials. **Services:** Interlibrary loans; copying; SDI; library open to public by appointment. **Automated Operations:** Computerized cataloging and serials. **Computerized Information Services:** DIALOG, SDC, BRS, Dow Jones News/Retrieval, APILIT, Tulsa. Performs searches for staff only. **Networks/Consortia:** Member of CORAL; AMIGOS. **Publications:** Newsletter, monthly - for internal distribution only. **Special Indexes:** Geology holdings (computer printout); serials list (computer printout); oil field index (computer printout).

★16537★
VALLEJO NAVAL AND HISTORICAL MUSEUM - LIBRARY (Hist)
734 Marin St.   Phone: (707) 643-0022
Vallejo, CA 94590   Dorothy E. Marsden, Libn.
Founded: 1980. **Staff:** Prof 1. **Subjects:** Local history; maritime history - general and of the Bay Area; Mare Island Naval Shipyard; naval philately. **Holdings:** 3000 books; Soland County Articles of Incorporation, 1852-1958; Soland County Historical Society notebooks. **Services:** SDI; library open to public by appointment. **Networks/Consortia:** Member of Bay Area Reference Center (BARC).

★16538★
VALLEY FORGE CHRISTIAN COLLEGE - LIBRARY (Rel-Theol)
                        Phone: (215) 935-0450
Phoenixville, PA 19460   Dorsey Reynolds, Libn.
Staff: Prof 1; Other 2. **Subjects:** Bible, theology (emphasis on Evangelical and Pentecostal doctrines), church history, Christian education. **Special Collections:** Pentecostalism. **Holdings:** 32,439 books. **Subscriptions:** 267 journals and other serials. **Services:** Interlibrary loans; copying; library open to public.

★16539★
VALLEY FORGE HISTORICAL SOCIETY - LIBRARY (Hist)
                        Phone: (215) 783-0535
Valley Forge, PA 19481   John F. Reed, Cur., Doc.
Founded: 1918. **Staff:** 2. **Subjects:** Revolutionary War. **Special Collections:** Washingtoniana. **Holdings:** 1000 books; 150 manuscripts. **Services:** Library open to public with restrictions. **Publications:** The Valley Forge Journal, semiannual.

★16540★
VALLEY GENERAL HOSPITAL - LIBRARY (Med)
400 S. 43rd St.   Phone: (206) 228-3450
Renton, WA 98055   Dr. Douglas R. Currin, Chm., Lib.Comm.
Founded: 1969. **Staff:** Prof 1. **Subjects:** Medicine, surgery and allied sciences. **Holdings:** 525 books; 60 bound periodical volumes. **Subscriptions:** 200 journals and other serials; 5 newspapers. **Services:** Interlibrary loans; library not open to public. **Computerized Information Services:** BRS. **Networks/Consortia:** Member of Seattle Area Hospital Libraries Consortium (SAHLC). **Publications:** Library News, quarterly. **Staff:** Teresa Y. Lu, Libn.; Lynne B. Graber, Libn.

★16541★
VALLEY HOSPITAL - LIBRARY (Med)
Linwood Ave.   Phone: (201) 447-8285
Ridgewood, NJ 07451   Wanda Borgen, Med.Libn.
Founded: 1963. **Staff:** 2. **Subjects:** Medicine, nursing, hospital management. **Holdings:** 1000 books; 3000 bound periodical volumes; 2 VF drawers of pamphlets. **Subscriptions:** 160 journals and other serials. **Services:** Interlibrary loans; copying; literature searches; library open to public with restrictions. **Networks/Consortia:** Member of Bergen-Passaic Health Sciences Library Consortium.

★16542★
VALLEY MEDICAL CENTER OF FRESNO - MEDICAL LIBRARY (Med)
445 S. Cedar Ave.   Phone: (209) 453-5030
Fresno, CA 93702   Vicky Christianson, Med.Libn.
Staff: Prof 1; Other 1. **Subjects:** Medicine, dentistry, nursing, hospital administration. **Holdings:** 5000 books and bound periodical volumes; cassette tapes in medical specialities. **Subscriptions:** 150 journals and other serials. **Services:** Interlibrary loans; copying; library open to public with restrictions.

★16543★
VALLEY NATIONAL BANK - LIBRARY/INFORMATION CENTER (Bus-Fin)
Box 71, A-315   Phone: (602) 261-2456
Phoenix, AZ 85001   J.F. Gorman, Mgr.
Founded: 1948. **Staff:** Prof 1. **Subjects:** Banking, business, economics, management. **Holdings:** 500 volumes. **Subscriptions:** 200 journals and other serials. **Services:** Library not open to public. **Computerized Information Services:** DIALOG, Dow Jones News/Retrieval.

★16544★
VALLEY NEWSPAPERS - LIBRARY (Publ)
600 S. Washington St.
Box 130   Phone: (206) 872-6674
Kent, WA 98031   Frances Wright, Libn.
Founded: 1970. **Staff:** 1. **Special Collections:** Bound volumes of Daily Record Chronicle, Daily News Journal, Daily Globe News and their predecessors. **Holdings:** Figures not available for books, microfilm, newspaper clippings, news photos, government documents, maps. **Subscriptions:** 6 newspapers. **Services:** Library not open to public.

★16545★
VALLEY PRESBYTERIAN HOSPITAL - LIBRARY FOR MEDICAL AND HEALTH SCIENCES (Med)
15107 Vanowen St.   Phone: (818) 902-2973
Van Nuys, CA 91405   Francine Kubrin, Libn.
Founded: 1959. **Staff:** Prof 1; Other 1. **Subjects:** General medicine, general surgery, nursing, hospital administration. **Holdings:** 4000 volumes; 500 audio cassettes; 1 vertical file drawer of pamphlets, bibliographies and reprints; 1 vertical file drawer of AV catalogs. **Subscriptions:** 350 journals and other serials. **Services:** Interlibrary loans; library not open to public. **Computerized Information Services:** MEDLINE, BRS.

★16546★
VALPARAISO UNIVERSITY - LAW LIBRARY (Law)
Wesemann Hall   Phone: (219) 464-5438
Valparaiso, IN 46383   Chris Kirkwood, Act.Dir.
Founded: 1879. **Staff:** Prof 3; Other 6. **Subjects:** Law. **Special Collections:** Indiana Supreme Court and Court of Appeals briefs, 1977 to present.

Holdings: 90,000 books; 5500 bound periodical volumes; CIS legislative histories, 1974 to present (microfiche); Supreme Court records and briefs, 1978 to present (microfiche). **Subscriptions:** 425 journals and other serials. **Services:** Interlibrary loans; copying; library open to lawyers. **Automated Operations:** Computerized cataloging. **Staff:** Sally Holterhoff, Doc.Libn.; Tim Watts, Ref.Libn.; Rich Mills, Cat.

★16547★
VALUATION RESEARCH CORPORATION - CORPORATE RESEARCH AND REFERENCE LIBRARY (Bus-Fin)
250 E. Wisconsin Ave.   Phone: (414) 271-8662
Milwaukee, WI 53202   Don F. Schwamb, Corp.Libn.
Staff: Prof 1; Other 2. **Subjects:** Appraisal/valuation, property assessment, real estate, accounting, taxation, industrial technology. **Special Collections:** Price indexes; machinery and equipment pricing files; real estate transactions; financial statements of corporations. **Holdings:** 2500 books; 200 bound periodical volumes; catalogs and price lists; annual and 10K reports for over 3500 firms. **Subscriptions:** 100 journals, serials and newspapers. **Services:** Interlibrary loans; copying; library open to public with restrictions and by prior notice. **Automated Operations:** Computerized cataloging. **Networks/Consortia:** Member of Library Council of Metropolitan Milwaukee, Inc. (LCOMM).

★16548★
VALUE LINE INC. - BUSINESS LIBRARY (Bus-Fin)
711 Third Ave.   Phone: (212) 687-3965
New York, NY 10017   Gloria Napoli, Chf.Libn.
Staff: Prof 1; Other 4. **Subjects:** Finance and economics. **Holdings:** Figures not available. **Subscriptions:** 89 journals and other serials. **Services:** Interlibrary loans; copying; library open to public with restrictions. **Automated Operations:** Computerized circulation. **Publications:** Business Library, daily. **Formerly:** Bernhard (Arnold) and Company, Inc.

VAN CLEEF (Noah) MEDICAL MEMORIAL LIBRARY
See: Illinois Masonic Medical Center - Noah Van Cleef Medical Memorial Library

VAN EVERA LIBRARY
See: Human Resources Research Organization

VAN GORDEN-WILLIAMS LIBRARY
See: Museum of Our National Heritage

★16549★
VAN HORNESVILLE COMMUNITY CORPORATION - OWEN D. YOUNG COLLECTION (Hist)
                    Phone: (315) 858-0030
Van Hornesville, NY 13475   Josephine Young Case, Pres.
Subjects: Development of electricity and radio, foreign affairs, rural and small colleges. **Special Collections:** Early days of radio collection; St. Lawrence University in Canton, NY; Owen D. Young Collection dealing with his activities as a rare book collector and breeder of Holstein-Friesian cattle. **Holdings:** 1085 boxes of correspondence, photographs, and clippings (1890-1967); file of newspaper clippings (1913-1967). **Services:** Copying; collection open by appointment to graduate students holding letters of recommendation.

VAN HOUTEN (Robert W.) LIBRARY
See: New Jersey Institute of Technology - Robert W. van Houten Library

VAN NOORD HEALTH SCIENCES LIBRARY
See: Pine Rest Christian Hospital

VAN NOY LIBRARY
See: U.S. Army Post - Fort Belvoir

VAN NUYS PUBLISHING COMPANY - LOS ANGELES DAILY NEWS
See: Los Angeles Daily News

VAN OOSTEN (John) GREAT LAKES FISHERY RESEARCH LIBRARY
See: U.S. Fish & Wildlife Service - John Van Oosten Great Lakes Fishery Research Library

VAN PELT LIBRARY
See: University of Pennsylvania

VAN STEENWYK (E.A.) MEMORIAL LIBRARY
See: Blue Cross of Greater Philadelphia - E.A. van Steenwyk Memorial Library

VAN TRUMP (James D.) LIBRARY
See: Pittsburgh History & Landmarks Foundation - James D. van Trump Library

VAN TYNE (Josselyn) MEMORIAL LIBRARY
See: Wilson Ornithological Society - Josselyn Van Tyne Memorial Library

VAN VOORHIS LIBRARY
See: Poetry Society of America

VAN WAGENEN (Jared, Jr.) LEARNING RESOURCE CENTER
See: SUNY - Agricultural and Technical College at Cobleskill - Jared van Wagenen, Jr. Learning Resource Center

★16550★
VAN WERT COUNTY LAW LIBRARY (Law)
Court of Common Pleas, 3rd Fl.   Phone: (419) 238-6935
Van Wert, OH 45891   Richard Atwood, Libn.
Staff: 1. **Subjects:** Law. **Holdings:** 14,000 volumes; Ohio law publications. **Services:** Library is open to bar members.

★16551★
VAN WYCK HOMESTEAD MUSEUM - LIBRARY (Hist)
Rte. 9, Box 133   Phone: (914) 896-9560
Fishkill, NY 12524   Ruth B. Polhill, Libn.
Founded: 1973. **Staff:** Prof 1. **Subjects:** Local and American history, early American crafts, genealogy, American Indian, biography. **Special Collections:** Holland Society of New York yearbooks, 1888-1931. **Holdings:** 700 books; 80 bound periodical volumes; 100 early military documents; clippings and early local newspapers; early business ledgers and schoolbooks. **Services:** Interlibrary loans; library open to public for research. **Publications:** Newsletter, monthly. **Remarks:** Maintained by Fishkill Historical Society, Inc.

VAN ZANDT (James E.) MEDICAL CENTER LIBRARY
See: U.S. Veterans Administration (PA-Altoona) - James E. Van Zandt Medical Center Library

★16552★
VANCOUVER ART GALLERY - LIBRARY (Art)
750 Hornby St.   Phone: (604) 682-5621
Vancouver, BC, Canada V6Z 2H7   Catherine Cowan, Libn.
Founded: 1931. **Staff:** Prof 1; Other 1. **Subjects:** Painting, sculpture, prints, drawings. **Special Collections:** Canadian exhibition catalogs, artists files, and museum collection catalogs. **Holdings:** 7000 books; 500 bound periodical volumes; 12,000 exhibition catalogs. **Subscriptions:** 125 journals and other serials. **Services:** Interlibrary loans; copying; library open to public for reference use only. **Publications:** Monthly bulletin; annual report. **Special Catalogs:** Checklist of biographical files - Canadian artists and artists working in Canada; artists exhibiting at the Vancouver Art Gallery.

★16553★
VANCOUVER BOARD OF TRADE - RESOURCE LIBRARY (Bus-Fin)†
5th Fl., 1177 W. Hastings St.   Phone: (604) 681-2111
Vancouver, BC, Canada V6E 2K3   Maureen W. Devine, Res.Libn.
Staff: Prof 1; Other 1. **Subjects:** Business, economics, international trade. **Special Collections:** International trade. **Holdings:** 350 books; 4 VF drawers of newspapers and pamphlets; 7 VF drawers of Statistics Canada publications; 5 VF drawers of annual reports and official publications; Business Opportunities Sourcing System (BOSS) of Canadian manufacturers and trading houses on microfiche. **Subscriptions:** 100 journals and other serials; 6 newspapers. **Services:** Copying; SDI; library open to public if material is not available elsewhere. **Networks/Consortia:** Member of Vancouver On-line Users Group (VOLUG); Central Vancouver Library Group. **Publications:** Annual Clerical Salary Survey; Laws in the Making, weekly summary of provincial government bills introduced in the legislature; Business Barometer, biweekly.

VANCOUVER COMMUNITY COLLEGE - VANCOUVER VOCATIONAL INSTITUTE
See: Vancouver Vocational Institute

VANCOUVER COURTHOUSE LIBRARY
See: British Columbia Law Library Foundation

VANCOUVER GENERAL HOSPITAL
See: University of British Columbia - Biomedical Branch Library

★16554★

VANCOUVER MEMORIAL HOSPITAL - R.D. WISWALL MEMORIAL LIBRARY (Med)
3400 Main St.
Box 1600   Phone: (206) 696-5143
Vancouver, WA 98668   Sylvia E. MacWilliams, Lib.Coord.
Founded: 1965. **Staff:** Prof 1. **Subjects:** Medicine, nursing. **Holdings:** 300 books. **Subscriptions:** 96 journals and other serials. **Services:** Interlibrary loans; library not open to public. **Automated Operations:** Computerized statistics. **Computerized Information Services:** MEDLARS. **Remarks:** Maintained by Southwest Washington Hospitals.

★16555★

VANCOUVER MUSEUMS & PLANETARIUM ASSOCIATION - LIBRARY AND RESOURCE CENTRE (Hist; Sci-Tech)
1100 Chestnut St.   Phone: (604) 736-4431
Vancouver, BC, Canada V6J 3J9   Norah J. McLaren, Libn.
Founded: 1968. **Staff:** Prof 1; Other 5. **Subjects:** Local history, decorative arts, ethnology, archeology, natural history, maritime history, astronomy. **Holdings:** 6500 books; maps. **Subscriptions:** 74 journals and other serials. **Services:** Library not open to public.

★16556★

VANCOUVER PUBLIC LIBRARY - BUSINESS & ECONOMICS DIVISION (Bus-Fin)
750 Burrard St.   Phone: (604) 682-5911
Vancouver, BC, Canada V6Z 1X5   Barbara Bell, Hd.
Founded: 1951. **Staff:** Prof 6; Other 13. **Subjects:** Industrial economics, transportation, management, marketing, labor, real estate. **Holdings:** 72,000 books and bound periodical volumes; 1500 trade directories; 20,000 corporation reports; 20,000 pamphlets; 51 cases of clippings. **Subscriptions:** 900 journals and other serials; 10 newspapers. **Services:** Interlibrary loans; copying; division open to public. **Automated Operations:** Computerized cataloging and circulation. **Networks/Consortia:** Member of Greater Vancouver Library Federation; Central Vancouver Library Group; Vancouver On-line Users Group (VOLUG). **Special Indexes:** Corporation card file; periodical indexing card file. **Staff:** Nancy Clegg, Libn.; Glenda Guttman, Libn.; Shelagh Flaherty, Libn.; Sheila Thompson, Libn.

★16557★

VANCOUVER SCHOOL OF THEOLOGY - LIBRARY (Rel-Theol)
6050 Chancellor Blvd.   Phone: (604) 228-9031
Vancouver, BC, Canada V6T 1X3   Elizabeth Hannon, Libn.
Staff: Prof 1; Other 5. **Subjects:** Biblical studies, Christianity, doctrinal and practical theology, denominations and sects, Judaism, women's studies. **Holdings:** 70,000 books; 3652 bound periodical volumes; 57 kits; 745 microfiche titles; 369 reels of microfilm; 39 phonograph records; 1361 cassettes and tapes; 74 filmstrips; 2982 slides; 17 maps. **Subscriptions:** 291 journals and other serials. **Services:** Interlibrary loans; copying; library open to public. **Publications:** Acquisitions list, monthly; periodical abstracts, monthly. **Staff:** Anne McCullum, Circ.Hd.; Mary Fankhauser, Cat.; Wayne Murphy, Acq.

★16558★

VANCOUVER TALMUD TORAH SCHOOL - LIBRARY (Rel-Theol)
998 W. 26th Ave.   Phone: (604) 736-7307
Vancouver, BC, Canada V5Z 2G1   Marylile Gill, Teacher/Libn.
Staff: Prof 1. **Subjects:** Hebraica and Judaica. **Holdings:** 5000 books; phonograph records; filmstrips; audio cassettes; kits; transparencies; study prints. **Subscriptions:** 50 journals and other serials. **Services:** Interlibrary loans; library open to public with restrictions.

★16559★

VANCOUVER TEACHERS' PROFESSIONAL LIBRARY (Educ)
Teacher Centre, 123 E. 6th Ave.   Phone: (604) 874-2617
Vancouver, BC, Canada V5T 1J6   Linda Dunbar, Lib.Techn.
Founded: 1921. **Staff:** 2. **Subjects:** Education. **Holdings:** 15,000 books; 500 pamphlets; 650 microfiche. **Subscriptions:** 282 journals and other serials. **Services:** Interlibrary loans; borrowing restricted to staff of Vancouver School Board. **Computerized Information Services:** DIALOG.

★16560★

VANCOUVER VOCATIONAL INSTITUTE - LIBRARY (Sci-Tech; Bus-Fin)
250 West Pender St.   Phone: (604) 681-8111
Vancouver, BC, Canada V6B 1S9   Ross M. Henderson, Campus Libn.
Founded: 1974. **Staff:** Prof 2; Other 6. **Subjects:** Electricity and electronics, engineering, graphic arts, mechanics, beauty culture, food trades, business and commerce, practical nursing. **Special Collections:** Electricity and electronics (800 volumes); business and commerce (600 volumes); food

trades (1300 volumes); nursing (1200 volumes). **Holdings:** 15,000 books; 600 pamphlet files; 200 AV items; 205 films. **Subscriptions:** 166 journals and other serials. **Services:** Interlibrary loans; copying; library open to public with restrictions. **Automated Operations:** Computerized cataloging. **Computerized Information Services:** DIALOG, UTLAS. Performs searches on cost recovery basis. Contact Person: Frieda Wiebe. **Networks/Consortia:** Member of British Columbia Union Catalogue (BCUC). **Remarks:** Maintained by Vancouver Community College. **Staff:** Frieda Wiebe, Pub.Serv.Libn.

★16561★

VANDALIA HISTORICAL SOCIETY - JAMES HALL LIBRARY (Hist)
Little Brick House
621 St. Clair St.   Phone: (618) 283-0024
Vandalia, IL 62471   Mary Burtschi, Dir.
Staff: Prof 3. **Subjects:** Illinois and local history. **Special Collections:** James Hall Collection, 1793-1868; Abraham Lincoln Collection, 1834-1839; biographies of Vandalia authors, artists and statesmen; Joseph Charles Burtschi Collection; Mary Burtschi Collection; Burtschi family archives, 1775-1975. **Holdings:** 10 books; photographs; manuscripts; reports; letters; scrapbooks. **Services:** Library open to public by appointment. **Staff:** Josephine Burtschi, Archv./Act.Libn.

VANDAMM AND WHITE STUDIOS ARCHIVES
See: New York Public Library - Performing Arts Research Center - Billy Rose Theatre Collection

VANDENBERG AIR FORCE BASE (CA)
See: U.S. Air Force - Western Space and Missile Center

VANDERBILT NATL. HISTORIC SITE
See: U.S. Natl. Park Service - Roosevelt-Vanderbilt Natl. Historic Sites

★16562★

VANDERBILT (R.T.) COMPANY, INC. - LIBRARY (Sci-Tech)
33 Winfield St.   Phone: (203) 853-1400
East Norwalk, CT 06855   Jane Wilson, Libn.
Founded: 1956. **Staff:** Prof 1. **Subjects:** Organic chemistry, rubber, plastics, ceramics, paint, mineralogy. **Holdings:** 10,000 books; 4800 bound periodical volumes; 1500 technical reports; 1000 reprints; 22 VF drawers of technical data; 1200 reels of microfilm; Chemical Abstracts and Official Patent Gazette (on microfilm). **Subscriptions:** 130 journals and other serials; 10 newspapers. **Services:** Interlibrary loans; copying; library open to public by appointment. **Networks/Consortia:** Member of Southwestern Connecticut Library Council (SWLC). **Publications:** Monthly Accessions Bulletin.

★16563★

VANDERBILT UNIVERSITY - ALYNE QUEENER MASSEY LAW LIBRARY (Law)
School of Law   Phone: (615) 322-2568
Nashville, TN 37203   Igor I. Kavass, Dir.
Staff: Prof 6; Other 6. **Subjects:** Law. **Holdings:** 167,000 books and bound periodicals; microforms; 44,488 documents. **Subscriptions:** 2600 journals and other serials. **Services:** Interlibrary loans; library open to public for reference use only. **Computerized Information Services:** LEXIS, Westlaw. **Staff:** Doris M. Bieber, Libn.; Howard A. Hood, Legal Info.Spec.

VANDERBILT UNIVERSITY - GEORGE PEABODY COLLEGE FOR TEACHERS
See: Peabody (George) College for Teachers of Vanderbilt University

★16564★

VANDERBILT UNIVERSITY - JEAN AND ALEXANDER HEARD LIBRARY - CENTRAL DIVISION - ARTS LIBRARY (Art)
419 21st Ave., S.   Phone: (615) 322-3485
Nashville, TN 37203   Jack Robertson, Arts Libn.
Staff: Prof 1; Other 1. **Subjects:** Art and architectural history, photography, landscape architecture, aesthetics, art criticism. **Holdings:** 30,000 books; 4200 bound periodical volumes; 2500 auction and sale catalogs; 2500 items in art picture study collection; 18 VF drawers. **Subscriptions:** 190 journals and other serials. **Services:** Interlibrary loans; copying; library open to public for reference use only. **Computerized Information Services:** DIALOG, OCLC. **Networks/Consortia:** Member of SOLINET; ARLIS. **Publications:** Vanderbilt University Fine Arts Theses, 1970-1980: Subject Index and Abstracts, decennial - available upon request. **Special Indexes:** Index of artists and subjects represented in major auctions at Sotheby Parke Bernet (card).

★16565★

VANDERBILT UNIVERSITY - JEAN AND ALEXANDER HEARD LIBRARY - CENTRAL DIV. - SARA SHANNON STEVENSON SCI. LIB. (Sci-Tech)
419 21st Ave. S.   Phone: (615) 322-2775
Nashville, TN 37203
Staff: Prof 3; Other 4. **Subjects:** Biology, chemistry, engineering, geology,

mathematics, physics, astronomy. **Special Collections:** Foreign and U.S. Geological Survey Collections. **Holdings:** 190,000 books and bound periodical volumes; 190 boxes of microcards of Landmarks of Science I and II; 96 drawers of microfiche of AEC Reports through 1971; 8 drawers of microfiche of NASA Reports, 1976 to present; 648 reels of microfilm of U.S. Patent Official Gazette, 1872 to present; 23 reels of microfilm of U.S. Patent Official Gazette Trademarks, 1971 to present; 20 reels of microfilm of U.S. Annual Report of the Commissioner of Patents, 1790-1871; 26 drawers of microfiche of miscellaneous materials. **Subscriptions:** 2650 journals and other serials. **Services:** Interlibrary loans; copying; library open to public with visitor registration forms and IDs. **Computerized Information Services:** DIALOG, OCLC. **Networks/Consortia:** Member of SOLINET. **Staff:** Mary Brockman, Ref.Libn.; Paul Murphy, Ref.Libn.

★16566★
VANDERBILT UNIVERSITY - JEAN AND ALEXANDER HEARD LIBRARY - DIVINITY LIBRARY (Rel-Theol)
419 21st Ave., S.   Phone: (615) 322-2865
Nashville, TN 37203   Dorothy Ruth Parks, Dir.
Founded: 1894. **Staff:** Prof 2; Other 1. **Subjects:** Religion and theology. **Special Collections:** Judaica Collection; memorabilia. **Holdings:** 130,000 volumes; microforms. **Subscriptions:** 889 journals and other serials. **Services:** Interlibrary loans; copying; library open to public. **Automated Operations:** Computerized cataloging, acquisitions, serials and reference services. **Computerized Information Services:** BRS, OCLC. Performs searches on cost recovery basis. Contact Person: William Hook. **Networks/Consortia:** Member of SOLINET. **Special Catalogs:** Library Guide, annual; Subject bibliographies for each graduate area in the Divinity School. **Staff:** Nancy R. Braun, Circ.Supv.; William Hook, Ref.Libn.

★16567★
VANDERBILT UNIVERSITY - JEAN AND ALEXANDER HEARD LIBRARY - DIVINITY LIBRARY - KESLER CIRCULATING LIBRARY (Rel-Theol)
419 21st Ave., S.   Phone: (615) 322-2865
Nashville, TN 37203   Dorothy Ruth Parks, Dir.
Founded: 1940. **Staff:** Prof 1; Other 1. **Subjects:** Religion. **Services:** Mail circulation of books to ordained ministry; library open to public with restrictions. **Special Catalogs:** Accession lists distributed to members periodically. **Remarks:** Kesler Circulating Library is a continuing education service of the Divinity Library and utilizes its holdings. Membership is open to clergy engaged in ministry (except those based in academic institutions whose needs are met by interlibrary loan) in the continental United States and Canada; nondenominational; free membership upon application. **Staff:** Nancy R. Braun, Circ.Supv.

★16568★
VANDERBILT UNIVERSITY - JEAN AND ALEXANDER HEARD LIBRARY - DYER OBSERVATORY (Sci-Tech)
Sta. B
Box 1803   Phone: (615) 373-4897
Nashville, TN 37235   Ellen Ellis, Libn.
Founded: 1953. **Staff:** Prof 1. **Subjects:** Astronomy, astrophysics. **Holdings:** 3800 books; 5000 bound periodical volumes; 8500 unbound reprints; 35 theses; 1100 slides; 4200 photographs of star fields. **Subscriptions:** 340 journals and other serials. **Services:** Interlibrary loans; observatory open to public by appointment. **Publications:** Arthur J. Dyer Observatory Reprints, irregular. **Remarks:** The library is located at 1000 Oman Dr., Brentwood, TN 37027.

★16569★
VANDERBILT UNIVERSITY - JEAN AND ALEXANDER HEARD LIBRARY - EDUCATION LIBRARY (Educ; Info Sci)
Box 325   Phone: (615) 322-8095
Nashville, TN 37203   Mary Beth Blalock, Act.Dir.
Staff: Prof 2; Other 5. **Subjects:** Education, psychology, special education, physical education, library and information sciences, curriculum materials. **Holdings:** 226,306 books; 566 reels of microfilm; 265,470 microfiche; 10,641 microcards; 729 cassettes; 1158 games and kits. **Subscriptions:** 1305 journals and other serials. **Services:** Interlibrary loans; copying; computer search service; library open to visiting scholars for reference use only. **Automated Operations:** Computerized cataloging and acquisitions. **Computerized Information Services:** OCLC. **Networks/Consortia:** Member of SOLINET. **Staff:** Pamela Estes, Hd.Ref.Libn.

★16570★
VANDERBILT UNIVERSITY - JEAN AND ALEXANDER HEARD LIBRARY - EDUCATION LIB. - PEABODY COLL. OF BOOKS ON CHILDREN (Educ)
Box 325   Phone: (615) 322-8095
Nashville, TN 37203   Pamela Estes, Libn.
Founded: 1969. **Staff:** Prof 1; Other 1. **Subjects:** Child study, child and

adolescent psychology, special education, child psychiatry, social problems of children, children in art, history and literature. **Special Collections:** Books by and about Jean Piaget (250 papers, unbound). **Holdings:** 12,500 books and serials; VF on 600 subjects related to children. **Subscriptions:** 70 journals and other serials. **Services:** Interlibrary loans; copying; collection open to public for reference use only. **Computerized Information Services:** OCLC. **Networks/Consortia:** Member of SOLINET. **Special Catalogs:** Subject catalog on materials by and about Piaget (card). **Special Indexes:** Author and title index of Piaget papers (card).

★16571★
VANDERBILT UNIVERSITY - JEAN AND ALEXANDER HEARD LIBRARY - MUSIC LIBRARY (Mus)
                                     Phone: (615) 322-8222
Nashville, TN 37203   Shirley Marie Watts, Libn.
Founded: 1948. **Staff:** Prof 1; Other 1. **Subjects:** Music. **Special Collections:** Seminar in piano teaching (lectures, master classes, recitals, 1970-1976; 213 tapes). **Holdings:** 10,593 books and bound periodical volumes; 11,547 scores; 9240 phonograph records; 1329 reels of tapes; microforms. **Subscriptions:** 150 journals and other serials. **Services:** Interlibrary loans; copying; library open to public for reference use only.

★16572★
VANDERBILT UNIVERSITY - JEAN AND ALEXANDER HEARD LIBRARY - SPECIAL COLLECTIONS DEPARTMENT (Rare Book; Hist)
21st Ave., S.   Phone: (615) 322-2807
Nashville, TN 37203   Marice Wolfe, Hd.
Founded: 1936. **Staff:** Prof 1; Other 1. **Subjects:** Tennessee history, Southern politics, Southern literature. **Special Collections:** Vanderbilt Collection (Vanderbilt published materials); Sevier Collection (Tennessee history and general rare books); Rand Collection (fine bindings, rarities); Jesse Wills Collection (fugitive/agrarian manuscripts and letters); Vanderbilt archives; W.T. Bandy Center for Baudelaire Studies. **Holdings:** 20,000 books; Vanderbilt theses and dissertations; 1000 cubic feet of manuscripts; 1500 cubic feet of archives. **Services:** Copying; department open to public for reference use only.

★16573★
VANDERBILT UNIVERSITY - JEAN AND ALEXANDER HEARD LIBRARY - TELEVISION NEWS ARCHIVES (Aud-Vis)
                                     Phone: (615) 322-2927
Nashville, TN 37203   James P. Pilkington, Adm.
Founded: 1968. **Staff:** Prof 1. **Subjects:** Television news. **Special Collections:** Network evening news programs since August 5, 1968 on videotape; Presidential speeches and press conferences; Democratic and Republican National Conventions; Watergate hearings; impeachment debates and more recent events. **Holdings:** Videotape (10,000 hours). **Services:** Interlibrary loans; copying; archives open to public. **Publications:** Television News Index and Abstracts, monthly.

★16574★
VANDERBILT UNIVERSITY - JEAN AND ALEXANDER HEARD LIBRARY - WALKER MANAGEMENT LIBRARY (Bus-Fin)
401 21st Ave. S.   Phone: (615) 322-2970
Nashville, TN 37203   Shirley Hallblade, Dir.
Founded: 1970. **Staff:** Prof 4; Other 6. **Subjects:** Management and business, corporate information. **Special Collections:** Career planning and placement resources. **Holdings:** 15,500 books; 2000 bound periodical volumes; 450 AV items; 30,000 microforms; 3000 corporate reports. **Subscriptions:** 750 journals and other serials. **Services:** Interlibrary loans; copying; library open to public with restrictions on borrowing materials; video production; supervision of student computer facilities. **Computerized Information Services:** DIALOG, NEXIS, OCLC. Performs searches on cost recovery basis. **Networks/Consortia:** Member of SOLINET. **Staff:** Danny Sulkin, Spec.; Carol Dickerson, Ref.Libn.; Sylvia Graham, Ref.Libn.; Vicki Watkins, Ref.Libn.

VANDERBILT UNIVERSITY - MEDICAL CENTER - BIOMEDICAL COMPUTING TECHNOLOGY INFORMATION CENTER
See: Biomedical Computing Technology Information Center

★16575★
VANDERBILT UNIVERSITY - MEDICAL CENTER LIBRARY (Med)
                                     Phone: (615) 322-2292
Nashville, TN 37232   T. Mark Hodges, Dir.
Founded: 1906. **Staff:** Prof 9; Other 18. **Subjects:** Health sciences. **Special Collections:** History of Medicine; History of Nutrition (Goldberger-Sebrell Pellagra Collection; Lydia J. Roberts Collection; Helen S. Mitchell Collection; E. Neige Todhunter Collection); Moll Hypnosis Collection; Vanderbilt Medical Faculty Manuscripts; Archives of Vanderbilt University Medical Center.

Holdings: 43,028 books and theses; 80,811 bound periodical volumes; 8599 government publications; 1558 AV items; 2667 microforms; 314 linear feet of manuscripts. **Subscriptions:** 1429 journals and other serials. **Services:** Interlibrary loans (fee); copying; SDI; library open to public with restriction on borrowing. **Automated Operations:** Computerized cataloging and ILL. **Computerized Information Services:** MEDLINE, BRS, DIALOG. **Networks/Consortia:** Member of Southeastern/Atlantic Regional Medical Library Services. **Publications:** Catalist, quarterly; Nutrition History Notes, quarterly; Current Serials List, annual. **Staff:** Byrd S. Helguera, Assoc.Dir.; Frances H. Lynch, Asst.Dir., Tech.Serv.; Mary H. Teloh, Spec.Coll.Libn.; Mary Charles Lasater, Monographs Libn.; Judy Orr, Hd.Libn., Ref. & Res.Serv; Carol E. Lewis, Ref.Libn.; Susan Way, Ref.Libn.; Gayle Grantham, Circ.Supv.; Sharon Helton, ILL Asst.; Dr. William J. Darby, Honor.Cur.; Dr. Harry S. Shelley, Honor.Cur.

★16576★
VANDERBURGH COUNTY LAW LIBRARY (Law)
City-County Courts Bldg., Rm. 207   Phone: (812) 426-5175
Evansville, IN 47708   Shirley Roll, Libn.
Founded: 1900. **Staff:** Prof 1. **Subjects:** Law. **Holdings:** 12,000 volumes. **Services:** Copying; library open to public with restrictions. **Remarks:** Maintained by Vanderburgh County and Evansville Bar Association.

★16577★
VANDERCOOK COLLEGE OF MUSIC - HARRY RUPPEL MEMORIAL LIBRARY (Mus)
3209 S. Michigan Ave.   Phone: (312) 225-6288
Chicago, IL 60616   Peter L. Eisenberg, Libn.
Founded: 1967. **Staff:** Prof 1; Other 1. **Subjects:** Music and music education, education. **Special Collections:** Performance Library (12,000 items). **Holdings:** 18,493 books; 1718 phonograph records; 2787 scores; 8 VF drawers of pamphlets; 6200 reels of microfilm; dissertations. **Subscriptions:** 81 journals and other serials. **Services:** Interlibrary loans; copying; library open to public for reference use only. **Networks/Consortia:** Member of Chicago Library System.

VANIER (Georges P.) LIBRARY
See: Concordia University - Loyola Campus - Georges P. Vanier Library

★16578★
VANIER INSTITUTE OF THE FAMILY - RESOURCE & INFORMATION CENTRE (Soc Sci)
151 Slater St., Suite 207   Phone: (613) 232-7115
Ottawa, ON, Canada K1P 5H3   Susan L. Campbell, Libn./Res.
Founded: 1968. **Staff:** Prof 1. **Subjects:** Family, communications, learning, informal economy, social policy, alternative lifestyles. **Holdings:** 3600 books; 20 VF drawers of pamphlets, dissertations and documents. **Subscriptions:** 220 journals and other serials. **Services:** Interlibrary loans; copying; center open to public with restrictions. **Special Catalogs:** Varieties of Family Lifestyles: Selected Annotated Bibliography Phase 1 - Innovative Lifestyles; Perspectives on Learning: A Selected Annotated Bibliography.

VANIER SCIENCE & ENGINEERING LIBRARY
See: University of Ottawa

VAREY (Vida B.) LIBRARY
See: Plymouth Congregational Church - Vida B. Varey Library

★16579★
VARIAN ASSOCIATES - EIMAC DIVISION - TECHNICAL LIBRARY (Sci-Tech)†
301 Industrial Way   Phone: (415) 592-1221
San Carlos, CA 94070   Merald Shrader, Hd., Engr.
Founded: 1955. **Subjects:** Electronics, electron devices, metals, ceramics, chemistry. **Holdings:** 5700 books; 2350 bound periodical volumes; 5800 pamphlets; 6300 technical reports. **Subscriptions:** 170 journals and other serials. **Services:** Interlibrary loans; library not open to public. **Computerized Information Services:** DIALOG.

★16580★
VARIAN ASSOCIATES - TECHNICAL LIBRARY (Sci-Tech)
611 Hansen Way   Phone: (415) 493-4000
Palo Alto, CA 94303   Joan Murphy, Mgr., Lib.Serv.
Founded: 1961. **Staff:** Prof 3; Other 3. **Subjects:** Electronics, chemistry, instrumentation, applied mathematics, physics. **Holdings:** 14,000 books; 30,000 bound periodical volumes; 23,000 technical reports. **Subscriptions:** 734 journals and other serials; 10 newspapers. **Services:** Interlibrary loans; copying; SDI; library open to public by appointment for reference. **Computerized Information Services:** DIALOG, RLIN. **Networks/Consortia:** Member of South Bay Cooperative Library System. **Publications:** Technical

Library Bulletin, monthly. **Special Catalogs:** Corporate bibliography (database). **Staff:** Sue Whisenhunt, Sr.Libn.; Donna Farmer, Libn.

★16581★
VARIAN ASSOCIATES - TECHNICAL LIBRARY (Sci-Tech)†
Salem Rd.   Phone: (617) 922-6000
Beverly, MA 01915   Katherine R. MacGregor, Libn.
Founded: 1961. **Staff:** Prof 1. **Subjects:** Microwave engineering, semiconductors, masers, cesium engineering. **Holdings:** 1000 books; 355 bound periodical volumes; government reports. **Subscriptions:** 75 journals and other serials. **Services:** Interlibrary loans; library not open to public. **Publications:** Newsletter, monthly - for internal distribution only.

★16582★
VARIAN CANADA INC. - TECHNICAL LIBRARY (Sci-Tech)†
45 River Dr.   Phone: (416) 877-0161
Georgetown, ON, Canada L7G 2J4   Rhonda Barber, Libn.
Founded: 1958. **Staff:** Prof 2. **Subjects:** Microwave electronics, metallurgy, chemical analysis, metal working, tool design, management. **Holdings:** 530 books. **Subscriptions:** 60 journals and other serials; 5 newspapers. **Services:** Interlibrary loans; library not open to public. **Staff:** Harry V. Haylock, Supv.

★16583★
VASSAR BROTHERS HOSPITAL - MEDICAL LIBRARY (Med)
Reade Pl.   Phone: (914) 454-8500
Poughkeepsie, NY 12601   Mrs. Howard A. Wilson, Med.Libn.
Founded: 1951. **Staff:** Prof 1. **Subjects:** Internal medicine, surgery, cardiology, pulmonary medicine, orthopedics. **Holdings:** 1425 books; 450 bound periodical volumes; 8 VF drawers of pamphlets, flyers and reports. **Subscriptions:** 72 journals and other serials. **Services:** Interlibrary loans; copying (limited); library open to students by appointment. **Networks/Consortia:** Member of Southeastern New York Library Resources Council (SENYLRC).

★16584★
VASSAR COLLEGE - ART LIBRARY (Art)
                                             Phone: (914) 452-7000
Poughkeepsie, NY 12601   Janet Clarke-Hazlett, Art Libn.
Staff: Prof 1. **Subjects:** Western European art and architecture, ancient through contemporary; American art. **Holdings:** 34,800 books and bound periodical volumes. **Subscriptions:** 180 journals and other serials. **Services:** Interlibrary loans; library open to public with restrictions. **Automated Operations:** Computerized cataloging. **Networks/Consortia:** Member of Southeastern New York Library Resources Council (SENYLRC).

★16585★
VASSAR COLLEGE - GEORGE SHERMAN DICKINSON MUSIC LIBRARY (Mus)
                                             Phone: (914) 452-7000
Poughkeepsie, NY 12601   Sabrina L. Weiss, Music Libn.
Founded: 1908. **Staff:** Prof 2; Other 3. **Subjects:** Music. **Special Collections:** Chittenden Pianoforte Library; historical editions and collected works. **Holdings:** 16,529 books and bound periodical volumes; 30,000 music scores; 25,000 LP recordings. **Services:** Interlibrary loans; library open to public with restrictions. **Computerized Information Services:** OCLC. **Staff:** Susan Grimm, Music Cat.

VAUGHAN (John) LIBRARY/LEARNING RESOURCES CENTER
See: Northeastern Oklahoma State University - John Vaughan Library/ LRC

VEDDER MEMORIAL LIBRARY
See: Greene County Historical Society

VEEDER (Borden S.) LIBRARY
See: St. Louis Children's Hospital - Borden S. Veeder Library

★16586★
VEGETARIAN INFORMATION SERVICE, INC. - INFORMATION CENTER (Agri)
Box 5888   Phone: (301) 530-1737
Bethesda MD 20814   Dr. Alex Hershaft, Libn.
Founded: 1976. **Staff:** 4. **Subjects:** Vegetarianism, diet and health, treatment of farm animals, animal rights. **Holdings:** 100 volumes; clipping files. **Subscriptions:** 20 journals and other serials. **Services:** Center open to serious scholars of vegetarianism and animal rights.

★16587★
VELSICOL CHEMICAL CORPORATION - RESEARCH AND DEVELOPMENT DEPARTMENT - LIBRARY (Sci-Tech)
341 E. Ohio St., 3rd Fl.   Phone: (312) 670-4771
Chicago, IL 60611   June M. Snyder, Libn.
Founded: 1940. **Staff:** 1. **Subjects:** Insecticides, plastics, paint, herbicides, analytical and organic chemistry. **Holdings:** 4000 books; 2000 bound periodical volumes; 500 other volumes. **Subscriptions:** 200 journals and other serials. **Services:** Library not open to public.

★16588★
VENABLE BAETJER & HOWARD - LIBRARY (Law)
2 Hopkins Plaza   Phone: (301) 752-6780
Baltimore, MD 21201   John S. Nixdorff, Libn.
Staff: Prof 1; Other 1. **Subjects:** Law - tax, labor, corporate, securities, environmental, trusts and estates, real estate. **Holdings:** 24,000 books; 900 bound periodical volumes. **Subscriptions:** 80 journals and other serials; 5 newspapers. **Services:** Interlibrary loans; copying; SDI; library open to public with restrictions. **Computerized Information Services:** LEXIS, DIALOG. **Remarks:** Maintains a branch library in Washington, DC.

★16589★
VENANGO COUNTY LAW LIBRARY (Law)
Court House
Corner 12th & Liberty Sts.   Phone: (814) 437-6871
Franklin, PA 16323   Julia I. McNamara, Law Libn.
Founded: 1922. **Staff:** Prof 4. **Subjects:** Pennsylvania and United States laws and court reports. **Holdings:** 20,000 volumes. **Services:** Library open to public for reference use only, circulation for lawyers only.

★16590★
VENTURA COUNTY HISTORICAL SOCIETY - LIBRARY & ARCHIVES (Hist)
100 E. Main St.   Phone: (805) 653-0323
Ventura, CA 93001   Patricia Sales, Res.Libn.
Founded: 1913. **Staff:** Prof 1. **Subjects:** Local history. **Holdings:** 2000 volumes; 10,000 photographs. **Subscriptions:** 45 journals and other serials. **Services:** Copying; photograph reproduction; library open to public. **Publications:** Newsletter, monthly; Ventura County Historical Society Quarterly.

★16591★
VENTURA COUNTY LAW LIBRARY (Law)
800 S. Victoria Ave.   Phone: (805) 654-2695
Ventura, CA 93009   Naydean L. Baker, Law Libn.
Founded: 1891. **Staff:** Prof 1; Other 5. **Subjects:** Law. **Holdings:** 45,396 books and bound periodical volumes; 105 reels of microfilm of U.S. Statutes; 1075 cassettes; 4555 microfiche. **Subscriptions:** 366 journals and other serials. **Services:** Library open to public for reference use only.

★16592★
VENTURA COUNTY RESOURCE MANAGEMENT AGENCY - TECHNICAL LIBRARY (Env-Cons)
800 S. Victoria Ave.   Phone: (805) 654-2480
Ventura, CA 93009   Evelyn Adams, Tech.Libn.
Staff: 1. **Subjects:** Environment, planning, air and water pollution, sanitation, public health, building and safety, transportation. **Holdings:** 7500 reports and documents. **Subscriptions:** 80 journals and other serials. **Services:** Library open to public for reference use only.

★16593★
VENTURA COUNTY STAR-FREE PRESS - LIBRARY (Publ)
Box 6711   Phone: (805) 656-4111
Ventura, CA 93006   Sara J. Riley, Libn.
Staff: Prof 1. **Subjects:** Newspaper reference topics. **Holdings:** 100 books; newspapers on microfilm, 1897 to present; county government documents; photograph files; clippings. **Subscriptions:** 13 journals and other serials. **Services:** Copying; library open to professionals and journalists. **Special Catalogs:** Divided card file: subject and byline, crime/law suits, accidents; index to county news items. **Remarks:** Library located at 5250 Ralston, Ventura, CA 93003.

★16594★
VERBEX CORPORATION - LIBRARY (Sci-Tech)
Two Oak Park   Phone: (617) 275-5160
Bedford, MA 01730   Frances Schutzberg, Tech.Libn.
Staff: Prof 1. **Subjects:** Speech recognition. **Holdings:** 1000 books; 750 technical reports; 1500 technical reports on microfiche; 2000 reprints. **Subscriptions:** 100 journals and other serials; 8 newspapers. **Services:** Interlibrary loans; copying; library open to public by appointment.

Computerized Information Services: DIALOG. **Remarks:** Verbex Corporation is a division of Exxon Enterprises.

VERMONT EDUCATIONAL RESOURCE CENTER (VERC)
See: Vermont State Department of Education

VERMONT ENVIRONMENTAL CENTER
See: Vermont Institute of Natural Sciences

★16595★
VERMONT HISTORICAL SOCIETY - LIBRARY (Hist)
Pavilion Bldg., 109 State St.   Phone: (802) 828-2291
Montpelier, VT 05602   Mrs. Reidun D. Nuquist, Libn.
Staff: Prof 2; Other 1. **Subjects:** Vermont history and Vermontiana, New England general and local history, genealogy. **Special Collections:** Vermont imprints; Harold G. Rugg Collection of Vermontiana. **Holdings:** 40,000 books and bound periodical volumes; 1000 maps; 30,000 photographs; 200 reels of microfilm; manuscripts; pamphlets; broadsides; phonograph records. **Subscriptions:** 220 journals and other serials. **Services:** Interlibrary loans (limited); copying; library open to public. **Publications:** Vermont History, quarterly; Vermont History News, 6/year - distributed to members. **Staff:** Karl B. Bloom, Asst.Libn.

★16596★
VERMONT INSTITUTE OF NATURAL SCIENCES - LIBRARY (Env-Cons)
Church Hill Rd.   Phone: (802) 457-2779
Woodstock, VT 05091   Sarah B. Laughlin, Dir.
Staff: Prof 14. **Subjects:** Environmental research, natural history. **Special Collections:** Natural history slides (40,000); Billings-Kittredge Herbarium Collection. **Holdings:** 2500 books; 90 bound periodical volumes; 2000 pamphlets in vertical file. **Subscriptions:** 55 journals and other serials. **Services:** Library open to public for reference use only; members may borrow. **Publications:** Vermont Natural History, annual; newsletter, bimonthly; Bird Records, quarterly. **Remarks:** Includes the holdings of Vermont Environmental Center. **Staff:** Jane Westover, Libn.; Nancy Withington, Rsrcs.Ctr.Coord.

★16597★
VERMONT LAW SCHOOL - LIBRARY (Law)
Chelsea St.   Phone: (802) 763-8303
South Royalton, VT 05068   W. Leslie Peat, Law Libn.
Founded: 1973. **Staff:** Prof 4; Other 4. **Subjects:** Law. **Holdings:** 56,200 books; 9600 bound periodical volumes; 34,100 volumes in microform. **Subscriptions:** 1120 journals and other serials; 10 newspapers. **Services:** Interlibrary loans; copying; library open to public for reference use only. **Computerized Information Services:** Westlaw, OCLC. **Networks/Consortia:** Member of New England Law Library Consortium (NELLC). **Staff:** Catherine Freese, Asst.Libn./Pub.Serv.; Victoria Weber, Asst.Libn./Acq.; Ann McHugo, Assoc.Libn./Tech.Serv.

★16598★
VERMONT STATE AGENCY OF ADMINISTRATION - PUBLIC RECORDS DIVISION (Hist)
State Administrative Bldg.   Phone: (802) 828-3288
Montpelier, VT 05602   A. John Yacavoni, Asst.Dir.
Staff: Prof 1; Other 16. **Subjects:** Vermont town and city land records prior to 1850, Vermont town vital records prior to 1850, Vermont probate record volumes prior to 1850. **Special Collections:** Field forms and draft material of Historical Records Survey inventories of Vermont town records and church records; Vermont Vital Record File, 1760-1954 (939 cubic feet). **Holdings:** 780 boxes of archival holdings; 19,700 reels of microfilm; 22,650 boxes of semiactive records center material. **Services:** Copying; records are open to public. **Publications:** Information Bulletin, monthly - to Vermont town and city clerks and treasurers.

★16599★
VERMONT STATE DEPARTMENT OF EDUCATION - VERMONT EDUCATIONAL RESOURCE CENTER (VERC) (Educ)
120 State St.   Phone: (802) 828-3124
Montpelier, VT 05602   David D. Joslyn, Libn.
Subjects: Education. **Special Collections:** ERIC microfiche (complete set); Vermont Educational Resource Base (VERB; 450 educational materials on microfiche). **Holdings:** Figures not available for books, pamphlets and newsletters. **Subscriptions:** 30 journals and other serials. **Services:** Interlibrary loans; copying; SDI; center open to public. **Computerized Information Services:** BRS. **Publications:** Computer Bits, 9/year - to Vermont schools. **Special Catalogs:** RAP (Resource Agent Program) catalog of free workshops. **Special Indexes:** VERB Index (with abstracts to collection holdings).

★16600★
VERMONT STATE DEPARTMENT OF LIBRARIES (Info Sci)
State Office Bldg. Post Office   Phone: (802) 828-3261
Montpelier, VT 05602   Patricia E. Klinck, State Libn.
Founded: 1970. **Staff:** Prof 16; Other 42. **Subjects:** Law, Vermontiana, general. **Holdings:** 547,000 books; films; filmstrips; microfilms; records; tapes; state and federal documents. **Services:** Interlibrary loans; copying; library open to public. **Computerized Information Services:** DIALOG, SDC, BRS, ERIC, OCLC. **Networks/Consortia:** Member of NELINET; Vermont Resource Sharing Network. **Publications:** Biennial Report; Department of Libraries News; Checklist of Available Vermont State Publications. **Special Catalogs:** Union Catalog of total holdings of libraries throughout the state, including colleges and universities (author-title card catalog). **Remarks:** The Department of Libraries, consisting of three divisions and five regional libraries, was formed by the merger of Vermont State Library and the Vermont Free Public Library Service. There are regional libraries in Dummerston, Berlin, Rutland, Georgia and St. Johnsbury. Department is located at 111 State St., Montpelier, VT 05602.

★16601★
VERMONT STATE HOSPITAL - AGENCY OF HUMAN SERVICES LIBRARY (Med)
103 S. Main St.
Waterbury, VT 05676   Susan Maywood, Chf.Libn.
Staff: Prof 1. **Subjects:** Psychiatry, public health, psychology, medicine, alcohol and drug abuse, corrections. **Holdings:** 10,000 books; 2000 bound periodical volumes; 30 cassettes; 60 cases of pamphlets; 45 boxes of government documents; **Subscriptions:** 200 journals and other serials. **Services:** Interlibrary loans; library open to hospital affiliates - depending on nature of material needed. **Networks/Consortia:** Member of Hospital Library Development Services (HLDS). **Publications:** Union lists of books and journals.

★16602★
VERMONT STATE OFFICE OF THE SECRETARY OF STATE - VERMONT STATE PAPERS (Hist)
Redstone Bldg.
27 Terrace St.   Phone: (802) 828-2363
Montpelier, VT 05602   D. Gregory Sanford, State Archv.
Founded: 1777. **Staff:** Prof 2. **Subjects:** Governors' official papers, surveyors' general papers, municipal corporations charter records, legislative committee records, original acts and resolves, Vermont state papers, 1744-1920, election records. **Special Collections:** Vermont/New Hampshire Boundary Case (30 feet); Vermont Bicentennial Commission (30 feet); Order of Women Legislators (2 feet); various state officers' papers (20 feet). **Holdings:** 500 books; 250 volumes of bound manuscripts; 60 volumes of maps, surveys and charters; 500 cartons of manuscript material; 60 boxes of original acts and resolutions; 57 boxes of legislative committee records. **Services:** Copying; material is available for research; will answer correspondence pertaining to archival material; open to public. **Publications:** State Papers of Vermont. **Special Catalogs:** Inventories for manuscript collections. **Staff:** Julie P. Cox, Asst. State Archv.

★16603★
VERMONT TECHNICAL COLLEGE - HARTNESS LIBRARY (Sci-Tech)
          Phone: (802) 728-3391
Randolph Center, VT 05061   Dewey F. Patterson, Lib.Dir.
Staff: Prof 1; Other 5. **Subjects:** Dairy management; agribusiness; engineering - civil, electrical, electronics, electromechanical and mechanical; surveying; architecture and building. **Holdings:** 47,000 books. **Subscriptions:** 425 journals and other serials; 8 newspapers. **Services:** Copying; library open to public with restrictions.

★16604★
VERNER, LIIPFERT, BERNHARD & MC PHERSON - LIBRARY (Law)†
1660 L St., N.W., Suite 1000   Phone: (202) 452-7495
Washington, DC 20036   May Haruye Yoneyama, Law Libn.
Staff: Prof 3; Other 2. **Subjects:** Law - international, administrative, commercial; legislation. **Special Collections:** Aviation collection; surface transportation collection. **Holdings:** 10,000 books; 129 audio cassettes; 455 microforms; work/product collection. **Subscriptions:** 254 journals and other serials; 30 newspapers. **Services:** Interlibrary loans; copying; library open to public by appointment. **Computerized Information Services:** LEXIS, Mead Data Central (MDC), Disclosure Inc., Accountants, Index, New York Times Information Service. **Networks/Consortia:** Member of Metropolitan Washington Library Council. **Publications:** VLBM Weekly; Inside VLBM, biweekly - both for internal distribution only. **Staff:** Anne Wargo, Asst.Libn.; Mike McDonald, Asst.Libn.

★16605★
VERSATEC - TECHNICAL INFORMATION CENTER (Sci-Tech; Comp Sci)
2805 Bowers Ave.   Phone: (408) 988-2801
Santa Clara, CA 95051   Sharon Tyler, Tech.Info.Spec.
Founded: 1982. **Staff:** Prof 1. **Subjects:** Electronics, computer science, paper. **Holdings:** 400 books. **Subscriptions:** 37 journals and other serials. **Services:** Interlibrary loans; center not open to public. **Automated Operations:** Computerized cataloging and serials. **Computerized Information Services:** DIALOG. **Networks/Consortia:** Member of Xerox PARC Libraries Network. **Remarks:** Versatec is a division of Xerox Corporation.

★16606★
VESTERHEIM GENEALOGICAL CENTER/NORWEGIAN-AMERICAN MUSEUM - LIBRARY (Area-Ethnic)
4909 Sherwood Rd.   Phone: (608) 271-8826
Madison, WI 53711   Gerhard B. Naeseth, Libn.
Founded: 1975. **Staff:** Prof 1. **Subjects:** Norwegian-American genealogy and history. **Holdings:** 525 books; 60 notebooks. **Services:** Copying; library open to public by appointment. **Publications:** Norwegian Tracks, quarterly - to members.

★16607★
VESTIGIA - LIBRARY (Soc Sci)
56 Brookwood Rd.   Phone: (201) 347-3638
Stanhope, NJ 07874   Robert E. Jones, Pres.
Staff: 2. **Subjects:** Unexplained phenomena. **Holdings:** 250 books and bound periodical volumes. **Subscriptions:** 53 journals and other serials; 6 newspapers. **Services:** Library open to public with restrictions. **Publications:** Vestigia Newsletter, annual. **Staff:** Dorothy Larkin, Libn./Exec.Sec.; Susan Balsley, Libn.

★16608★
VETCO OFFSHORE, INC. - TECHNICAL LIBRARY (Energy; Sci-Tech)
250 W. Stanley Ave.
Box 1688   Phone: (805) 653-2500
Ventura, CA 93001   Larry Markworth, Tech.Libn.
Founded: 1982. **Staff:** Prof 1. **Subjects:** Engineering - offshore, mechanical, and petroleum; metallurgy; welding; nondestructive examination. **Special Collections:** National Standards Association vendor catalogs (6000 on microfiche). **Holdings:** 500 books; 3 VF drawers of industrial and governmental engineering standards; 2 VF drawers of U.S. mechanical and design patents; 3 VF drawers of engineering periodical reprints (arranged by subject); 56 VF drawers of internal engineering reports and project files. **Subscriptions:** 60 journals and other serials. **Services:** Interlibrary loans; copying; library open to public by appointment and with restrictions. **Automated Operations:** Computerized cataloging and serials. **Computerized Information Services:** DIALOG, BRS, SDC. Performs searches on cost recovery basis. **Networks/Consortia:** Member of CLASS. **Special Catalogs:** Government and Industry Codes, Regulations, Standards and Specifications Held in the Technical Library (computer printout). **Also Known As:** Its Engineering Library.

VETERANS AFFAIRS CANADA
See: Canada - Veterans Affairs Canada

★16609★
VETERANS HOME OF CALIFORNIA - LINCOLN MEMORIAL LIBRARY (Mil)
          Phone: (707) 944-4279
Yountville, CA 94599
Founded: 1886. **Staff:** Prof 3; Other 16. **Subjects:** Spanish American War, World Wars I and II. **Special Collections:** Spanish American War Museum. **Holdings:** 37,265 books; 353 bound periodical volumes. **Subscriptions:** 160 journals and other serials; 55 newspapers. **Services:** Interlibrary loans; copying; library open to public for reference use only; members, employees and family may borrow. **Publications:** Observation Post, monthly - by Post Fund Services. **Staff:** Phyllis Bush, Asst.Libn.; Suzel Ho, Asst.Libn.

VICK MEMORIAL LIBRARY
See: Baptist Bible College

★16610★
VICKSBURG HOSPITAL, INC. - MEDICAL LIBRARY (Med)*
3311 I-20 Frontage Rd.   Phone: (601) 636-2611
Vicksburg, MS 39180   Dinnie K. Johnston, Med.Libn.
Founded: 1975. **Staff:** Prof 1. **Subjects:** Medicine, surgery, nursing, patient education. **Holdings:** 534 books; 1610 bound periodical volumes; 60 VF folders; 45 cassettes; 9 slide sets; 20 microforms; 2 video cassettes. **Subscriptions:** 70 journals and other serials. **Services:** Interlibrary loans; copying; library open to public upon approval by hospital administrator.

Networks/Consortia: Member of Central Mississippi Council of Medical Libraries.

VICKSBURG NATL. MILITARY PARK
See: U.S. Natl. Park Service

★16611★
VICKSBURG & WARREN COUNTY HISTORICAL SOCIETY - MC CARDLE LIBRARY (Hist)
Old Court House Museum   Phone: (601) 636-0741
Vicksburg, MS 39180   Blanche Terry, Res.Dir.
Founded: 1948. Staff: Prof 2. Subjects: Confederacy, local history, genealogy. Holdings: 2000 volumes. Services: Copying; library open to public with restrictions.

VICTOR (Michael, II) ART LIBRARY
See: Springfield Art Association - Michael Victor II Art Library

★16612★
VICTORIA COLLEGE/UNIVERSITY OF HOUSTON, VICTORIA - LIBRARY - SPECIAL COLLECTIONS (Hist)
2602 N. Ben Jordan   Phone: (512) 576-3157
Victoria, TX 77901   Dr. S. Joe McCord, Lib.Dir.
Special Collections: Local history (6000 volumes; 10,000 slides; photographs); Regional Historical Resource Depository (175 feet of archival materials; 175 reels of microfilm); 95 cubic feet of other archival materials. Services: Interlibrary loans; copying; collections open to public. Automated Operations: Computerized cataloging and circulation. Computerized Information Services: DIALOG, MEDLARS; DataPhase Automated Library Information System (internal database). Networks/Consortia: Member of AMIGOS Bibliographic Council, Inc.

★16613★
VICTORIA CONSERVATORY OF MUSIC - LIBRARY (Mus)
839 Academy Close   Phone: (604) 386-5311
Victoria, BC, Canada V8V 2X8   Larry de la Haye, Libn.
Founded: 1969. Staff: 2. Subjects: Music - instrumental, vocal. Special Collections: Collection of 78 r.p.m. recordings; 19th-century music (325 pieces). Holdings: 2000 books; 25,000 bound periodical volumes. Subscriptions: 51 journals and other serials. Services: Interlibrary loans; copying; library open to public with restrictions. Staff: Ann Calder, Asst.Libn.

★16614★
VICTORIA GENERAL HOSPITAL - HEALTH SCIENCES LIBRARY (Med)
                                           Phone: (902) 428-3497
Halifax, NS, Canada B3H 2Y9   Joyce A. Kublin, Libn.
Founded: 1972. Staff: Prof 1; Other 2. Subjects: Medicine, surgery, psychiatry, nursing, hospital administration. Holdings: 2000 books; 37 slide-tape programs. Subscriptions: 200 journals and other serials. Services: Interlibrary loans; copying; SDI; library open for reference use only to health sciences students of Dalhousie University. Computerized Information Services: DIALOG, MEDLARS. Networks/Consortia: Member of Nova Scotia On-Line Consortium. Publications: Acquisitions list, bimonthly - distributed to hospital staff and interested libraries.

★16615★
VICTORIA GENERAL HOSPITAL (North) - HEALTH SCIENCES LIBRARY (Med)*
35 Helmecken Rd.   Phone: (604) 727-4212
Victoria, BC, Canada V8Z 6R5   George E.A. Zizka, Libn.
Founded: 1945. Staff: Prof 1. Subjects: Medicine, nursing and allied health sciences. Holdings: 5500 books; AV items. Subscriptions: 125 journals and other serials. Services: Interlibrary loans; copying; SDI; library open to public by application and approval. Staff: Doreen Isherwood, Lib.Asst.

★16616★
VICTORIA GENERAL HOSPITAL (South) - GERIATRIC MEDICINE AND GERONTOLOGY (Med)†
841 Fairfield Rd.   Phone: (604) 388-9121
Victoria, BC, Canada V8V 2VD   George E.A. Zizka, Health Sci.Libn.
Founded: 1982. Staff: Prof 1; Other 1. Subjects: Geriatric medicine, social gerontology, aging, long-term care. Holdings: 550 books; 50 bound periodical volumes; government reports. Subscriptions: 20 journals and other serials. Services: Interlibrary loans; copying; library open to public.

★16617★
VICTORIA MEDICAL SOCIETY/ROYAL JUBILEE HOSPITAL - LIBRARY (Med)
1900 Fort St.   Phone: (604) 595-9723
Victoria, BC, Canada V8R 1J8   Johann van Reenen, Libn.
Founded: 1922. Staff: Prof 1; Other 1. Subjects: Clinical medicine and psychiatry, history of medicine, medical biographies, geriatrics. Holdings: 3000 books; 5000 bound periodical volumes; 150 cassette tapes. Subscriptions: 450 journals and other serials. Services: Interlibrary loans; library open to public with restrictions. Computerized Information Services: MEDLARS. Publications: Library Newsletter, quarterly.

★16618★
VICTORIA TIMES-COLONIST - LIBRARY (Publ)
P.O. Box 300   Phone: (604) 382-7211
Victoria, BC, Canada V8W 2N4   Corinne Wong, Libn.
Founded: 1955. Staff: Prof 1; Other 4. Subjects: Newspaper reference topics. Holdings: 5000 volumes; newspaper clipping and photograph collection; newspapers on microfilm; newspaper indexes. Services: Library for staff use only. Remarks: Times-Colonist is owned by Canadian Newspapers Ltd.

★16619★
VICTORIA UNION HOSPITAL - MEDICAL LIBRARY (Med)
1200 24th St., W.   Phone: (306) 764-1551
Prince Albert, SK, Canada S6V 5T4   Joan I. Ryan, Med.Rec.Libn.
Staff: 1. Subjects: Medicine, surgery and gynecology. Holdings: 225 books; 350 bound periodical volumes. Subscriptions: 13 journals and other serials. Services: Library open to hospital personnel only.

VICTORIA UNIVERSITY
See: University of Toronto

VICTORIA UNIVERSITY - UNITED CHURCH OF CANADA
See: United Church of Canada - Central Archives

VICTORIAN PERIODICAL LIBRARY
See: American Life Foundation and Study Institute - Americana Research Library

★16620★
VICTORY MEMORIAL HOSPITAL - MEDICAL LIBRARY (Med)
1324 N. Sheridan Rd.   Phone: (312) 688-3000
Waukegan, IL 60085   Helen Hewitt, Med.Lib.Tech.
Founded: 1969. Staff: Prof 1. Subjects: Medicine, nursing, hospitals. Holdings: 514 books and bound periodical volumes; 150 pamphlets. Subscriptions: 45 journals and other serials. Services: Interlibrary loans; library not open to public. Networks/Consortia: Member of Lake County Consortium.

★16621★
VIDEO FREE AMERICA - LIBRARY (Art)
442 Shotwell St.   Phone: (415) 648-9040
San Francisco, CA 94110   Joanne Kelly, Co-Dir.
Founded: 1970. Staff: 1. Subjects: Video, dance, individual artists. Holdings: 500 volumes. Subscriptions: 100 journals and other serials. Services: Library open to public by appointment.

VIDEO INN LIBRARY
See: Satellite Video Exchange Society

★16622★
VIDEO TAPE NETWORK, INC. - LIBRARY (Aud-Vis)
33 E. 68th St.   Phone: (212) 570-1200
New York, NY 10021   John A. Friede, Pres.
Founded: 1968. Subjects: Videotape programs - documentaries, music entertainment, comedy entertainment, minority issues, feminist issues, sports. Holdings: 300 videotape programs.

★16623★
VIGO COUNTY HISTORICAL SOCIETY - HISTORICAL MUSEUM OF THE WABASH VALLEY - LIBRARY (Hist)
1411 S. 6th St.   Phone: (812) 235-9717
Terre Haute, IN 47802   Judy Calvert, Libn.
Founded: 1958. Staff: Prof 1; Other 3. Subjects: Local history. Holdings: Figures not available. Services: Library open to public by permission. Publications: Leaves of Thyme, quarterly.

★16624★
VIGO COUNTY PUBLIC LIBRARY - SPECIAL COLLECTIONS (Hist)
One Library Square   Phone: (812) 232-1113
Terre Haute, IN 47807   Clarence Brink, Coord., Ref.Serv.
Staff: Prof 3; Other 3. **Subjects:** State and local history, genealogy. **Special Collections:** Baertich Collection (6 VF drawers); family files (18 VF drawers); community affairs (94 VF drawers); local club and association records (26 boxes); Dr. Charles N. Combs Memorabilia (1 box); Eugene V. Debs Collection (2 boxes); Jane Dabney Shackelford Collection (1 box); Joseph Jenckes Collection (1 box); Theodore Dreiser/Paul Dresser Collection (1 box); J.A. Wickersham Scrapbook (1 box); League of Women Voters of Terre Haute Collection; Rotary Club of Terre Haute Collection. **Holdings:** 7300 books; 1285 bound periodical volumes; 287 maps and charts. **Subscriptions:** 54 journals and other serials. **Services:** Copying; library open to public for reference use only. **Automated Operations:** Computerized cataloging. **Computerized Information Services:** OCLC. **Networks/Consortia:** Member of INCOLSA. **Publications:** Surname Index, irregular. **Special Catalogs:** Main Special Collections (card); Community Archives (card). **Staff:** Lois Harris, Spec.Coll.Libn.; Nancy Sherrill, Geneal.Libn.

★16625★
VIGO COUNTY SCHOOL CORPORATION - INSTRUCTIONAL MATERIALS CENTER (Educ)
3000 College Ave.   Phone: (812) 238-4354
Terre Haute, IN 47803   Georgia R. Cole, Coord.
Founded: 1966. **Staff:** Prof 2; Other 8. **Subjects:** Materials for curriculum, professional education. **Holdings:** 19,540 books; 16,703 transparency masters; 382 framed art prints; 939 slides; 2521 16mm films; 372 8mm films; 882 filmstrips; 3030 sound filmstrips; 632 tapes; 12,617 transparencies; 195 disc recordings; 217 videotapes; 40 realia; 207 charts; 3 maps; 63 pieces of sculpture; 57 program instructions; 44 videodiscs. **Subscriptions:** 17 journals and other serials. **Services:** Copying; center open to public with restrictions. **Automated Operations:** Computerized cataloging. **Computerized Information Services:** OCLC. **Networks/Consortia:** Member of INCOLSA. **Publications:** Catalog of the Instructional Materials Center, biennial with annual supplement; occasional bibliographies. **Special Catalogs:** Book catalog of holdings. **Staff:** Lorraine E. Brett, Cat.

VILLA ANNESLIE ARCHIVES
See: Polish Nobility Association

VILLANOVA UNIVERSITY ARCHIVES
See: Villanova University - Library Science Library

VILLANOVA UNIVERSITY - AUGUSTINIAN HISTORICAL INSTITUTE
See: Augustinian Historical Institute

★16626★
VILLANOVA UNIVERSITY - LIBRARY SCIENCE LIBRARY (Info Sci)
Graduate Dept. of Library Science   Phone: (215) 645-4672
Villanova, PA 19085   Carolyn C. Walsh, Libn.
Staff: Prof 3; Other 1. **Subjects:** Library and information sciences, children's and young adult's literature, archives, computer science. **Special Collections:** Philadelphia Authors and Illustrators (200 items). **Holdings:** 14,000 books. **Subscriptions:** 220 journals and other serials. **Services:** Interlibrary loans; copying; library open to public for reference use only. **Publications:** Pennsylvania Authors at a Glance; Philadelphia Children's Authors and Illustrators at a Glance. **Special Catalogs:** Annotated Bibliography of Periodical Holdings (book). **Staff:** Barbara A. Daebeler, Asst.Libn.; Carol A. Kare, Cat.

★16627★
VILLANOVA UNIVERSITY - PULLING LAW LIBRARY (Law)
Garey Hall   Phone: (215) 645-7020
Villanova, PA 19085   Alan Holoch, Dir./Asst.Prof.
Founded: 1953. **Staff:** Prof 7; Other 8. **Subjects:** Law. **Special Collections:** Church and State; corrections. **Holdings:** 258,000 volumes and microform equivalents. **Subscriptions:** 2700 journals and other serials. **Services:** Interlibrary loans; copying; library open to public for reference use only. **Computerized Information Services:** LEXIS, Westlaw, DIALOG, NEXIS. Performs searches for law school students and faculty. **Networks/Consortia:** Member of Mid-Atlantic Law Library Cooperative (MALLCO). **Staff:** Maura Buri, Per.Libn.; Nada Cail, Cat.; Elizabeth Devlin, Asst.Dir./Rd.Serv.; Janet Dreher, Acq./Doc.Libn.; Rosette Littman, Cat.; Marcia K. Sapowith, Ref.Libn.; Regina A. Smith, Asst.Libn., Rd.Serv.; Walter Champion, Asst.Ref.Libn.

★16628★
VILLE MARIE SOCIAL SERVICE CENTRE - LIBRARY (Soc Sci)
4018 St. Catherine, W.   Phone: (514) 989-1885
Montreal, PQ, Canada H3Z 1P2   Janet Sand-Steinhouse, Libn.
Founded: 1976. **Staff:** Prof 1. **Subjects:** Social services, family, youth, aged. **Holdings:** Government publications. **Subscriptions:** 65 journals and other serials. **Services:** Interlibrary loans; copying; SDI; library open to public by appointment. **Networks/Consortia:** Member of McGill Medical and Health Libraries Association (MMHLA). **Also Known As:** Centre de services sociaux Ville Marie.

VILLE DE MONTREAL - SERVICE DE L'URBANISME
See: Montreal City Planning Department

★16629★
VINCENNES UNIVERSITY - BYRON R. LEWIS HISTORICAL LIBRARY (Hist)
                                            Phone: (812) 885-4330
Vincennes, IN 47591   Robert R. Stevens, Dir.
Founded: 1967. **Staff:** Prof 1; Other 2. **Subjects:** Political, social, economic and general history of Lower Wabash; university archives; oral history of Depression Era; genealogy. **Holdings:** 6000 books and bound periodical volumes; manuscripts; photographs; maps; broadsides; newspapers; pamphlets. **Subscriptions:** 12 journals and other serials. **Services:** Limited area and genealogical research; library open to public.

VINCENT (D.J.) MEDICAL LIBRARY
See: Riverside Methodist Hospital - D.J. Vincent Medical Library

VINCENT (G. Robert) VOICE LIBRARY
See: Michigan State University - G. Robert Vincent Voice Library

VINCENT (John) ARCHIVE
See: University of California, Los Angeles - Music Library

★16630★
VINELAND HISTORICAL AND ANTIQUARIAN SOCIETY - LIBRARY (Hist)
108 S. 7th St.
Box 35   Phone: (609) 691-1111
Vineland, NJ 08360   Joseph E. Sherry, Libn.
Founded: 1864. **Staff:** Prof 1. **Subjects:** Genealogy and local history. **Special Collections:** Sheppard Genealogical Papers; Autograph Collection. **Holdings:** 5000 books; bound local newspapers, 1861-1935; 1 VF drawer of pamphlets; 8 boxes of documents; census material on microfilm. **Services:** Copying; library open to public for reference use only on a limited schedule. **Publications:** The Vineland Historical Magazine, annual - free to members, for sale to others.

★16631★
THE VINEYARD - REAL ESTATE, SHOPPING CENTER & URBAN DEVELOPMENT INFORMATION CENTER (Bus-Fin)
50 W. Shaw Ave.   Phone: (209) 222-0182
Fresno, CA 93704   Richard Erganian, Info.Dir.
Staff: Prof 2; Other 1. **Subjects:** Real estate, shopping centers, urban and regional planning, architecture, mortage financing, market research, landscaping. **Special Collections:** Shopping center, hotel and mixed use development. **Holdings:** 4500 books; 210 bound periodical volumes; 2000 other cataloged items; 30 real estate transcripts; 20 shopping center development transcripts; 10 appraisal tapes and cassettes; 5 income property reports and transcripts. **Subscriptions:** 250 journals and other serials; 25 newspapers. **Services:** Library open to real estate developers. **Special Catalogs:** Real Estate Information Sources. **Formerly:** O.K. Supermarket - Real Estate & Shopping Center Development Information Center. **Staff:** Aram Long, Staff Libn.

★16632★
VINNELL CORPORATION - CORPORATE/PROGRAM DEVELOPMENT LIBRARY (Mil)*
10530 Rosehaven St., Suite 600   Phone: (703) 385-4544
Fairfax, VA 22030   Sylvia A. Keys, Libn.
Founded: 1932. **Staff:** 1. **Subjects:** Military art and science, military education, vocational/technical education, job corps, specialized marketing information on Saudi Arabia and Southeast Asia. **Special Collections:** Photographs of corporate projects and personnel, 1932 to present (3000). **Holdings:** 250 books; 3000 proposals, reports, contracts; 20,000 military documents; 5000 other government documents; 1500 curriculum resources; 200 slides, cassettes, microfiche. **Subscriptions:** 75 journals and other serials; 5 newspapers. **Services:** Copying; SDI; library open to other library staffs. **Automated Operations:** Computerized cataloging. **Publications:** In-house user's manual. **Staff:** Alvin Rosendorf, Asst.Libn.

★16633★
VINSON & ELKINS - LAW LIBRARY (Law)
First City Tower
Houston, TX 77002
Phone: (713) 651-2678
Karl T. Gruben, Libn.
Founded: 1917. **Staff:** Prof 3; Other 7. **Subjects:** Law - Texas, environmental, foreign and international, oil and gas. **Holdings:** 75,000 books; 1500 bound periodical volumes; microforms; audio cassettes; U.S. and Texas documents. **Subscriptions:** 300 journals and other serials. **Services:** Interlibrary loans; copying; library open to researchers with approval of librarian. **Computerized Information Services:** DIALOG, SDC, LEXIS, Westlaw. **Staff:** David Blythe, Asst.Libn.; Loretta Pitts, Cat.

★16634★
VIRGIN ISLANDS - DEPARTMENT OF CONSERVATION & CULTURAL AFFAIRS - BUREAU OF LIBRARIES AND MUSEUMS (Hist)
Box 390
St. Thomas, VI 00850
Phone: (809) 774-3407
Dr. Henry C. Chang, Dir.
Founded: 1920. **Staff:** Prof 17; Other 61. **Subjects:** General and reference topics. **Special Collections:** Von Scholton Collection (Caribbean, West Indian and Virgin Island materials; 14,000 volumes; periodicals and newspapers; dissertations and manuscripts; maps and documents); Virgin Islands archives, 1655-1933 on microfilm; microfilm of newspapers 1770 to present. **Holdings:** 119,000 books; U.N., U.S. and Virgin Islands government documents depository; manuscripts; clippings; archival materials; ephemera. **Subscriptions:** 354 journals and other serials. **Services:** Interlibrary loans; copying; microfilming; library open to public. **Networks/Consortia:** Member of Virgin Islands Library & Information Network (VILINET). **Publications:** Annual Reports, Virgin Islands Government Documents, quarterly; Information newsletter, bimonthly; Caribbeana, union acquisitions list, irregular; occasional papers. **Special Catalogs:** Union List of Periodicals and Newspapers (book); Union Title File (card). **Special Indexes:** Local Newspaper index (card). **Remarks:** An additional telephone number is (809) 774-0630. **Staff:** June A.V. Lindqvist, Cur., Von Scholton Coll.; Martin Gerbens, Hd., Caribbean Coll.

★16635★
VIRGINIA BAPTIST HISTORICAL SOCIETY - LIBRARY (Hist; Rel-Theol)
University of Richmond
Box 34
Richmond, VA 23173
Phone: (804) 285-6324
Fred Anderson, Exec.Dir.
Staff: Prof 2; Other 2. **Subjects:** History - Virginia Baptist, Baptist, Virginia State, Confederate, Colonial Virginia. **Special Collections:** Church manuscripts (2400). **Holdings:** 12,000 books; 650 bound periodical volumes; 95 VF drawers of manuscripts, documents, papers, diaries, journals. **Subscriptions:** 12 journals and other serials. **Services:** Copying; library open to public by appointment. **Publications:** Virginia Baptist Register, annual - by subscription and membership; The Chronicle, quarterly - by membership. **Special Indexes:** Index to Virginia Baptist Register; index to The Religious Herald, 1828-1874 (card).

★16636★
VIRGINIA BAPTIST HOSPITAL - BARKSDALE MEDICAL LIBRARY (Med)
3300 Rivermont Ave.
Lynchburg, VA 24503
Phone: (804) 522-4608
Anne M. Nurmi, Libn.
Staff: Prof 1. **Subjects:** Obstetrics and gynecology, pediatrics, internal medicine. **Holdings:** 2032 books; 2213 bound periodical volumes; 115 filmstrips and cassette tapes. **Subscriptions:** 82 journals and other serials. **Services:** Interlibrary loans; copying; library open to public for reference use only. **Computerized Information Services:** MEDLINE. **Networks/Consortia:** Member of Southeastern/Atlantic Regional Medical Library Services; Lynchburg Area Library Cooperative.

★16637★
VIRGINIA BEACH PUBLIC LIBRARY SYSTEM - MUNICIPAL REFERENCE LIBRARY (Soc Sci)
Municipal Ctr.
Virginia Beach, VA 23456
Phone: (804) 427-4644
Kathleen G. Hevey, Municipal Ref.Coord.
Founded: 1972. **Staff:** Prof 1; Other 2. **Subjects:** Virginia Beach, collective bargaining for public employees, public administration. **Special Collections:** Governmental and community affairs scrapbooks; Library Department's Professional Collection. **Holdings:** 2064 books and documents; 126 bound periodical volumes; 563 vertical files; 2048 microfiche. **Subscriptions:** 106 journals and other serials; 10 newspapers. **Services:** Interlibrary loans; copying; SDI; library open to public with restrictions. **Automated Operations:** Computerized cataloging, acquisitions and circulation. **Computerized Information Services:** DIALOG, Local Government Information Network (LOGIN). **Publications:** Book Shelf - for internal distribution only. **Special Indexes:** Scrapbooks Index; newspaper clippings index (card).

★16638★
VIRGINIA BEACH PUBLIC LIBRARY SYSTEM - ROBERT S. WAHAB, JR. PUBLIC LAW LIBRARY (Law)
Municipal Ctr.
Virginia Beach, VA 23456-9002
Phone: (804) 427-4419
Robert P. Miller, Jr., Law Lib.Coord.
Staff: Prof 2. **Subjects:** Law. **Special Collections:** Prisoners' Collection (25 volumes). **Holdings:** 7391 books; 200 bound periodical volumes; 5 scrapbooks of legal materials; 4 VF drawers of pamphlets. **Subscriptions:** 25 journals and other serials. **Services:** Interlibrary loans; copying; library open to public for reference use only. **Special Indexes:** Subject indexes of vertical file information and law reviews. **Staff:** Terry R. Mathieson, Law Lib.Assoc.

★16639★
VIRGINIA CENTER FOR PSYCHIATRY - MEDICAL LIBRARY (Med)
301 Fort Lane
Portsmouth, VA 23704
Phone: (804) 393-0061
Renee E. Mansheim, Med.Libn.
Staff: Prof 1. **Subjects:** Psychiatry, psychology, clinical social work, adjunct therapies, nursing, alcoholism. **Holdings:** 1000 books; 450 bound periodical volumes; 215 audio cassettes; 15 video cassettes; 86 AV materials. **Subscriptions:** 90 journals and other serials. **Services:** Interlibrary loans; copying; library open to public with administrative approval. **Formerly:** Portsmouth Psychiatric Center.

★16640★
VIRGINIA CHEMICALS, INC. - LIBRARY (Sci-Tech)
3340 W. Norfolk Rd.
Portsmouth, VA 23703
Phone: (703) 483-7213
Barbara Smith, Libn.
Staff: Prof 2. **Subjects:** Chemistry, chemical engineering, textiles, pulp and paper. **Holdings:** 2000 books; 3000 bound periodical volumes. **Subscriptions:** 82 journals and other serials. **Services:** Library not open to public. **Computerized Information Services:** DIALOG.

★16641★
VIRGINIA COMMONWEALTH UNIVERSITY - JAMES BRANCH CABELL LIBRARY - SPECIAL COLLECTIONS (Hum)
901 Park Ave.
Richmond, VA 23284
Phone: (804) 257-1108
Daniel A. Yanchisin, Spec.Coll.Libn.
Founded: 1966. **Staff:** Prof 2; Other 2. **Subjects:** Contemporary Virginia authors and American poetry; 20th-century American cartoons and caricatures; book art. **Special Collections:** James Branch Cabell Collection of books, notes and manuscripts (3000 volumes); Poetry Society of Virginia Memorial Collection (325 volumes); Richmond Authors (200 volumes); Giacomini Collection (Samuel Johnson and James Boswell; 500 volumes); Adele Clark Suffrage Collection (100 feet); New Virginia Review Library (600 books and current periodicals); Richmond YWCA Records (30 feet); Virginia Nurses Association Archives (80 feet). **Holdings:** 6600 books; 1200 feet of manuscripts; 1100 theses; university archives. **Services:** Copying; collections open to public. **Automated Operations:** Computerized cataloging and serials. **Computerized Information Services:** BRS, OCLC. **Networks/Consortia:** Member of SOLINET.

★16642★
VIRGINIA COMMONWEALTH UNIVERSITY - MEDICAL COLLEGE OF VIRGINIA - TOMPKINS-MC CAW LIBRARY (Med)
MCV Sta., Box 667
Richmond, VA 23298
Phone: (804) 786-0823
William J. Judd, Dir., Univ.Lib.Serv.
Founded: 1913. **Staff:** Prof 8; Other 26. **Subjects:** Medicine, dentistry, pharmacy, nursing, basic sciences, allied health sciences. **Holdings:** 202,600 bound volumes; 2700 microforms; institutional archives. **Subscriptions:** 3577 journals and other serials; 5 newspapers. **Services:** Interlibrary loans; SDI; library open to public. **Automated Operations:** Computerized cataloging, serials and circulation. **Computerized Information Services:** DIALOG, MEDLINE, BRS, NLM, OCLC. Performs searches on cost recovery basis. Contact Person: Hilary Stoddard. **Networks/Consortia:** Member of SOLINET. **Publications:** Monthly Statistical Report; Library Handbook. **Staff:** Prudence Clark, Coll.Dev.Libn.; Judy Robinson, ILL; Hilary Stoddard, Online Serv.; Jodi Koste, Archv.; Faye Williams, Lrng.Rsrcs.Ctrs.; Virginia Crowe, Pub.Serv.

★16643★
VIRGINIA ELECTRIC AND POWER COMPANY - LIBRARY AND INFORMATION SERVICES (Sci-Tech; Energy)
One James River Plaza
Box 26666
Richmond, VA 23233
Phone: (804) 771-3657
Jeanne E. Varteressian, Supv.
Founded: 1937. **Staff:** Prof 4; Other 3. **Subjects:** Electric power, nuclear power, environment, fuel resources, engineering, management. **Holdings:** 19,000 books; 960 bound periodical volumes; 200 shelves of government and industry reports; 40 shelves of pamphlets and clippings; 18 shelves of standards; 7000 microforms, including industry standards. **Subscriptions:**

1000 journals and other serials; 185 newspapers. **Services:** Interlibrary loans; copying; library open to public by appointment. **Automated Operations:** Computerized cataloging, acquisitions and circulation. **Computerized Information Services:** DIALOG, SDC, Dun & Bradstreet Corporation. Contact Person: Linda G. Royal, 771-1981. **Staff:** Ann B, Flanagan, Info.Spec.; Linda G. Royal, Assoc.Info.Spec.; Mary Ann Dvorak, Asst.Info.Spec.; Sheila D. Hedgecock, Asst.Info.Spec.

★16644★
VIRGINIA HISTORIC LANDMARKS COMMISSION - ARCHIVES (Hist)
221 Governor St.   Phone: (804) 786-3143
Richmond, VA 23219
Subjects: Architecture and history of buildings, structures, and sites in Virginia, 1600s to present. **Holdings:** 35,000 files; 142,000 photographs. **Services:** Copying; archives open to public.

★16645★
VIRGINIA HISTORICAL SOCIETY - LIBRARY (Hist)
428 North Blvd.
Box 7311   Phone: (804) 358-4901
Richmond, VA 23221   Paul C. Nagel, Dir.
Founded: 1831. **Staff:** Prof 7; Other 3. **Subjects:** Virginiana and 16th-19th century Americana. **Special Collections:** Confederate imprints; 17th- and 18th-century English architecture. **Holdings:** 250,000 books and bound periodical volumes; 4 million manuscripts; prints and engravings; maps and printed ephemera; sheet music; newspapers; paintings. **Subscriptions:** 225 journals and other serials. **Services:** Copying; library open to public. **Publications:** Virginia Magazine of History and Biography, quarterly; Occasional Bulletin, semiannual. **Staff:** Howson W. Cole, Libn.; Virginius C. Hall, Jr., Assoc.Dir.,Lib.Serv.; Robert F. Strohm, Asst.Dir., Adm.

★16646★
VIRGINIA INSTITUTE OF MARINE SCIENCE LIBRARY (Sci-Tech)
                                            Phone: (804) 642-2111
Gloucester Point, VA 23062   Susan O. Barrick, Lib.Dir.
Founded: 1953. **Staff:** Prof 2; Other 2. **Subjects:** Marine biology and ecology, oceanography, aquaculture. **Special Collections:** Sport fishing collection; rare books. **Holdings:** 12,050 books; 19,550 bound periodical volumes; 500 volumes of VIMS Archives. **Subscriptions:** 1500 journals and other serials. **Services:** Interlibrary loans; copying; library open to public. **Automated Operations:** Computerized cataloging and serials. **Computerized Information Services:** DIALOG, OCLC. **Networks/Consortia:** Member of SOLINET. **Publications:** VIMS Publications List, annual; VIMS Contributions, annual; Chesapeake Bay Bibliography (book and online); Library Acquisitions List, bimonthly. **Remarks:** The library also serves the Graduate School of Marine Science of the College of William and Mary. **Staff:** Janice Meadows, Cat./ILL.

★16647★
VIRGINIA-MARYLAND REGIONAL COLLEGE OF VETERINARY MEDICINE - LIBRARY (Med)
Virginia Polytechnic Inst. & State Univ.
CVM, Phase II   Phone: (703) 961-7666
Blacksburg, VA 24061   Naomi V. Tuttle, Veterinary Med.Lib.Asst.
Founded: 1980. **Staff:** Prof 1; Other 2. **Subjects:** Veterinary medicine - clinical, preclinical. **Holdings:** 1370 books; 500 bound periodical volumes; 300 slide sets and video cassettes. **Subscriptions:** 194 journals and other serials. **Services:** Interlibrary loans; SDI; library open to public. **Automated Operations:** Computerized cataloging, acquisitions, serials and circulation. **Computerized Information Services:** DIALOG, MEDLARS. **Remarks:** Veterinary Medicine Library is a member of the Virginia Polytechnic Institute & State University library system.

★16648★
VIRGINIA MILITARY INSTITUTE - PRESTON LIBRARY (Sci-Tech)
                                            Phone: (703) 463-6228
Lexington, VA 24450   James E. Gaines, Hd.Libn.
Founded: 1839. **Staff:** Prof 4; Other 13. **Subjects:** Engineering, liberal arts. **Special Collections:** Civil War period; Virginia Military Institute archives. **Holdings:** 268,927 volumes; 86,721 government documents. **Subscriptions:** 805 journals and other serials; 31 newspapers. **Services:** Interlibrary loans; copying; library open to public. **Computerized Information Services:** DIALOG, OCLC. **Networks/Consortia:** Member of SOLINET. **Publications:** Friends of Preston Library Newsletter; annual report. **Special Indexes:** Library Guide. **Staff:** Wylma P. Davis, Ref.Libn.; John M. Robson, Asst.Ref.Libn.; David A. Badertscher, Tech.Serv.Libn.

★16649★
VIRGINIA MUSEUM OF FINE ARTS - LIBRARY (Art)
Boulevard & Grove Ave.
Box 7260   Phone: (804) 257-0827
Richmond, VA 23221   Betty A. Stacy, Libn.
Founded: 1936. **Staff:** Prof 4. **Subjects:** Art history, decorative arts, painting, sculpture, theater. **Special Collections:** John Barton Payne Collection; John Koenig (theater) Collection; Ellen Bayard Weedon (Oriental) Collection; Gordon Strause Collection; Ike Bana Society Collection; John G. Hayes Decorative Arts Collection. **Holdings:** 46,000 books; 1200 bound periodical volumes; VF drawers of clippings; 728 boxes of museum publications; 660 boxes of auction catalogs. **Subscriptions:** 200 journals and other serials. **Services:** Copying; library open to public for reference use only. **Staff:** Margaret Burcham, Lib.Asst.

VIRGINIA NATIONAL BANK
See: Sovran Bank, N.A.

VIRGINIA NURSES ASSOCIATION ARCHIVES
See: Virginia Commonwealth University - James Branch Cabell Library - Special Collections

★16650★
VIRGINIA POLYTECHNIC INSTITUTE AND STATE UNIVERSITY - ARCHITECTURE LIBRARY (Art)
Cowgill Hall   Phone: (703) 961-6182
Blacksburg, VA 24061   Robert E. Stephenson, Arch.Libn.
Staff: Prof 1; Other 4. **Subjects:** Architecture, art, urban affairs and planning, building construction, landscape architecture. **Holdings:** 48,075 books and bound periodical volumes; 2464 microforms; 1823 files of planning materials; 17,000 architecture slides. **Subscriptions:** 475 journals and other serials. **Services:** Interlibrary loans; copying; library open to public. **Automated Operations:** Computerized circulation. **Computerized Information Services:** DIALOG, OCLC. **Networks/Consortia:** Member of SOLINET. **Publications:** New Acquisitions List, monthly - available upon request. **Special Catalogs:** Planning vertical file catalog (card).

★16651★
VIRGINIA POLYTECHNIC INSTITUTE AND STATE UNIVERSITY - CAROL M. NEWMAN LIBRARY (Sci-Tech; Agri)
                                            Phone: (703) 961-5593
Blacksburg, VA 24061   Thomas A. Souter, Act.Dir.
Founded: 1872. **Staff:** Prof 56; Other 108. **Subjects:** Agricultural sciences, architecture, biological and physical sciences, engineering, humanities, social sciences. **Special Collections:** Archive of Norfolk & Western Railway; Archive of Southern Railway Predecessors; Sherwood Anderson book collection; History of Technology; Southwest Virginiana; Western Americana. **Holdings:** 1.6 million books and bound periodical volumes; 115,000 maps; 3.6 million microforms; 6000 phonograph records; 125 audiotapes; 58 videotapes. **Subscriptions:** 23,000 journals and other serials; 78 newspapers. **Services:** Interlibrary loans; copying; library open to public. **Automated Operations:** Computerized cataloging, acquisitions, serials and circulation. **Computerized Information Services:** DIALOG, OCLC, MEDLARS, CAS Online, Virginia Tech Library System (VTLS). Performs searches on cost recovery basis. Contact Person: Glenn Lowry, 961-6617. **Networks/Consortia:** Member of SOLINET. **Publications:** Detailed Documentation of Virginia Tech Library System (VTLS). **Staff:** Marilyn Norstedt, Hd., Hum.Dept.; Germaine C. Linkins, Bibliog.Serv.Libn.; Paul D. Metz, User Serv.Dept.; Shirley R. Glazener, Hd., Acq.Dept.; Donald J. Kenney, Hd., Gen.Ref.Dept.; Harry M. Kriz, Hd., Sci./Tech.Dept.; Mary R. Hinkle, Hd., Soc.Sci.Dept.; Glenn Lowry, Sys.Libn.

★16652★
VIRGINIA POLYTECHNIC INSTITUTE AND STATE UNIVERSITY - CENTER FOR THE STUDY OF SCIENCE IN SOCIETY - LIBRARY (Sci-Tech)
Price House   Phone: (703) 961-7687
Blacksburg, VA 24061   Ann LaBerge, Asst.Dir.
Staff: 2. **Subjects:** Science and technology studies; history - science, technology. **Special Collections:** Richard Schallenberg Collection (history of science and technology). **Holdings:** 1100 books; unbound periodicals, reports, and manuscripts. **Subscriptions:** 17 journals and other serials. **Services:** Library open to public.

★16653★
VIRGINIA POLYTECHNIC INSTITUTE AND STATE UNIVERSITY - GEOLOGY LIBRARY (Sci-Tech)
3040 Derring Hall   Phone: (703) 961-6101
Blacksburg, VA 24061   John D. Crissinger, Geology & Map Libn.
Staff: Prof 1; Other 1. **Subjects:** Geology of Virginia. **Holdings:** 33,000 books and bound periodical volumes; 350 reels of microfilm; 10,000

microfiche; 10,000 maps; 38,000 aerial photographs. **Subscriptions:** 500 journals and other serials. **Services:** Interlibrary loans; copying; library open to public. **Automated Operations:** Computerized circulation. **Computerized Information Services:** DIALOG, OCLC. Performs searches on cost recovery basis. **Networks/Consortia:** Member of SOLINET. **Publications:** New Acquisitions List, bimonthly - free upon request. **Staff:** Ethel Shrader, Asst.Libn.

VIRGINIA POLYTECHNIC INSTITUTE AND STATE UNIVERSITY - VETERINARY MEDICINE LIBRARY
See: Virginia-Maryland Regional College of Veterinary Medicine - Veterinary Medicine Library

★16654★
VIRGINIA STATE DEPARTMENT OF CONSERVATION & ECONOMIC DEVELOPMENT - NATIONAL CARTOGRAPHIC INFORMATION CENTER (Sci-Tech)
Virginia State Division of Mineral Resources Library
Box 3667
Charlottesville, VA 22903   Avon L. Hudson, Libn.
Staff: 1. **Subjects:** Geology, mineral resources, remote sensing. **Holdings:** 4050 books; 3248 bound periodical volumes; 470 theses; 5750 maps; 21,500 pamphlets; microforms. **Subscriptions:** 54 journals and other serials. **Services:** Center open to public for reference use only.

★16655★
VIRGINIA STATE DEPARTMENT OF CORRECTIONS - ACADEMY FOR STAFF DEVELOPMENT - LIBRARY (Soc Sci)
500 N. Winchester Ave.
Box 2215   Phone: (703) 943-3141
Waynesboro, VA 22980   Elizabeth A. Robson, Libn.
Staff: Prof 1; Other 1. **Subjects:** Criminal justice, management, psychology, juvenile delinquency, family therapy, training and development. **Holdings:** 4300 books; 69 bound periodical volumes; 295 16mm films; 148 filmstrips; 155 videotapes; 8 VF drawers; 2 VF drawers of clippings. **Subscriptions:** 67 journals and other serials. **Services:** Interlibrary loans; copying; library open to public by appointment.

★16656★
VIRGINIA STATE DEPARTMENT OF CRIMINAL JUSTICE SERVICES - LIBRARY (Law)
805 E. Broad St.   Phone: (804) 786-8478
Richmond, VA 23219   Stephen E. Squire, Libn.
Founded: 1982. **Staff:** Prof 1. **Subjects:** Criminal and juvenile justice - planning and evaluation; crime prevention programs; domestic violence. **Holdings:** 5300 volumes; 6 VF drawers; 45 microfiche. **Subscriptions:** 197 journals and other serials. **Services:** Interlibrary loans; copying; library open to public by appointment. **Networks/Consortia:** Member of Criminal Justice Information Exchange. **Publications:** Current Newsletters and Periodicals List, irregular - distributed upon request; List of Acquisitions, weekly - for internal distribution only.

★16657★
VIRGINIA STATE DEPT. OF EDUCATION - DIVISION OF MANAGEMENT INFORMATION SERVICES - DATA UTILIZATION & REPORTING (Educ)
Box 6Q   Phone: (804) 225-2101
Richmond, VA 23216   Dr. Jan L. Harris, Supv.
Founded: 1960. **Staff:** Prof 2; Other 1. **Subjects:** Educational research and statistics. **Holdings:** Statistical reports and documents. **Services:** Copying; library open to public. **Publications:** Facing Up, annual; Membership Report, annual; School Census, triennial.

★16658★
VIRGINIA STATE DEPARTMENT OF GENERAL SERVICES - DIVISION OF CONSOLIDATED LABORATORY SERVICES LIBRARY (Sci-Tech)
1 N. 14th St., Rm. 274   Phone: (804) 786-1155
Richmond, VA 23219   Susan Childress
Founded: 1963. **Subjects:** Chemistry. **Holdings:** 2794 books; 524 bound periodical volumes. **Services:** library not open to public.

★16659★
VIRGINIA STATE DEPARTMENT OF TRANSPORTATION SAFETY - FILM LIBRARY (Trans; Aud-Vis)*
300 Turner Rd.   Phone: (804) 276-9600
Richmond, VA 23225   Nancy T. Arrowood, Film Libn.
Founded: 1968. **Staff:** Prof 2. **Subjects:** Transportation and highway safety. **Special Collections:** Films on all phases of highway safety. **Holdings:** 900 books; 1000 films. **Subscriptions:** 20 journals and other serials. **Services:** Interlibrary loans; library open to public within the state of Virginia. **Special**

Catalogs: Film Catalog. **Staff:** Betty Stargardt, Film Libn.

★16660★
VIRGINIA STATE DIVISION OF LEGISLATIVE SERVICES - REFERENCE LIBRARY (Soc Sci)
State Capitol, Box 3-AG   Phone: (804) 786-1861
Richmond, VA 23208
Founded: 1972. **Staff:** Prof 2. **Subjects:** Energy, taxation, juvenile delinquency, crime, children, economics. **Special Collections:** Historical state reports, Acts of Assembly and journals. **Holdings:** Figures not available. **Services:** Copying; library open to public. **Computerized Information Services:** Legislative Information System (internal database).

★16661★
VIRGINIA STATE LAW LIBRARY (Law)
Supreme Court Bldg., 2nd Fl.
100 N. Ninth St.   Phone: (804) 786-2075
Richmond, VA 23219   Gail Warren, State Law Libn.
Staff: 3. **Subjects:** Law. **Holdings:** 71,500 books; 8500 bound periodical volumes. **Subscriptions:** 329 journals and other serials. **Services:** Copying; library open to public with restrictions. **Remarks:** Maintained by Virginia Supreme Court.

★16662★
VIRGINIA STATE LIBRARY (Hist; Soc Sci)
12th & Capitol St.   Phone: (804) 786-8929
Richmond, VA 23219   Donald Haynes, State Libn.
Founded: 1823. **Staff:** Prof 54; Other 83. **Subjects:** Virginiana, English history, American literature, Southern and Confederate history, genealogy, social sciences, U.S. history, English literature. **Special Collections:** Virginia newspapers; Virginia public records; Virginia maps; Confederate imprints. **Holdings:** 600,000 volumes; 85,592 maps; 29.1 million manuscripts; 169,072 reels of microfilm. **Subscriptions:** 1430 journals and other serials; 110 newspapers. **Services:** Interlibrary loans; copying; library open to public. **Automated Operations:** Computerized cataloging and circulation. **Computerized Information Services:** OCLC. **Networks/Consortia:** Member of SOLINET. **Publications:** Virginia Cavalcade, quarterly - by subscription; Virginia State Library Publications - by subscription and exchange. **Special Catalogs:** CAVALIR, statewide union list (microfiche). **Staff:** Dr. Louis H. Manarin, State Archv.; Jane M. Pairo, Asst. State Archv.; Connis O. Brown, Asst. State Archv.; William J. Hubbard, Dir., Lib.Serv.; William R. Chamberlain, Asst.Dir., Gen.Lib.; Nolan T. Yelich, Dir., Adm.Serv.; Dr. Jon K. Kukla, Asst.Dir., Pubn.

★16663★
VIRGINIA STATE LIBRARY FOR THE VISUALLY AND PHYSICALLY HANDICAPPED (Aud-Vis)
1901 Roane St.   Phone: (804) 786-8016
Richmond, VA 23222   Constance J.M. Tracy, Reg.Libn.
Founded: 1959. **Staff:** Prof 2; Other 15. **Subjects:** General. **Holdings:** 1800 large-type books; 60,000 talking books; 55,000 cassettes. **Subscriptions:** 46 journals and other serials. **Services:** Interlibrary loans; copying; volunteer tape recording program; library open to blind and physically handicapped; open to the rest of the public for reference use only. **Automated Operations:** Talking Book Machine inventory. **Networks/Consortia:** Member of National Library Service for the Blind & Physically Handicapped (NLS). **Publications:** Newsletter, quarterly. **Special Catalogs:** Catalog of large print holdings (book). **Staff:** Paulette Thomas, Libn.

★16664★
VIRGINIA STATE OFFICE OF EMERGENCY & ENERGY SERVICES - ENERGY INFORMATION AND SERVICES CENTER (Energy)
310 Turner Rd.   Phone: (804) 745-3245
Richmond, VA 23225   Kathy Erickson, Supv.
Founded: 1975. **Staff:** Prof 2; Other 1. **Subjects:** Energy. **Holdings:** 9000 books; 2000 subject files. **Subscriptions:** 122 journals and other serials. **Services:** Center open to public with restrictions. **Staff:** Barbara Dawson, Res.Spec.; Jennifer Snead, Res.Spec.

★16665★
VIRGINIA STATE TRUCK AND ORNAMENTALS RESEARCH STATION - LIBRARY (Agri)
1444 Diamond Springs Rd.   Phone: (804) 464-3528
Virginia Beach, VA 23455   Amy DesRoches, Libn.
Founded: 1920. **Staff:** 1. **Subjects:** Horticulture, soils, entomology, pesticides, farming. **Holdings:** 5450 books and bound periodical volumes. **Subscriptions:** 62 journals and other serials. **Services:** Library open to public for reference use only.

★16666★
VIRGINIA STATE UNIVERSITY - JOHNSTON MEMORIAL LIBRARY - SPECIAL COLLECTIONS (Educ)
Box JJ   Phone: (804) 520-6171
Petersburg, VA 23803   Catherine V. Bland, Dir., Lib.Serv.
Founded: 1882. **Special Collections:** U.S. government depository; black studies; instructional materials; manuscripts. **Holdings:** Figures not available. **Services:** Interlibrary loans; copying; library open to public with restrictions. **Automated Operations:** Computerized cataloging. **Computerized Information Services:** OCLC. **Networks/Consortia:** Member of SOLINET.

★16667★
VIRGINIA STATE WATER CONTROL BOARD - LIBRARY (Env-Cons)
2111 N. Hamilton St.
Box 11143   Phone: (804) 257-6340
Richmond, VA 23230   Patricia G. Vanderland, Libn.
Founded: 1974. **Staff:** Prof 1. **Subjects:** Water, water pollution, waste water, groundwater, toxins in water, environment. **Special Collections:** Virginia State Water Control Board publications (185); Environmental Protection Agency publications (2500). **Holdings:** 5000 books; 150 bound periodical volumes; 6000 pamphlets and reprints; 1800 unbound reports; 6300 microforms; government publications on water and environment. **Subscriptions:** 101 journals and other serials. **Services:** Interlibrary loans; copying; library open to public for reference use only. **Publications:** Acquisitions List, quarterly.

★16668★
VIRGINIA THEOLOGICAL SEMINARY - BISHOP PAYNE LIBRARY (Rel-Theol)
Seminary Rd. & Quaker Ln.   Phone: (703) 370-6602
Alexandria, VA 22304   J.H. Goodwin, Libn.
Founded: 1823. **Staff:** Prof 2; Other 3. **Subjects:** Theology. **Holdings:** 100,000 volumes. **Subscriptions:** 420 journals and other serials. **Services:** Interlibrary loans; copying; library open to public for reference use only. **Computerized Information Services:** OCLC. **Networks/Consortia:** Member of Washington Theological Consortium; CAPCON. **Staff:** Josephine Dearborn, Asst.Libn.

★16669★
VIRGINIA UNION UNIVERSITY - WILLIAM J. CLARK LIBRARY - SPECIAL COLLECTIONS (Soc Sci)
1500 N. Lombardy St.   Phone: (804) 257-5820
Richmond, VA 23220   Verdelle V. Bradley, Libn.
Founded: 1865. **Special Collections:** Black Experience (9905 volumes). **Services:** Interlibrary loans; copying; collections open to public with special permit for reference use only. **Computerized Information Services:** OCLC. **Networks/Consortia:** Member of CCLC.

★16670★
VIRGINIAN-PILOT & LEDGER-STAR - LIBRARY (Publ)
150 W. Brambleton Ave.   Phone: (804) 446-2242
Norfolk, VA 23510   Ann Kinken Johnson, Hd.Libn.
Founded: 1947. **Staff:** Prof 1; Other 4. **Subjects:** Newspaper reference topics. **Services:** Library not open to public except for brief reference questions by phone. **Special Indexes:** Index to Virginian-Pilot and Ledger-Star, 1947 to present. **Remarks:** Kirn Memorial Library (Norfolk Public Library) has copies of the newspapers on microfilm and is equipped to make copies.

★16671★
VISION INFORMATION PROGRAM, INC. (Med)*
Box 1208   Phone: (812) 332-4207
Bloomington, IN 47401   Dr. Gordon G. Heath, Pres.
Founded: 1960. **Subjects:** Vision characteristics of optometric patients. **Holdings:** 80,000 vision certificates; 120,000 microfilm copies of certificates. **Remarks:** Organization is concerned with the sale (and subsequent handling) of registered vision certificates to practicing optometrists for issuance to their patients; certificates are microfilmed for permanent record, and the recorded data are punched on IBM cards for statistical studies of vision characteristics.

★16672★
VISITING NURSE ASSOCIATION OF CHICAGO - LIBRARY (Med)
310 S. Michigan Ave.   Phone: (312) 663-1810
Chicago, IL 60604   Sarah Redinger, Libn.
Staff: Prof 1; Other 1. **Subscriptions:** Nursing, medicine. **Special Collections:** Patient Education literature (500 titles). **Holdings:** 2000 books; unbound periodicals. **Subscriptions:** 100 journals and other serials. **Services:** Interlibrary loans; copying; library open to public by appointment only. **Automated Operations:** Computerized cataloging and ILL. **Computerized Information Services:** OCLC. **Networks/Consortia:** Member of Greater

Midwest Regional Medical Library Network (Region 3); Chicago Library System.

★16673★
VISITING NURSE SERVICE, INC. - LIBRARY (Med)
328 E. Lakeside St.   Phone: (608) 257-6710
Madison, WI 53715   Ruth M. Hanson, Exec.Dir.
Subjects: Nursing, public health, physical and speech therapy, occupational therapy, home health aids, mobile meals, social work. **Holdings:** Figures not available. **Services:** Library open to employees and students only.

★16674★
VISUAL COMMUNICATIONS - ASIAN PACIFIC AMERICAN PHOTOGRAPHIC ARCHIVES (Area-Ethnic)
244 S. San Pedro St., Rm. 309   Phone: (213) 608-4462
Los Angeles, CA 90012   Nancy Araki, Exec.Dir.
Staff: 8. **Subjects:** Asian American studies. **Holdings:** 300,000 historical and contemporary photographs and slides. **Services:** Copying; library open to public by appointment - for reference use only. **Automated Operations:** Computerized photo indexing.

★16675★
VITERBO COLLEGE - ZOELLER FINE ARTS LIBRARY (Art; Mus)
815 S. Ninth   Phone: (608) 784-0040
La Crosse, WI 54601
Founded: 1970. **Staff:** 5. **Subjects:** Music, art, theater. **Holdings:** 4625 books; 1050 bound periodical volumes; 9500 musical scores; 2988 recordings; 250 tapes; 1100 plays. **Subscriptions:** 48 journals and other serials. **Services:** Library open to public with restrictions. **Networks/Consortia:** Member of Wisconsin Interlibrary Services (WILS).

★16676★
VITRO CORPORATION - LIBRARY (Sci-Tech)
14000 Georgia Ave.   Phone: (301) 231-2553
Silver Spring, MD 20910   James R. Griffin, Dept.Hd.
Founded: 1948. **Staff:** Prof 7; Other 22. **Subjects:** Missiles and spacecraft, systems engineering, management, data processing, electronic engineering, ships, underwater acoustics, antisubmarine warfare. **Holdings:** 9246 books; 1135 bound periodical volumes; 44,156 technical manuals and reports; 19,790 technical correspondence; 1,262,000 engineering drawings (1mm microfilm); Standards and Specifications (650,000 hard copy and on microfilm); 270 nautical charts. **Subscriptions:** 874 journals and other serials; 15 newspapers. **Services:** Interlibrary loans; copying; library open to public by appointment. **Automated Operations:** Computerized cataloging and circulation. **Computerized Information Services:** DIALOG, SDC, DTIC, Government-Industry Data Exchange Program (GIDEP). **Networks/Consortia:** Member of Interlibrary Users Association (IUA); Metropolitan Washington Library Council. **Publications:** List of new drawings and technical correspondence, daily - for internal distribution only; list of new technical reports, weekly - for internal distribution only; list of new books, monthly - for internal distribution only. **Special Indexes:** Indexes to drawings of ballistic missiles, guided missiles, missile engineering; technical correspondence index; books, technical reports and manuals index on COM (internal distribution only). **Formerly:** Automation Industries, Inc. - Vitro Laboratories Division - Administrative Support Department Library. **Staff:** Mary Ann Foohey, Group Supv.; Jay D. Tebo, Asst. Group Supv.; Eileen F. Cole, Ref.Libn.; Kathryn J. Cuskelly, Ref./ILL Libn.; Mary C. Wardlow, Ext.Libn.; Louis M. Morris, Ref./ Circ.Sect.Ldr.; Cheryl C. Slobodian, Cat.

VIVIAN (R.G.) ARCHIVE
See: U.S. Natl. Park Service - Chaco Center - Library

★16677★
VIVITAR CORPORATION - TECHNICAL LIBRARY
1630 Stewart St.
Santa Monica, CA 90406
Founded: 1975. **Subjects:** Photography, optics, engineering, mathematics, manufacturing, design. **Holdings:** 700 books; 200 bound periodical volumes. **Computerized Information Services:** Online systems. **Remarks:** Presently inactive.

★16678★
VIZCAYA GUIDES LIBRARY (Art)
3251 S. Miami Ave.   Phone: (305) 579-2808
Miami, FL 33129   Joy Mason, Lib.Chm.
Staff: 5. **Subjects:** Decorative arts, architecture, furniture, 15th-19th century history. **Special Collections:** James Deering - house, furnishings, gardens (folios; manuscripts; photographs; records; ledgers). **Holdings:** 2000 books; 85 bound periodical volumes; 15,000 slides. **Services:** Library open to

staff and guides.

VODGES (A.W.) LIBRARY OF GEOLOGY AND PALEONTOLOGY
See: San Diego Society of Natural History - Natural History Museum Library

VOGEL (Dr. Philip J.) LIBRARY
See: White Memorial Medical Center - Courville-Abbott Memorial Library

VOLCK (William H.) MUSEUM
See: Pajaro Valley Historical Association - William H. Volck Museum

VOLTA BUREAU LIBRARY
See: Alexander Graham Bell Association for the Deaf

★16679★
VOLTAIRE SOCIETY - LIBRARY (Hum)*
1837 N. Azalea St., Basswood
Okeechobee, FL 33472   R.L. Marchfield, Pres.
Staff: Prof 1; Other 1. **Subjects:** Atheism, health, religion and anti-religion, philosophy, animal kingdom. **Special Collections:** Voltaire's plays and works; books about Voltaire (30 volumes); Life Nature Library. **Holdings:** 550 books; 1000 bound periodical volumes. **Services:** Library open to local residents only. **Publications:** How to Stay Alive & Healthy with Diabetes, and How to Avoid Getting It.

★16680★
VOLTARC TUBES INC. - LIBRARY (Bus-Fin)
74 Linwood Ave.   Phone: (202) 255-2633
Fairfield, CT 06430   Evlyn Perkins, Libn.
Staff: Prof 1; Other 1. **Subjects:** Lamp manufacturing. **Holdings:** 500 books; 5 VF drawers of patents; 5 VF drawers of clippings. **Subscriptions:** 60 journals and other serials. **Services:** Copying; library open to public by appointment.

★16681★
VOLUNTARY ACTION CENTER OF THE ST. PAUL AREA - LIBRARY (Soc Sci)
518 Bremer Bldg.
419 N. Robert St.   Phone: (612) 227-3938
St. Paul, MN 55101   Maggi Davern, Exec.Dir.
Founded: 1975. **Subjects:** Management of volunteer programs. **Holdings:** 500 books and bound periodical volumes. **Subscriptions:** 18 journals and other serials. **Services:** Copying; library open to public.

★16682★
VOLUNTEER - THE NATIONAL CENTER FOR CITIZEN INVOLVEMENT - LIBRARY (Soc Sci)
1111 N. 19th St., Suite 500   Phone: (703) 276-0542
Arlington, VA 22209   Sharee Morris, Mgr., Info.Serv.
Founded: 1974. **Staff:** 1. **Subjects:** Volunteerism, leadership, administration, fundraising. **Holdings:** 10,000 published and unpublished documents in the field of volunteerism and citizen participation. **Subscriptions:** 50 journals and other serials. **Services:** Free library research service for associates; fee for nonassociates; training tours for use of the library. **Publications:** Volunteer Readership. **Formerly:** Located in Boulder, CO.

★16683★
VOLUSIA COUNTY LAW LIBRARY (Law)*
Courthouse Annex, Rm. 207
125 S. Orange Ave.   Phone: (904) 258-7000
Daytona Beach, FL 32014   Rae Mastropierro, Law Libn.
Staff: Prof 1. **Subjects:** Law. **Holdings:** 25,000 books and periodicals. **Services:** Copying; library open to public. **Remarks:** This library maintains branch libraries in DeLand and New Smyrna Beach.

★16684★
VOLUSIA COUNTY SCHOOL BOARD - RESOURCE LIBRARY (Educ)
729 Loomis Ave.
Box 1910   Phone: (904) 255-6475
Daytona Beach, FL 32015   Loretta O. Wright, Rsrc. Media Spec.
Founded: 1967. **Staff:** Prof 1; Other 1. **Subjects:** Education - in all subjects for K-12. **Special Collections:** Suitcase Museums (60). **Holdings:** 10,000 books; 96 bound periodical volumes; 12,000 audiovisual items and microfiche; 52 VF drawers; 4000 pamphlets. **Subscriptions:** 133 journals and other serials. **Services:** Interlibrary loans; library not open to public. **Special Catalogs:** Printed materials and nonprint media catalogs, supplement 2/year.

VON KLEINSMID LIBRARY
See: University of Southern California

VON RANKE (Leopold) LIBRARY
See: Syracuse University - George Arents Research Library for Special Collections

VOUGHT CORPORATION
See: LTV Aerospace and Defense Company

★16685★
VSE CORPORATION - TECHNICAL LIBRARY (Sci-Tech)
2550 Huntington Ave.   Phone: (703) 960-4600
Alexandria, VA 22303   Merriel T. Whitehead, Libn.
Founded: 1965. **Staff:** Prof 1. **Subjects:** Engineering, physics, mathematics, environment. **Holdings:** 3500 books; 2000 vendor catalogs; Visual Search Microfilm file on military and federal specifications, standards, handbooks and design engineering. **Subscriptions:** 75 journals and other serials. **Services:** Interlibrary loans; library not open to public. **Publications:** New Acquisitions, monthly - for internal distribution only. **Special Indexes:** Consolidated Master Cross Reference List; Cataloging Handbook H4-1 and H4-2 (all on microfiche).

★16686★
VSE CORPORATION - TECHNICAL LIBRARY (Sci-Tech)†
1417 N. Battlefield Blvd.   Phone: (804) 449-0608
Chesapeake, VA 23320   Patricia L. Alderman, Tech.Libn.
Founded: 1980. **Staff:** Prof 1. **Subjects:** U.S. Navy ships, marine engineering. **Special Collections:** AFS (auxiliary fast stores) ships (800 technical manuals, 7600 drawings). **Holdings:** 1400 books; 400 vendor catalogs; 5000 aperture cards of drawings; 1600 drawings; 1000 microfiche. **Services:** library not open to public. **Special Catalogs:** Technical manuals, specifications and test procedures catalog; catalog of drawings (both on cards). **Special Indexes:** Technical manuals bibliography lists.

W

★16687★
WABASH COUNTY HISTORICAL MUSEUM - HISTORICAL LIBRARY (Hist)
Memorial Hall   Phone: (219) 563-5058
Wabash, IN 46992   Jack Miller, Cur.
Founded: 1923. Staff: 2. Subjects: Indiana and Wabash County history, Civil War. Holdings: 1940 books; newspapers; manuscripts and documents. Services: Library open to public for research on premises.

★16688★
WABCO - CONSTRUCTION AND MINING EQUIPMENT - ENGINEERING TECHNICAL LIBRARY (Sci-Tech)
2301 N.E. Adams St.   Phone: (309) 672-7143
Peoria, IL 61639   Marilyn G. Kopp, Libn.
Founded: 1965. Staff: 1. Subjects: Engineering, welding, soil, mathematics, steel, metals and alloys. Holdings: 3500 books; 500 bound periodical volumes; 11 VF drawers of society papers. Subscriptions: 178 journals and other serials. Services: Library not open to public. Remarks: WABCO is the acronym for Westinghouse Air Brake Company.

★16689★
WACO-MC LENNAN COUNTY LIBRARY - SPECIAL COLLECTIONS DEPARTMENT (Hist)
1717 Austin Ave.   Phone: (817) 754-4694
Waco, TX 76701   Sue Kethley, Libn.
Staff: Prof 2; Other 2. Subjects: Texas and local history, genealogy. Holdings: 10,632 books; 14,135 bound periodical volumes; 4543 reels of microfilm; 3699 microfiche. Subscriptions: 413 journals and other serials; 11 newspapers. Services: Copying; department open to public. Automated Operations: Computerized cataloging. Networks/Consortia: Member of AMIGOS Bibliographic Council, Inc. Publications: Heart of Texas Records, quarterly - by subscription. Staff: Dorothy Progar, Dir., Libs.; Bill Parton, Assoc.Dir.; Marsha Westfall, Assoc.Dir.

★16690★
WADDELL AND REED, INC. - RESEARCH LIBRARY (Bus-Fin)
Box 1343   Phone: (816) 283-4072
Kansas City, MO 64141   Betty J. Howerton, Hd.Libn.
Founded: 1962. Staff: Prof 1; Other 3. Subjects: Stock market, industries, corporation statistics, investments, mutual funds, economics. Holdings: 700 books; 75 bound periodical volumes; 3000 corporate files; 300 government documents; 42,000 10K and 10Q reports on microfiche. Subscriptions: 200 journals and other serials; 40 newspapers. Services: Library open to public for reference use only, with limited access to corporation files.

WADEWITZ (E.H.) MEMORIAL LIBRARY
See: Graphic Arts Technical Foundation - E.H. Wadewitz Memorial Library

★16691★
WADHAMS HALL SEMINARY - COLLEGE LIBRARY (Rel-Theol)
Riverside Dr.   Phone: (315) 393-4231
Ogdensburg, NY 13669   Jonas Barciauskas, Hd.Libn.
Founded: 1924. Staff: Prof 2; Other 1. Subjects: Scholastic philosophy, ascetical theology, classical languages, ecclesiastical history, undergraduate arts. Holdings: 72,426 books; 14,033 bound periodical volumes; 868 reels of microfilm; 1929 records; 1166 tapes. Subscriptions: 650 journals and other serials. Services: Interlibrary loans; copying; library open to public. Networks/Consortia: Member of North County Reference and Research Resources Council (NCRRRC). Publications: Monthly Acquisitions List; Patron's Brochure. Staff: Sr. Helen Martin, Ref.Libn.Vivian Lalonde, ILL.

★16692★
WADLEY INSTITUTES OF MOLECULAR MEDICINE - RESEARCH INSTITUTE LIBRARY (Med)†
9000 Harry Hines Blvd.   Phone: (214) 351-8648
Dallas, TX 75235   Kathryn Manning, Libn.
Founded: 1956. Staff: Prof 1. Subjects: Cancer, microbiology, hematology, biochemistry, immunology, genetics, interferon. Holdings: 10,527 books and bound periodical volumes; 73 dissertations; 225 reprints; 6 VF drawers of unbound material. Subscriptions: 235 journals and other serials. Services: Interlibrary loans; copying; SDI; library open to all medical personnel. Computerized Information Services: MEDLINE. Networks/Consortia: Member of Dallas-Tarrant County Consortium of Health Science Libraries. Publications: Journal Clinical Hematology and Oncology, quarterly - distributed to interested medical personnel and libraries. Remarks: An additional

telephone number is (214) 351-8649.

★16693★
WADSWORTH ATHENEUM - AUERBACH ART LIBRARY (Art)
600 Main St.   Phone: (203) 278-2670
Hartford, CT 06103   John W. Teahan, Libn.
Staff: Prof 2. Subjects: Fine arts, museology, art education. Special Collections: Watkinson Collection (3000 volumes); Lewitt Collection of artists' books. Holdings: 20,000 books and bound periodical volumes; 32 VF drawers; 200 feet of shelved boxes of museum files; 120 feet of shelved sales catalogs; 15 feet of shelved bookplates. Subscriptions: 125 journals and other serials. Services: Interlibrary loans; copying; library open to public for reference use only. Special Indexes: Index to Wadsworth Atheneum Bulletin; Index to Wadsworth Atheneum Exhibitions, 1910 to present. Staff: Catherine C. Knapp, Asst.Libn.

WADSWORTH MEDICAL LIBRARY
See: U.S. Veterans Administration (CA-Los Angeles)

★16694★
WAGNER COLLEGE - HORRMANN LIBRARY (Hum)
631 Howard Ave.   Phone: (718) 390-3401
Staten Island, NY 10301   Y. John Auh, Chf.Libn.
Founded: 1883. Staff: Prof 5; Other 9. Subjects: Literature, chemistry, bacteriology, education, philosophy, religion, nursing, economics, history, biology, art, physics, sociology. Special Collections: U.S. Government documents depository; Edwin Markham Collection (10,000 volumes includings poems, prose, clippings, Markham's works in translation, musical settings, recordings and a line by line index to his poems). Holdings: 275,000 books; 63,000 bound periodical volumes; 17,500 documents; 28,000 serials; 1629 masters' theses; ERIC collections, 1968 to present; 12 VF drawers; 105,000 microform cards of old English literature. Subscriptions: 1203 journals and other serials; 24 newspapers. Services: Interlibrary loans; copying; library open to public with library card subscription. Automated Operations: Computerized cataloging. Networks/Consortia: Member of METRO. Publications: Markham Review, quarterly. Special Catalogs: Periodical Handbook; Library Handbook. Staff: Maria Soos, Hd.Cat.Gunvor Jensen, Asst.Libn.; Louise Santoro, Asst.Libn.; Richard Palumbo, Ref.Libn.

★16695★
WAGNALLS MEMORIAL LIBRARY (Hist)
150 E. Columbus St.   Phone: (614) 837-4765
Lithopolis, OH 43136   Jerry W. Neff, Exec.Dir.
Founded: 1924. Staff: 9. Special Collections: Books written by and belonging to Mabel Wagnalls-Jones; local history; letters written by O. Henry to Mabel Wagnalls-Jones; paintings by John Ward Dunsmore. Subscriptions: 150 journals and other serials. Services: Library not open to public. Networks/Consortia: Member of CALICO. Staff: Marilyn Stebelton, Prog.Coord.; Mrs. Jo Riegel, Hd.Libn.

★16696★
WAGNER FREE INSTITUTE OF SCIENCE - LIBRARY (Sci-Tech)*
17th St. & Montgomery Ave.   Phone: (215) 763-6529
Philadelphia, PA 19121   John Graham, Dir.
Staff: 2. Subjects: Natural and physical sciences. Holdings: 25,000 volumes; 150,000 bound periodical volumes and pamphlets. Subscriptions: 10 journals and other serials. Services: Interlibrary loans; library open to public.

WAGNER-KEVETTER LIBRARY
See: Carter (William) College & Evangelical Theological Seminary

WAGNER (Robert F.) LABOR ARCHIVES
See: New York University - Tamiment Library

WAHAB (Robert S., Jr) PUBLIC LAW LIBRARY
See: Virginia Beach Public Library System - Robert S. Wahab, Jr. Public Law Library

WAHLQUIST LIBRARY
See: San Jose State University

WAHLSTROM (Magnus) LIBRARY
See: University of Bridgeport - Magnus Wahlstrom Library

WAIKIKI AQUARIUM
See: University of Hawaii

★16697★
WAINWRIGHT GENERAL HOSPITAL - MEDICAL LIBRARY (Med)
Box 820   Phone: (403) 842-3324
Wainwright, AB, Canada T0B 4P0   Loretta Haire, Health Rec.Adm.
Staff: 1. **Subjects:** Medicine. **Holdings:** 260 books. **Subscriptions:** 20 journals and other serials. **Services:** Library not open to public.

★16698★
WAKE COUNTY MEDICAL CENTER - MEDICAL LIBRARY (Med)
3000 New Bern Ave.   Phone: (919) 755-8528
Raleigh, NC 27610   Karen K. Grandage, Dir., Med.Lib.
Staff: Prof 3; Other 1. **Subjects:** Medicine, pediatrics, orthopedics, nursing, hospital administration, related health care subjects. **Special Collections:** Staff development/training collection; Clinical Pastoral Education. **Holdings:** 5870 books; 2988 bound periodical volumes; 2500 AV programs. **Subscriptions:** 289 journals and other serials. **Services:** Interlibrary loans (fee); copying; library open to public with permission of librarian. **Computerized Information Services:** MEDLARS, BRS. Performs searchs on cost recovery basis. **Networks/Consortia:** Member of North Carolina Area Health Education Centers Program (AHEC) - Library and Information Services Network; Resources for Health Information (REHI). **Staff:** Christiana E. Jordan, Asst.Med.Libn.; Beverly Richardson, Wake AHEC Libn.; Shelia Edwards, Lib.Techn.

★16699★
WAKE FOREST UNIVERSITY - BABCOCK GRADUATE SCHOOL OF MANAGEMENT - LIBRARY (Bus-Fin)
Box 7689, Reynolda Sta.   Phone: (919) 761-5414
Winston-Salem, NC 27109   Jean B. Hopson, Lib.Dir.
Founded: 1970. **Staff:** Prof 1; Other 4. **Subjects:** General management. **Holdings:** 14,094 books; microforms. **Subscriptions:** 283 journals and other serials. **Services:** Interlibrary loans; copying; library open to public. **Automated Operations:** Computerized cataloging. **Computerized Information Services:** OCLC, DIALOG. **Networks/Consortia:** Member of SOLINET. **Publications:** Management periodicals in university collections.

★16700★
WAKE FOREST UNIVERSITY - BAPTIST COLLECTION (Rel-Theol)
University Library   Phone: (919) 761-5472
Winston-Salem, NC 27109   John R. Woodard, Jr., Dir.
Founded: 1885. **Staff:** Prof 1; Other 1. **Subjects:** North Carolina Baptist history, Wake Forest University history. **Special Collections:** Manuscript records of 100 North Carolina Baptist churches; microfilm records of 810 North Carolina Baptist churches. **Holdings:** 10,245 books; 1573 bound periodical volumes; 305 private collections (personal papers); 1304 reels of microfilm; vertical file of North Carolina churches; biography file of North Carolina ministers. **Services:** Copying; will answer correspondence relating to Baptist history; collection open to public. **Publications:** Newsletter, bimonthly; Special Bulletins, irregular. **Special Indexes:** Computer-produced index to Biblical Recorder, the North Carolina Baptist newspaper.

★16701★
WAKE FOREST UNIVERSITY - BOWMAN GRAY SCHOOL OF MEDICINE - COY C. CARPENTER LIBRARY (Med)
300 S. Hawthorne Rd.   Phone: (919) 748-4691
Winston-Salem, NC 27103   Michael D. Sprinkle, Dir.
Founded: 1941. **Staff:** Prof 12; Other 22. **Subjects:** Medicine. **Holdings:** 29,218 books; 74,380 bound periodical volumes; 3834 AV items; 5123 microforms. **Subscriptions:** 1967 journals and other serials. **Services:** Interlibrary loans; copying; SDI; library open to public for reference use only. **Automated Operations:** Computerized cataloging. **Computerized Information Services:** MEDLINE, DIALOG, BRS, OCLC; internal database. **Networks/Consortia:** Member of SOLINET. **Publications:** Folio (newsletter), monthly - for internal distribution only. **Staff:** Sherry Anderson, Assoc.Dir.; Nancy Ekstrand, Asst.Dir.; Faye Foltz, Hd., Ser.Sect.; Carolyn Parker, AV/Acq.Libn.; Rebecca Johnston, Hd.Cat.; Betty Ladner, Clinical Res.Libn.; Madeline Perez, Archv.; Deborah McMaster, Drug Lit.Spec.; Cheryl Whicker, Adm.Sec.

★16702★
WAKE FOREST UNIVERSITY - LAW LIBRARY (Law)
Reynolda Sta., Box 7206   Phone: (919) 761-5438
Winston-Salem, NC 27109   Kenneth A. Zick, II, Dir.
Founded: 1894. **Staff:** Prof 5; Other 4. **Subjects:** Law. **Holdings:** 93,335 books; 1683 bound periodical volumes; 260,710 microfiche; 4173 reels of microfilm. **Subscriptions:** 1500 journals and other serials; 9 newspapers. **Services:** Interlibrary loans; copying; library open to public. **Automated Operations:** Computerized cataloging, acquisitions, serials and ILL. **Computerized Information Services:** Westlaw, OCLC. **Staff:** Vivian L.

Wilson, Law Libn.; Donna H. Laroussini, Rd.Serv.Libn.; Edward Waller, Tech.Serv.Libn.; Mary Jo Brachen, Media Serv.Libn.

WAKSMAN INSTITUTE OF MICROBIOLOGY LIBRARY
See: Rutgers University, The State University of New Jersey

WALDMANN (John & Bertha E.) MEMORIAL LIBRARY
See: New York University - Dental Center - John & Bertha E. Waldmann Memorial Library

★16703★
WALDO COUNTY LAW LIBRARY (Law)
Waldo County Courthouse
73 Church St.   Phone: (207) 338-2512
Belfast, ME 04915   William Anderson, Libn.
Staff: 3. **Subjects:** Law. **Holdings:** 5000 volumes. **Services:** Library open to public.

★16704★
WALDO GENERAL HOSPITAL - MEDICAL LIBRARY (Med)
10560 5th, N.E.
Box 25167   Phone: (206) 364-2050
Seattle, WA 98125   Janet Schnall, Consulting Libn.
Founded: 1967. **Subjects:** Medicine, osteopathy. **Holdings:** 525 books. **Subscriptions:** 55 journals and other serials. **Services:** Library not open to public.

WALDO LIBRARY
See: Western Michigan University

WALFORD (Lionel A.) LIBRARY
See: U.S. Natl. Marine Fisheries Service - Sandy Hook Laboratory - Lionel A. Walford Library

★16705★
WALKER ART CENTER - STAFF REFERENCE LIBRARY (Art)
Vineland Pl.   Phone: (612) 375-7680
Minneapolis, MN 55403   Rosemary Furtak, Dir.
Founded: 1950. **Staff:** 1. **Subjects:** Contemporary art, art history, architecture, design, graphics, photography, painting, sculpture. **Special Collections:** One-man artist catalogs, 1940 to present; Walker Art Center Film Study Collection; Edmund R. Ruben Film Study Collection. **Holdings:** 5000 books; 550 bound periodical volumes; 25,000 catalogs; AV tapes, films, slides; 14 vertical files. **Subscriptions:** 110 journals and other serials. **Services:** Library open to graduate students upon request from their instructors; visiting personnel from other museums and scholars with advance notice. **Publications:** Design Quarterly; Walker Art Center exhibition catalogs.

WALKER (Donald S.) LABORATORY
See: Sloan-Kettering Institute for Cancer Research - Donald S. Walker Laboratory

WALKER (E.F.) MEMORIAL LIBRARY
See: First Baptist Church - E.F. Walker Memorial Library

WALKER (Elisha) STAFF LIBRARY
See: New York Infirmary Beekman Downtown Hospital - Elisha Walker Staff Library

WALKER (Hastings H.) MEDICAL LIBRARY
See: Hawaii State Department of Health - Hastings H. Walker Medical Library

WALKER (Henry B., Jr.) MEMORIAL ART LIBRARY
See: Evansville Museum of Arts and Science - Library

★16706★
WALKER (Hiram) HISTORICAL MUSEUM - REFERENCE LIBRARY (Hist)
254 Pitt St., W.   Phone: (519) 253-1812
Windsor, ON, Canada N9A 5L5   Alan Douglas, Cur.
Founded: 1958. **Staff:** Prof 1; Other 2. **Subjects:** Local history. **Holdings:** 900 books; 29 bound periodical volumes; 327 units of archives; 429 maps; 2800 photographs; 183 reels of microfilm; 1800 sheets of microfiche. **Subscriptions:** 26 journals and other serials. **Services:** Interlibrary loans (through Windsor Public Library); copying; library open to public. **Remarks:** Maintained by the Windsor Public Library Board.

WALKER MANAGEMENT LIBRARY
See: Vanderbilt University - Jean and Alexander Heard Library

★16707★
WALKER MANUFACTURING CO. - LIBRARY (Bus-Fin)
1201 Michigan Blvd.
Racine, WI 53402   Dennis Otwaska, Supv., Adm.Serv.
Staff: 1. **Subjects:** Automotive industry, business management. **Holdings:** 300 books; 50 bound periodical volumes; 3000 other cataloged items. **Services:** Library not open to public.

★16708★
WALKER MEMORIAL HOSPITAL - LIBRARY (Med)
Box 1200   Phone: (813) 453-7511
Avon Park, FL 33825-1200   Monica Lescay, Dir., Med.Rec./Libn.
Subjects: Medicine and allied health sciences. **Holdings:** Figures not available. **Services:** Interlibrary loans; library not open to public. **Staff:** Betty Collins, Asst.Libn.

★16709★
WALKER MUSEUM - LIBRARY
Fairlee, VT 05045
Subjects: Art, architecture, classical archeology, music, theater. **Special Collections:** Japanese 18th century illustrated books (25 volumes); 15th-16th century calligraphy (10 volumes); Persian lithographed Shah Nameh. **Holdings:** 1000 books; 100 paintings, Civil War letters, woolen industry records. **Remarks:** Presently inactive.

★16710★
WALL STREET JOURNAL - LIBRARY (Bus-Fin; Publ)
22 Cortlandt St.   Phone: (212) 285-5075
New York, NY 10007   Lottie Lindberg, Libn.
Founded: 1903. **Staff:** Prof 1; Other 12. **Subjects:** Finance, business, investments. **Holdings:** Figures not available for books; clippings file of the Wall Street Journal. **Services:** Library not open to public. **Computerized Information Services:** Dow Jones News/Retrieval. **Special Indexes:** Wall Street Journal Index, monthly with annual cumulation; Barron's Index, annual.

★16711★
WALLA WALLA COLLEGE - CURRICULUM LIBRARY (Educ)
Smith Hall   Phone: (509) 527-2221
College Place, WA 99324   Camille Wood, Dir.
Founded: 1963. **Staff:** Prof 1; Other 4. **Subjects:** Vocational guidance, curriculum, social sciences, mathematics, science, health and physical education, language arts, administration. **Special Collections:** Teaching kits; career information files; Standardized Test File (83 titles); children's literature (9950 volumes). **Holdings:** 28,525 books and bound periodical volumes; 13,000 pamphlets; 475 phonograph records; 3580 pictures; 150 maps and globes; 200 theses; 351 cassettes; 909 filmstrips; 208 transparencies; 1435 slides; 551 realia. **Subscriptions:** 11 journals and other serials. **Services:** Copying; library open to public with valid library cards.

★16712★
WALLA WALLA COLLEGE - SCHOOL OF NURSING PROFESSIONAL LIBRARY (Med)
10345 S.E. Market   Phone: (503) 251-6115
Portland, OR 97216   Shirley A. Cody, Libn.
Founded: 1960. **Staff:** Prof 1; Other 1. **Subjects:** Nursing - administration, medical-surgical, parent-child, public health, psychiatric and mental health. **Holdings:** 8000 books; 750 bound periodical volumes; 60 tape cassettes; 6 VF drawers of clippings; 2000 pamphlets; 20 slide-tape sets; 40 video cassettes; 51 filmstrips. **Subscriptions:** 125 journals and other serials. **Services:** Interlibrary loans; copying; library open to public with librarian's permission and to employees of Portland Adventist Medical Center.

★16713★
WALLA WALLA COUNTY LAW LIBRARY (Law)
Court House   Phone: (509) 529-9520
Walla Walla, WA 99362   Ben R. Forcier, Jr., Libn.
Staff: 1. **Subjects:** Law. **Holdings:** 30,000 volumes. **Services:** Library not open to public.

WALLACE (James A.) LIBRARY
See: Memphis Mental Health Institute - James A. Wallace Library

WALLACE (Lila Acheson) LIBRARY
See: Juilliard School - Lila Acheson Wallace Library

WALLACE (Lou) LIBRARY
See: Tennessee State Department of Agriculture - Lou Wallace Library

WALLACE MEMORIAL LIBRARY
See: Rochester Institute of Technology

★16714★
WALLINGFORD HISTORICAL SOCIETY, INC. - LIBRARY (Hist)
Box 73   Phone: (203) 269-6257
Wallingford, CT 06492   Peter P. Hale, Pres.
Staff: 1. **Subjects:** Local history, genealogy. **Holdings:** 450 books. **Services:** Library open to public by appointment. **Remarks:** Located at 180 S. Main St., Wallingford, CT 06492.

WALLOPS FLIGHT CENTER
See: U.S. NASA

WALLS (W.J.) HERITAGE HALL ARCHIVES
See: Hood Theological Seminary - Livingstone College - Library

WALNUT CANYON NATL. MONUMENT
See: U.S. Natl. Park Service

★16715★
WALNUT CREEK HISTORICAL SOCIETY - SHADELANDS RANCH HISTORICAL MUSEUM - HISTORY ROOM (Hist)
2660 Ygnacio Valley Rd.   Phone: (415) 935-7871
Walnut Creek, CA 94598   Beverly C. Clemson, Musm.Dir.
Founded: 1972. **Subjects:** Walnut Creek history. **Special Collections:** Joseph Reddeford Walker; Albert and Bessie Johnson; Seely-Hodges letters, 1852-1881 (94); Hiram Penniman family; bound collection of Walnut Kernel newspapers (37 years). **Holdings:** 500 books; 62 bound periodical volumes; 6 VF drawers of maps, manuscripts, files, records; 1300 photographs; 25 tapes; 120 unbound newspapers. **Services:** History room open to public by appointment. **Publications:** Shadelands News, quarterly - to members. **Staff:** Carl Lindeken, Hist.Res.

WALPOLE (Lewis) LIBRARY
See: Yale University - Lewis Walpole Library

★16716★
WALSH COLLEGE OF ACCOUNTANCY AND BUSINESS ADMINISTRATION - LIBRARY (Bus-Fin)
3838 Livernois   Phone: (313) 689-8282
Troy, MI 48084   Gloria B. Ellis, Lib.Dir.
Founded: 1965. **Staff:** Prof 2; Other 2. **Subjects:** Accounting, auditing, investments, business law, economics, money and banking, taxation, data processing and statistics. **Special Collections:** Annual reports of 1300 companies. **Holdings:** 15,000 books and bound periodical volumes; 500 pamphlets; 350 ultrafiche; 60 C.P.A. audiotapes. **Subscriptions:** 350 journals and other serials; 11 newspapers. **Services:** Interlibrary loans; copying; library open to alumni and accountants.

★16717★
WALSH YOUNG - LIBRARY (Law)
1500 Guinness House   Phone: (403) 263-8490
Calgary, AB, Canada T2P 0Z8   Susan L. Ross, Libn.
Staff: Prof 1. **Subjects:** Law. **Holdings:** Figures not available. **Services:** Interlibrary loans; copying; library open to public with restrictions. **Computerized Information Services:** QL Systems.

WALSON ARMY HOSPITAL
See: U.S. Army Hospitals

★16718★
WALTER, CONSTON & SCHURTMAN, P.C. - LAW LIBRARY (Law)
90 Park Ave.   Phone: (212) 210-9526
New York, NY 10016   Nina Cerny, Hd.Libn.
Staff: Prof 1. **Subjects:** Law - corporate, international, German. **Special Collections:** German law (German, French and English materials). **Holdings:** 10,000 books. **Services:** Interlibrary loans; copying; library open to public with lawyer's permission. **Automated Operations:** Computerized cataloging, acquisitions, serials and circulation. **Computerized Information Services:** Westlaw. Performs searches on subscription basis. Contact Person: P. Johrden, Attorney, 697-5640. **Networks/Consortia:** Member of Law Library Association of Greater New York.

WALTER HAMPDEN - EDWIN BOOTH THEATER COLLECTION AND LIBRARY
See: Hampden-Booth Theatre Library

WALTER (Jim) RESEARCH CORPORATION
See: Jim Walter Research Corporation

WALTER (Joseph C., Jr. and Elizabeth C.) GEOLOGY LIBRARY
See: University of Texas, Austin - Geology Library

WALTER LIBRARY
See: University of Minnesota

★16719★
WALTERS ART GALLERY - LIBRARY (Art)
600 N. Charles St.   Phone: (301) 547-9000
Baltimore, MD 21201   Muriel L. Toppan, Ref.Libn.
Staff: Prof 1; Other 1. Subjects: Art - European, Greek, Roman, Egyptian, medieval; manuscripts; sculpture. Holdings: 75,000 books; 9000 bound periodical volumes; 700 rare books; 782 illuminated manuscripts; 1400 incunabula. Subscriptions: 700 journals and other serials. Services: Copying; library open to scholars and students by appointment. Publications: Walters Art Gallery Bulletin, monthly; journal, annual; annual report. Staff: Lilian M.C. Randall, Kpr. of Mss.

WALTERS (Raymond) COLLEGE
See: University of Cincinnati - Raymond Walters College

★16720★
WALTHAM HOSPITAL - MEDICAL LIBRARY (Med)
Hope Ave.   Phone: (617) 899-3300
Waltham, MA 02154   Alison Coolidge, Libn.
Staff: Prof 1; Other 1. Subjects: Medicine, surgery, psychiatry, nursing, hospital administration. Holdings: 1000 books; 1600 bound periodical volumes; 400 cassettes; 2 VF drawers of pamphlets; 1200 volumes of unbound periodicals. Subscriptions: 153 journals and other serials. Services: Interlibrary loans; copying; SDI; library open to public by permission. Computerized Information Services: Online systems. Networks/Consortia: Member of Consortium for Information Resources (CIR).

★16721★
WALTON LANTAFF SCHROEDER & CARSON - LAW LIBRARY (Law)
900 Alfred I. DuPont Bldg.   Phone: (305) 379-6411
Miami, FL 33131   Daniel Linehan, Libn.
Founded: 1934. Subjects: Law. Holdings: 22,000 volumes. Services: Library open to attorneys with prior permission.

WALWORTH COUNTY - LAKELAND COUNSELING CENTER
See: Lakeland Counseling Center

★16722★
WANDERER PRESS - LIBRARY (Rel-Theol)
201 Ohio St.   Phone: (612) 224-5733
St. Paul, MN 55107   Kathleen E. Walsh, Info.Mgr.
Staff: Prof 1. Subjects: Catholic religion, theology and philosophy. Special Collections: Papal Encyclicals, 1740 to present; The Wanderer newspaper, 1867 to present. Holdings: 2000 books; 25 reels of microfilm. Subscriptions: 50 journals and other serials; 50 newspapers. Services: Interlibrary loans; library open to public by appointment.

★16723★
WANG INSTITUTE OF GRADUATE STUDIES - LIBRARY (Sci-Tech; Comp Sci)
Tyng Rd.   Phone: (617) 649-9731
Tyngsboro, MA 01879   Eileen Baker, Libn.
Founded: 1980. Staff: Prof 1; Other 2. Subjects: Software engineering, computer programming languages and methodology, advanced mathematics, management and business, computer science. Holdings: 2500 books and conference proceedings; 500 technical reports. Subscriptions: 275 journals and other serials. Services: Interlibrary loans; copying; SDI; library open to public for reference use only. Automated Operations: Computerized cataloging; automated internal records. Computerized Information Services: DIALOG, BRS, OCLC. Networks/Consortia: Member of NELINET.

WANGENHEIM ROOM
See: San Diego Public Library

WANGENSTEEN (Owen H.) HISTORICAL LIBRARY OF BIOLOGY AND MEDICINE
See: University of Minnesota - Biomedical Library

★16724★
WAPORA, INC. - LIBRARY
6900 Wisconsin Ave.
Chevy Chase, MD 20815
Defunct

★16725★
WAR MEMORIAL MUSEUM OF VIRGINIA - RESEARCH LIBRARY (Mil; Hist)
9285 Warwick Blvd.   Phone: (804) 247-8523
Newport News, VA 23607   Eliza E. Embrey, Libn.
Staff: 1. Subjects: Military history. Special Collections: Rare books and documents on Spanish-American War, Civil War, World Wars I and II; uniform regulations; military manuals. Holdings: 14,000 books; 200 bound periodical volumes; 700 newspapers; 5000 items in historical files; 300 microfiche; 350 films; 25 oral history tapes. Subscriptions: 60 journals and other serials. Services: Library open to public for research use. Special Catalogs: Film catalog.

WARBURG PARIBAS BECKER, INC.
See: A.G. Becker Paribas, Inc.

WARD (Clarence) ART LIBRARY
See: Oberlin College - Clarence Ward Art Library

WARD MEMORIAL LIBRARY
See: Sacred Heart Seminary

WARDEN WOODS CAMPUS RESOURCE CENTRE
See: Centennial College of Applied Arts & Technology

WARE (E.G.) LIBRARY
See: Garden Grove Historical Society - E.G. Ware Library

WARNE CLINIC
See: Pottsville Hospital and Warne Clinic

WARNE (Thomas) HISTORICAL MUSEUM AND LIBRARY
See: Madison Township Historical Society - Thomas Warne Historical Museum and Library

WARNER BROS. INC. ARCHIVES
See: Princeton University - William Seymour Theatre Collection

WARNER BROTHERS LIBRARY
See: University of Wisconsin, Madison - Wisconsin Center for Film and Theater Research

★16726★
WARNER-EDDISON ASSOCIATES, INC. - INFORMATION SERVICE (Info Sci; Comp Sci)
238 Broadway   Phone: (617) 661-8124
Cambridge, MA 02139   Elizabeth Bole Eddison, Pres.
Founded: 1973. Staff: Prof 9; Other 10. Subjects: Information science and sources, computer science, business, thesauri. Holdings: Figures not available. Services: Service not open to public. Automated Operations: Computerized cataloging and acquisitions. Computerized Information Services: OCLC; INMAGIC data management software. Networks/Consortia: Member of NELINET. Publications: Words That Mean Business: 3000 Terms for Access to Business Information, 1981 - for sale.

WARNER HOUSE LIBRARY
See: Constitution Island Association, Inc.

★16727★
WARNER-LAMBERT CANADA INC. - LIBRARY (Med)†
2200 Eglinton Ave., E.   Phone: (416) 750-2360
Scarborough, ON, Canada M1K 5C9   Edna Allen, Libn.
Staff: 1. Subjects: Medicine, pharmacy, advertising and marketing. Special Collections: Clinical papers, promotional reprints, product information (current, historical). Holdings: 1500 books; 600 bound periodical volumes; 6000 nonbook items; vertical files; 600 tapes; 1500 microfiche; 500 archive files. Subscriptions: 245 journals and other serials. Services: Interlibrary loans; copying (both by special request); library open to public by special request. Computerized Information Services: MEDLINE, TOXLINE, CAN/OLE, SDC. Special Indexes: Product Information.

★16728★

WARNER-LAMBERT CANADA INC. - TECHNICAL INFORMATION CENTRE (Sci-Tech)
2200 Eglinton Ave., E.   Phone: (416) 750-2402
Scarborough, ON, Canada M1K 5C9   Susan W. Underdown, Tech.Libn.
Founded: 1970. **Staff:** Prof 1. **Subjects:** Pharmaceuticals, chemistry, quality control, microbiology. **Holdings:** 1000 books; 300 bound periodical volumes; 1550 microfiche; 8 VF drawers of technical directions and research reports; 1 drawer of patents. **Subscriptions:** 73 journals and other serials. **Services:** Interlibrary loans; copying; center open to public by appointment. **Computerized Information Services:** SDC, BRS, NLM, CAN/OLE, DIALOG, Pergamon InfoLine Ltd. **Networks/Consortia:** Member of Sheridan Park Association.

★16729★

WARNER-LAMBERT COMPANY - CORPORATE LIBRARY (Sci-Tech; Med)
170 Tabor Rd.   Phone: (201) 540-2875
Morris Plains, NJ 07950   Nedra Behringer, Mgr., Corp.Lib.
Founded: 1945. **Staff:** Prof 7; Other 5. **Subjects:** Pharmaceuticals, medicine, pharmacology, chemistry, microbiology, dentistry, business. **Holdings:** 21,000 books; 21,000 bound periodical volumes; microfilm. **Subscriptions:** 500 journals and other serials. **Services:** Interlibrary loans. **Computerized Information Services:** Online systems. **Staff:** Verdelle B. Jones, Asst.Lib., Tech.Proc.; Edith B. Chapman, Sr.Lit.Sci.; Linda Warren, Supv., Lib.Oper.; Arlene F. Drucker, Sr.Lit.Sci.; Barbara R. Eckhardt, Sr.Lit.Sci.; Eric N. Goldschmidt, Sr.Lit.Sci.

★16730★

WARNER-LAMBERT/PARKE-DAVIS - RESEARCH LIBRARY (Sci-Tech; Med)†
2800 Plymouth Rd.   Phone: (313) 994-3500
Ann Arbor, MI 48105   Katherine Owen, Mgr.
Founded: 1885. **Staff:** Prof 10; Other 4. **Subjects:** Chemistry, pharmacology, medicine, toxicology, microbiology, pathology. **Holdings:** 17,478 books; 11,710 bound periodical volumes; 3500 microfilm cassettes; 203 pamphlets; 56,400 computerized and indexed product documents; 2356 translations; 2603 reprints. **Subscriptions:** 715 journals and other serials. **Services:** Interlibrary loans (limited); copying; SDI; translations; reprints; library open to public by permission. **Automated Operations:** Computerized serials and cataloging. **Computerized Information Services:** DIALOG, SDC, BRS, NLM; PARDLARS (literature citations on company products; internal database). **Networks/Consortia:** Member of Greater Midwest Regional Medical Library Network (Region 3); Metropolitan Detroit Medical Library Group (MDMLG). **Staff:** Barbara K. Becker, Supv.; Audrone V. Vaitiekaitis, Cat.Serv.; Sharon Lehman, Supv., Lit.Serv.

★16731★

WARNER, NORCROSS & JUDD - LIBRARY (Law)
900 Old Kent Bldg.   Phone: (616) 459-6121
Grand Rapids, MI 49503   Dianne Vander Kooy, Libn.
Staff: Prof 1. **Subjects:** Law. **Holdings:** 9000 books; 700 bound periodical volumes. **Subscriptions:** 154 journals and other serials. **Services:** Interlibrary loans; library open to public with special permission. **Computerized Information Services:** LEXIS, DIALOG.

★16732★

WARNER-PACIFIC COLLEGE - OTTO F. LINN LIBRARY (Rel-Theol)
2219 S.E. 68th Ave.   Phone: (503) 775-4368
Portland, OR 97215   Dr. William M. Orr, Gen.Lib.Adm.
Founded: 1937. **Staff:** Prof 3. **Subjects:** Religion, natural and applied science, education, business, economics, social and behavioral science, music, health, physical education. **Special Collections:** Church of God Collection (Anderson, Indiana). **Holdings:** 52,500 books; 3000 bound periodical volumes; 40 theses and dissertations; 1500 AV items relating to core program. **Subscriptions:** 250 journals and other serials; 5 newspapers. **Services:** Interlibrary loans; copying; library open to public. **Computerized Information Services:** Online systems. **Special Catalogs:** Headquarters of Union Catalog and Teletype Services. **Staff:** Richard Kelly, Tech.Serv.Libn.; Marilyn Neu, Circ.Libn.

WARNER RESEARCH COLLECTION
See: Burbank Public Library

★16733★

WARNER & STACKPOLE - LAW LIBRARY (Law)*
28 State St.   Phone: (617) 523-6250
Boston, MA 02109   Brian J. Harkins, Libn.
Staff: Prof 1; Other 1. **Subjects:** Law. **Holdings:** 10,000 books. **Services:** Library not open to public.

★16734★

WARNOCK HERSEY PROFESSIONAL SERVICES LTD. - LIBRARY (Sci-Tech)
128 Elmslie St.   Phone: (514) 366-3100
LaSalle, PQ, Canada H8R 1V8   Andre Blain, Gen.Mgr.
Founded: 1954. **Staff:** Prof 1. **Subjects:** Chemistry, concrete, engineering, pollution. **Holdings:** 1600 books. **Subscriptions:** 75 journals and other serials. **Services:** Interlibrary loans; copying; library open to public by appointment.

★16735★

WARREN COUNTY HISTORICAL SOCIETY - LIBRARY AND ARCHIVES (Hist)
Box 427   Phone: (814) 723-1795
Warren, PA 16365   Mrs. Conrad Brunke, Libn.
Staff: 2. **Subjects:** History - local, state, Indian; genealogy; Quaker records; local authors. **Special Collections:** Harold C. Putnam Collection including material on local history and the inland rivers of the eastern United States (95 linear feet); Joseph Wick Collection including background and history of construction of the Kinzua Dam (9 linear feet); Byron Barnes Horton Collection including history of the Barnes, Hortons and related families in New England and Pennsylvania (37 linear feet). **Holdings:** 2000 books; 300 VF boxes of material from local and area families and businesses; 250 boxes of magnetic tapes. **Subscriptions:** 14 journals and other serials. **Services:** Copying; library open to public with restrictions.

★16736★

WARREN COUNTY HISTORICAL SOCIETY - MUSEUM AND LIBRARY (Hist)
105 S. Broadway
Box 223   Phone: (513) 932-1817
Lebanon, OH 45036   Victoria Visintainer, Dir.
Founded: 1940. **Staff:** Prof 1; Other 35. **Subjects:** Local history, genealogy, archeology, Warren County data (court, census, school and church records), Shaker records, agriculture. **Special Collections:** Shaker Library. **Holdings:** 1200 volumes; 1526 family files; 600 general county information files; 75,000 index cards of county residents; 350 reels of microfilm of court records, church census, newspapers, school records; 24 volumes of cemetery, marriage and birth records; 87 bound copies of Ohio Historical Society quarterlies. **Subscriptions:** 20 journals and other serials. **Services:** Copying; library open to public. **Publications:** Historicalog, monthly.

★16737★

WARREN COUNTY LAW LIBRARY (Law)†
500 Justice Dr.   Phone: (614) 932-4040
Lebanon, OH 45036   Barbara Bronson, Libn.
Staff: 2. **Subjects:** Law. **Holdings:** 15,000 volumes. **Services:** Library open to public. **Staff:** Thomas Essex, Asst.Libn.

★16738★

WARREN GENERAL HOSPITAL - MEDICAL STAFF LIBRARY (Med)
667 Eastland Ave., S.E.   Phone: (216) 399-7541
Warren, OH 44484   Nancy L. Bindas, Med.Libn.
Founded: 1965. **Staff:** 1. **Subjects:** Medicine, surgery and allied sciences. **Holdings:** 401 books; 250 bound periodical volumes; 340 Audio-Digest tapes and cassettes; 220 videotapes. **Subscriptions:** 41 journals and other serials. **Services:** Interlibrary loans; library not open to public.

★16739★

WARREN HOSPITAL - MEDICAL LIBRARY (Med)
185 Roseberry St.   Phone: (201) 859-1500
Phillipsburg, NJ 08865   Mary K. Shipley, Staff Sec.
Staff: 1. **Subjects:** Medicine. **Holdings:** 3000 books. **Subscriptions:** 35 journals and other serials. **Services:** Library not open to public.

★16740★

WARREN LIBRARY ASSOCIATION - LIBRARY (Mus; Hist)
205 Market St.   Phone: (814) 723-4650
Warren, PA 16365   Mary Elizabeth Richardson, Ref.Libn.
Founded: 1873. **Staff:** Prof 6; Other 25. **Special Collections:** Petroleum history (450 items); popular American sheet music of show tunes, 1834-1955 (3590 items); Warren County newspapers on microfilm, 1824 to present. **Holdings:** 139,223 volumes; 4762 AV items; 460 historic Warren County photographs; 14,929 federal and state documents. **Subscriptions:** 311 journals and other serials; 17 newspapers. **Services:** Interlibrary loans (none on sheet music); copying; library open to public. **Automated Operations:** Computerized cataloging and ILL. **Computerized Information Services:** OCLC, DIALOG. **Networks/Consortia:** Member of Pittsburgh Regional Library Center (PRLC). **Publications:** Directory of Organizations, Warren County, PA, annual; Seneca District Films, annual - on request. **Staff:** Ann Lesser, Dir.; Helen F. Mason, Adult Serv.Libn.; Barbara Tubbs, ILL.

WARREN (Louis A.) LINCOLN LIBRARY & MUSEUM
See: Lincoln National Life Foundation - Louis A. Warren Lincoln Library and Museum

WARREN (S.D.) COMPANY
See: Scott Paper Company - S.D. Warren Company

★16741★
WARREN STATE HOSPITAL - MEDICAL LIBRARY (Med)
Box 249   Phone: (814) 723-5500
Warren, PA 16365   Daryl G. Ellsworth, Libn.
Founded: 1930. **Staff:** Prof 1; Other 1. **Subjects:** Psychiatry, neurology, psychology, medicine, sociology. **Holdings:** 15,500 books; 8600 bound periodical volumes; 1200 audio cassettes. **Subscriptions:** 245 journals and other serials. **Services:** Interlibrary loans; copying; library open to professional and preprofessional users. **Automated Operations:** Computerized cataloging and serials. **Computerized Information Services:** OCLC. **Networks/Consortia:** Member of Pennsylvania Union List of Serials (PAULS); Western Institutional Library Cooperative; Erie Area Health Information Library Cooperative. **Publications:** Acquisition List, quarterly.

WARRINGTON (Betty) MEMORIAL
See: Krotona Institute of Theosophy - Krotona Library - Betty Warrington Memorial

★16742★
WARSAW HISTORICAL SOCIETY - LIBRARY (Hist)*
15 Perry Ave.
Warsaw, NY 14569
Founded: 1939. **Subjects:** Wyoming County history, Civil War history. **Holdings:** 450 books; 100 years of local newspapers bound by years; local publications. **Services:** Library not open to public, except for announced open house.

WARTBURG THEOLOGICAL SEMINARY - AMERICAN LUTHERAN CHURCH - ARCHIVES
See: American Lutheran Church - Archives

WARTIME PROPAGANDA COLLECTION
See: Springfield City Library

★16743★
WARWICK PUBLIC LIBRARY - CENTRAL CHILDREN'S LIBRARY (Educ)
600 Sandy Lane   Phone: (401) 739-5440
Warwick, RI 02886   Alice E. Forsstrom, Hd. of Children's Serv.
Staff: Prof 1; Other 2. **Subjects:** Children's literature. **Special Collections:** Live animals for loan (12); educational toys (165). **Holdings:** 21,909 books. **Subscriptions:** 10 journals and other serials. **Services:** Interlibrary loans; copying; library open to public. **Networks/Consortia:** Member of Western Interrelated Library System. **Remarks:** Special collections are loaned to parents for their children's use.

★16744★
WASCANA HOSPITAL - HEALTH SCIENCES LIBRARY (Med)
Ave. G & 23rd Ave.   Phone: (306) 359-9230
Regina, SK, Canada S4S 0A5   Darlene Jones, Dir.
Staff: 2. **Subjects:** Rehabilitation, gerontology, pediatrics. **Holdings:** 2000 books; 950 bound periodical volumes. **Subscriptions:** 80 journals and other serials. **Services:** Interlibrary loans; copying; library open to public with restrictions. **Computerized Information Services:** Online systems. **Staff:** Lily Walter, Libn.

★16745★
WASCANA INSTITUTE OF APPLIED ARTS AND SCIENCES - RESOURCE & INFORMATION CENTRE (Med; Agri)
4635 Wascana Pkwy.
Box 556   Phone: (306) 565-4321
Regina, SK, Canada S4P 3A3   Pran Vohra, Supv./Chf.Libn.
Founded: 1972. **Staff:** Prof 3; Other 11. **Subjects:** Nursing, health sciences, dental nursing, agriculture, business. **Holdings:** 33,459 books and AV materials. **Subscriptions:** 511 journals and other serials; 8 newspapers. **Services:** Interlibrary loans; copying; SDI; center open to public for reference use only. **Networks/Consortia:** Member of Health Sciences Library Council. **Remarks:** Includes holdings of libraries at St. John Street Campus, Albert South Campus, Maxwell Crescent Campus and branch libraries in North Battleford, Yorkton, Moose Jaw and Weyburn. **Staff:** Florence Duesterbeck, Asst.Libn.; Miss Singh, Libn.

WASH INFORMATION CENTER
See: U.S. Agency for International Development - Water and Sanitation for Health Project

WASHBURN OBSERVATORY
See: University of Wisconsin, Madison

★16746★
WASHBURN UNIVERSITY OF TOPEKA - SCHOOL OF LAW LIBRARY (Law)
1700 College Ave.   Phone: (913) 295-6688
Topeka, KS 66621   John E. Christensen, Dir.
Founded: 1903. **Staff:** Prof 6; Other 7. **Subjects:** Law. **Special Collections:** U.S. Government documents depository, 1972 to present; Kansas documents depository. **Holdings:** 106,239 bound volumes; 36,434 volumes on microfiche; CIS microfiche, 1974 to present; U.S. Supreme Court records and briefs on microfiche, 1974 to present. **Subscriptions:** 2541 journals and other serials. **Services:** Interlibrary loans; library open to public with restrictions. **Computerized Information Services:** BRS, Commerce Clearing House Electronic Legislative Search System (ELSS), Westlaw, Auto-Cite, Kansas Legislative Information System, RLIN, DIALOG, LEXIS, OCLC. Performs searches for students and faculty. **Networks/Consortia:** Member of Mid-America Law School Library Consortium; Bibliographical Center for Research, Rocky Mountain Region, Inc. (BCR). **Staff:** Jan Brown, Doc.Libn.; Virgie Smith, Cat.; David Ensign, Asst.Libn.; Dorothea Warren, Ref.Libn.; Glen Peter Ahlers, Asst.Libn.

★16747★
WASHINGTON ADVENTIST HOSPITAL - MEDICAL LIBRARY (Med)
7600 Carroll Ave.   Phone: (301) 891-5261
Takoma Park, MD 20012   Loraine Sweetland, Libn./Supv.
Founded: 1928. **Staff:** Prof 1; Other 1. **Subjects:** Medicine, nursing. **Holdings:** 4600 volumes. **Subscriptions:** 261 journals and other serials; 6 newspapers. **Services:** Interlibrary loans; copying; SDI; library open to public for reference use only. **Automated Operations:** Computerized cataloging. **Publications:** Report on acquisitions, semiannual - distributed to hospital departments.

WASHINGTON ANALYTICAL SERVICES CENTER
See: EG&G, Inc.

★16748★
WASHINGTON ARCHAEOLOGICAL RESEARCH CENTER - LIBRARY (Sci-Tech)
Washington State Univ.
Commons Hall 322   Phone: (509) 335-8566
Pullman, WA 99164   Alice Gronski, Rec.Libn.
Founded: 1973. **Staff:** 1. **Subjects:** Archeology in Washington and the Pacific Northwest, anthropology, cultural resources management. **Holdings:** Figures not available; maps; photographs and slides. **Services:** Library open to public for reference use only.

★16749★
WASHINGTON AREA WOMEN'S CENTER - WAWC FEMINIST LIBRARY & ARCHIVES
1638 R St., No. 2
Washington, DC 20009
Subjects: Feminism, lesbianism, sexism. **Special Collections:** Lesbian Heritage archives, 1960 to present. **Holdings:** 1123 books; oral histories and Feminist Radio Network tapes. **Remarks:** Presently inactive.

★16750★
WASHINGTON BIBLE COLLEGE/CAPITAL BIBLE SEMINARY - OYER MEMORIAL LIBRARY (Rel-Theol)
6511 Princess Garden Pkwy.   Phone: (301) 552-1400
Lanham, MD 20706   Carol A. Satta, Dir., Lib.Serv.
Founded: 1949. **Staff:** Prof 1; Other 2. **Subjects:** Theology (evangelical), Bible, Christian education, missions and evangelism, Greek and Hebrew language studies, church history. **Holdings:** 39,000 books; 803 bound periodical volumes; 628 filmstrips; microforms; 627 cassette tapes; 1153 phonograph records; 133 transparency files; 612 religious teaching aid files; 580 VF folders of pamphlets. **Subscriptions:** 263 journals and other serials; 5 newspapers. **Services:** Interlibrary loans; copying; library open to public with restrictions.

WASHINGTON (Booker T.) NATL. MONUMENT
See: U.S. Natl. Park Service - Booker T. Washington Natl. Monument

★16751★
WASHINGTON CATHEDRAL FOUNDATION - CATHEDRAL RARE BOOK LIBRARY (Rel-Theol; Rare Book)
Mount St. Alban, N.W.
Washington, DC 20016   Irwin H. Wensink, Chm., Lib.Comm.
Founded: 1965. **Subjects:** Biblical texts, liturgies, church history, theology, church music, ecclesiastical art and architecture. **Special Collections:** Carson Collection of American Bishops (manuscript material in the hand of most of the Bishops of the Protestant-Episcopal Church). **Holdings:** 4000 books and manuscripts. **Services:** Library open to public by appointment. **Special Catalogs:** Catalogs of special exhibitions.

WASHINGTON COLLEGE OF LAW
See: American University

WASHINGTON COUNTY FREE LIBRARY
See: Western Maryland Public Libraries Regional Library

★16752★
WASHINGTON COUNTY HISTORICAL ASSOCIATION - MUSEUM LIBRARY (Hist)
14th & Monroe Sts.   Phone: (402) 468-5740
Fort Calhoun, NE 68023   Genevieve Slader, Libn./Cur.
Founded: 1938. **Staff:** 2. **Subjects:** Local and state history, family histories. **Special Collections:** Artifacts and copies of military records of Fort Atkinson, 1819-1827; pioneer documents and letters; Lorenzo Crounse Personal Papers (Governor of Nebraska, 1893). **Holdings:** 500 books; 30 bound periodical volumes; 96 maps and atlases; 54 school reports; 60 manuscripts (letters, genealogies, pioneer reminiscences); 1500 photographs; 23 photograph albums; 1100 clippings. **Services:** Interlibrary loans; copying; library open to public for reference use only. **Publications:** The Story of Fort Atkinson, pamphlet - for sale. **Staff:** Catharine C. Frahm, Dir.

★16753★
WASHINGTON COUNTY HISTORICAL AND MUSEUM SOCIETY - LE MOYNE HOUSE LIBRARY (Hist)
LeMoyne House
49 E. Maiden St.   Phone: (412) 225-6740
Washington, PA 15301   Nancy Berry Saxon, Dir.
Founded: 1900. **Staff:** Prof 1. **Subjects:** County histories, county biographies, Pennsylvania archives, family genealogies. **Special Collections:** Marriage records; cemetery records; county atlas and maps. **Holdings:** 3200 books; old newspapers. **Services:** Library open to public for reference use only.

★16754★
WASHINGTON COUNTY HISTORICAL SOCIETY - LIBRARY (Hist)
Stevens Memorial Musm.
307 E. Market St.
Salem, IN 47167   Lulie Davis, Sec.-Libn.
Founded: 1914. **Staff:** 1. **Subjects:** Genealogy, history, religion, biography and antiques. **Special Collections:** Newspapers, 1819 to present; Antiques Magazine (50 volumes); The Christian Record, 1843-1884; Quaker Genealogies - Hinshaw and local (Blue River). **Holdings:** 2000 books; 75 bound periodical volumes; 266 folders of genealogies; 36 cemetery record books; 300 church records; 2 Justice of Peace books; 13 survey records of Washington County (1923); 25 files of marriage affidavits, applications and certificates; 1 file of deeds; booklets of clubs and lodges; 61 diaries; 34 account books; 34 township books; war and school records. **Subscriptions:** 10 journals and other serials. **Services:** Copying; microreader; library open to public.

★16755★
WASHINGTON COUNTY HOSPITAL - WROTH MEMORIAL LIBRARY (Med)
King & Antietam Sts.   Phone: (301) 824-8801
Hagerstown, MD 21740   Myra Binau, Coord., Lib.Serv.
Founded: 1953. **Staff:** Prof 1; Other 2. **Subjects:** Medicine, nursing and related health subjects. **Holdings:** 5000 books and bound periodical volumes; 8 VF drawers of pamphlets and clippings. **Subscriptions:** 178 journals and other serials. **Services:** Interlibrary loans; copying; library open to public for reference use only. **Networks/Consortia:** Member of Mid-Atlantic Regional Medical Library Program (MARMLP).

★16756★
WASHINGTON COUNTY LAW LIBRARY (Law)
Court House   Phone: (301) 791-3115
Hagerstown, MD 21740   Elizabeth F. Wilkinson, Libn.
Staff: Prof 1. **Subjects:** Law. **Holdings:** Figures not available. **Subscriptions:** 18 journals and other serials. **Services:** Library not open to public.

★16757★
WASHINGTON COUNTY LAW LIBRARY (Law)
Court House
201 Putnam St.
Marietta, OH 45750   Patricia Wheeler, Libn.
Staff: Prof 2. **Subjects:** Law. **Holdings:** Figures not available. **Services:** Library open to public for reference use only. **Computerized Information Services:** Westlaw. Performs searches on subscription basis. **Remarks:** The library may be reached through (614) 373-6623.

★16758★
WASHINGTON COUNTY LAW LIBRARY (Law)†
Courthouse   Phone: (503) 648-8880
Hillsboro, OR 97123   Ann Karlen, Libn.
Founded: 1926. **Staff:** 1. **Subjects:** Law. **Holdings:** 15,000 volumes. **Services:** Copying; library open to public.

★16759★
WASHINGTON COUNTY LAW LIBRARY (Law)
Court House   Phone: (412) 228-6747
Washington, PA 15301   Jane M. Fulcher, Law Libn.
Founded: 1867. **Staff:** 1. **Subjects:** Law. **Holdings:** 16,000 volumes. **Services:** Library open to public.

★16760★
WASHINGTON COUNTY MUSEUM OF FINE ARTS - LIBRARY (Art)
City Park, Box 423   Phone: (301) 739-5727
Hagerstown, MD 21740   Mabert E. Fox, Exec.Sec.
Founded: 1931. **Subjects:** Art, art history. **Holdings:** 1200 volumes. **Services:** Interlibrary loans; library open to public for reference use only.

★16761★
WASHINGTON COUNTY MUSEUM LIBRARY (Hist)
602 N. Main St.   Phone: (612) 439-5956
Stillwater, MN 55082   Judith Payne, Cur.
Staff: 2. **Subjects:** History - Washington County, Minnesota, St. Croix River Valley. **Holdings:** 100 volumes. **Services:** Library open to public for reference use only. **Remarks:** Maintained by Washington County Historical Society.

★16762★
WASHINGTON COUNTY MUSEUM - LIBRARY (Hist)
17677 N.W. Springville Rd.   Phone: (503) 645-6606
Portland, OR 97229   Dr. Robert W. Keeler, Cur. of Coll.
Staff: 2. **Subjects:** History, anthropology, cultural resources management. **Special Collection:** Washington County Collection (manuscripts, pamphlets and ephemera). **Holdings:** 100 books; 10,000 photographs; 30 reels of microfilm of Washington County newspapers; 100 cubic feet of manuscript materials; 20 oral history tapes; 3 cubic feet of clippings; 10 reels of microfilm of Washington County archival materials. **Services:** Interlibrary loans; copying; library open to public for reference use only. **Networks/ Consortia:** Member of Washington County Cooperative Library Services (WCCLS).

★16763★
WASHINGTON COUNTY TOY LENDING LIBRARY (Educ)
223 N. 4th St.
Stillwater, MN 55082   Zantha LaFon-Horstmann, Coord.
Staff: Prof 1; Other 1. **Subjects:** Infant, preschool, and elementary educational toys and games. **Holdings:** 800 toys. **Services:** Library open to public. **Special Catalogs:** Toy catalog. **Staff:** Carol Woodward, Coord.

WASHINGTON FOUNDATION CENTER
See: Foundation Center - Washington Branch Library

★16764★
WASHINGTON GAS LIGHT COMPANY - CORPORATE LIBRARY (Bus-Fin; Energy)†
6801 Industrial Rd.   Phone: (703) 750-7927
Springfield, VA 22151   Jan Magnusson, Corp.Libn.
Founded: 1944. **Staff:** Prof 2; Other 1. **Subjects:** Gas technology, chemistry, physics, accounting, personnel administration, management. **Special Collections:** Company history. **Holdings:** 30,000 volumes. **Subscriptions:** 820 journals and other serials. **Services:** Interlibrary loans; copying; telecopying; library open to public on a limited basis. **Automated Operations:** Computerized cataloging. **Computerized Information Services:** DIALOG, OCLC. **Networks/Consortia:** Member of CAPCON. **Publications:** New in the Library, monthly. **Staff:** Victoria Harriston, Asst.Corp.Libn.

WASHINGTON (George) UNIVERSITY
See: George Washington University

★16765★
WASHINGTON HOSPITAL CENTER - MEDICAL LIBRARY (Med)
110 Irving St., N.W., Rm. 2A-21   Phone: (202) 541-6221
Washington, DC 20010   Marilyn Cook, Dir.
Founded: 1958. **Staff:** Prof 3; Other 4. **Subjects:** Medicine, nursing, allied health sciences. **Holdings:** 14,000 books; 16,000 bound periodical volumes; 1100 volumes on microfilm; 900 AV items; 1 file drawer of pamphlets. **Subscriptions:** 750 journals and other serials. **Services:** Interlibrary loans; library not open to public. **Automated Operations:** Computerized cataloging. **Computerized Information Services:** MEDLINE, DIALOG, OCLC, BRS. **Networks/Consortia:** Member of District of Columbia Health Sciences Information Network (DOCHSIN). **Publications:** News Log, monthly - for internal distribution only. **Staff:** Anne Swedenberg, Asst.Med.Libn.; Nancy L. Terry, Asst.Med.Libn.

★16766★
WASHINGTON HOSPITAL - HEALTH SCIENCES LIBRARY (Med)
155 Wilson Ave.   Phone: (412) 225-7000
Washington, PA 15301   Mary D. Leif, Libn.
Staff: Prof 1; Other 2. **Subjects:** Medicine, nursing, paramedicine. **Holdings:** 7500 books; 1500 bound periodical volumes; 1500 AV programs; 20 VF drawers of pamphlets and clippings. **Subscriptions:** 217 journals and other serials. **Services:** Interlibrary loans; copying; library open to public for reference use only. **Computerized Information Services:** MEDLINE. Performs searches on cost recovery basis. **Networks/Consortia:** Member of Southeast Pittsburgh Consortium.

★16767★
WASHINGTON & LEE UNIVERSITY - LAW LIBRARY (Law)
Lewis Hall   Phone: (703) 463-3157
Lexington, VA 24450   Sarah K. Wiant, Dir.
Staff: Prof 5; Other 9. **Subjects:** Law. **Special Collections:** Extensive early Virginia legal materials; annotated codes and statutes for all states, territories and possessions, federal government; records and briefs of U.S. Supreme Court, 4th U.S. Circuit Court of Appeals and Virginia Supreme Court; U.S. Government document depository; John W. Davis papers. **Holdings:** 221,709 volumes; microforms; 11,357 documents; 482 AV materials. **Subscriptions:** 4140 journals and other serials; 18 newspapers. **Services:** Interlibrary loans; copying; classroom videotaping; library open to public. **Automated Operations:** Computerized cataloging. **Computerized Information Services:** LEXIS, Westlaw, OCLC. **Publications:** Acquisitions List, monthly; Law Library Users Guide, annual; bibliographies on current legal issues. **Staff:** Terry Lee Beckwith, Assoc.Libn.; Jean Eisenhauer, Acq.Libn.; John P. Bissett, Cat.Libn.; Judy Stinson, Doc./Ref.Libn.

WASHINGTON LIBRARY FOR THE BLIND AND PHYSICALLY HANDICAPPED
See: Seattle Public Library

WASHINGTON (Mary Ball) MUSEUM AND LIBRARY, INC.
See: Mary Ball Washington Museum and Library, Inc.

★16768★
WASHINGTON (Mary) HOSPITAL - MEDICAL LIBRARY (Med)
2300 Fall Hill Ave.   Phone: (703) 373-4110
Fredericksburg, VA 22401   Joan S. Bulley, Med.Libn.
Staff: Prof 1; Other 1. **Subjects:** Medicine, nursing, biomedical sciences. **Holdings:** 500 books; 2200 bound periodical volumes. **Subscriptions:** 149 journals and other serials. **Services:** Interlibrary loans; copying; current awareness (limited); library open to public with restrictions. **Computerized Information Services:** MEDLARS. Performs searches on cost recovery basis.

WASHINGTON MEMORIAL LIBRARY
See: Middle Georgia Regional Library

★16769★
WASHINGTON METROPOLITAN AREA TRANSIT AUTHORITY - OFFICE OF PUBLIC AFFAIRS - LIBRARY (Trans)
600 Fifth St., N.W., Rm. 2G-02   Phone: (202) 637-1052
Washington, DC 20001   Michaela M. Cohan, Libn.
Founded: 1965. **Staff:** Prof 1. **Subjects:** Mass transit; transit in the Washington, DC area; environmental impact of rail transit; commuter railroads. **Special Collections:** WMATA documents (750 items); documentation on transit systems in U.S. and abroad. **Holdings:** 1100 books; 650 MF documents; 600 internal reports; 39 pamphlet boxes of materials from other transit systems; 23 pamphlet boxes of WMATA public hearings. **Subscriptions:** 18 journals and other serials. **Services:** Interlibrary loans;

copying; library open to public for reference use only.

★16770★
WASHINGTON MUTUAL SAVINGS BANK - INFORMATION CENTER & DIETRICH SCHMITZ MEMORIAL LIBRARY (Bus-Fin)
Box 834   Phone: (206) 464-4494
Seattle, WA 98111   Marcella C. Gaar, Info.Off.
Founded: 1970. **Staff:** Prof 1; Other 1. **Subjects:** Banking and finance, economics, investments, management, real estate. **Special Collections:** Seattle History (15 volumes); History of Washington State (6 volumes). **Holdings:** 2500 books; 300 reports; 10 VF drawers of annual reports; 6 VF drawers of ephemera and reports; 100 tapes and films; videotapes. **Subscriptions:** 210 journals and other serials; 12 newspapers. **Services:** Interlibrary loans; library open to public for reference use by request. **Computerized Information Services:** DIALOG. **Remarks:** Library is located at 1101 2nd Ave., Seattle, WA 98101.

★16771★
WASHINGTON NATIONAL INSURANCE COMPANY - INFORMATION RESOURCES CENTER (Bus-Fin)
1630 Chicago Ave.   Phone: (312) 866-3651
Evanston, IL 60201   Joy M. Blackburn, Libn.
Founded: 1956. **Staff:** Prof 2; Other 1. **Subjects:** Insurance - life, health, group; management; pensions. **Holdings:** 5800 books; 300 serials; 20 VF drawers; 750 reels of microfilm; 135 AV cassettes; 32 motion picture titles; company annual reports; Best's Insurance Reports, 1912 to present; proceedings of insurance associations. **Subscriptions:** 180 journals and other serials. **Services:** Interlibrary loans; SDI; center open for reference use only to qualified users. **Automated Operations:** Computerized cataloging, acquisitions, serials and circulation. **Computerized Information Services:** DIALOG, SDC, BRS, Dow Jones News/Retrieval, OCLC. **Networks/Consortia:** Member of ILLINET. **Publications:** Information Bulletin, daily; Acquisitions Bulletin, monthly - both distributed to all Home Office personnel; Handbook; Periodicals Holdings List; AV Cassette and Film Lists. **Staff:** Robin Manuel, Sr.Lib.Asst.

WASHINGTON NATL. RECORDS CENTER
See: U.S. Natl. Archives & Records Service

WASHINGTON NEWS BUREAU SOUND ARCHIVE
See: Broadcast Pioneers Library

★16772★
WASHINGTON PARK ZOO - LIBRARY (Sci-Tech)
4001 S.W. Canyon Rd.   Phone: (503) 226-1561
Portland, OR 97221   Warren J. Iliff, Dir.
Staff: Prof 1. **Subjects:** Zoology, animal husbandry, veterinary medicine, biology. **Special Collections:** Periodicals of zoos. **Holdings:** 500 books. **Subscriptions:** 100 journals and other serials. **Services:** Library open to public for reference use only. **Staff:** Janice Hixson, Animal Mgt.Sec.

★16773★
WASHINGTON POST - LIBRARY (Publ)
1150 15th St., N.W.   Phone: (202) 334-7341
Washington, DC 20071   William Hifner, Libn.
Founded: 1933. **Staff:** Prof 8; Other 16. **Subjects:** Newspaper reference topics. **Holdings:** 20,000 books; 6 million newspaper clippings; 30,000 pamphlets and documents; maps; pictures; microfilm. **Subscriptions:** 85 journals and other serials; 10 newspapers. **Services:** Interlibrary loans (fee); copying; library open to bonafide newspaper representatives only. **Computerized Information Services:** NEXIS.

★16774★
WASHINGTON PSYCHOANALYTIC SOCIETY - ERNEST E. HADLEY MEMORIAL LIBRARY (Med)
4925 MacArthur Blvd., N.W.   Phone: (202) 338-5453
Washington, DC 20007   Mary W. Allen, Libn.
Staff: Prof 1; Other 2. **Subjects:** Psychoanalysis, psychiatry, psychology, clinical and behavioral research. **Holdings:** 3200 books; 950 bound periodical volumes; 1200 unbound journals; 950 reprints. **Subscriptions:** 50 journals and other serials. **Services:** Interlibrary loans; copying; library open to professionals in psychoanalysis, psychiatry and psychology.

★16775★
WASHINGTON PUBLIC POWER SUPPLY SYSTEM - LIBRARY (Energy)
3000 George Washington Way
Box 968   Phone: (509) 372-6337
Richland, WA 99352   Betty J. Hodges, Lib.Spec.
Staff: 2. **Subjects:** Engineering standards, nuclear power, power

transmission. **Holdings:** 8600 books; 3800 standards; 2800 reports. **Subscriptions:** 174 journals and other serials. **Services:** Interlibrary loans; copying; library open to public with restrictions.

WASHINGTON STAR LIBRARY
See: District of Columbia Public Library - Washingtoniana Division

★16776★
WASHINGTON STATE ATTORNEY GENERAL'S LIBRARY (Law)
Temple of Justice   Phone: (206) 753-2681
Olympia, WA 98504   Phil Bunker, Law Libn.
Staff: Prof 1. **Subjects:** Law, consumer protection, crime prevention. **Special Collections:** Attorney General's formal and informal opinions written on the State Constitution with card index. **Holdings:** 11,500 books; 1620 bound periodical volumes; 145 boxes of Washington State Supreme Court briefs. **Subscriptions:** 25 journals and other serials; 12 newspapers. **Services:** Interlibrary loans; library not open to public. **Publications:** A.G. Reports; Annual Law Enforcement Salary Survey; miscellaneous brochures, irregular. **Remarks:** Offices also maintained in Seattle, Spokane and Tacoma. Figures include holdings for all locations.

★16777★
WASHINGTON STATE DEPARTMENT OF COMMERCE AND ECONOMIC DEVELOPMENT - TOURISM DEVELOPMENT DIVISION (Aud-Vis)
101 General Administration Bldg.   Phone: (206) 753-5600
Olympia, WA 98504   Leslie Sluman, Dir.
Founded: 1957. **Subjects:** Promotional material on Washington State. **Holdings:** Maps and brochures. **Services:** Materials are freely available for promotional use.

★16778★
WASHINGTON STATE DEPARTMENT OF ECOLOGY - TECHNICAL LIBRARY (Env-Cons)
PV-11   Phone: (206) 459-6150
Olympia, WA 98504
Staff: 1. **Subjects:** Water resources and quality, air quality, solid waste, environmental legislation, waste treatment, shorelines management. **Special Collections:** Publications of this department and predecessor agencies. **Holdings:** 4000 books; 12,000 other items. **Services:** Interlibrary loans; copying; library open to public. **Publications:** Selected New Additions to Ecology Library, bimonthly - for internal distribution only. **Remarks:** A Water Resources Information System is available for state-wide access and referral services. This library is a branch of the Washington State Library.

★16779★
WASHINGTON STATE DEPARTMENT OF NATURAL RESOURCES - DIVISION OF GEOLOGY AND EARTH RESOURCES - LIBRARY (Energy)
Bldg. One, Rowe 6
4224 6th Ave., S.E.   Phone: (206) 753-3647
Lacey, WA 98503   Connie J. Manson, Sr.Libn.
Founded: 1901. **Staff:** Prof 1. **Subjects:** Geology, mining, mineral resources. **Holdings:** 14,500 volumes; 12,000 state and federal documents; 500 technical reports; 1300 theses; 1300 U.S. Geological Survey topographic quadrangles of Washington; 1500 maps; vertical files. **Subscriptions:** 100 journals and other serials. **Services:** Copying; library open to public for reference use only. **Special Catalogs:** Subject bibliographies; Theses on Washington Geology, 1980 with updates. **Special Indexes:** Index to Geologic and Geophysical Mapping of Washington, 1984.

★16780★
WASHINGTON STATE DEPARTMENT OF REVENUE - RESEARCH AND INFORMATION DIVISION (Law; Bus-Fin)
414 Gen.Adm.Bldg. AX-02   Phone: (206) 753-5516
Olympia, WA 98504   Gary O'Neil, Dir. of Res.
Staff: 14. **Subjects:** Washington state and local government taxation and public finance, economic analysis and forecasting of revenues, analysis of tax legislation, dissemination of tax information. **Holdings:** Data series are maintained including collections and other statistics for state tax sources; publications and federal reports containing data on economic indicators. **Services:** Documents available to public for reference use only.

★16781★
WASHINGTON STATE DEPARTMENT OF TRANSPORTATION - LIBRARY (Trans; Plan)
Transportation Bldg.   Phone: (206) 753-2107
Olympia, WA 98504   Barbara Russo, Libn.
Founded: 1968. **Staff:** Prof 1; Other 2. **Subjects:** Transportation administration; highway transportation; public transit including the world's largest ferry system; rail and air transportation in the areas of planning,

design, construction, maintenance, operations and safety. **Special Collections:** Comprehensive plans for cities and counties of Washington. **Holdings:** 1075 books; 7555 reports; 1000 microfiche; 880 comprehensive plans. **Subscriptions:** 300 journals and other serials. **Services:** Interlibrary loans; copying; library open to public for reference use only. **Computerized Information Services:** DIALOG, SDC, OCLC. **Networks/Consortia:** Member of WLN. **Remarks:** This library is a branch of the Washington State Library.

★16782★
WASHINGTON STATE DEPARTMENT OF VETERANS AFFAIRS - STAFF & MEMBER LIBRARY (Med)
Washington Veterans' Home   Phone: (206) 876-7512
Retsil, WA 98378   Cherie J. Mastro, Staff Libn.
Founded: 1975. **Staff:** Prof 1; Other 3. **Subjects:** Geriatric medicine and nursing, long term care, autism, mental retardation, child welfare and abuse, gerontology. **Special Collections:** Aging (30 volumes); autism (38 volumes); mental retardation (35 volumes). **Holdings:** 4858 books; 1172 large print books. **Subscriptions:** 40 journals and other serials. **Services:** Interlibrary loans; library not open to public.

★16783★
WASHINGTON STATE ENERGY OFFICE - LIBRARY (Energy)
400 E. Union St.   Phone: (206) 754-0778
Olympia, WA 98504   Ginger Alexander, Libn.
Founded: 1978. **Staff:** Prof 1; Other 1. **Subjects:** Energy conservation, resources and planning; alternative sources of energy. **Holdings:** Figures not available. **Services:** Interlibrary loans; SDI (for state agencies); library open to public. **Networks/Consortia:** Member of WLN. **Publications:** Washington State Energy Use Profile, 1960-1981; Current Energy Research and Development in Washington State, 1981; WSEO Newsletter.

★16784★
WASHINGTON STATE HISTORICAL SOCIETY - LIBRARY (Hist)
315 N. Stadium Way   Phone: (206) 593-2830
Tacoma, WA 98403   Frank L. Green, Libn.
Founded: 1940. **Staff:** Prof 2. **Subjects:** Washington State history, Pacific Northwest history. **Special Collections:** Asahel Curtis negative collection. **Holdings:** 15,000 books; 200,000 pictures; 4000 manuscripts; 3000 pamphlets; 1017 reels of microfilm. **Subscriptions:** 35 journals and other serials. **Services:** Copying; research by mail; library open to public. **Staff:** Jeanne Engerman, Asst.Libn.

★16785★
WASHINGTON STATE LAW LIBRARY (Law)
Temple of Justice   Phone: (206) 753-6524
Olympia, WA 98504   C.E. Bolden, Dir.
Founded: 1920. **Staff:** Prof 4; Other 9. **Subjects:** Anglo-American law, government, jurisprudence. **Holdings:** 210,000 books; 10 VF drawers of pamphlets; 40 volumes of maps; 1400 volumes of appellate briefs. **Subscriptions:** 750 journals; 10 newspapers. **Services:** Interlibrary loans; copying; library open to public. **Automated Operations:** Computerized cataloging, acquisitions and serials. **Computerized Information Services:** DIALOG, Westlaw, SDC, Washington Legislative Information System, InstaCite. Performs searches free of charge and on cost recovery basis. Contact Person: Arthur J. Ruffier. **Networks/Consortia:** Member of WLN. **Publications:** Washington State legal documents - on exchange basis; Selected Recent Acquisitions List, bimonthly - free upon request. **Special Indexes:** Index to Washington State Attorney General Opinions. **Staff:** Arthur J. Ruffier, Ref.; James Tsao, Chf. of Tech.Serv.; Cora Morley Eklund, Cat.

★16786★
WASHINGTON STATE LIBRARY (Hist; Soc Sci)
State Library Bldg.   Phone: (206) 753-5592
Olympia, WA 98504   Roderick G. Swartz, State Libn.
Founded: 1853. **Staff:** Prof 47; Other 80. **Subjects:** Public administration, applied sciences, medicine and health, behavioral sciences, transportation, ecology, energy. **Special Collections:** Pacific Northwest History (15,100 items); Washington authors (5725 items). **Holdings:** 390,822 books; 63,000 bound periodical volumes; 818,450 U.S. documents; 209,100 Washington state documents; 144,900 other state documents; 29,600 reels of microfilm; 110,000 microfiche; 58 VF drawers; 4861 titles of films, video and audio cassettes, other AV materials. **Subscriptions:** 4835 journals and other serials; 172 newspapers. **Services:** Interlibrary loans; copying; library open to public. **Automated Operations:** Computerized cataloging, acquisitions and interlibrary loan search. **Computerized Information Services:** DIALOG, SDC, BRS, MEDLINE, Washington Legislative Information System. **Networks/Consortia:** Member of WLN; RLG. **Publications:** List of publications - available on request. **Special Catalogs:** Periodicals Holdings (microfiche); Washington State Publications (microfiche); AV Catalog (microfiche); Washington Authors

(pamphlet); Recent Books and Pamphlets About Washington (pamphlet); Washington Library Network Resource Directory (microfiche). **Staff:** Nancy Zussy, Dp. State Libn.Gene Bismuti, Chf., Info.Serv.Div.; O.F. Van Jepmond, Dir., WLN; Mary Moore, Chf., Lib.Plan.& Dev.Div.; Kristy Commes, Chf., Spec.Serv.Div.; Janet Blumberg, Chf., Tech.Serv.Div.

★16787★

WASHINGTON STATE LIBRARY - EASTERN STATE HOSPITAL LIBRARY (Med)

Box A   Phone: (509) 299-4276
Medical Lake, WA 99022   Mary E. Mims, Libn.
Founded: 1968. **Staff:** Prof 1; Other 1. **Subjects:** Psychiatry, nursing, medicine, mental health, social work. **Holdings:** 1535 books; 3 VF drawers. **Subscriptions:** 66 journals and other serials. **Services:** Interlibrary loans; copying; library open to public. **Networks/Consortia:** Member of WLN.

★16788★

WASHINGTON STATE LIBRARY - LAKELAND VILLAGE BRANCH LIBRARY (Med)

Box 200   Phone: (509) 299-5089
Medical Lake, WA 99022   Kathy Butler, Inst.Libn.
Founded: 1968. **Staff:** Prof 1; Other 1. **Subjects:** Mental retardation, medicine. **Holdings:** 997 books; 500 bound periodical volumes; 66 files of pamphlets. **Subscriptions:** 66 journals and other serials. **Services:** Interlibrary loans; copying; library open to public. **Networks/Consortia:** Member of WLN.

★16789★

WASHINGTON STATE LIBRARY - RAINIER SCHOOL STAFF LIBRARY (Med)
Rainier School
Box 600   Phone: (206) 829-1111
Buckley, WA 98321   Lynn Red, Module Supv.
Staff: Prof 1; Other 1. **Subjects:** Mental retardation, developmental psychology, institutionalization, deaf/blind/retarded handicapped. **Holdings:** 3000 books; 1596 bound and unbound periodical volumes; 100 boxes of pamphlets; 15 boxes of periodical, book and film catalogs in the field of retardation. **Subscriptions:** 163 journals and other serials; 30 newspapers. **Services:** Interlibrary loans; copying (limited); SDI; library open to public. **Computerized Information Services:** MEDLINE. **Networks/Consortia:** Member of WLN. **Publications:** Bibliographies, irregular.

★16790★

WASHINGTON STATE LIBRARY - WESTERN STATE HOSPITAL - STAFF LIBRARY (Med)

                                                      Phone: (206) 756-9635
Fort Steilacoom, WA 98494   Neal Van Der Voorn, Libn.
Founded: 1956. **Staff:** Prof 1; Other 2. **Subjects:** Psychiatry, clinical psychology, mental health, psychiatric nursing, psychiatric social work, medicine. **Holdings:** 5200 books; 375 tapes; 12 VF drawers of clippings, bibliographies and pamphlets; 3700 audiotapes. **Subscriptions:** 254 journals and other serials. **Services:** Interlibrary loans; copying; library open to public if material is not available elsewhere. **Networks/Consortia:** Member of WLN. **Publications:** In Touch, monthly - for hospital staff and residents. **Remarks:** The hospital's residents' collection contains an additional 11,000 volumes.

★16791★

WASHINGTON STATE OFFICE OF SECRETARY OF STATE - DIVISION OF ARCHIVES AND RECORD MANAGEMENT (Hist)
Archives & Records Ctr.
12th & Washington   Phone: (206) 753-5467
Olympia, WA 98504   Sidney McAlpin, State Archv.
Staff: Prof 7; Other 16. **Subjects:** State and local government records. **Special Collections:** Governors' Papers, 1854-1980; land records, 1858 to present; election returns; incorporation records, 1854 to present; Supreme Court records, 1854 to present; water rights, 1917 to present; legislative records, 1854 to present; state agency records, 1900 to present. **Holdings:** 6000 bound public records; 30,000 cubic feet of state and local archives; 120,000 cubic feet of records; 60,000 reels of microfilm. **Services:** Copying; research; library open to public. **Automated Operations:** Computerized cataloging. **Computerized Information Services:** Spindex Archival Control System (internal database). **Publications:** General Guide to the Washington State Archives; list of other publications - available on request. **Staff:** David Owens, Dp. State Archv.; Dwight Ellenwood, Rec.Anl.; Everett Evans, Microfilm Supv.; Wayne Lawson, Rec.Ctr.Mgr.; David Hastings, Asst. State Archv.; Pat Hopkins, Res.Archv.; Michael Saunders, Local Rec.; James Moore, Regional Archv.; Tim Eckert, Regional Archv.; Tim Fredrick, Regional Archv.; Jay Rae, Regional Archv.

★16792★

WASHINGTON STATE SCHOOL FOR THE DEAF - LEARNING RESOURCE CENTER (Educ)
611 Grand Blvd.   Phone: (206) 696-6223
Vancouver, WA 98661   James Randall, Dir.
Staff: Prof 5; Other 2. **Subjects:** Elementary and secondary education. **Special Collections:** Education for the deaf (professional books; 500 titles). **Holdings:** 10,672 books; 60 bound periodical volumes; VF drawers; 243 videotapes; 2853 filmstrips; 713 film loops; 211 microfiche; 27 charts. **Subscriptions:** 89 journals and other serials. **Services:** Interlibrary loans; copying; library open to those in the field of education of the deaf. **Staff:** Mary Moffitt, Libn.; Wanda Forcht, Libn.; Nancy Fahey, Instr. Media Spec.

★16793★

WASHINGTON STATE SUPERINTENDENT OF PUBLIC INSTRUCTION - RESOURCE INFORMATION CENTER (Educ)
Old Capitol Bldg., Fg-11   Phone: (206) 753-6731
Olympia, WA 98504   Mrs. Bobbie J. Patterson, Coord.
Staff: Prof 1; Other 1. **Subjects:** Education, curriculum materials, current trade books. **Holdings:** 200 books; complete ERIC collections. **Subscriptions:** 250 journals and other serials. **Services:** Interlibrary loans (limited); center open to teachers, school administrators, state agencies and colleges in Washington, for reference use only. **Computerized Information Services:** DIALOG, BRS. **Staff:** Shirley Dallas, Info.Spec.

★16794★

WASHINGTON STATE UNIVERSITY - EDUCATION LIBRARY (Educ)
130 Cleveland Hall   Phone: (509) 335-1591
Pullman, WA 99164-2110   Barbara Kemp, Hd., Hum./Soc.Pub.Serv.
Staff: Prof 2; Other 2. **Subjects:** Education. **Holdings:** 31,000 books; 9700 bound periodical volumes; 16 cabinets of ERIC microfiche; 4 cabinets of microfilm of journals; 12 VF cabinets; 2 cabinets of microfilm of monographs; 4 VF cabinets of tests; 850 masters' projects; 500 kits, tapes and records. **Subscriptions:** 825 journals and other serials. **Services:** Interlibrary loans (fee); copying; SDI; library open to public by registration and library card. **Automated Operations:** Computerized cataloging, acquisitions and circulation. **Computerized Information Services:** DIALOG; internal database. Performs searches on cost recovery basis. Contact Person: Carolyn Hook, 335-2691. **Networks/Consortia:** Member of WLN. **Publications:** List of recent acquisitions, monthly. **Staff:** Carolyn Hook, Ref./Coll.Dev.Libn.; Vicki Hohner, Supv.

WASHINGTON STATE UNIVERSITY - INTERCOLLEGIATE CENTER FOR NURSING EDUCATION
See: Intercollegiate Center for Nursing Education

★16795★

WASHINGTON STATE UNIVERSITY - MANUSCRIPTS, ARCHIVES, & SPECIAL COLLECTIONS (Hist; Hum)
                                                      Phone: (509) 335-6691
Pullman, WA 99164-5610   John F. Guido, Hd.
Staff: Prof 4; Other 5. **Subjects:** History - Pacific Northwest, agriculture, veterinary medicine; 20th-century literature; wildlife and recreation. **Special Collections:** Leonard and Virginia Woolf Library; Bloomsbury authors; Pacific Northwest Agricultural History Archives; Veterinary History; Pacific Northwest authors and presses; Pacific Northwest Composers; university archives; Angling. **Holdings:** 15,000 volumes; manuscripts; photographs; audiotapes; maps; broadsides; theses and dissertations. **Services:** Copying; collections.

★16796★

WASHINGTON STATE UNIVERSITY - OWEN SCIENCE AND ENGINEERING LIBRARY (Sci-Tech)
                                                      Phone: (509) 335-2671
Pullman, WA 99164-3200   Elizabeth P. Roberts, Hd.
Founded: 1892. **Staff:** Prof 5; Other 16. **Subjects:** Pure and applied sciences with special emphasis on agriculture, engineering, biological sciences, chemistry and mathematics. **Special Collections:** Mycology; plant pathology. **Holdings:** 361,559 books and bound periodical volumes; 28 cabinets of microfilm; 43 cabinets of microfiche. **Subscriptions:** 17,614 journals and other serials. **Services:** Interlibrary loans; copying; library open to public. **Automated Operations:** Computerized cataloging, acquisitions, circulation and bibliographic file. **Computerized Information Services:** DIALOG, SDC, BRS, MEDLARS, DOE/RECON. **Networks/Consortia:** Member of WLN; CRL. **Special Indexes:** Environmental Impact Statements Index; Index to Abstracts and Index Section; Palouse Bibliography (all print-outs). **Remarks:** Maintains an Agricultural Sciences Branch Library.

★16797★

WASHINGTON STATE UNIVERSITY - PRIMATE RESEARCH CENTER LIBRARY (Sci-Tech)

Pullman, WA 99164

Phone: (509) 335-1507
Francis A. Young, Dir.

Founded: 1957. **Staff:** Prof 1; Other 1. **Subjects:** Psychology, ophthalmology, optometry, neurophysiology, biophysics. **Holdings:** 1758 books; 2400 bound periodical volumes; 38 VF drawers of reprints and preprints. **Subscriptions:** 81 journals and other serials. **Services:** Library not open to public.

★16798★

WASHINGTON STATE UNIVERSITY - VETERINARY MEDICAL/PHARMACY LIBRARY (Med)

170 Wegner Hall
Pullman, WA 99164-6512

Phone: (509) 335-9556
Vicki F. Croft, Hd.

Staff: Prof 2; Other 3. **Subjects:** Veterinary and human medicine, pharmacy and pharmacology. **Holdings:** 14,000 books; 27,000 bound periodical volumes. **Subscriptions:** 1025 journals and other serials. **Services:** Interlibrary loans; copying; library open to public. **Automated Operations:** Computerized cataloging, acquisitions and circulation. **Computerized Information Services:** DIALOG, SDC, BRS, NLM. **Networks/Consortia:** Member of WLN; CLASS. **Staff:** Deborah Ludwig, Libn.; Kathleen Schmidt, Ser.Supv.; Elizabeth Edwards, Circ.Supv.

WASHINGTON STATE UNIVERSITY - WASHINGTON ARCHAEOLOGICAL RESEARCH CENTER

See: Washington Archaeological Research Center

★16799★

WASHINGTON THEOLOGICAL UNION - LIBRARY (Rel-Theol)

9001 New Hampshire Ave.
Silver Spring, MD 20903-3699

Phone: (301) 439-0551
Carol R. Lange, Libn.

Staff: Prof 2; Other 4. **Subjects:** Theology. **Special Collections:** Franciscana; Carmelitana; Augustiniana. **Holdings:** 131,000 volumes. **Subscriptions:** 330 journals and other serials. **Services:** Interlibrary loans; copying; library open to public. **Networks/Consortia:** Member of Washington Theological Consortium. **Publications:** Consortium Guide to Library Resources, updated as needed.

★16800★

WASHINGTON UNIVERSITY - ART & ARCHITECTURE LIBRARY (Art)

Steinberg Hall
Box 1061
St. Louis, MO 63130

Phone: (314) 889-5268
Imre Meszaros, Hd., Hum.Serv.

Founded: 1879. **Staff:** Prof 1; Other 4. **Subjects:** Art history, classical archeology, architecture, costume design, fine art techniques, East Asian art, building technology, urban planning and design, landscape architecture. **Special Collections:** East Asian Collection (1361 volumes on Oriental art); Bryce Collection (576 volumes on architectural history); Sorger Collection (243 volumes on historical costume; 2 VF drawers of plates); Eames and Young Collection (273 volumes on architectural history); rare books (2471 volumes). **Holdings:** 63,332 books and bound periodical volumes; 52 VF drawers of pamphlets and clippings. **Subscriptions:** 457 journals and other serials. **Services:** Interlibrary loans; copying; library open to public for reference use only. **Automated Operations:** Computerized cataloging. **Computerized Information Services:** BRS, DIALOG, SDC. **Networks/Consortia:** Member of St. Louis Regional Library Network. **Special Catalogs:** Washington University Art and Architecture Library List of Serials. **Staff:** Julie Arnott, Supv.

★16801★

WASHINGTON UNIVERSITY - BIOLOGY LIBRARY (Sci-Tech)

Life Sciences Bldg.
St. Louis, MO 63130

Phone: (314) 889-5405
Betty S. Galyon, Libn.

Staff: 3. **Subjects:** Genetics, mycology, embryology, neurosciences, molecular biology, botany. **Holdings:** 40,497 books and bound periodical volumes. **Subscriptions:** 400 journals and other serials. **Services:** Interlibrary loans; copying; library open to public. **Automated Operations:** Computerized cataloging. **Computerized Information Services:** OCLC. **Publications:** Monthly acquisitions list - sent to other science libraries. **Staff:** Charlotte Ellis, Sr.Asst.; Cecile Guenther, Circ.Reserve Asst.

★16802★

WASHINGTON UNIVERSITY - BUSINESS ADMINISTRATION LIBRARY (Bus-Fin)

School of Business Adm., Prince Hall
St. Louis, MO 63130

Phone: (314) 889-6334
Magda Buday, Bus.Libn.

Founded: 1925. **Staff:** Prof 2; Other 2. **Subjects:** Accounting, personnel, advertising, marketing, management, finance, production, administration, business and government, economics, organization psychology, quantitative business analysis. **Holdings:** 19,090 books; 190 dissertations; 201,766 disclosures on microfiche. **Subscriptions:** 200 journals and other serials. **Services:** Interlibrary loans; copying; library open to public for reference use only.

★16803★

WASHINGTON UNIVERSITY - CENTER FOR THE STUDY OF DATA PROCESSING - CSDP LIBRARY (Comp Sci)

Cupples I, Rm. 15
Skinker & Lindell Blvds.
St. Louis, MO 63130

Phone: (314) 889-5366
Barbara Luszczynska, Lib.Assoc.

Staff: Prof 1; Other 6. **Subjects:** Data processing, programming languages, systems analysis and design, software engineering, communications. **Holdings:** 3125 books; 415 bound periodical volumes; 51 staff seminar notebooks; 1 vertical file drawer of miscellaneous materials; 78 slides of computer-generated graphics. **Subscriptions:** 196 journals and other serials; 9 newspapers. **Services:** Interlibrary loans; library open to public for reference use only. **Automated Operations:** Computerized cataloging. **Publications:** Library Update, bimonthly.

★16804★

WASHINGTON UNIVERSITY - CHEMISTRY LIBRARY (Sci-Tech)

Louderman Hall
St. Louis, MO 63130

Phone: (314) 889-6591
Eileen Horn, Chem.Libn.

Founded: 1905. **Staff:** 2. **Subjects:** Chemistry - organic, inorganic, physical, biophysical; spectroscopy. **Holdings:** 24,384 books and bound periodical volumes; 327 theses; 454 microfiche. **Subscriptions:** 265 journals and other serials. **Services:** Interlibrary loans; copying; library open to public with restrictions. **Computerized Information Services:** DIALOG, SDC, BRS, NIH-EPA Chemical Information System, CAS Online. Performs searches on cost recovery basis plus surcharge.

★16805★

WASHINGTON UNIVERSITY - COMPUTER LABORATORIES REFERENCE ROOM (Comp Sci; Med)

700 S. Euclid Ave.
St. Louis, MO 63110

Phone: (314) 362-2275
Monica Shieh, Res.Libn.

Founded: 1968. **Staff:** Prof 1. **Subjects:** Computer science, biomedical engineering, electrical engineering, mathematics. **Holdings:** 2200 books; 754 bound periodical volumes. **Subscriptions:** 90 journals and other serials. **Services:** Interlibrary loans; copying; library open to public for reference use only.

★16806★

WASHINGTON UNIVERSITY - DENTISTRY LIBRARY (Med)

School of Dental Medicine
4559 Scott Ave.
St. Louis, MO 63110

Phone: (314) 454-0385
Carol Murray, Libn.

Founded: 1928. **Staff:** Prof 2; Other 3. **Subjects:** Dentistry and related subjects, basic sciences. **Special Collections:** McKellop's Collection (historical dental literature). **Holdings:** 17,000 volumes. **Subscriptions:** 300 journals and other serials. **Services:** Interlibrary loans; library open to public for reference use only.

★16807★

WASHINGTON UNIVERSITY - DEPARTMENT OF SPECIAL COLLECTIONS (Rare Book; Hum)

Olin Library
St. Louis, MO 63130

Phone: (314) 889-5495
Holly Hall, Hd.

Founded: 1962. **Staff:** Prof 2; Other 3. **Subjects:** 19th- and 20th-century English and American literature; history of printing and book arts; semeiology; Americana; St. Louis political and social welfare history; 16th-century French literature, especially Pierre de Ronsard. **Special Collections:** Contemporary American and British writers; distinguished faculty and alumni papers; university records. **Holdings:** 36,384 books and bound periodical volumes; 5000 ephemera; 250,000 manuscript items; 3000 cubic feet of archival records. **Subscriptions:** 50 journals and other serials. **Services:** Copying; collections open to public with restrictions. **Automated Operations:** Computerized cataloging. **Publications:** Occasional exhibit catalogs. **Special Catalogs:** Special subject area catalogs (card). **Special Indexes:** Manuscript index (card); registers and special finding aids to manuscript collections and archives. **Staff:** Timothy Murray, Cur., Mss.

★16808★

WASHINGTON UNIVERSITY - DEPARTMENT OF TECHNOLOGY AND HUMAN AFFAIRS - LIBRARY (Sci-Tech)

Box 1106
St. Louis, MO 63130

Phone: (314) 889-5494
Eric P. Rusten, Staff Assoc.

Staff: Prof 2. **Subjects:** Appropriate technology, international development, energy, environmental quality, educational communications, remote sensing. **Special Collections:** International development (1100 documents); remote sensing of natural resources (2900 documents); science, technology and society (700 documents); Center for Development Technology reports (complete set, 175 documents). **Holdings:** 11,000 books; 5000 microfiche; 3000 periodical and newspaper articles; 2000 technical reports. **Subscriptions:** 70 journals and other serials. **Services:** Interlibrary loans; library open to public with restrictions. **Automated Operations:** Computerized cataloging. **Special Indexes:** KWIC Subject Listing of Documents in Collection.

★16809★
WASHINGTON UNIVERSITY - EARTH AND PLANETARY SCIENCES LIBRARY (Sci-Tech)
Wilson Hall
St. Louis, MO 63130
Phone: (314) 889-5406
Deborah Hartwig, Libn.
Staff: Prof 1. **Subjects:** Geology, geophysics, geochemistry, mineralogy, geomorphology, petrology, sedimentation, structural geology, paleontology, planetary science. **Special Collections:** State Geological Survey Publications. **Holdings:** 25,852 books and bound periodical volumes; 8078 documents; 947 reprints; 392 pamphlets; 76,716 maps. **Subscriptions:** 249 journals and other serials. **Services:** Interlibrary loans; copying; library open to qualified users for reference. **Automated Operations:** Computerized cataloging and acquisitions. **Publications:** Monthly acquisitions list.

★16810★
WASHINGTON UNIVERSITY - EAST ASIAN LIBRARY (Area-Ethnic; Hum)
Box 1061
St. Louis, MO 63130
Phone: (314) 889-5155
Sachiko Morrell, Libn.
Founded: 1964. **Staff:** Prof 1; Other 1. **Subjects:** East Asia - language and literature, history, philosophy and religion, art history, social science, performing arts. **Special Collections:** Rare book collection; Robert S. Elegant Collection (4 cabinets of clippings, magazines, news releases during Chinese cultural revolution). **Holdings:** 88,350 books; 7840 bound periodical volumes; 134 boxes of microfilm; 1 cabinet of pamphlets; Taiwan Government documents. **Subscriptions:** 181 journals and other serials; 11 newspapers. **Services:** Interlibrary loans; copying; library open to public. **Publications:** Guide to Library Resources for Chinese Studies, 1978; Resource Sources for Chinese and Japanese Studies, 1976; List of Serials related to Chinese and Japanese Studies, 1973.

★16811★
WASHINGTON UNIVERSITY - EDWARD MALLINCKRODT INSTITUTE OF RADIOLOGY LIBRARY (Med)
510 S. Kingshighway Blvd.
St. Louis, MO 63110
Phone: (314) 362-2978
Harriet Fieweger, Libn./Sec.
Staff: 1. **Subjects:** Diagnostic and therapeutic radiology. **Holdings:** 849 books; 1017 bound periodical volumes; reprints and reports. **Subscriptions:** 41 journals and other serials. **Services:** Interlibrary loans; copying; library open to public for reference use only.

★16812★
WASHINGTON UNIVERSITY - GAYLORD MUSIC LIBRARY (Mus)
6500 Forsyth
St. Louis, MO 63130
Phone: (314) 889-5560
Susanne Bell, Music Libn.
Founded: 1947. **Staff:** Prof 1; Other 4. **Subjects:** Music. **Special Collections:** Sheet Music (51,000 pieces). **Holdings:** 66,955 books, bound periodical volumes and scores; 12,449 phonograph records; 4114 tapes. **Subscriptions:** 200 journals and other serials. **Services:** Interlibrary loans; copying; library open to visiting scholars for research. **Special Indexes:** Title index to popular sheet music collection (cards); Composer Index to vocal and piano sheet music collection (cards).

★16813★
WASHINGTON UNIVERSITY - GEORGE WARREN BROWN SCHOOL OF SOCIAL WORK - LIBRARY & LEARNING RESOURCES CENTER (Soc Sci)
Box 1196
St. Louis, MO 63130
Phone: (314) 889-6633
Michael E. Powell, Dir.
Staff: Prof 1; Other 1. **Subjects:** Social work, family therapy, child welfare. **Holdings:** 32,525 books and bound periodical volumes; 2000 government documents; 1525 theses/dissertations; 4122 pamphlets; 112 reels of microfilm; 11 films, filmstrips, slides; 321 recording discs and tapes. **Subscriptions:** 530 journals and other serials; 10 newspapers. **Services:** Interlibrary loans; copying; library open to those with library cards. **Publications:** Acquisitions list, quarterly.

★16814★
WASHINGTON UNIVERSITY - MATHEMATICS LIBRARY (Sci-Tech)
Cupples I, Rm. 15
Skinker & Lindell Blvds.
St. Louis, MO 63130
Phone: (314) 889-5366
Barbara Luszczynska, Lib.Assoc.
Staff: Prof 1. **Subjects:** Advanced mathematics. **Holdings:** 337 books; 2640 bound periodical volumes. **Subscriptions:** 83 journals and other serials. **Services:** Interlibrary loans; library open to public for reference use only.

★16815★
WASHINGTON UNIVERSITY - PFEIFFER PHYSICS LIBRARY (Sci-Tech)
Lindell & Skinker Blvds.
St. Louis, MO 63130
Phone: (314) 889-6215
B.M. Eickhoff, Physics Libn.
Staff: 2. **Subjects:** Astrophysics, atomic and nuclear physics, solid state physics, high energy particles, low temperature physics, cosmic rays, quantum mechanics, physical electronics, plasma physics, chemical physics, mathematics, mathematical physics, electronics, electrical and communications engineering, science history, astronomy, space physics. **Holdings:** 26,335 books and bound periodical volumes. **Subscriptions:** 197 journals. **Services:** Interlibrary loans; copying; library open to public for reference use only.

★16816★
WASHINGTON UNIVERSITY - REGIONAL PLANETARY IMAGE FACILITY - LIBRARY (Sci-Tech)
Dept. of Earth & Planetary Sciences
Campus Box 1169
St. Louis, MO 63130
Phone: (314) 889-5679
Betty L. Weiss, Libn./Data Mgr.
Staff: Prof 1. **Subjects:** Planetary geology, space exploration missions, remote sensing, image processing. **Special Collections:** Space mission photographs and videodiscs. **Holdings:** 700 books; 1200 digital tapes; microfiche sets. **Subscriptions:** 15 journals and other serials. **Services:** Copying; library open to public by appointment. **Computerized Information Services:** Better Image Retrieval Programs - BIRP (internal database). Contact Person: Dr. Edward Guinness.

★16817★
WASHINGTON UNIVERSITY - SCHOOL OF LAW - FREUND LAW LIBRARY (Law)
Mudd Bldg.
Box 1120
St. Louis, MO 63130
Phone: (314) 889-6459
Bernard D. Reams, Jr., Law Libn.
Staff: Prof 6; Other 9. **Subjects:** Law, taxation, urban affairs, international law. **Special Collections:** U.S. Supreme Court and Missouri Supreme Court Briefs; Ashman British Collection; Neuhoff Rare Book Collection; U.S. and Missouri documents depository. **Holdings:** 284,914 volumes; 325,792 microfiche; 54 microcards; 5222 reels of microfilm; 304 cassette tapes. **Subscriptions:** 2432 journals and other serials; 14 newspapers. **Services:** Interlibrary loans; copying; library open to members of the Law Library Association. **Automated Operations:** Computerized cataloging. **Computerized Information Services:** LEXIS, Westlaw, Commerce Clearing House Electronic Legislative Search System (ELSS). Performs searches on cost recovery basis. Contact Person: Margaret McDermott. **Networks/ Consortia:** Member of St. Louis Regional Library Network; Mid-America Law School Library Consortium. **Publications:** Select acquisitions list, quarterly - by request; bi-annual bibliography series - price by request. **Special Indexes:** Index to legislative histories (card). **Staff:** James M. Murray, Assoc. Law Libn.; Margaret Goldblatt, Ser.Libn.; Carol J. Gray, Doc.Libn.; Margaret McDermott, Ref./Rd.Serv.Libn.; Sue Burkholder, Cat.Libn.

WASHINGTON UNIVERSITY - SCHOOL OF MEDICINE - DEPARTMENT OF PEDIATRICS - ST. LOUIS CHILDREN'S HOSPITAL
See: St. Louis Children's Hospital

★16818★
WASHINGTON UNIVERSITY - SCHOOL OF MEDICINE - DEPARTMENT OF PSYCHIATRY LIBRARY (Med)
4940 Audubon Ave.
St. Louis, MO 63110
Phone: (314) 362-2454
Founded: 1963. **Staff:** Prof 1; Other 1. **Subjects:** Psychiatry, biochemistry, neurochemical pharmacology. **Holdings:** 1000 books; 20,000 bound periodical volumes; 3 VF drawers of department reprints. **Subscriptions:** 99 journals and other serials. **Services:** Library not open to public.

★16819★
WASHINGTON UNIVERSITY - SCHOOL OF MEDICINE LIBRARY (Med)
660 S. Euclid Ave.
St. Louis, MO 63110
Phone: (314) 362-7080
Prof. Susan Y. Crawford, Dir.
Founded: 1910. **Staff:** Prof 17; Other 32. **Subjects:** Medicine. **Special**

Collections: Becker Ophthalmological Collection, C.I.D. - Max A. Goldstein Collection in Speech and Hearing (both printed); William Beaumont, Joseph Erlanger, Leo Loeb, Evarts Graham, Helen Treadway Graham, E.V. Cowdry, Wendell Scott, school's early records (all manuscripts). **Holdings:** 75,000 books; 119,000 bound periodical volumes; 2500 feet of archives; 18,000 nonprint items. **Subscriptions:** 2410 journals and other serials. **Services:** Interlibrary loans; copying; clinical librarianship; library open to public. **Automated Operations:** Computerized cataloging, acquisitions, serials and circulation. **Computerized Information Services:** DIALOG, OCLC, BRS, SDC, NLM, PHILSOM; BACS (internal database); computer-assisted instruction. **Networks/Consortia:** Member of Midcontinental Regional Medical Library Program; St. Louis Regional Library Network. **Publications:** Library Guide, annual; Selection and Acquisitions Manual; Archives Manual; Library Newsletter; Annual Report. **Staff:** Cheryl Reuby, Hd., Tech.Serv.; Barbara Halbrook, Assoc.Dir.; Elizabeth Kelly, Hd., Access Serv.; Christopher Hoolihan, Rare Bk.Libn.; Millard F. Johnson, Jr., Res.Assoc.; Paul Anderson, Archv.

WASHINGTON'S HEADQUARTERS STATE HISTORIC SITE
See: New York State Bureau of Historic Sites

★16820★
WASHOE COUNTY LAW LIBRARY (Law)
Court House
Box 11130   Phone: (702) 785-4188
Reno, NV 89520   Sandra Marz, Law Lib.Dir.
Founded: 1915. **Staff:** Prof 2; Other 4. **Subjects:** Law. **Special Collections:** Nevada gambling, water rights and Indian law. **Holdings:** 29,245 books; 2514 bound periodical volumes, 1274 volumes in microform; 79 cassettes. **Subscriptions:** 224 periodicals. **Services:** Interlibrary loans; copying; library open to public for reference use only. **Automated Operations:** Computerized cataloging, acquisitions and serials. **Computerized Information Services:** Westlaw, DIALOG, RLIN; internal database. **Networks/Consortia:** Member of LAWNET; CLASS. **Publications:** Acquisitions list, monthly. **Staff:** Wilma Smith, Asst.Libn.

★16821★
WASHOE MEDICAL CENTER - MEDICAL LIBRARY (Med)
77 Pringle Way   Phone: (702) 785-5693
Reno, NV 89520   Sherry A. McGee, Dir., Med.Lib.
Founded: 1941. **Staff:** Prof 1; Other 1. **Subjects:** Medicine, nursing, allied health sciences. **Holdings:** 1574 books; 4339 bound periodical volumes. **Subscriptions:** 195 journals and other serials. **Services:** Interlibrary loans; copying; library open to public for reference use only. **Computerized Information Services:** MEDLARS. Performs searches on cost recovery basis. **Networks/Consortia:** Member of Northern California and Nevada Medical Library Group. **Publications:** Medical Library News, quarterly - to hospital staff, local libraries and other interested persons.

★16822★
WASHTENAW COMMUNITY COLLEGE - LEARNING RESOURCE CENTER - SPECIAL COLLECTIONS (Educ)
4800 Huron River Dr.   Phone: (313) 973-3300
Ann Arbor, MI 48106   Adella B. Scott, Dir. of LRC
Founded: 1965. **Special Collections:** Women in Higher Education; Washtenaw County Genealogy Collection; college archives. **Services:** Interlibrary loans; copying; collections open to public. **Automated Operations:** Computerized cataloging. **Computerized Information Services:** DIALOG. **Networks/Consortia:** Member of Michigan Library Consortium (MLC); Washtenaw-Livingston Library Network. **Publications:** Acquisitions List.

★16823★
WASHTENAW COUNTY METROPOLITAN PLANNING COMMISSION - LIBRARY (Plan)
Court House, Rm. 305
Box 8645   Phone: (313) 994-2435
Ann Arbor, MI 48107   Eve Wuttke, Asst.Dir.
Founded: 1949. **Staff:** 1. **Subjects:** Planning, census of population and housing, recreation, statistics, transportation, water sewage and drainage, conservation, urban growth and renewal, zoning ordinances, land use plans, development plans, subdivision ordinances. **Holdings:** 5000 books and bound periodical volumes. **Subscriptions:** 15 journals and other serials. **Services:** Copying; library open to public with permission.

WASON COLLECTION
See: Cornell University

WASSERMAN PUBLIC AFFAIRS LIBRARY
See: University of Texas, Austin

WATAUGA COUNTY HOSPITAL
See: Northwest Area Health Education Center - NW AHEC Library (Boone, NC)

★16824★
WATER INFORMATION CENTER, INC. (Env-Cons)
The North Shore Atrium
6800 Jericho Tpke.   Phone: (516) 921-7690
Syosset, NY 11791   Fred Troise, Vice-Pres.
Founded: 1959. **Subjects:** Ground water, water supply, conservation, pollution, chemistry of water, water laws. **Holdings:** 500 books; 2000 bound periodical volumes; 3000 technical reports. **Subscriptions:** 40 journals and other serials. **Services:** Answers general and semi-technical questions, especially on ground water, by phone or mail as a free public service; center not open to general public. **Publications:** Water Newsletter, semimonthly; Ground Water Newsletter, semimonthly; International Water Report, quarterly - available by subscription; Bibliographies: Water Publications of State Agencies; Geraghty & Miller's Groundwater Bibliography; The Water Atlas of the United States; Climates of the States; Ground Water Pollution in Europe; Water Resources of the World; Sources of Information in Water Resources. **Remarks:** Associated with Geraghty & Miller, Inc., groundwater consultants.

★16825★
WATER POLLUTION CONTROL FEDERATION - LIBRARY (Env-Cons)
2626 Pennsylvania Ave., N.W.   Phone: (202) 337-2500
Washington, DC 20037   Berinda J. Ross, Asst.Mgr., Tech.Serv.
Founded: 1928. **Staff:** Prof 1. **Subjects:** Water pollution control, water supply and resources, wastewater treatment and disposal, sludge treatment and disposal, collection systems, environmental engineering. **Holdings:** 2000 books; 300 bound periodical volumes. **Subscriptions:** 35 journals and other serials. **Services:** Interlibrary loans; copying; library open to public for reference use only. **Publications:** Journal WPCF; newsletters; Manuals of Practice; Special Publications; Surveys.

★16826★
WATER QUALITY ASSOCIATION - RESEARCH COUNCIL LIBRARY (Sci-Tech)
4151 Naperville Rd.   Phone: (312) 369-1600
Lisle, IL 60532   Douglas R. Oberhamer, Exec.Dir.
Staff: 15. **Subjects:** Water quality, water conditioning, home water supply, water usage, industrial water conditioning, water softening, water pollution, geographic water data. **Special Collections:** U.S. Government publications on water quality and usage; water conditioning industry publications; International Water Quality Symposia Proceedings, 1965-1968, 1970, 1972. **Holdings:** 1000 books; industry papers; manuscripts; clippings; committee reports and pamphlets. **Subscriptions:** 40 journals and other serials. **Services:** Copying; library open to public for reference use only. **Formerly:** Located in Lombard, IL. **Staff:** Maureen Hertel, Adm.Mgr.

WATER AND SANITATION FOR HEALTH PROJECT
See: U.S. Agency for International Development

★16827★
WATERBURY AMERICAN-REPUBLICAN - LIBRARY (Publ)
389 Meadow St.   Phone: (203) 574-3636
Waterbury, CT 06722   Mary B. Fuller, Libn.
Founded: 1926. **Staff:** Prof 1; Other 1. **Subjects:** Newspaper reference topics. **Holdings:** 1000 books; clippings; photographs and negatives; newspapers on microfilm, 1884 to present. **Subscriptions:** 25 newspapers. **Services:** Copying; library open to public with restrictions.

WATERBURY BAR LIBRARY
See: Connecticut State Library - Law Library at Waterbury

★16828★
WATERBURY HOSPITAL HEALTH CENTER - HEALTH CENTER LIBRARY (Med)
64 Robbins St.   Phone: (203) 573-6136
Waterbury, CT 06720   Mrs. M.F. Carmichael, Lib.Dir.
Staff: Prof 2; Other 1. **Subjects:** Medicine, nursing and allied health sciences. **Holdings:** 3045 books; 6300 bound periodical volumes; 4 VF drawers of clippings, pamphlets, bibliographies; 18 videotapes; 5 drawers of audiotapes. **Subscriptions:** 270 journals and other serials. **Services:** Interlibrary loans; copying; SDI; library open to public with permission of librarian. **Computerized Information Services:** MEDLARS. **Networks/Consortia:** Member of Northwestern Connecticut Health Science Library Consortium.

Staff: Joan Ruszkowski, Asst.Libn.

★16829★
WATERBURY STATE TECHNICAL COLLEGE - HELEN HAHLO LIBRARY (Sci-Tech)
1460 W. Main St.   Phone: (203) 575-8106
Waterbury, CT 06708   John Kiernan, Jr., Hd.Libn.
Founded: 1964. **Staff:** Prof 2; Other 1. **Subjects:** Electrical technology, data processing, chemical technology, mechanics, metallurgy, tools and manufacturing, industrial management. **Holdings:** 8836 books; 80 folders of pamphlets; 251 reels of microfilm. **Subscriptions:** 94 journals and other serials; 5 newspapers. **Services:** Interlibrary loans; copying; library open to public with restrictions. **Networks/Consortia:** Member of Region One Cooperating Libraries Service Unit for Northwestern Connecticut. **Staff:** Denise Ivain, Lib.Asst.

★16830★
WATERFORD HOSPITAL - HEALTH SERVICES LIBRARY (Med)
Waterford Bridge Rd.   Phone: (709) 364-0269
St. John's, NF, Canada A1E 4J8   Maisie Young, Libn.
Founded: 1969. **Staff:** 1. **Subjects:** Psychiatry, nursing, medicine, social work, psychology, pharmacology. **Holdings:** 2300 books; unbound periodicals; annual reports; manuscripts; pamphlets; AV items. **Subscriptions:** 104 journals and other serials. **Services:** Interlibrary loans; copying; library open to public by request.

★16831★
WATERLOO HISTORICAL SOCIETY - LIBRARY (Hist)
Box 552, Sta. C   Phone: (519) 743-0271
Kitchener, ON, Canada N2G 4A2   Erich Schultz, Pres.
Founded: 1912. **Subjects:** Waterloo County history. **Special Collections:** Early issues of Waterloo County newspapers. **Holdings:** Figures not available. **Services:** Copying; library open to public. **Publications:** Waterloo Historical Society Annual Volume - available with membership. **Special Indexes:** Index to annual volumes.

★16832★
WATERLOO LIBRARY AND HISTORICAL SOCIETY (Hist)†
31 E. Williams St.   Phone: (315) 539-3313
Waterloo, NY 13165   Elizabeth A. Stetz, Libn.
Founded: 1875. **Staff:** Prof 1; Other 1. **Subjects:** Local history, antiques. **Holdings:** 20,000 books; 800 bound periodical volumes; pictures; maps; diaries; letters; organization minute books; 1000 town and county records. **Subscriptions:** 50 journals and other serials. **Services:** Interlibrary loans (limited); library open to public with permission of librarian. **Networks/Consortia:** Member of Finger Lakes Library System.

★16833★
WATERS ASSOCIATES INC. - INFORMATION RESOURCE CENTER (Sci-Tech)
Maple St.   Phone: (617) 478-2000
Milford, MA 01757   Carla J. Clayton, Mgr., Tech.Info.Serv.
Founded: 1978. **Staff:** Prof 1; Other 1. **Subjects:** Chemistry, engineering. **Special Collections:** High performance liquid chromatography. **Holdings:** 800 books; 400 bound periodical volumes. **Subscriptions:** 120 journals and other serials. **Services:** Interlibrary loans; copying; center open to public with restrictions. **Automated Operations:** Computerized cataloging. **Computerized Information Services:** DIALOG, BRS, OCLC, NEXIS, Pergamon InfoLine Ltd. **Networks/Consortia:** Member of NELINET.

★16834★
WATERTOWN HISTORICAL SOCIETY - ARCHIVES
919 Charles St.
Watertown, WI 53094
Subjects: First kindergarten, Margarethe Meyer Schurz, Carl Schurz, Octagon houses, local history. **Holdings:** 100 volumes; photographs; clippings. **Remarks:** Presently inactive.

★16835★
WATERTOWN HISTORICAL SOCIETY INC. - LIBRARY (Hist)
22 DeForest St.
Oakville, CT 06779   Florence Crowell, Cur.
Staff: Prof 1; Other 1. **Subjects:** Genealogy, local history, state history, local authors. **Special Collections:** Collection of diaries of town's residents; state manuals; town reports; files on Watertown's history. **Holdings:** 1200 books; 40 bound periodical volumes; Town Times on microfilm, 1947-1975. **Services:** Copying; library open to public by appointment. **Automated Operations:** Computerized acquisitions. **Staff:** John F. Pillis, Pres.

★16836★
WATERVILLE HISTORICAL SOCIETY - LIBRARY AND ARCHIVES (Hist)
64 Silver St.   Phone: (207) 872-9439
Waterville, ME 04901
Founded: 1903. **Subjects:** History - local, regional, state; Civil War. **Special Collections:** Diaries, 1753-1955; early textbooks (200); 19th-century apothecary. **Holdings:** 1520 books; local newspaper, 1853-1906; early account books; old documents and letters; maps; old photographs. **Services:** Archives open to public with restrictions. **Also Known As:** Redington Museum.

★16837★
WATKINS WOOLEN MILL STATE HISTORIC SITE - RESEARCH LIBRARY (Hist)*
Rte. 2, Box 270M   Phone: (816) 296-3357
Lawson, MO 64062   Ann M. Matthews, Historic Site Adm.
Staff: Prof 2; Other 3. **Subjects:** 19th-century textile industry and farming. **Holdings:** 500 books; 2000 bound periodical volumes; 5000 pamphlets and letters. **Services:** Library open to public for reference use only on request. **Remarks:** Maintained by Missouri State Division of Parks & Historic Preservation.

WATKINSON LIBRARY
See: Trinity College

WATSON (Arthur R.) LIBRARY
See: Baltimore Zoo - Arthur R. Watson Library

★16838★
WATSON CLINIC - MEDICAL LIBRARY (Med)
Box 1429   Phone: (813) 687-4000
Lakeland, FL 33802   Cheryl Dee, Med.Libn.
Founded: 1945. **Staff:** Prof 1; Other 2. **Subjects:** Medicine. **Holdings:** 1500 books; 3000 bound periodical volumes; 550 cassettes. **Subscriptions:** 250 journals and other serials. **Services:** Interlibrary loans; copying; library open to public by permission.

WATSON (Eugene P.) LIBRARY
See: Northwestern State University of Louisiana - Eugene P. Watson Library

WATSON (John Brown) MEMORIAL LIBRARY
See: University of Arkansas, Pine Bluff - John Brown Watson Memorial Library

WATSON LIBRARY
See: University of Kansas

WATSON (Thomas J.) LIBRARY
See: Metropolitan Museum of Art - Thomas J. Watson Library

WATSON (Thomas J.) LIBRARY OF BUSINESS AND ECONOMICS
See: Columbia University - Thomas J. Watson Library of Business and Economics

WATSON (Thomas J.) RESEARCH CENTER LIBRARY
See: IBM Corporation - Thomas J. Watson Research Center Library

WATSTORE
See: U.S. Geological Survey - Water Resources Division - Natl. Water Data Storage & Retrieval System

WATT (Donald B.) LIBRARY
See: Experiment in International Living - School for International Training - Donald B. Watt Library

WATTS SCHOOL OF NURSING
See: Durham County Hospital Corporation

★16839★
WAUKEGAN HISTORICAL SOCIETY - JOHN RAYMOND MEMORIAL LIBRARY (Hist)
1917 N. Sheridan Rd.   Phone: (312) 336-1859
Waukegan, IL 60087
Staff: Prof 1; Other 4. **Subjects:** Local history. **Special Collections:** Waukegan authors. **Holdings:** 1338 books; 3 bound newspapers; 12 VF drawers of pamphlets; 4 drawer case of slides; 1 cabinet of maps and posters; 4 portfolios of old newspapers; 4 VF drawers of photographs; 1 VF drawer of material on landmark buildings; 3 VF drawers of ephemera. **Services:** Interlibrary loans; copying; library open to public. **Publications:**

Historically Speaking, monthly - to members. **Special Indexes:** Index to books, photographs and slides (card). **Staff:** Eleanor Moore, Co-Libn.; Eloise Daydif, Co-Libn.

★16840★
WAUKEGAN NEWS-SUN - LIBRARY (Publ)
100 Madison St.   Phone: (312) 689-6969
Waukegan, IL 60085   Barbara Apple, Libn.
Staff: Prof 1; Other 1. **Subjects:** Newspaper reference topics. **Holdings:** 850 books; 1666 reels of microfilm; photographs and newspaper clippings. **Subscriptions:** 15 journals and other serials; 25 newspapers. **Services:** Library not open to public. **Special Indexes:** News-Sun Microfilm Index (book); Editorial Index (card; book).

★16841★
WAUKESHA COUNTY HISTORICAL MUSEUM - RESEARCH CENTER (Hist)
101 W. Main St.   Phone: (414) 548-7186
Waukesha, WI 53186   Jean Penn Loerke, Musm.Dir./Hist.
Staff: Prof 2; Other 2. **Subjects:** Local history and genealogy. **Special Collections:** Pioneer Notebooks (unpublished information on early pioneers of city and county; 82 volumes). **Holdings:** 2700 books; 87 bound periodical volumes; 1 VF drawer of cemetery records; 1 VF drawer of census records; 40 VF drawers of newspaper clippings; 11,000 photographs; 10,000 negatives; 1800 slides. **Subscriptions:** 36 journals and other serials; 7 newspapers. **Services:** Copying; center open to adults for reference use only. **Publications:** Primary Bibliography for Research in Waukesha History; Family History Research in Waukesha County; list of other publications - available on request. **Staff:** Terry Becker, Res.Techn.

★16842★
WAUKESHA COUNTY TECHNICAL INSTITUTE - WCTI LIBRARY (Educ)
800 Main St.   Phone: (414) 691-5316
Pewaukee, WI 53072   Ruth Ahl, District Libn.
Staff: Prof 1; Other 6. **Subjects:** Nursing, business, real estate, food service, automobiles. **Special Collections:** Archives. **Holdings:** 32,904 books; 3573 unbound periodicals; 823 reels of microfilm; 103 films; 102 videotapes; ERIC documents; SAMS Photofact Service. **Subscriptions:** 422 journals and other serials; 33 newspapers. **Services:** Interlibrary loans; copying; library open to public for reference use only. **Automated Operations:** Computerized cataloging and circulation. **Computerized Information Services:** DIALOG, WCIS, SIRS, NEWSBANK. Performs free searches. **Networks/Consortia:** Member of Library Council of Metropolitan Milwaukee, Inc. (LCOMM); Wisconsin Interlibrary Services (WILS). **Publications:** WCTI film holdings list, annual; WCTI periodical holdings list, annual.

★16843★
WAUKESHA FREEMAN - NEWSPAPER LIBRARY (Publ)
200 Park Pl.   Phone: (414) 542-2501
Waukesha, WI 53186   Steven Walter, Mng.Ed.
Staff: 1. **Subjects:** Current events. **Holdings:** Story clippings; pictures, headshots and negatives; bound volumes, 1859 to present, in storage; newspapers, 1859 to present, on microfilm; city directories; college and high school yearbooks. **Services:** Library not open to public except to look at recent newspaper issues.

★16844★
WAUKESHA MEMORIAL HOSPITAL - MEDICAL LIBRARY (Med)
725 American Ave.   Phone: (414) 544-2150
Waukesha, WI 53186   Linda Oddan, Med.Libn.
Founded: 1958. **Staff:** Prof 1; Other 1. **Subjects:** Medicine, nursing, hospital administration. **Holdings:** 1900 books; 3100 bound periodical volumes; 9 VF drawers of pamphlets. **Subscriptions:** 190 journals and other serials. **Services:** Interlibrary loans; copying; library open to public with restrictions. **Computerized Information Services:** DIALOG, MEDLINE. **Networks/Consortia:** Member of Greater Midwest Regional Medical Library Network (Region 3); Southeastern Wisconsin Health Sciences Library Consortium (SWHSL).

★16845★
WAUSAU INSURANCE COMPANIES - LIBRARY (Bus-Fin)
2000 Westwood Dr.   Phone: (715) 847-8504
Wausau, WI 54401   Douglas H. Lay, Dir., Lib.Serv.
Founded: 1935. **Staff:** Prof 2; Other 3. **Subjects:** Insurance, industrial safety and health. **Holdings:** 15,000 books; 130 bound periodical volumes; 185 VF drawers of clippings. **Subscriptions:** 357 journals and other serials; 17 newspapers. **Services:** Interlibrary loans; library open to serious students and researchers. **Automated Operations:** Computerized journal routing. **Computerized Information Services:** DIALOG. **Networks/Consortia:** Member of Wisconsin Valley Library Service. **Publications:** Bookshelf,

monthly; In Fact, quarterly - both for internal distribution only. **Staff:** Donna S. Nuernberg, Ref.Libn.

WAY & WILLIAMS COLLECTION
See: University of North Carolina, Greensboro

WAYLAND (John W.) LIBRARY
See: Harrisonburg-Rockingham Historical Society and Museum - John W. Wayland Library

★16846★
WAYNE COMMUNITY COLLEGE - LEARNING RESOURCE CENTER (Bus-Fin; Sci-Tech)
Caller Box 8002   Phone: (919) 735-5151
Goldsboro, NC 27530   Dr. Shirley T. Jones, LRC Dean
Founded: 1957. **Staff:** Prof 7; Other 7. **Subjects:** Agriculture and natural resources, health occupations, dental occupations, business, liberal arts, engineering, mechanical vocations, aerospace maintenance technology, mathematics. **Special Collections:** Local genealogy collection. **Holdings:** 35,526 books; 31,053 microforms; 15,729 audiovisual materials. **Subscriptions:** 233 journals and other serials; 9 newspapers. **Services:** Interlibrary loans; copying; media production; center open to public. **Staff:** Dot Elledge, Dir., Lib.Serv.; Malcalm Shearin, Dir., Media Prod.; Sue Potter, Dir., Directed Stud.

★16847★
WAYNE COUNTY CIRCUIT COURT - LAW LIBRARY (Law)†
1407 City-County Bldg.   Phone: (313) 224-5265
Detroit, MI 48226   Kathleen M. Friedman, Law Libn.
Staff: Prof 1. **Subjects:** Law. **Holdings:** 14,400 books; 270 bound periodical volumes. **Subscriptions:** 20 journals and other serials. **Services:** Interlibrary loans; library open to judges and attorneys while in court.

★16848★
WAYNE COUNTY GENERAL HOSPITAL - MEDICAL LIBRARY (Med)*
2345 Merriman   Phone: (313) 274-3000
Westland, MI 48185
Founded: 1949. **Staff:** Prof 2; Other 2. **Subjects:** Biological sciences. **Holdings:** 3464 books; 6000 bound periodical volumes; 343 Audio-Digest tapes. **Subscriptions:** 222 journals and other serials. **Services:** Interlibrary loans; copying; library open to public for reference use only. **Networks/Consortia:** Member of Greater Midwest Regional Medical Library Network (Region 3).

★16849★
WAYNE COUNTY HISTORICAL MUSEUM - LIBRARY (Hist)
1150 North A St.   Phone: (317) 962-5756
Richmond, IN 47374   S. Anne Burcham, Dir.
Founded: 1930. **Staff:** Prof 3. **Subjects:** Local and Quaker history. **Special Collections:** Gaar Williams Collection (Chicago Tribune cartoonist); Victorian valentines (500); World War I posters. **Holdings:** 1000 books; 50 scrapbooks; records of the museum. **Subscriptions:** 15 journals and other serials. **Services:** Copying; library open to public for reference use only. **Also Known As:** Julia Meek Gaar Wayne County Historical Museum. **Staff:** Don A. Goodwell, Curator.

★16850★
WAYNE COUNTY HISTORICAL SOCIETY MUSEUM - LIBRARY (Hist)
21 Butternut St.   Phone: (315) 946-4943
Lyons, NY 14489   Marjory Allen Perez, County Hist.
Founded: 1949. **Staff:** 3. **Subjects:** Wayne County history and genealogy, western New York history. **Holdings:** 1800 volumes; 20 VF drawers of clippings, archives, pictures, pamphlets and scrapbooks. **Services:** Copying (limited); library open to public for reference use only. **Publications:** The Aesthetic Heritage of a Rural Area, 1978. **Special Indexes:** History of Pioneers Settlement of Phelps and Gorham Purchase. **Staff:** Fred H. Rollins, Dir.

★16851★
WAYNE COUNTY LAW LIBRARY ASSOCIATION (Law)
Wayne County Courthouse   Phone: (216) 262-5561
Wooster, OH 44691   Betty K. Schuler, Libn.
Founded: 1903. **Subjects:** Law. **Holdings:** 17,000 volumes; microfiche. **Services:** Copying; library open to public with restrictions. **Computerized Information Services:** LEXIS.

★16852★

WAYNE HISTORICAL MUSEUM - HISTORICAL COMMISSION ARCHIVES (Hist)
No. 1, Town Sq.   Phone: (313) 722-0113
Wayne, MI 48184   Mildred Hanchett, Dir./Supv.
Subjects: Local history. **Staff:** 2. **Holdings:** Clippings; manuscripts; documents; maps; genealogical material; cemetery inscriptions; church, school and local government records; local biographies; photographs. **Services:** Archives open to public.

★16853★

WAYNE PRESBYTERIAN CHURCH - LIBRARY (Rel-Theol)
125 E. Lancaster Ave.   Phone: (215) 688-8700
Wayne, PA 19087   Natalie Veitch, Libn.
Staff: Prof 1; Other 2. **Subjects:** Bible study, Christian education, biography, fine arts, sociology. **Special Collections:** Hymnals. **Holdings:** 4500 books; records; cassettes, filmstrips; 13 rapid reading program portfolios; 70 college catalogs. **Subscriptions:** 10 journals and other serials. **Services:** Library open to public with restrictions.

★16854★

WAYNE STATE COLLEGE - U.S. CONN LIBRARY (Educ)
200 E. 10   Phone: (402) 375-2200
Wayne, NE 68787   Dr. Jack Middendorf, Dir.
Founded: 1910. **Staff:** Prof 7; Other 7. **Subjects:** Education, literature, social science. **Holdings:** 100,000 book titles; 3500 AV materials; 45,000 government documents (selective depository); 350,000 microform titles, including ERIC microfiche collection. **Subscriptions:** 850 journals and other serials. **Services:** Interlibrary loans; copying; AV media production; library open to public. **Computerized Information Services:** DIALOG. **Networks/ Consortia:** Member of Northeast Library System; Postsecondary Educational Learning Resource Centers of Nebraska (PELARCON). **Publications:** ConnFormation, monthly - to faculty. **Staff:** Janet Brumm, Tech.Serv.; Carole Schmidt, Instr.Rsrcs.; Carol Singer, Govt.Docs./Bibliog.Instr.; Elizabeth Thoelke, Coll.Dev.; Joyce Thierer, Pub.Serv.; Richard Urwiler, AV Media Serv.

★16855★

WAYNE STATE UNIVERSITY - ARCHIVES OF LABOR AND URBAN AFFAIRS/UNIVERSITY ARCHIVES (Soc Sci)
Walter P. Reuther Library   Phone: (313) 577-4024
Detroit, MI 48202   Philip P. Mason, Dir.
Staff: Prof 12; Other 12. **Subjects:** American labor, urban affairs, civil rights, civil liberties, social reform, history of Wayne State University. **Special Collections:** Inactive files of United Auto Workers, American Federation of Teachers, The Newspaper Guild, United Farm Workers, Industrial Workers of the World, Air Line Pilots Association, Congress of Industrial Organizations and American Federation of State, County and Municipal Employees; personal papers of labor, political and community leaders. **Holdings:** 11,000 books; 2600 bound periodical volumes; 48,000 linear feet of archives; 500,000 still photographs; 6000 audiotapes; 200 oral histories. **Subscriptions:** 200 journals and other serials. **Services:** Copying; archives open to qualified researchers. **Publications:** Newsletter, 3/year. **Special Catalogs:** A Guide to the Archives of Labor History and Urban Affairs, Wayne State University Press, 1974. **Staff:** Malvina Abonyi, Archv.; Patricia Bartkowski, Archv.; Sandra Van Doren, Archv.; Lawrence Halsted, Archv.; Margery Long, Archv.; Dione Miles, Archv.; Warner Pflug, Asst.Dir.; Patricia Painter, Archv.; Joan Rabins, Archv.; Thomas Featherstone, Archv.; Carolyn Davis, Archv./Libn.

★16856★

WAYNE STATE UNIVERSITY - ARTHUR NEEF LAW LIBRARY (Law)
468 W. Ferry Mall   Phone: (313) 577-3925
Detroit, MI 48202   Georgia A. Clark, Law Libn.
Founded: 1927. **Staff:** Prof 5; Other 6. **Subjects:** Law and related fields. **Special Collections:** Depository for U.S. Government documents (82,643); Michigan Legal Collection; 6th Circuit Court of Appeals records and briefs; Alwyn V. Freeman International Law Collection; U.S. and Michigan Supreme Courts Records and Briefs. **Holdings:** 165,587 books; 31,220 bound periodical volumes; 428,259 microcards and microfiche; 661 reels of microfilm; 283 cassette tapes. **Subscriptions:** 4750 journals and other serials; 13 newspapers. **Services:** Interlibrary loans; copying (limited); library open to public. **Automated Operations:** Computerized cataloging and acquisitions. **Computerized Information Services:** LEXIS, Westlaw, NEXIS, OCLC. Performs searches on cost recovery basis. Contact Person: Stuart Yoak. **Publications:** Law Library News, semimonthly; Recent Acquisitions List, semimonthly - both primarily for faculty distribution. **Staff:** Marianne Maher, Acq.Libn.; Lida Keem, Ser.Libn.; Margaret Heinen, Rd.Serv.Libn.; Stuart Yoak, Ref.Libn.

★16857★

WAYNE STATE UNIVERSITY - EDUCATION LIBRARY (Educ; Info Sci)
                                             Phone: (313) 577-4035
Detroit, MI 48202   Theodore Manheim, Hd.
Founded: 1949. **Staff:** Prof 5; Other 5. **Subjects:** Education, library science, juvenile and adolescent literature. **Special Collections:** Eloise Ramsey Collection of Literature for Young People (10,000 items); NML microfiche college catalog collection; Rosenbach Collection of Early American Children's Books (906 microforms); Rhoda Kellogg Child Art Collection (255 microforms); Educational Testing Service Tests in Microfiche, sets A-I; Fearon-Pitman Curriculum Development Library, 1978 to present (microfiche); William S. Gray Research Collection in Reading, 1884-1981 (microfiche); Michigan Occupational Information System (microfiche); Health, Physical Education and Recreation Microform Publications (complete set) **Holdings:** 296,615 books; 18,146 bound periodical volumes; ERIC microfiche (complete set); 11,372 government documents; 7607 curriculum guides; 35 VF drawers of pamphlets and clippings. **Subscriptions:** 1148 journals and other serials. **Services:** Interlibrary loans; copying; library open to public for reference use only. **Automated Operations:** Computerized cataloging and serials listing. **Computerized Information Services:** Online systems. **Networks/Consortia:** Member of Michigan Library Consortium (MLC). **Staff:** Karen Bacsanyi, Ref.Libn.; Betty Borgman, Ref.Libn.David Rosenbaum, Ref.Libn.Gloria Sniderman, Ref.Libn.

★16858★

WAYNE STATE UNIVERSITY - FOLKLORE ARCHIVE (Hum; Area-Ethnic)
448 Purdy Library   Phone: (313) 577-4053
Detroit, MI 48202   Janet L. Langlois, Dir.
Founded: 1939. **Staff:** 2. **Subjects:** Oral, customary and material culture of urban occupational and ethnic groups. **Special Collections:** International Library of African Music (authentic tribal music); Ivan Walton Collection of Michigan Folklore (Great Lakes folk music); Michigan State University Collection of Folk Narrative; Southern Upland Folklife Oral Histories (Southern whites in Detroit). **Holdings:** 7000 separate collections of 3000 manuscripts, 1000 audiotape recordings, 2000 phonograph records, popular publications, videotapes, slides, photographs, file cards. **Services:** Copying; archive open to public. **Publications:** Annual Report; annotated holdings lists; Archive Study Series.

★16859★

WAYNE STATE UNIVERSITY - G. FLINT PURDY LIBRARY (Hum; Soc Sci)
                                             Phone: (313) 577-4040
Detroit, MI 48202   K.L. Kaul, Hd.
Founded: 1973. **Staff:** Prof 11; Other 17. **Subjects:** Humanities, social sciences. **Special Collections:** Leonard N. Simons Collection (Detroit and Michigan History). **Holdings:** 750,658 books; 127,278 bound periodical volumes; 308,269 documents (leaflets and bulletins only); 396,247 microforms. **Subscriptions:** 4917 journals and other serials; 30 newspapers. **Services:** Interlibrary loans; copying; library open to public for reference use only. **Automated Operations:** Computerized cataloging and serials. **Computerized Information Services:** DIALOG, BRS. Performs searches on cost recovery basis. **Networks/Consortia:** Member of Michigan Library Consortium; Southeastern Michigan League of Libraries. **Publications:** (WSU) Library leaflets; undergraduate guides to library use. **Staff:** Howard Sullivan, Coll.Dev.; E. Baxter, U.N. Doc.; W. Schram, Lib.Instr.; B. Hopkins, U.S. Doc.; Monica Collier, Microforms; Don Breneau, Ref.Coll.Dev.; R. Nuffer, Ref.; L. Spang, Searcher; W. Hulsker, Found.Ctr.Coll.

WAYNE STATE UNIVERSITY - INSTITUTE OF GERONTOLOGY
See: Institute of Gerontology

★16860★

WAYNE STATE UNIVERSITY - SCHOOL OF MEDICINE - VERA PARSHALL SHIFFMAN MEDICAL LIBRARY (Med)
4325 Brush St.   Phone: (313) 577-1088
Detroit, MI 48201   Faith Van Toll, Act.Med.Libn.
Founded: 1970. **Staff:** Prof 6; Other 16. **Subjects:** Clinical medicine, pharmacy and allied health sciences. **Holdings:** 58,416 books; 101,121 bound periodical volumes. **Subscriptions:** 2130 journals and other serials. **Services:** Interlibrary loans; copying; library open to public with restrictions. **Automated Operations:** Computerized acquisitions. **Computerized Information Services:** NLM, BRS, DIALOG. **Publications:** Report Series, infrequently. **Staff:** Ruth Taylor, Assoc.Libn.; Anaclare F. Evans, Cat./Hd., Tech.Serv.; Janet Zimmerman, DC3 Libn.; Andrea Sperlbaum, Coord., Pub.Serv.; Diane Landsiedel, Ser. Control Libn.

★16861★
WAYNE STATE UNIVERSITY - SCIENCE LIBRARY (Sci-Tech)
5048 Gullen Mall   Phone: (313) 577-4066
Detroit, MI 48234   Emerson Hilker, Hd.
Staff: Prof 5; Other 9. **Subjects:** Chemistry, biology, mathematics, engineering, computer science, physics, geology, nursing. **Special Collections:** Samuel Cox Hooker Chemistry Collection. **Holdings:** 186,052 books; 129,831 bound periodical volumes; 134,643 government documents; 59,127 microfiche; 1509 reels of microfilm; 455 microcards; 7546 maps. **Subscriptions:** 2535 journals and other serials. **Services:** Interlibrary loans; copying; library open to public with restrictions. **Automated Operations:** Computerized cataloging. **Computerized Information Services:** DIALOG, BRS, SDC. **Networks/Consortia:** Member of Michigan Library Consortium; Southeastern Michigan League of Libraries. **Publications:** Recent Additions List. **Special Catalogs:** Union List of Serials in Southeastern Michigan (ULOSSUM). **Staff:** Mary Velliky, Ref.Libn.; William Hulsker, Ref.Libn.; Jean Monroe, Ref.Libn.; Dr. James R. Ruffner, Ref.Libn.

WCRB LIBRARY
See: Charles River Broadcasting Company

WE CARE ABOUT SPECIAL CHILDREN MOBIL RESOURCE LIBRARY
See: North Shore University Hospital - Office of Health Education

WEAN MEDICAL LIBRARY
See: Trumbull Memorial Hospital

WEATHER SERVICE NUCLEAR SUPPORT OFFICE
See: U.S. Natl. Weather Service

WEAVER (Annie Belle) SPECIAL COLLECTIONS
See: West Georgia College - Irvine Sullivan Ingram Library - Annie Belle Weaver Special Collections

WEAVER (Jennie E.) MEMORIAL LIBRARY
See: First United Methodist Church - Jennie E. Weaver Memorial Library

WEBB (Del E.) MEMORIAL LIBRARY
See: Loma Linda University - Del E. Webb Memorial Library

WEBB (Del E.) MEMORIAL MEDICAL INFORMATION CENTER
See: Eisenhower Medical Center - Del E. Webb Memorial Medical Information Center

★16862★
WEBB INSTITUTE OF NAVAL ARCHITECTURE - LIVINGSTON LIBRARY (Sci-Tech)
Crescent Beach Rd.   Phone: (516) 671-0439
Glen Cove, NY 11542   Fred H. Forrest, Libn.
Founded: 1931. **Staff:** Prof 1; Other 1. **Subjects:** Naval architecture, marine engineering, engineering, science, literature, history, fine arts, philosophy, religion, social science. **Holdings:** 38,625 books and bound periodical volumes; 5020 engineering reports; 1180 phonograph records; 420 reels of microfilm; clippings and archives of W.H. Webb. **Subscriptions:** 350 journals and other serials; 6 newspapers. **Services:** Interlibrary loans; copying; library open to public by appointment. **Publications:** Accession list, quarterly. **Remarks:** The Center for Maritime Studies is located at the institute.

WEBB MEMORIAL LIBRARY
See: Penrose Hospital

★16863★
WEBER COUNTY LAW LIBRARY (Law)
Municipal Bldg.   Phone: (801) 399-8466
Ogden, UT 84401   Grace A. Rost, Libn.
Founded: 1896. **Staff:** Prof 1. **Subjects:** Law. **Holdings:** 11,500 volumes. **Services:** Copying; library open to public with restrictions.

WEBER MEMORIAL LIBRARY
See: San Antonio Community Hospital

WEBSTER (Daniel) COLLEGE
See: Daniel Webster College

WEBSTER (Jerome P.) LIBRARY OF PLASTIC SURGERY
See: Columbia University - Health Sciences Library

WEBSTER (John P.) LIBRARY
See: First Church of Christ Congregational - John P. Webster Library

WEBSTER MEDICAL LIBRARY
See: Evanston Hospital

★16864★
WEBSTER (Noah) FOUNDATION & HISTORICAL SOCIETY OF WEST HARTFORD - LIBRARY (Hist)
227 S. Main St.   Phone: (203) 521-5362
West Hartford, CT 06107   Elliott W. Hoffman, Dir.
Founded: 1970. **Staff:** Prof 4. **Subjects:** Noah Webster, local history, the Congregational Church in Connecticut, local architecture and preservation, Connecticut colonial life and culture. **Special Collections:** Noah Webster Collection (rare books; manuscripts; letters); rare book collection (200); West Hartford town records. **Holdings:** 800 books; 10 VF drawers of West Hartford archives and tax records; 6 VF drawers of pictures, clippings, scrapbooks, letters. **Subscriptions:** 22 journals and other serials. **Services:** Interlibrary loans; copying; library open to public with restrictions. **Publications:** Noah Webster, David C. Sargent, 1976; From Colonial Parish to Modern Suburb: A Brief Appreciation of West Hartford, Nelson R. Burr, 1976 - for sale; The Spectator, quarterly - to members. **Staff:** Chris Watson, Libn.

★16865★
WEBSTER & SHEFFIELD - LIBRARY (Law)
One Rockefeller Plaza   Phone: (212) 957-9800
New York, NY 10020   Christine Wierzba, Libn.
Staff: Prof 2; Other 3. **Subjects:** Law - corporate, antitrust, public finance, securities, taxation, real property. **Holdings:** 14,500 books; 350 bound periodical volumes; microfilm. **Subscriptions:** 48 journals and other serials; 6 newspapers. **Services:** Interlibrary loans; library not open to public. **Computerized Information Services:** LEXIS, Disclosure Inc., DIALOG. **Networks/Consortia:** Member of Law Library Association of Greater New York. **Staff:** Christine Graesser, Asst.Libn.

★16866★
WED ENTERPRISES - RESEARCH LIBRARY (Art)
1401 Flower St.   Phone: (818) 956-7263
Glendale, CA 91201   Joen B. Kommer, Mgr., Lib.Serv.
Staff: Prof 3; Other 2. **Subjects:** Architecture, art, design, history, travel, costume. **Special Collections:** Selected NTIS Reports; Stanford Research Institute Reports. **Holdings:** 22,000 books; clippings file; 50 internal reports on Disney World and Disneyland. **Subscriptions:** 500 journals and other serials. **Services:** Library not open to public. **Computerized Information Services:** NEXIS, DIALOG. **Special Indexes:** Magazine Index (card). **Also Known As:** Walt E. Disney Enterprises. **Staff:** Mona Martin, Asst.Mgr..; Aileen Kutaka-Barkley, Info.Spec.

WEEKS (I.D.) LIBRARY
See: University of South Dakota - I.D. Weeks Library

WEHRLE (A.T.) MEMORIAL LIBRARY
See: Pontifical College Josephinum - A.T. Wehrle Memorial Library

WEIGEL (Paul) LIBRARY OF ARCHITECTURE AND DESIGN
See: Kansas State University - Paul Weigel Library of Architecture and Design

WEINBERG (Rabbi Dudley) LIBRARY
See: Congregation Emanu-El B'ne Jeshurun - Rabbi Dudley Weinberg Library

★16867★
WEINBERG & GREEN, ATTORNEYS-AT-LAW - LIBRARY (Law)
100 S. Charles St.   Phone: (301) 332-8620
Baltimore, MD 21201   Sally J. Miles, Libn.
Staff: Prof 2; Other 3. **Subjects:** Law. **Holdings:** 20,000 books; 200 bound periodical volumes. **Subscriptions:** 80 journals and other serials. **Services:** Interlibrary loans; copying; SDI; library open to serious researchers by appointment. **Computerized Information Services:** LEXIS, New York Times Information Service. **Publications:** Acquisitions List, monthly - for internal distribution only. **Staff:** Jacqueline Greismann, Asst.Libn.

WEINBERG (Jack) LIBRARY
See: Illinois State Psychiatric Institute - Jack Weinberg Library

WEINBERG (Max and Edith) LIBRARY
See: Temple Israel - Max and Edith Weinberg Library

★16868★
WEINBERG NATURE CENTER - LIBRARY (Sci-Tech)
455 Mamaroneck Rd.
Scarsdale, NY 10583
Phone: (914) 723-4784
Peter J. Woodcock, Naturalist/Dir.
Founded: 1958. **Subjects:** Botany, ornithology, forestry, geology, environmental education. **Holdings:** 550 books. **Subscriptions:** 25 journals and other serials. **Services:** Library open to public for reference use only. **Remarks:** Maintained by Village of Scarsdale.

WEINER LIBRARY
See: Fairleigh Dickinson University

WEINER (Norman D.) PROFESSIONAL LIBRARY
See: Friends Hospital - Norman D. Weiner Professional Library

WEINLOS MEDICAL LIBRARY
See: Misericordia Hospital

WEINREICH LIBRARY AND ARCHIVES OF YIDDISH LINGUISTICS
See: Yivo Institute for Jewish Research - Library and Archives

★16869★
WEINSTEIN (Robert) MARITIME HISTORICAL COLLECTION (Aud-Vis)
1253 S. Stanley Ave.
Los Angeles, CA 90019
Phone: (213) 936-0558
R. Weinstein, Owner
Subjects: Sailing ships of all countries and trades. **Holdings:** 250,000 items including original and copy photographs, glass negatives, clippings, post cards.

★16870★
WEIR (Paul) COMPANY - LIBRARY (Energy)
20 N. Wacker Dr., Suite 2828
Chicago, IL 60606
Phone: (312) 346-0275
Mary A. Vacula, Libn./Info.Spec.
Staff: Prof 1; Other 1. **Subjects:** Coal, coal geology, mining engineering and laws, coal and mineral benefication. **Holdings:** 1000 books; 18 shelves of technical reports; 24 shelves of foreign publications; 36 shelves of state publications. **Subscriptions:** 153 journals and other serials. **Services:** Interlibrary loans; library not open to public. **Networks/Consortia:** Member of Chicago Library System. **Publications:** Acquisitions lists, monthly with annual cumulation - free upon request.

WEIS (Theofield G.) LIBRARY
See: Columbia Union College - Theofield G. Weis Library

WEISBERG (Alex F.) LIBRARY
See: Temple Emanu-El - Alex F. Weisberg Library

★16871★
WEISS (Louis A.) MEMORIAL HOSPITAL - L. LEWIS COHEN MEMORIAL MEDICAL LIBRARY (Med)
4646 N. Marine Dr.
Chicago, IL 60640
Phone: (312) 878-8700
Iris Sachs, Med.Libn.
Staff: Prof 1. **Subjects:** Medicine, pre-clinical sciences. **Holdings:** 1100 books; 800 bound periodical volumes. **Subscriptions:** 131 journals and other serials. **Services:** Interlibrary loans; copying; library open to public with restrictions. **Computerized Information Services:** NLM. **Networks/Consortia:** Member of Metropolitan Consortium; ILLINET; Greater Midwest Regional Medical Library Network (Region 3).

★16872★
WELBORN, DUFFORD, BROWN & TOOLEY - LAW LIBRARY (Law)
1700 Broadway
Denver, CO 80290-1199
Phone: (303) 861-8013
Cori Arsenault, Firm Libn.
Staff: Prof 1. **Subjects:** Real estate; taxation; law - oil and gas, environmental resources, mining, water. **Holdings:** Figures not available for books. **Subscriptions:** 91 journals and other serials. **Services:** Interlibrary loans; copying; library open to other law librarians. **Networks/Consortia:** Member of Colorado Consortium of Law Libraries. **Publications:** Library Newsletter, bimonthly - for internal distribution only. **Special Indexes:** Index to local court rule changes (card).

WELCH LIBRARY
See: Ohio Poetry Therapy Center

WELCH (William H.) MEDICAL LIBRARY
See: Johns Hopkins University - William H. Welch Medical Library

★16873★
WELD COUNTY DISTRICT COURT - LAW LIBRARY (Law)†
Weld County Court House
Greeley, CO 80631
Phone: (303) 356-4000
Joy W. Ahlborn, Libn.
Founded: 1924. **Staff:** Prof 1. **Subjects:** Law. **Holdings:** 18,000 books; 265 bound periodical volumes; 12,100 reports; 650 laws; 1050 texts. **Services:** Copying; library open to public.

★16874★
WELDER (Rob & Bessie) WILDLIFE FOUNDATION - LIBRARY (Sci-Tech)
Box 1400
Sinton, TX 78387
Phone: (512) 364-2643
J.G. Teer, Dir.
Founded: 1948. **Staff:** Prof 1; Other 1. **Subjects:** Agriculture, science and technology, environment and conservation, wildlife and ornithology. **Special Collections:** Alexander Westmore Library (4781 volumes). **Holdings:** 5749 books; 1225 bound periodical volumes; 150 dissertations and theses. **Subscriptions:** 226 journals and other serials. **Services:** Interlibrary loans; copying; library open to public by appointment. **Publications:** Welder Contributions. **Staff:** Vaunda Boscamp, Libn.

★16875★
WELDING INSTITUTE OF CANADA - LIBRARY (Sci-Tech)
391 Burnhamthorpe Rd. E.
Oakville, ON, Canada L6J 6C9
Phone: (416) 487-5415
Bruce F. Bryan, Info.Off. & Res.Engr.
Founded: 1973. **Staff:** Prof 1; Other 1. **Subjects:** Welding, nondestructive testing. **Holdings:** 400 books; 500 bound periodical volumes; 3 VF drawers. **Subscriptions:** 40 journals and other serials. **Services:** Interlibrary loans; copying; SDI; library open to institute members for reference use.

WELDON (D.B.) LIBRARY
See: University of Western Ontario - D.B. Weldon Library

★16876★
WELLESLEY COLLEGE - ARCHIVES (Educ)
Wellesley College
Wellesley, MA 02181
Phone: (617) 235-0320
Wilma R. Slaight, Archv.
Staff: Prof 1; Other 1. **Subjects:** Wellesley College, women's education. **Holdings:** 3000 linear feet of archival material. **Services:** Copying; archives open to public. **Computerized Information Services:** OCLC. **Networks/Consortia:** Member of NELINET; Boston Library Consortium.

★16877★
WELLESLEY COLLEGE - ART LIBRARY (Art)
Jewett Arts Center
Wellesley, MA 02181
Phone: (617) 235-0320
Katherine D. Finkelpearl, Art Libn.
Founded: 1883. **Staff:** Prof 1; Other 1. **Subjects:** Art history with strengths in Western European, American, Far Eastern and classical art and architecture; photography. **Holdings:** 32,010 volumes. **Subscriptions:** 125 journals and other serials. **Services:** Interlibrary loans; library not open to public. **Automated Operations:** Computerized cataloging. **Computerized Information Services:** OCLC. **Networks/Consortia:** Member of NELINET; Boston Library Consortium.

★16878★
WELLESLEY COLLEGE - MARGARET CLAPP LIBRARY - SPECIAL COLLECTIONS (Hum; Hist)
Wellesley College
Wellesley, MA 02181
Phone: (617) 235-0320
Anne Anninger, Spec.Coll.Libn.
Staff: Prof 1; Other 2. **Special Collections:** English Poetry Collection (including Robert and Elizabeth Barrett Browning; 12,000 volumes); Durant Collection (19th-century America; 10,000 volumes); Plimpton Collection (15th- and 16th-century Italian literature; 1200 volumes); Book Arts Collection (4600 volumes); Alcove of North American Languages (Indian languages; 280 volumes); Elbert Collection (slavery and Reconstruction; 800 volumes); Juvenile Collection (1000 volumes); John Ruskin Collection (900 volumes); Guy Walker Collection (illustrated books; 350 volumes). **Holdings:** 41,000 books; 20 linear feet of manuscripts and autographs. **Services:** Copying; collections open to public.

★16879★
WELLESLEY COLLEGE - MUSIC LIBRARY (Mus)
Jewett Arts Center
Wellesley, MA 02181
Phone: (617) 235-0320
Ross Wood, Music Libn.
Founded: 1904. **Staff:** Prof 1; Other 1. **Subjects:** Music. **Holdings:** 20,787 volumes; 11,498 sound recordings. **Subscriptions:** 204 journals and other serials. **Services:** Interlibrary loans; library open to public. **Automated Operations:** Computerized cataloging. **Computerized Information Services:** OCLC. **Networks/Consortia:** Member of NELINET; Boston Library Consortium; Boston Area Music Libraries (BAML).

★16880★

WELLESLEY COLLEGE - SCIENCE LIBRARY (Sci-Tech)
Science Ctr.   Phone: (617) 235-0320
Wellesley, MA 02181   Irene S. Laursen, Science Libn.
Founded: 1976. **Staff:** Prof 1; Other 2. **Subjects:** Biological sciences, chemistry, computer science, geology, mathematics, physics, psychology. **Holdings:** 82,606 books and bound periodical volumes. **Subscriptions:** 614 journals and other serials. **Services:** Interlibrary loans; copying; library open to public with restrictions. **Automated Operations:** Computerized cataloging. **Computerized Information Services:** OCLC, DIALOG. **Networks/Consortia:** Member of NELINET; Boston Library Consortium.

★16881★

WELLESLEY HOSPITAL - LIBRARY (Med)
160 Wellesley St., E.   Phone: (416) 966-6617
Toronto, ON, Canada M4Y 1J3   Verla E. Empey, Dir.
Founded: 1967. **Staff:** Prof 1; Other 4. **Subjects:** Medicine, nursing and hospital administration. **Holdings:** 10,810 books; 8301 bound periodical volumes; 2 VF drawers of bibliographies; 2 VF drawers of staff publications; 1300 AV items; 4 VF drawers. **Subscriptions:** 332 journals and other serials. **Services:** Interlibrary loans; copying; library open to public by appointment. **Computerized Information Services:** MEDLARS. Performs free searches.

★16882★

WELLINGTON COUNTY BOARD OF EDUCATION - EDUCATION LIBRARY (Educ)
500 Victoria Rd., N.   Phone: (519) 822-4420
Guelph, ON, Canada N1E 6K2   R.E. Monkhouse, Educ. Media Cons.
Founded: 1973. **Staff:** Prof 2; Other 5. **Subjects:** School librarianship, educational psychology, teaching, children's literature, curriculum support materials, special education. **Holdings:** 14,000 books; 300 bound periodical volumes; 24 drawers of current clippings. **Subscriptions:** 700 journals and other serials. **Services:** Interlibrary loans; copying; SDI; periodical reprint and routing services; current awareness services; library open to public with prior arrangement. **Computerized Information Services:** DIALOG, QL Systems, Info Globe, New York Times Information Service, BRS, CAN/OLE. Performs free searches. Contact Person: Paola Rowe. **Publications:** T-L Talk; Selection Aids; Educational Aids - all for internal distribution only. **Staff:** Paola Rowe, Educ.Libn.

★16883★

WELLINGTON MANAGEMENT COMPANY - RESEARCH LIBRARY (Bus-Fin)
Box 823   Phone: (215) 647-6000
Valley Forge, PA 19482   Jeanne Wilmer, Libn.
Staff: Prof 1; Other 1. **Subjects:** Corporate finance, industry. **Holdings:** 72 shelves of annual reports and financial information. **Subscriptions:** 60 journals and other serials; 15 newspapers. **Services:** Interlibrary loans; library open to public by appointment. **Remarks:** Library located at 1300 Morris Dr., Wayne, PA 19087.

★16884★

WELLS FARGO BANK - HISTORY DEPARTMENT 921 (Hist)
475 Sansome St.   Phone: (415) 396-4157
San Francisco, CA 94111   Grace A. Evans, Hist.Spec.
Subjects: Wells Fargo and Company history, California gold rush and mining, staging and western transportation, history of banking and finance, San Francisco history, Californiana. **Special Collections:** Photographic Collection; Wiltsee Memorial Collection of Western Stamps, Franks and Postmarks. **Holdings:** 3600 books. **Subscriptions:** 15 journals and other serials. **Services:** Department open to qualified researchers.

★16885★

WELLS FARGO BANK - LIBRARY 888 (Bus-Fin)
475 Sansome St.   Phone: (415) 396-3744
San Francisco, CA 94163   Alice E. Hunsucker, Asst.V.P./Mgr.
Founded: 1930. **Staff:** Prof 3; Other 3. **Subjects:** Banking, finance, economics. **Holdings:** 50,000 volumes. **Subscriptions:** 1200 journals and other serials; 22 newspapers. **Services:** Interlibrary loans; copying; library open to public for reference use only. **Automated Operations:** Computerized serials and circulation. **Computerized Information Services:** DIALOG, SDC, Dow Jones News/Retrieval, RLIN. **Publications:** New Acquisitions, monthly - for internal distribution only. **Remarks:** An additional telephone number is 396-7909. **Staff:** Linda Aldrich, Ref.Libn.; Paul North, Tech.Serv./Ref.

WELSH (W. Keith) LIBRARY
See: North York General Hospital - W. Keith Welsh Library

★16886★

WENDER, MURASE & WHITE - LIBRARY (Law)
400 Park Ave.   Phone: (212) 832-3333
New York, NY 10022   Karen A. Shea, Libn.
Staff: Prof 1; Other 2. **Subjects:** Law. **Special Collections:** Japanese, tax and foreign law. **Holdings:** 10,000 books; 300 bound periodical volumes; 9 VF drawers. **Subscriptions:** 65 journals and other serials; 12 newspapers. **Services:** Interlibrary loans; copying; SDI; library open to public with restrictions. **Computerized Information Services:** LEXIS, New York Times Information Service. **Publications:** Weekly Acquisitions List.

★16887★

WENHAM HISTORICAL ASSOCIATION AND MUSEUM - COLONEL TIMOTHY PICKERING LIBRARY (Hist)
132 Main St.   Phone: (617) 468-2377
Wenham, MA 01984   Eleanor E. Thompson, Dir.
Founded: 1952. **Staff:** 3. **Subjects:** Local history, decorative arts, fashions and costumes, herbals and horticulture, agriculture, domestic and farm animals, genealogy and town histories. **Special Collections:** Book collection of Massachusetts Society for Promoting Agriculture, founded 1792. **Holdings:** 2000 volumes; photographs and maps. **Services:** Library open to public with restrictions.

★16888★

WENNER-GREN FOUNDATION FOR ANTHROPOLOGICAL RESEARCH - LIBRARY (Soc Sci)
1865 Broadway   Phone: (212) 957-8750
New York, NY 10023-7596   Annetherese Hirth, Off./Prog.Mgr.
Founded: 1941. **Subjects:** Cultural and physical anthropology, archeology. **Holdings:** 3000 volumes. **Subscriptions:** 96 journals and other serials. **Services:** Interlibrary loans; library open by appointment. **Publications:** Viking Fund Publications in Anthropology; Current Anthropology; annual report of the foundation.

WENRICH MEMORIAL LIBRARY
See: Landmark Society of Western New York

★16889★

WENTWORTH INSTITUTE OF TECHNOLOGY - LIBRARY (Sci-Tech)
550 Huntington Ave.   Phone: (617) 442-9010
Boston, MA 02115   Ann Montgomery Smith, Dir. of Libs.
Founded: 1954. **Staff:** Prof 6; Other 3. **Subjects:** Aeronautics, electronics, electrical and mechanical engineering technology, architecture. **Special Collections:** Richard H. Lufkin Memorial Library (10,000 volumes). **Holdings:** 55,000 books and bound periodical volumes; 86 magazines and newspapers on microfilm; 100 microfiche. **Subscriptions:** 400 journals and other serials. **Services:** Interlibrary loans; library not open to public. **Automated Operations:** Computerized serials. **Computerized Information Services:** DIALOG. **Networks/Consortia:** Member of Fenway Library Consortium. **Staff:** Barbara Coffey, Assoc.Libn.; Michael Logan, Tech.Serv.Libn.; Lynn Robinson, Libn.; Priscilla Brondie, Circ.; Michael Roudette, Archv.

★16890★

WENTWORTH (T.T., Jr.) MUSEUM - LIBRARY (Hist)
8382 Palafox Hwy.
Box 806   Phone: (904) 438-3638
Pensacola, FL 32594   T.T. Wentworth, Jr., Pres.
Founded: 1958. **Staff:** 2. **Subjects:** History of Florida, Escambia County, Pensacola. **Special Collections:** Rare books on Florida, Pensacola and U.S. history. **Holdings:** 3000 books; 30 bound periodical volumes; 100 scrapbooks; 6000 newspapers, manuscripts, pictures, miscellaneous material and Fort Pickens material on microfilm. **Subscriptions:** 15 journals and other serials; 8 newspapers. **Services:** Library open to public with restrictions.

WENTZ (A.R.) LIBRARY
See: Lutheran Theological Seminary - A.R. Wentz Library

WENTZEL MEDICAL LIBRARY
See: Manatee Memorial Hospital

WERNER (Lillie B.) HEALTH SCIENCES LIBRARY
See: Rochester General Hospital - Lillie B. Werner Health Sciences Library

★16891★

WERTHEIM AND COMPANY, INC. - RESEARCH LIBRARY (Bus-Fin)†
200 Park Ave.   Phone: (212) 578-0427
New York, NY 10166   Joanne Johannessen, Libn.
Founded: 1927. **Staff:** Prof 1; Other 2. **Subjects:** Finance, business, economics, industrial statistics. **Special Collections:** Robert Fisher Manuals of

Obsolete Companies; historical stock price records. **Holdings:** 400 books; clippings for corporation records and industry files; 350 reels of microfilm; 58,000 microfiche; 10 VF drawers of pamphlets. **Subscriptions:** 50 journals and other serials; 12 newspapers. **Services:** Interlibrary loans; library open to clients and students, by appointment. **Publications:** Acquisitions List, weekly - for internal distribution only.

★16892★
WESCHCKE (Carl L.) LIBRARY (Rec)
1661 Woodbury Dr.
Woodbury, MN 55125
Phone: (612) 739-2490
Carl L. Weschcke, Pres.
Subjects: Astrology, Tantra, occultism, alchemy, witchcraft, Tarot. **Special Collections:** Bondage fetishism. **Holdings:** 20,000 books; 200 bound periodical volumes. **Subscriptions:** 25 journals and other serials. **Services:** Library open to public with written application. **Remarks:** The library is associated with Llewellyn Publications.

★16893★
WESLEY BIBLICAL SEMINARY - LIBRARY (Rel-Theol)
Box 9938
Jackson, MS 39206
Phone: (601) 957-1315
Wayne W. Woodward, Dir. of Lib.Serv.
Staff: Prof 1; Other 1. **Subjects:** Theology. **Holdings:** 26,894 books; 24 bound periodical volumes. **Subscriptions:** 171 journals and other serials. **Services:** Interlibrary loans; copying; library open to public.

★16894★
WESLEY MEDICAL CENTER - H.B. MC KIBBIN HEALTH SCIENCE LIBRARY (Med)
550 N. Hillside
Wichita, KS 67214
Phone: (316) 685-2151
Jan Braden, Dir., Lib.Serv.
Founded: 1956. **Staff:** Prof 4; Other 6. **Subjects:** Medicine and nursing. **Holdings:** 31,000 books; 9100 bound periodical volumes; 12,000 pamphlets; 3034 AV aids. **Subscriptions:** 501 journals and other serials. **Services:** Interlibrary loans; copying; library open to public with physician's approval. **Computerized Information Services:** MEDLINE; internal database. **Networks/Consortia:** Member of Wichita Area Health Science Libraries. **Staff:** Malcolm Germann, Libn.; Leslie James, Libn.; Jane Tanner, Libn.

WESLEY THEOLOGICAL SEMINARY
See: United Methodist Church

★16895★
WESLEY UNITED METHODIST CHURCH - LIBRARY (Rel-Theol)
721 King St.
La Crosse, WI 54601
Phone: (608) 782-3018
Ms. Johnie Wardwell, Libn.
Founded: 1966. **Staff:** Prof 1; Other 5. **Subjects:** Religion, philosophy, literature, children's collection, social sciences, fine arts. **Holdings:** 2400 books; 84 filmstrips; 33 phonograph records; 2 VF drawers of pamphlets, study guides. **Services:** Library open to public.

★16896★
WESLEYAN CHURCH - ARCHIVES & HISTORICAL LIBRARY (Rel-Theol)
Box 2000
Marion, IN 46952
Phone: (317) 674-3301
Paul W. Thomas, Dir.
Staff: 2. **Subjects:** History of the Wesleyan church. **Holdings:** 5000 books; conference minute books; journals; photographs; correspondence. **Services:** Interlibrary loans; copying; library open to public.

★16897★
WESLEYAN UNIVERSITY - ART LIBRARY (Art)
Davison Art Center
301 High St.
Middletown, CT 06457
Phone: (203) 347-9411
Richard H. Wood, Libn.
Subjects: Art. **Special Collections:** Renaissance art and architecture; print reference materials; 20th-century art. **Holdings:** 21,000 volumes. **Subscriptions:** 125 journals and other serials. **Services:** Interlibrary loans; library open to public with permission.

★16898★
WESLEYAN UNIVERSITY - LIBRARY - SPECIAL COLLECTIONS (Art; Hum)
Phone: (203) 347-9411
Middletown, CT 06457
Elizabeth A. Swaim, Spec.Coll.Libn./Archv.
Founded: 1831. **Staff:** Prof 1; Other 1. **Subjects:** English and American literature and civilization, history of printing, Methodistica, Wesleyan University and Middletown history. **Special Collections:** Henry Bacon papers (architecture; 50 feet); Wilbur O. Atwater papers (agricultural chemistry; 13.5 feet); Gorham Munson and social credit (33 feet). **Holdings:** 20,000 books; 600 feet of manuscripts and archives. **Services:** Copying; collections open to public by appointment.

★16899★
WESLEYAN UNIVERSITY - LIBRARY - WORLD MUSIC ARCHIVES (Mus)
Phone: (203) 347-9411
Middletown, CT 06457
Chris Montgomery, Music Libn.
Founded: 1965. **Staff:** Prof 1. **Subjects:** Ethnomusicology, non-Western music, Western nonclassical music. **Special Collections:** Music of North American Indians (especially Navajo ceremonial music), Java (music and language), Bali, Philippines, Japan, Korea, China, South India, British Isles, Greece, Afghanistan, Iran, Turkey and West Africa. **Holdings:** 2600 audiotapes; 1000 sound discs; 120 videotapes; 4 VF drawers of indices, translations and transcriptions. **Services:** Copying; archives open to public by appointment. **Networks/Consortia:** Member of NELINET.

★16900★
WESLEYAN UNIVERSITY - PSYCHOLOGY DEPARTMENT LIBRARY (Soc Sci)
Judd Hall
Middletown, CT 06457
Phone: (203) 347-9411
Shirley Schmottlach, Lib.Asst.
Founded: 1910. **Staff:** Prof 1. **Subjects:** Psychology, psychoanalysis, behavioral sciences, neurosciences. **Holdings:** 9851 books; 4649 bound periodical volumes; 146 bound theses. **Subscriptions:** 180 journals and other serials. **Services:** Interlibrary loans; copying; library open to public with restrictions.

★16901★
WESLEYAN UNIVERSITY - SCIENCE LIBRARY (Sci-Tech)
Phone: (203) 347-9411
Middletown, CT 06457
William Calhoon, Sci.Libn.
Founded: 1972. **Staff:** Prof 1; Other 4. **Subjects:** Astronomy, biology, chemistry, geology, mathematics, physics. **Special Collections:** History of Science (early editions; 888 volumes). **Holdings:** 125,725 volumes; 112,792 maps. **Subscriptions:** 996 journals and other serials. **Services:** Interlibrary loans; copying; library open to public with permission. **Computerized Information Services:** DIALOG, BRS.

★16902★
WESLEYAN WOMEN'S CENTER - LIBRARY (Soc Sci)
287 High St.
Wesleyan Station, Box WW
Middletown, CT 06457
Phone: (203) 347-9411
R. Rosenthal, Libn.
Founded: 1979. **Staff:** 6. **Subjects:** Women - health, history, sports, fiction and poetry. **Holdings:** 300 books; 3 drawers of subject files; directories. **Subscriptions:** 15 journals and other serials; 30 newsletters. **Services:** Library open to public. **Formed by the Merger of:** Wesleyan Women's Coalition - Library and Women's Studies Collective Library.

★16903★
WEST ALLIS MEMORIAL HOSPITAL - MEDICAL LIBRARY (Med)
8901 W. Lincoln Ave.
West Allis, WI 53227
Phone: (414) 546-6162
Joan A. Clausz, Med.Libn.
Staff: Prof 1. **Subjects:** Medicine. **Holdings:** 500 books; 900 bound periodical volumes. **Subscriptions:** 100 journals and other serials. **Services:** Interlibrary loans; library not open to public. **Computerized Information Services:** BRS. **Networks/Consortia:** Member of Southeastern Wisconsin Health Sciences Library Consortium (SWHSL).

★16904★
WEST BEND GALLERY OF FINE ARTS - LIBRARY (Art)
300 S. 6th Ave.
West Bend, WI 53095
Phone: (414) 334-9638
Thomas Lidtke, Exec.Dir.
Staff: Prof 1. **Subjects:** Art history and techniques. **Special Collections:** Letters, sketches, and documents of Carl von Marr, 1850-1936. **Holdings:** 250 books. **Services:** Copying; library open to public for reference use only. **Special Catalogs:** Carl von Marr catalog.

★16905★
WEST CENTRAL GEORGIA REGIONAL HOSPITAL - THE LIBRARY (Med)
3000 Schatulga Rd.
Box 12435
Columbus, GA 31995-7499
Phone: (404) 568-5236
Linda A. Sears, Libn., Sr.
Founded: 1974. **Staff:** Prof 1; Other 1. **Subjects:** Mental health. **Holdings:** 3229 books; 329 bound periodical volumes; 2705 journals and newsletters; 1883 AV materials; 2496 pamphlets; 300 LATCH materials. **Subscriptions:** 53 journals and other serials. **Services:** Library open to public for reference use only. **Networks/Consortia:** Member of Health Science Libraries of Central Georgia; Georgia Library Information Network (GLIN); Georgia Department of Human Resources Library Consortium; Southeastern/Atlantic Regional Medical Library Services.

★16906★
WEST CENTRAL MINNESOTA HISTORICAL CENTER - LIBRARY (Hist)
University of Minnesota, Morris　　　　　　Phone: (612) 589-2211
Morris, MN 56267　　　　　　　　　　Dr. Wilbert H. Ahern, Dir.
Founded: 1973. **Staff:** 2. **Subjects:** Ethnicity in west central Minnesota, agribusiness, Minnesota politics and government, oral history, church history. **Special Collections:** Stevens County Census Computerization Project; The Great Depression in West Central Minnesota; Powerline Construction Oral History Project. **Holdings:** 650 linear feet of local history materials; oral history cassettes; microfilm. **Services:** Copying; library open to public. **Remarks:** The center is maintained by the University of Minnesota, Morris.

★16907★
WEST CHESTER UNIVERSITY - FRANCIS HARVEY GREEN LIBRARY - SPECIAL COLLECTIONS (Educ; Hist)
　　　　　　　　　　　　　　　Phone: (215) 436-3456
West Chester, PA 19383　　R. Gerald Schoelkopf, Spec.Coll.Libn./Archv.
Founded: 1871. **Staff:** Prof 1; Other 1. **Subjects:** Botanical history, history of Chester County and Pennsylvania, Chester County and Pennsylvania authors, physical education. **Special Collections:** William Darlington Library (rare scientific and botanical materials); Chester County Cabinet Library; Philips Autograph Library; Shakespeare folios; Ehinger Library (historical material on physical education; 581 items); Chester County collection; university archives (350 boxes). **Holdings:** 9100 books; 200 bound periodical volumes; 5 folio drawers; 40 VF drawers; 100 magnetic tapes; 6 boxes of microfilm; 70 oral history tapes. **Services:** Interlibrary loans; copying; library open to public for reference use, with borrowing privileges by special arrangement. **Automated Operations:** Computerized cataloging. **Computerized Information Services:** DIALOG, BRS, SDC, OCLC. **Networks/Consortia:** Member of PALINET & Union Library Catalogue of Pennsylvania; Tri-State College Library Cooperative (TCLC); Interlibrary Delivery Service of Pennsylvania (IDS); State System of Higher Education Libraries Council (SSHELCO). **Special Catalogs:** Computerized periodical list. **Formerly:** West Chester State College.

★16908★
WEST CHESTER UNIVERSITY - SCHOOL OF MUSIC LIBRARY (Mus)
Francis Harvey Green Library　　　　　Phone: (215) 436-2430
West Chester, PA 19383　　　Ruth Weidner, Music Libn./Assoc.Prof.
Founded: 1960. **Staff:** Prof 1; Other 1. **Subjects:** Music history, opera, instrumental music, jazz, contemporary music, American music. **Holdings:** 24,000 scores; 20,000 phonograph records (33 1/3 rpm). **Services:** Interlibrary loans; copying; library open to public with restrictions. **Automated Operations:** Computerized cataloging. **Computerized Information Services:** OCLC, DIALOG, BRS, SDC. **Networks/Consortia:** Member of PALINET & Union Library Catalogue of Pennsylvania; Tri-State College Library Cooperative (TCLC); Interlibrary Delivery Service of Pennsylvania (IDS); State System of Higher Education Libraries Council (SSHELCO). **Publications:** Acquisitions Lists, irregular. **Special Indexes:** Song title file; record analytic file; piano music file; women composers; early music file.

★16909★
WEST COAST BIBLE COLLEGE - MC BRAYER LIBRARY - HUGHES MEMORIAL RESEARCH PENTECOSTAL CENTER (Rel-Theol; Educ)
6901 N. Maple Ave.　　　　　　　　Phone: (209) 299-7201
Fresno, CA 93710　　　　　　　　Edward E. Call, Hd.Libn.
Staff: Prof 1; Other 1. **Subjects:** Religion, philosophy, literature, psychology, social science, science, commercial education, education, arts. **Special Collections:** Pentecostal Studies research; Studies in 7th Day Adventism; Studies in Christian Scientism. **Holdings:** 28,461 books; 44 bound periodical volumes; microfilm; AV items. **Subscriptions:** 272 journals and other serials; 7 newspapers. **Services:** Interlibrary loans; copying; center open to public.

★16910★
WEST COAST LESBIAN COLLECTIONS, INC. (Soc Sci)
Box 23753　　　　　　　　　　　Phone: (415) 465-8080
Oakland, CA 94623
Staff: 3. **Subjects:** Lesbian culture. **Holdings:** 1000 books; 200 bound periodical volumes; organizational and personal manuscripts; unpublished research papers; photographs; ephemeral material. **Subscriptions:** 25 journals and other serials; 16 newspapers. **Services:** Copying; collections open to public by appointment. **Publications:** In the Life, semiannual - to members and by exchange. **Special Catalogs:** Guides to manuscript holdings.

★16911★
WEST COAST UNIVERSITY - ELCONIN CENTER LIBRARY (Sci-Tech; Comp Sci)
440 Shatto Pl.　　　　　　　　　　Phone: (213) 487-4433
Los Angeles, CA 90020　　　　　　Nancy K. Dennis, Dir. of Lib.
Staff: Prof 2. **Subjects:** Management, engineering, computer science.

Holdings: 7000 books; unbound periodicals. **Subscriptions:** 150 journals and other serials; 7 newspapers. **Services:** Interlibrary loans; copying; library open to public with restrictions. **Computerized Information Services:** DIALOG. Performs searches on cost recovery basis. **Staff:** Jeraldine Byrne, Acq.Libn.

★16912★
WEST END COLLEGIATE CHURCH - LIBRARY
West End Ave. at 77th St.
New York, NY 10024
Subjects: Religion. **Holdings:** 150 volumes. **Remarks:** Presently inactive.

★16913★
WEST END SYNAGOGUE - LIBRARY (Rel-Theol)
3810 West End Ave.　　　　　　　　Phone: (615) 269-4592
Nashville, TN 37205　　　　　　　　Annette R. Levy, Dir.
Staff: Prof 1. **Subjects:** Judaica, children's literature, Yiddish. **Holdings:** 4400 books. **Services:** Interlibrary loans; copying; library open to public.

★16914★
WEST GEORGIA COLLEGE - IRVINE SULLIVAN INGRAM LIBRARY - ANNIE BELLE WEAVER SPECIAL COLLECTIONS (Hist; Mus)
　　　　　　　　　　　　　　　Phone: (404) 834-1370
Carrollton, GA 30118　　　　　Myron W. House, Spec.Coll.Libn.
Founded: 1933. **Staff:** Prof 1. **Subjects:** West Georgia College archives, history of western Georgia, sacred harp music. **Special Collections:** Fourth District A & M School Collection (144 items; 19 volumes); Irvine S. Ingram papers (22 feet); J. Ebb Duncan papers (4 feet); oral history collection (50 audio cassettes; 2 video cassettes). **Holdings:** 1384 volumes; 11,724 clippings, letters, photographs and maps; 73 feet of manuscript collections. **Services:** Copying; collections open to public.

★16915★
WEST JERSEY HOSPITAL, EASTERN DIVISION - STAFF MEDICAL LIBRARY (Med)
Evesham Rd.　　　　　　　　　　Phone: (609) 795-3000
Voorhees, NJ 08043　　　　　　　Jean I. Belsterling, Med.Libn.
Founded: 1976. **Staff:** Prof 1. **Subjects:** Medicine, nursing, patient education. **Holdings:** 1000 books; 1500 bound periodical volumes; 35 AV items. **Subscriptions:** 135 journals and other serials. **Services:** Interlibrary loans; copying; SDI; library open to public for reference use only. **Networks/Consortia:** Member of Southwest New Jersey Consortium for Health Information Services; New Jersey Library Network Services.

★16916★
WEST LIBERTY STATE COLLEGE - ELBIN LIBRARY (Educ; Bus-Fin)
　　　　　　　　　　　　　　　Phone: (304) 336-8035
West Liberty, WV 26074　　　　　　Donald R. Strong, Libn.
Founded: 1932. **Staff:** Prof 5; Other 8. **Subjects:** Education, economics, business. **Special Collections:** Krise Rare Book Collection (400 volumes); college archives (10 filing drawers; 130 file boxes; 43 volumes). **Holdings:** 180,000 books; 27,801 bound periodical volumes; 42,000 pamphlets, clippings and pictures; 8000 recordings and tapes; 30,000 microforms; 3237 reels of microfilm; 2109 filmstrips and slides. **Subscriptions:** 1150 journals and other serials; 15 newspapers. **Services:** Interlibrary loans; copying; library open to public. **Computerized Information Services:** DIALOG. Performs searches on cost recovery basis. **Networks/Consortia:** Member of Pittsburgh Regional Library Center (PRLC). **Publications:** Accessions List, monthly; Handbook. **Staff:** Philip Ross, Acq.Libn.; Jeanne Schramm, Ref.Libn.; Beverly Bond, Cat./Ser.; Mrs. Francis Stewart, AV Libn.; Laurence Williams, Media Spec.

WEST (Roscoe L.) LIBRARY
See: Trenton State College - Roscoe L. West Library

WEST (Roy O.) LIBRARY
See: De Pauw University - Archives of De Pauw University and Indiana United Methodism

★16917★
WEST SUBURBAN HOSPITAL MEDICAL CENTER - WALTER LAWRENCE MEMORIAL LIBRARY (Med)
Erie at Austin　　　　　　　　　　Phone: (312) 383-6200
Oak Park, IL 60302　　　　Julia B. Faust, Dir. of Lib. & Info.Serv.
Founded: 1978. **Staff:** Prof 1; Other 2. **Subjects:** Clinical medicine, nursing. **Holdings:** 3000 books; 10 VF drawers; 600 audiotapes; 300 videotapes. **Subscriptions:** 350 journals and other serials; 5 newspapers. **Services:** Interlibrary loans; copying; SDI; library open to public by appointment. **Computerized Information Services:** MEDLINE, SDC. **Networks/Consortia:** Member of Greater Midwest Regional Medical Library Network (Region 3);

Metropolitan Consortium; Suburban Library System (SLS); Rush Affiliates Information Network (RAIN). **Publications:** Library News, quarterly - distributed in-house and to colleagues upon request.

★16918★

WEST TENNESSEE HISTORICAL SOCIETY - LIBRARY (Hist)
Memphis State University
Box 111046   Phone: (901) 458-4696
Memphis, TN 38111
Founded: 1935. **Staff:** Prof 1; Other 2. **Subjects:** Western Tennessee, Memphis and regional history. **Holdings:** 1000 books; 80 cubic feet of 19th- and early 20th-century manuscripts, scrapbooks and articles including archives of the society and its predecessor organizations, 1857 to present. **Subscriptions:** 10 journals and other serials. **Services:** Copying; library open to public. **Publications:** West Tennessee Historical Society Papers, annual. **Special Indexes:** Composite indexes to WTHS Papers and Guide to West Tennessee Historical Society Publications. **Remarks:** Library is part of Memphis State University - Brister Memorial Library - Mississippi Valley Collection. **Staff:** Dr. John E. Harkins, Supv.Archv.

★16919★

WEST TEXAS STATE UNIVERSITY - CORNETTE LIBRARY - SPECIAL COLLECTIONS (Hist)
W.T. Sta., Box 748   Phone: (806) 656-2761
Canyon, TX 79016   Dr. John G. Veenstra, Univ.Libn.
Founded: 1910. **Staff:** Prof 2; Other 3. **Special Collections:** Sheffy Collection (Southwestern Americana; 2070 items); American history; English history; government documents (17,773 bound; 538,420 unbound; 65,954 microforms). **Services:** Interlibrary loans; copying; collections open to public for reference use only. **Automated Operations:** Computerized cataloging. **Computerized Information Services:** OCLC, BRS, DIALOG. **Networks/Consortia:** Member of AMIGOS Bibliographic Council, Inc.; Harrington Library Consortium. **Staff:** A. Nall, Doc.Libn.; F. Hendrickson, Spec.Coll.

WEST VIRGINIA HISTORICAL SOCIETY
See: West Virginia State Department of Culture and History - Archives and History Library

WEST VIRGINIA PULP AND PAPER COMPANY
See: Westvaco Corporation

★16920★

WEST VIRGINIA SCHOOL OF OSTEOPATHIC MEDICINE - WVSOM LIBRARY (Med)
400 N. Lee St.   Phone: (304) 645-6270
Lewisburg, WV 24901-0827   Donna M. Hudson, Libn.
Staff: Prof 1; Other 4. **Subjects:** Medicine. **Holdings:** 9500 books; 1500 bound periodical volumes; 4000 AV materials. **Subscriptions:** 345 journals and other serials; 5 newspapers. **Services:** Interlibrary loans; copying; library open to public with restrictions. **Computerized Information Services:** MEDLINE. Performs searches on cost recovery basis; free searches for staff and students. **Publications:** WVSOM Newsletter, monthly.

★16921★

WEST VIRGINIA SCHOOLS FOR THE DEAF AND BLIND - WV SCHOOL FOR THE BLIND LIBRARY (Aud-Vis)
                                          Phone: (304) 822-3521
Romney, WV 26757   Leslie Durst, Libn.
Founded: 1963. **Staff:** Prof 2; Other 1. **Holdings:** 14,000 talking books; 150 magnetic tapes; 2881 braille books; 3050 print books; 500 commercial sound recordings. **Subscriptions:** 60 journals and other serials; 8 newspapers. **Services:** Library open to the blind or physically handicapped. **Networks/Consortia:** Member of National Library Service for the Blind & Physically Handicapped (NLS). The library is a sub-regional library in the system. **Staff:** Donna See, Libn.

★16922★

WEST VIRGINIA STATE ATTORNEY GENERAL - LAW LIBRARY (Law)
Rm. 26E, State Capitol   Phone: (304) 348-2021
Charleston, WV 25305
Staff: Prof 2. **Subjects:** Law. **Holdings:** 8678 volumes. **Services:** Library not open to public. **Computerized Information Services:** Westlaw. **Publications:** Biennial Report & Opinions of Attorney General - for sale. **Staff:** Alice E. Knight, Libn.; Deborah J. Dickerson, Libn.

★16923★

WEST VIRGINIA STATE BOARD OF VOCATIONAL EDUC. - DIV. OF VOCATIONAL REHABILITATION - STAFF DEVELOPMENT LIBRARY (Med)
Rehabilitation Center   Phone: (304) 768-8861
Institute, WV 25112   Mrs. Jo Skiles, Libn.
Staff: Prof 1. **Subjects:** Physical and vocational rehabilitation, behavioral sciences, management, medicine. **Special Collections:** Division of Vocational Rehabilitation research and development projects (52). **Holdings:** 10,432 books; 4300 monographs, reports and projects; 112 16mm films; 32 slides and cassettes; 30 videotapes. **Subscriptions:** 78 journals and other serials. **Services:** Interlibrary loans; copying; library open to public with restrictions. **Special Catalogs:** Film catalog.

★16924★

WEST VIRGINIA STATE COMMISSION ON AGING - LIBRARY (Soc Sci)
State Capitol   Phone: (304) 348-2241
Charleston, WV 25305   Eleanor M. Keenan, Libn.
Staff: Prof 1. **Subjects:** Gerontology. **Holdings:** 7695 books; 7 shelves of newsletters, reports, bulletins; 5 VF drawers of pamphlets; 5 VF drawers of clippings. **Subscriptions:** 34 journals and other serials. **Services:** Interlibrary loans; library open to public. **Publications:** Annual progress report; occasional brochures.

★16925★

WEST VIRGINIA STATE DEPARTMENT OF AGRICULTURE - PLANT PEST CONTROL & LABORATORY SERVICES DIVISION LIBRARY (Agri)
Capitol Bldg.   Phone: (304) 348-2212
Charleston, WV 25305   Maria Gyulahazi, Libn.
Staff: Prof 1; Other 1. **Subjects:** Entomology, plant pathology, regulatory control analysis, agriculture, chemistry. **Holdings:** 3000 books; 300 bound periodical volumes; 216 boxes of pamphlets. **Subscriptions:** 55 journals and other serials. **Services:** Interlibrary loans; library open to public by appointment.

★16926★

WEST VIRGINIA STATE DEPARTMENT OF CULTURE AND HISTORY - ARCHIVES AND HISTORY LIBRARY (Hist)
Cultural Center, Capitol Complex   Phone: (304) 348-0230
Charleston, WV 26505   Rodney A. Pyles, Dir.
Founded: 1905. **Staff:** Prof 4; Other 8. **Subjects:** West Virginia archives, history, genealogy; U.S. history; Civil War history; colonial history. **Special Collections:** Governors' papers (1500 linear feet); agency records; state documents; county records; newspapers (microfilm and clippings). **Holdings:** 100,000 books; 25,000 bound periodical volumes; 3000 linear feet of state archives; 25,000 reels of microfilm; 24 VF drawers of clippings. **Subscriptions:** 250 journals and other serials; 100 newspapers. **Services:** Copying; library open to public for reference use only. **Publications:** West Virginia History, quarterly; Checklist of State Publications, quarterly. **Remarks:** Includes the holdings of the West Virginia Historical Society. **Staff:** Mary M. Jenkins, Hd.Libn.; Carol Warner, Per./Doc.Libn.

★16927★

WEST VIRGINIA STATE DEPARTMENT OF EDUCATION - EDUCATIONAL MEDIA CENTER (Educ)
1900 Washington St., Rm. B346   Phone: (304) 348-3925
Charleston, WV 25305   Carolyn R. Skidmore, Lib.Dir.
Founded: 1963. **Staff:** Prof 3; Other 2. **Subjects:** Education. **Special Collections:** State Department of Education Publications; ERIC department publications. **Holdings:** 2500 books; 50 state education directories; 20 cabinets of ERIC microfiche; 4 VF drawers of publishers' catalogs; 1373 16mm films; 779 35mm filmstrips. **Subscriptions:** 200 journals and other serials. **Services:** Interlibrary loans; copying; center open to public for reference use only. **Special Catalogs:** Selection aids; catalogs of films. **Staff:** Francis Vickers, Media Ck.

★16928★

WEST VIRGINIA STATE DEPARTMENT OF HEALTH - STATE HYGIENIC LABORATORY - LIBRARY (Med)
167 11th Ave.   Phone: (304) 348-3530
South Charleston, WV 25303   Jennifer J. Graley, Stenographer
Staff: 1. **Subjects:** Public health. **Holdings:** 500 books. **Subscriptions:** 12 journals and other serials. **Services:** Library open to public with director's permission.

★16929★

WEST VIRGINIA STATE DEPARTMENT OF HIGHWAYS - RIGHT OF WAY DIVISION LIBRARY (Trans; Law)
1900 Washington St., E.   Phone: (304) 348-3195
Charleston, WV 25305
Founded: 1963. **Staff:** 1. **Subjects:** Real estate appraisal, law (eminent

domain), highway severance and research studies, building costs, right of way operating manuals. **Holdings:** 1400 volumes; 2 VF drawers of pamphlets; 200 slides; appraisal cassette tapes. **Subscriptions:** 20 journals and other serials. **Services:** Library open to public with permission. **Special Catalogs:** Appraisal subjects on cards.

★16930★
WEST VIRGINIA STATE DEPARTMENT OF NATURAL RESOURCES - DIVISION OF WATER RESOURCES - LIBRARY
1201 Greenbrier St.
Charleston, WV 25311
Subjects: Water, pollution, legislation. **Special Collections:** Environment Reporter (12 volumes). **Holdings:** State water basin studies and water quality reports; Environmental Protection Agency water pollution control reports and water resources planning; water resources data; journals of Water Pollution Control Federation; developing documents for proposed effluent limitations guidelines; economic analyses of proposed effective limitations; chemical and environmental engineering magazines. **Remarks:** Presently inactive.

★16931★
WEST VIRGINIA STATE DEPARTMENT OF WELFARE - LIBRARY
307 Jefferson St.
Charleston, WV 25305
Defunct. Holdings absorbed by West Virginia State Library Commission - Reference Library.

★16932★
WEST VIRGINIA STATE GEOLOGICAL AND ECONOMIC SURVEY - LIBRARY (Sci-Tech)
Box 879   Phone: (304) 292-6331
Morgantown, WV 26505   Ruth I. Hayhurst, Libn.
Founded: 1897. **Staff:** Prof 1. **Subjects:** Geology, petroleum, coal, oil, gas, related sciences. **Holdings:** 5567 books and bound periodical volumes; 8231 pamphlets. **Subscriptions:** 20 journals and other serials. **Services:** Copying; library open to staff only.

★16933★
WEST VIRGINIA STATE LEGISLATIVE REFERENCE LIBRARY (Law)
Rm. 206 W, Capitol Bldg.   Phone: (304) 348-2153
Charleston, WV 25305   Mary Del Cont, Libn.
Founded: 1957. **Staff:** Prof 1. **Subjects:** Legislation, law, education, government and finance, taxation. **Holdings:** 3150 volumes; 7 VF drawers of legislative reports from other states; 3 VF files of reports of Council of State Governments; 4 VF drawers of newspaper clippings. **Subscriptions:** 37 journals and other serials. **Services:** Interlibrary loans; library open to public. **Publications:** Reports of the Legislative Auditor's Office.

★16934★
WEST VIRGINIA STATE LIBRARY COMMISSION - FILM SERVICES DEPARTMENT (Aud-Vis)
Science and Cultural Ctr.   Phone: (304) 348-3976
Charleston, WV 25305   Steve Fesenmaier, Film Libn.
Founded: 1976. **Staff:** Prof 2; Other 4. **Special Collections:** Appalachia (100 films); astronomy (10 films); women (50 films); feature films (800); Les Blank Collection (15 films); foreign feature films (50); black history and culture (100 films). **Holdings:** 3400 16mm sound films. **Subscriptions:** 12 journals and other serials. **Services:** Interlibrary loans within state; department open to public. **Networks/Consortia:** Member of Educational Film Library Association. **Publications:** WVLC Film Services Newsletter, quarterly - distributed to WV public libraries. **Special Indexes:** Pickfick Papers II and supplements; filmographies on energy, women, Appalachia, features. **Remarks:** Conducts state and local film workshops and annual film festival. **Staff:** Frani Fesenmaier, Asst.Hd.

★16935★
WEST VIRGINIA STATE LIBRARY COMMISSION - REFERENCE LIBRARY (Soc Sci; Info Sci)
Science and Cultural Center   Phone: (304) 348-2045
Charleston, WV 25305   Karen E. Goff, Ref.Libn.
Founded: 1929. **Staff:** Prof 2; Other 5. **Subjects:** Political science, public administration, social welfare, economics. **Holdings:** 76,929 volumes; 500 West Virginia reports and publications; 14,384 reels of microfilm of periodicals; 78,853 microfiche; U.S. Government documents depository. **Subscriptions:** 711 journals and other serials. **Services:** Interlibrary loans; copying; library open to public. **Computerized Information Services:** DIALOG, SDC, New York Times Information Service. **Publications:** West Virginia Library Commission Newsletter, quarterly. **Special Indexes:** Charleston Newspaper Index, annual. **Remarks:** Includes the holdings of the former West Virginia State Department of Welfare - Library.

★16936★
WEST VIRGINIA STATE SUPREME COURT OF APPEALS - STATE LAW LIBRARY (Law)
E-404 Capitol Bldg.   Phone: (304) 348-2607
Charleston, WV 25309   Richard Rosswurm, Supreme Court Law Libn.
Founded: 1863. **Staff:** Prof 1; Other 4. **Subjects:** Law. **Special Collections:** State Constitutional Convention Debates; G.O.P. Collection; English and Canadian law; West Virginia documents. **Holdings:** 70,000 books; 500 bound periodical volumes; 2500 pamphlets; microfiche; records and briefs of U.S. Supreme Court, 1963 to present. **Subscriptions:** 504 journals and other serials. **Services:** Interlibrary loans; copying; library open to public. **Computerized Information Services:** Westlaw. **Publications:** Annual Report to the State Supreme Court; Recent Acquisitions, irregular; Recent Government Documents. **Special Catalogs:** Periodical Holdings. **Staff:** Marjorie Price, Asst. Law Libn.

★16937★
WEST VIRGINIA UNIVERSITY - COLLEGE OF BUSINESS AND ECONOMICS - BUREAU OF BUSINESS RESEARCH (Bus-Fin)
Box 6025   Phone: (304) 293-5837
Morgantown, WV 26506   Stanley J. Kloc, Act.Dir.
Staff: Prof 3; Other 18. **Subjects:** Business, economics, West Virginia economy, small business. **Holdings:** 2000 volumes; Association for Business and Economic Research, U.S. Department of Commerce Regional Economic Information System, and Conference Board publications. **Subscriptions:** 208 journals and other serials. **Services:** Bureau open to public. **Computerized Information Services:** U.S. Bureau of Economic Analysis database. Performs searches on cost recovery basis.

★16938★
WEST VIRGINIA UNIVERSITY - CREATIVE ARTS CENTER - MUSIC LIBRARY (Mus)
                                           Phone: (304) 293-4505
Morgantown, WV 26506   Ruby M. Canning, Supv.
Staff: Prof 1; Other 12. **Subjects:** Music. **Special Collections:** Frye Jazz Collection (3500 pre-1940 phonograph records). **Holdings:** 11,000 books and bound periodical volumes; 12,300 music scores; 850 reels of microfilm; 95 titles on microcards; 6300 phonograph records. **Services:** Interlibrary loans; library open to public with restrictions.

★16939★
WEST VIRGINIA UNIVERSITY - LAW LIBRARY (Law)
Law School
Box 6130   Phone: (304) 293-5309
Morgantown, WV 26506-6130   William E. Johnson, Law Libn./Professor
Staff: Prof 3; Other 4. **Subjects:** Law. **Holdings:** 141,100 volumes. **Subscriptions:** 1205 journals and other serials. **Services:** Copying. **Computerized Information Services:** Westlaw. **Staff:** Carol S. Davis, Sr.Cat.Libn.

★16940★
WEST VIRGINIA UNIVERSITY MEDICAL CENTER - CHARLESTON DIVISION - LEARNING RESOURCES CENTER (Med)
3110 Mac Corkle Ave., S.E.   Phone: (304) 347-1285
Charleston, WV 25304   Patricia Powell, Libn.
Staff: Prof 2; Other 4. **Subjects:** Medicine, nursing. **Holdings:** 12,000 books; 15,000 bound periodical volumes; 2000 AV items. **Subscriptions:** 525 journals and other serials. **Services:** Interlibrary loans; copying; center open to public. **Automated Operations:** Computerized cataloging. **Computerized Information Services:** OCLC, MEDLINE. **Networks/Consortia:** Member of Pittsburgh Regional Library Center (PRLC). **Publications:** Acquisitions list, monthly - by request; AV holdings list. **Remarks:** Includes the holdings of Charleston Area Medical Center - General Division - Medical Library.

★16941★
WEST VIRGINIA UNIVERSITY - MEDICAL CENTER LIBRARY (Med)
Basic Sciences Bldg.
Box 6306   Phone: (304) 293-2113
Morgantown, WV 26506-6306   Robert Murphy, Dir.
Founded: 1954. **Staff:** Prof 5; Other 11. **Subjects:** Medicine, dentistry, pharmacy, nursing. **Special Collections:** Medicine in West Virginia; occupational health. **Holdings:** 41,000 books; 116,000 bound periodical volumes; 400 dissertations and theses; 3660 reels of microfilm containing 342 titles; 5610 microfiche containing 2263 titles; 2500 slides and films. **Subscriptions:** 2100 journals and other serials. **Services:** Interlibrary loans; copying. **Computerized Information Services:** DIALOG, BRS, SDC, OCLC. Performs searches on cost recovery basis. Contact Person: Marge Abel. **Staff:** Marge Abel, Asst.Dir.; Jean Allyson McKee, Tech.Serv.; Diane Morton, Pub.Serv.; Beth Haugh, AV Serv.

★16942★
WEST VIRGINIA UNIVERSITY - WEST VIRGINIA AND REGIONAL COLLECTION (Hist)
University Library   Phone: (304) 293-3240
Morgantown, WV 26506   George Parkinson, Cur.
Founded: 1925. **Staff:** Prof 3; Other 5. **Subjects:** Appalachian, regional, state and local history and genealogy. **Holdings:** 27,000 volumes; 22,310 reels of microfilm; 12,000 linear feet of manuscripts including 3000 collections, photographs, oral histories, folk music and archival materials.

★16943★
WEST VIRGINIA WESLEYAN COLLEGE - ANNIE MERNER PFEIFFER LIBRARY (Hist)
College Ave.   Phone: (304) 473-8013
Buckhannon, WV 26201   Benjamin F. Crutchfield, Jr., Dir., Lib.Serv.
Founded: 1890. **Staff:** Prof 3; Other 7. **Subjects:** History of Methodist Church in West Virginia; history of Upshur County, West Virginia; Lincolniana. **Special Collections:** Pearl S. Buck Manuscripts (68 Hollinger boxes; 200 file envelopes). **Holdings:** 130,000 books and bound periodical volumes; 12,000 unbound periodicals; 4122 volumes in microform; 5580 nonprint items. **Subscriptions:** 651 journals and other serials; 20 newspapers. **Services:** Interlibrary loans; copying (limited); library open to public for reference use only. **Special Catalogs:** Media Catalog; Bibliography of Latin America; Afro-American Bibliography. **Staff:** Judith R. Martin, Cat.; Mary P. Thiedeman, Hd., Ref.

★16944★
WEST VOLUSIA MEMORIAL HOSPITAL - MEDICAL LIBRARY (Med)
Box 509   Phone: (904) 734-3320
De Land, FL 32721   Marjorie E. Cook, Med.Libn.
Staff: 1. **Subjects:** Medicine and allied fields. **Holdings:** 597 books; 150 bound periodical volumes; 2 Audio-Digest subscriptions. **Subscriptions:** 78 journals and other serials; 9 newspapers. **Services:** Interlibrary loans; copying; library open to public with permission. **Publications:** Newsletter - for internal distribution only.

WESTCHESTER ACADEMY OF MEDICINE
See: New York Medical College and the Westchester Academy of Medicine

★16945★
WESTCHESTER COUNTY HISTORICAL SOCIETY - LIBRARY (Hist)
75 Grasslands Rd.   Phone: (914) 592-4338
Valhalla, NY 10595   Elizabeth G. Fuller, Libn.
Founded: 1874. **Staff:** Prof 1. **Subjects:** Genealogy and history of Westchester County and New York State, history of New York City. **Special Collections:** French scrapbooks (43); Barron picture collection (New York City and the Revolutionary War; 225 volumes). **Holdings:** 5000 books; 350 bound periodical volumes; 8 VF drawers of manuscripts; 6 VF drawers of photographs; 12 VF drawers of clippings; 10 drawers of maps. **Subscriptions:** 27 journals and other serials. **Services:** Copying; library open to public.

★16946★
WESTCHESTER COUNTY MEDICAL CENTER - HEALTH SCIENCES LIBRARY (Med)
                                                      Phone: (914) 347-7033
Valhalla, NY 10595   Charlene Sikorski, Med.Libn.
Founded: 1925. **Staff:** Prof 1. **Subjects:** Medicine, nursing, psychiatry, psychology, dentistry. **Holdings:** 12,000 volumes. **Subscriptions:** 150 journals and other serials. **Services:** Interlibrary loans; copying; library open to public with permission of librarian. **Publications:** Acquisitions List, quarterly; Orientation and Information Manual.

WESTCHESTER MEDICAL CENTER LIBRARY
See: New York Medical College and the Westchester Academy of Medicine

★16947★
WESTCOAST TRANSMISSION COMPANY LIMITED - LIBRARY (Energy)
1333 W. Georgia St., 14th Fl.   Phone: (604) 664-5517
Vancouver, BC, Canada V6E 3K9   Beatrice P. Yakimchuk, Libn.
Staff: Prof 2; Other 1. **Subjects:** Energy regulation and law. **Special Collections:** History of Westcoast Transmission Company (20 books; 2 drawers of clippings). **Holdings:** 6000 books; 1200 annual reports; 12 VF drawers; 4 VF drawers of clippings; 200 other cataloged items. **Subscriptions:** 200 journals and other serials; 20 newspapers. **Services:** Interlibrary loans; copying; library open to public with restrictions. **Computerized Information Services:** DIALOG. **Staff:** Louise Barre, Asst.Libn.

★16948★
WESTERLY HOSPITAL - MEDICAL LIBRARY (Med)
Wells St.   Phone: (401) 596-4961
Westerly, RI 02891   Natalie V. Lawton, Libn.
Founded: 1956. **Staff:** Prof 1. **Subjects:** Medicine, surgery. **Holdings:** 838 books; 525 bound periodical volumes. **Subscriptions:** 52 journals and other serials. **Services:** Interlibrary loans; copying; library open to public for reference use only by request. **Networks/Consortia:** Member of Association of Rhode Island Health Sciences Librarians (ARIHSL).

WESTERN ARCHEOLOGICAL AND CONSERVATION CENTER
See: U.S. Natl. Park Service

★16949★
WESTERN CANADIAN UNIVERSITIES - MARINE BIOLOGICAL SOCIETY - DEVONIAN LIBRARY (Sci-Tech)
Bamfield Marine Sta.   Phone: (604) 728-3301
Bamfield, BC, Canada V0R 1B0   Christine Milliken, Libn.
Staff: 1. **Subjects:** Marine biology and ecology, biological oceanography, invertebrate zoology, phycology. **Special Collections:** K.D. Hobson Collection (reprints on polychaetes). **Holdings:** 2300 books; 925 bound periodical volumes; 1200 unbound journals; 1100 Canada, Fisheries and Aquatic Science Reports; 32 VF drawers of reprints; 62 dissertations. **Subscriptions:** 37 journals and other serials. **Services:** Interlibrary loans; copying; library open to public with restrictions.

★16950★
WESTERN CAROLINA UNIVERSITY - HUNTER MEMORIAL LIBRARY - SPECIAL COLLECTIONS
                                                      Phone: (704) 227-7474
Cullowhee, NC 28723   James B. Lloyd, Cur. of Spec.Coll.
Founded: 1953. **Special Collections:** Appalachia (2000 volumes); spider behavior (200 volumes). **Services:** Interlibrary loans; copying; collections open to public. **Automated Operations:** Computerized cataloging and serials. **Computerized Information Services:** DIALOG, OCLC; Online Manuscript Search Service (internal database). Performs free searches. **Networks/Consortia:** Member of SOLINET.

★16951★
WESTERN CENTER ON LAW AND POVERTY, INC. - LIBRARY (Soc Sci)
3535 W. 6th St.   Phone: (213) 487-7211
Los Angeles, CA 90020   Michelle Epstein, Coord. of Lib.Serv.
Staff: Prof 1; Other 1. **Subjects:** Poverty, education, consumer protection, discrimination, employment, housing, health, welfare. **Holdings:** 5000 books; pamphlets; pleadings; reprints. **Subscriptions:** 60 journals and other serials. **Services:** Interlibrary loans; center open to public with restrictions. **Computerized Information Services:** DIALOG, LEXIS; internal database. **Networks/Consortia:** Member of CLASS.

★16952★
WESTERN CENTER - LIBRARY (Med)
333 Curry Hill Rd.   Phone: (412) 745-0700
Canonsburg, PA 15317   Nicholas L. Liguori, Libn.
Founded: 1962. **Subjects:** Medicine, psychology, special education. **Holdings:** 1020 volumes. **Subscriptions:** 82 journals and other serials. **Services:** Library open to public with restrictions.

WESTERN COLLEGE OF VETERINARY MEDICINE
See: University of Saskatchewan

★16953★
WESTERN CONNECTICUT STATE UNIVERSITY - RUTH A. HAAS LIBRARY - SPECIAL COLLECTIONS (Educ)
181 White St.   Phone: (203) 797-4052
Danbury, CT 06810   Katherine J. Sholtz, Dir. of Lib.Serv.
Founded: 1903. **Staff:** Prof 10. **Special Collections:** Connecticut and Fairfield County history; Instructional Media Center; government documents (1700 linear feet). **Services:** Interlibrary loans; copying; collections open to public for reference use only. **Automated Operations:** Computerized cataloging. **Computerized Information Services:** OCLC, DIALOG, BRS. Performs searches on cost recovery basis. **Networks/Consortia:** Member of NELINET. **Publications:** Library Handbook.

★16954★
WESTERN CONSERVATIVE BAPTIST SEMINARY - CLINE-TUNNELL LIBRARY (Rel-Theol)
5511 S.E. Hawthorne Blvd.   Phone: (503) 233-8561
Portland, OR 97215   R.A. Krupp, Lib.Dir.
Founded: 1927. **Staff:** Prof 3; Other 4. **Subjects:** Religion, theology and

psychology. **Special Collections:** Oregon Baptist history. **Holdings:** 50,000 books; 2330 bound periodical volumes; 4 VF drawers of pamphlets; 6450 AV items. **Subscriptions:** 760 journals and other serials; 10 newspapers. **Services:** Interlibrary loans; copying; library open to public by registration and with limited loan privileges. **Automated Operations:** Computerized cataloging. **Computerized Information Services:** DIALOG, OCLC. **Publications:** Bibliography of Recent Acquisitions - distributed to faculty and limited number of libraries. **Staff:** Karen Peterson, Cat.Libn.; Betty Lu Johnstone, Rd.Serv.Libn.

★16955★
WESTERN COSTUME COMPANY - RESEARCH LIBRARY (Hist)
5335 Melrose Ave.   Phone: (213) 469-1451
Los Angeles, CA 90038   Nancy S. Kinney, Dir. of Res.
Staff: Prof 2. **Subjects:** Clothing, military and civilian uniforms, insignia, medals and decorations, police uniforms, occupational clothing, sports clothing, ecclesiastical clothing, folk dress. **Special Collections:** Sears, Roebuck and Montgomery Ward clothing catalogs, 1895 to present (70). **Holdings:** 12,000 volumes; 107 VF drawers; 800 volumes of wardrobe photographs from 20th Century-Fox films, 1930-1975. **Subscriptions:** 60 journals and other serials. **Services:** Copying; library open to public (fee). **Special Indexes:** Index of clothing, especially uniforms, as worn by world police and military, occupational groups, the clergy, ethnic groups and characters from literature, plays, movies and television.

★16956★
WESTERN CURRICULUM COORDINATION CENTER (WCCC) - RESOURCE CENTER (Educ)
1776 University Ave., Wist 216   Phone: (808) 948-6496
Honolulu, HI 96822   Gail M. Urago, Libn.
Staff: Prof 1; Other 4. **Subjects:** Vocational education and guidance. **Holdings:** 15,000 books; 4 VF drawers of pamphlets and clippings; 335 microfiche; 30 films; 100 filmstrips; 62 kits. **Services:** Interlibrary loans; center open to public with restrictions. **Computerized Information Services:** Internal database. **Publications:** Curriculum Materials in the Western Curriculum Coordination Center, 1980 - for sale; subject bibliographies for AV materials in the collection. **Special Catalogs:** Special Groups (minorities and women); productivity; small engines; energy. **Remarks:** Center is sponsored by U.S. Dept. of Education. It serves American Samoa, Arizona, California, Guam, Hawaii, Nevada, Northern Marianas, Trust Territory of the Pacific Isles.

WESTERN DEVELOPMENT AND LABORATORIES
See: Ford Aerospace & Communications Corp.

WESTERN ELECTRIC COMPANY, INC.
See: AT & T Bell Laboratories & Technologies; AT & T Technologies, Inc.

★16957★
WESTERN EVANGELICAL SEMINARY - GEORGE HALLAUER MEMORIAL LIBRARY (Rel-Theol)
4200 S.E. Jennings Ave.   Phone: (503) 654-5182
Milwaukie, OR 97222   Gary Metzenbacher, Dir. of Lib.
Founded: 1947. **Staff:** Prof 2; Other 7. **Subjects:** Religion, theology, philosophy, ethics, marriage, family. **Holdings:** 39,674 books; 2013 bound periodical volumes; 19 filmstrips; 498 cassette tapes; 203 magnetic tapes; 73 reels of microfilm; 19 phonograph records; 150 maps; 308 multimedia kits; 11 videotapes; 82 volumes on microfiche. **Subscriptions:** 446 journals and other serials; 8 newspapers. **Services:** Interlibrary loans; copying; library open to public. **Automated Operations:** Computerized cataloging. **Computerized Information Services:** DIALOG, OCLC. Performs searches on cost recovery basis. **Networks/Consortia:** Member of Clackamas County Cooperative Library System. **Publications:** Selected List of Books Processed, quarterly; Bulletin of the George Hallauer Memorial Library, quarterly - both for internal distribution only; Reference Tools for Theological Students, irregular. **Staff:** Patricia Kuehne, Asst.Dir.

WESTERN FEDERATION OF MINERS ARCHIVES
See: University of Colorado, Boulder - Western Historical Collection & University Archives

★16958★
WESTERN GEOPHYSICAL COMPANY OF AMERICA - R & D LIBRARY (Sci-Tech)
Box 2469   Phone: (713) 789-9600
Houston, TX 77001   Ching-Cheng C. Ting, R & D Libn.
Founded: 1968. **Staff:** 1. **Subjects:** Geophysics, mathematics, geology, computer science, physics, engineering. **Holdings:** 4600 books; 800 bound periodical volumes; technical reports; maps; government documents. **Subscriptions:** 103 journals and other serials. **Services:** Interlibrary loans;

library not open to public. **Computerized Information Services:** New England Research Application Center (NERAC), DIALOG. Performs searches on cost recovery basis. **Publications:** New books list, quarterly. **Remarks:** The library is located at 10001 Richmond Ave., Houston, TX 77042.

★16959★
WESTERN HIGHWAY INSTITUTE - RESEARCH LIBRARY (Trans)
1200 Bayhill Dr., Suite 112
San Bruno, CA 94066   Mae Frances Moore, Libn.
Founded: 1970. **Staff:** Prof 1. **Subjects:** Transportation, highways and bridges, trucking. **Holdings:** 1500 books. **Subscriptions:** 20 journals and other serials. **Services:** Interlibrary loans; copying; library open to public with restrictions.

★16960★
WESTERN HISTORICAL MANUSCRIPT COLLECTION/STATE HISTORICAL SOCIETY OF MISSOURI MANUSCRIPTS JOINT COLLECTION (Hist)
University of Missouri
23 Ellis Library   Phone: (314) 882-6028
Columbia, MO 65201   Nancy Lankford, Assoc.Dir.
Founded: 1943. **Staff:** Prof 12; Other 4. **Subjects:** History - Missouri, political, economic, agricultural, urban, labor, black, women's, frontier, religious, literary, social, science, steamboating. **Special Collections:** WPA HRS for Missouri; Missouri Constitutional Convention of 1943; World War II letters; colonial and pre-statehood papers of Ste. Genevieve. **Holdings:** Over 13 million items. **Publications:** Guide to the Western Historical Manuscripts Collection, 1952; supplement, 1956. **Special Indexes:** Finding aids (index, shelf list and chronological file). **Remarks:** The collection contains the manuscript holdings of both the University of Missouri and the State Historical Society of Missouri. Offices are located in the libraries of the four branches of the University of Missouri. Materials may be loaned among the four branches. **Staff:** Lynn Wolf Gentzler, Asst.Dir.; Laura Bullion, Sr.Mss.Spec.; Cynthia Stewart, Sr.Mss.Spec.; Darrell D. Garwood, Mss.Spec.; William G. Priest, Mss.Spec.; Paula Quirk, Mss.Spec.; Sharon L. Fleming, Mss.Spec.; Randy Roberts, Mss.Spec.; Claudia Lane Powell, Doc.Consrv.Spec.; Thomas D. Norris, Mss.Spec.

★16961★
WESTERN HISTORICAL MANUSCRIPT COLLECTION/STATE HISTORICAL SOCIETY OF MISSOURI MANUSCRIPTS JOINT COLLECTION (Hist)
University of Missouri
General Library 212
5100 Rockhill Rd.   Phone: (816) 276-1543
Kansas City, MO 64110   Gordon O. Hendrickson, Assoc.Dir.
Staff: Prof 2. **Subjects:** Kansas City history and architectural records, civic and political leadership, history of citizen action groups. **Holdings:** 2200 cubic feet of manuscripts. **Services:** Copying; collection open to public with restrictions. **Remarks:** This collection contains the manuscript holdings of both the University of Missouri and the State Historical Society of Missouri. Offices are located in the libraries of the four branches of the University of Missouri. Materials may be loaned among the four branches. **Staff:** David L. Boutros, Ms.Spec.

★16962★
WESTERN ILLINOIS UNIVERSITY - CENTER FOR WEST CENTRAL ILLINOIS REGIONAL STUDIES (Hist)
     Phone: (309) 298-2411
Macomb, IL 61455   Dr. John Hallwas, Dir.
Founded: 1979. **Staff:** Prof 1; Other 1. **Subjects:** West central Illinois regional authors and history. **Special Collections:** Tom Railsback papers; Elton Fawks papers; Illinois Regional Archives Depository Collection (court records for the region). **Holdings:** 12,000 books; 6000 photographs; 10,000 VF items; 750 linear feet of records. **Services:** Copying; SDI; center open to public. **Computerized Information Services:** OCLC. **Publications:** Western Illinois Regional Studies.

★16963★
WESTERN HISTORICAL MANUSCRIPT COLLECTION/STATE HISTORICAL SOCIETY OF MISSOURI MANUSCRIPTS JOINT COLLECTION (Hist)
University of Missouri
Rm. G-3 Library   Phone: (314) 341-4874
Rolla, MO 65401-0249   Mark C. Stauter, Assoc.Dir.
Staff: Prof 2. **Subjects:** History - Missouri, the Ozarks, mining and technology. **Special Collections:** Historical records of St. Joe Minerals Corporation (46 volumes); historical records of American Zinc Company (151 boxes). **Holdings:** 125 historical manuscript collections. **Services:** Interlibrary loans; copying; collection open to public. **Remarks:** This collection contains the manuscript holdings of both the University of Missouri and the State Historical Society of Missouri. Offices are located in the libraries of the four branches of

the University of Missouri. Materials may be loaned among the four branches. **Staff:** John F. Bradbury, Jr., Mss.Spec.

★16964★

WESTERN HISTORICAL MANUSCRIPT COLLECTION/STATE HISTORICAL SOCIETY OF MISSOURI MANUSCRIPTS JOINT COLL. (Hist; Soc Sci)
University of Missouri
Thomas Jefferson Library
8001 Natural Bridge Rd.   Phone: (314) 553-5143
St. Louis, MO 63121   Anne R. Kenney, Assoc.Dir.
Founded: 1968. **Staff:** Prof 3; Other 1. **Subjects:** History - state and local, women's, Afro-American, education, immigration; socialism; 19th-century science; ecology; peace; religion; Missouri politics; social reform and welfare. **Special Collections:** Socialist Party of St. Louis and Missouri (16 boxes); Paul W. Preisler Collection (50 boxes); Arthur W. Proetz Collection (1000 negatives and prints from 1890); Oral History Program (650 tapes); League of Women Voters of Missouri (59 boxes); Women's Historical Collections; St. Louis Local History Collection; Papers of Dr. Thomas A. Dooley, Margaret Hickey, Ernest and Deverne Calloway, Theodore Lentz, Alberta Slavin, Rep. William Hungate and Rep. James Symington; Archives of Academy of Science of St. Louis; Coalition for the Environment; Committee for Environmental Information; KETC-TV; Metropolitan Church Federation; Sierra Club - Ozark Chapter. **Holdings:** 2500 linear feet of manuscripts, photographs, oral history tapes and university archives. **Services:** Interlibrary loans (limited); copying of tape recordings and photographs; library open to public with restricted circulation. **Remarks:** This collection contains the manuscript holdings of both the University of Missouri and the State Historical Society of Missouri. Offices are located in the libraries of the four branches of the University of Missouri. Materials may be loaned among the four branches. **Staff:** Patricia L. Adams, Sr.Ms.Spec.

★16965★

WESTERN ILLINOIS UNIVERSITY - GEOGRAPHY & MAP LIBRARY (Geog-Map)
                                              Phone: (309) 298-1171
Macomb, IL 61455   John V. Bergen, Map Libn.
Founded: 1968. **Staff:** Prof 1; Other 1. **Subjects:** Maps of Illinois, U.S. topographic maps, thematic maps, geography, area or regional studies. **Special Collections:** Federal and state depositories; U.S. Geological Survey (50,000 maps); Defense Mapping Agency (30,000 maps); Illinois (10,000 maps; 12,000 air photographs, atlases and plat books). **Holdings:** 2500 books; 500 periodical volumes; 3000 atlases; 141,000 maps; 13,000 air photos; 1000 pamphlets; 60 theses; 120 map information catalogs. **Subscriptions:** 75 journals and other serials. **Services:** Interlibrary loans (limited); copying; library open to public.

★16966★

WESTERN ILLINOIS UNIVERSITY - LIBRARIES (Educ)
                                              Phone: (309) 298-2411
Macomb, IL 61455   Patricia A. Gogeen, Dir.
Founded: 1900. **Staff:** Prof 23; Other 34. **Subjects:** Elementary and secondary education, American history, English literature, psychology, political science. **Special Collections:** Icarian materials; music and physical sciences collection; audiovisual, art and education exhibits. **Holdings:** 465,000 books; 70,000 bound periodical volumes; 350,000 government documents; 12,000 volumes of special collections; 380,000 microforms; 1000 linear feet of university archives. **Subscriptions:** 4000 journals. **Services:** Interlibrary loans; library open to public. **Automated Operations:** Computerized circulation. **Computerized Information Services:** CDC, OCLC. **Staff:** Carol Covey, Ser.Libn.; Donna Goehner, Acq.Libn.Delmus E. Williams, Asst.Dir.; Allie Wise Gondy, Music Libn.; Roy Chang, Cat.Libn.;Lowell Oxtoby, AV Libn.; Mr. Helio Nardo, Asst.Cat.Libn.; Donald MacVean, Ref.Libn.; Kenneth Smejkal, Phys.Sci.Libn.; Martha Swanson, Asst.Cat.Libn.; Eugene Moushey, Ref.Libn.; Frank Goudy, Ref.Libn.; William Sanders, Exhibits & Arts Libn.; Ronald Rayman, Ref.Libn.; Esther Nelson, Ref.Libn.; Gordana Rezab, Archv./Spec.Coll.; Dorothy Montgomery, Circ.Libn.

★16967★

WESTERN ILLINOIS UNIVERSITY - MUSIC LIBRARY (Mus)
204 Browne Hall   Phone: (309) 298-1105
Macomb, IL 61455   Allie Wise Goudy, Music Libn.
Staff: Prof 1; Other 1. **Subjects:** Classical music. **Holdings:** 7000 books; 5000 bound periodical volumes; 4600 volumes of scores; 3800 phonograph records. **Subscriptions:** 100 journals and other serials. **Services:** Copying; library open to public. **Computerized Information Services:** DIALOG, OCLC. **Publications:** Guides to the collection. **Special Indexes:** Bibliographies and indexes of early music recordings, ethnic recordings, music education recordings; composers' biographies.

★16968★

WESTERN INTERSTATE COMMISSION FOR HIGHER EDUCATION - LIBRARY (Educ)
Drawer P   Phone: (303) 497-0284
Boulder, CO 80302   Karon M. Kelly, Dir.
Founded: 1955. **Staff:** Prof 1; Other 3. **Subjects:** Higher education, mental health and human services, nursing, corrections, minority education. **Holdings:** 7000 books and documents; 1000 volumes of unbound periodicals; 2000 documents on microfiche. **Subscriptions:** 280 journals and other serials; 10 newspapers. **Services:** Interlibrary loans; copying; library open to public. **Computerized Information Services:** DIALOG, BRS. **Publications:** Acquisitions List, monthly; Infolines, bimonthly.

WESTERN JEWISH HISTORY CENTER
See: Magnes (Judah L.) Memorial Museum

★16969★

WESTERN KENTUCKY UNIVERSITY - DEPARTMENT OF SPECIAL COLLECTIONS - FOLKLORE, FOLKLIFE & ORAL HISTORY ARCHIVES (Soc Sci)
Kentucky Bldg.   Phone: (502) 745-2592
Bowling Green, KY 42101   Patricia M. Hodges, Archv.
Staff: Prof 1. **Subjects:** Folklore, folk songs and music, social folk customs, traditional arts, regional oral history. **Holdings:** 3500 cassettes and tapes; 2000 manuscripts; collections of folk songs, beliefs, speech, correspondence. **Services:** Copying (limited); archives open to public.

★16970★

WESTERN KENTUCKY UNIVERSITY - DEPT. OF SPECIAL COLLECTIONS - KENTUCKY LIBRARY AND MUSEUM/UNIVERSITY ARCHIVES (Hist)
                                              Phone: (502) 745-2592
Bowling Green, KY 42101   Riley Handy, Hd., Spec.Coll.Dept.
Founded: 1931. **Staff:** Prof 6; Other 10. **Subjects:** Rare Kentuckiana, Mammoth Cave, Kentucky writers, Civil War, Shakers, Ohio Valley. **Special Collections:** Journals and writers of South Union Shaker Colony; Alice Hegan and Cale Young Rice Collection; McGregor Collection. **Holdings:** 25,000 books; 1250 bound periodical volumes; 48 VF drawers; 3300 photographs; 300 land grants; 2000 postcards; 435 prints; Kentucky census on microfilm, 1810-1900; 350 titles of Kentucky sheet music; scrapbooks; broadsides; maps. **Services:** Copying (limited); library open to public for research and reference. **Publications:** Occasional house organs. **Special Indexes:** Current Kentucky periodicals index. **Staff:** Constance A. Mills, Ref.Libn.; Virginia Pearson, Ref.Libn.; Elaine Harrison, Mss.Libn.; Helen Knight, Univ.Archv.; Nancy Baird, Ref.Libn.; Diane Alpert, Cur./Adm.Off.; Doug Nesbit, Pub.Info.Off.; Nancy Solley, Ref.Libn.; Debbie Smith, Musm. Registrar; Vicky Kohn, Asst.Cur. of Educ.; Bob Brigl, Asst.Cur., Exhibits.

★16971★

WESTERN LIFE INSURANCE COMPANY - LIBRARY (Bus-Fin)
Box 43271   Phone: (612) 738-4589
St. Paul, MN 55164   Carole Steele, Libn.
Founded: 1978. **Staff:** Prof 1; Other 1. **Subjects:** Insurance, management. **Holdings:** 300 books; annual statements. **Subscriptions:** 120 journals and other serials; 8 newspapers. **Services:** Library not open to public.

★16972★

WESTERN MARYLAND PUBLIC LIBRARIES - REGIONAL LIBRARY (Bus-Fin; Educ)
100 S. Potomac St.   Phone: (301) 739-3250
Hagerstown, MD 21740   Mary S. Mallery, Regional Libn.
Staff: Prof 2; Other 5. **Subjects:** Small business; home building, maintenance, and repair; antiques and collectibles; Civil Service and vocational tests; small scale farming. **Holdings:** 40,968 books; 300 reels of microfilm; 1385 16mm films; 1907 audio cassettes; 1000 automobile, truck, and motorcycle repair manuals; 246 video cassettes. **Services:** Interlibrary loans; copying; library open to public with restrictions. **Automated Operations:** Online 16mm film booking system. **Networks/Consortia:** Member of Maryland Interlibrary Loan Organization (MILO). **Remarks:** Library is maintained by the Washington County Free Library. **Staff:** Darlene Mann, Ref.Libn.; Ralph E. DeVore, Pub.Rel.Dir.; Lawrence Springer, AV Libn.

★16973★

WESTERN MEDICAL CENTER - MEDICAL LIBRARY (Med)
1001 N. Tustin Ave.   Phone: (714) 835-3555
Santa Ana, CA 92705   Evelyn Simpson, Dir., Med.Lib.
Staff: Prof 1; Other 2. **Subjects:** Medicine, nursing, surgery. **Holdings:** 4800 books; 5000 bound periodical volumes; 2300 Audio-Digest tapes (9 specialties); video cassettes. **Subscriptions:** 260 journals and other serials. **Services:** Interlibrary loans; copying; SDI; library open to public with

restrictions. **Computerized Information Services:** Online systems.

★16974★
WESTERN MEMORIAL REGIONAL HOSPITAL - HEALTH SCIENCE LIBRARY
(Med)†
West Valley Rd.
Box 2005   Phone: (709) 634-5101
Corner Brook, NF, Canada A2H 6J7   Walter S. MacPherson, Libn.
Founded: 1968. **Staff:** Prof 1; Other 1. **Subjects:** Medicine, nursing and paramedical fields. **Holdings:** 2500 books; 1150 bound periodical volumes. **Subscriptions:** 167 journals and other serials. **Services:** Interlibrary loans; copying; library open to public.

★16975★
**WESTERN MICHIGAN UNIVERSITY - ARCHIVES AND REGIONAL HISTORY
COLLECTIONS** (Hist)
                                                   Phone: (616) 383-1826
Kalamazoo, MI 49008   Wayne C. Mann, Dir.
Founded: 1957. **Staff:** Prof 2; Other 4. **Subjects:** History of Western Michigan University, local and regional history, genealogy. **Holdings:** 7000 books; 15,000 linear feet of manuscripts, photographs and other archival materials. **Subscriptions:** 20 journals and other serials. **Services:** Copying; collection open to public. **Special Indexes:** Comprehensive index to historic photographs. **Staff:** Peter Schmidt, Faculty Assoc.; Phyllis Burnham, Mss.Cat.

★16976★
WESTERN MICHIGAN UNIVERSITY - BUSINESS LIBRARY (Bus-Fin)
                                                   Phone: (616) 383-1926
Kalamazoo, MI 49008   David H. McKee, Hd.Libn.
Founded: 1958. **Staff:** Prof 3; Other 8. **Subjects:** Management, marketing, finance, accounting, business information systems, commercial law. **Holdings:** 33,04l books; 14,570 bound periodical volumes; 400 theses on microfilm; 25,000 corporate annual reports; 24 linear feet of business material; 300 linear feet of government documents; 24,366 other cataloged items. **Services:** Interlibrary loans; copying; library open to public. **Automated Operations:** Computerized circulation. **Computerized Information Services:** DIALOG, BRS, SDC; OLLI, CLSI (internal databases). Performs searches on cost recovery basis; consultant fee for nonuniversity personnel. **Networks/Consortia:** Member of Michigan Library Consortium (MLC). **Publications:** Guide to Business Library Materials series; New Acquisitions List.

★16977★
**WESTERN MICHIGAN UNIVERSITY - CENTER FOR WOMEN'S SERVICES -
LIBRARY** (Soc Sci)
331 Ellsworth Hall   Phone: (616) 383-6097
Kalamazoo, MI 49008   Karen Lason, Lib.Cons.
Staff: Prof 1; Other 1. **Subjects:** Women - health, financial status, careers, discrimination; displaced homemakers; nontraditional students and jobs; reentry women; equal pay for equal work. **Special Collections:** Local history of women's groups and causes, and of sex bias case in textbooks in public schools. **Holdings:** 1000 books; 9 VF drawers of clippings. **Subscriptions:** 20 journals and other serials. **Services:** Copying; library open to community members.

★16978★
WESTERN MICHIGAN UNIVERSITY - DOCUMENTS LIBRARY (Info Sci)
Waldo Library   Phone: (616) 383-4952
Kalamazoo, MI 49008   Michael McDonnell, Ref.Libn., Maps & Docs.
Founded: 1963. **Staff:** Prof 1; Other 2. **Subjects:** U.S. Government publications, 1963 to present; U.N. and Michigan documents. **Special Collections:** 19th Century Serial Set (microcard). **Holdings:** 390,000 documents. **Services:** Interlibrary loans; copying; library open to public. **Automated Operations:** Computerized cataloging. **Computerized Information Services:** DIALOG, OCLC, BRS; OLLI (internal database). Performs searches on cost recovery basis. **Networks/Consortia:** Member of Southwest Michigan Library Cooperative (SMLC).

★16979★
WESTERN MICHIGAN UNIVERSITY - EDUCATIONAL LIBRARY (Educ)
3300 Sangren Hall   Phone: (616) 383-1666
Kalamazoo, MI 49008   David Netz, Hd.Libn.
Founded: 1964. **Staff:** Prof 3; Other 4. **Subjects:** Educational research; higher, secondary and elementary education; educational psychology; educational tests and measurement; educational law; comparative education. **Special Collections:** ERIC documents (210,000 titles; 260,000 microfiche); Curriculum Development Library (10,000 microfiche); children's and young people's books (2510); textbooks (10,000 elementary and secondary); curriculum guides (2500 elementary and secondary). **Holdings:** 50,305 books; 10,306 bound periodical volumes; 6000 pamphlets; 2500 books on

microfilm; 500 producers' catalogs; 4400 audiovisual materials. **Subscriptions:** 600 journals and other serials. **Services:** Interlibrary loans; copying; library open to public with restrictions on circulation. **Automated Operations:** Computerized circulation. **Computerized Information Services:** DIALOG, BRS, SDC; OLLI (internal database). **Publications:** News, Views and Reviews; bibliographies and study guides; Education Library Link - all to College of Education Faculty. **Formerly:** Its Educational Resources Center. **Staff:** Helen J. Healy, Libn.; Patricia VanderMeer, Libn.

★16980★
**WESTERN MICHIGAN UNIVERSITY - HARPER C. MAYBEE MUSIC & DANCE
LIBRARY** (Mus; Art)
3008 Dalton Center   Phone: (616) 383-1817
Kalamazoo, MI 49008   Gregory Fitzgerald, Hd.Libn.
Founded: 1949. **Staff:** Prof 1; Other 1. **Subjects:** Music, dance. **Special Collections:** American vocal sheet music collection (1000 titles); WMU School of Music performance archives (800 tapes). **Holdings:** 10,395 books; 2901 bound periodical volumes; 12,212 scores; 9900 phonograph records and tapes; 144 reels of microfilm; 79 microfiche; 1250 other cataloged items. **Subscriptions:** 101 journals and other serials. **Services:** Interlibrary loans; copying; library open to public with restrictions on borrowing. **Automated Operations:** Computerized circulation. **Publications:** Guides to collection and catalogs; Recent Acquisitions, quarterly; newsletter, irregular - to faculty and staff. **Special Indexes:** Index to song collections; index to jazz recordings. **Formerly:** Its Music Library.

★16981★
**WESTERN MICHIGAN UNIVERSITY - INSTITUTE OF CISTERCIAN STUDIES
LIBRARY** (Rel-Theol)
Hillside West   Phone: (616) 383-1969
Kalamazoo, MI 49008   Beatrice H. Beech, Hd.
Founded: 1973. **Staff:** Prof 1; Other 1. **Subjects:** Cisterciansia, history, monasticism. **Special Collections:** Editions of Bernard of Clairvaux (400 volumes); medieval manuscripts; incunabula; early 16th-18th century books. **Holdings:** 6500 books; 336 bound periodical volumes; 82 manuscripts. **Services:** Interlibrary loans; copying; library open to public.

★16982★
**WESTERN MICHIGAN UNIVERSITY - INST. OF PUBLIC AFFAIRS - ENV.
RESOURCE CENTER FOR COMMUNITY INFO.** (Env-Cons; Plan)
                                                   Phone: (616) 383-3983
Kalamazoo, MI 49008
Staff: 1. **Subjects:** Environment, public policy, community planning. **Holdings:** 8 VF drawers of cataloged items. **Services:** Copying; center open to public for reference use only.

★16983★
WESTERN MICHIGAN UNIVERSITY - MAP LIBRARY (Geog-Map)
Waldo Library   Phone: (616) 383-4952
Kalamazoo, MI 49008   Michael McDonnell, Ref.Libn., Maps & Docs.
Founded: 1968. **Staff:** Prof 1; Other 2. **Subjects:** Domestic and foreign maps, antique maps of special historical interest, U.S. Geological Survey, TOPCOM, Coast and Geodetic Service, U.S. Forest Service, Soil Conservation Service, national parks, city maps, topographic maps, aeronautical and nautical charts. **Special Collections:** Climatological data; historical maps and atlases; soil surveys; gazetteers. **Holdings:** 200 books; 50 bound periodical volumes; 1200 atlases; 158,960 maps. **Services:** Copying; library open to public. **Automated Operations:** Computerized cataloging. **Computerized Information Services:** OCLC, DIALOG, BRS; OLLI (internal database). Performs searches on cost recovery basis. **Networks/Consortia:** Member of Southwest Michigan Library Cooperative (SMLC). **Special Catalogs:** Michigan Atlases - A Union List, 1971.

★16984★
WESTERN MICHIGAN UNIVERSITY - PHYSICAL SCIENCES LIBRARY (Sci-
Tech)
3376 Rood Hall   Phone: (616) 383-4943
Kalamazoo, MI 49008   Beatrice Sichel, Hd.Libn.
Founded: 1971. **Staff:** Prof 1; Other 1. **Subjects:** Mathematics, physics, geology, computer science, astronomy. **Holdings:** 39,334 books; 18,679 bound periodical volumes; 2397 geological maps; 83 reels of microfilm; 764 microfiche. **Subscriptions:** 551 journals and other serials. **Services:** Interlibrary loans; copying; library open to public. **Automated Operations:** Computerized circulation. **Computerized Information Services:** DIALOG, MATHFILE; OLLI (internal database). Performs searches on cost recovery basis.

WESTERN MINERAL RESOURCES LIBRARY
See: U.S. Geological Survey

★16985★
WESTERN MISSOURI MENTAL HEALTH CENTER - LIBRARY (Med)†
600 E. 22nd St.   Phone: (816) 471-3000
Kansas City, MO 64108   Ellen Bull, Med.Libn.
Founded: 1954. Staff: Prof 1. Subjects: Psychiatry, psychology, social science, psychological testing, psychoanalysis, drugs and alcohol. Special Collections: Works of Sigmund Freud. Holdings: 3200 books; 74 unbound periodical titles; 332 cassette tapes; phonograph records. Subscriptions: 79 journals and other serials. Services: Interlibrary loans; copying; library open to public with permission. Networks/Consortia: Member of Midcontinental Regional Medical Library Program.

★16986★
WESTERN MONTANA CLINIC - LIBRARY (Med)
501 W. Broadway   Phone: (406) 721-5600
Missoula, MT 59807   Patricia A. Manlove, Libn.
Staff: Prof 1. Subjects: Medicine. Holdings: 500 books; 165 bound periodical volumes. Subscriptions: 165 journals and other serials. Services: Interlibrary loans; copying; library open to public with restrictions. Computerized Information Services: Online systems. Networks/Consortia: Member of Pacific Northwest Regional Health Sciences Library Service (PNRHSLS).

★16987★
WESTERN MONTANA SCIENTISTS' COMMITTEE FOR PUBLIC INFORMATION - MONTANA ENVIRONMENTAL LIBRARY (Env-Cons)
Jeanette Rankin Hall
Univ. of Montana   Phone: (406) 243-2282
Missoula, MT 59812   William D. Tomlinson, Dir.
Founded: 1966. Staff: Prof 2; Other 3. Subjects: Air and water pollution, water resources, energy, fuels, pesticides and herbicides, radiation and hazardous materials, environment, conservation, chemical reference. Holdings: 5100 books; 51,000 reprints; 2000 subject files of newspaper, Congressional Record and Federal Register clippings; 19,000 35mm slides; 100 black and white prints. Subscriptions: 25 journals and other serials; 5 newspapers. Services: Interlibrary loans; library open to public. Automated Operations: Computerized cataloging, acquisitions, serials and circulation. Computerized Information Services: Internal database. Staff: Jean G. Parodi, Res.Spec.

★16988★
WESTERN MUSEUM OF MINING & INDUSTRY - LIBRARY (Sci-Tech)
1025 Northgate Rd.   Phone: (303) 598-8850
Colorado Springs, CO 80908   Bob Lincoln, Cur. of Educ.
Staff: Prof 1; Other 1. Subjects: Mining, metallurgy, electrical and mechanical engineering. Holdings: 5000 books; 400 bound periodical volumes; 45 other items; 16 boxes of pamphlets; 10 boxes of magazines; microfilm of early engineering periodicals. Services: Interlibrary loans; library open to members and scholars. Publications: Newsletter; Annual Report.

WESTERN NEW ENGLAND COLLEGE - MASSACHUSETTS COLLEGE OF PHARMACY & ALLIED HEALTH SCIENCES
See: Massachusetts College of Pharmacy & Allied Health Sciences

★16989★
WESTERN NEW ENGLAND COLLEGE - SCHOOL OF LAW LIBRARY (Law)
1215 Wilbraham Rd.   Phone: (413) 782-3111
Springfield, MA 01119   Donald J. Dunn, Law Libn.
Founded: 1973. Staff: Prof 6; Other 7. Subjects: Law. Holdings: 40,000 books; 70,000 bound periodical volumes. Subscriptions: 700 journals and other serials; 8 newspapers. Services: Interlibrary loans; copying; library open to public. Automated Operations: Computerized cataloging. Computerized Information Services: LEXIS. Networks/Consortia: Member of Cooperating Libraries of Greater Springfield, A CCGS Agency. Publications: Monthly List of New Acquisitions; Contents Pages of Legal Periodicals - both for internal distribution only. Staff: Bonnie White, Assoc. Law Libn.; Susan C. Wells, Hd., Tech.Serv.; Howard E. Polonsky, Hd., Rd.Serv.; Michele Dill, Ref.Libn.; Christine Archambault, Cat.Libn.

WESTERN NEW YORK FORUM FOR AMERICAN ART
See: SUNY - College at Buffalo - Burchfield Center-Western New York Forum for American Art

★16990★
WESTERN NEW YORK GENEALOGICAL SOCIETY, INC. - LIBRARY (Hist)
Box 338   Phone: (716) 649-4440
Hamburg, NY 14075   Donald C. Shaw, Dir.
Subjects: Genealogy and local history. Special Collections: McCabe Collection. Holdings: 350 books; 1500 unbound periodicals; 650 pamphlets, paperbacks, manuscripts, articles; genealogical society publications; 250 reels of microfilm. Services: Library open to public for reference use only. Publications: The Journal, quarterly.

★16991★
WESTERN ONTARIO BREEDERS, INC. - LIBRARY (Agri)
Hwy. 59 N.
P.O. Box 457   Phone: (519) 539-9831
Woodstock, ON, Canada N4S 7Y7   Howard D. Start, Dir.
Founded: 1946. Subjects: Livestock breeding, veterinary science. Holdings: 425 books and bound periodical volumes; breed journals; sire directories; sales catalogs. Subscriptions: 35 journals and other serials; 6 newspapers. Services: Library not open to public.

★16992★
WESTERN OREGON STATE COLLEGE - LIBRARY (Educ)
234 Monmouth Ave.   Phone: (503) 838-1220
Monmouth, OR 97361   Dr. Clarence Gorchels, Dir.
Founded: 1856. Staff: Prof 5; Other 7. Subjects: Education, liberal arts, special education. Special Collections: John C. Higgins Memorial Collection of Pacific Northwest History and Culture. Holdings: 179,000 books and bound periodical volumes. Subscriptions: 1506 journals and other serials; 83 newspapers. Services: Interlibrary loans; copying; library open to public for reference use only. Staff: Ms. Zillah Paeth, Hd.Acq.Libn.Lotte Larsen, Hd., Ref. & Lib.Instr.; Howard Hill, Hd.Cat.; Roy V. Bennett, Ref./Doc. & ILL.

WESTERN PENNSYLVANIA BOTANICAL SOCIETY LIBRARY
See: Carnegie Museum of Natural History - Library

★16993★
WESTERN PENNSYLVANIA GENEALOGICAL SOCIETY - LIBRARY (Hist)
4338 Bigelow Blvd.   Phone: (412) 681-5533
Pittsburgh, PA 15213   Helen M. Wilson, Libn.
Staff: Prof 2. Subjects: Genealogy, local history. Holdings: 370 books and bound periodical volumes; 76 archival items; 8 VF drawers of local obituaries; 28 VF drawers of clippings; 15 feet of newsletters; 800 pages of obituaries of persons born in Pennsylvania but living elsewhere. Services: Interlibrary loans; copying; library open to public. Publications: Quarterly; Jots From The Point; list of additional publications - available upon request. Special Indexes: Genealogical Surname Index. Remarks: The genealogical collection is housed at the Historical Society of Pennsylvania. Staff: Ruth S. Reed, Archv.

★16994★
WESTERN PENTECOSTAL BIBLE COLLEGE - LIBRARY (Rel-Theol)
Box 1000   Phone: (604) 853-7491
Clayburn, BC, Canada V0X 1E0   Rev. Laurence M. Van Kleek, Libn.
Founded: 1941. Staff: Prof 1; Other 3. Subjects: Humanities, social sciences, Bible, doctrinal and practical theology, world religions and cults, missions. Special Collections: Archive for Pentecostal Studies, includes Action, 1970 to present; Pentecostal Testimony, 1920-1940, 1942 to present. Holdings: 21,740 books; 221 bound periodical volumes; 23 filmstrips; 287 audio recordings; 820 microforms; 297 pamphlets; 50 clippings; 66 yearbooks. Subscriptions: 235 journals and other serials. Services: Copying; library open to public. Publications: WPBC Library Bulletin, bimonthly - distributed to faculty, staff and administration. Special Indexes: Indexes to denominational periodicals (mimeographed). Remarks: Library is located at 35235 Straiton Rd., Clayburn, BC V0X 1E0.

WESTERN PHILATELIC LIBRARY
See: Friends of the Western Philatelic Library

WESTERN PSYCHIATRIC INSTITUTE AND CLINIC
See: University of Pittsburgh

★16995★
WESTERN PUBLISHING COMPANY, INC. - CORPORATE TRAINING CENTER LIBRARY (Publ)
1220 Mound Ave.   Phone: (414) 633-2431
Racine, WI 53404   Richard H. Popp, Mgr., Corp. Training
Founded: 1950. Staff: 1. Subjects: Graphic arts, production, management, sales, education. Special Collections: Graphic Arts (past and present; 700 bound volumes). Holdings: 1904 books; 1000 pamphlets; 1500 unbound graphic arts magazines; 91 graphic arts films; 13,806 training slides in

graphic arts; 580 graphic arts transparencies; 182 CCTV tapes. **Services:** Copying; library open to public by appointment. **Special Catalogs:** Audiovisual catalog, annual update. **Remarks:** Library materials exist basically for teaching and reference in the field of graphic arts.

★16996★
WESTERN RESERVE HISTORICAL SOCIETY - LIBRARY (Hist)
10825 E. Blvd.   Phone: (216) 721-5722
Cleveland, OH 44106   Kermit J. Pike, Dir.
Founded: 1867. **Staff:** Prof 12; Other 5. **Subjects:** Ohio history, American genealogy, Civil War, slavery and abolitionism, ethnic history, American Revolution. **Special Collections:** Wallace H. Cathcart Shaker Collection; William P. Palmer Civil War Collection; David Z. Norton Napoleon Collection. **Holdings:** 218,800 books; 25,000 volumes of newspapers; 50,000 pamphlets; 5 million manuscripts; 26,000 reels of microfilm. **Subscriptions:** 322 journals and other serials; 50 newspapers. **Services:** Interlibrary loans; copying; library open to public. **Special Catalogs:** Catalogs to manuscript, genealogy and Shaker collections (all on cards). **Staff:** Charles Sherrill, Hd.Ref.Libn.; Dennis I. Harrison, Cur. of Mss.; Marian Sweton, Hd.Cat.

★16997★
WESTERN RESERVE PSYCHIATRIC HABILITATION CENTER - STAFF LIBRARY (Med)
1756 Sagamore Rd.
Box 305   Phone: (216) 467-7131
Northfield, OH 44067   Pearlie McAlpine, Libn.
Staff: 1. **Subjects:** Psychiatry, psychiatric nursing, psychology, social service. **Holdings:** 500 books. **Subscriptions:** 55 journals and other serials. **Services:** Interlibrary loans; library not open to public.

★16998★
WESTERN AND SOUTHERN LIFE INSURANCE CO. - LIBRARY (Bus-Fin)
400 Broadway   Phone: (513) 629-1393
Cincinnati, OH 45202   Virginia Custer, Libn.
Founded: 1952. **Subjects:** Business, insurance, recreation. **Holdings:** 3538 volumes; 4 VF drawers.

WESTERN SPACE AND MISSILE CENTER
See: U.S. Air Force

★16999★
WESTERN STATE HOSPITAL - MEDICAL LIBRARY (Med)
                                                  Phone: (405) 766-2311
Fort Supply, OK 73841   Vi Thomas, Lib.Techn.
Founded: 1950. **Staff:** Prof 1. **Subjects:** Substance abuse, psychiatry, geriatrics, psychology. **Holdings:** 2943 books; 23 bound periodical volumes; 50 boxes of booklets, pamphlets and reports; 43 slide sets; 74 cassettes; 37 records; 169 filmstrips; 27 films. **Subscriptions:** 73 journals and other serials; 35 newspapers. **Services:** Interlibrary loans; copying; library open to public for reference use only. **Automated Operations:** Computerized cataloging and circulation. **Remarks:** Maintains a patients' library of 6327 volumes.

★17000★
WESTERN STATE HOSPITAL - MEDICAL LIBRARY (Med)
Box 2500   Phone: (703) 885-9387
Staunton, VA 24401   Richard D. Wills, Libn.
Staff: Prof 1; Other 1. **Subjects:** Psychology, psychiatry, general medicine, nursing. **Holdings:** 3600 books; 600 bound periodical volumes. **Subscriptions:** 117 journals and other serials. **Services:** Interlibrary loans; library open to public.

★17001★
WESTERN STATE HOSPITAL - PROFESSIONAL LIBRARY (Med)
Russellville Rd.
Box 2200   Phone: (502) 886-4431
Hopkinsville, KY 42240   Margaret Crim Riley, Libn.
Staff: Prof 1; Other 1. **Subjects:** Psychiatry, psychology, nursing, medicine, social work, management. **Holdings:** 2500 books; 240 bound periodical volumes; 29 films, 92 filmstrips and 50 cassettes relating to mental health care. **Subscriptions:** 58 journals and other serials. **Services:** Interlibrary loans; copying; library open to public with restrictions.

WESTERN STATE HOSPITAL - STAFF LIBRARY
See: Washington State Library

★17002★
WESTERN STATE UNIVERSITY - COLLEGE OF LAW - LIBRARY (Law)†
1111 N. State College Blvd.   Phone: (714) 738-1000
Fullerton, CA 92631   Frank Phillips, Univ.Libn.
Staff: Prof 3; Other 16. **Subjects:** Law, California law. **Holdings:** 47,000 books; 244 other cataloged items; 500 tape cassettes; 20,000 microforms. **Subscriptions:** 700 journals and other serials; 12 newspapers. **Services:** Interlibrary loans; copying; library open to public for reference use only. **Staff:** Judith Runyon Leyva .

★17003★
WESTERN STATE UNIVERSITY - COLLEGE OF LAW - LIBRARY (Law)
2121 San Diego Ave.   Phone: (619) 297-9700
San Diego, CA 92110   Karla M. Randich, Asst.Prof./Libn.
Staff: Prof 2; Other 10. **Subjects:** Law. **Holdings:** 35,000 books; 5000 bound periodical volumes; 20,000 volumes in microform; 150 videotapes; 100 audiotapes. **Subscriptions:** 250 journals and other serials; 10 newspapers. **Services:** Interlibrary loans; library open to public. **Computerized Information Services:** LEXIS. **Staff:** Christine M. Cheff, Ref. & Pub.Serv.Libn.

★17004★
WESTERN STATES CHIROPRACTIC COLLEGE - W.A. BUDDEN MEMORIAL LIBRARY (Med)
2900 N.E. 132nd Ave.   Phone: (503) 256-3180
Portland, OR 97230   Kay Irvine, Hd.Libn.
Staff: Prof 2; Other 10. **Subjects:** Chiropractic, obstetrics, neurology, orthopedics, roentgenology. **Holdings:** 3000 books; 1000 bound periodical volumes. **Subscriptions:** 352 journals and other serials. **Services:** Interlibrary loans; copying; library open to public. **Computerized Information Services:** DIALOG, MEDLINE. Performs searches on cost recovery basis. **Networks/Consortia:** Member of Chiropractic Library Consortium (CLIBCON); Oregon Health Sciences Libraries Association (OHSLA); Portland Area Health Sciences Librarians. **Special Indexes:** Index to Chiropractic Literature. **Staff:** Sandra Loveland, Dir., Instr. Media Ctr.

★17005★
WESTERN THEOLOGICAL SEMINARY - BEARDSLEE LIBRARY (Rel-Theol)
                                                  Phone: (616) 392-8555
Holland, MI 49423   John R. Muether, Libn.
Staff: Prof 2; Other 2. **Subjects:** Theology. **Holdings:** 82,000 books; 4000 bound periodical volumes; 350 linear feet of archives; 3200 slides; 2060 microforms. **Subscriptions:** 591 journals and other serials. **Services:** Interlibrary loans; copying; library open to public with restrictions. **Automated Operations:** Computerized cataloging. **Networks/Consortia:** Member of Michigan Library Consortium. **Publications:** Reformed Review, 3/year. **Staff:** Colleen Slager, Acq./ILL.

★17006★
WESTERN UNION CORPORATION - LIBRARY (Sci-Tech)†
One Lake St.   Phone: (201) 825-5850
Upper Saddle River, NJ 07458   Alice Critchley, Libn.
Founded: 1921. **Staff:** Prof 1; Other 1. **Subjects:** Telecommunications, telegraphy, electronics, satellites. **Special Collections:** History of telegraphy. **Holdings:** 11,000 books; 3000 bound periodical volumes; 300 monographs. **Subscriptions:** 175 journals and other serials. **Services:** Interlibrary loans; copying; library open to public.

★17007★
WESTERN WASHINGTON UNIVERSITY - CENTER FOR PACIFIC NORTHWEST STUDIES (Hist)
Bellingham, WA 98225   Dr. James W. Scott, Dir.
Staff: 4. **Subjects:** History - Washington, Pacific Northwest, business. **Holdings:** 500 books; 100 bound periodical volumes; 600 volumes of bound newspapers; 300 cubic feet and 200 linear feet of business records; 90 cubic feet of manuscripts and personal collections; 4500 photographs and negatives. **Services:** Copying; center open to public for reference use only. **Publications:** Occasional Papers series. **Special Catalogs:** Guide to the Collections.

★17008★
WESTERN WASHINGTON UNIVERSITY - DEPARTMENT OF GEOGRAPHY AND REGIONAL PLANNING - MAP LIBRARY (Geog-Map)
Arntzen Hall 101   Phone: (206) 676-3272
Bellingham, WA 98225   Karl Thompson, Act. Map Cur.
Founded: 1957. **Staff:** Prof 1; Other 9. **Subjects:** Maps, atlases. **Special Collections:** Maps emphasizing the Pacific Northwest, Canada, Mexico and Circum-Pacific. **Holdings:** 670 atlases; 172,000 maps; 20,600 aerial photographs; 55 globes. **Services:** Copying; library open to public for

reference use only.

WESTERN WASHINGTON UNIVERSITY - HUXLEY COLLEGE OF ENVIRONMENTAL STUDIES
See: Huxley College of Environmental Studies

★17009★
WESTERN WISCONSIN TECHNICAL INSTITUTE - LIBRARY (Sci-Tech)
6th & Vine Sts.　　　　　　　　　　Phone: (608) 785-9142
La Crosse, WI 54601　　　　　　　　Thuan T. Tran, Hd.Libn.
Founded: 1966. **Staff:** Prof 2; Other 3. **Subjects:** Technology, health occupations, business administration, distributive education, adult education, home economics, agriculture. **Holdings:** 25,000 books and bound periodical volumes; 2000 reels of microfilm; 1200 microfiche; 8 VF drawers of pamphlets. **Subscriptions:** 450 journals and other serials; 30 newspapers. **Services:** Interlibrary loans; copying; bibliographic and reference services for faculty and students; library open to public. **Staff:** Annette Neiderkorn, Ref.Libn.

★17010★
WESTERNERS INTERNATIONAL, A FOUNDATION - LIBRARY (Hist)
College Sta., Box 3485
Tucson, AZ 85722　　　　　　　　　Carolyn Nelson, Libn.
Founded: 1944. **Staff:** 3. **Subjects:** Western history. **Holdings:** 500 volumes; publications, documents and correspondence of more than 100 local units called "Corrals" devoted to research and popularization of Western history. **Subscriptions:** 20 journals and other serials. **Services:** Copying; library open to public with restrictions. **Publications:** Buckskin Bulletin, quarterly - distributed to all members of local "Corrals" free; by subscription to others.

WESTFORNET-BERKELEY SERVICE CENTER
See: U.S. Forest Service - Pacific Southwest Forest & Range Experiment Station

WESTGATE FRIENDS LIBRARY
See: Society of Friends - Ohio Yearly Meeting

WESTHOLLOW RESEARCH CENTER LIBRARY
See: Shell Development Company

WESTINGHOUSE AIR BRAKE COMPANY
See: WABCO

★17011★
WESTINGHOUSE CANADA LTD. - ELECTRONICS DIVISION LIBRARY (Sci-Tech)†
777 Walker's Lane
P.O. Box 5009　　　　　　　　　　Phone: (416) 528-8811
Burlington, ON, Canada L7R 4B3　　　　E. Jackson, Libn.
Staff: Prof 1. **Subjects:** Electronics and electrical engineering, data processing. **Holdings:** 2000 books; trade literature from 1000 manufacturers; 1000 reports; 8000 military, government and commercial specifications and standards; 25 VF drawers of pamphlets; 200 reels of microfilm. **Subscriptions:** 150 journals and other serials; 15 newspapers. **Services:** Interlibrary loans; copying; library open to public for reference use only, on request. **Publications:** Library Bulletin, irregular - for internal distribution only.

★17012★
WESTINGHOUSE ELECTRIC CORPORATION - BETTIS ATOMIC POWER LABORATORY - LIBRARY (Energy)†
Box 79　　　　　　　　　　　　Phone: (412) 462-5000
West Mifflin, PA 15122-0079　　　　Mary Louise Frazee, Libn.
Founded: 1949. **Staff:** Prof 4; Other 3. **Subjects:** Nuclear power. **Holdings:** 44,000 books and bound periodical volumes; internal technical reports and correspondence; Atomic Energy Commission reports. **Subscriptions:** 300 journals and other serials. **Services:** Interlibrary loans; library not open to public. **Remarks:** The Westinghouse Electric Corporation operates under contract to the U.S. Department of Energy.

★17013★
WESTINGHOUSE ELECTRIC CORPORATION - DEFENSE & ELECTRONIC CENTER - TECHNICAL INFORMATION CENTER (Sci-Tech)
MS 1204, Box 1693　　　　　　　　Phone: (301) 765-2858
Baltimore, MD 21203　　　　　　　　Joan L. Doerr, Supv.
Founded: 1961. **Staff:** Prof 3; Other 5. **Subjects:** Electronic communication engineering, systems engineering. **Holdings:** 11,000 books; 2000 bound periodical volumes; 100,000 technical reports on microfilm. **Subscriptions:**

450 journals and other serials. **Services:** Interlibrary loans; center not open to public. **Computerized Information Services:** DIALOG, SDC, BRS, DOE/RECON, DTIC.

★17014★
WESTINGHOUSE ELECTRIC CORPORATION - ELECTRICAL SYSTEMS DIVISION - TECHNICAL LIBRARY (Sci-Tech)†
1501 S. Dixie　　　　　　　　　　Phone: (419) 226-3121
Lima, OH 45804　　　　　　　　　Russel J. Heine, Tech.Pub.Anl.
Staff: 1. **Subjects:** Electrical and electronic engineering. **Holdings:** 2200 books; 1100 bound periodical volumes; 8000 technical reports; 600 patents. **Subscriptions:** 100 journals and other serials. **Services:** Library not open to public. **Computerized Information Services:** Mechanized retrieval.

★17015★
WESTINGHOUSE ELECTRIC CORPORATION - LAMP DIVISIONS - ENGINEERING LIBRARY (Sci-Tech)†
1447 Chestnut Ave.　　　　　　　　Phone: (201) 926-7940
Hillside, NJ 07205
Staff: Prof 1. **Subjects:** Electric lamps, optics, luminescence, inorganic chemistry, metals and materials, metallurgy. **Holdings:** 2500 books; 8400 bound periodical volumes; 14 VF drawers of patents and disclosures; 15 VF drawers of technical reports; 5 VF drawers of translations; 15 VF drawers of files. **Subscriptions:** 185 journals and other serials. **Services:** Interlibrary loans; library not open to public. **Computerized Information Services:** Online systems.

★17016★
WESTINGHOUSE ELECTRIC CORPORATION - LIBRARY 3-S-14
700 Braddock Ave.
East Pittsburgh, PA 15112
Defunct. Merged with Westinghouse Electric Corporation - Steam Turbine Generator Division - Technical Library to form its Steam Turbine Generator Division - Library.

★17017★
WESTINGHOUSE ELECTRIC CORPORATION - MEDIUM POWER TRANSFORMER DIV. - SHARON ENGINEERING LIBRARY†
469 Sharpsville Ave.
Sharon, PA 16146
Subjects: Electrical and mechanical engineering, insulation theory, physics. **Holdings:** 1050 books; 250 bound periodical volumes; 800 issued patents; 2000 patent disclosures. **Remarks:** Presently inactive.

★17018★
WESTINGHOUSE ELECTRIC CORPORATION - NAVAL REACTOR FACILITY LIBRARY (Sci-Tech)
Box 2068
Idaho Falls, ID 83401　　　　　　　　Coy E. Stewart, Libn.
Founded: 1956. **Staff:** Prof 1; Other 7. **Subjects:** Atomic power. **Holdings:** 4000 books; 58,000 documents and technical reports. **Subscriptions:** 52 journals and other serials. **Services:** Library not open to public.

★17019★
WESTINGHOUSE ELECTRIC CORPORATION - NUCLEAR ENERGY SYSTEMS - ADVANCED REACTORS DIVISION - LIBRARY (Sci-Tech)†
Waltz Mill Site
Box 158　　　　　　　　　　　Phone: (412) 722-5301
Madison, PA 15663　　　　　　　　Ann Chernega, Lib.Mgr.
Founded: 1967. **Staff:** Prof 2; Other 2. **Subjects:** Fast reactor technology, nuclear enginering and fuels, energy policy, metallurgy. **Special Collections:** Advanced coal conversion collection (coal gasification/liquefaction). **Holdings:** 7100 books; 3400 bound periodical volumes; Department of Energy reports (20,000 hard copy; 720 microfiche file drawers). **Subscriptions:** 332 journals and other serials. **Services:** Interlibrary loans; copying; library open to public by special arrangement. **Automated Operations:** Computerized cataloging and serials. **Computerized Information Services:** DOE/RECON, DIALOG, New York Times Information Service, SDC; internal database. **Publications:** Waltz Mill Library Services; ARD Library Bulletins, weekly - for internal distribution only. **Special Indexes:** Technical record book index (computer printout); internal ward reports index (computer printout). **Staff:** Kathleen L. Horvat, Tech.Libn.

★17020★
WESTINGHOUSE ELECTRIC CORPORATION - OFFSHORE POWER SYSTEMS LIBRARY (Energy)†
7960 Arlington Expy.
Box 8000　　　　　　　　　　　Phone: (904) 724-7700
Jacksonville, FL 32211　　　　　　Minnie G. Thurston, Supv., Lib.Serv.
Founded: 1972. **Staff:** Prof 1. **Subjects:** Nuclear power, environment,

engineering. **Holdings:** 5600 books; 150 bound periodical volumes. **Subscriptions:** 150 journals and other serials; 10 newspapers. **Services:** Interlibrary loans; library not open to public.

★17021★
WESTINGHOUSE ELECTRIC CORPORATION - RESEARCH AND DEVELOPMENT CENTER - RESEARCH LIBRARY (Sci-Tech)
1310 Beulah Rd.   Phone: (412) 256-1610
Pittsburgh, PA 15235   Anita Newell, Mgr.
Founded: 1923. **Staff:** Prof 3; Other 4. **Subjects:** Chemistry, ceramics, electrical engineering, electronics, mathematics, magnetics, mechanical engineering, mechanical sciences, metallurgy, nuclear sciences, space sciences, physics. **Holdings:** 50,000 volumes. **Subscriptions:** 650 journals and other serials. **Services:** Library open to public by special arrangement.

★17022★
WESTINGHOUSE ELECTRIC CORPORATION - STEAM TURBINE GENERATOR DIVISION - LIBRARY (Sci-Tech; Comp Sci)
The Quadrangle   Phone: (305) 281-2171
Orlando, FL 32817   Tena Crenshaw, Libn.
Founded: 1983. **Staff:** Prof 1; Other 1. **Subjects:** Engineering, mathematics, computers, management, metallurgy. **Holdings:** 3500 books; 600 bound periodical volumes; 7500 other cataloged items. **Subscriptions:** 250 journals and other serials. **Services:** Interlibrary loans; library not open to public. **Automated Operations:** Computerized circulation. **Computerized Information Services:** DIALOG, BRS; internal database. **Publications:** New Books Listing, monthly; Newly Issued STGD Reports, monthly. **Formed by the Merger of:** Westinghouse Electric Corporation - Library 3-S-14 and its Steam Turbine Generator Division - Technical Library.

★17023★
WESTINGHOUSE ELECTRIC CORPORATION - STEAM TURBINE GENERATOR DIVISION - TECHNICAL LIBRARY
Lester Branch
Box 9175
Philadelphia, PA 19113
Defunct. Merged with Westinghouse Electric Corporation - Library 3-S-14 to form its Steam Turbine Generator Division - Library.

★17024★
WESTINGHOUSE ELECTRIC CORPORATION - TAMPA DIVISION - ENGINEERING LIBRARY
6001 S. Westshore Blvd.
Box 19218
Tampa, FL 33616
Defunct

★17025★
WESTINGHOUSE ELECTRIC CORPORATION - WATER REACTOR DIVISIONS - INFORMATION RESOURCE CENTER (Sci-Tech)
Box 355   Phone: (412) 373-4200
Pittsburgh, PA 15230   Cynthia A. Hodgson, Mgr.
Founded: 1955. **Staff:** Prof 11; Other 8. **Subjects:** Nuclear technology, engineering and industry, business management and marketing. **Special Collections:** Productivity; career planning. **Holdings:** 50,000 books and bound periodical volumes; 300,000 technical reports in microform; 25,000 technical reports and documents; 500 videotapes; 3000 pamphlets. **Subscriptions:** 650 journals and other serials. **Services:** Interlibrary loans; copying; center open to public by appointment only. **Automated Operations:** Computerized cataloging, serials and circulation. **Computerized Information Services:** DIALOG, BRS, DOE/RECON, NEXIS, Dow Jones News/Retrieval, Dun & Bradstreet Corporation, INVESTEXT, Dialcom, Inc., Newsshare; Techline (internal database). **Networks/Consortia:** Member of Pittsburgh Regional Library Center (PRLC). **Special Indexes:** KWOC Indexes to videotapes and films, Nucleonics Week 1968-80, Selected Public Information on Nuclear Energy (SPINDEX), TMI related information. **Formerly:** Its Nuclear Energy Systems. **Staff:** Barbara Spiegelman, Sr.Info.Spec.; Karen Commings, Sr.Info.Spec.; Esther Nathanson, Sr.Info.Spec.; Honey Marchetti, Info.Spec.; Bobbi Kendig, Info.Spec.

★17026★
WESTINGHOUSE ELECTRIC CORPORATION - WESTINGHOUSE NUCLEAR TRAINING CENTER - INFORMATION RSRC. CENTER (Energy; Sci-Tech)†
505 Shiloh Blvd.   Phone: (312) 872-4585
Zion, IL 60099   Pat O'Rear, Info.Spec.
Founded: 1970. **Staff:** 1. **Subjects:** Nuclear power, physics. **Holdings:** 500 books; 600 technical manuals; 150 videotapes; 5000 slides; 300 microfiche. **Subscriptions:** 25 journals and other serials; 6 newspapers. **Services:** Interlibrary loans; center not open to public.

★17027★
WESTINGHOUSE ELECTRIC CORPORATION - WIPP TECHNICAL LIBRARY (Sci-Tech)
Box 40039   Phone: (505) 766-3030
Albuquerque, NM 87196   Elaine K. Bickerstaff, Libn.
Staff: Prof 1; Other 1. **Subjects:** Nuclear waste disposal, geology. **Special Collections:** U.S. Department of Energy Waste Isolation Pilot Plant (WIPP) materials. **Holdings:** 150 books; 3500 technical reports; 2000 slides; 36 folders of news clippings. **Subscriptions:** 29 journals and other serials; 5 newspapers. **Services:** Interlibrary loans; library not open to public. **Automated Operations:** Computerized cataloging. **Computerized Information Services:** DIALOG. **Publications:** What's New in the Library, monthly - for internal distribution only.

★17028★
WESTINGHOUSE HANFORD COMPANY - FUEL SYSTEMS INFORMATION CENTER
Box 1970
Richland, WA 99352
Defunct

★17029★
WESTLAKE COMMUNITY HOSPITAL - LIBRARY (Med)
1225 Superior St.   Phone: (312) 681-3000
Melrose Park, IL 60160   Carol D. Strauss, Libn.
Staff: Prof 1. **Subjects:** Medicine, nursing, hospitals, health administration. **Holdings:** 750 books; 50 bound periodical volumes; 6 VF drawers of pamphlets. **Subscriptions:** 90 journals and other serials. **Services:** Interlibrary loans; SDI; library open to public for reference use only. **Networks/Consortia:** Member of Metropolitan Consortium; Suburban Library System (SLS).

★17030★
WESTMINSTER ABBEY - LIBRARY (Rel-Theol)
Mission, BC, Canada V2V 4J2   Boniface Aicher, O.S.B., Libn.
Subjects: Theology, church history, scripture. **Holdings:** 25,000 books; 2000 bound periodical volumes; 3000 microfiche. **Subscriptions:** 70 journals and other serials; 15 newspapers. **Services:** Copying; library open to public with restrictions.

★17031★
WESTMINSTER CHOIR COLLEGE - TALBOTT LIBRARY (Mus)
Hamilton Ave. at Walnut Ln.   Phone: (609) 921-3658
Princeton, NJ 08540   Sherry L. Vellucci, Dir., Lib.Serv.
Staff: Prof 6; Other 4. **Subjects:** Music - choral, organ, church. **Special Collections:** Choral music performance collection (over 3500 titles in multiple copy); Music Education Resource Center. **Holdings:** 25,000 books and bound periodical volumes; 17,000 music scores; 1000 microforms; 7000 sound recordings. **Subscriptions:** 135 journals and other serials. **Services:** Interlibrary loans (fee); copying; library open to public with a fee for circulation for area residents. **Automated Operations:** Computerized cataloging. **Computerized Information Services:** OCLC. **Networks/Consortia:** Member of PALINET & Union Library Catalogue of Pennsylvania. **Staff:** Jeanette Jacobson, Asst.Libn./Cat.; Nancy A. Wicklund, Asst.Libn.; Mary Benton, Acq.Libn.; Jane Nowakowski, Choral Libn.; Marilyn Quinn, Media Libn.

★17032★
WESTMINSTER COLLEGE - WINSTON CHURCHILL MEMORIAL AND LIBRARY (Hist)
7th & Westminster Ave.   Phone: (314) 642-3361
Fulton, MO 65251-1299   Warren M. Hollrah, Musm.Mgr./Coll.Archv.
Staff: 3. **Subjects:** Sir Winston Churchill. **Special Collections:** Sir Christopher Wren; World War II; 20th-century Anglo/American documents. **Holdings:** 1100 books; 530 reels of microfilm. **Services:** Library open to public with restrictions. **Automated Operations:** Computerized cataloging. **Publications:** Memorial Memo, 3/year. **Remarks:** An alternate phone number is 642-6648.

★17033★
WESTMINSTER INSTITUTE FOR ETHICS AND HUMAN VALUES - LIBRARY (Soc Sci)
361 Windermere Rd.   Phone: (519) 673-0046
London, ON, Canada N6G 2K3   Gwen Fraser, Asst. for Pub.Educ.
Staff: Prof 1. **Subjects:** Ethics - bioethics, legal, business and professional, philosophical; morality and population. **Holdings:** 704 books and bound periodical volumes; journal article and newspaper clipping files. **Subscriptions:** 34 journals and other serials. **Services:** Copying; library open to public for reference use only. **Publications:** Westminster Affairs (newsletter), quarterly - free upon request. **Remarks:** The Westminster Institute for Ethics and Human Values is sponsored by Westminster College and the University of

Western Ontario. It is a private, nonprofit organization conducting interdisciplinary research and educational programs.

WESTMINSTER LAW LIBRARY
See: University of Denver - College of Law

★17034★
WESTMINSTER PRESBYTERIAN CHURCH - JOHN H. HOLMES LIBRARY (Rel-Theol)
4991 Cleves Warsaw Pike   Phone: (513) 921-1623
Cincinnati, OH 45238   Emma Reeves, Libn.
Founded: 1948. **Subjects:** Bible, philosophy, children's books, devotional materials, religious education, family living. **Holdings:** 5038 books. **Subscriptions:** 10 journals and other serials. **Services:** Library open to public.

★17035★
WESTMINSTER PRESBYTERIAN CHURCH - LIBRARY (Rel-Theol)
4400 N. Shartel   Phone: (405) 524-2204
Oklahoma City, OK 73118   J. Richard Hershberger, Assoc. Minister
Founded: 1950. **Staff:** Prof 1; Other 1. **Subjects:** Religion, church history, biography. **Holdings:** 1200 books and bound periodical volumes. **Services:** Library open to public with restrictions.

★17036★
WESTMINSTER PRESBYTERIAN CHURCH - LIBRARY (Rel-Theol)*
2040 Washington Rd.   Phone: (412) 835-6630
Pittsburgh, PA 15241   Mrs. R.L. Hutchison, Libn.
Staff: Prof 2. **Subjects:** Religion, West Pennsylvania history. **Holdings:** 4000 books. **Services:** Library not open to public.

★17037★
WESTMINSTER PRESBYTERIAN CHURCH - LIBRARY (Rel-Theol)
2701 Cameron Mills Rd.   Phone: (703) 549-4766
Alexandria, VA 22302   Esther M. Cook, Libn.
Founded: 1956. **Staff:** Prof 1; Other 2. **Subjects:** Religion. **Holdings:** 2100 books; phonodiscs; audiotapes. **Subscriptions:** 11 journals and other serials. **Services:** Library open to public.

★17038★
WESTMINSTER THEOLOGICAL SEMINARY - MONTGOMERY LIBRARY (Rel-Theol)†
Chestnut Hill   Phone: (215) 887-5511
Philadelphia, PA 19118   Robert J. Kepple, Libn.
Founded: 1929. **Staff:** Prof 3; Other 3. **Subjects:** Biblical studies, theology, church history, patristics. **Special Collections:** Bible texts and versions (1000); Reformed theology of 16th-20th centuries (2500 items). **Holdings:** 80,000 books; 10,000 bound periodical volumes; 600 reels of microfilm. **Subscriptions:** 800 journals and other serials. **Services:** Interlibrary loans; copying; library open to public. **Automated Operations:** Computerized cataloging and acquisitions. **Computerized Information Services:** OCLC, BRS. **Networks/Consortia:** Member of PALINET & Union Library Catalogue of Pennsylvania; Southeastern Pennsylvania Theological Libraries Association (SEPTLA). **Remarks:** Library located at Willow Grove Ave. & Church Rd., Glenside, PA 19038. **Staff:** Dennis Pakala, Cat.; Grace Mullen, Archv./Pub.Serv.

★17039★
WESTMORELAND COUNTY HISTORICAL SOCIETY - CALVIN E. POLLINS MEMORIAL LIBRARY (Hist)
Museum of Art Building
221 N. Main St.   Phone: (412) 836-1800
Greensburg, PA 15601   Linda E. Forish, Adm.Sec.
Staff: 3. **Subjects:** Local history, genealogy, fine and decorative arts, archeology. **Special Collections:** Early West Pennsylvania manuscript collections dealing with local area and individuals. **Holdings:** 1200 books; 4 VF drawers; 12,000 documents; 20 reels of microfilm; 500 slides; 400 architectural drawings of Westmoreland County. **Services:** Copying; library open to public on a fee basis. **Special Indexes:** Archival holdings indexes; Westmoreland County History, A Union List and Bibliography (paperback book available for sale); indexes and photos to fine and decorative arts collections.

★17040★
WESTMORELAND HOSPITAL - LIBRARY AND HEALTH RESOURCE CENTER (Med)
532 W. Pittsburgh St.   Phone: (412) 832-4088
Greensburg, PA 15601-2282   Janet C. Petrak, Libn.
Founded: 1959. **Staff:** Prof 1; Other 1. **Subjects:** Medicine, nursing, surgery. **Special Collections:** History of nursing; Clinical Pastoral Education Program Support Collection. **Holdings:** 3685 books; 1499 bound periodical volumes.

Subscriptions: 348 journals and other serials. **Services:** Interlibrary loans; copying; library open to public for reference use only. **Networks/Consortia:** Member of Southeast Pittsburgh Consortium. **Publications:** Library & Health Resource Center Newsletter.

★17041★
WESTMORELAND MUSEUM OF ART - ART REFERENCE LIBRARY (Art)
221 N. Main St.   Phone: (412) 837-1500
Greensburg, PA 15601   Jeannine Earley, Musm.Asst.
Founded: 1958. **Staff:** 1. **Subjects:** American and European artists and styles, American architecture, techniques of materials, history. **Holdings:** 10,200 books; 75 bound periodical volumes; 28,000 exhibition catalogs; 15,000 museum exchange bulletins and reports; 50,000 exhibition brochures. **Subscriptions:** 45 journals and other serials. **Services:** Copying; library open to public for reference use only. **Publications:** Monthly brochures on exhibitions.

WESTON CLINICAL SCIENCE CENTER LIBRARY
See: University of Wisconsin, Madison - Center for Health Sciences Libraries

★17042★
WESTON COUNTY HISTORICAL SOCIETY - ANNA MILLER MUSEUM - LIBRARY (Hist)
Box 698   Phone: (307) 746-4188
Newcastle, WY 82701   Helen Larsen, Musm.Dir.
Staff: 2. **Subjects:** Wyoming and Western history; U.S. Congress. **Special Collections:** Frank W. Mondell, Wyoming Congressman, 1898-1922 (300 volumes of Congressional Record; Senate documents; reports). **Holdings:** 400 books; 50 bound periodical volumes; periodicals, 1860 to present; 100 items of ephemera, local history, clippings, pamphlets, booklets, manuscripts; 1400 local history photographs; 30 oral history tapes. **Subscriptions:** 10 journals and other serials. **Services:** Copying; library open to public with restrictions.

WESTON OBSERVATORY
See: Boston College

★17043★
WESTON RESEARCH CENTRE - INFORMATION RESOURCE CENTRE (Food-Bev)
1047 Yonge St.   Phone: (416) 922-5100
Toronto, ON, Canada M4W 2L3   Lusi Wong, Info.Mgr.
Founded: 1976. **Staff:** Prof 1; Other 2. **Subjects:** Food science, chemical analysis, microbiology, packaging, the senses. **Holdings:** 1600 books and bound periodical volumes; 12 VF drawers of patents, manuscripts, pamphlets and clippings. **Subscriptions:** 200 journals and other serials. **Services:** Interlibrary loans; copying; SDI; center open to public by appointment only. **Computerized Information Services:** DIALOG, BRS, QL Systems, CAN/OLE, Questel, Info Globe. Performs searches on cost recovery basis. **Networks/Consortia:** Member of Sheridan Park Association. **Publications:** Frontiers, monthly - to clients. **Special Indexes:** Index of internal reports.

★17044★
WESTON (Roy F.), INC. - TECHNICAL INFORMATION CENTER AND LIBRARY (Env-Cons; Energy)†
Weston Way   Phone: (215) 692-3030
West Chester, PA 19380   Margo Dinniman, Sr.Info.Spec.
Founded: 1963. **Staff:** Prof 1; Other 1. **Subjects:** Pollution, waste, environmental science, planning, design engineering, energy. **Holdings:** 2000 books; 700 bound periodical volumes; 10,000 documents; 2500 microfiche. **Subscriptions:** 120 journals and other serials. **Services:** Interlibrary loans; copying; microfiche reader-printer; library open to public by request. **Computerized Information Services:** DIALOG, SDC, DTIC, MEDLARS; internal database. **Publications:** From the Library - for internal distribution only.

★17045★
WESTON SCHOOL OF THEOLOGY - LIBRARY (Rel-Theol)
99 Brattle St.   Phone: (617) 868-3450
Cambridge, MA 02138   James Dunkly, Dir.
Founded: 1922. **Staff:** Prof 5; Other 4. **Subjects:** Theology, papal and conciliar documents, New Testament, Jesuitica. **Special Collections:** Arabic Collection (4000 volumes). **Holdings:** 248,000 volumes. **Subscriptions:** 872 journals and other serials. **Services:** Interlibrary loans; copying; library open to public with restricted circulation. **Automated Operations:** Computerized cataloging. **Computerized Information Services:** OCLC. **Networks/Consortia:** Member of NELINET; Boston Theological Institute Libraries. **Remarks:** The Weston School of Theology Library is a Jesuit theologate library which shares facilities with the Episcopal Divinity School. The Episcopal

Divinity School was formed by the merger of the Episcopal Theological School and the Philadelphia Divinity School - William Bacon Stevens Library. The Yarnall Library of Theology (Philadelphia Divinity School) is now maintained by the University of Pennsylvania Van Pelt Library. **Staff:** Lois Neve, Circ.Libn.; Sandra Boyd, Ref.Libn.; Sherrie Tuck, Acq.Libn.; Clifford Wunderlich, Tech.Serv.Libn.

★17046★
WESTPOINT PEPPERELL - RESEARCH CENTER - INFORMATION SERVICES LIBRARY (Sci-Tech)
3300 23rd Dr.
Box 398   Phone: (205) 756-7111
Valley, AL 36876   Philip D. Lawrence, Jr., Supv., Info.Serv.
Founded: 1944. **Staff:** Prof 1; Other 2. **Subjects:** Textiles, chemistry, electronics, textile testing, dyeing, fire retardancy, environmental pollution, engineering, industrial hygiene. **Holdings:** 9000 books; 3000 bound periodical volumes; 15 VF drawers of research reports; 4 VF drawers of patents; 4 VF drawers of reprints; 4000 microfiche; 4 VF drawers of catalogs, brochures and manufacturing technical data. **Subscriptions:** 200 journals and other serials; 10 newspapers. **Services:** Interlibrary loans; copying; SDI; library open to students. **Computerized Information Services:** DIALOG, SDC, NLM, NIH-EPA Chemical Information System, Questel. Performs searches on cost recovery basis. **Publications:** Recent Accessions, quarterly - distributed to technical supervisors.

★17047★
WESTRECO, INC. - FOOD RESEARCH AND DEVELOPMENT - LIBRARY (Food-Bev)
555 S. Fourth St.
Box 274   Phone: (315) 598-1234
Fulton, NY 13069   Janice Burns, Res.Libn.
Founded: 1955. **Staff:** Prof 1. **Subjects:** Confectionery industry; food processing; chemistry - industrial, physical, analytical; chemical engineering. **Special Collections:** Chocolate; cocoa. **Holdings:** 1200 books; 10,000 unbound periodical volumes; 20 VF drawers of pamphlets, articles, clippings and newsletters. **Subscriptions:** 50 journals and other serials. **Services:** Interlibrary loans; library not open to public. **Remarks:** Westreco, Inc. was established to conduct research activities in the U.S. for the Nestle companies. **Formerly:** Nestle Company, Inc. - Technical Services Division - Library.

★17048★
WESTRECO, INC. - TECHNICAL LIBRARY (Food-Bev)
Boardman Rd.   Phone: (203) 355-0911
New Milford, CT 06776   Jean Trapani, Mgr., Info.Serv.
Staff: Prof 2; Other 1. **Subjects:** Food science, analytical chemistry, nutrition. **Special Collections:** Company reports and files on food technology and agricultural research. **Holdings:** 3000 books; 1500 bound periodical volumes; 1000 patents; 15 VF drawers of pamphlets; 70 reels of microfilm of company records; metal corrosion articles; Pineapple Research Institute reports. **Subscriptions:** 150 journals and other serials. **Services:** Interlibrary loans; library open to public for reference use only by arrangement. **Computerized Information Services:** DIALOG, SDC, NEXIS, HAZARDLINE. **Networks/Consortia:** Member of Southwestern Connecticut Library Council (SWLC). **Special Indexes:** Index to company reports (book); Termatrex index to company reports and files. **Staff:** Linda Fontaine, Libn.

WESTSIDE HOSPITAL LIBRARY
See: U.S. Veterans Administration (IL-Chicago)

★17049★
WESTVACO CORPORATION - INFORMATION SERVICES CENTER (Sci-Tech)
Box 5207   Phone: (803) 744-8231
North Charleston, SC 29406   Elizabeth de Liesseline, Info.Spec.
Staff: Prof 2; Other 2. **Subjects:** Papermaking, pulping, forestry, utilization of by-products. **Holdings:** 9000 books and bound periodical volumes; 50,000 company reports; 15,000 patents; 2000 clippings. **Subscriptions:** 150 journals and other serials. **Services:** Interlibrary loans; center not open to public. **Computerized Information Services:** SDC, DIALOG. **Publications:** Reports Bulletin, monthly. **Also Known As:** West Virginia Pulp and Paper Company. **Staff:** Barbara McDonald, Info.Spec.

★17050★
WESTVACO CORPORATION - LAUREL RESEARCH LIBRARY (Sci-Tech)
Johns Hopkins Rd.   Phone: (301) 792-9100
Laurel, MD 20707   Marie Liang, Res.Libn.
Founded: 1967. **Staff:** Prof 1. **Subjects:** Chemistry - paper, polymer, organic, colloidal; paper physics; biotechnology; corrosion. **Special Collections:** Specialized collection of books, periodicals and bibliographies on

paper chemistry and physics. **Holdings:** 2500 books; 2500 bound periodical volumes. **Subscriptions:** 110 journals and other serials; 5 newspapers. **Services:** Interlibrary loans; library not open to public. **Computerized Information Services:** SDC, DIALOG. **Networks/Consortia:** Member of Baltimore-Washington Interlibrary Loan Association.

★17051★
WESTVIEW CHRISTIAN REFORMED CHURCH - LIBRARY (Rel-Theol)
2929 Leonard St., N.W.   Phone: (616) 453-3105
Grand Rapids, MI 49504   Beatrice Dahnke, Libn.
Founded: 1900. **Staff:** Prof 1; Other 1. **Subjects:** Religion. **Holdings:** 1965 books. **Services:** Library not open to public.

★17052★
WESTVILLE CORRECTIONAL CENTER - STAFF LIBRARY (Med; Law)
Box 473   Phone: (219) 785-2511
Westville, IN 46391   Catherine M. Mohlke, Dir., Lib.Serv.
Founded: 1954. **Staff:** 1. **Subjects:** Psychiatry, psychology, criminology, penology, social work, rehabilitation, community corrections. **Holdings:** 2500 books; 5 VF drawers of clippings, reprints, articles, staff writings. **Subscriptions:** 20 journals and other serials. **Services:** Interlibrary loans; copying; library open to the academic community and health science consortium members for reference use by special arrangement. **Networks/Consortia:** Member of La Porte, Porter, Starke Health Science Libraries Consortium; Greater Midwest Regional Medical Library Network (Region 3). **Publications:** Serials Holding Catalog of LPS Consortium; New Acquisitions Lists - for internal distribution only. **Special Catalogs:** Film Catalog; Cassette Catalog (both book).

★17053★
WESTWOOD FIRST PRESBYTERIAN CHURCH - WALTER LORENZ MEMORIAL LIBRARY (Rel-Theol)
3011 Harrison Ave.   Phone: (513) 661-6846
Cincinnati, OH 45211   Marian B. McNair, Libn.
Founded: 1957. **Staff:** Prof 1; Other 9. **Subjects:** Religion, curriculum materials, children's books, fiction, biography. **Special Collections:** Henderson Collection (107 books from 1800s, recorded in Library of Congress). **Holdings:** 3800 books; 3 VF drawers; 290 filmstrips, cassettes, records, slides; Presbyterian College bulletins. **Subscriptions:** 12 journals and other serials. **Services:** Interlibrary loans; library open to public. **Publications:** Library Bulletin, monthly; Christian holidays; bibliographies for church school and adult study groups; Sponsored Workshops for Church Libraries in Cincinnati Presbytery.

★17054★
WETHERSFIELD HISTORICAL SOCIETY - OLD ACADEMY MUSEUM LIBRARY (Hist)
150 Main St.   Phone: (203) 529-7656
Wethersfield, CT 06109   C. Douglas Alves, Jr., Dir.
Founded: 1932. **Staff:** Prof 2; Other 15. **Subjects:** Wethersfield history, genealogy, maritime history. **Holdings:** 800 books; 15 bound periodical volumes; 1000 other cataloged items; 5000 manuscripts. **Services:** Copying; library open to public. **Publications:** Wethersfield Newsletter, quarterly; Local History, annual.

WETMORE (Alexander) LIBRARY
See: Welder (Rob & Bessie) Wildlife Foundation - Library

WEY MEMORIAL LIBRARY
See: Arnot-Ogden Memorial Hospital

★17055★
WEYERHAEUSER (Charles A.) MEMORIAL MUSEUM - LIBRARY (Hist)
Box 239   Phone: (612) 632-4007
Little Falls, MN 56345   Jan Warner, Exec.Dir.
Founded: 1975. **Staff:** Prof 1; Other 2. **Subjects:** Local history of Morrison County. **Special Collections:** Microfilm of Swanville News (defunct local newspaper); microfilm of Minnesota State Census (every ten years, 1865-1904); Works Progress Administration (WPA) Biographies of Morrison County; microfilm of Pierz Journal; microfilm of Motley Mercury and Motley Register. **Holdings:** 800 books. **Services:** Interlibrary loans; copying; library open to public for reference use only. **Publications:** News & Notes, quarterly. **Remarks:** Maintained by the Morrison County Historical Society.

★17056★
WEYERHAEUSER COMPANY - ARCHIVES (Sci-Tech)
                                                Phone: (205) 924-5051
Tacoma, WA 98477   Donnie Crespo, Archv.
Staff: Prof 2; Other 2. **Subjects:** Weyerhaeuser Company, forest products,

logging, lumber manufacturing, pulp/paperboard, Pacific Northwest. **Holdings:** 1000 cubic feet and 128 linear feet of archival material including correspondence and office files, 1900 to 1983, ledgers, journals, annual and financial reports, biographical files, speeches of company executives and personnel, company publications, minute books of the company, photographs of company facilities and operations, photographs of logging in the Northwest, films, oral history interviews, artifacts and memorabilia, maps. **Services:** Copying (limited); archives open to public with restrictions. **Publications:** Weyerhaeuser Company Archives, 1981; The White River Lumber Company, 1979; Clemons Tree Farm, 1981; Weyerhaeuser Timber Company History 1900-1950. **Special Catalogs:** Shelf lists; content notes; descriptive catalogs. **Staff:** Pauline Larson, Asst.Archv.

★17057★
WEYERHAEUSER COMPANY - CORPORATE LIBRARY (Bus-Fin)
CH 1-W   Phone: (206) 924-3030
Tacoma, WA 98477   Karin H. Williams, Mgr., Corp.Lib.
Founded: 1952. **Staff:** Prof 4; Other 4. **Subjects:** Business, economics, forestry, finance, law/tax, management, marketing. **Special Collections:** Annual reports of major national and foreign companies (5000 cataloged items); Conference Board collection; Stanford Research Institute collection. **Holdings:** 10,000 books; 8 drawers of maps; 4 VF drawers. **Subscriptions:** 450 journals and other serials; 40 newspapers. **Services:** Interlibrary loans; library open to public with preference given to employees. **Computerized Information Services:** DIALOG, SDC, BRS, Info Globe, NEXIS, LEXIS, Dow Jones News/Retrieval. **Networks/Consortia:** Member of WLN. **Publications:** Bulletin of new services and holdings, monthly. **Remarks:** Maintains a Law/Tax Library and a Marketing & Economic Research Library. **Staff:** Carolyn Burns, Supv., Tech.Serv.; Linda McBroom, Bus.Libn.; Carol Orion, Bus.Libn.

★17058★
WEYERHAEUSER COMPANY - SFRD TECHNICAL INFORMATION CENTER (Sci-Tech)
Box 1060   Phone: (501) 624-8536
Hot Springs, AR 71901   Memory R. Froncek, Info.Spec.
Staff: 1. **Subjects:** Forestry and related subjects. **Holdings:** 5000 pamphlets. **Subscriptions:** 75 journals and other serials. **Services:** Center open to public with restrictions. **Formerly:** Its Southern Forestry Research Library.

★17059★
WEYERHAEUSER COMPANY - TECHNICAL INFORMATION CENTER (Sci-Tech)
                                          Phone: (206) 924-6265
Tacoma, WA 98477   L.W. Martinez, Mgr.
Founded: 1957. **Staff:** Prof 7; Other 6. **Subjects:** Wood and wood products, plastics, coatings, adhesives, paper chemistry, chemical engineering. **Holdings:** 20,000 books; 30,000 reports. **Subscriptions:** 803 journals and other serials. **Services:** Interlibrary loans; copying (both limited); SDI; center open to public by permission. **Automated Operations:** Computerized cataloging and serials. **Computerized Information Services:** DIALOG, SDC. **Publications:** Accession list, monthly - limited circulation; Journal Holdings list, annual. **Special Catalogs:** Journal subject list (computer printout).

★17060★
WEYERHAEUSER COMPANY - WESTERN FORESTRY RESEARCH CENTER - LIBRARY (Sci-Tech)
Box 420   Phone: (206) 736-8241
Centralia, WA 98531   Donna Loucks, Libn.
Founded: 1954. **Staff:** Prof 1; Other 1. **Subjects:** Forestry, biology, zoology, ecology, herbicides, pesticides, agronomy, genetics, physiology, dendrology. **Holdings:** 3000 books; 1000 bound periodical volumes; 40,000 reports; 200 dissertations. **Subscriptions:** 150 journals and other serials. **Services:** Copying; library open to public for reference use only. **Automated Operations:** Computerized cataloging and serials. **Computerized Information Services:** DIALOG, SDC; internal database. **Publications:** Weyerhaeuser Forestry Paper, irregular.

WEYERHAEUSER LIBRARY
See: Macalester College

★17061★
WHALE CENTER - EXTINCT SPECIES MEMORIAL FUND - LIBRARY (Env-Cons)
3929 Piedmont Ave.   Phone: (415) 654-6621
Oakland, CA 94611   Kathy Bertolucci, Hd.Libn.
Staff: Prof 2. **Subjects:** Whales and whaling - commercial and aboriginal; International Whaling Commission; marine sanctuaries; whale habitat; outer-continental shelf (OCS) lease sales. **Special Collections:** International Whaling Commission documents and reports. **Holdings:** 500 books; 75 bound periodical volumes; 14 VF drawers. **Services:** Copying; library open to public for reference use only. **Publications:** Newsletters; action alerts; special publications on whaling; ethics; research. **Staff:** Anthony J. Pettinato, Asst.Libn.

★17062★
WHALE PROTECTION FUND - ENVIRONMENTAL EDUCATION RESOURCE LIBRARY (Env-Cons)
624 Ninth St., N.W.   Phone: (202) 737-3600
Washington, DC 20001   Twig C. George, Educ.Coord.
Founded: 1979. **Staff:** Prof 15. **Subjects:** Whales, wildlife, energy, ecology. **Holdings:** 700 books; 9 films. **Subscriptions:** 40 journals and other serials. **Services:** Copying; library open to public for reference use only. **Publications:** Whale Report, quarterly; Seal Report; Sea Turtle Report, both irregular.

★17063★
WHALING MUSEUM SOCIETY, INC. - LIBRARY (Env-Cons; Hist)
Main St.
Box 25   Phone: (516) 367-3418
Cold Spring Harbor, NY 11724   Robert D. Farwell, Exec.Dir.
Founded: 1936. **Staff:** Prof 6. **Subjects:** Whaling, whales, Cold Spring Harbor, marine mammal conservation, coastwise trade under sail, scrimshaw. **Special Collections:** Manuscript collections on whales, whaling and Cold Spring Harbor (thousands of documents). **Holdings:** 800 books; 10 drawers of archives; 6 drawers of photographs and prints; 12 reels of microfilm of logbooks. **Subscriptions:** 12 journals and other serials. **Services:** Copying; library open to public with written application to director. **Publications:** A Whaling Account (newsletter); annual reports; pamphlets; miscellaneous publications; bibliographies. **Staff:** Edith DeLaney, Libn./Archv.

★17064★
WHATCOM/ISLAND HEALTH SERVICES - LIBRARY (Med)
3201 Ellis St.   Phone: (206) 734-5400
Bellingham, WA 98225   Betty Jo Jensen, Med.Libn.
Founded: 1975. **Staff:** Prof 1. **Subjects:** Medicine. **Holdings:** 600 books. **Subscriptions:** 80 journals and other serials. **Services:** Library not open to public. **Computerized Information Services:** MEDLINE. **Remarks:** The library is divided between St. Joseph and St. Luke's Hospitals. Street address and telephone listed above are for St. Joseph Hospital. St. Luke's Hospital's street address and telephone are 809 E. Chestnut St., 734-8300.

★17065★
WHEAT RIDGE REGIONAL CENTER - EMPLOYEE'S LIBRARY (Med)
10285 Ridge Rd.   Phone: (303) 424-7791
Wheat Ridge, CO 80033   Clara Ann Glover, Dir.
Staff: Prof 2; Other 2. **Subjects:** Mental retardation, behavior modification, developmental disabilities, child development, psychology, sociology, medicine. **Holdings:** 1145 books; 200 pamphlets. **Subscriptions:** 28 journals and other serials. **Services:** Library not open to public. **Networks/Consortia:** Member of Central Colorado Library System (CCLS). **Formerly:** Colorado State Home and Training School - Staff Library.

★17066★
WHEATON COLLEGE - BILLY GRAHAM CENTER - ARCHIVES (Rel-Theol)
Wheaton, IL 60187   Robert Shuster, Dir.
Staff: Prof 2; Other 4. **Subjects:** North American Protestant missions and evangelistic work. **Special Collections:** Records of Africa Inland Mission, Evangelical Foreign Mission Association, Billy Graham Evangelistic Association, China Inland Mission, South America Mission and National Religious Broadcasters; papers of Herbert J. Taylor, Paul Rader, R.A. Torrey and Billy Sunday. **Holdings:** 250 archival and manuscript collections; 15,000 photographs; 6000 audiotapes; 1200 reels of microfilm. **Services:** Copying; archives open to public. **Publications:** From the Graham Center Archives, semiannual - free upon request. **Special Indexes:** Guides to special collections. **Staff:** Paul Ericksen, Assoc.Archv.

★17067★
WHEATON COLLEGE - BILLY GRAHAM CENTER - LIBRARY (Rel-Theol)
                                          Phone: (312) 260-5194
Wheaton, IL 60187   Ferne L. Weimer, Dir.
Staff: Prof 3; Other 4. **Subjects:** Christian evangelism and missions; history of revivalism; American church history; Celtic church history; patristics. **Special Collections:** Joint IMC/CBMS Missionary Archives (microfiche); Council for World Mission Archives (microfiche); Moravian Missions to the Indians (microfilm); Early American Imprints; Pamphlets in American History. **Holdings:** 53,000 books; 3500 bound periodical volumes; 1000 theses and dissertations; microforms; imprints and pamphlets. **Subscriptions:** 375 journals and other serials. **Services:** Interlibrary loans; copying; SDI; library open to public with restrictions. **Automated Operations:** Computerized

cataloging. **Computerized Information Services:** OCLC. **Publications:** Occasional papers of conferences; occasional short bibliographies. **Staff:** Nancy Schelkopf, Tech.Serv.; John Thompson, Tech.Serv.

★17068★
WHEATON COLLEGE - BUSWELL MEMORIAL LIBRARY (Rel-Theol; Hum)
501 E. Seminary   Phone: (312) 682-5101
Wheaton, IL 60187   P. Paul Snezek, Dir.
Founded: 1860. **Staff:** Prof 9; Other 11. **Subjects:** American history, religion and theology, American and English literature, science, education. **Special Collections:** Wheaton College archives; Korea; Mormonism; Hymnals; Ngbak Tribe; C.S. Lewis; Owen Barfield; G.K. Chesterton; George Macdonald; Dorothy Sayers; J.R.R. Tolkien; Charles Williams; Madeleine L'Engle; Malcolm Muggeridge; Frederick Buchner; Paul Bunyan; Charles Dickens; Everett Mitchell; Robert H. Siegall; Norman Stone; Kenneth Taylor; David Winter; Hans Rookmacher; Ronald Allyson. **Holdings:** 224,862 books; 34,897 bound periodical volumes; 199,268 microforms; 17,058 documents; 2444 tapes; 6799 music scores; 4803 phonograph records. **Subscriptions:** 1506 journals and other serials; 25 newspapers. **Services:** Interlibrary loans; copying; library open to visiting scholars. **Automated Operations:** Computerized cataloging. **Computerized Information Services:** DIALOG, OCLC. **Networks/Consortia:** Member of ILLINET; Libras, Inc. **Publications:** Collegii Bibliotheca; Library Handbook. **Staff:** Jonathan Lauer, Hd., Pub.Serv.; Sharon Vance, Hd., Tech.Serv.; Virginia Powell, Music/Educ./AV Libn.; Daniel Bowell, Asst., Pub.Serv.; Lyle Dorsett, Cur., Wade Coll.; Daniel Smith, Hd., Media Serv.; William Favata, Lib.Sys. Designer.

★17069★
WHEATON COLLEGE - LIBRARY - FINE ARTS COLLECTION (Art; Mus)
                                                             Phone: (617) 285-7722
Norton, MA 02766   Faith Dickhaut Kindness, Fine Arts Libn.
Founded: 1960. **Staff:** 1. **Subjects:** Art, music. **Holdings:** 24,000 volumes (including scores); 4600 phonograph records; 72,000 slides; 10,000 photographs. **Subscriptions:** 118 journals and other serials. **Services:** Interlibrary loans; copying; library open to public for reference use only. **Automated Operations:** Computerized cataloging. **Computerized Information Services:** OCLC. **Networks/Consortia:** Member of NELINET; Southeastern Massachusetts Cooperating Libraries (SMCL). **Remarks:** The Music Library is located in Watson Hall; the Art Collection is located in the Main Library. The Art Department slide and photograph collections are housed in Watson Hall.

★17070★
WHEATON COMMUNITY HOSPITAL - MEDICAL LIBRARY (Med)
401 12th St., N.   Phone: (612) 563-8226
Wheaton, MN 56296   Diana Johnson, Dir.
Staff: 1. **Subjects:** Medicine. **Holdings:** Figures not available. **Subscriptions:** 90 journals and other serials. **Services:** Interlibrary loans; copying; library open to public with restrictions. **Networks/Consortia:** Member of Valley Medical Network.

★17071★
WHEATON HISTORICAL ASSOCIATION - LIBRARY & RESEARCH OFFICE (Hist; Sci-Tech)
Wheaton Village   Phone: (609) 825-6800
Millville, NJ 08332   Gay Le Cleire Taylor
Staff: 3. **Subjects:** Glass history and manufacture, American glass, European glass, Victorian life, antiques, American architecture. **Special Collections:** Charles B. Gardner Library (200 glass photographs and documents; 53 framed glass documents; 75 glass books). **Holdings:** 700 books; 25 bound periodical volumes; 100 personal papers of T.C. Wheaton; 35 newspapers and pamphlets; 20 glass ledgers and indentures; 200 photographs of glass factories; 2000 glass slides. **Subscriptions:** 12 journals and other serials. **Services:** Copying; library open to public by appointment.

WHEELER (John M.) LIBRARY
See: Harkness (Edward S.) Eye Institute - John M. Wheeler Library

★17072★
WHEELING HOSPITAL, INC. - HENRY G. JEPSON MEMORIAL LIBRARY (Med)
Medical Pk.   Phone: (304) 243-3308
Wheeling, WV 26003   Rosella M. Saseen, Med.Libn.
Founded: 1936. **Staff:** Prof 1; Other 1. **Subjects:** Medicine, nursing, allied health sciences. **Holdings:** 2200 books; 118 bound periodical volumes; 612 cassettes; 5 VF drawers; pamphlet file. **Subscriptions:** 113 journals and other serials. **Services:** Interlibrary loans; library open to public with restrictions. **Computerized Information Services:** MEDLINE. **Networks/Consortia:** Member of Southeastern/Atlantic Regional Medical Library

Services.

★17073★
THE WHEELMEN - LIBRARY
1479 Guinea Ln.
Warrington, PA 18976
Defunct

★17074★
WHEELRIGHT MUSEUM - LIBRARY (Area-Ethnic)†
704 Camino Lejo
Box 5153   Phone: (505) 982-4636
Santa Fe, NM 87501   Susan McGreevy, Dir.
Founded: 1937. **Staff:** 6. **Subjects:** Navaho and other Indians (religion, history, arts), comparative religions, the Southwest. **Holdings:** 1885 books; 2281 bound periodical volumes; 1000 Navaho ceremonial art archives; 100 Navaho myths in manuscript; 3000 Navaho ceremonial music recordings; 1000 Navaho sandpaintings on slides; 100 music and prayer tapes. **Subscriptions:** 10 journals and other serials. **Services:** Interlibrary loans; library open to students and researchers. **Publications:** Navaho Figurines Called Dolls; Introduction to Navaho Sandpaintings.

★17075★
WHIDDEN MEMORIAL HOSPITAL - LIBRARY (Med)
103 Garland St.   Phone: (617) 389-6270
Everett, MA 02149   Selma W. Eigner, Libn.
Staff: Prof 1. **Subjects:** Medicine, nursing, allied health sciences. **Holdings:** 1500 books; 115 bound periodical volumes; 4 shelves of clippings and pamphlets. **Subscriptions:** 69 journals and other serials. **Services:** Interlibrary loans; copying; library open to public for reference use only. **Networks/Consortia:** Member of Massachusetts Health Sciences Library Network (MAHSLIN).

★17076★
WHIRLPOOL CORPORATION - TECHNICAL INFORMATION CENTER (Sci-Tech)
Monte Rd.   Phone: (616) 926-5323
Benton Harbor, MI 49022   Clifford L. Tierney, Mgr.
Founded: 1964. **Staff:** Prof 2; Other 2. **Subjects:** Mechanical and electrical engineering, polymer science, food technology. **Holdings:** 8000 books. **Subscriptions:** 402 journals and other serials. **Services:** Interlibrary loans; center open to public on request. **Automated Operations:** Computerized cataloging and circulation. **Computerized Information Services:** DIALOG, NLM; WIN (Whirlpool Information Network; internal database). **Networks/Consortia:** Member of Michigan Library Consortium (MLC); Berrien Library Consortium. **Publications:** WIN Alert, monthly - for internal distribution only. **Staff:** Gene Heileman, Tech.Libn.

WHITAKER (John C.) LIBRARY
See: Forsyth Memorial Hospital - John C. Whitaker Library

WHITAKER (Mae M.) LIBRARY
See: St. Louis Conservatory and Schools for the Arts (CASA) - Mae M. Whitaker Library

★17077★
WHITE AND CASE - LIBRARY (Law)
14 Wall St.   Phone: (212) 732-1040
New York, NY 10005   John J. Banta, Chf. Law Libn.
Founded: 1901. **Staff:** Prof 5; Other 7. **Subjects:** Law. **Holdings:** 35,000 volumes. **Services:** Interlibrary loans; library not open to public. **Computerized Information Services:** LEXIS, Westlaw, DIALOG. Contact Person: Jim Bonacorda. **Remarks:** White and Case maintains branch libraries at their offices in London, Paris, Hong Kong, Singapore, Stockholm, New York City (280 Park Ave.), Washington, DC and Palm Beach, FL. **Staff:** Jim Bonacorda, Asst.Libn.; Janet Marforio, Tax Libn.; Ray Marano, Br.Libn.; Jane Towell, Br.Libn.; Sara Wagschal, Cat.

WHITE (Charles E.) MEMORIAL LIBRARY
See: University of Maryland, College Park - Libraries - Charles E. White Memorial Library

WHITE (E.G.) RESEARCH CENTER
See: Andrews University - James White Library

WHITE (G.W. Blunt) LIBRARY
See: Mystic Seaport, Inc. - G.W. Blunt White Library

★17078★
WHITE HAVEN CENTER - STAFF LIBRARY (Med)
Oley Valley Rd.   Phone: (717) 443-9564
White Haven, PA 18661   Frances M. McSpedon, Libn.
Founded: 1972. **Staff:** Prof 1. **Subjects:** Mental retardation, developmental disabilities. **Holdings:** 1600 books; 1 vertical file. **Subscriptions:** 75 journals and other serials. **Services:** Interlibrary loans; library open to the public through interlibrary loan. **Networks/Consortia:** Member of Health Information Library Network of Northeastern Pennsylvania (HILNNEP).

WHITE (James Herbert) LIBRARY
See: Mississippi Valley State University - James Herbert White Library

WHITE (James) LIBRARY
See: Andrews University - James White Library

WHITE (John G.) COLLECTION OF FOLKLORE, ORIENTALIA, & CHESS
See: Cleveland Public Library - John G. White Collection of Folklore, Orientalia, & Chess

★17079★
WHITE MEMORIAL MEDICAL CENTER - COURVILLE-ABBOTT MEMORIAL LIBRARY (Med)
1720 Brooklyn Ave.   Phone: (213) 268-5000
Los Angeles, CA 90033   Joyce Marson, Dir.
Founded: 1920. **Staff:** Prof 2; Other 2. **Subjects:** Medicine, nursing, dietetics, paramedicine. **Special Collections:** Library of Dr. Philip J. Vogel. **Holdings:** 44,000 volumes; 8 VF drawers of pamphlets; tapes; phonograph records; filmstrips. **Subscriptions:** 450 journals and other serials. **Services:** Interlibrary loans; copying; library open to public for reference use only. **Computerized Information Services:** MEDLINE. **Networks/Consortia:** Member of Pacific Southwest Regional Medical Library Service (PSRMLS). **Staff:** Mary E. Flake, Asst.Libn.

★17080★
WHITE MEMORIAL MEDICAL CENTER - NEUROLOGY LIBRARY
1720 Brooklyn Ave.
Los Angeles, CA 90033
Defunct

★17081★
WHITE PLAINS HOSPITAL - BERTON LATTIN MEMORIAL MEDICAL LIBRARY (Med)
E. Post Rd. at Davis Ave.   Phone: (914) 681-1231
White Plains, NY 10601   Joan Giordano, Mgr., Med.Lib.
Staff: Prof 1; Other 1. **Subjects:** Medicine, nursing, allied health fields. **Holdings:** 600 books; 2300 bound periodical volumes; VF of allied health subjects. **Subscriptions:** 100 journals and other serials. **Services:** Interlibrary loans; copying; library open to public for reference use only. **Computerized Information Services:** MEDLINE. Performs free searches. **Networks/Consortia:** Member of Health Information Libraries of Westchester (HILOW). **Publications:** Medical Library News, quarterly - for internal distribution only.

★17082★
WHITE RIVER VALLEY HISTORICAL SOCIETY MUSEUM - LIBRARY (Hist)
918 H St., S.E.   Phone: (206) 939-2783
Auburn, WA 98002   LaVerna J. Conrad, Libn.
Founded: 1970. **Staff:** Prof 1; Other 3. **Subjects:** Local Northwest history and genealogy, history of local industries. **Special Collections:** Histories of pioneer families. **Holdings:** 400 volumes; 25 boxes of pamphlets; 10 maps; 25 cassette tapes. **Services:** Library open to public for reference use only.

WHITE (Robert J.) LAW LIBRARY
See: Catholic University of America - School of Law - Robert J. White Law Library

WHITE (Robert M.) MEMORIAL LIBRARY
See: Paoli Memorial Hospital - Robert M. White Memorial Library

WHITE SANDS MISSILE RANGE
See: U.S. Army

WHITE (William Allen) LIBRARY
See: Emporia State University - William Allen White Library

WHITE (William M.) BUSINESS LIBRARY
See: University of Colorado, Boulder - William M. White Business Library

★17083★
WHITE & WILLIAMS - LIBRARY (Law)
1234 Market St.   Phone: (215) 854-7126
Philadelphia, PA 19107   Margaret S. Fallon, Libn.
Staff: Prof 1; Other 2. **Subjects:** Law. **Holdings:** 13,500 volumes. **Subscriptions:** 80 journals and other serials. **Services:** Interlibrary loans; library not open to public. **Computerized Information Services:** LEXIS.

WHITEFORD MEMORIAL LIBRARY
See: Foreign Services Research Institute

WHITEHALL LIBRARY
See: Stonington Historical Society

WHITEHEAD (Alfred) MEMORIAL MUSIC LIBRARY
See: Mount Allison University - Alfred Whitehead Memorial Music Library

WHITESHELL NUCLEAR RESEARCH ESTABLISHMENT
See: Atomic Energy of Canada, Ltd. - WNRE Library

★17084★
WHITMAN COLLEGE - EELLS NORTHWEST COLLECTION AND NORTHWEST ARCHIVES (Hist)
Penrose Memorial Library
345 Boyer St.   Phone: (509) 527-5191
Walla Walla, WA 99362   Lawrence L. Dodd, Cur. of Mss. & Spec.Coll.
Subjects: History of the city of Walla Walla, Walla Walla County, Whitman College (1804 to present), and the Pacific Northwest. **Special Collections:** Papers of American Board of Commissioners for Foreign Missions-affiliated missionaries in the Pacific Northwest; missionary activities on the Skokomish Indian Reservation, 1874-1907; photographs and manuscripts of Indians of the Pacific Northwest coast; Walla Walla area business records; Whitman College archives; photographs of Walla Walla area. **Holdings:** 6000 books; 800 periodicals. **Services:** Interlibrary loans; copying; library open to public with restrictions. **Automated Operations:** Computerized cataloging and acquisitions. **Computerized Information Services:** Spindex III (Historical Records of Washington State).

★17085★
WHITMAN & RANSOM - LIBRARY (Law)
522 Fifth Ave.   Phone: (212) 575-5800
New York, NY 10036
Founded: 1920. **Staff:** Prof 2; Other 2. **Subjects:** Law, corporate law. **Special Collections:** Japanese Law (1600 volumes). **Holdings:** 9000 volumes. **Services:** Interlibrary loans; copying; library open to public with restrictions. **Computerized Information Services:** DIALOG, LEXIS. **Staff:** Gena M. Eisenberg, Asst.Libn.

★17086★
WHITMAN (Walt) BIRTHPLACE ASSOCIATION - LIBRARY AND MUSEUM (Hum)
246 Walt Whitman Rd.   Phone: (516) 427-5240
Huntington Station, NY 11746   Betsy Vondrasek, Cur.
Founded: 1949. **Staff:** 5. **Subjects:** Books by and about Walt Whitman. **Special Collections:** Translations and studies in foreign languages including Japanese and Catalan. **Holdings:** 350 books; artifacts; plaques; portraits; scrapbooks; rare monographs; catalogs; pamphlets; bibliographies; letters; broadsides; photostats of manuscripts; file of Walt Whitman Review. **Services:** Library open to public for reference use only. **Publications:** Broadsides of Whitman prose and poetry - for sale; West Hills Review - A Walt Whitman Journal, annual - by subscription.

★17087★
WHITMAN (Walt) HOUSE - LIBRARY (Hist)
330 Mickle St.   Phone: (609) 964-5383
Camden, NJ 08103   Eleanor Ray, Caretaker
Founded: 1920. **Staff:** 1. **Subjects:** Walt Whitman. **Holdings:** 175 books. **Services:** Library open to public on a limited basis.

★17088★
WHITNEY COMMUNICATIONS CORPORATION - RESEARCH LIBRARY (Publ)
Time & Life Bldg., Rm. 4600
110 W. 51st St.   Phone: (212) 582-2300
New York, NY 10020   Christine P. Leamon, Res.Dir.
Founded: 1970. **Staff:** Prof 2. **Subjects:** Publishing, finance, business, broadcasting. **Special Collections:** New York Herald Tribune historical material. **Holdings:** 100 VF drawers of corporate records and archives of Whitney Communications Corporation. **Subscriptions:** 75 journals and other serials. **Services:** Library open by appointment to members of SLA.

★17089★
WHITNEY (Eli) MUSEUM - LIBRARY (Rec)
Route 139							Phone: (203) 488-2157
North Branford, CT 06471				Merrill K. Lindsay, Pres.
Staff: Prof 1. **Subjects:** Antique arms. **Special Collections:** Photo archive (8000 transparencies of American and European arms and private collections); arms auction and sales catalogs, 1900 to present. **Holdings:** 1200 books. **Subscriptions:** 24 journals and other serials.

WHITNEY INFORMATION SERVICES
See: General Electric Company - Corporate Research & Development

WHITNEY LIBRARY
See: New Haven Colony Historical Society

★17090★
WHITNEY MUSEUM OF AMERICAN ART - LIBRARY (Art)
945 Madison Ave.					Phone: (212) 570-3649
New York, NY 10021					May FitzGerald, Libn.
Subjects: American art, particularly of the 20th century. **Holdings:** 18,000 volumes; 79 VF drawers of clippings on American artists. **Subscriptions:** 47 journals and other serials. **Services:** Library open by appointment to qualified researchers only.

★17091★
WHITTAKER CORPORATION - TASKER SYSTEMS DIVISION - TECHNICAL LIBRARY (Sci-Tech)
1785 Voyager Ave.
Box 8000						Phone: (818) 341-3010
Simi Valley, CA 93063					Orlean A. Hinds, Libn.
Staff: Prof 1. **Subjects:** Engineering, management, mathematics. **Holdings:** 1500 books; military specifications and standards; patents; 12,000 unbound reports; 6000 reports on microfiche and microfilm. **Subscriptions:** 165 journals and other serials. **Services:** Library not open to public. **Computerized Information Services:** DIALOG. **Remarks:** An alternate telephone number is (805) 584-8200. **Formerly:** Located in Chatsworth, CA.

WHITTEN CENTER LIBRARY & MEDIA RESOURCE SERVICES
See: South Carolina State Department of Mental Retardation

★17092★
WHITTIER COLLEGE - DEPARTMENT OF GEOLOGY - FAIRCHILD AERIAL PHOTOGRAPH COLLECTION (Aud-Vis)†
							Phone: (213) 693-0771
Whittier, CA 90608					Dallas D. Rhodes, Dir.
Founded: 1965. **Staff:** 1. **Subjects:** Aerial photographs, primarily of California, 1927-1965. **Special Collections:** Fairchild Collection including 1500 flights (300,000 prints; 100,000 negatives; 500 photo-mosaic flight indexes; 500 orthophoto maps). **Services:** Interlibrary loans (fee); collection open to public on a fee basis. **Special Indexes:** Inventory of flights (looseleaf); Flight Index Maps.

★17093★
WHITTIER COLLEGE - SCHOOL OF LAW - LIBRARY (Law)
5353 W. 3d St.					Phone: (213) 938-3621
Los Angeles, CA 90020				J. Denny Haythorn, Dir./Assoc.Prof.
Staff: Prof 6; Other 7. **Subjects:** American law. **Holdings:** 113,436 volumes; 365 cassettes. **Subscriptions:** 1343 journals and other serials; 19 newspapers. **Services:** Interlibrary loans; copying; library open to attorneys, law students and others wishing to use legal research materials. **Automated Operations:** Computerized cataloging. **Computerized Information Services:** Westlaw, LEXIS, DIALOG, RLIN. **Networks/Consortia:** Member of CLASS. **Publications:** Whittier Law Review, quarterly - by subscription. **Staff:** Lindy R. Carll, Ref.; Rosanne Krikorian, Asst.Dir.; Christa Gowan, Ser.; Carol Heron, Tech.Serv.; Virbala Thaker, Govt.Doc.

★17094★
WHITTIER HOME ASSOCIATION - LIBRARY (Hist)
86 Friend St.					Phone: (617) 388-1337
Amesbury, MA 01913				Debra Moore, Cur.
Subjects: John Greenleaf Whittier. **Holdings:** Figures not available. **Services:** Library open to public for reference use only on a limited schedule and for a fee. **Remarks:** The library at the Whittier home consists of books, pamphlets, newspapers, letters and other documents which belonged to poet and abolitionist John Greenleaf Whittier. It is now being cataloged for the first time and will be available to visitors.

WHITTIER (N. Paul) HISTORICAL AVIATION LIBRARY
See: San Diego Aero-Space Museum - N. Paul Whittier Historical Aviation Library

★17095★
WHITWORTH COLLEGE - SCIENCE LIBRARY (Sci-Tech)†
							Phone: (509) 489-3550
Spokane, WA 99251
Founded: 1955. **Staff:** 1. **Subjects:** Chemistry, physics, geology, biology. **Holdings:** 2850 books; 1700 bound periodical volumes; 60 filmstrips; 750 microcards; 3 VF drawers of supply and book catalogs; 100 pamphlets. **Subscriptions:** 66 journals and other serials. **Services:** Interlibrary loans; copying; library open to public for reference use only.

WHORTON (John L.) MEDIA CENTER
See: First Baptist Church - John L. Whorton Media Center

WHYTE (John A.) MEDICAL LIBRARY
See: Delaware Valley Medical Center - John A. Whyte Medical Library

WHYTE (Peter and Catharine) FOUNDATION - ARCHIVES OF THE CANADIAN ROCKIES
See: Archives of the Canadian Rockies

WIBBERLEY (Harold E., Jr.) LIBRARY
See: Brazilian-American Cultural Institute, Inc. - Harold E. Wibberley, Jr. Library

★17096★
WICHITA ART ASSOCIATION, INC. - REFERENCE LIBRARY (Art)
9112 E. Central					Phone: (316) 686-6687
Wichita, KS 67206					Irma Hobbs, Chm., Lib.Comm.
Founded: 1920. **Staff:** Prof 1; Other 4. **Subjects:** Art. **Holdings:** 3000 volumes. **Services:** Library open to public for reference use only.

★17097★
WICHITA ART MUSEUM - LIBRARY (Art)
619 Stackman Dr.					Phone: (316) 264-6251
Wichita, KS 67203					Lois F. Crane, Libn.
Founded: 1935. **Staff:** Prof 1; Other 2. **Subjects:** American art, general art history. **Holdings:** 2500 books; 13 VF drawers; 4000 slides. **Subscriptions:** 27 journals and other serials. **Services:** Library open to public for reference use only.

★17098★
WICHITA EAGLE-BEACON - LIBRARY (Publ)
825 E. Douglas					Phone: (316) 268-6575
Wichita, KS 67203					Sally Stratton, Chf.Libn.
Founded: 1912. **Staff:** Prof 2; Other 4. **Subjects:** Newspaper reference topics. **Holdings:** 400,000 clippings; 200,000 photographs; pamphlets; maps; microfilm. **Services:** Library not open to public.

★17099★
WICHITA FALLS STATE HOSPITAL - PATIENTS AND MEDICAL LIBRARY (Med)
Box 300						Phone: (817) 692-1220
Wichita Falls, TX 76307				Grace E. Smith, Libn.
Staff: 1. **Subjects:** Psychiatry, psychology, surgery and nursing, philosophy, anatomy, education, forensic medicine, history of medicine. **Special Collections:** Bassett Collection (anatomy); Baker and Baker Collection (neurology). **Holdings:** 3500 books; 50 bound periodical volumes; 1050 AV aids; 200 pamphlets; 100 medical reports. **Subscriptions:** 65 journals and other serials; 15 newspapers. **Services:** Interlibrary loans; copying; library open to nursing schools and social workers in local nursing homes. **Networks/Consortia:** Member of TALON.

★17100★
WICHITA GENERAL HOSPITAL - MEDICAL LIBRARY (Med)*
1600 8th St.					Phone: (817) 723-1461
Wichita Falls, TX 76301				Marge Bohack, Hd.Libn.
Founded: 1915. **Subjects:** Medicine, nursing. **Holdings:** 2500 books; 450 bound periodical volumes; 4 VF drawers of pamphlets; 100 medical journals; 50 nursing journals. **Subscriptions:** 42 journals and other serials. **Services:** Interlibrary loans; library not open to public.

★17101★
WICHITA PUBLIC LIBRARY - BUSINESS AND TECHNOLOGY DIVISION (Bus-Fin; Sci-Tech)
223 S. Main
Wichita, KS 67202
Phone: (316) 262-0611
Larry DePiesse, Hd.
Founded: 1950. **Staff:** Prof 3; Other 5. **Subjects:** Aeronautics, petroleum, geology, economics, mathematics, taxes, finances, firearms, automobiles, business management. **Holdings:** 25,000 volumes; Patent Gazette, 1872 to present, on microfilm; 20,589 pamphlets; 2452 auto repair manuals; 1180 telephone directories. **Subscriptions:** 304 journals and other serials; 6 newspapers. **Services:** Interlibrary loans; copying. **Automated Operations:** Computerized cataloging and circulation. **Computerized Information Services:** DIALOG. **Publications:** Occasional book lists and bibliographies. **Staff:** Jimmie Hooper, Asst.Dept.Hd.; Jayne Young, Asst. II.

WICHITA SCOUTING CO-OP, INC.
See: Oil Information Library of Wichita Falls

★17102★
WICHITA-SEDGWICK COUNTY HISTORICAL MUSEUM - LIBRARY & ARCHIVES (Hist)
204 S. Main
Wichita, KS 67202
Phone: (316) 265-9314
Robert A. Puckett, Dir.
Staff: 2. **Subjects:** Local and state history. **Special Collections:** Complete collection of Wichita city directories, 1874 to present; M.C. Naftzger Collection (books on Wichita and Kansas history). **Holdings:** 600 books; 50 bound periodical volumes; 75 other cataloged items; 6 VF drawers of clippings. **Services:** Copying; library open to public with restrictions. **Publications:** Heritage, quarterly.

★17103★
WICHITA STATE UNIVERSITY - DEPARTMENT OF CHEMISTRY - LLOYD MC KINLEY MEMORIAL CHEMISTRY LIBRARY (Sci-Tech)
1845 Fairmount
Wichita, KS 67208
Phone: (316) 689-3120
B. Jack McCormick
Founded: 1926. **Staff:** 1. **Subjects:** Chemistry. **Holdings:** 6000 books; 8000 bound periodical volumes; 1000 volumes of periodicals on microcards. **Subscriptions:** 130 journals and other serials. **Services:** Interlibrary loans; library open to public for reference use only.

WICHITA STATE UNIVERSITY - INTERNATIONAL REFERENCE ORGANIZATION IN FORENSIC MEDICINE AND SCIENCES
See: International Reference Organization in Forensic Medicine and Sciences

★17104★
WICHITA STATE UNIVERSITY - SPECIAL COLLECTIONS (Hist)
1845 Fairmount
Wichita, KS 67208
Phone: (316) 689-3590
Michael T. Kelly, Cur.
Staff: Prof 1; Other 1. **Subjects:** State and local history, congressional papers, radical pamphlets, history of printing, slavery and abolitionism, university archives, history of hypnotism/mesmerism. **Holdings:** 4500 books and bound periodical volumes; 150 Kansas maps; 625 linear feet of manuscript collections and pamphlets; 2400 theses; 108 linear feet of archives. **Services:** Interlibrary loans; copying; collections open to public. **Special Catalogs:** Manuscript registers.

★17105★
WICHITA STATE UNIVERSITY - THURLOW LIEURANCE MEMORIAL MUSIC LIBRARY (Mus)
Walter Duerksen Fine Arts Center
Wichita, KS 67208
Phone: (316) 689-3029
David L. Austin, Music Libn.
Founded: 1926. **Staff:** Prof 1; Other 1. **Subjects:** Music. **Special Collections:** Kansas Music Teachers' Association Archives; Thurlow Lieurance Archives. **Holdings:** 14,350 books; 12,000 phonograph records; 475 tape recordings; 15,500 music scores. **Services:** Interlibrary loans; library open to public. **Automated Operations:** Computerized cataloging. **Networks/Consortia:** Member of AMIGOS Bibliographic Council, Inc.

★17106★
WIDE WORLD PHOTOS, INC. (Aud-Vis)
50 Rockefeller Plaza
New York, NY 10020
Phone: (212) 621-1930
Jim Donna, Gen. Sales Mgr.
Staff: Prof 35. **Subjects:** News and feature pictures on all subjects. **Special Collections:** Glass negatives from the former New York Times - Wide World files (900,000). **Holdings:** 50,000,000 news and feature type pictures. **Services:** Pictures for newspaper and commercial use; photography assignments, distribution and transmission of pictures; print and reproduction fees charged.

WIDENER LIBRARY
See: Harvard University - History of Science Library

WIDENER UNIVERSITY - DELAWARE COUNTY HISTORICAL SOCIETY
See: Delaware County Historical Society

WIDENER UNIVERSITY - DELAWARE LAW SCHOOL
See: Delaware Law School of Widener University

WIDENER UNIVERSITY - LINDSAY LAW LIBRARY
See: Lindsay Law Library

★17107★
WIDENER UNIVERSITY - WOLFGRAM MEMORIAL LIBRARY (Hum)
17th & Walnut Sts.
Chester, PA 19013
Phone: (215) 499-4066
Theresa Taborsky, Lib.Dir.
Founded: 1821. **Staff:** Prof 10; Other 16. **Subjects:** Arts and sciences, behavioral sciences, education, economics and management, engineering, nursing. **Special Collections:** Wolfgram Collection (English literature). **Holdings:** 120,500 books; 32,000 bound periodical volumes; 5200 reels of microfilm; 8400 microfiche; 3000 recordings; 200 16mm films; 25 videotapes. **Subscriptions:** 1750 journals and other serials; 16 newspapers. **Services:** Interlibrary loans; copying; library open to public with restrictions. **Automated Operations:** Computerized cataloging, acquisitions and serials. **Computerized Information Services:** BRS, DIALOG, VU/TEXT, OCLC. Performs searches on cost recovery basis. Contact Person: Maria Varki, 499-4080. **Networks/Consortia:** Member of PALINET & Union Library Catalogue of Pennsylvania; Tri-State College Library Cooperative (TCLC); Interlibrary Delivery Service of Pennsylvania (IDS); Consortium for Health Information & Library Services (CHI). **Publications:** WolfGRAMS, 4/year - to academic community. **Remarks:** The Wolfgram Memorial Library houses the collections of the Delaware County Historical Society and the Lindsay Law Library. **Staff:** V. Emerson, Ref.Serv.H. Domenech, Archv.; K.J. Kim, Pub.Serv.; D. Medzie, Acq; D. Nutty, AV; P. O'Neill, Ref; M. Varki, Ref.; C. Wisneski, Media Ctr.

★17108★
WIDETT, SLATER & GOLDMAN P.C. - LIBRARY (Law)
60 State St.
Boston, MA 02109
Phone: (617) 227-7200
Sarah G. Connell, Hd. Law Libn.
Staff: Prof 1; Other 2. **Subjects:** Law - corporation, real estate, securities, antitrust, government contracts, banking, estate planning, family, hospital, probate, tax, bankruptcy, education, labor. **Special Collections:** Memoranda of Law Archives (200 legal memoranda). **Holdings:** 12,000 books; 500 bound periodical volumes. **Subscriptions:** 400 journals and other serials; 10 newspapers. **Services:** Interlibrary loans; copying; SDI; library open to public with restrictions. **Computerized Information Services:** LEXIS, Disclosure Inc. **Publications:** WS&G Library News - to all attorneys. **Special Catalogs:** Catalog to Memoranda of Law Archives (card).

WIENER (William E.) ORAL HISTORY LIBRARY
See: American Jewish Committee - William E. Wiener Oral History Library

WIGGANS (R. Glen) MEMORIAL LIBRARY
See: Norwalk Hospital - R. Glen Wiggans Memorial Library

★17109★
WIGGIN AND DANA - LIBRARY (Law)*
195 Church St.
New Haven, CT 06508
Phone: (203) 789-1511
Kathleen A. Ingraham, Libn.
Staff: 1. **Subjects:** Law. **Holdings:** 11,104 books; **Services:** Library not open to public. **Computerized Information Services:** LEXIS.

★17110★
WIGHT CONSULTING ENGINEERS, INC. - TECHNICAL LIBRARY (Sci-Tech)†
127 S. Northwest Hwy.
Barrington, IL 60010
Phone: (312) 381-1800
Sally M. Trainer, Sec.
Staff: Prof 1; Other 2. **Subjects:** Water, sanitary engineering, city planning, transportation, environment, industrial waste. **Holdings:** 1800 books; 400 bound periodical volumes; 50 directories. **Subscriptions:** 30 journals and other serials; 5 newspapers. **Services:** Interlibrary loans; copying; library open to public upon request.

★17111★
WILBERFORCE UNIVERSITY - REMBERT-STOKES LEARNING CENTER - ARCHIVES AND SPECIAL COLLECTIONS (Hist)
Phone: (513) 376-2911
Wilberforce, OH 45384
Jean Mulhern, Chf.Libn.
Staff: Prof 2; Other 4. **Subjects:** African Methodist Episcopal (A.M.E.) Church history; books by and about blacks, 19th century; history of Wilberforce

University. **Special Collections:** A.M.E. Church conference minutes; papers of Bishop Reverdy Cassius Ransome, university president W.S. Scarbrough, and Wilberforce professor Milton S.J. Wright. **Holdings:** 2000 books; 250 bound periodical volumes; 10,000 other cataloged items. **Services:** Copying; library open to public by appointment. **Networks/Consortia:** Member of Dayton-Miami Valley Consortium (DMVC). **Special Catalogs:** Printed guides to some parts of collection.

WILBOUR LIBRARY OF EGYPTOLOGY
See: Brooklyn Museum

WILBUR COLLECTION OF VERMONTIANA
See: University of Vermont

★17112★
WILBUR SMITH AND ASSOCIATES - LIBRARY (Plan)
1301 Gervais St.
Box 92   Phone: (803) 738-0580
Columbia, SC 29202   Jasper Salmond, Info.Dir.
Founded: 1972. **Staff:** Prof 2. **Subjects:** Transportation, planning, architecture, civil engineering, economics, energy. **Holdings:** 15,000 books; speeches; vertical file. **Subscriptions:** 50 journals and other serials. **Services:** Interlibrary loans; library open to public with restrictions. **Publications:** Acquisitions list; Federal Register Report, both monthly - for internal distribution only.

WILCOCK (Peter) LIBRARY
See: Camsell (Charles) General Hospital - Peter Wilcock Library

WILCOX COLLECTION OF CONTEMPORARY POLITICAL MOVEMENTS
See: University of Kansas

★17113★
WILCOX (G.N.) MEMORIAL HOSPITAL & HEALTH CENTER - MEDICAL LIBRARY (Med)*
3420 Kuhio Hwy.   Phone: (808) 245-4811
Lihue, HI 96766
Founded: 1971. **Staff:** 1. **Subjects:** Medicine. **Special Collections:** Doctors of Hawaii - in memoriam (5 volumes). **Holdings:** 400 books; 35 bound periodical volumes; 150 cassette tapes. **Subscriptions:** 70 journals and other serials. **Services:** Interlibrary loans; copying; library open to public. **Networks/Consortia:** Member of Pacific Southwest Regional Medical Library Service (PSRMLS). **Publications:** Ka Moolelo - The Tale (hospital newsletter), 10/year - to hospital personnel and national and state distribution.

WILCOX LIBRARY
See: William Penn College

★17114★
WILDERNESS LEADERSHIP INTERNATIONAL - OUTDOOR LIVING LIBRARY
Wilderness Leadership Center
Box 770
North Fork, CA 93643
Founded: 1970. **Subjects:** Wilderness survival, edible wild plants, camping, mountaineering, homestead skills, health. **Holdings:** 3344 books; 300 magazine articles, pamphlets and reprints; films and slide-tape programs. **Remarks:** Presently inactive.

★17115★
WILDLIFE MANAGEMENT INSTITUTE - LIBRARY (Env-Cons)
1101 Fourteenth St., N.W., Suite 725   Phone: (202) 347-1774
Washington, DC 20005   Richard E. McCabe, Dir.Pubns.
Staff: Prof 18. **Subjects:** Wildlife and conservation. **Special Collections:** Complete Transactions of North American Wildlife and Natural Resources Conference; all Proceedings of American Game Conference; American Game Bulletin, complete run. **Holdings:** 1000 volumes. **Subscriptions:** 50 journals and other serials. **Services:** Library open to public with restrictions. **Special Indexes:** 40-year cumulative index to Transactions of North American Wildlife and Natural Resources Conference.

WILDLIFE RESEARCH CENTER
See: U.S. Fish & Wildlife Service

★17116★
WILDWOOD HISTORICAL COMMISSION - WILDWOOD LIBRARY OF NEW JERSEY HISTORY (Hist)
4400 New Jersey Ave., Rm. 214   Phone: (609) 522-2444
Wildwood, NJ 08260   Ethel T. Holmes, Attendant
Founded: 1962. **Subjects:** State and local history, American history.

Holdings: 1200 books; 2300 bound periodical volumes; 1400 school records; newspapers, 1899 to present; city records; clippings; photographs. **Services:** Library open to public on limited schedule.

★17117★
WILEY (John) AND SONS, INC. - LIBRARY
605 Third Ave.
New York, NY 10158
Founded: 1965. **Special Collections:** Books published by John Wiley and Sons, subsidiaries and divisions. **Remarks:** Presently inactive.

★17118★
WILFRID LAURIER UNIVERSITY - LIBRARY (Hum)
75 University Ave., W.   Phone: (519) 884-1970
Waterloo, ON, Canada N2L 3C5   Erich R.W. Schultz, Univ.Libn.
Founded: 1911. **Staff:** Prof 13; Other 40. **Subjects:** Humanities, business and economics, social work. **Holdings:** 410,000 books; 16,200 serial titles; 130,000 government documents; 86 VF drawers of annual reports, pamphlets, clippings; 16,200 reels of microfilm; 59,000 microcards; 250,000 microfiche; 6500 recordings; 3800 cassettes; 39,500 slides. **Subscriptions:** 5200 journals and other serials; 30 newspapers. **Services:** Interlibrary loans; copying; library open to public. **Automated Operations:** Computerized cataloging, acquisitions, circulation, serials and government documents. **Computerized Information Services:** DIALOG, SDC, BRS, CAN/OLE, Info Globe, International Development Research Centre (IDRC). **Publications:** Bibliographies; Annual Report; WLU Extension Catalogue; Serials List; CODOC. **Staff:** Dr. W. Sirskyj, Cat.; Mrs. Brooke Skelton, Cat.; Brian Flood, Cat.; Vera Zub, Cat.; Howard Parkinson, Circ.Libn.; Diane Wilkins, Ser.Libn.; Richard Woeller, Govt.Doc.Libn.; Joan Mitchell, Bibliog.; John Arndt, Ref./Coll.Libn.; John McCallum, Ref./Coll.Libn.; Diane Peters, Ref./Coll.Libn.; Herbert Schwartz, Sys.; Norma McClenaghan, Hd., Acq.Dept.

★17119★
WILKES-BARRE GENERAL HOSPITAL - HOSPITAL LIBRARY (Med)
Auburn & River Sts.   Phone: (717) 829-8111
Wilkes-Barre, PA 18764   Rosemarie Kazda Taylor, Dir., Lib.Serv.
Founded: 1935. **Staff:** Prof 1; Other 1. **Subjects:** Medicine, nursing and related subjects, hospital administration. **Holdings:** 2962 books; 160 titles on microfilm; AV items; 5 VF drawers of pamphlets; periodicals. **Subscriptions:** 401 journals and other serials. **Services:** Interlibrary loans; copying; SDI; library open to health personnel. **Computerized Information Services:** MEDLARS, DIALOG. Performs searches on cost recovery basis. **Networks/Consortia:** Member of Northeastern Pennsylvania Bibliographic Center (NEPBC); Health Information Library Network of Northeastern Pennsylvania; Greater Northeastern Regional Medical Library Program. **Special Indexes:** Medical Index, monthly - for internal distribution, area libraries and by request.

★17120★
WILKES-BARRE LAW AND LIBRARY ASSOCIATION (Law)*
Courthouse, Rm. 23   Phone: (717) 822-6712
Wilkes-Barre, PA 18711   Lawrence H. Sindaco, Libn.
Staff: Prof 3. **Subjects:** Law. **Holdings:** 30,000 books; 200 bound periodical volumes. **Subscriptions:** 20 journals and other serials. **Services:** Copying; library open to those directly engaged in the legal profession. **Publications:** Luzerne Legal Register, weekly.

★17121★
WILKES COLLEGE - EARTH AND ENVIRONMENTAL SCIENCES READING ROOM (Sci-Tech; Env-Cons)
Box 111   Phone: (717) 824-4651
Wilkes-Barre, PA 18766   Brian Redmond, Chm.
Staff: 3. **Subjects:** Earth sciences, environmental sciences, urban planning, astronomy. **Special Collections:** Local acid mine drainage; local coal mining. **Holdings:** 1000 books; 100 bound periodical volumes; 2000 pamphlets; 2000 maps. **Subscriptions:** 20 journals and other serials. **Services:** Interlibrary loans; reading room open to public with written permission. **Publications:** Department Research Series. **Special Indexes:** Computerized listing of map collection.

★17122★
WILKES COLLEGE - INSTITUTE OF REGIONAL AFFAIRS - LIBRARY (Soc Sci)
165 S. Franklin St.
Box 111   Phone: (717) 824-4651
Wilkes-Barre, PA 18766   Dr. Andrew Shaw, Jr., Dir.
Staff: Prof 4; Other 2. **Subjects:** Government - local, state, in-service training; economic development; legislative reference (state). **Special Collections:** Flood Recovery Collection, 1972 (records of Flood Recovery Task Force, Inc.). **Holdings:** 5000 books; 2000 bound periodical volumes; 3000 pamphlets, studies, reports; 20 file cabinets of news clippings; 500

maps. **Subscriptions:** 256 journals and other serials. **Services:** Interlibrary loans; library open to public. **Publications:** IRA Newsletter, monthly - public service. **Staff:** Dorothy Schlingman .

WILKES LIBRARY
See: Strayer College

WILKINS (Merle) EDUCATION RESOURCE CENTER
See: Baptist Hospital - Medical Library

WILKINS (Walter L.) BIO-MEDICAL LIBRARY
See: U.S. Navy - Naval Health Research Center - Walter L. Wilkins Bio-Medical Library

★17123★
WILL COUNTY HISTORICAL SOCIETY - ARCHIVES (Hist)
803 S. State St.   Phone: (815) 838-5080
Lockport, IL 60441   Rose Bucciferro, Cur.
Subjects: History of Will County, Illinois, and the Illinois and Michigan Canal (1830-1935); genealogy. **Holdings:** 350,000 archival items including property records, surname files, biographies, and cemetery records. **Services:** Copying; archives not open to public. Manual search services available by written request on a fee basis.

★17124★
WILL ROGERS LIBRARY (Hist)†
121 N. Weenonah   Phone: (918) 341-1564
Claremore, OK 74017   Geraldine Warmack, Libn.
Founded: 1936. **Staff:** 2. **Subjects:** Will Rogers, American Indians. **Holdings:** 24,533 books; 188 bound periodical volumes; 5 VF drawers of clippings and pamphlets. **Subscriptions:** 36 journals and other serials; 5 newspapers. **Services:** Interlibrary loans; copying; library open to public.

★17125★
WILLAMETTE UNIVERSITY - LAW LIBRARY (Law)
250 Winter St., S.E.   Phone: (503) 370-6386
Salem, OR 97301   Richard F. Breen, Jr., Law Libn.
Founded: 1883. **Staff:** Prof 3; Other 4. **Subjects:** Law. **Holdings:** 92,000 volumes. **Subscriptions:** 2200 journals and other serials; 7 newspapers. **Services:** Interlibrary loans; copying; library open to public. **Automated Operations:** Computerized cataloging. **Computerized Information Services:** Westlaw, OCLC. **Staff:** Mary Edith Gilbertson, Acq.Libn.; Lysa Hall, Law Cat.

WILLARD (Frances E.) MEMORIAL LIBRARY
See: National Woman's Christian Temperance Union - Frances E. Willard Memorial Library

★17126★
WILLARD LIBRARY OF EVANSVILLE - SPECIAL COLLECTIONS DEPARTMENT (Hist)
21 First Ave.   Phone: (812) 425-4309
Evansville, IN 47710   Joan M. Elliott, Spec.Coll.Libn.
Subjects: History and genealogy of Evansville, Vanderburgh County, and the surrounding areas in Indiana, Illinois, and Kentucky, 1800 to present. **Special Collections:** Records of Willard Library and its predecessors; Southwest Indiana Historical Society collection; Vanderburgh Historical and Biographical Society collection; papers of Annie Fellows Johnston (author), Albion Fellows Bacon (social reformer), Norman A. Shane, Sr. (businessman and civic leader); radio newscast scripts; U.S. Weather Service, Evansville Station, records; photographic collection of local persons and subjects. **Holdings:** 70 linear feet of personal papers, city, township, and county records. **Services:** Copying; center open to public.

★17127★
WILLARD PSYCHIATRIC CENTER - HATCH LIBRARY (Med)
Hatch Bldg.   Phone: (607) 869-3111
Willard, NY 14588   Helen Bunting, Sr.Libn.
Founded: 1869. **Staff:** Prof 1. **Subjects:** Psychiatry, medicine, psychology, health sciences, nursing. **Holdings:** 3300 books; 1200 bound periodical volumes; 12 cubic feet of medical files. **Subscriptions:** 80 journals and other serials; 8 newspapers. **Services:** Interlibrary loans; copying; library open to public with director's written permission. **Computerized Information Services:** New York State Library Data Base (internal database). **Networks/Consortia:** Member of South Central Research Library Council (SCRLC); Finger Lakes Library System.

★17128★
WILLET STAINED GLASS STUDIOS - LIBRARY (Art)
10 E. Moreland Ave.   Phone: (215) 247-5721
Philadelphia, PA 19118   Helene Weis, Libn.
Founded: 1890. **Staff:** Prof 1. **Subjects:** Stained glass (historic and contemporary process), art. **Holdings:** 1000 volumes; 14,750 photographs; 20,000 slides; 4500 microforms; pictures and clippings. **Subscriptions:** 30 journals and other serials. **Services:** Interlibrary loans; copying; library open to qualified persons.

★17129★
WILLIAM H. RORER, INC. - RESEARCH LIBRARY (Sci-Tech; Med)
500 Virginia Dr.   Phone: (215) 628-6358
Fort Washington, PA 19034   Catherine M. Heslin, Info.Sci.
Founded: 1962. **Staff:** Prof 2; Other 1. **Subjects:** Organic chemistry, biochemistry, pharmacology, medicine, pharmacy. **Holdings:** 6000 books; 1000 reels of microfilm; 20 reports on microfiche. **Subscriptions:** 300 journals and other serials. **Services:** Interlibrary loans; library open to medical and other health professionals. **Computerized Information Services:** DIALOG, SDC, NLM.

★17130★
WILLIAM M. MERCER, LTD. - INFORMATION CENTRE (Bus-Fin)
1 First Canadian Pl., 56th Fl.
P.O. Box 59   Phone: (416) 868-2989
Toronto, ON, Canada M5X 1G3   Laurence Pellan, Libn.
Founded: 1974. **Staff:** Prof 2. **Subjects:** Employee benefits, pensions, financial planning, strategic planning, salary administration, executive compensation, group insurance benefits. **Holdings:** 1500 books. **Subscriptions:** 150 journals and other serials; 5 newspapers. **Services:** Interlibrary loans; copying; center open to public at librarian's discretion and by appointment only. **Automated Operations:** Computerized serials circulation lists. **Computerized Information Services:** Infomart. **Staff:** Janice Green, Libn.

★17131★
WILLIAM M. MERCER, INC. - LIBRARY INFORMATION CENTER (Bus-Fin)
3303 Wilshire Blvd.   Phone: (213) 386-7840
Los Angeles, CA 90010   Robert C. Costello
Subjects: Employee benefits, health insurance, life insurance, social security, disability insurance, pensions. **Special Collections:** Employee Benefit Collection. **Holdings:** 300 books; 50 VF drawers of reports, clippings and legal documents. **Subscriptions:** 640 journals and other serials; 25 newspapers. **Services:** Interlibrary loans; library open to public with restrictions. **Computerized Information Services:** DIALOG; MRLIN (internal database). **Publications:** Library Browser, monthly.

★17132★
WILLIAM M. MERCER, INC. - LIBRARY/INFORMATION CENTER (Bus-Fin)
200 Clarendon St.   Phone: (617) 421-0367
Boston, MA 02116   Holly W. Garner, Mgr., Info.Serv.
Staff: Prof 2; Other 1. **Subjects:** Pensions, health care benefits, compensation, consulting. **Holdings:** 450 books; 500 bound periodical volumes; 18 VF drawers of subject files; reports. **Subscriptions:** 100 journals and other serials; 10 newspapers. **Services:** Interlibrary loans; library open to other librarians. **Computerized Information Services:** DIALOG. **Publications:** Library Browser, monthly - to consultants and clients; Of Interest, bimonthly - to consultants. **Special Indexes:** Computerized Report Index.

★17133★
WILLIAM PATERSON COLLEGE OF NEW JERSEY - SARAH BYRD ASKEW LIBRARY - SPECIAL COLLECTIONS (Hist)
300 Pompton Rd.   Phone: (201) 595-2116
Wayne, NJ 07470   Robert Lopresti, Docs./Spec.Coll.Libn.
Founded: 1924. **Special Collections:** New Jerseyana (1500 volumes); first and limited editions of American and English authors (525); autograph collection (100 volumes); miscellany (120 volumes). **Services:** Interlibrary loans; copying; collections open to public for reference use only. **Automated Operations:** Computerized cataloging, acquisitions and circulation. **Computerized Information Services:** DIALOG, BRS, OCLC. **Networks/Consortia:** Member of PALINET & Union Library Catalogue of Pennsylvania. **Publications:** New Books list, monthly.

★17134★
WILLIAM PENN COLLEGE - WILCOX LIBRARY - SPECIAL COLLECTIONS (Rel-Theol)
                                                            Phone: (515) 673-8311
Oskaloosa, IA 52577   Marion E. Rains, Libn.
Staff: Prof 2; Other 3. **Subjects:** Quakers - history, biography and genealogy.

Holdings: 1998 books; 350 bound periodical volumes; cemetery records on microfilm; clippings; scrapbooks; pictures. **Subscriptions:** 10 journals and other serials. **Services:** Interlibrary loans; copying; collections open to public. **Computerized Information Services:** OCLC. **Networks/Consortia:** Member of Southeast Iowa Academic Libraries (SIAL); Bibliographical Center for Research, Rocky Mountain Region, Inc. (BCR). **Publications:** William Penn College: A Product and a Producer, 1973. **Staff:** Edward Goedeken, Tech.Proc.Libn.

WILLIAMS BROTHERS CANADA LIMITED
See: Swan Wooster Consultants Limited

★17135★
WILLIAMS BROTHERS ENGINEERING COMPANY - TECHNICAL INFORMATION CENTER (Sci-Tech; Energy)†
6600 S. Yale Ave.   Phone: (918) 496-5020
Tulsa, OK 74177   Kay Kittrell, Mgr.
Staff: Prof 2. **Subjects:** Pipeline engineering, petroleum industry, energy technology, environmental engineering, energy statistics. **Special Collections:** Liquid natural gas historical/technical data; pipeline maps. **Holdings:** 5000 books; 10,000 company reports; 487 reels of microfilmed association standards; 200 maps; 200 VF drawers of clippings and reprints. **Subscriptions:** 140 journals and other serials. **Services:** Copying; center open to public with restrictions. **Publications:** Newsletter, quarterly - for internal distribution only. **Special Catalogs:** Technical Reports Catalog (card); catalog of published papers of company personnel (card). **Staff:** Sara Seaman, Tech.Libn.

★17136★
WILLIAMS (C.S.) CLINIC - LIBRARY (Med)
901 Helena St.   Phone: (604) 368-5211
Trail, BC, Canada V1R 3X4   Dr. L. Simonetta, Lib.Chm.
Subjects: Medicine and related fields. **Holdings:** 500 books; 1000 bound periodical volumes. **Subscriptions:** 10 journals and other serials. **Services:** Library open to area doctors only.

★17137★
WILLIAMS COLLEGE - CENTER FOR ENVIRONMENTAL STUDIES - LIBRARY (Env-Cons)
                                          Phone: (413) 597-2500
Williamstown, MA 01267   Nancy E. Hanssen, Doc. & Env.Stud.Libn.
Founded: 1972. **Staff:** Prof 1; Other 1. **Subjects:** Berkshire County natural resources, planning and local history; agriculture; energy; forestry; pollution; environmental law; historic preservation. **Holdings:** 2000 books; 960 bound periodical volumes; 4300 U.S. Government documents; 3000 reports, manuals, local government documents. **Subscriptions:** 160 journals and other serials. **Services:** Copying; library open to public with restrictions.

★17138★
WILLIAMS COLLEGE - CHAPIN LIBRARY (Rare Book; Hum)
Stetson Hall, 2nd Fl.
Box 426   Phone: (413) 597-2462
Williamstown, MA 01267   Robert L. Volz, Custodian
Founded: 1923. **Staff:** Prof 2; Other 1. **Special Collections:** Incunabula (550 volumes); English literature before 1700 (1500 volumes); English 18th- and 19th-century first editions (1800 volumes); Americana (1600 volumes); History of Science (500 volumes); Ornithology (250 volumes); Classical and European literature (1500 volumes); Bibles and liturgical books (300 volumes); Aldine Press (135 volumes); Graphic Arts and private press books (3000 volumes); Walt Whitman (600 items); William Saroyan (250 items); Edwin Arlington Robinson (300 items); Samuel Butler (1000 items); Rudyard Kipling (700 items); Joseph Conrad (140 items); Theodore Roosevelt (200 items); William Faulkner (450 items); pre-1600 codices (40 volumes); historical and literary manuscripts (1400 items); prints of historical subjects (500 items); English 17th- and 18th-century broadside ballads (130 items). **Holdings:** 30,000 volumes. **Subscriptions:** 25 journals and other serials. **Services:** Copying; library answers correspondence requests for bibliographical information; library open to public with restrictions. **Automated Operations:** Computerized cataloging. **Publications:** Exhibition handlists; The Graphic Art of C.B. Falls, 1982. **Special Catalogs:** Short-Title List of Books in the Chapin Library, 1939; special card file for printers - place of printing, date of imprint, binders; watermarks in incunabula; provenance; maps and illustrations; catalog of the collection of Samuel Butler (of Erewhon) in the Chapin Library, 1945; Book Decoration in America: 1890-1910, 1979. **Remarks:** Library sponsors lectures, exhibitions, arranges seminars for advanced courses. **Staff:** Wayne G. Hammond, Asst.Libn.

WILLIAMS (E.K.) LAW LIBRARY
See: University of Manitoba - E.K. Williams Law Library

★17139★
WILLIAMS INTERNATIONAL - LIBRARY (Sci-Tech)
2280 W. Maple Rd.
Box 200   Phone: (313) 624-5200
Walled Lake, MI 48088   Lydia O. Johnstone, Hd.Libn.
Staff: Prof 1; Other 1. **Subjects:** Aerodynamics, gas turbine engines, metallurgy. **Holdings:** 1000 books; 5000 documents. **Subscriptions:** 40 journals and other serials. **Services:** Interlibrary loans; library not open to public. **Computerized Information Services:** Online systems.

WILLIAMS (John R., Sr.) HEALTH SCIENCES LIBRARY
See: Highland Hospital of Rochester - John R. Williams, Sr. Health Sciences Library

THE WILLIAMS (Kemper and Leila) FOUNDATION - HISTORIC NEW ORLEANS COLLECTION
See: Historic New Orleans Collection

★17140★
WILLIAMS-KUEBELBECK & ASSOCIATES, INC. - LIBRARY (Bus-Fin)
611 Veterans Blvd., Suite 205   Phone: (415) 365-7202
Redwood City, CA 94063   Nancy Jane Myers, Libn.
Founded: 1972. **Staff:** Prof 1. **Subjects:** Real estate market, fiscal impact analysis. **Special Collections:** Marina Development (125 volumes). **Holdings:** 75 books; 1500 unbound reports. **Subscriptions:** 98 journals and other serials. **Services:** Interlibrary loans; library not open to public. **Computerized Information Services:** DIALOG. **Publications:** Newsletter, monthly; bibliographies - both for internal distribution only. **Special Catalogs:** Internal reports catalog (card).

WILLIAMS (Paul) MEMORIAL RESOURCE CENTER
See: Investigative Reporters and Editors, Inc. - Paul Williams Memorial Resource Center

WILLIAMS (Roger) GENERAL HOSPITAL
See: Roger Williams General Hospital

WILLIAMS (Roger) PARK
See: Roger Williams Park

WILLIAMS (Samuel C.) LIBRARY
See: Stevens Institute of Technology - Samuel C. Williams Library

WILLIAMS (T.F.) HEALTH SCIENCES LIBRARY
See: Monroe Community Hospital - T.F. Williams Health Sciences Library

WILLIAMSON (Dr. George S.) HEALTH SCIENCES LIBRARY
See: Ottawa Civic Hospital - Dr. George S. Williamson Health Sciences Library

WILLIAMSON LIBRARY
See: Railroad Enthusiasts New York Division, Inc.

★17141★
WILLIAMSPORT AREA COMMUNITY COLLEGE - SLOAN FINE ARTS LIBRARY (Art)
1005 W. 3rd St.   Phone: (717) 326-3761
Williamsport, PA 17701   Kate D. Hickey, Dir., Lib.Serv.
Founded: 1969. **Subjects:** Art, architecture. **Holdings:** 2500 volumes. **Services:** Interlibrary loans; copying; library open to public.

★17142★
WILLIAMSPORT HOSPITAL - LEARNING RESOURCES CENTER (Med)
777 Rural Ave.   Phone: (717) 322-7861
Williamsport, PA 17701-3198   Michael Heyd, Dir.
Staff: Prof 1; Other 1. **Subjects:** Medicine, nursing and related fields. **Special Collections:** Old medical textbooks dating back to 1850. **Holdings:** 3869 books; 4567 bound periodical volumes; 238 filmstrip/cassette programs; 252 slide/cassette programs; 61 video cassette programs; 150 audio cassette programs; 3 16mm films. **Subscriptions:** 230 journals and other serials. **Services:** Interlibrary loans; copying; reference and bibliographic information; center open to public for reference use only. **Computerized Information Services:** MEDLARS. Performs searches on cost recovery basis. **Networks/Consortia:** Member of Susquehanna Library Cooperative; Central Pennsylvania Health Sciences Library Association (CPHSLA).

WILLIS (Jeannie) MEMORIAL LIBRARY
See: Mc Gill University - Religious Studies Library

★17143★
WILLKIE FARR & GALLAGHER - LIBRARY (Law)
153 E. 53rd St.   Phone: (212) 935-8000
New York, NY 10022   Marilyn E. Maney, Hd.Libn.
Staff: Prof 6; Other 8. Subjects: Law - corporate, tax, real estate, trusts and estates, general. Holdings: 36,000 books; 250 bound periodical volumes; 10 drawers of annual reports; 5 cabinets of microforms. Subscriptions: 175 journals and other serials. Services: Interlibrary loans. Automated Operations: Computerized cataloging. Computerized Information Services: DIALOG, SDC, Dow Jones News/Retrieval, NEXIS, LEXIS, CDC, Bureau of National Affairs, Inc. (BNA), OCLC. Staff: Mindy J. Myers, Asst.Libn.; Maryann O'Donnell, Cat.; Karenn Carpenter, Ref.Libn.; Mike Gottfried, Ref.Libn.; Nancy Moskowitz, Ref.Libn.

★17144★
WILLMAR PUBLIC SCHOOLS - COMMUNITY EDUCATION TOY LIBRARY
(Educ)
c/o Pioneer Land Library System
410 S.W. 5th St.   Phone: (612) 235-3162
Willmar, MN 56201   Linda Cogelow, Coord.
Staff: 2. Holdings: 350 toys; baby furniture. Services: Library not open to public. Publications: Brochures listing hours, toy inventory, rules; irregular.

★17145★
WILLMAR STATE HOSPITAL - LIBRARY (Med)
Box 1128   Phone: (612) 235-3322
Willmar, MN 56201   Linda Bjornberg, Libn.
Founded: 1917. Staff: Prof 1. Subjects: Alcoholism, psychiatric nursing, mental retardation. Special Collections: Brandes Memorial Library (special collection of books on alcoholism). Holdings: 2000 books. Subscriptions: 63 journals and other serials. Services: Interlibrary loans; copying; library open to public with restrictions. Networks/Consortia: Member of Minnesota Department of Human Services Library Consortium.

WILLS (Bob) MEMORIAL ARCHIVE OF POPULAR MUSIC
See: Panhandle-Plains Historical Museum - Research Center

★17146★
WILLS EYE HOSPITAL AND RESEARCH INSTITUTE - ARTHUR J. BEDELL MEMORIAL LIBRARY (Med)
Ninth & Walnut Sts.   Phone: (215) 928-3288
Philadelphia, PA 19107   Fleur Weinberg, Libn.
Founded: 1832. Staff: Prof 1; Other 2. Subjects: Ophthalmology - clinical, historical. Special Collections: Ophthalmic history. Holdings: 2500 books; 7600 bound periodical volumes; 200 Wills Quarterly Conference Papers; 2 VF drawers of Wills staff reprints; 5 VF drawers; 250,000 audiotapes, cassettes, slides; 78 video cassettes. Subscriptions: 125 journals and other serials. Services: Interlibrary loans; library open to public by appointment. Computerized Information Services: NLM.

★17147★
WILMER, CUTLER & PICKERING - LAW LIBRARY (Law)
1666 K St., N.W.   Phone: (202) 872-6183
Washington, DC 20006   Elaine Mitchell, Dir. of Info.Serv.
Staff: Prof 4; Other 9. Subjects: Law - antitrust, corporate, securities, tax, administrative. Special Collections: Collection of legislative histories and bound Senate and House reports. Holdings: 35,000 books; 1500 bound periodical volumes. Subscriptions: 1200 journals and other serials; 15 newspapers. Services: Interlibrary loans; copying; library open to public with restrictions. Automated Operations: Computerized cataloging and serials. Computerized Information Services: LEXIS, New York Times Information Service, DIALOG, SDC, Dow Jones News/Retrieval, OCLC. Staff: Teresa Llewellyn, Dp.Dir.; Barclay Inge, Leg.Spec.

WILMER MEMORIAL MEDICAL LIBRARY
See: Abington Memorial Hospital

WILMER OPHTHALMOLOGICAL INSTITUTE
See: Johns Hopkins University

★17148★
WILMETTE HISTORICAL MUSEUM - LIBRARY (Hist)
565 Hunter Rd.   Phone: (312) 256-5838
Wilmette, IL 60091
Founded: 1950. Staff: 1. Subjects: History and institutions of the village of Wilmette. Holdings: 350 books; 120 bound periodical volumes; 4000 photographs; 30 VF drawers of archival material. Services: Library open to public with restrictions.

★17149★
WILMINGTON AREA HEALTH EDUCATION CENTER - HEALTH SCIENCES LIBRARY (Med)
2131 S. 17th St.   Phone: (919) 343-0161
Wilmington, NC 28402-9990   Ms. Spencer Kearns Sexton, Libn.
Staff: Prof 2; Other 4. Subjects: Internal medicine, nursing, oncology, cardiology, surgery, obstetrics and gynecology, allied health sciences. Holdings: 2500 books; 2000 bound periodical volumes; AV software. Subscriptions: 200 journals and other serials. Services: Interlibrary loans; copying; SDI; library open to public for reference use only. Computerized Information Services: BRS, NLM. Networks/Consortia: Member of North Carolina Area Health Education Centers Program (AHEC) - Library and Information Services Network. Staff: Jocelyn C. Bass, Asst.Libn.

★17150★
WILMINGTON COLLEGE - CURRICULUM MATERIALS CENTER (Educ)*
Phone: (513) 382-6661
Wilmington, OH 45177   George Winsor, Prof. of Educ.
Founded: 1962. Staff: 2. Subjects: Education. Holdings: 2000 books; filmstrips; records; maps and globes; vertical files. Services: Interlibrary loans; copying; center open to public. Staff: Larry Kroah, Libn.

★17151★
WILMINGTON MEDICAL CENTER (Delaware Division) - MEDICAL STAFF LIBRARY (Med)
501 W. 14th St.
Box 1668   Phone: (302) 428-2201
Wilmington, DE 19899   Helen St. Clair, Med.Libn.
Founded: 1965. Staff: Prof 2; Other 2. Subjects: Medicine. Holdings: 3500 books; 5000 bound periodical volumes. Subscriptions: 250 journals and other serials. Services: Interlibrary loans; copying; library open to public for reference use only. Automated Operations: Computerized cataloging. Computerized Information Services: BRS, MEDLINE, OCLC. Networks/Consortia: Member of Wilmington Area Biomedical Library Consortium (WABLC); Delaware Library Consortium. Staff: Diane Wolf, AV Libn.

★17152★
WILMINGTON NEWS-JOURNAL COMPANY - LIBRARY (Publ)
831 Orange St.   Phone: (302) 573-2038
Wilmington, DE 19899   Charlotte Walker, Chf.Libn.
Founded: 1955. Staff: Prof 4; Other 2. Subjects: Newspaper reference topics. Special Collections: Company archives. Holdings: 15000 books; 92 VF drawers of photographs and art; city directories; 10 million clippings. Subscriptions: 150 journals and other serials; 10 newspapers. Services: Copying; library open to public with restrictions. Staff: Dorothy Brown, Sr.Libn.; Helen Carnell, Libn.; Eva Donaldson, Libn.; Cecilia James, Libn.

★17153★
WILMINGTON STAR-NEWS NEWSPAPERS, INC. - LIBRARY (Publ)
1103 S. 17th St.
Box 840   Phone: (919) 343-2309
Wilmington, NC 28402   Shirley A. Moore, Libn.
Staff: Prof 1; Other 1. Subjects: Newspaper reference topics. Holdings: Wilmington Star and News, 1925 to present, on microfilm; local clipping files on microfilm. Services: Library open to public on a limited basis.

WILMOT (Lorette) Library
See: Nazareth College of Rochester - Lorette Wilmot Library

★17154★
WILSHIRE BOULEVARD TEMPLE - SIGMUND HECHT LIBRARY (Rel-Theol)†
3663 Wilshire Blvd.   Phone: (213) 388-2401
Los Angeles, CA 90010   Mitzi Weinstein, Libn.
Staff: Prof 1; Other 1. Subjects: Judaica, Bible, philosophy, religion, Jewish history, education, language and literature, arts, sociology. Special Collections: World War, 1939-1945: trials of the major war criminals (complete set). Holdings: 16,000 books and bound periodical volumes; 100 pamphlets; 12 VF drawers of uncataloged pamphlets; 100 filmstrips. Subscriptions: 15 journals and other serials. Services: Interlibrary loans; library open to public for reference use only.

WILSON (Charles S.) MEMORIAL HOSPITAL
See: United Health Services/Wilson Hospital

★17155★
WILSON COUNTY HISTORICAL SOCIETY - MUSEUM LIBRARY (Hist)
420 N. 7th   Phone: (316) 378-3965
Fredonia, KS 66736   Bonnie Forbes, Musm.Cur.
Founded: 1962. **Staff:** 2. **Subjects:** The West; Kansas; pioneer life; plains agriculture - tools, equipment, facilities. **Special Collections:** Original set of the Offical Records of the Civil War. **Holdings:** 400 books; 300 bound periodical volumes; 1050 indexed pictures; 68 indexed notebooks of clippings; 15 notebooks of clipped obituaries from last 40 years in Wilson County; 110 reels of microfilm of Wilson County newspapers; books of grade school local history essays, 1983-1984. **Services:** Copying; library open to public for reference use only. **Publications:** Newsletter, 4/year.

WILSON (Cunningham) LIBRARY
See: St. Vincent's Hospital - Cunningham Wilson Library

WILSON (Curtis Laws) LIBRARY
See: University of Missouri, Rolla - Curtis Laws Wilson Library

WILSON (Edmund) LIBRARY
See: University of Tulsa - Mc Farlin Library - Rare Books and Special Collections

★17156★
WILSON FOODS, INC. - RESEARCH LIBRARY (Food-Bev)†
4545 Lincoln Blvd.   Phone: (405) 525-4781
Oklahoma City, OK 73105   Joy Jones
Staff: 2. **Subjects:** Chemistry, food science. **Holdings:** 600 books. **Subscriptions:** 70 journals and other serials; 12 newspapers. **Services:** Library not open to public.

★17157★
WILSON, IHRIG & ASSOCIATES - LIBRARY (Sci-Tech)
5776 Broadway   Phone: (415) 658-6719
Oakland, CA 94618   Thomas Mugglestone, Libn.
Staff: Prof 1. **Subjects:** Acoustics theory; acoustics - building, industrial, and general; rapid transit noise and vibration. **Holdings:** 500 books; 2000 reports; 1800 articles and reprints. **Subscriptions:** 47 journals and other serials. **Services:** Interlibrary loans (limited); copying; library open to public by appointment. **Automated Operations:** Computerized cataloging. **Computerized Information Services:** DIALOG. Performs searches on cost recovery plus professional fee basis.

WILSON LIBRARY
See: University of Minnesota

★17158★
WILSON MEMORIAL HOSPITAL - LIBRARY/LEARNING CENTER (Med)
1705 S. Tarboro St.   Phone: (919) 399-8253
Wilson, NC 27893   Marian H. Spencer, Lib.Dir.
Founded: 1964. **Staff:** Prof 1; Other 2. **Subjects:** Medicine, nursing and allied health fields. **Holdings:** 2827 books and bound periodical volumes; 1018 video cassettes; 252 slide sets; 396 filmstrips. **Subscriptions:** 90 journals and other serials. **Services:** Interlibrary loans; copying; library open to public with restrictions. **Networks/Consortia:** Member of North Carolina Area Health Education Centers Program (AHEC) - Library and Information Services Network. **Special Catalogs:** Audiovisual Catalog.

WILSON MEMORIAL LIBRARY
See: Aldersgate College

WILSON (Miriam B.) FOUNDATION - OLD SLAVE MART MUSEUM
See: Old Slave Mart Museum

★17159★
WILSON ORNITHOLOGICAL SOCIETY - JOSSELYN VAN TYNE MEMORIAL LIBRARY (Sci-Tech)
Museum of Zoology
University of Michigan   Phone: (313) 764-0457
Ann Arbor, MI 48109   William A. Lunk, Chm. of Lib.Comm.
Founded: 1930. **Staff:** 1. **Subjects:** Ornithology. **Holdings:** 1700 books; 2400 bound periodical volumes; 700 boxes of pamphlets and reprints; 250 translations; 70 dissertations; 50 sound recordings. **Subscriptions:** 193 journals and other serials. **Services:** Interlibrary loans; direct mail loan service to members of Wilson Ornithological Society; library open to University of Michigan staff and students. **Staff:** Janet G. Hinshaw, Libn.

WILSON RECORDINGS COLLECTION
See: University of British Columbia

★17160★
WILSON (Thomas) CENTER - MEDICAL AND PROFESSIONAL LIBRARY
Mount Wilson Lane
Mount Wilson, MD 21112
Defunct

★17161★
WILSON (Woodrow) BIRTHPLACE FOUNDATION, INC. - RESEARCH LIBRARY & ARCHIVES (Hist)
20 N. Coalter St.
Box 24   Phone: (703) 885-0897
Staunton, VA 24401   Dr. Katharine L. Brown, Exec.Dir.
Founded: 1973. **Staff:** Prof 2. **Subjects:** Life and times of President Woodrow Wilson; international affairs during World War I period; Wilson family members; American government, 1902-1921. **Special Collections:** Katherine C. Brand Collection (Life and Times of Woodrow Wilson; 500 volumes); Wallace M. McClure Collection (Woodrow Wilson and International Affairs; 1000 volumes). **Holdings:** 4000 books; 150 bound periodical volumes; 1000 pamphlets; 1000 pieces of Woodrow Wilson and family manuscripts; 10 boxes of period newspaper clippings; 20 boxes of period photographs; 12 drawers and 20 boxes of institutional archives. **Subscriptions:** 20 journals and other serials. **Services:** Library open to public on request. **Staff:** Gertrude Middendorf, Libn.

★17162★
WILSON (Woodrow) INTERNATIONAL CENTER FOR SCHOLARS - LIBRARY (Soc Sci)
Smithsonian Institution Bldg.   Phone: (202) 357-2567
Washington, DC 20560   Zdenek V. David, Libn.
Founded: 1970. **Staff:** Prof 2; Other 2. **Subjects:** U.S. history and politics, American studies, Latin American studies, Russian studies, East Asian studies, international security. **Special Collections:** Russian/Soviet Collection of the Kennan Institute (4000 volumes). **Holdings:** 16,000 books, documents and bound periodical volumes; 8 VF drawers. **Subscriptions:** 600 journals and other serials; 25 newspapers. **Services:** Interlibrary loans; copying; library open to public for reference use only. **Publications:** Bibliographies, irregular. **Remarks:** The center is an autonomous branch of the Smithsonian Institution.

WILSON (Woodrow) MEMORIAL LIBRARY
See: United Nations Headquarters - Dag Hammarskjold Library

WILSON (Woodrow) SCHOOL OF PUBLIC AND INTERNATIONAL AFFAIRS
See: Princeton University - Woodrow Wilson School of Public and International Affairs

★17163★
WILTON HISTORICAL SOCIETY, INC. - LIBRARY (Hist)
249 Danbury Rd.   Phone: (203) 762-7257
Wilton, CT 06897
Subjects: Connecticut and Wilton history and genealogy. **Special Collections:** Connecticut and New England maps. **Holdings:** 500 volumes; manuscript collection. **Services:** Copying; library open to public for reference use only. **Remarks:** Library is housed at the Wilton Public Library.

WINCHELL LIBRARY OF GEOLOGY
See: University of Minnesota - Geology Library

★17164★
WINCHESTER HISTORICAL SOCIETY - ARCHIVE (Hist)
225 Prospect St.
Box 206   Phone: (203) 379-8433
Winsted, CT 06098   Pauline Fancher, Cur.
Subjects: Local history. **Holdings:** Figures not available for books, photographs, maps and documents; 5000 glassplate negatives. **Services:** Archive open to public for reference use only by appointment. **Remarks:** Curator can be reached at 379-6269.

★17165★
WINCHESTER MEMORIAL HOSPITAL - HEALTH SCIENCES LIBRARY (Med)
South Stewart St.   Phone: (703) 665-5124
Winchester, VA 22601   Beth A. Layton, Libn.
Staff: Prof 1. **Subjects:** Medicine, nursing, allied health sciences. **Holdings:** 400 books; 2000 bound periodical volumes. **Subscriptions:** 100 journals and other serials. **Services:** Interlibrary loans; copying; library open to public by appointment. **Computerized Information Services:** MEDLARS. Performs searches on cost recovery basis. **Publications:** Library News, monthly - for

internal distribution only.

WINCHESTER REPEATING ARMS COMPANY ARCHIVES
See: Buffalo Bill Historical Center - Harold Mc Cracken Research Library

★17166★
WINDELS, MARX, DAVIES & IVES - LIBRARY (Law)
51 W. 51st St.   Phone: (212) 977-9600
New York, NY 10019   Huguette Streuli, Libn.
Staff: Prof 2; Other 1. **Subjects:** Law - corporate, international, securities, tax, trusts and estates, banking. **Holdings:** 18,000 books; 550 bound periodical volumes. **Subscriptions:** 185 journals and other serials; 10 newspapers. **Services:** Interlibrary loans; library open to public with restrictions. **Computerized Information Services:** LEXIS, DIALOG, NEXIS, Dow Jones News/Retrieval, National Automated Accounting Research System (NAARS). **Publications:** Library Newsletter, bimonthly.

★17167★
WINDSOR COALITION FOR DEVELOPMENT - THIRD WORLD RESOURCE CENTRE (Soc Sci)★
125 Tecumseh, W.   Phone: (519) 252-1517
Windsor, ON, Canada N8X 1E8   Sr. Gabrielle Morin, SNJM, Coord. of Rsrcs.
Staff: 2. **Subjects:** Aids to social action and development education, disarmament and arms trade, foreign relations, human rights, natural resources. **Holdings:** 1100 books; 194 reports and manuscripts; 30 vertical file boxes of articles; 32 simulation games; 34 filmstrips and slide shows; 45 kits. **Subscriptions:** 62 journals and other serials; 7 newspapers. **Services:** Copying; center open to public. **Publications:** Newsletter, 5/year.

★17168★
WINDSOR HISTORICAL SOCIETY, INC. - LIBRARY (Hist)
96 Palisado Ave.   Phone: (203) 688-3813
Windsor, CT 06095   Robert T. Silliman, Dir.
Founded: 1923. **Staff:** Prof 1; Other 12. **Subjects:** Local history, genealogy, biography. **Special Collections:** Account books; Bibles; Northeast history; history and genealogy of 1633 founding families; history of 20 daughter towns which were once part of Windsor. **Holdings:** 3000 books; 50 bound periodical volumes; 3000 other cataloged items; documents and historic pictures concerning Windsor and its people; 100 ephemeral files. **Services:** Copying; library open to public for reference use only.

WINDSOR PUBLIC LIBRARY - HIRAM WALKER HISTORICAL MUSEUM
See: Walker (Hiram) Historical Museum

★17169★
WINDSOR STAR - LIBRARY (Publ)
167 Ferry St.   Phone: (519) 256-5511
Windsor, ON, Canada N9A 4M5   Mary Jane Handy, Libn.
Founded: 1935. **Staff:** Prof 1; Other 2. **Subjects:** Newspaper reference topics. **Holdings:** 300 books; one million clippings; 1.5 million pictures; 5000 maps; 7 VF drawers of pamphlets; 24 drawers of microfilm of Windsor Star, 1893 to present; 200 other cataloged items. **Services:** Copying; library open to public with restrictions.

★17170★
WINE INSTITUTE - LIBRARY (Food-Bev)
165 Post St.   Phone: (415) 986-0878
San Francisco, CA 94108   Joan V. Ingalls, Libn.
Founded: 1934. **Staff:** Prof 1. **Subjects:** Wine and winemaking, viticulture. **Special Collections:** California wine industry clippings and brochures. **Holdings:** 3100 books and bound periodical volumes. **Subscriptions:** 100 journals and other serials. **Services:** Library not open to public except by special permission.

★17171★
WINE MUSEUM OF SAN FRANCISCO - CHRISTIAN BROTHERS RARE WINE BOOKS LIBRARY
633 Beach St.
San Francisco, CA 94109
Defunct. Holdings absorbed by Seagram Museum - Library & Archives.

★17172★
WINEBRENNER THEOLOGICAL SEMINARY - LIBRARY (Rel-Theol)
701 E. Melrose Ave.
Box 478   Phone: (419) 422-4824
Findlay, OH 45839-0478   Oscar C. Schultz, Jr., Hd.Libn.
Founded: 1942. **Staff:** Prof 2; Other 3. **Subjects:** Church history, Old and New Testament, contemporary theology, homiletics, Christian education and practical theology, Christian ministries. **Special Collections:** Church of God

old and rare books; Church of God history; John Winebrenner materials. **Holdings:** 28,500 books; 1350 bound periodical volumes; 286 other items; 8 VF of pamphlets. **Subscriptions:** 125 journals and other serials. **Services:** Interlibrary loans; copying; library open to public. **Automated Operations:** Computerized cataloging. **Computerized Information Services:** OCLC. **Staff:** Florence Cook, Cat.

★17173★
WINEDALE HISTORICAL CENTER - LIBRARY (Hist)
Box 11   Phone: (409) 278-3530
Round Top, TX 78954   Gloria Jaster, Off.Supv.
Staff: 1. **Subjects:** Historic sites, furniture, decorative arts, agriculture. **Holdings:** 835 books; 75 bound periodical volumes; 200 other cataloged items; historic preservation documentation. **Subscriptions:** 38 journals and other serials. **Services:** Interlibrary loans; copying; library open to public for reference use only. **Publications:** Quid Nunc (newsletter), quarterly - to friends of Winedale, members and museums. **Remarks:** Administered by the University of Texas, Austin.

★17174★
WINFIELD STATE HOSPITAL AND TRAINING CENTER - PROFESSIONAL AND MEDICAL LIBRARY (Med)
                                          Phone: (316) 221-1200
Winfield, KS 67156   Janis Beecham, Lib.Ck.
Staff: Prof 1. **Subjects:** Mental retardation, psychology, medicine, social work and welfare, education and special education, nursing. **Holdings:** 2100 books; 189 bound periodical volumes; 146 AV programs; 476 unbound periodical volumes; 398 indexes and abstracts in volumes; 15 theses; 3000 pamphlets and clippings. **Subscriptions:** 70 journals and other serials. **Services:** Interlibrary loans; copying; library open to public. **Networks/Consortia:** Member of Midcontinental Regional Medical Library Program.

WINN LIBRARY
See: Gordon College

★17175★
WINNEBAGO COUNTY LAW LIBRARY (Law)
Courthouse Bldg., Suite 306
400 W. State St.   Phone: (815) 987-2514
Rockford, IL 61101   Roberta S. McGaw, Libn.
Founded: 1975. **Staff:** Prof 1; Other 1. **Subjects:** General legal material; federal, Illinois and Wisconsin law. **Holdings:** 16,000 volumes and microfiche. **Subscriptions:** 26 journals and other serials. **Services:** Interlibrary loans; copying; library open to public. **Networks/Consortia:** Member of Northern Illinois Library System (NILS). **Remarks:** The Winnebago County Law Library is an agency of the Winnebago County Board.

★17176★
WINNEBAGO MENTAL HEALTH INSTITUTE - MEDICAL LIBRARY (Med)
Box 9   Phone: (414) 235-4910
Winnebago, WI 54985-0009   Mary Campfield, Dir. of Lib.Serv.
Founded: 1873. **Staff:** Prof 1; Other 1. **Subjects:** Psychiatry, psychology, social service, counseling, hospital administration, nursing, sociology. **Holdings:** 6000 books and bound periodical volumes; 8 VF drawers of pamphlets; 400 cassette tapes; 15 videotapes. **Subscriptions:** 183 journals and other serials. **Services:** Interlibrary loans; copying; library open to public. **Networks/Consortia:** Member of Fox River Valley Area Library Consortium; Fox Valley Library Council.

★17177★
WINNIPEG ART GALLERY - CLARA LANDER LIBRARY (Art)
300 Memorial Blvd.   Phone: (204) 786-6641
Winnipeg, MB, Canada R3C 1V1   David W. Rozniatowski, Libn.
Founded: 1912. **Staff:** Prof 2. **Subjects:** History of art and painting, drawing, sculpture, ceramics, prints, architecture, antiques and photography. **Special Collections:** Canadiana (Eskimo and Indian art). **Holdings:** 15,200 books; 720 bound periodical volumes; 8500 exhibition catalogs; 844 reports; 666 folders of bulletins; 7000 folders of biographies of artists; 136 binders of archives. **Subscriptions:** 40 journals and other serials. **Services:** Interlibrary loans; copying; library open to public; gallery membership is necessary for loan privileges. **Publications:** Exhibition catalogs. **Special Catalogs:** Index to collection (punched cards).

★17178★
WINNIPEG BIBLE COLLEGE/WINNIPEG THEOLOGICAL SEMINARY - LIBRARY (Rel-Theol)
                                          Phone: (204) 284-2923
Otterburne, MB, Canada R0A 1G0   Karen Friesen, Libn.
Staff: Prof 3; Other 25. **Subjects:** Theology, Old and New Testament.

Holdings: 29,820 books; 936 bound periodical volumes; 1183 tapes; 436 phonograph records; 399 volumes in microform; 580 choral music items; 92 media kits. **Subscriptions:** 240 journals and other serials. **Services:** Interlibrary loans; copying; library open to public. **Staff:** Audrey Adrian-Neufeld, Asst.Libn.; Martha Loeppky, Lib.Techn.

★17179★
WINNIPEG CLINIC - LIBRARY (Med)
425 St. Mary Ave.   Phone: (204) 957-1900
Winnipeg, MB, Canada R3C 0N2   S. Loeppky, Libn.
Staff: 1. **Subjects:** Medicine. **Holdings:** Figures not available. **Subscriptions:** 110 journals and other serials. **Services:** Interlibrary loans; copying; library open to public with restrictions.

★17180★
WINNIPEG DEPARTMENT OF ENVIRONMENTAL PLANNING - LIBRARY (Plan)†
395 Main St.   Phone: (204) 985-5174
Winnipeg, MB, Canada R3B 3E1   Mrs. A. Thiesson, Libn.
Founded: 1960. **Staff:** Prof 1; Other 2. **Subjects:** City planning, local government, real estate trends, urban economics, geography. **Holdings:** 6600 books; pamphlets; 400 slides; 3050 reports; maps; microfiche. **Subscriptions:** 40 journals and other serials. **Services:** Interlibrary loans; library open to public with restrictions on some material.

★17181★
WINNIPEG FREE PRESS - LIBRARY (Publ)
300 Carlton St.   Phone: (204) 943-9331
Winnipeg, MB, Canada R3C 3C1   Mrs. E. Langer, Libn.
Founded: 1923. **Staff:** 6. **Subjects:** Newspaper reference topics. **Special Collections:** Selected Canadian and Manitoba government documents. **Holdings:** 6800 volumes. **Subscriptions:** 125 journals and other serials. **Services:** Interlibrary loans; library not open to public.

★17182★
WINNIPEG HEALTH SCIENCES CENTRE - LIBRARY SERVICES (Med)
700 McDermot Ave.   Phone: (204) 787-2743
Winnipeg, MB, Canada R3E 0T2   Barbara Greeniaus, Dir., Lib.Serv.
Founded: 1981. **Staff:** Prof 1; Other 4. **Subjects:** Medicine, surgery, pediatrics, nursing, allied health sciences, hospital administration. **Holdings:** 8000 books; 300 bound periodical volumes; 1000 slides. **Subscriptions:** 400 journals and other serials. **Services:** Interlibrary loans; copying; SDI; library open to public with restrictions. **Computerized Information Services:** MEDLARS. **Networks/Consortia:** Member of Manitoba Health Libraries Association (MHLA).

★17183★
WINNIPEG SCHOOL DIVISION NO. 1 - TEACHERS LIBRARY AND RESOURCE CENTRE (Educ)
1180 Notre Dame Ave.   Phone: (204) 943-3541
Winnipeg, MB, Canada R3E 0P2   Gerald R. Brown, Chf.Libn.
Staff: Prof 4; Other 27. **Subjects:** Education and audiovisual education, library science, Canadiana, Manitobiana. **Special Collections:** Historical curriculum texts. **Holdings:** 15,206 books; 873 bound periodical volumes; 4216 AV items; 27 VF drawers; 261 reels of microfilm; 1977 titles of 16mm films; 112 titles of videotapes. **Subscriptions:** 326 journals and other serials. **Services:** Interlibrary loans; copying; center open to public with restrictions. **Publications:** Newsletter, monthly. **Special Catalogs:** 16mm Film Catalog; Community Resources Catalog. **Staff:** Jean Baptist, Cons., Lib. Media Serv; M. Green, Hd., Tech.Serv.; Anne Hicks, Cat.; Corinne Tellier, Ref.Libn.

★17184★
WINNIPEG SOCIAL PLANNING COUNCIL - LIBRARY (Soc Sci)
412 McDermot Ave.   Phone: (204) 943-2561
Winnipeg, MB, Canada R3A 0A9   E. T. Sale, Exec.Dir.
Subjects: Social welfare policy in Manitoba, Canada and other selected areas. **Holdings:** Figures not available for books; studies; reports. **Services:** Library open to public.

WINNIPEG THEOLOGICAL SEMINARY
See: Winnipeg Bible College/Winnipeg Theological Seminary

★17185★
WINONA MEMORIAL HOSPITAL - HEALTH SCIENCES LIBRARY (Med)†
3232 N. Meridian   Phone: (317) 927-2248
Indianapolis, IN 46208   Karen A. Davis, Med.Libn.
Founded: 1971. **Staff:** Prof 1. **Subjects:** Medicine, nursing, hospital administration, allied health sciences. **Holdings:** 1335 books; 1980 bound periodical volumes; 3 VF drawers of pamphlets. **Subscriptions:** 155 journals

and other serials. **Services:** Interlibrary loans; library not open to public. **Automated Operations:** Computerized cataloging. **Computerized Information Services:** BRS. **Networks/Consortia:** Member of Central Indiana Health Science Library Consortium (CIHSLC); Central Indiana Area Library Services Authority (CIALSA); Greater Midwest Regional Medical Library Network (Region 3); INCOLSA.

★17186★
WINROCK INTERNATIONAL - LIBRARY (Agri)†
Petit Jean Mountain, Rte. 3   Phone: (501) 727-5435
Morrilton, AR 72110   Joan Newton, Libn.
Staff: 2. **Subjects:** Animal agriculture, ruminant livestock, range management, public policy, appropriate technology systems. **Holdings:** 3000 books; 50 bound periodical volumes; 200 reports on microfiche; 2000 government documents; 10,000 slides; 12 VF drawers of miscellaneous material. **Subscriptions:** 416 journals and other serials; 10 newspapers. **Services:** Interlibrary loans; copying; library open to public for reference use only. **Computerized Information Services:** Online systems.

★17187★
WINSTON-SALEM FOUNDATION - FOUNDATION CENTER REGIONAL LIBRARY (Soc Sci)
229 First Union Bldg.   Phone: (919) 725-2382
Winston-Salem, NC 27101   Sara N. Willard, Libn.
Subjects: Foundations. **Special Collections:** North Carolina Foundation IRS Returns. **Holdings:** 35 volumes; 250 annual reports; source book profiles. **Services:** Copying; library open to public. **Also Known As:** Donors Forum of Forsyth County.

★17188★
WINSTON-SALEM JOURNAL AND SENTINEL - REFERENCE DEPARTMENT (Publ)
418 N. Marshall   Phone: (919) 727-7275
Winston-Salem, NC 27102   Marilyn H. Rollins, Ref.Dept.Mgr.
Founded: 1947. **Staff:** Prof 4; Other 3. **Subjects:** Newspaper reference topics. **Holdings:** 1219 books; 50 bound periodical volumes; 3000 pamphlets; 1.7 million newspaper clippings; 265,000 photographs; 18,000 negatives; 1738 reels of microfilm of newspapers; 6 VF drawers of reports. **Subscriptions:** 188 journals and other serials; 53 newspapers. **Services:** Copying; department open to students for academic research by appointment. **Remarks:** Published by the Piedmont Publishing Company.

★17189★
WINSTON-SALEM STATE UNIVERSITY - O'KELLY LIBRARY - SPECIAL COLLECTIONS (Educ)
                                          Phone: (919) 761-2128
Winston-Salem, NC 27110   Mae L. Holt, Dir. of Lib.Serv.
Founded: 1922. **Special Collections:** Curriculum Materials Center Collection (28,005 items); Black Studies Collection; School of Nursing Library. **Services:** Interlibrary loans; copying; library open to public. **Automated Operations:** Computerized cataloging (records). **Computerized Information Services:** OCLC. **Networks/Consortia:** Member of SOLINET. **Publications:** Library Handbook; List of New Books Added Monthly. **Staff:** Lois Leggett, Spec.Coll.Libn.

★17190★
WINSTON & STRAWN - LIBRARY (Law)
One 1st National Plaza   Phone: (312) 558-5740
Chicago, IL 60603   Donna M. Tuke, Chf.Libn.
Founded: 1857. **Staff:** Prof 3; Other 2. **Subjects:** Law - securities, antitrust, corporate, tax, labor, real estate. **Holdings:** 30,000 volumes. **Subscriptions:** 250 journals and other serials. **Services:** Interlibrary loans; copying; library open to lawyers and other professionals for reference use only. **Automated Operations:** Computerized cataloging. **Computerized Information Services:** LEXIS, DIALOG, New York Times Information Service, OCLC. **Networks/Consortia:** Member of ILLINET. **Publications:** Library Bulletin, monthly - to all attorneys. **Staff:** Nell Ingalls, Asst.Libn.

★17191★
WINTER HAVEN HOSPITAL - J.G. CONVERSE MEMORIAL MEDICAL LIBRARY (Med)
200 Ave. F., N.E.   Phone: (813) 293-1121
Winter Haven, FL 33881   Henry Hasse, Lrng.Rsrcs.Spec.
Founded: 1957. **Staff:** Prof 2; Other 1. **Subjects:** Medicine, nursing, allied health sciences, community mental health. **Holdings:** 1230 books; 1002 bound periodical volumes; 10 file boxes of pamphlets; 33 audio cassettes; 37 video cassettes. **Subscriptions:** 120 journals and other serials. **Services:** Interlibrary loans; copying; library open to public for reference use only. **Computerized Information Services:** MEDLARS. Performs searches on cost

recovery basis. Contact Person: Kathy Miller. **Staff:** Cheryl Dee, Cons.; Kathy Miller, Asst.Libn.

★17192★
WINTER PARK MEMORIAL HOSPITAL - MEDICAL STAFF LIBRARY (Med)†
200 N. Lakemont Ave.   Phone: (305) 646-7049
Winter Park, FL 32792   Patricia N. Cole, Med.Libn.
Staff: Prof 2; Other 1. **Subjects:** Medicine and surgery. **Holdings:** 3109 books; 3237 bound periodical volumes; 150 feet of shelves of unbound periodicals; 1450 tapes; 1 VF drawer of pamphlets. **Subscriptions:** 195 journals and other serials. **Services:** Interlibrary loans; copying; bibliographic and reference services for staff doctors and nurses, and for students at local colleges and universities; library open to public for reference use only with permission of administration. **Publications:** Report to Chairman of Library Committee, bimonthly; New Acquisitions List, monthly - both for internal distribution only.

WINTER (William) MARINE LIBRARY
See: College of Insurance - Insurance Society of New York - Library

WINTHROP LABORATORIES
See: Sterling Drug, Inc.

★17193★
WINTHROP, STIMSON, PUTNAM AND ROBERTS - LIBRARY (Law)
40 Wall St.   Phone: (212) 530-7567
New York, NY 10005   Nancy J. Haab, Libn.
Founded: 1948. **Staff:** Prof 3; Other 4. **Subjects:** Law, public utilities. **Holdings:** 30,000 volumes. **Subscriptions:** 40 journals and other serials. **Services:** Interlibrary loans; library not open to public. **Staff:** Faya Cohen, Asst.Libn.

WINTON HILL TECHNICAL CENTER
See: Procter & Gamble Company

★17194★
WIRE ASSOCIATION INTERNATIONAL - TECHNICAL INFORMATION CENTER (Sci-Tech)
1570 Boston Post Rd.
Box H   Phone: (203) 453-2777
Guilford, CT 06437   Deborah Rutter, Tech.Info.Mgr.
Staff: Prof 1; Other 1. **Subjects:** Wire technology, metallurgy, manufacturing engineering. **Special Collections:** Complete run of Wire Journal (indexed, abstracted); complete run of Wire and Wire Products (48 volumes; indexed, abstracted). **Holdings:** 600 books; 80 bound periodical volumes. **Subscriptions:** 13 journals and other serials. **Services:** Interlibrary loans; copying; center open to public with restrictions. **Computerized Information Services:** DIALOG, Pergamon Infoline Ltd.; internal database. Performs searches on fee basis. **Networks/Consortia:** Member of Southern Connecticut Library Council (SCLC). **Publications:** 1-3 Wire Association Conference Proceedings, annual; Technical Report, annual. **Special Indexes:** Wire Index (hardcopy of internal database holdings), updated every 2 years.

★17195★
WISCONSIN ALUMNI RESEARCH FOUNDATION - LIBRARY (Bus-Fin)
614 N. Walnut St.
Box 7365   Phone: (608) 263-2848
Madison, WI 53707   Lila N. Hillyer, Libn.
Founded: 1948. **Staff:** 1. **Subjects:** Finance, investment, licensing (patents), foundation history. **Holdings:** 500 books; 400 bound periodical volumes; 100 reprints; 200 VF drawers and 25 shelves of correspondence, clippings, pamphlets, reprints, reports; 115 VF drawers and 25 shelves of licensing, development, educational files; 60 VF drawers and 30 shelves of financial and investment files. **Subscriptions:** 26 journals and other serials. **Services:** Library open to University of Wisconsin staff who have obtained clearance from the managing director of the foundation. **Staff:** John R. Pike, Mng.Dir.

WISCONSIN ARCHITECTURAL ARCHIVE
See: Milwaukee Public Library

WISCONSIN AREA RESEARCH CENTER ARCHIVES
See: University of Wisconsin, Oshkosh - University Libraries and Learning Resources - Special Collections

WISCONSIN CENTER FOR FILM AND THEATER RESEARCH
See: University of Wisconsin, Madison

WISCONSIN CENTER FOR FILM AND THEATRE RESEARCH - MANUSCRIPT COLLECTION
See: State Historical Society of Wisconsin - Archives Division

★17196★
WISCONSIN CONSERVATORY OF MUSIC - LIBRARY (Mus)
1584 N. Prospect Ave.   Phone: (414) 276-5760
Milwaukee, WI 53202-2394   Brian Jonathan Gerl, Dir.
Founded: 1968. **Staff:** Prof 1; Other 2. **Subjects:** Music. **Holdings:** 26,000 books and scores; 5500 sound recordings. **Subscriptions:** 35 journals and other serials. **Services:** Interlibrary loans; copying; library open to public for reference use only. **Automated Operations:** Computerized cataloging and ILL. **Networks/Consortia:** Member of Library Council of Metropolitan Milwaukee, Inc. (LCOMM). **Publications:** Facsimile reprint of 12 Landler for Two Guitars, Opus 55, by Mauro Giuliani.

WISCONSIN DISSEMINATION PROGRAM (WDP)
See: Wisconsin State Department of Public Instruction

★17197★
WISCONSIN GAS COMPANY - CORPORATE AND LAW LIBRARY (Energy; Law)
626 E. Wisconsin Ave.   Phone: (414) 291-6666
Milwaukee, WI 53202   Carolyn A. Simpson, Coord. of Regulatory Info
Founded: 1930. **Staff:** Prof 1; Other 1. **Subjects:** Natural gas, public utility regulation law, engineering, gas industries, corporation law. **Holdings:** 2100 books; 520 bound periodical volumes; 6 VF drawers of pamphlets. **Subscriptions:** 190 journals and other serials; 5 newspapers. **Services:** Interlibrary loans; copying; SDI; library open to public by appointment. **Automated Operations:** Computerized cataloging, acquisitions, serials and circulation. **Computerized Information Services:** DIALOG, SDC. **Networks/Consortia:** Member of Library Council of Metropolitan Milwaukee, Inc. (LCOMM); American Gas Association Library Services Committee.

★17198★
WISCONSIN HOSPITAL ASSOCIATION - MEMORIAL LIBRARY (Med)†
5721 Odana Rd.   Phone: (608) 274-1820
Madison, WI 53719   Pat Craven, Libn.
Staff: Prof 1. **Subjects:** Health care and statistics, hospital administration, health careers, medical education, labor relations, long term care programs, hospital law and regulations. **Holdings:** 2200 books. **Subscriptions:** 40 journals and other serials. **Services:** Interlibrary loans; copying; library open to public for reference use only. **Networks/Consortia:** Member of South Central Wisconsin Health Planning Area Cooperative.

★17199★
WISCONSIN INDIANHEAD TECHNICAL INSTITUTE, NEW RICHMOND CAMPUS - LEARNING RESOURCE CENTER (Sci-Tech)
1019 S. Knowles Ave.   Phone: (715) 246-6561
New Richmond, WI 54017   David D. Hartung, Libn.
Founded: 1969. **Staff:** Prof 1; Other 2. **Subjects:** Agriculture, business, general education, health occupations, home economics, trade and industry. **Special Collections:** Curriculum Library (1300 volumes; 350 AV items). **Holdings:** 7800 books; 3860 AV items. **Subscriptions:** 160 journals and other serials; 16 newspapers. **Services:** Interlibrary loans; center open to public. **Networks/Consortia:** Member of Technical Information Exchange. **Also Known As:** Indianhead Technical Institute. **Staff:** Valerie Peltier, AV Techn.

★17200★
WISCONSIN INDIANHEAD TECHNICAL INSTITUTE, SUPERIOR CAMPUS - LIBRARY (Bus-Fin; Sci-Tech)†
600 N. 21st St.   Phone: (715) 394-6677
Superior, WI 54880   Donald Rantala, LRC Spec.
Founded: 1950. **Staff:** Prof 1; Other 2. **Subjects:** Nursing, mechanical design, electronics, business, data processing, marketing and advertising. **Holdings:** 8000 books; 1500 pamphlets; 25 maps; theses; microfilm; slides; cassettes. **Subscriptions:** 150 journals and other serials; 25 newspapers. **Services:** Copying; library open to public with restrictions. **Also Known As:** Indianhead Technical Institute. **Staff:** Eleanor Johnson, Asst.Libn.

★17201★
WISCONSIN INFORMATION SERVICE (Soc Sci)
161 W. Wisconsin Ave., Rm. 7071   Phone: (414) 276-0760
Milwaukee, WI 53203   Judith H. Cohen, Dir.
Staff: Prof 2; Other 4. **Subjects:** Human services, especially in health and social work. **Special Collections:** Files on 1100 Milwaukee area human service agencies. **Services:** Service open to public by appointment. **Publications:** WIS data reports, monthly. **Special Indexes:** Alphabetical and

numerical lists of agencies. **Staff:** Alice C. Henry, Asst.Dir.

WISCONSIN JEWISH ARCHIVES
See: State Historical Society of Wisconsin - Archives Division

★17202★
WISCONSIN LUTHERAN SEMINARY - LIBRARY (Rel-Theol)
6633 W. Wartburg Circle   Phone: (414) 242-2331
Mequon, WI 53092   Rev. Martin O. Westerhaus, Libn.
Founded: 1863. **Staff:** Prof 2; Other 2. **Subjects:** Theology, church history. **Holdings:** 33,150 books; 2150 bound periodical volumes. **Subscriptions:** 265 journals and other serials. **Services:** Interlibrary loans; copying; library open to public with restrictions. **Staff:** Rev. Robert M. Oswald, Tech.Serv.

WISCONSIN REGIONAL PRIMATE RESEARCH CENTER
See: University of Wisconsin, Madison

★17203★
WISCONSIN SCHOOL FOR THE DEAF - JOHN R. GANT LIBRARY (Educ; Aud-Vis)
309 W. Walworth Ave.   Phone: (414) 728-6477
Delavan, WI 53115   Betty E. Watkins, Libn.
Founded: 1852. **Staff:** Prof 1. **Subjects:** Books of high interest-low vocabulary, professional library, K-12 general collection. **Special Collections:** Education of the deaf; captioned films for the deaf (1100). **Holdings:** 6000 books; 1700 filmstrips; 150 film loops; 500 microfiche; 16 drawers of transparencies. **Subscriptions:** 89 journals and other serials. **Services:** Interlibrary loans; copying; library open to public with librarian's permission. **Publications:** Wisconsin Times, monthly - for patrons.

★17204★
WISCONSIN STATE BOARD OF VOCATIONAL, TECHNICAL & ADULT EDUCATION - RESEARCH COORDINATING UNIT RESOURCE CTR. (Educ)
4802 Sheboygan Ave., HFSOB, 7th Fl.
Box 7874   Phone: (608) 266-3705
Madison, WI 53707   Roland J. Krogstad, Dir.
Founded: 1967. **Staff:** Prof 2; Other 1. **Subjects:** Education - vocational, technical, adult. **Holdings:** 500 books; 3300 research reports; 1000 curriculum materials; 150,000 ERIC documents on microfiche. **Services:** Copying; center open to public. **Publications:** Bits about Research (newsletter), annual - distributed to RCU directors and clients in vocational education. **Special Indexes:** Loose-leaf index of ERIC descriptors.

★17205★
WISCONSIN (State) DEPARTMENT OF DEVELOPMENT - LIBRARY (Plan)
123 W. Washington Ave.
Box 7970   Phone: (608) 266-2423
Madison, WI 53707   Judith Royster, Libn.
Staff: Prof 1. **Subjects:** Housing, economic and community development, small business, local government, tourism. **Special Collections:** Local, county, and regional planning commission reports; departmental archives. **Holdings:** 10,000 books. **Subscriptions:** 150 journals and other serials; 6 newspapers. **Services:** Interlibrary loans; copying; library open to public. **Automated Operations:** Computerized cataloging. **Networks/Consortia:** Member of Madison Area Library Council. **Publications:** DOD Library Briefs, monthly - available upon request.

★17206★
WISCONSIN STATE DEPARTMENT OF EMPLOYEE TRUST FUNDS - LIBRARY (Bus-Fin)
201 E. Washington Ave., Rm. 171
Box 7931   Phone: (608) 266-7387
Madison, WI 53707   John R. Wendorf, Prog.Asst./Libn.
Staff: Prof 1. **Subjects:** Pensions, insurance, social security. **Special Collections:** Collections of historical materials on various state pension and retirement programs; pamphlets of other states' retirement systems; legislative history on retirement bills (10 VF drawers). **Holdings:** 125 books; 2 VF drawers of clippings; 2000 manuscripts and documents. **Subscriptions:** 41 journals and other serials. **Services:** Interlibrary loans; copying; library open to public. **Automated Operations:** Computerized cataloging and acquisitions. **Publications:** Library summary of new acquisitions, monthly.

★17207★
WISCONSIN STATE DEPARTMENT OF HEALTH & SOCIAL SERVICES - LIBRARY (Soc Sci)
1 W. Wilson St., Rm. 655
Box 7850   Phone: (608) 266-7473
Madison, WI 53707   Mary Gusse Sanchez, Libn.
Staff: Prof 1; Other 2. **Subjects:** Public health and welfare, corrections,

community services, mental health, vocational rehabilitation. **Holdings:** 10,000 books; 401 bound periodical titles; 75 pamphlet boxes. **Subscriptions:** 347 journals and other serials. **Services:** Interlibrary loans; SDI; library open to public. **Automated Operations:** Computerized cataloging. **Computerized Information Services:** LEXIS. **Publications:** Acquisition list, monthly - free upon request.

★17208★
WISCONSIN STATE DEPARTMENT OF INDUSTRY, LABOR & HUMAN RELATIONS - JOB SERVICE LIBRARY (Soc Sci)
201 E. Washington Ave.
Box 7944   Phone: (608) 266-2832
Madison, WI 53707   Janet D. Pugh, Libn.
Staff: Prof 1; Other 1. **Subjects:** Labor, employment, demographics. **Holdings:** 10,000 books; government documents. **Subscriptions:** 80 journals and other serials. **Services:** Interlibrary loans; library open to public for reference use only. **Publications:** Acquisition List, monthly - to interested persons. **Special Catalogs:** Annotated Directory of Labor Market Information.

★17209★
WISCONSIN STATE DEPARTMENT OF JUSTICE - LAW LIBRARY (Law)
123 W. Washington, Rm. 349
Box 7857   Phone: (608) 266-0325
Madison, WI 53707   Michael F. Bemis, Law Libn.
Founded: 1969. **Staff:** Prof 2; Other 1. **Subjects:** Wisconsin law, general law. **Special Collections:** Antitrust law; consumer protection; law enforcement and criminology; drugs; environmental protection. **Holdings:** 25,000 books and bound periodical volumes; 3 VF drawers of legal form and precedence files; department and division publications. **Subscriptions:** 30 journals and other serials; 20 newspapers. **Services:** Library not open to public, but arrangements may be made with librarian for use of materials. **Computerized Information Services:** LEXIS, NEXIS. **Publications:** Information bulletins, irregular - for internal distribution only. **Special Indexes:** Index digest to opinions of the Attorney General of Wisconsin, 1845-1972 (book with update on computer microfiche card). **Staff:** Sara Paul, Asst. Law Libn.

★17210★
WISCONSIN STATE DEPARTMENT OF NATURAL RESOURCES - BUREAU OF RESEARCH - TECHNICAL LIBRARY (Env-Cons)
3911 Fish Hatchery Rd.   Phone: (608) 266-9725
Fitchburg, WI 53711   Rose B. Smith, Libn.
Staff: Prof 2. **Subjects:** Fish, wildlife, water resources. **Holdings:** 1350 books; 374 bound periodical volumes; unbound reports; dissertations; documents; reprints; bureau publications. **Subscriptions:** 60 journals and other serials. **Services:** Interlibrary loans; copying; library open to public for reference use only. **Computerized Information Services:** DIALOG. Performs searches on cost recovery basis. **Networks/Consortia:** Member of Wisconsin Interlibrary Services (WILS). **Publications:** Acquisition list, irregular - for internal distribution only; periodical holdings lists, irregular.

★17211★
WISCONSIN STATE DEPARTMENT OF NATURAL RESOURCES - LIBRARY (Env-Cons)
Box 7921   Phone: (608) 266-8933
Madison, WI 53707   Patricia Parsons, Dept.Libn.
Staff: Prof 1; Other 2. **Subjects:** Environmental protection, air pollution, solid waste and water quality management, natural resources, fish and wildlife. **Holdings:** 4200 books; 100 bound periodical volumes; 4500 other cataloged items. **Subscriptions:** 151 journals and other serials. **Services:** Interlibrary loans; library open to public for reference use only. **Networks/Consortia:** Member of Madison Area Library Council; Wisconsin State Agency Librarians Council.

★17212★
WISCONSIN STATE DEPARTMENT OF NATURAL RESOURCES - MAC KENZIE ENVIRONMENTAL EDUCATION CENTER (Env-Cons)
Rte. 2, Box 825   Phone: (608) 635-4498
Poynette, WI 53955   Robert Wallen, Prog.Spec.
Staff: 1. **Subjects:** Natural resources, natural sciences, environment. **Holdings:** 600 books; 12 VF drawers of pamphlets and clippings; 2500 color slides. **Subscriptions:** 10 journals and other serials. **Services:** Center open to public with restrictions.

★17213★
WISCONSIN STATE DEPARTMENT OF NATURAL RESOURCES - SOUTHEAST DISTRICT LIBRARY (Env-Cons)
2300 N. 3rd St.   Phone: (414) 562-9536
Milwaukee, WI 53212   Kathleen Schultz, Libn.
Staff: Prof 1. **Subjects:** Pollution and quality of air and water, fish and

wildlife, solid waste management, parks and recreation, forestry. **Special Collections:** Departmental publications (technical bulletins, research reports, surface water reports; 325); Environmental Protection Agency documents (650). **Holdings:** 2100 books; 35 bound periodical volumes. **Subscriptions:** 79 journals and other serials; 14 newspapers. **Services:** Interlibrary loans; copying; SDI; library open to public for reference use only.

★17214★
WISCONSIN STATE DEPARTMENT OF PUBLIC INSTRUCTION - D.P.I. LIBRARY (Educ)
125 S. Webster St., 3rd Fl.
Box 7841
Madison, WI 53707
Phone: (608) 266-2529
Marjorie D. Westergard, Libn.
Founded: 1968. **Staff:** Prof 1. **Subjects:** Educational administration, handicapped children, curriculum development, public administration. **Special Collections:** Wisconsin Public School curriculum materials. **Holdings:** 1000 books; 300 pamphlets; 1981-1982 curriculum development library on microfiche; 234,000 ERIC microfiche (complete); tests on microfiche. **Subscriptions:** 300 journals and other serials. **Services:** Interlibrary loans; copying; library open to public for reference use only. **Automated Operations:** Computerized cataloging. **Computerized Information Services:** DIALOG, BRS; WIRE (human resources database). **Networks/Consortia:** Member of Madison Area Library Council (MALC); Wisconsin State Agency Librarians Council. **Publications:** New Acquisitions, monthly.

★17215★
WISCONSIN STATE DEPARTMENT OF PUBLIC INSTRUCTION - SCHOOL FOR THE VISUALLY HANDICAPPED - LIBRARY (Aud-Vis)
1700 W. State St.
Janesville, WI 53545
Phone: (608) 755-2967
Jean Wolski, Libn.
Founded: 1850. **Staff:** Prof 1. **Subjects:** General. **Special Collections:** Braille and talking books. **Holdings:** 3132 books; 288 items in a tactile materials center; 50 disc recordings; 1 VF drawer of pamphlets; 2892 braille books; 5395 talking books; 65 filmstrips; 80 tape recordings. **Subscriptions:** 60 journals and other serials. **Services:** Library services restricted to the visually handicapped.

★17216★
WISCONSIN STATE DEPARTMENT OF PUBLIC INSTRUCTION - WISCONSIN DISSEMINATION PROGRAM (WDP) (Educ)
125 S. Webster St.
Box 7841
Madison, WI 53707
Phone: (608) 266-2127
Dianne Hopkins, Dir.
Founded: 1977. **Staff:** Prof 2. **Subjects:** Education and related social sciences, research, professional improvement, instructional materials, educational technology, library and information science. **Holdings:** ERIC microfiche collection; 300 journals; 3000 monographs. **Services:** Program open to public. **Computerized Information Services:** BRS, DIALOG; Wisconsin Information Resources for Educators (WIRE; online file of Wisconsin resource people, networks and organizations). Performs searches on fee basis. **Publications:** WDP Brochure and request form - on request; WDP Newsletter; subject bibliographies. **Staff:** Nancy Ahlquist, Search Anl./Libn.; Carolyn Folke, Search Anl./Libn.

★17217★
WISCONSIN STATE DEPARTMENT OF TRANSPORTATION - LIBRARY (Trans; Plan)
4802 Sheboygan Ave., Rm. 901
Box 7913
Madison, WI 53707
Phone: (608) 266-0724
Cordell Klyve, Libn.
Founded: 1961. **Staff:** Prof 1; Other 1. **Subjects:** Transportation planning, highways, urban transit, Wisconsin urban planning, transportation economics. **Special Collections:** Transportation (Highway) Research Board. **Holdings:** 4300 books; 200 unbound periodical volumes; 9500 reports and 300 pamphlets. **Subscriptions:** 200 journals and other serials. **Services:** Interlibrary loans; copying; library open to public. **Networks/Consortia:** Member of Madison Area Library Council (MALC). **Publications:** Recent Acquisitions, monthly - distributed to Department of Transportation staff and others upon request.

★17218★
WISCONSIN STATE DIVISION FOR LIBRARY SERVICES - REFERENCE AND LOAN LIBRARY (Hum)
2109 S. Stoughton Rd.
Madison, WI 53716
Phone: (608) 266-1081
Sally J. Drew, Dir.
Founded: 1895. **Staff:** Prof 8; Other 21. **Subjects:** Literature, history, biography, geography, religion, education, political science, music, recreation. **Holdings:** 167,000 volumes; 13,221 phonograph records; 4700 reels of microfilm of periodicals; 600 AV items; 13,934 Wisconsin and federal documents; 995 mixed media kits; 3894 audiotapes; 111 films; 968 videotapes; 5110 reels of microfilm; 5170 pamphlets; 185 video discs. **Subscriptions:** 700 journals and other serials. **Services:** Interlibrary loans; copying; library is the state resource center for public and school libraries; other resource center libraries are searched for needed material to which requests are then referred. **Automated Operations:** Computerized cataloging. **Computerized Information Services:** OCLC. **Networks/Consortia:** Member of WILS. **Publications:** Manual for Interlibrary Loan Service; Selected lists of holdings. **Special Catalogs:** Large Type; Kid Stuff, a catalog of materials for children's programs in public libraries; Viz 2, a catalog of films, filmstrips, videotape and other audiovisual materials; About Libraries, a catalog of nonbook materials about libraries and librarianship (all book form). **Staff:** Virginia Potter, Ref.Supv.; Janice Lang, Tech.Serv.Supv.; Reid Harrsch, Acq./Bibliog.Serv.Libn.; Mary Struckmeyer, IL; Willeen Tretheway, AV Libn.

★17219★
WISCONSIN STATE - FOND DU LAC COUNTY LAW LIBRARY (Law)
Court House
Fond du Lac, WI 54935
Phone: (414) 921-5600
Mary E. Scharf, Law Libn.
Staff: 1. **Subjects:** Law. **Holdings:** 10,000 volumes. **Services:** Library open to public with restrictions.

★17220★
WISCONSIN STATE JOURNAL - LIBRARY (Publ)
Box 8058
Madison, WI 53708
Phone: (608) 252-6112
Ronald J. Larson, Hd.Libn.
Staff: Prof 1; Other 1. **Subjects:** Local news and history, state news, state government, University of Wisconsin news. **Special Collections:** Clips on Joseph McCarthy; anti-war demonstration photographs, 1965-1972, at University of Wisconsin, Madison. **Holdings:** Newspaper clippings and microfilm; subject and people photograph files. **Services:** Copying; library open to public with restrictions. **Automated Operations:** Computerized reference directory.

WISCONSIN STATE LAW LIBRARY
See: Wisconsin State Supreme Court

★17221★
WISCONSIN STATE LEGISLATIVE REFERENCE BUREAU (Soc Sci)
State Capitol, Rm. 201 North
Madison, WI 53702
Phone: (608) 266-0341
H. Rupert Theobald, Chf., Lib. & Ref.Sects.
Founded: 1901. **Staff:** Prof 12; Other 7. **Subjects:** State government - public administration, taxation, finance, education, public welfare, labor, conservation, energy, pollution, public health, agriculture, industrial development, motor vehicle regulation, highway finance and development, legislative procedure, courts, civil rights, civil service, civil defense; federal and local governments. **Special Collections:** Wisconsin session laws, statutes, legislative journals and Supreme Court reports, 1848 to present; opinions of the Attorney General, 1904 to present; Blue Books, 1858 to present; bound volumes of legislative bills, 1897 to present; archival depository of departmental reports in separate collection of state documents; legislative bill drafting records, 1927 to present. **Holdings:** 100,000 volumes, including an extensive number of unbound and microfiche volumes of clippings. **Subscriptions:** 300 journals and other serials. **Services:** Interlibrary loans; copying; library open to public. **Computerized Information Services:** LEXIS, NEXIS; access to National Conference of State Legislatures' Library Information Services (LIS); ATMS (bill histories), STAIRS (Wisconsin statutes; internal databases). **Publications:** Research Bulletins; Informational Bulletins; Wisconsin Briefs; Wisconsin Facts; Comparative Facts, all irregular; Wisconsin Blue Book, biennial. **Special Indexes:** Index to legislation introduced in the Wisconsin Legislature since 1897; State Document Catalog. **Staff:** Patricia V. Robbins, Dir. of Ref. & Lib.; Mina Waldie, Supv.Libn.; Rose Arnold, Libn.; Rosemary Lucas, Libn.; Marian Rogers, Libn.; Larry Barish, Res.Anl.; Peter Cannon, Res.Anl.; Amy Hague, Res.Anl.; Dick Pazen, Res.Anl.; Clark Radatz, Res.Anl.; Richard Roe, Res.Anl.; Gary Watchke, Res.Anl.

★17222★
WISCONSIN STATE MEDICAL SOCIETY - LIBRARY (Med)
330 E. Lakeside St.
Box 1109
Madison, WI 53701
Phone: (608) 257-6781
Mary Angell, Mng.Ed./Libn.
Staff: 1. **Subjects:** Medicine. **Holdings:** 125 volumes. **Subscriptions:** 158 journals and other serials. **Services:** Library not open to public. **Publications:** Wisconsin Medical Journal, monthly - to members of the Wisconsin State Medical Society.

★17223★

WISCONSIN STATE OFFICE OF THE COMMISSIONER OF INSURANCE - LIBRARY (Bus-Fin)
Box 7873   Phone: (608) 266-3585
Madison, WI 53707   Jan Angell
Staff: Prof 1. **Subjects:** Insurance and its law. **Special Collections:** Wisconsin Insurance Report, 1895-1979. **Holdings:** 1000 books; 1400 bound periodical volumes; 35 cubic feet of unbound periodicals. **Subscriptions:** 30 journals and other serials. **Services:** Library open to public with restrictions. **Remarks:** The library is located at 123 W. Washington Ave., 7th Fl.

★17224★

WISCONSIN STATE - RACINE COUNTY LAW LIBRARY (Law)
730 Wisconsin Ave.   Phone: (414) 636-3862
Racine, WI 53403   Lawrence E. Flynn, Ck. of Courts
Founded: 1850. **Subjects:** Law. **Holdings:** 16,500 books; Wisconsin Briefs on microfiche. **Services:** Copying; library open to public.

★17225★

WISCONSIN STATE SUPREME COURT - WISCONSIN STATE LAW LIBRARY (Law)
Box 7881   Phone: (608) 266-1424
Madison, WI 53707   Marcia J. Koslov, State Law Libn.
Founded: 1836. **Staff:** Prof 5; Other 4. **Subjects:** Law. **Holdings:** 130,000 volumes; 8350 documents; 3000 reels of microfilm; 6000 microfiche. **Subscriptions:** 470 journals and other serials. **Services:** Copying; library open to public for reference use only. **Staff:** Dennis Austin, Dp. Law Libn.; M. Elaine Sharp, Asst.Libn./Tech.Serv.; Cheryl A. O'Connor, Asst.Libn./Rd.Serv.

★17226★

WISE COUNTY HISTORICAL COMMISSION ARCHIVE (Hist)
1602 S. College
Box 427   Phone: (817) 627-5586
Decatur, TX 76234   Rosalie Gregg, Exec.Dir.
Staff: 2. **Subjects:** Wise County history, family histories, cemetery records. **Special Collections:** Wise County Messenger and Decatur News (microfilm); Wise County, Tennessee and Virginia census records; Civil War; Presidents; Texas Heritage Project; county histories. **Holdings:** Figures not available for books; microfiche. **Services:** Copying; archive open to public for reference use only; will answer mail inquiries. **Publications:** Newsletter, monthly.

★17227★

WISE (Isaac M.) TEMPLE - RALPH COHEN MEMORIAL LIBRARY (Rel-Theol)
8329 Ridge Rd.   Phone: (513) 793-2556
Cincinnati, OH 45236   Judith S. Carsch, Libn.
Staff: Prof 1. **Subjects:** Judaica, Holocaust. **Holdings:** 15,000 books. **Subscriptions:** 23 journals and other serials. **Services:** Library open to public with restrictions.

★17228★

WISHARD (William N.) MEMORIAL HOSPITAL - PROFESSIONAL LIBRARY/ MEDIA SERVICES (Med)†
1001 W. 10th St.   Phone: (317) 630-7028
Indianapolis, IN 46202   Jana Bradley, Dir.
Staff: Prof 5; Other 8. **Subjects:** Medicine, nursing, health care administration. **Special Collections:** Emergency medical services (100 volumes). **Holdings:** 5000 books; 7500 bound periodical volumes; 315 VF items; 500 AV items; 20 folders of historical file of Health and Hospital Corporation. **Subscriptions:** 375 journals and other serials. **Services:** Interlibrary loans; copying; current awareness service; library open to public for reference use only. **Automated Operations:** Computerized cataloging. **Computerized Information Services:** OCLC, DIALOG, BRS, SDC, NLM. **Networks/Consortia:** Member of Central Indiana Health Science Library Consortium; Greater Midwest Regional Medical Library Network (Region 3); INCOLSA. **Publications:** Media Tips, monthly - for internal distribution only. **Staff:** Kirsten Quam, Tech.Serv.Coord.; Frances Bischoff, Media Serv.Coord.; Christine Foster, Libn./Search Anl.; John Welby, Prod.Spec.

WISTAR INSTITUTE OF ANATOMY AND BIOLOGY
See: University of Pennsylvania

WISWALL (R.D.) MEMORIAL LIBRARY
See: Vancouver Memorial Hospital - R.D. Wiswall Memorial Library

★17229★

WITCO CHEMICAL CORPORATION - GOLDEN BEAR DIVISION - QC/R & D LIBRARY (Sci-Tech)
Ferguson & Manor Rds.
Box 5446   Phone: (805) 393-7110
Oildale, CA 93388   Euthene Snell, Libn.
Founded: 1948. **Staff:** 2. **Subjects:** Petroleum refining, lubricants, asphalt pavements, rubber, emulsions, instrumental analyses. **Holdings:** 2200 books; 670 bound periodical volumes; 5 catalogs; 5 VF drawers of internal technical reports; preprints; reprints; instrumental scans; 5 VF drawers of patents, technical documents, product development information; 5 VF drawers of government and industry specifications, qualifications and contracts. **Subscriptions:** 47 journals and other serials. **Services:** Copying; library open to public by appointment.

★17230★

WITCO CHEMICAL CORPORATION - LIBRARY (Sci-Tech)
3200 Brookfield   Phone: (713) 433-7281
Houston, TX 77045   Helen K. Kim, Tech.Libn./Res.Chem.
Staff: Prof 1. **Subjects:** Chemistry and applied technology. **Holdings:** Figures not available for books and bound periodical volumes; reprints; reports; technical abstracts. **Subscriptions:** 96 journals and other serials. **Services:** Library not open to public. **Computerized Information Services:** SDC. **Publications:** Current Notes, monthly - for internal distribution only.

★17231★

WITCO CHEMICAL CORPORATION - RICHARDSON GROUP - LIBRARY (Sci-Tech)*
2701 W. Lake St.   Phone: (312) 344-4300
Melrose Park, IL 60160   Candi Strecker, Libn.
Staff: Prof 1. **Subjects:** Polymers, emulsions, chemicals, rubber and graphic arts materials. **Holdings:** 2000 books; 1000 bound periodical volumes; patents. **Subscriptions:** 100 journals and other serials. **Services:** Interlibrary loans; copying; library open to public with permission. **Computerized Information Services:** DIALOG, SDC. **Networks/Consortia:** Member of Suburban Library System (SLS).

★17232★

WITCO CHEMICAL CORPORATION - TECHNICAL CENTER LIBRARY (Sci-Tech)
100 Bauer Dr.   Phone: (201) 337-5812
Oakland, NJ 07436   Miss Jo Therese Smith, Mgr., Info.Serv.
Founded: 1967. **Staff:** Prof 1. **Subjects:** Chemistry, chemical engineering, petroleum chemistry. **Special Collections:** Petroleum technology; surfactant technology. **Holdings:** 8000 books; 7000 bound periodical volumes; 15 VF drawers of patents, pamphlets and reprints; 5 drawers of patents and journals on microfiche. **Subscriptions:** 180 journals and other serials. **Services:** Interlibrary loans; library not open to public. **Computerized Information Services:** DIALOG, CAS Online. **Publications:** Research News; New Acquisitions, both irregular.

WITHERSPOON (John) LIBRARY
See: Princeton University - Rare Books and Special Collections

★17233★

WITHLACOOCHEE REGIONAL PLANNING COUNCIL - LIBRARY (Plan)
1241 S.W. 10th St.   Phone: (904) 732-3307
Ocala, FL 32674-2798   Vivian A. Whittier, Res.Asst.
Staff: Prof 1. **Subjects:** Statistics, planning, land use, water, energy, criminal justice. **Holdings:** 4000 bound periodical volumes; 190 films; maps; technical reports. **Subscriptions:** 19 journals and other serials. **Services:** Copying; library open to public with restrictions on lending materials. **Publications:** Data Subscription Service (reports), quarterly; Bulletin; Final Inspection Report, biannual. **Special Catalogs:** WRPC Publications List; film catalog (booklet). **Remarks:** Most library materials are concerned with Citrus, Hernando, Levy, Marion and Sumter counties.

WITT (Rabbi Louis) MEMORIAL LIBRARY
See: Temple Israel - Rabbi Louis Witt Memorial Library

WITTE MEMORIAL MUSEUM
See: San Antonio Museum Association - Libraries

★17234★

WITTENBERG UNIVERSITY - THOMAS LIBRARY (Rel-Theol)
                                                Phone: (513) 327-7016
Springfield, OH 45501   Betty Beatty, Act.Dir.
Founded: 1846. **Staff:** Prof 6; Other 11. **Subjects:** Lutheran Church, Martin Luther, Reformation. **Special Collections:** Baltasar Gracian y Morales

Collection; Wilhelm C. Berkenmeyer Colonial Parish Library (226 volumes); Susan V. Russell Tape Library (religious sermons); Archives, Ohio Synod Lutheran Church in America; University Archives; 19th-century Ohio newspapers; Lutheran Reformation; 19th-century American literature (1500 volumes); Cyril F. DosPassos Collection of Lepidoptera (2500 volumes); diaries, papers and etchings of Walter Tittle, American artist, 1883-1965; correspondence, manuscripts and books of Dr. Martin C. Fischer, University of Cincinnati professor; Geiger Family Papers, 1870-1910. **Holdings:** 250,000 books; 35,000 bound periodical volumes; 14,000 phonograph records; 1400 AV materials; 35,000 volumes of Library of American Civilization and English Literature on microfiche; 3000 volumes on East Asia. **Subscriptions:** 1268 journals and other serials; 16 newspapers. **Services:** Interlibrary loans; copying; library open to public. **Automated Operations:** Computerized cataloging, acquisitions and serials. **Computerized Information Services:** DIALOG, BRS, OCLC. **Networks/Consortia:** Member of OHIONET; Southwest Ohio Council for Higher Education (SOC). **Publications:** Library publications, irregular - to friends of the library. **Special Indexes:** Indexes to Martin C. Fischer, Walter Tittle and Geiger Family Papers collection; University Archives index (card). **Staff:** Al La Rose, Hd.Ref.Libn.; Ronald L. Cain, Hd., AV Serv.Velma Layman, Circ.Libn.; Patricia Yvan, Cat.Libn.; Regina Entorf, Hd., Instr.Serv./Doc.; Kathleen Schulz, Ref. & Per.Libn.

WNYC ARCHIVES
See: New York Public Library - Performing Arts Research Center - Rodgers & Hammerstein Archives of Recorded Sound

★17235★
WOFFORD COLLEGE - SANDOR TESZLER LIBRARY - ARCHIVES (Hist)
N. Church St.   Phone: (803) 585-4821
Spartanburg, SC 29301   Herbert Hucks, Jr., Archv.
Staff: Prof 1. **Subjects:** History of Wofford College, its alumni and faculty. **Holdings:** 1415 books; 565 bound periodical volumes; 850 cataloged items; manuscripts of books by faculty members; tape recordings of "From Dr. Snyder's Study" (1948-1949 broadcasts over local radio station WSPA; manuscripts, tapes and broadcasts contained in 28 legal size filing cabinet drawers); college catalogs; yearbooks; college journals; alumni and faculty publications; Old Gold and Black (student newspaper); memorabilia and photographs. **Services:** Copying; archives open to public for reference use only.

★17236★
WOFFORD COLLEGE - SANDOR TESZLER LIBRARY - LITTLEJOHN RARE BOOK ROOM (Rare Book)
N. Church St.   Phone: (803) 585-4821
Spartanburg, SC 29301   Frank J. Anderson, Libn.
Founded: 1854. **Subjects:** South Caroliniana; private presses, including Wofford Library Press; 16th- and 17th-century books; Folio Society publications; 19th- and 20th-century children's books. **Special Collections:** Matthew Carey Collection (100 volumes); Haynes Brown Hymnal Collection (800 volumes). **Holdings:** 10,000 books; 1000 bound periodical volumes. **Services:** Room open to public by appointment with supervision. **Publications:** Special Collections Checklists, Numbers 1-7; Wofford Bibliopolist.

WOFSY (Alan) FINE ARTS
See: Alan Wofsy Fine Arts

WOJNIAK MEMORIAL HOSPITAL
See: Evangelical School of Nursing

WOLBACH (John G.) LIBRARY
See: Harvard University - Observatory Library

★17237★
WOLF, BLOCK, SCHORR & SOLIS-COHEN - LIBRARY (Law)
Packard Bldg., 12th Fl.   Phone: (215) 977-2000
Philadelphia, PA 19102   John Duckett, Libn.
Founded: 1913. **Staff:** Prof 2; Other 2. **Subjects:** Law - corporate, real estate, labor, litigation. **Special Collections:** Tax law. **Holdings:** 14,000 volumes. **Subscriptions:** 75 journals and other serials. **Services:** Interlibrary loans; library open to public by appointment. **Computerized Information Services:** LEXIS. **Staff:** Lisa McLean, Asst.Libn.

★17238★
WOLFE (Harvey G.) LIBRARY (Mil)
Box 3514   Phone: (818) 241-7284
Glendale, CA 91201   Douglas L. Evans, Libn.
Founded: 1954. **Staff:** Prof 2. **Subjects:** Espionage, sabotage, military intelligence, secret services, secret societies, cryptography. **Holdings:** 8500

books; 3500 clippings. **Subscriptions:** 20 journals and other serials; 12 newspapers. **Services:** Library serves as a reference source for television and motion picture industries and certain governmental agencies; library not open to public.

WOLFE (Max & Beatrice) LIBRARY
See: Beth Tzedec Congregation - Max & Beatrice Wolfe Library

★17239★
WOLFEBORO HISTORICAL SOCIETY - PLEASANT VALLEY SCHOOLHOUSE - LIBRARY & FIRE ENGINE MUSEUM (Hist)
S. Main St.   Phone: (603) 569-4997
Wolfeboro, NH 03894   Harrison D. Moore, Pres.
Staff: 1. **Subjects:** Local history and genealogy, 19th-century fire engines. **Holdings:** 300 books; maps; scrapbooks of local events; town reports; old school records. **Services:** Library open to public by appointment.

WOLFGRAM MEMORIAL LIBRARY
See: Widener University

WOLFGRAM MEMORIAL LIBRARY - LINDSAY LAW LIBRARY
See: Lindsay Law Library

WOLFNER MEMORIAL LIBRARY FOR THE BLIND & PHYSICALLY HANDICAPPED
See: Missouri State Library

WOLFSON (Isaac N.) LIBRARY
See: Letchworth Village Developmental Center - Isaac N. Wolfson Library

WOMACK ARMY COMMUNITY HOSPITAL
See: U.S. Army Hospitals

★17240★
WOMAN'S GENERAL HOSPITAL - MEDICAL LIBRARY (Med)
1940 E. 101st St.   Phone: (216) 421-3100
Cleveland, OH 44106   Dzwinka Komarjanski, Circuit Libn.
Staff: Prof 1. **Subjects:** Medicine. **Holdings:** 470 books. **Subscriptions:** 45 journals and other serials. **Services:** Interlibrary loans; copying (limited); library open to hospital personnel only. **Computerized Information Services:** MEDLINE.

WOMAN'S WAY - RESOURCE CENTER
See: Young Women's Christian Association of Marin - Resource Center

★17241★
WOMEN ARTISTS NEWS - ARCHIVES (Art)
Grand Central Sta., Box 3304   Phone: (212) 666-6990
New York, NY 10163   Rena Hansen, Adm.
Subjects: Art, women artists. **Holdings:** 24 VF drawers of archival material on women in the arts. **Subscriptions:** 25 journals and other serials. **Services:** Copying; archives open to public by appointment. **Publications:** Women Artists News, bimonthly; Guide to Women's Art Organizations, biennial; Voices of Women (criticism, poetry, graphics); Women Artists of the World (essays, photographs and reproductions of art works of women artists worldwide). **Remarks:** Published by Midmarch Associates. **Staff:** Cynthia Navaretta, Exec.Dir.

★17242★
WOMEN & INFANTS HOSPITAL OF RHODE ISLAND - HEALTH SCIENCES INFORMATION CENTER (Med)
50 Maude St.   Phone: (401) 274-1100
Providence, RI 02908   Christine Chapman, Libn.
Founded: 1884. **Staff:** Prof 1; Other 2. **Subjects:** Obstetrics, gynecology, pediatrics. **Holdings:** 2000 books; 1650 bound periodical volumes. **Subscriptions:** 185 journals and other serials. **Services:** Interlibrary loans; copying; SDI; center open to public with permission. **Computerized Information Services:** NLM. Performs searches on cost recovery basis. **Networks/Consortia:** Member of Greater Northeastern Regional Medical Library Program; Association of Rhode Island Health Sciences Librarians (ARIHSL).

★17243★
WOMEN'S ACTION ALLIANCE, INC. - LIBRARY (Soc Sci)
370 Lexington Ave., Suite 603   Phone: (212) 532-8330
New York, NY 10017   Jane Ordway, Info.Serv.Coord.
Founded: 1975. **Staff:** Prof 1. **Subjects:** Women's issues - child care, sex discrimination, marriage, divorce, family, health, employment, affirmative action, reproductive rights, legislation, organizations and centers. **Special**

Collections: Maintains files of national women's organizations and women's centers state by state. **Holdings:** 2000 books; 2000 bound periodical volumes; 40 VF drawers. **Subscriptions:** 200 journals and other serials. **Services:** Interlibrary loans; library open to public by appointment. **Automated Operations:** Computerized cataloging. **Publications:** List of publications - available upon request; financial aid letter. **Special Indexes:** Employment resource list for New York City.

★17244★
WOMEN'S CAREER CENTER - LIBRARY (Soc Sci)
30 N. Clinton Ave.   Phone: (716) 325-2274
Rochester, NY 14604   Sarah I. Hartwell, Coord. of Info. & Rsrcs.
Staff: Prof 1. **Subjects:** Vocational guidance, career change, career management and development. **Holdings:** 600 books; 55 file boxes of clippings, pamphlets and annual reports. **Subscriptions:** 30 journals and other serials. **Services:** Interlibrary loans; copying; library open to public.

★17245★
WOMEN'S CENTER OF SOUTHEASTERN CONNECTICUT - LIBRARY (Soc Sci)*
120 Broad St.
Box 572   Phone: (203) 447-0366
New London, CT 06320   Jessica S. Owaroff, Libn.
Staff: Prof 1. **Subjects:** Feminism, violence against women, health, women's issues. **Holdings:** 500 books; 25 bound periodical volumes; vertical files. **Subscriptions:** 15 journals and other serials; 5 newspapers. **Services:** Copying; library open to public for reference use only.

★17246★
WOMEN'S COLLEGE HOSPITAL - MEDICAL LIBRARY (Med)
76 Grenville St.   Phone: (416) 966-7468
Toronto, ON, Canada M5S 1B2   Margaret Robins, Med.Libn.
Founded: 1955. **Staff:** Prof 1; Other 3. **Subjects:** Dermatology, diabetes, perinatal medicine, obstetrics and gynecology. **Holdings:** 3000 books; 3000 periodical volumes; 410 tapes; 175 video cassettes; 110 cassette tape sets. **Subscriptions:** 205 journals and other serials. **Services:** Interlibrary loans (fee); library not open to public. **Networks/Consortia:** Member of Toronto Medical Libraries Group.

★17247★
WOMEN'S COLLEGE HOSPITAL - PSORIASIS EDUCATION AND RESEARCH CENTRE (Med)
60 Grosvenor St.   Phone: (416) 964-0247
Toronto, ON, Canada M5S 1B6   Dr. R. Schachter, Dir.
Founded: 1976. **Staff:** Prof 1. **Subjects:** Psoriasis, occupational skin health. **Holdings:** Reprint articles from MEDLINE. **Services:** Copying; SDI; center open to public for reference use only.

★17248★
WOMEN'S EQUITY ACTION LEAGUE - NATIONAL INFORMATION CENTER ON WOMEN AND THE MILITARY (Mil)
805 15th St., N.W., Suite 822   Phone: (202) 638-1961
Washington, DC 20005   Carolyn Becraft, Proj.Dir.
Staff: Prof 3; Other 2. **Subjects:** Women and the military, military families, veterans, retired military personnel, registration and the draft, employment and utilization. **Holdings:** 37 books; 107 reports; 9 VF drawers of clippings and articles. **Services:** Copying; library open to public.

★17249★
WOMEN'S HISTORY RESEARCH CENTER, INC. - NATIONAL CLEARINGHOUSE ON MARITAL RAPE (Soc Sci)
2325 Oak St.   Phone: (415) 548-1770
Berkeley, CA 94708   Laura X, Exec.Dir.
Staff: Prof 1; Other 1. **Subjects:** Rape - marital, date, cohabitation, legislation; marital rape legislation. **Special Collections:** Spousal rape. **Holdings:** 20 books; 800 files of clippings, reports, newsletters, studies, research and dissertations. **Subscriptions:** 10 journals and other serials. **Services:** Copying; clearinghouse open to public with restrictions. **Publications:** Bibliographic Guide to the Files on Marital Rape; Newsletter; Summary of Greta Rideout's Story; pamphlet; sociolegal case chart.

★17250★
WOMEN'S HISTORY RESEARCH CENTER, INC. - WOMEN'S HISTORY LIBRARY (Hist)
2325 Oak St.   Phone: (415) 548-1770
Berkeley, CA 94708   Laura X, Dir.
Founded: 1968. **Staff:** Prof 2; Other 20. **Subjects:** Women's health and mental health, women and law, black and Third World women, female artists, children, films by and/or about women, Soviet women. **Special Collections:**

International Women's History Archive (850 titles on microfilm). **Holdings:** 2000 books; 300 tapes; 54 reels of microfilm on health and law; 90 reels of microfilm of women's periodicals in Herstory Collection. **Services:** Library not open to public; library holdings available on microfilm. **Publications:** Directory of Films by and/or about Women; Female Artists Directory; Health, Law and Herstory microfilm - all for sale.

★17251★
WOMEN'S INTERNATIONAL NETWORK (Soc Sci; Publ)
187 Grant St.   Phone: (617) 862-9431
Lexington, MA 02173   Fran P. Hosken, Ed.
Subjects: Women's development and health, women's economic development. **Special Collections:** Feminine genital mutilation. **Holdings:** Figures not available. **Subscriptions:** 40 journals and other serials; 10 newspapers. **Publications:** WIN News, quarterly; list of additional publications - available on request.

★17252★
WOMEN'S MOVEMENT ARCHIVES (Soc Sci)
Sta. Q, P.O. Box 928   Phone: (416) 597-8865
Toronto, ON, Canada M4T 2P1   Sandra Fox, Proj.Mgr.
Staff: 3. **Subjects:** Women's political groups; lesbian groups; women's conferences, festivals, demonstrations, issues. **Holdings:** 250 books; 250 periodicals and newsletters; 450 group files; individual files.

★17253★
WOMEN'S RESOURCE AND ACTION CENTER - SOJOURNER TRUTH WOMEN'S RESOURCE LIBRARY (Soc Sci)
130 N. Madison   Phone: (319) 353-6265
Iowa City, IA 52242   Kathy Lorz, Staff Libn.
Staff: Prof 1; Other 5. **Subjects:** Feminism. **Special Collections:** Complete holdings of Ain't I A Woman, feminist periodical published 1970-1973. **Holdings:** 700 books. **Subscriptions:** 25 journals and other serials. **Services:** Library open to public. **Publications:** Women's Resource & Action Center News, monthly - by subscription and free local distribution.

★17254★
WOOD COUNTY HISTORICAL SOCIETY - HISTORICAL MUSEUM LIBRARY (Hist)
13660 County Home Rd.   Phone: (419) 352-0967
Bowling Green, OH 43402   Lyle Fletcher, Archv.
Founded: 1955. **Staff:** Prof 1. **Subjects:** History of Wood County, Ohio. **Holdings:** 150 books; maps; papers. **Services:** Library open to public. **Publications:** The Black Swamp Chanticleer, monthly. **Special Indexes:** Index of surnames in Leeson-Evers History of Wood County; Surname Index of the Pioneer Scrap Book of Wood County and the Maumee Valley by Charles Evers; index for 4 wood county atlases: Historical Atlas of the World (Wood County edition) 1875, Lucas and Part of Wood Counties, Ohio 1871, Atlas of Wood County 1886 and Atlas of Wood County 1912.

★17255★
WOOD COUNTY LAW LIBRARY (Law)
County Office Bldg., 1st Fl.   Phone: (419) 353-3921
Bowling Green, OH 43402   Marianne Mason, Law Libn.
Staff: 2. **Subjects:** Law. **Holdings:** 17,000 books; 1500 bound periodical volumes; 250 volumes of law opinions; tapes. **Subscriptions:** 230 journals and other serials. **Services:** Interlibrary loans; copying; library open to public. **Computerized Information Services:** Westlaw.

★17256★
WOOD GUNDY INC. - LIBRARY (Bus-Fin)
100 Wall St.   Phone: (212) 344-0633
New York, NY 10005   Anne Bowman
Staff: Prof 1. **Subjects:** Investment securities. **Holdings:** Figures not available.

★17257★
WOOD GUNDY LTD. - LIBRARY (Bus-Fin)
Royal Trust Tower
P.O. Box 274   Phone: (416) 869-8100
Toronto, ON, Canada M5K 1M7   Anne Baumann, Libn.
Founded: 1964. **Staff:** Prof 1; Other 4. **Subjects:** Corporations and industry, investments, accounting, economics. **Special Collections:** Wood Gundy publications (145 binders); financial statements of private Canadian companies (8000 microfiche). **Holdings:** 5000 volumes. **Subscriptions:** 434 journals and other serials; 310 Statistics Canada titles. **Services:** Interlibrary loans; copying. **Computerized Information Services:** Info Globe, DIALOG, Dow Jones News/Retrieval. **Publications:** Acquisitions list, monthly; list of Wood Gundy Research Reports, quarterly; periodicals list, annual - all for

internal distribution only. **Special Indexes:** Index of Wood Gundy research reports, 1976 to present.

WOOD (John Penman) LIBRARY OF NATIONAL DEFENSE
See: University of Pennsylvania - John Penman Wood Library of National Defense

WOOD (General Leonard) ARMY COMMUNITY HOSPITAL
See: U.S. Army Hospitals - General Leonard Wood Army Community Hospital

WOOD LIBRARY-MUSEUM OF ANESTHESIOLOGY
See: American Society of Anesthesiologists

WOOD LIBRARY OF ZOOLOGY AND ORNITHOLOGY
See: Mc Gill University - Blacker/Wood Library of Zoology and Ornithology

WOOD NEPAL LIBRARY
See: American-Nepal Education Foundation

WOOD (Samuel J.) LIBRARY
See: Cornell University - Medical College - Samuel J. Wood Library

WOOD TECHNICAL LIBRARY
See: U.S. Army Medical Research Institute of Chemical Defense

WOODBERRY POETRY ROOM
See: Harvard University

★17258★
WOODBURY COUNTY BAR ASSOCIATION - LAW LIBRARY (Law)
7th & Douglas Sts.
Woodbury County Courthouse, 6th Fl.   Phone: (712) 279-6609
Sioux City, IA 51101   Susan M. Dunn, Libn.
Staff: Prof 1; Other 1. **Subjects:** Law - state, general. **Holdings:** 12,000 volumes. **Services:** Copying; library open to public. **Computerized Information Services:** Westlaw.

★17259★
WOODBURY UNIVERSITY - LIBRARY (Bus-Fin; Art)
1027 Wilshire Blvd.   Phone: (213) 482-8491
Los Angeles, CA 90017   Dr. Everett L. Moore, Dir., Lib.Serv.
Founded: 1884. **Staff:** Prof 3; Other 5. **Subjects:** Economics, international business, art, architecture, interior decoration, management. **Holdings:** 54,110 books; 1587 bound periodical volumes; 18,407 microforms; 3901 slides, filmstrips, cassettes and films. **Subscriptions:** 485 journals and other serials; 12 newspapers. **Services:** Interlibrary loans; copying; library open to public for reference use only. **Remarks:** Library is located at 1034 Wilshire Blvd., Los Angeles, CA.

★17260★
WOODHULL MEDICAL AND MENTAL HEALTH CENTER - HEALTH SCIENCES LIBRARY (Med)
760 Broadway, Rm. 3A160   Phone: (718) 963-8397
Brooklyn, NY 11206   Leon Elveson, Med.Libn.
Prof 1; Other 2. **Subjects:** Medicine, nursing and allied health sciences. **Holdings:** 500 books; 400 bound periodical volumes. **Subscriptions:** 200 journals and other serials. **Services:** Interlibrary loans; copying. **Networks/Consortia:** Member of Brooklyn-Queens-Staten Island Health Sciences Librarians (BQSI). **Formed by the Merger of:** Jewish Hospital and Medical Center of Brooklyn - Greenpoint Hospital Affiliation and Cumberland Hospital.

★17261★
WOODLAKE LUTHERAN CHURCH - LIBRARY (Rel-Theol)
7525 Oliver Ave., S.   Phone: (612) 866-8449
Richfield, MN 55423   Jean Ellefson, Church Libn.
Founded: 1959. **Staff:** Prof 1; Other 12. **Subjects:** Religion and religious teaching, books of interest to adults and youth. **Holdings:** 5192 volumes; recordings; art. **Services:** Library not open to public.

★17262★
WOODLAND PARK ZOOLOGICAL GARDENS - LIBRARY (Sci-Tech)*
5500 Phinney Ave., N.   Phone: (206) 625-4550
Seattle, WA 98103   Mary C. Hopkins, Libn.
Founded: 1971. **Staff:** Prof 1; Other 1. **Subjects:** Mammals and birds (wild and captive), reptiles, amphibians, ecology, sociobiology, animal husbandry, state and federal wildlife legislation. **Holdings:** 759 books; pamphlets; microforms. **Subscriptions:** 21 journals and other serials. **Services:** Library

open to public for reference use only.

WOODMAN ASTRONOMICAL LIBRARY
See: University of Wisconsin, Madison - Washburn Observatory

★17263★
WOODMEN ACCIDENT & LIFE COMPANY - LIBRARY (Bus-Fin)
1526 K St.
Box 82288   Phone: (402) 476-6500
Lincoln, NE 68501   Virgene K. Sloan, Libn.
Founded: 1969. **Staff:** Prof 1. **Subjects:** Health and life insurance, law, office management, data processing, accounting, finance, economics. **Holdings:** 3500 books; 60 films and filmstrips; 20 VF drawers of clippings, reports, policy forms, pamphlets; 40 videotapes; 300 audio cassettes. **Subscriptions:** 125 journals and other serials. **Services:** Library not open to public. **Special Indexes:** Index of company magazine and bulletins (card).

WOODRUFF HEALTH SCIENCE LIBRARY
See: Northside Hospital

WOODRUFF LIBRARY
See: Emory University

WOODRUFF (Robert W.) Library
See: Atlanta University Center - Robert W. Woodruff Library

WOODS (D.S.) EDUCATION LIBRARY
See: University of Manitoba - D.S. Woods Education Library

WOODS, GORDON
See: Clarkson, Gordon/Woods, Gordon

★17264★
WOODS HOLE OCEANOGRAPHIC INSTITUTION - RESEARCH LIBRARY (Sci-Tech)
          Phone: (617) 548-1400
Woods Hole, MA 02543   Carolyn P. Winn, Res.Libn.
Founded: 1932. **Staff:** Prof 2; Other 9. **Subjects:** Oceanography; marine geology, chemistry and biology; ocean engineering; marine policy. **Special Collections:** Institution Archives and Data Collection (12,000 AV tapes; 160,000 underwater photographs; 11,000 charts and atlases; 3000 films; 10,000 slides). **Holdings:** 12,000 books; 20,000 bound periodical volumes; 20,000 technical reports; 250,000 reprints. **Subscriptions:** 1500 journals and other serials. **Services:** Interlibrary loans; copying; library open to public by permission of librarian. **Computerized Information Services:** DIALOG, BRS, DOE/RECON, CAS Online. Performs searches on cost recovery basis. Contact Person: Colleen Hurter. **Networks/Consortia:** Member of New England On-Line Users Group (NENON). **Publications:** Monthly accession announcement; WHOI report bibliography, annual; Collected Reprints, annual - by exchange. **Special Indexes:** Oceanographic Index. **Remarks:** Library is jointly maintained with the Marine Biological Laboratory, where the library's holdings are housed. **Staff:** William Dunkle, Data Libn.

★17265★
WOODSIDE RECEIVING HOSPITAL - STAFF RESOURCE LIBRARY/PATIENTS' LIBRARY (Med)
800 E. Indianola Ave.   Phone: (216) 788-8712
Youngstown, OH 44502   Carol L. Homrighausen, Libn.
Founded: 1978. **Staff:** Prof 1. **Subjects:** Psychiatry, psychiatric nursing, mental illness, mental health, social services, psychotherapy. **Special Collections:** The Psychoanalytic Study of the Child (14 volumes); large print collection (90 volumes); patients' library (includes the Yale Shakespeare). **Holdings:** 5952 books; 31 bound periodical volumes; 255 boxes of archives; 150 reports; 2000 pamphlets; 22 documents; 200 phonograph records; 10 drawers of filmstrips and cassette tapes; 400 items in picture files; 219 dissertations. **Subscriptions:** 105 journals and other serials; 11 newspapers. **Services:** Interlibrary loans; library open to visiting state staff and relatives of institution staff. **Networks/Consortia:** Member of Northeastern Ohio Universities College of Medicine (NEOUCOM). **Publications:** Public relations posters and flyers, monthly; acquisitions update, monthly. **Special Catalogs:** Research bibliography catalogs.

WOODSON (Carter G.) LIBRARY
See: Association for the Study of Afro-American Life and History, Inc. - Carter G. Woodson Library

WOODSON RESEARCH CENTER
See: Rice University

WOODSTOCK COLLEGE ARCHIVES
See: Georgetown University - Special Collections Division - Lauinger
   Memorial Library

★17266★
WOODSTOCK HISTORICAL SOCIETY, INC. - JOHN COTTON DANA LIBRARY
   (Hist)
26 Elm St.   Phone: (802) 457-1822
Woodstock, VT 05091   John Martin, Pres.
Staff: 3. **Subjects:** Woodstock history, antiques, Vermont history,
Woodstock genealogy. **Special Collections:** Charles Dana's Account Books
(102 volumes); old Woodstock newspapers. **Holdings:** 2500 books; 51 bound
periodical volumes; 500 pamphlets; 41 maps; 250 VF folders of papers and
manuscripts; account books and records of Woodstock merchants. **Services:**
Library open to public with restrictions. **Publications:** Woodstock's U.S.
Senator Jacob Collamer, 1944; Something About Old Woodstock, 1952; The
Vermont Heritage of George Perkins Marsh, 1960; My Grandmother's and
Other Tales, 1968 - all for sale; The Dana House Collection, 1974; Hiram
Powers, Vermont Sculptor, 1974.

★17267★
WOODSTOCK THEOLOGICAL CENTER - LIBRARY (Rel-Theol)
Georgetown University
Box 37445   Phone: (202) 625-3120
Washington, DC 20013   Thomas A. Marshall, S.J., Libn.
Staff: Prof 2; Other 2. **Subjects:** Roman Catholic theology, patristics,
Jesuitica, Catholic Americana. **Special Collections:** Rare Jesuitica; Teilhard de
Chardin Collection. **Holdings:** 166,000 books; 30,000 bound periodical
volumes; 11,800 rare books; 984 reels of microfilm; 1683 microfiche.
Subscriptions: 600 journals and other serials. **Services:** Interlibrary loans;
copying; library open for special scholarly research. **Networks/Consortia:**
Member of Consortium of Universities of the Washington Metropolitan Area.
Staff: William J. Sheehan, C.S.B., Asst.Libn.

★17268★
WOODVIEW-CALABASAS PSYCHIATRIC HOSPITAL - LIBRARY (Med)
25100 Calabasas Rd.   Phone: (818) 888-7500
Calabasas, CA 91302   Ching-Fen Wu Tsiang, Libn.
Founded: 1968. **Staff:** Prof 1. **Subjects:** Psychiatry, nursing, general
medicine. **Holdings:** 2000 books; 500 bound periodical volumes.
Subscriptions: 25 journals and other serials. **Services:** Interlibrary loans;
library open to medical staff.

★17269★
WOODVILLE STATE HOSPITAL - PROFESSIONAL LIBRARY (Med)†
                                              Phone: (412) 279-2000
Carnegie, PA 15106   Mary Thompson, Libn.
Founded: 1967. **Staff:** Prof 1. **Subjects:** Psychiatry, psychology, behavioral
sciences, psychiatric nursing, medicine. **Holdings:** 2500 books and bound
periodical volumes. **Subscriptions:** 107 journals and other serials. **Services:**
Interlibrary loans; copying (limited); library open to local mental health
professionals. **Networks/Consortia:** Member of Greater Northeastern
Regional Medical Library Program. **Publications:** Bulletin of recent acquisitions
- for internal distribution only.

WOODWARD BIOMEDICAL LIBRARY
See: University of British Columbia

★17270★
WOODWARD-CLYDE CONSULTANTS, EASTERN REGION - WCC LIBRARY
   (Sci-Tech)
201 Willowbrook Blvd.   Phone: (201) 785-0700
Wayne, NJ 07470   Aida R. Green, Libn.
Staff: Prof 1. **Subjects:** Geotechnical engineering, geology, hydrogeology.
Special Collections: Geologic Atlas of the United States (197 folios).
Holdings: 2000 books; 3000 maps. **Subscriptions:** 52 journals and other
serials. **Services:** Interlibrary loans; copying; library open to public for
reference use only by appointment. **Computerized Information Services:**
DIALOG, SDC, National Water Data System. Performs searches on cost
recovery basis.

★17271★
WOODWARD-CLYDE CONSULTANTS - ENVIRONMENTAL SYSTEMS
   DIVISION - INFORMATION CENTER (Env-Cons)†
One Walnut Creek Center
100 Pringle Ave.   Phone: (415) 945-3000
Walnut Creek, CA 94596   Harriet Annino, Libn.
Founded: 1973. **Staff:** Prof 1. **Subjects:** Environmental impact, oil pollution,
air quality, water quality, energy, environment. **Holdings:** 500 books; 3000

reports. **Subscriptions:** 150 journals and other serials. **Services:** Interlibrary
loans; copying; center open to public on request.

★17272★
WOODWARD-CLYDE CONSULTANTS - LIBRARY/INFORMATION CENTER
   (Sci-Tech)
203 N. Golden Circle Dr.   Phone: (714) 835-6886
Santa Ana, CA 92705   Ute Hertel, Rec.Mgr./Libn.
Staff: Prof 1. **Subjects:** Geology, engineering, geophysics, waste disposal,
environmental sciences. **Holdings:** 5000 books; 500 bound periodical
volumes; 400 WCC reports; 15 file cabinets of maps; 1 file cabinet of
reprints; microfiche. **Subscriptions:** 60 journals and other serials. **Services:**
Interlibrary loans; copying; library open to public by appointment.
Publications: New Book List, quarterly. **Special Catalogs:** Project files
catalog (card).

★17273★
WOODWARD-CLYDE CONSULTANTS, WESTERN REGION - INFORMATION
   CENTER (Sci-Tech)†
One Walnut Creek Center
100 Pringle Ave.   Phone: (415) 945-3000
Walnut Creek, CA 94596   Anne T. Harrigan, Libn.
Founded: 1965. **Staff:** Prof 1; Other 1. **Subjects:** Soil mechanics,
earthquake engineering, geology, seismology. **Holdings:** 2500 books; 6000
reports; 5000 unbound periodicals; 8 VF drawers of pamphlets.
Subscriptions: 250 journals and other serials. **Services:** Interlibrary loans;
copying; SDI; center open to public on request. **Computerized Information
Services:** Online systems. **Publications:** Acquisitions List, monthly - for
internal distribution only.

★17274★
WOODWARD GOVERNOR CO. - WOODWARD LIBRARY (Sci-Tech)
5001 N. Second St.   Phone: (815) 877-7441
Rockford, IL 61101   Ben Schleicher, Adm.Serv.Supv.
Founded: 1957. **Staff:** 2. **Subjects:** Prime movers, aircraft, governors,
locomotives, electricity and machine shop practices. **Holdings:** 1200
volumes; 10 VF drawers of technical papers; 1 VF drawer of bulletins.
Subscriptions: 150 journals and other serials. **Services:** Interlibrary loans;
copying; library open to public for reference use only by request. **Publications:**
Prime Mover Control - monthly. **Staff:** Mabel Beaumont, Libn.

WOODWARD (Roy J.) MEMORIAL LIBRARY OF CALIFORNIANA
See: California State University, Fresno - Henry Madden Library -
   Department of Special Collections

★17275★
WOODWARD STATE HOSPITAL SCHOOL - STAFF LIBRARY (Med)
                                              Phone: (515) 438-2600
Woodward, IA 50276   Joy Averill, Libn.
Founded: 1962. **Staff:** 1. **Subjects:** Mental retardation, pediatrics, dentistry,
psychology, special education, nursing, recreation, medicine, social work.
Holdings: 4539 books; 8 VF drawers of pamphlets and reprints; 15 16mm
films. **Subscriptions:** 64 journals and other serials. **Services:** Interlibrary
loans; library open to public for reference use only. **Networks/Consortia:**
Member of Polk County Biomedical Consortium (PCBC); Central Iowa
Network.

WOOLAROC MUSEUM
See: Phillips (Frank) Foundation, Inc.

WOOLF (Leonard and Virginia) LIBRARY
See: Washington State University - Manuscripts, Archives, & Special
   Collections

WOOLWORTH CENTER OF MUSICAL STUDIES
See: Princeton University - Phonograph Record Library

★17276★
WORCESTER ART MUSEUM - LIBRARY (Art)†
55 Salisbury St.   Phone: (617) 799-4406
Worcester, MA 01608   Kathy L. Berg, Libn.
Founded: 1896. **Staff:** Prof 3; Other 1. **Subjects:** Fine arts, art history.
Holdings: 38,000 volumes; 50 shelf feet of exhibition catalogs; 160 shelf
feet of sale and dealer catalogs. **Subscriptions:** 90 journals and other serials.
Services: Interlibrary loans; copying; library open to public for reference use
only. **Networks/Consortia:** Member of Worcester Area Cooperating Libraries
(WACL). **Special Indexes:** Card index to Worcester Art Museum objects
published in Worcester Art Museum publication (by accession number). **Staff:**
Anne P. Walsh, Asst.Libn.; Cynthia Bolshaw, Slide Libn.

★17277★

WORCESTER CITY HOSPITAL - MEDICAL LIBRARY (Med)
26 Queen St.
Phone: (617) 799-8186
Worcester, MA 01610
Timothy D. Rivard, Med.Libn.
Founded: 1937. **Staff:** Prof 1; Other 1. **Subjects:** Medicine and allied subjects. **Holdings:** 1500 books; 4500 bound periodical volumes. **Subscriptions:** 200 journals and other serials. **Services:** Interlibrary loans; copying; use of library for reference may be requested. **Networks/Consortia:** Member of Central Massachusetts Consortium of Health Related Libraries (CMCHRL).

★17278★

WORCESTER COUNTY HORTICULTURAL SOCIETY - LIBRARY (Sci-Tech)
30 Elm St.
Phone: (617) 752-4274
Worcester, MA 01608
Wanda H. Sandberg, Libn.
Staff: 2. **Subjects:** Horticulture (specializing in fruit culture). **Holdings:** 5000 books; 1000 bound periodical volumes; 300 seed, tool, plant and equipment catalogs. **Subscriptions:** 25 journals and other serials. **Services:** Library open to public.

WORCESTER DISTRICT MEDICAL SOCIETY
See: University of Massachusetts Medical School & Worcester District Medical Society

★17279★

WORCESTER FOUNDATION FOR EXPERIMENTAL BIOLOGY - GEORGE F. FULLER LIBRARY (Sci-Tech)
222 Maple St.
Phone: (617) 842-8921
Shrewsbury, MA 01545
Melinda Saffer, Lib.Dir.
Founded: 1945. **Staff:** Prof 2; Other 2. **Subjects:** Molecular biology, chemistry, biochemistry, physiology, pharmacology, neurobehavioral sciences. **Holdings:** 8000 books; 25,000 bound periodical volumes; 4 VF drawers of chemical patents; 4 VF drawers of subject bibliographies; 4 VF drawers of clippings. **Subscriptions:** 858 journals and other serials. **Services:** Interlibrary loans; copying; SDI; library open to staffs and students of institutions of higher education in the community. **Computerized Information Services:** DIALOG, SDC, BRS, MEDLARS. **Networks/Consortia:** Member of New England On-Line Users Group (NENON); Central Massachusetts Consortium of Health Related Libraries (CMCHRL). **Publications:** Monthly Acquisitions list; Periodicals list, annual; bibliographies. **Special Catalogs:** Collected reprints of Worcester Foundation authors (book); catalog of bound company annual reports, 1945 to present (book).

★17280★

WORCESTER HAHNEMANN HOSPITAL - MEDICAL LIBRARY (Med)
281 Lincoln St.
Phone: (617) 792-8567
Worcester, MA 01605
Roger S. Manahan, Libn.
Staff: Prof 1. **Subjects:** Medicine. **Special Collections:** Dr. Hahnemann's Collection of Historic Medical Texts (150). **Holdings:** 230 books; 440 bound periodical volumes. **Subscriptions:** 54 journals and other serials. **Services:** Interlibrary loans; copying; library open to public for reference use only. **Computerized Information Services:** MEDLINE. Performs searches on cost recovery basis. **Networks/Consortia:** Member of Worcester Area Cooperating Libraries (WACL).

★17281★

WORCESTER HAHNEMANN HOSPITAL - SCHOOL OF NURSING LIBRARY (Med)
281 Lincoln St.
Phone: (617) 792-8567
Worcester, MA 01605
Roger S. Manahan, Libn.
Founded: 1900. **Staff:** Prof 1. **Subjects:** Nursing and related subjects. **Special Collections:** Historical nursing books. **Holdings:** 2000 books; 800 bound periodical volumes; AV items; 50 tape recordings; 8 drawers of pamphlets and reports; 20 models; 25 maps and charts; 400 slides; 50 filmstrips and recordings; 12 motion picture films. **Subscriptions:** 29 journals and other serials. **Services:** Interlibrary loans; copying; library open to public for reference use only.

★17282★

WORCESTER HISTORICAL MUSEUM - LIBRARY (Hist)
39 Salisbury St.
Phone: (617) 753-8278
Worcester, MA 01609
Jessica S. Goss, Hd.Libn.
Founded: 1875. **Staff:** Prof 1; Other 2. **Subjects:** Local history. **Holdings:** 20,000 volumes; photographs; maps; manuscripts; ephemera. **Services:** Copying (limited); library open to public on a limited schedule. **Networks/Consortia:** Member of Worcester Area Cooperating Libraries (WACL).

★17283★

WORCESTER LAW LIBRARY (Law)
County Court House
Phone: (617) 756-2441
Worcester, MA 01608
Mary A. Terpo, Law Libn.
Founded: 1842. **Staff:** Prof 1; Other 3. **Subjects:** Law. **Holdings:** 98,000 volumes; periodicals; 10 VF drawers of pamphlets; Reporter series on ultrafiche; Federal Register and State Session Laws on microfiche; Massachusetts Supreme Judicial Court Records and Briefs on microfiche. **Services:** Interlibrary loans; copying; library open to public. **Publications:** Annual Report, 1844 to present. **Remarks:** Part of the Massachusetts State Trial Court; Marnie Warner, Law Library Coordinator.

★17284★

WORCESTER POLYTECHNIC INSTITUTE - GEORGE C. GORDON LIBRARY (Sci-Tech)
West St.
Phone: (617) 793-5411
Worcester, MA 01609
Albert G. Anderson, Jr., Hd.Libn.
Founded: 1865. **Staff:** Prof 9; Other 12. **Subjects:** Engineering, chemistry, environmental science, computer science, physics, life sciences, biomedicine, mathematics, city planning, history of science and technology. **Special Collections:** WPI Archives; History of Engineering. **Holdings:** 225,104 books; 39,251 bound periodical volumes; 13,009 technical reports; 2066 maps; 125 boxes and 25 files of archives; 8 VF drawers; 702,911 microfiche (NASA, American Engineering Council (AEC), NASA Test Support); 2200 recordings; 5200 videotapes, audio cassettes, film loops. **Subscriptions:** 1300 journals and other serials; 25 newspapers. **Services:** Interlibrary loans; copying; microfiche copying; transparencies made; library open to qualified users. **Automated Operations:** Computerized cataloging. **Computerized Information Services:** OCLC. **Networks/Consortia:** Member of NELINET; Worcester Area Cooperating Libraries (WACL). **Publications:** New Acquisitions list, monthly; Library Handbook. **Staff:** Carmen Brown, Hd., Pub.Serv./Ref.; Helen Shuster, Hd., Tech.Serv.; Cornelia Pomeroy, Circ.; Diana Johnson, Ref./ILL; Christina Yuan, Ref.; Donald Richardson, Tech. Reports; Lora Brueck, Spec.Coll.; Joanne Williams, Ref.

★17285★

WORCESTER PUBLIC LIBRARY - REFERENCE AND READER SERVICES (Soc Sci; Sci-Tech; Hum)
Salem Sq.
Phone: (617) 799-1655
Worcester, MA 01608
Penelope B. Johnson, Hd.
Staff: Prof 18; Other 2. **Subjects:** History, art, music, social and political science, literature, travel, science and technology, business, religion, architecture. **Special Collections:** Worcester Collection. **Holdings:** 376,369 books; 58,612 bound periodical volumes; 317,329 government documents; 7000 recordings; Massachusetts State documents. **Subscriptions:** 959 journals and other serials; 63 newspapers. **Services:** Interlibrary loans; copying; services open to public. **Automated Operations:** Computerized cataloging, acquisitions and circulation. **Computerized Information Services:** OCLC. **Networks/Consortia:** Member of Central/Western Massachusetts Automated Resource Sharing (C/W MARS). **Staff:** Paul Pelletier, Hd., Bus., Sci. & Tech.; Jane Peck, Hd., Hum. & Fine Arts; Leonard Lucas, Hd., Soc.Sci. & Hist.; Nancy Gaudette, Worcester Coll.Libn.

★17286★

WORCESTER STATE COLLEGE - LEARNING RESOURCES CENTER (Educ)
486 Chandler St.
Phone: (617) 793-8027
Worcester, MA 01602
Bruce Plummer, Dir.
Founded: 1874. **Staff:** Prof 7; Other 17. **Subjects:** Education, humanities. **Special Collections:** Education Resources Collection (11,000 elementary and secondary textbooks; 1200 curriculum guides; 1000 tests); Children's Collection (8500 juvenile volumes). **Holdings:** 152,000 books; 2000 bound periodical volumes; 45,000 microforms; 15,000 16mm films; 8mm film loops; slides; phonograph records; tapes; video cassettes. **Subscriptions:** 850 journals and other serials; 10 newspapers. **Services:** Interlibrary loans; copying; television and photography studios; center open to public. **Computerized Information Services:** DIALOG. Performs searches on cost recovery basis. **Networks/Consortia:** Member of Worcester Area Cooperating Libraries (WACL); Central/Western Massachusetts Automated Resource Sharing (C/W MARS). **Publications:** Learning Resources Center Location Guide, given to users as needed. **Staff:** Betsey Brenneman, Acq.; Krishna Das Gupta, Tech.Serv.; Daniel Dick, Ref.; Ruth Greenslit, Circ.; Pamela McKay, Per.Ruth Webber, Cat.

★17287★

WORCESTER TELEGRAM AND GAZETTE, INC. - LIBRARY (Publ)
20 Franklin St.
Phone: (617) 793-9240
Worcester, MA 01613
Sharon C. Carter, Libn.
Founded: 1913. **Staff:** 7. **Subjects:** Newspaper reference topics; biography. **Special Collections:** Local and state history and biography. **Holdings:** 374

books; 250,000 clippings; 192,300 graphics; Worcester Telegram, 1884 to present, on microfilm; Evening Gazette, 1866 to present, on microfilm. **Services:** Copying; library open to public on written request only.

★17288★
WORCESTER VOCATIONAL SCHOOLS - GEORGE I. ALDEN LIBRARY (Educ)
26 Salisbury St.   Phone: (617) 799-1945
Worcester, MA 01608
Founded: 1963. **Staff:** Prof 1; Other 2. **Subjects:** Optometry, vocations and careers. **Holdings:** 7000 books. **Subscriptions:** 73 journals and other serials. **Services:** Library open to public with restrictions.

WORDEN SCHOOL OF SOCIAL SERVICE
See: Our Lady of the Lake University

★17289★
WORK IN AMERICA INSTITUTE, INC. - LIBRARY (Soc Sci)
700 White Plains Rd.   Phone: (914) 472-9600
Scarsdale, NY 10583   Ellen Daniels, Mgr., Info.Serv.
Staff: Prof 2; Other 1. **Subjects:** Productivity, quality of working life, work innovations and design, personnel management. **Special Collections:** Publications of the former National Center for Productivity and Quality of Working Life (50 volumes). **Holdings:** 2000 books; 2200 file documents; 20,000 subject files of clippings, unpublished reports and technical documents. **Subscriptions:** 203 journals and other serials. **Services:** Library open to public by appointment. **Special Indexes:** Subject Headings Index. **Staff:** Cynthia Rubino, Libn.

★17290★
WORKER'S COMPENSATION BOARD OF ONTARIO - HOSPITAL & REHABILITATION CENTRE - MEDICAL LIBRARY (Med)
115 Torbarrie Rd.   Phone: (416) 244-1761
Downsview, ON, Canada M3L 1G8   Catherine W. Wilson, Libn.
Staff: 1. **Subjects:** Physical medicine, rehabilitation psychology, orthopedics, neurology, psychiatry, psychology, physical and occupational therapy. **Holdings:** 1700 books; 220 bound periodical volumes; videotapes; cassettes; slides; 16mm films. **Subscriptions:** 117 journals and other serials. **Services:** Interlibrary loans; library not open to public.

★17291★
WORKING OPPORTUNITIES FOR WOMEN - RESOURCE CENTER (Soc Sci)
2344 Nicollet Ave., Suite 140   Phone: (612) 874-6636
Minneapolis, MN 55404   Kate Wulf, Dir.
Subjects: Women - assertiveness, careers, motherhood, minorities. **Holdings:** 600 books; 7 resource files; 2 shelves of educational bulletins. **Subscriptions:** 12 journals and other serials. **Services:** Copying; center open to public for reference use only.

WORKSHOP IN POLITICAL THEORY & POLICY ANALYSIS
See: Indiana University

★17292★
WORLD AFFAIRS COUNCIL OF NORTHERN CALIFORNIA - LIBRARY (Soc Sci)
312 Sutter St., Suite 200   Phone: (415) 982-2541
San Francisco, CA 94108   Lone C. Beeson, Hd.Libn.
Founded: 1947. **Staff:** Prof 2. **Subjects:** International relations, foreign policy, political science, economics, modern history. **Special Collections:** Newsletters and press releases from various embassies and information centers; U.S. Department of State documents. **Holdings:** 6000 books; 200 documents; 3000 pamphlets; 300 cassette tapes; maps. **Subscriptions:** 40 journals and other serials; 5 newspapers. **Services:** Copying; library open to public with restrictions on borrowing. **Publications:** Booknotes, monthly - distributed to members. **Staff:** Edith Malamud, Circ.Libn.

★17293★
WORLD ARCHEOLOGICAL SOCIETY - INFORMATION CENTER (Hist)
Lake Rd. 65-48
Star Rt. Box 445   Phone: (417) 334-2377
Hollister, MO 65672   Ron Miller, Dir.
Founded: 1971. **Staff:** Prof 2. **Subjects:** Archeology, anthropology and art history of the world; Biblical archeology; museum science. **Special Collections:** Steve Miller Library of American Archaeology (1100 publications); democracy club; publications commendations; Bible repair project. **Holdings:** 6500 volumes; 7500 item clipping file; 2000 photographs, tapes and slides. **Subscriptions:** 30 journals and other serials; 6 newspapers. **Services:** Center not open to public. **Publications:** W.A.S. Newsletter, irregular - sent to W.A.S. members, exchange organizations and to individuals who send in clippings, newspapers and books. **Staff:** Mrs. Steve Miller,

Asst.Dir.

★17294★
WORLD ASSOCIATION OF DOCUMENT EXAMINERS - WADE LIBRARY (Law)
111 N. Canal St.   Phone: (312) 930-9446
Chicago, IL 60606   Lee Arnold, Libn.
Founded: 1973. **Staff:** Prof 2; Other 3. **Subjects:** Handwriting, documents, paper and ink, law, trial procedure, psychology. **Holdings:** 5000 books. **Subscriptions:** 75 journals and other serials; 25 newspapers. **Services:** Library not open to public. **Publications:** WADE Exchange, monthly; WADE Journal, quarterly. **Staff:** Martha Lindberg, Libn.

WORLD BANK
See: International Monetary Fund/World Bank

★17295★
WORLD BANK LAW LIBRARY (Law)
1818 H St., N.W. (E-743)   Phone: (202) 477-2128
Washington, DC 20433   Linda L. Thompson, Law Libn.
Founded: 1975. **Staff:** Prof 1; Other 1. **Subjects:** Law - international, foreign, comparative; arbitration; administrative tribunals. **Holdings:** 15,000 books. **Subscriptions:** 150 journals and other serials. **Services:** Interlibrary loans; library open to public for reference use only on request. **Computerized Information Services:** LEXIS.

★17296★
WORLD BOOK INC.- RESEARCH LIBRARY (Publ)
Merchandise Mart Plaza   Phone: (312) 341-8777
Chicago, IL 60654   Mary Kayaian, Hd., Lib.Serv.
Founded: 1920. **Staff:** Prof 2; Other 3. **Subjects:** General reference, biography, statistics. **Holdings:** 22,000 volumes; 300 VF drawers of pamphlets and clippings; 40,000 photographs and slides; college catalogs; 3000 maps; 400 government publications. **Subscriptions:** 600 journals and other serials; 6 newspapers. **Services:** Interlibrary loans; library not open to public. **Automated Operations:** Computerized cataloging. **Computerized Information Services:** DIALOG. **Networks/Consortia:** Member of ILLINET.

★17297★
WORLD DATA CENTER A - GLACIOLOGY INFORMATION CENTER (Sci-Tech)
CIRES, Campus Box 449
University of Colorado   Phone: (303) 492-5171
Boulder, CO 80309   Ann M. Brennan, Info.Spec.
Founded: 1957. **Staff:** Prof 1; Other 1. **Subjects:** All aspects of snow and ice, including snow cover, avalanches, glaciers, sea, river, lake ice, polar ice sheets, permafrost, paleoglaciology, ice physics. **Special Collections:** Historical glacier photograph collections (1880s-1960s). **Holdings:** 3000 books and technical reports; 7500 reprints. **Subscriptions:** 70 journals and other serials. **Services:** Interlibrary loans; copying; SDI; will answer requests for information by correspondence; center open to public. **Automated Operations:** Automated bibliographic file of holdings. **Computerized Information Services:** DIALOG; Citation Data Base, Glacier Photo Index (internal databases). Performs searches on cost recovery basis. Contact Person: Claire Hanson. **Publications:** Quarterly accessions list - free.

★17298★
WORLD DATA CENTER A - METEOROLOGY (Sci-Tech)
Natl. Environmental Satellite, Data & Info.Serv.
Natl. Climatic Data Ctr.
Federal Bldg.   Phone: (704) 258-2850
Asheville, NC 28801   Dr. L. Ray Hoxit, Act.Dir.
Founded: 1957. **Staff:** Prof 2. **Subjects:** Meteorology, solar radiation, ozone, atmospherics. **Special Collections:** Synoptic Meteorological data for International Geophysical Year and International Quiet Solar Year; USSR radiosonde data on microfilm; rocketsonde data on magnetic tape; Global Atmospheric Research Program Atlantic Tropical Experiment and Global Weather Experiment data on magnetic tape. **Holdings:** 1200 reels of microfilm; 1600 magnetic tapes; 10 cabinets of other data. **Services:** Data available at cost of reproduction to any inquirer. **Publications:** High Altitude Meteorological Data (on microfilm). **Remarks:** Center is sponsored by the U.S. National Oceanic and Atmospheric Administration.

★17299★
WORLD DATA CENTER A - OCEANOGRAPHY (Sci-Tech)
Natl. Oceanic and Atmospheric Adm.   Phone: (202) 634-7249
Washington, DC 20235   James Churgin, Dir.
Founded: 1957. **Staff:** Prof 2; Other 2. **Subjects:** Physical and chemical oceanographic data, biological oceanographic data, current data, sea surface

data. **Special Collections:** Oceanographic data from the International Geophysical Year, the International Indian Ocean Expedition and other international cooperative oceanographic expeditions and projects. **Holdings:** Oceanographic data on log sheets, machine listings and in publications for more than 770,000 stations. **Services:** Copying; utilizes Automatic Data Processing (ADP) facilities of the National Oceanographic Data Center; facility open to qualified scientists and persons interested in oceanography. **Publications:** Catalogue of Data, annual; Catalogue of Accessioned Publications, annual; reports of oceanographic data exchange, annual.

★17300★
WORLD DATA CENTER A - ROCKETS & SATELLITES - NATIONAL SPACE SCIENCE DATA CENTER (NSSDC) (Sci-Tech)
Code 630.2, Goddard Space Flight Ctr.   Phone: (301) 344-6695
Greenbelt, MD 20771   Dr. James I. Vette, Dir.
Subjects: Space science. **Special Collections:** Satellite and space probe experimental data. **Holdings:** 472,949 volumes; 30,000 microfiche; 68,292 tapes; 35,000 reels of microfilm; 1,676,500 linear feet of photographs. **Services:** Copying; SDI; center open to public by appointment. **Automated Operations:** Computerized cataloging, acquisitions and files. **Computerized Information Services:** Internal databases.

★17301★
WORLD DATA CENTER A - SOLAR-TERRESTRIAL PHYSICS (Sci-Tech)
Natl. Oceanic and Atmospheric Adm.
E/GC2
325 Broadway   Phone: (303) 497-6323
Boulder, CO 80303   Joe H. Allen, Dir.
Founded: 1957. **Staff:** Prof 9; Other 16. **Subjects:** Geomagnetism, ionospheric phenomena, solar and interplanetary phenomena, aurora, airglow, cosmic rays. **Special Collections:** Largest collection of solar-terrestrial data in the world. **Holdings:** 18.2 million feet of 35mm film; station booklets; 6500 magnetic tapes; punched cards; microfiche. **Services:** Copying; library open to public. **Automated Operations:** Computerized cataloging and circulation. **Computerized Information Services:** Online systems. **Publications:** Catalogs of data (by discipline, periodically); Solar-Geophysical Data, monthly; UAG-Report Series, intermittent. **Remarks:** This data center includes the holdings of the former Instrumental Aurora, Solar Activity, Cosmic Rays, Airglow and Ionosphere, and Geomagnetism World Data Centers. **Also Known As:** National Geophysical Data Center, Solar-Terrestrial Physics Division.

WORLD HEALTH ORGANIZATION - PAN AMERICAN HEALTH ORGANIZATION
See: Pan American Health Organization

★17302★
WORLD HUNGER EDUCATION SERVICE - LIBRARY (Soc Sci; Agri)
1317 G St., N.W.   Phone: (202) 223-2995
Washington, DC 20005   Dr. Patricia L. Kutzner, Exec.Dir.
Founded: 1976. **Staff:** Prof 3; Other 1. **Subjects:** World food problems, agricultural policy, appropriate technology, poverty. **Holdings:** 300 books; government publications; Washington Post clippings; unbound reports; pamphlets; documents. **Subscriptions:** 110 journals and other serials. **Services:** Library open to public for reference use only. **Publications:** Hunger Notes, monthly - by subscription; Who's Involved with Hunger; AV Guide to Politics of Hunger.

★17303★
THE WORLD INSTITUTE FOR ADVANCED PHENOMENOLOGICAL RESEARCH AND LEARNING - LIBRARY AND ARCHIVES (Hum)
348 Payson Rd.   Phone: (617) 489-3696
Belmont, MA 02178   Marie Lynch
Subjects: Phenomenology. **Holdings:** 500 books. **Subscriptions:** 15 journals and other serials. **Services:** Library open to public with restrictions. **Publications:** Phenomenology Information Bulletin: A Review of Philosophical Ideas and Trends.

★17304★
WORLD JEWISH GENEALOGY ORGANIZATION - LIBRARY (Rel-Theol; Hist)
1533 60th St.
Box FF
Brooklyn, NY 11219   Phone: (718) 435-0500
                                                 Rabbi N. Halberstam, Libn.
Staff: 1. **Subjects:** Judaica. **Holdings:** 10,000 books. **Services:** Library not open to public. **Publications:** Bibliography and biography journal devoted to genealogy. **Formerly:** Menorah Institute.

★17305★
WORLD LIFE RESEARCH INSTITUTE - LIBRARY (Sci-Tech)
23000 Grand Terrace Rd.   Phone: (714) 825-4773
Colton, CA 92324   Bruce W. Halstead, Lib.Dir.
Founded: 1959. **Staff:** Prof 2; Other 2. **Subjects:** Marine biotoxins, venomous snakes, plant and insect biotoxins, dangerous marine animals, herbal and medicinal plants, biomedical history, biologically-active natural products. **Holdings:** 7000 books and bound periodical volumes; 50 manuscripts; 18,000 reprints and pamphlets; bibliographic references on biotoxins; 4000 maps and pictures of poisonous plants and animals. **Subscriptions:** 20 journals and other serials. **Services:** Copying; library open to public by appointment. **Publications:** Monographs on poisonous plants and animals; handbooks on immunology and nontoxic medical therapies. **Special Indexes:** Plant and animal poisons.

★17306★
WORLD MODELING ASSOCIATION - WMA LIBRARY (Bus-Fin)
Box 100   Phone: (914) 737-8512
Croton-on-Hudson, NY 10520   Ruth Tolman, Pres.
Staff: 3. **Subjects:** Fashion - careers, modeling and merchandising; personal development. **Special Collections:** Photographic and Professional Modeling Collection. **Holdings:** 275 books and bound periodical volumes; 28 manuscripts; clippings. **Subscriptions:** 18 journals and other serials. **Services:** Copying; library open to public by mail inquiry only. **Publications:** Who's Who in Modeling - to school career guidance centers and individuals. **Staff:** Kathy Miller, Libn.

WORLD MUSIC ARCHIVES
See: Wesleyan University - Library

WORLD PEACE FOUNDATION LIBRARY
See: Tufts University - Fletcher School of Law & Diplomacy - Edwin Ginn Library

★17307★
WORLD PEACE THROUGH LAW CENTER - ARCHIVES (Hist; Law)
1000 Connecticut Ave., N.W., Suite 800   Phone: (202) 466-5428
Washington, DC 20036
Subjects: International law, human rights, international trade, law and technology, aviation and outer space, nuclear arms control. **Holdings:** Figures not available. **Services:** Archives not open to public. **Publications:** The World Jurist (newsletter), bimonthly; Law/Technology (journal), quarterly; publications directory.

★17308★
WORLD PEACE THROUGH LAW CENTER - INFORMATION CENTER
1000 Connecticut Ave., N.W., Suite 800
Washington, DC 20036
Subjects: International law, law and technology, human rights, international trade, nuclear arms control. **Holdings:** 50 books and bound periodical volumes; U.N. documents. **Automated Operations:** Computerized circulation. **Publications:** List of publications - available on request. **Remarks:** Presently inactive.

WORLD STUDENT CHRISTIAN FEDERATION - ARCHIVES
See: Yale University - Divinity School Library

★17309★
WORLD TRADE CENTRE TORONTO - LIBRARY (Bus-Fin)
60 Harbour St.   Phone: (416) 863-2153
Toronto, ON, Canada M5J 1B7   Wendy Vosberg, Dir.
Founded: 1978. **Staff:** Prof 1. **Subjects:** Importing and exporting, Canadian industries, customs administration, shipping. **Holdings:** 1200 books; 12 VF drawers of clippings and annual reports. **Subscriptions:** 300 journals and other serials. **Services:** Copying; library open to public with restrictions. **Computerized Information Services:** DIALOG, BRS, New York Times Information Service, Info Globe. **Remarks:** The World Trade Centre is under the auspices of the Toronto Harbour Commissioners.

★17310★
WORLD UNIVERSITY ROUNDTABLE - WORLD UNIVERSITY LIBRARY (Rel-Theol)
711 E. Blacklidge Dr.
Sun Sta., Box 40638
Tucson, AZ 85719   Phone: (602) 622-2170
                                        Howard John Zitko, Act.Libn.
Founded: 1947. **Staff:** Prof 1; Other 1. **Subjects:** Metaphysics, esoteric science, holistic healing, UFO phenomena, pre-history, Oriental religions. **Special Collections:** Rare books in religious philosophy. **Holdings:** 15,000 books; 250 bound periodical volumes; 100 boxes of unbound magazines,

dissertations, essays, paperbacks; 1000 other cataloged items. **Subscriptions:** 27 journals and other serials. **Services:** Library not open to public. **Publications:** World University Library, occasional - to members and the general public.

★17311★
WORLD VISION INTERNATIONAL - INFORMATION RESOURCE CENTER (Rel-Theol)
919 W. Huntington Dr.   Phone: (213) 574-9017
Monrovia, CA 91016   Mary H. Janss, Res.Assoc.
Founded: 1970. **Staff:** 2. **Subjects:** World Christianity, missions, hunger refugees and unreached people. **Holdings:** 3500 books; 90 periodical titles; 7 simulation games; 36 VF drawers of geographic material on each country; 21 VF on North American mission organizations; 7 VF drawers. **Subscriptions:** 325 journals and other serials. **Services:** Copying (limited); center open to public with restrictions. **Automated Operations:** Computerized cataloging. **Computerized Information Services:** DIALOG, The Source. **Publications:** World Vision, in-house magazine. **Special Indexes:** Computerized AUTOLIB index to book collection organization files.

★17312★
WORLD WITHOUT WAR COUNCIL - MIDWEST LIBRARY (Soc Sci)
421 S. Wabash   Phone: (312) 236-7459
Chicago, IL 60605   Robert Woito, Pubn.Dir.
Staff: Prof 1; Other 2. **Subjects:** International relations and organizations, arms race and disarmament, human rights, nonviolence, world economic development, crises issues, area studies, ethics and war. **Holdings:** 2000 books; reference files on organizations in war/peace field. **Subscriptions:** 10 journals and other serials. **Services:** Library open to public. **Publications:** Newsletter, quarterly - free upon request.

★17313★
WORLD ZIONIST ORGANIZATION - AMERICAN SECTION - ZIONIST ARCHIVES AND LIBRARY (Area-Ethnic)
515 Park Ave.   Phone: (212) 753-2167
New York, NY 10022   Sylvia Landress, Dir. & Libn.
Founded: 1939. **Staff:** Prof 5; Other 2. **Subjects:** Israel, Zionism, Middle East, history of the Jews and Jewish life. **Holdings:** 50,000 books and pamphlets; 50,000 photographs; 977 reels of microfilm; slides; filmstrips; nonmusical and musical recordings; symphonic scores; folk music; maps and posters; 137 VF drawers of archival material. **Subscriptions:** 400 journals and other serials. **Services:** Interlibrary loans; copying; library open to public. **Staff:** Esther Togman, Asst.Dir. & Libn.; Ruth Fergenson, Libn.; Judy Wallach, Libn.

WORLDWIDE CHURCH OF GOD - AMBASSADOR COLLEGE
See: **Ambassador College**

WORTH (Sol) ETHNOGRAPHIC FILM ARCHIVE
See: **University of Pennsylvania - Annenberg School of Communications - Library**

★17314★
WORTHINGTON HISTORICAL SOCIETY - LIBRARY (Hist)
50 W. New England Ave.   Phone: (614) 885-1247
Worthington, OH 43085   Lillian Skeele, Libn.
Staff: Prof 1. **Subjects:** Local history and genealogy, historic preservation, decorative arts, pioneer crafts, dolls, lace-making. **Holdings:** 750 books. **Services:** Library open to public by appointment.

WQED LIBRARY
See: **Metropolitan Pittsburgh Public Broadcasting, Inc.**

★17315★
WRATHER PORT PROPERTIES, LTD. - ARCHIVES AND RESOURCE CENTER (Trans; Hist)
RMS Queen Mary
Box 8
Long Beach, CA 90801   Phone: (213) 435-4747
                    Richard Gano, Dir., Exhibits
Founded: 1967. **Staff:** Prof 3. **Subjects:** RMS Queen Mary. **Special Collections:** Ship's Logs (145); Radio, Engines, Boilers and Steam Logs; memoranda, letters and reports, papers for stores, crew, cargo and drydocking (17 VF drawers and 200 linear feet). **Holdings:** 100 books; 2500 photographs; 20 VF drawers of plans for mechanical and utilities installations; 250 menus; 45 passenger lists; 350 memorabilia, pamphlets, booklets, souvenirs. **Services:** Center not open to public; requests for materials should be addressed to the Exhibits Department. **Remarks:** Ninety percent of the material in the library was found on the ship. **Staff:** Bill Winberg, Hist.

★17316★
WRIGHT INSTITUTE - GRADUATE DIVISION LIBRARY (Soc Sci)
2728 Durant Ave.   Phone: (415) 841-9230
Berkeley, CA 94704   Lorraine D. Kos, Libn.
Staff: Prof 1; Other 1. **Subjects:** Psychology, sociology, education, research methodology, Third World psychology. **Special Collections:** Dr. Abraham Maslow Collection (his complete private collection donated by his widow). **Holdings:** 10,000 books; 152 Wright Institute dissertations. **Subscriptions:** 36 journals and other serials. **Services:** Interlibrary loans; library open to public only through faculty members' approval. **Computerized Information Services:** DIALOG. Performs searches on cost recovery basis.

WRIGHT (J.M.) TECHNICAL SCHOOL
See: **Connecticut State Board of Education - J.M. Wright Technical School**

WRIGHT (John Shepard) MEMORIAL LIBRARY
See: **Indiana Academy of Science - John Shepard Wright Memorial Library**

WRIGHT-PATTERSON AIR FORCE BASE (OH)
See: **U.S. Air Force: Hospital Medical Center - Medical Library; Institute of Technology; Museum - Research Division Library; Wright Aeronautical Laboratories; Wright-Patterson Technical Library**

★17317★
WRIGHT STATE UNIVERSITY - ARCHIVES & SPECIAL COLLECTIONS (Hist)
                    Phone: (513) 873-2092
Dayton, OH 45435   Dr. Patrick B. Nolan, Hd. of Archv.
Staff: Prof 5; Other 4. **Subjects:** Aeronautics history, Wright Brothers, Ohio and local history, genealogy, Abraham Lincoln. **Special Collections:** Early Aviation (1000 volumes); Miami Valley history (3000 volumes); Abraham Lincoln (500 volumes); university archives (100 cubic feet); manuscripts (1000 cubic feet). **Holdings:** 4100 books and bound periodical volumes; 30 cubic feet of Wright Brothers Papers; 24 cubic feet of James M. Cox Papers; 100 cubic feet of labor union records; 200 cubic feet of local business records; 40 cubic feet of local church records. **Services:** Copying; collections open to public for reference use only. **Automated Operations:** Computerized cataloging. **Networks/Consortia:** Member of Southwest Ohio Council for Higher Education (SOC); Ohio Network of American History Research Centers. **Special Catalogs:** Inventories or registers for manuscript collections; computer guide and COM catalog to local government records. **Staff:** Robert H. Smith, Jr., Archv.; Dorothy Smith, Ref. & Proc.Spec.; Phyllis Steele, Local Rec.Spec.

★17318★
WRIGHT STATE UNIVERSITY - HEALTH SCIENCES LIBRARY (Med)
3640 Colonel Glenn Hwy.   Phone: (513) 873-2266
Dayton, OH 45435   Mary Ann Hoffman, Act. Health Sci.Libn.
Founded: 1974. **Staff:** Prof 7; Other 23. **Subjects:** Medicine, human anatomy, microbiology, physiology, psychology, biochemistry, human growth, genetics, cardiology, nursing. **Special Collections:** Ross A. McFarland Collection in Aerospace Medicine and Human Factors Engineering; Aerospace Medical Association Archives; H.T.E. Hertzburg Collection in Anthropometry. **Holdings:** 24,870 books; 39,470 bound periodical volumes; 871 AV programs. **Subscriptions:** 1287 journals and other serials. **Services:** Interlibrary loans; copying; SDI; library open to public with restrictions. **Automated Operations:** Computerized cataloging and serials. **Computerized Information Services:** MEDLINE, DIALOG; Ohio Health Audiovisuals On-line Catalog (internal database). **Networks/Consortia:** Member of Southwest Ohio Council for Higher Education; Greater Midwest Regional Medical Library Network (Region 3); OHIONET; Biomedical Communications Network; Miami Valley Association of Health Sciences Libraries. **Publications:** Ross Armstrong McFarland; Health Sciences Library Update - to users. **Special Catalogs:** Periodical holdings in the Health Sciences Library. **Remarks:** This library contains holdings of the Fels Research Institute - Jennie May Fels Memorial Library. **Staff:** R. Taylor Putney, Coord., Pub.Serv.; Monica Yunag, Coord., Coll.Dev./Access.

WRIGHT (W. Howard) RESEARCH CENTER
See: **Schenectady Chemicals, Inc. - W. Howard Wright Research Center**

★17319★
WRIGLEY (Wm., Jr.) COMPANY - CORPORATE LIBRARY (Bus-Fin)
410 N. Michigan Ave.   Phone: (312) 644-2121
Chicago, IL 60611   Linda Hanrath, Corp.Libn.
Founded: 1978. **Staff:** Prof 1; Other 1. **Subjects:** Business, chewing gum industry. **Special Collections:** Company history (5 VF drawers). **Holdings:** 300 volumes; 12 VF drawers. **Subscriptions:** 100 journals and other serials.

Services: Interlibrary loans; library open to public with restrictions. **Networks/Consortia:** Member of Chicago Library System.

★17320★
WRIGLEY (Wm., Jr.) COMPANY - QUALITY ASSURANCE BRANCH LIBRARY (Sci-Tech)
3535 S. Ashland Ave.　　　　　　　　Phone: (312) 523-4040
Chicago, IL 60609　　　　　　　　Elizabeth R. Cibulskis, Tech.Libn.
Staff: Prof 1. **Subjects:** Quality assurance. **Holdings:** 250 titles. **Services:** Interlibrary loans; copying; SDI; library open to public with restrictions. **Remarks:** The Research & Development Library, located at the same address, staffs and services the Quality Assurance Branch Library.

★17321★
WRIGLEY (Wm., Jr.) COMPANY - RESEARCH & DEVELOPMENT LIBRARY (Sci-Tech)
3535 S. Ashland Ave.　　　　　　　　Phone: (312) 523-4040
Chicago, IL 60609　　　　　　　　Elizabeth R. Cibulskis, Tech.Libn.
Founded: 1972. **Staff:** Prof 1. **Subjects:** Chewing gum, food science and technology, flavors, chemistry, packaging, chemical engineering. **Special Collections:** Chewing gum patent file (19th century to present; 1300 patents). **Holdings:** 1400 books; 310 volumes of unbound periodicals; 7 VF drawers of clippings and brochures; 5 VF drawers of catalogs and trade literature. **Subscriptions:** 130 journals and other serials. **Services:** Interlibrary loans; copying; SDI; library open to public by appointment. **Computerized Information Services:** DIALOG, New England Research Application Center (NERAC). **Publications:** New Patents, monthly; Lab Library Letter, monthly - both for internal distribution only. **Special Catalogs:** Catalogs of chemicals and instruments (card). **Special Indexes:** Subject index to patents; index to equipment manuals (both card).

WROTH MEMORIAL LIBRARY
See: Washington County Hospital

WSAZ-TV NEWS FILM ARCHIVE
See: Marshall University - James E. Morrow Library - Special Collections

★17322★
W2ZI HISTORICAL WIRELESS MUSEUM - HISTORICAL WIRELESS LIBRARY
19 Blackwood Drive
Trenton, NJ 08628
Defunct. Collection disbursed to New England Wireless & Steam Museum, Inc. - Library, Antique Wireless Association, Inc. - Library and Radio Hall of Fame.

★17323★
WUESTHOFF MEMORIAL HOSPITAL - MEDICAL LIBRARY (Med)
110 Longwood Ave.
Box 6　　　　　　　　　　　　Phone: (305) 636-2211
Rockledge, FL 32955　　　　　　　Nancy A. Hanson, Med.Libn.
Staff: Prof 1; Other 2. **Subjects:** Medicine, surgery, nursing, allied health sciences. **Holdings:** 2082 books; 946 bound periodical volumes; 783 audio cassettes; 49 slide carrousels; 4 VF drawers of pamphlets. **Subscriptions:** 137 journals and other serials. **Services:** Interlibrary loans; copying; library open to public with administrative approval.

WUPATKI-SUNSET CRATER LIBRARY
See: U.S. Natl. Park Service

★17324★
WYANDOT COUNTY HISTORICAL SOCIETY - WYANDOT MUSEUM - LIBRARY (Hist)
130 S. 7th St.　　　　　　　　　Phone: (419) 294-3857
Upper Sandusky, OH 43351　　　　　　　Garnett Hudson, Cur.
Subjects: Wyandot Mission, Indian artifacts. **Holdings:** 500 books. **Services:** Library open to public for reference use only.

★17325★
WYANDOTTE COUNTY HISTORICAL SOCIETY AND MUSEUM - HARRY M. TROWBRIDGE RESEARCH LIBRARY (Hist)
631 N. 126th St.　　　　　　　　Phone: (913) 721-1078
Bonner Springs, KS 66012　　　　　　　Stephen J. Allie, Archv.
Founded: 1956. **Staff:** Prof 1; Other 5. **Subjects:** Wyandotte County and Kansas City history, Wyandotte and Delaware Indians. **Special Collections:** Proceedings of Congresses of mid-19th century; bound magazines and school texts of the late 19th century; Early, Conley and Farrow Family Collections, 1763-1960 (30 cubic feet of papers, books, photographs). **Holdings:** 3000 books; 1000 bound periodical volumes; clippings; microfilm. **Subscriptions:** 10 journals and other serials. **Services:** Copying; library open to public.

★17326★
WYANDOTTE COUNTY LAW LIBRARY (Law)
County Courthouse
710 N. 7th St.　　　　　　　　　Phone: (913) 342-4225
Kansas City, KS 66101　　　　　　Rita Hollecker Kancel, Law Libn.
Founded: 1925. **Staff:** 2. **Subjects:** Law. **Special Collections:** Blackstones Commentaries, 1761 (4 volumes). **Holdings:** 17,000 books. **Subscriptions:** 12 journals and other serials. **Services:** Copying; library open to students with recommendation of an attorney.

WYCLIFFE COLLEGE
See: University of Toronto

WYETH LABORATORIES DIVISION
See: American Home Products Corporation

★17327★
WYLE LABORATORIES - TECHNICAL INFORMATION LIBRARY (Sci-Tech)
128 Maryland St.　　　　　　　　Phone: (213) 322-1763
El Segundo, CA 90245　　　　　　　Linda Rogers, Res.Libn.
Staff: Prof 1. **Subjects:** Noise control, acoustics. **Holdings:** 12,000 books; 50 bound periodical volumes. **Subscriptions:** 25 journals and other serials. **Services:** Interlibrary loans; copying; library open to public. **Automated Operations:** Computerized cataloging. **Computerized Information Services:** DIALOG.

★17328★
WYMAN PARK HEALTH SYSTEM, INC. - MEDICAL LIBRARY (Med)
3100 Wyman Park Dr.　　　　　　　Phone: (301) 338-3572
Baltimore, MD 21211-2895　　　　　Laurie A. Conway, Med.Libn.
Founded: 1947. **Staff:** Prof 1; Other 1. **Subjects:** Medicine, nursing, pharmacology, dentistry. **Holdings:** 2172 books; 4757 bound periodical volumes; 200 AV items. **Subscriptions:** 98 journals and other serials. **Services:** Interlibrary loans; library not open to public. **Computerized Information Services:** NLM. **Networks/Consortia:** Member of Baltimore Consortia for Resource Sharing.

WYOMING GEOLOGICAL SURVEY
See: Geological Survey of Wyoming

★17329★
WYOMING HISTORICAL AND GEOLOGICAL SOCIETY - BISHOP MEMORIAL LIBRARY (Hist)
49 S. Franklin St.　　　　　　　　Phone: (717) 823-6244
Wilkes-Barre, PA 18701　　　　　　　Margaret E. Craft, Libn.
Founded: 1858. **Staff:** Prof 3; Other 1. **Subjects:** Wyoming Valley and Pennsylvania history. **Special Collections:** Manuscripts (1750-1950) relating chiefly to the Wilkes-Barre region of the Susquehanna Valley and the Wyoming Valley (1500 cubic feet). **Holdings:** 5000 books; 500 bound periodical volumes; 900 reels of microfilm of Wilkes-Barre newspapers, 1797-1950; 2500 photographs. **Subscriptions:** 15 journals and other serials. **Services:** Copying; library open to public. **Publications:** Susquehanna Company Papers; Proceedings and Collections, irregular; Newsletter. **Special Catalogs:** Unpublished guides to manuscript collections.

★17330★
WYOMING STATE ARCHIVES MUSEUMS & HISTORICAL DEPARTMENT (Hist)
Barrett Bldg.　　　　　　　　　Phone: (307) 777-7518
Cheyenne, WY 82002　　　　　　　Robert D. Bush, Dir.
Staff: 70. **Subjects:** Wyoming and Western history; collection, preservation and interpretation of historical, ethnological and archeological materials. **Holdings:** 6500 volumes; 38,500 reels of microfilm of Wyoming newspapers, 1867 to present, National Archives materials, scrapbooks, manuscripts; maps and plats; documents; letters; ledgers; diaries; research collections; census records; oral histories; folklore; AV materials; government records (territorial and state). **Subscriptions:** 75 journals and other serials. **Services:** Copying; department open to public for reference use only with staff member present. **Publications:** Annals of Wyoming, semiannual; Wyoming History News, 6/year; calendar of Wyoming history; Buffalo Bones, Stories from Wyoming's Past. **Special Indexes:** Indexes to Annals of Wyoming, 1897-1974; Inventory of WPA Manuscripts Collection; Oral History index. **Staff:** Bill Barton, Hd., Hist.Res.Div.; Mike Mayfield, Hd., Musm.Div.; Julia Yelvington, Hd., Archv.Div.

★17331★
WYOMING STATE DEPARTMENT OF ECONOMIC PLANNING AND DEVELOPMENT - LIBRARY (Energy; Plan)
Barrett Bldg.   Phone: (307) 777-6430
Cheyenne, WY 82002   Anne W. McGowan, Lib.Mgr.
Staff: Prof 1. **Subjects:** Energy and economic development, land use planning, water development, Wyoming statistics, mineral development. **Holdings:** 500 books; 5000 documents and reports. **Subscriptions:** 105 journals and other serials. **Services:** Interlibrary loans; copying; SDI; library open to public. **Publications:** New to the Library, bimonthly column in newsletter - free upon request.

★17332★
WYOMING (State) DEPARTMENT OF EDUCATION - INSTRUCTIONAL RESOURCE CENTER (Educ)
Hathaway Bldg.   Phone: (307) 777-6254
Cheyenne, WY 82002   Jack Prince, Coord., Instr.Rsrcs.
Staff: Prof 1; Other 1. **Subjects:** K-12 science, mathematics, social studies, language arts, arts; education. **Special Collections:** ERIC microfiche collection. **Holdings:** 300 books; 100 education newsletters; 20 professional journals; 100 computer software diskettes. **Subscriptions:** 50 journals and other serials. **Services:** Interlibrary loans; center open to residents of Wyoming. **Networks/Consortia:** Member of Special Net. **Publications:** Wyoming Educator (newsletter), monthly - for internal distribution only. **Special Indexes:** ERIC Index to Resources in Education (book).

★17333★
WYOMING STATE DEPARTMENT OF HEALTH & SOCIAL SERVICE - PUBLIC HEALTH FILM LIBRARY (Med; Aud-Vis)
Hathaway Bldg., Rm. 518   Phone: (307) 777-7363
Cheyenne, WY 82002   Cindy G. Stephens, Film Libn.
Staff: Prof 1; Other 1. **Subjects:** Nursing, mental health, childbirth education, venereal diseases, dental health, school health. **Special Collections:** Drivers education; Rape Prevention; Family Violence. **Holdings:** 600 16mm films. **Services:** Library open to public with restrictions. **Special Catalogs:** Film Library Catalog. **Remarks:** Library is part of the Division of Health and Medical Services.

★17334★
WYOMING STATE HOSPITAL - MEDICAL LIBRARY (Med)*
Box 177   Phone: (307) 789-3464
Evanston, WY 82930   Charles D. Bright, Supv.
Staff: Prof 2; Other 2. **Subjects:** Psychiatry, medicine, nursing, social work, psychology. **Holdings:** 2500 books and bound periodical volumes. **Subscriptions:** 160 journals and other serials; 34 newspapers. **Services:** Interlibrary loans; copying; library open to public with restrictions. **Staff:** William L. Matchinski, Inst.Prog.Lib.Spec.

★17335★
WYOMING STATE LAW LIBRARY (Law)
Supreme Court Bldg.   Phone: (307) 777-7509
Cheyenne, WY 82002   Albert W. St.Clair, Law Libn.
Founded: 1897. **Staff:** Prof 3. **Subjects:** Law. **Holdings:** 65,240 volumes. **Subscriptions:** 425 journals and other serials. **Services:** Interlibrary loans; copying; library open to public.

★17336★
WYOMING STATE LIBRARY (Hist)
Supreme Court & State Library Bldg.   Phone: (307) 777-7281
Cheyenne, WY 82002   Wayne H. Johnson, State Libn.
Founded: 1871. **Staff:** Prof 10; Other 21. **Subjects:** Wyoming, Western Americana, North American Indians, library science, cookbooks, art and architecture. **Special Collections:** Large print books (2983). **Holdings:** 151,556 books; 1208 bound periodical volumes; 18 VF drawers of U.S., Wyoming and foreign materials; regional depository for U.S. Government publications (1 million); depository for Wyoming publications (4000). **Subscriptions:** 400 journals and other serials; 54 newspapers. **Services:** Interlibrary loans; copying; library open to public. **Automated Operations:** Computerized cataloging, acquisitions and circulation. **Computerized Information Services:** BRS, DIALOG. **Networks/Consortia:** Member of Bibliographical Center for Research, Rocky Mountain Region, Inc.; Health Sciences Information Network (HSIN); Wyoming Library Network. **Publications:** Annual Report; Annual Report of Wyoming Public Library Service; Outrider (newsletter); Wyoming Library Roundup. **Special Catalogs:** Wyoming Union List of Serials; Large Print catalog; Directory of Wyoming Libraries; Wyoming Library Laws. **Staff:** Mary Sue Streeper, Chf., Bibliog.Serv.; Gwen Rice, Chf., Ref. & ILL; Jerome B. Frobom, Chf., Govt.Pubn.; Corky Walters, Chf., Coll.Dev. & Educ.; Helen E. Higby, Lib.Dev.Off.; Shirley Sedgwick, Chf., Acq.; Donna Jo Best, Chf., Bus.Off.; Linn Rounds, Pub.Info.Off.; Jerry Krois, Chf., Lib. Automation.

★17337★
WYTHEVILLE COMMUNITY COLLEGE - KEGLEY LIBRARY - SPECIAL COLLECTIONS (Hist)
1000 E. Main St.   Phone: (703) 228-5541
Wytheville, VA 24382   Anna Ray Roberts, Coord., Lib.Serv.
Staff: Prof 2; Other 2. **Subjects:** Southwest Virginia history and genealogy. **Holdings:** 500 books; 86 bound periodical volumes; 300 historical maps; 500 oral history interviews; data on 70 local cemeteries; 4 VF drawers; 90 volumes of family history; 100 volumes of local history; 65 reels of microfilm; 1000 newspapers. **Services:** Copying; collections open to public. **Staff:** Timothy D. Smith, Asst.Libn.

X

★17338★
XAVIER SOCIETY FOR THE BLIND - NATIONAL CATHOLIC PRESS AND LIBRARY FOR THE VISUALLY HANDICAPPED (Aud-Vis)
154 E. 23rd St.
New York, NY 10010
Anthony F. LaBau, Dir.
Holdings: 1500 books in braille; 300 books in large type; 550 books on cassette. **Services:** Multiple copies of books and periodicals in all three forms available on free loan. **Publications:** Newsletter, weekly; Catholic Review, monthly (braille, large print and cassette).

★17339★
XAVIER UNIVERSITY OF LOUISIANA - COLLEGE OF PHARMACY - LIBRARY (Med)†
Palmetto & Pine Sts.
Phone: (504) 483-7428
New Orleans, LA 70125
Yvonne C. Hull, Libn.
Staff: Prof 1; Other 1. **Subjects:** Pharmacy, pharmacology, medicinal chemistry, pharmacognosy, clinical pathology, toxicology, drug interaction, public health, history of pharmacy. **Special Collections:** Collection of volumes dealing with medical and pharmaceutical information from the 19th century (150); antique chemical handbooks and pharmacopeias are included. **Holdings:** 4000 books; 2800 bound periodical volumes; 250 audio cassettes; 10 records; 3 films. **Subscriptions:** 100 journals and other serials. **Services:** Interlibrary loans; copying; SDI (limited); library open to public for reference use only. **Networks/Consortia:** Member of New Orleans Consortium. **Remarks:** Library has initiated a Drug Information Center in cooperation with V.A. Hospital of New Orleans.

★17340★
XEROX CORPORATION - DIABLO SYSTEMS, INC. - TECHNICAL LIBRARY (Sci-Tech)
Box 5030, MS 319
Phone: (415) 498-7921
Fremont, CA 94537
Sally Turk, Tech.Info.Spec.
Staff: Prof 1; Other 1. **Subjects:** Engineering, electronics. **Holdings:** 300 books; 80 bound periodical volumes. **Subscriptions:** 90 journals and other serials. **Services:** Interlibrary loans; library not open to public. **Computerized Information Services:** DIALOG, RLIN; internal database. **Networks/Consortia:** Member of CLASS. **Publications:** Library bulletin, bimonthly; yearly holdings list. **Remarks:** The library is a branch of the Xerox Corporation - Palo Alto Research Center.

★17341★
XEROX CORPORATION - EL SEGUNDO TECHNICAL LIBRARY (Comp Sci)
701 S. Aviation Blvd., A3-25
Phone: (213) 536-5222
El Segundo, CA 90245
Marilyn Durkin, Tech.Libn.
Founded: 1968. **Staff:** Prof 2; Other 3. **Subjects:** Computer science, electronics, microelectronics, management, marketing, telecommunications. **Holdings:** 4800 books; 1200 bound periodical volumes; 3000 reports and conference proceedings. **Subscriptions:** 280 journals and other serials; 15 newspapers. **Services:** Interlibrary loans; copying (limited); SDI. **Automated Operations:** Computerized cataloging and serials. **Computerized Information Services:** DIALOG, OCLC, Environmental Health Services, BRS, SDC; internal databases. **Networks/Consortia:** Member of OCLC Pacific Network; CLASS. **Publications:** What's New in the Library, quarterly - to management and professionals; Journal Holdings, annual.

★17342★
XEROX CORPORATION - GINN AND COMPANY LIBRARY (Educ; Publ)
191 Spring St.
Phone: (617) 861-1670
Lexington, MA 02173
Constance J. LeBeau, Libn.
Founded: 1867. **Staff:** Prof 1; Other 1. **Subjects:** English, reading, mathematics, science, social science, education, home economics, testing. **Special Collections:** Complete first editions of every title published by Ginn and Company in all subject areas. **Holdings:** 40,000 books; 9 filing cabinets of pamphlets and dissertations; 1000 microfiche. **Subscriptions:** 200 journals and other serials. **Services:** Library not open to public.

★17343★
XEROX CORPORATION - INFORMATION PRODUCTS DIVISION - LIBRARY SERVICES (Sci-Tech)
1341 W. Mockingbird Ln.
Phone: (214) 689-6027
Dallas, TX 75247
Marjorie A. Henderson, Mgr., Lib.Serv.
Staff: Prof 1; Other 3. **Subjects:** Business machines, electronic typing systems, communication equipment. **Special Collections:** Word processing; document creation centers; facsimile transmission. **Holdings:** 2000 books; 600 reports. **Subscriptions:** 500 journals and other serials; 10 newspapers. **Services:** Interlibrary loans; copying; SDI; library open to public by appointment. **Automated Operations:** Computerized cataloging, acquisitions, serials and circulation. **Computerized Information Services:** DIALOG, SDC, BRS, LEXIS, NewsNet,Inc. **Publications:** Periodicals received; current acquisitions; Keystroke, bimonthly. **Special Catalogs:** Holdings (book catalog). **Formerly:** Its Office Systems Division.

★17344★
XEROX CORPORATION - LAW LIBRARY (Law)
Phone: (203) 329-8700
Stamford, CT 06904
Geraldine McColgan Brown, Hd.Libn.
Founded: 1969. **Staff:** Prof 1; Other 1. **Subjects:** Law, business. **Holdings:** 15,000 volumes; 2 VF drawers of pamphlets; 6 drawers of cassette tapes; 6 drawers of annual reports; 2 drawers of foreign materials; 10 drawers of microfiche. **Subscriptions:** 350 journals and other serials; 10 newspapers. **Services:** Interlibrary loans; copying; library open to public by appointment at discretion of librarian. **Computerized Information Services:** SDC, Dow Jones News/Retrieval, LEXIS, Auto-Cite, DIALOG, Westlaw; internal databases. **Networks/Consortia:** Member of Southwestern Connecticut Library Council.

★17345★
XEROX CORPORATION - PALO ALTO RESEARCH CENTER - TECHNICAL INFORMATION CENTER (Comp Sci; Info Sci)
3333 Coyote Hill Rd.
Phone: (415) 494-4042
Palo Alto, CA 94304
Giuliana A. Lavendel, Mgr.
Founded: 1971. **Staff:** Prof 7; Other 9. **Subjects:** Computer and information science, physics, material science, electronics, psychology, education. **Special Collections:** Information systems and materials. **Holdings:** 12,000 books; 5000 bound periodical volumes; 10,000 external reports; 50,000 Xerox reports; microfilm; microfiche. **Subscriptions:** 600 journals and other serials. **Services:** Interlibrary loans; copying; SDI; center open to public by previous arrangement. **Automated Operations:** Computerized cataloging, serials and circulation. **Computerized Information Services:** DIALOG, SDC, BRS, Dow Jones News/Retrieval, RLIN; internal database. **Networks/Consortia:** Member of South Bay Cooperative Library System (SBCLS); CLASS. **Publications:** Library Bulletin, monthly; holdings list, annual; Update, weekly. **Special Catalogs:** Report list catalog. **Staff:** M. Alice Wilder, Supv., User Network; Katherine S. Jarvis, Tech.Info.Spec.; Maia Pindar, Tech.Info.Spec.

XEROX CORPORATION - R.R. BOWKER COMPANY
See: Bowker (R.R.) Company

★17346★
XEROX CORPORATION - TECHNICAL INFORMATION CENTER (Sci-Tech)
Box 305
Phone: (716) 422-3505
Webster, NY 14580
Michael D. Majcher, Mgr., Tech.Info.Ctr.
Founded: 1960. **Staff:** Prof 17; Other 16. **Subjects:** Xerography, electrophotography, reprography, electronics, chemistry, physics, photography, materials and processes, computer science. **Special Collections:** Corporation Technical Archives. **Holdings:** 35,000 books; 12,500 bound periodical volumes; 30,000 internal reports; 20,000 external reports; 90 VF drawers; 5100 reels of microfilm; 25,000 microfiche; 1.5 million patents. **Subscriptions:** 1800 journals and other serials. **Services:** Interlibrary loans; SDI; Xerox Telecopier Facsimile Service; center open to public by appointment. **Automated Operations:** Computerized cataloging, acquisitions, serials and circulation. **Computerized Information Services:** OCLC, Predicasts, Inc., DIALOG, SDC, BRS, New York Times Information Service, Dow Jones News/Retrieval, NIH-EPA Chemical Information System. **Networks/Consortia:** Member of Rochester Regional Research Library Council (RRRLC). **Publications:** TIC Users Guide; Internal Reports Accession List; Current Awareness Bulletin. **Special Catalogs:** C.O.M. Catalogs; online catalogs. **Remarks:** Includes the holdings of the former Xerox Corporation - Xerox Square Library. **Staff:** T.J. Morey, Mgr., Tech.Serv.; Cecelia E. Rice, Pub.Serv.; F. Bell, Database/Indexing Serv.

★17347★
XEROX CORPORATION - UNIVERSITY MICROFILMS INTERNATIONAL - LIBRARY (Publ)
300 N. Zeeb Rd.
Phone: (313) 761-4700
Ann Arbor, MI 48106
Joseph J. Fitzsimmons, Pres.
Founded: 1938. **Staff:** Prof 5. **Subjects:** Early English printed books, incunabula, early American printed books, early English and American periodicals, out-of-print books. **Holdings:** 500,000 dissertations; 113,000 out-of-print books; 13,000 periodicals on microfilm. **Services:** Library not open to public. **Computerized Information Services:** DATRIX (doctoral research information; internal database). **Publications:** UMI Newsletter; Serials in Microform Catalog; Series Reel Guides and Indexes; Special Bibliographies; Dissertation Abstracts International; Masters Abstracts;

Monograph Abstracts; American Doctoral Dissertations. **Special Catalogs:** Books on Demand Catalog. **Special Indexes:** Comprehensive Dissertation Index. **Staff:** Anita Werling, Mgr., Coll.Dev.

XEROX CORPORATION - VERSATEC
See: Versatec

★17348★

XEROX CORPORATION - XEROX EDUCATION PUBLICATIONS - LIBRARY (Educ)
245 Long Hill Rd.   Phone: (203) 347-7251
Middletown, CT 06457   Harriet S. Osburn, Hd.Libn.
Staff: Prof 4. **Subjects:** Education, current affairs, social studies, language arts, reading. **Holdings:** 15,750 books; 137 drawers of news releases, clippings, pamphlets; 2200 microforms; 137 VF drawers of photographs and illustrations; 2 VF drawers of cartoons; 500 volumes of curriculum guides. **Subscriptions:** 400 journals and other serials; 10 newspapers. **Services:** Library open to public for reference use only. **Computerized Information Services:** NEXIS. **Networks/Consortia:** Member of Southern Connecticut Library Council (SCLC). **Staff:** Robert Cumming, Asst.Libn.; Maryellen Renn, Photograph Libn.; Gloria Denert, Photograph Libn.

★17349★

XEROX CORPORATION - XEROX SQUARE LIBRARY
Xerox Sq. 105
Rochester, NY 14644
Defunct. Holdings absorbed by Xerox Corporation - Technical Information Center.

XEROX ELECTRO-OPTICAL SYSTEMS
See: Xerox Special Information Systems

★17350★

XEROX RESEARCH CENTRE OF CANADA - TECHNICAL INFORMATION CENTRE (Sci-Tech)
2660 Speakman Dr.   Phone: (416) 823-7091
Mississauga, ON, Canada L5K 2L1   Betty A. Bassett, Mgr., Tech.Info.Ctr.
Founded: 1974. **Staff:** Prof 1; Other 2. **Subjects:** Electrochemistry, polymer chemistry, colloid chemistry, surface science, electrophotography, xerography, control engineering, paper science, materials science. **Special Collections:** Internal technical reports (60,000). **Holdings:** 10,000 books; 8000 bound periodical volumes; 2000 reels of microfilm; 65,000 microfiche. **Subscriptions:** 500 journals and other serials; 8 newspapers. **Services:** Interlibrary loans; copying; SDI; center open to public by appointment. **Automated Operations:** Computerized cataloging and current awareness service. **Computerized Information Services:** DIALOG, SDC, BRS, CAS Online, Info Globe, CAN/OLE, Occupational Health Services, Inc., Pergamon InfoLine Ltd., UTLAS. **Networks/Consortia:** Member of Sheridan Park Association. **Publications:** TIC Update, monthly; Serials Holdings List, annual. **Special Catalogs:** Library Catalog (microfiche), quarterly.

★17351★

XEROX SPECIAL INFORMATION SYSTEMS - TECHNICAL LIBRARY (Sci-Tech; Comp Sci)
250 N. Halstead St., M/S 1369   Phone: (818) 351-2351
Pasadena, CA 91109   Frances A. Piatt, Libn.
Founded: 1983. **Staff:** Prof 1. **Subjects:** Optics, lasers, computers and computer languages. **Holdings:** 1500 books; 500 bound periodical volumes. **Subscriptions:** 150 journals and other serials. **Services:** Interlibrary loans; library not open to public. **Automated Operations:** Computerized circulation and serials. **Computerized Information Services:** DIALOG, BRS. **Formerly:** Xerox Electro-Optical Systems.

Y

★17352★
YADKIN COUNTY HISTORICAL SOCIETY - LIBRARY (Hist)
Yadkin County Public Library
E. Main St.
Box 1250   Phone: (919) 679-8792
Yadkinville, NC 27055   Mildred Matthew, Pres.
Founded: 1972. **Subjects:** Local and North Carolina history. **Special Collections:** Family genealogies of Surry and Yadkin counties. **Holdings:** 750 volumes; 14 boxes of clippings and manuscripts; 5 reels of microfilmed census data. **Services:** Copying; library open to public for reference use only. **Automated Operations:** Computerized cataloging and acquisitions. **Special Catalogs:** Catalog of newspaper clippings, family genealogies (card).

★17353★
YAKIMA COUNTY LAW LIBRARY (Law)
Yakima County Court House   Phone: (509) 457-5452
Yakima, WA 98901   Linda Von Essen, Law Libn.
Founded: 1932. **Staff:** Prof 1. **Subjects:** Law. **Holdings:** 16,500 volumes. **Services:** Interlibrary loans; copying; library open to public with restrictions. **Automated Operations:** Computerized acquisitions.

★17354★
YAKIMA VALLEY GENEALOGICAL SOCIETY - LIBRARY (Hist)
Box 445   Phone: (509) 248-1328
Yakima, WA 98907   Ellen Brzoska, Libn.
Founded: 1967. **Staff:** Prof 2; Other 18. **Subjects:** Genealogy, family history, Yakima County and central Washington history. **Special Collections:** Abstracts from old bound newspapers, 1884-1925; Daughters of the American Revolution, Daughters of Washington Pioneers collections. **Holdings:** 2000 volumes; 3000 bound periodical volumes; 100,000 cards of Yakima County cemetery file; 50,000 cards of Klickitat County, Kittitas County cemetery files; 8 VF drawers of reports, clippings, pamphlets and documents; 200 reels of microfilm and cassette tapes; 100 family history interview sheets. **Subscriptions:** 200 journals and other serials. **Services:** Interlibrary loans; copying; library open to public for reference use only. **Publications:** Yakima Valley Genealogical Society Bulletin, quarterly. **Remarks:** The library is located at N. 3rd and East B St., Yakima, WA. **Staff:** Eugenia Flickinger, Libn.

★17355★
YAKIMA VALLEY MUSEUM AND HISTORICAL ASSOCIATION - ARCHIVES (Hist)
2105 Tieton Dr.   Phone: (509) 248-0747
Yakima, WA 98902   Frances A. Hare, Archv.
Subjects: Area history and development, Yakima Indians, pioneers, irrigation history. **Special Collections:** Apple and pear box labels; William O. Douglas Collection (1500 books; slides; films; photographs). **Holdings:** 3316 books; 4000 photographs; clipping file; documents; manuscripts. **Services:** Copying; archives open to public for reference use only. **Remarks:** Includes the holdings of the Gannon Museum of Wagons.

YALE CENTER FOR BRITISH ART
See: Yale University

★17356★
YALE CLUB OF NEW YORK CITY - LIBRARY (Hum)
50 Vanderbilt Ave.   Phone: (212) 661-2070
New York, NY 10017   David T. Dale, Libn.
Founded: 1897. **Staff:** Prof 1; Other 1. **Subjects:** Literature, history, travel, biography, social sciences, art, music. **Special Collections:** Yale memorabilia and publications. **Holdings:** 45,000 volumes. **Subscriptions:** 100 journals and other serials. **Services:** Library not open to public.

YALE COLLECTION OF HISTORICAL SOUND RECORDINGS
See: Yale University

★17357★
YALE UNIVERSITY - AMERICAN ORIENTAL SOCIETY LIBRARY (Area-Ethnic)
Sterling Memorial Library, Rm. 329   Phone: (203) 436-1040
New Haven, CT 06520   Mary Ann T. Itoga, Libn.
Founded: 1842. **Staff:** Prof 1. **Subjects:** Oriental civilizations - language, literature, history, culture. **Holdings:** 21,179 volumes. **Subscriptions:** 115 journals and other serials. **Services:** Collection open only to members of the society, Yale University personnel and visiting scholars on application.

Networks/Consortia: Member of RLG; CRL; CTUW Project.

★17358★
YALE UNIVERSITY - ANTHROPOLOGY LIBRARY (Sci-Tech)
Kline Science Library
Box 6666   Phone: (203) 436-0874
New Haven, CT 06511   Richard J. Dionne, Libn.
Staff: 1. **Subjects:** Anthropology. **Holdings:** 7600 books; 8400 bound periodical volumes. **Subscriptions:** 180 journals and other serials. **Services:** Interlibrary loans; copying; library open to public with permission. **Networks/Consortia:** Member of RLG; CRL; CTUW Project.

★17359★
YALE UNIVERSITY - ART AND ARCHITECTURE LIBRARY (Art)
Art & Architecture Bldg.
Yale Sta., Box 1605A   Phone: (203) 436-2055
New Haven, CT 06520   Nancy S. Lambert, Libn.
Staff: Prof 3; Other 8. **Subjects:** History of art, architecture, city planning, painting, sculpture, graphic arts. **Special Collections:** Faber Birren Collection on color (books; photographs). **Holdings:** 80,000 volumes; 340 boxes of exhibition catalogs; 55 VF drawers of pamphlets; 30 VF drawers of city planning material; 251,000 slides; 162,000 photographs. **Subscriptions:** 450 journals and other serials. **Services:** Interlibrary loans; copying (both limited); library open to public for reference use only; Special Borrower's Card for which there is a fee. **Networks/Consortia:** Member of RLG; CRL; CTUW Project. **Staff:** Helen Chillman, Slide Libn.

★17360★
YALE UNIVERSITY - ARTS OF THE BOOK COLLECTION (Hum)
Sterling Memorial Library   Phone: (203) 436-2200
New Haven, CT 06520   Gay Walker, Cur.
Founded: 1967. **Staff:** Prof 1; Other 2. **Subjects:** Typography, book illustration and design, calligraphy, bookbinding, private presses and fine printing. **Special Collections:** Caricature; trade cards; Western Americana prints; engraved views of Vienna; historic printing material including the Bibliographical Press, containing four presses and an extensive collection of printing types; engraved woodblocks; special archives of Fritz Kredel, Fritz Eichenberg and Carl P. Rollins. **Holdings:** 12,000 books; 9000 prints; type specimens; archive of student printing, including masters' theses from School of Graphic Design at Yale. **Services:** Interlibrary loans; copying; collection open to public. **Automated Operations:** Computerized cataloging and acquisitions. **Networks/Consortia:** Member of RLG; Association of Research Libraries (ARL); CTUW Project.

★17361★
YALE UNIVERSITY - BABYLONIAN COLLECTION (Hist)
Sterling Memorial Library
120 High St.   Phone: (203) 432-4725
New Haven, CT 06520   William W. Hallo, Cur.
Founded: 1912. **Staff:** Prof 5. **Subjects:** Assyriology; cuneiform; Sumerian, Akkadian, Hittite, Mesopotamian literature, archeology and history; Semitics. **Special Collections:** Cuneiform texts from the collections of E.I. David, E.J. Banks, J.P. Morgan, Edwin T. Newell, General Theological Seminary. **Holdings:** 6000 books; 1000 bound periodical volumes; 1000 reprints; 30,000 cuneiform tablets and inscriptions; 3000 cylinder seals and stamp seals; 1000 other Ancient Near Eastern artifacts. **Subscriptions:** 25 journals and other serials. **Services:** Library open to public upon application to the curator. **Networks/Consortia:** Member of RLG; CRL; CTUW Project. **Publications:** Yale Oriental Series - Babylonian Texts; Yale Oriental Series - Researches; Babylonian Inscriptions in the Collection of James B. Nies, Yale University; Goucher College Cuneiform Inscriptions; Babylonian Records in the Library of J. Pierpont Morgan; Yale Near Eastern Researches. **Remarks:** This library includes "the largest collection of cuneiform tablets and cylinder seals in the U.S.A." **Staff:** Gary Beckman, Asst.Cur.; Harvey Weiss, Archeology Adv.; Ulla Kasten, Musm.Ed.; B.R. Foster, Assyriologist.

★17362★
YALE UNIVERSITY - BEINECKE RARE BOOK AND MANUSCRIPT LIBRARY (Rare Book; Hist)
Wall & High Sts.   Phone: (203) 436-8438
New Haven, CT 06520   Ralph Franklin, Dir.
Founded: 1963. **Staff:** Prof 9; Other 27. **Subjects:** Alchemy and the occult; Afro-American arts and letters; American, British and European history and literature; British economic tracts; Congregationalism; exploration and travel; French illustrated books; German literature; Greek and Latin literature; history of education; history of printing; incunabula; Judaica; Latin America; Native American History and Languages; Near Eastern manuscripts; newspapers (early British and American); ornithology; Oxford; papyri; playing cards; pre-1600 manuscripts; Russian books and manuscripts; sporting books; Theatre

Guild; theology; Tibet; Western Americana. **Special Collections:** Leonie Adams, Aldus Manutius, Matthew Arnold, Asch, Joel Barlow, Barrie, Baskerville, Baskin, William Beckford, S.V. Benet, W.R. Benet, Boccaccio, Boswell, Hermann Broch, Browning, Buchan, Burney, Byron, Cabell, Carlyle, Rachel Carson, Sir Winston Churchill, Barrett Clark, Coleridge, Conrad, Cooper, Walter Crane, Defoe, Dickens, Hilda Doolittle, Norman Douglas, Muriel Draper, Katherine Dreier, Dryden, Jonathan Edwards, George Eliot, Maria Edgeworth, Arthur Davison Ficke, Fielding, Vardis Fisher, John Gould Fletcher, Paul Leicester Ford, Garrick, Jean Giono, Gissing, Goethe, Herman Hagedorn, Hutchins and Neith Boyce Hapgood, Hardy, Marsden Hartley, John Hersey, Hogg, Paul Horgan, Langston Hughes, Joseph Ireland, Washington Irving, Robinson Jeffers, James Weldon Johnson, Samuel Johnson, Joyce, Kafka, Kipling, Landor, D.H. Lawrence, Sinclair Lewis, Mabel Luhan, George Macdonald, William McFee, MacLeish, Norman MacLeod, Thomas Mann, F.T. Marinetti, Marquand, Masefield, Mencken, Meredith, Milton, George Moore, Sir Thomas More, Robert Nathan, O'Neill, James Gates Percival, Pope, Ezra Pound, James Purdy, Dorothy Richardson, Samuel Richardson, Rilke, Bruce Rogers, Ruskin, Shakespeare, Sheridan, Spenser, Gertrude Stein, Leo Stein, Stevenson, Stieglitz, Ezra Stiles, Swinburne, Tennyson, Thackeray, Tocqueville, Toklas, Trollope, Van Vechten, Walton, Robert Penn Warren, Rebecca West, Edith Wharton, Whitman, Wilder, William Carlos Williams, Edmund Wilson, Kurt Wolff, Wordsworth, Richard Wright, Eleanor Wylie. **Holdings:** 500,000 books, pamphlets and periodical volumes; 2 million manuscripts. **Services:** Copying; library open to public. **Networks/Consortia:** Member of RLG; CRL; CTUW Project. **Staff:** Marjorie G. Wynne, Res.Libn.; George Miles, Cur./W.Amer.; Stephen Parks, Cur./Osborn Coll./Mss.; Christa Sammons, Cur./German Coll.; David E. Schoonover, Cur./Amer.Lit.; Patricia Howell, Pub.Serv.Libn.; Suzanne Rutter, Tech.Serv.Libn.

★17363★

YALE UNIVERSITY - BENJAMIN FRANKLIN COLLECTION (Hist)
Sterling Memorial Library, Rm. 230
Yale Sta., Box 1603A
New Haven, CT 06520   Phone: (203) 436-8646
           Dorothy W. Bridgwater, Asst.Libn.
Founded: 1935. **Subjects:** Books, manuscripts, portraits, medals and other apparatus relating to Benjamin Franklin and the American Revolution. **Holdings:** Figures not available. **Subscriptions:** 10 journals and other serials. **Services:** Copying; collection open to public for reference use only. **Networks/Consortia:** Member of RLG; CRL; CTUW Project. **Special Catalogs:** Catalog of printed material and manuscripts in the collection (card).

★17364★

YALE UNIVERSITY - CLASSICS LIBRARY (Hum)
Phelps Hall, 344 College St.   Phone: (203) 436-1130
New Haven, CT 06520   Carla M. Lukas, Libn.
Founded: 1892. **Staff:** Prof 1. **Subjects:** Greek and Latin classical literature, ancient history, art, archeology, papyrology. **Holdings:** 19,642 volumes. **Subscriptions:** 138 journals and other serials. **Services:** Interlibrary loans; copying; library open to public by permission. **Networks/Consortia:** Member of RLG; CRL; CTUW Project.

★17365★

YALE UNIVERSITY - COLLECTION OF THE LITERATURE OF THE AMERICAN MUSICAL THEATRE (Theater; Mus)
Sterling Memorial Library, Rm. 226   Phone: (203) 436-1822
New Haven, CT 06520   Richard Warren, Jr., Cur.
Founded: 1954. **Subjects:** Musical shows produced on Broadway for profit. **Holdings:** Books; theater programs; pamphlets and clippings; phonograph records; sheet music and scores. **Services:** Collection open to public for reference use only by appointment. **Networks/Consortia:** Member of RLG; CRL; CTUW Project.

★17366★

YALE UNIVERSITY - COLLECTION OF MUSICAL INSTRUMENTS - LIBRARY (Mus)
15 Hillhouse Ave.
Box 2117   Phone: (203) 436-4935
New Haven, CT 06520   Richard Rephann, Dir.
Founded: 1900. **Staff:** 3. **Subjects:** Organology. **Holdings:** 200 books; 200 pamphlets; 500 files in archives on each instrument in collection. **Services:** Library open to public by appointment. **Networks/Consortia:** Member of RLG; CRL; CTUW Project. **Publications:** Checklist, catalog data sheets, phonograph recording. **Special Indexes:** Checklist of the Yale University Collection of Musical Instruments. **Remarks:** The books in the library of the collection are officially part of the J.H. Jackson Music Library of Yale University but are permanently located at the collection.

★17367★

YALE UNIVERSITY - COWLES FOUNDATION FOR RESEARCH IN ECONOMICS - LIBRARY (Bus-Fin)
30 Hillhouse Ave.   Phone: (203) 436-0249
New Haven, CT 06520   Karlee Gifford, Libn.
Founded: 1932. **Staff:** Prof 1. **Subjects:** Economic theory, mathematical econometrics, macroeconomic theory, microeconomic theory, monetary theory, game theory. **Holdings:** 6000 books; 2500 bound periodical volumes; 3000 reprints and unpublished articles; 600 Cowles Foundation papers. **Subscriptions:** 160 journals and other serials. **Services:** Interlibrary loans; copying; permission to use library may be requested from director. **Networks/Consortia:** Member of RLG; CRL; CTUW Project.

★17368★

YALE UNIVERSITY - DIVINITY SCHOOL LIBRARY (Rel-Theol)
409 Prospect St.   Phone: (203) 436-8440
New Haven, CT 06510   Stephen L. Peterson, Divinity Libn.
Founded: 1932. **Staff:** Prof 6; Other 13. **Subjects:** History of doctrine, biblical studies, missions, theology. **Special Collections:** Historical Library of Missions (90,000 items); archives of the Student Volunteer Movement (230 linear feet); archives of the World Student Christian Federation (225 linear feet); papers of American missionaries in China (400 linear feet); papers of John R. Mott (100 linear feet); missions pamphlet collection (225 linear feet); Historical Sermons Collection (75 linear feet); United Board for Christian Higher Education in Asia (205 linear feet); Council for World Mission (23,000 microfiche); Methodist Missionary Society (8700 microfiche); American Home Missionary Society (385 reels of microfilm); International Missionary Council/Conference of British Missionary Societies (2500 microfiche). **Holdings:** 330,000 books and bound periodical volumes; 250 linear feet of other personal papers and archives collections. **Subscriptions:** 1200 journals and other serials. **Services:** Interlibrary loans; copying; library open to public on a fee basis. **Automated Operations:** Computerized cataloging. **Networks/Consortia:** Member of RLG; CRL; CTUW Project. **Staff:** John Bollier, Asst.Libn.; Viola Day Mullin, Hd., Tech.Serv.; Paul Stuehrenberg, Cat.Libn.; Rolfe Gjellstad, Ser.Libn.; Martha Smalley, Archv.; Micheline Nilsen, Circ.Supv./ILL.

★17369★

YALE UNIVERSITY - EAST ASIAN COLLECTION (Area-Ethnic)
Sterling Memorial Library   Phone: (203) 436-4810
New Haven, CT 06520   Hideo Kaneko, Cur.
Staff: Prof 7; Other 10. **Subjects:** East Asian languages and literature, history, art, politics, government, economics, law, social conditions, religion, education, humanities and social sciences. **Holdings:** 233,310 volumes in Chinese; 134,183 volumes in Japanese; 4520 volumes in Korean; 4877 reels of microfilm. **Services:** Interlibrary loans; copying; collection open to qualified outside users. **Networks/Consortia:** Member of RLG; CRL; CTUW Project. **Remarks:** Includes holdings of the Sinological Seminar Library. **Staff:** Antony Marr, Assoc.Cur.; Boksoon Hahn, Hd.Cat.Libn.; Mitsuko Ichinose, Prin.Cat./Ref.Libn.; Hsiao-Chiang Chen, Prin.Cat.Libn.; Sekiko McDonald, Prin.Cat.Libn.; Huei-Ju Chang, Sr.Cat.Libn.

★17370★

YALE UNIVERSITY - ECONOMIC GROWTH CENTER COLLECTION (Soc Sci)
140 Prospect St.   Phone: (203) 436-3412
New Haven, CT 06520   Billie I. Salter, Libn. for Social Sci.
Founded: 1961. **Staff:** Prof 3; Other 5. **Subjects:** Economic data sources and surveys focusing primarily on the developing countries. **Holdings:** 47,636 books and bound periodical volumes. **Subscriptions:** 3765 journals and other serials. **Services:** Interlibrary loans; copying; collection open to public for reference use only, circulation limited to card holders. **Computerized Information Services:** RLIN. **Networks/Consortia:** Member of RLG; CRL; CTUW Project. **Special Catalogs:** Shelf list arranged by country and subdivided by subject. **Remarks:** The library became a special collection within the Social Science Library in 1977. **Staff:** Edita R. Baradi, Acq.Libn.; Nenita A. Fernandez, Cat.Libn.

★17371★

YALE UNIVERSITY - ELIZABETHAN CLUB COLLECTION (Hum)
459 College St.   Phone: (203) 436-8535
New Haven, CT 06511   Stephen R. Parks, Libn.
Founded: 1911. **Subjects:** Elizabethan drama, 16th and 17th century. **Holdings:** 300 volumes, before 1700. **Services:** Copying; collection open to public by arrangement. **Networks/Consortia:** Member of RLG; CRL; CTUW Project. **Publications:** Newsletter, annual - to members. **Remarks:** Readers may consult Elizabethan Club volumes, by arrangement, in the Beinecke Library.

★17372★

YALE UNIVERSITY - ENGINEERING AND APPLIED SCIENCE LIBRARY (Sci-Tech; Comp Sci)
Becton Ctr., 15 Prospect St.   Phone: (203) 432-4539
New Haven, CT 06520   Elizabeth Hayes, Hd.
Founded: 1969. **Staff:** 2. **Subjects:** Applied sciences, engineering, computer sciences. **Holdings:** 32,000 books and bound periodical volumes. **Subscriptions:** 455 journals and other serials. **Services:** Interlibrary loans; copying; library open to qualified users. **Networks/Consortia:** Member of RLG; CRL; CTUW Project.

★17373★

YALE UNIVERSITY - FORESTRY LIBRARY (Env-Cons)†
205 Prospect St.
22 Sage Hall   Phone: (203) 436-0577
New Haven, CT 06511   Joseph A. Miller, Libn.
Founded: 1900. **Staff:** Prof 1; Other 3. **Subjects:** Forestry, environmental studies, ecology, biology, natural resources management, conservation, wildlife, land use, planning. **Holdings:** 125,000 books and bound periodical volumes, including government documents and reports; 175 newsletter titles; 800 dissertations; 300 maps; 800 microforms. **Subscriptions:** 900 journals and other serials. **Services:** Interlibrary loans; copying; library open to public for reference use only. **Networks/Consortia:** Member of RLG; CRL; CTUW Project. **Special Catalogs:** Dictionary Catalog, 12 volumes, published in 1962. **Also Known As:** Henry S. Graves Memorial Library.

★17374★

YALE UNIVERSITY - GEOLOGY LIBRARY (Sci-Tech)
Box 6666   Phone: (203) 436-2480
New Haven, CT 06511   Harry D. Scammell, Libn.
Staff: Prof 1; Other 2. **Subjects:** Geology, paleontology, oceanography, meteorology. **Holdings:** 97,000 volumes; 166,593 maps, including U.S. Geological Survey geologic and topographic series; 14,000 reprints. **Subscriptions:** 2509 journals and other serials. **Services:** Interlibrary loans; copying; library open to public with permission. **Networks/Consortia:** Member of RLG; CRL; CTUW Project.

★17375★

YALE UNIVERSITY - INDOLOGICAL AND LINGUISTIC SEMINAR - LIBRARY (Hum)
302 Hall of Graduate Studies
320 York St.   Phone: (203) 436-1862
New Haven, CT 06520   Prof. Stanley Insler, Chm.
Subjects: Indology, descriptive linguistics, historical linguistics. **Special Collections:** Bequest of Franklin Edgerton; Edward E. Salisbury, Professor of Sanskrit. **Holdings:** 5000 books; 500 bound periodical volumes; 500 offprints. **Services:** Library open to public by appointment. **Networks/Consortia:** Member of RLG; CRL; CTUW Project.

★17376★

YALE UNIVERSITY - JOHN HERRICK JACKSON MUSIC LIBRARY (Mus)
98 Wall St.   Phone: (203) 436-8240
New Haven, CT 06520   Harold E. Samuel, Libn.
Founded: 1917. **Staff:** Prof 4; Other 10. **Subjects:** Music. **Special Collections:** Complete manuscripts and papers of Richard Donovan, Lehman Engel, Henry Gilbert, Thomas de Hartmann, Charles E. Ives, J. Rosamond Johnson, Armin Loos, Leo Ornstein, Horatio Parker, Quincy Porter, Carl Ruggles, David Stanley Smith, Alec Templeton; Virgil Thomson; Kurt Weill; Lowell Mason Collection of Church Music (10,000 items); Marc Pincherle Collection of musical iconography (1200 items). **Holdings:** 100,000 volumes; 20,000 pieces of sheet music; 14,000 phonograph records; microfilm. **Subscriptions:** 1000 journals and other serials. **Services:** Interlibrary loans; copying; library open to public for reference use only. **Networks/Consortia:** Member of RLG; CRL; CTUW Project. **Staff:** Victor Cardell, Asst.Libn.; Helen Bartlett, Hd.Cat.Monica Slomski, Cat.

★17377★

YALE UNIVERSITY - KLINE SCIENCE LIBRARY (Sci-Tech)
Kline Biology Tower, Rm. C-8   Phone: (203) 436-3710
New Haven, CT 06520   Richard J. Dionne, Sci.Libn.
Staff: Prof 3; Other 10. **Subjects:** Biological sciences, physics, chemistry, conservation, oceanography. **Special Collections:** Evans Collection (bryology and lichenology). **Holdings:** 175,000 books and bound periodical volumes; 193,256 hard copies, microfiche and microcards in the AEC depository. **Subscriptions:** 1659 journals and other serials. **Services:** Interlibrary loans; copying; SDI; library open to qualified users with permission of librarian. **Computerized Information Services:** Online systems. **Networks/Consortia:** Member of RLG; CRL; CTUW Project. **Staff:** Elizabeth E. Ferguson, Ref.Libn.; Corrine B. Coe, Acq.Libn.

★17378★

YALE UNIVERSITY - LAW LIBRARY (Law)
127 Wall St.   Phone: (203) 436-2215
New Haven, CT 06520   Morris L. Cohen, Libn.
Staff: Prof 14; Other 26. **Subjects:** Anglo-American law, foreign and comparative law, international law. **Special Collections:** Blackstone Collection. **Holdings:** 660,000 volumes. **Subscriptions:** 9000 journals and other serials. **Services:** Interlibrary loans; copying; library open to qualified users. **Automated Operations:** Computerized cataloging. **Computerized Information Services:** LEXIS, Westlaw. **Networks/Consortia:** Member of RLG; New England Law Library Consortium (NELLC); CRL; CTUW Project. **Staff:** Gene Coakley, Faculty Serv.Libn.Carl Lamers, Foreign Law Libn.; Robert E. Brooks, Hd.Ref.Libn.; Nelly E. Ermili, Hd., Acq.Dept.; Frances B. Woods, Hd., Cat.Dept.; J. Michael Hughes, Asst.Ref.Libn.; Mary Jane Kelsey, Adm.Serv.Libn.; Margaret Chisholm, Pub.Serv.Libn.; Martha Clark, Circ.Libn.

★17379★

YALE UNIVERSITY - LEWIS WALPOLE LIBRARY (Hist)
154 Main St.   Phone: (203) 677-2140
Farmington, CT 06032   Catherine Jestin, Libn.
Staff: Prof 2; Other 2. **Subjects:** Horace Walpole, Earl of Orford; 18th century caricatures and cartoons; 18th century English history; Wilmarth Sheldon Lewis; Strawberry Hill and Twickenham; William Mason; Thomas Gray; Thomas Chatterton. **Special Collections:** Horace Walpole's Library, 1717-1797 (1255 volumes; 1500 manuscripts); Strawberry Hill Press (500 volumes); 18th century satiric prints (8339); Sir Charles Hanbury Williams papers, 1708-1759 (93 volumes); Edward Weston papers, 1703-1770 (25 volumes); Keppel Family papers (9 volumes); Henry Seymour Conway papers, 1721-1795 (14 volumes). **Holdings:** 26,190 books; 1810 bound periodical volumes; 330 bound manuscripts; 35 linear feet of manuscripts; 37,000 prints, drawings and paintings. **Subscriptions:** 18 journals and other serials. **Services:** Copying; library open to scholars by appointment. **Automated Operations:** Computerized cataloging. **Networks/Consortia:** Member of RLG. **Staff:** Joan Sussler, Cur.

★17380★

YALE UNIVERSITY - MANUSCRIPTS AND ARCHIVES (Hist)
Sterling Memorial Library   Phone: (203) 432-4695
New Haven, CT 06520   Katharine Morton, Hd.Libn.
Founded: 1701. **Staff:** Prof 14; Other 9. **Subjects:** Yale history; Connecticut history; religion; World War I and II diplomacy; 19th century science and technology; Progressive Period; 20th century journalism, law, and political writing. **Special Collections:** Papers of Chester Bowles, Henry L. Stimson, Edward M. House, Jerome Frank, Walter Lippmann, Benjamin Silliman, John Lindsay and Dwight Macdonald; Crawford Theater Collection (modern drama); Contemporary Medical Care and Health Policy Collection; University Archives. **Holdings:** 31,600 books; 51,500 bound periodical volumes; 175,000 photographs; 27,861 reels of microfilm; 25,000 linear feet of manuscripts. **Services:** Copying; archives open to public. **Special Catalogs:** Card catalog for manuscripts. **Special Indexes:** Registers or indexes to manuscript collections. **Staff:** Judith A. Schiff, Chf.Res.Archv.; Patricia Stark, Ref.Archv.; John Dojka, Univ.Archv.

★17381★

YALE UNIVERSITY - MAP COLLECTION (Geog-Map)
Sterling Memorial Library, Map Rm.   Phone: (203) 436-8638
New Haven, CT 06520   Barbara B. McCorkle, Cur. of Maps
Founded: 1932. **Staff:** Prof 1; Other 1. **Subjects:** Historical map collection covering the entire world. **Special Collections:** E.L. Stevenson Collection (glass plates of early maps); Horace Brown Collection of early New England maps; Karpinski-Thorne Collection of rare and early atlases. **Holdings:** 2500 atlases; 185,000 maps. **Services:** Copying; collection open to public for reference use only. **Networks/Consortia:** Member of RLG; CRL; CTUW Project. **Staff:** Margit E. Kaye, Sr.Lib.Spec.

★17382★

YALE UNIVERSITY - MATHEMATICS LIBRARY (Sci-Tech)
12 Hillhouse Ave.
Yale Sta., Box 2155   Phone: (203) 436-0725
New Haven, CT 06520   Paul J. Lukasiewicz, Mathematics Libn.
Staff: 1. **Subjects:** Pure mathematics. **Holdings:** 12,400 books; 12,740 bound periodical volumes. **Subscriptions:** 306 journals and other serials. **Services:** Interlibrary loans; library open to public for reference use only. **Networks/Consortia:** Member of RLG; CRL; CTUW Project.

★17383★

YALE UNIVERSITY - MEDICAL LIBRARY (Med)
333 Cedar St.   Phone: (203) 785-5354
New Haven, CT 06510   Bella Z. Berson, Act.Med.Libn.
Founded: 1814. **Staff:** Prof 10; Other 27. **Subjects:** Medicine, nursing, public health, allied health sciences. **Special Collections:** History of medicine (60,000 volumes); George Milton Smith Collection of early ichthyology (700 volumes); Edward Clark Streeter Collection of early weights and measures (350 volumes and 3000 artifacts); Clement C. Fry Collection of medical prints and drawings (1400 items); medical and scientific incunabula. **Holdings:** 328,025 volumes; 150 manuscript codices before 1600; 120,000 foreign medical theses. **Subscriptions:** 2565 journals and other serials. **Services:** Interlibrary loans; copying; SDI; library open to public with restrictions. **Computerized Information Services:** NLM, DIALOG, RLIN, BRS. **Networks/ Consortia:** Member of RLG; CRL; CTUW Project; Greater Northeastern Regional Medical Library Program. **Publications:** Users' Guide, irregular, Subject Bibliography, irregular. **Staff:** Ferenc A. Gyorgyey, Med.Hist.Libn.; R. Kenny Fryer, Hd., Ref.Libn.; Alicja Krenta, Hd.Acq.Libn.; Doris Sosensky, Hd., Circ.

★17384★

YALE UNIVERSITY - OBSERVATORY LIBRARY (Sci-Tech)
260 Whitney Ave., J.W. Gibbs Laboratory
Box 6666   Phone: (203) 436-3460
New Haven, CT 06511   Ann Dallavalle, Lib.Serv.Asst.
Founded: 1871. **Staff:** 3. **Subjects:** Astronomy, astrophysics, celestial mechanics, physics, mathematics. **Special Collections:** Extensive collection of domestic and foreign observatory publications. **Holdings:** 9000 books; 6000 bound periodical volumes; 800 shelf feet of observatory reprints. **Subscriptions:** 120 journals and other serials. **Services:** Interlibrary loans; copying; library open to public for reference use only. **Networks/Consortia:** Member of RLG; CRL; CTUW Project. **Publications:** Transactions of Yale University Observatory; Bright Star Catalog, 4th edition; Supplement to the Bright Star Catalog, 1983; Tables of the Motion of the Moon; General Catalog of Trigonometric Stellar Parallaxes and supplement 1963; The Evolution of Galaxies and Stellar Populations, 1977. **Staff:** Mary Albee, Bus.Mgr.

★17385★

YALE UNIVERSITY - ORNITHOLOGY LIBRARY (Sci-Tech)
310 Bingham Lab., Peabody Museum
170 Whitney Ave.
Box 6666   Phone: (203) 436-8547
New Haven, CT 06511   Eleanor H. Stickney, Sr.Musm.Asst.
Founded: 1959. **Staff:** Prof 1. **Subjects:** Ornithology. **Special Collections:** William R. Coe Collection. **Holdings:** 8500 books; 2000 bound periodical volumes; 15,000 reprints. **Subscriptions:** 140 journals and other serials. **Services:** Interlibrary loans; copying; library open to public by permission. **Networks/Consortia:** Member of RLG; CRL; CTUW Project.

★17386★

YALE UNIVERSITY - SCHOOL OF DRAMA LIBRARY (Theater)
222 York St.
Yale Sta., Box 1903A   Phone: (203) 436-2213
New Haven, CT 06520   Pamela C. Jordan, Libn.
Staff: 1. **Subjects:** Plays by American, British, and foreign playwrights; history of the theater; theater architecture; drama criticism; costume and set design; stage lighting; acting; direction; production. **Special Collections:** Abel Thomas (1200 books); Rockefeller Prints Collection (80,000 photos); George Pierce Baker Collection; slide collections; History of Costume (1188 slides); Architecture, Interiors and Furnishings (1893 slides). **Holdings:** 23,000 books; 1200 bound periodical volumes; 550 production books; 412 masters' theses; 127 dissertations; 76 scrapbooks of clippings. **Subscriptions:** 60 journals and other serials; 12 newspapers. **Services:** Interlibrary loans; copying; listening station; circulation limited to Yale University card holders. **Networks/Consortia:** Member of RLG; CRL; CTUW Project.

★17387★

YALE UNIVERSITY - SEMITIC REFERENCE LIBRARY (Area-Ethnic)†
314 Sterling Memorial Library
Yale University Library
New Haven, CT 06520   Edward A. Jajko, Near East Bibliog.
Founded: 1930. **Subjects:** Comparative Semitics; Hebrew, Arabic and other Semitic languages (except Akkadian). **Holdings:** 1500 volumes. **Networks/ Consortia:** Member of RLG; CRL; CTUW Project.

★17388★

YALE UNIVERSITY - SLAVIC & EAST EUROPEAN COLLECTIONS (Hum; Area-Ethnic)
Sterling Memorial Library   Phone: (203) 436-0230
New Haven, CT 06520   Tatiana Rannit, Cur.
Founded: 1961. **Staff:** Prof 1; Other 4. **Subjects:** East Europe - social sciences, humanities, linguistics, history. **Special Collections:** Joel Sumner Smith; Harrison Thomson; Mikhail Rostovtseff; George Vernadsky; Vasilii Tutcheff; Pilsudski archives (microfilm). **Holdings:** 232,200 books in Slavic and East European languages alone; 67,165 bound periodical volumes; 2 VF drawers of clippings; 38 archival collections; 20,154 titles on microfilm and microfiche; 142 shelves of pamphlet volumes; 1.75 aisles of Free Europe material. **Subscriptions:** 331 journals and other serials; 66 newspapers. **Networks/Consortia:** Member of RLG; CRL; CTUW Project.

★17389★

YALE UNIVERSITY - SOCIAL SCIENCE LIBRARY (Soc Sci)
140 Prospect St.
Yale Sta., Box 1958   Phone: (203) 436-3412
New Haven, CT 06520   Billie I. Salter, Libn. for Social Sci.
Founded: 1972. **Staff:** Prof 8; Other 13. **Subjects:** Administrative sciences, business, economics and economic development, finance, health services administration, management, political science, sociology. **Special Collections:** Economic Growth Center Collection (government reports, surveys, statistical yearbooks, bulletins focusing on developing countries and their economies; 47,636 volumes); Social Science Data Archive (490 machine-readable data files of political and social surveys, voting records and economic data sources); Roper Center Archives (public opinion polls; 64 drawers). **Holdings:** 61,000 volumes; corporate reports of New York Stock Exchange, selected other domestic companies and 2000 foreign firms; 5 drawers of subject files; 14 drawers of political polls. **Subscriptions:** 2158 journals and other serials. **Services:** Interlibrary loans; copying; library circulation limited to card holders only. **Automated Operations:** Computerized cataloging. **Computerized Information Services:** DIALOG, RLIN, BRS, SDC. **Networks/Consortia:** Member of RLG; CRL; CTUW Project. **Publications:** Social Science Data Archive's Directory of Data Holdings and Services. **Staff:** Anthony A. Angiletta, Soc.Sci.Bibliog.; Joan Bernstein, Staff Res.Spec./Prog.; JoAnn L. Dionne, Ref.Libn. & Data Archv.; Judith O. Carnes, Ref.Libn. & Coll.Dev.; Cesar Rodriguez, Acq.Libn.; Edita R. Baradi, Acq.Libn.; Nenita A. Fernandez, Cat.Libn.

★17390★

YALE UNIVERSITY - SOUTHEAST ASIA COLLECTION (Area-Ethnic)
Sterling Memorial Library   Phone: (203) 436-1092
New Haven, CT 06520   Charles R. Bryant, Cur.
Staff: Prof 2; Other 2. **Subjects:** Southeast Asia (Burma, Thailand, Laos, Vietnam, Cambodia, Philippines, Malaysia, Brunei, Singapore, Indonesia) - social sciences and humanities. **Holdings:** 185,000 books and bound periodical volumes. **Subscriptions:** 750 journals and other serials. **Services:** Interlibrary loans; copying. **Automated Operations:** Computerized cataloging, acquisitions and serials. **Networks/Consortia:** Member of RLG; CRL; CTUW Project; Southeast Asia Microform Project (SEAM). **Publications:** Checklist of Southeast Asian Serials (published in 1968). **Staff:** Miss Lian Tie Kho, Libn.

★17391★

YALE UNIVERSITY - STERLING CHEMISTRY LIBRARY (Sci-Tech)
225 Prospect St.   Phone: (203) 436-3397
New Haven, CT 06520   Deborah Paolillo, Hd.
Founded: 1923. **Subjects:** Chemistry and biochemistry. **Holdings:** 13,400 books and bound periodical volumes. **Subscriptions:** 200 journals and other serials. **Services:** Interlibrary loans; copying; library open to public with restrictions. **Networks/Consortia:** Member of RLG; CRL; CTUW Project.

★17392★

YALE UNIVERSITY - YALE CENTER FOR BRITISH ART - PHOTO ARCHIVE (Art)
2120 Yale Sta.   Phone: (203) 432-4097
New Haven, CT 06520   Dr. Anne-Marie Logan, Libn./Photo Archv.
Staff: 3. **Subjects:** British art - paintings, drawings, prints and sculpture, 1500-1945 (emphasizing works dating before 1900). **Special Collections:** Photographs after works by British artists and foreigners working in Great Britain (100,000 black/white photographs); British School photographs in the Witt Collection, Courtauld Institute, London (4000 microfiche); Harold Jennings Collection (60 volumes containing 150,000 prints, photographs and reproductions after paintings, drawings and prints of British sitters). **Services:** Copying; archive open to public. **Computerized Information Services:** Internal database. **Special Indexes:** Subject thesaurus of British Art (20,000 terms); Artist authority list for British Artists (4500 names); Computerized Census of British Art in North American Collections (in progress).

★17393★

YALE UNIVERSITY - YALE CENTER FOR BRITISH ART - RARE BOOK COLLECTION (Art; Rare Book)
2120 Yale Sta.
New Haven, CT 06520
Phone: (203) 432-4099
Joan M. Friedman, Cur. of Rare Bks.
Staff: Prof 2; Other 3. **Subjects:** British illustrated books, 15th-19th centuries; visual arts in Great Britain, 17th-19th centuries. **Special Collections:** Major J.R. Abbey Collection of Color-Plate Books. **Holdings:** 20,000 rare books and serials. **Services:** Copying; collection open to public. **Automated Operations:** Computerized cataloging. **Computerized Information Services:** RLIN. **Special Catalogs:** Computerized catalog of illustrators, graphic techniques, provenance, imprints, bookbinding and chronology. **Staff:** Elisabeth R. Fairman, Cat.Libn.

★17394★

YALE UNIVERSITY - YALE CENTER FOR BRITISH ART - REFERENCE LIBRARY (Art)
1080 Chapel St.
Yale Sta., Box 2120
New Haven, CT 06520
Phone: (203) 432-4097
Dr. Anne-Marie Logan, Libn./Photo Archv.
Staff: Prof 1; Other 1. **Subjects:** British art - painting, drawings, prints, sculpture and architecture, 1500-1945. **Special Collections:** Sotheby sales catalogues, 1734-1980; Victoria and Albert Museum oils, watercolors, architectural drawings and miniatures; British Museum Satirical Prints; British Museum's Turner Bequest; Huntington Library drawings (all on microfilm). **Holdings:** 9000 books; 1000 bound periodical volumes; 870 reels of microfilm; 7300 microfiche. **Subscriptions:** 60 journals and other serials. **Services:** Copying; library open to public. **Automated Operations:** Computerized cataloging. **Computerized Information Services:** DIALOG; internal database. **Networks/Consortia:** Member of RLG.

★17395★

YALE UNIVERSITY - YALE COLLECTION OF HISTORICAL SOUND RECORDINGS (Hist)
Sterling Memorial Library
New Haven, CT 06520
Phone: (203) 436-1822
Richard Warren, Jr., Cur.
Founded: 1960. **Staff:** Prof 1; Other 2. **Subjects:** Phonograph recordings of historical interest in the fields of concert music, jazz, drama, politics, literature, documentary from the end of the 19th century to the present, with emphasis on history of performance practice in the arts. **Holdings:** 100,000 sound recordings; catalogs; lists; books; photographs; autograph letters, manuscripts, and other documents relating to the history of phonograph recording. **Subscriptions:** 20 journals and other serials. **Services:** Collection open to public for reference use only by appointment. **Networks/Consortia:** Member of RLG; CRL; CTUW Project. **Special Indexes:** The Rigler & Deutsch Record Index - a National Union Catalog of Sound Recordings - Part I; An Index to 78rpm Sound Recordings in ARSC/AAA member libraries.

★17396★

YAMAHA MOTOR CORPORATION USA - YAMAHA R&D MINNESOTA - RESEARCH LIBRARY (Sci-Tech; Bus-Fin)
1255 Main St.
Coon Rapids, MN 55433
Phone: (612) 755-2743
William B. Seath, Info.Mgr.
Founded: 1979. **Staff:** Prof 1; Other 2. **Subjects:** Engineering, business and management. **Special Collections:** Patent records; Society of Automotive Engineers papers; snowmobile laws; snowmobile accident records. **Holdings:** 475 books; 40 bound periodical volumes; 9 VF drawers. **Subscriptions:** 100 journals and other serials; 5 newspapers. **Services:** Interlibrary loans; library not open to public. **Computerized Information Services:** Access to online systems.

★17397★

YARDNEY ELECTRIC CORPORATION - TECHNICAL INFORMATION CENTER (Sci-Tech)†
82 Mechanic St.
Pawcatuck, CT 06379
Phone: (203) 559-1100
Pamela J. Lochner, Libn.
Founded: 1960. **Staff:** Prof 1. **Subjects:** Batteries, electrochemistry, chemistry, electrical engineering, metallurgy, plastics. **Holdings:** 1000 books. **Subscriptions:** 10 journals and other serials. **Services:** Center not open to public.

★17398★

YARMOUTH COUNTY HISTORICAL SOCIETY - RESEARCH LIBRARY AND ARCHIVES (Hist)
P.O. Box 39
Yarmouth, NS, Canada B5A 4B1
Phone: (902) 742-5539
Helen Hall, Archv.
Staff: 1. **Subjects:** Local history and genealogy, shipping. **Holdings:** 1300 books; manuscripts; maps; charts; clippings; pictures. **Services:** Copying; library open to public. **Publications:** Brochure, annual; Early Vital Records of the Township of Yarmouth, N.S. **Special Indexes:** Index to Shipping of Yarmouth, N.S.

★17399★

YASODHARA ASHRAM SOCIETY - LIBRARY (Rel-Theol)
Box 9
Kootenay Bay, BC, Canada V0B 1X0
Phone: (604) 227-9224
Dawn Spickler, Libn.
Staff: Prof 1. **Subjects:** Yoga, religious and spiritual philosophy, Eastern religions, Western psychology. **Special Collections:** Extensive collection of works of Swami Sivananda Saraswati, many not elsewhere available in North America. **Holdings:** 3500 books; 400 Eastern magazines. **Services:** Library open to registered guests of the society. **Publications:** Ascent (journal of the society), 3/year.

★17400★

YAVAPAI COUNTY LAW LIBRARY (Law)†
County Courthouse, Fl. 4
Prescott, AZ 86301
Phone: (602) 445-7450
Richard Corson, Law Libn.
Staff: 2. **Subjects:** Law. **Holdings:** 11,986 books and bound periodical volumes. **Services:** Library open to public for reference use only. **Staff:** Marla Lett, Asst.Libn.

YEATES (Jasper) LAW LIBRARY CoLLECTION
See: Lancaster County Historical Society - Library

★17401★

YELLOWSTONE-BIGHORN RESEARCH ASSOCIATION - LIBRARY (Sci-Tech)
Red Lodge, MT 59068
Founded: 1936. **Subjects:** Geology. **Special Collections:** N.H. Darton's personal collection. **Holdings:** 2300 volumes; geological manuscripts, reprints and maps; herbarium contains plants from Montana and Wyoming: 81 families, 381 genera, 1028 species.

YELLOWSTONE LIBRARY AND MUSEUM ASSOCIATION
See: U.S. Natl. Park Service

YERKES OBSERVATORY LIBRARY
See: University of Chicago

YERKES REGIONAL PRIMATE CENTER
See: Emory University

★17402★

YESHIVA TORAH VODAATH AND MESIFTA - TORAH VODAATH LIBRARY (Rel-Theol)
425 E. Ninth St.
Brooklyn, NY 11218
Phone: (718) 941-8000
Founded: 1918. **Staff:** Prof 1; Other 2. **Subjects:** Biblical exegesis, Talmud (and novellae on), Rabbinical responsa, Halachic literature, liturgy and homiletic literature, Jewish history, Hebrew and Yiddish literature, Hasidic literature. **Holdings:** 23,500 books; 575 bound periodical volumes; 600 unbound periodicals; 280 unbound pamphlets. **Subscriptions:** 65 journals and other serials. **Services:** Copying; library open to public. **Staff:** Pincus Schwartz, Asst.Libn.; Samuel Laufer, Asst.Libn.

★17403★

YESHIVA UNIVERSITY - ALBERT EINSTEIN COLLEGE OF MEDICINE - D. SAMUEL GOTTESMAN LIBRARY (Med)
1300 Morris Park Ave.
Bronx, NY 10461
Phone: (212) 430-3108
Charlotte K. Lindner, Dir. of Lib.
Founded: 1955. **Staff:** Prof 7; Other 15. **Subjects:** Biochemistry, cell biology, medicine, molecular biology, pharmacology, physiology, genetics, anatomy, oncology, pathology, psychiatry, immunology. **Special Collections:** Gresser Collection (ophthalmology). **Holdings:** 63,735 books; 84,925 bound periodical volumes; 40 VF drawers of archives; 25,155 issues; 210 dissertations. **Subscriptions:** 2345 journals and other serials. **Services:** Interlibrary loans; copying; SDI; library open to public with restrictions. **Automated Operations:** Computerized cataloging. **Computerized Information Services:** MEDLARS, BRS. **Networks/Consortia:** Member of Medical Library Center of New York (MLCNY). **Publications:** Acquisitions List, bimonthly. **Staff:** Florence Schreibstein, Asst.Libn./Chf.Per.Libn.; Clara Dunleavy, Chf.Ref.Libn.; Elsie Herzberg, Chf. of Circ.Dept.; Rachline Habousha, Asst.Ref.Libn.; James Swanton, Chf.Cat.; Norma Nelson, Asst.Ref.Libn.;Norman Flores, Circ.Lib.

★17404★

YESHIVA UNIVERSITY - ALBERT EINSTEIN COLLEGE OF MEDICINE -
   DEPARTMENT OF ANESTHESIOLOGY - LIBRARY (Med)
Eastchester Rd. & Morris Park Ave.
Bldg. J, Rm. 1226
Bronx, NY 10461   Agnes Klein, Adm.
Subjects: Anesthesiology. Holdings: 200 books; 500 bound periodical
volumes; 110 slide/tape sets. Subscriptions: 30 journals and other serials.
Services: Library not open to public.

★17405★

YESHIVA UNIVERSITY - ALBERT EINSTEIN COLLEGE OF MEDICINE - DEPT.
   OF PSYCHIATRY - J. THOMPSON PSYCHIATRY LIB. (Med)
Bronx Municipal Hospital Center
NR 2E7A   Phone: (212) 430-5571
Bronx, NY 10461   Silvia Davidson, Libn.
Staff: Prof 1; Other 1. Subjects: Psychiatry, psychoanalysis, social work,
philosophy, history, literature, theology, arts. Holdings: 8000 books; 1988
bound periodical volumes; 6 VF drawers of reprints; 82 masters'
dissertations. Subscriptions: 110 journals and other serials. Services:
Interlibrary loans; library not open to public.

★17406★

YESHIVA UNIVERSITY - ALBERT EINSTEIN COLLEGE OF MEDICINE -
   SURGERY LIBRARY (Med)
Jacobi Hospital, Rm. 613
Pelham Pkwy. & Eastchester Rd.   Phone: (212) 430-5800
Bronx, NY 10461
Founded: 1965. Subjects: Surgery and medicine. Holdings: 571 books;
1448 bound periodical volumes; 2 drawers of reprints. Subscriptions: 21
journals and other serials. Services: Interlibrary loans; preparation of
bibliographies for department members; library not open to public. Remarks:
Jacobi Hospital is located in the Bronx Municipal Hospital Center.

★17407★

YESHIVA UNIVERSITY - HEDI STEINBERG LIBRARY (Rel-Theol)
Stern College for Women
245 Lexington Ave.   Phone: (212) 481-0570
New York, NY 10016   Edith Lubetski, Hd.Libn.
Founded: 1954. Staff: Prof 3; Other 2. Special Collections: Judaica and
Hebraica (10,000 volumes). Holdings: 73,000 volumes. Services:
Interlibrary loans; copying; library open to public for reference use only.
Networks/Consortia: Member of METRO.

★17408★

YESHIVA UNIVERSITY - MENDEL GOTTESMAN LIBRARY OF HEBRAICA
   AND JUDAICA (Area-Ethnic)
500 W. 185th St.   Phone: (212) 960-5382
New York, NY 10033   Pearl Berger, Hd.Libn.
Founded: 1920. Staff: Prof 3; Other 2. Subjects: Rabbinics; Bible and
Jewish commentaries; Hebrew and cognate languages; Jewish history,
philosophy and literature. Special Collections: Vatican Collection; Lehman
Collection (both on microfilm). Holdings: 140,000 books; 20,000 bound
periodical volumes; 1050 reels of microfilm; 2800 microfiche; 1000
manuscripts. Subscriptions: 600 journals and other serials. Services:
Interlibrary loans; copying; library open to public for reference use only.
Automated Operations: Computerized cataloging. Computerized
Information Services: OCLC. Networks/Consortia: Member of METRO.

★17409★

YESHIVA UNIVERSITY - POLLACK LIBRARY - LANDOWNE-BLOOM
   COLLECTION (Soc Sci)
500 W. 185th St.   Phone: (212) 960-5378
New York, NY 10033   Pearl Berger, Hd.Libn.
Founded: 1975. Subjects: Aging, Jewish social welfare. Holdings: 12,000
books; 10,000 pamphlets and documents; 1490 dissertations in microform.
Services: Interlibrary loans; copying; collection open to public for reference
use only. Automated Operations: Computerized cataloging. Computerized
Information Services: OCLC. Networks/Consortia: Member of METRO.

★17410★

YIVO INSTITUTE FOR JEWISH RESEARCH - LIBRARY AND ARCHIVES
   (Area-Ethnic)
1048 Fifth Ave.   Phone: (212) 535-6700
New York, NY 10028   Marek Web, Chf.Archv.
Founded: 1925. Staff: Prof 14; Other 15. Subjects: Yiddish language,
literature, drama and folklore; East European Jewry; European Jewry in the
19th and 20th centuries; Jewish history; Jewish immigration to the U.S.; Jews
under Nazi rule. Special Collections: Rare books; Rabbinics; Vilna Collection

of periodicals; Nazi literature; Jewish music; archives of Jewish organizations;
archives of ghettoes and concentration camps; captured Nazi documents;
manuscripts of Yiddish writers; Weinreich Library and Archives of Yiddish
Linguistics; Landsmanshaft Archive. Holdings: 315,000 volumes; 8500 linear
feet of manuscript collections, records of institutions, individual collections,
general records of the Yivo archives, photograph collections, art collections;
30 linear feet of tapes and recordings; microfilm: library - 2000 reels,
archives - 2400 reels. Subscriptions: 486 journals and other serials.
Services: Interlibrary loans; copying; library open to public on a limited
schedule. Publications: News of the Yivo, 3/year - sent to members;
bibliographies on certain subjects (mimeographed). Special Catalogs: Library
catalogs for special collections; guide to major collections in the Yivo
Archives; archives' inventories and registers of individual collections. Staff:
Dina Abramowicz, Chf.Libn.; Jack Weinstein, Adm.Libn.; Stanley Bergman,
Assoc.Libn.;Bella Hass Weinberg, Cons.; Itzek Gottesman, Archv.; Fruma
Mohrer, Archv.; Eleanor Mlotek, Archv.; Rosaline Schwartz, Dir., Pub.Prog.;
Samuel Norich, Exec.Dir.; Hannah Fryshdorf, Asst.Dir.

YMCA
See: Young Men's Christian Association

YONGE (P.K.) LABORATORY SCHOOL
See: University of Florida - P.K. Yonge Laboratory School

YONGE (P.K.) LIBRARY OF FLORIDA HISTORY
See: University of Florida - P.K. Yonge Library of Florida History

★17411★

YONKERS GENERAL HOSPITAL - MEDICAL LIBRARY (Med)
127 Ashburton Ave.   Phone: (914) 965-8200
Yonkers, NY 10701   Lucila R. Samson, Med.Libn.
Founded: 1965. Staff: Prof 1. Subjects: Internal medicine, surgery,
gynecology, pathology, psychiatry, pediatrics. Holdings: 800 books; 300
bound periodical volumes; 3 VF drawers of pamphlets; cassettes.
Subscriptions: 45 journals and other serials. Services: Interlibrary loans;
copying; library open to public. Networks/Consortia: Member of Health
Information Libraries of Westchester (HILOW); Greater Northeastern Regional
Medical Library Program.

★17412★

YONKERS HISTORICAL SOCIETY - LIBRARY (Hist)
Hudson River Museum
511 Warburton Ave.   Phone: (914) 969-5622
Yonkers, NY 10701   Olga C. Kourre, Libn.
Founded: 1952. Subjects: History of Yonkers, Westchester County and
Hudson River; local authors. Holdings: 400 books; manuscripts; documents.
Services: Library open to public for reference use only.

★17413★

YONKERS PUBLIC LIBRARY - FINE ARTS DEPARTMENT (Art; Mus)
1500 Central Park Ave.   Phone: (914) 337-1500
Yonkers, NY 10710   Joan W. Stevenson, Dept.Hd.
Founded: 1962. Staff: Prof 3; Other 9. Subjects: History of art, painting,
sculpture, architecture, graphic arts, crafts, music, performing arts,
photography and film arts, antique collecting. Holdings: 13,500 books;
15,000 recordings; 1000 cassettes; 7550 pieces of sheet music; 2000
slides; 3 file drawers of film catalogs; 17 file drawers of pictures; 5 file
drawers of clippings. Subscriptions: 55 journals and other serials. Services:
Interlibrary loans; copying; library open to public with restrictions on
borrowing. Networks/Consortia: Member of Westchester Library System.
Staff: Valerie Schneer, Ref.Libn.; Lois Herzberg, Ref.Libn.

★17414★

YONKERS PUBLIC LIBRARY - INFORMATION SERVICES - TECHNICAL &
   BUSINESS DIVISION (Bus-Fin; Sci-Tech)
7 Main St.   Phone: (914) 476-1255
Yonkers, NY 10701   Marta Schwarz, Dept.Hd.
Founded: 1938. Staff: Prof 6. Subjects: Business and finance,
transportation, engineering, aeronautics, automobiles, building trades,
plumbing and heating, mathematics, physics, chemistry. Special Collections:
Annual and 10K reports of most corporations; telephone directories of U.S.
cities; state, business and biographical directories. Holdings: 19,500 books;
107 bound periodical volumes; Official Patent Gazette, 1925 to present;
7000 government depository publications; 17,000 pamphlets. Subscriptions:
240 journals and other serials. Services: Interlibrary loans; copying; library
open to public.

★17415★

YORK BOROUGH BOARD OF EDUCATION - PROFESSIONAL LIBRARY (Educ)
2 Trethewey Dr.   Phone: (416) 653-2270
Toronto, ON, Canada M6M 4A8
Founded: 1971. **Staff:** Prof 1; Other 2. **Subjects:** Education, sociology.
Holdings: 15,000 books; 75 files of unbound reports; 1500 filmstrips and
media kits; 50 drawers of pamphlets and clippings; 200 reels of microfilm;
4000 microfiche. **Subscriptions:** 300 journals and other serials; 6
newspapers. **Services:** Interlibrary loans; copying; SDI; library open to public.
Automated Operations: Computerized cataloging. **Computerized
Information Services:** BRS, Info Globe, SDC, DIALOG. **Networks/Consortia:**
Member of Professional Education Libraries Cataloguing Network (PEL).
Publications: New Books, 6/year; Current Magazine Contents - both for
internal distribution only. **Staff:** Pat Steenbergen, Libn.; Sheila Moll, Libn.

★17416★

YORK COUNTY LAW LIBRARY (Law)
Court House   Phone: (717) 854-0754
York, PA 17401   Gail A. Davis, Libn.
Founded: 1872. **Staff:** Prof 1; Other 1. **Subjects:** Law. **Holdings:** 30,000
volumes. **Services:** Interlibrary loans; copying; library open to public for
reference use only.

★17417★

YORK COUNTY PLANNING COMMISSION - LIBRARY (Plan)
118 Pleasant Acres Rd.   Phone: (717) 757-2647
York, PA 17402   Trudy Stockton, Libn.
Staff: 1. **Subjects:** Planning, land utilization, transportation, recreation,
utilities, natural resources, statistics, housing, social and health planning,
computerized information systems. **Holdings:** 6000 books and pamphlets;
tapes. **Subscriptions:** 60 journals and other serials. **Services:** Interlibrary
loans; copying; library open to public. **Publications:** Planning Commission
Newsletter, quarterly - to interested citizens and municipal officials; Housing
Newsletter, biennial; Transportation Newsletter, biennial. **Remarks:** Library is
an affiliated data center of the Pennsylvania State Data Center, which was
established to facilitate the dissemination of census data.

★17418★

**YORK-FINCH GENERAL HOSPITAL - DR. THOMAS J. MALCHO MEMORIAL
LIBRARY** (Med)
2111 Finch Ave., W.   Phone: (416) 744-2583
Downsview, ON, Canada M3N 1N1   Mona Kakoschke, Med.Libn.
Staff: Prof 1. **Subjects:** Medicine, nursing, hospital administration. **Holdings:**
1000 books. **Subscriptions:** 156 journals. **Services:** Interlibrary loans; library
not open to public. **Computerized Information Services:** MEDLARS.
Networks/Consortia: Member of Toronto Health Libraries Association.

★17419★

YORK HOSPITAL - HEALTH SCIENCES LIBRARY (Med)
15 Hospital Dr.   Phone: (207) 363-4321
York, ME 03909   Darryl Hamson, Med.Libn.
Staff: 1. **Subjects:** Medicine, nursing, hospital administration. **Holdings:** 338
books; 353 bound periodical volumes. **Subscriptions:** 85 journals and other
serials. **Services:** Interlibrary loans; copying; library open to professionals in
community. **Computerized Information Services:** NLM. Performs free
searches. **Networks/Consortia:** Member of Health Science Library and
Information Cooperative of Maine; Health and Medical Information
Cooperative of Southern Maine. **Publications:** Classified Information
(newsletter), monthly - for internal distribution only.

★17420★

YORK HOSPITAL - LIBRARY (Med)
1001 S. George St.   Phone: (717) 771-2495
York, PA 17405   Barbara H. Bevan, Libn.
Founded: 1962. **Staff:** Prof 2; Other 4. **Subjects:** Medicine, nursing, health
education. **Special Collections:** Health Education Resource Shelf (100 books;
pamphlets; periodicals); Chaplaincy Collection (150 books). **Holdings:** 7422
books; 5503 bound periodical volumes. **Subscriptions:** 393 journals and
other serials. **Services:** Interlibrary loans; copying; SDI; library open to public
with restrictions on borrowing. **Computerized Information Services:** BRS,
MEDLARS; internal database. Performs searches free and on cost recovery
basis. Contact Person: Beth A. Evitts. **Networks/Consortia:** Member of
Central Pennsylvania Health Sciences Library Association; University of
Pennsylvania Affiliated Librarians. **Publications:** Library Letter, irregular.
Special Indexes: Periodical list (book and online); Health Education Books in
Hospital & Public Libraries (book and online). **Staff:** Beth A. Evitts, Asst.Libn.

★17421★

YORK RESEARCH CORPORATION - LIBRARY (Env-Cons)†
One Research Dr.   Phone: (203) 325-1371
Stamford, CT 06906   Barbara A. Goodhouse, Libn.
Founded: 1969. **Staff:** Prof 1. **Subjects:** Pollution - air, water; chemistry;
industrial hygiene; solid wastes; engineering. **Holdings:** 1800 books.
Subscriptions: 90 journals and other serials. **Services:** Interlibrary loans;
copying; SDI; library open to public by appointment. **Networks/Consortia:**
Member of Southwestern Connecticut Library Council (SWLC).

★17422★

YORK TECHNICAL COLLEGE - LIBRARY (Sci-Tech)
U.S. 21 Bypass   Phone: (803) 324-3130
Rock Hill, SC 29730   Amanda Yu, Libn.
Founded: 1964. **Staff:** Prof 1; Other 1. **Subjects:** Industrial arts, business,
health sciences, engineering, liberal arts. **Holdings:** 19,439 books; 21,672
microforms; 25,702 slides; 3334 cassette tapes; 2530 transparencies;
1623 filmstrips. **Subscriptions:** 225 journals and other serials; 13
newspapers. **Services:** Interlibrary loans; copying; library open to residents of
area.

★17423★

**YORK UNIVERSITY - CENTRE FOR RESEARCH ON LATIN AMERICA AND
THE CARIBBEAN - CERLAC-LARU DOCUMENTATION CENTRE** (Soc Sci)
204B Founders College
4700 Keele St.   Phone: (416) 667-3085
Downsview, ON, Canada M3J 1P3   Peter Landstreet, Dp.Dir., CERLAC.
Staff: Prof 1; Other 1. **Subjects:** Latin America and the Caribbean - sociology,
economics, political science, history; Canadian-Latin American/Caribbean
relations. **Special Collections:** Research reports and working papers from
Latin American social science research centers in Argentina, Brazil, Chile,
Ecuador, Mexico, Peru, Uruguay, Venezuela, and Costa Rica; reviews of the
Organization for Economic Cooperation and Development (OECD) pertaining to
Latin America; United Nations information and statistics; Brazilian government
documents. **Holdings:** Figures not available for books; government research
reports on microfilm and microfiche; Spanish, Portuguese, and Italian journals.
Subscriptions: 40 journals and other serials. **Services:** Copying; center open
to public by appointment. **Publications:** List of publications - available upon
request. **Remarks:** Includes holdings of the Latin America Research Unit
(LARU).

★17424★

YORK UNIVERSITY - DEPARTMENT OF VISUAL ARTS - SLIDE LIBRARY (Art;
Aud-Vis)
Fine Arts Phase II, Rm. 274   Phone: (416) 667-3749
Toronto, ON, Canada M3J 1P3   Michele Metraux, Coord.
Staff: Prof 3; Other 4. **Subjects:** Painting, sculpture, architecture. **Special
Collections:** Germain Bazin Collection of Photographs; Theodore A. Heinrich
Slide Collection. **Holdings:** 170,000 35mm slides. **Subscriptions:** 35 journals
and other serials. **Services:** Library open to faculty. **Staff:** Donna McFarlane,
Asst. Slide Libn.; Lillian Szczepaniak, Slide Lib.Ck.

★17425★

**YORK UNIVERSITY - FACULTY OF ARTS - PROGRAMME IN ENGLISH AS A
SECOND LANGUAGE - ESL RESOURCE COLLECTION** (Educ)
306 Strong College
4700 Keele St.   Phone: (416) 667-3926
Downsview, ON, Canada M3J 1P3   Merlin Homer, ESL Coord.
Staff: 1. **Subjects:** Canadian multiculturalism, English as a second language.
Holdings: 225 books; 45 bound periodical volumes; 1 box of ESL abstracts
files; 1 box of ESL publishers' catalogs; 1 VF drawers of resource materials
for teaching English as a second language at college level; 1 VF drawers of
ESL teacher education resources; 1 VF drawers of guides in foreign languages.
Services: Collection open to public with coordinator's permission.

★17426★

YORK UNIVERSITY - FACULTY OF ARTS - WRITING WORKSHOP LIBRARY
(Educ)
208 Strong College
4700 Keele St.   Phone: (416) 667-3737
Downsview, ON, Canada M3J 1P3   Sylvia Meade, Adm.Sec.
Subjects: Composition, how to write and teach special subjects. **Holdings:**
1100 books; 100 bound periodical volumes. **Services:** Interlibrary loans;
library open to students and faculty.

★17427★

YORK UNIVERSITY - FACULTY OF EDUCATION - EDUCATION CENTRE
  (Educ)*
S166 Ross Bldg.
4700 Keele St.   Phone: (416) 667-2395
Downsview, ON, Canada M3J 1P3   Prof. Laura Ford, Supv.
Founded: 1974. **Staff:** Prof 1; Other 1. **Subjects:** Education. **Holdings:**
10,891 books; 716 kits; 846 filmstrips; 380 phonograph records. **Services:**
Center not open to public.

★17428★

YORK UNIVERSITY - FILM LIBRARY (Aud-Vis)
Scott Library
4700 Keele St.   Phone: (416) 667-2546
Downsview, ON, Canada M3J 2R2   Kathryn Elder, Libn.
Founded: 1970. **Staff:** Prof 1; Other 3. **Holdings:** 1348 16mm film titles;
921 video cassettes. **Services:** Films loaned to other Ontario universities.
Automated Operations: Computerized cataloging. **Special Catalogs:**
Annotated catalog with subject index (book). **Remarks:** The Film Library
provides film reference service and obtains films from outside rental sources.

★17429★

YORK UNIVERSITY - GOVERNMENT DOCUMENTS/ADMINISTRATIVE
  STUDIES LIBRARY (Bus-Fin; Info Sci)
113 Administrative Studies Bldg.
4700 Keele St.   Phone: (416) 667-2545
Downsview, ON, Canada M3J 2R6   Vivienne Monty, Libn.
Staff: Prof 3; Other 7. **Subjects:** Documents of the governments of Canada,
Great Britain, United States; documents of United Nations, Organization for
Economic Cooperation and Development, European Communities;
management; public administration; capital markets; corporations;
administrative behavior; arts management; executive development. **Holdings:**
200,000 documents (83,000 bound); 9500 reels of microfilm; 1 million
microfiche and microcards; 2000 volume reference collection; 15,000 bound
periodical volumes; microfiche data file on Canadian and American companies
from the mid-1950s to 1972 (U.S. companies) and to the present for
Canadian companies. **Subscriptions:** 600 journals and other serials; 12
newspapers. **Services:** Interlibrary loans; copying; library open to public.
Automated Operations: Computerized cataloging and acquisitions.
Computerized Information Services: SDC, DIALOG, CAN/OLE, BRS, QL
Systems, New York Times Information Service, Info Globe, International
Development Research Centre. **Staff:** Anne Cannon, Asst.Hd.; D.K. Varma,
Adm.Stud.Libn.

★17430★

YORK UNIVERSITY - INSTITUTE FOR SOCIAL RESEARCH - DATA BANK
  (Soc Sci)
4700 Keele St.   Phone: (416) 667-3026
Downsview, ON, Canada M3J 2R6   Prof. Gordon Darroch
Founded: 1968. **Staff:** Prof 11; Other 6. **Subjects:** Social sciences with
Canadian focus; survey research - by mail, telephone or interview,
questionnaire design, measurement, programming and data analysis. **Services:**
Facility open to public with restrictions. **Computerized Information Services:**
Data archives (internal database). Contact Person: John Tibert. **Special
Catalogs:** Canadian Social Science Data Catalogue. **Formerly:** Its Institute for
Behavioural Research.

★17431★

YORK UNIVERSITY - LAW LIBRARY (Law)
4700 Keele St.   Phone: (416) 667-3939
Downsview, ON, Canada M3J 2R5   Prof. B.J. Halevy, Libn.
Founded: 1892. **Staff:** Prof 5; Other 23. **Subjects:** Law. **Holdings:** 236,580
books; 69,420 volumes on microfilm. **Subscriptions:** 2446 journals and other
serials. **Services:** Interlibrary loans; copying; library open to public with fee for
borrowing. **Automated Operations:** Computerized cataloging. **Computerized
Information Services:** QL Systems. **Publications:** Acquisitions list, monthly;
Cataloging Information Service. **Staff:** Bonnie Preece, Hd., Acq.; Elizabeth
Srinivasagam, Hd., Rd.Serv.; Monica Perot, Hd., Circ.; Judy Ginsberg, Hd.,
Cat.; Marianne Rogers, Ref.Libn.

★17432★

YORK UNIVERSITY - LISTENING ROOM (Mus)
Scott Library, Rm. 409
4700 Keele St.   Phone: (416) 667-3694
Downsview, ON, Canada M3J 2R2   Julie Stockton, Hd.
Founded: 1970. **Staff:** Prof 1; Other 2. **Subjects:** Music and theater. **Special
Collections:** CBC Ideas Collection (1530 reels of tape). **Holdings:** 10,262
books and scores; 10,463 phonograph records; 2500 tapes. **Services:**
Copying; room open to public. **Publications:** Handbook.

★17433★

YORK UNIVERSITY - MAP LIBRARY (Geog-Map)
Scott Library, Rm. 115
4700 Keele St.   Phone: (416) 667-3353
Downsview, ON, Canada M3J 2R2   Janet Allin, Hd.
Founded: 1970. **Staff:** Prof 1; Other 1. **Subjects:** Geography, cartography.
Holdings: 3600 books and atlases; 81,000 maps; 120 wall maps; clipping
file; pamphlet file; 3700 air photos; file of articles on cartography; maps on
slides. **Subscriptions:** 30 journals and other serials. **Services:** Interlibrary
loans; copying; library open to public. **Remarks:** Location of Canadian Ports
Collection material.

★17434★

YORK UNIVERSITY - SPECIAL COLLECTIONS (Rare Book; Hum)
Scott Library, Rm. 305
4700 Keele St.   Phone: (416) 667-2457
Downsview, ON, Canada M3J 2R2
Founded: 1965. **Staff:** 1. **Subjects:** Canadian history and literature, 20th
century British literature. **Special Collections:** Auden; Day-Lewis; Isherwood;
MacNeice; Spender; the Sitwells; Marsh; MacLeish. **Holdings:** 12,000 books;
Canadian pamphlets. **Services:** Copying; collections open to public.
Automated Operations: Computerized cataloging and acquisitions.

★17435★

YORK UNIVERSITY - STEACIE SCIENCE LIBRARY (Sci-Tech; Comp Sci)
4700 Keele St.   Phone: (416) 667-3927
Downsview, ON, Canada M3J 2R3   Brian B. Wilks, Sci.Libn.
Founded: 1970. **Staff:** Prof 1; Other 6. **Subjects:** Mathematics, chemistry,
computer science, physics, biology. **Holdings:** 56,000 books; 49,250 bound
periodical volumes; 25,000 microforms. **Subscriptions:** 1800 journals and
other serials. **Services:** Interlibrary loans; copying; CAN/SDI profiling and
editing; library open to public for reference use only. **Automated Operations:**
Computerized cataloging, acquisitions and circulation. **Computerized
Information Services:** DIALOG, BRS, SDC, CAN/OLE, QL Systems,
MEDLARS, New York Times Information Service, Info Globe. **Staff:** Anne
Benincasa, Circ.Supv.

★17436★

YORK UNIVERSITY - UNIVERSITY ARCHIVES (Hist; Hum)
105 Scott Library
4700 Keele St.   Phone: (416) 667-3306
Downsview, ON, Canada M3J 2R2   Hartwell Bowsfield, Univ.Archv.
Founded: 1960. **Staff:** Prof 1; Other 1. **Special Collections:** Papers of Louis
Applebaum (40 feet); Bill Bissett (23 feet); Harry Crowe (50 feet); William
Esdaile (7 feet); Joseph O. Goodman (100 feet); Allan Grossman (60 feet);
Margaret Laurence (12 feet); Norman Levine (15 feet); Roy Mitchell (3 feet);
Mavor Moore (30 feet); Northern Journey (6 feet); Sitwell Family (9 feet);
Vaughan Township, Ontario (45 feet); Lady Victoria Welby (17 feet); Canadian
Broadcasting Corporation TV Drama Scripts (423 feet); multiple listings of the
Toronto Real Estate Board, 1953-1982 (368 feet); Province of Ontario Land
Registry Books, 1796-1956 (916 feet); Toronto Telegram Photograph
Collection, 1920-1971 (889 feet). **Holdings:** 3234 feet of manuscripts; 713
feet of university records; 1427 theses. **Services:** Copying; archives open to
public with restrictions. **Publications:** Accession Bulletin, irregular - for
internal distribution only.

YOSEMITE NATL. PARK
See: U.S. Natl. Park Service

YOUNG (Arthur) & COMPANY...
See: Arthur Young & Company...

★17437★

YOUNG, CONAWAY, STARGATT & TAYLOR - LIBRARY (Law)
Rodney Sq. N., 11th Fl.
Box 391   Phone: (302) 571-6680
Wilmington, DE 19899-0391   Grace L. Simmons, Libn./Rec.Mgr.
Staff: Prof 1; Other 1. **Subjects:** Law. **Holdings:** 10,000 books.
Subscriptions: 79 journals and other serials. **Services:** Library open to area
attorneys.

YOUNG (Howard) MEDICAL CENTER
See: Howard Young Medical Center

★17438★

YOUNG MEN'S CHRISTIAN ASSOCIATION OF METROPOLITAN HARTFORD,
  INC. - CAREER COUNSELING CENTER LIBRARY (Educ)
160 Jewell St.   Phone: (203) 522-4183
Hartford, CT 06103   Dr. William N. Goodwin, Dir.
Staff: Prof 1; Other 1. **Subjects:** Career counseling, colleges. **Special**

Collections: College catalogue collection (1600 on microfiche); chronicle occupational briefs (800 titles). **Holdings:** 1000 books; 3000 bound periodical volumes. **Subscriptions:** 25 journals and other serials; 15 newspapers. **Services:** Copying; library open to public.

★17439★
YOUNG MEN'S CHRISTIAN ASSOCIATIONS OF THE UNITED STATES OF AMERICA - YMCA HISTORICAL LIBRARY (Soc Sci)
101 N. Wacker Dr.   Phone: (312) 977-0031
Chicago, IL 60606   Ellen Sowchek, Libn.
Founded: 1880. **Staff:** Prof 1; Other 1. **Subjects:** History of the YMCA movement in the United States, Canada, and abroad; religion; social group work; religious education; physical education. **Special Collections:** Early Young Men's Societies, 1712-1850. **Holdings:** 6000 books; 2000 bound periodical volumes; 3000 reports, manuscripts, dissertations; 5000 pamphlets; 2.5 million boxed documents; 125 reels of microfilm; 3000 photographs; bibliographical notes prepared for YMCA histories. **Subscriptions:** 35 journals and other serials. **Services:** Interlibrary loans; copying; bibliographic services for researchers; library open to persons engaged in legitimate research projects. **Formerly:** National Council of the Young Men's Christian Associations of the U.S., located in New York, NY.

★17440★
YOUNG MEN'S MERCANTILE LIBRARY ASSOCIATION - LIBRARY (Hist)†
414 Walnut St.   Phone: (513) 621-0717
Cincinnati, OH 45202   Jean M. Springer, Exec.Dir.
Subjects: History. **Holdings:** 200,000 volumes. **Services:** Library not open to public.

YOUNG MEN'S PHILANTHROPIC LEAGUE
See: Jewish Guild for the Blind

YOUNG MEN'S AND YOUNG WOMEN'S HEBREW ASSOCIATION
See: 92nd Street Young Men's and Young Women's Hebrew Association

★17441★
YOUNG (Morris N. & Chesley V.) MNEMONICS LIBRARY (Soc Sci)
270 Riverside Dr.   Phone: (212) 233-2344
New York, NY 10025   Morris N. Young, M.D., Dir.
Founded: 1953. **Staff:** 2. **Subjects:** Memory and related subjects, memory aids, mnemonics. **Holdings:** 5000 items; books; pamphlets; manuscripts; prints; articles; records; cassettes; games; 15,000 index cards on subject. **Services:** Copying; library open to accredited researchers by appointment. **Publications:** Bibliography of Memory; How to Develop an Exceptional Memory; How to Read Faster and Remember More; The Magic of a Mighty Memory; William Stokes: Magician of Memory; The Magic of a Powerful Memory.

★17442★
YOUNG RADIATOR COMPANY - LIBRARY (Sci-Tech)†
2825 Four Mile Rd.   Phone: (414) 639-1011
Racine, WI 53404   Sandra Kraft, Libn.
Founded: 1945. **Subjects:** Competitive heat transfer material, specifications and data. **Holdings:** 600 books and bound periodical volumes; 300 magazines; 1450 catalogs and 5700 folders (cataloged); 10 volumes of patents; 1 VF drawer of clippings; 5 VF drawers; house organs; annual reports. **Subscriptions:** 250 journals and other serials. **Services:** Interlibrary loans; copying; library open to public with restrictions.

YOUNG AND RUBICAM, INC. - FRYE-SILLS, INC.
See: Frye-Sills, Inc.

★17443★
YOUNG AND RUBICAM INTERNATIONAL - LIBRARY (Bus-Fin)
285 Madison Ave., 10th Fl.   Phone: (212) 953-3075
New York, NY 10017   Celestine G. Frankenberg, Dir. of Lib.Serv.
Founded: 1953. **Staff:** Prof 4; Other 3. **Subjects:** Advertising, marketing. **Special Collections:** Company histories; annual reports; cookbooks; art books; picture collection; competitive advertisers file. **Holdings:** 5000 volumes. **Subscriptions:** 250 journals and other serials. **Services:** Interlibrary loans; library not open to public. **Computerized Information Services:** NEXIS, DIALOG.

YOUNG (Whitney M., Jr.) MEMORIAL LIBRARY OF SOCIAL WORK
See: Columbia University - Whitney M. Young, Jr. Memorial Library of Social Work

★17444★
YOUNG WOMEN'S CHRISTIAN ASSOCIATION OF MARIN - RESOURCE CENTER (Soc Sci)
1000 Sir Francis Drake Blvd.
San Anselmo, CA 94960   Bonnie Rose Hough, Coord.
Staff: Prof 1; Other 3. **Subjects:** Career planning, women's movement, county resources, political issues, health, counseling. **Holdings:** 300 books; 10 VF drawers; 2 scrapbooks; 130 tapes. **Subscriptions:** 90 journals and other serials; 5 newspapers. **Services:** Center open to public for reference use only. **Formerly:** Woman's Way - Resource Center.

YOUNG WOMEN'S CHRISTIAN ASSOCIATION OF MONTREAL
See: Montreal Young Women's Christian Association

★17445★
YOUNG WOMEN'S CHRISTIAN ASSOCIATION - NATIONAL BOARD - LIBRARY (Soc Sci)
726-730 Broadway
New York, NY 10003   Elizabeth D. Norris, Libn./Hist.
Founded: 1959. **Staff:** Prof 1; Other 1. **Subjects:** Women, racism, sexism, civil rights, women's health, youth, voluntarism. **Special Collections:** Womans Press Publications, 1918-1952 (2500 volumes). **Holdings:** 10,000 books; 25 VF drawers of subject files, clippings, pamphlets, reports and catalogs. **Subscriptions:** 175 journals and other serials. **Services:** Interlibrary loans; copying; library open to students and scholars by referral. **Publications:** New Library Books, monthly - for internal distribution only.

YOUNG WOMEN'S HEBREW ASSOCIATION
See: 92nd Street Young Men's and Young Women's Hebrew Association

★17446★
YOUNGSTOWN HOSPITAL ASSOCIATION - HEALTH SCIENCES LIBRARY (Med)
345 Oak Hill Ave.   Phone: (216) 747-0751
Youngstown, OH 44501   Christine S. Roeder, Supv., Health Sci.Lib.
Staff: Prof 2; Other 1. **Subjects:** Clinical medicine, science and nursing. **Holdings:** 1868 books; 5541 bound periodical volumes; Audio-Digest tapes. **Subscriptions:** 216 journals and other serials. **Services:** Interlibrary loans; copying; library open to college students with librarian's permission. **Automated Operations:** Computerized cataloging. **Computerized Information Services:** MEDLINE. **Networks/Consortia:** Member of Northeastern Ohio Universities College of Medicine. **Staff:** Patricia Augustine, Med.Libn.

YOUNGSTOWN AND MAHONING COUNTY PUBLIC LIBRARY
See: Public Library of Youngstown and Mahoning County

YOUTH LIBERATION ARCHIVE
See: Temple University - Central Library System - Contemporary Culture Collection

★17447★
YOUTH NETWORK COUNCIL, INC. - CLEARINGHOUSE (Soc Sci)
104 N. Halsted St.   Phone: (312) 226-1200
Chicago, IL 60606   Denis Murstein, Adm.Dir.
Founded: 1972. **Staff:** Prof 2; Other 1. **Subjects:** Alternative youth services, runaway youth, adolescent sexuality, substance abuse, grantsmanship, juvenile justice, community development, public relations. **Holdings:** 500 books; 80 VF drawers of pamphlets; Federal Register, 1978 to present. **Subscriptions:** 60 journals and other serials; 10 newspapers. **Services:** Interlibrary loans; copying; clearinghouse open to public by appointment. **Publications:** Newsline Journal, quarterly - by subscription; Reachout, Resource Guide to Substance Abuse in Metropolitan Chicago; Youth Employment & Training Guide; A Guide to Advocacy for Youth - all for sale.

★17448★
YOUTH RESOURCES, INC. - LIBRARY (Agri; Soc Sci)
14580 Mission St.
Box DD   Phone: (714) 327-2639
Cabazon, CA 92230   Paul J. Marks, Pres.
Subjects: Forestry, agriculture, conservation, youth training, work experience education, self-supporting nonprofit organizations, nonmedical health and remedies, human settlements, Christian studies. **Holdings:** 127 books and bound periodical volumes; 12 VF drawers of reports, manuscripts and letters. **Subscriptions:** 12 journals and other serials. **Services:** Library not open to public. **Formerly:** Its Agri-Silviculture Institute Library.

★17449★
YPSILANTI REGIONAL PSYCHIATRIC HOSPITAL - STAFF LIBRARY (Med)
Box A   Phone: (313) 434-3400
Ypsilanti, MI 48197   Penny Kirkman, Dir., Lib.Serv.
Staff: 1. **Subjects:** Activity therapy, psychiatry, nursing, psychology, social work, medicine, neurology. **Holdings:** Figures not available. **Services:** Interlibrary loans; library not open to public. **Special Catalogs:** Audio Visual Media (card).

YUKON CHAMBER OF MINES
See: British Columbia and Yukon Chamber of Mines

★17450★
YUKON TERRITORY - DEPARTMENT OF TOURISM, RECREATION AND CULTURE - YUKON ARCHIVES (Hist)
Box 2703   Phone: (403) 667-5321
Whitehorse, YT, Canada Y1A 2C6   Miriam McTiernan, Territorial Archv.
Founded: 1972. **Staff:** Prof 4; Other 3. **Subjects:** Yukon history and current development; Klondike gold rush; Yukon native people; northern pipelines; Alaska Highway. **Special Collections:** Yukon Record Group I (central records of Yukon Government, 1894-1951; 475 meters); Dawson Mining Recorder (placer and quartz mining records, 1894-1971; 200 meters); White Pass and Yukon Route Records (transportation company records, 1898-1960; 25 meters). **Holdings:** 11,000 books; 215 bound periodical volumes; 900 meters of territorial, municipal and federal government records; 300 meters of private manuscripts and corporate records; 350 reels of microfilm; 5000 pamphlets; 8000 maps; 20,000 photographs; 160 films. **Subscriptions:** 100 journals and other serials; 35 newspapers. **Services:** Copying; duplication of photographs and maps; Public Reading Room open to public. **Publications:** Information pamphlet. **Special Indexes:** Visual finding aids for photographs; inventories of government, private and corporate records; pamphlet collection. **Formerly:** Its Department of Tourism, Heritage & Cultural Resources. **Staff:** Charles Maier, Archv.; Diane Chisholm, Archv.; Eileen Edmunds, Libn.

★17451★
YUMA COUNTY LAW LIBRARY (Law)
219 W. 2nd St., Court House   Phone: (602) 782-4534
Yuma, AZ 85364   Anna Margaret Sibley, Libn.
Staff: Prof 1. **Subjects:** Law. **Holdings:** 12,000 volumes. **Services:** Library not open to public.

YUMA PROVING GROUND
See: U.S. Army

YWCA
See: Young Women's Christian Association

Z

★17452★
ZACHRY (H.B.) COMPANY - CENTRAL RECORDS AND LIBRARY (Bus-Fin)
Box 21130   Phone: (512) 922-1213
San Antonio, TX 78285   Janice Burger, Libn.
Staff: 1. **Subjects:** Construction specifications, industrial relations, tax laws, electronic data processing, accounting procedures, building codes. **Holdings:** 1500 books; 60 bound periodical volumes; film; maps. **Subscriptions:** 135 journals and other serials. **Services:** Interlibrary loans; copying; library maintained for company personnel, but brief inquiries handled; library open to public by permission.

ZACKRISON (H.B.) MEMORIAL LIBRARY
See: U.S. Army - Construction Engineering Research Laboratory - H.B. Zackrison Memorial Library

ZAHN INSTRUCTIONAL MATERIALS CENTER
See: Temple University - Central Library System - Zahn Instructional Materials Ctr./Social Adm. Lib.

ZALE LIBRARY
See: Bishop College

★17453★
ZANESVILLE ART CENTER - LIBRARY (Art)
620 Military Rd.   Phone: (614) 452-0741
Zanesville, OH 43701   Mrs. Joseph Howell, Libn.
Staff: 4. **Subjects:** Art history, art techniques, aesthetics, world art, antiques. **Holdings:** 6000 books; 3000 filmstrips and slides. **Subscriptions:** 11 journals and other serials. **Services:** Library open to public. **Publications:** Monthly Bulletin.

★17454★
ZATOR COMPANY - LIBRARY
56 Boylston St.
Cambridge, MA 02138
Defunct

★17455★
ZEIGLER COAL COMPANY - BUSINESS LIBRARY
2700 River Rd., Suite 400
Des Plaines, IL 60018
Subjects: Coal, environmental law. **Holdings:** 1500 volumes. **Remarks:** Presently inactive.

ZEISL (Erich) ARCHIVE
See: University of California, Los Angeles - Music Library

★17456★
ZEITLIN PERIODICALS COMPANY, INC. - LIBRARY (Publ)
817 S. La Brea Ave.   Phone: (213) 933-7175
Los Angeles, CA 90036   Stanley Zeitlin, Pres.
Founded: 1925. **Staff:** Prof 7; Other 12. **Special Collections:** Back-issue periodicals. **Holdings:** 2 million periodicals. **Services:** Library open to public by appointment. **Publications:** Catalogs, irregular.

★17457★
ZEITLIN & VER BRUGGE, BOOKSELLERS - LIBRARY (Rare Book)†
815 N. La Cienega Blvd.   Phone: (213) 655-7581
Los Angeles, CA 90069   Jacob Israel Zeitlin, Pres.
Subjects: History of science and medicine, art and art history, Americana, books and printing, photography, first and limited editions. **Special Collections:** Bibliographical Reference Library (3000 volumes). **Holdings:** 30,000 books. **Subscriptions:** 10 journals and other serials. **Services:** Library open to public by appointment. **Publications:** Rare book and art catalogs, quarterly.

★17458★
ZELLER (George A.) MENTAL HEALTH CENTER - PROFESSIONAL LIBRARY (Med)
5407 N. University   Phone: (309) 691-2200
Peoria, IL 61614   Barbara Haun, Libn.
Founded: 1967. **Staff:** Prof 1; Other 1. **Subjects:** Psychiatry, psychology, community mental health, mental retardation, geriatrics, special education, sociology, general medicine. **Holdings:** 3000 books; 800 bound periodical volumes; 4 VF drawers. **Subscriptions:** 52 journals and other serials. **Services:** Interlibrary loans; copying; library open to students and professionals in the field. **Networks/Consortia:** Member of Heart of Illinois Library Consortium; ILLINET; Illinois Valley Library System; Illinois Department of Mental Health and Developmental Disabilities Library Services Network. **Publications:** New Book List, monthly - for internal distribution only. **Remarks:** Maintained by Illinois State Department of Mental Health and Developmental Disabilities.

ZELLER (Max and Lore) Library
See: Jung (C.G.) Institute of Los Angeles, Inc. - Max and Lore Zeller Library

★17459★
ZENITH ELECTRONICS CORPORATION - TECHNICAL LIBRARY (Sci-Tech)
1000 N. Milwaukee Ave.   Phone: (312) 391-8452
Glenview, IL 60025   Ruby Chu, Hd.Libn.
Staff: Prof 1; Other 1. **Subjects:** Physics, mathematics, electronics, engineering, chemistry. **Holdings:** 10,500 books; 5000 bound periodical volumes; pamphlet file. **Subscriptions:** 300 journals and other serials. **Services:** Interlibrary loans; library not open to public. **Computerized Information Services:** Online systems. **Formerly:** Zenith Radio Corporation - Engineering Library.

ZIFF-DAVIS PUBLISHING COMPANY - PSYCHOLOGY TODAY
See: American Psychological Association - Psychology Today Library

★17460★
ZIFF-DAVIS PUBLISHING COMPANY - TRANSPORTATION DIVISION - LIBRARY (Publ; Rec)
One Park Ave.   Phone: (212) 503-5300
New York, NY 10016   Amelia Schwartz, Dir., Lib.Serv.
Founded: 1972. **Staff:** Prof 1. **Subjects:** Travel and tourism. **Holdings:** 3000 books; 120 bound periodical volumes; VF drawers; 27,000 microjackets. **Subscriptions:** 80 journals and other serials. **Services:** Reader-printer retrieval of Travel Weekly articles; library open to public by appointment.

ZIMPRO INC.
See: Sterling Drug, Inc.

★17461★
ZINC INSTITUTE - INFORMATION SERVICE (Sci-Tech)
292 Madison Ave.   Phone: (212) 578-4750
New York, NY 10017   Mary W. Covington, Mgr., Info.Serv.
Staff: Prof 1. **Subjects:** Production and use of zinc and zinc alloys and products; galvanization; building construction; die casting. **Special Collections:** Proceedings of International Galvanizing Conferences. **Holdings:** 1500 volumes; 30 VF drawers. **Subscriptions:** 200 journals and other serials. **Services:** Interlibrary loans; services open to public by appointment. **Computerized Information Services:** DIALOG, SDC.

★17462★
ZION MENNONITE CHURCH - LIBRARY (Rel-Theol)
149 Cherry Lane   Phone: (215) 723-5605
Souderton, PA 18964   Gwen N. Hartzel, Chm., Lib.Comm.
Founded: 1945. **Staff:** 6. **Subjects:** Bible, Mennonite Church history, books for children and young people. **Holdings:** 5000 books. **Services:** Interlibrary loans; library open to public.

ZION NATL. PARK
See: U.S. Natl. Park Service

ZIONIST ARCHIVES AND LIBRARY
See: World Zionist Organization - American Section

ZIONIST YOUTH MOVEMENT
See: Hashomer Hatzair-Zionist Youth Movement

ZISKIND MEMORIAL LIBRARY
See: Temple Beth-El

★17463★
ZITTRER, SIBLIN, STEIN, LEVINE - LIBRARY (Bus-Fin)
4115 Sherbrooke St., W.   Phone: (514) 933-1112
Montreal, PQ, Canada H3Z 1K9   Norman Daitchman
Subjects: Accounting, auditing, tax. **Holdings:** 200 books. **Subscriptions:** 10 journals and other serials. **Services:** Library not open to public.

ZIV LIBRARY OF TELEVISION PROGRAMS
See: University of Wisconsin, Madison - Wisconsin Center for Film and Theater Research

★17464★
ZOECON CORPORATION - LIBRARY (Sci-Tech)
975 California Ave.
Box 10975   Phone: (415) 857-1130
Palo Alto, CA 94303   Carolyn A. Erickson, Libn.
Staff: Prof 2; Other 2. **Subjects:** Organic chemistry, invertebrate biochemistry, general biology, botany and plant genetics, entomology and pest control. **Holdings:** 5500 books; 2500 bound periodical volumes; 10,000 reprints; 900 cartridges of microfilm; 4000 microfiche. **Subscriptions:** 300 journals and other serials. **Services:** Interlibrary loans; copying; library open to public by request. **Computerized Information Services:** DIALOG, SDC, NLM; internal database. **Networks/Consortia:** Member of CLASS. **Staff:** Jean L. LuValle, Asst.Libn.

ZOELLER FINE ARTS LIBRARY
See: Viterbo College

★17465★
ZOOLOGICAL SOCIETY OF CINCINNATI - MEDIA CENTER (Sci-Tech; Aud-Vis)
3400 Vine St.   Phone: (513) 281-3700
Cincinnati, OH 45220   MiMi Hilarius, Media Ctr.Coord.
Founded: 1977. **Subjects:** Zoology, biology, natural history, environmental science, botany. **Special Collections:** Zoological Realia. **Holdings:** 3100 books; 100 bound periodical volumes; 3500 slides; 20 educational kits; 1200 vertical files. **Subscriptions:** 20 journals and other serials. **Services:** Center open to public for reference use only on a limited schedule.

★17466★
ZOOLOGICAL SOCIETY OF PHILADELPHIA - LIBRARY (Sci-Tech)
34th St. & Girard Ave.   Phone: (215) 243-1100
Philadelphia, PA 19104   Alyssa N. Scheuermann, Libn.
Staff: Prof 1. **Subjects:** Zoology, ornithology, mammalogy, herpetology, ichthyology, natural history, zoos and zoo management. **Holdings:** 3000 books; 75 bound periodical volumes; archival material; reports; theses. **Subscriptions:** 250 journals and other serials. **Services:** Interlibrary loans; copying; library open to public by appointment. **Publications:** Monthly report - for internal distribution only.

★17467★
ZOOLOGICAL SOCIETY OF SAN DIEGO - ERNST SCHWARZ LIBRARY (Sci-Tech)
San Diego Zoo
Box 551   Phone: (619) 231-1515
San Diego, CA 92112   Michaele M. Robinson, Libn.
Founded: 1916. **Staff:** Prof 2; Other 1. **Subjects:** Zoology, taxonomy, ethology, zoological medicine, natural history, horticulture. **Special Collections:** Charles E. Shaw Herpetological Library (300 books; 5000 reprints); Ernst Schwarz reprint collection (2000). **Holdings:** 9000 books; 4000 bound periodical volumes; 15,000 reprints; 60 boxes of zoo annual reports and guidebooks; 54 linear feet of Zoological Society archives. **Subscriptions:** 680 journals and other serials; 8 newspapers. **Services:** Interlibrary loans; library not open to public. **Computerized Information Services:** DIALOG. **Networks/Consortia:** Member of CLASS; San Diego Greater Metropolitan Area Library & Information Agency Council (METRO). **Publications:** Acquisitions list, monthly - distributed to staff; Serials Holding List, updated annually. **Staff:** Janet S. Lombard, Asst.Libn.

ZUG MEMORIAL LIBRARY
See: Elizabethtown College

ZYLMAN (Jacob D.) MEMORIAL LIBRARY
See: Fairfax Hospital - Jacob D. Zylman Memorial Library

APPENDIX A
NETWORKS AND CONSORTIA

Appendix A

Networks and Consortia

All libraries in this directory were asked for information concerning the networks and consortia in which they participate. This appendix is a geographic list by state of over 800 cooperative organizations and their addresses based on the responses given by librarians. These groups range in scope and sophistication from local informal arrangements to larger regional and national organizations.

Questionnaires were mailed to all networks and consortia in the eighth edition and newly formed organizations reported to us. In cases where no separate address for the group could be found, the address of the reporting member library is given. Names of contact persons are included when known.

Networks well known by their acronym, such as NELINET or MINITEX, are listed under it; others appear under their complete name. When a network is known by more than one name, that information is noted in the entry and the variant name or acronym can be found in the cumulative index arranged in alphabetical order at the end of the Appendix.

United States

ALABAMA

★N1★
ALABAMA CENTER FOR HIGHER EDUCATION (ACHE)
c/o J.F. Drake Memorial Learning
Resources Center
Alabama A & M University
Box 489   Phone: (205) 859-7309
Normal, AL 35762
Address and phone are those of member library.

★N2★
ALABAMA CONSORTIUM FOR THE DEVELOPMENT OF HIGHER EDUCATION (ACDHE)
1500 E. Fairview Ave.
Montgomery, AL 36106
Defunct

★N3★
ALABAMA HEALTH LIBRARIES ASSOCIATION MEDICAL LIBRARY PROGRAM †
Box 17059   Phone: (205) 272-8781
Montgomery, AL 36193   Willette W. Vaughan, Coord.

★N4★
ALABAMA LIBRARY EXCHANGE, INC. (ALEX)
Box 443   Phone: (205) 536-3177
Huntsville, AL 35804   Lee E. Pike, Dir.

★N5★
ALABAMA LIBRARY INFORMATION NETWORK (ALIN)
Alabama Public Library Service
6030 Monticello Dr.   Phone: (205) 277-7330
Montgomery, AL 36130   Anthony W. Miele, Dir.

★N6★
ALABAMA SOCIETY FOR HOSPITAL LIBRARY MANAGERS
c/o Medical Library
Northeast Alabama Regional Medical Center
400 E. Tenth St.
Box 2208   Phone: (205) 235-5877
Anniston, AL 36202   Priscilla B. Lloyd, Libn.

★N7★
COUNCIL OF HEALTH SCIENCES LIBRARY DIRECTORS
c/o Lister Hill Lib. of the Health Sciences
University of Alabama
University Sta.   Phone: (205) 934-5460
Birmingham, AL 35294   Richard B. Fredericksen
Address and phone are those of member library.

★N8★
JEFFERSON COUNTY HOSPITAL LIBRARIANS' ASSOCIATION
2010 Brookwood Medical Center Dr.   Phone: (205) 877-1131
Birmingham, AL 35209   Lucy Moor, Med.Libn.
Address rotates annually.

★N9★
MARINE ENVIRONMENTAL SCIENCES CONSORTIUM (MESC)
Dauphin Island Sea Lab Library
Box 369-370   Phone: (205) 861-2141
Dauphin Island, AL 36528   George Crozier, Coord.

★N10★
NORTH ALABAMA BIOMEDICAL INFORMATION NETWORK (NABIN)
Medical Library
University of Alabama in Huntsville
Huntsville, AL 35899   Joy Graham, Interim Dir.

ALASKA

★N11★
ALASKA LIBRARY NETWORK
c/o Alaska State Library
Pouch G
Juneau, AK 99811

ARIZONA

★N12★
ARIZONA RESEARCH INFORMATION CENTER (ARIC)
c/o Tucson Public Library
Box 27470   Phone: (602) 791-4393
Tucson, AZ 85726   Carol Ann Rott, Coord.
Formerly: Pima Regional Library Service (PRLS).

★N13★
ARLIS
c/o Heard Museum Library
22 E. Monte Vista Rd.   Phone: (602) 252-8840
Phoenix, AZ 85004   Mary E. Graham, Libn.

★N14★
CONSORTIUM FOR INTERNATIONAL DEVELOPMENT INFORMATION
    NETWORK (CIDNET)
Arid Lands Information Center
University of Arizona
845 N. Park Ave.   Phone: (602) 621-7897
Tucson, AZ 85719   Elaine Cook, Mgr.

★N15★
MARICOPA BIOMEDICAL LIBRARIANS (MABL)
c/o Health Science Library
Good Samaritan Medical Center
Box 2989   Phone: (602) 257-4353
Phoenix, AZ 85062
Address and phone are those of member library.

★N16★
NATIONAL PLANETARY IMAGE LIBRARIES
c/o Space Photography Laboratory
Department of Geology
Arizona State University   Phone: (602) 965-7029
Tempe, AZ 85287   Prof. Ronald Greeley

ARKANSAS

★N17★
ARKANSAS AHEC CONSORTIA
c/o Medical Library
Sparks Regional Medical Center
1311 S. I St.   Phone: (501) 440-4179
Fort Smith, AR 72901   Grace Anderson, Dir., Med.Lib.

★N18★
HENDERSON-OUACHITA LIBRARY CONSORTIUM
c/o Henderson State University Library
Box 632
Arkadelphia, AR 71923
Address is that of member library.

CALIFORNIA

★N19★
AREAWIDE LIBRARY NETWORK (AWLNET)
2420 Mariposa St.   Phone: (209) 488-3229
Fresno, CA 93721   Sharon Vandercook, Ref.Coord.
Affiliated with the San Joaquin Valley Library System.

★N20★
BAY AREA EDUCATION LIBRARIES
c/o Library and Archives
Far West Laboratory for Education
Research and Development
1855 Folsom St.   Phone: (415) 565-3065
San Francisco, CA 94103
Address and phone are those of member library.

★N21★
BAY AREA LIBRARY AND INFORMATION NETWORK (BALIN)
125 14th St.
Oakland, CA 94612
A multi-type library organization affiliated with the Bay Area Library and
Information System (BALIS).

★N22★
BAY AREA LIBRARY AND INFORMATION SYSTEM (BALIS)
125 14th St.   Phone: (415) 839-6001
Oakland, CA 94612   Kathryn Page, Act.Sys.Coord.

★N23★
BAY AREA REFERENCE CENTER (BARC)
San Francisco Public Library
Civic Center   Phone: (415) 558-2941
San Francisco, CA 94102   Fauneil McInnis, Dir.

★N24★
BAY AREA TRANSPORTATION INFORMATION NETWORK
c/o Assn. of Bay Area Governments Library
Metropolitan Transportation Commission
101 8th St.   Phone: (415) 849-3223
Oakland, CA 94607
Address and phone are those of member library.

★N25★
BCG SYSTEMWIDE INFORMATION RESOURCE NETWORK
West Coast Information Center
Boston Consulting Group
2180 Sand Hill Rd.
Menlo Park, CA 94020

★N26★
BECHTEL INFORMATION NETWORK
c/o Bechtel Central Library
50 Beale St.   Phone: (415) 768-5306
San Francisco, CA 94119

★N27★
CALIFORNIA STATE UNIVERSITY SYSTEM
c/o University Library
California State Polytechnic University
3801 W. Temple Ave.   Phone: (714) 598-4671
Pomona, CA 91768
Address and phone are those of member library.

★N28★
CALINET
c/o Edward L. Doheny Memorial Library
University of Southern California
University Park   Phone: (213) 743-2924
Los Angeles, CA 90089-0182   Lynn F. Sipe, Coord.
Also Known As: California Library Network.

★N29★
CENTRAL ASSOCIATION OF LIBRARIES (CAL)
Stockton-San Joaquin County Library
605 N. El Dorado St.   Phone: (209) 944-8650
Stockton, CA 95202   Janet Kase, Dir.

★N30★
CENTRAL CALIFORNIA MEDICAL LIBRARY GROUP
c/o Medical Library
Merced Community Medical Center
301 E. 13th St.
Box 231   Phone: (209) 385-7058
Merced, CA 95340   Betty Maddalena, Coord.
Address and phone are those of member library.

★N31★
CLASS
1415 Koll Circle, Suite 101   Phone: (408) 289-1756
San Jose, CA 95112   Ron Miller, Exec.Dir.
Also Known As: California Library Authority for Systems & Services.

★N32★
COASTAL HEALTH LIBRARY INFORMATION CONSORTIUM (CHLIC)
c/o Library
California Polytechnic State Univ.   Phone: (805) 546-2273
San Luis Obispo, CA 93407   Paul Scott, Pres.
Address rotates periodically.

★N33★
CONSUMER HEALTH INFORMATION COOPERATIVE (CHIC)
c/o Wadsworth Medical Library
U.S. Veterans Administration
Wilshire & Sawtelle Blvds.   Phone: (213) 824-3102
Los Angeles, CA 90073
Address and phone are those of member library.

★N34★
CONSUMER HEALTH INFORMATION PROGRAM AND SERVICES (CHIPS)
Carson Regional Library
151 E. Carson St.   Phone: (213) 830-0909
Carson, CA 90745   Rose Erikson, Coord.

★N35★
COOPERATING LIBRARIANS IN CLAREMONT (CLIC)
c/o The Claremont Colleges   Phone: (714) 621-8045
Claremont, CA 91711   Patrick Barkey, Dir.

★N36★
ENERGY LIBRARIANS OF THE BAY AREA
c/o Library of the Environment
Peninsula Conservation Foundation   Phone: (415) 328-5313
Palo Alto, CA 94306
Address and phone are those of member library.

★N37★
49-99 COOPERATIVE LIBRARY SYSTEM
Stockton-San Joaquin County Pub.Lib.
605 N. El Dorado St.   Phone: (209) 944-8650
Stockton, CA 95202   Janet Kase, Dir.
Address and phone are those of member library.

★N38★
HEALTH INFORMATION TO COMMUNITY HOSPITALS (HITCH)
c/o Norris Medical Library
University of Southern California
2025 Zonal Ave.   Phone: (213) 224-7414
Los Angeles, CA 90033   Nelson J. Gilman, Dir.

★N39★
HEWLETT-PACKARD LIBRARY/INFORMATION NETWORK
Corporate Library
Hewlett-Packard Company
1501 Page Mill Rd.   Phone: (415) 857-3092
Palo Alto, CA 94304

★N40★
INLAND EMPIRE ACADEMIC LIBRARIES COOPERATIVE (IEALC)
c/o Chaffey Community College
5885 Haven Ave.   Phone: (714) 987-1737
Alta Loma, CA 91701   Phyllis Smith, Coord.
Address rotates biennially.

★N41★
INLAND EMPIRE MEDICAL LIBRARY COOPERATIVE
c/o Medical Library
San Bernardino Community Hospital
1500 W. 17th St.   Phone: (714) 887-6333
San Bernardino, CA 92411
Address and phone are those of member library.

★N42★
JOINT UNIVERSITY OF CALIFORNIA MAP LIBRARY MANAGEMENT GROUP
Map and Imagery Laboratory Library
University of California   Phone: (805) 961-2779
Santa Barbara, CA 93106   Larry Carver, Dept.Hd.

★N43★
KAISER PERMANENTE LIBRARY SYSTEM (KPLS)
c/o Health Sciences Library
Kaiser Permanente Medical Center
4647 Zion Ave.   Phone: (619) 563-2190
San Diego, CA 92120
Address and phone are those of member library.

★N44★
KERN HEALTH SCIENCE LIBRARIES CONSORTIUM
c/o Kern Health Science Library
1830 Flower St.   Phone: (805) 326-2227
Bakersfield, CA 93305

★N45★
LOS ANGELES COUNTY HEALTH SCIENCES LIBRARIANS GROUP
c/o Medical Libraries
Los Angeles County/USC Med.Ctr.
1200 N. State St.   Phone: (213) 226-7006
Los Angeles, CA 90033
Address and phone are those of member library.

★N46★
MARIN CONSORTIUM FOR HIGHER EDUCATION
Box 2212
San Rafael, CA 94902
Defunct

★N47★
MARIN LIBRARY NETWORK (MLN)
c/o Marin Community College   Phone: (415) 485-9470
Kentfield, CA 94904   Cal Kurzman, Dean, LRC

★N48★
MEDICAL LIBRARY CONSORTIUM OF SANTA CLARA VALLEY
c/o Health Science Library
San Jose Hospital
675 E. Santa Clara   Phone: (408) 998-3212
San Jose, CA 95112   Joan Gerteis, Chm.
Chairmanship and address rotate bienially. Also Known As: Santa Clara County
Medical Library Consortium.

★N49★
MEDICAL LIBRARY GROUP OF SOUTHERN CALIFORNIA AND ARIZONA
  (MLGSCA)
Box 4615
Irvine, CA 92716-4615

★N50★
METROPOLITAN COOPERATIVE LIBRARY SYSTEM (MCLS)
2235 N. Lake Ave., Suite 106   Phone: (818) 798-1146
Altadena, CA 91001   Holly Millard, Sys.Dir.

★N51★
MONTEREY BAY AREA COOPERATIVE LIBRARY SYSTEM (MOBAC)
MPC Library Bldg.   Phone: (408) 646-4256
Monterey, CA 93940   Helen Gottlober, Coord.

★N52★
MOUNTAIN VALLEY LIBRARY SYSTEM
Sacramento Public Library
828 I St.   Phone: (916) 444-0926
Sacramento, CA 95814   Mark R. Parker, Coord.

★N53★
NORTH BAY COOPERATIVE LIBRARY SYSTEM (NBCLS)
725 Third St.   Phone: (707) 544-0142
Santa Rosa, CA 95404-4480   Linda J. Knutson, Adm.

★N54★
NORTH STATE COOPERATIVE LIBRARY SYSTEM (NSCLS)
257 N. Villa St.   Phone: (916) 934-2173
Willows, CA 95988   James H. Kirks, Jr., Coord.

★N55★
NORTHERN CALIFORNIA AND NEVADA MEDICAL LIBRARY GROUP
c/o The Library
University of California   Phone: (415) 666-2533
San Francisco, CA 94702   Jacqueline Wilson, Pres.
Address rotates annually.

★N56★
NURSING INFORMATION CONSORTIUM OF ORANGE COUNTY (NICOC)
Medical Library
Western Medical Center
1001 N. Tustin Ave.   Phone: (714) 533-6220
Santa Ana, CA 92705   Evelyn Simpson, Co.Dir.

★N57★
OCLC PACIFIC NETWORK
Ninth & Dartmouth   Phone: (714) 621-8046
Claremont, CA 91711
Formerly: OCLC/Western.

★N58★
ORANGE COUNTY LIBRARIES ASSOCIATION (OCLA)
c/o Technical Information Center
American McGaw
Box 25080   Phone: (714) 660-2505
Santa Ana, CA 92799-5080   Carol DeLape, Coord.

★N59★

PACIFIC SOUTHWEST REGIONAL MEDICAL LIBRARY SERVICE (PSRMLS)
Biomedical Library
University of California   Phone: (213) 825-1200
Los Angeles, CA 90024   Gloria Werner
Region 7 of the Regional Medical Library Program serving AZ, CA, HI and NV.

★N60★

PENINSULA LIBRARY SYSTEM
c/o Business Section
San Mateo Public Library
55 W. Third Ave.   Phone: (415) 574-6955
San Mateo, CA 94402
Address and phone are those of member library.

★N61★

PRIVATE LAW LIBRARY ASSOCIATION OF SAN FRANCISCO
c/o Brobeck, Phleger & Harrison - Library
Spear St. Tower
1 Market Plaza   Phone: (415) 442-1054
San Francisco, CA 94105
Address and phone are those of member library**Formerly:** San Francisco Law
Librarians.

★N62★
RLG
Jordan Quadrangle   Phone: (415) 328-0920
Stanford, CA 94305   La Vonne Gallo, Mgr.
Operates the Research Libraries Information Network (RLIN).**Also Known As:**
Research Libraries Group, Inc.

★N63★

SACRAMENTO AREA HEALTH SCIENCES LIBRARIANS GROUP (SAHSL)
5380 Elvas Ave.   Phone: (916) 452-2671
Sacramento, CA 95819   K.D. Proffit, Libn.
Address rotates annually.

★N64★

SAN BERNARDINO, INYO, RIVERSIDE UNITED LIBRARY SERVICES
    (SIRCULS)
312 W. 20th St., Suite D   Phone: (714) 882-7577
San Bernardino, CA 92405

★N65★

SAN DIEGO GREATER METROPOLITAN AREA LIBRARY & INFORMATION
    AGENCY COUNCIL (METRO) †
c/o San Diego County Public Library
5555 Overland Ave.   Phone: (619) 278-8090
San Diego, CA 92123   Debra Miller, Dir.

★N66★

SAN DIEGO AND IMPERIAL COUNTIES COMMUNITY COLLEGES LEARNING
    RESOURCES COOPERATIVE
c/o Miramar College
10440 Black Mountain Rd.   Phone: (619) 469-8900
San Diego, CA 92126   Carolyn F. Norman, Coord.
Address rotates annually.**Formerly:** San Diego Area Community Colleges
Learning Resources Cooperative.

★N67★

SAN FERNANDO VALLEY MEDICAL LIBRARY GROUP
c/o American Bio-Science Laboratories
7600 Tyrone Ave.   Phone: (818) 989-2520
Van Nuys, CA 91405   Lois Mackey, Chm.
Address rotates annually.

★N68★

SAN FRANCISCO BIOMEDICAL LIBRARY NETWORK
Enge Medical Library
Children's Hospital of San Francisco
Box 3805
San Francisco, CA 94119

★N69★

SAN FRANCISCO CONSORTIUM
513 Parnassus Ave., Suite S-224   Phone: (415) 666-2407
San Francisco, CA 94143   Malcolm S.M. Watts, M.D., Exec.Sec.

★N70★

SAN JOAQUIN VALLEY LIBRARY SYSTEM (SJVLS)
2420 Mariposa St.   Phone: (209) 488-3185
Fresno, CA 93721   Sharon Vandercook

★N71★

SAN MATEO COUNTY HOSPITAL LIBRARY CONSORTIA
c/o San Mateo County Dept. of Health Serv.Lib.
225 37th Ave.   Phone: (415) 573-2520
San Mateo, CA 94403
Address and phone are those of member library.

★N72★

SERRA COOPERATIVE LIBRARY SYSTEM
c/o San Diego County Library, Bldg. 15
5555 Overland Ave.
San Diego, CA 92123

★N73★

THE SOURCE NETWORK
c/o Architecture & Urban Planning Lib.
Southern California Institute of Architecture
1800 Berkeley St.   Phone: (213) 829-3482
Santa Monica, CA 90404   Rose Marie Rabin

★N74★

SOUTH BAY AREA REFERENCE NETWORK
Division Library
Litton Applied Technology
645 Almanor Ave.   Phone: (408) 773-7059
Sunnyvale, CA 94088-3478   Doron Dula, Libn.

★N75★

SOUTH BAY COOPERATIVE LIBRARY SYSTEM (SBCLS)
2635 Homestead Rd.   Phone: (408) 984-3278
Santa Clara, CA 95051   Craig Conover, Coord.

★N76★

SOUTH STATE COOPERATIVE LIBRARY SYSTEM †
c/o Los Angeles County Public Library
7400 E. Imperial Hwy.
Box 7011   Phone: (213) 922-7538
Downey, CA 90241   Vicki Jenkins, Coord.

★N77★

SOUTHEAST HOSPITAL LIBRARIANS GROUP
c/o Health Science Library
Downey Community Hospital
11500 Brookshire Ave.   Phone: (213) 869-3061
Downey, CA 90241
Address and phone are those of member library.

★N78★

SOUTHERN CALIFORNIA ANSWERING NETWORK (SCAN)
Los Angeles Public Library
630 W. 5th St.   Phone: (213) 626-7555
Los Angeles, CA 90071   Evelyn Greenwald, Dir.

★N79★

SOUTHERN CALIFORNIA CONSORTIUM
c/o Downey Historical Society Museum Library
12458 Rives Ave.
Box 554   Phone: (213) 862-2777
Downey, CA 90241
Address and phone are those of member library.

★N80★

SOUTHERN CALIFORNIA FILM CIRCUIT (SCFC)
4819 Regalo Rd.   Phone: (213) 348-8767
Woodland Hills, CA 91364   William J. Speed, Adm.

★N81★

TOTAL INTERLIBRARY EXCHANGE (TIE)
Box 771   Phone: (805) 654-2643
Ventura, CA 93002   Phyllis Maggeroli, Coord.

★N82★
TRANSPORTATION PLANNING SUPPORT INFORMATION SYSTEM (TPSIS)
Division of Transportation Planning
California Dept. of Transportation
1120 N St.   Phone: (916) 322-7760
Sacramento, CA 95814   Les Jones, Res.Mgr. I

★N83★
TRANSPORTATION RESEARCH SERVICES INFORMATION NETWORK
   (TRISNET)
c/o Institute of Transportation Studies Library
University of California
412 McLaughlin Hall
Berkeley, CA 94720
Address is that of member library.

★N84★
UNIVERSITY OF CALIFORNIA CHICANO INFORMATION MANAGEMENT
   CONSORTIUM
c/o Chicano Studies Library
University of California
3408 Dwinelle Hall   Phone: (415) 642-3859
Berkeley, CA 94720
Address and phone are those of member library.

★N85★
WESTFORNET
Pacific S.W. Forest-Range Experiment Sta.
U.S. Forest Service
1960 Addison St.
Box 245   Phone: (415) 486-3173
Berkeley, CA 94701   Theodor B. Yerke
Also Known As: Western Forest Information Network.

★N86★
XEROX PARC LIBRARIES NETWORK
3333 Coyote Hill Rd.   Phone: (415) 494-4040
Palo Alto, CA 94304   Giuliana Lavendel, Coord.

COLORADO

★N87★
ARKANSAS VALLEY REGIONAL LIBRARY SERVICE SYSTEM
205 W. Abriendo Ave.   Phone: (303) 542-2156
Pueblo, CO 81004   Stephen K. Ooton, System Dir.

★N88★
BIBLIOGRAPHICAL CENTER FOR RESEARCH, ROCKY MOUNTAIN REGION,
   INC. (BCR)
1777 S. Bellaire, Suite G-150   Phone: (303) 691-0550
Denver, CO 80222   David Brunell, Exec.Dir.
See also the library listing for this network in the main section.

★N89★
CENTRAL COLORADO LIBRARY SYSTEM (CCLS)
3805 Marshall St., Suite 204
Wheat Ridge, CO 80033   Gordon C. Barhydt, Dir.

★N90★
COLORADO ALLIANCE OF RESEARCH LIBRARIES (CARL)
3840 York St., Unit J   Phone: (303) 571-2270
Denver, CO 80205   Ward Shaw, Exec.Dir.

★N91★
COLORADO CONSORTIUM OF LAW LIBRARIES
Box 13,363   Phone: (303) 691-5400
Denver, CO 80201   Dorothy Norbie, Pres.

★N92★
COLORADO COUNCIL OF MEDICAL LIBRARIANS
c/o Lutheran Medical Center Library
8300 W. 38th Ave.   Phone: (303) 425-8662
Wheat Ridge, CO 80038   Susan Higginbotham, Pres.
Address rotates annually.

★N93★
COLORADO LIBRARY NETWORK (COLONET)
Colorado State Library
1362 Lincoln St.   Phone: (303) 866-5442
Denver, CO 80203

★N94★
DENVER AREA HEALTH SCIENCES LIBRARY CONSORTIUM
c/o Assoc. of Operating Room Nurses Library
10170 E. Mississippi   Phone: (303) 755-6300
Denver, CO 80231   Sara Katsh, Coord.
Address rotates annually.

★N95★
HIGH PLAINS REGIONAL LIBRARY SYSTEM
2227 23rd Ave.   Phone: (303) 330-7691
Greeley, CO 80631   Nancy Knepel, Coord.

★N96★
PATHFINDER REGIONAL LIBRARY SERVICE SYSTEM
South First & Uncompahgre   Phone: (303) 249-1078
Montrose, CO 81401

★N97★
PEAKS AND VALLEYS (MEDICAL) LIBRARY CONSORTIUM
c/o Arkansas Valley Regional
Library Service System
205 W. Abriendo   Phone: (303) 542-2156
Pueblo, CO 81004   Steve Ooton, Pres.
Address rotates annually.

★N98★
PLAINS AND PEAKS REGIONAL LIBRARY SERVICE SYSTEM †
Broadmarket Sq.
1761 S. 8th St., H-2
Colorado Springs, CO 80906   Mary Jeanne Owen, Dir.

★N99★
SOCIAL SCIENCE EDUCATION CONSORTIUM
Resource & Demonstration Center
855 Broadway   Phone: (303) 492-8155
Boulder, CO 80302

★N100★
SOUTHWEST REGIONAL LIBRARY SERVICE SYSTEM (SWRLSS) †
201 12th St., Drawer B   Phone: (303) 247-4782
Durango, CO 81301   S. Jane Ulrich, Dir.

★N101★
THREE RIVERS REGIONAL LIBRARY SERVICE SYSTEM
Box 97   Phone: (303) 984-2887
New Castle, CO 81647   Donna Good, Dir.

CONNECTICUT

★N102★
BIBLIOMATION
925 Broad St.   Phone: (203) 367-0189
Bridgeport, CT 06604   Michael J. Simonds, Exec.Dir.

★N103★
CAPITOL AREA ASSOCIATION OF MEDICAL LIBRARY DIRECTORS
   (CAAMLD) †
c/o V.A. Hospital Medical Library
555 Willard Ave.   Phone: (203) 666-6951
Newington, CT 06111   Julie Lueders
Formerly: Capitol Area Health Consortium Libraries.

★N104★
CAPITOL REGION LIBRARY COUNCIL
275 Windsor St.   Phone: (203) 549-0404
Hartford, CT 06120   Dency Sargent, Exec.Dir.

★N105★
CONNECTICUT ASSOCIATION OF HEALTH SCIENCE LIBRARIES (CAHSL)
c/o Health Sciences Library
New Milford Hospital
21 Elm St.   Phone: (203) 355-2611
New Milford, CT 06776   Susan E. Hays, Pres.
Address rotates annually.

★N106★
CTUW PROJECT †
c/o University of Connecticut Library   Phone: (203) 486-2220
Storrs, CT 06268   Norman Stevens, Hd.

★N107★
HARTFORD CONSORTIUM FOR HIGHER EDUCATION
30 Elizabeth St.   Phone: (203) 236-1203
Hartford, CT 06105   Ruth W. Billyou, Coord.

★N108★
HEALTH INFORMATION LIBRARIES OF WESTCHESTER (HILOW)
c/o Health Sciences Library
Stamford Hospital
Shelburne Rd.
Box 9317   Phone: (203) 325-7522
Stamford, CT 06904   Joanna Faraday, Pres.
Address rotates annually.

★N109★
**INFORMATION NETWORK FOR MATERIALS EFFECTING DEVELOPMENT
     (INFORMED)**
c/o Save the Children Library
48 Wilton Rd.   Phone: (203) 226-7271
Westport, CT 06880   Nancy Faesy, Chm.
Address rotates annually.

★N110★
MOLENET
Molesworth Institute
143 Hanks Hill Rd.   Phone: (203) 429-7051
Storrs, CT 06268   Basil Fotherington-Thomas, Dir.

★N111★
NORTHEASTERN CONNECTICUT HOSPITAL LIBRARY CONSORTIUM
c/o Medical Library
Manchester Memorial Hospital
71 Haynes St.   Phone: (203) 646-1222
Manchester, CT 06040   Anna Salo, Coord.
Address rotates annually.

★N112★
**NORTHWESTERN CONNECTICUT HEALTH SCIENCE LIBRARY
     CONSORTIUM**
24 Hospital Ave.
Danbury, CT 06810   Maryanne Witters

★N113★
**REGION ONE COOPERATING LIBRARIES SERVICE UNIT FOR
     NORTHWESTERN CONNECTICUT**
c/o Silas Bronson Library
267 Grand St.   Phone: (203) 756-6149
Waterbury, CT 06702   Leo N. Flanagan

★N114★
SOUTHEASTERN CONNECTICUT LIBRARY ASSOCIATION (SECLA)
Avery Point   Phone: (203) 445-5577
Groton, CT 06340   James R. Benn, Dir.

★N115★
SOUTHERN CONNECTICUT LIBRARY COUNCIL †
2901 Dixwell Ave.   Phone: (203) 248-5898
Hamden, CT 06518   Sherry W. Hupp, Regional Coord.

★N116★
**SOUTHWESTERN CONNECTICUT HEALTH SCIENCE LIBRARY
     CONSORTIUM**
Shelburne Rd.
Box 9317
Stamford, CT 06904
Inactive

★N117★
SOUTHWESTERN CONNECTICUT LIBRARY COUNCIL (SWLC)
Bridgeport Public Library
925 Broad St.   Phone: (203) 367-6439
Bridgeport, CT 06604   Ann Neary, Coord.

★N118★
UNITED TECHNOLOGIES LIBRARY SYSTEM
c/o Library
United Technologies Research Ctr.   Phone: (203) 727-7120
East Hartford, CT 06108   Irving H. Neufeld, Chf.
Address and phone are those of member library.

DELAWARE

★N119★
COUNCIL OF HISTORICAL LIBRARIES OF DELAWARE (CHILD)
Hagley Museum & Library
Box 3630   Phone: (302) 658-2400
Wilmington, DE 19807   R.D. Williams, Dir.

★N120★
DELAWARE LEARNING RESOURCE SYSTEM (DLRS)
c/o Education Resource Center
University of Delaware
012 Wilard Hall   Phone: (302) 738-2235
Newark, DE 19711   Janet Dove, Dir., E.R.C.

★N121★
DELAWARE LIBRARY CONSORTIUM
Delaware Law School
Concord Pike
Box 7475
Wilmington, DE 19803   Jacqueline R. Paul, Coord.

★N122★
KENT LIBRARY NETWORK (KLN)
c/o Delaware Tech and Community College
Terry Campus   Phone: (302) 736-5404
Dover, DE 19901   Joe Gates, Asst.Libn.
Address rotates biennially.

★N123★
LIBRARIES IN THE NEW CASTLE COUNTY SYSTEM (LINCS)
c/o Delaware Academy of Medicine
1925 Lovering Ave.   Phone: (302) 656-1629
Wilmington, DE 19806   Gail Gill, Coord.

★N124★
LINCK
c/o Medical Library
Governor Bacon Health Center   Phone: (302) 834-9201
Delaware City, DE 19706
Address and phone are those of member library.

★N125★
MEDICAL INFORMATION CONSORTIUM OF KENT & SUSSEX (MEDICKS)
c/o Medical Library
Beebe Hospital
Drawer 226
Lewes, DE 19958
Inactive

★N126★
WILMINGTON AREA BIOMEDICAL LIBRARY CONSORTIUM (WABLC)
Delaware Academy of Medicine
1925 Lovering Ave.   Phone: (302) 656-1629
Wilmington, DE 19806   Gail P. Gill

DISTRICT OF COLUMBIA

★N127★
ASSOCIATION OF RESEARCH LIBRARIES (ARL)
1527 New Hampshire Ave., N.W.   Phone: (202) 232-2466
Washington, DC 20036   Shirley Echelman, Exec.Dir.

★N128★ †
CAPCON †
1776 Massachusetts Ave., N.W., Rm. 412   Phone: (202) 785-0700
Washington, DC 20036   Joseph B. Ford, Exec.Dir.
Also Known As: Capitol Consortium Network.

★N129★
CHRISTIAN COLLEGE COALITION
1776 Massachusetts Ave., N.W.   Phone: (202) 293-6177
Washington, DC 20036   John R. Dellenback, Pres.

★N130★
**CONSORTIUM OF ACADEMIC HEALTH SCIENCES LIBRARIES OF THE
   DISTRICT OF COLUMBIA**
c/o Dahlgren Memorial Library
Georgetown Univ. Medical Center
3900 Reservoir Rd.
Washington, DC 20007   Naomi C. Bweung
Address is that of member library.

★N131★
**CONSORTIUM OF UNIVERSITIES OF THE WASHINGTON METROPOLITAN
   AREA**
1346 Connecticut Ave., N.W., Suite 531   Phone: (202) 466-2628
Washington, DC 20036   Dr. Darrell Lemke, Coord., Lib.Prog.

★N132★
CRIMINAL JUSTICE INFORMATION EXCHANGE
c/o National Institute of Justice
633 Indiana Ave., N.W.   Phone: (202) 724-5883
Washington, DC 20004   Kyle Kramer, Coord.

★N133★
**DISTRICT OF COLUMBIA HEALTH SCIENCES INFORMATION NETWORK
   (DOCHSIN)**
c/o Sturges Memorial Library
Group Health Assn. of America
624 9th St., N.W., Suite 700   Phone: (202) 737-4311
Washington, DC 20001
Address and phone are those of member library.

★N134★
ERIC
Dissemination & Improvement of Practices
National Institute of Education
U.S. Dept. of Education   Phone: (202) 254-5500
Washington, DC 20208-1101   Charles W. Hoover, Chf.
Also Known As: Education Resources Information Center.

★N135★
FEDLINK
Federal Library Committee
Library of Congress   Phone: (202) 287-6454
Washington, DC 20540   Milton Megee, Coord.
Also Known As: Federal Library and Information Network.

★N136★
INTERNATIONAL ROAD FEDERATION (IRF)
525 School St., S.W.
Washington, DC 20024
IRF is one of the offices in the U.S. cooperating with the International Road
Research Documentation.

★N137★
METROPOLITAN WASHINGTON LIBRARY COUNCIL
Council of Governments
1875 I St., N.W., Suite 200   Phone: (202) 223-6800
Washington, DC 20006   Mollyne Honor-Forte, Dir.

★N138★
NASA LIBRARY NETWORK (NALNET) †
Scientific & Technical Info. Branch
NASA Headquarters   Phone: (202) 755-3544
Washington, DC 20546

★N139★
**NATIONAL LIBRARY SERVICE FOR THE BLIND & PHYSICALLY
   HANDICAPPED (NLS)**
Library of Congress
1291 Taylor St., N.W.   Phone: (202) 287-5100
Washington, DC 20542   Frank Kurt Cylke, Dir.
Regional and subregional libraries in this network are listed in Appendix B. See
also the library listing for this network in the main section.

★N140★
**NATIONAL NATURAL RESOURCES LIBRARY AND INFORMATION SYSTEM
   (NNRLIS)**
Natural Resources Library
U.S. Dept. of the Interior
18th and C Sts., N.W.   Phone: (202) 343-5821
Washington, DC 20240   Philip M. Haymond, Coord.
See also the library listing for this network under U.S. Dept. of the Interior -
Natural Resources Library in the main section.

★N141★
NATIONAL STANDARD REFERENCE DATA SYSTEM (NSRDS)
Office of Standard Reference Data
U.S. Natl. Bureau of Standards   Phone: (301) 921-2228
Washington, DC 20234   Dr. David R. Lide, Jr., OSRD Chf.

★N142★
REHABILITATION INFORMATION ROUND TABLE (RIR)
c/o National Rehabilitation Information Center   Phone: (202) 635-5826
Washington, DC 20017   Mark X. Odum, Adm.Coord.

★N143★
VALNET
Library Division 142D
Veterans Administration
810 Vermont Ave., N.W.   Phone: (202) 389-2711
Washington, DC 20420   Karen Renninger, Chf., Lib.Div.
Also Known As: Veterans Administration Library Network.

★N144★
WASHINGTON AREA HOSPITALS MEDLINE CONSORTIUM
c/o Health Sciences Library
Providence Hospital
1150 Varnum St., N.E.   Phone: (202) 269-7144
Washington, DC 20017   Sr. Frances Healy

★N145★
WASHINGTON THEOLOGICAL CONSORTIUM
487 Michigan Ave., N.E.
Washington, DC 20017   Dr. Daniel F. Martensen, Coord.

FLORIDA

★N146★
FLORIDA COMCAT
c/o Orange County Library System
10 N. Rosalind St.   Phone: (305) 425-4694
Orlando, FL 32801   John Claytor, Adm.
Also Known As: Florida Computer-Output-Microform Catalog.

★N147★
FLORIDA LIBRARY INFORMATION NETWORK (FLIN)
State Library
R.A. Gray Bldg.   Phone: (904) 487-2651
Tallahassee, FL 32301-8021   Robert Gorin, Hd., Loans

★N148★
FLORIDA UNION LIST OF SERIALS (FULS)
Library West
University of Florida Libraries
Gainesville, FL 32611
Defunct

★N149★
**INTERNATIONAL ASSOCIATION OF MARINE SCIENCE LIBRARIES AND
   INFORMATION CENTERS (IAMSLIC)**
c/o Harbor Branch Foundation, Inc.
R.R. 1, Box 196   Phone: (305) 465-2400
Fort Pierce, FL 33450   Kristen L. Metzger, Pres.
Address rotates annually.

★N150★
LAWNET
Legal Information Center
College of Law
University of Florida   Phone: (904) 392-0417
Gainesville, FL 32611   Betty Taylor, Chm.

★N151★
PALM BEACH COUNTY HEALTH SCIENCES LIBRARY CONSORTIUM
Richard S. Beinecke Medical Library
Good Samaritan Hospital
Box 3166   Phone: (305) 655-5511
West Palm Beach, FL 33402   Linda O'Callaghan, Asst.Med.Libn.
Address rotates annually.

★N152★
REGIONAL ECONOMIC INFORMATION NETWORK
c/o Research & Information Library
Tampa Bay Regional Planning Council
9455 Koger Blvd.   Phone: (813) 577-5151
St. Petersburg, FL 33702
Address and phone are those of member library.

★N153★
ATLANTIC HEALTH VENTURES, INC.
780 W. Granada Blvd., Suite 106   Phone: (904) 677-6031
Ormand Beach, FL 32019   Alex Gyarfas, Circuit Med.Libn.
Formerly: Shared Hospital Services of Florida, Inc.

★N154★
SOUTH FLORIDA ONLINE SEARCHERS
c/o Otto G. Richter Library
University of Miami
Box 248214   Phone: (305) 284-4900
Coral Gables, FL 33124   Lyn MacCorkle, Coord.
Address rotates annually.

★N155★
TAMPA BAY LIBRARY CONSORTIUM
c/o Jim Walter Research Corp. Library
10309 9th St., N.   Phone: (813) 576-4171
St. Petersburg, FL 33702
Address and phone are those of member library.

★N156★
TAMPA BAY MEDICAL LIBRARY NETWORK
Medical Center Library
University of South Florida
12901 N. 30th St.
Box 43   Phone: (813) 974-2775
Tampa, FL 33612   Sarah Harmon, Coord.

★N157★
U.S. NATL. OCEANIC & ATMOSPHERIC ADMINISTRATION -
    SOUTHEASTERN AREA RESOURCES COOPERATIVE (NOAASARC)
c/o NOAA Miami Library
4301 Rickenbacker Causeway   Phone: (305) 361-4428
Miami, FL 33149
Address and phone are those of member library.

★N158★
WEST COAST LIBRARY CONSORTIUM (WELCO)
c/o Selby Public Library
1001 Blvd. of the Arts   Phone: (813) 366-7303
Sarasota, FL 33577   Joan Hopkins, Pres.
Address rotates annually.

GEORGIA

★N159★
ATLANTA HEALTH SCIENCE LIBRARIES CONSORTIUM
Medical Library
Georgia Baptist Medical Center
300 Boulevard N.E.   Phone: (404) 653-4603
Atlanta, GA 30312   Fay E. Boyer, Coord.
Address rotates annually.

★N160★
ATLANTA LAW LIBRARIES ASSOCIATION
c/o Macey and Zusmann
1794 Peachtree St.   Phone: (404) 894-7200
Atlanta, GA 30309   Pat Strougal, Chm.

★N161★
ATLANTA ONLINE USERS GROUP (AOUG)
c/o Library Services
Georgia Power Company
Box 4545   Phone: (404) 526-6856
Atlanta, GA 30302   Kitty Manning, Coord.

★N162★
CCLC
159 Ralph McGill Blvd., Suite 602   Phone: (404) 659-6886
Atlanta, GA 30365   Hillis D. Davis, Dir.
Also Known As: Cooperative College Library Center, Inc.

★N163★
CENTRAL GEORGIA ASSOCIATED LIBRARIES †
c/o Nola Brantly Memorial Library
721 Watson Blvd.   Phone: (912) 923-0128
Warner Robins, GA 31093   Evelyn Merk, Chm.

★N164★
EAST GEORGIA LIBRARY TRIANGLE
Georgia Southern College
Landrum Box 8074   Phone: (912) 681-5115
Statesboro, GA 30460   Kenneth G. Walter, Chm.

★N165★
GEORGIA DEPARTMENT OF HUMAN RESOURCES LIBRARY CONSORTIUM
4770 N. Peachtree Rd.   Phone: (404) 393-7076
Atlanta, GA 30338   Beth Donaldson, Coord.

★N166★
GEORGIA HEALTH SCIENCES LIBRARY ASSOCIATION (GHSLA)
Medical Library
Georgia Baptist Medical Center
300 Boulevard, N.E.   Phone: (404) 653-4603
Atlanta, GA 30312   Fay E. Boyer, Chm.
Address rotates annually.

★N167★
GEORGIA INTERACTIVE NETWORK FOR MEDICAL INFORMATION
c/o Medical School Library
Mercer University   Phone: (912) 744-2515
Macon, GA 31207   Jocelyn Rankin, Coord.
Also Known As: GAIN.

★N168★
GEORGIA LIBRARY INFORMATION NETWORK (GLIN)
Division of Public Library Services
Georgia Department of Education
156 Trinity Ave., S.W.
Atlanta, GA 30303   Faye Elmore, Cons.

★N169★
HEALTH SCIENCE LIBRARIES OF CENTRAL GEORGIA (HSLCG)
c/o Medical Library
Mercer Univ. School of Medicine   Phone: (912) 744-2515
Macon, GA 31207   Jocelyn Rankin

★N170★
LESBIAN CIRCLE OF INDEXERS
c/o Southeastern Lesbian Archives
Atlanta Lesbian Feminist Alliance
Box 5502   Phone: (404) 523-7786
Atlanta, GA 30307   Alea Feall, Libn.

★N171★
SMOKY MOUNTAIN CONSORTIUM
c/o Mac Willis, Coord.
Reinhardt College
Waleska, GA 30183

★N172★
SOLINET
400 Colony Sq. Plaza Level
1201 Peachtree St., N.E.   Phone: (404) 892-0943
Atlanta, GA 30361   Frank P. Grisham, Exec.Dir.
Also Known As: Southeastern Library Network.

★N173★
SOUTH GEORGIA ASSOCIATED LIBRARIES
c/o Brunswick Junior College
Brunswick, GA 31523

Phone: (912) 264-7270
J. Allen Spivey, Sec./Treas.

★N174★
SOUTHFORNET
c/o Science Library
University of Georgia
Athens, GA 30602
Also Known As: Southern Forest Information Network.

Phone: (404) 546-2477
Virginia Rutherford, Coord.

★N175★
**SOUTHWEST GEORGIA HEALTH SCIENCE LIBRARY CONSORTIUM
     (SWGHSLC)**
c/o Medical Library
Colquitt County Memorial Hospital
Box 40
Moultrie, GA 31776

Phone: (912) 985-3420
Susan Danner

★N176★
UNIVERSITY CENTER IN GEORGIA, INC. †
c/o Georgia State University
University Plaza
Atlanta, GA 30303

Phone: (404) 658-2668
Charles B. Bedford, Dir.

IDAHO

★N177★
BOISE VALLEY HEALTH SCIENCES LIBRARY CONSORTIUM
c/o Health Sciences Library
St. Alphonsus Regional Medical Center
Boise, ID 83706
Address is that of member library.

★N178★
SOUTHEAST IDAHO HEALTH INFORMATION CONSORTIUM
c/o Health Science Library
Idaho Falls Consolidated Hospital
2525 S. Boulevard Ave.
Idaho Falls, ID 83401

Phone: (208) 529-7128
Colleen C. Winward, Pres.

ILLINOIS

★N179★
**AMERICAN HOSPITAL SUPPLY CORPORATION - INFORMATION SERVICES
     NETWORK**
Information Center
American Critical Care
1600 Waukegan Rd.
McGaw Park, IL 60085

Phone: (312) 473-3000
Marlene Galante Kozak, Mgr.

★N180★
**AREAWIDE HOSPITAL LIBRARY CONSORTIUM OF SOUTHWESTERN
     ILLINOIS (AHLC)**
c/o St. Joseph's Hospital
915 E. Fifth St.
Alton, IL 62002
Address rotates annually.

Phone: (618) 463-5151
Betty Byrd, Coord.

★N181★
BUR OAK LIBRARY SYSTEM
405 Earl Rd.
Shorewood, IL 60436

★N182★
CAPITAL AREA CONSORTIUM
Prevention Resource Center
901 S. Second St.
Springfield, IL 62703
Address rotates biennially.

Phone: (217) 525-3456
Viesta Morris, Coord.

★N183★
CAPITOL AREA CONSORTIUM OF HEALTH SCIENCE LIBRARIES
Health Science Library
St. Mary's Hospital
1800 E. Lake Shore Dr.
Decatur, IL 62525

Phone: (217) 429-2966
Laura L. Brosamer, Libn.

★N184★
CHAMPAIGN-URBANA CONSORTIUM
c/o Library
Sarah Bush Lincoln Health Center
Box 372
Matoon, IL 61938
Address rotates annually.

Phone: (217) 258-2525
Florence Heyduck, Libn.

★N185★
CHICAGO ACADEMIC LIBRARY COUNCIL (CALC)
Roosevelt University Library
430 S. Michigan Ave.
Chicago, IL 60605
Address rotates annually.

Adrian Jones, Chm.

★N186★
CHICAGO AREA THEOLOGICAL LIBRARY ASSOCIATION (CATLA)
c/o Jesuit-Krauss-McCormick Library
1100 E. 55th St.
Chicago, IL 60615
Address and phone are those of member library.

Phone: (312) 667-3500

★N187★
CHICAGO ASSOCIATION OF LAW LIBRARIES (CALL)
30 W. Washington
Chicago, IL 60602

Phone: (312) 670-2955
Nancy Tuohy, Pres.

★N188★
CHICAGO CLUSTER OF THEOLOGICAL SCHOOLS (CCTS)
1100 E. 55th St.
Chicago, IL 60615
Defunct

★N189★
CHICAGO LIBRARY SYSTEM
c/o Chicago Public Library
425 N. Michigan, Rm. 1344
Chicago, IL 60611

Eva R. Brown, Lib.Sys.Dev.Off.

★N190★
CHICAGO AND SOUTH CONSORTIUM
Health Sciences Library
St. Joseph Hospital
333 N. Madison St.
Joliet, IL 60435

Phone: (815) 725-7133
Cathy Siron, Coord.

★N191★
CONSORTIUM OF PSYCHOANALYTIC LIBRARIES
Chicago Institute for Psychoanalysis
Chicago, IL 60601

Phone: (312) 726-6300
Glenn Miller, Coord.

★N192★
CORN BELT LIBRARY SYSTEM
1809 W. Hovey Ave.
Normal, IL 61761

Phone: (309) 452-4485
Henry Meisels, Dir.

★N193★
COUNCIL OF WEST SUBURBAN COLLEGES
Box 471
Lisle, IL 60532

Phone: (312) 971-0960

★N194★
CRL
6050 S. Kenwood Ave.
Chicago, IL 60637
See also the library listing, Center for Research Libraries, for this network in
the main section.

Phone: (312) 955-4545
Donald B. Simpson, Dir./Chf.Exec.Off.

★N195★
CUMBERLAND TRAIL LIBRARY SYSTEM †
12th & McCawley Sts.   Phone: (618) 662-2741
Flora, IL 62839   Glenn Dockins

★N196★
DUPAGE LIBRARY SYSTEM
127 S. First St.
Box 268   Phone: (312) 232-8457
Geneva, IL 60134   Carol Morrison, Coord.

★N197★
EAST CENTRAL NETWORK FOR CURRICULUM COORDINATION (ECNCC)
Sangamon State University
E22   Phone: (217) 786-6375
Springfield, IL 62708   Ruth Patton, Coord.

★N198★
FOX VALLEY HEALTH SCIENCE LIBRARY CONSORTIUM
Medical Library
Central DuPage Hospital
0 N. 025 Winfield Rd.   Phone: (312) 682-1600
Winfield, IL 60190   Dorothy Rowe, Coord.

★N199★
GREAT RIVER LIBRARY SYSTEM (GRLS)
515 York St.   Phone: (217) 223-2560
Quincy, IL 62301   Travis E. Tyer, Exec.Dir.

★N200★
GREATER MIDWEST REGIONAL MEDICAL LIBRARY NETWORK
Library of the Health Sciences
Health Sciences Center
Univ. of Illinois at Chicago
1750 W. Polk St.   Phone: (312) 996-2464
Chicago, IL 60612
Region 3 of the Regional Medical Library Program serving IA, IL, IN, KY, MI, MN, ND, OH, SD, WI.

★N201★
HEART OF ILLINOIS LIBRARY CONSORTIUM (HILC)
Learning Resource Center
Carl Sandburg College
2232 S. Lake Storey Rd.   Phone: (309) 344-2518
Galesburg, IL 61401   Sandy Wallace, Coord.
Address rotates biennially.

★N202★
ILLINET
Illinois State Library
275 Centennial Bldg.   Phone: (217) 782-7848
Springfield, IL 62703
Also Known As: Illinois Library & Information Network.

★N203★
ILLINOIS DEPARTMENT OF MENTAL HEALTH AND DEVELOPMENTAL DISABILITIES LIBRARY SERVICES NETWORK (LISN)
Professional Library
Zeller Mental Health Center   Phone: (309) 691-2200
Peoria, IL 61614

★N204★
ILLINOIS HEALTH LIBRARIES CONSORTIUM
Meat Industry Information Center
Natl. Livestock & Meat Board
444 N. Michigan Ave.
Chicago, IL 60611   William D. Siarny, Jr., Coord.

★N205★
ILLINOIS STATE DATA CENTER COOPERATIVE (ISDCC)
Ilinois State Bureau of the Budget
605 Stratton Office Bldg.
524 S. 2nd St.   Phone: (217) 782-5414
Springfield, IL 62706

★N206★
ILLINOIS VALLEY LIBRARY SYSTEM
c/o Medical Staff Library
Graham Hospital Association
210 W. Walnut St.   Phone: (309) 647-5240
Canton, IL 61520
Address and phone are those of member library.

★N207★
JUDAICA LIBRARY NETWORK OF CHICAGO
c/o Norman and Helen Asher Library
Spertus College of Judaica
618 S. Michigan Ave.   Phone: (312) 922-9012
Chicago, IL 60605   Richard W. Marcus, Coord.

★N208★
KASKASKIA LIBRARY SYSTEM
306 N. Main St.   Phone: (618) 235-4220
Smithton, IL 62285   Edgar W. Chamberlin, Exec.Dir.

★N209★
LAKE COUNTY CONSORTIUM
Fohrman Library
Condell Memorial Hospital
900 Garfield   Phone: (312) 362-2900
Libertyville, IL 60048   Emily I. Bergmann, Coord.
Formerly: North Shore Library Consortium.

★N210★
LIBRAS INC.
c/o Elmhurst College Library
190 Prospect Ave.   Phone: (312) 583-2700
Elmhurst, IL 60126   Dorothy-Ellen Gross, Pres.
Formerly: LIBRAS Academic Library Cooperative.

★N211★
LINCOLN TRAIL LIBRARIES SYSTEM
1704 W. Interstate Dr.   Phone: (217) 352-0047
Champaign, IL 61820   Jan Beck Ison, Exec.Dir.
Member of ILLINET.

★N212★
METROPOLITAN CONSORTIUM
Stromberg Library
Swedish Covenant Hospital
5145 N. California Ave.   Phone: (312) 878-8200
Chicago, IL 60625   Jan Zibrat, Coord.
Also Known As: Chicago Metropolitan Consortium.

★N213★
MIDWEST UNIVERSITIES ENERGY CONSORTIUM
c/o Documents Center
Energy Resources Center
University of Illinois at Chicago
Box 4348   Phone: (312) 996-4490
Chicago, IL 60680

★N214★
NORTH SUBURBAN LIBRARY SYSTEM (NSLS)
200 W. Dundee Rd.   Phone: (312) 459-1300
Wheeling, IL 60090   Dr. Elliott E. Kanner, Rsrcs.Coord.

★N215★
NORTHERN ILLINOIS LIBRARY SYSTEM (NILS)
4034 E. State St.   Phone: (815) 229-0330
Rockford, IL 61108   Ralph Johnson, Coord.

★N216★
QUAD CITY AREA BIOMEDICAL CONSORTIUM
c/o Moline Public Hospital
635 Tenth Ave.   Phone: (309) 757-3107
Moline, IL 61265   Connie Santarelli, Coord.
Address rotates biennially.

★N217★
RESOURCE SHARING ALLIANCE OF WEST CENTRAL ILLINOIS
515 York St.   Phone: (217) 223-2560
Quincy, IL 62301   Travis E. Tyer, Pres.
Also Known As: ALLIANCE.

★N218★
RIVER BEND LIBRARY SYSTEM
Box 125   Phone: (309) 799-3155
Coal Valley, IL 61240   Mary Root, Coord.
Member of ILLINET.

★N219★
ROLLING PRAIRIE LIBRARY SYSTEM (RPLS)
345 W. Eldorado St.   Phone: (217) 429-2586
Decatur, IL 62522   Robert F. Plotzke, Exec.Dir.

★N220★
RUSH AFFILIATES INFORMATION NETWORK (RAIN)
c/o West Suburban Hospital Library
Erie at Austin   Phone: (312) 383-6200
Oak Park, IL 60302   Julia Faust, Coord.
Address rotates annually.

★N221★
SANGAMON VALLEY ACADEMIC LIBRARY CONSORTIUM (SVAL)
c/o Lumpkin Library
Blackburn College   Phone: (217) 854-3231
Carlinville, IL 62626   Robert L. Underbrink, Adm.

★N222★
SHAWNEE LIBRARY SYSTEM
c/o Energy Center
Shawnee Solar Project, Inc.
808 S. Forest   Phone: (618) 457-8172
Carbondale, IL 62901
Address and phone are those of member library.

★N223★
STARVED ROCK LIBRARY SYSTEM
c/o Nelson Library of Health Sciences
Perry Memorial Hospital
530 Park Ave., E.   Phone: (815) 875-2811
Princeton, IL 61356
Address and phone are those of member library.

★N224★
SUBURBAN LIBRARY SYSTEM (SLS)
125 Tower Dr.   Phone: (312) 325-6640
Burr Ridge, IL 60521   Lester L. Stoffel, Exec.Dir.

★N225★
U.S. TOY LIBRARY ASSOCIATION
5940 W. Touhy Ave.   Phone: (312) 763-7350
Chicago, IL 60648
Formerly: U.S. Toy Lending Libraries located in Cincinnati, OH.

★N226★
UPSTATE CONSORTIUM OF MEDICAL AND ALLIED LIBRARIES IN
    NORTHERN ILLINOIS
c/o Medical Library
St. Anthony Hospital
5666 E. State St.   Phone: (815) 226-2000
Rockford, IL 61108   Nancy Dale, Coord.
Address rotates biennially.

★N227★
WEST CENTRAL CONSORTIUM (WCC)
St. Mary Hospital
1415 Vermont St.   Phone: (217) 223-1200
Quincy, IL 62301   Carol Dennis
Address rotates annually.

INDIANA

★N228★
AREA 2 LIBRARY SERVICES AUTHORITY (ALSA 2)
209 Lincolnway E.   Phone: (219) 255-2562
Mishawaka, IN 46544   Martha Stratton, Coord.

★N229★
CENTRAL INDIANA AREA LIBRARY SERVICES AUTHORITY (CIALSA)
1100 W. 42nd St.   Phone: (317) 926-6561
Indianapolis, IN 46208   Judith Wegener, Exec.Dir.

★N230★
CENTRAL INDIANA HEALTH SCIENCE LIBRARY CONSORTIUM
c/o V.A. Medical Center Library
1481 W. Tenth St.   Phone: (317) 635-7401
Indianapolis, IN 46202   Judith Alfred, Chf., Lib.Serv.
Address rotates periodically.

★N231★
EAST CENTRAL INDIANA HEALTH SCIENCES LIBRARY CONSORTIUM
c/o Ball Memorial Hospital Library
2401 University Ave.   Phone: (317) 747-3204
Muncie, IN 47303   Kay McKibben, Coord.
Address and phone are those of member library.Formerly: Health Science
Library Consortium of East Central Indiana.

★N232★
EASTERN INDIANA AREA LIBRARY SERVICES AUTHORITY (EIALSA)
R.R. 1, Box 76-A   Phone: (317) 378-0216
Daleville, IN 47332   Jeanne D. Strother, Interim Adm.

★N233★
EVANSVILLE AREA HEALTH SCIENCES LIBRARIES CONSORTIUM
c/o St. Mary Medical Ctr. Library
3700 Washington Ave.   Phone: (812) 479-4151
Evansville, IN 47750   E. Jane Saltzman, Coord.

★N234★
FOUR RIVERS AREA LIBRARY SERVICES AUTHORITY
Old Vanderburgh Co.Ct. House, Rm. 210 Phone: (812) 425-1946
Evansville, IN 47708   Ida L. McDowell, Coord.

★N235★
INCOLSA
1100 W. 42nd St.   Phone: (317) 926-3361
Indianapolis, IN 46208   Barbara E. Markuson, Exec.Dir.
Also Known As: Indiana Cooperative Library Services Authority.

★N236★
INDIANA STATE DATA CENTER
Indiana State Library
140 N. Senate Ave.   Phone: (317) 232-3735
Indianapolis, IN 46204   Sharon K. Lyons, Coord.

★N237★
INDIANAPOLIS LAW CATALOGING CONSORTIUM
c/o School of Law Library
Indiana University
735 W. New York St.   Phone: (317) 264-4028
Indianapolis, IN 46202   Wendell Johnting
Formed in cooperation with Indiana University - School of Law Library and
INCOLSA.

★N238★
NORTHEAST INDIANA HEALTH SCIENCES LIBRARIES
c/o Hospital Library
U.S. Veterans Administration
1600 Randalia Dr.   Phone: (219) 743-5431
Fort Wayne, IN 46805
Address and phone are those of member library.

★N239★
NORTHEASTERN INDIANA HEALTH SCIENCE LIBRARY CONSORTIUM
Caylor-Nickel Clinic
311 S. Scott St.   Phone: (219) 824-3500
Bluffton, IN 46714   Pat Niblick, Coord.
Address and phone are those of member library.

★N240★
NORTHWEST INDIANA AREA LIBRARY SERVICES AUTHORITY (NIALSA)
1919 81st Ave. W.   Phone: (219) 736-0631
Merrillville, IN 46410   Bill Crowley, Adm.

★N241★
NORTHWEST INDIANA HEALTH SCIENCE LIBRARY CONSORTIUM
c/o School of Medicine
Indiana University
3400 Broadway   Phone: (219) 980-6550
Gary, IN 46408   Rachel Feldman, Libn.

★N242★
SOUTHEASTERN INDIANA AREA LIBRARY SERVICES AUTHORITY (SIALSA)
718 Third St.   Phone: (812) 372-0691
Columbus, IN 47201   Martha J. McDonald, Dir.

★N243★
STONE HILLS AREA LIBRARY SERVICES AUTHORITY (SHALSA) †
911 E. 2nd St.   Phone: (812) 334-8347
Bloomington, IN 47401   Sara Laughlin

★N244★
TRI-ALSA
304 Central Bldg.
203 W. Wayne St.   Phone: (219) 424-6664
Fort Wayne, IN 46802   Jane Raifsnider, Coord.
Also Known As: Area 3 Library Services Authority.

★N245★
WABASH VALLEY AREA LIBRARY SERVICES AUTHORITY
222 S. Washington St.   Phone: (317) 362-4235
Crawfordsville, IN 47933   Judy Greeson, Adm.
A multitype library network.

IOWA

★N246★
BI-STATE ACADEMIC LIBRARIES (BI-SAL)
c/o Marycrest College Library
Davenport, IA 52804   Sr. Joan Sheil, Coord.

★N247★
CENTRAL IOWA NETWORK (CIN)
4715 Grand Ave.   Phone: (515) 277-0220
Des Moines, IA 50312
An electronic mail network for interlibrary loan and reference.**Formerly:**
Central Iowa Regional Library System (CIRLS).

★N248★
DUBUQUE AREA LIBRARY CONSORTIUM
St. Joseph Unit Library
Mercy Health Center
Dubuque, IA 52001

★N249★
IOWA LIBRARY INFORMATION TELETYPE EXCHANGE (ILITE)
State Library
Historical Bldg.
E. 12th & Grand   Phone: (515) 281-4326
Des Moines, IA 50319   Martha Richardson, Dir.

★N250★
IOWA UNION LIST OF SERIALS
State Library of Iowa
Historical Bldg.
12th & Grand St.   Phone: (515) 281-4326
Des Moines, IA 50319   Martha Richardson, Dir.

★N251★
LINN COUNTY LIBRARY CONSORTIUM (LCLC)
1026 "A" Ave., N.E.   Phone: (319) 369-7358
Cedar Rapids, IA 52402   Sally Harms, Coord.

★N252★
NORTHEAST IOWA ACADEMIC LIBRARIES (NEIAL) †
c/o Ficke-Laird Library
University of Dubuque   Phone: (319) 353-3707
Dubuque IA 52002   Duncan Brockway, Exec.Dir.

★N253★
POLK COUNTY BIOMEDICAL CONSORTIUM (PCBC)
c/o Library
Des Moines Area Community College
2006 S. Ankeny Blvd.   Phone: (515) 964-6573
Ankeny, IA 50021   Diana Messersmith, Coord.
Address rotates biennially.

★N254★
SIOUXLAND HEALTH SCIENCE LIBRARY CONSORTIUM
c/o Library-Media Center
St. Lukes Regional Medical Center
2720 Stone Park Blvd.   Phone: (712) 279-3156
Sioux City, IA 51104
Address and phone number are those of member library.

★N255★
SOUTHEAST IOWA ACADEMIC LIBRARIES (SIAL)
Iowa Wesleyan College
Mt. Pleasant, IA 52641   Patricia Newcomer
Address rotates biennially.

KANSAS

★N256★
**ASSOCIATED COLLEGES OF CENTRAL KANSAS LIBRARIES COMMITTEE
(ACCK)**
105 E. Kansas Ave.   Phone: (316) 241-5150
McPherson, KS 67460   Rowena Olsen, Chm., Lib.Comm.

★N257★
KANSAS LIBRARY NETWORK
Kansas State Library
State Capitol, 3rd Fl.   Phone: (913) 296-3296
Topeka, KS 66612   Vee Friesner, Exec.Dir.

★N258★
KIC INTERLIBRARY LOAN NETWORK
Kansas State Library
State Capitol, 3rd Fl.   Phone: (913) 296-3296
Topeka, KS 66612   Bruce L. Flanders, Dir., ILL
KIC is an acronym for Kansas Information Circuit.

★N259★
MID-AMERICA LAW SCHOOL LIBRARY CONSORTIUM
1700 College
Topeka, KS 66621   John Christensen, Chm.
Address rotates with chairmanship.

★N260★
NORTHEAST KANSAS LIBRARY SYSTEM (NEKL)
10000 W. 75th St., Suite 130   Phone: (913) 831-4996
Shawnee Mission, KS 66204   Glen L. Plaisted, Coord.

★N261★
SOUTH CENTRAL KANSAS LIBRARY SYSTEM (SCKLS)
901 N. Main   Phone: (800) 362-2615
Hutchinson, KS 67501   Leroy M. Gattin, Jr., Coord.

★N262★
SOUTHEAST KANSAS LIBRARY SYSTEM †
218 E. Madison   Phone: (316) 365-6976
Iola, KS 66749   Ray Willson, Adm.

★N263★
STATE SERVICES
A.R. Dykes Library - Outreach Program
Univ. of Kansas Medical Ctr.
2100 W. 39th St.   Phone: (816) 588-7313
Kansas City, KS 66103   Carolyn McCown Anderson, Hd.
A toll-free telephone number is 1-800-332-4193.

★N264★
WICHITA AREA HEALTH SCIENCE LIBRARIES
c/o H.B. McKibbin Health Science Lib.
Wesley Medical Center
550 N. Hillside   Phone: (316) 685-2151
Wichita, KS 67214
Address and phone are those of member library.

KENTUCKY

★N265★
**EASTERN KENTUCKY HEALTH SCIENCE INFORMATION NETWORK
(EKHSIN)**
c/o Camden-Carroll Library
Morehead State University   Phone: (606) 784-4301
Morehead, KY 40351   Bonnie McNeely, Libn.
Address is that of member library.

★N266★
KENTUCKY COOPERATIVE LIBRARY INFORMATION PROJECT (KENCLIP)
Kentucky Dept. for Libraries and Archives
Box 537   Phone: (502) 875-7000
Frankfort, KY 40602-0537   Linda L. Sherrow, Br.Mgr.

★N267★
KENTUCKY EDUCATIONAL INFORMATION CENTER (KEIC)
3113 Lexington Rd.   Phone: (502) 588-3197
Louisville, KY 40206   A. Scott Kochenrath, Sr.Couns.

★N268★
KENTUCKY HEALTH SCIENCES LIBRARY CONSORTIUM
c/o V.A. Hospital Library
800 Zorn Ave.   Phone: (502) 895-3401
Louisville, KY 40202   James F. Kastner, Pres.

★N269★
KENTUCKY UNION LIST OF SERIALS (KULS)
Ekstrom Library
University of Louisville
2301 S. 3rd St.   Phone: (502) 588-5931
Louisville, KY 40292   Janet Dakan

★N270★
LOCOLS
c/o Information Center
Meidinger, Inc.
2600 Meidinger Tower, Louisville Galleria
Louisville, KY 40202
Defunct

★N271★
STATE ASSISTED ACADEMIC LIBRARY COUNCIL OF KENTUCKY (SAALCK) †
c/o Western Kentucky University Lib.   Phone: (502) 745-2904
Bowling Green, KY 42101   Earl Wassam, Dir., Lib.Serv.
Address rotates annually.

★N272★
TEAM-A LIBRARIANS
c/o Southern Baptist Theological Seminary
2825 Lexington Rd.   Phone: (502) 897-4807
Louisville, KY 40280   Dr. Ronald F. Deering
Also Known As: Theological Education Association of Mid-America Librarians.

LOUISIANA

★N273★
BAYOULAND LIBRARY SYSTEM
301 W. Congress
Box 3427   Phone: (318) 261-5793
Lafayette, LA 70502   Gary Gilreath, Dir.

★N274★
COMMUNITY MEDICAL LIBRARY CONSORTIUM
Earl K. Long Hospital Medical Library
5825 Airline Hwy.   Phone: (504) 358-1089
Baton Rouge, LA 70805   Elaine P. O'Connor, Coord.

★N275★
GREEN GOLD LIBRARY SYSTEM †
Box 21523   Phone: (318) 226-5897
Shreveport, LA 71120   James R. Pelton

★N276★
HEALTH SCIENCES LIBRARY ASSOCIATION OF LOUISIANA
c/o Medical Library
V.A. Medical Center   Phone: (318) 473-0010
Alexandria, LA 71301
Address and phone are those of member library.

★N277★
LOUISIANA GOVERNMENT INFORMATION NETWORK (LAGIN)
Louisiana State Library
Box 131   Phone: (504) 342-4920
Baton Rouge, LA 70821   Judith I. Boyce, Coord.

★N278★
LOUISIANA STATE ARCHIVAL SYSTEM
Louisiana State Archives & Rec.Serv.
Off. of the Secretary of State
Box 44125   Phone: (504) 342-5440
Baton Rouge, LA 70804

★N279★
LOUISIANA STATE UNIVERSITY SYSTEM INTERLIBRARY NETWORK (LSU SINET)
Louisiana State University Library   Phone: (504) 388-2138
Baton Rouge, LA 70803   Paul G. Wank

★N280★
NEW ORLEANS AREA HEALTH SCIENCE LIBRARIES
c/o Hospital Library Services
Touro Infirmary
1401 Foucher St., 10th Fl., M Bldg.
New Orleans, LA 70115
Address is that of member library.

★N281★
TRAIL BLAZER LIBRARY SYSTEM †
1800 Stubbs Ave.   Phone: (318) 387-1950
Monroe, LA 71201   Harris Agnes

MAINE

★N282★
AROOSTOOK HEALTH INFORMATION AND RESOURCE CONSORTIUM (AHIRC)
R.A.I.S.E.
Box 1238   Phone: (207) 764-7178
Presque Isle, ME 04769
See also the library listing for this network in the main section under Northern Maine RAISE.

★N283★
HEALTH AND MEDICAL INFORMATION COOPERATIVE OF SOUTHERN MAINE (HAMIC)
c/o Osteopathic Hospital
335 Brighton Ave.
Portland, ME 04102
Address rotates annually.

★N284★
HEALTH SCIENCE LIBRARY AND INFORMATION COOPERATIVE OF MAINE (HSLIC)
V.A. Medical Center
Box 395   Phone: (207) 622-7566
Togus, ME 04330

★N285★
MAINE REGIONAL LIBRARY SYSTEM
Maine State Library
LMA Bldg., Sta. 64   Phone: (207) 289-3328
Augusta, ME 04333   Benjamin Keating
The Maine Regional Library System includes the Bangor Public Library, the Portland Public Library and the Maine State Library as Area Reference and Resource Centers.

★N286★
NORTH ATLANTIC HEALTH SCIENCE LIBRARIES (NAHSL)
c/o Maine Medical Center Library
22 Bramhall St.   Phone: (207) 871-4079
Portland, ME 04102
Address and phone are those of member library.

★N287★
SEACOAST REFERENCE LIBRARIES CONSORTIUM
c/o Old Gaol Museum Library
Lindsay Rd. & York St.
York, ME 03909
Defunct

★N288★
SIX COUNTY HOSPITAL LIBRARY CONSORTIUM (SCHLC)
Down East Community Hospital
Upper Court St.   Phone: (207) 255-3356
Machias, ME 04654   Charles E. Hilt, Chm.
Address may rotate.**Formerly:** Five County Hospital Library Consortium.

MARYLAND

★N289★
BALTIMORE CONSORTIA FOR RESOURCE SHARING
Medical Library
Provident Hospital   Phone: (301) 578-2351
Baltimore, MD 21215   Bertha G. Wilson, Act.Dir., Lib.Serv.

★N290★
BALTIMORE-WASHINGTON INTERLIBRARY LOAN ASSOCIATION
c/o Laurel Research Library
Westvaco Corporation
Johns Hopkins Rd.   Phone: (301) 792-9100
Laurel, MD 20707   Maria Liang, Res.Libn.

★N291★
BETHESDA MILITARY MEDICAL LIBRARY GROUP
c/o AFFRI Library, N. Pope
Natl. Naval Medical Command   Phone: (301) 295-0428
Bethesda, MD 20814

★N292★
CANCER COMMUNICATIONS NETWORK
9000 Rockville Pike
Blair Bldg., Rm 629   Phone: (301) 427-8656
Bethesda, MD 20205   Judith Stein, Proj.Off.

★N293★
CONSORTIUM OF HEALTH SCIENCES LIBRARIES OF THE EASTERN SHORE
c/o Health Sciences Library
Memorial Hospital
S. Washington St.   Phone: (301) 822-1000
Easton, MD 21601
Address and phone are those of member library.

★N294★
INTERLIBRARY USERS ASSOCIATION (IUA)
c/o Engineering & Physical Sci.Lib.
University of Maryland   Phone: (301) 454-4281
College Park, MD 20742   Herbert N. Foerstel, Pres.
Address rotates with president.

★N295★
LAW LIBRARY ASSOCIATION OF MARYLAND (LLAM)
c/o Semmes, Bowen & Semmes Library
10 Light St., 11th Fl.   Phone: (301) 539-5040
Baltimore, MD 21202
Address rotates annually.

★N296★
MARYLAND ASSOCIATION OF HEALTH SCIENCE LIBRARIANS
Medical Chirurgical Faculty of
the State of Maryland
1211 Cathedral St.   Phone: (301) 539-0872
Baltimore, MD 21201
Address and phone are those of member library.

★N297★
MARYLAND AND D.C. CONSORTIUM OF RESOURCE SHARING (MADCORS)
Saul Schwartzback Memorial Library
Prince George's General Hosp. & Med.Ctr.   Phone: (301) 341-2440
Cheverly, MD 20785
Address rotates biennially.

★N298★
MARYLAND INTERLIBRARY LOAN ORGANIZATION (MILO)
Enoch Pratt Free Library
State Library Resource Ctr.
400 Cathedral St.   Phone: (301) 396-5328
Baltimore, MD 21201   Eleanor Jo Rodger, Chf., Network Serv.

★N299★
MID-ATLANTIC REGIONAL MEDICAL LIBRARY PROGRAM (MARMLP)
National Library of Medicine
8600 Rockville Pike   Phone: (301) 496-5955
Bethesda, MD 20209   Maxine K. Hanke, Coord.
Defunct. Absorbed by Southeastern/Atlantic Regional Medical library
Services.

★N300★
NATIONAL LIBRARY OF MEDICINE (NLM)
8600 Rockville Pike   Phone: (301) 496-4777
Bethesda, MD 20209   Becky Lyon-Hartmann, Coord.
See also the library listing for this network in the main section.

★N301★
SOUTHEASTERN/ATLANTIC REGIONAL MEDICAL LIBRARY SERVICES
Health Science Library
University of Maryland
111 S. Greene St.   Phone: (301) 528-2855
Baltimore, MD 21201   Carol G. Jenkins, Exec.Dir.
Region 2 of the Regional Medical Program serving AL, DC, FL, GA, MD, MS,
NC, SC, TN, VA and WV. A toll-free telephone number is (800) 638-6093.

★N302★
STATE AGENCY LIBRARY ASSOCIATION OF MARYLAND (SALAM)
c/o Maryland State Law Library
Courts of Appeal Bldg.
361 Rowe Blvd.
Annapolis, MD 21401-1697
Defunct

★N303★
**U.S. NATL. OCEANIC & ATMOSPHERIC ADMINISTRATION LIBRARY &
   INFORMATION NETWORK**
c/o Library & Info.Serv. Division
Camp Springs Center
5200 Auth Rd.
Camp Springs, MD 20233
Inactive

MASSACHUSETTS

★N304★
AREA HEALTH EDUCATION CENTER STATEWIDE PROGRAM (AHEC)
c/o Medical School at Worcester
University of Masschusetts
55 Lake Ave., N.   Phone: (617) 856-3255
Worcester, MA 01605   Michael Huppert, Dir.

★N305★
ASSOCIATION OF BOSTON LAW LIBRARIANS
c/o Gaston Snow & Ely Barlett
One Federal St.   Phone: (617) 426-4600
Boston, MA 02110   Gina Lynch, Coord.
Address and phone are those of member library.

★N306★
BOSTON AREA MUSIC LIBRARIES (BAML)
c/o Farber Library
Brandeis University   Phone: (617) 647-2517
Waltham, MA 02254   Robert Evensen, Coord.

★N307★
BOSTON BIOMEDICAL LIBRARY CONSORTIUM
c/o Health Science Library
Mt. Auburn Hospital
330 Mt. Auburn St.   Phone: (617) 492-3500
Cambridge, MA 02138   Cherie Haitz, Chm.
Address rotates annually.

★N308★
BOSTON GROUP OF GOVERNMENT LIBRARIES (BOGGL)
State Transportation Library
10 Park Plaza   Phone: (617) 973-7151
Boston, MA 02116   Toby Pearlstein
Address rotates annually.

★N309★
BOSTON LIBRARY CONSORTIUM
Boston Public Library, Rm. 339
666 Boylston St.
Boston, MA 02117
Phone: (617) 262-0380
Ann C. Schaffner, Coord.

★N310★
BOSTON THEOLOGICAL INSTITUTE LIBRARIES
45 Frances Ave.
Cambridge, MA 02138
Phone: (617) 495-5780
Clifford Wunderlich, Coord.

★N311★
CENTER FOR MASSACHUSETTS DATA
Executive Office for Commun. & Dev.
100 Cambridge St.
Boston, MA 022022
Phone: (617) 727-3253
Charles J. McSweeney, Coord.

★N312★
**CENTRAL MASSACHUSETTS CONSORTIUM OF HEALTH RELATED
LIBRARIES (CMCHRL)**
c/o Medical School Library
University of Massachusetts
Worcester, MA 01605
Phone: (617) 856-2206
Faith Anttila, Adm.

★N313★
**CENTRAL/WESTERN MASSACHUSETTS AUTOMATED RESOURCE
SHARING (C/W MARS)**
Oral History Collection
Shea Memorial Library
American International College
1000 State St.
Springfield, MA 01109
Phone: (413) 737-7000
Dr. F. Knowlton Utley, Lib.Dir.

★N314★
COMMUNITY HEALTH INFORMATION NETWORK (CHIN)
Health Sciences Library
Mt. Auburn Hospital
330 Mt. Auburn St.
Cambridge, MA 02138
Phone: (617) 492-3500
Cherie Haitz, Lib.Dir.

★N315★
CONSORTIUM FOR INFORMATION RESOURCES (CIR)
C.G. Tedeschi Library
Framingham Union Hospital
115 Lincoln St.
Framingham, MA 01701
Phone: (617) 879-7111
Sandra Clevesy, Adm.

★N316★
**COOPERATING LIBRARIES OF GREATER SPRINGFIELD, A CCGS AGENCY
(CLGS)**
c/o Learning Resources Center
Holyoke Community College
303 Homestead Ave.
Holyoke, MA 01040
Phone: (413) 538-7000
Elizabeth Sheehan, Dir.

★N317★
DIGITAL LIBRARY NETWORK
555 Virginia Rd., VR03-3/W5
Concord, MA 01742
Phone: (617) 264-3433
Joyce Ward, Coord.

★N318★
EASTERN MASSACHUSETTS REGIONAL LIBRARY SYSTEM
c/o Boston Public Library
Copley Sq.
Boston, MA 02117
Phone: (617) 536-4010
Mary A. Heneghan, Regional Adm.

★N319★
ESSEX COUNTY COOPERATING LIBRARIES (ECCL)
Peabody Institute Library
15 Sylvan St.
Danvers, MA 01923
Phone: (617) 774-0557
Nicolas McAuliffe, Coord.
Address rotates biennially.

★N320★
FENWAY LIBRARY CONSORTIUM (FLC)
c/o Sawyer Library
Suffolk University
8 Ashburton Pl.
Boston, MA 02108
Phone: (617) 723-4700
Edmund G. Hamann, Coord.
Address rotates biennially.

★N321★
GOETHE INSTITUTE LIBRARIES
c/o Goethe Institute Boston
170 Beacon St.
Boston, MA 02116
Phone: (617) 262-6050
Dorothee Burney, Libn.

★N322★
GTE LIBNET
GTE Laboratories Library
40 Sylvan Rd.
Waltham, MA 02254
Phone: (617) 890-8460

★N323★
HILC, INC.
c/o Five Colleges, Inc.
97 Spring St.
Amherst, MA 01002
Dora Tudryn, Adm.Asst.
HILC includes the libraries of Amherst, Hampshire, Mount Holyoke and Smith
Colleges and the University of Massachusetts.

★N324★
**MASSACHUSETTS CONFERENCE OF CHIEF LIBRARIANS IN PUBLIC HIGHER
EDUCATIONAL INSTITUTIONS (MCCLPHEI)**
Library - Learning Resource Center
Cape Cod Community College
West Barnstable, MA 02668
Phone: (617) 362-2131
Greg M. Masterson, Pres.
Address and presidency rotate annually.

★N325★
MASSACHUSETTS HEALTH SCIENCES LIBRARY NETWORK (MAHSLIN)
c/o Mack Memorial Library
Salem Hospital
81 Highland Ave.
Salem, MA 01970
Phone: (617) 741-1200
Jennie McGee, Pres.
Address rotates annually.

★N326★
MASSACHUSETTS MENTAL HEALTH LIBRARIANS CONSORTIUM
c/o Staff Library
Hogan Regional Center
Box A
Hathorne, MA 01937
Phone: (617) 774-5000
Bonnie Stecher, Coord.

★N327★
MERRIMACK INTERLIBRARY COOPERATIVE (MILC) †
c/o The Brook School
1160 Great Pond Rd.
North Andover, MA 01845
Phone: (617) 686-6101
Kathleen O'Doherty

★N328★
MOTOROLA LIBRARY NETWORK
c/o Corporate Library
Codex Corporation
20 Cabot Blvd.
Mansfield, MA 02048
Doris Friedeborn
Address is that of member library.

★N329★
NELINET
385 Elliot St.
Newton, MA 02164
Phone: (617) 969-0400
Ms. Laima Mockus, Exec.Dir.
Also Known As: New England Library Information Network.

★N330★
NEW ENGLAND ON-LINE USERS GROUP (NENON)
c/o George F. Fuller Library
Worcester Foundation for
Experimental Biology
222 Maple St.
Shrewsbury, MA 01545
Phone: (617) 842-8921
Address and phone are those of member library.

★N331★
**NORTHEAST CONSORTIUM OF COLLEGES AND UNIVERSITIES IN
MASSACHUSETTS (NECCUM)**
300 Hampshire St.
Lawrence, MA 01841
Phone: (617) 686-3183
Diana Strange, Exec.Dir.

★N332★
NORTHEASTERN CONSORTIUM FOR HEALTH INFORMATION (NECHI) †
c/o Medical Library
Cutler Army Hospital   Phone: (617) 796-6750
Fort Devens, MA 01433   Lesley Seidel

★N333★
ROUTE 128 LIBRARIANS GROUP
c/o Information Center
International Data Corporation
5 Speen St.   Phone: (617) 872-8200
Framingham, MA 01701
Address and phone are those of member library.

★N334★
SOUTHEASTERN ASSOCIATION FOR COOPERATION IN HIGHER
    EDUCATION IN MASSACHUSETTS (SACHEM)
c/o Swain School of Design Library
100 Madison St.
New Bedford, MA 02740
Address is that of member library.

★N335★
SOUTHEASTERN MASSACHUSETTS CONSORTIUM OF HEALTH SCIENCE
    LIBRARIES (SEMCO) †
c/o Learning Resource Center
Cape Cod Community College   Phone: (617) 362-2131
West Barnstable, MA 02668   Adrienne Latimer

★N336★
SOUTHEASTERN MASSACHUSETTS COOPERATING LIBRARIES (SMCL)
Bridgewater State College   Phone: (617) 697-8321
Bridgewater, MA 02324   Owen T.P. McGowen, Coord.

★N337★
WELEXACOL
c/o Horn Library
Babson College   Phone: (617) 235-1610
Babson Park, MA 02157
Address rotates annually. Also Known As: Wellesley-Lexington Area
Cooperating Libraries.

★N338★
WESTERN MASSACHUSETTS HEALTH INFORMATION CONSORTIUM
c/o Medical Library
Berkshire Medical Center
725 North St.   Phone: (413) 499-4161
Pittsfield, MA 01201   Jutta Ludhe, Co-Chm.

★N339★
WORCESTER AREA COOPERATING LIBRARIES (WACL)
Worcester State College
486 Chandler St.   Phone: (617) 754-3964
Worcester, MA 01602

MICHIGAN

★N340★
BERRIEN LIBRARY CONSORTIUM
Andrews University   Phone: (616) 471-7771
Berrien Springs, MI 49104   William Hessel, Pres.

★N341★
CAPITOL AREA LIBRARY NETWORK (CALNET)
Library Service Center
407 N. Cedar St.   Phone: (517) 676-2147
Mason, MI 48854   Kathleen M. Scripter, Contact Person

★N342★
COUNCIL ON RESOURCE DEVELOPMENT (CORD)
c/o Oakland County Law Library
1200 N. Telegraph Rd.   Phone: (313) 858-0011
Pontiac, MI 48053   Richard Beer, Dir., Law Lib.
Address rotates annually.

★N343★
DETROIT AREA LIBRARY SERVICE (DALS)
Detroit Public Library
4420 Woodward Ave.
Detroit, MI 48202

★N344★
DETROIT ASSOCIATED LIBRARIES REGION OF COOPERATION
c/o Detroit Public Library
5201 Woodward Ave.   Phone: (313) 833-4036
Detroit, MI 48202   Lesley C. Loke, Coord.

★N345★
DGP CONSORTIUM (Detroit, Grosse Pointe)
c/o Health Science Library
Bon Secours Hospital
468 Cadieux Rd.   Phone: (313) 343-1619
Grosse Pointe, MI 48230
Address and phone are those of member library.

★N346★
FLINT AREA HEALTH SCIENCE LIBRARY NETWORK (FAHSLN)
Hurley Medical Center
1 Hurley Plaza   Phone: (313) 766-0454
Flint, MI 48502   Marilyn Schleg, Pres.
Address rotates periodically.

★N347★
GRAND RAPIDS AREA UNION LIST OF SERIALS (GRAULS)
c/o VanZoeren Library
Hope College
Holland, MI 49423

★N348★
HEALTH INSTRUCTIONAL RESOURCES ASSOCIATION (HIRA)
1101 W. University Dr.   Phone: (313) 652-5338
Rochester, MI 48063   Lucy Lee, Chm.

★N349★
KALAMAZOO ET AL (KETAL)
Waldo Library
Western Michigan University   Phone: (616) 383-4961
Kalamazoo, MI 49008   Carl Sachtleben, Adm.

★N350★
LAKELAND AREA LIBRARY NETWORK (LAKENET)
c/o Lakeland Library Cooperative
60 Library Plaza, N.E.   Phone: (616) 456-4426
Grand Rapids, MI 49503   Harriet Field, Coord.

★N351★
LIBRARY COOPERATIVE OF MACOMB (LCM)
16480 Hall Rd.   Phone: (313) 286-5750
Mt. Clemens, MI 48044   CoraEllen DeVinney, Dir.

★N352★
MACOMB AREA LIBRARIES HEALTH INFORMATION CONSORTIUM
    (MALHIC)
c/o Medical Library East
St. Joseph Hospital
215 North Ave.   Phone: (313) 286-8100
Mt. Clemens, MI 48043   Sandra Cryderman, Coord.

★N353★
METROPOLITAN DETROIT MEDICAL LIBRARY GROUP (MDMLG)
c/o Shiffman Medical Library
Wayne State University
4325 Brush St.
Detroit, MI 48201

★N354★
MICHIGAN AREA SERIAL HOLDINGS CONSORTIUM (MASH)
Bay Medical Center
Health Sciences Library
1900 Columbus Ave.
Bay City, MI 48706
Defunct. Absorbed by Michigan Health Sciences Libraries Union List of Serials.

★N355★
MICHIGAN DATABASE USERS GROUP
c/o Professional Development Rsrc.Ctr.
Lansing Community College
419 N. Capitol, Box 40010
Lansing, MI 48901
Address is that of member library.

★N356★
MICHIGAN HEALTH SCIENCES LIBRARIES ASSOCIATION
c/o Burns Health Sciences Library   Phone: (616) 348-4500
Petoskey, MI 49770   Ray Kelly, Pres.
Address rotates annually.

★N357★
MICHIGAN HEALTH SCIENCES LIBRARIES UNION LIST OF SERIALS
South Macomb Hospital Library
11800 12 Mile Rd.
Warren, MI 48093   Lynn Sorensen-Sutton
Absorbed the former Michigan Area Serial Holdings Consortium (MASH).

★N358★
MICHIGAN LIBRARY CONSORTIUM (MLC)
6810 S. Cedar St., Suite 8   Phone: (517) 694-4242
Lansing, MI 48910   Kevin C. Flaherty, Exec.Dir.

★N359★
MID-MICHIGAN HEALTH SCIENCES LIBRARIES (M-MHSL)
c/o Clinical Center Library, A137
Michigan State University   Phone: (517) 353-3037
East Lansing, MI 48824-1313   Leslie M. Behm, Chm.
Address rotates biennially.

★N360★
MID-PENINSULA LIBRARY COOPERATIVE
c/o Medical Center Library
U.S. Veterans Administration
East H St.   Phone: (906) 774-3300
Iron Mountain, MI 49801   Phyllis E. Goetz, Chf., Lib.Serv.

★N361★
NORTHLAND LIBRARY COOPERATIVE
316 E. Chisholm   Phone: (517) 356-1622
Alpena, MI 49707   Sue Williams, Coord.

★N362★
OAKLAND COUNTY UNION LIST OF SERIALS (OCULS)
1200 N. Telegraph Rd.   Phone: (313) 858-0738
Pontiac, MI 48053   Phyllis Jose, Libn.

★N363★
OTTAGON HOSPITAL LIBRARY CONSORTIA
c/o Hospital and Medical Staff Library
Holland Community Hospital
602 Michigan Ave.
Holland, MI 49423
Address is that of member library.

★N364★
PONTIAC-ALLEN PARK-DETROIT CONSORTIUM (PAD)
c/o Medical Library
Hutzel Hospital
4707 St. Antoine   Phone: (313) 494-7179
Detroit, MI 48201   Caryl L. Scheuer
Address and phone are those of member library.

★N365★
SAULT AREA INTERNATIONAL LIBRARY ASSOCIATION (SAILA)
c/o Lake Superior State College Library   Phone: (906) 635-2402
Sault Ste. Marie, MI 49783   Charles E. Nairn, MI Coord.
SAILA is an international organization serving both Sault Ste. Marie, MI, and Sault Ste. Marie, ON.

★N366★
SISTERS OF MERCY HEALTH CORPORATION AV-LIBRARY GROUP
Learning Resource Center
Sisters of Mercy Health Corporation
28550 Eleven Mile Rd.   Phone: (313) 478-9900
Farmingham Hills, MI 48018   Patricia Tavidian, Coord.

★N367★
SOUTHEASTERN MICHIGAN LEAGUE OF LIBRARIES (SEMLOL) †
c/o Purdy Library
Wayne State University   Phone: (313) 577-4040
Detroit, MI 48202   Avram Rosenthal, Chm.

★N368★
SOUTHWEST MICHIGAN LIBRARY COOPERATIVE (SMLC)
200 S. Kalamazoo St.   Phone: (616) 657-4698
Paw Paw, MI 49079   Dr. Alida L. Geppert, Dir.

★N369★
UNION LIST OF SELECT SERIALS OF MICHIGAN
c/o Oakland University Library
Rochester, MI 48063
Defunct

★N370★
UP HEALTH SCIENCES LIBRARIES CONSORTIUM
c/o Health Sciences Library
Marquette General Hospital
420 W. Magnetic   Phone: (906) 228-9448
Marquette, MI 49855
Address and phone are those of member library.

★N371★
UPPER PENINSULA OF MICHIGAN AV CONSORTIUM (UPMAC)
c/o Education Department
Marquette General Hospital
420 W. Magnetic   Phone: (906) 228-9440
Marquette, MI 49855   Susan Berry, Coord.
Also Known As: Upper Peninsula Medical AV Consortium (UPMAC).

★N372★
UPPER PENINSULA REGION OF LIBRARY COOPERATION, INC. (UPRLC)
217 N. Front St.   Phone: (906) 228-9510
Houghton, MI 49855

★N373★
VALLEY REGIONAL HEALTH SCIENCES LIBRARIANS †
c/o Saginaw Health Science Library
1000 Houghton   Phone: (517) 771-6837
Saginaw, MI 48602   Cindy Anderson, Pres.

★N374★
WASHTENAW-LIVINGSTON LIBRARY NETWORK (WLLN)
Washtenaw County Library
4133 Washtenaw Ave.   Phone: (313) 971-6056
Ann Arbor, MI 48107   Mary Croteau, Lib.Dir.

★N375★
WAYNE/OAKLAND LIBRARY FEDERATION (WOLF)
33030 Van Born Rd.   Phone: (313) 326-8910
Wayne, MI 48184   Leo T. Dinnan, Dir.

★N376★
WHITE PINE LIBRARY CONSORTIUM
c/o Special Collections
Grace A. Dow Memorial Library
1710 W. St. Andrews Dr.   Phone: (517) 835-7151
Midland, MI 48640   Rosemarie Byers, Dir.
Address and phone are those of member library.

MINNESOTA

★N377★
AREA HEALTH EDUCATION CENTER OF MINNESOTA (AHEC)
c/o University of Minnesota
1342 Mayo, 420 Delaware St., S.E.
Minneapolis, MN 55455
Defunct

★N378★
ARROWHEAD LIBRARY SYSTEM
701 11th St., N.   Phone: (218) 741-3840
Virginia, MN 55792   Kenneth R. Neilson, Dir.

★N379★
ARROWHEAD PROFESSIONAL LIBRARIES ASSOCIATION (APLA)
College of St. Scholastica   Phone: (218) 723-6198
Duluth, MN 55811   Mary Ellen Braafladt, Coord.
Address rotates annually.

★N380★
CAPITOL AREA LIBRARY CONSORTIUM (CALCO) †
Legislative Reference Library
111 State Capitol   Phone: (612) 296-3398
St. Paul, MN 55155   Linda Feist, Pres.

★N381★
CENTRAL MINNESOTA LIBRARIES EXCHANGE (CMLE)
c/o Learning Resources
St. Cloud State University   Phone: (612) 255-2950
St. Cloud, MN 56301   Patricia E. Peterson, Coord.

★N382★
COOPERATING LIBRARIES IN CONSORTIUM (CLIC)
c/o James J. Hill Reference Library
80 W. Fourth St.   Phone: (612) 277-9531
St. Paul, MN 55102   Jan Chittenden, Coord.

★N383★
HONEYWELL INFORMATION NETWORK (HIN)
c/o Honeywell Technology Strategy Ctr.
1700 W. Hwy 36   Phone: (612) 378-5639
Roseville, MN 55113   Denise F. Cumming, Info.Spec.
Address rotates annually.

★N384★
MEDI-SOTA LIBRARY CONSORTIUM
Canby Community Hospital
District 1   Phone: (507) 223-7277
Canby, MN 56220   Janet Fransen, Coord.

★N385★
METRONET
228 Metro Square Bldg.
7th & Robert Sts.   Phone: (612) 224-4801
St. Paul, MN 55101
Metronet was created to foster cooperation among all types of libraries and media centers in a seven county area.

★N386★
METROPOLITAN LIBRARY SERVICES AGENCY (MELSA)
Griggs-Midway Bldg.
1821 University Ave.   Phone: (612) 645-5731
St. Paul, MN 55104   W.M. Duncan, Dir.

★N387★
MINITEX
33 Wilson Library
University of Minnesota
309 19th Ave., S.   Phone: (612) 376-3926
Minneapolis, MN 55455   William DeJohn, Dir.
See also the library listing for this network in the main section.Also Known As: Minnesota Interlibrary Telecommunications Exchange.

★N388★
MINNESOTA DEPARTMENT OF HUMAN SERVICES LIBRARY CONSORTIUM
Oak Terrace Nursing Home
14500 County Rd. 67   Phone: (612) 934-4100
Minnetonka, MN 55345   Susan Ager, Coord.

★N389★
MINNESOTA INFORMATION NETWORK FOR EDUCATORS (MINE)
State Department of Education
Capitol Square Bldg., Rm. 501
St. Paul, MN 55101
Defunct

★N390★
MINNESOTA ONLINE USERS GROUP
c/o Super Valu
Box 990   Phone: (612) 828-4000
Eden Prairie, MN 55440   Linda Canfield, Chm.
Address rotates annually.

★N391★
MINNESOTA REGIONAL RESEARCH CENTERS (MRRC)
1500 Mississippi St.
St. Paul, MN 55101
Defunct

★N392★
MINNESOTA STATE UNIVERSITY SYSTEM PROJECT FOR AUTOMATED LIBRARY SYSTEMS
Memorial Library
Mankato State University   Phone: (507) 389-6201
Mankato, MN 56001
Address and phone are those of member library.

★N393★
MINNESOTA THEOLOGICAL LIBRARIES ASSOCIATION (MTLA)
c/o Luther-Northwestern Seminary Lib.
2375 Como Ave.
St. Paul, MN 55108
Address is that of member library.Formerly: Consortium of Minnesota Seminary Libraries.

★N394★
NORTH COUNTRY LIBRARY COOPERATIVE (NCLC)
c/o Arrowhead Library System   Phone: (218) 741-3840
Virginia, MN 55792   Nancy Alsop, Coord.

★N395★
NORTHERN LIGHTS LIBRARY NETWORK (NLLN)
Box 246 - Graystone Complex   Phone: (218) 847-3427
Detroit Lakes, MN 56501   Joan Larson, Coord.

★N396★
SOUTHCENTRAL MINNESOTA INTER-LIBRARY EXCHANGE (SMILE)
Box 3031   Phone: (507) 389-1425
Mankato, MN 56001   Lucy Lowry, Coord.

★N397★
SOUTHEAST LIBRARY SYSTEM (SELS)
334 16th St., S.E.   Phone: (507) 281-1404
Rochester, MN 55904   Marilyn Igel, Coord.

★N398★
SOUTHEASTERN LIBRARIES COOPERATING (SELCO) †
ESC Bldg., Rm. 12
334 16th St., S.E.   Phone: (507) 288-5513
Rochester, MN 55904   Raymond Ogden, Exec.Dir.

★N399★
SOUTHWEST AREA MULTI-COUNTY MULTI-TYPE INTERLIBRARY EXCHANGE (SAMMIE)
BAC 504
Southwest State University   Phone: (507) 532-9013
Marshall, MN 56258   Nancy Alsop, Coord.

★N400★
TRI-COLLEGE UNIVERSITY LIBRARY CONSORTIUM
Livingston Lord Library
Moorhead State University   Phone: (218) 236-2922
Moorhead, MN 56560   Darrel M. Meinke, Coord.

★N401★
TWIN CITIES BIOMEDICAL CONSORTIUM (TCBC)
Hennepin County Medical Center Lib.
701 Park Ave.
Minneapolis, MN 55415   Patty Williams, Coord.
Address rotates annually.

★N402★
TWIN CITIES STANDARDS COOPERATORS
J. J. Hill Reference Library
Fourth & Market St.   Phone: (612) 227-9531
St. Paul, MN 55102   Patricia Ricci, Coord.

★N403★
WASECA INTERLIBRARY RESOURCE EXCHANGE (WIRE)
University of Minnesota Technical
College Library   Phone: (507) 835-1000
Waseca, MN 56093   Kathryn Rynders, Chm.
Produces Waseca Union List of Serials (WULS) and Waseca AV Listing (WAVL) (both computer generated).

MISSISSIPPI

★N404★
CENTRAL MISSISSIPPI COUNCIL OF MEDICAL LIBRARIES
c/o Luther Manship Medical Library
St. Dominic-Jackson Memorial Hospital
969 Lakeland Dr.   Phone: (601) 982-0121
Jackson, MS 39216
Address and phone are those of member library.

★N405★
CENTRAL MISSISSIPPI LIBRARY COUNCIL
Jackson Metropolitan Library
301 N. State St.
Jackson, MS 39201
Address is that of member library.

★N406★
COASTAL MISSISSIPPI LIBRARY COOPERATIVE (CMLC)
Biloxi Public Library
217 Lameuse St.   Phone: (601) 374-0330
Biloxi, MS 39530   Mary Reiman, Chm.
Address rotates annually.

★N407★
MISSISSIPPI BIOMEDICAL LIBRARY CONSORTIUM †
c/o V.A. Medical Center Library
1500 E. Woodrow Wilson   Phone: (601) 362-4471
Jackson, MS 39216   Sherry Laughlin, Pres.

MISSOURI

★N408★
ASSEMBLIES OF GOD LIBRARY CONSORTIUM
c/o Cordas C. Burnett Library
Assemblies of God Graduate School
1445 Boonville Ave.   Phone: (417) 862-2781
Springfield, MO 65802
Address and phone are those of member library.

★N409★
KANSAS CITY LIBRARY NETWORK, INC. (KCLN)
c/o Medical Library
St. Luke's Hospital
44th & Wornall Rd.   Phone: (816) 932-2333
Kansas City, MO 64111   Karen Horst, Pres.

★N410★
KANSAS CITY METROPOLITAN LIBRARY NETWORK (KCMLN)
3675 S. Noland Rd., Suite 215   Phone: (816) 461-7001
Independence, MO 64055

★N411★
KANSAS CITY REGIONAL COUNCIL FOR HIGHER EDUCATION (KCRCHE)
912 E. 63rd St.   Phone: (816) 361-4143
Kansas City, MO 64110   Stanley Love, Pres.

★N412★
KANSAS CITY THEOLOGICAL LIBRARY ASSOCIATION
c/o William Broadhurst Library
Nazarene Theological Seminary
1700 E. Meyer Blvd.   Phone: (816) 333-6255
Kansas City, MO 64131   William C. Miller, Libn.

★N413★
LIBRARIES OF THE UNIVERSITY OF MISSOURI INFORMATION NETWORK (LUMIN)
522 Clark Hall
University of Missouri-Columbia   Phone: (314) 882-7233
Columbia, MO 65211   James F. Corey, Lib.Sys.Dir.

★N414★
MID-MISSOURI LIBRARY NETWORK (MMLN)
100 W. Broadway
Box 1267   Phone: (314) 442-7115
Columbia, MO 65205   Frederick Raitnel, Dir.

★N415★
MISSOURI LIBRARY NETWORK CORPORATION
333 Kirkwood Rd.   Phone: (314) 965-7030
St. Louis, MO 63122   Mary Ann Mercante, Exec.Dir.

★N416★
MISSOURI STATEWIDE INTERLIBRARY LOAN NETWORK
Missouri State Library
Truman Office Bldg.
Box 387   Phone: (314) 751-3615
Jefferson City, MO 65101   Darla Parkes, Ref. & ILL Libn.

★N417★
NORTHEAST MISSOURI LIBRARY NETWORK
Pickler Library, Rm. 105
Northeast Missouri State University   Phone: (816) 785-4542
Kirksville, MO 63501   Bronwyn France, Coord.
This is a 42-member multi-type library network.**Also Known As:** NEMO
Library Network.

★N418★
NORTHWEST MISSOURI LIBRARY NETWORK †
1904 North Belt Hwy.   Phone: (816) 364-3386
St. Joseph, MO 64507   James Minges, Coord.

★N419★
ST. JOSEPH AREA LIBRARY COOP †
c/o Northwest Missouri Library Network
1904 North Belt Hwy.   Phone: (816) 364-3386
St. Joseph, MO 64507

★N420★
ST. LOUIS REGIONAL LIBRARY NETWORK
9929 Manchester Rd., Suite 258   Phone: (314) 968-2489
St. Louis, MO 63122   Dr. Arthur R. Taylor, Adm.

★N421★
SOUTHWEST MISSOURI LIBRARY NETWORK †
c/o Springfield-Greene County Library
397 E. Central   Phone: (417) 869-4621
Springfield, MO 65802   Shannon Roy, Coord.

★N422★
SPRINGFIELD GREEN COUNTY LIBRARY NETWORK
c/o Main Post Library
Bldg. 1607   Phone: (314) 368-5431
Ft. Leonard Wood, MO 65473-5000   Christine M. Reser, Chf.Libn.

MONTANA

★N423★
BILLINGS AREA HEALTH SCIENCES INFORMATION COOPERATIVE (BAHSIC)
c/o Library
South Central Montana Regional
Mental Health Center
1245 N. 29th St.   Phone: (406) 252-5658
Billings, MT 59101   ElRene A. Dorn, Libn.
Address and phone are those of member library.

★N424★
BUTTE AREA LIBRARY ASSOCIATION
106 W. Broadway
Butte, MT 59701

★N425★
HELENA AREA HEALTH SCIENCES LIBRARY CONSORTIUM (HAHSLC)
c/o Medical Reference Library
Shodair Children's Hospital
Box 5539   Phone: (406) 442-1980
Helena, MT 59604   Suzy Holt, Info.Rsrcs.Spec.

★N426★
MONTANA HEALTH SCIENCES INFORMATION NETWORK
c/o Renne Library
Montana State University   Phone: (406) 994-4882
Bozeman, MT 59717   Thomas A. Bremer, Coord.

★N427★
MONTANA INFORMATION NETWORK EXHCANGE (MINE) †
c/o Montana State Library
1515 E. 6th Ave.   Phone: (406) 449-3004
Helena, MT 59620

NEBRASKA

★N428★
HASTINGS AREA LIBRARIANS
c/o First Presbyterian Church Library
7th at Lincoln Ave.   Phone: (402) 462-5147
Hastings, NE 68901   Joyce Ohlsen, Dir.
Address and phone are those of member library.

★N429★
LINCOLN HEALTH SCIENCE LIBRARY GROUP
624 Peach St.   Phone: (402) 476-2811
Lincoln, NE 68501   Mary Root, Pres.
Address rotates annually.

★N430★
METROPOLITAN OMAHA HEALTH SCIENCE LIBRARIANS GROUP
  (MOHSLG)
c/o Nursing Library
Bishop Clarkson School of Nursing
333 S. 44th St.
Omaha, NE 68131
Defunct

★N431★
MIDCONTINENTAL REGIONAL MEDICAL LIBRARY PROGRAM
McGoogan Library of Medicine
University of Nebraska Med.Ctr.
42nd & Dewey Ave.   Phone: (402) 559-4326
Omaha, NE 68105   Carolyn Anne Reid, Assoc.Dir.
Region 4 of the Regional Medical Library Program serving CO, KS, MO, NE, UT
and WY.

★N432★
NEBASE
Nebraska Library Commission
1420 P St.   Phone: (402) 471-2045
Lincoln, NE 68508   Pat Gildersleeve, Coord.

★N433★
NEBRASKA LIBRARY LOAN & INFORMATION EXCHANGE (NELLIE)
Nebraska Library Commission
1420 P St.   Phone: (402) 471-2045
Lincoln, NE 68508   John Kopischke, Dir.

★N434★
NORTHEAST LIBRARY SYSTEM
c/o Columbus Public Library   Phone: (402) 563-1016
Columbus, NE 68601
Formerly: Northern Library Network.

★N435★
POSTSECONDARY EDUCATIONAL LEARNING RESOURCE CENTERS OF
  NEBRASKA (PELARCON)
c/o U.S. Conn Library
Wayne State College
200 E. 10   Phone: (402) 375-2200
Wayne, NE 68787
Address and phone are those of member library.

NEVADA

★N436★
INFORMATION NEVADA
Nevada State Library
Capitol Complex   Phone: (702) 885-4178
Carson City, NV 89710   Danna G. Sturm, Coord.

★N437★
U.S. DEPARTMENT OF AGRICULTURE DOCUMENT DELIVERY SERVICE
c/o Life and Health Sciences Library
Fleischmann College of Agriculture Bldg.
University of Nevada   Phone: (702) 784-6616
Reno, NV 89557   Betty Hulse, Lib.Asst. II

★N438★
WESTERN COUNCIL OF STATE LIBRARIES †
c/o Nevada State Library
Capitol Complex   Phone: (702) 885-5130
Carson City, NV 89710   Sharon W. Turgeon, Pres.

NEW HAMPSHIRE

★N439★
CHIEF OFFICERS OF STATE LIBRARY AGENCIES IN THE NORTHEAST
  (COSLINE)
New Hampshire State Library
20 Park St.
Concord, NH 03301   Shirley G. Adamovich, State Libn.

★N440★
MERRIMACK VALLEY/LAKES REGION HEALTH SCIENCE LIBRARIANS
c/o Health Science Library
Catholic Medical Center
100 McGregor St.   Phone: (603) 668-3545
Manchester, NH 03102   Marcia Allen, Libn.

★N441★
NASHUA AREA MATERIALS EXCHANGE (NAME)
c/o Daniel Webster College Library
University Dr.   Phone: (603) 883-3556
Nashua, NH 03063
Address is that of member library.

★N442★
NEW HAMPSHIRE AUTOMATED INFORMATION SYSTEMS BOARD
20 Park St.   Phone: (603) 271-2392
Concord, NH 03301   Shirley G. Adamovich, State Libn.

★N443★
NEW HAMPSHIRE COLLEGE & UNIVERSITY COUNCIL, LIBRARY POLICY
  COMMITTEE (NHCUC)
Notre Dame College Library
2321 Elm St.   Phone: (603) 669-3432
Manchester, NH 03104   Douglas W. Lyon, Coord.

★N444★
URBAN PUBLIC LIBRARY CONSORTIUM
c/o Fine Arts Department
Manchester City Library
405 Pine St.   Phone: (603) 624-6550
Manchester, NH 03104
Address and phone are those of member library.

NEW JERSEY

★N445★
AT & T BELL LABORATORIES LIBRARY NETWORK
Crawfords Corner Rd.   Phone: (201) 949-3456
Holmdel, NJ 07733   F.H. Spaulding, Dir.
Formerly: Bell Laboratories Library Network.

★N446★
BERGEN COUNTY COOPERATIVE LIBRARY SYSTEM (BCCLS)
368A Paramus Rd.   Phone: (201) 652-8806
Paramus, NJ 07652   Lila Cohen, Sys.Adm.

★N447★
BERGEN-PASSAIC HEALTH SCIENCES LIBRARY CONSORTIUM
c/o Medical Library
Holy Name Hospital
718 Teaneck St.   Phone: (201) 833-3014
Teaneck, NJ 07666   Margaret DeMarrais, Chm.
Address rotates biennially.

★N448★
CENTRAL JERSEY HEALTH SCIENCE LIBRARIES ASSOCIATION
c/o Health Science Library
St. Joseph Medical Center
601 Hamilton Ave.   Phone: (609) 559-5068
Trenton, NJ 08629   Harold Boyer, Chm.

★N449★
CONSORTIUM OF EAST NEW JERSEY
c/o Nancy Thompson Library
Kean College of New Jersey   Phone: (201) 527-2017
Union, NJ 07083   Barbara Simpson, Dir.

★N450★
COSMOPOLITAN BIOMEDICAL LIBRARY CONSORTIUM (CBLC)
c/o Health Sciences Library
Mountainside Hospital   Phone: (201) 429-6240
Montclair, NJ 07042   Patricia Regenberg, Pres.
Address rotates annually.

★N451★
COUNTY OF ESSEX COOPERATING LIBRARIES (CECLS)
Upsala College Library
345 Prospect St.   Phone: (201) 266-7295
East Orange, NJ 07019   Karen Lee, Coord.

★N452★
GPUNC SYSTEM LIBRARIES
c/o GPU Nuclear Headquarters Library
100 Interpace Pkwy.   Phone: (201) 263-6184
Parsippany, NJ 07054   Jan Thompson, Libn.
Formerly: GPU Nuclear Libraries Network.

★N453★
HEALTH SCIENCE LIBRARIES OF NEW JERSEY
Center for Health Affairs
746-760 Alexander Rd., CN-1   Phone: (609) 452-9280
Princeton, NJ 08540   Cheryl Newman, Pres.
Presidency rotates annually.

★N454★
JEWISH LIBRARY ASSOCIATION OF DELAWARE VALLEY
c/o Beth Israel Congregation Library
1015 E. Park Ave.   Phone: (609) 691-0852
Vineland, NJ 08360
Address and phone are those of member library.

★N455★
MEDICAL RESOURCES CONSORTIUM OF CENTRAL NEW JERSEY
   (MEDCORE)
c/o Medical Library
Hoeschst-Roussel Pharmaceuticals
Rte. 202-206, N.   Phone: (201) 231-3177
Somerville, NJ 08876   Barbara Boyajian, Pres.

★N456★
MONMOUTH-OCEAN BIOMEDICAL INFORMATION CONSORTIUM
Medical Library
Monmouth Medical Center
3rd & Pavilion Ave.   Phone: (201) 870-5170
Long Branch, NJ 07740   John Conway, Dir.

★N457★
NEW JERSEY ACADEMIC LIBRARY NETWORK
c/o Music Branch Library
Wilson Bldg. 615
Glassboro State College   Phone: (609) 445-7306
Glassboro, NJ 08028   Marjorie Travaline, Libn.

★N458★
NEW JERSEY LIBRARY NETWORK
State Library
185 W. State St.   Phone: (609) 292-2992
Trenton, NJ 08625-0520   Robert A. Drescher, Coord.

★N459★
NEW JERSEY STATE LIBRARY REGIONAL FILM CENTERS
c/o South Jersey Regional Film Library
Echelon Urban Center
Laurel Rd.   Phone: (609) 772-1642
Voorhees, NJ 08043   Katherine Schalk-Greene, Dir., Lib.
Address and phone are those of member library.

★N460★
PARTNERS FOR LEARNING (PFL)
Health Science Library
Elizabeth General Medical Center
925 E. Jersey St.
Elizabeth, NJ 07021   Catherine Boss, Proj.Dir.
Address is that of member library.

★N461★
PHUY
c/o Speer Library
Princeton Theological Seminary
Box 111
Princeton, NJ 08540
This is a consortium composed of Princeton, Harvard, Union and Yale divinity
collections. Inactive.

★N462★
PINELANDS CONSORTIUM
c/o Deborah Heart & Lung Center
1 Trenton Rd.
Brown Mills, NJ 08015   Carol Harris

★N463★
SOCIETY FOR COOPERATIVE HEALTHCARE AND RELATED EDUCATION
   (SCHARE)
MacKay Library
Union County College   Phone: (201) 276-5710
Cranford, NJ 07016   Carol Dreyer, Coord.

★N464★
SOUTH JERSEY LIBRARY ASSOCIATION
c/o Beth Israel Congregation Library
1015 E. Park Ave.   Phone: (609) 691-0852
Vineland, NJ 08360
Address and phone are those of member library.

★N465★
SOUTHWEST NEW JERSEY CONSORTIUM FOR HEALTH INFORMATION
   SERVICES
Cooper Hospital/University Medical Ctr.
One Cooper Plaza   Phone: (609) 964-0140
Camden, NJ 08103   Marge LaRue, Coord.

★N466★
TRENTON AREA REFERENCE LIBRARIES
c/o Information Resource Center
New Jersey State Dept.
of Env. Protection
190 W. State St. (CN-402)
Trenton, NJ 08625   JoAnn Post, Coord.

NEW MEXICO

★N467★
DEPARTMENT OF INTERIOR LIBRARIES AND INFORMATION SERVICE
Chaco Center Library
U.S. Natl. Park Service
Box 26176   Phone: (505) 766-3545
Albuquerque, NM 87125   Thomas C. Windes, Supv.Archeo.

★N468★
NEW MEXICO CONSORTIUM OF BIOMEDICAL LIBRARIES
Los Lunas Hospital & Training School
Box 1269   Phone: (505) 865-9611
Los Lunas, NM 87031   Sarah Morley, Coord.

★N469★
NEW MEXICO INFORMATION SYSTEM (NEMISYS)
New Mexico State Library
325 Don Gaspar   Phone: (505) 827-2033
Santa Fe, NM 87503   Harold L. Bogart, Coord.

NEW YORK

★N470★
AMERICAN EXPRESS COMPANY LIBRARY CONSORTIUM
c/o Card Information Center
American Express Company
American Express Plaza   Phone: (212) 323-4146
New York, NY 10004
Address and phone are those of member library.

★N471★
ASSOCIATED COLLEGES OF THE ST. LAWRENCE VALLEY, INC. (ACSLV)
Raymond Hall
SUNY - College at Potsdam   Phone: (315) 265-2790
Potsdam, NY 13676   Judy C. Chittenden

★N472★
ASSOCIATION OF LAW LIBRARIES OF UPSTATE NEW YORK
c/o Emory A. Chase Memorial Library
Greene County Court House
Box 65   Phone: (518) 943-3130
Catskill, NY 12414
Address and phone are those of member library.

★N473★
BILINGUAL EDUCATION TELECOMMUNICATIONS NETWORK (BETNET)
c/o Resource Library and Info. Unit
Office of Bilingual Education
131 Livingston St., Rm. 204   Phone: (718) 858-5505
Brooklyn, NY 11201
Address and phone are those of member library.

★N474★
BROOKLYN EDUCATIONAL & CULTURAL ALLIANCE
26 Court St., Suite 1403   Phone: (718) 852-4400
Brooklyn, NY 11234   Howard B. Hornstein, Exec.Dir.

★N475★
BROOKLYN-QUEENS-STATEN ISLAND HEALTH SCIENCES LIBRARIANS (BQSI)
c/o Coney Island Hospital
2601 Ocean Pkwy.   Phone: (718) 615-4299
Brooklyn, NY 11235   Ronnie Joan Mark, Act.Pres.
Address and presidency rotate.

★N476★
CAPITOL DISTRICT LIBRARY COUNCIL FOR REFERENCE & RESEARCH RESOURCES (CDLC)
91 Fiddlers Lane   Phone: (518) 785-0798
Latham, NY 12110   Charles D. Custer, Exec.Dir.
See also the library listing for this network in the main section.

★N477★
CENTRAL NEW YORK LIBRARY RESOURCES COUNCIL (CENTRO)
763 Butternut St.   Phone: (315) 478-6080
Syracuse, NY 13208   James M. Turner, Jr., Exec.Dir.

★N478★
CHAUTAUQUA-CATTARAUGUS LIBRARY SYSTEM
106 W. 5th St.   Phone: (716) 484-7135
Jamestown, NY 14701   Murray L. Bob, Adm.

★N479★
CLINTON-ESSEX-FRANKLIN LIBRARY SYSTEM
Box 570   Phone: (518) 563-5190
Plattsburgh, NY 12901   Stanley A. Ransom, Adm.

★N480★
CONSORTIUM OF ALTERNATIVE CENTERS OF CONTEMPORARY ART
c/o Franklin Furnace Archives, Inc.
112 Franklin St.
New York, NY 10013
Defunct

★N481★
CONSORTIUM OF FOUNDATION LIBRARIES
c/o Carnegie Corporation of New York
437 Madison Ave.   Phone: (212) 371-3200
New York, NY 10022   Patricia Haynes, Chm.

★N482★
COUNCIL OF ARCHIVES AND RESEARCH LIBRARIES IN JEWISH STUDIES (CARLJS)
122 E 42nd St., Suite 1512   Phone: (212) 490-2280
New York, NY 10168   Abraham Atik, Coord.
Affiliated with the World Council on Jewish Archives, Jerusalem.

★N483★
DOWNSTATE DEVELOPMENTAL CENTER LIBRARIES
c/o Library
Letchworth Village Development Ctr.
Thiells, NY 10984
Defunct

★N484★
EDUCATIONAL FILM LIBRARY ASSOCIATION
c/o Audiovisual Resource Center
Cornell University
8 Research Park   Phone: (607) 256-2091
Ithaca, NY 14850   Carol Doolittle, AV Coord.
Address and phone are those of member library.

★N485★
FAUL
757 Ostrom Ave.
Syracuse, NY 13210
Defunct

★N486★
FINGER LAKES LIBRARY SYSTEM
314 N. Cayuga St.   Phone: (607) 273-4074
Ithaca, NY 14850   Richard Panz, Dir.

★N487★
GENERAL FOODS INFORMATION NETWORK
250 North St.   Phone: (914) 335-1040
White Plains, NY 10625   Theresa Maylone, Adm.
Coordinator rotates annually.

★N488★
GREATER NORTHEASTERN REGIONAL MEDICAL LIBRARY PROGRAM
New York Academy of Medicine Library
2 E. 103rd St.   Phone: (212) 876-8763
New York, NY 10029   Kay Mills Due, Assoc.Dir.
Region 1 of the Regional Medical Library Program serving CT, DE, ME, MA, NH, NJ, NY, PA, RI, VT and PR.

★N489★
HEALTH RESOURCES COUNCIL OF CENTRAL NEW YORK (HRCCNY)
c/o Upstate Medical Center
SUNY
766 Irving Ave.   Phone: (315) 473-4580
Syracuse, NY 13210   Peter Uva, Pres.
Address rotates annually.

★N490★
INDEPENDENT RESEARCH LIBRARY ASSOCIATION (IRLA)
New York Public Library
5th Ave. & 42nd St.   Phone: (212) 930-0708
New York, NY 10018

★N491★
INTERSHARE
57 Willoughby St.
Brooklyn, NY 11201
Defunct. Absorbed by METRO (New York Metropolitan Reference and Research Library Agency).

★N492★
LAW LIBRARY ASSOCIATION OF GREATER NEW YORK
c/o Davis Polk & Wardwell
One Chase Plaza   Phone: (212) 530-4266
New York, NY 10005   Nuchine Nobari, Hd.Libn.
Address rotates annually.

★N493★
LIBRARY CONSORTIUM OF HEALTH INSTITUTIONS IN BUFFALO (LCHIB)
Health Sciences Library
Stockton Kimball Tower
SUNY at Buffalo   Phone: (716) 831-3351
Buffalo, NY 14214   Randy Wheeler, Dir., Consortium
Consortium consists of eight teaching hospital libraries and the university's
Health Sciences Library.

★N494★
LIBRARY EXCHANGE AND RESOURCES NETWORK (LEARN)
Utica/Marcy Psychiatric Center
1213 Court St.
Utica, NY 13502   Tom Smith, Coord.
Address is that of member library.

★N495★
LIBRARY INFORMATION AND ONLINE NETWORK (LIONS)
c/o New York Public Library
20 W. 53rd St.   Phone: (212) 621-0661
New York, NY 10019   Robert Goldstein, Coord.

★N496★
LONG ISLAND LIBRARY RESOURCES COUNCIL (LILRC)
Box 31   Phone: (516) 286-0400
Bellport, NY 11713   Herbert Biblo, Exec.Dir.
See also the library listing for this network in the main section.

★N497★
LONG ISLAND MEDIA CONSORTIUM
c/o Nassau Community College Library
Stewart Ave.   Phone: (516) 222-7413
Garden City, NY 11530   Arthur Friedman, Chm.

★N498★
MANHATTAN-BRONX HEALTH SCIENCES LIBRARY GROUP †
c/o Medical Library
V.A. Medical Center
408 First Ave.   Phone: (212) 686-7500
New York, NY 10010   Thomas Williams, Chm.

★N499★
MEDICAL LIBRARY CENTER OF NEW YORK (MLCNY)
5 E. 102nd St., 7th Fl.   Phone: (212) 427-1630
New York, NY 10029   William D. Walker, Coord.
See also the library listing for this network in the main section.

★N500★
MEDICAL & SCIENTIFIC LIBRARIES OF LONG ISLAND (MEDLI)
c/o Shell Library
Nassau Academy of Medicine
1200 Stewart Ave.   Phone: (516) 832-2320
Garden City, NY 11530   Pamela Kerns, Pres.

★N501★
MEDSHARE
Medical Library
Brookhaven Memorial Hospital
101 Hospital Rd.
Patchogue, NY 11772
Defunct

★N502★
METRO
57 Willoughby St.   Phone: (718) 852-8700
Brooklyn, NY 11201   Joan Neumann, Exec.Dir.
Also Known As: New York Metropolitan Reference and Research Library
Agency.

★N503★
MID-YORK LIBRARY SYSTEM
1600 Lincoln Ave.   Phone: (315) 735-8238
Utica, NY 13502   Alfred C. Hasemeier, Adm.

★N504★
MONROE COUNTY LIBRARY SYSTEM
115 South Ave.   Phone: (716) 428-7347
Rochester, NY 14604   Linda M. Bretz

★N505★
NASSAU-SUFFOLK LIBRARY CONSORTIA
c/o Art & Architecture Library
New York Institute of Technology
Wheatley Rd.   Phone: (516) 686-7579
Old Westbury, NY 11568   Stephen H. Van Dyke, Libn.

★N506★
NETWORK FOR CONTINUING MEDICAL EDUCATION (NCME)
15 Columbus Circle   Phone: (800) 223-0272
New York, NY 10023   Kristin Kramer, Coord.

★N507★
NEW YORK STATE INTERLIBRARY LOAN NETWORK (NYSILL)
Division of Library Development
New York State Library
Cultural Education Center   Phone: (518) 474-7890
Albany, NY 12230   Jane G. Rollins, Assoc., Lib.Serv.

★N508★
NEW YORK UNIVERSITY, NEW SCHOOL, COOPER UNION CONSORTIUM
c/o Raymond Fogelman Library
New School for Social Research
65 Fifth Ave.   Phone: (212) 741-7902
New York, NY 10003
Address and phone are those of member library.

★N509★
NORTH COUNTRY REFERENCE AND RESEARCH RESOURCES COUNCIL
   (NCRRRC)
Box 568   Phone: (315) 386-4569
Canton, NY 13617   Richard H. Kimball, Exec.Dir.

★N510★
NORTHERN NEW YORK HEALTH INFORMATION COOPERATIVE
c/o North Country Reference &
Research Resources Council
Box 568
Canton, NY 13617

★N511★
RAMAPO CATSKILL LIBRARY SYSTEM
619 North St.   Phone: (914) 343-1131
Middletown, NY 10940   Alfred L. Freund, Adm.

★N512★
REGIONAL CONFERENCE OF HISTORICAL AGENCIES
c/o Library & Archives
National Soaring Museum
Harris Hill, R.D. 3   Phone: (607) 734-3128
Elmira, NY 14903
Address and phone are those of member library.

★N513★
RESEARCH LIBRARY ASSOCIATION OF SOUTH MANHATTAN
c/o Bobst Library
New York University
70 Washington Sq., S.
New York, NY 10012   Carlton C. Rochell

★N514★
ROCHESTER ONLINE USERS GROUP
Rush Rhees Library
University of Rochester   Phone: (716) 275-4437
Rochester, NY 14627   Michael Poulin, Co-Chm.
Address rotates annually.

★N515★
ROCHESTER REGIONAL RESEARCH LIBRARY COUNCIL (RRRLC)
339 East Ave., Rm. 300   Phone: (716) 232-7930
Rochester, NY 14604   Janet M. Welch, Dir.

★N516★
SAVE CONSORTIUM
c/o Ellis Hospital Medical Library
1101 Nott St.
Schenectady, NY 12308   Dorothy E. Brandon, AV Coord.
Also Known As: Shared Audio Visuals/Equipment Consortium.

★N517★
SOUTH CENTRAL RESEARCH LIBRARY COUNCIL (SCRLC)
DeWitt Bldg.
215 N. Cayuga St.   Phone: (607) 273-9106
Ithaca, NY 14850   Janet E. Steiner, Exec.Dir.

★N518★
SOUTHEASTERN NEW YORK LIBRARY RESOURCES COUNCIL (SENYLRC)
9 Collegeview Ave.   Phone: (914) 471-0625
Poughkeepsie, NY 12603   Ruth Brown Chamberlain, Exec.Dir.
Maintains the Southeastern Bibliographic Center (SEBC).

★N519★
SUFFOLK COOPERATIVE LIBRARY SYSTEM
627 N. Sunrise Service Rd.
Bellport, NY 11713   Robert N. Sheridan, Dir.

★N520★
SUNY/OCLC LIBRARY NETWORK
Central Administration
State University of New York
State University Plaza   Phone: (518) 474-1685
Albany, NY 12246   Glyn T. Evans, Dir.

★N521★
THREE R'S COUNCIL, ITHACA
c/o Medical Center Library
U.S. Veterans Administration   Phone: (607) 776-2111
Bath, NY 14810   Norma Haskins, Chf., Lib.Serv.
Address and phone are those of member library.

★N522★
UNION CATALOG OF MEDICAL MONOGRAPHS
c/o Medical Library, Area 3-I
Equitable Life Assurance Society of the U.S.
1285 Avenue of the Americas   Phone: (212) 554-2935
New York, NY 10019
Address and phone are those of member library.

★N523★
WESTCHESTER LIBRARY SYSTEM
8 Westchester Plaza   Phone: (914) 592-8214
Elmsford, NY 10523   Maurice J. Freedman, Dir.

★N524★
WESTERN NEW YORK HEALTH SCIENCES LIBRARIANS (WNYHSL)
Information Dissemination Service
Health Science Library
SUNY at Buffalo
3435 Main St.   Phone: (716) 831-3351
Buffalo, NY 14214   Michele Farrell, Pres.

★N525★
WESTERN NEW YORK LIBRARY RESOURCES COUNCIL (WNYLRC)
Lafayette Sq.   Phone: (716) 852-3844
Buffalo, NY 14203   Joyce D. Everingham, Exec.Dir.

NORTH CAROLINA

★N526★
AREA HEALTH CONSORTIUM FOR SHARING HEALTH INFORMATION
c/o Learning Resource Center
Technical College of Alamance
Box 623   Phone: (919) 578-2002
Haw River, NC 27258   Ronald J. Plummer, Coord., Lib.Serv.
Address is that of member library.

★N527★
ASSOCIATION FOR POPULATION/FAMILY PLANNING LIBRARIES AND
   INFORMATION CENTERS - INTERNATIONAL
c/o Carolina Population Center Library
University Square - East, 300A   Phone: (919) 962-3006
Chapel Hill, NC 27514   Gloria A. Roberts, Pres.
Also Known As: APLIC-International.

★N528★
CAPE FEAR HEALTH SCIENCES INFORMATION CONSORTIUM
c/o Medical Library
Womack Army Hospital
U.S. Army Hospitals   Phone: (919) 396-0205
Fort Bragg, NC 28307   Cecilia C. Edwards, Med.Libn.
Address rotates annually.

★N529★
CHARLOTTE AREA EDUCATIONAL CONSORTIUM
c/o Abbot Vincent Taylor Library
Belmont Abbey College   Phone: (704) 825-3711
Belmont, NC 28012
Address is that of member library.

★N530★
COOPERATING RALEIGH COLLEGES CONSORTIUM (CRC)
Meredith College
Box X-120   Phone: (919) 829-8538
Raleigh, NC 27607-5298   Dr. Rosalie P. Gates, Dir.

★N531★
METROLINA LIBRARY ASSOCIATION
Information Resource Center
Duke Power Company
Box 670
Cornelius, NC 28031   E. Butler Scarborough, Pres.

★N532★
NCCC UNION COM CATALOG PROJECT
c/o Learning Resource Center
Central Carolina Technical College
1105 Kelly Dr.   Phone: (919) 775-5401
Sanford, NC 27330   Linda S. Halstead, Proj.Dir.

★N533★
NORTH CAROLINA AREA HEALTH EDUCATION CENTERS PROGRAM -
   LIBRARY AND INFORMATION SERVICES NETWORK
Health Sciences Library, 223H
University of North Carolina   Phone: (919) 962-0700
Chapel Hill, NC 27514   Lynne Siemers, Liaison Libn.

★N534★
NORTH CAROLINA CENTER FOR INDEPENDENT HIGHER EDUCATION, INC.
   (NCCIHE)
1300 St. Mary's St., 4th Fl.   Phone: (919) 832-5817
Raleigh, NC 27605   Gwenn H. Reynolds, Coord.

★N535★
NORTH CAROLINA INFORMATION NETWORK (IN-WATS)
Interlibrary Services Branch
Division of State Library
109 E. Jones St.   Phone: (919) 733-3683
Raleigh, NC 27611   Sue Farr, Hd.

★N536★
NORTH CAROLINA INTERLIBRARY LOAN NETWORK
North Carolina State Department of
Cultural Resources
109 E. Jones St.   Phone: (919) 733-2570
Raleigh, NC 27611   David N. McKay, State Libn.

★N537★
NORTHWEST AHEC LIBRARY INFORMATION NETWORK †
Northwest Area Health Education Center
Bowman Gray School of Medicine   Phone: (704) 322-0662
Winston-Salem, NC 27103   Phyllis Gillikin, Coord.
Formerly: Northwest Area Health Center Consortium.

★N538★
RESOURCES FOR HEALTH INFORMATION (REHI)
Medical Library
Wake County Medical Center
3000 New Bern Ave.   Phone: (919) 755-8529
Raleigh, NC 28610   Beverly Richardson, Wake AHEC Libn.
Chairmanship rotates irregularly.

★N539★
ROCKINGHAM COUNTY HEALTH INFORMATION CONSORTIUM
c/o Martha Davis, Director
Rockingham County Public Library
527 Boone Rd.
Eden, NC 27288

★N540★
TRIANGLE RESEARCH LIBRARIES NETWORK (TRLN)
c/o D.H. Hill Library
North Carolina State University
Box 7111   Phone: (919) 737-2843
Littleton, NC 27695

NORTH DAKOTA

★N541★
NORTH DAKOTA NETWORK FOR KNOWLEDGE
North Dakota State Library
Liberty Memorial Bldg.
Capitol Grounds   Phone: (701) 224-2490
Bismarck, ND 58505

★N542★
NORTH DAKOTA STATE LIBRARY TELETYPE NETWORK
c/o Memorial Library - Special Collections
Minot State College   Phone: (701) 857-3200
Minot, ND 58701   Ronald J. Rudser, Dir.

★N543★
NORTHERN PLAINS CONSORTIUM FOR EDUCATION
Jamestown College   Phone: (701) 253-2505
Jamestown, ND 58401   Donald T. Cannon, Dir.

★N544★
NORTHWEST AREA HEALTH EDUCATION CENTER CONSORTIUM
c/o Angus L. Cameron Medical Library
Trinity Medical Center
20 4th Ave., S.W.   Phone: (701) 857-5435
Minot, ND 58701
Also Known As: Northwest AHEC Consortium.

★N545★
VALLEY MEDICAL NETWORK (VMN)
c/o TNI Medical Library
700 First Ave. S.   Phone: (701) 235-5354
Fargo, ND 58103   Diane Nordeng, Coord.
Address and coordinator rotate annually.

OHIO

★N546★
ART RESEARCH LIBRARIES OF OHIO (ARLO)
Toledo Art Museum
Box 1013
Toledo, OH 43697
Inactive

★N547★
BIOMEDICAL COMMUNICATIONS NETWORK
c/o Health Sciences Library
Wright State University
3640 Glenn Hwy.   Phone: (513) 873-2266
Dayton, OH 45435   Audrey J. Kidder, Health Sci.Libn.
Address and phone are those of member library.

★N548★
CALICO †
c/o Wagnalls Memorial Library
150 E. Columbus St.   Phone: (614) 837-4765
Lithopolis, OH 43136   Jo Riegel, Pres.
Also Known As: Columbus Area Library and Information Council of Ohio.

★N549★
CANTON-MASSILLON BRS CONSORTIA
c/o Medical Library
Doctors' Hospital Inc. of Stark County
400 Austin Ave., N.W.   Phone: (216) 837-7371
Massillon, OH 44646
Address and phone are those of member library.

★N550★
CENTRAL OHIO HOSPITAL LIBRARY CONSORTIUM
Riverside Methodist Hospital
3535 Olentangy River Rd.   Phone: (614) 261-5230
Columbus, OH 43214   Ms. Jo Yeoh, Coord.

★N551★
CINCINNATI AREA HEALTH SCIENCES LIBRARY ASSOCIATION (CAHSLA)
231 Bethesda Ave.
Mail Location 574   Phone: (513) 872-5541
Cincinnati, OH 45267   Stephena Harmony, Coord.
Address rotates annually.

★N552★
CINCINNATI ONLINE CONSORTIUM FOR LIFE SCIENCES (COCLS)
James N. Gamble Institute of Med.Res.
2141 Auburn Ave.   Phone: (513) 369-2540
Cincinnati, OH 45219   Lisa McCormick, Res.Libn.
Address rotates biennially.

★N553★
CINCINNATI ONLINE USERS GROUP
Medical Library
Good Samaritan Hospital
3217 Clifton Ave.   Phone: (513) 872-2433
Cincinnati, OH 45220   Roaslie Zajac, Med.Libn.

★N554★
CLEVELAND AREA METROPOLITAN LIBRARY SYSTEM (CAMLS)
11000 Euclid Ave., Rm. 309   Phone: (216) 368-2642
Cleveland, OH 44106-1799   Nancy Wareham, Exec.Dir.

★N555★
COMMITTEE FOR LIBRARY COOPERATION (CLC)
c/o Jerome Library
Bowling Green State University   Phone: (419) 372-2856
Bowling Green, OH 43402   Dwight F. Burlingame, Dean of Libs.
Address rotates annually.

★N556★
CONSORTIUM FOR HEALTH EDUCATION IN APPALACHIA OHIO (CHEAO)
P.O Drawer 825   Phone: (614) 593-5526
Athens, OH 45701   Kathleen D. Connick, Coord.

★N557★
CONSORTIUM OF UNIVERSITY FILM CENTERS (CUFC)
c/o Audio Visual Services
330 KSU Library
Kent State University   Phone: (216) 672-3456
Kent, OH 44242   John Kerstetter, Act.Exec.Dir.

★N558★
DAYTON AREA MEDLINE CONSORTIUM
c/o Health Sciences Library
St. Elizabeth Medical Center
601 Miami Blvd., W.   Phone: (513) 229-6061
Dayton, OH 45408
Address and phone are those of member library.

★N559★
GREATER CINCINNATI LIBRARY CONSORTIUM (GCLC)
3333 Vine St.
Cincinnati, OH 45220   Carrie Conlin, Exec.Dir.

★N560★
HEALTH SCIENCE LIBRARIANS OF NORTHWEST OHIO (HSLNO)
c/o Burns Health Sciences Library
Mercy Hospital
2238 Jefferson Ave.
Toledo, OH 43624
Address is that of member library.

★N561★
LAKE ERIE MEDICAL LIBRARIANS ASSOCIATION
c/o Medical Staff Library
St. Joseph Hospital
205 W. 20th St.
Lorain, OH 44052
Address is that of member library.

★N562★
MEDICAL LIBRARY ASSOCIATION OF NORTHEASTERN OHIO
c/o Medical Library
St. Lukes Hospital
11311 Shaker Blvd.   Phone: (216) 368-7691
Cleveland, OH 44104
Address and phone are those of member library.

★N563★
MIAMI VALLEY ASSOCIATION OF HEALTH SCIENCES LIBRARIES
Health Sciences Library
Wright State University
3640 Colonel Glenn Hwy.   Phone: (513) 873-2003
Dayton, OH 45435
Address and phone are those of member library.

★N564★
MIAMI VALLEY LIBRARIES (MVL) †
c/o Milton Union Public Library
560 S. Main St.   Phone: (513) 698-5515
West Milton, OH 45383   Martha Coulton
Formerly: Miami Valley Library Organization (MILO).

★N565★
MIAMI VALLEY UNION LIST
c/o Medical Center Library
U.S. Veterans Administration
3200 Vine St.
Cincinnati, OH 45220   Cynthia R. Sterling, Libn.
Address is that of member library.

★N566★
NEOMAL †
c/o Oberlin College Library   Phone: (216) 775-8285
Oberlin, OH 44074   William A. Moffett, Chm.

★N567★
NOLA REGIONAL LIBRARY SYSTEM
25 E. Boardman St.
Youngstown, OH 44503   Theresa Trucksis, Proj.Coord.

★N568★
NORTH CENTRAL LIBRARY COOPERATIVE
27 N. Main St.   Phone: (419) 526-1337
Mansfield, OH 44902   Mike Snyder, Dir.

★N569★
NORTHEASTERN OHIO UNIVERSITIES COLLEGE OF MEDICINE (NEOUCOM)
Basic Medical Sciences Library
Rootstown, OH 44272   Karen Brewer, Lib.Dir.
Also Known As: Council of Hospital Librarians.

★N570★
NORTHWEST LIBRARY DISTRICT (NORWELD)
c/o Wood County District Public Library
251 N. Main St.   Phone: (419) 352-2903
Bowling Green, OH 43402   Allan Gray, Coord.

★N571★
NORTHWEST OHIO CONSORTIUM (NOC) †
c/o Anthony Wayne Library
Defiance College   Phone: (419) 784-4010
Defiance, OH 43512   Maxie J. Lambright, Chm.

★N572★
OHIO-KENTUCKY COOPERATING LIBRARIES - UNION LIST OF SERIALS
Wright State University Library   Phone: (513) 873-3034
Dayton, OH 45435   Kathryn Chilson, Hd., Ser.Dept.
Formerly: Union List of Serials Miami Valley, Cincinnati and Northern Kentucky.

★N573★
OHIO NETWORK OF AMERICAN HISTORY RESEARCH CENTERS
1982 Velma Ave.
Columbus, OH 43211
Also Known As: Network of American History Research Centers. Inactive.

★N574★
OHIO NETWORK OF MEDICAL HISTORY COLLECTIONS
c/o Historical Division
Cleveland Health Sciences Library
11000 Euclid Ave.   Phone: (216) 368-3648
Cleveland, OH 44106   Dr. Patsy A. Gerstner, Chf.Cur.

★N575★
OHIO REGIONAL ASSOCIATION OF LAW LIBRARIES
Law School Library
University of Dayton
300 College Pk.   Phone: (513) 229-2314
Dayton, OH 45469

★N576★
OHIO VALLEY AREA LIBRARIES (OVAL) †
State Route 93 W.   Phone: (614) 384-2103
Wellston, OH 45692   Linda Harfst, Adm.

★N577★
OHIONET
1500 West Lane Ave.   Phone: (614) 486-2966
Columbus, OH 43221   Ronald Diener, Exec.Dir.
Also Known As: Ohio Library Network.

★N578★
SOUTHEASTERN OHIO LIBRARY ORGANIZATION (SOLO)
Regional Library Service Ctr.
Rte. 4   Phone: (614) 783-3795
Caldwell, OH 43724

★N579★
SOUTHWEST OHIO COUNCIL FOR HIGHER EDUCATION (SOC)
1810 Harvard Blvd.   Phone: (513) 278-9105
Dayton, OH 45406   Dr. Pressley C. McCoy, Pres.
Formerly: Dayton-Miami Valley Consortium (Library Division) (DMVC).

★N580★
WEST CENTRAL OHIO ONLINE USERS GROUP
c/o Medical Library
Educational Resources Center
Miami Valley Hospital
One Wyoming St.   Phone: (513) 223-6192
Dayton, OH 45409
Address and phone are those of member library.

★N581★
WESTERN OHIO REGIONAL LIBRARY DEVELOPMENT SYSTEM (WORLDS)
640 W. Market St.   Phone: (419) 227-9370
Lima, OH 45801   Mrs. J. Schneider, Coord.

OKLAHOMA

★N582★
GREATER OKLAHOMA CITY AREA HEALTH SCIENCES LIBRARY CONSORTIUM (GOAL)
c/o Norman Regional Hospital Library
Box 1308   Phone: (405) 321-1700
Norman, OK 73070   Michelynn McKnight, Coord.
Address rotates annually.

★N583★
OKLAHOMA HEALTH SCIENCES LIBRARY ASSOCIATION (OHSLA)
c/o Medical Library, 142D
V.A. Medical Center   Phone: (918) 683-3261
Muskogee, OK 74401   Larry L. Shea, Pres.
Address and presidency rotate annually.

★N584★
OKLAHOMA SPECIAL COLLECTIONS AND ARCHIVES NETWORK (OSCAN)
c/o McFarlin Library
University of Tulsa
600 S. College Ave.   Phone: (918) 592-6000
Tulsa, OK 74104   Toby Murray, Pres.
Address rotates annually.

★N585★
OKLAHOMA TELECOMMUNICATIONS INTERLIBRARY SYSTEM (OTIS)
Oklahoma Dept. of Libraries
200 N.E. 18th St.   Phone: (405) 521-2502
Oklahoma City, OK 73105   Mary Hardin, ILL Libn.

★N586★
TULSA AREA LIBRARY COOPERATIVE (TALC)
400 Civic Center   Phone: (918) 581-5328
Tulsa, OK 74103   Carol Hughes, Coord.

OREGON

★N587★
CAREER INFORMATION SYSTEM (CIS)
University of Oregon
1787 Agate St.   Phone: (503) 686-3872
Eugene, OR 97403   Dr. Bruce McKinlay, Dir.

★N588★
CLACKAMAS COUNTY COOPERATIVE LIBRARY SYSTEM
c/o George Hallauer Memorial Library
Western Evangelical Seminary
4200 S.E. Jennings Ave.   Phone: (503) 654-5182
Milwaukie, OR 97222   Gary Metzenbacher, Lib.Dir.

★N589★
LANE-DOUGLAS CONSORTIA
c/o Douglas ESD
1871 N.E. Stephens   Phone: (503) 440-4755
Roseburg, OR 97470   Jim Heath, Chm.
Address rotates biennially.

★N590★
OREGON HEALTH INFORMATION NETWORK (OHIN)
Oregon Health Sciences Univ.Lib.   Phone: (503) 225-8026
Portland, OR 97207   Steve Teich, Coord.

★N591★
OREGON HEALTH SCIENCES LIBRARIES ASSOCIATION (OHSLA)
c/o Health Sciences Lib. & Info.Ctr.
Salem Hospital
665 Winter St., S.E.
Box 14001   Phone: (503) 370-5559
Salem, OR 97309   Susan Dyer, Health Sci.Libn.
Address and phone are those of member library.

★N592★
OREGON ONLINE USERS GROUP (OOUG)
c/o Arthur Andersen & Co.
111 S.W. Columbia, Suite 1400   Phone: (503) 226-1331
Portland, OR 97201   Judy R. Weinsoft, Libn.

★N593★
PORTLAND AREA HEALTH SCIENCES LIBRARIANS
c/o Health Sciences Library
Eastmoreland General Hospital
2900 S.E. Steele St.   Phone: (503) 234-0411
Portland, OR 97202
Address and phone are those of member library.

★N594★
SOUTHERN OREGON LIBRARY FEDERATION (SOLF)
Jackson County Library
413 W. Main St.   Phone: (503) 776-7285
Medford, OR 97501   Celeste Fransiskeano

★N595★
WASHINGTON COUNTY COOPERATIVE LIBRARY SERVICES (WCCLS)
17880 S.W. Blanton St.
Box 5129   Phone: (503) 642-1544
Aloha, OR 97006   Donna M. Selle, Coord.

★N596★
WASHINGTON-OREGON REGIONAL LIBRARY DEVELOPMENT (WORLD)
c/o Professional Library
Portland Public Schools
Box 3107
Portland, OR 97208
Defunct

PENNSYLVANIA

★N597★
ASSOCIATED COLLEGE LIBRARIES OF CENTRAL PENNSYLVANIA (ACLCP)
c/o Messiah College Library   Phone: (717) 766-2511
Grantham, PA 17027   Roger Miller, Chm.

★N598★
ASSOCIATION FOR LIBRARY INFORMATION (AFLI)
Duquesne Library   Phone: (412) 434-6138
Pittsburgh, PA 15219   Paul J. Pugliese, Exec.Dir.

★N599★
BERKS COUNTY LIBRARY ASSOCIATION
Box 7545
Reading, PA 19603   Kathryn A. Joffred, Pres.

★N600★
CENTRAL PENNSYLVANIA CONSORTIUM (CPC)
Dickinson College   Phone: (717) 245-1490
Carlisle, PA 17013

★N601★
CENTRAL PENNSYLVANIA HEALTH SCIENCES LIBRARY ASSOCIATION (CPHSLA)
c/o Medical Library
Lancaster General Hospital   Phone: (717) 299-5511
Lancaster, PA 17604   Claudette Strohm, Pres.
Address rotates annually.

★N602★
CENTRAL PENNSYLVANIA SLA USERS GROUP
c/o Communications Center
Hershey Foods Corporation
1025 Reese Ave.   Phone: (717) 534-5106
Hershey, PA 17033
Address and phone are those of member library.

★N603★
CONFEDERATION OF STATE & STATE RELATED INSTITUTIONS †
c/o Central Professional Library
Norristown State Hospital   Phone: (215) 631-2948
Norristown, PA 19401

★N604★
CONSORTIUM FOR HEALTH INFORMATION & LIBRARY SERVICES (CHI)
15th St. & Upland Ave.   Phone: (215) 447-6163
Chester, PA 19013   Kathleen Vick, Exec.Dir.

★N605★
COOPERATING HOSPITAL LIBRARIES OF THE LEHIGH VALLEY AREA (CHL) †
Allentown Hospital
17th and Chew Sts.   Phone: (215) 821-2405
Allentown, PA 18102   Karen Weston

★N606★
DELAWARE VALLEY INFORMATION CONSORTIUM (DEVIC)
c/o Medical Library
Rolling Hill Hospital
60 E. Township Line Rd.   Phone: (215) 663-6328
Elkins Park, PA 19117   Dee Disardina, Coord.
Address rotates with coordinator.

★N607★
ERIE AREA HEALTH INFORMATION LIBRARY COOPERATIVE (EAHILC)
Metro Health Center
252 W. 11th St.   Phone: (814) 455-3961
Erie, PA 16301   Judith Gustafson

★N608★
GREATER PHILADELPHIA LAW LIBRARY ASSOCIATION UNION LIST
c/o Clark, Ladner, Fortenbaugh & Young
1818 Market St., 32nd Fl.   Phone: (215) 241-1883
Philadelphia, PA 19103   Carol C. Haas, Coord.

★N609★
**HEALTH INFORMATION LIBRARY NETWORK OF NORTHEASTERN
   PENNSYLVANIA (HILNNEP)**
c/o Moses Taylor Hospital Library
745 Quincy Ave.   Phone: (717) 969-4057
Scranton, PA 18510   JoAnn Babish, Chm.
Address rotates biennially.

★N610★
HEALTH INFORMATION RESOURCES CONSORTIUM (HI RESCU)
Somerset State Hospital Library
Box 631   Phone: (814) 445-6501
Somerset, PA 15501-0631   Eve Kline, Libn.

★N611★
INTERLIBRARY DELIVERY SERVICE OF PENNSYLVANIA (IDS)
c/o Pittsburgh Regional Library Ctr.
Chatham College   Phone: (412) 441-6409
Pittsburgh, PA 15232   Dr. Scott Bruntjen, Adm.
Also Known As: Pennsylvania Interlibrary Delivery System.

★N612★
LAUREL HIGHLANDS HEALTH SCIENCES LIBRARY CONSORTIUM (LHHSLC)
c/o Library, Rm. 209
University of Pittsburgh at Johnstown   Phone: (814) 266-9661
Johnstown, PA 15904   Heather Brice, Dir.

★N613★
LEHIGH VALLEY ASSOCIATION OF INDEPENDENT COLLEGES, INC. (LVAIC)
Moravian College   Phone: (215) 691-6131
Bethlehem, PA 18018   Galen Godbey

★N614★
LIBERTY MUTUAL LIBRARY SYSTEM
c/o Business Reference Library
Liberty Mutual Insurance Co.
600 Grant St.   Phone: (412) 391-6555
Pittsburgh, PA 15222

★N615★
MID-ATLANTIC LAW LIBRARY COOPERATIVE (MALLCO)
c/o Law Library
University of Pittsburgh
3900 Forbes Ave.   Phone: (412) 434-6293
Pittsburgh, PA 15260   Jenni Parrish, Dir.
Address and phone are those of member library.

★N616★
NORTHEASTERN PENNSYLVANIA BIBLIOGRAPHIC CENTER (NEPBC)
D. Leonard Corgan Library
King's College
14 W. Jackson St.   Phone: (717) 826-5841
Wilkes-Barre, PA 18711   Terrence Mech, Dir.

★N617★
NORTHEASTERN PENNSYLVANIA INDEPENDENT COLLEGES
c/o Marywood College
Learning Resource Center
2300 Adams Ave.
Scranton, PA 18509
Address is that of member library.

★N618★
NORTHWEST INTERLIBRARY COOPERATIVE OF PENNSYLVANIA (NICOP)
Erie County Library System
3 S. Perry Sq.   Phone: (814) 452-2333
Erie, PA 16501   Michele M. Ridge, Chm.
Address rotates biennially.

★N619★
PALINET & UNION LIBRARY CATALOGUE OF PENNSYLVANIA
3401 Market St., Suite 262   Phone: (215) 382-7031
Philadelphia, PA 19104   James G. Schoenung, Exec.Dir.
See also the library listing for this network in the main section, under
Pennsylvania Area Library Network.**Also Known As:** Library Catalogue of
Pennsylvania; PALINET/ULC.

★N620★
PENNSYLVANIA UNION LIST OF SERIALS (PAULS)
Somerset State Hospital Library
Box 631   Phone: (814) 445-6501
Somerset, PA 15501-0631

★N621★
**PHILADELPHIA AREA REFERENCE LIBRARIANS INFORMATION EXCHANGE
   (PARLIE)**
Drexel University Library   Phone: (215) 895-2755
Philadelphia, PA 19104   Margorie Rothberg, Chm.
Address rotates biennially.

★N622★
PITTSBURGH COUNCIL ON HIGHER EDUCATION †
3814 Forbes Ave.   Phone: (412) 683-7905
Pittsburgh, PA 15213   Donn C. Neal, Exec.Dir.

★N623★
PITTSBURGH-EAST HOSPITAL LIBRARY COOPERATIVE
St. Francis Medical Center
45th St. and Penn Ave.   Phone: (412) 622-4772
Pittsburgh, PA 15201   Elizabeth McCulloch, Pres.
Address and presidency rotate irregularly.

★N624★
PITTSBURGH REGIONAL LIBRARY CENTER (PRLC)
Beatty Hall
Chatham College   Phone: (412) 441-6409
Pittsburgh, PA 15232   Dr. Scott Bruntjen, Exec.Dir.

★N625★
PITTSBURGH REGIONAL MEDICAL LIBRARY GROUP
c/o Uniontown Hospital
500 W. Berkeley St.   Phone: (412) 430-5178
Uniontown, PA 15401
Address and phone are those of member library.

★N626★
SOUTHEAST PITTSBURGH CONSORTIUM
c/o Medical Staff Library
Latrobe Area Hospital
West Second Ave.   Phone: (412) 537-1275
Latrobe, PA 15650

★N627★
**SOUTHEASTERN PENNSYLVANIA THEOLOGICAL LIBRARIES ASSOCIATION
   (SEPTLA)**
c/o Lutheran Theological Seminary
7301 Germantown Ave.   Phone: (215) 248-4616
Philadelphia, PA 19119   David Wartluft, Chm.
Address rotates biennially.

★N628★
STATE SYSTEM OF HIGHER EDUCATION LIBRARIES COUNCIL (SSHELCO)
c/o West Chester State College   Phone: (215) 436-2747
West Chester, PA 19380
Formerly: Council of Pennsylvania State College and University Library
Directors (COPSCAULD).

★N629★
SUBSTANCE ABUSE LIBRARIANS & INFORMATION SPECIALISTS (SALIS)
c/o Medical Library
Eagleville Hospital
Box 45   Phone: (215) 539-6000
Eagleville, PA 19408
Address and phone are those of member library.

★N630★
SUSQUEHANNA LIBRARY COOPERATIVE
c/o Mansfield State College Library   Phone: (717) 662-4071
Mansfield, PA 16933   Larry Nesbit, Chm.

★N631★
THREE VALLEY ON-LINE USERS GROUP
c/o Communications Center
Hershey Foods Corporation
1025 Reese Ave.   Phone: (717) 534-5106
Hershey, PA 17033
Address and phone are those of member library.

★N632★
TRI-COUNTY LIBRARY CONSORTIUM
New Castle Public Library
207 E. North St.   Phone: (412) 658-6659
New Castle, PA 16101

★N633★
TRI-STATE COLLEGE LIBRARY COOPERATIVE (TCLC)
Rosemont College Library
Rosemont, PA 19010   Jude D. O'Shea

★N634★
UNIVERSITY OF PENNSYLVANIA AFFILIATED LIBRARIANS
c/o Fox Chase Cancer Center
7701 Burholme Ave.   Phone: (215) 728-2710
Philadelphia, PA 19111   Jane Bosley, Libn.
Address rotates annually.

★N635★
UNIVERSITY OF PITTSBURGH AREA HEALTH EDUCATION CENTER
  PROGRAM (AHEC)
Loeffler Bldg., 3rd Fl.
121 Meyran Ave.
Pittsburgh, PA 15260
Defunct

★N636★
WEBNET, INC.
c/o Pittsburgh Regional Library Center
Chatham College   Phone: (412) 441-6409
Pittsburgh, PA 15232   Joan M. Mitchell, Pres.
Also Known As: Western Pennsylvania Buhl Network.

★N637★
WESTERN INSTITUTIONAL LIBRARY COOPERATIVE
c/o Somerset State Hospital Library
Box 631   Phone: (814) 445-6501
Somerset, PA 15501   Eve Kline, Coord.

PUERTO RICO

★N638★
CONSORCIO EDUCATIVO DEL OESTE - RECINTO CIENCIAS MEDICAS
Ramon Emeterio Betances Medical Lib.
Puerto Rico Department of Health
Box 1868
Mayaguez, PR 00708   Myrna Y. Ramirez, Libn.
Address is that of member library.

RHODE ISLAND

★N639★
ASSOCIATION OF RHODE ISLAND HEALTH SCIENCES LIBRARIANS
  (ARIHSL) †
c/o Women and Infants Hospital
50 Maude   Phone: (401) 274-1100
Providence, RI 02908   Christine Chapman

★N640★
CONSORTIUM OF RHODE ISLAND ACADEMIC AND RESEARCH LIBRARIES,
  INC. (CRIARL)
University of Rhode Island Library   Phone: (401) 792-2666
Kingston, RI 02881-0803   Arthur P. Young, Chm.

★N641★
RHODE ISLAND AUTOMATED LIBRARY CONSORTIUM
c/o Rhode Island Department of
State Library Services
95 Davis St.   Phone: (401) 277-2726
Providence, RI 02908   Dorothy B. Frechette, Proj.Coord.
Address and phone are those of member library.

★N642★
RHODE ISLAND INTERRELATED LIBRARY NETWORK
95 Davis St.   Phone: (401) 277-2726
Providence, RI 02908   Dr. Fay Zipkowitz, Dir.

★N643★
WESTERN INTERRELATED LIBRARY SYSTEM
c/o Warwick Public Library
600 Sandy Lane
Warwick, RI 02886-3998

SOUTH CAROLINA

★N644★
AREA HEALTH EDUCATION CENTER OF SOUTH CAROLINA
c/o Health Sciences Library
Spartanburg General Hospital
101 E. Wood St.   Phone: (803) 573-6220
Spartanburg, SC 29303   Fay J. Towell, Dir., Lib.Serv.

★N645★
CHARLESTON HIGHER EDUCATION CONSORTIUM (CHEC)
171 Ashley Ave.   Phone: (803) 792-3628
Charleston, SC 29425

★N646★
COLUMBIA AREA MEDICAL LIBRARY ASSOCIATION (CAMLA)
Professional Library
William S. Hall Psychiatric Institute
Box 202   Phone: (803) 758-5370
Columbia, SC 29202   Neeta N. Shaw, Coord.

★N647★
CONSORTIUM OF SOUTHERN BIOMEDICAL LIBRARIES, INC. (CONBLS)
c/o Library
Medical University of South Carolina
171 Ashley Ave.   Phone: (803) 792-2374
Charleston, SC 29425   Warren A. Sawyer, Pres.
Address rotates periodically.

★N648★
HEALTH COMMUNICATIONS NETWORK
Division of Continuing Education
Medical Univ. of South Carolina
171 Ashley Ave.   Phone: (803) 792-4435
Charleston, SC 29425   Tessa Hooker, Prog.Info.Coord.

★N649★
NCR LIBRARY NETWORK
Technical Library
NCR Corporation
3325 Platt Springs Rd.   Phone: (803) 796-9250
West Columbia, SC 29169   Trudy Katz Cook, Coord.

SOUTH DAKOTA

★N650★
AREA HEALTH EDUCATION CENTER OF SOUTH DAKOTA (AHEC)
c/o School of Medicine
University of South Dakota   Phone: (605) 677-5403
Vermillion, SD 57069   Donald G. Brekke, AHEC Proj.Dir.

★N651★
CENTRAL SOUTH DAKOTA HEALTH SCIENCE LIBRARY CONSORTIUM
c/o Medical Library
St. Mary's Hospital
803 E. Dakota Ave.   Phone: (605) 224-3178
Pierre, SD 57501   DeAnn DeKay Hilmoe, Coord.
Address and phone are those of member library.

★N652★
COLLEGES OF MID-AMERICA CONSORTIUM
c/o Norman B. Mears Library
Sioux Falls College
1501 S. Prairie Ave.   Phone: (605) 336-2850
Sioux Falls, SD 57101   Jane B. Kolbe, Dir.

★N653★
NORTH CENTRAL UNIVERSITY CENTER (NCUC)
1600 S. Minnesota   Phone: (605) 336-5555
Sioux Falls, SD 57105   Dr. Thomas Kilian

★N654★
SOUTH DAKOTA HOSPITAL LIBRARY ASSOCIATION
Medical Library
U.S. Veterans Administration
Box 5046
Sioux Falls, SD 57116
Defunct

TENNESSEE

★N655★
**ASSOCIATION OF MEMPHIS AREA HEALTH SCIENCES LIBRARIES
(AMAHSL)**
Center for the Health Sciences Library
University of Tennessee
800 Madison Ave.   Phone: (901) 528-5634
Memphis, TN 38163

★N656★
EAST TENNESSEE ONLINE USERS GROUP
c/o Research Laboratories
Tennessee Eastman Co., B150b
Kingsport, TN 37662   M. Gail Preslar
Address rotates annually.

★N657★
GREATER MEMPHIS CONSORTIUM
c/o Lewis Memorial Library
Memphis Academy of Arts
Overton Park
Memphis, TN 38112
Address is that of member library.

★N658★
HEALTH EDUCATION LIBRARY PROGRAM (HELP)
Medical Library
Erlanger Medical Center
975 E. 3rd St.   Phone: (615) 778-7498
Chattanooga, TN 37403   Margarette Koplan, Coord.

★N659★
KNOXVILLE AREA HEALTH SCIENCES LIBRARY CONSORTIUM (KAHSLC)
c/o Ag/Vet Medical Library
University of Tennessee   Phone: (615) 974-4728
Knoxville, TN 37996-4500   Mary H. Daniels, Pres.
Address rotates annually.

★N660★
TRI-CITIES AREA HEALTH SCIENCES LIBRARIES CONSORTIUM
Quillen-Dishner Coll. of Med.Lib.
East Tennesee State University
Box 23290A   Phone: (615) 928-6426
Johnson City, TN 37614   Janet Fisher, Asst. Dean

TEXAS

★N661★
AMIGOS BIBLIOGRAPHIC COUNCIL, INC.
11300 N. Central Expy., Suite 321   Phone: (214) 750-6130
Dallas, TX 75243   Louella V. Wetherbee, Exec.Dir.

★N662★
APLIC CENSUS NETWORK
c/o Population Research Center
1800 Main Bldg.
University of Texas   Phone: (512) 471-5514
Austin, TX 78712   Doreen S. Goyer, Libn.
Address and phone are those of member library.

★N663★
**ASSOCIATION FOR HIGHER EDUCATION OF NORTH TEXAS - LIBRARY
COMMITTEE (AHE)**
Box 830688   Phone: (214) 231-7211
Richardson, TX 75083   John Hall, Coord., Lib.Prog.

★N664★
ASSOCIATION OF VISUAL SCIENCE LIBRARIANS
c/o College of Optometry
University of Houston
4901 Cullen Blvd.   Phone: (713) 749-3548
Houston, TX 77004   Suzanne Ferimer, Chm.
Address rotates biennially.

★N665★
CIRCUIT RIDER HEALTH INFORMATION SERVICE (CRHIS)
c/o Library
Victoria College/Univ. of Houston
2602 N. Ben Jordan   Phone: (512) 576-3151
Victoria, TX 77901-5699   Susan Johnston, Libn.
Address and phone are those of member library.

★N666★
COASTAL BEND HEALTH SCIENCES LIBRARY CONSORTIUM
Memorial Medical Center
2606 Hospital Blvd.
Box 5280   Phone: (512) 881-4198
Corpus Christi, TX 78405   Robert Polanco, Coord.

★N667★
COUNCIL OF RESEARCH & ACADEMIC LIBRARIES (CORAL)
Box 290236   Phone: (512) 696-2606
San Antonio, TX 78280-1636   Robert Houze, Exec.Dir.

★N668★
DALLAS AREA METROPLEX PROJECT (DAMP)
c/o Library/Media Services
Life Planning/Health Services
2727 Oaklawn, Suite 228   Phone: (214) 522-0290
Dallas, TX 75219   Bola Odumosu, Med.Rec.Adm.

★N669★
DALLAS ASSOCIATION OF LAW LIBRARIANS (DALL)
c/o Gardere & Wynne
1500 Diamond Shamrock Tower   Phone: (214) 747-7211
Dallas, TX 75201   Linda Gardner, Coord.
Address rotates annually.

★N670★
**DALLAS-TARRANT COUNTY CONSORTIUM OF HEALTH SCIENCE
LIBRARIES**
c/o Learning Resources Center
School of Nursing
Baylor University
3700 Worth St.
Dallas, TX 75246   Jody Guenther, Coord.
Address rotates annually.

★N671★
DEL NORTE BIOSCIENCES LIBRARY CONSORTIUM
University of Texas
El Paso, TX 79968
Phone: (915) 533-6094
Esperanza A. Moreno, Adm.

★N672★
EAST TEXAS HIGHER EDUCATION LIBRARY INFORMATION EXCHANGE
2100 S. Mobberly
Box 7001
Longview, TX 75601
Defunct

★N673★
HARRINGTON LIBRARY CONSORTIUM
c/o Learning Resource Center
Amarillo College
Box 447
Amarillo, TX 79105
Phone: (806) 376-5111
George Huffman, Dir.

★N674★
HEALTH ORIENTED LIBRARIES OF SAN ANTONIO (HOLSA)
c/o UT Health Science Center Library
7703 Floyd Curl Dr.
San Antonio, TX 78284
Phone: (512) 691-6271
Rajia Tobia, Pres.

★N675★
HOUSTON AREA LAW LIBRARIANS INTERLIBRARY LOAN
c/o Houston City Legal Dept.Lib.
City Hall, 4th Fl.
Box 1562
Houston, TX 77063
Phone: (713) 222-5151
Mary Vela-Creixell, Law Libn.

★N676★
HOUSTON AREA LIBRARY SYSTEM
Houston Public Library
500 McKinney Ave.
Houston, TX 77002
Phone: (713) 222-4704
Amy Mollberg, Coord.

★N677★
HOUSTON AREA RESEARCH LIBRARY CONSORTIUM (HARLIC)
Texas Medical Center Library
Jones Library Bldg.
Houston Academy of Medicine
Houston, TX 77030
Phone: (713) 797-1230
Richard Lyders, Pres.
Address and presidency rotate biennially.

★N678★
HOUSTON MUSIC LIBRARIANS' CONSORT (HMLC)
c/o Houston Public Library
500 McKinney Ave.
Houston, TX 77002
Phone: (713) 224-5441
Marcia Schemper, Mus.Libn.
Address rotates annually.

★N679★
HOUSTON ONLINE USERS GROUP (HOLUG)
c/o Business and Technical Library
Hughes Tool Company
Box 2539
Houston, TX 77001
Phone: (713) 924-2990
Melody Morningstar,, Div.Libn.
Address rotates annually.

★N680★
KERRVILLE AREA HEALTH SCIENCES LIBRARIES
c/o Health Sciences Library
U.S. Veterans Administration
Kerrville, TX 78028
Phone: (512) 896-2020
Address and phone are those of member library.

★N681★
METROPLEX COUNCIL OF HEALTH SCIENCE LIBRARIANS
Information Center
Nuclear Medical Laboratories
1800 Hurd Dr.
Box 2860
Irving, TX 75061
Phone: (214) 659-1100
Address and presidency rotate annually.

★N682★
NORTHEAST TEXAS LIBRARY SYSTEM (NETLS)
625 Austin
Garland, TX 75040
Phone: (214) 494-7192
Elizabeth Crabb, Coord.

★N683★
NORTHEAST TEXAS ONLINE USERS GROUP (NETOUG)
Mesquite Public Library
Mesquite, TX 75149
Phone: (214) 285-6369

★N684★
SAN ANTONIO ONLINE USERS GROUP
Funding Information Center
507 Brooklyn
San Antonio, TX 78215
Phone: (512) 227-4333
Candes Chumney, Exec.Dir.

★N685★
**SOUTH CENTRAL ACADEMIC MEDICAL LIBRARIES CONSORTIUM
(SCAMEL)**
c/o Health Sciences Library
Texas College of Osteopathic Medicine
Camp Bowie at Montgomery
Fort Worth, TX 76107
Phone: (817) 735-2464
Bobby R. Carter, Treas.

★N686★
TALON
Health Science Center Library
University of Texas
5323 Harry Hines Blvd.
Dallas, TX 75235
Phone: (214) 688-2085
James "Pat" Craig, Coord.
Region 5 of the Regional Medical Library Program. TALON is an acronym for the five states served by the program - TX, AR, LA, OK and NM.**Also Known As:** South Central Regional Medical Library Program.

★N687★
TALON-LAW
c/o Law Library
University of Houston
University Park
Houston, TX 77004
Address is that of member library.

★N688★
TAMU CONSORTIUM OF MEDICAL LIBRARIES
Administration Bldg.
College of Veterinary Medicine
Texas A & M University
College Station, TX 77843
Phone: (713) 845-7427
Virginia Algermissen, Dir.

★N689★
TEXAS CHURCH LIBRARY ASSOCIATION
c/o Media Library
First Baptist Church
Box 85
Abilene, TX 79604
Phone: (915) 673-5031
Address and phone are those of member library.

★N690★
**TEXAS DEPARTMENT OF MENTAL HEALTH & MENTAL RETARDATION
LIBRARY ASSOCIATION**
Central Office Library
Box 12668
Austin, TX 78711
Address is that of member library.

★N691★
TEXAS STATE LIBRARY COMMUNICATIONS NETWORK
Texas State Library
Box 12927
Austin, TX 78711
Phone: (512) 475-3564
Edward Seidenberg

UTAH

★N692★
CONFERENCE OF INTERMOUNTAIN ARCHIVISTS (CIMA)
300 Rio Grande
Salt Lake City, UT 84101
Phone: (801) 533-5808
Loretta Hefner, Coord.

★N693★
UTAH COLLEGE LIBRARY COUNCIL
2150 South 300 West
Salt Lake City, UT 84115
Phone: (801) 533-5875
Amy Owen, Exec.Sec.

★N694★
UTAH HEALTH SCIENCES LIBRARY CONSORTIUM
c/o Clinical Library
University Medical Center
University of Utah
Salt Lake City, UT 84132
Address rotates annually.
Phone: (801) 581-4686
Joan Stoddart, Chm.

VERMONT

★N695★
HOSPITAL LIBRARY DEVELOPMENT SERVICES (HLDS)
Dana Medical Library
University of Vermont
Burlington, VT 05405
Phone: (802) 656-2200
Carolyn Walters Fox

★N696★
NORTH COUNTRY CONSORTIUM
c/o Information Center
Northeastern Vermont Regional Hospital
Hospital Drive
St. Johnsbury, VT 05819
Phone: (802) 748-8141
Eleanor B. Simons, Coord.

★N697★
VERMONT/NEW HAMPSHIRE HEALTH SCIENCE LIBRARIES
c/o Health Science Library
Rutland Regional Medical Center
Allen St.
Rutland, VT 05701
Phone: (802) 775-7111
Address and phone are those of member library.

★N698★
VERMONT RESOURCE SHARING NETWORK
c/o Vermont Dept. of Libraries
State Office Bldg.
Montpelier, VT 05602
Phone: (802) 828-3261
Sybil B. McShane, Coord.

★N699★
VERMONT UNION CATALOG
Reference Service Unit
Vermont Dept. of Libraries
State Office Bldg.
Montpelier, VT 05602
Phone: (802) 828-3261
Sybil B. McShane, Hd., Ref.Serv.

VIRGIN ISLANDS

★N700★
VILINET
c/o Bureau of Libraries
Box 390
St. Thomas, VI 00801
Phone: (809) 774-3407
Also Known As: Virgin Islands Library & Information Network.

VIRGINIA

★N701★
AMERICAN GAS ASSOCIATION LIBRARY SERVICES COMMITTEE
American Gas Association
1515 Wilson Blvd.
Arlington, VA 22209
Phone: (703) 841-8416
Steven J. Dorner, Mgr., Industry Info.Serv.

★N702★
COMMITTEE ON INFORMATION HANG-UPS
c/o Natl. Technical Information Service
5285 Port Royal Rd.
Springfield, VA 22161
Phone: (703) 487-4624
Ruth S. Smith, Coord.

★N703★
CONSORTIUM FOR CONTINUING HIGHER EDUCATION IN NORTHERN VIRGINIA - LIBRARY NETWORKING COMMITTEE
4210 Roberts Rd.
Fairfax, VA 22032
Phone: (703) 323-2155
Charlotte Wilhelmi, Consortium Dir.

★N704★
GE LIBRARIES NETWORK
c/o General Electric Company
Industrial Electronics Information Ctr.
Box 8106
Charlottesville, VA 22906

★N705★
LYNCHBURG AREA LIBRARY COOPERATIVE
Campbell County Public Library
Rustberg, VA 24588
Address rotates annually.
Phone: (804) 847-0961
Elizabeth Hamilton, Coord.

★N706★
NORTHERN VIRGINIA HOSPITAL LIBRARIES
c/o Doctors' Library
Arlington Hospital
1701 N. George Mason Dr.
Arlington, VA 22205
Address and phone are those of member library.

★N707★
RICHMOND AREA LIBRARIES COOPERATIVE
c/o E. Claiborne Robins School of
Business Library
University of Richmond
Richmond, VA 23173
Phone: (804) 285-6394
Address and phone are those of member library.

★N708★
SHENANDOAH VALLEY INDEPENDENT COLLEGE LIBRARY COOPERATIVE
Eastern Mennonite College
Harrisonburg, VA 22801
Address rotates annually.
Phone: (703) 433-2771
Jim Lehman

★N709★
SOUTHWESTERN VIRGINIA HEALTH INFORMATION LIBRARIANS
c/o Library Services, 142D
V.A. Medical Center
Salem, VA 24153
Address rotates biennially.
Phone: (703) 982-2463
Jean Kennedy, Pres.

★N710★
TIDEWATER HEALTH SCIENCES LIBRARIES (THSL)
Patient Library
V.A. Medical Center
Hampton, VA 23667
Address rotates annually.
Phone: (804) 722-9961
Maggie Demchuk, Coord.

★N711★
TRALINET
ATLS, Bldg. 117
Fort Monroe, VA 23651
Phone: (804) 727-4291
James H. Byrn, Dir.
Also Known As: U.S. Army Training & Doctrine Command (TRADOC) Library & Information Network.

★N712★
VIRGINIA TIDEWATER CONSORTIUM FOR CONTINUING HIGHER EDUCATION
Crittenton Hall
768 W. 52nd St.
Norfolk, VA 23508
Dr. Lawrence Dotolo

★N713★
VIRGINIA UNION LIST OF BIOMEDICAL SERIALS (VULBS)
Claude Moore Health Sciences Library
Univ. of Virginia Medical Center
Box 234
Charlottesville, VA 22908
Phone: (804) 924-5521

★N714★
**WESTERN REGION CONSORTIUM FOR CONTINUING & HIGHER
  EDUCATION IN VIRGINIA, LIBRARIANS' NETWORKING COMMITTEE**
c/o Carol Neuman Library
Virginia Polytechnic Institute &
State University
Blacksburg, VA 24061
Defunct

WASHINGTON

★N715★
COUNCIL ON BOTANICAL HORTICULTURAL LIBRARIES
Pierce Rhododendron Library
Rhododendron Species Foundation
2525 S. 336th St.
Box 3798   Phone: (206) 927-6960
Federal Way, WA 98063-3798   Mrs. George Harrison, Chm.

★N716★
COUNCIL OF SPOKANE AREA LIBRARIES (COSAL)
c/o Spokane County Library District
N. 2901 Argonne Rd.   Phone: (509) 924-4122
Spokane, WA 99206   Michael Wirt, Dir.
Address rotates annually.

★N717★
EWNIC
c/o Spokane Medical Library
W. 35 8th Ave.   Phone: (509) 747-5777
Spokane, WA 99204   Lisa Veium, Dir.

★N718★
HEALTH INFORMATION NETWORK SERVICES (HINS)
Box 1067
Everett, WA 98026   Shirley Lewis, Coord.
A joint service of Providence Hospital and General Hospital of Everett, WA.

★N719★
HEMINGER (Ross A.) HEALTH SCIENCES LIBRARY CONSORTIUM
c/o Central Washington Hospital
1211 Rosewood
Box 1887   Phone: (509) 662-1511
Wenatchee, WA 98801   Jane Belt, Med.Libn.
Address and phone are those of member library.

★N720★
**PACIFIC NORTHWEST REGIONAL HEALTH SCIENCES LIBRARY SERVICE
  (PNRHSLS)**
Health Sciences Library
University of Washington   Phone: (206) 543-8262
Seattle, WA 98195   Gerald J. Oppenheimer, Dir.
Region 6 of the Regional Medical Library Program serving AK, ID, MT, OR and
WA.

★N721★
PIERCE COUNTY MEDICAL LIBRARY CONSORTIUM
315 S. K St.
Box 5277   Phone: (206) 572-5340
Tacoma, WA 98405   Marion Von Bruck, Coord., Lib.Serv.
See also the library listing for this network in the main section.

★N722★
PUGET SOUND LAW LIBRARIANS
c/o Preston, Thorgrimson, Ellis & Holman
2000 IBM Bldg.
Box 2927   Phone: (206) 623-7580
Seattle, WA 98111   Margaret Chillingworth, Libn.

★N723★
SEATTLE AREA HOSPITAL LIBRARY CONSORTIUM (SAHLC)
Medical Library
Group Health Eastside
2700 152nd, N.E.   Phone: (206) 883-5431
Redmond, WA 98052   Mary Lumsden, Pres.
Address rotates annually.

★N724★
SEATTLE ENGINEERING LIBRARIANS ROUNDTABLE
c/o R.W. Beck Associates Library
Tower Bldg.
7th Ave. and Olive Way   Phone: (206) 622-5000
Seattle, WA 98101   Enid Slivka, Coord.

★N725★
SISTERS OF PROVIDENCE LIBRARY CONSORTIUM
c/o Health Sciences Library
St. Elizabeth Medical Center   Phone: (509) 575-5000
Yakima, WA 98902
Address and phone are those of member library.

★N726★
WASHINGTON MEDICAL LIBRARIANS' ASSOCIATION
c/o Reference Library
Swedish Hospital Medical Center
747 Summit Ave.   Phone: (206) 292-2484
Seattle, WA 98104   Jean C. Anderson, Chf.Libn.

★N727★
WLN
Washington State Library   Phone: (206) 459-6518
Olympia, WA 98504   "Van" Van Jepmond, Dir.
Also Known As: Washington Library Network.

WEST VIRGINIA

★N728★
HUNTINGTON HEALTH SCIENCE LIBRARY CONSORTIUM
Health Science Libraries
Marshall Univ. School of Medicine   Phone: (304) 696-6426
Huntington, WV 25701   Edward Dzierzak, Chm.

★N729★
**NORTH-CENTRAL AREA CONSORTIUM FOR HEALTH INFORMATION
  RESOURCES (NACHIR)**
United Hospital Center Library   Phone: (304) 624-2230
Clarksburg, WV 26301   Brenda Curry, Coord.

★N730★
WEST VIRGINIA BIOMEDICAL INFORMATION NETWORK
Medical Center Library
West Virginia University   Phone: (304) 293-2113
Morgantown, WV 26506   Diane Morton, Coord.

★N731★
WEST VIRGINIA LIBRARY COMMISSION UNION CATALOG
c/o Harpers Ferry Center Library
U.S. National Park Service   Phone: (304) 535-6371
Harpers Ferry, WV 25425   David Nathanson, Chf.Libn.

WISCONSIN

★N732★
**CONSORTIA OF HEALTH AUDIOVISUAL RESOURCES OF MADISON
  (CHARM)**
Mendota Mental Health Institute
301 Troy Dr.   Phone: (608) 244-2411
Madison, WI 53704   Marge Grinnell, Libn.
Address rotates annually.

★N733★
COUNCIL OF WISCONSIN LIBRARIES, INC. (COWL)
Memorial Library, Rm. 464
728 State St.
Madison, WI 53706

★N734★
FOX RIVER VALLEY AREA LIBRARY CONSORTIUM
St. Vincent Hospital
835 S. Van Buren St.   Phone: (414) 432-8621
Green Bay, WI 54305   Margaret Warpinski, Coord.
Address rotates biennially.

★N735★
FOX VALLEY LIBRARY COUNCIL
225 N. Oneida St.
Appleton, WI 54911   Rick Krumwiede, Chm.

★N736★
FOX VALLEY ON-LINE USERS GROUP
c/o Neenah Technical Center
James River Corporation
1915 Marathon Ave.
Box 899
Neenah, WI 54956

★N737★
GREAT LAKES REGIONAL MEDICAL LIBRARY NETWORK
c/o Health Sciences Library
St. Mary's Hospital
2323 N. Lake Dr.
Box 503   Phone: (414) 289-7000
Milwaukee, WI 53201   Carolyn J. Barloga, Libn.

★N738★
LIBRARY COUNCIL OF METROPOLITAN MILWAUKEE, INC. (LCOMM)
814 W. Wisconsin Ave.   Phone: (414) 271-8470
Milwaukee, WI 53233   Carole Engel, Exec.Dir.

★N739★
MADISON AREA LIBRARY COUNCIL (MALC)
1922 University Ave.   Phone: (608) 231-1052
Madison, WI 53705   Kathryn Wright, Coord.

★N740★
MILWAUKEE DOWNTOWN LAW LIBRARIANS
c/o Quarles & Brady Library
780 N. Water St.   Phone: (414) 277-5000
Milwaukee, WI 53202
Address and phone are those of member library.

★N741★
NORTH EAST WISCONSIN INTERTYPE LIBRARIES (NEWIL)
c/o Nicolet Federated Library System
515 Pine St.   Phone: (414) 497-3468
Green Bay, WI 54301   Mary Schmidt, Contact Person

★N742★
NORTHERN WISCONSIN HEALTH SCIENCE LIBRARIES COOPERATIVE
c/o Learning Resource Center
School of Nursing
St. Joseph's Hospital
611 St. Joseph's Ave.   Phone: (715) 387-7374
Marshfield, WI 54449   Margaret Allen, Coord.
Address rotates annually.

★N743★
OCLC MUSICAL RECORDINGS ANALYTICS CONSORTIUM (OMRAC)
c/o Music Library
Golda Meir Library
University of Wisconsin
Box 604   Phone: (414) 963-5529
Milwaukee, WI 53201   Richard E. Jones, Coord.

★N744★
SISTERS OF ST. MARY - SYSTEM WIDE LIBRARY CONSORTIUM
c/o St. Mary's Hospital Medical Center
707 S. Mills St.   Phone: (608) 258-6532
Madison, WI 53715

★N745★
SOUTH CENTRAL WISCONSIN HEALTH PLANNING AREA COOPERATIVE
c/o Library
St. Mary's Hospital Medical Center
707 S. Mills St.
Madison, WI 53715   Joan M. Zweifel, Coord.

★N746★
SOUTHEASTERN WISCONSIN HEALTH SCIENCE LIBRARY CONSORTIUM
  (SWHSL)
c/o Health Science Learning Ctr.
St. Francis Hospital
3237 S. 16th St.   Phone: (414) 647-5156
Milwaukee, WI 53215   Joan Yanicke, Coord.

★N747★
STATE HISTORICAL SOCIETY OF WISCONSIN - AREA RESEARCH CENTER
  NETWORK
816 State St.
Madison, WI 53706

★N748★
TECHNICAL INFORMATION EXCHANGE
c/o Learning Resource Center
Wisconsin Indianhead Technical Institute   Phone: (715) 246-6561
New Richmond, WI 54017
Address and phone are those of member library.

★N749★
WEST CENTRAL WISCONSIN HOSPITAL LIBRARY CONSORTIUM
Luther Hospital
1221 Whipple St.
Eau Claire, WI 54701
Inactive

★N750★
WESTERN WISCONSIN COUNCIL OF LIBRARIES
Indianhead Federated Library System
3501 Golf Rd.
Eau Claire, WI 54701   Nancy Hunt, Coord.

★N751★
WESTERN WISCONSIN HEALTH SCIENCES LIBRARY CONSORTIUM
c/o Health Sciences Library
St. Francis Medical Ctr.
615 S. 10th St.   Phone: (608) 785-0940
La Crosse, WI 54601   Sr. Louise Therese Lotze, Lib.Supv.
Address rotates annually.Formerly: Western Wisconsin Consortium.

★N752★
WISCONSIN INTERLIBRARY SERVICES (WILS)
464 Memorial Library
728 State St.
Madison, WI 53706   Kathryn Schneider-Michaelis, Dir.

★N753★
WISCONSIN LIBRARY NETWORK
c/o Reference and Resource Center
Zimpro Inc.
Sterling Drung Inc.
Military Rd.   Phone: (715) 359-7211
Rothschild, WI 54474
Address and phone are those of member library.

★N754★
WISCONSIN STATE AGENCY LIBRARIANS COUNCIL
c/o D.P.I. Library
Department of Public Instruction
125 S. Webster St.
Box 7841
Madison, WI 53707
Address is that of member library.

★N755★
WISCONSIN VALLEY LIBRARY SERVICE
400 First St.   Phone: (715) 847-5535
Wausau, WI 54401   Heather Eldred, Sys.Adm.

★N756★
WISCONSIN VTAE LIBRARY TECHNICAL INFORMATION EXCHANGE
  NETWORK
c/o Madison Area Technical College
211 N. Carroll St.   Phone: (608) 266-5025
Madison, WI 54303   Jan Jeffcott, Libn.
Address rotates annually.

WYOMING

★N757★
HEALTH SCIENCES INFORMATION NETWORK (HSIN)
c/o Science & Technology Lib.
University of Wyoming
Univ. Sta., Box 3262
Laramie, WY 82071

★N758★
MUDDY MOUNTAIN HEALTH SCIENCES LIBRARY CONSORTIUM
c/o Converse County Memorial Hospital
S. 5th and Oak   Phone: (307) 358-2122
Douglas, WY 82633   Barbara Widhalm, Coord.
Address rotates annually.

★N759★
NORTHEASTERN WYOMING MEDICAL LIBRARY CONSORTIUM
c/o Griffith Memorial Library
Sheridan College
Box 1500   Phone: (307) 674-6446
Sheridan, WY 82801   Niki Conca, Coord.

★N760★
SOUTHEAST WYOMING HEALTH SCIENCE LIBRARY CONSORTIUM
3200 West C   Phone: (307) 532-5413
Torrington, WY 82240

★N761★
SPECIAL NET
c/o Instructional Resource Center
Wyoming State Dept. of Education
Hathaway Bldg.   Phone: (307) 777-6254
Cheyenne, WY 82002   Jack Prince, Coord., Instr.Rsrcs.
Address and phone are those of member library.

★N762★
WYOMING LIBRARY NETWORK
c/o Wyoming State Library
Supreme Court & State Library Bldg.   Phone: (307) 777-7281
Cheyenne, WY 82002
Address and phone are those of member library.

Canada

ALBERTA

★N763★
ALBERTA GOVERNMENT LIBRARIES' COUNCIL
c/o Alberta Environment Library
Oxbridge Pl., 14th Fl.
9820 106th St.   Phone: (403) 427-6132
Edmonton, AB T5K 2J6   Marilyn Corbett, Chm.
Address rotates annually.

★N764★
ALBERTA INFORMATION ASSOCIATION
c/o Library
AMOCO Canada Petroleum Co., Ltd.
444 7th Ave., S.W., Rm. 1013   Phone: (403) 233-1451
Calgary, AB T2P 0Y2   F.M. Drummond, Chm.

★N765★
SCITECH
Library Services
Alberta Research Council
4445 Calgary Trail South   Phone: (403) 438-1666
Edmonton, AB T6H 5R7

BRITISH COLUMBIA

★N766★
ASSOCIATION OF BRITISH COLUMBIA ARCHIVISTS
c/o Anglican Church of Canada Archives
6050 Chancellor Blvd.   Phone: (604) 228-9031
Vancouver, BC V6T 1X3
Address and phone are those of member library.

★N767★
ASSOCIATION OF CANADIAN ARCHIVISTS
c/o Anglican Church of Canada Archives
6050 Chancellor Blvd.   Phone: (604) 228-9031
Vancouver, BC V6T 1X3
Address and phone are those of member library.

★N768★
CENTRAL VANCOUVER LIBRARY GROUP
Coopers & Lybrand
1111 W. Hastings St.   Phone: (604) 661-5700
Vancouver, BC V6E 3R2   Cathy Carter, Libn.
Address rotates annually.

★N769★
GOVERNMENT LIBRARIES ASSOCIATION OF BRITISH COLUMBIA (GLABC)
P.O. Box 834
Victoria, BC V8W 2P9

★N770★
HEALTH SCIENCES LIBRARY NETWORK
Woodward Biomedical Library
University of British Columbia
2198 Health Sciences Mall   Phone: (604) 228-3639
Vancouver, BC V6T 1W5   Jane Price, Coord.

★N771★
VANCOUVER ON-LINE USERS GROUP (VOLUG)
P.O. Box 48616, Bentall Sta.   Phone: (604) 683-8521
Vancouver, BC V7X 1A3   Patricia B. Daum, Coord.

MANITOBA

★N772★
COUNCIL OF PRAIRIE UNIVERSITY LIBRARIES (COPUL)
Brandon University Library   Phone: (204) 727-9642
Brandon, MB R7A 6A9   M. Nichols, Coord.

★N773★
MANITOBA HEALTH LIBRARIES ASSOCIATION (MHLA)
Medical Library
University of Manitoba
770 Bannantyne   Phone: (204) 786-4342
Winnipeg, MB R3E 0W3   Michael Tennenhouse, Pres.
Address rotates annually.

NOVA SCOTIA

★N774★
ASSOCIATION OF ATLANTIC UNIVERSITIES LIBRARIANS COUNCIL
c/o Library
Technical University of Nova Scotia
Barrington & Bishop St.
Box 1000
Halifax, NS B3J 2X4   Iain Bates, Libn.

★N775★
NOVA SCOTIA ON-LINE CONSORTIUM
c/o C. Webb
Health Sciences Library
Dalhousie University   Phone: (902) 424-5442
Halifax, NS B3H 4H7

ONTARIO

★N776★
ASSOCIATION OF COMMUNITY INFORMATION CENTRES IN ONTARIO
89 Wyndham St., N., Suite 201   Phone: (519) 836-2511
Guelph, ON N1H 4E9   Paul Young, Exec.Dir.

★N777★
BIBLIOCENTRE
80 Cowdray Court   Phone: (416) 299-1515
Scarborough, ON M1S 4N1   Doug Wentzel, Dir.

★N778★
CANADA - NATIONAL RESEARCH COUNCIL - CANADA INSTITUTE FOR SCIENTIFIC & TECHNICAL INFORMATION (CISTI)
Montreal Rd.   Phone: (613) 993-1600
Ottawa, ON K1A 0S2   Norma Burns, Exec.Asst.
See also the library listing for this network in the main section.

★N779★
CANADIAN TRANSPORTATION RESEARCH INFORMATION SYSTEM (CTRIS)
Library & Information Centre
Transport Canada
Tower C, Place de Ville   Phone: (613) 992-4529
Ottawa, ON K1A 0N5

★N780★
CHIROPRACTIC LIBRARY CONSORTIUM (CLIBCON)
Canadian Memorial Chiropractic College
1900 Bayview Ave.   Phone: (416) 482-2340
Toronto, ON M4G 3E6   J. Claire Callaghan, Coord.

★N781★
CONSEIL CANADIEN DE RECHERCHES URBAINES ET REGIONALES
251 Laurier Ave., W.
Ottawa, ON K1P 5J6
Defunct

★N782★
EDUCATION LIBRARIES SHARING OF RESOURCES NETWORK (ELSOR)
45 York Mills Rd.   Phone: (416) 489-3332
Willowdale, ON M2P 1B6   Carol Williams, Coord.

★N783★
HAMILTON/WENTWORTH DISTRICT HEALTH LIBRARY NETWORK
Health Sciences Library
McMaster University
1200 Main St., W.   Phone: (416) 525-9140
Hamilton, ON L8N 3Z5   Linda Panton, Coord.

★N784★
LAKE ERIE REGIONAL LIBRARY SYSTEM (LERLS)
380 Saskatoon St.   Phone: (519) 453-9100
London, ON N6H 1G4   Sam Coghlan, Dir.

★N785★
LIBRARIANS AND INFORMATION SPECIALISTS IN ADDICTIONS (LISA)
c/o Addiction Research Foundation
33 Russell St.   Phone: (416) 595-6144
Toronto, ON M5S 2S1
Address and phone are those of member library.

★N786★
NORTHWESTERN ONTARIO MEDICAL PROGRAMME - LIBRARY NETWORK
Health Sciences Library
McMaster University   Phone: (416) 525-9140
Hamilton, ON L8N 3Z5   Peter Maurer, Coord.

★N787★
O.H.A. REGION 9 HOSPITAL LIBRARIES GROUP
c/o Williamson Health Sciences Lib.
Ottawa Civic Hospital
1053 Carling Ave.   Phone: (613) 725-4450
Ottawa, ON K1Y 4E9   Mabel C. Brown, Coord.

★N788★
ONTARIO COUNCIL OF UNIVERSITY LIBRARIES (OCUL)
c/o Mills Memorial Library
McMaster University   Phone: (416) 525-9140
Hamilton, ON L8S 4L6   Graham Hill, Chm.
Address rotates biennially.

★N789★
ONTARIO GOVERNMENT LIBRARIES' COUNCIL (OGLC)
P.O. Box G.M.S. 40
Queen's Park
Toronto, ON M7A 1N8   R. Brian Land, Chm.

★N790★
ONTARIO TECHNOLOGY CENTRES TIS NETWORK
Ontario Centre for Microelectronics
1150 Morrison Dr.   Phone: (613) 596-6690
Ottawa, ON K2H 9B8   Brian Silcoff, Mgr., Tech.Info.Serv.

★N791★
PROFESSIONAL EDUCATION LIBRARIES CATALOGUING NETWORK (PEL)
c/o Information Centre
Ministry of Education
Mowat Block, 13th Fl.
Queen's Park   Phone: (416) 965-4581
Toronto, ON M7A 1L2   Elizabeth Horak, Chm.

★N792★
SHELL CANADA TECHNICAL INFORMATION SYSTEM
Shell Research Centre Library
Oakville Research Centre
Shell Canada Ltd.
P.O. Box 2100   Phone: (416) 827-1141
Oakville, ON L6J 5C7   Mr. Lan C. Sun, Libn.

★N793★
SHERIDAN PARK ASSOCIATION
2275 Speakman Dr.   Phone: (416) 823-6160
Mississauga, ON L5K 1B1   Ms. E. Gordon, Coord.

★N794★
SOUTH CENTRAL REGIONAL LIBRARY SYSTEM (SCRLS)
220 Dundurn St., S.   Phone: (416) 525-2610
Hamilton, ON L8P 4K7   June E. Wilson, Dir.

★N795★
TORONTO AREA ACCOUNTING LIBRARIANS (TAAL)
c/o Clarkson Gordon/Woods Gordon Lib.
Toronto Dominion Centre
Box 251   Phone: (416) 864-1234
Toronto, ON M5K 1J7   Karen Melville, Libn.

★N796★
TORONTO HEALTH LIBRARIES ASSOCIATION
c/o Thistletown Regional Centre Lib.
Ontario Ministry of Community &
Social Service
51 Panorama Court   Phone: (416) 741-1210
Rexdale, ON M9V 4L8   Joy Shanfield, Libn.

★N797★
TORONTO MEDICAL LIBRARIES GROUP
c/o Library
Ontario Cancer Institute
500 Sherbourne St.   Phone: (416) 924-0671
Toronto, ON M4X 1K9   Carol Morrison, Pres.

★N798★
WELLINGTON COUNTY HEALTH LIBRARY NETWORK
c/o Conestoga College of
Applied Arts & Technology
70 Westmount Rd.   Phone: (519) 824-2950
Guelph, ON N1H 5H7   Joy Weiss, Coord.

QUEBEC

★N799★
AGRICULTURE CANADA NETWORK OF LIBRARY SERVICES
c/o Agriculture Canada Res. Station
2560 Hochelaga Blvd.
Ste. Foy, PQ G1V 2J3
Address is that of member library.

★N800★
**ASSOCIATION DES BIBLIOTHEQUES DE LA SANTE AFFILIEES A
L'UNIVERSITE DE MONTREAL (ABSAUM)**
c/o Bibliotheque de la Sante
Universite de Montreal
C.P. 6128, Succursale A   Phone: (514) 343-6890
Montreal, PQ H3C 3J7   Lise Lambert, Sec.

★N801★
ASSOCIATION DES CARTOTHEQUES CANADIENNES
Service des bibliotheques - Cartotheque
Universite de Sherbrooke   Phone: (819) 565-4507
Sherbrooke, PQ J1K 2R1   Diane Quirion-Turcotte

★N802★
ASTED
7243 Rue Saint-Denis   Phone: (514) 271-3349
Montreal, PQ H2R 2E3   Lise Brousseau
Also Known As: Association pour l'Avancement des Sciences et des
Techniques de la Documentation.

★N803★
CREPUQ
East Tower, Rm. 1817
2 Complexe Desjardins   Phone: (514) 288-8524
Montreal, PQ H5B 1B3   Richard Perusse

★N804★
MC GILL MEDICAL AND HEALTH LIBRARIES ASSOCIATION (MMHLA)
c/o Maimonides Geriatric Centre
5795 Caldwell Ave.   Phone: (514) 481-2927
Montreal, PQ H4W 1W3   Sheindel Bresinger, Coord.
Address rotates biennially.

★N805★
MONTREAL HEALTH LIBRARIES ASSOCIATION
Medical Library
Sir Mortimer B. Davis Jewish General Hosp.
3755 Cote St. Catherine Rd.   Phone: (514) 342-3111
Montreal, PQ H3T 1E2   Arlene Greenberg, Pres.

★N806★
OTTAWA-HULL AREA LIBRARY DELIVERY SERVICE
Federal Libraries Liaison Office
25 Eddy St., 9th Fl.   Phone: (613) 997-9780
Hull, PQ K1A 0N4
Formerly: Council of Federal Libraries: Ottawa-Hull Area Library Delivery
Service.

★N807★
RIBLIN
c/o CREPUQ
East Tower, Rm. 1817
2 Complexe Desjardins   Phone: (514) 288-8524
Montreal, PQ H5B 1B3   Onil Dupuis, Coord.

★N808★
SIGIRD
Centre d'Information sur le
Ressources en Education Economique
Universite du Quebec
P.O. Box 8891   Phone: (514) 282-7703
Montreal, PQ H3C 3P3

SASKATCHEWAN

★N809★
ASSOCIATION OF SASKATCHEWAN GOVERNMENT LIBRARIES (ASGL)
c/o Saskatchewan Agriculture Library
3085 Albert St.
Regina, SK S4S 0B1   Helene Stewart, Coord.
Address rotates annually.

All numbers refer to networks and consortia listed in geographic order in Appendix A.   An asterisk before an entry number indicates that a cross reference has been made from this title.

APPENDIX B
REGIONAL AND SUBREGIONAL LIBRARIES
FOR THE BLIND AND PHYSICALLY HANDICAPPED

Appendix B

Regional and Subregional Libraries for the Blind and Physically Handicapped

In cooperation with a network of regional and subregional libraries, the Library of Congress provides free library services to persons who are unable to read or use standard printed materials because of visual or physical impairment. Books and magazines in recorded form (talking books) or in braille are delivered to eligible readers by postage-free mail and are returned in the same manner. Specially designed phonographs and cassette players are also loaned free to persons borrowing talking books.

This list contains three elements: the addresses, telephone numbers, and names of libraries in charge of each of the regional and subregional libraries in the network. The regional library or libraries listed under each state provide a full range of library services to handicapped readers. In many states, readers receive talking books through subregional libraries, which are local public libraries having collections of current materials and direct access to the resources of their regional libraries. In addition, they offer their handicapped readers reference and reader's advisory services.

Regional libraries are listed after the state heading. Subregional libraries within the state are listed next, arranged alphabetically by the city in which they are located. Some states contain more than one regional library. In this case, a remark is added to the entry to signify which portion of the state is served by a particular regional library.

American citizens certified eligible for such services who reside in foreign countries receive library service from:

National Library Service for the Blind and Physically Handicapped
Library of Congress
1291 Taylor Street, N.W.
Washington, DC 20542
Phone: (202) 287-5100

ALABAMA

ALABAMA REGIONAL LIBRARY FOR THE BLIND & PHYSICALLY HANDICAPPED
Alabama Public Library Service   Phone: (205) 277-7330
Montgomery, AL 36130   Mr. Hulen E. Bivins
TDD number is 272-0830. The toll-free telephone number for state residents is (800) 392-5671.

PUBLIC LIBRARY OF ANNISTON & CALHOUN COUNTY - LIBRARY FOR THE BLIND & HANDICAPPED
Box 308   Phone: (205) 237-8501
Anniston, AL 36201   Mrs. Deenie M. Culver

HOUSTON-LOVE MEMORIAL LIBRARY - DEPARTMENT FOR THE BLIND & PHYSICALLY HANDICAPPED
Box 1369   Phone: (205) 793-9767
Dothan, AL 36301   Mary Sue Carte

HUNTSVILLE SUBREGIONAL LIBRARY FOR THE BLIND & PHYSICALLY HANDICAPPED
Box 443   Phone: (205) 536-0022
Huntsville, AL 35804   Joyce L. Smith

ALABAMA INSTITUTE FOR DEAF AND BLIND - LIBRARY FOR THE BLIND & PHYSICALLY HANDICAPPED
525 N. Court St.   Phone: (205) 362-1054
Talladega, AL 35160   Gloria S. Lemaster

TUSCALOOSA PUBLIC LIBRARY - SUBREGIONAL LIBRARY FOR THE BLIND & PHYSICALLY HANDICAPPED
1801 River Rd.   Phone: (205) 345-5820
Tuscaloosa, AL 35401   Barbara B. Jordan

ALASKA

ALASKA STATE LIBRARY - SERVICES FOR THE BLIND & PHYSICALLY HANDICAPPED
650 W. International Airport Rd.   Phone: (907) 561-1003
Anchorage, AK 99502   Antoinette Shalkop

ARIZONA

ARIZONA STATE LIBRARY FOR THE BLIND & PHYSICALLY HANDICAPPED
1030 N. 32nd St.   Phone: (602) 255-5578
Phoenix, AZ 85008   Richard C. Peel
The toll-free telephone number for state residents is (800) 255-5578.

FLAGSTAFF CITY-COCONINO COUNTY PUBLIC LIBRARY - SPECIAL SERVICES
324 W. Aspen   Phone: (602) 774-0270
Flagstaff, AZ 86001   Kathy Winkel

PRESCOTT TALKING BOOK LIBRARY
215 E. Goodwin   Phone: (602) 445-8110
Prescott, AZ 86301   Ms. Jan Marr

1621

ARKANSAS

ARKANSAS STATE LIBRARY FOR THE BLIND & PHYSICALLY HANDICAPPED
One Capitol Mall　　　　　　　　　　Phone: (501) 371-1155
Little Rock, AR 72201　　　　　　　　　Cleotta Mullen

OZARKS REGIONAL LIBRARY - LIBRARY FOR THE BLIND & HANDICAPPED, NORTHWEST
217 E. Dickson St.　　　　　　　　　　Phone: (501) 442-6253
Fayetteville, AR 72701　　　　　　　　Rachel Anne Ames

FORT SMITH PUBLIC LIBRARY FOR THE BLIND & HANDICAPPED
61 S. 8th　　　　　　　　　　　　　　Phone: (501) 783-0229
Fort Smith, AR 72901　　　　　　　　　　Mary Nigh

CROWLEY RIDGE REGIONAL LIBRARY - LIBRARY FOR THE BLIND & PHYSICALLY HANDICAPPED, NORTHEAST
315 W. Oak　　　　　　　　　　　　Phone: (501) 935-5133
Jonesboro, AR 72401　　　　　　　　　　Ruth Ball

CLOC REGIONAL LIBRARY - LIBRARY FOR THE BLIND & HANDICAPPED, SOUTHWEST
Box 668　　　　　　　　　　　　　Phone: (501) 234-1991
Magnolia, AR 71753　　　　　　　Christine McDonald

CALIFORNIA

BRAILLE INSTITUTE OF AMERICA, INC. - LIBRARY
741 N. Vermont Ave.　　　　　　　　Phone: (213) 663-1111
Los Angeles, CA 90029　　　　　　　　Phyllis Cairns
This regional library serves southern California. The toll-free telephone number for residents within the service area is (800) 252-9486.

CALIFORNIA STATE LIBRARY - BRAILLE & TALKING BOOK LIBRARY
600 Broadway　　　　　　　　　　Phone: (916) 322-4090
Sacramento, CA 95818　　　　　　Mrs. Marion Bourke
This regional library serves northern California. The toll-free telephone number for residents within the service area is (800) 952-5666.

FRESNO COUNTY FREE LIBRARY - BLIND AND PHYSICALLY HANDICAPPED SERVICES
770 N. San Pablo Ave.　　　　　　　Phone: (209) 488-3217
Fresno, CA 93728　　　　　　　　　　Mike Starry
TDD number is 488-3209.

SAN FRANCISCO PUBLIC LIBRARY FOR THE BLIND & PRINT HANDICAPPED
3150 Sacramento St.　　　　　　　　Phone: (415) 558-5035
San Francisco, CA 94115　　　　　　Martha Heverly
TDD number is 864-1112.

COLORADO

COLORADO STATE LIBRARY - SERVICES FOR THE BLIND & PHYSICALLY HANDICAPPED
1313 Sherman St.　　　　　　　　Phone: (303) 866-2081
Denver, CO 80203　　　　　　　　　Carol Reeder
The toll-free telephone number for state residents is (800) 332-5852.

CONNECTICUT

CONNECTICUT STATE LIBRARY - LIBRARY FOR THE BLIND & PHYSICALLY HANDICAPPED
198 West St.　　　　　　　　　　Phone: (203) 566-2151
Rocky Hill, CT 06067　　　　　　Ms. Dale Wierzbicki
The toll-free telephone number for state residents is (800) 842-4516.

DELAWARE

DELAWARE STATE DIVISION OF LIBRARIES - SPECIAL SERVICES
43 S. Dupont Hwy.
Box 639　　　　　　　　　　　　Phone: (302) 736-4748
Dover, DE 19901　　　　　　　　　Mr. Lee Steele
The toll-free telephone number for state residents is (800) 282-8676.

DISTRICT OF COLUMBIA

DISTRICT OF COLUMBIA REGIONAL LIBRARY FOR THE BLIND & PHYSICALLY HANDICAPPED
901 G St., N.W., Rm. 215　　　　　　Phone: (202) 727-2142
Washington, DC 20001　　　　　　Grace J. Lyons
TDD number is 727-2255.

FLORIDA

FLORIDA STATE DIVISION OF BLIND SERVICES - LIBRARY FOR THE BLIND & PHYSICALLY HANDICAPPED
Box 2299　　　　　　　　　　　Phone: (904) 252-4722
Daytona Beach, FL 32015　　　　　Donald J. Weber
TDD number is 252-4722. The toll-free telephone number for state residents is (800) 342-5627.

MANATEE COUNTY CENTRAL LIBRARY - TALKING BOOK SERVICE
1301 Barcarrota Blvd., W.　　　　　Phone: (813) 748-5555
Bradenton, FL 33505　　　　　　　　Mary Peach

BROWARD COUNTY TALKING BOOK LIBRARY
100 S. Andrews Ave.　　　　　　　Phone: (305) 765-5999
Fort Lauderdale, FL 33301　　　　　Joann Block
TDD number is 357-7413.

JACKSONVILLE PUBLIC LIBRARY - TALKING BOOK LIBRARY
2809 Commonwealth Ave.　　　　　Phone: (904) 388-6135
Jacksonville, FL 32205　　　　　Gloria E. Zittrauer

MIAMI-DADE PUBLIC LIBRARY SYSTEM - DADE COUNTY TALKING BOOK LIBRARY
150 N.E. 79th St.　　　　　　　　Phone: (305) 751-8687
Miami, FL 33138　　　　　　　　Barbara L. Moyer
TDD number is 758-6599.

ORLANDO PUBLIC LIBRARY - TALKING BOOK SECTION
10 N. Rosalind Ave.　　　　　　　Phone: (305) 425-4694
Orlando, FL 32801　　　　　　　　Dan Kennedy
TDD number is 425-5668.

TAMPA-HILLSBOROUGH COUNTY PUBLIC LIBRARY SYSTEM - TAMPA SUBREGIONAL LIBRARY
900 N. Ashley St.　　　　　　　　Phone: (813) 223-8349
Tampa, FL 33602　　　　　　　Jeannette Martin
TDD number is 223-8858.

PALM BEACH COUNTY PUBLIC LIBRARY SYSTEM - TALKING BOOKS
3650 Summit Blvd.　　　　　　　Phone: (305) 686-0895
West Palm Beach, FL 33406　　　　Ms. Pat W. Soule

GEORGIA

GEORGIA STATE LIBRARY FOR THE BLIND & PHYSICALLY HANDICAPPED
1050 Murphy Ave., S.W.　　　　　Phone: (404) 656-2465
Atlanta, GA 30310　　　　　　　Jim DeJarnatt

DOUGHERTY COUNTY PUBLIC LIBRARY - ALBANY TALKING BOOK CENTER
2040 Newton Rd.　　　　　　　　Phone: (912) 439-1685
Albany, GA 31701　　　　　Kathryn R. Sinquefield

ATHENS REGIONAL LIBRARY - TALKING BOOK CENTER
435 N. Lumpkin St.   Phone: (404) 354-2625
Athens, GA 30601   Janet Wright
TDD number is 354-2620.

**AUGUSTA-RICHMOND COUNTY PUBLIC LIBRARY - TALKING BOOK
    CENTER**
425 9th St.   Phone: (404) 724-8255
Augusta, GA 30901   Gary Swint

SOUTHWEST GEORGIA REGIONAL LIBRARY - TALKING BOOK CENTER
Shotwell & Monroe Sts.   Phone: (912) 246-3895
Bainbridge, GA 31717   Laura S. Harrison

**BRUNSWICK-GLYNN COUNTY REGIONAL LIBRARY - TALKING BOOK
    CENTER**
208 Gloucester St.   Phone: (912) 264-7360
Brunswick, GA 31523   Ruby Y. Myers

CHATTAHOOCHEE VALLEY REGIONAL LIBRARY - TALKING BOOK CENTER
Bradley Dr.   Phone: (404) 327-0211
Columbus, GA 31995   Crawford B. Pike

OCONEE REGIONAL LIBRARY - TALKING BOOK CENTER
806 Highland Ave.   Phone: (912) 275-3322
Dublin, GA 31021   Katharine O'Brien

CHESTATEE REGIONAL LIBRARY - TALKING BOOK CENTER
322 Oak St., Suite 5   Phone: (404) 535-5738
Gainesville, GA 30501   David Thompson

CHEROKEE REGIONAL LIBRARY - TALKING BOOK CENTER
305 S. Duke St.   Phone: (404) 638-2992
Lafayette, GA 30728   Robert L. Manning

WASHINGTON MEMORIAL LIBRARY - TALKING BOOK CENTER
1180 Washington Ave.   Phone: (912) 744-0877
Macon, GA 31201   Rebecca M. Sherrill

SARA HIGHTOWER REGIONAL LIBRARY - TALKING BOOK CENTER
606 Broad St.   Phone: (404) 291-6030
Rome, GA 30161   Sadie Jenkins

C.E.L. REGIONAL LIBRARY - TALKING BOOK CENTER
2002 Bull St.   Phone: (912) 234-5127
Savannah, GA 31499   Linda Field
The toll-free telephone number for residents within the service area is (800)
342-4455.

SOUTH GEORGIA REGIONAL LIBRARY - TALKING BOOK CENTER
110 W. Central Ave.   Phone: (912) 333-5210
Valdosta, GA 31601   Frank Bonney

GUAM

**GUAM TERRITORIAL LIBRARY FOR THE BLIND & PHYSICALLY
    HANDICAPPED**
Nieves M. Flores Memorial Library
254 Martyr St.   Phone: (671) 472-6417
Agana, GU 96910   Pauline V. Concepcion
This is a Hawaiian subregional library.

HAWAII

HAWAII STATE LIBRARY FOR THE BLIND & PHYSICALLY HANDICAPPED
402 Kapahulu Ave.   Phone: (808) 732-7767
Honolulu, HI 96815   Lydia S. Ranger

IDAHO

IDAHO STATE LIBRARY - BLIND & PHYSICALLY HANDICAPPED LIBRARY
325 W. State St.   Phone: (208) 334-2117
Boise, ID 83702   Evva L. Larson
The toll-free telephone number for state residents is (800) 233-4931.

ILLINOIS

**ILLINOIS REGIONAL LIBRARY FOR THE BLIND & PHYSICALLY
    HANDICAPPED**
1055 W. Roosevelt Rd.   Phone: (312) 738-9210
Chicago, IL 60608   James Pletz

SHAWNEE LIBRARY SYSTEM
Greenbriar Rd.   Phone: (618) 985-3713
Carterville, IL 62918   Joan Laskaris

**CHICAGO LIBRARY SERVICE FOR THE BLIND & PHYSICALLY
    HANDICAPPED**
1055 W. Roosevelt Rd.   Phone: (312) 738-9200
Chicago, IL 60608   Mari Beth Lefere

RIVER BEND LIBRARY SYSTEM - TALKING BOOKS PROGRAM
Box 125   Phone: (309) 799-3155
Coal Valley, IL 61240   Dee Canfield

LEWIS AND CLARK LIBRARY SYSTEM
R.R. 4, Box 368   Phone: (618) 656-3216
Edwardsville, IL 62025   Mary Lou Kampwerth
The toll-free telephone number for residents within the service area is (800)
642-9545.

CUMBERLAND TRAIL LIBRARY SYSTEM
12th & McCawley   Phone: (618) 662-2679
Flora, IL 62839   Susan Amos

WESTERN ILLINOIS LIBRARY SYSTEM
1518 S. Henderson   Phone: (309) 343-2380
Galesburg, IL 61401   Ronald Winner

**DU PAGE LIBRARY SYSTEM - SUBREGIONAL LIBRARY FOR VISUALLY &
    PHYSICALLY DISABLED PEOPLE**
127 S. 1st St.   Phone: (312) 232-8457
Geneva, IL 60134   Sharon Hoffman

**NORTH SUBURBAN AND SUBURBAN LIBRARY SYSTEM - SUBURBAN
    AUDIO VISUAL SERVICE FOR THE BLIND & PHYSICALLY HANDICAPPED**
920 Barnsdale Rd.   Phone: (312) 352-7671
LaGrange Park, IL 60525   Leon L. Drolet, Jr.

**CORN BELT, LINCOLN TRAIL AND ROLLING PRAIRIE LIBRARY SYSTEMS -
    SERVICE TO THE BLIND & PHYSICALLY HANDICAPPED**
1809 W. Hovey Ave.   Phone: (309) 454-2711
Normal, IL 61761   Clara E. Castelo
The toll-free telephone number for residents within the service area is (800)
322-9164.

**STARVED ROCK LIBRARY SYSTEM - SUBREGIONAL LIBRARY FOR THE
    BLIND & PHYSICALLY HANDICAPPED**
900 Hitt St.   Phone: (815) 434-7537
Ottawa, IL 61350   Karen L. Odean
The toll-free telephone number for residents within the service area is (800)
892-7882.

ILLINOIS VALLEY LIBRARY SYSTEM
845 Brenkman Dr.   Phone: (309) 353-4115
Pekin, IL 61554   Valerie Brenkman

GREAT RIVER LIBRARY SYSTEM - TALKING BOOK LIBRARY
515 York St.   Phone: (217) 223-2560
Quincy, IL 62301   Karen Gray
The toll-free telephone number for residents within the service area is (800)
252-0889.

NORTHERN ILLINOIS LIBRARY SYSTEM
4034 E. State St.   Phone: (815) 229-0330
Rockford, IL 61108   Mr. Chris Anthon

**BUR OAK LIBRARY SYSTEM - SERVICES FOR THE BLIND & PHYSICALLY
   HANDICAPPED**
405 Earl Rd.   Phone: (815) 729-2039
Shorewood, IL 60436   Mary Moss

KASKASKIA LIBRARY SYSTEM
Box 325   Phone: (618) 235-4220
Smithton, IL 62285   Beverly J. Sanders

INDIANA

**INDIANA STATE LIBRARY - DIVISION FOR THE BLIND & PHYSICALLY
   HANDICAPPED**
140 N. Senate Ave.   Phone: (317) 232-3684
Indianapolis, IN 46204   Barney R. McEwen
The toll-free telephone number for state residents is (800) 622-4970.

BARTHOLOMEW COUNTY LIBRARY
536 5th St.   Phone: (812) 379-1277
Columbus, IN 47201   Elizabeth Ann Booth

**ELKHART PUBLIC LIBRARY - BLIND & PHYSICALLY HANDICAPPED
   SERVICES**
300 S. Second St.   Phone: (219) 522-2665
Elkhart, IN 46516   Kay McCarroll

**EVANSVILLE-VANDERBURGH COUNTY PUBLIC LIBRARY - TALKING BOOKS
   SERVICE**
22 South East Fifth   Phone: (812) 428-8235
Evansville, IN 47708   Barbara Shanks

ALLEN COUNTY PUBLIC LIBRARY - READERS' SERVICES DEPARTMENT
Box 2270   Phone: (219) 424-7241
Fort Wayne, IN 46801   Paul Deane

LAKE COUNTY PUBLIC LIBRARY - TALKING BOOK SERVICE
1919 W. 81st Ave.   Phone: (219) 769-3541
Merrillville, IN 46410   Joanne Panusuk
TDD number is 769-3541, ext. 240. The toll-free telephone number for
residents within the service area is (800) 552-8950.

IOWA

IOWA STATE COMMISSION FOR THE BLIND - LIBRARY
4th & Keosauqua   Phone: (515) 283-2601
Des Moines, IA 50309   Catherine Ford
The toll-free telephone number for state residents is (800) 362-2587.

KANSAS

**KANSAS STATE LIBRARY - DIVISION FOR THE BLIND & PHYSICALLY
   HANDICAPPED**
ESU Memorial Union
1200 Commercial   Phone: (316) 343-7124
Emporia, KS 66801   Caroline G. Longmoor
The toll-free telephone number for state residents is (800) 362-0699.

**CENTRAL KANSAS LIBRARY SYSTEM HEADQUARTERS - TALKING BOOK
   SERVICE**
1409 Williams   Phone: (316) 792-2393
Great Bend, KS 67530   Ms. Jerri Robinson
The toll-free telephone number for residents within the service area is (800)
362-2642.

**SOUTH CENTRAL KANSAS LIBRARY SYSTEM - TALKING BOOK
   SUBREGIONAL LIBRARY**
901 N. Main   Phone: (316) 663-5441
Hutchinson, KS 67501   Ms. Bert Newton
The toll-free telephone number for residents within the service area is (800)
362-2615.

**NORTH CENTRAL KANSAS LIBRARY SYSTEM - MANHATTAN PUBLIC
   LIBRARY FOR THE BLIND & PHYSICALLY HANDICAPPED**
Juliette & Poyntz   Phone: (913) 776-4741
Manhattan, KS 66502   Frank Carroll
The toll-free telephone number for residents within the service area is (800)
432-2796.

NORTHWEST KANSAS LIBRARY SYSTEM
408 N. Norton   Phone: (913) 877-5148
Norton, KS 67654   Clarice Howard
The toll-free telephone number for residents within the service area is (800)
432-2858.

TOPEKA PUBLIC LIBRARY - TALKING BOOKS
1515 W. 10th St.   Phone: (913) 233-2040
Topeka, KS 66604   Marlene F. Hendrick
TDD number is 233-3277. The toll-free telephone number for residents
within the service area is (800) 432-2925.

WICHITA PUBLIC LIBRARY - TALKING BOOKS DEPARTMENT
223 South Main   Phone: (316) 262-0611
Wichita, KS 67202   Betty C. Spriggs
TDD number is 262-3972. The toll-free telephone number for residents
within the service area is (800) 362-2869.

KENTUCKY

KENTUCKY LIBRARY FOR THE BLIND & PHYSICALLY HANDICAPPED
300 Coffee Tree Rd.
Box 818   Phone: (502) 875-7000
Frankfort, KY 40602   Adam Ruschival
The toll-free telephone number for state residents is (800) 372-2968.

NORTHERN KENTUCKY TALKING BOOK LIBRARY
502 Scott St.   Phone: (606) 491-7610
Covington, KY 41011   Alice Manchikes

LOUISVILLE FREE PUBLIC LIBRARY - TALKING BOOK LIBRARY
301 W. York St.   Phone: (502) 587-1069
Louisville, KY 40203   Maxine Harris Surratt
TDD number is 589-7924.

LOUISIANA

**LOUISIANA STATE LIBRARY - SECTION FOR THE BLIND & PHYSICALLY
   HANDICAPPED**
760 Riverside, N.   Phone: (504) 342-4943
Baton Rouge, LA 70802   Richard Smith
The toll-free telephone number for state residents is (800) 543-4702.

MAINE

**MAINE STATE LIBRARY - LIBRARY SERVICES FOR THE BLIND &
   PHYSICALLY HANDICAPPED**
State House, Sta. 64   Phone: (207) 289-3959
Augusta, ME 04333   Louise Hinkley
The toll-free telephone number for state residents is (800) 452-8793.

BANGOR PUBLIC LIBRARY
145 Harlow St.   Phone: (207) 947-8336
Bangor, ME 04401   Judith Leighton
The toll-free telephone number for residents within the service area is (800)
432-7860.

CARY LIBRARY
107 Main St.
Phone: (207) 532-3967
Houlton, ME 04730
Norma Watson

LEWISTON PUBLIC LIBRARY
105 Park St.
Phone: (207) 783-2331
Lewiston, ME 04240
Muriel Landry

PORTLAND PUBLIC LIBRARY - TALKING BOOKS DEPARTMENT
5 Monument Sq.
Phone: (207) 773-4761
Portland, ME 04101
Janice Littlefield
The toll-free telephone number for residents within the service area is (800) 442-6384.

WATERVILLE PUBLIC LIBRARY
73 Elm St.
Phone: (207) 872-5433
Waterville, ME 04901
Edna M. Rasco

MARYLAND

MARYLAND STATE LIBRARY FOR THE BLIND & PHYSICALLY HANDICAPPED
1715 N. Charles St.
Phone: (301) 659-2668
Baltimore, MD 21201
Lance Finney
The toll-free telephone number for state residents is (800) 492-5627.

PRINCE GEORGE'S COUNTY MEMORIAL LIBRARY - TALKING BOOK LIBRARY
6530 Adelphi Rd.
Phone: (301) 779-9330
Hyattsville, MD 20782
Shirley J. Bean

MONTGOMERY COUNTY DEPARTMENT OF PUBLIC LIBRARIES - SERVICE FOR THE PHYSICALLY HANDICAPPED
99 Maryland Ave.
Phone: (301) 279-1679
Rockville, MD 20850
Martha Spencer
TDD number is 871-1570.

MASSACHUSETTS

MASSACHUSETTS REGIONAL LIBRARY FOR THE BLIND & PHYSICALLY HANDICAPPED
Perkins School for the Blind
175 N. Beacon St.
Phone: (617) 924-3434
Watertown, MA 02172
Patricia Kirk
The toll-free telephone number for state residents is (800) 852-3133.

WORCESTER PUBLIC LIBRARY - TALKING BOOK LIBRARY
Salem Sq.
Phone: (617) 799-1730
Worcester, MA 01608
Marlene Temsky
TDD number is 799-1724. The toll-free telephone number for residents within the service area is (800) 922-8326.

MICHIGAN

LIBRARY OF MICHIGAN - LIBRARY FOR THE BLIND & PHYSICALLY HANDICAPPED
Box 30007
Phone: (517) 373-1590
Lansing, MI 48909
Margaret Wolfe
This regional library serves the entire state of Michigan except Wayne County. The toll-free telephone number for residents within the service area is (800) 992-9012.

WAYNE COUNTY REGIONAL LIBRARY FOR THE BLIND & PHYSICALLY HANDICAPPED
33030 Van Born Rd.
Phone: (313) 274-2600
Wayne, MI 48184
Barbara Goral
This regional library serves only Wayne County. TDD number is 326-1080.

NORTHLAND LIBRARY COOPERATIVE - BLIND & PHYSICALLY HANDICAPPED LIBRARY
316 E. Chisholm
Phone: (517) 356-4444
Alpena, MI 49707
Susan S. Williams

WASHTENAW COUNTY LIBRARY - LIBRARY FOR THE BLIND & PHYSICALLY HANDICAPPED
Box 8645
Phone: (313) 971-6059
Ann Arbor, MI 48107
Mary Udoji

WILLARD SUBREGIONAL LIBRARY
7 W. Van Buren
Phone: (616) 968-8166
Battle Creek, MI 49016
Margaret E. Ritz

DOWNTOWN DETROIT SUBREGIONAL LIBRARY FOR THE BLIND & PHYSICALLY HANDICAPPED
121 Gratiot Ave.
Phone: (313) 224-0580
Detroit, MI 48226
Alva Fuquay
TDD number is 224-0584.

FARMINGTON COMMUNITY LIBRARY - OAKLAND COUNTY SUBREGIONAL LIBRARY FOR THE BLIND & PHYSICALLY HANDICAPPED
32737 W. Twelve Mile Rd.
Phone: (313) 553-0300
Farmington Hills, MI 48018
Carole Hund
TDD number is 553-0320.

MIDEASTERN MICHIGAN LIBRARY CO-OP - BLIND & PHYSICALLY HANDICAPPED LIBRARY
G-4195 W. Pasadena Ave.
Phone: (313) 732-1120
Flint, MI 48504
Joyce Wheat

KENT COUNTY LIBRARY SYSTEM - KENT COUNTY LIBRARY FOR THE BLIND & PHYSICALLY HANDICAPPED
775 Ball, N.E.
Phone: (616) 774-3262
Grand Rapids, MI 49503
Linda Waltman
TDD number is 531-6800.

UPPER PENINSULA LIBRARY FOR THE BLIND & PHYSICALLY HANDICAPPED
217 N. Front St.
Phone: (906) 228-7697
Marquette, MI 49855
Suzanne Dees
The toll-free telephone number for residents within the service area is (800) 562-8985.

MACOMB LIBRARY FOR THE BLIND & PHYSICALLY HANDICAPPED
16480 Hall Rd.
Phone: (313) 286-6660
Mt. Clemens, MI 48044
Margaret Hachey

MUSKEGON COUNTY LIBRARY FOR THE BLIND & PHYSICALLY HANDICAPPED
635 Ottawa St.
Phone: (616) 724-6257
Muskegon, MI 49442
Ruth Garver

BLUE WATER LIBRARY FEDERATION - BLIND & PHYSICALLY HANDICAPPED LIBRARY
210 McMorran Blvd.
Phone: (313) 982-3600
Port Huron, MI 48060
Stanley K. Arnett

SOUTHWEST MICHIGAN LIBRARY FOR THE BLIND & PHYSICALLY HANDICAPPED
300 Library Lane
Phone: (616) 323-3714
Portage, MI 49002
Ann Niedzielski
The toll-free telephone number for residents within the service area is (800) 554-0054.

GRAND TRAVERSE AREA LIBRARY FOR THE BLIND & PHYSICALLY HANDICAPPED
322 Sixth St.
Phone: (616) 941-2311
Traverse City, MI 49684
Carol Hubbell

MINNESOTA

MINNESOTA LIBRARY FOR THE BLIND & PHYSICALLY HANDICAPPED
Braille and Sight Saving School
Phone: (507) 332-3279
Faribault, MN 55021
Myrna Wright
The toll-free telephone number for state residents is (800) 722-0550.

MISSISSIPPI

MISSISSIPPI STATE LIBRARY COMMISSION - SERVICE FOR THE HANDICAPPED
5455 Executive Pl.   Phone: (601) 354-7208
Jackson, MS 39209   JoEllen Ostendorf

MISSOURI

WOLFNER MEMORIAL LIBRARY FOR THE BLIND & PHYSICALLY HANDICAPPED
1221 Locust St.   Phone: (314) 241-4227
St. Louis, MO 63103   Pennie D. Peterson
The toll-free telephone number for state residents is (800) 392-2614.

MONTANA

MONTANA STATE LIBRARY - DIVISION FOR THE BLIND & PHYSICALLY HANDICAPPED
1515 E. Sixth Ave.   Phone: (406) 449-2064
Helena, MT 59620   Darleen Tiensvold
The toll-free telephone number for state residents is (800) 332-3400.

NEBRASKA

NEBRASKA STATE LIBRARY COMMISSION - LIBRARY FOR THE BLIND & PHYSICALLY HANDICAPPED
1420 P St.   Phone: (402) 471-2045
Lincoln, NE 68508   David Oertli
The toll-free telephone number for state residents is (800) 742-7691.

NORTH PLATTE PUBLIC LIBRARY - BLIND & PHYSICALLY HANDICAPPED PROGRAM
120 W. 4th St.   Phone: (308) 532-6424
North Platte, NE 69101   Brenda Behsman
This subregional library may be called collect.

NEVADA

NEVADA STATE LIBRARY - TALKING BOOK PROGRAM
Capitol Complex   Phone: (702) 885-5160
Carson City, NV 89710   Mrs. Leslie M. Hester
The toll-free telephone number for state residents is (800) 992-0900, ext. 5160.

CLARK COUNTY LIBRARY DISTRICT - SPECIAL SERVICES
1401 E. Flamingo Rd.   Phone: (702) 733-7810
Las Vegas, NV 89109   Ann Langevin
TDD number is 732-0730.

NEW HAMPSHIRE

NEW HAMPSHIRE STATE LIBRARY- DIVISION OF LIBRARY SERVICES TO THE HANDICAPPED
17 S. Fruit St.   Phone: (603) 271-3429
Concord, NH 03301   Eileen Keim

NEW JERSEY

NEW JERSEY LIBRARY FOR THE BLIND & HANDICAPPED
2300 Stuyvesant Ave.   Phone: (609) 292-6450
Trenton, NJ 08618   Marya Hunsicker
TDD number is 633-7251. The toll-free telephone number for state residents is (800) 792-8322.

NEW MEXICO

NEW MEXICO STATE LIBRARY FOR THE BLIND & PHYSICALLY HANDICAPPED
325 Don Gaspar   Phone: (505) 827-3829
Santa Fe, NM 87503   Mr. Jerry Wise
The toll-free telephone number for state residents is (800) 432-5515.

NEW YORK

NEW YORK STATE LIBRARY FOR THE BLIND & VISUALLY HANDICAPPED
Cultural Education Center
Empire State Plaza   Phone: (518) 474-5935
Albany, NY 12230   Jane Summers
This regional library serves the entire state of New York except New York City and Long Island. The toll-free telephone number for state residents is (800) 342-3688.

NEW YORK PUBLIC LIBRARY - LIBRARY FOR THE BLIND & PHYSICALLY HANDICAPPED
166 Ave. of the Americas   Phone: (212) 925-1011
New York, NY 10013   Barbara Nugent
This regional library serves only New York City and Long Island.

SUFFOLK COOPERATIVE LIBRARY SYSTEM - READING FOR THE HANDICAPPED
627 N. Sunrise Service Rd.   Phone: (516) 286-1600
Bellport, NY 11713   Julie Klauber
TDD number is 286-4546.

NASSAU LIBRARY SYSTEM - TALKING BOOKS
900 Jerusalem Ave.   Phone: (516) 292-8920
Uniondale, NY 11553   Lorna Bertino
TDD number is 579-8585.

NORTH CAROLINA

NORTH CAROLINA LIBRARY FOR THE BLIND & PHYSICALLY HANDICAPPED
Dept. of Cultural Resources
1811 North Boulevard   Phone: (919) 733-4376
Raleigh, NC 27635   Charles H. Fox
The toll-free telephone number for state residents is (800) 662-7726.

NORTH DAKOTA

SOUTH DAKOTA STATE LIBRARY FOR THE HANDICAPPED
State Library Bldg.   Phone: (701) 781-2604
Pierre, SD 57501   Daniel W. Boyd
North Dakota is served by the South Dakota Regional Library. The toll-free telephone numbers for North Dakota residents are (800) 843-9948 and (800) 843-7927.

OHIO

OHIO LIBRARY FOR THE BLIND & PHYSICALLY HANDICAPPED
800 Vine St., Library Sq.   Phone: (513) 369-6074
Cincinnati, OH 45202   Carol Heideman
This regional library serves southern Ohio. TDD number is 369-6072. The toll-free telephone number for residents within the service area is (800) 582-0335.

CLEVELAND PUBLIC LIBRARY - LIBRARY FOR THE BLIND & PHYSICALLY HANDICAPPED
325 Superior Ave.   Phone: (216) 623-2911
Cleveland, OH 44114   Jacqueline H. Goodin
This regional library serves northern Ohio. TDD number is 566-8294. The toll-free telephone number for residents within the service area is (800) 362-1262.

OKLAHOMA

OKLAHOMA REGIONAL LIBRARY FOR THE BLIND & PHYSICALLY HANDICAPPED
1108 N.E. 36   Phone: (405) 521-3514
Oklahoma City, OK 73111   Bill E. McIlvain

TULSA CITY-COUNTY LIBRARY SYSTEM - SPECIAL SERVICES
400 Civic Center   Phone: (918) 592-7920
Tulsa, OK 74103   Ellen Ontko
TDD number is 592-7968.

OREGON

OREGON STATE LIBRARY - SERVICES FOR THE BLIND & PHYSICALLY HANDICAPPED
555 13th St., N.E.   Phone: (503) 378-3849
Salem, OR 97301   Kathleen McHarg
The toll-free telephone number for state residents is (800) 452-0292. The toll-free telephone number for Portland residents is (503) 224-0610.

PENNSYLVANIA

FREE LIBRARY OF PHILADELPHIA - LIBRARY FOR THE BLIND & PHYSICALLY HANDICAPPED
919 Walnut St.   Phone: (215) 925-3213
Philadelphia, PA 19107   Michael P. Coyle
This regional library serves eastern Pennsylvania. The toll-free telephone number for residents within the service area is (800) 222-1754.

CARNEGIE LIBRARY OF PITTSBURGH - LIBRARY FOR THE BLIND & PHYSICALLY HANDICAPPED
4724 Baum Blvd.   Phone: (412) 687-2440
Pittsburgh, PA 15213   Sue O. Murdock
This regional library serves western Pennsylvania. The toll-free telephone number for residents within the service area is (800) 242-0586.

PUERTO RICO

PUERTO RICO REGIONAL LIBRARY FOR THE BLIND & PHYSICALLY HANDICAPPED
520 Ponce de Leon Ave.
Stop 8 1/2, Puerta de Tierra   Phone: (809) 723-2519
San Juan, PR 00901   Carmen Rodriguez

RHODE ISLAND

RHODE ISLAND STATE DEPARTMENT OF STATE LIBRARY SERVICES - REGIONAL LIBRARY FOR THE BLIND & PHYSICALLY HANDICAPPED
95 Davis St.   Phone: (401) 277-2726
Providence, RI 02908   Barbara L. Wilson
The toll-free telephone number for state residents is (800) 662-5141.

SOUTH CAROLINA

SOUTH CAROLINA STATE LIBRARY - DIVISION FOR THE BLIND & PHYSICALLY HANDICAPPED
700 Knox Abbott Dr.   Phone: (803) 758-2726
Cayce, SC 29033   Frances Case
The toll-free telephone number for state residents is (800) 922-7818.

SOUTH DAKOTA

SOUTH DAKOTA STATE LIBRARY FOR THE HANDICAPPED
State Library Bldg.
800 N. Illinois   Phone: (605) 773-3514
Pierre, SD 57501   Daniel W. Boyd
The toll-free telephone number for state residents is (800) 592-1841. This regional library also serves North Dakota.

TENNESSEE

TENNESSEE REGIONAL LIBRARY FOR THE BLIND & PHYSICALLY HANDICAPPED
Tennessee State Library & Archives
403 Seventh Ave., N.   Phone: (615) 741-3915
Nashville, TN 37219   Miss Francis H. Ezell
TDD number is 255-6956. The toll-free telephone number for state residents is (800) 342-3308.

TEXAS

TEXAS STATE LIBRARY - DIVISION FOR THE BLIND & PHYSICALLY HANDICAPPED
Box 12927, Capitol Sta.   Phone: (512) 475-4758
Austin, TX 78711   Mr. Dale Propp
The toll-free telephone number for state residents is (800) 252-9605.

UTAH

UTAH STATE LIBRARY COMMISSION - DIVISION FOR THE BLIND & PHYSICALLY HANDICAPPED
2150 S. 300 W., Suite 16   Phone: (801) 533-5855
Salt Lake City, UT 84115   Gerald A. Buttars
The toll-free telephone number for state residents is (800) 662-5540. This regional library also serves Wyoming. The toll-free telephone number for residents in Wyoming and other western states is (800) 453-4293.

VERMONT

VERMONT STATE DEPARTMENT OF LIBRARIES - SPECIAL SERVICES UNIT
                                     Phone: (802) 828-3273
Montpelier, VT 05602   Josephine Hess

VIRGIN ISLANDS

VIRGIN ISLANDS REGIONAL LIBRARY FOR THE BLIND & PHYSICALLY HANDICAPPED
Lagoon Complex No. 3
Frederiksted   Phone: (809) 772-2250
St. Croix, VI 00842   Michael John Herz

VIRGINIA

VIRGINIA STATE LIBRARY FOR THE VISUALLY & THE PHYSICALLY HANDICAPPED
1901 Roane St.   Phone: (804) 786-8016
Richmond, VA 23222   Constance J. Moore
TDD number is 786-8863. The toll-free telephone number for state residents is (800) 552-7015.

ALEXANDRIA LIBRARY - TALKING BOOK SERVICE
John Adams Ctr.
5651 Rayburn Ave.   Phone: (703) 998-5463
Alexandria, VA 22311   Patricia Bates

FAIRFAX COUNTY PUBLIC LIBRARY - SPECIAL SERVICES
6209 Rose Hill Dr.   Phone: (703) 971-0030
Alexandria, VA 22310   Jeanette A. Studley
TDD number is 978-2209.

**ARLINGTON COUNTY DEPARTMENT OF LIBRARIES - TALKING BOOK
    SERVICE**
1015 N. Quincy St.   Phone: (703) 527-4777
Arlington, VA 22201   Mary M. Bergin
TDD number is 525-3086.

**HAMPTON SUBREGIONAL LIBRARY FOR THE BLIND & PHYSICALLY
    HANDICAPPED**
107 E. Howard St.   Phone: (804) 727-6630
Hampton, VA 23663   Mary Sue Newman

**NEWPORT NEWS PUBLIC LIBRARY SYSTEM - LIBRARY SERVICE FOR THE
    BLIND & PHYSICALLY HANDICAPPED**
112 Main St.   Phone: (804) 877-9488
Newport News, VA 23601   Julie Hewin Byrd
TDD number is 599-6475.

ROANOKE CITY PUBLIC LIBRARY SYSTEM
706 S. Jefferson St.   Phone: (703) 981-2921
Roanoke, VA 24011   Rebecca S. Cooper

STAUNTON PUBLIC LIBRARY - TALKING BOOK CENTER
19 S. Market St.   Phone: (703) 885-6215
Staunton, VA 24401   Ann Fairman

VIRGINIA BEACH PUBLIC LIBRARY - SPECIAL SERVICES DIVISION
936 Independence Blvd.   Phone: (804) 464-9175
Virginia Beach, VA 23455   Marilyn W. Mortensen
TDD number is 464-9136.

WASHINGTON

**WASHINGTON REGIONAL LIBRARY FOR THE BLIND & PHYSICALLY
    HANDICAPPED**
821 Lenora St.   Phone: (206) 464-6930
Seattle, WA 98129   Ms. Jan Ames
The toll-free telephone number for state residents is (800) 542-0866.

WEST VIRGINIA

**WEST VIRGINIA LIBRARY COMMISSION - SERVICES FOR THE BLIND &
    PHYSICALLY HANDICAPPED**
Science & Cultural Ctr.
Greenbrier & Washington Sts.   Phone: (304) 348-4061
Charleston, WV 25305   Nell Laraway
The toll-free telephone number for state residents is (800) 642-8674.

**KANAWHA COUNTY PUBLIC LIBRARY - SERVICES FOR THE BLIND &
    PHYSICALLY HANDICAPPED**
123 Capitol St.   Phone: (304) 343-4646
Charleston, WV 25301   Jay Pauley

**CABELL COUNTY PUBLIC LIBRARY - SERVICES FOR THE BLIND &
    PHYSICALLY HANDICAPPED**
455 9th St. Plaza   Phone: (304) 523-9451
Huntington, WV 25701   Suzanne L. Marshall

**PARKERSBURG & WOOD COUNTY PUBLIC LIBRARY - SERVICES FOR THE
    BLIND & PHYSICALLY HANDICAPPED**
3100 Emerson Ave.   Phone: (304) 485-6564
Parkersburg, WV 26101   Ms. Kim Flanigan

WEST VIRGINIA SCHOOL FOR THE BLIND
                                      Phone: (304) 822-3521
Romney, WV 26757   Donna See

OHIO COUNTY PUBLIC LIBRARY
52 16th St.   Phone: (304) 232-0244
Wheeling, WV 26003   Rosalie Galloway

WISCONSIN

**WISCONSIN REGIONAL LIBRARY FOR THE BLIND & PHYSICALLY
    HANDICAPPED**
814 W. Wells St.   Phone: (414) 278-3045
Milwaukee, WI 53233   Ms. Corliss Rice
The toll-free telephone number for state residents is (800) 242-8822.

BROWN COUNTY LIBRARY - SPECIAL SERVICES DIVISION
515 Pine St.   Phone: (414) 497-3473
Green Bay, WI 54301   Angela Basten
TDD number is 432-1758.

WYOMING

**UTAH STATE LIBRARY COMMISSION - DIVISION FOR THE BLIND &
    PHYSICALLY HANDICAPPED**
2150 S. 300 W., Suite 16   Phone: (801) 533-5855
Salt Lake City, UT 84115   Gerald A. Buttars
Wyoming is served by the Utah regional library. The toll-free number for
residents of Wyoming and other western states is (800) 453-4293.

APPENDIX C
PATENT DEPOSITORY LIBRARIES

Appendix C

Patent Depository Libraries

The libraries listed below have been designated as patent depositories by the U.S. Patent and Trademark Office and are open for public use. Each of the patent depository libraries offers the publications of the patent classification system (i.e., *The Manual of Classification, Index to the U.S. Patent Classification, Classification Definitions,* etc.) and provides technical staff assistance to aid individuals in gaining effective access to patent information.

Depending upon the library, the patents may be available in bound volumes, in microform, on computer, or in some combination thereof. Facilities for making copies are generally provided for a fee. Not all depository libraries have equally complete collections, however. Some libraries have available the entire patent collection dating back to 1790, while other libraries have collections of much more limited scope. Therefore it is advisable to contact the particular library in advance about its collection size and hours of service to the public in order to ensure that a meaningful search in the chosen area of technology can be conducted.

With one exception, as noted in the list following, the collections are organized in patent number sequence.

Alabama

Auburn University Libraries
Auburn University, AL 36849
(205) 826-4500

Birmingham Public Library
2100 Park Place
Birmingham, AL 35203
(205) 254-2551

Alaska

Anchorage Municipal Libraries
524 W. 6th
Anchorage, AK 99501
(907) 264-4481

Arizona

Arizona State University Libraries
Tempe, AZ 85287
(602) 965-3417

Arkansas

Arkansas State Library
1 Capitol Mall
Little Rock, AR 72201
(501) 371-1526

California

Los Angeles Public Library
630 W. Fifth St.
Los Angeles, CA 90071
(213) 626-7555

California State Library
Library-Courts Building
Box 2037
Sacramento, CA 95809
(916) 445-2585

San Diego Public Library
City Administration Building
202 C St.
San Diego, CA 92101
(619) 236-5800

*Sunnyvale Public Library
Patent Information Clearinghouse
665 W. Olive Ave.
Sunnyvale, CA 94086
(408) 738-5585

Colorado

Denver Public Library
3840 York St.
Denver, CO 80205
(303) 571-2000

Delaware

University of Delaware, Newark
Library
Newark, DE 19711
(302) 451-2231

Florida

Broward County Main Library
Government Documents Department
100 S. Andrews Ave.
Fort Lauderdale, FL 33301
(305) 357-7444

Miami-Dade Public Library
One Biscayne Blvd.
Miami, FL 33132-2585
(305)579-5001

Georgia

Georgia Institute of Technology
Price Gilbert Memorial Library
Atlanta, GA 30332
(404) 894-4510

Idaho

University of Idaho
Library
Moscow, ID 83843
(208) 885-6534

Illinois

Chicago Public Library
425 N. Michigan Ave.
Chicago, IL 60611
(312) 269-2900

Illinois State Library
Centennial Building
Springfield, IL 62706
(217) 782-2994

Indiana

Indianapolis-Marion County
  Public Library
Box 211
Indianapolis, IN 46206
(317) 269-1700

Louisiana

Louisiana State University
Troy H. Middleton Library
Baton Rouge, LA 70803
(504) 388-2217

Maryland

University of Maryland Libraries
College Park, MD 20742
(301) 454-3011

Massachusetts

University of Massachusetts
Physical Sciences Library
Graduate Research Center
Amherst, MA 01003
(413) 545-1370

Boston Public Library
Copley Square
Boston, MA 02117
(617) 536-5400 Ext: 366

Michigan

University of Michigan
University Library
818 Harland Hatcher Library—South
Ann Arbor, MI 48109
(313) 764-9356

Detroit Public Library
5201 Woodward Ave.
Detroit, MI 48202
(313) 833-1000

Minnesota

Minneapolis Public Library and
  Information Center
300 Nicollet Mall
Minneapolis, MN 55401
(612) 372-6500

Missouri

Linda Hall Library
5109 Cherry St.
Kansas City, MO 64110
(816) 363-4600

St. Louis Public Library
1301 Olive St.
St. Louis, MO 63103
(314) 241-2288 Ext: 301

Montana

Montana College of Mineral Science
and Technology
Butte, MT 59701
(406) 496-4126

Nebraska

University of Nebraska, Lincoln Libraries
106 Love Library
Lincoln, NE 68588
(402) 472-2526

Nevada

University of Nevada, Reno
Library
Reno, NV 89557-0044
(702) 784-6533

New Hampshire

University of New Hampshire
University Library
Durham, NH 03824
(603) 862-1540

New Jersey

Newark Public Library
5 Washington St.
Box 630
Newark, NJ 07101-0630
(201) 733-7800

New Mexico

University of New Mexico
General Library
Albuquerque, NM 87131
(505) 277-4241

New York

New York State Library
Cultural Education Center
Empire Plaza
Albany, NY 12230
(518) 474-5930

Buffalo and Erie County Public Library
Lafayette Square
Buffalo, NY 14203
(716) 856-7525

New York Public Library
The Research Libraries
Fifth Ave. & 42nd St.
New York, NY 10018
(212) 930-0800

North Carolina

North Carolina State University
D.H. Hill Library
Box 7111
Raleigh, NC 27695-7111
(919) 737-2843

Ohio

Public Library of Cincinnati and
Hamilton County
Library Square
800 Vine St.
Cincinnati, OH 45202-2071
(513) 369-6000

Cleveland Public Library
325 Superior Ave.
Cleveland, OH 44114-1271
(216) 623-2800

Ohio State University Libraries
1858 Neil Ave. Mall
Columbus, OH 43210
(614) 422-6151

Toledo-Lucas County Public Library
325 Michigan St.
Toledo, OH 43624
(419) 255-7055

Oklahoma

Oklahoma State University
Edmund Low Library
Stillwater, OK 74078
(405) 624-6313

Pennsylvania

Alliance College
Cambridge Springs, PA 16403
(814) 398-4611

Franklin Institute Library
20th & Race Sts.
Philadelphia, PA 19103
(215) 448-1284

Carnegie Library of Pittsburgh
4400 Forbes Ave.
Pittsburgh, PA 15213
(412) 622-3100

Pennsylvania State University Libraries
E 505A Pattee Library
University Park, PA 16802
(814) 865-0401

Rhode Island

Providence Public Library
150 Empire St.
Providence, RI 02903
(401) 521-7722

South Carolina

Medical University of South Carolina
Library
170 Ashley Ave.
Charleston, SC 29425
(803) 792-2374

Tennessee

Memphis and Shelby County Public
   Library and Information Center
1850 Peabody Ave.
Memphis, TN 38104
(901) 725-8855

Texas

University of Texas, Austin
General Libraries
PCL 3.220
Austin, TX 78713
(512) 471-3811

Texas A&M University
Sterling C. Evans Library
College Station, TX 77843-5000
(409) 845-8111

Dallas Public Library
1515 Young St.
Dallas, TX 75201
(214) 749-4100

Rice University
Fondren Library
Box 1892
Houston, TX 77251-1892
(713) 527-4022

Utah

University of Utah
Marriott Library
Salt Lake City, UT 84112
(801) 581-8558

Washington

University of Washington
M171 Suzzallo Library, FM-25
Seattle, WA 98195
(206) 543-1760

Wisconsin

University of Wisconsin, Madison
Kurt F. Wendt Engineering Library
215 N. Randall Ave.
Madison, WI 53706
(608) 262-7980

Milwaukee Public Library
814 W. Wisconsin Ave.
Milwaukee, WI 53233
(414) 278-3000

APPENDIX D
FEDERAL INFORMATION CENTERS

Appendix D

Federal Information Centers

The Federal Information Centers exist primarily to assist persons by answering questions concerning the federal government. A telephone call or letter to the nearest center will get a direct answer to a query or put the individual in touch with the proper federal agency that can be of assistance. Addresses and telephone numbers are listed below. Persons living in a location without a direct telephone line must place a long distance call to the center nearest to them.

Alabama

Residents of Alabama may write to:

Federal Bldg. & U.S. Courthouse
75 Spring St., S.W.
Atlanta, GA 30303

or call:

Birmingham
(205) 322-8591

Mobile
(205) 438-1421

Alaska

Federal Bldg. & U.S. Courthouse
701 C St.
Box 33
Anchorage, AK 99513
(907) 271-3650

Arizona

Residents of Arizona may write to:

Government Information Center
880 Front St.
San Diego, CA 92188

or call:

Phoenix
(602) 261-3313

Arkansas

Residents of Arkansas may write to:

Lanham Federal Bldg.
819 Taylor St.
Fort Worth, TX 76102

or call:

Little Rock
(501) 378-6177

California

Federal Bldg.
300 N. Los Angeles St.
Los Angeles, CA 90012
(213) 688-3800

Federal Bldg. & U.S. Courthouse
650 Capitol Mall
Sacramento, CA 95814
(916) 440-3344

Government Information Center
880 Front St.
San Diego, CA 92188
(619) 293-6030

Federal Bldg. & U.S. Courthouse
450 Golden Gate Ave.
Box 36082
San Francisco, CA 94102
(415) 556-6600

or call:

Santa Ana
(714) 836-2386

Colorado

Federal Center
Box 25006
Denver, CO 80225
(303) 236-7181

or call:

Colorado Springs
(303) 471-9491

Pueblo
(303) 544-9523

Connecticut

Residents of Connecticut may write to:

Federal Bldg., Rm. 2-110
26 Federal Plaza
New York, NY 10278

or call:

Hartford
(203) 527-2617

New Haven
(203) 624-4720

Florida

Cramer Federal Bldg., Rm. 105
144 First Ave., S.
St. Petersburg, FL 33701
(813) 893-3495

or call:

Fort Lauderdale
(305) 522-8531

Jacksonville
(904) 354-4756

Miami
(305) 350-4155

Orlando
(305) 422-1800

Tampa
(813) 229-7911

West Palm Beach
(305) 833-7566

Georgia

Federal Bldg. & U.S. Courthouse
75 Spring St., S.W.
Atlanta, GA 30303
(404) 221-6891

Hawaii

Federal Bldg.
300 Ala Moana Blvd.
Box 50091
Honolulu, HI 96850
(808) 546-8620

Illinois

Kluczynski Federal Bldg., 33rd Fl.
230 S. Dearborn St.
Chicago, IL 60604
(312) 353-4242

Indiana

Residents of Indiana may write to:

Federal Bldg., Rm. 7411
550 Main St.
Cincinnati, OH 45202

or call:

Gary
(219) 883-4110

Indianapolis
(317) 269-7373

Iowa

Residents of Iowa may write to:

U.S. Post Office & Courthouse
215 N. 17th St.
Omaha, NE 68102

or call:

(800) 532-1556

Kansas

Residents of Kansas may write to:

Federal Bldg., Rm. 2616
1520 Market St.
St. Louis, MO 63103

or call:

(800) 432-2934

Kentucky

Residents of Kentucky may write to:

Federal Bldg., Rm. 7411
550 Main St.
Cincinnati, OH 45202

or call:

Louisville
(502) 582-6261

Louisiana

Residents of Louisiana may write to:

Federal Bldg. & U.S. Courthouse
515 Rusk Ave.
Houston, TX 77002

or call:

New Orleans
(504) 589-6696

Maryland

Residents of Maryland may write to:

Federal Bldg., Rm. 1232
600 Arch St.
Philadelphia, PA 19106

or call:

Baltimore
(301) 962-4980

Massachusetts

McCormack P.O. & Courthouse, Rm. 812
Boston, MA 02109
(617) 223-7121

Michigan

McNamara Federal Bldg., Rm. M-25
477 Michigan Ave.
Detroit, MI 48226
(313) 226-7016

or call:

Grand Rapids
(616) 451-2628

Minnesota

Residents of Minnesota may write to:

Kluczynski Federal Bldg., 33rd Fl.
230 S. Dearborn St.
Chicago, IL 60604

or call:

Minneapolis
(612) 349-5333

Missouri

Federal Bldg., Rm. 2616
1520 Market St.
St. Louis, MO 63103
(314) 425-4106

Residents of other Missouri locations
may call (800) 392-7711

Nebraska

U.S. Post Office & Courthouse
215 N. 17th St.
Omaha, NE 68102
(402) 221-3353

Residents of other Nebraska locations
may call (800) 642-8383

New Jersey

Residents of Northern New Jersey may write to:

Federal Bldg., Rm. 2-110
26 Federal Plaza
New York, NY 10278

Residents of Southern New Jersey
may write to:

Federal Bldg., Rm. 1232
600 Arch St.
Philadelphia, PA 19106

or all residents of New Jersey may call:

Newark
(201) 645-3600

Trenton
(609) 396-4400

New Mexico

Residents of New Mexico may write to:

Lanham Federal Bldg.
819 Taylor St.
Fort Worth, TX 76102

or call:

Albuquerque
(505) 766-3091

New York

Federal Bldg.
111 West Huron St.
Buffalo, NY 14202
(716) 846-4010

Federal Bldg., Rm. 2-110
26 Federal Plaza
New York, NY 10278
(212) 264-4464

or call:

Albany
(518) 463-4421

Rochester
(716) 546-5075

Syracuse
(315) 476-8545

North Carolina

Residents of North Carolina may write to:

Federal Bldg. & U.S. Courthouse
75 Spring St., S.W.
Atlanta, GA 30303

or call:

Charlotte
(704) 376-3600

Ohio

Federal Bldg., Rm. 7411
550 Main St.
Cincinnati, OH 45202
(513) 684-2801

or call:

Akron
(216) 375-5638

Cleveland
(216) 522-4040

Columbus
(614) 221-1014

Dayton
(513) 223-7377

Toledo
(419) 241-3223

Oklahoma

Residents of Oklahoma may write to:

Lanham Federal Bldg.
819 Taylor St.
Fort Worth, TX 76102

or call:

Oklahoma City
(405) 231-4868

Tulsa
(918) 584-4193

Oregon

Green-Wyatt Federal Bldg., Rm. 318
1220 S.W. 3rd Ave.
Portland, OR   97204
(503) 221-2222

Pennsylvania

Federal Bldg., Rm. 1232
600 Arch St.
Philadelphia, PA 19106
(215) 597-7042

or call:

Pittsburgh
(412) 644-3456

Rhode Island

Residents of Rhode Island may write to:

McCormack P.O. & Courthouse, Rm. 812
Boston, MA 02109

or call:

Providence
(401) 331-5565

Tennessee

Residents of Tennessee may write to:

Federal Bldg. & U.S. Courthouse
75 Spring St., S.W.
Atlanta, GA 30303

or call:

Chattanooga
(615) 265-8231

Memphis
(901) 521-3285

Nashville
(615) 242-5056

Texas

Lanham Federal Bldg.
819 Taylor St.
Fort Worth, TX 76102
(817) 334-3624

Federal Bldg. & U.S. Courthouse
515 Rusk Ave.
Houston, TX 77002
(713) 229-2552

or call:

Austin
(512) 472-5494

Dallas
(214) 767-8585

San Antonio
(512) 224-4471

Utah

Residents of Utah may write to:

Federal Center
Box 25006
Denver, CO 80225

or call:

Salt Lake City
(801) 524-5353

Virginia

Residents of Virginia may write to:

Federal Bldg., Rm. 1232
600 Arch St.
Philadelphia, PA 19106

or call:

Norfolk
(804) 441-3101

Richmond
(804) 643-4928

Roanoke
(703) 982-8591

Washington

Residents of Washington may write to:

Green-Wyatt Federal Bldg., Rm. 318
1220 S.W. 3rd Ave.
Portland, OR 97024

or call:

Seattle
(206) 442-0570

Tacoma
(206) 383-5230

Wisconsin

Residents of Wisconsin may write to:

Kluczynski Federal Bldg., 33rd Fl.
230 S. Dearborn St.
Chicago, IL 60604

or call:

Milwaukee
(414) 271-2273

APPENDIX E
FEDERAL JOB INFORMATION CENTERS

Appendix E

Federal Job Information Centers

The Office of Personnel Management operates Federal Job Information Centers in the cities listed below. The centers provide general information on federal employment, explain how to apply for specific jobs, and supply application materials. Those seeking information are invited to telephone, write, or visit.

Alabama

Southerland Bldg.
806 Governors Dr., S.W.
Huntsville, AL 35801
(205) 453-5070

Alaska

Federal Bldg.
701 C St.
Box 22
Anchorage, AK 99513
(907) 271-5821

Arizona

U.S. Postal Service Bldg.
522 N. Central Ave.
Phoenix, AZ 85004
(602) 261-4736

Arkansas

Federal Bldg., 3rd Fl.
700 W. Capitol Ave.
Little Rock, AR 72201
(501) 378-5842

California

Linder Bldg.
845 S. Figueroa
Los Angeles, CA 90017
(213) 688-3360

1029 J St., Rm. 202
Sacramento, CA 95814
(916) 440-3441

880 Front St.
San Diego, CA 92188
(714) 293-6165

211 Main St., 2nd Fl.
San Francisco, CA 94105
(415) 974-9725

Colorado

1845 Sherman St.
Denver, CO 80203
(303) 837-3509

Connecticut

Federal Bldg., Rm. 613
450 Main St.
Hartford, CT 06103
(203) 722-3096

District of Columbia

1900 E St., N.W.
Washington, DC 20415
(202) 737-9616

Florida

Federal Bldg. & U.S. Courthouse
80 N. Hughey Ave.
Orlando, FL 32801
(305) 420-6148 or 6149

Georgia

Russell Federal Bldg., 9th Fl.
75 Spring St., S.W.
Atlanta, GA 30303
(404) 221-4315

Guam

Pacific News Bldg., Rm. 308
238 O'Hara St.
Agana, GU 96910
(671) 344-5242

Hawaii

Honolulu (and Island of Oahu):

Federal Bldg., Rm. 1310
300 Ala Moana Blvd.
Honolulu, HI 96850
(808) 546-8600

Illinois

55 E. Jackson, Rm. 1401
Chicago, IL 60604
(312) 353-5136

Indiana

46 E. Ohio St., Rm. 124
Indianapolis, IN 46204
(317) 269-7161

Iowa

210 Walnut St., Rm. 191
Des Moines, IA 50309
(515) 284-4545

In Scott & Pottawattamie Counties
call (402) 221-3815

Kansas

One-Twenty Bldg., Rm. 101
120 S. Market St.
Wichita, KS 67202
(316) 269-6106

In Johnson, Leavenworth and
Wyandotte Counties
call (816) 374-5702

Louisiana

F. Edward Hebert Bldg., Rm. 849
610 South St.
New Orleans, LA 70130
(504) 589-2764

Maryland

Garmatz Federal Bldg.
101 W. Lombard St.
Baltimore, MD 21201
(301) 962-3822

Massachusetts

3 Center Plaza
Boston, MA 02108
(617) 223-2571

Michigan

477 Michigan Ave., Rm. 565
Detroit, MI 48226
(313) 226-6950

Minnesota

Federal Bldg.
Ft. Snelling
St. Paul, MN 55111
(612) 725-4430

Mississippi

100 W. Capitol St., Suite 335
Jackson, MS 39260
(601) 960-4585

Missouri

Federal Bldg., Rm. 134
601 E. 12th St.
Kansas City, MO 64106
(816) 374-5702

Old Post Office, Rm. 400
815 Olive St.
St. Louis, MO 63101
(314) 425-4285

Nebraska

U.S. Courthouse & Post Office Bldg.,
Rm. 1010
215 N. 17th St.
Omaha, NE 68102
(402) 221-3815

New Hampshire

McIntyre Federal Bldg., Rm. 104
80 Daniel St.
Portsmouth, NH 03801
(603) 436-7220 Ext: 762

New Jersey

Peter W. Rodino, Jr., Federal Bldg.
970 Broad St.
Newark, NJ 07102
(201) 645-3673

In Camden call (215) 597-7440

New Mexico

Federal Bldg.
421 Gold Ave., S.W.
Albuquerque, NM 87102
(505) 766-5583

New York

Jacob K. Javits Federal Bldg.
26 Federal Plaza
New York, NY 10278
(212) 264-0422

James N. Hanley Federal Bldg.
100 S. Clinton St.
Syracuse, NY 13260
(315) 423-5660

North Carolina

Federal Bldg.
310 New Bern Ave.
Box 25069
Raleigh, NC 27611
(919) 755-4361

Ohio

Federal Bldg.
200 W. 2nd St.
Dayton, OH 45402
(513) 225-2720

Oklahoma

200 N.W. 5th St., Rm. 205
Oklahoma City, OK 73102
(405) 231-4948

Oregon

Federal Bldg.
1220 S.W. 3rd St.
Portland, OR 97204
(503) 221-3141

Pennsylvania

Federal Bldg., Rm. 168
Harrisburg, PA 17108
(717) 782-4494

Wm. J. Green, Jr., Federal Bldg.
600 Arch St.
Philadelphia, PA 19106
(215) 597-7440

Federal Bldg.
1000 Liberty Ave.
Pittsburgh, PA 15222
(412) 644-2755

Puerto Rico

Federico Degetau Federal Bldg.
Carlos E. Chardon St.
Hato Rey
San Juan, PR 00918
(809) 753-4209

Rhode Island

Pastori Federal Bldg., Rm. 310
Kennedy Plaza
Providence, RI 02903
(401) 528-5251

South Carolina

Federal Bldg.
334 Meeting St.
Charleston, SC 29403
(803) 724- 4328

Tennessee

100 N. Main St., Suite 1312
Memphis, TN 38103
(901) 521-3956

Texas

1100 Commerce St., Rm. 6B4
Dallas, TX 75242
(214) 767-8035

701 San Jacinto St., 4th Fl.
Houston, TX 77002
(713) 226-2375

643 E. Durango Blvd.
San Antonio, TX 78206
(512) 229-6611

Virginia

Federal Bldg., Rm. 220
200 Granby Mall
Norfolk, VA 23510
(804) 441-3355

Washington

Federal Bldg.
915 2nd Ave.
Seattle, WA 98174
(206) 442-4365

West Virginia

Federal Bldg.
500 Quarrier St.
Charleston, WV 25301
(304) 343-6181 Ext: 226

APPENDIX F
UNITED NATIONS DEPOSITORY LIBRARIES

Appendix F

United Nations Depository Libraries

The following list contains the names of libraries in the United States and Canada that house United Nations documents and publications. Fifty-seven libraries are designated depositories for the United Nations and its organizations. Users are advised to contact a particular library directly to ascertain the extent of its holdings. The entries are arranged geographically by state or province and city. Within each city, the entries are arranged alphabetically according to the name of the parent institution or library.

UNITED STATES

California

University of California, Berkeley
General Library
Government Documents Department
Berkeley, CA 94720
(415) 642-3287

Los Angeles Public Library
630 W. Fifth St.
Los Angeles, CA 90071
(213) 626-7461

University of California, Los Angeles
University Research Library
405 Hilgard Ave.
Los Angeles, CA 90024
(213) 825-3135

Stanford University Libraries
Stanford, CA 94305
(415) 497-9108

Colorado

Denver Public Library
Government Publications Division
1357 Broadway
Denver, CO 80203
(303) 571-2140

Connecticut

Yale University
Seeley Mudd Library
Public Documents Rm.
New Haven, CT 06520
(203) 436-0176

District of Columbia

Library of Congress
Washington, DC 20540
(202) 287-5000

United Nations Information Centre
1889 F St., N.W.
Washington, DC 20006
(202) 296-5370

Florida

Nova University Law Library
3100 S.W. 9th Ave.
Ft. Lauderdale, FL 33315
(305) 522-2300

Florida State University
Robert Manning Strozier Library
Documents Department
Tallahassee, FL 32306
(904) 644-6061

Hawaii

University of Hawaii
Public Services - Government Documents,
   Maps & Microforms
Hamilton Library
2550 The Mall
Honolulu, HI 96822
(808) 948-8230

Illinois

Library of International Relations
77 S. Wacker Dr.
Chicago, IL 60606
(312) 567-6803

University of Chicago
Regenstein Library
1100 E. 57th St.
Chicago, IL 60637
(312) 962-7874

Northwestern University Library
Government Publications Department
1935 Sheridan Rd.
Evanston, IL 60201
(312) 492-3130

University of Illinois
Education and Social Sciences Library
100 Main Library
1408 W. Gregory Dr.
Urbana, IL 61801
(217) 333-2305

Indiana

Indiana University Libraries
Bloomington, IN 47405
(812) 335-3403

Indiana University
School of Law Library
735 W. New York St.
Indianapolis, IN 46202
(317) 264-4028

Iowa

University of Iowa Libraries
Government Publications Department
Iowa City, IA 52242
(319) 353-3318

Kansas

University of Kansas Libraries
Lawrence, KS 66045
(913) 864-4662

Kentucky

University of Kentucky
Margaret I. King Library
Government Publications Department
Lexington, KY 40506-0039
(606) 257-3139

Louisiana

Louisiana State University
Troy H. Middleton Library
Business Administration/Documents Department
Baton Rouge, LA 70803
(504) 388-2570

Maryland

Johns Hopkins University
Milton S. Eisenhower Library
Government Publications/Maps/Law Library
Charles & 34th Sts.
Baltimore, MD 21218
(301) 338-8360

Massachusetts

Boston Public Library
Government Documents, Microtext, Newspapers
Copley Square
Box 286
Boston, MA 02117
(617) 536-5400

Harvard University
Harvard College Library
Government Documents Division
Cambridge, MA 02138
(617) 495-2479

Michigan

University of Michigan
Harlan Hatcher Graduate Library
Ann Arbor, MI 48109
(313) 764-9373

Minnesota

University of Minnesota
Government Publications Division
409 Wilson Library
309 19th Ave., S.
Minneapolis, MN 55455
(612) 373-7813

Nevada

University of Nevada, Reno
University Library
Government Publications Department
Reno, NV 89557
(702) 784-6579

New Jersey

Princeton University
Pliny Fisk Library
Princeton, NJ 08544
(609) 452-3211

New York

Cornell University
Olin Library
Ithaca, NY 14853
(607) 256-4144

Columbia University
Law School Library
435 W. 116th St.
New York, NY 10027
(212) 280-3737

Council on Foreign Relations, Inc.
58 E. 68th St.
New York, NY 10021
(212) 734-0400

New York Public Library
Economic and Public Affairs Division
5th Ave. & 42nd St., Rm. 228
New York, NY 10018
(212) 930-0750

New York University
Bobst Library
United Nations Collection
70 Washington Sq., S.
New York, NY 10012
(212) 598-3609

North Carolina

University of North Carolina, Chapel Hill
Wilson Library
Documents Section
Bldg. 024A
Chapel Hill, NC 27514
(919) 962-1301

Ohio

Cleveland Public Library
Social Sciences Department
325 Superior Ave.
Cleveland, OH 44114-1271
(216) 623-2860

Pennsylvania

University of Pennsylvania
Charles Patterson Van Pelt Library
3420 Walnut St./CH
Philadelphia, PA 19104
(215) 898-7555

Puerto Rico

Catholic University of Puerto Rico
School of Law
Monsignor Juan Fremiot Torres
    Oliver Law Library
Ave. Las Americas
Ponce, PR 00732
(809) 844-4150

University of Puerto Rico
Biblioteca General
Box C
Rio Piedras, PR 00931
(809) 764-0000

Rhode Island

Brown University
John D. Rockefeller, Jr. Library
Documents Department
Providence, RI 02912
(401) 863-2167

Tennessee

Joint Universities Libraries
Nashville, TN 37203
(615) 322-2834

Texas

University of Texas, Austin Library
Documents Collection
General Libraries, PCL 2.400
Austin, TX 78712
(512) 471-3813

Utah

University of Utah
Marriott Library
Documents Department
Salt Lake City, UT 84112
(801) 581-8394

Virginia

University of Virginia
Alderman Library
Government Documents
Charlottesville, VA 22901
(804) 924-3133

Washington

University of Washington Libraries
Government Documents Center
Seattle, WA 98195
(205) 543-1760

CANADA

Alberta

University of Alberta Library
Government Publications
Edmonton, AB T6G 2J8
(403) 432-3776

British Columbia

University of British Columbia
University Library
Government Publications
   & Microforms Division
Vancouver, BC V6T 1W5
(604) 228-2584

Manitoba

Manitoba Legislative Library
200 Vaughan St., Main Fl.
Winnipeg, MB R3C 1T5
(204) 946-7214

New Brunswick

University of New Brunswick
Harriet Irving Library
Government Documents Department
Box 7500
Fredericton, NB E3B 5H5
(506) 453-4752

Nova Scotia

Dalhousie University Library
Documents Section
Halifax, NS B3H 4H8
(902) 424-3649

Ontario

Queen's University at Kingston
Documents Library
Douglas Library
Kingston, ON K7L 5C4
(613) 547-6992

University of Ottawa
Bibliotheque Morisset
Institute for International Cooperation
65 Hastey St.
Ottawa, ON K1N 9A5
(613) 231-6892

Canadian Institute of International
   Affairs Library
15 King's College Circle
Toronto, ON M5S 2V9
(416) 979-1851

University of Toronto Library
Government Publications Division
Toronto, ON M5S 1A5
(416) 978-3931

Quebec

McGill University
McLennan Library
Government Documents Department
3459 McTavish St.
Montreal, PQ H3A 1Y1
(514) 392-4959

Universite de Montreal
Bibliotheque des sciences humaines et
   sociales periodiques
Case Postale 6202, Succursale A
Montreal, PQ H3C 3T2
(514) 343-7424

Universite Laval Bibliotheque
Services des Documents Officiels
Ste. Foy, PQ G1K 7P4
(418) 656-3343

Saskatchewan

University of Saskatchewan
Murray Memorial Library
Government Publications Department
Saskatoon, SK S7N 0W0
(306) 343-3141

APPENDIX G
REGIONAL GOVERNMENT DEPOSITORY LIBRARIES

Appendix G

Regional Government Depository Libraries

Free information from the Federal Government on a broad range of subjects is available to all Americans through the U.S. Government Printing Office Depository Library Program. Fifty regional depositories receive every unclassified Government publication of interest to the public, and have undertaken the responsibility of retaining this material permanently, in paper or microfiche format. Interlibrary loan and reference services are also porvided. A listing of regional depositories with their addresses and telephone numbers follows.

Alabama

Auburn University, Montgomery Library
Documents Department
Montgomery, AL 36193
(205) 279-9110 Ext: 253

University of Alabama Library
Reference Department/Documents
Box S
University, AL 35486
(205) 348-6046

Arizona

Arizona State Department of Library,
   Archives & Public Records
State Capitol, 3rd Fl.
1700 W. Washington
Phoenix, AZ 85007
(602) 255-4121

University of Arizona Library
Government Documents Department
Tucson, AZ 85721
(602) 621-4871

Arkansas

Arkansas State Library
Documents Service Section
One Capitol Mall
Little Rock, AR 72201
(501)371-2090

California

California State Library
Government Publications Service
Library & Courts Bldg.
914 Capitol Mall
Box 2037
Sacramento, CA 95809
(916) 322-4572

Colorado

University of Colorado, Boulder
Norlin Library
Government Publications
Campus Box 184
Boulder, CO 80309
(303) 492-8834

Denver Public Library
Government Publications Department
1357 Broadway
Denver, CO 80203
(303) 571-2131

Connecticut

Connecticut State Library
231 Capitol Ave.
Hartford, CT 06106
(203) 566-4971

Florida

University of Florida Libraries
Documents Department
Library West
Gainesville, FL 32611
(904) 392-0366

Georgia

University of Georgia Libraries
Government Documents Department
Athens, GA 30602
(404) 542-8949

1659

Appendixes

Hawaii

University of Hawaii
Hamilton Library
Government Documents Collection
2550 The Mall
Honolulu, HI 96822
(808) 948-8230

Idaho

University of Idaho Library
Documents Section
Moscow, ID 83843
(208) 885-6344

Illinois

Illinois State Library
Government Documents
Centennial Bldg.
Springfield, IL 62756
(217) 782-5012

Indiana

Indiana State Library
Serials Section
140 N. Senate Ave.
Indianapolis, IN 46204
(317) 232-3686

Iowa

University of Iowa Libraries
Government Publications Department
Iowa City, IA 52242
(319) 353-3318

Kansas

University of Kansas
Spencer Research Library
Documents Collection
Lawrence, KS 66045
(913) 864-4662

Kentucky

University of Kentucky
Margaret I. King Library
Government Publications Department
Lexington, KY 40506
(606) 257-3139

Louisiana

Louisiana State University
Troy H. Middleton Library
Government Documents Department
Baton Rouge, LA 70803
(504) 388-2570

Louisiana Tech University
Prescott Memorial Library
Documents Department
Tech Sta., Box 10408
Ruston, LA 71272
(318) 257-4962

Maine

University of Maine, Orono
Raymond H. Fogler Library
Tri-State Regional Documents Depository
Orono, ME 04469
(207) 581-1680

Maryland

University of Maryland, College Park
McKeldin Library
Documents Division
College Park, MD 20742
(301) 454-3034

Massachusetts

Boston Public Library
Government Documents Section
Copley Square
Box 286
Boston, MA 02117
(617) 536-5400 Ext: 226

Michigan

Detroit Public Library
5201 Woodward Ave.
Detroit, MI 48202
(313) 833-1409

Library of Michigan
Government Documents
735 E. Michigan Ave.
Box 30007
Lansing, MI 48909
(517) 373-0640

Minnesota

University of Minnesota
Government Publications Library
409 Wilson Library
309 19th Ave., S.
Minneapolis, MN 55455
(612) 373-7813

Mississippi

University of Mississippi
J.D. Williams Library
Documents Department
University, MS 38677
(601) 232-5857

Montana

University of Montana
Maureen & Mike Mansfield Library
Documents Department
Missoula, MT 59812
(406) 243-6700

Nebraska

Nebraska State Library Commission
Federal Documents Department
1420 P St.
Lincoln, NE 68508
(402) 471-2045

Nevada

University of Nevada, Reno Library
Government Publications Department
Reno, NV 89557
(702) 784-6579

New Jersey

Newark Public Library
U.S. Documents Division
5 Washington St.
Box 630
Newark, NJ 07101
(201) 733-7812

New Mexico

University of New Mexico
General Library
Government Publications & Maps Dept.
Albuquerque, NM 87131
(505) 277-7180

New Mexico State Library
325 Don Gaspar Ave.
Santa Fe, NM 87501
(505) 827-3800

New York

New York State Library
Documents Control
Cultural Education Center, 6th Fl.
Empire State Plaza
Albany, NY 12230
(518) 474-5563

North Carolina

University of North Carolina, Chapel Hill
Wilson Library
BA/SS Division Documents
Chapel Hill, NC 27514
(919) 962-1151

North Dakota

North Dakota State University Library
Government Documents Department
Fargo, ND 58105
(701) 237-7008

Ohio

State Library of Ohio
Documents Section
65 S. Front St.
Columbus, OH 43215
(614) 462-7051

Oklahoma

Oklahoma State Department of Libraries
Government Documents
200 N.E. 18th St.
Oklahoma City, OK 73105
(405) 521-2502

Oklahoma State University Library
Documents Department
Stillwater, OK 74078
(405) 624-6546

Oregon

Portland State University Library
Box 1151
Portland, OR 97207
(503) 229-3673

Pennsylvania

Pennsylvania State Library
Government Publications Section
Walnut St. & Commonwealth Ave.
Box 1601
Harrisburg, PA 17105
(717) 787-3752

Texas

Texas State Library
Public Services Department
1201 Brazos
Capitol Sta., Box 12927
Austin, TX 78711
(512) 475-2996

Texas Tech University Library
Documents Department
Lubbock, TX 79409
(806) 742-2268

Utah

Utah State University
Merrill Library and Learning Resources
   Center, UMC-30
Documents Department
Logan, UT 84322
(801) 750-2682

Virginia

University of Virginia
Alderman Library
Government Documents
Charlottesville, VA 22901
(804) 924-3133

Washington

Washington State Library
Documents Section
Olympia, WA 98504
(206) 753-4027

West Virginia

West Virginia University Library
Government Documents Section
Box 6069
Morgantown, WV 26506
(304) 293-3640

Wisconsin

State Historical Society of Wisconsin Library
Government Publications Section
816 State St.
Madison, WI 53706
(608) 262-4347

Milwaukee Public Library
Documents Division
814 W. Wisconsin Ave.
Milwaukee, WI 53233
(414) 278-3017

Wyoming

Wyoming State Library
Supreme Court & State Library Bldg.
Cheyenne, WY 82002
(307) 777-6344

SUBJECT INDEX

Abbreviations

(State, Province and Territory)

AL	Alabama	NB	New Brunswick
AK	Alaska	NH	New Hampshire
AB	Alberta	NJ	New Jersey
AS	American Samoa	NM	New Mexico
AZ	Arizona	NY	New York
AR	Arkansas	NF	Newfoundland
BC	British Columbia	NC	North Carolina
CA	California	ND	North Dakota
CO	Colorado	NT	Northwest Territories
CT	Connecticut	NS	Nova Scotia
DE	Delaware	OH	Ohio
DC	District of Columbia	OK	Oklahoma
FL	Florida	ON	Ontario
GA	Georgia	OR	Oregon
GU	Guam	PA	Pennsylvania
HI	Hawaii	PE	Prince Edward Island
ID	Idaho	PQ	Quebec
IL	Illinois	PR	Puerto Rico
IN	Indiana	RI	Rhode Island
IA	Iowa	SK	Saskatchewan
KS	Kansas	SC	South Carolina
KY	Kentucky	SD	South Dakota
LA	Louisiana	TN	Tennessee
ME	Maine	TX	Texas
MB	Manitoba	UT	Utah
MD	Maryland	VT	Vermont
MA	Massachusetts	VI	Virgin Islands
MI	Michigan	VA	Virginia
MN	Minnesota	WA	Washington
MS	Mississippi	WV	West Virginia
MO	Missouri	WI	Wisconsin
MT	Montana	WY	Wyoming
NE	Nebraska	YT	Yukon Territory
NV	Nevada		

SUBJECT INDEX

Entries 1-10009, Part 1 ● Entries 10010-17467, Part 2

Entries are arranged geographically under each subject. Geographic two-letter codes may be found on the opposite page.

Aeronautics (Continued)
14715; **NM** 13981, 14146; **NY** 23, 500, 501, 1326, 2069, 4539, 5535, 6245, 7307, 7756, 9253, 9547, 10856, 10857, 10928, 12530, 13976, 14387, 16141; **NC** 9773; **ND** 13924; **OH** 3071, 5138, 5384, 11523, 13251, 13970, 13983, 13984, 14496; **OK** 347, 7040, 9704, 13937, 14385; **ON** 2233, 2235, 2253, 2257, 2267, 2590, 3789, 16302; **PA** 1548, 4973, 5158, 10641, 14713; **PQ** 99, 1950, 2321, 6587, 10926; **TN** 840, 1088, 14723, 16224; **TX** 1339, 5130, 6121, 12825, 13403, 13417, 13593, 13875, 13882, 13911, 13933, 13934, 14724; **VA** 78, 106, 1010, 6498, 13980, 14131, 14495, 14500; **WA** 1545, 12375, 13074, 13916; **WI** 1496

Aeronautics, Commercial: AB 2312; **CT** 15029; **DC** 107, 14191, 14370; **NJ** 14390; **NY** 101; **PQ** 99; **TX** 346

Aeronautics—History: AL 14003; **CA** 372, 2997, 9896, 12113, 12134, 16197; **CO** 3884, 13866; **CT** 3366; **DC** 14519; **FL** 4337; **IL** 108; **IA** 114; **MA** 13871; **NM** 224; **NY** 3225, 3654, 7327; **OH** 17317; **WI** 4513

Aeronautics—Law and legislation: CA 5903, 12945, 15307; **DC** 107, 3558, 14191, 14388; **GA** 14389; **IL** 7512; **LA** 3929; **NY** 1222, 2716, 5591, 13172; **PQ** 6587, 7735

Aeronautics—Safety measures: NJ 14390; **OH** 1095; **VA** 14131

Aerosols: NM 7613

Aerospace engineering: CA 11517; **CT** 1091; **DC** 2552; **MD** 283, 3300, 10046; **MN** 15800; **OH** 15379; **OK** 15996; **PA** 12634; **TX** 7631, 16241; **VA** 6042; **WI** 16438

Aerospace medicine See: Space medicine

Africa: AB 90; **CA** 12940, 15286; **DC** 6143, 7357, 7376, 12598, 14817; **IL** 6855, 9942; **LA** 670; **MI** 2655, 8463; **NH** 10833; **NY** 87, 9546, 13179; **OH** 10111; **OK** 7212; **ON** 7087; **PQ** 3316, 15077; **SC** 8983; **WI** 16428

Africa—History: CA 1994; **IL** 9942; **PA** 13313

Africa, North: CO 508; **DC** 8488

Africa, South See: South Africa

Africa, West: MI 8464

African art See: Art, African

African Methodist Episcopal Zion Church: OH 10548, 17111

Africana: BC 12520; **CA** 1994; **DC** 6144; **IL** 2827; **MA** 1583, 1603; **NY** 86

Afro-Americans (See also Blacks): AL 141, 13207; **CA** 15344; **DC** 6143, 6144, 14519; **GA** 995, 1000, 3005; **IL** 2827, 4106, 6855; **MA** 13057; **NY** 3488, 13135; **NC** 1369; **OK** 7212; **ON** 3267; **PA** 2798, 7416, 16069; **SC** 10212; **TX** 13415; **VA** 16351; **WA** 12376

Afro-Americans in business: DC 6145

Afro-Americans—History: AL 10954, 13715; **CA** 7563; **CT** 3572, 13641; **DC** 6144; **GA** 1000, 7063; **IL** 4106, 6855; **IN** 6348, 6374; **LA** 670; **ME** 15674; **MD** 3271, 10968; **MA** 8352; **MO** 7418, 14632, 16960, 16964; **NY** 1795, 9546, 11183; **OH** 91, 10111, 17111; **PA** 1377, 2798, 7356, 13313, 16069; **TN** 4755; **TX** 1480, 7773, 13415; **VA** 14594; **WA** 12376

Afro-Americans in medicine: DC 6141; **TN** 8172

Afro-Americans in the performing arts: CA 15298; **MI** 3919; **NY** 5763

Afro-Americans—Religion: DC 6146; **GA** 1001

Afro-Americans—Social life and customs: DC 15463, 15464; **LA** 670; **MD** 10968; **NY** 9546; **PA** 16069

Aged (See also Gerontology): AZ 10775; **DC** 9114; **IN** 6357; **MS** 8647; **NJ** 9660; **ON** 2346, 3574; **OR** 10343; **WI** 7983, 15021

Agricultural chemicals: BC 16616; **CT** 13801, 16898; **MI** 1236; **MO** 8682, 14400; **NJ** 432, 4845, 10579; **NY** 12983; **OH** 10912; **PA** 11540; **TN** 5416

Agricultural economics: AB 171, 7774; **CA** 12939, 13075, 15221, 15243, 15270; **CT** 2606; **DC** 6601, 14265; **IL** 761, 2802, 3821, 6283, 15553; **IA** 10788; **MB** 15678; **MI** 8448, 15741; **MN** 15837; **OH** 694, 10108, 10136; **ON** 2112, 2190, 10263; **PQ** 2128; **SK** 2116, 12243; **TX** 16253; **WI** 16450

Agricultural engineering: AZ 14263; **CA** 2898; **IL** 15553, 15570; **MB** 15684; **MD** 14266; **MN** 15837; **MO** 15852; **NY** 96; **ON** 11431; **PA** 12865; **SK** 2133, 16154

Agricultural machinery: AL 14254; **CA** 4844; **IL** 3821, 6608; **IA** 6814, 8517; **MD** 14266; **SK** 10921, 12273; **TX** 13454

Agricultural marketing See: Produce trade

Agriculture (See also Farm management): AL 130, 13362; **AB** 2117, 2123, 2124, 4555, 7774, 10216, 15142; **AK** 15113; **AZ** 801, 15155, 15166; **BC** 15197; **CA** 2000, 2612, 4060, 12982, 12984, 13784, 13825, 14185, 15221, 15256, 15279, 15324; **CO** 3182, 5485, 14247; **CT** 3367; **DE** 4098, 15444; **DC** 3362, 5457, 6556, 14269; **FL** 15465, 15466, 15467, 15468, 15469, 15484, 15497; **GA** 19, 4913, 14259, 15501, 15502, 15508; **HI** 5798, 9708; **ID** 14258, 15550; **IL** 3791, 3821, 12776, 13240, 15553; **IN** 267, 4312, 6623, 11129; **IA** 6688; **KS** 6942, 6952; **KY** 1820, 15639; **LA** 7585, 7599, 16213, 16214; **MB** 2125, 2136, 15678; **MD** 2503, 14266; **MA** 874, 10213; **MI** 8437, 8470; **MN** 301, 2451, 4165, 4511, 4614, 8592, 15833, 15837, 15844; **MS** 8641; **MO** 636, 4585, 4762, 6929, 8682, 8745; **NE** 10228, 15881; **NV** 15900; **NB** 2119, 9359; **NH** 15911; **NJ** 432, 11624; **NY** 282, 3489, 3491, 3511, 6692, 7495, 11493, 13084, 13085, 13086, 13087, 13088, 13124; **NC** 2943, 9249, 9752, 9772, 9773, 11389; **ND** 9792, 9803; **NS** 9973; **OH** 10094, 10107, 10108; **OK** 10186; **ON** 2112, 2120, 2126, 2190, 2889, 6976, 10263, 11431, 15512, 15513, 16282; **OR** 10339, 10359; **PA** 3851, 4579, 6532, 10647, 12865; **PE** 2118; **PR** 16105; **PQ** 2129, 3292, 6474, 7450, 7739, 11164; **SC** 3035; **SD** 12715; **SK** 2131, 10921, 12243, 12274, 16745; **TN** 5416, 13342, 13364, 16217; **TX** 13373, 13378, 13426, 16874; **VT** 16603; **VA** 16651; **WA** 16796; **WI** 611, 7125, 8557, 16467, 17009; **WY** 16497

Agriculture, Cooperative: IL 6283; **ND** 9792

Agriculture—History: CA 12172; **IL** 9867, 12209, 15553; **IA** 8517; **MA** 16887; **MO** 16837, 16960; **NE** 14646; **OK** 10194; **PA** 10604; **TX** 333; **VA** 16651; **WI** 12966

Agronomy See: Agriculture

Aiken, Conrad: GA 5248; **NY** 13126

Air conditioning (See also Refrigeration): IL 11316; **KY** 290; **NJ** 6654; **NY** 2498; **PA** 1570; **WI** 6843

Air defense: NY 7511; **TX** 13994

Air Force—History See: United States Air Force—History

Air—Pollution: BC 2188; **CA** 1971, 4412, 4419, 15302; **CT** 17421; **DC** 4390, 4399, 8400; **IL** 4408; **IA** 6681; **KY** 290; **MI** 4401; **MN** 35, 8621, 15842; **MO** 4385; **NV** 15898; **NJ** 4366, 4928; **NY** 4624, 5079; **NC** 4393, 4400; **OH** 1249; **ON** 2187, 10278; **PA** 102, 4972, 10612, 10637; **TN** 14566; **TX** 13418; **UT** 9748; **WI** 17211, 17213

Air-ships (See also Balloons): CA 915, 16200; **OH** 127, 5384

Air travel: AB 2312; **CA** 111; **NY** 10482, 13602; **ON** 2315; **WA** 16781

Airplanes (See also Helicopters): AB 1960, 9915; **CA** 5127, 7460, 9675, 9895, 12113, 13804; **CT** 4004; **FL** 13894; **MD** 14796; **MO** 14141; **OH** 11523, 13983; **OK** 14385; **PA** 11460; **PQ** 1094; **TX** 13908; **WI** 4513

Airplanes—Jet propulsion: GA 11545; **NY** 5160

Airplanes—Motors: IN 1361; **MA** 5136; **NY** 1326, 4539; **OH** 5138, 13984

Antitrust law (Continued)
DC 1952, 3558, 7081, 9128, 13060, 14304, 14339, 14398, 17147; GA 297, 3089, 7065; IL 2717, 5030, 11570, 17190; MA 17108; MI 3014; MO 12489; NY 1951, 3771, 3931, 4034, 6176, 6960, 9129, 10507, 12521, 16865; OH 5137; PA 1426, 5114; TX 843; VA 6213; WI 4850, 17209

Apiculture See: Bee culture

Apollo Lunar Missions: TX 5141

Appalachia: DC 739; GA 4951; KY 1376, 7455, 8829, 14609, 15650; NC 742, 15931, 16950; TN 2507, 4180; VA 4345, 14594; WV 7998, 16934

Appliances, Electric See: Electric apparatus and appliances

Applied art See: Art industries and trade

Appraisal See: Assessment

Appropriate technology: DC 14817, 17302; GA 12286; ME 13597; MO 16808; MT 9081; OK 4172

Aquaculture: AL 1042; AK 157, 15119, 15120; AZ 15155; AR 14402; BC 15197; CA 745; CT 14551; FL 4792, 15471; HI 10062; IL 15578; ME 15672; NS 3544; OK 4414; PR 16113; RI 16126; SC 12703; SK 12254; TX 14558; VA 16646; WA 7124; WV 14405

Aquariums: CA 745; HI 15530; NY 10380

Aquatic animals: NJ 14556; SC 8167; WA 14552

Arab countries—History: CT 5688; MA 6482; NY 7273; OH 10143; UT 16329

Arbitration (See also Negotiation): DC 17295; NY 353, 1231; ON 2280

Archeology: AL 14683; AB 15219; AZ 664, 8977, 11098, 14696, 14698; BC 1734; CA 12127, 13026, 14697; CO 14661; CT 495, 17364; DC 2474, 5706, 12589; GA 3245; ID 15544; IL 15369; IA 12206, 14616, 15616; KY 10418; LA 7595; ME 4587; MB 7909; MD 11946; MA 1604, 4164, 5753, 5902, 8089, 10556; MI 3915; MO 5824, 10426, 11873, 15859, 17293; NE 14662; NJ 750, 6479, 9434, 10985; NM 8972, 12183, 12313, 14589, 14591, 14602, 14603, 14634, 15920; NY 562, 1788, 3216, 6208, 8373, 8374, 8708, 9030, 9523, 9554, 11191, 12978, 16888; OH 10048, 10127, 13539, 14666, 15382; ON 2252, 11599, 16276; PA 2487, 4906, 5006, 16058, 17039; PQ 11160; SD 10408; TN 8225; TX 11411, 13377, 13408; UT 1696; WA 12370, 16748

Archery: CO 3876

Architecture: AL 1039, 5942, 13713; AB 189, 990, 15214; AZ 804, 15150; AR 15170; BC 15193, 16336; CA 150, 722, 2044, 3735, 4467, 5282, 5321, 5506, 5848, 6957, 8004, 8348, 8782, 10034, 10526, 12760, 12932, 13720, 15239, 15288, 15289, 15290, 15312, 16186, 16866, 17259; CO 3161, 12558, 15396; CT 3565, 5689, 16898, 17359; DC 502, 2552, 3978, 6137, 7384, 9155, 9278, 12559; FL 4780, 5964, 11391, 15472, 16678; GA 5240, 5241, 10892; HI 3713; ID 15547; IL 537, 855, 2822, 5661, 6773, 9061, 10014, 10681, 10927, 13466, 15589; IN 1142, 4386, 5940, 6348, 15979; IA 3890, 12955; KS 6948, 15630; KY 12853, 15644, 15657; LA 7584, 13686, 13695; ME 10214; MB 15679; MD 4379, 6827, 15695; MA 763, 1553, 1574, 1591, 2082, 2787, 4971, 5716, 6842, 8055, 8088, 8089, 10547, 12237, 12576, 12658, 13823, 16877, 16889; MI 3570, 3902, 3912, 5293, 7257, 8450, 9899, 15734, 15749; MN 8572, 8575, 15783, 15815, 16705; MO 1894, 5847, 11888, 13145, 13230, 16800; NE 6880, 15879; NV 15905; NH 3752, 9402; NJ 9424, 10985, 10997, 11613; NM 15918, 15921, 15925; NY 25, 541, 1664, 1789, 1855, 2711, 3206, 3467, 3496, 3641, 6113, 7204, 8370, 8935, 9494, 9495, 9510, 9639, 9645, 10515, 10518, 10924, 11191, 11342, 11486, 12364, 12557, 12594, 12668, 12978, 13094, 13112, 13116, 13180, 13215, 13749, 14327, 16142, 16584, 17413; NC 9776; ND 9800; NS 13235; OH 1071, 3049, 3054, 3063, 3236, 3712, 3775, 6036, 7077, 7135, 7720, 8417, 10048, 10124, 10155, 11072, 12087, 13538, 15378; OK 1368, 6152, 16007; ON 2230, 2281, 16311, 16400, 17424; OR 503, 7350, 16013; PA 987, 2479, 2486, 4992, 10634,

Architecture (Continued)
10718, 10722, 10799, 12196, 12885, 13315, 16049, 17041; PQ 1288, 2581, 2582, 7146, 7239, 7722, 8952, 15051; RI 1815, 7050, 11045, 11397, 16125; SC 3034, 3035, 17112; TN 8213, 8223, 16564; TX 1073, 1289, 3620, 3697, 6840, 8819, 10763, 12097, 15540, 16230, 16246; VA 764, 3153, 5807, 16350, 16645, 16650, 16651; WA 13591, 16361, 16395; WI 7831, 8555, 8558, 16449

Architecture, Church See: Church architecture

Architecture and the handicapped: DC 13986; NY 6646; ON 9212; PA 5655

Architecture, Islamic: MA 5712, 8089

Architecture, Naval See: Naval architecture

Arctic regions (See also Polar regions): AB 769, 4019, 5317, 10484; AK 161, 162, 14124, 14128, 15115, 15121, 15124; CA 1302, 10063; MB 6162; NJ 5313; NY 4514; ON 2210, 2252, 2275, 5617; PQ 2198; TX 4519; VT 2621; WA 14116

Area studies: AZ 14079; CA 8780, 14129; DC 653, 14470; KS 15634; NY 13179; OH 10121; PA 4881; TX 14085; UT 16324; VT 4512; WI 472

Arid regions agriculture: AZ 15144; CA 15324; PQ 7737

Aristotle: PA 16061

Arizona: AZ 783, 784, 785, 791, 795, 797, 2520, 2640, 3525, 8707, 9295, 9860, 9861, 10779, 10780, 13915, 15150, 15152, 15168; CA 12820; TX 4306

Arkansas: AR 816, 818, 820, 821, 823, 1374, 3612, 4076, 5090, 6865, 10390, 12815, 15172, 15178

Armament: ID 15545; VT 5140

Armenia—History: DC 831; MA 832

Arms and armor: CA 14008; CT 17089; KY 14106; MA 5902; PA 10721; VA 14104

Arms control (See also Disarmament): DC 5058, 13991; MA 5703; VA 9185

Art, African: AZ 13678; CO 3869; DC 12598; IN 6383; LA 9449; MD 1156; MA 7326; NY 1787; NC 9757; OK 7212; SC 10212

Art, American: AL 1467, 8794; CA 767, 4661, 15040, 15312; CT 7680, 9357; DE 3832, 4105; DC 3481, 9154, 9155, 9156, 12588, 12590, 12611, 12612, 12613; KS 17097; KY 15657; ME 4587; MD 1156; MA 55, 1753, 3015, 9736, 16877; MI 1397, 6912; MN 8602; NJ 11613; NM 8973; NY 166, 341, 481, 766, 1787, 4509, 6985, 7977, 8942, 9037, 13105, 13737, 13776, 16584, 17090; NC 11377, 15953; OH 1922; ON 851; PA 1661, 5004, 17041; SC 3201; TN 6200, 13338; TX 857, 2510, 12096; VT 8954; WV 6207; WY 1847

Art, Ancient: CT 17361; DC 2558, 9156; KY 15657; MA 8964; NY 1788, 3216

Art and art history: AL 1467, 1469; AB 12745; AZ 10743, 13678, 15148; AR 15170; BC 16336, 16552; CA 847, 1384, 1432, 1979, 3601, 3973, 4282, 4661, 5282, 5321, 7484, 7488, 7533, 7548, 8140, 8234, 9676, 9957, 10526, 12126, 12128, 12180, 12216, 12932, 13720, 15289, 15290, 15343, 16186, 16866, 17259, 17457; CO 3161, 3869, 15396; CT 5685, 7682, 10462, 15514, 16693, 16897, 17359, 17364; DE 4105; DC 2558, 3480, 3481, 3978, 5706, 5708, 9152, 9153, 9156, 12589, 12612; FL 3637, 7458, 7869, 8405, 8960, 9954, 11438, 11439, 15725; GA 992; HI 6060, 15527; ID 1552, 15547; IL 855, 6310, 12774, 15356, 15359, 15589; IN 846, 848, 4506, 6382, 6383, 6407, 6426, 15991; IA 2574, 3763, 3890, 12535, 15601; KS 15630, 17096; KY 5813, 12853, 15647, 15657; LA 9449; ME 10887; MB 17177; MD 1156, 4379, 6828, 8027, 15696, 16719, 16760; MA 854, 858, 1387, 1575, 2787, 3015, 5088, 5712, 8055, 8963, 8964, 12576, 16877, 17069, 17276; MI 2601, 3570, 3902, 3912, 4766, 4770, 5442, 6912, 6977, 8450, 15734, 15749, 15751; MN 8572, 8574, 10807, 15784, 16705; MO 6924, 6928, 9327, 9328, 10901, 11873, 11888, 12890, 15859, 16800, 17293;

Astronomy (Continued)
11210, 11582, 11599, 16277; **PA** 4973, 10650, 11290, 13153, 13321, 16056, 16070; **PR** 3490, 16116; **PQ** 15075; **TN** 16565, 16568; **TX** 14497, 16255; **VA** 14495, 16353; **WA** 16390; **WV** 16934; **WI** 15374, 16471

Astrophysics: **BC** 2260, 2261; **CA** 1984, 2475, 4469, 5529, 12948, 14490, 15315; **CO** 1135, 9082, 14574, 15408, 15411; **CT** 17384; **DE** 15453; **DC** 2476, 14765; **HI** 15520; **IL** 64, 15364, 15587; **IN** 15982; **MA** 554, 5735, 8066, 8083, 12592, 13683; **MN** 15823; **MO** 16815; **NH** 8910; **NJ** 6479, 10977; **NY** 3228, 13796, 14491; **NC** 4119; **OH** 10118; **OK** 16006; **ON** 2266, 16277; **PQ** 15075; **TN** 16568; **WI** 15374, 16471

Atheism: **FL** 16679; **TX** 12661

Athletics: **PQ** 15066

Atlanta (GA): **GA** 993, 996

Atlantic City (NJ): **NJ** 1003

Atlases See: Maps and atlases

Atomic power: **CA** 1668, 4308, 5135, 5153, 6015; **CO** 11511; **CT** 572, 3251; **DC** 2977, 14522; **FL** 17020; **GA** 9997, 12805; **ID** 4285, 17018; **IL** 3266, 17026; **MD** 1036; **MA** 2081; **MI** 2989, 15770; **NV** 4288; **NJ** 5404, 5406, 5407, 11092, 11093; **NM** 12198, 15222; **NY** 1770, 3413, 7103, 11473; **NC** 4111; **OH** 5386, 8755, 9714; **ON** 1033, 2391; **PA** 5408, 10002, 14473, 17012; **VA** 1109, 16643; **WA** 16775

Atomic power—Law and legislation: **CA** 1303; **CT** 572; **DC** 14812; **IL** 11503; **MD** 1036; **MN** 8587; **TX** 5577

Atomic power—Security measures: **NY** 1771, 1772, 5291; **ON** 1035; **TN** 10023; **WI** 7199

Atomic transition probabilities: **DC** 14525

Atomic weapons: **CO** 13914; **DC** 5058, 14243; **NV** 11378; **NM** 7517, 12198, 14311, 15222; **PA** 9041

Auden, Wystan Hugh: **ON** 17434

Audio-visual materials: **AL** 1472; **AB** 15213, 15217; **AZ** 15160; **BC** 1723, 1737, 1885, 7211, 12279, 15189; **CA** 4028, 7549, 13881, 15240, 15289; **CO** 15395, 15397; **CT** 15424; **DC** 3979, 5457, 7379, 9152, 9158, 14516, 14517; **FL** 4828, 7652, 8406; **GA** 5237; **GU** 4779; **HI** 5778, 5786, 5791; **IL** 856, 2809, 2826, 6293, 9822, 9864; **IN** 267, 6421, 11126; **KY** 8829, 12751; **ME** 7854; **MD** 4377, 15705; **MA** 5712, 8961; **MI** 8462, 15460, 15751, 15772; **MN** 8575, 8599, 8612, 10027, 12001, 15785, 15813; **MS** 8645; **MO** 11891; **MT** 1452; **NE** 15888; **NB** 15906; **NH** 15914; **NJ** 12721; **NY** 396, 1532, 1540, 1853, 3491, 3729, 4275, 5014, 9025, 9074, 9143, 9517, 9637, 11492, 13052, 13182, 13189, 16622; **NF** 9663; **NC** 9752; **NS** 9980; **OH** 3782, 7004, 10088, 11077; **OK** 10185; **ON** 229, 6328, 8392, 10247, 12291, 16278; **OR** 10888, 10889, 16022, 16026; **PA** 2482, 4996, 7918, 10636, 10707, 10722, 11910, 14095, 16102; **PE** 10958; **PQ** 1445, 15052, 15083; **RI** 1815, 16125; **TN** 2628, 16573; **TX** 6130, 9825, 15537, 16243; **UT** 12076, 16321, 16325, 16527; **VA** 3152; **WA** 2682, 12381, 16363; **WI** 11461, 16424, 16432, 16463, 16479; **WY** 17333

Auditing (See also Accounting): **AB** 13577, 13578; **BC** 10944; **CA** 3471, 3472, 7238, 10561, 10947, 14441; **DC** 3473, 3857, 14439; **FL** 4820, 10945; **IL** 3470, 6311, 10560; **MA** 14438; **MN** 3858; **NY** 505, 3856, 10562, 10950; **ON** 2365, 3650, 10951; **PA** 3860; **PQ** 10563; **TX** 10564

Augustinians: **MD** 16799; **PA** 1058

Auroras: **CO** 17301

Austen, Jane: **NY** 1067

Australia: **DC** 1076; **NY** 1077

Australian literature: **BC** 15195

Austria: **DC** 7364; **NY** 1078

Authors: **AL** 16168; **AB** 15220; **CA** 7553, 7557, 12164, 15351,

Authors (Continued)
16041; **CO** 9286; **CT** 3370; **FL** 5964, 8409, 15495; **GA** 8489; **IL** 2825, 2826, 10014; **IN** 6364; **IA** 2573, 6685, 12963, 15619; **KY** 4197, 7607, 15658; **ME** 1625, 7865; **MA** 15714; **MI** 5071; **MN** 8585; **MS** 15845; **MO** 9460, 11889; **NV** 15905; **NH** 3753; **NJ** 9658, 10995, 11619; **NY** 3853, 5995, 13185; **OH** 10164, 11074, 16274; **ON** 9205; **TN** 16165; **TX** 15542

Autism: **AB** 218; **DC** 9254; **IN** 6379; **ME** 10783; **MA** 6990; **MN** 5299; **WA** 11802

Automatic control: **AZ** 8871; **CA** 9893; **IA** 8744; **MA** 5538; **NY** 3252; **NC** 6542; **PA** 7288; **PQ** 7749; **WI** 4237

Automation (See also Robots, Industrial): **IL** 12502; **IA** 8744; **MA** 4950; **MI** 5178, 12651, 13805; **NY** 6253; **NC** 6542; **OH** 2952; **ON** 1176; **PQ** 12499; **TX** 3297

Automobile industry and trade: **CA** 9707; **MI** 280, 1086, 2097, 3920, 5189, 8473, 8864, 8866, 9947, 12205, 13805; **NY** 5185; **PA** 11507; **WI** 16707

Automobiles: **AB** 11385; **CA** 9707, 12134; **CO** 3024, 3877; **FL** 6706; **IN** 1037; **KS** 17101; **MI** 3920, 6155, 11572; **MN** 9079; **MO** 1080; **NV** 5660; **NY** 1794, 4970; **ON** 732, 2324, 3579; **PA** 2, 4993, 13169; **SK** 12273; **VA** 371; **WA** 12375; **WI** 4138

Automobiles—History: **IN** 1507, 6424; **MI** 1085, 3920, 4771, 5863, 8865, 12565; **ON** 732; **PA** 2, 13169; **VA** 371

Automobiles—Rearview mirrors: **MI** 4032

Automobiles—Safety measures: **DC** 14538; **MI** 8867

Automotive engineering: **AZ** 5092; **CA** 92, 1084, 7562; **DC** 14538; **IL** 12779, 13657; **MD** 4378, 7809; **MA** 3526; **MI** 280, 2895, 3924, 4238, 4401, 4874, 5177, 5180, 5181, 5184, 5190, 7257, 8865, 11514, 14138; **MN** 8587, 10233, 13509; **NY** 13088; **NC** 8795; **OH** 6449; **OK** 10192; **ON** 2590; **OR** 6232; **PA** 1845, 10641, 12634; **TX** 3699; **WI** 7819

Aviation See: Aeronautics

Aviation law See: Aeronautics—Law and legislation

Aviation medicine: **AL** 13993; **FL** 14712; **GA** 14389; **NJ** 14714; **OK** 14385; **ON** 2165; **PQ** 6587

Aviation safety See: Aeronautics—Safety measures

Avocados: **CA** 15324

Babson, Roger Ward: **MA** 1110

Babylonia: **CT** 17361; **NJ** 10995

Bach, Johann Sebastian: **CA** 7349; **DC** 7380; **IL** 422; **OH** 1134

Bacon, Francis: **CA** 4954, 10742, 12133; **NS** 3676

Bacteriology (See also Microbiology): **AK** 14419; **CA** 15228; **FL** 5393, 15484; **IL** 15594; **MD** 652, 15697; **MT** 14545; **NY** 4876, 16694; **ON** 2107, 3365, 16282, 16301, 16308; **SK** 2268

Baden-Powell, Lord Robert: **ON** 1634, 1635; **TX** 1633

Bahaism: **IL** 1116

Baking: **IL** 617; **KS** 504; **MB** 2109; **NY** 3786

Ballet (See also Dancing): **MA** 5751; **NY** 9540

Ballistics: **CO** 15456; **MD** 14705

Balloons (See also Air-ships): **CA** 915; **DC** 12597; **MA** 13871

Baltic literature: **NY** 9548

Baltimore (MD): **MD** 13, 1147, 1148, 1149, 3271, 4377, 10557

Balzac, Honore de: **IL** 15373

Band music: **AL** 13660; **AR** 10390; **DC** 14486; **MD** 13588, 15703;

Biography (Continued)
ON 7088, 8386, 8388, 10383; PA 5006, 5764, 5965; PQ 11151; RI 11035; TX 5914, 12100, 13459; WA 12379, 13202

Biological chemistry: AB 2124; CA 315, 482, 546, 1312, 3108, 7253, 8269, 10004, 11308, 12072, 12465, 12938, 13177, 13196, 13612, 15227, 15228, 15295, 15306, 15324, 17464; CT 1543, 14551, 17391; DE 4087, 4103; DC 9072; FL 440, 4819, 6852; HI 15521; IL 11149, 14256, 15558; IN 11119, 11120, 15982; KS 6941, 12621; LA 7582, 13687; MD 5421, 14092; MA 1651, 4286, 5696, 5748, 7946, 8060, 8067, 8092, 17279; MI 8453, 16505; MN 13510, 15836; NH 15911; NJ 2099, 5993, 8271, 10978, 10979; NY 398, 2959, 3100, 3207, 3213, 3512, 3934, 4225, 7096, 8050, 8203, 13125, 13190, 17403; NC 1907, 11389; OH 1244, 5298, 7007, 10110, 15536; ON 2114, 2147, 16282; PA 488, 8272, 10650, 13311, 13314, 14248, 16054, 16068, 16074, 17129; PQ 6474, 12540; SK 16156; TN 10017, 16222; TX 7688, 16238, 16268, 16692; WA 14555; WI 10700, 15042

Biological control systems: GA 4350

Biological systems: VA 7044

Biology (See also Botany; Natural history; Zoology): AL 12804, 15108; AB 2124, 2169, 15130, 15214; AK 14548, 15116; BC 2192; CA 684, 1993, 7253, 7259, 12072, 12142, 12146, 12353, 12465, 12938, 12982, 15228, 15279, 15281, 15293, 15306, 15324, 15336, 15354, 16040, 16203, 17464; CO 9192, 15414; CT 15515, 16901, 17373, 17377; DE 4096; DC 2555, 5228, 9247; FL 751, 4791, 4819, 4832, 15484; GA 4354, 4395, 4641; ID 15550; IL 2799, 7173, 9944, 12367, 12785, 15364, 15557, 15599; IN 4314, 6376, 6413, 11129, 15986; KS 15633; KY 15640; LA 13694; ME 8889; MB 2125, 15689; MD 5301, 14266, 14542; MA 1614, 1651, 5696, 8092, 9009, 12575, 16880, 17279; MI 8470, 8482, 15769, 16861; MN 2455, 12334, 15787, 15834, 15837; MO 8518, 16801; NE 10228; NV 15900; NB 15909; NH 15911; NJ 1710, 8273, 10978, 11624, 12722, 14855; NM 12790; NY 59, 1774, 1794, 3207, 3489, 3644, 4876, 11186, 11193, 11499, 13002, 13092, 13124, 13190, 16135, 17403; NC 9772, 15951; NS 3683; OH 1246, 3044, 3046, 3047, 4391, 7456, 8418, 10050, 10110, 10128, 15388, 17465; OK 10186; ON 7237, 7795, 11195, 16282, 16416, 17435; OR 10891, 16029; PA 2481, 4079, 4975, 10647, 10711, 12585, 13149, 13311, 16045, 16074, 16081, 16094; PR 16116; PQ 7724, 15056, 15086; SD 12715; TN 10021, 10025, 16565; TX 7688, 12793, 13451, 16268; UT 14036; VA 16343, 16354; WA 3722, 5361, 16387, 17095; WI 1355, 7987

Biology—Classification: MI 15767; PA 10642

Biology, Freshwater See: Freshwater biology

Biology, Marine See: Marine biology

Biomass energy: AZ 15162; CO 12671; IL 6303; MI 6875; MT 9081; ON 2263; PR 2603; PQ 4883

Biomedical engineering: CA 15300; DC 9072; FL 6852; IL 13613, 13614; MD 14090, 14417; MN 13510; NH 3746; NY 5839; PA 2483; TX 6567

Biomedicine See: Medicine, Biochemic

Biometric research: DC 9072; TN 1461

Bionics: IN 8527; MD 13592; MA 3521; NY 4290; PA 4079; SK 2268

Biosciences See: Life sciences

Biotechnology See: Bionics; Human engineering

Birds: AB 2160; CA 1970, 5489, 6577, 12110; CO 3874, 14413; CT 3368, 13641, 17385; DE 3838; DC 12609; FL 8955, 14617; IL 2799, 4653, 6310, 15557; IN 4160; KS 15622; LA 9955; MB 3863; MD 1048, 1159, 3662; MA 8052, 15716; MI 6910, 6913, 8427, 15736, 15767, 17159; MN 15786; MS 8640; NJ 9057; NY 562, 1794, 3503, 3504, 12469; NC 15948; ON 2252, 7237, 16312; PA 2487, 17466; PQ 6755, 7723; SC 16174; SK 2159; TN 3636; TX 16874; WA 12375

Birds, Protection of: CA 6577

Birmingham (AL): AL 7424, 7427

Birth control: CA 15345; DC 10869, 10871; FL 4827; HI 4187, 6496; IN 10811, 10816; MD 6831, 9098; MA 12578; MI 15773; MN 10814; MO 10809; NY 3212, 6636, 10813, 10868, 13857; NC 931, 2492, 4569; OH 10812; ON 10373; PA 10815; TX 7395, 10810; WA 10870; WI 10817

Birth defects: DE 4087; MD 6987; MA 7185; NY 7933, 9563

Birth, Multiple: IL 2632

Black, Hugo La Fayette: AL 15107

Black literature See: Literature—Black authors

Black studies See: Blacks—Study and teaching

Blackfoot Indians See: Siksika Indians

Blacks (See also Afro-Americans): AL 141, 13714; AK 13895; AR 15179; CA 10038; DC 6863; GA 1000; IL 4106; MN 8580; NJ 9657; NY 86, 3488, 12978; OH 91; TN 4755; TX 10923

Blacks in art: MO 11888

Blacks—Study and teaching: AL 130, 4777; CA 15344; DC 3981, 11861; IL 6991; IN 15981; MO 5668; NJ 9660; NY 1795, 3647, 7494, 9546, 9632, 13859; NC 9752, 17189; OH 2523, 10111, 10548; ON 16407; PA 731, 4193, 7416, 13328; SC 13633; VA 5631, 16666, 16669

Blake, William: CA 15335; NY 58; TN 384

Blind (See also Braille; Talking books): AZ 4930; BC 15188; CA 10037; CO 3159, 3166; CT 3393; FL 4815; GA 5251; ID 6268; IL 4086, 6294; KY 7017; MA 10680; MI 8446; MN 8601, 8622; MO 8674; NM 9438; NY 467, 468, 3219, 5840, 6796, 9259, 9463, 9492, 9535; OH 10105; OK 10181; ON 2385; OR 10350; PA 10409; PQ 6471; VA 16663; WA 12382; WI 17215

Bloch, Ernest: CA 1505

Blood: CA 6485; ME 4931; PA 6767

Blood pressure: MD 5904

Boats and boating: CT 8999; ME 3818; MA 7950, 10430; NY 13055, 13493; TN 10431; VA 7953; WA 16374

Bogan, Louise: MA 669; OH 8420

Bonaparte, Napoleon: FL 4833; IL 3797; OH 16996; PA 4980; PQ 7727

Bonds (See also Securities; Stocks): AZ 10066; NY 1105

Book exchanges See: Exchanges, Literary and scientific

Book industries and trade (See also Publishers and publishing): BC 15204; CA 15252; IL 3797; ME 1625; MD 15706; MI 15759; NJ 4; NY 1627, 4968, 5530, 9280; OH 3068; ON 2327, 2328, 8381; PA 16097, 16098, 16100; PQ 7736; TX 16246; VA 6501

Book-plates: CA 2995, 16150; IL 8537; KY 15657; LA 13696; MN 8575; NH 3753; NY 7494, 8942; ON 11212; TX 4919

Bookbinding: CA 1559; CT 17360; DC 7383; MA 5552, 16878; NY 5530; NC 15948; NS 3678; ON 16312

Books, Condensed: NY 11284

Books—Conservation and restoration: DC 7383

Books, Illustrated See: Illustrated books

Boots and shoes—Trade and manufacture: PA 4862

Borax: CA 14150

Boston (MA): MA 1575, 1583, 1592, 1596, 1616, 3597, 8089, 8115

Botanical gardens: AL 1466; AZ 3893; CA 11246, 15229; IL 2803;

Chemistry (Continued)
12367, 12785, 12922, 12923, 12997, 13613, 14469, 15364, 15558, 15599, 16587, 17459; **IN** 1137, 1708, 1926, 4314, 6370, 6378, 6413, 6623, 8527, 11120; **IA** 666, 3486, 15602; **KS** 6941, 15633, 17103; **KY** 889, 8009, 13808, 15641; **LA** 4057, 4485, 7582, 14260; **MD** 232, 5301, 6597, 7702, 8011, 12342, 14006, 14037, 14266, 14542, 15697, 17050; **MA** 286, 668, 874, 1651, 1947, 3867, 4950, 4971, 5103, 5300, 5704, 8067, 8092, 9009, 9391, 10840, 11268, 12575, 12866, 13685, 14087, 14101, 14421, 15718, 16833, 16880, 17279, 17284; **MI** 1236, 3896, 4053, 4054, 4061, 4062, 4874, 5190, 8453, 12300, 15742, 16505, 16730, 16861; **MN** 2455, 5173, 5853, 6053, 7806, 13504, 13508, 13509, 15791; **MS** 5869; **MO** 7419, 7876, 8518, 16804; **MT** 1012; **NE** 10228, 15883; **NV** 15902; **NB** 15909; **NH** 3747, 15912; **NJ** 288, 435, 1123, 2942, 4845, 5068, 5551, 5593, 5990, 7047, 7689, 8271, 8273, 8696, 8700, 9268, 9712, 10029, 10683, 10975, 10979, 11617, 12907, 12908, 13064, 13998, 14038, 14108, 16729, 17232; **NM** 15222; **NY** 59, 282, 1100, 1234, 1774, 1794, 2770, 2941, 3022, 3213, 3512, 3644, 4228, 4232, 4362, 4876, 5144, 5168, 6258, 7103, 9547, 9966, 9996, 10592, 10655, 11186, 11193, 11476, 11499, 12637, 12983, 13002, 13092, 13101, 13109, 13125, 13190, 13237, 13763, 13765, 13793, 14315, 16135, 17047; **NC** 448, 1881, 1909, 4115, 9752, 11389, 15943; **ND** 9802, 15966; **NS** 31, 2254; **OH** 829, 1108, 1246, 2442, 2527, 2728, 2766, 4051, 4391, 4644, 5201, 7007, 7077, 7456, 7718, 8134, 8719, 8755, 9714, 10050, 10115, 10912, 11005, 11085, 12340, 12356, 13001, 13970, 13984, 15388; **OK** 9184, 10191, 10429, 10739, 15995, 17156; **ON** 1934, 1935, 1936, 2080, 2113, 2167, 2291, 2961, 4049, 4092, 4480, 7237, 7795, 7803, 10302, 11197, 13754, 16283, 16299, 16416, 16728, 17435; **OR** 10331, 10891, 14174, 16029; **PA** 104, 488, 837, 1016, 1026, 2481, 2485, 4079, 4383, 4859, 4976, 5287, 5314, 5571, 5872, 6871, 7117, 7804, 8564, 10613, 10650, 10653, 10711, 10726, 10916, 11148, 12585, 13070, 13149, 13314, 13670, 14176, 14248, 14778, 14850, 16046, 16075, 17021; **PR** 16116; **PQ** 2170, 6332, 6853, 7749, 8274, 9720, 11145, 13755, 15062, 15086, 16734; **SC** 3035, 6724, 12285, 13836; **SD** 12715, 16177; **SK** 12270, 16163; **TN** 2759, 8010, 8226, 10021, 10025, 10219, 12974, 16565; **TX** 1015, 1018, 4058, 4075, 4101, 4104, 4231, 4304, 4529, 5210, 5284, 5563, 6153, 6261, 8753, 9711, 10913, 11362, 12467, 12468, 12793, 12825, 13065, 13138, 13369, 13405, 15539, 16238, 17230; **UT** 6564, 14036; **VT** 6249, 16332; **VA** 1010, 3146, 6276, 10730, 14785, 16345, 16640, 16658, 16764; **WA** 1254, 6718, 11330, 16367, 17095; **WV** 1413, 9269, 10911, 13767, 14317; **WI** 289, 1355, 5812, 6524, 6857, 7057, 7125, 7987, 16437, 16468; **WY** 14316, 16497

Chemistry, Analytic (See also Spectrum analysis): **AB** 5650; **CA** 15295; **CT** 667, 17048; **DC** 14415; **FL** 15477; **GA** 4348; **IL** 15558; **IN** 4052, 11120, 15982; **LA** 5573; **MA** 484, 1117, 5419, 8539; **MI** 3027; **MN** 15791; **NJ** 1123; **NY** 678; **OH** 11571, 15377; **ON** 2259, 2291, 5559, 5992, 16283; **OR** 13244; **PA** 11655, 16075; **PQ** 6086; **TN** 11002; **WI** 7154, 16437

Chemistry, Food See: Food—Composition

Chemistry—History: **CA** 15295; **PA** 16048

Chemistry, Inorganic: **FL** 15477; **IL** 8857, 15558; **IN** 1946, 15982; **MD** 5421; **MO** 16804; **NY** 3213, 10055; **OH** 14468; **ON** 16283; **PA** 10918; **WI** 16437

Chemistry, Organic: **CA** 315, 4151, 13177, 13196, 15231, 15295, 17464; **CT** 7466, 10695, 13801, 16562; **FL** 12341, 15477; **GA** 4348; **IL** 129, 1286, 8857, 10917, 14256, 15558; **IN** 11120, 15982; **KY** 2588; **MD** 5421; **MA** 484, 5155, 5419, 8067, 8754; **MN** 4247, 15791; **MS** 15850; **MO** 10690, 16804; **NJ** 393, 3936, 5993, 6600, 9268, 10000, 10579, 12302, 13769; **NY** 59, 437, 1709, 3213, 4362, 5157, 9952, 10055, 10654, 12296; **NC** 1907, 2943, 8007; **OH** 886, 2509, 4341, 5387, 7633, 14468; **ON** 4090, 13799, 16283; **PA** 419, 3603, 8272, 16075, 17129; **PQ** 1101; **TN** 4223, 11002; **TX** 2584; **VA** 285, 3724; **WV** 1568; **WI** 16437

Chemistry, Textile See: Textile chemistry

Cherokee Indians: **GA** 2776, 5917; **OK** 2775, 5297, 9853, 16011

Chesapeake Bay: **MD** 2778, 8035

Chess: **CA** 7548; **CO** 3155; **NY** 1789, 9523, 14094; **NC** 7134;

Chess (Continued)
OH 3067; **PA** 5006

Chest medicine See: Medicine, Thoracic

Chesterton, Gilbert Keith: **IL** 17068; **IN** 15990; **NY** 9299; **ON** 16310; **SK** 16161

Chewing gum: **IL** 1255, 17319, 17320, 17321

Cheyenne Indians: **KS** 1418

Chicago (IL): **IL** 2808, 2812, 2815, 2817, 2825, 5953, 7169, 10013, 11551

Chicanos See: Mexican Americans

Chickasaw Indians: **MS** 14668; **OK** 10177

Child abuse: **BC** 15037; **CA** 8402; **DC** 2636, 3030, 14348; **FL** 10784; **IA** 6678; **MA** 9393; **NY** 4145; **ON** 2847; **WI** 16463

Child development: **CA** 3442, 4577, 6491, 6897, 8402, 11238, 11334, 11639; **CT** 5278; **DE** 10755; **DC** 2855; **FL** 13619, 15480; **IL** 2632, 4433, 4452, 6514, 7310, 15575; **IN** 4507, 5307, 6381; **IA** 2841; **KS** 4359; **MB** 15681; **MI** 5271, 6506; **MN** 3547, 12006, 13590; **NY** 1182, 2843, 3233, 3451, 3491, 9520; **ND** 12731; **OH** 2611, 10132; **OK** 11239; **ON** 3854, 16303; **PQ** 7729; **RI** 1639; **SC** 13633; **TN** 16570

Child psychology: **CA** 11334; **CT** 3380; **MN** 8588; **NJ** 9656; **NY** 942, 3451, 6780, 11188; **NC** 15935; **OH** 3059, 11660; **ON** 13479, 16303; **PQ** 6076, 6079, 6105, 8802, 15076; **RI** 1639; **TN** 16570

Child welfare: **BC** 1731; **CA** 16204; **CO** 3168; **CT** 3380; **DC** 599, 6854; **FL** 10784; **IL** 15035, 15371; **IN** 6414; **KY** 7023; **MA** 1578, 9393; **MS** 8647; **MO** 16813; **NY** 942, 2843, 12854; **ON** 3854; **PA** 67, 2842, 16065, 16099; **PQ** 2710; **SK** 12256; **TX** 13428

Children: **CA** 2844; **CT** 12287; **MA** 41; **NE** 4593; **NM** 7220; **NY** 9094, 14198

Children—Care and hygiene: **NJ** 6851; **NC** 2491

Children, Exceptional See: Exceptional children

Children, Gifted See: Gifted children

Children's literature (See also Story-telling): **AL** 7428, 15104; **AB** 15135, 15213; **AZ** 13679, 15158; **AR** 820; **BC** 15189, 15207; **CA** 3000, 5023, 7551, 10475, 10672, 10858, 12143, 12164, 12936, 15236, 15252, 15320, 15328, 15335; **CO** 53, 15415; **CT** 3370, 11654, 12769; **DE** 6639; **DC** 3983, 7361, 7385; **FL** 4830, 4833, 15473, 16184; **GA** 2068, 4346; **HI** 1703, 5784, 15526; **IL** 2826, 4740, 6293, 6315, 9103, 9703, 12343, 15373, 15569; **IA** 15604; **KS** 4360, 6942, 15622; **MD** 12071; **MA** 4477, 5768, 12577, 16878, 17286; **MI** 2655, 3917, 4743, 4773, 5448, 15759, 16857; **MN** 54, 3133, 7807, 11565, 15792, 15826; **MS** 16211; **MO** 9917, 11890, 14121, 15870; **NE** 3311; **NH** 15917; **NJ** 6774, 8843; **NM** 15927; **NY** 541, 1182, 1779, 2845, 4190, 7503, 9515, 9519, 10764, 11982, 13043, 13106, 13126, 13227, 16140; **NC** 741, 9754, 15949, 15955, 15956; **NS** 8896; **OH** 3061, 8420, 10122, 11073, 15443; **OK** 10187, 16004; **ON** 9199, 9202, 10275, 13559, 13560, 13562, 16415, 16882; **OR** 16030; **PA** 1510, 2478, 2788, 5005, 5828, 16098, 16626; **PR** 16108; **PQ** 7736; **RI** 16743; **SC** 1537, 17236; **SK** 16122; **TN** 13712; **TX** 3707, 5914, 6132, 10923, 13457; **WA** 2679, 2682, 15422, 16369; **WI** 16426, 16439, 16453, 16462, 16479

Children's plays—Presentation, etc.: **ON** 16312

Chilean literature: **CT** 15425

Chimes (See also Bells; Carillons): **MI** 5553

China: **AZ** 15164; **BC** 15185; **CA** 2459, 12142, 15230, 15235, 15313; **CT** 17369; **DC** 5224, 7360, 9122, 14537, 14742; **IL** 15361; **KS** 15624; **MD** 15698; **MA** 4477, 5722, 5727; **MI** 15735; **MN** 4576, 8513, 15797; **NJ** 10983, 11612; **NY** 2874, 3210, 3520, 11789, 16134; **NS** 15655; **OH** 10120; **PA** 16079; **TX** 16231

China—History: **CA** 7552; **HI** 5769; **MA** 2872; **MN** 8514

Chinese Americans: CA 2875, 7552, 15224; HI 5769; PA 2873

Chippewa Indians: MN 8598, 14637

Chiropody See: Podiatry

Chiropractic (See also Naturopathy): CA 7392, 7523, 10472, 10521; IL 9101; IA 10471; MN 9926; MO 3037, 7468; NY 9466; ON 2377; OR 17004; PA 7304; SC 12477; TX 13388

Chocolate and cocoa: NY 17047; PA 5883

Choctaw Indians: MS 14668

Choral music: IL 15585; IN 6419; KY 12753; MA 11337; MI 6566; NJ 17031; NY 10846, 16139; OH 7011, 11072; ON 10245; PA 5003; TX 3827

Christian art and symbolism: FL 11438; NJ 10980; NY 1850, 3216, 5934, 12055; OK 4747; PQ 10326

Christian education: AL 12737; AB 1206, 8918, 10922; AZ 496; CA 10438, 12112; CO 9297; DE 3966; FL 4732, 4786, 7646, 7652; GA 2517; ID 1549; IL 8812; IN 4915, 5415; KY 7016; MD 4194, 16750; MA 5389; MI 4734, 5409, 5476; MN 3962, 7648; MO 2647, 2887, 2938, 4683, 8328, 9298, 10426; NE 2890; NM 5289; NC 6063, 10758; ND 13639; OH 17172, 17234; ON 706, 10243; OR 8931; PA 375, 3961, 7192, 10708, 16538, 16853; SC 1535; SK 1687; TN 3741, 12293; TX 4671; WA 7647, 11033

Christian Reformed Church: IA 4036; MI 2075

Christian Science: CA 16909; MA 4705, 7505

Chromatographic analysis: IL 12502; MD 14151; MA 16833; NY 1100; PA 5888, 11655

Chronic diseases: NY 3103, 5358, 14952

Chumachan Indians: CA 7476, 12217

Chumash Indians See: Chumachan Indians

Church architecture: MA 421; NY 13749

Church of the Brethren: IL 1416, 2905; IN 5415; KS 7805; PA 1673, 4317, 11366; VA 1684

Church of Christ, Scientist See: Christian Science

Church of England: AB 704; BC 707; DC 4956; IL 5093; KY 4422; NY 5200; ON 702, 703, 706, 708, 16314; PQ 705

Church of God: IN 693; ND 9906; OH 17172; OR 16732

Church of Jesus Christ of Latter-Day Saints See: Mormon Church

Church of the Nazarene: MO 9298

Church of the New Jerusalem See: New Jerusalem Church

Church schools: AB 2105, 2413, 4860, 12025; BC 16994; CA 1412, 6026, 7518, 7624, 10836, 12175; CO 9297; CT 11654; DC 7964; FL 1187; IL 1063, 7626; IN 11983; IA 5422; KS 7805, 11937; MB 8240; MA 1388, 13156; MI 3150, 5443, 11311; MN 3136, 5353; MO 1186, 2644; NH 11677; NY 6108; ND 8015; OH 10085; PA 30, 1185, 8826; PQ 10933; RI 1223; SC 3187, 5061; SK 236; TN 12796; TX 333, 824, 4671, 7632, 12828; VA 4203; WV 16943

Church and state: FL 4632; MD 662; NY 525; OH 4633; PA 16627; TX 1276, 12661

Church and synagogue libraries See: Libraries, Church and synagogue

Churchill, Sir Winston Leonard Spencer: CT 17362; DC 4375; IL 15588; MO 17032; OH 11074

Cincinnati (OH): OH 2947, 2950, 5487, 8416, 11074

Cinema See: Moving-pictures

Circus: CA 7548, 15345; CT 1680; IL 6315; MA 5751; MI 3919, 4770; NJ 10998; NY 6275, 9539, 12676; OH 2962; ON 8395; PA 5008, 5976; TN 8231; TX 12099; WI 2963

Cistercians (See also Benedictines): KY 5281; MI 16981

Cities and towns—Study and teaching: CA 11247, 12144, 15302; CT 5524, 15423, 15428; DC 11248, 14165, 16513, 16515; IL 12786, 15559; KS 15621; MD 11321; MA 8088; MI 8475, 16855; MN 7914; MO 16817; NJ 10997; NY 6199; OH 15375; ON 6565, 7796, 16281; PA 5478, 13328, 16072; PQ 15051, 15090; SK 12250; VA 9732; WI 8553

Citizenship: NY 9482

Citrus fruits: CA 1102, 10858, 13075, 13076, 15279, 15324, 15335; FL 14251, 15469

City government See: Municipal government

City planning (See also Land use—Planning; Open spaces; Regional planning; Urban renewal): AB 188, 1964, 4264, 15214; AZ 804, 10750, 13676, 15150; BC 5492, 10964; CA 3735, 5319, 7558, 8004, 8399, 10317, 12114, 12223, 12760, 13022, 14332, 15239, 15246, 15288, 16186, 16205; CO 1622; CT 5679, 17359; DC 6137, 12559, 14324, 16513, 16515; FL 4822, 8412; GA 991, 8351, 14329; HI 6062; IL 2812, 8316, 9061, 9849, 12560, 12831, 15559, 16514, 17110; IN 1142, 4386, 4916, 15979; IA 12955; KS 15631; KY 7337, 15644, 15657, 15667; LA 13686; MB 15679, 17180; MD 1149, 2635, 6824, 8029, 15695; MA 1574, 1600, 5716, 14326, 14630, 17284; MI 3923, 8475, 13631, 15734; MN 1228, 8353, 8584, 15783; MO 6925, 13145, 13230; NJ 9431, 10996, 10997, 11616; NY 2981, 3206, 3493, 3496, 3641, 5875, 9494, 9570, 10516, 11014, 11016, 11259, 11320, 11342, 12978, 14327; NC 5513; NS 9979; OH 123, 2947, 3070, 3073, 8417, 9844, 10124, 15378; ON 1534, 2220, 2281, 2283, 5613, 8389, 8396, 9832, 11008, 12292, 13553, 16035, 16311; OR 7205, 10883, 16013; PA 255, 8789, 10705, 10799, 12741, 16049; PR 16109; PQ 1288, 7146, 7239, 7722, 11161, 15051; SC 3034, 4776, 5517, 17112; SK 11317; TN 7110, 9021; TX 3709, 9787, 14330, 15540, 16230; VA 4543, 16650; WA 8940, 12378, 16361, 16781; WI 2980, 16443, 16483

Civil defense: DC 14443; IL 1640; MD 9132; WI 17221

Civil engineering: AL 11609; AB 8725; BC 7715; CA 1668, 3721, 3735, 6596, 6725, 6986, 7559, 7766, 8004, 12759, 12937, 14028, 14034, 14775, 15234, 15262, 15300; CO 2901; CT 5689; DC 2552, 14103; FL 4780, 4791, 13946, 14020; GA 3717, 14031, 14033; IL 2804, 4838, 5640, 10884, 14013, 14027, 15570; IN 11125, 15983; KS 6954; KY 15654, 15660; MB 7906, 15684; MD 3718, 14705; MA 4971, 8064, 13253, 13684, 13823, 14023, 15718; MI 3924, 8456; MN 15800; MO 1894, 13145, 14029, 15852; NE 14024; NV 15899; NB 15907; NH 9408, 15915; NJ 1896, 10919, 10981; NM 13981; NY 618, 3022, 3205, 3494, 3644, 4224, 4369, 7888, 10516, 12364, 13190, 13215; NC 4110, 4122; ND 15970; NS 13235; OH 4370, 7720, 10124, 15379, 15389; OK 1368, 10191, 15996; ON 39, 2281, 2283, 2315, 11008, 11198, 16293, 16410; OR 14026, 14312; PA 1128, 2483, 4079, 10716, 13315, 14025, 14739, 16064, 16073; PQ 7749; SC 17112; SK 16154; TN 13364, 14022; TX 1018, 4522, 6123, 7465, 14015, 14016, 14035, 16241; VT 16603; WA 3722, 14032; WV 13759, 14018

Civil law: AL 8702; AB 172; CA 49, 1823, 3605, 7623, 15251; DC 11071, 14345; LA 7588, 13690; MI 3941, 8736; NY 7293; ON 2308, 10266, 12516, 16034; PA 3283, 6769, 10713; PR 2561, 6557, 11108, 16112; PQ 2723, 7735; TX 117

Civil liberty See: Liberty

Civil rights: AL 7424, 13207, 13715; AB 187, 6630; CA 1265, 1977, 8175, 8401, 10458, 12761; DC 3981, 5031, 5059, 6147, 6190, 6611, 9130, 14196, 14341, 14382, 17307; GA 3005, 7063, 12802, 15507; IN 15981; LA 670; MI 16855; MN 9232; NY 362, 522, 525, 728, 2631, 6607, 7149, 9575, 11353, 17445; OH 15098, 15392, 15442; ON 10283, 17167; PA 7157; PQ 15088; TX 16259; WI 17221

Civil service: DC 14813; NY 6526, 9473, 9560, 10239; WI 17221

Civil War (See also Confederate States of America): AL 7426, 7427,

Civil War (Continued)
8703, 8984; **AR** 816, 14673; **CA** 1460, 7411, 8140, 10056,
15345; **CO** 15458; **CT** 12074, 13641; **DC** 7384, 14519;
FL 5962; **GA** 996, 5917, 14625, 14652, 15505; **IL** 1643, 1868,
2808, 2825, 3761, 6307, 7169, 7785; **IN** 5966, 6348, 7414,
16687; **KS** 4901; **KY** 16970; **LA** 7570, 7585, 13696; **ME** 16836;
MD 12071, 14577, 14585; **MA** 1597, 8144; **MI** 7311, 8734,
15778; **MN** 8005; **MS** 16211; **MO** 3025, 6727, 8663, 11831,
15867; **NJ** 1007, 12413; **NY** 1792, 4636, 4940, 5972, 6179,
7891, 9487, 10248, 13776, 16742; **OH** 1317, 1341, 5806,
7772, 16996; **PA** 5288, 5956, 8529, 10623, 13777, 14633;
SC 12695, 14626, 16174; **TN** 7412, 12485, 12796, 14584,
14688, 14691; **TX** 5674, 5923, 6132, 6765, 11415, 11561,
14508; **VA** 2529, 3325, 4914, 5941, 11225, 12883, 13034,
13514, 13821, 14586, 14631, 14660, 14675, 14680, 16648,
16651, 16725; **WA** 13202; **WV** 7998, 14643, 14644, 16926;
WI 5431, 11219, 16489

Clarinet music: **CT** 15516

Classical literature: **CT** 17364; **DC** 2550, 5699; **IL** 15560; **MA** 5845,
10732, 17138; **MI** 3150; **MN** 15793; **NY** 3208, 13181;
OH 3068, 10117, 15382; **ON** 16314; **PA** 4193; **PQ** 4021,
12395; **TX** 16239

Classification: **MD** 15711

Clays: **GA** 13475; **NJ** 4366

Cleaning and dyeing industry: **MD** 6597

Clemens, Samuel Langhorne (Mark Twain): **CA** 3478, 7557, 15226;
CT 2648, 7972, 13031; **HI** 15529; **MO** 7971, 7973, 7974,
12964; **NY** 1857; **OH** 11074; **PA** 5005; **TX** 6132, 12085;
WI 16456

Cleveland, Grover: **NJ** 10995; **NY** 1850

Cleveland (OH): **OH** 3066, 3070

Climatology (See also Meteorology): **AB** 2143; **BC** 2141; **CO** 2901,
15406; **FL** 15724; **IL** 13947; **MB** 2139; **MD** 14492; **MO** 14565,
14702; **NH** 3747; **NJ** 13492, 14569; **NC** 14575; **NS** 2138;
ON 2140, 15512; **PQ** 2142; **TN** 14566; **UT** 9748

Clocks and watches (See also Horology): **NY** 1865; **ON** 2369;
PA 9066; **WA** 12375

Clothing and dress (See also Costume; Fashion): **CA** 16955;
IL 15575; **IN** 11124; **MA** 14101; **NY** 13609; **OH** 10132;
WA 16382

Clothing trade: **CA** 7322; **NY** 317, 6618; **OR** 1238; **VA** 6537

Club management: **DC** 3083

Coal (See also Fuel): **BC** 1732, 1740; **CO** 5568, 11527, 14454;
IL 6505, 12786, 16870; **KY** 15645, 15654; **MA** 2081; **MT** 8315,
9877; **NJ** 7128; **NY** 9577; **ND** 15969; **OH** 10096; **ON** 4017,
11440; **OR** 9331; **PA** 1487, 3398, 4948, 5296, 7067, 7117,
10612, 10640, 14176, 14850; **TN** 16221; **TX** 1558, 4840;
WV 13137, 14317, 16932; **WY** 13165, 14316

Coast Guard: **CT** 14192; **NJ** 5864; **NY** 14195; **NS** 2313

Coastal engineering: **FL** 14731, 15478; **MA** 8068; **MS** 14041;
NS 3544; **OR** 10060; **PA** 14025; **VA** 14017

Coasts: **AK** 15124; **CA** 14678; **DC** 14578; **FL** 4804, 12716, 14020;
MD 14588; **NY** 9570; **NC** 14598

Coatings, Protective See: Protective coatings

Cobalt: **ON** 4307

Coccidioidosis: **CA** 14869

Cocoa and chocolate See: Chocolate and cocoa

Coconuts: **NY** 930

Cody, William Frederick (Buffalo Bill): **CO** 1848, 3885; **WY** 1847

Coffee: **GA** 3090; **IN** 6220; **NJ** 5167

Cohan, George M.: **NY** 8958

Coinage and money: **DC** 6627, 14199; **NY** 12913; **WI** 6576

Cold regions See: Polar regions

Collective bargaining (See also Labor and laboring classes):
CA 2026; **HI** 5770; **MN** 15808; **NJ** 9421; **NY** 317, 460, 1231,
9092, 9590, 10364, 11014; **ON** 2214; **VA** 16637; **WI** 6604

Collective settlements: **IN** 6373; **ME** 13861; **OH** 3287; **PA** 10625

College fraternities See: Students' societies

Colleges See: Universities and colleges

Colloids: **ME** 4847; **MD** 17050; **MI** 34; **OH** 11005; **ON** 2259, 17350;
TN 11002

Colonial Williamsburg See: Williamsburg (VA)

Colonization: **CO** 4904; **NY** 7277

Color: **CT** 17359; **MD** 12342; **NY** 4227; **PA** 419

Colorado: **CO** 53, 895, 1620, 1621, 3154, 3155, 3156, 3158, 3160,
3173, 3531, 3882, 4896, 5494, 7170, 7442, 8982, 10767,
10790, 11050, 12184, 12768, 13618, 14113, 15417

Colorado River: **AZ** 10909; **CA** 2015

Colum, Padraic: **NY** 13093

Combustion: **CA** 3094; **DC** 14526; **IN** 5179; **MA** 9878; **TN** 3250;
TX 1945, 2584; **VA** 12327

Comic books, strips, etc.: **CA** 12150; **IA** 6688; **MI** 8472; **NY** 3254,
8956, 9685; **OH** 1632, 10138

Commerce and trade (See also Foreign trade and employment):
AL 14275; **AB** 178, 194; **AK** 14272; **AZ** 474, 14296; **BC** 1732,
15195, 16553; **CA** 1169, 7520, 7550; **CT** 5686, 14287;
DC 2721, 4516, 5029, 6751, 14201, 14305, 14398, 14475;
FL 4803, 8407, 14289; **GA** 4604, 14273, 14303; **HI** 1173,
2720, 5783; **IL** 2535, 2802, 14280; **IN** 6355; **IA** 14284;
LA 7569, 14293; **MB** 7902; **MD** 14274; **MA** 8105, 14276;
MI 14285; **MN** 14291; **MO** 6929, 14300; **NB** 9360; **NJ** 3948;
NY 4651, 6881, 9561, 14277, 14294; **NC** 14286; **NS** 3679,
5596; **OH** 14281, 14282; **OK** 10168; **ON** 2287, 2290, 2354,
2363, 4515, 6151, 8382, 10282, 17309; **OR** 10875; **PA** 14295,
14297; **PR** 14302; **PQ** 8799, 11167; **SK** 12259; **TN** 14292;
TX 12794, 14283, 14288; **UT** 14301; **VA** 11381, 14299;
WA 16378; **WV** 14278; **WI** 14290

Commercial law (See also Banking law; Bankruptcy; Business law,
etc.): **CA** 7550, 7634; **DE** 11416; **DC** 627, 6624, 14340, 16604;
MI 8531, 16976; **ON** 2163, 2348, 5378, 5379, 13488; **PQ** 2723;
RI 65

Commercial statistics: **DC** 14305; **MN** 7913; **NY** 4127; **OK** 15994

Commodity exchanges: **DC** 3263; **IL** 2802, 2810; **MN** 2451

Common law: **AL** 12089; **CA** 15278; **NB** 15908; **ON** 2308, 16034;
PR 16112; **PQ** 7735

Common Market countries See: European Economic Community
countries

Communes See: Collective settlements

Communicable diseases (See also Epidemiology; Public health):
DC 14144; **GA** 14189, 14190; **IN** 6354; **LA** 13687; **MD** 14092,
14763; **MT** 14545; **NY** 9026, 9563; **TX** 13427

Communication (See also Journalism; Mass media; Radio
broadcasting; Telecommunication; Television broadcasting):
AZ 8871; **CA** 284, 1087, 1531, 5543, 11515, 13256, 13725;
CO 8914, 15457; **CT** 1913; **DC** 7081, 14470; **FL** 4155, 4826;
GA 14134; **HI** 5799, 6495; **IL** 4439, 8870, 15564; **IN** 14135;
IA 11508; **KS** 15626; **LA** 979; **MD** 6278, 17013; **MA** 683, 4339,
5538, 6914, 11264, 16594; **MI** 12205; **MN** 15801; **MO** 9222;
NJ 959, 960, 961, 11273, 11365; **NY** 452, 963, 5148, 9495,
9547, 9631, 13227, 13721, 17088; **NC** 6242, 15949; **OH** 964;

Education (Continued)
IN 6381, 6429, 11128; IA 416, 6679, 8019, 15978; KS 6952, 15631; KY 4196, 7022, 8829, 8947, 15642; LA 7600, 9452, 9934, 12740; ME 16208; MB 1657, 3141, 7896, 7897, 15681, 17183; MD 1151, 3204, 4446, 8032, 10969, 15708; MA 1599, 1601, 1607, 1686, 2085, 4758, 6111, 7340, 8352, 9690, 15670, 17286, 17342; MI 698, 3921, 3925, 7814, 7837, 15460; MN 1052, 8586, 8588, 8608, 12006, 15799, 15813; MS 8644, 8657, 15848; MO 7418, 11896, 15870; MT 8766; NE 16854; NV 15903; NB 9361, 15050, 15906; NH 9406, 10833; NJ 6964, 9421, 9652, 9656, 9847, 12413, 12509, 13625; NM 9444; NY 86, 1182, 1532, 1540, 1795, 1852, 3113, 4583, 4626, 4873, 4875, 5306, 5659, 6652, 9520, 9529, 9536, 11070, 11488, 12975, 13085, 13095, 13103, 13106, 13108, 13112, 13118, 13183, 13227, 16140, 16694; NC 9752, 15949; ND 3940, 8015, 9797; NS 8896, 9980, 9989; OH 3072, 3246, 7004, 10113, 10122, 10123, 11075, 12430, 12970, 13543; OK 2670, 9933, 10187, 10193, 12834; ON 2408, 4189, 5303, 5612, 7179, 7236, 8710, 9751, 9828, 10250, 10258, 10275, 10276, 10573, 11201, 12289, 13552, 13719, 16292, 16411, 16417, 17415, 17427; OR 7354, 10340, 10886, 12800, 16732, 16992; PA 3004, 4994, 7132, 10628, 10643, 10646, 10796, 11356, 11558, 12487, 13308, 13329, 16096; PR 16106; PQ 2684, 2685, 3313, 3334, 7728, 11158, 11165, 15067, 15081, 15082; SC 10760, 12701; SD 3673; SK 12247, 12271, 16122, 16153; TN 10016, 16569; TX 2967, 3706, 4297, 12828, 13396, 13412, 16243; UT 16521; VT 2532, 16599; VA 239, 828, 4546, 10972, 16348; WA 2679, 2682, 12377, 16369, 16379, 16792, 16794; WV 736, 7999, 16916, 16927; WI 3469, 7830, 16426, 16427, 16462, 16488, 16490, 17216

Education—Accreditation See: Accreditation (Education)

Education, Adult See: Adult education

Education—Curricula: AL 15104; AB 4268, 15135, 15213; AZ 15160; AR 820; BC 1884, 16338; CA 1928, 2059, 5023, 7538, 10315, 10475, 12168, 12222, 12935, 15261, 16189; CO 3886; DE 15452; FL 7958, 15492, 16403; IL 2801, 9104, 15569; IN 6372, 6401, 16625; IA 15604; KY 15642; ME 7855; MB 1657, 7896, 17183; MD 8790, 15708; MA 1607, 5717, 7340, 8321, 12066, 17286; MI 698, 4206, 7814, 7837, 8503, 10041, 15772, 16857, 16979; MN 7914, 8588; MS 15848; MO 15870; NE 6966, 15888; NJ 6774, 6963; NM 4210, 15927; NY 4436, 11792, 12975, 13095, 13106, 13118, 16140; NF 9663; NC 741, 2749, 17189; OH 2956, 4441, 8318, 9051, 10122, 15443, 17150; OK 10187; ON 4487, 8398, 16411, 16882; PA 1510, 4257, 6410, 7132, 11356; PQ 7728, 11034; RI 14734; TN 16569; TX 2967, 16267; UT 12076; VA 11428; WA 2679, 16369, 16711, 16793; WI 16462, 16479, 17199, 17214; WY 17332

Education, Elementary: AB 4268; AZ 10745; CA 2602; CO 12734; CT 4191; FL 5986, 7958; GA 5237; IL 4433, 16966; IA 15604; ME 7855; MD 15708; MI 8461, 15772, 16979; MN 3307, 8608; MO 5668; NH 729; NC 9765; ON 2351, 8398, 16038; PA 10703, 11352; PQ 15087; SD 1491; TN 13712; TX 16267; WI 16479; WY 17332

Education, Experiential See: Non-formal education

Education, Higher: AL 15104; AB 170; CA 2046, 16151, 16189; CO 2563, 16968; DC 369, 426, 921, 2894, 3304, 4435, 14851; FL 4798, 15480; GA 12803; IL 15593; KY 7019; MA 9380; MI 7215, 15772, 16979; MN 8608; MO 923, 2887; NJ 2470, 4281; NY 1231, 3540, 5012, 6512, 9092, 13103, 13229; ON 16313; PQ 938, 2295, 15080; VA 10068

Education—History: AL 15104; DC 9179; IL 9103; IN 6381; MA 12065; NY 16140; ON 10258, 16292

Education, International See: International education

Education, Jewish See: Jews—Education

Education, Preschool: CA 2602, 6026, 8778, 10315, 16189; CO 12734; IL 4433; MD 15708; MN 3785; ON 16303

Education, Religious See: Religious education

Education, Rural: NM 4440

Education, Secondary: AB 4268; AK 15117; CO 12734; CT 4191; FL 7958; IL 16966; IA 15604; ME 7855; MD 15708; MI 15772,

Education, Secondary (Continued)
16979; MN 8608; NJ 2470; NC 9765; ON 2351, 8398, 16038; PA 10703, 11352; SD 1491; TX 16267; WI 16479; WY 17332

Education, Urban: MA 5717; NY 4445

Education, Year-round: CA 9123

Educational exchanges, International: NY 6512

Educational facilities See: School facilities

Educational law and legislation: MI 16979; NJ 9421

Educational media See: Teaching—Aids and devices

Educational research: AB 15133; AK 15117; CA 3445, 4577, 9123, 12822; DC 9179; FL 7958; MA 8108; MI 8461, 16979; NV 15903; ON 2408, 8397; OR 9923; PA 11356; PQ 2685; TN 8224; VT 4512; VA 16657; WI 17216

Educational technology: CO 6763; FL 4825; GA 14134; MI 15772; NJ 4281; ON 10258; VA 14140; WA 6447; WI 17216

Educational television See: Television in education

Educational tests and measurements: CA 516, 3622, 4577; DE 6639; IL 15569; IA 416; MA 1607, 4277, 4496, 5717, 6645, 9737, 17286; MI 16857, 16979; NJ 4279, 4280, 4444; NY 4875, 11792; NC 3262; ON 10258; PA 10703; VA 359; WA 16794; WI 16462

Egyptology: AZ 10743; IL 15369, 15370; LA 15929; NY 1788; PA 4084; TX 12792

Eichenberg, Fritz: CT 17360

Eisenhower, Dwight David: KS 14821; NY 3225; PA 14633

Eisenhower, Mamie Doud: IA 4295

Elastomers: MN 13506; TX 4102

Elections: CA 2983; CT 15436; DC 4601, 11350, 14839; MI 9165

Electric batteries See: Storage batteries

Electric engineering: AL 13716, 14098; AB 336, 1961, 4267, 8725; AK 15118; AZ 6050, 14119; BC 1104, 2168; CA 1668, 1983, 5899, 7559, 7766, 12122, 12197, 12529, 12758, 12937, 15262, 15300, 15350; CO 9083, 16988; CT 5129, 6711, 9724, 9845, 9960, 17397; DC 2552, 3268, 8921, 10904, 14391, 14777; FL 4155, 4791, 4793, 5397, 8873; GA 3435; HI 5795; IL 945, 1542, 3265, 4517, 4838, 6043, 6052, 8515, 15566, 15567, 15570; IN 978, 11125, 14730, 15983; KY 15654, 15660; ME 2654; MB 7906, 15684; MD 4289; MA 681, 3947, 8064, 8079, 8486, 8677, 8679, 9854, 11265, 11270, 11275, 13684, 15718, 16889; MI 4874, 7257, 7279, 8456, 17076; MN 6053, 12860, 13508, 15800; MO 1894, 13145, 15852, 16805, 16815; NV 4288, 15899; NB 15907; NH 3746, 5152, 15915; NJ 973, 1332, 1896, 11092, 11274, 12527, 14010, 14038; NM 13874; NY 1363, 3022, 3205, 3252, 3494, 3644, 4224, 5151, 5192, 5535, 6257, 7888, 9577, 10856, 12530, 13190, 16141; NC 4110, 4122; ND 15970; NS 2166, 13235; OH 4370, 10124, 15379, 15389, 17014; OK 1368, 10174, 10191, 15996; ON 39, 80, 2171, 2262, 2281, 2320, 2360, 10256, 11202, 16293, 16410, 17011; OR 5897, 10449, 10885, 14312; PA 2483, 3774, 4079, 5405, 8355, 10716, 11277, 11512, 12857, 13315, 14778, 16063, 16073, 17021; PQ 1938, 1950, 6227, 8804; SK 12268, 16154; TN 13364; TX 1018, 4522, 5574, 7465, 12825, 13397, 13403, 14015, 14088, 16241; VT 16603; VA 5146, 11213, 12861; WI 260, 4237, 8560, 10406, 12905

Electric meters: NH 5152

Electric power: AB 4267; CA 1307, 4308; CO 10823; DC 4258, 4602, 9244; FL 13212; IN 6428; MA 13024; MI 3899; MN 10389; NJ 5404; NY 7500, 10324, 11473; NC 4111; OH 3043, 13533; PA 5408; VA 16643

Electric railroads (See also Transportation): CA 539; CT 3371; IL 6292; MI 4147; NY 11235; OR 10330; PA 11237

Episcopal Church See: Protestant Episcopal Church in the U.S.A.

Erie County (NY): NY 1850

Erie County (PA): PA 8313, 10623

Erosion See: Soil conservation

Eskimos (See also Indians of North America): AK 9716, 15114; BC 15195; MB 6161, 17177; NS 3684; ON 2210, 8387; VT 2621

Esperanto: CA 4472; DC 4471; OR 16030

Essences and essential oils: NJ 3105, 6600; NY 5038

Essex County (MA): MA 4477

Estate planning: CA 1161; FL 12570; MA 17108; NY 1877, 6176; ON 5378; RI 65

Estonia: DC 7364; ON 7235

Ethics (See also Bioethics; Medical ethics; Professional ethics): CO 6282; DC 5231; IL 8137; MN 15821; NY 5759; ON 17033

Ethics, Medical See: Medical ethics

Ethnic groups—Canada: AB 2353, 13734; MB 13730; ON 8387; PQ 2295; SK 13735

Ethnic groups—United States: CA 894, 6464, 7482; GA 4913; IL 9850, 10436; LA 15929; MA 3626; MI 15765; MN 6696, 15807; NE 15893; NH 9019; NY 2616, 11189, 11190; OH 7006, 13733, 16996; OK 16012; PA 1133, 8313, 16072, 16091; TX 16232; WA 16397; WI 12967

Ethnology: AZ 5822, 14696, 14698; BC 1734; CA 12127; CO 14661; CT 6185; DC 12602, 12610; MB 7909; MA 5388, 5753, 10555; MI 3571; NE 14663; NJ 9653; NM 14602, 15920; NY 4514, 6208, 8371; PA 16058; PQ 15091; SD 1512; TN 8225

Ethnomusicology: CA 15254, 15311; CO 3880; CT 16899; DC 7359; FL 15731; IL 9943; IN 6375, 6385; MB 15686; MN 15820; NY 3224, 9464; ON 11209; TX 16236, 16244

Europe: CA 12140, 12142, 12940; DC 4494, 7373; IL 15574; MA 5698; MN 15810; MO 6655; PQ 15058

Europe, Central See: Central Europe

Europe, Eastern: CA 12940; CT 17388; DC 5224; IL 1160; MI 7808; NY 3230, 11228; OH 10091, 10121; PQ 10843

European Economic Community countries: DC 4494; MA 1579; NY 4495; PQ 15058

European literature: DC 7367; MA 5172; ON 8388

Euthanasia: IL 661

Evangelical Covenant Church: IL 4497

Evangelical Synod Church: MO 4498

Evangelical United Brethren (See also United Methodist Church): MN 13849; OH 15031; PA 13839; VA 12470

Everglades: FL 14617

Evolution: CA 6494; MA 15716; NC 15951; VA 16352

Excavation: MS 14046

Exceptional children: ME 15671; OH 11076; WI 9887

Exceptional children—Education: AL 15104; BC 1730; CA 2602, 6491, 10315; CO 1624, 6763, 12734; FL 13077, 16183; IL 6297, 8948; IN 6365; IA 5327, 15604; ME 1263, 15671; MD 15708; MA 4758, 5997, 5998, 8112, 8117; MI 7837, 8474; MO 5668; NJ 6203, 9656; NM 9172; NY 1532, 6186, 7317, 9467, 9820, 11070, 11976; OH 10105, 15096; ON 8397, 8398, 9182, 13479, 16882; OR 16992; PA 3004, 4215, 4329, 10609, 16952; PR 16111; PQ 7728, 7729, 11034, 15087; SC 12697,

Exceptional children—Education (Continued) 12698; SD 1491; TN 10552, 12767, 13712, 16569, 16570; TX 16267; VA 2677, 4434; WI 3469

Exchange programs, International See: Educational exchanges, International

Exchanges, Literary and scientific: DC 15044

Exhibitions: IL 2825; MD 15695; MA 1597, 5716

Exploration See: Voyages and travels

Explosives: CA 14801; DE 4098, 5589, 5871; DC 14152; IN 14803; MD 14737, 14769, 14795; MN 6046; NJ 13998; NM 12198; ON 1934; PA 1026; TX 6779, 8046; UT 5867; VA 14802

Factory and trade waste See: Solid waste

Fairs: CA 2054

Falconry: CO 13866

Fall River Line: MA 4565

Family (See also Stepfamily): CA 507, 1974; IL 4570, 15575; IN 11124; MN 9117; NM 13818; NY 36, 4572, 12424, 12996, 17243; NC 15963; OH 10149; ON 16578; PA 7989, 16099; PQ 2710, 12539; TX 941

Family medicine: AB 15218; CA 12294; CT 10536; IN 1138; LA 5497; ME 15910; MO 11951; NJ 6204, 6988; NY 5910; ON 3116; PA 4866; TX 16270; VA 11447; WY 16493

Family planning See: Birth control

Family violence: BC 15037; DC 2636

Far East See: East Asia

Fargo (ND): ND 9803

Farm machinery See: Agricultural machinery

Farm management (See also Agriculture): MN 4511; NY 96; VT 16603

Farms (See also Agriculture): MD 2503, 16972; NM 860

Farrell, James Thomas: OH 8420

Fashion (See also Clothing and dress; Costume): BC 15193; CA 4589, 4590, 10519, 16955; MA 8055; MN 8572; NY 3317, 4591, 8369, 10518, 10925, 13609; ON 5217; OR 1238; TX 1261, 3701

Fashion models See: Models, Fashion

Fasteners: PA 12904

Father's rights: AZ 12534; PA 2842

Fats See: Oils and fats

Faulkner, William: LA 13696, 15929; MA 12577, 17138; MS 15845; NY 14094; OH 11074, 16274

Federal government: AL 1471; CA 2530, 14510, 14511; CO 14509; CT 3383, 13722; DC 2836, 9194, 13862, 14383, 14513, 14514, 14519; FL 8408; GA 14505; IL 2817, 14506; MD 3363, 14520; MA 14502; MN 8578; MO 14507; NJ 14503; NY 11791; NS 3679; OH 3062; ON 2274, 14472; PA 14504; TX 1273, 14508; UT 16525; WA 14512; WI 17221

Federal Reserve Banks: CA 4621, 4714; DC 4623; GA 4604; IL 4607; MA 4605, 4606; MN 4613, 4614; MO 4611, 4612, 4620; NY 4616, 4617; OH 4609; PA 4608, 4618; TX 4610; VA 4619

Feminism: AL 1474; FL 9003; GA 998; IL 9945; IA 17253; MD 15707; NY 13478; PA 7104, 13316; PQ 15091; WI 16478

Fencing: MI 8471; PA 8926

Fermentation: IL 14256; MO 709; SK 2268; WI 15042

Fermi, Enrico: IL 15373

Fertilizers and manures: AL 13362; DC 4646; FL 4790; MD 14266

Festivals: FL 6599

Fetishism: MN 16892

Fiber optics: AZ 8874; MN 6641; NJ 951, 5124; NC 12501; PQ 1348

Fiberglass See: Glass fibers

Fibers (See also Cotton; Wool): CA 6919; DE 4098; MO 8745; NJ 2587, 13462; NC 9771; OH 5387; TX 8753, 16253; VA 4093

Fiedler, Arthur (American orchestra conductor): MA 1611

Field, Eugene: CO 3884; MO 4652, 12964

Fillmore, Millard: NY 1850, 13115

Films See: Moving-pictures

Filters and filtration: MA 8539; MN 4029; NY 10468

Finance (See also Banks and banking): AL 15100; AB 3020; BC 3256; CA 1239, 1300, 1975, 2438, 7776, 10525, 11643, 12192, 12943, 15308, 16188, 16885; CO 12926, 13806, 15418; CT 84, 4656, 5682, 15423, 17389; DC 14395, 14476; FL 4820; GA 993; IL 1, 2813, 4109, 6965, 11503, 12992, 15357, 15563; IN 6377; IA 15603; KS 17101; LA 13693; MB 15677; MD 50; MA 1594, 10946; MI 3910, 9070, 15459, 15756, 16976; MN 15788; NJ 4657, 5455, 9655, 10992, 11055; NM 15928; NY 548, 1184, 1232, 1791, 1807, 1851, 3017, 3232, 3663, 3807, 3951, 4030, 4031, 4063, 4067, 4695, 5164, 5356, 6699, 7048, 7054, 7263, 7429, 7502, 7778, 7810, 7923, 7948, 8320, 9521, 9638, 9642, 10239, 10432, 10464, 10465, 12392, 12454, 12455, 12927, 16145, 16548, 16710; OH 8133, 10119, 11087; ON 2173, 2174, 2176, 2348, 7813, 8382, 10569, 11602, 16297, 16414; PA 10638, 11507, 14849, 16055, 16083, 16883; PQ 3326, 3649, 4241, 7732, 11155, 11159, 13069; TX 399, 5575, 11413; VA 4544, 8691, 15033, 16131, 16347; WA 11240, 11656, 12371, 16364, 17057; WI 16473

Finance, Public: DC 8937, 13221, 14165, 14374, 16513; HI 5782; IL 8316; KY 7028; MB 7900; MA 1589; MS 15846; NJ 11616; NY 2607, 5801, 6526; OH 10104; ON 2290, 2407, 10290, 10295; PA 10602, 10603; PR 11111, 16118; RI 11396; SC 16169; TX 16259; WA 12378, 16780; WI 17221

Fine arts See: Arts

Finland: DC 7364; MN 10781

Finland—History: MI 4663; ON 7179

Finnish Americans: MI 4662; MN 15826

Finnish literature: MA 4758; ON 7235

Fire insurance See: Insurance, Fire

Firearms (See also Ordnance): AL 1473; CA 4664; CT 11340, 17089; DC 9242, 14152; KS 17101; MD 14151; OK 3770; ON 10291; TX 5923; UT 1822; WV 6207, 14643; WY 1847

Fires and fire prevention: AK 14425; AZ 5604; BC 2152; CA 3096; CT 6439, 14194; DC 14367, 14517, 14526; FL 13206; IL 6280, 6289, 6773; KY 4198; MD 9132; MA 4532, 5154, 9144, 9385; MN 11996, 15802; NY 1794, 3123, 9569; NS 4665; ON 2282, 10292; PQ 929; RI 270; WA 16375; WI 5098

Fireworks: IN 14803; PA 16048; TX 6779

Fish and fisheries (See also Salmon): AK 157, 14404, 14432, 14548, 14563, 15116, 15119; AR 14402; BC 2192, 2197; CA 745, 1970, 2050, 14561, 14562; CT 8999, 14551; FL 4809, 8325, 14020, 14559, 14560; GA 5254; IL 12457; ME 7862; MB 2193; MD 4243, 6443, 14554, 14572; MA 8093, 14553; MI 8441, 14403, 15736, 15767; MN 14411, 15786, 15839; MS 5561, 8640; MO 14400; NE 9312; NB 1024, 2191; NJ 14556; NY 561, 562, 10380, 14412; NF 2196, 3117; NC 15930; NS 1318, 2199, 3544, 3675; OK 15993; ON 2194,

Fish and fisheries (Continued)
2200; OR 3148, 10060, 10341, 10356; PA 10619, 17466; PQ 2195, 2198, 11164; RI 16126, 16130; SC 12703; SK 12254; TN 13359; TX 14558; WA 7124, 14399, 14555, 16373; WV 14405; WI 14406

Fish and game: BC 1725; CA 2050, 8818; CT 3370; DC 9242; FL 6606; GA 5254; MI 2655; NH 15917; NS 3675; PA 16100; PQ 11170; VT 559; VA 3144, 9265, 16646; WI 17210, 17211, 17213

Fisher, Dorothy Canfield: VT 16335

Fisheries See: Fish and fisheries

Fishes See: Fish and fisheries

Fishing See: Fish and game

Fitzgerald, F. Scott and Zelda: MN 12003; PA 5288

Flags: AL 411; KS 3082; MA 4760; NY 9550; PA 9145; VA 14078

Flavor: FL 12341; IL 17321; NJ 6600

Flight instrumentation See: Electronics in aeronautics

Flight safety See: Aeronautics—Safety measures

Flint (MI): MI 4774, 12565

Flood control: CA 9334, 10317, 15269, 15321; FL 4821; MS 14021, 14043; NV 14187; TN 13364; TX 14016; VA 14017, 14457

Floor coverings: NJ 3336

Florida: FL 1803, 2920, 4788, 4803, 4813, 4814, 4815, 4833, 4902, 5109, 5598, 5925, 5944, 5945, 5948, 5962, 5964, 6742, 7163, 8354, 8409, 10318, 10662, 10847, 11905, 12021, 12969, 13005, 13905, 14601, 14617, 15479, 15493, 15727, 16184, 16890

Flowers: AL 1466; IL 465; MO 8662; OH 10107; ON 2992; TN 8212

Flowers, Wild See: Wild flowers

Fluid mechanics: CA 1982, 6230, 11517, 11520, 14490; CO 3179; CT 1091, 2732; ID 4285; IN 5179; MA 8063; MN 4029, 15825; NH 3586; NJ 6459, 7755, 14569; NY 4273, 8681; OH 2769, 9726; PA 16064; TX 1876; VA 14495

Fluid power technology: ON 2590; WI 8560, 9146

Flying saucers: AZ 72, 13729, 17310; CA 9189; FL 13013; IL 9188; WV 12844

Folk art: AB 13734; CA 3566, 13658, 15322; DC 9154; HI 15527; NM 8974; NC 12771; OH 3064; PA 5976; SK 13735; TN 2628; VA 10, 3153

Folk-lore (See also Mythology): AL 8984; AZ 13679; AR 10427, 15172; CA 15298, 15320, 15322; CO 15458; DC 3990, 7358, 7359; FL 4812; HI 5790; ID 3122; IL 15571; IN 6384, 6385, 6423; KS 4899, 6934; KY 7015, 14609, 16969; LA 16212, 16213; ME 15673; MI 3917, 10043, 16858; MN 8586; MS 8016, 15845; MO 11890; NE 15893; NB 15049; NM 8974; NY 1795, 8705, 9515, 9523, 9548, 9578, 11490, 13116; NF 8204, 9670; OH 3067, 3072, 3781; ON 2252, 8394, 13562; OR 16018; PA 2478, 4999, 7067, 10601, 10604, 16047; PQ 12629; TN 2628, 4180; TX 16226, 16236, 16242; UT 1690; VA 11225

Folk music: AL 15109; AZ 15161; CA 15322; CO 3880, 15412; DC 7359; IN 6375, 6384; KY 12753, 16969; ME 15673; MN 15820; MO 12895, 15393; NY 9541, 16139; NC 15946; PA 16047; SD 499; TN 2628; WI 16457

Food: CA 8138, 12939; CT 9001; DC 7274, 13058; IL 11149, 12915, 15575; MA 8070, 15718; MI 17076; MN 4165, 15833, 15837; MO 11241; NB 9370; NJ 5163, 7431; NY 678, 4659, 6692; OH 6449, 11571, 12340, 17043; ON 2208, 16301, 17043; PR 16105; PQ 7739, 11164; WA 16373; WI 5812, 8128

Food, Chemistry of See: Food—Composition

Friends, Society of See: Society of Friends

Frontier and pioneer life: IN 9871; IA 4036; KS 2878, 12664; MT 14639; NM 15925; NY 2883; TX 2505, 4895, 13454; WI 12966

Frost, Robert: CA 12164; CT 13641; MA 669, 1605, 6872; NH 3753, 10832, 15917; NY 9635; NC 15948

Fruits and vegetables (See also Horticulture): BC 2132; CA 14264; DE 11010; FL 14251, 15466; LA 16214; NY 3511; NS 2122; ON 2135, 10262; VA 13827

Fuel (See also Coal): CA 2794; IL 6306, 6505; IN 1361; MI 8867; NJ 14715; NY 4369; OH 14496; ON 2257; PA 3398; TX 4303, 11226; VA 16643

Fuel pumps: IA 3830

Fund raising: CA 2983, 4934, 10580, 15036; CT 1649; DC 3539; GA 994; IL 15035; MA 906; NY 2620, 3029, 9080; VI 3143; VA 15034; WI 7984

Funeral rites and customs See: Undertakers and undertaking

Fur trade: AB 5317; CA 16041; MB 6161; MN 14637; MO 8663, 8665; MT 8758; NM 2506; SD 12710; WA 14628

Furnaces: OH 8504; PA 14647

Furniture: CA 4282, 10034; CT 7680; FL 16678; IL 5661; MI 3902, 5447, 5876, 6977; NC 5062; OR 1238; SC 2744

Future resources See: Forecasting

Future worlds See: Forecasting

Gaidoz, Henri: IN 6385

Gallup polls: CT 15436

Gambling: NV 15895, 16820; ON 10260

Game See: Fish and game

Games: MD 9747; NY 11181; PA 5006

Gandhi, Mohandas Karamchand (Mahatma): CA 1980; DC 6342; NY 3420

Gardening (See also Horticulture): AR 480; DC 5707; MN 8616; MS 6737; OH 5084; PA 2484; TN 8212; TX 3690; VA 13514; WA 21, 12374

Gardner, Isabella Stewart: MA 5088

Garfield, James Abram: OH 5106, 7165

Garibaldi, Giuseppe: NY 5089

Garland, Hamlin: CA 16198

Gas industry (See also Gas, Natural): CO 8690; IL 10666; MN 8591; NE 6658; NJ 11092; NY 7500, 10324; ON 2238, 10839, 13775; PA 10667; TX 4303, 7480, 13333, 13395, 13409, 13666; VA 470, 16764; WV 3194

Gas manufacture and works: IL 6505; NY 6881; ON 10839; SK 12268; VA 470

Gas, Natural: AL 12680; AB 219, 2414, 2415, 13598; BC 1104; CA 10447, 12759; DC 583, 4602, 6341; IL 5095; KY 13399; MA 2081, 3248, 6772; MI 8430; MO 10486; NE 6658; NV 2712; OH 3193, 3414; OK 6660, 9184, 10738; ON 3427, 10251; PQ 11175, 13601; TX 3195, 3826, 4303, 6743, 10166, 12808, 13606, 16536; UT 8915; VA 470; WI 17197

Gas, Natural—Law and legislation: AB 219, 15212; AR 8943; CO 16872; LA 6874; NY 1877; TX 1917, 3400, 16633; WV 3194

Gas—Research: NY 13763; OH 1249

Gas turbines: CT 1091

Gases, Liquified See: Liquified gases

Gastroenterology: CA 8291; NY 1859; OH 11723

Gay Liberation Movement See: Homosexuality

Gearing: VA 471

Gears See: Gearing

Gems: CA 5116; IL 7454; KY 5813; NY 1865; ON 2369; VA 14449

Genealogy: AL 411, 1041, 7427, 8703, 10954, 12090; AZ 791, 2926, 2928, 8707; AR 816, 3612, 5090; BC 1714; CA 2040, 2041, 2916, 2930, 2931, 2936, 3600, 4066, 5025, 7487, 7555, 7845, 10527, 10858, 12130, 12212, 12214, 12653, 12686, 13700; CO 3882, 5495, 10790, 12914, 13618; CT 1680, 3373, 3383, 4550, 5335, 5396, 5973, 6344, 7001, 8491, 9373, 9420, 12675, 13028, 13035, 16714, 16835, 17163; DE 3845, 5957; DC 3980, 7366, 7385, 9157, 9257; FL 2920, 2933, 2937, 8411, 10321, 10662, 10847, 11905, 12969; GA 995, 2776, 3559, 5118, 5239, 5249, 8489; HI 2921, 5788, 9255; ID 2935, 6264; IL 1495, 2724, 4324, 5073, 6307, 6698, 7963, 8878, 9661, 12726, 17123; IN 266, 5985, 6363, 13525, 16624, 16629, 16754, 17126; IA 1967, 5534, 6670, 6682, 12963, 17134; KS 6938, 7423, 8516, 11435, 14605; KY 4197, 4655, 7012, 7015, 9261, 10419; LA 7575, 7577, 16213; ME 394, 7856, 7865, 10214; MD 5120, 6828, 8026, 8039, 8042, 8525, 8786, 13803; MA 351, 1599, 1648, 2909, 3817, 4477, 5768, 5963, 6504, 6872, 9351, 9387, 9750, 12339, 13048; MI 2912, 2922, 2989, 3909, 4774, 5117, 5449, 7995, 8499, 9810, 10031, 16822, 16975; MN 1522, 5011, 7151, 8579, 8596, 8598, 9961; MS 7233, 8643, 16211, 16611; MO 3025, 5825, 6578, 7107, 8665, 8832, 11702, 11892; MT 2918, 5475; NE 3658, 4209, 9316, 16752; NV 2914, 2923; NB 9368, 10208; NH 32, 395, 7883, 8171, 9402, 9412, 10893, 17239; NJ 1003, 2435, 2927, 3631, 5121, 5313, 5331, 5586, 5959, 5967, 6201, 8727, 8842, 9262, 9423, 9432, 11619, 13141, 13623, 16630; NM 2908; NY 253, 1799, 1854, 2565, 2760, 2772, 3147, 3532, 4144, 4175, 4252, 4636, 5203, 5206, 6004, 6179, 6180, 6210, 7494, 7824, 9486, 9550, 9578, 9586, 10202, 10240, 11141, 11491, 11869, 12308, 12326, 12405, 16945, 16990, 17304; NF 9670; NC 2534, 2747, 8629, 9759, 13148, 16846; ND 12965, 15967; NS 17398; OH 262, 2911, 3066, 3660, 3783, 5501, 6157, 10087, 10088, 10877, 11079, 12798, 12970, 13541, 13710, 16996, 17314, 17317; OK 10178; ON 2275, 5324, 7312, 9830, 10254, 12515; OR 2915, 5119, 13512; PA 1842, 2078, 2480, 3002, 4448, 5053, 5122, 5951, 5952, 5955, 5965, 5975, 5976, 7153, 7196, 7282, 7299, 8735, 9375, 9833, 10601, 11364, 13140, 16735, 16753, 16993, 17039; PE 10960; PQ 3132, 11151, 12399; RI 11392; SC 1969, 6181, 10578, 12692; SD 12710; SK 12261; TN 2756, 7109, 8220, 13354; TX 320, 1291, 2733, 2913, 2924, 3703, 4305, 4922, 6128, 12100, 13438, 16689; UT 1702, 2917, 2929, 3303; VT 1371, 16595, 17266; VA 337, 4545, 4966, 8014, 9730, 16662, 17337; WA 2932, 2934, 7324, 12379, 12555, 13897, 17354; WV 1560, 10204, 16926; WI 6994, 8556, 8739, 8742, 11219, 12967, 16420, 16486, 16489, 16606; WY 2925

Genetic engineering: CA 4005; NY 4290; TX 7688

Genetics: CA 12072, 12938; CT 9389; DC 2474; GA 5252; IL 2862, 15557; IN 15986; ME 6734; MA 5696, 12496; MN 15836; MO 16801; MT 12488; NJ 10978; NY 3100, 3207, 4876, 9579, 13190, 17403; NC 15942, 15951; OH 10110, 17318; ON 2108; PA 13311, 16068; PQ 7724, 8800, 15057; TX 16258, 16692; VT 16334; VA 16344

Geochemistry: CA 1990, 12933; CO 15402; DC 2473; GA 15510; IL 15572; IN 6387; IA 15607; MN 15803; MO 15854; MT 8757; NJ 13254; NY 3220, 13184, 14458, 16143; OK 15997; ON 2203; WA 11518, 14579

Geodesy: DC 14242; FL 14573; MD 14572; OH 10141; ON 2184; VA 14040

Geographical names See: Names, Geographical

Geography (See also Maps and atlases): AZ 801; BC 15195; CA 15334, 15350; CT 6185; DC 3984, 7368, 9161, 14242; GA 5262; IL 7389, 11250, 12777, 12786, 15582, 16965; IN 6386; KS 15628; MI 3915; MN 7807; NH 10831; NJ 5624; NM 15926; NY 3219, 4514, 9523, 11182, 13179; OH 3066,

Geography (Continued)
13539; ON 2184, 2203, 2457, 7794, 8386, 16035, 16306, 16409, 17433; OR 7352, 16024; PA 10611, 13323; PQ 7740, 15068; TN 14723; UT 16324; WA 16377; WI 472, 16445

Geology (See also Mineralogy; Paleontology): AL 5213, 15108; AB 215, 671, 2202, 2427, 2790, 4019, 5560, 6040, 6221, 8689, 9722, 12463, 13072, 13575, 13598, 13785, 15214; AK 12665, 14173, 14336; AZ 1014, 14446, 14676, 15145, 15159, 15166; AR 8944; BC 1724, 1746, 2201, 2722, 6523, 10804, 13242, 15205; CA 1022, 1301, 1970, 1990, 2037, 2793, 2998, 3716, 3721, 4464, 4841, 5283, 5632, 7036, 7289, 8718, 10057, 10075, 11347, 12137, 12146, 12667, 12933, 13782, 13783, 13784, 14447, 15233, 15234, 15277, 15303, 15334, 15339, 15350, 16203, 16519, 17272, 17273; CO 328, 1013, 1366, 1797, 2795, 3160, 3167, 3401, 3874, 5568, 8690, 13334, 14179, 14444, 14619, 15402; CT 12305, 16901, 17374; DE 3847; DC 2473; FL 4808, 4832; GA 4354, 4641, 13475, 14031; ID 15550; IL 2799, 5640, 6306, 9937, 12923, 15364, 15572, 15599; IN 6370, 6373, 6387, 11127; IA 15607; KS 4900, 6936, 6937, 15628, 15633, 17101; KY 7020, 15643; LA 674, 7583, 12920; ME 10009; MB 7909, 15684; MD 2074, 3718, 15699; MA 5713, 8080, 12575, 15716, 16880; MI 8459, 8482, 15745, 15769, 16861, 16984; MN 2455, 8595, 12334, 15803; MS 8642, 14046, 16210; MO 7419, 8671, 15854, 15869, 16809; MT 8315, 8757, 17401; NE 15887; NV 2712, 14180, 14318, 15901; NB 9370, 15909; NH 3747, 14007; NJ 3453, 9422, 10982, 11624, 17270; NM 9437, 9442, 14460, 14600, 15222, 17027; NY 562, 1794, 1862, 3217, 9547, 9674, 10467, 13092, 13101, 13127, 13184, 14459, 16143; NF 9665; NC 9755, 15936; ND 15971; NS 31, 9982, 13235; OH 3193, 7010, 8418, 10101, 10133, 10146, 15380; OK 366, 675, 7041, 10168, 10175, 10191, 10198, 10739, 13701, 15997; ON 1705, 2203, 5354, 6335, 6336, 7237, 7795, 8393, 9862, 10286, 11203, 11440, 11599, 16285, 16416; OR 2897, 10342, 10891, 14608, 16029; PA 29, 254, 1834, 2481, 2487, 3416, 4977, 10611, 10640, 14176, 16050; PR 16116; PQ 7749, 11166, 11636, 12631, 15069, 15086; SC 12700; SD 12709; SK 12270, 16155; TN 8227, 13343, 16565; TX 672, 887, 1275, 3086, 3399, 3826, 4075, 4519, 4921, 5046, 5212, 5284, 5536, 5567, 6127, 7640, 7700, 8483, 8500, 8687, 8695, 10166, 10657, 12306, 12464, 12793, 13065, 13335, 13375, 13419, 13789, 16234, 16245, 16958; UT 16323; VA 473, 14449, 16653, 16654; WA 3722, 11518, 14462, 16387, 16779, 17095; WV 14317, 16932; WI 1355, 8559, 16446; WY 5565, 14316, 16494

Geomagnetism See: Magnetism, Terrestrial

Geophysics: AB 2427, 2790, 8689, 13785, 15214; AK 14336, 15118; AZ 12410; CA 1990, 12933, 13783, 14490, 15233, 15303, 15334, 17272; CO 1366, 2795, 3160, 3167, 9082, 15402; DC 2473, 2474, 2476; HI 5771; IL 9937, 15572; IN 6387; IA 15607; MD 14572; MA 554, 1584, 8072, 12592; MN 15803; MO 16809; MT 8757; NJ 10982; NY 3217, 3220, 13184; NC 15936; OH 2504, 15390; OK 10175, 15997; ON 2181, 2203, 16287; PQ 12631; TX 1018, 2792, 3399, 4519, 8500, 8687, 10657, 12464, 13065, 13335, 16245, 16249, 16958; WA 12435, 16387; WI 16446; WY 16494

George, Henry: CA 5219

Georgia: GA 995, 996, 2068, 2776, 3559, 5234, 5236, 5238, 5239, 5249, 5250, 5251, 5255, 5259, 5260, 5262, 5917, 7139, 7620, 8489, 14625, 14652, 15503, 15505, 15506, 15507, 16914

Geothermal resources: AK 15118; CA 5268, 5269, 11347, 13600; CO 15456; OR 10885; TX 11226; UT 13366

Geriatrics (See also Gerontology): AL 14862; AB 4265, 5376; BC 1729, 16616, 16617; FL 1270; IL 8245; MN 10027; NJ 1381; NY 3103, 8363, 8731, 12358, 14952, 14961, 17409; ON 3574, 11972, 12018; PA 4534, 4864, 10717; PQ 2694, 2697; SD 14990; WA 16782; WI 11495

German Americans: CO 3180, 5495; IL 15577; KS 4319; PA 4980, 5273, 7282, 8926; VA 4203; WI 8549

German language: ON 10257

German literature: CA 5340; CT 15425; GA 5338; IL 5337, 15373; MB 5274; MD 6830; MA 5339; NY 5336; ON 5342, 5343; PA 5273; PQ 5341

Germany: CA 5340; DC 7364; GA 5338; MA 5339, 5698; NY 5272; ON 5342

Germany—History: CA 5340, 15335; GA 5338; MA 5339; NY 247, 5336, 13118; NC 2516; ON 5342; PA 5273; PQ 5341

Gerontology (See also Aged): AZ 10775; BC 16616; CA 507, 894, 4013, 12220, 14874, 16190; CO 1405; CT 3379, 5681; DC 367, 515, 920, 3986, 9119, 14196, 14886; FL 14889; IL 15035, 15598; MD 410, 9174; MA 1608, 3656; MI 6506, 6507, 15774; MN 14934; NE 7838; NH 3745; NJ 1381; NY 3233, 6581, 8050, 8363, 11550; OH 15384; ON 12043; PA 4973, 5471, 10714, 10717, 16099; PQ 2697, 6078, 7848; RI 11402; SK 4315, 12688; TN 4179, 13340; TX 9825; VA 5498, 9044, 9162; WA 16782; WV 16924; WI 16464

Gershwin, George and Ira: NY 8958; TN 4755

Gifted children (See also Exceptional children): CO 3886; ME 15671; OH 9052, 11076; RI 9150; VA 4434; WA 16369

Gilbert and Sullivan: NY 5196

Girl Scouts: GA 5305; NY 5306

Girls: IN 5307

Glaciology: AB 295, 769; AK 15118; CO 15406, 17297; MT 14635; OH 10133

Glass: CA 5506; LA 9449; NJ 17071; NY 1262, 3523, 9556; OH 733, 5837, 7343, 7344, 10416, 13542; PA 10916; VA 2896; WV 6207, 10076

Glass fibers: PA 10914

Glass manufacture: MA 8092; NY 3522, 13465; OH 686, 5149, 10415; ON 4020; PA 1756

Glass painting and staining: PA 4992, 17128

Glass, Pressed See: Pressed glass

Gliding and soaring: NY 9253

Goethe, Johann Wolfgang von: CT 17362; DC 12350; IL 15373; NY 5336

Gogarty, Oliver St. John: PA 1840

Gold: NY 5344

Gold Rush (California): CA 2037, 12226, 16884

Gold Rush (Klondike): WA 16396; YT 17450

Golf: CA 2988; KS 5360; NJ 14463

Gore, Christopher: MA 5390

Goudy, Frederic William: CT 2648; DC 7385; NY 11477

Government See: Federal government; Municipal government; Political science; State and provincial government

Governors (Machinery): IL 17274

Graham, Billy: IL 17066; KY 12752; MN 5427

Grain: AB 2117; CA 14264; IL 761; KS 6943, 6944; MB 2109, 13828; MN 2451, 15836; NY 6712; ON 2126; PE 2118; PQ 2128, 6435; SK 2133

Grain—Harvesting: KS 6943

Grain—Milling: KS 6944

Grand Canyon: AZ 9861, 14636

Grant, Ulysses Simpson: IL 12778

Grants See: Subsidies

Graphic arts (See also Lithography; Photography; Printing):

Health insurance See: Insurance, Health

Health—Law and legislation: **CA** 12220; **DC** 14843; **GA** 297; **MD** 14418; **MA** 622; **MN** 8600; **MO** 11903; **PA** 6090

Health maintenance organizations (HMO) (See also Group medical practice): **CO** 8159; **DC** 5532; **NY** 9471; **OR** 6892

Health manpower See: Medical personnel

Health services administration: **AB** 15138; **CA** 6899; **CO** 3873; **DC** 6145, 13041; **HI** 15523; **IL** 3295; **MB** 7905; **MD** 6834, 14776; **MA** 8090, 8110, 14323; **MN** 8611; **MS** 15850; **NJ** 5819, 15723; **NY** 6198; **OH** 2608, 7046, 10161; **ON** 2204; **PA** 1923, 4863, 13224; **PE** 10961; **PQ** 15054; **TN** 8172; **TX** 13992; **VA** 939; **WI** 16435, 17201

Hearing and deafness: **AB** 217; **AZ** 10744; **CA** 2024, 6114, 6115, 10037; **CO** 3159, 15414; **CT** 9927; **DC** 238, 5074, 5075, 13884; **FL** 4796; **IL** 6293; **IN** 6365; **KS** 6518; **KY** 7018; **MN** 580; **MO** 2650, 11881, 16819; **NY** 467, 5840, 7341, 9535, 11478, 11480, 11976; **OH** 3048; **ON** 2361, 16406; **OR** 4489, 10350, 10351; **PA** 4530; **PQ** 6541, 7752, 15054; **TN** 8232; **WA** 16792; **WI** 5098, 17203

Heart—Diseases: **AB** 202; **FL** 8413; **MI** 14932; **NJ** 3810; **NY** 11749; **TX** 478, 13427

Heat engineering: **MA** 4152; **OH** 8504; **ON** 2265, 12448

Heat transfer See: Heat transmission

Heat transmission: **CA** 5091; **ID** 4285; **PA** 16064; **WI** 17442

Heating: **NJ** 6654; **NY** 2498; **OH** 8504; **WI** 6843

Heavy particles (Nuclear physics) (See also Particles (Nuclear physics)): **TN** 10018

Hebraica See: Jewish literature

Hebrew language: **DC** 7357; **MD** 16750; **TX** 12792

Helicopters: **CA** 6174, 14008; **CT** 15030; **FL** 11309; **MD** 13723; **MO** 14141; **PA** 1548; **TX** 1339; **VA** 479, 14131

Hematology (See also Blood): **CA** 13612; **IN** 4052; **ON** 27, 10244; **TN** 16222; **TX** 16692

Hemingway, Ernest: **CA** 1442, 15340; **IL** 10014; **MA** 12577, 14826; **OH** 11074

Henry, O. See: Porter, William Sidney (O. Henry)

Heraldry: **AL** 411; **CA** 3600, 5582; **CO** 3882; **DC** 3980, 7366; **FL** 8411, 10321; **GA** 8489; **IN** 266; **MA** 1599, 4760, 6504, 8964; **MI** 5449; **MO** 11892; **NM** 2908; **NY** 1854, 9550, 9586; **OH** 3066; **TX** 3703; **VA** 14078

Herbicides (See also Pesticides): **IL** 16587; **SK** 2127

Herpetology See: Reptiles

Hibernation: **MD** 6609

High energy physics See: Nuclear physics

High temperatures: **CA** 12672; **IN** 13757; **OH** 13766

Higher education See: Education, Higher

Highway engineering (See also Traffic engineering): **AB** 195; **AK** 160; **CA** 1084, 2030, 2031, 2033, 2035, 16959; **CO** 3171; **DC** 9039, 14370; **IL** 3013; **IN** 6359; **IA** 6680; **MD** 8040; **MA** 8115; **MI** 8443; **MN** 8615; **NH** 9408; **NY** 9568; **ON** 10294, 11462; **OR** 10346; **SK** 12250; **TN** 13348; **TX** 2511, 16237; **VA** 5807; **WA** 16781; **WV** 16929

Highway law: **DC** 14393

Highway safety See: Traffic safety

Hindu literature: **CA** 1029, 1980, 15265; **NY** 16134

Historic buildings—Conservation and restoration: **AB** 203; **AZ** 15150; **AR** 823; **BC** 1734; **CA** 1977, 5319; **DC** 9278; **FL** 5944; **GA** 14649; **IN** 5940; **KY** 6761, 15644; **LA** 7584, 13686; **MD** 5622; **MA** 2082, 2787; **MI** 9899; **NE** 4015; **NY** 1832, 7204, 8935, 9570, 9596; **ND** 12965; **OH** 1628, 8416; **OR** 10883, 16013; **PA** 4448; **TX** 12094; **VA** 16644; **WA** 6758; **WI** 5947

Historic sites (See also Monuments): **DC** 14629; **KS** 14622; **KY** 14581; **MD** 14585; **MA** 14658, 14684, 14686; **MO** 16837; **MT** 14592, 14639; **NJ** 14615; **NY** 9555, 10200, 12405, 14682; **NC** 14599, 14664; **ON** 2270; **PA** 14583, 14624, 14647; **TN** 14584, 14691; **TX** 14620; **VA** 14587, 14675; **WA** 14628; **WY** 14621

Historical society libraries: **AK** 2869, 3483, 13550, 16534; **AZ** 783, 784, 2520, 10780, 12437; **AR** 1374, 4076, 5090; **BC** 7115; **CA** 497, 982, 1976, 1977, 2755, 2875, 3828, 4066, 4299, 5019, 5086, 5838, 5960, 7164, 7818, 7941, 8779, 8822, 9010, 9340, 10466, 10522, 11443, 12107, 12124, 12125, 12214, 12226, 12232, 12517, 12545, 16590, 16715; **CO** 895, 1620, 3156, 11050, 11529, 12184; **CT** 2430, 3078, 3102, 3373, 3728, 3742, 4550, 5396, 5973, 7435, 7682, 7829, 7917, 8491, 9373, 9420, 9435, 11525, 12074, 12522, 12675, 12917, 13028, 13035, 13571, 16714, 16864, 17054, 17163, 17164, 17168; **DE** 5957; **DC** 3196; **FL** 4788, 4902, 5598, 5925, 5948, 5962, 7163, 10662, 10847, 11690, 11905, 12021; **GA** 996, 2776, 5234, 5239, 7620; **HI** 5796, 8123; **ID** 1557, 6264, 6265, 7223, 16512; **IL** 1065, 1868, 2808, 3104, 3891, 4504, 5051, 5326, 5912, 5968, 6307, 6922, 6979, 7785, 7825, 7963, 8878, 10077, 10669, 13164, 16561, 16839, 17123; **IN** 261, 1225, 1494, 4173, 5052, 5625, 5860, 5966, 5985, 6348, 6350, 7993, 9871, 11140, 13525, 16623, 16754; **IA** 318, 2573, 2774, 12963; **KS** 1918, 3008, 4319, 4901, 6938, 7423, 8516, 11436, 13481, 17155, 17325; **KY** 5678, 7015, 7823; **ME** 700, 2090, 3818, 7856, 10214, 10575, 16836; **MD** 6797, 8026, 8786, 13852; **MA** 696, 888, 1316, 1433, 1648, 2432, 2763, 2786, 3817, 4035, 4124, 4565, 4568, 4756, 5963, 7339, 7684, 7871, 7885, 7932, 8061, 8142, 8144, 9036, 9750, 9835, 9836, 10205, 10206, 10553, 10769, 11214, 12204, 12339, 15669, 17282; **MI** 1266, 3861, 4663, 4961, 6109, 7311, 7981, 7995, 8045, 8499, 8734, 9899, 10031, 16852; **MN** 717, 1522, 1811, 2518, 3026, 3456, 3537, 3610, 3671, 5011, 5377, 5461, 5854, 6084, 6701, 6921, 7114, 7151, 7270, 8005, 8596, 8597, 8598, 8599, 9701, 9734, 9840, 10224, 10388, 10781, 10866, 11242, 11409, 12795, 12818, 16761, 16906; **MS** 16611; **MO** 1047, 1524, 3101, 5824, 6727, 6845, 8663, 8664, 8832, 11702; **MT** 2521, 8758; **NE** 45, 3658, 4015, 9313, 9314, 9315, 9316, 9317, 12476, 16752; **NV** 9342; **NH** 8171, 9399, 9402, 10686, 12070, 17239; **NJ** 1007, 1379, 1878, 2088, 2435, 3576, 3631, 5331, 5586, 5967, 6201, 7836, 8727, 8843, 9235, 9423, 9455, 10003, 10530, 12059, 12896, 13141, 16906, 17254; **NY** 61, 1064, 1799, 1850, 2565, 2760, 2772, 3189, 3532, 3932, 4190, 4252, 4474, 4636, 4940, 5206, 5503, 5958, 5961, 5969, 5970, 5972, 6179, 6210, 6757, 6862, 7269, 7494, 7824, 8490, 8708, 8785, 9236, 9487, 9696, 10202, 10236, 10248, 10382, 10425, 11141, 11341, 11475, 11547, 11869, 12233, 12297, 12308, 12325, 12326, 12407, 12469, 12614, 12676, 12813, 12976, 12987, 13053, 13524, 16742, 16832, 16850, 16945, 17412; **NC** 13148, 17352; **ND** 12965, 12991; **NS** 17398; **OH** 262, 2950, 3007, 5106, 5479, 6157, 7165, 7186, 7508, 10088, 10089, 10584, 10877, 13209, 16736, 16996, 17254, 17314, 17324; **OK** 2347, 10176, 10178, 13702; **ON** 7312, 11698, 16831; **OR** 3191, 6877, 10330, 10334, 12799; **PA** 46, 1842, 2078, 2091, 2783, 3002, 3190, 3530, 3581, 3630, 3833, 4448, 5053, 5276, 5502, 5766, 5951, 5952, 5954, 5955, 5956, 5965, 5975, 5976, 7153, 7193, 7196, 7282, 7299, 8257, 8521, 8735, 8933, 9692, 9833, 10215, 10601, 10620, 10621, 10622, 10623, 10624, 10625, 10626, 10627, 10718, 10932, 11232, 12486, 12620, 13140, 13773, 16539, 16735, 16753, 17039, 17329; **PQ** 1758, 7437, 8637, 12628, 12629; **RI** 1706, 9677, 10691, 11392, 11394; **SC** 3674, 3743, 12692; **TN** 3970, 11526, 16918; **TX** 3695, 6765, 13372, 13386; **UT** 16522; **VT** 2531, 16595, 17266; **VA** 4966, 5677, 11465, 11497, 12883, 16635, 16645; **WA** 4217, 5971, 6758, 7089, 7324, 12555, 16784, 17082; **WV** 5500, 10204; **WI** 4041, 6994, 8549, 8739, 11219, 11441, 11496, 12281, 12422, 12967, 16841; **WY** 17042

History: **AL** 1041; **AB** 15129, 15137, 15219; **AR** 15179; **BC** 10559, 15195, 16555; **CA** 11, 2041, 2054, 2595, 7487, 7555, 10038, 11786, 16150; **CT** 5687, 17362, 17364; **DC** 3984, 4851, 6833, 7367, 14368; **GA** 5248; **HI** 5788; **ID** 15551; **IL** 2820, 5953,

History (Continued)
6285, 7172, 9661, 15560, 15574; **KS** 15622; **KY** 8829, 14000; **MD** 4382; **MA** 1599, 5724, 11835, 14193; **MI** 3915, 8466; **MN** 7807, 8579, 12005, 15810, 15829; **MO** 9918, 11882; **NJ** 4077, 6479, 10995; **NM** 15920; **NY** 1792, 1854, 3208, 3209, 3225, 5196, 9523, 9530, 9583, 9688, 11182, 11489, 13179, 17356; **NC** 4117; **OH** 3066, 10131, 11079, 13539, 17440; **ON** 8386; **OR** 7352; **PA** 4257, 5006; **PQ** 15077; **RI** 11035; **SC** 2744, 14120; **TX** 3706, 12100, 13459; **UT** 1697, 16324; **WI** 7983

History of medicine See: Medicine—History

History, Military See: Military history

Hitler, Adolf: DC 6622, 7385

Hockey: MN 14466; **ON** 5987

Holmes, Sherlock (See also Doyle, Sir Arthur Conan): CA 12150, 12164; **IL** 6285; **MN** 15829; **NM** 1801; **NC** 15948; **ON** 8388

Holocaust, Jewish: CA 6016, 6787; **DC** 13306; **FL** 2639; **IL** 3360, 5829; **MI** 13296; **MN** 6789, 8581; **MO** 1757; **NE** 6795; **NJ** 1404, 4167, 13285, 13305; **NY** 523, 528, 1533, 1870, 2610, 6804, 10498, 13265, 13266, 13277, 17410; **OH** 1529, 3039, 17227; **ON** 7228; **PA** 5642; **PQ** 6807; **RI** 13271; **TN** 6785; **WA** 13280

Home delivery of books See: Direct delivery of books

Home economics: AB 15142; **CT** 3384; **FL** 4832; **GA** 19, 4913, 15508; **IL** 15575; **IN** 11124; **KS** 6942; **MN** 15837; **NE** 15881; **NB** 15906; **NJ** 1320, 2099; **NY** 11193, 11493; **NS** 8896; **OH** 10132; **OK** 10186; **ON** 6976; **PA** 6410; **SK** 16163; **WI** 7832, 16467, 16490

Homeopathy: AZ 413; **CA** 15342; **NY** 8498; **OH** 6217; **PA** 5590; **PQ** 7748

Homestead law: CA 4163; **NE** 14646

Homesteading See: Homestead law

Homosexuality (See also Lesbianism): AL 7190; **CA** 2007, 6041, 6478, 10234; **DC** 9130; **FL** 9003; **MD** 300; **MA** 1759; **NY** 2904, 5100, 6607; **ON** 2358; **PA** 5101; **TX** 6233; **WI** 16478

Hoover, Herbert: CA 2997; **IA** 14825

Hopi Indians: AZ 8977; **KS** 1418

Hopkins, Gerard Manley: WA 5361

Hops: OR 10355

Horology (See also Clocks and watches): CT 408; **GA** 5236; **OH** 657; **PA** 9066

Horse-drawn vehicles: NY 8985

Horse-racing: CA 1995; **KY** 6968; **NV** 15895; **NY** 6813, 13659; **ON** 2410, 2412

Horses: AZ 746; **CA** 1995, 2045, 2066; **CO** 747; **CT** 15425; **KY** 6968; **MN** 15833; **MO** 1047; **NV** 15900; **NY** 3491, 6813, 13088, 13659; **ON** 2410, 2412, 6194; **PA** 16059, 16066; **TX** 642, 10478; **VA** 660, 9265; **WI** 7183

Horticulture (See also Organic gardening): AL 1466; **AB** 2117, 2124; **BC** 2132; **CA** 7524, 11246, 12211, 13044, 15229, 15324; **CO** 3182, 3870, 6087; **DC** 5707, 14501; **FL** 4541, 15467, 15468, 15483, 15484, 15497; **GA** 996, 4641; **ID** 884; **IL** 2803, 8855, 15553; **IN** 11129; **KY** 15639; **LA** 603, 16214; **MD** 3662, 5937; **MA** 5695, 6842, 17228; **MI** 3901, 15762; **MN** 8624, 15811, 15837, 15844; **MO** 8662, 8704; **NY** 1778, 3492, 5085, 5911, 6088, 7495, 9465, 10820, 13087, 16138; **NF** 2130; **NC** 15942; **ND** 9801; **OH** 3772, 5084, 6000, 7076, 10108, 12344; **ON** 2126, 2135, 2992, 6194, 9698, 10262, 16282; **PA** 2484, 3851, 7504, 10605, 13308, 13322, 16057; **SC** 1767; **TN** 4003, 8212, 13339, 16218; **TX** 3690; **VA** 489, 9727, 16344, 16665; **WA** 11408; **WI** 5098

Hosiery: NC 9054

Hospital libraries (See also Hospitals—Administration; Medicine; Nursing; Surgery, etc.):

AL 1196, 1197, 1202, 2497, 4531, 6032, 6732, 9715, 9837, 11041, 12048, 12719, 12729, 15101

AB 1962, 2106, 4265, 6019, 8569, 8635, 11178, 11580, 12083, 16697

AZ 5375, 7078, 7938, 8327, 10746, 10747, 11838, 11848, 11925, 11953, 12351, 13677

AR 813, 12045, 12846, 15177

BC 1883, 7430, 11594, 15186, 15192, 15203, 16615, 16617

CA 298, 680, 1213, 1267, 1798, 1866, 1978, 2579, 2638, 2850, 2851, 2859, 3279, 3280, 3535, 3733, 3734, 3767, 4012, 4024, 4065, 4296, 4333, 4468, 5020, 5310, 5318, 5369, 5881, 5982, 6010, 6012, 6022, 6095, 6212, 6430, 6818, 6891, 6897, 6898, 6899, 6900, 6901, 6902, 6903, 6905, 6906, 7039, 7231, 7483, 7528, 7529, 7531, 7535, 7539, 7943, 8187, 8198, 8255, 8288, 8291, 8323, 8912, 9890, 10369, 10377, 10444, 10495, 10583, 10859, 11245, 11446, 11695, 11745, 11754, 11755, 11775, 11780, 11801, 11826, 11849, 11866, 11907, 11919, 11942, 11963, 12047, 12093, 12105, 12109, 12156, 12169, 12176, 12193, 12224, 12228, 12418, 12442, 12506, 12762, 13570, 15275, 16542, 16545, 16973, 17079

CO 1405, 1623, 2848, 3879, 7671, 8192, 8307, 8941, 9192, 9789, 10510, 10661, 10879, 10907, 10934, 11528, 11556, 11685, 11738, 11807, 11915, 11938, 12030, 13163

CT 1112, 1679, 2577, 3727, 4549, 5102, 5681, 6096, 7886, 8314, 8496, 8897, 9356, 9447, 9672, 9959, 9967, 10499, 11506, 11744, 11808, 11952, 12053, 12440, 12918, 15424, 16828

DE 1485, 11448, 11746, 17151

DC 2444, 2855, 3199, 3977, 5232, 5491, 11038, 12498, 16765

FL 1191, 1192, 1270, 1424, 1539, 2578, 3276, 4009, 4752, 4789, 5370, 5392, 5599, 5900, 6005, 6345, 7181, 7880, 8188, 8292, 8413, 8903, 9817, 10367, 11647, 11688, 11747, 11850, 11909, 11955, 13213, 15421, 15486, 15534, 16185, 16708, 16944, 17191, 17192, 17323

GA 752, 2424, 2666, 3584, 3790, 4835, 5235, 5247, 8152, 9897, 9912, 10759, 11851, 11854, 12718, 15535

GU 5546

HI 5779, 5927, 6895, 11748, 13038, 17113

ID 1455, 1958, 6263, 11670, 11929

IL 244, 303, 1056, 1891, 2454, 2649, 2806, 2862, 2881, 3237, 3284, 3318, 3457, 3458, 3814, 4255, 4325, 4505, 5072, 5363, 5428, 5462, 5859, 5931, 6020, 6029, 6290, 6456, 6738, 7144, 7174, 7184, 7515, 7629, 7665, 7668, 7801, 7935, 8185, 8200, 8245, 8278, 8286, 8289, 8344, 8345, 8424, 8898, 9909, 9914, 9962, 10010, 10479, 10531, 10682, 11007, 11254, 11367, 11423, 11451, 11502, 11557, 11605, 11674, 11679, 11684, 11687, 11689, 11722, 11728, 11730, 11742, 11765, 11766, 11776, 11803, 11813, 11814, 11944, 11954, 12510, 12706, 12724, 13157, 13160, 16620, 16871, 16917, 17029

IN 1138, 2513, 2564, 3011, 3278, 3802, 6463, 7666, 7959, 8197, 8337, 11699, 11719, 11781, 11828, 11852, 11858, 11930, 11973, 12049, 12690, 17185, 17228

IA 269, 1750, 1882, 3764, 4272, 6673, 6674, 8279, 8284, 8285, 11815, 11830, 11927, 11928

KS 1415, 2576, 11047, 11757, 11827, 12450, 13029, 15629, 16894

KY 5366, 6083, 6191, 6193, 6801, 7603, 7612, 9710, 10402, 11681, 11707, 11725, 11727, 11817, 12058

Hospital libraries (Continued)
WY 8194

Hospitals—Administration: **AB** 184, 204, 1962; **BC** 1715, 1729; **CA** 6890; **CT** 5522; **DC** 14143, 14887; **FL** 1192; **IL** 412, 490, 491, 1891, 5877, 11605; **IN** 1138, 2667; **IA** 6671; **KY** 9710; **ME** 2653; **MB** 1653; **MA** 1755; **MI** 1554, 15743; **MN** 5611, 8600, 11244; **MO** 2540; **NY** 3498, 4334, 6093, 8776, 13831, 14961; **ND** 7669; **OH** 122, 2608; **OK** 1199; **ON** 10255, 10280; **PA** 6090; **PQ** 4625; **RI** 11393; **TN** 6092; **TX** 13427; **VA** 939; **WI** 17198

Hospitals—Design and construction: **CA** 6957, 8162, 13022; **IL** 5877; **MA** 10547; **MN** 5611

Hospitals, Military: **AL** 13956, 14066, 14071; **AK** 13957, 14052; **AZ** 14055; **CA** 13950, 13958, 14065; **CO** 14060, 14061; **DC** 13952, 14074; **FL** 13959; **GA** 14058, 14070; **HI** 14072; **IL** 13953, 13960; **KS** 14062; **KY** 14054; **LA** 14053; **MA** 14057; **MS** 13954; **MO** 14064; **NE** 13951; **NJ** 14073; **NM** 13961; **NY** 13962; **NC** 14076; **OH** 13955; **OK** 13963; **TX** 13964, 13965, 13967, 13968, 14056, 14059, 14075; **VA** 14063, 14067; **WA** 13966, 14068, 14069

Hospitals, Naval and marine: **CA** 14744, 14745, 14746, 14750; **FL** 14747, 14748, 14749; **IL** 14751; **MD** 14776; **NC** 14752; **PA** 14753; **RI** 14754; **TN** 14755; **TX** 14756; **VA** 14757, 14771; **WA** 14758

Hospitals—Planning: **MN** 5611; **WI** 12742

Hospitals, Veterans': **AL** 14860, 14861, 14862, 14863; **AZ** 14864, 14865, 14866; **AR** 14867, 14868; **CA** 14869, 14870, 14871, 14872, 14873, 14874, 14875, 14876, 14877, 14878, 14879; **CO** 14880, 14881; **CT** 14882, 14883; **DE** 14884; **DC** 14888; **FL** 14889, 14890, 14891, 14892, 14893; **GA** 14894, 14895, 14896; **ID** 14897; **IL** 14898, 14899, 14900, 14901, 14902, 14903; **IN** 14904, 14905, 14906; **IA** 14907, 14908, 14909; **KS** 14910, 14911, 14912; **KY** 14913, 14914; **LA** 14915, 14916, 14917; **ME** 14918, 14919; **MD** 14920, 14921, 14922; **MA** 14923, 14924, 14925, 14926, 14927; **MI** 14928, 14929, 14930, 14931, 14932; **MN** 14933, 14934; **MS** 14935; **MO** 14936, 14937, 14938, 14939; **MT** 14940, 14941; **NE** 14942, 14943, 14944; **NV** 14945; **NH** 14946; **NJ** 14947, 14948; **NM** 14949; **NY** 14950, 14951, 14952, 14953, 14954, 14955, 14956, 14957, 14958, 14959, 14961, 14962; **NC** 14963, 14964, 14965, 14966; **ND** 14967; **OH** 14968, 14969, 14970, 14971, 14972; **OK** 10196, 14973, 14974; **OR** 14975, 14976, 14977; **PA** 14978, 14979, 14980, 14981, 14982, 14983, 14984, 14985; **PR** 14986; **RI** 14987; **SC** 14988; **SD** 14989, 14990, 14991; **TN** 14992, 14993, 14994, 14995; **TX** 14996, 14997, 14998, 14999, 15000, 15001, 15002, 15003, 15004, 15005; **UT** 15006; **VT** 15007; **VA** 15008, 15009, 15010; **WA** 15011, 15012, 15013, 15014, 15015; **WV** 15016, 15017, 15018, 15019; **WI** 15020, 15021, 15022; **WY** 15023, 15024

Hotel administration See: Hotel management

Hotel management: **CA** 2985; **DC** 6107; **IL** 10491; **IN** 11124; **MI** 8451, 9947; **MN** 2461; **NY** 3517, 3647, 10489, 10544; **OH** 5988; **RI** 6860; **TN** 6001; **TX** 9949, 10490

House construction: **DC** 9053; **MD** 16972

Household management See: Home economics

Housing: **AB** 185, 1964, 4264; **BC** 15037; **CA** 1975, 4248, 4603, 5209, 7316, 8399, 9168, 12223, 14332, 15246, 15304; **CT** 15423; **DC** 3976, 8854, 9118, 9196, 14324, 14325, 16513, 16515; **FL** 13211; **GA** 14329; **IL** 5488, 8316, 15576; **IN** 4711; **ME** 16208; **MB** 7903; **MD** 1147; **MA** 1600, 14326; **MI** 5205, 8475; **NJ** 10994, 11616; **NY** 2981, 6526, 9574, 14327; **NC** 9763; **OH** 6117, 8422, 9842; **ON** 2220, 2346, 6565, 8389, 10285, 13553; **PA** 42, 6118, 14328, 17417; **SC** 5517; **SK** 11317; **TN** 7110, 8222; **TX** 14330; **WI** 17205

Houston (TX): **TX** 5663, 6126, 6133, 15542

Howells, William Dean: **CA** 16198; **NY** 247; **OH** 8420, 10164, 16274

Hubbard, Elbert: **AZ** 9861; **NY** 1064, 1857

Hudson River Valley: **NY** 166, 3189, 5503, 12564, 17412

Hughes, James Langston: **NY** 11183

Huguenots—History: **NY** 6179, 6180, 6182; **SC** 6181

Human ecology: **BC** 13855; **CA** 16202; **DC** 15463; **MI** 8470; **NY** 3489, 8935; **NC** 4114; **ON** 1863; **WA** 6225

Human engineering: **CA** 6183, 14804; **CT** 4131; **OH** 13984, 17318; **ON** 2165; **PA** 14713; **VA** 6189, 14104

Human growth: **NJ** 4444

Human relations See: Interpersonal relations

Human resources See: Manpower

Human rights See: Civil rights

Human services (See also Public welfare): **CO** 15457; **IL** 2807; **MD** 898; **MO** 8673; **NY** 3121; **TX** 6129, 13428; **VA** 9162

Human settlements See: Land settlements

Humanism: **FL** 4632; **OH** 4633; **TX** 12661

Humanities: **AB** 2105, 15136; **AR** 724; **BC** 15195; **CA** 1993, 2575, 2995, 2996, 3138, 3935, 12140, 15279; **CO** 13866; **CT** 6018; **DC** 2558, 7367, 7382, 9137; **GA** 15505; **IL** 856, 7172, 9784, 12774, 12783; **IN** 11136; **IA** 5422; **MB** 15687; **MA** 1593, 5388, 8075, 17285, 17286; **MI** 16859; **MO** 6924, 11893, 11898; **NJ** 6964, 9657; **NY** 3209, 3214, 3225, 3646, 9546, 11343, 13106, 13181, 13495; **NC** 9169; **OH** 1503, 10091, 10142; **OK** 2670, 10189; **ON** 7178, 7235, 9199, 9200, 9211, 11601, 11868, 15513, 16036, 16310, 16315, 16399, 17118; **OR** 10348; **PA** 6532, 8926, 13140; **PQ** 2581, 3316, 6471, 11160, 15077; **TX** 7271, 16246; **UT** 1694; **WI** 7986, 16427, 16448

Humor See: Wit and humor

Hungarian Americans: **IN** 7121

Hungary: **DC** 7364; **IN** 7121; **NY** 493

Hunger: **CA** 17311; **DC** 17302; **IN** 5033; **NY** 8020

Hunt, Richard Morris: **DC** 502

Hunting See: Fish and game

Hurricanes: **FL** 14568, 15478

Huxley, Aldous: **CA** 15298, 15345; **CO** 15415; **IN** 1140; **NH** 3753; **NY** 13112; **ON** 16312; **TX** 15542

Hydraulic engineering: **CA** 6986, 7289, 11258, 13636; **CO** 3179, 3182; **IL** 14027; **LA** 7573; **MB** 7906; **MA** 5154, 15669; **MN** 8924; **MS** 14021, 14043, 14046; **ON** 2161, 2257; **OR** 2900; **PA** 6110, 11512; **PQ** 6227, 12617; **TX** 2511; **VA** 14017; **WA** 14032

Hydrodynamics: **CA** 1982; **MA** 8068; **NY** 4273

Hydrography: **DC** 14242

Hydrology (See also Water-supply): **AL** 5213; **AZ** 14263, 15166; **BC** 1103; **CA** 1989, 2015, 3452, 4464, 10063, 10317, 12114, 14019, 14028; **CO** 3179, 15406; **FL** 4821; **GA** 14031; **IL** 6316; **IN** 14455; **IA** 3830; **LA** 7573; **MA** 8068, 14023; **MN** 1220, 14030, 15803, 15825, 15840; **MS** 8642; **MO** 15854; **NV** 14187, 14318, 15897; **NH** 14007; **NJ** 17270; **NM** 9437, 14460; **NY** 14458; **OH** 9281, 10114; **OK** 15997; **ON** 4635, 6616, 11008; **SK** 2272, 12248; **TX** 14448; **UT** 9748; **WA** 11518; **WI** 14456

Hygiene, Industrial See: Industrial hygiene

Hymns: **CA** 2996; **CO** 6282; **GA** 4349; **IL** 7402, 17068; **IN** 5395, 8243; **KY** 12753; **MA** 421, 1613; **MN** 7645; **MO** 3310, 7655; **NJ** 4077; **NY** 13790; **NC** 8827; **OH** 13648; **ON** 16315; **PA** 10802, 10932, 11366; **SC** 17236; **TX** 6231, 12788, 12829

Hypertension: **IL** 12367

Hypnotism: AZ 4447; CA 494; KS 17104; MN 1131; MO 3801; NY 6529, 10496; PQ 2367; TN 16575

Ibis: WI 6592

Iceland: CA 10477; DC 7364; MB 15680; MN 12818; NY 3501

Ichthyology See: Fish and fisheries

Iconography See: Christian art and symbolism

Idaho: ID 1557, 3122, 6265, 6266, 6267, 7223, 7334, 8976, 10421, 15552, 16512

Illinois: IL 1065, 1642, 1868, 2724, 2725, 2808, 2817, 3104, 3891, 4324, 4504, 5051, 5073, 5326, 5912, 5968, 6307, 6309, 6312, 6698, 6922, 6979, 7169, 7410, 7626, 7785, 7825, 7963, 8878, 9867, 10013, 10077, 10502, 10669, 12209, 12726, 15577, 16561, 16839, 16962, 17123, 17148

Illiteracy See: Literacy

Illumination of books and manuscripts (See also Paleography): IN 11126; NJ 10985; NY 5027, 9549; PA 5005, 16085

Illustration, Medical See: Medical illustration

Immigration See: Emigration and immigration

Immunochemistry: NY 1315

Immunology: CA 383, 482, 2987, 3108, 4005, 12353, 12941, 13612, 15228; CO 9192; DC 14144; NJ 8271; NY 6873, 9579, 13662, 17403; NC 1314; ON 2107, 3365, 10244, 16308; PA 8272, 16068; PQ 7730; SC 8167; TN 16222; TX 16692; WA 6009

Incunabula: CA 6209, 12136, 15291; CT 13641; DC 7385; IL 2825; MD 16719; MA 17138; MI 15746, 17347; MO 11889; NJ 10995; NY 3523; NC 15948; PA 3126, 11701, 12036, 16100

Indexing: OH 7227; PA 8484

India: CA 15265; CT 17375; DC 6342; MN 15782; NY 3420, 16134; OH 3067; TX 16231

Indiana: IN 261, 266, 1140, 1143, 1225, 1494, 1507, 2864, 3397, 3971, 4173, 4506, 4964, 5052, 5625, 5860, 5966, 5985, 6348, 6356, 6362, 6363, 6364, 6369, 6398, 6408, 6423, 6463, 7993, 9871, 10806, 11140, 13525, 14657, 16623, 16624, 16629, 16687, 16754, 16849, 17126; KY 3555

Indians of North America (See also Eskimos; name of specific tribes, e.g., Creek Indians): AB 177, 5317, 15129, 15134; AK 13550, 14689; AZ 496, 5822, 8707, 9295, 10747, 15148; BC 15195; CA 2040, 7555, 7944, 10033, 10477, 12136, 12820, 14511, 15255, 15276, 15287; CO 3869, 4904; CT 495, 13641; DC 3030, 7359, 12605, 14337; FL 498; IL 9002; IN 6394, 8967; IA 12963; KS 14622; KY 12853; LA 13689; MB 6162, 7907; MA 2865, 5043, 12656; MN 9170; MS 14668; MO 11831; MT 14635; NE 14662; NB 15906; NJ 1682, 1879, 3576, 10995; NM 4440, 6480, 11536, 12832, 14634, 15925; NY 128, 2624, 5691, 11182; ND 8627, 15967; NS 3684; OH 1113, 1227, 9933, 16011, 17124; ON 2210, 3267, 6218, 7235, 8387, 9209, 16216; OR 4045; PA 586, 4257, 5006, 7299, 16058; PQ 12626; SD 1054, 1492, 12538, 14590, 16180; SK 1260, 12263, 12264, 12269; TX 322; UT 16330; WA 12649, 14671, 16394, 17355; WI 7929; WY 1847, 14621, 17336

Indians of North America—Art: DC 14335; MB 17177; NE 6880; NM 6480; OK 10729, 10734; OR 10882; TX 12096, 13441; WA 12961

Indians of North America—History: AK 2869; AZ 784, 7940, 12437; AR 821, 14673; BC 9006; CA 497, 7203, 7476, 7875, 12127; CO 3161, 8982, 9291; CT 6344; DC 12610, 14519; ID 14670; IL 6307, 9002, 9661; IN 9871; KS 6934, 6938; MB 6161; MI 1477, 7177, 8738; MN 8005, 8583, 8597, 8598, 14677; MO 15867; MT 1486, 8758, 14610; NE 3658, 9316; NJ 5313, 8770; NM 8975, 12313, 17074; NY 2566, 6208; OH 14666; OK 2775, 5297, 10176, 10177, 10860, 16012, 16319; OR 3148; SD 499, 12710; TN 13045, 16225; TX 10487, 13083; WI 5983

Indians of North America—Legal status, laws, etc.: AZ 7937, 15151; CO 9291; DC 14334, 14345; MT 15878; NV 16820; NM 15924; NC 15944; OK 16003, 16317; ON 9209; SD 16181; SK 12244

Indonesia: CA 15265; MN 4576; NY 3519

Industrial arts (See also Vocational education): AB 12744; BC 16560; CA 4028, 7565, 10040, 12146; CT 3378, 5689, 9960, 16829; GA 12806; IL 1641, 2838; IN 6415; KS 4765; KY 8829; MA 1591, 4758, 17288; MN 4134, 7912, 8590, 12010; NH 9415, 9416; NY 8711, 17414; NF 3139; NC 2645, 8795, 13234, 16846; ND 9798; NS 9985; OK 10192; ON 248, 2590, 3328, 4139, 4575, 5218, 7622, 8710, 9695, 11633, 11867, 11868, 12542; OR 10335; PA 8534; PQ 2582; SC 4778, 5521, 13063, 13633, 13637, 17422; SD 16182; SK 6974, 16745; TN 7111; TX 13446, 13448; WI 1496, 3995, 7819, 7832, 8544, 8545, 8823, 9846, 12827, 17009, 17199, 17200

Industrial design See: Design, Industrial

Industrial development: DC 14537; MB 7902; MD 1146; MS 8651; MO 8670; NS 9979; ON 10282; PQ 11167; TN 13344; TX 13434; WI 17221

Industrial engineering: CA 12937, 15262, 15300; GA 6509, 6510; IL 7100; IN 11125; KY 15660; MA 15718; MI 5333; MO 15852; NB 9370; NY 3022, 3205, 3494, 4226, 13190; NS 13235; OH 15379; OK 11524, 15996; ON 16293; PA 16073; PQ 7749; SK 12270; VA 13238

Industrial hygiene (See also Medicine, Industrial): AL 17046; AZ 12079; BC 1745; CA 2026, 2060, 15247, 15260; CO 7927; CT 17421; DC 14367; ID 14364; IL 9245; MD 8037, 14047; MA 8074, 8109; MI 3027, 15774; NJ 436, 4526; NY 3516, 5079, 9641; NT 9925; OH 10103, 14540, 15377; OK 4172; ON 2342, 4090, 4092, 5558, 10280, 16301; PA 2944, 6436, 8565, 14365, 16076; PQ 2213, 6522, 9720, 11157; SK 12252; TN 10025; VA 11665; WA 14366; WV 14564, 16941; WI 16845

Industrial management (See also Management): CA 14779; GA 5240; IL 5804; NJ 13011; NY 4232; NC 11386, 11387; PA 10916; PQ 10926; TN 8010; WI 8560, 12571

Industrial medicine See: Medicine, Industrial

Industrial relations (See also Labor and laboring classes): AB 187; CA 15248, 15308, 15316; CO 6598, 8916; CT 15429; DC 457, 1873, 9131, 14547; FL 4782; HI 5770; IL 6461, 12426, 15579; IN 11130; MB 15677; MD 15709; MA 5729, 8071, 15713; MI 5189, 8465, 8867, 13805, 15756; MN 15808; NJ 10984, 11623; NY 460, 1231, 3507, 5635, 7922, 9095, 9521, 10364, 14356; NC 3320; NS 9981; OH 8505; ON 2145, 2212, 2214, 2280, 2373, 5217, 6151, 6329, 9884, 10252, 10283, 10297, 11204, 16280, 16297, 16414; PA 16055, 16083; PQ 1327, 2409, 3334, 4241, 7732, 7734, 7868, 15077; TX 5576, 13789, 17452; WI 16447

Industrial research See: Research, Industrial

Industrial safety: AB 221; AZ 12079; BC 1745; CA 3096, 14780, 15247, 16194; CO 14363; CT 83, 5683; DE 4098; DC 6617, 14367; FL 4794; ID 14364; IL 631, 1640, 9245, 13657; MD 8037; MA 8065; MN 11996; NJ 4528, 6654; NY 518, 3507, 3516, 9564, 9569, 10654; NT 9925; OH 10103, 10415, 14540; OK 4172; ON 2293, 2342, 4092, 4887, 6432, 10283, 10297; PA 2944, 4972, 8565, 14365; PQ 929, 2213, 11157; TX 4840, 13398, 14015; VA 11665; WA 14366; WV 14564; WI 6969, 16845

Industrial wastes See: Solid waste

Industry: BC 16556; CA 10525, 12134; CT 1761; DC 14305; GA 993; IL 4723; MI 4772; MN 3447; NB 9369; NY 778, 1794, 2753, 4695, 7502, 7758, 8319, 12927, 13485, 16891; OH 3780; ON 2287, 17309; PA 16883

Infantry: GA 14077

Infectious diseases See: Communicable diseases

Information retrieval (See also Documentation): AR 15174; CA 520,

Information retrieval (Continued)
3301, 3935, 16503; DC 2553, 6446, 7382; MA 6454; NJ 944;
NY 6243, 6245, 6333; OH 2766, 6449; OK 16318; ON 16284;
PA 6532, 8484, 16077, 16090, 16098; WA 6447

Information science: AZ 6050; CA 7464, 10445, 13192, 15252,
16189, 17345; CO 6448; DC 620, 7365, 9179, 13974, 14471;
FL 4830; GA 1002, 4346; IL 4722, 9821, 15581; IN 6400;
LA 7589; MD 897, 6444, 14541, 15693, 15694; MA 1553,
6914, 8103, 12518, 16726; MI 15766; NJ 3298; NY 4436,
6452, 7503, 11794, 12332, 12850; NF 9671; NC 2490;
OH 2526, 10065; ON 9204, 16415; PA 9141, 10595, 16063,
16098; PQ 7736, 12630; RI 11405; TN 14320, 16569;
TX 13437, 13439; VA 5880, 10819, 14246; WI 16453

Information storage and retrieval systems (See also Computers;
Programming (Electronic computers)): BC 1741; CA 6569,
11521, 13236, 17345; CO 2563, 15418; DC 620, 14536;
MD 6451, 7064, 14541; MI 15759; MN 8617; MO 15855;
NY 5165; ON 1347; PA 16090; VA 13238

Infra-red technology: CA 6173; CT 1215; MA 6047; MI 4415, 4416;
OH 2949, 10118; WA 12871

Ink: MI 1235; NJ 15027

Inorganic chemistry See: Chemistry, Inorganic

Insect control—Biological control (See also Insecticides):
CA 15221, 15238

Insecticides (See also Pesticides): GA 14262; IL 16587

Insects: AB 201, 2151; BC 2132, 2134, 2152, 15208; CA 1970,
2025, 12984, 14250, 15221, 15238, 15279, 15324, 15327,
17464; CT 3367; DC 12604, 13999; FL 4802, 4819, 15466,
15468, 15469, 15484, 15497; GA 5258, 14262; HI 1478;
ID 14258, 15550; IL 3438, 15557, 15578; IN 11129, 15986;
KY 15639; MB 15678; MD 6465, 14266; MA 15716; MI 15767;
MN 15779, 15839; NE 15881; NH 15911; NJ 432; NY 562,
3495, 4876, 7495; NF 2150; NC 9772, 13753; NS 2122;
OH 7456, 10110; OK 10186; ON 2110, 2113, 2135, 2147;
PA 29, 2487, 10642; PE 2118; PQ 2129, 2148, 7739; SK 2131;
VA 16665; WV 16925

Instructional materials See: Teaching—Aids and devices

Instrumentation See: Scientific apparatus and instruments

Insulation (Heat): PA 2713

Insurance: AB 6547; BC 6543; CA 3894, 4038, 4581, 4666, 6438,
6544, 12162, 17131; CO 15418; CT 82, 84, 3439, 10748,
13611, 15437; DC 10412; GA 4425; IL 292, 3084, 5886, 6975,
12681, 12962; IN 639; IA 7080, 7674; KS 4358, 12388;
LA 3929; MA 1429, 3260, 6548, 7347, 7348, 8099, 8100,
12971, 13066; MN 475, 9932, 11995, 11996, 16971; MO 6929,
9055, 10201; NE 8997, 10228; NJ 9655, 11053, 11057;
NY 517, 3123, 4426, 7992, 8364, 9521, 9537, 13229, 13583,
16532; OH 9290, 11078, 16998; ON 2174, 2217, 2964, 3330,
11059, 11306, 13067, 13547; PA 417, 513, 2477, 2944, 3151,
4993, 6163, 7346, 8993, 10588, 16055; PQ 3895, 5280, 6434,
7141, 11159, 13069; RI 270, 8377; TX 13860; VT 9216;
WA 11656, 16364; WI 6604, 8403, 12409, 16473, 16845

Insurance, Fire: MA 6548, 9385; NY 518; ON 10268

Insurance, Health: CA 1998; CO 5483; CT 3372; DC 427, 5532;
FL 1514; IL 1183, 1513, 16771; ME 13780; MB 5484;
MD 14844; MA 6815; MI 15743; MO 1520; NE 17263; NY 1515,
8995, 8996, 9471; NC 1516; ON 3613; PA 1519, 1521, 10596;
PQ 3527, 6723; VA 1517; WA 5533; WI 98, 9930

Insurance law: AZ 7330, 10066; CA 49, 4666, 13605; CT 85;
DC 13143; FL 4805; GA 3329; IL 291, 292, 3823, 6975, 7512;
MB 5484; MI 3941; MO 9055; NY 517, 13172; ON 6327;
WI 9929, 17223

Insurance, Life: CO 5483; CT 3372, 3374, 7393; DC 22, 427;
GA 3329, 7394; IL 8538, 16771; IN 11361; ME 13780;
MB 5484; MA 6815, 9390; MN 7649; NE 17263; NY 6037,
8995, 8996, 9500; ON 3613, 3614, 6327, 7926, 8252, 8994,
9742, 13068; PA 418, 4650, 11049; PQ 6723; TX 11052;
WI 98, 9931

Insurance—Mathematics: GA 3329; IL 5886; MB 15677; MA 12971;
MO 9055; NY 3123; ON 3330, 3613, 8252; PA 11049;
PQ 13069, 13584; WI 98

Insurance, Property and casualty: IL 12433; NJ 3621; NY 2494,
6545

Insurance, Social See: Social security

Insurance, Unemployment: MI 8438

Intelligence service: DC 2618, 5233, 14233; VA 830

Intensive care See: Critical care medicine

Interior decoration: AZ 804; AR 15170; CA 722, 1432, 4590, 5848,
8782, 10034, 12128, 17259; CT 10462, 17386; DC 12559;
FL 11439, 12766, 15472; IL 5661, 10681, 15575; KY 15644;
LA 7584; MB 15679; MI 4770, 5876; MN 15783; MO 5847;
NY 3317, 4591, 6113, 9494, 9510, 12557; NC 5062; OH 6036,
15378; OK 16007; OR 7350, 16013; PA 4992; TX 12097;
WI 8555, 10463

Internal medicine (See also Endocrinology; Gastroenterology):
CO 3176; FL 14893; IN 1138; KS 14911; MD 6837; MI 11940,
14931; MT 14940; NJ 4371; OH 1421

Internal revenue law: DC 14474; IL 3095

International business enterprises: CA 7461, 10454, 12943, 16188,
17259; DC 10412; MO 8254; NY 1914, 4459, 7925, 8320,
9638, 13587, 13856, 13858; ON 2287, 16414, 17309;
PA 10638, 16055; PQ 7732; TX 12794; VA 12842; WA 16364;
WI 16473

International cooperation: CA 16205; DC 2599, 6617, 10363;
MO 16808; ON 6594, 9209; PQ 2154

International education: AL 6573; CA 8780, 16189; CT 15438;
MO 923; NJ 5328; NY 13103; PA 16096

International educational exchanges See: Educational exchanges,
International

International finance: CA 8780; DC 6625; MI 15756; NY 4617,
4872, 6881, 7925, 8833, 12075, 12322; ON 1172, 4515;
PA 16080; PQ 11584

International law: BC 16337; CA 7506, 7623, 15251, 15278;
CO 13865, 15409; CT 15184, 17378; DC 621, 655, 935, 1952,
4879, 5225, 5230, 6624, 6833, 7371, 7372, 10412, 14304,
14305, 14368, 14369, 14388, 14843, 16604, 17295, 17307;
FL 9992, 12570, 15488, 15728; GA 3089, 7065; IL 3459, 7389,
7695, 8127, 9939, 15365; IN 6405; IA 4072; KS 6940;
LA 7588; MA 1579, 5728, 9855, 13681; MI 5188, 15757,
16856; MN 15812; MS 15849; MO 16817; NE 3592; NY 362,
916, 1125, 1688, 3771, 9482, 10434, 11331, 11489, 11793,
13858, 16718, 17166; NS 3682; OH 2525, 10090, 12909,
15392, 16273; ON 2189, 2402, 11205, 16295; PA 3939,
16044; PR 6557, 16112; PQ 6587, 15058; RI 14800;
SD 16181; TX 3400, 12794, 16257, 16633; VA 5222, 14806,
16342

International organization: CA 12940, 15244, 15330; DC 1006;
IL 7389; MI 15757; NY 3541, 13858; OH 15098

International relations: AZ 14079; BC 10559; CA 7563, 10454,
11247, 13922, 14129, 14770, 15249, 16205, 17292;
CO 12331; DC 449, 1006, 1775, 4494, 4882, 5233, 6833,
7362, 10362, 14107, 14368, 14470, 14537, 17162; FL 14132;
GA 14077; HI 6495, 10435; IL 7389, 17312; IN 15984;
LA 6610; MD 14711; MA 5700, 5703, 5725, 5726, 13681;
MI 3923; MO 6655, 8254, 13854; NJ 961, 9660, 10999;
NY 1795, 3225, 3541, 5012, 9521, 9688, 11489, 13721,
13858, 14048; OH 3040; ON 2189, 2216, 2222, 2223, 2226,
2368, 2458, 8394, 14472, 17167; PA 4881, 7157, 14145,
16084; PQ 15058; RI 14800; TX 9950; VA 607, 7994, 9185,
13193, 13672, 13980, 13990, 17161; WI 16482

International trade See: Commerce and trade

International visitors See: Visitors, Foreign

Interpersonal relations: DC 15464; NJ 6774; NY 3219, 3646;

Interpersonal relations (Continued)
   PQ 2708; SC 14120; TX 14133

Inuit See: Eskimos

Inventions: NJ 14615; ON 2364

Investment banking (See also Banks and banking): CA 1106, 2438,
   7550, 11560, 12192, 12943; DC 6665, 8854, 10412, 14837;
   IL 9885; MA 4649, 11139; MN 6273; NY 1396, 3663, 4081,
   4240, 4868, 4872, 5123, 7924, 8319, 8320, 8838, 10464,
   11051, 11336, 12075, 12322, 14858; ON 8501, 11602,
   13067, 17257; PA 4993, 5000; VA 6490

Investments, Foreign (See also International law): IL 1127

Ion exchange: MA 6668

Ionization: DC 14528

Ionosphere: CO 17301

Iowa: IA 318, 1846, 1967, 2573, 2774, 4071, 5534, 6670, 6682,
   6685, 6688, 7275, 11143, 12963, 15616, 15978

Ireland: IL 11941; MA 6694; MN 3137; NJ 12413; NY 6690, 11788;
   PQ 3316

Ireland—History: AL 12090; MA 1583; NJ 12414; PA 2788

Irish Americans: IL 6693; MA 6694; MI 10043; NY 521, 11788

Irish literature: BC 15207; CA 12936; FL 15495; GA 4355; IL 6693,
   12778; KS 15622; KY 15658; ME 3099; MA 1583; NJ 12414;
   NY 4878, 7268, 13118; ON 11212, 16312; PA 1840, 2788

Iron (See also Steel): MA 14686; NC 8509; ON 4017, 9876;
   PA 2495, 3184, 14647

Irving, Washington: CT 17362; NY 12564

Isherwood, Christopher William: ON 17434

Islam: CO 508; DC 97; IN 9740; MA 5701; NY 6477; OH 10143;
   PQ 7733

Islamic architecture See: Architecture, Islamic

Islands: CA 12217

Isotope separation: TN 8010

Israel: CA 1650, 1871, 6793; FL 2639, 13284, 15485; IL 9703;
   MD 6783; MA 1402, 5826, 13302; MI 8508, 13296; MN 8911;
   NE 6795; NJ 1404; NY 528, 3421, 9741, 13286, 17313;
   OH 1529; ON 7228; PA 4084, 5828; PQ 1528

Italian Americans: NY 2616, 9512

Italian language: NY 9512

Italian literature: CA 12165; MA 16878; NY 3226, 6707; ON 16312;
   PA 16061; PQ 6708

Italy: DC 7364; NY 3226, 6707, 9512; PQ 6708

Italy—History: CA 12165; IL 15588; MA 6709; MI 8471; NY 5089;
   PQ 6708

Ives, Charles Edward: CT 17376

Jackson, Andrew: TN 13352, 13354

Jackson, Thomas Jonathan ("Stonewall"): VA 5941

James Bay (PQ): PQ 12626

James, Jesse: MO 6727; TN 13365

Japan: AB 3423; AZ 15164; BC 15185; CA 12142, 15235, 15313;
   CT 17369; DC 5224, 6751, 7360; FL 8839; IL 15361;
   KS 15624; KY 7032; MD 15698; MA 4867, 5722, 5727;
   MI 15735; MN 4576, 15797; NE 3593; NJ 910, 10983, 11612;
   NY 3210, 3422, 3520, 6752, 11789, 16134; OH 10120;

Japan (Continued)
   PA 16079; TX 16231

Japanese Americans: CA 6484, 15298; FL 8839

Jarrell, Randall: NC 15960

Jay family: NY 6756

Jazz music: AR 811; CT 3369, 13641; FL 15731; IL 9784, 15367;
   LA 13697; MA 1385; MI 3903, 6566; MO 15393; NJ 5311,
   10990, 11622; NY 13099; PA 5002, 7919, 16908; VA 13989;
   WV 16938; WI 16484

Jeffers, Robinson: CA 10056, 15345, 16150

Jefferson, Thomas: DC 7385; MO 8663, 8665, 14651; VA 2676,
   3145

Jesuits: CA 2001, 16151; DC 5233, 17267; IL 6778; MA 17045;
   MI 3150; MO 11899, 11900; NY 7268; NC 4116; ON 6218;
   PQ 3290, 3291; SK 2104; WA 5361, 12649; WI 7986

Jewelry (See also Gems): CA 5116; NY 1865; ON 2369; RI 11045,
   16127

Jewish literature: AL 13287; AZ 13273; BC 16558; CA 1650, 3343,
   5832, 6787, 6793, 13290; CO 15458; CT 3352, 13283;
   DC 13306; FL 13276, 13284, 13289, 13292, 13298; IL 2830,
   3350, 3356, 3360, 9703, 13299, 13630, 15373; MD 10165;
   MA 3353, 5826, 13272, 13291, 13302, 13307; MI 3341, 3345,
   6786, 8508, 13270, 13296; MN 6782, 13293; MO 1757,
   13297; NE 6795; NJ 3344, 13267, 13275, 13285; NY 247,
   1398, 3348, 3359, 5833, 6781, 6808, 7277, 9524, 13264,
   13265, 13266, 13268, 13274, 13277, 13279, 13286, 13288,
   13294, 13303, 17304, 17402, 17407, 17408; NC 15948;
   ND 13269; OH 3039, 3342, 4554, 10506, 13260, 13295,
   13300, 17227; ON 95, 6788, 7228; PA 721, 3346, 3355, 4084,
   4994, 5642, 7851, 10079, 10080, 13261; PQ 6807; RI 13271,
   13282; TN 6785, 16913; TX 2884, 3339, 13281, 13451;
   WA 13280; WI 3347, 3358

Jewish music See: Music, Jewish

Jews: BC 16558; CA 1871; IL 12870; MD 6783, 6797; NJ 8851;
   NY 522, 523, 527, 528, 3543, 6806, 9524, 9706, 9741, 11355,
   17304, 17409, 17410; PA 116, 4084

Jews, Canadian: MB 2370; ON 2372, 9199; PQ 2371, 6807

Jews—Education: CA 1871, 6793; FL 2639; MD 1155, 9330;
   MA 5826; MI 8508; NY 1533, 1870, 6791, 6792, 13265;
   OH 13260; PA 116, 5467, 5468, 11292

Jews, German: NY 1115

Jews—History: CA 1650, 1871, 6016, 6793, 7844, 7845, 9193,
   10585; CO 11529; FL 2639, 13292, 15485; IL 9816; IN 6350;
   MB 2370; MA 526; MI 3341; MN 54, 6782; MO 1757; NE 6795;
   NJ 13304, 13305; NY 247, 1398, 1870, 2610, 5756, 6798,
   6804, 6808, 9524, 9705, 9706, 9818, 13264, 13277, 17313,
   17402, 17408, 17410; OH 10506, 13260; ON 7228; PA 3349,
   3355, 11292; PQ 1528; RI 11394; SC 2744; TN 6794, 13301;
   TX 13278

Jews, Russian: CA 1265, 7844; MA 5826; MN 6789; NY 2626, 9112

Johnson, Andrew: TN 13354, 14584

Johnson, Lyndon Baines: TX 14659, 14827

Johnson, Samuel: NV 15905; NY 3514; NC 15948; VA 16641

Journalism (See also Communication): CA 15245; FL 4783;
   IL 12774; IN 6390; KS 15626; MI 3914; MN 15801; MO 6663,
   15857; NY 1430, 3231, 13088, 13181; NS 15655; OH 10134;
   PA 4999, 13320; VA 571; WI 16458

Joyce, James: CT 17362; IL 12778; KS 6951, 15622; NY 3514,
   7268, 13100; TX 12792

Judaica See: Jewish literature

Judaism: AL 13287; BC 16557, 16558; CA 5832, 9193, 10585,

Language and languages (Continued)
FL 8410; HI 5788, 6495; ID 15547; IL 2824, 9120, 13258, 15560, 15584; IN 15990; LA 9453; MD 6828, 14084; MA 16878; MI 3913, 3917, 15748; MN 8582, 15818; MO 14309; NJ 9657; NY 382, 1793, 1855, 3208, 5850, 8705, 9516, 9523, 9533, 11184, 11490, 13181; NC 3635; OH 3064, 3067, 7005, 10117, 13540, 15382; OK 10189; ON 2269, 8387, 9206, 10257; OR 7352; PA 4999, 9062; PQ 4880; TX 3707, 13875, 14085; UT 16329; WA 12380; WI 7833

Lasers and masers: AL 14097; CA 7464, 9893, 9894, 10453, 11517, 11522, 17351; CO 3179; CT 15028; MA 1089, 8087; MI 7099; MN 6641; NM 13981; NY 71, 1326; ON 2265; WA 12871

Latin America: CA 2995, 6664, 10039, 12215, 12940, 16202; DC 5706, 6143, 6556, 6556, 7369, 7375, 7378, 10362, 14817, 17162; FL 12039, 13906, 13919, 14114, 14132, 15487; IL 12777, 15574; IN 6392; KS 15622; LA 13689; MD 24; MA 10481; MI 8463; MO 6655, 15872; NY 3653, 5935, 13126, 13179; OH 10113, 10136; ON 2323, 7087, 17423; PA 6410, 11559, 16087; PQ 15091; TX 4423, 16232; VA 12187

Latvia: DC 7364

Laubach, Frank C.: NY 7230

Law—Canada:

AB 173, 174, 1370, 1482, 1888, 6515, 7243, 7244, 8047, 8542, 11180, 15139, 16717

BC 1717, 1718, 1719, 1720, 1864, 3768, 4588, 4989, 6543, 11607, 15196

FL 3666

MB 7245

MI 5191, 15462

NB 1224, 10473, 15048

NF 7246, 9664

NS 3682, 9974, 9975

OH 13535

ON 1501, 1502, 1705, 2098, 2175, 2215, 2216, 2237, 2289, 2308, 2359, 2374, 3552, 3553, 3614, 4091, 4478, 4592, 4986, 5378, 5379, 5615, 7249, 7698, 7797, 8494, 10259, 10266, 10273, 10300, 11205, 12516, 13037, 13488, 13572

PQ 1221, 1328, 2718, 2723, 3895, 5280, 7735, 7790, 10074, 11152, 11168, 11469, 15045, 15088

SD 16181

SK 7247, 7248, 8820, 12244

WV 16936

Law, Civil See: Civil law

Law, Corporation See: Corporation law

Law, Criminal See: Criminal law

Law enforcement: AB 193; CA 12365; DC 14224, 14348, 14381, 14517; FL 458, 4806; IL 12782; IN 6351, 6403; IA 6672; KY 4198; ME 7854; MD 1158, 14349; MI 357, 8460; MN 6641, 8594; MO 7418; NC 2645, 9766; ON 2298; PA 10652; VA 14343; WI 5098, 17209

Law—Great Britain: AZ 800; DC 7372; KS 15632; MA 1390, 4566, 4974, 5628, 5629; MI 15462; MO 16817; NE 3592; NY 9600, 13794; SD 16181; WV 16936

Law—History and criticism: CA 5509, 16195; DC 7371; FL 9992; IN 6405; NY 9613; OH 12203; PA 3080, 7193, 13332; PQ 7735

Law, International See: International law

Law, Maritime See: Maritime law

Law, Military See: Military law

Law, Mining See: Mining law

Law, Ocean See: Ocean law

Law reform: AB 6515; ON 2215

Law, Russian See: Russian law

Law, Space See: Space law

Law—Study and teaching: AL 12089, 15103, 15107; AB 15216; AZ 800, 15151; AR 15171, 15175; BC 15196, 16337; CA 2067, 5323, 5350, 5509, 7417, 7623, 7719, 9279, 10671, 12149, 12171, 12838, 12945, 15251, 15267, 15278, 15307, 15341, 15656, 16148, 16149, 16152, 16195, 16405, 17002, 17003, 17093; CO 13865, 15409, 15454; CT 15184, 15430, 17378; DE 3837; DC 380, 655, 730, 935, 2559, 5225, 5230, 6147; FL 4829, 9992, 13007, 15488, 15728; GA 997, 4352, 5263, 8264, 15504; ID 15549; IL 3796, 6287, 6817, 7628, 9939, 12775, 15365, 15580; IN 6391, 6405, 15985, 16546; IA 4072, 15612; KS 15632, 16746; KY 9872, 15646, 15663; LA 7588, 7630, 12809, 13690; ME 15676; MB 15683; MD 15182, 15692; MA 1579, 5728, 9394, 9855, 13056, 16989; MI 3463, 3898, 15462, 15757; MN 5621, 8676, 15812; MS 8639, 15849; MO 11903, 15861, 15865, 16817; MT 15878; NE 3592, 15884; NV 9195; NB 15908; NJ 11621, 11629, 12415; NM 15924; NY 1786, 3221, 3505, 4877, 5996, 9496, 9497, 9644, 10434, 13097, 13186, 13794; NC 2103, 4123, 9753, 15944, 16702; ND 15975; OH 2443, 2525, 3074, 10090, 10137, 15099, 15392, 15440, 16273; OK 10169, 10314, 16003, 16317; ON 11205, 16034, 16295, 16412, 16418, 17431; OR 7323, 16023, 17125; PA 533, 3939, 4135, 7421, 13332, 16044, 16088, 16627; PR 2561, 16112; PQ 7735, 15065; SC 16170; SD 16181; SK 16157; TN 8230, 16220, 16563; TX 1277, 9102, 11979, 12727, 12794, 13414, 13453, 15541, 16257; UT 1695, 16326; VT 16597; VA 3145, 5222, 16133, 16342, 16767; WA 5362, 16119, 16384; WV 16939; WI 7985, 16451; WY 16495

Law—United States:

AL 140, 1132, 3691, 6759, 7209, 7822, 8702, 8787, 13208, 15106

AB 1888, 7784

AK 158

AZ 1806, 3091, 3092, 4503, 5295, 5526, 7330, 7937, 8716, 10066, 10777, 17400, 17451

AR 819, 8943, 12386

CA 49, 145, 146, 296, 316, 985, 1126, 1161, 1162, 1168, 1751, 1823, 1911, 1927, 1956, 2016, 2017, 2018, 2019, 2020, 2027, 2028, 2029, 2040, 2051, 2530, 2598, 3444, 3462, 3605, 3829, 4298, 4759, 5022, 5292, 5323, 5350, 5470, 5499, 5605, 5758, 5846, 5903, 5921, 6136, 6195, 6326, 6667, 6691, 6867, 6887, 7035, 7059, 7068, 7202, 7225, 7250, 7399, 7448, 7467, 7506, 7521, 7530, 7543, 7634, 7705, 7706, 7881, 7942, 8235, 8256, 8777, 8848, 8849, 8934, 9168, 9279, 9341, 9896, 10231, 10319, 10372, 10441, 10446, 10543, 10692, 10772, 10803, 10827, 11444, 11445, 11611, 11640, 12108, 12115, 12116, 12117, 12118, 12152, 12157, 12171, 12173, 12185, 12191, 12213, 12221, 12225, 12391, 12443, 12473, 12505, 12546, 12670, 12682, 12952, 13144, 13243, 13468, 13482, 13605, 13642, 13699, 13706, 14351, 15330, 16591

CO 53, 568, 3164, 3178, 3769, 3872, 4300, 6003, 6013, 11060, 11467, 12472, 13807, 13865, 14338, 16872

CT 331, 3385, 3386, 3387, 3388, 3389, 3390, 3391, 3392, 10218, 13611, 13762, 15184, 17109

DE 3192, 3837, 3846, 3849, 4097, 5870, 9374, 17437

DC 66, 772, 841, 937, 1207, 1873, 2447, 3098, 3263, 3558, 3611, 3975, 4064, 4622, 5029, 5304, 5999, 7081, 7362, 7371, 7372, 8835, 8847, 9183, 10540, 10664, 10765, 11071, 11538, 12446, 12452, 12999, 13060, 13973, 14107, 14268, 14305, 14319, 14324, 14334, 14337, 14340, 14346, 14369,

Lee, Robert Edward: **VA** 3325, 13034, 14587

Legal aid: **DC** 9240; **IL** 9099; **NY** 2627, 7293, 7294

Legal education See: Law—Study and teaching

Legal ethics: **DC** 380

Legal medicine See: Medical jurisprudence

Legal services, Prepaid See: Prepaid legal services

Legislation: **AL** 1044; **AB** 207; **AK** 163; **CA** 1021, 7521, 14441; **DC** 772, 3364, 11069, 11350, 14467, 14839, 16604, 17147; **IL** 6308, 6817, 14835; **IN** 6362; **MI** 8434; **NY** 8524, 11487; **ON** 7249, 14472; **PA** 10628, 14440, 16044; **PQ** 11152; **UT** 16323; **VA** 13672

Legislative reference: **AK** 162; **BC** 1720; **CA** 2043; **CT** 3383; **DE** 3846; **DC** 14813; **FL** 4818; **HI** 5782; **IL** 6308; **IA** 6684; **KS** 6939; **KY** 7031; **LA** 7574; **ME** 7864; **MD** 1148, 8034; **MI** 8445; **MN** 8619; **MO** 8672; **MT** 8764; **NB** 9367; **NJ** 9433; **NM** 9443; **NY** 9473, 9580, 9585; **NF** 9668; **NC** 9767; **NS** 9986; **OK** 10183; **ON** 10259; **PA** 10629, 17122; **RI** 11407; **SK** 12265; **TN** 13351; **TX** 13436; **VA** 16660; **WV** 16933; **WI** 8553, 17221

Leisure (See also Recreation): **CO** 15399; **IL** 15554; **MD** 12071; **ON** 16399, 16401; **OR** 16021; **PA** 7240

Lenses, Contact See: Contact lenses

Lenski, Lois: **AR** 820; **FL** 4833; **KS** 4360; **NY** 13106; **NC** 15956; **OK** 16004

Leprosy: **HI** 5779; **LA** 14830; **NJ** 536; **NY** 3723

Lesbianism (See also Homosexuality): **AL** 7190; **CA** 2007, 16910; **CT** 5690; **FL** 9003; **GA** 998; **MA** 1615, 1759; **NY** 5100, 7315; **ON** 2358, 17252; **PA** 5101; **TN** 10199; **TX** 6233

Lewis and Clark Expedition: **MO** 8663, 8665, 14651; **MT** 8758; **PA** 586

Lewis, Fielding: **VA** 6980

Lewis, Sinclair: **CA** 16198; **DC** 7385; **MN** 7331, 7807, 15829; **OH** 11074

Lewis, Wyndham: **NY** 3514, 13100

Lexicography (See also Encyclopedias and dictionaries): **MI** 5071

Liability (Law): **CA** 5758; **MA** 622; **NY** 6883; **PA** 11255

Liberty: **CA** 8175, 15312; **MI** 16855; **NY** 405, 522, 525, 5012, 9526; **TX** 9948

Liberty of the press: **CA** 8175, 15345; **MO** 15853; **VA** 571

Libraries, Church and synagogue: **AL** 4676, 4729, 13287; **AB** 11713; **AZ** 4741, 11934, 13273; **AR** 4670; **CA** 3343, 4675, 4708, 4726, 4731, 4742, 4748, 10209, 12112, 13290, 13643, 13654; **CO** 1057, 4344, 4730; **CT** 1408, 3352, 4704, 4707, 11697, 12707, 13283; **DC** 2796, 8909, 9229, 13306; **FL** 1399, 4233, 4689, 4732, 9781, 10523, 11455, 13263, 13276, 13284, 13289, 13292, 13298; **GA** 12011; **HI** 11705; **IL** 1403, 2830, 3350, 3356, 3360, 4733, 4740, 4746, 9823, 10400, 11770, 11998, 12387, 13299; **IN** 251, 2888, 4719, 5009, 10203, 10504; **IA** 4716; **KS** 8242; **KY** 2646, 4047, 4638; **LA** 1530, 4720, 13663; **MD** 10165, 10931; **MA** 1402, 3337, 3353, 4677, 4705, 4706, 4710, 10423, 13272, 13291, 13302, 13307; **MI** 1476, 1912, 3341, 3345, 3357, 4678, 4702, 4709, 4728, 4734, 4735, 4743, 4886, 8202, 13270, 13296, 17051; **MN** 54, 1401, 2641, 4254, 4679, 4717, 5413, 6033, 8892, 8911, 10011, 10403, 11990, 13293, 13645, 15821, 17261; **MS** 2662, 4680, 4681, 4688; **MO** 1409, 2071, 4682, 4683, 4697, 4698, 6164, 13297, 13477, 13653; **NE** 4736; **NJ** 1404, 3344, 3577, 3595, 13267, 13275, 13285, 13304, 13305, 13652; **NM** 4420, 4691, 4750, 6322, 13818; **NY** 2537, 2673, 3147, 3348, 3359, 4703, 4745, 10498, 13264, 13265, 13266, 13268, 13274, 13277, 13279, 13286, 13288, 13294, 13303; **NC** 4684, 4690, 4694; **ND** 13269; **OH** 94, 3342, 5906, 6886, 10506, 13295, 13300, 13817, 17034, 17053, 17227; **OK** 4747, 11760, 17035; **ON** 95, 1411; **OR** 4737; **PA** 721, 1400,

Libraries, Church and synagogue (Continued)
1410, 2463, 2885, 3338, 3346, 3349, 3355, 4176, 4699, 4718, 4738, 4749, 5275, 5642, 5762, 5915, 7042, 7851, 10079, 10080, 11310, 13261, 16853, 17036, 17462; **RI** 13271, 13282; **SD** 1425, 4685; **TN** 4701, 13301, 16913; **TX** 2663, 2907, 3339, 3596, 4174, 4672, 4673, 4674, 4686, 4687, 4692, 4727, 4739, 4744, 5913, 5914, 9812, 13278, 13281, 13616; **VA** 4693, 4700, 11370, 12013, 17037; **WA** 882, 10829, 13280, 15422; **WV** 4725; **WI** 883, 1417, 3347, 3358, 6065, 8883, 9814, 10404, 10971, 13646, 16895

Libraries, Rural: **PA** 3003

Libraries, Special: **MI** 5071; **NY** 12850

Library consortia See: Library cooperation

Library cooperation: **IL** 2625; **MD** 7064; **NY** 2436, 9791; **OH** 10065

Library humor: **CT** 8714

Library information networks See: Library cooperation

Library science (See also Bibliography): **AL** 134; **AB** 1959, 15136; **AZ** 15158; **BC** 15204; **CA** 7557, 15252, 16189; **CT** 3383; **DC** 538, 2553, 9179, 15044; **FL** 4830, 12969; **GA** 1002, 4346; **ID** 6267; **IL** 537, 1933, 2819, 4086, 9821, 12773, 12781, 15581, 15593; **IN** 6363, 6400; **IA** 6685, 15613; **LA** 7589; **MB** 17183; **MD** 6444, 8032, 15693; **MA** 8103, 10955, 12518; **MI** 3914, 15759, 15772, 16857; **MN** 8609, 15799; **MS** 8649; **NV** 9345; **NB** 9364; **NJ** 9433; **NM** 9444; **NY** 1627, 3222, 4436, 5802, 7503, 10924, 11794, 12332, 12850, 13089; **NC** 9754, 9759, 15949; **ND** 9797; **NS** 9989; **OH** 2526, 2766, 6771, 10065, 11075; **OK** 10183, 10189; **ON** 7178, 8385, 9199, 9204, 10267, 16296, 16415, 16882; **OR** 10348; **PA** 3003, 3004, 4994, 7132, 7438, 16097, 16098, 16626; **PR** 16108; **PQ** 7736, 15053; **RI** 11405; **SK** 12269; **TN** 16569; **TX** 3707, 12101, 13437, 13439, 13457; **VA** 5880, 10972; **WI** 16453; **WY** 17336

Lie detectors and detection: **NY** 9276

Life insurance See: Insurance, Life

Life-saving: **CA** 14478; **MA** 14596; **NC** 14597

Life sciences: **AZ** 801; **CA** 7534, 12911, 14490, 14741, 15257, 15350, 16200; **CT** 17377; **DC** 13974; **FL** 13877; **IL** 2813, 6280; **IN** 6370; **MD** 6838, 8011; **MA** 8057, 17284; **MI** 3924, 8470; **MO** 15860; **NJ** 288, 1464, 4484; **NY** 4334, 9537, 13793; **NC** 9769; **OH** 9852, 12028; **ON** 2266, 11601; **PA** 1462, 2485, 6532, 10647; **TX** 6119, 13869; **VA** 14246, 14807, 16343; **WI** 16467

Light metals (See also Aluminum): **OH** 1247; **ON** 227

Lighter-than-air (LTA) craft See: Air-ships

Lighting See: Lamps and lighting

Limericks: **IN** 6384

Limestone: **IN** 6352

Limnology: **AK** 15119; **CO** 14454; **MB** 2193; **MA** 9377; **MI** 8478, 14571, 15736, 15770; **MN** 15803, 15839; **NY** 6502; **OH** 10114, 10128; **OK** 15993; **ON** 2161, 6615; **PA** 16094; **PQ** 11170; **WI** 14406, 16436, 16472

Lincoln, Abraham: **CA** 7411, 15345; **CO** 3155; **CT** 15183; **DC** 7378, 7385, 12350; **GA** 1000; **IL** 1643, 2808, 6285, 6307, 9784, 15373, 15574, 16561; **IN** 1924, 6392, 7414, 14657; **IA** 5438; **KS** 1129, 6951, 11937; **KY** 1376, 12853, 14581; **MA** 1605; **MI** 3909, 10043; **MO** 8663, 9841; **MT** 8767; **NJ** 1508; **NY** 8566; **OH** 17317; **PA** 4980, 8529, 13777, 14633; **RI** 1819; **TN** 7412, 12796; **TX** 7271; **WA** 13202; **WV** 16943; **WI** 7986

Lind, Jenny: **PA** 644; **TX** 12099

Lindsay, Vachel: **IL** 7410

Linguistics (See also Language and languages): **BC** 15195; **CA** 11332, 14308, 15350, 16193; **CT** 5757, 17375; **DC** 4438, 5233, 5706, 12610; **HI** 15524; **IL** 2824, 12774, 15584; **MA** 8075; **MI** 15748; **MN** 15795; **NJ** 910; **NM** 15920; **NY** 8705,

Maryland (Continued)
11946, 12071, 13205, 15702

Masers See: Lasers and masers

Mason, George: VA 5579

Masonry (See also Building materials): AB 2709

Masons (Secret order) See: Freemasons

Mass media: HI 6495; IL 12783; IN 14135; NY 8349, 13185; ON 2155, 16278; PA 16042; PQ 2958, 11173; WI 12966, 16458

Mass transit See: Urban transportation

Massachusetts: MA 519, 696, 888, 1316, 1433, 1648, 1754, 2082, 2432, 2763, 2786, 3306, 3597, 3817, 4035, 4124, 4283, 4565, 4568, 4756, 4867, 5508, 5768, 5939, 5963, 6731, 6872, 7339, 7616, 7684, 7871, 7885, 7932, 8061, 8113, 8114, 8142, 8144, 9036, 9351, 9387, 9737, 9750, 9835, 9836, 10205, 10206, 10213, 10422, 10553, 10554, 10688, 11214, 12204, 12339, 12658, 13015, 13048, 14596, 14684, 15669, 15715, 16887, 17282, 17285, 17287

Materials: AB 5641, 5650; AZ 12410; CA 2033, 5091, 5977, 7253, 7259, 11516, 11517, 11520, 12937, 15300, 16200; CO 6918; CT 15029, 15426; DE 15446; FL 14142, 15481; GA 7463; ID 4285; IL 391, 775, 3821, 3822, 6280, 13657, 15570; IA 666; ME 4647; MD 8011; MA 3944, 4137, 8064, 8092, 11268, 12884, 13253, 14087; MI 5178, 8456, 12651, 14138; MN 6250, 13504, 15800; MO 1365, 11887; NH 15915; NJ 288, 4527; NM 12198, 15222; NY 3494, 5151, 8139, 13128, 13763; NC 4122, 14130; NS 2166; OH 1359, 2952, 10140, 15379; ON 5094; OR 10331, 14174; PA 633, 2483, 11767, 14850, 16064; PQ 2264; TN 3250; TX 5130, 9713; VA 11384, 14794

Materials handling: CA 4844; MD 3; OH 13519; OR 6232

Materials—Thermal properties: IN 11122

Mathematics: AL 15108; AB 15131, 15214; AZ 7091, 15166; AR 15169; BC 15200, 15205; CA 92, 1900, 1993, 2998, 4869, 4870, 5266, 6169, 7253, 7259, 9303, 12146, 12946, 14708, 14725, 15225, 15277, 15300, 15310, 15334, 15338, 15340, 15350, 15354, 16193, 16203; CO 810, 9083, 14574, 15411; CT 11654, 15515, 16901, 17382, 17384; DE 15453; DC 2552, 3991, 5228, 9247, 13974, 14529, 14765; FL 4791, 4832, 12867, 17022; GA 4354; IL 1953, 8870, 9941, 9944, 12785, 15364, 15567, 15583, 17459; IN 1926, 6402, 11131, 11133, 14730, 15987; IA 15614; KS 15637, 17101; KY 15651, 15658, 15660; LA 12740, 13691; MB 15689; MD 1565, 14037, 14492, 15694, 15699; MA 57, 370, 1614, 1651, 3120, 5714, 5715, 5731, 6568, 8079, 8086, 8092, 8677, 9009, 12866, 13683, 15718, 16723, 16880, 17284; MI 8120, 8476, 8482, 15761, 15771, 16505, 16861, 16984; MN 7806, 15798, 15817; MO 7419, 15858, 16814; NE 10228, 15889; NH 15915; NJ 947, 950, 4523, 6479, 6497, 10986, 11625, 13011, 14010; NM 15222; NY 1774, 1794, 1858, 3022, 3223, 3230, 3508, 3644, 3646, 4876, 6257, 6258, 7103, 9537, 9547, 9633, 11186, 11193, 11499, 13101, 13132, 13187, 16135; NC 4119, 15932; ND 15973; NS 31, 13235; OH 2527, 4370, 5138, 8418, 10141, 13984, 15383; OK 2670, 10191, 15995; ON 2080, 2307, 7237, 7795, 11207, 16307, 16399, 16400, 16416, 17435; OR 4775, 10891, 16025; PA 2483, 4079, 6486, 7303, 10646, 10649, 13149, 13318, 16056, 16070, 16089, 17021; PR 16116; PQ 7742, 7749, 15071, 15086; RI 1818; SC 3035, 12285; TN 10021, 16224, 16565; TX 2792, 4154, 5130, 12793, 13405, 13451, 16241, 16255, 16266, 16683; UT 16328; VA 720, 5195, 6498, 7044, 9121, 14089, 14785, 14794, 16353; WA 1254, 16372, 16385; WI 289, 7987, 16455; WY 16497

Mather, Cotton, Increase, and Richard: MA 421

Maurepas, Jean, Comte de: NY 3514

Meat industry and trade: AZ 5527; IL 9217, 13168; NE 14252; WI 8128

Mechanical engineering: AL 13716; AB 336, 8725; CA 1668, 1809, 3096, 3735, 5091, 7253, 7766, 11146, 11258, 12197, 12528, 12759, 12937, 15025, 15262, 15350, 16608; CO 2901, 6918,

Mechanical engineering (Continued)
9083, 16988; CT 1091, 5689, 9960; DC 8921, 14103, 14777; FL 4791, 8873, 12867; IL 1542, 2536, 2804, 13657, 15570; IN 11125, 13757, 15983; IA 8744; KS 1547, 6954; KY 15654, 15660; MB 7906, 15684; MD 10046, 14705; MA 5154, 8064, 13253, 13684, 13823, 15718, 16889; MI 3924, 4238, 4874, 5190, 7257, 8456, 17076; MN 15800; MO 1894, 8743, 13145, 15852; NV 15899; NB 15907; NH 3746, 15915; NJ 1896, 6459, 8698, 13604; NY 3022, 3205, 3494, 3644, 4224, 4369, 5151, 7888, 8139, 8681, 13190, 13765; NC 4110, 4122, 11388; ND 15970; NS 2166, 2313, 5879, 13235; OH 4370, 10124, 13667, 15379, 15389; OK 1368, 10191, 15996; ON 39, 2257, 2281, 2320, 5094, 11208, 16293, 16410; OR 14312; PA 2483, 3774, 4079, 5405, 11512, 12865, 13315, 14778, 16064, 16073, 17021; PQ 1938, 2170, 7749, 10926; SK 16154; TN 8010, 13364; TX 1018, 4522, 6972, 7465, 12825, 13403, 13404, 14015, 14088, 16241; VT 16603; VA 5146, 12861; WV 13759; WI 8560, 10406

Mechanization: OH 8334

Medical care (See also Long-term care of the sick): CA 1518, 12220, 13022; CO 8159; DC 551, 9114, 14321, 14322; FL 1514; HI 15523; IL 490, 492, 1513, 3295, 15371; ME 8148; MD 14776, 14834, 14844; MA 5744, 5746, 8060; MN 13247; MO 1520, 15855; NE 7838; NJ 6856; NY 1515, 2614, 4659, 6850, 9563; ON 2204, 10280, 10297; OR 6892; PA 1521, 12902, 16045; PQ 3527; TN 6092; TX 13977; WA 16393; WI 12742, 17198

Medical communication See: Communication in medicine

Medical devices See: Medical instruments and apparatus

Medical economics: CA 1518, 1998, 11247; DC 551, 5532; IL 550, 1513; MD 14844; MA 5746; MI 15741; MS 8650; MO 1520; NJ 6856; NY 1515, 6093, 8364, 9563; NC 1516; ON 10250, 10255, 10261; PA 1519; PQ 11163

Medical education (See also Paramedical education): AL 15101; AB 15218; AK 15116; BC 15210; CA 7539, 10448, 15273, 15282, 15284, 15293, 15336, 15337, 15342; CO 15419, 15420; CT 5681, 15424; DC 911, 5232, 14887; FL 6740, 15486, 16185; IL 15596, 15597, 15598; IA 15608; KS 15629; KY 15652, 15661; ME 7859, 15910; MB 15685; MD 6838, 15691; MI 5657, 6215, 15733; MN 15787, 15834; MO 6334, 11964, 15856, 15864, 15871; NE 15894; NV 15904; NJ 6856; NM 15923; NY 9488, 13051, 13114; NF 3140; NC 8913, 15937; OH 3038, 9852, 17318; OK 16001; ON 5610, 16032; PA 5277; SK 16156; TN 16219, 16222, 16575; TX 13869, 16227, 16265; UT 16331; WA 6558, 16380, 16381; WV 13830

Medical electronics See: Electronics in medicine

Medical emergencies See: Emergency medical services

Medical ethics: CA 6530; DC 5231; GA 11854; MA 3120; NY 5759; PA 8276, 11286

Medical group practice See: Group medical practice

Medical illustration: CT 17383; FL 15730; IL 9938, 9962, 15373; ME 8282; MD 9213; MA 5748; NY 9462; PQ 7748; TX 16272

Medical instruments and apparatus: MD 14090, 14417; MN 1131; NJ 4142; PA 4338

Medical jurisprudence: AR 817; CA 1162, 1518, 3605, 5022, 10322; DC 937; FL 7878; KS 6640; MD 6838; MA 622, 5748; MI 51; MN 15834; NY 5591, 6816, 7769, 9475, 9602; OH 2525; ON 10261, 10291; PA 363; PQ 3527; TX 17099

Medical laws and legislation: AZ 10066; IL 1127; MD 10047; MA 1612; PA 3939, 4863

Medical personnel: CO 8159; IA 6677; NJ 6856; NY 9197

Medical records: CA 8146; IL 552

Medical research (See also Medicine, Experimental): AR 724; CA 10474, 13612, 14741, 14873, 14877, 15257, 15282; CT 9389, 14789; DC 9258, 14144; FL 8413; GA 14189; HI 15521; IL 3237; KS 5885, 12621; ME 4931; MB 15680; MD 9175, 9213, 14092, 14763; MA 4286; NJ 6519, 12907;

Medical research (Continued)
NM 7613; NY 477, 6873, 8050, 9477, 13120; OH 5080;
ON 3365, 10281, 16286; PA 1541, 7213, 16054; PQ 3077,
12540; TX 6528; VA 14807

Medical school libraries: AL 15110, 16167; AB 15138; AZ 15147;
AR 15176; CA 12944, 16192; CT 17383; DE 3831; DC 5223,
6141; FL 15729, 15730; GA 4353, 8154, 8265, 8830; IL 9938,
11605, 12772, 15532, 15562; IN 6406; IA 16031; LA 7593,
13694; MD 6836, 6837, 14859; MA 5744, 5748, 12887,
13682, 15719; MI 15763, 16860; MN 8129; MO 15533, 16819;
NE 3591; NH 3745; NJ 11624, 15720, 15721, 15722, 15723;
NY 3509, 8905, 9462, 9501, 13098, 13130, 13136, 13795,
16147, 17403, 17404, 17405, 17406; NF 8205; NC 4120,
4169, 16701; ND 15976; NS 3685; OH 7045, 8155, 10129,
10156; OK 10312, 16010; ON 2224, 11196; OR 10333;
PA 5590, 6768, 8156, 10639, 10709, 13330, 16045, 16081;
PR 10861, 16115; PQ 7743, 15055, 15095; SC 8166, 16172;
SD 16178; TN 4181, 8172; TX 6119, 13977, 16270, 16271,
16272; VT 16333; VA 4216, 16354, 16642; WV 8000, 16920;
WI 8158, 16435

Medical social work: CO 4907; MI 3908; NC 2777; WI 16673

Medical sociology See: Social medicine

Medical statistics: AZ 790; CA 2060; DC 551; IA 6677; MD 9087

Medical technology: MA 8090; MO 15855; NV 15900; NY 13128;
NS 9985; ON 13558; PA 12885; TN 8172; TX 623

Medicine (See also Hospital libraries; names of medical specialties,
e.g., Gastroenterology): AK 15122; BC 3127, 17136; CA 144,
5266, 7473, 7532, 11308, 12294; CO 3873, 13867; CT 5522,
5684, 8526; DE 4103; DC 9166, 12336, 14143, 14886, 14887;
FL 16838; IL 579, 6008, 12776, 13732; IA 1882; ME 7861,
9873; MB 17179; MD 8153, 9213, 14542, 14707; MA 286,
5896; MI 2737, 8470, 16730; MN 11244, 13510; MS 8652;
MO 340, 7961; MT 5474; NJ 1313, 5990, 10365, 16729;
NY 437, 1774, 2658, 3644, 7692, 8161, 9029, 9499, 9587,
9966, 11471, 11499, 13190, 13237; NC 4598; OH 3044, 3045,
3046, 4051; OK 10182; ON 2255, 2376, 2939, 9965, 16301,
16416; PA 14239, 16952; PR 11106; PQ 8, 1101, 1908, 3527,
4627, 8274; RI 11395; SC 16511; TN 826, 1319; TX 1280,
1436, 11362, 13407, 13449, 13450, 13977; WA 10762,
16798; WI 9930, 17222

Medicine, Biochemic: AK 15116; CA 2987, 3659, 15260; DE 6260;
HI 15521; IL 431, 7144, 7629, 11605, 13613, 15562; IN 1544;
IA 14253; LA 13687; ME 2653; MD 7444, 9213, 14091;
MA 872, 17284; MI 3275, 16505; MN 15787; MO 16805;
NJ 8693, 12302; NM 15222; NY 437, 8161, 13002; NC 1314;
OH 9951; OR 10336; PA 4338, 13315; TX 12817; VA 5195

Medicine, Clinical: AZ 7939; BC 16617; CA 1973, 1978, 5849,
11641, 12188, 13177, 15284, 15336; FL 12738, 14748;
IL 550, 1891, 15364; IN 11132; ME 15910; MA 3521; MI 8454,
16504, 16860; MO 4320, 11883; NY 1351, 3218, 4334, 4525,
8164, 9501, 10696, 13003; NC 2750; ND 11147; OH 7391,
10129, 11452; ON 27, 7793; PA 6532, 7804; PQ 3077;
RI 8632; TX 13376, 13394; WA 5533, 12878; WV 8000;
WI 3198; WY 4571, 16493

Medicine, Environmental See: Environmental health

Medicine, Experimental (See also Medical research): OH 10129,
12028; PQ 7730

Medicine—History: AL 15110; AB 15138; BC 3127, 15210, 16617;
CA 6749, 7473, 7532, 8912, 11826, 12944, 15282, 15293,
15342, 16192, 17457; CO 3873; CT 5684, 9356, 17383;
DC 5232, 14074; FL 15730; GA 8154; IL 415, 550, 6588, 8424,
12772, 15364, 15596; IN 6392; IA 15608; ME 6983;
MB 15685; MD 6838, 8153, 9213, 15691; MA 5748, 9379,
9691, 12887, 15719; MI 5862, 15733; MN 8129, 15787;
MO 11883; NE 15894; NJ 8262; NM 15923; NY 3218, 3500,
6805, 7313, 9462, 9488, 9489, 9501, 9640, 11474, 13098,
13130, 13136, 16147; NF 8205; NC 3549, 4120, 15937;
ND 15976; NS 3685; OH 3047, 6799, 15375, 15386; ON 27,
3574, 16612, 16407; OR 10333; PA 3126, 5590, 10606,
13330, 16081; PR 16115; PQ 7748; RI 11395; SC 8166;
SD 16178; TN 4181, 4453, 16575; TX 1280, 16268, 16271,
16272; VT 16333; WA 16380; WV 7998; WI 8158, 8543,
11753, 16435

Medicine, Industrial: AB 221; BC 1745; DE 4095; GA 365; MD 5215;
NY 4225, 4525; ON 2342; PQ 2213; TX 11939

Medicine, Legal See: Medical jurisprudence

Medicine, Military (See also Medicine, Naval): DC 14143;
MD 14859; OH 13955; ON 2224, 2229; PA 14239; TX 13992

Medicine, Naval: MD 14707, 14763

Medicine, Physical (See also Rehabilitation): CA 12224; IL 11327;
MI 11328; NY 6581; ON 17290; PQ 6473; WV 16923; WI 3648

Medicine, Preventive (See also Public health): CA 2060, 7526,
11013, 14745; IA 6689; MB 7901; MA 5744; MI 15774;
ON 2224; PA 5817; PQ 15054; RI 11403

Medicine—Study and teaching See: Medical school libraries

Medicine, Submarine See: Submarine medicine

Medicine, Thoracic (See also Heart—Diseases; Respiratory
organs—Diseases): CA 1213; MD 6838; MO 8667; NY 11749;
NC 14963; ON 12445; PQ 8801; TX 12102

Medicine, Transportation See: Transportation medicine

Medicine, Veterinary See: Veterinary medicine

Medieval history See: Middle Ages—History

Melchior, Lauritz: NE 3725

Melville, Herman: CA 2995; HI 15529; IL 9661; NH 3753; UT 1700

Membranes (Technology): LA 5573

Memory (See also Mnemonics): MI 7155; NY 3229, 17441

Memphis (TN): TN 2628, 8220

Mencken, Henry Louis: KS 15622; KY 15658; MD 13205; NH 3753;
NY 1793; PA 5288

Mennonites (See also Amish; Anabaptists): CA 8241; IN 907, 5949,
8243; KS 1418, 8242; MB 8240, 8246; OH 1526; ON 3403;
PA 7196, 8244, 8534, 11366, 17462; VA 4203

Menopause: FL 15475

Mental health (See also Psychiatry and psychoanalysis): AB 191;
BC 1729; CA 7527; CO 16968; IL 6514; IN 2615; IA 6678;
MB 7901; MD 8033, 14831, 14832, 14833; MA 8101;
MI 15755, 15764; MS 8646; MO 15855; NV 9343; NJ 2499,
4177; NY 60, 3233, 4145, 5802, 8249, 9474, 9593; OH 10098,
10149; PA 5590, 6525; PR 11104; TX 8251, 13411, 13429,
16247; VT 16601; VA 9220; WI 7180, 16463

Mental health facilities:

AB 205, 206, 208, 209

AZ 787, 794

AR 817, 1375

BC 11458

CA 983, 2042, 2076, 4560, 5099, 7210, 7217, 8379, 9011,
10541, 10880, 12684, 13020, 17268

CO 1422, 3176, 4907, 17065

CT 302, 3396, 4323, 5602, 6516

DE 3848, 5402

DC 11729

FL 689, 4816, 4817, 12717

GA 2668, 5252, 5423, 16905

HI 5781

Mental health facilities (Continued)

IL 304, 2828, 4002, 4310, 6313, 6741, 7716, 7817, 12532, 13523, 17458

IN 2667, 4507, 7469, 7835, 8949, 9376, 10044, 12833

IA 3001, 5327, 6340, 8250, 8893

KS 6847, 7219, 9958, 10379, 10520, 13551, 17174

KY 4213, 10398, 17001

LA 2652, 12733

ME 1165, 10783

MB 1654, 7895, 11671, 12393

MD 1765, 3617, 4212, 11566, 12886, 12897

MA 1602, 5997, 5998, 7420, 7787, 8097, 8112, 8143, 13219

MI 3908, 7155, 9900, 10028, 10782, 13615, 17449

MN 718, 1647, 2086, 4578, 4637, 8821, 11252, 12015, 17145

MO 1504, 5056, 11834, 11886, 16985

MT 12705

NE 1287, 5760, 9731

NV 9343

NH 9403

NJ 690, 4475, 4535, 5528, 6203, 6861, 13624

NM 7568, 9441

NY 1458, 1861, 2437, 2651, 3568, 3589, 4326, 5403, 5653, 6159, 7069, 7070, 8498, 9592, 9594, 10549, 10768, 11188, 11485, 12051, 16530, 16531, 17127

NF 16830

NC 1802, 4037, 13739

ND 9796, 12731

OH 989, 2084, 3058, 3238, 3779, 4567, 7401, 9843, 10898, 11660, 16997, 17265

OK 2669, 16999

ON 3018, 5616, 6219, 7075, 10237, 10957, 11179, 12031

OR 4211, 10347

PA 274, 3738, 4001, 4215, 5032, 5671, 5765, 7232, 8157, 10614, 10615, 10617, 10725, 10727, 16103, 16741, 17078, 17269

PQ 4046, 6071, 6076, 6077, 12539

RI 1921

SC 1828, 5520, 5607

SK 11061

TN 8215

TX 15, 1074, 12103, 13367, 17099

UT 16523

VT 1666

VA 2665, 2677, 4214, 12836, 16639, 17000

WA 16787, 16790

WI 1812, 6993, 8236, 8551, 8554, 11495, 12811, 17176

Mental health facilities (Continued)

WY 17334

Mental hygiene See: Mental health

Mental retardation: AB 8425, 15130; CA 2023, 10880, 12684; CT 9786; FL 13077; GA 5423; IL 8948, 12436; IA 17275; KS 17174; ME 15671; MB 7895; MD 6987; MA 12496; MI 10028; MS 8646; NE 1287, 9309; NJ 6203, 9815; NM 7568; NY 1800, 3568, 7317, 8740, 9595, 10235; OH 9843, 15096; ON 5616, 8380, 9182, 10271, 10272, 10957; PA 4329, 17078; PQ 8798; SC 12697, 12698; TN 826; TX 8251, 13429; VT 1656; WA 16788, 16789; WI 9887

Mental tests See: Educational tests and measurements

Merchandising See: Advertising and marketing

Merchant marine: MD 13607; NY 553, 13122, 14488; NS 7966; VA 7953

Merton, Thomas: KY 1349, 5281; MA 1583; MO 6998

Metabolism: CA 14873; MD 9175; ON 16286

Metal castings: OR 10929

Metal powders See: Powder metallurgy

Metal-working machinery: OH 2952

Metallurgy (See also Metals; names of specific metals, e.g., Aluminum): AL 14183; AB 5641, 12480; AZ 1014, 15166; BC 2168, 3255, 10804; CA 4841, 4869, 6889, 7766, 8718, 11258, 11542, 16608; CO 329, 11511, 15415, 16988; CT 326, 332, 909, 3251, 9960, 10221, 10222, 11340, 13460, 15426, 17194; DC 14521, 14530; FL 17022; GA 12839; ID 4285; IL 1017, 1569, 2536, 3438, 3575, 10217, 13889, 15570; IN 1946, 6462, 7145, 13757; IA 666, 6687; KY 6251, 15654; MD 7809, 8011; MA 4137, 14087; MI 325, 4054, 4238, 8456, 8480, 8482; MN 14184, 15800; MO 14181, 15869; NV 13526, 14180, 15901; NJ 878, 947, 1538, 4527, 4528, 6458, 6459; NY 1772, 3205, 4369, 5144, 5151, 6590, 7103, 7920, 9547, 10592, 12851, 12925, 13190, 13997; NC 5572; OH 624, 829, 1826, 3071, 5156, 5984, 7718, 8334, 9714, 10140, 11348, 13667, 13766, 15379; OK 10736, 15996; ON 227, 1296, 2080, 2180, 3257, 4016, 4307, 4562, 4563, 6337, 9874, 10302, 11200, 12995, 16293; OR 4466, 6232, 14174; PA 259, 313, 1427, 1428, 1944, 2481, 2483, 2495, 4859, 6110, 6871, 7980, 11767, 14778, 14850, 16048, 16073, 17021; PQ 228, 2264, 9718, 9720, 11145, 12499; RI 13232; SC 12285; TN 3250, 8010, 10021; TX 2092, 6178; UT 14182; VA 11384; WA 1254; WV 9269; WI 260, 289, 11376

Metallurgy, Powder See: Powder metallurgy

Metals (See also Metallurgy): CA 1298, 6888, 6889, 6919, 16579; CT 15028, 15029; DC 14521; GA 12839; IL 6280, 10217, 16688; MD 980; MI 3924; MO 9717; NY 1773, 4659, 9674, 12355, 13763; OH 624, 1247, 6325, 7765; ON 4563, 9721; PA 312, 1845, 8564; WI 7154, 12571

Metals—Finishing (See also Electroplating): MI 10232

Metaphysics: AK 10741; AZ 17310; CA 6666, 11018, 12167, 12950, 13819; FL 13013, 13471; TX 4470; VA 15038

Meteorites: AZ 798

Meteorology: AL 14097; AK 15118; AZ 15157; BC 2141; CA 2898, 4869, 10063, 10064, 12948, 14736; CO 9083, 15406; CT 17374; DC 14517; FL 14568, 14573, 15724; GA 4641; IL 6316, 13947, 15364; IN 11127; KS 6949; MB 2139; MD 14572; MA 554, 1584, 4418, 5103, 5715, 7946, 8072, 8080, 13871; MS 8641; MO 14702; NV 14703, 15898; NH 8910; NJ 13492, 14569; NY 2069, 5079, 13127, 14491; NC 4113, 4393, 14575, 17298; NS 2138; ON 2140; PA 10640; PQ 2142, 7744; TX 6533, 13374, 16241; UT 9748

Methodist Church See: United Methodist Church

Metric system: MD 569; ON 2218

Mexican Americans: AZ 799, 3525; CA 7563, 8401, 8402, 10039,

Mexican Americans (Continued)
12182, 12936, 15232, 15296, 15347; **CO** 12032; **DC** 3304; **IL** 15584; **IN** 15981; **NM** 4440; **TX** 941, 6126, 16232, 16261, 16264

Mexico: CA 12215; **DC** 7378; **LA** 13689; **NM** 15925

Mexico—History: AZ 784; **CA** 2041, 14595, 15226; **LA** 13689; **TX** 4306, 14604, 16229, 16232, 16261, 16264

Mice: ME 6734

Michener, James Albert: CO 15977; **MD** 13205

Michigan: MI 1258, 1266, 1397, 2655, 2752, 2989, 3808, 3861, 3909, 3928, 4774, 4961, 5449, 5450, 6109, 6695, 7177, 7311, 7892, 7981, 7995, 8045, 8130, 8434, 8444, 8446, 8447, 8482, 8499, 8734, 9810, 9899, 10031, 10766, 10789, 12441, 15765, 16852, 16859, 16975

Microbiology (See also Bacteriology): AL 14416, 15108; **AB** 201; **AK** 15116; **CA** 383, 2715, 3081, 8124, 8269, 13196, 15257, 15293; **CO** 3182, 3477; **CT** 9001, 9995, 11419; **GA** 14189; **IL** 1286, 7123, 13613, 14256, 15557; **IN** 6376, 6623, 8527, 15986; **IA** 6689; **KY** 15640; **MD** 652, 14092, 15697; **MA** 5733, 5748, 8539, 15716; **MI** 16730; **MO** 8247; **NE** 15880; **NJ** 2099, 11630, 12302; **NY** 1709, 14257; **NC** 1314; **OH** 10110; **ON** 2208, 7148, 10281, 16728, 17043; **PA** 487, 14248, 16076; **TX** 13138, 16258, 16692; **WI** 10700, 15042

Microcomputers: CA 744, 6552; **MI** 15772; **OH** 6450

Microelectronics: CA 556, 11522; **MD** 283; **MN** 3448; **NY** 6281; **OH** 5398; **OR** 6553

Micronesia: GU 15511; **HI** 15528

Microprocessors: CA 5815, 6551, 13256; **CT** 5143; **IL** 1542; **PA** 8484

Micropublishing: CA 16503; **MD** 922; **NY** 6452; **OH** 1341; **ON** 3267

Microscope and microscopy: IL 7704; **LA** 14260; **MA** 8092; **NY** 1262, 13772

Microwave circuits: MD 283

Microwaves: BC 8485; **CA** 1087, 6714, 11263, 12948; **CT** 691; **MA** 8486, 16581; **NY** 5148; **OH** 686; **ON** 2311, 16582; **VA** 6621

Middle Ages—History: DC 5708; **IN** 15988; **MN** 11773; **NH** 11677; **NJ** 10995; **NY** 4878, 13090; **ON** 3115, 16309, 16310; **PA** 16051; **PQ** 4021; **SK** 2104

Middle East See: Near East

Migraine: ON 8523

Migration, Internal: FL 4827

Milhaud, Darius: CA 8541

Military art and science (See also Naval art and science): AL 13876, 14003, 14096; **AB** 2169; **AK** 14124, 14128; **AR** 13912; **BC** 11600; **CA** 6920, 11247, 11246, 13881, 13938, 13940, 14008, 14129, 14480, 14482, 14716, 15350; **CO** 12331, 13866, 14113; **DC** 6555, 6622, 11248, 14107, 14229, 14537; **FL** 13894, 13906, 14114, 14132, 14787; **GA** 14077, 14111, 14126, 14134, 14485; **HI** 13903; **IN** 13900, 14135; **KS** 14009, 14125; **KY** 14000; **MD** 14105; **MA** 13902, 14080, 14087; **MI** 14137, 14138; **MS** 13907, 13971; **MO** 13942, 14121; **NH** 13931; **NJ** 14115; **NM** 13909, 14139; **NY** 14048, 14094, 14117; **NC** 14112; **ND** 13979; **NS** 2221; **OK** 13878, 14049; **ON** 2222, 2223, 2226, 2233, 2235, 11590, 11596; **OR** 10891; **PA** 4881, 14095, 14145, 16053; **PQ** 2170, 2228; **RI** 14734, 14800; **SC** 2966, 13926, 14120; **TX** 13899, 13911, 13994, 14118; **VA** 720, 1283, 3824, 10819, 12912, 13193, 13990, 14051, 14083, 14086, 14089, 14104, 14110, 14127, 14140, 14236, 14244, 14481, 14704, 16632; **WA** 13897, 14116, 14122; **WV** 14643

Military assistance: DC 5059; **NC** 14082; **PA** 9041

Military communications See: Communications, Military

Military education—Aids and devices: FL 14797; **VA** 16632

Military engineering: BC 2380; **CA** 4848, 14034; **DC** 14103; **IL** 13996; **MA** 14193; **ON** 2235; **VA** 1949, 14004, 14039

Military history (See also Naval history): AL 13949, 14002, 14005; **AK** 14124; **AZ** 14079; **AR** 821; **CA** 372, 625, 4664, 13887, 14100, 14129, 14226, 14482; **DC** 6622, 9164, 13879, 14107, 14229, 14483, 14537; **FL** 13919, 14132; **GA** 14077, 14123, 14126, 14625; **HI** 13903, 13941, 14099, 14484; **IL** 2428, 4909; **IN** 14803; **KS** 14009, 14188, 14622; **KY** 14106, 14914; **MD** 14050, 14105, 14727; **MA** 688, 1605, 5902, 8094, 12656; **MI** 5071, 14137; **MN** 8597; **MO** 13942; **MT** 8758; **NE** 9314; **NV** 13927; **NH** 4309, 10558; **NJ** 14011; **NM** 13904, 13909, 14627; **NY** 1850, 4912, 10207, 14093, 14094, 14117, 14195, 16551; **NC** 4168, 14112; **NT** 2236; **OH** 14972; **OK** 14049; **ON** 4908, 8386; **PA** 10624, 14095, 14624; **PQ** 11763; **RI** 1819, 14800; **SC** 2965; **TN** 14723; **TX** 4897, 5923, 13875, 13911, 13994, 14133, 14620, 16263; **VT** 9968; **VA** 2529, 3325, 5195, 7994, 9185, 13910, 13980, 14001, 14039, 14078, 14086, 14140, 14481, 16648, 16725; **WA** 4905, 13916, 14607; **WI** 12967

Military intelligence: AZ 14079; **CA** 17238; **CO** 13914; **DC** 14233, 14761; **VA** 14081

Military law: DC 11071, 14223, 14805; **IN** 14135; **ON** 2237; **VA** 14083, 14806

Military medicine See: Medicine, Military

Military psychology See: Psychology, Military

Military research (See also Ordnance research): CA 14245; **TX** 12824

Military transportation See: Transportation, Military

Military vehicles See: Vehicles, Military

Milk (See also Dairy products): IL 445; **MD** 14266

Millay, Edna St. Vincent: CT 13641; **DC** 7378; **RI** 16128

Miller, Henry: CA 15298; **IL** 12778; **MN** 15829

Milton, John: AB 15129; **IL** 15588; **IN** 6392; **ON** 16407

Mime (See also Pantomime): NY 557; **ON** 13561

Mineral industries: BC 15201; **DC** 558, 14178; **MD** 14175; **MT** 8757

Mineralogy: CO 1013, 14444, 15402; **CT** 16562; **FL** 4808; **IL** 6306, 15572; **IA** 15607; **KY** 15643; **MA** 5713; **MI** 8480; **MN** 15803; **MS** 8642; **MO** 16809; **NV** 15901; **NJ** 878, 10982; **NY** 3217, 16143; **OH** 10101; **ON** 2180; **PA** 1834, 2487, 5302, 10640, 16048; **PQ** 6474; **SD** 12709; **TX** 1670, 4056, 4921, 16234, 16245; **VA** 14449

Miners: BC 9006; **CO** 15417

Mines and mineral resources: AB 180, 8725; **AK** 159, 14173; **AZ** 792, 1014, 10656, 15145, 15159; **BC** 1724, 1746, 2722, 3255, 10804, 13242, 15201; **CA** 1298, 1957, 2037, 4060, 4841, 7036, 7766, 8718, 9350, 10517, 14150, 16519; **CO** 327, 328, 1013, 1366, 1797, 2901, 3156, 3157, 3160, 3401, 3715, 3885, 5568, 7931, 11527, 13334, 14179, 14363, 14444, 16988; **CT** 332, 7000, 13460; **DC** 558, 14337; **ID** 15550; **IL** 16870; **IN** 6387; **KS** 6936; **KY** 15645; **MD** 14175; **MA** 8064; **MI** 6109, 8482; **MN** 6696, 9840, 14184, 15800; **MO** 8671, 14181, 15869; **MT** 8315, 8757, 14171; **NV** 15901; **NM** 9437, 14172; **NY** 3205, 9674; **NS** 2433, 9992, 13235; **OH** 1252; **OK** 3402; **ON** 1296, 2080, 2180, 2183, 3866, 4562, 6335, 6336, 7237, 9721, 9862, 9874, 10286, 11200, 11440; **OR** 9331; **PA** 1026, 3416, 7067, 10612, 14176; **PQ** 3292, 9720, 11166, 12447; **SD** 12709; **TX** 4075, 5420; **VA** 14449, 16654; **WA** 14462, 16779; **WV** 13137, 14564; **WY** 5214, 13165, 14168, 16499

Mining law: AZ 4503; **CA** 15251; **CO** 330

Minneapolis (MN): MN 6084, 8579, 8579, 8584

Minnesota: MN 717, 1310, 1522, 1811, 2518, 2656, 3026, 3456,

Noise pollution (Continued)
ON 10278; **PQ** 15045

Non-destructive testing: **CA** 16608; **MA** 14087; **NE** 9321; **ON** 16875; **TX** 12824

Non-formal education: **AZ** 12837; **CO** 919; **MI** 8468; **NY** 11070; **PA** 5478, 16096

Non-profit corporations See: Corporations, Nonprofit

Non-wage payments: **CA** 17131; **DC** 4357; **KY** 8173; **MA** 9390, 17132; **NJ** 7133; **NY** 4426, 6618; **OH** 12497; **ON** 13585, 17130; **PQ** 6723, 13197, 13584; **TX** 10568; **WI** 6604, 11333

Norfolk (VA): **VA** 9730

North Africa See: Africa, North

North Atlantic Treaty Organization (NATO): **DC** 1006

North Carolina: **NC** 1516, 2534, 2747, 4168, 5511, 5554, 8629, 9758, 9761, 10210, 11578, 13148, 14597, 14598, 14599, 14664, 15931, 15947, 15965, 17352

North Dakota: **ND** 940, 8627, 9797, 9803, 12965, 12991, 15967

North-West Mounted Police See: Royal Canadian Mounted Police

Northern regions See: Polar regions

Northwest, Pacific: **BC** 1735, 11600, 15207; **ID** 6265, 6267, 15544, 15552; **OR** 3202, 7353, 8131, 10334, 13512, 16030, 16992; **WA** 4217, 5971, 12374, 12379, 13202, 13897, 14628, 16394, 16395, 16396, 16748, 16784, 16786, 16795, 17007, 17056, 17084, 17355

Northwest Territories (Canada): **AB** 15128; **NT** 9924

Northwest Territory (U.S.) See: Old Northwest

Norway: **DC** 7364; **MN** 12685

Norwegian Americans: **IA** 7643, 9963; **MN** 9961, 12685; **WI** 16606

Nova Scotia: **NB** 8881; **NS** 3677, 9986, 9987, 9990, 17398

Nuclear energy See: Atomic power

Nuclear engineering: **AL** 13716; **CA** 1304, 1307, 10517, 12758, 15262, 15350, 16200; **CO** 6918; **CT** 572; **DC** 8921, 14777; **FL** 4794, 17020; **ID** 773, 4365; **IL** 573, 775, 3265, 4838, 15570; **IN** 11125; **KY** 15660; **MD** 1305, 10001; **MA** 8092, 13823; **MI** 3924; **MO** 15852; **NJ** 1896, 11093; **NY** 1772, 1774, 3205, 3494, 4239, 5291, 7103, 16141; **OH** 1252, 8755, 13667, 15379; **OK** 15996; **ON** 1030, 10256; **OR** 10885; **PA** 4542, 8564, 17019, 17025; **PQ** 900; **SC** 2764; **TN** 13364; **TX** 5574; **WI** 16438

Nuclear facilities—Law and legislation See: Atomic power—Law and legislation

Nuclear fusion: **CA** 5066; **MA** 8084; **MI** 7099

Nuclear medicine: **CA** 15306; **IL** 12502; **MD** 6821, 13988, 14414; **MA** 1117, 8057, 9391; **MI** 11940; **NY** 2959, 11825; **PA** 13331; **SK** 12275; **TN** 10017

Nuclear physics: **AB** 15140; **CA** 10453, 10754, 12931, 15315; **CO** 15411; **IL** 573, 4640, 15587; **IN** 11133, 15982; **IA** 666; **KS** 6949; **MA** 8066, 13683; **MN** 15823; **NY** 1770, 3228, 4876; **OH** 10118, 15390; **OK** 16006; **PA** 7980, 16092; **PQ** 7751; **TN** 10022; **VA** 3146, 14785

Nuclear reactors (See also Atomic power): **AL** 4394; **CA** 5066, 5135, 6015; **CT** 3251; **GA** 3717; **IL** 3714; **MI** 15770; **NJ** 11094; **ON** 1030; **PA** 17019; **PQ** 1032; **TN** 10023

Nuclear safeguards See: Atomic power—Security measures

Nuclear sciences: **CA** 4287, 7253, 7259, 11146, 15300; **CT** 12305; **DC** 14243; **ID** 4285; **IL** 775, 12236; **KY** 8009; **MB** 1034; **MI** 15770; **MO** 15860, 16815; **NV** 14318, 14703; **NM** 12198; **NY** 6245, 7103, 7307; **OH** 1108, 5386; **ON** 1033, 1035, 4307,

Nuclear sciences (Continued)
4635; **PA** 17021, 17025; **PR** 16114; **SC** 12285; **TN** 10021, 10022; **TX** 5130; **UT** 6564; **VA** 1109; **WA** 1254

Nuclear weapons See: Atomic weapons

Nudism: **CA** 4331, 6848

Numerical analysis: **NY** 13187; **ON** 16284

Numismatics (See also Coinage and money): **CA** 13740; **CO** 574; **DC** 6627; **NH** 9999; **NY** 575; **OH** 3066; **ON** 2392; **PA** 4982; **PQ** 11151, 12624; **TX** 16239

Nursing (See also Nursing school libraries; Psychiatric nursing): **AB** 169; **AK** 151; **BC** 1716, 11325; **CA** 7473, 12146, 12174; **CO** 927, 16968; **CT** 5522; **DC** 2555; **FL** 6740; **GA** 365; **IL** 11803, 12785, 15562, 15596, 16672; **IN** 11132; **IA** 6671, 8019; **KY** 4196; **LA** 9934; **MB** 7893; **MD** 8301, 9213, 11816; **MA** 4758; **MI** 8470, 16861; **MN** 1423, 11244, 15787; **MO** 7418, 15864; **NV** 15900; **NB** 9358; **NH** 9418; **NM** 15923; **NY** 529, 3644, 6198, 8161, 9029, 9197, 9590, 10433, 13087, 13088, 13092, 13098, 13104, 13130, 13795; **NF** 8205; **NC** 2645, 4598; **OH** 3044, 3046, 8155, 10129; **OK** 1113, 10182, 10190, 10312, 16001; **ON** 248, 2393, 2593, 7178, 7793, 8709, 9751, 10297, 11326, 16301; **OR** 10333; **PA** 1836, 10647, 12902, 13330, 16045; **PQ** 8807, 10329, 15082; **SC** 8166; **SD** 10940; **SK** 16156, 16745; **TX** 6119, 13449, 13456, 13992, 16271, 16272; **VT** 2532; **WA** 6558; **WI** 5098, 7987, 16673

Nursing—History: **AL** 1200, 12048; **CT** 9356; **LA** 9934; **MD** 6838; **MA** 1577, 1606, 7873, 9378, 9691; **MN** 11481; **NJ** 4372; **NY** 529, 9488, 13227; **OH** 15384; **PA** 1836, 11911, 17040; **TX** 1070, 13456; **WA** 6558; **WI** 3197

Nursing school libraries: **AL** 1200, 11041; **AB** 4861, 11581; **AR** 1198; **CT** 11743; **FL** 4784, 4831, 6736; **GA** 9838; **IL** 4500, 5429, 6291, 7668, 8245, 11502, 11680, 11750, 11943; **IN** 10511, 11726, 11857; **IA** 6675, 8001; **LA** 2738, 10391, 12750; **ME** 4202; **MD** 8025, 12886; **MA** 1577, 7873, 9378, 11733, 17281; **MI** 1931, 5587, 5862; **MO** 1216, 1875, 6803, 8346, 8661, 11779, 11924; **NE** 1830; **NJ** 2882, 4372, 5843, 6775, 8263, 8919, 10396; **NY** 1407, 3200, 9197, 11732, 11841, 11913, 12052; **NF** 5412; **NC** 4140, 8312, 17189; **ND** 13650; **NS** 11936; **OH** 1062, 3804, 4330, 4558, 6800, 11040, 11721, 13664, 15384; **ON** 3323; **OR** 4332, 16712; **PA** 16, 1660, 2789, 4294, 4963, 5112, 6747, 7214, 8302, 8303, 8304, 9848, 10607, 10939, 11287, 11579, 11911, 11931, 12439; **PQ** 7746; **TN** 1203, 4454, 8341, 11975; **TX** 5852, 5878, 6214, 8342, 8343, 16265; **VA** 3118, 3795, 8196, 11424; **WI** 3197, 4256, 11856

Nutrition (See also Food industry and trade): **AZ** 12837; **BC** 1729, 15210; **CA** 546, 2060, 2468, 3659, 8138, 10004, 10943, 15256; **CT** 6184, 9001, 12287, 17048; **DC** 596, 7274, 13058, 14415; **GA** 3090; **HI** 15523; **IL** 1286, 3668, 7123, 9217, 11149, 13168, 15575; **IN** 1708, 2664, 5033, 6623, 11124; **KY** 15639; **MD** 14267, 15705; **MA** 8070, 8092, 13682; **MI** 3288, 5271, 6971, 8449; **MO** 8247, 10685, 11241; **NE** 15881; **NJ** 2099, 3563, 5163; **NY** 477, 2614, 3489, 3491, 5168, 6712, 13227, 14412; **NC** 15935; **OH** 3044, 3046, 10018, 10132, 11571; **ON** 2112, 2377, 7073; **PA** 4079, 5883, 7304; **PQ** 6435, 15054; **RI** 6860; **SK** 12249; **TN** 16575; **TX** 16238; **VA** 14086; **WA** 16387

Nutrition policy: **CT** 2606; **DC** 6601, 17302; **MI** 3288

Obstetrics: **DC** 414, 3199; **HI** 6955; **MD** 6835; **MN** 15814; **NY** 8119; **NS** 5414; **PA** 6768, 7841; **PQ** 11604; **RI** 17242

Occult sciences (See also Magic; Witchcraft): **CA** 7561, 11065, 12133, 13472; **CO** 5115; **IL** 6476, 13470, 15569; **MI** 5071; **MN** 16892; **NY** 10496; **OH** 3067; **PA** 11568; **RI** 8331; **TX** 4470

Occupational health See: Industrial hygiene

Occupational retraining: **MN** 8608; **NJ** 9429; **NY** 4626; **OK** 9096; **WV** 16923

Occupational safety See: Industrial safety

Occupational therapy (See also Rehabilitation): **AR** 813; **CT** 9967; **MD** 576; **MA** 8097; **ON** 8709; **PQ** 2706, 6473; **TN** 10017; **TX** 13456; **WI** 16673

Ocean engineering (See also Marine sciences): BC 1738; CA 745, 1992, 12227, 14766; MD 14572; MA 8064, 8093, 17264; MS 14767; NF 8207; OH 5401; TX 4842

Ocean law: DC 14706; OR 10060; VA 16342

Ocean travel: WA 5592

Oceania: AS 4630; CA 5582, 10443, 10456, 15351; DC 9650, 14817; GU 4779, 15511; HI 1703, 5787, 5796, 10435, 15528; IN 1924

Oceanography (See also Coasts; Marine biology): AL 7947; AK 157, 14548, 15119, 15120; BC 2168, 6523, 16949; CA 684, 2053, 2793, 3716, 10063, 10485, 12359, 12941, 13782, 13784, 14561, 14562, 14725, 14766, 15269, 15339, 15340, 16187; CO 9083, 14574, 15402; CT 5129, 17374, 17377; DE 15449; DC 12593, 14570, 14578, 17299; FL 4791, 4792, 5644, 9993, 14560, 14573, 15724; GA 15510; HI 5771, 6653, 10062, 14550, 15530; IL 9937, 15364, 15572; IN 11127; ME 7862, 15672; MD 14572, 15699, 15712; MA 1253, 5715, 5732, 7946, 8072, 8080, 14553, 17264; MS 5561, 14767; NJ 14569; NY 3220, 3518, 3644, 13127, 14618; NC 4118, 14557, 14575, 15930, 15936; NS 1318, 3544; OK 15997; OR 10359; PR 16113; PQ 2195, 2198, 7747; RI 11269, 16130; SC 1230; TX 8699, 13335, 13374, 13380, 16245, 16249; VA 9680, 14709, 16646; WA 14555, 14579, 16373; WI 16436, 16446

O'Connor, Flannery: GA 5236

Office management: DC 13041; NE 17263; NY 13223; VA 13040

Ohio: OH 262, 1211, 1317, 1628, 2950, 3007, 3556, 3660, 3783, 4965, 5106, 5501, 5806, 5932, 6157, 7002, 7165, 7186, 7388, 7508, 7772, 8416, 10087, 10088, 10089, 10104, 10154, 10164, 10584, 10805, 10877, 12798, 12970, 13209, 13541, 13710, 14666, 15375, 16695, 16736, 16996, 17254, 17314, 17317, 17324

Ohio Valley: IL 15373; KY 16970; OH 8420, 11074; PA 16078

Oil (Petroleum) See: Petroleum

Oil sands: AB 214, 13174, 13175; WY 14316

Oil-shales: CO 4417, 14454, 15456; KY 15645; MN 14184; WY 14316

Oil spills: CA 15350, 17271; CO 4417; DC 14397; MA 8093; MI 12872

Oil well drilling: CA 6324, 12227; KS 6937; OK 9184; TX 9713, 10166, 13419, 13445

Oil well drilling fluids See: Drilling muds

Oil well logging: CT 12305; TX 5105, 5212

Oil wells: CA 2013, 10075

Oils, Essential See: Essences and essential oils

Oils and fats: IL 761, 12915, 13168; LA 14260; MN 2451; NJ 3105, 3936, 7319; NY 3786; TX 692

Oklahoma: OK 1227, 2347, 3590, 8965, 9933, 10176, 10178, 10183, 10488, 13702, 16011, 16012

Old Northwest: IN 3397, 6348; MI 2655, 3909, 5449, 15778; MT 8767; OH 2950; OR 7353

Olson, Charles: BC 12520; CT 15425

Olympic games (See also Sports): CA 4713, 7548; IN 9275; NY 13116; OK 9285; PQ 2394

Ombudsman: AB 210, 6630

O'Neill, Eugene: CT 4491, 17362; NH 3753; OH 11074

Ontario: MB 16419; ON 1662, 4908, 5617, 6218, 7088, 7178, 7179, 7312, 7479, 9830, 9832, 10242, 10259, 10289, 10293, 11698, 12515, 16215, 16408, 16706, 16831

Open spaces (See also City planning; Parks; Recreation areas; Regional planning): IL 10307, 13632; NY 11016

Opera: CA 566, 7488, 15254; CT 3369; DC 7380; FL 15474; IL 2823; IN 6395; MI 8467; MN 15820; MO 11878; NY 2661, 3510, 6882, 8375, 9541, 9542, 13093, 13180; NC 15946; OH 10049, 10144, 12314; ON 2395, 8390, 16413; PA 8534, 16908; TX 3701, 12104, 12791; UT 12810; WA 16386

Operations research (See also Systems engineering): CA 12937, 12946, 14770, 15262; DC 13873, 14231; GA 7463; MA 873, 5746; MI 8451; NM 14139; NY 3232, 3494, 16145; NC 15932; ON 16414; PA 16055; PQ 4241, 7732, 15070; VA 720, 3302, 5195, 6498, 7044, 14012, 14704

Ophthalmology: AL 4531, 6732; AZ 11838; CA 275, 2162, 4018, 6891, 12757, 12944, 14746, 15258, 15293; FL 14890, 15729, 15730; IL 8245; LA 5497, 13582, 14830; MD 6839; MA 577, 5743, 9381, 11368; MO 6619, 15871, 16819; NH 3745; NJ 9425; NY 1262, 2542, 5651, 9259, 9485, 17403; OH 10151, 12035, 15385; OK 10179, 15999; ON 16275; OR 5365; PA 4530, 4962, 10598, 12295, 17146; PQ 7743, 7748; TN 12767; TX 233; WA 16797; WV 8000

Optics: AL 13993; AZ 15163, 15166; CA 2162, 5128, 9894, 17351; CO 6240; CT 10310, 10677, 10793; IL 1953, 15587; MA 577, 1117, 5154, 6047, 6710; MI 5131, 7099; MN 6057; NH 7113; NJ 12207, 13046, 17015; NM 9263, 14146; NY 1262, 4232, 12868, 13114, 16146; OH 2949, 5298, 7344; ON 2265; PA 16063; TX 4156, 15538; VA 11213; WA 12871

Optics, Electronic See: Electron optics

Optometry: AL 15110; CA 12757, 15258; DC 342; IL 6286; IN 16671; MA 9381, 17288; MI 4642; MO 6619, 15871; NJ 9425; NY 1262, 13114; OH 10129, 10151; ON 16400; PA 10598; PQ 15074; TN 12767; TX 15538

Oral history: AL 7424, 13714, 13949, 15109; AZ 15149; AR 6865; CA 4634, 7762, 7845, 9219, 12124, 15226, 15298, 15312, 15353; CO 1621, 4896; CT 5523; DC 7358, 7359, 7367, 14742; FL 4902, 5944, 5948, 5962, 10662; GA 995; HI 15519; ID 1557, 6265, 7223; IL 2724, 10013, 10502, 11553, 12209; IN 6364, 6398, 10806, 16629; IA 2573; KS 4899; KY 4200, 7455, 14609, 15666, 16969; LA 7577, 13697; ME 15673; MD 14759, 14760; MA 519, 2787, 5507, 5508, 7339, 8077, 11222, 14826; MI 4774, 5863, 10789; MN 2656, 3610, 7270, 8514, 9785, 9840, 9916, 12795, 12818, 16906; MO 1524, 14824, 16964; MT 15875; NJ 11622, 13625; NM 7517, 15925; NY 523, 3225, 9540, 9646, 11355, 14690; NF 8204; NC 4884; ND 15967; OH 10088, 12652, 13541; OK 10176, 16011; ON 249; OR 16018; PA 418, 8313, 13317, 13773, 14095, 14633, 16072; RI 11036, 16127; SD 499; TN 4755, 8231, 14640; TX 1279, 4186, 6126, 9826, 10487, 13373, 14827, 16242, 16261; VA 825, 4345; WA 4217, 7324, 12555; WV 7998, 14018, 14643; WI 16489

Orchestra: CA 8987; DC 646; KY 15665

Orchestral music: AR 10390; BC 16339; DC 3987; MD 15703; MA 2740, 9857; MI 3927, 6566, 8467; MN 8603, 15820; NY 9522, 9541, 10846; OH 10144; ON 9288; PA 3652, 4995, 10724; PR 3411; PQ 2322; TX 12104; VA 5221, 11426; WI 1323

Orchids: CA 12146; MA 5734

Ordnance (See also Firearms): AZ 14147; CA 74, 4848; CT 4004; DC 14519; FL 14731; GA 14485; IL 13996; MD 3, 14105, 14737, 14769; MI 5131; MN 6045; NM 14139; NY 13997; OK 14049; PA 9041; PQ 11593

Ordnance, Naval: CA 14766, 14790, 14791, 14801; CT 14798; DC 14706, 14743, 14777; FL 14797; KY 14768; MD 14795; MA 14840; RI 14799; VA 14802

Ordnance research: IL 13996; MN 6046; NJ 13998; NM 13981; NY 13997; VA 6498

Oregon: CA 3828; OR 3191, 4045, 5119, 6877, 7207, 7353, 10334, 10348, 10352, 12799, 12800, 13512, 16030, 16762

Organ: CA 649, 15332; FL 13009; OH 10144; PA 5288

Philippine Islands: CA 12730; MI 15746, 15765

Philosophy: AB 15211; AZ 12029, 17310; BC 15195; CA 1395, 2575, 2595, 2622, 5049, 6666, 7561, 7624, 10040, 10742, 11018, 11786, 12950, 13819, 15340, 16201, 16909; DC 2558, 3988, 4022, 7964, 10054, 12012, 12350, 13846; FL 11771; HI 5790; ID 15547; IL 2820, 6778, 15574; KY 3354, 12754; MA 5199, 5741, 6645; MI 3921, 4133, 11653; MN 8586, 8593, 11773, 12004, 12009, 15829; MO 3305, 8328, 11898, 11978; MT 2501; NE 3593; NH 9412; NM 12026; NY 1795, 1852, 3227, 5833, 9458, 9523, 9530, 10532, 11187, 11488, 11860, 13181, 16691, 16694, 16862; NC 2516; ND 8015; NS 15655; OH 10085, 10131, 13543; ON 3115, 8394, 10052, 12020, 15094, 16216, 16305, 16312, 16314; OR 7352, 16957; PA 4994, 10802, 11701; PQ 2581, 4021, 7750, 12395, 15045, 15078; SK 2104, 11703; TN 5648; TX 3707, 11977, 12101; WA 12380, 16389; WI 4023, 7833, 7986, 10469, 11989

Philosophy, Oriental: BC 15185, 17399; CA 654, 1980, 6484, 10742; IL 13470; NY 11789, 13835; WA 16371

Philosophy of science See: Science—Philosophy

Phonograph records See: Sound recordings

Phosphates: FL 4790; ON 4429

Photoelectricity: NJ 12207

Photogrammetry: AB 2160; MD 14572; MN 15840; MS 14767; NY 11562; ON 2184, 2265, 10294, 11206; VA 628, 14040

Photograph collections: AL 7424; AK 687, 15115; AZ 785, 2640; CA 1023, 1295, 5019, 5086, 5960, 7564, 9219, 10753, 10858, 12125, 12163, 15242, 15317, 15325, 16674; CO 1620, 3156, 8982, 10767; CT 12917, 17392; DC 1749, 5233, 6144, 7384, 9156, 9160, 12613, 14229, 14269, 14325, 14409, 14434, 14514, 14743, 14845; FL 4813, 5948, 8409, 13627; HI 5796; IL 2822, 5953, 10014, 10824, 13466, 15359; IN 5940; KS 15627, 15636; KY 7012, 10419, 15657, 15662; LA 13689; MB 15680; MD 10557; MA 858, 1587, 1596, 5697, 8081, 8089, 12658; MI 5450, 15751; MN 7114, 8599; MO 8664, 11888; MT 15875; NE 9316, 10230; NJ 4903; NM 8975; NY 481, 562, 908, 1079, 1430, 3107, 3215, 3216, 3493, 3627, 4493, 4629, 4952, 5206, 5325, 5330, 5458, 5585, 5934, 6697, 7052, 7327, 8020, 8210, 8368, 8370, 8726, 8920, 8968, 8969, 10200, 10751, 10752, 10757, 11339, 12491, 13017, 17106; ND 12965; OH 2548, 3054, 3066, 10109; OK 16011; ON 2247, 2252, 5987, 13036, 13557, 13564, 17424; OR 12799, 16030; PA 1808, 2480, 5004, 5956, 7191, 11468, 16072; PQ 2389; SD 10408; SK 12257; TX 1279, 16226; VA 4545, 5665, 16535; WA 5971, 12374, 12961, 13202, 16396; WI 16427

Photography (See also Space photography): AL 8794; AB 12745; AZ 15149; CA 847, 1340, 1432, 1796, 3138, 3601, 5128, 5321, 7519, 10034, 10519, 10526, 12160, 15298, 15325, 15335, 15343, 16186; CO 15396, 15415; CT 10462, 15514; DC 3481, 12612, 14743; FL 4832; GA 992; IL 856, 12779, 15356, 15564, 15589; IN 6382; KS 15630; KY 15644, 15662; LA 9449; MB 15679; MD 1156, 8027; MA 854, 4971, 5697, 6710, 8055, 10840, 12658, 12892, 16877; MI 3570, 3912, 15734; MN 15784, 16705; MO 6924; NH 3752; NJ 1902, 4100, 7047, 9654, 13046, 13620; NM 1789, 3230, 4221, 4227, 4228, 4232, 4952, 6582, 6583, 6626, 8970, 9511, 9526, 9528, 10518, 11191, 11480, 11486, 12318, 13180, 16142, 17346, 17413; NS 9976; OH 3236, 10155, 11072, 12889, 13538; ON 2249; OR 7350; PA 6961, 13320, 13327; TN 13338, 16564; TX 2510, 3701, 8962, 11411, 12097, 16246; VA 5221, 13514; WI 8546, 8552, 16458

Photography, Aerial: AB 181, 15143; AZ 15159; BC 1726, 15191; CA 14452, 15352, 17092; CO 14450; DC 14515; FL 15489; GA 15509; IL 15366, 15582; LA 7573; MN 7914; MO 12819; NY 3515, 9572; NS 3683; OK 10194; ON 1752, 2185, 11206, 16035; OR 16024; PQ 7740, 15089, 15092, 15093; SC 16171; SK 16123; TN 13361; VA 14451; WA 16383; WI 16433

Photography, Stereoscopic: CA 13000; PA 9270

Physical education and training: AL 15104; AB 15136; DC 4443; IL 15554, 15593, 17439; IN 6388; MB 15681; MA 12894; MI 16857; NY 13104, 13108; NC 9749, 15958; ON 12881; PA 4178, 16907; PQ 7728, 15066; SC 9064; SK 16153;

Physical education and training (Continued) TN 16569; TX 16267; VA 348; WI 16427

Physical medicine See: Medicine, Physical

Physical therapy: AR 813; CA 7392; NB 8722; NY 6198; ND 15976; ON 8709; PQ 6790; WI 3648, 16673

Physicians' assistants: VA 344

Physics: AL 14097, 14098, 15108; AZ 7091, 7617, 8869; AR 15169, 15173; BC 2168, 15205; CA 1340, 1904, 1983, 1993, 2475, 2998, 4870, 5266, 5543, 6166, 6168, 6169, 6170, 6172, 6173, 6255, 6920, 7259, 7446, 8636, 10754, 11520, 11522, 11635, 12197, 12948, 14801, 15259, 15277, 15315, 15334, 15338, 15340, 15354, 16040, 16200, 16203, 17345; CO 1135, 9083, 11511, 14574, 15408, 15411; CT 439, 10222, 13800, 15028, 15515, 16901, 17377, 17384; DE 4096, 5873, 15453; DC 2476, 2557, 5228, 13974, 14521, 14765, 14772; FL 4832, 15481, 15494; GA 4354; ID 773, 4285; IL 775, 6277, 7173, 9863, 9944, 12785, 12922, 15364, 15566, 15587, 15599, 17026, 17459; IN 1926, 6370, 6402, 11133; IA 15617; KS 6949, 15633; KY 13808, 15641, 15660; MD 1565, 6823, 8011, 14037, 14492, 14542, 14705, 15699; MA 57, 577, 668, 874, 1090, 1614, 1651, 5715, 5736, 8079, 8083, 8092, 9854, 10840, 11268, 12575, 12866, 13683, 14087, 14101, 14421, 15668, 15718, 16880, 17284; MI 8469, 15771, 16861, 16984; MN 2455, 6053, 7806, 15823; MO 7419, 16815; NE 10228, 15891; NV 4288, 15902; NB 15909; NH 3747, 15913; NJ 947, 1332, 6479, 9268, 10986, 11627, 14038; NM 9263, 15222; NY 59, 501, 512, 1774, 3022, 3228, 3512, 3644, 4228, 4232, 5144, 6243, 6258, 7103, 9743, 10856, 11193, 11499, 11562, 13092, 13101, 13132, 13188, 13793, 14315, 14491, 16146; NC 4119, 15932; ND 15973; OH 1246, 2527, 5386, 7007, 8719, 8755, 10050, 10118, 12028, 13970, 13984, 15390; OK 10191, 16006; ON 1033, 1935, 2080, 2167, 2265, 7237, 7795, 11210, 16287, 16416, 17435; OR 4775, 10331, 10891, 11301, 13244, 14174, 16029; PA 957, 2481, 2483, 4079, 4973, 4978, 5158, 10633, 10650, 10916, 13149, 13321, 16056, 16070, 16092, 17021; PR 16116; PQ 2170, 7749, 15075, 15086; SC 3035, 12285; SK 16159; TN 10021, 16224, 16565; TX 4154, 5105, 8753, 12793, 13405, 16255, 16958; VT 16332; VA 1109, 3146, 6498, 14495, 14794, 14807, 16358, 16764; WA 1254, 16372, 16390, 17095; WI 289, 1355, 6857, 7987, 16459; WY 14316, 16497

Physics, High energy See: Nuclear physics

Physics—History: MN 15823; NY 512; PA 586

Physics, Plasma See: Plasma (Ionized gases)

Physics, Terrestrial See: Geophysics

Physiology: CA 2060, 12938, 15228; FL 4819; IL 15364, 15557, 15594; IN 6393, 9376; IA 6689; MD 14542; MA 5696, 5733; MI 1931; NY 3218, 3229, 4876, 8050; NC 15951; ON 16286; PA 16054; PR 16116

Phytopathology See: Plant diseases

Piaget, Jean: DE 10755; TN 16570

Piano music: CA 7962; DC 7380; IL 15585; IN 6395; MD 15704; NY 9542, 16585; OH 10144; TN 16223

Pierce, Franklin: NH 9402

Pigments (See also Dyes and dyeing): MD 12342; OH 13001

Pikes Peak region: CO 10767, 10790

Pilgrims (New Plymouth Colony): MA 10769, 10825

Pioneering See: Frontier and pioneer life

Pipe: SK 12267

Pipe lines: AB 199, 200; AK 152; CA 1302; DC 4602; MI 15769; OK 17135; ON 10839, 13599; PQ 13601; TX 8483, 8694; YT 17450

Pitcairn Islands: CA 5582, 10456

Pittman, Key (Senator): WA 12555

Pittsburgh (PA): PA 2480, 5975, 10796, 10799, 16091

Place-names See: Names, Geographical

Planets (See also Satellites): AZ 15167; CA 15303; MA 8080; MO 16816; TX 7640, 16249

Planning: AZ 795; CA 1644, 11637, 15304; FL 11391, 15499, 17233; IA 15609; LA 7578; MD 714, 15181; MA 763, 8115; MI 4764, 8452, 10032; MO 5847, 13230; MT 8762; NC 9763; OH 7720, 15378; OR 10344; PA 1844, 17417; TN 1226, 8219, 8222; TX 3620; VA 10819

Planning, City See: City planning

Planning, Regional See: Regional planning

Planning, Urban See: City planning; Urban renewal

Plant diseases: AB 201; BC 2132, 2134, 2137; CA 7524; FL 4802, 15466, 15468, 15483, 15497; HI 5798; IL 15578; MB 2125, 2136; MD 6465; MN 15779, 15837, 15842; NY 7889; NF 2130; NS 2122; OH 10108; ON 2113; PA 16057; PE 2118; PQ 2111, 2128, 2148; SD 12715; SK 2131; WA 16796; WV 16925; WI 16460

Plasma (Ionized gases): MA 1089, 8087; NJ 10991; NY 16144

Plastic surgery See: Surgery, Plastic

Plastics: CA 6319; CO 5097; CT 392, 667, 8749, 11534, 13800, 13801, 16562; DE 4098; IL 6052, 9875, 13614, 14469, 16587; MD 980, 14795; MA 1947, 5155, 8754, 15668; MI 4054; MN 2730, 3455, 13506; MO 8745; NJ 2586, 2587, 3336, 5068, 7689, 8686, 10821, 13769, 14108; NY 2941, 6632, 8685; NC 10220; OH 127, 4668, 5201, 5381, 5382, 5387, 6325, 8747, 10416; OK 723, 10739; ON 3428, 4088, 4089, 4132, 10855; PA 1756, 8683, 10910, 11540, 11541, 13241; PQ 2264, 9883, 13755; SC 5417; WA 17059; WV 1568; WI 6746

Plath, Sylvia: MA 12577

Playwrights See: Dramatists

Plumbing: ON 637; SK 12267

Plymouth (MA): MA 10769; NH 10833

Plywood (See also Wood): VA 5649; WA 589; WI 4888

Podiatry: CA 1973, 5369; DC 590; IL 12312; IA 11302, 16031; MD 7667; NJ 11984; NY 9480; OH 10082; PA 10599, 10600; WI 9355

Poe, Edgar Allan: PA 5005; VA 16535

Poetry: AK 16534; AZ 15165, 15168; BC 12520; CA 1437, 7554, 7557, 15279, 15320, 15335, 15340, 16150; CO 9014; FL 4833, 15495; IN 1140, 1924; KS 6951, 15622; MB 15680; MA 669, 5754, 16878; MI 3917; MN 8582; MO 15867; NH 3751; NJ 8772, 9657; NY 81, 3645, 5995, 9523, 9706, 10835, 13093, 13100, 13134; NC 15954; OH 10092, 10125, 10164, 15381, 16274; ON 7791; PA 4999, 13316, 16100; RI 1819; VA 16641; WA 12380; WI 16425

Point-of-purchase advertising See: Advertising, Point-of-sale

Poisons (See also Toxicology): MD 14420

Poland: CA 10841; CT 2648; DC 7364; IL 10844; KS 15634; MD 10845; NH 3943; NY 5919, 10774, 10842; PA 276, 6025; PQ 10843

Polar regions: AB 903, 15128, 15214; AK 14173, 15115; BC 15207; CO 15406; DC 9161, 14706; IL 12786; NH 3753, 14007; NT 2211, 2236; OH 10133; ON 7237, 10839; PQ 7744, 7747, 7753; VT 2621

Police, Royal Canadian Mounted See: Royal Canadian Mounted Police

Police—Study and teaching: AL 14096; CT 3376; DC 14348; GA 12284; IL 9946; IN 6351; IA 6672; KY 4198; ME 7854; MD 1158, 8043, 14349; MN 8612; MO 11884; NY 6816, 9032, 9476; OH 5988; OK 10190; ON 10299, 10300, 11592; WI 9846, 16452

Poliomyelitis: NH 3745

Polish Americans: IL 10844

Polish art See: Art, Polish

Polish literature: IL 10844; KS 15634; PA 276, 6025; PQ 10843; WI 4955

Political extremism See: Political rights

Political parties: CA 15316; DC 3865; TX 11256

Political rights: AZ 9861; CA 2056; KS 15638; MI 8471; PA 5013; TX 9948

Political science (See also Constitutional law): AL 13876; AB 207, 15137; BC 1720; CA 2595, 7563, 10458, 12135, 12147, 12940, 13176, 13922, 13928, 15249, 15263, 15330, 16205, 17292; CT 13722, 17389; DC 449, 1775, 3990, 4494, 4882, 5224, 5233, 6833, 7362, 8877, 14107, 14368, 14383, 14537, 14839, 17162; GA 5259, 14077; ID 15551; IL 2820, 7333, 7389, 12777, 15569, 15574, 16966; IN 6403, 11128; IA 15611; KS 6939, 14009, 15638; KY 14000; MB 7908; MD 15180; MA 5729, 8071; MI 3923; MN 8579; NJ 9433, 9433, 10999; NY 2979, 3219, 4938, 9458, 11187, 11791, 13087, 13183, 13858, 14048; NC 14082, 15941; NS 3679, 9986; OH 3072, 10085, 10131, 11078, 15440; OK 10193, 14049; ON 2189, 2226, 2273, 8394, 10259; OR 13033; PA 4178, 7157, 13309, 14145; PQ 11152, 15079; SC 12701; SK 12265; TX 3706, 9948; UT 16322, 16324; WA 16391; WV 16935; WI 16440

Politics, Practical: AL 1040; CA 6535, 11349, 15244, 15274, 15312, 15316; CT 3383; DC 2836, 3364, 3865, 9689, 11350; GA 12802; KY 15650; MA 14826; MI 9165; MN 8596; MS 8654; MO 14824, 15867; NJ 10994, 11619; NY 2569, 9688; ON 2216; PQ 11160, 15091; TX 9950, 14827

Polk, James Knox: TN 10849, 13354

Pollution: AB 182, 200, 12954; AK 15119; AR 814; BC 1725, 1738, 2188; CA 1989, 4244, 4388, 4389, 4412, 15271, 16592, 17271; CO 4402, 4411, 4417; CT 667, 4039, 14194; DC 3407, 14345; FL 4804; GA 4407; HI 5795; IL 4408, 5418, 6305, 12236; MB 7899; MD 14006, 14090, 14410; MA 4403, 5103, 8053, 13823; MI 3027, 6913, 12872; MN 4029; MO 4410; MT 16987; NY 4290, 4405, 7870, 8567, 9641; NC 10220; ND 15972; OH 4391, 10102; OK 4414; ON 1934, 2114, 2186, 4635, 6274, 10302, 12995; OR 4396; PA 10002, 17044; PQ 11166, 11170, 16734; SK 12248; TN 840; TX 1876, 11226, 14015, 16259; UT 14182; WA 4413, 14579; WI 11376, 13004

Polo: VA 9265

Polychlorinated biphenyl (PCB): CA 15271

Polymers and polymerization: CA 1093, 11257, 15231; CT 439, 667, 1324, 7466, 8749, 10310, 11534; DE 4098; FL 6812, 8752; IL 2771, 3799, 5418, 8857, 12922, 13760, 17231; IN 15982; KY 2588; LA 5573; MD 5391, 14417, 17050; MA 12, 484, 1947, 5419, 8754, 14087, 15718; MI 4062, 8433, 17076; MN 13504, 13505, 13506, 13508; NJ 288, 393, 1233, 2587, 3936, 4484, 8686, 10000, 10821, 10975, 13064, 13769, 15027; NY 281, 2941, 5157, 8685, 10055, 12296, 12983; NC 448, 1314, 4094, 9771, 10220; ND 9802; OH 404, 686, 886, 4644, 4668, 5380, 5381, 5382, 7633, 12340, 14468; OK 10739; ON 2259, 4132, 10855, 13497, 17350; PA 104, 837, 4099, 7117, 7513, 8683, 10853, 10910, 10914; SC 483, 5417, 10854; TN 4223, 11002; TX 4102, 11362; VA 285, 4093, 6537; WV 1568, 8684

Pomo Indians: CA 7164

Pope, Alexander: NY 3514

Popular culture: CA 2056, 12150, 15298; IL 9850; MI 8472; OH 1632, 3069; PA 16100

Popular literature: **DC** 3989; **FL** 16184

Population (See also Census; Demography): **CA** 7520, 11434, 12147, 12756, 12939, 16202; **DC** 10869, 10871, 13863, 14165; **FL** 4827; **GA** 5260; **HI** 4187, 6496, 15523; **IN** 5033, 10811; **IA** 6677, 15610; **KS** 6950, 15621; **MD** 6831, 6835; **MA** 5702; **MI** 15773; **MN** 10814, 15781; **MO** 10809; **NJ** 10989, 10994; **NY** 3212, 6636, 10813, 10868, 13857; **NC** 931, 2492, 4114, 4569; **OH** 10812; **ON** 2307; **PA** 10815, 16060; **RI** 1817; **TX** 7395, 10810, 13434, 16256; **VA** 3757; **WA** 1251, 10870; **WI** 10817, 16434, 16442

Porter, Katherine Anne: **MD** 15701, 15706

Porter, William Sidney (O. Henry): **NC** 5511; **OH** 16695

Portraits, Medical See: Medical illustration

Portsmouth (NH): **NH** 10893

Portugal: **DC** 7369, 7375; **MA** 10899; **NY** 5934, 5935; **PA** 6410

Portugal—History: **CA** 13728; **DC** 2556

Postage-stamps—Collectors and collecting: **AL** 7425; **CA** 5035, 6647, 6753, 10858, 13740, 16884; **FL** 12655; **IL** 75, 2893, 3110; **IN** 7414; **LA** 12638; **MA** 2450; **NJ** 9057; **NY** 3111, 10728; **OH** 3060; **PA** 585, 4982, 4993

Postal cards: **CA** 2054, 12128, 12163; **CT** 8714; **NH** 8171; **NJ** 10973; **PA** 3864; **RI** 6638; **VA** 9730; **WI** 7911

Postal service: **DC** 14818; **MA** 2450; **ON** 2145

Postal service—History: **IL** 3110; **NE** 6722; **PA** 585

Potawatomi Indians: **IN** 5052

Potter, Beatrix: **PA** 5005

Poultry: **KS** 6951; **MD** 14266; **NY** 3489; **NS** 2122; **OH** 10108; **WI** 16461

Pound, Ezra: **BC** 12520; **CA** 15335; **CT** 17362; **ID** 15552; **OH** 16274; **RI** 16128

Poverty (See also Public welfare): **AL** 13714; **CA** 16951; **DC** 17302; **IN** 5033; **MN** 8607; **NY** 8020, 9470; **OH** 2523; **ON** 2346; **WI** 3286, 16447

Poverty research: **GA** 3005

Powder metallurgy (See also Metallurgy): **NJ** 8330; **OH** 6325; **ON** 4136; **PA** 3184

Powell, John Wesley: **AZ** 10909

Power-plants: **BC** 1103; **CA** 7711; **CO** 13023, 14186; **CT** 15028; **FL** 4793; **NJ** 4928; **PA** 13824; **TX** 1306, 4871; **WA** 16775

Power resources (See also Fuel): **AL** 9901, 12680; **AB** 180, 199, 200, 769, 2427, 6040, 9972, 10689; **AK** 14310, 15124; **AZ** 793, 15152; **BC** 1732, 1744, 16947; **CA** 43, 76, 2038, 2899, 4163, 4244, 4245, 4308, 4388, 5066, 5091, 5348, 6569, 7259, 7558, 10057, 10058, 10440, 10447, 10581, 11215, 11299, 11510, 11635, 12223, 12942, 13081, 13192, 13673, 15237, 15302, 15306, 15334, 17271; **CO** 3179, 11466, 12671, 13023; **CT** 1913, 3251, 11297, 13834; **DC** 2977, 3362, 4602, 4926, 6259, 6517, 7780, 9035, 9128, 12337, 13863, 14313, 14314, 14337; **FL** 4797, 13212, 15481; **GA** 5246, 9997, 12286, 12805; **HI** 5795; **ID** 773; **IL** 5083, 5095, 6283, 6303, 8316, 15595; **IN** 6358, 6377; **IA** 15609; **KS** 6933, 6942; **KY** 15644, 15645, 15654; **LA** 7572, 7707; **ME** 7867, 16208; **MD** 2635, 4594, 10001, 14705; **MA** 1940, 2081, 2739, 3248, 4364, 6772, 8064, 8073, 9386, 9392, 11261, 11437; **MI** 3430, 8430; **MN** 301, 4836, 6058, 8610, 9879, 9880, 15800; **MO** 10486, 16808; **MT** 8762, 9877, 16987; **NE** 10229; **NV** 2712, 14318; **NB** 9366; **NH** 9401, 9405; **NJ** 4553, 8696, 11092; **NM** 9442, 15222; **NY** 447, 1774, 2605, 3494, 4290, 4405, 4659, 7285, 8567, 8692, 9129, 9138, 9587, 10324, 13178, 13371, 16141; **NC** 2493; **ND** 15972; **NS** 3544, 3680, 9982; **OH** 3043, 10086, 10096, 12356; **OK** 7041, 10172, 10174, 13701, 17135; **ON** 2180, 2183, 2238, 2263, 2889, 4307, 4480, 5558, 6151, 10251, 13599; **OR** 9331, 9920,

Power resources (Continued)
10342, 10449, 10885, 14312, 16019; **PA** 2483, 5564, 5571, 10589, 10716, 12196, 13824, 16073, 17044; **PR** 2603; **PQ** 1938, 6227, 6228, 6229, 11166, 12626; **SC** 12699; **TN** 13363, 14320, 14566; **TX** 1558, 2976, 3699, 5212, 5536, 6123, 11096, 13375, 13395, 16235; **UT** 13366; **VI** 3142; **VA** 1283, 3146, 4363, 6661, 8678, 16660, 16664; **WA** 1254, 16372, 16378, 16783, 16786; **WI** 4888; **WY** 5214, 17331

Power resources—Research: **AL** 5213, 12804; **AZ** 15162; **CA** 3273, 4287, 7253, 12759; **CT** 5065; **DC** 77; **ID** 4285; **IL** 774, 6505; **IN** 1141; **IA** 666; **MA** 1584; **NE** 6658; **NM** 9436, 12198; **NY** 5144; **OK** 9184, 10739; **PA** 4973, 5158, 5296; **TN** 13364; **TX** 6743; **UT** 16323; **VA** 8691; **WY** 14316

Precious metals: **NJ** 4366; **RI** 13232

Prepaid legal services: **DC** 9240

Pre-Raphaelites (Art): **AZ** 808; **DE** 3832

Presbyterian Church: **AZ** 11934; **IL** 7703; **KY** 7610; **MS** 11314; **MO** 3557; **NJ** 1508, 1508, 10976; **NY** 4250; **NC** 5950; **ON** 16305; **PA** 9888, 10932, 11313; **PQ** 10933; **TX** 1072; **VA** 13791

Preschool education See: Education, Preschool

Preservation of books See: Books—Conservation and restoration

Presidents—United States: **DC** 7378, 14383; **GA** 14820; **IA** 14825; **KS** 14821; **MA** 14826; **MI** 14823; **MO** 14824; **NY** 2633, 3646, 14822; **OH** 5806; **TN** 16573; **TX** 14827, 14828

Press, Underground See: Underground press

Presses, Private See: Private presses

Preventive medicine See: Medicine, Preventive

Primates: **CA** 15273; **GA** 4356; **LA** 13687; **MD** 7444; **MA** 5733; **OR** 10336; **TX** 12817; **WA** 16392, 16797; **WI** 16475

Primitive art See: Art, Primitive

Prince Edward Island: **NB** 8881; **PE** 10960, 10962, 16104

Printing (See also Graphic arts): **CA** 1559, 15226, 15279, 15312, 15345, 17457; **CO** 3884; **CT** 10793, 15514, 17360; **DC** 7385; **FL** 5466, 15495; **GA** 15506; **IL** 9060, 15373, 15564; **KY** 15657; **ME** 12347; **MD** 8022; **MA** 4283, 5724, 9737; **MN** 4134, 8574, 13507; **NJ** 10995; **NY** 540, 7494, 11477, 11479, 11480, 13126; **OH** 11074, 12928; **ON** 8118, 8384, 9210, 13562; **PA** 5006, 5465, 16098; **PR** 11110; **PQ** 7727; **RI** 16128; **TX** 4185, 16229; **VA** 719, 16352; **WI** 7819

Printing—History: **CA** 1977, 11576, 12136, 12164; **CO** 3155; **CT** 3370, 13641, 16898, 17360; **IL** 9661, 15373; **KS** 15622, 17104; **MA** 1652, 12577; **MI** 6910; **MO** 11889, 16807; **NV** 15905; **NJ** 4, 10995; **NY** 1857, 3222, 5530, 7503, 10924, 11477, 13093, 13185, 15394; **NC** 15959; **OH** 2526, 7008, 16274; **ON** 16312; **PQ** 7736; **RI** 1816; **TX** 3702, 12792, 13379; **UT** 1700; **VA** 3144

Prints: **CA** 7533, 7548; **DC** 7384; **IL** 7333; **IN** 1924; **MA** 1575, 1596, 12892; **MI** 8450; **MO** 9328, 10901; **NY** 540, 8020, 8368, 8370, 8956, 9511, 9586, 10764, 11181, 11191; **ON** 2249; **PA** 4992, 5004, 8816, 10635; **PQ** 7727

Prisons: **DC** 11000; **NY** 6816

Private presses: **AB** 15129; **AZ** 808; **CA** 1559, 12136, 15345, 16150; **CO** 15415; **CT** 13641; **DC** 7385; **IL** 6315, 12778; **ME** 1240; **MA** 1605, 17138; **MI** 6910; **MN** 15829; **NH** 3753; **NJ** 10995; **NY** 1857, 5995, 10697, 11185, 11477; **NC** 15959; **ON** 8384, 16399, 16415; **PA** 2486; **SC** 17236; **WI** 16425

Probate law and practice: **CA** 7059; **CO** 4300; **MA** 5383, 17108; **MI** 3941; **OH** 7997

Process control: **CA** 1985; **OH** 33; **PA** 4751

Produce trade: **CA** 15243; **FL** 14251; **IA** 10788; **NC** 13753; **OH** 10107; **PA** 4579; **SK** 12243; **VA** 13827

Productivity of labor See: Labor productivity

Products liability: **DC** 3426; **IL** 1127; **MA** 11369; **MO** 12489; **NY** 5635, 13586; **OH** 5137

Professional ethics: **IL** 2630

Profit-sharing: **NY** 13583

Programmed instruction (See also Computer-assisted instruction): **MI** 5851; **NY** 4436

Programming (Electronic computers) (See also Computers; Information storage and retrieval systems): **BC** 2168; **CA** 744, 1905, 3301, 5815, 5892, 6246, 6552, 7525, 8636, 13192, 13195, 14710; **CO** 6240; **CT** 5143; **FL** 12766; **IL** 6043, 12235; **KY** 15651; **MA** 681, 4150, 11270, 16723; **MN** 6250; **MO** 16803; **NV** 4288; **NH** 3949; **NJ** 962, 1335; **NY** 6243, 7949, 13975; **ON** 1863, 2231, 6237; **OR** 13245, 13246; **PA** 4751, 12857, 16077; **SK** 12258; **VT** 6249; **VA** 6252, 14012; **WA** 16368

Propaganda: **CA** 12940; **DC** 14470, 14471; **KS** 15638; **MA** 12893; **VA** 7994; **WI** 16458

Propellants: **CA** 14801, 15025; **DC** 14809; **MD** 6822, 14769; **VA** 1011

Propellants, Rocket See: Rockets (Aeronautics)—Fuel

Propulsion, Flight See: Airplanes—Motors

Prosthesis: **IL** 9936; **IN** 1544; **NY** 14960; **TX** 6567; **VA** 578

Protective coatings (See also Corrosion and anti-corrosives; Paint; Thin films): **CA** 2986; **DC** 14530; **IL** 3799, 11610; **IN** 13473; **MI** 1235; **MN** 13505; **NJ** 2587, 8686, 10000, 15027; **NY** 10857, 12925, 13464; **OH** 4645, 9726, 12340; **PA** 4099, 7129, 7513; **VA** 11382; **WA** 17059

Protest literature: **PA** 13316

Protestant churches: **MA** 5705

Protestant Episcopal Church in the U.S.A.: **CA** 12317, 13643; **CT** 11022; **IL** 1642, 11027; **IN** 11020; **MA** 11024, 17045; **MO** 11031; **NY** 5200, 11025, 11030; **OR** 11023; **PA** 11021; **SC** 3674; **SD** 11026; **TN** 16165, 16166; **TX** 4423, 11019, 11029; **UT** 11028; **WA** 11032, 11033

Proust, Marcel: **IL** 15584, 15588

Provincial government See: State and provincial government

Psoriasis: **ON** 17247

Psychiatric nursing: **MI** 3908; **NV** 9343; **NY** 1861

Psychiatry and psychoanalysis (See also Mental health): **AL** 14862; **AZ** 14866; **AR** 14868; **BC** 1730; **CA** 2005, 2023, 3279, 5310, 5849, 5881, 5982, 6749, 6908, 7547, 8912, 9339, 12161, 12353, 12763, 14741, 14745; **CO** 3873, 15420; **CT** 2577, 4549, 6516, 7397, 9967, 14882, 14883, 15439; **DC** 592, 16774; **FL** 6740, 14889, 14890; **GA** 5247, 14895; **IL** 63, 2809, 4885, 6514, 14900, 14903, 15596; **IN** 2513, 14905, 14906, 17052; **IA** 14909; **KS** 8238, 8239, 14911; **KY** 14913; **LA** 9450; **ME** 14918; **MB** 1654; **MD** 1765, 14831, 14832, 14833, 14922, 15690; **MA** 1590, 1602, 9691, 11433, 14926, 14927; **MI** 3908, 8436, 14928, 14930; **MN** 10027, 11244; **MO** 8666, 14937, 16818, 16985; **NE** 9309; **NJ** 2499, 4475, 9815, 14948; **NM** 14949; **NY** 36, 1407, 1861, 2437, 2617, 4145, 6540, 6581, 6720, 6780, 7069, 7096, 7497, 8358, 9029, 9230, 9489, 9490, 9505, 9592, 9593, 10902, 11474, 13119, 14950, 14954, 14956, 14958, 14959, 14961, 16147, 16946, 17405; **NC** 2777, 14966; **ND** 9338; **NS** 9984; **OH** 2955, 3059, 14968, 14969; **ON** 16406; **PA** 3930, 4001, 4158, 6525, 8157, 10615, 10702, 14980, 14983; **PR** 11105; **PQ** 2399, 2698, 2699, 2700, 6069, 6072, 6073, 7721; **SC** 1828; **SD** 12708; **SK** 12262; **TN** 14994; **TX** 6119, 13411, 15005, 16270; **UT** 15006; **VT** 1666, 16601; **VA** 15010; **WA** 11063, 15013; **WI** 11495, 15021; **WY** 15024

Psychiatry and religion: **NY** 6540; **PA** 12647; **SC** 5520; **WI** 2546

Psychical research: **CA** 6445, 11569, 12167; **FL** 13013; **MB** 15680;

Psychical research (Continued) **MO** 12875; **NE** 9309; **NJ** 16607; **NY** 629, 10496, 10497; **NC** 4942, 11062; **OH** 3072; **RI** 8331; **TX** 8562, 12792; **VA** 749, 933

Psychoanalysis See: Psychiatry and psychoanalysis

Psychology (See also Child psychology): **AB** 15219; **AZ** 12837, 15154; **BC** 1730, 1731; **CA** 514, 516, 1460, 1974, 2005, 2006, 2007, 2008, 2575, 2602, 3335, 6521, 6884, 6908, 7561, 9339, 10040, 13176, 14804, 15236, 15299, 16193, 17316; **CO** 15414; **CT** 4131, 15439, 15515, 16900; **DE** 10755; **DC** 515, 594, 3988, 6483, 6854, 9179, 14764; **FL** 11771, 15480; **GA** 4354; **IL** 44, 63, 2820, 4452, 4570, 4885, 9103, 12773, 12781, 15569, 16966; **IN** 6413, 8337, 11134; **IA** 15618; **KS** 8239; **MB** 231, 1654; **MD** 13988, 14833; **MA** 5738, 8085, 12575, 16880; **MI** 1931, 3908, 3921, 15755, 15764; **MN** 8586, 15799; **NH** 729; **NJ** 4279, 4475, 9815, 10993, 11624; **NY** 682, 779, 1795, 3229, 6199, 6527, 9230, 9458, 9530, 9592, 10497, 11187, 11193, 11488, 13092, 13227; **NC** 2600, 2777; **NS** 3683; **OH** 10092, 10123, 10156, 15097; **OK** 10193, 12834; **ON** 6216, 8394, 9828, 10258, 10275, 11201, 11211, 13552; **OR** 7352, 10337; **PA** 4158, 4979, 4994, 10615, 11064, 16074; **PR** 2452, 16106; **PQ** 2700, 2708, 7729, 15067, 15086; **TN** 16569; **TX** 3706, 8562, 13969, 16247; **UT** 16324; **VT** 1666; **VA** 593, 6189, 10972, 16343; **WA** 7062, 12377, 16380, 16797; **WI** 3469; **WY** 16497

Psychology, Forensic: **NY** 1781

Psychology, Military: **CA** 14008; **CT** 14789; **PA** 14145; **TX** 14133

Psychology, Physiological: **MA** 5738; **NJ** 10993

Psychopharmacology: **CA** 6908; **IL** 6313; **MD** 14831, 14833; **MI** 7155; **NE** 9309; **NJ** 5990; **NY** 3934, 7096; **PQ** 4046, 7721; **TX** 13411

Psychotherapy: **CT** 4323; **IL** 15371; **IN** 4507; **NJ** 10993; **NY** 6527; **NC** 12732; **UT** 345; **WI** 16464

Psychotropic drugs: **DC** 14517

Public administration: **AL** 134, 1044; **AB** 207; **AR** 8350; **BC** 1721; **CA** 2040, 5349, 7556, 12119, 12144, 13898, 15246, 15274, 16205; **DC** 6145, 7362, 8877, 9196, 13862, 14270, 14383, 14813; **FL** 4818, 10366; **GA** 12283; **HI** 5782, 6062; **ID** 6267, 15546; **IL** 8316; **IN** 6377; **KS** 6939, 15631; **KY** 7031, 15667; **LA** 1869, 7579, 11067; **MD** 15180; **MA** 8116, 14438; **MI** 3918, 3923, 15737; **MN** 5856, 8584, 15824; **MS** 15847; **MT** 8764, 15877; **NV** 9345; **NJ** 9432, 10994; **NM** 9444; **NY** 2979, 3498, 6526, 6816, 9521, 9560, 10873, 11066, 13183, 13185; **NC** 15939; **NS** 9981; **OH** 3070, 10104, 10119, 11084, 12970; **ON** 2173, 2279, 2280, 10250, 10259, 17429; **OR** 16014; **PA** 10602, 10644, 10646, 16084; **PR** 11103, 11111, 16118; **PQ** 11165, 15079; **RI** 11399; **SD** 16179; **TN** 8231; **TX** 3709, 11413, 16259; **UT** 16322; **VA** 16637; **WA** 12378, 16786; **WV** 16935; **WI** 8553, 17221

Public finance See: Finance, Public

Public health (See also Communicable diseases; World health): **AL** 139, 15110; **AB** 191; **AK** 14829; **AZ** 790, 15147; **BC** 1729; **CA** 2060, 7526, 7562, 12146, 12174, 12188, 12219, 15260, 15293; **CO** 3879; **CT** 3382, 17383; **DC** 10480, 14321; **FL** 4465, 6740, 16185; **GA** 5253, 14189; **HI** 15523; **IL** 15596; **IN** 6354; **KY** 7023; **ME** 7859; **MB** 7901; **MD** 6838, 8033, 9213, 10966, 14832, 14834; **MA** 1610, 5746, 5748, 8110; **MI** 3923, 8442, 15774; **MN** 8611, 15787; **MS** 8645; **MO** 2540, 15871; **NV** 3006; **NB** 9363; **NJ** 9427, 9428; **NY** 398, 3218, 4525, 8732, 9027, 9474, 9477, 9563, 10868, 13114, 13831; **NC** 9762, 15937; **OH** 121; **OK** 16001; **ON** 2204, 10280, 10281, 16406; **PA** 256, 4294, 5821, 16076; **PR** 11104, 16115; **PQ** 6067, 11162; **RI** 11403; **SC** 12696; **SK** 12249; **TN** 9022, 13346, 13347; **TX** 1070, 13383, 13427, 16259; **VT** 16601; **WA** 12373, 16380, 16786; **WV** 16928; **WI** 17207, 17221; **WY** 17333

Public hygiene See: Public health

Public interest groups: **DC** 4941

Public interest law: **HI** 7292; **IL** 7295; **PA** 3283; **TX** 4184

Public lands: **DC** 14334; **FL** 4810; **NE** 14646

Public opinion: AK 15123; BC 15190; CT 15427; IL 15368; IA 15611; NY 5667; NC 15941; WI 16458

Public opinion polls: CA 15266; CT 15436, 17389; DC 1874; IL 15592; KS 15621; KY 15667; NJ 11365; NY 3487, 5667; NC 15941; ON 17430

Public policy: BC 1721; CA 1981; DC 14439, 16513; GA 3005; IL 2630; MA 5726; MI 15737, 16982; NY 3219, 13089; OR 13033; PA 5013; TX 16259; VA 13672

Public relations: DC 3539; IL 8003, 15564; IN 14135; MI 5189; MO 15857; NY 52, 966, 975, 1910, 6715, 11089

Public utilities: AL 133, 12680; AB 213, 2414, 2415, 4267; AK 14310; AZ 12079; BC 1104, 1744; CA 1304, 1307, 2038, 7559, 9127, 10440, 12122; CO 658, 11090; CT 9845, 11297; DE 3192; DC 597, 4258, 4602, 4926, 9128, 10904, 14314, 14391, 14837; FL 4793, 4794; GA 5246; HI 5794, 5795; IL 3265, 4109, 10666, 11570, 12236; IN 6428; ME 2654; MB 7906; MD 1154, 1305; MA 3248, 13823; MI 3429, 3430, 3899, 8430; MN 8591, 9879, 9880, 10389; MO 13774; MT 8759; NE 6658; NB 9366; NH 9405; NJ 5404, 5406, 5407, 11092, 12062; NY 447, 971, 1618, 3413, 3951, 4239, 7285, 7500, 9129, 9577, 10324, 11331, 11473, 12927, 13025, 17193; NC 2493; NS 9988; OH 3043, 3414, 10086, 10093, 11095, 13533; OK 10174, 11091; ON 2238, 2359, 2360, 3427, 10256, 13775; OR 10449, 10885; PA 5405, 8355, 10608, 10667, 10716; PQ 8804, 11175; SK 12268; TN 13363; TX 3698, 4871, 5198, 5574, 5576, 6123, 6127, 11096, 12835, 13395, 13666; UT 8915; VT 2675; VA 470; WA 1309, 11115; WI 3670, 17197

Public welfare (See also Social service): AL 134; AZ 788; BC 1731, 15199; CA 12084, 15264, 15316; CO 3168; DC 367, 599, 6149, 7362, 14321; FL 4818; IN 6414; KS 6935; KY 7023; ME 7861, 16208; MB 2178, 7901, 17184; MD 1148, 5820; MA 12519, 14323; MN 15828; MS 8647; NJ 8729; NY 60, 1795, 3225, 3645, 4875, 6199, 9470, 13089, 17409; NC 4169; NS 3684; OH 2523; ON 2204, 2346, 3282, 8394, 10271; OR 16014; PA 5821, 13329; PR 16111; TX 16259; VA 15034; WA 16393; WV 16935; WI 3286, 17207, 17221

Public welfare—Law: IL 9099; NY 2627; PA 10713

Public works: AB 189; CA 6725; IL 600; TX 14016

Publishers and publishing (See also Book industries and trade; Newspaper libraries): AZ 12534; BC 917; CA 11, 56, 1162, 15252, 16503; CT 5524, 5531, 10536; DC 594, 9689, 14811; FL 7095, 13619; IL 3569, 3754, 4361, 6855, 11250, 12343, 12919, 15564, 17296; IN 6392, 12280; MD 11371; MA 57, 6111, 12518, 17342; MI 5071, 15759; MN 902; NY 373, 481, 529, 912, 1098, 3317, 3853, 4260, 5659, 5802, 6652, 7758, 7839, 9280, 9523, 9684, 9688, 9969, 10424, 10494, 10675, 12310, 12332, 13513, 13515, 17088, 17460; NC 15949, 15962; OH 8318; ON 2327, 2328, 4658, 5303, 7813, 9205, 9874, 12728, 16296; PA 2541, 7651, 12902, 13322, 16098; PQ 11285; TN 13853; TX 16246; VA 571, 8426, 13514; WI 16995

Puerto Rico: CT 15425, 15435; IL 11100; NY 1572, 3640, 10070; PR 11101, 11102, 11103, 11109, 16107, 16110, 16111, 16114, 16117

Pulp See: Wood-pulp

Puppets and puppet-plays (See also Mime): MI 3902; NY 9539; ON 10301, 13561; PQ 7727

Purchasing: DC 14805; NJ 9059

Pyle, Howard: DE 3832; PA 1661, 5005

Pyrotechnics See: Fireworks

Quacks and quackery: PA 7304

Quakers See: Society of Friends

Quality control: FL 8752; IL 17320; ON 2406, 16728; TX 12824; VA 386; WI 630, 15042

Quality of working life (See also Labor productivity): DC 14270;

Quality of working life (Continued)
TX 591

Quebec, Northern See: Northern Quebec

Quebec (Province): PQ 1758, 2580, 3112, 3131, 3132, 6470, 7437, 8637, 11151, 11153, 11160, 11230, 12396, 12399, 12628, 12629, 15081, 15092

Race relations: AL 13714; DC 6854; MA 8352; NY 9110; NC 12732; TN 13341

Rachmaninoff, Sergei W.: DC 7380

Rackham, Arthur: KY 15658; MO 11890; PA 5005

Radar: AZ 8871; CA 776, 3623, 5194, 6166, 6171, 6714, 8636, 10485, 11522, 12529, 13982, 14725; FL 11335; MI 4415; NJ 7462, 11274, 14390; NY 5139, 5147, 7511, 12868; VA 11213, 13669

Radiation chemistry: IN 15989; NJ 13254

Radiation—Effect on...: MD 14534; MI 7099, 15770; NV 11378, 14318; TN 10019

Radiation—Safety measures: AL 14005; IN 13473; MD 14414; MA 8074; ON 2208; PA 10612; SC 2764; TN 10024

Radio: CA 15298, 15317, 16196; DC 12600, 14516; IL 2821, 12779; NJ 11280; NY 735, 1794; OH 3068; ON 8395; RI 9398; WI 16474

Radio astronomy: MA 8087; NY 563; ON 16277; PR 3490; VA 9233

Radio broadcasting (See also Television broadcasting): AZ 9745; CA 9744, 10676, 12662, 15245, 15319; CO 11229; CT 5687; DC 1749, 7370, 7379, 9050, 9231; FL 4783; KY 7608; MD 5351; MA 765; MN 15801; NY 387, 2568, 2569, 3225, 9073, 9075, 9076, 9539, 11227; OH 1631, 10386; ON 2155, 2330, 2332, 2336, 2338; OR 5346; PQ 2329, 2331, 11230; TN 8229; UT 1692; VT 2734

Radio waves: MD 6278

Radioactive waste disposal: CA 4464; MB 1034; MD 1036; NV 14318; NM 12823, 14311, 17027; NY 1773; OH 1252; SC 2764; TN 10023; WA 1251, 11518

Radiobiology: MD 12608, 13988, 14414; NM 7613; NY 8203; TN 16225

Radiochemistry: AL 4394; VA 14457

Radiography: NJ 7691; ON 8709; TX 12824

Radioimmunoassay: NY 1315

Radioisotopes: NY 2959; ON 1031; PQ 8274

Radiology: AK 14052; CO 3182; IL 11231; MD 6821, 14414; MA 14421; MI 8885; MO 16811; NJ 10410; NY 1271, 7888, 11825; OK 1113; PA 13331; PQ 8806; TX 5852; WV 10163

Radiopharmaceuticals: NY 2959

Radiotherapy: BC 2422; ON 10244

Railroads (See also Transportation): AB 1960; CA 2002, 2047, 10056; CO 3158, 3885, 4904, 8982, 14372; DC 609, 913, 14370, 14836; GA 5239; IL 601, 6292, 7172, 9661; IN 6348, 9234; MD 2782, 9078; MA 13027, 15669; MI 7995; MN 3610, 5922, 8596; MS 16211; MO 11882; MT 10501; NE 6722, 13787, 14663, 15893; NV 9347, 15905; NJ 9235, 9553; NY 5192, 6777, 9236, 11235; NC 9772; OH 262, 1317, 5806, 7388; OK 2347; ON 2275, 2366, 2387, 16508; OR 5245; PA 307, 1845, 5161, 7093, 11237, 12741, 14583; PQ 2388, 2389, 2396, 2400; SK 12273; TX 11236, 12789; VA 2779, 4384, 16352, 16651; WA 16781; WI 6916, 8487

Railroads, Electric See: Electric railroads

Railroads—Models: NJ 9553; WI 6916

Raleigh, Sir Walter: **NC** 15947

Ranch life: **AB** 13016; **CA** 12635; **TX** 10487, 13454

Rape: **CA** 17249; **NY** 9094; **WI** 6885

Rapid transit See: Urban transportation

Rare books (See also Incunabula): **AL** 15109; **AK** 15127; **AR** 12815, 15172; **CA** 6209, 12136, 12164, 12936, 13044, 15226, 15228, 15235, 15298, 15308, 17457; **CT** 3370, 13641, 17393; **DC** 7385, 14706, 14765, 15463, 16751; **FL** 4833, 11438, 13284, 15495; **GA** 14077, 15506; **HI** 15529; **IL** 3458, 3797, 9936, 9943, 12778, 15373, 15588; **IN** 6369, 10203, 15990; **IA** 15619; **KS** 2878, 4360; **KY** 1376, 2687, 7032, 15644, 15658; **LA** 7596, 13696; **ME** 1166, 1240, 4587; **MB** 13730, 15680; **MD** 1155, 6827, 15706, 16719; **MA** 1575, 1583, 1597, 5088, 5724, 8077, 12577, 15715, 17138; **MI** 4133, 15735, 15746; **MN** 8129, 9734, 12003, 15829; **MS** 16211; **MO** 11889, 11900, 11978; **NE** 3591; **NH** 3753; **NJ** 10995; **NM** 15925; **NY** 58, 1857, 3230, 3514, 3523, 7891, 9544, 9549, 9586, 9636, 10697, 10764, 13093, 13100, 13101, 13108, 13115, 13126, 13136, 13185, 13772; **NC** 15948; **NS** 3677; **OH** 1421, 3067, 5834, 7388, 10048, 10154, 11074, 15375; **OK** 15998, 16004; **ON** 9210, 11212, 16036, 16312; **OR** 16030; **PA** 2486, 5005, 8534, 10639, 12487, 13222, 16061, 16098, 16100; **PR** 2453, 16117; **PQ** 7727, 11763; **RI** 11035, 16128; **SC** 17236; **TN** 6177; **TX** 3702, 7271, 9827, 12101, 16264; **VA** 242, 5579

Rare earths See: Earths, Rare

Rather, Dan (Broadcast journalist): **MA** 1605

Rauschenbush, Walter: **NY** 378

Rayburn, Sam (Senator): **TX** 11256

Reactors (Nuclear physics) See: Nuclear reactors

Read, Sir Herbert: **BC** 16340

Reading: **DE** 6639; **DC** 3989, 9179; **IL** 4439, 9103, 12343; **ME** 7280; **MI** 16857; **MN** 10413; **NY** 7230, 7436, 9536, 11982, 13095; **NC** 3262; **PQ** 7729; **TX** 13455

Reagan, Ronald: **CA** 11349

Real estate See: Real property

Real property: **AZ** 10066; **CA** 1911, 4248, 5220, 7316, 7399, 7506, 8849, 12162, 13726, 15246, 15304, 16631, 17140; **CO** 15398, 15418, 16872; **CT** 15423; **DC** 614, 3098, 14395, 16515; **IL** 3095, 6571, 9061, 11291, 12659, 16514, 17190; **MA** 17108; **MI** 3014, 6059, 8451; **MN** 11243; **MO** 7226; **NY** 3517, 3931, 5028, 5113, 5516, 6869, 6960, 7201, 7769, 9643, 10432, 12427, 16865, 17143; **NC** 5514; **ON** 112, 4592; **OR** 6878; **PA** 1426, 2477, 5000, 13312, 16055, 17237; **PQ** 11161; **TX** 6866, 8946, 12098; **VA** 1563, 6213; **WA** 4927, 16364; **WI** 352, 11333, 16473, 16547

Realism in art: **NY** 81

Rearview mirrors See: Automobiles—Rearview mirrors

Recombinant DNA: **CA** 15257

Recording, Magnetic See: Magnetic recorders and recording

Recordings, Sound See: Sound recordings

Records management: **CA** 6612, 15252; **NH** 9409; **ON** 10242

Recreation (See also Leisure): **CA** 2050, 14028; **CO** 14656; **CT** 5685; **DC** 3987; **GA** 14649; **IL** 9133; **IN** 390, 6388; **MA** 12894; **MN** 15840; **MO** 14029; **MT** 15877; **NM** 14172; **NY** 13108; **NC** 9749; **ON** 7178, 10269, 10270, 12881; **OR** 16021; **TX** 14016; **VA** 9238; **WI** 8555, 16466

Recreation—Administration: **AB** 190; **CT** 9927; **NE** 9312; **OR** 16021

Recreation areas (See also Parks): **GA** 14649

Red Cross: **DC** 602; **ON** 2402

Redwood: **CA** 11300

Reed, Walter (General): **VA** 16354

Reformation: **CA** 5509; **IL** 7703; **IN** 8243; **MO** 2623, 3310; **NJ** 4077; **OH** 17234; **PA** 7677, 12330; **PQ** 10933; **UT** 1700

Reformed Church: **MO** 4253, 4498; **NJ** 9372; **NY** 6004; **NC** 5950; **PA** 4499, 17038

Refractories industry: **CA** 6889; **MD** 5193; **MA** 9953; **OH** 5150, 5156; **ON** 9956; **PA** 5643

Refrigeration (See also Air conditioning): **IL** 11316; **MD** 11315; **MN** 13474; **NY** 2498; **PA** 1570

Refugees: **CA** 17311; **MN** 15807; **NY** 14197

Regional planning (See also City planning; Open spaces): **AL** 138, 9780; **AB** 15214; **AR** 8350; **BC** 5492, 15193; **CA** 148, 2031, 7558, 8399, 12186, 12683, 15239, 15274, 15316, 16205, 16592; **CO** 11099, 12768; **CT** 3542; **DE** 3843; **DC** 739, 6517, 8400; **FL** 5109, 7879, 8354, 12716, 13211; **HI** 5780; **IL** 5488, 8316, 9849, 12831, 13632, 15559; **IN** 1142, 6418; **IA** 12955; **KS** 6948; **KY** 7609; **MD** 5622, 5820, 8029, 8036, 10967, 11321; **MA** 5716, 8088, 8105, 17137; **MI** 12735, 13631, 16823; **MO** 4188; **NE** 10227, 15879; **NJ** 3629, 8493; **NY** 2659, 3493, 5875, 6526, 9031, 9570, 11320, 13738; **NS** 3544, 3545; **OH** 3661, 8422, 9842, 9844; **OK** 16007; **ON** 40, 6565, 8396, 10285, 16311; **OR** 7205; **PA** 3836, 7301, 8260, 10646, 16049; **PE** 10961; **PR** 16109; **PQ** 2286, 11174, 12626; **RI** 11399; **SC** 4776; **SK** 12250; **TN** 2757, 13355; **TX** 9787, 13383, 16259; **WA** 3012, 11114; **WI** 12743, 16443

Rehabilitation (See also Medicine, Physical; Occupational retraining; Occupational therapy): **AB** 5376; **AZ** 8327; **CT** 4192, 5102; **DC** 9239; **FL** 4815; **GA** 4350; **IL** 11327, 15598; **MB** 12639; **MD** 8031; **MA** 7185, 8101; **MI** 8474, 11328; **MN** 3554; **NE** 7838; **NY** 5358, 5839, 6186, 6581, 6646, 7070, 14960; **OK** 9096; **ON** 2397, 2403, 2404, 7073, 9182, 10271, 11196, 17290; **PA** 5655, 7840, 11289; **PQ** 2706, 6473, 6541, 6790; **SK** 4315; **TX** 6528, 13429; **WV** 16923; **WI** 17207

Reinhardt, Max: **NY** 13093

Reinsurance: **KS** 4358; **NY** 2494; **ON** 8252

Reliability (Engineering): **MD** 781; **MI** 5131; **NY** 5139; **OH** 5401; **TX** 14088

Religion and law: **DC** 2559

Religion and psychiatry See: Psychiatry and religion

Religion and theology (See also Bible; names of specific churches, e.g., Baptists): **AB** 15211; **BC** 15195; **CA** 1102, 1460, 2575, 6666, 7126, 12084, 13472; **CT** 6; **DC** 2550, 2558, 2560; **GA** 1001, 13530; **IL** 3308, 12783, 17068; **IN** 2545, 13225; **KY** 3354; **MB** 16419; **MI** 698, 10399; **MN** 1052, 5427, 8586; **MO** 11344, 11345, 11893; **MT** 2501; **NE** 3311, 3593; **NY** 1792, 1852, 4250, 9530, 11353, 11488, 11686, 12080, 13185; **NS** 15655; **OH** 6038, 8922, 11075; **ON** 10052, 11323, 16315; **PA** 4994; **PQ** 2341, 4880, 7868, 10326, 15078; **RI** 11036; **SD** 10940; **SK** 2104; **TN** 16566, 16567; **TX** 12101, 12792; **VA** 1645, 15038; **WA** 12380; **WI** 9016

Religions: **AK** 10741; **BC** 16994; **CA** 5425, 7561, 10742, 13819; **DC** 3988; **HI** 5790; **IL** 1116, 2820, 8137; **KY** 5281, 12754; **MD** 9330; **MA** 5199; **MI** 3921, 4728; **MN** 12004; **NY** 3106, 6030, 6477, 11338, 13835; **OH** 3067; **PQ** 2705, 7750; **WA** 7647

Religious art See: Art and religion

Religious education: **AB** 9673, 9738, 9905; **CA** 16909; **CO** 6282; **CT** 6018; **FL** 5986; **IL** 4343, 6778, 7402, 17439; **IN** 8828; **KY** 7013; **MB** 15687, 15688; **MD** 3204; **MI** 8508, 11311; **MN** 3307, 8593, 9782, 10012; **MO** 2886; **NJ** 9847; **NY** 10005; **NC** 6891; **ND** 9906; **NS** 11980; **ON** 2686, 6216, 8398, 15094, 16216; **OR** 9907; **PA** 12647; **PQ** 3290, 8720; **TX** 3686, 3688; **WA** 9908; **WV** 737

Religious Society of Friends See: Society of Friends

St. Louis (MO): MO 8663, 8665, 11877, 11888, 11892, 14651, 16807, 16964

Sales management: DC 6107; IL 3754; NY 12068

Sales promotion (See also Advertising and marketing): IL 1264

Saline water conversion: LA 5573; MA 13024; PQ 7737

Salmon: BC 6631; CA 14562; NB 1024; NS 2199; WA 14399, 16373

Salvage (Waste, etc.): AZ 14263; BC 1738; CA 2025, 3273, 15321; CT 667; FL 2902, 5109; IL 5493; MA 2094; MN 6641; NY 8681; ON 2187, 4635; PA 1431, 10002; TN 16221; UT 4291; WI 3185, 11363

Samizdat See: Underground literature—Russia

San Antonio (TX): TX 3760, 12094

San Diego (CA): CA 12124, 12125, 12129, 12145

San Francisco (CA): CA 9219, 12155, 12163, 12166, 12635, 14129

Sandburg, Carl: IL 15588; NC 14599; PA 3938

Sandoz, Mari: NE 15893

Sanger, Margaret: MA 12578

Sanitary engineering: CA 2898, 2899, 6986, 7536, 11258; GA 4395; IL 5493, 17110; MD 14047; MA 13684; MT 5981; NC 8817; OH 7720; OK 4414; ON 2161; TX 13708; VA 13864

Sanskrit literature: CA 15265; MN 15782; NY 6477, 16134

Santayana, George: ON 16399

Saraswati, Sivananda (Swami): BC 17399

Saroyan, William: CA 2054, 5021; MA 17138

Saskatchewan: SK 1260, 12239, 12257, 12261, 12269

Satellites (See also Planets): AZ 7137, 15167; CA 76; DC 3268, 5226; MD 3269; MA 12592; NJ 17006; ON 2311; PQ 12845

Savannah (GA): GA 5239

Savings and loan associations See: Building and loan associations

Sawyer, Ruth: MN 3133

Scandinavia: CA 2996; IA 7643; MN 15826; WA 9725

Scandinavia in art: MN 15784

Scandinavian Americans: CA 1996; MN 1052, 8598, 9916

Scaticook Indians: CT 7000

Schnitzler, Arthur: NY 13093

Schoenberg, Arnold: CA 842

Scholarships: IN 9187; VA 10068

School discipline: PA 9093

School facilities: DE 3841; NV 15903; NY 25; OR 4432

School management and organization: AL 4777; CA 3445, 10315, 12168; DE 3841; DC 9246; MD 6832; NY 11070; ON 16292; OR 4432; PQ 11034, 15067; SC 1537; TX 16267; VA 4278; WI 17214

Schumann, Robert: NY 12323

Schwenkfelder Church: PA 12330

Science fiction: AZ 15168; CA 12150, 15335; CO 810; KS 15622; LA 13696; MA 8091; MN 8604; MO 15872; NV 605; NM 4210; NY 13185; NC 5554; OH 15442; ON 13563; PA 13325, 16100; TX 13379; WI 16425

Science—History: AZ 15168; BC 15210; CA 1993, 2041, 2475, 2997, 12142, 12146, 12936, 15226, 17457; CT 1887, 15515, 16901, 17380; DE 15447; DC 12588, 12600, 12601, 14074; FL 15495; IL 15364, 15588; IN 6392; IA 6688; KS 15622, 15633; KY 15660; MD 6828; MA 1652, 3120, 5723, 8075, 8077, 8081, 17138, 17284; MI 6910, 8466, 8470, 8471, 15746; MO 7419; NJ 6479, 14615; NY 512, 3223, 3500, 9547, 10857, 11343, 13190; NC 15943; OH 3071, 10154; OK 16002; ON 2253, 16312, 16407; OR 10891; PA 29, 586, 4973, 16048; RI 1816, 1819; SC 16174; SD 16177; UT 16329; VA 16652; WA 16387; WI 16456

Science information See: Communication in science

Science—Philosophy: CA 7126, 12072, 12142, 12950; DC 13974; MN 15819; NY 512; OH 4628; PA 16100; PQ 15045; SD 16177; VA 6603

Science policy See: Science and state

Science research See: Research

Science and state: DC 7362, 14814; HI 5780; MA 5729, 8065; OK 16009; ON 2219, 2294; VA 16652

Science—Study and teaching: CA 15261; DC 9247, 9248; IL 8979; MA 8065, 8980; OH 4441, 4628; TN 13045

Science and technology (See also Engineering; Technological innovations; specific names of sciences, e.g., Biology): AL 130; AB 9859, 15142, 15214; AZ 801, 15166; BC 1716; CA 2000, 2058, 2065, 2996, 2997, 3935, 7392, 7562, 10040, 12134, 12911, 14770; CO 3877, 13866; CT 1681, 1761, 4639, 5686, 6018, 17372; DC 354, 3991, 7382, 7386, 9038, 9247, 12336, 12337, 12609, 13863, 14107, 14529; FL 4832, 8407; GA 993, 4641, 5240, 15508; HI 5780, 5783; ID 15550; IL 2813, 6289, 8515, 8979, 11503, 12776, 13745, 15599; IN 265, 4506, 6346, 6349, 6413, 6420, 11136; IA 15606; KS 6942; KY 7336; LA 9452; MB 15689; MD 4378, 13592, 14711; MA 1598, 3120, 5714, 8077, 8980, 9009, 13871; MI 3571, 4772, 5863; MN 5922, 8587, 12000; MO 6929, 11887, 11897, 13748, 16808; NE 15881; NV 11379; NH 9415, 9418; NJ 910, 1313, 3298, 6964, 8845, 9424, 9659, 10973, 12413, 13011, 13621; NY 1794, 1858, 7758, 9495, 9537, 9587, 9589, 10675, 10924, 11186, 11343, 11354, 11480, 11482, 11493, 13087, 13092, 13101, 13112, 13190, 13772, 13858, 14222, 17414; NC 9769, 9773, 9774; NS 3683; OH 127, 3071, 3780, 4069, 4965, 8418, 10142, 11085, 11087, 13542; OK 2670; ON 2255, 2356, 4139, 7178, 7237, 7795, 8393, 9200, 10304, 11601, 11513, 16039, 16301, 16400; OR 7354, 10348, 10891, 16029, 16732; PA 4993, 7303, 8926, 13140, 16090, 16696; PR 16111, 16116; PQ 2582, 3314, 3315, 8141; RI 1818, 11046; SC 10325, 10760; TN 8221, 9024; TX 3699, 4920, 6124, 6127, 7271, 7687, 12098, 13378, 13768, 16266; UT 1698; VT 4537; VA 11384, 11427, 14244, 14816, 16359, 16651; WA 12375, 16379, 16786, 16796; WV 13082; WI 7832, 8557; WY 16497

Scientific apparatus and instruments: CA 1311, 5891, 13982, 14008; CO 6918; CT 10677; DC 14529; IN 1544, 4483; NH 7113; NY 1774, 3252; PA 6054, 11512; PQ 1094; TX 4522

Scotland: FL 4833; IL 7172; MN 3137; NY 606

Sculpture: AB 12745; CA 5321, 15289; CT 3565, 17359; DC 12590; IA 3890; KY 15657; MD 8022, 16719; MA 2787, 8055; MI 3902; NY 5550, 9510, 9556, 16142, 17413; NC 15961; OH 3063; OK 15992; ON 8656, 17424; RI 1815; TX 9693; VA 16649; WA 16362; WI 8546, 8555

Sealing (Technology) (See also Plastics; Welding): CT 7466; MI 12985

Seattle (WA): WA 5971, 12374, 16770

Secondary education See: Education, Secondary

Securities (See also Bonds; Stocks): AL 7209; BC 1208; CA 2022, 5903, 6867, 7059, 7506, 7634; DC 1952, 7081, 13060, 14837; FL 4820; GA 297, 10908, 12388; IL 1127, 3095, 5030, 6959, 8127, 14838, 17190; KS 12388; MB 11417; MA 5383, 8099, 12354, 17108; NE 1118; NJ 1939, 7637; NY 1394, 1824, 1877, 1951, 3130, 3807, 3931, 3951, 4014, 4153, 5028, 6176, 6970, 8838, 10308, 11331, 12075, 12427, 12455, 12521, 12573, 12616, 12927, 16710, 16865, 17166, 17256; ON 3614,

Securities (Continued)
7789, 13565; **PA** 13032; **TX** 117, 399, 1917, 6859, 12794; **WA** 4376; **WI** 11150, 11333

Seed industry and trade: **DC** 608, 14501; **ID** 884; **MD** 14266; **WA** 21

Seismology (See also Earthquakes; Volcanoes): **BC** 6523; **CA** 1987, 3825, 11635, 15233, 15234; **CO** 17301; **DE** 3847; **DC** 2476; **IL** 2804; **MA** 1584, 8080; **NY** 1772, 4876; **OH** 2504; **OK** 10175; **ON** 2181; **TX** 16249

Selenology See: Moon

Self-actualization: **MI** 6475; **PA** 12315

Self-defense: **WI** 6885

Semiconductors: **AZ** 1899, 6549, 8874; **CA** 69, 556, 1019, 1904, 4538, 6170, 6551, 11520, 12508; **CT** 10677; **IN** 5182; **MA** 3945, 5540, 11268, 16581; **MN** 6056; **NJ** 11280; **NY** 6281; **OR** 5897, 6553; **TX** 8872, 13406

Seminole Indians: **FL** 10318

Semitic history See: Jews—History

Semitic languages: **CT** 17387; **DC** 2560; **IL** 5093, 15370; **NJ** 10976; **NY** 5833, 9524, 17408; **PA** 4084

Sendak, Maurice: **PA** 11559

Serial publication of books: **NY** 9508

Servants of Mary (Roman Catholic Order): **IL** 10328

Seton, Ernest Thompson: **TX** 1633

Seventh-Day Adventists (See also Adventists): **AB** 2413; **CA** 7473, 16909; **DC** 12421; **MD** 3204, 11371; **MI** 698; **NE** 13771; **TN** 12796

Seventh-Day Baptists: **NY** 247; **WI** 12422

Sex: **CA** 2062, 6478; **IL** 10824; **IN** 6398, 7079, 10811, 10816; **MN** 10814; **MO** 10809; **NY** 6527, 10813, 12210, 12424; **NC** 15935; **OH** 10812; **PA** 10815; **PQ** 15083; **TX** 10810; **WI** 10817

Sex crimes (See also Rape): **CA** 6536

Sexism: **CA** 8248; **NJ** 12509; **NY** 17445

Shakers: **DE** 4105; **KY** 5678, 16970; **ME** 13861; **MA** 5043, 12429; **NY** 1857, 5995, 9543, 12431; **OH** 16736, 16996; **PA** 5502

Shakespeare, William: **CA** 4954, 12133, 12432; **CT** 17362; **DC** 4375, 4851, 7385; **IL** 15588; **KS** 11937; **MD** 15705; **MA** 5388; **MI** 15746; **NH** 3751, 3753; **NC** 15948; **OH** 3068; **ON** 13036, 16312; **PA** 16052, 16907; **UT** 12810; **WI** 588

Shale, Black: **KY** 15643

Shale oils See: Oil-shales

Shaw, George Bernard: **MA** 12577; **NY** 3514; **NC** 15948; **PA** 1840

Shellfish: **GA** 5254; **MD** 14554; **PQ** 7723

Shells: **IN** 6394

Ship-building: **CA** 11459, 14780, 14790; **CT** 8999; **DC** 14777; **HI** 14781; **ME** 7858; **MD** 2074; **MA** 5134; **NY** 9547, 14487; **NC** 9756; **PA** 14783; **VA** 7953; **WI** 7911

Shipping: **BC** 7967; **CA** 7877, 7965, 10064, 12662; **DC** 14370, 14397; **FL** 10483; **ME** 1625, 2090; **MA** 683, 8096; **MI** 1266; **NB** 9368; **NJ** 12357; **NY** 12987, 13122; **ON** 2315; **OR** 10875; **RI** 1706; **TX** 13382; **VA** 7953

Shipwrecks: **NY** 4175, 13055; **OH** 5479; **TX** 10392

Shock (Physiologic): **IL** 613

Shoemaking See: Boots and shoes—Trade and manufacture

Shop practice See: Machine-shop practice

Shopping centers (See also Retail trade): **CA** 16631; **NY** 6591

Shrimps: **TX** 14558

Sibelius, Jean: **IN** 1924

Sickle cell anemia: **DC** 6141; **NY** 2543

Sierra Nevada Mountains: **CA** 12504

Sight See: Vision

Sign language: **FL** 4796; **ME** 1263; **MO** 11881

Silent films: **NJ** 268, 4903

Silica and silicates: **PA** 10918

Silver: **CO** 15415; **CT** 6643; **DC** 12511

Simulation methods: **CA** 7471; **FL** 11309

Single parents: **PA** 2842

Sioux Indians: **SD** 12710

Sisterhoods: **CA** 4025; **IL** 6098, 9251; **KY** 12057; **MN** 12551; **NY** 12552; **PA** 12548; **WA** 12550; **WI** 7983

Skis and skiing: **MI** 9252

Slavery (See also Underground railroad): **AR** 15179; **CA** 2062; **CT** 13031; **DC** 3981, 15464; **IN** 7414; **KS** 17104; **LA** 7585; **MD** 10968; **MA** 8144, 10554, 16878; **MI** 2655; **MN** 8580, 8585; **MO** 7418; **NY** 3514, 6756; **OH** 16996; **PA** 8529, 10932, 13151; **SC** 10212; **TX** 13415; **WI** 16440

Slavic languages and literature: **BC** 15195; **IL** 6285, 15590; **KS** 15634; **NY** 9548, 13179; **OH** 10121, 10130; **ON** 16415; **PA** 12562

Slavs—History: **CO** 16207; **IL** 15590; **PA** 12562; **TX** 12563

Slides (See also Audio-visual materials): **DE** 4105; **DC** 9153; **IN** 6383, 6426; **MO** 9327; **NM** 15918; **OH** 3054; **ON** 10293; **PA** 2482, 13327; **PE** 3327; **SC** 3034; **TN** 8223

Sloan, John: **DE** 3832

Slovakia: **IL** 12567; **OH** 4696, 12568

Small arms See: Firearms

Small business: **CA** 1644, 12192; **DC** 14841; **GA** 5264, 5916; **IL** 459; **LA** 9839; **MD** 16972; **MA** 1594, 9699; **NY** 1791, 4127, 9095; **ON** 2355; **PA** 2477; **PQ** 4600; **SK** 12259; **TN** 3465; **WA** 12371; **WV** 16937; **WI** 5490, 16466, 17205

Small presses See: Little presses

Smell and taste: **PA** 8724

Smith, Margaret Chase (Senator): **ME** 12586

Smoking (See also Tobacco): **DC** 9013, 13527; **KS** 543; **MD** 10071; **NY** 477; **PQ** 2411; **WA** 12303

Soap (See also Detergent, Synthetic): **AZ** 834; **NJ** 3105, 7319, 11373; **OH** 11003, 11004, 11006

Soap box derbies: **OH** 6644

Soaring (Aeronautics) See: Gliding and soaring

Social change: **DC** 2599; **MA** 5697, 12067; **PA** 13316

Social insurance See: Social security

Social interaction: **NY** 9110, 9575

Social medicine: **GA** 4354; **NY** 8775; **ON** 10261

Social protest movements: MI 15746; PA 13316; WI 16483

Social sciences: AB 15136, 15217, 15219; BC 15190, 15195; CA 11, 1993, 2049, 2996, 3935, 6766, 7563, 12135, 12147, 15279, 15305; CO 13866, 15407; CT 6, 5687, 17389; DC 1874, 3990, 7382, 11248, 14517; FL 7095, 12969; GA 993; HI 5789, 5790, 15524; ID 15551; IL 6309, 9866, 12777, 12782, 12786, 14835, 15569; IN 6423, 6463, 11136; IA 8019; KS 15621; KY 7026; LA 11833; MB 3141; MA 20, 11223; MI 16859; MN 8586, 12005; MS 6737; MO 11882, 11893; NE 16854; NJ 477, 1795, 3121, 3208, 3214, 3487, 3646, 4873, 9521, 9546, 9583, 9584, 11187, 11343, 11498, 11608, 13136, 13183, 13185, 13858, 16862; OH 3072, 3783, 4985, 10085, 10142, 12970, 13543; ON 248, 9199, 9200, 9211, 11601, 15513, 16036, 16315, 17430; OR 7354, 10348; PA 731, 5006, 6410, 6532, 8926; PR 2452, 16111; PQ 2295, 2684, 3316, 7868, 15077, 15082; TN 8221; TX 3706, 12100; UT 1699; VA 9732, 11427, 14807, 16651; WA 1251, 9908, 14122; WI 7833, 16440

Social sciences—Study and teaching: CO 4442; IN 6401; NY 6160

Social security: CT 15439; DC 14322, 14842, 14843; MD 14844; MI 6506, 6507; NY 3225, 3507, 6850; PQ 11176, 15088; WI 16483, 17206

Social service (See also Medical social work; Public welfare): AB 191, 1965, 4270; BC 15037, 15199; CA 15036, 16204; CT 15439; DC 599, 6149; GA 5252; IL 6809, 7627, 13811, 15035, 15371, 15569, 17439; IN 2513, 6414; IA 6678; KS 6935; MB 7901; MD 9063; MA 1578, 12519; MI 15775; MN 15828; MO 8673, 16813; MT 2501; NB 9363; NJ 8729; NY 60, 3233, 4572, 4875, 6199, 6780, 9470, 9595, 12080, 12081; NS 9983; OH 2523, 7002, 10092, 10149; ON 2593, 3282, 17118; OR 16014; PA 13329, 16065, 16099; PQ 2698, 2710, 7746, 11162, 11163, 16628; RI 11404; SK 12256; TX 10393, 13428; VA 15034; WA 16393; WI 2546, 16464, 17201

Social welfare See: Public welfare

Socialism: CT 15183, 15425; KS 15638; NY 685, 9646; WI 16422, 16483

Society of Friends: DC 12643; IL 15577; IN 4161, 8243, 10806, 13751, 16849; IA 17134; KS 5034; MD 4763, 13205; MA 9351; NY 118, 12645; NC 4116, 5554; OH 12646; ON 12642; PA 5764, 10577, 12647, 13151, 13152, 13222, 16735; RI 12644

Society of Jesus See: Jesuits

Society of St. Vincent de Paul: MO 12660

Sociology: AB 8425, 15137; CA 10040, 12147, 15263, 17316; CT 15439, 17389; DC 515, 1874, 3990, 14196; GA 5253; IL 2820, 3032, 12777, 15368, 15569; IN 11128; IA 15611; MD 4382; MA 5749; MI 3923; NY 1795, 1852, 3219, 9458, 9530, 11187, 13183; NS 3684; OH 11075; OK 10193; ON 8394, 9828, 10299, 17415; PA 4178; PQ 2685; TX 3706; UT 16324; WA 12377; WI 16447

Soft drinks See: Carbonated beverages

Softball (See also Baseball): OK 324

Software See: Programming (Electronic computers)

Soil conservation: AZ 14261; MS 8653; TX 3406

Soil science: AB 215, 2151; AK 15113; BC 2134; CA 3452, 6596, 6725, 17273; CO 3182, 14444; FL 15467, 15497; ID 14258; IA 12669; ME 12787; MB 15678; MN 1220, 15831, 15837; MS 14044, 14045, 14046; NE 9321; NB 2119; NJ 3453; NY 13109; NC 4113; ON 2114; PQ 2129, 15045; SK 2133, 12255; TX 5046; VA 16665; WI 611

Solar energy: AL 14498; AB 216; AZ 801, 5092, 15162; CA 1668, 2038, 3273, 4467, 11299, 13081; CO 11466, 12671; DC 2977, 2978; FL 4787, 4797; IL 6302, 10407, 12451; IN 1141; MD 3; MA 1574, 8701; MI 6875; MT 299, 9081; NH 9401; NJ 950; NY 9493; OH 10096; OK 10739; ON 2263; OR 10885; PA 3408, 4948, 4972, 4973, 13824, 14473; PR 2603; PQ 7737; TN 9024, 13363, 16221; VT 9395; VA 6661

Solar houses: DC 2978

Solar radiation: MD 12608; NC 17298

Solid state physics: CA 1019, 1983, 5891, 5894, 15315; DC 14532; IL 15587; IN 15982; MN 15823; NJ 10981, 11282; NM 12198; ND 15973; OH 15390; PA 956, 16092; PQ 7751

Solid waste: CA 4244, 4412; CO 4402; DC 4399, 16825; FL 2902, 4804; GA 4407; IL 3013, 4408, 5493; IA 6681; ME 6876; MD 14090; MA 4166, 4364, 4403; MI 10032; MN 8621; MO 4410; NB 9362; NY 4387; OH 4391, 12087; OK 4172; ON 10278; OR 4396; PA 1431, 10612, 12196; TX 4409; WA 16778

Sonora Desert: AZ 14672

Sound recordings (See also Audio-visual materials): AZ 15161; BC 15209; CA 10458, 12947, 15332, 16199; CO 15412; CT 15516, 17395; DC 6575, 7379, 7380; FL 15731; IL 9865, 9943, 15585; IN 6375; LA 7590; MB 2333; MD 13588, 15704; MA 2740; MI 8458; MN 15820; MO 15393; NH 3750; NJ 10990; NY 2571, 3504, 3510, 9518, 9542, 11294, 13117, 13182, 13185; NS 2334; OH 1631, 7005, 15376; ON 2277, 2336, 2337, 16298; PA 3249; PQ 1447, 2335; TN 3550, 8228

Sound recordings—History: CA 7203; CT 17395; DE 3844; NY 734; OH 10386; PA 5002; SC 3114

Sousa, John Philip: DC 14486; MD 13588

South Africa: AL 13207; CA 1994

South America See: Latin America

South Asia: AZ 15164; BC 15185; DC 7360; HI 15517; IL 15372, 15555, 15556; KS 6947; MN 5620, 15782; TX 16231

South Carolina: SC 1767, 1969, 2089, 2489, 2744, 2745, 2965, 2966, 3114, 3743, 5061, 10212, 10578, 12691, 12692, 12695, 12701, 13549, 16173, 17236

South Dakota: ND 15967; SD 499, 1054, 1492, 3665, 3673, 12538, 12710, 12711, 12712, 14590, 16179, 16180

South Sea Islands See: Oceania

Southeast Asia See: Asia, Southeastern

Southern States: AL 7427, 10954, 12090; GA 4355, 5917; LA 7585, 13696; MS 8654; NY 15394; NC 9759, 15950; TN 13352, 13354, 16165, 16572; TX 4305; VA 3325, 16360, 16662

Southwest: AZ 664, 783, 784, 785, 791, 797, 5822, 8977, 12437, 14672, 14695, 14696, 15148, 15168; CA 2459, 2995, 7534, 12479; CO 3161, 3531, 4904; MD 24; NM 224, 5289, 5755, 8971, 8975, 9439, 9444, 13885, 13904, 13909, 14491, 14602, 15925, 17074; NY 9523; OK 5297, 9184, 16011, 16012; TX 319, 322, 3695, 4306, 4895, 10487, 13454, 13994, 16264, 16919

Soviet Union: AK 161; CA 11247, 12940; CO 12331; DC 5224, 7364, 17162; MA 5742; NE 15893; NY 3219, 9548, 11228, 13545; VA 7044

Soviet Union—History: CA 2062; KS 15634; NY 3230

Soviet Union—Languages: NJ 910; NY 13545

Soybean: CA 12843; IL 12915; IN 2664; MO 636

Space colonies: AZ 7137

Space flight (See also Astronautics): AL 14498; NY 1326; PA 14847; SK 14846; TX 11415

Space law: MS 15845; OK 16003; PQ 7735

Space medicine (See also Aviation medicine): CA 14489; FL 14712; OH 13955, 13984, 17318; PA 14713; TX 13869

Space photography: AZ 807, 15167; MO 16816; PA 14847; TX 7641

Space sciences (See also Astronautics; Astronomy; Geophysics): **AL** 14097, 14498, 15112; **AZ** 14446; **CA** 76, 1992, 4869, 4870, 6166, 7713, 11521, 12873, 14490, 15279, 16200; **CO** 1135, 8006; **CT** 15028; **DC** 13974, 14493; **FL** 14494; **IL** 64; **IN** 6417, 6420; **MD** 6823, 13252, 17300; **MA** 1090, 5735, 6047, 8079; **MI** 3924; **MN** 6045, 6057; **MS** 14499; **NY** 501, 3494, 4236, 5535, 11483, 11562; **OH** 4370, 13251, 13667, 14496; **OK** 7040, 11524; **PA** 276, 5158, 14847, 17021; **TX** 7640, 13403, 14497; **UT** 5867

Space vehicles: **CA** 5127; **CO** 8006; **NY** 5160; **TX** 14497

Spain: **CA** 2459, 12215; **DC** 7369, 7375; **NY** 5934, 5935; **PA** 6410; **PR** 16110

Spain—History—Civil war: **CA** 15340; **MA** 1652

Spanish America See: Latin America

Spanish-American War: **CA** 16609; **DC** 14519; **VA** 16725

Spanish civil war See: Spain—History—Civil war

Spanish language: **CT** 15425; **ON** 10257; **VT** 4512; **WI** 16465

Spanish literature: **CA** 10039, 15340; **DC** 7369; **IL** 2824; **NY** 1793, 5933, 5935; **PA** 16061, 16100; **TX** 13451, 16264; **WI** 16465

Spanish missions: **TX** 10392, 13386

Special education See: Exceptional children—Education

Special libraries See: Libraries, Special

Specifications (See also Standardization): **CA** 5329; **CT** 3319; **DC** 14531; **IL** 13614; **ON** 17011; **TX** 11509

Specifications, Military See: Standards, Military

Spectrum analysis (See also Chemistry, Analytic): **CA** 1311; **IL** 15599; **MD** 14175, 15697; **MA** 279, 8092; **MN** 15791; **MO** 16804; **PA** 11655, 16070, 16075; **TN** 4754

Speech: **CA** 15350; **CT** 5757; **DC** 238; **IL** 4439, 12774, 12783, 15569; **IN** 11128; **KS** 6518; **MA** 3651, 4339, 16594; **MN** 3135; **MO** 16819; **NJ** 6497; **NY** 11976, 13227; **OH** 10126

Speech, Disorders of: **CO** 15414; **DC** 5074; **FL** 4796; **IL** 8948; **IA** 15608; **ME** 15671; **MA** 4339; **MO** 11881; **NV** 15900; **NY** 6198, 11193; **PQ** 7752; **TN** 8232; **TX** 16260

Speleology (See also Caves): **AL** 9264; **UT** 14693

Spender, Stephen: **ON** 17434

Spices: **MD** 7702; **MI** 6917

Spiders: **CA** 12146; **NC** 16950

Spinal cord—Wounds and injuries: **CO** 13163; **NY** 14957, 14960; **ON** 2397; **PA** 5655

Sports (See also Athletics; Olympic games; names of specific sports, e.g., Baseball): **AL** 1041, 14848; **CA** 4713, 7548, 9215; **FL** 8405; **HI** 5786; **IL** 635, 3797, 15554; **IN** 15990; **LA** 9451; **MD** 4379; **MI** 3909, 3914; **MN** 12004, 12005; **NY** 1854, 9523, 11181, 11221, 11490, 13515, 15394; **NC** 9749; **NS** 9978; **OH** 1632, 11075, 13538; **ON** 10269, 12881, 16401; **PA** 5006, 12882; **PQ** 2394; **VA** 9265; **WI** 7833, 8555

Sports medicine: **AL** 14848; **CA** 1973, 2638; **CO** 14815; **FL** 6648; **IN** 6388; **MD** 13778; **MO** 11916; **NJ** 5614; **NY** 9551, 11193; **OH** 11723; **ON** 2377, 12881

Springs (Mechanism): **CT** 909

Stagecoaches See: Coaching (Transportation)

Stained glass See: Glass painting and staining

Stainless steel See: Steel, Stainless

Stamp-collecting and stamp-collectors See: Postage-stamps—Collectors and collecting

Standard Reference Data Program See: National Standard Reference Data System

Standardization: **CA** 5329, 7470, 7562; **DC** 3426, 14527, 14529, 14531; **FL** 14494; **IL** 2813, 12369, 13745; **MD** 9266; **MA** 1940; **MN** 10233; **MO** 7419, 8743; **NJ** 9659; **NM** 14146; **NY** 638, 1794; **OH** 3071, 13667; **ON** 2406, 12929; **OR** 10340; **PA** 633, 13824; **TX** 3699, 11509; **VA** 471; **WA** 14366; **WI** 8557, 16438

Standards, Military: **AB** 9915; **CT** 3319; **MD** 9266; **MO** 4340; **NY** 4473, 7103; **OH** 14234; **OR** 4775; **PA** 11460; **VA** 4157; **WI** 14232

State and provincial government: **AB** 183, 210; **AK** 156, 162; **AZ** 791; **AR** 818; **BC** 1720; **CA** 2040, 15244; **DC** 13862; **FL** 12969; **GA** 5259; **HI** 5782; **ID** 6265, 6267; **IL** 6309, 6311; **IN** 6356; **IA** 6685; **KY** 3548, 7024, 7031; **LA** 7575, 11067; **ME** 7864; **MD** 8042; **MA** 8113, 8114, 8116; **MI** 8446, 8460, 15737; **MN** 2656; **MS** 15847; **MO** 8673; **MT** 8764; **NV** 9345; **NB** 9369; **NH** 9404, 9412; **NJ** 9432; **NM** 9444; **NY** 2979; **NC** 9759, 15939; **ND** 9797; **OH** 10104; **OK** 10183; **ON** 9209, 10242, 10295; **OR** 10348; **PA** 10603, 10630; **PQ** 11165; **RI** 11396; **SC** 12701, 16169; **SD** 16179; **TX** 1273, 13412, 13436, 13437; **UT** 16520; **VT** 16600, 16602; **WA** 16786, 16791; **WI** 17221

Staten Island (NY): **NY** 12976, 12978

Statistics: **AB** 196, 2299, 15131, 15132; **BC** 2305; **CA** 12946, 15225, 15266, 15277; **DC** 427, 14165; **IL** 9941, 14357, 15364, 15583; **IN** 11131; **IA** 6677; **KS** 15623; **KY** 15651, 15660; **MB** 2306, 15689; **MD** 3363, 15694; **MA** 5714, 5729, 5750, 15718; **MI** 8476, 15459, 15761; **MN** 15830; **MS** 8651; **MO** 15858; **NJ** 948, 949, 10986, 11625; **NY** 3223, 3332, 4226, 4876, 13858, 14356, 16135; **NF** 2303; **NC** 15932; **NS** 2300; **OH** 10141; **ON** 2304, 2307, 3331, 6453, 16297; **PA** 10649, 13318, 16055, 16089; **PQ** 2301, 7732, 7742, 11167; **SK** 2302; **TX** 13969; **UT** 16323; **VA** 5195, 14089, 14704; **WA** 16385; **WI** 16455

Statutes: **AB** 8542; **AR** 8943; **CA** 14167; **DC** 14319; **FL** 3666; **IL** 4085; **MB** 7908; **MA** 5629; **MI** 3429; **MO** 8746; **OH** 2525, 7827; **ON** 2289; **TX** 5576, 5901; **VT** 1497

Steam: **MA** 11437; **NJ** 4928; **PA** 9662; **RI** 9398

Steamboats: **ID** 8976; **IA** 11143; **LA** 7585; **MO** 16960; **NJ** 8727; **NY** 12987; **OH** 11074; **TN** 8220; **VT** 16335; **WI** 10381, 16427

Steel (See also Iron; Metallurgy): **NJ** 8862; **NC** 8509; **OH** 1247, 13519; **ON** 4017; **PA** 3184, 6871, 7636, 14237, 14849, 14850

Steel industry and trade: **IL** 6461; **ON** 4016; **PA** 1427, 1428, 6870, 14849

Stein, Gertrude: **CA** 2995, 15298

Steinbeck, John: **CA** 1442, 12069, 12181, 12936; **IN** 1140; **MN** 15829

Steiner, Rudolph: **ON** 727

Stennis, John C. (Senator): **MS** 8654

Stepfamily (See also Family): **NY** 12996

Stereoscopic photography See: Photography, Stereoscopic

Sterilization (Bacteriology): **NJ** 4484; **PA** 640

Sterilization (Birth control) See: Birth control

Stevenson, Robert Louis: **AS** 4630; **CA** 12512; **PA** 5005

Stockbridge (MA): **MA** 13015

Stocks (See also Bonds; Investment banking): **CO** 12926; **DC** 11298, 14837; **IL** 14838; **MB** 11417; **MD** 16588; **MA** 1594, 4649; **MO** 16690; **NM** 407; **NY** 641, 1824, 3806, 3951, 5113, 5227, 9630, 10308, 12927, 13586, 16891; **ON** 1893, 7789, 13565; **PQ** 9333; **TX** 399, 6866

Stockton (CA): **CA** 5588

Stokowski, Leopold: **PA** 3652

Stonehenge (Megalithic monument): **CA** 13026

Storage batteries: **CT** 17397; **IL** 5399; **MA** 4137; **OH** 13756;
ON 4136; **WI** 6844, 11260

Storks: **WI** 6592

Story-telling: **FL** 4812; **MN** 3133; **MO** 11890; **ON** 13561; **TN** 9271

Stoves: **UT** 13030

Stowe, Harriet Beecher: **CT** 13031; **MA** 9036, 11222

Strains and stresses (Mechanics): **OH** 10930

Stratford Festival: **ON** 13036

Stress (Physiology): **AB** 202; **CA** 6530, 14741

Strindberg, August S.: **MN** 15826

Strip mining: **PA** 10612; **WV** 13137

Structural engineering: **AB** 2709; **CA** 1809, 2898, 3096, 3735,
3825, 7766, 9702, 11258, 12759, 15234; **DC** 14773; **HI** 3713;
IL 2804, 3013, 5640, 10884, 14013; **MA** 14023; **MO** 13145;
MT 5981; **NJ** 1896; **NY** 4224, 10516, 12364; **OH** 3712;
OR 2900; **PA** 1128, 7302; **TX** 8699, 8819

Studebaker automobile: **IN** 3971

Students' societies: **DC** 14851; **IL** 7320; **IN** 9187; **MI** 9746; **NY** 9741

Study abroad programs See: Educational exchanges, International

Sturbridge (MA): **MA** 10213

Submarine boats: **CA** 745; **CT** 5129, 14810; **NH** 14782; **WI** 7911

Submarine geology: **BC** 2201; **FL** 14573, 15724; **MA** 17264;
NY 3518; **PA** 254; **PQ** 7747; **TX** 16249

Submarine medicine: **CT** 14789

Submarine warfare: **CA** 284; **CT** 14798; **MD** 16676; **RI** 11269,
14799; **VA** 14709

Subsidies: **CO** 3881; **IL** 4033; **OH** 4932; **TX** 3709, 5060

Suffrage: **CA** 16150; **CT** 13031; **DC** 7385, 9284, 14629; **MA** 12578;
NY 467, 4936; **NC** 15963; **VA** 16641

Sugar: **DC** 13058; **HI** 7681; **NY** 678; **PA** 4973

Sugar beet: **CO** 632

Sugar—Manufacture and refining: **HI** 5798

Suggestion systems: **IL** 9065

Suicide: **AB** 2379; **CA** 4013; **NY** 4145; **OH** 14968

Sulphur: **DC** 13061

Sunday, William Ashley (Billy): **IN** 5415; **TX** 7271

Supreme courts See: Courts of last resort

Surface mining See: Strip mining

Surgery (See also Shock (Physiologic)): **AZ** 7939; **CA** 144; **CO** 927;
IL 415; **MD** 14763; **MA** 610; **MI** 1930; **NY** 1948, 17406;
OK 16000; **PA** 1835; **PQ** 7730; **TN** 12404; **TX** 1070; **WV** 1942

Surgery, Plastic: **AL** 4531; **CA** 3108, 11755; **LA** 14830; **NJ** 11692;
NY 3218, 9485; **OH** 13955; **PA** 7305

Surrealism: **IL** 855

Survey research See: Public opinion polls

Surveying: **BC** 7715; **DC** 14103; **FL** 4810; **MD** 14572; **ON** 10268;

Surveying (Continued)
PQ 11166; **VT** 16603

Sweden: **AB** 13159; **DC** 13161; **MN** 645; **NY** 13158; **PA** 644

Swedenborgianism: **MA** 13155, 13156; **NY** 13154; **OH** 16517;
PA 30

Swedish Americans: **IL** 13164, 13166; **MN** 645; **PA** 644

Sweeteners: **IL** 12915; **NY** 10673

Swift, Jonathan: **NY** 3514; **ON** 7791; **PA** 16061

Swimming: **FL** 6648

Synagogue libraries See: Libraries, Church and synagogue

Synthetic fabrics: **GA** 7058; **PQ** 6853

Synthetic fibers See: Textile fibers, Synthetic

Synthetic fuels: **MA** 13024; **TX** 1018

Syracuse (NY): **NY** 10240

System analysis: **AR** 15174; **CA** 776, 1171, 3301, 5194, 10445,
13192; **DC** 14231; **GA** 5242; **MD** 781; **MA** 6454; **MO** 16803;
NY 4428; **VA** 14704

Systematics (Biology) See: Biology—Classification

Systems, Communication See: Telecommunication systems

Systems engineering (See also Operations research): **AR** 958;
CA 76, 7470, 7471, 11215, 12528; **IL** 952; **MD** 16676, 17013;
MA 8677; **NJ** 1336; **NY** 5192, 12868; **ON** 1346; **PA** 14713,
16063, 16063; **TX** 6254; **VA** 8678, 13669

Tactics (See also Military art and science): **OH** 1250

Tagore, Rabindranath: **DC** 6342

Talking books (See also Braille): **BC** 15188; **CA** 1646, 12135,
13469; **DE** 3840; **DC** 7381; **GA** 5251; **ID** 6268; **IA** 6676;
KY 7025; **MN** 8601, 8622; **MO** 8674, 11345; **NE** 9319;
NJ 11293; **NY** 6796, 9492, 9545, 9582, 11490; **NC** 9760;
OK 10180, 10181; **ON** 2385, 9212; **OR** 10349; **PA** 4998,
10409; **PQ** 2386, 6471; **UT** 16526; **VA** 16663; **WA** 12382;
WV 16921; **WI** 17215

Taoism: **NY** 11789

Tar sand See: Oil sands

Tariff: **DC** 13595, 14224, 14475; **NJ** 1331; **NY** 1027, 14222,
14225; **PQ** 2288

Taste and smell See: Smell and taste

Tattooing: **CA** 13718

Taxation: **AL** 8702, 12543; **AB** 197, 198, 3020, 13577; **AZ** 805,
8716, 10066, 12618; **AR** 8945; **BC** 1208, 10944, 13580;
CA 49, 865, 1161, 2012, 3471, 3472, 3605, 5219, 5323, 5350,
5758, 5903, 6691, 6867, 7059, 7506, 7634, 8849, 10231,
10525, 10561, 10947, 11640, 12138, 13579, 13726, 16188,
16195; **CO** 13807, 16872; **CT** 866, 13518, 13762; **DE** 11416;
DC 1952, 3098, 3473, 3558, 3611, 5304, 7081, 8847, 9272,
10566, 10765, 13060, 13143, 13221, 13862, 14201, 14350,
14374, 14474, 14853, 17147; **FL** 4146, 7878, 9992, 10785,
10945, 12570, 15488; **GA** 297, 7065, 10908; **IL** 870, 875,
1127, 3095, 5030, 5459, 6571, 6817, 6959, 7695, 7708,
8127, 11570, 12426, 17190; **KS** 17101; **ME** 16208; **MD** 16588;
MA 867, 1372, 1612, 3474, 4457, 5383, 8099, 8116, 10946,
17108; **MI** 3014, 4149, 5191, 8531, 15737, 16716; **MN** 3858,
8614, 10567, 11243, 15794; **MO** 5515, 7226, 8670, 8673,
11903, 12489, 16817; **NE** 1118, 15884; **NJ** 6202, 7133, 7637;
NY 505, 876, 1222, 1618, 1688, 1951, 3475, 3771, 3856,
3931, 4458, 4524, 5028, 5113, 5516, 5635, 6176, 6960,
6970, 7502, 7769, 8524, 8836, 9571, 9638, 10225, 10432,
10507, 10539, 10735, 10950, 10953, 11144, 12427, 12521,
16865, 17143, 17166; **NC** 5514; **OH** 3036, 7997, 10099,
10414; **OK** 2975; **ON** 112, 869, 2098, 2292, 2310, 2407, 3614,

Taxation (Continued)
4592, 5378, 7797, 10290, 11587, 12516; **OR** 10345; **PA** 417, 1499, 3860, 4949, 9834, 10628, 11255, 13032, 17237; **PQ** 3019, 3895, 7790, 10563, 11171, 13197, 13584, 17463; **RI** 65, 5928; **SD** 16181; **TN** 13356; **TX** 117, 863, 1119, 1917, 6859, 6866, 10564, 10568, 12794, 17452; **VA** 1563, 3145, 13220, 16660; **WA** 4927, 16780, 17057; **WV** 16933; **WI** 352, 4850, 8423, 9929, 11150, 11333, 17221

Tea: **IN** 6220; **NJ** 7431

Teachers, Training of: **AB** 220; **BC** 1886; **CA** 2602, 3445, 10315, 15261; **DC** 4443; **FL** 7958, 16183; **IL** 9104, 9120; **IN** 6361, 6372, 6429, 16625; **MD** 5041, 12071, 15708; **MO** 9918; **NE** 3311; **NH** 6967, 9400; **NJ** 9652; **NY** 9637, 9889, 13189; **NS** 9980; **OH** 4441, 15443; **ON** 2408, 5612, 8398, 16038, 16417, 16882; **PA** 3004; **PQ** 15087; **SK** 16153; **TN** 16569; **TX** 4182, 4185, 7632; **VA** 9121; **WI** 16426

Teaching—Aids and devices: **CA** 5023, 9994, 12143; **FL** 4828, 16403; **MI** 15772; **NJ** 5312; **NM** 9171; **NY** 4436; **OH** 10122; **PA** 13329, 16102; **PQ** 11158; **SK** 16153; **WA** 4218

Technical assistance: **DC** 13863; **NY** 429, 4873

Technological innovations: **CA** 12873; **ON** 2364

Technology See: Science and technology

Technology assessment: **CT** 5065; **DC** 14814; **OK** 16009

Technology—History: **CA** 2041; **DE** 5589; **DC** 12600, 12601; **KY** 15660; **MA** 8075, 8077; **NY** 9547; **OK** 16002; **VA** 16652

Technology transfer: **CO** 15455

Teilhard de Chardin: **DC** 17267; **MN** 15821; **NY** 647

Telecommunication (See also Communication): **AL** 12704; **AZ** 14119; **AR** 958; **BC** 8485; **CA** 776, 1531; **CO** 969, 972, 14574; **CT** 5125, 6711, 10793; **DC** 361, 967, 3268, 3270, 5226, 14231, 14391; **FL** 11217, 13042; **GA** 953, 3435, 12338; **IL** 945, 952, 1338, 4517, 6284; **IN** 978; **MD** 2445, 3269, 3996; **MA** 871, 954, 3526, 5540, 8321; **MI** 8428; **MS** 13907; **MO** 12830; **NJ** 944, 946, 947, 948, 949, 950, 968, 970, 973, 1331, 1332, 1333, 1334, 1335, 1336, 1337, 5124, 11272, 11276, 13516, 17006; **NY** 452, 965, 971, 3434, 4290, 4428, 6715, 12868; **NC** 974, 12501; **NS** 7968; **OH** 955, 6719, 10065, 10081; **ON** 1329, 1346, 1347, 2155, 2171, 2172, 2311, 2387, 9884, 10294, 13249; **PA** 956, 957; **PQ** 1327, 1348, 9883, 12845; **TX** 9322, 9881, 13945

Telecommunication—History: **IL** 6284

Telecommunication systems: **IL** 1640; **NY** 5139; **VA** 3441

Telegraph: **CA** 12662; **NJ** 17006; **NY** 735; **RI** 9398

Telemeter: **CA** 13982; **ON** 2311; **TX** 14497

Telephone: **AZ** 977, 5542; **BC** 1743; **CA** 5197; **GA** 3435; **HI** 5799; **IL** 5539, 6284; **KS** 8966; **MI** 8428; **NJ** 587, 951; **NY** 975; **NC** 12501; **OH** 10081; **ON** 1329; **PQ** 1327, 1328, 1330, 1348; **TX** 5198

Television: **CA** 3788, 6011, 12142, 12166, 15298, 15317, 16196; **IL** 2821, 12779; **IN** 6420, 11281; **NJ** 11280; **NY** 735, 1794; **ON** 2277, 8395; **PA** 5008, 11277; **WI** 16474

Television advertising: **AZ** 15153; **MA** 41

Television broadcasting (See also Radio broadcasting): **AZ** 9745; **CA** 462, 12662, 15245, 15285; **CT** 2570, 5687; **DC** 463, 1749, 7370, 7379, 9050, 11068; **FL** 4783; **MA** 41; **MN** 15801; **NY** 387, 2568, 2569, 4274, 9073, 9075, 9076, 9539, 13259; **ON** 2155, 2172, 2330, 2332, 2338, 2339, 2991, 13719, 17436; **PA** 8376, 13635; **PQ** 2248, 2329, 2331, 11230; **TN** 16573; **VT** 2734

Television, Cable See: Community antenna television

Television in education: **DC** 361, 11068; **ON** 13719

Temperance (See also Alcohol and alcoholism): **IL** 9283; **IN** 6220;

Temperance (Continued)
MI 15765; **OH** 10088; **ON** 230; **PA** 13151

Tennessee: **TN** 2756, 4180, 7109, 8216, 8220, 11526, 13352, 13354, 13355, 13358, 13364, 13365, 14584, 14640, 16165, 16225, 16572, 16918

Tennis: **NY** 11221, 11795; **RI** 6649

Tennyson, Alfred, Lord: **AL** 12090; **OH** 10154; **ON** 16315

Teratology See: Abnormalities (Animals and plants)

Terrestrial magnetism See: Magnetism, Terrestrial

Terrorism: **DC** 2618; **FL** 14132

Testing (See also Specifications; Standardization): **AZ** 14147; **DC** 14773; **FL** 14142; **NE** 9321; **NJ** 14855; **UT** 6564; **VA** 14104

Tests and measurements See: Educational tests and measurements

Texas: **TX** 321, 1073, 1279, 1291, 2505, 2733, 3604, 3695, 3696, 3708, 3760, 4182, 4185, 4186, 4306, 4895, 4897, 4922, 5663, 5674, 5923, 6128, 6132, 6133, 6765, 6866, 8048, 9826, 9827, 10392, 10487, 11236, 11256, 11415, 11561, 12085, 12092, 12096, 12100, 12170, 12792, 12956, 12998, 13372, 13373, 13379, 13386, 13408, 13412, 13436, 13437, 13438, 13440, 13441, 13442, 13454, 13892, 13933, 14659, 15542, 16226, 16229, 16233, 16234, 16242, 16261, 16612, 16689, 17173, 17226

Text-books: **AB** 15135; **AZ** 10745; **CA** 9994, 12143, 15328, 16189; **FL** 16403; **ID** 6269; **MB** 15681; **MA** 1601, 5717, 6111, 17286; **NJ** 13625; **NY** 5659, 6437, 13106, 13108, 13113, 13189, 13227; **OH** 8318, 15443; **ON** 5303, 16292; **PA** 2788, 10574, 10796; **PR** 16106; **TN** 13712; **WA** 2679

Text-books—History: **FL** 16184

Textile chemistry: **NJ** 3936; **NC** 368, 3320, 9771, 12200; **SC** 8536; **VA** 285, 1114, 6537

Textile fabrics (See also Fibers): **AL** 8751, 17046; **CA** 7533; **CT** 1324; **DC** 648, 13461; **FL** 438, 8752; **IL** 12369, 15575; **LA** 14260; **MD** 6597; **MA** 8322, 14101, 15669; **MN** 13508, 13509; **MO** 6924, 16837; **NE** 15881; **NJ** 2840, 13462; **NY** 4591, 7618, 10055, 12594; **NC** 448, 1881, 2748, 4094, 9771, 9772; **OH** 6449; **ON** 4088, 4089, 10302; **OR** 10338; **PA** 2609, 3603, 10712, 11540, 12346; **PQ** 6853; **RI** 11046, 12561; **SC** 3035, 6006, 6724, 8536, 10822, 13836; **TN** 4223; **VA** 3724, 9274, 16640; **WA** 16382, 16387

Textile fibers, Synthetic: **DE** 5871; **GA** 7058; **NJ** 13462; **NC** 4094; **OH** 10415; **ON** 4090; **SC** 8750; **VA** 1114

Thanatology See: Death

Theater (See also Drama): **AZ** 808; **CA** 1867, 1977, 1979, 6481, 7488, 7557, 8987, 12936; **CT** 3370, 5687, 17362, 17386; **DC** 4851, 6139, 7370; **FL** 8405, 15474; **HI** 5786; **IL** 2822, 7626, 12774, 13466, 15571; **IN** 6398; **KY** 15647, 15658; **ME** 1562; **MD** 8027; **MA** 669, 1585, 1597, 4339, 5724, 5751, 12579; **MI** 3919, 4770, 15746; **MN** 2868, 3135, 5581; **MO** 8665; **NH** 3753; **NJ** 10995, 10998; **NY** 277, 339, 557, 1789, 5627, 6650, 6882, 8958, 9326, 9522, 9539, 11181, 13091, 13093, 16138; **NC** 15940, 15948; **NS** 9978; **OH** 3068, 4965, 6651, 10126, 10150, 11072, 13538, 15376, 15442; **ON** 8395, 17432; **OR** 7352; **PA** 3657, 4980, 4999, 5008, 5275, 10710, 16100; **PQ** 3409, 9273; **TX** 3701, 4919, 12791, 16244, 16246; **UT** 12810; **VA** 5221, 16350, 16649; **WA** 3524, 16370; **WI** 588, 7831, 8555, 12966, 16474, 16675

Theater, Musical See: Musical theater

Theology See: Religion and theology

Theology—Study and teaching: **AB** 9738; **AK** 11764; **BC** 9904, 16557, 17030; **CA** 1999, 5049, 5347, 5425, 5832, 6585, 8241, 10438, 11786, 11992, 12317; **CO** 2880, 3871, 3888, 12032; **CT** 5688, 12033, 17368; **DC** 3129, 4022, 4958, 6146, 10054, 11861, 12012, 13846, 17267; **FL** 7646, 11771, 12039; **GA** 3203; **IL** 1416, 2547, 2833, 3954, 5093, 5829, 6285, 6538, 7675, 7703, 8137, 9813, 11941, 12870, 13644; **IN** 693, 907,

Theology—Study and teaching (Continued)
2545, 2892, 3312, 5415, 11983, 13751; **IA** 10306, 12320; **KS** 2643; **KY** 881, 4422, 7342, 7610, 12751, 12752, 12753, 12754; **LA** 9448, 11833; **ME** 1166; **MB** 17178; **MD** 16750, 16799; **MA** 697, 1613, 5389, 5705, 5845, 10867, 11787, 17045; **MI** 2075, 5409, 5443, 6475, 8432, 11653, 11784, 17005; **MN** 1414, 1419, 3607, 7645, 7648, 11773, 12009, 15032; **MS** 11314, 16893; **MO** 901, 3305, 3310, 3557, 4253, 6998, 8520, 9298, 11978, 12008; **NE** 5410; **NJ** 4077, 6320, 9372, 10976; **NY** 2883, 3106, 5200, 5833, 6808, 8021, 8261, 8894, 9632, 10532, 11696, 11860, 12055, 12400, 13790, 16691; **NC** 2516, 4116, 6063; **ND** 940; **NS** 1025; **OH** 890, 986, 1503, 5834, 8347, 10548, 11945, 13648, 15031, 17172; **OK** 10311, 10740; **ON** 2642, 3115, 10243, 11691, 12020, 15094, 16316; **OR** 16954, 16957; **PA** 1441, 2072, 4193, 4501, 7198, 7676, 7677, 8017, 10802, 11292, 11312, 11313, 11701, 11712, 12034, 17038; **PR** 4502; **PQ** 5451, 5452, 12395, 12398; **SC** 7678; **SD** 1512, 9739; **SK** 2326, 11703, 12016, 16158, 16160, 16161; **TN** 379, 5648, 6841, 8233, 16166; **TX** 941, 1072, 1205, 2884, 3710, 4423, 10053, 11977, 12829, 13385, 13392; **VA** 13791, 16668; **WA** 4561; **WI** 4023, 7986, 11652, 11693, 11759, 11871, 11989, 17202

Theosophy (See also Anthroposophy): **CA** 7126, 12167, 13469, 13472; **FL** 13471; **IL** 13470; **NY** 13835

Thermal engineering See: Heat engineering

Thermodynamics: **AL** 14183; **CA** 7460, 7713; **DC** 14523, 14532; **GA** 11545; **NJ** 4928; **OK** 9184; **OR** 14174; **PA** 7980; **TX** 1945, 13381; **UT** 5905; **VA** 12327; **WI** 16468

Thermophysical properties See: Materials—Thermal properties

Thin films (See also Protective coatings): **ND** 15973; **OH** 5398

Third World See: Underdeveloped areas

Thomas, Dylan: **NY** 13100

Thompson, Stith: **IN** 6385

Thomson, Virgil: **CT** 17376; **MO** 15863

Thoracic medicine See: Medicine, Thoracic

Thoreau, Henry David: **ME** 15674; **MA** 13489; **RI** 1819

Tibet: **AK** 10741; **CT** 17362; **NY** 3520, 7934

Tidal waves See: Tsunamis

Tin: **OH** 13521

Tissue culture: **MD** 652; **NY** 6873, 8567

Titanium: **NV** 13526; **OR** 10929; **PA** 3184

Tobacco (See also Smoking): **DC** 13527, 14152; **KY** 1820; **MD** 10071, 14151; **NJ** 5455; **NY** 9509, 13528; **NC** 7398, 7516, 9778, 11386, 11387, 11389; **OH** 3067; **PQ** 2411, 6331, 6332; **VA** 386, 9274, 10730

Toilet preparations (See also Cosmetics): **NJ** 1710, 6851, 7319

Tolkien, John Ronald Reuel: **IL** 17068; **PA** 10513; **WI** 7983

Tolstoy, Leo: **NY** 13545

Tools (See also Agricultural machinery): **PA** 4162, 10626

Topography (See also Maps and atlases): **AB** 15143; **CA** 14452, 15348; **CO** 14450; **DC** 14242; **GA** 15509; **LA** 7573; **NJ** 9422, 10996; **NY** 9525, 13131; **OH** 7010; **ON** 1752, 8386; **PA** 10611, 10648, 13323, 16050; **TN** 13361; **TX** 13375; **WI** 16433

Toponymy See: Names, Geographical

Toronto (ON): **ON** 2990, 2991, 12292

Toscanini, Arturo: **NY** 9541

Tourist trade (See also Travel): **AB** 194; **BC** 1716; **CO** 15399; **DC** 14857; **NY** 3517, 17460; **ON** 2285, 2405, 10293; **PQ** 2690,

Tourist trade (Continued)
11167; **SK** 12259; **WI** 17205

Town planning See: City planning

Toxicology: **AB** 171, 201; **AK** 14419; **CA** 2791, 4151, 15260, 15271, 17305; **CO** 7927; **CT** 12986; **DE** 4095; **DC** 4390, 14367, 14415; **FL** 4781; **GA** 14190, 14259; **IL** 3759, 4408, 6280, 10917; **IA** 6689; **MD** 5215, 5301, 14047, 14091, 14418; **MA** 872, 4286, 4364, 4403, 8074; **MI** 15774, 16730; **NJ** 288, 436, 4526, 8693; **NM** 7613; **NY** 2770, 4225, 9563, 11790; **NC** 9180; **OH** 14540, 15377; **ON** 2208, 2342, 5992, 6274, 10291; **PA** 6436, 10613, 14365, 16076; **TN** 9214, 10025; **TX** 4409, 12466, 15539; **WI** 5812, 14406

Toy libraries: **CA** 2459, 3442, 11238, 11639; **IL** 7310; **KS** 4359; **MI** 10766; **MN** 3785, 6234, 10413, 11565, 12474, 13590, 16763, 17144; **NM** 7220; **NY** 7619; **OH** 15096; **OK** 11239; **PA** 2079, 10674; **RI** 16743

Track-athletics: **IN** 9275

Tractors: **IL** 2536

Trade See: Business; Commerce and trade

Trade-marks (See also Copyright; Patents): **CA** 7321, 13080; **DC** 14201, 14340; **IL** 12507; **MN** 5174; **NH** 10533; **NJ** 8270; **NY** 6960, 13226, 13586, 14856

Trade-unions: **CA** 6620; **DC** 88, 13826; **IA** 15603; **MD** 6440, 7642, 15700; **MI** 8465, 16855; **NY** 9564; **ON** 2212, 2373, 7792

Trades See: Industrial arts

Traffic engineering (See also Highway engineering): **CA** 2033, 6811; **DC** 6539, 9040; **FL** 15496; **IL** 6304, 15573; **ME** 7863; **MD** 8040; **MI** 8443, 8460; **MN** 8615; **NY** 7094; **ON** 13567; **PA** 10651; **TN** 1226; **TX** 8819; **VA** 6810; **WA** 16781

Traffic safety: **BC** 6543; **CA** 1084, 2010; **DE** 3842; **DC** 6539, 6546, 9040, 14538; **IL** 9245, 9946; **ME** 7863; **MI** 8460, 8867, 15776, 15777; **MN** 8612; **MO** 1080, 8518; **NY** 9568; **NC** 15938; **ON** 2293, 2324, 10294, 13596; **PA** 4972, 8868, 10651; **TX** 13398; **VA** 371, 4384, 16659

Training devices See: Military education—Aids and devices

Transcendentalism: **MA** 13489

Translations: **CA** 11332; **MA** 5721; **NJ** 910; **ON** 2296; **PA** 4586; **PQ** 2297; **SK** 16120

Transplantation of organs, tissues, etc.: **AL** 1196; **MD** 14763

Transportation (See also Air travel; Electric railroads; Railroads): **AL** 9901; **AB** 2312, 5104; **AK** 160; **AZ** 13727; **BC** 16556; **CA** 1084, 2030, 2031, 2032, 2034, 2035, 3735, 6811, 8399, 10565, 11642, 12106, 12159, 12756, 15250, 15304, 16959; **CO** 15418; **DC** 913, 1209, 3611, 4926, 6546, 6579, 9040, 10566, 13863, 14370, 14476, 14836; **FL** 4811, 4818, 11632, 15496; **GA** 5257; **HI** 5783; **IL** 2829, 6304, 9849, 9946; **IN** 11125; **IA** 6680, 15609; **KY** 15654; **ME** 16208; **MD** 2782, 4594, 9078, 11321, 13607, 15710; **MA** 2739, 8064, 8115, 12658, 14371; **MI** 3918, 5205, 8443, 8475, 8864, 8866, 10032, 12735, 15747, 16823; **MN** 1228, 9840; **MO** 1080, 9222, 15868; **NE** 13787; **NB** 15907; **NJ** 9235, 10996; **NY** 7094, 9547, 9573, 9588, 10516, 10873, 12514, 17414; **NC** 13608; **ND** 9805; **NS** 9979; **OH** 123, 126, 2660, 8422, 9842, 10100, 15379; **OK** 13701; **ON** 40, 2156, 2315, 2317, 2387, 10294, 13567, 13568; **OR** 10346, 16014; **PA** 5748, 7093, 10618, 10651, 16055, 17417; **PQ** 2318, 2396, 15060; **RI** 6638; **SC** 17112; **TN** 1226, 13348, 16221; **TX** 7631, 12096, 12789, 13378, 13380, 13708, 16237; **VA** 1283, 6810, 16659; **WA** 1545, 5971; **WI** 3732, 6969, 17217

Transportation, Air See: Air travel

Transportation, Automotive—Freight: **AL** 650; **CA** 16959; **IL** 6608; **MI** 5042; **MO** 5133; **OH** 126; **VA** 651; **WA** 7033

Transportation—Law and legislation: **DC** 598, 12452, 14388; **NY** 6970

Transportation, Marine See: Shipping

Transportation, Military: VA 14001, 14140

Transportation, Urban See: Urban transportation

Transvestism: CA 6750

Traumatology: OR 4332; PA 7305

Travel (See also Ocean travel; Tourist trade; Voyages and travels):
BC 1733, 1737, 15207; CA 7555, 10038, 11300, 13720;
CO 15399; CT 5687; DE 3850; DC 634, 3984, 9161, 12593,
14857; HI 5788; IN 6369; MD 4382; MA 6488; MI 3915, 10399;
MN 8579, 8598, 9079, 12004, 12005; MO 1080, 7969, 7970;
MT 8761; NJ 5126, 9658; NY 1788, 1792, 1854, 9552, 11182,
11489, 17356, 17460; OH 3066, 11079, 13539, 15375;
OK 10170; ON 2285; PA 5006, 5211; PQ 99; SC 16174;
TX 1028, 3706, 6132, 10490, 12100; VA 371; WA 12379;
WI 7833

Tree ring research See: Dendrochronology

Trees: OR 6433; WA 17060

Tropical medicine: FL 5393; HI 5772, 5779; NH 3745; OH 13955;
PR 16115

Tropics: FL 14142

Trucking industry See: Transportation, Automotive—Freight

Truman, Harry S: MO 14824

Tsunamis (See also Earthquakes): FL 15478; HI 6653

Tuba music: IN 1144

Tuberculosis (See also Medicine, Thoracic): CA 1213; CO 9192;
DE 1485; GA 9912; HI 5779; ON 10272, 12445

Tumors (See also Cancer): CA 12224; MA 1556; MN 15814;
MO 4320; NJ 9651; NY 398, 2542, 17403; ON 11853

Tungsten: CT 326; OH 5156

Tunnels: NY 3205

Turbines: CA 5091, 12672; IL 5186; IN 5179; MA 5136, 9878;
MI 17139; NH 3586; NJ 7755, 13604; NY 5160; OH 13251;
PA 15026; PQ 10926

Turkey: CT 15425; DC 8488; NY 360, 13707

Twain, Mark See: Clemens, Samuel Langhorne (Mark Twain)

Tydings, Millard E.: MD 15700

Typography See: Printing

UFOs See: Flying saucers

Ukraine: AB 12056, 13734; CO 13736; IL 13732; MB 13730;
MA 5721; NY 12484, 13731; OH 13733; ON 12054; PA 7916,
12562; SK 8712, 13735

Ulcers: CA 2634; ND 11147; OH 6217

Underdeveloped areas: AL 13362; CA 10458, 12939; CT 17370,
17389; DC 596, 6625, 7367, 10411, 10412, 14817; IL 7389;
KS 6947; MA 5725, 6482, 7408, 12067; MN 15821; NY 429,
8020, 11183, 13478, 14198; ON 6594, 7087, 13552; PQ 7725;
WI 16450

Underground construction: MN 15831

Underground literature—Russia: NY 11228; WI 16456

Underground press: CT 15425; DC 7367; MD 300; MI 10043;
NY 11353; OH 1341; PA 13316, 16042; WI 16439

Underground railroad: PA 13313

Undertakers and undertaking: CA 12153; IL 9149; MA 9388;

Undertakers and undertaking (Continued)
OH 2948; ON 6194

Underwater acoustics: CT 5129, 14798; FL 14731, 14774;
MD 16676; NY 4273; NS 2166; RI 11269; VA 13669

Underwater demolition See: Naval tactics

Underwater weapons See: Ordnance, Naval

Underwater welding and cutting: OH 748

Unemployment insurance See: Insurance, Unemployment

Unidentified flying objects See: Flying saucers

Union of Soviet Socialist Republics (USSR) See: Soviet Union

Unions See: Trade-unions

Unitarianism: IL 8137; MA 5705, 13802

United Brethren See: Evangelical United Brethren

United Church of Canada: AB 12025; MB 16419; NS 13815;
ON 13813, 13814

United Church of Christ: CT 13816; LA 670; PA 4499, 7198

United Kingdom See: Great Britain

United Methodist Church: AL 1475, 6205; CA 12317, 13842;
CT 16898; DC 13846; GA 4349, 4355; IL 5093, 13837; IN 3798;
KS 1129, 13840; KY 881, 7032; MD 13852; MA 1613, 13845;
MN 13849; MS 1954; MT 13848; NE 13841; NJ 4077, 13838;
NY 4250; NC 4112, 4116; OH 8347; PA 13839, 13843;
SC 13851; SD 13844; TN 13853, 16510; TX 12788, 12792,
13850; WV 16943; WI 1417, 13847

United Nations: DC 7367; GA 15503; IL 7389; IN 6405; KS 15623;
MD 6829; MA 1592, 8071, 13681; MI 8455; MO 13854;
NJ 5328, 10994; NY 1795, 3221, 3541, 9647, 13858;
OH 3072; ON 2368, 17429; WI 16482

United States Air Force—History: AL 13949; CA 13898; CO 13866;
DC 100, 14519; HI 13941; NM 13885; OH 13972; TX 13892,
13933

United States—Armed Forces—History: CA 14226; DC 14229;
TX 13882

United States—Armed Forces—Women: AL 14096; DC 17248;
WA 4905

United States Congress: AZ 15156; DC 3361, 3364, 11069, 14304,
14467, 14839; GA 15507; IL 3968; MD 3363; MI 8455;
NY 2633; OH 3062; TX 1273, 11256; WY 17042

United States—History (See also Americana; specific regions of the
U.S.): AL 1040; AZ 15156; AR 821; CA 1460, 12479, 12686,
12940, 13887; CO 4904, 14656; DC 5233, 7366, 7367, 7378,
12350, 12601, 12636, 14513, 14514, 14516, 14519, 14629,
14839, 17162; FL 10538, 14611; GA 14652; IL 2808, 2825,
15574, 17068; IN 2864, 11128; IA 14825; KS 15631;
LA 12740, 13896; MD 6828, 8026; MA 351, 1575, 1597, 8113,
8978, 14826, 16878; MI 8466, 8734; MN 8597, 8598;
MO 8663, 8665, 11892, 14824; NJ 10995, 11619; NY 481,
1850, 3214, 3215, 4912, 6756, 8708, 9523, 9530, 9550,
9586, 13043, 13776, 14822; NC 8629; OH 5806, 7008, 10088,
11074; OK 5297, 13939; PA 586, 1483, 3765, 4982, 5013,
5965, 6745, 7356, 13777, 14095, 14648; PQ 11763; RI 1816;
SC 13549; TN 12485, 13352, 13354; TX 12789, 13882,
13994, 14827, 16919; VA 242, 3144, 6501, 13034, 16352,
16360, 16662, 17161; WV 14643, 16926; WI 12967, 16483

United States Marine Corps: HI 14479, 14484; VA 14481

United States Marine Corps—History: DC 14519

Universalist Church: MA 5705, 13802

Universities and colleges (See also Education, Higher): CA 12951;
CO 15977; DE 15445; FL 15498; GA 7139, 15500; HI 15525;
IL 9935, 15593; IN 6412, 15980; KS 6952, 15636; KY 15665;

Universities and colleges (Continued)
MD 15700; MI 16975; MN 8586, 15832; MT 8768; NH 15917; NY 15394, 16549; NC 15950; ND 15967; PA 16043, 16071; SC 16175; TN 16165, 16225; WA 16398; WI 16429

Universities and colleges—Alumni: DC 3539

Uranium: BC 1739; CO 11527; KS 6936; NM 12823; ON 3866, 4307, 11440; PQ 11636

Urban education See: Education, Urban

Urban planning See: City planning

Urban renewal (See also City planning): AZ 13680; AR 8350; DC 3976, 14324; GA 14329; MD 1147, 1149, 15181; MA 1600, 14326; NY 14327; OH 3070; ON 2220, 8396, 10285; PA 42, 10705, 14328; TX 14330

Urban studies See: Cities and towns—Study and teaching

Urban transportation: AB 195, 1964; CA 539, 10323, 12159, 12764, 15283; CO 11322; DE 3842; DC 598, 9039, 14370, 14373, 16769; GA 991, 8351; IL 2834; IN 6359, 6389; IA 6680; ME 7863; MA 683, 8115; MI 8443; MN 8353; MO 4188; NY 6526, 10873; NC 13608; OH 984; ON 8389, 9832, 11462, 16516; PA 5161, 7093, 10872, 12741; PQ 2388, 8810; VA 8678; WA 8940, 16781; WI 17217

Urbanization: FL 4827

Urology: IL 15596; LA 13687; OH 6035

Utah: UT 1690, 1700, 12810, 16330, 16520, 16522, 16525

Utilities See: Public utilities

Utopias in literature: MO 15872; PA 13325

Vacuum technology: IL 8875; IN 11278; MI 4032; NJ 12207; NY 12851

Valley fever See: Coccidioidosis

Vanderbilt families: NY 14682

Vegetable oils See: Oils and fats

Vegetables See: Fruits and vegetables

Vegetarianism: MD 16586; NY 710

Vehicles (See also Automobiles): NV 5660

Vehicles, Military: CA 4848; KY 14106; MI 5131; ON 2232; VA 14004

Verbal aggression: WI 7874

Vermont: NY 13116; VT 1371, 2425, 2531, 2532, 5426, 12458, 12460, 16335, 16595, 16598, 16600, 16602, 17266

Vertical/short takeoff and landing aircraft (V/STOL) See: V/STOL aircraft

Veterans: DC 14885, 14886, 14887; IN 535; ON 2319; WI 5431

Veterans' hospitals See: Hospitals, Veterans'

Veterinary medicine: AL 1045, 13717, 13956; AB 171, 2124; AK 151, 15116; CA 2066, 15273, 15279, 17467; CO 3182, 8841; DE 15444; FL 5394, 15486; GA 14189, 15508; IL 656, 15594; IN 4312, 11135; IA 6688, 6689, 14253; KS 1282, 6942, 6951, 6953; KY 15639; LA 7598, 13687; MD 13988, 14266; MA 4286, 13682; MI 8437, 8470, 8471, 8477; MN 8624, 15834, 15843, 15844; MS 8652; MO 10378, 10731, 11241, 15862; MT 8769; NJ 432; NM 13961; NY 711, 3497, 9563, 14257; NC 2645, 9779; OH 3052, 8155, 10152; OK 10195; ON 2107, 2112, 10264, 10265, 15513, 16991; OR 10359, 12063, 16772; PA 10647, 16059, 16066; PQ 11164, 15072; RI 11395; SK 16164; TN 1319, 16217; TX 13376, 13967, 13968, 13992; VA 16647; WA 16795, 16798; WI 16467

Vibration: CA 17157; CO 4367; DC 14773; MD 14705; NH 14782;

Vibration (Continued)
OH 10930; PA 7513

Victorian literature See: Literature, Victorian

Video games: CA 981

Videotape recorders and recordings: BC 12279; CA 6011, 16621; DC 463; IL 9822; NY 725, 9280, 11294, 16622

Vietnam: CA 7552, 12730, 14728; CO 3181; OK 16319; TX 16263

Violence research: ID 15545; VA 3824

Virgin Islands: VI 3142, 16634

Virginia: KY 4655; LA 9955; MD 4763; VA 242, 337, 825, 3144, 3153, 4543, 4545, 4966, 5221, 5579, 5677, 6980, 8014, 8741, 9730, 10896, 11225, 11465, 11497, 12883, 13034, 13049, 13980, 14631, 14675, 16351, 16635, 16637, 16644, 16645, 16651, 16653, 16662, 17337

Virology: CA 15257; FL 5394; GA 14189; IN 4052; KY 15640; MT 14545; NY 6873, 9477, 9579; ON 2107, 3365, 10244

Vision: IL 6286; IN 6397, 16671; MO 6619; NY 3229, 4227, 8050, 13114

Visitors, Foreign: DC 6656

Vivisection: DC 9258; IL 9045

Vocal music: BC 16613; IL 15585; MI 8467, 16980; MN 15820; NY 3510; OH 8906, 10049, 10144; ON 8390; PA 612, 5003; PQ 2322; WI 12657

Vocational education (See also Industrial arts): AL 15104; AZ 7940; CA 7482; DC 3982, 9167, 14517; FL 4825, 10787; GA 5063; HI 16956; IL 2838, 6085, 9910, 12208; IN 6367, 6415; KS 4765; KY 7336; ME 12787; MA 4758, 8117, 17288; MN 716, 8590, 15838; NE 9310; NH 9415, 9416, 9417; NJ 6962, 8773, 9656, 11626; NM 12832; NY 1833, 6160, 9531, 9532, 9564, 13086, 13104, 13135; NC 4894, 5556; ND 9798; NS 5601; OH 4430, 5805, 5988, 9089, 10147; OK 10184; ON 5218, 10276; OR 9923, 10340, 10351; PA 1377, 3128, 6858; PQ 3313, 15087; SC 4778, 10325, 10760, 13063, 13633, 13637; SD 9106; TX 9949; VA 16632; WV 7999; WI 3995, 5098, 7183, 8510, 12827, 16842, 17204; WY 16500

Vocational guidance (See also Counseling): CO 14113; CT 17438; HI 16956; MD 4380; MI 8438; MN 15822; MT 15876; NY 2533, 4510, 4626, 6186, 9531, 9564, 10239, 11505, 12663; OR 16015, 16016; SK 12242; TX 13875; WA 12377, 16711

Volcanoes (See also Seismology): CA 14655; HI 14645

Volleyball: IN 1140

Voltaire: FL 16679; ON 16312

Voluntarism: DC 367, 602; MN 15828, 16681; NY 924; VA 15034, 16682

Voyages and travels (See also Travel): CA 2041, 10443, 12217; CT 15183, 17362; DC 14706; FL 14611; HI 1478, 5796; KS 8012, 15622; MB 6162; MD 6827, 6828; MI 6910, 15778; MN 8583; NY 4514, 9544; NT 2236; OK 10176; ON 8386, 16407; OR 10334, 16030; PA 987, 8926; PQ 7727; RI 11035; VA 16352; WA 16394

V/STOL aircraft: CT 15030; PA 1548; VA 14131

Wabash Valley (IN): IN 16623, 16629

Wages: IL 5804, 5886; KY 8173; MA 17132; NY 6618, 7922; ON 13585; PA 5803

Wales: MN 3137

Wallace, Irving: WI 16486

Walpole, Horace: CT 17379